THE NEW ILLUSTRATED
ENCYCLOPEDIA
OF KNOWLEDGE

THE NEW
ENCYCL
OF KNOW

ILLUSTRATED

OPEDIA

VLEDGE

PORTLAND HOUSE

NEW YORK

THE NEW ILLUSTRATED ENCYCLOPEDIA OF KNOWLEDGE
Executive Editor Stephen P. Elliott

1986 edition published by Portland House, distributed by
Crown Publishers, Inc.

Library of Congress Cataloging-in-Publication Data

New illustrated encyclopedia of knowledge.

Rev. ed. of: The Random House encyclopedia.
New rev. ed. c1983.
1. Encyclopedias and dictionaries. 1. Portland
House (Firm) II. Random House encyclopedia.
AG5.N35   1986   031   86-12248
ISBN 0-517-61879-6

Manufactured in the United States of America

h g f e d c b a

PREFACE

THE NEW ILLUSTRATED ENCYCLOPEDIA OF KNOWLEDGE gives you, in easy-access, A-Z form, the basic information you need about more than 16,000 individual subjects in the fields of biography, politics, humanities, science, geography, natural history, law, languages, sports, literature, music and a host of other topics. Containing hundreds of thousands of separate facts and more than 800 illustrations, it provides the inquiring reader with up-to-the-minute answers about the world we live in and summarizes all that is significant from the past.

Biographies include the world's great political and military leaders, artists, writers, scientists and inventors. They give a person's full name, life dates, nationality and occupation or main claim to fame – all in the first sentence for rapid access to the basic information. Articles on places give their location, history, modern significance and population. The major cities of every country, selected on the basis of population and historical importance or interest, are included.

Articles on things – animal, vegetable, mineral or abstract – begin with a definition, often enlarged by means of examples to explain how they fit into the area of knowledge of which they are part. These articles reflect the language of our times, from scientific concepts such as "computer language" to artistic movements such as "Cubism" and activities such as "basketball".

ARRANGEMENT

Subjects are arranged in strict alphabetical order no matter how many words a title contains and that system continues up to the punctuation mark. Thus *Confederate States of America* precedes *Confederation of Canada,* which in turn precedes *Confederation of the Rhine.* Words in parentheses are not taken into account. Names beginning with *Mc, St,* or *SS* are alphabetized as if they were spelled out (ie, *Mac, Saint* or *Saints*).

Titled persons with the same name are listed in the order of saints, popes, emperors, kings; untitled persons with the same surname and given names are listed chronologically by birth date. Where persons, places and things have the same name, they are listed in that order. Places with the same name are listed by the alphabetical position of their countries; thus Athens, Greece, precedes Athens, Georgia (United States). Cities of the same name in the United States are alphabetized by states; thus Columbus, Georgia, precedes Columbus, Ohio.

Equivalent metric weights and measures are given in parentheses.

A

Aachen (Aix-la-Chapelle), city in W West Germany, 40mi (64km) WSW of Cologne, near Belgian and Dutch borders; noted for hot sulfur baths used to treat rheumatism, gout, and skin disorders, also used by Romans in AD 1st century; probable birthplace of Charlemagne; site of medieval imperial diets and church councils. Taken by France 1794, city surrendered to Prussia 1815; occupied by Allies 1918–30; first major German city to fall to Allies in WWII (October 1944); important industrial center and railroad junction. Industries: steel, textiles, machinery, rubber goods. Pop. 242,000.

Aalto, Alvar (1899–1976), Finnish architect and furniture designer. His unique handling of floor levels and his use of natural materials and irregular forms can be seen in both his public buildings and private residences. His work includes the municipal library at Viipuri (1927–35), the sanitorium at Paimio (1929–33), the Baker House at the Massachusetts Institute of Technology (1947–48), Säynätsalo town hall group (1950–52), and Finlandia House, Helsinki (1971). His well-known furniture designs are characterized by curved strips of laminated wood.

Aardvark, nocturnal, naked or sparsely haired mammal of central and southern Africa that lives on termites and ants picked up with its sticky foot-long (30cm) tongue. Length: to 5ft (1.5m); weight: to 150lbs (68kg). It is the only species in the order Tubulidentata.

Aardwolf, rare nocturnal mammal that lives in open or bush country in Southern and East Africa. It has soft, black-striped yellow-gray underfur and coarse outer fur forming a crest along the back, and a long, bushy tail. It eats termites and other insects. Overall length: 26in (64cm). Family Hyaenidae; species *Proteles cristata.*

Aaron, in the Bible, older brother of Moses and first high priest of Israel. He acted as spokesman for Moses and performed many miracles. During Moses' stay on Mount Sinai, he built the golden calf and led in its worship. His tribe, the Levites, were priests of Israel.

Abaca. *See* Manila Hemp.

Abacus, a mathematical tool used in Asia and the Middle East for solving problems of addition and subtraction. A simple device made up of beads strung on wire in units of 10, it has been used in various forms for thousands of years. The Chinese abacus dates from the 12th century.

Abadan, city in SW Iran, on Abadan Island in Persian Gulf; important center of Middle East oil; pipeline terminus; site of the first oil refinery (1913) built by the Anglo-Iranian Oil Company. Pop. 306,000.

Abalone, seashore gastropod mollusk with a single flattened spiral shell perforated by a row of respiratory holes, found on Mediterranean, E Atlantic, and Pacific shores and off coasts of S Africa and Australia. It has a large fleshy foot and sensory projections on the underside. Length: 12in (30cm). Family Haliotidae; species include *Haliotis rufescens.*

Abbadids, Moorish dynasty that ruled Seville, Spain, from 1023 to 1091. After the collapse of the Córdoba caliphate, the cadi of Seville proclaimed himself king as Abbad I in 1023. His son Abbad II succeeded him in 1042 and made Seville the strongest kingdom in southern Spain. His successor Abbad III, who became king in 1069, was a patron of the arts. He was overthrown and forced into exile in 1091 by the Almoravids. *See also* Almoravids.

Abbas (died 652), uncle of the Prophet Mohammed and of the caliph Ali. A rich merchant in Mecca, he gave his name to the famous dynasty of Muslim caliphs, the Abbasid.

Abbasids, Muslim dynasty that held the caliphate from 750 to 1258. They traced their descent from Abbas, the uncle of Mohammed. The family came to power by defeating the Umayyads, who were exiled to Spain. The Abbasids moved the caliphate from Damascus to Baghdad, where it achieved great splendor, particularly under Harun al-Rashid and al-Mamun. After the family's downfall in 1258, one member escaped to Cairo, where the dynasty continued to be recognized until the 16th century.

Abbey, a complex of buildings that makes up a religious community, the center of which is the abbey church, and the whole of which is directed by an abbot or abbess. Since the fall of monasticism in England, often only the church remains. A famous example is Westminster Abbey.

Abbey Theatre, theater erected on Abbey St., Dublin (1904), by Annie E.F. Horniman to house the Irish National Theatre Society, presenting Irish actors in Irish plays. In 1924, with a government subsidy, the Abbey became the national theater of Ireland. Works by W.B. Yeats, Lady Gregory, J.M. Synge, and Sean O'Casey have been introduced there by such actors as Sara Allgood, Arthur Sinclair, and Barry Fitzgerald.

Abbott, Berenice (1898–), US photographer, b. Springfield, Ohio. Working in Paris, first as assistant to Man Ray, she made superb portraits of writers and artists of the 1920s. She began her celebrated studies of New York City here in 1929. From 1958 she photographed scientific phenomena.

Abbott, (Sir) John (1821–93), lawyer, educator, and prime minister of Canada (1891–92). Dean of McGill Law School, he was a Conservative legislator ousted during the Pacific Scandal of 1873. In 1880 he was reelected to parliament and later succeeded John Macdonald as prime minister. *See also* Pacific Scandal of 1873.

ABC Mediation, arbitration conducted by Argentina, Brazil and Chile to settle a dispute between Mexico and the United States when President Wilson landed Marines at Vera Cruz (1914).

Abd al-Hamid II (1842–1918), Ottoman sultan (1876–1909), nephew of Abd al-Aziz. He reigned after his brother, Murad V, became insane. He suspended the constitution, executing Midhat Pasha. Russia forced him to sign the Treaty of San Stefano (1878). He sought German aid to save the empire. A revolt of the Young Turks led to his ouster. Mohammed V succeeded.

Abd al-Malik (646–705), fifth Umayyad caliph (685–705), son of Marwan I. With Gen. al-Hajjaj, he defeated the rival caliph, Abdullah ibn-al-Zubayr, battled Byzantine forces, and united Islam. He reformed government and secured Arabic as the official language. Walid I succeeded.

Abd-el-Krim (1885–1963), Rif leader in Morocco. In 1921–22 his Rif tribesmen captured Spanish outposts. In 1925 he attacked French Morocco and was defeated by combined French-Spanish troops. He surrendered in 1926, but escaped to Egypt to lead a new independence movement.

Abdomen, in vertebrates, that portion of the body between the chest and the pelvis, containing the abdominal cavity, and the abdominal viscera, including most of the digestive organs. In arthropods it is the posterior part of the body, containing the reproductive organs and part of the digestive system.

Abdul-Jabbar, Kareem (1947–), US basketball player, b. Lewis Alcindor in New York City. After leading his University of California, Los Angeles, team to three NCAA championships (1967–69), he joined the Milwaukee Bucks in the National Basketball Association (1969) and then (1975) the Los Angeles Lakers. Considered his era's best player, he was named most valuable player a record six times.

Abdullah (1882–1951), king of Jordan (1946–51), son of Hussein. In 1921, after aiding Britain in World War I, he became emir of Trans-Jordan. He lost control of Hejaz to Ibn Saud. In World War II he resisted the Axis. He fought Israel, annexed land, and signed an armistice (1949). He was assassinated in Jerusalem, and Talal ascended the throne.

Abel, in Genesis, second son of Adam and Eve, killed by his brother Cain.

Abelard, Peter (1079–1142), French philosopher, regarded as the founder of the University of Paris. In *Sic et Non (Yes and No)* he proposed reconciling discrepancies among Christian authorities through dialectic. His opponents advocated faith above logic and twice had him condemned as a heretic. He is best known for his tragic love affair with Héloise, for which he was attacked and emasculated. He became a monk; Héloise entered a convent.

Aberdeen, town of Aberdeenshire, in NE Scotland: university and cathedral city: important docks and fish market; main port for North Sea petroleum developments. Industries: papermaking, shipbuilding, engineering, textiles. Pop. 182,006.

Aberdeen Angus, jet black breed of beef cattle originally developed in Scotland. Small and naturally hornless, they yield excellent meat. Not as common as Shorthorn or Hereford breeds, they are gaining in popularity in the United States, Canada, New Zealand, and Argentina. *See also* Beef Cattle, Cattle.

Abernathy, Ralph (David) (1926–), US clergyman and civil rights leader, b. Linden, Ala. He succeeded Dr. Martin Luther King, Jr., as leader of the Southern Christian Leadership Conference upon King's assassination (1968) and served for more than a decade, continuing to promote the nonviolent civil rights movement that King initiated. He organized the Montgomery bus boycott (1955) and the Poor People's March on Washington (1968). Abernathy was also chairman of the Atlanta branch of Operation Breadbasket, the economic arm of the SCLC. *See also* Southern Christian Leadership Conference.

Aberration, any of various defects in lens and mirror images arising when light is not incident at or near the center of the system. Spherical aberration occurs when rays from the object falling on the periphery of a lens or mirror are not brought to the same focal point as rays at the center; the image is thus blurred. Chromatic aberration occurs in lens images due to the different colors of the dispersed light being brought to different focal points; the image is thus falsely colored.

Aberration of Light, apparent slight change of position of a celestial object, such as a star, due to the effect of the orbital motion around the sun of the earth, and thus an observer, on the direction of arrival of the light. A telescope must be inclined by an angle of up to about 20″ to accommodate this.

Abidjan, capital city of the Ivory Coast, on the Ebrie Lagoon; popular tourist resort; site of the University of Abidjan (1963) and the Museum of the Ivory Coast; major center of communication, transportation, administration, commerce. Industries: soap, lumber, textiles, chemicals, beer. Pop. 850,000.

Abigail, two biblical figures, one being the wife of sheep and goat owner Nabal. She persuaded David not to retaliate for Nabal's refusal to give him a share of wool. She later became David's wife. The other was step sister of David, wife of Jether, and mother of Amasa.

Abilene, city in NW central Texas, 152mi (246km) WSW of Fort Worth; seat of Taylor co. Settled as a railway junction, it was named after Abilene, Kansas, because of the cattle driven there; site of Hardin-Simmons University (1891), Abilene Christian College (1906), and McMurry College (1923). Industries: agriculture, ranching, oil refining. Founded 1881; inc. 1882. Pop. (1980) 98,315.

Abington School District v. Schempp (1963), US Supreme Court case that ruled unconstitutional a law requiring bible readings in public schools, citing First Amendment restriction on laws "respecting an establishment of religion."

Ablation, in aerospace technology, the wearing away of the outer surface of a material by flaking, chipping, melting, or vaporization. Nose cones and leading edges of re-entry capsules and missiles are equipped with ablating material to remove excess heat. Good ablating materials such as quartz and teflon have low thermal conductivity, high melting points, high specific heat, and high heats of vaporization and fusion; they often create an insulating layer of vapor to protect the spacecraft further.

Ablation, in geology, a measure of glacial loss through melting, evaporation, wind erosion, or calving (formation of icebergs). Sometimes used in geomorphology

Aardvark

Aberdeen Angus

Abruzzi, Italy

to mean the loss of surface or rock by wind or water action.

Abnaki, or **Wabanaki,** tribe of Algonkian-speaking North American Indians of the Eastern Woodlands group. They inhabited NE New England, to which they apparently fled as refugees from English colonists. Later most of them went to New Brunswick, Canada, where their descendents live today. In history they were famous as the people who inhabited the fabled Norumbega.

Abnormal Psychology, division of psychology concerned with behavior disorders, eg, psychotic disorders such as schizophrenia, psychoneurotic problems such as phobias, personality disorders, and problems caused by brain damage or mental retardation. Unlike clinical psychology and psychiatry, abnormal psychology focuses on basic theory rather than on treatment. *See also* Clinical Psychology; Psychiatry.

Abolitionism, 19th-century movement to end slavery in the United States. Although antislavery sentiment went back as far as the 1690s, when the Quakers began speaking out against it, the first antislavery society was not founded until 1775. Many other such societies were established during the Revolutionary War. The efforts of Thomas Jefferson resulted in the outlawing of slavery in the Northwest Territory (1787). The United States Constitution (1788) prohibited the slave trade. Several states passed legislation abolishing slavery in the 1780s. In 1808 the further importation of slaves was prohibited by Congress. In 1817 the American Colonization Society was formed to transport free blacks to a colony in Africa. This solution was denounced by Benjamin Lundy, William Lloyd Garrison and other influential abolitionists of this period. The Missouri Compromise (1820) prohibited new slave states above the 36°30′ north latitude. In 1833 the American Anti-Slavery Society was formed in Philadelphia. Active in this group were Arthur and Lewis Tappan, Theodore Dwight Weld and James G. Birney. The Underground Railroad, with such conductors as Harriet Tubman, helped fugitive slaves reach freedom. From the 1840s ex-slave Frederick Douglass was an abolitionist speaker. Efforts to elect abolitionist Birney president, as candidate of the Liberty party (1840, 1844), failed, as did the Free Soil party with former Pres. Martin Van Buren as candidate (1848). Sectional disputes intensified, and the Compromise of 1850 attempted to appease both North and South. Harriet Beecher Stowe's *Uncle Tom's Cabin* (1852) increased antislavery sentiment. During the 1850s the abolitionists concentrated on helping fugitive slaves. The Emancipation Proclamation (1863) weakened slavery, but it was not ended until the 13th Amendment to the US Constitution (1865). *See also* Garrison, William Lloyd; Missouri Compromise.

Abominable Snowman, legendary creature of the Himalayas. The Sherpa natives describe it as longhaired, able to walk erect, with apelike facial features. Several expeditions have attempted to find concrete evidence for the Yeti, as he is called by the Sherpas, but all have failed.

Abortion, the termination of a pregnancy before the fetus is viable. An abortion, in which the fetus is expelled from the womb, can be either spontaneous or induced and occurs before the 28th week following conception and usually during the first twelve weeks. A spontaneous abortion, often called a miscarriage, can result from a number of factors including disease and injury. Induced abortion procedures include vacuum suction, dilation and curettage, hysterotomy, and saline injection. Many religions have condemned in-

duced abortion but it became illegal in practice only in the 19th century. Efforts to legalize abortion have increased in response to the rapid expansion of world population, pressure from women's rights movements, and a high maternal death rate from illegal abortions. Many states of the United States liberalized their laws and, in 1973, the U.S. Supreme Court decision, *Roe v. Wade,* restricted states' rights regarding the prohibition of abortion, but opponents continue to press for prohibition by constitutional amendment.

Abraham, in the Bible, son of Terah and founder of Jewish nation. He was commanded by God to move to Canaan and transmit God's blessing to all people of the earth. Childless, his wife Sarah gave him her maid Hagar who bore Ishmael. A rivalry grew between the two women when Sarah bore Isaac several years later.

Abraham, Plains of, located in Quebec City, Canada, the site of the decisive battle of the French and Indian War. After the battle in 1759, during which generals Wolfe and Montcalm, the British and French commanders, were slain, the way was clear for British dominance in E Canada.

Abrasion, in geology, mechanical wearing down of rock surface by wind, water, glacial movements, tides, or currents. *See also* Erosion.

Abrasives, hard and rough substances used in grinding and polishing objects by abrading their surfaces. Some abrasives are used as fine powders, others in larger fragments with sharp, cutting edges. Most natural abrasives are minerals, eg diamond, garnet, emery, corundum, pumice, flint, and quartz. Crushed steel and powdered glass are also used. Synthetic abrasives include silicon carbide, aluminum oxide, and synthetic diamonds.

Abruzzi, mountainous region in central Italy, on the Adriatic Sea; self-governing since 1965; capital is Aquila; comprised of the provinces of Chieti, Pescara, Teramo, and Aquila. Industries: textiles, food processing, agriculture, livestock. Pop. 1,552,556.

Absalom, several biblical figures, most notably the third son of David. He murdered his brother Ammon for the rape of their sister. Plotting to seize the throne that would soon be Solomon's, he was killed by David's general, Joab. Another was the father of Matthias and Jonathan.

Abscissa, distance of a point from the y axis in a Cartesian coordinate system; the x coordinate when the position of a point is expressed as the ordered pair (x,y).

Absolute Zero, the temperature at which all parts of a system are at the lowest energy permitted by the laws of quantum mechanics. At this temperature ($-273°C$) the entropy of the system is also zero, although the total energy may be non-zero. The system has only one energy state available to it, and if isolated remains in that state forever.

Absolution, in religion, a formal act by a member of the clergy through which sins are forgiven, as in the sacrament of penance. The authority is derived from God, and grace is given to those qualified. It may be received following a private confession or a public ceremony.

Absolutism, government with unlimited power vested in one individual or group. First used to describe 18th-century European monarchies that claimed divine right to power. *See also* Divine Right.

Absorbent, substance with the power to absorb large quantities of other substances. Absorbents are usually porous materials: examples are activated charcoal and zeolites. They have many uses, including separating, purifying, decolorizing, and deodorizing.

Abstract Art, loosely used term commonly applied to 20th-century art styles. It has been used to cover two contrary schools. The first is the reduction or abstraction of natural forms to simpler, stylized ones, as in the works of Paul Klee, Paul Cézanne, and Jean Louis Forain. The second is the construction from non-representational basic forms of art objects that are intended to be appreciated for what they are, and not as representations. It can be subdivided into romantic and organic artists, including Wassily Kandinski, Joan Miró, Jean Arp, and Franz Kline, and classical and geometric artists, including Kazimir Malevich, Piet Mondrian, and Ben Nicholson. *See also* Abstract Expressionism.

Abstract Expressionism, US art movement most active in the late 1940s and early 1950s. It had worldwide acclaim and imitation. The paintings were generally large, abstract (with some figurative elements), asymmetrical in composition, with loose painterly brushwork and dramatic coloring. The artists laid great stress on the process of painting, some regarding it as a ritual. Stressing spontaneity and free expression, they revolted against prescribed technical procedures, traditional aesthetic canons, and the idea of a finished art product. They included Willem de Kooning, Jackson Pollock, Mark Rothko, and Robert Motherwell.

Abu Bakr (573–634), first Muslim caliph, successor of Mohammed. His daughter, Aisha, married Mohammed, with whom he went on the Hegira. The Orthodox chiefs secured him as caliph (632). He subjugated the hostile tribes of Arabia with the help of Gen. Khalid ibn-al-Walid. He united the Arabian peninsula and urged conquests in Iraq, Persia, and Syria. He was instrumental in extending Islam as a world religion. In 634 Omar succeeded him.

Abu Dhabi, sheikdom on S coast of Persian Gulf; capital is Abu Dhabi. Founded by the Al Bu Falah family in the 18th century; signed a peace treaty with Great Britain 1820 and made a British protectorate 1892; became a member of the independent federation United Arab Emirates when it was formed in 1971. Main industry is oil, discovered 1958. Area: 26,000sq mi (67,340sq km). Pop. 235,662. *See also* United Arab Emirates.

Abu-Simbel, (Ipsambul or Abu Sunbul), village in S Egypt on the Nile River; site of two famous temples built by Ramesses II in the 13th century BC. In the early 1960s, the United Nations funded a project to cut up the huge statues of Ramesses II and the temples and move them inland, safe from the rising waters caused by the construction of the Aswan High Dam.

Abydos, ruined ancient city of Egypt, 50mi (80.5km) NW of Thebes; site of temples built from 1st to 25th dynasty. One of the temples contains tablets listing the names of ancient Egyptian rulers, which has aided in reconstructing the succession of Egyptian pharaohs. A famous temple of Osiris was built here by Ramesses II on top of another temple 2,000 years older.

Abydos, ancient city in Phrygia, Asia Minor, opposite Sestos at the narrowest point of the Dardanelles. Near here Xerxes I built a bridge of boats (480 BC), the Athenian fleet defeated the Spartan (411 BC), and Maslamah crossed his army (716–17).

Abyssal Animals, animals living at deepest ocean depths in low temperatures, darkness, and high pressure. They include crustaceans, fish, jellyfish, and squid. Adaptations for their environment include extended fins to detect food and warn of predators and expansible mouths, gullets, and stomachs to eat food as large as themselves. Often fluorescent and sometimes blind, they scavenge for fragments sinking from upper levels.

Abyssal Zone, the division of the ocean that begins at about the 2000-m (6,600-ft) depth and includes the rest of the deep ocean. The water temperature ranges from 41° to 30°F (5° to −1°C). The zone has no light so there are no seasons and no plants, but there are many forms of life like glass sponges, sea lilies, lamp shells, and grenadiers. The bottom is covered by deposits of biogenic oozes and non-biogenic sediments (red clays).

Abyssinian Cat, exotic, short-haired domestic cat breed, probably developed from the Kaffir cat. It has a wedge-shaped head; green, gold or hazel almond-shaped eyes; broad-based pointed ears; and a long, tapered tail. Its ruddy brown or brick colored coat has black-tipped hairs. The Red variety lacks black pigment. *See also* Kaffir Cat.

Acacia, evergreen shrubs and trees native to Australia and widely distributed in tropical or subtropical regions. They have small leaves and yellow or white flowers. Some species have thorns. Grown mainly as ornamentals, some are grown for gum arabic or other gums used in tanning, soap, and medicine. Height: 4–60ft (1.2–18m). Family Leguminosae; genus *Acacia.*

Académie Française, French literary academy. Established by Cardinal Richelieu in 1634, the Académie Française remains an influential institution. Its aim is to identify writing of literary distinction and to uphold the purity of the national language. Most of the great French writers have in the past belonged to the Académie.

Acadia, early term for what is now the Maritime Provinces of E Canada and the coastal region of N Maine. The area was first settled with Europeans in 1604 by Sieur De Monts. Early settlements such as Port Royal were attacked by British and colonial American forces over the issues of the fur trade and sea routes. In 1755 many of the French settlers were deported for refusing a loyalty oath to Britain. British dominance was complete by 1763, and the area developed profitable fishing and farming industries.

Acanthocephala, phylum of spiny-headed parasitic worms once thought to be Nematodes. They are identified by a retractible spiny proboscis and an elongated, cylindrical body. The young are parasitic in insects and the adults in vertebrates, attaching themselves to the intestinal lining. Length: about 1ft (30.5cm). Species include *Echinorhyncus.*

Acanthus, thistlelike, perennial plant found in N South America, Africa, Mediterranean region, India, and Malaya. It has lobed leaves often spiny, and white or colored flower spikes. The 20 species include bear's breeches *(Acanthus mollis),* with large, oval leaves and rose, white, or bronze flower spikes. Other species include *Justicia americana,* or water willow, with slender, willowlike leaves and pale violet or purple and white flower clusters. *A. spinosis,* with curled leaves, is the pattern for the ornamentation on the capital of the Corinthian column.

Acapulco, city in S Mexico, 190mi (306km) SSW of Mexico City, on the Pacific coast; winter resort noted for beautiful scenery, deep-sea fishing, lavish hotels, entertainment. It was an important port for 250 years linking Spain and the Philippines as "Manila Galleons" made annual trips to and from Manila. Coconuts and bananas are grown in area. Founded 1550 by Spanish. Pop. 456,700.

Acceleration, rate of change of velocity. *Average* acceleration $\bar{\mathbf{a}}$ of a body changing from velocity $\mathbf{v}_1$ to $\mathbf{v}_2$ in time t is $(\mathbf{v}_2 - \mathbf{v}_1)/t$. *Instantaneous* acceleration $\mathbf{a}$ is the value approached by $\bar{\mathbf{a}}$ as t becomes small. *See also* Velocity.

Accelerator, in economics, a more sophisticated form of the multiplier. According to this concept, as incomes are created and GNP levels increase, businessmen become more optimistic about the future and tend to increase their investment in new plant and equipment as well as planned inventory changes. This in turn further stimulates the increasing income levels, which results in an even higher GNP. *See also* Multiplier.

Accelerator, Electrostatic, type of particle accelerator in which a constant high voltage is applied between a pair of electrodes in an evacuated tube. Charged particles are accelerated in the electric field between the electrodes, gaining an energy eV, where e is the electron charge and V the applied voltage. The Van de Graaff generator (developed 1929) and the Cockcroft-Walton generator (1932) can be used as high-voltage sources. The energy of heavy ions can be doubled if two accelerators are used in tandem: negative ions are accelerated then stripped of some electrons; the resulting positive ions are accelerated by the second machine. *See also* Accelerators, Particle.

Accelerator, Field, type of particle accelerator in which charged particles are accelerated by use of alternating electric fields in an evacuated chamber. The particles must enter the high-frequency field as it begins increasing (negative particles) or decreasing (positive particles) for maximum energy increase. The path of the particles may be straight, as in linear accelerators, or curved, as in the cyclotron, synchrotron, and betatron. With a circular path the particles make many revolutions; the long path length allows greater energy increase. Magnetic fields are used to focus the particles into a narrow stable beam and to maintain the required curvature of the beam. As the particle velocity rises a relativistic increase in mass occurs. This causes beam instability in the cyclotron, limiting the final energy, but has been overcome in the high-energy synchrotron, betatron, and synchrocyclotron.

Accelerator, Particle, device in which charged elementary particles, such as electrons or protons, are accelerated to very high velocities and thus acquire very high energies. Accelerators have an evacuated chamber in which the particles move, acceleration being provided by motion in electric and magnetic fields. Electrostatic devices are relatively simple, having electrodes operating at a very high potential difference. In field accelerators an electric field produces the acceleration, the particles being kept in a stable narrow beam by magnetic fields. Accelerators are used in cancer treatment, in the production of radioactive isotopes for medicine, research, and technology, in sterilizing food, and so on. Very large expensive high-energy accelerators are used in nuclear physics to produce other particles, such as mesons, neutrinos, and antiparticles, by directing the accelerated beams at stationary targets or by causing two similar energetic beams to collide. The highest energies—hundreds of billions of electron volts (GeV)—are obtained with proton synchrotrons. Study of the reactions and decay processes of these particles provides information on nuclear forces and the basic nature of matter. *See also* Accelerator, Electrostatic; Accelerator, Field.

Accelerometer, a device to measure acceleration. A simple accelerometer is a plumb bob attached to the accelerating object—its angle with the vertical indicates the magnitude of the acceleration. A more sophisticated version, such as is used in ballistic missiles, is an electromechanical device that translates forces of acceleration into electrical current.

Acclimatization, adjustment of an organism to a new environment, climate or circumstances. It involves a gradual, natural change permitting an organism to exploit new regions. Plant and animal species acclimatize differently.

Accordion, musical instrument with organlike tone produced by air from a bellows vibrating reeds. The melody is played on a piano-type keyboard, with chordal accompaniment controlled by buttons. Invented (1822) by Friedrich Buschmann in Germany, the accordion is used in folk music of America, central Europe, and eastern Europe.

Accounting, profession whose objective is to provide relevant financial information in a usable form in order that such groups as management, governmental units, and the investing public can make rational decisions.

Accra, capital city of Ghana, W Africa, on the Gulf of Guinea. Est. 17th century, around three fortresses: James Fort (British), Crèvecoeur (Dutch), and Christiansburg Castle (Danish); taken by British in the 19th century; made capital of the Gold Coast Colony 1876; transportation and educational center; site of University of Ghana (1948) and the Defense Commission of the Organization of African Unity. Industries: textiles, food products, shoes, chemicals. Pop. 700,000.

Accretion, in geology, the building up of beaches and shorelines. Wave action and currents may add to some coastlines by transporting material from erosion zones. Deltas built up by river systems are accreted land created by the deposition of suspended materials.

Acculturation, that process of cultural change that occurs when one society meets another. There are two main types of acculturation. Free acculturation results from friendly interchange, and the acceptance of cultural change on the part of the changed society. Directed acculturation occurs when a society, through domination, forces another to change.

Acestes, in Vergil's *Aeneid,* a king of Sicily. Son of a Sicilian river god, Crimisius, and a Trojan woman, Segesta, he was the mythical founder of the city of Segesta. Aeneas was entertained by Acestes on his way to Italy and left many Trojans with him.

Acetaldehyde, colorless volatile flammable liquid (formula CH_3CHO) made by the partial oxidation of ethanol or catalytic oxidation of ethylene. Properties: sp. gr. 0.783; melt. pt. −185.8°F (−121°C); boil. pt. 69.44°F (20.8°C). *See also* Aldehyde.

Acetaminophen, ingredient used as a substitute for or in combination with aspirin in many over-the-counter drugs. It has fever-reducing and pain-killing properties.

Acetate, salt or ester of acetic acid; that is, a compound containing the ion CH_3COO^- or the group CH_3COO^-. Cellulose acetate is a material made by the action of acetic anhydride on cellulose. It is used in synthetic acetate fibers, in lacquers, and in acetate film.

Acetic Acid, colorless corrosive low-melting solid (formula CH_3COOH) made by the oxidation of ethanol, either by catalysis or by the action of bacteria. It is the active ingredient in vinegar, and has many uses in the organic chemicals industry. Properties: sp. gr. 1.049; melt. pt. 61.89°F (16.604°C); boil. pt. 244.4°F (117.9°C). *See also* Carboxylic Acid.

Acetone, colorless flammable sweet-smelling liquid (formula CH_3COCH_3) made by oxidizing isopropyl alcohol. It is a basic raw material for the manufacture of many organic chemicals and a widely used solvent. Properties: sp. gr. 0.79; melt. pt. −139.63°F (−95.35 °C); boil pt. 133.16°F (56.2°C).

Acetylcholine, chemical compound released by certain nerve cells that serves as a transmitter in nerve conduction. Following stimulation of a nerve cell, acetylcholine is released at the point of contact (synapse) between it and the cell it innervates, causing that effector cell to act; such as stimulation of muscle contraction, or stimulating another nerve cell to conduct.

Acetyl Coenzyme A (Co A), acetyl derivative of coenzyme A, a sulfur-containing nucleotide, that is a precursor in the metabolism of fatty acids, carbohydrates, and proteins, being an important intermediate in the Krebs' cycle. Coenzyme A functions as a carrier of the 2-carbon acetyl group, which is attached to the sulfur group.

Acetylene, colorless flammable gaseous hydrocarbon (formula HC:CH), made by the action of water on calcium carbide or by breakdown of other hydrocarbons. It is used in high-temperature oxyacetylene cutting flames, and as a raw material for making some organic chemicals. Properties: melt. pt. −113.44°F (−80.8°C).

Achaean League, two confederations of Greek city-states formed in the area of the Peloponnesus called Achaea. The first, founded sometime in the 5th century BC for mutual protection against pirates, lasted through the 4th century BC. The second, founded in 280 BC to drive out the Macedonians, ended up warring with Sparta, siding with Rome in 198 BC. In 146 BC Rome subjugated and dissolved the league.

Achaemenids (*c.* 500–331 BC), Persian dynasty, descendants of Achaemenes who ruled in the province of Pars in SW Iran. The Greeks corrupted "Parsa" to "Persis" and used it for the whole kingdom. The rulers included Cyrus the Great, Cambyses, Smerdis, Darius I, Xerxes I, Artaxerxes I, Xerxes II, Sogdianus, Darius II, Artaxerxes II, Artaxerxes III, Arses, and Darius III, who was murdered fleeing from Alexander the Great (331 BC).

Achebe, Chinua (1930–), Nigerian writer. His novels deal primarily with a search for identity in modern Africa and with the effect of change on people's lives. *Things Fall Apart* (1958) depicts life in an African village before and after the arrival of missionaries.

Achernar, or **Alpha Eridani,** bluish-white main-sequence star in the constellation Eridanus. Characteristics: apparent mag. +0.47; absolute mag. −1.6; spectral type B5; distance 75 light-years.

Acheron, in Greek mythology, a river of the underworld. One of five rivers that surrounded Hades, the realm of Pluto. Charon carried the souls of the dead across either the Acheron or the Styx.

Dean Acheson

Acorn worm

Acropolis

Acheson, Dean (1893–1971), US statesman, b. Middletown, Conn. After serving as assistant secretary of state (1941–45) and undersecretary (1945–47), he became secretary of state (1949–53) under President Truman. Strongly anti-communist, he helped develop such postwar policies as the Marshall Plan, the Truman Doctrine, and North Atlantic Treaty Organization (1949). He encouraged support for Nationalist China and UN involvement in Korea. His advice was sought by Presidents Kennedy, Johnson and Nixon. He wrote *Present at the Creation* (1969), which won a Pulitzer Prize (1970).

Achilles, son of Peleus and Thetis; hero of Homer's *Iliad.* Achilles was the bravest and the greatest Greek hero of the Trojan war. Legend held him invulnerable from weapons because he had been dipped in the River Styx at birth, save for one heel by which he was held. Achilles chose to win glory and die young at Troy. During the fighting an arrow shot by Paris struck his heel, slaying him.

Achilles' Tendon, strong elastic band of connective tissue joining bone to muscle that connects the gastrocnemius muscle of the calf of the leg to the heel bone, or calcaneus.

Acid, chemical compound containing hydrogen that can be replaced by a metal or other positive ion to form a salt. Acids dissociate in water to yield hydrogen ions (H^+): the solutions are corrosive, have a sharp taste, and give a red color to litmus indicator. Strong acids, such as hydrochloric acid (HCL), are fully dissociated into ions; weak acids, such as acetic acid (CH_3COOH), are partially dissociated. *See also* Base.

Acid Number, or value, number of milligrams of potassium hydroxide necessary to neutralize the free fatty acids in one gram of a specified substance. The acid number is used to measure the fatty acid content of fats, oils, etc.

Acidosis, abnormal condition in which the acid-base balance of the blood is upset, with the blood becoming too acidic (pH below 7). May be caused by kidney malfunction, diabetes, or other diseases. Symptoms include weakness and malaise.

Acid Rain, rain that is highly acidic because of sulfur oxides, nitrogen oxides, and other air pollutants dissolved in it. Normal rain is slightly acidic, with a pH of 6. (The pH scale ranges from 1 for extremely acidic to 14 for extremely basic or alkaline, with 7 being neutral.) Acid rain may have a pH value as low as 2.8. Acid rain can severely damage both plant and animal life. Certain lakes, for example, have lost all fish and plant life because of acid rain.

ACLU. *See* American Civil Liberties Union.

Acmeism, movement in Russian poetry in the 1910s and 1920s led by N.S. Gumilev and S.M. Gorodetsky. The Acmeists, writing in a clear, precise style, rejected the mysticism and impressionism of the Symbolist movement. Acmeism produced several important poets, including Osip Mandelstam and Anna Akhmatova.

Acne, inflammatory disease of the sebaceous, or oil-producing, glands of the skin, probably caused by a hormonal imbalance and resulting in skin lesions ranging from mild blackheads and papules to infected cysts. It is extremely common at puberty, usually disappearing by 18, but sometimes persisting or periodically recurring in middle age, when a related dis-

order—acne rosacea—characterized by red blotchy (flushlike) acnelike lesions may occur.

Acoma, Queres-speaking tribe of Pueblo Indians inhabiting a rock mesa 357ft (109m) high in Valencia, N.M.; the town name is Ako. First mentioned by Fray Marcos de Niza in 1539 as Acus, the town was entered by Coronado the following year. Next to Oraibi, it is regarded as the oldest continuously inhabited town in the United States. The tribe, noted for fine pottery, numbers approximately 2,000.

Aconcagua, mountain in W Argentina, in the Andes Mountains on Chilean border, 70mi (112km) WNW of Mendoza; highest peak in Western Hemisphere, 22,834ft (6,959m); first climbed by members of Fitzgerald expedition 1897.

Aconite, a flowering plant of the genus *Aconitum,* family Ranunculaceae, also called monkshood, friar's cap and wolfsbane. Its roots provide the alkaloid aconitine, which is used in modern times for medical purposes; in ancient times it was used as poison.

Acorn Worm, solitary, wormlike, marine animal found worldwide to depths of 10,000ft (3000m). The head-end of the burrowing or foraging adult has a proboscis and collar. Food is filtered from seawater entering the mouth and leaving through gill slits. Length: .75in–7.5ft (2cm–2.3m). A common genus is *Balanoglossus;* there are 100 species. Class Enteropneusta.

Acoustic Waves. *See* Sound.

Acre (Akko), seaport town in N Israel, on Bay of Acre, 10mi (16km) N of Haifa; Phoenician city captured by Arabs AD 638; ruled at different times by Egypt, Assyria, Persia, and Macedonia; from 1200–1291, it grew and prospered as center of Christian power. It was taken by British 1918; became part of Israel 1948; is center of Bahai religion. Industries: fishing, steel rolling. Pop. 33,900.

Acromegaly, condition in which there is an overproduction of pituitary growth hormones in an adult, causing enlarged hands, feet, and facial features.Also known as Marie's syndrome, it is often caused by a pituitary tumor. Treatment of the tumor arrests continued abnormal growth of the extremities.

Acrophobia, irrational fear of high places, usually accompanied by obsessional thoughts of falling or jumping. Persons suffering from acrophobia often feel dizzy and nauseated (at times, nearly paralyzed) when they look down from a high place.

Acropolis, area in ancient Greek communities situated on the highest topographical point and used as the location of the chief religious and municipal buildings. The hilltop site was regarded as the home of the gods. The Acropolis of Athens was the district atop the rocky hill near the center of the city, commanding a view of the bay and Aegean Sea at Piraeus. Of the original structures that survive, the most significant are the Propylaea, gateway to the Acropolis; the Parthenon, chief shrine to Athena; the Erechtheum, a shrine to agricultural deities; and the small Temple of Athena Nike. Most of the architecture and sculpture was completed at the time of Cimon and Pericles, and much of it still stands, despite invasion, erosion, and removal of treasures to museums. *See also* Elgin Marbles, Erechtheum Carvings, Parthenon.

Acrylic, one of a group of synthetic, short-chain unsaturated carboxylic acid derivatives comprising many plastics and thermoplastic resins. Variations in rea-

gents and processes of formation yield either hard and transparent, or soft and resilient products. Its transparency, toughness, and dimensional stability make it useful for molded structural parts, jewelry, adhesives, coating compounds, and textile fibers.

Acrylic-Resin Paint, a synthetic plastic type of paint, in wide use since the 1960s. It dries rapidly and serves as a vehicle for any kind of pigment. It is capable of the transparent brilliance of water colors as well as the density of oil paints and stands up well under heat and humidity.

ACTH. *See* Adrenocorticotropic Hormone.

Actin, fibrillar protein involved in cellular contractile processes. It is most prevalent in muscle cells, where it reacts with myosin to form actomyosin. *See also* Actomyosin.

Acting, representing a character in a performance on stage or before cameras. In ancient Greece acting had to be highly stylized because plays were performed in vast outdoor arenas. The actors (all male) wore platform sandals and large masks. The Romans held acting in low esteem; slaves performed farces. The tragedies of Seneca were written to be read aloud, not performed. Acting all but disappeared in Western Europe in the early Christian era. The first signs of revival were the crude religious pageants of the Middle Ages and the somewhat later trade guild pageants. The actors were all amateurs, members of the church or guild. Italy produced the first modern professional acting in the Commedia dell' arte, in which the players improvised situations based on standard plot outlines. Shakespeare's actors were professionals. Their style of acting was broad and exaggerated. During the Restoration period in England a more naturalistic style of acting evolved. Female roles were now played by women. The greatest impact on 20th-century acting was from the theories of the Russian director Konstantin Stanislavski. He encouraged the actor's total psychological identification with the character. The Actors' Studio, New York City, applied and expanded upon Stanislavski's theories in developing the method school of acting. Film and TV made new and different demands on actors, but offered new areas in which to work.

Actinide Elements, group of radioactive elements with atomic numbers from 89 to 103; actinium (89), thorium, protactinium, uranium, neptunium, plutonium, americium, curium, berkelium, californium, einsteinium, fermium, mendelevium, nobelium, and lawrencium (103). Each element is analogous to the corresponding lanthanide element (eg thorium is a close analogue of cerium). The most important member of the group is uranium, because of its use as a nuclear fuel; the transuranic elements (neptunium to lawrencium) do not occur in nature and only plutonium, because of its use in nuclear weapons, has any importance.

Actinium, radioactive metallic element (Symbol Ac) of the actinide group, discovered first (1899) by André Debierne. It is found associated with uranium ores. Ac^{227}, a decay product of U^{235}, is a beta emitter. Properties: at. no. 89; sp. gr. 10.07 (calc.); melt. pt. 1922°F (1050°C); boil. pt. 5792°F(3200°C): most stable isotope Ac^{227} (half-life 21.6 yr). *See also* Actinide Elements.

Actinomycosis, fungus (*Actinomyces israelii*) infection, more common in men. Produces multiple, draining, pus-filled abscesses and sinus tracts, most often in the neck and face region, causing a "lumpy jaw" appearance, but also affecting other parts of the body.

Treatment consists of draining abscesses and administering antimicrobial agents.

Actium, Battle of (31 BC), naval clash in which the fleet of Octavian, commanded by Agrippa, defeated the fleets of Mark Antony and Cleopatra. Antony deserted his forces, and Octavian captured the majority of his ships. Antony's army surrendered a week later, making Octavian sole ruler of the Roman Empire.

Act of Congress, bill or resolution passed into law by both the US Senate and House of Representatives.

Act of Union (1841), legislation uniting French-speaking Lower Canada and English-speaking Upper Canada as proposed by Lord Durham. It gave equal representation to each sector. The subsequent council to Lord Sydenham, the governor, included both conservative and reform elements and established a parliament for the province that raised the issue of responsible self-government as opposed to British dominance. *See also* Lower Canada; Upper Canada.

Actomyosin, the complex of the proteins actin and myosin. This forms the basic unit of contraction in muscle cells.

Acton, John Emerich Edward Dalberg, 1st Baron (1834–1902), English historian, b. Italy. One of the most influential historians in Europe during the late 18th century, he never completed a book. While teaching at Cambridge University (1895–1902), however, he planned the *Cambridge Modern History* and his lectures and essays were collected in various volumes after his death. He was a Roman Catholic who was a strong liberal in religion and politics and an avid supporter of Liberal Prime Minister William Gladstone. Acton was a member of the House of Commons (1859–65) and received a peerage through Gladstone in 1869.

Acts of the Apostles, book of the New Testament, claims the same author as the Gospel of Luke. It was written for a believing community. Many see it written around 85 AD as a sequel. It covers the early church from Christ's resurrection through Paul's missionary work.

Acupuncture, Chinese medical treatment in which long, thin needles are inserted into specific points on the body to relieve pain, to alleviate physical disorders, and to provide anesthesia during surgery. Acupuncture was first described in the *Nei-ching* (c.2700 BC) and is based on the *yin-yang* theory of balances and the belief that the acupuncture points on the body are connected with the various organs of the body. Illness is an imbalance; treatment with acupuncture transmits impulses to the brain and then to the desired organ, restoring balance and health. The relationship of these points and the actual mechanism of acupuncture is not accounted for by current knowledge of nerve anatomy and physiology. However, Chinese doctors claim a 90% effectiveness rate for the method as well as safety and few side effects. Acupuncture began to be used in the West in the 1950s.

Adad, also **Hadad,** in Babylonian mythology, the rain god, bringer of storms, giver of waters, and protector of the harvest. In his role of war god he became the destroyer whose whirlwinds, thunderbolts, and droughts brought havoc to the enemy. In the Babylonian myth of the flood Adad appears as the storm god. With Sin and Shamash, he formed a powerful triangle of the pantheon.

Adalbert, Saint (956?–997), first bishop of Prague. He was elected bishop in 983 and came into increasing conflict with the ruling powers of Bohemia over what he saw as an insincere attitude toward the church. In 994 he left to become a missionary in Prussia, where he was murdered.

Adam, in the Bible, first man and progenitor of all mankind, created by God in his own image. He and his wife, Eve, were cast out of the Garden of Eden for sinning. They had three sons, Cain, Abel, and Seth.

Adam, Robert (1728–92), Scottish architect and designer. He developed a refined neoclassical style that was highly influential in England and abroad. He designed interiors and furniture to harmonize with the exterior of his buildings. A notable example of his work is Luton Hoo mansion, Bedfordshire, England (1768–75).

Adams, Abigail (1744–1818), Wife of Pres. John Adams and mother of Pres. John Quincy Adams, b. Abigail Smith at Weymouth, Mass. Very active in her husband's political career, her many letters have since become an important source for the history of US society. She strongly supported equal education for women and spoke out frequently against slavery.

Adams, Ansel (1902–84), US photographer, b. San Francisco. Concentrating on the scenic grandeur of the Western United States, Adams has produced magnificent prints that are widely exhibited and reproduced. A cofounder of the *f*/64 group, he has been instrumental in forming museum and university photographic departments and is a celebrated teacher. He wrote the *Basic Photo-Books* series of technical manuals (1968). His most recent books, *Ansel Adams, Images 1923–1974* (1975) and *The Portfolios of Ansel Adams* (1977) are overall views of his life's work. A 1979 exhibit at the Museum of Modern Art marked a 50-year career.

Adams, Henry (Brooks) (1838–1918), US author, b. Boston. A direct descendant of Presidents John Adams and John Quincy Adams, he was secretary to his father, Charles Francis Adams, Sr., first (1860–61) while the latter was in Congress and then (1861–68) when he was US minister to Britain. Returning to the United States, he taught history at Harvard University (1870–77). He resigned his teaching position and settled in Washington, D.C., devoting himself to writing. His works include the muckraking *Chapters of Erie* (articles written earlier with his brother Charles Francis Adams, Jr., and published in book form in 1886); *Democracy* (1880) and *Esther* (1884), topical novels; the monumental *History of the United States Under the Jefferson and Adams Administrations* (9 vols., 1889–91); *Mont-Saint-Michel and Chartres* (privately printed 1904, published 1913), reflections on medieval culture; *The Education of Henry Adams* (privately printed 1906, published 1918), a brilliant autobiographical work; and *The Degradation of the Democratic Dogma* (essays written earlier and published posthumously in 1919 by his brother Brooks Adams). His elegant but pessimistic theories of history and his ironic view of himself influenced writers of the 1920s.

Adams, John (1735–1826), 2nd President of the United States, b. Braintree (now Quincy), Mass., graduate, Harvard, 1755. In 1764, he married Abigail Smith; they had five children, one of whom was John Quincy Adams. Adams practiced law in Braintree and Boston. He opposed the Stamp Act and became involved in anti-British politics, partly through the influence of his more radical cousin, Samuel Adams. After 1774, he was a member of the First and Second Continental Congresses, where he distinguished himself as a moderate revolutionist. He helped Thomas Jefferson draft the Declaration of Independence and sponsored George Washington as commander of the armed forces.

In 1777 he was sent as commissioner to France and spent most of the next decade in Europe. He was in France and the Netherlands during the Revolution and was one of the drafters of the Treaty of Paris (1783), which ended the war. In 1785 he became the first US minister to Great Britain, where he tried to reestablish normal trade relations. Frustrated in those efforts, he asked to be recalled in 1788.

In 1789, Adams was chosen vice president. His eight years in that office were distinguished but personally frustrating to him. Washington's administration, which began as nonpartisan, soon separated into factions. Adams acted as mediator between the conservative faction, led by Alexander Hamilton, and the liberal faction, led by Thomas Jefferson. Naturally a conservative, Adams moved closer to the conservative, or Federalist, faction. He was the Federalist candidate for president in 1796, running against Jefferson. Adams won by a small margin and Jefferson was elected vice president.

Adams's four years in office were marked by his efforts to steer a middle course between the pro-French faction of the Jeffersonians and the Federalists, who were violently anti-French. Only Adams's calm diplomacy (particularly in the XYZ Affair) avoided open war with France. His administration was not a popular success, however, and he was defeated for re-election by Jefferson. He retired to Quincy, where he died on July 5, 1826.

Career: First and Second Continental Congresses (1774–77); US commissioner and minister to France, the Netherlands, and Great Britain (1777–89); vice president (1789–97); president (1797–1801).

Adams, John Quincy (1767–1848), 6th president of the United States, b. Braintree (now Quincy), Mass., son of president John Adams and Abigail Smith Adams. As a young boy he accompanied his father on European diplomatic missions, and at the age of 14 he was secretary to the US minister to Russia. He graduated from Harvard in 1787 and read for the law. President Washington named him minister to the Netherlands in 1794. While in Europe he married Louisa Catherine Johnson; they had four children, one of whom was Charles Francis Adams (1807–86). In 1797 his father named him minister to Prussia. In 1803 he was elected to the US Senate as a Federalist. His independence alienated him from his party, however, and he resigned in 1808. He became minister to Russia in 1809, and in 1814 he was one of the commissioners that drew up the Treaty of Ghent, which ended the War of 1812. He became minister to Great Britain in 1815, and in 1817 President Monroe named him secretary of state. He is ranked as one of the most successful secretaries in US history; the Monroe Doctrine was his most enduring contribution. In the presidential election of 1824, Adams was the candidate of the almost extinct Federalists and ran against Andrew Jackson, Henry Clay, and William H. Crawford. Jackson polled the most votes, but the election was decided in the House of Representatives. Clay threw his support to Adams, who was elected. The Jacksonians charged them with a corrupt bargain, an accusation that only increased when Adams named Clay his secretary of state. Adams was not a natural politician; he had a cold and aloof personality, and he refused to enter into the political deals that were the norm of the era. As a result, his administration was not a successful one. He ran for reelection in 1828, again with Jackson as his opponent. The campaign was one of the dirtiest in US history, with both sides making unproved charges. Jackson won an overwhelming victory, and Adams retired, embittered, to Quincy. Three years later, however, he was elected to the House of Representatives, where he served with great distinction until his death at the age of 81.

Career: Minister to the Netherlands (1794–97), Prussia (1797–1800), Russia (1809–13), Great Britain (1815–17); US Senate (1803–08); secretary of state (1817–24); president (1825–29); US House of Representatives (1831–48).

Adams, Samuel (1722–1803), American Revolutionary patriot and signer of Declaration of Independence. b. Boston, Mass. As a member and clerk of the Massachusetts legislature (1765–74), he was the chief radical spokesman for revolution. He helped form the Sons of Liberty, the Committees of Correspondence, and led the 1765 Stamp Act protest and the Boston Tea Party (1773). He was a delegate to both sessions of the Continental Congress.

Adam's Apple, frontal protuberance in the neck, especially prominent in men, formed by the apex of the triangular-shaped larynx.

Adamson, Robert (1821–48), Scottish pioneer photographer. Working with David Octavius Hill from 1843 to 1848, he made celebrated calotypes of many prominent Scots and of Edinburgh and rural scenes.

Adams-Onís Treaty (1819), agreement between the United States and Spain, negotiated by Sec. of State John Quincy Adams and Spanish Minister Luis de Onís. Spain gave up its land east of the Mississippi River and its claims to the Oregon Territory and the United States assumed debts of $5,000,000 and gave up claims to Texas.

Adana, city in S Turkey, on Seyhan River; 30mi (48km) from Mediterranean coast; capital of Adana prov.; held by Egyptians 1832–40; scene of Armenian massacre 1909; occupied by French 1919–21. Industries: tobacco, textiles, grains, explosives. Founded *c.* 66 BC as Roman colony and military station. Pop. 347,000.

Adapa, mythological Babylonian hero. He was the fisherman son of the god of wisdom, Ea. Adapa was given the gift of great knowledge and intelligence by his father. When he was offered immortality by the sea gods in exchange for his knowledge, he refused, marking the fall of man.

Adaptation, the capacity of an organism or population of organisms to fit into its environment in such a way that it is able to continue to survive and reproduce itself. This capacity is usually achieved through development of characteristics that help the organism adapt; they are usually considered characteristics that can be inherited and passed on to successive generations. *See also* Adaptive Radiation.

Adaptive Radiation, divergent adaptation, a simultaneous divergence of several populations of one parent type into different forms, each suited to a different environmental condition. If a species emerges and becomes distributed over several types of surroundings, the populations of each area may develop specialized features suited to the new environments.

Addams, Jane (1860–1935), US social reformer, b. Cedarville, Ill. She co-founded (1889) Hull House, a social settlement that served as a community center for the poor in Chicago, and was instrumental in the settlement movement across the country. Active in the women's suffrage movement, she was also co-recipient of the Nobel Peace prize (1931). Her works include

John Adams

John Quincy Adams

Samuel Adams

Twenty Years at Hull House (1910), *A New Conscience and an Ancient Evil* (1912), and *The Second Twenty Years at Hull House* (1930).

Addax, large, powerful antelope found in the Sahara Desert. Grayish with black tuft on forehead, both sexes bear long, ribbed horns in open spiral. They have splayed hooves for moving on sand. Almost extinct due to hunting, it derives most of its water from succulent plants. Length: to 78in (2m); height: to 4ft (1.2m) at shoulder; weight: to 264lb (120kg). Family Bovidae; species *Addax maculatus*.

Addiction, use of drugs in such a way that they become essential to the individual. Characteristics of addiction usually include an overwhelming urge to continue taking the drug regardless of the means of obtaining it; a tendency to increase the dose; and a psychological and/or a physiological dependence.

Addis Ababa (Addis Abeba), capital and largest city in Ethiopia; central section is 8,000ft (2,440m) above sea level; administrative and communications center; site of university (1950), National Theater and Library (1944), international airport; headquarters of Organization of African Unity. Founded 1887; scene of Italian-Ethiopian treaty (1896) that recognized Ethiopian independence; occupied by Italy 1936; liberated by British 1941. Industries: tanneries, textiles, breweries. Pop. 1,161,267.

Addison, Joseph (1672–1719), English poet, essayist, and politician. His essays, in the periodicals the *Tatler* (1709–11) and the *Spectator* (1711–12 and 1714) in which he collaborated with Richard Steele, cover literature, philosophy, politics, and morals. Addison wrote largely for the educated middle classes. His poetry includes the verse tragedy "Cato" (1713). *See also* Steele, Richard.

Addison's Disease, condition in which there is decreased activity of the adrenal glands, resulting in skin bronzing, weakness, weight loss, digestive disturbances, and sometimes emotional changes. Usually successfully treated by cortisone administration. *See also* Adrenal Glands.

Addition, arithmetical operation signified by +, interpreted, for natural numbers, as the number of members of a set produced by combining other sets. The numbers added together are the addends; the result is the sum. *See also* Arithmetical Operations.

Adelaide, town in Australia, at the mouth of the Torrens River on Gulf St. Vincent; capital of South Australia state; cultural and governmental center; site of the University of Adelaide (1874), Flinders University (1966), and the Natural History Museum (1895); noted for its churches and cathedrals; major port in South Australia. Exports: fruit, wine, wheat. Industries: machinery, chemicals, textiles, electronic equipment. Founded 1836; inc. 1840. Pop. 899,300.

Adélie Coast (Land), region in Wilkes Land, E Antarctica between George V Coast and Clarie Coast. Captain Jules Dumont d'Urville of France sighted the area (1840), and named it for his wife; Douglas Mawson, an Australian geologist explored it 1911–14 and 1929–31; under French rule from 1938. In 1955, the French Southern and Antarctic Territories were formed by combining Adélie Coast with several islands in Indian Ocean; site of meteorological-scientific bases since 1956. Area: 150,000sq mi (388,500sq km).

Aden, seaport city and capital of People's Democratic Republic of Yemen, on the Gulf of Aden, 100mi (161km) E of the Red Sea. A Roman trading port, its importance diminished with the discovery of the cape route around Africa to India (15th century); occupied by Ottoman Turks 1538 until *c.* 1839, when it was taken by Britain; governed until 1937 as part of India; made a free port 1850, greatly increasing its importance and trade with opening of Suez Canal 1869; made a crown colony 1935; surrounding territory became Aden Protectorate 1937; joined the British-sponsored Federation of South Arabia 1963; opposition by Aden nationalists, resulted in creation of the independent republic (1967), with Aden as capital since 1968. Industries: cigarettes, soap, oil refining, salt. Pop. 225,000.

Aden, Gulf of, W arm of Indian Ocean between Yemen and the Somali Republic, E Africa; connects with Red Sea on W via Bab al-Mandab; part of the Mediterranean Sea–Indian Ocean trade route. Length: 550mi (886km).

Adenauer, Konrad (1876–1967), German political figure. Lord high mayor of Cologne (1917–33), he was twice imprisoned by the Nazis. He helped create the Christian Democratic Union, the dominant postwar party, and was its leader (1946–66). In 1949 he was elected the first chancellor of the Federal Republic of Germany. As chancellor, he promoted German reconstruction, led Germany to membership in NATO (1955), campaigned for European unity and establishment of the Common Market. He resigned as chancellor in 1963.

Adenine, organic compound of the purine group, a group of nitrogen-containing compounds found in combined form in the nucleic acids.

Adenoids, mass of lymphoid tissue found in the upper part of the throat behind the nose. They can become infected, swollen, interfering with breathing and speaking, and are sometimes removed, often with the tonsils.

Adenosine Triphosphate (ATP), nucleotide consisting of adenine, D-ribose, and three phosphate groups. Hydrolysis of ATP to give ADP (adenosine diphosphate) or AMP (adenosine monophosphate) and phosphate is accompanied by a large change in free energy. This hydrolysis is coupled to a phosphorylation reaction in biological systems to provide the energy needed for a number of processes. ATP is synthesized from ADP, for example in photosynthesis using energy derived from sunlight.

Adhesive, substance used for joining materials together. Many types of adhesive exist, including animal and vegetable products and synthetic resins. Adhesives are generally applied as colloidal sols, which change, in position, to gels holding the surfaces by cohesion and adhesion.

Adiabatic Process, process involving a thermodynamic change in a system, without any gain or loss of heat or mass into or out of the system, and resulting from the expansion or compression of the gas or fluid composing it. As a parcel of air rises in the atmosphere, for example, with decreasing pressure it expands and becomes cooler, and as an air parcel falls it is compressed and becomes warmer, without gaining or losing heat or mass from outside.

Adirondack Mountains, circular mountain group located in NE New York; extends from Mohawk Valley (S) to the St Lawrence River (N); site of many scenic lakes, gorges and waterfalls. Much of the area has been set aside as Adirondack State Park; noted famous resort areas, including Lake Placid and Lake George, are located here. Highest point is Mt Marcy, 5,344ft (1,630m).

Adjutant Stork, or Marabou, large scavenging bird found in Africa, India, and SE Asia, named for its militarylike gait. With white, black, and gray plumage and unattractive throat pouches, it feeds on carcasses. Length: 2–5ft (61–152 cm). Species *Leptoptilos dubius*.

Adler, Alfred (1870–1937), Austrian psychiatrist. After working with Sigmund Freud (1902–11), Adler broke with him to found his own school, "individual psychology." Contrary to Freud's emphasis on the sex drive, Adler postulated strivings for social success and power as fundamental in human motivation. Individuals develop problems and maladjustments when they cannot surmount feelings of inferiority acquired in childhood. Adler's concept of the "creative self" stressed the positive, active role the individual plays in shaping his own goals and personality.

Admetus, mythical king of Pharae, a city in Thessaly. He aroused the ire of Artemis, who ruled that he would die young. Apollo arranged his longevity if someone would die for him. Admetus's wife Alcestis took his place in death. However, Hercules went to her grave, outwrestled Death, and returned her to life.

Administrative Law, regulates the powers, procedures, and acts of administrative agencies of the executive branch of government. It applies to the organization, power, duties, and functions of these public agencies.

Admirable Crichton, The (1902), a comic satire by British playwright J.M. Barrie which examines the criteria for class distinctions. Crichton, a butler, is shipwrecked on an island with his employers. His skill and inventiveness quickly make him a leader, reversing the previous master-servant relationship.

Admiralty Islands, volcanic island group, NW of New Guinea in Bismarck Archipelago, SW Pacific Ocean; territory of New Guinea. Manus Island, largest of the group and site of the principal port Lorengau, is surrounded by approx. 40 smaller islands. Industries: pearls, copra. Discovered 1616 by Dutch seaman William Schouten. Area: approx. 800sq mi (2,072sq km). Pop. 27,600.

Admiralty Law. See Maritime Law.

Ado-Ekiti, city in SW Nigeria, 20mi (32km) SSW of Ilaro; taken by British 1894; site of phosphate deposits. Industries: cacao, indigo, dyeing, cotton weaving, palm oil, textiles, brick, poultry. Crops: yams, rice. Founded *c.* 15th century. Pop. 213,000.

Adolescence, life stage from puberty to the start of adulthood. As boys and girls move into their teens they experience rapid body changes and problems of emotional and social adjustment. *See also* Puberty.

Adolf of Nassau (1250?–98), king of Germany (1292–98). He was elected successor to the Hapsburg Rudolf I in 1292, despite Rudolf's attempts to secure the crown for his son Albert. Adolf increased his lands and power so rapidly that the frightened electors deposed him in 1298 in favor of Albert I. Adolf was killed in the ensuing conflict.

Adonis, in Phoenician and Greek mythology, a youth loved by Aphrodite for his beauty. After Adonis was killed by a wild boar, Zeus allowed him to spend a third of the year with Aphrodite, a third with Persephone, queen of the underworld, and a third of his time as he wished.

Adoption, act of a person taking to himself as his child one who is not by fact or law his child. It is an institution or practice followed throughout the world, and in ancient times often involved the adoption of an adult male in order to continue a family line. Modern laws call for an investigation into the suitability of the proposed parent(s) and for the consent of a child over 12 or 14 years.

Adrenal Glands, pair of small, caplike, endocrine glands situated above the kidneys. Each consists of a cortex, or outer layer, and medulla, or inner part. Essential to human life, the cortex produces many steroids, including cortisone, that regulate the blood's salt and water balance and the function of certain white blood cells. The medulla produces two hormones: adrenaline (epinephrine), during emergency or stress, that increases the immediate energy supply, blood pressure, heart rate, and peripheral vasodilation; and noradrenaline (norepinephrine) that transmits nerve impulses and constricts peripheral vasodilation.

Adrenaline, or epinephrine, chief hormone secreted by the adrenal medulla in man. It stimulates the nervous system, raises metabolism, increases cardiac rate and output, and increases blood pressure when released naturally or injected intravenously. When given as a drug it may have side effects such as anxiety, headache, dizziness, and weakness. It is often given to treat anaphylactic shock. *See also* Norepinephrine.

Adrenocorticotropic Hormone (ACTH), protein hormone secreted by the anterior lobe of the pituitary. It stimulates the adrenal cortex to release steroid hormones. It is used to test adrenal function, and as an anti-inflammatory agent.

Adrian IV, Roman Catholic pope (1154–59), b. Nicholas Breakspear (*c.* 1100), the only English pope. In 1152 he served as a papal legate to Scandinavia and was successful in organizing the Church there. In 1155 he crowned emperor Frederick I Barbarossa, but relations with the emperor were not always amicable. In 1156 peace was made with Sicily and an alliance grew between the papacy and William I.

Adrian, Edgar Douglas (1889–1977), English physiologist. His important discoveries concerning the function of nerve cells, including the "all-or-none" law, earned him part of the 1932 Nobel Prize in physiology or medicine.

Adrianople, Treaty of (1829), pact signed at Edirne (formerly Adrianople), Turkey, at the termination of the Russo-Ottoman War (1828–29). The treaty gave Russia the islands controlling the mouth of the Danube and the Black Sea coast of the Caucasus, and it opened the Dardanelles and Bosporus to Russian shipping.

Adriatic Sea, extension of the Mediterranean Sea, bordered by Italy (W) and Yugoslavia and Albania (E); extends 500mi (805km) SE from the Gulf of Trieste to the Strait of Otranto. Noted for clear, blue water and mild climate, it is a popular tourist region; Italian coast is low and straight, Yugoslav coast is rocky and indented, with many small islands. Width: 60–140mi (96–225km). Depth: 4,000ft (1,220m).

Adsorption, taking up by a solid or liquid of a gas or liquid in contact with it. The amounts adsorbed and the rate of adsorption depend on the nature of the structure exposed, the chemical identities and concentrations of the substances involved, and the temperature. Silica gel and active carbon can take up great volumes of gas.

Adventists, Christians concerned with the imminent Second Coming of Christ. Through him, the evil in the world will be destroyed. William Miller (1782–1849) formed the first organized movement in the United States in 1831. His followers were called Millerites or Second Adventists. Controversies over dates of the Coming led groups to split. *See also* Seventh-Day Adventists.

Advice and Consent, legislative power granted to the Senate by Article II, Section 2, of the US Constitution. The Senate must approve all presidential appointments and foreign treaties.

Aediles, magistrates of ancient Rome. The six aediles (three patricians and three plebeians), whose office lasted from 494 BC to AD *c.* 235, maintained public facilities, supervised public festivities, and enforced traffic and market regulations.

A.E.F. *See* American Expeditionary Force.

Aegean Sea, extension of the Mediterranean Sea between Greece and Turkey, bounded by Crete on the S; connected to the Black Sea and Sea of Marmara by the Dardanelles; contains many islands, mostly of Greece; in ancient times it was divided into the Thracian Sea, Icarian Sea, Myrtoan Sea, and Sea of Crete. Ancient name Archipelago now applies to any island group. Length: 400mi (644km). Width: 200mi (322km).

Aegis, in Greek mythology, the shield made for Jupiter by Vulcan. He carried thunder with it. Athena held it as a sign of authority when she went on missions for her father. In its center was the head of Medusa, which was said to have had the power of turning men to stone.

Aegisthus, in Greek legend, the son of Thyestes. Together they killed Atreus, king of Mycenae, father of Agamemnon and Menelaus. Aegisthus and his father held Mycenae until it was later recovered by Agamemnon. During the Trojan war Aegisthus seduced Agamemnon's wife, Clytemnestra, and murdered Agamemnon upon his return from Troy.

Aehrenthal, Count von Alois Lexa (1854–1912), statesman of Austria-Hungary. He served as ambassador to Romania (1895) and Russia (1899) before becoming foreign minister (1906–12). In this capacity he showed short-sightedness and substantial lack of ability, managing to alienate Italy, Russia, and most other European nations in the critical years before World War I.

Aemilian Way, ancient Roman road constructed by Marcus Aemilius Lepidus in 187 BC. An extension of the Flaminian Way, it began at Arminum (Rimini) and terminated at Placentia (Piacenza). Later lengthened to Mediolanum (Milan), it chiefly served the military.

Aeneas, in Greek mythology, the son of Anchises and Aphrodite. Active in the defense of Troy, he was removed by Poseidon from the city since he was destined to rule over the survivors of Troy. Aeneas led the Trojans westward to Italy. The Romans accepted Aeneas and his Trojan company as their ancestors.

Aeneid, poem written by the Roman poet Vergil between 30 and 19 BC. Written in 12 books, the *Aeneid* recounts the legendary founding of the town of Lavinium by the Trojan Aeneas. The *Aeneid* resembles the writings of Homer in both form and concepts: the first six books have been called "Vergil's *Odyssey*" and the last six, his *Iliad.* The two themes of Rome's destiny and human suffering are contained in the character of Aeneas who tries in spite of human limitations to fulfill the divine mission. The *Aeneid* was regarded by Romans as their national epic and the study of Vergil's works was widespread.

Aeolian Formation. *See* Eolian Formation.

Aeolians, ancient Greeks whose late Bronze Age members founded Lesbos and other settlements at the end of the second millennium BC. They were noted for genius in music and poetry.

Aeolis (Aeolia), ancient region in NW Asia Minor, extending from the entrance of the Hellespont (now the Dardanelles) on the Aegean Sea, to the Hermus River (now Gediz River) where Aeolian Greeks built cities before 1000 BC. Aeolis was considered a collective term for the cities rather than a geographical unit; the 12 southern cities formed the Aeolian League (8th century BC).

Aequi, ancient tribe in Italy. They expanded their territory from the central regions westward to occupy areas near modern Tivoli, Palestrina, and the Alban Hills. They returned to their original regions by 431 BC, allied with Rome, and attained Roman citizenship by the 1st century BC.

Aeration, artificial method of bringing air into direct contact with a fluid. Compressed air, furnishing oxygen to promote bacterial action, is blown into a reagent tank in the treatment of sewage. Aeration is also used in the fermentation and soft drink industries, as well as in the manufacture of penicillin and other antibiotics.

Aerobe, an organism that can grow in the presence of free atmospheric oxygen. Some aerobes can live with or without oxygen and are called facultative anaerobes.

Aerodynamics, science of air in motion and the forces acting on bodies, such as aircraft, in motion through the air. The designer of a flyable aircraft must consider four fundamental factors and their relationships: weight of the aircraft and load, lift to overcome the pull of gravity, drag or the forces that retard motion, and thrust, the driving force. Understanding of these forces is complicated by their non-uniform behavior in the various regimes of modern flight.

Aeronautical Engineering, activity encompassing the design and construction of aircraft, their systems and performance in subsonic, supersonic, and hypersonic regimes of flight. By using such tools as the wind and shock tunnels, experimental evidence can be gathered on behavior of materials and designs as if in flight. Computers allow rapid solutions to theoretical problems that once could only be flight-tested. To understand new phenomena requires knowledge of thermodynamics, fluidics, and chemistry since flights in the hypersonic range involve physical and chemical changes not previously encountered by machines. Aeronautical engineering requires a comprehensive scientific background. *See also* Aerodynamics.

Aeronautics, science of the operation of aircraft. Airplanes, gliders, rotorcraft, and balloons share some principles of flight but are unique in others. Free balloons and dirigibles go aloft by displacing air with a gas or hot air. Free balloons have no means of propulsion, but dirigibles use aircraft engines. Rotorcraft utilize lift provided by a rotating wing or rotor. The helicopter propels itself forward by tilting the plane of rotation of its powered rotor, while the gyroplane or autogyro's rotor free-wheels, making it necessary to gain forward motion by using an engine-driven propeller. Gliders and airplanes use lifting wings. The glider dives for forward motion and lift. The airplane uses a second source of lift, the propeller, to pull itself forward, or moves in a reaction to the expulsion of hot gases. *See also* Aircraft.

Aeronomy, the study of the earth's upper atmosphere, including its composition, density, temperature, and chemical reactions, as recorded by sounding rockets and earth satellites.

Aerosol, (1) suspension of liquid or solid particles in a gas. Mist comprises about 10^{15} water droplets suspended in a liter of air; airborne bacteria or dust (which we call smoke) are solid-based aerosols. (2) Pressurized spray container for packaging deodorant, insecticide, paint, etc. Fluorocarbons, often used as propellants in such aerosols, may be harmful to the ozone layer.

Aerospace Medicine, a division of medical science that studies the medical aspects and problems of human beings in space. An organization of medical personnel and scientists concerned with space study, called the Aerospace Medical Association (ASMA), was formed in the United States in 1959, as an outgrowth of the Aero Medical Association formed in 1929.

Aeschylus (525–456 BC), Greek dramatist. The earliest known writer of tragedies whose plays exist in complete form, he was also the first to include more than one character in a play. Seven of his works survive: *The Suppliants, The Persians, The Seven Against Thebes, Prometheus Bound,* and the *Oresteia* trilogy *(Agamemnon, The Chöephoroe,* and *The Eumenides).* They are characterized by impressive language, and moral and religious themes. *See also* Oresteia.

Aesculapius, in Greek mythology, son of Apollo and the nymph Coronis. The first physician, he became so skilled that he could restore the dead to life. In art he is portrayed as a strong youth bearing a serpent entwined around a staff.

Aesir, principal race of the Nordic gods. Three of these, Woden (Odin), Thor (Donar), and Tyr (Tiw), and a few others were the object of a cult that extended throughout the lands inhabited by the Teutons. Secondary to the Aesir was a race of Teutonic gods known as the Vanir.

Aesop (*c.* 620–560 BC), Greek fabulist. A former slave, he was the reputed creator of numerous short tales about animals, all illustrating human virtues and failings. Aesop supposedly died in Delphi, where he angered citizens and was thrown off a cliff. *See also* Fable.

Aesop's Fables, short animal tales designed to convey a moral lesson, eg *The Hare and the Tortoise* teaches "slow and steady wins the race," and *The Fox and the Crow* cautions against trusting flatterers. Ascribed by tradition to a slave in the 6th century BC, a collection of the tales accompanied by 185 "clear and lively woodcuts" was translated and printed by William Caxton in 1484.

Aesthetics, study of beauty and of standards of value in judging beauty, especially in art. The term was first used in the 18th century to describe a science whose

Aeronautics: First Aircraft Flight

Afghan hound

Pamir Afghanistan

object is beauty, although philosophizing about the arts dates from the writings of Plato and earlier. In the 18th century, G. W. F. Hegel employed the term in its present sense. In the 20th century, aesthetics has come to be regarded as a science independent of philosophy, studying works of art, human behavior toward art, and the enjoyment of art.

Aetolian League, a federal state organized from loose Greek tribes in 370 BC. It was normally hostile to Macedonia, but was Rome's first Greek ally. Later hostile to Rome, it was forced to be a subject ally in 189 BC.

Afars and the Issas, French Territory of the. *See* Djibouti.

Affenpinscher, small German "monkey dog" (toy group) known since the 17th century in Europe. This sturdy, terrier-type dog's rounded head, short-pointed muzzle, and small, pointed, erect ears accented by a prominent chin and bushy whiskers, moustache, and eyebrows give it a distinctive expression. The body is medium-length; legs are straight; and the tail is cut short and carried high. The black coat is hard, wiry, and short, except on the legs and face, where it is more shaggy. Average size: 8–10in (20–25cm) high at shoulder; 7–8lb (3–3.5kg). *See also* Toy Dog.

Afghan Hound, aristocratic hunting dog (hound group) originating in Sinai Peninsula 4000–3000 BC and later established in Afghanistan. Aloof and dignified, it has a long, slender head and jaws; long, hanging ears; level back; arched loins; long, straight legs with large feet; and long, tapered tail with ring or curve at end. The thick, silky coat, which may be any color, is short and smooth on the back and longer over the rest of the dog. There is a long topknot on the head. Average size: 24–28in (61–71cm) high at shoulder; 50–60lb (22.6–27kg). *See also* Hound.

Afghanistan, Republic of, nation in W central Asia. Landlocked and mountainous, during the 19th century it served as a buffer state between Russia and the British empire in India, and remained staunchly nonaligned until Soviet involvement began during the late 1970s.

Land and Economy. Mountains of sedimentary rock over a metamorphic base separate N from S and cover 60% of the land. Peaks over 20,000ft (6,100m) rise in the E Hindu Kush. In the N, steppes slope down to the Amu Darya River; the S is covered by the Registan and other deserts (41,000sq mi; 106,190sq km). Arid in summer, cold in winter, the country has poor agricultural conditions, yet 80% of the people live by farming and herding. Minerals are difficult to find and mine. Small factories produce cloth and clothing, while families weave rugs and make pottery.

People. Local languages show most people to be descended from Persians, Tatars, and Mongols. Islam is the national religion, and the people belong mostly to the Sunnite sect. Many were once nomads, but today 90% lead a settled life, with 10% located in cities. Government programs bring education to more youngsters than religious schools once did, but only about 12% of the men and 6% of the women are literate.

Government. Afghanistan is ruled as a one-party people's republic. Babrak Karmal, installed in office in 1979 in a coup with Soviet military backing, serves as prime minister and president of the revolutionary council.

History. Trade routes through the area in ancient times brought Persian (Iranian) traders, who gradually became dominant. The Pushtuns among them grew especially strong, although Arabs, Turks (Tatars), and Mongols left lasting influences. Afghans, descended

from the Pushtuns, began to unite in the 17th century. The British exerted pressure from India in the 19th century, until they held control. After WWI, local tribes rebelled, and in 1921 Britain recognized the country as an independent monarchy. While King Mohammed Zahir Shah was in Europe (1973), the military took control of the government. The government remained unstable, however, and Soviet influence increased. Soviet forces invaded in 1979, establishing a virtual puppet government, despite international protests. Nearly 3,000,000 Afghanis fled into neighboring Pakistan, and fighting continues between Soviet troops and Afghani anti-occupation guerrilla forces.

PROFILE

Official name: Republic of Afghanistan
Area: 250,775sq mi (649,507sq km)
Population (1975): 12.7 million
 Density, 50 per sq mi (19 per sq km)
Chief cities: Kabul, the capital; Kandahar,
Government: People's Republic
Gross national product (1975): $2,100,000,000
Trading partners (major): USSR

Africa, continent mostly in Eastern and Northern hemisphere straddling the equator. Of the continents, only Asia is larger.

Land. Africa forms a giant plateau between the Atlantic and Indian oceans. Its highest features include the Atlas and Ahaggar mts (NW), the Ethiopian Highlands (E), and the Drakensberg Mts (SE). Mt Kilimanjaro has the continent's highest peak, 19,340ft (5,899m). A huge sunken strip in the SE is known as the East African (or Great) Rift Valley. The Sahara, largest desert in the world, stretches across the N, covering more than 25% of the continent. The Kalahari and Namib are smaller deserts in the S and SW. Of islands near Africa, Madagascar (Malagasy Republic) is the world's fourth largest.

Lakes and Rivers. The Rift valley holds such major lakes as Rudolf, Nyasa, and Tanganyika; Lake Victoria, in the E, is Africa's largest, 26,828sq mi (69,485sq km); Lake Chad lies in the central N. The Nile, longest river in the world, 4,150mi (6,682km), flows from Lake Victoria. Other major rivers are the Niger, Congo, and Zambezi.

Climate and Vegetation. Only a N strip and the S end of Africa extend beyond the tropics. Much of the continent is hot and, outside the desert areas, humid. The strip along the equator receives more than 100in (254cm) of moisture a year in places, which helps produce a thick rain forest. The forest gives way to areas of acacia and brush and finally to grasslands, or savannas. The deserts receive little moisture, but grassy oases occur where springs and mountain streams provide water.

Animal Life. Ostriches live in the deserts, while vultures range over a wide area. The grasslands and brush support giraffes, rhinoceros, zebras, many types of antelopes, and lions. Elephants live from the plains to the forests, as do some giraffes, rhinoceros, zebras, many types of antelopes, and lions. Gorillas and chimpanzees remain in the jungles. Hippopotamuses are in the E rivers, and crocodiles remain numerous in places. Pythons are the largest snakes, but mambas and cobras are more dangerous to man.

People. The original inhabitants of Africa were dark-skinned peoples who hunted, fished, and gathered roots, fruits, and nuts. N of the Sahara, they were replaced by Arabs; S of the Sahara, Negroid types still predominate. Farming and herding support more than 85% of Africa's peoples. The pygmies of the rain forest continue as gatherers and hunters, as do the Bushmen and Hottentots of the SW deserts. The unusually tall Masai and Watusi of E Africa live by herding cattle and sheep.

Economy. The Arabs cultivate olives, figs, dates, and grains. S of the Sahara the principal commercial agricultural crops are rubber, cocoa, coffee, and peanuts. Copper, bauxite, gold, and diamonds are mined. Various governments since the 1960s have nationalized some European-founded industries. Most rivers have cataracts suitable to run hydroelectric or industrial plants. With the exception of South Africa, African countries have developing economies. During the late 1970s and early 1980s, Africa (excluding the oil exporters) was plagued by severe payments deficits from inflation and oil price increases and by decreasing food output. Famines have occurred periodically due to droughts in the arid Sahel zone south of the Sahara, and from war and dislocation in Ethiopia, Somalia, and Uganda.

History. Egyptian civilization existed 6,000 years ago, and Phoenicians settled on Africa's Mediterranean coast about 1000 BC, but Roman forces later conquered them and Egypt. As Roman influence lessened, the kingdom of Ghana developed in W Africa. About AD 650, Arabs advanced W from the Arabian Peninsula. Below the Sahara, the Mali kingdom replaced that of Ghana during the 11th century. Portuguese began exploring the Atlantic coastline in the 15th century. Europeans came to seek gold and gems but between 1600–1800 captured blacks for the slave trade. The discovery of diamonds (1866) and gold (1886) in South Africa and the opening of the Suez Canal (1869) helped bring outsiders. During the late 19th century, European nations raced to build African empires. Most African countries have received independence since 1950. With the institution of black majority rule in Zimbabwe (formerly Rhodesia) in 1980, South Africa became the only country with a white minority government and was under increasing international pressure to abolish apartheid and to relinquish control of Namibia. Famine, aggravated by prolonged drought, received worldwide attention during the 1980s. Instability and ethnic conflicts are widespread, and the Communist and Western powers continue to compete for influence.

PROFILE

Area: 11,677,239sq mi (30,244,049sq km)
 Largest nations: Sudan, Algeria, Zaire—each over 900,000sq mi (2,331,000sq km)
Population: 442,000,000
 Density, 31 per sq mi (15 per sq km)
 Most populous nations: Nigeria 82,503,000; Egypt, 40,983,000; Ethiopia, 29,710,000
Chief cities: Cairo, Egypt; Alexandria, Egypt; Kinshasa, Zaire; Casablanca, Morocco; Johannesburg, South Africa; Algiers, Algeria; Lagos, Nigeria
Industries (major products): iron, steel, petroleum products, rubber, chemicals, fertilizers, textiles, foodstuffs
Agriculture (major products): dates, grapes, figs, wheat, corn, rice, barley, sorghum, cocoa, coffee, tea, vegetables, cotton
Minerals (major): gold, diamonds, bauxite, uranium, copper, iron ore, cobalt, manganesse coal, petroleum, natural gas

African Languages, languages spoken on the African continent. These include the Afro-Asiatic or Semitic languages in N and Ethiopia, such as Arabic, Cushitic, Berber. Others are the sub-Saharan, black, or Afro-African, which divided into three major families—Sudanic in central and E Africa, Niger-Kordofanian in equatorial, and Khoisan in the SW. English, Spanish, French, Portuguese, and Afrikaans show colonial presence. The original alphabets were non-Roman, but many were first rendered by Europeans into modified Roman with diacritics for unique sounds—clicks or tones.

African Methodist Episcopal Church, second largest Methodist group in the United States. Objecting to the church's racial discriminatory policy, a group withdrew from the Methodist Episcopal Church in 1787. The first AME church was dedicated in 1793 in Philadelphia. Richard Allen was the first bishop; formal organization followed in 1816. Its doctrines are those of traditional Methodist churches. There are approximately 1.1 million members. *See also* Methodist Church.

African Methodist Episcopal Zion Church, formed in 1796 by a group of black members of the John Street Church (Methodist Episcopal) in New York City who protested racial discrimination. The name was approved in 1848, and James Varick was the first bishop. The church spread rapidly throughout the northern states, and some churches developed in the South. Missionary activity and education are stressed. There are approximately 900,000 members.

African Music, the music of the black African people south of the Sahara, distinguished by great variety, subtlety, and complexity. It is performed in association with traditional occasions, such as festivals, marriages, funerals, religious rites and celebrations, and cult ceremonies, and also as part of private or recreational activities. Work songs and songs in traditional styles to suit social, religious, or seasonal occasions are part of the culture and may vary widely in character from people to people or area to area. The intricate rhythmic, melodic, and harmonic patterns are in many ways unlike those familiar in traditional Western music. The instruments used include gourds, rattles, serapers, xylophones, slitdrums, bells, and plucked instruments of various kinds. Drums, moreover, are used for transmitting messages ("talking drums") as well as for music. The music of black Africa has played an unmistakable part in the development of jazz, the spirituals of American blacks, and many of the characteristic dances of Latin America.

African Violet, tropical African flowering house plant. The velvety, rounded leaves grow in spreading rosettes centered by purple or white blossoms with yellow stamens. Red stems and leaf undersides are common. Care: bright indirect light, warm temperature, humid air, well-drained soil (1 part potting soil, 2 parts peat moss, 1 part sand) kept barely moist with tepid water. Propagation is by leaf cuttings or crown divisions. Height: 4–6in (10–15cm). Family Gesneriaceae; genus *Saint paulia.*

Afrikaners, or Boers, people of mainly Dutch descent inhabiting the Republic of South Africa. They first settled around the Cape in the 17th century and were joined by French Huguenot refugees. Tension between them and the British led first to the Great Trek (1835–40), in which the Afrikaners moved inland, establishing the Orange Free State and the Transvaal, and later to the Boer War (1899–1902), won by Britain. The Afrikaners control political power in South Africa, and their Calvinism and concern with "purity of blood" has led to the republic's policy of apartheid.

Afro-African Languages, languages native to the African continent and spoken by, or derived from, languages natively spoken by black African or Negroid peoples. The term is used sometimes to distinguish the three major families of sub-Saharan African languages from the Semitic or Afro-Asiatic languages of Arabic countries. Many black Africans speak Semitic tongues, and among themselves the three southern families differ at least as greatly as European and Oriental languages differ.

Afterbirth, the placenta and fetal membranes expelled from the uterus after childbirth.

Afterimage, image formed as an aftereffect of staring at a bright spot or pattern. Often the color of the afterimage is the complement of the original stimulus. The "spots" one sees after a flashbulb fires are afterimages.

Agamemnon, Greek king of Mycenae, brother of Menelaus. He led the siege of Troy. When Troy fell Agamemnon returned home with his captive Cassandra, but was slain by his wife Clytemnestra and her lover Aegisthus. His death was avenged by his children Orestes and Electra.

Agar, complex substance extracted from certain seaweeds; a colloidal powder forming a rigid gel in solution. It is used as a thickening agent in ice cream, an emulsifier, adhesive, and support medium for growing bacterial cultures.

Agassiz, Jean Louis Rodolphe (1807–1873), US naturalist, b. Switzerland. He worked to make science available to the public. Known also for his work in geology and ichthyology, Agassiz made significant studies in the classification of animals, especially fossil forms, and in the movement and distribution of glaciers. From 1836–1837 he explored glaciers, and in 1839 proved through experimentation that glaciers move. His *Études sur les glaciers* (1840) proposed the theory of an ice age, in which glaciers covered most of northern Europe. His general zoological classification, *Nomenclator Zoologicus* (1842–1846), aroused interest in the study of fossils and introduced order into what had been zoological chaos. He began lecturing and writing scientific essays in America in 1846, and in 1861 he became a US citizen.

Agassiz, Lake, glacial lake of ancient North America; about 700mi (1,130km) long by 200mi (320km) wide and covered parts of Saskatchewan, Ontario, Manitoba, North Dakota, and Minnesota. Formed by glacial blockage of various rivers, the lake existed as much as 2,000,000 years ago in the Pleistocene Epoch, and was named after Louis Agassiz in 1879.

Agate, a fine-grained variety of chalcedony, a silica mineral, that is essentially quartz. It occurs in bands of various colors, or blended in clouds or mosslike patterns. Semiprecious in quality, agate is frequently used for jewelry. *See also* Quartz.

Agave, short-stemmed, succulent flowering plant of the family Agavaceae found in tropical, subtropical, and temperate areas. All have narrow, lance-shaped leaves clustered at the plant base. Many have large flower clusters. The century plant *(Agave americana)* of SW North America is a well-known stemless plant with a 40-ft (12-m) stalk topped by a flower cluster. Each plant produces a flower spike once a year or less frequently, after which the leaves die, leaving the roots to produce a new plant. Other species are sisal hemp *(A. sisalana)* and the many species of yucca. Some species contain a sap that produces an intoxicant when fermented. There are fewer than 250 species in the wild, but many others are cultivated commercially or for decoration.

Agee, James (1909–55), US author, b. Knoxville. A writer for *Fortune* magazine and a film critic for *Time* and *The Nation,* he also wrote poetry and novels. His works include *Let Us Now Praise Famous Men* (1941; with Walker Evans), a bitter account of sharecroppers in Alabama during the Depression, and *A Death in the Family* (1957). *See also* Death in the Family, A; Evans, Walker.

Agena. *See* Beta Centauri.

Agency Shop, employment situation in which the worker need not be a member of a union before or after employment, but nevertheless must pay the recognized union in the plant an amount of money, usually equal to union dues. The idea is that the worker should pay part of the cost of union representation.

Agent Orange, a herbicide used extensively by the United States during the Vietnam War to defoliate jungles in order to reveal enemy encampments or installations. Claims that Agent Orange causes birth defects and cancer are disputed. However, there is strong evidence that dioxin, a contaminant found in trace amounts in Agent Orange, causes cancer and other illnesses. Agent Orange is composed of 2,4-dichlorophenoxyacetic acid and 2,4,5-trichlorophenoxyacetic acid.

Agglomerate, coarse volcanic rock that includes both rounded and angular fragments in a finer matrix, thus combining the characteristics of conglomerates and breccias. Charles Lyell coined the term in 1831. *See also* Breccia; Conglomerate.

Agglutination, clumping of bacteria or red blood cells by antibodies that react with antigens on the cell surface. *See also* Antigen.

Aggregate, any building or construction material used to form concrete by mixing with cement, lime, gypsum, or other adhesive. It provides desirable qualities such as volume and resistance to wear. Examples are sand, crushed and broken stone, pebbles, and boiler ashes. Fine aggregates are used to make thin and smooth structural members; coarse aggregates are used for more massive elements.

Aggregate Consumption, total amount that consumers will spend on goods and services during the year. Economists assume that this amount will vary directly with the level of real GNP, stock of liquid assets, population size, and other variables. This aggregate consumption is a portion of GNP. *See also* Gross National Product.

Aggregate Demand, total demand for goods and services in the economy. It is composed of consumption (by households) plus investment (by business) plus government expenditures plus net exports (net foreign demand for goods and services; exports less imports). The dollar volume of aggregate demand depends upon the level of GNP, disposable income, and other aggregate measures of income and wealth as well as expectations about future economic conditions such as employment and inflation.

Aggregation, treatment of a number of terms in a mathematical expression as a single unit, denoted by enclosing the terms in parentheses or placing a bar above them. Thus in $7(x^2 = 2)$ the whole term, $x^2 = 2$, is multiplied by 7.

Aggression, deliberate act that inflicts pain or suffering on another individual. Aggression in animals is regarded as instinctual by ethologists. The question of the origins of human aggression is controversial, however. Some regard it as instinctual; others, entirely learned; still others, as a mix. Modern psychologists suggest imitation as an important way children acquire aggressive behaviors.

Agincourt, village in N France, 33mi (53km) W of Arras; scene of defeat of French army by Henry V of England in 1415 during the Hundred Years War. Although the French were more heavily armored, English archers with longbows decimated the French ranks; battle is central to Shakespeare's *Henry V.*

Agnew, Spiro Theodore (1918–   ), US vice president, b. Baltimore, Md. He was elected chief executive of Baltimore co (1962) and governor of Maryland (1966). Richard M. Nixon's running mate on the Republican ticket (1968), Agnew served as vice-president (1969–73). His forceful, picturesque language made him a popular speaker. In 1973 he was indicted on bribery, conspiracy, and tax charges for actions he allegedly took while governor of Maryland. He pleaded no contest to charges of tax evasion and resigned on Oct. 10, 1973. He was subsequently disbarred (1974) and became an international trade consultant.

Agni, fire-god in Vedic mythology, revered as god of the home in his domestic aspect and appearing in lightning and the sun as a nature deity. He functioned as a messenger between men and the gods when he carried consumed offerings of the sacrificial altars to the heavens.

Agnosticism, theory of religious knowledge, associated with English rationalist Thomas Huxley (1825–95), that it is impossible either to demonstrate or to refute God's existence, on the basis of available evidence.

Agoraphobia, morbid fear of open places, a term derived from the Greek *agora* (marketplace). Afflicted persons are apt to show signs of acute panic when alone in an open or public place.

Agouti, medium-sized, herbivorous rodent of Central and South America and West Indies. Hunted as food by man and other animals, they have short ears, long legs, tiny tails, and coarse fur that ranges from orange to brown to black. They sit erect when eating, holding food with their front paws. Family Dasyproctidae. *See also* Paca.

Agra, city in India, on Yamuna River. Established 1560 by Mogul emperor Akbar as the site for his capital; under reign of Shah Jahan, the Taj Mahal was built (1648) as the tomb and memorial to his wife Mumtaz Mahal; city's importance declined steadily when the Mogul empire moved its headquarters to Delhi (1658); annexed to British Empire (1802), it was capital of the North West prov. during the mid-19th century; site of Akbar's fort (1566) and tomb, the Pearl Mosque, and the Great Mosque—all magnificent examples of Mogul architecture. Industries: glass, shoes, textiles, tourism. Founded 1560. Pop. 637,785. *See also* Taj Mahal.

Agranulocytosis, acute and serious illness caused by chemicals or hypersensitivity to drugs in which infection-barrier granulocytes (a type of white blood cell) rapidly disappear, causing rapid and often overwhelming infection, usually starting at oral mucous membranes.

Agrarian Laws, Roman, legislation in ancient Rome by which public lands, usually confiscated from cities and states defeated in battle, were assigned to tenants. They were attempts to rectify the gross imbalance between lands held by the rich and the minimal share held by the poor. The principal enactments of these laws occurred in 367 BC, 233 BC, 133 BC, 123 BC, 82 BC, and 43 BC, but all of them were generally ignored or gotten around. The edict of Domitian (*c.* AD 82),

Spiro T. Agnew

Agouti

Agra, India: Taj Mahal

granting public lands permanently to those who currently held them, kept them in the hands of the wealthy.

Agrarian, or **Agricultural, Revolution,** a change in attitudes and methods of farming that took place in England in the 18th century. With greater commerce came an increased market for food. Legal reallocation of land ownership (the "enclosure" movement) made for more compact and economical farms. Use of machinery, such as Jethro Tull's seed drill, began. Systems of crop rotation were instituted. Beginning before the industrial revolution, the transformation took over a century to complete and can be regarded both as a prelude to and a part of industrialization.

Agribusiness, the total agricultural industry, or sector, including producing farm products, processing them, and marketing the finished good, as well as production of agricultural machinery and supplies for the farm.

Agricola, Gnaeus Julius (37–93), Roman general; conqueror and governor of Britain. As governor (c.78–85), he Romanized Britain without oppression and expanded Roman influence to Wales and part of Scotland. His enlightened rule was described by Tacitus, his son-in-law.

Agricultural Adjustment Act (1933), New Deal legislation of President Franklin Roosevelt designed to increase the purchasing power of farmers by balancing production with consumption. It set up the Agricultural Adjustment Agency (AAA), which provided subsidies for lower production and penalized overproduction. The production control features of the AAA were declared unconstitutional (1936) by the US Supreme Court.

Agricultural Engineering, division of agricultural science including some mechanical engineering, construction, hydraulics, and soil mechanics. Engineering is responsible for irrigation, machine design, and changes in applications of various techniques.

Agriculture, science of cultivating the soil and raising plant and animal life for human survival. Since Neolithic times (7000 BC), agriculture has been an essential way of life. Modern technology has raised farming from the self-survival level to a commercial level where a disproportionately small number of people feed almost the world's entire population. Areas improved by advanced technology include: irrigation, drainage, conservation, sanitation, plant and animal breeding, fertilization, pesticides, soil analysis, animal nutrient requirements, food preservation, and transportation. Biological and physical scientists and engineers are constantly developing new methods, raising production to an ever greater scale.

Mechanization, significant since the 18th century, has increased productivity, reduced manual labor, and replaced draft animals, in most countries, by machines. Specialization is the modern trend, with soil, climate, and topography determining the crop or animal raised: grain is raised on large, flat or rolling fields; truck farms and dairies are located adjacent to large cities for easier marketing; livestock is raised near its food source. See also Agribusiness, Irrigation, Slash-and-Burn Cultivation.

Agriculture, Department of (USDA), US cabinet level department within the executive branch. It is directed by the secretary of agriculture, who is a cabinet member. It accumulates and makes available agricultural information. It engages in research, education, conservation, marketing, regulatory work, agricultural adjustment, surplus disposal, and rural development. The department's activities are primarily directed to-

ward increasing the efficiency, production, and profit of the agricultural industry. Among its more important agencies are the Food and Nutrition Service, Soil Conservation Service, Forest Service, and Federal Crop Insurance Corporation. It was established in 1862.

Agrigento, formerly Girgenti; city in S Sicily, Italy; capital of Agrigento prov. It was founded c. 580 BC as Acragas or Akragas by Greek colonists from Gela; prospered until conquered by the Cathaginians in 406 BC; captured by Romans in 210 BC, and commerce improved. Greek ruins remain, including temples to Hera and Zeus. Industries: agricultural trade, mining. Pop. 51,682.

Agrippa, Marcus Vipsanius (63–12BC), Roman general, adviser to Roman emperor Augustus. After Caesar's death in 44 BC, Agrippa was influential in Augustus' attainment of the throne, commanding two naval battles in 36 BC against Sextus Pompeius and helping to defeat Mark Antony at Actium in 31 BC. Agrippa was appointed consul three times, married the emperor's daughter, and became heir-designate.

Agrippina II, Julia Agrippina (AD 15?–59), daughter of Vipsania Agrippina, and mother of Nero, who became a Roman emperor. When her uncle Claudius became emperor, she married him and persuaded him to name Nero as his heir-designate. In AD 54 she murdered Claudius, and Nero gained the throne. Nero had her killed in AD 59.

Agronomy, the science of improving methods of soil management in the interest of agriculture. The science revolves around studies of particular plants, soils, and the interrelationship of the two. Agronomy has resulted in disease-resistant plants, selective breeding, and chemical fertilizers.

Aguascalientes, city in central Mexico, 364mi (586km) NW of Mexico City; capital of Aguascalientes state; health resort, noted for mineral springs; built above ancient, advanced tunnel system of unknown origin. Industries: textiles, smelting, processed food. Founded 1575 as Spanish military base. Pop. 238,700.

Aguilar v. Texas (1964), US Supreme Court case in which the court declared that a search warrant was only valid when it had been issued by a magistrate who had studied an affidavit and determined there was a probable cause. The decision ruled out the use of hearsay evidence as a basis for a warrant.

Aguinaldo, Emilio (1869–1964), Filipino leader. Leader of the 1896 insurrection against Spain, he was exiled to Hong Kong, but returned with the outbreak of the Spanish-American War (1898) to fight for independence. He set up the Philippine Republic with himself as president, resisting the US occupation forces until 1901. After swearing allegiance to the United States, he retired to private life until 1935 when he ran unsuccessfully for the presidency. In 1945 he was accused of collaborating with the Japanese during World War II. After a brief imprisonment he was released. In 1950 he became a member of the Philippine Council of State.

Ahab (died c. 853 BC), king of Israel (c. 874–853 BC), son and successor of Omri. He secured peace between his northern kingdom and Tyre by marrying Jezebel. With Benhadad he withstood Shalmaneser III at Karkar on the Orontes (c. 854 BC). Elijah told him to banish idols. He fought Benhadad for land east of Jordan and was killed. His son Ahaziah succeeded him.

Ahaz (died c. 727 BC), king of Judah (c. 735–725 BC), son of Jotham. With the aid of Tiglath-pileser III of

Assyria, he beat back the forces of Pekah of Israel and Rezin of Damascus. The prophet Isaiah opposed his alliance with Assyria. His son Hezekiah succeeded him.

Ahidjo, Ahmadou (1924–   ), first president of the United Republic of Cameroon. After serving in the territorial government of the French Cameroons, he managed to attain independence for his country (1960) and union with the new independent former British Cameroons (1961) while maintaining close ties with France. He forced the uniting of all political parties in 1966. He was re-elected president in 1980 for the fifth consecutive term, but resigned in 1982. Cameroon generally prospered under his leadership.

Ahmadabad, city in W India, on Sabarmati River; capital of Gujarat state; Mahatma Gandhi located his school for training freedom fighters at nearby Sabarmati Ashram; site of Indian National Congress headquarters; transportation and cultural center of the state, with numerous magnificent mosques, temples, and tombs; noted for its cotton. Founded 1412. Pop. 1,741,522.

Ahriman, or **Angra Mainyu,** Zoroastrian principle of evil and unrighteousness standing in opposition to the God, Ahura Mazda. Like God, Ahriman is pure spirit and has with him subsidiary evil spirits such as lust and heresy. Born of infinite time along with Ahura Mazda, nevertheless, Ahriman will be defeated. See also Ahura Mazda; Zoroastrianism.

Ahura Mazda, in Zoroastrianism, the only God and creator. Later called Ohrmazd, Ahura Mazda was pure goodness. Evil was attributed to an opposing principle, Ahriman. Ahura Mazda will defeat Ahriman in the end. The six Bounteous Immortals springing from Ahura Mazda are godly aspects that can be shared in by righteous men. See also Ahriman; Zoroastrianism.

Ahvenanmaa Islands (Aland Islands), archipelago belonging to Finland, in the Baltic Sea, between Finland and Sweden; fewer than 100 of the 7,000 islands are habitable. Colonized by Sweden 12th century, they were ceded to Russia 1809; became part of Finland 1917; unsuccessfully petitioned at end of WWI to be returned to Sweden; made autonomous and neutral under Finland's sovereignty. Area: 581sq mi (1,505sq km). Pop. 21,010.

Aïda (1871), tragic opera in four acts by Guiseppe Verdi, libretto in Italian by Verdi and Antonio Ghislanzoni, from a plot by Egyptologist Mariette Bey. The opera was commissioned for the opening of the Suez Canal (1869), but was not completed in time. The plot concerns an Egyptian hero, Rhadames (tenor), who spurns the hand of Princess Amneris (mezzo-soprano) for the love of an Ethiopian slave, Aïda (soprano). Jealousy and patriotism contribute to the death of the lovers, who are buried alive together.

AIDS. See Autoimmune Disease.

Aiken, Conrad (1889–1973), US poet, novelist, and critic, b. Savannah, Ga. His work, characterized by introspection and subtle imagery, includes *Selected Poems* (1929; Pulitzer Prize 1930), *Brownstone Eclogues and Other Poems* (1942), and *Ushant* (1952), an autobiography.

Aikido, martial art based on an ancient Japanese system of self-defense. Unlike some other martial art forms, where force is met with counter-force, Aikido employs the technique of avoiding action by giving way to an opponent's force, thereby causing the attacker to have a temporary loss of balance. Aikido also is used as a competitive fighting sport.

Ailanthus, or tree of heaven, paradise tree, Chinese sumac; deciduous, weedlike tree native to China but naturalized in America and Europe. It is tolerant of air pollution, thrives in any soil or climate, and resists most insects and diseases. The fern-shaped leaves grow to 3ft(9cm). Greenish-yellow male and female flowers are borne on separate trees. The nine species include *Ailanthus altissima.* Height: 50–75ft (15–23m). Family Simaroubaceae.

Aileron, hinged control surface on the outboard trailing edge of each wing of an airplane. By rotating the control wheel, the pilot deflects the ailerons down or up in opposite directions to increase or decrease lift, causing the airplane to roll or bank.

Aintab. *See* Gaziantep.

Ainu, aboriginal people, inhabiting Hokkaido (northern Japan) and Sakhalin, and formerly also found in the Kuril Islands. Racially distinct from the Japanese, Ainus possess certain Caucasoid features, notably profuse body and facial hair. Traditionally hunters, fishermen, and trappers, they practice animism and are famed for their bear cult.

Air Conditioning, process of controlling the flow, temperature, and humidity of air, at times including odor and dust removal, in homes, industry, and transportation facilities. Cooling and reduction of humidity is accomplished by refrigeration in summer. In winter the process is reversed by the injection of steam or warm water into heated air. Control of odors and dust is obtained through the use of air filters. Finally, air motion by fans ensures adequate removal of undesired air and replenishment with conditioned air.

Aircraft, machine that derives its lift from the reaction of the mass of air acted upon by fixed wings or rotor, or that rises as the result of being lighter than the surrounding air. Airplanes—heavier-than-air craft with fixed wings and engines—are classified on the basis of intended use, number of engines, type of landing gear, and wing configuration. Rotorcraft—the helicopter that uses a powered rotor for lift and thrust, and the gyroplane that uses a free-wheeling rotor and separate thrust engine—are a second category. Gliders—fixed-wing, powerless craft—comprise a third group; and lighter-than-air craft—rigid, semi-rigid—a fourth. *See also* Dirigible.

Aircraft Carrier, ship designed to carry aircraft and constructed so that aircraft can be launched from and landed on it. A modern nuclear carrier has a flight deck some 1000-ft (300-m) long. Weighing 75,000 tons and with a 4,500 man crew, a nuclear carrier can carry 90 aircraft and launch one per minute with each of four steam catapults. On the big carriers the landing deck is angled to port so that launching and landing operations may be carried on simultaneously.

Aircraft Engine, powerplant, single or in series, that provides energy to take off and maintain flight. Reciprocating engines in general use are gasoline fueled and air cooled. Jet engines that require special fuels are the turbojet and turbofan, which compress air before mixing fuel and utilize the expanding gas of combustion for propulsion. The simpler ramjet uses no compressor or turbine.

Air-Cushion Vehicle, often termed ground-effect vehicle or hovercraft; machine capable of hovering several inches to a few feet above ground or water and of motion forward, backward, or laterally. It accomplishes this by the use of power-driven fans rotating on vertical axes that force air through movable louvres to control direction. It is used as a recreation vehicle and has been experimented with by the military.

Airedale Terrier, working dog (terrier group) bred in northern England's Aire River Valley and brought to United States about 1881. Largest of the terriers, this wiry-coated, black and tan dog has a long, flat head squared off by chin whiskers. Ears are V-shaped and folded. Long straight legs appear massive because of their thick coat. The short tail is carried straight up. Standard size: 23in (58cm) high at shoulder; 45lb (20kg). *See also* Terriers.

Airfoil, any shape or surface such as a wing, tail, or propeller blades on an airplane that has as its major function the deflection of airflow to produce a pressure differential or lift. An airfoil typically has a leading and trailing edge, a chord, and upper and lower camber.

Air Force, Department of the, US government agency. It is responsible for providing an air force that is capable, in conjunction with the other armed forces, of preserving the peace and security of the United States. The department is separately organized under the authority, direction, and control of the secretary of defense. Est. 1947, subsequent legislation 1949.

Air Force, United States (USAF), one of the three major military services established under the Department of Defense in the National Security Act of 1947. It began as the Aeronautical Division of the Army in 1907, became the Aviation Section of the Signal Corps in 1914, the Air Service in 1918, the Army Air Corps in 1926, and the Army Air Forces in 1941. The United States has relied heavily on its air arm since World War I and in such non-war situations as the Berlin Airlift (1948–49) and the Cuban Missile Crisis of 1962.

Airglow, faint permanent glow of the Earth's upper atmosphere resulting from the recombination of molecules, such as oxygen, nitrogen, and chemical impurities, that have been ionized during daytime by ultraviolet radiation from the sun and possibly by cosmic-ray and solar-wind particles.

Airlock, the hermetically sealed passageway connecting airless environment (for example, outer space) with ship cabin or space station work area. Entry is made through an outer door, which must be closed before inner door opens to preserve inner atmosphere.

Air Mass, a large body of the atmosphere nearly homogeneous horizontally in temperature, pressure, and vapor content and therefore in weather effects. High and low pressure zones on weather maps correspond to air masses, covering large areas horizontally although only a few miles vertically. Fronts, or frontal zones, occur between air masses, whose movement brings the weather. Air masses are often classified in terms of origin as polar (cold) or tropical (warm), maritime (wet, over oceans) or continental (dry, over land). *See also* Circulation, Atmospheric; Front, Weather.

Air Pollution, contamination of the atmosphere by any solid, liquid, or gaseous substances except for water. Natural pollutants include salt crystals from oceans, dust and gases from volcanoes, and pollen and spores from plants. Artificial pollutants include smokes and gases from industrial, automotive, municipal, and household activities. The United States, Canada, and 32 East and West European countries signed an accord to curb airborne pollutants in 1979.

Sources. In the United States, 60% of the air pollution is estimated to come from motor vehicles, 17% from industry and space heating, 14% from power plants, and 9% from incineration. Particularly harmful substances polluting air include carbon monoxide and dioxide, hydrocarbons, nitrogen and sulfur oxides, and fine smoke and dust particles, to all of which motor vehicles make a substantial contribution. Pollution often persists and accumulates with temperature inversions leading to pollution disasters, especially with fog.

Effects. Air pollution affects the health, particularly of those with respiratory difficulties like asthma, chronic bronchitis, and emphysema. Its economic costs are estimated at $10 billion a year in the United States alone. Many nations now have clean-air laws to prevent or diminish air pollution. *See also* Fluorocarbons; Inversion.

Air Pressure, the pressure exerted by air, usually within an enclosed space. *See also* Atmospheric Pressure.

Airship, power-driven lighter-than-air craft able to control its direction of motion. A rigid airship or zeppelin maintains its form with a framework of girders covered by a rubber fabric. Nonrigids have no internal structure. Only the pressure of the contained helium maintains the shape. A semirigid airship utilizes a rigid or jointed keel to stiffen the rubberized envelope.

Air Traffic Control, system of aircraft guidance to provide for safe, orderly movement. It consists of ground and local control, from the tower, concerned with traffic at the airport; arrival and departure control operating from radar rooms that directs stacking and separation and funnels traffic to or from the runways; and a system of en route control that allows controllers to "hand off" flights that reach the limits of their radar observation.

Aisha (611–678), the favorite of the 12 wives of the Prophet Mohammed, daughter of abu-Bakr. She married young, collected over 2000 sayings of Mohammed and his companions (hadiths), and incited an unsuccessful uprising against Ali. *See also* Mohammed.

Aisne, river in France; rises near Vaubecourt, flows NW and W from Argonne Forest to join Oise River near Compiègne. In WWI the plateau along the river near Craonne was scene of bitter trench warfare. Length: 175mi (282km).

Aix-en-Provence, city in SE France, 17mi (27km) N of Marseille near mineral springs; site of a popular spa, university (1409), 13th–14th-century Cathedral of Saint-Sauveur; cultural center; home of painter Paul Cézanne. Industries: wine making equipment, electrical apparatus, farming. Founded 123 BC by Romans. Pop. 114,014.

Aix-la-Chapelle, Treaty of (1748), diplomatic agreement between France and Britain ending the War of the Austrian Succession (1740–48) (known in America as King George's War). The treaty did little to settle the causes of the conflict as it simply called for the mutual restitution of conquests made during the war. *See also* Austrian Succession, War of the.

Ajaccio, seaport town and capital of Corsica, France, on the Gulf of Ajaccio, an inlet of Mediterranean Sea. Napoleon was born here and his home is a national museum; occupied by Italians in WWII. Industries: sardine fishing, shipbuilding, cigars, wax. Founded 1492 by Genoese colonists. Pop. 51,770.

Ajax, name given to two legendary heroes who fought on the Greek side during the Trojan war. The Greater Ajax was the son of Telamon, king of Salamis. The Lesser Ajax was the son of Oileus, king of Locris.

Ajax (*c.*447 BC), Greek tragedy thought to be Sophocles' earliest surviving play. In it Ajax goes mad when the armor of Achilles is awarded to Odysseus instead of to him, angers the gods, and dies. Ajax is considered the hero of the work because he exemplifies the Greek code of honor.

Ajman ('Ujman), sheikdom in United Arab Emirates, in E Arabia, on the Persian Gulf; consists of the town of Ajman and two mountain villages. Formerly a British protectorate, it joined the United Arab Emirates 1971. Main industry is oil production. Area: approx. 100sq mi (259sq km). Pop. 21,566.

Ajuga, commonly called bugle or bugle-weed, a European perennial herbaceous plant of the mint family. It is widespread as a weed in North America but varieties are used for borders and in rock gardens.

Akan, African people who settled in Ghana, Togo, and the eastern Ivory Coast (*c.*1000–1700). They have matrilineal clan groupings and ancestor worship; yams are the staple of their diet.

Akbar (1542–1605), Mogul emperor of India (1556–1605). Succeeding his father, he conquered Gujarat, Bengal, Kashmir, Sind, and Quandahar. He reformed the government, centralized the financial system, and won loyalty to the throne and unity among his non-Muslim people.

Akhenaton (Ikhnaton) (*d.c.*1362 BC), ancient Egyptian king of the 18th dynasty (*r.c.*1379–1362 BC). He succeeded his father, Amenhotep III. His name at accession was Amenhotep IV. Renouncing the old gods, he introduced worship of the sun god, Aten, and established a new capital at Akhetaton (modern Tell-el-Amarna). After his death, however, Egypt rejected solar worship. His wife was Nefertiti. *See also* Amenhotep IV.

Akita, city in NW Honshu, Japan, on the Sea of Japan; capital of Akita prefecture; site of castle-fort (733) and university (1949); important export center. Akita prefecture contains the largest oil field and copper mines in Japan; agricultural region. Oil refining is the major industry. Crops: rice, tobacco, fruit. Pop. 261,000.

Akita, Japanese hunting dog (working group) bred in Akita prefecture in the 17th century; brought to United States in 1937 by Helen Keller. It has a broad, triangular head; small pointed, wide-set ears carried erect; a long body; muscular legs; and large, curled tail. The straight, harsh double coat of any color stands straight out and is shorter on head, legs, and ears. Average size: 20–27in (51–69cm) high at shoulder; 75–110lb (34–50kg). The Akita is considered a symbol of good health by Japanese and has been designated a national treasure by the Japanese government. *See also* Working Dog.

Akron, city in NE Ohio, on Little Cuyahoga River, 35mi (56km) SE of Cleveland; seat of Summit co, Ohio and Erie Canal opened here in 1827 and spurred growth of area. Home of abolitionist John Brown is preserved as a museum. City has a dirigible airdock; site of world's first rubber factory, est 1869 by Dr. B. F. Goodrich, Institute of Rubber Research, and University of Akron (1913). Industries: rubber, plastics, transportation

Aircraft carrier: USS Nimitz

Ajaccio, Corsica

Mobile, Alabama

equipment. Settled *c.* 1825; inc. as village 1836; chartered as city 1865. Pop. (1970) 237,177.

Alabama, state in SE United States, in the Deep South's Cotton Belt. In the Civil War, it was one of the six original states of the Confederacy.

Land and Economy. Roughly the N half lies in the Appalachian Highlands, which have deposits of coal and other minerals; the remainder is in the Gulf Coastal Plain, which is crossed by the Black Belt, a wide strip of rich soil, valuable for farming. The Mobile River, flowing S to the Gulf of Mexico, and its tributaries, the Alabama and the Tombigbee, form the chief river system. On the Tennessee River in the N are three hydroelectric power dams and a Tennessee Valley Authority nuclear power plant. Traditionally agrarian, the economy has been altered by industrial growth concentrated in urban areas, where the majority of the population lives. Birmingham is a leading steel center.

People. The 19th-century settlers were immigrants from other states or black slaves who worked cotton plantations before the Civil War. The migration from rural areas to urban centers was long and slow.

Education and Research. There are about 60 institutions of higher education. The University of Alabama and Auburn University are state-supported. At Huntsville, NASA's George C. Marshall Space Flight Center is a focus of rocket and missile research.

History. Spanish explorers visited Alabama in the 16th century, but the first white settlers were the French, in 1701. Great Britain acquired the region from France in 1763 and ceded most of it to the United States after the American Revolution (1783). Some of the S, then part of Florida, was in Spanish hands until 1812. In 1817, the Territory of Alabama was created. Alabama seceded on Jan. 11, 1861; Montgomery was the first Confederate capital. Alabama was readmitted to the Union in June 1868. During the 1960s the state was a center of civil rights activities, and Gov. George C. Wallace achieved national prominence as a proponent of segregation. An independent presidential candidate in 1968, Wallace withdrew from national politics in 1972 after an assassination attempt left him partially paralyzed, but was reelected governor in 1982.

PROFILE

Admitted to Union: 1819; rank, 22nd
US Congressmen: Senate - 2; House of Representatives - 7
Population: 3,890,061 (1980); rank, 22nd
Capital: Montgomery, pop. (1980) 178,157
Chief cities: Birmingham, 284,413; Mobile, 200,452; Huntsville, 142,513
State Legislature: Senate, 35 members; House of Representatives, 105
Area: 51,609sq mi (133,667sq km); rank, 29th
Elevation: Highest, Cheaha Mt, 2407ft (734m); lowest, sea level
Industries (major products): iron and steel products, chemicals, processed foods, paper and paper products, textiles
Agriculture (major products): cotton, poultry, cattle
Minerals (major): coal, stone, petroleum
State nicknames: Heart of Dixie, Yellowhammer State
State motto: "We Dare Defend Our Rights"
State bird: Yellowhammer (Flicker)
State flower: Camellia
State tree: Southern Pine

Alabama, or **Alibamu,** Muskogean-speaking tribe of North American Indians. Their ancient home was the upper Alabama River; they moved around widely in the Southeast, eventually to Louisiana and Polk co, Tex., where their 500 descendants today inhabit a reservation area with the closely related Koasati.

Alabama Claims, demands by the US government for indemnity from Britain for damage done to Northern ships by the Confederate cruiser Alabama and other Confederate ships constructed and outfitted in England during the US Civil War. By the Treaty of Washington (May 1871), Britain agreed to submit the claims to arbitration. The United States was later awarded (1872) $15.5 million in gold for direct damages.

Alabaster, a compact, massive variety of gypsum, snow-white and translucent in nature. May be dyed or heated and made opaque. Used for statuary and ornaments for centuries. *See also* Gypsum.

Al-Alamein (El Alamein or **Al-'Alamayn),** village in N Egypt, 65mi (105km) W of Alexandria; Allied forces, led by British Gen. Bernard Montgomery, in November 1942 pushed Axis powers back across Libya into E Tunisia; this led to defeat of Axis efforts to take Alexandria and Suez Canal during WWII.

Alameda, city in W California, on island near E shore of San Francisco Bay, 6mi (10km) E of San Francisco; site of naval air base, commercial airports; Industries: manufacture of borax, aircraft parts, pumps. Inc. 1854. Pop. 63,852.

Alamo, mission building in San Antonio, called "the cradle of Texas liberty." Here, in February 1836, about 180 Texans, led by William Travis, Davy Crockett, and Jim Bowie, held out until overwhelmed by several thousand Mexicans under General Santa Anna on March 6. Six weeks later at San Jacinto, Texans went into battle shouting "Remember the Alamo." They then defeated Santa Anna's army in the final battle for Texas independence.

Alamogordo, city in SW New Mexico, 85mi (137km) NE of Sacramento, California; seat of Otero co; site of White Sands Missile Range, where the first atomic bomb was exploded June 16, 1945, and Holloman Air Force Base; trade center. Industries: lumber, tourism. Founded 1898; inc. 1912. Pop. (1970) 24,024.

Alanbrooke, Alan Francis Brooke, 1st Viscount (1883–1963), English military commander, b. France. As chief of the imperial general staff (1941–46), he directed British tactics against Germany and coordinated Anglo-American strategy with Eisenhower.

Alarcón, Pedro Antonio de (1833–91), Spanish novelist. His literary career reflected his transition from a staunch anticleric to a devout Roman Catholic. Wounded in the Moroccan campaign, he wrote a journal of his war experiences (1859–60) but gained international fame upon the publication of the short novel *The Three-Cornered Hat* (1874).

Alaric (*c.*370–410), king of the Visigoths (395–410). His forces conquered Thrace, Macedonia, and Greece and occupied Epirus (395–96). He invaded Italy in 401 and 408 and engineered the siege (408) and sack (410) of Rome. The city was plundered relatively lightly, but the power of the Roman Empire was irredeemably diminished. He planned an invasion of Sicily and Africa, but his fleet was demolished in a storm. He died shortly thereafter.

Alaska, state in NW United States, separated from the continental United States by the province of British Columbia, Canada. It is the largest state in area and the smallest in population.

Land and Economy. About 25% of Alaska lies N of the Arctic Circle. The Alaska Range in the S central area includes the highest peaks in North America. The chief river is the Yukon, flowing E to W to the Bering

Sea. The Aleutian Island chain, which has active volcanoes, extends 1,700mi (2,737km) SW and W. The Alexander Archipelago, containing hundreds of islands, is in the SE. Alaska's natural resources, especially fish, timber, and petroleum, are the base of its economy. Vast oil deposits in the Brooks Range in the N are tapped via a pipeline which runs 800mi (1,288km) from Prudhoe Bay on the Arctic Ocean to Valdez on the S coast. Construction of the line brought thousands of workers to the state. Tourism is a major revenue source.

People. The population has more than tripled since WWII. Most people came from other parts of the United States. Their average age is younger than in other states. About 17% of the population is of Eskimo or Indian extraction.

Education and Research. There are nine institutions of higher education; some carry on research in meteorology and in testing materials and techniques under extreme climatic conditions.

History. Vitus Bering, a Danish navigator serving Russia, made the first recorded landing in July 1741. Russian hunters followed, and a monopoly company exported furs until wasteful slaughter of animals decimated the supply. The United States purchased Alaska from Russia on Oct. 18, 1867, for $7.2 million, less than 2 cents an acre. Fishing drew settlers, and after gold was discovered in the 1890s the population doubled in 10 years. Self-government was granted gradually but the first territorial legislature did not meet until 1913. In WWII, after Japanese forces occupied Attu and Kiska in the Aleutians, Alaska was developed as a major military area. The development of North Slope oil deposits and completion of the Alaska oil pipeline (1977) transformed the economy, although, in the mid-1980s, a worldwide oil glut meant lower oil prices and a downturn in the economy. The controversial Alaska lands bill, approved by the federal government despite Alaskan opposition in 1980, protected over 1,000,000 acres (400,000 hectares) of wilderness from unregulated development.

PROFILE

Admitted to Union: 1959; rank 49th
US Congressmen: Senate, 2; House of Representatives, 1
Population: 400,481 (1980); rank, 50th
Capital: Juneau, (1980) 19,528
Chief cities: Anchorage, 173,017; Fairbanks, 22,645; Ketchikan, 7,198
State legislature: Senate, 20 members; House of Representatives, 40
Area: 586,400sq mi (1,518,776sq km); rank, 1st
Elevation: Highest, Mt McKinley, 20,320ft (6,198m); lowest, sea level
Industries (major products): processed foods (fish), forest products (pulp)
Minerals (major): petroleum, natural gas
State nickname: None
State motto: "North to the Future"
State bird: Yellow Ptarmigan
State fish: King Salmon
State flower: Forget-me-not
State tree: Sitka Spruce

Alaska Highway, road connecting Dawson Creek, British Columbia, with Fairbanks, Alaska; built by the United States April-November 1942 to link military installations in Alaska with US proper by protected land route. Length: 1,523mi (2,452m).

Alaskan Boundary Dispute (1902–03), dispute between the United States and Britain, representing Canada, over possession of the inlets between Alaska and Canada after the Klondike gold strike. It was settled by a six-man panel in favor of the United States.

Alaskan Brown Bear, or Kodiak bear, omnivorous brown bear of Kodiak Island and adjacent areas on Alaskan mainland. Length: over 8ft (2.5m); weight: to 1715lb (772kg). Species *Ursus arctos.*

Alaskan Malamute, Arctic sled dog (working group) for pulling heavy freight; named after Eskimo tribe. This substantial dog has a broad head and large bulky muzzle; wedge-shaped ears erect at alert; brown, almond-shaped eyes; strong, compact body; straight, heavy-boned legs; and fox brush tail. The short to medium-length thick, coarse coat ranges from light gray to black with white. There is a characteristic face mask marking. Average size: 25in (64cm) high at shoulder; 85lb (38kg). *See also* Working Dog.

Alaska Purchase (1867), transfer of the Russian territory of Alaska to the United States for $7,200,000. Many Americans regarded Alaska as a frozen wasteland and the purchase was called "Seward's Folly" after Secretary of State William Seward, who negotiated the purchase.

Alaska Range, mountain range located in S central Alaska; extends in a semi-circular shape from the Alaska Peninsula to the Yukon. The highest point is Mt McKinley, 20,320ft (6,198m).

Alba (or Alva), Fernando Alvarez de Toledo, Duke of (1508–82), Spanish general and regent of the Netherlands. He joined the Spanish army in 1524. In 1547 he was instrumental in the victory of Mühlberg over John Frederick, Elector of Saxony. In 1567, Philip II appointed him regent of Netherlands. He ruthlessly suppressed Protestant and nationalist opposition. Thousands of people, including Counts Egmont and Hoorn, were executed. In 1572 the Dutch rose up in armed rebellion. Alba was unable to quell it completely. He was recalled to Spain in 1573. After years of being out of favor, in 1580 he led a successful invasion of Portugal.

Albacore, long-finned tuna of warm seas. Cigar-shaped with a large tail sharply divided into two lobes, it has a long pectoral fin. A fast swimmer, it is an important commercial and game fish; albacore white meat is canned. Length: 3ft (91cm); weight: 40–80lbs. (18–36kg). Family Scombridae; species *Thunnus alalugna.*

Alba Longa, city of ancient Latium near Lake Albano, 12mi (19km) SE of modern Rome; believed to have been built *c.* 1152 BC by Ascanius (son of Aeneas); reputedly Latium's most powerful city as head of Latin League, and mother city of Rome; traditional birthplace of Romulus and Remus; modern site of papal summer residence Castel Gandolfo, on Lake Albano. Only tombs (over 3,000 years old) remain of ancient city.

Albania (Shqipëri), People's Socialist Republic of, small independent nation of the Balkan Peninsula in SE Europe. Since WWII, Albania has been a Communist state, although it remains isolated from other Communist nations, and despite its developing economy, has an official economic policy of "self-reliance."

Land and Economy. Albania lies on the Adriatic Sea, bordered by Yugoslavia (N and E) and by Greece (S). The interior of the country consists of high mountain ranges and highland plateaus. In the N are the rugged, forbidding North Albanian Alps; the limestone surface rocks do not support good soil. The most fertile lands are found in the valleys of the S. Several W-flowing rivers drop through narrow, deeply cut valleys down to the coastal lowlands. Few Albanians live in these marshy coastal plains. Durres is the only notable seaport. The Soviet-styled economy is about evenly divided between agricultural production and industrialization. Substantial industrial progress has been achieved since WWII, and farm output has increased much faster than population.

People. The population is exceptionally homogeneous; about 97% is of Albanian ethnic origin. The two major tribal groups are the Gegs of the N and the Tosks of the S. The Albanian language is spoken by both groups, but the dialect of the Tosks is the official language. All religious activities are strongly discouraged by the Communist government. Two-thirds of the people are Muslims of the Sunni and Bektashi sects; the remainder are Christians of the Eastern Orthodox and Roman Catholic churches. Nearly a million ethnic Albanians live in Yugoslavia.

Government. The constitution is styled on the Soviet model, and provides for a legislature (the People's Assembly), an executive branch (the Presidium), and an independent judiciary. True power lies, however, in the politburo and central committee of the Albanian Workers' party.

History. The Albanians are descended from the Illyrians, who settled the Balkan Peninsula in the pre-Christian era. For centuries the Albani tribe resisted the influence of the Romans and the Byzantines. The Turks gained control over the Albanians in the 15th century, and the Islamic religion penetrated all but the most mountainous regions. A national revival began in the 19th century and culminated in Albanian independence (1912). The Communist party, formed in WWII, with Enver Hoxha as its head, seized power in 1944, establishing close ties with Yugoslavia until 1948, when Albania became a satellite of the USSR. After breaking off with the USSR in 1961, Albania allied itself with China, but all ties were formally ended in 1978. Since then the country has established trade agreements with Greece and Yugoslavia and, with Hoxha's death and Ramiz Alia's succession to the party leadership in 1985, has made tentative overtures to expand its international ties.

PROFILE

Official name: People's Socialist Republic of Albania
Area: 11,100sq mi (28,749sq km)
Population: 2,600,000; *Density,* 234 per sq mi (90 per sq km)
Chief cities: Tirana (capital); Durres; Shkoder
Government: Communist
Religion: Muslim, Eastern Orthodox
Language: Albanian (official)
Monetary unit: Lek
Gross national product: $1,200,000,000
Per capita income: $520
Industries (major products): food processing, textiles, petroleum products, cement
Agriculture (major products): corn, wheat, tobacco
Minerals (major): coal, chromium, copper
Trading partners (major): People's Republic of China, Czechoslovakia, Poland, East Germany

Albany, city in SW Georgia on Flint River; seat of Dougherty co; industrial and trade center for agricultural region. Crops: pecans, peanuts, cotton. Industries: airplane manufacturing, pharmaceuticals, meat packing, cotton milling. Inc. 1841. Pop. (1980) 73,934.

Albany, city and capital of New York, on the W bank of the Hudson River, 145mi (234km) N of New York City; seat of Albany co. Henry Hudson first visited the area in 1609 as he explored the river; Dutch traders built Fort Nassau here 1614, which was destroyed by flood 1617 and replaced by Fort Orange 1624; captured by English 1664 and renamed Albany; scene of 1754 Albany Congress; after the Revolutionary War, it replaced New York City as state capital (1797); site of Schuyler Mansion (1762), Ten Broeck Mansion (1798), Cherry Hill (1768, home of Van Rensselaer descendants until 1963), University of Albany (1844), state capitol (1871), and Albany Law School, Medical College, and College of Pharmacy. Industries: brewing, meat packing, chemicals, brushes, textiles. Settled 1614, 2nd-oldest permanent settlement in 13 colonies; inc. 1686. Pop. (1980) 101,727.

Albany Congress (1754), colonial conference to discuss Indian relations. Representatives from New Hampshire, Massachusetts, Rhode Island, Connecticut, New York, Pennsylvania, and Maryland met in Albany, N.Y., at British urging to gain the loyalty of the Iroquois Indians against the French. A treaty was negotiated. At this meeting Benjamin Franklin also proposed a Plan for Union of the colonies, which would have coordinated and centralized defense, Indian relations, and westward expansion. It was approved by the Congress but rejected by both Britain and the individual colonial governments.

Albatross, large, oceanic bird of Southern Hemisphere famed for strong flying power. It has long, thick, hooked bill, short tail, webbed toes, long wings, and thick feathers. Known to eat ship throwaways, it feeds mainly on marine animals. After elaborate courtship, the females lay a single chalky egg in a small nest on an isolated island. Length: 4–11ft (122–335cm). Family Diomedeidae.

Albedo, the fraction of light or other radiation striking a surface or body, like the ground, that is reflected by it, the remainder being absorbed. Expressed as a percentage, bare ground has an average albedo of 10 to 20%, fresh snow 80 to 85%, and the whole earth, viewed from satellites, 36%.

Albee, Edward Franklin (1928–   ), US dramatist, b. Washington, D.C. His best known play is *Who's Afraid of Virginia Woolf?* (1962). Other of his clever, biting commentaries on American life include the one-act plays *The Zoo Story* (1959) and *The Sandbox* (1960), and the full-length plays *Tiny Alice* (1965), *A Delicate Balance* (1967, Pulitzer Prize), *Seascape* (1975), and *The Lady from Dubuque* (1980).

Albers, Josef (1888–1976), German painter, poet, and art teacher. He helped to develop color field painting and op art. He studied at the Bauhaus, and in 1933 he came to the United States. His most famous work, dealing with color relationships, is "Homage to the Square," a series of paintings begun in 1949. *See also* Color Field Painting; Op Art.

Albert I (1875–1934), king of Belgium (1909–34). Son of Philip, Count of Flanders, he succeeded his uncle, Leopold II, and restored confidence in the throne. In 1914 he led the Belgian resistance, holding the Germans while the Allied defense formed. He led the Belgian and French forces in the final general offensive through Belgium (1918). After the war, he devoted himself to the task of reconstruction.

Albert II (1397–1439), king of Germany (1438–39), king of Bohemia and Hungary (1438–39); founder of the Hapsburg German succession. He succeeded his father as Albert V, duke of Austria (1404–39), and as duke proved a capable reorganizer. His short reign as king was marked by unrest in Hungary and Bohemia and a war with the Turks in which he was killed.

Albert I, called Albert the Bear (1100–70), first margrave of Brandenburg (1150–70). His hold on Brandenburg was always tenuous, but he contributed greatly to the Christianizing and Germanizing of NE Germany.

Albert III, called Albert the Bold (1443–1500), Duke of Saxony. Founder of the Albertine line, he ruled Saxony jointly with his older brother, Ernest (1464–85). When the dominions were apportioned, Albert received eastern and western parts, including Meissen.

Albert, Lake (Albert Nyanza), lake in E central Africa on the border between Zaire and Uganda. The Semliki River and the Victoria Nile empty into Lake Albert; the Albert Nile flows from it; discovered 1864 by Samuel Baker. Length: 100mi (161km); width: 19mi (31km); max. depth: 168ft (51m).

Alberta, province of W Canada, bordered on the S by the state of Montana.

Land and Economy. Except where the Rocky Mountain ranges lie along part of the W boundary, Alberta is part of the high plains of central North America, with a few hills and deep river valleys. The principal rivers are the Athabasca, Peace, Saskatchewan, and Milk. Lesser Slave Lake is the largest of the many lakes; Lake Louise, in the Rockies, is noted for its beauty. The fertile plains support vast wheat farming and livestock raising, and the oil and natural gas fields of central Alberta make a major contribution to the economy. Manufacturing is mostly concentrated in the areas of Edmonton and Calgary.

People. Settlement did not begin on a large scale until the late 19th century, when immigrants came from other Canadian provinces, the United States, and Europe. The character of the population stabilized, and now more than 80% was born in the province.

Education. The University of Alberta, at Edmonton, and the universities of Calgary and Lethbridge are the centers of higher education. There are a number of junior colleges.

History. The area was part of a huge territory granted in 1670 by Charles II of England to the Hudson's Bay Co., a fur-trading enterprise. In 1870 the government of Canada bought the region from the company. Farming pioneers arrived, and a transcontinental railroad was completed across the S part in 1885. The area was part of the North West Territories and was governed from the Canadian capital in Ottawa, but in 1882 this was divided into four districts, Alberta being one. In 1905 it was admitted to the Confederation as a province along with Saskatchewan. Natural gas was discovered as early as 1914, but rich oil fields found after WWII were a major stimulus to the economy. During the late 1970s and early 1980s conflicts between Alberta and the federal government over provincial autonomy and oil revenues gave rise to an Albertan secessionist movement and threatened Canadian unity.

PROFILE

Admitted to Confederation: Sept. 1, 1905; rank, 8th
National Parliament Representatives: Senate, 6; House of Commons, 19
Population: 1,838,037
Capital: Edmonton, 491,359
Chief cities: Edmonton; Calgary, 530,816; Lethbridge, 51,668; Red Deer, 39,370
Provincial Legislature: Legislative Assembly, 75 members
Area: 255,285sq mi (661,188sq km); rank, 4th
Elevation: Highest, Mt Columbia, 12,294ft (3,750m); lowest, Slave River, 686ft (209m)
Industries (major products): petroleum products, processed foods (meat), chemicals, fabricated metals
Agriculture (major products): wheat, cattle, dairy products, hogs, poultry
Minerals (major): petroleum, natural gas, sulfur
Floral emblem: wild rose

Albania

Edward Albee

Louisa May Alcott

Albert Nile, river in Uganda, the section of the Nile River that drains Lake Albert and flows N through NW Uganda; site of the Nimule Dam, part of Equatorial Nile Project to increase water power. Length: 130mi (209km).

Albert of Saxe-Coburg-Gotha (1819–61), prince consort of Queen Victoria. The son of Ernest I, duke of Saxe-Coburg-Gotha, Albert married his first cousin Victoria in 1840. Although at first unpopular in Britain because he was not English, he gradually gained acceptance through his promotion of science and the arts, his influence on diplomatic affairs, and his devotion to the queen. He suggested the International Exhibition of 1851. In world affairs he counseled for a restrained approach to the Trent Affair (1861), which helped to avoid a war with the United States.

Albertus Magnus (1206–80), German theologian. Exposed to Aristotle's philosophy at Padua, he became a Dominican (1223) and Bishop of Regensburg (1260). Albertus wrote *Books on the Sentences* and a *Summa Theologiae,* the second essentially repetitive of the Aristotelian Scholasticism of the first. Thomas Aquinas was one of his pupils. He was beatified in 1622.

Albigenses, followers of the Catharist heresy in southern France (Languedoc) during the 12th and 13th centuries who threatened the political power of the Roman Catholic Church. Pope Innocent III called for a crusade against them. The French crown used the crusade to conquer Languedoc in 1229.

Albinism, hereditary absence of pigment from the skin, hair, and eyes. The hair is snow white, and the eyes, which are often extremely sensitive to light, are pink with red pupils. In partial, or piebald, albinism, only certain areas are affected, producing white spotting or white forelock, for example.

Alboin (died 573), Germanic Lombard king who conquered northern Italy. Coming from Noricum and Pannonia (now in Austria and Hungary), he led his people across the Alps to conquer north and central Byzantine Italy. He established Pavia as capital of the new Lombard kingdom (572).

Albumin, group of soluble proteins that occur in many animal tissues and fluids. Principal forms are egg albumin (ovalbumin), milk albumin (lactalbumin), and blood albumin (serum albumin).

Albuquerque, Affonso de (1453–1515), Portuguese admiral and founder of the Portuguese empire in the East. He made his first trip to India in 1503 and went again in 1506, this time as governor. He explored the Madagascar and East African coasts and built forts throughout the East. He took control of Malacca, Calicut, the Malabar Coast, Ceylon, and Goa, which he made the Portuguese capital in the East (1510). The victim of political intrigue, he was recalled in 1515, but died before leaving Goa.

Albuquerque, city in W central New Mexico, on Upper Rio Grande River; seat of Bernalillo co; largest city in New Mexico. Founded by Spanish 1706, it served as a military post until 1870; newer city section was founded 1880; noted health resort. It is the site of Old Town Plaza (1706), Church of San Felipe de Neri (1706), University of New Mexico (1889), University of Albuquerque (1940). Industries: nuclear research and development, food processing, railroad shops. Inc. 1890. Pop. (1980) 331,767.

Alcaeus (c.600 BC), Greek lyric poet who wrote political songs, hymns, and love songs. He was widely imitated by Horace and others, but only fragments of his poems have survived.

Alcestis (438 BC), Greek tragedy by Euripides. The work is best known for its strong characterization of its noble heroine. Alcestis takes her husband's place in Hades so that he may live. Heracles brings her back alive, and husband and wife are reunited.

Alchemy, primitive form of chemistry practiced in Western Europe in the Middle Ages, popularly supposed to involve a search for the Philosopher's Stone —an agent capable of transmuting base metals into gold. In fact, alchemy was a more general study involving a combination of practical chemistry, astrology, philosophy, and mysticism, based on the concept of the unity of matter and analogous ideas of the unity of man with the universe. Similar movements existed in China and India. In Western Europe, alchemy was practiced from early Christian times until the 17th century. *See also* Paracelsus, Philippus Aureolus; Phlogiston Theory.

Alcibiades (450–404 BC), Athenian general and statesman, ward of Pericles, intimate of Socrates, related to Plato. After the disastrous Sicilian campaign which he inspired, he temporarily aided Sparta. Regaining position in Athens, he was defeated at Notium in 407.

Alcman (c.650 BC), chief lyric poet of Sparta. A former slave from Sardis, he is regarded as the founder of erotic poetry. He abandoned the hexameter and wrote in varied, simple meters. Among his known work, surviving in fragments, is the poem "Parthenion" (a choir song for girls), which was found in Egypt in 1855, on a 1st-century papyrus.

Alcmene, in Greek mythology, the mother of Hercules by Zeus. She was betrothed to Amphitryon, Prince of Thebes, who had avenged the death of her brothers. While he was away Zeus came to Alcmene disguised as Amphitryon. Iphicles was the son of Alcmene and Amphitryon.

Alcohol, member of a class of organic compounds characterized by the presence of a hydroxyl (-OH) group bound to a hydrocarbon group. Ethanol, C_2H_5OH, is the commonest example. Alcohols can be oxidized to aldehydes, as in $C_2H_5OH + 0 \rightarrow CH_3CHO$ (acetaldehyde). Further oxidation gives a carboxylic acid: $CH_3CHO + 0 \rightarrow CH_3COOH$ (acetic acid). They react with acids to give esters: thus, ethanol and acetic acid give ethyl acetate, $C_2H_5OH + CH_3COOH \rightarrow C_2H_5OOCCH$. Their systematic names are formed using the suffix -ol.

Alcoholics Anonymous, organization that seeks to help alcoholics help themselves, with the ultimate goal of rehabilitation. Founded in 1935, it has local autonomous groups in more than 90 countries. Membership is open to anyone who has the desire to stop drinking, and the group works on a shared-experience and help method.

Alcoholism, an illness marked by excessive use and preoccupation with alcohol that interferes with a person's health and ability to work and function in society. Extremely common, it is the number-one drug problem in many parts of the world. Alcohol is a depressant drug that produces changes in behavior even in moderate doses, but it is with repeated heavy use that serious problems occur. The illness develops insidiously and is sometimes hard to recognize, but signs such as frequent drunkenness, a great change in personality when drinking, a person's forgetting what he or she said or did when drinking, and sickness and problems at home or at work because of drinking signal the beginning of a serious problem. Alcoholism causes damage to many parts of the body and can result in cirrhosis of the liver, stomach and intestinal inflammation, and muscle damage as well as severe damage to the brain and nervous system, manifested by alcoholic blackouts, psychotic episodes and other illnesses. It is not known why some people become alcoholics, but a combination of psychological, hereditary, biochemical, familial, and cultural factors are probably interwoven to produce susceptibility. The illness is treated—very often successfully—in a variety of ways, many involving counseling or psychotherapy. Drugs that make a person physically sick immediately after taking alcohol are also sometimes used to produce alcohol aversion.

Alcott, Amos Bronson (1799–1888), American philosopher, teacher, reformer, and important member of the New England Transcendentalists; b. near Wolcott, Conn. He established a series of progressive schools for children, the last of which was the Temple School in Boston, and was influential in founding the utopian community, Fruitlands, in Massachusetts. He was the father of the author Louisa May Alcott.

Alcott, Louisa May (1832–88), US author, b. Germantown, Pa. She is best known for her books for children. Her first published book was *Flower Fables* (1854), a collection of fairy stories. Family debts led her to write the autobiographical novel *Little Women* (1868). Its great success led her to write *An Old-Fashioned Girl* (1870), *Little Men* (1871), *Jo's Boys* (1886), and others.

Alcuin (735–804), scholar and cleric from Northumbria in Britain, trained at cathedral school at York. Invited to set up a palace school in court of Charlemagne, he became a central figure of the Carolingian Renaissance. His prolific writings include a corrected text of the Vulgate Bible. *See also* Carolingian Renaissance.

Aldebaran, or **Alpha Tauri,** red giant star in the constellation Taurus. Characteristics: apparent mag. + 0.78; absolute mag. −0.2; spectral type K5; distance 65 light-years.

Aldehyde, member of a class of organic compounds characterized by the presence of the group =CO:H. The simplest example is formaldehyde, HCOH, used as a preservative. Aldehydes can be made by oxidizing simple alcohols. They are generally reducing agents, being oxidized to carboxylic acids, and also form addition and condensation compounds with many reagents. Their systematic names are formed using the suffix -al (ethanal, CH_3CHO). *See also* Alcohol.

Alden, John (c. 1599–1687), American settler, b. England. A signer of the Mayflower Compact and organizer of Plymouth Colony, he settled in Duxbury, Mass, in 1627. Traditionally, he is known as the first Pilgrim to set foot on Plymouth Rock, and as the man who won the hand of Priscilla Mullens after first wooing her for his friend, Miles Standish, an event dramatized in Henry Wadsworth Longfellow's poem, "The Courtship of Miles Standish." He wed Priscilla in 1625 and they had 11 children. He served as the governor's assistant (1623–41, 1650–86), twice serving as deputy governor.

Alder, ornamental trees and shrubs of the birch family native to the Northern Hemisphere and W South America. They have toothed leaves and woody cones that remain on branches after nuts are released. The scaly bark is used in dyeing and the wood is used in bridges because it resists underwater rot. The red, speckled, and European alders are well-known species. They are short-lived trees and usually among the first to appear in denuded areas. There are 30 species. Family Betulaceae; genus *Alnus. See also* Birch.

Aldhelm (Ealdhelm) (?639–709), English cleric and poet, saint of the Roman Catholic Church. He became abbot of Malmesbury *c.*675 and first bishop of Sherborne in 705. He established numerous monasteries and churches.

Aldosterone, mineralocorticoid hormone secreted by the adrenal cortex. It regulates the salt and water balance of the body.

Aldrin, Edwin ("Buzz") (1930–), US astronaut, b. Glen Ridge, N.J. Aldrin piloted the Gemini XII orbital rendezvous space flight (November 1966) and the lunar module for the first lunar landing (July 1969). Following Neil Armstrong, he was the second man on the moon.

Aldrin, brown solid chlorinated naphthalene derivative (formula $C_{12}H_8Cl_6$) widely used as a contact insecticide. It is insoluble in water and is used as an emulsion or powder. It is also incorporated into plastic cable coverings to make them resistant to termites.

Aleichem, Sholom (1859–1916), pseud. of Solomon Rabinowitz, Yiddish novelist, dramatist, and short story writer. Born in Russia, he emigrated to the United States. He portrayed the oppressed Russian Jews with humor and compassion. His works include *The Old Country* (trans. 1946) and *The Milkman (Tevye)* (1945), adapted as the musical *Fiddler on the Roof* (1964). He helped found the Yiddish Art Theater and was influential in establishing Yiddish as a literary language.

Alemanni, or **Alamanni,** loose confederation of ancient Germanic tribes. First mentioned in 213 as unsuccessfully attacking the Romans between the Elbe and the Danube, by the 5th century they were settled in what is now Alsace, Baden, and NE Switzerland. In 496 they were defeated by Clovis I of the Franks, and by 536 they were completely subjugated to Frankish rule. They were converted to Christianity in the 7th century. From their name came the French and Spanish names for Germany: Allemagne and Allemania.

Alembert, Jean le Rond d' (1717–83), French mathematician, scientist, and writer who conducted important studies on fluid dynamics, celestial mechanics, and partial differential equations. In 1780 he published an eight-volume work on his mathematical studies. He also wrote articles for Diderot's *Encyclopédie,* which he helped to edit.

Aleppo (Halab), second-largest city in Syria, approx. 70mi (113km) E of Mediterranean Sea; captured by Arabs from the Byzantines in AD 638; captured by Ottoman Turks (1517), became a great commercial center. Importance declined in late 19th century, after the completion of the Suez Canal; became part of Syria in 1924; site of 12th-century Byzantine citadel, the Great Mosque (715), university (1960) and institute of music; mentioned by Shakespeare in *Macbeth.* Industries: pistachio nuts, fruit, cotton, silk, cement. Pop. 710,636.

Aleut, distant branch of the Eskimo people occupying the Aleutian Peninsula and Shumagin Islands. They are divided into two major groups—the Unalaska and Atka. First discovered by Vitus Bering in 1741, they were forced into service as fur hunters and front-line attackers of other native peoples as far south as California. They numbered about 16,000, a number reduced to less than 1500 a century later due to brutal treatment. They were noted as excellent hunters of sea otters, blue foxes, and seals, and the women weave superb baskets of sea-grass. Today, approximately 5000 Aleut people live in scattered villages throughout SW Alaska. *See also* Eskimo.

Aleutian Islands, chain of volcanic islands, reaching from the Alaska Peninsula 1,200mi (1,932km) toward the USSR's Komandorski Islands. The main island groups are the Fox, Andreanof, Rat, and Near islands. The islands were discovered 1741 by the Danish explorer Vitus Bering for Russia and were purchased by the United States in 1867. The Japanese occupied some of the islands in WWII. Inhabited mainly by Eskimos, there is some agriculture, but the chief industries are fishing and fur hunting. Pop. (approx.) 8,000.

Aleutian Range, volcanic mountain system in S Alaska, on E Alaskan Peninsula, extends S to Aleutian Islands; site of Mt Katmai, 6,715ft (2,015m), and Katmai National Monument, a recreational facility in a volcanic area, including Valley of Ten Thousand Smokes. Length: approx. 700mi (1,127km).

Alewife, marine commercial fish found in N Atlantic and also landlocked in large freshwater lakes. Canned or salted as "river herring," it is gray-green with dark horizontal side stripes. Length: 15in (38.1cm); weight: 14oz (.4kg). Family Clupeidae; species *Pomolobus pseudoharengus.*

Alexander III, Roman Catholic pope (1159–81), b. Orlando Bandinelli. He was not the choice of Holy Roman Emperor Frederick I and an antipope, Victor IV, was elected. A schism persisted for 17 years, ending with the Lombard League victory over Frederick at the battle of Legano. Alexander decreed that the College of Cardinals be solely responsible for papal elections.

Alexander VI, Roman Catholic pope (1492–1503), b. Rodrigo Borgia (*c.*1431). Winning the papacy by promises and bribes, his reputation for poisoning his enemies grew with his drive for power. Many in the College of Cardinals were his relatives. He was more concerned with the arts and increasing the power of his office than with reform.

Alexander I (1777–1825), Russian tsar (1801–25). After repulsing Napoleon's attempt to conquer Russia (1812), he led his troops across Europe and into Paris (1814). During the first part of his reign, he introduced administrative and educational reforms with the advice of Mikhail Speranski. Later, however, under the influence of Alexis Ararchev, he instituted reactionary measures, including the establishment of military colonies. Under the influence of various mystical groups, he helped form the Holy Alliance with other European powers. He was named constitutional monarch of Poland in 1815 and also annexed Finland, Georgia and Bessarabia to Russia.

Alexander II (1818–81), Russian tsar (1855–81). He was known as the "Tsar Liberator" for his emancipation of the serfs in 1861. His reign saw the end of the Crimean War (1856), but under the influence of Pan-Slavism he warred with Turkey (1877–78) and gained much influence in the Balkans. He sold Alaska (1867), but expanded the eastern part of the empire. He brutally put down a revolt in Poland (1863). In 1881 he was assassinated by revolutionaries.

Alexander III (1845–94), Russian tsar (1881–94). Under the influence of Pobedonostsev, procurator of the Holy Synod, he introduced reactionary measures limiting local government; censorship of the press was enforced and arbitrary arrest and exile became common. Ethnic minorities were persecuted. In 1889, land captains appointed by the government limited the rights of the peasants. The three principles of orthodoxy, autocracy, and nationalism were the basis of his reign. Toward the end of his career, he formed an alliance with France.

Alexander III (1241–86), king of Scotland (1249–86). He repelled a Norwegian attack on the Western Isles (1263) and purchased the Norwegian possessions of Hebrides and Man (1266). He promoted peace with England and Norway and furthered Scottish unity, prosperity, and independence.

Alexander I (1888–1934), king of the Serbs, Croats, and Slovenes (1921–29) and king of Yugoslavia (1929–34). In his efforts to forge a united country from the rival national groups and ethnically divided political parties he created an autocratic police state. He was assassinated.

Alexander Nevski (*c.* 1220–1263), Russian ruler and national hero, grand prince of Vladimir, the political center of Russia at this time. He paid voluntary tribute to the Mongols who in turn appointed him grand prince, after he had been prince of Novgorod (1238–52). He defeated the Swedes on the Neva (1240, hence the name "Nevski"), and the Teutonic Knights on Lake Peipus (1242). He was canonized in 1547.

Alexander of Tunis, Harold Rupert Leofric George, 1st Earl (1891–1969), English military commander. He directed the successful British offensive in Egypt and Libya (1942) and was Eisenhower's deputy in the victorious Tunisian campaign (1943) before becoming commander in chief of Allied forces in Italy. After the war he was governor-general of Canada (1946–52) and British minister of defense (1952–54).

Alexander Severus, Marcus Aurelius (208?–235), Roman emperor (222–35). A boy of 14 when he came to power, he remained throughout his reign under the influence of his mother, Mamaea. As a military leader, he fought the newly established Persian Sassanid Empire (231–33), and restored the Roman frontier in the Near East. On the Rhine and Danube frontiers, he chose to buy peace from the Germans rather than to fight. His troops interpreted this policy as cowardice. They rebelled, killed Alexander and Mamaea, and plunged the empire into decades of military anarchy.

Alexander the Great (Alexander III of Macedonia) (356–323 BC), the greatest general in ancient history. Tutored by Aristotle, he took the throne at age 20, destroying rivals and consolidating power in Greece. In spring 334 he began the Persian expedition, conquering West Asia Minor and storming the island of Tyre (332), his greatest military victory. He subdued Egypt and occupied Babylon, marching north in 330 to occupy Media and then conquering central Asia in 328. In 327 he invaded India. He then set about consolidating his empire but died of apparently natural causes at 32. Deified, a legend in his own time, he was buried in a golden coffin in Alexandria.

Alexandria (Al-Iskandariyah), chief port and 2nd-largest city in Egypt, on the W extremity of the Nile Delta, between Lake Maryut and Mediterranean Sea. Founded 332BC by Alexander the Great, it became part of the Roman Empire in 30BC. Muslims took over in AD 642, and city declined until construction of the Mahmudiyah Canal in 1819 when trade revived and city began to flourish; site of university, several museums, zoological park, botanical gardens, and a 25,000-seat stadium; it is also Middle East headquarters for the World Health Organization. Industries: petroleum refining, textiles, paper, plastics. Pop. 2,201,000.

Alexandria, city in N Virginia, 6mi (10km) S of Washington, D.C.; settled early 18th century; site of Carlyle House (1752); Gadsby's Tavern (1752) used by George Washington; Christ Church (1767). Industries: fertilizers, chemicals, machinery. Est 1748 by Virginia House of Burgesses; inc. 1779. Pop. (1980) 103,217.

Alexandrian Library, Egyptian library founded 290BC by Ptolemy Soter of Alexandria and enriched by successive rulers. Destroyed by Saracen armies under Caliph Omar in 638, it is thought the collection reached 700,000 volumes.

Alexandrine, 12-syllable line in poetry. Its name is probably derived from French medieval poetry about Alexander the Great. The most noted use of alexandrine is in classical French tragedy. Famous occurrences in English are Drayton's *Polyolbion* (1613–22) and the last line of the stanza form used in Spenser's *The Faerie Queene* (1589; 1596).

Alexis (1629–76), Russian tsar (1645–76). He established a new code of laws (1648). His war with Poland (1654–67) led to the reunification of the Ukraine with Russia. He suppressed a peasant rebellion led by Stenka Razin (1670–71) and supported Patriarch Nikon's church reforms. This led to the formation of the Old Believers, who refused to accept these reforms. Western culture began to influence the arts during his reign.

Alexius I Comnenus (1048–1118), Byzantine emperor (1081–1118), founder of the Comnenian dynasty. This soldier-emperor came to the throne at a time when Byzantium was virtually destroyed, having lost vast territories to foreign invaders. During the 37 years of his reign, Alexius held off the Normans from their threatened attack on Constantinople; turned the force of the western armies of the First Crusade to his own advantage by using them to reconquer parts of Anatolia; and defeated the Patzinaks and Seljuk Turks.

Alexius II Comnenus (1168?–1183), Byzantine emperor (1180–83). The death of his father, Manuel I Comnenus, left 12-year-old Alexius the victim of unscrupulous adults. The unpopular regency of his Latin mother, Mary of Antioch, was overthrown by his uncle, Andronicus Comnenus. Andronicus, after having himself crowned as Alexius' co-emperor, had the boy strangled and his body thrown into the sea.

Alfalfa, or lucerne, deep-rooted perennial plant native to Europe and naturalized in the United States. It has small leaflets and purple flower clusters. Valued for its ability to restore nitrogen to the soil, it is grown as fodder, pasture, and a cover crop. Height: 1–3ft (30–91cm). Family Leguminosae; species *Medicago sativa.*

Alfonsín Foulkes, Raúl (1927–), Argentine president (1983–). He became active in the Radical Civic Union (UCR) while attending the National University of La Plata. Elected a local UCR representative at 24, he rose rapidly, winning election to the national parliament in 1963. Defeated in his bid for nomination as a presidential candidate in 1972, he remained politically active until the military takeover of the government (1976). In 1982 he assumed the leadership of the UCR. Elected president in an upset victory, he moved to improve Argentina's human rights record, introduce fiscal and monetary reforms, and reduce labor unrest.

Aleppo, Syria: Byzantine citadel

Alewife

Algeria

Alfonso I (1112–85), first king of Portugal (1139–85). He was the son of Henry of Burgundy, count of Portugal. After his father's death (1112), his mother acted as regent until 1128, when Alfonso deposed her. He fought ceaselessly from about 1130 to 1139 against the kings of León and Castile and against the Moors. Upon conquering Lisbon in 1147, he styled himself king, a title later ratified by Castile and the pope. He was succeeded by his son Sancho I.

Alfonso III (1210–79), king of Portugal (1248–79). He was the son of Alfonso II and the brother of Sancho II, whom he succeeded. He seized power in 1245 after Sancho was deposed by the pope. He removed the last vestiges of Moorish power from Portugal and reached an agreement with the king of Castile, whose illegitimate daughter he married. Diniz, who succeeded Alfonso, was born of this union.

Alfonso VI (c.1030–1109), Spanish king of León (1065–1109) and of Castile (1072–1109). He inherited León from his father, and after the assassination of his brother Sancho II of Castile, he took over that crown. He further consolidated his power in Spain by taking Galicia from his brother García in 1072. He made his capital city of Toledo a great cultural center. The exploits of El Cid took place during his reign.

Alfonso VIII (1155–1214), Spanish king of Castile (1158–1214). He was the son of Sancho III, whom he succeeded at age three. After much fighting for the regency, he took control in 1166. He fought both Moors and fellow Christian kings. In 1212, however, he forged a coalition with the Christian kings and won an important victory over the Almohads. He married Eleanor, daughter of Henry I of England. Their son, Henry I, succeeded to the throne.

Alfonso X (the Wise) (1221–84), Spanish king of Castile and León (1252–84). He was the son and successor of Ferdinand II. He continued his father's wars against the Moors, but his chief ambition was to become Holy Roman emperor. A dissident group of German nobles named him anti-king (to Richard, Earl of Cromwell) but papal opposition kept him in Spain. Alfonso's credentials as a scholar were impressive; he wrote a landmark codification of the law and histories of Spain and the world. He was patron to Jewish, Moorish, and Christian scholars, philosophers, and scientists. In 1282, his son, Sancho IV, rebelled and took most of his kingdom away. Alfonso died two years later in Seville, the only city that still remained loyal to him.

Alfonso XIII (1886–1941), king of Spain (1886–1931). He was the posthumous son of Alfonso XII, and his mother Maria Christina acted as regent until 1902. Although personally popular, Alfonso was unable to cope with the various demands of Catalan and Basque nationalists, socialists, right-wingers, and republicans. In 1923 he turned to the right-wing dictator, Gen. Miguel Primo de Rivera. That government fell in 1930, and in 1931 Alfonso was forced to abdicate in favor of a republic.

Alfred (849–99), king of Wessex (871–99), called Alfred the Great. Warrior, scholar, and lawgiver, he saved Wessex from the Danes and laid the foundations of a united English kingdom. Youngest of four successively reigning sons of king Ethelwulf, he inherited a weak throne. After the Danish invasion of Wessex (878), he escaped to Athelney, returning a few weeks later to defeat the Danes at Edington and recover the kingdom. To strengthen Wessex against future attack, he built a fleet, constructed forts, and reorganized the army. He furthered political stability by publishing a code of laws, commissioned English translations of

Christian Latin authors, encouraged scholarship, and founded schools.

Algae, a large and diverse group of essentially aquatic plants found in salt and fresh waters everywhere in the world. All algae make their own food by photosynthesis, and algae are the primary source of food for mollusks, fish, and other aquatic animals. Algae are directly important to man as a food (especially in Japan), as fertilizers, and as sources of agar, carrageenin, and alginic acid. Algae range in size from microscopic plants such as the green pond scums to huge brown kelps sometimes more than 150ft (46m) long. The smallest algae are variously shaped single-celled organisms, some of which can move about by means of whiplike "arms" called flagellae. Many single-celled algae cluster together in colonies. Larger many-celled algae—including the many familiar seaweeds—grow in a wide variety of shapes, including cords, ruffled sheets, and intricately branched structures resembling some land plants. However, even the most advanced algae do not have true roots, stems, and leaves like those of the higher plants. The chief kinds of algae are classified in five botanical divisions: blue-green algae (Cyanophyta), golden algae (Chrysophyta), brown algae (Phaeophyta), green algae (Chlorophyta), and red algae (Rhodophyta). See also Seaweed; Thallophyte.

Algarve, southernmost province of Portugal; bounded by Baixo Alentejo prov. (N), Atlantic Ocean (S and W), and Guadiana River (E); capital is Faro. First occupied by Phoenicians, then Moors, who were overcome by Alfonso III in 1250. Products: fruits, tuna, and sardines. Area: 1,958sq mi (5,071sq km). Pop. 316,200.

Algebra, generalized form of arithmetic in which symbols replace numbers. Thus $3 + 5 = 8$ is a statement in arithmetic; $x + y = 8$ is one in algebra, involving variables x and y. Higher algebras also exist in which the entities are not necessarily numbers nor are the rules those of arithmetic. An example is Boolean algebra, which can be applied to sets (and also to logical propositions). It involves such concepts as the union and intersection of subsets of a given set. See also Mathematics.

Algebraic Function, function that is expressible using algebraic terms and operations. For instance, $3x^3 + x$ is an algebraic function, as contrasted with $\log x$, which is a transcendental function expressed by a convergent series.

Algebraic Operations, the operations of ordinary algebra: that is, the arithmetical operations addition, subtraction, multiplication, and division. Operations that involve infinite series and functions such as $\log x$ are not algebraic—they depend on the use of limits. The term algebraic is also applied to arithmetical operations carried out with due regard to sign. Thus, the algebraic sum of a and $-b$ is $a - b$, the algebraic product of $-a$ and $-b$ is $+ab$, etc. See also Arithmetical Operations.

Algeciras (Algeciros), seaport city in S Spain, on the Bay of Algecira in Andalusia; first Spanish town conquered by Moors, 711; taken by King Alfonso XI of Castile in 1344. Algeciras suffered much destruction during war between Moors and Spaniards; was rebuilt in 1704 by Spaniards; important resort area and port of entry from NW Africa. Pop. 81,662.

Algeria (Algérie), independent nation in North Africa. Influenced over the years by succeeding Arab and French colonization, this mostly Muslim country has

nationalized land and industry. The country is governed under a one-party socialist system.

Land and economy. Located in NW Africa, with 640mi (1025km) of coastline on the Mediterranean Sea between Tunisia and Morocco, neighbors include Libya (E), Niger (SE), Mali and Mauritania (SW). Two Atlas mountain chains determine its climate. In the N the Tellian chain runs parallel to the coast and is fertile with moderate climate and sufficient rain. The S Saharan range, a high plateau with less rainfall, separates the N from the Sahara Desert. Oil found in 1957 accounts for 70% of exports; natural gas is plentiful. Sixty percent of the population is engaged in agriculture, and a third of the national income is derived from its crops—cereals, fruits, wine, plus livestock and olive oil. The lack of skilled workers hindered production, and a system of worker-managed plants and farms was instituted (1967–71) to develop nationalized properties.

People. Descendants of invaders from Phoenicia, Rome, Arab lands, Turkey, and France, mixed with the indigenous Berber tribes, make up modern Algeria. Arabs brought their language, the official tongue, as well as their Islamic religion. There are about 50,000 foreign technicians and teachers in the country. There are some 45,000 Catholics, plus small Protestant and Catholic communities.

Government. A strong, central government controls the country, with policy making in the hands of the National Revolutionary Council. Rule is by decree.

History. Conquered by Carthage in 146BC, then Rome, and later the Arabs in the 7th century, the territory was colonized by France in 1830, and annexed as an overseas department with representation in the French assembly; control remained in French hands. The Algerian push for equal political rights led to a terrorist revolt in 1954 initiated by the Nationalist Liberation Front (FLN). In 1962, following six years of war and after a referendum on self-determination, independence was granted. In 1963, Premier Ahmed Ben Bella was deposed in a bloodless coup by Col. Houari Boumedienne. Following his death in 1978 he was replaced by Col. Benjedid Chadli. During the early 1980s, Algeria supported the Polisario guerrilla independence movement in the Western Sahara.

PROFILE

Official name: Democratic and Popular Republic of Algeria
Area: 919,590sq mi (2,381,738sq km)
Population: 16,200,000
Density: 18 per sq mi (7 per sq km)
Chief cities: Algiers (capital); Oran; Constantine
Government: Republic
Religion: Islam
Language: Arabic
Monetary unit: Dinar
Gross national product: $13 billion
Per capita income: $780
Industries: wine, olive oil, natural gas, petroleum products, leather goods
Agriculture: wheat, barley, corn, oats, flax, tobacco, olives, dates, citrus fruits, cattle
Minerals: oil, iron, zinc, lead, mercury, coal, copper
Trading partners: France (major), United States, European Common Market, USSR

Algiers (Alger or **Al-Jaza'ir),** city and capital of Algeria extends 10mi (16km) along W side of Algiers Bay; North Africa's chief port on the Mediterranean; first settled by Phoenicians, became a Roman colony (Icosium) 2nd century BC. Turks ruled 1518; base for Barbary pirates for 300 years; later became capital and trade center of French colony of Algeria; surrendered to Allies 1942; Algerian rebellion occurred 1954; independence was proclaimed 1962. City contains the National Library, university (1909), astronomical observatory, Jardin d'Essai Park, the Casbah (a 16th-century Turkish citadel), and the Great Mosque (1660). Industries: iron ore, flour, wine, tobacco, vegetables, paper, fishing, tourism. Pop. 1,839,000.

Algonkin or **Algonquin,** large tribe that gave its name to the Algonkian language, distributed throughout North America. The Algonkin people occupied the Ottawa River area around AD 1600 at which time they numbered about 6000. They were driven from their home by the Iroquois and were eventually absorbed into other related tribes in Canada.

Algorithm, a simple mathematical procedure of computation that involves computing columns of figures separately, and carrying or borrowing from one column to the next, or of positioning rows of figures in a rote manner so as to derive an answer by inspection. The procedure has been attacked because it rests upon mechanical procedures, rather than an understanding of an operation's logical structure. The term is also used in computer science with reference to the method of a computer in following an established series of specific steps in the solution of a problem.

Alhambra, Moorish palace and citadel overlooking Granada, Spain. Actually a series of buildings and gardens, the Alhambra was begun in 1248 by the Moorish rulers of Granada. It is the finest example of Moorish architecture in Spain and is regarded as one of the architectural masterpieces of the world. The buildings fell into disrepair after the expulsion of the Moors in 1492 but extensive restoration work has been done since the 19th century.

Ali (600?–61), fourth Muslim caliph (656–61), son of Abu Talib, the Prophet Mohammed's uncle. A faithful follower of the Prophet, Ali married his daughter Fatima and was expected to become caliph when he died. However, 3 other caliphs ruled, and 24 years passed before he succeeded Othman, another son-in-law of Mohammed. Ali crushed a revolt in Iraq, but was not able to suppress Muawiyah, Mohammed's secretary who was now governor of Syria. When Ali was murdered by fanatics, his son Hasan succeeded him, but abdicated under pressure by Muawiyah. The division in Islam between the Sunni and the Shiites began at this time. Ali, his sons Hasan and Husain, and his wife Fatima are venerated by the Shiites who claim Ali was the rightful heir to Mohammed.

Ali, Muhammad (1942–   ), US boxer, b. Cassius Clay in Louisville, Ky. He won the Olympic light-heavyweight championship (1960) and then beat Sonny Liston for the world's heavyweight championship (1964). Boxing authorities took away Ali's title (1967) after he refused induction into the US Army. He was cleared of all charges (1970) and returned to the ring, regaining the world's title by defeating George Foreman (1974). He came out of retirement several times, losing and regaining the world's heavyweight title in bouts with Leon Spinks (1978) and losing to Larry Holmes (1980).

Alicante, city in SE Spain; capital of Alicante prov., former site of Roman naval base; scene of execution of José Antonio Primo de Rivera, Falangist leader (1936); important Mediterranean port. Exports: esparto, fruit, oil, wine, cereals. Industries: clay products, tobacco, textiles, automobile engines. Area: (prov.) 2,264sq mi (5,864sq km). Pop. (city) 184,716; (prov.) 920,105.

Alice's Adventures in Wonderland (1865), book by Lewis Carroll. In a carefully constructed world of nonsense, a young girl, Alice, encounters such characters as the White Rabbit, the Dodo, the Caterpillar, the Cheshire Cat, the March Hare, the Mad Hatter, and the Red Queen. Although scholars have debated the allegorical significance of these characters for years, they have remained marvelously resistant to adult interpretation.

Alien and Sedition Acts (1798), US legislation designed to curb criticism of the government. War with France seemed a real possibility, and critics of the Federalist party's policies were outspoken. Many of the severest critics were refugees from Europe. The Naturalization Act required 14 years residency for citizenship instead of the previous 5-year requirement. The Alien Act authorized the president to deport foreigners who were considered dangerous. The Alien Enemies Act enabled the deportation or confinement of foreign citizens during war. The most notorious was the Sedition Act, which was carried out in a partisan manner. It outlawed conspiracies against the government and allowed prosecution of those who wrote and published "false, scandalous or malicious" items against the government. Republicans attacked the laws and by 1802, only the Alien Enemies Act was still in force.

Alienation, in psychology, the state of being alienated or diverted from normal functions. The alienated person is estranged and withdrawn from contact with the real world. The term is also used in anthropology and sociology to indicate powerlessness or social isolation.

Aligarh, city in N central India, between Ganges and Yamuna rivers; center of Muslim culture with establishment of Aligarh Muslim University (1920) and Aligarh Movement under Sayyid Ahmad Khan. The movement sought to teach Muslims participation in political life, resulting in separatist All-India Muslim League. Industries: cotton mills, agricultural market. Pop. 254,008.

Alimentary Canal, digestive tract that begins with the mouth cavity, continues into the esophagus to the stomach, small intestine, and large intestine, or colon, and ends at the anus. It is about 30ft (9m) long. *See also* Digestive System.

Aliphatic Compound, any chemical compound of an organic class in which the atoms are not linked to form rings, including the alkanes, alkenes, and the alkynes. It is one of the major structural groups of organic molecules.

Alkali, soluble substance that reacts with acids to make salts. Strong alkalis include the hydroxides of the alkali metals sodium, potassium, rubidium and cesium, as well as ammonium hydroxide, made when ammonia is dissolved in water. The carbonates of these metals and ammonium carbonate form weak alkalis.

Alkali Elements, univalent metals forming Group IA of the periodic table: lithium, sodium, potassium, rubidium, and cesium. They are all soft silvery-white metals, which rapidly tarnish in air and react violently with water to form solid hydroxides. The hydroxides are very soluble in water, forming strongly basic solutions. The electropositive properties and high reactivity of these elements is due to the single electron in their outer electron shells.

Alkaline-Earth Elements, bivalent metals forming Group IIA of the periodic table: beryllium, magnesium, calcium, strontium, barium, and radium. They are all light, soft, and highly reactive. All, except magnesium, react vigorously with cold water to form hydroxides. Magnesium will only react with hot water and its hydroxide is less soluble than those of the other alkaline earths. The oxides and hydroxides are strongly basic. Radium is important for its radioactivity.

Alkaloid, member of a class of complex nitrogen-containing organic compounds found in certain plants. Alkaloids are usually tertiary amines. They are often bitter and highly poisonous substances, important because of their physiological activity. Examples are atropine, codeine, morphine, nicotine, quinine, and strychnine.

Alkyds, polyesters, generally of phthalic acid and glycerol. The solid resins are molded at high speed under low pressure and cured quickly. They are used widely in industrial products where insulating properties, strength, and stability over a wide range of voltage, temperature, and humidity are important. Examples are vacuum-tube bases and automotive ignition parts. *See also* Polyester.

Allah, Arabic name of God. The one and only God of Islam, Allah is the omnipresent and merciful rewarder. Unreserved surrender to Allah, as preached in the Koran, is the very heart of the Muslim faith. Beyond human conceptualization, Allah is at once formidable and benevolent. *See also* Islam; Koran.

Allahabad, city in N central India, at junction of Yamuna and Ganges rivers; pilgrimage center because of Hindu belief that goddess Saraswati joined the two rivers at this point; site of Magh Mela fair, a religious celebration held every 12th year; site of University of Allahabad (1887), one of the oldest in India; agricultural trade center. Pop. 513,997.

Allegheny Mountains, mountain range, extends from Pennsylvania through Maryland, Virginia, and West Virginia; contains large quantities of coal and timber. Highest point is Spruce Knob, W.Va., 4,860ft (1,482m).

Allegheny River, river with its source in N central Pennsylvania; flows NW to New York, then SW through Pennsylvania to Pittsburgh, where it meets the Monongahela and forms the Ohio River. Length: 325mi (523km).

Allegory, literary work in either prose or verse in which more than one level of meaning is expressed simultaneously. The fables of Aesop and of La Fontaine, which give human meaning to animal behaviors, are simple allegories. Other examples are the 15th-cen-

tury anonymous play *Everyman;* 16th-century Edmund Spenser's *Faerie Queene;* 17th-century John Bunyan's *A Pilgrim's Progress.* Allegory can also be found in the works of John Dryden, Alexander Pope, and Jonathan Swift (18th-century); and in such later authors as Henry James, Franz Kafka, D.H. Lawrence, and William Faulkner.

Allele, one of a pair of genes at the same location on a pair of chromosomes. *See* Genes.

Allen, Ethan (1738–89), US frontiersman and Revolutionary War soldier, b. Litchfield, Conn. He moved to the New Hampshire grants (now Vermont) in 1768 and became commander of the Green Mountain Boys, a volunteer militia. Allen and his troops, with sympathizers from Connecticut and Massachusetts, captured Fort Ticonderoga, May 10, 1775.

Allenby, Edmund Henry Hynman, 1st Viscount (1861–1936), English military commander. A distinguished cavalry officer, he defeated the Turkish forces in Palestine and Syria (1917–18), capturing Jerusalem, Damascus, and Aleppo. He served as British high commissioner in Egypt (1919–25).

Allende Gossens, Salvador (1908–73), president of Chile (1970–73). He died in a military coup on Sept. 11, 1973. Candidate of the Popular Unity coalition, he was the first democratically elected Marxist head of state in Latin America. A medical doctor and active member of the Socialist party from its formation in 1933, he was senator from 1945 and unsuccessfully ran for the presidency in 1952, 1958, and 1964.

Allentown, city in E Pennsylvania on Lehigh River; seat of Lehigh co. The Liberty Bell was brought here for safekeeping in 1777; city was a munitions headquarters for Continental Army during Revolutionary War. In the Pennsylvania Dutch region, city is site of Muhlenberg College (1848), Cedar Crest College (1867), Allentown College of St Francis de Sales, and a branch of Pennsylvania State University. Industries: clothing, truck and bus bodies, beer. Founded 1762; inc. as borough 1811, as city 1867. Pop. 103,758.

Allergy, hypersensitive reaction exhibited to certain substances not normally considered distressing. Substances may include such diverse materials as pollen, animal dander, fungus, household dust, occasionally foods, and increasingly drugs, penicillin being a common allergen. The most typical allergic reactions are sneezing and reddening of eyes and mucous tissues (hay fever), wheezing and shortness of breath (asthma), and skin eruptions and itching (eczema). Certain childhood allergies, particularly to food, diminish with age; other allergies do not appear until adulthood. Although the tendency to allergic reactions is frequently hereditary, the specific allergy is not. In one family, a parent may react to pollen by sneezing, one child to dust by shortness of breath, another child to cat hair with eczema. Emotional state is apparently also a factor in the onset of some allergic reactions. In some cases, such as so-called penicillin shock in children, acute allergic reactions can be fatal. Treatment of allergic symptoms usually requires identification of the allergen, its removal from the environment if possible, or alternately a course of desensitization to the substance. Certain drugs are useful in relieving acute symptoms. *See also* Asthma; Eczema; Hay Fever.

Alliance, in international relations, an agreement for furtherance of mutual or similar aims between states or other parties, usually arrived at by formal treaty. Related terms include pact, organization, league, and union. The North Atlantic Treaty Organization (NATO) is an alliance.

Alligator, crocodilian similar to family Crocodylidae members, but it has a broader head and more obtuse snout. Each summer the female alligator lays 20–70 goose-sized eggs on shore in a mounded nest of leaves and mud and remains nearby to guard them. The American alligator (*Alligator mississipiensis*) is found only in SE United States. Length: to 19ft (6m). The almost extinct smaller Chinese alligator (*Alligator sinensis*) is restricted to the Yangtze-Kiang river basin. Length: to 6ft (1.8m). It has no webbing between its toes. Family Alligatoridae. *See also* Crocodile.

Alliteration, close repetition of consonant sounds within a line of verse or prose. Predominant in Old English poetry, then revived in the 14th century, alliteration is also found in some modern poetry: for example, in this line from W.H. Auden: "By the waters of waking I wept for the weeds." . . .

Allium, bulbous herbs native to temperate to warm regions of the Northern Hemisphere. They are noted for their odor, characteristic of some species, such as garlic, onion, shallot, and chives. The leaves are mostly

Ethan Allen

Allosaurus

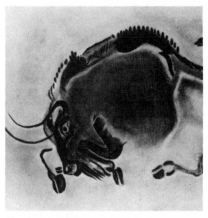

Altamira cave painting

hollow and the small flowers grow in clusters. Often grown as ornamentals, the flowers are usually rose, lilac, purple, or white, with some reddish, yellowish, greenish, or blue. Family Liliaceae.

Allosaurus, or **Antrodemus,** dinosaur that ranged North America during Late Jurassic-Early Cretaceous period. A biped with powerful hindlimbs and small, three-fingered clawed forelimbs. A hunting carnivore, it may have also been a scavenger. Length: to 35ft (10.5m); weight: 2 tons.

Allotrope, one of two or more distinct physical forms of an element, occurring in the liquid, gaseous, or, more usually, solid state. Examples are the existence of molecular oxygen and ozone, white and gray tin, and graphite, diamond, and other forms of carbon.

Alloy, a mixture of two or more metals. Alloys are generally hard and brittle and have a lower melting point than their constituents (those with the lowest melting point are called eutectic mixtures). Properties are frequently different from those of constituent elements and alloys may be considerably stronger than pure metals. Most are prepared by mixing when molten. Some mixtures, combining metal with another, non-metallic substance, such as in steel, are also referred to as alloys.

All Saints Day, in Christian churches, a day that celebrates all the saints of the church. The holiday is November 1 in the West and the first Sunday after Pentecost in the East. The festival was known as All Hallows in medieval England, and the eve of the day is celebrated in the United States as Halloween, primarily a children's holiday.

Allspice, or **pimento**, aromatic tree native to West Indies, Mexico, and Central America. Small white flower clusters produce berry-like, brown, spicy fruits ¼in (6.4mm) in diameter and with the combined flavors of nutmeg, cloves, and cinnamon. They are dried and used as a spice, in perfumes, and in medicine. Height: to 40ft (12m); family Myrtaceae; species *Pimenta officinalis.*

Alluvium, general term that describes the sediments —sand, silt, and mud—deposited by flowing water along the banks, delta, or flood-plain of a river or stream. Fine-textured sediments that contain organic matter form soil.

Alma-Ata, formerly Vernyi or Vyernyi; largest city and capital of Kazakhstan, USSR, near China border; also capital of Alma-Ata oblast; site of Turkistan-Siberian rail terminus, two universities (1934 and 1945); commerce center. Industries: food processing, lumber, machinery, tobacco. Founded 1854 as Russian fortress. Pop. 890,000.

Al Mansura (El Mansura), city in S Egypt, on Damietta River; capital of Daqahliya governorate; scene of battle (1250) in which Crusaders, led by Louis IX (France), were defeated by Mameluke (Egypt). Industries: cotton, wool processing, dairying, woodworking. Pop. 212,300.

Almeria, city in SE Spain, on the Gulf of Almeria; capital of Almeria prov.; former Moorish naval base, taken by Christians 1489; site of Gothic cathedral, ruins of Moorish fort; important Mediterranean seaport. Exports: grapes, esparto, iron. Industries: chemicals, metalwork. Area: (prov.) 3,388sq mi (8,775sq km). Pop. (city) 114,510; (prov.) 375,004.

Almohads, Berber Muslim dynasty (1147–1269) in North Africa and Spain, followers of a monotheistic reform in Islam. Mohammed ibn-Tumart set about to purify Islam and oust the Almoravids. Later Abd-al-Mumim, Yusuf II, and Yakub I seized Morocco and Spain. In 1212 Alfonso VII of Castile routed them at Navas de Tolosa, and in 1269 their capital Marrakesh fell to the Merenid dynasty.

Almond, a tree, apparently native to S Asia, resembling the related peach, although larger and longer-living. The almond tree flowers around March north of the equator, and is grown widely. Leading exporters in the 1970s of nuts, almond oil, and meal were Italy, Spain, Morocco, Portugal, and Iran, in addition to the United States. Species *Prunus amygdalus. See also* Peach.

Almoravids, Berber dynasty that ruled in Morocco and Moorish Spain in the 11th and 12th centuries. Yusuf ibn-Tashfin was the dynasty's greatest ruler. After conquering Morocco (c. 1062), they founded Marrakesh. In 1086 Yusuf went to the aid of the petty Moorish kings in Spain. Shocked at the worldly Spanish Muslims, the puritanical Almoravids returned in 1090 and conquered virtually all of Muslim Spain. By 1107, however, Almoravid power was destroyed in both Morocco and Spain by the even more puritanical Almohads.

Aloe, a genus of African house plants that have fleshy leaves with spiny edges. They grow in dense rosettes and have drooping red or yellow flower clusters. Care: direct sunlight, well-drained soil (equal parts potting soil and sand) kept dry between waterings. Propagation is by suckers. Width: 4–10in (10–25cm). Family Liliaceae.

Alp Arslan (1029–72), sultan of the Seljuk Turks (1063–72). His conquest of Armenia and attacks on Syria, Cilicia, and Cappadocia severely weakened the military position of the Byzantine Empire. After a decisive victory over the Byzantines at the Battle of Manzikert (1071), Turkish domination of Asia Minor was assured.

Alphabet, writing system based, ideally, on the principle of one symbol for one phoneme. It was refined by the Greeks, but experimenting had been done from 1800 BC to 1300 BC. The alphabet allows a written language that makes the spread of information and culture possible and allows the storage of knowledge. The tools of writing greatly influenced the letter forms.

Alpha Centauri, or **Rigil Kent,** binary star in the constellation Centaurus, and the nearest stellar system to the Sun. It has two components, Alpha Centauri A (yellow dwarf) and Alpha Centauri B (orange dwarf), orbited by a third faint companion, Proxima (red dwarf). Characteristics: apparent mag. 0.0 (A), +1.4 (B), +10.7 (Proxima); absolute mag. +4.4 (A). +5.8 (B), +15.1 (Proxima); spectral type G2 (A), K1 (B), M5 (Proxima); distance 4.3 light-years. *See also* Beta Centauri.

Alpha Rays, or **Alpha Particles,** stable, positively charged particles emitted spontaneously by certain radioactive isotopes (undergoing alpha decay), discovered by Pierre and Marie Curie and Ernest Rutherford and identified as nuclei of helium (two protons, two neutrons). Their penetrating power is low compared with that of beta particles but they cause intense ionization along their track. Their energy, characteristic of the emitting radioisotope, lies between 2 million and 12 million electronvolts. *See also* Radioactivity.

Alpha Waves, recording of one type of brain activity, which occurs when the subject is awake but relaxed, often with his eyes closed. Alpha activity is rhythmic with a typical 8 to 12 hertz wave. Alpha activity can be conditioned by positive reinforcement enabling some people to achieve a calm bodily state at will. *See also* Brain Waves.

Alphorn, or **Alpine Horn,** primitive musical instrument, consisting of a long wooden tube, one end of which rests on the ground. The composer Rossini used one of the typical herdsmen's melodies played on it by the Alpine herdsmen of Switzerland in the overture to his opera *William Tell.*

Alpine Plants, small plants found on rocky slopes and mountain meadows above the treeline. They include Alpine forget-me-not (*Myosotis alpestris*), Drummond's willow (*Salix drummondiana*), Alpine harebell (*Campanula lasicarpa*), and others. The term is frequently applied to all mountain plants. Alpines, such as creeping juniper, are used chiefly in rock gardens. May be found at altitudes up to 5,000ft (1,525m).

Alps, mountain system of S central Europe, extends from Gulf of Genoa on the Mediterranean Sea to NW and W Yugoslavia. It occupies parts of Switzerland, Italy, France, Austria, Germany, and Yugoslavia; traversed by many gaps and passes. It is the origin of many geological terms associated with mountains and glaciers; noted for scenery, ski slopes, and lakes; year-round tourist attraction. Important source of hydroelectric power; it also provides grazing and farming land in its valleys. Highest peak is Mt Blanc, 15,771ft (4,810m). Length: 660mi (1,063km).

Alsace-Lorraine, region in E France composed of Bas-Rhin and Haut-Rhin depts.; territory of Belfort and Moselle. Bounded by Luxembourg (N), Germany (N and E), and Switzerland (S); separated from Germany by the Rhine River; region has been traditional source of friction between France and Germany. France lost region (except for Belfort) to Germany at end of Franco-Prussian War (1871); restored to France after WWI, lost again during WWII, and returned to France at end of war. Area is rich in iron ore, contains steel plants and textile mills.

Altaic Languages, family of languages spoken by about 80 million people in Turkey, Iran, the Soviet Union, Mongolia, and parts of China. It consists of three branches: the Turkic languages, the Mongolian languages, and the Tungusic languages, a small group spoken in the Soviet Union and China. Turkish is the most important of the Altaic languages. They are named after the Altai Mountains where they are believed to have originated.

Altair, or **Alpha Aquilae,** the brightest star in the constellation Aquila; a white star of the first magnitude. Characteristics: apparent mag. +0.75; absolute mag. +2.1; spectral type A7; distance 16 light-years.

Altamira, Cave Paintings of (c. 14,000–9500 BC), paintings and engravings in prehistoric caves west of Santander, northern Spain. They were discovered in 1879 but not accepted as genuine until the early 20th century. The roof of the caves' lateral chamber is covered with animal paintings, including bison, boars, and horses, executed in vivid black, red, and violet, as well as eight engraved anthropomorphic figures and hand prints and outlines.

Alternating Current. *See* Current, Electric.

Alternation of Generations, two-generation cycle by which some plants reproduce. The asexual (sporophyte) form produces spores that in turn grow into the sexual (gametophyte) form. The gametophyte produces the egg cell (fern) or capsule (moss) that grows into another sporophyte. The moss gametophyte consists of the protonema, or moss plant. The fern gametophyte is the prothallus or familiar fern plant. *See also* Fern; Gametophyte; Moss.

Althing, Icelandic parliament and oldest European legislative assembly. It was first convened at Thingvellir, near Reykjavik, in 930. The 60 members (40 in the lower house and 20 in the upper house) are elected by proportional representation for four-year terms. The two houses act on occasion as a United Althing, as in 1944, when the assembly voted independence from Denmark.

Altitude, in astronomy, angular distance of a celestial body from the horizon, measured in degrees along a vertical circle passing through the body. Altitude and azimuth form a coordinate system for giving astronomical positions.

Altitude Sickness, deficiency of oxygen in the blood and tissues that occurs at high altitudes and produces symptoms such as dizziness, palpitations, headache, nosebleed, and nausea.

Altruism, helping behavior that does not involve any selfish motives or obvious gain for the helper. Psychologists have identified several factors that may be important for the development of altruism, including the capacity for empathy and opportunities to observe altruistic models or parents.

Alum, any of several compounds, the most important of which medicinally are potassium or aluminum alum, used as astringents and styptics.

Aluminum, common metallic element (symbol Al) of group IIIA of the periodic table, first obtained in pure form by Friedrich Wöhler (1827). It is the most common metal in the earth's crust; the chief ore is bauxite (a hydrated oxide), from which the metal is extracted by electrolysis. Alloyed with other metals, it is extensively used in machined and molded articles, particularly where light materials are required, as in aircraft. Chemically it is a reactive metal, protected from oxidation by a passive layer of oxide. Properties: at. no. 13; at. wt. 26.9815; sp. gr. 2.699; melt. pt. 1220.38°F (660.21°C); boil. pt. 4473°F (2467°C); most common isotope Al^{27} (100%).

Aluminum Processing, the two-step process in the production of the pure metal from bauxite, its chief ore. Bauxite is first refined to obtain pure alumina (Al_2O_3), which is smelted to produce aluminum. The Bayer process, involving digestion, clarification, precipitation, and calcination is the most common refining process yielding half the original amount of ore. Smelting involves dissolving alumina in melted cryolite and passing a current through the mixture to yield pure aluminum and carbon dioxide (the Hall-Heroult process). *See also* Aluminum.

Alyssum, wild flower native to Europe and found along roads and in waste lands of the United States. They have lance-shaped leaves, often covered with pale down and white or yellow flowers. Species include annual *Alyssum alyssoides;* perennial golden tuft *A. saxatile;* and biennial *A. petracum.* Height: 1–2ft (30–61cm). Family Cruciferae.

Alzheimer's Disease, a degenerative brain disease, also called Pre-senile Dementia, usually occurring in adults aged 40-60. It results in a gradual atrophy of the brain and increased difficulty in physical and intellectual functions; its first symptoms include irrationality and loss of memory and orientation leading to a total breakdown of mental activity. There is no specific treatment for this disease.

Amado, Jorge (1912–), Brazilian novelist. His works, which abound in violence and stark realism, explore the plight of Brazil's poor. He occasionally writes lyrically about pastoral Brazil, but his main concern is poverty. *Sweat* (1934) and *Land of Violence* (1942) are typical. The musical play *Sarava* (1979) was based on his novel *Dona Flor and Her Two Husbands* (1969).

Amagasaki, city in S Honshu, Japan, on Osaka Bay; site of 16th-century castle; damaged by US air raids 1945. Industries: iron, steel, chemicals, textiles. Pop. 553,696.

Amalgam, solid or liquid alloy of mercury with other metals. Most metals will dissolve in mercury, although iron is an exception.

Amalgamation, Ore, an old and still-used process of recovering gold and silver from their ores by the use of mercury. The mercury forms an alloy (called amalgam) with the precious metals. This is then recovered and processed to obtain the pure metal.

Amana Society, religious community in Iowa. Founded in Germany, the group was persecuted and fled to the United States in 1842. Seven villages in Iowa were settled in 1855. Specializing in wool and wood handicrafts, it is one of the most successful communal communities.

Amanita, large genus of widely distributed mostly poisonous mushrooms. In contrast to common mushrooms, amanitas usually have long stalks and have the prominent remains of a veil in a fleshy ring under the cap and at the bulbous base.

Amaranth, heavy-looking plant from tropics of E Asia. Flowers, densely clustered in spikes or tassels, are often hidden by colorful foliage. Among 800 species is annual foxtail *Amaranthus caudatus* with a crimson-purple flower. Height: 1–3ft (30–90cm). Family Amarantaceae.

Amarillo, city in NW Texas, 65mi (105km) E of New Mexico in the Texas Panhandle; seat of Potter co; first white visitors were explorers with Francisco Coronado's expedition; settled after the Civil War, its economy and population boomed with discovery of natural gas (1918) and oil (1921). Industries: gas, oil, grains, cattle. Inc. 1899. Pop. (1980) 149,230.

Amaryllis, any of more than 800 species of perennial herbs found mostly in the tropics and subtropics. All have bulbs or underground stems with narrow grass-like leaves and showy, lilylike flowers. The petals are attached to the seed receptacle and the fleshy fruits are kidney-shaped. Family Amaryllidaceae.

Amati, family of Italian violinmakers in Cremona in the 16th and 17th centuries, including **Andrea** (*c.*1520–78), the founder of the Cremona school of violinmaking, his two sons **Antonio** (*c.*1550–1638) and **Girolamo** (1551–1635), and Girolamo's son **Nicolò** (1596–1684) and grandson **Girolamo** (1649–1740).

Amazon, greatest river of South America, and 2nd longest river in the world, draining the vast rain forest of N central South America. Its drainage basin includes the N 75% of Brazil and substantial portions of Colombia, Ecuador, Guyana, Peru, and Venezuela. Carrying the greatest volume of water of any river in the world, the Amazon is the central artery of an extensive river system; major tributaries are the Madeira, Purus, Juruá, Ucayeli, Marañon, Napa, Putumayo, Japurá, and Negro rivers; the Marañon is regarded as the headstream of the Amazon proper. Although swampy flood banks accompany the river's path, the great Selvas (rain forest and drainage basin) is thickly vegetated terra firma, producing hardwoods and rubber, a region of approx. 2,053,318sq mi (5,318,094sq km) flanked by the Brazilian Highlands (S), Andes Mts (W), and Guiana Highlands (N).

Cultivation of the region has been limited to the sporadic harvesting of natural products; lumbering has been hindered by the absence of pure stands of valuable woods, the rain forest encouraging growth of a wide variety of flora, side by side, across the entire region. The basin is sparsely inhabited, chiefly by Brazilians; the vast majority of these settlers reside along the floodbank, while a small Indian population lives and hunts in the greater expanses of the rain forest.

The Amazon is navigable as far W as Iquitos, Peru, or more than 2,000mi (3,220km) inland; the Brazilian government has begun a major program to develop the natural resources of the hinterland in step with the economically advanced E coast of Brazil. The river was first descended from Peru in 1541 by the Spaniard Francisco de Orellana. Length (including Marañon River, headstream): approx. 3,900mi (6,279km).

Amazonas, vast lowland region in N central South America, drained by the Amazon River system; bounded by the Pakaraima and Acarai Mts (N), Cordillera Oriental and Andes Mts (W), and Serra Das Pasecis and S Brazilian highlands (S); includes districts in S Venezuela, SE Colombia, N Peru, and central NW Brazil (largest). Total area of basin: over 750,000sq mi (1,942,500sq km).

Amazons, in Greek legend, a race of female warriors. They lived on the banks of the River Thermodon in Asia Minor. At the siege of Troy the Amazons fought as allies of the Trojans. Here their queen Penthesilia was slain by Achilles after she had killed many Greek warriors.

Amber, hard, yellow-to-brown, translucent fossil resin, found in alluvial soils, in lignite beds, or on seashores, especially near the Baltic Sea, where large deposits represent extinct flora 50,000,000 years old. May be rods or irregular nodules. Fossil insects and plants found as inclusions. Deeply colored amber takes a fine polish and is prized as a gem.

Amberfish, or **amberjack,** marine food and game fish found in tropical and subtropical waters. Fast swimming, this blunt-headed fish is blue and silver with bronze stripe along its side. The young have bright golden bands along the sides. Length: 5–6ft (1.5–1.8m); weight: 120lb (54kg). Family Carangidae; Species *Seriola dumerli.*

Ambergris, musky, gray, waxy substance formed in intestines of sperm whales, used in perfumes as a fixative for flower scents.

Amblyopia, partial or sometimes total loss of vision in the absence of any signs of eye abnormalities, usually due to nonuse of one eye. It may be acquired or congenital. In small children, the condition is termed lazy eye and is often the result of strabismus, in which one eye focuses on the object while the other turns inward. Treatment consists of exercising the problem eye; surgery may also be required.

Amboise, town in France on Loire River, 15mi (24km) E of Tours. Renaissance château with two towers stands over the town; once used by French kings, it later became a prison. A Huguenot conspiracy here in 1560 failed, but three years later the Edict of Amboise guaranteed religious freedom to Huguenot nobility and gentry; site of vineyards. Pop. 11,116.

Ambrose, Saint (*c.*340–97), bishop of Milan, who resisted imperial demands to surrender Milan's churches to the Arians. He refused to compromise his orthodox position, and acquired a reputation for administrative skill and eloquence. Augustine mentions Ambrose as instrumental in his own conversion. He was also the author of works on theology and ethics that greatly influenced the thought of the Western Church.

Ambrosia, in Greek and Roman mythology, magical substance eaten by gods. The gods kept their immortality by bathing in it or rubbing it into their skin. Without ambrosia a god became weak. A mortal who ate it became strong and immortal. Sometimes it was mixed with nectar as a drink.

Ambystoma, North American mole salamander. Most hide underground except for breeding. Used in laboratories, they have a sturdy build and broad head. Length: to 13in (33cm). Best known of about 25 species are the marbled, spotted, and tiger salamanders. Family Ambystomidae. *See also* Salamander.

Ameba, rhizopod protozoan that has constantly changing, irregular shape. Found in ponds, damp soil, or animal intestinal tracts, it consists of a thin unit membrane covering, large nucleus, food and contractile vacuoles, and fat globules. It is almost transparent; reproduction is by fission. Length: to 0.1in (3mm). Class Rhizopoda (Sarcodina); species include common *Ameba proteus* and *Entameba histolytica,* which causes amebic dysentery.

Ameboid Motion, method of locomotion of amebas, other protozoa, and other animal cells, including white blood cells. When a cell area is stimulated, the outer tube of "gel" protoplasm extends outward in one direction forming a false foot, or pseudopod, and the inner liquid "sol" flows in that direction, carrying the whole cell with it.

Amendment, Constitutional, procedure to change or modify the US Constitution according to Article V of the document. Upon the recommendation of two-thirds of both houses of Congress, a proposed amendment may be submitted to the legislatures of the states or to special state conventions. Three-fourths of the states must approve in order for the amendment to be approved. *See also* Constitution, U.S.

Amenhotep II, ancient Egyptian king (1448–20 BC), co-regent (1446–48 BC), son and successor of Thutmose III. He crushed an uprising in Syria, defended the frontier as far as the Euphrates, invaded Nubia, and erected temples to Amon at Karnak. Thutmose IV succeeded.

Amenhotep III, ancient Egyptian king (1417–1379 BC), and successor of his father, Thutmose IV. The XVIII dynasty peaked in his reign. Despite raids from the Bedouins and Hittites, he maintained peace throughout the empire. He built the 623-ft (190-m)-long Temple of Luxor, concluded the 1000-ft (305-m)-long Great Temple of Amon, promoted sculpture, and celebrated games. His wife, Queen Tiy, helped with state affairs. Akhenaton succeeded him.

Amberfish

Amboise, France

American saddle horse

Amenhotep IV. *See* Akhenaton.

Amenorrhea, absence of menstruation. Abnormal in a nonpregnant, nonlactating woman between the ages of puberty and menopause.

American Bar Association, organization whose members are attorneys admitted to the bar of any state in the United States. The association maintains a library and specialized committees varying from maritime law to "Education About Communism and Its Contrast with Liberty Under Law." Founded 1878. Members: about 160,000.

American Civil Liberties Union (ACLU), organization dedicated to defending "the rights of man set forth in the Declaration of Independence and the Constitution." Its activities vary from test court cases and opposition to repressive legislation to public protest on inroads of rights. It has defended people and organizations throughout the political spectrum, which has often made its activities controversial. The ACLU maintains a library and specialized committees, and its publications include *Civil Liberties.* Members: about 200,000. Founded 1920.

American Expeditionary Force (A.E.F.), World War I US army contingent sent to Europe (1918) under command of Maj. Gen. John J. Pershing. He preserved its identity and integrity when Allied field commanders wanted to integrate the US troops into the existing defense structure. The A.E.F. was a conscripted army led by professional soldiers.

American Federation of Labor (AFL), US labor organization. It was founded of craft unions (skilled workers) consolidated into a single federation while each union maintained its autonomy. The AFL was organized in 1886 at a trades union convention in Columbus, Ohio. Samuel Gompers, its first president, served for 37 years (1886–1924). The AFL advocated strikes to gain goals of fair wages and hours, collective bargaining with employer and written contract. With decline of Knights of Labor, AFL grew into leading US union organization. It merged with the CIO in 1955. *See also* Gompers, Samuel.

American Federation of Labor and Congress of Industrial Organizations, The (AFL–CIO), US labor organization. It is a federation of over 125 national and international labor unions, combining both craft and industrial workers. Established in 1955, it combined in a merger the American Federation of Labor (AFL) and Congress of Industrial Organizations (CIO). The merger healed a 20-year breach between the two unions. George Meany was elected president and continued in office until his retirement (1979), when he was succeeded by Lane Kirkland. During the 1970s public employee and service industry unions became a major element in the organization's membership. Although each union within the federation is fully autonomous, the ultimate governing body of the AFL-CIO is an Executive Council made up of the president, vice presidents, and secretary-treasurer, elected at its convention held every two years. *See also* American Federation of Labor; Congress of Industrial Organizations.

American Foxhound, versatile hunting dog (hound group) used in packs or individually to trail by scent; ancestors brought to US in 17th–18th centuries. It has a long, slightly domed head and square-cut muzzle; low-set, long, hanging ears; large hound eyes; a moderately long body with slightly arched loin; medium length legs; and slightly curved, brush tail. The close, hard coat can be any color. Average size: 22–25in

(56–63.5cm) high at shoulder; 60–70lb (27–32kg). *See also* Hound.

American Medical Association (AMA), a federation of 54 state and territorial medical associations, founded in 1847 for the promotion of medical standards of education and ethics. The AMA also develops programs to provide scientific information to the profession and health-education materials to the public. There are about 210,000 members.

American Revolution (1775–81), conflict that established the independence of the 13 American colonies from Britain.
  Background. In 1760, King George III became king of England, and in 1763 the Peace of Paris ended the Seven Years War and in North America the French and Indian War. The peace confirmed Britain's dominion of North America, as the French surrendered Canada. Great Britain, faced with an expanding empire and a large debt, sought to tax the colonies and enforce existing trade laws. Writs of assistance (general search warrants), effective 1761, were strongly opposed in Massachusetts. Following the Sugar Act of 1764, British Parliament passed the Stamp Act of 1765, which called for stamps on all legal documents, newspapers, and cards. Colonists protested against these measures, using "no taxation without representation" as a rallying cry, and Sons of Liberty groups were formed. Parliament repealed the Stamp Act in 1766 but passed the Declaratory Act asserting the crown's right to legislate for the colonies. The Townshend Acts of 1767 set a duty on imported tea, glass, and paper with the revenue to be used to pay royal officials in the colonies. In 1768, British troops arrived. Hatred for the troops in Boston erupted in a brawl March 1770, dubbed the Boston Massacre, in which five citizens were killed. Duties were dropped on all imports except tea. A truce continued until the announcement in 1772 that Massachusetts officials would be paid by the crown, placing them under British control. Unrest grew and in 1772–73, to keep in touch, committees of correspondence were formed in Massachusetts and other colonies. Aroused by the British Tea Act of 1773, designed to aid financially the East India Co., colonists disguised as Indians boarded ships in Boston harbor on December 16 and dumped the tea. This resistance led to disiplinary action through the Intolerable Acts, which closed the port of Boston, deprived Massachusetts of most of its rights, and provided that persons accused of a capital crime be tried in England. To enforce these acts Gen. Thomas Gage, in charge of British troops, was appointed the colony's governor. In response to the Intolerable Acts, the First Continental Congress met in Philadelphia on Sept. 5, 1774. The colonial delegates rejected the Intolerable Acts and set up the Continental Association, which provided for nonimportation of all British goods and for nonexportation to Britain.
  War for Independence. In 1774 militia groups called Minutemen formed in the Boston area. General Gage detailed British troops to destroy militia stores at Concord. Alerted, 77 armed Minutemen met the British on April 19, 1775, on the Lexington Green. An unidentified shot brought on the clash that killed eight Americans. The British continued to Concord, destroyed supplies but were attacked by the militia at Concord Bridge, and harassed by colonials on the return march to Boston. Colonial reinforcements arrived in Boston, and the town was soon under siege. These troops before Boston became the Continental Army, and on June 15, the Second Continental Congress made George Washington commander in chief. Before his arrival in Cambridge on July 3, the Battle of Bunker Hill took place on June 17. Americans were driven from their hasty entrenchments but inflicted heavy losses on the British. On October 10, Gen. William Howe re-

placed Gage as British commander. The British evacuated Boston on March 17, 1776, and Washington proceeded to New York City. During 1775–76 the Americans waged an unsuccessful campaign against the British in Canada.
  The Declaration of Independence, adopted on July 4, 1776, made the break with Britain decisive and followed efforts to resolve differences with the crown. Militarily, the colonials did poorly, and after a series of defeats Washington retreated from New York to Pennsylvania. Crossing the Delaware River on Christmas 1776, he surprised and captured the British outpost at Trenton on December 26; on Jan. 3, 1777, he defeated the British at Princeton, improving American morale. The British, attempting to divide the colonies, mounted a three-pronged assault that focused on New York State. Gen. John Burgoyne, descending along Lake Champlain from Canada, was to be joined by Col. Barry St. Leger, advancing eastward in the Mohawk Valley. They were to meet with General Howe's forces moving N from New York City. The strategy failed when Burgoyne was defeated and surrendered his army at Saratoga on Oct. 17, 1777, and St. Leger had been defeated at Oriskany on August 6. A turning point in the war, it influenced France to recognize the colonies. Howe, instead of advancing up the Hudson, occupied Philadelphia. Washington's army, ill-fed and in rags, spent the winter of 1777–78 at Valley Forge, Penn., where they reorganized.
  In 1778 the French alliance was signed. In June Sir Henry Clinton replaced Howe as commander of the British forces. On Dec. 29, the British captured Savannah, and the focus of the war shifted to the South. In 1779, Spain joined the war against England, and George Rogers Clark with his Virginians conquered the old Northwest. In 1780, General Cornwallis was given command of the southern campaign. On September 23, a plot of Benedict Arnold to surrender West Point to Clinton was revealed, but Arnold escaped. British control in South Carolina weakened, and in August 1781, Cornwallis was pushed to Yorktown, Va. The French fleet entered Chesapeake Bay in September, Washington and the Comte de Rochambeau's French and American forces joined the Marquis de Lafayette at Williamsburg, Va. Finding himself bottled up, Cornwallis surrendered his army Oct. 19, 1781, ending the British military efforts in the United States. The remaining British troops stayed in New York City until the official end of the war on Sept. 3, 1783, when the Treaty of Paris was signed. *See also* individual battles and biographies; Boston Massacre; Continental Congress, First; Declaration of Independence; Intolerable Acts; Paris, Treaty of.

American River, river in N California, flows SW into the Sacramento River at Sacramento. Discovery of gold at Sutter's Mill on river in 1848 spurred California gold rush. Length: 30mi (48km).

American Saddle Horse, light horse breed for park or show riding developed in Kentucky, Tennessee, and Virginia for transportation over long distances. Known as a breed since 1891, this easy-riding horse has a refined head, long neck, short rounded back, and high-set tail. Colors are bay, brown, chestnut, gray, black, and golden. Height: 60–64in (152–163cm) at shoulder; weight: 1000–1200lb (450–545kg).

American Samoa, E part of Samoa island group in S Pacific Ocean; US territory; comprised of islands of Tituila (including capital, Pago Pago), Sand, Rose, Swains, and the Manua group. Under control of native chiefs until *c.* 1860, the islands were granted to United States 1899 by treaty with former co-administrators, Germany and Great Britain; a constitution (1960) allows local legislature. Exports: canned fish, copra, cacao, local crafts. Area: 76sq mi (197sq km). Pop. 27,769.

American Short-haired Cat, or domestic short-haired, domestic cat breed with a broad head, short face, powerful body, broad chest, strong legs, and thick tail. Its coat is short, fine, and dense. Color varieties are black, white, blue, cream, blue-cream, tortoiseshell, calico, and tabby.

American Staffordshire Terrier, well-muscled dog (terrier group) originally used as pit bull, or fighting dog. Brought to United States around 1870 as the Staffordshire Terrier, the heavier American version was registered as a separate breed in 1972. It has a powerful head, cropped or uncropped ears, deep chest, and short body. Legs are moderately long; the short tail tapers to a point; and the short, stiff coat can be any color or colors. Average size: 18–19in (46–48cm) high at shoulder. *See also* Terrier.

American System, formula advocated by Henry Clay and John C. Calhoun about 1824. Calling for high tariffs and highway construction, the policy also advocated the establishment of a national bank.

American Tobacco Case (1911), Supreme Court decision against the tobacco monopoly. The court declared only "undue" restraint of trade was forbidden. It allowed reorganization of the company and weakened the Sherman Antitrust Act.

American Water Spaniel, working gun dog (sporting group) developed in midwestern US. A dog that springs game and retrieves. It has a long head and square muzzle; long, low-set, lobular ears; sturdy body; medium-length legs; and a long, curved tail. The distinctive, closely curled coat is feathered on the legs and tail; colors are solid liver or dark chocolate. Average size: 15–18in (38–46cm) high at shoulder; 28–45lb (13–20.5kg). *See also* Sporting Dog.

Americium, radioactive metallic element (symbol Am), first of the actinide group, made by Glenn Seaborg and others by neutron bombardment of plutonium. Am^{241} is used as a source of gamma rays. Properties: at. no. 95; sp. gr. 13.67; melt. pt. 1821°F (995°C); boil. pt. 4725°F (2607°C); most stable isotope Am^{243} (7.37×10^3 yr). *See also* Actinide elements.

Amethyst, transparent, violet variety of crystallized quartz, containing more iron oxide than other varieties, found mainly in Brazil, Uruguay, Ontario and North Carolina. Valued as a semiprecious gem since ancient times. *See also* Quartz.

Amharic, a language of the Semitic or Hamito-Semitic family. Original to the province of Amhara and Shoa, it has been the official language of Ethiopia since *c.* 1300 and has many words from the ancient Ghiz tongue, which was the official language at the time of the conversion to Christianity in 335.

Amherst, Jeffrey (Baron) (1717–97), British general in America. During the last French and Indian War (1754–63), he was named commander-in-chief of British forces (1758). His victories included Louisbourg (1758), Crown Point and Ticonderoga (1759) and Montreal (1760). He was made a field marshal and baron after his conquest of Canada.

Amiens, city in France, on Somme River, 72mi (116km) N of Paris; known as Samarobriva in pre-Roman times; became part of French crown lands in 1185. Taken by Germany during Franco-Prussian War, WWI and WWII; site of 13th-century Cathedral of Notre Dame, the largest church in France and one of the finest examples of Gothic architecture. Industries: machinery, chemicals, textiles. Pop. 135,992.

Amiens, Treaty of (1802), diplomatic agreement between Britain, France, Spain, and the Netherlands inaugurating a 14-month interval of peace during the Napoleonic wars. France recovered most of her colonies but evacuated Naples. Britain withdrew from Egypt but retained Trinidad and Ceylon. The insecure peace ended in May 1803.

Amin, Idi (*c.* 1925–), president of Uganda (1971–). He joined the British army in the colony of Uganda and became commander of independent Uganda's army in 1966. He staged a military coup in 1971, overthrowing Milton Obote. In 1972 he expelled about 80,000 Asian Ugandans. In the same year he also withstood a pro-Obote attack from Tanzania. He was elected president of the Organization of African Unity in 1975. Amin's erratic behavior inspired several attempted coups, and in l979 his government was overthrown. Amin fled the country.

Amine, member of a class of organic compounds derived from ammonia by replacing hydrogen atoms with organic groups. Methylamine, $CH_3 NH_2$, is a primary amine (one hydrogen replaced). Replacement of two hydrogens gives a secondary amine and three hydrogens gives a tertiary amine. Amines have a characteristic ammoniacle odor: they are produced in the putrefaction of organic matter. Like ammonia they are weakly basic. *See also* Alkaloid.

Amino Acid, acid containing at least one carboxyl group (-COOH) and at least one amino group (NH_2). These acids are of great biological importance as they link together to form proteins. They have the general formula $R{\cdot}CH(NH_2)COOH$ and link together to form the peptide structure -NH-CO- by condensation of the -NH_2 group of one acid and the -COOH of another. Proteins are cross-linked polypeptides consisting of hundreds or thousands of amino acids. Some 20 amino acids occur in proteins; not all organisms are able to synthesize all of them. Essential amino acids are those that an organisms has to obtain ready-made from its environment. There are 8 such essential amino acids for man.

Amish, conservative Protestant sect, members of the old order Amish Mennonite Church. Descendants of the followers of Jakob Ammann, a 17th-century Mennonite leader who advocated strict community conformity, they started arriving in E Pennsylvania *c.* 1720. Today about 70,000 Amish are dispersed in 50 or so communities in the United States and Canada. They live as simply and self-sufficiently as possible, shunning modern conveniences such as electricity and automobiles. *See also* Mennonites.

Amistad Case. In 1839, slaves, led by a man named Cinque, overpowered their owners on the *Amistad,* a Spanish slave ship. The ship landed in the United States and Abolitionists forced the case to the Supreme Court, where former Pres. John Quincy Adams argued for the slaves, who were set free in 1841.

Amman, capital city of Jordan, 50mi (81km) ENE of Jerusalem. In Biblical times it was the chief city of the Ammonites and known as Rabbath Ammon; rebuilt in *c.* 200 BC by Ptolemy II Philadelphus and renamed Philadelphia; prospered after 30 BC as part of the Roman Empire. Chosen as the capital in 1921, it is the administrative, commercial, and transportation center of Jordan; site of University of Jordan (1962). Industries: textiles, tobacco, cement, leather. Pop. 615,000.

Ammeter, instrument for measuring electric current. In the most accurate type (moving coil) for direct current, the current to be measured passes through a coil suspended in a magnetic field, causing deflection of a needle attached to the coil. The other main type (moving iron) can be used with both direct and alternating current. In this the coil is fixed and the passage of the current causes two pieces of soft iron to become magnetized; the mutual repulsion between them causes a needle to move.

Ammonia, colorless nonflammable pungent gas (formula NH_3) manufactured by the Haber Process. It is the most important nitrogen compound because of its production in fixing nitrogen for fertilizers. The gas dissolves in water to form an alkaline solution: ammonium salts contain the ion NH_4^+. Properties: melt. pt. −107.86°F (−77.7°C); boil pt. −28.03°F (−3.35°C).

Ammonoid, any of an extinct group of shelled cephalopod mollusks. They are believed to be descended from the nautiloids (of which the pearly nautilus is the only surviving form). Common as fossils in marine rocks of Devonian to Cretaceous ages, ammonoid shells are either straight or coiled and served as protective as well as hydrostatic devices that could be adjusted by varying the air pressure for different water depths. The many chambers of which each is composed are joined by highly convoluted walls that appear as complex suture lines on the surface.

Amnesia, loss of memory; more particularly, partial or complete inability to recall. When the amnesia is selective (only certain unpleasant memories are eliminated), it is usually psychogenic. Organically caused amnesias are usually unrelated to specific details of experience. In retrograde amnesia memory loss extends back in time from the point of onset (eg, a head injury).

Amnesty, official act of pardon granted by the head of government to violators of a national law. Amnesty may be absolute or conditional. If absolute, it absolves the violator of all offenses. If conditional, it stipulates the offender must meet certain obligations to obtain the pardon.

Amnesty International, organization whose efforts are directed in behalf of political prisoners around the world; founded in 1961 by a London lawyer, Peter Benenson. It had 170,000 members in 107 nations in 1977, when it was awarded the Nobel Peace Prize. Funded by private donations, it champions the rights of individuals who are detained especially for political or religious reasons. Advocating nonviolence, Amnesty called for the "universal ratification of international human rights covenants" on its 20th anniversary in 1981.

Amniotic Fluid, liquid filling the amnionic cavity which protects the fetus from injury. This fluid is released at delivery when the membranes rupture.

Amon. *See* Amun.

Amorphous Substance, solid substance in which the atoms or molecules have no regular order. Amorphous substances are noncrystalline; the term does not refer to outward appearance but to internal structure. Charcoal, lamp black, and similar forms of carbon are examples. Glasses are also amorphous; characteristically they have no definite melting point but soften over a temperature range, and may be regarded as supercooled liquids.

Amos, biblical author and third of the 12 minor prophets. During the reign of Uzziah, King of Judah (*c.* 8th century BC), he criticized the wickedness of the Hebrews.

Amoy (Xiamen, or **Hsia-men),** seaport city in SE China, on Amoy and Ku-lang islands on Formosa Strait. An important port, it flourished after being opened for foreign trade (1842); because of its proximity to Taiwan, it had great strategic importance after Communists took control of Chinese mainland (1949). Pop. 400,000.

Ampère, André-Marie (1775–1836), French physicist, mathematician and prodigy. He was professor of chemistry and physics at Bourg and later mathematics professor at Ecole Polytechnique in Paris. The founder of electrodynamics (now called electromagnetism), he performed numerous experiments with currents and magnetism. He was the first to derive electricity measuring techniques, and he also constructed the precursor of the galvanometer. Ampère's law is a mathematical description of the magnetic force between two electric currents. His name is also commemorated in the unit of electric current measurement (ampere). *See also* Electrodynamics.

Amphetamines, drugs that stimulate the central nervous system. They are used in medicine to treat certain psychiatric disorders, to depress appetite in certain weight-loss cases, and in special circumstances where temporary stimulation and prevention of fatigue are absolutely necessary. The drugs, including Benzedrine and Dexedrine, popularly known as "pep pills," are an increasing drug-abuse problem. After the immediate stimulating effects wear off, the user may experience fatigue and depression. The drugs may also cause apprehension, insomnia, dizziness, headache, digestive disturbances, confusion and even psychotic episodes and convulsions. A particularly severe form of amphetamine abuse involves injecting the amphetamine (then called "speed").

Amphibia, class of terrestrial to aquatic vertebrates between fish and reptile on the evolutionary scale. Amphibians have smooth, slimy, moist skin with a network of blood vessels to aid in respiration. Most adults have limbs with digits. Body temperature is determined by environment. Because amphibian eggs are shell-less, they are laid in water or humid surroundings to prevent drying out. There is generally an aquatic larval stage. All adults are carnivorous, but larvae are frequently herbivorous. The class consists of three living orders: Caudata—salamander and siren (sometimes sirens are classified separately as Trachystomata); Anura or Salientia—frog and toad; and Apoda—wormlike caecilian. There are about 2500 living amphibian species.

Amphibious Warfare, the strategy and tactics of employing sea-launched land forces against coastal military objectives. Seaborne assaults are used to bypass enemy defenses and seize key objectives and often serve as the prelude to major overseas land campaigns. Specialized amphibious equipment ranges from large helicopter carriers and tank landing ships, to small amphibious vehicles and assault boats.

Amphibole, any of some 30 complex rock-forming mineral varieties characterized by their double-chain silicate (SiO_4) structure. They all contain water (as OH ions) and usually Ca,Mg,Fe. Found in igneous and metamorphic rocks. Form wedge-shaped fragments on cleavage. Orthorhombic or monoclinic crystals often needle-like or fibrous. Common varieties are

American water spaniel

Roald Amundsen

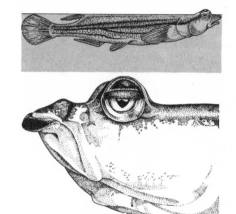

Anableps

hornblende, tremolite, actinolite and anthophyllite. Some varieties are used in commercial asbestos.

Amphioxus, or lancelet, marine, fish-shaped animal living in coarse gravel on warm sea bottoms. It has a well-developed notochord, but no enlarged head region or brain; segmented body muscles; a pharynx with gill slits; rudimentary eyes; and tentacles around its mouth to strain food from water. Length: to 3in (8cm). There are 25 species. Subphylum Cephalochordata; genus *Branchiostoma*.

Amphipod, or scud, mainly marine crustaceans, though some are freshwater and a few, such as the beach flea, are semi-terrestrial. They have laterally compressed bodies and two compound eyes. Some are parasitic. Length: .125–5.5in (.32–14cm).

Amphisbaenid, cylindrical, mostly legless, burrowing reptile found in tropical America and Africa. They resemble earthworms having rings of scales around their bodies and tails. They have no external ear openings and no left lung. Only a few have short front legs. Length: 12in (30cm). The worm lizard *Rhineura floridana* is found in Florida. Formerly considered lizards, the 100 species are now classified as a Squamata suborder. Family Amphisbaenidae. *See also* Lizard.

Amphitrite, in Greek mythology, the goddess of the sea, wife of Poseidon. She fled to Atlas after refusing Poseidon's proposal of marriage, but was returned to Poseidon by a dolphin. As a reward, he transformed it into the constellation Dolphin.

Amphitryon. *See* Alcmene.

Amplifier, device for increasing the voltage (voltage amplifier) or the current (power amplifier) of an electrical signal. In both cases the energy required to amplify the signal is obtained from a source other than the signal. The amplification device formerly used was the triode (or pentode) electron tube, but tubes have been almost completely replaced by the lighter, smaller, and more economical transistor.

Amplitude Modulation (AM), process in which a signal wave (the modulating wave) alters the intensity (amplitude) of a carrier wave, in order to transmit information. Sidebands are produced above and below the carrier frequency relative to the signal's value.

Amritsar, city in NW India; capital of Amritsar district in Punjab state; est by Ram Das, 4th Sikh Guru. Guru Arjan built the Golden Temple, located in the middle of a lake, which attracts many Sikh pilgrims; center of Sikh empire and religion. Industries: carpets, textiles, embroideries. Founded 1577. Pop. 432,663.

Amsterdam, capital and largest city in Netherlands; divided by Amstel River and linked to the North Sea by the North Sea Canal. Dutch East India Co. (1602) brought the city to a peak in prosperity and a great influx of European refugees. Its commerce and importance declined with capture by French 1795 and British blockade during Napoleonic Wars; surrendered to Germany in WWII; site of church (1334), 16th-century city hall, Royal Palace, National Museum (1808), Rembrandt's house; Olympic Games (1928); seat of University of Amsterdam (1632), Free Reformed University (1880). Industries: exporting, fishing, diamond cutting, iron, steel, railroad cars, sugar and oil refining, food processing, chemicals, glass, paper, rubber, ships, cars, aircraft. Chartered *c.* 1300. Pop. 752,500.

AMU. *See* Atomic Mass Unit.

Amu Darya (Jayhun), chief river in central Asia; rises in Pamir Mts; flows NW down Hindu Kush slopes onto plain below Termez, USSR; forms boundary between Tadzhik SSR and NE Afghanistan; flows W and NW through E Turkmen SSR and W of Uzbek SSR, into swampy delta at Aral Sea. Chief tributaries are Vakhsh, Kafirnigan, Surkhab (N), and Kunduz (S). Ancient name was Oxus; crossed by Alexander in 328 BC; navigable for 930mi (1,497km). Length: approx. 1,600mi (2,576km).

Amulet, object or emblem worn to ward off danger, ensure good fortune, or increase personal power. A rabbit's foot or St. Christopher's medal is an amulet. *See also* Fetish.

Amun, or Amon, ancient Egyptian deity of reproduction or of the animating force. He is represented as a ram or as a ram-headed man, or a goose or snake, and often as a crowned king. Amun was worshiped at Thebes in the 12th dynasty, then later as a powerful national god renamed Amun-Ra, identified with the sun. Amun's temples are at Luxor, Karnak, and Thebes. *See also* Amun-Ra.

Amundsen, Roald (1872–1928), Norwegian explorer and discoverer of the South Pole. From 1903–06, he sailed through the Northwest Passage and, from his observations, was able to locate the exact position of the North Magnetic Pole. His next expedition took him to the Antarctic, and in December 1911, one month ahead of Captain Robert Scott, another explorer, he reached the South Pole. In his later years, he conducted an exploration of the north polar regions by air (1926). Throughout most of his life, Amundsen was a well-known lecturer and writer. His books include *North West Passage* (1908), *The South Pole* (1912), *The North East Passage* (1918–20), and *My Life as an Explorer* (1927).

Amun-Ra (Amun-Re), in 18th-dynasty Egypt, the national god, patronized by the pharaohs. Amun of Thebes became identified with the sun god Ra, and emerged as Amon-Ra, only to be cast down when Akhenaton proclaimed worship of the single god Aton, the solar disk, as the state religion. *See also* Amun.

Amur (Hei-lung Chiang), river in NE Asia, at Soviet-Chinese border, formed by confluence of Shilka and Argun rivers; flows SE forming 1,000-mi (1,611-km) border between Manchuria and Soviet Union subdivisions, then flows NE, through Far Eastern USSR, before entering N end of Tatar Strait, of the Pacific. Chief ports are Soviet cities Khabarovsk, Komsomolsk, Nikolayevsk. Valley region was settled by Russians 1847. Length: approx. 1,800mi (2,898km).

Amylase, digestive enzyme secreted by the salivary glands (salivary amylase, or ptyalin) and the pancreas (pancreatic amylase, or amylopsin). It aids in digestion by breaking down starch into simple sugars.

Amyotrophic Lateral Sclerosis, or Gehrig's disease, a disease of middle life primarily affecting men, with no known cause, brought to public attention by its affliction of baseball player Lou Gehrig. Symptoms are gradual weakness and atrophy of the muscles of the hands, then arms and legs, with some spasticity. There is no known cure.

Anabaptists, ancestors of today's Baptists, active during the Middle Ages. Seeking to maintain the purity of the early Christian churches, they insisted on rebaptism, as infant baptism is not in accord with the New Testament. Scripture, rather than the church, was held

supreme. For four centuries, Anabaptists grew in numbers in Europe. *See also* Baptists.

Anabasis, Xenophon's account in seven books of the Greek expedition under Cyrus the Younger against Artaxerxes of Persia, and the subsequent retreat and adventures of the Greek mercenaries (401–399 BC).

Anableps, or four eyes, freshwater fish found from S Mexico to N South America. A band of skin divides its eyes into halves for simultaneous vision above and below the water surface. Young (1–5) are born alive at one time. Length: 6–8in (15–20cm). Family Anablepidae; species *Anableps*.

Anabolism, constructive metabolic process that turns food into living tissue in living organisms. *See also* Metabolism.

Anaconda, South American snake, related to the boa. It is mainly aquatic, a good climber, and feeds on mammals and birds near riverbanks. Color is olive-green with black blotches and rings. Length: to 25ft (7.6m). Family Boidae; species *Eunectes murinus*.

Anacoustic Zone, or "zone of silence," the region above 100 miles altitude where distance between air molecules becomes greater than the wavelength of sound, so that no sound waves can be propagated. With increasing height, high-frequency (short-wavelength) sounds disappear first, and only lower tones can be heard.

Anacreon (*c.*570–485 BC), Greek author. His main themes were wine, love, and merry living. Expressive in style, he wrote lyrics, elegies, and epigrams. Little of his work has survived, although he was often imitated.

Anaerobe, an organism that cannot grow in the presence of free atmospheric oxygen. Bacteria of this type are a problem in canning since they can grow under vacuum.

Anagram, a word or group of words whose letters have been transposed to produce other words, as "time" and "mite" from the word "emit." A sophisticated anagram would be a transposition of letters producing a word or phrase that bears some logical relation to the original.

Anaheim, city in S California, 16mi (26km) E of Long Beach; site of Disneyland, Anaheim Stadium and Convention Center; 8th most populous city in Calif. Industries: electronic equipment, fruit canning, greeting cards. Founded in 1857 by Germans; inc. 1870. Pop. (1980) 221,847.

Analgesic, drug that relieves pain. It may be narcotic, such as morphine or cocaine, or it may be nonnarcotic, such as the commonly used aspirin and acetanilid and phenacetin compounds.

Analog Computer, computer that solves scientific and technical problems by accepting a set of continuously varying quantities, which reflect variations in the physical quantities under consideration, and that manipulates them, usually electronically, as required. *See also* Computer, Electronic.

Analogy, in literature, a method of verbal comparison, from a term originally used by the Greeks to mean similarity in proportional relationships (as A is to B, so C is to D). It is a method used to heighten illumination, as in comparing a known thing or circumstance to another, or in defense in argumentation.

Analytic Geometry, or coordinate geometry, branch of geometry in which a position is represented by numbers in some coordinate system, and lines, curves, and surfaces can be represented by algebraic equations. The geometric properties can then be studied by the methods of algebra. It was first introduced by René Descartes in the 17th century; analytic geometry in Cartesian coordinate systems is also called Cartesian geometry. *See also* Mathematics.

Anaphylaxis, or **anaphylactic shock,** an acute, serious allergic reaction that occurs after a person eats, inhales, or is injected with a substance (antigen), such as penicillin, insect venom, or certain foods, to which he has been previously sensitized and against which he has developed antibodies. Second exposure to the offending substance can lead to paleness, faintness, palpitations, hives, swelling, difficulty in breathing, and, if untreated, shock.

Anarchism, political theory that regards all forms of government as evil, coercive, and unnecessary. Anarchism advocates a social order based on liberty and voluntary cooperation. Zeno of Citium (*c.* 334–262 BC), the founder of stoicism, is regarded as the father of anarchism. In the 19th century Mikhail Bakunin advocated politically active, violent anarchism. Fear of anarchism, supposedly spread by foreign agitators, remained strong in the United States well into the 20th century.

Anastasia (*c.* 1901–?18), grand duchess of Russia, the youngest daughter of the last emperor, Nicholas II, presumably murdered together with other members of the royal family in July 1918. Since 1920, several women have claimed to be Anastasia, the legal heir to the Romanov fortune held in Swiss banks. None of the claimants has proven legitimate.

Anatolia. *See* Asia Minor.

Anatomy, that branch of biological science that studies the structure of an organism. The study of anatomy can be divided in several ways. On the basis of the size of the structures studied, there is gross anatomy, studying structures with the naked eye; microscopic anatomy, studying finer detail with a light microscope; submicroscopic anatomy, studying even finer structural detail with an electron microscope; and molecular anatomy, studying with sophisticated instruments the molecular makeup of structures. Microscopic and submicroscopic anatomy involve two closely related sciences: histology, the study of tissue that makes up a body organ, and cytology, the study of cells that make up a tissue. Anatomy can also be classified according to the organism or type of organism studied, for example, plant anatomy, invertebrate anatomy, vertebrate anatomy, human anatomy. Developmental anatomy, or embryology, is the study of the origin, development, and relationship of various body parts. The study of the structure of any body part is intimately connected with the function or activity of that organ, the study of which is physiology. *See also* Physiology.

Anaxagoras of Clazomene (*c.* 500–428 BC), Greek philosopher, the most important before Socrates. He was the teacher of Euripides, Pericles, and, possibly, Socrates. He believed that all matter was composed of "seeds" or minute particles. He explained the true cause of eclipses. Toward the end of his life he was exiled from Athens for his "impious" teaching that the sun was a white-hot stone and the moon was composed of earth and merely reflected the sun's rays.

Anaximander (611–547 BC), Greek scientist and philosopher credited as the author of the first geometric model of the universe. His fame rests chiefly on his doctrine of a single world-principle, the starting point and origin of the cosmic process, which he identified as *apeiron* or "the infinite."

Ancestor Worship, worship and propitiation of the spirits of dead relatives. Ancestral spirits are worshiped to win benefits or avoid evils. Ancestor worship is based on the belief that spirits of the dead continue to live in the natural world and have the power to do good or evil. In the past, ancestor worship flourished in China, ancient Rome, and elsewhere, and it is still practiced in Melanesia.

Anchorage, seaport city, in S central Alaska, at head of Cook Inlet base of Kenai Peninsula, 470mi (757km) S of Fairbanks; state's oil supply center; location of army post, airport, salmon canneries; scene of severe earthquake (1964). Founded 1914. Pop. (1980) 173,017.

Anchovy, marine schooling fish found worldwide in temperate and tropical seas. Silvery fish with setback mouths, there are more than 100 species including the common Atlantic *Anchoa mitchilli.* Length: 5–9in (13–23cm). Family Engraulidae.

Andalusia, largest administrative region in S Spain, bounded by the Strait of Gibralter in the Mediterranean Sea (S), Portugal (W), Estremadura, New Castile, and Murcia provinces (N and E); divided into eight modern provinces 1833. Settled by Phoenicians 1100 BC, and taken by Romans 3rd century BC, it peaked under Moors (when it was called al-Andalus) 8th–13th centuries; fell to Nationalist forces during Spanish Civil War (1936–39). A popular resort area, it is a fertile region with large mineral deposits. Crops: wheat, corn, barley, grapes, olives, sugar, citrus fruit. Area: 33,675sq mi (87,218sq km). Pop. 5,971,277.

Andaman and Nicobar Islands, union territory in India, E of Bay of Bengal; island chain made up of the Andaman Islands (S) and Nicobar Islands (N); capital is Port Blair. The Andamans, consisting of about 175 islands, were used as British penal colony from 1858; the 19 Nicobar islands became a British possession in 1869. The two island groups were joined administratively in 1872 under British control until 1942 when occupied by Japan (1942–45); passed to India 1947. Exports: lumber, copra. Andaman Islands, area: 2,508sq mi (6,496sq km). Nicobar Islands, area: 707sq mi (1,831sq km). Total pop. 100,000.

Andaman Sea, branch of the Indian Ocean, in S Asia; bordered by Andaman and Nicobar Islands (W), Burma (N), Malay Peninsula (E), Sumatra (S); Rangoon, main port, is on the Gulf of Martaban, a NW inlet. Length: 600mi (966km). Width: 400mi (644km).

Andersen, Hans Christian (1805–75), Danish author of many fairy tales, notably "The Ugly Duckling," "The Little Mermaid," "Thumbelina," "The Swineherd," "The Emperor's New Clothes," "The Constant Tin Soldier," and "The Little Match Girl." The tales were first translated into English in 1846 by Mary Howitt, who called the book *Wonderful Stories for Children. See also* Fairy Tale.

Anderson, Marian (1902–), US contralto, b. Philadelphia. She established her reputation as a singer touring America and Europe in recitals (1925–35). Forbidden in 1939 by the Daughters of the American Revolution to perform at Constitution Hall, Washington, D.C., she was sponsored by Eleanor Roosevelt in a concert at the Lincoln Memorial. She made her Metropolitan Opera debut in 1955 as Ulrica in Verdi's *Un Ballo in Maschera,* marking the first appearance of a black singer in a leading role at the opera hall. In 1978 she received a special gold medal authorized by Congress for her contribution to the arts.

Anderson, Maxwell (1888–1959), US dramatist, b. Atlantic, Pa. At first a journalist, he turned full time to playwriting with the success of *What Price Glory?* (1924), an antiwar comedy written with Laurence Stallings. In 1933 he won a Pulitzer Prize for *Both Your Houses,* a satire on the US Congress. He wrote a number of plays in verse, most successfully *Winterset* (1935), a tragedy based on the Sacco-Vanzetti case, and *High Tor* (1937), a romantic comedy. He also wrote many historical dramas including *Elizabeth the Queen* (1930) and *Valley Forge* (1934). He wrote the librettos for the Kurt Weill musicals *Knickerbocker Holiday* (1938) and *Lost in the Stars* (1940).

Andersonville Prison, historic prison in Andersonville, SW Georgia; used by the Confederacy to confine Union prisoners. Harsh conditions led to death of 12,000 soldiers. Est. 1970 as a national historic site. Area: 495 acres (200 hectares).

Andes, mountain range in South America, along Caribbean and Pacific coasts; extends through Venezuela, Colombia, Ecuador, Peru, Bolivia, Chile, and Argentina; one of the world's longest and highest mt ranges; formerly inhabited by the Incas. Aconcagua, in Argentina, is the highest peak, 22,835ft (6,965m). Hazardous air currents, rough terrain, and low temperatures have made transportation and communication extremely difficult. Most of its inhabitants have depended on subsistence farming and mineral products. Mineral exploitation is a major commercial concern of Andean countries. Length: 5,000mi (8,050km).

Andesite, named for a type of lava common in the Andes Mountains, an extrusive igneous rock similar to rhyolite in structure and similar to diorite in its composition. It contains feldspar and ferromagnesian minerals. *See also* Igneous Rocks.

Andorra, small state situated high in the E Pyrenees between France and Spain. Although the several high mountain valleys have poor soil, they support large flocks of sheep. The increasing tourist trade supplements the traditional livestock raising. Andorra La Vieja is the main town; the people are Catalan-speaking and Roman Catholic. Area: 179sq mi (464sq km). Pop. 26,558.

Andrássy, (Count) Gyula (1823–90), Hungarian statesman and diplomat. An ardent nationalist, he joined the abortive rebellion of 1848 against Austria and escaped execution by remaining in exile until 1857. When the dual monarchy was formed, he became first prime minister for Hungary (1867). From 1871 to 1879, he was minister of foreign affairs for the Austro-Hungarian Empire, which he represented at the Congress of Berlin in 1878. His plan for Austria, occupation of Bosnia and Herzegovina, was accepted by the powers. His son was also a Hungarian diplomat.

Andrew, Prince (1960–), second son of Queen Elizabeth II and Prince Philip, Duke of Edinburgh; fourth in succession to the British throne. In 1986 he married Sarah Ferguson, a commoner.

Andrew, in the New Testament, son of Jonah, brother of Simon Peter, and one of the first disciples of Jesus.

Androcles, Roman slave supposed to have lived *c.* AD 20, who ran away from his master and hid in a cave. He took a thorn from the paw of a suffering lion. Later Androcles faced the same lion in the Roman Arena. The lion recognized Androcles and refused to harm him.

Androgen, general name for masculinizing hormones secreted principally by the testes. *See also* Testosterone.

Andromeda, evergreen shrub of the heath family, with narrow leaves and pink, bell-shaped flowers.

Andromeda Galaxy (M 31; NGC 224), great spiral galaxy in Andromeda, the nearest major external galaxy to our own Milky Way system. It is larger than the Milky Way Galaxy, but resembles it closely, and also possesses satellite systems similar to the Magellanic Clouds. Distance 2,000,000 light years. *See also* Spiral Galaxy.

Andropov, Yuri Vladimirovich (1914–84), Soviet political leader and first secretary of the Communist party (1982–84). He became an alternate member of the Politburo in 1967, the same year in which he was appointed to head the KGB, the secret police, and a voting member in 1973. He was a strong advocate of Soviet intervention in Czechoslovakia in 1968 and in Poland in 1981. After the death of Leonid Brezhnev in 1982, Andropov was elected first secretary of the Communist Party and president of the Soviet Union.

Andros, (Sir) Edmund (1637–1714), British colonial governor. He served as proprietary governor of New York (1674–81), and became the royal governor of the Dominion of New England (1686–89) ruling all the colonies north of New Jersey. He was also lieutenant governor of Virginia (1692–97).

Androsterone, steroid hormone with masculinizing effects. It is obtained from the testes and from male urine and controls the growth and function of male sexual organs and the production of secondary male sexual characteristics, such as the growth and distribution of hair.

Anechoic Chamber, or dead room, room designed to be echo-free so that it can be used in acoustic laboratories to measure sound reflection and transmission. The walls, floor, and ceiling must be insulated and all surfaces covered with an absorbent material, such as asbestos fiber, often over inward-pointing pyramid shapes to reduce reflection. To reduce standing waves the room is usually asymmetrical. *See also* Echo.

Anemia, an abnormal condition in which there is a decrease in the amount of the pigment hemoglobin in the red blood cells or a decrease in the number of red blood cells. Anemia may be caused by excessive blood loss, by a decrease in production of hemoglobin or red blood cells, or by excessive destruction of hemoglobin or red blood cells. Symptoms of anemia include fatigue, weakness, pallor, often vague gastrointestinal signs, and if the anemia is severe, faintness and palpitations. There are several types of anemia. In *iron-deficiency anemia* hemoglobin production is deficient because of a deficiency in the iron necessary for hemoglobin production. It is most commonly caused by chronic blood loss—from a minor disorder such as hemorrhoids or from serious diseases such as ulcers or cancer. *Pernicious anemia* is an impairment of the body's ability to absorb vitamin B_{12}, a vitamin necessary for normal red blood cell maturation. Deficiencies in other substances, such as folic acid or other B vitamins, may also decrease red blood cell produc-

Marian Anderson

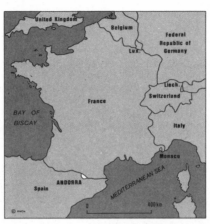

Andorra

Yuri V. Andropov

tion. In the *hemolytic anemias* there is excessive destruction of red blood cells. Such destruction may be due to hereditary abnormalities (such as sickle-cell anemia) or from nonhereditary conditions such as drug reactions or the production of antibodies to one's own red blood cells. Bone marrow is the site of red blood cell production and diseases of the bone marrow, due to radiation, drugs or chemicals, cancer, etc., may also produce anemia. *See also* Sickle-cell Anemia.

Anemometer, an instrument using rotating cups, vanes, or propellers to measure the speed or force of the wind; wind or weather vanes indicate the direction from which the wind comes.

Anemone, or pasqueflower, perennial plant found worldwide. It has sepals resembling petals and numerous stamens and pistils covering a central knob. Two or three deeply toothed leaves appear in a whorl midway up the stem. Many are wildflowers, including the North American wood anemone *(Anemone quinquefolia)*, a low delicate plant with five sepals; Japanese anemone *(Anemone japonica)*, an autumn-blooming species grown in gardens; and pasqueflower *(Anemone patens)*, with large white or blue flowers appearing before the foliage. There are 150 species. Family Ranunculaceae. *See also* Buttercup.

Anesthesia, state of insensibility or loss of sensation produced by disease or various anesthetics used during surgical procedures. During general, or total, anesthesia the entire body becomes insensible and the individual sleeps; in local anesthesia only a specific part of the body is rendered insensible and the patient remains conscious. Local anesthetics, such as spinals, are injected into the spinal fluid and cause loss of sensation to part of the spinal area or the entire area below the injection level; nerve blocks affect only the pathway of a particular nerve; and others affect only small areas, such as the nose or bladder. Well-known anesthetic agents include nitrous oxide, a weak agent also called laughing gas; cyclopropane, a strong and widely used agent; ether and chloroform, volatile agents once widely used but now largely replaced; injected barbiturate agents for short, relatively painless procedures; and relaxants for relaxing muscles for proper surgical manipulation. All anesthetic agents can produce undesirable and even dangerous effects and the choice, dose, and effects of each agent must be carefully considered for each patient.

Anesthesiology, branch of medicine involving the use of anesthetic agents to prevent pain during surgical and other procedures and care of the anesthetized patient.

Aneto, Pico de, highest peak in the Pyrenees in NE Spain, in the Maladeta group, S of the French border. Height: 11,168ft (3,406m).

Aneurysm, localized saclike enlargement of an artery, most commonly the aorta. It is caused by weakening of the artery wall and produces pain and pressure on surrounding tissues and hemorrhage if it ruptures.

Angel Falls, waterfall in SE Venezuela, in the Guiana Highlands; highest uninterrupted waterfall in world, 3,212ft (980m).

Angelfish, marine reef fish found in shallow tropical waters. Its deep body is laterally compressed and marked and colored brightly. Length: to 2ft (61cm). Family Chaetodontidae; species includes yellow and blue Queen *Holacanthus ciliaris*.

Angelico, Fra (1400–55), Italian painter, b. Guido di Pietro. His works of religious subjects, mostly traditional altarpieces, reflect a strong classical influence. He became a Dominican monk around 1421, and much of his work consisted of mural painting in the monastery of S. Marco in Florence, which he entered in 1439. His most famous work is a series of 35 paintings for the doors of a silver chest in the church of SS. Annunziata, Florence.

Anger, human emotion ranging in intensity from annoyance to rage, usually evoked by a threatening but nonfeared stimulus, and often leading to aggression. *See also* Aggression; Emotion.

Angers, city in France, on the Marne River, 165mi (266km) SW of Paris; capital of Maine-et-Loire dept.; called Julio-Magus in Roman times. Invaded by Norse in 9th century, and by the English in 12th and 15th centuries; Huguenots took city in 1585; site of 12th-century Cathedral of St Maurice, and slate quarries. Industries: liqueur distillation, leather goods, rope. Pop. 163,191.

Angevins, medieval dynasty that became the Plantagenets, a line of English kings begun when Henry II (Count of Anjou) ascended the throne in 1154. The Angevins retained the crown until 1399.

Angina Pectoris, type of heart disease characterized by a distinctive anxiety-producing pain or feeling of tightness in the chest or back, often extending to the arm and sometimes to the jaw area or other parts of the body. It is often precipitated by walking outdoors, exposure to cold or wind, or emotional excitement. It is caused by a temporary decrease in blood and oxygen to a part of the heart, usually as a result of a narrowing or closure of a coronary artery. It is treated symptomatically, most often with nitroglycerine. Any underlying causes are corrected if possible.

Angioma, common, localized lesion of the skin and underlying tissue caused by enlargement of blood or lymph vessels. So-called portwine stains and strawberry marks are types of angiomas.

Angiosperms, flowering plants that have seeds enclosed in an ovary. There are more than 250,000 species of angiosperms, including the majority of garden plants and most deciduous shrubs and trees. All existing seed-bearing plants are divided into two groups: angiosperms and gymnosperms (conifers and their relations), which have seeds borne on open scales. Angiosperms occur in every land area of the earth and are abundant in rivers and freshwater lakes. *See also* Gymnosperm.

Angkor, ancient site in NW Cambodia, covering an area of 40sq mi (104sq km); contains ruins of several capitals of the Khmer Empire, which flourished for six centuries; first capital founded by Yasovarman I, centered around the temple of Phnom Bak Kheng; site of the Angkor Wat (temple) complex (1113–50), one of the largest structures of worship in the world. Angkor Thom, the last capital (12th–13th centuries), centered around the Bayon, a Buddhist temple; site was abandoned 1434. Discovered by French 1860.

Angle, measure of the inclination of two straight lines or planes to each other. One complete revolution is divided into 360 degrees or 2π radians. One degree may be subdivided into 60 minutes, and one minute into 60 seconds.

Anglerfish, marine fish found in temperate and tropical seas. It is characterized by movable rod with lure (actually a modified ray of the dorsal fin) positioned on the head to attract prey. Most have a flattened head and wide mouth with hanging flaps of skin fringing the body. The 225 species include goosefish, monkfish, batfish, and frogfish. Order Lephiiformes.

Angles, a Germanic tribe from a district now called Angeln in Schleswig-Holstein. In the 5th century, with neighboring tribes, the Jutes and Saxons, they invaded England, settling in Mercia, Northumbria, East and Middle Anglia. Tacitus (1st century AD) described them as worshippers of the Scandinavian deity Nerthus. Bede, in *Ecclesiastical History* (731), described their conquest. The name England derives from their name (Angle-Land).

Anglesite, a sulfate mineral, lead sulfate ($PbSO_4$). Usually found together with cerussite in hydrothermal veins as an alternation product of galena. Orthorhombic system tabular or prismatic crystals; also massive or stalactitic. Colorless, white or gray; hardness 2.5–3; sp gr 6.4.

Anglicanism, beliefs in accordance with the teachings of the Church of England. It has been identified as the "Anglican Communion" since the 19th century. Developing since Henry VIII's separation from the Roman Catholic Church (1534), it is based on scriptural and ecclesiastical authority. The governing function is episcopal, and worship is liturgical. Elements of both Roman Catholicism and Protestantism are contained in the theology. The decision (1978) not to ordain women caused sharp divisions within the church. In 1982, diplomatic ties with the Roman Catholic Church were restored. *See also* Church of England.

Anglo-Saxon Architecture (fl.449–1066), architectural style found in several small churches in the southeast and north of England and characterized by long and short stonework, square apses, either aisles or side chambers called *porticus*, pilaster strips, and distinctive timber work. Anglo-Saxon architecture is difficult to distinguish from the Roman ruins it was often built on or from, and many wooden structures are lost.

Anglo-Saxon Chronicle, main source of British history of the Anglo-Saxon period. Compiled in the late 9th century, it traces the history of Britain from the Roman Conquest to the reign of Alfred the Great.

Anglo-Saxons, peoples of Germanic origin who settled in England beginning in the mid-5th century, supplanting the Celts. The term itself was first used in the early 9th century to distinguish the Saxon settlers in England from the Old Saxons of northern Germany. After the Norman Conquest (1066) "Anglo-Saxon" became synonymous with "English."

Angola, independent nation in W Africa. Also known as Portuguese West Africa until 1975 independence, it is a Bantu nation rich in oil, coffee, and diamonds. It has been torn by a nationalist civil war.

Land and economy. Located in both the equatorial and tropical climate zone, it is divided into two sections: Angola proper is S of the Congo River, bordered by Zaire (N and NW), Zambia (E), Namibia (South West Africa) (S), and the Atlantic Ocean (W). The Angolan exclave of Cabinda, a rain forest, is separated from Angola by Zaire. Central Angola is largely the Bie plateau, 3,000–5,000ft (915–1,525m) above sea level; hydroelectric power is generated by the plateau's falls and rapids. The Mocamedes Desert is in the S. Main rivers are the Cuanza and Cunene; Luanda and Lobito are the principal ports. Varying altitudes, cold ocean currents, and low rainfall result in a tropical N and semi-arid S. The most important economic development came with the 1966 discovery of oil off Cabinda and expansion of the Cassinga iron mines. Coffee is the main cash crop, and diamonds are a principal industry. By the late 1970s much of the economy had been nationalized.

People. Angolans are almost entirely Bantu black Africans divided into four tribes: Ovimbundu (33%), Bankongo (24%), Kimbundu (25%), and Chokwe (8%). A version of Bantu is spoken by most tribes; Portuguese is common to the country. Most people follow traditional tribal religions. The literacy rate is 15%.

Government. The MPLA (Movemento Popular do Libertacão de Angola) is the sole legal political party. The head of state, José Eduardo dos Santoas (1979–   ), is president of the republic and party, commander of the armed forces, and chairman of the cabinet. A 206-member National People's Assembly was elected in 1980.

History. Portuguese explorer Diego Cao landed in 1483, befriending the African kingdom. Portugal remained in power, with the exception of the 1641–48 Dutch occupation. Angola was a primary source of slaves for Brazilian plantations in the New World. After WWII nationalist Angolans sought autonomy, and uprisings continued until a new Portuguese government offered independence in 1975. A power struggle between Soviet-backed forces and Cubans against South African and Western-backed factions emerged. The violent civil war caused most of the whites to leave the country, the economy to decline, and a secession move by Cabinda. The country officially became independent on Nov. 11, 1975. By 1976 the Soviet-supported MPLA controlled the government. Angola continues to receive military and economic support from the USSR and Cuba. Angola has supported black liberation movements in neighboring countries, including Zimbabwe (formerly Rhodesia) and Namibia (Southwest Africa); South African forces have sporadically attacked black Namibian guerrilla bases in Angola. In 1985, the US began aiding the Angolan anticommunist forces.

PROFILE

Official name: People's Republic of Angola
Area: 481,351sq mi (1,246,700sq km)
Population: 6,580,000
Density: 14 per sq mi (5per sq km)
Chief cities: Luanda (capital); Huambo; Lobito
Government: people's republic
Religion: Indigenous tribal religions
Language: Portuguese (national)
Monetary unit: Escudo
Gross national product: $2,980,000,000
Per capita income: $492
Industries: food processing, bottling and brewing, cement, glass, paper, cotton, footwear, soap
Agriculture: coffee, corn, sugar, cotton, wheat, tobacco, sisal, fish, cattle
Minerals: diamonds, petroleum, iron, copper, manganese, sulphur, phosphates
Trading partners: Portugal, Federal Republic of Germany, United States, United Kingdom

Angora Cat, long-haired domestic cat breed with round head, short body, short tail, and short, strong legs. It is also called Turkish and Ankara cat after its place of origin. Its large eyes are wide-set—one is blue and one is yellow. Not a Persian, its silky fine coat is usually white. Smoke and Black varieties have yellow eyes. A purebred Angora is usually deaf.

Angora Goat, domestic goat native to Turkey, now found worldwide. Its body is covered with long, silky hair (mohair) important in the textile industry. *See also* Goat.

Angostura Bark, bark of a South American tree *Galipia officinalis,* known also as cusparia bark. It has been used in the past to treat fevers, but is now used as an aromatic bitter.

Angstrom, Anders Jon (1814–74), Swedish astronomer and physicist, one of the founders of the science of spectroscopy. In 1861 he began to use the spectroscope and photographic plates to study the solar system. His experiments proved that the sun contains hydrogen, and in 1869 he was able to map the entire solar spectrum. Units of the wavelength of light are named for him (angstrom unit).

Ångström Unit, or **Ångström,** unit of length, equal to 10^{-10} meter or 0.1 nanometer, used to express the wavelength of light and ultraviolet radiation, interatomic and intermolecular distances, etc. Symbol: A.

Anguilla, island in British West Indies; one of Leeward Islands, 60mi (97km) NW of St Christopher; part of St Christopher Nevis-Anguilla group, associated with Great Britain. Anguilla left the union in 1967, claiming political and economical discrimination, but returned in

1971 and, in 1976, became an internal self-governing state associated with Britain. Industries: tourism, livestock, mining, fishing. Area: 35sq mi (91sq km). Pop. 6,500.

Angular Acceleration, rate of change of angular velocity. Average angular acceleration of a body whose angular velocity changes from ω_1 to ω_2 over a time t is $(\omega_2-\omega_1)/t$. Instantaneous angular acceleration is value approached by ω as t becomes small. The direction of the angular acceleration vector is perpendicular to the plane of motion. The tangential acceleration a_T of a particle at a distance r from a fixed point is directly proportional to the magnitude of its angular acceleration: $a_T = r\omega$.

Angular Distance, in astronomy, apparent distance on the celestial sphere between two celestial bodies measured along an arc of a great circle passing through them with the observer at the center. Angular distance of the Pointers (Ursa Major) is 5°.

Angular Momentum, the product of the moment of inertia I and angular velocity ω of a body or system of particles. Usually denoted by **L,** angular momentum is a vector quantity that is conserved (remains constant) at all times.

Angular Velocity, the rate of change of a body's angular position relative to a fixed point. Average angular velocity $\bar{\omega}$ of a body moving from angle θ_1 to θ_2 in time t is $(\theta_2 - \theta_1)/t$. Instantaneous angular velocity ω is the value approached by $\bar{\omega}$ in succeeding instants (mathematically, as t goes to zero). The direction associated with the angular velocity of a body is perpendicular to the plane of its motion. The speed v of a body at a distance r from a fixed point is directly proportional to the magnitude ω of its angular velocity: $v = r\omega$. *See also* Velocity.

Anhwei (Anhui), prov. in E central China divided by Wan Mts into two areas: N is an extensive plain area with limited agriculture due to cold winters; S has a sub-tropical climate and produces tea. Capital is Hofei, 90mi (145km) W of Nanking. Industries: steel, iron, coal, copper, rice, Hsuan paper, India ink. Area: 54,015sq mi (139,899sq km). Pop. 35,000,000.

Anhydride, chemical compound derived from a specified compound by abstraction of water. Thus sulfur trioxide, SO_3, is the anhydride of sulfuric acid: it reacts with water thus, $SO_3 + H_2O \rightarrow H_2SO_4$. The organic anhydrides contain the group -CO-O-CO- and give carboxylic acids with water: acetic anhydride, for example, gives acetic acid thus, $CH_3CO \cdot O \cdot COCH_3 + H_2O \rightarrow 2\ CH_3COOH$.

Anhydrite, a sulfate mineral, calcium sulfate ($CaSO_4$), usually found in sedimentary rocks associated with salt beds. Readily takes up water from gypsum. Crystallizes in orthorhombic system, usually forming massive deposits. Colorless when pure; glassy or pearly luster; hardness 3–3.5; sp gr 3. *See also* Gypsum.

Aniline, colorless oily liquid (formula $C_6H_5NH_2$) made by reduction of nitrobenzene. It is an important starting material for making organic compounds, particularly dyestuffs. Properties: sp. gr. 1.02; melt. pt. 20.66°F (−6.3°C); boil. pt. 363.43°F (184.13°C). *See also* Amine.

Animal, living organism of the animal kingdom, distinguishable from members of the plant kingdom by characteristics such as the power of locomotion, well-defined body shape, limited growth, and inability to produce own food. Higher animals, such as the vertebrates, are easily distinguished from plants, but simpler forms are more difficult. Some one-celled organisms could be assigned to either category. Protozoa, sponges, jellyfish, segmented worms, arthropods, mollusks, echinoderms, and chordates are the major phyla.

Animal Classification, systematic grouping of animals into categories based on shared characteristics. The first major classification was by Aristotle. The method now used was devised by Carolus Linnaeus, a Swedish botanist, in the 1750s. All modern classification is based upon evolutionary relationships.

Of a two-part Latin name, the first part indicates genus, the second, species. A species is composed of animals capable of interbreeding in nature. A genus includes all similar and related species. The family takes in all like genera, and an order all related families. Similar orders are grouped in a class and related classes make up a phylum. Twenty separate phyla comprise the Animal Kingdom. For example, Dog: phylum Chordata; class Mammalia; order Carnivora; family Canidae; genus *Canis;* and species *familiaris. See also* Animal.

Animal Husbandry, division of agriculture concerned with selection, breeding, production, management, and marketing of farm animals. The primary subjects of animal husbandry are beef and dairy cattle, hogs, sheep, horses, and poultry. Factors affecting animal husbandry include acreage, soil, market location, feed availability, state of markets, and climate.

Animism, belief that the universe is filled with spirits capable of exerting a malignant or beneficial effect. Every natural object and phenomenon, whether tree, stream, or storm, is regarded as possessing life, consciousness, and a spirit. When animals and plants die their spirits live on, and, if an animal is killed improperly, its spirit can inflict harm. These beliefs are widespread in primitive religions. *See also* Fetish; Mana; Shaman; Taboo; Totem.

Anise, annual herb native to Egypt and widely cultivated for its small, ridged licorice-flavored seeds. It has small white flowers. Height: to 2.5ft (76cm). Family Umbelliferae; species *Pimpinella anisum. See also* Carrot.

Anjou, region and former province of W France, bounded N by Maine River, E by Touraine, SE by Saumurols, S by Poiton, and W by Brittany; under control of England in 1154, Italy in 1246, and a succession of counts; Louis XI annexed it to French crown in 1480. An agricultural area known for its Vouvray and Saumur wines, it is watered by the Loire River.

Ankara, formerly Angora; capital city of Turkey and of Ankara prov., in W central Turkey, at junction of Cubuk and Ankara rivers; processing and agricultural trade center, on railroad line, especially noted for angora wool and mohair production; site of University of Ankara (1946), Middle East Technical University (1956), Hacettepe University (1967), and airport. Ancient town (Ancyra) was important commercial center, becoming Roman provincial capital (Galatia Prima); flourished under Augustus; captured by Tamerlane 1402. Ankara declined until establishment of Turkish national government there 1920. Industries: textiles, foodstuffs, cement and tiles, leather goods, metal works. Pop. 1,522,350.

Ankylosaurus, armored ornithischian dinosaurs of Cretaceous age (71–136 million years ago) of W United States and Canada. A low-set herbivore with short, massive legs and hooved feet, its leathery skin covering on its back and sides was armor-plated with bony nodules and plates arranged in geometric rows. Its tail ended in a bony club much like the head of a mace. Length: 15ft (5m); width: 6ft (1.8m); height: 4ft (1.2m).

Annaba, formerly Bône; seaport and dept. capital in NE Algeria, at the E foot of the Edough Range. City was founded by Carthaginians, flourished as wealthy Roman port of Hippo Regius until *c.* AD 300 and was plundered by Vandals 431; rebuilt by Arabs in 7th century; center of Christianity and home of St Augustine, 396–430. Industries: phosphates, chemicals, cork, barley, ironworks. Pop. 152,006.

Anna Karenina (1873–76), realist novel by Count Leo Tolstoi in which he explores the themes of marriage, social order, and responsibility. The passionate but adulterous and ultimately ruinous love affair between Anna Karenina and Count Vronsky is contrasted with the conventional marriage of Levin and Kitty.

Annam (Anam), former kingdom on E coast of Indochina, that now lies within the country of Vietnam; N boundary is 1954 demilitarized zone and dividing line of N and S Vietnam republics; extends 800mi (1,288km) on narrow strip between S China Sea (E) and Annamese Cordillera (W); capital was Hue. Ancient empire fell to China 214 BC and regained self-government; ruled by China AD 939–1428; French obtained missionary and trade agreements 1787, but disputes led to French seizure beginning 1858 and protectorate was est 1883–84. During WWII it was occupied by Japanese; in 1945 it became autonomous state of Vietnam (comprised of Tonkin, Annam, and Cochin China); heavy and lengthy fighting centered around Hue in 1968 Tet offensive of Vietnam War. Industries: textiles, rice, fish processing. Area: approx. 58,000sq mi (150,220sq km).

Annapolis, seaport city and capital of Maryland on S bank of Severn River 22mi (35km) SSE of Baltimore; seat of Anne Arundel co. Founded 1649 by Puritans from Virginia seeking asylum from religious persecution, who est. (1650) a boatyard on the Severn River; served as temporary national capital (1783–84); scene of signing of the peace treaty with England (1784) ending Revolutionary War in Senate Chamber of the State House (still standing); site of St John's College (1696), US Naval Academy (1845), the Old Treasury (1695),

Anise

Ankylosaurus

Queen Anne

Maryland's oldest building, and more than 80 pre-Revolutionary buildings. In 1965 the "old city" of Annapolis, laid out in 1696 when the colony's capital was moved here from St Mary's, was declared a national historic site. Industries: seafood packaging, boatyards, plastics, concrete products. Named Providence at founding 1649; changed to Annapolis 1695; chartered by Queen Anne 1708; inc. as city 1796. Pop. (1980) 31,740.

Annapurna, mountain range in the Himalayan system, N central Nepal. Annapurna I (E) rises to 26,502ft (8,083m); it was scaled 1950 by French expedition led by Maurice Herzog; 11th-highest peak in the world. Annapurna II (W) rises to 26,041ft (7,943m).

Ann Arbor, city in S Michigan on the Huron River, 36mi (58km) W of Detroit; seat of Washtenaw co; research, educational, medical center; site of the University of Michigan (1817). Industries: computers, scientific instruments, automotive parts. Founded 1824 by pioneers from Virginia and New York; inc. 1851. Pop. (1980) 107,316.

Anne (1665–1714), queen of Great Britain and Ireland (1702–14). The second daughter of James II, she was the last reigning Stuart, and after the Act of Union (1707) first reigning monarch of the united kingdom of England and Scotland. She was dependent on her successive favorites, Sarah, duchess of Marlborough, and Abigail Masham, but presided over an age of military success and cultural distinction. No child survived from her marriage (1683) with George, prince of Denmark. She was succeeded by George, elector of Hanover in 1714.

Anne, Princess (1950–), only daughter of Great Britain's Elizabeth II; a noted competitive horsewoman. She married (1973) Lt. Mark Phillips.

Annealing, slow heating and cooling of a metal, alloy, or glass to release internal stresses, dislocations, or vacancies that may have been introduced during mechanical shaping such as rolling or extruding, to increase the material's workability and durability. Machine tools, wire, and sheet are annealed during manufacture.

Annelida, phylum of segmented worms. All have encircling grooves usually corresponding to internal partitions of the body. A digestive tube, nerves, and blood vessels run through the entire body, but each segment has its own set of excretory ducts. Annelids form an important part of the diet of many animals. There are more than 6000 species. The three main classes are Polychaeta, marine worms; Oligochaeta, freshwater or terrestrial worms; and Hirudinea or leeches.

Anne of Cleves (1515–57), fourth wife of Henry VIII. Her marriage (1540) was a political alliance joining Henry with the German Protestants, and was declared null after only six months. Pensioned by Henry, Anne remained in England until her death.

Annihilation, conversion of an elementary particle and its antiparticle, on collision, into radiation. The mass of the two particles is converted directly into energy in the form of gamma rays. An electron and positron annihilate to produce two gamma-ray photons, travelling in opposite directions to conserve momentum. Each has an energy of 0.51 MeV, which is equivalent to the rest mass of the electron or positron.

Annual, plants that complete their life cycle in one growing season. They are used in summer flower beds, window boxes, pots, or winter greenhouses. Popular garden annuals include zinnias, nasturtiums,

sweet peas, and petunias. Some plants may be started indoors and others sown in place. Some self-seed, such as baby's breath and marigolds. *See also* Biennial; Perennial.

Annual Ring, or growth ring, concentric circles visible in cross-sections of woody stems or trunks. Representing the annual growth of the cambium layer, each ring consists of an inner spring (xylem) layer and an outer summer (phloem) layer. The growth of summer wood is thick-walled, providing contrast between the rings. Used to determine the approximate age of trees, the thickness of these rings reveals the environmental conditions during a tree's lifetime.

Anoa, or dwarf water buffalo, three smallest species of wild buffalo, native to Celebes and Philippines. The young are covered with yellow woolly hair; adults are almost hairless with black or brown skin blotched with white. Their short horns are straight and ringed. Height: to 41in (104cm) at shoulder. Family Bovidae; genus *Anoa. See also* Buffalo; Ox.

Anode, the positive electrode of an electrolytic cell or electron tube (sometimes called the *plate*). It is the electrode by which electrons leave a system. *See also* Electrolysis.

Anodizing, the subjection of a metal such as aluminum or magnesium to electrolytic action by making it the anode of a cell, then coating the metal with a protective film.

Anole, arboreal lizard found in warm regions of North and South America and the West Indies. Enlarged finger and toe pads enable it to cling to surfaces. It is best known for its ability to change from brown to yellow and several shades of green. Males have an expandable dewlap. The familiar green anole, American chameleon, is found in S United States and Caribbean. Length: 5–18in (13–46cm). There are 200 species. Family Iguanidae; genus *Anolis. See also* Lizard.

Anomalistic Period, time taken for a celestial body to make one complete revolution around another, starting and finishing at the same orbital point, such as perihelion or perigee. It is slightly longer than the sidereal period. For the Moon it equals 27.55455 days; for the Earth it is 365.25964 days.

Anomaly, a deviation from the expected value, as in "gravity anomaly." The gravity anomalies are the direct result of the deviation of the earth from the perfect theoretical ellipsoidal form. A meterological anomaly means a local reading of temperature or rainfall that differs from the expected. An oceanographic anomaly is an unexplained temperature or degree of salinity.

Anopheles Mosquito, bloodsucking arthropod, the principle vector of human malarias. The female needs a blood meal prior to laying its eggs, and during feeding releases malaria organisms into the victim's bloodstream.

Anorexia Nervosa, abnormal loss of appetite and refusal to eat, occurring almost exclusively among young women in their teens and twenties and probably of psychological origin. It results in emaciation, deficiency symptoms, amenorrhea, and other disorders.

Anorthosite, rock similar to gabbro, but made up almost entirely of plagioclase feldspar and containing little or no pyroxene. Anorthosite is an intrusive rock, but its origin is uncertain. Large areas of this otherwise uncommon rock occur in New York, Minnesota, Can-

ada, Norway, and the Soviet Union. *See also* Igneous Rock; Plagioclase.

Anoxia, general term for acute or chronic deficiency of oxygen in the tissues. It can occur at high altitudes or as a result of underlying disease (eg, lung or heart malfunction) or toxic agents. Symptoms include troubled breathing, rapid pulse, and cyanosis.

Anschluss, German word for the unification of Austria and Germany. Outlawed by treaty at the close of World War I, expressly to limit the strength of Germany, the Anschluss was nevertheless favored by Germans of all political persuasions, including Communists and Socialists as well as rightists. Unification finally took place through a show of force under Hitler (1938). The union was dissolved by the Allies in 1945 and Austria again became an independent state.

Anshan (An-shan), city in Manchuria, China, 60mi (97km) SW of Mukden. The hub of China's iron and steel production, iron mining dates from 10th century. Industries: blast furnaces, cement, coke ovens, steel converters. Pop. 1,500,000.

Ant, insect of the order Hymenoptera. Representatives range from 0.04 to 1.2in (1–30mm) in length and are found worldwide. They live as social insects, feeding on plants, nectar, and other insects. Most representatives are wingless, except at times of dispersal. Family Formicidae. *See also* Army Ant; Carpenter Ant; Fire Ant; Honey Ant.

Antaeus, in Greek mythology, the giant of Libya, the son of the sea god Poseidon and Gaea. All strangers passing through his land had to wrestle him, and since he derived strength when thrown by touching his mother Gaea (Earth), he never lost. Hercules discovered his secret and crushed him to death high off the ground.

Antakya, formerly Antioch; city in S Turkey, approx. 20mi (32km) E of Mediterranean coast, on Orontes River; capital of Hatay prov.; founded *c.* 300 BC by Seleucus I; became commercial rival of Alexandria; defeated by Pompey (64 BC); important Roman commercial and cultural center; early Christian center; conquered by Persians (538), Arabs (638), Byzantine Empire (969), Seljuk Turks (1085), army of the First Crusade (1098); severely damaged by earthquake 1872; transferred to Syria 1920; restored to Turkey 1939. Modern city occupies small part of ancient site; remains of aqueduct, theater, castle, and thick walls still visible. Industries: olives, tobacco, cotton, grain. Pop. 57,855.

Antarctica, fifth-largest continent, surrounding the South Pole and surrounded by the Antarctic Ocean, which is actually the southernmost section of the Atlantic, Pacific, and Indian oceans. Almost entirely within the Antarctic Circle and perpetually snow-covered, it holds strategic and scientific interest for the rest of the world. No humans live permanently on Antarctica. Scientists visit for purposes of research and exploration but leave when their work is accomplished.
 Land. Shaped roughly like an open fan, with the Antarctic Peninsula as a handle, the continent is a snowy desert covering about 5,250,000sq mi (13,597,500sq km). The land is a high plateau, having an average elevation of 6,000ft (1,830m). Mountain ranges occur near the coasts. The interior, or South Polar Plateau, lies beneath about 8,000ft (2,440m) of snow, an accumulation of tens of thousands of years. Mineral deposits exist in the mountains, but exploiting them has not become practical. Coal may be plentiful, but the known deposits of copper, nickel, gold, and iron

will not pay the expenses of unearthing and exporting them.

Seas and Glaciers. Most continents have lakes and rivers, but the rivers of Antarctica are frozen, inching toward the sea, and instead of lakes there are large bodies of water along the coasts. The great Beardmore Glacier creeps down from the South Polar Plateau and loses itself in the Ross Ice Shelf. This shelf of ice is that part of the Ross Sea that never thaws, and the Ross Sea is the part of the Antarctic Ocean that makes up the S extremity of the Pacific Ocean. The southernmost part of the Atlantic is that portion of the Antarctic Ocean known as the Weddell Sea.

Climate and Vegetation. Antarctica remains cold all year, with only a few coastal areas being free of snow or ice in summer—December to February. On most of the continent the temperature remains below freezing, and in August it has been recorded at nearly −130° F (−54°C). Precipitation generally amounts to only 7–15in (17.5–38cm) of snow a year, but melting is less than that, allowing a buildup over the centuries. Nevertheless, mosses manage to survive on rocks along the outer rim of the continent. Certain algae grow on the snow, while other algae appear in pools of fresh water when melting occurs.

Animal Life. The best known Antarctic animals are penguins, especially the emperor and Adélie. Whales, such as the blue and finback, live in the icy waters, as do a few species of hair seals.

History. Islands associated with the great S continent were sighted in the 18th century, and in 1820 Nathaniel Palmer, an American hunting fur seals, reached what is now called the Antarctic Peninsula. Explorers from several nations provided claims to sections of the continent for their countries, but the United States recognizes none of these. Charles Wilkes of the United States explored enough of the coast between 1838 and 1840 to prove a continent existed, and James Clark Ross of England made coastal maps about the same time. Toward the end of the 19th century, exploration reached inland until a race for the South Pole developed. Roald Amundsen of Norway won, reaching the pole on Dec. 14, 1911. The airplane brought a new era of exploration, and Richard E. Byrd of the United States became the best-known of the airborne polar explorers. In the 1970s scientists from a dozen nations studied the continent and its past. International treaties help control the activities on and around Antarctica.

Antarctic Circle, the southernmost parallel, 66.5° south of the equator, at which the sun neither sets on the day of summer solstice (December 22) nor rises on the day of winter solstice (June 21). *See also* Arctic Circle; Solstice.

Antarctic Current, a continuous eastward-moving ocean current encircling the earth around Antarctica. It moves the water from one ocean to another, a process completed every 1800 years.

Antares, or **Alpha Scorpii,** red supergiant star in the constellation Scorpius. It apparently has a smaller green companion orbiting it. Characteristics: apparent mag. 0.92; absolute mag. − 4.5; spectral type M1; distance 400 light-years.

Anteater, usually nocturnal, toothless, insect-eating mammal that lives in forests of tropical America. It has a long tapered snout, a long sticky tongue for capturing insects, and long claws for ripping open ant and termite nests. Length: 7–60in (18–152cm). Family Myrmecophagidae. *See also* Edentate; Pangolin.

Antelope, hollow-horned, bovid ruminants found throughout the Old World, except in Madagascar, Malaya, and Australasia; most occur in Africa. They range from rabbit-size to ox-size. Horns of varying shapes are borne by both sexes in some species, only males in others. All are two-horned except the chousingha or four-horned antelope. Most females bear a single young each year. Family Bovidae. *See also* Bovidae; Ruminant.

Antenna, or (especially in Britain) **aerial,** the part of a radio system from which the signal is radiated into space (transmitting antenna) or by which it is received from space (receiving antenna). The shape and structure of the antenna depend on the frequency of the radiation and the directional requirements of the system. For example, a beam antenna is required to transmit a radar beam while a simple wire may suffice for an amplitude-modulated radio receiver.

Anthony, or **Antony, Saint** (*c.* AD250–350), known as the first Christian monk. Born of Christian parents in Egypt, he withdrew into complete solitude to practice ascetic devotion at the age of 20. The monastic ideal, outlined in the *Life of St. Antony* attributed to St. Athanasius, attracted many. At his death Christian monasticism was well established.

Anthony, Susan Brownell (1820–1906), US reformer and woman suffragist, b. Adams, Mass. She organized the first woman's temperance association. In the 1850s, she lectured against slavery and for women's rights. After the Civil War, she opposed giving the vote to freed black men without enfranchising women and with Elizabeth Cady Stanton she organized the National Woman Suffrage Association (1869). It later became (1890) the National American Woman Suffrage Association and she was its president 1892–1900. In 1979, a $1 Susan B. Anthony coin was released, the first to honor an American woman. *See also* Woman Suffrage.

Anthozoa, or flower animals, also called Actinozoa, a class of coelenterates characterized by columnar body, top mouth surrounded by tentacles, and bottom disc for sliding or holding. There is no medusa stage. Included are sea anemones, corals, and sea pens. Subphylum Cnidaria.

Anthracnose, any of various fungal plant diseases that attack several important crops and are characterized by blisters or ulcerlike lesions of dead tissues, on fruit, leaves, and twigs. The lesions are often dark and sunken, or grayish with rust-colored edges. Spores of anthracnose fungi are commonly transmitted by insects, seeds, and rain.

Anthrax, contagious disease, chiefly of grass-eating mammals (but also affecting man, swine, dogs, and captive wild animals), caused by the microbe *Bacillus anthracis.* Animals catch the disease from contaminated feed and water and from certain insects in which the microbe may live for years. The symptoms of the fatal disease are staggering, bloody discharge, and convulsions. The disease can be prevented by vaccine and treated with arsenicals and antibiotics.

Anthropoid Apes, tailless primates including gibbons and larger great apes—orangutans, chimpanzees, and gorillas. Apes are the largest and—except for man—the most intelligent primates. Family Pongidae. *See also* Primates.

Anthropoidea, suborder of primates including monkeys, apes, and human beings. Anthropoids have flatter, more manlike faces and larger brains and are larger size than prosimian primates. *See also* Primates.

Anthropology, science of man in his physical and sociocultural aspects. It is concerned with the whole chronological and geographic range of human societies. However, there has been an emphasis on microstudies of small autonomous (frequently pre-literate) groups since to explore the range of human physical and sociocultural diversity it is important to examine societies whose isolation implies an original group of institutions. Modern anthropology stems from the first half of the 19th century when the first systematic racial classification was made and an interest in cultural evolutionism followed the publication in 1859 of Darwin's *Origin of Species. See also* Ethnography; Ethnology.

Antibes, resort town in S France, on the Riviera, 11mi (18km) SW of Nice. Founded by Greek colonists, it was called Antipolis; contains ruins of a later Roman settlement and 16th–17th-century fortifications. Industries: tourism, oranges, olives, wines, perfumes. Founded 340 BC. Pop. 56,309.

Antibiotic, a chemical produced by a microorganism—for example, by specific strains of certain bacteria or molds—that is capable, in dilute solutions, of stopping the growth of or destroying bacteria and some other disease-causing microorganisms. The introduction of antibiotics, since about the time of World War II, has revolutionized medical science, making possible the control and in some cases the virtual elimination of once widespread and often fatal diseases, including typhoid, plague, cholera, and tuberculosis.

Antibiotics are selective—that is, effective against only specific microorganisms; those effective against a large number of microorganisms are known as broad-spectrum antibiotics. Antibiotics in general are bacteriostatic, inhibiting the growth of sensitive bacteria. Some others dissolve or kill sensitive bacteria. Some important antibiotics are penicillin, the first widely used antibiotic, effective against many staphylococcal infections, including bronchitis and tonsillitis; streptomycin, effective against tuberculosis, and some lung, liver, and urinary infections; and the tetracyclines, effective against many bacterial and rickettsial infections. Some bacteria, once sensitive to certain antibiotics, have become resistant to them, posing a serious threat to continued antibiotic therapy and giving impetus to a constant search for new antibiotics.

Antibody, or immunoglobulin, globular protein of the blood that reacts specifically with foreign substances or organisms that enter an animal, rendering it immune to them. Preformed antibodies can be injected for immediate protection, for example, injection of tetanus antitoxin.

Anticline, in geology, an upward fold in sedimentary rocks that results in a tilting of the stratifications. In a simple anticline, the oldest rocks are domed at the center of the formation; the newer layers of sedimentary deposition are layered over the dome. *See also* Folding.

Anticoagulant, substance that prevents or counteracts coagulation, or clotting. Heparin is a commonly used blood anticoagulant.

Antidiuretic, an agent that inhibits the discharge of urine from the body. An antidiuretic hormone (ADH)—vasopressin—is secreted by the posterior pituitary gland and acts to increase water retention by the kidneys.

Antidote, remedy or other agent used to counter the effects of a poison. Antidotes are specific, depending on the poison ingested.

Antietam, Battle of (Sept. 16–17, 1862), Civil War engagement, also known as Sharpsburg, fought in Sharpsburg, Md. Gen. George McClellan's 75,000 Union soldiers made five assaults on Gen. Robert E. Lee's 40,000 Confederates. Each side lost over 12,000 men. Neither side won, but Lee was forced to give up his Maryland campaign and retreat to Virginia.

Antifreeze, substance dissolved in a liquid to lower its melting point and thus prevent it freezing in cold weather. The antifreeze used in car radiators is usually ethylene glycol (ethane diol, HOC_2H_4OH), to which is added corrosion inhibitors and antifoaming agents.

Antigen, any substance or organism which, when injected into the body, induces the formation of antibodies that will react specifically with that antigen. *See also* Antibody.

Antigone, in Greek mythology, daughter of Oedipus and Jocasta, king and queen of Thebes. She accompanied Oedipus until his death, tried to prevent her brother Polynices from attacking Thebes, and committed suicide after she was condemned to death by Creon for defying his prohibition against burying Polynices. Sophocles' tragedy *Antigone* (*c.* 442 BC) is notable for its noble characterization of its heroine.

Antigua and Barbuda, independent island nation in Caribbean, which includes the islands of Antigua, Barbuda, and Redonda. Although cotton, fruit, and vegetables are cultivated, tourism constitutes the mainstay of the economy. Antigua was discovered by Christopher Columbus in 1493. Early French and Spanish settlements failed, and the island was finally colonized by Britain in 1632. Granted self-rule in 1967 and full independence in 1981, the new nation faced high unemployment and a separatist movement on Barbuda. Pop. 75,000; area 171 sq mi (443 sq km); capital: St. John's.

Antihistamine, drug that counteracts or otherwise prevents the effects of histamine, a natural substance released by the body in response to injury or more often as part of an allergic reaction, which produces symptoms such as sneezing, runny nose, burning eyes.

Anti-Lebanon Mountains (Al-Jabal ash Shargi), mountain range along E coast of Lebanon. Highest peak is Mt Hermon, 9,232ft (2,816m). Part of the range forms the Lebanon-Syria border.

Antilogarithms, numbers having specified numbers as their logarithm. Thus the antilogarithm (or antilog) of 0.4771 is 3, because $\log 3 = 0.4771$ (to 4 places of decimals). *See also* Logarithms.

Antimatter, matter identical to ordinary particles in all except charge. Antiparticles such as positrons (the antielectron), antiprotons, and antineutrons, are produced in many reactions but instantly collide with other particles and disappear. Since the photon is its own antiparticle, the possibility exists that distant stars or galaxies are made up of antimatter. Data collected by high altitude ballons in 1979 suggested that the upper atmosphere has a flow of antimatter.

Antimissile Missile, or **antiballistic missile (ABM),** a defensive missile designed to intercept and destroy incoming ballistic missiles. Its usefulness is questionable because of short warning times, high speeds of attack missiles, the possibility of decoys, and

Susan B. Anthony

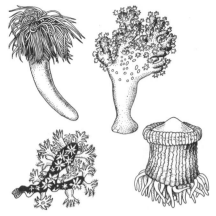

Anthozoa

Aoudad

the need to limit warhead size for explosions over a nation's own territory. *See also* Ballistic Missile.

Antimony, toxic metallic element (symbol Sb) of group V of the periodic table, known from early times. Commonest ore is stibnite (a sulfide). It is used in some alloys, particularly in hardening lead for batteries, type metal, etc. The element has two allotropes: a silvery metallic form and an amorphous gray form. Properties: at. no. 51; at. wt. 121.75; sp. gr. 6.684; melt. pt. 1,166.9 °F (630.5°C); boil. pt. 2,984°F (1,640°C); most common isotope Sb[121] (57.25%).

Antioch. *See* Antakya.

Antiochus III, the Great (242–187 BC), king of Syria (223–187 BC), son of Seleucus II. After his defeat at Rafa (217 BC) by Ptolemy IV, he invaded Egypt (212–202 BC), seizing land from Ptolemy V with the help of Philip V of Macedon. He recaptured Palestine, Asia Minor, and the Thracian Cheronese. The Romans overwhelmed him at Thermopylae (191 BC) and at Magnesia (190 BC). The rebuilt Seleucid empire shrank when he gave up all possessions west of the Taurus. Seleucus IV succeeded him.

Antiope, in Greek legend, two figures. One was the mother of Amphion and Zethis by Zeus. The other was the wife of Theseus and the daughter of a queen of the Amazons and Ares, god of war.

Antioxidant, chemical additive designed to reduce oxidation. Antioxidants are used to prevent fatty foods becoming rancid, deterioration of rubber, formation of gums in gasoline, etc. Most are organic amines and phenols, functioning by terminating the free-radical chain reaction causing oxidation. Sulfur dioxide and ascorbic acid are often used as antioxidants for foodstuffs.

Antiparticles. *See* Elementary Particles and Antiparticles.

Antipope, one who falsely claims to be pope, or whose election to pope was later declared unsanctioned by the Roman Catholic Church. Clement III (Guibert of Ravenna), Benedict III (Pedro de Luna), and Felix V (Amadeus VIII) were among the 36 antipopes.

Anti-Semitism, prejudice against Jews. Since ancient times, Jews were persecuted for religious reasons. They refused to worship idols or emperors. Almost from the beginning of the Christian era they were accused of being Christ's crucifiers. Denied access to other professions, Jews of the Middle Ages turned to moneylending and other professions looked upon with contempt, thus inadvertently adding economic prejudice. The growing nationalism of the nineteenth century further isolated the Jews who now became looked upon as racially separate or inferior. Tyrants such as Tsar Alexander II of Russia in the late 19th century and Adolf Hitler in the 20th century drew upon all these separate currents of anti-Semitism to strengthen their own positions. After World War II, anti-Zionism among the Arabs and the Soviet Union added a new, political dimension to anti-Semitism.

Antiseptic, substance that destroys disease-causing and other organisms on the surface of the body. Most are toxic if taken internally. Among the commonly used antiseptics are alcohol, iodine, and chlorine.

Antitoxin, antibody produced by the body in response to toxins. They are specific and neutralize the toxin. Antitoxin serums are used to treat and prevent bacterial diseases, such as tetanus and diphtheria.

Antler, bony outgrowth on the skull of male deer shed annually. In temperate-zone species, antlers begin to grow in early summer. They are soft, well supplied with blood, and covered with thin, velvety skin. Later, the blood recedes and the dried skin is rubbed off. Antlers then serve as sexual ornaments and weapons until shed the following spring. First-year males grow short spikes. More branches (points) are added each year until maturity is reached. *See also* Deer; Horn.

Ant Lion, or **doodlebug,** larvae of ant lion fly, found worldwide, with larger ones in the tropics. They have large, sickle-shaped jaws and dig conical pits in dry sand or dust, feeding on ants that fall in. Adults are soft-bodied with 2.8–7in (7–18cm), finely veined wings. Family Myrmeleontidae. *See also* Lacewing; Neuroptera.

Antofagasta, city in N Chile, on the Pacific Ocean; capital of Antofagasta prov.; founded 1870 by Chileans to utilize nitrates in the Desert of Atacoma. The War of the Pacific began in 1879 when Chilean troops moved into the city; Bolivia relinquished both city and province to Chile after the war. Industries: copper, nitrates, foundries, ore refineries. Pop. 149,720.

Antoninus Pius (86–161 AD), Roman emperor (138–61). The adopted son of Hadrian, he was made consul (120) and later sent as proconsul to Asia. His peaceful reign saw the promotion of art and science, the construction of public works and fine buildings, legal reform, and new provisions for orphans. In Britain Agricola built the Wall of Antoninus (142–43). Antoninus' constant companion was his wife's nephew, Marcus Aurelius, who eventually became emperor himself.

Antony, Mark (*c.* 83–30 BC), Roman military and political leader. In spite of his wild youth, he proved an able soldier. Julius Caesar had him appointed a quaestor in 52 BC and a tribune in 49 BC. He fought with Caesar against Pompey at the battle of Pharsala (48 BC). After Caesar's assassination (44 BC), Antony roused the populace against the conspirators and drove them from Rome. His relations with Octavian were uneasy, but he was finally given control over Asia after defeating the last of the conspirators at Philippi in 42 BC. He then met and fell in love with Cleopatra. In 40 BC he married Octavian's sister, Octavia, as a peace gesture, but by 37 BC he had deserted her and was living openly with Cleopatra in Alexandria. In 36 BC he married Cleopatra. Octavian stripped him of his authority and sent a fleet to destroy him. Antony and Cleopatra's fleets were defeated off Actium in 31 BC. Antony killed himself upon Octavian's entry into Alexandria.

Antony and Cleopatra (*c.* 1606), a tragedy by William Shakespeare in which Antony, one of Rome's great triumvirate, is bewitched by the charms of Cleopatra, Queen of Egypt. His obsession with her causes him to neglect his country and antagonize his allies, and finally costs him his power and his life. Like many Elizabethan plays, the drama deals with the dangers of pride.

Antron. *See* Nylon.

Antwerp (Antwerpen, Anvers), port city in N Belgium, on the Scheldt River, 23mi (37km) N of Brussels; capital of Antwerp prov. Antwerp rose to commercial prominence in the 15th century as English merchants moved their headquarters here; it was the seat of the world's first stock exchange (1460). Its commercial importance was influenced by the closing of the Scheldt River by the Treaty of Westphalia (1648) and its reopening (*c.* 1803) and improvement by Napoleon

I; by 1863, Antwerp was considered one of the world's major ports; site of State University Center (1965), Royal Museum of Fine Arts (1880–90), zoological gardens, 14th-century Cathedral of Notre Dame, ancient city walls. Industries: oil refining, food processing, shipyards, diamond cutting. Chartered 1291. Pop. 209,200.

Anu, in Assyro-Babylonian mythology, the supreme god of the pantheon, chief of the triad of the sons of Anshar, Anu, Ea, and Enlil. Anu is the sky-god, enthroned in heaven as the ruler of destiny, and the creator of spirits and demons from cold and rain and darkness. Anu ruled with Bel as the two principle Mesopotamian deities.

Anubis, jackal-headed god of the ancient Egyptians.

Anxiety, emotional state marked by apprehension or dread in which a specific focus is usually lacking. Anxiety is manifested by restlessness, rapid heart beat, tremor, sweating, and irregular breathing (sometimes accompanied by a feeling of constriction or suffocation).

Aorta, the largest artery in the body. Oxygenated blood passes from the heart's left ventricle through a set of semilunar valves to the aorta. Just outside the heart, the aorta curves into an aortic arch and branches to form the arteries that carry the oxygenated blood to all parts of the body except to the lungs. *See also* Artery; Heart.

Aoudad, or **Barbary Sheep,** wild sheep found in N African rocky hills and now introduced into SW United States. It has a uniform reddish-brown coat and long, soft mane on throat and chest. Both sexes have large, backward-pointed horns. It can be crossbred with domestic goats. Length: to 75in (1.9m). Family Bovidae; species *Ammotragus lervia. See also* Sheep.

Apache, an Athabascan-speaking tribe of North American Indians inhabiting Arizona, New Mexico, and Oklahoma. Divided into four primary bands—the White Mountain, San Carlos, Jicarilla, and Mescalero—they migrated from the Northwest about 1000 AD with the Navajo but separated to form a distinct tribal group. They retained their earlier nomadic raiding customs, which brought them into military conflict with the Mexicans and US citizens, notably under Cochise and Geronimo. They lived in brush wickiup dwellings and are noted for their basketry. The total population is approximately 15,000.

Apache Wars, series of battles in Arizona, New Mexico, Texas, and Oklahoma between Apache Indians and whites. One Indian leader, Cochise, made peace in 1872, but another, Geronimo, fought until 1886. Atrocities occurred on both sides.

Apartheid, the Republic of South Africa's policy of racial separation. Meaning "apartness" in Afrikaans, the policy was made official by Daniel F. Malan after his Nationalist party took power in 1948. Based on the doctrine of white supremacy, apartheid severely limits all aspects of the lives of South Africa's blacks (70% of the population), holding them in economic and political subservience. South Africa left the British Commonwealth in 1961 in response to antiapartheid pressures. Violent opposition to apartheid accelerated during the 1980s and attracted worldwide attention.

Apatite, a phosphate mineral, calcium phosphate with hydroxyl, fluorine, and chlorine. Found in igneous rocks and sedimentary deposits. Hexagonal system prismatic or tabular crystals; also in granular aggregates or massive crusts. White, if pure, but often green, brown, yellow or blue; hardness 5, sp gr 3.1–3.4. Frequently beautiful as a gem, but usually too soft for cutting and polishing. Varieties called asparagus stone (green) or moroxite (blue) are gems.

Ape, variety of primates composed of gibbons (family Hylobatidae), gorillas, orangutans, and chimpanzees (family Pongidae), all of the order Primate. They differ from monkeys in that they are brachiators—they swing by their arms—whereas monkeys are true quadrapeds. Ranging in size from 3 ft (1 m) tall and 25 lb (11 kg) to 6 ft (1.8 m) tall and 400 lb (180 kg), apes have hooklike hands with an opposable thumb, long powerful arms, and almost inflexible backs with 3 lumbar vertebrae, as compared with 6–7 in monkeys. Gibbons and orangutans are native to Asia, mainly arboreal, and generally live in small groups. Gorillas and chimpanzees are native to Africa, found mainly in ground habitats, and live in large groups.

Apennines (Appennino), mountain range extending length of Italian peninsula; a continuation of the Pennine Alps. Unselective deforestation over the years has caused deep erosion and landslides; site of numerous hydroelectric plants, sheep and goat grazing. Highest point is Mt. Corno, 9,560ft (2,916m). Length: 840mi (1,352km).

Apex, in astronomy, point on the celestial sphere, located in the constellation Hercules, toward which the sun appears to be moving. As the sun slowly orbits the galactic center, nearby stars, as seen from the earth, appear to move away from it due to the sun's relative velocity.

Aphasia, condition usually associated with an organic brain disorder involving the loss or impairment of ability to communicate through language. May involve loss of ability to communicate by speech, writing, or symbols or the inability to comprehend language. Often clinically expressed through vague and confused speech. *See also* Brain Disorders.

Aphid, or plant louse, soft-bodied insect found worldwide. It transmits virus diseases of plants. Winged or wingless, these insects suck plant juices and are often found in large numbers in one location. Females reproduce with or without mating, resulting in one to several generations per year. Length: to 0.2in (5mm). Family Aphididae. *See also* Homoptera.

Aphorism, concise sentence expressing an important truth. Hippocrates published his famous series of precepts under the title *Aphorisms.* One of these, translated later by Chaucer, is: "The life so short, the craft so long to learn."

Aphrodite, Greek goddess of love, beauty, and fruitfulness. Identified by the Romans as Venus. Daughter of Zeus and Dione. Her husband was designated as Hephaestus (Vulcan), although she loved many gods and legendary mortals. Among these were Mars, Adonis, whose death left her brokenhearted, and Anchises, who was the father of Aeneas. Statues of her include Venus de Milo (Paris) and Aphrodite of Cnidus (Rome).

Apia, capital and chief port of Western Samoa, on N coast of Upolu Island; UN trust territory until 1962, when Samoa became independent country; site of geophysical observatory and agricultural college. Industries: cacao, coffee, lumber, handcrafts. Pop. 30,-593.

Apocalyptic Literature, a literary genre, most prevalent in Judaic and Christian works from about 200 BC to 200 AD, which incorporated great acts of God along with overwhelming catastrophies such as plagues or famines. The works were popular among religiously persecuted groups, and showed the forces of God winning for the faithful.

Apocrypha, certain writings of the Old Testament not considered canonical by Jews and Protestants but generally included in the Roman Catholic canon. The Apocrypha consists of the following books: First Esdras, Second Esdras, Tobit, Judith, Wisdom, Ecclesiasticus, Baruch, the Prayer of Manasses, First Maccabees, Second Maccabees. Also included are the following parts of books: Esther 10.4 to 16.24 and Daniel 3.24–90, 13, and 14. In Roman Catholic bibles, these works are considered deuterocanonical, except for First and Second Esdras (numbered Third and Fourth Esdras in Catholic bibles) and the Prayer of Manasses. Those works are considered pseudoepigraphical and are usually placed in an index at the end of the Old Testament. The term "apocryphal" is also sometimes used to identify certain spurious New Testament writings. *See also* New Testament; Old Testament.

Apogee, point in the orbit about the earth of the moon or an artificial satellite, at which the body is farthest from the earth. *See also* Perigee.

Apollinaire, Guillaume (1880–1918), originally named Guillaume de Kostrowitzky, French poet, writer, and art critic. A leading figure in avant-garde circles, he championed Cubism and Futurism and contributed to several literary journals. His poetry, varying from the lyrical to the modernist, includes *Alcools* (1913) and the typographically experimental *Calligrammes* (1918). Other works are a collection of short stories, *L'Hérésiarque et cie* (1910), and a play, *Les Mamelles de Tirésias* (1918).

Apollo, Greek god, second to Zeus. Deity of the sun, archery, agriculture, patron of farmers, poets, physicians, founder of cities, and giver of laws. He was the son of Zeus and Leto, twin to Artemis. In the Trojan war he sided with Troy, sending a plague against the Greeks. In art and sculpture he is represented as a partially draped figure with a bow and quiver, shepherd's crook, sometimes accompanied by an animal sacred to him.

Apollonius of Rhodes (3rd century BC), Greek poet. Born in Alexandria, Apollonius spent his later life in Rhodes. A pupil of Callimachus, he disagreed with the views of his teacher on epic poetry. Apollonius is best known as author of the epic poem *Argonautica.*

Apollo Program, US project to send men to the Moon. Initiated in May 1961 by President John Kennedy, it achieved its objective on July 21, 1969, when Neil Armstrong set foot on the lunar surface. The program terminated with the successful Apollo-Soyuz linkup in space during July 1975, having placed over 30 astronauts in space and 12 on the Moon.

Apostle, in Christianity, the 12 original disciples of Jesus. The term was extended to include the major missionaries of the early church, including Paul and Barnabas, and later missionaries, including Patrick of Ireland, to previously pagan nations.

Apostles' Creed, a formulated expression of beliefs used in Western Christianity as far back as the 2nd century. The creed is not the work of the apostles. Simple in form, it deals with the three persons of the Trinity.

Apostolic Succession, doctrine in Orthodox, Roman Catholic, and Anglican churches that the ministry is continued from the apostles of Christ. The basis of the historical church is guaranteed continuity usually in the rank of bishop.

Apotheosis, act of deifying a human being. The Greeks elevated founders of cities and colonies to the status of gods after death. The Romans deified Romulus, Caesar, Augustus, and others. After Christianity became the official religion of the Roman Empire, emperors could not be deified.

Appalachian Mountains, mountain system extending from E Canada SW to Alabama. Includes the White Mts, Green Mts, Catskills, Alleghenies, Blue Ridge, and Cumberland Mts. The highest point is Mt Mitchell in Yancey co, N.C., 6,684ft (2,039m).

Appaloosa, western breed of horse developed by the Nez Percé Indians of NW United States. A strong-backed horse, it is bay, chestnut, black, or gray with a distinctive white mark over loin, rump, and hips containing spots of body color. Tail and mane are thin. Height: at least 56in (142cm) at shoulder; weight 1100lb (495kg).

Apparent Movement, or illusory movement, phi phenomenon, or the marquee effect, occurs when two or more stimuli are turned on and off in rapid succession; if they are lights, a spot of light appears to jump from one location to another. Motion pictures, which are really a series of sequential still pictures, are an example of apparent movement.

Appeals, Courts of, system directly beneath the US Supreme Court, created (1891) to relieve work load of Supreme Court. There are 11 Courts of Appeals, 1 in the District of Columbia and 10 circuits distributed throughout the United States. Each court has from three to nine judges but cases are generally heard before three judges. There is no original jurisdiction. Appeals are brought from administrative agencies and the US Tax Court and District Courts. Most often they act as courts of last resort.

Appeasement, policy where one government grants unilateral concessions to another to forestall a political, economic, or military threat. Appeasement of Germany at Munich (1938) at the expense of Czechoslovakia is considered a classic example.

Appendicitis, inflammation of the appendix probably caused by obstruction of the organ. Symptoms include general abdominal distress, followed by more severe pain in the lower right abdomen. Nausea and vomiting usually follow. Acute appendicitis is usually treated only by surgical removal of the appendix. A ruptured appendix can cause peritonitis and death. *See also* Peritonitis.

Appendix, small, fingerlike organ located near the junction of the small and large intestines, usually in the lower right quarter of the abdomen. It has no known function but often becomes inflamed, necessitating surgical removal.

Appian Way, ancient military road in Italy, constructed 312 BC by the censor Appius Claudius Caecus. It was the chief highway to Greece and the East, connecting Rome with Capua; later extended to Beneventum, Tarentum and Brundisium; portions remain today. A new, parallel Appian Way was built in 1784. Length: approx. 350mi (564km).

Apple, common name for the most widely cultivated fruit tree of temperate climates. Derived from the *Malus pumila* native to SE Europe and SW Asia, apples are propagated by budding or grafting. More than 7,000 varieties have been recorded in the United States alone. From the flowers, which require cross-pollination to produce a desirable fruit, the fleshy fruit develops in a variety of sizes, shapes and acidities; generally roundish, 2–4in (5–10cm) in diameter and some shade of yellow, green, or red. A mature tree may yield up to 30 bushels of fruit in a single growing season. Of the total world production, Europe produces 50% to 60% of the annual crop with the United States adding another 16% to 20%. Japan, Korea, China, India, Australia, New Zealand, Argentina and Chile are also important producers. More than 80% of the U S annual crop is used as fresh fruit; less than 10% is used for vinegar, juice, jelly, and apple butter; almost 10% is canned. Family Rosaceae.

Apple Maggot, or railroad worm, black and yellow fly, 0.16 to 0.24in (4–6mm) long, with spotted wings. It is a serious pest of apples and blueberries throughout North America. The larvae leave brown trails through the inside of the fruit. Family Tephritidae, species *Rhagoletis pomonella. See also* Diptera.

Applied Mathematics, study of physical phenomena using mathematical methods. In one sense the subject is simply the application of mathematical tools in science or engineering. More generally, it is a body of knowledge and theory with a mathematical structure including the abstract entities and formal rules of 'pure' mathematics together with physical measurable quantities and physical laws. It includes such topics as mechanics, fluid mechanics, statistics, quantum theory, and relativity theory. *See also* Mathematics.

Applied Psychology, use of psychological theory in fields as diverse as the design of spacecraft, classroom learning, industrial relations, personnel counseling, consumer education, military training, and mental health.

Appomattox, town in Virginia, 18mi (29km) E of Lynchburg; near Appomattox Court House National Historical Park; seat of Appomattox co; nearby is site of Gen. Lee's surrender to Union forces under Gen. Grant (Apr. 9, 1865). Industries: tobacco marketing, lumber, flour milling, batteries, clothes. Inc. 1925. Pop. (1970) 1,400.

Apprenticeship, learning a craft or trade from a skilled worker in exchange for assisting in the work for a specified time period. Known since ancient times, the practice became highly structured in medieval Europe under the supervision of the guilds. Today, apprenticeship programs sponsored by unions or professional organizations are regulated by governmental agencies.

Apricot, a stone-fruit tree cultivated throughout temperate regions, thought to have originated in China. Large, spreading trees with dark green leaves and white blossoms bear the yellow or yellowish-orange fruit that is eaten fresh or preserved. Species *Prunus armeniaca.*

April, fourth month of the year. The name may be derived from the Latin word *aperire* ("to open"). It has 30 days. The birthstone is the diamond.

Apteryx. *See* Kiwi.

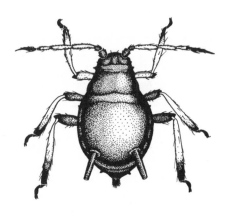

Aphid

Appomattox Court House: Lee surrenders to Grant

Arab-Israeli Wars: Israeli troops in Lebanon

Apuleius, Lucius (c. 125–170), Roman writer. His prose narrative *The Golden Ass* (or *Metamorphoses*) is the only classical Latin novel that has survived in its entirety. He also wrote philosophical treatises influenced by Neoplatonism and Eastern mysticism. *See also* Golden Ass, The.

Aqaba, Gulf of, NE arm of the Red Sea between the Sinai Peninsula, Egypt, and Saudi Arabia; entrance is through the Strait of Tiran. Gulf has played important role in Arab-Israeli conflicts; it was blockaded by Arabs 1949–56, and again in 1967 when Israel held strategic points along Strait of Tiran to guarantee open passage for ships. Length: 100mi (161km).

Aquaculture. *See* Fish Culture.

Aquamarine. *See* Beryl.

Aquarium, vessel for keeping fish in captivity, ranging from small bowls to large public aquariums. Fish were kept in captivity as early as 2500 BC in Sumeria, and ancient Romans kept marine fish in large pools connected to the sea. Indoor aquariums were developed by Sung Dynasty (960–1278) Chinese who kept goldfish in porcelain vessels. The earliest large public aquarium was the Fish House at Regent's Park, London, in 1850. The New York Aquarium opened in 1896. There are now about 100 large aquariums in the United States, including the Marinelands in Florida and California. Home aquariums usually hold 10–15 gal (38–57l) of water. Equipment such as thermostatic heater, air pump, filter, plants, and sand or gravel is needed to provide proper balance between fish, water, oxygen, and temperature. *See also* Tropical Fish.

Aquarius, or the **Water Bearer,** equatorial constellation situated on the ecliptic between Capricornus and Pisces; the eleventh sign of the zodiac. It contains the Saturn Nebula (NGC 7000), the globular cluster M2 (NGC 7089), and the Helix Nebula (NGC 7293). Brightest star Beta Aquarii. Astrological sign for the period Jan. 20–Feb. 18.

Aquatic Animals, animals living in water, including minute zooplankton, crustaceans, fish, and mammals. Physical factors affecting their growth include temperature, light intensity, and available carbon dioxide, oxygen, and dissolved materials.

Aquatic Mammal, mammal that spends all or most of its life in water. They evolved from land-living ancestors. Some, notably whales (including dolphins and porpoises) and sirenians, have adapted completely to a life in water and no longer leave the water to breed. Their forelimbs are modified into flippers and they have lost their hind limbs and developed a tail fin. Seals are almost as adapted for aquatic life as whales but retain functional hind limbs and leave the water to breed. Other partially aquatic mammals include the beaver, muskrat, and water rat (rodent); otter (carnivore); and water shrew and desman (insectivore).

Aquatic Plant. *See* Hydrophyte.

Aquatint, type of etching that produces transparent tones. The copper plate, bitten by acid through a porous ground of granulated resin, becomes textured, and produces a speckled tone when printed. *See also* Printmaking.

Aqueous Solution, solution in which water is the solvent. Water dissolves many polar substances, that is, ionic compounds and covalent compounds with molecular dipoles, because the water molecules themselves are polar, with negative charge on the oxygen atom.

They tend to cluster around positive ions (solvation), making the solution energetically favorable. *See also* Electrolytic Solution.

Aquifer, an underground formation that is an economically significant water source. An aquifer might be sand or gravel, or any other type of permeable rock layer that holds and delivers water to streams, springs, or wells. The water source may be glacial and the aquifer system may be extensive. *See also* Hydrology; Water Table.

Aquinas, Thomas (c. 1225–74), Roman Catholic theologian, philosopher, and saint. He joined the Dominican order, followed Albertus Magnus to Paris in 1245, and thereafter refused ecclesiastical dignities in order to preach and work on his *Summa Theologica* (1266–73). Revelation, he argued, could not conflict with reason, and while separate, they rested on the one absolute Truth. In the *Summa Catholicae Fidei contra Gentiles*, he defined theology as the queen of the sciences. The *Summa* was to systematize all human knowledge by reconciling Aristotle and Christianity. Philosophically, he maintained the real existence of Universals. Aquinas was canonized in 1323.

Aquino, Corazon (1933–), Philippines political figure, president (1986–). After graduating from Mt. St. Vincent College in New York City, she met and married Benigno Aquino, a political activist opposed to Philippines Pres. Ferdinand Marcos. A political novice, Mrs. Aquino became a candidate for president after members of the Marcos-controlled military reputed to be responsible for her husband's assassination were acquitted. Following an election marked by widespread reports of fraud and voter harassment by Marcos supporters and massive public demonstrations against him, Marcos stepped down and left the country. Mrs. Aquino became president, promising economic and political reforms.

Aquitaine, historical region of SW France; Toulouse was the capital. Under the Romans it was called Aquitania and became an integral part of the Roman Empire, including all land between Pyrenees Mts and Garonne River. The Romans were followed by the Visigoths and then the Franks. Independent for a time, it belonged to France and then England until early 13th century when all but Gascony (S part) was returned to France. At end of Hundred Years War in 1453 all of Aquitania was inc. into France.

Arab, peoples of many nationalities found predominantly in the Middle East and North Africa, who share a common heritage in the religion of Islam and their language (Arabic). The majority of the population is either agriculturalist or city-dwelling; the remainder practice pastoralism, raising camels, sheep, and goats. The patriarchal family is the basic social unit in a strongly traditionalist culture that has been little affected by external influences, although wealth from oil is bringing rapid modernization.

Arabia, peninsular region in SW Asia, bordered by Persian Gulf (E), Arabian Sea (S), Syrian Desert (N), and Red Sea (W); unified by Muslims in 7th century; dominated by Ottoman Turks after 1517. Husayn led successful revolt against the Turks and founded independent state in Hejaz region. The Saud family defeated Husayn in a violent siege and founded Saudi Arabia in 1925. Great Britain held protectorates, but after WWII British influence declined greatly and other independent states emerged in the region. Area: 1,000,000sq mi (2,590,000sq km). Pop. 17,800,000.

Arabian, oldest horse breed, developed for endurance in the Arabian deserts. Source of all light horse breeds, this slender horse has a refined head, deep quarters, and short back with one less lumbar and one or two less tail vertebrae than other breeds. Its sleek coat is bay, gray, chestnut, black, or white, with black skin and white marks only on head and legs. Height: 56–61in (142–155cm) at shoulder; weight: 850–1100lb (385–500kg).

Arabian Desert, mountainous desert in E Egypt bordered by Nile Valley (W), Red Sea and Gulf of Suez (E); extends along E coast of Egypt, merging with Nubian Desert in S. Oil is produced in N; granite, sandstone, and porphyry found in the mountains are used for building stones. Nomadic tribes inhabit the desert; site of 3rd-century monastery of St Anthony. Area: 86,000sq mi (222,740sq km).

Arabian Nights, The, also called **A Thousand and One Nights** and originally **Alf Layla Wa Layla,** tales of a variety of origins—Arab legends, Indian and Persian fairy tales, and Egyptian love stories—compiled in written form as long ago as the 15th century in the colloquial Arabic language from the oral tradition. In the Western versions Scheherazade tells one tale nightly of such heroes as Aladdin, Ali Baba, or Sinbad to postpone her death by her master's hand. The tales throw some light on Arabic life in the 9th through 16th centuries.

Arabian Sea, NW arm of Indian Ocean, bordered by Somalia and Arabian Peninsula (W), India and Malabar Coast (E), Indian Ocean (S). Two main branches are off to the NW: Gulf of Aden connecting with Red Sea, and Gulf of Oman joining with Persian Gulf. Indus River is the largest river emptying into the sea; major medieval trade route between Arab kingdoms and Chinese empire passed through Arabian Sea and Persian Gulf. Length: 1,800mi (2,898km).

Arabic, a Semitic language. Classical Arabic is the language of the Moslem scriptures, the Koran. With many colloquial variations, the written form is understood in all Moslem countries across North Africa to Iraq. Original to the Arabian Peninsula, it spread with Islamic conquests in the 7th and 8th centuries. Estimated number of speakers now is 90 million.

Arabic Numeral, one of the symbols 0, 1, 2, 3, 4, 5, 6, 7, 8, and 9, used in the common notation for writing numbers in the decimal system. *See also* Numeral.

Arab-Israeli Wars (1948–49, 1956, 1967, 1973–74). Tension and armed conflict between Israel and the Arab States have existed since 1920, when Britain received a League of Nations mandate for Palestine. The first full-scale war was set off by Israeli independence on May 14, 1948. From 1945–1948 the Israelis had made substantial gains against Palestinian Arabs. The 1948–49 war clearly showed the Arab opposition to Israeli independence, on territory the Arabs considered as theirs. During 1948 Arab troops from Egypt, Iraq, Lebanon, Syria, and Transjordan (modern Jordan) invaded Israel. Initial gains by the Arabs were soon halted and a cease-fire was established on Jan. 7, 1949. From 1949 to 1956 truce was enforced by UN security forces. In October 1956 the Israeli armed forces under the direction of Moshe Dayan launched an attack into the Sinai Peninsula. Israel was supported by France and Britain, who were alarmed by the nationalization of the Suez Canal. International opinion forced a cease-fire in November; Israel surrendered territorial gains after it had been guaranteed access to the Gulf of Aqaba on its southern border. In 1967, Egyptian President Nasser closed the Gulf of Aqaba to

Israel, and in retaliation Israel launched a massive air attack, and in the ensuing Six Day War Israel captured the Sinai Peninsula, the Golan Heights on the Syrian border, and the Old City of Jerusalem. Intermittent hostilities continued until 1973, when the Arab states began active preparations for war. Egyptian and Syrian forces attacked on Oct. 6, 1973, on Yom Kippur, a Jewish holiday. Israel managed to push back Egypt and Syria only after losing many men and much equipment. A tentative cease-fire was established by October 25, but fighting continued until 1974. In 1979, Egypt and Israel signed a peace treaty and Israel began a phased withdrawal from the Sinai. Sporadic fighting between Israeli troops and Palestine Liberation Organization (PLO) guerrillas continued in S Lebanon until mid-1982, when Israel launched an invasion that culminated with the PLO's withdrawal from Lebanon. A multi-nation UN force was sent to Lebanon to preserve a cease-fire. By the mid-1980s, despite conflict between Israeli troops and Shiite guerrillas in S Lebanon, most Israeli forces were withdrawn.

Arab League, name given to the League of Arab States formed in 1945 to give a collective political voice to the Arab nations. Members include Algeria, Bahrain, Djibouti, Egypt, Iraq, Jordan, Kuwait, Lebanon, Libya, Mauritania, Morocco, Oman, Qatar, Saudi Arabia, Somalia, Sudan, Syria, Tunisia, United Arab Emirates, People's Democratic Republic of Yemen, and Yemen Arab Republic; in 1975 the league recognized Palestine as an independent state with full membership in the league. The most important attempts have been made by the league in terms of Arab economic life. In 1953 they set up an Arab Telecommunications Union, in 1954 a postal union was organized, and in 1959 a financial organization (Arab bank) was developed. The Arab Common Market was formed in 1965 and opened to all Arab members in 1973. Political unity, however, has been hampered by a split among the members concerning pro-Western activities. Following the Egyptian-Israeli peace treaty of 1979, Egypt was suspended from the league, whose headquarters were temporarily moved from Cairo to Tunis, Tunisia.

Arachnida, worldwide class of arthropods including spiders, ticks, mites, scorpions, and harvestmen. All have four pairs of jointed legs, two body regions (cephalothorax and abdomen), and chelicerate jaws. They lack antennae and wings. *See also* Harvestman; Mite; Scorpion; Spider; Tick.

Arafat, Yasir (1929–), leader of the Palestine Liberation Organization (PLO), one of the first Palestinians to advocate guerrilla war against Israel. In 1974 he was recognized by Arab leaders as the "sole legitimate representative of the Palestinian people." Arafat's status and that of the PLO were enhanced by UN recognition of the PLO, his membership (1981) on the Islamic peace commission, and his agreement to try to settle Arab-Israeli differences by more peaceful means during the second half of the 1980s.

Aragón, region in NE Spain, bordered by the Pyrenees Mts (N), the Iberian Mts (S), Catalonia (E), and Old Castile (W); formerly part of ancient Roman province of Hispania Tarraconensis. In 1479 the Kingdom of Aragón became part of Spain; Aragón retained its own government, currency, and military forces until the 18th century; agricultural region. Crops: grapes, wheat, sugar beets. Industries: textiles, chemicals, iron, marble, limestone. Area: 18,382sq mi (47,609sq km). Pop. 1,152,708.

Aragonite, a carbonate mineral, calcium carbonate ($CaCO_3$), formed under special conditions, generally in caverns and hot springs. Readily converts to calcite (another mineral of $CaCO_3$). Orthorhomic system groups of needle-like crystals or massive deposits, twinning common. Glassy white; hardness 3.5–4; sp gr 2.9.

Aral Sea (Aral'skoje More), formerly Khorezmiyskoye More; 4th-largest inland body of water in the world, in central Asian USSR, in SW Kazakhstan and NW Uzbekstan; has no outlet, many small islands; fed by rivers Syr Darya (NE) and Amu Darya (S); generally shallow and only slightly saline, indicating geographically recent separation from Caspian Sea, 175mi (282km) to the E. Population along shores is sparse, concentrated mostly in NE Aralsk-Kazalinsk. Settled by Russians in 1840s. Area: approx. 26,000sq mi (67,340sq km).

Aramaic, Biblical Semitic language, the original language of parts of the Old Testament. After the Babylonian captivity, it was the common written and spoken language of the Middle East until replaced by Arabic. Minor dialects persist.

Aran Islands, group of three small islands in Northern Ireland, at entrance to Galway Bay. Chief islands are Inishmore, Inishman, Inisheer; site of pre-Christian ruins. Area: 18sq mi (47sq km). Pop. 2,269.

Arapaho, Algonkian-speaking tribe of North American Indians. Their original home was in the Red River valley; they moved across the Missouri River and split into two groups. After the Treaty of Medicine Lodge (1847) one group joined the Southern Cheyennes in Oklahoma, while the northern band went onto Wind River Reservation with the Shoshone. A Plains tribe, they joined with the Cheyenne in raiding migrating white settlers. Their population today is approximately 3000.

Ararat, Mount (Büyük Ağri Daği), mountain in E extremity of Turkey, 10mi (16km) from Iranian border; 20mi (32km) from USSR; has two extinct volcanic peaks; named for 9th century BC kingdom founded there; earthquake (1840) destroyed last settlement; traditional landing place of Noah's Ark (Genesis 8:4); boundary treaties with Russia (1921) and Iran (1932) locate mountain completely in Turkey; first climbed by Friedrich Parrot 1829. Great Ararat rises 17,000ft (5,185m); Little Ararat rises 13,000ft (3,965m).

Araucaria, genus of evergreen tree native to the Southern Hemisphere. They have scale-like leaves, whorled branches, and seed-bearing cones. Family Pinaceae. *See also* Norfolk Island Pine, Monkey Puzzle Tree.

Arawakan, a family of American Indian languages spoken in northern South America, mainly in Colombia, Venezuela, and Peru, but also in Brazil, Guyana, and Surinam. Taino, an Arawakan language now extinct, was once the dominant language of the islands in the Caribbean. The English word "hurricane" comes from this language.

Arbitrage, process whereby currency, securities, goods, or gold are purchased in one country's market and sold in another market for a profit, which is possible when there are differences among the exchange rates or interest rates in various countries. *See also* Exchange Rate.

Arbitration, settling disputes by seeking and accepting third-party decisions. Arbitration is rarely compulsory; success is dependent upon both parties to the dispute accepting the arbitrator's decision. The United Nations International Court of Justice has had limited success in arbitrating disputes between nations.

Arboriculture, scientific cultivation of trees and shrubs used for decoration and shade. Aspects of growth studied include pruning; transplanting; tree removal; treatment of wounds, cavities, and other damage; controlling insects; and diagnosing ailments. Early Egyptians were the first to transplant trees properly and correct treatments of wounds were known in ancient Greece. Arboriculture includes growing timber trees (silviculture) and fruit trees (pomology).

Arborvitae, common name for six species of the genus *Thuja,* a resinous, evergreen conifer of the Cypress family (Cupressaceae) native to North America and E Asia. It grows in the form of trees or shrubs, with thin outer bark, fibrous inner bark, and a characteristically flattened branch.

Arbutus, trees and tall shrubs native to the Mediterranean region and W North America. They have dark green, leathery leaves, and reddish brown bark. The urn-shaped flowers are white, red, or pink, and the strawberry-like fruit is red or orange. Family Ericaceae.

Arc (geometric), portion of a curve. For a circle, the length *(s)* of an arc is the product of the angle (θ) it subtends at the center, measured in radians, and the radius *(r)*: that is, $s = r\theta$.

Arcadia, ancient region in Peloponnesus, Greece; completely surrounded by mountains. Chief city, Megalopolis, was center of political activity and capital of the Arcadian Confederacy; destroyed during Greek War of Independence (1821–29). Founded 370BC.

Arch, in construction, a rigid, upward curved span between two points of support, usually functioning in the bearing of great weight, as in a bridge or ceiling. The triumphal arches of the Romans are an example of arch use for decoration, rather than support. True arches have been used for at least 6,000 years; uncurved arches, with one large stone leaning on another, have neolithic origins.

Archaeopteryx, first known bird, it was preserved in Jurassic deposits in Europe. Raven-sized and fully feathered, its skeleton resembled a reptile's rather than a modern bird's. It had no beak, but jaws with teeth. It was capable only of weak, flapping flight.

Archangel (Archangel'sk), city in Russian SFSR, USSR; capital of Archangel'sk oblast; port at head of Dvina Gulf and Northern Dvina delta; contains large harbor (often ice-bound); site of monastery of Archangel Michael (1685–99). City was opened to European trade *c.* 1600 by Boris Godunov, and it prospered as only Russian port until 1703; received Allied convoys during WWII. Industries: shipbuilding, lumber milling, paper production. Settled 10th century by Northmen. Pop. 398,000.

Arch Bridge, a bridge that uses arched spans to bear the weight of the bridge superstructure as well as its load. Arch bridges thrust outward as well as down at the ends and are said to be under compression. Arch bridges date back at least 2000 years to still-standing Roman edifices.

Archeology, scientific study of former human life and activities through material remains (fossils, artifacts, buildings). Archeologists' work includes: retrieval of the remains from the ground or seabed; recording and interpreting the circumstances in which objects were found (their level in the soil, association with other objects); thorough examination and description of their finds; and hence the building up of a picture of the culture that produced the objects. In the study of cultures that developed the art of writing, written remains supplement other material, but archeology increasingly relies on the aid of various scientific techniques to increase knowledge about the past.

Archerfish, fish found in brackish waters of SE Asia and Australia. It is yellowish-green to brown with dark markings and catches insect prey by spitting water "bullets." Length:to 8in (20cm). Family Toxotidae; 5 species including *Toxotes jaculatrix.*

Archery, sport involving the use of a bow and arrow. The object is to accumulate points by shooting a specified number of arrows in a target that consists of five concentric circles, the innermost circle being the "bull's-eye." Other than target-shooting, the three other divisions of archery are field, flight, and crossbow. Archery was the prime military weapon used before the advent of gunpowder and was revived as a sport in England in 1676 by Charles II. Its popularity grew after the Grand National Archery Association, the sport's first governing body, was formed in England in 1861.

Archimedes (287–212 BC), Greek mathematician and inventor. He is known for his studies in geometry, physics, hydrostatics, and mechanics. He is credited with discovering the principle (Archimedes' principle) that an object immersed in fluid will lose in weight an amount equal to the weight of the fluid displaced. He also invented a mechanical device (Archimedes' screw) that raises water and calculated the value of π. Several legends surround his life, one of which is that he discovered Archimedes' principle while sitting in his bath watching the water his body displaced. It is said that he ran all the way home shouting "Eureka!" (I have found it), forgetting even to dress. His works include *On the Sphere and Cylinder, On Spirals, On Floating Bodies,* and *On the Method of Mechanical Theorems.*

Archimedes' Principle, the observation that a body in a fluid is buoyed up by a force equal to the weight of the displaced fluid. The principle is said to have occurred to Archimedes in his bath as he puzzled over how to tell a golden crown from one alloyed with silver.

Archimedes' Screw, a machine used for raising water, thought to have been invented by Archimedes in the 3rd century BC. The most common form of the machine is a cylindrical pipe enclosing a helix, inclined at a 45° angle to the horizontal with its lower end in the water. When the machine rotates, water moves up through the pipe.

Archipelago, a sea or a marine area in which many islands are clustered, or the islands themselves. *See also* Atoll; Coral Reef.

Architecture, A work of architecture is a stable construction that meets the practical and aesthetic needs of a civilized people. Both an art and a technique, its quality is a determining factor of that society's quality of life. *See also* Gothic architecture.

Architrave, in classic architecture, the beam that is the lowest piece in the entablature (the architrave, frieze, and cornice), above the colonnade of a building and below the roof. Although very plain in Doric architecture, other styles compose it of several horizontal layers and bands.

Archer fish

Arctic tern

Argentina

Archives, documentary materials accumulated by an institution and preserved for their historical and literary value. The concept of archives located independently of a library reached full development during the French Revolution.

Arctic, Area N of the Arctic Circle (lat. 66° 30′ N); includes the Arctic Ocean, Greenland, and the northernmost regions of Asia, Europe, and North America. These lands partially surround the ice-covered Arctic Ocean and vary from low coastal plains to high ice plateaus and mountains; most of the area is dominated by tundra, poorly drained lowlands. Sparsely populated, the region has been inhabited for centuries by people mainly of the Mongoloid race. The main groups include the Eskimo of Greenland, North America, and E Siberia, the Samoyeds of W USSR, the Chukchi of E USSR, and the Lapps of Europe. Hunting, fishing, reindeer herding, and handcrafts are the chief sources of support. Various Arctic regions contain vast resources of minerals; however, most are inaccessible. The Arctic regions of the USSR are the most developed. The Arctic regions were first explored by Norsemen (9th–12th centuries); exploration continued in the 16th and 17th centuries by the Dutch and English in search of the Northwest or Northeast Passage to the Orient. The English navigators Henry Hudson discovered the Hudson Bay in 1610 and William Baffin explored Baffin Bay in 1616. Russian exploration was led by the Danish navigator Vitus Bering, who discovered the Bering Straits 1728. British naval officer John Franklin, lost in an Arctic expedition (1845–48), is credited with the discovery of the Northwest Passage. US exploration began 1850; the first official US scientific expedition was 1881–82; US explorer Robert E. Peary was the first man to reach the North Pole (1909). The first air flight over the North Pole was accomplished by US explorers Richard E. Byrd and Floyd Bennett and Norwegian explorer Roald Amundsen. The USSR established the first drifting scientific station (1937). During WWII the US Air Force set up several air bases and meteorological stations in Alaska, Canada, and Greenland. The US atomic-powered submarine, the Nautilus, accomplished the first submerged crossing of the North Pole (1958). Since then, Canada, the United States, and the USSR have developed new ice-breakers that may permit year-round Arctic navigation and economic exploitation, especially of minerals.

Arctic Circle, the northernmost parallel, 66.5° north of the equator, at which the sun neither sets on the day of summer solstice (June 21) nor rises on the day of winter solstice (December 22). *See also* Antarctic Circle; Solstice.

Arctic Ocean, ocean N of Arctic Circle, between North America and Eurasia; almost totally landlocked, bordered by Greenland (SW), Canada and Alaska (NW), USSR (N and NE), Norway (SE); connected to Pacific Ocean by Bering Strait, and to Atlantic Ocean by Davis Strait and Greenland Sea. The smallest ocean, it includes Barents, Beaufort, Chukchi, Greenland, and Norwegian seas. There is animal life (plankton) in all Arctic water and polar bears, seals, and gulls up to 88° N. Area: 5,400,000sq mi (13,986,000sq km).

Arctic Tern, seabird whose migrations are longest of any bird—from summer breeding areas in the far north to wintering areas in Antarctica. It has gray, black, and white feathers and a bright bill and feet. Gregarious, it nests in colonies and lays eggs (1–4) in a sandy scrape nest. Length: 17in (43cm). Species *Sterna paradisaea*.

Arcturus, or **Alpha Boötis,** red giant star in the constellation Boötes. Characteristics: apparent mag. −0.06; absolute mag. −0.3; spectral type K2; distance 36 light-years.

Ardennes (Forest of Ardennes), wooded plateau area in SE Belgium, N Luxembourg, and Ardennes dept in N France, E and S of Meuse River. Chief cities are Liège and Namur; scene of heavy fighting in both world wars, especially in the Battle of the Bulge, Dec. 1944–Jan. 1945. A well-preserved forest, wild game is abundant and cleared areas support farming and grazing. Population is sparse.

Area, measure of the amount of surface of a plane figure or body; given in square units (cm², in², etc). The area of a rectangle of sides *a* and *b* is *ab;* the areas of triangles and other polygons can be determined using trigonometry. Areas of curved figures and surfaces can be determined by using integral calculus.

Ares, Greek god of war (Roman, Mars). He was the son of Zeus and Hera and the lover of Aphrodite. Ares' activities were making war and love. In the Trojan war he sided with the Trojans, whose leader, Hector, he favored with his personal protection. Among his offspring were Fear, Rout, and Cynus, who was slain by Hercules. In art Ares is often represented as a stalwart figure armed with a helmet, shield, and spear.

Argali, or **Marco Polo sheep,** wild sheep native to the mountains of Cen. Asia. The largest of all sheep, it has 75-in (1.9-m) curved horns. Height: 4ft (1.2m) at shoulder; weight: 300lb (135kg). Family Bovidae; species *Ovis ammon. See also* Sheep.

Argenteuil, city in N France, on the Seine River; developed around a 7th-century convent, which was destroyed during the French Revolution; site of shrine in Saint-Denis Basilica (1866) containing the Seamless Tunic, traditionally believed worn by Christ. Industries: metalworks, furniture, airplane and railroad parts, chemicals. Pop. 103,141.

Argentina, republic in South America occupying most of S part of the continent. In the Americas only Canada, the United States, and Brazil are larger. Most people, Spanish-speaking and Roman Catholic, come from European backgrounds. In some ways underdeveloped, Argentina prospers when labor and political unrest and weather permit.

Land and Economy. The Andes stretch down W Argentina, separating it from Chile. Several peaks reach above 20,000ft (6,100m), and Aconcagua is the highest mountain in the Americas, 22,834ft (6,964m). N Argentina has a hot, humid savanna area, the Chaco, covered with grasses and occasional trees. Central Argentina is the plains, or pampas, region where livestock and cereal grains thrive in the temperate climate. S Argentina, cold and mountainous, is sheep country. Numerous rivers border or cross Argentina, with the Paraná and Uruguay joining to form a wide estuary, the Rio de la Plata. Minerals, largely unexploited, occur in the mountains. The country is second to Venezuela among petroleum producers of Latin America and has large natural gas pockets. During WWI and II, Argentina industrialized but still imports many manufactured goods. Exports, including beef, are mainly agricultural.

People. Wandering Indian tribes occupied the land until Spaniards drove them out or mixed with and absorbed them. A large mestizo population resulted; these people of mixed blood became the gauchos, or cowboys, of the pampas. Late in the 19th century Europeans—Italians, Spaniards, and Germans particularly—flocked to the country. Their descendants and the mestizos have gradually lost much of their separate identities. About 68% of the people lives in urban areas, with more than 35% in Buenos Aires.

Government. Following the military coup in 1976, the constitution was suspended, and a three-man junta took control. The junta pledged to return the country to a democratic government and beginning in 1980 allowed some political parties to operate.

History. Under the viceroyalty of Peru, Argentina suffered by being distant from Lima, but in 1776 Spain formed the viceroyalty of La Plata with headquarters in Buenos Aires. When Napoleon went to war with Spain in 1808, independence movements spread, and Argentina became free in 1816. Political coups caused turmoil throughout Argentine history. In 1946, Col. Juan Perón, after gaining popularity with labor, won the presidency. He became a dictator, but in 1955 the army overthrew him. From exile he rebuilt his strength and regained the presidency in 1973, with his third wife, Isabel, as vice president. He died in 1974, and she became Latin America's first woman president, but a financial scandal, inflation, and guerrilla warfare between leftists and rightists weakened her regime, and she was removed from power in 1976. Under the rightist military regime that replaced Isabel Perón, severe repression occurred, and thousands of political prisoners disappeared. An economic reorganization plan based on free-market principles, launched in 1976, helped to reduce a yearly inflation rate then exceeding 300% and provide economic stability. In 1982, Argentine troops occupied the Falkland Islands (Islas Malvinas), long claimed by Argentina. Britain quickly sent a task force that recaptured the islands, which led to changes in Argentina's government leadership.

PROFILE

Official name: Republic of Argentina
Area: 1,100,000sq mi (2,849,000sq km)
Population: 26,740,000
Density, 23per sq mi (9per sq km)
Chief cities: Buenos Aires (capital); Rosario; Córdoba
Government: Republic
Gross national product (1978 est): $45,000,000,000
Per capita income $1,536.
Industries (major products): iron, steel, cars, machinery, petroleum products.
Agriculture (major products): beef, wheat, corn, grapes, sorghum, oats, wool.
Minerals (major): petroleum, natural gas, lead, zinc, tin, manganese, iron, copper, beryl.
Trading partners (major): European Common Market, Brazil, United States.

Arginine, essential amino acid (NH₂C(NH)·NH(CH₂)₃CH·NH₂·COOH). *See* Amino Acid.

Argon, gaseous nonmetallic element (symbol Ar) of the noble-gas group, discovered (1894) by Lord Rayleigh and Sir William Ramsay. Argon is present in the Earth's atmosphere (0.94% by volume) and is obtained by the fractionation of liquid air. It is used in electric-light bulbs, fluorescent tubes, arc welding, and semiconductor preparation. The element forms no compounds. Properties: at. no. 18; at. wt. 39,948; density 1.7837 g dm⁻³; melt. pt. −308.6°F (−189.2°C); boil. pt. −302.3°F (−185.7°C); most common isotope Ar⁴⁰ (99.6%). *See also* Noble Gases.

Argonaut, predaceous, ocean-dwelling cephalopod mollusk found worldwide. Related to the octopus, it has eight suckered arms. Two of the female's arms are modified to secrete a coiled, paper-thin, ridged shell that is actually an egg case. The shell-less male has a specialized tentacle (hectocotylus) to hold sperm. It detaches and independently crawls into female's mantle. Female length: 6m (15.2cm); shell length: 8in (20.3cm). Male length: 1in (2.5cm). The paper nautilus (*Argonauta argo*) is best known of the six species. Family Argonautidae. *See also* Cephalopod.

Argonauts, in Greek legend, 50 heroes who sailed the ship *Argo* to Colchis, a kingdom at the eastern end of the Black Sea, in search of the Golden Fleece. Their leader was Jason, husband of Medea. Many adventures and tragedies characterized their wanderings. The Golden Fleece symbolized a kingdom promised Jason when he returned with it.

Argus, name of several figures in Greek legend. One was a giant with 100 eyes, half of which remained open at all times. Another Argus was the shipbuilder who built the ship *Argo* for Jason and became a crew member.

Aria, in music, a solo song with instrumental accompaniment; also a lyrical instrumental piece. It is an important element of opera, and is also found in cantatas and oratorios. The term originated in the 17th century when Giulio Caccini published a series of songs with continuous accompaniment, which he termed arie (singular, aria).

Arianism, theological stance heretical to Christianity based on the teachings of Arius (*c.*250–336). Arius taught that Christ was a created being, and not divine. Since the Son had a definite beginning, he is mortal, and as such can have no direct knowledge of God. The Council of Nicaea (325) condemned Arianism. *See also* Nicaea, Councils of.

Aries, or **the Ram,** northern constellation situated on the ecliptic and lying southeast of Triangulum. As the first sign of the Zodiac, it formerly contained the First Point of Aries, the intersection of the ecliptic and the equator marking the vernal equinox. Owing to precession this has now shifted westward into Pisces. Brightest star: Alpha Arietis (Hamal). Astrological sign for the period Mar. 21–Apr. 19.

Ariosto, Ludovico (1474–1533), Italian Renaissance poet and dramatist. A statesman, diplomat, and administrator for the d'Este family, his real interest was literature. His plays were the first to imitate Latin comedy in the vernacular. His most famous work is the epic poem *Orlando Furioso* (1532).

Aristocracy, system in which a privileged class exercises political control over society. Historically, the term describes a hereditary nobility. Its contemporary usage includes any ruling group or class, especially those characterized by wealth.

Aristophanes (*c.* 448–380 BC), Greek writer of comedies. Eleven of his more than 40 plays survive; they are the only extant comedies from his time. All follow the same basic plan: realistic characters become involved in absurd situations. Graceful choral lyrics frame caustic personal attacks. A conservative, Aristophanes attacked Euripides' innovations in drama, Socrates' philosophical radicalism, and Athens' expansionist policies. His most noted plays are *The Clouds* (423), *The Birds* (414), *Lysistrata* (411), and *The Frogs* (405).

Aristotle (384–322 BC), Greek philosopher, Plato's disciple for 19 years. After Plato's death, he opened his first school in Asia Minor. Having educated Philip of Macedon's son Alexander between 343 and 334 BC, Aristotle returned to Athens to open a school in the Lyceum. Upon Alexander's death (323), Aristotle, accused of impiety, fled to Euboea where he died a year later. Moving away from Plato's theory of the Forms, he developed the theory of the Unmoved Mover. Among his works are *De Anima, Metaphysics,* and *Nicomachean Ethics.*

Arithmetic, simple calculations and reckoning using numbers and such operations as addition, subtraction, multiplication, and division. The study of arithmetic usually involves learning procedures for operations such as long division, extraction of square roots, etc. More fundamental study of the integers is a branch of higher mathematics—number theory. *See also* Mathematics.

Arithmetical Operations, the commonly used operations of arithmetic: addition, subtraction, multiplication, and division. The procedures of arithmetic were put on a formal axiomatic basis by Guiseppe Peano in the late 19th century. Using certain postulates, including that there is a unique natural number, 1, it is possible to give formal definition of the set of natural numbers and the arithmetical operations. Thus, addition is interpretable in terms of combining sets: in $2 + 7 = 9$, 9 is the cardinal number of a set produced by combining sets of 2 and 7. Multiplication can be thought of as repeated additions: subtraction and division are the inverse operations of addition and multiplication. The operations can be extended to negative, rational, and irrational numbers.

Arithmetic Mean, or average, number obtained from a set of numbers by dividing their sum by the number of members in the set. Thus for numbers *a, b, c,* and *d,* the arithmetic mean is $(a + b + c + d)/4$. *See also* Geometric Mean.

Arithmetic Progression, sequence of numbers in which each term is produced by adding a constant term to the preceding one. Thus it has the form $a, a + d, a + 2d, \ldots$ An example is the progression 1, 3, 5, etc. Here d is called the common difference. The sum of such a progression, $a + (a + d) + (a + 2d) + \ldots$, is an arithmetic series. For n terms it has a value $n/2[2a + (n-1)d]$.

Arius (*c.*250–336), an heretical priest, noted for his asceticism. He supported a subordinationist teaching about the person and nature of Christ: the Son is a perfect creature, but inferior to the Father and less than divine. In 325 the Council of Nicaea condemned him.

Arizona, state in SW United States, bordered on the S by Mexico.

Land and Economy. The Colorado Plateau, at elevations of 4500 - 10,000ft (1,373 - 3,050m) occupies the N part of the state. It is cut by many steep canyons, notably the Grand Canyon of the Colorado River, which is a national park. The Colorado is the principal river, flowing about 700mi (1127km) through the state and along its W boundary. Hoover Dam in the NW created Lake Mead for irrigation and water supply to distant points. Other scenic landmarks are Monument Valley, the Painted Desert, and the Petrified Forest. The Mexican Highlands, a mountain mass running NW to SE, separates the plateau from the Sonoran Desert region in the SW and S. Arizona's mineral resources and its grazing and farming land have long been mainstays of the economy. Mining and agriculture are still important, but since the 1950s manufacturing has been the most profitable sector. Tourism is a major source of income.

People. Between 1950 and 1970, Arizona's population more than doubled, and in the 1970s its annual growth rate was more than 35%; new residents came from all parts of the United States. Arizona is a popular retirement region because of its healthful climate. Nearly 80% of the population is classed as urban. Arizona has more Indians than any other state, remnants of the 15 aboriginal tribes.

Education and Research. There are nine institutions of higher education. The Lowell Observatory at Flagstaff and the Kitt Peak National Observatory at Tucson are leading centers of astronomical research.

History. Spanish explorers visited the region in 1539–40, and Jesuit missionaries taught the Indians after 1690. The area became part of Mexico, which kept it after winning independence from Spain in 1821. At the end of the Mexican War (1848), Mexico ceded most of the present state to the United States and in 1853 land in the SW was acquired from Mexico by the Gadsden Purchase. Arizona became a US territory in 1863. Major growth began after WWII, and rapid population increases and development of high technology industries continuing into the 1980s placed a strain on resources, especially scarce water supplies.

PROFILE

Admitted to Union: 1912; rank, 48th
US Congressmen: Senate - 2; House of Representatives - 4
Population: 2,717,866 (1980); rank, 29th
Capital: Phoenix, pop. 764,911 (1980)
Chief cities: Tucson, 330,537; Scottsdale, 88,364; Tempe, 106,743
State legislature: Senate, 30 members; House of Representatives, 60
Area: 113,909sq mi (295,024sq km); rank, 6th
Elevation: Highest, Humphreys Peak, 12,670ft (3864m); lowest, 100ft (31m) on Colorado River
Industries (major products): machinery (electrical, non-electrical), electronic components
Agriculture (major products): cotton, citrus fruits, cattle, sheep
Minerals (major): copper, gold, silver, molybdenum
State nickname: Grand Canyon State
State motto: Ditat Deus (God Enriches)
State bird: Cactus Wren
State flower: Saguaro Cactus Blossom
State tree: Paloverde

Ark, Noah's, according to Genesis 6:14–16, the floating house Noah was ordered to build and live in with his family and one pair of all living creatures during the Flood. 450ft (137m) long and 75ft(22.8m) wide, it was believed to have come to final rest on Mount Ararat. *See also* Ararat.

Arkansas, state in the S central United States; one of the 11 Confederate states in the Civil War.

Land and Economy. In the E and S the land is low, providing excellent soil for farming, while rugged hills of moderate height mark the W and N. All the drainage flows into the Mississippi River, which forms the E boundary. The state's principal river is the Arkansas, flowing SE across the central area. Forests are extensive and contribute largely to the economy. Agriculture is important, but manufacturing is expanding. Hot Springs National Park is a major attraction in the tourist industry.

People. Most residents are descended from immigrants who moved westward from the S Atlantic states after 1815. A rural way of life in isolated communities prevailed generally until after WWII, but by 1970 half the population was classed as urban.

Education. There are more than 20 institutions of higher education. The University of Arkansas is state-supported, and there are seven state colleges.

History. Spaniards visited the region in 1541, and by 1673 Frenchmen descended the Mississippi as far as the Arkansas River. In 1682 the Sieur de la Salle claimed all the Mississippi valley for France. Four years later the French made a settlement, later called Arkansas Post, on the lower Arkansas River. Their missionaries and traders were active until 1762, when France ceded the area to Spain. Returned to France in 1800, it passed to the United States by the Louisiana Purchase in 1803. It was made part of Missouri Territory in 1812 and became a separate territory in 1819. Arkansas was the 9th state to secede and join the Confederacy in 1861. It rejoined the Union in 1868. Development of the state's resources proceeded slowly until the 1950s.

PROFILE

Admitted to Union: 1836; rank, 25th
US Congressmen: Senate - 2; House of Representatives - 4
Population: 2,285,513 (1980); rank, 33rd
Capital: Little Rock, 158,461 (1980)
Chief cities: Fort Smith, 71,384; North Little Rock, 64,419; Pine Bluff, 56,576
State legislature: Senate, 35 members; House of Representatives, 100
Area: 53,104sq mi (137,539sq km); rank, 27th
Elevation: Highest, Magazine Mt, 2823ft (861m); lowest, Ouachita River, 55ft (17m)
Industries (major products): wood products, chemicals, processed aluminum ore
Agriculture (major products): cotton, poultry, rice, timber
Minerals (major): bauxite (aluminum ore), petroleum, natural gas
State nickname: Land of Opportunity
State motto: Regnat Populus (The People Rule)
State bird: Mockingbird
State flower: Apple Blossom
State tree: Shortleaf Pine

Ark of the Covenant, according to Jewish tradition, the portable wooden gold-adorned chest containing the two stone tablets on which the Ten Commandments were inscribed. Regarded as the most sacred shrine of ancient Israel, it symbolized God's covenant with His chosen people. Only the high priest could look upon it; no one could touch it. The tabernacle built by King Solomon to house it was destroyed in 586 BC and no further record of the original Ark remains. In today's synagogues, the Holy Ark is a closet or recess in which the congregation's sacred scrolls are kept.

Arkwright, (Sir) Richard (1732–92), English textile industrialist and inventor. His use of power machinery and the factory production system was innovative. In 1764 he began work on his spinning frame, which he patented in 1769.

Arles, town in S France, on Rhone River 45mi (72km) NW of Marseille. Romans called it Arelate and connected it to the Mediterranean Sea by canal in 103 BC; counts of Savoy and King Charles VI of France acquired it in 14th century; contains remains of a 2nd-century Roman amphitheatre, now used for bullfights, and 12th–14th century Montmajour abbey. Industries: boat building, metal working, sulfur refining. Pop. 50,345.

Arlington, city in N Texas, 13mi (21km) E of Fort Worth; site of University of Texas at Arlington (1895). Industries: automobiles, rubber products, machinery. Founded 1876; inc. 1883. Pop. (1980) 160,123.

Arlington, city in N Virginia, across Potomac River from Washington, D.C.; site of Arlington National Cemetery, Tomb of the Unknown Soldier, the Pentagon, and Marymount College (1950). Originally a part of the District of Columbia, it was made a co of Virginia in 1847. Pop. (1980) 152,599.

Arizona: Chiricahua National Monument

Louis Armstrong

Benedict Arnold

Arlington Heights, city in NE Illinois; NW suburb of Chicago; race track is nearby. Industries: publishing, nursery farming. Pop. (1980) 66,116.

Arlington National Cemetery, national cemetery in Virginia, opposite Washington, D.C., on the S bank of the Potomac River; former estate of Robert E. Lee; site of Tomb of the Unknown Soldier, memorial amphitheater, and graves of many servicemen and prominent Americans. Area: 408acres (165hectares). Est. 1864.

Arm, technically, that part of the body comprised of the upper part of the limb extending from the shoulder joint to the elbow. In popular usage the term has come to mean both the arm and the forearm.

Armada, Spanish, fleet sent in 1588 by the Catholic Philip II of Spain against the Protestant Elizabeth I of England. The Armada, under the command of the Duke of Medina Sidonia, consisted of 130 ships. It sailed up the English Channel, where it was met by a fast, modern English fleet. Badly beaten in the fight and hampered by the weather, the Armada was unable to land in England. It tried to get back to Spain by sailing around Scotland. Storms destroyed it, and its survivors were forced to surrender. The destruction of the Armada marked the decline of Spanish power and the consequent rise of English power.

Armadillo, nocturnal mammal found from Texas to Argentina. Noted for the armor of bony plates that protects its back and sides; when attacked, some species roll into a ball so that no vulnerable parts are exposed. It eats insects, carrion, and plants. Length: 5–40in (12.7–101cm). Family Dasypodidae.

Armageddon, from the Hebrew *har megiddo,* "hill of Megiddo"; according to Revelation 16:16, the place where the final battle between the demonic kings of the earth and the forces of God will be fought at the end of the world. The strategically situated Palestinian city of Megiddo was historically the scene of many battles in Biblical times.

Armagnac, region in SW France; formerly part of old province of Gascony; agricultural area, famous for brandy. Once part of the Roman Empire, it became a countship in the 10th century; annexed by France 1607.

Armaments. *See* Weapons.

Armenia, ancient kingdom of W Asia, now divided between Iran, Turkey, and USSR; centered in the mountainous region SE of Black Sea and SW of Caspian Sea; the Euphrates and Araks rivers have their sources in this historical political battlefield. Strategically located between Europe and Asia, it has been the scene of repeated battles for more than 3,000 years. It enjoyed prosperity under Tigranes the Great 95–56 BC; under Roman and Byzantine rule until AD 1046 when it fell to Turkey; ravaged by Mongol forces (13th century); divided between Ottomans and Persia (1620), the latter part coming under Russian rule 1828–29; Turkish Armenians' fight for independence began in 1894 and culminated in almost total destruction of Armenian population by 1915. Armenia's declaration of independence (1917) was opposed by Russia and Turkey. Russo-Turkish Treaty (1921) established present boundaries.

Armenian Language, Indo-European language spoken in the Armenian, Georgian, and Azerbaijan Soviet Socialist Republics and in parts of Turkey, central Europe, and North and South America. It is the single remaining survivor of a distinct part of the Indo-European language group.

Armenian Soviet Socialist Republic, smallest constituent republic of USSR, in the S Caucasus Mts. Republic occupies E part of ancient Armenia; borders Georgian SSR (N), Iran (S), Azerbaijan SSR (E), and Turkey (W); a mountainous region, it rises to 13,432ft (4,097m) at Mt Aragats. Yerevan is capital; other major cities are Leninakan and Kirovakan. Araks and its tributary Razdan are the chief rivers; Lake Sevan has fishing industry; Araks valley is agricultural region. Products: cotton, fruit, rice, tobacco. Area: approx. 11,500sq mi (29,785sq km). Est. 1921; made a constituent republic 1936. Pop. 2,950,000.

Arminianism, liberal Calvinism mixed with humanism, named after its founder, Jacobus Arminius (1560–1609). Reason and faith should not be contradictory. The sacraments are merely signs of union, and Christ's death is only an example of God's punishment of sin. It was later to influence the development of deism and pietism.

Armor, (1) Protective clothing and headgear usually made of metal or thick leather used to prevent injury to warriors in battle. Employed since antiquity, body armor, except for the helmet, ceased to be of use in Europe in the 17th century. (2) Metal plating on warships or armored vehicles that is at least strong enough to deflect small arms fire. Warships were first armored in the mid-19th century, vehicles during World War I. (3) Military units having a high concentration of armored vehicles such as tanks, armored personnel carriers, and mechanized artillery.

Armory Show, international exhibition of modern art held at the 69th Armory, New York City, Feb. 17–March 15, 1913. It later traveled to Chicago and Boston. Originally the show was intended to exhibit radical US artists, but the European section created a greater controversy. The show introduced Impressionism, Post-Impressionism, Fauvism, and Cubism to the less aesthetically developed US viewers. It forced US artists to discard academicism and was the beginning of modern art in the United States.

Arms Control, activity undertaken by powerful nations to prevent one from destroying the other in warfare, especially with nuclear weapons. The nations attempt to maintain a balance of power by regulating each other's stockpiling of weapons. Not the same as "disarmament," which means to give up or reduce the military establishment of a nation.

Armstrong, (Daniel) Louis (1900–71), US jazz trumpeter, singer, and bandleader, b. New Orleans. "Satchmo" rose to prominence in the 1920s in Chicago and in Harlem cabarets. After that he made numerous world tours, appeared in films, and made many recordings with other jazz musicians and bands. His unique, gruff vocal style produced several hit recordings including "Hello Dolly" (1964).

Armstrong, Neil (Alden) (1930–), US astronaut, b. Wapokoneta, Ohio. He was the first man to walk on the moon (July 21, 1969). Selected a NASA astronaut in 1962, he was the command pilot for the Gemini XIII orbital flight. In 1978 he received the new Congressional Space Medal of Honor.

Army, United States, the ground service of the US armed forces. It consists of approximately 785,000 personnel under the president, who is commander in chief of the armed forces, and the general supervision of the secretary of the army and his advisor, the Army chief of staff, who is the Army's highest ranking officer. The Army chief of staff is a member of the Joint Chiefs of Staff. The department of the Army is charged with the organization, training, and equipping of these forces, but not their military employment. The army also provides assistance in disaster relief, conducts research into weapons development, carries on training at civilian colleges, and administers the US Military Academy at West Point, among other services. The Army has 16 active divisions and helps to maintain 8 National Guard and 12 reserved divisions; major overseas commands are the Seventh Army in Europe and the Eighth Army in Korea. The Continental Army existed from 1775, but the first regular standing was authorized by Congress in 1785. The war department was established in 1789. The department of war became the department of the Army in 1947, and in 1949 it became a part of the Department of Defense. The US Army has taken part in all major wars between the War of 1812 and the Vietnam conflict. A draft was occasionally employed and was used in peacetime after World War II. In 1973, Congress established an all-volunteer Army. For the first time in the history women were among the 1980 graduates at West Point. Draft registration resumed in 1980 for men only. *See also* Defense, Department of; Joint Chiefs of Staff.

Army Ant, or **Driver Ant,** highly predaceous, tropical and subtropical ant found in both hemispheres. Ranging in size from 0.13 to 1.75in (3.25–43.75mm) in length, they move en masse hunting for food and migrating. Family Formicidae. Subfamily Dorylinae. *See also* Ant; Hymenoptera.

Armyworm, moth caterpillar that travels in hordes, destroying crops as they go. The best known armyworm is the orange-, brown-, and yellow-striped *Pseudaletia unipuncta.* Length: 1.5in (38mm). Outbreaks of this caterpillar occur annually east of the Rocky Mountains in the United States. Family Noctuidae.

Arnica, a large genus of perennials of the composite family, native to the Northern Hemisphere. It has daisy-like flower heads. *Arnica montana* was formerly used for treating sprains.

Arno, river in Italy; rises in the Apennines Mts; flows W to the Ligurian Sea below Pisa; site of flood control works, some planned by Leonardo da Vinci; failed to prevent serious flooding of Florence in 1966, which resulted in major damage to city's art treasures. Length: 150mi (242km).

Arnold, Benedict (1741–1801), Revolutionary War officer and traitor, b. Norwich, Conn. He was placed in command of Philadelphia after being wounded at the battle of Saratoga. In 1780, he was given command of West Point, a fort he proposed to deliver to the British for a sum of money. The plan failed, and Arnold fled. He was made a brigadier general by the British and led raids on New London, Conn., and Virginia. He died in London.

Arnold, Matthew (1822–1888), English poet and critic. The son of Thomas Arnold, he held the Oxford chair in poetry (1857–67). His writings include literary criticism, such as *Essays in Criticism* (series 1, 1865; series 2, 1888), and social commentary, such as *Culture and Anarchy* (1869). His poems include "Sohrab and Rustum" and "The Scholar Gypsy" (1853) and "Thyrsis" and "Dover Beach" (1867).

Arnulf (*c.*850–99), king of the East Franks (887–99); last Carolingian Holy Roman emperor (896–99). He gained the kingdom of the East Franks by defeating his uncle Emperor Charles III. He decisively defeated the Norsemen at Louvain in 891. He invaded Italy (894), captured Rome (895), and was crowned Holy Roman Emperor there (896).

Aromatic Compound, organic chemical compound that contains atoms of carbon joined to form a ring-shaped molecule.

Arouet, François-Marie. *See* Voltaire.

Arp, Jean (Hans) (1887–1966), French sculptor, painter, and poet. He was a pioneer in the field of abstract art and a leader in European avant-garde movements in the first half of the 20th century. In Zurich during World War I he was a founder of the Dada movement and in the 1920s joined the Surrealists. He first sculpted in the early 1930s. His works are marked with a simple exuberance, of which *Mountain, Table, Anchors, Navel* (1925) and *Human Concretion* (1935) are typical examples. *See also* Abstract Art; Dada; Surrealism.

Árpád (died 907), semi-legendary Magyar chief, national hero of Hungary, founder of the Árpád dynasty. In 895 the invading Magyars under Árpád seized control of Pannonia. Árpád conquered Moravia, raided the Italian peninsula, and also attacked Germany. During constant wars with the Bulgarians and Walachians, he greatly extended his territory. By 896, the Magyars controlled what is now called Hungary.

Arrest, the act of placing a person in custody or under restraint, most usually because he is suspected of committing or has committed a crime. In civil proceedings, an arrest is made for the purpose of holding a person to a demand made against him.

Arrhythmia, an irregularity in the pace or force of the heartbeat. Various abnormalities include atrial tachycardia (fast heartbeat), atrial flutter, and atrial fibrillation, in which there is erratic and ineffective atrial contraction. In the course of normal activity, the heart rate of a healthy person will have some variety.

Arrowhead, or swamp potato, marsh plant found in tropical and temperate America. Its leaves are arrow-shaped and flowers are small, white, and cup-shaped on long stems. Species include common arrowhead *Sagittaria latifolia.* Family Alismataceae.

Arrowroot, tropical and subtropical perennial plant found in wet habitats of North and South America. Leaves are lance-shaped and flowers are usually white. Among 350 species are West Indian *Maranta arundinacea* whose rhizomes yield an easily digested starch. Family Marantaceae.

Arrowworm, wormlike, marine invertebrate common in warm waters. They are transparent and dart-shaped with thin fins and pairs of spiny hooks for jaws. They eat plankton and small animals. Length: 0.1–4in (3mm–10cm). There are 50 species. Phylum Chaetognatha.

Arsenic, toxic metalloid element (symbol As) of group V of the periodic table, probably obtained by Albertus Magnus (1250). Chief ores are realgar and orpiment (both sulfides) and mispickel (arsenopyrite, FeSAs). Arsenic is used for hardening lead and in semiconductors. Two allotropes are known: a gray metallic form and a yellow nonmetallic form. Properties: at. no. 33; at. wt. 74.9216; melt. pt. 1503°F (817°C); sublimes 1135°F (613°C); most common isotope As^{75} (100%).

Arsenopyrite, a sulfide mineral, iron arsenide-sulfide (FeAsS); the major ore of arsenic. Found with precious metal ores in high-temperature veins. Monoclinic system prismatic crystals or granular masses. Metallic white-gray; hardness 5.5–6; sp gr 6.

Arson, crime, the intentional burning of the property of another. In most places arson is divided into degrees, with the heaviest punishment meted for actions which endanger life.

Art Deco, decorative style, also known as *moderne.* First promoted in Paris in 1925, it flourished in the late 1920s through the 1930s. It sought to create for mass production sleek, linear decorative and industrial designs expressive of modern technology. Glass, semiprecious stones, and man-made materials such as ferro-concrete and plastics were favored.

Artemis, Greek goddess, daughter of Zeus and Leto, twin sister of Apollo (Roman, Diana). She was a virgin who assisted in childbirth and protected the young of humans and animals. She was goddess of the hunt, deity of light, associated with the moon. *See also* Diana.

Arteriosclerosis, several diseases of the arteries, including atherosclerosis, the most common form. It is caused by deposits of fatty materials and sometimes calcium on the arterial walls, narrowing the passage for blood, with the calcium also decreasing elasticity of the arteries. There are usually no overt symptoms until the disease in well advanced. Serious cases can lead to coronary disturbance, in which case symptoms may include exrcruciating chest pains radiating to the arms or neck (angina pectoris). So-called senile forgetfulness or confusion may occur if brain vessels are involved. There is evidence that predisposition to the disease is hereditary and that it is more likely to strike cigarette smokers, sedentary persons, or those with high-fat diets. Prevention and control of arteriosclerosis through low fat/low cholesterol diet and exercise is currently favored. If an aneurysm or obstruction in the artery is identifiable, surgery may be indicated. Anticoagulant drugs are sometimes effective on a short-term basis. See also Aneurysm; Angina Pectoris; Atherosclerosis.

Artery, a blood vessel that carries blood away from the heart. The pulmonary artery carries deoxygenated blood to the lungs, but all other arteries carry oxygenated, usually bright red, blood to the various tissues of the body. Artery walls are thick, elastic, and muscular, and they pulsate as they carry blood through the body. They are protected and usually embedded in muscle; a cut artery is serious, causing quick blood loss.

Artesian Water, results from a formation in which an aquifer exists between layers of impervious rock. The water in the aquifer is under sufficient pressure to rise to the surface wherever possible. It does so naturally in bubbling springs or in dug wells that need no pumping. The name indicates the region in France (Artois) where such wells exist. *See also* Aquifer; Hydrology.

Arthritis, an inflammation of the joints. Its most common form, rheumatoid arthritis, occurs most frequently in middle-aged women. The cause is unknown, although physical and emotional stress may trigger symptoms. Symptoms may begin with aching and stiffness developing into pain in the joints affected. Persons with chronic rheumatoid arthritis may show swelling of hands and wrists, perhaps deformities of hands and fingers. The disease is rarely totally disabling. Treatment includes prescribed exercise, particularly of the affected joints, diet, rest, and salicylates (aspirin) to reduce pain. The most severe cases may require surgery or other types of medication. Other forms of arthritis may result from staphylococcal or gonococcal infection. *See also* Rheumatism.

Arthropod, members of the largest animal phylum, Arthropoda. Living forms include crustaceans, arachnids, centipedes, millipedes, and insects. The more than 800,000 species are thought to have evolved from annelids. All have a hard outer skin of chitin that is attached to the musculature on the inside. The body is divided into segments, modified among different groups, with each segment originally carrying a pair of jointed legs for walking or swimming. They have well-developed digestive, circulatory, and nervous systems. Landforms use tracheae for respiration.

Arthur, semilegendary British king said to have united British tribes against the invading Saxons after the Roman withdrawal. He is usually considered as having lived in the 6th century, although this is not borne out by the *Anglo-Saxon Chronicle.* He became the focus for many medieval legends and romances and became an important figure in English literature.

Arthur, Chester Alan (1830–86), 21st President of the United States, b. Fairfield, Vt.; graduate, Union College, 1848. In 1859 he married Ellen Lewis Herndon; they had three children. A lawyer in New York City, Arthur became a faithful lieutenant of Roscoe Conkling, the Republican state boss. In 1871, President Grant named Arthur collector of customs for New York, a powerful patronage–dispensing office. He was removed in 1878 by President Hayes, thereby setting off a bitter dispute between Conklin's Stalwarts and the Half-Breeds, or supporters of James G. Blaine. The two factions stalemated the 1880 Republican convention. They finally compromised by naming James A. Garfield for president and Arthur for vice president. The ticket won the election with a narrow popular majority.

In July 1881, Garfield was shot by an assassin. He died on Sept. 19 and Arthur became President. His administration belied his background as a party hack. It was honest and efficient and made a serious effort to reform the spoils system. He was denied renomination in 1884 by his party, which nominated Blaine.

Career: collector of customs, port of New York (1871–78); vice president (1881); President (1881–85).

Arthurian Romance, in literature, the numerous medieval stories based on the largely apocryphal life of King Arthur of Britain and his knights. Arthur was probably a real chieftain who flourished in the 6th century. He is mentioned in several ancient chronicles. His feats combine the courage of a human general and the mystical powers of a god. An early written form of the legend appears in the *Historia* of Geoffrey of Monmouth (12th century). It was developed further by the Norman writer Wace (12th century). The legend also spread to France, where it was popularized in the writings of Chrétien de Troyes (12th century). A major Arthurian work is Thomas Malory's *Morte d'Arthur* (1485). Modern works have also been based on the legend.

Artichoke, or globe artichoke, tall, thistlelike perennial plant native to the Mediterranean region, widely grown in warm regions for the large, edible, immature flower heads. It has spiny, lobed or fernlike leaves and its flowers, if allowed to mature, are blue or white. Height: 3–5ft (0.9–1.5m). Family Compositae; species *Cynara scolymus.*

Articles of Confederation (1781–89), the first constitution of the United States. This document formally joined the 13 colonies for the first time under a central government. The Articles, proposed by Richard Henry Lee and drafted by a committee headed by John Dickinson, were in force until superseded by the US Constitution in 1789. Submitted to the Continental Congress in 1776 and adopted the next year, the Articles were not ratified by all the states until 1781. There was controversy over whether each state would be represented by one delegate or would be represented according to population and whether taxation would be based on population or land value. There was also much dispute over the disposition of the western lands. In the final form, the Articles gave each state one vote, based taxes on the value of surveyed land, and prevented the US government from interfering with a state's western territory. The US government provided for in the Articles of Confederation was weak because it lacked the power to tax, to force the states to obey its laws, or to regulate trade. The desire for a stronger government led to the Constitutional Convention of 1787. *See also* Constitution of the United States.

Artificial Gravity. *See* Gravity, Artificial.

Artificial Insemination, the induction of semen without sexual intercourse by using an instrument to inject seminal fluid into the vagina or uterus. Among the first successful insemination experiments on mammals were those of Italian physiologist Lazzaro Spallanzani (1729–99). The artificial impregnation of livestock makes available proven sires at low cost. In human reproduction the semen may be from the husband of the woman inseminated or from an anonymous donor. The world's first test tube baby, a healthy girl, was born in 1978 in England as the result of an experiment in which an embryo was fertilized outside the womb.

Artificial Kidney, a popular term for a device operating outside the body that removes from the blood the substances ordinarily removed by a properly functioning natural kidney and excreted in the urine. *See also* Dialysis.

Artificial Limb, a man-made limb or segment thereof used to replace a limb or part of a limb lost by amputation and often to perform its functions.

Artificial Satellite. *See* Satellite, Artificial.

Artificial Sweetener. *See* Sweetener, Artificial.

Artillery, projectile-firing weapons with a carriage or mount. An artillery piece is generally one of four types —gun, howitzer, mortar, or missile launcher. Modern artillery is classified according to caliber ranging from under 120mm for light artillery, to over 210mm for very heavy. The exact origin of artillery is unknown, although it appears to have been used in Europe and the Near East in the 14th century. Used by the Turks to take Constantinople in 1453, it became an important weapon in the 15th century. Advances in the 19th century, including smokeless powder, elongated shells, rifling, and rapid-fire breach loading, made artillery indispensable on the battlefield.

Artiodactyla, order of mammals characterized by hoofs with an even number (2 or 4) of toes. It includes giraffes, hippopotamuses, deer, cattle, hogs, sheep, goats, camels, and water buffaloes. Mostly of Old World origin, artiodactyls are now found worldwide. They range in size from the 8-lb (3.6-kg) mouse deer to the 4.5-ton hippopotamus.

Art Nouveau, decorative art movement that spread throughout Western Europe and, to some extent, to the

Chester Alan Arthur

Artichoke

Arthur Ashe

United States from the 1880s to about 1910. Architecture, painting, sculpture, graphic arts, furniture, textiles, and jewelry were all influenced by the style's fluid, undulating lines; symbolic themes; and exotic, dreamlike designs. Some of the most successful practitioners of art nouveau were architect Antonio Gaudi, one of the most original artists of the movement; Hector Guimard, who designed the entrances to the Paris *métro*; René Lalique, jewelry designer; Louis Tiffany, glassware designer; Alphonse Mucha and Aubrey Beardsley, graphic designers and artists.

Aruba, island in Netherlands Antilles, off the coast of NW Venezuela. Industries: tourism, phosphates, oil refining. Area: 69sq mi (179sq km). Pop. 61,788.

Arum, flowering succulent plants, native to Europe. The wild and cultivated species have large, veiny leaves and dense flowers on a short stem surrounded by a spathe. Complex natural insect traps are formed by these flowers. These plants contain calcium oxalate that produces a burning sensation in the mouth and throat when eaten. Common species are the jack-in-the-pulpit, calla lily, skunk cabbage, and philodendron. Family Araceae.

Aryans, Land of The. *See* Iran.

Asbestos, fibrous naturally occurring mineral used in insulating and fireproofing materials. Asbestos is used in the form of wool, fabric, and various asbestos-cement compounds. Several types exist; they are varieties of amphibole, pyroxene, and chrysotile minerals. The form known as blue asbestos (amosite) has certain advantages over the other white forms, but can cause a serious lung condition (asbestosis), or "white lung disease." Exposure to asbestos has been linked to lung cancer.

Ascension Island, volcanic island in S Atlantic Ocean, midway between Africa and South America; governed by British Colony of St Helena; discovered 1501 by Portuguese explorer João da Nova; site of US missile and satellite tracking station; only settlement is Georgetown. (1976 est.) Pop. 1,113.

Asceticism, self-denial of bodily pleasures and worldly pursuits indulged in for religious purposes, typically to heighten spiritual awareness. It is practiced in some form in most religions, and in Christianity it is regarded as an imitation of Christ. The commonest form of ascetic discipline—and the form most often practiced by lay persons—is fasting.

Asclepius. *See* Aesculapius.

Ascorbic Acid. *See* Vitamin C.

Asexual Reproduction, reproduction of organisms characterized by the lack of meiosis and fusion of two gamete nuclei. It occurs in several forms: fission (bacteria, protozoa); budding (hydra); spore formation (yeast); vegetative reproduction (strawberries); regeneration (planaria); and parthenogenesis (honeybees).

Asgard, in Scandinavian mythology, the domain of the gods. The Aesir resided here in splendid mansions. Chief of these was Valhalla, home of Woden, where the heroes slain in battle were carried in triumph.

Ash, genus of deciduous trees found in northern temperate regions. The wood is elastic, strong, and shock resistant, used for tool handles, baseball bats. About one-half of the 70 species are American, including *Fraxinus americana,* the white ash, found from Nova Scotia to Texas; black ash, *F. nigra;* and the green ash,

F. pennsylvanica lanceolata. Others are manna ash, *F. ornus,* the flowering ash of southern Europe and Asia Minor, and the European ash, *F. excelsior,* which grows to 140ft (43m) tall. Family Oleaceae.

Ashanti, Negroid people of S and central Ghana. In the 18th century they established a powerful empire, based on trade in slaves with the Dutch and British. Conflicts with the British throughout the 19th century were finally resolved in 1902, when the Ashanti territories were declared a British Crown colony. Ashanti society is matrilineal and traditionally agricultural, plantain, bananas, manioc, yams, and cocoa being the chief crops. Ashantis bear allegiance to a paramount chief, whose capital is at Kumasi and who is advised by his mother or sister. Ashanti religion is animist and includes ancestor-worship; their crafts include weaving.

Ashcan School (*c.*1907), group of US painters, also called The Eight, who revolted against the National Academy and aestheticism and painted realistic city scenes (including ashcans) and ordinary people. They included Robert Henri, George Luks, William Glackens.

Ashcroft, Dáme Peggy (1907–), leading British actress. After her debut in 1926, she covered the classical repertoire from Shakespeare (notably as Desdemona in *Othello* in 1930) to Pinter. In 1968 she became a director of the Royal Shakespeare Company with whom she appeared both at Stratford-upon-Avon and in London. She received an Academy Award (1985) for her appearance in *A Passage to India* (1984).

Ashe, Arthur Robert (1943–), US tennis player, b. Richmond. He won the US (1968), Australian (1970), and Wimbledon (1975) singles championships. Heart surgery (1979) ended his career, but he became the US Davis Cup team captain (1980–85).

Asheville, city in W North Carolina, 100mi (161km) WNW of Charlotte, on the Swannanoa River near Great Smoky Mts National Park; site of Vanderbilt estate, Colburn Mineral Museum, Asheville-Biltmore College (1927); birthplace of Thomas Wolfe. Industries: tourism, tobacco processing, lumber, electronic equipment, textiles, glass. Founded 1794; inc. 1797; chartered as city 1835. Pop. (1980) 53,281.

Ashkenazim, Jews who originally settled in NW Europe, as distinguished from the Sephardim, Jews who settled in Spain and Portugal.

Ashkhabad (Aschabad), formerly Poltoralsk; city in central Asian USSR, near Iranian border; capital of Turkmen SSR; fertile oasis region; site of university (1950), museum, agricultural, medical, and teachers' colleges; crossed by Trans-Caspian Railroad. Industries: vineyards, orchards, cotton, silk, motion pictures. Founded 1881 as fortress (Askhabad). Pop. 309,000.

Ashoka, emperor of India (*c.*274–136 BC). His reign is known from engravings on rocks and from traditions in Sanskrit literature. He was referred to as Piyadassi, "benevolent aspect." One of his edicts suppressed a royal hunt and stressed the sanctity of animal life. He was a lay Buddhist and his son converted Ceylon, present day Sri Lanka, to that faith.

Ashur, national god of the Assyrians. A god of battle, depicted as eagle-headed and winged, usually combined with the solar disk surmounted by a warrior, he is identified with Baal of the city of Ashur, a storm god, and has similarities to Jahweh of the early Israelites.

Ashurbanipal, or **Assurbanipal,** king of Assyria (669–627 BC). Noted as the last great king of Assyria, under his reign Assyria reached its highest level in art, architecture, literature, and science, although the period was beset with warfare. He abandoned control of the Nile Valley in 654 BC, but conquered several Phoenician cities and suppressed a Babylonian revolt led by his half-brother (648 BC), slaughtering many inhabitants in retaliation. By 639 BC the Elamite kingdom had been absorbed by Assyria. Ashurbanipal assembled the first systematically organized library in the Near East. More than 20,000 tablets and fragments of the library, the chief sources of knowledge of ancient Mesopotamia, are now in the British Museum. Constant warfare so weakened his empire that his two sons, who ruled briefly after his death, could not preserve it. Assyria succumbed to the Medes and the Persians a few years later.

Asia, largest continent of the world, entirely in the Eastern Hemisphere. It extends above the Arctic Circle and, at Singapore, almost to the equator, with much of Indonesia and smaller islands lying below that line.

Land. Asia is separated from Europe by an imaginary line along the Ural Mountains, Caspian Sea, Caucasus Mountains, and Black Sea. Its vast area includes some barely habitable regions—the frozen N; the Arabian and central deserts, of which the Gobi is one of the largest in the world, est at 500,000sq mi (1,295,000sq km); and the world's tallest mountains, including the Himalaya, Karakoram, and Kunlun. The highest peak is Everest, at 29,028ft (8,854m).

Lakes and Rivers. Major lakes fall mostly across the center of Asia and include the Caspian—partly in Europe—the Aral Sea, and lakes Balkhash and Baikal. Many rivers flow from the mountains, with the Yangtze being Asia's longest, 3,434mi (5,526m); others are the Lena, Mekong, Yellow, Indus, Brahmaputra, and Ganges.

Climate and Vegetation. Asia experiences temperature extremes, with warm days and cold nights, hot summers and cold winters. In the S peninsulas the climate is hot and, except in SW Asia, moist. Coniferous forests cover much of the N 25% of the continent, while tropical rain forests thrive in the S central, SE, and island regions. Steppe areas border the central mountain and desert sections, and grasslands occur in E Asia.

Animal Life. Monkeys are numerous, but unique apes are the orangutan of SE islands and the gibbon of Malaysia. Probably best-loved is China's giant panda, which is related to the raccoon. Less exotic mammals include bears, wolves, leopards, tigers, camels, and elephants. Ducks, quail, owls, vultures, doves, wrens, and hundreds of other birds abound. Nests of cliff swallows are collected for bird's-nest soup, and mynas can be taught to imitate speech. Dangerous reptiles include crocodiles, kraits, cobras, and pythons.

Economy. Agriculture is important to most countries. Rice forms the major crop in the E and S, while wheat and barley grow to the W and N. Taiwan and Japan are highly industrialized, with India, Turkey, and S. Korea becoming steadily more so. Petroleum exports support several Middle Eastern countries and Indonesia.

People. Asia, with half the world's population, has many peoples, sometimes classed in two major categories. The Mongoloid peoples live in the E half of Asia; the Caucasians, whether light-skinned (as in parts of the USSR), dark-skinned (as in India), or in between (as in the Arab lands), inhabit the W half. Major languages are Indo-Aryan, Sino-Tibetan, Ural-Altaic, Malayan, and Semitic. Hinduism has the most adherents, followed by Islam, Confucianism, Buddhism, Shintoism, Christianity, Taoism, and Judaism.

History. About 3000 BC the Sumerians developed a type of character-figure writing (cuneiform), and in another 1,500 years the Phoenicians developed an alphabet. Between 600 and 500 BC both Buddha and Confucius flourished, and the Persian Empire came into existence. Early in the 7th century AD, China became the world's most advanced region, and the Arabs began to spread Islam. To free the Holy Land from Islamic control, Europeans launched numerous Crusades, which brought about an increased knowledge of and interest in Asia. Genghis Khan controlled much of Asia before his death in 1227, and his grandson Kublai Khan encouraged the arts as well as war. In the mid-15th century, Turks replaced remnants of the Roman Empire with the Ottoman Empire. After Vasco da Gama reached India, and Ferdinand Magellan proved that man could sail round the globe, Asia's isolation began to end. The British, French, Dutch, Spanish, and Portuguese gained footholds, which started crumbling when the Spanish-American War took the Philippines out of European control. Japan proved itself a world power in the Russo-Japanese War early in the 20th century and continued on a path of belligerency until its defeat in WWII. Since then former colonies have gained independence. Conflicts between Communist and Western powers centered in SE Asia, with wars in Korea (1950–53) and Vietnam (1954–75). The area remains troubled by war and instability, creating a serious refugee problem in the late 1970s and early 1980s. The major focus of geopolitical concern has shifted to the Middle East, where Israel has fought sporadically with its Arab neighbors since 1948; a peaceful solution in the near future seems unlikely. Tensions increased in 1979, with an Islamic fundamentalist revolution in Iran and Soviet intervention in Afghanistan. After years of self-imposed isolation the People's Republic of China has emerged as a major world power.

PROFILE

Area: 17,000,000sq mi (44,030,000sq km)
Largest nations: USSR, Asian (6,500,000sq mi; 16,835,000sq km); China, People's Republic of (3,700,000sq mi; 9,583,000sq km); and India (1,246,880sq mi; 3,229,419sq km)
Population: 2,461,000,000
Density, 142per sq mi (55per sq km). *Most populous nations,* China, People's Republic of, 933,030,000; India, 638,390,000; Japan, 114,900,000
Chief cities: Tokyo, Japan; Shanghai, China; Peking, China; Bombay, India; Djakarta, Indonesia, Hong Kong

Asia Minor (Anatolia), great peninsula of extreme W Asia, bordered by Black Sea (N), Mediterranean (S), and Aegean Sea (W); the famous waterway comprised of the straits of Bosporus and Dardanelles passes through this region, and with the Taurus Mts in the S and Anatolian Plateau spreading through the remainder of the area, it comprises most of Turkey; the scene of political struggles since ancient times.

Asian Literature, creative writings from the peoples of Asia. It can be separated into five divisions: (1) the ancient Middle East; (2) the Arabic and Persian literatures that followed in the area of the ancient Middle East and also went beyond it; (3) India; (4) China and Japan; and (5) Southeast Asia. There is no overall unifying characteristic of Asian literature.

The Hebrew Old Testament makes the literature of the ancient Middle East the most important to the Western world. In Arabic literature lyric poetry, such as the verses in the Koran, is the most significant form. The Persians were known for their epic poetry. In Indian writing religious feelings predominate; the mundane and the secular are linked. The Hindu epic *Mahabharata* typifies this fact. Chinese literature emphasizes philosophy as expressed in lyric poetry. The anthology *Shih Ching* is an example. Poetry and drama have dominated in Japan; brevity, as in 17-syllable *haiku,* is the soul of wisdom in Japanese poetry. Southeast Asia has the most diverse literature.

Asmara (Asmera), city in N Ethiopia, 40mi (64km) SW of Mesewa; capital of Eritrea prov.; occupied by Italy 1889; capital of Italian colony 1936–1941, when it was captured by British; became part of Ethiopia 1962; site of University of Asmara (1958); fertile region where fruits, vegetables, coffee and oil seeds are grown. Industries: breweries, ceramics, textiles. Pop. 276,355.

Asmodeus, Prince of Demons in Hebrew mythology. In Talmudic literature he was the adversary of King Solomon, who compelled him to help build the temple in Jerusalem. Asmodeus later borrowed Solomon's magic ring, with which he flung the king into a faraway land, assumed his shape, reigned in his stead, and committed the sins attributed by scripture to Solomon.

Asp, or asp viper, S European viper characterized by an upturned snout. It varies in color, but is mostly brown-red with dark spots. It feeds on rodents, birds, lizards, and earthworms and is aggressive when disturbed. The asp Cleopatra used to commit suicide was probably another species of N African viper or Egyptian cobra. Length: to 30in(76cm). Family Viperidae; species *Vipera aspis. See also* Viper.

Asparagine, white crystalline soluble amino acid ($NH_2CO{\cdot}CH_2CH{\cdot}NH_2{\cdot}COOH$) that occurs in leguminous plants. *See* Amino Acid.

Asparagus, perennial plants primarily native to Africa. They have tuberous or fleshy roots, scale-like leaves, small greenish flowers, and are grown for their decorative greenery or as a garden vegetable. *Asparagus officinalis,* an erect perennial of Europe and Asia, is grown widely in the United States for its edible, tender shoots. Family Liliaceae.

Asparagus Fern, house plant native to S Africa with feathery foliage growing on long, cascading stems, upright plumes, or horizontal triangular branchlets. Care: bright indirect light, barely moist soil (equal parts loam, peat moss, sand). Propagation is by root division or seeds. Family Liliaceae; genus *Asparagus.*

Aspartic Acid, white crystalline amino acid ($COOH{\cdot}CH_2{\cdot}CH{\cdot}NH_2{\cdot}COOH$) that occurs in sugar beets. *See* Amino Acid.

Aspen, several trees *(Populus)* of the willow family, known for their oval leaves that quake in even gentle breezes, owing to their slender, flattened petioles. Native to temperate Eurasia, North Africa, and North America, they grow to 90ft (27m).

Asphalt, naturally occurring black or brown semisolid bitumens, used mainly for road covering and roofing. Asphalts are found in deposits in many parts of the world, including Trinidad, Venezuela, and in Alabama and Texas. They were probably produced by chemical change of mineral oils and consist of colloidal suspensions of coal-like material in heavy oil.

Asphyxiation, cause of death resulting from lack of oxygen in air breathed. Common causes of asphyxiation are drowning and smoke inhalation.

Aspidistra, or cast-iron plant, a genus of durable house plants native to China with arching, oval leaves. Care: indirect light, barely moist soil (equal parts loam, peat moss, sand). Propagation is by root division. Height: to 3ft (91cm). Family Liliaceae.

Aspirin, or **acetylsalicylic acid,** white crystalline substance made from salicylic acid; an extensively used antipyretic and analgesic drug taken for headache, rheumatic pain, fever, etc.

Asquith, Herbert Henry. *See* Oxford and Asquith, Herbert Henry Asquith, 1st Earl of.

Ass, wild equine found in African and Asian desert and mountain areas. Smaller than the horse, it has a short mane and tail, large ears, small hooves, and dorsal stripes. It brays instead of neighing. Gestation period is 12 months; one colt is born. Male is called a jack; female a jennet or jenny. The three African races (species *Equus asinus*) are Nubian (now extinct), North African, and the rare Somali. Height: 3–4.5ft (91.5–137cm) at shoulder. Asian races, *Equars hemion,* are the Kiang, Ghorkar, and Onager. Family Equidae. *See also* Kiang; Onager.

Assad, Hafez al (1928–), president of Syria. He attended the Syrian Military Academy and rose through the ranks to become a general. He was minister of defense (1965–70). After a coup d'état in 1970 he was elected president.

Assam, state in NE India, almost cut off from the main body of India by Bangladesh (SW) and Nepal (W); capital is Shillong; ruled by Ahom empire 1400–1825; passed to Britain 1826 through the Treaty of Yandabo; became self-governing province 1937; provided home for Hindu refugees from Muslim East Pakistan 1959–60, 1971. Industries: tea, rice, sugar cane, timber, oil. Area: 30,000sq mi (77,700sq km). Pop. 17,810,000.

Assassin, secret Muslim sect founded *c.*1090 by Hasan ibn-al-Sabbah. It quickly gained control of the Muslim world by spreading terror. The members were organized into two classes with the highest class as devotees. They were used as instruments of assassination, sometimes sacrificing their own lives. The order was noted in the tales of Marco Polo and the crusaders, who brought the term "assassin" to Europe. It derives from the alleged use of hashish by terrorists seeking ecstatic visions.

Assassin Bug, large, often brightly colored bug found worldwide. Most species feed on other insects but some feed on man and rodents. Length: 0.25–1.33in (6–34mm). Family Reduviidae. *See also* Kissing bug.

Assemblies of God, largest Pentecostal religious sect in the United States, founded by preachers of the Church of God in Hot Springs, Ark., in 1914. In 1916 it was incorporated and titled General Council of Assemblies of God. There are about 600,000 members at present. *See also* Pentecostalism.

Assimilation, a blending of cultures that occurs when different groups live closely together and merge their ways of life. European immigrants to the United States in the 19th and early 20th centuries became assimilated. They adopted American ways but also added some of their customs and attitudes to American life style. *See also* Pluralism.

Assiniboine Indians, nomadic North American Indian tribe. Their language was Siouan, and they were related to the Dakotas, although they migrated westward from Minnesota to Saskatchewan and the Lake Winnepeg area. Their culture is that of the Plains Indians. They were peaceful trading partners of the Hudson's Bay Company, and their trade helped to destroy the French monopoly among tribes of that region. Today they are about 5,000 in number, with 4,000 on reservations in Montana and 1,000 living in Canada.

Assisi, town in central Italy, overlooking the Tiber and Topino rivers; developed from ancient town of Asisium; birthplace of St Francis; site of medieval castle, cathedral (1140), and the famous St Francis' Basilica. Industries: manufacturing, tourism. Pop. 24,002.

Associative Law, rule of combination in mathematics in which the result of two or more operations on terms does not depend on the way in which they are grouped. Thus, normal addition and multiplication of numbers follows the associative law, since $a + (b + c) = (a + b) + c$, and $a \times (b \times c) = (a \times b) \times c$.

Assonance, imperfect rhyme, where the stressed vowels in the words agree, but the consonants do not. Examples are: "hulks, exults"; "penitent, reticence"; "neck, met." Commonly found in medieval ballads, assonance has also been used as a literary device by such poets as John Milton, Alfred Tennyson, Gerard Manley Hopkins, and Dylan Thomas.

Assumption, generally accepted principle on which a subject is built. *See also* Postulate.

Assurbanipal. *See* Ashurbanipal.

Assyria, ancient empire of the Middle East. It took its name from the city of Assur, or Ashur, which was located on the Tigris River near the modern city of Mosul, Iraq. At its height, the Assyrian Empire comprised the modern nations of Iraq, Syria, Jordan, Israel, and Egypt; and it included parts of Saudi Arabia, Armenia, and Asia Minor (Turkey). The Assyrian Empire had its beginning in the 3rd millennium BC, reached its zenith between the 9th and 7th centuries BC, and thereafter went into swift decline. In 612 BC its capital city, Nineveh, was captured by a combined force of Medes, Babylonians, and Scythians, and Assyria lost its hegemony. Later Assyria was absorbed into the Persian Empire.

The Assyrians were a Semitic people who adapted parts of the Babylonian and Hittite religions; their chief god was Ashur, and their kings were regarded as deities. The Assyrians gradually increased their power until the 12th century BC, when their first great king, Tiglath-pilesar I (died *c.*1077 BC), conquered Babylonia and parts of Armenia and Asia Minor. In the 9th century Ashurnazirpal II further expanded the empire and established efficient control over the conquered territories. An exceedingly warlike people, the Assyrians continued to increase their territories under such rulers as Shalmaneser III (died 824 BC), Tiglath-Pilesar III (died 727 BC), Sargon (died 705 BC), Sennacherib (died 681 BC), and Esar-Haddon (died 669 BC).

Ashurbanipal (died 627 BC) was the last great Assyrian king. Under his rule Assyrian art—particularly its great bas-relief sculpture—and Assyrian learning reached their greatest development. The luxuriance of Ashurbanipal's court at Nineveh was of legendary proportions. The cost of maintaining his huge armies, added to the sumptousness of his court, fatally weakened the empire. Two of his sons ruled briefly after his death, but with the capture of Nineveh in 612 BC, the empire fell into ruin.

Assyrian Architecture (*fl.* 1250–612 BC), architectural style derived from Babylonian architecture. Temples and ziggurats were significant structures, but palaces became even more important. The Assyrians used multicolored ornamental brickwork, and the high

Asp

Assassin bug

Astrology

plinths or dados at the bases of their buildings were often carved with low-relief sculpture. Interiors were similarly decorated with continuous friezes. The cities of Ashur, Ninevah, Nimrud, and Khorsabad were the sites of the greatest Assyrian palaces.

Assyro-Babylonian Mythology, described a cosmic order of heaven, earth, and an underworld and populated it with some 4000 deities and demons to direct the physical and spiritual activities of the world. The complex stories dealing with the Mesopotamian pantheon are generally regarded as literary entertainments or interesting explanations of natural occurrences and religious rituals, having little effect on the daily lives or religious activities of the people. As in the later state religion of the Greeks of the Golden Age, the mythology is an important part of the culture in the arts, but is not an integral part of the liturgy of the priests or church.

Astarte, also **Ashtart** or **Ashtoreth,** Phoenician goddess of fertility and love, equivalent to Ishtar of the Assyro-Babylonians and Aphrodite of the Greeks. She is represented by a crescent, perhaps symbolic of the moon or the horns of a cow. The dove, gazelle, and myrtle were sacred to her.

Astatine, radioactive element (symbol At) of the halogen group, first made (1940) by bombarding bismuth with alpha particles. It is made only in trace amounts. Properties: at. no. 85; melt. pt. 482°F (250°C); boil. pt. 662°F (350°C); most stable isotope At^{210} (half-life 8.3hr). *See also* Halogen elements.

Aster, a genus of mostly perennial, leafy-stemmed plants native to the Americas and Eurasia. Popular garden plants, asters usually bear daisylike flowers in clusters. The outer rays are white, blue, pink or purple and the inner disks are yellow, turning darker with age. Family Compositae.

Asteroid, minor planet or planetoid, any of several thousand small celestial objects orbiting the sun in the region between Mars and Jupiter. Ranging in diameter from only a few kilometers to several hundred, asteroids may be the remains of a planet that broke up or failed to attain a stable existence. *See also* Ceres.

Asthenosphere, portion of the earth's upper mantle extending from 60–120mi (97–193km) below the surface. *See also* Crust, Earth; Mantle.

Asthma, recurring seizures of shortness of breath or breathlessness accompanied by wheezing or whistling sound. Difficulty in breathing is caused by the inability to force air out of the lungs; inhalation is not impaired. Asthma is designated as cardiac, non-allergic bronchial, and allergic bronchial, the last by far the most common. Some hereditary factors are attached to allergic bronchial asthma. Bronchial attacks may be excited by allergens such as pollen, molds, and dust, less frequently by foods and drugs. Acute attacks frequently occur at night, may be prolonged and culminate in coughing and expectoration of sputum. Drugs are sometimes prescribed to contain acute attacks, but elimination of, or desensitization to, stimulus is the treatment of choice. *See also* Allergy.

Astor, John Jacob (1763–1848), US merchant and fur trader, b. Germany. Arriving penniless in the United States, Astor became a successful businessman in New York City and then went into the China trade. In 1808 he founded the American Fur Co. and after the War of 1812 developed a monopoly on the US fur trade. He retired from the fur trade in 1834 and concentrated on land investment.

Astor, Nancy Witcher (Langhorne), Viscountess (1879–1964), British politician, the first woman elected to the House of Commons, serving 1919–45, b. United States. A Conservative, she advocated temperance, educational reform, women's and children's welfare. In the 1930s, she and her husband William Waldorf Astor became, at their estate Clivedon, the center of a group of influential proponents of appeasement toward Nazi Germany.

Astrakhan (Astrachan), port city in SE European USSR; on Caspian Sea and Voly River delta, approx. 800mi (1,288km) SE of Moscow; capital of Astrakhan oblast; site of USSR's largest fisheries; a railroad, airline, oil shipping, and trade center; site of walled kremlin (c. 1550). City developed in the 13th century under Mongols; near site of ancient Khazar city of Itil (8th–10th centuries); Tartar stronghold until capture 1554–56 by Ivan IV (the Terrible); in 1917–20 civil war the city remained in Russian hands, becoming a base for Caspian Sea conquest of 1920. Exports: oil, rice, timber, fruit. Pop. 472,000.

Astrobiology. *See* Exobiology.

Astrogeology, study of rocks, craters, and other surface features of the Moon, Mars, and other planets. Includes on site and laboratory studies of Moon rocks, seismological data (Moon only), photographic mappings, magnetic field measurements, and micrometeorite data.

Astrology, pseudoscientific study of the influence supposedly exercised by celestial bodies upon the lives of men. Originating in Babylon some 3000 years ago, it sought by means of essentially arbitrary rules to work out man's personal fate according to the motions and positions of the Sun, Moon, and planets at the time of his birth. For this purpose, accurate observational records began to be kept, which eventually provided the impetus for transforming the superstition of astrology into the exact science of astronomy.

Astronaut (Russian: Cosmonaut), person who navigates or rides in a space vehicle; also, a person selected for a training program to fly in space vehicles. Most astronauts are former test pilots. The first man in space was Yuri Gagarin, Soviet Union, 1961. The first man on the Moon was Neil Armstrong, United States, 1969. The first woman in space was Valentina Tereshkova, Soviet Union, June 16, 1963.

Astronomical Unit (symbol A.U.), astronomical unit of length used for distance measurements within the solar system, equal to the mean distance of the Earth from the Sun. 1 A.U. is equal to 92.957 million mi (149.60 million km).

Astronomy, branch of science that has been studied since ancient times and is now concerned with the universe and its contents in terms of the relative motions of celestial bodies, their positions on the celestial sphere, physical and chemical structure, evolution, the phenomena occurring on them, etc. The main branches are celestial mechanics, astrophysics, cosmology, and astrometry. Waves of all regions of the electromagnetic spectrum can now be studied either with ground-based instruments or, where no atmospheric window exists, by observations and measurements made from satellites, space probes, and rockets. These instruments include telescopes, associated photographic and spectrographic equipment, and other detecting and analyzing devices, which are often coupled to a computer in order to process measurements and other information rapidly. *See also* Astronomy, Radio; Black Hole; Comet; Constellation; Eclipse,

Solar; Galaxy; Moon; Planet; Pulsar; Quasar; Solar System; Star; Sun; Telescope, Radio.

Astronomy, Gamma-Ray, branch of astronomy concerned with the study of gamma rays from space. Gamma rays cannot penetrate the Earth's atmosphere and must therefore be detected by equipment carried in satellites, etc. The Sun is the principal source of gamma rays.

Astronomy, Infrared, branch of astronomy concerned with detecting infrared (IR) waves from space, determining their source, and studying the IR spectrum of such sources. Most IR radiation is absorbed by the Earth's atmosphere apart from a few narrow longwavelength bands and the band adjacent to the visible region; thus most studies must be made from satellites, rockets, or balloons. The Sun is an important IR source. Thousands of other IR sources are now known. These are mainly stars with low surface temperatures, some of which are only in an early development stage. Very strong IR sources exist in Cygnus, the Orion Nebula and at the galactic center. IR techniques are used to study planetary atmospheres, stellar evolution, galactic structure, and in many other fields.

Astronomy, Optical, oldest branch of astronomy, in which reflecting and refracting telescopes and other optical equipment are used in detecting and studying light sources in the universe. Sources include celestial bodies, such as the planets and their satellites, that reflect light from a nearby star and bodies, such as stars and star systems (galaxies), that emit light. The entire visible spectrum can penetrate the Earth's atmosphere for ground-based telescopic studies. However, due to atmospheric disturbances, pollution, background light from the night sky, clouds, etc, observatories are often in mountainous or other isolated regions and many observations are made from satellites, space probes, and high-flying aircraft.

Astronomy, Radar, branch of astronomy in which radar pulses reflected back to Earth from celestial bodies inside the solar system are studied for information concerning the distance from Earth of the bodies, their orbital motion, and large surface features.

Astronomy, Radio, relatively new branch of astronomy in which radio telescopes and other equipment are used to detect radio waves from space and determine their source and energy spectrum. Radio wavelengths of about 8mm to over 20m can pass through the Earth's atmosphere without ionospheric reflection. Radio astronomy studies this wavelength band and the resulting view of the radio universe differs from that of the visible universe, although radio sources can often be identified with visible light sources. The most powerful radio sources include the Sun; interstellar clouds of hot hydrogen, such as the Orion Nebula; discrete sources, mainly supernova remnants and pulsars, such as the Crab Nebula; quasars; and radio galaxies. There is also a weak isotropic background radio emission centered on the 21cm emission of hydrogen.

Astronomy, Ultraviolet, branch of astronomy concerned with detecting ultraviolet (UV) waves from space, determining their source, and studying the UV spectrum of such sources. An atmospheric window exists for high-wavelength UV waves (200–400 nanometers), which can thus be studied from the ground. Lower wavelengths must be studied from satellites and rockets. The Sun is an important UV source; other discrete sources include the Orion Nebula and the intense Wolf-Rayet stars.

Astronomy, X-ray, branch of astronomy concerned with detecting X-rays from space, determining their source, and studying the spectrum of X-ray energies emitted. X-rays are absorbed by the Earth's atmosphere so that detecting instruments, such as Geiger counters and specially designed telescopes, must be carried in satellites or rockets. X-ray sources include the Sun, whose emission originates mainly in the corona, and the Crab Nebula. Other Galactic sources occur in the constellations Scorpio, Cygnus, and Centaurus. Extragalactic sources include the radio source Cygnus A and the radio galaxy M87 in Virgo.

Astrophysics, branch of astronomy concerned with the physical and chemical nature of stars and other celestial bodies and with their evolution. Many branches of science, including nuclear physics, plasma physics, relativity, and spectroscopy, are used in predicting properties and features of celestial bodies and in interpreting the information obtained from astronomical studies in all sections of the electromagnetic spectrum.

Asturias, Miguel Angel (1899–1974), Guatemalan novelist. He won the Nobel Prize for literature in 1967. His most famous novel, *El Señor Presidente* (1946), condemns dictatorship. It was based on conditions in his own country but has been praised for its universality. In it he criticizes the change from a rural, natural world to an urbanized community dominated by a dictator. Among his other novels are *Hombres de maíz* (1949), about the takeover of Indian land for maize-growing profits, and a trilogy criticizing US economic control of banana plantations.

Asturias, former kingdom in northwestern Spain, coextensive with the modern Oviedo province. The indigenous Iberian people were conquered by the Romans in the 2nd century BC. When the Moors overran Spain in the 8th century, the Christian nobles fled to the Asturian mountains. One of them, Pelayo, founded (*c.* 718) the kingdom of Asturias; it was from this first Christian kingdom that the gradual reconquest of Spain began. In the 10th century it became the kingdom of Asturias and León, and three centuries later it became part of the kingdom of Castile.

Asunción, capital and largest city of Paraguay, in S Paraguay, on E bank of Paraguay River at the junction with Pilcomayo River; chief river port and administrative, industrial, and cultural center of Paraguay; site of Pantéon Nacional (tomb for national heroes), La Encarnación (church), National University (1889), Catholic University (1960); scene of "comuneros" rebellion against Spanish rule 1731; occupied by Brazil 1868–76. Industries: meat packing, textiles, food products. Founded 1536 as trade outpost and Jesuit mission. Pop. 400,000.

Aswan, city in SE Egypt, on the E bank of the Nile River just below Lake Nasser and the Aswan High Dam which impounds it; capital of Aswan governorate. An ancient Egyptian settlement called Syene, meaning "market place," the city was of strategic importance to the Egyptians and Greeks because it controlled shipping and communication from above the first cataract of the Nile. The modern city is a commercial and tourist center that has benefited greatly from the construction of the Aswan High Dam (completed 1970). Although some archeological treasures were lost in the impounding of Lake Nasser, the temples of Abu-Simpel were saved; the rocky terrain is the site of ancient Egyptian and Greek temples and monuments. Industries: steel, textiles, tourism. Pop. 246,000.

As You Like It (*c.* 1599), a comedy by William Shakespeare about the wicked Duke Frederick and his brother, Duke Senior. Banished from power, Duke Senior establishes a new court under nature's laws in the Forest of Arden. The intricate plot resolves both a star-crossed love affair as well as the political feud.

Atabrine, quinacrine hydrochloride, an antimalarial drug. It is a yellow, bitter compound.

Atahualpa (1500–33), Incan ruler of Peru. The son of Huayna Capac, he fought for control of the Incan realm with Huáscar, his half-brother, whom he defeated in 1532, the year Francisco Pizarro arrived in northern Peru. Atahualpa later was taken prisoner by Pizarro and executed.

Atamasco Lily, or **zephyr lily,** North American bulb plant growing wild in wet woods and clearings. The large waxy flower faces upward and is pink or white. Leaves are long, slim, and channeled. Height: 6–15in (15–38cm). Family Amaryllidaceae; species *Zephyranthes atamasco.*

Atatürk, Kemal (1881–1938), Turkish leader and founder of modern Turkey. As a youth he joined the Young Turks, a liberal movement that sought to establish a government independent of Ottoman rule. He fought against the Italians in Tripolitania (1911) and served with distinction in World War I. In 1919 he organized the Turkish Nationalist party in E. Anatolia and formed an army. In 1919 he announced the aims of an independent Turkish state and in 1921–22 he expelled the Greeks from Anatolia. He abolished the sultanate (1922) and proclaimed the republic in 1923. Elected president in 1923 and reelected in 1927, 1931, and 1935, he instituted reforms touching on virtually every aspect of national life.

Athabasca Lake, lake in W central Canada, on N Alberta-Saskatchewan border; 4th-largest lake in Canada; drains into the Slave River. Fort Chipewyan built in 1788 is preserved at W end of lake; gold and uranium deposits nearby. Area: 3,120sq mi (8,081sq km).

Athabascan, or **Athapascan,** also known as Slave Indians, tribe and language family of North American Indians inhabiting NW Canada. They were forced north to the Great Slave Lake and Fort Nelson by the Cree. Their common name, Slave, derives from the domination and forced labor exacted by the Cree. The Athabascan tribe has always been closely linked to the Chipewyan people, and some authorities regard the two as one extended group. Today some 25,000 Athabascan Indians live in NW Canada. The Athabascan language, which derives from the tribe, covers the largest geographical area of all North American Indian groups; speakers extend from the Cree in Canada to the Tolowa and Hupa in California and the Navajo and Apache of the Southwest. No accurate count exists, but the Athabascan-speaking tribes of North America would probably approximate well over 250,000.

Athanasian Creed, a Christian profession of faith that explains the teachings of the church on the Trinity and the incarnation. It is accepted as the authoritative profession in the Roman Catholic and Anglican churches.

Athanasius, Saint (*c.* 297–373), Christian theologian, Doctor of the Church. As patriarch of Alexandria, he confuted the Arians—and Arius himself—both during and after the Council of Nicaea (325). In *Discourses against the Arians* (357) he represented the Trinity as composed of three Persons in one Nature. During the tumultuous Arian controversy, when he was twice forced into exile, he steadfastly upheld the Nicene Creed and maintained thereby the essential divinity of Christ. He is no longer credited with writing the Athanasian Creed. Feast: May 2. *See also* Arianism; Nicene Creed.

Atheism, a system of thought developed around the denial of God's existence. Atheism, so defined, first appeared during the Enlightenment, the age of reason. In ancient Greece, it meant refusal to worship the state deities.

Athena, Greek goddess of war and crafts (Roman, Minerva). She was born fully grown and armed from the head of Zeus. As the goddess of war, she aided the Greeks in the Trojan War. As goddess of crafts, she inspired the ship *Argo* and the wooden horse by Epius. Athens was named in her honor.

Athens (Athínai), capital city of Greece, SW of Saronic Gulf; capital of Attica department. The ancient city built on the Acropolis was the greatest center of art and culture in Greece; gained significant power during Persian Wars (500–449 BC); city prospered from 468 to 429 BC under Cimon and Pericles, during which time Aeschylus, Sophocles, Euripides, and Socrates produced their finest work; defeated by Sparta in the Peloponnesian Wars (431–404 BC). Under Alexander the Great, Athens gained some independence; it declined under Roman control (from 228 BC). After Greek War of Independence (1821–30), Athens regained former standing as a cultural and commercial center. Most noted artistic treasures are the Parthenon (432 BC), a temple to Athena; Parthenos, a Doric structure created by Ictinus and Callicrates; the Erechtheum (408 BC), a temple of Athena, Poseidon, and Erechtheus; and the Theater of Dionysus (*c.* 500 BC), the oldest Greek theater. Modern Athens and its port of Piraeus form a major transportation and economic hub of the Mediterranean. Industries: shipbuilding, paper mills, machinery, textiles, breweries, chemicals, glass, tourism. Pop. metro area: 2,540,000 est.

Atherosclerosis, most common form of arterial disease. An early stage of arteriosclerosis, it is a thickening of artery walls. *See also* Arteriosclerosis.

Athlete's Foot, a contagious, fungus-caused infection usually appearing first between the last two toes. Itching, macerated skin and blisters are usual symptoms.

Áthos, Mount, mountain peak in NE Greece, on S Athos peninsula. Inhabited since 9th century by an independent community of monks of St Basil; made theocratic republic 1927 and placed under Greek suzerainty. Height: approx. 6,670ft (2,034m).

Atlanta, industrial city in NW central Georgia; state capital; seat of Fulton co; distribution, commercial, cultural, and financial capital of the SE United States. The land was ceded to Georgia 1821 by Creek Indians and was settled 1833; by 1837, it was founded as the town at the end of the Western and Atlantic Railroad line and named Terminus; served as a Confederate supply depot and communications center during the Civil War; on Sept. 2, 1864, it fell to Gen. Sherman who devastated the city by fire on November 15. The city was rapidly rebuilt into an important industrial and commercial center; it was made temporary state capital 1868 and, by popular vote, permanent capital 1877. In the 20th century, Atlanta grew to become one of the major US cities; it was one of the first southern cities to desegregate its schools successfully; Maynard Jackson was installed as Atlanta's first black mayor in 1974. It is the site of capitol building (1899), city hall (1929), Cyclorama Building, High Museum of Art, Oakland Cemetery, Fort Walker, Atlanta Campaign National Historic Site, Kennesaw Mt National Battlefield Park, grave of Martin Luther King, Jr., many government, military, and business institutions, Atlanta Stadium (1966) hosting the professional football team, Atlanta Falcons, and baseball team, Atlanta Braves. Among its educational institutions are Emory University (1836), Georgia Institute of Technology (1885), Atlanta University (1865), Morehouse College (1867), and Georgia State University (1913). Industries: textiles, furniture, chemicals, glass, paper, lumber, iron and steel, leather, electronics, aluminum, candy, farm equipment, flour, automobile and aircraft assembly, printing, publishing, food processing. Inc. 1843 as Marthasville; renamed Atlanta 1845; reinc. 1847. Pop. (1980) 425,022.

Atlantic Charter (Aug.14, 1941), agreement between Winston Churchill and Franklin D. Roosevelt outlining the common aims of their governments in international affairs. They renounced territorial aggrandizement and called for self-determination for all people in selecting their governments. Among other points, they called for freedom of the seas, the abandonment of force in foreign policy, and greater international cooperation in improving worldwide economic and social conditions to free all people from fear and want.

Atlantic City, city in SE New Jersey, 60mi (97km) SE of Philadelphia, on Absecon Island; built on a 10mi (16km) sandbar in Atlantic Ocean; developed after railroad was constructed in 1854; site of 4-mi (6-km) boardwalk (1896); modern convention and tourist center. In 1976 casino gambling was legalized and Atlantic City experienced an increase in tourism after the first casinos opened in 1978. Settled 1790 as a fishing village; inc. 1854. Pop. (1980) 40,199.

Atlantic Ocean, second largest of the world's oceans, separates North and South America from Europe and Africa. Divided into the N Atlantic and S Atlantic at about 5°N latitude, it has two separate current systems; N system circulates clockwise; S counterclockwise. Area: 32,000,000sq mi (82,880,000sq km). Width: approx. 2,500mi (4,025km). Length: approx. 8,000mi (12,880km). Greatest known depth: Milwaukee Deep, in the Puerto Rican trench, 30,246ft (9,225m).

Atlantis, legendary island in the Atlantic Ocean, W of the Rock of Gibraltar. Plato wrote about Atlantis in his dialogues (the "Timaeus" and the "Critias") and described their highly developed society before the island was destroyed by an earthquake and overtaken by the sea. The name Atlantis is synonymous with Utopia, and groups trying to discover the island's site are continually active.

Atlas, in Greek mythology, the son of the Titan Iapetus and the nymph Clymene and brother of Prometheus. According to Homer, he was a marine being who supported the pillars that divided heaven and earth. According to Hesiod, he was one who, having warred against Zeus, was condemned to hold up the heavens.

Atlas, collection of maps or charts, usually found in book form, and often containing pictures, indexes of placenames, and facts of interest. It may be world or regional, and contain such information as climate, boundaries, geology, history, and population. The term comes from the custom of placing a picture of the Greek god Atlas holding up the earth in the frontispiece of books of maps.

Atlas Mountains, mountain system in NW Africa; extends 1,500mi (2,415km) from the coast of SW Morocco to the coast of N Tunisia; consisting of several

Mount Athos, Greece: monastery

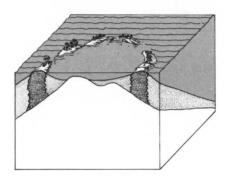

Atoll

Attica, Greece

ranges, the highest peak, Toubkal, 13,671ft (4,170m), is found in the Grand Atlas range in W Morocco; rich in minerals, the mountains have fertile, well-watered farmland on the N and drier, grass-covered slopes on the S.

Atmosphere, the whole envelope of air, composed of a variety of gases, surrounding the earth or other celestial body and held to it by gravitational attraction. The physics, chemistry, and dynamics of atmospheric processes are studied in the attempt to understand, predict, and control events affecting weather, climates, and pollution. *Composition.* A mixture of the heavier gases in the atmosphere lies near the earth. About 95% of the atmosphere by mass is below the 15-mi (25-km) altitude. Dry air is composed largely of nitrogen (78.1%), oxygen (20.9%), and about 0.9% of inert argon gas, with varying amounts of water vapor added near the earth. The remaining 0.1% of the atmosphere consists of traces of carbon monoxide and dioxide, other pollutants like sulfur and nitric dioxides, and more inert gases like krypton, xenon, and the fluorocarbons. Further from the earth are lighter gases like atomic oxygen, helium, and hydrogen. *Atmospheric shells.* The atmosphere can be conceived as a series of concentric shells in which the earth is nested. In the shell nearest the earth, the troposphere, ranging up 5 to 7mi (8 to 11km) above the surface, the mixture of the air's gases and dust with water vapor creates all the clouds, precipitation, and weather. The colder stratosphere, the next shell, from 5 to 25mi (8 to 40km), contains the jet streams, clear conditions, and ozone concentrated in its upper regions. Above, to a height of 50mi (80km), is the mesosphere, in which many chemical reactions occur, powered by sunlight. The temperature climbs steadily in the thermosphere above, which gives way to the exosphere at about 185mi (300km), from which helium and hydrogen may dart off into space. The ionosphere, the shell of ions or charged particles affected by the magnetic field, ranges from about 30mi (48km) out into the Van Allen belts.

Atmospheric Pressure, the pressure exerted by the atmosphere because of its gravitational attraction to the earth or other body, measured by barometers and usually expressed in units of inches (or millimeters) of mercury. Standard atmospheric pressure at sea level is 29.92 inches (760 millimeters) of mercury, and the column of air above each square inch of earth's surface weighs about 14.7 pounds (6.7kg). With an atmosphere composed largely of carbon dioxide, the surface atmospheric pressure of Venus is 95 times that of the earth.

Atoll, ring of coral rising from the ocean floor in warm areas of strong sunlight. Most atolls are built on the top of submarine volcanoes that have been eroded. The coral that is above sea level is usually surrounded on the ocean side by a reef of submerged coral, which on larger atolls may have other tiny islands in among the underwater formations.

Atom, smallest particle of matter that can take part in a chemical reaction, every element having its own characteristic atoms. The atom, once thought indivisible, consists of a tiny central positively charged nucleus, identified by Ernest Rutherford (1911), around which orbit electrons. The number of electrons in an atom (atomic number) and their configuration determines its chemical properties. The nucleus contains tightly packed protons and neutrons, the number of protons equaling the electron number in a neutral atom. Removal of an atomic electron produces a charged ion. The orbits of the electrons were first described in the (Niels) Bohr atom (1913), using quantum mechanics. An electron of a particular energy can only

occupy one of a number of permitted orbits, termed energy levels. Given sufficient energy an electron can jump from one energy level to a higher one. It can also return to a lower level, emitting radiant energy in the form of a photon of a specific frequency. Wave mechanics has since modified the concept of fixed orbits. *See also* Atomic Number; Atomic Weight; Nucleus, Cell; Subatomic Particles.

Atomic Battery, or **nuclear battery,** device that converts energy from radioactive particles into electrical current. Common sources include tritium (H_3) and Krypton-85, both emitters of beta particles.

Atomic Bomb. *See* Nuclear Weapon.

Atomic Clock, the most accurate device for measuring time, based on atomic or molecular events of known frequency (the reciprocal of time). In the cesium clock, used to define the second, the frequency used is that of the radiation (9,192,631,770 hertz) absorbed when cesium-133 atoms change between two different energy states in a magnetic field. The accuracy is better than one part in 10^{13}. In the ammonia clock the frequency of vibration (23,870 Hz) of the nitrogen atom is used.

Atomic Energy. *See* Nuclear Energy.

Atomic Mass Number, or nucleon number, the total number of protons and neutrons (nucleons) in the nucleus of a particular atom. The isotopes of an element have different mass numbers although their atomic numbers are identical.

Atomic Mass Unit (AMU), unit of mass, used to express atomic weights, defined since 1961 as 1/12th the mass of the most abundant isotope of carbon, carbon-12 (6 electrons, 12 protons + neutrons). It is equal to 1.6605×10^{-27} kg.

Atomic Number, number of protons in the nucleus of a neutral atom of an element or number of electrons moving around that nucleus. It determines the chemical properties of an element and its position in the periodic table. Isotopes of an element all have the same atomic number.

Atomic Radius, radius of an atom when it can be considered as if it were a small hard sphere. Thus, effective radii of atoms can be measured from experiments on probabilities of atomic collisions. In fact, most of the volume occupied by an atom is "empty space," and the electron distribution can be described only by a probability. No absolute geometric meaning can be given to the atomic radius; its value depends on the circumstances in which it is used. For example, radii can be ascribed to atoms in different types of chemical bond.

Atomic Spectrum, spectrum of sharp lines characteristic of the element involved and produced by the radiation emitted when electrons jump between energy levels of the atom. *See also* Atom.

Atomic Weight, the average mass of the atoms in a particular specimen of an element (usually taken to be the natural isotope composition), given in atomic mass units. It is the ratio of the mass of the atom in question to 1/12th the mass of the carbon-12 atom.

Atonality, in music, the practice of organizing a composition in terms of timbre and rhythm and the 12 tones of the chromatic scale without reference to a tonal center, as in Arnold Schoenberg's *Pierrot Lunaire* (1912).

Atonement, in religion, process by which a sinner moves toward union with God, through prayer, sacrifice, and the cleansing of one's deeds and thoughts. It is a theme that is apparent in some form in most religions, modern and ancient.

Atonement, Day of. *See* Yom Kippur.

ATP. *See* Adenosine Triphosphate.

Atrium, interior court of a Roman house, partially roofed, onto which the dwelling rooms opened. The term is also applied to the entrance court of early Christian churches.

Atrophy, in medicine, refers to the shrinking of a cell, tissue, or organ. It may be associated with a number of pathological conditions, most commonly muscular diseases.

Atropine, poisonous alkaloid (formula $C_{17}H_{23}O_3N$) obtained from certain solanaceous plants, such as *Atropa belladona* (deadly nightshade). It is used medically as an anti-spasmodic, and for dilating the pupil of the eye.

Attenborough, Richard (1923–), British actor, director, and producer. He began his professional acting career while attending the Royal Academy of Dramatic Arts. After wartime service in the RAF he acted in films such as *Brighton Rock* (1947) and *The Gift Horse* (1952). He produced and appeared in *Seance on a Wet Afternoon* (British Academy Award for best actor, 1964). He directed *Oh, What a Lovely War* (1969) and *Young Winston* (1972) and produced and directed *Gandhi* (1983), which won 8 Academy Awards.

Attica (Attiki), department in central Greece, bounded by the Aegean Sea (E), Saronic Gulf (S), Gulf of Cornith (W), Euboea Island and Voiotia dept. (N); capital city is Athens. According to legend, Cecrops, a mythical king, divided the region into 12 independent colonies, united by Theseus under administrative control of Athens (700 BC); Cleisthenes, a politician of Athens, reformed the aristocratic rule, classifying people into 10 tribes based on topographical divisions. Industries: lead mining, marble quarrying, cattle, shipping, tourism. Area: 1,305sq mi (3,375sq km). Pop. 2,060,000. *See also* Athens.

Attila (c. 406–53), known as the Scourge of God, king of the Huns (434–53), coruler with his elder brother Bleda until he murdered him in 445. Theodosius II, Roman emperor of the East, was compelled to pay him tribute. Nevertheless, Attila invaded the Balkan peninsula (441–43), destroying cities and demanding and receiving a threefold increase in his tribute. After Emperor Valentinian III of the West refused to pay tribute Attila invaded Gaul (451). Allied with the Ostrogoths and Vandals, he fought a great battle at Châlons-sur-Marne against the Roman general Aëtius who was supported by the Visigoths. Attila suffered heavy losses but was still able to invade Italy the next year. He was met at the gates of Rome by Pope Leo I whose majestic presence is said to have prevented the city's destruction. With his army suffering from disease and lack of provisions, he recrossed the Alps and died before he could once again invade Italy.

Attis, Greek shepherd who was loved by Cybele, goddess of the earth, fertility, and wild nature. In a jealous rage Cybele caused Attis to lose his senses. In this deranged state Attis castrated himself and died. Cybele transformed him into a pine tree, which became sacred to her. She changed his blood into violets.

Attitude, Spacecraft, orientation with respect to a given set of axes. Three variables specify attitude: *pitch,* the angle with the horizontal made by the long axis of the spacecraft; *yaw,* the angle through which the bow turns left or right of the "forward" direction; and *roll,* the angle of rotation about the long axis.

Attitudes, sets of beliefs, values, and feelings in an individual that are consistent across different situations and circumstances. Studies of attitudes in social psychology have focused primarily on the process of attitude change, especially under circumstances where the individual is confronted with persuasion. The effectiveness of a persuasive attempt depends on many factors, including the believability of the source (persuader), the nature of the persuasive message (eg, whether strong arguments come first or last), and personality characteristics of the receiver or target of the persuasive attempt (eg, older subjects are usually less gullible). Of special concern to both sociologists and psychologists are prejudice and discrimination, cases in which increased knowledge of attitude formation and change might benefit society.

Attlee, Clement (Richard), 1st Earl (1883–1967), English politician, prime minister (1945–51). His experience as a social worker in London's East End convinced him to dedicate his life to social improvement through politics. He joined the Fabian Society (1907) and the Labour party (1908). First elected to Parliament in 1922, he served the first (1924) Labour government and the second (1929–31) becoming postmaster general. In 1935 he became leader of the Labour party. He served in Winston Churchill's wartime coalition government (1940–45) and became prime minister himself with the 1945 Labour victory. Under his leadership, the Bank of England, all utilities, the railroads, and the coal and iron and steel industries were nationalized. The National Health Service and other social reforms were instituted. India, Pakistan, Burma, Ceylon, and Palestine were granted their independence. The Labour party was narrowly defeated in 1951. Attlee continued as head of the party in opposition until his retirement in 1955.

Attorney General of the United States, chief US law officer. He heads the US department of justice and is a cabinet member. The attorney general represents the country in legal matters and gives advice and opinions to the president and to the heads of the executive departments when requested. The office was established in 1789. *See also* Justice, Department of.

Attucks, Crispus (1723?–70), American patriotic figure, supposedly a fugitive slave who had worked 20 years as a merchant seaman. Unarmed seamen and Boston dockworkers were taunting British troops guarding customs officers when the troops opened fire, killing Attucks and four others in the "Boston Massacre."

Atum, ancient Egyptian deity pictured as a human being and identified with the sun god Re. Atum was the god of creation according to the priests of Heliopolis, an important religious center of Egypt.

Atwood, Margaret (Eleanor) (1939–), Canadian author and critic. Her first volume of poetry, *Double Persephone,* was published in 1961, the year she graduated from the University of Toronto. Since then she has won international acclaim for her considerable output of poetry, short stories, children's books, and literary criticism, as well as novels, including *Bodily Harm* (1982) and *The Handmaid's Tale* (1986). Her major themes include feminism, politics, and human rights. She is also noted for her commitment to bringing wider attention to the work of Canadian authors.

Auckland, largest city in New Zealand, on an isthmus of NW North Island; chief port and capital of Auckland prov.; served as capital of New Zealand 1841–1865 and now is chief base of New Zealand's navy; site of the War Memorial Museum, University of Auckland (1882), many extinct volcanoes. Industries: shipyards, canneries, chemicals. Pop. 797,406.

Auden, W(ystan) H(ugh) (1907–73), US author, b. England. His works encompass social and political commentary. He went to the United States in 1939 and from 1956–61 taught poetry at Oxford University. His works, showing great technical skill, include *The Age of Anxiety* (1947; Pulitzer Prize, 1948).

Auditory Nerve, the eighth cranial nerve. It transmits sound impulses from the cochlea of the inner ear to the auditory cortex of the brain. It also functions in the maintenance of balance. *See also* Cranial Nerves.

Audubon, John James (1785–1851), US ornithologist and artist, b. Les Cayes, Santo Domingo (now Haiti). He painted all of the species of birds in the United States known in the early 19th century. He met with little success in the United States, supporting himself by sidewalk portraiture. In 1826 he sent his work to Europe, where it was published as *The Birds of America* in four volumes (1827–38). After publication Audubon became a great success and proceeded to publish *Ornithological Biography* (5 vols., 1831–39) and *A Synopsis of the Birds of North America* (1839). Today Audubon's works remain both popular and respected for their beauty and accuracy.

Augean Stables, in Greek legend, a series of filthy stalls belonging to King Augeas of Elis. As one of his 12 labors Hercules had to clean them in one day. He diverted the waters of the Alpheus and Peneus rivers through the stables, washing away all the filth. The expression is a synonym for a dirty or untidy place.

Augsburg, city in S West Germany, on the Lech River; a free imperial city in 1276; became a prosperous banking and commercial center in 15th and 16th centuries; Augsburg Confessions (1530), a basic profession of Lutheran beliefs, were presented to Imperial Diet here; noted for cathedral started in 994, a 17th-century town hall, and 16th-century Fuggerie (residence for poor). Industries: textiles, clothing, motor vehicles. Founded *c.* 15 BC by Romans. Pop. 247,700.

Augsburg, Peace of, agreement reached by the Diet of the Holy Roman Empire meeting in Augsburg, Germany, on Sept. 25, 1555, that ended the conflict between Roman Catholics and Lutherans within the empire. It was the first permanent legal recognition of Lutheranism in Germany. Each prince was to decide whether Roman Catholicism or Lutheranism was to be practiced in his lands. Dissenters were allowed to sell their lands and move. Free cities and imperial cities were open to both Catholics and Lutherans. The rights of other Protestant sects, including Calvinists, were not considered.

Augsburg Confessions, summation of the Lutheran faith, formulated in 1530. Martin Luther and Philipp Melanchthon collaborated on its development. First presented to the Holy Roman Emperor Charles V, it was given to theologians of the Roman Catholic church for consideration; they renounced it. A bond among Lutheran churches, it became a model for later statements of religious beliefs. Its moderate language and temperate tone showed loyalty to Christian traditions.

August, eighth month of the year. Named after the Roman Emperor Augustus, it has 31 days. The birthstone is the sardonyx or carnelian.

Augusta, city at head of navigation of Savannah River in E Georgia; seat of Richmond co; resort area, scene of annual Masters golf tournament; trade center; former capital of Georgia (1785–95). Industries: brick and clay products, textiles, chemicals, wood and paper products. Settled 1735; inc. 1798. Pop. 47,532.

Augusta, capital city in S central Maine, on Kennebec River, 35mi (56km) from the Atlantic Ocean; site of Plymouth Colony trading post, Fort Western (1628; a museum since 1754); capitol was designed by Charles Bulfinch; site of James G. Blaine's 19th-century home, now governor's mansion. A dam built across the Kennebec River 1837 converted Augusta from a shipping center to a manufacturing city. Industries: tourism, lumber, shoes, textiles, paper products. Inc. 1797; chartered as city 1849. Pop. (1980) 21,819.

Augustine, Saint (354–430), Christian theologian and philosopher. Augustine's *Confessions* gives us an intimate psychological self-portrait of a spirit in search of ultimate purpose. This he believed he found in his conversion to Christianity (386), which took place only after worldly and philosophical confusion. As bishop of Hippo (North Africa) from 396–430, he defended Roman Catholic orthodoxy against the Manichaeans, the Donatists and the Pelagians. According to the doctrine of his *Enchiridion* (421), he tended to emphasize the corruption of human will, and the freedom of the divine gift of grace. The *City of God* (426), perhaps his most enduring work, was a model of Christian apologetic literature. Of the Four Fathers of the Latin Church, which also included Ambrose, Jerome and Gregory, Augustine is considered the greatest.

Augustus, Gaius Julius Caesar Octavianus (Octavian) (63 BC–AD 14), first Roman emperor (27 BC–AD 14). The adopted son of Julius Caesar, he went to Rome after Caesar's assassination in 44 BC to avenge his death. He secured the consulship and made an alliance with Anthony and Lepidus, the Second Triumvirate, which defeated his enemies. At Philippi (42 BC) Anthony and he defeated Brutus and Cassius. With Agrippa's aid, he beat Pompeius (36 BC) on the Mediterranean. At the battle of Actium (30 BC) Agrippa's victory over Anthony consolidated power of Octavian at Rome. In 29 BC the Senate voted him emperor. The title "Augustus" was conferred upon him in 27 BC, but he called himself "the first citizen." As emperor, he sought no more conquests and fostered colonization. He reorganized the empire, made taxation more equitable; rebuilt roads, temples, and the Forum; took general censuses; set up good fire, police, and military protection; and encouraged art, literature, and education. His only defeat occurred when his legions under Varus were massacred by the German troops of Arminius (AD 9).

His reign is called the Augustan Age, the time of Vergil, Ovid, Livy, Horace, Maecenas. Roman civilization developed under his world peace *(Pax Romana).* Tiberius, his stepson, succeeded him.

Auk, squat-bodied seabird of colder Northern Hemisphere coastlines. The flightless great auk *(Pinguinus impennis),* called the Atlantic penguin, became extinct in the 19th century; height: 30in (76cm). The razor-billed auk is typical of living species. Family Alcidae. *See also* Razor-billed Auk.

Aurangzeb (1618–1707), last of the great Mogul emperors of India (1658–1707). In 1658 he had his father, Shah Jahan, imprisoned and crowned himself emperor. In the first part of his reign, he strengthened his empire; under him the empire reached its apex. Toward the end of his reign, however, he alienated many of his subject peoples, especially the Hindus and the Deccan.

Aurelian (Lucius Domitius Aurelianus) (212?–75), Roman emperor (270–75). His victories against the Germanic invaders of Italy, his reconquest of Palmyra, and his recovery of Gaul and Britain earned him the title of "Restorer of the World." In Rome he established the Unconquered Sun God as the protective deity of the empire.

Auricle, also known as atrium, each of the upper two chambers of the four-chambered heart. They are comparatively thin-walled since they only pump blood down into the muscular ventricles of the heart. *See also* Heart.

Auriga, or **the Charioteer,** northern constellation situated northeast of Taurus. Auriga contains several open clusters, including M36 (NGC 1960). Brightest star Alpha Aurigae (Capella).

Aurochs, or **Urus,** extinct wild ox, the longhaired ancestor of modern domesticated cattle. Once found throughout forests of Africa, Europe and SW Asia, it became extinct in 1627. Back-breeding experiments in Germany have produced an animal resembling ancient species. Family Bovidae; species *Bos primigenius.*

Aurora, suburban city in NE central Colorado, 5mi (8km) E of Denver in Adams and Arapahoe cos. Inc. 1903. Pop. (1980) 158,588.

Aurora, city in NE Illinois, 37mi (60km) W of Chicago; site of Aurora College (1893). Industries: chemicals, glass, transportation equipment. Inc. 1857. Pop. (1980) 81,293.

Aurora, a sporadic radiant display appearing in shifting, colored rays, streamers, or draperies in the night sky. Most frequent in zones around the earth's poles and called aurora borealis to the north and aurora australis to the south, auroras are caused by interactions of charged particles from the sun with the earth's magnetic field.

Austen, Jane (1775–1817), English novelist. A clergyman's daughter, she led an uneventful life but wrote six novels of great craftsmanship, insight, and wit: *Sense and Sensibility* (1811), *Pride and Prejudice* (1813), *Mansfield Park* (1814), *Emma* (1816), *Persuasion* (1818), and *Northanger Abbey* (1818). *See also* individual novels.

Austin, Stephen (1793–1836), US pioneer, b. Wythe County, Va. On his father's death in 1821, he took up his father's grant in the Spanish territory that was to become Texas. He settled the first English-speaking colony there and was followed by many other successful colonists. Mexico opposed this colonization, and Austin went to Mexico City to argue his case, but was arrested. On his return in 1835, he became a leader in the fight for Texas independence.

Austin, city in S central Texas, 75mi (121km) NE of San Antonio, on both sides of the Colorado River; capital of Texas and seat of Travis co; served as capital of the Republic of Texas 1839, which was temporarily moved to Houston 1842–45 because of insurgent Mexican occupation of San Antonio and Indian invasions; after Texas was admitted to the United States 1845, it

Aurochs

Australia

Austria

served as temporary capital until 1870 when it was made the permanent seat of government. Austin's industrial growth was spurred 1934 with the harnessing of the Colorado River for hydroelectricity and the initiation of flood control projects. It is the site of the capitol building (1885), old land office (1857), governor's mansion (1856), French embassy (1840), and home of author O. Henry; educational institutions include University of Texas (1881); nearby are many recreational facilities and Bergstrom Air Force Base; convention center; commercial and distribution center for diversified farming region. Industries: electronics, glass, furniture, food processing, bricks, tiles, machinery, wood and metal products. Settled 1835 as Waterloo; inc. 1839 and renamed in honor of Stephen F. Austin. Pop. (1980) 345,496.

Australasia, geographical term for the islands of New Zealand, New Guinea, and Australia, in the S Pacific Ocean; sometimes used synonomously with Oceania, including the Malay Archipelago and Polynesia to the NE.

Australia, independent nation in the S Pacific Ocean occupying the continent of Australia. First settled by the British, it has received large influxes of immigrants since WWII. The standard of living is among the highest in the world.
   Land and Economy. The smallest, most arid continent, it is located below the SE Asian archipelago, bisected by the Tropic of Capricorn and bounded on the E by the Pacific Ocean, W by the Indian Ocean, and includes the State of Tasmania. Most of the country is a low plateau with a flat and arid center. Its 12,000-mi (19,320-km) coast contains the Great Barrier Reef, largest coral reef in the world. The SE section is 500,000sq mi (1,295,000sq km) of fertile plain. The low ranges (Great Dividing Range and Australian Alps) mainly parallel the E coast with moderate chains in the W and central sections. Most are rounded foothills with no glaciers and little snow. The highest is Mt Kosciusko, 7,316ft (2,231m). Darling, its longest river, has been dry for as long as 18 months. Rainfall is sufficient on the E coast, the SE and SW; the interior receives less than 10in (26cm) annually. Water supply and conservation are continuous problems. An unpredictable climate results from its latitude and long coastline exposed to the tradewinds. Although agriculture accounts for most of its export income, there has been rapid industrial growth. About 19% of the work force is in manufacturing, 6% in agriculture. Wool and meat are major products. Australia produces 30% of the world's wool supply and is the largest exporter of beef, second of lamb. Over half of its large wheat crop is exported. Mineral exports have been rising, especially since the 1965 discovery of iron ore. Oil and gas were found 1965–68 and uranium 1972–74. By the early 1980s minerals comprised one-third of export revenues.
   People. Until 1788 there were 350,000 aborigines in the country. As European, predominantly British, settlements grew, indigenous peoples declined to 144,-381 in 1976. Now each state is responsible for those aborigines in its region, but they face considerable discrimination. Many Chinese came before the 1901 restriction act, and since WWII, 2,300,000 immigrants, 50% British and many from central European countries, have entered. Two-thirds of the population is in the SE (New South Wales and Victoria), one-third in Sydney and Melbourne. English is the official language. Literacy is 98.5%.
   Government. Fully independent within the British Commonwealth, Australia is governed by a prime minister, the leader of the majority party in the elected House of Representatives, and an elected, bicameral parliament. Its three main parties are Australian Labor party (trade unions), Liberal party (moderates and

business), and Country party (conservative and agriculture).
   History. Early discovery of Australia was delayed by the colossal size of the Pacific Ocean. In 1577, Sir Francis Drake, looking for spices and trade, turned N to Peru. It was not until 1605–06 that Dutch explorer William Jansz sailed close to Queensland; he was probably the first European to see the coast, which he described as desolate, with black savages. In 1642, Abel Janszoon Tasman circumnavigated the continent, reaching Tasmania and New Zealand. Englishman James Cook, sailing around Cape Horn in 1768, was the first European to reach the E coast, and in 1770, finding it favorable for settlement, he took possession for Britain. Many early settlers were convicts; 19th-century policy emancipated them, and immigration was encouraged. Six colonies were created: New South Wales (1823), Tasmania (1825), Western Australia (1838), Southern Australia (1842), Victoria (1851), and Queensland (1859). These were united under the Commonwealth of Australia Act of 1900. The first parliament met in 1901. The Statute of Westminster Adoption Act of 1942 gave Australia complete autonomy. Since then Australia has emerged as a leader in Asian and Pacific affairs. Malcolm Fraser, leader of the Liberal party and prime minister from 1975 to 1983, faced labor unrest, rising unemployment, and inflation that ultimately led to his defeat. His successor, Robert J. Hawke of the Australian Labour Party, although pledging national reconciliation, had to deal with escalating financial problems.

PROFILE

Official name: Commonwealth of Australia
Area: 2,967,909sq mi (7,686,884sq km)
Population: 13,232,600
   Density: 5 per sq mi (2 per sq km)
Chief cities: Canberra (capital); Sydney; Melbourne; Adelaide; Brisbane
Government: Federal republic
Religion: Anglican, 31%; Catholic, 12%; Methodist, 8½%; Presbyterian, 8%
Language: English
Monetary unit: Australian dollar
Gross national product: $32,000,000,000
Per capita income: $2,484
Industries: wool, iron, steel, textiles, electrical and radio equipment, drugs, chemicals, metal products, aircraft, ships, automobiles, meat products, machinery
Agriculture: cattle, sheep, wheat, fruits, sugar
Minerals: uranium, coal, gold, copper, iron, silver, lead, tin, bauxite, petroleum, gas, nickel
Trading partners: United Kingdom, United States, Japan, People's Republic of China

Australian Aborigines (officially: Native Australians), peoples who inhabited Australia prior to European settlement. Decimated by the early European settlers, they numbered about 144,000 in the late 1970s, about 45,000 of whom were of pure descent, and were organized into about 500 tribes. They are traditionally nomadic, living by hunting and gathering in small scattered groups. Their society is patrilineal, and polygamy is widespread, as is both male and female circumcision, the latter playing an important part in initiation ceremonies. Their culture is traditionally rich in carving and painting and their religion includes a remarkable and diverse mythology.

Australian Alps, mountain range in Victoria and New South Wales, SE Australia; part of Great Dividing Range, which forms the watershed between the Murray River system and streams flowing into the Tasman Sea; site of numerous resort areas and forest re-

serves; first explored 1839–40. Highest peak is Mt Kosciusko, 7,316ft (2,231m), highest point in Australia.

Australian Antarctic Territory, external territory of Australia in Antarctica, including all territory and islands (except Adélie Land). Claimed 1933. Area: 2,360,000sq mi (6,112,400sq km).

Australian Cattle Dog, herding dog, also called Australian heeler because it herds livestock by nipping their heels. This dog has a V-shaped head and prick ears. The body is covered with a short, harsh coat colored mottled blue with tan or red speckle. Average size: 18–20in (46–51cm) high at shoulder; 33lb (15kg).

Australian Kelpie, herding dog, also called Australian collie. It has a V-shaped head, prick ears, almond-shaped eyes, and brush tail. The short, dense coat can be solid black, red, fawn, liver, smoke blue, black and tan, or red and tan. Average size: 18–20in (46–51cm) high at shoulder; 30lb (13.5kg).

Australoid Race, one of the major human racial groupings, often subdivided into pygmy (Negrito) and full-sized peoples. Full-sized Australoids have heavy skin pigmentation; large jaws and prominent brow ridges; wavy to curly hair; and hair distribution and stature similar to Caucasoids. The term usually covers the Australian and Tasmasian aborigines and associated populations. See also Negrito Subrace.

Australopithecus, or "southern ape," name given to race of extinct near-men whose fossilized bones, dating back to about 3,000,000 years ago, have been found in South Africa. The Australopithecines had teeth more human than ape-like, and like man could move and stand fully erect without the help of their arms. They are therefore classified as hominids (men), and are possibly direct ancestors of modern man. See also Pithecanthropus.

Austrasia, Germanic N and E part of the Frankish kingdom during the Merovingian period of French history. Divided into the semi-independent regions of Austrasia, Neustria, and Burgundy in the 6th and 7th centuries, the lands were reunited under the Austrasian Pepin family just in time to ward off the Arab crossing of the Pyrenees. From this new foundation sprang the Carolingian empire of Charlemagne.

Austria, Republic of, nation in central Europe. It was once the center of an extensive empire under the royal house of Hapsburgs. As its capital, Vienna was long one of the world's great cities.
   Land and Economy. About 70% of Austria lies in the E Alps. The mountains, composed primarily of crystalline rock and limestone, comprise three longitudinal ranges: the Northern Limestone Alps, the Central Alps, and the Southern Limestone Alps. The highest peak is the Grossglockner, 12,461ft (3,801m). The rivers Inn, Salzach, and Enns flow N into the Danube. The Drava River drains the S mountains. Austria's spectacular mountain scenery attracts tourists and sports enthusiasts from all over the world. The Austrian economy is that of a prosperous modern industrial nation. Large industrial concentrations have developed around the cities of Vienna, Linz, and Graz. Austria is landlocked; its chief waterway is the Danube, and the most fertile lands lie in the Danubian Plain. The nation's largest industrial firms, commercial banks, oil and heavy industry concerns were nationalized by the government in 1946.
   People. The Austrians are descended from a variety of peoples, including Germans, Slavs, and Mediterraneans. The people are 98% German-speaking; the various dialects are related to the Bavarian group of

dialects. Almost 90% of the people are Roman Catholic, while 6% are Protestant. The majority lives in the city and works in industry. One-fifth of the entire population lives in Vienna.

Government. The constitution separates the federal government into executive, legislative, and judiciary branches. Power is wielded chiefly by the legislature—the Federal Assembly; this body consists of the Federal Council (Bundesrat) and the National Council (Nationalrat). The head of government is the chancellor. He and his ministry are responsible to the National Council. Austria's major political parties are the Socialist party, whose leader Bruno Kreisky became chancellor in 1970, and the more conservative People's party.

History. The founding of Austria—or *Österreich,* the "eastern realm"—is generally traced to Otto I, 10th-century emperor of the Holy Roman Empire. Vienna became the capital in 1140. After 1278, Austria became identified with the powerful House of Hapsburg. The Austrian branch of the Hapsburgs united with the crowns of Hungary and Bohemia, establishing what later became the Austrian Empire. In 1867 the dual monarchy of Austria-Hungary was created; it lasted until WWI. In 1918 the Hapsburgs were overthrown and Austria was est. as a republic. Germany seized Austria in 1938, uniting the two countries. Defeated in WWII, Austria was partitioned into four zones by the Allies. Austria became a member of the United Nations in 1955, the year the Allies ended their occupation. In the same year the Federal Assembly approved a measure declaring Austria to be "permanently neutral," a policy the country continues to follow.

PROFILE

Official name: Republic of Austria
Area: 32,375sq mi (83,851sq km)
Population: 7,500,000
Density: 232per sq mi (89per sq km)
Chief cities: Vienna (capital), 1,600,000; Graz, 250,000; Linz, 200,000; Salzburg, 130,000
Government: Federal republic
Religion (major group): Roman Catholic
Language (official): German
Monetary unit: Schilling
Gross national product: $58,000,000,000
Per capita income $6,360
Industries (major products): chemical products, heavy machinery, vehicles, textiles, electrical equipment, steel
Agriculture (major products): wheat, rye, potatoes, dairy products
Minerals (major): lignite, graphite, iron, copper, magnesite, natural gas
Trading partners (major): West Germany, Italy, Switzerland

Austrian Empire, all lands controlled by the Hapsburg dynasty, beginning in 1804, when Holy Roman Emperor Francis II, reacting to Napoleon I's assumption of the title of emperor, proclaimed himself Francis I, emperor of Austria. Under Francis I and Metternich, the Austrian empire successfully thwarted change at home and encouraged peace abroad. Nationalist movements and calls for constitutional government were ignored until the 1848 revolution in Paris touched off similar revolts throughout the empire—in Vienna, Bohemia, Hungary, and the Italian provinces. They were put down and a constitution enacted (but never put into effect).

Under Prince Felix Schwarzenberg and Emperor Francis Joseph, authoritarian rule continued until Austria's humiliating war with Prussia in 1866. Loss of land and prestige forced the emperor to negotiate with the Hungarian nationalist leaders, and the compromise or *Ausgleich* of 1867 was worked out. Thereafter the term "empire of Austria" was applied only to the non-Hungarian Hapsburg territories, and the area as a whole was called the Austro-Hungarian or Dual Monarchy. *See also* Austro-Hungary; Austro-Prussian War.

Austrian Succession, War of the (1740–48), name for what was actually several related wars: the war for the Austrian succession itself, in which France supported Spain's claim to part of the Hapsburg domains; the first and second Silesian Wars, in which Frederick II of Prussia took Silesia from Austria; and the war between France and Britain over colonial possessions (known as King George's War). *See also* King George's War.

Austro-Hungary (1867–1918), reorganization of the Austrian Empire as the dual monarchy of the Empire of Austria and the Kingdom of Hungary. After its defeat in the Austro-Prussian War (1866), Austria was compelled to grant greater autonomy to Hungary. The *Ausgleich,* or compromise, of 1867 created the dual monarchy. The Emperor of Austria and the King of Hungary would be the same person, but each nation would have its own parliament and premier and control its internal affairs. Only foreign affairs would be controlled by a central government. The *Ausgleich* did not take into consideration the nationalistic desires of Slavic, Italian, and other minorities, nor did it please Hungarians who wanted complete autonomy or Austrians who would have preferred a realignment with other German states. The death of the first Emperor-King, Francis Joseph, in 1916 and serious setbacks in the war led to the inevitable collapse of the dual monarchy. Czechoslovakia and Hungary declared their independence in 1918, Emperor Charles abdicated, and Austria was declared a republic.

Austronesian Languages, or Malayo-Polynesian languages, include Malay, Indonesian, Tagalog, Malagasy, and numerous other languages spoken in Indonesia, the Philippines, New Guinea, and the islands of the Pacific Ocean. There are four branches: Indonesian, Melanesian (which includes Fijian), Micronesian (which includes Chamorro, spoken on Guam), and the Polynesian languages, which include Maori, Tongan, Tahitian, and Samoan. There are about 175 million speakers in all.

Authoritarianism, political philosophy that concentrates power in the hands of a person or small group not responsible to the people. Authoritarian systems deify the state and are based on antidemocratic principles. Classic examples are Germany under Hitler, Italy under Mussolini, and Spain under Franco.

Autism, Infantile, disorder of young children characterized by failure to relate to others, failure to use language normally, and ritualistic and repetitive patterns of behavior such as excessive rocking or spinning. The autistic child seems to withdraw into a private world. The causes of autism are not known, but some experts believe such children have a disorder that affects their ability to understand language and to form concepts.

Autoimmune Disease, any one of a group of disorders caused by antibodies produced specifically to direct attacks against the body's own tissues. One such disease in which autoimmunity is believed involved is systemic lupus erythematosus (SLE), an inflammation of the connective tissue occuring most often in young women. Another, acquired immune deficiency syndrome (AIDS), causes infections and rare types of cancer. Discovered in the 1980s, AIDS affects primarily male homosexuals and users of intravenous drugs. Although medical advances have been made, there is no known cure, and the disease is fatal. The occasional presence of so-called auto-antibodies in an individual does not necessarily indicate autoimmune disease.

Autolycus, in Greek mythology, son of the Greek god Hermes and mortal Chione. He received from his father the gift of rendering what he touched invisible. In this way he was able to commit numerous thefts until Sisyphus, whose oxen he had stolen, caught him.

Automobile. The first automobile was built by the Frenchman N.J. Cugnot in 1769. Cugnot's vehicle was steam-powered, designed to haul artillery, and achieved about 2mph (3.2kph). In 1862, J.J.E. Lenoir built the first gas-fueled internal combustion two-stroke engine. In 1876, German inventor N.A. Otto built the first four-stroke engine, the prototype of modern automobile engines. By 1885 Karl Benz and Gottlieb Daimler had founded an automobile industry in Germany. Seven years later, the Duryea brothers, J. Franklin and Charles, created the first American gasoline-powered auto; it achieved 10mph (16kph). By 1910 there were some 80 manufacturers in North America, but not until 1913, when Henry Ford introduced mass-production techniques, was production commercially feasible for the mass market.

Autonomic Nervous System, portion of the nervous system that is entirely efferent in action and that experiences widespread effects during emotional episodes. It includes both central and peripheral nervous system elements, and its actions affect the glands and organs of the body. It is subdivided into the *sympathetic nervous system,* which predominates during periods of strong emotion (eg, anger or fright), and the *parasympathetic nervous system,* which predominates during periods of relative emotional calm.

Autumnal Equinox, equinox occurring when the sun crosses the celestial equator, moving toward the southern hemisphere, on about September 23. The crossing point on the equator is the First Point of Libra, now actually situated in the constellation Virgo, which is diametrically opposite the First Point of Aries.

Auvergne, region and former prov. of S France, now divided into depts of Puy-de-Dôme and Cantal. In Roman times it was conquered by Julius Caesar after the fall of the Gallic leader Vercingetorix. It has a scenic chain of inactive volcanoes running N to S, and many examples of Romanesque architecture.

Auxin, plant hormone produced in growing tips of roots and stems. Auxins accelerate plant growth by stimulating cell enlargement and interacting with other hormones. Actions include cell elongation in response to geotropism and phototropism; cambial growth; fruit drop and leaf fall; and plant part dominance. Types include natural indoleacetic acid and synthetic auxins used commercially. *See also* Gibberellin.

Avalanche, tumbling down of a mass of snow. An avalanche is most likely on a hill of slope greater than 35°. The snow that moves may be dry, from recent snowfall; wet, thawed, or wet with rain; or slab, wind-packed, wind-driven snow. Any steep slope with 12in (30cm) or more of new snow may avalanche as a result of weather change or slope disturbance due to vibration.

Avars, Mongolian people who settled near the Volga River about 461. While one group remained there, another moved into the Danube River basin in the 6th century, occupying Dacia, what is now modern-day Romania. Their domain extended from the Volga to the Baltic Sea, and they exacted huge tributes from the Byzantine Empire during this time. The Avars were finally crushed by Charlemagne in 795.

Avatar, a "descent" or incarnation of God. The original idea was that from time to time God manifests himself in order to restore virtue. In Hindu tradition, Vishnu had ten important avatars. Avatars appear also in Buddhist and Jain traditions.

Average, in statistics, the one score that most typifies an entire set of scores. It may be the arithmetic mean of the scores (the sum of the scores divided by their number), the mode (the one score that occurs most often), or the median (the score that divides the set of scores into upper and lower halves). Most often the "average" is the arithmetic mean.

Averrhoës, medieval Latin name for Abu-al-Walid Ibn Rushd (1126–98), foremost Islamic philosopher in Spain. Appointed *qadi,* or judge, in Seville in 1169 and later in Córdoba, he became physician to the Caliph of Marrakesh in 1182. Banished (1184–99) to a small village near Seville for advocating reason over religion, he returned to favor shortly before his death. His major work, *Incoherence of the Incoherence,* defends Neoplatonism and Aristotle.

Aversion Therapy, or aversive conditioning, use of learning or conditioning procedures to develop aversive responses to certain situations or to unwanted habits. The therapy consists of pairing a noxious stimulus such as an electric shock or bad-tasting substance with the performance of the unwanted behavior (eg, overeating or smoking) until an aversion to that behavior is developed.

Aviary, enclosure, usually spacious enough for flight, for the observation and/or breeding of captive birds. It is generally made of wire-mesh. Large flight cages are usually found in zoos, though private homes sometimes have a room or porch set aside. Natural planted surroundings are preferred, although difficult to maintain.

Avicenna, Latin name of Abu Ali Ibn Sina (980–1037), influential Persian philosopher and physician. A royal physician to Persian princes, he attempted to reconcile his own Neo-Platonic mysticism with Islamic doctrine. Among his many works are the *Shifa (Recovery),* a collection of treatises on Aristotelian logic, metaphysics, and natural science, and the *Canon,* a medical compendium.

Avignon, city in SE France, 50mi (81km) NNW of Marseilles at the confluence of the Rhone and Durance rivers. A thriving city under Roman rule, it declined in the 5th and 6th centuries. In 1316 work on the Papal Palace was begun. The massive, fortress-type palace has a great hall with incomparable acoustics, gardens, and beautifully carved tomb of John XXII, with its Romanesque cathedral, Notre Dame des Doms. Papacy held Avignon until 1791 when it was annexed to France. Industries: wine, grain, leather. Pop. 93,024.

Ávila, city in central Spain, on Adaja River, 53mi (85km) WNW of Madrid; capital city of Ávila prov., religious center noted for medieval architecture, including Cathedral of San Salvador, Basilica of San Vicente, and 11th-century wall; birthplace of St Teresa. City was taken from the Moors in 1088 by Alfonso VI of León and Castile. Industries: flour milling, tanning, woolen goods. Area: (prov.) 3,110sq mi (8,055sq km). Pop. (city) 31,000; (prov.) 203,798.

Aviz, dynasty that ruled Portugal from 1385 to 1580. It was founded by John I, who was grand master of

Avignon, France: papal palace

Aye-aye

Azores

Aviz, a knightly order. The dynasty's rule coincided with the most glorious period of Portuguese history. Its last ruler was Henry the cardinal-king.

Avocado, fruit of the avocado tree that is green to dark purple and pear-shaped. Its soft, greenish flesh surrounds a single large seed and has a nutty flavor; weight: to 4lb (2kg). Or, many varieties of a single species (*Persea americana)* of a tall or spreading tree with elliptical leaves native to Mexico, Central America, and W South America, cultivated worldwide.

Avocet, graceful, long-legged, black-patterned, white wading bird. It sweeps its long, upcurved bill through shallow water for food. It performs a mass courtship rite that includes specific head movements. Spotted, olive eggs (4) are laid in a rootlet-lined ground scrape, usually near water. Length: 18in (44cm). Genus *Recurvirostra.*

Avogadro, (Lorenzo Romano) Amedeo, Conte di Quaregna e Ceretto (1776–1856), Italian physicist and chemist. Avogadro's law, stating that equal volumes of gases at the same pressure and temperature contain the same number of molecules, led him to hypothesize that nitrogen and oxygen are diatomic molecules (an idea accepted after his death).

Avogadro's Number, or **Avogadro's Constant,** a constant (symbol L) equal to 6.022×10^{-23} /mol, giving the number of atoms or molecules present in one mole of a substance. It is both the ratio of the universal gas constant to Boltzmann's constant and of Faraday's constant to the charge of the electron. *See also* Mole.

Avon River, either of two rivers in England. Bristol, or Lower Avon, rises in Cotswold Hills, Gloucestershire, and flows S and W through Bristol to enter Severn Estuary at Avonmouth. Length: 75mi (121km). Warwickshire, or Upper Avon, rises in Northamptonshire, and flows SW through Stratford-on-Avon to join Severn River at Tewkesbury. Length: 96mi (155km).

Axiom, accepted assumption used as a basis for deductive reasoning. *See* Axiomatic Method; Postulate.

Axiomatic Method, method of mathematical reasoning based on logical deduction from assumptions (axioms). The method is fundamental to the philosophy of modern mathematics; it was used by the Greeks and formalized early this century by the great German mathematician David Hilbert. In an axiomatic system certain undefined entities (terms) are taken and described by a set of axioms. Other, often unsuspected, relationships (theorems) are then deduced by logical reasoning. Seen in this light, mathematics is a purely abstract system with no connection with the physical world. Applications of mathematics are those in which objects or measurements in the physical world can be identified with the terms of the system. For instance, the points, lines, and angles of Euclidean geometry are connected by postulates, and theorems, such as the Pythagorean theorem, can then be deduced. This geometry describes measurements of position, distance, and angle in space.

Axis, in astronomy, imaginary line about which a planet or star rotates and which passes through the poles of the body. The time taken for one complete rotation gives the length of day on that planet.

Axis Deer, or **chital, hog deer,** small deer native to India, Indochina, and Philippine Islands. They are bright reddish- or yellowish-brown with white spots and have three-tined antlers. Hog deer are stockier than the others. Indian axis deer congregate in herds of 100 or more. Length: to 5ft (1.5m); weight: to 1000lb (450kg). Family Cervidae; genus *Axis. See also* Deer.

Axis Powers, term applied to Germany and Italy after they signed the Rome-Berlin Axis in October 1936 and to Japan, which joined them in the Tripartite Pact (Sept. 27, 1940). Minor Axis powers were Hungary and Romania (1940) and Bulgaria (1941).

Axon, that part of a nerve cell, or neuron, that carries a nerve impulse beyond and away from the cell body, carrying, for example, an impulse for movement to a muscle. There is only one axon per neuron. The axon is often long and usually unbranched. Its central part, or axis cylinder, is surrounded with a fatty, pearly myelin sheath (white matter) in all peripheral nerves and in all central nerves, except those of the brain and spinal cord. Those in peripheral nerves are covered by an additional delicate sheath, a neurillemma, that functions to regenerate damaged nerves. *See also* Neuron.

Ayatollah, an honorific title, meaning "gift of God" or "reflection of God," bestowed upon a Muslim leader who has attained significant distinction and, often, political influence. *See also* Khomeini, Ayatollah.

Aye-Aye, small, primitive, squirrellike primate of Madagascar's bamboo forests. Nocturnal and tree-dwelling, it is dark brown to black and has long, narrow, bony fingers with claws. Its diet includes insects, fruit, and other plant foods. Length: 16in (40.6cm) excluding tail. Species *Daubentonia madagascarensis.*

Ayers Rock, rock in SW Northern Territory, Australia. The largest monolith in the world, it is oval shaped and composed of a composite mass of clastic sedimentary rock; included in Ayers Rock-Mt Olga National Park (est. 1958). Discovered by Sir Henry Ayers (1872). Height: 1,143ft (349m). Length: 4mi (6km). Width: 1.5mi (2.4km).

Aymará, major tribe of South American Indians, occupying the highlands of Bolivia and Peru. By 1500 they were brought into the Inca Empire, subsequently being overcome by the Spanish in 1542. The Aymará instigated a revolt in 1780 in which they unsuccessfully sought to overthrow the Spaniards. Their culture is marked by excellence in textiles, pottery, and metalwork. Today the Aymará population is approximately 600,000.

Ayrshire, common breed of dairy cattle originally from Scotland, introduced widely in Canada and to a lesser extent in the United States, South Africa, and New Zealand. Medium-sized and gracefully built, they are predominantly red, brown, and white, with black markings. Their milk production is below Holsteins' but greater in butterfat content. *See also* Dairy Cattle; Dairy Farming.

Azalea, shrubs and small trees native to temperate regions of Asia and North America. Mostly deciduous, they have leathery leaves, and showy, funnel-shaped flowers of red, pink, magenta, orange, yellow, and white, sometimes variegated. Family Ericaceae; genus *Rhododendron. See also* Rhododendron.

Azerbaijan Soviet Socialist Republic (Azerbajdžanskaja), constituent republic in SE European USSR, in E Transcaucasia; bordered by Dagestan Autonomous Republic (N), Iran and the Aras River (S), Caspian Sea (E), and Armenian Republic (W). Baku is the capital and major industrial center. The republic includes Nakhichevan Autonomous Republic and Nagorno Karabakh Autonomous Oblast; site of Baku University, Azerbaijan Academy of Sciences. Region was known to ancients as Albania, and was dominated by Arabs, Turks, and Mongols; ceded by Persia to Russia (1813, 1828). After Bolshevik Revolution, Azerbaijan joined Armenia and Georgia to form anti-Bolshevik group; proclaimed independence but was taken by Red Army 1920. Soviet rule was est and region became member of Transcaucasian SFSR 1922; became separate constituent republic 1936. Industries: chemicals, building materials, carpets, agriculture, oil and other mineral processing. Area: 33,436sq mi (86,599sq km). Pop. 5,865,000.

Azimuth, angle between the vertical plane on which a celestial body is located and the plane of the meridian. It is measured, in astronomy, eastward from the north point of the observer's horizon and in navigation and surveying westward from the south point. Altitude and azimuth form a coordinate system for giving astronomical position.

Azores, island group of Portugal in N Atlantic Ocean, approx. 900mi (1,450km) W of Portugal; includes three island groups of nine main islands: Sao Miguel and Santa Maria (E); Terceira, Graciosa, Sao Jorge, Faial, and Pico (center); Flores and Corvo (W). Crops: grapes, tea, pineapples, oranges, grains, tobacco, vegetables. Industries: tourism, wine, basket weaving, pottery. First visited by Portuguese 1427–37; settled 1450. Pop. 336,100.

Azov, Sea of (Azovskoye More), N arm of Black Sea, between Ukrainian SSR (N) and Rostov oblast and Krasnodar Krai (E); Crimea is SW; connected with Black Sea by Kerch Strait; narrows in NE to form Gulf of Taganrog. A shallow sea with only slight salinity, it is fed by the Don, Mius, Kalmius, Yeya, and Kuban rivers (E). Fishing center is on its E coast. Area: 14,520sq mi (37,607sq km).

Aztec, Indian civilization that rose to a position of dominance in the central valley of Mexico (*c.*1450). A warlike group with an excellent military organization, the Nahua, or Aztecs, settled near the western shore of Lake Texcoco (*c.*1325). They established a tribute-collecting empire, which included most of modern Mexico and went as far south as Guatemala. Their state was theocratic, placing emphasis on a number of deities; worship included human sacrifice. At the time of the Spanish conquest, Aztec society was in the process of changing from a clan-based system to a highly stratified one based on the exploitation of labor. Using the discontent of the satellite tribes, Hernán Cortés was able to recruit the Indian allies necessary for his defeat of the Aztecs in 1521.

Aztec Architecture was based on that of the cultures they subdued, especially that of the Toltecs. The Aztecs excelled in engineering. Their capital, Tenochtitlán (1325), built on an island, depended on dikes, causeways, and canals. It stood for 200 years.

Azurite, a carbonate mineral, basic copper carbonate. Found in oxidized portion of copper ore veins, often as earthy material with malachite. Hardness 3.5–4; sp gr 3.77–3.89. Crystal brilliant and transparent blue, too soft for good gemstone. Used by ancients as pigment in wall painting.

B

Baal, Phoenician god of fertility. Second in importance to El, he was identified with the Greek god Zeus. Every seven years Baal would fight Mot, god of sterility. If Baal won, there would be seven years of good harvests; if Mot won, there would be seven years of famine.

Baalbek (Ba'labakk), town in E Lebanon, 35mi (56km) NW of Damascus. An early Phoenician settlement, Greeks occupied it 331 BC and renamed it Heliopolis (city of the sun); colonized by the Romans 1st century BC. Noted for Greek and Roman architecture, it is site of Temple of Jupiter built during Nero's reign (AD 54–68) and the Temple of Bacchus (AD 100). Pop. 11,700.

Babbage, Charles (1792–1871), British mathematician, professor at Cambridge. He worked out the first actuarial tables and planned a calculating machine, the forerunner of the modern computer, the construction of which he failed to complete.

Babbitt Metal, any alloy containing a high tin content as well as copper and antimony, specifically an alloy invented by Isaac Babbitt in 1839 as bearing material for steam engines. Some or most of the tin content may be replaced by lead.

Babel, Tower of, according to Genesis 11:1–9, a tall building built in the Babylonian city of Babel to reach heaven. God made the workers' speech incomprehensible to one another, scattered them over the earth, and thus stopped the building of the tower.

Baber (1483–1530), first Mogul ruler of India (1526–30). He became ruler of Fergana, a principality in C Asia in 1495. He struggled with various relatives for Samarkand but lost all holdings and settled in Kabul, from where he gained control of Delhi and Agra, establishing Mogul rule in India.

Babeuf, François Emile (1760–97), called "Gracchus," political activist in the French Revolution. He supported land reform and the Constitution of 1793. He was guillotined by the Directory after an attempted insurrection. His *Manifesto of Equals* (1796), favoring the use of secrecy and force, influenced later socialists.

Baboon, large African monkey with doglike face. They have cheek pouches for carrying food, and males have huge canine teeth up to 2in (5cm) long. The buttocks have callouslike pads surrounded by brilliantly colored naked skin. Walking on all fours, they are day-active, ground dwellers that travel in families and larger troops led by old males, usually in open, rocky country. They eat a wide variety of plant foods, insects, and other small animals. Baboons are aggressive fighters, and several old males can usually fight off a leopard—probably their main enemy. Weight: 30–90lb (14–41kg). Genus *Chaeropithecus* (or *Papio*). *See also* Monkey.

Babylon, an ancient city of Mesopotamia located on the Euphrates River about 55mi (89km) S of present-day Baghdad. Settled since prehistoric times, it was made the capital of Babylonia by Hammurabi in the 18th century BC. The city was completely destroyed in 689 BC by the Assyrians under Sennacherib. After restoration it flourished and became noted for its hanging gardens, one of the seven wonders of the world, and its sensual living. In 275 BC the city was abandoned when the Seleucid dynasty built a new capital at Seleucia.

Babylonia, ancient empire of Mesopotamia. City states, including Ur and Lagash, existed in the area since the 3rd millennium BC. The first empire centered in the city of Babylon was est. by Hammurabi *c.* 1955–13 BC. Toward the end of the 18th century BC the city was sacked by the Hittites, and early in the next century the empire was taken over by the Kassites, an originally nomadic people from Elam. The first Babylonian empire fell to the Assyrians *c.*722–626 BC. Nabopolassar reestablished an independent Babylonia in 625 BC. With the Persians and Medes as allies, he captured the Assyrian capital, Nineveh. In 538 BC the second Babylonian empire fell to the Persians.

Babylonian and Neo-Babylonian Architecture, architectural style that flourished from 3000 to 1250 BC and whose chief buildings were temples. As architectural complexes developed around them, the temples were generally raised on platforms. Cities developed from several temple groups, and the elevation of the central temple formed a ziggurat ("holy mountain"). The city of Babylon included the colored and glazed Ishtar Gate, Nebuchadnezzar's citadel palace, and the famous Hanging Gardens.

Babylonian Captivity (586–538BC), period from the fall of Jerusalem when Jewish leaders were deported to Babylon until the fall of Babylon itself to the Persians and the return of the Jews to Israel.

Babylonian Captivity (1309–77), exile of popes at Avignon. As choice of the French king, Pope Clement V set up court in Avignon, a papal see in French territory, beginning a line of French popes under the influence of the king. The term, first used metaphorically by the Italian scholar Petrarch, is a reference to the 48-year-long Babylonian captivity of the Jews from the period of the fall of Jerusalem (586 BC) to the return of the Jews to Israel (538 BC). The papal court returned to Rome with Pope Gregory XI in 1377, but two French antipopes, Clement VII and Benedict XIII, lived at Avignon during the Great Schism (1378–1417).

Bacchanalia, festivals in ancient Greece in honor of Bacchus. They were marked by much drinking and revelry and were often riotous and licentious. The celebrants, known as Bacchantes, originally were women, but later men were included. They wore fawn skins, ivy on their heads, and carried pine cone–topped staffs.

Bacchus, Roman god of wine, similar to the Greek god Dionysus. He was the son of Jupiter and Semele. Reared by nymphs, shepherds, and satyrs, he learned the secrets of cultivating grapes and making wine. His worship led to riotous revelry and debauchery. *See also* Dionysus.

Bach, Johann Sebastian (1685–1750), German Baroque composer. He held a series of successive court positions as organist and music director and had 20 children, four of whom were also composers. Though only a few of his works were published during his lifetime, Bach brought contrapuntal forms to their highest expression and is unequaled in his ability to interweave melodies with the highly constrictive rules of Baroque harmony and counterpoint. His greatest works include masterpieces for the organ (chorale preludes, fugues, toccatas, etc); the six *Brandenburg Concertos* for chamber orchestra; over 200 cantatas; church music, such as the *Mass in B Minor;* violin sonatas; harpsichord and violin concertos; and numerous works for the harpsichord, such as *The Well-Tempered Clavier,* six *Partitas,* and *The Art of the Fugue,* incomplete at his death.

Bachelor's Button, or cornflower, popular, hardy garden annual grown almost worldwide. It has gray-green foliage and blue, purple, pink, or white flowers. Height: 3ft (0.9m). Family Compositae; species *Centaurea cyanus.*

Bacillus, genus of aerobic, gram-positive, spore-forming bacteria present in the soil. One species, *B. anthracis,* causes anthrax pathogenic to man. *See also* Bacteria.

Backgammon, game of strategy and luck usually involving two players. There is a specially marked board divided into two halves, each containing 12 alternately colored points. Each player receives 15 disks that are arranged in a predetermined order (US version) on the boards. Each move is determined by the throw of dice, and the first player to successfully move all 15 pieces around the board into his "home" or "inner board," and then off the board, wins the game.

Bacon, Francis (1561–1626), English philosopher and statesman. He rose swiftly under James I, being appointed attorney general (1613); lord keeper (1617)—a post his father, Nicholas, had held under Elizabeth I; and finally lord chancellor (1618). But he was forced to resign his offices (1621), charged with venality. Neither official responsibilities nor dismissal impeded his philosophical effort to break the hold of Aristotelian logic in favor of an inductive empiricism. Nature, he affirmed, could be understood only by systematic experimentation, and controlled only by being understood. He entertained the notion of cataloging all useful knowledge in his *Advancement of Learning* (1605) and *Novum Organum* (1620). *The New Atlantis* (1627) discusses his philosophy as practiced in an imaginary nation.

Bacon, Francis (1910–), British painter, b. Dublin. His satiric works emphasize the repulsive, horrible aspects of human life. His works often mimic religious art, as in his variations of the Velázquez portrait of Pope Innocent X and his Black Triptychs—three triptychs on the suicide of his closest friend.

Bacteria, one-celled microscopic organisms of the plant kingdom (class Schizomycetes) that are capable of free living since they possess all the metabolic processes necessary for growth and reproduction. They are present virtually everywhere, and some can live even in the absence of free oxygen. They can be classified according to (1) shape: cocci (round or oval); bacilli (rod shaped); and spirilla (curved rods); (2) need for oxygen; (3) ability to take up Gram's stain (gram negative or positive); and (4) ability to utilize various metabolites. Some bacteria form spores, hardened protective cases, which permit them to survive harsh environments, even for centuries. Bacteria are a major cause of human disease, and many ways to control them have been devised. Common protective measures include sterilization with high heat (121°C), such as pasteurization to kill pathogenic bacteria in milk, and exposure to chemical disinfectants. Some bacteria and yeasts produce compounds that kill other bacteria, and these have been isolated and used as antibiotics, such as penicillin. The body can produce antibodies to some bacteria to kill them. Bacteria are useful in the production of cheese, alcoholic beverages, and drugs. Through the use of recombinant DNA techniques developed in the 1970s, they can produce such substances as interferon, beta-endorphin, and growth hormone in commercial quantities when the genes for these substances are inserted into the bacterial genetic material.

Bacteriology, branch of microbiology that studies the characteristics and action of bacteria.

Bacteriophage, a virus that infects bacteria, a so-called phage or bacterial virus. The virus is used to study the chemical processes of heredity.

Badajoz, city in SW Spain, on the Guadiana River, near Portuguese border; capital of Badajoz prov.; an ancient fortress city that flourished under Moorish rule; site of ruins of Moorish citadel and 13th-century cathedral; important trade center. Area: (prov.) 8,360sq mi (21,652sq km). Pop. (city) 101,710; (prov.) 687,599.

Baden-Baden, town in SW West Germany, 18mi (29km) SW of Karlsruhe in the Black Forest; site of 3rd-century Roman garrison, Roman mineral bath remains. Now a health resort and spa, it has many hotels, villas, walks, and parks. Pop. 49,400.

Baden-Powell of Gilwell, Robert Stephenson Smyth Baden-Powell, 1st Baron (1857–1941), British soldier and founder of the Scout movement. He held Mafeking against the Boers (1899–1900). From 1910, he devoted himself to the Scout movement.

Badger, burrowing, nocturnal mammals found in Eurasia, North America, and Africa. They have flattened, stocky bodies with short legs and tails. Carnivores, they also eat insects and plants. Eurasian badgers *(Meles meles)* are the largest and have gray bodies with black and white striped heads. American badgers *(Taxidea taxus)* are smaller and have gray-brown to red fur with a white head stripe. Length: 16–28in (40.6–71cm); weight: 22–44lb (10–20kg). Family Mustelidae.

Badlands, horizontally bedded sediment in an arid or semi-arid area. The infrequent and heavy rains cause rapid runoff and the result is severe erosion. The terrain is characterized by steep gullies and almost no vegetation. *See also* Desert; Erosion.

Badminton, game for two to four persons. It is the national sport of Malaysia, Singapore, and Indonesia, and is popular in the United States and Canada. It enjoyed popularity in England in the 1870s after it was brought over from India (where it was called *poona*), and the rules were changed. The game is similar to tennis, and the object is to volley, with light rackets, a shuttlecock or bird (a cork base to which feathers are attached) until it is missed by an opponent or hit out of bounds. The court used for singles (indoors and out) is 17 by 44 feet (5.2 by 13.4m); for doubles it is 20 by 44 feet (6.1 by 13.4m). The net is 5 feet (1.5m) high in the center.

Baedeker, Karl (1801–59), German publisher, best known for a series of guidebooks to various cities which aimed to eliminate the need for guided tours. The first French editions appeared in 1846; English editions appeared in 1861.

Baekeland, Leo Hendrik (1863–1944), US chemist, b. Belgium. He invented a type of photographic paper capable of being developed under artificial light. He also invented the first of the thermosetting plastics—Bakelite—a substance that led to the development of the plastics industry.

Francis Bacon

Bahamas

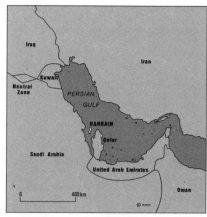

Bahrain

Baffin, William (1584–1622), English navigator and explorer. From 1612–16, he led several expeditions in search of the Northwest Passage, one of which led to the discovery of the bay between Greenland and Canada (since named for him). He was the first to determine longitude at sea by using lunar observation.

Baffin Island, largest and easternmost island in the Canadian Arctic Archipelago of the Northwest Territory; separated from Labrador by Hudson Strait; 5th-largest island in the world; mostly mountainous terrain. Population is almost entirely Eskimo. S area visited 1576–78 by Martin Frobisher, English explorer. Named for William Baffin who visited N part of island in 1616. Length: 1,000mi (1,610km). Width: 500mi (805km). Pop. 3,387.

Baghdad, capital city of Iraq, on the Tigris River; est 762 as capital of Abbaside caliphate, it grew to be a cultural and financial center. Hub of caravan trade between India, Persia, and the West; destroyed by the Mongols 1258; in the early 20th century Iraq gained independence from Turks, and Baghdad became capital (1921); modern administrative, transportation, and educational center. Industries: oil refineries, textiles, gold and silverware, food processing. Pop. 2,800,000.

Baghdad Railway, rail line linking Europe and the Middle East. In 1902 a German firm was granted permission by the Ottoman Empire to extend the line through Turkey to Baghdad. Great Britain and France objected to this "Berlin to Baghdad" linkup, seeing it as a threat to their own imperialist interests in the Middle East. They sought every means possible of stopping the construction. The resulting tension was a contributing factor to the hostility leading up to World War I.

Bagpipe, musical instrument with reed pipes connected to a windbag held under the arm and filled by mouth or bellows. Chanter pipes have finger holes for melody, with drone pipes producing monotone accompaniment. Bagpipes, originating in Greece or Asia, are associated with Scotland and Ireland but are also played elsewhere in rural Europe.

Bagworm, moth caterpillar that partially conceals itself in a cocoon of silk strands and leaf and twig bits. The common bagworm (*Thyridopteryx ephemeraeformis*) attacks trees and shrubs, especially arbovitae and cedar. Family Psychidae.

Baha'ism, religion founded (1863) by Bahaullah as an outgrowth of Babism. Headquartered in Haifa, Israel, this rapidly growing religion has centers throughout the world. Baha'ism seeks world peace through the unification of all religions. It stresses a simple life dedicated to serving others. It recognizes Bahaullah as the latest prophet of God. *See also* Babism; Bahaullah.

Bahamas, Commonwealth of the, independent archipelago in Atlantic Ocean, SE of Florida and NE of Cuba. It is comprised of 700 islands, 2,000 cays, and numerous coral reefs stretching over a 700-mi (1,127-km) area.

The rocky terrain of the islands provides little chance for agricultural development. The subtropical climate averages between 70–90°F (21–32°C). Tourism is the mainstay of the economy; commercial fishing, salt, rum, cement, oil refining, and handicrafts are important industries, of which large amounts are exported. There is an international airport at Nassau, the capital of the Bahamas, on New Providence Island. Special tax laws make the Bahamas an international banking haven.

Of the native population, over 90% is African or of mixed Afro-European stock. The majority lives on New Providence Island, in or near Nassau, earning a living

from the tourist, fishing, or handicraft industries. The Church of England is the predominant religion with a see at Nassau since 1861. Education is compulsory between ages 6 and 14; Queens College is in Nassau.

Ruled as a crown colony since the 18th century, the Bahamian political parties demanded a degree of independence in 1962; by 1963, a new constitution was drawn up providing for a parliamentary form of government. In 1973, the Bahamas became an independent nation; the monarch of England and governor-general remain titular heads of state; a prime minister serves as head of government.

San Salvador Island is traditionally believed to be the first stop of Christopher Columbus in his quest of the New World (1492). Partially settled by England's Eleutherian Adventurers (1648), the islands' development was hampered by numerous pirate and buccaneer bases. Charles II granted the islands to six lords proprietors of Carolina in 1670; this proved unsuccessful because of numerous pirate and Spanish attacks. The British crown, represented by Capt. Woodes Rogers, assumed complete and direct control by 1729, expelling militants and restoring civil order. Held briefly by Spain (1782) during American War of Independence, the islands were given back to England by the Treaty of Versailles (1783) in exchange for E Florida. In 1834, the lords proprietors had relinquished all their authority to the crown and slavery was abolished. The Bahamas were used extensively during WWII by both American and British forces for training and air bases.

PROFILE

Official name: Commonwealth of the Bahamas
Area: 5,380sq mi (13,934sq km)
Population: 225,000
Chief islands: Grand Bahama, Abaco, Eleuthera, New Providence, Andros, Cat, San Salvador (Watlings), Exuma, Long, Crooked, Acklins, Mayaguana, Inagua
Religion: Church of England, Baptist, Roman Catholic, and Methodist
Language: English (official)
Monetary unit: Bahamian dollar

Bahaullah (1817–92), Persian religious leader, b. Mirza Husayn Ali Nuri, founder of Baha'ism. He became a Babist in 1850 and suffered with them in their persecution. In 1863 he broke with the Babists, declaring himself Bahaullah ("The Glory of Allah"), the Promised One foretold by Bab. His work, the *Katabi Ikan (The Book of Certitude)* is the Baha'i holy book. *See also* Babism; Baha'ism.

Bahia, state in E central Brazil; capital is Salvador. Industries: minerals, cattle, carnuba wax, lumber, cacao, tobacco, sugar distilling, cotton milling. Area: 216,612sq mi (561,025sq km). Declared province of Brazil 1823, state 1889. Pop. 8,438,900 est.

Bahrain (Al-Bahrayn), island state in the Persian Gulf off the coast of Saudi Arabia. The economy is dependent upon petroleum. The nation consists of the islands of Bahrain, Sitrah, Al-Muharraq, Umm Na'sān, and about 30 smaller ones. The terrain is generally flat and only on the main island does the altitude rise above 330ft (100m). Summers are hot and humid, and most rainfall is limited to the cooler winter months. Soils are fertile once irrigated; because of the lack of surface water much of the supply has to be raised by artesian wells. In the irrigated areas fruit and vegetables are the main crops; livestock is unimportant. Although Bahrain has produced petroleum from oilfields in the center of Bahrain Island for over 40 years it derives most of its income from refining Saudi oil that is piped from Dhahran to Sitrah. Traditional industries of dhow building and pearling are being replaced by industries serving a more affluent populace. Two major developments of

the 1970s have been the smelting of bauxite and the development of Mīna' Salmān as a free port for the S Persian Gulf. Bahrain has also become an international financial center. The country is ruled by a royal family assisted by a cabinet. The 1972 constitution calling for a national assembly was suspended in 1975.

History. Bahrain was conquered by the Muslims in 7th century, by the Portuguese in 16th century, and by Persians in 17th. In 1861, Bahrain became a British Protectorate, and until 1971, Britain was responsible for its defense and foreign affairs. Since 1782 the Al Khalifah family has ruled the state.

PROFILE

Official Name: State of Bahrain
Area: 240sq mi (622sq km).
Population: 364,082.
Density: 1,517 per sq mi (585 per sq km).
Chief cities: Manama (capital), 94,697; Al-Muharraq, 44,567.
Government: Hereditary emirate
Religion: Islam
Gross national product: (1977) $630,000,000.
Trading partners (major): Japan, Saudi Arabia.

Baikal (Baykal, Bajkal), Lake, Asia's largest fresh water lake and world's deepest lake, in S Siberia, USSR, near Mongolian border, chiefly within Buryat ASSR; fed by Barguzin, Selenga, and many other rivers. Angara River is sole outlet; bordered by mountain ranges Baikal (W), Barguzin (E), Khamar-Daban (S). Contains 27 islands, has moderating influence on climate of the region; site of large hydroelectric project. Its center section reaches depth of 5,710ft (1,742m). Length: 395mi (636km). Width: (max.) 49mi (79km).

Baja California (Lower California), peninsula in NW Mexico, extends 800mi (1,288km) SSE between Mexico and the United States; S half is the territory of Baja California Sur; N half comprises the state of Baja California, which has the highest standard of living in Mexico; most important crop is long-staple cotton; main industry is the assembling of imported materials. Discovered 1535 by the Spanish; separated from Alta California, United States, 1772; formation of Baja state 1951. Pop. (state) 1,434,000; (territory) 123,786.

Bakelite, trade name for a thermosetting resin consisting of phenol or cresol condensed with formaldehyde; used for insulating purposes and in making plastic products. The trade name is also applicable to a wide range of thermoplastic resins. Named after L. H. Baekeland.

Baker Island, small atoll in central Pacific Ocean, near the equator, SW of Hawaii. Discovered 1832 by US Capt. Michael Baker; became US Territory 1936. Area: 1sq mi (2.6 sq km).

Bakersfield, city in S central California, at the S end of the San Joaquin valley; seat of Kern co; gold discovered in 1885 and petroleum in 1889; important oil refining center. Industries: plastics, drugs, processed foods. Inc. 1898. Pop. (1980) 105,611.

Baker v. Carr (1962), landmark US Supreme Court decision holding that apportionment of state legislatures and redistricting to assure proper representation were proper issues to be decided in federal courts. The court overruled *Colegrove* v. *Green* (1946) and limited the "political question" doctrine to cases involving separation of powers questions and deference to the executive.

Baking Powder, mixture used in baking as a substitute for yeast. Baking powders generally contain sodium bicarbonate mixed with an acid constituent, such as tartaric acid, cream of tartar, or calcium phosphate, so that carbon dioxide is produced, thus giving a spongy texture during baking.

Bakke Case, US Supreme Court case (1978) involving Allan Bakke, who was refused admission (1972) to the University of California at Davis medical school, despite his excellent academic record. He sued the university on a charge that he had been passed over in favor of less qualified applicants who were admitted to increase the number of minority students. In 1978, the Supreme Court ruled that Bakke had been a victim of reverse discrimination and must be admitted to the university.

Baku, city and capital of Azerbaijan (Azerbajdžanskaja) SSR, USSR; important oil shipping port on W coast of Caspian Sea. City encircles Baku Bay and is a major Soviet industrial and cultural center. Commercial oil production began in the 1870s and now the port handles tremendous volume of oil and oil products shipping. City is site of Azerbaijan Academy of Sciences, cultural institutions, 13th-century fortress of Bad-Kube, 11th-century mosque, 12th-century Maiden's Tower. Baku was trade and craft center in medieval times; prospered under Shirvan Shahs 15th century; Persians ruled 1509–1723; annexed by Russia 1806. Pop. 1,465,000 est.

Bakunin, Mikhail (1814–76), Russian political philosopher. He was converted to violent revolution while in Paris (1848), and was active in radical politics. His position, known as revolutionary anarchism, repudiates all forms of governmental authority as fundamentally at variance with human freedom and dignity. In *God and the State* (1882) Bakunin recognized natural law alone as consistent with liberty. *See also* Anarchism.

BAL (British Anti-Lewisite), oily liquid used as an antidote for poisoning caused by organic arsenic compounds and heavy metals, including mercury and gold.

Balaam, in the Bible, Midianite prophet called by Balek, king of Moab, to curse the Israelites wandering in the wilderness. Commanded by an angel of God, through his donkey, he blessed them instead.

Balakirev, Mili Alekseyevich (1837–1910), Russian composer. One of the "Russian Five" dedicated to advancing Russian nationalism in 19th-century music, his best-known compositions are *Islamey* (begun in 1866, but not completed until 1882) and incidental music to *King Lear* (1858–61).

Balaklava (Balaclava), section of city of Sevastopol, in Ukrainian SSR, USSR; site of ancient Greek city. A medieval Genoese settlement, it was taken by Turks 1475. Balaklava was scene of charge of the Light Brigade (1854) during Crimean War. Industries: limestone quarrying, fishing, health resort. Inc. 1957 into Sevastopol. Pop. 145,000.

Balaklava, Battle of (1854), inconclusive action fought during the Crimean War by English, French, and Turkish troops resisting a Russian attack on their supply port of Balaklava. It is famous for the gallant but disastrous charge of Lord Cardigan's Light Brigade of cavalry.

Balance of Payments, overall surplus or deficit that occurs as a result of the exchange of all goods and services between countries. A country with a balance of payments deficit incurs a debt that will require that arrangements be made for future payment or the exchange of gold between countries. Balance of payments deficits, if continual, can be a serious problem, because they will cause an outflow of gold. Such a drain in turn leads to pressure for devaluation in order to correct the deficit situation. A country with a balance of payments surplus is in a favorable position, but it may be under international pressure to revalue (ie, lower the price of gold) in order to adjust the imbalance.

Balance of Power, system in international affairs in which nations seek to keep peace and order by maintaining an approximate equilibrium of power among rivals, thereby preventing any single one from having a marked advantage.

Balance of Trade, surplus or deficit incurred by a country; the difference between the sum of its imports and the sum of its exports.

Balanchine, George (1904–83), US ballet dancer and choreographer, b. Georgi Balanchivadze in Russia. Trained at the Imperial Ballet School, St Petersburg, he left Russia in 1924 and became a principal dancer and choreographer for Diaghilev's Ballets Russes in Paris.

He moved to the United States in 1933 and was director of the Metropolitan Opera ballet (1934–37). A founder of the School of American Ballet (1934), he became the first artistic director of the New York City Ballet in 1948. Works he has choreographed include *The Prodigal Son* (1929), *The Nutcracker* (1954), *Don Quixote* (1965) and *Slaughter on Tenth Avenue* for the musical *On Your Toes* (1936).

Balaton, Lake, lake in W Hungary, 55mi (89km) SW of Budapest; many shoreline resorts; largest lake in central Europe. Area: 232sq mi (601sq km).

Balboa, Vasco Núñez de (c.1475–1519), Spanish conquistador and discoverer of the Pacific Ocean. He went to Hispaniola in 1500 and in 1510 to Darién (Panama), where he ousted its governor, Martín Fernández de Enciso, and took control. With a group of Indians he crossed the isthmus and discovered, in September 1513, the Pacific. Before that news reached Spain, the king dispatched Pedro Arias de Ávila to take charge of Darién. Arias had treason charges brought against Balboa and had him executed in 1519.

Bald Cypress, deciduous tree growing in shallow water in SE United States. They have woody growth (knees) on the roots that grow above water and lose their feathery, light green needles in autumn. Height: to 15ft (4.6m). Family Taxodiaceae; species *Taxodium distichum*.

Bald Eagle, or **American Bald Eagle,** large eagle, also the national emblem of the United States, found along North American wetlands particularly in Alaska and Florida. A sea eagle, it feeds on fish and small animals. It is brown with a white head and tail and yellow bill. Although protected by law since 1940 (1953 in Alaska), it readily succumbs to pesticides and is now endangered. Length: 40in (102cm). Species *Haliaetus leucocephalus*. *See also* Eagle.

Balder, Scandinavian God of sunlight, beauty, brightness, and wisdom, the son of Woden and Frigg. Through the treachery of Loki, god of evil, Balder was killed by an arrow made of mistletoe. Of all the Aesir, pantheon of the gods in Asgard, he was the fairest and most amiable.

Baldness, or **Alopecia,** the absence of hair from the skin where hair normally is present. Causes include hereditary disease, old age, nutritional deficiencies, and pregnancy. In some cases, hair will grow back normally; in others, loss is permanent. Premature baldness, loss of hair in late adolesence or early adulthood, occurs most often in males and is believed hereditary.

Baldwin I (1058–1118), king of Jerusalem (1100–18). A military leader of the First Crusade (1096–99), he demanded and received the crown of Jerusalem in 1100. He consolidated and strengthened the Latin states of the Middle East.

Baldwin II (died 1131), king of Jerusalem (1118–31). His cousin, Baldwin I, appointed him Count of Edessa (1100–18). He was captured by the Seljuk Turks in 1104 and held until ransomed in 1108. He then recaptured Edessa from his regent, Tancred. He was again captured by the Turks (1123–24) while king of Jerusalem. After release, he expanded his kingdom. He was succeeded by his son-in-law, Fulk of Anjou.

Baldwin, James (1924–), US author, b. New York City. A novelist, essayist, and playwright, he was born in Harlem, where he preached in storefront churches as a youth. He lived in Paris (1948–56). His works deal with race relations and with sexuality. They include the novel *Go Tell It on the Mountain* (1953); the books of essays *Notes of a Native Son* (1955), *Nobody Knows My Name* (1961), *The Fire Next Time* (1963), and *Just Above My Head* (1979); and the play *Blues for Mister Charlie* (1964).

Baldwin, Robert (1804–58), Canadian statesman. A leader of the movement for representative, cabinet government for Canada. With Louis LaFontaine (representing the French of lower Canada), he shared the first premiership of united Canada (1841–43). They were returned to power (1847–51). He advocated co-operation between French and British Canadians, organized an effective system of municipal government for Ontario, reorganized the court system, and secularized the University of Toronto.

Baldwin, Stanley, 1st Earl Baldwin of Bewdley (1867–1947), British Conservative statesman. He ran the family iron business until elected to Parliament (1908). He became chancellor of the exchequer (1922–23), and although his handling of the US debt was criticized, he succeeded Bonar Law as prime minister (1923–24). Becoming prime minister again (1924–29), he weathered the general strike (1926). While

prime minister for the third time (1935–37), he had to deal with the abdication crisis (1936).

Balearic Islands, resort islands in the W Mediterranean, off the coast of Spain; comprises Baleares prov., Spain; capital is Palma; formerly occupied by Iberians, Phoenicians, Greeks, Carthaginians, Romans, and Byzantines. The Moors established an independent kingdom in the 11th century, and its pirate inhabitants harassed Mediterranean coastal cities. The islands are part of Catalonia, which became an autonomous region in 1980. The chief islands are Minorca, Ibiza, and Majorca. Industries: tourism, silver filigree, olive oil, wine, fruit. Area: 1,936sq mi (5,014sq km). Pop. (city) 234,098; (prov.) 558,287.

Balfour, Arthur James Balfour, 1st Earl of (1848–1930), British Conservative statesman. His time as prime minister (1902–05) was marked by party friction. He was an energetic leader of the opposition (1906–11) and first lord of the admiralty (1915–16). In 1917 he issued the Balfour Declaration in favor of founding a Jewish nation in Palestine. He played a major role in postwar European agreements.

Balfour Declaration, letter written by British Foreign Secretary Arthur Balfour to the British Zionist Federation in 1917 pledging cooperation for the settlement of Jews in Palestine. Jews were admitted when the area, a province of the Ottoman Empire, became a British mandate after World War I. In 1948 British forces withdrew and the state of Israel was proclaimed.

Bali, island province of Indonesia, off E tip of Java between Bali Sea and Indian Ocean; capital is Denpasar. Under Javanese control from AD 1000, it was a Dutch possession 1908–1949; occupied by Japanese during WWII; center of Majaphit Hinduism religion and culture; famous for natural beauty and native culture; popular tourist resort. Industries: rice, cassava, copra, meat processing. Area: 2,171sq mi (5,623sq km). Pop. 2,247,000.

Balkan Mountains, major mountain range of Balkan Peninsula in Bulgaria; extends from E Yugoslavia through central Bulgaria to the Black Sea; constitutes a continuation of the Carpathian Mts. Rich in minerals, serves as climatic barrier for inland region; includes Shipka Pass at an altitude of approx. 4,000ft (1,220m). Highest peak is Botev, 7,794ft (2377m).

Balkan States, group of countries in SE Europe, on the Balkan Peninsula, consisting of Albania, Bulgaria, Greece, Romania, Turkey, and Yugoslavia.

Balkan Wars (1912–13), two successive wars involving Balkan powers. In the first, the members of the Balkan League (Serbia, Bulgaria, Greece, and Montenegro) won most of the Ottoman Empire's European territory. In the second, Serbia, Greece, and Romania quarreled with Bulgaria over the distribution of conquests in Macedonia.

Ballad, narrative poem of strong rhythm and simple language, suitable for singing. Ballads are of two types: folk and literary. Early folk ballads, such as "Barbara Allen" and "Lord Randal," were anonymous, transmitted orally in song, and altered as repeated from generation to generation, resulting in many versions of the same story. Literary ballads are later poets' skilled imitations of the anonymous popular form. An example is Samuel Taylor Coleridge's "The Rime of the Ancient Mariner."

Ballade, poem comprised of three stanzas of seven or eight lines each, concluding with an envoy addressed to a prominent person, which serves as a summary or dedication. The same line ends each stanza and the envoy. Only three or four rhymes recur. Derived from Old French poetry, the ballade form is exemplified in "Ballade to Queen Elizabeth" by Henry Austin Dobson.

Ballard, James Graham (1930–), British science fiction writer. His first story was *Prima Belladonna* (1956). It was followed by novels such as *The Wind from Nowhere* (1962), *The Drought* (1965), *The Crystal World* (1965), *Crash* (1970), and *High Rise* (1974).

Ballet, theatrical art form in which stylized dancing to music conveys a story or theme. It evolved from Renaissance court spectacles. The first formal ballet, *La Ballet Comique de la Reine,* was performed at the French court of Catherine de Medicis in 1581. Thoinot Arbeau wrote the first treatise on ballet, *Orchésographie* (1588). Louis XIV, who himself performed in ballet, founded the French Royal Ballet Academy in 1661. The first ballet for public performance was not commissioned until early in the 18th century. Jean Georges Noverre was the most influential choreographer and theorist of the 18th century. His *Lettres sur la Danse*

George Balanchine

James Baldwin

Honoré de Balzac

et les Ballets (1760) insisted that meaningless gestures and masks be replaced by a more naturalistic style. The performance of *La Sylphide* in Paris (1832) set the model for the romantic ballets of the 19th century. Toward the end of the 19th century Russian ballet began emphasizing technique and virtuosity. In 1909, Sergei Diaghilev and his Ballets Russes revolutionized ballet with dynamic choreography and dancing. The mid-20th century saw a melding of elements of classical ballet and modern dancing.

Ballet Comique de la Reine, La, ballet by Baldassario Belgiojoso produced in 1581, the first ballet as we know the art form today. A lavish spectacle, it lasted five hours and cost 3.6 million gold francs. The libretto was published and used as one of the first books on ballet.

Ballet Russe de Monte Carlo, the name of several ballet companies that succeeded the Diaghilev Ballets Russes, which disbanded after Sergei Diaghilev's death in 1929. Under the management of René Blum and Col. Vasili de Basil from 1932, who vied for control, the company toured the United States under impresario Sol Hurok's sponsorship. In 1938 Léonide Massine and Blum formed a new, separate company. George Balanchine and Michel Fokine, among others, have been associated with this company. *See also* Diaghilev, Sergei.

Ballets Russes, dance company founded in 1909 in Paris by Sergei Diaghilev with Michel Fokine as chief choreographer. The company revitalized and reshaped ballet by bringing together some of the greatest, most innovative dancers (Anna Pavlova, Nijinsky), choreographers (Léonide Massine, Bronislava Nijinska, George Balanchine), composers (Stravinsky, Debussy, Richard Strauss), and artists as set and costume designers (Picasso, Chagall, Matisse). The company disbanded after Diaghilev's death in 1929, but many of its members then joined the Ballet Russe de Monte Carlo.

Ballista, large crossbowlike firing device used by the Romans and other ancient armies to hurl rocks and other missiles at enemy formations and fortifications.

Ballistic Missile, self-propelled missile that traverses most of its trajectory in the earth's outer atmosphere under the influence of gravity alone. Ballistic missiles equipped with thermonuclear warheads and dispersed in ground-based hardened silos or in nuclear submarines are the supreme military weapon of modern times. *See also* Intercontinental Ballistic Missile; Intermediate Range Ballistic Missile; Missile.

Ballistics, study of projectile motion. *Exterior* ballistics includes the study of gravitational forces, atmospheric friction, variation of the direction and strength of the gravitational field with height, variation of the temperature and density of the atmosphere with height, curvature of the earth's surface, and change in the velocity of sound with altitude. *Interior* ballistics deals with events inside the gun barrel or rocket engine: propulsion systems, gas pressure changes, effect of spinning (rifling) on stability, and strength of materials.

Balloon, bag of tough, light material filled with heated air or buoyant gas, lighter than air so as to rise and float in the atmosphere. It is non-powered and flies only where the wind takes it. Balloons have been used for meteorology, communications, military observation, upper-air research, and for sport flying.

Balloon Fish. *See* Porcupine Fish.

Ballooning, sport in which participants ascend and travel in a basket-like gondola suspended from a balloon filled with hot air or hydrogen. The basic principle of the hot-air balloon, first tried out successfully in 1783 in France by two brothers, Joseph and Jacques Etienne Montgolfier, is to heat the air inside the balloon. As the heated air expands, it becomes lighter than the surrounding air and tends to rise. The use of hydrogen for ballooning was begun in 1766 by Henry Cavendish, who showed that hydrogen was seven times lighter than air.

In 1783, the first manned flight with a hot-air balloon was achieved by Pilatre de Rozier. Later on in the year, three men successfully made the first ascent with a hydrogen-filled balloon. Ballooning reached the height of its popularity in the early part of the 20th century with such notable events as the annual James Gordon Bennett Cup race. Although declining in popularity after World War II, the sport enjoyed a resurgence in the 1970s with the application of modern techniques.

Ballot, object used to cast a vote. The word derives from the Italian *ballotta,* "little ball." Since 5th-century BC Athens, balls were used to cast votes: white for yes, black for no. Today, the usual ballot, a sheet of paper, is being replaced by the voting machine.

Balsa, evergreen tree native to tropical America. Its light, buoyant wood is used for rafts and airplane models. Leaves are heart-shaped and the whitish or greenish flowers are bisexual. Height: to 80ft (24m). Family Bombacaceae; species *Ochroma lagopus. See also* Kapok.

Balsam, aromatic resin obtained from plants. Or, healing preparations, especially those with benzoic and cinnamic acid added to the resin. Or, balsam-yielding trees, such as the balsam fir and balsam poplar. Also numerous species of tropical succulent plants of the family Balsaminaceae that are sprawling, waterside forms with thin leaves and pendent flowers. *Impatiens* is the most common North American genus.

Balsam Fir, evergreen tree native to NE North America. It has flat needles and 2.5in (6.3cm) cones. It is often grown for pulpwood and Christmas trees. Height: to 70ft (21.3m). Family Pinaceae; species *Abies balsamea.*

Baltic Sea, arm of the Atlantic Ocean in N Europe, connected with the North Sea by Kattegat and Skagerrak; bordered by Denmark, Sweden, Finland, USSR, Poland, East Germany, and West Germany. The Kiel Canal links the Baltic to the North Sea and the White Sea; Baltic Canal links it to the White Sea; partially frozen in the winter. Area: 160,000sq mi (414,400sq km).

Baltimore, major US seaport city, in N central Maryland, 40mi (64km) NE of Washington, D.C., on the Patapsco River estuary; largest city in Maryland. Acquired by the Maryland legislature 1729, it developed into a shipbuilding center and major exporter of flour and tobacco. Baltimore served as the meeting place for the Continental Congress (December 1776–March 1777) during the British occupation of Philadelphia in the American Revolution, and inspired Francis Scott Key to write "The Star Spangled Banner" during the British bombardment of Fort McHenry (Sept. 13–14, 1814); it flourished during both world wars as demand for ships and industrial produce increased. It is the site of the home and grave of Edgar Allen Poe, Lee-Jackson Memorial, Pimlico racetrack, Westminster Church, Municipal Museum (1813), Flag House Museum, Lexington Market (1803), Fort McHenry National Monument (est. 1939), Cathedral of the Assumption of the Blessed Virgin (1806, 1st U.S. Roman Catholic cathedral), London Park and Baltimore National cemeteries, Washington Monument (1815, earliest memorial to George Washington); and home of National Football League's Baltimore Colts and American Baseball League's Baltimore Orioles. Urban renewal during the mid-20th century created Charles Center and a complex of office, apartment, and retail buildings, Inner Harbor. Numerous institutions of higher education including Johns Hopkins University (1876). Industries: steel, shipbuilding, shipyards, aerospace, electrical insulators, chemicals, copper and sugar refining, printing, publishing. Settled mid-17th century by the Barons of Baltimore; town est. 1729; inc. 1745 as town, 1797 as city. Pop. (1980) 786,775.

Baltimore Oriole, American songbird named because its colors are the same as the coat of arms of the Baltimore family, founders of Maryland. The male has black head, neck, back, and wings and orange breast, rump, and outer tail feathers. Females, olive above and yellow below, build long slender weed-and-bark nests slung from twigs in a high tree. Length: to 8in (20cm). Species *Icterus galbula.*

Baluchitherium, extinct genus of giant rhinoceros believed to have been the largest land mammal ever to have existed, and known from fossil deposits of Late Oligocene and Early Miocene age in Asia.

Balzac, Honoré de (1799–1850), French novelist. Balzac began writing thrillers in a Paris attic before his spectacular failure as a publisher. His first success was *Les Chouans* (1829), and many great novels followed in his grand scheme *The Human Comedy.* They include *Eugénie Grandet* (1833), *Le Père Goriot* (1835), and *La Cousine Bette* (1847).

Bamako, picturesque capital city of Mali, on the Niger River, 90mi (145km) NE of the Guinea border; site of schools of medicine, administration, and engineering; leading center of Muslim learning 11th–15th centuries; occupied by French 1883; made capital of French Sudan 1908. Industries: shipping, textiles, meat, metal products. Pop. 380,000.

Bamberg, city in West Germany on Regnitz River, 31mi (50km) N of Nürnberg; capital of powerful ecclesiastical state 1007–1802, when it joined Bavaria; site of 12th-century church, bishops' palaces (1571–76), observatory. Industries: textiles, machinery, beer. Pop. 73,800.

Bamboo, tall, treelike grass found worldwide in tropical and subtropical regions, mostly in SE Asia. The hollow, woody stems grow in branching clusters from a thick rhizome and the leaves are stalked blades. It is used for construction materials and household implements. Some bamboo sprouts are eaten. The pulp and fiber go into paper production. Height to 120ft (37m). There are 1000 species. Family Gramineae; subfamily Bambusoidae. *See also* Grass.

Banana, long, curved, yellow or reddish fruit of the banana plant consumed worldwide. It has soft, creamy flesh. Or, treelike plant found in tropical areas worldwide. It is propagated from sprouts growing from the perennial root or rhizome. The large annual stem is topped with a crown of long, broad leaves. A spike of yellow, clustered flowers grows from the crown center. This spike bends downward and becomes bunches of 50–150 fruits or hands of 10–20. After fruiting, the plants die. Those used for cooking are called plantain. Height: to 40ft (12m). Over 100 varieties are cultivated. Family Musaceae; genus *Musa. See also* Plantain.

Band, a group of musicians playing primarily woodwind, percussion, and brass instruments, or a specifically designated group of instruments, as in a string band or brass band. Famous bandmasters and composers, such as Patrick S. Gilmore and John P. Sousa, helped to elevate the quality of the band in the United States.

Banda, Hastings (Kamuzu) (*c.* 1902–), president of Malawi (1966–). He studied medicine in the United States and practiced in England before returning to Africa (1953). He became a nationalist political leader, guiding Nyasaland to independence as Malawi and to membership in the British Commonwealth (1964) and establishing an autocratic presidency (1966). He was criticized by other black African leaders for dealing with South Africa.

Bandaranaike, Sirimavo (Ratwatte Dias) (1916–), prime minister of Sri Lanka (formerly Ceylon)(1960–77). She became the world's first female prime minister in 1960, after her husband, the former premier, was assassinated in the previous year. Her Sri Lanka Freedom party was defeated in 1965, but returned to power in 1970. In 1971 she put down an uprising led by the Marxist People's Liberation Front. In 1972 a new constitution was adopted and the country's name was officially changed to Sri Lanka. Under Mrs. Bandaranaike, the nation has pursued socialist and neutralist policies.

Banda Sea, section of the Pacific Ocean, surrounded by the Malay Islands, Indonesia, linking the Indian and Pacific Oceans; bounded by Buru and Ceram (N), Kai and Aru (E), Tanimbar Islands (S), Timor (SW), Celebes (NW). Length: 600mi (966km). Width: 300mi (483km).

Bandung, city in Indonesia, 110mi (177km) SE of Djakarta; capital of West Java prov.; scene of historic Asian-African Conference (1955), Nuclear Research Center (1964). Industries: food processing, canning, tea, quinine, textiles. Founded 1810. Pop. 1,200,000.

Bandung Conference (1955), meeting in Bandung, Indonesia, of representatives of 28 nonaligned countries of Africa and Asia and China to show united opposition to colonialism and to gain recognition for the "Third World." *See also* Third World.

Baneberry, any of about 10 species of perennial plants (genus *Actaea*) of the buttercup family found throughout the temperate Northern Hemisphere. All have poisonous berries appearing in fall. The North American white baneberry *(A. alba)* has sharply toothed leaflets and white berries with black eyes. Height: to 2ft (61cm).

Bangalore (Bangalur), city in S central India, 180mi (290km) W of Madras; capital of Mysore state; est 1537 by Mysore dynasty, it was besieged and occupied by Hyder Ali (1758) but later restored to former rulers by British defeat (1791) of Tippoo Sahib, Hyder Ali's son. Britain ruled Mysore 1831–81, retaining Bangalore as military headquarters until 1947; 5th-largest city in India; industrial and transportation center. Pop. 1,653,779.

Bangkok (Krung Thep), capital city of Thailand, on the Chao Phraya river, 25mi (40km) above the Gulf of Siam; capital of Phra Nakhon prov. Commercial, financial, transportation, and cultural center; hub of major rice-growing region; site of Grand Palace walls, Wat Phra Kaew (royal Buddhist temple), several universities, national theater and museum; headquarters of UN Economic Commission for Asia and the Far East. The capital of Siam and stronghold against Burmese until destroyed 1767; capital changed to Thon Buri (1769) until King Rama I renamed Bangkok capital in 1782. Industries: textiles, food processing, sawmills, oil refining, shipyards. Pop. 4,000,000.

Bangladesh (Bengal Nation), independent nation in Asia. It is a low-lying plain formed by the Ganges and Brahmaputra rivers. Its monsoon climate, which gives it the highest rainfall in the world, and its location in the cyclone belt combine to produce devastating floods; a weak economy has generated periodic famine.

Land and Economy: The world's eighth-most populous nation, it is bisected by the Tropic of Cancer. Its coastline borders the Bay of Bengal with India and Burma adjacent. Raw jute and jute manufacture account for 90% of foreign earnings. Offshore oil was found in 1974. Although over 80% of the people are farmers and rice is the major crop, the country is not self-sufficient in food; it depends on foreign aid. Land productivity, disease, famine, and the birth rate are long-term problems. It is estimated that the present population of 73,700,000 will rise to 175,000,000 by the year 2000.

People: 98% of the people are Bengali and speak Bengali, the official language; the rest include Urdu-speaking Muslim immigrants from India and tribal peoples. Islam is the religion of 85% of the people with the balance made up of Hindus, Buddhists, Christians, and animists. The literacy rate is 26%.

Government: A president, elected to a five-year term, leads the government. He selects the cabinet from the 330-member parliament, 300 of whom are elected and 30 of whom are women appointed to the body.

History: A melting pot of Dravidians, Aryans, Mongolians, Arabs, Persians, and Turks, the region of Bangladesh was ruled by Hindu and Buddhist dynasties until the British assumed control in the 18th century. In 1947, India and Pakistan gained independence. Pakistan was divided into two sections, East (now Bangladesh) and West, two areas nearly 1,000 miles (1,610km) apart. In the mid-1960s, Sheikh Mujibur Rahman emerged as the spokesman for East Pakistan autonomy. In 1971 he organized a provisional independent government, and civil war erupted. Bengali forces assisted by Indian troops defeated West Pakistan, and on March 16, 1971, Bangladesh emerged as a separate nation. Mujibur Rahman was killed in a 1975 coup d'état, and the military assumed control of the government, returning it to an elected government in 1979 with Gen. Ziaur Rahman as president. He was assassinated in an unsuccessful military coup attempt in 1981, and in 1982, following political instability, martial law was established by army leaders. Restrictions eased by the mid-1980s.

PROFILE

Official name: People's Republic of Bangladesh
Area: 55,126sq mi (142,776sq km)
Population: 85,000,000
Density: 1,360per sq mi (525per sq km)
Chief cities: Dacca (capital); Khulna; Chittagong
Government: Republic
Religion: Islam
Language: Bengali
Monetary unit: Taka
Gross national product: $7,730,000,000
Per capita income: $85
Industries (major products): jute products, cotton textiles, wood products, processed foods
Agriculture (major products): jute, rice, sugar cane, tea, oilseeds, fish, forests, cotton
Trading partners (major): US, UK, USSR, and Japan

Bangor, city in S Maine, at the confluence of Penobscot and Kenduskeag rivers. Settled 1769 as Sunbury, it was occupied by British during War of 1812; important port of entry. Industries: tourism, shoes, paper, tools, lumber, printing. Inc. as town 1791, as city 1834. Pop. (1980) 31,643.

Bangui, capital city of Central African Republic; a port on the Ubangi River, near the Zaire border; nation's chief port of international trade. Industries: textiles, food products, shoes, beer, soap. Founded 1889 by French. Pop. (including suburbs) 350,000.

Banjo, musical instrument with from four to nine strings; drum-like body; and long, fretted neck, strummed with pick. Probably of Arabic or Spanish origin, it was brought to America by slaves.

Bank of England, England's central banking institution, founded in 1694 and situated in Threadneedle Street, City of London. Nationalized in 1944, it regulates foreign exchange, issues bank notes, advises the government on monetary matters, and acts as the government's financial agent.

Bank of the United States, First (1791–1811), national bank established under Alexander Hamilton's plan to put the United States on a solid economic basis. The bank conducted business for the government. It was soundly operated, but state banking interests defeated its rechartering.

Bank of the United States, Second, national bank chartered in 1816. This bank, modeled on Alexander Hamilton's First Bank, was chartered by Congress although there was much opposition to giving it the power to establish local branches that would compete with state-chartered banks. Maryland unsuccessfully carried its challenge to the Supreme Court in the case of *McCulloch* v. *Maryland* (1819). President Andrew Jackson opposed the bank and vetoed its rechartering, so it went out of existence in 1836.

Bankruptcy, legal procedure whereby a business may be liquidated under the direction of the court system. A bankruptcy petition is normally filed only when a business determines that its obligations so far outweigh its net worth and future opportunities that it will be impossible for the business to survive.

Banneker, Benjamin (1731–1806), US scientist, b. Elliott, Md. He was a mathematician, astronomer, surveyor, and clock-maker. In 1791 he became the first black presidential appointee when George Washington appointed him to the District of Columbia Commission to survey the site of the new capital.

Bannister, Roger (Gilbert) (1929–), English athlete. An Oxford graduate, he was the first man to run the mile in less than four minutes. He accomplished the feat on May 6, 1954, in a time of 3 minutes, 59.4 seconds. He received his medical degree at St. Mary's Hospital Medical School (1954) and subsequently became a well-known physician and government sports advisor.

Bannock, a Shoshonean-speaking tribe that broke off from the Northern Paiute and settled in SE Idaho, where they acquired many Nez Percé and Shoshoni traits. They are primarily noted for their role in the Bannock War of 1878. The bulk of the tribe—some 500 individuals—share Fort Hall, Idaho, with the Shoshoni tribe.

Bannockburn, town in central Scotland, scene of battle (1314) in which Robert Bruce defeated the English under Edward II. Pop. 3,887.

Banting, (Sir) Frederick Grant (1891–1941), Canadian physician. He shared the 1923 Nobel Prize in physiology or medicine for his work in extracting the hormone insulin from the pancreas, thus making it possible to give insulin to diabetes mellitus sufferers.

Bantu Languages, languages variously grouped with the Benue-Niger or Niger-Kordofanian families of African languages. They form the largest group of languages spoken from the Congo Basin to South Africa. Swahili or Kingwana is the most widely used of these. With Lingala, Zulu, Luganda, and others they total over 30 million speakers.

Banyan, evergreen tree of E India whose branches send down aerial shoots that take root, forming new trunks. These trunks of a single tree can cover an area up to 2000ft (610m) in circumference. It has dark green, oval leaves and produces small, round fruits. Height: to 100ft (30m). Family Moraceae; species *Ficus benghalensis.*

Baobab, tropical tree native to Africa, Madagascar, and N Australia. It has a stout trunk containing water storage tissue, and short, stubby branches with sparse foliage. Fiber from its bark is used in making rope. Its gourdlike fruit has edible pulp. Height: to 75ft (23m); trunk diameter: 30ft (9m). Family Bombacaceae; species *Adansonia digitata.*

Baptistry, part of a church or related separate building used for baptism. Based on the early baptistry in the Lateran basilica at Rome, many were octagonal. Baptistries remained even after immersion was no longer practiced.

Baptists, members of a Protestant denomination who profess a personal religion based on the principle of religious liberty. With no official creed and no hierarchy, individual churches are autonomous. Historically, they developed from the Reformation Anabaptists. They continue to practice baptism of believers only through immersion. Insisting on freedom of thought and expression, they developed a democratic government. The Baptist World Alliance, an advisory group, convenes every five years. Baptists comprise one-third of Protestants in the United States. *See also* Anabaptists.

Bar, a unit of pressure, corresponding to the pressure of a column of mercury one meter high. Atmospheric pressure is about .76 bars, or 760 millibars. A millibar is also called a torr, after the Italian Torricelli, an early inventor of the barometer.

Barabbas, in the New Testament, convicted felon in prison at the time of Jesus' trial before Pilate. The people, given a choice of which prisoner to set free, convinced Pilate Barabbas should be released and Jesus crucified.

Baranof Island, island off SE Alaska, W Alexander Archipelago. It is named for Russian trader Aleksandr Baranov. Area: 1,597sq mi (4,136sq km).

Baranov, Aleksandr Andreevich (1746–1819), Russian fur trader in Alaska. After heading an earlier Russian fur trading company in the Kodiak Islands, Baranov became (1799) head of the Russian-American Company. He greatly expanded Russian penetration of North America—eventually establishing posts as far south as Fort Ross, north of San Francisco—and brought great profits to the company.

Barbados, independent island state in West Indies, in Windward Islands group, E of St Vincent: Settled by

Bangladesh

Banyan

Barbados

British 1627; independent since 1966; member of Organization of American States, Commonwealth of Nations, and the United Nations. Industries: tourism, sugar cane, molasses, rum, fishing. Highest point is Mount Hillaby, 1,104ft (336m). Pop. 253,000.

Barbarians. *See also* Alans; Angles; Burgundians; Franks; Gepids; Huns; Ostrogoths; Saxons; Sueves; Thuringians; Vandals; Visigoths.

Barbarossa. *See* Frederick I.

Barbary Ape, tailless, yellowish-brown, apelike monkey native to Algeria, Morocco, and Gibraltar. It is the size of a small dog. The Gibralter Barbary apes are the only wild monkeys in Europe. Species *Macaca sylvana*. *See also* Macaque.

Barbary Coast, waterfront section of San Francisco, California; known for corruption that flourished during 1890–1917; named after the notorious Barbary Coast of North Africa.

Barbary Sheep. *See* Aoudad.

Barbary States, coastal region in N Africa, consisting of Tripoli, Tunisia, Algeria, and Morocco; part of Libya until Roman domination in AD 42; independent Muslim states 7th–15th centuries; pirate states under Turkish control (16th–19th centuries); notorious for Mediterranean raids. Several wars reduced their power, and France gained control of Algeria, Morocco, and Tunisia by 1912. Now independent states: Libya (1951), Morocco and Tunisia (1956), Algeria (1962).

Barbed Wire, a form of fencing patented (1867) by Joseph F. Glidden. First marketed in 1874, the metal wire had barbs spaced every few inches. This simple product changed the history of the west by allowing the fencing of cattle ranges to contain livestock and prevent damage to property by cattle.

Barbel, or Barb, freshwater fish of W Asia and S central Europe. A game and food fish, it has an elongated body, flattened underside, and two pairs of fleshy mouth whiskers. Length: 19.7–35.4in (50–90cm); Weight: to 49lb (22kg). Family Cyprinidae; species *Barbus barbus*.

Barber, Samuel (1910–81), US composer, b. West Chester, Pa. Using a basically conservative, post-Romantic style, Barber has composed works in many forms, including chamber music; two symphonies; a *Piano Concerto* (1962, Pulitzer Prize 1963); and two operas, *Vanessa* (1958, Pulitzer Prize 1959) and *Antony and Cleopatra* (1966). *See also* Romantic Music.

Barber of Seville, The (1816), 3-act comic opera by Gioacchino Antonio Rossini, Italian libretto by Cesare Sterbini, after Pierre Beaumarchais' play satirizing aristocratic foibles. Performed first in Rome, it was a failure, but had a successful performance in New York (1819). Figaro (baritone) is a clever, boastful barber of 17th-century Spain who helps Count Almaviva (tenor) to win Rosina (soprano) in spite of the efforts of her guardian Bartolo (bass) to marry her for her dowry.

Barberry, thorny shrub widespread in northern temperate regions. Leaves and small, yellow flowers appear at same time in spring. The small, red fruit is a favorite of birds. Height: 7ft (2m). Among the 300 species are the American *Berberis canadensis*, European *B. vulgaris*, and Japanese *B. thunbergii*. Family Berberidaceae.

Barbet, brightly colored tropical bird, related to the toucan and honeyguide, known for its annoying sounds. They are stocky, coarse looking birds, with heavy bills, beardlike bristles, and short legs. They feed mainly on fruit. They excavate a cavity in a tree limb leading to a chamber where white eggs (2–5) are laid. Length: 4–13in (10–33cm). Family Capitonidae.

Barbiturates, drugs used to induce sleep or sedation. Among the common barbiturates are phenobarbital, secobarbital (Seconal), pentobarbital (Nembutal). When taken in prescribed doses, they are safe, effective medical agents, but barbiturates are also dangerous drugs: in large doses they are addictive, and when combined with other drugs such as alcohol or tranquilizers can produce unexpected unconsciousness and death.

Barbizon School, school of painting that derives its name from a village 30 miles southeast of Paris near the forest of Fontainebleau. A group of artists, led by Théodore Rousseau, gathered there (*c.*1830–80) to discuss art and to paint what was simple and commonplace in nature. Many artists visited. Millet, Courbet, Daumier, and Corot were inspired to do searching landscapes there.

Barbour, John (*c.*1316–1395), Scottish poet. About 1375 he wrote *The Bruce*, Scottish literature's earliest epic, describing Scotland's fight for independence from England. It combines patriotic sentiment with historical accuracy.

Barcelona, seaport city in NE Spain, between Besos and Llobregat rivers on the Mediterranean Sea, 385mi (620km) NE of Madrid; capital of Barcelona prov. In 1714 Philip V of Spain captured the city; taken by French during Napoleonic Wars (1808–13). Barcelona has been the center of anarchist and separatist movements since 19th century. Industries: breweries, sawmills, furniture, petroleum. Founded 3rd century BC by Carthaginian Barca family. Pop. 2,000,000.

Barents, Willem (died 1597), Dutch navigator and explorer. He commanded several expeditions in search of a Northeast Passage. The arctic sea northeast of Scandinavia bears his name.

Barents Sea, part of Arctic Ocean, E of USSR and N of Norway; named for Dutch navigator Willem Barents. Main ports of Murmansk and Vardø are ice-free.

Barge, flat-bottomed boat used to transport cargo in inland waterways. Originally, goods were moved on unpowered (dumb) barges pulled by horses along towpaths. With the advent of powered barges, whole assemblies of interconnected powered and dumb barges were used on natural waterways. Today, barges that can haul 10,000 tons are towed by high-powered tugs for short voyages.

Bargello, Italian national art museum, Florence. It originated as the Palazzo del Podestà in 1255, and was converted into a prison in 1574 and into a museum in 1857–65. It is known for important Renaissance sculptures including Davids by Michelangelo, Donatello, and Verrocchio; bronzes by Cellini and Pollaiuolo; Giotto's portrait of Dante; and terra-cottas by Della Robbia.

Bari, port city in S Italy; capital of Bari prov. and Apulia region; an important Roman colony, it was later ruled by Saracens, Byzantines, Normans, Germans, and Venetians; embarkation point for Crusaders; joined Italy 1860; site of 11th-century cathedral, Norman castle, and archeological museum. Industries: food processing, oil refining, boatbuilding, textiles. Pop. 384,722.

Barite, a sulfate mineral, barium sulfate ($BaSO_4$). In sedimentary rocks and as gangue material in ore veins in limestone. Orthorhombic system tabular crystals or masses. Radiating clusters of crystals are called "barite roses." Colorless, white or yellow; hardness 3–3.5; sp gr 4.5.

Barium, common metallic element (symbol Ba) of the alkaline-earth group, discovered 1808 by Sir Humphrey Davy. Chief sources are heavy spar (sulfate) and witherite (carbonate). The barium atoms are opaque to X rays, and barium sulfate is taken internally to permit X-ray examination of the intestines. Properties: at. no. 56; at. wt. 137.34; sp. gr. 3.5; melt. pt. 1337 °F (726°C); boil. pt. 2984°F (1641°C); most common isotope Ba[138] (71.66%). *See also* Alkaline-earth Elements.

Bark, outer protective covering of a woody plant stem. It is made up of several layers. As food-conducting cells die, they become the inner layer. The cork layer, waxy and waterproof, is the thickest layer and hardens into the tough, often-fissured outer covering. Lenticels, spongy areas, allow the stem to breathe. In smooth-barked trees, the cork layer is active for the life of the tree; in rough-barked trees, the outer cork layer dies and cracks as the stem diameter increases. *See also* Cork.

Bark Beetle, or engraver beetle, small brown to black beetle that tunnels through inner bark and wood of trees. The tunnels of some form species-characteristic, engraving-like patterns. Family Scolytidae.

Barkley, Alben William (1877–1956), US vice president and political leader, b. Graves co, Ky. He served as a US representative (1913–27) and senator (1927–49; 1954–56) and was instrumental in securing passage of New Deal legislation. He was also Senate majority leader (1937–47). Under Pres. Harry Truman, he was vice president (1949–53).

Barley, cereal grass, native to Asia and Ethiopia, widely cultivated since 5000 BC. Three cultivated species are: *Hordeum vulgare*, favored in United States; *H. distichum*, commonly grown in Europe; and *H. irregulare*, or irregular barley, grown in Ethiopia. Barley is used as food for humans and animals, and in making malt beverages. Family Gramineae. *See also* Grass.

Bar Mitzvah, Jewish ceremony in which a young male (traditionally 13 years and 1 day) is initiated into the adult religious community by reading from the Torah as part of the worship service. A parallel ceremony, the Bat Mitzvah, for girls has been introduced in some synagogues and temples.

Barnabus, Christian apostle of the first century, originally named Joseph. Barnabus accompanied Paul (Saul) on two proselytizing missions to Cyprus and the European mainland. A rift developed between the two religious leaders; Paul replaced Barnabus as head of the Antioch church.

Barnacle, sessile crustacean living mostly on rocks and floating timber. Some are commensal on whales, turtles, and fish. There are also parasitic species. The free-swimming larvae settle permanently on their heads and their carapace becomes covered with a number of calcareous plates. The shrimplike adult stands on its head and uses its feet to kick food into its mouth. Two main types are those with stalks (goose barnacles) and those without stalks (acorn barnacles). There are 800 living species. Subclass Cirripedia. *See also* Crustacean.

Barnard, Christiaan (1922–), South African surgeon. On Dec. 3, 1967, he was the first to perform a human heart transplant and in 1974 he was the first to implant a second heart in a patient and to link the circulations of the two hearts so they worked together as one.

Barnard's Star, red dwarf star in the constellation Ophiuchus. It was discovered by US astronomer E. E. Barnard in 1916, and is remarkable for having the greatest proper motion of any star so far observed. A companion body, perhaps an orbiting planet, with a mass 15 times that of Jupiter, was detected near it in 1963. Characteristics: apparent mag. 9.5; absolute mag. 13.2; spectral type M5; distance 6.0 light-years.

Barnaul, city in Russian SFSR, USSR, on Ob River; capital of Altai Krai; industrial and trade center serving surrounding agricultural and mining area; site of agricultural and teachers' colleges. Founded 1738. Pop. 531,000.

Barn Owl, owl with a heart-shaped, monkeylike face and long legs mostly found in the Eastern Hemisphere. The widely distributed common barn owl *(Tyto alba)* lives in old buildings where its acute hearing helps it locate rodents and other prey in total darkness; other barn owls hunt during the day, except the nocturnal bay owl *(Phodilus badius)* of Asian forests. Family Tytonidae. *See also* Owl.

Barn Swallow, swift-flying, highly migratory swallow, commonly summering in the Northern Hemisphere and wintering in S Southern Hemisphere. It is generally steel blue above, chestnut to salmon to white below, and has a deeply forked tail. It feeds on insects and builds a mud-and-straw, feather-lined nest in a barn or other building for its brown- or purple-spotted white eggs (4–6). Length: 6–7in (15–17.5cm). Species *Hirundo rustica.*

Barnum, Phineas Taylor (1810–91), US showman and promoter, b. Bethel, Conn. A superb publicist, he established (1842) the American Museum in New York City, where he presented the dwarf Tom Thumb, a bearded lady, and other "freaks." In 1850 he brought Jenny Lind to the United States for a concert tour. After a temporary retirement from show business, he opened (1871) in Brooklyn, N.Y., his circus, billed as "The Greatest Show on Earth." He later merged (1881) with a rival to form Barnum and Bailey.

Baroda, city in W India, between Mahi and Narbada rivers; headquarters of the Gaikwars (18th century) who enhanced it with gardens and picturesque buildings; site of Baroda University (1949) and the State Museum and Picture Gallery (1894). Industries: cotton textiles, chemicals, pottery. Pop. 467,422.

Barometer, an instrument for measuring atmospheric pressure in order to predict probable local weather changes resulting from approaching fronts and air masses. Mercury and aneroid barometers are two basic types, and barographs are barometers recording changes in atmospheric pressure. *See also* Atmospheric Pressure.

Barons' War (1263–67), struggle between Henry III of England and his barons. Breaking his pledge to rule through a council of barons (1261), Henry provoked war (1263). Rejecting arbitration by Louis IX of France, the barons, under Simon de Montfort, defeated Henry at Lewes (1264) and summoned a parliament (1265). The royalists' victory at Evesham (1265) eventually ensured the barons' submission without securing their constitutional aims.

Baroque Architecture, architecture characterized by exuberant decoration, curvaceous forms, an emphasis on grand or superhuman scale, and a sense of movement. It flourished in the 17th and early 18th centuries and changed character according to the country in which it was used. Many buildings were designed to evoke a specific emotional response from those who entered. In the 18th century in England, France, and Italy a greater sense of restraint and classicism prevailed; for these exceptions the term "Baroque Classicism" is used.

Baroque Art, style of art from late 16th to early 18th centuries, between Mannerism and Rococo. The term is from the French, meaning odd or curious, and until the 19th century, Baroque art was thought of as absurd and grotesque. Italian Baroque is generally divided into three periods: Early (from 1585), High (from 1625), and Late (1675–1715). The style is characterized by a concern for balance and wholeness. To achieve a unified effect, parts of a large painting are subordinate to the whole, and paintings and sculpture are subordinate to the building they decorate.

Baroque art is also known for its high technical virtuosity and its reproduction of reality, ie, in the color and texture of an object. It is dynamic and attempts to involve the spectator in a specific dramatic moment. Strong opposites are evident, eg, light against dark, mass against void, and strong diagonals and curves. The aim is for the total effect, and often tricks of scene painting, such as false perspective and *trompe l'oeil,* are used to produce it. The sculpture and architecture of Bernini dominated High Baroque. His masterpieces include the Piazza before St. Peter's and his marble group "Ecstasy of St. Teresa." In painting, Cortona's "The Rape of the Sabines" and his famous ceilings exemplify the style. Rubens, Rembrandt, Van Dyck, Velázquez, and Murillo painted in the Baroque style.

Baroque Music, music composed from roughly 1600 to 1750. The period is notable for the development of contrapuntal (polyphonic) music culminating in the masterpieces of J. S. Bach and Handel, the development of opera, oratorio, and cantata featuring solo singers, and the emergence of many purely instrumental forms of music such as the fugue, sonata, concerto, suite, toccata, passacaglia, and chaconne. Many composer-musicians were employed and patronized by royal courts of Europe. Some of the other major composers of this period include Monteverdi, Vivaldi, and Scarlatti from Italy, Lully, Couperin, and Rameau from France, Buxtehude and Telemann from Germany, and Purcell from England. Though German by birth, Handel spent much of his highly successful career in England. *See also* Cantata; Opera; Oratorio; Polyphony.

Barque, standard merchant ship in the North Atlantic during the second half of the 19th century, characterized by two square-rigged masts and a third with fore-and-aft sails.

Barracouta, or snoek, atun, South African mackerel, commercial food fish found in tropical and temperate marine waters. A snake (deep-sea) mackerel, it has a laterally compressed body, elongated lower jaw, and two dorsal fins. Length: 3.3ft (lm); weight: 8.8–13.2lb (4–6kg). Family Gempylidae; species *Thyrsites atun.*

Barracuda, marine fish found in tropical Atlantic and Pacific. Known to attack man, it has a large mouth with razor sharp teeth; its olive green body is elongated. Length: to 6ft. (183cm.); weight: 3–50lbs.(1.4–23kg.). Family Sphyraenidae; species 20, including Great *Sphyraena barracuda.*

Barranquilla, city and port in N Colombia, on Magdalena River; capital of Atlántico dept. In 1935 the river channel was deepened to accommodate ocean-going vessels; rich agricultural region; site of two universities. Industries: canneries, flour mills, petrochemicals. Founded 1629. Pop. 661,920.

Barras, Paul, Vicomte de (1755–1829), French leader, important member of the Directory during the Revolution, 1795–99. He influenced Napoleon's rise to power. Napoleon became suspicious of him, however, and intermittently kept Barras out of France.

Barred Owl, North American owl with barred, brown plumage and a strident call. Length: 1.3–1.7ft (40–52cm). Species *Strix varia. See also* Owl.

Barred Spiral Galaxy, type of spiral galaxy in which the arms extend from opposite sides of an elongated central section resembling a bar. Barred spiral galaxies are graded in three groups, SBa to SBc, according to increasing openness of their spiral arms. *See also* Galaxy; Spiral Galaxy.

Barrel Cactus, barrel-shaped cactus of North America. Most have stout, hooked spines and obvious ribs. Flowers, varying in color, are usually fragrant. Many smaller species with showy blooms are kept as houseplants. Family Cactaceae; genera *Ferocactus*—height: to 10ft (3m)—and *Echinocactus*—height: to 2ft (61cm). *See also* Cactus.

Barrel Organ, mechanical musical instrument developed in 15th-century Holland. Pins on a rotating drum control organ pipes fed from a wind chest. Mozart wrote three compositions for it; a portable modification, the hurdy-gurdy, is used by street musicians.

Barrie, (Sir) James Matthew (1860–1937), Scottish dramatist and novelist. His novel, *The Little Minister* (1891), established his reputation as a novelist, but after the production of his play *Walker, London* (1892) he devoted himself to the theater, writing mostly light dramas. *Peter Pan* (1904), *Dear Brutus* (1917), and *Mary Rose* (1920) were sentimental fantasies for children. Among his other plays were *The Professor's Love Story* (1895), *Quality Street* (1903), *The Admirable Crichton* (1903), and *What Every Woman Knows* (1908).

Barrier Reef, a long narrow coral reef lying roughly parallel to the shore but separated from it by a large deep lagoon. The Great Barrier Reef of Australia is the most famous.

Barrow, village in Alaska; the northernmost US community, it is 9mi (14km) SW of Point Barrow. US Navy operates Arctic Research Laboratory nearby. Whaling is chief industry. Pop. (1980) 2,207.

Barrymores, acting family, known as the "royal family of the American stage." **Maurice** (1847–1905) was the patriarch of the clan, b. Herbert Blythe in Agra, India. He gave up a career in law to be an actor, making his stage debut in a London production of *London Assurance* (1872). In 1875 he went to the United States where he joined Augustin Daly's stock company and married Georgiana Drew, daughter of a US acting family. Their children—**Lionel** (1878–1954), **Ethel** (1879–1959), and **John** (1882–1942)—all b. Philadelphia, were raised in the tradition of the theater. Lionel made his debut at age 6. At 15 he returned to the stage in Sheridan's *The Rivals.* After studying painting in Paris for 3 years he starred in *Peter Ibbitson* (1917), *The Copperhead* (1918), and *The Jest* (1919). He won an Academy Award for *Free Soul* (1931). He made many films and starred in the "Dr. Kildare" series on radio and film. Ethel made her stage debut at age 14, after giving up plans to be a pianist. Her stage roles included *A Doll's House* (1905), *Trelawney of the Wells* (1911), and *The Corn Is Green* (1942). She won an Academy Award for *None but the Lonely Heart* (1944). John, known as the "Great Profile," made his stage debut at 11 in *Magda.* After a long and successful stage career that covered modern and classical roles, he went to Hollywood where he starred in *Beau Brummel* (1924), *Don Juan* (1926), *Grand Hotel* (1932), and *Dinner at Eight* (1933). The three Barrymore children co-starred in *Rasputin and the Empress* (1932).

Barter, exchange of one good or service for another without the benefit of money as a medium of exchange. A barter agreement among countries calls for exchange of stated amounts of goods.

Barth, John (1930–), US author, b. Cambridge, Md. A professor of English, he has written several novels. His works are complex and imaginative. They include *The End of the Road* (1958), *The Sot-Weed Factor* (1960), *Giles Goat-Boy* (1966), and *Chimera* (1972), three novellas for which Barth won the 1973 National Book Award in fiction, *Letters* (1979), and *Sabbatical: A Romance* (1982).

Barth, Karl (1886–1968), Swiss theologian. A leading thinker of 20th-century Protestantism, he tried to lead theology back to principles of the Reformation and to emphasize the revelation of God through Jesus Christ. His school has been called dialectical theology or theology of the word. In 1935 he was deported from Germany for his anti-Nazi stance. His works include *Epistle to the Romans* (1918) and the four-volume *Church Dogmatics* (1932–62).

Bartholdi, Frédéric Auguste (1834–1904), French sculptor. He is well known for the Statue of Liberty in New York Harbor, dedicated in 1886. His best work is the "Lion of Belfort" in Belfort, France.

Bartholomew, according to the New Testament, one of the 12 apostles of Christ. It has been conjectured that he might be identical with Nathanael.

Bartlett, Josiah (1729–95), American patriot and a signer of the Declaration of Independence, b. Amesbury, Mass. After a successful medical practice, he served variously as chief justice of the New Hampshire superior court (1788–90), chief executive of the state, and then governor (1793–94).

Bartók, Béla (1881–1945), Hungarian composer. With Zoltán Kodály, Bartok amassed a definitive collection of Hungarian folk music that became the basis of many of his compositions. His early works exhibited a preference for dissonance and avoided sentimentality. Later works display more attention to melody and a mastery of orchestration. His orchestral works contain a number of masterpieces including *Music for Strings, Percussion, and Celesta* (1936), *Violin Concerto No. 2* (1938), and *Concerto for Orchestra* (1943). His six string quartets have been regarded as the finest since Beethoven. He was also a piano virtuoso and composed many piano pieces, including *Mikrokosmos,* a six-volume set of progressive piano pieces. *See also* Kodály, Zoltán.

Barton, Clara (Clarissa Harlowe) (1821–1912), US educator and humanitarian, b. Oxford, Mass. She taught school (1836–54) before establishing a very successful free school in New Jersey. During the Civil War she traveled with the Union Army to nurse the

P.T. Barnum

Ethel and John Barrymore

Clara Barton

wounded, provide supplies, and search for the missing. She went abroad (1869) to do similar work in the Franco-Prussian War with the International Red Cross. When she returned to the United States, she founded the American National Red Cross (1881) and campaigned for US ratification of the Geneva Convention (1882). She was responsible for the "American Amendment" at the Geneva Convention (1884), which provided for the Red Cross to be active in peacetime emergency work, such as floods, hurricanes, and other natural disasters.

Baruch, the personal scribe used by the biblical prophet Jeremiah in transcribing his first and second scrolls. Baruch went into hiding with Jeremiah after the prophesies were read to Jehoiakim, king of Judah, who burned them. God ordered the scrolls rewritten. His name was given to the Book of Baruch.

Baryon, member of a subgroup of hadrons, all of which have half-integral spin. They include the proton and neutron (nucleons) and the long-lived hyperons. A quantum number, the baryon number, may be assigned as $+1$ for baryons, -1 for antibaryons, and 0 for mesons. In any nuclear reaction the baryon number must remain constant: baryons cannot be created or destroyed except in pairs of baryons and antibaryons. *See also* Hadron; Meson; Quark.

Basalt, hard, fine-grained igneous rock, which may be intrusive or extrusive. The most common rock found in volcanic lava, its color can be dark green, brown, dark gray, or black. Its composition is chiefly plagioclase, feldspar, and pyroxene, and it often has a glassy appearance. *See also* Igneous Rocks; Plagioclase.

Base, chemical compound that can react with an acid to form a salt (and water). Most bases are oxides or hydroxides of metals or are compounds, such as ammonia, that yield hydroxide ions in water. Soluble bases are also called alkalis. Bases give solutions that contain hydroxide ions (OH^-) and give a blue color to litmus paper. Strong bases, such as caustic soda ($NaOH$), are fully dissociated into ions; weak bases, such as ammonia (NH_3), are partially dissociated in solution. *See also* Acid.

Base (geometric), side opposite the vertex of a triangle from which an altitude is drawn. The area of a triangle is one half the product of the base and the height. *See also* Triangle.

Baseball, sport popular in the United States (where it is the national game), Japan, the Caribbean, and Latin America. The top US professional teams are divided into the American and National Leagues. It is played by two opposing teams of nine players each—a pitcher, catcher, four infielders, and three outfielders.
　Rules. Except for a 1973 American League ruling that allows a designated hitter to bat for the pitcher without having to play the field, players may not return to the game once they are replaced. There are usually four umpires in a game who rule on all aspects of play. A regulation game is divided into nine innings; each team having three outs in an inning and runs being scored each time a player completes a circuit of four bases. Games tied at the end of nine innings are played until there is a winner, except for curfew limits or rain delays, in which case the game, from the point it ended, is rescheduled. The home team always bats last, except if it is leading after the visitors have completed their half of the ninth inning, in which case it has won the game, and there is no need to bat. In the United States, the two leagues are the American and National. The American League of 14 teams is composed

of the Baltimore Orioles, Boston Red Sox, California Angels, Chicago White Sox, Cleveland Indians, Detroit Tigers, Oakland Athletics, Kansas City Royals, Minnesota Twins, Milwaukee Brewers, New York Yankees, Seattle Mariners, Texas Rangers, and Toronto Bluejays. The National League of 12 teams is composed of the Atlanta Braves, Chicago Cubs, Cincinnati Reds, Houston Astros, Los Angeles Dodgers, Montreal Expos, New York Mets, Philadelphia Phillies, Pittsburgh Pirates, St. Louis Cardinals, San Diego Padres, and San Francisco Giants. The teams in each league are divided into two divisions. Each team plays a 162-game schedule, and the winner of each division competes in a best-three-out-of-five playoff series. The winners then compete in a World Series (held annually since 1905), a best-four-out-of-seven series, to decide the champion.
　History. Baseball is believed to have its roots in the English game of rounders, played in the 19th century. Although credit is given to Abner Doubleday for inventing baseball in Cooperstown, N.Y. (the site of the Baseball Hall of Fame), in 1839, the claim is refuted by some authorities. In 1846, Alexander J. Cartwright, a surveyor, established a set of rules and the guidelines to the playing field, which included having the bases 90 feet (27.4m) apart. The game was further enhanced by a set of playing rules written in 1858 by Henry Chadwick.
　After the Civil War, when the game was popular with Union soldiers, the first professional team, the Cincinnati Red Stockings, began playing in 1869. Their success led to the formation of the first professional league, the National Association, which began in 1871 and gave way to the National League in 1876. Other professional leagues were formed, but none survived except for the American League, which began play as a major league in 1901.

Basel (Bâle, or **Basle),** city in NW Switzerland, on the Rhine River; capital of Basel canton; joined the Swiss Confederation 1501; site of cathedral where Erasmus is buried, medieval gates, 16th-century town hall, 15th-century university, and annual Swiss Industries Fair. Industries: publishing, silk textiles, food produce, metal goods. Pop. 192,800.

Basel, Council of, Roman Catholic Church council convoked at Basel in 1431. It instituted church reforms and conciliated the Hussites in Bohemia. Conflict with Pope Eugene IV over conciliar authority led the pope to denounce the council in 1437. In 1439, the council declared Eugene deposed and chose an antipope, Amadeus of Savoy, as Pope Felix V. Felix resigned in 1449 and the council was dissolved.

Basenji, ancient, deerlike, barkless hunting dog (hound group) originating in central Africa. It has a flat head with rounded muzzle and wrinkled forehead; small, pointed erect ears; and almond-shaped eyes. The short body is deep-chested; legs are long and strong; and the high-set tail is curled tightly over to the side. Its short, silky coat can be chestnut red, black, or tan. Feet, chest, and tip of tail are white. Average size: 17in (43cm) high at shoulder; 24lb (11kg). *See also* Hound.

Basil I, Byzantine emperor (r. 867–86) and founder of the Macedonian dynasty. The son of a provincial peasant, Basil was befriended by Emperor Michael III, who assisted him in his rise to power. After Michael designated him as co-emperor, Basil had his former patron murdered and assumed sole power in Byzantium. Basil's most effective policies concerned the conversion of the Bulgars to Orthodox Christianity rather than to Roman Catholicism; military campaigns against the

Paulician religious sect in Asia Minor; and an attempted revision of Roman legal codes.

Basil II (958?–1025), Byzantine emperor (976–1025), surnamed Bulgaroctonus ("Bulgar-slayer"). One of Byzantium's ablest rulers, Basil presided over the apogee of the empire. He is best known for his military victory over the Bulgarian tsar Samuel in 1014, which brought the entire Balkan peninsula under Byzantine control. During Basil's reign, the empire's sphere of influence was further enlarged by the conversion of Kievan Russia to Orthodox Christianity.

Basil, common name for *Ocimum basilicum,* an annual of the tropics. An aromatic herb of the mint family with white or purple flowers, its dried leaves are used for seasoning.

Basilica, Roman, long halls used as commercial markets and courtrooms, related in plan to the Greek temple. Basilicas were typically rectangular, with colonnades and one or more apses. The earliest examples date from the 2nd century BC and were next to the Forum.

Basilica Church, the earliest type of Christian church, first erected *c.* 312 AD under Constantine. A long colonnaded hall, with altar at the east end and entrance at the west, was characteristic. Plain exteriors contrasted with richly decorated interiors.

Basilisk, semi-aquatic lizard found in trees near streams of tropical America. It has a compressed greenish body, whiplike tail, crest on its back, and an inflatable pouch on its head. It can run over water in a two-legged fashion, and eats plants and insects. Length: to 20in (51cm). Family Iguanidae; genus *Basiliscus.*

Basin, Oceanic, one of two major provinces of the deep ocean floor, lying at over 2km (1.2mi) in depth. The mid-ocean ridges is the other province. Together they constitute 56% of the earth's surface. The deep ocean basin is underlain by a thin crust, about 7km (4.3mi) thick, and is covered by thin sediment and dotted by low abyssal hills.

Basketball, fast-action ball game, most popular in the United States, where it is played professionally. It is also played extensively in Europe, Latin America, and Asia. It is played by two teams of five persons each, usually indoors, on a court a maximum of 94 feet (28.7m) in length and 50 feet (15.2m) in width. At each end of the court is a backboard to which a metal ring is attached, 18 inches (45.7cm) in diameter and 10 feet (3m) above the floor. Bottomless netting is usually attached to the rim. The five players consists of two guards, two forwards, and a center, with free substitution permitted.
　Rules. Players may pass, dribble, roll, or throw the ball, but may not run with it. The object is to advance the ball to the team's own basket and attempt to score by shooting the ball through the top of the basket. Each field goal counts two points, and free throws (shots taken as the result of penalties) count as one point. Professionals, who play four 12-minute quarters, are allowed to commit six fouls before being eliminated from a game. Collegians, who play two 20-minute halves, are allowed five fouls. If a contest ends in a tie, five-minute quarters are played until the deadlock is broken.
　History. Basketball was invented in 1891 by Dr. James Naismith, a physical education instructor at the YMCA college in Springfield, Mass. Professional basketball began in 1896 in New York City, but did not reach its popularity as a spectator sport until 1954,

when the game was greatly enhanced by the "24-second rule" (professional only), requiring that a team shoot within 24 seconds or lose possession of the ball. The most popular major basketball league today is the National Basketball Association, which began in 1949 with the merger of the National Basketball League and the Basketball Association of America. Another major league, the American Basketball Association, was formed in 1961. Four of its teams were incorporated into the NBA in 1976, and the rest disbanded. The game is a major sport at colleges and high schools in the United States. The most popular of all post-season collegiate tournaments is the National Collegiate Athletic Association championships, begun in 1939. The sport has been a part of the Olympic Games since 1936.

Basques, people inhabiting N Spain and SW France in the W foothills of the Pyrenees, numbering approximately 900,000. They are of unknown origin, and their language has no known relationship with any other language. Traditionally farmers, shipbuilders, and sailors, they possess a fierce independence that led to bloody clashes with the Spanish government and acts of terrorism in their fight for regional autonomy in the 1970s. Terrorism continued despite the granting of home rule in 1980.

Basra (Al-Basrah), port city in Iraq, on the Shatt al-Arab River; capital of Basra prov: second in importance to Baghdad during Abbasid dynasty (750–1258); destroyed by Mongols 13th century and rebuilt 8mi (13km) from original site. Under Ottoman Empire (17th century), it was opened as a port to European traders; harbor was renovated by British in WWI and used as a supply route to Russia during WWII. Industries: oil, grains. Exports: dates. Founded 638. Pop. 915,000.

Bass, marine and freshwater food and game fish. The marine striped bass *(Roccus saxatilis)* is found along the Atlantic coast of North America and is a major game fish. Length: 6ft (183cm); weight: 125lb (56kg). Smallmouth bass *(Micropterus dolomieu)* and large-mouth bass *(Micropterus salmoides)* are found in North American fresh waters. Weight: 12–25lb (5–11kg). The black bass *(Centropristis striatus)* is a valuable food fish. Length: to 2ft (61cm); weight: 8lb (3.5kg). Another marine bass, the channel bass or red drum *(Sciaenops ocellata)*, is an important food and game fish of the American Atlantic. Length: 5ft (152.4cm); weight: 75lb (34kg). Order Perciformes.

Bass Clarinet, woodwind musical instrument (sometimes metal) ranging 3 octaves, one below the B*b* clarinet. It has a single-reed mouthpiece bent horizontally and a bell bent upward. It is used in symphony orchestras. *See also* Clarinet.

Basse Terre, town in British West Indies, on St Kitts Island in Leeward Islands group; capital of St Kitts-Nevis; commercial center. Founded 1627. Pop. 15,897.

Basse-Terre, seaport town in French West Indies; capital of French dept. of Guadeloupe; important import-export center serving surrounding agricultural region. Founded 1643. Pop. 15,690.

Basset Horn, musical instrument resembling a bass clarinet without the horizontal mouthpiece. It was used by Mozart in *The Magic Flute* and *The Marriage of Figaro* and by Richard Strauss in *Salome* and *Electra.* It is usually replaced today by the alto clarinet. *See also* Bass Clarinet; Clarinet.

Basset Hound, hunting dog (hound group) originating in France several centuries ago. It has a large, domed head; deep, heavy muzzle; hanging lips; and dewlaps. The low-set, very long ears hang in folds; eyes are sad. A long, level body is set on short, heavy-boned legs; the long tail is carried up. Coat is hard and short; colors are white, tan, and black. Skin is loose and elastic. Average size: 12–15in (30–38cm) high at shoulder; 25–50lb (11–23kg). The basset is used for trailing game by scent over rough terrain. *See also* Hound.

Bassoon, main bass instrument of symphony orchestra woodwinds, with a range of 3 octaves corresponding to the cello. It has a double-reed mouthpiece and a conical bore, the tube bending back on itself to reduce length. Bassoons are used extensively in modern symphonic and chamber music.

Bass Strait, channel in SE Australia connecting the Indian Ocean and the Tasman Sea; Melbourne is on its NW coast; important fishing industry. Discovered by George Bass (1798). Length: 185mi (266km). Width: 80–150mi (129–241km).

Bastille, 14th-century fort and prison in Paris. Because political prisoners were traditionally incarcerated there, it became a symbol of royal oppression. On July 14, 1789, a Parisian mob stormed it, captured the ammunition stored there, and released its prisoners (only seven, none of them political). Its governor was killed, its troops surrendered, and the fort was destroyed. This action marked the beginning of the French Revolution, and its anniversary (July 14) is celebrated as the major French holiday.

Bastogne, town in SE Belgium, 23mi (37km) N of Arlon; held by US troops during the Battle of the Bulge (1944) when Germans were driven back (1945); highway and railroad junction. Pop. 6,816.

Basutoland. *See* Lesotho.

Bat, only mammal that can fly rather than glide. Bats are nocturnal and found in all tropical and temperate regions. Most are brown, gray, or black. The bat's wing is formed by a sheet of skin stretched over a frame of greatly elongated "arm" and "hand" bones. Bats are able to fly and hunt in complete darkness by a kind of sonar, which uses echoes of the bat's own supersonic squeaks to locate obstacles and prey. Many bats live largely on insects, some are carnivorous, some live on flower nectar and pollen, and one group—the flying foxes—subsists on fruit. They are generally small, ranging in length from 0.75–15in (2–38cm). The 178 genera of bats make up the order Chiroptera.

Bataan, province of the Philippines, on peninsula of Luzon Island, extending S from W central coast, shielding Manila Bay from South China Sea. Densely forested on W side, population is concentrated along E bay; scene of heavy fighting during WWII between American-Philippine forces and Japanese forces. Crops: rice, sugar cane. Pop. 214,131.

Batan (Batanese Islands), island group between Luzon Island, Philippines, and Formosa Island; the northernmost prov. of the Philippines, is comprised mainly of Zitberat, Y'ami, and Batan islands; capital is Basco, on Batan Island. Industries: sugar cane, rice, coal mining. Area: 80sq mi (207sq km). Pop. 11,425.

Batavi, or **Batavians,** Germanic tribe living in the Rhine-Meuse delta area of what is now Netherlands about the time of Christ. Noted as warriors, they served in the Roman army. About 70 AD, Claudius Civilis led them in an unsuccessful revolt against Roman rule. In the 4th century they were displaced by the Salian Franks.

Batavian Republic (1795–1806), name for the Netherlands after its conquest by the French. The principal accomplishment of the republic was the beginning of social and political modernization. In 1806 it became the Kingdom of Holland, ruled by Louis Bonaparte.

Bateson, William (1861–1926), English biologist. He founded and named the science of genetics. His experiments served as a foundation for the modern understanding of heredity. Bateson translated much of Gregor Mendel's pioneering work on plant mutation and was instrumental in bringing it recognition as well as extending, through his own experiments, Mendel's theories to animals.

Batfish, bottom-dwelling, marine angler fish of W Atlantic and E Pacific. Flat-bodied and scaleless, it has large armlike pectoral fins. Length: to 15in (38.1cm). Family Ogocephalidae; species 60, including short-nosed *Ogocephalus nasutus. See also* Anglerfish.

Bath, city in SW England, on the River Avon, 10mi (16km) SE of Bristol. Hot springs discovered here by Romans in 1st century have been used to treat rheumatism, arthritis, and gout. In the 18th century the city became a fashionable resort area, and appeared in much contemporary British literature; fine examples of Georgian architecture remain; site of homes of Admiral Nelson, William Pitt, Charles Dickens. Each June the Bath Festival features music, drama, sports. Industries: printing, electrical engineering, paint, tourism, soap. Chartered 1189. Pop. 84,300.

Batholith, huge mass of igneous material that reaches the earth's surface. A batholith is so considered if it has an exposed surface of about 40 sq mi (104 sq km). It may have been originally an intrusive igneous structure, which eventually became surface material as a result of erosion.

Baths, public bathing facilities. At first they were probably related to religious ritual. Baths existed in ancient Egypt and the Indus River Valley. The classical Greeks built elaborate public baths. These were copied and further embellished with mosaics and gilt details by the Romans. Water was brought by aqueduct from reservoirs and heated in pipes. The grandest Roman baths, now in ruin, were built by three emperors: Titus (80), Caracalla (212–35), and Diocletian (302). Even more richly designed baths were built later in Islamic nations, including the baths of the Alhambra in Granada, Spain, built in the 14th century.

Bathsheba, in the Bible, wife of Uriah the Hittite and, later, wife of David, who arranged Uriah's death in battle. Solomon was one of her sons by David.

Baths of Caracalla, Roman baths (thermae) built at Rome (211–17 AD). The huge enclosure included gardens, a stadium, and lecture rooms as well as the *tepidarium* (warm lounge), *caldarium* (hot room), and *frigidarium* (cooling room with open-air swimming pool).

Bathurst (Banjul), capital of the Republic of Gambia, W Africa, in W Gambia on St Mary's Island where Gambia River enters the Atlantic Ocean; port and economic center of Gambia. Industries: peanut processing, shipping of skins, hides, beeswax. Founded 1816 by British as a trading post. Pop. 36,570.

Bathymetric Chart, a map that shows the topography of the sea bottom. Contour lines connect all known and extrapolated points at the same depth below sea-level. Data are obtained by sounding techniques, especially echo sounding, sonar, and underwater television. *See also* Sonar.

Batik, technique for decorating textiles by covering with molten wax the portions of a design that are to remain undyed, dyeing the exposed area, removing the wax, rewaxing, and redyeing. The process is repeated for each color desired. The technique was originally developed in Malaya.

Bat Mitzvah. *See* Bar Mitzvah.

Baton Rouge, capital city of Louisiana, in SE central section, on the Mississippi River, 78mi (126km) WNW of New Orleans; seat of East Baton Rouge parish; farthest-inland deep water port on the Gulf of Mexico; ceded to Britain by France 1763, and to United States with Louisiana Purchase (1803); site of large petrochemical complex, Louisiana State University, and Southern University. Industries: natural gas, chemicals, plastics, wood products. Settled 1719; inc. 1817; became capital 1849. Pop. (1980) 219,486.

Battenberg, German princely family. In the 19th century, the titles prince and princess of Battenberg were bestowed on the morganatic grandchildren of the grand duke of Hesse-Darmstadt. One of them, Louis Battenberg (1854–1921), became an English admiral, was created marquess of Milford Haven, and married a granddaughter of Queen Victoria. During World War I, the English branch of the Battenbergs anglicized the name to Mountbatten. Prince Philip, Duke of Edinburgh, is a Mountbatten.

Battery, a collection of cells that convert different types of energy, usually chemical, into direct current electrical energy. Primary batteries, such as those in a flashlight, cannot be re-charged, unlike storage batteries, which are re-charged when a current in the reverse direction restores the original chemical state. The lead and sulfuric acid battery, used in the automobile, is most common.

Battle of. . . . *See* second part of name.

Battleship, most powerful type of naval warship during the late 19th and early 20th centuries, displacing from 10,000 to over 75,000 tons. Battleships combined the thickest armor and the most powerful naval guns. In addition to their main armament, housed in huge armored turrets, most were armed with smaller batteries for combating lighter enemy warships, and, later, automatic weapons for protection against aircraft. During World War II the striking power of the battleship was surpassed by that of the aircraft carrier. The few surviving battleships are limited to amphibious support missions. *See also* Aircraft Carrier.

Batu Khan (died 1255), Mongol leader who defeated Russia in 1240 and also controlled Hungary, Poland, and Bohemia. His invasion was made easier by the lack of unity among the Russian rulers. He planned to invade Europe, but returned to the East to choose a successor to head the Mongol empire (1241).

Batumi (Batum), seaport city in SW Georgian SSR, USSR, on the Black Sea; capital of Adzhar ASSR; major port and trade center, near Turkish border; site of oil pipeline and Soviet naval base. City was site of ancient Greek colony of Batis; medieval hold of Georgia; possession of Turks 16th century–1878, when it was annexed to Russia. Industries: oil refining and shipping, food processing, engineering works. Pop. 118,000.

Basset hound

Bayeaux tapestry: detail

Beak: red-tailed hawk

Baudelaire, Charles (1821–67), French poet and critic, precursor of Symbolist poetry. He contributed to reviews and translated Edgar Allan Poe. Baudelaire was charged with obscenity on the publication of his volume of poetry *Les Fleurs du Mal* (1857). His critical works include *Curiosités esthétiques* (1868) and *L'Art Romantique* (1869).

Baudouin (1930–), king of Belgium (1951–). He succeeded his unpopular father, Leopold III, who abdicated in his favor. He granted independence to the Belgian Congo (1960) and encouraged the formation of the Common Market.

Bauhaus, school for architects and artists founded at Weimar, Germany, in 1919 by Walter Gropius. Such diverse talents as Marcel Breuer, Paul Klee, Wassily Kandinsky, Lázló Moholy-Nagy, and Ludwig Mies van der Rohe worked together to produce a distinctly modern approach to design. The Bauhaus style emphasized craftsmanship and its architecture, in particular, was severely functional. The Bauhaus, which moved to Dessau in 1925, aroused opposition from the traditionalists, and it was closed by the Nazis in 1933. Most of its members moved to the United States, where Chicago became the center of the Bauhaus style.

Bauhinia, genus of evergreen shrubs, trees, and woody climbing vines, native to tropical and subtropical areas of the world. They are grown for their showy flowers and foliage. Family Leguminosae.

Bavaria (Bayern), largest state of West Germany; bounded by East Germany (N), Hesse and Baden-Württemberg (W), Austria (S), Czechoslovakia (E); Munich is the capital. Part of Roman Empire until 5th century; taken by Charlemagne 788; part of Holy Roman Empire 10th century; ruled by Wittelsbach family 1180–1918, who joined it to Second German Empire in 1871; became republic 1918; constitution was abolished 1933; came under W Germany as state of Bavaria 1946; agricultural region. Industries: tourism, glass, porcelain, Bavarian beer. Area: 27,239sq mi (70,549sq km). Pop. 10,810,400.

Bayamón, town in NE central Puerto Rico; first municipality in Puerto Rico to be settled; industrial and residential suburb of San Juan. Crops: coffee, tobacco, fruit, sugar. Founded 1772. Pop. (municipality) 154,440; (town) 146,363; (city) 205,800.

Bayberry, North American shrub with evergreen, aromatic leaves, naked flowers, and small fruits covered with a greenish-white wax used in making bayberry candles and perfumed soap. Height: to 35ft (11m). Family Myricaceae; species *Myrica cenifera*.

Bayeux Tapestry (11th–12th century), actually an embroidery, in the Bayeux Museum, Bayeux, France. Depicting in more than 70 scenes the Norman Conquest of England (1066), it is 230ft by 20in (70m by 51cm). Traditionally it is attributed to Queen Matilda, wife of William the Conqueror, but is probably of a somewhat later date. As well as a fine work of art, it is an important source of the costuming and military history of the time.

Bay of Pigs Invasion (1961), an unsuccessful effort by Cuban exiles to overthrow Premier Fidel Castro by invading the south coast of Cuba near the Bay of Pigs. About 1500 Cubans, trained, equipped, and transported by the United States, were involved. President Kennedy, after an initial denial, accepted US responsibility for the invasion attempt, which became a propaganda benchmark for both Cuba and Cuban exiles.

Bayonne, port town in SW France, at confluence of Nive and Adour rivers, near Bay of Biscay. Taken by English in 1199; French since 1451. A citadel dating from 1633–1707 overlooks the harbor and city. Industries: shipbuilding, distilling, chocolates. Pop. 44,706.

Bayonne, city in NE New Jersey, on a 3-mi (5-km) peninsula between New York Bay and Newark Bay; site of huge oil refineries (since 1875), US naval supply depot. Industries: chemicals, metal products, textiles, yacht building. First visited by Henry Hudson in 1609; settled by Dutch and English 1656; inc. 1869. Pop. (1980) 65,047.

Bayonne Decree (1808), order issued by Napoleon to seize all US ships in French-controlled ports. It was issued in the wake of the US embargo acts.

Bayou, a lake or sluggish stagnant stream, with an almost imperceptible current, that follows a winding course through alluvial lowlands, coastal swamps, marshes, or river deltas. The term is localized to the lower Mississippi River basin.

Bayreuth, city in S West Germany, 41mi (66km) NE of Nürnberg, on Roter Main River; belonged to branch of the Hohenzollern family (1248–1791); taken by Prussia 1791; ceded to Bavaria 1810; scene of annual Bayreuth Festival of Wagnerian music held in Festspielhaus (opera house designed by Wagner). Industries: textiles, metals, machinery. Founded 1194. Pop. 66,-900.

Baytown, city in SE Texas, 22mi (35km) ESE of Houston; location of shipyard dating to Civil War. Industries: oil, rubber products, petrochemicals. Settled 1864. Pop. (1980) 56,923.

Bazaine, François Achille (1811–88), French military officer and marshal of France. He served in the Crimean War (1854–56) and in Mexico (1863). Created marshal in 1864, he commanded French troops in the Franco-Prussian War (1870–71). His incompetence led to the disaster at Sedan, in which Emperor Napoleon III and his army were captured. Convicted of treason in 1873—for intrigues with the Germans during the war—Bazaine escaped and lived thereafter in exile. *See also* Franco-Prussian War.

Bazille, Jean-Frédéric (1841–70), French painter. A patron and member of the Impressionists, he was influential to that movement's growth. He worked with Monet and Renoir and gained his first success with his *Family Reunion,* shown in the Paris Salon of 1868. He died in the Franco-Prussian War. *See also* Impressionism.

BBC (British Broadcasting Corporation), state-financed radio and television network. Its directors are appointed by the government, but in terms of policy and content, the BBC is largely independent. It was set up in 1927 to replace the British Broadcasting Company that had been in operation since 1922. Its first director-general (1927–38) was Lord Reith, whose philosophy of the BBC as an instrument of education and civilization has greatly shaped the policies of the corporation.

BCG, or *Bacillus Calmette-Guerin,* a vaccine against tuberculosis, named for its discoverers, the French bacteriologists Albert Calmette and Camille Guerin.

Beach, the gently sloping zone of the shore, covered by sediment, sand, or pebbles, that extends from the low-water line to the limit of highest storm waves. The sediment is derived from erosion or river alluvium.

Waves washing on the beach move the sediment back and forth so the heavier pebbles remain on the beach and the sand works down into the water.

Beach Flea, or sand hopper, semi-terrestrial amphipod crustacean that hides in burrows in wet sand or in seaweed. Its legs are modified for hopping. Length: to 1in (2.5cm). Family Talitudidae.

Beach Grass, perennial grass found on sandy coasts of Europe, N Africa, and North America. It grows in tufts, has rolled, spikelike leaves, and long, cylindrical flower clusters. Because the tough underground stems spread, it is planted to combat beach erosion. Height: to 3ft (91cm). Family Gramineae; genus *Ammophila. See also* Grass.

Beacon, Aircraft, low frequency and medium frequency radio transmission. The location of the radio transmitter is indicated on navigation charts. A pilot is able to fly to the transmitter, or he can use it to determine his position by checking indications on his automatic direction finder.

Beaded Lizard. See Gila Monster.

Beagle, hunting dog (hound group) used in packs to chase and follow small game. Of ancient origin; modern breed dates from mid-19th-century England. One of the most popular breeds, it has a long, slightly domed head with a medium-length, square-cut muzzle. Low-set, hanging ears are long and broad; the wide-set, large eyes have a soft expression. A short-backed, muscular body is set on medium-length legs. The brush tail is carried up. The white, tan, and black coat is close and hard. Average size: two varieties—to 13in (33cm) high at shoulder; and over 13in but not over 15in (38cm); 20–40lb (9–18kg). *See also* Hound.

Beak, or bill, horny or stiff animal mouthparts that are projecting or pointed. Beaks are found among cephalopods, some insects, some fish, and all egg-laying mammals, turtles, and birds. Bird bills are adapted to many functions: grasping, preening, seed cracking, piercing, tearing, sieving, nectar-sipping, stabbing, and display.

Beaked Whale, small to medium toothed whale with distinct beak. Ranging from solitary to gregarious, they make rapid deep dives for food fish and cephalopods. Length: 13–43 ft (4–13m). Family, Hyperoodontiade. *See also* Whale.

Bean, plants grown for their edible seeds and seed pods, including broad, string, snap, kidney, and scarlet runner beans. The broad bean *(Vicia faba)* is native to Asia, and is grown mainly in Canada and Europe as fodder. The string bean *(Phaseolus vulgaris)* is native to tropical South America and is common in the United States. There are several varieties cultivated. Its long pod or kidney-shaped seeds are eaten as vegetables. *Phaseolus vulgaris humilis* is a bush type. Both types have varieties of yellow, green, or wax pods. The scarlet runner *(Phaseolus coccineus)* has scarlet, rather than white or lilac, flowers and shorter, broader seeds. Family Leguminosae. *See also* Lima Bean; Soybean.

Bear, large, omnivorous, and nocturnal mammals with stocky bodies, thick coarse fur, and short tails. Bears are native to the Americas and Eurasia. The sun bear is the smallest, the Alaskan brown bear the largest. They have poor sight, fair hearing, and an excellent sense of smell. Except for the fish- and seal-eating polar bear, they eat a wide variety of plant and animal foods. They often kill their prey with a powerful blow by the forepaw. In cold regions, all except the polar bear spend most of the winter hibernating. Length: 4–10ft (1.2–3m); weight: 100–1715lb (45–780kg). Order Carnivora; family Ursidae; there are 6 species. *See also* grizzly bear.

Bear Flag Revolt (1846), uprising by US settlers in California. During the Mexican War, a group of US emigrants in Mexico's territory of California proclaimed the Republic of California at Sonoma in June and raised the "bear flag," which showed a grizzly bear facing a red star. The republic lasted until US troops arrived in July and replaced the bear flag with the American.

Bearings, the supporting elements, usually of specially resistant metals, that permit connected members of machines to rotate or move in a straight line relative to one another without allowing them to separate in the direction in which the load is applied. To minimize friction, surfaces of bearings are generally lubricated. The surfaces may also be separated by balls confined to a race (ball bearings) or by rollers (roller bearings).

Béarn, historical region of SW France, in the Pyrenees; formerly part of Roman Aquitania; now part of Pyrénées-Atlantiques dept. In the 6th century Bearn was controlled by Gascony; it became a county in the 9th century. In 1290 Béarn passed to the count of Foix, who became king of Navarre; in 1484 it passed to the house of Albret. In 1620 Béarn was united with the French crown, administered by the parliament of Navarre. Main industry is cattle breeding.

Beat Generation, term referring to a group of US writers in the 1950s who rejected middle-class values and commercialism. Originally centered in New York, where many of them first met, the group included poets Allen Ginsberg, Gregory Corso, and Lawrence Ferlinghetti and novelists Jack Kerouac and William Burroughs. When Ferlinghetti moved to San Francisco, his City Lights Press became publisher to many of the Beat writers.

Beatification, act in the Roman Catholic Church by which the pope authorizes the public veneration of a deceased individual. It is a step toward canonization. The title "Blessed" is given.

Beatitudes, group of blessings spoken by Jesus at the opening of the Sermon on the Mount, as recorded most fully in Matthew 5:3–12.

Beaton, Sir Cecil Walter Hardy (1904–80), British photographer, costume and stage designer, and writer. He began his career in the 1920s as a fashion photographer, and took up stage designing in the 1930s. His WWII photographs recorded the endurance of wartime hardship by the British people. His film and stage designs include *Gigi* (film, 1951), *My Fair Lady* (stage, 1956; film, 1964), and *Coco* (1969). Beaton's books include *The Wandering Years* (1962) and *Memoirs of the 40s* (1973).

Beatrix, Queen (1938–), Queen of The Netherlands. Born Beatrix Wilhelmina Armgard, she was the first child of then Crown Princess Juliana and Prince Bernhard. Beatrix became heir presumptive to the throne in 1948 at the time of her mother's accession. Her 1966 marriage to West German diplomat Claus von Amsberg was controversial, but her right was preserved. She became queen in 1980 when her mother, citing age, abdicated in her favor.

Beaufort, Henry (*c.* 1374–1447), English statesman and prelate, illegitimate son of John of Gaunt. As chancellor to Henry IV and Henry V, Beaufort considerably influenced English domestic and foreign policy. Guardian of Henry VI (1422), he controlled England in the 1430's, and endeavored to conclude peace with France. As bishop of Winchester from 1404 he completed the cathedral.

Beaufort, Margaret, Countess of Richmond and Derby (1443–1509), English heiress, patroness of learning. By Edmund Tudor, Earl of Richmond (married 1455), she became the mother of the future Henry VII.

Beaufort Sea, part of the Arctic Ocean NE of Alaska, W of Arctic Archipelago; first explored by Canadian Vilhjalmur Stefansson (1915). Maximum depth: approx. 15,000ft (4,575m).

Beaufort Wind Scale, a scale of numbers from 0 to 17 corresponding to stages in wind force and speed, with names and descriptions of the resultant land or sea effects. The Beaufort number 0 means calm, wind less than 1 mile per hour, with smoke rising vertically. Beaufort 3 means light breeze, 8–12 miles per hour, with leaves in constant motion. Beaufort 11 is storm, 64–72 miles per hour, and Beaufort 12–17 is hurricane, 73–136+ miles per hour with devastation.

Beauharnais, Alexandre, Vicomte de (1760–94), French general who served in the American Revolution. In 1789 he was a deputy of the nobility in the revolutionary French States-General. As commander of the army of the Rhine in 1793, he was held responsible for the surrender at Mainz and was guillotined. His wife, Josephine, later married Napoleon.

Beauharnais, Eugène de (1781–1824), French general, son of Napoleon's wife Josephine. A lieutenant of his stepfather at the battles of Marengo and Lützen, he was later adopted by Napoleon and made (1805) viceroy of Italy. After Napoleon's downfall, he lived in Bavaria as the duke of Leuchtenberg.

Beauharnais, Joséphine de. *See* Josephine.

Beaujolais, former province of France on W bank of Saône River, north of Lyon; formed around the small village of Beaujeu; Lyon is the industrial hub of this area. Known for Beaujolais wine.

Beaumont, (Sir) Francis (1584–1616), English dramatist who in collaboration with John Fletcher from about 1606 to 1616 produced romantic tragicomedies, including *The Knight of the Burning Pestle, Philaster, A Maid's Tragedy, A King and No King,* and *The Scornful Lady* (1613). Although contemporaries of Shakespeare, Beaumont and Fletcher were more influenced by Ben Jonson.

Beaumont, port city in SE Texas, 73mi (118km) E of Houston; seat of Jefferson co; first settlers were French and Spanish fur trappers and explorers; population boom occurred in 1901 after discovery of oil. Industries: oil refinering, paper, lumbering, sulfur, rice milling. Settled 1835; inc. 1881. Pop. (1980) 118,102.

Beauregard, Pierre Gustave Toutant de (1818–93), Confederate Civil War general, b. near New Orleans, La. He served in the Mexican War and was superintendent of West Point when war broke out in 1861. On April 14, 1861, he forced the Union surrender of Ft. Sumter, S.C., in the first action of the war. He also served as a commander at Bull Run (1861), at Shiloh (1862), and in the Carolinas (1864–65). He was active in Louisiana government after the war.

Beauvais, town in France, 42mi (68km) NW of Paris. It was noted for making Gobelin tapestries; the factory was destroyed in WWII and never rebuilt; site of the unfinished cathedral of St Pierre. Industries: building materials, machinery, blankets. Founded by Romans. Pop. 56,725.

Beauvoir, Simone de (1908–86), French novelist and essayist. *She Came to Stay* (1943) and *The Mandarins* (1954) are portraits of the Existentialist intellectual circle of which she was a member and of her close companion, Jean-Paul Sartre. Her best known work remains the lengthy feminist essay *The Second Sex* (1949). Other significant works include *The Prime of Life* (1960), *A Very Easy Death* (1964), and *The Coming of Age* (1972).

Beaver, large rodent with fine brown to black fur, webbed hind feet, and a broad scaly tail; lives in streams and lakes of Europe and North America. Although the flesh is edible, beavers are hunted mostly for their fur which, after the coarse hairs have been removed, is highly valuable. Beavers eat parts of trees, shrubs, and plants. They build lodges of trees and branches above water level and construct dams and canals of stones, sticks, and mud. Length: to 4ft (1.2m); weight: to 70lb (32kg). Species *Castor fiber.*

Beaverbrook, (William) Max(well) Aitken, 1st Baron (1879–1964), Canadian born British politician and proprietor of mass-circulation newspapers. A successful financier by 1907, he moved to England entered Parliament (1910). He gained control of the *Daily Express* (1916) and the *Evening Standard* (1923), founded the *Sunday Express* (1918) and invigorated popular journalism. In 1936 he tried to prevent Edward VIII's abdication, and in WWII he was a minister in Churchill's cabinet. A fervent imperialist, he backed the Suez campaign in 1956 and opposed Britain's bid to join the European Economic Community.

Becket, Thomas à (1118?–70), English clergyman and statesman. A friend of Henry II, he was appointed chancellor of England (1155) and vigorously pursued the interests of the crown. In 1162 he became archbishop of Canterbury. Resigning the chancellorship that year, he thenceforth devoted his energies exclusively to church affairs. Bitter conflict with Henry over clerical privileges and the independence of ecclesiastical courts followed, and Becket fled from England seeking papal support. Returning unsubdued to Canterbury after six years' exile, he was murdered there by four of Henry's knights. He was acclaimed a martyr and canonized (1173).

Beckett, Samuel (1906–), Irish novelist and playwright. Living in Paris since 1937, he writes in both English and French. His bleak mastery of theater of the absurd is shown in such plays as *Waiting for Godot* (1952), *Endgame* (1957), *Krapp's Last Tape* (1958), and *Not I* (1973). He is concerned with alienated individual consciousness in his novels, such as *Murphy* (1938), *Malone Dies* (1951), *Molloy* (1951), and *Watt* (1953). He received the Nobel Prize for literature in 1969. *See also* Theater of the Absurd.

Becquerel, Antoine Henri (1852–1908), French physicist. He was professor of physics at the Paris Museum of Natural History (a post held by his father and grandfather before him) and later at the Ecole Polytechnique. He is remembered for his accidental discovery of radioactivity in uranium salts, for which he shared a Nobel Prize (1903) with Pierre and Marie Curie. His other work was concerned with the rotation of the plane of polarized light in a magnetic field.

Bed Bug, broad, flat, wingless bug found worldwide. It feeds by sucking blood from birds, animals, and man. Length: to 0.25in (6mm). Family Cimicidae; species *Cimex lectularius.*

Bede (*c.* 673–735), called the Venerable Bede, monk and scholar from Northumbria in Britain who spent his entire life in the monastery of Jarrow near Whitby. The most important of his many works on science, grammar, history, and theology is the *Ecclesiastical History of the English Nation,* which covers the period from Caesar's conquest to 731.

Bedford, John of Lancaster, Duke of (1389–1435), third son of Henry IV of England. Lieutenant of England during much of Henry V's absence in France, he became regent of France and protector of England (1422). He administered France justly and was successful in the renewed fighting after 1427 but failed at the siege of Orléans (1429). He was responsible for Joan of Arc's execution (1431).

Bedlam, institution for the insane, founded as the priory of St. Mary of Bethlehem, London (1247), converted *c.* 1400 to a hospital, and incorporated as a royal foundation (1547). The word "Bedlam" is a corruption of "Bethlehem."

Bedlington Terrier, graceful, lamblike breed of dog (terrier group) established 1870, brought to United States about 1890. First called gypsy's dog, the Bedlington terrier has a pear-shaped head; filbert-shaped, hanging ears; long legs; and a gracefully curved 9–11 in (23–28cm) tail. The coat, usually trimmed to 1in (2.5cm) for show, can be blue, liver, blue and tan, liver and tan, sandy, or sandy and tan. Average size: 16.5in (42cm) high at shoulder; 17–23lb (8–11kg). *See also* Terrier.

Bedouin, nomadic people of Arab culture and Muslim faith, inhabiting the deserts of the Middle East. Traditionally they live in tents, moving with their herds of camels, goats, sheep, or sometimes cattle across vast areas of arid land in pursuit of the sparse grazing. Their society is patrilineal and they are proverbial for their hospitality, honesty, and fierce independence and courage. Although true Bedouin despise manual labor and city life, many have succumbed to 20th-century economic pressures and taken up employment in the towns.

Bedsore, ulcerous sore caused by prolonged pressure against the skin, occurring most often in bedridden patients. Bedsores may be prevented by cleanliness and relief of pressure.

Bed-wetting, or enuresis, the unintentional voiding of urine at night by children. Protracted enuresis may be due to delayed maturation of bladder capacity or control, and often disappears with maturity. True enuresis appears to be more closely related to a child's general health and emotional state than to organic dysfunction, hence successful treatment is increasingly oriented to careful planning and patience on the part of parents. Drugs or psychiatric treatment are occasionally prescribed.

Bee, any member of the insect Superfamily Apoidea. They are distinguished from other members of the Order Hymenoptera by the presence of specially adapted hairs, which allow for the collection of pollen. They all feed their young honey and pollen, rather than animal food. The body is usually quite hairy and the hairs are multi-branched or plumose. Honey and bumblebees are social insects forming colonies; many other bees are solitary. Found worldwide, they are im-

Beaver

Henri Becquerel

Henry Ward Beecher

portant pollinators, with some living in other bees' colonies. *See also* Bumblebee; Carpenter Bee; Honeybee.

Beech, deciduous tree native to the northern hemisphere. All have wide-spreading branches, smooth gray bark, and alternate, coarse-toothed, green leaves. Male flowers hang from thin stems and pairs of female flowers hang on hairy stems and develop into triangular, edible nuts enclosed by burs. The American beech *(Fagus grandifolia)* is an important timber tree used for furniture and tool handles; height: 80ft (24m). There are 10 species. Family Fagaceae.

Beecham, (Sir) Thomas (1879–1961), English conductor. He founded the New Symphony Orchestra in 1905, the Royal Philharmonic in 1919, and the London Symphony in 1932, becoming its permanent conductor. He introduced the operas of Richard Strauss into England and was widely known as an interpreter of such composers as Frederick Delius and Jean Sibelius.

Beecher, Henry Ward (1813–87), US clergyman, b. Litchfield, Conn. Claiming to be the recipient of special revelation, he became a passionate preacher. Of wide influence, he campaigned against slavery and for woman suffrage. He edited the *Independent,* a Congregational journal, and later, the *Christian Union.*

Bee Eater, tropical Eastern Hemisphere bird that swoops to catch its favorite prey, bees and wasps. They have long curved beaks; bright, often greenish, plumage; and long tails. They nest in large colonies and build tunnels to their egg chambers where white eggs (2–5) are laid and incubated by both parents. Length: 6–15in (15–38cm). Family Meropidae.

Beef Cattle, breeds of domesticated cattle raised primarily for meat. Larger than dairy cattle, they are chunky and rectangular in appearance and convert most of their food into flesh. Beef production includes three distinct agricultural types: breeding, ranching, and feeding. Some farmers do all three, but the modern trend is toward specialization. Breeds include Aberdeen Angus, Brahman, Charolais, Hereford, Longhorn, and Shorthorn. *See also* Animal Husbandry; Cattle.

Bee Fly, gray to black fly, 0.6 to 1in (15–25mm) long, found worldwide. The adult feeds on flower nectar; the larvae are parasitic on other insects. Family Bombyliidae, genus *Bombylius. See also* Diptera.

Beefsteak Fungus, a species of arboreal mushroom, *Fistulina hepatica,* also called ox-tongue or poor man's beefsteak, that is common on hardwoods, especially oak. Wedge-shaped, it has a cap 2–10in (5–25cm) broad with spore-bearing tubes on the underside. When present, the stem is horizontal. Young beefsteak fungi look and feel like meat; the flesh oozes red juice. It is edible and mycophagists rate it from fair to good.

Beer, alcoholic beverage produced by brewing and fermentation of a cereal extract (malt), which is flavored with a bitter substance (hops). Ingredients also include water, sugar, and yeast. The alcohol content of beer ranges from about 1.5 to 8.3 grams per cc. Among the types of beer are ales, which are pale or brown in color; stouts, very dark brown and bitter; and porter, a sweeter stout. Beer is especially popular in the United States, Great Britain, and Germany.

Beerbohm, Sir Max (1872–1956), British caricaturist and drama critic. His writings include *A Christmas Garland* (1912), parodies on contemporary writers, and *Around Theatre* (1930; 1953). He also wrote a novel,

Zuleika Dobson (1911), an amusing satire set in Oxford. Some of his caricatures were published in *Rossetti and His Circle* (1922).

Be'er Sheva' (Beersheba), city in S Israel, 45mi (72km) SW of Jerusalem; capital of Southern District; site of oracle, important during Biblical times; controlled by Britain 1922–47; site of Negev Institute for Arid Zone Research; industrial, commercial, educational, and transportation center. Industries: chemicals, glass. Pop. 96,500.

Beet, vegetable originating in Europe and parts of Asia. It is cultivated in most cool areas. Its leaves are green or red, and edible but it is grown for the thick, red or gold root. Beets should have sandy loam in a sunny area. Some varieties are eaten as a vegetable, others are a source of sugar, and some are used as fodder. Family Chenopodiaceae; species *Beta vulgaris. See also* Sugar Beet.

Beethoven, Ludwig van (1770–1827), German composer, b. Bonn. A virtuoso pianist, Beethoven gradually became deaf, making a concert career impossible. Despite his deafness, he composed many masterpieces that place him in the forefront of all composers. He is often regarded as the last Classical and the first Romantic composer. He was a master of orchestral form.

His early works are in the classic tradition of Haydn and Mozart, with whom he studied. His middle period (1801–1814), despite increasing deafness, produced his Third and Fifth symphonies, the "Emperor" *Piano Concerto No. 5,* the *Violin Concerto,* and the "Appassionata" *Piano Sonata No. 23.* In his last period, composing in total deafness, Beethoven produced his last five string quartets, the *Missa Solemnis,* and the Ninth Symphony, which many critics regard as the greatest symphony ever composed, and which was the first symphony to use singers and a chorus. His one opera, *Fidelio* (1805, revised 1814), is also highly regarded.

Beetle, insects characterized by horny front wings that serve as protective covers for the membranous hind wings and are not used in flight. They are widely distributed on every continent except Antarctica. Most beetles live on land, but some are aquatic. They are usually stout-bodied, and their mouthparts are adapted for biting and chewing. Poor flyers, exoskeletons give them protection against bodily injury and drying up, a serious problem for most insects. Beetles are the most numerous group of insects, and over 300,000 species have been described. Most feed on plants, some are predators of small animals, including other insects, and some are scavengers. Beetles undergo complete metamorphosis. Their larvae, called grubs, usually have three pairs of legs, but grubs of weevils or snout beetles are legless. Unlike caterpillars, grubs have distinct heads, usually dark in color. Length: 0.02–7.5in (0.5mm–19cm). Order Coleoptera. *See also* Insect.

Beeton, Mrs. (1836–65), compiler of *Mrs. Beeton's Household Management* (1861), probably the world's most famous cook book. It was originally published in monthly parts between 1860 and 1861.

Beggar's Opera, The, opera with libretto by John Gay and popular music of the day arranged by J.C. Pepusch, first performed in England in 1728. It was very popular in its time, is one of the few successful "ballad" operas, and formed the basis of the 20th-century comic opera *The Threepenny Opera* (1928).

Begin, Menachem (1913–), prime minister of Israel, b. Russian Poland. Fleeing the Germans in 1939, he was sentenced to eight years in a slave-labor camp for his Zionist associations but was released in 1941 to

fight in the new Polish army. He entered Palestine in 1942 and became Palestinian paramilitary commander (1943) against the British. Begin became prime minister in 1977 and worked with Egyptian President Anwar Sadat to reach an accommodation between their two countries. Begin and Sadat shared the Nobel Peace Prize for 1978. Winning reelection by a narrow margin in the 1981 parliamentary elections, Begin continued to maintain a hard line on Israel's security interests and on Israeli-occupied Judea, Samaria, and Gaza, but his popularity fell during Israel's 1982 invasion of Lebanon, and he resigned in 1983.

Begonia, family of plants, shrubs, or trees native to tropical America and SE Asia. Those popular as house plants have various sized and shaped leaves; white, pink, or red flowers; and often hairy stems. There are three types: rex with ornamental leaves of green, red, and silver combinations; rhizomatus with fleshy, creeping stems and glossy leaves; and basket with trailing stems and brightly colored leaves. Male and female flowers are separate but on the same plant. Care: bright indirect sunlight, humid air, well-drained soil (equal parts loam, peat moss, perlite, sand). Propagation is by stem and leaf cuttings or division of rhizomes. Family Begoniaceae; genus *Begonia.*

Behaviorism, school of psychology that emphasizes studying observable acts using the methods of the natural sciences, particularly laboratory experiments. Early behaviorists objected to explanations of behavior that involved references to mind, will, or feelings. They studied actions that could be observed objectively, measured, and counted. Behaviorists try to explain learning as simple conditioning. Leading American behaviorists are John B. Watson and B.F. Skinner.

Behavior Modification, or Behavior Therapy, treatment of psychological disorders by using principles and methods from learning theory. Such treatment assumes that abnormal or undesirable behavior is learned, as are other behaviors, through conditioning and reinforcement. Therapy is designed to reward and encourage desirable, constructive behaviors while unwanted or abnormal behaviors are ignored or punished. For example, an overaggressive child's behavior might be modified as follows: when the child behaves destructively, isolate him (a time-out period); reward constructive behavior (quietness, cooperation) with praise, affection, or even candy immediately after the behavior occurs; punish intolerable instances of aggression with withdrawal of privileges. Behavior therapy is used to treat such diverse problems as alcoholism, juvenile delinquency, and the behaviors of the mentally retarded and behaviorally disturbed. *See also* Behaviorism; Learning Theory; Reinforcement.

Behring, Emil Adolph von (1854–1917), German bacteriologist and pioneer immunologist. In 1901 he was awarded the first Nobel Prize in physiology or medicine for his work on serum therapy, especially for developing a diphtheria antitoxin.

Beijing. *See* Peking.

Beirut (Bayrut), capital city of Lebanon, on the E shore of the Mediterranean Sea; was ancient Phoenician city of Berytus; prospered in 1500 BC as a trade center and later as an important commercial colony of the Roman Empire and site of a prominent law school (AD 3). City was captured by the Arabs 635 and by the Ottoman Turks 1516; taken by France in WWI (1918); extensively damaged in 1975–76 civil war; major center of trade, culture, finance; site of Lebanese, French, American, and Arab universities. Industries: shipping, food processing, textiles. Pop. 702,000.

Belau (formerly Palau), self-governing island group in the Caroline Islands of the W Pacific, consisting of about 200 islands, only 8 of which are inhabited. A Spanish possession 1710–1898, it was then held by Germany until 1914, when Japan occupied the islands. At the end of WWII control passed to the United States, which administered them as part of the US Trust Territory of the Pacific Islands. Self-government was instituted in 1981, and termination of the Trust Territory bringing full independence is scheduled for the early 1980s. Most of the inhabitants are Micronesian, engaged in subsistence agriculture. Commercial fishing and copra processing are also important economic activities. Capital: Koror; area: 189sq mi (460sq km); pop. 14,800.

Belaúnde Terry, Fernando (1912–), president of Peru (1963–68; 1980–85). Before becoming involved in politics (1944), he was a noted architect. He formed his own political party, Popular Action (1956), and in 1963 won election as president. A military coup in 1968 removed him, but disenchantment with left-wing military rule returned him to the presidency in 1980. His administration was plagued by leftist guerrilla activities in the early 1980s.

Belém, seaport city in N Brazil, on Pará River, 90mi (145km) from Atlantic Ocean; capital of Pará state; site of governor's palace (1762), and Belém University of Pará (1957). Industries: sawmills, shipyards, brick. Exports: rubber, Brazil nuts, pepper. Founded 1615. Pop. 565,097.

Belfast, capital and largest city of Northern Ireland, at the mouth of the River Lagan on Belfast Lough; seat of County Antrim. It is the site of a Norman castle, Cathedral of Ste Anne, Queens University (1845), Victoria College (1854), National Museum and Art Gallery; scene of much fighting between Catholics and Protestants since the 19th century; noted as center of Irish linen industry. Industries: tobacco, food processing, shipbuilding, textiles, aircraft. Founded 1177; inc. 1613 by James I of England; became capital of Northern Ireland 1920. Violence between Roman Catholics and Protestants in the 1970s and 1980s often paralyzed the city. Pop. 374,300.

Belgae, Germanic and Celtic tribes who banded together about 2000 years ago and lived in what is now Belgium, the Netherlands, Germany, and northern France. The German tribes overcame and mixed with the Celts, producing a nation that Julius Caesar called the bravest of the Gauls. Caesar conquered them in 57 BC. Many Belgae crossed over to and settled in Britain.

Belgian, draft horse breed developed in Belgium from Flemish type horse and introduced in the United States in 1886. A patient, powerful horse, it has a massive, wide, deep and low-set body. Colors are bay, chestnut, and roan, all with flaxen mane and tail and white face blaze. Height 62–68in (157–173cm) at shoulder; weight: 1900–2200lb (855–990kg).

Belgian Malinois, sheepherding dog (working group) bred in Belgium about 1898. A square, elegant dog, it has a flat head with pointed muzzle; triangular, erect ears; deep-chested, level-backed body; straight, medium-length legs; and long tail. The short, straight coat, colored rich fawn to mahogany, is longer around the neck, on the tail, and on back of thighs. Average size: 22–26in (56–66cm) high at shoulder; 50–60lb (23–27kg). *See also* Working Dog.

Belgian Sheepdog, sheepherding dog (working group) developed in Belgium 1891–98 and also called Gronendael. It has a flat head with pointed muzzle; triangular, erect ears; level, firm body; medium-length, straight legs; and long tail. Its abundant black coat is long and straight with shorter hair on head, ears, and lower legs. Average size: 21–26in (53–66cm) high at shoulder; 50–60lb (22.5–27kg). *See also* Working Dog.

Belgian Tervuren, shepherd dog (working group) bred in Belgium about 1885. It has a long head with pointed muzzle; erect, triangular ears; level back; medium-length, straight legs; and long tail. The long, harsh coat is shorter on head, ears, and lower legs. Color is rich fawn to russet mahogany with black overlay and face mask. Average size: 22–26in (56–66cm) high at the shoulder; 50–60lb (22.5–27kg). *See also* Working Dog.

Belgium (Belgique, or België), Kingdom of, a small, densely populated nation of W Europe. The people are of Flemish, French, and German background; all three languages are in current usage. The country, which is a constitutional monarchy, has one of the world's most highly developed economies.

Land and Economy. Belgium is a country of coastal lowlands and gently undulating plains rising to the hills of the Ardennes in the S. Flanders, the coastal area bordering the North Sea, is a flat, moist plain traversed by many rivers and canals. Belgium's central plain, lying between Flanders and the Meuse River, is a fertile farming region; most industry is situated here, as is a majority of the country's population. The Ardennes is a rocky, wooded plateau unsuitable for farming. The climate is maritime, with damp, foggy winters and mild summers. Industry is focused in the cities along the Scheldt and Meuse rivers; both are important coal regions. For centuries, Belgium has been famed for its textiles, linens, and lace. Other important industries include chemical, coal, metallurgical, glassware, furniture, and sugar refining. The economy depends upon extensive importation of raw materials, and foreign export markets for its manufactured products. Only 7% of the population is engaged in agriculture. Antwerp and Ghent are major European seaports.

People. Belgians may be divided roughly into two major language-groups. N of Brussels the people are mostly Flemings; the official language is Flemish, which is similar to Dutch. The Belgians of the S are called Walloons; the official language, Walloon, is a dialect of French. The city of Brussels is officially bilingual. The country is overwhelmingly Roman Catholic.

Government. The king is the head of state and commander-in-chief of the armed forces. The ministers of government are leaders of the dominant party in parliament, and are appointed by the king. Government policy is carried out by the prime minister and his cabinet. The leading political parties are the Social Christian, Socialist, and Liberal. Voting in national elections is compulsory for all Belgians 21 years and older.

History. During the Middle Ages many textile manufacturing and trade centers developed in the area that is now Belgium. The French united the small states of the region in the 14th century, and included them in the duchy of Burgundy. After 1477, the Austrian and Spanish branches of Hapsburgs controlled the area for more than 300 years. Belgium and the Netherlands were united after the Congress of Vienna (1815). The Belgians revolted and founded a constitutional monarchy 1831 under Prince Leopold of Saxe-Coburg. Belgium colonized Africa's Congo region in the 19th century. In both world wars the country was overrun and occupied by German forces. It joined the North Atlantic Treaty Organization (NATO) in 1949. Belgium was instrumental in conceiving and forming the European Economic Community. Continuous political conflicts between the Flemings and Walloons have resulted in unstable governments. Plans for regional autonomy began in 1971, but have proceeded slowly, partly because the status of Brussels remains unresolved.

PROFILE

Official name: Belgium, Kingdom of
Area: 11,781 sq mi (30,513sq km)
Population: 9,855,110
Density: 836per sq mi (323per sq km)
Chief cities: Brussels (capital); Antwerp; Ghent
Government: constitutional monarchy
Religion (major): Roman Catholic
Languages: Flemish, French, German
Monetary unit: Belgian franc
Gross national product: $67,200,000,000
Industries (major products): chemicals, glass, textiles
Agriculture (major products): wheat, barley, sugar beets, potatoes
Minerals (major): coal, iron, copper
Trading partners (major): West Germany, France, Netherlands, United States

Belgrade (Beograd), capital city of Yugoslavia, at the junction of the Sava and Danube rivers; settled by Celts, Illyrians, and Romans. In 1929 it became part of Yugoslavia, and suffered much damage during German occupation in WWII; center of cultural, economic, and political activities of Yugoslavia; site of 16th-century Darjah Mosque, museums, palaces, and Serbian Academy of Science. Industries: chemicals, metals, machine tools, textiles. Pop. 1,209,360.

Belize (British Honduras), independent country and member of the Commonwealth of Nations in Central America, bounded by the Caribbean Sea (E), Mexico (N), and Guatemala (S and W). The terrain is mostly low with swampland along the coast, rising inland to the country's highest point, Victoria Peak, approx. 3,700ft (1,130m), and heavily forested in S regions. The main industry is timber, followed by fishing and tourism. Only a small portion of the land is farmed. Chief products include: sugar cane, citrus fruits, coconuts, maize, rice, yams, and beans. The people, predominantly English-speaking, are of black African descent and are concentrated around Belmopan, the capital, and Belize, the principal port. Spanish-speaking Mayan Indian descendants live in northern regions. Originally part of the Mayan civilization, the area was settled *c.* 1638 by British logcutters from Jamaica. Constantly contested by Spain until 1798, it came under the administration of Jamaica, 1862–84. Belize adopted a new constitution in 1960 and gained internal self-government in 1964. Guatemala has claimed Belize since 1859 and independence was slowed because of the colony's need of protection. In 1981 independence was granted, and Britain agreed to leave troops in the new country. Its constitution provides for a parliamentary system, headed by a prime minister, and a bicameral legislature.

PROFILE

Official name: Belize
Area: 8,866sq mi (22,963sq km)
Population: 144,657
Chief cities: Belmopan (capital), Belize
Government: Parliamentary democracy
Language: English

Belize, town in Belize, Central America; 50mi (81km) NW of Belmopan; formerly the country's capital, now the largest city and principal port; almost totally destroyed in a hurricane (1961). Industries: sawmilling, rice hulling; trade center for lumber, fruit, coconuts. Pop. 39,887.

Bell, Alexander Graham (1847–1922), US inventor of the telephone and educator of the deaf, b. Scotland. He was educated at Edinburgh and London and worked with his father, inventor of the Visible Speech System for educating the deaf. The family moved to Canada in 1870, and Bell began teaching his father's system in New England. He opened a training school in Boston in 1872 and taught speech at Boston University from 1873–77. His work in the transmission of sound by electricity led to the first demonstration of the telephone in 1876. He founded the Bell Telephone Co. in 1877. Among his other inventions were the photophone, an instrument for transmitting sound by light vibrations (1880), and the wax cylinder record for phonographs.

Belladonna, poisonous herb *(Atropa belladonna)* that has a sap used medicinally to enlarge the pupil of the eye and whose roots and leaves contain the antispasmodic pain-relieving drug atropine. *See also* Atropine.

Belladonna Lily, South African bulb plant cultivated for its fragrant rose-pink flowers. Family Amaryllioacene species *Amaryllis belladonna.*

Bellbird, tropical American cotinga with a loud bell-like call. The black-winged bellbird *(Procnias averano)* of Trinidad and N South America has fleshy growths hanging from its chin and throat. The Central American three-wattled bellbird *(Procnias tricarunculata)* has whiplike wattles around its bill.

Belleau Wood, Battle of (June 2–July 7, 1918), World War I Allied victory in France in which the US 2nd Division, spearheaded by its Marine brigade, checked German attacks west of Château-Thierry. The Americans counterattacked and recaptured the village of Bouresches and the southern edge of Belleau Wood.

Belle Isle, Strait of, channel in Canada separating Newfoundland and SE Labrador; ice-locked November–June; northernmost entrance to the Gulf of St. Lawrence. Length: 35mi (56km). Width: 15mi (24km).

Bellerophon, in Greek legend, the son of Glaucus, king of Corinth and grandson of Sisyphus. lobates sent him to slay the fire breathing dragon Chimera. On his way Bellerophon captured and tamed the winged horse Pegasus, and by riding above the dragon he was able to kill it with bow and arrows.

Bellevue, city in W Washington, on Lake Washington; E suburb of Seattle; population increased with the completion of the Floating Bridge to Seattle. Industries: electronic components, concrete, prefabricated homes. Settled 1880; inc. 1953. Pop. (1980) 73,903.

Bellflower, annual, perennial, or biennial plants native to northern temperate regions and tropical mountains and now cultivated in gardens. All have bell-shaped flowers of white, blue, or pink, alternate leaves, and milky sap. Well-known are the blue, biennial Canterbury bells *(Campanula medium)* and tall *Campanula americana* found in moist woodlands of the United States; height: to 6ft (1.8m). There are 300 species. Family Campanulaceae.

Bellingham, city in NW Washington, 18mi (29km) S of Canadian border, on Puget Sound; formed from combination of four towns in 1903. Industries: farming, lumber, fishing, processed foods. Founded 1852; inc. 1904. Pop. (1980) 45,794.

Bellini, Giovanni (*c.*1430–1516), Italian painter. He was the genius of the Venetian High Renaissance and the greatest of the Venetian Madonna painters. In his early works, executed in the family workshop, his treatment of nature was precise and realistic, in 15th-cen-

Belgium

Alexander Graham Bell

Saul Bellow

tury fashion, but it gradually became poetic and monumental, as did his handling of color and light. He frequently included landscapes as background, as in his portraits of the Doges. In his graceful, gentle allegorical paintings and his altarpieces (such as that for San Giobbi), he often used architectural settings, within which the figures were bathed in light and atmosphere. In *St. Jerome,* one of his later, highly innovative works, the saint is seated in a landscape and seen through an arch before which the other life-sized figures stand. The greatest teacher of his generation, his pupils included Giorgione, Titian, Palma Vecchio, and Sebastiano del Piombo. In midcareer he began using oils instead of tempura, thereby establishing their predominance in Venetian painting.

Belloc, (Joseph) Hilaire (Pierre) (1870–1953), English author, b. France. A versatile writer, he is remembered chiefly for his light verse, especially *Cautionary Tales* (1907). He wrote several satirical novels in collaboration with G.K. Chesterton. He was an earnest Catholic and a Liberal member of Parliament (1906–10).

Bellow, Saul (1915–), US author, b. Lachine, Canada. Reared in Chicago, he taught English and creative writing at various universities. A novelist, short story writer, and playwright, his first novel, *The Dangling Man,* appeared in 1944. Subsequent novels include *The Adventures of Augie March* (1953), *Henderson the Rain King* (1959), *Herzog* (1964), *Mr. Sammler's Planet* (1970), and *The Dean's December* (1982); a collection of short stories, *Him with His Foot in His Mouth,* appeared in 1984. Bellow won three National Book Awards for fiction (1954, 1965, 1971). He was awarded the Pulitzer Prize for *Humboldt's Gift* (1975) and the 1976 Nobel Prize in literature.

Bellows, George (1882–1925), US illustrator and painter, b. Columbus, Ohio. A member of the Ashcan School, he painted many fine portraits, as well as depictions of prize fights, street scenes, prayer meetings, and rallies. *See also* Ashcan School.

Bell's Palsy, form of neuritis characterized by complete paralysis of one side of the face. Recovery may be spontaneous; surgery is indicated rarely.

Bellwort, perennial woodland plant native to Canada and the United States. They have fleshy root stalks, light green leaves, and yellow, bell-shaped flowers. Family Liliaceae; genus *Uvularia.*

Belmopan, capital of Belize, 41mi (66km) SW of city of Belize. Made capital 1970. Pop. 2,700.

Belo Horizonte, city in E Brazil, 200mi (322km) N of Rio de Janeiro; capital of Minas Gerais state; first planned city in South America; site of University of Minas Gerais (1927), and the Catholic University of Minas Gerais (1959). Industries: mineral ores, diamonds, textiles, iron, steel. Founded 1897. Pop. 1,-106,722.

Belorussian (Belorusskaja) Soviet Socialist Republic (White Russia), constituent republic in W central European USSR; bordered by Lithuanian and Latvian republics (N), the Ukraine (S), Russian Soviet Federal Socialists Republic (E), Poland (W). Since 1944, Belorussian SSR comprises 12 oblasts; population is 80% Belorussian, 20% Russian, Polish, and Jewish. Minsk is capital. Region was colonized by East Slavic tribes 5th–8th centuries; passed to Russia 1772, 1793. The republic proclaimed independence 1918 but was taken by Red Army 1919; site of Soviet-Polish War 1919–20. Treaty of Riga (1921) gave W part to Poland

and E part to USSR (1922); W section was inc. into USSR 1939. Only the Ukrainian Republic and Belorussia of the 15 union republics of USSR have separate UN seats. Industries: lumber, potatoes, grains, flax, sugar beets, electrical equipment, textiles, chemicals. Area: 80,154sq mi (207,599sq km). Pop. 9,468,-000.

Belshazzar, in the Bible, son of Nebuchadnezzar and last king of Babylon. Daniel prophesied the conquering of Babylon by Cyrus and Belshazzar was slain the same night.

Beluga, or white whale, small, toothed Arctic whale that is milky white when mature. It preys on fish, squid, and crustaceans and is, in turn, prey for killer whales. Its curlewlike cry is easily audible. Length: to 17ft (5m). Species: *Delphinapterus leucas. See also* Whale.

Benares. *See* Varanasi.

Bendjedid, Chadli (1929–), Algerian president (1979–). Leaving the French Army in 1954, he joined the guerrilla forces during the Algerian revolution. Allied with Houari Boumedienne in the coup that overthrew Ben Bella in 1965, Bendjedid served on the Revolutionary Council. He was elected president in 1979, following Boumedienne's death (1978).

Bends, or decompression sickness, nitrogen saturation of the tissues brought on by an increase, followed by a swift decrease, in atmospheric pressure. It is most common in divers and tunnel workers. Symptoms are pains in the joints, particularly the knees. Treatment consists of proper decompression and recompression procedures, and administration of oxygen.

Benedict, Saint. *See* Benedict XI.

Benedict XI, Roman Catholic pope (1303–04), b. Niccolo Boccasini (*c.*1240). A member of the Benedictine order, he was made a cardinal in 1298 and served on missions to England and France. He was noted for his sanctity and administrative abilities. In 1638, he was beatified by Pope Clement XII.

Benedict XV, Roman Catholic pope (1914–22), b. Giacomo della Chiesa (1854). During World War I, he strived for peace among nations, stressing pacifist idealism. He tried to unite all Roman Catholics, made changes in the Curia, and published a new Code of Canon Law.

Benedictines, Roman Catholic monastic order founded in the 6th century by St. Benedict. The first monastery was at Monte Cassino, Italy. Benedictine monasteries, which follow St. Benedict's rule, later spread all over the world.

Benelux Economic Union, European economic union, forerunner of the European Common Market. The 50-year treaty creating this economic union of Belgium, the Netherlands, and Luxembourg was signed in 1958 to replace an earlier customs union formed in 1948. The treaty went into effect Nov. 1, 1960.

Beneš, Eduard (1884–1948), Czechoslovak statesman. A disciple of Tomaš Masaryk, he actively promoted Czech independence during World War I and became the first foreign minister of the newly created state (1918–35). He was delegate to the Paris peace conference; member of the council of the League of Nations; chief proponent of the Little Entente. Beneš was elected president of Czechoslovakia in 1935. After resigning in Sept. 1938 to protest German occupation of the Sudetenland, he headed the Czech government-

in-exile from London. He returned in 1945; was reelected president in 1946; but resigned in 1948 after the Communist takeover.

Benevento, city in SW Italy, NE of Naples; capital of Benevento prov. Est. as Malies by the Samnites, it was an important Roman town on the Appian Way. Manfred, King of Naples and Italy, was killed here 1266; site of Lombard-Saracenic cathedral and Trajan's Arch (Porta Aurea). Industries: agricultural machinery, optical instruments, bricks. Pop. 62,131.

Bengal, region in India, partitioned in 1947, including West Bengal state, India, and Bangladesh, and combined delta of the Ganges and Brahmaputra rivers; ruled by King Gopala (AD 750) who founded Pal dynasty, spreading Buddhism and prosperity through region; followed by Senas, a Hindu people, in the late 11th century; invaded by Mohammed Khalji in 12th century, who reorganized region under Muslims; Akbar, Mongol emperor, ruled from 1576, when Bengal became the richest region in empire. Conquered by British 1757, it became center of British Indian Empire with Calcutta as capital city; made an autonomous region (1937) with present boundaries secured in 1947. Area: 77,442sq mi (200,575sq km).

Bengal, Bay of, NE inlet of the Indian Ocean, bounded by India and Sri Lanka (W), India and Pakistan (N), Burma (E), Indian Ocean (S); many principal rivers empty into the Bay, including Ganges, Brahmaputra, Kirstna, Mahanadi; major ports on its shores are: Madras, Calcutta, Akyab, Chittagong, Visakhapatnam, Trincomalee. Length: approx. 1,300mi (2,093km). Width: 1,000mi (1,610km).

Bengali, a major language of the Indian subcontinent. It is spoken by virtually all of the 85 million inhabitants of Bangladesh, and by 45 million more in the Indian province of East Bengal. Bengali belongs to the Indic branch of the Indo-European family of languages. In number of speakers it ranks sixth or seventh in the world.

Benghazi (Banghazi), city in Libya, on the NE shore of the Gulf of Sidra, 400mi (644km) E of Tripoli; city has been conquered and ruled by the Romans, Vandals, Byzantines, Arabs, and Turks (16th century to 1911); the Italians, using Benghazi as a colonizing headquarters in the 1930s, developed it into a seaport, naval and air base, and WWII supply base. An important administrative city in Libya, it is commercial and industrial center for Cyrenaica prov. Industries: shipping, construction, oil, food processing. Founded by the Greeks 6th century BC. Pop. 325,000.

Ben-Gurion, David (1886–1973), Israeli political figure, prime minister (1948–53, 1955–61, 1961–63), b. as David Green in Poland. Ben-Gurion was the prime figure in the establishment of the state of Israel. He emigrated to Palestine (1906). Expelled by the Turks during World War I, he returned when the British took control. Encouraging Jewish immigration in the 1920s and 1930s in the hopes of bringing about a Jewish national homeland, he became (1935) head of the Zionist Executive, a worldwide organization. Though he called for the Jews of Palestine to fight for independence (1939), he cooperated with the British during World War II.

After the war he led the struggle against the British until independence (1948). He became the new state's first prime minister and led it through a war with Arab states (1948–49). After resigning (1953), he returned to the government as defense minister (1953) and soon became prime minister again (1955), leading Israel through another conflict with the Arabs (1956).

Resigning (1961), he quickly returned to the premiership. After retiring (1963), he continued his political involvement, forming a splinter party from the dominant Mapai party, which he had helped found (1929) and led. His books include *Rebirth and Destiny of Israel* (1954), *Israel: Years of Challenge* (1965), and *Memoirs* (1970).

Benin, independent nation of W Africa, formerly called Dahomey. Once a French protectorate, it is a country of 40 ethnic tribal groups and a low-level economy.

Land and Economy. Located in the bulge on the S side of W Africa, Benin is bordered by Nigeria, Toga, Upper Volta, and Niger, with 75 mi (121km) on the Gulf of Guinea. The coast is hot and humid, and there are two rainy and two dry seasons; average annual rainfall is 32in (813mm). Benin has three plateaus, one fertile, another of bare rocks, and a third with streams flowing to the Volta and Niger rivers and including the Atakora range. The E section is a plain. Subsistence agriculture is the economic base. Palm products and cotton account for half of export revenues.

People. The leading class in Benin is composed of male-line descendants of the Aja (Fons, or Dahomey) who had established the early kingdom. Trained for civil service by the French, they are the best educated; literacy is 25% among school-age children. In the N are the nomadic Fulani and the Somba tribe, hunters with no political organization; E are Baribas. 90% of the population is rural, and 65% practices animist religion. French is the common language.

Government. Benin has been under military rule since 1970. The constitution of 1977 instituted a national assembly, whose members belong to the sole legal political party, the Benin People's Revolutionary Party.

History. Benin's history dates back to three principalities—Allada, Porto-Novo, and Dahomey—in the S area who were being pushed by the N Kingdom of Abomey in the 16th century. Dahomey was the most aggressive, pushing N and selling slaves. In 1863 the king of Porto-Novo sought French protection. By 1892 France had subjugated all groups and made them protectorates as part of French West Africa. The 1956 Overseas Reform Act expanded civil rights, and in 1960 the country became independent as Dahomey. The official name was changed to Benin in 1976. Economic and regional rivalries have caused numerous military coups d'état and changes of government since 1960. The Marxist-Leninist military government in power since 1972 relaxed its authority somewhat during the late 1970s and improved relations with France.

PROFILE

Official name: People's Republic of Benin
Area: 43,483sq mi (112,621sq km)
Population: 3,377,000
Density: 78per sq mi (30per sq km)
Chief cities: Porto-Novo (capital); Cotonou
Government: Military
Religion: Animist, Christian, and Moslem (Muslim)
Language: French (official)
Monetary unit: CFA franc
Gross national product: $540,000,000
Per capita income: $170
Industries: food processing, including beer, palm oil
Agriculture: peanuts, cotton, coffee, tobacco
Minerals: petroleum
Trading partners: France (major), other members of European Common Market, United States, Canada

Benin, Kingdom of, West African state from *c.* 1400–1897. It established friendly relations with Portugal, sending an ambassador in the 16th century, and carrying out an extensive trade in pepper, cloth, ivory, palm products, and slaves. Benin was subjugated by Great Britain in 1897–98 and is now a part of Nigeria.

Benin City, city in S Nigeria, 150mi (242km) E of Lagos, on a branch of the Benin River; capital of Mid-Western state; an administrative, trade, and cultural center during 13th–18th centuries; excavations have uncovered art treasures of this period. Industries: rubber processing, mining, lumber, yams, coconut palms. Pop. 127,000.

Benitoite, a ring silicate mineral, barium titanium silicate, found only in San Benito County, Calif. Hexagonal system tabular, triangular crystals. Glassy blue to white; hardness 6–6.5; sp gr 3.6. Valuable gemstone when transparent, without flaws, and of good color.

Benjamin, in Genesis, youngest son of Jacob, born to Rachel who died during childbirth. His tribe settled between Judah and Ephraim. According to the New Testament, the apostle Paul descended from this tribe.

Benn, Anthony Neil Wedgwood (Tony) (1925–), British Labour politician. He was elected to Parliament in 1950 and in 1963 disclaimed his hereditary peerage in order to remain in the House of Commons. He failed to win reelection from Bristol in 1983, but won the seat from Chesterfield in 1984. He was Postmaster-General (1964–66), Minister of Technology (1966–70), and Secretary of State for Energy (1975–79). He wrote *Arguments for Socialism* (1979).

Bennett, Enoch Arnold (1867–1931), British author. He documented realistically the provincial life of England's industrial Midlands, where he was born, in his novels of the "Five Towns", such as *Anna of the Five Towns* (1902), *The Old Wives' Tale* (1908), and the trilogy *Clayhanger* (1910), *Hilda Lessways* (1911), and *These Twain* (1916).

Ben Nevis, mountain in W Scotland, in Inverness-shire, near Fort William, overlooking Glen Nevis; highest point in the British Isles, 4,406ft (1,344m).

Bentham, Jeremy (1748–1832), English philosopher, jurist, and social reformer. Trained as a lawyer but never practicing, Bentham developed the theory of utilitarianism based on the premise that "the greatest happiness of the greatest number" should be the object of individual and government action. This philosophy was spelled out in his *Introduction to the Principles of Morals and Legislation* (1789). His followers were responsible for much of England's early reform legislation. *See also* Utilitarianism.

Benthic Division, all of the ocean bottom from the high-tide line to the greatest depths. It is divided into two main systems, the littoral and the deep-sea. The littoral system is divided into eulittoral and sublittoral zones and the deep-sea into the bathyal and abyssal zones.

Benthos, the forms of life on the ocean floor. They include sessile animals like sponges and barnacles, creeping forms like crabs and snails, and burrowing ones like clams and worms. The term "benthos" is also applied to the deepest part of the ocean. *See also* Benthic Division.

Benton, Thomas Hart (1889–1975), US painter, b. Neosho, Mo. He was a leader of the regionalist movement and was famous for his paintings of rural and small-town life and for his many murals (including those for the Truman Library in Independence, Mo.). He was also the teacher of Jackson Pollock.

Benz, Karl (1844–1929), German pioneer of the internal combustion engine. After some success with an earlier two-stroke engine, Benz built a four-stroke in 1885 that, first applied to a tricycle, achieved great success when installed in a four-wheel vehicle in 1893. Benz was the first to make and sell light, self-propelled vehicles built to a standardized pattern. Hundreds of vehicles had been built by the turn of the century.

Benzene, colorless volatile sweet-smelling flammable liquid hydrocarbon (formula C_6H_6) obtained in petroleum refining. Benzene is the simplest aromatic hydrocarbon having a structure containing a hexagonal ring of unsaturated carbon atoms (benzene ring). It is a raw material for manufacturing many organic chemicals and is also a useful solvent. Properties: sp. gr. 0.879; melt. pt. 41.9°F (5.5°C); boil. pt. 176.18°F (80.1°C).

Benzoic Acid, colorless crystalline weak carboxylic acid (formula C_6H_5COOH) made from toluene. Properties: sp. gr. 1.266 (at 15°C); melt. pt. 252.32°F (122.4°C); boil. pt. 480.2 (249°C).

Beothuk, now-extinct people once inhabiting Newfoundland, perhaps the first Indians seen by white explorers. They were noted for their custom of painting their bodies with red ochre. Only a handful survived among the English colonists, and in time these apparently crossed the Belle Isle Strait and became intermixed with the Naskapi.

Beowulf (?8th century), Old English epic poem. It tells how the murderous monster Grendel terrorizes King Hrothgar's Danish domains until Beowulf, a Swedish prince, kills it by tearing off its arm. Grendel's mother seeks revenge, but Beowulf kills her in an underwater battle. Fifty years later the aged Beowulf, now king of Sweden, fights and slays a fire-breathing dragon, but dies of his wounds.

The poem's unknown author used already ancient material—the gloomy folklore, violent history, and harsh morality of the pagan Germanic peoples before their migration to England—to construct a lyrical tragedy infused with the newer and gentler sentiments of Christianity. It is written in long, alliterative lines with four strongly emphasized syllables. Metaphors are frequently used, but similes are rare.

Berbers, Caucasoid African people, believed to originate from the E Mediterranean, who constitute the basic population of Morocco, Algeria, and Tunisia. Their traditional livelihood is by subsistence farming, the chief crops being grain, vegetables, and fruit, with some animal husbandry, especially among the nomadic tribes. Typical Berber houses are single-story, built of stone, with a few small windows to minimize heat penetration. Each village or nomadic tribe is governed by decisions taken at meetings which all respectable and healthy adult men attend.

Berchtesgaden, town in West Germany, 10mi (16km) S of Salzburg, Austria, in the Bavarian Alps. Salt mined since the 12th century; site of Adolf Hitler's villa retreat, Berghof (1938); bombed by Allies Mar. 1945; popular resort. Pop. 39,800.

Berchtold, (Count) Leopold von (1863–1942), Austro-Hungarian statesman. As foreign minister (1912–15), he was responsible for the ultimatum sent to Serbia (1914) after the assassination of Archduke Francis Ferdinand at Sarajevo, which was the immediate cause of World War I.

Berengar II (*c.* 900–966), self-styled king of Italy (950–61) and protagonist in the career of Otto the Great. When Berengar attacked Pope John XII, Otto came to pope's defense and was crowned Holy Roman Emperor (962). Subsequent negotiations between John and Berengar ended in Otto deposing John and imprisoning Berengar.

Berg, Alban (1885–1935), Austrian composer. A student of Arnold Schoenberg, Berg composed his relatively few works in a complex, highly individualized style based on Schoenberg's 12-tone system. His opera *Wozzeck* (1923) is regarded as one of the masterpieces of 20th-century opera. He also composed a *Violin Concerto* (1935) and began another opera, *Lulu,* which was unfinished at his death.

Bergama, town in W Turkey, 50mi (81km) N of Izmir; site of ancient Greek city (Mysia); former capital of Pergamum kingdom (3rd century BC); political and cultural center of the East for nearly four centuries; early center of Christianity; commercial center under Byzantine and Ottoman empires. Industries: carpets, iron, silver and copper mining. Crops: tobacco, olives. Pop. 24,121.

Bergamo, city in N Italy; capital of Bergamo prov. Est. by Gauls, it became a Roman town; destroyed by Attila; joined Italy 1859; site of Romanesque cathedral, baptistry (1340). Industries: textiles, cement. Pop. 127,390.

Bergen, port city in SW Norway, on the North Sea; capital of Hordaland co; 3rd-largest city in Norway; industrial and cultural center; site of University of Bergen (1948), National Theater (1850), several museums and art galleries, Rosencrantz Tower (1562), Haakonshallen (13th-century Viking hall). Industries: shipbuilding, electrical equipment, textiles, processed fish. Founded in the 11th century, Bergen was Norway's chief city and the residence of several medieval kings. Pop. 213,594.

Bergen-Belsen, village in Lower Saxony, West Germany. It was the site of a Nazi concentration camp, liberated by the British Army in April 1945. More than 50,000 prisoners, most of them Jews, were freed, but thousands of those died soon after from the effects of imprisonment.

Bergman, (Ernst) Ingmar (1918–), Swedish stage and film writer-director. With a versatile company of artists and a strong personal vision, he has created dark allegories, sex satires, and complex studies of human relationships. His major films include *The Seventh Seal* (1956), *Wild Strawberries* (1957), *The Virgin Spring* (1959), *Persona* (1965), *Scenes from a Marriage* (1974), *The Magic Flute* (1975), *The Serpent's Egg* (1978), *Autumn Sonata* (1978), and *Fårö Document 1979* (1980).

Bergman, Ingrid (1915–82), Swedish actress whose acclaimed stage performances—*Joan of Lorraine* (1946), *Liliom* (1940), and *Anna Christie* (1941)—led to a long and varied film career in Hollywood. She won Academy Awards for *Gaslight* (1944), *Anastasia* (1956), and *Murder on the Orient Express* (1974). Other films include *Casablanca* (1942), *The Inn of the Sixth Happiness* (1958), and *Autumn Sonata* (1978). She also starred in the television drama *A Woman Called Golda* (1982).

Bergschrund, either one deep and wide crevasse in a glacier, or a series of parallel and narrow ones. The breaks are produced by tension within the ice, often at the point where the moving ice separated from the immobile or apron ice. The formation is more common in old or retreating glaciers.

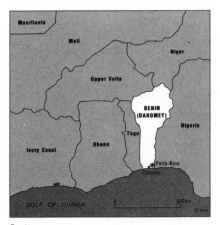

Benin

Ingmar Bergman

Irving Berlin

Bergson, Henri (1859–1941), French philosopher of evolution. He saw the world as a struggle between man's life force (élan vital) and the material. Man perceives the material through the use of his intellect while the life force is perceived through intuition. It is through intuition that one perceives the reality of time. He received the Nobel Prize for literature in 1927. Among his many works are *Time and Free Will* (1889), *Laughter* (1901), *Creative Evolution* (1907), and *The Creative Mind* (1934).

Beriberi, disease caused by deficiency of Vitamin B_1 and other vitamins, frequently brought on by a diet of polished rice. Symptoms are weakness of legs, then arms. Therapeutic doses of B complex vitamins are the treatment.

Bering (Beringa) Island, island in E USSR, in SW Bering Sea, off the coast of Kamchatka peninsula; largest of the Komandorski group; flat and barren lands suffer severe windstorms; named for Vitus Bering, Danish navigator who served Russia and died here 1741; chief town is Nikolskoye. Width: approx. 15mi (24km). Length: approx. 55mi (89km).

Bering Sea, northernmost reach of Pacific Ocean, bounded by Siberia (NW), Alaska (NE), and separated from the Pacific Ocean by the Aleutian Island chain; connected with Arctic Ocean via the Bering Strait; icelocked in winter months. Exploration by Russia by Danish navigator Vitus Bering in early 18th century led to international recognition of great fur-seal resource. Sale of Alaska to the United States in 1867 precipitated the Fur-Seal Controversy (1881). Area: approx. 878,000sq mi (2,274,020sq km).

Bering Strait, strait at N extreme of Bering Sea, separating W Alaska from extreme E Siberia and connecting Bering Sea (S) with the Arctic Ocean (N); named after Vitus Bering, Danish explorer who served Russia. Width: approx. 55mi (89km).

Berkeley, city in W California, N of Oakland; originally a land grant from Spain to Peralta family in 1820; annexed to the United States 1853 and named Oceanview; name changed in 1866 to Berkeley; site of Armstrong College (1918), the University of California (1868), Lawrence Radiation Laboratory (atomic research), Lawrence Hall of Science. Industries: food processing, chemicals, metal products. Founded 1853; inc. 1878. Pop. (1980) 103,328.

Berkelium, radioactive metallic element (symbol Bk) of the actinide group, first made (1949) by alpha-particle bombardment of Am^{241}. Properties: at. no. 97; most stable isotope Bk^{247} (1.4×10^3 yr). *See also* Actinide Elements.

Berlin, Irving (1888–), US composer of musicals and over 1000 popular songs, b. Israel Baline in Russia. His successful Broadway musicals include *Annie Get Your Gun* (1946) and *Call Me Madam* (1950). Two highly successful films are *Easter Parade* (1948) and *White Christmas* (1954). His many popular songs include "Alexander's Ragtime Band," "White Christmas," and "God Bless America."

Berlin, city in East Germany, on the Spree and Havel rivers; former capital of Germany. Core of the city developed from two Wendish villages of Berlin and Kölln which merged in 1307. It was nearly destroyed in the Thirty Years' War (1618–48) but was rebuilt. In the 17th century a canal connecting the Oder and Spree rivers helped it as a great trading center; it developed as an 18th-century industrial center and in 1871 became the capital of the German Republic. Before its virtual de-

struction in WWII, it was the 2nd-largest city in Europe and 5th-largest in the world.

In July 1945, Berlin was divided into four sectors: British, French, US, and Russian. Tension and distrust between Russia and the three Western powers resulted in Berlin Blockade by Russia in 1948. Massive US airlift made the blockade ineffective, and it was lifted in 1949. After this, the Russians organized the Democratic Republic of Germany (East Germany) with East Berlin as its capital. In 1951, West Berlin became one of the states of the German Federal Republic (West Germany). Further tension between the United States and Russia developed during the East Berlin rebellion of 1953 and led to the erection (1961) of East Germany's Berlin Wall, which was an attempt to stem the flow of refugees out of East Berlin. *See also* Berlin, East; Berlin, West.

Berlin, Conference of (1884–85), meeting of the major European nations, the United States, and Turkey in Berlin to discuss the problems of West African colonization and arrange for free trade along the Niger and Congo rivers. The conference affirmed British claims on Nigeria and Belgian claims on the Congo, but other agreements on trade and political neutrality proved untenable in the years to follow.

Berlin, Congress of (1878), meeting of European states after the Russo-Turkish war, which Russia won. It overrode the Treaty of San Stefano by which Russia had received large areas in the Caucasus and gained independence for Serbia, Montenegro, and Bulgaria, and semi-independence for Bosnia and Hercegovina. At the congress, German chancellor Otto von Bismarck established the Treaty of Berlin, which limited Russia's naval power, divided Bulgaria, and allowed Austria-Hungary to occupy Bosnia and Hercegovina.

Berlin, East, city and capital of East Germany; site of state opera, Humboldt University (formerly Frederick William University), and St. Hedwig's Cathedral. On the site of the Royal Palace is Marx-Engels Square. In the Soviet Military Cemetery is a massive statue of a Soviet soldier, built partly from the remains of Hitler's Chancellery. A fine zoo and many museums are also here, Moscow-designed apartment buildings line Karl Marx Allee, the sector's showcase. Erection of the Berlin Wall in 1961 put the famous Brandenburg Gate totally in Soviet zone. Industries: clothing, electrical goods, chemicals. Pop. 1,098,000.

Berlin, West, city and state of West Germany, more than 100mi (161km) inside East Germany. The main street, Kurfürstendamm, runs through the heart of city, and contains cafés, theaters, hotels, and night clubs; site of Tiergarten Park, Olympic Stadium, Dahlem Gallery, Benjamin Franklin Hall, and Dahlem Free University (1948). Industries: electrical goods, clothing, machinery, foodstuffs. Pop. 1,984,800.

Berlin Airlift (1948–49), an operation put into effect by the United States and Great Britain after the USSR closed all roads and rail lines between West Germany and Berlin, cutting off supply routes to the city. The 11-month airlift, in 272,264 flights, provided basic necessities to blockaded Berlin.

Berlin Decree (1806), act by Napoleon directed against the British blockade of European ports. It placed Britain under a French blockade.

Berlin Wall, barrier built between East and West Berlin by the East Germans (1961). The fortified and heavily guarded wall cut off movement and communication between West Berlin and the rest of East Germany except at official crossing sites.

Berlioz, Hector (1803–1869), French Romantic composer who astounded his contemporaries with innovative orchestral writing in such works as *Symphonie fantastique* (1830), *Harold in Italy,* for viola and orchestra (1834), and *Roméo et Juliette* (1839). He also wrote grandiose operas, including *Les Troyens* (1859). *See also* Romanticism in Music.

Bermuda, formerly Somers Islands; 300 islets and islands constituting British crown colony, 570mi (918km) SE of Cape Hatteras, North Carolina; includes larger islands of St George, Somerset, Bermuda, and Ireland; capital is Hamilton, on Bermuda Island. It became part of the crown in 1684 and was granted internal self-government in 1968; site of U.S. naval and air force base. Industries: tourism, perfume, ship repairing, pharmaceuticals, textiles, cut flowers. Area: 21sq mi (54sq km). Pop. 53,500.

Bermuda Grass, perennial grass native to the Mediterranean region and grown in North America as lawn and pasture grass. It has short, flat leaves, flower spikes at stem tips, and creeping rhizomes. Height: to 16in (40cm). Family Gramineae; species *Cynodon dactylon.*

Bern, capital city of Switzerland, on Aare River, 59mi (95km) SW of Zurich; capital of Bern canton; became part of Swiss Confederation in 1353; accepted the Reformation in 1528; during French Revolutionary Wars, Bern was occupied by French troops (1798); noted for medieval architecture, 15th-century town hall, Gothic cathedral, and university. Industries: precision instruments, chemicals, chocolate, tourism. Founded 1191 as military post. Pop. 149,800.

Bernadette of Lourdes (1844–79), b. Bernadette Soubirous. The daughter of a poor French miller, she began to see visions of the Virgin Mary (1858) who revealed to her the healing shrine of Lourdes. In 1866 she became a member of the Sisters of Notre Dame at Nevers.

Bernadotte, (Count) Folke (1895–1948), Swedish diplomat. In June 1948, as head of the Swedish Red Cross, he was appointed UN mediator to negotiate a truce between the newly created state of Israel and the Arab countries. On Sept. 17, while negotiating a permanent armistice, he was killed by Israeli partisans in Jerusalem.

Bernadotte Dynasty, family of Béarn, France. In 1810 Jean Baptiste Bernadotte (1763?–1844) was chosen crown prince to succeed the childless Charles XIII of Sweden who had adopted him. The son of a French lawyer, he rose from the ranks in Napoleon's army. Under his leadership Sweden acquired Norway from Denmark. He became King Charles XIV in 1818, founding the present Swedish dynasty. King Carl XVI Gustav, Sweden's king, is the seventh ruler of the Bernadotte dynasty.

Bernard of Clairvaux (1091–1153), French mystic and religious leader. He was abbot of the Cistercian monastery of Clairvaux (1115–53). Under his direction, nearly 100 new monasteries were founded. In 1130 he became a churchman of international importance during a contested papal election and afterward became an adviser to several popes. He actively fought heresy and advocated the Second Crusade (1146). His devotion to the Virgin Mary and the Infant Christ greatly influenced his contemporaries and the future direction of the Roman Catholic Church.

Bernese Mountain Dog, Swiss draft dog and pet (working group) brought to Switzerland 2000 years ago by Roman soldiers. A hardy dog, it has a flat head with strong muzzle, hanging lips, and dewlaps; short, compact body; sturdy legs; and thick, medium length tail. The silky, long, slightly wavy coat is jet black with russet brown and white marks. Average size: 23–27.5in (58.5–70cm) high at shoulder; 50–70lb (23–32kg). *See also* Working Dog.

Bernhardt, Sarah (1844–1923), original name Rosine Bernard, French actress of legendary international stature, known as the greatest tragedienne of her day. Her superb potrayals in *King Lear* (1867), *Ruy Blas* (1867), *Phèdre* (1874), and *Hernani* (1877) earned her the title "divine Sarah." She also toured Europe and the United States, managed the Theatre Sarah Bernhardt in Paris (1899) where she played Hamlet, made two silent films (1912), and continued acting even after a leg amputation (1914).

Bernini, Gianlorenzo (1598–1680), Italian architect and sculptor. He dominated sculpture in his time, but his reputation failed when the Baroque style went out of favor. It has since been regained. Early portraits—psychological studies—include the "Vigevano" bust (1617–18), the "Montoya" bust (*c.*1621), and "Bellarmine" bust (1622). Later works, including "Francis I d'Este" (1650–51) and "Louis XIV" (1665), represent portrait bust in the ultimate Baroque style.

His architectural work was largely executed in his later career, and many of his most important plans and designs were never executed. In 1637 he designed the facade towers for St. Peter's, Rome, but the project ended in disaster because of technical problems and nearly ruined his career. His design for the square of St. Peter's (1662–64) is a masterpiece. He was commissioned to design the new Louvre in 1665, but the plan, though influential, was never realized. He designed several churches, including S. Andrea al Quirinale in Rome (1658–70), the Palazzo di Montecitorio (1650), and the S. Maria dell' Assunzione in Arrica (1662–64). His artistic aim, to express the mysteries of the Catholic religion with artistic clarity, is best realized in the sculpture "Ecstasy of St. Theresa" (1645–52) in Santa Maria della Vittoria, Rome. *See also* Baroque Art.

Bernoulli, Daniel (1700–82), Swiss mathematician and member of a famous family of mathematicians. His book on hydrodynamics indicated that fluid pressure decreases as the velocity of fluid flow increases. This statement is Bernoulli's Equation. He also attempted the first statement of the kinetic theory of gases.

Bernoulli's Equation, the relation between the work done on a moving liquid by pressure forces and its change in kinetic and potential energy. Generally stated in the form $p + \frac{1}{2} v^2 + gy = \text{constant}$, where p is the pressure, v the velocity, g the density, and y the height of the fluid at any point. The equation makes it possible to measure the velocity of a liquid by measuring its pressure at two points, as with a manometer or Pitot tube.

Bernstein, Leonard (1918–), US conductor, composer, and pianist, b. Lawrence, Mass. He debuted in 1943 and was associated with the New York Philharmonic Orchestra as a conductor (1955–58) and as music director (1958–69), after which he devoted a great deal of time to composing and writing. During his tenure with the New York Philharmonic he became well known and popular both as a conductor and as a musician. His compositions include three symphonies, ballets, and music for the Broadway shows *Candide* (1956) and *West Side Story* (1957).

Berry, historic region and former prov. in central France; originally a settlement of the Bituriges Cubi, part of Roman Aquitaine, it was purchased by French Crown 1101; made a duchy 1360; returned to France 1601; a prov. until 1789, when France was divided into depts.; cattle farming region; chief city is Bourges.

Berry, small, fleshy fruit containing many seeds. It consists of an outer skin, fleshy middle, and inner membrane enclosing the seeds. Often juicy and edible, a true berry comes from a flower ovary with petals attached underneath (superior ovary). Berries include tomato, grape, eggplant, and red pepper; citrus fruits are modified berries. False berries are fruits formed from the matured ovary wall and other flower parts, often the floral tube. They can be distinguished from true berries by flower remnants left on the fruit (cranberry).

Berthier, Louis Alexandre, Prince de Wagram (1753–1815), Napoleon's trusted assistant and chief of staff of the Grande Armée, sovereign prince of Neuchâtel. He fought during the American and French revolutions, Napoleon's first reign (when he acquired his titles), and served Louis XVIII until Napoleon's reappearance.

Berthollet, Claude Louis, Comte (1748–1822), French chemist. He discovered the structure of ammonia, showed the bleaching ability of chlorine, and predicted the law of mass action, though his views were ignored on this subject. He was made a senator and a count by Napoleon.

Bertillon Measurement, system of measuring human physical characteristics (eg length of middle finger), evolved originally by Alphonse Bertillon (1853–1914) for criminal identification, and now used extensively by physical anthropologists.

Beryl, a ring silicate mineral, beryllium aluminum silicate. Hexagonal system, usually prismatic hexagonal crystals; glassy white, blue, yellow, green, pink; hardness 8; sp gr 2.6–2.8. Gemstone varieties are aquamarine (pale blue-green) from Brazil; emerald (deep green) from Colombia; and morganite (pink) from Madagascar. Cut stones have little brilliance, but are valued for intense color.

Beryllium, metallic element (symbol Be) of the alkaline-earth group, first isolated (1828) by Friedrich Wöhler. It occurs in many minerals including aquamarine and emerald (both forms of beryl). The metal is used in certain alloys that combine lightness with rigidity. Beryllium and its oxide are also used as moderators in nuclear reactors. Properties: at. no. 4; at. wt. 9.01218; sp. gr. 1.85; melt. pt. 2332°F (1279 °C); boil. pt. 5378°F (2972°C); most common isotope Be^9 (100%). *See also* Alkaline-earth Elements.

Berzelius, Baron Jöns Jakob (1779–1848), Swedish chemist, one of the founders of modern chemistry. His accomplishments include the discovery of the elements cerium, selenium, and thorium; the isolation of the elements silicon, zirconium, and titanium; the determination of atomic weights; and the devising of a modern system of chemical symbols. He prepared the first table of atomic weights, and he contributed to the founding of the radical theory. *See also* Periodic Table.

Besançon, city in E France, at the foot of the Jura Mountains; contains ruins of a Roman arch, aqueduct, and theater; became part of France 1676. University of Besançon opened 1691. Industries: textiles, food processing, clock- and watchmaking. Pop. 126,187.

Bessarabia, historical region in SW European USSR; primarily in Moldavian SSR and the Ukraine, it forms passageway from Russia to Danube valley. Kishinev is capital. Greek colonists settled Black Sea coast 7th century BC; site of Roman colony Dacia until *c.* AD 4th century when Goths, Huns, Avars, and Magyars invaded; by 7th century Slavs had settled in the region. Kievan Russians held control 9th–11th centuries; it was included in Moldavia 1367; ceded to Russia 1812; proclaimed autonomous republic 1917; renounced Soviet ties 1918 and declared independent Moldavian republic (united with Romania); forced to inc. into USSR 1940 (confirmed 1947). Crops: grapes, grains, tobacco, sugar beets, fruit. Area: 17,600sq mi (45,584sq km).

Bessel, Friedrich Wilhelm (1784–1846), German mathematician and astronomer. A self-taught astronomer, by the age of 26 he was appointed by Frederick William III of Prussia to build an observatory at Königsberg, where he remained for the rest of his life as director. In 1818 he produced a new star catalogue and in 1838 he measured the parallax of 61 Cygni, giving the first measurement of a star's distance. He worked out the general method of mathematical analysis involving the functions that bear his name.

Bessemer Process, the first method for mass-producing steel. Carbon and other impurities are removed from molten pig-iron with a blast of air forced through the molten metal in a Bessemer converter. After most carbon is removed, some is restored to desired proportions, along with manganese, with the addition of ferromanganese when the metal is poured into a large ladle. Ingot molds are then filled with the steel from the ladle. Invention of the process is credited to Henry Bessemer, an English engineer who obtained the first patent in 1855, and to William Kelly, an American inventor whose patent was issued in 1857.

Best, Charles Herbert (1899–1978), Canadian physiologist, b. W. Pembroke, Me. He participated in the discovery of insulin in 1921 with F.G. Banting. From 1929–65 he was head of the department of physiology at the University of Toronto and chief of the Banting-Best department of medical research after Banting's death (1941).

Beta Centauri, or **Agena,** or **Hadar,** bluish-white giant star in the constellation Centaurus. It is associated with a 9th-magnitude companion. Characteristics: apparent mag. 0.61; absolute mag. −4.3; spectral type B1; distance 300 light-years.

Beta Crucis, or **Mimosa,** blue-white subgiant star in the constellation Crux (Southern Cross). Characteristics: apparent mag. +1.28; absolute mag. −4.0; spectral type B0; distance 370 light-years.

Beta Rays, or **Beta Particles,** particles emitted spontaneously by certain radioactive isotopes (undergoing beta decay), discovered and identified as energetic electrons by Antoine Becquerel (1876). They cause ionization along their path and have fairly high penetrating power. Their energy, ranging from 0.003 million to 13 million electronvolts, is characteristic of the emitting isotope. Beta decay results from the breakdown of a neutron in the nucleus to a proton, an electron, and an antineutrino. *See also* Radioactivity.

Betatron, field accelerator in which electrons move in a circle inside a toroidal vacuum chamber. Acceleration is induced by the changing magnetic flux of an electromagnet. Energies can reach 300 MeV.

Betelgeuse, or Alpha Orionis, red supergiant star and the second-brightest star in the constellation Orion. It is a pulsating variable whose diameter fluctuates between 330 and 460 solar diameters. Characteristics: apparent mag. +0.85 (mean); absolute mag. −5.5 (mean); spectral type M2; distance 650 light-years.

Betel Nut Palm, also areca, tall slender palm tree native to Malaya; planted throughout Southeast Asia and the Pacific islands. Height: to 100ft (30.5m). It has small feather-shaped leaves. Its seeds are chewed as a stimulant or narcotic. Family Palmaceae, species *Areca catechu.*

Bethany (Al-'Ayzariyah), town in Jordan, 2mi (3km) E of Jerusalem, at foot of Mt of Olives; Biblical home of Mary, Martha, Lazarus; traditional site of the Ascension of Jesus and Jesus' raising of Lazarus from the dead.

Bethe, Hans Albrecht (1906–), US nuclear physicist, b. Strassburg, Germany (now Strassbourg, France). He helped to develop the atomic bomb, although his major scientific contribution has been in the field of stellar energy processes. He determined the source from which the sun and stars derive their energy. He was honored in 1961 with the Fermi award for his work with atomic energy, and in 1967 with a Nobel Prize for his work on stellar energy production and his contributions to the nuclear reaction theory, and in 1976 with the Niels Bohr Gold Medal for his work on the peacetime use of atomic energy.

Bethel (Baytin), archeological site and village in Jordan, 11mi (18km) N of Jerusalem; as city of ancient Palestine it preceded Jerusalem as a Jewish shrine; traditional site of Jacob's dream of ladder reaching to heaven; occupied by Israel 1967.

Bethesda, city in W central Maryland, 7mi (11km) from Washington, D.C.; site of research center of National Institutes of Health (1939), Naval Medical Center (1942), and National Cancer Institute. Settled in late 17th century by Scottish, English, and Irish, it was named for the Bethesda Presbyterian Church, which they built in 1820. Pop. (1970) 71,621.

Bethlehem (Bayt Lahm), town in Jordan, 5mi (8km) SSW of Jerusalem; traditional birthplace of Jesus Christ; early home of King David; site of Biblical massacre of the Innocents (Matt. 2:16) and Church of the Nativity built by Constantine (AD 326), oldest Christian church still in use. Under Ottoman Empire 1571–1915, and then part of British Palestine mandate until 1948, it was inc. into Jordan 1950; occupied by Israelis since 1967 war. Tourism and sale of religious souvenirs are principal industries. Pop. 16,313.

Bethlehem, city in E Pennsylvania on the Lehigh River, 5mi (8km) E of Allentown; site of Lehigh University (1865), Moravian College (1807). Bach Choir performs here at annual festival. Industries: steel, cement. Settled 1740 by Moravians; inc. 1917. Pop. (1980) 70,419.

Bethune, Mary McLeod (1875–1955), US educator, b. Mayesville, S.C. The daughter of former slaves, she began teaching in 1895. In 1904 she established the Daytona Normal and Industrial Institute for Negro Girls in Florida. In 1923 it became Bethune-Cookman College, of which she was president until 1942. Active in national affairs, she founded the National Council of Negro Women and was director of Negro affairs in the National Youth Administration (1936–44).

Betjeman, John (1906–84), English poet. He became Poet Laureate in 1971. His verse, traditional in form, was concerned with the details and oddities of English

Leonard Bernstein

Bethlehem

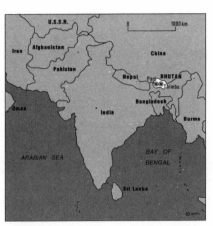
Bhutan

domestic life. *Summoned by Bells* (1960) was a verse autobiography of his early years. He was also a noted authority on Victorian and Edwardian architecture.

Betony, common name for colorful herbs of the mint family including *Stachys grandiflora* and *S. officinalis.* Flowers of this perennial from Asia Minor are white or purple arranged in showy clusters.

Bet Sh'ean, town in NE Israel, in Jordan River valley, 18mi (29km) SE of Nazareth; excavations have revealed settlements (c. 3,000–2,000 BC); important center in the 18th and 19th Egyptian dynasties; mentioned in the Bible as Beth-shan; one of ten cities of Decapolis; taken by Arabs AD 636; some early structures remain. Modern town was settled 1949 by Israelis. Produces textiles. Pop. 11,900.

Bevan, Aneurin (1897–1960), British socialist statesman. An active trade unionist, he became a Labour member of Parliament (1929) and gradually assumed leadership of the Labour party left wing, whose views he expressed in the *Tribune,* which he edited (1940–45). As minister of health (1945–51), he inaugurated the National Health Service. His book *In Place of Fear* was published in 1952.

Bevatron, an elementary-particle accelerator, similar to a synchrotron, that accelerates particles into the billion-electron-volt (BeV) range. *See also* Synchrotron.

Bevin, Ernest (1884–1951), British trade unionist and socialist statesman. Organizer of the Dockers' Union (1910–21) and general secretary of the Transport and General Workers' Union (1921–40), Bevin planned the general strike (1926) and later criticized Labour's failure to overcome unemployment. He was minister of Labour and National Service (1940–45), and as foreign secretary (1945–51) he assisted in Europe's economic recovery and helped establish the North Atlantic Treaty Organization.

Beyle, Marie Henri (1783–1842). *See* Stendhal.

Bezique, card game for two or more players. Most popular is the two-handed version that is played with 64 cards. Bezique for three requires a 96 card pack and for four a 128 card pack. The game was developed in France and England in the 1860s and was the principal inspiration for pinochle. The cards in each suit rank ace, 10, king, queen, jack, 9, 8, 7. The twos to the sixes are disregarded. Each player is dealt eight cards; another card is turned up to establish trump. A player other than the dealer leads and the others follow, playing any card they desire. Cards are drawn from the deck after each trick. The highest card or trump wins the trick, and the game continues until all cards, from the hand and deck, have been played.

Bhagavad Gita, or "The Song of the Lord," popular episode in the sixth book of the Hindu epic, the *Mahabharata.* Probably composed shortly before the Christian era, the Gita presents Krishna as the Supreme God who, if worshiped, will save men. The Gita begins with a battle between two related but hostile clans. The archer Arjuna, seeking his relatives in the opposing army, hesitates until Krishna reminds him of his duty to fight. Devotion and faith toward the Lord is the central theme of the episode. *See also* Hinduism; Krishna; Mahabharata.

Bhavnagar (Bhaunagar), city in W India, on Gulf of Cambay (Khambhat); chief port of Kathiawar Peninsula; capital of former princely state of Bhaunagar; site

of two colleges of Gujarat University. Industries: textiles, bricks, tiles. Exports: cotton, grain, oilseeds. Founded 1723. Pop. 222,462.

Bhutan, a monarchy with an advisory council and 130-member national assembly. Located in the Himalayas, on NE border of India, it is bounded by Tibet and China (N), Assam and India (E), Assam and West Bengal (S), and Sikkim and Tibet (W). The official capital is Thimbu; traditional capital is Punakka.

Eight high mountain ranges, including the Himalayas, cross the country; the highest peak is Kula Kangri, 24,784ft (7,559m). Torrential annual rain storms, with an average fall of 200–250in (508–635cm), are recorded.

The people of Bhutan are predominantly Bhutias. Their religion is a form of Buddhism closely related to Tibetan Buddhism. The language, basically Tibetan, is Dzongka. They are mainly farmers of small plots; rice is the chief crop. Yaks, pigs, sheep, cattle, and tanguns (a breed of pony) are raised. Handicrafts of metal, wood, and leather are produced.

In the 9th century the original inhabitants of Bhutan were conquered by Tibetan soldiers who ultimately became the present Bhutians. China took the country in 1720; in 1772 relations with Britain began, and in 1864, Britain occupied part of S Bhutan; portions were annexed to India in 1865. By a 1910 treaty Britain agreed that it would subsidize Bhutan and manage its foreign affairs. When India gained its independence in 1949, it assumed Britain's role with Bhutan, while Bhutan managed its own internal affairs. A Chinese threat to the country in the 1960s caused India to close the Tibetan-Bhutanese border, and Bhutan built up a small army. In 1971, Bhutan joined the United Nations.

Government is conducted by a monarch and small advisory council. In 1954 a national assembly was formed; 25% of its 130 members is appointed by the king; the remainder is composed of village headmen, elected for five-year terms. The present ruler is Singhi Wangchuk, who succeeded his father in 1972.

PROFILE

Official name: Kingdom of Bhutan
Area: 18,147sq mi (47,001sq km)
Population: 1,600,000
Chief cities: Thimbu (official capital); Punakha (traditional capital); Paro Dzong
Religion: Buddhism
Language: Dzongka; Druk-ke (a Tibetan dialect)

Bhutto, Zulfikar Ali (1928–79), Pakistani political leader. A protégé of Ayub Khan, he held several cabinet posts between 1958–63 before becoming foreign minister. Critical of the agreement ending the war with India, he left the government and formed the opposition Pakistan People's party (1967). After the 1970 election he refused to cooperate with Mujibur Rahman's Awami League, which had won a majority in the legislature. Civil war resulted. After Bangladesh (East Pakistan) gained independence, Bhutto became president of what remained of Pakistan (1971). Under a new constitution (1973), he became prime minister. In 1977 he was overthrown and in 1979 convicted and executed for murder.

Biafra, former state in W Africa, formed from East-Central, South-Eastern, and River states of Nigeria. After it was est May 30, 1967, by Ibos, all economic aid was cut off by Nigeria. War broke out July, 1967; overwhelmed by numerous Nigerian attacks, Biafra's land size was reduced, oil fields (its main source of income) were lost, and its people suffered high casualties; secessionist attempt ended Jan. 15, 1970, when Biafra was reincorporated into Nigeria.

Biafra, Bight of, wide bay off coasts of Cameroon and Equatorial Guinea, W Africa; in E part of Gulf of Guinea; contains island of Fernando Pó.

Bialystok, city in NE Poland, approx. 100mi (161km) NE of Warsaw; capital of Bialystok prov.; manufacturing center. Industries: metal, textiles. Founded 1310. Pop. 166,600.

Biarritz, town in SW France, near Spanish border on Bay of Biscay. Native population is Basque; popular resort area since 1838 with mild climate, mineral waters, and beaches. Pop. 27,653.

Biathlon, sport that involves skiing and target shooting, popular in Scandinavia. Each competitor is required to ski 20 kilometers (12.4 miles), stopping four times during the race to fire at a fixed target with a rifle. A miss results in penalty time being added to the race time. The competitor with the lowest corrected time wins.

Bible, sacred scriptures of Judaism and Christianity. It is regarded as the source of divine revelation and of prescriptions and prohibitions for moral living. The Hebrew Bible, or Old Testament, excluding the Apocrypha, is accepted as sacred by both Jews and Christians. The Roman Catholic Church and Eastern Orthodox Church each accept parts of the Apocrypha as sacred, while Jews and Protestants do not. The New Testament is accepted as sacred only by Christians. *See also* Apocrypha; New Testament; Old Testament.

BOOKS OF THE BIBLE
(King James Version)
Old Testament

Genesis	Ecclesiastes
Exodus	Song of Solomon
Leviticus	Isaiah
Numbers	Jeremiah
Deuteronomy	Lamentations
Joshua	Ezekiel
Judges	Daniel
Ruth	Hosea
I Samuel	Joel
II Samuel	Amos
I Kings	Obadiah
II Kings	Jonah
I Chronicles	Micah
II Chronicles	Nahum
Ezra	Habakkuk
Nehemiah	Zephaniah
Esther	Haggai
Job	Zechariah
Psalms	Malachi
Proverbs	

New Testament

Matthew	I Timothy
Mark	II Timothy
Luke	Titus
John	Philemon
Acts	Hebrews
Romans	James
I Corinthians	I Peter
II Corinthians	II Peter
Galatians	I John
Ephesians	II John
Philippians	III John
Colossians	Jude
I Thessalonians	Revelation
II Thessalonians	

Bibliography, system of listing books, described and arranged for easy reference and study. Swiss naturalist Konrad von Gesner (1516–65) is credited with the first modern bibliography, *Universal Bibliography,* a listing of all living and deceased Latin, Greek, and Hebrew writers, published in 1545.

Bibliothèque Nationale, national library of France, located in Paris. The oldest in the world still in existence, it dates from the reign of Charles V (1364–80). First opened to the public in 1692, it receives a copy of every publication printed in France. The library is divided into nine departments, including books, coins, maps, and manuscripts.

Bicameral System, legislative system having two chambers or branches. Its origin dates back to the House of Commons and House of Lords in the English Parliament. Bicameralism refers to the structure of the legislature, not its method of operation.

Bichir, primitive bony fish found in African fresh waters. Elongated with large horny scales, it has 5–18 flaglike finlets along its back and a two-part swim bladder for breathing air at the water surface. Length: 2–3ft (61–91cm). There are 11 species including Congo *Polypterus weeksi.* Family Polypteridae. *See also* Osteichthyes.

Bichon Frise, French-Belgian dog (nonsporting group) descended from water spaniel. Popular in ancient times as item of barter; common street or circus dog in 1880s. It has a broad, round head; longish muzzle; and pronounced nose. Ears are dropped; a long body is set on strong-boned legs; and the tail is curved to lie over the back. The long, silky, loosely curled coat gives the dog a powder puff appearance; colors are solid white or white with cream, apricot, or gray. Average size: 8–12in (20.5–30.5cm) high at shoulder. *See also* Nonsporting Dog.

Bicycle, a light, two-wheeled steerable vehicle, propelled by human power, first made by Karl von Drais in Germany (1816) and developed as an important means of transportation and recreation in many countries. Englishman J.K. Starley demonstrated the first successful chain drive in 1885. Today most bicycles have a "diamond frame" invented in 1893, coaster or friction brakes, a drive system providing 1 to 18 possible ratios, inflatable tires, light-weight alloy wheels, and myriad accessories.

Bicycle Racing, sport, most popular in Europe and the United States, involving a variety of events, from the sprint to the internationally known Tour de France (begun in 1903), where the world's best cyclists compete annually in a road race more than 2,000 miles (3,220km) long. Racing in the United States was most popular during the 1920s and 1930s, when Madison Square Garden in New York City held six-day races. The sport in the United States suffered with the advent of the automobile and, unlike Europe, is only now conducted on an amateur level. Bicycle racing, a regular event at the Olympic Games, first blossomed with the invention of the pneumatic tire in 1888 by John Dunlop, an English veterinary surgeon.

Biedermeier Style, a phase of German art (1816–48) characterized by simplicity, orderliness, and sober realism. The name is derived from a humorous literary character, a symbol of middle-class conservatism. Furniture of this style was well designed, using local materials and naturalistic stenciled decorations.

Bien-hoa, manufacturing city in S Vietnam, 20mi (32km) NNE of Saigon; former capital of Cambodia; site of US air base in Vietnam war. Pop. 82,506.

Biennial, plant that lives two years, producing flowers and seeds the second year. Some biennial seeds planted in early spring will blossom that same year. Most biennials are sown from June to August and bloom the following year. Popular garden biennials include foxglove, Canterbury bells, and wallflower. Some biennial garden plants seem perennial because they reseed themselves. *See also* Annual; Perennial.

Bienville, Jean Baptiste Le Moyné, Sieur de (1680–1768), French colonizer of Louisiana, b. Canada. In 1698, he accompanied his brother, Sieur d'Iberville, from Canada to the mouth of the Mississippi River. He founded Mobile (1710) and New Orleans (1718) and was the governor of Louisiana (1701–12, 1717–26, 1733–43).

Bigamy, in English and US law, criminal offense of entering into a second marriage when a first marriage is still in effect. Bigamy is also the state of a man having two wives or a woman two husbands.

Big-Bang Theory of Universe, cosmological theory postulating that at some time in the past all the matter of the universe was concentrated at near infinite density at one point and was subsequently hurled in all directions at great velocity by a cataclysmic explosion. Matter, evolved into galaxies, nebulae, etc, is still receding but with time the velocity has decreased. The universe thus has a finite size and age. The recently discovered microwave cosmic background radiation is thought to be the remnant radiation of the big bang and is thus evidence for this theory. *See also* Hubble Constant.

Big Dipper. *See* Ursa Major.

Bighorn Mountains, mountain range in N central Wyoming, reaching 120mi (193km) into S Montana, E of the Bighorn River; contains Bighorn National Forest. Highest point is Cloud Peak, 13,175ft (4,018m).

Bighorn Sheep, or Rocky Mountain sheep, wild sheep, native to mountains of W North America, closely related to Siberian forms. Living in herds of about 50, their great climbing ability is aided by elastic foot pads. The largest curved horns so far measured reached 50in (1.3m). Height: 3.5ft (1.07m) at shoulder; weight: up to 300lb (136kg). Family Bovidae; species *Ovis canadensis. See also* Sheep.

Bignonia, a genus of woody vines native to North America and Japan that have small disks at ends of tendrils for climbing, compound leaves, and showy, yellow or reddish tubular flowers. The cross vine or trumpet flower *(B. capreolata)* grows in S United States. Family Bignoniaceae.

Bihár, state in NE India; bordered by Nepal (N), West Bengal state (E), Orissa and Madhya Pradesh states (S), Uttar Pradesh state (W); capital is Patna. Known in ancient times as Magadha, it was center of the Maurya (4th and 3rd centuries BC) and Gupta (AD 4th and 5th centuries) dynasties; drained by Ganges River, it is a rich agricultural area and produces a majority of the country's mica, coal, copper, and iron ore. Area: 67,198sq mi (174,043sq km). Pop. 56,387,296.

Bikini Atoll, formerly Escholtz Island; group of about 30 islets in W central Pacific Ocean; part of Ralik Chain (Marshall Islands), US-administered UN trust territory; scene of US atomic and hydrogen bomb tests 1946–1958; island was declared safe for habitation 1969 but unsafe 1978 because of high residual radioactivity levels. Residents were forced to leave the island. Area: 2sq mi (5sq km).

Bilateralism, agreement between two states to jointly pursue common interests. Bilateral agreements pertain to political, military, economic, technical, and cultural matters. Mutual benefit is generally the key to such agreements. Accordingly, agreements involve both great and small powers.

Bilateral Monopoly, market situation in which there is a pure monopoly on both the buyer's and seller's side, ie, there is a single purchaser of a good and a single seller of this good. An example of a bilateral monopoly would be a union selling the services of its workers to only one employer.

Bilbao, city in N Spain on the Nervión River, near the Bay of Biscay; capital city of Vizcaya prov.; important commercial center and seaport. Industries: chemicals, steel, shipbuilding. Founded *c.* 1300. Pop. 410,490.

Bildungsroman, German "educational novel," of which the prototype is Goethe's *Wilhelm Meister,* where an artistic temperament is taught by experience how to come to terms with reality. Gottfried Keller's *Der Grüne Heinrich* (1854–55) is the last direct example, while Thomas Mann's *The Magic Mountain* (1924) is a good example of an ironical parody of this traditional form.

Bile, complex mixture of substances secreted by the liver, stored in the gall bladder, and released into the intestine, where it aids in the absorptive process during digestion.

Bile Acids, group of steroid acids present in bile. In man the commonest is cholic acid ($C_{24}H_{40}O_5$), which is conjugated by its carboxyl group to the amino groups of the amino acids glycine and taurine. The bile acids are emulsifiers for fats and fat-soluble vitamins, thus promoting their absorption by the intestine.

Bilirubin, reddish-yellow bile pigment. It consists of a breakdown product of hemoglobin conjugated to glucuronic acid for excretion.

Bill, draft of a proposed law. It requires legislative action before it can become law. A bill before either house of the US Congress requires the approval of both houses to become a law.

Billbug, weevil that is pest of grasses and cereal crops. They have long snouts, or bills. The common corn billbug (genus *Sphenophorus*) is best known. Family Curculionidae.

Billiards, game most popular in the United States and England. It has several variations, played either with 3 balls (billiards) or 15 balls (pocket billiards). In billiards the standard table is 6 by 12 feet (1.8 by 3.66m), with 6 pockets (English) or no pockets (United States), where scoring is by caroms only. Pocket billiards is the more popular game in the United States. The table is 9 by 4.5 feet (2.7 by 1.4m), with 6 pockets. A cue ball is used along with 15 consecutively numbered balls. The object is to make a continuous run of 14 balls, leaving the 15th on the table. The 14 balls are then racked again, and the ball that remained from the previous game is used to scatter the racked balls. Players shoot until they miss sinking a ball, and the first player to score 150 points (one point for each ball) is the winner.

Billings, city in S central Montana, on Yellowstone River; seat of Yellowstone co; site of Eastern Montana College (1927), Rocky Mountain College (1883); nearby are Custer National Forest and Yellowstone National Park, and Inscription Cave (discovered 1937), containing ancient Indian writings. The Yellowstone Museum has Indian artifacts and relics of the area's history. Industries: oil refining, sugar refining, meat packing, flour milling, vegetable canning. Founded 1882 during construction of Northern Pacific Railroad; inc. 1885. Pop. (1980) 66,798.

Bill of Exchange, unconditional written order from one party to another calling on him to pay on demand, or at some specified future date, a sum of money to some particular person, or to bearer. A check is a bill of exchange.

Bill of Rights, name given to the first 10 amendments to the US Constitution. These amendments were passed by Congress and ratified by the states in 1791, only four years after the signing of the Constitution. They were added because many in the United States feared tyranny by the new government, and several states were willing to ratify the Constitution only after George Washington promised to add such a list of liberties. Among the protections of the Bill of Rights are the freedom of worship, of speech, of the press, and of assembly; the right to bear arms; freedom from unreasonable search and seizure; the right to a speedy trial by jury; and protection from self-incrimination. Powers not granted specifically to the federal government were reserved for the states. *See also* Constitution of the United States.

Bill of Rights (1689), British statute enshrining the constitutional principles established after James II's abdication (1688) and accepted by William and Mary as a condition of their ascending the throne. It excluded Roman Catholics from the succession, set out the subject's political and civil rights, and effectively guaranteed parliamentary supremacy over the crown.

Billy the Kid (1859–81), US outlaw, also known as William H. Bonney, b. Henry McCarty in New York City. He moved to New Mexico in 1873 with his mother and stepfather. After killing a man in 1877, he took the alias William H. Bonney. In 1878 he killed a sheriff and led a gang of cattle rustlers. He was captured in 1880, tried, and sentenced to death. He admitted to 21 murders. He escaped jail, but was caught and killed by Sheriff Pat F. Garrett of Lincoln co, N. Mex.

Biloxi, city in SE Mississippi, on small peninsula between Biloxi Bay and Mississippi Sound on the Gulf of Mexico. New Biloxi was founded in 1719 and was the capital of French Louisiana until 1722, when New Orleans replaced it; site of "Beauvoir," last home of Jefferson Davis (1852–54), the Biloxi Light House (1848), and Ship Island (off the coast), a Union Fort in the Civil War. Industries: tourism, fishing, boatbuilding. Inc. 1896. Pop. (1980) 49,311.

Bimetallism, policy of defining the money of a country in terms of two metals, usually gold and silver, making each of them legal tender, and defining each of them in terms of the other. Bimetallism has not worked well and has not been used in recent years because the value of the metals changes with respect to each other.

Binary Star, stellar system consisting of two separate stars orbiting around a common center of gravity. Visual binaries are those whose component stars can be distinguished with the naked eye or through a tele-

Bichon frise

Bighorn sheep

Billy the Kid

scope; spectroscopic binaries are visually unresolvable but show redshifts and blueshifts in their spectra as the individual stars move toward or away from the observer. *See also* Double Star; Eclipsing Variable.

Binding Energy, energy that must be supplied to an atomic nucleus in order to split it into its constituent nucleons (neutrons and protons). A nucleus must be supplied with its binding energy before it will undergo fission (except in the case of radioactive decay). The mass of a nucleus is slightly less than the mass of its constituent particles. According to Einstein's law, $E = mc^2$, this difference in mass is equivalent to the energy released when the nucleons bind together. This is the energy source of the hydrogen bomb and the fusion reactor. *See also* Fission, Nuclear.

Binghamton, city in S central New York at the confluence of the Chenango and Susquehanna rivers. Harpur College of the State University of New York is here. Industries: shoes, electronic equipment. Inc. 1867. Pop. (1980) 55,860.

Binoculars, optical instrument, for use with both eyes simultaneously, that produces a magnified image of a distant object or scene. It consists of a pair of identical telescopes, one for each eye, both containing an objective and eyepiece lens and a system, usually of prisms, to form an erect image.

Binomial Nomenclature, scientific system of giving each organism a two-part, Latin name. The first part is the genus and the second part the species, for example, *Homo sapiens* is the binomial name for humans. This system was developed by Swedish botanist Carolus Linnaeus in the 18th century.

Binomial Theorem, rule for expanding an expression of the form $(x + y)^n$, where n is a positive integer, as a series. This is given by $x^n + n\,x^{n-1}y + \frac{n(n-1)}{2}\,x^{n-2}y^2 + \frac{n(n-1)(n-2)}{3!}\,x^{n-3}y^3 \ldots y^n$. If n is not a positive whole number the series becomes infinite (the binomial series).

Biochemistry, study of the chemical compounds and reactions occurring in living matter. It includes the isolation and identification of natural products of plants and animals—fats, proteins, hormones, enzymes, etc.—together with study of the complex reactions of these in metabolism.

Biodegradability, property of a substance that allows microorganisms to break it down into stable, simple compounds such as water and carbon dioxide. This property is utilized in refuse disposal.

Bioelectricity, electricity originating in living plants or animals. Different electrical potentials are built up within the organism. Bioelectricity caused by ionic separation across a membrane is associated with nerve impulses and muscle contractions.

Bioengineering, science of applying engineering techniques to the problems of medicine and biology. Also, the engineering of devices to aid or replace defective or insufficient body organs, for example, artificial limbs and hearing aids.

Biofeedback, from "biological feedback," monitoring of internal bodily states by using sensitive electronic instruments. People are trained to control internal functioning through operant conditioning. Using biofeedback, people can learn to consciously control their heart rate, blood pressure, and brain-wave patterns. The method holds promise for treating headaches, hy-

pertension, and other problems related to the activities of the autonomic nervous system. *See also* Autonomic Nervous System.

Biogenetic Law, or recapitulation theory, principle that the stages that an organism goes through during embryonic development reflect the stages of that organism's evolutionary development.

Bioko Island (formerly Fernando Po), island in Bight of Biafra, off coast of W Africa; province of Equatorial Guinea; contains fertile volcanic farmland. Exports: cacao, coffee, copra. Malabo is capital and country's largest city. Discovered 1472 by Fernâo do Po, a Portuguese navigator; ceded to Spain 1778. Area: 779sq mi (2,018sq km); pop. (island) 80,000.

Biology, study or science of life, including botany, zoology, ecology, morphology, physiology, cytology, histology, genetics, embryology, and microbiology. These sciences deal with life and living things, including origin, history, makeup, development, function, and relationships of living things to each other and their environment. Biology is also the study of how life perpetuates itself and the differences between the living and not living.

Bioluminescence, production of light, without heat, by living organisms. Its biological function is varied: in some species (fireflies) it is a recognition signal in mating; in others (squids) it is a method of diverting predators for protection; and in many deep-sea fish it is simply a form of illumination. The light-emitting substance (luciferin) in most species is an organic molecule that emits light when it is oxidized by molecular oxygen in the presence of an enzyme (luciferase). Each species has different forms of luciferin and luciferase. Some jellyfish do not require an enzyme, light being emitted by a protein (photoprotein) when it is acted upon, in some species, by a calcium ion, in others, by molecular oxygen.

Biome, extensive community of animals and plants whose makeup is determined by soil and climatic conditions. Characteristically, there is distinctive, dominant vegetation, such as tundra, desert, or jungle.

Biophysics, study of biological problems in terms of the laws and techniques of physics. Subjects studied include: the structure and function of such complex biological molecules as proteins and nucleic acids using X-ray diffraction methods; the conduction of electricity by nerves in terms of the action potentials created by the flow of sodium and potassium across the sheaths of nerve fibers; the transport of molecules across cell membranes using radioactive tracers and other physical methods; muscle contraction using electron microscopy and X-ray diffraction; energy transformations in living organisms; and the function of hormones in the body using radioisotopes as tracers. Applied biophysics is concerned with the design of biomedical instruments as well as the diagnosis and treatment of cancer using scanning techniques and radiotherapy.

Biosphere, or zone of life, portion of the earth from its crust to the surrounding atmosphere, encompassing all living organisms. It is self-sufficient except for energy from the sun and extends a few miles above and below sea level.

Biotin, member of the vitamin B complex (formula $C_{10}H_{16}O_3N_2S$) that occurs in small quantities in most cells. *See also* Vitamin; Vitamin H.

Biotite, one of the mica group of common rock-forming minerals. It is potassium and magnesium-iron aluminum silicate $[K(Fe,Mg)_2 (Si_3Al)O_{10} (OH)_2]$. Common in igneous and metamorphic rocks. Monoclinic system tabular prismatic crystals, grains and scaly masses. Splits into elastic sheets. Black, dark green or brown; glassy. *See also* Mica.

Birch, any of about 40 species (genus *Betula*) of trees and shrubs native to cooler areas of the Northern Hemisphere. The smooth, resinous bark peels off in papery sheets. The double-toothed leaves are oval or triangular with blunt bases and arranged alternately on branches. The male catkins droop while smaller female catkins stand upright and develop into conelike clusters with tiny one-seeded nuts. Some well-known species are gray, sweet, and yellow birch. The American white or paper birch *(Betula papyrifera)* has clear white striped bark that peels naturally. It was formerly used for canoes and wigwam coverings by Indians. Height: to 80ft (24m). Family Betulaceae.

Bird, 8600 species of feathered vertebrates occupying every conceivable habitat from deserts and tropics to polar wastes. They are warm-blooded and have forelimbs modified to wings, hindlimbs for walking, and jaws elongated into a toothless beak. They lay eggs in nests, incubate the eggs, and care for young. They feed on seeds, nectar, fruit, and carrion and hunt insects and large prey. Sight is the dominant sense, with smell being the poorest. Size ranges from the 2.5in (6.4cm) bee hummingbird to the royal albatross with a wingspread of 11.5ft (3.5m), and the 8ft (2.4m) tall ostrich. Several extinct flightless birds were even bigger. Of the 27 orders, the perching birds include more species than all others combined.

The bird body is constructed primarily for flight with all its parts modified accordingly. There are several flightless groups of large land birds: ostrich, rhea, emu, cassowary, kiwi, and penguin. Flightless members of typically flighted groups also occur, such as the rail and cormorant. Birds are descended from thecodont reptiles with the first fossil bird, *Archaeopteryx*, dating from late Jurassic times. Class Aves.

Bird Banding, practice of ringing a bird's leg with a light aluminum band for identification. Birds are released after banding. This practice is helpful in unravelling bird migration and distribution, life spans, and territorial requirements. Ornithologists share records on a worldwide basis. *See also* Ornithology.

Bird Migration, periodic movement from one climatic zone or region to another, usually for feeding or breeding purposes. Few birds remain in the same locality for the entire year. They generally gather in flocks before migrating and use the colder part of their range for breeding. Distances traveled range from the Arctic tern's 22,000-mile (35,400-km) annual flight from pole to pole to the short altitudinal and local movements of tropical species. Migration is triggered by internal drives tied to the reproductive cycle and keyed by changes in day length, temperature, and food supply. Directional clues used during migratory journeys include innate factors, use of the sun and stars as a compass, and geographic features.

Bird of Paradise, brightly colored, ornately plumed, perching bird of N Australia, New Guinea forests, and nearby areas. They generally have stocky bodies, rounded wings, short legs, and squarish tails. The males' plumes—wirelike, twisted, threadlike, or pennantlike—are black, orange, red, yellow, blue, or green and become erect during elaborate courtship displays and rituals. Pinkish streaked eggs (1–2) are laid in a cup-shaped nest of twigs, stems, and leaves on a branch. Length: 5–40in (12.5–102cm). Family Paradisaeidae.

Bird-of-Paradise Flower, ornamental plant native to S Africa. It grows from rhizomes and has stiff, leathery, oblong leaves. The flowers are brilliant orange and blue held in a boat-shaped, green bract. Height: to 5ft (1.5m). Family Musaceae; species *Strelitzia reginae.*

Birds, The (414 BC), Greek comedy by Aristophanes. Disgusted with their world, a group of men persuade the birds to create a city halfway between heaven and earth in which they will have complete control of gods and men. An amusing fantasy, it illustrates man's eternal search for an ideal society.

Birmingham, city in NW England; 2nd-largest British city; known for manufacture of cheap goods known as "Brummagem ware." Industries: cars, bicycles, chemicals, electrical equipment, chocolate (in suburb Bournville), guns, machine tools, plastic goods. Pop. 1,084,-600.

Birmingham, industrial city and port of entry in N central Alabama, in Jones Valley; seat of Jefferson co; largest city in Alabama. Originally a cotton-growing area, it was founded 1871 by Elyton Land Co. in conjunction with Louisville and Nashville Railroad. It is the site of Samford University (1842), Birmingham-Southern College (1856), Daniel Payne College (1889), Miles College (1907). Industries: iron, steel, metalworking, fabricated metals, construction and transportation equipment. Inc. 1871. Pop. (1980) 284,413.

Birth Control Pill, also often called Oral Contraceptive, a pill containing estrogen and progesterone hormones that prevents ovulation and thus the possibility of pregnancy. A widely used method of birth control, it has been associated with some serious and some minor side effects and should be prescribed on an individual basis.

Birthmark, or nevus, an area of pigment, usually red, purple, yellow, or brown, appearing on the skin at birth or shortly after. Some are caused by concentrations of melanin, others (strawberry marks) by raised blood vessels. Most birthmarks fade or disappear with maturity.

Birth Order, sequence of birth of children in a family. Psychologists have studied the effects of birth order on personality development, noting, for example, that parents may be overanxious with the first and overspoiling with the youngest. Parent attitudes are more important than birth order itself.

Birth Rate, statistical system for determining the number of births in a given area, age group, socioeconomic stratum, or time period. The most common type is the crude birth rate, or the number of births per 1000 population per year.

Biscay, Bay of, inlet of Atlantic Ocean, SW of France and N of Spain; noted for strong currents and sudden, violent storms. Chief ports: Bilbao, San Sebastián, Santander in Spain; Bayonne, Brest, La Rochelle, Saint-Nazaire in France. Resort area is along French coast; site of important sardine fishing grounds.

Biscayne Bay, inlet of the Atlantic Ocean on the E coast of Dade co, SE Florida. Miami is on its NW shore and the island of Biscayne Key is on the NE. Biscayne National Monument at S end of bay. Shallow, narrow inlet is 40mi (64km) long.

Bisection, Angle, geometrical construction to cut an angle into two equal parts. An arc is drawn, with its center at the vertex, cutting the sides of the angle at two points. Two arcs of equal radius are then drawn from these points, and a straight line drawn from their point of intersection to the vertex, thus bisecting the angle.

Bishop, title for a rank within the ministry of the Christian church. Duties of the bishop include the general control of a particular diocese.

Bishops' Wars (1639, 1640), campaigns by Charles I of England against the Scots. Charles aimed to strengthen episcopacy by imposing English church ritual on Scotland; the 1638 Covenant pledged the Scots to defend presbyterianism. By the treaty of Ripon (1640), Charles was forced to pay an indemnity to the invading Scots.

Bismarck, Otto von (1815–98), German statesman. Born into a wealthy Prussian family, he dedicated his life to building, by any means, a strong, unified Germany under Prussian leadership. He entered the Prussian parliament in 1847 and served until he was appointed Prussian minister to the German diet (1851–59). Between 1859–62 he was ambassador to Russia and, in 1862, ambassador to France. In 1862 William I named him premier of Prussia. He quickly dissolved the parliament and expanded the army. In 1864, jointly with Austria, he seized Schleswig-Holstein from Denmark in a brief war. In 1866 he forced Austria into the Austro-Prussian (Seven Weeks) War. Austria was discredited as Prussia's rival among the German states, Schleswig-Holstein was granted outright to Prussia, and the Northern German Confederation was formed. Bismarck then turned to uniting the German states against France. Victory in the Franco-Prussian War (1870–71) brought the southern German states into the Prussian-led confederation. In 1871 William I was proclaimed German emperor and Bismarck the first chancellor. Bismarck now turned to alliances rather than wars to foster German interests. In 1872 he formed the Three Emperors' League with Austro-Hungary and Russia. He presided over the 1878 Congress of Berlin, which established spheres of influence in the Balkans, and the 1884 Berlin Conference that did the same for Africa. In 1879 he dissolved the Three Emperors' League by forming the Triple Alliance with Austro-Hungary and Italy. His one major failure was his 1871–78 *Kulturkampf* campaign against the Roman Catholic Church and the Catholic Center party. He dealt more successfully with the socialists. When repressive measures instituted in 1878 failed, he himself introduced sweeping social reforms. Between 1883–87, Germany became the first nation to institute a comprehensive social security system and to establish child and woman labor laws. Throughout his years as chancellor, Bismarck encouraged industrialization at home and colonization overseas. He found it difficult to work with William II, who came to power in 1888. In 1890 the "Iron Chancellor" was forced to resign and went into retirement.

Bismarck, city and capital of North Dakota, in S central part of state over-looking Missouri River; seat of Burleigh co. Lewis and Clark stayed near here 1804–05. Camp Greeley (later Fort Hancock) was built in 1872 to protect workers on Northern Pacific Railroad. Industries: livestock raising, dairying, woodworking. Inc. 1873. Pop. (1980) 44,485.

Bismarck Archipelago, volcanic island group off NE New Guinea, SW Pacific Ocean; comprised of New Britain (largest), New Ireland, Lavongai, Admiralty Islands, Duke of York Islands, Massau Islands, Vitu Islands, and many smaller islands. Australia administered the archipelago as a part of UN Trust Territory of New Guinea from 1947 until 1975 when it became a part of Papua New Guinea. Products: shellfish, coconuts. Founded 1616. Area: 19,173sq mi (49,658sq km). Pop. 176,471.

Bismuth, metallic element (symbol Bi) of group V of the periodic table, first identified as a separate element in 1753. The chief ores are bismite (oxide) and bismuth glance (sulfide). Bismuth expands when it solidifies, a property exploited in several bismuth alloys used in making castings. Properties: at no. 83; at. wt. 208.-9806; sp. gr. 9.75; melt. pt. 520°F (271.3°C); boil. pt. 2840°F (1561°C); most common isotope Bi^{209} (100%).

Bison, two species of wild oxen formerly ranging grasslands and open woodlands over most of North America and all of Europe. Once numbering in millions, the American bison is now almost extinct in the wild. The Wisent (European Bison) was reduced to two herds by the 18th century. Both are now found in parks. Head, neck, and shoulder hair is long and shaggy with a beard on the chin and shorter hair on the rest of the body. They have heavy heads, short necks, humped shoulders, short, upcurving horns. The American is more massive and shaggier than the European. Length: to 137in (3.5m); height: to 117in (3m); weight: to 2970lb (1336kg). Family Bovidae; species American *Bison bison,* Wisent *Bison bonasus. See also* Buffalo.

Bissau (Bissao), largest city and capital of Guinea-Bissau, W Africa, on Bissau Island; former colonial capital (1942–74); administrative and military center. Founded 1687 by Portuguese as fortified post and trade center; a free port since 1869. Crops: palm oil, peanuts, copra, hardwoods, rubber. Pop. 75,000.

Bithynia, ancient region of NW Asia Minor. Originally occupied by Thracians, it was inc. into the Persian Empire by Cyrus the Great in the 6th century BC. The Bithynians never submitted to Alexander the Great or his successor. It evolved into a strong, independent kingdom until several weak leaders led to its rapid decline. In 74 BC, according to the will of its last king, Nicomedes IV, it became a Roman province.

Bitterling, freshwater fish native to Asia Minor and central Europe. Deep-bodied, its fin rays are not true spines. Female deposits eggs into mantle cavities of clams and mussels for breeding. Length: to 3.5in (8.9cm). Family Cyprinidae; species *Rhodeus sericeus.*

Bittern, solitary heronlike wading bird found in marshes around the world. Heavy-bodied, it is brownish with streaks and spots and easily hides itself in swamplands. During mating, males snap their bills and make gulping noises. The female lays white or brownish eggs (3–6). Length: 10in–3ft (25–91cm). Family Ardeidae.

Bitterroot, perennial native to mountainous North America from Montana to British Columbia and south into California, with fleshy leaves, short stalks and red blossoms. The starchy root was a food of the American Indian. Family Portulacaceae; species *Lewisia rediviva.*

Bittersweet, woody climbing plant found in moist thickets. The entire plant is toxic. The pointed leaves have a lobe at the base on each side; the violet or purple flowers produce coral red berries. Height: to 12ft (3.7m). Family Solanaceae; species *Solanum dulcamara.*

Bivalve, 20,000 living species of mollusks. Characteristically their soft parts are enclosed by two hinged shells (valves) closed by powerful muscles. Most are marine but there are many freshwater forms. The majority burrow in mud or sand; some attach themselves to solid objects; and many bore into wood or rocks. Included are clams, cockles, scallops, oysters, mussels, and lucines. They are headless and have a hatchet-shaped foot for digging and sometimes eyes lining the mantle edge. Usually two siphons circulate water for extracting food particles. Sexes are generally separate, but some are hermaphroditic. Classification varies but is usually based on variations of gill arrangement. Length: 1/6in–4ft (2mm–1.2m). Class Pelecypoda. *See also* Mollusk.

Bizerte (Binzert or Bizerta), fortified city and seaport in N Tunisia, N Africa, on Mediterranean Sea. Northernmost city in Africa, it has harbor with channel to Lake of Bizerte; site of German base in WWII and French naval base to 1963. Industries: fish processing, olive oil, flour mills, oil refining, cement, brick and tile production, ship repair. Founded by Phoenicians. Pop. 62,000.

Bizet, Georges (1838–75), French romantic composer. His opera *Carmen* (1875), though unsuccessful when first performed, has become one of the most popular operas ever. Bizet also composed other operas and two successful orchestral pieces, a *Symphony in C* (1855) and the *L'Arlesienne Suites* (1872).

Black, Hugo (LaFayette) (1886–1971), US jurist and senator, b. Harlan, Ala. A US Senator from Alabama (1927–37), he sponsored the Wages and Hours bill (1937), investigated merchant-marine subsidies (1933) and vigorously supported New Deal legislation. Appointed an associate justice of the US Supreme Court in 1937, he favored a broad interpretation of the Constitution, and wrote numerous dissents defending civil rights and liberties. In the late 1960s, however, he voted to uphold state criminal laws.

Black and Tan Coonhound, hunting dog (hound group) used to trail possum and raccoon by scent. A descendant of the 11th-century English Talbot hound, it has an oval-shaped head and long, square muzzle; low-set hanging ears; a level-backed body; medium-length, straight legs; and long tail carried freely. The short, dense, coal black coat is marked with rich tan. Standard size: 25–27in (63.5–68.5cm) high at shoulder; 70–85lb (32–38kg). *See also* Hound.

Black and Tan Terrier. *See* Manchester Terrier.

Black Ape, or Celebes ape, Celebes crested macaque, tailless, tree-dwelling, medium-sized monkey found chiefly on N Celebes Island. It has a small crest of hair and is mostly black or dark brown. Species *Cynopithecus niger. See also* Monkey.

Black Bass, black sea bass, or sea bass, marine food fish found well offshore in N Atlantic. Length: 2ft (61cm); Weight: to 8lb (3.6kg). Family Serranidae; species *Centropristis striatus. See also* Bass.

Black Bear, bear found in North America and Asia. The American black bear lives in forested areas from Canada to C Mexico. It is usually black and eats a wide variety of plant and animal foods, including carrion. It is usually timid and avoids man. Length: 5–6ft (1.5–1.8m); weight: 265–330lb (120–150kg). Species *Euarctos americanus.* The Asiatic black bear lives in bush or forest areas of E and S Asia. Smaller than the American black bear, it has a white crescent marking on the chest. It is aggressive and sometimes kills livestock and humans. Species *Selenarctos thibetanos. See also* Bear.

Otto von Bismarck

Hugo Black

Harry Blackmun

Blackbeard (died 1718), English pirate, b. Edward Teach. In 1716 he began attacking shipping off the West Indies, the Spanish Main, and the coasts of Carolina and Virginia. His career ended when his 40-gun warship, *Queen Anne's Revenge,* was attacked by two sloops sent by the governor of Virginia, and he was killed.

Blackberry, or bramble, fruit-bearing bushes, native to the northern temperate regions. Having erect or trailing prickly stems and leaves of oval, toothed leaflets, the blossoms are white, pink, or red, and the edible berries are black or dark red. Family Rosaceae; genus *Rubus.*

Blackbird, American bird, the male having black or blackish plumage. The typical red-winged blackbird *(Agelaius phoeniceus)* has a straight bill, long pointed wings, and rounded tail. They feed on insects and sometimes, in flocks, become crop pests. Nesting in colonies, the female builds a nest for the eggs (2–7) and the male helps care for the young. Length: 8–10in (20–25cm). Family Icteridae.

Blackbody, an ideal body that absorbs all incident radiation and reflects none. Such a body would look black; hence the name. The study of blackbodies has been an extremely important part of the history of physics. Wien's Law, Stefan's Law, and Planck's Law of Blackbody Radiation grew out of this study, as did Planck's discovery of quantum mechanics.

Blackbuck, or Indian antelope, medium-sized, long-horned antelope native to the open plains of India. Females and young are fawn colored and males are dark, becoming almost black at maturity. Underparts are white with white on muzzle and around eyes. Only males carry long, annulated, spiral horns. They are hunted for sport by trained cheetahs. Length: to 47in (1.2m); height: to 32in (81cm) at shoulder. Family Bovidae; species *Antilope cervicapra.*

Black Death, an outbreak of plague, thought to be bubonic plague, which ravaged most of Western Europe during the 14th century and at 10-year intervals throughout the Middle Ages. Carried by the infected fleas of the black rat, the plague came west from Kaffa, a grain port in the Crimea, in 1346. It had reached England and Italy by 1348 and Germany, Scandinavia, and Poland by 1349–50. The Black Death took about one third of the population of Europe in the first three years, and perhaps a total of half before the worst epidemics ceased. The results were a widespread decline in morality, a decline in the achievements of monasteries, political discontent, a labor shortage, and in Germany, the massacre of thousands of Jews, who were blamed for the plague. *See also* Bubonic Plague.

Black-eyed Susan, or yellow daisy, annual or biennial North American plant. It has hairy leaves and daisylike flowers with golden-yellow rays and purplish-brown disks. Height: 3ft (0.9m). Family Compositae; species *Rudbeckia hirta.*

Blackfish, or tautog, marine food and game fish of the North Atlantic. It is black or greenish. Length: to 3ft (91.5cm); weight: 22lb (10kg). Family Labridae; species *Tautoga onitis.*

Black Fly, or buffalo gnat, yellow to gray, blood sucking fly, 0.04 to 0.2in. (1–5mm) long, found in north temperate and subarctic areas. The larvae are found in fast-running water. Some diseases are carried by this fly, but the bite alone may be severe enough to disable a man. Family Simuliidae. *See also* Diptera.

Blackfoot, or **Blackfeet**, one of the largest and most warlike North American Indian tribes; actually a confederation of three Algonquian-speaking subdivisions: the Siksika, or Blackfoot proper; the Kainah; and the Pikuni. Their nomadic Plains traits were intensified with the acquisition of the horse. They originally occupied a vast area in Saskatchewan, Alberta and N Montana and are among the few Indians still occupying their old homelands. Today there are approximately 6250 Blackfoot in the United States and 3500 in Canada.

Black Forest (Schwarzwald), heavily forested mountain range in SW West Germany, between Rhine and Neckar rivers to Swiss border; source of Danube and Neckar rivers with many lakes and mineral springs. Range is a popular tourist attraction, famous for cuckoo clocks and music boxes. Industries: lumbering, cattle. Highest peak is Feldberg, approx. 4,898ft (1,494m). Length: 90mi (145km).

Black Hawk War (1832), war between the Sac and Fox Indians and the United States. Black Hawk was a Sac chief who opposed the forced treaty of 1831. Fighting bravely against superior numbers of US volunteers, Black Hawk was finally defeated at the Battle of Bad Axe (1832).

Black Hills, mountain cluster in W South Dakota and NE Wyoming; named for the dark pines that appear black from afar. Gold was discovered (1874) by an exploratory mission led by General Custer; site of Homestake Mine, largest U.S. gold mine; uranium, mica, silver, and feldspar are also mined. Tourist areas include 2 national forests, Wind Cave National Park, Custer State Park, Jewel Cave National Monument, and Mt Rushmore National Memorial. Highest peak is Harvey Peak, S. Dak., 7,242ft (2,209m). *See also* Mount Rushmore.

Black Hole, postulated end-product of the total gravitational collapse of a massive star into itself following exhaustion of its nuclear fuel, the collapsed matter inside being crushed to unimaginably high density. It is an empty region of totally distorted space that acts as a center of gravitational attraction; matter is drawn toward it and once inside cannot escape. Its boundary (the event horizon) is a demarcation line, rather than a material surface, defining the area from which no matter, light, or other radiation can escape. Suspected but unconfirmed black holes include Cygnus-XI.

Blackjack, card game for two or more players, using a regular deck. Each player, including the dealer, receives two cards; the dealer's second card is turned face up. The object is to get more points than the dealer but less than 22. Aces count as 11 or 1, picture cards as 10, and all others count their face value. All players may take additional cards, but any total over 21 automatically loses. The dealer may not take any cards if his two-card total is 17 or extra cards add up to 17. If the dealer's total is 16, or reaches 16, he must take an additional card.

Blacklists, a labor practice in which certain people are excluded from employment. During the late 19th and early 20th centuries, blacklisting was sometimes used by employers against those employees who were union organizers or agitators, preventing them from gaining employment in a particular industry. It was also practiced during the 1940s and 1950s to boycott entertainers thought to have been associated with the Communist party.

Blackmun, Harry A(ndrew) (1908–   ), US jurist and lawyer, b. Nashville, Ill. A practicing attorney (1934–59), law instructor, and Mayo Clinic counsel (1950–59) he was appointed in 1959 to the US Circuit Court of Appeals. In 1970 he was nominated an associate justice of the US Supreme Court by Richard Nixon. Blackmun's nomination was confirmed unanimously in June 1970. He is considered moderately liberal on civil rights issues and a conservative on matters of criminal law.

Black Muslims, US religious movement, officially called the Nation of Islam, founded in Detroit in 1930 by W. D. Fard. After Fard's disappearance in 1934, Elijah Muhammad took over leadership and moved to Chicago. The Muslims adhere strictly to the Koran's moral codes, forbidding alcohol, drugs, gambling, and smoking. Women are subservient to men. The Muslims maintain their own schools, farms, and businesses, living as independently as possible from the larger society. In the 1960s, Malcolm X carried the Muslim message to a larger, more sophisticated audience. Suspended from the church in 1963, he was assassinated in 1965. Muhammed Ali is a leading lay spokesman for the movement. Total membership is kept secret. Elijah Muhammad died in 1975 and was succeeded by his son Wallace, who called for radical changes in the movement, including the welcoming of whites into the movement and the promotion of women to leadership positions.

Black Oak, North American timber tree with lobed, reddish leaves and dark, blocky bark. Height: to 80ft (24m). Family Fagaceae; species *Quercus velutina.*

Blackout, Physiological, total obscuration of vision encountered by test pilots and astronauts during heavy acceleration; caused by insufficient oxygen supply to the eye. Blackout is the opposite of *redout,* a reddish haze caused by engorged blood vessels in the eye, which is encountered at zero-g or negative-g conditions.

Blackpool, city in NW England, on Irish Sea coast, 28mi (45km) N of Liverpool; vacation resort, attracting 8,000,000 visitors annually; Noted for illuminations and 520ft (157m) tower. Pop. 147,000.

Black Prince. *See* Edward.

Black Sea, inland sea between Europe and Asia, connected to the Aegean Sea by the Bosporus, Sea of Marmara, and the Dardanelles; surrounded by USSR (N and E), Turkey (S), Bulgaria and Romania (W). It is a major USSR sea outlet, yielding large quantities of anchovies, carp, mullet, bream, and gobies. Area: 159,600sq mi (413,364sq km).

Black Snake, or black rat snake, wide-ranging North American rat snake, also called pilot or mountain black snake. A good climber, it is shiny black, sometimes with small, light spots between scales, and has a paler belly. Length: to 6ft (183cm). Family Colubridae; species *Elaphe obsoleta. See also* Colubrid.

Black Spot, any of various plant diseases, mostly caused by fungi, that form black spots on leaves, including apple scab, apple anthracnose, peach scab, and black spot of roses. Rose black spot, caused by the fungus *Diplocarpon rosae,* is the worst rose disease in North America.

Blackstone, (Sir) William (1723–80), English jurist and legal scholar. As a fellow of All Souls College at Oxford (1753), he introduced the first law curriculum in an English university and became the first Vinerian Professor of Law at Oxford (1758). Elected to Parliament (1761), he was the first solicitor-general to Queen

Charlotte Sophia (1763). He was knighted and appointed a Justice of the Common Pleas in the same year (1770). His book *Commentaries on the Laws of England* still serves as the foundation for much of the English and US legal practice.

Black Volta (Volta Noire), chief headstream of the Volta River in W Africa; rises in Upper Volta, flows S to join the White Volta River, forming the Volta River; forms part of W boundary of Ghana. Length: 840mi (1,352km).

Black Walnut, deciduous tree *Juglans nigra* of the walnut family growing to 150ft (46m). A native of E and Central United States, it is grown for ornament, timber, and nuts.

Blackwell, Elizabeth (1821–1910), US physician, b. England. In 1847, she began to study medicine at the Geneva Medical School in New York after being denied admission to several other schools. She graduated (1849) at the head of her class, becoming the first woman doctor in the United States. She pioneered in obtaining medical education for women in the United States and established the New York Infirmary (1857) which combined health services and medical training. In 1869 she emigrated to England to continue her teaching and writing.

Black Widow Spider, American black spider with red markings, often hour-glass shaped, underneath. It is poisonous, resulting in symptoms similar to appendicitis. The female eats its mate and bites. The male does not bite or feed. Several closely related species are found worldwide. Length: to 0.6in (15mm). Family Theridiidae; species *Latrodectus mactans. See also* Spider.

Bladder, Urinary, a large pouch in which urine is stored. Urine, a kidney secretion containing waste products and water extracted from the blood, is passed through two narrow tubes, the ureters, to the bladder, where it is stored until the pressure becomes too great and nervous impulses signal that the bladder has to be emptied. Urine leaves the bladder through the urethra.

Bladderwort, matlike, aquatic plant found in bogs or ponds. It has feathery, threadlike leaves with small bladders. Upright stems bear purple or dark pink flowers. Species include purple *Utricularia purpurea* and butterwort *Pinguicula.* Family Lentibulariaceae.

Blaine, James Gillespie (1830–93), US public official, *b.* West Brownsville, Pa. An influential Maine Republican, he served as a state legislator (1858–62), a congressman (1863–76), speaker of the house (1869–75), and US senator (1876–81). He ran for president in 1884 but lost the election to the Democratic candidate, Grover Cleveland, partly because of the defection of reform Republicans (Mugwumps). He served as secretary of state (1881; 1889–92).

Blake, William (1757–1827), English poet, painter, and engraver. He was apprenticed to an engraver (1772) and studied at the Royal Academy (1778). A friend of William Godwin and Thomas Paine, he supported the French Revolution. His work is characterized by the prophetic and mystical visions he experienced. *Poetical Sketches* (1783) was followed by *Songs of Innocence* (1789), *The Marriage of Heaven and Hell* (1790), and *Songs of Experience* (1794). His prophetic books, portraying his private mythologies, include *The Book of Urizen* (1794), *The Four Zoas* (1797), *Milton* and *Jerusalem* (1804). In addition to his own works, Blake illustrated *The Book of Job* and Dante's *Divine Comedy.*

Blanc, Mont, highest peak in the Alps, and the 2nd-highest peak in Europe; on the French-Italian border; scaled in 1786; popular resort area. The 7-mi (11-km) Mt Blanc tunnel is cut through its base. Height: 15,771ft (4,810m).

Blanche of Castile (1187?–1252), queen of France. She was the granddaughter of Eleanor of Aquitaine and Henry II of England. Her marriage to Louis VIII (1200) was meant to reconcile the Capets and the Plantagenets. She became queen in 1223 and served as regent for her son Louis IX (1226–36, 1248–52), and co-regent with another son Alphonse (1250–52).

Blanching, bleaching plant parts by protection from sun to improve color and texture, usually for vegetables. Celery is blanched by mounding earth around the stalks. Endive and cauliflower are blanched by tying the outside leaves over the heads.

Blank Verse, unrhymed verse, especially iambic pentameter or unrhymed heroic; widely used in English dramatic and epic poetry. The Earl of Surrey introduced blank verse into England in the 16th century with his translation of the *Aeneid.* The form was used by Christopher Marlowe, William Shakespeare, John Milton, William Wordsworth, and Alfred Tennyson, among others. *See also* lamb.

Blantyre, city in S Malawi, SE Africa, in the Shire Highlands; commercial center of Malawi. Industries: textiles, cement, food processing. Founded 1876; merged with Limbe to form one city 1956. Pop. 228,520.

Blarney, village in SW Republic of Ireland, in central Cork. It is noted for 15th-century castle containing the Blarney Stone, said to endow anyone who kisses it with "the blarney" (fluent persuasive speech). Pop. 932.

Blast Furnace, smelting furnace in which iron ore is made into pig iron; it is also used in smelting other metals, such as copper, lead, and tin. A blast of compressed air, supplied from the bottom of the furnace, provides combustion for smelting the ore. The furnace used in iron production is usually a cylindrical steel structure, narrow at the top and bottom. As the metal becomes molten, it sinks to the bottom where it is tapped.

Blastomycosis, infectious, fungus-caused disease usually centered in the lungs, which can spread to the skin. Untreated, it may be fatal.

Blastula, embryo at the developmental stage that consists of a hollow, cavity (blastocoele) surrounded by one or more spherical layers of cells. Commonly called the hollow ball of cells stage, it follows the morula stage in embryonic development.

Bleach, substance used to remove the color from textiles, paper, etc. Most bleaches act by oxidizing the pigment. Chlorine, or compounds such as calcium and sodium hypochlorites, are commonly used. Other oxidizing bleaches are hydrogen peroxide, used for hair, and sodium perborate. For some applications reducing agents, such as sulfur dioxide, are employed.

Bleeding. *See* Hemorrhaging.

Bleeding Heart, ornamental perennial plant with feathery leaves, arched stems, and clusters of heart-shaped, rose-red flowers. Height: to 2ft (60cm). Family Fumariaceae; species *Dicentra spectabilis.*

Blenheim, village in S West Germany, on Danube River, 23mi (37km) NNW of Augsburg; scene of English victory over French and Bavarians in War of Spanish Succession. (1704). Pop. 900.

Blenny, marine fish of shallow and offshore waters of all tropical and temperate seas. Scaleless, with a long dorsal fin, it is olive green with varicolored markings. Length: to 4in (10.2cm). Family Blenniidae; species 300, including fringehead *Blennius tentacularis.*

Blepharitis, inflammation of the border of the eyelid, sometimes accompanied by ulceration and discharge.

Blériot, Louis (1872–1936), French aircraft designer and aviator who was the first man to fly across the English Channel (1909). The flight from Calais to Dover took 37 minutes. As a designer Blériot was responsible for a number of design innovations, including a system by which the pilot could operate elevators and ailerons by remote control. In World War I he built the noted SPAD fighters.

Bleuler, Paul Eugen (1857–1939), Swiss psychiatrist, pioneer in the diagnosis and treatment of psychoses. He coined the term *schizophrenia* and, unlike his predecessors, attributed the symptoms to psychological rather than physiological origins.

Bligh, William (1754–1817), British admiral. Captain of HMS *Bounty* (1787), Bligh survived the famous mutiny (1789), sailing nearly 4,000 miles (6,400km) in the ship's longboat. After service at Camperdown (1797) and Copenhagen (1801) he was governor of New South Wales (1805–08).

Blight, a term applied either to the yellowing, browning, and withering of plant tissues caused by various diseases, or to the diseases themselves. Blights may be caused by microorganisms, such as bacteria and fungi, or by environmental factors such as drought. Common blights induced by microorganisms include fire blight and bean blight, caused by bacteria, and spinach blight (mosaic), caused by a virus. Blight diseases typically affect leaves more severely than other plant parts. Control of blight depends on its cause. Blights caused by microorganisms, for example, are controlled by good sanitation; by growing blight-resistant varieties; and by spraying with various fungicides and antibiotics.

Blindfish, or Blind Cave Fish, freshwater fish found mainly in cave waters of North America. Usually white, it ranges from being blind, with no or imperfect eyes, to having sight. Length: to 3in (7.6cm). Family Characidae; species includes Mexican *Astyanax jordani* and Family Amblyopsidae; species Ozark *Amblyopsis rosae.*

Blindness, in the United States is defined as corrected vision not exceeding 20/200 on the standard Snellen eye chart. Blindness occurs most frequently in persons over 55, with the greatest percentage caused by senile cataract (clouding of the lens) and glaucoma (hardening of the eye due to pressure within the eyeball). Other causes of blindness include infectious disease such as tuberculosis, measles, or syphilis; diseases such as diabetes; nutritional deficiencies; injuries; and congenital anomalies, which include inherited defects. Blindness as a result of disease and accident is being reduced rapidly with progress in research, early diagnosis, and accident prevention programs. Education for the blind includes not only Braille reading and guide dog training, but also active sports, and classes and vocational training aimed at enabling the visually impaired to function as independently as possible in sighted society.

Blind Snake, burrowing, wormlike, termite-eating, legless reptile with rudimentary eyes. They have vestiges of pelvic girdles. The Typhlopidae (blind snakes) found worldwide tropically are considered legless lizards. The Leptotyphlopidae (slender blind snakes) range from S Central United States to Argentina and are also found in Africa and Asia. Length: 4–12in (102–305mm). *See also* Lizard; Reptile; Snake.

Blind Spot, small area of the retina of the eye where there is no visual reception. It is the area where optic nerve processes converge and where blood vessels enter and leave the eye.

Blister Beetle, medium-sized, cylindrical-bodied beetle that secretes blister-producing cantharidin. Formerly used as a diuretic and aphrodisiac, cantharidin was made from the dried European blister beetle known as the Spanish fly *(Lytta vesicatoria).* Family Meloidae.

Blitzkrieg, (from German, "lightning war"), mode of warfare characterized by a sudden, overwhelming attack with powerful force. The blitzkrieg tactic was effectively used by the German forces in their invasion of Poland in September 1939.

Blixen, Karen. *See* Dinesen, Isak.

Block and Tackle. *See* Pulleys and Hoists.

Block Mountain, an uplift that is the result of block faulting. This is one type of fault in which the crustal portions of the earth are broken into structural blocks of different elevations and positions. *See also* Orogeny.

Bloemfontein, city and judicial capital of Republic of South Africa, 295mi (475km) W of Durban; capital of Orange Free State province; seat of appellate division of the Supreme Court. Dutch farmers settled in area early 19th century; site of modern city was selected as a fort by Major Douglass Warden 1846; major educational center with two US observatories nearby; site of University of Orange Free State (1855). Industries: furniture, glassware, metal works. Founded 1846. Pop. 182,000.

Blois, town in N central France on Loire River; capital of Loir-et-Cher dept. In 10th century the counts of Blois were most powerful feudal lords of France; town was a favorite royal residence. Industries: wheat, vegetables, wine. Pop. 51,950.

Blood, a fluid tissue composed of plasma in which are suspended several types of individual cells. Blood volume in a healthy individual is about 5.8 qts (5.5 liters) of which 54% is plasma, and 46% is composed of cells. Blood transports oxygen, water, nutrients, body metabolites, and internal secretions, and contains all the factors necessary for clotting. The blood cells fall into two major classes: erythrocytes or red blood cells, and leukocytes or white blood cells. The red blood cells carry oxygen; the white blood cells serve as scavengers which phagocytose foreign objects, such as bacteria and cellular debris that may be present in the blood stream. Normal red cells count is about 4.8–5.4 million per cubic centimeter, while the normal white count is about 5000 cells per cubic centimeter. Platelets, small disks filled with granules, which participate in blood clotting, are also present in numbers around 2–3,000,000 per cubic centimeter. Disease states exist in which one or more of the constituents are present in

Black widow spider

Bloodhound

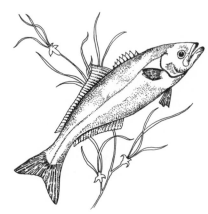

Bluefish

abnormal amounts; for example, too few red cells as in anemia, or too many white cells as in leukemia.

Blood Clotting, a protective physiological mechanism to prevent loss of blood due to injury or other causes of hemorrhage. A tight fibrous meshwork forms at the site of injury through a complex series of interrelated reactions involving about 20 blood-borne factors. At the injury site, platelets gather, releasing thromboplastin, which converts prothrombin to thrombin; thrombin is involved in splitting fibrinogen to fibrin, which polymerizes with other fibrin molecules to form a clot, plugging the break. Normal clotting time is 8 to 15 minutes. Hemophilia is the congenital absence of one of these factors, resulting in excess bleeding. Abnormal clot formation blocking a vessel is called thrombosis.

Bloodhound, hunting dog (hound group) that trails by scent; known as early as 3rd century in Europe. Evidence uncovered by the bloodhound is acceptable in courts of law. It has a long, tapering, narrow head with loose, hanging lips and wrinkled skin. The low-set ears are very long and hang in folds; eyes are deep-set. The strong-backed body is set on large, muscular legs; a long, tapering tail is carried up. The short coat can be black, red and tan, or tawny. Average size: 25–27in (63.5–68.5cm) high at shoulder; 80–110lb (36.5–50kg). *See also* Hound.

Blood Poisoning, or **Bacteremia,** the prolonged invasion of the bloodstream with pathogenic bacteria. Symptoms may include a relatively sudden onset of chills and fever, nausea, vomiting, change in the character of a wound, skin eruptions. Bacteria may enter through lesions in the skin or follow an infectious disease. Antibiotics are the usual treatment.

Blood Pressure, the pressure exerted on the walls of the arteries by the blood; a function of the elastic resistance of the artery (diastolic pressure) and cardiac output (systolic pressure). An average adult pressure is 120/80 mm Hg. systolic/diastolic pressure.

Bloodroot, plant found in the fertile woods of E United States. A low-growing perennial, the white or pink blooms appear before the leaves. Its alkaloid, sanguinarine, is used in medicine. Family Papaveraceae; species *Sanguinaria canadensis.*

Blood Type. Erythrocytes, or red blood cells, are grouped into several types because of genetically determined antigens located on their surface. For example, the ABO system consists of four major types: A or B, A and B, or neither (O), depending on the presence or absence of these factors. Knowledge of blood type is important with respect to transfusions and tissue or organ transplants; and has medico-legal uses, especially in assignment of paternity.

Blood Vessel, closed tubelike processes that carry blood throughout the body. There are three major types of blood vessels: arteries, which carry blood away from the heart; veins, which carry blood to the heart; and capillaries, the smallest blood vessels, where gases and dissolved substances diffuse in and out of the blood. *See also* Artery; Capillary; Vein. *See also* arteries; capillaries; veins.

Bloomfield, town in NE New Jersey, 4mi (6km) NNW of Newark; served as Revolutionary War supply point; site of Bloomfield College (1868). Industries: pharmaceuticals, petrochemicals, electrical equipment. Settled 1660; inc. 1900. Pop. (1980) 47,792.

Bloomington, city in S central Indiana, 45mi (72km) SW of Indianapolis; seat of Monroe Co. A heavily for-

ested region, it also has limestone quarries; site of Indiana University (1820). Inc. 1878. Pop. (1980) 51,-646.

Bloomington, city in SE Minnesota; suburb adjacent to Minneapolis; business center. Industries: electronics, computers, farm equipment. Inc. 1953. Pop. (1980) 81,831.

Bloomsbury Group, British intellectual group that met in the homes of members in the Bloomsbury Square area of London between 1904–39. It included Clive and Vanessa Bell, E. M. Forster, Roger Fry, John Maynard Keynes, Lytton Strachey, and Leonard and Virginia Woolf. The group's philosophy, "the creation and enjoyment of aesthetic experience," was influenced by the philosopher G. E. Moore.

Blowfish. *See* Puffer.

Blowfly, greenbottle fly, or bluebottle fly, black, blue, or green fly, 0.25 to 0.45in (6–11mm) long, found worldwide. The larvae usually feed on dead animals or meat-containing garbage. This fly's habits resemble those of the housefly. Family Calliphoridae. *See also* Housefly.

Blowgun, or blowpipe, weapon consisting of a tube through which a pellet or poisoned dart is ejected by force of breath. It is widely used by South and Central American and Southeast Asian people for hunting small game, and is highly efficient in forest zones, and where accuracy is valued above range.

Bluebell, or harebell, blue bellflower developed in England and widely cultivated in gardens. Other unrelated plants are also called bluebells. Height: 6–20in (15–51cm). Family Campanulaceae; species *Campanula rotundifolia.*

Blueberry, deciduous evergreen shrub native to E North America. There are two types: the cultivated highbush, grown commercially, prefers acid, damp soil; the wild lowbush prefers sandy, acid soil. Family Ericaceae; genus *Vaccinium.*

Bluebird, North American thrush found in open woodlands and cultivated areas feeding on insects, often in orchards and farmyards. They have thin bills, stocky bodies, and forked tails. Males are bluish above and females grayish. Pale blue eggs (4–6) are laid in a grass-and-weed-lined nest in a hole in a tree or fence post. Length: 7in (17.8cm). Genus *Sialia.*

Bluebonnet, or Texas bluebonnet, annual wild-flower of Texas, easily grown in United States. It has blue flower spikes and blooms in late spring. Height: to 1ft (30cm). Family Leguminosae; species *Lupinus subcarnosus.*

Blue-Collar Worker, a person involved in physical labor that results in the production of goods and services. Factory workers and farmers are blue-collar workers.

Blue Crab, swimming food crab prized along Atlantic and Gulf coasts. They are scavengers in brackish water near mouths of rivers. The body extends on each side to a long, sharp spine. After molting, the shell is soft. Its last pair of legs is flat and oarlike. Length: 6in (15cm). Family Portunidae; species *Callinectes sapidus. See also* Crustacean; Decapod.

Bluefish, schooling marine food and game fish found throughout tropical and temperate seas, except the C and E Pacific. Fished commercially, it is blue-green

with a black blotch on each side. Length: to 4ft (121.9cm); weight: to 27lb (12.2kg). Family Pomatomidae; species *Pomatomus saltatrix.*

Bluegill, or bluegill sunfish, North American freshwater fish found in still water lakes and ponds. Ice-fished in winter, it is marked by 5–7 vertical bars on each side. Length: to 15in (38.1cm); Weight: 41lb (1.8kg). Family Centrachidae; species *Lepomis macrochirus.*

Blue-green Algae, widely distributed group of primitive microscopic algae (division Cyanophyta) found in virtually every environment, including oceans, barren rocks, glaciers, and hot springs. The characteristic blue-green color results from the presence of a blue pigment in addition to green chlorophyll. Dense growths of blue-green algae produce the "blooms" that give eutrophic ponds and lakes a muddy green color. In existence for more than 2 billion years, some are single cells, others occur in threadlike rows of cells. All lack a definite nucleus. They resemble bacteria.

Blue Jay, E North American bird known for its loud "jay-jay" call. It has a large head crest, rounded wings, long tail, and bright blue, black, and white plumage. It builds a bulky nest, high above ground in dense evergreen thickets, for its olivey eggs (3–6). Length: 10–12in (25–30cm). Species *Cyanocitta cristata.*

Blue Nile, (Al-Bahr Al-Azraq), river in NW Ethiopia; rises in Lake Tana, flows S and W into the Sudan, merging with White Nile to form the Nile River; site of Roseires and Sennar dams, built for irrigation. Length: 1,000mi (1,610km). *See also* Nile.

Blueprint, a photographic reproduction (using cyanide salts) with white lines against a blue background, frequently employed in drafting. The paper is coated with a solution of ammonium ferric citrate and potassium ferricyanide and exposed to intense light under the transparent sheet of material to be copied. When washed, the copy emerges, stable to light.

Blue Rider (Blaue Reiter), loosely organized group of artists formed in Munich, Germany, in 1911 by the abstract expressionist Wasily Kandinski. Influenced by cubism, the group tried to stress in their paintings inner impulses and to provoke a personal response from their viewers. The group included Aleksey von Jawlensky, Paul Klee, Franz Marc, and August Macke.

Blue Ridge Mountains, E and SE range of the Appalachian Mountains, extending from S Pennsylvania into Georgia, includes Black Mountains, Unaka Mountains, Great Smoky Mountains, and South Mountain. A narrow ridge 10mi wide (16km) in N, widens to 70mi (113km) in North Carolina. Heavily forested with few lakes; people live in valleys on small farms. Site of Great Smoky Mountains National Park in North Carolina and Shenandoah National Park in Virginia; Appalachian Trail takes hikers across top of range. Industries: timbering, apple growing, tourism. Highest peak is Mount Mitchell, N.C., 6,684ft (2,039m).

Blues, style of jazz-folk music that developed in the late 19th century and that was first popularized in the United States by W.C. Handy. A blues song typically involves 12 measures, in a minor key, with flatted 3rd and 7th chords (the "blue" notes). Blues songs are often slow and sad, expressing despair for a lost lover. Blues songs were a large part of early American jazz and still influence many jazz and folk artists today.

Bluet, or Quaker ladies, small tufted, perennial plant native to North America with small leaves and white or blue flowers. Family Rubiaceae; species *Houstonia caerulea.*

Blue Whale, slate-blue whalebone whale hunted almost to extinction. It summers in the arctic and Antarctica and winters in warmer seas. The largest animal that ever lived, its 4-ton tongue is as large as an elephant. Length: to 100ft (30m); weight: 150 tons. Species *Sibbaldus musculus.*

Blum, Leon (1872–1950), French statesman and political leader. He served in the Chamber of Deputies (1919–40) as a leader of the Socialist party where he introduced sweeping social reforms. He was premier (1935, 1936–37) and vice premier (1938–39), leading the opposition to the Munich Pact. Interned by the Vichy government (1941–45) he was released by the Allies. He headed the caretaker government (1946–47) prior to the elections held by the new Fourth Republic.

Blumenbach, Johann Friedrich (1752–1840), German physiologist and comparative anatomist, often called the father of physical anthropology. His research in the measurement of craniums suggested for the first time the importance of utilizing comparative anatomy in the study of human history. Blumenbach proposed five families of man: Caucasian, Mongolian, Malayan, Ethiopian, and American.

B'nai B'rith, Jewish service organization, founded in New York City in 1843. Open to any Jew who follows its precepts of love and brotherhood, its name means "sons of the Covenant." It is the oldest and largest Jewish service organization in the world, with over half a million members. It sponsors the Hillel Foundation on college campuses and combats anti-Semitism through the Anti-Defamation League (founded 1913).

Boa, constricting snake mostly restricted to the New World. All bear their young live. The boa constrictor *(Constrictor constrictor)* of American tropics grows to 12ft (3.7m). Smaller species are the iridescent rainbow boa and emerald tree boa. Most are arboreal but some are subterranean. The rosy boa and rubber boa of W United States are small, terrestrial forms. Family Boidae.

Boadicea (died 62 AD), British queen of the Iceni in East Britain. She was the wife of King Prasutagus, who, on his death, left his daughters and the Roman emperor as co-heirs. The Romans seized his domain and Boadicea led a revolt against them. Defeated, she took poison. The name more properly appears as Bonduca and Boudicca.

Boas, Franz (1858–1942), US anthropologist, first professor of anthropology at Columbia University (1899–1936), b. Germany. He was a scholar of the cultures and languages of the American Indians, of statistical physical anthropology, and of descriptive and theoretical linguistics. Important works include *Primitive Art* (1927), *Anthropology and Modern Life* (rev. ed. 1932), *The Mind of Primitive Man* (rev. ed. 1938), and *Race and Democratic Society* (1945), a collection of essays.

Boating, sport, popular world-wide, that includes yachting, motorboating, rowing (crew racing), canoeing and iceboating. Races are held with each type of craft, and rowing, yachting, and canoeing are included in the Olympic Games. The most prominent boating competitions include the International Challenge Cup (canoe sailing), the International Team Trophy (power cruisers), the Harmsworth Trophy and Gold Cup (motorboating), the Ice Yacht Challenge Pennant of America (iceboating), and the America Cup races (yachting).

Boaz, in the Bible, Bethlehemite related to Naomi's husband Elimelech. He married their daughter-in-law Ruth, inheriting her deceased husband's estates.

Bobcat, or wild cat, red lynx, vicious, short-tailed cat found throughout swamp, forest, and chaparral areas of United States, S Canada, and Central America. Its reddish-brown coat has black spots and underparts are white. The gestation period is 50–60 days and 2–4 young are born. It feeds on rodents and jack rabbits. Length: body—25–30in (63.5–76.2cm); tail-5in (12.7cm). Family Felidae; species *Lynx rufus. See also* Cat; Lynx.

Bobolink, American songbird that nests in Canada and N United States and winters in S South America. Males have a tawny neck, buff back, and black underparts. Females lay brown-spotted eggs (4–6) in a simple ground nest. Length: to 7in (17.8cm). Species *Dolichonyx oryzivorus.*

Bobsledding, one of the fastest and most dangerous of winter sports. Two- or four-men teams ride in an open steel-bodied vehicle with sledlike runners on an icy, snow-covered downhill course that is steeply banked with twisting inclines. The competition bobsled, for a four-man crew, weighs 489 pounds (220kg), and 356 pounds (160kg) for the two-man crew. Bobsledding, which followed tobogganing, was developed at St. Moritz, Switzerland, in the late 19th century and was first included in the winter Olympic Games in 1924. The only bobsled course in the United States is at Mt. Van Hoevenberg in Lake Placid, New York, site of the 1932 winter Olympic Games. *See also* Tobogganing.

Boccaccio, Giovanni (1313–75), Italian poet and prose writer. His first work, the *Filocopo,* is sometimes considered the first European novel, but he is best known for the *Decameron* and for *Fiammetta,* the partly autobiographical story of a young man's first love affair. He knew and imitated the older Dante, and with his friend Francesco Petrarch he is considered one of the founders of the Italian Renaissance. *See also* Decameron.

Boccie, a ball game, popular in Italy and in Italian communities throughout South America, Australia, and the United States. It can be played indoors or outdoors, uses a playing area that averages 60 by 10 feet (18 by 3m), with boarded sides and ends. The surface is covered with sand or soil. There are two to four players on a team, and four balls for each team. After a smaller wooden ball (jack) is thrown toward the end of the enclosure, the players, in turn, try to bring their ball to a position closest to the jack, by throwing the ball underhand. A player may use the side boards or any surface of the playing area in an attempt to move their opponent's ball away from the jack or to protect the position of his ball. One point is awarded for each ball that is closer to the jack than an opponent's. A game is 12 points.

Boccie was played in ancient Rome. The English version, called *bowles,* was played in the 12th century, and the German game, *keglers,* began in the 14th century. The game is governed by the Unione Federazioni Italiane Bocce, founded in Turin in 1898.

Bochum, city in West Germany, 10mi (16km) E of Essen; site of church (1599), Ruhr University (1965), planetarium (1964); commercial and transportation center. Industries: steel, iron, automotive, textiles, chemicals, machinery. Chartered 1321. Pop. 413,400.

Bock, Hieronymus (*c.* 1480–1554), German botanist. Often considered the founder of modern botany, he constructed a system of plant classification based on physical characteristics. His description of German plants, *Neu Kreutterbuch* (1539), was a vast improvement on earlier herbals.

Bode's Law, empirical numerical relationship for the mean distances of the planets from the sun. It is named for German astronomer Johann Bode, who popularized it in the late 18th century. If the number 4 is added to 0, 3, 6, 12, 24, 48, 96, 192, and each sum is divided by 10, the figure arrived at is the mean distance in astronomical units of the planets from the sun beginning with Mercury and including the asteroid belt. The law works for those planets known in the 18th century. It does not work for Neptune and Pluto, discovered in the 19th century.

Bodhista, bodhisatta, or bodhisatva, in Hinayana Buddhism, an individual who is about to reach Nirvana, such as Gautama prior to his enlightenment. In Mahayana Buddhism, this is an individual on the verge of enlightenment who delays his salvation in order to help mankind. *See also* Buddhism; Nirvana.

Bodleian Library, founded in 1602 at the University of Oxford in England. It served as a deposit library for 150 years until the British Museum opened. Its collection has grown to 2.5 million volumes and, in the central and dependent libraries, can accommodate 17,000 readers.

Bodoni, Giambattista (1740–1813), Italian printer, one of the originators of the first modern, Roman style, type face. He published editions of Homer, Virgil, and Horace in the new type face. His editions were considered particularly elegant, although there were numerous typographical errors.

Boeotia, department in central Greece, bounded by Attica, Megaris, Gulf of Corinth (S), Phocis (Wand NW), Atlantic channel and the Euripos (E), and Locres Opuntia (N); capital is Levádhia; site of 19th-century excavations by Heinrich Schliemann, revealing the Treasury of Minyas (1250 BC). The Boeotian League (7th century BC), headed by Thebes, defeated the Spartans; and Thebes dominated until destroyed by Alexander the Great 336 BC. Area: 1,225sq mi (3,173sq mi). Pop. 114,288.

Boer, Dutch word meaning farmer. Name used to identify Dutch- and Huguenot-descended inhabitants of the Republic of South Africa. More correctly called Afrikaner. *See also* Afrikaners.

Boer War, or **South African War** (1899–1902), conflict between Britain and the Transvaal (South African Republic) and Orange Free State. The British had gradually laid claim to South African lands in the 19th century, and their mining operations and control of commerce created great resentment among the Boers, white residents of Dutch, German, and Huguenot descent. War broke out in late 1899. After initial victories the Boer forces were repeatedly defeated by the reinforced British. Failing at conventional warfare, the Boers carried out an extensive guerrilla campaign that the British crushed with concentration camps and dragnets. An uneasy truce was arranged (Treaty of Vereeniging, 1902), and the Union of South Africa was formed in 1910.

Boethius (Anicius Manlius Severinus) (*c.* 475–525), Roman statesman and philosopher under the Emperor Theodoric. He attempted to eliminate governmental corruption, but was finally imprisoned on a charge of conspiracy. In prison at Ticinum, where he was subsequently tortured and executed, he wrote *On the Consolation of Philosophy,* a dialogue based on Neoplatonist and Aristotelian principles. *See also* Neoplatonism.

Bogarde, Dirk (1921–), British film actor, real name Derek Niven van den Bogaerde. He made his film debut in *Esther Waters* (1947) and after his success in *The Blue Lamp* (1950) became a leading British film star. His later and most notable films include *Victim* (1961), *The Servant* (1963), *Darling* (1965), *Accident* (1967), *Death in Venice* (1971), and *Despair* (1979). He published his autobiography in 1976.

Bogart, Humphrey (DeForest) (1899–1957), US film actor, b. New York City. He is acclaimed for roles requiring a complex of qualities: toughness, cynicism, sexual magnetism, heroic integrity, and honor. His films include *The Petrified Forest* (1936), *The Maltese Falcon* (1941), *Casablanca* (1942), *The Big Sleep* (1946), *Treasure of the Sierra Madre* (1948), *The African Queen* (1951), for which he won an Academy Award as best actor, and *The Caine Mutiny* (1954).

Boghead Coal. *See* Coal.

Bogomils, 10–15th century heretical Christian sect, founded by Bogomil, a priest. This starkly ascetic group originated in Bulgaria *c.* 950, spread to other Slavic countries and to France, influencing the Albigensian heresy. Bogomils believed that the power of evil (Satan, God's first and fallen son) or materialism was uppermost in the world but with the redeeming help of God's second son (Christ), this bondage could be broken and evil destroyed. Called the "Beloved of God," these "Old Believers" comprised the bulk of Christians in Bulgaria, despite continued persecution.

Bogotá, capital city of Colombia; in central Colombia, 300mi (483km) N of the equator. Known as "Athens of the South," it is a cultural, educational, and financial center of Colombia; has fine examples of Spanish colonial architecture. Founded 1538 by the Spanish near the center of a Chibcha Indian culture; in 1830 it became the capital of New Granada, later called Colombia. Industries: tobacco products, sugar, flour, textiles. Pop. 2,855,065.

Bohemia, historic region, now refers to W Czechoslovakia. From 950–1526 it was part of the Holy Roman Empire; under the rule of the Hapsburgs, it became part of Austria-Hungary (1526). It secured its independence following WWI, becoming the core of the new country of Czechoslovakia. Munich Pact (1938) removed the Sudetanland from Czechoslovakia and annexed it to Germany; the pre-1938 boundaries were restored in 1945. Made a prov. of Czechoslovakia 1945, it was dissolved in 1949, and rezoned 1968.

Bohr, Niels (1885–1962), Danish physicist. He worked with J.J. Thomson and Ernest Rutherford before being appointed professor at the University of Copenhagen. He used the quantum theory to explain the structure of the atom. He escaped from German-occupied Denmark (1943) and helped to develop the atom bomb in the United States. After the war he returned to Copenhagen and worked for international cooperation. He was awarded a Nobel Prize in physics in 1922 for his work on atomic structure. *See also* Quantum Theory.

Franz Boas

Bolivia

Heinrich Boll

Boiling Point, the temperature at which a substance changes phase from liquid to vapor or gas.

Boise, capital and largest city of Idaho, in valley of the Boise River; seat of Ada co; trade center for agricultural region of SW Idaho and E Oregon. Crops: sugar beets, potatoes, alfalfa, onions. Industries: steel, sheet metal, furniture, electrical equipment, lumber products. Founded 1863 as supply center for gold miners; inc. 1864; reinc. 1961 to annex suburbs. Pop. (1980) 102,451.

Boise River, river in SW Idaho, formed from three forks that rise in the Sawtooth Mts and flow together approx. 15mi (24km) E of Boise, then W past Boise to Snake River at Oregon line. The river is used in Idaho irrigation projects. Length of river from point of convergence is 60mi (97km).

Bokassa I (1921–), Emperor of the Central African Empire (1977–79). Jean-Bédel Bokassa came to power in 1966 in a military coup. After serving as president (1966–77) of the Central African Republic, he crowned himself emperor in an elaborate ceremony and changed the name of the country. A 1979 coup, with military aid provided by the French government, removed Bokassa, who went into exile, and replaced him with his cousin David Dacko.

Bola, or bolas, missile hunting weapon of South American Indians, consisting of three or more stone balls held together with thongs, and thrown in such a manner as to entangle the legs of the prey. The bola is used predominantly in the open country of the Patagonian and Pampas zones.

Boleslav I, called the Mighty (died 1025), Polish ruler (992–1025), first to be crowned king of Poland (1025). Starting from a small principality on the Vistula River, he established Polish dominion from the Oder and Neisse rivers to the Dnieper and from Western Pomerania to the Carpathian Mountains. Bohemia recognized him as a duke (1003). The Christian church was firmly established. At his death, Poland was one of the strongest states of Europe.

Boletus, a genus of terrestrial mushrooms whose spore-bearing parts are tubes instead of gills. They have a fleshy central stem and cap. Of the many species, several are edible. Poisonous ones either turn blue when bruised, have red tube mouths, or both.

Boleyn, Anne (1507–36), second wife of Henry VIII of England. Henry, who was tiring of Queen Catherine of Aragon and wanted a male heir, became infatuated with her. The pope's refusal to grant a divorce led to Henry's break with Rome. The archbishop of Canterbury annulled his marriage to Catherine and he married Anne (1533). Anne gave birth to the future Queen Elizabeth but no sons. Henry, tiring of her, had her beheaded on charges of adultery and incest.

Bolide, or fireball, large unusually bright meteor.

Bolingbroke, Henry St. John, Viscount (1678–1751), English political philosopher and statesman. A Tory member of Parliament (1701), he achieved power under Queen Anne (1713) but continued in opposition during the Hanoverian succession. His *Idea of a Patriot King* (1749) was thought to have influenced the "philosophes," to whom his skepticism presumably appealed. See also Philosophes.

Bolívar, Simón (1783–1830), the central figure in the South American independence movement in both its political and military phases. He took part in the fer-

ment that arose in Latin America following the Napoleonic invasion of Spain, and was instrumental in the creation of two short-lived republican governments in Venezuela (1810–14). Twice defeated by royalist forces, Bolívar went into exile (1815), but returned to the mainland the next year. By 1819 he had achieved some successes on the battlefield in eastern and southern Venezuela. In that year, Gran Colombia was created and Bolívar became its president. Military victories in Peru, Bolivia, and Ecuador followed. At a time when sovereignty was becoming a reality, Bolívar no longer believed that a system founded on representative and republican principles was feasible. He came to feel that Latin America was unprepared for democratic government. In the end, Bolívar became completely disillusioned, believing America to be ungovernable.

Bolívar. See Ciudad Bolívar.

Bolivia, Republic of, landlocked nation in W central South America, with extremes in altitude, climate, and wealth.
   Land and Economy. Bolivia has three regions: mountains in the center and along the W border; a great plateau—the altiplano—stretching between them; and a N and E plains area (68% of the country). The Bolivian Andes contain deposits of tin and silver, major supports of the economy. The altiplano has an average altitude of 12,000ft (3,660m), and, although cold and dry, provides the best living conditions. There Indians raise potatoes, beans, and cereal grains. Entirely in the S tropics, Bolivia has hot, humid lowlands in the N and E, and in the SE has a share of the dry Gran Chaco prairie. Oil from the S should prove of great value. La Paz, seat of most government functions, has textile, footwear, and other light industries, while the second city, Cochabamba, produces foodstuffs and cigarettes. Sucre, the official capital, is the judicial center. The largest source of foreign exchange is the illegal export of dried coca (from which cocaine is derived).
   People. About 55% of the people are Indians of the Quechua and Aymara tribes, and another 31% are of Spanish and Indian blood. The whites, Spanish-speaking and Catholic, control government, mining, and industry, while the mestizos perform labor duties and farm; the Indians, mostly illiterate, live by farming.
   Government. Formally a republic with a president, Senate, and Chamber of Deputies elected by all adults, Bolivia was ruled by the military 1971–82. Although elections for a civilian government were held in 1980, a right-wing military government assumed control. Elections in 1982 returned the government to civilian control.
   History. Tiahuanaco Indians settled beside Lake Titicaca, highest major lake in the world, about the time of Christ. Later, the Incas ruled the region for 200 years, until the Spanish arrived in the 1530s. Bolivian rebellions against Spain started in the 18th century, but independence came only in 1825 when Antonio José de Sucre defeated the Europeans. Bolivia's borders developed as the country split from Peru (1839), lost land leading to the Pacific to Chile (1883), and lost a war with Paraguay (1935) over the Chaco. Despite repeated attempts during the 1970s, Bolivia has not obtained a corridor through Chile to the Pacific Ocean. Under the right-wing military junta that assumed power in 1980 with the aid of Argentina, a period of severe repression began. The military's inability to solve economic problems hastened the return to civilian rule in 1982. In 1985, with the economy deteriorating, a new austerity program created further worker unrest.

PROFILE

Official name: Republic of Bolivia
Area: 424,163sq mi (1,098,581sq km)

Population: 5,570,105
   Density, 13per sq mi (5per sq km)
Chief cities: Sucre, official capital; La Paz, seat of government
Government: Republic
Gross national product: $1,700,000,000
Trading partners (major): Brazil, Argentina

Böll, Heinrich (1917–85), German novelist and short-story writer. His works include *Where Were You, Adam?* (1950), *Acquainted with the Night* (1953), *The Clown* (1963), *Absent Without Leave* (1964), *Group Portrait with Lady* (1971), *The Lost Honor of Katharina Blum* (1975), *Fursorgliche Belagerung* (1979), and *The Safety Net* (1982). A concern for catholic authenticity pervaded his work, but his humorously satirical short stories were perhaps his finest achievement. Böll won the Nobel Prize for literature in 1972.

Boll Weevil, small, gray, long-snouted beetle common in Mexico and SE and SC United States. Adults and larvae feed on the cotton plant, especially the bolls, and are serious crop pests. There are usually 4–6 generations each year. Species *Anthonomus grandis. See also* Weevil.

Bollworm, or pink bollworm, caterpillar destructive to cotton in many parts of the world. The bollworm is pinkish or cream colored. Besides attacking green cotton bolls, it feeds on okra, hollyhock, hibiscus, and related plants. Length: 0.5in (12mm). Species *Pectinophora gossypiella.*

Bologna, city in N central Italy, at foot of Apennines; capital of Bologna prov. and Emilia-Romagna region. The ancient Etruscan town of Felsina, it became a free commune 12th century; site of 11th-century university, Church of San Petronio (1390), and the Palazzo Comunale (13th, 15th, 16th centuries); transportation center. Industries: chemicals, food processing, electric motors. Pop. 484,406.

Bolsheviks, group led by V.I. Lenin that obtained a brief majority in the early 20th-century Russian Social Democratic party, but then lost power to the Mensheviks. In the 1917 November Revolution, however, the Bolsheviks played such an important role that the revolution carries their name. By 1918 the break with the Mensheviks was total and the Bolsheviks formed the Russian Communist party. The Bolsheviks stressed absolute party loyalty and were generally hesitant to compromise on any issue.

Bolton, city in NW England, 11mi (18km) NW of Manchester; spinning frame (1769) and spinning mule (1779) were invented here. Industries: textiles, chemicals. Pop. 263,300.

Bolzano (Bozen), city in N Italy; capital of Bolzano prov.; important regional commercial center since the Middle Ages; it became Italian 1918. Heavily damaged in WWII, many landmarks remain, including the cathedral, 14th-century Franciscan church, and medieval houses. Industries: tourism, engineering, textiles, wine. Pop. 106,857.

Boma, port city in W Zaire, equatorial Africa, on Congo estuary, 60mi (96km) E of Atlantic Ocean; commercial center; capital of Congo Free State (1887–1908) and of Belgian Congo until 1923. Exports: lumber, cacao, bananas. Founded as slave market in 16th century. Pop. 79,000.

Bomb, an explosive that is planted (mine), concealed (booby trap), thrown (grenade), projected (mortar shell), flown (buzz bomb). It is most frequently an explosive dropped (aerial bomb) such as atomic bomb, or fragmentation bomb. *See also* Nuclear Weapon.

Bombardier Beetle, ground beetle found in North America and Europe. It fights off predators by bombarding them with an irritating gas. Each discharge of gas makes a sound like a tiny popgun. Genus *Brachinus.*

Bombay, largest city in India; capital of Maharashtra state; located on an island off W coast, it is second only to Calcutta as India's leading port. It was ceded to England by Portugal 1661 as part of Catherine Braganza's dowry to Charles II; annexed by East India Co. 1708; dock and transportation facilities expanded in late 19th century; after 1941, population grew due to immigration and increasing birth rate. City was enlarged through rezoning 1951; cultural, educational, trade, and financial center; site of University of Bombay (1857), Indian Institute of Technology (1958). Industries: chemicals, textiles. Exports: cotton, manganese. Founded 1534. Pop. 5,970,575.

Bona Dea, Roman deity of fruitfulness in earth and in women, also known as Damia. Women celebrated her cult with a mysterious festival forbidden to men. The dedication day of her temple was May 1.

Bonaparte, family of Italian origin living in Corsica (also spelled Buonaparte). **Carlo** (1746–85), a lawyer, and **Maria Letizia Ramolina** (1750–1836), known as Madame Mère, were parents of a large family whose members were raised to distinction by their second and famous son, Napoleon I. **Joseph** (1768–1844), the eldest son, became king of Spain (1808–13). **Charles Lucien Jules Laurent** (1775–1840), the third son, known as Prince Canino, opposed Napoleon's despotic rule and lived in exile in Italy. **Maria Anna Elisa (Elisa)** (1777–1820) became Duchess of Tuscany. **Louis** (1778–1846) was created King of Holland in 1806. He married Hortense de Beauharnais. Their son became Napoleon III. **Maria Paulina (Pauline)** (1780–1825) was first married to General LeClerc and later to Prince Camillo Borghese. **Carolina (Caroline)** (1782–1839) married Joachim Murat, a marshal of France, who became king of Naples. *See also* Napoleon I; Napoleon II; Napoleon III.

Bonaparte, Joseph (1768–1844), king of Spain, b. Corsica. He was the eldest brother of Napoleon I. He participated in the Italian campaign (1797) and later served as diplomat for the First Republic of France. Napoleon made him king of Naples (1806), and he was appointed king of Spain in 1808, serving until 1813. After Napoleon's defeat at Waterloo, he resided in the United States (1815–32).

Bonaparte, Louis (1778–1846), King of Holland (1806–10), brother of Napoleon Bonaparte and father of Charles Louis Napoleon, later Napoleon III of France. He accompanied his brother in the Italian and Egyptian campaigns. Became a general in 1804; governor of Paris 1805. Forced by Napoleon to take the Dutch throne, he worked to restore the economy and promote the welfare of the Dutch, but the French Continental System was ruinous to Dutch trade. Napoleon felt he was too lenient and the conflict led Louis to abdicate (1810). He assumed the title of Comte de St-Leu. Holland was annexed to France.

Bonaparte, Napoleon. *See* Napoleon I.

Bonapartism, domestic reforms and governmental centralization carried out by Napoleon Bonaparte (1769–1821) during his rule in France.

Bonaventure (*c.*1217–74), Italian theologian and Roman Catholic saint. In 1254 he became head of the Franciscan school in Paris. In 1257 he was elected minister general of the order. Three varieties of theology, he claimed, correspond to 3 stages of mind in the consideration of God: the senses, reason, and last, pure mind. Unlike Aquinas, he did not favor Aristotelianism, but rather a more mystical and Platonic turn of mind is clear in his *Itinerary of Mind and God.*

Bond, Ionic. *See* Ionic Bond.

Bonds, promissory notes guaranteeing the repayment of a specific amount of money on a particular date at a particular fixed rate of interest. Bonds may be issued by corporations, states, cities, or the federal government. The quality of the bond and the interest rate paid on it will be determined by the length of time the loan will be outstanding and the risk involved. Thus the federal government would normally pay a lower rate of interest on its bonds than would cities because US bonds are relatively risk-free. A very healthy corporation could normally pay a lower interest rate than a less secure business.

Bonds, Chemical. *See* Chemical Bonds.

Bone, a type of connective tissue that forms the framework, or skeleton, of the body, protects the internal organs, serves as lever for muscles, stores calcium and phosphorus, and in its marrow produces red and white blood cells. Bone is surrounded by membrane, the periosteum, the outer layer of which serves for the attachment of ligaments, tendons, and muscles; the inner layer contains osteoblasts for bone growth. Bone itself is composed of a strong, dense, outer compact layer and a lighter, porous, inner spongy layer that contains the bone marrow. All bone contains a hard, calcium-containing matrix, which is arranged in layers, or lamellae, that are generally arranged concentrically around a Haversian canal, a canal containing a blood vessel. Bone cells, or osteocysts, each in a space called a lacuna, occur between lamellae and are linked to one another and to the blood vessels by canaliculi. Bone formation is called ossification. *See also* Skeletal System.

Bonefish, marine game fish found in shallow, warm waters. A bottom feeder, it has a pointed head covered with thick cartilage, a receding mouth, and silvery coloring. Length: 3.5ft (106.7cm); Weight: 18lb (8.2kg). Family Albulidae; species *Albula vulpes, Dixonia hemoptera.*

Bongo, large Central African antelope living in dense, humid forests. Both sexes carry spirally twisted horns. It has a reddish coat with vertical white stripes along its sides, erect mane and large ears. Height: to 55in (1.4m) at shoulder; weight: to 484lb (220kg) Family Bovidae; species *Boocerus Taurotragus eurycerus.*

Bonheur, Rosa (1822–99), French painter and sculptor. She was best known and very popular in her time for her sympathetic and accurate depictions of animals. She first exhibited at the Paris Salon of 1841 with two animal paintings and later with sculpture. Her works include *The Horse Fair* (1853).

Boniface (*c.*680–754), English missionary, a Roman Catholic saint. Called the Apostle of Germany, he left England in 716 to convert the pagan Germans. For his success he was rewarded with the Archbishopric of Mainzin (745). In 754, however, he was martyred by pagans in Friesland.

Boniface IX, Roman Catholic pope (1389–1404) b. Pietro Tomacelli (*c.* 1345). Elected pope during the Great Schism, he excommunicated Clement VII, the antipope. He tried, unsuccessfully, to strengthen Rome's position during the schism. He decreed the feast of the Visitation.

Bonito, marine tuna found in all warm and temperate waters, usually in large schools. Canned commercially, it is blue-black and silver. Length: to 3ft (91cm); Weight: 12lb (5.4kg). Family Scombridae; species includes *Bonito bonite.*

Bonn, capital city of Federal Republic of Germany (West Germany), on the Rhine River, 13 mi (21km) S of Cologne; residence of electors of Cologne (1238–1794); awarded to Prussia by Congress of Vienna (1815); site of 11th-century Romanesque cathedral, Poppelsdorf Castle (1715–30), Rathas (city hall, 1837) university (1786); birthplace of Beethoven; chosen as capital of West German state 1949. Industries: publishing, aluminum, electrical materials, stoneware, chemicals, insurance. Founded AD 1st century as Roman camp. Pop. 238,500.

Bonnard, Pierre (1867–1947), French painter. His early work, mainly of domestic scenes, was in the style of Paul Gauguin and Paul Sérusier. He received favorable reviews for his entries in the Salon des independents, Paris, in 1891, and a year later, for *The Terrasse Family.* Other notable works include *Luncheon* (1927) and his masterpiece, *Figure Before a Fireplace* (1917).

Bonnie Prince Charlie. *See* Stuart, Charles Edward.

Bonsai, Japanese gardening art of dwarfing woody plants and shrubs by pruning and restraining root growth. True bonsai are outdoor plants and need a dormant period during winter. Bonsai plants are most easily formed from plants with a substantial, tapering trunk, naturally twisted branches, and small leaves. The tree or shrub is shaped so the lower trunk is bare of branches; the middle is bare in front; and the top is surrounded. Branch shape is controlled by wiring. Container shape should complement. Practiced for centuries in the Orient, bonsai has been popular in the United States since World War II.

Bonus Army (1932), group of unemployed veterans that marched on Washington D.C. and demanded cash payment of bonus certificates. The 17,000 veterans camped out during June and July until President Hoover sent regular troops under Douglas MacArthur to disperse them. In 1936, the veterans were given cashable bonds.

Booby, seabird found in colonies on tropical and subtropical islands. They have bright faces, long necks, cone-shaped bills, and webbed feet. Expert fliers, they dive for fish. Most lay 2–3 eggs. Length: 26–40in (65–100cm). Genus *Sula.*

Book Louse, or **bookworm,** transparent to white, usually wingless insect found worldwide. It feeds on molds in dusty places with high temperature and humidity, such as shelves, books, and behind loose wallpaper. Length: to 0.04in (1mm). Family Liposcelidae; genus *Liposcelis.*

Book of Common Prayer, official service book for the Church of England. First prepared in 1549 under the direction of Archbishop Thomas Cranmer to simplify the services of the recently formed church. Many editions and revisions have been issued since the first text.

Book of Mormon, The, sacred work of the Church of Jesus Christ of Latter-Day Saints (Mormons). Mormons hold it in equal esteem with the Bible. First published in 1830, it is supposedly the translation of golden tablets revealed to Joseph Smith, the church's founder, by the angel Moroni in Palmyra, N.Y. It tells the story of a Hebrew tribe that sailed to America (*c.*600 BC) across the Pacific and then split into two groups. One group, the Lamanites, lost their beliefs and became savages. They were the ancestors of the American Indians. The others, the Nephites, developed a great culture. Jesus Christ appeared among them, and his teachings and the history of the tribe were written down by the prophet Mormon and his son Moroni on the gold tablets. The Lamanites, however, eventually destroyed the Nephites (*c.* AD 400). Smith claimed that he returned the tablets to the angel after showing them to 11 witnesses. *See also* Mormons.

Book of the Dead, a collection of Old Egyptian texts dating from the 16th century BC and after. The papyrus texts, which were of many different kinds, were placed in the tombs of the dead in order to help them combat the dangers of the underworld.

Boolean Algebra. *See* Algebra.

Boomerang, missile weapon, evolved by the Australian aborigines for hunting and warfare. Essentially a modified throwing stick, the boomerang is shaped with a pronounced curve or angle, enabling the skilled thrower to make it describe a circle in the air and return to him. Non-returning boomerangs are also found.

Boone, Daniel (1734–1820), US trailblazer and pioneer, b. Oley Township, Pa. In 1775, Boone blazed the Wilderness Road and founded Boonesboro in Kentucky. During the Revolution, he was captured by Indians. He escaped in 1778 and reached Boonesboro in time to prevent its capture. He lost his Kentucky lands because of faulty titles, and then moved to Missouri, where he again lost his land, but Congress restored part of it.

Booth, John Wilkes (1838–65), US actor and assassin of President Lincoln, b. Bel Air, Md. A successful actor who often appeared with his brothers Edwin and Junius Brutus, he was a Confederate sympathizer. On April 14, 1865, at Ford's Theater in Washington, D.C., he fatally shot President Lincoln, who died shortly thereafter. Unsuccessful attempts on the lives of members of Lincoln's cabinet were made by co-conspirators. Booth escaped but was trapped in a barn, where he died. The assassination infuriated the North and contributed to the severity of Reconstruction.

Booth, William (1829–1912), English religious leader, founder (1878) and first general of the Salvation Army. *See also* Salvation Army.

Boothia Peninsula, peninsula in Northwest Territory, Canada; northernmost part of North American mainland. Almost uninhabited, it was discovered and explored by British explorer John Ross 1829–33. Area: 12,483sq mi (32,331sq km).

Borage, hairy, annual herb, native to the E Mediterranean region and cultivated in Europe and North America for bee-feeding, salads, and flavoring. It has rough, oblong leaves and drooping clusters of bright blue flowers. Height: to 2ft (60cm). Family Boraginaceae; species *Borago officinalis.*

Borate, one of a class of inorganic compounds that are salts of boric acid (H_3BO_3) or of more complex oxyacids of boron. Many borate minerals exist: the

Daniel Boone

John Wilkes Booth

Aleksandr Borodin

most important are borax, colemanite, and kernite, all used as sources of boron compounds.

Borax, the most common borate mineral, hydrous sodium borate. Occurs in large deposits in dried-up salt lakes in arid regions. Monoclinic system prismatic crystals, crusts and masses. Colorless or white; transparent or opaque; hardness 2–2.5; sp gr 1.7. Many commercial uses such as in ceramics, in agricultural chemicals, as water softener.

Bordeaux, seaport city in SW France, on the W bank of the Garonne River; capital of Gironde dept. Although 60mi (97km) from open ocean, it is an excellent deepwater port. In 4th century it was a thriving metropolis of the Roman province of Aquitania Secunda; the English held it 1154–1453 and developed its trade; site of 18th-century buildings, vestige of a 3rd-century Roman amphitheatre and the Gothic cathedral of St. André; famous for wines and brandies. Industries: shipbuilding, textiles, soap, glass, beer. Pop. 226,281.

Borden, (Sir) Robert Laird (1854–1937), Canadian prime minister (1911–20). A lawyer, historian, and educator, he headed the Conservative party after 1901. Borden worked for civil service reform, public telephone and telegraph ownership, and imperial preferential trade, while attacking economic reliance on the United States. He cooperated with Henri Bourassa's nationalist faction, railroad interests, and industrialists, and he represented Canada at the Washington Disarmament Conference (1921) and the League of Nations. He wrote extensively on Canada's history, constitution, and jurisprudence.

Border Collie, oldest sheepherding purebred dog with great speed and strength. The head is similar to that of the old-fashioned collie with a slightly blunted, short muzzle and broad skull. The black or black and white coat is wavy and can be long or short. Average size: 18in (45.5 cm) high at shoulder; 45lb (20.5kg). *See also* Collie.

Border States, those slave-holding states where there was strong anti-slavery sentiment, including Delaware, Kentucky, Maryland and Missouri, and West Virginia, which remained in the Union. They were called border states because they shared a border with the Confederate States. President Abraham Lincoln, anxious not to lose these states to the South, excluded them from the Emancipation Proclamation (1863).

Border Terrier, working dog (terrier group) purebred since the 18th century in the border country of northern England and Scotland. The border terrier's hunting ability is shown in its otter-shaped head; straight, muscular legs; and narrow body. Ears are V-shaped, dropped forward. The short tail is carried up. The short, dense, harsh coat is blue and tan, grizzle and tan, or red. Average size: 12in (30cm) high at shoulder; 13–15lb (6–7kg). *See also* Terrier.

Bore, Tidal, a turbulent, wall-like wave of water that rushes up a narrowing estuary, bay, or tidal river. It seems to be caused by a combination of the incoming tidal wave, the slope and shape of the channel, and the river flow.

Boreal Forest, wooded zone with a cold, dry climate and poor sandy soil, including the Northern Hemisphere just below the Arctic tundra, high mountain regions, and SE United States. It is characterized by the predominance of coniferous trees such as pine, fir, spruce, and hemlock.

Borges, Jorge Luis (1899–), Argentine writer, the best-known Argentine author of the 20th century. His huge output of work has become a frame of reference for all Latin American writers. Most famous for his short stories—including the collections *El hacedor* (1960), and *El libro de arena* (1975)—he also wrote books of poetry and essays. His stories often use elaborate puzzles to dramatize what he believes is the extreme difficulty of achieving knowledge. Despite this skepticism, he writes with humor and awe about our attempts to unravel life's mysteries.

Borghese, noble Italian dynasty, originating in 13th-century Siena and moving to Rome in the 1500s. **Camillo** became Pope Paul V (1605). His nephew **Scipione Caffarelli**, a cardinal (died 1633, patron of artist Bernini), was responsible for the construction of the Villa Borghese. Other family members furthered dynastic wealth by obtaining principalities and marrying into the Orsini and Aldobrandini families. **Camillo** (1775–1832) won infamy by selling the Borghese art collection to his brother-in-law, Napoleon.

Borgia, family, notorious in 15th- and 16th-century Italian politics. From Spain the family went to Rome with first Borgia pope, **Calixtus III** (1455–58). His nephew **Rodrigo** became **Pope Alexander VI** (1492) and was the father of the infamous **Cesare** (c. 1475–1507) and **Lucrezia** (1480–1519). By alliances with the French, use of papal influences, strategic marriages, and treachery, the family sought political control over the Papal states and throughout central Italy. Alexander's death in 1502, Cesare's illness at the same time, and the election of Borgia enemy Giuliano della Rovere as Pope Julius II conspired to defeat Borgia aspirations.

Borgia, Cesare (c. 1475–1507), major figure in Italian politics while his father was Pope Alexander VI. In 1498 he secured French military assistance for an assault on central Italy. His ruthlessness in the successful campaigns through 1502 won him the reputation that caused Machiavelli to cite him as the example of the new "prince." His political fortunes collapsed with Alexander's death (1502), his own illness, and the election of a Borgia enemy as Pope Julius II.

Borgia, Lucrezia (1480–1519), daughter of Pope Alexander VI and sister of Cesare Borgia. Her 1493 marriage to Giovanni Sforza, lord of Pesaro, was annulled by Alexander in 1497 when the alliance it had created proved unworkable. The 1498 marriage to Alfonso, nephew of Alfonso II of Naples, ended with Alfonso's murder by Cesare's henchman when that tie threatened the alliance with France. After the collapse of Borgia aspirations in 1503, she lived the art patron's quiet life at the court of Ferrara with husband, Alfonso d'Este.

Boric Acid, also known as orthoboric acid or boracic acid, H_3BO_3, a white crystalline compound. It is weakly acidic and water soluble. It occurs naturally in the hot lagoons of Tuscany, Italy. Boric acid is used as a mild antiseptic, particularly when diluted in water, as an eyewash. It is also used as the solid in dusting powders.

Boris Godunov (1874), opera in prologue and four acts by Modest Mussorgsky, Russian libretto by the composer based on Alexander Pushkin's play and Nikolai Karamzin's histories. Of several versions, Nicolai Rimsky-Korsakov's orchestration is the best known, although Mussorgsky's original scoring is being revived. The plot is a series of scenes from Russian history (1598–1605).

Borlaug, Norman Ernest (1914–), US agronomist, b. Cresco, Iowa. He was awarded the Nobel Peace Prize in 1970 for his accomplishments in the "green revolution," developing an improved wheat seed and a higher-yielding rice.

Bormann, Martin (1900–45), German National Socialist leader. He joined the Nazi party in 1925 and was important in the party hierarchy. In 1941 he succeeded Rudolf Hess as deputy fuehrer. Although reported dead in 1945, he was sentenced to death in absentia by the Nuremberg war crimes tribunal. In 1973 the West German government declared him dead, a suicide in 1945, when his skeleton was identified.

Born, Max (1882–1970), British physicist, b. Breslau, Germany. A physics professor at Gottingen University, he left Germany in 1933 and went to Great Britain, where he later became professor at the University of Edinburgh. For his work in quantum mechanics, the basis of atomic and nuclear physics, he received the 1954 Nobel Prize.

Borneo, island in the Malay Archipelago, SE Asia. Largely undeveloped, Borneo is the world's 3rd-largest island, divided into four political regions: Sarawak state (W) and Sabah state (N) are Malaysian; Brunei state (NW) is a British protectorate; Kalimantan state (E, central, and S) which covers 70% of the island, is part of Indonesia. Borneo was colonized by Chinese in the 7th century, followed by Malays; Spanish, Portuguese, Dutch, and English trade started in the 16th and 17th centuries; by 1888, Sabah, Brunei, and Sarawak were declared British protectorates; the remainder were claimed by Dutch; present divisions were fixed in 1963. Industries: agriculture, forestry, fishing, oil and coal extraction. Area: 287,000sq mi (743,330sq km). Pop. 6,000,000.

Bornholm, island group in extreme E Denmark, in the Baltic Sea. After Germany's surrender in May, 1945, German forces made a desperate stand here, but Soviet troops forced their surrender. Bornholm is largest island. Industries: farming, fishing, handicrafts. Pop. 47,126.

Bornite, or peacock ore, a sulfide mineral, copper iron sulfide (Cu_5FeS_4); common copper ore in intrusive igneous rocks and metamorphic rocks. Cubic system, rarely as crystals, frequently in masses. Bronze with purple iridescent tarnish; metallic; opaque; hardness 3; sp gr 5.

Borodin, Aleksandr (1834–87), Russian composer. He was one of the "Russian Five," composers who promoted Russian nationalism in music in the 19th century. His most popular work is the *Polovtsian Dances* from his opera *Prince Igor* (begun 1869). He also composed three symphonies.

Borodino, town in Russian SFSR, USSR, on the Kolocha River, 70mi (113km) WSW of Moscow; battlefield site of 1812 Napoleonic Wars where Russians under Mikhail Kutuzov were defeated, thus opening Moscow to Napoleon's army.

Boron, nonmetallic element (symbol B) of group III of the periodic table, first isolated (1807) by Sir Humphry Davy. It occurs in several minerals, notably borax and the chief ore, kernite. Amorphous boron, an impure powder, is made by reducing the oxide with magnesium. Pure boron is obtained as a hard crystalline material by decomposing boron tribromide vapor on a hot metal filament. The element is used in semiconductor devices and the stable isotope B^{10} is a good neutron absorber, used in nuclear reactors and particle counters. Properties: at. no. 5; at. wt. 10.81; sp. gr. 2.34 (cryst.), 2.37 (amorph.); melt. pt. 4172°F (2300°C); most common isotope B^{11} (80.22%).

Borromeo, Carlo (1538–84), Italian church reformer and Roman Catholic saint. He was created cardinal by his uncle Pius IV (1560), and then Archbishop of Milan. His tenure was remarkable for administrative and spiritual reform. He lived simply, insisted on an educated clergy, and urged the reconvening of the Council of Trent. During the plague of 1576–78 he heroically administered to the needs of the populace.

Borromini, Francesco (1599–1667), Italian architect. His Baroque palace and church designs were based on geometric modules rather than on the proportions of the human body and had tremendous influence in Italy and northern Europe. A notable example of his work is S. Carlo alle Quattro Fontane in Rome (begun 1634).

Borstal System, British method for rehabilitation of juvenile offenders, ages 16–21. The system derives its name from the first institution, which was established for boys, at Borstal, England, in 1902. It emphasizes training, residential-type living, and individual attention. The system was later extended to girls.

Borzoi, hunting dog (hound group) that relies on sight and speed; also called Russian wolfhound. An elegant dog dating from 17th-century Russia, it has a slightly domed, long, narrow head; long, powerful jaws; small, fine ears laid back on the neck; a deep but narrow-chested body; gracefully curved back; long legs; and a long, curved tail. The long, silky coat is flat, wavy, or curly; it is short and smooth on the head, ears, and front of legs. The coat can be any color. Average size: 26–31in (66–81cm) high at shoulder; 75–105lb (34–47.5kg). *See also* Hound.

Bosch, Jerome (Hieronymus van Aeken) (*c.* 1450–1516), Flemish painter. He portrayed fantastic creatures in strange worlds. His archaic and highly individualistic style is explained in part by his artistic isolation and his adherence to heretic Protestant sects. His concern with the evils that constantly beset mankind is depicted in *Garden of Earthly Delights;* his anti-Church attitude, in *Adoration of the Kings. Hay-Wain* is a good example of his style—flat figures in rich dress in a panoramic view.

Bosnia, constituent republic in central Yugoslavia on the Sava River; comprises the regions of Bosnia (N) and Hercegovina (S), in the Dinaric Alps; Sarajevo is the capital. First settled by the Serbs, became powerful independent country by the 12th century; taken by Turks in 1463, then ruled by Hungary, Germany, and finally Yugoslavia in 1946. Industries: lumber, corn, tobacco, cotton, wheat, grapes, copper, iron ore, lignite, manganese, hydroelectricity. Area: 19,741sq mi (51,129sq km). Pop. 3,746,000.

Bosporus, narrow strait joining Sea of Marmara with Black Sea, separating European and Asian Turkey; scenic banks are lined with villas and old castles; important strategic and commercial passage; controlled by Turks since 1452; refortified after Montreux Convention of 1936. Length: 19mi (30km). With Dardanelles Strait at SW end of Sea of Marmara, Bosporus creates a water route from the Black Sea to the Aegean Sea. *See also* Dardanelles.

Bossier City, city in NW Louisiana, across the Red River from Shreveport; site of ruins of Confederate Fort Smith; Barksby Air Force Base nearby; center of large oil- and gas-producing area. Inc. 1907. Pop. (1980) 49,969.

Boston, seaport city and capital of Massachusetts, in E part of state at mouth of Charles and Mystic rivers on Massachusetts Bay; seat of Suffolk co; largest city in New England. Founded 1630 by John Winthrop and Puritans as the main colony of the Massachusetts Bay Co., it was named for the town in Lincolnshire, England. Seeking religious freedom, the colony soon developed into a stronghold of Puritanism and a leader in the opposition to Britain's taxation and trade restrictions; it was the scene of several events leading to the outbreak of the American Revolution: the Boston Massacre (March 5, 1770), the Boston Tea Party (Dec. 16, 1773), and the Battle of Bunker Hill (June 17, 1775). Boston contains the 17th-century home of Paul Revere, Old North Church (1723), Old South Meetinghouse (1729), Faneuil Hall (1742), and the Old State House (1748). It was the birthplace of US Unitarianism at King's Chapel (1785) and is the site of the mother church of Christian Science (1894); the YMCA was started here (1851) seven years after it was founded in Britain; the Roman Catholic Archdiocese of Boston is the 2nd-largest in the United States; from 1830–65 city was center of an abolitionist movement.

A noted educational center, Boston is the site of the Boston Public Latin School (1635), and of numerous colleges, including Mass. College of Pharmacy (1823), Boston University (1839), Mass. State College at Boston (1852), New England Conservatory of Music (1867), Mass. College of Art (1873), Burdett College (1879), Emerson College (1880), Wheelock College (1889), Northeastern University (1898), Wentworth Institute (1904), Simmons College (1899), Suffolk University (1906), Emmanuel College (1919). Harvard University (1636), Tufts University (1858), Brandeis University (1848), Radcliffe College (1879), and Mass. Institute of Technology (1860) are nearby. Cultural facilities include the Boston Museum of the Fine Arts, the Isabella Stewart Gardner Museum, Boston Public Library, and Boston Symphony Orchestra. Leading medical centers and research facilities are here; Boston is also the home of the Red Sox (American League baseball team), the Celtics (National Basketball Association team), and the Bruins (National Hockey League team). Industries: apparel, chemicals, publishing, shipbuilding, electronic equipment, fishing, wool processing. Inc. as city 1822. Pop. (1980) 562,994.

Boston, Siege of (1775–76), Revolutionary War conflict. British troops in Boston were surrounded by American colonial forces. The siege began in April 1775 when the British retreated to Boston after the battles at Lexington and Concord. It ended in March 1776 when American troops, under the command of George Washington, captured Dorchester Heights and the British under Gen. William Howe evacuated Boston and sailed to Nova Scotia.

Boston Massacre (1770), riot by American colonists angered over the quartering of troops in private homes. It was put down by British soldiers and resulted in the death of five civilians, including Crispus Attucks. The riot was used as a propaganda device by Sam Adams. The soldiers were tried for murder, defended by John Adams, and acquitted.

Boston News-Letter, first successful American newspaper, published 1704–1776. Founded by John Campbell, it was edited by him until 1722. In 1708 the first illustration in a colonial newspaper appeared in it.

Boston Tea Party (1773), protest by a group of Bostonians, disguised as Indians, against the Tea Act and the policy of "taxation without representation." Tea from ships was thrown into Boston harbor after Gov. Thomas Hutchinson refused to let the ships return to England without unloading. *See also* Tea Act.

Boston Terrier, native American breed (nonsporting group) bred in Boston about 1870 from English bulldog and white English terrier. Its square head is flat on top. The muzzle is square, short, and wide. Ears are natural bat shape or cropped. Large eyes are wide-set. The short body is wide-chested. Wide-set legs are medium-long. The short, low-set tail is either straight or screw-shaped. Characteristic coloring of the short, smooth, fine coat is brindle with a specific pattern of white marks. Average size: three classes—under 15lb (7kg); 15–20lb (7–9kg); 20–25lb (9–11.5kg). *See also* Nonsporting Dog.

Boswell, James (1740–95), Scottish biographer and author. He traveled widely in Europe, meeting Voltaire and Jean Jacques Rousseau. His early works include *Account of Corsica* (1768) and *Journal of a Tour to the Hebrides* (1785), an account of his travels with Samuel Johnson. A friend of Johnson and fellow member of the Literary Club, his *Life of Johnson* (2 vols., 1791) is one of the greatest English biographies.

Bosworth Field, English battleground 12 miles (19.3km) W of Leicester, site of the concluding battle of the Wars of the Roses (1485). There the Lancastrians, under the future Henry VII, defeated and killed the Yorkist Richard III.

Botanical Garden, large garden preserve for display, research, and teaching purposes. Wild and cultivated plants from all climates are maintained outdoors and in greenhouses. Although organized gardens date from ancient Rome, the first botanical gardens were est during the Middle Ages. In the 16th century, gardens existed in Pisa, Bologna, Padua, and Leiden. Aromatic and medicinal herbs were arranged in rows and still exist in the Botanical Garden of Padua. The first US botanical garden was est. by John Bartram in Philadelphia in 1728. Famous botanical gardens include the Royal Botanical Gardens in Kew (near London) est. 1759; Botanical Gardens of Berlin-Dahlem 1646; and Botanical Gardens in Schönbrunn, Vienna 1753.

Botany, the study of plant life. It includes the classification, structure, physiology, reproduction, and evolution of plants; also plants in relation to their environment and the economic aspects of their use by man. The chief subdivisions of botany are taxonomy, morphology, physiology, and genetics. Plants have always been important to man and necessary to human life. Primitive man depended on plant life for food, warmth, and shelter. Man learned to cultivate wild plants and discovered those that would grow from seed and those that were weeds. He studied plant composition, proper breeding methods, and treatment of diseases. As botanists learned more about plants, they began to catalog all known plants instead of only those with medicinal virtues. The first authentic work in botany is credited to Theophrastus, a pupil of Aristotle, about 300 BC.

Botany Bay, bay of the Tasman Sea in New South Wales, Australia; discovered by Capt. James Cook in 1770. Fed by the Georges and Woronora rivers, it is about 5mi (8km) across and 1mi (1.6km) wide at its mouth.

Botfly, warble fly or cattle grub, stout black and white to gray fly, 0.35 to 0.7in (9–18mm) long, an ectoparasite of many animals; found worldwide. The larvae enter through small wounds and grow under the skin. Damage to the skin is caused by infection of the exit hole. Family Oestridae. *See also* Diptera.

Botha, Pieter W(illem) (1916–), South African prime minister (1978–). Politically active from the age of 20, he held several important positions before succeeding John Vorster as prime minister. Botha formed the multiracial advisory council on constitutional change in 1980, the first institution of its kind in South Africa. Replacing the upper house of parliament, it consists of whites, mixed-race, and Indians although no blacks were among its numbers. He also established the Southwest Africa Territorial Force in 1980 to defend the disputed territory of Namibia.

Bothnia, Gulf of, chief arm of the Baltic Sea; north of Ahvenanmaa Islands, between Sweden (W) and Finland (E); freezes part of the year; contains lumber shipping ports. Length: approx. 400mi (644km). Width: 50–150mi (8–241km).

Bothwell, James Hepburn, 4th Earl of (?1535–78), Scottish nobleman, third husband of Mary, Queen of Scots. He made many enemies in Scotland's turbulent politics but won the queen's affection by loyally supporting her. When her husband Lord Darnley was murdered (1567), Bothwell was implicated; nevertheless, Mary married him. The nobles rebelled, and Bothwell fled abroad. He died insane in a Danish prison.

Botswana, Republic of, formerly Bechuanaland Protectorate; republic in S Africa bounded by Namibia (N and W), Zimbabwe (NE), Republic of South Africa (S and SE). It was the first British high commission territory to attain independence (1966); the main legislature is a National Assembly.

The terrain is a tableland rising to a mean elevation of 3,300ft (1,007m). In the S and SW the enormous Kalahari Desert expands N into bush lands. The Okavango River basin, located in the NW, has industrial potential as source for an irrigation project. Although varying from N to S, the average annual rainfall is 18in (457mm), and the climate is subtropical. Only 4% of the land is used for agricultural purposes (corn, sorghum, peanuts). Important sources of income have included wages from Botswanans working in the mines and industries of Zimbabwe and the Republic of South Africa. Botswana has developed its copper and diamond industries since their discovery in 1969–70, and now diamond exports are a leading source of foreign exchange.

The majority of Botswana's population belongs to its eight principal tribes: Bamangwato, Bakwena, Bangwaketse, Batawana, Bakgatla, Bamalete, Barolong, Batlokwa. These people are mainly pastoral, with low literacy rates and health standards. There is a shortage of indigenous industrial workers. Christianity and tribal beliefs constitute the main religions. English is the official language, with Tswana as the main African language.

A British protectorate was est. in the N in 1884–85 at the insistence of the Botswana tribes as a safeguard against occupation by Boers and Matabeles. British Bechuanaland was est. the same year, as a crown colony lying S of the Molopo River. Ten years later the S area was annexed to Cape of Good Hope colony, with the N region remaining a protectorate until its independence in 1966. Sir Seretse Khama, leader of the independence movement, served as the country's first president until his death in 1980, when he was succeeded by former vice-president Dr. Quett Masire. During the 1980s, Botswana continued to decrease ties with South Africa.

PROFILE

Official name: Republic of Botswana
Area: 231,804sq mi (600,372sq km)
Population: 791,000

Boston, Massachusetts: Christian Science Center

Bottle-nosed whale

Clara Bow

Chief cities: Gaborone (capital); Serowe; Kanye; Molepolole
Religion: Tribal, Christianity
Language: English (official), Tswana, Setswana
Monetary unit: South African rand

Botticelli, Sandro (c. 1445–1510), Italian painter. Influenced by Piero Pollaiuolo, he worked with him on a series of *Seven Virtues* (1470; Uffizi, Florence). In Florence he was patronized by the leading families, including the Medicis, whose portraits he included in *Adoration of the Magi* (Uffizi, Florence). In 1481 he went to Rome to assist in the decoration of the Sistine Chapel. After his return to Florence, he painted a number of mythological pictures, including *Birth of Venus* and *Pallas Subduing a Centaur* (both, Uffizi, Florence). He is known for his masterful use of color, graceful lines, and poignant themes.

Bottle-nosed Whale, beaked whale found in Atlantic waters. Its nose resembles the neck of a bottle and it usually travels in small groups. Length: 30ft (9m). Species *Hyperoodon ampullatus* (N Atlantic); *Hyperoodon planifrons* (S Atlantic). *See also* Beaked Whale; Whale.

Botulism, form of food poisoning caused by a bacterial toxin so lethal that death can occur within hours, apparently from respiratory paralysis. Early symptoms include lassitude, disturbance of vision, sometimes though not always with nausea and vomiting. The most frequent source of botulism is home-canned foods. Hospitalization is necessary.

Boucher, François (1703–70), French painter, decorator, and engraver. A follower of the Rococo style of the Louis XV period, he was immensely popular and widely imitated all over Europe. He painted historical, mythological, genre, and landscape works, executing over 1,000 paintings, 10,000 drawings, and 180 engravings, of which the Wallace Collection of London holds the largest part. *See also* Rococo.

Bougainville, largest island of Solomon Island group, in W Pacific Ocean, E of New Guinea; territory of Papua, New Guinea. The Emperor Mountains run through the middle section; contains rich soil, many harbors. Discovered 1768 by Louis de Bougainville, the island was under German control 1882, taken by Australia 1914, occupied by Japan during WWII, and retaken by Australia 1945. Crops: coconuts, coffee, cacao. Exports: copra, rubber. Area: 3,880sq mi (10,049sq km). Pop. 70,000.

Bougainvillea, tropical, flowering woody vine often grown as garden plant in warm climates. Its inconspicuous flowers have showy purple or red bracts. It was named after explorer Louis de Bougainville who collected it near Rio de Janiero. Family Nyctaginaceae; species *Bougainvillea spectabilis*.

Bouguer Anomaly, the observation that the gravity measured on a great rock mass, such as a mountain range, is greater than the average. This is due to the gravitational force exerted by the rock mass itself.

Boulder, city in N central Colorado, seat of Boulder co, 25mi (40km) NW of Denver; site of University of Colorado (1876) and National Bureau of Standards. Industries: tourism, space research, agriculture, mining. Settled 1858; inc. 1871. Pop. (1980) 76,685.

Boulder Fern, or hayscented fern, lacy, North American fern of dry woodlands and open pastures. The brittle, yellowish-green fronds have haylike aroma. It has a slender, rapidly growing rootstock. Height: to 3ft

(9km). Family Cyatheaceae; species *Dennstaedtia punctilobula*.

Boulogne-sur-Mer, seaport town in France, on the English Channel; one of the leading fishing ports of France; in AD 53 the Romans sailed from here to conquer Britain. During WWI it was a British base, and during WWII it was a German submarine base. Industries: canning, shipbuilding. Pop. 49,276.

Bouncing Bet, common name for a herbaceous plant of the pink family, native to Europe and W Asia and naturalized in North America. The stocky upright perennial growing to about 3ft (91cm) bears clusters of large pink or white blooms in late summer. Family Caryophyllaceae; species *Saponaria officinalis*. *See also* Pink.

Boundary-layer Flow, the behavior of a fluid in the region immediately next to a solid body immersed in the fluid. In this region, layers of the fluid "slide" over one another, and the measure of this internal friction, viscosity, becomes the determining characteristic of the flow.

Bourbon, House of, European dynastic family, the various branches of which are longtime rulers of France, Spain, and several independent Italian states. The Bourbons were descendants of the Capetians, the royal family that ruled France from 987 to 1328. In 1272, Robert of Clermont, a descendant of Louis IX, married Beatrice of Bourbon, a great heiress, and their son Louis was created duc de Bourbon in 1327. The ducal title continued until 1527 when the Bourbon lands were seized by the crown and the title eliminated. In the meantime, a cadet branch, the Bourbon-Vendôme line, was adding important fiefs to its holdings, including the kingdom of Navarre. Thus, when Henry of Navarre became king of France as Henry IV in 1589, the Bourbons became France's ruling family. They continued to rule until the French Revolution. Two members of the family, Louis XVIII and Charles X, ruled during the Bourbon Restoration (1814–30) and Louis Philippe, who ruled from 1830–48, was of the Bourbon-Orleans line, a cadet branch. Descendants of that line continued to be pretenders to the French crown.

The Bourbons became the ruling family of Spain in 1700 when Philip V, grandson of Louis XIV of France, assumed the throne, an act that brought on the War of the Spanish Succession. Except for brief periods, his descendants continued to rule Spain until 1931, when the Second Republic was declared. The republic, in turn, was replaced by the Nationalist government of Francisco Franco. His hand-picked successor, Juan Carlos I, who became king upon Franco's death (1975), was a Bourbon. The Bourbon rulers of Naples, the Two Sicilies, and Parma were all descended from the Spanish Bourbons.

Bourbonnais, former territory in central France, most of which corresponds to the present dept. of Allier. It was gradually put together by the counts of Bourbon, who became known as the Archimbaud dynasty. One of their members, Beatrice of Bourbon, married Robert (1256–1318), son of Louis IX of France, and thus gave the name "Bourbon" to the French royal family. Bourbon became a duchy in 1327 and was attached to the French crown in 1531.

Bourgeois Gentleman (1670), satirical comedy by French dramatist Molière about M. Jourdain, a wealthy bourgeois whose desire to be considered a gentleman becomes an obsession and finally a delusion. The play contains Molière's typical social satire as well as brilliantly realized characters.

Bourgeoisie, the middle class. Originally it referred to the artisans and craftsmen who lived in medieval French towns. The Industrial Revolution greatly increased their number and importance. They divided into the *haute bourgeoisie* (captains of industry and bankers) and the *petite bourgeoisie* (managers and tradesmen). Karl Marx credited the bourgeoisie with being instrumental in overthrowing feudalism but condemned them as reactionary capitalists who held down the proletariat. Among many intellectuals, especially those who were once called bohemian, the bourgeoisie is stereotyped as selfish, materialistic, mediocre, and unimaginative.

Bourges, city in central France, 122mi (195km) S of Paris; capital of Cher dept. Caesar captured it 52 BC; it later became the capital of the Roman prov. of Aquitania Prima; a medieval trade, banking, and financial center; site of 13th-century Cathedral of St Etienne. Town is now a market center for the surrounding agricultural area. Pop. 80,379.

Bourguiba, Habib (c. 1903–), Tunisian political figure, president (1957–). In 1934 he founded the Neo-Destour party. In the next two decades he was often imprisoned by the French rulers of Tunisia for his nationalist activities. During his years of liberty he traveled abroad several times promoting the cause of Tunisian independence. In 1954 he began the negotiations that culminated in independence in 1956. Premier (1956–57), he deposed the bey and became the president (1957). In foreign policy he has favored negotiations between the Arab states and Israel. In 1974 he agreed to a plan for merger of Tunisia and Libya, but the plan has not been acted upon. In 1975 he was made president for life.

Bouvier des Flandres, a cattle-driving dog (working group) bred in southwestern Flanders and northern France. A powerful dog, it has a medium-long, flat head; arched brow; and wide, deep muzzle. The high-set, erect ears are cropped to points. The body is short; the legs appear heavy because of coat; the high-set tail is docked. The fawn to black coat is rough and unkempt with characteristic eyebrows, mustache, and beard. Average size: 23.5–27.5in (59.5–70cm) high at shoulder; 60–70lb (27–32kg). *See also* Working Dog.

Bovidae, family of horned ruminants consisting of 49 genera and about 115 species that are found worldwide. They feed on grass or other plants and most are gregarious and nomadic. Included are antelopes, buffalo, cattle, goat, and sheep. The earliest fossil record of this family is from Miocene times.

Bow, Clara (1905–65), US silent film star, b. Brooklyn, N.Y. Known as the "It" girl, she was a vivacious comedienne who personified the flapper in *Dancing Mothers*, *Mantrap* (1926), *It* (1927), and *The Wild Party* (1929). Her much publicized wild personal life and difficulty in adjusting to sound films led to a sharp decline in her popularity and her early retirement.

Bow and Arrow, missile weapon comprising a length of wood, horn, etc., flexed and held in tension by a string, and a pointed shaft, usually flighted with feathers and tipped. Developed probably in the Upper Paleolithic, the bow and arrow is still almost universally used by primitive communities for hunting and warfare. The weapon's efficacy is often increased by steeping the arrowheads in poison. *See also* Archery.

Bowdler, Thomas (1754–1825), English editor. He is noted for his expurgated version of Shakespeare, *The Family Shakespeare*, which first appeared in 1818. He also published an expurgated edition of Gibbon's *His-*

tory of the Decline and Fall of the Roman Empire (1826). The term *bowdlerize,* meaning to omit indelicate sections, is derived from his name.

Bowel. *See* Colon.

Bowerbird, forest bird of New Guinea and Australia. The male builds a complicated and brightly ornamented bower to attract the female. After mating, the female lays her eggs (1–3) in a cup-shaped nest. Adults, mainly terrestrial, have short wings and legs and variously colored plumage. Length: 10–15in (25–38cm). Family Ptilonorhynchidae.

Bowfin, or mudfish, dogfish, gringle, grindle, primitive bony fish found in fresh waters of E United States and Canada. Its long cylindrical body has a characteristic long spineless dorsal fin. The head is covered with bony plates, the body with heavy scales. A well-developed swim bladder enables it to survive for 24 hours out of water. Family Amiidae; Species *Amia calva. See also* Osteichthyes.

Bowie, James (*c.*1796–1836), US frontiersman and hero of the Texas Revolution, b. Logan, Ky. He moved to Texas from Louisiana in 1828 and married the daughter of the Mexican vice governor. But by 1832 he had joined the US colonists who opposed the Mexican government. Appointed a colonel in the Texas army (1835), he fought in several battles before being killed at the Alamo. The invention of the bowie knife has been attributed to him.

Bowling, indoor sport in which a ball is rolled down a wooden alley in an attempt to knock down a set of maple pins. The most popular form of the game, which includes duckpins, rubberband duckpins, and candlepins, is tenpins, played with a large, heavy ball and ten 15-inch (38.10cm) pins set up in a triangular form at the target end of the alley. A regulation alley measures 41 to 42 inches (104–107cm) and 60 feet (18.3m) from the foul line to the center of the headpin. The ball, which has two to three finger holes, weighs from 10 to 16 pounds (4.5 to 7.2kg).

A game is divided into 10 frames, with a maximum of 2 throws for each frame. Each downed pin counts as one point. Knocking all the pins down on the first ball is called a strike and scores 10 points plus the total of the next two throws. Toppling all the pins on the second ball is called a spare and scores 10 points plus the total of the next throw. The highest score possible is 300, made by 12 consecutive strikes.

History. Bowling, which existed as early as 5200 BC, was introduced in the United States by the Dutch in the 19th century. The sport began to flourish in the 1950s with the introduction of the automatic pinsetter. The American Bowling Congress, formed in 1895, includes over 5,000,000 members.

Bowling Green, industrial city in SW Kentucky, 95mi (153km) SW of Louisville; seat of Warren co; agriculture area. Industries: meat packing, tobacco processing, tool and die making. Founded 1789. Pop. (1980) 40,450.

Box, evergreen tree or shrub found in tropical and temperate regions in Europe, North America, and W Asia. The shrub is popular for topiary and box lumber is used for musical instruments. It has dark green, oval glossy leaves and pale brown ridged bark. One female flower is surrounded by several male flowers; none have petals. The 100 species include English or common *Buxus semepervirens* and larger *Buxus balearica* that grows to 80ft (24m).

Box Elder, deciduous tree native to temperate North America. A rapidly growing tree, its leaves are oblong and pointed. The flowers are yellowish-green with different sexes on separate trees. Height: to 70ft (21m). Family Aceraceae; species *Acer negundo.*

Boxer, German police dog (working group) originally used for bullbaiting and dogfighting; named for its fighting style of using paws like man boxing. A sturdy, square-built dog, it has a slightly arched head and square muzzle with lower jaw protruding, wrinkles, and black mask. High-set, erect ears are cropped to points. A short body is set on medium-long straight legs. The docked tail is carried up. A short, shiny coat is fawn and brindle. Average size: 21–25in (53.5–63.5cm) high at shoulder; 60–75lb (27–34kg). *See also* Working Dog.

Boxer Rebellion (1900), violent Chinese uprising to oust all foreigners from China. Forces led by secret society of Boxers (Righteous and Harmonious Fists) that murdered Europeans and Chinese Christians besieged Peking's foreign legation enclave for two months. An eight-nation expeditionary force put down the uprising, and in 1901 a treaty was signed allowing the stationing of troops in China and the resumption of trade.

Boxing, sport of fist fighting, also known as pugilism and prize fighting. It is a contest between two participants in a roped-in square (ring). The ring area measures from 18 to 24 feet square (5.5 to 7m), and extends two to three feet (.61 to .91m) beyond the ropes. The surface is padded and covered with canvas, and three ropes, supported to posts at each corner, form the ring's boundaries. Boxers, who fight according to weight, are classified into eight divisions. These are flyweight (112lb, 50kg), bantamweight (118lb, 85kg), featherweight (126lb, 57kg), lightweight (135lb, 60.7kg), welterweight (147lb, 66.1kg), middleweight (160lb, 72kg), light-heavyweight (175lb, 79kg), and heavyweight (unlimited). For amateurs, a light-welterweight (139lb, 63kg), and light-middleweight (156lb, 70kg) class is included. Boxers wear trunks with a protective cup underneath, a fitted mouthpiece, high soft-soled shoes, and leather gloves. Professional fighters use 8-ounce (227-gram) gloves, and amateurs use 12-ounce (340-gram) gloves. Professional bouts can be 4, 6, 8, 10, 12, or 15 rounds of 3 minutes duration with a 1-minute rest in-between. Amateur bouts are scheduled for three rounds of two minutes each. A fight is enforced by a referee in the ring, and ends when there is a knock-down (where a boxer is unable to get to his feet by the count of 10), or a technical knockout (one fighter is too seriously injured to continue). If both fighters finish the scheduled rounds, a decision is awarded by the officials, usually the referee and two judges

History. Boxing, one of the oldest athletic endeavors, dates from 4000 BC. The more modern form of boxing emerged in England in 1719 where the contestants fought without gloves. The bare-knuckle era came to a close in 1889 when the boxing rules introduced in 1865 by John Sholto Douglas, 8th Marquis of Queensbury, were standardized.

Box Turtle, turtle native to United States and Mexico with a hinge across the undershell, enabling front and back portions to close completely against the upper shell. All species have domed shells. They are terrestrial and eat animal and vegetable matter. Length: 5–6in (127–153mm). Family Emydidae; genus *Terrapene. See also* Turtle.

Boyars, higher nobility of Russia until Peter the Great, who abolished the title. The most influential members belonged to a council that advised the tsar in affairs of state. During the medieval period, the boyars struggled to take power from the princes. In reaction, Ivan the Terrible attacked the boyars in the 16th century and confiscated their estates. By the 17th century their power had declined.

Boycott, attempt to change a policy or practice by refusing to deal with the originator of the policy. The term originated in 1880 when Irish tenant farmers refused to work for, supply, or speak with a man named Charles Boycott who was an agent of their landlord. A labor strike is technically a form of boycott. A *primary boycott* is directed against the party with whom the dispute exists; a *secondary boycott* is directed at a third party (eg, one of a manufacturer's suppliers) to get him to bring pressure on the first party. Secondary boycotts in labor disputes are illegal under the Taft-Hartley Act (1947).

Boyle, Richard, 1st Earl of Cork (1566–1643), English settler in Ireland. He settled in Ireland in 1588, acquiring vast estates including Walter Raleigh's (1602). Employing English settlers, he improved the land, built mills, established new towns, ironworks and other industries. In 1629 he was appointed a lord justice of Ireland and in 1631 he became Ireland's Lord high treasurer. Between 1633–41, he struggled with Thomas Wentworth, Earl of Strafford, lord deputy of Ireland, for influence at court and in Ireland. He finally triumphed over Strafford. Two of his sons were Robert Boyle, the scientist, and Roger Boyle, 1st Earl of Orrey.

Boyle, Robert (1627–91), English scientist, often regarded as the father of chemistry, and an advocate of the experimental approach to science. Working at Oxford, with Robert Hooke as his assistant, he made an efficient vacuum pump with which he was able to establish that the volume of a gas is inversely proportional to its pressure at a constant temperature. He freed experimental science from much alchemical superstition, introducing the modern concept of an element (which forms compounds). He worked to characterize acids and alkalies, and he showed the importance of air in sound propagation. After leaving Oxford he moved to London, becoming a founding fellow of the Royal Society.

Boyle's Law, the observation that the volume of a gas at constant temperature is inversely proportional to the pressure. First stated by Robert Boyle around 1660, the discovery was spurred by Boyle's invention of a vacuum pump allowing him to reduce pressures to levels never before achieved. Boyle's Law is a special case of the Ideal Gas Law: $pV = NkT$. *See also* Ideal Gas Law.

Boyne, Battle of the (1690), engagement that took place near Drogheda, Ireland, in which the forces of the Protestant William III defeated those of the Catholic James II.

Boyne River, river in E Republic of Ireland; rises in Bog of Allen in Kildare, and flows NNE through Meath into Irish Sea below Drogheda; scene of Battle of the Boyne (1690) fought 3mi (5km) W of Drogheda. Length: 70mi (113km).

Boy Scouts, a world-wide organization for boys which stresses outdoor knowledge and good citizenship and operates without racial, religious, political, or class distinction. The Boy Scouts are divided into community groups called troops, which are subdivided into patrols. Scouts can advance through several grades and can earn merit badges for proficiency in various activities. There are three classes of scouts; tenderfoot, first and second class. The Cub Scouts and Explorer Scouts are affiliated organizations for boys under 12 and for older teenagers (including girls) respectively. The organization was founded in Great Britain in 1908 by Sir Robert Baden-Powell. It was incorporated in the United States in 1910, and headed by James E. West, 1911–43. Its US publications include: *Boy's Life, Scouting Magazine,* and *Exploring Magazine.*

Boysenberry, perennial bramble, related to loganberries but hardier and more productive, having a larger, less acidic berry. Most berries are frozen and shipped, but some are eaten fresh, canned, or made into preserves. Family Rosaceae; genus *Rubus. See also* Loganberry.

Brabant, ancient duchy covering area in S Netherlands and N Belgium; independent in 12th century, became part of Netherlands in 19th century. Settled in 5th century by Franks.

Brachiopoda, or lamp shell, small animal phylum identified by two-valved shell, a stalk in some species, and a characteristic ciliated lophophore—a tentacle-like organ used for feeding. Similar in appearance to bivalve mollusks, the brachipod valves are dorsal and ventral rather than right and left. Reproduction is sexual. Among some 260 species are *Lingula* (oldest known animal genus) and *Terebratulina.*

Brachiosaurus, giant vegetarian sauropod dinosaur living in North America and E Africa during Jurassic times. It was unique, having larger forelimbs than hind limbs. This was probably a useful adaptation for standing in water with only its nostrils, on top of its head, above the surface. It was the heaviest of all dinosaurs. Weight: 80ton (72t). *See also* Sauropoda.

Bracken, or brake fern, weedy fern *(Pteridium aquilinum)* found in temperate and tropical areas throughout the world. It has a perennial black rootstock that extends underground and sends up 15-ft (4.-6m) fronds at intervals. The leaves are coarse, triangular, and used as fodder.

Bracket Fungus, or **Shelf Fungus,** any of a large family (Polyporaceae) of common arboreal fungi that have spore-bearing tubes under the cap. Bracket fungi are usually hard and leathery or woodlike and have no stems. They often cover old logs and their parasitic activity may kill living trees. Some are edible when young.

Bract, modified leaf found on a flower stalk or the flower base. Bracts are usually small and scalelike. In some species they are large and brightly colored as in the dogwood and poinsettia.

Braddock, Edward (1695–1755), British military commander. He was given command of all British forces in North America in 1755 against the French. He cut the first road westward from Cumberland, Md., through the Allegheny mountains. Leading a force to attack Ft. Duquesne (Pittsburgh, Pa.), he was mortally wounded during an ambush by French and Indians near Duquesne.

Bradford, William (1590–1657), colonial governor and signer of Mayflower Compact. A Pilgrim, he came to America on the Mayflower (1620), and was elected governor of Plymouth Colony (1621), serving almost continually until his death. He helped draw up a body of laws for the colony (1636) and provided firm leadership through difficult times. His *History of Plimoth Plantation, 1620–46,* is the basis for all accounts of the Plymouth Colony. *See also* Mayflower Compact; Pilgrims; Plymouth Colony.

Boxer

William Henry Bragg

Johannes Brahms

Bradford, city in N England, in Aire Valley, 9mi (14km) W of Leeds; former center of Yorkshire woolen industry. Industries: textiles and textile machinery. Pop. 460,600.

Bradley, Omar Nelson (1893–1981), US general, b. Clark, Mo. He graduated from the US Military Academy and later taught there. In World War II he commanded the II Corps in North Africa and the invasion of Sicily (1943), led the 1st Army in the Normandy invasion (1944), and took over the 12th Army Group in Germany (1944). After the war, he served as chief of staff of the US Army (1948–49) and was appointed first chairman of the joint chiefs (1949–53). He retired from the military in 1953.

Brady, Mathew B. (1823–96), pioneer US photographer, b. Warren co, N.Y. After studying daguerreotypy with Samuel F.B. Morse, he became the leading US portraitist of his day. President Lincoln was a frequent subject. Brady organized a staff of photographers to make a record of the Civil War when that conflict broke out. Much of his work is in the Library of Congress. He died alone and forgotten in a hospital charity ward.

Bradycardia, arrhythmic heartbeat defined by a pulse of less than 60 per minute. Sometimes associated with hemorrhaging, it is also common in healthy athletes.

Braganza, dynasty that ruled Portugal from 1640 until the monarchy was abolished in 1910; a collateral branch ruled as emperors of Brazil from 1822 to 1889. The dynasty was founded by the Duke of Braganza, who ruled (1640–56) as John IV. During the Napoleonic Wars, the royal family fled to Brazil, then a Portuguese colony. When Brazil declared its independence in 1822, it was ruled by Pedro I, the son of John VI of Portugal. The monarchy was overthrown in 1889.

Bragg, (Sir) William Henry (1862–1942), English physicist. With his son, William Lawrence, he worked on the determination of crystal structure by X-ray diffraction and was responsible for Bragg's law. He was awarded a Nobel Prize in 1915 jointly with his son.

Brahe, Tycho (1546–1601), Danish astronomer. Educated in law at Copenhagen and Leipzig, he became interested in astronomy and devoted himself to improving observational techniques, later building an observatory on the island of Ven (1576). The most accurate observer of his time, he discovered a nova (1572) and did much to advance the Copernican theory. His calculations were later used by Johannes Kepler.

Brahma, creator god in Hinduism. First mentioned in the *Brahmanas,* he is one of the three gods in the Trimurti. Although Brahma is equal to the gods Vishnu and Shiva, he has not been the object of a special devotional cult, and there is only one temple devoted to him, at Pushkar in India. *See also* Brahmanas.

Brahman, highest ranking hereditary group of the traditional Indian caste system. Their ancient function was as priests and religious leaders. Brahmans took their status from their seer progenitors who in Hindu belief gained supernatural powers through piety and learning.

Brahmanism, an Indian religion characterized by acceptance of the *Veda* as divine revelation. The *Brahmanas,* the major texts of this religion, are the ritualistic books comprising the greater portion of Vedic literature. As Brahmanism developed, the *Upanishads* became important texts also. With time, deities of post-Vedic origin were worshiped and the influence of Brahman priests diminished. A newer, popular form of

Brahmanism emerged. "Hinduism" is the customary term for this modern phase of development. *See also* Hinduism; Upanishads; Veda.

Brahmaputra, important river in SE Asia; rises as the Matsang River in N Himalayan Mts, Tibet; flows across SE Tibet as Tsangpo River; continues S to Assam, India, as the Dihang River. It becomes known as Brahmaputra from Sadiya S to Bangladesh where it joins the Jamuna River, sharing the Ganges Delta in the Bay of Bengal. Length: 1,800mi (2,900km); navigable for last 800mi (1,288km).

Brahms, Johannes (1833–1897), German romantic composer. Encouraged by his friends Robert and Clara Schumann, he began to earn his living as a composer at age 30. He followed classical models of form and was a master of contrapuntal harmony. He composed in all major musical forms except opera. Among his greatest works are the *German Requiem* (1868), the *Variations on a Theme of Haydn* (1873), the *Violin Concerto in D* (1878), and two piano concertos. His songs, including *Schicksalslied* (1868), and chamber music are also highly regarded. His first symphony did not appear until 1876, but was followed by three others. They are among the finest symphonies of the Romantic period. *See also* Romanticism in Music.

Braided Stream, an old riverbed that has gradually created a network or series of interconnected channels or braids. Or, a river fed by meltwater, carrying considerable suspended material from the parent glacier.

Braille, Louis (1809–52), French inventor of the Braille system of reading for the sightless, who was himself blinded at the age of three. While a scholar, and later a teacher, at the Institute of Blind Youth in Paris, Braille developed a system of embossed dots to enable the blind to read by touch. This was published first in 1829, and a more complete form appeared in 1837. In 1932, a form known as Standard English Braille became accepted for worldwide use.

Brain, principal structure of the central nervous system, composed primarily of neurons and their supporting cells. The human brain is about the size of two clenched fists held tightly together, and it is distinguishable by an extremely convoluted outer covering or cortex. The brain develops from a structure called the neural tube and when fully developed it retains hollow recesses (ventricles) to circulate cerebrospinal fluid. The cortex is an elaborate thickening at the front of the "tube"; a second thickening further back forms the cerebellum. The forward area, the forebrain, is followed by the midbrain and the hindbrain. These areas are covered by the cerebral cortex, which has identifiable features called lobes (frontal, temporal, parietal, and occipital), each of which is associated with one or more behaviors, eg, sight.

In addition to regulating observable behavior, the brain governs the organ systems of the body. It is now known that there is no one center in the brain for activity; brain functions are much more complex and usually involve many diffuse relationships. *See also* individual parts of the brain; Central Nervous System.

Brain Damage, term used to describe the cause of almost any loose set of symptoms, such as disturbances of speech or movement, which might have roots in injury to the brain. It is most often connected to children who exhibit physical or social symptoms of retardation. Causes may be related to delayed or incomplete brain development, brain trauma suffered during or after birth, psychiatric or social disturbances,

or diseases such as epilepsy. Treatment depends on accurate diagnosis. *See also* Cerebral Palsy; Epilepsy.

Brain Disorders, mental disturbances in which the central feature is an impairment of brain tissue function. They should be distinguished from functional, or psychogenic, mental disturbances in which the primary cause does not involve an impairment of brain function. Brain disorders are associated with impairment of memory, orientation, comprehension, and judgment, and also by shallowness of emotional expression. These symptoms may vary widely in severity depending mostly upon the extent of underlying brain impairment. Secondary personality changes are often observed in these disorders, depending upon such factors as the strength and type of personality and the amount of psychological and social stress present.

Organic brain disorders are divided into acute and chronic types depending upon the reversibility of the brain function disturbance. Acute disorders are temporary and generally the result of a disruption of brain function rather than the destruction of brain tissue, as in the chronic disorders. Acute brain disorders may be caused by such things as infection, drug or alcohol intoxication, and brain trauma. Chronic brain disorders include such things as congenital defects, hereditary diseases, senility, and brain damage. *See also* Brain Damage; Senility.

Brain Storage, in psychology, the capacity of the mind (brain) to store information (memories). The term is most often used in physiological theories of changes that occur in the brain when information is learned. *See also* Memory.

Brain Trust, group of advisors to Pres. Franklin D. Roosevelt. An unofficial cabinet, it was instrumental during the early years of the New Deal (1933–35) in developing social and economic policies. Prominent brain-trusters included Raymond Moley, Adolf A. Berle, Jr., and Rexford G. Tugwell.

Brainwashing, technique used to alter a person's basic beliefs and attitudes without the person's consent. Such techniques involve attempts to render a victim's beliefs so useless that he substitutes new values and beliefs for the old ones. Sometimes used against war or political prisoners, specific procedures have included removal from peer group, starvation and physical abuse, threats of death, and forced confessions and self-recriminations—all designed to make a captive dependent on his captors and receptive to new ideas. Acceptance of the new ideas is rewarded. Brainwashing has different effects on different individuals. A person's background may enable him to withstand substantial stress, as revealed by Korean War POWs. Religious cults have been accused of brainwashing adherents

Brain Waves, output of the electrical activity of selected areas of the brain. A brain-wave recording is called an electroencephalogram (EEG), which is taken by placing electrodes on the scalp, amplifying their output, and recording the result. Typical EEG patterns correspond to several activity or consciousness states; eg, alpha activity is registered by persons who are resting but conscious. This activity can be conditioned through positive reinforcement, with the reinforcer simply a light that goes on when alpha activity occurs.

Braking, Atmospheric, drag exerted on a vehicle as it reenters the earth's atmosphere and encounters increased air densities. This friction slows and heats the vehicle. Orbital calculations and materials design are influenced by this factor. It includes the concept of "skipping" into and out of the atmosphere repeatedly to slow down safely.

Bramante, Donato (1444–1514), Italian painter and architect. His Roman buildings, eg, Sta. Maria dele Pace and the circular Tempietto of S. Pietro, stand as classic examples of High Renaissance style. His most important work is the basilica of St. Peter's, Rome.

Brampton, town in S Ontario, Canada, 21mi (34km) NW of Toronto; seat of Peel co; noted for greenhouses; important dairy region. Industries: automobiles, optical goods, soap. Inc. 1873. Pop. 102,459.

Bran, skin or husk of grains of wheat, rye, or other cereal grasses. It is separated from the kernels and used for animal feed and for roughage in the human diet. *See also* Grass.

Branching, growth extension of vascular plants. A branch, developing from the stem, consists of the branchlet, previous year's growth, and the twig, new growth. The terminal bud at the twig end forms a new twig during the next growing season, as do lateral buds in leaf axils along the twig. Types of branching include: tillering—branches produced from the plant base (cereals and grasses); ex-current—single main shaft and smaller, lateral branches (conifers); deliquescent—spreading branches (deciduous trees); and columnar—unbranched stem (coconut and palms).

Brancusi, Constantin (1876–1957), French sculptor. His primitive style is revealed in a series of wooden sculptures begun in 1914, which include "Prodigal Son" (1914), "Sorceress" (1916), and "Chimera" (1918). In 1919, his controversial "Bird in Space" was not permitted to enter the United States as a work of art but instead was taxed on its value as raw metal. This decision was later reversed in a suit filed by Brancusi, and the sculpture is now housed in the Museum of Modern Art, New York City. Other works include "The Kiss" (1908), "Prometheus" (1911), "Sculpture for the Blind" (1924; Philadelphia Museum of Art), and "Flying Turtle" (1943).

Brandeis, Louis D(embitz) (1856–1941), US jurist and lawyer, b. Louisville, Ky. A Boston lawyer (1879–1916) known as the "people's attorney," he opposed high utility rates and railroad monopolies, supported wages-and-hours laws and inexpensive life insurance. An advisor to President Wilson, he was instrumental in creating the Federal Reserve Act (1913) and Clayton Anti-Trust Act (1914). His appointment as associate justice of the US Supreme Court (1916–39) aroused much criticism. The first Jew to sit on that court, he was noted for his dissents favoring civil liberties and social welfare legislation and for his use of sociological facts to support his opinion. His opinion in *Whitney* v. *California* (1927) is considered a milestone in the defense of unpopular expression.

Brandenburg, former state in NE Germany, now part of East Germany. It formed the nucleus for the kingdom of Prussia; Berlin and Potsdam are the chief cities. The March of Brandenburg, as it was called, was founded in 1134 by Albert I the Bear, who brought in settlers from the lower Rhineland. It came under the rule of the Hohenzollerns in 1411, and in 1417 Frederick I became the first elector of Brandenburg. Joachim II, who ruled 1535–71, converted to Lutheranism. Frederick William the Great Elector ruled 1640–88 and greatly increased its territory. His successor, Frederick II, became the first king of Prussia in 1701. *See also* Hohenzollern Dynasty.

Brandenburg, port city in central East Germany, on Havel River, 38mi (61km) SW of Berlin. Present city evolved from the 1715 union of a Wendish village founded in 1170 on S bank of Havel and a German settlement founded in 1196 on N bank. A third part of the town is on an island in the river and is the site of a 12th–14th-century cathedral. Industries: steel, tractors, textiles. Pop. 93,660.

Brando, Marlon (1924–), US film star, renowned for his "method" style of acting. His first major film success was in *A Streetcar Named Desire* (1951). Other notable films included *The Wild One* (1954), *On the Waterfront* (1954), *One-eyed Jacks* (1961), *Mutiny on the Bounty* (1962), *The Godfather* (1971), *Last Tango in Paris* (1972), *The Missouri Breaks* (1976), and *Apocalypse Now* (1979).

Brandt, Willy (1913–), German statesman, b. Herbert Frahm. A member of the Social Democratic party, he fled to Norway and then to Sweden during the Nazi reign. It was while in exile that he adopted Willy Brandt as a pseudonym. He returned to Germany after World War II and was elected mayor of West Berlin in 1957. In 1969 he became chancellor of West Germany. He initiated a program of cooperation with the Communist bloc nations. In 1971 he was awarded the Nobel Peace prize. He resigned in 1974 after a close aide was exposed as an East German spy. He headed the Independent Commission on International Development Issues (the Brandt Commission) (1977–).

Brant, Northern Hemisphere coastal bay marine goose with stocky, dark-colored body, white collar, and rump feathers. It feeds on roots and shellfish and nests in the far north, laying white eggs (3–5). Length: 2ft (0.6m); weight: 3lb (1.4kg). Genus *Branta*.

Brantford, city in SE Ontario, Canada, approx. 60mi (97km) SE of Toronto, on the Grand River; named for Mohawk Indian chief Joseph Brant who est the Six Nations of the Iroquois tribes here 1784, for which organization the city is still headquarters; home of Alexander Graham Bell. Industries: agricultural and construction equipment, machinery, truck bodies, lumber, paper, furniture. Pop. 66,950.

Braque, Georges (1882–1963), French painter, printmaker, and sculptor. He was a pioneer of modern art. His earliest work precurses cubism (*Large Nude, Landscape at L'Estague, Houses at L'Estague,* 1907–09). *Head of a Woman* (1909) and *Violin and Palette* (1909–10) are transitional works between early and analytic cubism, which influenced later modern art. Later he moved to collages, and after World War I his style became flatter and his color stronger (*The Table,* 1918). *Woman with a Mandolin* (1937) typifies his more diverse style of the 1930s and 40s, while *The Echo* (1956) shows the brighter colors of his later work. *See also* Cubism.

Brasília, capital of Brazil; city is in W central Brazil, 580mi (934km) NW of Rio de Janeiro. Constitution of 1891 referred to moving the capital inland from Rio de Janeiro, but it was not until 1956 that construction was begun; in 1957 city was laid out in shape of an airplane by Lúcio Costa, Brazilian architect; extremely modern public buildings were designed by Oscar Niemeyer. In 1960 the capital was formally moved; site of presidential palace, cathedral, university. Pop. 272,002.

Brass, an alloy of copper and zinc. Often small amounts of other metals, such as tin, are added to make the alloy more resistant to corrosion. Brass is yellow in color. It is used for plumbing and lighting fixtures, electrical fittings, and ornamental metalwork.

Brasses, type of gravestone consisting of an engraved, rectangular brass sheet mounted on a polished stone slab. A two-dimensional figure of the deceased was engraved on the brass against a hatched background. This form of funeral monument was introduced into Western Europe early in the 13th century, and the greatest number of brasses (over 7000) have survived in England. They are an important source of information on medieval English armor and costumes.

Brassica, genus of 40 species of plants, including mustard, cabbage, cauliflower, broccoli, and turnip. They have flower clusters at the plant top, long, beaded seedpods, and leaves with thick midribs. Charlock *(Brassica kaber)* is bristly with lobed leaves; height 1–2ft (30.5–61cm). Field Mustard *(B. rapa)* is a succulent plant with gray-green, lobed leaves; height: 24–32in (61–81.3cm). *B. japonica* is the source of edible mustard greens. Family Cruciferae.

Bratislava, city in S central Czechoslovakia, on W bank of Danube River, 30mi (48km) E of Vienna; capital of Slovakia, became part of Hungarian kingdom after 10th century, and part of Czechoslovakia in 1918. Now a shipping and manufacturing center, it has a pipeline carrying oil from USSR. Pop. 340,902.

Bratsk, city in E Siberian Russian SFSR, USSR; comprised of eight settlements separated by forests on the Angara River; site of enormous hydroelectric plant and ruins of Cossack watchtowers. Industries: metallurgy, cellulose, construction. Founded 1631 by Cossacks. Pop. 209,000.

Braun, Eva (1912–45), mistress of Adolf Hitler. A photographer's assistant, she met Hitler about 1936 and lived with him thereafter. So far as is known, she never exercised any political influence. She and Hitler were married in Berlin the day before they committed suicide together.

Braun, Wernher von. *See* Von Braun, Wernher.

Brave New World (1932), satiric novel by Aldous Huxley. The novel presents a future totalitarian society with technologically developed leisure industries, genetic manipulation, and sterile promiscuity.

Braxton, Carter (1736–97), a signer of the Declaration of Independence, b. Newington, Va. He furnished ships for the Revolutionary War, and was a member of the Continental Congress (1775–76; 1777–83; 1785) and also served in the Virginia Council of State (1786–91; 1794).

Brazil (Brasil), Federative Republic of, largest nation of South America and third-largest in the Western Hemisphere. A country of sophisticated cities and undeveloped rain forests, it lures tourists and fortune seekers in spite of economic and political difficulties.

Land and Economy. About 65% of Brazil is a high plateau of crystalline and stratified rocks sloping W toward the Paraguay River and N to the Amazon. The Amazon basin, covered with a thick rain forest, stretches along the equator and forms the major lowland. Near the Atlantic coast the Brazilian Highlands rise to more than 9,000ft (2,745m). The most N part of Brazil is in the Guiana Highlands. A wealth of minerals—iron ore, manganese, lead, gem stones, marble—waits to be extracted. About 60% of the people raise cereal grains or help on large ranches, and coffee and other plantations. Manufacturing has developed since WWII, although heavy machinery, fuels, and some other goods are imported. The government is implementing a controversial development program in the Amazonian Basin.

People. Some Indians of the Amazon and the high mountains maintain their heritage, but those of the central plateau have mixed with Europeans, as have descendants of blacks brought as slaves. Perhaps 60% of the people are of European, especially Portuguese, descent, and 35% have mixed blood. Portuguese is the major language, and more than 90% of the population is Roman Catholic. School expansion and adult education in the 1960s reduced illiteracy, but about 40% of the people still cannot read or write.

Government. Formally a republic with a president, Senate, and Chamber of Deputies, Brazil came under military control in 1964. In 1980 independent political parties were allowed to operate and, by 1985, the country was returned to civilian government.

History. The Portuguese claimed Brazil in 1500 and started settlements after 1530. During Europe's Napoleonic Wars the Portuguese royal family escaped to Rio de Janeiro. Some members remained to rule when peace returned to Europe and, to prevent local unrest, declared Brazil's independence in 1822. Dom Pedro II held the Brazilian throne for half a century. Turmoil following the abolition of slavery led to the Emperor's departure for Europe in 1889, when Brazil became a republic. Since then civil strife and political upheavals have alternated with short periods of stability. The military regime, although repressive, reduced political unrest. By the early 1980s, however, Brazil's dramatic economic growth had been replaced by a spiraling trade deficit, a yearly inflation rate exceeding 100%, and heavy dependence on imported oil. The return to civilian government in 1985 failed to halt Brazil's economic woes.

PROFILE

Official name: Federative Republic of Brazil
Area: 3,286,478sq mi (8,511,965sq km)
Population: 122,879,000
Chief cities: Brasília, the capital; São Paulo; Rio de Janeiro
Government: Military regime
Gross national product: $70,000,000,000
Per capita income: $700
Industries (major products): foodstuffs, textiles, lumber, paper, steel, chemicals, transportation equipment
Agriculture (major products): coffee, corn, wheat, cacao, tobacco, sugar cane, fruits
Minerals (major): iron ore, coal, silver, oil, gold
Trading partners: United States, European Common Market, Argentina, Venezuela, Japan

Brazil Current, warm current of S Atlantic Ocean; a branch of S Equatorial current; flows S along E coast of South America.

Brazilian Highlands, region in E Brazil, S of Guiana Highlands; landforms are separated by two river systems, the Paraná-Paraguay and the Amazon. The highest peak in Brazil, Pico da Bandeira, 9,482ft (2,892m), lies in the SE section.

Brazil Nut, seed of an evergreen South American tree found particularly along the Amazon River and Rio Negro. It has 2-ft (61-cm) leathery leaves and grows to 150ft(46m) tall. Cream yellow flowers produce a thick-walled fruit 4–6in (10.2–15.2cm) in diameter. Inside the fruit are 12–25 large, 3-sided seeds—the Brazil nut of commerce. Family Myrtaceae; species *Bertholletia excelsa.*

Brazing, process in which metallic parts are joined by the fusion of alloys that have lower melting points than the parts themselves. The filler material is either pre-placed or fed into the joint as the parts are heated.

Louis Brandeis

Brazil

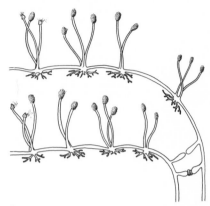

Bread mold

Brazed joints are highly reliable and used extensively in the rocket and aircraft industry.

Brazza, Pierre Paul François Camille Savorgnan de (1852–1905), French explorer, b. near Rome, Italy. He explored the Ogowe River in West Africa for the French government in the late 1870s and 1880s. He founded Brazzaville (Congo) and established a French protectorate over the kingdom of Makoko. From 1886–98 he was governor general of the French Congo.

Brazzaville, capital and largest city of the Republic of the Congo, Africa, on Stanley Pool on the Congo River; former capital of French Equatorial Africa (1910–1958); and a base of the Free French forces during WWII; a major port on the Congo River; connects by rail to the country's main seaport, Pointe-Noire. Industries: beverages, tanning, construction, textiles, tobacco. Founded 1880 by the French explorer Savorgnan de Brazza. Pop. 290,000.

Bread Mold, any of several hundred species of fungi (order Mucorales) found in soil and organic matter that have distinctive, usually black, spores. The familiar species, *Rhizopus nigricans,* forms a dense wooly growth on bread, fruits, and vegetables.

Breadroot, or Indian breadroot, perennial plant native to the prairies of W North America. It has an edible tuberous root, small oval leaves, and blue and whitish flower spikes. Height: to 1.5ft (46cm). Family Leguminosae; species *Psoralea esculenta.*

Breakbone Fever. See Dengue.

Breakspear, Nicholas. See Adrian IV.

Bream, freshwater minnow of E and N Europe. Fished commercially in the Baltic Sea region, its high-set body is black and silver. Length: 19.7–27.6in (50–70cm). Weight: 8.8–13.2lb (4–6kg). Family Cyprinidae; species *Abramis brama. See also* cichlid.

Breast, either of a pair of glandular organs that in the female produce and secrete milk to nourish newborn young. In the male they are rudimentary and nonfunctional. The human female breast, which develops during adolescence, is made up of about 20 irregularly shaped lobes separated by connective tissue and fat tissue. Lactiferous ducts lead from each lobe to the nipple, a small cone-shaped structure in the center of the breast, surrounded by an areola, a pigmented area that is pinkish before pregnancy, brownish after. *See also* Lactation.

Breastbone. See Sternum.

Breath Holding, a common response to stress in children under the age of four, associated with violent crying and temper tantrums. Since it produces a lack of oxygen, breath holding can lead to dizziness and fainting. Children rarely engage in breath holding after age six.

Breathing, or respiration, a two-stage process during which oxygen-laden air is drawn into the lungs by contraction of muscles of the chest wall which expand the lungs; upon relaxation, the lungs recoil, expelling carbon dioxide–laden air. *See also* Respiratory System. *See also* respiration.

Brébeuf, (Saint) Jean de (1593–1649), missionary and patron saint of Canada, b. France. Ordained a Jesuit in 1623, Brébeuf traveled extensively after 1625 among the Hurons of Georgian Bay and Lake Huron.

Caught between the British and Indians, he was tortured to death by the Iroquois. His translations from the Hurons are found in *The Jesuit Relations.* He was canonized in 1930.

Breccia, general term that describes a rock formed by the cementation of sharp-angled fragments in a matrix of a material that may be different from or similar to that of the fragments. Their origin varies. Some are formed in fault zones, some in talus slopes, and others are volcanic in origin.

Brecht, Bertolt (1898–1956), German dramatist, b. as Eugen Berthold Friedrich Brecht. Among his notable works, most depicting a world of struggle and suffering in a uniquely bittersweet manner, are: *In the Jungle of Cities* (1923), *Edward II* (1924), *A Man's a Man* (1926), *The Threepenny Opera* (with music by Kurt Weill, 1928), *The Rise and Fall of the City of Mahogonny* (with music by Kurt Weill, 1930), *St. Joan of the Stockyards* (1932), *The Seven Deadly Sins of the Petty Bourgeoisie* (with choreography by George Balanchine and music by Kurt Weill, 1933), *The Private Life of the Master Race* (1937), *Mother Courage and Her Children* (with music by Paul Dessau, 1941), *The Good Woman of Setzuan* (with music by Paul Dessau, 1943), *Galileo* (English version, 1947), *The Caucasian Chalk Circle* (1st version, with music by Paul Dessau, 1948), *Schweyk in the Second World War* (with music by Hans Eisler, 1956), and *The Resistible Rise of Arturo Ui* (published posthumously, 1957).

After Hitler came to power (1933), Brecht lived abroad, first in Scandinavia, then in the United States. After appearing under subpoena before the House Un-American Activities Committee (1947), he returned to Europe, first to Switzerland, then to East Berlin. There he directed the Berliner Ensemble and tested his dramatic theories, such as the *Verfremdungs-Effekt* (alienation or distancing effect, devices reminding the audience that the theater is not reality). His plays move from realism to expressionism in what he called epic theater, an attempt to merge social with aesthetic concerns.

Breckinridge, John Cabell (1821–75), US vice president, b. Lexington, Ky. He was a major in the Mexican War and a congressman (1851) until elected vice president under James Buchanan (1856). Defeated as a pro-slavery presidential candidate in 1860 by Abraham Lincoln, he became a Confederate general and secretary of war in Jefferson Davis' cabinet (1865).

Breda, city in S Netherlands, 14mi (23km) W of Tilburg, on Merk River; site of Compromise of Breda (1566) marking Dutch rebellion against Philip II of Spain and the Inquisition. Industries: fruit canning, textiles, machinery. Chartered 1252. Pop. 118,086.

Breeder Reactor, a nuclear fission reactor in which more fissile material is produced than is consumed. *See* Fission Reactor.

Breeding, changing or promoting certain genetic characteristics through careful selection and combination of the parent stock. Breeding may be a crossing or inbreeding to produce the desired type of offspring.

Breisgau, historic region in SW West Germany, E of the Rhine River and NE of Basel, Switzerland; region was held successively from Middle Ages by the Dukes of Zähringen, the counts of Kyberg and Urach, and the Hapsburgs; ceded to duchy at Baden 1810 and became part of state of Baden-Württemberg 1951. The region was autonomous and wealthy in 18th century, at which time its area was approx. 1,000sq mi (2,590sq km).

Bremen, port city in N West Germany on Weser River; capital of state of Bremen est. 1947; virtually independent until 18th century; part of French empire 1810–13; joined North German Confederation 1866; site of WWII naval base. Industries: food processing, beer, textiles, iron, steel, shipbuilding. Founded *c.* 782. Pop. 570,700.

Bremerhaven, seaport city in W Germany, on the N bank of Weser River as it flows into the North Sea; first regular ship service between United States and continental Europe was est. here 1847; West Germany's largest fishing port. Founded 1827; inc. 1851. Pop. 142,700.

Bremerton, city in W Washington, 15mi (24km) SW of Seattle, on Puget Sound; named for William Bremer who founded the townsite and est. the Puget Sound Naval shipyard, the most important industry in the city. Founded 1891; inc. 1901. Pop. (1980) 36,208.

Brennan, William J(oseph), Jr. (1906–), US jurist, b. Newark, N.J. A judge of the New Jersey Superior Court (1949–50) and the New Jersey Supreme Court (1952–56), he was appointed an ad interim associate justice of the US Supreme Court by Eisenhower in 1956. His appointment was confirmed by the Senate in March 1957. Considered a moderate liberal and a civil rights advocate, his opinion in *New York Times* v. *Sullivan* (1964) limited the scope of state libel laws. He also defended civil liberties in his opinions on the law of obscenity.

Brenner Pass, lowest of main Alpine passes, connecting Bolzano, Italy, with Innsbruck, Austria. The first road to traverse Alps was built across this pass 1772. During WWII, Hitler and Mussolini met here several times. Elevation: 4,495ft (1,371m). Length: 59mi (95km).

Brescia, city in N Italy; capital of Brescia prov. Sacked by Attila 452, it repeatedly changed rulers, passing to Austria 1814, and joining with Italy 1859. The city contains the Roman bronze *Winged Victory,* the 13th-century Broletto, and the Loggia (15th-16th century); transportation and agricultural center. Industries: firearms, vehicles, textiles. Pop. 215,260.

Brest, seaport city on Atlantic coast of France, near tip of Brittany; contains an excellent natural harbor and the chief French naval base on the Atlantic Ocean. During WWII, Germany had a huge submarine base here; site of a national engineering school. Industries: electronic equipment, clothing. Pop. 172,176.

Brest, formerly Brest-Litovsk; city in Belorussian (Belorusskaja) SSR, USSR; capital of Brest oblast; river transport center at confluence of Bug and Muchavec rivers; site of teachers college, signing of Polish Orthodox and Roman Catholic church union (1596). Founded 1017 by East Slavs; conquered 1241 by Mongols, 1319 by Lithuania; under Polish rule 1569; sacked by Swedes 1657; annexed by Russia 1795; under Polish rule 1919–39, then returned to Russia. Industries: food processing, lumbering, textiles. Pop. 167,000.

Brest-Litovsk, Treaty of (1918), peace treaty between Russia and Germany in World War I. The terms were harsh, and Russia had to give up its Baltic provinces and the Ukraine. Trotsky was against signing the treaty, but the Germans increased their offensive and, fearing the new Bolshevik state would be destroyed, Lenin accepted the terms. The treaty was annulled by the Soviets after Germany was defeated.

Bretigny, Treaty of (1360), diplomatic agreement between England and France. Edward III of England abandoned his claim to the French throne. In return his vast holdings in southwestern France were freed from French sovereignty. The treaty was soon broken on both sides, and the Hundred Years War resumed.

Breton, language spoken in Brittany, on the northwest coast of France. A Celtic language, it is most closely related to Welsh, the area where it was originally spoken. It is rapidly dying out in favor of French.

Bretton Woods Conference (1944), United Nations' Monetary and Financial Conference meeting at Bretton Woods, N.H. Representatives of the 44 United Nations agreed to establish the International Monetary Fund and the International Bank for Reconstruction and Development.

Breuer, Marcel (1902–81), US architect and designer, b. Hungary. He studied and taught at the Bauhaus from 1920 to 1928, during which time he designed his famous tubular steel chair. In 1937 he went to Harvard University to teach architecture. A leading exponent of the International style, he practiced with Walter Gropius (1938–41), combining Bauhaus internationalism with New England regionalism in several houses, including his own at Lincoln, Mass. (1939). He also designed the UNESCO Building, Paris (1953–58; with Pier Nervi and Bernard Zehrfuss), St. John's Abbey, Collegeville, Minn. (1953–61), the I.B.M. Research Center in La Gaude, France, and the Whitney Museum of American Art, New York City (completed 1966).

Brewing. *See* Fermentation.

Brewster, William (1567–1644), pilgrim religious leader, signatory of the Mayflower Compact. He withdrew from the Anglican church (1606) forming the Separatists, who, due to persecution, fled from England to Holland (1608), where they became known as Pilgrims. He returned to England to help organize the Pilgrim migration on the *Mayflower* 1620. He was a leader of the church at Plymouth and influential in management of the colony. *See also* Mayflower Compact.

Brezhnev, Leonid (1906–82), Soviet political leader. He was active in the Ukrainian Communist party after 1931, and in 1935 he graduated from the Dneprodzerzhinsk Metallurgical Institute as an engineer. He rose steadily in party posts, and in 1952 he became secretary to the central committee of the Soviet Communist party. In 1957 he became a member of the presidium (later politburo) of the central committee. He helped plan the downfall of Nikita Khrushchev in 1964 and soon emerged as one of the two chief rulers of the Soviet Union, sharing power with Alexei N. Kosygin. Brezhnev was named first secretary and Kosygin was premier. Brezhnev's power steadily eclipsed that of Kosygin, however, and by the late 1960s, Brezhnev was acknowledged as the sole ruler, although Kosygin remained as premier. Brezhnev's tenure in office was marked by a vigorous foreign policy. He became president in 1977. In 1968 he sent Soviet troops into Czechoslovakia to put down an uprising. That action caused him to enunciate the "Brezhnev doctrine," which stated the Soviet intention of intervening in the domestic affairs of any of the Soviet bloc countries if Communism became threatened there. He pursued a policy of détente with the West, particularly with the United States, and signed various treaties and trade agreements with the Western powers. At the same time he pursued an aggressive policy furthering Soviet—and Communist—interests in Africa and the Middle East. In 1979 he sent Soviet troops into Afghanistan and, in 1981, threatened intervention in Poland's internal affairs. Soviet relations with the Communist government of China continued to deteriorate under his leadership.

Brian Boru (926–1014), king of Ireland (1002–14). Originally a clan princeling in Munster, he unified all Ireland. He was murdered after winning a great victory over the Norse at Clontarf. Norse power in Ireland was destroyed forever, but Ireland fell into chaos with Brian Boru's death.

Briand, Aristide (1862–1932), French statesman. A lawyer, he entered the Chamber of Deputies (1902) as a Socialist and helped to draft the law (1905) for the separation of the Roman Catholic Church and the state. He first became premier in 1909–10 and was also premier in WWI (1915–17). An advocate of peace and internationalism, he was awarded the Nobel Peace prize (1926). As foreign minister 1925–32, he was the author of the Locarno Pact (1925) and the Kellogg-Briand Pact (1928). *See also* Kellogg-Briand Pact.

Briard, French sheep dog (working group) dating from at least 12th century. It has a long, wide head and muzzle; high-set, thick ears carried flat against the head or cropped; deep- and broad-chested body; strong-boned legs; and long tail carried with a crook at the end. The long coat is coarse and hard and can be any uniform color but white. Average size: 22–27in (56–68.5cm) at shoulder; 70–80lb (32–36.5kg). *See also* Working Dog.

Brick, any baked or fired, rectangular or prismatic, mass of clay used for construction. Sun dried brick was used 5000 years ago in Egypt and Babylonia. The modern US building brick measures 2¼ × 3¾ × 8in (5.7 × 9.5 × 20.3cm). It is made from ground clay in machines that either mold bricks or cut off an extruded section of stiff clay to make a complete brick. It is then conveyed into a continuously operating kiln.

Bridge, any structure providing a continual passage over a body of water, roadway, or valley for man, vehicles, pipelines or power transmission lines. Bridges are prehistoric in origin, the first probably being logs that fell across a desired path. Today, bridges come in a great variety of forms, depending upon span, function and area—moveable bridges, pontoon bridges, overpasses, causeways, aqueducts, suspension bridges and cantilever bridges.

Bridge, card game for four players with a regular deck. It is derived from whist and is one of the most popular card games in the English-speaking world. The game has several versions, but the most popular since 1925 is contract bridge. This version is, except for the scoring, the same as auction bridge, in which each player bids for the right to name trump. With the four players pairing off into partners, the entire deck is dealt (13 cards per player) and the bidding begins. After the bid is won, the partner of the player who won the bid lays his hand face up on the table. The bidder then plays off this hand and his own to try to win the number of tricks bid plus six other tricks. The cards rank from ace down to two; in bidding, suits rank spades, hearts, diamonds, and clubs. Cards must be played in order of suit, and then with trump.

Bridgeport, city in SW Connecticut, 17mi (27km) SW of New Haven, on Long Island Sound; port of entry and chief industrial city in Connecticut. Industries: electrical appliances, firearms, helicopters. Settled 1639, grew as a fishing community; inc. 1836. Pop. (1980) 142,546.

Bridger, James ("Jim") (1804–81), US fur trader, hunter, trapper, b. Richmond, Va. He discovered the Great Salt Lake (1824), South Pass through the Rockies, and the area now Yellowstone Park. In 1843 he built Fort Bridger in southwest Wyoming to supply the settlers traveling on the Oregon Trail. He helped plan stagecoach routes, scouted for the army against the Indians, and then in 1857 against the Mormons.

Bridges, Calvin Blackman (1889–1938), US geneticist, b. Schuyler Falls, N.Y. He helped to prove the chromosomal basis of heredity and sex. Work with Thomas Hunt Morgan on the fruit fly *(Drosophila)* proved that heritable variations were traced to observable changes in the chromosomes. These experiments resulted in the construction of "gene maps," which proved the chromosome theory of heredity.

Brie, historical region in N central France, E of Paris; in Middle Ages it comprised a county; located mainly in Seine-et-Marne dept., it is famous for vineyards and Brie cheese.

Brig, 18th-century development of the brigantine, slightly larger and with three to four sails on each of two main masts.

Brigantine, small, two-masted sailing ship appearing in the 17th century.

Brighton, city in S England, on the English Channel, 48mi (77km) S of London; popular holiday resort. City was popularized in the 19th century when the Prince Regent's royal pavilion was rebuilt here (1817). Pop. 159,000.

Brigid, Saint (453–523), Irish holy woman. The city of Kildare, according to legend, takes its name from Saint Brigid's cell, which she established in an oak tree, hence Kil-dara, "the church of the oak." She is said to have performed numerous miracles and is recognized as one of the patron saints of Ireland.

Brindisi, city in S Italy; capital of Brindisi prov.; a Roman naval station; Virgil died here 19 BC. Conquered by Normans 1071; one of major embarkation ports for Crusaders; site of Roman column marking terminus of Appian Way, and medieval castle of Frederick II; commercial center. Industries: food processing, chemicals, wine. Pop. 80,357.

Brine Shrimp, small branchiopod crustacean related to fairy shrimp and found in salt lakes throughout the world. It can live in high concentrations of brine and swims belly-up. It has no carapace and has stalked, compound eyes and a long tail. Length: 0.5in (13mm). *See also* Crustacean; Fairy Shrimp.

Brisbane, (Sir) Thomas Makdougall (1773–1860), British astronomer and colonial administrator. He served in the British army for many years. He was governor of New South Wales (1821–25) in Australia, there establishing an observatory near Sydney in 1822. He founded another observatory in Scotland in 1841. Brisbane, Australia, is named for him.

Brisbane, seaport city in E Australia, on the Brisbane River; capital of Queensland state; site of Renaissance-style Parliament House (1869), University of Queensland (1909); major shipping and rail center. Exports: wool, meat, sugar, coal. Industries: oil refineries, food processing, textiles, shipbuilding, automotive assembly. Settled 1824 as a penal colony; became capital in 1859. Pop. 703,000.

Bristol, city in SW England, on the River Avon, 7mi (11km) from mouth of Bristol channel; important seaport since the 12th century; site of Brunel's Clifton Suspension Bridge (1845), crossing the Avon NW of Bristol. Imports: wine, fruit, grain, tobacco. Industries: aircraft, footwear, tobacco, chocolate, chemical products. Pop. 425,203.

Bristol, industrial city in N Connecticut, 15mi (24km) SW of Hartford; site of American Clock and Watch Museum. Industries: clock-making, tools. Settled 1727; inc. 1911. Pop. (1980) 57,370.

Britain, Battle of (August-October, 1940), the German air offensive against Britain. Saturation bombing of military installations, factories and land and sea transportation sites by the Luftwaffe was to be a prelude to a German invasion. Britain resisted valiantly, destroying over 1500 German bombers, and invasion plans were abandoned.

Britannia Metal, alloy primarily of tin (94%) with a small amount of copper (1%) and antimony (5%). Britannia metal is silver white in color and similar to pewter and is used widely in making domestic tableware, such as silverware, teapots, and other items.

British Columbia, prov. in W Canada, on the Pacific Ocean, bordered on the S by the states of Washington, Idaho, and Montana, and in the extreme NW by the state of Alaska.

Land and Economy. British Columbia is mountainous; many ranges of the Rocky Mts run S to N, with deep river valleys among them. The Pacific coastline is broken by inlets with hundreds of islands, of which Vancouver Island in the SW is the most important. Vast forests cover much of the country and yield the timber that is a mainstay of the economy. Commercial fishing is a major industry along the coast. Manufacturing is centered in the cities of the SW; agriculture is largely confined to the valleys. The mountain and coast scenery attracts a profitable tourist trade.

People. The cities of the S and the S end of Vancouver Island contain more than 70% of the pop. The majority came from other Canadian provinces, and trace their origins primarily to the British Isles.

Education. There are three universities supported by the prov.—the University of British Columbia, at Vancouver; Simon Fraser University at Burnaby, a Vancouver suburb; and the University of Victoria. Notre Dame University at Nelson is a Roman Catholic institution.

History. Capt. James Cook of Britain landed on the coast in 1778. Russians and Spaniards sought to exploit the fur trade, and in 1794 the British government sent Capt. George Vancouver to take possession of the land. Other British explorers pushed W from Canada, and the region came to be called New Caledonia. In 1846, the S boundary with the United States was fixed, and in 1849 Vancouver Island became a British colony. It was united with New Caledonia as British Columbia in 1866, and became a province of Canada in 1871. Although the first transcontinental railroad was completed in 1885, the province encountered economic difficulties during the early 20th century. With the discovery of oil and natural gas in 1951, rapid development took place, and British Columbia is now one of Canada's wealthiest provinces.

PROFILE

Admitted to confederation: July 20, 1871; rank, 6th
National Parliament representatives: Senate, 6; House of Commons, 23
Population: 2,562,600
Capital: Victoria, 62,551
Chief cities: Vancouver, 396,563; Victoria; New Westminster, 38,393

Leonid Brezhnev

Benjamin Britten

Louis Victor de Broglie

Provincial legislature: Legislative Assembly, 55 members
Area: 366,255sq mi (948,600sq km); rank, 3rd
Elevation: Highest, 15,300ft (4,663m), Mt Fairweather; lowest, sea level
Industries (major products): lumber, paper and pulp, processed foods
Agriculture (major products): cattle, poultry, vegetables, fruits
Minerals (major): copper, asbestos, coal, gold, silver, lead, zinc
Floral emblem: flowering dogwood

British Empire, overseas territories ruled by Great Britain. The empire originated in the late 16th century with the commercial activities of the chartered companies, eg, the British East India Company. *The First Empire.* Commercial ventures (sugar and tobacco plantations), missionary activities, and slave trading led to creation of British colonies in the Caribbean and N America in the 17th century. Loss of thirteen American colonies led to the demise of the First Empire (1783) and transfer of control of the colonies from the crown to Parliament. *The Second Empire.* British expansion was renewed in the 19th century and colonies were acquired in the Far East, Australia, Africa, and elsewhere. By World War I, the empire included about one-fourth of the world's pop. and land surface. A trend toward self-government ultimately resulted in independence for most colonies and the formation of the Commonwealth of Nations. *See also* Commonwealth of Nations.

British Indian Ocean Territory, island colony in Indian Ocean, composed of Chagos Archipelago, Farquhar Atoll, Desroches Island, Aldabra Islands; est. 1965 by Britain in an effort to remain in a strategic position between Africa and Asia. Industries: coconuts, fishing. Area: 31sq mi (80sq km). Pop. 560.

British Isles. *See* Great Britain.

British Museum, national repository, London, established by an Act of Parliament as a storehouse of knowledge for the benefit of the "learned and curious." It was opened in 1759. Its original purpose was historical and scientific rather than aesthetic. The nucleus of the original collection was donated by Sir Hans Sloane in 1753. Later additions included the Rosetta Stone and the Phrygian and Elgin Marbles. The Museum includes the National Museum of Archaeology, the Department of Ethnology, the Museum of Natural History, and the Department of Prints and Drawings, which houses an album of Dürer's drawings, works by Rembrandt and Rubens, a sketchbook by Bellini, 20 drawings by Michelangelo, and 20,000 drawings by Turner.

British North America Act (1867), legislation of the British parliament creating the Dominion of Canada from the provinces of Nova Scotia, New Brunswick, and Canada. The act provided for a constitution, a bicameral parliament, the reestablishment of Ontario and Quebec as separate provinces, and a legal system for Canada. Education and property law were left to the provinces, with the central government to control foreign policy and criminal law.

British Somaliland, British protectorate in E Africa. Formed in 1884–87, it was united with Italian Somaliland as the independent state of Somali in 1960.

British Thermal Unit (BTU), the amount of heat energy necessary to raise the temperature of a pound of water from 63°F to 64°F. One BTU is the equivalent of 778.3 foot-pounds, 252 calories, or 1055 joules.

British West Indies, those islands in the West Indies, between the Caribbean Sea (W), Gulf of Mexico (NW), and Atlantic Ocean (E), that do not have independent status and are associated with the United Kingdom. The five dependent territories are the British Virgin Islands, Cayman Island, Montserrat, Anguilla, and Turks and Caicos Islands. St. Kitts-Nevis is an Associated State with internal self-government, while the United Kingdom retains control over defense and foreign affairs. In 1958, ten British territories formed the West Indies Federation; it dissolved in 1962 and its former members began seeking independence separately.

Brittany (Bretagne), region and former prov. in NW France, jutting into Atlantic Ocean and bounded on N by English Channel. Prehistoric megaliths (huge stones) indicate an ancient race may have inhabited the area *c.* 2500–1800BC; earliest known people were Celts from British Isles (*c.* 8th century BC.). Romans conquered the area 56BC, withdrew in the 5th and 6th centuries. From 10th century Brittany was involved in a series of battles with England or France until 1532 when it became part of France. Industries: tourism, fishing, farming, orchards.

Brittany Spaniel, gun dog (sporting group) bred in France; of ancient lineage; first tailless specimen bred about 100 years ago. This rugged but graceful dog has a medium-length head and muzzle, tapering to a fawn, tan, or pink nose. The short, leafy ears are set high and lie flat; legs are long and graceful; and the tail, when present, is docked. The dense, flat coat is dark orange and white and lightly feathered on the legs. Average size: 17.5–20.5in (44.5–52cm) high at shoulder; 30–40lb (13.5–18kg). *See also* Sporting Dog.

Britten, Benjamin (1913–76), English composer. Although he composed in all forms, Britten was primarily known for his operas, which rank him as the foremost English opera composer of the 20th century. His operas include *Peter Grimes* (1945), *The Rape of Lucretia* (1946), *Albert Herring* (1947), *A Midsummer Night's Dream* (1960), and *Death in Venice* (1973). His most popular nonoperatic work was the *Young Person's Guide to the Orchestra* (1946), a set of variations displaying the different sounds of the orchestra.

Brittle Star, or serpent star, marine echinoderm with small central disc body and long, sinuous arms, which break off easily and are reproduced by regeneration. Class Ophiuroidea; species include phosphorescent *Amphipholis* and a small *Ophiactis.*

Brno (Brunn), city in central Czechoslovakia, 115mi (185km) SE of Prague; site of Gothic Cathedral of St Paul and 13th-century castle; scene of a yearly international trade fair. Industries: armaments, machinery. Founded 10th century. Pop. 335,918.

Broadbill, stocky, brightly colored bird of tropical Africa and Asia. With a flattened bill, short neck and legs, and strong feet, it feeds mainly on insects and other small animals. The female lays spotted white eggs (2–4) in a woven root-and-grass nest suspended over water. Length: 5–11in (12–28cm). Family Eurylaimidae.

Broadside, single sheet of paper printed on one side. Popular ballads of the 16th and 17th centuries were printed on broadsides for sale in public places where they were also sung or recited.

Broccoli, variety of cauliflower with large, lobed leaves and thick stems. Tiny green or purple flowers form 9-in (23-cm) compact heads that are eaten. It

matures in 60–70 days. Family Cruciferae; species *Brassica oleracea.*

Brocket Deer, or càriacu, small deer ranging from S Mexico to Paraguay. Stout with slender limbs and an arched back, they are timid and live alone or in pairs in wooded areas. Their antlers are usually simple spikes. Length: to 3ft (91cm); weight: to 46lb (21kg). Family Cervidae; genus *Mazama;* There are 10 species.

Brockton, city in E Massachusetts; historic museum, junior college. Industries: shoes, textiles, machinery. Settled *c.* 1700, it was part of Bridgewater until 1821; inc. 1881. Pop. (1980) 95,172.

Broglie, (Prince) Louis Victor de (1892–), French physicist. He became professor of physics at the University of Paris. He is responsible for the concept that all elementary particles have an associated wave and for the formula that predicts this wavelength. With Erwin Schrödinger he later developed the form of quantum mechanics called wave mechanics, for which he was awarded a Nobel Prize in 1929.

Broglie Family, French noble family. They were naturalized French subjects originating from Italy. The Broglies had distinguished military careers in Louis XIV's armies and the diplomatic corps. **François Marie II** (1671–1745), 1st Duc de Broglie, led Louis XIV's armies in Flanders, Germany, Italy. He was made marshall of France (1734). **Victor** (1785–1870), 3rd Duc de Broglie, was a distinguished statesman, serving as minister of the interior and foreign affairs and president of the council (1835).

Bromeliad, any of 2,000 species of tropical American plants of the family Bromeliaceae (order Bromeliales); some of which are epiphytic, some terrestrial herbs, some subshrubs. All have basal leaves and flowers in dense spikes, panicles, or heads with large bracts. Most familiar of the family are the pineapple (*Ananas comosus*) and Spanish moss (*Tillandsia usneoides*).

Bromide, salt of hydrobromic acid, or an organic compound containing bromide. The bromides of ammonium, sodium, potassium, and certain other metals are used medically as sedatives. Silver bromide is light-sensitive and is used in photography.

Bromine, nonmetallic element (symbol Br) of the halogen group, first isolated in 1826. It is extracted by treating sea water or natural brines with chlorine. The element is a red-brown volatile liquid used in making a range of commercially useful compounds. Chemically it resembles chlorine but is less reactive. Properties: at. no. 35; at. wt. 79.904; sp. gr. 3.12; melt. pt. 19.04°F (−7.2°C); boil. pt. 137.8°F (58.78°C); most common isotope Br^{79} (50.54%). *See also* Halogen Elements.

Bronchi (sing. **Bronchus**), the two branches into which the trachea (windpipe) divides, with one branch leading to each lung. The bronchi divide treelike into smaller and smaller branches, called bronchioles, as they spread through the lung. They eventually open into the lung's air sacs and alveoli where the gases of air and blood are exchanged. *See also* Lungs.

Bronchiectasis, enlargement of one or more bronchial tubes usually resulting from bronchitis or tuberculosis. Symptoms are coughing and copious expectoration.

Bronchitis, inflammation of the bronchial tubes caused most frequently by irritation of the lungs from chemicals or pollutants or by disease. Symptoms include coughing and expectoration of mucus. Medication relieves symptoms; a warm, dry climate improves the condition.

Brontë, Anne (1820–49), English novelist. The youngest of the Brontë sisters, she became a governess, an experience reflected in *Agnes Grey* (1847). Her other novel is *The Tenant of Wildfell Hall* (1848).

Brontë, Charlotte (1816–55), English novelist. Her personal life was unhappy. She was born into genteel poverty; her mother, four sisters, (two of them, Emily and Anne, also novelists), and dissolute brother died early; her love for a married man was unrequited; she died in childbirth within a year of her marriage. Her four novels—*The Professor* (written 1846, published 1857), *Jane Eyre* (1847), *Shirley* (1849), and *Villette* (1853)—are works of remarkable passion and imagination. *See also* Jane Eyre.

Brontë, Emily (1818–48), English novelist and poet. She was the sister of Charlotte and Anne Brontë, also novelists. Her love for her native Yorkshire moors and her insight into human passion are manifested in her poetry and in her only novel, *Wuthering Heights* (1847).

Brontosaurus, or Apatosaurus, best-known of huge North American sauropods of Jurassic times (136–190 million years ago). Supported on four elephantine limbs and bearing a long neck and tail, this giant had a small head with feeble, peglike teeth that probably served for shoveling in soft, aquatic vegetation. Length: 80ft (24m); weight: over 40 tons. *See also* Sauropoda.

Bronx, The, residential borough of New York City, N.Y., on S end of a peninsula bordered by the Hudson River (W), Harlem River (SW), East River (S), Long Island Sound (E); connected to boroughs of Manhattan and Queens by a network of bridges. Site of numerous educational institutions, the Bronx Zoo, and Yankee Stadium. Founded by Jonas Bronck for the Dutch West India Co. 1641. Inc. as part of New York City 1898. Pop. (1980) 1,169,115.

Bronze, traditionally an alloy of copper and tin containing no more than 33% tin. It has long been used in art for sculpting. Other substances are often added, such as aluminum (aircraft parts, tubing), silicon (marine hardware, chemical equipment) and phosphor (springs, electrical parts). Bronze is noted for its strength, hardness, resistance to corrosion, and malleability.

Bronze Age, period from the early fourth millennium BC onward, in which man learned to make bronze artifacts and to use the wheel and the ox-drawn plow. The resulting growth of technology and trade occasioned the rise of the first civilizations in Sumer and Egypt. *See also* Iron Age.

Bronze Sculpture, sculpture of bronze. Bronze is strong, enduring, and has great tensile strength, a desirable property in sculpture, making possible free extension or protrusion of unsupported parts of a figure and permitting a large mass to be balanced on a narrow base. Bronze can convey the effect of plastic (modeling), glyptic (carving), or toreutic (metalworking), depending upon the nature of the original. For example, Renaissance and modern bronzes reflect a plastic technique because they are cast from originals modeled in clay. Early Greek bronzes reflect a glyptic technique because their originals were carved wood.

There are two main types of cast objects, solid and hollow. In primitive cultures solid casts were used, but this is only effective for small objects. The invention of hollow casting allowed for the production of monumental works, lighter in weight, and for free-standing parts to be cast separately and then assembled. In solid casting a model of the object is executed in wax, which is then coated with clay. Firing hardens the clay mold and melts the wax model, which flows out. Molten bronze, which is poured into the mold, cools, and when the clay mold is broken, the bronze cast is free. The cast is then perfected by chasing, reworking small details, and polishing. There are two methods of hollow casting: the *cire-perdue* or "lost-wax" process and sand casting. The former is used for art; the latter, primarily in industry and for small pieces of large works. In the *cire-perdue* method, the wax model must be hollow, so it is produced on a core of clay. The clay core is attached to an outer clay mold by iron bars so it remains in place when the wax model is melted out. The space once occupied by wax is now filled with molten bronze. Large casts are made in pieces and attached later. The final removal and reworking is the same as for solid casts. Cellini used the original model to make an intermediate plaster mold that could be used to make many wax models. Thus many reproductions or replicas could be made from one model.

When bronze is exposed to air it develops a patina, a hard protecting surface. A natural patina, taking

many years, forms from copper carbonate (light greenish) or copper sulfate (brownish black). Often an artificial patina is produced by the sculptor. Bronze casting is extremely old, going back to the third millennium BC and bronze has been a popular medium for art throughout history. Some master bronze sculptors include Donatello, Ghiberti, Cellini, Verrocchio, Rodin, Epstein, Brancusi, and Lipchitz. Chinese and Japanese bronzes are equally noteworthy.

Brooke, Rupert (Chawner) (1887–1915), English poet. The patriotism of his early war poems and his good looks made him a contemporary legend, though both his criticism and poetry suggest a more complex personality than the naïve hero. He died on a hospital ship without having experienced actual warfare.

Brookeborough, Basil Stanlake Brooke, 1st Viscount (1888–1973), prime minister of Northern Ireland (1943–63). He was elected to the Northern Ireland Parliament (1929) and served as provincial minister of agriculture (1933–41) and of commerce (1941–45) before becoming prime minister. He developed the economy and improved relations with the Republic of Ireland, although he was an uncompromising supporter of Northern Ireland's inclusion in Great Britain.

Brook Farm, utopian community, founded 1841 in W Roxbury, Mass. Led by George Ripley, a former Unitarian minister, members tried to combine thinking with working and to give equal pay to all; many famous people of the time participated, including Nathaniel Hawthorne, Charles Dana, Ralph Waldo Emerson; experiment was abandoned in 1847 due to unproductive land and lack of water power for industries. Original farm started with 15 members, 200 acres (81 hectares), and 4 buildings; site is now marked by a bronze plaque.

Brookline, residential town in E Massachusetts; suburb of Boston; birthplace of President John F. Kennedy, now a national historic site; site of antique auto museum and Hebrew College. Settled 1630s; inc. 1705. Pop. (1980) 55,062.

Brooklyn, borough of New York City, New York; seat of and coextensive with Kings co, in SW extremity of Long Island; separated by East River from Manhattan, to which it is connected by the Brooklyn (1883), Manhattan (1909), and Williamsburg (1903) bridges; subway tunnels, and the vehicular Brooklyn-Battery Tunnel; it is connected to Staten Island by the Verrazano-Narrows Bridge (1964). Brooklyn was scene of Revolutionary War Battle of Long Island during which British Tories defeated the patriots and gained control of Long Island, Aug. 27, 1776. The borough is the site of Brooklyn College (1930), Packer Collegiate Institute (1845), Pratt Institute (1887), Long Island University (1926), St Francis College (1858), St Joseph's College for Women (1916), New York City Community College of Applied Arts and Sciences (1946), Kingsborough Community College (1963), Prospect Park, Marine Park, and Coney Island. Industries: shipbuilding, brewing, paint, varnish, building equipment. First sighted 1524 by Giovanni da Verrazano, Florentine navigator; founded by Dutch and Walloons (1636–37). First settlement in 1645 was called Breuckelen; inc. as village 1816, as city 1834; became borough 1898. Area: 71sq mi (184sq km). Pop. (1980) 2,230,936.

Brooks Range, mountain range across N Alaska, from Kotzebue Sound to the border of Canada; separates Arctic Ocean coastal plain from the Yukon basin; barren, rugged, uninhabited. Highest peak is Mt Michelson 9,239ft (2,818m).

Brook Trout. See Char.

Broomcorn, cultivated variety of sorghum. The tall grass panides are used for brooms and brushes. *See also* Sorghum.

Brothers Karamazov, The (1879–80), psychological novel by Fyodor Dostoevski, about Fyodor Karamazov and his four sons; Dimitri, a good-for-nothing, Ivan, an atheistic intellectual, Alyosha, who is studying for the priesthood under the elder, Zossima, and the illegitimate Smerdyakov, an epileptic. Their relationships become increasingly complex—Fyodor and Dimitri both love Grushenka, while Ivan loves Dimitri's betrothed, Katerina. The drama lies in the murder of the father by the sons, symbolizing man's revolt against his heavenly father.

Brougham, Henry Peter, 1st Baron Brougham and Vaux (1778–1868), British political figure, b. Scotland. In the House of Commons (1810–12, 1815–30) he fought for press freedom, the abolition of slavery, legal reform, and public education. As chancellor (1830–34), he reformed legal procedure and helped pass the Re-

form Act (1832). He was a founder of the University of London (1828) and designed the brougham carriage.

Brouwer, Adriaen (c. 1605–38), Flemish painter. Influential in the development of Dutch and Flemish painting, he is noted for his depictions of peasant life and for his humorous treatment of figures sleeping, drinking, smoking, and fighting (eg, *The Smokers,* Metropolitan Museum of Art, New York City).

Brown, Edmund Gerald, Jr. (Jerry) (1938–), b. San Francisco, Calif. After graduating from Yale University Law School in 1964, he became involved in Democratic politics. He was elected California's secretary of state in 1970 and became governor of California in 1975. Brown ran unsuccessfully for the Democratic presidential nomination in 1976 and 1980 and for the U.S. Senate in 1982.

Brown, John (1800–59), US anti-slavery crusader, b. Torrington, Conn. He led the Pottawatomie Massacre (1856) in Kansas in which five alleged slaveowners were killed. In an attempt to provoke a slave rebellion in Virginia he raided a government arsenal at Harper's Ferry in October 1859, but he was captured by a company of marines commanded by Robert E. Lee. After being tried for insurrection, treason, and murder, he was convicted and hanged at Charlestown (now in W. Va.) on Dec. 2, 1859.

Brown, Lancelot "Capability" (1715–83), English landscape gardener who revolutionized garden and parkland layout in the 1700s. He designed or remodelled nearly 150 estates, including gardens at Blenheim and Kew. He worked to achieve casual effects, with scattered groups of trees and gently rolling hills. He earned his nickname from a habit of saying that a place had "capabilities of improvement".

Brown, Robert (1773–1858), Scottish botanist. He went on an expedition to Australia (1801–05) and returned to England with valuable botanical collections. He described the flora of Australia in *Prodomus florae Novae Hollandiae et Insulae Van Diemen* (1810), a classic of systematic botany. In 1831 he described and named the nucleus of the plant cell, one of his pioneering observations. He is best known for establishing, in *A Brief Account of Microscopical Observations* (1829), that minute particles suspended in a liquid or gas are continuously in motion. This movement has since been called "Brownian movement." *See also* Brownian Movement.

Brown Algae, a group of almost exclusively marine algae (division Phaeophyta) that includes the largest seaweeds, the kelps, some of which are more than 150ft (46m) long. Like familiar higher plants but unlike most other algae, brown algae have complex structures including rootlike holdfasts to anchor them to the ocean floor; air-filled bladders to help them float; and other organs resembling stems and leaves.

Brown Bear, brown colored bears including the grizzly and Alaskan brown, or Kodiak, bears. Originally found in most of Eurasia and W North America, they are now rare except in Alaska and Canada. The largest of all bears, some are carnivores, some herbivores, and some omnivores. Length: over 8ft (2.4m); weight: 300–1,715lb (135–772kg). Species *Ursus arctos. See also* Bear.

Brownian Movement, rapid and random movement of particles suspended in a fluid, observable up to a particle size of 3×10^{-3}mm, caused by the thermal kinetic energy of its environment. The diffusion of pollutants through the atmosphere, and the movement of "holes" (minute regions of positive electrical charge) through a semiconductor are examples.

Browning, Elizabeth Barrett (1806–61), English poet. The wife of Robert Browning, she lived in Florence from 1847. She began writing poetry at an early age. *The Battle of Marathon* was published privately in 1820 and was followed by *The Seraphim and Other Poems* (1838) and *A Drama of Exile* (1845). The 1850 edition of her poetry included *Sonnets from the Portuguese. Aurora Leigh* (1856) was her last important poem.

Browning, Robert (1812–89), English poet. He is noted for his use of the dramatic monologue, as in "My Last Duchess" and "Soliloquy of the Spanish Cloister," both published in *Bells and Pomegranates* (1846). While living in London (1832–46), he wrote the volumes *Paracelsus* (1835), *Sordello* (1840), and other works as well as *Bells and Pomegranates*, a collection that also includes the narrative poem "Pippa Passes" and the dramatic lyric "Home Thoughts from Abroad." In 1846 he married Elizabeth Barrett and moved to Italy, where he lived until she died in 1861. While there he published the volumes *Christmas-Eve and Easter Day* (1854) and *Men and Women* (1855), which includes

Brooklyn Museum

John Brown

Brown bear

"Love Among the Ruins" and "Fra Lippo Lippi." Returning to London, he became popular with *Dramatis Personae* (1864) and *The Ring and the Book* (1864–69), a series of dramatic dialogues that many consider his masterpiece. His later works include *Dramatic Idyls* (2 vols., 1879–80).

Brown Rot, any of various chiefly fungal plant diseases characterized by decay and browning of tissues. The worst cause of brown rot is the fungus *Monilivia fructicola,* which attacks peaches and other stone fruits after harvesting.

Brown Snake, wide-ranging North American Secretive snake. Dekay's snake of NE United States lives in moist woods, swamps, and city parks and lots. Brownish with two parallel rows of black spots down its back, its young have a yellow collar. Length: to 13in (33cm). Family Colubridae; species *Storeria dekayi. See also* Snake.

Brownsville, port city in S Texas, 25mi (40km) W of Gulf of Mexico; seat of Cameron co; est. as a military post by Gen. Zachary Taylor, who named it Fort Brown for Major Jacob Brown. Industries: food processing, chemicals, fishing. Founded 1846. Pop. (1980) 84,997.

Brown Swiss, rugged breed of dairy cattle originally from the mountains of Switzerland. Found in the United States, they are more common in Italy, Austria, and Hungary. Brown, they sometimes have a gray stripe along the back. They produce more milk than Ayrshires but the butterfat content is the same. One of the oldest breeds, it was once also used for meat and as a draft animal. *See also* Dairy Cattle.

Brown-tail Moth, tussock moth caterpillar that is a serious pest of many fruit and deciduous shade trees, especially in the New England states, New Brunswick, and Nova Scotia. It is dark brown and hairy, with tufts of white hairs along each side. Length: 1.5in (38mm). Species *Nygmia Phaeorrhoea.*

Brown v. Board of Education (of Topeka) (1954), landmark US Supreme Court decision that overturned the "separate but equal" doctrine of public education established in *Plessy v. Ferguson* (1896). The court, led by Chief Justice Earl Warren, declared that racial segregation in schools "deprived the children of the minority group of equal educational opportunities" and found separate facilities to be "inherently unequal" and in violation of the Constitution's equal protection clause. This decision gave impetus to the later civil rights movement of the 1960s.

Brown v. Board of Education (1955), US Supreme Court decision that sought to implement the desegregation ruling of *Brown v. Board of Education of Topeka* (1954). The court declared that local courts had to fashion equitable remedies to fit local circumstances and instructed them to do so "with all deliberate speed." *See also* Brown v. Board of Education of Topeka (1954).

Broz, Josip. *See* Tito.

Bruce, Blanche Kelso (1841–98), US political figure, b. Farmville, Va. He was a US Senator from Mississippi (1875–81), the first black to serve a full term. He fought for the civil rights of blacks, Indians, and Asians in the United States and served as Register of the Treasury Department (1881, 85–89) and as Recorder of Deeds (1889).

Bruce, Edward (died 1318), Scottish king of Ireland (1315–18). He helped his brother, Robert I, become

Scotland's king. In Ireland he led the Irish against their English overlords, before being killed in battle.

Bruce, Robert. *See* Robert I (of Scotland).

Brucellosis, or undulant fever, disease passed from animal to man often in unpasteurized milk; often fatal if undiagnosed. Symptoms include headache, weakness, remittent fever. Pasteurization of milk and destruction of infected animals have made the disease rare.

Brucite, a secondary hydroxide mineral, magnesium hydroxide [Mg(OH)$_2$], derived from periclase (MgO). In marbles and serpentine metamorphic rocks. Hexagonal system plates and fibrous masses. Pearly white to red; transparent and waxy; hardness 2.5; sp gr 2.4.

Brücke, Die, loose association of German painters, founded in Dresden (1905) by Ernst Kirchner, Karl Schmidt-Rottluff, and Erich Heckel. They thought of their art as a bridge between the current academic style of painting and a freer style of expression. Using broken lines, angular forms, and intense colors, they produced emotionally expressive woodcuts and paintings.

Bruckner, Anton (1824–1896), Austrian Romantic composer. An intensely religious man, Bruckner composed mostly religious works and nine symphonies infused with religious feeling. Closer in style to the symphonies of Schubert than to those of Beethoven, Bruckner's symphonies contain scherzos second only to those found in Beethoven's symphonies, and his last three symphonies were major achievements of Romantic music. *See also* Romanticism in Music.

Brueghel, Jan the Elder (1568–1625), Flemish painter. He painted religious and mythological subjects, landscapes, and still lifes in the Mannerist style. His early work borrowed subjects from his father (Pieter the Elder) and other contemporaries. Later and more original works include a painting of the "Four Elements" (c.1609) and an exquisite landscape, "Village Street" (1611). *See also* Mannerism.

Brueghel, Pieter the Elder (Peasant Brueghel) (c. 1525–69), Flemish painter. He was one of the greatest of Netherlandish painters, whose style, untouched by the conventional, was nearly impressionistic. He was a great artist of action and movement, and his works depict generalized forms often with a satirical approach. His work developed most obviously in his treatment of the landscape. Early works use the landscape solely as background, transitional works separate the foreground from middleground, and later works develop the landscape into a unified whole, with fewer and smaller figures present. An example of his early work is "Children's Games"; "Peasant Wedding" is in his mature style. His paintings fall into roughly three categories, all of which overlap—the fantasy or allegory, the genre, and the Biblical. Representative paintings include, respectively, "Fall of the Rebel Angels" (1562), "Return of the Herd," and "Massacre of the Innocents."

Brueghel, Pieter the Younger (1564–1638), Flemish painter. His country and religious works are sometimes copied from, and always in the tradition of, his father (Pieter the Elder). His nickname "Hell" derived from his depictions of hell.

Bruges (Brugge), city in NW Belgium, 55mi (89km) WNW of Brussels; capital of West Flanders prov.; 14th-century commercial and financial center of N Europe; dukes of Burgundy resided here and founded Order of

Golden Fleece (1429). City is built on a network of canals, for which the city is called "City of Bridges." Industries: shipbuilding, food processing, tourism. Founded 865. Pop. 119,718.

Brummell, George Bryan (1778–1840), English social dandy called Beau Brummell; noted for his wit and style of dress. As a close friend of the prince of Wales (later George IV), Brummell greatly influenced English men's fashions. Gambling debts caused him to flee to France, where he lived in poverty and died insane in an asylum at Caen.

Brundage, Avery (1887–1975), US sportsman, b. Detroit. He was a staunch advocate of keeping "professionalism" out of amateur sports, and served as president of the International Olympic Committee (1952–72).

Brunei, sultanate in N Bornea, SE Asia; under British protection; capital is Bandar Seri Begauan; influenced by Chinese (10th–11th centuries); Brunei kings ruled island 15th–16th centuries; their power diminished during trade with western European nations; by 1888, it was ruled by Britain; in 1963 Brunei became a protectorate with sultan's power reinstated and in 1979 an agreement was signed for eventual independence. Oil was discovered 1929, and the island now enjoys highest standard of living in SE Asia. Area: 2,226sq mi (5,765sq km). Pop. 162,400.

Brunel, (Sir) Marc Isambard (1769–1849), British engineer, b. France. A refugee from the French Revolution, he came to New York City in 1793 and was chief engineer of New York. He went to England in 1799, where he invented machinery for making ships' blocks. He was responsible for the construction of the Thames Tunnel (1825–43) and was knighted in 1841.

Brunelleschi, Filippo (1377–1446), Italian architect. His systematic use of perspective and his engineering skill made completion of the octagonal ribbed dome of the Florence Cathedral possible. His other architectural achievements include Ospedale degl' Innocenti and the Church of San Lorenzo, both in Florence.

Brunhild, a beautiful princess in ancient Germanic literature. She was a Valkyrie, whom Odin banished from Valhalla for disobeying his rule. On earth, she could only marry a man stronger than herself. Siegfried fulfilled this condition, but wooed her for another. When Brunhild discovered this trickery, Siegfried was killed.

Brunswick, city in E West Germany on Oker River, 90mi (145km) SSE of Hamburg; capital of Lower Saxony state; site of crossroads of ancient trade routes, St Balsius Cathedral (1173–94), and Dankwarderode fortress (1175), technical university; member of Hanseatic League (13th century). Industries: pianos, optical equipment, food products, printing. Founded 861; made city 12th century. Pop. 223,700.

Brussels (Bruxelles), city in central Belgium, 26mi (42km) S of Antwerp; capital of Belgium, and of Brabant prov. Est. as a military post in the 10th century, it prospered and became the center of the wool industry; capital of Netherlands (1530) under Hapsburg empire; scene of World's Fair (1958). Industries: textiles, chemicals, electrical equipment, brewing. Founded c. 900. Pop. 1,050,787.

Brussels Griffon, small, distinctive Belgian dog (toy group) derived from the Affenpinsoher and the Belgian street dog. It has an upturned, black nose set between prominent eyes, a domed forehead, and protruding chin. Small, high-set ears are cropped or natural. The body is short; legs are medium-length and wide-set; the docked tail is held high. There are two types of coat: rough (wiry, but not shaggy, with a fringe around the face) and smooth. Colors are reddish brown and black or solid black. Average size: 8in (20cm) high at shoulder; 8–10lb (3.5–4.5kg). *See also* Toy Dog.

Brussels Sprouts, cabbage-related plant first grown in Belgium. Leaves grow from the top of a thick, erect stalk and stem buds develop into miniature, globular heads that are eaten as a vegetable. It matures in 85–90 days. Height: 22in (55.9cm). Family Cruciferae; species *Brassica oleracea gemmifera.*

Brut (*c.* 1205), early Middle English verse history of Britain by Layamon from the supposed arrival of Brutus, son of Aeneas, to the time of Cadwalader (*c.* 689). Based on the works of Geoffrey of Monmouth and Robert Wace, the *Brut* contains the earliest mention in English of King Arthur, King Lear, and Cymbeline. It is the first significant work in Middle English.

Brutus, Lucius Junius (*fl.* late 6th century BC), a founder of the Roman Republic. He led the Romans in the expulsion of the last Tarquin king (510 BC) after the rape of his kinswoman Lucrece by the king's son. He is reputed to have executed his own two sons for plotting to restore the Tarquins.

Brutus, Marcus Junius (*c.*85–42 BC), Roman political figure, one of the principal assassins of Julius Caesar. First siding with Pompey, he was forgiven by Caesar and made governor of Cisalpine Gaul (46 BC). He turned against Caesar after the murder of Cato, his uncle. After Caesar's murder (44 BC), he went to Greece, where he raised an army and with Cassius engaged in battle with Marc Antony and Octavian. Defeated at Philippi (42 BC), he committed suicide.

Bryan, William Jennings (1860–1925), US lawyer and politician, b. Salem, Ill. A former Democratic Congressman (1891–95) and a leading advocate of the free coinage of silver, Bryan made the "Cross of Gold" speech at the 1896 Democratic convention which won him the presidential nomination; he lost to William McKinley. Nominated again in 1900, he ran on a chiefly anti-imperialist platform and was again defeated by McKinley. He was defeated in his third try in 1908 by William Howard Taft. He helped Woodrow Wilson win the Democratic nomination in 1912 and became Wilson's secretary of state. He resigned in 1915, believing Wilson's foreign policy to be leading the country into World War I.

In his later years, Bryan became a religious fundamentalist. He favored prohibition and opposed the teaching of evolution. He acted as prosecuting attorney in the Scopes "monkey" trial in 1925, opposing Clarence Darrow, who was attorney for the defense. Bryan won the case but died five days after its conclusion. *See also* Free Silver; Scopes Trial.

Bryant, William Cullen (1794–1878), US poet and editor, b. Cummington, Mass. He began to write poetry as a youth; his first book of *Poems* appeared in 1821. It contained some of his most famous verse, including *Thanatopsis* and "To a Waterfowl." Although he studied and practiced law, he dropped it in 1825 when he became coeditor of *New York Review.* In 1826 he began working for the New York *Evening Post,* soon rising to editor (1829) and part-owner. Under his leadership the *Post* emerged as a powerful liberal organ, advocating abolition and free trade. Bryant also continued to write poetry, primarily nature poetry. Later volumes of his work include *The Fountain* (1842), *A Forest Hymn* (1860), and *Thirty Poems* (1864).

Bryophyte, a group of small green plants (division Bryophyta) consisting of the mosses and liverworts. Bryophytes grow on damp surfaces exposed to light, including rocks and tree bark, and are found in nearly every land habitat from the Arctic to the Antarctic. They lack specialized tissues for transporting water, minerals, and food; instead, these materials diffuse slowly from cell to cell through the plant. In the typical bryophyte life cycle a relatively conspicuous green sexual stage alternates with an inconspicuous nongreen asexual (spore-bearing) stage that is dependent on the sexual stage for food. *See also* Alternation of Generations.

Bryozoa, phylum of moss animals, also called sea mats and corallines. These plantlike, marine animals live in branching colonies. Each animal has a protective case, U-shaped digestive tract, and ciliated feeding tentacles. The body is formed of two cell layers. Reproduction is by budding. Species include *Alcyonidium;* length: 11.8in (300mm) and *Bugula;* length: 2.8in (70mm).

Bubastis, ancient city in the Nile Delta of Egypt. Dating back to the VI dynasty (2420–2258 BC), it gained importance when the pharaohs of the XIX dynasty (1320–1200 BC) moved their capital to the Delta. Bubastis itself served as capital during the XXII (945–745 BC) and XXIII (745–718 BC) dynasties. The city declined following the second Persian conquest (343 BC). It was noted as the center of worship of the cat-headed (or lion-headed) goddess Bast. According to Herodotus, it also held an annual Saturnalia.

Bubble Chamber, instrument for detecting and identifying charged particles, such as the proton. It consists of a large chamber in which a liquid, usually hydrogen or helium, is kept just above its boiling point by pressure. Any energetic ionizing particle passing through the liquid will ionize it. If the pressure is suddenly reduced, allowing the liquid to reach its boiling point, a line of tiny bubbles begins to form along this ionized path. These tracks are photographed before the pressure is restored, particles being identified by the nature of the tracks, their curvature in an applied magnetic field, and by the tracks of their decay products. *See also* Cloud Chamber.

Buber, Martin (1878–1965), Jewish philosopher, theologian, and political activist, b. Vienna. An early, ardent Zionist, from 1901 he edited *Die Welt,* the Zionist weekly. He edited *Der Jude,* the leading journal of German-speaking Jewish intellectuals (1916–24). He defiantly opposed the Nazis in Germany until forced to migrate to Palestine in 1938, where he became a professor of social philosophy at Hebrew University. His most important published work is *I and Thou* (1923), which discusses the relationship between man and God.

Bubonic Plague, disease usually transmitted to humans by fleas from rats. Symptoms include chills and fever, followed by vomiting, diarrhea, headache, and inflammation and swelling of lymph nodes, especially in the region of the groin. Sanitation is the preventive measure. *See also* Plague.

Bucaramanga, commercial city in N central Colombia, in the E Andes highlands; many colonial monuments. Crops: coffee, tobacco, cacao. Founded 1622. Pop. 340,783.

Bucephalus, horse of Alexander the Great. It accompanied Alexander on his major campaigns. When Bucephalus died (326 BC) in India, Alexander had him buried on the banks of the Hydaspes River (now Jhelum River) and built the city of Bucephalia in his memory. The city was across from the modern city of Jhelum in Pakistan.

Buchan, John, 1st Baron Tweedsmuir (1875–1940), British author and statesman. He was famous for his adventure novels, which included *The Thirty-Nine Steps* (1915) and *Sick Heart River* (1941). He also wrote a four-volume history of WWI and biographies of Julius Caesar, Walter Scott, and Oliver Cromwell. He served as Governor-General of Canada from 1935 until his death.

Buchanan, James (1791–1868), 15th President of the United States, b. near Mercersburg, Pa.; graduate, Dickinson College, 1809. He never married. A Pennsylvania lawyer, he began his political career as a Federalist and later became a conservative Democrat.

A strong secretary of state under President Polk, he settled the Oregon dispute with Great Britain, but the dispute with Mexico over Texas resulted in the Mexican War. In 1853, President Pierce named him minister to Great Britain. While in that post, he negotiated the ill-fated Ostend Manifesto, which would have authorized the United States to take Cuba by force if necessary.

As the Democratic presidential candidate in 1856, he was the narrow winner over John C. Fremont, the Republican, and Millard Fillmore, the candidate of the Whigs and Know-Nothings. His presidency was marked by the rising animosity between the proslavery and the antislavery states. His attempt to maintain the "sacred balance" between North and South pleased no one, and the South moved closer and closer to secession. He reluctantly supported the federal garrison at Fort Sumter because of his fear that it would precipitate war. He was right: the Civil War began only weeks after he left office.

Career: House of Representatives, 1821–31; Minister to Russia, 1832–34 and Great Britain 1853–56; U.S. Senate, 1834–45; Secretary of State, 1845–49; President, 1857–61.

Bucharest (Bucuresti), capital and largest city of Romania, on Dimbovita River; became capital 1862; occupied by Germans 1916–18; under Nazi control 1940–44; site of 17th-century Metropolitan Church, theaters, museums, two universities, and seat of patriarch of Romanian Orthodox Church; major industrial and communications center. Industries: food processing, textiles, chemicals, automobiles, metal working, oil refining. Founded 15th century as fortress. Pop. 1,588,592.

Buchenwald, village in SW East Germany near Weimar. It was the site of one of the most notorious German concentration camps for the imprisonment of Jews, est. 1937 by the Nazis; taken in April 1945 by US troops, who found extreme examples of starvation and torture.

Buck, Pearl (1892–1973), U.S. novelist, b. Hillsboro, W.Va. The daughter of missionaries, she was raised in China, which is the setting for many of her novels. A prolific writer, her first book appeared in 1930. The following year *The Good Earth* was published. A novel about Chinese peasants, it won her the Pulitzer Prize in 1932. Other works include *Sons* (1932), *The Mother* (1934), *A House Divided* (1935), and *Dragon Seed* (1942). In 1938 she was awarded the Nobel Prize in literature.

Buckeye. *See* Horse Chestnut.

Buckingham Palace, London residence of British sovereigns since 1837. Formerly belonging to the dukes of Buckingham, it was purchased by George III (1761) and remodeled by the architect John Nash in 1825 into a 600-room palace. Sir Aston Webb redesigned the east front in 1913. The celebrated changing of the guard takes place daily when the sovereign is in residence.

Buckwheat, dicotyledonous grain plant native to Asia and cultivated worldwide and well adapted to cool and arid places. This grain is important as poultry and livestock food. Bees make a dark honey of its pollen. Common buckwheat *(Fagopyrum esculentum)* is branched and has swollen sheaths where heart-shaped leaves are attached; white bisexual flowers; and triangular seeds enclosed by brown rind. Height: to 3ft (1m). Tartarian buckwheat *(F. tataricum)* has seeds with toothed edges. Its flour, unsatisfactory for bread, is used in pancakes. Hulled kernels are called groats. Family Polygonaceae.

Budapest, capital city of Hungary, on the Danube River; formed by inc. of Buda and Pest, 1872. Buda became the capital of Hungary 1361; by 1800, Buda's importance was waning and Pest became Hungary's more important city. After union of two cities, Budapest became one of two capitals of Austro-Hungarian monarchy; by 1917 it was Hungary's leading commercial center as well as its cultural hub. In 1918 it was declared capital of independent country of Hungary; Russia seized control 1948; city was scene of unsuccessful uprising against Russian control in 1956. Industries: flour milling, iron and steel products, tourism. Settled AD100 by Romans. Pop. 2,070,966.

Buddenbrooks (1901), novel by Thomas Mann (with his elder brother Heinrich). Showing the influences of Friedrich Nietzsche and Richard Wagner, the story depicts the decline of a wealthy merchant family, caused by an increase in spiritual and artistic refinement and culminates in the death of the last heir.

Buddha, name given to Siddhartha Gautama (*c.* 563–*c.*483 BC), the founder of Buddhism. Buddha, in Sanskrit, means "the enlightened one." Born into a noble family of the Himalayan foothills, at the age of 29 he left his family to become a wandering ascetic. After six years of meditation and fasting, he obtained enlightenment while seated under the holy tree Bodh Gaya. For the rest of his life he traveled throughout N India preaching his message. *See also* Buddhism.

Buddhism, religion founded in India *c.*528 by Siddhartha Gautama, the Buddha. Buddhism is based on Four Noble Truths: existence is suffering; the cause of suffering is craving and attachment; cessation of suffering is possible through Nirvana; Nirvana is attained through the Eightfold Path, which consists of the proper views, resolve, speech, action, livelihood, effort, mindfulness, and concentration. Today there are more than 160 million Buddhists in the world, concentrated most heavily in Burma, Ceylon, Indochina, and Japan.

Budding, or gemmation, form of asexual reproduction that produces a new organism from an outgrowth of the parent. Buds break from the parent (hydra) or remain attached. Several freshwater sponges form gemmules (internal buds) that escape from the parent during unfavorable conditions and open to form new sponges when conditions are favorable.

Budding, in horticulture, grafting buds on woody plants to produce more vigorous plants or to dwarf, particularly in stone fruit trees. It is done with varieties of the same, or closely related, species. A bud and small piece of bark are cut from a shoot of new growth and inserted into a T-shaped cut on the understock with the

William Jennings Bryan

James Buchanan

Bulgaria

bud touching the cambium layer. It is then tied in place. Budding is most successful when done in spring.

Budgerigar. *See* Parakeet.

Buena Park, city in S California, W of Anaheim; most important industry is tourism; site of Knott's Berry Farm and a wax museum of movie stars. Inc. 1953. Pop. (1980) 64,165.

Buena Vista, Battle of (Feb. 1847), Mexican War battle, in which US troops under Gen. Zachary Taylor were attacked by General Santa Anna's Mexican army. After two indecisive days, Santa Anna withdrew, giving the United States control of northern Mexico.

Buenos Aires, capital of Argentina, in E central Argentina, on estuary of the Río de la Plata, 150mi (242km) W of Atlantic Ocean. Colonized 1536 by Pedro de Mendoza who named it Santa María del Buen Aire; he abandoned it because of indian attacks; refounded by Juan de Garay 1580. In 1854, a constitution was drawn up, and Buenos Aires began challenging other provinces for control of the government. In 1880, city was detached from Buenos Aires prov. and set up as a separate federal district and capital of Argentina; political, commercial, industrial center; site of University of Buenos Aires (1821). Industries: tourism, textiles, meat processing, flour mills, metal works. Pop. 8,925,000.

Buerger's Disease, inflammation of arteries and veins often accompanied by thrombosis. Causes are unknown although men 20–45 are most susceptible. Symptoms are numbness, tingling, pain. Treatment is rest and exercise. *See also* Thrombosis.

Buffalo, industrial city and port of entry in W New York, on E shore of Lake Erie; seat of Erie co. Settled 1803 by Holland Land Co., its industrial growth was spurred as W terminus of newly opened Erie Canal (1825); scene of assassination of President McKinley at 1901 Pan-American Exposition and of inaugural oath of Theodore Roosevelt. It is site of McKinley Monument, Theodore Roosevelt Inaugural National Historic Site, Albright-Knox Art Gallery, Canisius College (1870), D'Youville College (1908), State University of New York at Buffalo (1867). Industries: flour milling, automobiles, chemicals, railroad shops. Inc. 1832. Pop. (1980) 357,870.

Buffalo, common name for several wild or domesticated oxen of Asia and Africa. It is a misnomer for American bison. Family Bovidae. *See also* Anoa; Ox; Water Buffalo.

Buffalo Fish, freshwater fish found in large rivers of the Mississippi Valley. Brownish to bluish-green, this sucker is a bottom feeder. Length: 10in–3ft. (25–90cm); weight: average 2–3lbs (0.9–1.4 kg), many are 20–30lbs (9–14kg). Family Catostomidae; species: bigmouth *Ictiobus cyprinellus*, smallmouth *Ictiobus bubalus*.

Buffer Solution, solution to which a moderate quantity of a strong acid or a strong base can be added without making a significant change to the pH. Buffer solutions usually consist of a mixture of a weak acid and one of its salts, a mixture of an acid salt and its normal salt, or a mixture of two acid salts.

Bugle, brass wind instrument resembling a small trumpet without valves, capable only of natural tones (C-F-A-C). Because its penetrating tones carry great distances, it is used for military signaling, as in call to arms, reveille, retreat, and taps. *See also* Trumpet.

Bug River, two rivers in E Europe. Southern Bug River rises in hills of Ukrainian SSR, USSR, flows SE to Black Sea and is navigable for less than 100mi (161km). Length: 530mi (853km). Western Bug River rises in hills ENE of Zoluchev, in Ukrainian SSR, USSR, flows NW to Brest, forming part of Soviet-Polish border, and is navigable for 300mi (483km). Length: 484mi (779km).

Bujumbura, formerly Usumbura; capital city and chief port of Burundi and Bujumbura prov., SE central Africa, on tip of Lake Tanganyika in W Burundi; administrative, commercial, and manufacturing center; site of University of Bujumbura (1961), airport. Est. as German military post 1897, city was made capital of Belgian Ruanda-Urundi after WWI; remained capital when Burundi proclaimed independence 1962. Industries: tourism, textile, soap, agricultural products. Pop. 160,000.

Bukavu, formerly Costermansville; port city in E Zaire, Equatorial Africa, at S end of Lake Kivu; capital of Kivu region; administrative and trade center. Industries: food processing, tourism. Founded 1901. Pop. 180,-633.

Bukhara (Buchara), city in W Uzbek SSR, USSR; capital of Bukhara oblast; site of 10th-century mausoleum of Ismail Samanid, minaret of Kalyan (1127), the Ulugbek (1417–18), oldest Muslim school in central Asia. City was under Arabs 7th-9th century when it became Islamic center; capital of Persian Samanid state 10th century; under Turks and Mongols 12th-15th centuries; made a protectorate of Russia 1868. Industries: natural silk, natural gas, handicrafts, textiles, rugs. Pop. 147,000.

Bukharin, Nikolai Ivanovich (1888–1938), Soviet Communist theoretician. He joined the Bolsheviks in 1906 and was deported in 1911. In Cracow he collaborated with Lenin on the newspaper *Pravda*. He returned to Russia in 1917, opposed the Brest-Litovsk Treaty, and supported Stalin's position in 1924 against rapid industrialization. In 1937, he was accused of being a Trotskyite. He was executed in the 1938 purges.

Bulawayo, city in SW Rhodesia, central S Africa, 240mi (384km) SW of Salisbury; site of a Matabelle revolt (1896); nearby are 18th-century ruins of Khami, 2nd-largest city in Rhodesia, and major industrial center. Industries: textiles, motor vehicles, cement. Founded by British 1893. Pop. 318,000.

Bulb, underground bud that produces a plant. It consists of a short, underground stem and enlarged, fleshy leaf scales. Food is stored in the scales, which are layered in a series of rings (onion) or loosely attached to the stem (some lilies). Bulbs produce smaller bulbs in the axils of the outer leaf scales. When mature, these offsets can be planted, producing new flowering-sized bulbs.

Bulbul, noisy songbird of tropical and subtropical Africa and Asia. They have rounded wings and long, dull-colored plumage with some having crests. They feed on fruits and insects. The female lays spotted white or pink eggs (2–4) in a cup-shaped nest in a tree or bush. Length: 7in (17.5cm). Family Pycnonotidae.

Bulfinch, Charles (1763–1844), US architect, b. Boston. He is particularly noted for his public buildings, including the State House in Boston; University Hall at Harvard, Cambridge, Mass; and Massachusetts General Hospital, Boston. From 1818–30 he completed the building of the Capitol in Washington, D.C.

Bulgaria (Bâlgarija), People's Republic of, nation of the Balkan Peninsula in SE Europe. Since WWII, the country has been one of the Communist bloc nations under the domination of the Soviet Union. Bulgaria was part of the Ottoman Empire for 500 years. The Bulgarian language is a Slavic tongue.

Land and Economy. The Balkan Mts traverse the country from W to E, dividing Bulgaria into two separate geographic regions. N of the mountains lies the Danube Plain, a tableland of limestone and loess reaching N to the Danube River. S of the Balkan range lies the extensively farmed Maritsa Valley. Sofia, the capital city, is situated in the mountains in W central Bulgaria, with convenient access to both the Danube and Maritsa regions. Bulgaria has one of the least developed economies in Europe. The Communist regime which gained power after WWII established a centrally planned, Soviet-style economy. Agriculture was collectivized, and the chief emphasis was put on developing industry. The pattern of foreign exports shifted steadily from farm to manufactured products. In its effort to develop necessary electric power and heavy industry, consumer goods were neglected. Living standards remained low. Bulgaria receives substantial economic assistance from the Soviet Union.

People. The Bulgars who invaded and settled what is now Bulgaria in the 7th century were a non-Slavic people. Today's Bulgarian tongue derives not from the Bulgars but from the Slavs they conquered and by whom they were assimilated. The Bulgarian language is written in the Cyrillic alphabet. Most Bulgarians belong to the Bulgarian Orthodox Church. A minority of less than 10% is Muslim. As elsewhere, there is a constant movement in the population from the farming villages to the manufacturing centers.

Government. Bulgaria styles itself a people's republic, but the Bulgarian Communist party wields dictatorial power in the country. A national assembly elected by the people functions only to approve party policies and decrees. The national assembly elects from its members a presidium, of which the chairman is given the title of president.

History. In the early Middle Ages the Bulgarian kingdom became a powerful state, reaching from the Black Sea to the Adriatic. A golden age of art and culture culminated with the rule of the 10th-century Bulgarian emperor Simeon I. The Ottoman Turks conquered Bulgaria 1396 and ruled for five centuries. The beginnings of modern Bulgaria are traced to demands for political independence in the 19th century. In WWI, Bulgaria allied with Germany, hoping to regain lost territories in the Balkans. Defeated, Bulgaria suffered economic and political crises through the 1920s and 1930s. Economic progress was achieved with Germany's help in the 1930s; the two nations were allied in WWII. The Soviet Union invaded Bulgaria in 1944. Two years later a Communist regime was established, with Georgi Dimitrov as premier, until his death in 1949. Since 1954, Todor Zhivkov has been the country's leader, maintaining close ties to the Soviet Union.

PROFILE

Official name: People's Republic of Bulgaria
Area: 42,823sq mi (110,912sq km)
Population: 8,864,000
 Density: 207per sq mi (80per sq km)
Chief cities: Sofia (capital); Plovdiv; Varna
Government: Communist
Religion: Bulgarian Orthodox Church
Language: Bulgarian (official)
Monetary unit: Leva
Gross national product: $20,900,000,000
Per capita income: $2,280
Industries (major products): steel, cement, fertilizer, textiles, processed foods

Agriculture (major products): wheat, corn, tobacco, barley, sugar beets
Minerals (major): iron ore, copper, lead, zinc, petroleum
Trading partners (major): Soviet Union, East Germany, Italy

Bulgars, Turaien people living on the Black Sea. Part of their population moved to present day Bulgaria and, in the 9th century, the rest emigrated to the Volga region, which later became a major Russian economic center in the Middle Ages. They adopted the Moslem faith and were ruled by the Mongols in the 13th century. At the beginning of the 15th century, they became subjects of the Muscovite state.

Bulge, Battle of the, final German offensive in World War II. The US lines were thin along the border of France and Germany when the Germans launched an attack in December 1944. US forces rallied, holding at Bastogne, and the Germans were thrown back.

Bulldog, English bullbaiting breed (nonsporting group) several centuries old. No longer a vicious fighter, its distinctive large head has a short, turned-up muzzle; large nose set between the eyes; projecting lower jaw; and hanging lips. High-set ears fold over and back. The large body has muscular shoulders; broad chest; and short, stout legs. The short tail is straight or screw-shaped and carried low. A short, straight, fine coat can be a red or other color brindle; solid white, red, or fawn; or piebald. Skin is soft and loose. Average size: 13–15in (33–38cm) at shoulder; 50lb (22.5kg). *See also* Nonsporting Dog.

Bullfighting, sport popular in Mexico, Columbia, Peru, Venezuela, Ecuador, and Spain, where it is the national sport. A bullfight usually includes six bulls and three matadors, who are assigned two bulls each on the basis of a lot chosen the morning of the fight. Each matador, whose role it is to kill the bull, has five assistants. These include two picadors, who are mounted on armored horses, and three *peones* or *banderilleras.* A bullfight takes place in three stages so that the bull can be sufficiently weakened (his head hanging low) so a clean kill can be made. In the first stage, the picadors stab the bull four times with their lances *(pics)* (this number varies according to the condition of the bull) to weaken the charging bull. The *peones* then come out and, while on the run, plant the banderillas (barbed sticks) on the withers of the bull behind the neck muscles, a maneuver to anger the bull so that it will charge the matador. The matador then enters the arena with a sword and small red cape (muleta). Before attempting to kill the bull—by thrusting the sword into the bull's heart through the top of the neck—the matador makes several daring passes with his muleta. Depending upon the matador's performance, he may be awarded the tail or ears of the bull.

Bullfrog, or American bullfrog, aquatic frog, native to the United States, living in lakes and ponds. It is green or green with brown markings above. It has a loud, bass voice and is famous for its jumping ability. Length: to 8in(20cm). Family Ranidae; species *Rana catesbiana. See also* Frog.

Bullhead, freshwater catfish originally found throughout E United States. Now farmed as food, it has been introduced in Europe and Hawaii. It has four pairs of fleshy mouth whiskers and a square tail. Length: to 24in (61cm); weight: to 8lb (3.6kg). Family Ictaluridae; species include yellow *Ictalurus natalis* and brown *Ictalurus nebulosus.*

Bull-mastiff, guard and watchdog (working group) developed in England from a cross of 60% mastiff and 40% bulldog; also called gamekeeper's night dog. A powerful dog, it has a large head with broad, deep muzzle, wrinkles, and hanging lips. V-shaped ears are carried close to the cheeks; body is compact; wide-set legs are straight and well-boned; the tapered tail is set high. A short, dense coat is red, fawn, or brindle. Average size: 25–27in (63.5–68.5cm) high at shoulder; 110–130lb (50–59kg). *See also* Working Dog.

Bull Run, First Battle of (July 21, 1861), Civil War engagement, also called Manassas, fought near Manassas, Va., not far from Washington D.C. Undertrained Union troops commanded by Gen. Irvin McDowell, at first successful, were eventually routed by Confederate troops under Gen. P.G.T. Beauregard, reinforced by Gen. Thomas J. Jackson, who earned his nickname "Stonewall" at the battle.

Bull Run, Second Battle of (Aug. 28–30, 1862), Civil War battle, also called Manassas. On the old battleground of 1861, 48,000 Confederates under Gen. Robert E. Lee beat 75,000 Union soldiers under Gen. John Pope, so that once more, Lee threatened Washington D.C. Union losses were 16,000 to the Confederates' 9000. Pope was dismissed as commander of the Union army, and Gen. George McClellan, the former commander, was given command again.

Bull Snake, nonpoisonous snake found in Central and W United States and Mexico. Its powerful body is yellow marked with dark splotches. It kills by constriction. Length: to 5ft (1.5m). Family Colubridae; species *Pituophis melanoleucus. See also* Snake.

Bull Terrier, a sport dog (terrier group) recognized in two varieties—the white ("White Cavalier") and the colored. In the past this strongly built, active dog was used in dog pits and for bear baiting. Its large, oval head has a characteristic downface profile; ears are small and erect; the dark eyes are sunken and triangular. The bull terrier has a broad-chested body; big-boned legs; and a short tapering tail. A short, flat, harsh coat is pure white in the white variety and any color but white in the colored. Average size: 19–23in (48.5–56cm) high at shoulder, 30–36lb (135–165kg). *See also* Terrier.

Bülow, Bernhard, Prince von (1849–1929), German statesman and imperial chancellor from 1900–09. A careful conservative in domestic affairs, his facile mobility in foreign affairs heightened European tensions before World War I. He was forced to resign in 1909 because of imperial disfavor.

Bulrush, grasslike herbs *(Scirpus)* of the sedge family. Growing to 9ft (2.7m), their stalks are tipped with headlike clusters of flowers. They prefer damp, boggy places of Europe, Africa, and North America.

Bultmann, Rudolf (Karl) (1884–1976), German theologian. He is one of the most controversial and influential New Testament scholars of the 20th century. His existentialist interpretations, which systematically demythologize the New Testament, are found in *The Theology of the New Testament* (1951).

Bumblebee, robust, black and yellow to orange bee, usually 0.75in (19mm) or more in length. It usually builds its nest in deserted mouse or bird nests. Found worldwide, they are important pollinators of clover, due to their very long tongues. Family Apidae, tribe Bombini. *See also* Bee.

Bunche, Ralph Johnson (1904–71), US statesman, b. Detroit. He headed the political science department at Howard University from 1929 until World War II, when he became chief research analyst for the Office of Strategic Services. Following two years in the State Department (1944–46) he joined the United Nations as director of the trusteeship division. As secretary of the Palestine Commission, he brought peace to the Holy Land, for which he was awarded the Nobel Peace Prize (1950). In 1957 he became UN undersecretary for special political affairs. From 1967 until his death, he was undersecretary general of the United Nations.

Bundesrat, upper house of the West German and Austrian parliaments. In West Germany, it is composed of voting representatives elected by the 10 federal states and of non-voting West Berliners, serving four-year terms. The Bundesrat acts on measures sent from the Bundestag, the lower house. Historically, the Bundesrat acted as the chief executive organ of the German Confederation (1815–66). *See also* Bundestag.

Bundestag, 496-member lower house of the West German parliament, responsible for initiating legislation, ratifying the most important treaties, and electing the West German chancellor. With an equal number of representatives from the state parliaments, the Bundestag elects the federal president. There are also 22 non-voting members from West Berlin. *See also* Bundesrat.

Bunker Hill, Battle of, Revolutionary War battle that took place on June 17, 1775, on Boston's Charlestown peninsula. The first major battle of the Revolution, it actually was fought south of Bunker Hill on Breed's Hill, where the Americans built hasty fortifications. Technically defeated, the Americans earned a moral victory by inflicting heavy losses on the British.

Bunsen, Robert Wilhelm (1811–99), German chemist, professor at Marburg and later at Heidelberg. His early work on organic arsenicals caused him the loss of an eye in an explosion and also severe poisoning. When he recovered he widened his scope, designing several calorimeters, a carbon-zinc electric cell (Bunsen cell), a grease-spot photometer, and contributed to the development of the gas burner associated with his name. He discovered an arsenic poisoning antidote, and studied the properties of magnesium. With his assistant Gustav Kirchhoff, he devised the science of spectroscopy, using it to discover two new elements (cesium and rubidium).

Bunsen Burner, gas burner widely used in science laboratories. It is named for its inventor, Robert W. Bunsen. The burner is a 5-in (13-cm) upright tube, usually of brass, attached to a gas source. It has an adjustable valve at its base to admit air. The flame is smokeless and intense.

Bunting, brightly colored finch found almost worldwide. These birds with canarylike bills build cup-shaped nests for pale spotted eggs (2–6). Males of the New World genus *Passerina* are brightly colored; length 5in (12.5cm). Females are smaller and duller. Buntings of the Old World genus *Emberiza* are slightly larger and dull colored with streaks. The circumpolar snow bunting *(Plectrophenax nivalis nivalis)* is almost white. Family Fringillidae.

Bunyan, John (1628–88), English preacher and author. A Parliamentarian soldier during the English Civil War, he became a Puritan minister in 1655 and twice suffered imprisonment for his nonconformist religious activities. His writings, popular and colloquial in style, include *Grace Abounding* (1666), and *The Pilgrim's Progress* (1678). *See also* Pilgrim's Progress, The.

Bunyan, Paul, US folk hero. Tales of the giant lumberjack and his Blue ox, Babe, appeared in the mid-19th century lumber camps, telling of a giant able to cut miles of trees with a swing of his ax and crediting him with the creation of the Rocky Mountains and the Grand Canyon. Babe helped shape the land by drinking rivers dry.

Buoyancy, the upward force experienced by an object in a fluid. The object actually encounters pressure from all sides, but the pressure on its lower part is greatest because of the increasing depth of the fluid. Thus the resultant of all these forces is a force acting upward. This upward force is equal to the weight of the water displaced. *See also* Archimedes' Principle.

Burbank, Luther (1849–1926), US horticulturist, b. Lancaster, Mass. Through the scientific development of numerous useful varieties of fruits, grains, and flowers, he helped to elevate plant breeding to a modern science. On his world famous experimental farm in Santa Rosa, Calif., Burbank utilized revolutionary breeding methods to develop more than 800 new strains and varieties of plants, including 113 new varieties of plums and prunes, 10 new berries, and 50 varieties of lilies. His method, which consisted of obtaining good seedlings by gathering multiple crosses of foreign and native strains that were then grafted onto mature plants, allowed for a speedy assessment of hybrid characteristics, aiding both the study of genetics and the development of plants for commercial use.

Burbank, city in S California, 10mi (16km) NW of Los Angeles; site of movie and television studios; chief industry is aircraft manufacture. Inc. 1911. Pop. (1980) 84,625.

Burbot, freshwater codfish found around the North Pole to Eurasia and North America; also in Great Lakes. A slender fish, it spawns in winter. Length: to 32in (81.3cm); weight: 12lb (514kg). Family Gadidae; species *Lota lota.*

Burdock, weedy herb found throughout Europe, North Africa, and North America. It has large, basal leaves and thistlelike purple flowerheads covered by stiff, hooked bracts. The common or lesser burdock, *Arctium minus,* is a biennial with reddish-purple flowers. Height: to 9ft(2.7m). Family Compositae.

Burdwan, city in NE India, on Damodar River; site of ancient temples and palaces. Industries: rice and oilseed milling, trade center, tools, cutlery. Pop. 152,239.

Bureaucracy, body of appointive government officials who implement and often influence public policy. Characterized by an administrative hierarchy resembling a pyramid, bureaucracies are ranked from the top down, according to responsibilities, duties, and qualifications. Bureaucracy is popularly associated with "red tape" and with functioning by rigid and arbitrary routine.

Burger, Warren Earl (1907–), chief justice of the US Supreme Court (1969–86), b. St. Paul, Minn. In 1931 he received a law degree and began practicing and teaching law. He was assistant attorney general in charge of the civil division of the department of justice (1953–56). He served as judge of US Court of Appeals in Washington, D.C. (1956–69) and was then appointed by Pres. Richard M. Nixon as chief justice of the Supreme Court (1969). Before the appointment, he was active in criminal law reform and critical of many Warren Court decisions on criminal cases. A conservative, his court

Ralph Bunche

Luther Burbank

Warren Burger

restrained and sometimes reversed liberal decisions of the Warren Court. In *Harris* v. *New York* (1971) the Court reversed *Miranda* v. *Arizona,* thereby legalizing the use of a suspect's statement, made while in police custody, for trial purposes. The ruling on the Federal Election Campaign Act of 1974 (1976) upheld most of the act, but stated that the commission that would administer federal political-matching funds must be appointed by the president rather than Congress. In *Gregg* v. *Georgia* (1976) capital punishment for murder was declared constitutional, but other crimes do not warrant the death penalty (*Coker* v. *Georgia*:1977). *Regents of the University of California* v. *Bakke* (1978) dealt with reverse racial discrimination and affirmative action programs. He retired in 1986.

Burgess, Anthony (John Burgess Wilson) (1917–), English novelist and critic. Malaya, where he lived (1954–59), is the setting for a trilogy—*Time for a Tiger* (1956), *The Enemy in the Blanket* (1957), and *Beds in the East* (1959). In later novels he shows an interest in projecting social trends in linguistic effects, and in religious symbolism, as in *A Clockwork Orange* (1962); other works include *1985* (1978), *Man of Nazareth* (1979), *Earthly Powers* (1980), *On Going to Bed* (1982), *The End of the World News* (1983), and *Enderby's Dark Lady* (1984).

Burgos, city in N Spain, 130mi (209km) N of Madrid; capital of Burgos prov.; capital of kingdom of Castile (9th-16th centuries); home and burial place of El Cid; served as capital of Gen. Francisco Franco's regime during Civil War (1936–39); site of Gothic cathedral (1221), Church of San Esteban, and Arco de Santa Maria; important trade and tourist center. Industries: fabrics, soap, furniture, shoes, wine. Founded 884. Pop. 119,915.

Burgoyne, John (1722–92), British general during the Revolutionary War. He served in Boston (1775) and Canada (1776). Campaigning in New York State, he secured Crown Point and Ft. Ticonderoga, but was forced to surrender his forces at Saratoga, Oct. 17, 1777.

Burgundy, historical region of France that now includes depts. of Yonne, Côte-d'Or, Saône-et-Loire, Ain, and Nièvra; contains numerous medieval Romanesque churches; Dijon is its historical capital. A rich agricultural region, it has been known for its wine since 50 BC. Burgundy's golden age began in 1361 when France's John II made his son, Philip the Bold, duke of Burgundy. These dukes dominated French politics in the early 15th century. Their last reigning duke, Charles the Bold, unsuccessfully challenged power of Louis XI in 1465; Burgundy as a state ceased to exist after 1477 when Louis XI made it part of the crown lands.

Burgundy, School of, group of Flemish panel painters and miniaturists who worked at Dijon between 1390 and 1420. Their work was intended for Chartreuse de Champmol near Dijon, but their style of realism remained Flemish. The master of Flemalle and the Van Eyck brothers have their roots here.

Burke, Edmund (1729–97), Irish political figure and author. He became secretary to British prime minister Rockingham and entered Parliament (1765). He attacked increasing royal power and supported the parliamentary process. With Charles J. Fox he sought wiser treatment for the Catholics and Americans. As forces' paymaster (1782–83) he reduced crown patronage. He instigated the impeachment of Warren Hastings in an attempt to reform India's government (1788). Burke believed in liberty based on order, with

change being gradual. His *Reflections on the Revolution in France* (1790) shows his horror at the radicalism of the French Revolution, and he broke with Fox over the reform question (1791).

Burkino Faso. *See* Upper Volta.

Burlesque, in the United States, a type of popular entertainment accenting sex and comedy and devised by Michael Bennett Leavitt (1865). The peak in its popularity was the 1900s and it spawned dozens of famous comics and singers. After World War I, to compete with films, it introduced the striptease.

Burlington, city in N central North Carolina, 18mi (29km) E of Greensboro; site of Elon College. Industries: textiles, hosiery, yarn. Inc. 1893. Pop. (1980) 37,-266.

Burlington, city in NW Vermont, on Lake Champlain; seat of Chittenden co; scene of British naval attack in War of 1812; birthplace of John Dewey; burial place of Ethan Allen. Largest city in the state, it is site of University of Vermont and Trinity College. Industries: metallurgy, missile parts, textiles, wood products. Settled 1773; inc. 1865. Pop. (1980) 37,712.

Burma (Myanma), an isolated socialist republic in SE Asia. Its greatest asset is its mineral wealth. The famous WWII Burma Road supply line to China from 1938–42 ran through the country.

Land and economy. Circled by barriers of imposing mountain ranges to the N, E, and W (Saramati is 15,000ft (4,575m) above sea level), Burma has been isolated from outside contact; its forests and rivers have discouraged travel within the country. The Irrawaddy River is its economic lifeline and major transportation system. Rangoon is its chief port. Burma's monsoon climate results in yearly rainfall of 30in (76cm) in the central dry zone to 200in (508cm) on the coast. An agricultural country, it once led the world in rice exports, but shifting world markets have lowered sales. Exports are lead and zinc ore, precious stones, lumber. The chief import is industrial machinery.

People. Burmans comprise the main ethnic group with smaller groups of Karens, Chins, and Kachins. Eighty-five percent practice Theravada Buddhism. Burmese is the principal language. Education is free from primary school to college. Traditional Buddhist schools exist in the rural areas. Literacy is 64%.

Government. According to the constitution of 1973 the president heads the 29-member State Council, the chief government body. The People's Assembly consists of 464 elected members, from the Burma Socialist Programme Party, the sole legal political party.

History. Kublai Khan's Mongols invaded in 1287 and started centuries of warring dynasties until 1824, when Burma was annexed to British India. In 1937 a constitution allowed some self-government. Occupied by the Japanese in WWII, it suffered great devastation until 1945 when Burmese Nationalist and Allied troops liberated the country. With independence in 1948, Burma became a parliamentary democracy. In 1962, Gen. Ne Win grabbed power from elected premier U Nu and set Burma on a socialist path with a neutral foreign policy. Uprisings by Communist guerrillas and pressures from ethnic minorities —especially Muslims in Arakan province—are its most pressing problems. In 1974, Ne Win was elected president of a civilian government, relinquishing the post to San Yu in 1981.

PROFILE

Official name: Socialist Republic of the Union of Burma
Area: 261,789sq mi (678,034sq km)

Population: 33,310,000;
  Density: 127per sq mi (49per sq km)
Chief cities: Rangoon (capital); Mandalay; Moulmein
Government: Socialist republic
Religion: Buddhist (major)
Language: Burmese
Monetary unit: Kyat
Gross national product: $5,140,000,000
Per capita income: $82
Industries: processed food, textiles, tobacco, and wood products
Agriculture: rice, cotton, teak, rubber, sesame, millet
Minerals: petroleum, lead, silver, tin, tungsten, zinc, rubies, sapphires, jade
Trading partners: Singapore, Indonesia, Japan, European Common Market

Burma Road, major ground transportation route into Nationalist China during World War II. Closed by Japanese pressure, the road from the railhead at Lashio, Burma, to Siakwan in Yunnan prov., China, was reopened by Allied forces in 1945. Until then China's links with the outside were primarily by air.

Burmese, the official language of Burma, spoken by about three-fourths of the population, or some 25 million people. It belongs to the Tibeto-Burman branch of the Sino-Tibetan family of languages.

Burmese Cat, short-haired domestic cat breed developed in the United States during the 1930s. Not an oriental type, it has a round head, yellow or gold almond-shaped eyes, wide-set ears, and a thick, muscular body. The flat, satinlike coat of this dainty, affectionate cat is solid sable brown. Varieties are Blue and Champagne.

Burnet, common name for perennials native to the north temperate zone. The leaves, comprised of serrated leaflets, are sometimes used in salads when young. Small individual flowers are bunched along tall spikes. Conspicuously long stamens give the spikes a feathery look. The American burnet grows to 5ft (1.5m). Family Rosaceae; genus *Sanguisarba*.

Burns, Robert (1759–96), the national poet of Scotland. The son of a tenant farmer, he began to write poetry in 1783. In 1786 he published *Poems, Chiefly in the Scottish Dialect* to raise money to emigrate to Jamaica. The huge success of this volume led him to change his plans and move to Edinburgh, where he became the chief attraction of literary and social circles. A second, expanded edition of his poems appeared in 1787. In 1788 he left Edinburgh, married, and settled on a farm in Ellisland where he remained until 1791, when he obtained a post in the excise office at Dumfries. He died after an attack of rheumatic fever. In his poetry he combined Scottish dialect and folk idiom with the craftmanship of the finest British poets. He added new vitality to English poetry, which had grown stilted. He wrote nearly 300 songs set to ancient Scottish airs, including "Auld Lang Syne," "Flow Gently, Sweet Afton," and "Comin' Thro' the Rye." His lyric poems, such as "To a Mouse" and "To a Louse," were often satiric, yet playful, as were such longer poems as "The Cotter's Saturday Night" and "Tam o'Shanter."

Burns, damage to body tissue by heat, chemicals, electricity, or radiation. First-degree burns involve only the superficial skin, second- and third-degree burns penetrate progressively deeper. Treatment includes relief of pain, control of infection, prevention of shock.

Burr, Aaron (1756–1836), vice president of the United States, b. Newark. A Revolutionary War veteran and senator from New York (1791–97), he ran for vice president on Thomas Jefferson's Democratic-Republican ticket in 1800. Burr and Jefferson were tied in the electoral college but Jefferson was elected president with Alexander Hamilton's support. Hamilton's public attacks on Burr led to a duel in which Burr killed Hamilton (1804). His political career ended by this duel, Burr engaged with Gen. James Wilkenson in an apparent conspiracy to establish an independent republic in the Southwest. He was tried for treason but was acquitted (1807) and spent the rest of his career practicing law.

Burro, Spanish word for ass, small domesticated ass used as a pack animal in SW United States and in Mexico. A long-eared, sturdy animal derived from the Nubian wild ass, it is brown, gray, or black. Many are now feral. Family Equidae; species *Equus asinus asinus. See also* Ass.

Bursa, formerly Brusa, city in NW Turkey, approx. 13mi (21km) SE of Sea of Marmara; capital of Bursa prov.; ancient city of Prusa founded by King Prusias; now a rail terminus and trade center. Industries: textiles (especially silk), carpets, tiles, tobacco, rice, grains. Pop. 346,084.

Bursitis, inflammation of a sac or cavity usually near a joint. Cause may be injury or disease. It is characterized by pain, swelling, limited motion.

Burton, Harold H(itz) (1888–1964), US jurist, mayor of Cleveland (1935–40) and US senator from Ohio (1941–45), b. Jamaica Plain, Mass. He was appointed associate justice of the US Supreme Court in 1945, where he shared the views of judges Vinson and Frankfurter favoring judicial restraint, the loyalty oath, and other civil liberty restrictions. He did, however, side with the liberal wing on civil rights decisions, most notably *Brown* v. *Board of Education* (1954). After retiring in 1958, he served occasionally on the court of appeals in Washington, D.C.

Burton, (Sir) Richard Francis (1821–90), English explorer and specialist on the Orient. In 1853, disguised as an Afghan pilgrim, he made a pilgrimage to Medina and Mecca, being one of the first Europeans to visit those cities. On his second trip to East Africa with John Speke in 1858, he discovered Lake Tanganyika. From 1861 until his death, he served in the British diplomatic service. The author of more than 30 travel books, he was best known for his translation of the Oriental tales, the "Arabian Nights."

Burundi, republic in E central Africa, headed by a president, bordered by Rwanda (N), Tanzania (E), Lake Tanganyika (SW), and Zaire (W). The capital is Bujumbura. Located near the equator, the country has two wet and two dry seasons with an annual rainfall of 31–57in (79–145cm); prolonged droughts have often resulted in serious famines. The lowlands of the W (Ruzizi River Valley and E shore of Lake Tanganyika) rise rapidly into mountains from 7,000–9,000ft (2,135–2,745m) and then fall into lower plateaus of 4,500–6,000ft (1,373–1,830m), where most of the population is concentrated. A predominantly agricultural economy (41% of land is arable) supports widespread subsistence farming. Coffee is the main export crop; cotton and tea are also exported; some cattle are raised. Cassiterite (tin) is the chief mineral. The Hutu or Bahutu comprise 86% of population and are mainly farmers. The Tutsi (Watutsi) are cattle raisers and warriors and account for 12% of inhabitants; they enjoy higher social status than the Hutu. Elementary schools enroll about 40% of children in this age group; few go on to secondary or college education.

In the 19th century the country was ruled by a king (Tutsi). Burundi and Rwanda joined German East Africa in 1890. Germany actually began to rule in 1897. During WWI Belgium occupied the country, and in 1919 the League of Nations made it a Belgian mandate. In 1946 it became the UN trust territory of Ruanda-Urundi. In 1962 it became a separate independent country. Since then it has suffered many power struggles between Hutu and Tutsi. Following an uprising in 1972, more than 150,000 Hutu were killed by the Tutsi-dominated army. In 1976 the military assumed control of the government.

PROFILE

Official name: Republic of Burundi
Area: 10,747sq mi (27,835sq km)
Population: 4,100,000
Chief cities: Bujumbura (capital); Gitega
Religion: Christianity and tribal
Language: Kirundi and French
Monetary unit: Burundi franc

Burying Beetle, or carrion beetle, medium-sized beetle found in all temperate regions. They bury and lay their eggs in dead mice, frogs, birds, and other small animals. Genus *Necrophorus.*

Bury Saint Edmunds, market town in S England; farming region. St Edmund, last king of the Angles, was buried here 903. Industries: sugar refining, brewing, agricultural machinery. Pop. 25,629.

Bush, George Herbert Walker (1924–), US vice president, political leader, and diplomat, b. Milton, Mass. The son of US Sen. Prescott S. Bush, George Bush moved to Texas and established a successful career in the oil industry after service in World War II and graduation from Yale (1948). In 1966 he was elected to the House of Representatives from Texas. Losing a campaign for the Senate in 1970, he was appointed US ambassador to the United Nations by Pres. Richard M. Nixon. Bush was US liaison officer to the People's Republic of China under Pres. Gerald Ford (1974) and was head of the CIA (1976–77) before returning to private industry. In 1980, after campaigning unsuccessfully against Ronald Reagan for the Republican presidential nomination, he was selected by Reagan as his running mate and elected vice president in 1980.

Bush Baby, or galago, primitive squirrellike primate of African forests and bushlands. They are usually gray or brown with a white stripe between the eyes. Bush babies are gregarious, nocturnal, tree dwellers, often domesticated as pets. Genera *Galago, Euoticus. See also* Primates.

Bushido, or Way of the Samurai, a code of conduct in Japan not unlike the chivalric codes of European knights. It stressed complete loyalty to one's master, bravery, and a hard spartan life-style. Unlike European knights, however, Samurai were encouraged to take pride in their literary and educational accomplishments.

Bushmaster, largest New World pit viper, found in Central America and N South America. It has large venom glands and long fangs and is gray and brown with a bold diamond pattern. Length: to 12ft (3.7m). Family Crotalidae; species *Lachesis muta. See also* Pit Viper.

Bushmen, or San, Khoisan-speaking people of southern Africa; characteristically of short stature, with a leathery yellowish skin and large buttocks. Until recently they had a hunting and gathering culture, with little value for material possessions. However, only a few thousand still follow traditional ways, mostly in the Kalahari region; others have become assimilated into white and Bantu agricultural society as hired laborers.

Bushrangers, bandits who terrorized the Australian outback in the 19th century. Many were escaped convicts, others were adventurers who after 1850 attacked gold convoys. The notorious Kelly gang was wiped out in 1880.

Business Cycles, patterned movements of the economy consisting of recurring periods of prosperity and recession. Normally measured by the industrial production of the economy, a business cycle may be divided into four phases: depression, recovery, prosperity, and recession. Depression is the turning point of the lower portion of the business cycle; prosperity is the turning point of the upper portion. Recession and depression are usually associated with rising unemployment and decreases in consumer buying power. Recovery and prosperity are normally associated with low unemployment, expanding consumer purchasing power, and rising prices. The short-run business cycle consists of seasonal fluctuations in the economy as well as short periods of expansion and contraction. The long-run business cycle involves major movement of the economy over many years.

Bustard, shy, heavy-bodied, ostrichlike bird of Eastern Hemisphere grasslands and semideserts that flies strongly and runs swiftly. It has a thick bill, a long neck and legs, gray or brown plummage with white spots on top and black spots below. It feeds on small animals, and lays eggs (1–5) in a ground depression. Height: 14.5–52in (37–132cm). Family Otididae.

Butadiene (1,3-butadiene), gaseous flammable hydrocarbon (formula $CH_2{:}CHCH{:}CH_2$) made from butenes or by cracking naphtha. It is copolymerized with styrene to produce synthetic rubbers. Properties: sp. gr. 0.62; melt. pt. −164.03°F (−108.91°C); boil. pt. 24.06°F (−4.41°C).

Butane, gaseous flammable colorless hydrocarbon (C_4H_{10}), obtained as a byproduct of petroleum refining. It is used as a fuel gas and in the manufacture of synthetic rubber. Properties: melt. pt. −217.03°F (−138.35°C); boil. pt. 31.1°F (−0.5°C).

Butler, Samuel (1835–1902), English satiric novelist, scientific writer, and translator. Emigrated to New Zea-

land in 1859. Returning to England, he wrote *Erewhon* (1872), *The Way of All Flesh* (1903), travel books, articles on Homer, and several works opposing Darwin's theory of evolution.

Butte, city in SW Montana, in plateau of Rocky Mts; seat of Silver Bow co; site of Montana College of Mineral Science and Technology (1893), headquarters of Deer Lodge National Forest. Industries: silver, copper, and manganese mining. Founded 1864; inc. as town 1876; as city 1879. Pop. 37,205.

Butte, hard rock remnant covering soft sediment in an arid region. When wind and water erosion wear away softer rock on the slopes of a hill, the resulting formation is a columnar structure with nearly vertical sides.

Buttercup, or crowfoot, herbaceous flowering plant distributed worldwide. Numerous stamens and pistils form a button or bushy cluster at the flower center and leaves are palmate and deeply cut. The common buttercup (*Ranunculus acris*), found in fields and meadows, is an erect, hairy plant with glossy yellow flowers. Height: to 3ft (91cm). Family Ranunculaceae.

Butterfish, marine commercial fish found along Atlantic and Pacific coasts. A favorite sport fish for panfrying, it is silvery-gray or blue with dark spots. Length: 12in (30.5cm); weight: 1.25lb (0.57kg). Family Stromateidae; species includes Atlantic *Peprilus triacanthus* and California pompano *Peprilus simillimus.*

Butterfly, day-active, usually brightly colored insect. The butterfly is distinguished from the moth by its slender body and knobbed antennae. It holds its wings vertically when at rest. Order Lepidoptera; family Papilionoidea. *See also* Lepidoptera.

Butterfly Fish, tropical marine fish found around coral in shallow waters. A popular aquarium fish, it has a disc-shaped, compressed body with extended snout. Colors and patterns are bright and varied. Length: 6–8in (15.2–20.3cm). Family Chaetodontidae; species includes common *Chaetodon ocellatus.*

Butternut, a deciduous tree *Juglans cinerea* of the Walnut family, native to E North America, growing to 90ft (27m). The fruit is ovalish, and the nut is furrowed, oily, and sweet.

Butterwort, any of a large group (genus *Pinguicula* of the family Lentibulariaceae) of carnivorous bog plants that capture and digest insects in a sticky secretion ("butter") on their leaves. Butterworts are stemless and bear single white, purple, or yellow flowers on a leafless stalk.

Buzzard, slow-moving hawk with broad, rounded wings, fan-shaped tail, sharp hooked beak, and sharp talons. The common European buzzard (*Buteo buteo*) is brown above and mottled with white below. North American representatives include the red-shouldered hawk (*Buteo lineatus*) and red-tailed hawk (*Buteo jamaicensis*). In the Western Hemisphere the term "buzzard" is often used for the turkey vulture (*Cathartes aura*). Length: 23–32in (59–81cm). Genus *Buteo.*

Byrd, Richard Evelyn (1888–1957), naval officer and polar explorer, b. Winchester, Va. He entered the Navy (1912), retired (1916), and was recalled and trained as an aviator (1917). With copilot Floyd Bennett, he led the first flight over South Pole (1926) and the first of five North Pole expeditions (1928). He spent five months alone in Antarctica (1934), publishing experiences in *Alone* (1938). His last Antarctic trip (1955–56) was in preparation for US participation in the International Geophysical Year.

Byrd, William (1543–1623), English musician, who became the greatest composer of the Elizabethan period. A lifelong Roman Catholic, Byrd was appointed by Elizabeth I to be joint organist of the Chapel Royal with Thomas Tallis, whom he succeeded (1585). With Tallis, he was granted a monopoly to print music. Byrd was master of all the musical forms of his day, important for his madrigals, the body of distinguished church music that he wrote for both Catholic and Anglican services.

Byrnes, James F(rancis) (1879–1972), US lawyer and statesman, b. Charleston, S.C. A US congressman (1911–25) and senator (1931–41) from South Carolina, appointed associate justice of the US Supreme Court by Franklin D. Roosevelt in 1941, he resigned in 1942 to direct the Office of Economic Stabilization. US secretary of state (1945–47) and delegate to the UN (1953), he was governor of South Carolina (1951–55), advocating segregation and states' rights.

Byron, George Gordon Noel Byron, 6th Baron (1788–1824), English poet. Lord Byron is as much

Burundi

George Bush

Richard Byrd

remembered for his flamboyant, romantic life as for his poetry. He was born with a club foot and as a child suffered poverty and abuse from his unstable mother. At the age of 10, he inherited the title and estates of a great-uncle. His first collection of poems, published in 1807, was badly received; but with *English Bards and Scotch Reviewers* (1809), a satirical work, his reputation was made. In 1812 he published the first of two cantos of *Childe Harold's Pilgrimage*. It was a brilliant success, and Byron immediately became the literary and social lion of London. Identified with the romantic, idealistic hero of his poem, Byron was widely regarded as the personification of the romantic poet; the term "Byronic hero" was coined as much to describe him as the protagonists of his poems. Byron embarked on a series of love affairs, most notoriously one with Lady Caroline Lamb, wife of William Lamb (later Lord Melbourne). He apparently also had homosexual affairs and a liaison with his half sister. In 1815 he married Annabella Milbanke, but the marriage lasted only a year, primarily because of the rumors of Byron's varied sex life. The scandals of his personal life increased, and Byron left England for Italy.

Despite a life of dissipation in Italy and Switzerland, Byron produced a large body of work, including Cantos III and IV of *Childe Harold* (1816, 1817), *The Prisoner of Chillon* (1816), *Beppo* (1818), *Mazeppa* (1819), and *Don Juan* (1819–24). He became interested in the cause of the Greek independence fighters against Turkish domination. He went to Greece to fight with them but contracted brain fever and died shortly after his arrival. In his own day, Byron was highly regarded as a lyric poet and was ranked with Percy Bysshe Shelley and John Keats as the great trio of English Romanticism. Modern critics, however, tend to regard his satirical works more highly than his lyrical poems. *Don Juan* is generally regarded as his masterpiece.

Byzantine Architecture, architecture characterized by the use of the dome to cover polygonal and square churches, baptistries, and tombs and dating from the 5th century. The plan is typically central rather than longitudinal, and the central dome, surrounded by groupings of smaller or semi-domes, is supported by means of pendentives. Construction is of brick arranged in decorative patterns and mortar. Interiors are faced with marble slabs, colored glass mosaics, gold leaf, and fresco decoration. Typically the head and shoulders of Christ are depicted in the dome, the four Evangelists in the pendentives, and the Virgin and Child in the east-facing apse. Byzantine architecture remained unusually conservative for more than a thousand years and influenced church building in Russia, Italy, Greece, and elsewhere.

Byzantine Empire, known also as the East Roman Empire, or Medieval Greek Empire. The history of the Byzantine Empire spanned the long period from AD 330 when its capital city of Constantinople was est. by the Roman Emperor Constantine the Great, to the year 1453, when the same city was captured by the Ottoman Turks.

Location. Constantinople, a well-fortified city on the Bosporus, commanded one of the most important routes between the European and Asian continents. The city was the heart of the empire, whose outer boundaries were constantly changing, as it annexed foreign territories and was in turn invaded. It generally comprised large parts of Anatolia, or Asia Minor, and the Balkans, as well as (during periods of expansion) S Italy and Ravenna, Greece, Syria, Egypt, and portions of Spain and the N African coast.

Culture. Though the Byzantines considered themselves the heirs of the Roman Empire (and referred to themselves as Romans), their society was a mixture of many elements. The traditions of imperial Rome

shaped their governmental institutions; the language and customs of classical Greece molded their cultural life; and Orthodox Christianity determined their religion.

Government and History. The Byzantine state was, in theory, a continuation of the Roman Empire. While the Roman Empire in the West had fallen into decline after the Germanic invasions, imperial traditions remained in effect in the East. The Emperor Justinian I (r.527–65) reconquered the territory of the old Roman Empire, and codified the Roman law. Under the Heraclian emperors (610–717), the empire defeated its Persian enemies, but also saw the rise of the Arab threat. During the age of the Iconoclastic Controversy (717–867), the Isaurian and Amorian rulers dealt with severe internal crises. The Macedonian epoch (867–1081) is known as the Golden Age of the Byzantine Empire, for it was a time of territorial consolidation and cultural flowering. The emperors of the Comnenian and Angelian dynasties (1081–1204) witnessed both an expansion of Byzantine power and the threatening advance of the crusading armies of W Europe. The crusaders ruled Byzantium during the dominion of the Latin Empire of Constantinople (1204–61). Michael VIII, restorer of the Greek Empire, founded the Palaeologan dynasty (1261–1453). When, in 1453, Constantinople fell to the Turkish forces of Sultan Muhammad II, the Byzantine Empire came to an end.

Byzantium. *See* Constantinople; Istanbul.

C

Cabal, advisers to Charles II of England during the period 1667–73. Chosen by the king to replace the earl of Clarendon, who had been impeached as lord chancellor, the initials of the five members—Clifford, Arlington, Buckingham, Ashley Cooper, Lauderdale—spelled "cabal." They plotted with the king to bring about religious toleration for Dissenters (including Catholics) against the wishes of Parliament. However, the 1672 Declaration of Indulgence produced an uproar causing all high-ranking Catholics (including two in the Cabal) to resign, thus ending the Cabal.

Cabala, or Kabbala, form of Jewish mysticism. It holds that every word, letter, number, even accent of the Bible contains mysteries to be interpreted. The earliest extant cabalist work is the *Sefir Yezirah* (Book of Creation), dating from about the 3rd century AD. This work contains monologues attributed to Abraham to which numerology was applied to explain creation. Cabalism spread throughout Europe in the 13th century and is still practiced by some Hasidic Jews.

Cabaret Theater, a form of entertainment, usually held in a cafe setting, characterized by intimate rapport between entertainer and audience and simple production values, and often producing satire and avant-garde humor. In pre-Hitler Germany it was linked with advanced politics and art and influenced the works of Bertolt Brecht.

Cabbage, vegetable cultivated for over 2000 years. Its large, green or reddish-purple leaves have fleshy midribs and form round, compact heads; diameter: 6–9in (15.2–22.9cm); weight: 4–6lb (1.8–2.7kg). A cool weather crop, it matures in 60–75 days. If grown during hot weather, it often goes to seed. Chinese cabbage

(Brassica pekinensis) has a milder taste and 18in (45.7cm) cylindrical heads. Family Cruciferae; species *Brassica oleracea capitata.*

Cabbage Palm, several palms whose young leaves are eaten as a vegetable. Among them are cabbage palmetto *(Sabal palmetto)*, a 90ft (27m) tall palm native to SE United States; *Roystonea oleracea*, also called palmiste, a 120ft (37m) tall West Indian palm; and the Australian *Livistona australis*, which grows to 80ft (24m). Family Palmaceae.

Cabeza de Vaca, Álvar Núñez (c.1490–c.1557), Spanish explorer. Leaving Spain in 1527, he was shipwrecked the following year off the Texas coast. He and three other survivors were the first Europeans to explore the American Southwest, as recorded in his *The Shipwrecked Men* (1542). His *Comentarios* (1555) recounts hardships endured in South America, where he served unsuccessfully as governor of Paraguay (1541–42) and opened a trail from Brazil to Paraguay.

Cabinda (Kabinda), port town in Angola, SW Africa, 35mi (56km) N of Congo River; capital of Cabinda, an autonomous Angolan district. Exports: palm, timber, oil, cacao. Pop. 81,265.

Cabinet, body of official advisers to a nation's chief executive; usually the heads of the government's administrative departments. Its power differs in various political systems. In the United States, it exercises only the authority the president chooses to give it.

Cabinet Government, system in which the legislature establishes the administrative government and provides the leadership. The chief executive is usually a prime minister selected by the party with a majority in the legislature. The system originated in 18th-century England with the development of parliamentary supremacy and party government.

Cabinetmaking, skill of furniture making and interior woodwork finishing. Cabinetmaking reached its height in the 18th century, the golden age of furniture design, under the masters Thomas Chippendale, George Hepplewhite, Thomas Sheraton, the Adam brothers, and Duncan Phyfe, an immigrant from Scotland working in America. Cabinets can be divided into a large number of classes according to their shape, style, period, and country of origin; but their common characteristics are that they contain a series of drawers and pigeonholes. In its rudimentary form the cabinet was an oblong box, with or without feet, small enough to rest on a table, filled with drawers and closed with doors, and used for safeguarding jewels, precious stones, and money. During the Renaissance cabinets became more elaborate and architectural until they became one of the most sumptuous pieces in the household.

The basis of the cabinet was wood, carved, polished, or inlaid, sometimes embellished with ivory, tortoiseshell, and cut and polished precious stones. Doors and drawers were sometimes painted with classical or mythological scenes. During the 16th and 17th centuries a popular form actually recreated a tiny palatial interior behind folding doors. Armoires, which consisted of two pieces, one on top of the other, originated with the Flemish cabinetmakers and spread to France and England. A glass-fronted cabinet for china and glass was highly favored by the English during the Georgian period.

Cable, George Washington (1844–1925), US short story writer and novelist, b. New Orleans. A leader of the local color movement, a number of his stories of Louisiana appeared in a collection, *Old Creole Days* (1879). His novels include *The Grandissimes* (1880), about early 19th-century Louisiana, *Madame Delphine* (1881), and *Bonaventure* (1888). *See also* Local Color.

Cabot, John (c.1450–98), navigator and explorer, b. Giovanni Caboto in Italy. He was employed by Henry VII and sailed in the *Mathew* from Bristol in search of a western route to India. He landed at Cape Breton Island or Newfoundland (1497). On his second voyage (1498) he presumably reached Greenland and sailed on to Chesapeake Bay. His discovery served as the basis of English claims in North America.

Cabot, Sebastian (*c.* 1476–1557), Italian navigator and explorer. The son of John Cabot, he explored the Americas for England and Spain. He founded and directed the expeditions of the Merchant Adventurers of London, which initiated Russian-English commerce with a treaty.

Cabral, Pedro Álvares (*c.* 1467–*c.* 1520), Portuguese navigator. In 1500 King Manuel sent him with a fleet of ships to the East Indies. Unaccountably, he sailed westward and discovered Brazil, which he claimed for Portugal.

Cabrillo, Juan Rodríguez (died 1543), Portuguese explorer in Spanish service. He discovered California (1542) while exploring the west coast of Mexico. He landed at Point Loma Head, San Diego Bay (now in Cabrillo National Monument), then sailed up to San Francisco Bay.

Cacao, or chocolate tree, tropical and subtropical evergreen tree found in South and Central America. Its seeds are the source of chocolate and cocoa. It has long, leathery, oval leaves and yellow flower clusters, and reddish, woody fruits, each containing about 50 flat cacao beans. Height: 40ft(12m). Family Sterculiaceae; species *Theobroma cacao.*

Cáceres, city in W central Spain, on Cáceres River; capital of Cáceres prov.; site of many Roman and Moorish remains. Industries: cloth, pottery, leather, stock raising, wine. Area: (prov.) 7,701sq mi (19,946sq km). Pop. (city) 56,064; (prov.) 457,777.

Cacomistle, or ring-tailed cat, nocturnal, omnivorous member of the raccoon family native to SW United States and Mexico. Agile tree-climbers, they have gray to brown fur with black bands on bushy tails. They make good pets, being especially good rat hunters. Length: 14.5in (36.8cm); weight: to 2.5lb. (1.1kg). Family Procyonidae; species *Bassariscus astutus* (or *Jentinkia sumichrasti*).

Cactus, dicotyledonous succulents found throughout the Western Hemisphere, the majority in hot, arid regions. These leafless plants are thick, fleshy, and spiny. The swollen green joints of the stem function as leaves. A layer of wax over the stem helps control evaporation of moisture and roots are adapted to absorb water. Large cuplike blossoms have many stamens and stigmas in the center. Some well known species are barrel cactus, saguaro, prickly pear, and cereus. There are over 1000 species. Family Cactaceae.

Caddis Fly, mothlike insect found worldwide. It is an important fish food. Adults have long antennae and hold their wings tentlike. The larvae are found in ponds and streams, building cases or nets to live in. Length: 1in (25mm). Order Trichoptera.

Caddo, language family and confederation of related US Indian tribes once occupying the region of Louisiana, Arkansas, Texas, and Oklahoma. They were closely related to the Natchitoches, Adai, Hasinai, and Eyeish peoples, all of whom are now extinct. About 1,000 members of the various Caddoan bands live on the Witchita Reservation in SW Oklahoma.

Cade, Jack (died 1450), Irish rebel who led the 1450 disturbance in Kent and Sussex (Cade's Rebellion) against Henry VI. Claiming to be a Mortimer, cousin of the Duke of York, and captain of Kent, he issued a manifesto listing administrative reforms, and in May and June marched with 40,000 followers on London. They maintained order for two days, and then began pillaging the city. Cade, with a price on his head, escaped but was killed in Sussex.

Cadillac, (Sieur) Antoine de la Mothe (1658–1730), French colonial adminstrator. Arriving in Canada (1683), he engaged in Indian fighting (1684–87), and commanded the post at Michilimackinac (1694–97). He founded Detroit (1701) and served as its commandant (1704–10). He was governor of Louisiana (1713–16) until he fell into political disfavor and was imprisoned briefly in the Bastille.

Cádiz, seaport city in SW Spain, on the Bay of Cádiz; capital of Cádiz prov. Conquered by Carthaginians, Romans, Goths, Moors; Columbus departed from Cádiz in his 2nd journey to the New World (1495); site of 13th-century cathedral, art and archaeological museums, tomb of composer Manuel de Falla. Industries: chemicals, paper, textiles, salt, shipbuilding, fishing. Founded 1100 BC by Phoenicians. Pop. 135,743.

Cádiz, Gulf of, wide inlet of Atlantic Ocean, on SW coast of Spain; extends for 200mi (322km) from Cape Saint Vincent, Portugal, SE to Gibraltar; the Guadalquivir and Guadiana rivers flow into it.

Cadmium, metallic element (symbol Cd) of group IIB of the periodic table, first isolated (1817) by Friedrich Stromeyer. It is found in greenockite (sulfide) but the chief source is as a by-product in the extraction of zinc. Its main use is as a protective electroplated coating. Chemically it resembles zinc. Properties: at. no. 48; at. wt. 112.4; sp. gr. 8.65; melt. pt. 609.6°F (320.9°C); boil. pt. 1409°F (765°C); most common isotope Cd^{114} (28.86%).

Cadmus, in Greek mythology, a prince of Phoenicia. Cadmus and his brothers were sent to find their sister Europa, who had been carried off by Zeus. After a fruitless search, Cadmus founded and settled in a town he named after himself. After eight years of proving himself to the gods, he was crowned king of Cadmia, later called Thebes.

Caduceus, in classical times, a herald's wand or staff, a badge showing that the bearer was a sacred person not to be molested. Its original form was in all probability a straight branch from the top of which two twigs grew. These twigs were then pulled back and twined around the branch. Later the twigs were represented as snakes. Thus the caduceus is often snake-entwined.

Caecilian, limbless, underground burrowing amphibian resembling oversized earthworm, found in Central and South America, Asia, and Africa. Possessing minute, often useless, eyes, it has a sensory tentacle in a groove above the nose on each side of the head. The male has an organ for internal fertilization of the female. There are live-bearing and egg-laying species. Length: to 4.5ft (1.4m). There are 75 species. Order Gymnophiona; family Caeciliidae. *See also* Amphibia.

Caecum, blind end or pouch at the junction of the small and large intestines and to which is attached the appendix. *See also* Colon.

Caedmon (*fl.* 670), earliest-known English poet. According to Bede, he was an illiterate herdsman of Whitby Abbey who was commanded in a vision to turn the scriptures into poetry. Although credited with many other Old English poems, his sole surviving work is probably the brief "Hymn to Creation."

Caen, city and port in N France, on the Orne River; capital of Calvados dept.; important since 11th century, when William the Conqueror resided here. Many architectural masterpieces were destroyed in WWII; its university (1432) was rebuilt, and the 11th-century Abbaye Aux Hommes (burial place of William the Conqueror), Abbaye aux Dames, and Church of St Nicholas were preserved. Industries: iron ore mining, textiles, automobiles, electronic gear. Pop. 110,262.

Caernarvon (Caernarfon), historic town in NW Wales, on Menai Strait; formerly county town of Caernarvonshire, which became part of Gwynedd in 1974; site of Roman fortress ruins (AD 70–80); castle built by Edward I (1283) in which his son Edward II (or Edward of Carnarvon) was born 1284. He was crowned first Prince of Wales here in 1301; Princes of Wales are now invested here. Industries: tourism, slate exporting, oil importing. Pop. 9,253.

Caesar, (Gaius) Julius (*c.*104–44 BC), Roman general and political figure. Of patrician birth, he married Cornelia, daughter of Cinna, a colleague of Marius, popular party leader who granted Caesar a priesthood (87 BC) that was later proscribed by Sulla (82BC). After Sulla's death Ceasar became military tribune and leader of the popular party against the Senate. As pontifex maximus (63 BC) he directed reforms that resulted in the Julian calendar. He fought in Spain, returning to form the First Triumvirate (60 BC) with Pompey and Crassus. An effective mediator, he instituted agrarian reforms, created a plebeian-patrician coalition, and successfully waged the Gallic Wars (58–49 BC), emerging as one of history's greatest military commanders. He secured Roman dominance of Gaul and Britain.

When his rivalry with Pompey caused the Senate to demand that he dissolve his army, he refused and crossed the Rubicon River to engage in civil war. He defeated Pompey's forces at Pharsalus (48 BC) and, pursuing Pompey to Egypt, met Cleopatra, who later bore him a son. He conquered Pharnaces II of Pontus and wrote of the victory "Veni, vidi, vici" ("I came, I saw, I conquered"). Returning to Rome, he became dictator but refused royal title. Resentment against him mounted, and he was assassinated in the Senate on the Ides of March (44 BC) in a conspiracy led by Cassius and Marcus Brutus. He bequeathed his wealth and power to his grandnephew Octavian, who, with Mark Antony, avenged his murder. Historians debate Caesar's character but laud his military genius, statesmanship, and writings, *The Gallic Wars* and *Civil War.*

Caesarea, ancient city in Israel, on Mediterranean Sea, 22mi (35km) S of Haifa; was a Roman capital in Palestine, given to King Herod by Octavian 30 BC; site of St Paul's imprisonment AD 57–59; scene of massacre of Jews demanding Roman citizenship AD 66; fortified 1251 by Louis IX; destroyed by Saracens 1291; noted for ancient Roman theater.

Caesium. *See* Cesium.

Caesura, pause in a line of verse, occuring near the middle and generally indicating a pause in the meaning. The caesura is found in Greek and Latin prosody as well as in English-language prosody.

Caffeine, a stimulant found in several plants, used in many common beverages, including coffee, tea, cola drinks, and in some medicines.

Cage, John (1912–), US composer, b. Los Angeles. His daring experiments and innovations received attention (eg, pianos "prepared" with objects on their strings to alter pitch and tone; adding chance events to music). Compositions for prepared piano include *Bachanale* (1938) and *Sonatas and Interludes* (1946–48).His 10-hour composition, *Empty Voices*, was first performed in 1979.

Cagliari, port city in Sardinia, Italy; capital of Cagliari prov. and of Sardinia region. Founded by Phoenicians, it was independent in the Middle Ages; vital naval and air bases on island were destroyed by Allied bombing in WWII. Historical landmarks include Roman amphitheater, Cathedral of St Cecilia (1257–1312), 5th- and 6th-century Christian church. Exports: lead, zinc, salt. Industries: agriculture, salt extraction, cement. Pop. 236,931.

Caguas, city in E central Puerto Rico; fertile agricultural area; major industrial center. Industries: sugar refining, textiles, coffee. Pop. 107,500.

Caiman, or cayman, alligatorlike reptile of Central and South America. Most abundant are the spectacled caimans with curved ridges of bone connecting the eye sockets. The black caiman *(Melanosuchus niger)* is the largest, reaching a length of 15ft (4.6m). Smooth-fronted caimans are the smallest and have especially heavy armor. Family Alligatoridae. *See also* Alligator.

Cain, in Genesis, firstborn son of Adam and Eve and brother of Abel. Because God accepted Abel's offering in preference to his own, Cain murdered Abel in anger. Banished to the wilderness, he and his family lived thereafter as nomads.

Cairn Terrier, small working dog (terrier group) bred in Scotland and first shown in United States in 1916. Used to rout fox and badgers, the cairn has a short, broad head, small pointed and erect ears; a medium-long, level body; short legs; and a short tail carried up. Its hard, weather-resistant coat is any color but white. Its ears, muzzle, and tail tip are darker than the coat. Average size: 10in (25cm) high at shoulder; 14lb (6.3kg). *See also* Terrier.

Cairo, capital city of Egypt; a port on the Nile River; includes two islands in the Nile, Zamalik and Rawdah, linked to the mainland by bridges. Cairo was founded AD 969 and includes Old Cairo, a Roman fortress city. Built on high ground to avoid Nile floods, it flourished and replaced Alexandria as the capital in 1863; site of the sphinx and pyramids of Giza (dating from 3000 BC), over 400 museums, temples, palaces, and mosques. Industries: tourism, textiles, iron, steel, sugar refining, cigarettes. Pop. 5,517,000.

Caisson, a watertight structure or chamber used in excavation or construction. It accommodates workmen underwater and also facilitates removal of excavated materials. Frequently used in underwater tunnels, where it acts as a shell for the building of a foundation. Open caissons or pneumatic caissons using air pressure to support the excavation may be used.

Calabria, region of S Italy, comprising the "toe" of the Italian "boot"; includes the provinces of Catanzaro,

Sebastian Cabot

Calamity Jane

John C. Calhoun

Cosenza, and Reggio di Calabria; capital is Catanzaro. Region was center of Greek colonization; fortunes declined under Roman rule; it was repeatedly invaded; conquered by Giuseppe Garibaldi 1860. Economic development has been slow due to the rugged terrain, poor communications, earthquakes, and feudal landholding conditions. Industries: hydroelectric power, agriculture, livestock, quarrying. Area: 5,822sq mi (15,079sq km). Pop. 2,048,901.

Caladium, genus of tropical American plants commonly grown for their brilliantly colored, variegated, arrow-shaped leaves. Leaf colors combine green, red, pink, silver, and white. It grows from a tuberous rhizome (underground stem) that can be stored. Family Aracea.

Calah, ancient city in Assyria, S of Ninevah, founded 13th century BC by Shalmaneser I. It is the same city as Nimrud. In 880 BC it was used as the capital of Assyria by Ashurnasirpal II; and is mentioned in the Book of Genesis. Excavations have uncovered palaces of Ashurnasirpal II and Shalmaneser III, ivories, sculpture, and the black obelisk of Shalmaneser III.

Calais, city in N France, on the Strait of Dover. A major commercial center and seaport since Middle Ages, it fell into English hands in 1347; a Rodin monument commemorates the legend of six burghers who offered their lives to save the town; city was returned to French rule 1558. Industries: lace making, chemicals, paper. Pop. 79,369.

Calamine, a pinkish, odorless powder of zinc oxide and some ferric oxide, dissolved in mineral oils and used in skin ointments to treat such disorders as chicken pox, poison ivy, and skin rashes.

Calamity Jane (1857–1903), US frontier figure, b. as Martha Jane Canary in Princeton, Mo. After working in western mining and railroad camps, she became associated with the US Cavalry as a guide and scout in the Black Hills area and was in Deadwood, S.D., during the gold rush there. Dime novels presented her as a crusader against evil romantically attached to Wild Bill Hickok. In actuality she was a heavy-drinking, rough-and-tumble character who wore men's clothing and was expert with a rifle and on a horse. Drifting around the West, she married (1891) a man named Clinton Burke, but he soon left her. She then appeared in Wild West shows. There are various explanations for her nickname. One is that she warned people that to offend her was to "court calamity."

Calcination, process of heating solids to high temperatures, but below their fusion point, in order to remove volatile substances, oxidize a portion of their mass (roasting), or render them friable. Lead, zinc, calcium, copper, and iron ores calcine to agglomerated oxides, which may be used as colored pigments or as intermediates in metal extraction.

Calcite, a carbonate mineral, calcium carbonate ($CaCO_3$). Found in all types of occurrences and with all classes of rocks. It is the main constituent of limestone. Hexagonal system varied crystals from rare tabular to prismatic or needlelike, also microcrystalline to coarse. Glassy white, fluoresces red, pink, yellow; hardness 3; sp gr 2.7. Transparent variety used in optical instruments.

Calcium, common metallic element (symbol Ca) of the alkaline-earth group, first isolated (1808) by Sir Humphrey Davy. It occurs in many rocks and minerals, notably limestone (carbonate) and gypsum (sulfate), and in bone. The metal has few commercial applica-

tions but calcium compounds are widely used. Chemically it is a reactive element, combining readily with oxygen, nitrogen, and other nonmetals. Properties: at. no. 20; at. wt. 40.08; sp. gr. 1.55; melt. pt. 1558°F (848°C); boil. pt. 2709°F (1487°C); most common isotope Ca^{40} (96.95%). *See also* Alkaline-Earth Elements.

Calcium Carbonate, white insoluble compound (formula $CaCO_3$) that occurs as marble, chalk, limestone, calcite, etc. It is used in the manufacture of cement and lime, and as a constituent of antacids and dentifrices. Properties: sp. gr. 1.49–1.66 (calcite); decomposes at 1648°F (898°C).

Calculus, branch of higher mathematics involving the operations of differentiation and integration. Calculus is often considered to have two parts—differential calculus and integral calculus—both concerned with the limiting values of a function as a variable tends to approach zero. Differential calculus enables the calculation of the rate at which one quantity changes with respect to another. It is used in finding slopes of curves, velocities, accelerations, etc. Integral calculus is used in finding the areas enclosed by curves, and in solving related problems. *See also* Mathematics.

Calculus, a "stone," often a calcium compound, usually in the urinary system. Excruciating pain is the chief symptom. Spontaneous expulsion is frequent.

Calcutta, city in E India; capital of West Bengal state; 2nd-largest city and chief port in India; former capital of British India (1773–1912); site of the Maidan (a park with statues of famous men), St Paul's Cathedral, Ochterlony Monument, the Kalighat (a Hindu temple). Calcutta is the world's largest jute-milling center; transportation hub. Industries: electrical equipment, cotton textiles, food processing. Exports: mineral ores, tea, hides, chemicals. Founded c. 1690. Pop. 7,031,382.

Caldecott, Randolph (1846–86), English illustrator of children's books. The popularity of his illustrations of Washington Irving's books led to his being asked to illustrate a pair of children's books in color: *The House That Jack Built* and *John Gilpin*, based on William Cowper's ballad, both published in 1878. Caldecott followed these with 14 other titles. The Caldecott Medal has been awarded annually since 1938 to the artist of the most distinquished US-published illustrated book for children.

Calder, Alexander (1898–1976), US sculptor, b. Philadelphia. He gained recognition with his miniature circus and toys made of wire and wood, which he exhibited at the Salon des Humoristes, Paris, 1927. In 1926 he executed his first wire sculpture, "Josephine Baker." Influenced by Joan Miró and Pieter Mondrian he created the mobile, a kinetic sculpture with parts that move either by motors or air currents. His first mobile was "Dancing Torpedo Shape." The term *mobile* was given to Calder's moving sculptures by Marcel Duchamp; Jean Arp coined the term *stabile* to apply to similar work that did not move. In later years, Calder became increasingly occupied with monumental stabiles, such as "Ticket Window" (1965; Lincoln Center for the Performing Arts, New York City) and "Man," executed for the 1967 Montreal Expo.

Caldera, volcanic basin, usually large and shallow, the result of subsidence of a volcanic summit. This is due to the migration of magma under the earth's crust. Caldera of extinct volcanoes, if fed by snow, springs, or ice, may become crater lakes.

Caldwell, Erskine (1903–), US author, b. Coweta co, Ga. His novels and short stories about the South often deal with people down on their luck and are noted for their mixture of humor, sex, and violence. His works include the novels *Tobacco Road* (1932) and *God's Little Acre* (1933), a number of other novels, and several collections of short stories, including *Stories of Life/North and South* (1983).

Calendar, a system by which the beginning and the divisions of the civil year are fixed. Days, weeks, and months are arranged in a definite order. Divisions are based on the movements of the earth and the appearances of the sun and moon. Ancient lunar calendars, based on the number of days between two full moons (29½ days), resulted in a lunar year of 354 days. In modern calendars, months are approximately one-twelfth of a solar year (365¼ days).

Calgary, city in SW Alberta, Canada, at the junction of the Box and Elbow rivers; site of the University of Calgary (1945) and Provincial Institute of Technology and Art (1916); industrial and commercial center. Industries: grain elevators, flour mills, livestock, wheat, lumber, brick, cement, oil refineries. Founded in 1875 as Northwest Mounted Police post; inc. 1893; government reorganized 1952. Pop. 530,816.

Calhoun, John Caldwell (1782–1850), US vice president and political leader, b. Abbeville District, S.C. After serving in the House of Representatives (1811–17), he was secretary of war (1817–25) under Pres. James Monroe. He was vice president (1825–32), under John Quincy Adams and Andrew Jackson, resigning over the nullification issue. Calhoun was elected to the Senate immediately and served there, except for a brief period as secretary of state under Pres. John Tyler (1844–45), until 1850. A staunch advocate of slavery, states' rights and nullification, he strongly influenced the South in the course that led to the Civil War.

Cali, city in W Colombia on Cali River; capital of Valle dept.; damaged in 1885 by earthquake. Cauca Valley Authority (1954) was established to develop flood control, land reclamation, and electric power; site of old aqueduct, cathedral, and two universities. Industries: tourism, tires, tobacco, textiles, paper. Founded 1536. Pop. 898,253.

Calicut (Kozhikode), seaport city in S India, on the Arabian Sea; capital of the Kozhikode district. Visited by Vasco de Gama 1498, it developed into European trading center with post est. by British East India Co. 1664; calico cloth (named for the city) was first exported to England in 17th century; ceded to Britain 1792, who held it until 1947, when India declared independence. Exports: coconuts, coffee, tea, spices, rubber, lumber. Pop. 333,980.

California, state in W United States, situated on the Pacific Ocean, the largest state in population and the 3rd-largest in area.

Land and Economy. In the W, the low Coast Ranges run N and S, paralleling the high Sierra Nevada in the E. Between these ranges lies the fertile Central Valley, drained by the Sacramento and San Joaquin rivers. In the SE are broad desert areas; the N is mountainous. With an all-year growing season and vast irrigation projects, the state is a leader in many crops. It also ranks high in commercial fisheries. Forests covering about 40% of the land support an important lumber industry. Mineral deposits include a variety of ores valuable in manufacturing, which is the largest sector of the economy. California factories make aircraft, aerospace equipment, electronic components, missiles, automobiles, communications equipment, chemical and petroleum products, cement, paper, and fibers. A year-round tourist industry is important to the state.

People. Between the 1950 and 1970 censuses, the population nearly doubled. About 90% of the people live in urban areas. Approximately the same proportion were born in the United States, with the remainder coming largely from Mexico, Canada, the British Isles, China, and Japan.

Education and Research. The University of California, with many branches, is world-famous. Among notable privately endowed institutions are Stanford University, California Institute of Technology, and the University of Southern California. There are more than 200 institutions of higher education. The Lick, Mt Wilson, and Palomar observatories are leaders in astronomical research. Other important facilities are the Scripps Institution of Oceanography and the Lawrence Radiation Laboratory.

History. Spanish sailors explored the coast in 1542, but the first settlement was in 1769, when Spaniards from Mexico founded a mission at San Diego. Other missions and military posts were established, and California was joined to Mexico, then a Spanish colony. The lands of the 21 Franciscan missions were broken up by law, and land grants created huge cattle ranches. Settlers came from the United States, and in 1846, early in the Mexican War, US forces occupied California, which was ceded to the United States at the war's end. After gold was discovered in 1848, the Gold Rush swelled the population from 15,000 to 250,000 in four years. In November 1849 the people voted California into the Union without approval of Congress, which did not come until Sept. 9, 1850. The opening of the Union Pacific Railroad in 1868 brought an era of great expansion. During and immediately after WWII the spread of manufacturing plants speeded the shift of economic emphasis from agriculture to industry, especially aerospace and electronics. In recent years two native sons have been elected to the presidency of the United States, Richard Nixon (elected 1968) and Ronald Reagan (elected 1980).

PROFILE

Admitted to Union: 1850; rank, 31st
US Congressmen: Senate—2; House of Representatives—43
Population: 23,668,562 (1980); rank, 1st
Capital: Sacramento, 275,741 (1980)
Chief cities: Los Angeles, 2,966,763; San Francisco, 678,974; San Diego, 875,504
State legislature: Senate, 40 members; Assembly, 80
Area: 158,693sq mi (411,015sq km); rank, 3d
Elevation: Highest, Mt Whitney, 14,494ft (4421m); Lowest, Death Valley, 282ft (86m) below sea level
Industries (major products): transportation equipment, processed foods, machinery (electrical and non-electrical), ordnance, metal products
Agriculture (major products): fruits, vegetables, nuts, poultry, cattle, dairy products
Minerals (major): petroleum, borax, asbestos
State nickname: Golden State (unofficial)
State motto: Eureka (I Have Found It)
State bird: Valley Quail
State flower: Golden Poppy
State tree: Redwood

California Current, Pacific Ocean current; flows S along W coast of North America; part of clockwise current of the entire North Pacific, carrying cool waters from the North Pacific current.

California Fan Palm, also desert palm of California, a stout-trunked palm native to the Colorado desert and cultivated as a decorative tree in California and Europe. Found in groves or clumps, its tall trunk is covered with a thick mat of dead leaves; leaves are fan-shaped and the black berry fruits were used as food by American Indians. Height: 50–75ft (15–23m). Family Palmaceae; species *Washingtonia filifera.*

Californium, radioactive metallic element (symbol Cf) of the actinide group, first made (1950) at the University of California, Berkeley, by alpha-particle bombardment of Cm^{242}. Properties: at. no. 98; most stable isotope Cf^{251} (8000yr). *See also* Transuranium Elements.

Caligula, Gaius Caesar (12–41), Roman emperor (37–41), nephew of Tiberius. The Senate and army made him emperor over the grandson of Tiberius. He became mentally disturbed, and his reign was cruel and absurd. His soldiers killed him and made Claudius I emperor.

Caliph, ruler of the Muslim community. Upon Mohammed's death in 632, Abu Bakr was designated the first Khalifat rasul-Allah ("successor of the Messenger of God"), or Caliph, by popular vote in Medina. Through the years, the center of the Caliphate was moved often. In 1517 the Ottoman sultan Selim I seized the title for himself and his dynasty. The Turkish republic abolished the title in 1924.

Calixtus I, Roman Catholic pope (217–22), and saint. Rising from slavery, his leniency with adulterers, murderers, and other sinners was condemned but became important in forming the church's penance doctrine.

Calixtus II, Roman Catholic pope (1119–24), b. the son of a French count of Burgundy. A spokesman for reformers within the church, he sponsored Gregorian reforms and opposed lay investiture. In 1122, he signed the Concordat of Worms achieving a compromise on this issue with Holy Roman Emperor Henry V.

Calla Lily, flowering plant native to S Africa and cultivated widely in greenhouses and as a house plant. The flower consists of a white showy spathe and yellow spadix. Height: to 2.5ft (76cm). Family Araceae; species *Zantedeschia elliottiana.*

Callaghan, Leonard James (1912–), British Labour politician. He entered Parliament as member for Cardiff South in 1945 and sat for Cardiff South-east from 1950. He was elected leader of the Labour Party and became Prime Minister in 1976, serving until 1979. He is the only Prime Minister in British history to have held all three of the major offices of state: Chancellor of the Exchequer (1964–67), Home Secretary (1967–70), and Foreign Secretary (1974–76).

Callao, seaport city on central W coast of Peru, approx. 8mi (13km) W of Lima. Center of international commerce, greater Callao is a province with departmental status. Industries: flour milling, brewing, sugar refining. Founded 1537 by Francisco Pizarro, the original city was destroyed by tidal wave and earthquake 1746. Pop. (greater Callao prov.) 320,700; (city) 296,721.

Callicrates, Greek architect in Athens, 5th century BC. Together with Ictinus, he erected the Parthenon (447–432 BC). He also designed the Temple of Athena Nike.

Calligraphy, art of fine writing. It differs from lettering, which uses mechanical aids such as the rule, compass, and square. Calligraphy is free hand, with a certain style, and with the components in proportion to each other and to the whole. In Europe there was a marked difference between the hands used for literary works, generally called uncials, rounded, easily inscribed letters, and those used for documents and letters, called cursive, which were more practical, regularized, and handsome. Within these classes several distinct styles were employed side by side. These distinctions are apparent in extant Greek examples. Fragments on papyrus from the 3rd century BC show a variety of cursive hands. Documents from the 2nd and 1st centuries BC show less breadth and spaciousness than the earlier samples, and the letters are rounder and more uniform in size. Several different types of Greek uncials were used in Roman times; among these was the "biblical hand," whose letters were square, heavy, upright, with thick and thin strokes well distinguished. This became the prevalent type of uncial during the Byzantine period. By this time papyrus had been replaced by vellum. During the 8th century the minuscule superseded the uncial for ordinary, commercial purposes. The Latin alphabet, used in calligraphy, developed like the Greek. Square or "rustic" capitals were used for literary works; a cursive form, which developed into uncial and minuscule cursive, was used for letter writing and documents. The minuscule cursive became the basis for medieval church and commercial writing, varying from nation to nation, and according to the purpose. Special hands were used by different classes, such as clerks, public scriveners, and notaries, and by papal and other chanceries. Intentional complexity was developed to prevent forgeries. During the Renaissance handbooks on calligraphy were developed, and from the 17th century, as English commerce spread, so did the English writing style. The 20th century has witnessed a revival of interest in the art of fine writing.

Callimachus (*c.*300–240 BC), Greek poet. Born in Cyrene, Callimachus was the most important Greek poet of the Hellenistic period. Among the best-known of his works were the *Aetia*, or *Causes*, a discussion of the origins of myths, legends, and rituals; and the *Lock of Berenice*, a celebration of the Egyptian Queen Berenice.

Callimachus, Athenian commander at the battle of Marathon (490 BC). He accepted Miltiades' decisive plan to meet the Persians in the field and was killed in the last stages of the battle.

Calliope, steam-operated musical instrument with a series of pipes or whistles played on a keyboard. Invented in America (*c.*1880) and named for the Greek Muse of Eloquence, it was often mounted on circus parade wagons.

Callisthenes of Olynthus (360?–?328 B.C.), Greek philosopher and historian. A nephew of Aristotle, he was chosen as historian of Alexander the Great's Asiatic expedition. He criticized Alexander's adoption of Oriental customs, was accused of plotting against him, and died in prison. He is considered the first historian to refer to the story of Alexander's divine birth. His works include a history of Greece from 387–357 and a history of the Phocian War.

Callisto, satellite of Jupiter; one of the Galilean satellites. Diameter 2795mi (4500km); mean distance from planet 1,168,000mi (1,881,000km); mean sidereal period 16.69 days.

Callistratus (died 355 BC), Athenian orator. Best known for his speech of 366, which is supposed to have inspired the orator Demosthenes. He also commanded Athenian forces sent to intervene in fighting between Thebes and Sparta in 378. He was later condemned, exiled to Macedonia, and then executed for Spartan sympathies. Callistratus was also the name of a mid-2nd century BC Greek author of commentaries on poets.

Callus, hard, thickened area of skin usually at a place on hands or feet where pressure is continual. A callus may be removed by chemicals or friction.

Caloric Theory of Heat. *See* Heat.

Calorie, the amount of heat necessary to raise one kilogram of water at atmospheric pressure from a temperature of 14.5°C to 15.5°C. The small calorie, written without a capital, is that amount of heat necessary to raise a gram of water through that temperature interval. Thus the Calorie is 1,000 times the size of the calorie.

Calorimeter, a device that measures the heat energy of a substance. The calorimeter consists of an insulated container filled with fluid, a stirrer, and a thermometer. When a known amount of the heated substance is placed in the calorimeter, it loses heat to the liquid. The stirrer distributes this heat evenly and the temperature change determines the heat energy of the substance.

Calpurnia (*fl.* 1st century BC), Roman noblewoman. A member of the prominent Piso family, she was Julius Caesar's last wife (married 59 BC). She is mentioned in Plutarch and appears as a character in Shakespeare's *Julius Caesar.*

Calvary, place where Jesus was crucified. Called Calvary by John, both Luke and Matthew refer to the site as Golgotha. The location has most often been thought to be near the Church of the Holy Sepulchre in Jerusalem, but a small hill called "Gordon's Calvary" has also been proposed as the actual site.

Calvert, Cecilius, 2nd Baron Baltimore (*c.* 1605–75), first proprietor of Maryland. He acquired the grant to the colony of Maryland (1632) after the death of his father, George Calvert. He was an absentee ruler, governing by deputies. A Roman Catholic, he managed to retain the colony through the Puritan Revolution in England, passing control to his son Charles.

Calvert, Charles, 3rd Baron Baltimore (1637–1715), second proprietor of Maryland. He was sent to Maryland by father, Cecilius, as a deputy governor (1661). He became proprietor after his father's death (1675). A Roman Catholic in a predominantly Protestant Maryland, he was autocratic and suppressed a revolt (1676). He went to England (1684) to debate a boundary controversy with William Penn. His charter was overthrown by a Protestant revolt (1689) and he never returned.

Calvin, John (1509–64), French theologian, a key figure of the Protestant Reformation; b. as Jean Chauvin. He first prepared for a career in the Catholic Church but then turned to the study of law and, later, the classics. Around 1533 he converted to Protestantism and began work on his *Institutes of the Christian Religion* (published 1536). In this work, frequently revised and expanded, he presented the basics of what came to be known as Calvinism. To avoid persecution, he traveled in France, Italy, and Switzerland. In 1536 he was persuaded to stay in Geneva, Switzerland, and advance the Reformation there. He began a thoroughgoing, austere revamping of the life of the city. Opposition to him emerged, and he was banished in 1538, but he was welcomed back in 1541 and remained there until his death. In 1541 his *Ecclesiastical Ordinances* provided a framework for church and civic life in what came to be called the "Protestant Rome." Regulation of con-

San Francisco, California: Fisherman's Wharf

Calligraphy

Cambodia: Angkorwat

duct in Geneva was extended to all areas of life. Economic development was promoted by emphasis on such virtues as thrift, industry, sobriety, and responsibility. Supposed witches and heretics (such as Michael Servetus, who was burned at the stake in 1553) were persecuted. Education was promoted. Calvin split with the Lutherans over the nature of the sacrament of the Lord's Supper and vigorously trained many French refugees to act as missionary pastors to that country. He also intrigued with various French nobles in the events that led to the Wars of Religion (1562–98). By the time of his death the brilliant and charismatic Calvin saw the beginnings of the great impact his doctrines were to have thoroughout Western Europe.

Calvinism, doctrines and attitudes derived from or strongly influenced by Protestant theologian John Calvin (1509–64) and advanced by the churches (Reformed and Presbyterian) established in his tradition. The term is used in several senses, ranging from the narrowly specific to the broadly general, from the theological and moral to the social and psychological. Rejecting papal authority and relying on the Bible as the source of religious truth, Calvinism stresses the utter sovereignty of God and the predestination of every person either to election—by irresistible grace—to bliss in harmony with God or to damnation in separation from him. It politically subordinates state to church and cultivates austere morality, family piety, business enterprise, education, and science.

The development of these doctrines, particularly predestination, and the rejection of consubstantiation regarding the sacrament of the Last Supper caused a split in Protestantism between the Lutheran church and what became the Reformed and Presbyterian churches. Jacobus Arminius (1560–1609) later posed an important challenge to Calvinism over the question of predestination, and his views were adopted by the Methodists and most Baptists. The influence of Calvinism spread rapidly, particularly in Switzerland, France, The Netherlands, England, Scotland, and what became the United States, and it had profound impact on the course of Western cultural history. In Britain and the United States it was part of the Puritan movement. Among important figures in its spread and development were John Knox (1505–72) in Scotland and Jonathan Edwards (1703–58) in what became the United States.

Calypso, in Greek mythology, the daughter of Atlas and Tethys. She reigned over the mythical island of Ogyaria. When Odysseus landed on the island during a storm, she kept him there for seven years. She bore him three sons, Latinus, Nausthinous, and Nausinous. Finally, Hermes was sent by Zeus, king of the gods, to have Odysseus released.

Camagüey, formerly Puerto Príncipe; city in E central Cuba; capital of Camagüey prov.; important agricultural trade center. Industries: exotic woods, cattle raising. Founded 1514. Pop. 197,720.

Camaldolites (Congregation of the Monk Hermits of Camaldoli), Roman Catholic religious order. They were founded as an offshoot of the Benedictines by St. Romuald at Camaldoli in Italy about 1012 during the monastic reform movement of that time. The order ideally sought to combine hermitages and monasteries, but separate establishments of each type were also made. The Camaldolites have a history of both scholarship and evangelization. They operate about 30 establishments today.

Camass, or bear grass, hardy, North American plant. The familiar camassia has long thin leaves, blue or white flowers, and edible bulbs. It grows from British Columbia to California. Family Liliaceae.

Cambium, layer of formative cells, only one cell thick, in woody plant stems and roots. This layer manufactures cells from spring until frost, increasing the diameter of the woody stem. It is located between the mature wood and bark, providing a zone of weakness enabling the bark to be peeled off.

Cambodia (Kampuchea), independent nation in SE Asia. Once an advanced artistic civilization, then part of French Indochina, it has been buffeted by regional and internal war.
Land and Economy. With Laos and Vietnam, Cambodia was once part of French Indochina. It is dependent on rice fields in the level central area formed by the Mekong River basin. Bordered by Thailand, Laos, Vietnam, and the Gulf of Thailand, its SE is covered with mountains and forests. The climate is tropical monsoon. Before WWII the economy was based on rice farming in a 75,000sq mi (200,000sq km) area, plus fishing and forestry. Since the war, the economy has suffered, and exports of rice and rubber have dropped.
People. Cambodians are descended from the Khmer, S Indian settlers who intermarried with Mongoloid tribes. Ethnic minorities include Chinese, Vietnamese, Cham-Malays, and Burmese. Hinayana Buddhism is the main religion, Khmer the common language. Monastery schools for primary education were always prevalent, and since independence secondary education has been open to almost all. Literacy is 85%.
Government and History. The 1976 constitution provides for a republic with a legislative assembly.
A vassal of the Funan empire (AD100–500), Cambodian lineage also includes Indian migrants from the sub-continent. Wealth came from rice and caravan trade tolls. In 802, Jayavarman took the throne, inaugurating a period of great art and architecture in a civilization still seen in the ruins of Angkor, the ancient capital. In 1863, France was asked to provide protectorate status to Cambodia, and in 1953 Cambodia declared its independence. US-Vietnam warfare increased tensions on the country, and in 1970 U.S.-backed Gen. Lon Nol took power from Prince Norodom Sihanouk. The country became the Khmer Republic, heavily dependent on US military and economic aid. On April 17, 1975 the Khmer Rouge (Communist National United Front) assumed authority. The new government under Prime Minister Pol Pot, which had close ties to China, initiated a radical reorganization of the country, depopulating the cities and forcing urban dwellers to labor in the countryside. By 1979—when as many as 3,000,000 people had died, most from starvation—insurgents backed by Vietnamese troops successfully defeated the Khmer Rouge and established a new Communist government, considered by many a Vietnamese puppet-government. The Pol Pot government went into exile in the N, and both sides claimed to be Cambodia's legitimate government. In 1981 a UN demand for withdrawal of Vietnamese troops was ignored. Three factions opposed to the Vietnamese-backed regime united in 1982 and gained significant international support. Area: 69,898sq mi (181,036sq km); Pop: 5,900,000.

Cambrian Period, the oldest period of the Paleozoic Era, lasting from about 570 million to 500 million years ago. It is the earliest geological system containing a large assortment of fossils. All the animal phyla, with the exception of the vertebrates, are represented in the seas. The land was barren. The most common forms were trilobites, brachiopods, sponges, and snails. Plant life consisted of seaweeds. See also Geologic time; Paleozoic Era.

Cambridge, city in E England, on River Cam, 48mi (77km) NE of London; important medieval river port; noted for 12th-century university containing many buildings of historic and architectural value. Industries: printing, cement, electronics. Pop. 98,519.

Cambridge, city in E Massachusetts, across the Charles River from Boston; seat of Middlesex co; site of Harvard University (1636), Radcliffe College (1879), Massachusetts Institute of Technology (1859), and Lesley College (1909); noted for Craig House (1759), Cooper-Frost-Austin house (c.1657), Episcopal Church (1761). Industries: printing, publishing, electronics, scientific instruments. Settled 1630; inc. 1846. Pop. (1980) 95,322.

Cambridge Platonists, group of Cambridge philosophers and theologians who advocated a revival of Neo-Platonism in the 17th century, especially Ralph Cudworth and Henry More. They claimed that the mind, or "Candle of the Lord," could achieve mystic union with God by virtue of eternal and immutable ideas. See also Neoplatonism.

Cambyses II (d. 522 BC), son of Cyrus the Great and King of Persia (529–522 BC), his main achievement was the conquest of Egypt. His other campaigns failed and turned him from a benevolent to a harsh ruler. He died in battle in Syria.

Camden, city in W New Jersey, on Delaware River opposite Philadelphia; seat of Camden co; developed around railroad (1834) into a commercial and shipbuilding center; home of Walt Whitman (1873–92). Industries: soup, pens, paper, wood products, electric and electronic goods. Settled c. 1681; inc. 1828. Pop. (1980) 84,910.

Camel, large, even-toed, cud-chewing, hoofed mammal. They are covered with dense shaggy brown or gray wool. Their broad, two-toed, padded feet, heavy eyelashes, and hairs in ears protect against sand. They are indispensible beasts of burden in desert areas, being able to survive on minimum food and water and to carry large loads. The one-humped dromedary, native from India to N Africa, is no longer found in the wild. The two-humped Bactrian, native to Chinese Turkistan and Mongolia, is widely domesticated in other areas. The dromedary is taller because of its longer legs, reaching 6.5ft (2.0m) at shoulder. Family Camelidae; genus Camelus. See also Artiodactyla; Ruminant.

Camellia, evergreen trees or shrubs native to Japan and popular as garden plants. They have oval, dark green leaves and waxy, roselike flowers of pink, red, white, or rose. Family Theaceae; species Camellia japonica.

Camelot, in English mythology, the place where King Arthur of England held his court. The popular legend found its way into Tennyson's The Idylls of the King, which, in turn, produced several other books, movies, and the Lerner and Loewe musical, Camelot.

Cameos, ornamental jewelry consisting of a carved stone such as onyx, sardonyx, or agate, usually circular or oval, affixed to a background of a different color. The decoration, usually white, is carved in raised relief. Cameos were a very common form of jewelry in the ancient world, and great care was used in choosing stones consisting of several variegated strata. Interest in them was revived in the Renaissance and continues to the present.

Camera, optical device of varying complexity for taking photographs, consisting essentially of a light-tight box in which photographic film can be positioned. Light from the scene being photographed is focused by a lens system onto the film when a shutter is opened for a brief period. The amount of light falling on the film is controlled by the shutter speed, often variable, and by the diameter of the lens (aperture), which can also often be varied using an adjustable diaphragm. A viewfinder indicates what will appear on the photograph. Many cameras also have a rangefinder, enabling a focused image to be produced for a given object distance, and a built-in exposure meter, used to determine correct combination of shutter speed and aperture for the prevailing light conditions.

Camera Lucida, apparatus for drawing and copying in perspective, developed in 1812 by W. H. Wollaston. A prism is set between the draftsman's eye and the paper in such a way that light is reflected from the object he is copying onto the paper.

Camera Obscura, optical apparatus consisting of a darkened chamber into which light is admitted through a convex lens. A portable version of this was used by 17th- and 18th-century artists to trace scenes from nature. By the 19th century it was reduced to a box, fitted with a lens and mirror, placed on a tripod, and surrounded by black curtains. It eventually developed into the modern camera.

Cameroon (Cameroun), Federal Republic of, nation in W Africa, extending from Gulf of Guinea approx. 700mi (1,125km) NE to Lake Chad. There are five major geographical regions. The coastal plain extends 10–50mi (16–81km) inland from the sea to the forest region; the climate is one of extreme heat and humidity, with an annual rainfall of over 360in (914cm). The mountain region of W Cameroon extends N to the edge of Lake Chad; this region has a mild climate with fertile soil; it is the site of Mt Cameroon, the highest peak in W Africa, rising, to 13,354ft (4,073m). The inland forest plateau is less humid than the coastal plain; it produces cacao, bananas, palm oil, rubber, and hardwood. The Adamawa plateau region forms a barrier between the N and S. The N Savanna plain extends from the Adamawa plateau region to Lake Chad; little rainfall and high temperatures produce little vegetation.

Cameroon's economy depends heavily on subsistence farming, although the export of oil from off-shore deposits began in 1978. About 80% of the population lives in E Cameroon. There are over 150 different ethnic groups. The major ethnic groups of E Cameroon are the Fulani and Kirdi (N), and Bamileke, Bulu, Bamoun, Ewondo, Beti, Douala, Bassa (S). W Cameroon ethnic groups include the Bakweri, Douala, Nigerians, Ibo, Ibibio, Ijaw, Ekoi, and Edo. Approx. half of all Cameroonians follow tribal animism; 35% Christianity; and 20% Islam. There are two educational systems: W Cameroon is modeled after the British system, and E Cameroon is based on the French system. In the S most school age children attend classes; in the N, more isolated region, only a little over 10% attends school. Cameroon has teacher training and technical education institutions. The Federal University in Yaounde has an enrollment of over 1,000 students.

The constitution of 1972 established a centralized government headed by an elected president with broad powers, who appoints the prime minister, cabinet, and provincial governors. Ahmadou Ahidjo, president since independence in 1960, was elected to his fifth consecutive term in 1980, but resigned in 1982. He was replaced by Paul Biya. The unicameral national assembly has 120 seats.

Before gaining independence, Cameroon had a history of foreign domination. The region was discovered in the 15th century by the Portuguese, but the Germans first est a protectorate of Cameroon 1884–1914. During WWI the territory was occupied by both British and French troops and was subsequently divided between the two nations as mandates under the League of Nations. After WWII, Cameroon became a UN trust territory governed by the same powers. The French territory achieved independence in 1960. The British portion joined the new nation the following year, and a federal government was established with power carefully divided between the two regions. Since the establishment of a fully integrated government in 1972, dissident groups have opposed the unitary structure.

PROFILE

Official name: United Republic of Cameroon
Area: 183,569sq mi (475,444sq km)
Population: 8,248,000
Chief cities: Yaoundé (capital), Douala, Edéa
Government: Republic
Religion: Animism (major); Christianity, Islam
Language: French, English (official)
Monetary unit: Franc CFA

Camisards, French Protestants of the Cévennes region who rebelled against Louis XIV (1702) after being systematically persecuted. Though small in number, they were at first successful under their leader, Jean Cavalier, but by 1711 their force was diminished and Protestantism had all but disappeared in France.

Camomile, or chamomile, any of several plants of the genera *Anthemis* and *Matricaria*. Flowers of the perennial European camomile are used to make a medicinal tea. This plant is also a popular groundcover. *M. chamomilla* is the annual false camomile. Family Compositae.

Camouflage, in military science, technique used to conceal personnel and equipment from observation by making them blend with their natural surroundings. Examples are nets used to break up angular silhouettes and colors reflecting local environments.

Campaign, Political, effort conducted by groups or parties to secure election of a candidate or candidates, or adoption of a program. Political campaign styles differ depending on the political system, but the goals are similar. Typically, campaigns require a large degree of organization, strategy, communications, and funding to succeed.

Campaign for Nuclear Disarmament (CND), mass-protest movement in Britain. It was founded by its president, Bertrand Russell and Canon John Collins in 1958. It organized an annual Easter march between the atomic research center at Aldermaston, Berkshire, and Trafalgar Square, London. In members and activity it has declined from its 1960 peak, when it influenced the Labour Party conference to pass a resolution in favor of unilateral disarmament.

Campania, region in S Italy, on Tyrrhenian Sea; includes provinces of Anellino, Benevento, Caserta, Napoli, and Salerno. Capital is Naples. Settled by Greeks and Etruscans, it prospered under Roman rule (4th century BC); conquered by Goths, Byzantines, Lombards, Normans; merged with Italy 1860. Chiefly mountainous; fertile plains produce fruit, grain, wine. Industries: metallurgy, chemicals, textiles, shipbuilding, tourism. Area: 5,249sq mi (13,595sq km). Pop. 5,346,-828.

Campanile, bell tower, often near but not attached to a church. They originated in the 6th century, and were the first church spires in Europe. A notable example is the campanile in Piazza San Marco, Venice.

Campbell, (Sir) Malcolm (1885–1948), English automobile and speedboat racer. He was the first man to reach a speed of 300mph (483kph), which he accomplished in his famed automobile *Bluebird* at the Bonneville (Utah) Salt Flats (1935). He then turned to speedboats and set a record by reaching 141mph (227km/h) (1939). He was knighted in 1931.

Campbell, (Mrs) Patrick, born Beatrice Stella Tanner (1865–1940), English actress for whom G. B. Shaw wrote the part of Eliza Doolittle in *Pygmalion* (1912). A distinguished actress, she and Shaw had a platonic affair recorded in a volume of letters later used as the basis for the play *Dear Liar* (1970).

Campbell-Bannerman, (Sir) Henry (1836–1908), British prime minister (1905–08), b. Scotland. Entering Parliament (1868), he held minor posts before becoming war secretary (1886) and reforming his department. As Liberal leader, he formed a strong reforming government (1905–08) before ill health forced his retirement.

Campeche, seaport in SE Mexico, on W coast of Yucatán Peninsula, on Gulf of Campeche; capital of Campeche state; site of pre-Colombian town. Exports: cotton, sugar cane, cigars, hides, tobacco. Industries: cigars, chocolate, tanning, distilling, shoes. Spain landed 1517; founded 1540. Pop. 337,000.

Camp Fire Girls, US organization placing its main emphasis on girls (ages 6–18), founded in 1910 by Luther Halsey Gulick and other educators "to stimulate and aid in the formation of habits making for health and character." In 1975 Camp Fire adopted a program called "A New Day" expanding membership to all youths from birth to age 21, adults and families. There are also boys clubs and co-ed clubs within Camp Fire. Publications include *The Camp Fire Leadership*. Membership: about 500,000.

Camphor Tree, evergreen tree native to Taiwan, Japan, China, Java, Sumatra, and Brazil. Camphor is obtained from its wood by distillation. Family Lauraceae; species *Cinnamomum camphora.*

Campinas, city in SE Brazil, 57mi (92km) NW of São Paulo. Industries: sugar refining, metal casting, coffee processing. Pop. 328,629.

Campion, Edmund (1540–81), English clergyman. Although he had strong Roman Catholic leanings, he became an Anglican deacon in 1568. While in Dublin, he wrote a *History of Ireland* (1571). He went to Europe in 1571 and was ordained a Catholic priest in 1578. In 1580 he returned to England to minister to the Catholics there, who were forbidden to practice their religion. He made many conversions. His pamphlet *Decem rationes* (1581) against the Protestants created a sensation. Arrested and tortured on the rack, he refused to recant his religious convictions. Condemned on trumped-up charges of treason, he was hanged, drawn, and quartered. He was beatified by the Catholic Church in 1886.

Campion, common name for the over 500 species of the large genus *Silene* of the pink family. Found mainly near the Mediterranean, certain species grow in central Europe and Great Britain.

Campobello, island in SW New Brunswick, Canada, at the entrance of Passamaquoddy Bay just off the coast of Maine; connected to Lubec, Me., by the Roosevelt Memorial Bridge (1962). Pres. Franklin D. Roosevelt maintained a summer home here; since 1964, administered by a joint US–Canadian Commission as an international park. Area: 2,722acres (1,102hectares).

Cam Ranh Bay, inlet of S China Sea, on E coast of S central Vietnam, between Phan Rang and Nha Trang; site of former French naval base and largest US base during Vietnam War. Length: 10mi (16km). Width: 20mi (32km).

Camus, Albert (1913–60), French novelist, playwright, and essayist, born in Algeria. After working in avant-garde theater and journalism, he became one of the leaders of the French Resistance. He achieved recognition with his first novel *The Stranger* (1942). Despite the recurrent themes of "the absurd" and mankind's powerlessness in his novels *The Plague* (1947) and *The Fall* (1956), and in essays (*The Rebel,* 1951), he committed himself to humanitarian values and received the Nobel Prize for literature in 1957.

Cana (Cana of Galilee), village in Israel, approx. 4mi (6km) NE of Nazareth; where Christ reportedly performed his first miracle by turning water into wine at a wedding.

Canaanites, Biblical name of the people who inhabited Palestine, lower Syria, and Lebanon, dating to the 3rd millennium BC. They occupied the ancient maritime territory of Phoenicia and were known as Phoenicians, the Greek word for "purple," because of their famous Tyrian purple dye acquired from shellfish.

Canada, independent nation in North America. A country rich in minerals and agriculture, it was settled by the French and English and became an independent Commonwealth country with a federal system of government, in which the provinces enjoy a large measure of autonomy.

Land and Economy. The 2nd-largest country in the world (after the USSR), Canada occupies the N half of the North American continent, stretching E and W from the Atlantic to Pacific oceans, N from the 49th parallel to the North Pole, including all the islands in the Arctic Ocean from W of Greenland to Alaska. It is divided into 10 provinces, which are (E–W): Newfoundland, Nova Scotia, Prince Edward Island, New Brunswick, Quebec, Ontario, Manitoba, Saskatchewan, Alberta, and British Columbia. Two territories—Northwest Territories and Yukon Territory—are in the NW. The outstanding geological feature is the Canadian Shield, a 1,850,000-sq-mi (4,791,500-sq-km) arc of Pre-Cambrian rock from Labrador around Hudson Bay to the Arctic islands. The Shield, site of once great mountain chains worn down and covered by the sea, contains valuable minerals—gold, silver, platinum, copper, nickel, cobalt, iron, and zinc—making Canada one of the most important mining countries in the world. The Shield's N portion is a treeless plain with permanently frozen subsoil; in its S section are forests. Extending from the Shield's W border to the Canadian Rockies are prairies more than 800mi (1,288km) wide that yield wheat, the dominant crop, and are centers of livestock raising. W Canada is a land of mountains with fishing, agriculture, and lumbering as important industries. With the development of major oil and natural gas deposits since the 1950s in the W, the now-dominant energy industry has resulted in dramatic economic growth there, and made Canada a major oil-producing country.The E provinces provide rich farm lands, forests, coal mines, and major fishing sources along the long coastline. Source of a route into the interior for early settlers, the St Lawrence-Great Lakes area is the

Cameroon

Albert Camus

Canada

most populous section of Canada as well as its economic and political center. It contains over 60% of the population. Abundant minerals have made Canada the world leader in the production of silver, nickel, potash, and zinc; second in gypsum, asbestos, uranium, and sulfur; third in gold, lead, and platinum; fourth in magnesium and fifth in copper. Timber is also valuable, and Canada is a world leader in newsprint production. The growth of manufacturing during the 1950s and 1960s changed Canada from a rural society to an industrial and urban country. Farming employs 7% of the working population. Mechanization has made it possible to export 30%–40% of its total agricultural production, accounting for 11% of total exports. Wheat is particularly important. Of the total fishing catch, 75% is exported.

People. Canada's indigenous Indians and Eskimos are descendants of the Mongoloid tribes who took the NW route from Asia across the Bering Strait 15,000–20,000 years ago. The Arctic region contains about 12,000 Eskimos. Today, 44% of the population is of British descent. About 30% is French, descended from the colonists who came to Canada in the 17th and 18th centuries, and now heavily concentrated in Quebec and New Brunswick. During the American Revolution many British loyalists fled to Canada from the United States, and after 1900 waves of immigrants from Germany, the Ukraine, and Italy settled on the prairie farmlands or the urban centers. Native Indians have been increasing in number, accounting for over 210,000, mostly living in the prairie states. During periods of US prosperity, emigration has brought Canadians S to work in the industrial cities. Forty-six percent of the population is Roman Catholic with the coalition United Church of Canada next (20%). Literacy is almost 100%.

Government. In its role as a member of the Commonwealth of Nations, Canada is both a constitutional monarchy and a democracy. Internally, there is a federal structure of the 10 provinces and 2 territories. The British monarch names a governor general who serves as symbol of the association with the Commonwealth. Parliament is divided into two houses. Members of the Senate are appointed by the governor general on the advice of the prime minister. Members of the House of Commons are elected. The executive branch includes a cabinet, headed by the prime minister, who is the leader of the party in power. Within each province the government is headed by a premier and parliament.

History. Rivalry between the French and the English marked Canada's early development. John Cabot, sailing for England, reached Newfoundland in 1497 and claimed possession for King Henry VII. In 1534, French explorer Jacques Cartier planted the French flag on the Gaspé Peninsula, and in 1604, Samuel de Champlain established the first French colony, Port Royal, in Nova Scotia; four years later he founded what is now the city of Quebec. French navigators traveled the St Lawrence and Hudson rivers, claiming large interior lands for France. Traders and missionaries penetrated the interior, and French officials made peace with the Indians, thus encouraging French immigration. Seeking a share of the lucrative fur trade, the British in 1670 est the Hudson's Bay Co. Continental war between France and England extended to the New World, and the 1759 defeat of French commander Montcalm brought the fall of Quebec; the 1763 Treaty of Paris gave Canada to Britain. In 1791 a constitutional act divided Canada into two sections—an English portion in what is now Ontario and a French portion in what is now Quebec. The next 40 years were marked by trade and expansion. Alexander Mackenzie, the first white man to cross the continent, reached the Arctic in 1789 and the Pacific in 1793. The United States invaded Canada during the War of 1812, which ended in

a stalemate with the Treaty of Ghent. French Canadians demanded political reform, and in 1840 Upper and Lower Canada were joined and self-government approved. Border questions between the United States and Canada were settled during the same period when the 49th parallel was accepted as the demarcation line. A movement to join the isolated colonies spread across the continent was spurred by promises to build a railway system linking the provinces and to provide future protection against US invasion, especially during the Civil War, when there was anti-British feeling in the United States. In 1867 the British North America Act joined four provinces—Quebec, Ontario, Nova Scotia, and New Brunswick—and provided for a parliamentary system. In 1869 Canada bought land from the Hudson's Bay Co., carving out of it the provinces of Manitoba (1870), Saskatchewan (1905), and Alberta (1905). Encouraged by a transcontinental railway promise, British Columbia joined the union in 1871 and Prince Edward Island in 1873. The last addition came in 1948 when Newfoundland became Canada's 10th province. Outstanding leaders during the drive for independence and the early years of confederation included John A. Macdonald, Wilfrid Laurier, and William Lyon Mackenzie King. Canada joined the Allies in WWII and after the war became a member of the United Nations. The Liberal party dominated politics from the early 1960s into the early 1980s, with first Lester Pearson and, from 1968–79 and again from 1980–84, Pierre Elliott Trudeau as prime minister. Progressive Conservative Brian Mulroney became prime minister in 1984.

During the late 1970s and early 1980s, Canada successfully weathered severe crises of national unity. In Quebec, four-fifths French-speaking, the militant Parti Québécois won the elections of 1976 on a secessionist platform, but in 1980 Quebec voters rejected a referendum on separate status. In 1979 Trudeau announced plans to repatriate the British North America Act, which functions as the Canadian constitution, but is amendable only by act of the British parliament. The provincial premiers were at first opposed to the move, but a compromise reached in 1981 was rejected only by Quebec and was signed into effect by Queen Elizabeth II in 1982.

PROFILE

Official name: Canada
Area: 3,851,809sq mi (9,976,185sq km)
Population: 23,900,000
   Density: 6per sq mi (2.3per sq km)
Chief cities: Ottawa (capital); Montreal; Toronto; Edmonton
Government: Constitutional monarchy with parliamentary system of government
Religion: Roman Catholic (major), Anglican, United Church
Language: English, French
Monetary unit: Canadian dollar
Gross national product: $245,800,000,000
Per capita income: $10,296
Industries: pulp and paper, petroleum products, iron, steel, motor vehicles, aircraft, machinery, chemicals, aluminum, fish canning
Agriculture: wheat, barley, oats, rye, potatoes, fish, cattle, forests
Minerals: oil, iron ore, gold, silver, platinum, copper, nickel, cobalt, zinc
Trading partners: United States, Japan, United Kingdom
   Following is a list of the prime ministers of Canada.

PRIME MINISTERS OF CANADA

John A. McDonald	1867–73
Alexander Mackenzie	1873–78
John A. McDonald	1878–91
John J.C. Abbot	1891–92
John S.D. Thompson	1892–94
Mackenzie Bowell	1894–96
Charles Tupper	1896
Wilfrid Laurier	1896–1911
Robert L. Borden	1911–20
Arthur Meighen	1920–21
W. L. Mackenzie King	1921–26
Arthur Meighen	1926
W. L. Mackenzie King	1926–30
Richard B. Bennett	1930–35
W. L. Mackenzie King	1935–48
Louis Stephen St. Laurent	1948–57
John George Diefenbaker	1957–63
Lester B. Pearson	1963–68
Pierre Elliott Trudeau	1968–79
Joe Clark	1979–80
Pierre Elliott Trudeau	1980–

Canada Goose, North American wild goose found in wide-ranging habitats, grazing on grasses or feeding on aquatic vegetation in streams and ponds. It has white cheek pouches and a long black neck. Nesting on stream banks or tundra, it lays white eggs (4–10). Length: 23–40in (58–100cm); weight: 3–14lb (1 1/3–6 1/3kg). Species *Branta canadensis. See also* Goose.

Canada Lynx, short-tailed cat found in forest swamp areas of Canada, Alaska, and NW United States. A valuable fur mammal, it has large feet and tufted ears and long thick fur that is grayish mottled with brown, white cheek hair, and black ear marks. The gestation period is 62 days and 1–4 young are born. It feeds on hares, rodents, and birds. Length: body—32–36in (81–91cm); tail—4in (10.2cm); weight: 15–30lb (6.7–13.5kg).

Canadian Pacific Railway, transcontinental railroad system in Canada. Privately owned, it stretches from Halifax, Nova Scotia, to Vancouver, British Columbia. It grew out of an agreement in 1871 between the Canadian federal government and British Columbia in which the federal government promised to build a transcontinental line if British Columbia joined the Canadian confederation. Construction was begun by the government but, following a political scandal (Pacific Scandal) and other difficulties, it was turned over to a private syndicate in 1880. The main line from Montreal to the Pacific coast was completed in 1885. *See also* Pacific Scandal.

Canadian River, river in SW United States; flows from S Colorado S and E across NE New Mexico and NW Texas to Arkansas River in Oklahoma. In mid-19th century river valley was part of pioneers' Fort Smith-Santa Fe Trail. Length: 906mi (1,459km).

Canadian Shield (Laurentian Highlands), great plateau of Canada, roughly outlining the Hudson Bay; extends from the Mackenzie River basin SE through S Ontario and S Quebec (passing through Great Lakes region of N central America), and NE to the Labrador Sea; this large geographic formation is characterized by numerous lakes and rivers and coniferous forests.

Canal, artificial waterway constructed for irrigation, drainage, navigation or in conjunction with hydroelectric dams. Many canals serve multiple purposes. The construction of canals is ancient; 4000 years ago, Nahrwn, 400ft (122m) wide and 200mi (322km) long, was built in ancient Mesopotamia. The longest canal able to accommodate large ships today connects the Baltic and White Seas in the USSR: it is 141mi (227km) long.

Canal Boat, flat-bottomed craft used on canalized natural inland waterways and artificial canals to transport goods. Barges are the best known. With the enlargement of formerly inadequate canal lock systems, large powered barges are economical transport units, especially in Europe.

Canaletto (1697–1768), Italian painter, b. Giovanni Antonio Canal. A landscapist, he is most famous for his views of Venice. He was very popular in the 1720s and 30s, especially with visiting Englishmen. He executed four views of Venice for Stephano Conti of Lucca (1725–26) and a large group of Roman scenes in the 1740s. After 1745 he went to England, where he painted many popular London views and landscapes.

Canary, popular cage bird found wild in the Azores and Canary and Madeira islands. These yellowish finches feed on fruits, seeds, and insects and lay spotted greenish-blue eggs in cup-shaped nests. The pure yellow varieties are larger than the wild canaries, and have been domesticated since the 16th century. They are taught various songs by exposing them to recordings. They breed poorly in captivity. Family Fringillidae; species *Serinus canarius.*

Canary Current, cold current of N Atlantic Ocean; flows SW from Spain along NW coast of Africa; joins North Equatorial current at approx. 20° N latitude.

Canary Islands, an island group in the N Atlantic Ocean, approx. 70mi (113km) off the NW coast of Africa. The Canary Islands constitute two provinces of Spain: Las Palmas, consisting of Gran Canaria, Lanzarote, Fuerteventura, Graciosa, Montana Clara, Alegranza, Roque de Ester, Roque del Oeste, Las Isla de Lobos; and Santa Cruz de Tenerife, consisting of Tenerife, La Palma, Gomera, Hierro. The chief cities are Santa Cruz de la Palma and Las Palmas. The area is 2,808sq mi (7,273sq km).

The islands are mountainous, warm, with little rainfall; efficient irrigation allows the development of numerous crops, including bananas, sugarcane, tobacco, tomatoes, nuts, citrus fruits, grapes, and vegetables. The islands' economy is based on the export of agricultural goods. A great quantity of grapes are grown for the manufacture and export of wine. Fishing, fish canning and salting are major industries. Because of the mild climate and beautiful scenery the tourist industry is growing rapidly.

The inhabitants are mostly Spanish immigrants; the original inhabitants, called Guanches, are believed to be of Berber stock. The Guanches have been entirely absorbed by the Spanish settlement.

In 1402 French explorer Jean de Bethencourt attempted unsuccessfully to conquer the islands. Henry III of Castile came to his aid, naming Bethencourt king of the islands, answerable only to Spain. In 1936, Francisco Franco began his revolt against the Spanish republic from the islands. Pop. 1,170,224.

Canasta, card game for two to six players. The game, a branch of the rummy family, is generally played by two sets of partners using two standard decks. The object is to accumulate points through various melding methods, similar to rummy. The cards have different point values, and 3000 points is usually the total needed to win. *See also* Rummy.

Canaveral, Cape, low sandy promontory extending E into Atlantic Ocean in E Florida; site of NASA's John F. Kennedy Manned Space Flight Center, main US launch site for space flights and long-range missiles; Patrick Air Force Base is nearby.

Canberra, capital city of Australia, in Australian Capital Territory, SE New South Wales, 155mi (248km) SW of Sydney on the Molonglo River. Settled *c.* 1824, it was chosen 1908 as the new site of Australia's capital. Designed 1911 by Chicago architect, Walter Burley Griffin, construction began 1913 but was interrupted by WWI and the Depression; by 1927, the capital and some governmental agencies were moved to Canberra; the first meeting of Parliament was held 1947. The transfer of nongovernmental activities to the area greatly spurred the city's development and construction increased with the est of National Capital Planning Commission (1958). By 1960s, Canberra was Australia's largest inland city. It is the site of Australian National University (1946), Canberra University College (1929), Royal Military College, Mt Stromlo Observatory, Parliament House, Yarralumla House (residence of governor-general), The Lodge (home of prime minister), Australian-American Memorial, and approx. 40 international embassies. The federal government is the major employer of Canberra's residents; tourism is a major industry. Pop. 133,100.

Cancer, unchecked growth of tissue spreading through the body, frequently causing death unless diagnosed and treated early. It may occur in virtually any organ, with lung cancer most frequent in men and breast cancer in women. Treatment of cancer can be surgical, chemical, by radiation, or a combination.

Cancer is regarded by many researchers as a multifactor disease with environmental factors, such as smoking, pollution, and exposure to occupation, chemical, and genetic factors, such as familial predisposition to certain cancers, implicated. Viruses also cause some cancers, such as Burkitt's lymphoma, and abnormal hormone levels are implicated in some breast cancers. Research in the 1980s has revealed the existence of cancer genes in cells; these are specific genes that trigger the transformation of healthy cells into cancer cells.

Cancer, or the Crab, northern constellation situated on the ecliptic between Gemini and Leo; the fourth sign of the zodiac. It contains two open clusters: M44, the Praesepe or Beehive Nebula (NGC 2632), and M67 (NGC 2682). Brightest star Beta Cancri. Astrological sign for the period June 22–July 22.

Candela, or new candle, basic unit of luminous intensity defined as the luminous intensity of a black body of surface area 1/60 square centimeter at the temperature of freezing platinum (1,769°C) and at atmospheric pressure. Symbol cd.

Candide (1759), short novel by Voltaire written as a satire of optimistic philosophical theories. A farcical yet horrific tale, it recounts the adventures of Candide, who has been taught to be thoroughly optimistic about life by his tutor, Pangloss. His journeys are beset by disaster and misfortune, but he relentlessly pursues his ideal in the form of the baron's daughter Cunégonde, who eventually adds to his disillusionment.

Candytuft, annual and perennial plants native to Spain and popular garden flowers. They have large, domelike clusters of white, red, or violet flowers. Species include annual rocket candytuft *(Iberis saxitilis);* annual candytuft *(I. umbellata);* and perennial evergreen candytuft *(I. sempervirens).* Height: to 18in (45.7cm). Family Cruciferae.

Cane, a grasslike plant *(Arundinaria gigantea)* growing in SW United States. With flat 1-ft (30-cm) leaves, it can grow to 25ft (7.6m) in damp swampy areas.

Canetti, Elias (1905–), Bulgarian-born British writer. He went to school in Switzerland and Germany and in 1929 received his doctorate in chemistry from the University of Vienna. Settling in Vienna, he wrote his only novel, *Die Blendung,* in 1935 (published in England as *Auto-da-Fé* (1946) and in the United States as *Tower of Babel* (1947)). He moved permanently to London in 1939. His other works include memoirs, *The Tongue Set Free: Remembrance of a European Childhood, The Torch in My Ear,* and *Kafka's Other Trial,* a study of the Central European scene. He received Germany's Georg Büchner prize in 1972. In 1981 he was awarded the Nobel Prize for literature.

Canidae, or dog family, chiefly meat-eating mammals that typically have long muzzles, large canine teeth, long legs, long tail, and blunt claws that cannot be retracted. It includes domestic and wild dogs, coyotes, wolves, jackals, and foxes. It is represented everywhere except Antarctica. Order Carnivora.

Canis Major, or the Great Dog, southern constellation situated south of Monoceros. It contains the bright open cluster M41 (NGC 2287). Brightest star Alpha Canis Majoris (Sirius).

Canker, ulcerous sore, especially around the mouth and lips. Causes may be from injury, allergy, or hormonal reaction. Healing is usually spontaneous.

Cankerworm, two small, slender moth caterpillars that feed on tree leaves. The spring *Paleacrita vernata* which also feeds on fruits, and the fall *Alsophila pometaria* are in the measuring worm family (Geometridae).

Canna, or Indian shot, flowering plant native to tropical America and Asia. Grown as an ornamental, it has large red, pink, yellow, or white flowers and large, broad leaves. Height: 1.5–5ft (46–152cm). Among 50 species is *Canna indica.* Family Cannaceae.

Cannae, ancient town in SE Italy, on the Ofanto River, between modern Barletta and Canosa; site of crushing defeat in 216 BC of Roman army by the Carthaginians under Hannibal. The Roman consul Lucius Aemilius Paulus died in the battle.

Cannes, resort city in SE France on French Riviera, 18mi (29km) SW of Nice; site of 16th- and 17th-century churches in the old part of city; scene of international film festival held each spring. Industries: textiles, shipbuilding. Pop. 71,080.

Cannibalism, eating human flesh as food or for ritual purposes. The practice was once very widespread and still exists in New Guinea and elsewhere. People are eaten to satisfy vengeance or hunger or as a means of acquiring their strength and powers.

Canning, George (1770–1827), English political figure. A follower of the younger Pitt, he entered Parliament in 1793 and was undersecretary for foreign affairs (1796–99), treasurer of the navy (1804–06), and foreign minister (1807–10). He resigned as foreign minister after bitter rivalry, including a duel, with Viscount Castlereagh. As president of the board of control for India (1816–20), he followed reform policies. After Castlereagh's death, he became foreign minister again (1822–27). A conservative himself, by supporting free trade and liberal movements abroad he shrewdly advanced Britain's interests. After his maneuverings in Latin America provoked the Monroe Doctrine, he stirred up British prejudice against the United States. On the domestic scene he innovated by deliberately appealing outside Parliament for public support for his policies. He became prime minister four months before his death.

Cannon, Joseph G. (1836–1926), Republican congressman (1873–91; 1893–1913; 1915–23), b. New Garden, N.C. Known as "Uncle Joe," Cannon was Speaker of the House (1903–11) who ruled with an iron hand, appointing all committees. He chaired the Rules Committee that determined priority of bills and created the arbitrary and partisan control of procedure called "Cannonism." Attempts to oust him (1909–10) failed, causing serious party rifts.

Cannon, cast metal tube used to fire and aim missiles propelled by the explosion of gunpowder in the cylinder. Cannon were first used in the 14th century. Major improvements in the 19th century included steel tubes, more powerful chemical propellants, breech-loading mechanisms, and standardized parts. By World War I, recoil devices were employed to absorb the shock of firing. *See also* Artillery; Howitzer.

Cano, Juan Sebastián del (*c.*1460–1526), Spanish navigator who was first to circumnavigate the globe. He commanded one of five vessels in Magellan's famous expedition and assumed control in 1521 after Magellan's death, returning to Spain in 1522.

Canoe, narrow, double-ended, shallow draft boat, propelled by paddles or sail, different forms of which are used on inland and offshore waters by communities all over the world. Canoes range in size from boats easily portable by one man to Maori "war canoes" 60ft (18m) long.

Canon Law, body of ecclesiastical law. In the Roman Catholic church, it is based on custom and regulations set forth by the founders of Christianity, with later additions of decrees of councils and popes and bishops. The most recent compilation of canon law, known as Codex juris canonici, was completed in 1918. It encompasses general universal laws, as well as local diocesan laws, and supersedes all prior compilations. A further revision, initiated in 1959, is now in progress.

Canopus, or **Alpha Carinae,** the second brightest star visible from earth. Canopus is a yellowish supergiant. Characteristics: apparent mag. −0.71; absolute mag. −5.5; spectral type FO; distance 300 light-years.

Canova, Antonio (1757–1822), Italian sculptor. A foremost neoclassical artist, his works include "Eurydice" (1773; Louvre, Paris), "Orpheus" (1776; Louvre, Paris), "Venus Victrix" (1804; Borghese Gallery, Rome), and the "Amor and Psyche" group (Louvre, Paris). Called to Paris in the early 1800s by Napoleon, he executed a bust of Napoleon from life, in addition to a number of other Napoleonic statues.

Cantaloupe, or muskmelon, trailing annual vine native to S Asia. Many varieties are cultivated in North America. It has roundish, hairy leaves and small, yellow flowers. The musky, netted fruit is globelike with yellow, white, or red flesh. The true cantaloupe *(Cucumis melo cantalupensis)* has a scaly rind unfamiliar to most people. Family Cucurbitaceae; species *Cucumis melo reticulatus. See also* Melon.

Cantata, musical work consisting of several pieces or movements sung by vocalists and chorus, often accompanied by an orchestra. Cantatas were composed mainly in the Baroque period by such masters as Alessandro Scarlatti, Rameau, and J.S. Bach, who composed over 200, most of them with religious texts. *See also* Baroque Music.

Canterbury, Archbishop of, primate of all England according to the doctrines of the Church of England. Residing in Canterbury, Kent, the archbishop also

Candytuft

Cannes, France

Canterbury, England

maintains a seat in Lambeth Palace, London. The archbishopric was established when Pope Gregory I sent (597) St Augustine to England on a mission to convert the Anglo-Saxons. During the Reformation, Archbishop Thomas Cranmer accepted the English crown's decision (1534) to make the English monarch, not the pope, head of the Church of England. Although no longer considered the head of all the separate dioceses in England, the archbishop presides as senior bishop over the Lambeth Conferences, which are held every 10 years by the Anglican communities.

ARCHBISHOPS OF CANTERBURY

Augustine	601–04
Lawrence (or Laurentius)	604–19
Mellitus	619–24
Justus	624–27
Honorius	627–53
Deusdedit	655–64
Theodore	668–90
Brihtwald (or Beorhtweald)	692–731
Tatwin (or Taetwine)	731–34
Nothelm	735–39
Cuthbert	740–60
Breguwine (or Bregowine)	761–64
Jaenbeorht (or Lambert, etc)	765–92
Ethelhard (or Aethelheard)	793–805
Wulfred	805–32
Feologeld (or Feolgild)	832
Ceolnoth	833–70
Ethelred (or Aethelred)	870–89
Plegmund (or Plegemund)	890–914
Aethelhelm	914–23
Wulfhelm	923–42
Odo (or Oda)	942–58
Aelfsige	959
Beorhthelm	959
Dunstan	960–88
Ethelgar (or Aethelgar)	988–90
Sigeric	990–94
Aelfric	995–1005
Aelfheah (or Alphege)	1005–12
Lyfing	1013–20
Ethelnoth (or Aethelnoth)	1020–38
Eadsige	1038–50
Robert of Jumièges	1051–52
Stigand	1052–70
Lanfranc	1070–89
Anselm	1093–1109
Ralph d'Escures (or Ralph de Turbine)	1114–22
William of Corbeil	1123–36
Theobald	1138–61
Thomas à Becket	1162–70
Richard	1174–84
Baldwin	1184–90
Hubert Walter	1193–1205
Stephen Langton	1207–28
Richard le Grant (or Richard of Wethershed)	1229–31
Edmund Rich	1233–40
Boniface of Savoy	1245–70
Robert Kilwardby	1273–78
John Peckham	1279–92
Robert de Winchelsea	1293–1313
Walter Reynolds	1313–27
Simon Meopham	1328–33
John de Stratford	1333–48
Thomas Bradwardine	1349
Simon Islip	1349–66
Simon Langham	1366–68
William Whittlesey (or Wittlesey)	1368–74
Simon of Sudbury	1375–81
William Courtenay	1381–96
Thomas Arundel	1396–1414
Henry Chichele (or Chicheley)	1414–43
John Stafford	1443–52
John Kempe	1452–54
Thomas Bourchier	1454–86
John Morton	1486–1500
Henry Dean	1501–03
William Warham	1504–32
Thomas Cranmer	1533–56
Reginald Pole	1556–58
Matthew Parker	1559–75
Edmund Grindal	1576–83
John Whitgift	1583–1604
Richard Bancroft	1604–10
George Abbot	1611–33
William Laud	1633–45
William Juxon	1660–63
Gilbert Sheldon	1663–77
William Sancroft	1678–91
John Tillotson	1691–94
Thomas Tenison	1695–1715
William Wake	1716–37
John Potter	1737–47
Thomas Herring	1747–57
Matthew Hutton	1757–58
Thomas Secker	1758–68
Frederick Cornwallis	1768–83
John Moore	1783–1805
Charles Manners Sutton	1805–28
William Howley	1828–48
John Bird Sumner	1848–62
Charles Thomas Longley	1862–68
Archibald Campbell Tait	1868–82
Edward White Benson	1883–96
Frederick Temple	1896–1902
Randall Thomas Davidson	1903–28
Cosmo Gordon Lang	1928–42
William Temple	1942–44
Geoffrey Francis Fisher	1945–61
Arthur Michael Ramsey	1961–74
Frederick Donald Coggan	1974–80
Robert Alexander Kennedy Runcie	1980–

Canterbury, cathedral city in SE England, on River Stour; market town trading in grain and hops. The present cathedral, built 11th-15th centuries, replaced St Augustine Abbey and a later cathedral that burned; it is the seat of the archbishop and primate of the Anglican Church. Murder of Thomas à Becket (1170) occurred in the cathedral and is commemorated by a tablet; after his canonization, Canterbury became a major pilgrimage center. Geoffrey Chaucer's *Canterbury Tales* (14th century) deal with these pilgrims. The 15th-century tower of the cathedral is 235ft (72m) high. City is also site of University of Kent at Canterbury (1964). Tourism is the chief industry. Founded AD 43. Pop. 115,600.

Canterbury Bells, biennial bellflower native to S Europe and widely cultivated. It has large spikes of cup-shaped pink, blue, or white flowers. Family Campanulaceae; species *Campanula medium. See also* Bellflower.

Canterbury Tales, The (*c.* 1388–1400), collection of narrative poems by Geoffrey Chaucer, each purporting to be told by one of a party of pilgrims to Canterbury. The pilgrims are described in a vivid "Prologue." The tales range from the courtly "The Knight's Tale" to the bawdy "The Miller's Tale," from the charming "The Nun's Priest's Tale" to the exuberant characterizations by narration in "The Wife of Bath's Tale" and "The Pardoner's Tale."

Cantilever (1) a projecting beam that is rigidly supported at one end with force applied at the free end, as in a diving board. Used in constructing balconies. (2) A bridge supported by two projecting beams, joined in the center by a connecting member and supported on piers and anchored by counterbalancing members.

Cantilever Bridge, form of girder bridge, characterized by a span that can be considered as two half-beams effectively anchored at one end and meeting (unsupported) in the middle. The Quebec Bridge (1918) has a main cantilever span 1,800ft (550m) long where it crosses the St Lawrence River.

Canto, major division of a long poem, such as the cantos comprising Dante's *Divine Comedy,* Edmund Spenser's *Faerie Queene,* and Lord Byron's *Don Juan.*

Canton (Guangzhou), largest city and port in S China, on Pearl River, 95mi (153km) from Hong Kong; capital of Kwangtung prov. From 300 BC, when it was conquered by the first emperor of the Ch'in dynasty, it has been an important trading port. It served as the headquarters (1911) of the revolutionary movement and the Nationalist party and as site of the Whampoa Military Academy, est 1924 and directed by Chiang Kai-shek; the Republic of China was declared here (1920s). Industries: textiles, paper, rubber products, shipbuilding, sugar refining, iron and steel production, furniture. Pop. 3,000,000.

Canton, city in E central Ohio, 20mi (32km) SSE of Akron; seat of Stark co; site of Malone College (1892), Walsh University (1960), National Football League Hall of Fame; was the home of President William McKinley who is buried here in National McKinley Memorial (1907). Industries: water softening equipment, forgings, steel, office equipment. Inc. 1854. Pop. (1980) 94,730.

Cantonese, one of the major dialects of Chinese. Within the Chinese People's Republic it is spoken by about 50 million people, mainly in the extreme southern provinces of Kwangtung and Kwangsi. It is also the dialect spoken by most Chinese in Southeast Asia and in the United States.

Cantor, singer who performs in a religious service. He may lead a choir or the congregation or sing the service himself in response to the rabbi, priest, or minister.

Cantos, The, long poetic work by Ezra Pound. Begun in 1915, it was intended to consist of 120 poems, or "cantos," of which a few remained unfinished at the time of Pound's death in 1972. Complex, erudite, and allusive, *The Cantos* is epic in scope, sweeping through the history of civilization (especially China, Renaissance Italy, and the United States) and ranging from the intensely lyrical and personal to the public and didactic. Much about the events of Pound's own life and his views on the arts and political economy is incorporated as are fragments from many literatures and even musical notes and Chinese characters. Particularly important for the work is material from the *Odyssey,* Ovid's *Metamorphoses,* and the *Divine Comedy.* The general theme of *The Cantos* is the search for exemplars of beauty and order.

Canute II (?994–1035), king of Denmark (1014–28), Mercia (1016), England (1017–35), and Norway (1028–29). He accompanied his father, Sweyn, on the Danish invasion of England (1013). After his father's death (1014) he withdrew to Denmark and was accepted as joint king with his brother until 1018, when he became sole king. He invaded England again (1015) and divided it (1016) with the English king Edmund Ironside. He was accepted as king of the whole country in 1017 after Edmund's death. His rule over England was a just and peaceful one. He restored the church to high position and codified English law. He also worked for good relations with Normandy, Aquitaine, and the Holy Roman Empire. His reign in Scandinavia was more turbulent. He conquered Norway (1028), made one son king of Denmark (1028), and made another son king of Norway (1029). Toward the end of his life he led an army into Scotland to stop Scottish invasions.

Canute IV (1043?–1086) "The Holy," king of Denmark (1080–86) and patron saint. A harsh king, he levied heavy taxes to benefit the church. Planning to invade England, he forced the peasants to mobilize but they rebelled, killing him at the Church of St. Alban at Odense. He was canonized in 1099. Feast: Jan. 19.

Canvasback Duck, North American diving duck that is a prized game bird. It has a chestnut head and neck, pale gray back, and black breast and tail. It lays large, greenish eggs (10). Length: 2ft (61cm); weight: 3lb (1.4kg). Species *Aythya valisneria. See also* Duck.

Canyon, deep, narrow depression in the earth's crust, either on land where it is the result of water erosion by a youthful river moving through arid terrain, or marine where its origin is not as clear. It may be the same as the canyon on land with subsidence of the entire riverbed and surrounding terrain or the result of marine currents, particularly turbidity currents.

Capacitance, or electrical capacity, ability of a capacitor to store electrical charge when there is a potential difference between its plates. The capacitance, *C,* of a capacitor is equal to the charge, *Q,* on either plate divided by the voltage between the plates, *V;* or $C = Q/V$. It is measured in farads.

Capacitor, or condenser, electrical device having the property of capacitance and consisting of a system of conductors (plates) separated by an insulator (dielectric). Simplest form has two parallel metal plates, each of area *A,* separated by a distance, *d,* which is filled with a dielectric of permittivity E. The capacitance, *C,* is equal to AE/d.

Cape Breton Island, rocky island in NE Nova Scotia, Canada; separated from the mainland by the Strait of Canso; site of Cape Breton Highlands National Park, numerous summer resorts, and North Barren, highest peak in Nova Scotia. Industries: lumbering, fishing, coal mining, pulp. Ceded from French to British 1763. Pop. 42,969.

Cape Buffalo, several races of large oxen, native to Africa south of the Sahara Desert. Brown to black, their hair is thick on the young, sparse on adults. Horns, recurved, meet at bases over the forehead, forming a helmet. It can run 35mph (56kph). Considered the most dangerous African game animal, its numbers have been greatly reduced because of hunting. Height: to 59in (150cm) at shoulder; weight: to 2000lb (900kg). Family Bovidae; species *Syncerus caffer. See also* Buffalo; Ox.

Cape Coast, city in S Ghana, W Africa, 75mi (121km) WSW of Accra; capital of Central Region; capital of the Gold Coast until replaced by Accra (1877). Industries: fishing, export trade. Settled 1610 by Portuguese. Pop. 51,764.

Cape Cod, sandy peninsula in SE Massachusetts, extends into the Atlantic Ocean in a hook shape, forming Cape Cod Bay; glacial origin. Presently a popular resort area, it was originally a haven for fishing, whaling, and salt making. The area facing the Atlantic is now major part of Cape Cod National Seashore.

Cape Colony, a colony founded by the British in 1806. The area was first occupied by black Africans and Boers and subsequently became a province of the Republic of South Africa. *See also* Cape Province.

Cape Horn, southernmost point in South America; sighted by Francis Drake in 1578; first rounded in 1616 by Willem Cornelis van Schouten; known for vicious westerly gales; clipper ship trade route to California in the 1850s.

Capek, Karel (1890–1938), Czech novelist, playwright, and essayist. After studying philosophy, he became a journalist. His works chiefly portrayed man's struggle against fate, especially in a scientific world. His writings included *R.U.R.,* a play about robots (1920), and the novel *War with the Newts* (1936).

Capelin, smelt-like, schooling marine fish found in Arctic and N Pacific. It is distinguished by long anal fin and tufted growths along its sides. Length: 5.9–7.9in (15–20cm). Family Salmonidae; species *Mallotus villosus.*

Capella, or **Alpha Aurigae,** spectroscopic binary star in the constellation Auriga, both of whose components are yellow giants. Characteristics: apparent mag. +0.09 (combined); absolute mag. +0.12 (Capella A), +0.37 (Capella B); spectral type G8 (Capella A), GO (Capella B); distance 45 light-years.

Cape Province, formerly Cape Colony; cape and province in the Republic of South Africa, bordered by Indian Ocean (SE) and Atlantic Ocean (W); unofficially known as Cape of Good Hope. Slaves were imported in 1658; however the British abolished slavery in 1834, 20 years after the cape was ceded to Britain. Diamonds were discovered in 1867. Parliamentary government est. 1872; joined with Union of South Africa in 1910; site of Stellenbosch, Cape Town, Rhodes, and Fort Hare universities. Industries: wool, diamonds, wine, asbestos. Area: 278,465sq mi (721,224sq km). Pop. 6,731,820.

Capercaillie, largest grouse of European evergreen forests. It is valued as a game bird. The male is mostly black with green reflections, red wattles over the eyes, and some white patches. The smaller female is brownish and lays yellowish eggs (5–8) in a ground-scrape nest after the male performs a trancelike courtship dance. They feed on vegetable matter. Length: 3ft (90cm). Species *Tetrao urogallus.*

Capet, surname given to King Hugh of France and his descendants (987–1328). Although originally an elective monarchy, the throne was passed from father to son for 15 generations by having the eldest son crowned during his father's lifetime. The Capetians gradually extended their rule from the two counties of Paris and Orleans to the whole of France. Philip Augustus, who reigned from 1180 to 1223, laid the foundations for the French monarchy by dispossessing the English king of Normandy, Anjou, and Maine. The dynasty's prestige was enhanced by the just reign of Louis IX.

Capetians, French royal family forming the third dynasty, it began with Hugh Capet, Duke of Francia, in 987 and ended with Charles IV in 1328, providing France with a total of 15 kings. Hugh Capet was elected king after the death of Louis V, the last of the Carolingians. The House of Capet effected alliance with the Church; dominance over the feudal forces, thus extending the king's rule over the entire country; and the beginnings of an administrative system. It was succeeded by Philip VI of the House of Valois.

Cape Town, capital city of the Republic of South Africa, and capital of Cape prov.; at the foot of the Table Mts. It is the site of Union Parliament, a 17th-century castle, and the National Historic Museum. Noted educational and tourist center, it includes the University of Cape Town and Table Mt aerial cableway. Industries: clothing, engineering equipment, motor vehicles. Pop. 1,108,000.

Cape Verde (Cabo Verde), island republic in E Atlantic Ocean, approx. 300mi (483km) W of Dakar, Senegal (W Africa). Formerly an overseas province of Portugal, the island group became independent on June 5, 1975, through the efforts of the African Party for the Independence of Guinea and Cape Verde, which is now the controlling party in the government. The archipelago is comprised of about 15 islands and islets, which are divided into two groups: the Windward Islands (N), including Boa Vista, Sal, São Nicolau, Santa Luzia, São Vicento, Santo Antão, Ilhéu Branco, and Ilhéu Raso; and the Leeward Islands (S), including São Tiago (the largest), Maio, Fogo, Brava, and the Ilheus do Rombo. Capital is Praia, on S São Tiago island.

The islands are of volcanic origin and are generally mountainous, containing deposits of coal and salt, important to the group's economy. Inhabitants are primarily Portuguese and African. The literacy rate is comparatively high and many Cape Verdian males leave the islands to work in Portugal or Africa. Mining, fishing, and farming are the chief occupations, but agricultural output of cash crops (coffee, tobacco, sugar cane, oranges, sisal, peanuts) and subsistence crops (cassava, sweet potatoes) has been hindered by recurrent droughts, including a severe one in 1975. Discovered 1455 by Alvise Ca Da Mosto serving Prince Henry of Portugal, the archipelago became part of Portugal in 1495 and was administered as a separate province of Portugal until its independence in 1975. Famine, triggered by drought beginning in 1984, caused major problems in the mid-1980s.

PROFILE

Official name: Republic of Cape Verde
Area: 1,557sq mi (4,033sq km)
Population: 319,000
Chief cities: Praia (capital); Mindelo
Religion: Roman Catholic
Language: Portuguese
Monetary unit: Cape Verdian escudo
Gross national product: $80,000,000.

Cape Verde Peninsula, peninsula in Republic of Senegal; westernmost projection of Africa. Discovered *c.* 1445 by Portuguese Navigator, Joao Fernandes; mostly dunes, limestone cliffs and marshes. Dakar, capital of Senegal, is on its S coast.

Cap-Haïtien, seaport town in N Haiti, West Indies, 95mi (153km) N of Port-au-Prince; capital of Nord dept.; settled by French, it served as capital of colonial Haiti 1697–1770; occupied 1791 by forces of Toussaint L'Overture, rebel slave leader; 1811–1820 was capital of kingdom of Henri Christophe who built the Sans Souci Palace and Citadelle La Ferrière, still standing. Exports: coffee, sugar. Pop. 50,000.

Capillarity, the elevation or depression of a liquid in a small open tube, called a capillary tube, inserted in the liquid. Capillarity is caused by the surface tension forces between the liquid and the tube material. *See also* Surface Tension.

Capillary, the smallest blood vessel in the body. The walls of capillaries consist of a single cell layer through which oxygen diffuses from the blood and carbon dioxide and dissolved wastes diffuse into the blood, turning it from its arterial bright red to its venous dark purplish.

Capital, in economics, factor of production that includes plant and machinery used in the production process. The rate of return on capital is normally referred to as the interest rate. Capital is fixed in the short run in that new plants and new equipment cannot be obtained in a specific short-run period. Capital is normally provided through the sale of stocks and bonds or other forms of debt.

Capital Gain, the difference between the buying price for a capital asset and a higher selling price. If a stock is purchased for $100 and is later sold for $120, a $20 capital gain has occurred. *Long-term* capital gains occur if the asset has been held more than six months. They are taxed at a more favorable rate than *short-term* capital gains in which the asset is held less than six months. The time requirements have been changed to 9 months for 1977 and to 12 months from 1978 on.

Capitalism, economic system characterized by private ownership of the means of production and by dependence upon the profit motive and the market direction of productive efforts. In a capitalistic system the owners of productive resources, by trying always to maximize the income earned by them, presumably ensure that the most effective use is made of all resources. As each resource owner searches for higher returns from his resources, he is forced to use them in the way consumers in general want them used, for this is the only way he can earn the maximum return. Under capitalism, government plays a relatively small part in the economy, regulating more than controlling. Producers and consumers are free to make most economic choices.

Capital Punishment, punishment of death for a person convicted of a criminal act. A United Nations' survey conducted in 1975 revealed that 103 of the 135 member states retained capital punishment. No one was executed in the United States from 1967 until 1977. After protracted litigation and circus-like publicity, convicted murderer Gary Gilmore was executed by a Utah firing squad to end the suspension of capital punishment in the United States.

Capitol, building in Washington, D.C., in which the US Congress convenes. President Washington laid the cornerstone in 1793. William Thornton was the original architect. Congress first met in the partially completed building in 1800. In 1814 it was burned to the ground by the British. Its restoration was supervised by Benjamin Latrobe and then Charles Bulfinch, who saw its completion in 1830. Under the direction of Thomas U. Walter it was greatly enlarged (1851–65), with the addition of the extended House and Senate wings and central dome. The building is approximately 750ft (229m) long and 350ft (107m) wide, with the dome reaching a height of 288ft (88m).

Capone, Al(phonse) (1899–1947), US gangster of the Prohibition era, b. Italy. He grew up in Brooklyn, N.Y. First a bodyguard to Johnny Torrio, Capone inherited the former's crime empire. In 1927, Capone's wealth was about $27,000,000, most derived from illegal liquor. He was eventually convicted of income tax evasion (1931) and imprisoned.

Capote, Truman (1924–84), US author, b. New Orleans. His first novel, *Other Voices, Other Rooms,* appeared in 1948. Other works include a novella, *Breakfast at Tiffany's* (1958), *The Grass Harp* (1951), *In Cold*

Cape Town, South Africa

Cape Verde

Capuchin

Blood (1965), with which Capote stated he had introduced a new literary genre, the nonfiction novel, and *Music for Chameleons* (1980).

Cappadocia, ancient plateau region of Asia Minor (modern E central Turkey); cuneiform tablets found at Kültepe record Assyria-Asia Minor trade before 1800 BC; part of Persian Empire (6th century BC); semi-independent kingdom (*c.* 225 BC); annexed as Roman province AD 17; early Christian center (AD 1st century).

Capri, Island of (Isola Di Capri), island in Bay of Naples, Italy. A favored Roman resort, the Roman Emperor Augustus resided here; it passed from French to British rule several times during the Napoleonic Wars; was returned to Kingdom of the Two Sicilies 1813. The Blue Grotto, a famous cavern on the coast, was rediscovered in 1826; site of ruins of two medieval castles. Industries: tourism, agriculture, fishing. Area: 4sq mi (10sq km). Pop. 7,725.

Capricornus, or the **Sea Goat,** southern constellation situated on the ecliptic between Sagittarius and Aquarius; the tenth sign of the zodiac. Usually referred to as Capricorn only for astrological purposes, this constellation contains the faint globular cluster M30 (NGC 7099). Brightest star: Delta Capricorni (Deneb Algiedi), an eclipsing binary. Astrological sign for the period Dec. 22–Jan. 19.

Caprivi Strip, narrow strip of land in NE South West Africa, bounded by Botswana (S), Zambia and Angola (N); named in honor of German Chancellor Leo von Caprivi, who wanted the land as outlet to Zambezi River; desert climate; some farming is done in the easternmost section of the strip, where the Zambezi River is used for irrigation. Length: 300mi (483km). Width: 50mi (81km).

Capsule, Spacecraft, the portion housing the astronauts or scientific payload of the mission. The capsule must be designed to withstand the heat, acceleration, shocks, vibration, spinning or tumbling, radiation, meteoritic impacts, vacuum and low temperatures of space while maintaining a stable environment for the passengers and instruments. The capsule contains the spacecraft controls, portholes, instruments to monitor the physical activities of the crew, TV cameras, ventilators, and hand grips. Capsules have double walls to protect against meteorites and highly reflecting exteriors.

Capuchin, also cebus or ring-tailed monkey, small monkey found from Honduras to N Argentina. Generally brown, yellowish, or gray, they are day-active tree dwellers. Omnivorous but preferring fruit, they are the most common pet monkeys in the United States and Europe. Species white-faced *Cebus capucinus,* weeper *C. apella,* white-fronted *C. albifrons,* black-capped *C. nigrivittatus. See also* Monkey.

Capuchins, a Roman Catholic religious order, begun by Matteo da Bascio in 1525 as a reform movement of the Franciscans. The pointed hood (in Italian, *capuccino*) of their habit provided them with their name. They also wear beards. The order is a strict one, emphasizing austerity. They played an important role in the Counter-Reformation, particularly in preaching and in foreign missions. In 1619 they were constituted an independent order, the Order of Friars Minor Capuchin. In 1622 they were instrumental in founding the Congregation of the Propagation of the Faith in Rome. One of the largest Catholic orders, they number about 15,000 friars today.

Capybara, largest living rodent, native to Central and South America. Semi-aquatic with webbed feet, it is big-bodied, short-legged, tiny-tailed, and nearly hairless. Length: 4ft (1.2m); weight: 110lb (50kg). Species *Hydrochoerus Lydrochaeris.*

Caracal, or Persian lynx, short-haired, long-eared carnivore of the cat family native to Africa and parts of Asia and India. Mainly nocturnal, caracals are quick and agile. They have slender, red-furred bodies and pointed ears tipped with black tufts. Length: 2.5ft(76cm); weight: to 40lb(18kg). Family Felidae; species *Felis caracal.*

Caracalla, Marcus Aurelius Antoninus (188–217 AD), Roman emperor (211–17). The son of Septimius Severus, he earned his name because he wore a Gallic tunic *(caracalla).* He resented sharing rule with his brother, Geta, whom he murdered along with 20,000 of Geta's supporters. He pacified the German frontier, planned further Persian conquests, and extended Roman citizenship to all free male inhabitants of the empire (212) in order to increase the income tax. He erected the Baths of Caracalla. Macrinus killed him in Asia and succeeded him as emperor.

Caracara, agile, diurnal bird of prey related to falcon found from S United States through South America. They are black and white and eat carrion and live animals. Length: 20–25in. (50–62.5cm). Family Falconidae.

Caracas, capital city of Venezuela, on Guaire River; under Spanish control until 1821; city almost destroyed by earthquake (1812); birthplace of Simón Bolívar, leader of revolts against Spain; site of Central University of Venezuela (1725), Plaza Bolívar, official center of city, equestrian statue of Simón Bolívar, and colonial cathedral (1614); oil boom in 1950s spurred city's growth. Industries: automobiles, oil, breweries, rubber goods. Founded 1567. Pop. 1,035,499.

Caramanlis, Constantine (1907–), president (1980–85) of Greece. A lawyer, he entered parliament in 1935 and served in cabinet posts after World War II. He became prime minister in 1955, promoting industrialization and a pro-West foreign policy, resigning in 1963 after quarreling with King Paul and going into exile. He returned in 1974 after seven years of military rule, forming a civilian government and scoring an impressive election victory. He served as prime minister until 1980, when he was elected president.

Caravaggio, Michelangelo Merisi da (1573–1610), Italian painter. His realistic and naturalistic style was in direct contrast to the late Mannerist style of his day. He attracted many admirers and followers for a time, but the movement died out after 1620, by which time his influence had been felt throughout Europe. His early works include the *Calling of St Matthew* and the *Martyrdom of St Matthew, Boy with a Basket of Fruit,* and *The Fortune Teller. Rest on the Flight into Egypt* (*c.* 1590–95) demonstrates Caravaggio's earlier graceful, lyrical, and delicate style, while *Raising of Lazarus* (1609) is typical of his later realistic style, marked by emotional intensity and angular drawing. Caravaggio's artistic manipulation of light enables his works to suggest a spirituality and religious feeling that his otherwise realistic rendering would deny.

Caraway, biennial herb native to Eurasia and cultivated for its small, brown, crescent seedlike fruit that is used for flavoring foods. It has feathery leaves and white flowers. Family Umbelliferae; species *Carum carvi.*

Carbide, inorganic compound of carbon with a more electropositive element. Boron and silicon both form hard carbides used as abrasives. Many transition metals also form carbides, in which the carbon atoms occupy interstitial positions in the metal lattice. Some electropositive metals form ionic carbon compounds. The best known is calcium carbide (CaC_2), which reacts with water to give acetylene.

Carbohydrate, organic compound of carbon, hydrogen and oxygen, in which the last two have the same proportions as in water. The simplest carbohydrates are the sugars, usually with five or six carbon atoms in each molecule. Glucose and fructose are naturally occurring sugars with the formula $C_6H_{12}O_6$, but with different structures. One molecule of each combines with loss of water to make cane sugar ($C_{12}H_{22}O_{11}$). Starch and cellulose have hundreds of glucose molecules linked together, in long lines in cellulose but branching in starch. *See also* Saccharide.

Carbolic Acid, solution of phenol (C_6H_5OH) in water, used as a disinfectant. *See also* Phenol.

Carbon, common nonmetallic element (symbol C) of group IV of the periodic table, known from earliest times. There are two crystalline allotropes: graphite, a soft black slippery solid, and diamond, a very hard gemstone. Various amorphous forms of carbon also exist. Industrial diamonds are used in rock drills and in cutting and polishing tools. Graphite is a solid lubricant and is also employed in electrodes, crucibles, and lead pencils. Amorphous carbon has many uses including as a pigment for inks, filler for rubber, and absorbent for decolorizing and deodorizing. Chemically carbon is notable for the vast number of compounds it forms with hydrogen and other nonmetals. Properties: at. no. 6; at. wt. 12.011; sp. gr. 1.9-2.3 (graphite), 3.15-3.53 (diamond); melt. pt. 6422°F (approx.) (3550°C); sublimes 6093°F (3367°C); most common isotope C^{12} (98.89%).

Carbonaceous Chondrite, a special kind of rare stony meteorite. *See also* Stony Meteorite.

Carbon Black, finely divided form of carbon made by incomplete combustion of natural gas or petroleum oil. It is used in both natural and synthetic rubber and in printing inks. Properties: sp. gr. 1.8–2.1; boil. pt. 7592°F (4200°C).

Carbon Cycle, circulation of carbon in the biosphere. Atmospheric carbon dioxide is changed to carbohydrates by plants during photosynthesis. Animals eat the plants and return carbon dioxide to the atmosphere by defecation and decomposition.

Carbon Dioxide, colorless odorless gas (formula CO_2) that occurs in the atmosphere (0.03%) and as a product of combustion of fossil fuels. In its solid form (dry ice) it is used to refrigerate foods, etc.; as a gas it is used in carbonated beverages, as a fire extinguisher, and to provide an inert atmosphere in welding. Properties: density 1.98 kg dm^{-3}; melt. pt. (5.2 atm) -69.9°F (-56.6°C); sublimes -109.5°F (−78.5°C).

Carbon Dwarf Star, very late type of red dwarf star belonging to either of two spectral classes designated N and R. The absorption lines in the spectra of these stars are due chiefly to carbon compounds and the surface temperatures involved range downward from about 2600°K to 1700°K.

Carboniferous Period, the fifth geologic division of the Paleozoic Era, lasting from 345 to 280 million years ago. Often divided into two periods: the Mississippian and the Pennsylvanian. It is called the "Age of Coal" because of extensive swampy forests that turned into most of today's coal deposits. Amphibians flourished and the first reptiles appeared. Land snails, scorpions, spiders, giant archaic dragonflies and cockroaches were common. Marine life including sea lilies and sharks abounded in warm, shallow inland seas; lobefins, lungfishes, and numerous primitive ray-finned fishes lived in fresh water. *See also* Geologic Time; Paleozoic Era.

Carbon Monoxide, colorless odorless highly poisonous gas (formula CO) formed during the incomplete combustion of fossil fuels and occuring in coal gas and the exhaust gas of internal-combustion engines. It is used in producer gas, in metallurgy, and in the manufacture of chemicals. Properties: density 1.25 kg dm^{-3}; melt. pt. −326°F (−199°C); boil. pt. −312.7°F (−191.5°C).

Carbon Tetrachloride, colorless nonflammable liquid with characteristic odor (formula CCl_4) prepared by the chlorination of methane or the catalytic reaction of carbon disulfide and chlorine. It is used as a refrigerant, insecticide, degreaser, and dry cleaning fluid. Properties: sp. gr. 1.59; melt. pt. −9.4°F (−23°C); boil. pt. 170.2°F (76.8°C).

Carborundum, trade name for silicon carbide (SiC) abrasives and refractories prepared by heating silica (SiO_2) with carbon in an electric furnace. It is used in grinding wheels, abrasive grains and powders, and valve-grinding compounds, and in refractory bricks and blocks. Nearly as hard as diamond, it slowly oxidizes at temperatures above 1,832°F (1,000°C).

Carboxylic Acid, member of a class of organic compounds containing the group CO·OH. The commonest example is acetic acid, CH_3COOH, present in vinegar. Carboxylic acids can be made by oxidizing an alcohol (an intermediate aldehyde is produced). Generally, they are weakly acidic; like other acids they form salts with bases and esters with alcohols. Esters of high-molecular weight carboxylic acids, such as stearic, lauric, and oleic acids, are present in animal and vegetable fats; for this reason carboxylic acids are often called fatty acids. The systematic names are formed using the suffix -oic (ethanoic acid, CH_3COOH). *See also* Alcohol.

Carburetor, device used in gasoline-powered internal-combustion engines to vaporize and mix fuel with air and inject the mixture into the engine inlet airstream in the correct ratio for proper combustion. Generally steady speed requires a ratio of 15:1 air to fuel. Richer ratios of 10:1 air to fuel are necessary for starting cold engines.

Carcassonne, town in S France, on Aude River, 57mi (92km) SE of Toulouse; capital of Aude dept. Originally fortified by the Romans in 1st century BC, old part of town is hilltop medieval fortress; Visigoths built towers in 6th century that are still intact; fortifications were added in 12th century. New city across river is a farm trading center. Industries: tourism, textiles, shoes, rubber. Pop. 43,616.

Carcinogen, substance or agent that causes cancer. Carcinogens include chemical agents, radiation, and some viruses. Many different chemical carcinogens have been identified in laboratory animals and a smaller number are definitely established for man. For example, beta-naphthylamine causes bladder cancer among workers in the dyestuffs industry, coal tar and coal-tar derivatives produce skin cancer, and carcinogenic hydrocarbons in tobacco smoke cause lung cancer.

Carcinoma, one of two major forms of cancer, a malignant growth of epithelial cells, which can push into surrounding tissues. *See also* Cancer; Sarcoma.

Cardamine, or bitter cress, genus of herb found in wet areas. The leaves, round or featherlike, are borne on long stalks; flower clusters are white and rose or purple; and seedpods are long and narrow. Species include spring cress *(C. bulbosa)*—height: to 18in (45.7cm); mountain water cress *(C. rotundifolia)*; and cuckooflower *(C. pratensis)*. Family Cruciferae.

Cardamom, herb from tropical India. A thick plant, it has white flowers with yellow and blue striped edges. The seeds are used as a spice and in medicine. Height: to 10ft (3m). Family Zingiberaceae; species *Elettaria cardamom.*

Cardiac Cycle, process by which the heart pumps blood. Blood enters the heart while it is relaxed (diastole), filling the atria and ventricles. Contraction (systole) of the ventricles forces blood out of the heart. At the end of this contraction, the ventricles again relax, and the heart starts to fill again, readying for the next cycle. *See also* Circulatory System; Heart.

Cardiff (Caerdydd), capital of Wales, and major port, in South Glamorgan on Severn estuary at mouths of rivers Taff, Rhymney, and Ely; seat of university college of South Wales and Monmouthshire (1893); site of 11th-century castle; administrative center for Mid and South Glamorgan. Industries: steel, shipbuilding, motor components, cigars, paper, chemicals, brewing. Pop. 284,000.

Cardigan Welsh Corgi, guard and cattle dog (working group) brought to British Isles over 3000 years ago by Celts. Related to the dachshund, it has a wide, flat head with medium-length, tapered muzzle; large, wide-set, erect ears, rounded at tips; long, strong body; short, slightly bowed legs; and long fox brush tail. The moderately long coat can be red, sable, black, tricolor, or blue merle—all with white marks. Average size: 12in (30.5cm) high at shoulder; 15–25lb (7–11.5kg). *See also* Working Dog.

Cardinal, rank in the hierarchy of the clergy of the Roman Catholic Church. Ranked after the Pope, most are bishops, nominated as cardinals by the Pope. The title of "Eminence" is used to refer to a Cardinal. With administrative functions, they reside in Rome unless they are bishops of foreign dioceses. A new pope is elected by the College of Cardinals. *See also* Cardinals, College of.

Cardinal, or redbird, North American songbird with a pleasant, clear, whistlelike song. The male has bright red plumage and crest and a thick orange-red bill. The female is duller in color. They feed on seeds, fruits, and insects. A loose, cup-shaped nest, lined with fine grass and hair, holds the pale blue, heavily spotted eggs (4) incubated by the female. The male helps feed the young. Length: to 9in (23cm). Family Fringillidae; species *Richmondena cardinalis.*

Cardinal Number, number expressing the content of a set but not the order of its members. Thus 6 is a cardinal number in "6 books". Two sets have the same cardinal number if their members can be put in one-to-one correspondence—a concept that allows the idea of cardinal numbers of infinite sets. The set of integers is said to have cardinal number X (aleph-null). The set of all real numbers cannot be put into one-to-one correspondence with aleph-null and is a "larger" infinite set. Other higher sets can be constructed leading to arithmetic of transfinite numbers.

Cardinals, College of, also known as the Sacred College, group of cardinals serving as advisors and counsellors to the pope. It is ranked highly in the Roman Curia, after the pope. During a vacancy in the papal office, the College of Cardinals controls the church and elects the new pope.

Cardiology, branch of medicine that deals with the diagnosis and treatment of the diseases and disorders of the heart and vascular system.

Cardozo, Benjamin Nathan (1870–1938), US jurist, b. New York City. In 1891 he was admitted to the bar and (1913) was elected to the New York Supreme Court. He was appointed by Herbert Hoover to the Supreme Court. He served as an associate justice (1932–38). Considered a liberal, he strove to simplify the law and to create an intermediary department between the legislature and the courts. His decisions on New Deal legislation were extremely influential.

Cargo Cult, millenarian religious and political movement in parts of Melanesia where natives have been suddenly confronted by white civilization. They expect their ancestors to return in planes or ships laden with modern goods and to free them from white control and the need to work. As part of the cult they prepare runways and landing areas for the expected cargoes.

Caria, ancient division of Asia Minor, in SW part of modern Turkey; ruled by Lydia (6th century), then Persia; conquered 334 BC by Alexander and later Syria, became part of Roman province 125 BC.

Carib, group of American Indians, relatively few in number, scattered over a large area of N South America. They speak dozens of related but different languages often loosely referred to as Carib, but more accurately known as the Cariban languages.

Caribbean Sea, extension of N Atlantic Ocean, bounded by South America, Central America, and the West Indies; location of 12 independent island republics. Main tributary rivers are: Magdalana and Atrato of Colombia; San Juan Grande and Coco of Nicaragua; and Motagua of Guatemala. Sea is crossed by international shipping lanes to Panama Canal. Area: 750,000sq mi (1,942,500sq km).

Cariboo Mountains, mountain range in E British Columbia, Canada, separated from main range of Rocky Mts by upper Fraser River; W foothills were scene of 1860 gold rush. Length: approx. 200mi (322km). Highest peak is Mt Sir Wilfred Laurier, 11,750ft (3,584m).

Caribou, or reindeer, large deer inhabiting N Canada, Alaska, E Siberia, Greenland, and Arctic Eurasia. Their thick coats have woolly underfur and the broad hooves can be splayed out for support in snow. Both males and females have antlers. Male antlers are long, sweeping beams with forward projecting brow tines. Gregarious, some formerly assembled in herds of thousands for fall migration. Some types are now almost extinct. They mate in September and October. The gestation period is eight months with 1–2 calves born. They eat grasses, sedges, leaves, lichens, and mosses. Height: 4ft(1.2m) at shoulder; weight: to 700lb (320kg). Family Cervidae; genus *Rangifer. See also* Deer.

Caricature, art history term meaning a charged or loaded portrait. The caricaturist attempts to convey the essence of his subject in a comic likeness. More generally, the term is used to denote a pictorial burlesque or ludicrous representation. The word and genre first appeared in the late 16th century. Bernini was a master caricaturist. Hogarth attempted to distinguish between depiction of character, his forte, and comic likeness, but the two traditions merged. Daumier, the 19th-century French political caricaturist, was a great master. In the 20th century many popular graphic artists have combined caricature with social and political satire.

Carina, or the Keel, extensive southern constellation situated south of Vela and Puppis. It contains the Keyhole Nebula (NGC 3372). Brightest star Alpha Carinae (Canopus).

Carleton, Guy, 1st Baron Dorchester (1724–1808), British military figure and colonial administrator, b. Ireland. Entering the British army in 1742, he saw service in North America during the French and Indian War, including at the Battle of the Plains of Abraham (1759). He became lieutenant governor of Quebec in 1766 and governor in 1768. He conciliated the French-Canadians, and his policies were confirmed by the Quebec Act passed by the British Parliament (1774). As British military commander in Canada in 1775, he defeated the Quebec campaign (1775–76) of the Americans in the Revolutionary War. Clashes with British officials then led to his retirement and departure from Canada (1778). In 1782, however, he returned as commander in chief of British forces in Canada. He was named a baron and governor in chief of British North America in 1786. Serving as governor until 1796, he advocated the federation of all British colonies in North America and promoted the Constitution Act of 1791.

Carlists, Spanish faction that favored the royal claims of Don Carlos (1788–1855) and his successors. When Ferdinand VII left the throne (1833) to his daughter, Isabella II, rather than his brother Carlos, civil war broke out. Isabella's forces finally won in 1840. Carlist sentiments persisted, however, and several uprisings (1860, 1869, 1872) failed, but the Carlists seized considerable territory in 1873. That uprising was ended in 1876, but Carlist sentiments—and Carlist pretenders—have persisted to the present.

Carloman, name of several members of the Frankish Carolingian dynasty, including **Carloman** (715–54), mayor of the palace of Austrasia; **Carloman** (828–880), king of Bavaria and Italy; and **Carloman** (died 884), who became sole ruler of the realm.

Carlos, or **Don Carlos** (1788–1855), Spanish prince and pretender to the throne. His elder brother Ferdinand VII changed Spanish law so that his daughter Isabella II could succeed him, which she did in 1833. Carlos was then proclaimed king by his partisans, known as Carlists, and civil war ensued. Isabella won in 1840, and Carlos went into exile. In 1845 he resigned his pretensions in favor of his son Don Carlos II. *See also* Carlists.

Carlsbad Caverns National Park, park in SE New Mexico. A series of limestone caves, 60,000,000 years old, are the largest yet discovered. The caverns are characterized by magnificent stalagmite and stalactite formations, and countless bats that swarm in the evenings, except in winter. Still not totally explored. Area: 46,753acres (18,935hectares). Est. 1930.

Carlyle, Thomas (1795–1881), Scottish philosopher, critic, and historian. An early study of German Romantics led to his translation of Goethe's *Wilhelm Meister* (1824). His most successful work, *Sartor Resartus* (1833–34), combined philosophy and autobiography.

Caricature: John Wayne in True Grit

Carnation

Andrew Carnegie

His histories include *The French Revolution* (3 vols. 1837), and a study of Frederick II of Prussia (6 vols. 1858–65). He was antidemocratic in his political thought and sought strong heroes or leaders, as expressed in a series of lectures *On Heroes, Hero Worship, and the Heroic in History* (1841).

Carmel, Mount, mountain ridge in NW Israel; extends 15mi (24km) from Esdraelon plain to Mediterranean Sea; home of the prehistoric Carmel man, a link between Neanderthal and modern man; associated with biblical prophets Elijah and Elisha; grapes for Mt Carmel wine are grown here; site of many monasteries and Jewish kibbutzim; Order of Carmelites founded here AD 1156. Height: 1,789ft (546m).

Carmelites, the "Order of Our Lady of Mount Carmel;" religious order founded by St Berthold in Palestine in 1154. The order of Carmelite Sisters was founded in 1452. The primitive rule of poverty, vegetarianism, and solitude, established by Albert of Vercelli in 1209, was revitalized in the "Teresian Reform" of St Teresa in the 16th century. Missionary work is stressed.

Carmen (1875), opera in 4 acts by Georges Bizet, French libretto by Henri Meilhac and Ludovic Halévy, after Prosper Mérimée's novel. The title role is for mezzo-soprano but is sometimes sung by soprano or contralto. Carmen, a femme fatale, induces Don José (tenor), a corporal of the guard, to join the gypsy smugglers, then deserts him for the toreador Escamillo (baritone) and meets her tragic death at the hands of Don José.

Carmina Burana, a manuscript collection of popular Latin songs from a 12th-century monastery in Bavaria. Probably composed and perpetuated by minstrels and students, many of the songs or poems tell of gambling and drinking, but some have moral or religious subjects. During the 18th century, several translations were published in Europe, and the lyrics were set to music by Carl Orff in 1935.

Carnap, Rudolph (1891–1970), German philosopher. A member of the Vienna Circle and recognized as a founder of logical positivism, he came to the United States from Europe in 1936. Coeditor of the *Journal of Unified Science* (formerly *Erkenntnis*) with Hans Reichenbach, he wrote extensively on the theory of probability, theory of knowledge, mathematical logic, and the philosophy of science.

Carnation, popular name for a perennial of European origin, now widely grown in greenhouses. A slender-stemmed herbaceous plant that grows to 5ft (1.5m), the carnation blooms from October to June. Each plant produces 18 to 24 blooms ranging in color from white to yellow, pink and red. In some varieties the petals are variegated. Carnations are grown commercially for cut flowers. Family Caryophyllaceae; species *Dianthus caryophyllus*.

Carnegie, Andrew (1835–1919), US industrialist and philanthropist, b. Scotland. He came to the United States as a boy and at 16 he became one of the first US telegraph operators, working for the Pennsylvania Railroad for 12 years (1853–65). Foreseeing the demand for iron and steel, he left the railroad and started the Keystone Bridge Works, and from 1873 he concentrated on steel. He bought oil fields, a railway, and steamships and by 1901, when his Carnegie Steel Co. was sold for $250 million to the US Steel Co. combine, it was producing 25% of the steel sold in the United States. He endowed 2,500 libraries and donated more than $350 million to foundations. In 1900 he founded the Carnegie Institute of Technology in Pittsburgh and in 1902 the Carnegie Institution of Washington, D.C.

Carnera, Primo (1906–1967), Italian boxer. Standing over 6ft 5in (195cm) tall and weighing 260lbs(117kg), he was the biggest man ever to win the heavyweight championship (1933) when he defeated Jack Sharkey. He lost the title to Max Baer (1934).

Carnic Alps (Alpi Carniche, Karnische Alpen), mountain range of the Eastern Alps, between S Austria and NE Italy, in Carniola region; year-round resort area. Highest peak is Mt Kellerwand, 9,217ft (2,811m).

Carnivora, an order of about 274 living species of mammals found worldwide (except for the Antarctic and some oceanic islands). They probably arose from insectivores during the Paleocene. Most are carnivorous, having teeth adapted for eating flesh, a simple stomach and short intestine, clawed toes, and a well-developed brain. The clavicles (collar bones) are lacking or are vestigial. Some of the best known are cats, dogs, bears, hyenas, weasels, raccoons, civets, and seals.

Carnivorous Plant. *See* Insectivorous Plant.

Carnot, Nicolas Léonard Sadi (1796–1832), French army officer and engineer. His major work, *Réflexions sur la puissance motrice du feu* (1824), provided the first theoretical background to the steam engine and introduced the concepts of reversible cycles and the second law of thermodynamics. He died of cholera at the age of 36 and his work was forgotten until it was revived by Lord Kelvin in 1848.

Carnot Cycle, the steps gone through by a heat engine (such as a steam or gasoline engine) that transform heat energy into mechanical work. All such engines extract heat at high temperature from some reservoir (the boiler or the gasoline); use the expansion of gases at that temperature to perform work such as moving a piston; and then reject waste heat into another reservoir, such as the atmosphere, at lower temperature. This process is often diagrammed on a pressure-volume graph. Such graphs allow comparison of the efficiencies of widely differing types of engines.

Carnotite, a secondary vanadate mineral, potassium uranium vanadate, an ore of uranium and radium important for atomic energy. Occurs in the Colorado Plateau, Australia, and Congo as yellow-green crusts or cavity fillings in sandstone and in fossilized wood. Finely crystalline (probably orthorhombic), dull or earthy; sp gr 3–5.

Carol I (1839–1914), prince of Romania (1866–81); first king (1881–1914). He aided Russia in the first Russo-Turkish War, 1877–78. Romanian independence and Carol's sovereignty were recognized by the Congress of Berlin in 1878; Carol was crowned in 1881. Romania was neutral during the First Balkan War (1912), but in the second it joined Serbia and Greece against Bulgaria. As a result, Romania became, by 1913, the strongest Balkan power. Carol preserved the neutrality of Romania at the start of World War I, but sympathized with the Germans.

Carol II (1893–1953), king of Romania (1930–40), grandnephew of Carol I. His 1917 morganatic marriage to Mme. Zizi Lambrino ended in divorce, and in 1921 he married Helen, a princess of Greece. In 1925 he renounced the throne to move to Paris with his mistress Magda Lupescu. He returned in 1930 and supplanted his son Michael as king, despite opposition of the Liberals and economic crisis conditions. Carol II supported the Romanian Fascist party. Anti-Jewish laws and rigid censorship were part of his program to become dictator, but German pressure forced him to abdicate in favor of his son Michael in 1940, leaving the real power in the hands of the dictator, Ion Antonescu.

Caroline Affair (1837), United States-Canadian altercation. In 1837, Canadian rebels, under William Lyon Mackenzie, took refuge on Navy Island, in the Niagara River. A US boat, the *Caroline*, which supplied the rebels, was captured, set on fire and sent over Niagara Falls by Canada's Capt. Andrew Drew. One US citizen was killed. The controversy's arbitration led to the Webster-Ashburton Treaty. *See also* Rebellion of 1837; Webster-Ashburton Treaty.

Caroline Islands, archipelago of more than 900 volcanic islands, coral islets, and reefs in W Pacific Ocean, N of the equator; part of US Trust Territory of the Pacific Islands since 1947; larger islands include Palau, Ponape, Truk, and Yap. Fishing is the main occupation; most natives are Micronesians. Exports: cacao, tapioca, dried bonito. Area: 830sq mi (2,150sq km). Pop. 66,900.

Caroline of Brunswick (1768–1821), queen of George IV of Britain. They were separated for most of their marriage, but on George's accession (1820) she claimed her rank of queen. The government introduced a divorce bill, but Caroline won public sympathy, the case was abandoned, and she retained her title, although she was prevented from entering Westminster Cathedral to attend his coronation.

Carolingian Renaissance, cultural revival in France and Italy under the encouragement of the Emperor Charlemagne (742–814). Having enlarged and enriched the Frankish kingdom and organized an efficient government, the illiterate monarch was able to gather notable educators and artists from all over his kingdom and beyond, including the British teacher Alcuin of York, who helped him found a palace school at Aachen. He promoted Catholicism, art, and learning by founding abbeys and encouraging church building. As the first Roman emperor in the West in over 300 years, he imposed a new culture in Europe, combining Christian, Roman, and Frankish elements. Although his renaissance declined along with his empire after his death, its influence remained until the later Middle Ages.

Carolingians, dynasty that governed in France from 751 to 987; in Germany from 751 to 911; and in Italy, sporadically, from 774 to 901. Their alliance with the popes and their strong administrative ability enabled the Carolingians to rule new kingdoms, transforming Europe from a group of tribes into feudal monarchies. Their empire was at its peak under Charlemagne, who was crowned "Emperor of the Romans" in 800.

Carotene, plant pigment with vitamin A activity; obtained from fruits and vegetables in the diet and converted by the eye into visual pigment, necessary for sight.

Carotenoid, one of a group of fat-soluble plant pigments ranging in color from yellow to red. Carotenoids also occur in some animal fats. They include three isomers of carotene, a red pigment that is converted in the liver into vitamin A.

Carothers, Wallace Hume (1896–1937), US chemist, b. Burlington, Iowa, who discovered the synthetic fiber now called nylon. He committed suicide before seeing its enormous success. *See also* Nylon.

Carp, freshwater food fish found in temperate waters. Farmed in Japan for low-cost protein, it has four fleshy mouth whiskers and is brownish or golden. Length: to 40in (101.6cm); Weight: 60lb (27.2kg). Family Cyprinidae; species includes common *Cyprinus carpio* and Asiatic grass carp *Ctenophrynogodon idella.*

Carpathian Mountains, mountain range in central and E Europe, beginning in E Czechoslovakia and extending NE to Polish-Czechoslovakian border; Northern Carpathians (Beskids and Tatra) run E along border and SE through W Ukraine, USSR; Southern Carpathians (Transylvania Alps) continue SW to Danube River; sparsely settled except for valleys in S regions. Industries: lumbering, mining, tourism. Highest peak is Gerlachovka, 8,737ft (2,665m) in Northern Carpathians. Length: 950mi (1,530km).

Carpenter Ant, large black ant, 0.25 to 0.75in (6.35 to 19mm) long, that makes its home in galleries in damp wood. It feeds on honeydew from aphids and not the wood in which it lives. It is found worldwide. Family Formicidae; Genus *Camponotus.*

Carpenter Bee, yellow and black to metallic bee, 0.25 to 1in (6–25mm) long, found worldwide. It makes its nest in plant stems or wood. The larger ones resemble bumblebees. Family Apidae, Subfamily Xylocopinae. *See also* Bee.

Carpentry, the craft and trade of cutting, working, and joining lumber for structural and functional purposes. Involved are basic house construction, the building of staircases, windows and doors, and furniture-making and decorative woodwork. Many specialized tools and techniques have been developed over the centuries.

Carpetbaggers, epithet used after the US Civil War to refer to Northern whites affiliated with the Republican party who went to the South to participate in or take personal advantage of Reconstruction. The name referred to the traveling bag, usually made of carpeting, in which people of the period often carried their belongings.

Carpet Beetle, small beetle whose larvae feed on rugs, upholstery, stored clothing, and other textile products. The best protection against them is frequent and thorough housecleaning. Genera *Anthrenus* and *Attagenus.*

Carracci, Lodovico (1555–1619), Italian painter. He dominated the artistic scene in Bologna as leader of the Carracci Academy, which included his cousins Agostino and Annibale Carracci. He made a strong contribution to Baroque art through such works as *Bargellini Madonna* (1588), *Preaching of St. John the Baptist* (1592), and *The Crucifixion* (1614) *See also* Baroque Art.

Carrack, small wooden sailing ship first appearing in the Middle Ages and characterized by one or two large square-rigged main masts, one or two smaller lateen mizzen or rear masts, and a rear rudder. One example was the *Santa Maria* of Christopher Columbus.

Carrara, formerly Apuania; city in central Italy; site of renowned marble quarries, used by Michelangelo. Notable landmarks include Pisan-style 12–14th-century cathedral, 13th-century castle. Chief industry is the production and exportation of marble. Pop. 70,125.

Carrier, in disease, any person, who in apparent good health harbors a disease that does not affect him, yet upon accidental contact, the disease can be transmitted with resultant full-blown infection.

Carrier Pigeon, a homing pigeon; any domestic pigeon used for racing or carrying messages and trained to return to its loft by being released at gradually increased distances. The name is also given to a breed of large pigeons with long wings, bare skin about the eyes, and a greatly developed cere, the fleshy covering at the base of the bill.

Carrier Wave, a high frequency electromagnetic wave modulated by sound or light signals in wireless transmission. The length and frequency of its carrier wave identifies each individual transmitter, so that a receiver can be tuned to its channel. To prevent interference, transmitter carrier waves are normally separated by clear channels of 10 kc frequency.

Carroll, Lewis (1832–98), pseud. of Charles Lutwidge Dodgson; English mathematician, photographer, and novelist. He is especially remembered for *Alice's Adventures in Wonderland* (1865) and its sequel, *Through the Looking-Glass* (1872), which have attracted much serious scholarly criticism as well as being popular children's classics. *See also* Alice's Adventures in Wonderland.

Carrot, a single species *(Daucus carota)* of herbaceous plant native to Afghanistan and cultivated widely. It has an edible taproot that is white, yellow, purple, or orange. It has fernlike leaves sheathed at the base and white, flat-topped flower clusters. Other members of the carrot family (Umbelliferae) are parsley, celery, anise, dill, caraway, and poison hemlock.

Carson, Kit (1809–68), US trapper, guide, and soldier; b. as Christopher Carson in Madison co, Ky. Raised in Missouri, in 1826 he ran away to Taos, N.M. He then made his living as a trapper, hunter, and guide throughout the Rockies and Sierras. He achieved fame for his work as guide for John C. Frémont's expeditions (1842–46) and was with Frémont in California when the Bear Flag Revolt took place in 1846. During the Mexican War he carried dispatches for Frémont and Gen. Stephen Kearny. In 1853 he was US Indian agent at Taos and in 1861 he became a colonel in the army and fought against Confederate and Indian forces. At the end of the war he was made a brigadier general and commanded at Fort Garland in Colorado (1866–67). In 1868 he was named superintendent of Indian affairs for Colorado Territory.

Carson, Rachel Louise (1907–1964), US biologist and science writer, b. Springdale, Pa. She is best known for her widely popular and influential books on pollution, wild life, and the sea. She made her career with the US Bureau of Fisheries, now the US Fish and Wildlife Service. In 1951 she published *The Sea Around Us,* a natural history of the sea, which subsequently won a National Book Award. *Silent Spring* (1962), about the dangers of pollution, had worldwide impact. Other works include *Under the Sea-Wind* (1941) and *The Edge of the Sea* (1955).

Carson City, capital of Nevada, 30mi (48km) S of Reno; coextensive with Ormsby co; founded as Eagle Station (1851), renamed for Kit Carson; experienced population and financial boom with the discovery of the Comstock Lode (1859); site of a branch of US Mint (1870–93), which houses a natural science and history museum. Industries: tourism, gambling. Inc. 1875. Pop. (1980) 32,022.

Cartagena, city and port in NW Colombia, on the Bay of Cartagena in the Caribbean Sea; good harbor; important city of Spanish America in the 17th century; became part of Colombia 1821. Principal oil port of Colombia; site of university (1824). Industries: oil refining, sugar, tobacco, hides, textiles, tourism. Founded 1533. Pop. 256,598.

Cartagena, major seaport city in SE Spain, on the Mediterranean Sea; Moors captured the city in the 8th century; recaptured by Spaniards in 13th century; destroyed by Francis Drake in 1585; site of medieval Castillo de la Concepción, and modern naval base. Industries: shipbuilding, lead, zinc, iron. Founded *c.* 255 BC by Carthaginians. Pop. 146,904.

Cartel, formal agreement among the producers of a good to fix the market price and to divide the market among the participants. Cartels ordinarily result in higher prices to consumers and extra profits for sellers. Unless specifically exempted, cartels are illegal in the United States. *See also* Sherman Antitrust Act.

Carter, James Earl, Jr. (Jimmy) (1924–), 39th president of the United States (1977–81), b. Plains, Ga. Carter attended the US Naval Academy, from which he graduated in 1946. He entered the Navy and was assigned to the nuclear submarine program under Adm. Hyman Rickover. In 1946 he married Rosalynn Smith; they had three sons and one daughter. Upon the death of his father in 1953, Carter resigned from the Navy and returned to Plains, where he took over the family peanut farming and processing business.

Carter served in the Georgia state senate, and in 1966 he entered the Democratic primary for governor. He was defeated but four years later he won both the Democratic primary and the general election. His four-year administration was noted for improved race relations and fiscal conservatism.

Carter entered the state primaries for president in 1976 and won the Democratic Party nomination. He and running mate Walter F. Mondale defeated the Republican ticket of Gerald Ford and Robert Dole. As president, Carter was admired for his courage and integrity but found wanting in leadership. The major accomplishments of his administration were in civil service reform, in the establishment of a national energy policy, and in the passing of significant environmental legislation. He gained prestige as mediator in the Israel-Egypt peace negotiations but suffered criticism for his restrained stance against Iran over the hostage issue, which was still unresolved on election day in 1980. The unsatisfactory state of the economy, the evident lack of direction in Washington, and Carter's personal aloofness all contributed to his overwhelming loss of the election to Ronald Reagan in 1980. He wrote *Keeping Faith* (1982).

Career: governor of Georgia (1971–75); president (1977–81).

Carteret, (Sir) George (c.1610–80), British proprietor in America. In England, he was a naval officer and a Royalist supporter, for which the king gave him a grant to American lands "to be called New Jersey." He was one of the eight original proprietors of Carolina (1663) and joint proprietor with Lord Berkeley of the province of New Jersey (1664). He also served as deputy treasurer of Ireland (1667–73).

Cartesian, doctrine of the 17th-century French philosopher René Descartes. Cartesians agreed with Descartes that all human knowledge could be established with mathematical certainty on the basis of indubitable first truths. The thinking self alone, working on its own clear and distinct ideas, could create a world. Matter (extended substance) and mind (thinking substance) constituted the fullness of reality, while the former, always in motion, was the sole object of scientific study. *See also* Cogito Ergo Sum; Descartes, René; Rationalism.

Cartesian Coordinate System, coordinate system in which the position of a point is specified by its distances from intersecting lines (the axes). In the simplest type —rectangular coordinates in two dimensions—two axes are used at right angles: the y axis and the x axis. The position of a point is then given by a pair of numbers (x,y). The abscissa, x, is the point's distance from the y axis, measured along the x axis, and the ordinate, y, is the distance from the x axis. The axes in such a system need not be at right angles. In three dimensions three axes are used, and a point has three coordinates, x, y, and z. *See also* Coordinate System.

Carthage, ancient seaport in N Africa, on tip of peninsula in Bay of Tunis; founded by Phoenician colonists, 9th century B.C.; fought the Punic Wars against Rome, Carthage was destroyed during the Third Punic War 149–146 B.C. Rebuilt by Caesar in 44 BC, it was the capital of the Vandals (439–533 AD), and was nearly destroyed by the Arabs (698). Louis IX (St. Louis) of France died there in 1270 of plague while on a crusade.

Carthusians, Christian religious order founded by St Bruno in 1084 at the Grande Chartreuse monastery near Grenoble, France. A strictly contemplative order, the monks are vowed to silence and solitude. The order includes nuns.

Cartier, Jacques (1491–1557), French explorer. Born of a wealthy family, Cartier probably accompanied Verrazano to New France in 1524. In 1534 he was sent by Francis I to find a northwest passage to the Spice Islands. He explored the Gulf of St. Lawrence, Newfoundland, New Brunswick, and, in a second voyage (1535), Quebec and Montreal. He established good relations with the Indians but lost favor with the French court. In 1541 he helped found a colony at Cap Rouge and then devoted the rest of his life to exploration and description of Canada, decimating his personal fortune.

Cartilage, a flexible supporting tissue composed of a nonliving matrix within which are living cartilage cells. Cartilage is comparatively soft. In man the ends of some bones and the nose, the ears, and the windpipe, remain cartilaginous throughout life.

Cartography, the ancient art and science of representing all or a portion of the earth's surface to some kind of scale, usually drawn or printed on a flat surface through the use of various kinds of projections. There are many kinds of maps, the most common being topographical. In civil engineering planning, relief maps are the clearest method for demonstrating the three-dimensional nature of the terrain. *See also* Map.

Cartoon, preparatory drawing for a tapestry, oil painting, fresco, or stained-glass window. The design, drawn in chalk, charcoal, pencil, or, in the case of the weaver's cartoon, in full color, was transferred by tracing with a stylus or pounding charcoal dust through tiny holes. The present use of *cartoon* as a humorous drawing is derived from a 19th-century competition for fresco designs for Parliament parodied in *Punch.* Animated, humorous motion pictures are also called cartoons.

Caruso, Enrico (1873–1921), Italian tenor, one of the most famous operatic singers of all time. He made his debut in Naples in 1894, and his fame began in 1902 when he sang at Monte Carlo. After his US debut at the Metropolitan Opera in 1903 in Verdi's *Rigoletto,* he remained at the Metropolitan for 17 years. He earned the Metropolitan much success and money, singing about 50 different roles and becoming the most ac-

Jimmy Carter

Enrico Caruso

George Washington Carver

claimed and highest paid singer in the world. He also appeared in the leading European opera houses and made many phonograph recordings.

Carver, George Washington (1864–1943), American agricultural chemist and experimenter, b. Diamond Grove, Mo. He is best known for his scientific research on the peanut, from which he derived more than 300 products. Born a slave, he attended Simpson College in Iowa and received a master's degree in science from Iowa State Agricultural College. In 1896 he became head of the department of agriculture at Tuskegee Institute in Alabama, where he devoted his research to developing products that might be utilized by the South, whose lands had been ravaged by the one crop system. He developed products from the peanut, sweet potato, and soy bean. His primary intent was to aid impoverished farmers, which he did in part through extensive lecture tours.

Cary, (Arthur) Joyce (Lunel) (1888–1957), British novelist, b. Northern Ireland. He left Oxford University to study art. His experiences in colonial political service in Nigeria (1913–20) are reflected in *Mister Johnson* (1939). He also wrote two trilogies, the first of which contains *The Horse's Mouth* (1944), his most famous novel.

Casablanca (Dar-el-Beida), seaport and largest city in Morocco, on W coast, on the Atlantic Ocean; subtropical climate; commercial, industrial and export center for approx. 60% of Morocco's trade. Built on site of ancient city of Anfa, which was destroyed by Portuguese 1468; occupied by French 1907; site of conference between Prime Minister Churchill and President Roosevelt, Jan. 1943. Industries: cement, chemicals, textiles, tobacco, food processing. Pop. 1,952,200.

Casablanca Conference (January 1943), meeting of US Pres. Franklin Roosevelt and British Prime Minister Churchill at Casablanca, North Africa. The Allied leaders pledged to fight until the Axis forces surrendered unconditionally.

Casanova, or **Casanova de Seingalt, Giovanni Jacopo** (1725–98), Italian adventurer and author. He studied for the priesthood but was expelled for immoral conduct; after serving as secretary to a Roman cardinal and serving in the Venetian army, he traveled throughout Europe, gaining a reputation for gambling, spying, and womanizing. Imprisoned in Venice (1755) he escaped and returned to Paris where his amorous deeds and charm led to financial and social success. He served as a spy for the Venetian Inquisition (1774–82) and retired as librarian for Count von Waldstein in Bohemia. His memoirs are world famous.

Cascade Range, mountain range in W United States; extends from NE California N across Oregon and Washington into Canada; site of Cascade Tunnel, 8mi (13km) railroad tunnel, longest in North America. Crater Lake National Park and Lake Chelan National Recreation area are in Cascades. Highest peak is Mt Ranier, 14,410ft (4,395m).

Case, the classification of nouns and pronouns according to their use in a sentence. The noun or pronoun is in the nominative case when it is used as the subject or subjective complement; it is in the objective (accusative) case when it is used as the direct or indirect object of a verb or preposition; it is in the possessive case when it indicates ownership or relationship.

Casement, (Sir) Roger (David) (1864–1916), Irish political figure. As a British consul (1895–1912), he gained international fame by exposing exploitation of

natives in the Congo and Peru. During World War I he sought German assistance for Irish independence. After he landed in Ireland from a German submarine, the British government executed him for treason. In an attempt to destroy his reputation, British agents circulated what purported to be his diary accounts of homosexual encounters. It has never been established whether the accounts were genuine.

Cashew, evergreen tree *(Anacardium occidentale)* of the sumac family, native to the West Indies. Growing to 40ft (12m), it has longish leaves and yellow-pink flowers. The kernel of the nut is popular for eating. Its gum is sometimes used in varnish.

Cashmere Goat. *See* Kashmir Goat.

Casimir III, called the Great (1309–70), king of Poland (1333–70), son of Ladislas I and last of the Piast dynasty. His enlightened rule encouraged education and the spread of culture. He also Westernized administration and published a new legal code. He added Galacia to his domain (1340), while abandoning Silesia and Pomerania. Called the "Peasants' King," he improved their conditions. German and Jewish refugees were protected. In 1364, the University of Cracow was established.

Casimir IV (1427–92), king of Poland (1447–92). The greatest cultural heights were reached during his reign. Casimir conducted a successful 13-year war against the Teutonic Knights (1454–66) and acquired West Prussia, Pomerania, and other lands from them by the terms of the 2nd peace of Thorn (1466). In 1467, he founded the Polish Sejm, or diet.

Casino, card game played by two to four players with a standard 52–card deck. The object of the game is to take the greatest number of cards and the greatest number of spades by either matching cards that are played on the table or by building upon the cards played on the table (placing a two on a seven for an eventual pickup with a nine).

Casper, city in N central Wyoming; seat of Natrona co; population boomed with discovery of oil 1890. Industries: oil refining, meat packing. Founded 1888; inc. 1889. Pop. (1980) 51,016.

Caspian Sea, shallow salt lake primarily in USSR; extreme S portion is on Iranian border; world's largest inland body of water; water level fluctuates according to evaporation and tributaries' conditions; mainly fed by the Volga River, also receives the Ural, Emba, Kura and Terek rivers; has no outlet. Chief USSR ports are Baku, an oil center, and Astrachan. An important trade route for centuries, it was a medieval Mongol-Baltic route for Asian goods; transportation and shipping route; supports fisheries and sealeries. Area: 144,000sq mi (372,960sq km).

Cassander (c.358–297 BC), king of Macedonia (316–297 BC), son of Antipater. He joined Alexander in Asia in 324. They disliked one another, but the tradition that he murdered Alexander is false although he did slay Alexander's mother, son, and widow. After Antipater's death, he tried to hold Macedonia and Greece against Antigonus' efforts to reunite Alexander's empire and defeated him in the Battle of Ipsus (301 BC).

Cassandra, in classical mythology, a Trojan skilled in the art of prophecy, but condemned by Apollo never to be taken seriously. Her warning that the Greeks would capture Troy went unheeded. She was raped by the Greek soldier Ajax, carried off by Agamemnon, and murdered by Clytemnestra and Aegisthus.

Cassatt, Mary (1845–1926), US painter and printmaker, b. Allegheny City, Pa. Influenced by Degas, her work generally depicts social and domestic scenes, most often involving fashionable women and children. Her works, also influenced by Oriental art, include the notable *The Morning Toilet* (1886), *The Lady at the Tea Table* (1885), and *Woman Sewing* (1886).

Cassava, or manioc, tapioca plant *(Manihot esculenta)*, a woody shrub or herb of the spurge family. A native of Brazil, it grows to 9ft (2.7m), and has small clustered flowers. The tuberous roots are poisonous, but when the juice is expelled, they become edible and are used for food.

Cassini, Giovanni Domenico (1625–1712), French astronomer, born in Italy. In France from 1669, he is chiefly remembered for being the first to detect the dark cleft between Saturn's two outer rings (Cassini's Division). He also discovered four of Saturn's moons.

Cassini's Division, a dark gap, discovered in 1675 by the French-Italian astronomer Giovanni Domenico Cassini, lying between rings A and B of the planet Saturn. (The A and B rings are the outer bright rings seen from the earth.) Until the flyby of the Voyager spacecraft in 1980, Cassini's Division had been thought empty, and dynamical explanations of why it necessarily had to be empty were widely accepted. Voyager revealed the presence of many thin, diffuse rings within the division.

Cassino, formerly San Germano; town in central Italy, on the Rapido River; built on ancient (866) Valsci town of Casinum; site of Monte Cassino (Benedictine abbey) which was medieval center of arts and learning; scene of savage fighting 1944 in which town and monastery were destroyed; later rebuilt; agricultural and commercial center. Chief industry is toys. Pop. 24,695.

Cassiopeia, northern circumpolar constellation situated in the Milky Way north of Andromeda and characterized by the W shape of its five most conspicuous stars. In addition to several clusters and variables, Cassiopeia contains two radio sources: Cassiopeia A, the remains of a supernova of 1700, and Cassiopeia B, the remnant of Tycho Brahe's supernova of 1572.

Cassiterite, an oxide mineral, tin oxide (SnO_2); the major ore of tin. Mined from placer deposits chiefly in Malay peninsula. Also in pegmatites and high-temperature veins. Tetragonal short prismatic crystals; often twinned, or masses and radiating fibres. Translucent black, yellow or white; hardness 6–7; sp gr 7.

Cassius Longinus, Gaius (died 42 BC), Roman general and political figure, leader of the assassins of Julius Caesar. A bitter, ascetic man of distinguished family, he campaigned under Crassus in Parthia (53 BC), saving the remnants of the defeated army. Siding with Pompey against Caesar, he was pardoned and promised the governorship of Syria. After organizing with Marcus Brutus the successful conspiracy against Caesar (44 BC), he fled to Macedonia where he and Brutus engaged in battle at Philippi (42 BC) with Mark Antony and Octavian, who sought to avenge Caesar's murder. Cassius committed suicide, erroneously believing the battle to be lost.

Cassowary, huge, powerful, flightless bird of rain forests of New Guinea, N Australia, and nearby islands. Adult has coarse black plumage, horny growth on a brightly colored head, short bill and legs, and sharp claws. The male incubates green eggs (3–8) in a platform nest on the forest floor. Length: 52–65in (1.3–

1.6m); weight: 40lb (63kg) or more. Species *Casuarius casuarius.*

Castanets, percussion instrument producing clicking sounds with two pairs of hinged hardwood shells attached to the player's thumbs. They are often played by Spanish dancers, often to guitar accompaniment.

Caste, a formal, rigid system of social stratification based on factors beyond individual control (eg, race, sex, or religious heritage) and sanctioned by tradition. This kind of system is called *ascriptive* because the individual is born into his or her position and cannot change it. The Hindu caste system in India and South Africa's apartheid are contemporary examples. *See also* Stratification.

Castel Gandolfo, town in central Italy, on Lake Albano; became realm of Holy See 1608; summer residence of Pope. The Villa Barberini houses the Vatican observatory. Industries: peaches, wine, fish. Pop. 4,623.

Castiglione, Giovanni Benedetto (1616–70), Italian painter and printmaker. He was the leading 17th-century Italian follower of the Dutch school as well as first known practitioner of monotype, or single-print technique. He was also among the first to make chiaroscuro woodcuts.

Castile, New, provincial region in Spain; captured by Castilian kings from Moors (1212). New Castile includes the provinces of Madrid, Toledo, Guadalajara, Cuenca, and Ciudad Real. Philip II made Madrid the capital of Spain in 1561. Chief products are olive oil and grapes. Pop. 5,164,026.

Castile, Old, provincial region in Spain; former county of the kingdom of Leon, ruled by Castilian kings. Castile and Aragón were united in 1479 by Isabella I of Castile and Ferdinand II of Aragón. Old Castile includes the provinces of Ávila, Logroño, Santander, Burgos, Segovia, Soria, Valladolid, and Palencia. Severe climate and poor soil allow only limited grain growing and sheep raising. Pop. 2,135,788.

Casting, Metal, forming metal materials by permitting molten metal to fill and solidify in molds of desired shapes. Most castings are made by pouring metal in sand and clay molds. Specialized processes, such as plastic molding, composite molding, investment casting (or lost wax process), and die casting permit greater dimensional accuracy, smoother surfaces, and finer detail.

Cast Iron, a general term that includes a number of irons, especially gray irons and pig irons (those directly out of the blast furnace). They cover a wide range of iron-carbon-silicon alloys containing from 1.7 to 4.5% carbon along with varying amounts of other elements. Gray iron (so-called because its fracture looks grayish) is the most widely used for casting automobile blocks, machinery parts, hollow ware, and many other products. *See also* Casting, Metal.

Cast Iron Architecture. Used in European structures since 1779, cast iron became most important with the development by James Bogardus of prefabricated iron skeletal frames in the latter 19th century. Cast iron architecture prefigured the skyscraper developed by the Chicago School, although steel became its main material.

Castle, a fortified residence of a king or noble in the Middle Ages. Built of earth or masonry, located on a site dominating its environs and usually surrounded by a water filled moat, castles were enclosed by high walls protecting those inside from attack or siege. Castles could be of regular or irregular shape, but almost all had common architectural elements for defensive purposes. Turrets were usually found at the angles of the wall and occasionally interspersed along the exterior walls. The walls were built thick enough to withstand bombardment and wide enough at the top to allow the defenders to group and maneuver behind the protection afforded by the parapets that capped them. Inside the walls were the residence, the stables, the arsenal, and the storage space for the daily provisions.

Castle Architecture, architecture resulting from the combination of feudal residences with fortresses, developed in the 9th century. Built on a defensible height, the main tower or keep was surrounded by a masonry palisade and a ditch. The main entrance was protected by drawbridge and portcullis. Later, fortifications were doubled by a second surrounding wall flanked by towers. The discovery of gunpowder ended the military usefulness of castle architecture.

Castlereagh, Robert Stewart, 2nd Viscount (1769–1822), British diplomat and politician, b. Ireland. While chief secretary of Ireland (1799–1801), he helped secure the passage of the Act of Union with Great Britain (1800). As British war secretary (1805–06, 1807–09), he opposed Napoleon vigorously but had to resign after a duel with George Canning, his great political rival. Castlereagh was a brilliant foreign secretary (1812–22), backing Wellington in war and helping secure a long-term peace in Europe at the Congress of Vienna (1814–15).

Castor and Pollux, in Greek and Roman legend, twin sons of Leda. The twins were inseparable; after Castor's death Pollux refused immortality. They were transformed into the constellation Gemini.

Castor Oil, a viscous, yellowish oil from the castor bean plant, sometimes used as a cathartic and for many industrial uses.

Castro, Fidel (1927–), Cuban revolutionary leader and prime minister (1959–). Protesting Fulgencio Batista's seizure of power (1952), Castro led an armed attack on the Moncada military barracks (July 26, 1953). Unsuccessful, Castro was captured and sentenced to 15 years in prison. Granted an amnesty in 1955, he went to Mexico, learned guerrilla tactics, and began his association with Che Guevara. Castro returned to Cuba in 1956 and set up his headquarters in the Sierra Maestra Mts. When the Batista regime collapsed in 1958, Castro capitalized on the power-vacuum and became de facto head of state. Within a few months he had consolidated his position and was able to rule without the support of traditional political groups. Pledged to the radical transformation of Cuban society, he declared himself a Marxist-Leninist in 1961. The unsuccessful Bay of Pigs invasion in 1961 by Cuban exiles, backed by the US government, enhanced Castro's prestige, but the success of the United States in forcing the Soviet Union to remove its missiles from Cuban soil in 1962 damaged his image as a Communist leader. Implacably hostile to the United States, he was forced to balance his allegiances between the Soviet Union and Communist China for a time. He remained firmly in power, however, and in the 1970s sent troops to African nations to expand Cuban influence. During the Carter administration (1977–81) some small steps were made in easing relations between Cuba and the United States, but during the mid-1980s, Castro's support of the leftist Nicaraguan government brought US criticism of him.

Cat, carnivorous mammals found on all continents except Australia and ranging in size from the common housecat to the Siberian tiger. Most cats walk on their toes and have short, rounded skulls; meat-eating teeth; and sharp retractile sickle-shaped claws. They have five toes on each front foot and four on each back foot. They have good nocturnal vision, acute hearing, and a well-developed sense of equilibrium. Most cats are nocturnal and solitary. The gestation period is about three months and 1–6 blind, helpless young are born.

Cats are descended from the same general evolutionary stock as civets and mongooses; the extinct sabertoothed cat appeared about 38 million years ago. Modern cats are classified into two main groups. The small felids—*Felini*— include 15 genera with 28 species ranging from the familiar domestic cat to the puma. The big felids—*Pantherini*— developed from the small cats. They include two genera: *Uncia* (snow leopard) and *Panthera,* with four species (leopard, jaguar, tiger, and lion). The throat anatomy of big cats enables them to roar.

The domestic cat *(Felis domesticus)* developed in Asia, Africa, and Europe, possibly from the Kaffir cat and the European wildcat. It was domesticated by the Egyptians and Indians sometime before 3000BC and was brought West by Phoenician sailors. Domestic breeds are divided into two groups: short-hairs, which include American, foreign or exotic, and Manx breeds; and longhairs, which include Persian and Angora breeds. Family Felidae.

Catacombs, early Christian (and some Jewish) subterranean cemeteries, often used as refuges from persecution and as shrines. The extensive catacombs of Rome are best known, but remains of others have been found in Europe, N Africa, and Turkey. Built between the 1st and 5th centuries, those in Rome are a complex of layered corridors as deep as 60ft (18m) below ground with burial niches, vaults, and rooms along the sides covered with inscribed tablets. Some were decorated with fresco. Plundered during the barbarian invasions, they were later largely forgotten until rediscovered in 1578. They are now maintained by the Vatican.

Catalan, Romance language spoken mainly in northeastern Spain (in the area known as Catalonia), but also in the Balearic Islands, Andorra, and southern France. There are about 6 million speakers in all.

Catalepsy, condition in which parts of the body remain in any position in which they are placed. Causes may be organic, psychological, or the result of hypnosis.

Catalonia, autonomous region in NE Spain, extends from French border S to Mediterranean Sea; includes Barcelona, Gerona, Lérida, and Tarragona. United with Aragón in 1137, Catalonia kept its own laws and language; became an important medieval trade center; declined after union of Castile and Aragón (1479); became a 20th-century center for the anarchist movement; in 1980, was made an autonomous region within Spain; site of several medieval castles. Industries: tourism, automobiles, airplanes, textiles. Crops: grapes, olives, cereals. Area: 12,332sq mi (31,940sq km). Pop. 5,122,567.

Catalpa, ornamental American and Asiatic tree that has large, heart-shaped leaves and showy white or purple flowers. The beanlike fruit pods contain many seeds. The common catalpa *(Catalpa bignonioides)* is sometimes called Indian bean. Height: to 60ft (18m). Family Bignoniaceae.

Catalysis, modification of the rate of a chemical reaction, by the addition of a substance, termed a catalyst, which is not consumed in the reaction. Catalytic action can reveal the reaction mechanism; many industrial processes rely on catalysis to accelerate reactions and occasionally to inhibit undesirable ones. Development of life forms is impossible without catalysis, for a series of strikingly specific-acting enzymes select and follow just one of a large number of metabolic pathways, acting much faster than nonbiological catalysts.

Catalyst, chemical compound that accelerates or inhibits the rate of a chemical reaction without itself being consumed. Inhibitors are commonly antioxidants, often used to prevent degradation of organic compounds, especially in air. Metals or their compounds catalyze by absorbing gases to their surface, forming intermediates that readily react to form the desired product, then product-forming while regenerating the original catalytic surface.

Catamaran, a swift, bridged-over, two-hulled craft, equipped with sails, popular in sport sailing. Originally, a raft of Indian and Indonesian waters developed for cargo carrying and for long voyages by Melanesian and Polynesian peoples.

Catania (Catana), port city in E Sicily, Italy, at foot of Mt Etna; capital of Catania prov.; ancient Catana was founded by Greeks 729 BC, and repeatedly invaded; it suffered devastating volcanic eruption 1669, earthquake 1693; city was rebuilt 18th century; site of Greek and Roman ruins, Norman Cathedral (1091), first Sicilian university (1434). Industries: chemicals, sulphur, textiles. Pop. 400,242.

Cataract, opacity of the lens of the eye usually a result of degenerative changes in old age or disease such as diabetes. Symptoms are gradual but painless loss of vision. The cataract may be removed surgically and corrective lenses prescribed.

Catastrophe Theory, a mathematical technique published in 1972 by the French mathematician René Thom. The theory concerns processes that do not always take place through continuously changing conditions but, instead, may at some point undergo a catastrophe—an event in which certain mathematical quantities change by a sudden, discontinuous leap. The technique is particularly useful for describing situations in which gradually changing motivations or inputs cause a sudden change in a system's behavior or output.

Catawba, one of the most powerful southern Siouan tribes of North American Indians, originally living in North Carolina and Tennessee. They were active on the colonists' side during the Revolution and as a reward were given land in York and Lancaster counties in South Carolina, where about 350 now reside; a few moved to Oklahoma. They are noted for their pottery and basketry.

Catboat, a broad-beamed, shallow-draft sailboat with a single mast placed forward and carrying a single large sail extended by a long boom; generally with a centerboard and very popular in sport sailing.

Caterpillar, wormlike larva of a butterfly or moth. Caterpillars have segmented bodies, short antennae, simple eyes, chewing mouthparts, and 5–8 pairs of legs, some with hooks or claws. Most have a few scattered hairs, but some are woolly looking. Nearly all feed on plants and plant products and many are serious farm and garden pests. *See also* Lepidoptera.

Fidel Castro

Cathedral: Salisbury, England

Catherine of Aragon

Catfish, freshwater and marine fish found worldwide in tropical and subtropical waters. Characterized by fleshy whiskers on the upper jaw, they are scaleless and some species have venomous spines. Length: to 4ft (121.9cm); Weight: 57lb (25.6kg). Order Siluriformes (also Cyriniformes); families include Sea, Marine, Electric, North American Freshwater, Clariid (Walking), Long-whiskered, and Upsidedown.

Catharsis, in psychology, expression of repressed feelings during the treatment of neurotic disorders. Sigmund Freud and Josef Breuer pioneered the "Cathartic Method," in which hypnotized patients were encouraged to remember and tell about repressed experiences. Though Freud later abandoned hypnosis, he retained the basic form of psychoanalytic treatment.

Cathedral Architecture. The early churches were basilicas. During the 11th and 12th centuries, massive domed and vaulted Romanesque architecture predominated. The great Gothic cathedrals of the 13th, 14th, and 15th centuries had ribbed vaults, pointed arches, and windows of stained glass that contributed to the sense of lightness and soaring space. *See also* Gothic Architecture; Romanesque Architecture.

Cather, Willa (1873–1947), US novelist and short-story writer, b. Winchester, Va. When a child, her family settled in Red Cloud, Nebr. She grew up among the immigrant farmers who became the subject of many of her books. She graduated from the University of Nebraska (1895) and served as managing editor of *McClure's Magazine* in New York (1908–12). Her fiction incorporates the pioneer traits she knew so well: love of the land, loyalty to family, ties to the past, and the constant struggle with nature. Operating within this framework in books usually set in the Midwest or Southwest, she created quiet works filled with strong characters who make life a noble thing. Her novels include *O Pioneers!* (1913), *My Ántonia* (1918), *A Lost Lady* (1923), *The Professor's House* (1925), and *Death Comes for the Archbishop* (1927).

Catherine II (1729–96), tsarina of Russia (1762–96). A German princess, she married Peter III in 1745. His mismanagement of government and his bad treatment of her led Catherine to organize a rebellion that ended in Peter's assassination. She was crowned tsarina in 1762. At the beginning of her reign, she was a liberal monarch and called meetings to discuss reforms. Threatened by the radical sentiments of the French Revolution, however, she became a reactionary. She imposed serfdom in the Ukraine, took part in the division of Poland among Russia, Prussia, and Austria (1795), cruelly suppressed the Pugachev Rebellion of 1773, and increased the privileges of the gentry in the Charter of 1785. A patroness of the arts, she corresponded with the French writers Voltaire and Diderot, wrote satires, and built palaces.

Catherine de Médicis (1519–89), queen of France. The daughter of Lorenzo de' Médici, she became queen of France (1547) as Henry II's consort. Perpetually threatened by various factions, she clung to power by trying to set rival groups against each other, or by attempting conciliation. Her tolerance of the Protestant Huguenots eventually gave way to dependence on the Roman Catholic Guise party, whose growing power she failed to control. She exerted great power during the reign of her son Charles IX (1560–74) and had some influence over her youngest son, Henry III (reigned 1574–89).

Catherine of Aragon (1485–1536), Spanish-born first queen of Henry VIII of England, whom she married in

1509. Their only living child was a daughter. Henry, wanting a male heir, used her former marriage (1501–02) to his brother Arthur as a pretext for divorce. Archbishop Cranmer declared their marriage null (1533). Despite continued harassment, Catherine refused to accept the Act of Succession (1534). This law placed the children of Henry's second wife, Anne Boleyn, in line to the throne.

Catherine of Siena (1347–80), Roman Catholic saint. She took orders in 1364, and was supposed to have received the *stigmata* or impression of Christ's wounds. Active politically, Catherine encouraged Pope Gregory XI to return to Rome from Avignon (1377).

Catherine of Valois (1401–37), queen of France, also called Catherine of France. The daughter of Charles VI of France, she became queen of England upon her marriage to King Henry V, according to the terms of the Treaty of Troyes (1420). A son, the future Henry VI, was born the next year, and in 1422 Henry V died. She then married Owen Tudor, and their son Edmund, Duke of Richmond, was the father of Henry VII, the first Tudor king.

Cathode, the negative electrode of an electrolytic cell or electron tube. It is the electrode from which electrons enter a system. *See* Electrolysis; Electron Tube.

Cathode Rays, radiation emitted by the cathode of an electron tube containing a low-pressure gas. The rays were identified (1897) by J. J. Thomson as streams of charged particles whose charge-to-mass ratio indicated an unknown extremely lightweight elementary particle, later called the electron. The electrons are emitted from the cathode as a result of the impact of positive gas ions formed in the tube.

Cathode Ray Tube, a type of vacuum tube used as a television picture tube and an oscilloscope. An electron gun shoots a beam of electrons, focused by a grid. This strikes a fluorescent screen to produce a spot of light. An electrostatic or magnetic field deflects the beam to particular spots on the screen. In a television picture tube, the deflecting plates are controlled by the incoming picture signals.

Catkin, drooping, scaly spike of unisexual flowers without petals, such as the pussy willow or poplar. This deciduous flower cluster is also typical of birches and some beeches.

Cat Nation. *See* Erie Indians.

Catnip, or catmint, common name for *Nepeta cataria*, an aromatic herb of the mint family. Introduced from Europe, it grows wild in North America. Cats are attracted to this perennial and are excited by its aroma.

Cato (the Elder), Marcus Porcius (234–149 BC), Roman statesman, orator, and writer. He served as an officer in the Second Punic War (191 BC). He held many important posts in Rome beginning in 204 BC, culminating in his appointment as censor in 184. As censor he worked to restore the old ideals of Rome—courage, honesty, and simple living. Cato urged the destruction of Carthage and lived to see the Third Punic War begin. His *On Agriculture* (c.160 BC) is the earliest fully extant Latin literary work. Fragments of his *Origines*, the first Latin history of Rome, remain.

Cato (the Younger), Marcus Porcius Cato Uticensis (95–46 BC), Roman patriot. Great-grandson of Cato the Elder, his support of Republican government and his opposition to Caesar led to the foundation of the first triumvirate. Military tribune of Macedonia (67) and

quaestor (65), he was tribune (62) and praetor (54). He favored Pompey against Caesar in 49 and when news of Caesar's victory reached him in Utica, he committed suicide in preference to surrender to Caesar.

CAT Scanner, computerized axial tomography, specialized diagnostic X-ray technique that measures the density of body tissues, thus producing via a computer a cross-section picture of human body organs. The technique was developed by Allan McLeod Cormack and Godfrey Newbold Hounsfield, who were awarded the 1979 Nobel Prize in medicine or physiology. Basically, the technique involves an X-ray beam that scans the density of body tissues and a linked computer that constructs a profile of these densities, which are then displayed on a screen. Scanning time for the patient is about 5 seconds. The CAT scanner is especially useful in diagnosing tumors, blood clots, hemorrhages, and heart and brain problems, thereby eliminating the need for exploratory surgery.

Cat's Eye. *See* Chrysoberyl.

Catskill Mountains, plateau of the Appalachian system in SE New York, on the W bank of the Hudson River. Highest peak is Slide Mt, 4,204ft (1,282m). Area of Rip Van Winkle legend, it abounds in forests, streams, and lakes; popular resort area near New York City metropolitan area.

Catt, Carrie Chapman Lane (1859–1947), U.S. reformer and suffragette, b. Ripon, Wis. Raised on the frontier, she moved to New York after her second marriage. She joined the National American Women Suffrage Association and became its president in 1900. Her "Winning Plan" meant working for suffrage through local political parties. Catt was also a founder of the Daughters of the American Revolution (DAR).

Cattail, tall marsh plants with long, erect leaves and stiff stems bearing fuzzy, brown, cylindrical flower spikes. The leaves of some species are used in making baskets or matting. Height: 3–9ft (1–3m). Species include common *Typha latifola*. Family Typhaceae.

Cattle, large ruminant mammals of the original Old World genus *Bos*. Included are domesticated cattle (*Bos taurus*), and domesticated zebu (*Bos indicus*). Other members are the wild and domesticated yak of Central Asia, the wild gaur and domesticated gayal of S Asia, and the wild banteng and koupray of Indochina. Young cattle are calves; females are heifers until they give birth and are then cows; males are bulls. Castrated males raised for beef are steers and when raised as draft animals, oxen. Horns, sometimes only on males, are permanent, hollow, and unbranched. The cheek teeth are high-crowned for grazing. A thick pad replaces the upper front teeth. In the wild, cattle congregate in small herds. They are raised primarily for meat and milk. Leather, glue, gelatin, and fertilizer are by-products. Before farm machinery, draft oxen were essential to agriculture. Cattle were domesticated about 8000 years ago in Anatolia. Height: 39–78in (1–2m) at shoulder; weight: 1100–2200lb (500–1000kg). *See also* Auroch; Beef Cattle; Dairy Cattle; Water Buffalo.

Cattle Brands, any of various marks made on the skin of cattle to permit easily recognizable identification. In the past, this was done with a hot iron stamp attached to a long handle. By pressing the burning iron against the thigh of a cow, the resulting scar made the pattern of the stamp. Today, branding is done with chemicals, tattooing, paint, tags, and notching. The practice of branding is 4000 years old, with its origin in Egypt.

Cattleya, tropical American, epiphytic orchid popular with florists and amateur gardeners. The large, showy flowers have two petals and a large lip surrounding the flower center. Colors range from white with yellow velvety markings to deep purple. Leaves are lance-shaped. There are 40 species and many varieties, including the white nun *(Cattleya skinnerii)* and the Brazilian *C. labiata* having up to seven flowers on each stem. Height: to 18in (45.7cm). Family Orchidaceae.

Catulus, Gaius Lutatius (*fl.*3rd century BC), Roman consul. In 241 BC he led the fleet that defeated the Carthaginians at the Battle of the Aegates Islands that ended the First Punic War.

Catullus, Gaius Valerius (died 54 BC), Roman poet. Of a wealthy family, Catullus spent most of his short life in Rome, where he became part of the literary society and attended the salon of Clodia. The beautiful Clodia was the most important influence of Catullus' life and the "Lesbia" of his most famous poems. His longer works are the poems *Attis* and *The Marriage of Peleus and Thetis,* but he is best known for his short love lyrics. *See also* Attis.

Cauca, river in W Colombia; rises in the Andes Mts, flows N to Magdalena River; lower course is navigable. Coffee is grown in its fertile valley. Length: 600mi (966km).

Caucasian Languages, family of languages, numbering about 40, spoken by over 5 million people in a small area of the Soviet Union between the Black and the Caspian seas. Georgian is the most important of these languages, accounting for over half of all the speakers. Others include Kabardian, Adygei, Abkhazian, Chechen, Ingush, Avar, Lezgin, and Dargin.

Caucasoid Race, one of the major human racial groupings. Physical characteristics include light skin pigmentation; narrow, high-bridged noses; hair varying between straight and curly; heavy body hair; and high incidence of the Rh-negative blood type. Since 1500 AD, Caucasoids have spread from their European, Near Eastern, and North African homelands, displacing aboriginal populations in many parts of the world.

Caucasus (Bol'voj Kavkaz), mountain system and region in SE European USSR, extends from Kuban River mouth on Black Sea SE to Apsheron Peninsula on the Caspian Sea. System includes two major regions: North Caucasia (steppes) and Transcaucasia; forms a natural barrier between Asia and Europe. The Georgian Military Road, Mamison and Daryal passes, and Ossetian Military Road are major traversing routes; major cities include Yerevan, Grozny, Baku (oil pipeline origin), Tbilisi, Ordzhonikidze. The range has been scene of invasions and migrations of Persians, Khazars, Arabs, Huns, Mongols, and Russians. Source of oil, iron, manganese, hydroelectric power; site of several tourist resorts along the Black Sea coast. Crops: cotton, fruits, grain. Highest peak is Mt Elbrus, 18,481ft (5,637m). Length: 750mi (1,208km).

Cauchon, Pierre (c.1371–1442), French bishop. As bishop of Beauvais, he presided over the trial of Joan of Arc who was captured in his diocese in 1430. Since he had been councilor of English King Henry VI and his regent in France, the Duke of Bedford, since 1422, he served English interests at the trial by obscuring the political aspects with inquisitorial procedure. He became bishop of Lisieux in 1432 and participated in the anti-papist Council of Basel in 1435.

Caucus, private meeting of political party members to select candidates, assess issues, or plan a campaign. In a legislative caucus, party members discuss leadership positions, issues, policies, and strategies.

Caudillo, type of political leader prevalent in Latin America during the 19th century. A civilian-on-horseback, he was supported by a paramilitary force. The aim of the caudillo band was to gain wealth, the tactic usually violence. Some caudillos dominated only very small areas, others an entire nation.

Cauliflower, plant of the cabbage family with a short, thick stem and large, lobed leaves. White or purplish flower clusters form tightly compressed 8in (20cm) heads that are eaten as a vegetable. In the garden, the heads are blanched, or kept white, by tying outer leaves over the head; some varieties are self-blanching, having leaves that grow over the head. It matures in 50–80 days. Family Cruciferae; species *Brassica oleracea italica.*

Caustic Soda. *See* Sodium Hydroxide.

Cauto River, longest river in Cuba; rises in Sierra Maestra; flows NW and W to Caribbean Sea, N of Manzanillo; navigable for small vessels. Length: 150mi (242km).

Cavalier, Jean (c1681–1740), French Huguenot general. At the age of 20, this baker of Anduze became the leader of the camisards, the white-shirted guerrillas who fought the army of Louis XIV for three years during the Huguenot revolt in Cévennes. He surrendered to Villars in 1704, and the revolt gradually ended. Cavalier served Savoy and then sailed to England where he became governor of the Isle of Wight.

Cavalier King Charles Spaniel, small hunting dog based on the 16th-century toy spaniel popular during the reign of England's Charles II and featured in paintings of the time. The modern breed, not considered a toy, has a flat skull with a short, tapered muzzle; wide-set ears and eyes; and a square, deep-chested body. The long, silky coat is black with tan marks or solid red. Average size: 12in (30.5cm) high at shoulder; 10–18lb (4.5–8kg). *See also* Spaniel.

Cavalier Poets, group of 17th-century English lyric poets, most of whom were courtiers at the court of Charles I and disciples of Ben Jonson. Their poetry is witty, amorous, and often bawdy. The leading cavalier poets were Robert Herrick, Thomas Carew, John Suckling, and Richard Lovelace.

Cavally, river in W Africa; rises in the Man Mts in W Ivory Coast; empties into the Gulf of Guinea; forms a section of the boundary between the Ivory Coast and Liberia. Length: 320mi (515km).

Cave, Edward (1691–1754), English printer and publisher, who produced the first modern English magazine. He wrote and published *The Gentleman's Magazine* (1731–54), a collection of news and political essays. One of his writers was Samuel Johnson.

Cave, a natural underground cavity, with an opening to the surface formed by ground water, underground streams, and ocean waves. The study of caves, called speleology, includes cave geology, hydrology, anthropology, and biology.

Cavell, Edith (1865–1915), English nurse. She established modern nursing in Belgium and later was killed by the Germans for aiding and sheltering Allied soldiers during World War I, an execution that aroused public outcry throughout much of the world.

Cavendish, Henry (1731–1810), English physicist and chemist. He discovered hydrogen and the composition of water, determined the composition of air, and estimated the Earth's mass and density by a method called the Cavendish experiment. He also determined nitric acid composition, the specific gravity of carbon dioxide and hydrogen, and stated the inverse square law for the interaction of charged particles. The Cavendish Laboratory at Cambridge is named after him.

Cavity, Dental, a localized wearing away of a tooth, beginning at the surface and progressing inward to the pulp. Microorganisms acting on sugars and starches and producing an excess of acid are believed to be the underlying cause. Prevention and treatment include proper diet, cleaning of teeth and filling of existing cavities.

Cavour, Camillo Benso, Conte di (1810–61), Italian (Piedmontese) statesman instrumental in uniting Italy under Savoy rule. A 19th-century liberal dedicated to liberty, progress, and moderation, he first was prime minister to Victor Emmanuel II in 1852. From 1856–60 he engineered Italian liberation from Austrian domination (with French aid), then the expulsion of the French from southern Italy (with Giuseppe Garibaldi's forces), and, finally, the neutralization of Garibaldi's influence in liberated regions. This allowed formation of kingdom of Italy in March 1861, three months before his death.

Cavy, South American rodents from which guinea pigs are descended. Most are small (under 2.2lb or 1kg), dark, nocturnal plant-eaters with short legs and no tail, but the Patagonian cavy has long legs and weighs up to 33lb (16kg). Family Caviidae. *See also* Guinea Pig.

Cawnpore. *See* Kanpur.

Caxton, William (1422–1491), the first English printer. He set up his printing press in 1476 at Westminster. He published over 100 books, 24 of them his own translations from French.

Cayenne, capital city of French Guiana, N central South America, on Cayenne Island in Cayenne River. Devil's Island is off the NW coast; site of Pasteur Institute (1940). Industries: sawmills, rum, gold, Founded by French 1664. Pop. 19,668.

Cayley, Sir George (1773–1857), English inventor who founded the science of aerodynamics and pioneered in aerial navigation. He built the first successful glider able to carry a man and developed the basic form of the modern airplane. He also founded the Regent Street Polytechnic Institute in London, invented the caterpillar tractor, and did research in scientific education and in land reclamation.

Cayman Islands, islands in British West Indies, 200mi (322km) NW of Jamaica, in NW Caribbean Sea; includes Grand Cayman, Little Cayman, and Cayman Brac. Capital is Georgetown on Grand Cayman. Industries: tourism, turtle and shark fishing, shipbuilding, coconuts, lumber. Discovered 1503 by Christopher Columbus; colonized 1734. Pop. 10,652.

Cayuga, major branch of the Five Nations of the Iroquois Confederacy, originally living around Lake Cayuga, N.Y., and Grand River in Ontario, Canada. The Cayuga joined the British during the Revolution and afterwards became widely scattered into Ohio, Wisconsin, and Oklahoma, where they joined the Seneca. Today there are approximately 550 in Oklahoma and 400 Cayuga in New York.

Cayuga Lake, lake in W central New York; longest of the Finger Lakes. At S end of lake is Taughaunock Falls with a drop of 215ft (66m). Along shore of lake are Wells College and Cornell University. Area: 38mi (61km) long by 1–3.5mi (1.6–5.6km) wide.

Ceauşescu, Nicolae (1918–), Romanian Communist party leader and statesman. Under a collective leadership with Ion Maurer and Chivu Stoica from 1961 Romania's growth rate was the highest in Eastern Europe. The country cooperated fully with the Soviet Union, and the land was collectivized. Beginning in 1965, under his leadership as Communist party secretary, economic problems with the USSR caused a resurgence of Romanian nationalist spirit. In 1965 Ceausescu succeeded as chief of the party upon the death of Premier Gheorghiu-Dej, and in 1967 he became president of the council (or chief of state) as well. He was formally designated president in 1974 and continued his policy of an independent Communist government.

Cebu, city in central Philippines, on central E coast of Cebu Island; capital of Cebu prov. A mountain range extends length of the island; rich agricultural area; site of oldest Spanish settlement in the Philippines (1565), Southwestern University (1950). Industries: hemp, tobacco, corn, sugar cane, rice, coconuts, coal. Discovered 1521 by Ferdinand Magellan. Pop. 418,517.

Cecil, (Edgar Algernon) Robert, first Viscount Cecil of Chelwood (1864–1958), English statesman. A Conservative member of Parliament (1906–23), he won the 1937 Nobel Peace Prize. After holding posts of undersecretary (1915) and assistant secretary of state (1918) and minister of blockade (1916), he helped draft the League of Nations covenant, was president of the League of Nations Union (1923–45), and represented Britain at several disarmament conferences. Works include *The Way of Peace* (1928) and *A Real Peace* (1941).

Cecil, William, 1st Baron Burghley (1520–98), chief minister of Elizabeth I of England. He was secretary of state (1550–53) under Edward VI but failed to win Mary's favor. On Mary's death Elizabeth made him again secretary of state (1558–72) and then lord high treasurer (1572–98). An able administrator, he helped the queen steer a moderate course between Catholicism and extreme Protestantism. He was an invaluable link between the queen and Parliament. In 1587 he was responsible for ordering the execution of Mary, Queen of Scots.

Cecilia, Saint (died 230?), patron saint of music and the blind. Her festival is celebrated on November 22. According to her legend, she converted her husband to Christianity and was martyred with him. She was reputed to accompany her devotions with music.

Cecropia Moth, large North American moth that is dark reddish-brown. It has no mouthparts and lives only the few days needed to mate and lay eggs. Cecropia caterpillars feed on tree and shrub leaves. Wing span: to 6in (15cm). Family Saturniidae; species *Hyalaphora cecropia. See also* Moth.

Cecrops, in Greek mythology, the founder of Athens. Cecrops, possessor of a man's body and a snake's tail, became the first king of Attica. He brought 12 Greek cities under his control, made Athena the patron deity, and acknowledged Zeus as the supreme god.

Cedar, evergreen tree native to North Africa and Asia, and grown in warmer temperate regions worldwide.

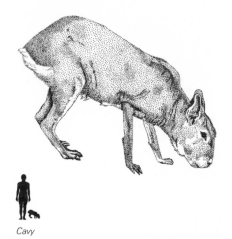

Cavy

Cayman Islands

Cedar waxwing

They have clustered needlelike leaves, oblong cones, and fragrant, durable wood. They are popular lawn trees. Height: 40–200ft (12–61m). Family Pinaceae; genus *Cedrus*.

Cedar Falls, city in NE Iowa, 6mi (10km) W of Waterloo, on the Cedar River; site of University of Northern Iowa (1876). Industries: pumps, golfing equipment, farm machinery. Inc. 1854. Pop. (1980) 36,322.

Cedar Rapids, city in E central Iowa, 105mi (169km) ENE of Des Moines; seat of Linn co; named for rapids on the Cedar River; site of Coe College (1851), Mount Mercy College (1875), and an art museum with a collection of works by Grant Wood. City is one of Iowa's chief industrial and commercial centers. Industries: cereals, machinery, paper, pharmaceuticals. Settled 1838; inc. as town 1849, as city 1856. Pop. (1980) 110,243.

Cedar Waxwing, small North American bird with red, waxy-looking flight feathers. It has brownish plumage, black eye patches, and a yellow-tipped tail. Migrating in large, compact flocks, it feeds on berries and blossoms. The female lays pale bluish-gray eggs (3–5) in a cup-shaped, twig-and-grass nest in a tree. Length: 8in (20cm). Species *Bombycilla cedrorum*.

Celadon, semi-transparent bluish or grayish-green glazes used in Chinese and Korean ceramics. Noteworthy are the celadon wares of the Sung period (10th–13th centuries). *See also* Porcelain.

Celandine, erect, branched herb, common in Britain and America. The plant has yellow sap, serrated leaves, and yellow flowers of about 1in (2.5cm) wide. Family Papaveraceae; species *Chelidonium majus*.

Celebes Sea, part of the Pacific Ocean between Philippines and Indonesia, SE Asia; bounded by Sulu Archipelago and Mindanao Island (N), Sangihe Island (E), Celebes Island (S), Borneo (W). Area: 165,000sq mi (427,350sq km).

Celery, biennial plant native to Europe and widely cultivated for its long stalks used as a vegetable or salad. Its seedlike fruits are used as food flavoring and in medicine. It has white flowers. Family Umbelliferae; species *Apium graveolens*.

Celesta, percussion instrument resembling a glockenspiel and played by keyboard, with a range from middle C up 4 octaves. Invented by Auguste Mustel in Paris (1868), its clear, tinkling tones were first used in symphonic orchestration by Tchaikovsky in "Dance of the Sugar Plum Fairy," from the *Nutcracker Suite* (1892). *See also* Glockenspiel.

Celestial Equator, great circle on the celestial sphere, lying midway between the celestial poles in the same plane as the earth's equator.

Celestial Mechanics, branch of astronomy concerned with the relative motions of celestial bodies that are associated in systems, such as the solar system or a binary star system, by gravitational fields. First developed by Isaac Newton in the 17th century on the basis of Kepler's laws and the law of gravitation, celestial mechanics (rather than general relativity) is usually sufficient to calculate the various factors determining the motion of planets, satellites, comets, stars, and galaxies around a center of gravitational attraction.

Celestial Sphere, imaginary sphere of infinite radius used for defining the positions of celestial bodies as seen from Earth, which lies at the center of the sphere.

The sphere rotates, once in 24 hours, about a line that is an extension of the Earth's axis. The position of a celestial body is the point at which a radial line through the body meets the surface of the sphere. It is given quantitatively in terms of coordinates, such as declination and right ascension or altitude and azimuth, referred to great circles on the sphere, such as the celestial equator, horizon, or ecliptic.

Celestine V, Roman Catholic pope (1294) and saint, b. Pietro di Murrone (c. 1215). A Benedictine monk, he was never in Rome as pope and became the first pope to abdicate when he was unable to adapt to the papacy. He was canonized by Pope Clement V in 1313.

Celestite, a sulfate mineral, strontium sulfate ($SrSO_4$), with distinctive pale blue, orthorhombic system tabular or elongate crystals. Chiefly in sedimentary rocks, also as gangue material in ore veins. Sometimes in fibrous veins and fine-grained deposits. Glassy white to pale blue; hardness 3–3.5; sp gr 4.

Celiac Disease, intestinal disturbance caused by intolerance to wheat and rye products. Symptoms include depression, abdominal distention, soft stools.

Cell, smallest unit of life that can exist and sustain itself independently. All living things are made up of one or more cells. In multicellular organisms, groups of specialized cells combine to form tissue, such as muscle or skin. Cells are capable of electrical activity (nerve cells) and of locomotion.

Most cells have a cell membrane that encloses the cytoplasm and nucleus. The cytoplasm, which is organized by a cytoskeleton, is the site of protein synthesis (in the endoplasmic reticulum) and energy production (in the mitochondria). The nucleus is enclosed in a nuclear membrane and contains the cell's genetic material in the chromosomes, thus governing much of the activity of the cytoplasm; it is also responsible for the reproduction of the cell. The cells of blue-green algae and bacteria (prokaryotes) do not have a nuclear membrane. Plant cells have a rigid cellulose cell wall and contain pigment-containing chloroplasts in their cytoplasm.

Cell, Chemical. *See* Battery; Cells, Electrochemical.

Cell Division, cell increase making it possible for an organism to grow. In some body parts, including lower skin layers, intestinal lining, and blood cells, this process continues throughout an individual's life. *See also* Mitosis.

Cellini, Benvenuto (1500–71), Italian goldsmith, sculptor, and author of a famous *Autobiography* (1558–62). As proud and unscrupulous as he was talented, he was often involved in brawls and scandals and was twice imprisoned. His best-known work as a goldsmith was an elaborate saltcellar for Francis I of France (1543). His "Nymph of Fontainebleau" (1543–44) a bronze relief, is the high point of the art of the School of Fontainebleau. He began to work with free-standing sculpture in 1545; his "Perseus and the Head of Medusa" is one of that craft's greatest achievements.

Cello or **Violoncello,** second largest of violin family of musical instruments, with a soft, mellow tone, one octave below the viola, and a range of 2½ octaves. The seated player, using a bow, holds the cello vertically, supporting it with his knees. Developed in the 16th century by Amati, cellos are used in symphony orchestras, string ensembles, and as solo instruments, notably by Pablo Casals.

Cellophane, flexible, transparent film made of regenerated cellulose and used mostly as a wrapping material. It is made by dissolving wood pulp or other plant material in an alkali, and then neutralizing the alkaline solvent with an acid. The precipitate is impregnated with glycerine, dried, and cut into sheets.

Cells, Electrochemical, devices from which electricity is obtained as a result of a chemical reaction. A cell consists of two electrodes (a positive anode and a negative cathode) immersed in a solution (electrolyte). The chemical reaction takes place between the electrolyte and one of the electrodes. In a primary cell, current is produced directly as a result of chemical action, whereas in a secondary cell (battery) the chemical reaction is reversible and the cell can be charged by passing a current through it.

Celluloid, a cheap, hard, synthetic plastic invented in 1870 and made by mixing cellulose nitrate with pigments and fillers in a solution of camphor or alcohol. When heated, the resulting compound is pliable and moldable. Highly flammable, it has been superseded by other plastics.

Cellulose, fibrous carbohydrate providing the structural framework of plant cell walls. The most abundant organic compound in the world, it is made up of glucose subunits. It is economically important as plant fibers (cotton), lumber, and wood pulp, and is obtained by treating wood to dissolve everything but the cellulose and is used in manufacturing paper products, rayon, and celluloid.

Cellulose Nitrate. *See* Nitrocellulose.

Cellulose Plastics, any of numerous thermoplastic (plastic when reheated) derivatives of the plant substance cellulose. Included are cellulose nitrate (or nitrocellulose), used in explosives and propellants; various cellulose acetates for making textile fibers and packaging films; and ethyl cellulose, used in the manufacture of shock-resistant materials.

Celsius, Anders (1701–44), Swedish astronomer noted for inventing the Celsius, or centigrade, thermometer (1742). He also published a collection of observations of the aurora borealis (1733).

Celsus, Aulus Cornelius (1st century AD), Roman encyclopedist, author of a comprehensive work covering several topics. Only the section dealing with medicine survived. *De medicina* is the most complete Roman medical text extant. Most of what is known about Hellenistic medical practices is based on Celsus' description.

Celtic Languages, group of languages spoken in parts of Great Britain, Ireland, and France, forming a subdivision of the Indo-European family. There are two branches: the Brythonic, which includes Welsh, Breton, and the extinct language Cornish; and Goidelic, which includes Gaelic and Manx, of the Isle of Man, which died out only recently. The Celtic languages were dominant in Britain until the 5th century AD when they began to be supplanted by the Germanic dialects of the invading Anglo-Saxons.

Celtic Mythology, stories of local deities of the Celtic tribes who were scattered throughout continental Europe and the British Isles. Each tribe had an omnipotent god, similar in attributes to Dagda, who possessed all-embracing power and whose cauldron was always full, signifying abundance. The world that the gods inhabited was seen in the myths as a reflection of the world of men. Female divinities seem to have been identified more closely with nature or with a local topographical feature.

Celts, group of people originating in Europe, chiefly in what is now Germany. There were many Celtic tribes, or peoples, speaking related languages as they spread from Germany and France to Belgium, Ireland, Scotland, and Wales. They also invaded Italy, Bohemia, and Russia. They were called Keltoi by the Greeks and Gauls by the Romans after Julius Caesar, whose war against them in 58 BC ended Celtic independence on the European continent. Celtic culture was rural, the economy largely local except for rather sophisticated metal production. Celtic religious and cultural leaders, called druids, practiced magic and Celtic ritual. Celtic culture and language can still be traced in Ireland, Scotland, Wales, and Brittany.

Cement, a fabricated substance that hardens and becomes adhesive after being applied in a plastic mass. In engineering, cement refers to a fine powder, consisting of gypsum, lime, plaster, or portland cement. Used to bind sand and gravel to form concrete, to unite structures, and to coat surfaces as a protection from chemicals.

Cement, Portland, a binding material used in concrete and mortar. It is made by heating a mixture of crushed chalk and clay to form a clinker, which is then crushed and packed into bags. When water is added to cement, it recrystallizes, the interlocking crystals of calcium silicate and calcium aluminate forming a hard mass on drying.

Cenis, Mont, pass on French-Italian border; one of the great invasion routes of Italian history; site of one of world's longest railroad tunnels, the first through the Alps, constructed 1857–70, connecting Turin, Italy, with Chambéry, France. Altitude: 6,831ft (2,083m).

Cenozoic Era, most recent major division of geologic time, beginning about 65 million years ago and extending through the present, called the Age of Mammals. It is subdivided into the Tertiary and Quaternary periods. It is the period during which the modern world with its characteristic geographical features and plants and animals developed. *See also* Geologic Time.

Censors, two magistrates of ancient Rome. They were elected for a five-year term to take the census (for taxation and military purposes); oversee public works, finance, and morals; and fill senate vacancies. The office lasted from 443 BC to the reign of Domitian (AD 81–96).

Censorship, the system whereby a government or other group claims the right to protect the public interest by influencing the release of any item of mass communication, such as books, newspapers, movies, and plays. Censorship can take on two forms; one where the government discourages or suppresses printed material, and one whereby the press is used as an instrument of a government or other group, with the press required to print materials provided by officials. In the United States, the First Amendment forbids abridgement of freedom of the press.

Census, survey conducted by a national government to collect facts about the society it governs. In addition to ascertaining up-to-date population counts, most censuses also seek information about marital status, age and sex of citizens, numbers of children, occupation, education, housing, and spoken language. The government may use this information as a basis for policy-making.

Centaur, in Greek mythology, one of a race of beings part horse and part man. They were the children of the Lapith king Ixion.

Centaurus, or **the Centaur,** extensive southern constellation situated north of Crux and Carina and containing the sun's nearest stellar neighbors, the stars of the Alpha Centauri system. The bright star Beta and the globular cluster Omega are also prominent.

Center of Gravity, point in or near a body or system of bodies through which passes the resultant force of all the gravitational forces acting on each particle of the body or system. It is thus the point at which the weight of the body may be considered to act. In a uniform gravitational field it is the same as the center of mass.

Center of Mass, the point in space associated with a rigid body or system of particles such that the acceleration of this point multiplied by the total mass of the system equals the sum of all the forces acting on the system. Isaac Newton first verified his law of gravity by assuming the earth and moon to attract each other as though they were point masses located at their centers.

Centigrade, a term for the temperature scale having 100 divisions between the freezing point of water (0 degrees) and boiling point (100 degrees). Now replaced by the term "Celsius" after the inventor of the scale. *See also* Temperature Scales.

Centimeter, unit of length defined as one hundredth part of a meter. *See* Weights and Measures.

Centipede, or hundred-legger, invertebrate animal found worldwide. Red to brown, they have one pair of legs per body segment, one pair of antennae, and little or no sight. Predacious, they feed mostly on other arthropods, but some inflict a painful bite. Living in dark places, they find their prey by touch and smell. Length: 1.2–6in (3–17mm). Class Chilopoda. *See also* Myriapoda.

Central, Cordillera, mountain range of the Andes in Colombia; one of three parallel systems: Oriental, Central, and Occidental. Highest peak is 19,020ft (5,801m).

Central African Republic, formerly Central African Empire, landlocked nation in central Africa, governed by an emperor. Bounded by Chad (N), Sudan (E), Zaire and Congo Republic (S), and Cameroon (W). The country is a great, well-watered plateau covered by savanna, except for an area of dense tropical forests (S) and a semi-desert area (NE). It has a humid climate with annual rainfall of 70in (178cm) in the Ubangi (Oubangui) River Valley, and 31in (79cm) in NE semi-desert. Subsistence agriculture provides the primary livelihood. Coffee and cotton are chief cash crops. The leading exports are diamonds, coffee, wood, and cotton. About 10% of the land is cultivated, and more than 80% is suitable for grazing.Approximately 80% of the population lives in rural areas. The country has no dominant tribe; most of the inhabitants migrated into the area during past 200 years to escape the slave trade. The four main ethnic groups are Azande, Yakoma, Sango, and Banziri. French is the official language, but Sango is spoken in all areas. The literacy rate is between 5% and 10%; about 45% of elementary-age school children attend school.

The French first occupied the area in 1887; in 1894 the colony of Ubangi-Shari was formed; it was administratively united with Chad in 1906 and made part of French Equatorial Africa in 1910. Forced labor by concessionaires to whom France had leased the territory led to rebellions in 1928, 1935, and 1946. Ubangi-Shari supported the Free French in WWII. At the end of the war France's attitude toward its colonies altered and they were given representation in French parliament. The first responsible government was created in 1957. In 1958 the colony voted to become a self-governing republic within the French community, and its name became Central African Republic. In 1960 it declared its independence, but the next six years saw a deterioration in the economy, and corruption and increasing inefficiency under President David Dacko. As the result of a bloodless coup Dec. 31, 1966–Jan. 1, 1967, Col. Jean-Bedel Bokassa took over the presidency, abrogated the constitution, and dissolved the National Assembly. In 1976, Bokassa adopted an Islamic name, transformed the republic into an empire, and proclaimed himself Emperor Bokassa I. Bokassa's rule became increasingly brutal, and he was deposed in a coup led by David Dacko and backed by France in 1979. Dacko, faced with continuing protests and demands for a multi-party political system, was replaced in 1981 by Gen. André Kolingba, who ran a strict military government despite promises to return to civilian rule.

PROFILE

Official name: Central African Republic
Area: 240,535sq mi (622,986sq km)
Population: 2,446,000
Chief cities: Bangui (capital); Bouar; Carnot
Religion: Tribal, Christian, Islam
Language: French (official), Sango
Monetary Unit: Franc CFA

Central America, geographical term for the narrow strip of land that connects North America to South America and divides the Caribbean Sea from the Pacific Ocean; it consists of Guatemala, El Salvador, Honduras, Nicaragua, Costa Rica, Belize, Panama. Highly developed by the Mayas, the region (excluding Panama) was conquered and ruled by the Spanish from the 16th century until 1839 when the confederation broke up and independent states were formed. The terrain is mostly mountainous; climate is tropical. The area enjoys an economic, ethnic, and geological unity; Spanish is the main language. Crops: bananas, coffee, cotton. Area: 276,400sq mi (715,876sq km).

Central Intelligence Agency (CIA), government agency established to coordinate intelligence activities of the several government departments and agencies in the interest of national security in the United States. The CIA works in an advisory capacity to the National Security Council in matters of national security. The agency has no police, subpoena, or law enforcement powers or internal security functions. The National Security Council may direct the CIA to perform other functions related to security. In the mid-1970s the CIA was attacked for abusing its powers, particularly in violating the restrictions against its operation within the United States. Founded 1947.

Central Nervous System (CNS), portion of the nervous system encased by the bony skull and spinal column, ie, the brain and the spinal cord.

Central Powers, the World War I coalition of Germany, Austria-Hungary, Bulgaria, and Turkey that fought the Allied Powers of Britain, France, Belgium, Russia, and, later, the United States.

Central Tendency, method of summarizing large groups of data into meaningful statistics. The basic measures of central tendency are the arithmetic mean, the median, and the mode. Each measure is useful under certain conditions, but the most commonly used is the arithmetic mean. *See also* Frequency Distribution.

Centrifugal Force, the apparent (but nonexistent) outward force felt by a person in curvilinear motion. For example, a bus turning left causes a passenger to experience a "force" to the right, but it is simply his own tendency to continue in a straight line conflicting with the bus' leftward acceleration.

Centrifuge, a mechanical device, usually a rapidly spun container, using centrifugal force to separate substances of varying density. Used in draining water (as in a washing machine), separating cream from milk, blood cells from whole blood, sugar from syrup and many other laboratory and industrial purposes.

Centriole, dense body forming central portion of the centrosome near the nucleus of a cell. It occurs in all cells except those of angiosperms and the sperm cells of ferns and gymnosperms. During mitosis and meiosis, centrioles divide before the rest of the cell, moving to either pole of the cell and forming the spindle.

Centripetal Force, the inward force on an object constraining it to move in a curvilinear path. The sun's gravitational force is also the centripetal force causing the earth's nearly circular motion. A mass m traveling with velocity v in an arc of a circle of radius r is acted upon by a centripetal force $F = mv^2/r$.

Centurion, military officer of ancient Rome. The commander of 1/60 part of a Roman legion, or 100 men, he usually rose from footsoldier and was well paid to maintain discipline. The 60 centurions of a legion were organized into 10 cohorts of six, chief among which was the first cohort.

Cephalic Index, measurement of the head, used in physical anthropology. The maximum width of the skull is divided by the maximum length, and the result expressed as a percentage: the classifications are dolichocephalic (long-headed; under 75%); mesocephalic, or mesaticephalic (medium; 75–80%); brachycephalic (short-headed; over 80%).

Cephalopod, predatory marine mollusk (including squid, cuttlefish, nautilus, octopus) having eight or more arms surrounding the mouth. Each has a well-developed nervous system permitting great speed and alertness; large eyes with image-forming ability equalling vertebrates'; and a mouth with a parrotlike beak. Most squirt inky fluid to confuse attackers. They move by jet-stream propulsion, squirting water from their mantle edge. Their heavily yolked eggs develop into larval young, resembling adults. The extinct ammonoids and belemnoids were once common cephalopods. There are 600 living species. *See also* Mollusk.

Cepheid Variable, type of regular pulsating variable star whose maximum luminosity is directly proportional to the time it takes to pass from one maximum brightness to the next. These objects, whose prototype is the star Delta Cephei in the northern constellation Cepheus, are generally very reliable in their light variations, thus allowing their distances to be very accurately measured. Classical Cepheids, of Population 1, have periods of one to fifty days. Their discovery in external galaxies has been a major aid in determining intergalactic distances. *See also* RR Lyrae Variable.

Ceramics, in art, objects made of moistened clay that have been shaped and then baked. Earthenware, terra-cotta, brick, tile, faience, majolica, stoneware, and porcelain are all ceramics. The clay consists largely of aluminum silicates derived from weathered rock or oc-

Central African Republic (formerly Empire)

Ceramics

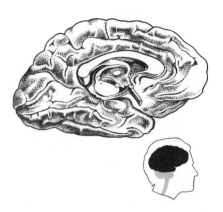

Cerebrum

curring in natural deposits and may contain iron oxide, sand, bone ash, grog (crushed pottery), petuntse (china stone), steatite, mica, or powdered flint, which are used to create different kinds of pottery and porcelain.

Clay may be shaped by hand, using a coil or slab technique, a mold, or a potter's wheel. Ceramic ware is ornamented by clay inlays, by relief modeling on the surface, or by incised, stamped, or impressed designs. A creamy mixture of clay and water (slip) can be used to coat the ware. After drying, ceramic ware is baked in a kiln, until it has hardened into its "biscuit" stage. Glaze, a silicate preparation applied to the clay surface and fused to it during firing, is used to make the pottery nonporous and to give it a smooth, colorful, decorative surface.

Primitive cultures of Africa, America, and the Pacific, as well as ancient Egypt and neolithic communities of Europe, were all familiar with terra-cotta vessels. In ancient Egypt they developed a faience with a glaze, and Mesopotamia and Persia used large architectural tiles with colorful glazes. In the 6th and 5th centuries BC the Greeks developed red, black, and white glazed pottery with figures and scenes on it, while the Romans used relief decoration on theirs. Persian, Syrian, and Turkish pottery with colorful glazes continued to be produced after the fall of Rome. In Spain, lusterware, the first sophisticated ceramics of the modern era, was produced by the 9th-century Moors. Italian majolica, Dutch delft, German Meissen, and English Wedgewood were further refinements of the product. Chinese porcelain dates from the T'ang dynasty, and Chinese stoneware goes back to about 3000 BC. In the 20th century there has been renewed interest in folk pottery.

Ceramics, in technology, articles made from inorganic compounds formed in a plastic condition and hardened by heating in a furnace. Earthenware is a porous ceramic made from kaolin, ball clay, and crushed flint. Porcelain is made from kaolin and feldspar, and heated to a higher temperature. It is nonporous and translucent. Special ceramics are made from pure aluminum oxide, silicon carbide, titanates, and other compounds.

Ceram (Seram) Sea, a section of W Pacific Ocean in central Moluccas, Indonesia, N of Banda Sea and S of Moluccas Sea. Area: approx. 20,000sq mi (51,800sq km).

Cerberus, in Greek mythology, a dog who guarded the entrance to Hades. He is represented as having three to fifty heads.

Cereal, any grain of the grass family (Poaceae), used for food, including wheat, corn, rice, rye, oats, and barley. Cereals are the principal food source for the world's population, directly or indirectly as feed for livestock.

Cerebellum, a part of the brain, often known as the "little brain." Somewhat butterfly shaped, the cerebellum is divided into two hemispheres, marked by parallel grooves. The cerebellum is concerned mainly with coordination of muscular activity, regulating muscle tone for proper posture and balance, and regulating voluntary muscular movements. It also modifies cerebral cortex activity. See also Brain.

Cerebral Cortex, covering structure of the brain, most highly developed in humans, which suggests that it governs the higher nerve activity usually termed the human intellect. The cortex has intricate connections with most other neural structures in the body.

Cerebral Hemorrhage, rupture of a blood vessel in the brain usually caused by arteriosclerosis, less often by injury or disease. Symptoms are headache, vomiting, then coma. Extensive hemorrhage is fatal; recovery from minor hemorrhage may take months.

Cerebral Palsy, disease caused by damage to the brain. The damage may result from disease or injury before birth, from difficulties during childbirth, or, in later life, from infection, circulatory diseases, or head injury. Symptoms include spastic movements of arms and legs, and sometimes convulsions. Signs of mental retardation, which accompany the disease in about one-third of the cases, may reflect difficulty in communication rather than acute retardation. Treatment includes speech and muscle training and use of orthopedic devices.

Cerebrospinal Fluid, fluid found in the subarachnoid space, between the arachnoid and the pia mater layers of the meninges, the membranes that protect the brain and spinal cord from shocks. A sample of the fluid taken by means of a spinal tap aids in the diagnosis of diseases affecting the meninges. See also Meninges.

Cerebrum, one of the major divisions of the brain, and that part that makes the human brain so different in activity and appearance from the brains of other animals. It is divided into two dome-shaped parts, the cerebral hemispheres, each of which is divided into four lobes: frontal, parietal, temporal, and occipital. Each hemisphere is made up of an outer dark grayish layer (gray matter) known as the cerebral cortex; cortical white matter, made up of nerve fibers; and gray basal ganglia that connect with other portions of the cerebrum and with other parts of the brain. The cerebral cortex, which is convoluted to increase its surface area, is the basis of the brain's intellectual capacity, the seat of learning and memory, and a center for associative functions, for many sensory perceptions, and for many motor activities. See also Brain.

Cerenkov, Pavel Alekseevich (1904–), Russian physicist. Working at the Institute of Physics of the Soviet Academy of Science, he discovered that light is emitted by charged particles traveling at very high speeds, a phenomenon known as the Cerenkov effect. He was awarded a Nobel Prize in 1958 jointly with I.M. Frank and I.Y. Tamm.

Cerenkov Radiation, bluish light emitted in a cone when energetic particles travel through a transparent medium of fairly high refractive index (such as water) at a speed that exceeds the velocity of light in that medium.

Ceres, in Roman mythology, goddess of food plants. She was often worshipped with the god Cerus.

Ceres, largest of the asteroids; the first to be sighted, discovered (1801) by Giuseppi Piazzi. Diameter 750mi (1200km); mean distance from Sun 257,000,000mi (413,770,000km); mean sidereal period 4.6 yr.

Cereus, cactus native to West Indies and E South America and found throughout North and South America. Its stems are long, cylindrical, ribbed, and may be treelike or trailing. The night-blooming cereus, found in Arizona, New Mexico, and Texas, is usually drab though it produces magnificent fragrant white flowers that open for only one night. It is often kept as a house plant. Height: to 8ft (2.4m). There are 25 species. Family Cactaceae; genus Cereus.

Cerium, metallic element (symbol Ce) of the lanthanide group, first isolated in 1803. Chief ore is monazite (phosphate). It is used in pyrophoric alloys and in catalysts and the oxide is used in incandescent mantles. Properties: at. no. 58; at. wt. 140.120; sp. gr. 6.7; melt. pt. 1463°F (795°C); boil. pt. 278°F (3468°C); most common isotope Ce^{140} (88.48%). See also Lanthanide Elements.

Cerumen. See Ear Wax.

Cervantes, Miguel de (1547–1616), Spanish novelist, poet, and dramatist. He went to Italy in 1569, in the service of a cardinal, was wounded in the Battle of Lepanto in 1571. While returning to Spain in 1575, he was captured and kept as a slave in Algiers. He was ransomed in 1580 and settled in Madrid. Cervantes' works include La Galatea (1585), Don Quixote de la Mancha (1605; 1615), and Novelas Ejemplares (1613). See also Don Quixote de la Mancha.

Cervera y Topete, Pascual (1839–1909), Spanish admiral, Count of Jerez, Marquis of Santa Ana. Minister of marine in 1892, he sailed at the head of the Spanish fleet May 19, 1898, to fight the Americans in the Spanish-American War. When he reached the harbor at Santiago, Cuba, he tried to run the American blockade; his ships were surrounded and sunk. Upon defeat he remarked, "Spain prefers honor without ships to ships without honor." Taken prisoner, he was returned to Spain (September 1898).

Cesalpino, Andrea (1519–1603), Italian physiologist and botanist. His De plantis (1583) was one of the first attempts to classify plants according to their flowers and fruits.

Cesium, or **Caesium,** rare metallic element of the alkali-metal group, discovered in 1860. Chief ore is pollucite (silicate). Cesium has few commercial uses. Chemically it is an extremely reactive electropositive element. The decay rate of the isotope Cs^{133} is used in defining the second. Properties: at. no. 55; at. wt. 132.9055; sp. gr. 1.87; melt. pt. 83.30°F (28.5°C); boil. pt. 1274°F (690.0°C); most common isotope Cs^{133} (100%). See also Alkali Elements; Atomic Clock.

Cesium Clock. See Atomic Clock.

Cetacea, order of mammals comprised of whales, including porpoise, dolphin, and the narwhal.

Ceuta, Spanish city in N Morocco, on the Strait of Gibraltar; a territory of Spain since 1580 and part of Cadiz prov. Built by the Phoenicians, it was in turn held by Carthaginians, Romans, Vandals, Byzantines, Arabs, and Portuguese. Forming one of the Pillars of Hercules, it is an important refueling port for ships. Industries: shipping, fishing, food processing. Pop. 67,187.

Cevennes, mountain range in S France, W of Rhône River, extends NE and SW from St Etienne to Canal du Midi, which separates the range from the Pyrenees. Mulberry, olive, and chestnut trees grow on the slopes. Highest peak is Mt Mézenc, 5,753ft (1,755m).

Ceylon. See Sri Lanka.

Cézanne, Paul (1839–1906), French painter. In 1861 he went to Paris to study art, where he met Camille Pissarro, who strongly influenced his development. He exhibited with the first Impressionist show of 1874: House of the Hanged Man (1873–74; Louvre, Paris) is characteristic of his Impressionist period. He later separated himself from the Impressionists, trying to paint what he saw in simple geometric shapes, using color and distortion, as in The Card Players (1890–92; S. C.

Clark Collection, New York City). His portraits, such as *Madame Cézanne* (*c.*1885; S. S. and V. White College, Ardmore, Pa.), are also geometrical studies. The *Bathers* (1898–1905; Philadelphia Museum of Art) incorporates a number of his methods of dealing with perspective. Cézanne is one of the most important influences on 20th–century art.

CGS System, system of units based on the centimeter, the gram, and the second. *See* Weights and Measures.

Chacabuco, Battle of (Feb. 12, 1817), the first major engagement in the War of Independence against Spain led by José de San Martín after he crossed the Andes from Argentina to Chile. The royalists withdrew with heavy losses from the Santiago area.

Chachalaca, noisy, long-tailed game bird found in brushlands and forest edges of S United States and Central and South America. These brownish, chicken-like birds may be a potential future meat source. The female lays white eggs (2) in a stick-and-leaf nest in a low tree. Length: 19.75in (50cm); weight: 1 1b (0.5kg). Genus *Ortalis.*

Chacma, black-faced, dark-furred baboon of E and S Africa. Species *Chaeropithecus ursinus. See also* Baboon.

Chaco, lowland plain in S central South America, having three principal divisions: Chaco Boreal in N Paraguay and S Bolivia; Chaco Central in NE Argentina; Chaco Austral in central Argentina. Most inhabitants reside in Argentine cities of Formosa and Resistencia. Industries: lumbering, cattle grazing, oil prospecting, tannin extraction. Area: 300,000sq mi (777,000sq km).

Chaco War, conflict between Paraguay and Bolivia over possession of the Chaco (1932–35). Bolivia, landlocked as a result of territory lost during the War of the Pacific, sought a route to the sea via the Rio de la Plata. The war cost 50,000 Bolivian and 35,000 Paraguayan lives. Most of the disputed territory was ceded to Paraguay by the 1938 peace treaty.

Chad, republic in N central Africa, completely landlocked; governed by a president. Capital is Ndjamena (formerly Fort Lamy). Bounded by Central African Republic (S), Sudan (E), Libya (N), and Cameroon, Niger, and Nigeria (W), it is 900mi (1,449km) from the nearest seaport. Almost entire N half of country is desert with an annual rainfall of approximately 8in (20cm). There is little human life here except for nomads. Below this a steppe zone with a rainfall of 30in (76cm) has more vegetation; palm trees thrive. This area slopes toward Lake Chad (W) where cattle are raised. The highest population concentration is in the semitropical savanna region in the S. Annual rainfall is 35–48in (89–22cm), and there is farming and fishing. From the late 1960s–1974 Chad suffered a severe drought, as did much of W Africa.

The people of the N region are predominantly Muslim tribes of Bedouin Arabs, Fulani, Tuareg, and Wadaians; herding is their main occupation. The S part of Chad has a predominantly black African population of Saras, Massa, and Moudang; they are mainly animists with some Christians. Agriculture is their main occupation. Hostile feelings between these two distinct civilizations have often erupted in violence and political instability since independence. Cotton accounts for 80% of Chad's exports; peanuts are the only other cash crop. Trade is chiefly with France.

The history of Chad has been traced by archaeological findings to the beginning of the Christian era; by the AD 4th century it was an important trading center. Various tribes attempted to take it, and by the 12th century a kingdom of Kanem existed within Chad. From the 16th–19th century it was controlled by Kanem and Bornu. Dissension during the 19th century weakened the states; foreign exploration of the area had begun and by 1913 Chad was conquered by France. In 1920 it was made a colony within the federation of French Equatorial Africa. After WWII it was granted its own territorial assembly and given representation in French parliament. In 1960 it became an independent republic.

By 1965 a one party system controlled the country and in 1966 a guerrilla war broke out. President Ngarta Tombalbaye requested French assistance under a defense pact with that country. The French withdrew in 1971 and warfare ceased in 1973. Tombalbaye was assassinated in 1975 and was succeeded by Felix Malloum. Malloum, unable to control increasing violence, fled the country in 1979; French troops arrived again and a transitional government was established. By early 1980, however, the truce was broken, and later in the year Libyan troops invaded the capital in support of Goukouni Oueddei. In 1981 a merger between the two countries was announced, but subsequently this was rejected by Chad; withdrawing Libyan forces were replaced by an Organization of African Unity (OAU) peace-keeping force. Hissene Habré succeeded Oueddei, who was overthrown in 1982. Civil war escalated in 1983, and Libyan troops loyal to Oueddei remained in control in certain sections of Chad through the mid-1980s.

PROFILE

Official name: Republic of Chad
Area: 495,754sq mi (1,284,000sq km)
Population: 4,405,000
Chief cities: Ndjamena, formerly Fort-Lamy (capital); Moundou; Fort-Archambault
Religion: Islam, animism, Christianity
Language: French (official)
Monetary unit: Franc CFA

Chad, Lake, lake in N central Africa; mainly in the Republic of Chad, partly in Nigeria, Cameroon, and Niger. Chief tributary is the Chari River. Depth (max): 25ft (7.6m). Depending on the season, surface of lake varies from 4,000–10,000sq mi (10,360–25,900sq km).

Chadic Languages, large sub-group of Afro-Asiatic or Semitic-related languages. They are found in N area of Nigeria and E to Republic of Chad. Hausa (Haoussa) is the largest member of this group. Unlike other Semitic-related African tongues, these, because of interaction with languages to south, are tone languages.

Chadwick, Florence May (1918–), US swimmer, b. San Diego, Calif. She was the first woman to swim the English Channel both ways. She broke the time record for swimming the Santa Catalina Channel and also crossed the Straits of Gibralter, the Dardanelles, and the Bosporous in record swimming time.

Chadwick, Sir James (1891–1974), English physicist. In 1932 he discovered the neutron by bombarding beryllium with alpha particles. For this work he was awarded a Nobel Prize in 1935. *See also* Neutron.

Chaeronea, ruined ancient city in E central Greece, NW of Thebes; scene of Philip II of Macedon's defeat of the united forces of Thebes and Athens (338BC); the massacre of the Thebans by Alexander, Philip's son; and Sulla's victory over the army of Mithridates VI of Pontus (86BC).

Chaetognatha, a phylum of about 50 species of marine invertebrates known as arrowworms. *See* Arrowworm.

Chagall, Marc (1887–1985), French painter, b. Russia. In 1910, he went to Paris from Russia. His paintings, often dreamlike with floating figures, are full of Russian folk lore and Jewish symbolism and are said to have influenced the Surrealists. His most recent work has been abstract designs for stained-glass windows and architectural decoration, including 12 stained-glass windows symbolizing the tribes of Israel (1962) in the Hadassah-Hebrew University Medical Center synagogue in Jerusalem and two vast murals (1966) for the Metropolitan Opera House, New York City, representing the sources and triumph of music. He was awarded the Legion of Honor in 1977.

Chagas' Disease, infectious disease transmitted by a protozoan parasite, *Trypanosoma cruzi,* in insect feces, primarily in South and Central America. Swelling at entry point (often the eye), fever and malaise are early symptoms; heart involvement is typical of the chronic form.

Chain, Sir Ernst Boris (1906–79), English biochemist, b. Germany. He shared the 1945 Nobel Prize in physiology or medicine for his part in "the discovery of penicillin and its therapeutic effect." Chain, working with Howard Florey and Alexander Fleming, helped to isolate and prepare penicillin for large-scale production. *See also* Florey, Howard.

Chain Reaction, a self-sustaining molecular or nuclear reaction in which the products of the reaction are required to sustain the reaction. *See* Fission, Nuclear.

Chalcedon, ancient Greek city in Bithynia, on the E shore of the Bosporus opposite ancient Byzantium (now Istanbul). Its site is now occupied by Kadikoy, Turkey. It was founded by Greeks from Megara (*c.* 680 BC) shortly before the founding of Byzantium; because its site was clearly less desirable than that of Byzantium, it was dubbed the "city of the blind." It vacillated between Spartan and Athenian interests, was ruled for a time by Persia, became part of Alexander the Great's empire, and came under Roman domination in 197 BC . Mithridates VI of Pontus inflicted a notable defeat on the Romans at Chalcedon in 73 BC. Frequently attacked by barbarians thereafter, it was the site of the Christian church's Council of Chalcedon in AD 451. It fell to Persia again in 616 and was destroyed by the Turks in 1075.

Chalcedony, fine-grained variety of quartz used by gem engravers and cut and polished as ornamental. Well-known varieties are agate (common, semiprecious; occurring in colored bands), bloodstone (dark green with bits of red jasper throughout), carnelian (translucent dark red with hematite dispersions), flint (opaque black, due to carbon inclusions), jasper (opaque and usually red due to a mixture of hematite), and onyx (striped).

Chalcidice (Khalkidhikí), department and peninsula in NE Greece forming three fingers in the Aegean Sea: Kassandra (W), Sithonia (central), Athos (E); originally inhabited by Thracians, Greeks est colonies 8th and 7th centuries BC; subsequently conquered by Macedonia and Rome. Industries: magnesite mining, agriculture, beehives. Pop. 73,850.

Chalcid Wasp, dark colored wasp, 0.08 to 0.12 in (2–3mm) long, with some less than 0.02 in (0.5mm); found worldwide. Most of the larvae are parasitic on other insect eggs and larvae. Superfamily Chalcidoidea. *See also* Hymenoptera.

Chalcis (Khalkís), town in E Greece, on Euboea Island; capital of Euboea prefecture; important commercial city of ancient Euboea, its residents founded settlements in Sicily, Italy, Macedonia, and Chalcidice; defeated by Athens 446 BC; annexed to Macedonia 338 BC; occupied by Venice AD 1209; besieged by Turks 1470; came under Greece 1830; Aristotle died here 332 BC. Industries: trade, soap, cement. Pop. 36,300.

Chalcocite, a sulfide mineral, copper sulfide (Cu_2S), and one of the chalcocite group, which also includes acanthite and stromeyerite. A major ore of copper found mainly in sulfur deposits. Orthorhombic system granular masses, or rare prismatic crystals, sometimes twinned. Metallic, dark gray, easily cut; hardness 2.5–3; sp gr 5.8.

Chalcopyrite, a sulfide mineral, copper iron sulfide ($CuFeS_2$); the most important copper ore. In sulfide veins and in igneous and contact metamorphic rocks. Tetragonal system sphenoidal or tetrahedral crystals, often twinned, and as masses. Brittle, metallic, brass-colored, opaque. Hardness 3.5–4; sp gr 4.3.

Chaldaean Dynesty. *See* Neo-Babylonian.

Chalk, natural calcium carbonate ($CaCO_3$) formed from the shells of minute marine organisms. It varies in properties and appearance, pure forms, such as calcite, containing up to 99% calcium carbonate. Blackboard chalk consists of calcium sulfate.

Challenger Expedition, first oceanographic expedition to circle the globe. The voyage of the 2300-ton steam corvette H.M.S. *Challenger* began December 1872, lasted till May 1876, and collected data that filled 50 large volumes, written by 76 authors over a 23-year period. Nearly every ocean was sounded and almost 4500 new species of animals were collected.

Chalmers, Thomas (1780–1847), Scottish churchman. He was a leader in the formation of the Free Church of Scotland (1843), which grew out of dissent within the Established Church over state interference in church matters.

Châlons-sur-Marne, city in NE France, on the Marne River, 95mi (153km) NE of Paris; capital of Marne dept.; scene of 451 defeat of Attila and the Huns by Actius; site of 13th-century Cathedral of St Etienne. Industries: champagne, wallpaper, electrodes, beer. Pop. 55,709.

Chamberlain, (Sir) (Joseph) Austen (1863–1937), English political figure. The son of Joseph Chamberlain and half brother of Neville Chamberlain, he entered upon a 45-year Parliamentary career in 1892. He was postmaster general (1902), chancellor of the exchequer (1903–05, 1919–21), secretary of state for India (1915–17), a member of the war cabinet (1918–19), lord privy seal (1921–22), Conservative party leader (1921–22), foreign secretary (1925–29), and first lord of the admiralty (1931). As foreign secretary he was one of the main architects of the Locarno Pact of 1925 by which France, Germany, and Belgium accepted their existing frontiers and Britain and France agreed to guarantee these frontiers. He received the 1925 Nobel Peace Prize (with Charles G. Dawes) for his work on the pact.

Chamberlain, Joseph (1836–1914), English political figure. A successful business career led to his election (1873) as reform mayor of Birmingham. He left that post after being elected to Parliament (1876). He served as Liberal president of the board of trade (1880–85) and president of the local government board (1886) but resigned (1886) and joined the Liber-

Chad

Neville Chamberlain

Chameleon

al-Unionists, who opposed Prime Minister Gladstone's home rule proposals for Ireland. As colonial secretary (1895–1903) in the Conservative/Liberal-Unionist government (1895–1906), Chamberlain advocated both social reform and a vigorous colonial policy. He was held responsible for the events that led to the Boer War (1899–1902). He resigned his post in 1903 to campaign for a tariff policy giving preference to products from British Empire countries. His advocacy of a departure from Britain's traditional policy of free trade split the Conservative/Liberal-Unionist bloc and led to its removal from office in 1906. That same year he suffered a stroke that incapacitated him until his death.

Chamberlain, (Arthur) Neville (1869–1940), English political figure. He was a son of Joseph Chamberlain and half-brother of Austen. From business he turned to municipal politics (1911) and entered Parliament as a Conservative (1918). From 1922 he held government posts whenever the Conservatives ruled, eventually becoming prime minister (1937–40). He sought peace through negotiation and by appeasing Hitler and Mussolini while Britain rearmed. German successes at the beginning of World War II brought about his resignation (1940).

Chamberlain, Owen (1920–   ), US physicist, b. San Francisco. After working on the development of the atom bomb, he became professor of physics at the University of California, Berkeley. With Emilio Segrè, using the Bevatron accelerator, he confirmed the existence of the antiproton, for which they were awarded a Nobel Prize for physics in 1959.

Chamberlain, Wilton Norman "Wilt" (1936–   ), US basketball player, b. Philadelphia. The greatest offensive player in pro basketball history, with a career total of 31,419 points. He played in the National Basketball Association for Philadelphia (1960–62, 1965–68), San Francisco (1963–65), and Los Angeles (1969–73). He was elected to the Basketball Hall of Fame in 1978.

Chamber Music, music in which one person plays each part, as opposed to orchestral music, where several people play each part. The number of players determines the name of the group. For example, a trio is composed of three players, a quartet of four players. Much chamber music is for string instruments only. In general, the emphasis is on the group's performance as a whole rather than on that of any individual player.

Chameleon, arboreal lizard found chiefly in Madagascar, Africa, and Asia. The common chameleon *(Chamaeleo chamaeleon)* ranges into Spain. It is characterized by its ability to change color. The compressed body has a curled, prehensile tail and bulging eyes that move independently. Many species have a helmet or horn on the head. They are egg-laying and eat insects and small birds. Length: 7–24in (17–60cm). There are 80 species. Family Chamaeleontidae. *See also* Lizard.

Chamois, nimble, goatlike ruminant inhabiting mountain ranges in Europe and Asia Minor. Close-set horns with backward hooked ends are worn by both sexes. It has coarse brown fur. Females and young gather in herds. Its skin is made into the familiar polishing chamois. Length: to 50in (1.3m); weight: 55–110lb (25–50kg). Family Bovidae; species *Rupicapra rupicapra.*

Chamomile. *See* Camomile.

Champagne, district of France, E of Paris, consisting mainly of Aube, Marne, Haute-Marne, and Ardennes depts. Major city is Reims where early French kings were crowned. Trade fairs in the 11th–13th centuries made the district a center of European trade and finance; scene of heavy fighting during WWI along Marne River. Area is rather arid and produces most of the world's champagne.

Champaign, city in E central Illinois; founded 1855 when the Illinois Central Railroad came through; site of University of Illinois at Urbana-Champaign (1867); fertile farm area. Industries: metal products, electrical equipment, academic apparel. Inc. 1860. Pop. (1980) 58,133.

Champlain, Samuel de (1567–1635), French explorer, founder of New France (Canada). In 1603 he went on an exploring and fur-trading expedition to the Gulf of St. Lawrence, where he explored the St. Lawrence River as far as the Lachine Rapids. He later (1604–07) led settlers to Port Royal (now Annapolis Royal, Nova Scotia) and explored the Atlantic coast from Nova Scotia to Martha's Vineyard, discovering Mt Desert Island and the larger Maine rivers. As lieutenant governor of New France, Champlain founded Quebec in 1608. He explored northern New York State, where he discovered Lake Champlain in 1609. He also explored the Ottawa River (1613) and the Great Lakes (1615). He served as governor of New France from 1633–35.

Champlain, Lake, lake separating New York State and Vermont, extending into Quebec, Canada; connects to the Hudson River by Champlain division of Barge Canal and serves as a link in the Hudson-St Lawrence waterway. Discovered by Samuel de Champlain 1609, scene of many historic battles in French and Indian Wars, American Revolution (including a naval conflict 1776), and the defeat of British in War of 1812 by Thomas MacDonough. Many resorts are on the lake making use of it for swimming, fishing, boating, and winter sports. Plattsburgh, NY, and Burlington, Vt, are its largest cities. Area: 490sq mi (1269sq km).

Champollion, Jean François (1790–1832), French Egyptologist. The first conservator of Egyptian antiquities for the Louvre, he is generally considered the creator of Egyptology. He was the leading figure in decoding the Rosetta Stone, the key to all Egyptian hieroglyphics.

Chan Chan, capital of the Chimu kingdom on the northern coast of Peru, which reached the height of its power between AD 1400 and 1450. Extensive adobe ruins remain. Chan Chan was the administrative center of the agricultural Chimu economy. After the Inca conquest (c. 1464), Chan Chan became an Inca provincial capital.

Chandelle, in aviation, a maximum-performance climbing turn with a 180° change in direction. It is used as a training maneuver to demonstrate coordination, speed sense, and planning since it requires arrival at the opposite heading as the bank becomes zero and the airspeed is just above the stall. *See also* Stall, Aircraft.

Chandigarh, city in NW India, at foot of Siwalik Hills; capital of Punjab and Haryana states. One of India's planned cities, designed by Swiss architect Le Corbusier, it was built up in the 1950s; seat of Punjab University (1947), site of garden of Pinjora, replica of Srinigar's Shalimar gardens. Pop. 233,004.

Chandragupta (321?–296 BC), founder of the Maurya Empire, the first great empire of India. He seized the throne of Magadha kingdom from the Nanda dynasty and extended their holdings to include much of northern India. He is believed to be the Sandrocottos of Greek literature of the time of Alexander the Great.

Chandragupta I (r. AD 320–335), Indian emperor. He inherited his kingdom from Ghatotkacha. He enlarged it through marriage to a princess of north Bihar. He was the first Indian ruler to use the title of emperor.

Changchun, city in central Manchuria, NE China; capital of Kirin prov.; site of first automobile plant in China. Industries: agricultural products, machinery, textiles, food processing. Pop. 1,200,000.

Chang Tang, arid desert plateau in central and N Tibet, W China, bounded by Trans-Himalayas (S) and Kunlunshanma (N); contains many fresh and saline lakes. Area: 210,000sq mi (543,900sq km).

Channel Islands, group of islands in SW end of English Channel, 30mi (48km) off W coast of France. Part of United Kingdom, the main islands are Jersey, Guernsey, Alderney, and Sark. Main towns are St Helier, Jersey, and St Peter Port, Guernsey. Group constitutes a popular holiday resort with mild climate and fertile soil. Industries: farming, tourism, fishing. Exports: agricultural and dairy products. Area: 75sq mi (194sq km). Pop. 126,156.

Chanson de Roland, French epic by an unknown author of the late 11th century, which describes the defeat of Charlemagne's rear guard at Roncevaux pass in the Pyrenees on Aug. 15, 778. Because of the treachery of Ganelon, the king's main forces do not arrive in time to save Roland (Hrodlandus, Margrave of Brittany). As in the typical *chansons de geste* (songs of great deeds), the poem alters historical fact in order to develop the personal and tragic elements of a situation. The structure consists of 10-syllable lines grouped in *laisses,* which all end in the same assonance. *See also* Chansons de Geste; Charlemagne.

Chansons de Geste, Old French epic poems of the 11th through 13th centuries, generally dealing with the military campaigns of Charlemagne and his lieutenants. These anonymously written narratives describe imaginary events in the lives of William of Orange, Girart de Rosillon, Roland, and others. *Chanson de Roland* is perhaps the best known of the works.

Chanterelle, a genus of medium-sized fleshy terrestrial mushrooms (Cantharellaceae), most of which are edible, especially *C. cibarius,* which has long been highly prized. It has an orange, funnel-shaped cap with prominent gills continuing down the stem.

Chanukah. *See* Hanukkah.

Chao Chi. *See* Hui Tsung.

Chao K'uang-yin (died 976), founder of the Chinese Sung dynasty (960–1279). He was a scholarly general who eliminated regional military control, established a paid army, and laid the basis for three centuries of cultural flourishing in Sung China.

Chaos, in early Greek cosmology, the representation of the emptiness of the universe and the darkness of the Underworld.

Chapala, Lake, largest lake in Mexico, 30mi (48km) S and SE of Guadalajara; resort noted for scenery and fishing. Area: 651sq mi (1,686sq km).

Chapbook, a forerunner of the inexpensive book or magazine. The chapbook was a cheap pamphlet that was sold by a chapman (peddler) between the 15th and 18th centuries. These small books were pulp fiction, newsletters, comics, and easy-to-read Bible stories, all designed for the common taste and education.

Chapel Hill, residential town in central North Carolina, at the edge of the Piedmont region, 11mi (18km) WSW of Durham; site of University of North Carolina (1789). Founded 1792; inc. 1851. Pop. (1980) 32,421.

Chaplin, (Sir) Charlie (1889–1977), English actor and filmmaker, b. Charles Spencer Chaplin. Widely rated the greatest comedian of the silent era and a brilliant mime, he toured the United States with a pantomime troupe in 1910 and worked for Keystone Studios (1914–16). In his short films, including *Tillie's Punctured Romance* (1914), *The Immigrant* (1917), and *A Dog's Life* (1918), he developed the Tramp—a jaunty, wistful, often pathetic soul in baggy pants, bowler, and moustache. In 1919, with D. W. Griffith, Mary Pickford, and Douglas Fairbanks, Sr., he founded United Artists Films, an independent production company. Among Chaplin's major features were *The Kid* (1920), *The Gold Rush* (1924), *The Circus* (1928), *City Lights* (1931), *Modern Times* (1936), *The Great Dictator* (1940), *Monsieur Verdoux* (1947), and *Limelight* (1952). Attacked for his politics and personal behavior, he left the United States in 1952 to settle in Switzerland. He was honored by the Academy of Motion Picture Arts and Sciences in 1973 and was knighted by Queen Elizabeth II in 1975.

Chapultepec, national park in central Mexico, SW of Mexico City, in rocky hill region; site of 18th-century castle; favorite resort area of Maximillian; stronghold during Mexican War, fell to United States (Sept. 8, 1847); scene of Inter-American conference (Feb. 21–Mar. 8, 1945) that passed Act of Chapultepec, a wartime tactic to insure assistance and solidarity in the Western Hemisphere.

Char, or brook trout, freshwater game fish found in coastal streams and isolated lakes in E North America and parts of Europe. It is speckled with buff or red spots and has white borders on ventral and anal fins. Length: to 31in (79cm); weight: 15lb (6.8kg). Family Salmonidae; species Arctic char *Salvelimus alpinus,* brook trout *Salvelimus fontinalis. See also* Osteichthyes.

Characin, or characid, freshwater tropical fish found from Texas to lower South America and in Africa. Popular home aquarium fish, characins have slender to fairly deep bodies and beautiful colorations. Length: 1in–5ft (2.5–152.4cm); Weight: to 125lb (56.7kg). Family Characidae; 1,000 species including silver dollar fish, piranha, neon tetra, and headstander.

Charbray. *See* Zebu.

Charcot, Jean Baptiste Étienne August (1867–1936), French explorer and physician. Son of the famous psychiatrist Jean Martin Charcot, he led two Antarctic expeditions. During the first (1903–05), he found that the Bismarck Strait connected with the sea east of the Graham coast; he also mapped the Palmer Peninsula's west coast. He tried to reach the South Pole in his 1908–10 expedition. He drowned when his ship *Pourquoi-Pas?* was wrecked off Iceland.

Charcot, Jean Martin (1825–1893), French physician, the "father of neurology." He did classic studies of hypnosis and hysteria and was teacher to Pierre Janet and Sigmund Freud. His work centered on how behavioral symptoms of patients related to diseases of the nervous system.

Chardin, Jean Baptiste Siméon (1699–1779), French painter. His paintings were careful, quiet, but always fresh and lively. He sold his work very cheaply and made many copies of popular pictures. Paintings of middle-class life were a fad in his lifetime, but he gave them up to go back to still-life pictures and finally to portraits painted with pastels.

Charioteer, The. *See* Auriga.

Charlemagne (742–814), king of the Franks, (768–814) and Holy Roman emperor (800–814). The eldest son of Pepin the Short, he inherited Neustria, the northwestern half of the Frankish kingdom, in 768 and annexed the other half upon his brother Carloman's death (771). Responding to threats against Rome and his own sovereignty, he led two armies into Italy and captured the Lombard throne (773). In reprisal to constant Saxon raids, he began a long (772–785) and brutal conquest of Saxony, finally securing it for Christianity and Frankish law. He also deposed the disloyal duke of Bavaria and defeated the Avars of the middle Danube (791–96,804), adding new lands to his empire. By 811 he had established the Spanish March, a Christian refuge in northern Spain. He was coronated emperor by Pope Leo III (800). A man of great power and enthusiasm, he initiated the intellectual, artistic, and ecclesiastical awakening known as the Carolingian Renaissance. His empire, though lacking sufficient economic and political structure to maintain unity after his death, had combined the Germanic peoples for the first time. He was canonized in 1165.

Charles V (1500–58), Holy Roman emperor (1519–58) and king of Spain as Charles I (1516–56). From his father, Philip I of Castile, he inherited the Netherlands in 1506. He grew up in Flanders, where he was born, under the guidance of his regent-aunt Margaret of Austria. He inherited Spain, Naples, Sicily, and Sardinia from his grandfather Ferdinand II in 1516. In 1517 he arrived for the first time in Spain, where he appointed foreign favorites to court positions and greatly increased taxes. He bribed the electors of the Holy Roman Empire into naming him (1520) successor to his grandfather Emperor Maximilian I. He left Spain for Germany in 1520, hoping to establish a universal empire. But his attempt failed, primarily because of three counterforces: the ambitions of Francis I of France in Italy, the threats of the Ottoman Turks, and the Protestant Reformation in Germany. Peace was made with France in 1529, but the long war had led to revolts in Spain (Comuneros, 1520–21), and by the Protestants in Germany (Sickingen's revolt, 1522–23; Peasants' War, 1524–26). Charles was able to hold off the Ottomans but was unable to push them back. Although in the Edict of Worms (1521) he had declared Martin Luther and his followers to be outlaws, the Protestants grew stronger. Charles became a leader of the Catholic Reformation as formulated at the Council of Trent (1545). As early as 1521, Charles had begun sharing rule of his vast empire with his brother Ferdinand, king of Bohemia and Hungary. He gave Ferdinand increasing power in Germany and returned to Spain in 1531. In 1554 and 1555 he ceded his Italian possessions and the Netherlands to his son Philip. He entered the monastery of Yuste, Spain, in 1556, ceding Spain to Philip. In 1558 he officially abdicated as Holy Roman emperor to be succeeded by Ferdinand.

Charles VI (1685–1740), Holy Roman emperor (1711–40) and king of Hungary, as Charles III. After an unsuccessful attempt to ascend to the Spanish throne that precipitated the War of the Spanish Succession, he became Holy Roman emperor. Retiring to his Austrian possessions, he lost much of his land in wars. He was able to secure his daughter Maria Theresa's succession only with much difficulty. He was the last of the Hapsburg male line.

Charles I (1887–1922), Austrian emperor (1916–18), and king (as Charles IV) of Hungary (1916–18), the last Hapsburg ruler. Grandnephew of Emperor Francis Joseph, on accession to the throne he sought a separate peace with the Allies and tried to hold the crumbling empire together. In 1918, Hungary and Czechoslovakia declared their independence, Charles abdicated and went into Swiss exile. In 1921 he twice attempted to regain the Hungarian throne. He was arrested and deported to Madeira, where he died.

Charles I (1600–49), king of England, Scotland, and Ireland (1625–49). Charles made an unpopular marriage in 1625 to Catholic Henrietta Maria of France. Until 1628 he was dominated by the 1st duke of Buckingham, who commanded an inglorious war against France (1626–30). Because it failed to finance the war, Charles dissolved Parliament three times in four years. In 1628 it forced him to assent to the Petition of Right, which, among other things, prohibited taxation without Parliament's consent. Charles then ruled without a parliament (1629–40). His arbitrary exactions antagonized the landed class and his High Church policies enraged the Scots, who revolted (1639). Almost bankrupt, Charles called the Short Parliament and then the Long Parliament in 1640. The latter gained many reforms and impeached his chief advisers.

In the Grand Remonstrance (1641) Parliament summarized the grievances against the king. Civil war broke out in 1642. With Scottish aid, the forces of Parliament crushed the king's troops at Naseby (1645) and Charles surrendered. Charles's intrigues during his imprisonment led to a second civil war in 1648, but Cromwell's army triumphed, and Charles was tried and beheaded.

Charles II (1630–85), king of England, Scotland, and Ireland (1660–85). Charles fled to France after his father's defeat in 1646. After his father's execution Charles was proclaimed king of Scots, and he unsuccessfully invaded England (1650–51). Thereafter Charles was in exile until Cromwell's death; he was proclaimed king of England in 1660.

In 1662 Charles issued the Declaration of Indulgence, which freed nonconformist Protestants and Catholics from interference, but Parliament forced him to withdraw it. He also attempted to circumvent Parliament's foreign policy by making secret agreements with Louis XIV of France and accepting covert subsidies from him. Titus Oates's accusations of a Popish Plot created national hysteria (1678–80), during which many Catholics were forced out of office. Charles dissolved the Parliament that passed the Habeas Corpus Act (1679) and successfully staved off Parliament's attempts to introduce bills preventing James, his brother and a professed Catholic, from succeeding to the throne, the Exclusion Crisis (1680–81). (Charles had married Catharine of Braganza in 1662, but they had no children.) Threatened by assassination in the Rye House Plot (1683), Charles died of a stroke in 1685.

Charles IV, called **Charles the Fair** (1294–1328), king of France (1322–28), successor of his brother Philip V. He increased royal revenues by debasing the coinage and levying taxes. He invaded Guienne (1324), a possession of England, and in 1327 England ceded most of the province to Charles and paid a large indemnity. The last king of the Capetian dynasty, he was succeeded by Philip VI of the Valois line.

Charles V, called **Charles the Wise** (1337–80), king of France (1364–80). An able ruler, he regained most of the territory previously lost to the English; stabilized the coinage; and took a stand against marauding free companies; strengthened royal authority; introduced standing army, powerful navy, fiscal reforms; established royal library; built Bastille. Placed severe economic burden on country through lack of practical budgeting. Succeeded by his son Charles VI.

Charles VI, called **Charles the Well-beloved or Charles the Mad** (1368–1422), king of France (1380–1422). Until 1388 he was controlled by his uncle Philip the Bold of Burgundy, whose policies drained the treasury and provoked uprisings. After ruling effectively for four years, Charles suffered the first of recurrent attacks of insanity. Philip and Louis d'Orleans, the king's brother, fought over control of the kingdom. Philip had Louis murdered in 1407 and allied himself with Henry V of England. Charles was compelled to sign the Treaty of Troyes (1420), which recognized Henry V as his successor.

Charles VII, called **the Well-Served** (1403–61), king of France (1422–61). The son of Charles VI, he reigned at the end of the Hundred Years' War. Excluded from throne by Treaty of Troyes; however, took power (1422) when Charles VI died. Ruled south of the Loire; Henry V of England controlled the north. Joan of Arc and Arthur III, Duke of Brittany, were two of his followers in the war against England. He was crowned (1429) at Rheims. Treaty of Arras (1435) won Burgundy as ally in 1440. A truce with England was signed, and England finally withdrew from Guienne (1453). He established heavy taxation, a standing army, and a permanent land tax. He was succeeded by his son Louis XI.

Charles IX (1550–74), king of France (1560–74). His mother Catherine de Médicis became regent when at the age of 10 he succeeded his brother Francis II, although her authority temporarily waned when in 1571 the young king fell under the influence of Gaspard de Coligny, leader of the Huguenots. Coligny and thousands of his followers were slain in the St Bartholomew's Day Massacre (1572), ordered by Charles at the instigation of his mother. He was succeeded by his brother Henry III.

Charles X (1757–1836), king of France (1824–30). Brother of Louis XVI and Louis XVIII, he fled France at the outbreak of the French Revolution in 1789. He remained in England until the Bourbon restoration (1814). He opposed the moderate policies of Louis XVIII. After the assassination of his son in 1820, his reactionary forces triumphed. Shortly after his accession, he signed a law (1825) indemnifying émigrés for land confiscated during the Revolution. In 1830 he dissolved the liberal chamber of deputies and issued the July Ordinance, which restricted suffrage and press freedom and dissolved the newly elected chamber. The people rose up in arms and Charles was forced to abdicate and flee. He designated his grandson Henry as successor, but the Duc d'Orléans, Louis Philippe, was selected.

Charles I (1226–85), king of Naples and of the Two Sicilies (1266–85), son of Louis VIII of France and Blanche of Castile. This prince, noted for restless ambition and harsh administration, was offered the throne by Pope Innocent IV and became one of the most powerful European rulers.

Charles II (1661–1700), king of Spain, Naples, and Sicily (1665–1700). He was the son and successor of Philip IV, and the last of the Spanish Hapsburgs. He was mentally incompetent and reigned under the re-

Charlie Chaplin

Charles II of England

Charles, Prince of Wales

gency of his mother, Mariana of Austria, and his illegitimate half-brother, John of Austria. During Charles's reign, Spain was greatly weakened by the War of Devolution and the War of the Grand Alliance. His death—and his will naming Philip of Anjou as his heir —set off the War of the Spanish Succession. *See also* Devolution, War of; Grand Alliance, War of; Spanish Succession, War of.

Charles III (1716–88), king of Spain (1759–88) and of Naples and Sicily (1735–59), the son of Philip V and Elizabeth Farnese. He conquered (1734) Naples and Sicily in the War of the Polish Succession and inherited the Spanish crown in 1759 from his half-brother Ferdinand VI. He then turned over Naples and Sicily to his son Ferdinand, who ruled as Ferdinand I of the Two Sicilies. Charles was a highly competent ruler. His reign was marked by the gaining of Louisiana from the French in 1763 and by the expulsion of the Jesuits in 1767. He was succeeded by his son Charles IV.

Charles IV (1748–1819), king of Spain (1788–1808), son and successor of Charles III. Unable to cope with the upheavals of Napoleon Bonaparte, Charles virtually turned over the government to his wife Maria Luisa and her lover Manuel de Godoy. Godoy formed an alliance with France, but Spain was nevertheless occupied by French troops in the Peninsular War. Charles was forced to abdicate in favor of his son Ferdinand VII, who in turn was forced from the throne by Napoleon. *See also* Godoy, Manuel de; Maria Luisa.

Charles XIV John (1763–1844), king of Sweden (1810–44). French by birth, his original name was Jean Baptiste Bernadotte. He fought in the French Revolution and was made a marshal of Napoleon. He was chosen by the Swedish legislature in 1810 to succeed Charles XIII, who had no heirs. By the Treaty of Kiel he forced Denmark to cede Norway to Sweden, and he became king of Norway as Charles III John (1818–44). He joined the Allies against Napoleon at the Battle of Leipzig in 1814. His subsequent reign brought peace and prosperity to Sweden.

Charles XVI Gustav (1946–), king of Sweden (1973–). Known as Carl, he ascended the throne after the death of his grandfather, King Gustav VI. His father, Prince Gustav Adolf, was killed in an air crash in 1947. A descendant of Marshal Bernadotte, he was a constitutional monarch with no political power and was an environmentalist, knowledgeable on international affairs, labor and industry. In 1976 he married Silva Sommerlath, a West German commoner, and visited the United States.

Charles, Prince of Wales (1948–), eldest son of Elizabeth II of Great Britain, heir to the British throne. Educated at Cambridge University (1967–70), he trained as an air force pilot before becoming a naval officer (1971–76). He was invested with the title Prince of Wales in 1969 and married in 1981 to Lady Diana Spencer. Their sons, William (1982–) and Henry (1984–), are second and third in line to the throne.

Charles, called **Charles the Bold** (1433–77), last reigning duke of Burgundy (1467–77), son and successor of Philip the Good. Aligned with England by marriage to Margaret, Edward IV's sister (1468), he was ruler of the Low Countries, Luxembourg, Burgundy, and Franche-Comte. He continued to conquer lands separating his possessions. He seized Lorraine in 1475, thereby alienating the Swiss, whom he subsequently attacked. He was defeated and killed by the Swiss in 1477. Continually at war with France throughout his reign, Burgundy's resistance to that country ended with his death.

Charles, Jacques Alexandre César (1746–1823), French physicist, inventor, and mathematician who was the first to use a hydrogen balloon. He discovered the law relating the expansion of a gas to its temperature rise. Gay-Lussac published this work some 15 years after Charles's discovery and it is alternately known as Charles's law or Gay-Lussac's law. He is credited with inventing a thermometric hydrometer and improving Fahrenheit's aerometer and Gravesande's hydrometer.

Charles Augustus (1757–1828), duke of Saxe-Weimar-Eisenach (1758–1828) and grand duke after 1815. Through his alliance with Frederick II of Prussia he achieved great influence in German affairs. He fought against Napoleon I in the Napoleonic Wars, but his duchy was forced to enter the Confederation of the Rhine in 1806. An important member of the Congress of Vienna, he was raised to the rank of grand duke by that body. He was a great patron of the arts; Goethe and Schiller were under his protection.

Charles' Law, the observation that the volume of a gas at constant pressure is directly proportional to its temperature. Discovered by the French scientist Jacques Charles around 1787, the law is a special case of the Ideal Gas Law. *See also* Boyle's Law; Ideal Gas Law.

Charles Martel (688–741), Frankish ruler, natural son of Pepin of Heristal, grandfather of Charlemagne. Upon the death of his father (714), he seized control of Austrasia and Neustria. He later conquered Burgundy, Aquitaine, and Provence and subjugated many German tribes across the Rhine. In 732 at Tours he halted the advance of the Muslims from Spain. He divided his kingdom between his sons Pepin the Short and Carloman.

Charleston, port city in SE South Carolina; seat of Charleston co; William Sayle and a group of English colonists settled nearby in 1670 at Albemarle Point; later for better defense they moved to Oyster Point and made their capital Charles Town, which was named for King Charles II, and served as capital until 1790. The first Civil War engagement was here at Fort Sumter; site of the First Ordinance of Secession (1860). Points of interest include the Dock Street Theater (1736), one of the first in the country; College of Charleston 1770; Fireproof Buildings (1826); Charleston Museum (1773); Slave Market Museum. Industries: foreign trade, chemicals, steel, tourism. Founded 1680; inc. 1783. Pop. (1980) 69,510.

Charleston, capital city of West Virginia, in W central part of state at junction of Elk and Kanawha rivers; seat of Kanawha co; city grew around Fort Lee; home of Daniel Boone. Industries: chemicals, glass, metal, timber, oil, coal. Founded 1788; inc. 1794. Pop. (1980) 63,968.

Charlevoix, Pierre Francois Xavier de (1682–1761), Canadian historian and explorer, b. France. He canoed up the St. Lawrence in 1721 to the Great Lakes and eventually reached New Orleans. He wrote the first general history of Canada (1744) and edited *Memoires de Trevoux*, a Jesuit journal.

Charlotte, city in S North Carolina; state's largest city and capital of Mecklenbourg co; site of two universities and three colleges; birthplace of Pres. James K. Polk; distribution center for agricultural products. Industries: cotton products, farm implements, oil refining, chemicals. Settled *c.* 1748; inc. 1768; occupied by British 1780. Pop. (1980) 314,447.

Charlotte Amalie, seaport and capital of the US Virgin Islands, on St Thomas Island; Danish architecture. Pop. 12,372.

Charlottesville, city in central Virginia, 70 mi (113km) W of Richmond; seat of Albemarle co; named for Queen Charlotte of Britain; site of University of Virginia (1819); Monticello, Thomas Jefferson's home; Ash Lawn, James Monroe's home. Industries: publishing, research, textiles. Founded 1762; inc. 1888. Pop. (1980) 45,010.

Charlottetown, capital of Prince Edward Island, Canada, in center of island overlooking Hillsborough Bay; site of University of Prince Edward Island (1969); major commercial and transportation center. Industries: food processing, fishing, tourism. Founded by French 1720; became capital 1765; inc. 1855. Pop. 17,063.

Charolais, creamy white breed of beef cattle, originally developed in France. In the United States it is sometimes crossbred with zebu. *See also* Beef Cattle; Zebu.

Charterhouse of Parma (1839), novel by Stendhal, narrating the adventures of Fabrizio del Dongo. His aunt, Sanseverina, sponsors him in a church career. After Fabrizio becomes archbishop of Parma, he has an affair with Clélia Conti who has earlier helped him escape from prison. The tragic death of their son and Clélia's death is followed by Fabrizio's retirement to a monastery (the Charterhouse) and death.

Chartism, British working-class movement for social and political reform, 1838–48. The Chartists sought the enactment of William Lovett's People's Charter, which called for the democratization of the ballot. Racked by factional disputes and unable to capitalize on the continental revolutions of 1848, the movement collapsed when plans to resettle industrial workers in the countryside failed.

Chartres, town in NW France, on the Eure River, 50mi (81km) SW of Paris; capital of Eure-et-Loir dept.; rich farming area. In ancient times Druids assembled here; early Christians built a basilica in 4th century on site now occupied by the 12th-13th century Gothic Cathedral of Notre Dame, whose stained glass and superb sculptures make it one of Europe's finest structures. Industries: woolens, leather, hosiery, radio and television parts. Pop. 41,251.

Charybdis, in Greek mythology, a whirlpool that dwelled opposite the monster Scylla in a Sicilian sea; the daughter of Poseidon and Earth. She had stolen the oxen of Hercules, for which Zeus changed her into a whirlpool whose vortex swallowed up ships, but failed to capture that of Odysseus. *See also* Scylla and Charybdis.

Chase, Salmon Portland (1808–73), chief justice of the US Supreme Court (1864–73), b. Cornish, NH. He is known as the defender of fugitive slaves. He organized the Liberty party (1841) and was founder of the Free-Soil party (1848). He served as US Senator (1849–55, 1860), and governor of Ohio (1855–59). He was secretary of the treasury (1861–64), during which time he supported the National Banking Act (1863). He was appointed chief justice by President Lincoln, succeeding Roger Taney. As chief justice, Chase reorganized the federal courts in the South, and presided over the Jefferson Davis trial (1867) and the Senate impeachment proceedings against President Johnson (1868). His dissenting opinion in the Slaughterhouse Cases (1873) became a position of the courts about the restrictive clause of the 14th Amendment. He also presided over *Hepburn* v. *Griswold* (1870), which made legal tender unconstitutional. The decision was reversed in the Legal Tender Cases (1871) despite his dissenting view.

Chase, Samuel (1741–1811), US jurist, b. Somerset co., Maryland. A signer of the Declaration of Independence and Maryland General Assemblyman (1764–84), he was appointed an associate justice of the US Supreme Court in 1796. A Federalist, impeached in 1804 for his conduct at the trials of two Jeffersonians, he won acquittal on the ground that holding opposing political views is not misconduct.

Chat, several species of warblers, including the North American yellow-breasted chat *(Icteria virens)* known for its mimicking ability, and the red-breasted chat *(Granatellus venustus)* of Central America. *See also* Warbler.

Chateau Architecture, fortified seigneurial residence that was the French equivalent of the English castle in medieval times. In the 15th century changes in methods of warfare and in the feudal system made the heavily fortified chateau obsolete. Lightly fortified, luxurious country houses, such as Amboise, Blois, Chambord, and Chenonceaux, mark the transition between medieval fortress and country mansion.

Chateaubriand, François-René, Vicomte de (1768–1848), the dominant literary figure of his generation and the founder of French Romanticism. For him, nature was savage and beautiful, man primitive and good, and God omnipotent and benevolent. A trip to the United States in 1791 influenced his writing; the landscapes and people he encountered in the wilds of America gave vent to his vivid imagination, reflected in works such as *Atala* (1801) and *Le génie du Christianisme* (1802).

Châteauroux, town in central France on the Indre River; capital of Indre dept.; grew around 10th-century castle built by lords of Déols; castle was replaced in 15th century by Chateau Raoul, which still stands. Industries: woolens, paper, agricultural machinery. Pop. 55,629.

Château Thierry, town in France, on E bank of Marne River, 47mi (76km) ENE of Paris; built on the side of a hill with ruins of old castle Thierry, reputedly built by Charles Martel. Jean de la Fontaine was born here 1621; his home is a museum. Industries: stone quarrying, musical instruments, yarn. Pop. 13,856.

Chatham, William Pitt, Ist Earl of. *See* Pitt, William, Ist Earl of Chatham.

Chattanooga, city in E Tennessee, on Tennessee River; seat of Hamilton co; originally a Cherokee territory, it later became a trading center called Ross' Landing; served as a Union military base during Civil War and was the scene of many battles including the Chattanooga and Chickamauga campaigns; since 1935, it has been headquarters for several divisions of the Tennessee Valley Authority. Industries: iron, steel, processed foods, synthetics, tourism. Settled 1835; inc. 1839. Pop. (1980) 169,565.

Chaucer, Geoffrey (*c.*1340–1400), the greatest of English medieval poets, strongly influenced by contemporaneous French and Italian writers. Born in London the son of a wine merchant, he served at court and on diplomatic missions before being appointed controller of customs in London (1374–86). His writings are remarkable for their range, narrative sense, power of characterization, and humor. They include *The Book of the Duchess, The House of Fame, The Parliament of Fowls, Troilus and Criseyde,* and *The Canterbury Tales. See also* individual works.

Chaus, or jungle cat, swamp lynx, striped yellowish to brownish cat found in scrub and mountain areas of S Asia, the Middle East, and NE Africa. Long-legged, it will interbreed with the domestic cat. Length: body—23.6–29.5in (60–75cm); tail—9.8–13.8in (25–35cm). Family Felidae; species *Felis chaus. See also* Cat.

Chavín, one of the earliest prehistoric culture periods in South America, lasting from *c.* 1000 to 200 BC Named for the Chavín de Huántar in N Peru, these people developed excellent stone sculpture, the earliest gold work yet found in the Americas, as well as some of the most remarkable ceramics, judged both by technology and esthetic form.

Checheno-Ingush (Ceceno-Ingusskaja) Autonomous Soviet Socialist Republic, administrative district in SE European USSR, in the N Caucasus; capital is Grozny. Formed in 1936 by merging the Chechen and Ingush autonomous areas, it was dissolved 1943–44 because of German collaboration in WWII: reunited 1957. Chief rivers are the Terek and Sunzha; whose valleys are the main source of agricultural products; Grozny oil field is a major source of Soviet oil; 40% of population is urban. Industries: oil refining, food processing, chemicals, oil field equipment, wine, cognac, fruit canning. Area: 7,452sq mi (19,301sq km). Pop. 1,169,000.

Checkers, game for two players. It originated in Europe in the 16th century. Each player uses 12 pieces (either red or black) and sets them on the board in a predetermined order. The board consists of 64 alternately colored squares (either red and black or white and black). All play is from the black squares. The players sit opposite one another and alternate in moving their pieces forward. Pieces are captured by jumping over opposing pieces, and the game ends when all of a player's pieces are removed from the board.

Checks and Balances, division of power provided for in the US Constitution among the legislative, executive, and judicial branches of government to ensure that no one has domination over the other two.

Cheetah, or hunting leopard, spotted cat found in hot, arid areas of Africa, Middle East, and India. A long-legged cat with blunt, nonretractable claws, its coat is tawny brown with round black spots. Capable of running over 55mph (88.5kph), it hunts gazelles and antelope by sight. Its gestation period is 90–95 days and 1–8 young are born. Length: body—55–59in (140–150cm); tail—23.6–31.5in (60–80cm); weight: 132lb (60kg). Family Felidae; subfamily Acinonchinae. Species include Asian *Acinonyx venatica;* African *Acinonyx jubatus,* and the striped *Acinonyx rex. See also* Cat.

Cheever, John (1912–82), US author, b. Quincy, Mass. A short story writer and novelist, his works deal with suburbanites. Among his works are *The Wapshot Chronicle* (1957), *The Wapshot Scandal* (1964), *Bullet Park* (1969), *Falconer* (1977), *The Stories of John Cheever* (1978), for which he was awarded the Pulitzer Prize, and *Oh What a Paradise It Seems* (1982).

Chefoo (Yantai, or Yen-tai), port city in E China, on N coast of the Shantung Peninsula; important fishing port, opened to foreign trade 1862; scene of Chefoo Convention (1876) which est. new Chinese ports for foreign trade. Pop. 180,000.

Cheiromancy. *See* Palmistry.

Chekiang, smallest province in E China, on E China Sea, including the Choushan archipelago; capital is Hangchow, the royal capital under the Southern Sung dynasty (12th–13th centuries); birthplace of Chiang Kai-shek, Nationalist Chinese leader. Industries: agriculture (in the N plain region), fishing (on the coast and in the archipelago), silk, food processing. Area: 39,305sq mi (101,800sq km). Pop. 31,000,000.

Chekov, or **Chekhov, Anton Pavlovich** (1860–1904), Russian playwright whose theatrical realism evolved with the Moscow Art Theatre under Constantin Stanislavski. Chekov depicted the frustrations of Russian society in the final years of tsarism. The characters of *The Sea Gull* (1896), *Uncle Vanya* (1899), *The Three Sisters* (1900), and, especially, *The Cherry Orchard* (1904) were created with such validity that they bridged the Bolshevik Revolution and remain favorites of Soviet theater and elsewhere.

Chelation, chemical reaction in which a single organic compound, termed a chelating agent, binds itself to a metal ion at more than one point. Tartaric acid, $(HO_2C\text{-}CHOH)_2$, and ethylenediamine, $(H_2NCH_2)_2$, are chelating agents. Such ligands are used as extractants in chemical separations and widely affect molecular environments such as hemoglobin in life processes.

Chelyabinsk (Cel'abinsk), industrial city in Russian SFSR, USSR, on Mias River; capital of Chelyabinsk oblast; metallurgical and industrial center; resettlement area for emigrants to Siberia in 19th century. Industries: food processing, iron, steel, textiles, chemicals. Founded 1658; chartered 1745. Pop. 1,019,000.

Chemical Bonds, forces holding atoms together in chemical compounds. In an isolated atom the electrons move around the positive nuclei. When atoms come together to form compounds, the total electrons move in the combined field of the nuclei, and a more stable configuration is produced (that is, one of lower energy). Usually chemists treat the forces between atoms as individual linkages between pairs of atoms. These are the chemical bonds, which are classified according to the way the electrons are distributed. A covalent bond is formed by sharing a pair of electrons between two atoms; when the electron pair is supplied by one of the atoms the link is a coordinate bond. Ionic bonds are produced by transfer of electrons to form ions, which bind by electrostatic attraction. In ionic, and to a lesser extent, coordinate bonds there is an unequal distribution of charge between the atoms. Such bonds are said to be polar. A bond produced by sharing one electron pair, or by transfer of one electron, is a single bond. Double and triple bonds can also form. In compounds it is often possible to assign an energy to a bond—equal to the energy to separate two parts of the molecule. This is the bond energy. *See also* Covalent Bond; Hydrogen Bond; Ionic Bond; Valence.

Chemical Cell. *See* Battery Cell.

Chemical Equation, representation of a chemical reaction, using symbols for the atoms of the elements. The equation shows how the atoms are rearranged as a result of the reaction: eg, $2H_2 + O_2 = 2H_2O$ is the equation representing the formation of water from hydrogen and oxygen. A knowledge of atomic weights enables the equation to be used to calculate the proportions in which the substances will react. In this example, 4 kg $[2 \times (1 + 1)]$ of hydrogen react with 32 kg (16 + 16) of oxygen to form 36 kg of water (at. wt. O=16, H=1).

Chemical Equilibrium, state of a reversible reaction when the concentrations of products and reactants are constant with time. The initial rate of a chemical reaction falls off as the concentrations of reactants decrease and the build-up of products causes the rate of the reverse reaction to increase. Equilibrium is the steady state occurring when these two rates are equal and reaction has apparently ceased. *See also* Equilibrium Constant.

Chemical Kinetics, branch of chemistry concerned with the measurement and study of reaction rate and its dependence on factors such as concentration and temperature. The term is also applied to the behavior of a particular reaction.

Chemical Nomenclature. Until the end of the 18th century the names of substances gave no indication of their composition. J. J. Berzelius (1779–1848) proposed the system now used, in which the name of a compound indicates the elements it contains and sometimes in what proportions. The naming of the elements themselves has been somewhat haphazard—some from Greek (eg iodine and chlorine), some from mythology (eg thorium and niobium), etc.

When two elements combine to form a compound the name of the second element is modified to end in *-ide* (hydrogen chloride). When more than one compound can be formed from the same elements a numerical suffix is used (eg carbon monoxide, carbon dioxide). The naming of chemical compounds (especially in organic chemistry) is now a precise discipline and many older names have been modified to comply with modern rules.

Chemical Reaction, process in which one or more chemical substances are converted into other substances. Reactions involve the formation or breaking of chemical bonds as the starting materials (the reactants) change into the final substances (the products). These changes characterize the mechanism of the reaction, which may be simple or may involve a complex sequence of steps. *See also* Chemical Equilibrium; Chemical Kinetics; Endothermic Reaction; Exothermic Reaction.

Chemical Symbols. The alchemists used symbols for some of the elements and John Dalton (1766–1844) devised a more extensive system. However, these have all been abandoned in favor of the system devised by J. J. Berzelius in 1811. In this system letters, or pairs of letters, are used to represent the atoms of an element (eg O for oxygen). Not all elements can be represented by their initial letters (11 elements start with the letter C), some require two letters (eg Cl for chlorine and Cd for cadmium). Several elements have symbols based on their Latin names, eg Na for sodium (natrium).

Chemical Warfare, military use of chemical weapons, such as poisonous gases, defoliants, and herbicides, over large areas.

Chemistry, branch of physical science concerned with the formation of compounds by chemical elements and with the structures and reactions of such compounds. Chemistry is essentially concerned with the electrons in atoms, in particular with the way atoms form chemical bonds. Nuclear properties and reactions are the province of physics.

The subject grew out of alchemy in the 17th and 18th centuries. Today it is a vast body of knowledge with a number of subdivisions. The main classification is into organic chemistry, the study of carbon compounds, and inorganic chemistry, the study of compounds of the other elements. Physical chemistry is concerned

Salmon P Chase

Geoffrey Chaucer

Anton Chekov

with the physical properties and behavior of compounds.

Chemistry is of immense commercial importance. Industrial chemistry, including chemical engineering, involves the study and development of equipment and processes for making useful chemicals and products, including fertilizers, cosmetics, explosives, pharmaceuticals, dyestuffs, paints, synthetic resins and fibers, and plastics. *See also* Alchemy; Biochemistry.

Chemotherapy, treatment of a disease by systematic drugs that specifically kill or impair disease-producing organisms in the body without damaging the patient. The term is often used to describe the treatment of cancer by drugs. Generally, it is the use of any drug to treat any disease. The concept of specific drug treatment was first introduced in the early 1900s by German bacteriologist Paul Ehrlich and greatly advanced after the mid-1930s with the development of sulfa drugs, antibiotics, and other modern drugs.

Chemurgy, the development of new chemical products for industry from organic raw materials, especially those of agricultural origin.

Chenab, one of "Five Rivers" of the Punjab, India; rises in the Indian Himalayas, flows through Jammu Kashmir and W central Punjab, Pakistan, to unite with the Sutlej to form the Panjnad River; supports extensive canal and irrigation systems. Length: 599mi (964km).

Chen-Chiang (Chinkiang, Zhenjiang), city in E China, on S bank of Yangtze River, 43mi (69km) NE of Nanking. First opened to foreign trade in 1859, it was a British concession until 1927, when it was returned to China; served as capital of Kiangsu prov. from 1928–49; site of Kiangsu medical college. Industries: silk, vinegar, paper products, tobacco, rice and flour milling. Pop. 250,000.

Chengchow. See Zhengzhou.

Chengdu (Chengtu), city in S central China, near Ching Kiang River, 170mi (274km) NW of Chungking; capital of Szechwan prov.; site of US air base 1944–45, university (1931), irrigation system over 2,000 years old; agricultural trade center. Industries: iron, steel, machinery, silk. Pop. 1,250,000.

Cheng Ho (1371–1433), Chinese admiral and diplomat. A member of a Mongol family, he was captured, castrated, and placed in the court of Emperor Yung Lo of the new Ming dynasty. In a series of seven extensive voyages (1405–33), conducted chiefly to increase trade, he helped broaden Chinese influence throughout the regions of the Indian Ocean. He explored areas of Africa and Asia almost a century before Western explorers.

Ch'eng I, or **Ch'eng Yi** (1033–1107), Chinese philosopher, founder of the Neo-Confucian School of Reason *(li),* which has been characterized as the school of "Platonic realism." He was originally a student of Chou Tun-i, and his work was given definite expression by Chu Hsi. *See also* Chu Hsi.

Cheng-te (Chengteh, or Chengde), city in NE China, on Luan River 110mi (177km) NE of Peking; former summer capital of Ch'ing Dynasty (1644–1911); site of many parks, lakes, palaces, and pavilions; distribution center for pharmaceuticals, lumber products, fruits. Pop. 200,000.

Chengtu. See Chengdu.

Ch'en Tu'hsiu (1879–1942), Chinese political leader. One of the founders of the Chinese literary renaissance of 1917, he helped found the Chinese Communist party, which he led from 1921–27. He was deposed by Mao Tse-tung in 1927, arrested in 1933, and pardoned in 1937.

Cheops. *See* Khufu.

Cherbourg, seaport in NW France, on English Channel, on N shore of Cotentin Peninsula. Founded as a Roman outpost, it was under English control periodically until 18th century; severely damaged during German occupation in WWII. Modern city is naval base, trade center, and seaside resort. Pop. 34,637.

Cherchell (Cherchel), town and port in N Algeria, on the Mediterranean Sea. Ancient city (Iol) was founded by Carthaginians; made capital of Mauretania 25 BC and renamed Caesarea. Important center of Greco-Roman culture after being taken by Rome AD 42 and it declined after being sacked by Vandals in 5th century; site of many Roman ruins, including baths and an amphitheater. Pop. 11,667.

Cherenkov, Pavel. *See* Cerenkov, Pavel Alekseevich.

Chernenko, Konstantin (Ustinovich) (1911–85), Soviet politician, general secretary of the Communist party and president of the Soviet Union (1984–85). The oldest man ever elected general secretary, he was widely considered to be an ineffective leader, holding office merely to bridge the gap between the aging conservative holdovers of the Brezhnev era and the younger technocrats such as Mikhail Gorbachev, who succeeded him. In failing health, he was often absent from public view, and he died without having made any major changes in Soviet policies.

Chernigov (Cernigov), port city in Ukrainian SSR, USSR, on Desna River; capital of Chernigov oblast. A Lithuanian city in 14th century, it passed to Russia in 16th century; under Polish rule part of 17th century; site of Spasski Cathedral and the Church of the Assumption in the Yelets Monastery (both 11th century). Industries: footwear, flour, textiles, musical instruments. Founded c. 907. Pop. 241,000.

Chernovtsy (Cernovcy), city in Ukrainian SSR, USSR, on Prut River, near Romanian border; capital of Chernovtsy oblast; cultural, commercial and industrial center; important Moldavian center in 14th century; occupied by Austria in 1775; part of Romania 1918–40; annexed to Russia in 1940. When it was occupied during WWII by Germans, Jewish population was executed. Industries: textiles, machines, wood processing, food preserving. Pop. 209,000.

Cherokee, second largest tribe of North American Indians; members of the great Iroquoian language family. They migrated south into the Appalachian region around Tennessee, Georgia, and the Carolinas. Smallpox introduced by white settlers caused the deaths of over one-half of the tribe. The Cherokee sided with the British during the Revolution, and as a result were forced to move west over the tragic Trail of Tears, further reducing their population. Today approximately 45,000 live in Oklahoma, while about 15,000 still remain in North Carolina, descendants of those few Indians who escaped into the hills. Another 15,000 reside throughout the United States. There are almost no full-blooded Cherokee today.

Cherry, widely grown fruit tree of the temperate regions, probably native to W Asia and E Europe. Three types of cherry trees, bearing the sweet, sour, or duke cherries, are grown for their edible fruit, which is almost globular, about 1in (2.5cm) in diameter and yellow to red to almost black in color. Sweet cherries are eaten fresh. All types are canned or frozen. The wood is prized for the manufacture of furniture. Family Rosaceae; genus *Prunus.*

Cherry Laurel, any of various evergreen shrubs native to SE Europe and grown ornamentally in the United States. Reaching to 18ft (5.4m), they have glossy leaves and white flowers. Family Rosaceae; genus *Prunus.*

Cherry Orchard, The (1904), 4-act drama, last and best known play of Anton Chekhov. At its premiere in the Moscow Art Theatre (1904), the author's wife Olga Knipper created the role of aristocrat Mme. Ranevskaya. A bankrupt family, symbol of decaying czarist society, fails to save its estate as their cherry orchard is cleared for commercial housing by new owner Lopakhin, enterprising son of a serf.

Chert, impure, brittle type of flint. A cryptocrystalline variety of silica, its color can be white, yellow, gray,or brown. It occurs mainly in limestones and dolomites, and its origin is unknown.

Chesapeake, city in SE Virginia; scene of the Battle of Great Bridge (1775); formed by union of South Norfolk with Norfolk co. 1963. Industries: farming, fertilizer, lumber, steel equipment. Inc. 1963. Pop. (1980) 114,226.

Chesapeake Bay, inlet of the Atlantic Ocean in Virginia (S) and Maryland (N) at the mouth of the Susquehanna River; divides the Delmarva Peninsula from E Maryland and E Virginia; fed by Patuxent, Rappahannock, James, and Chester rivers. Part of intercoastal waterway, it is linked to Delaware River by the Chesapeake and Delaware Canal. First permanent English settlement in present-day United States was at Jamestown, Virginia, on Chesapeake Bay (1607); in 1608 John Smith explored and charted the bay. US Naval Academy was built at Annapolis 1845. Baltimore, on the Patapsco River, arm of the bay, is Maryland's largest city. Length: 193mi (311km). Width: 3–30mi (5–48km).

Chesapeake Retriever, water-loving hunting dog (sporting group) developed from English stock shipwrecked off the Maryland coast. The head is broad with a short, pointed muzzle. Small ears hang loose, and yellowish eyes are wide-set. A medium-length body is slightly higher in the hindquarters; feet are webbed; and the tail is 12–15in (30.5–38cm) long. The thick, short dark brown to deadgrass color coat is particularly water- and cold-resistant. Average size: 23–26in (58.5–66cm) high at shoulder; 65–75lb (29.5–34kg). *See also* Sporting Dog.

Chess, board game for two players. Play is conducted on a square board of 64 alternately colored squares. Each player receives 16 chessmen, of one color. There are 8 pawns, 2 knights, 2 bishops, 2 rooks (or castles), 1 queen, and 1 king. The pieces are arranged in a predetermined order on the board, and each piece has a designated order of movement. The game is "pure" in that no luck or dice are involved. The object of the game is to trap, or checkmate, the opponent's king. It is believed that a version of the modern game originated in India in the 6th century.

Chester, port city in SE Pennsylvania, 14mi (22km) SW of Philadelphia on Delaware River; industrial and commercial center; site of Pennsylvania Military College (1821), Penn-Morton College, Crozer Theological Seminary (1867), Caleb Pusey House (1683), noted as the oldest English house in the state, Old Court House (1724), Pennsylvania's oldest civic building. Industries: shipbuilding, steel, automobiles, pharmaceuticals, electronics, oil refining, paper, textiles, chemicals. Settled 1644 by Swedish and Dutch settlers; inc. 1866. Pop. (1980) 45,794.

Chesterton, G(ilbert) K(eith) (1874–1936), English essayist, novelist, and poet. His Father Brown stories, concerning the detective work of a wordly wise priest, first appeared in 1911. He wrote many essays on social and political themes. His novels include *The Napoleon of Notting Hill* (1904) and *The Man Who Was Thursday* (1908). He became a Roman Catholic in 1922, after which he published *St. Francis of Assisi* (1923) and *St. Thomas Aquinas* (1933).

Chestnut, deciduous tree native to temperate areas of the northern hemisphere. It has lance-shaped leaves and furrowed bark. Male flowers hang in long catkins and female flowers are solitary or clustered at base of catkins. The prickly husked fruits open to reveal 2–3 nuts. The American chestnut *(Castanea dentata),* once common, has been almost wiped out by blight. Other species bearing single-nut fruits are called chinquapin. There are four species. Family Fagaceae. *See also* Chinquapin.

Chestnut Blight, a highly destructive disease that has nearly wiped out the American chestnut. The blight is caused by a fungus *(Endothia parasitica)* that produces cankers in the vital cambium layer of the stem and branches. Chinese and Japanese chestnuts are resistant to the disease.

Chevalier, Maurice (1888–1972), French singer and actor. A star of the French music halls, he first appeared in the United States in the operetta *Dédé* (1921). His manner was breezy and casual, he almost always appeared in a jauntily tipped straw hat to sing songs such as "Louise" and "Mimi." Among his films were the musicals *Gigi* (1958), *Can-Can* (1960), and *Fanny* (1961).

Cheviot Hills, range running SW-NE along English-Scottish border. Highest point is The Cheviot, 2,676ft (816m), in Northumberland. Length: 35mi (56km).

Chevrotain, or mouse deer, small, even-toed, hoofed mammal from C Africa and SE Asia. Resembling deer, they have small, hornless heads, pointed snouts, and slim legs. Most are brown with white spots and stripes. The males have small upper tusks. Height: 14in (35cm) at shoulder; family Tragulidae; genera *Hyemosuchus* and *Tragulus;* there are 7 species.

Cheyenne, capital city of Wyoming, 10mi (16km) N of Colorado border; seat of Laramie co; a leading town in the Old West, frequented by Calamity Jane, Buffalo Bill, and Wild Bill Hickok. Industries: packing plants, oil refineries. Founded 1867 by officers of US Army and Union Pacific Railroad; inc. 1869. Pop. (1980) 47,283.

Cheyenne, large Algonquian-speaking North American Indian tribe whose home was originally in Minnesota but who spread into the Red River region, the Platte, and into Wyoming. In the mid-18th century they allied with the Arapaho; about the same time they split evenly into the Northern and Southern Cheyenne. The Northern Cheyenne now live in Montana, around Tongue River, numbering about 2000; the Southern group made peace with their earlier enemies the Kiowa and settled in Oklahoma, where approximately 3500 Cheyenne-Arapaho now live. *See also* Arapaho.

Chiang Ch'ing (Jiang Qing) (1914–), the fourth wife of Chinese Communist leader Mao Tse-tung. A former Shanghai movie actress, she joined Mao in Yenan during the war against Japan. She emerged from relative obscurity in the 1960s to become a high-ranking party official and the leader of the Cultural Revolution faction. After Mao's death (1976), she came under strong political attack and, as one of the Gang of Four, was arrested in 1976 for attempting to seize power. She was sentenced to death (1981) but the sentence was suspended for two years and commuted to life imprisonment in 1983.

Chiang Ching-kuo (1909–), president of Nationalist China and elder son of Chiang Kai-shek, whom he succeeded as Taiwan's leader in 1975. Ching-kuo returned to China after spending 12 years in the Soviet Union and rose rapidly in the Nationalist government, becoming premier in 1972. He was elected president in 1978.

Chiang Kai-shek (1887–1975), key political leader in 20th-century China. He was head of the Nationalist Party (Kuomintang) and government from 1928 until his death. Successor to Sun Yat-sen, Chiang was a Japanese-trained military officer and the first commandant of the Whampoa Military Academy, whose graduates helped form his political power base. He consolidated his power from 1928, fighting rebellious warlords and opposing the Communists. During war with Japan (1937–45) he emerged as one of the "big four" global leaders. He was elected president of China in 1948 under a post-war constitution and retained the position after his government retreated to Taiwan in 1949. He married Soong Mei-ling in 1927 and became a Christian.

Chiaroscuro, art term for the opposition of light and dark in painting and graphics. Rembrandt and Caravaggio were skilled in its use.

Chiastolite, variety of andalusite, aluminum silicate (Al_2OSiO_4), found in metamorphic rocks. Orthorhombic system elongated prismatic crystals, which in cross-section show a black cross on a gray ground. Hardness 7.5; sp gr 3.1–3.2.

Chiba, city in Japan, on Tokyo Bay; capital of Chiba prefecture; important agricultural region; site of 8th-century Buddist temple, university (1949). Industries: textiles, paper. Pop. 659,000.

Chibcha, or **Muisca,** a late prehistoric culture in South America occupying the departments of Cundinamarca and Boyacá in Colombia; Bogotá and Tunja were the major centers. Between 1000–1541, when the Spaniards conquered the region, these people developed remarkable city-states; and with a total population of about 750,000 inhabitants, were one of the few to equal the Inca in political sophistication. Artistically, however, they produced inferior pottery, and their weaving and goldsmithing were inferior to that of their neighbors. The legend of El Dorado comes from the Chibcha custom of the king annually diving into Lake Guatavita covered with gold dust, which washed off in a sacrifical ceremony. In modern times, Chibcha refers to a contemporary American Indian language family whose speakers inhabit southern Panama and northern Colombia.

Chicago, city in NE Illinois, on SW shore of Lake Michigan; seat of Cook co and 2nd-largest US city, major industrial, commercial, cultural, and shipping center of the Midwest. A trading post under Jean Baptiste Point du Sable and John Kinzie in the late 1700s, it was site of Fort Dearborn military post 1803; with the construction of the Erie Canal and railroads, Chicago attracted more settlers. The River and Harbors Convention of 1847 attracted businessmen from outside the city, such as Cyrus McCormick, a manufacturer of farm equipment; settlers were put to work in newly established retail houses such as Marshall Field and Co., in the stockyards of Gurdon S. Hubbard's meat packing industry, and food processing plants. The city was the scene of the Chicago Fire (Oct. 8–10, 1871), the Haymarket Riot (labor uprising, 1886), and the Pullman Strike (1894). Chicago's Columbia Exposition (1893) introduced such contemporary ideas as electric transit systems and the commercial buildings of architects Louis H. Sullivan and Frank Lloyd Wright. Chicago became a noted cultural center in the late 19th and early 20th centuries, with the establishment of the Chicago Symphony Orchestra, a city opera company, and literary magazines. Chicago contains the largest railroad terminal in the world, and O'Hare International Airport, busiest US commercial airport; home of several professional sports teams: Chicago Cubs and Chicago White Sox (baseball), Chicago Bears (football), Chicago Black Hawks (hockey), and the Chicago Bulls (basketball); site of McCormick Place, convention center, Merchandise Mart, Museum of Science and Industry, Art Institute of Chicago, the Newberry Library, and the Library of International Relations; colleges include the University of Chicago (1890), Northwestern University (1851), University of Illinois (1946), Loyola University (1869), Chicago State University. Industries: steel, chemicals, machinery, plastics, furniture, metalworking, food processing. Inc. 1837. Pop. (1980) 3,005,072.

Chicago School of Architecture, late 19th-century US development of commercial building design that used the principle of metal framing to achieve great height in buildings. The all-steel skeleton, first employed here, became the standard method of skyscraper construction. Dankmar Adler, Louis Sullivan, Daniel Burnham, John Root, William Holabird, and Martin Roche were the main practitioners.

Chicanos, term used by Mexican-Americans to describe themselves. The term stems from the Aztec word "Meshicano." The term became popular in the late 1960s as a result of Cesar Chavez's efforts to organize migrant Mexican farm workers and also as a result of a 1967 land dispute that sought to have much of the southwestern United States returned to its original Mexican owners.

Chichén Itzá, chief city and shrine of the combined Toltec and Maya peoples in Yucatán, Mexico, between AD 11th and 13th centuries. Remains include temple-pyramids, an astronomical observatory, and a sacrificial well. After 1200 Chichén Itzá lost its preeminence to nearby Mayapan. Period of occupation *c.*600–1450.

Chichester, cathedral city in S England, 13mi (21km) NE of Portsmouth; market town for agriculture and livestock; many Roman architectural remains; site of Norman cathedral (begun 1090). Pop. 93,200.

Ch'i-ch'i-ha-erh (Qiqihaer, or Tsitsihar), city and port in China, on Nen River near Great Khingan Mts. Industries: locomotives, machine tools, paper products, cement. Founded 1691. Pop. 760,000.

Chichimec, name applied to the scattered, heterogeneous groups of Indians living to the north and west of the Toltec and Aztec empires of central Mexico. Hunters and warriors, they successfully resisted Aztec and Spanish domination.

Chickadee, any of several North American titmice whose calls resemble a whistled "chick-a-dee." Chickadees are small and plump, with short, rounded wings, stubby bills, dark caps and bibs, and light cheeks. The typical black-capped chickadee *(Parus atricapillus)* of E North America is an active, easily tamed bird that feeds on seeds and insects. It grows to about 5in (13cm). Its nests—often in tree stumps—hold 5 to 9 brown-speckled white eggs that hatch in 12 days. Family Paridae; genus *Parus. See also* Titmouse.

Chickasaw, small, fiercely independent and warlike North American Indian tribe closely related to the Muskhogean-speaking Choctaw, occupying N Mississippi-Tennessee lands from Memphis into neighboring Alabama. They were far more important in history than their numbers indicate; allied with the English, they were hostile to the French and Spanish but quite friendly with Americans. Being slaveholders, during the Civil War they joined the Confederacy with their Choctaw brothers, for which they were punished severely by the loss of their lands. About 6000 now live in Oklahoma.

Chicken, most important domesticated bird in the world. It is the major source of eggs and an important meat source, supporting a specialized and widespread food industry. Chickens are also raised for exhibitions and scientific use. These light-skeletoned birds have short weak wings, strong legs, chin wattles, and a head comb. Males are known as cocks; females as hens; and castrated males as capons. Various breeds have been developed for particular use. Some, such as Rhode Island, Wyandotte, and Plymouth Rock, are raised for meat and eggs. Others, such as White Plymouth Rock, Cornish, and Rock Cornish, mainly supply meat. The White Leghorn is an excellent egg producer. Miniature bantams, the long-tailed Japanese Yokohama, and others are raised for ornament. Species *Gallus domesticus.*

Chicken Pox, or varicella, contagious virus-caused disease usually of children. Early symptoms are mild headache, low fever, general malaise, followed within a day by small blisters surrounded by redness usually visible first on the torso. Recovery is rapid with little or no scarring. Antihistamine is often prescribed to relieve itching.

Chick-pea, also dwarf pea, garbanzo, chich, gram; bushy annual cultivated from antiquity in S Europe and Asia for its pealike seeds, it is now also grown in Africa and the Americas. Seeds are eaten boiled or roasted; sometimes ground as a coffee substitute. Family Leguminosae; species *Cicer arietinum.*

Chickweed, common name for a spreading annual, native to Europe and naturalized throughout temperate regions. Its drooping stems grow to about 12in (30cm). Having opposite oblong leaves about 2.5in (6cm) long, the small white flowers are about 0.5in (1.3cm) wide. Chickweed is a garden weed in North America. Family Caryophyllaceae; species *Stellaria media.*

Chicle, a natural gum, available in reddish-brown pieces and consisting of the coagulated milky juice of the sapodilla *(Achras zapota),* a fruit tree of tropical America. First tried as a substitute for rubber, chicle became the chief ingredient of chewing gum by the end of the 19th century. In the 1940s it began to be replaced by synthetics and now has little commercial value.

Chicopee, city in SW Massachusetts, at the confluence of the Chicopee and Connecticut rivers. Indus-

President and Madame Chiang Kai-shek

Lydia Maria Child

Chile

tries: rubber products, sporting goods, firearms, and machinery. Settled 1641; inc. 1890. Pop. (1980) 55,112.

Chicory, perennial weedy plant. Its leaves are used cooked or as salad greens and the fleshy roots are ground for mixing with or substituting for coffee. Chicory has bright blue, daisylike flowers. When grown only for its leaves, plant tops are cut off, forcing it to produce a leafy head that is sometimes called French endive. Height: 6ft (1.8m). Family Compositae; species *Chichorium intybus.*

Chi Cygni. *See* Cygnus.

Chiem (Chiemsee) Lake, largest lake in West Germany, 40mi (64km) ESE of Munich; outlet is Alz River. Contains three islands; the largest is site of a palace imitating Versailles, built in late 19th century by Louis II of Bavaria. Area: 31sq mi (80sq km).

Ch'ien Lung (1711–99), fourth Manchu emperor of China (1736–96). The Ch'ien Lung emperor helped China to the apex of its power under the Manchus, taking Tibet (1751) and other regions. He also encouraged literature and art, and brought China into closer contact with Europe and into a period of unmatched prosperity during which the population more than doubled.

Chigger, also called harvest mite, or red bug, tiny, red larva of some kinds of mites found worldwide. Adults lay eggs on plants and hatched larvae find a host animal or human, in whom their bites cause a severe rash and itching. Length: 0.01in (.25mm). Order Acarina; family Trombiculidae. *See also* Mite.

Chihuahua, largest state in Mexico, on North-Mexican Plateau; climate and terrain vary from cool mountains (W), mild (central), to arid desert (E); city of Chihuahua, the capital of the state, is site of beautiful colonial cathedral and is famous breeding center for miniature Mexican dogs named after city. Industries: zinc, lead, copper, gold mining, forestry, livestock raising, tourism, beans, cotton, coats, potatoes, fruit. Founded (state) 1560 as Spanish settlement; (city) 1700. Area: (state) 95,400sq mi (247,086sq km). Pop. (state) 1,730,012; (city) 363,850.

Chihuahua, tiny terrierlike dog (toy group) descended from the 9th-century Techichi, dog of the Central American Toltec Indians. It has an appledome skull; short, pointed nose; large, wide-set eyes; and large, erect ears. The level-backed body is set on straight legs with small feet. The long, sickle-shaped tail is held in a loop over the back. There are two types of coat: the smooth is soft, close, and glossy with a ruff on the neck; the long is flat or slightly curly, feathered on the feet and legs, with a large ruff around the neck and plumed tail. Coat may be any color. Average size: 5in (12.5cm) high at shoulder; to 6lb (2.5kg). *See also* Toy Dog.

Chikamatsu Monzaemon (1653–1725), Japanese dramatist, b. as Sugimori Nobumori. Writing mainly for the puppet theater, Chikamatsu wrote over 160 plays and is perhaps the greatest Japanese dramatist. His writings were mostly historical romances and domestic tragedies, including *The Love Suicides at Amijima* (1703) and *The Battles of Coxinga* (1715), which are still performed today.

Child, (Sir) John (died 1690), English colonial official. The first person to control all of the East India Company's Indian factories (1686–90), his use of military power to gain territory for the company and his un-

scrupulous behavior led to rebellion and war. He was deputy-governor of Bombay (1679–81) and president of Surat (1682–90). Child engaged in war with the Mogul emperor of Delhi and when Child's province, Surat, was seized, his removal was one of the peace conditions.

Child, Lydia Maria (1802–80), US author and reformer, b. Medford, Mass. During 1826–34 she edited *Juvenile Miscellany,* the first US children's periodical. An ardent abolitionist, she wrote *Appeal in Favor of That Class of Americans Called Africans* (1833) and edited the *National Anti-Slavery Standard* (1841–49). She was also an advocate of woman suffrage.

Child Development, study of the changes that occur in children from conception to adolescence. First called child psychology, the field first focused on such topics as weaning, feeding schedules, and toilet training. The scope is now broader, including all factors—hereditary and environmental, physical and emotional—that interact as children grow up. *See also* Developmental Psychology.

Childe Harold's Pilgrimage (1812–18), autobiographical, romantic poem by Lord Byron, divided into 4 cantos, in Spenserian stanzas. The poem tells of a young man's disillusionment with his easy life and his subsequent wanderings through Europe.

Childeric I (436–81), king of the Salian Franks (458–81). With Roman aid he defeated the Visigoths at Orléans (463). He later defeated the Saxons and the Alemanni (463). He was succeeded by his son, Clovis I. In 1653 his tomb was found at his capital near Tournai, Belgium.

Childeric II (653?–673), king of Austrasia (660–673). He was the last Merovingian king to attempt to rule independently of the Carolingian mayors of the palace. He seized Neustria and Burgundy from the mayors but was assassinated in the same year.

Childeric III Frankish king (r.741–751), last of Merovingians. Rule was entirely subject to control of the mayors of the palace, the Carolingians. Pepin the Short deposed Childeric (751).

Child Marriage, marriage in which one or both participants are children. Since sexual and romantic attachments are obviously low in such a case, the marriage is usually arranged so as to provide an economic and social link between two families or groups. *See also* Marriage.

Child Psychiatry, study and treatment of childhood behavioral disorders, including childhood schizophrenia, early infantile autism, adjustment reactions of childhood, mental retardation, and learning disabilities.

Child Psychology. *See* Child Development; Developmental Psychology.

Children's Crusade (1212), movement to regain the Holy Land from the Muslims. The crusade was preached by two 12-year-old boys, Stephen of France and Nicholas of Germany. Encouraged by beliefs in angelic guidance and miracles, thousands of boys and girls, followed by bands of adult vagabonds, headed toward Marseilles, intending to cross the Mediterranean to Palestine. Although Pope Innocent III tried to end the crusade, some of the German children actually reached the Holy Land, where they disappeared. The French children were offered free transportation to Jerusalem by Hugh the Iron and William of Posquères,

who took them instead to Africa and sold them as slaves.

Children's Literature, in English-speaking countries, emerged as a distinct form in the 18th century. John Newbery, an English author, was the first serious publisher of children's books. He published a collection of Mother Goose rhymes in 1765. (A translation of Charles Perrault's *Tales of Mother Goose* had appeared in 1729). Newbery also published *A Pretty Little Pocket Book* (1744) and *Little Goody Two Shoes* (1765). In the 19th century, romanticism encouraged the creation of works for children, including the folk tales of the brothers Grimm and the fairy stories of Hans Christian Andersen. With Edmund Evans's improvements in color printing methods (1865), picture books flourished, as did the great illustrators, Kate Greenaway, Randolph Caldecott, Howard Pyle, and Arthur Rackham. Many 19th-century works of fantasy and adventure—Robert Louis Stevenson's *Treasure Island* (1880), Lewis Carroll's *Alice's Adventures in Wonderland* (1865), and *Through the Looking Glass* (1872), Louisa May Alcott's *Little Women* (1868), and Mark Twain's *Adventures of Huckleberry Finn* (1885) —are still popular with children and adults. In the 20th century the output of children's literature has been huge. In the United States, the Newbery Medal is awarded for outstanding children's books; the Caldecott Medal, for the best picture book. The Carnegie and Greenaway Medals are awarded in Great Britain.

Chile, Republic of, nation in SW South America. Most of its history during the 20th century has been marked by political upheaval between leftists and rightists.

Land and Economy. Long (about 2,500mi; 4,025km) and narrow (average width, about 110mi; 177km), Chile occupies a plain between the Pacific Ocean and the Andes, where some peaks reach above 20,000ft (6,100m). The Atacama Desert, containing nitrate and copper deposits, occupies about 70,000sq mi (181,300sq km) of the N. Chile's central zone provides rich soils, but they must be irrigated to produce wheat, alfalfa, corn, beans, peas, and fruits. S Chile is wet and cold. Broken into a maze of islands and peninsulas, it produces petroleum and lumber, and offers good sheep-raising country.

People. Mostly mestizos and European—Spaniards, Britains, Germans—the people speak Spanish and are about 90% literate. The Mapuche (Araucanian) Indians make up less than 2% of the population and live mainly in the S. Most people belong to the Roman Catholic church, although many attend irregularly. About 65% live in urban communities.

Government. According to its constitution, Chile should have a president and a two-house legislature elected by citizens 21 and over who can read and write. But in 1973, the military overthrew the leftist government that had won control in 1970, disbanded the legislature, and ordered all political parties to become inactive.

History. In the mid-1500s, Pedro de Valdivia founded settlements in Chile and encouraged colonists to come there. José de San Martín and Bernardo O'-Higgins defeated the Spanish in Chile in 1818 and guaranteed the country independence. By winning a victory over Bolivia and Peru in 1883, Chile gained the Atacama Desert. In 1938 the people elected a left-of-center president, Pedro Aguirre Cerda, and from then on gradually moved further left. Salvador Allende was elected president in 1970 and was Latin America's first freely elected Marxist chief of state. His nationalization of industries, conservative position, and a disintegrating economy all contributed to the military coup in 1973 that resulted in his death. The military government, under the leadership of Augusto Pinochet Ugarte, has faced both domestic protests and international criti-

Chili

cism for persistent human rights violations. The nationalized economy under Allende has been reversed in favor of a free-market system.

Chili, hot red pepper raised commercially in Mexico and SW United States. Also called cayenne pepper, it is an annual with ovate leaves and white or greenish-white flowers that produce seedpods. When dried, this pod is ground into a condiment. Height: 1–6ft (30–82cm). Family Solanaceae; species *Capsicum frutescens.*

Chiltern Hills, range of chalk hills in S central England, extending NE from Goring Gap in the Thames Valley, through Oxfordshire, Buckinghamshire, and Bedfordshire, to the East Anglian heights; formerly densely wooded, yielding beech for furniture. Highest point is Coombe Hill, 852ft (260m). Length: 55mi (89km).

Chimaera, or **ratfish,** also rabbit fish, elephant fish, ghost shark, cartilaginous, deep water fish with short nose, long poison spine at dorsal fin, and ratlike tail. Its liver oil is used in precision equipment. Length: 3ft (91.4cm); weight: 35lb (16kg). Family Chimaeridae; species, about 28 including Pacific *Hydrolagus collei. See also* Chondrichthyes.

Chimbote, port city on coast of W central Peru, approx. 250mi (403km) NNW of Lima; suffered severe damage in 1970 earthquake. Industries: steel, fishing, fish meal. Pop. 159,045.

Chimkent (Čimkent), city in S Kazakh SSR (Central Asian) USSR, in W foothills of Tien Shan Mts; capital of Chimkent oblast; industrial center on Turkistan-Siberian railway; site of teachers' college and museum; founded 12th century as caravan center on Silk Road to China; Russia gained control 1864. Industries: fruit canning, lead smelting, natural gas, chemical and lead works. Pop. 303,000.

Chimney Swift, small, sooty brown bird with long tapering wings that breeds in E and C North America. It attaches its nest with gluey saliva to an inside vertical chimney wall. It feeds on insects. The female lays white glossy eggs (4–5). They migrate with their young to Central and South America for the winter. Length: 6–12in. (15–30cm). Species *Chaetura pelagica.*

Chimpanzee, gregarious, intelligent great ape of tropical Africa. Chimpanzees are mostly black and powerfully built. A smaller chimpanzee of the Congo region is sometimes classified as separate species. Chimpanzees often nest in trees but spend most waking time on ground searching for fruits and nuts. They are quite communicative and, in captivity, have learned a limited human vocabulary. Height: 4.5ft (1.3m); weight: 150lb (68kg). Species *Pan troglodytes, Congo Pan paniscus. See also* Primates.

China, History of, dates back more than 3,000 years. Skeletal fragments and pottery shards found in the 1923 excavations of limestone hills SW of Peking pointed to the existence of human life in the area 500,-000 years ago; 20,000 years ago evidence of modern man appeared. With marked ethnic and regional differences, an authentic, persistent culture appeared to develop from within the area in a pattern of exalted culture, invasion by barbarians leading to a period of decay and decline, and another high cultural plane once the invaders were expelled. The first recorded dynasty was the Shang (c.1600–1030 BC) with royal houses, carvings on stone, and script. Evidence of merchants first appeared in the Chou dynasty (1030–221 BC). Iron was used, astronomy analyzed, music developed, and Confucius lived. In the Ch'in dynasty (221–206 BC) the first centralized government was organized by an emperor, who burned antagonistic books, and construction of the Great Wall began. The peaceful Han dynasty (206 BC–AD 220) rivaled Rome in wealth, power, and prestige. Foreign trade flourished;

Buddhism emerged; and astronomy and literature were studied. Warfare, invasions, and Taoism appeared from 220–581, followed by a period of construction within the country in the Sui period (581–618). The first historical encyclopedia, scientific studies, and the only female emperor in Chinese history came in the T'ang dynasty (618–907). Printing emerged in the politically chaotic years of 907–960, and the Sung dynasty (960–1279) developed civil service examinations, paper currency, modern cities, trading ships, gunpowder, political parties, and the magnetic needle. Kublai Khan, founder of the Yuan dynasty (1264–1368), continued intellectual advances and building. Marco Polo wrote of his reign. A decline at the close of the Yuan period continued into the Ming dynasty (1368–1644); despots suppressed opposition. Paintings, porcelains, and rugs were produced, and Roman Catholic missionaries introduced Western culture. Conquest of China by Manchu peoples brought the Chi'ing (Manchu) dynasty (1644–1911), a period of European imperialist expansion to seek raw materials and markets for products and to trade in opium. The United States promoted the Open Door Policy, giving all nations equal access to China's trade. In the Boxer Uprising (1900) anti-Western Chinese attempted unsuccessfully to oust all foreigners. Reforms to save China by overthrowing the Manchus came too late. In 1911 the emperor abdicated. A republic was established with Sun Yat-sen its first president but in 1912 Sun resigned in favor of Yuan Shih-K'ai, whose repressive policies outlawed Sun's radical Kuomintang party. In 1921 Sun set up a rival government in Canton with aid from the newly formed Chinese Communist party and the USSR. Chiang Kai-shek led the Kuomintang army in victory, but then reversed Sun's policy of cooperation with the Communists and executed many leaders. In 1928, Chiang organized a Nationalist government in Nanking and received foreign recognition. The rival Communist government was set up in the early 1930s in Kiangsi; however, Chiang's opposition forced them on a Long March (1934) to Shensi prov. where they reorganized and spread their philosophy among the peasants. Mao Tse-tung emerged as their leader. At the end of World War II, full scale war broke out between the hostile factions as they fought for territory evacuated by the Japanese. Inflation, official corruption, and famine weakened the Nationalists and support shifted to the Communists. Peking fell to them in January 1949. Other major cities followed, and on Oct. 1, 1949, the Communists proclaimed a central people's government. The Nationalist government moved to Taiwan. Each government has since claimed to be the legitimate government of China, and does not recognize the other. In 1971 the United Nations recognized the People's Republic of China, unseating Taiwan, resulting in its loss of some international prestige. Any rapprochement between the two governments in the near future seems unlikely. *See also* China, People's Republic of; China, Republic of.

China (Zhongguo), People's Republic of, independent nation in Asia, also known as Communist China. With 22 provinces and 5 autonomous regions, China contains 20% of the world's population. It has passed through domestic and foreign wars to the present Communist government.
  Land and Economy. There are fertile plains and deltas in the E watered by three great rivers (Yangtze, Yellow, and Si). Mountains separate it from Manchuria and Mongolia on the N; the Himalayas on the S. China is the third-largest country in the world. It is the world's largest producer of rice and the third-largest coal producer. Eighty percent of its trade is with free-world countries, with major imports of machinery, fertilizer, and grains and exports of raw materials, agricultural products, and textiles.
  People. The largest ethnic group is Han Chinese (94%), and the national language is the Peking dialect of Mandarin Chinese. Religion has been discouraged by the state. In pre-Communist China there were Buddhists, Confucianists, Taoists, Muslims, and Roman Catholics. Two major goals have been control of population growth and the expansion of education.
  Government. The Constitution of the People's Republic (1978) theoretically provides that power be shared by the National People's Congress, its standing committee, and the party leadership. In fact, government reins are held by the Communist party structure.
  History. In the 1920s, when China was an unstable republic, Chiang Kai-shek organized the country under a coalition of Nationalists, Soviet advisors, and the Communists, an association lasting until 1927 when Chiang drove the Communists out. This precipitated the 1934–35 Long March to Shensi prov. where the Communists reorganized, spread their philosophy, and in 1949 defeated Chiang, who fled to Taiwan. On Oct. 1, 1949, the People's Republic of China was born under the leadership of Chairman Mao Tse-tung.
  Under Chairman Mao and Premier Chou En-lai, China long remained isolated from world economic and diplomatic affairs, although it took possession of

Tibet (1950) and fought in the Korean War. The Cultural Revolution of the late 1960s sought to revitalize revolutionary policies and was indicative of internal power struggles. China's admission to the United Nations in place of Taiwan (1971) showed China's increased importance in world affairs. The deaths of Mao and Chou, in 1976, led to internal disputes, with moderates emerging as the new leaders and discrediting left-wing elements led by Mao's widow, Chiang Ch'ing, and her associates, the so-called Gang of Four. By 1981 moderate Deng Xiaoping was firmly in control. He favored strong ties with the West, and in 1979 diplomatic relations with the United States were established. His program of rapid economic expansion, although curbed by inflation and rising foreign deficit, was somewhat successful and economic reforms were announced in the mid-1980s.

China, Republic of (Taiwan), independent state, also known as Nationalist China, primarily on the island of Taiwan, 90mi (145km) off SE coast of mainland China. The government was established by Gen. Chaing Kai-shek's Kuomintang government in 1948 after Communists captured the mainland. Taiwan is claimed by the People's Republic of China as one of its provinces.
  Land and Economy. Taiwan, 240mi (386km) long, also includes the Pescadores Island, Quemoy, and Matsu. Mountains cover the E; the W is fertile and cultivated. The climate is semi-tropical, and the country is in the typhoon and earthquake belt. Light manufacturing has replaced agriculture as the dominant factor in the economy.
  People. The Taiwanese are descended from migrating mainlanders, aboriginal Philippine tribes, and over 2,000,000 who came from mainland China since 1949. Mandarin is taught in schools, and Buddhism-Taoism is the principal religion. Literacy is 84%.
  Government. The 1947 constitution provided for elected National Assembly. After Chiang Kai-shek's death in 1975 power passed to his son, Chiang Ching-kuo. The nationalist Kuomingtang party dominates.
  History. Migrations came from the mainland in the 17th century, the Dutch (1624–61), several Chinese warring dynasties, and in 1895 the Japanese. The republic has administered the island since the Japanese surrendered at the end of WWII. Taiwan's international position declined in the 1970s with the loss of its UN seat to mainland China in 1971 and the increasing diplomatic recognition of the Communist regime. However, the economy continued to develop, and although hopes of decreased tension with the mainland grew after Chiang Kai-shek's death, in 1975, a quick resolution to the two states' differences seemed unlikely during the 1980s.

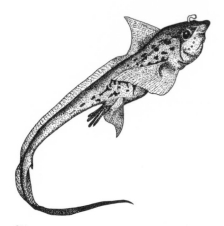

Chimaera

People's Republic of China

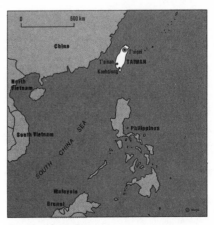

Republic of China (Taiwan)

China Clay, or kaolin, a fine white clay from weathered aluminous minerals that contain kaolinite as principal constituent. It remains white after firing and is used chiefly in manufacturing fine ceramics.

Chinch Bug, black insect, 0.17 to 0.2in (4.25–5mm) long, with white wings and red legs; a serious pest of grass, corn, wheat, and other grain in the eastern and central United States. Family Lygaeidae; species *Blissus leucopterus. See also* Hemiptera.

Chinchilla, small, soft-furred rodents native to South America that were hunted almost to extinction and are now bred in captivity for their fur, the most expensive of all animal skins. The fur is long and silky, silver to brown or blue gray with darker outer hairs, dense, and soft to the touch. Length: 9–15in (23–38cm); weight: 1–2lb (500–1000g). Family Chinchillidae.

Ch'in Dynasty (221–207 BC), the totalitarian state that unified all of China into a centralized area of control. It is noted for the building of the Great Wall and is infamous for the burning of books (213 BC) and persecution of scholars. It made legalist philosophy the basis for governmental control over the population. The English name for China stems from this time. *See also* Tsin Dynasty.

Chinese, language spoken by about 95% of the population of China and by many millions more in Taiwan, Hong Kong, Southeast Asia, and other countries. There are six major dialects, which are not mutually intelligible, of which the most important is Mandarin, spoken by about two-thirds of the population. Chinese is written in ideographs, which number in the thousands and date back several thousand years. It has twice as many speakers as any other language in the world. In 1979, the world was introduced to *Pinyin* (in use in mainland China since 1958), a new system for the spelling of Mandarin words in the Roman alphabet.

Chinese Architecture, architectural style that as early as the neolithic period used columns, not walls, to support roofs, faced houses south, and used bright colors. The characteristic Chinese roof with wide overhang and upturned eaves was probably developed in the Chou period (1027–c.256BC). The ground plan of temples and palaces—a walled complex with central axis—was established in the Han dynasty (202 BC–AD 220). In the same period, the practice of building residential units around a central courtyard containing an elaborately planned garden became standard. The pagoda derives from Buddhist influences, notably the Indian stupa, and dates from the 6th century.

Chinese Exclusion, series of laws to limit Chinese immigration into the United States. Skilled and unskilled Chinese laborers were barred from entering the United States by the Chinese Exclusion Act of 1882. Subsequent laws continued this policy, which was supported by labor leaders on racist and economic grounds. In 1943 Congress established an annual quota of 105 for immigration from China. The national origins quota system ended in the 1960s.

Chinese Lantern Plant, or winter cherry, perennial plant native to Japan and widely cultivated in gardens. The creeping stems bear large, ovate, long-stalked leaves and small white flowers that produce a red berry surrounded by a papery, lanternlike red calyx. Height: to 2ft (61cm). Family Solanaceae; species *Physalis.*

Chinese Literature. The oldest Chinese writing of any kind is found in the Shang dynasty (c.1600–c.1030 BC), but the oldest literature comes from the Chou dynasty (c.1030–221 BC). This period produced the canonical writings of Confucianism: the Five Classics, including the first poetry anthology *Shih ching* (Classic of Odes); and the Four Books, containing doctrinal writings, such as *The Book of Mencius.* Traditionally attributed to Confucius (c.551–479 BC), the *Shih ching* was probably in existence before his time. Also in this era Lao-tzu supposedly founded Taoism, a religious-magical reaction to the moral-political emphasis of Confucianism. During the Han dynasty (206 BC–AD 220), *fu* flourished; they were elaborate prose poems praising the dynasty. The golden age of Chinese literature arrived in the T'ang dynasty (618–907). Li Po, Wang Wei, and Tu Fu were the outsanding poets. In the Sung dynasty (960–1279) the novel, often historical, and the drama, stressing conflicts such as filial versus national loyalty, came into being. But the lyric poem has been the dominant form in Chinese literature. It is normally philosophical but with a quietness of tone and an emphasis on simple, routine experiences. In the first half of the 20th century the literature became greatly modernized. Under the Communists, strict censorship was imposed.

Chinese Music dates back at least 4000 years. Its importance was emphasized by Confucius (551–479 BC) and again later by the emperors of the Han dynasty (206 BC–AD 220). During the T'ang Dynasty (618–907) and the Sung Dynasty (960–1279), Chinese music entered its classical period; orchestras of 300 or more instruments were commonly used for ritual and court music. The Chinese tonal system is based on fifths. Chinese music may be generally classified into four types: sacred music, chamber music, folk music, and operatic music. Instruments used include those made of bamboo and wood, as well as metal bells and stone chimes.

Ch'ing Dynasty (1644–1911), also known as Manchu Dynasty, last great dynasty in China. The Manchus were tungusic tribesmen who invaded and took over Ming Dynasty China, keeping traditional Chinese patterns of rule but maintaining garrisons and separate quarters for themselves. They gradually became sinicized and provided China with a period of stability and prosperity until disrupted by Western imperialism. They were overthrown when the Chinese republic was founded. *See also* Manchu Dynasty.

Ch'ingtao (Qingdao, or Tsingtao), port city in E China, on Yellow Sea. Germany occupied city 1897 in retaliation for murder of two German missionaries by Chinese; leased as part of Shantung prov. from 1898 for 99 years. Modern city was constructed 1898–1914; Japan held it 1914–22 and 1938–45; site of US naval base 1945–49, when it fell to communists; seat of Shantung University (1926). Industries: textiles, food processing, tobacco, paper, diesel locomotives. Pop. 1,300,000.

Chinkiang. See Chen-Chiang.

Chino, city in S California, 30mi (48km) E of Los Angeles; site of state prison; business and processing hub for regional dairy and agricultural farms. Industries: mobile homes, textiles. Founded 1887; inc. 1910. Pop. (1980) 40,165.

Chinook, or Flathead (from their custom of deforming infant's heads as a beauty mark), American Indians living along the Pacific coast from the mouth of the Columbia River north to Grays Harbor in Washington. Though numbering less than 1000, the Chinook traveled widely and their language was used by many Indians and whites during the settlement period. Approxi-

mately 400 Chinook live on the Quinault and Warm Springs Reservations.

Chinquapin, deciduous tree native to United States and China. It has hairy leaves and twigs and single-seeded fruits. There are six species. Family Fagaceae; genus *Castanea.* Or, evergreen trees and shrubs native to E Asia and W United States. Family Fagaceae; genus *Castanopsis. See also* Chestnut.

Chios (Khios), island in E Greece, W of Turkey, in Aegean Sea; colonized by Ionians and occupied by Persians 494–79 BC; joined Delian League 478 BC; flourished under Byzantines AD 1st century; passed to Constantinople, Genoese, Ottomans, finally to Greece (1912); traditional birthplace of Homer. Industries: sheep and goats, figs, olives, marble quarries. Area: 350sq mi (907sq km). Pop. 53,942.

Chi Particles. *See* Quark.

Chipmunk, small, ground-dwelling squirrel native to North America and Asia. They carry food (nuts, berries, seeds) in cheek pouches and store it underground. Color varies but most are brown with one or more black-bordered, light stripes. Active tree-climbers in summer, they sleep much of the winter. Length: 5–6in (13–15cm) excluding tail. Family Sciuridae; genera *Eutamias* and *Tamias.*

Chippendale, Thomas (1718?–1779), English furniture designer and maker whose fame came not so much from his own works, although he was one of the great English craftsmen, as from the wide circulation of *The Gentleman and Cabinet-Maker's Director . . . ,* a trade catalogue illustrating the designs of his shop.

Chippewa, known in Canada as Ojibwa, the largest Algonquian-speaking tribe of North American Indians, inhabiting a region from Lake Superior and Lake Huron west to Turtle Mountain, North Dakota. The Chippewa drove the Sioux west onto the Plains, drove the Fox south, and repulsed the Iroquois. They were always a large tribe and today about 55,000 live along the United States-Canada border. In error, Longfellow based his poem Hiawatha upon Chippewa legend, even though the major character was Iroquois.

Chirac, (René) Jacques (1932–), French political figure, prime minister (1974–76, 1986–). A graduate of the Institut d'Études Politiques in Paris, he served as a military officer in Algeria, then did graduate work at the École Nationale d'Administration. He held several increasingly important civil service positions and was appointed to two cabinet posts before becoming premier in 1974. He resigned in 1976 and served as mayor of Paris from 1977, an office he retained after becoming prime minister a second time.

Chirico, Giorgio de (1888–1978), Greek-born Italian painter. Best known for disturbing landscapes and still lifes, mostly done before World War I, Chirico used exaggerated perspective in depicting empty and almost lifeless city spaces. Chirico founded "metaphysical painting," but later repudiated all modern art and studied the subjects and techniques of academic art.

Chiropractic, a type of medical practice based on the theory that the nervous system integrates all of the body's functions, including defense against disease, and that when the nervous system is impaired in any way—by, for example, "nerve interference" caused by even a slightly misplaced vertebra or other musculoskeletal part—there is decreased resistance to disease and pain. Chiropractors aim to remove nerve interference by manipulations of the musculoskeletal parts, particularly in the spinal region.

Chiru, or Tibetan antelope, medium-sized, slim-legged antelope native to plateaus of Tibet and considered sacred by Mongols. Its short, woolly hair is pale fawn with darker face and front of legs. Long, black, high-rising horns are carried only by males. It digs a deep depression as a shelter. Length: to 55in. (1.4m); height: to 32in (81cm) at shoulder. Family Bovidae; species *Fantholops hodgsoni. See also* Ruminant.

Chisholm v. Georgia (1793), first important US Supreme Court decision in which the court upheld the right of a citizen of one state to sue the government of another state. Strong opposition to this ruling led to the adoption of the 11th Amendment (1798), which overturned the decision.

Chital. *See* Axis Deer.

Chitimacha, tribe of Tunica-speaking North American Indians inhabiting the Grand River, Grand Lake, and Bayou Teche region in Louisiana. A strong tribe, they held off the French for many years. Today some 375 live around Charenton, La. Chitimacha basketry is highly prized for its color and intricacy of design.

Chiton, or coat of mail, simple mollusk found creeping on rocks along marine shores. Bilaterally symmetrical, its upper surface has eight overlapping shells; underneath are a large fleshy foot, degenerate head with mouth, gills, and mantle. Length: to 12in (30.5cm). Class Amphineura (or Polyplacophora); family Chitonidae; species include giant Pacific *Amicula stelleri.*

Chittagong, city in Bangladesh, S Asia, on Karnaphuli River; principal port of country and capital of Chittagong division; conquered 1666 by nawab of Bengal; ceded 1760 to British East India Co. Port facilities damaged 1971 in Indo-Pakistani War. Industries: jute, tea, oil, engineering works. Pop. 416,733.

Chivalry, code of ethics and behavior for knights in Western Europe between about the 11th and the 14th centuries. The term comes from the French word for knighthood, *chevalerie,* and the code was generally established by the 13th century. Combining Christian virtues and barbarian ferocity, a knight was expected to show unflinching courage, a passion for adventure, devotion to a lady of his choice, fair play, loyalty, generosity, and uprightness. He was expected to defend his lord, his lady, the Holy Church, and Christendom, as well as provide protection and show compassion for the weak and the injured. Although these virtues were probably rare in reality, the literature of the Middle Ages abounds with embodiments of the ideal.

Chives, perennial herb that smells like an onion, but does not have bulbous roots. The long hollow leaves have an onion-like flavor and are used as a seasoning. The flowers grow in rose-purple clusters. Family Liliaceae; species *Allium schoenoprasum.*

Chloral Hydrate, drug that in therapeutic doses produces natural-like sleep but with repeated use becomes addictive. Mixed with alcohol (as in a "Mickey Finn") or taken in large doses, it is dangerous and can result in death.

Chloramphenicol, widely known under the trade name Chloromycetin, an antibiotic effective against many disease-causing microorganisms. It should be used very cautiously because it can produce serious blood cell loss.

Chlorate, salt of chloric acid, containing the ion CLO_3^-. Chlorate salts are good oxidizing agents and sources of elemental oxygen. Sodium and potassium chlorates are used in explosives and also as weedkillers.

Chloride, salt of hydrochloric acid, or an organic compound containing chlorine. The best known example is common table salt, sodium chloride (NaCl).

Chlorine, common nonmetallic element (symbol Cl) of the halogen group, first discovered (1774) by Swedish chemist K.W. Scheele. It occurs in common salt (NaCl), carnallite, and sylvite. The element, a greenish-yellow gas which is extracted by electrolysis of brine, is extensively used in purifying drinking water, making wood pulp, and in the manufacture of a vast range of compounds. Chemically it is a reactive element, combining with most metals. Properties: at. no. 17; at. wt. 35.453; sp. gr. 3.214 g dm^{-3}; melt. pt. −149.76°F (−100.98°C); boil. pt. −30.28°F (−34.6°C); most common isotope Cl^{35} (75.53%). *See also* Halogen Elements.

Chloroform, colorless volatile sweet-smelling liquid (formula $CHCl_3$) prepared by the chlorination of methane or the action of bleaching powder on acetone, acetaldehyde, or ethanol. It is used in the manufacture of fluorocarbons, as an insecticide, solvent, and anesthetic. Properties: sp gr 1.48; melt. pt. −82.3°F (−63.5 °C); boil. pt. 142.2−F (61.2°C).

Chlorophyll, one of a group of pigments present in the chloroplasts of plants that absorb light for photosynthesis. Chlorophylls are responsible for the green color of plants; in some plants, however, the green color may be masked by the presence of other photosynthetic pigments. There are several types: chlorophyll A (formula $C_{55}H_{72}O_5N_4Mg$) is present in all photosynthetic plants except bacteria; chlorophyll B ($C_{55}H_{70}O_6N_4Mg$) occurs in higher plants and green algae; and chlorophylls C and D are present in some algae.

Chlorophyta. *See* Algae.

Chloroplast, the microscopic green structure within a plant cell in which photosynthesis takes place. The chloroplast is enclosed in a double membrane. Two pigments providing the green color (chlorophyll A and chlorophyll B) absorb the light energy that converts to chemical energy.

Chlorosis, in plant pathology, a yellowing or blanching of leaves of green plants caused by deficiencies of minerals, especially magnesium or potassium, or by plant parasites.

Chlorpromazine, widely known under trade name Thorazine, a synthetic drug, first developed as an antinauseant, but subsequently found to tranquilize, or calm, the central nervous system. Considered a major tranquilizer, it is used under close medical supervision in the treatment of schizophrenia and cases of severe anxiety or other mental illnesses.

Choanichthyes, subclaess of bony fish containing Crossopterygii (Coelacanth) and Dipnoi (lungfish). Most common during the Devonian period (345–395 million years ago), most members of this group are now extinct. They are characterized by bony skeleton, paired fins with a central skeletal axis, nostrils opening through the face and into the mouth, and a well-developed air bladder. Members of this group provided the evolutionary stock for amphibians. Class Osteichthyes.

Choctaw, one of the largest tribes of Muskhogean-speaking North American Indians, located in SE Mississippi and part of Alabama. An agricultural people closely related to the Chickasaw, they were generally at peace with the settlers, and remained neutral during the Revolution. As large slave-owners, they supported the South during the Civil War. A majority of the Choctaw moved to Oklahoma in 1830, where some 40,000 of their descendents still reside. *See also* Chickasaw.

Choiseul, Etienne Francois, Duc de (1719–85), French statesman. He fought with distinction in the War of Austrian Succession (1740–48), then entered the diplomatic service under Mme. de Pompadour's patronage. He served as ambassador to Rome (1754–57) and to Austria (1757–58), where he negotiated the marriage between Marie Antoinette and the future Louis XVI. As minister of foreign affairs (1758–70), he negotiated the Family Compact of 1761 between France, Spain, and other Bourbon rulers and the Treaty of Paris (1763) ending the Seven Years War. He annexed Lorraine in 1766 and Corsica in 1768. He supported the publication of the Encyclopédie in 1759 and aided suppression of the Jesuits in 1764. He was dismissed from court in 1770, mainly at the instigation of Mme. Du Barry.

Chola, south Indian dynasty. The Cholas established a kingdom in the areas around Tenjore and Tiruchirapalli and attacked Ceylon in the 2nd century, but were soon submerged by neighboring peoples. They rose again in the 9th century. Rajaraja I (*r.* 985–1014) and Rajendra I (*r.* 1014–44) extended their empire in India and attacked Ceylon. Rajendra I also organized a great naval expedition that attacked the Srivijaya empire in Sumatra. After this war the Chola empire dominated much of India, Ceylon, Southeast Asia, and what is now Indonesia. Revolts reduced the power of the empire in succeeding years, and the dynasty ended in 1279. Social and economic life and Hindu culture flourished under the Cholas, who built great monuments, temples, and irrigation systems. Village assemblies played an important role in local government in their state.

Cholecystitis, an inflammation of the gall bladder, most often associated with gallstones. In mild forms it produces indigestion, sometimes with nausea and vomiting, after eating fried or greasy foods. Severe or acute attacks usually require removal of the stone.

Cholera, acute disease caused by the bacteria *Vibrio cholerae* and occurring in epidemic form in tropical and subtropical areas with poor sanitation. Produces almost continuous, watery diarrhea, often accompanied by vomiting and muscle cramps; leads to severe dehydration. If untreated, more than half the victims die; but adequate care, including fluid replacement and antibiotics, can result in a very high recovery rate.

Cholesterol, white waxy sterol ($C_{27}H_{45}OH$) that occurs in plasma, blood cells, egg yolk, bile, etc, and is an important constituent of cell membranes. A diet rich in animal products may produce excess cholesterol in the blood, which is suspected of being a contributory factor in cardiovascular disease.

Choline, one of the B vitamins; necessary for the synthesis of fatty acids by the liver. Dietary sources are egg yolk, and some vegetable oils.

Cholinesterase, enzyme that breaks down the nerve transmitter acetylcholine at the nerve synapse. *See also* Acetylcholine.

Cholla, cactus characterized by cylindrical joints, native to North and South America. The tree cholla has loose, branching joints that cling to passers-by; height to 12ft (4m). The cane cholla has spectacular red flowers and persistent yellow fruit; height: to 8ft (2.5m). The Christmas cholla has clusters of olive-sized, red fruits that ripen in December; height: to 3ft (1m). Family Cactaceae; genus *Opuntia. See also* Opuntia.

Cholula (Cholula de Rivadabia), town in E central Mexico, 6mi (10km) W of Puebla; ancient center of Toltec and Aztec civilizations; city conquered and destroyed, and Indians massacred by Hernando Cortés (1519); site of ruins of famous pyramid Teocali de Cholula, sacred worship place to the Aztec god Quetzalcoatl, and several churches; popular tourist spot. Pop. 20,913.

Chondrichthyes, class of cartilaginous fish including Elasmobranchs (shark, ray, and skate) and Holocephali (chimaera). These marine fish have cartilaginous skeletons, well-developed lower jaw, paired fins, separate gill openings, no air bladder, bony teeth, and placoid scales. Fertilization is internal; males have specialized pelvic fins or claspers. The chimaera is intermediate in development between sharks and bony fish. It has separate anal and urogenital openings and the upper jaw is fused to the cranium, as in bony fish. Chondrichthyes developed during the late Devonian period (345 million years ago). There are about 600 living species.

Chondrule, spheroidal body, usually under 1/10in (3mm) embedded in a ground mass and common to chondrite stony meteorites. *See* Stony Meteorite.

Ch'ŏngjin, city in NE North Korea, on the Sea of Japan; controlled in the 1930s by Japan, which developed the Musan iron mines; severely damaged during the Korean War (1950–53). Industries: iron, steel, sardines. Pop. 200,000.

Chŏnju, city in South Korea, 120mi (193km) S of Seoul; burial place of the founder of the Yi dynasty; richest rice-growing and most densely populated region in South Korea. Industries: fans, paper, ginger. Pop. 262,816.

Chopin, Frédéric (1810–1849), composer and pianist, b. Poland of Polish and French parents. After 1831 he lived in Paris and had a long love affair with George Sand. Chopin is regarded as one of the greatest composers for the piano. His music is highly melodic, lyrical, romantic, and original, and important in the development of piano techniques. Although he composed two piano concertos and three piano sonatas, his best-known works are numerous short pieces—ballades, etudes, nocturnes, waltzes, preludes, impromptus. Polish nationalism inspired his mazurkas and polonaises.

Chord, in music, the simultaneous occurrence of three or more musical tones of different pitch. How notes are distributed and spaced within a chord is called chording. Depending on the placement of notes, chords can be broken down into the categories anomalous, characteristic, common, inverted, or transient. The study of harmony involves the functions of the various chords and classifies them as dominant, subdominant, and the diminished 7th, among others.

Chordate, vertebrates and some marine animals characterized by a rodlike, cartilaginous, supporting structure called a notochord at some point in their life cycle. Other shared features are gill slits, hollow nerve cord along the back, bilaterally symmetrical body, and segmented muscles and nerves. Chordates are subdi-

Chiru

Frederick Chopin

Chow Chow

vided into three subphyla: urochordates—tunicate or seasquirt; cephalochordates—amphioxus; and vertebrates that have a notochord surrounded and replaced by bony or cartilaginous vertebrae. Hemichordates are wormlike marine animals (acorn worm and pterobranch) sometimes classified as chordates but generally put in a separate phylum. Phylum Chordata. *See also* Acorn Worm; Amphioxus; Tunicate; Vertebrate.

Chorea, any of several diseases involving involuntary jerking movements of parts of the body. One form, Sydenham's chorea, or St. Vitus dance, occurs in children, more often in girls, and is characterized by irregular muscular movements and abrupt jerks. Usually accompanied by an emotional disorder, it is self-limiting, usually subsiding in a few weeks or months. It may be associated with rheumatic fever. Another form of chorea, Huntington's chorea, is a rare hereditary disease that starts in early middle life with jerky motions and lack of coordination and gradually progresses with mental deterioration, emotional outbursts, and grotesque movements occurring, and finally death. Other rarer forms of chorea may occur during serious illnesses or may be present at birth.

Chorus, term derived from the Greek work *choros,* meaning a sacred dance with singing. A chorus is a group of singers who perform choral music in operas, oratorios, or concerts. Large church choirs are called choruses. Most modern choral music is written for four-part harmony.

Chou Dynasty (1122–221 BC), longest and most famous of Chinese dynasties, noted for its achievements in government, literature, philosophy, and art. The founder, Wu Wang, overthrew the Shang dynasty. During the Spring and Autumn period (722–481 BC), Confucius and Lao Tze founded schools of thought that gave thrust to all subsequent Chinese culture. It was an age when Chinese culture expanded throughout most of present-day China.

Chou En-lai (Zhou Enlai) (1898–1976), the leading international spokesman and prime minister of the People's Republic of China from its founding in 1949 until his death. Educated in Japan and Europe, he rose to high position in the Communist party at an early age and remained its most skilled negotiator and international contact man. He participated in the famous Long March and represented the Communists in Chungking during World War II. His negotiating skills played a crucial role in the eventual Communist victory in China.

Chow Chow, ancient Chinese hunting dog (nonsporting group) brought to West in 1780. The only dog to have a blue-black tongue, its massive head has a short, broad muzzle and full, hanging lips. The small, erect ears tilt forward slightly. A short, compact body is set on heavy-boned legs. The tail is carried close to the back. The dense, coarse coat of any color stands straight out and forms a large ruff around the neck. Average size: 18–20 in (45.5–51cm) high at shoulder; 50–60lb. (23–27kg). *See also* Nonsporting Dog.

Chrétien de Troyes, romance writer of northern France (fl. *c.* 1160–1190), noted for his tales of King Arthur and his knights. Besides a number of translations of Latin poems, he wrote at least seven romances, including *Lancelot, Ywain,* and *Perceval.* Although he derived his subject matter from oral tradition and written sources, his contributions to romance literature include elaboration of plot structure and character development.

Christ. See Jesus Christ.

Christ, Churches of, once known as Campbellites, originated in the United States in 1811 by Alexander Campbell. An outgrowth of the Disciples of Christ, it derives unity from the Bible, the only basis of faith. It is a movement back to Scripture. There are about 2,-400,000 members. *See also* Disciples of Christ.

Christchurch, city on E South Island, New Zealand, at N base of Banks Peninsula; site of University of Canterbury (1873) and its associated School of Arts (1882). Industries: fertilizer, rubber, woolens, electrical goods, furniture. Founded 1850 as a Church of England settlement. Pop. 325,710.

Christian III (1503–59), king of Denmark and Norway (1534–59). The son of Frederick I, Christian was elected king in 1534. He established Lutheranism in Denmark in 1536, broke the power of the Hanseatic League, and instituted social and educational reforms.

Christian V (1646–99), king of Denmark and Norway (1670–99), son of Frederick III. Although a weak despot, his minister Griffenfeld made him absolute monarch. A statute book, *Christian V's Danish Law,* replaced old provincial laws.

Christian X (1870–1947), king of Denmark (1912–47) and Iceland (1919–44). He succeeded Frederick VIII. During his reign universal suffrage was established (1915) and social welfare policies were consolidated. He tried to remain neutral during WWI and heroically defied the Germans during occupation, 1940–45.

Christian Architecture, Early, architectural period (330–800) dominated by the basilica churches. Commonly erected over the burial place of the saint to whom the church was dedicated, they synthesize the features and materials of earlier Roman buildings, secular and sacred. Typically, closely spaced columns support a simple entablature, or more widely spaced columns carry semi-circular arches up to the sanctuary and apse.

Christianity, religion based on belief in Jesus Christ as the Son of God. God revealed himself to man through Christ, who is seen as a prophet. Numerous Christologies, or theological understandings of Christ, have been developed. The historical reality of his life is understood, although treated differently in relation to the understanding of Christ as divine. Through his redemptive act, salvation is possible for man to attain. Different churches vary on the process of salvation.

Christianity is an historical religion, based on Judaism and shaped by the Western world. The first division within Christianity was that between the Eastern and Western churches. During the 16th century, the Reformation in England, which began as a reform within the church, led to the development of Protestantism. The major Christian divisions are Orthodox, Roman Catholicism, and Protestantism. Ecumenical movements today are attempting to unite the Christian churches in an effort to make Christianity an active, positive force in the world. *See also* Protestantism; Roman Catholic Church.

Christian Science, religious movement founded by the American Mary Baker Eddy (1821–1910). Its followers believe that mankind's physical and moral problems can be solved by means of prayer. Instruction is based on the Bible and Mrs. Eddy's book *Science and Health with Key to the Scriptures.* Divine Mind is used as a synonym for God, and man, as the "image and likeness of God," is regarded as the complete and flawless manifestation of this Mind.

Christie, (Dame) Agatha (Miller) (1891–1976), English author. A prolific and popular writer of detective stories, her novels have intricate plots and are often set in an upper-class setting in England. Her most famous characters are Hercule Poirot, a cunning but eccentric Belgian detective, and Miss Jane Marple, an elderly English village spinster-sleuth. Her novels include: *The Mysterious Affair at Styles* (1920), which introduced Poirot; *The Murder of Roger Ackroyd* (1926), considered a classic of the detective genre; *Murder at the Vicarage* (1930), which introduced Marple; *Murder on the Orient Express* (1934); *And Then There Were None* (1940); and *Curtain* (1975), ending the Poirot series. She also wrote plays, including *The Mousetrap* (1952) and *Witness for the Prosecution* (1953). *The Mousetrap* holds a world's record for the longest continuous run at one theatre (from 1952). Some romantic novels by her appeared under the name Mary Westmacott.

Christmas, religious celebration commemorating the birth of Jesus Christ. It is celebrated on December 25 in the West and, for the most part, in the East. One exception in the East is the Armenian Church, which celebrates Christmas on Jan. 6.

Christmas Cactus, Brazilian hybrid cactus widely cultivated for its striking flowers. In the wild, this cactus grows on trees or shrubs but produces its own food. It is pollinated by hummingbirds. A popular house plant, it needs more moisture and less sun than other cactus. Family Cactaceae; genus *Schlumbergera.*

Christmas Carol, A (1843), sentimental story by Charles Dickens. Ebenezer Scrooge, a miser who thinks Christmas is an unnecessary expense, is converted by horrific visions of his past, present, and future. His subsequent generosity saves the life of Tiny Tim, the crippled son of his clerk, Bob Cratchit.

Christmas Fern, North American evergreen fern common on rocky slopes, wooded streambanks, and in swamps. Its lustrous, tapering, green leaves cascade from a central rootstock. Height: to 2.5ft (76cm). Family Aspleniaceae; species *Polystichum acrostichoides. See also* Fern.

Christmas Island, largest atoll in Pacific Ocean, S of Hawaii and N of the equator; in Line Islands; discovered 1777 by Capt. James Cook; annexed by Britain 1888; site of nuclear tests by Britain (1950s) and United States (1962); sovereignty claimed by Britain and United States. Area: 222sq mi (575sq km). Pop. 477.

Christophe, Henri (1767–1820), Haitian revolutionary leader, president (1807–11), and king (1811–20). Born a free black on the island of Grenada, he participated in the armed struggle against the French and fought a civil war with the partisans of the mulatto Pétion. Christophe ordered the construction of the Citadelle, a fort overlooking present-day Cap Haitien, which cost 20,-000 Haitian lives.

Christopher, Saint, patron of ferrymen. A vast quantity of legend has grown up about this early martyr, who possibly perished during Decius' persecution, *c.*250. One legend has it that he took up carrying travelers across a river as a work of charity, among whom was Christ in the form of a child. He is considered to be a legendary figure and is no longer officially recognized as a saint by the Roman Catholic Church.

Chromite, an oxide mineral, ferrous chromic oxide ($FeCr_2O_4$) and the only ore of chromium. Separates early from magma when igneous rocks first form.

Cubic system octahedral crystals and granular masses. Weakly magnetic; black, metallic and opaque; hardness 5.5; sp gr 5.1.

Chromium, metallic element (symbol Cr) of the first transition series, first isolated in 1798. Chief ore is chromite ($FeO.CrO_3$). Chromium is a dull gray metal but takes a high polish and is extensively used as an electroplated coating. It is also an ingredient of many special steels. Properties: at. no. 24; at. wt. 51.996; sp. gr. 7.19; melt. pt. 3434°F (1890°C); boil. pt. 4500°F (2,482°C); most common isotope Cr^{52} (83.76%). *See also* Transition Elements.

Chromosomes, threadlike bundles in the nuclei of the cells of bodies of organisms, containing the genes that determine the heredity of an individual. Chromosomes are arranged in pairs, and the number of pairs is constant within a given species. Humans normally have 46, arranged in 23 pairs; one of each pair is passed on to offspring during reproduction. *See also* Heredity.

Chromosphere, region of the sun's atmosphere closest to the solar surface (photosphere), extending upward for some 3100mi (5000km) and increasing in temperature from 4000°K to 1,000,000°K. The chromosphere merges into the tenuous corona and is the source of many solar phenomena, including flares, prominences, and spicules. *See also* Sun.

Chronicle Plays, a form of historical drama popular in England during the 1590s which used *The Chronicles of England, Scotland, and Ireland* by Raphael Holinshed (1577, 1587) as a principal source. Usually patriotic, the form includes Marlowe's *Edward II* and Shakespeare's *Richard* and *Henry* plays.

Chronicles, two historical books of the Old Testament. Called Paralipomenon in the Douai Bible, the two books can be divided into four sections: a lengthy genealogy from Adam to Saul; the fall of Saul and accession of David, with some instructions on worship; the reign of Solomon; the history of Judah from the division of the kingdom to the fall of Jerusalem and the Babylonian exile.

Chronometer, a portable time piece, usually having a detent escapement and compensation balance, beating half-seconds, for keeping accurate time. The atomic clock is the most precise instrument to date. *See also* Atomic Clock.

Chrysalis, intermediate or pupa stage in the life cycle of all true butterflies (except the satyr and panessian). It hangs, without a cocoon, on a silk pad from a stalk. *See also* Butterfly; Lepidoptera; Pupa.

Chrysanthemum, large genus of annual and perennial plants native to temperate Eurasia. Centuries of selective breeding have modified the original plain daisylike flowers. Most species, such as the florists' chrysanthemum *(C. morifolium),* have striking large white, yellow, bronze, pink, or red flower heads. Family Compositae.

Chrysoberyl, an oxide mineral, beryllium aluminum oxide ($BeAl_2O_4$). Found in beryllium-rich pegmatite dikes. Orthorhombic system rare crystals, prismatic or tabular. Transparent green, yellow, or brown; hardness 8.5; sp gr 3.69. Gem varieties are cat's eye and alexandrite. Bright yellow-green is most highly valued.

Chrysostum, Saint John (*c.* 345–407), theologian and Roman Catholic saint. He celebrated his conversion to Christianity (*c.* 368) by 10 years of solitary asceticism. Although consecrated archbishop of Constantinople (398), he continued to live with monastic symplicity. He offended the emperor and earned the veneration of the crowd by reviling his superiors for moral reprobation; he was banished in 404. Chrysostum is the author of voluminous homilies, commentaries, and letters.

Chuang-tzŭ (365?–290? BC), Chinese philosopher. His book is one of the most important works in Taoism. Preaching detachment from worldly desires, its quiet, contemplative outlook has strongly influenced the Chinese character.

Chub, freshwater carp found in flowing waters. It has a large head, wide mouth, and is gray-brown. Length: 4–12in (10–31cm). Family Cyprinidae; species includes *Hybopsis gracilis, Leuciscus cephalus.* Also, marine schooling fish found in warm seas, oval-shaped with a small mouth and bright colors. Family Kyphosidae; species yellow *Kyphosus incisor* and Bermuda *Kyphesus secatrix.*

Chuckwalla, flattened, desert-dwelling lizard of SW North America. It is dull-colored with loose side folds of skin and sometimes has red blotches or a banded tail. It eats creosote leaves, hides in rocky crevices, and inflates its body when threatened. Length: to 20in (50cm). Family Iguanidae; species *Sauromalus obesus. See also* Iguana.

Chuck-Will's-Widow, bird of E United States known for its nocturnal "chuck-will-widow" call. It has reddish-brown feathers marked with black and the male has white tail patches. It feeds mainly on insects. The female lays pinkish eggs (2) in dead leaves on the ground. Length: 12in (30cm). Species *Caprimulgus carolinensis.*

Chukchi, Paleo-Asiatic-speaking people, who inhabit the Chukchi peninsula in NE Soviet Union. They are divided into the seminomadic reindeer herders of the tundra, and a sedentary coastal group who practice fishing.

Chukchi Sea, part of Arctic Ocean, lies N of Bering Strait between Asia and North America, bounded W by Wrangel Island, S by NE Siberia, and NW by Alaska; distinguishable from the Arctic Ocean only by its oceanographic qualities (it is more saline); navigable August-September.

Chulalongkorn, Somdeth Phra Paraminda Maha (1853–1910), king of Siam as Rama V (1868–1910). He abolished slavery and the feudal system, modernized the courts, built railroads, and advanced education and technology. Educated in Europe himself, he appointed many Europeans to government posts. He often was in conflict with the French in neighboring Indochina who coveted his territory.

Chula Vista, city in S California, S of San Diego. Industries: citrus fruits, vegetables, aircraft parts, textiles. Inc. 1911. Pop. (1980) 83,927.

Ch'unch'ŏn, city in South Korea, on the Pukhan River, 45mi (72km) NE of Seoul; agricultural area. Crops: soybean, rice, millet. Pop. 120,517.

Chun Doo Hwan (1931–), South Korean president. Trained as a soldier at the Korean Military Academy, he joined the Special Forces in the United States after the Korean War and commanded the White House Division in Vietnam, rising to the general staff. Following the assassination in 1979 of President Park Chung Hee, he took control of the military in a coup and consolidated his power. In 1980, he was elected as South Korea's fifth president. His administration was plagued by financial scandals and by an increasingly active political opposition.

Chungking (Ch'ung-ching, Chongqing), city in S China, at junction of the Yangtze and Chialing rivers; former headquarters of the ancient Kingdom of Pa, overtaken by the state of Chin 4th century BC; wartime capital of China 1937–45 after Nanking was beseiged during Japanese invasion; transportation and shipping center. Industries: chemicals, steel, iron, silk, cotton textiles, plastics. Pop. 3,500,000.

Churches of God, US Protestant Pentecostal religious sect. It grew out of the Later Rain revival that began in the Great Smokey Mountains in 1886 under the leadership of R.G. Spurling and W.F. Bryant. They preached that a second rain of gifts of the Holy Spirit similar to the first Pentecostal would occur. Members practice speaking in tongues. There have been many splits in the church since its founding. Today about half a million people are members of various Churches of God sects.

Churchill, (Lord) Randolph Henry Spencer (1849–95), English political figure, father of Winston Churchill. He entered Parliament (1874) as a Conservative but attacked the Conservative old guard and campaigned for "Tory democracy." He became secretary of state for India (1885–86) and chancellor of the exchequer (1886). In an unsuccessful bid for more power, he resigned from office (1886) but returned to Parliament in 1892 and attacked William Gladstone's plans for Irish Home Rule.

Churchill, Sarah Jennings, Duchess of Marlborough. *See* Marlborough, Sarah Jennings Churchill, Duchess of.

Churchill, (Sir) Winston (Leonard Spencer) (1874–1965), English political figure and author, Britain's prime minister (1940–45, 1951–55). The son of Lord Randolph Churchill and Jennie Jerome, an American, he became a cavalry officer (1895). He served in campaigns in India (1896–98) and the Sudan (1898) and established a reputation as an author with his accounts of them. As a reporter in South Africa he was captured (1899) by the Boers but escaped and gained public attention that assisted in his election to the British Parliament in 1900 as a Conservative. Switching to the Liberals in 1904 to support free trade, he became undersecretary of state for the colonies (1906–08), president of the Board of Trade (1908–10), and home secretary (1910–11). As home secretary he suppressed labor unrest but also promoted social reforms. As first lord of the admiralty (1911–15), he expanded the British navy in preparation for war. The failure of the Dardanelles Campaign (1915), which he had strongly supported, brought about his resignation and return to active military service (1915–16).

He returned to political office as minister of munitions (1917–18), secretary of state for war and for air (1918–21), and colonial secretary (1921–22). As war secretary he insisted on British intervention against the Bolsheviks in Russia. As colonial secretary he promoted the formation of new Arab states while supporting a Jewish national homeland in Palestine and helped negotiate the establishment of the Irish Free State. Defeated in the election of 1922, he turned to writing his *The World Crisis* (5 vol., 1923–29), a history of World War I. He entered Parliament again in 1924, serving as Conservative chancellor of the exchequer (1924–29). As chancellor, he worsened economic conditions by returning Britain to the gold standard (1925), an act that contributed to the general strike of 1926. Out of office from 1929 to 1939, he continued in the public eye through his writings, his opposition to Indian nationalism, and his support of Edward VIII, and, above all, for his warnings of the danger posed by Nazi Germany.

The coming of World War II brought him back to government, first as first lord of the admiralty (1939–40) and then as prime minister (1940–45) and minister of defense (1940–45). An inspiring orator and phrasemaker, he proved a brilliant war leader as he mobilized Britain with "blood, toil, tears, and sweat" to meet its "finest hour," the dark days of the Battle of Britain. He established particularly close ties with US President Roosevelt; became the principal architect of the "grand alliance" among the United States, Britain, and the Soviet Union after 1941; and attended a series of vital international conferences at Casablanca, Teheran, Cairo, Quebec, and Yalta.

Shortly after the defeat of Germany in 1945, the Conservatives were defeated at the polls by the Labour party. Churchill then turned to warning against Communist expansion (coining the phrase "Iron Curtain" in 1946) and writing his highly regarded *The Second World War* (6 vol., 1948–53). Once more prime minister (1951–55) he ended rationing and the nationalization of the steel and auto industries but retained most of Labour's socialistic reforms and sought to maintain a special relationship between the United States and Britain. In 1953 he received the Nobel Prize in literature. He resigned his office in 1955 and then published another major historical work, *A History of the English-Speaking Peoples* (4 vol., 1956–58).

Churchill River, formerly Hamilton River, river in Newfoundland, Canada; rises in Ashuanipi Lake, in SW Labrador; flows through a series of lakes to the Atlantic Ocean, near Rigolet; large hydroelectric power station at Churchill Falls (300ft; 92m). Length: 600mi (966km).

Churchill River, river in NW Saskatchewan, Canada; flows from Methy Lake W to N through several lakes, into Hudson Bay at Churchill, N Manitoba; location of former fur trade route; hydroelectric power plant on upper course. Length: 1,000mi (1,610km).

Church of Christ, Scientist, or **Christian Science,** Protestant religion founded by Mary Baker Eddy (1821–1910) in Boston in 1879. Faith healing is central, as health is considered a spiritual reality. Membership totals are not published. *See also* Christian Science; Faith Healing.

Church Theater, drama that is either staged in or sponsored by a church. In the Middle Ages the Catholic Church was instrumental in reviving popular interest in drama, staging mystery and miracle plays as a means of both instruction and inspirational entertainment. With the Reformation, church participation in drama ceased, and not until the 20th century, with the 1929 Canterbury Festival of Music and Drama, did drama re-establish a place in religion.

Churn, a device for making butter. The old farm style dash churn consisted of a wooden cylindrical tub and lid with a wood plunger that was manually raised and dropped. Modern industrial churns are huge, barrel-shaped containers that agitate until all fat globules clump together to form butter. The remaining liquid, buttermilk, is drained off.

Churriguera, José Benito de (1665–1725), Spanish architect after whom a style of baroque, "Churrigueresque," is named. One of a family of artists who worked together in Madrid and Salamanca, José Churriguera combined the grand baroque of Rome with forms from local wood sculpture to produce an exuberant style characterized by twisted columns and ornate stucco decoration. His work was highly influential in

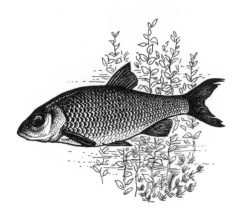
Chub

Winston Churchill

Ciliata

Spain and the colonies and imitations were often done by less judicious and skillful workers. Thus "Churrigueresque" is often used inaccurately to mean vulgar baroque.

Churrigueresque Style, extravagant Baroque architecture and ornamentation in Spain and Spanish America. It takes its name from José de Churriguera and his family, 17th-century Spanish architects and decorators. Churrigueresque was actually a term of opprobrium coined by neoclassical detractors.

Chyle, a fine emulsion of neutral fats found in lymph vessels in the intestine, which results from absorption of fats during digestion.

Chyme, the mixture of partially digested food and digestive juices present in the stomach during the digestive process.

CIA. *See* Central Intelligence Agency.

Cicada, or 17-year locust, or dog-day cicada, large, flylike insect found worldwide. A true locust makes a loud sound by rubbing a pair of plates on its abdomen together. Females lay eggs in tree twigs, often causing damage to the twigs. The dog-day cicada appear annually in July and August. The 17-year locust or periodical cicada appear every 13–17 years. Cicada larvae spend from 2 to 17 years in the ground feeding on roots. Length: to 2in (30mm). Family Cicadidae.

Cicero, Marcus Tullius, or **Tully** (106–43 BC), Roman political figure, philosopher, and orator. A leader of the senate, he exposed Catiline's conspiracy and prosecuted his supporters. Although he opposed Julius Caesar he took no part in his assassination. He attacked Marc Antony in the senate. When Octavian came to power, Antony persuaded him to have Cicero executed. Among his greatest speeches were *Orations Against Catiline* and the *Phillipics*, defenses of the republic in answer to Marc Antony. His Stoic philosophical works include *De Amicitia* (On Friendship) and *De officiis* (On Duty). He wrote a number of works on rhetoric. His many letters are a rich source of information on Roman life and politics.

Cicero, town in NE Illinois; suburb of Chicago; has over 150 factories in approx. 2sq mi (5sq km). Industries: communication and electronic equipment, printing presses, rubber goods. Founded 1857. Pop. (1980) 61,232.

Cid, The (died 1099) (Spanish: El Cid Campeador, "the lord champion"), Spanish national hero. His real name was Rodrigo, or Ruy, Díaz de Vivar. A knight in the service of the Christian kings of Castile and Navarre, he distinguished himself in wars against the Moors. In 1081, however, he was banished by Alfonso VI and went into service of the Moorish king of Zaragoza. Later he conquered Valencia and Murcia from the Moors and ruled them until his death. His deeds have been much romanticized in Spanish legend and literature. Pierre Corneille based his tragedy *Le Cid* on him.

Ciliata, class of protozoa found in fresh water, characterized by hairlike cilia used for locomotion and food collecting. Orders include the Holotrichs with cilia over the entire body *(Paramecium);* Spirotrichs with fused cilia around the mouth *(Stentor);* and Peritrichs, with cilia around the mouth and stalk for attachment *(Vorticella).*

Cilicia, ancient area of SE Asia Minor (now in Turkey), between the Taurus Mts and the Mediterranean. It was

dominated in succession by Assyria, Persia, Greece, Rome, Byzantium, the Arabs, Armenia, the Mamelukes, the Ottomans, finally becoming part of modern Turkey.

Cimabue, Giovanni, properly Cenni di Pepo (c.1240–c.1302), Italian painter who was an important transitional figure between the Byzantine style of painting and the great Florentine school of the 14th century. His best-known work is *Madonna and Child Enthroned with Angels and Prophets* now in the Uffizi Gallery, Florence. Much of Cimabue's work has been damaged by time or accident. The frescoes at the Church of St Francis at Assisi and the mosaics at the Cathedral of Pisa are in poor condition and the great *Crucifixion* at Santa Croce was severely damaged in the Florentine flood of 1966. Little is known of his life; he is said to have been the teacher of Giotto.

Cimbri, ancient Germanic tribe. The Cimbri fought successfully against Rome (113 BC) in Illyricum and later migrated to Gaul and Spain. They joined with the Teutones to take Italy but were vanquished by Roman forces under Marius and Catulus at Vercellae in 101 BC.

Cimon (507?–449 BC), Athenian statesman and soldier, his numerous military and political successes made him leader of the aristocrats opposing Themistocles and later Pericles. His greatest military success was destroying the Persian fleet c.466 BC.

Cinchona, trees native to the Andes Mountains and grown in South America, Indonesia, and Zaire. They are a source of quinine. Family Rubiaceae.

Cincinnati, city and port of entry in SW Ohio, across the Ohio River from Covington, Ky.; seat of Hamilton co; 3rd-largest city in Ohio. Originally named Losantiville, it grew around Fort Washington, est 1789 by the US government to quell Indian attacks; in 1790, its name was changed to Cincinnati (after the Revolutionary War Society of Cincinnati) and made co seat; served as first seat of Northwest Territory legislature. Known as the "Queen City" of the West, development was spurred by steamboat trade on Ohio River and the completion of the Miami Canal (1827), making the city a shipping center for farm products and meat. Before the Civil War, it was a terminus on the Underground Railroad. In order to compete with the growing cities of Chicago and St Louis, Cincinnati built its own railroad (1880) connecting with Chattanooga, Tenn.; it is still the only US city to own and lease its own railroad. It was scene of Cincinnati riots (1884), a result of corruption in politics and law enforcement; the reform movement won the 1924 election, ending the era of boss control. Cincinnati is the site of the Taft Museum (1820), Tyler Davidson Fountain (1871), Cincinnati Zoological Garden (1875), Eden Park; birthplace of President William H. Taft. Notable educational institutions include University of Cincinnati (1819), Ohio College of Applied Science (1828), Xavier College (1831), Hebrew Union College (1875). Industries: machine tools, soap products, playing cards, brewing, meat packing, cosmetics, automobiles, truck bodies, aircraft engines, radar, machinery, metal goods, furniture, candy, mattresses. Founded 1788; inc. 1802 as town, 1819 as city. Pop. (1980) 385,457.

Cincinnatus Lucius, or Titus Quinctius (c.519–438 BC), legendary Roman hero. Consul in 460, he was named dictator by the Senate in 458. He left his farm, defeated the Aequians in 16 days, and then renounced his post to return to his farm. According to legend, he was again called to the dictatorship in 439 to put down the traitor Spurius Melius.

Cinder Cone, truncated, conical structure composed largely of unconsolidated volcanic material, mostly ash. The cinder cone is a characteristic of a volcano that produces large amounts of gas and ash rather than lava and is tall rather than broad.

Cineraria, or florist's cineraria, perennial hothouse plant native to the Canary Islands. It has heart-shaped leaves and large clusters of white, pink, blue, or purple daisylike flowers. Family Compositae; species *Senecio cruentus. See also* Dusty Miller.

Cingulate Gyrus, protuberance or ridge between depressions on the surface of the cerebral cortex, part of the limbic system. *See also* Limbic System.

Cinna, Lucius Cornelius (c.130–84 BC), Roman political figure. After service in the Social War (90–88 BC), he became consul (87 BC). After Sulla left Rome for the war against Mithridates VI, Cinna repealed Sulla's laws and proposed full civil equality for the new Roman citizens of Italy. Conservatives allied with his fellow consul Gnaeus Octavius to expel Cinna from Rome. Cinna then allied with Marius, Sulla's rival, captured Rome and massacred Sulla's followers. After the death of Marius (86 BC) Cinna directed affairs, holding the consulship until his death. He suppressed dissent but instituted economic reforms and extended the franchise to all inhabitants of Italy. In 84 BC he mobilized to resist the returning Sulla, but his troops mutinied and killed him.

Cinnabar, a sulfide mineral, mercuric sulfide(MgS) and the major ore of mercury. Found in hydrothermal veins and volcanic deposits. Rhombohedral system columnar or prismatic crystals, often twinned, and as granular masses. Red; brilliant to dull; hardness 2–2.5; sp gr 8.1.

Cinnamon, light brown spice made from the dried inner bark of the cinnamon tree. Its delicate aroma and sweet flavor make it a common ingredient in baked foods. Once worth its weight in gold, it was also valued for religious rites and witchcraft. Or, a bushy evergreen tree native to India and Burma and now cultivated in West Indies and South America. Family Lauraceae; species *Cinnamomum zeylandicum.*

Cinnamon Fern, common North American fern found in wet places. Its woolly, cinnamon-colored, spore-bearing fronds are not as tall as the separately produced broad foliage fronds. It grows in bouquetlike clusters. It is a popular greenhouse plant. Height: to 4ft (120cm). Family Osmundaceae; species *Osmunda cinnamomea. See also* Fern.

Cinquefoil, any of various annual and perennial plants and shrubs, native to the temperate and arctic regions. The leaves are composed of three leaflets, and the small white, yellow, or red flowers consist of five petals. Family Rosaceae; genus *Potentilla.*

Cinque Ports, association of ports in SE England. The grouping of Dover, Hastings, Hythe, Romney, and Sandwich began under the Anglo-Saxons and was expanded by the Norman kings, who granted privileges in return for the ports providing ships during wartime. The association reached its height during the Hundred Years' War (1337–1453). After Henry VIII founded the royal navy, the ports' power declined.

Circassians, Muslim people native to the Caucasus Mountains. During the 19th century, they unsuccessfully resisted the Russian government's attempt to take over the Caucasus. They often figure in Russian literature, such as in Lermontov's *Hero of Our Times.*

Circe, in Greek legend, daughter of Helios and Perse. Known for her evil spells, she was able to change humans into wolves, lions, and swine. When Odysseus' ship landed on her island, all his men were turned into swine. Odysseus, protected by moly, a magic herb, forced Circe to restore his men to human form.

Circle, plane geometric figure that is the locus of points equidistant from a fixed point (the center). This distance is the radius (*r*). The area of a circle is πr^2 and its perimeter (circumference) is $2\pi r$. *See also* Conic.

Circuit, Electric, system of electric conductors and electronic components connected together so that they form a continuously conducting path. In modern electronic devices, circuits are often printed in copper onto a plastic card (printed circuit) to which the transistors, capacitors, and other elements are soldered. In even smaller devices, a chip of semiconductor is treated in such a way that it consists of a number of components connected together.

Circular Flow of Income, model of the economic system that depicts the relationships or flow of money and economic goods throughout the economy. As goods are produced by the business sector, they flow to the consumer sector. In return for such goods, the business is paid money. A circular flow also occurs with the factors of production. Land, labor, and capital flow from the consumers who own these resources to business firms that use them to produce goods. In return for the factors of production, the consumer sector is paid wages or income.

The exchange of goods produced by businesses for dollars from the consumer is accomplished through use of the market mechanism of supply and demand. Through supply and demand, the price of the goods as well as the quantity produced is determined.

Circulation, Atmospheric, the patterns of average flow of the atmosphere around the earth by means of which heat is transferred from zones with a surplus, like the tropics, to zones of heat deficit, like the poles. Explanations of the poleward circulation are found in convective cells, supplemented by large-scale eddies involving planetary waves, cyclones and anticyclones, low-pressure troughs, and high-pressure ridges. The eddies also take part in the longitudinal atmospheric circulation around the earth, with the earth's rotation maintaining easterly winds toward the equator and westerlies toward the poles. Narrow jet streams blow swiftly over middle latitudes, usually toward the west in the lower stratosphere, and move further poleward during the summer. Both poleward and longitudinal circulations are stronger in the winter than in the summer hemisphere. *See also* Cyclone; Easterlies; Hadley Cell; Jet Stream; Westerlies.

Circulatory System, the transportation system of the body, transporting oxygen and digested food to tissues throughout the body and carrying carbon dioxide and other waste materials to organs that remove wastes from the body. The circulatory system consists of closed blood vessels that carry the blood throughout the body propelled by the pumping action of the heart. In mammals, birds, and some reptiles there are two circulatory systems: the pulmonary (lung) circulation and the systemic (bodily) circulation, intimately related. In the circulation, blood enters the lungs, where it picks up oxygen and gives off carbon dioxide. The freshly oxygenated blood then flows through the pulmonary vein to the left auricle of the heart, then to the left ventricle, from which it is pumped through valves into the aorta, the largest artery in the body. The aorta branches into a network of arteries and finally capillaries, carrying oxygen to all parts of the body (including the heart itself). The blood picks up waste products in the capillaries, which join to form venules and eventually veins leading to one main vessel, the vena cava, which returns the deoxygenated blood to the heart's right auricle. The blood enters the right ventricle, from which it is pumped through the pulmonary artery to the lungs. *See also* Heart.

Circumcision, operation of cutting away the whole or part of the foreskin of the penis. There is a wide ethnic incidence of circumcision as a ritual, where it signifies either the formal introduction of a male into his group or the achievement of status. *See also* Puberty Rites.

Circumference, measure of the distance around a closed curve. For a circle it is equal to $2\pi r$, where r is the radius.

Circumpolar Star, any star that remains above the horizon during the entire 360 degrees of daily travel.

Circus Maximus, the oldest and largest of the Roman stadia used for horse and chariot races, it was 2,000ft (610m) long, 650ft (198m) wide, and seated 250,000 spectators. Erected, traditionally, in the 6th century BC by Tarquin the younger, first Etruscan king of Rome, it was substantially rebuilt and made an important resort by Julius Caesar. It no longer stands.

Cirque, bowl-shaped, eroded area around a snowbank or a glacier. The eroded area is usually cut into the bedrock by repeated freezing and thawing or it may be the result of glacial movement. Cirque lakes are water-filled formations, often fed by the retreating glacier that created them. *See also* Erosion; Glaciology.

Cirrhosis, serious disease in which bands of fibrous tissue form in the liver. The liver becomes hard, blood flow through the organ is impaired, and some liver cells die. Cirrhosis of the liver is one of the most common causes of death among middle-aged people. It is usually associated with alcoholism but may also be caused by certain tropical fungal food contaminants and occasionally as a result of viral hepatitis or some rare disorders. Generally a loss of appetite and general weakness are followed by signs of liver impairment: jaundice, spidery skin marks, tendency to bleed, and, in men, a loss of sexual functioning. Early treatment, particularly in alcohol-induced cases in which cessation of alcohol intake occurs, can arrest development of the disease. Otherwise, blood vessels leading to the liver become engorged, sometimes rupturing, and the liver no longer detoxifies harmful intestinal material, leading to serious, hard-to-treat, and often fatal consequences.

Cisalpine Gaul, ancient region of Gaul in present-day Italy. The name is derived from the Latin "on this side of the Alps." Divided into Cispadane Gaul ("this side of the Po River") and Transpadane Gaul, it was settled by the Gauls, 5th century BC, and then conquered (222 BC) and assimilated by the Romans. Julius Caesar granted its inhabitants Roman citizenship 49 BC.

Cisalpine Republic, N Italian state set up by Napoleon (1797) as a French dependency. It united the Italian states from Lombardy to Emilia for the first time in modern history. In 1805 it became the kingdom of Italy.

Cispadane Republic, government of the Italian region of Emilia est by Napoleon Bonaparte in early 1797, with its constitution based on that of Bologna. On July 17, 1797, Napoleon merged it with the Cisalpine Republic.

Cistercians, religious order of White Monks founded by St Robert of Molesmes in 1098, based on ideals of strict and primitive Benedictinism. A cloistered community dedicated to prayer and adoration, the Cistercians were noted agricultural pioneers and sheepherders. The 17th century brought the Strict Observance reform, whose supporters are popularly known as Trappists.

Cithara. *See* Kithara.

Citizen Kane (1941), US film. Produced and directed by Orson Welles from Herman J. Mankiewicz's screenplay and photographed by Gregg Toland, this film described the career of a newspaper tycoon markedly similar to William Randolph Hearst. It starred Welles, Everett Sloane, Joseph Cotton, and Agnes Moorehead. Abounding in cinematic innovations, it remains one of the most gripping films in the medium's history.

Citizenship, relationship in which a person is a member of a state, by birth or naturalization, and owes allegiance to it. Citizenship carries with it certain rights and duties. Modern countries determine the requirements for citizenship. The United States, for example, generally supports the rule of *jus soli,* and anyone born in the United States is a citizen. The United States also accepts children born abroad of US parents as citizens during their minority and they may retain citizenship if they fulfill certain conditions.

Citric Acid, colorless crystalline solid (formula $C_6H_8O_7$) having a sour taste and occurring free in lemons and limes. It is used for flavoring, in effervescent salts, and as a mordant. Properties: sp gr 1.54; melt. pt. 307.4°F (153°C).

Citrus Fruits, important fruits of the genus *Citrus* in the rue family. These include the orange, lime, lemon, grapefruit, kumquat, and tangerine. These subtropical trees or shrubs are widely cultivated wherever they can get plenty of sun and moisture. The flowers are usually white, waxy, and fragrant. The fruit is usually ovoid with a thick, aromatic rind. The interior is pulpy and juicy and is divided into segments that contain the seeds. Most citrus fruits contain a high amount of vitamin C.

City, in the United States, a term applied to municipalities governed under a charter granted by the state. In general, a political unit with a large, centralized population.

City of God, The, religious and philosophical work by Augustine of Hippo. Begun about two years after the Visigoths sacked Rome in 410 and completed in 426, it was a reply to charges that the influence of Christianity had caused the city's fall. The first 10 of the work's 22 books held that vices within the empire rather than Christianity brought about Rome's collapse. The remaining books elaborate an important Christian philosophy of history. In this view history from the fall of Adam to the end of time is seen as the development of two opposing powers, the city of God and the city of the world, a place of conflict and confusion. To one or the other of these cities all mankind must eventually belong. After the Last Judgment the city of God becomes Heaven and the city of the world Hell.

City-state, self-governing political unit comprised of an independent city and its adjacent hinterland. Historically, city-states have existed during three periods: the ancient city-states of Mesopotamia and Greece; those of Medieval and Renaissance Europe; and, to a limited extent, in the modern world. They represent an effective form of political organization to achieve physical and economic protection. Many, like ancient Athens and medieval Florence, flourished as commercial and cultural centers. They sometimes banded together to form maritime leagues or alliances for trading and protection. Although the nation-state is today the dominant political unit, several city-states persist as anomalies in the contemporary world. The most notable is Singapore.

Ciudad Bolívar, formerly Angostura; city and port in E Venezuela; capital of Bolívar state, on Orinoco River; site of longest suspension bridge in South America, the Angostura, 2,336ft (712m) long. Industries: wood products, leather. Founded 1764 as Angostura. Pop. 103,728.

Ciudad Juárez, city in N Mexico, on the Rio Grande; connected by bridge to El Paso, Tex.; site of Mission of Our Lady of Guadalupe (1659), and Museum of Art and History; named for Mexican President Benito Juárez (1888); commercial center. Industries: tourism, textiles. Pop. 570,000.

Ciudad Madero, city in E Mexico, N of Tampico; important center of petroleum industries. Pop. 121,782.

Ciudad Obregón, city in NW Mexico, 65mi (105km) SE of Guaymas; agricultural region. Industries: livestock, vegetables, flour milling, canning, copper mining. Pop. 152,834.

Ciudad Victoria, city in E central Mexico, 135mi (217km) NW of Tampico; agricultural and trading center; site of university (1956). Industries: mining, sugar cane, citrus fruit, livestock, tanning, textiles. Founded 1750. Pop. 94,304.

Civet, or **Civet Cat,** small, savage, catlike animal found in Africa, Asia, and S Europe. Related to the genet and mongoose, it has a small head and narrow body set on long legs. Its coat is brindled gray with black stripes and spots. The substance known as civet is a fatty secretion of the animal's scent glands, once important as a perfume base. Length: body—28in (7cm), tail—14in (35cm). Family Viverridae; species five, including African *Viverra civetta* and Asian *V. civettictis.*

Civil Disobedience, passive resistance to law or authority, usually associated with an act of conscience. The term originated with Henry Thoreau's essay "Resistance to Civil Government," (1849) in which he argued that disobeying a law is preferable to disobeying one's own conscience. It was associated in India with the nationalist supporters of Mohandas K. Gandhi and in the United States with the followers of Martin Luther King, Jr.

Civil Engineering, the field of engineering that deals with the creation, improvement, and protection of the communal environment, providing facilities for living, industry, and transportation, including large buildings, roads, bridges, canals, railroad lines, airports, water-supply systems, dams, harbors, docks, aquaducts, tunnels, and other constructions. Civil engineering requires a thorough knowledge of surveying, construction, material properties, soil properties, and hydraulics. Important divisions of the field are architectural, irrigation, transportation, soil and foundation, geodetic, hydraulic and coastal, and ocean engineering.

Civil Law, legal system derived from Roman Law prevalent in continental Europe and in the Western Hemisphere in Louisiana, Quebec Province, and Latin America. It is distinguished from common law, the sys-

Circus Maximus

Cirque: Rocky Mountains

American Civil War: Union troops at Petersburg, Virginia

tem generally adhered to in England and English-speaking countries. Civil law is based on a system of codes, the most famous of which is the Napoleonic Code (1804), and decisions are precisely worked out from general basic principles *a priori;* that is, the civil law judge is bound by the conditions of the written law and not by previous judicial interpretation. Civil law influences common law in the areas of jurisprudence, admiralty, testamentary and domestic relations, and is the basis for the system of equity. In common usage, the term civil law means regulations governing private legal affairs, and contrasts with public law and criminal law. *See also* Common Law; Law; Private Law; Roman Law.

Civil Rights Acts (1957, 1960, 1964, 1968), US legislation. The first of these acts established the Civil Rights Commission to investigate violations of the 15th Amendment. The 1960 Civil Rights Act enabled court-appointed federal officials to protect black voting rights. An act of violence to obstruct a court order became a federal offense. The Civil Rights Act of 1964, the strongest civil rights legislation since the Civil War, established as law equal rights for all citizens in voting, education, public accommodations, and in federally assisted programs. In 1968, a civil rights act was passed guaranteeing equal treatment in housing and real estate to all citizens.

Civil Rights and Liberties, basic individual rights and freedoms protected against infringement by government. In the United States, they include the rights to freedom of speech, press, religion, and assembly, as well as the rights to property and equal treatment under law. The US heritage stems from a series of English documents: the Magna Carta (1215); the Petition of Right (1628); and the Bill of Rights (1689). Together with the US Constitution (particularly the first 10 amendments) and the civil rights acts, they represent the basis for US civil rights and liberties. *See also* Civil Rights Acts.

Civil War, American (1861–65), conflict between the North (the Union) and 11 southern states (the Confederacy), sometimes known as the War Between the States. Its immediate cause was the secession of the southern states from the Union; northerners regarded the Union as indivisible, and the war was fought to resolve that issue. The more general cause was the question of slavery, an institution well established in the southern states but one that abolitionists were determined should not be extended to the new western states. Sectional differences between North and South, particularly economic ones, were at least as old as the nation, but by the 1850s slavery, abolition, and states' rights had created schisms that, despite efforts at compromise, seemed insoluble. Politically, the two sides had polarized: Northern abolitionists had coalesced into the new Republican party and southern states' righters remained in the Democratic party. The election in 1860 of the Republican candidate, Abraham Lincoln, was the virtual assurance of southern secession from the Union. On Dec. 20, 1860, South Carolina left the Union, quickly followed by Texas, Mississippi, Georgia, Florida, Louisiana, and Alabama. North Carolina, Virginia, Tennessee, and Arkansas seceded later. There was, in addition, secessionist sentiment in the border states, but all of them eventually stayed in the Union.

The war began on April 12, 1861, when South Carolina fired on Fort Sumter, the federal installation in Charleston harbor. Lincoln, newly inaugurated, recognized that as an act of war, and the battle was joined. The Confederate capital was established at Richmond, Va., and the Union army's first objective was to take that city. In the attempt, however—in the first Battle of

Bull Run (July 21, 1861)—Confederate troops scored a victory. Lincoln was forced to begin his long search for a military commander who would measure up to the able southern generals, particularly Robert E. Lee and Stonewall Jackson. The search finally ended with Ulysses S. Grant, who became commander of the West in October 1863 and supreme commander in March 1864. His ablest lieutenant was William T. Sherman.

In the meantime, the Confederates continued to pile up victories. Lee, replacing the wounded Joseph E. Johnston, won the Peninsular Campaign (April–June 1862). Stonewall Jackson carried off a brilliant campaign in the Shenandoah Valley (March–June 1862) and went on to win the Seven Days battle (June–July 1862) and the Second Battle of Bull Run (August 1862). Union superiority in both numbers and in material was beginning to be felt, however, and Union troops checked Lee's army in the Antietam campaign (September 1862), the battle of Fredericksburg (Dec. 13, 1862), and twice at Chancellorsville (December 1862 and May 1863). The Union victory in the Gettysburg campaign (June–July 1863) is generally considered the turning point of the war. By that time the vastly superior northern navy had effectively blockaded southern ports, thereby denying the Confederacy much needed trade with Europe. It was from such trade that the South had depended for much of its war materials. The war in the West took on increasing importance. Union strategy was to win the war by dividing the South, which was to be accomplished by taking control of the Mississippi, Tennessee, and Cumberland rivers. The first big Union victory was at Fort Donelson, on the Tennessee, on Feb. 16, 1862. General Grant was the Union commander. The Battle of Shiloh (April 1862) was less conclusive. Grant won a signal victory in the Vicksburg campaign (November 1862–July 1863), which, combined with the fall of Memphis (June 1862), gave the Union control of virtually all of the Mississippi. Confederate troops, under Braxton Bragg, almost defeated the Union forces in the Chattanooga campaign (November 1863), but the superior forces of the Union saved the day. By the end of 1863, Tennessee was restored to the Union.

In March 1864 Grant went east to become supreme commander. He confronted Lee's army in the Wilderness campaign (May–June 1864) and began the long siege of Petersburg, Va., the defense of which was vital to the survival of Richmond. General Sherman, meanwhile, won the Battle of Atlanta and began his destructive march through Georgia to the sea. He conquered Savannah in December 1864. He then moved north and won the battle of Five Forks (April 1, 1865), the last major battle of the war. That victory cut off the southern retreat route for Confederate troops in Richmond. Petersburg fell two days later, and Richmond was no longer defensible. Realizing the desperation of his position, Lee surrendered to Grant at Appomattox Courthouse on April 9, 1865. Other southern commanders quickly capitulated, and the war was over.

By almost any criterion, the Civil War was the most destructive in US history. The casualties were greater than those of any other war, and the physical destruction of the countryside was unprecedented. It caused the economic ruin of the South, and the Reconstruction policies after the war poisoned the relations between North and South for a century. The war, and Reconstruction, left a legacy of racial bitterness between white and black. *See also* Abolitionism; Reconstruction; Slavery.

Civil War, English (1642–48), conflict arising out of the struggle between Charles I and Parliament. When Charles ruled without Parliament (1629–40), divisions between the court and the people over religion, taxation, rights, and foreign policy were increased. A Scot-

tish revolt against church policy compelled Charles to summon the Long Parliament (1640) to raise funds. The Parliament impeached the king's closest advisers and in the Grand Remonstrance (1641) demanded church reform and greater parliamentary power. The king responded by attempting to arrest John Pym and other parliamentary leaders (1642). The king and parliament raised opposing armies.

The king and his royalist supporters held the north and west until the Scots joined the parliamentarians and defeated him at Marston Moor (1644). Parliament organized the New Model Army, making Oliver Cromwell second-in-command. The Royalists were decisively defeated at Naseby (1645) and Charles surrendered (1646). He escaped from custody (1647), formed an alliance with the Scots and began the Second Civil War (1648). The king's forces were swiftly defeated by Cromwell's army. Parliament, now firmly controlled by Cromwell, tried Charles and executed him for treason (1649). A Commonwealth, with Cromwell as leader, was declared.

Civil War, Spanish (1936–39), conflict between the Loyalists and Nationalists for control of Spain. Both sides began as loose alliances: the Loyalists, so-called because they were loyal to the government of the Second Republic, consisted of republicans, socialists, Communists, and Basque and Catalonian separatists. The Nationalists comprised the right-wing professional army, the more conservative faction of the Roman Catholic Church, monarchists, Carlists, and the great landowners.

The causes of the war began in 1931, when the monarchy was abolished and the Second Republic was instituted. The government made attempts to reform Spanish institutions and customs. Church and state were separated; land reform was begun; and military influence was controlled. All these measures were upsetting to the traditionalist forces of Spain, including the church, the landed interests, and the military.

The actual war began in July 1936, with an uprising of the Spanish army in Morocco. The commander there, Francisco Franco, soon emerged as the leader of the Nationalist side. The Nationalists quickly took control of the north of Spain, while the Loyalists held Madrid, Catalonia, and much of the south. Fighting, including aerial bombing of civilians, was intense and great suffering resulted.

Nazi Germany and Fascist Italy gave aid to the Nationalist forces, including both troops and supplies. The democracies, on the other hand, maintained strict neutrality, leaving only the Soviet Union to come to the aid of the Loyalists, which greatly strengthened the Communists within the Loyalist ranks. International brigades, mostly under Communist control, were formed and fought on the side of the Loyalists. The Nationalists made steady progress throughout 1937 and in late 1938 began a major assault on Catalonia. When Barcelona fell in January 1939, the Loyalist cause was doomed. On March 27, 1939, the Nationalists entered Madrid, and the war was over. More than 1,000,000 Spaniards had been killed, and more than 250,000 were forced into exile.

Civitavecchia, town in W central Italy, on Tyrrhenian Sea; chief port for Rome; sacked by Saracens 828; Pope Leo IV built walled mountain town 854; old site rebuilt under papal protection. Final construction of citadel was supervised by Michelangelo; site of naval arsenal built by Bernini 1508. Industries: cement, metallurgical works. Pop. 42,570.

Clairvoyance, the supernatural or extrasensory power to see objects or events actually removed in time and space from the observer, a form of extrasensory perception or ESP. *See also* Parapsychology; Precognition.

Clam, bivalve mollusk found mainly in marine waters. It is usually partially buried in sand or mud with its shells slightly open for feeding. With a large foot for burrowing, its flat body lies between two muscles for closing the shells and is covered by the mantle and has in- and out-current openings, elongated into siphons in some species. Class Pelecypoda. The largest species is Tridacna; Length: 5ft (152cm); Weight: 500lb (225kg). Edible clams include *Venus mercenaria,* quahog or hard shell clam of Atlantic coast, and *Mya arenaria,* the soft shell or gaper clam.

Clam Worm. *See* Nereis.

Clan, unilineal descent group, in which kinship is recognized either through the male line (patrilineal) or through the female line (matrilineal). *See also* Kinship; Matriarchy; Patriarchy.

Clarence, George, Duke of (1449–78), younger brother of Edward IV of England, b. Ireland. He joined his father-in-law, the earl of Warwick, in revolt against Edward (1469–70), but later rejoined his brother (1471). In 1478 he was accused of treason and murdered in the Tower of London before he stood trial.

Clarendon, Edward Hyde, 1st Earl of (1609–74), English statesman and historian. Initially critical of Charles I, he became a leading royal adviser (1641) and later worked for the Restoration. As Charles II's chief minister, his moderation made him unpopular. Forced into exile (1667), he wrote his *History of the Rebellion* about the English Civil War.

Clarendon, Constitutions of (1164), 16 articles issued by Henry II of England, limiting temporal and judicial powers of the church. The article requiring clerics convicted in church courts to be surrendered to secular courts for punishment was especially controversial. Archbishop Thomas à Becket initially accepted the articles, but later repudiated them. The ensuing quarrel led to Becket's murder.

Clarendon Code, four English statutes passed (1661–65) under Charles II's minister Clarendon to strengthen the established church. Nonconformist worship was hampered by restrictions on the size of gatherings and the movement of ministers. Municipal and church officers were required to be professed Anglicans. These laws reduced the strength of the Nonconformists, especially the Presbyterians.

Clarinet, woodwind musical instrument of ancient Asian origin, with end-blown cylindrical wood pipe and single-reed mouthpiece, commonly pitched B*b* (also A), with alto clarinet E*b*. Utilized for flexibility and tonal quality variations in different registers, it has a range of 3 1/2 octaves, from D below middle C. It has been used in symphony orchestras since the early 19th century and in jazz since around 1920.

Clark, George Rogers (1752–1818), American Revolutionary general, b. Albemarle County, Va. A militia captain in Lord Dunmore's War (1774), Clark was given a commission in the Virginia militia during the revolution by Gov. Patrick Henry. In 1778, he took the offensive in the Northwest Territory. After suffering great hardships, he and his men defeated the British at Kaskaskia, Ill. (1778), and Vincennes, Ind. (1779).

Clark, Joseph (Joe) (1939–), Canadian politician. He earned degrees from the University of Alberta and was on its political science faculty (1965–67). Active in Conservative Party affairs from 1957, he was president of the Progressive Conservative Student Federation from 1962 to 1965. A believer in free enterprise and limited government, he was first elected to Parliament in 1972. He became Canada's youngest prime minister in 1979, ousting Pierre Elliott Trudeau. After only nine months in office he lost his position to Trudeau in March 1980. He remained leader of the Progressive Conservative Party.

Clark, (Sir) Kenneth McKenzie (1903–83), English art historian. A professor at Oxford, he was director of the National Gallery in London (1934–45) and chairman of the Arts Council on Great Britain (1955–60). His writings include *Leonardo da Vinci* (2d ed. 1952), *Rembrandt and the Italian Renaissance* (1966), *The Romantic Rebellion* (1974), *Another Part of the Wood* (1975), and *Animals and Men* (1977). His television lecture series *Civilisation,* a cultural survey, was extremely popular.

Clark, Tom C(ampbell) (1899–1977), US jurist and lawyer, b. Dallas, Texas. A US Justice Department attorney (1937–45), he became US attorney general in 1945, and in 1949 was appointed an associate justice of the US Supreme Court. A civil rights advocate noted for his opinion upholding the provisions of the Civil Rights Act of 1964 requiring desegregation of public accommodations, he retired in 1967 when his son, Ramsey Clark, became attorney general.

Clark, William (1770–1838), US explorer who, with Meriwether Lewis, led an expedition of the Northwest Territory (1803–06), b. Caroline co, Va. In 1813 he became governor of Missouri Territory; from 1821 he served as superintendent of Indian affairs. *See also* Lewis and Clark Expedition.

Clarke, Arthur Charles (1917–), English science-fiction writer. He is noted for the solid scientific background in his works; many of the scientific predictions in his novels have become realities. His novels include *Childhood's End* (1953), *A Fall of Moondust* (1961), *Voices from the Sky* (1965), *Imperial Earth* (1976), and *2010; Odyssey Two* (1982). The film *2001: A Space Odyssey* (1968) was based on his short story "The Sentinel."

Clarksville, city in NW Tennessee; seat of Montgomery co; site of Austin Peay State University. Industries: agriculture, cattle raising, tobacco, meat packing. Inc. 1855. Pop. (1980) 54,777.

Class, Social, a system of social stratification that organizes groups of people on the basis of shared characteristics. Social scientists have long argued about the basis for class distinctions. Socialist thinkers believe capital and access to the means of production are the basic factors; others state that status is crucial; a third group claims a group's relationship to political power determines its class position. The concept of social class is fundamental to the understanding of social organization. *See also* Status.

Classical Music, music composed from roughly 1750 to 1820. At this time musical styles were characterized by emotional restraint, the dominance of homophonic methods (ie, melodies with accompaniment), and clear structures and forms underlying the music. During this period instrumental music crystallized into the forms of concerto, sonata, symphony, and string quartet. The piano became the most popular keyboard instrument, replacing the harpsichord. The greatest composers of this period—all from Vienna—were Haydn, Mozart, Beethoven, and Schubert, who are among the greatest who have ever lived. Also important in this period were reformations in opera introduced by Gluck. *See also* Opera; Polyphony.

Classicism in Art, art history term used to describe both an aesthetic attitude and an artistic tradition. The artistic tradition refers to the classical antiquity of Greece and Rome, its art, literature, and criticism, and the subsequent periods that looked back to Greece and Rome for their prototypes, viz., Carolingian Revival, Renaissance, and neoclassicism. The aesthetic use of the term suggests the classical characteristics of clarity, order, balance, unity, symmetry, and dignity. The concept is also used in a comparative sense to describe those works that exhibit the salient features of a given style.

Classic Revival, art and architecture in the style of the ancient Greeks and Romans. In general, the style reflects a simplicity, harmony, and balance. The Italian Renaissance and the neoclassic style in England and the United States in the early 19th century are examples of classic revival.

Classification, Biological, or taxonomy, organization of plants and animals into categories based on similarities of appearance, structure, evolution, or habit. The categories, ranging from the most inclusive to the exclusive, are kingdom, phylum, class, order, family, genus, species, and sometimes variety. There are also subphyla, subfamilies, etc., in some categories. *See also* Taxonomy.

Classification, Library, process of organizing materials in a collection according to a system. Widespread interest in classification developed during the late 19th century, a period of great growth for libraries. The Dewey Decimal System is the most used worldwide.

Classification of Animals. *See* Animal Classification.

Claudianus, Claudius (*c.*370–404), last important Latin poet in the classical tradition. An Alexandrian, Claudianus came to Italy and mastered Latin. His poems, falling into three groups, include panegyrics along with the mythological epic *De raptu Proserpinae.*

Claudius I (10 BC–AD 54), Roman emperor (41–54), son of Drusus, nephew of Tiberius. He was the first emperor chosen by the army, a situation that angered the Senate. He made conquests in Germany, added Britain as a province of Rome (43), absorbed Mauritania, Thrace, and Judea into the empire, and built the harbor at Ostia and the Claudian aqueduct. His wives and enemies maligned his ability. Agrippina, his fourth wife, poisoned him and secured the emperorship for her own son by a former marriage, Nero.

Clausius, Rudolf Julius Emanuel (1822–88), German physicist. He is regarded as the founder of thermodynamics and, using the work of Carnot, was the first to state explicitly the second law. He also introduced the concept of entropy.

Claves, Cuban musical instrument consisting of two round hardwood sticks beaten together to produce a percussion accompaniment for popular and folk tunes.

Clavichord, earliest stringed musical instrument with mechanical action controlled by a keyboard. Introduced in the 12th century, it was used extensively from the 16th to 18th century. J. S. Bach composed his series "The Well-Tempered Clavier" (1722) for this instrument with its soft, delicate, expressive tone.

Clavicle, or collarbone, thin slightly curved bone attached by ligaments to the top of the sternum. The collarbone and shoulder blade make up the shoulder, or pectoral girdle, linking the arm to the axis of the body.

Clavier, generic term for stringed musical instruments played with a keyboard, such as the harpsichord, Clavichord, and later the pianoforte.

Clay, Cassius. *See* Ali, Muhammad.

Clay, Henry (1777–1852), US statesman, b. Hanover co, Va. A lawyer, he practiced in Lexington, Ky., after 1797. He served in both the US House of Representatives (1811–14; 1815–21; 1823–25), where he was several times speaker, and in the US Senate (1831–42; 1849–52). He was one of the "war hawks" who favored the War of 1812. He ran for president in 1824, and when the election went to the House of Representatives, he threw his support to John Quincy Adams, who was elected. When Adams named Clay secretary of state (1825–29), the charge of "corrupt bargain" was widely made. One of the founders of the Whig party, he ran against Andrew Jackson, a bitter political enemy, in 1832. He continued to oppose the Jacksonians in Congress. He ran for president again in 1844 as a Whig but was defeated by James Polk. Clay's last years in the Senate were spent trying to work out a compromise between the slave-owning states of the South and the free northern states. The Compromise of 1850 was one result of those efforts. *See also* Compromise of 1850; War of 1812; Whigs.

Clay, group of aluminum silicate rocks of various compositions, including kaolinite and halloysite, usually mixed with some quartz, calcite, or gypsum. It is formed by the weathering of granite or other igneous rocks containing feldspar. Soft when wet, it hardens on firing and is used to make pottery, stoneware, tiles, bricks, and molds, and as a filler for paper, rubber, and paint.

Clayton Anti-Trust Act (1914), US legislation to strengthen the Sherman Anti-Trust Act (1890). It prohibited corporate practices not previously covered, including price discrimination, interlocking directorates, tying contracts, and holding stock in competitive firms. It exempted trade unions from restraint of trade clauses.

Clayton-Bulwer Treaty (April 1850), agreement between the United States and Great Britain negotiated by Sec. of State John M. Clayton and Sir Henry Bulwer. Among the treaty's provisions were joint control and protection of any ship canal that might be built in Central America, guaranteed neutrality and security of such a canal, and pledges not to occupy or colonize any part of Central America.

Cleanthes (*c.* 331–232 BC), Greek philosopher. A disciple of Zeno of Citium, he was the second head of the Stoic school. Of the fragments of his works that survive, the principal one is the philosophical poem "Hymn to Zeus." More than did Zeno, he stressed the transcendency of God. *See also* Stoicism.

Clear-air Turbulence (CAT), the turbulence encountered by aircraft at high altitudes, often associated with the jet stream, even though the atmosphere is devoid of clouds.

Clear Lake, either of two lakes in California: 1) A fresh water lake in W California, 80mi (130km) N of San Francisco; largest within the state; recreational area. Length: 25mi (40km). Width: 1–10mi (2–16km). 2) A vast reservoir in NE California, 10mi (16km) S of Ore-

Henry Clay

Georges Clemenceau (left): at the front, World War I

Grover Cleveland

gon border; the Lost River flows out of it NW to Oregon.

Clearwater, residential city, W Florida peninsula, 18mi (29km) NW of St Petersburg; seat of Pinellas co. Industries: citrus fruits, fishing. Settled as Clear Water Harbor in 1841; inc. 1891. Pop. (1980) 85,450.

Clearwing Moth, small, day-flying moth that has transparent hindwings and looks like a wasp. Clearwing caterpillars bore into the roots and stems of trees and shrubs. Family Aegeriidae. *See also* Moth.

Cleft Palate, congenital deformity in which there is an opening in the palate, or roof of the mouth, causing direct communication between the nasal and mouth cavities. It is often associated with harelip, an opening of the upper lip. Cleft palate results from a defect in embryonic development and can range in severity from a small opening to complete separation of the palates and opening of part of the gum tissue. Normal treatment includes special feeding for the first year, then surgical correction of the deformity, followed by special dental care and speech therapy if necessary.

Cleisthenes, the name of two Greek statesmen. The first was tyrant of Athens *c.*600–580 BC; the second, his grandson, was in power 508–506, completely changing the administrative divisions of Athens and leaving behind the state power of ostracism. He is thought of as the creator of Athenian democracy.

Cleistogamous Flower, small, closed self-fertilizing flowers. Cleistogamous fertilization takes place within a flower that does not open. It ensures seed production when normal cross-pollination fails. Sweet violet, oxalis, and impatiens are examples.

Clematis, genus of about 250 species of perennial, mostly climbing shrub found worldwide. Many have attractive flowers or flower clusters. Leaves are usually compound. Well-known species are woodbine and old-man's-beard. Family Ranunculaceae.

Clemenceau, Georges (1841–1929), French political figure. While a medical student in Paris he helped found and wrote for republican journals and was jailed briefly in 1862 for these activities. Between 1865–1869 he lived in the United States. Shortly after returning to France he participated in the founding of the Third Republic. He served in the chamber of deputies from 1876 to 1893. He was also highly influential through newspaper articles he wrote. Having made many powerful enemies, he was defeated for reelection in 1893. He then dedicated himself to journalism for the next decade. He was an early, ardent defender of Alfred Dreyfus. In 1902 he was elected to the senate and in 1906 became premier. As premier he settled the first Moroccan crisis, enforced the new law separating church and state, and strengthened France's alliance with Great Britain. He broke with the socialists over his harsh measures against striking miners. His cabinet fell in 1909. Back in the senate he attacked Germany and urged military preparedness. In November 1917 he formed a coalition government that restored French morale and led to victory. Representing France at the Paris Peace Conference he clashed with Woodrow Wilson over concern for French security. His government was defeated in 1920 and he retired from the senate.

Clemens, Samuel Langhorne. *See* Twain, Mark.

Clement I, Roman Catholic pope (88?–97?) and saint. His primary concern was church organization. He remained under constant observation by civil authorities

until his martyrdom for refusing to pledge allegiance to the Roman emperor.

Clement III, Roman Catholic pope (1187–91), b. Paolo Scolari. After the fall of Jerusalem to Saladin in 1187, he preached the Third Crusade. He made the Scottish church dependent on Rome (1188).

Clement VII, antipope (1378–94) during the Great Schism. He had served as a papal legate under Pope Gregory XI. He remained convinced of the legitimacy of his election as pope. *See also* Great Schism.

Clement of Alexandria (150?–?220), Greek church father. His full name was Titus Flavius Clemens. He studied in Alexandria, Egypt, where he founded a school that became a center of learning. Several writings have survived, including his *Hortatory Address to the Greeks,* the *Paedagogue,* the treatise *Who Is the Rich Man That Shall Be Saved?,* and the *Hypotyposes.* For Clement, Christian truth is joined to Greek philosophy while his work paves the way for specifically Christian doctrine.

Cleopatra (69–30 BC), queen of Egypt (51–30 BC). In 48 BC, with the aid of Julius Caesar, she overthrew her husband-brother coruler Ptolemy XII. She became Caesar's mistress, followed him to Rome, and bore him a son, Caesarion. After Caesar's assassination (44 BC), she fled Rome. She won the affections of Marc Antony and with him returned triumphantly to Egypt (42 BC). In 36 BC they were married. This outraged Octavian Caesar; he decided to destroy them. In 31 BC Antony and Cleopatra's fleets were destroyed at Actium. They fled back to Alexandria where Antony killed himself. Cleopatra surrendered to Octavian, but was unable to win him over. She killed herself with an asp.

Clermont-Ferrand, capital city of Puy-de-Dôme dept. in S central France; scene of council in 1095 that initiated the Crusades. Industries: rubber goods, chemicals, linen, machinery. Founded by Romans. Pop. 161,203.

Cleveland, (Stephen) Grover (1837–1908), 22nd and 24th President of the United States, b. Caldwell, N.J. In 1886 he married Frances Folsom; they had five children. A lawyer in Buffalo, N.Y., Cleveland was elected mayor of that city (1881). His reputation as a reformer led to his nomination and election as Democratic governor of New York. He quickly achieved a national reputation, and the Democrats chose him as their presidential candidate (1884). He won a narrow victory over James G. Blaine.

His first term was marked by an attempt to reform the civil service and by his advocacy of a low tariff; both issues had strong opponents in both parties. He ran for re-election in 1888 but was narrowly defeated by Benjamin Harrison, the Republican candidate and an advocate of a high tariff.

In 1892, he was nominated again, and this time he decisively defeated Harrison. The Panic of 1893 raised the issue of free coinage of silver, which was supported by the radical or free-silver Democrats. An economic conservative, Cleveland opposed free coinage and secured the repeal of the Sherman Silver Purchase Act, which enraged the radical Democrats. In 1894, he broke the Pullman Strike in Chicago by the use of federal troops. The free-silver Democrats prevailed at the 1896 convention and nominated William Jennings Bryan.

He was essentially a moderate in foreign policy. Cleveland broadened the interpretation of the Monroe Doctrine in the Venezuela Boundary Dispute with Great Britain. He refused to annex Hawaii after a US-

backed faction overthrew the monarchy, and he discouraged those who wanted to take Cuba from Spain.

Career: Mayor, Buffalo, N.Y., 1881; New York Governor, 1883–85; President, 1885–89, 1893–97.

Cleveland, city and port of entry in NE Ohio, at mouth of Cuyahoga River on Lake Erie; seat of Cuyahoga co; largest city in Ohio. A leading ore port and Great Lakes shipping point, it is also an iron and steel center; site of Case Western Reserve University (1826), John Carroll University (1886), Cleveland State University (1923), Cuyahoga Community College (1963), and the Cleveland Institute of Art and the Fine Arts Garden; home of the Cleveland Symphony Orchestra, and Play House (1916), which operates three repertory theaters; parks total 2,000acres (800hectares) and include a large zoo; the city's *Plain Dealer* newspaper is nationally known. John D. Rockefeller was educated in Cleveland and started his oil dynasty here in 1870 by forming Standard Oil Co. The National Aeronautics and Space Administration maintains a large research center here. Industries: chemicals, oil refining, garments, food processing. Founded 1796 by Moses Cleaveland; chartered as city 1836. Pop. (1980) 573,822.

Cleveland Bay, light horse breed developed in Cleveland district of Yorkshire, England, for riding, driving, and farm use. Large for a light horse, it is always solid bay with black legs. Height: 64in (160cm) at shoulder; weight: 1150–1400lb (521.6–635kg).

Cleveland Heights, city in N Ohio; E suburb of Cleveland; just W of city are Case Western Reserve University (1826), Cleveland Museum of Art, and Ursuline College (1871). Inc. 1921. Pop. (1980) 56,438.

Click Beetle, or skipjack, snapping beetle, beetle that turns over by snapping its body and throwing itself into the air. It makes an audible click in the process. Its long, cylindrical larvae are called wireworms. Family Elateridae. *See also* Wireworm.

Cliff Dwellers, Pueblo Indians of the US Southwest, who lived in masonry houses built into the sides of cliffs (about AD 1000). Hand-hewn stone bricks and adobe mortar were the main construction materials. Ceilings had large crossbeams placed on laths of small branches, plastered over. Buildings were four to five stories high with each story set back, making terraces. By the end of the 13th century, the Pueblos had left their cliff dwellings for small villages further south. *See also* Mesa Verde; Pueblo Indians.

Clifton, city in NE New Jersey on Passaic River, 9mi (14km) N of Newark. Industries: steel, textiles, chemicals, electronics. Settled 1640 as fur trading post; inc. 1895. Pop. (1980) 74,388.

Climate, the totality of weather behavior over periods of decades or centuries, investigated by climatologists. Macroclimates cover broad climatic regions around the globe; microclimates involve climatic conditions of a small area like a lawn or a field. Solar radiations reaching the earth vary with the seasons over broad regions, determining the torrid (tropical), temperate, and frigid (polar), or similar, climatic zones. Land and sea characteristics, like mountain ranges and ocean currents, as well as the general atmospheric circulation contribute also to the mean temperatures and precipitation, as well as vegetative cover, that defines smaller climatic regions. W. Köppen's climate classification, for example, basically involves mean temperature, precipitation, and vegetative distributions as affected by these other factors. C. W. Thornthwaite's analysis of climates emphasizes the measurement of potential evapotranspiration, the amount of moisture, if available, removed from the land by both evaporation from surfaces and transpiration by plants. *See also* Climate Control; Weather.

Climate Control, the prediction and control of climatic changes. Evidence over thousands of years from tree rings, Earth strata, pollen counts, and Greenland and Antarctic ice cores, from many past glaciations, and even from weather data of the last 100 years has indicated vast changes in climates. Some evidence exists of a worldwide warming during the first four decades of this century, since followed by a cooling trend. But the causes, single or multiple, for these changes are as yet undetermined. They have been attributed variously to variations in solar output, in Earth's orbital path or axis of rotation, in the Earth's atmosphere (caused by changes in amount of volcanic or meteoric dust or carbon dioxide or ozone), in ocean currents, or in snow cover or vegetation cover. Until climatic changes can be explained, climates cannot be controlled, although changes have been proposed employing such techniques as shifting ocean currents or melting polar ice by darkening it. *See also* Climate; Weather Modification.

Climatology, the study by scientists (climatologists) of the earth's climates with the aim of identifying their conditions, including characteristic temperature, pressure, winds, precipitation, and vegetation, and eventually determining their causes and ultimate control. *See also* Meteorology.

Climbing Fern, or Hartford fern, delicate North American fern with 3ft (91cm) vinelike leaves in rows on a twining stem. Sterile leaflets are palmately lobed and sporiferous leaflets are forked. Family Schizaeaceaea; species *Lygodium palmatum. See also* Fern.

Climbing Perch, tropical freshwater fish found in SE Asia. Not a true perch, it is popular with home aquarists. It is gray-brown or green and uses extended gill covers to "walk" on land for short distances. Length: to 10in (25.4cm). Family Anabantidae; species *Anabas testudineus.*

Clinical Psychology, field psychology concerned with diagnosis and treatment of behavior disorders, from failures in adjustment to severe mental illness. Clinical psychologists may work with psychiatrists, but they are not required to have medical degrees. *See also* Abnormal Psychology; Psychiatry.

Clinton, George (1739–1812), US statesman, b. Little Britain, N.Y. An early patriot and delegate to the Second Continental Congress, he was briefly a brigadier general in the Revolution and then was elected governor of New York (1777). He served to 1795 and later supported Thomas Jefferson, whose vice president he became in 1804. Reelected in 1808, he died in office.

Clinton, (Sir) Henry (1738?–95), English general. Sent to the American colonies in 1775, he served under Generals Howe and Burgoyne at Boston in May and Bunker Hill in June; he participated in the Battle of Long Island in August 1776. In 1778 he succeeded Howe as commander-in-chief and in 1780 captured Charleston and the southern army. He resigned his post in 1782 and two years later served as governor of Gibralter. His son, Sir Henry Clinton (1771–1829), was one of Wellington's favorite officers, serving in the Peninsular War (1811) and at Waterloo (1815).

Clipper Ship, three-masted commercial vessel built during the first half of the 19th century primarily for speed, and characterized by a long slim hull and many sails. One of the fastest, the American *Flying Cloud,* sailed from New York to San Francisco via Cape Horn in 89 days.

Clive, Robert, Baron Clive of Plassey (1725–74), English soldier and colonial administrator. He went to India as an official of the British East India Company in 1843. He was taken prisoner when Madras was recaptured by the Bengalese in 1746, but escaped. He used guerrilla tactics to take and hold Arcot in the struggle between the French and British East India companies (1751). Appointed governor of Fort St. David (1755), in 1757 he recaptured Calcutta and defeated the Bengalese at the Battle of Plassey. He governed Bengal until 1760, when he returned to England. He was governor of Bengal again 1765–67, but had to return to England to answer charges of embezzling state funds. He was acquitted by Parliament in 1772.

Cloaca, common cavity into which intestinal, urinary, and genital tracts open in fish, reptiles, birds, and some primitive mammals.

Cloisonné, type of enameling technique used in Byzantine art. It reached its apex in Western art during the 10th and 11th centuries. The design is constructed out of wires soldered to a plate, and the cells (cloisons) thus formed are filled with a colored vitreous paste which, when fired, turns into colored glass.

Cloister, an uncovered quadrangle surrounded by a covered walk. An open colonnade forms the side of the walk facing the quadrangle; the other side is bounded by the inner walls of surrounding buildings. Notable examples are at Oxford University and St. John Lateran Church, Rome.

Clone, the descendants of a single cell—a pure cell line. In plants, a clone is the set of plants obtained from a single original plant by means of vegetative propagation such as budding, grafting, or taking cuttings. In animals, asexual reproduction of one parent often produces a set of individuals that form a clone. Cloning is also a technique of genetic manipulation in which a particular gene is isolated from a cell's genetic material for study. The technique of cloning is also used to produce hybridomas, a monoclonal cell line derived from fused plasmocytoma and immune lymphocyte cells. Because the immunological reactivity of such a cell line can be chosen, hybridomas are valuable in immunological and embryological studies.

Clontarf, town in E Republic of Ireland, on N shore of Dublin Bay; suburb of Dublin. Irish forces under Brian Boru defeated the Danes here 1014; site of Clontarf Castle (1835).

Clotaire I (*c.* 497–561), Frankish king. On the death of his father, Clovis I, in 511 he received a share of the Frankish kingdom with his capital at Soissons. In 524 he divided the share of his deceased brother Clodomir with another brother Childebert I. In 531 he conquered and divided Thuringia with his brother Theodoric. He and Childebert seized and divided Burgundy in 534. Their attack against the Visigoths of Spain was repulsed (542). Clotaire became the sole king of the Franks after the death of Theodoric's heir (555) and of Childebert (558).

Clotaire II (died 629), Frankish king. He succeeded his father, Chilperic I, as king of Neustria (584). Upon the death of his cousin Theodoric II (613), he became king of Austrasia, thus becoming king of all the Franks. In 614 he had to make concessions to the nobles, including the establishment of the position of mayor of the palace, that would in the long run destroy the power of the Frankish kings.

Clothes Moth, small moth whose larva attacks woolen fabrics, furs, and leather. The most destructive of the three species is the case-making *Tinea pellionella.* It builds and lives in a small portable case. Family Tineidae. *See also* Moth.

Cloud, a visible mass of tiny water droplets or ice particles in the atmosphere, formed by condensation of water vapor around condensation nuclei. Other clouds may consist of dust or smoke particles dense enough to be visible. Clouds are classified in many groups by meteorologists according to their appearance and formation. Cirrus clouds are white and filmy or curly, usually high in altitude and formed of ice crystals. Cumulus clouds are white, piled-up masses of clouds at low or middle altitudes, with flat bases and rounded outlines above. Stratus clouds are relatively low, gray clouds stretched out horizontally in layers. Nimbostratus clouds are dark and gray, accompanied usually by precipitation. Cumulonimbus clouds are exceptionally dense with a flat base, developing rapidly vertically with an anvil head or plume to form the familiar thundercloud yielding lightning, thunder, and usually heavy precipitation, sometimes hail. *See also* Condensation.

Cloud Chamber, or **Expansion Chamber,** instrument for detecting and identifying charged particles, such as the proton, based on a device invented by C. T. Wilson (1895). It consists of a chamber containing saturated gas or air. If the gas is cooled quickly by adiabatic expansion, any energetic ionizing particle passing through the gas will leave a line of droplets along its path. The liquid drops form on the ions left in the wake of the particle. Particles can be identified by the nature of the tracks, their curvature in an applied magnetic field, and by the tracks produced by decay products. *See also* Bubble Chamber.

Clouded Leopard, small, rare cat found in forests of India, SE Asia, Sumatra, and Borneo. A nocturnal prowler, its coat is ochre yellow marked with dark stripes and spots. It is an expert climber and has the longest canine teeth of any cat. The gestation period is 90 days and 2–4 young are born. Length: body—29.5–41.4in (75–105cm); tail—27.5–35.4in (70–90cm); weight: 50lb (23kg). Family Felidae; species *Leo nebulosa.*

Cloud Seeding, the technique of adding particles to clouds to alter their natural development, usually to initiate or increase their precipitation. Granulated solid carbon dioxide and silver iodide crystals have been used to promote the formation of precipitation in clouds by providing condensation nuclei. Mixed results have been obtained from many cloud-seeding experiments, and the technique is not yet under predictable control. *See also* Weather Modification.

Clove, aromatic, evergreen tree native to the Molucca Islands and the source of the cloves of commerce. Small purple flower clusters are dried to produce cloves. Height: to 40ft (12m). Family Myrtaceae; species *Eugenia aromatica.*

Clover, generally low growing annual, biennial, and perennial plants. Primarily native to temperate and warm regions of the Northern Hemisphere. The leaves have three leaflets, seldom four, and the dense flower clusters are white, red, purple, pink, or yellow. Clover nectar is used by bees for making honey. These plants restore nitrogen to the soil and are used for forage and in lawn seed mixtures. Family Leguminosae; genus *Trifolium.*

Clovis I, or **Chlodowech** (465–511), Salian king of the Frankish kingdom that dominated much of western Europe in the early Middle Ages. Clovis invoked the aid of his wife Clotilda's god during a battle near Cologne. Victorious, he and his troops were baptized. He divided his kingdom among his sons shortly before his death.

Clovis III (682–95), Merovingian king of Neustria and Burgundy. His rule marked the end of the Merovingians' power; his kingdom was actually controlled by Pepin II, Carolingian mayor of the palace of Austrasia.

Clownfish, or clown triggerfish, marine fish found in shallow Indo-Pacific waters. It has a compressed body, leathery skin, a spine in its dorsal fin, and has blue and green streaks on black, with an orange mouth. Family Balistidae; species *Balistoides conspicillium, Balistoides niger.* Also orange, brown, and white Indo-Pacific damselfish. Length: to 6in (15.2cm). Family Pomacentridae; species *Amphiprion percula.*

Clubfoot, congenital deformity in which the foot twists inward and downward, looking somewhat like a club. It occurs in about one out of 1000 births, usually in males. It can be corrected by placing the foot in casts to make its position normal or by surgical intervention. In a few cases clubfoot occurs after birth as the result of neurological or muscular disease.

Club Moss, any of about 200 species (genus *Lycopodium,* order Lycopodiales) of small evergreen seedless plants, which, unlike the more primitive true mosses, have specialized tissues for transporting water, food, and minerals. The stems of some species are erect, while those of other species (the ground pines) creep along the ground and bear erect branches.

Cluj, city in NW central Romania, on Somesul River in Transylvania; formerly part of Austria-Hungary, became Romanian in 1920; noted for 14th-century Gothic church and botanical gardens. Industries: chemicals, electrical equipment, machinery. Founded 12th century by German colonists. Pop. 222,429.

Clumber Spaniel, slow-working finder and retriever breed of dog (sporting group) originally bred in England by Duke of Newcastle at Clumber Park. A sedate, heavy-looking dog with a thoughtful expression, it has a massive head with upper lips overhanging the lower jaw. Long, broad ears hang close to the head. The long, low body is set on short, heavy legs. The tail is carried low. A silky, feathered coat is lemon or orange with white. Average size: about 17in (43cm) high at shoulder; 55–65lb (25–29.5kg). *See also* Sporting Dog.

Cluniac Order, or **Order of Cluny,** Roman Catholic religious order. Founded by William the Pious, Duke of Aquitaine, in 910 at the Monastery of Cluny near Mâcon, France, it was known almost from its beginning for its high standards, reflected in strict Benedictine rule, stress on splendid and solemn worship, importance of personal spiritual life, and sound economics with independent lay control. Its influence spread throughout southern France and Italy, reaching its height in the 12th century. The monastery at Cluny survived until 1790.

Cluny, town in E central France, in Saône-et-Loire dept.; noted for Benedictine Abbey of Cluny and for Cluny lace. Founded 910 by St Berno, a Burgundian monk. Pop. 4,000.

Cluster, Stellar, any of innumerable collections of gravitationally associated stars occurring within galax-

Clipper ship

Clumber spaniel

Coblenz, West Germany

ies. Stellar clusters are of two main types: open, or galactic, clusters and globular clusters. Open clusters, usually found in the spiral arms of galaxies, consist of up to several thousand young stars belonging to Population I; globular clusters, much more concentrated, are found in the halo surrounding the centers of galaxies and consist of old Population II stars running into the millions.

Cluster Variable. See RR Lyrae Variable.

Clyde River, river in Scotland; rises in Southern Uplands; flows NE, then NW, passing over the Falls of Clyde near Lanark, and widening into the Firth of Clyde at Dumbarton; noted for shipbuilding yards below Glasgow. Length: 106mi (171km).

Clydesdale, draft horse breed developed in Clyde River Valley, Scotland, from Flemish and English horses. It was introduced in the United States during the 1870s. A massive horse with distinctive style and action, it has characteristic long hair below its knees. Colors are bay or brown with white marks. Height: 64–68in (163–173cm) at shoulder; weight: 1700–1900lb (710–860kg).

Clymer, George (1739–1813), American patriot and a signer of the Declaration of Independence and the US Constitution, b. Philadelphia, Pa. A successful merchant, he attended the Continental Congress (1776–78; 1780–83) and later worked to promote penal reform in Pennsylvania.

Clytemnestra, wife of Agamemnon, Greek king of Mycenae, who led the siege of Troy. After the fall of Troy, Agamemnon returned home with his captive Cassandra, where he was slain by Clytemnestra and her lover Aegisthus. The Greek poet Aeschylus attributes the murder to Clytemnestra alone. The murder was avenged by Agamemnon's son Orestes.

Cnidaria, or **Coelenterata,** a phylum consisting of about 9000 species of aquatic invertebrates. Included are corals, hydras, jellyfish, sea anemones, sea pens, sea fans, and sea whips.

Cnidus (Cnidos), ancient Greek city of Caria, SW Asia, on tip of Resadiye Peninsula, Turkey; independent city and member of Dorian Hexapolis; ruled by Persians 540 BC; noted for wealth, temples, and statues; important trade center; site of a medical school and the statue Aphrodite by Praxiteles.

Coachwhip Snake, or whipsnake, slender agile snake ranging from United States to N South America. It varies in color but is frequently brown and striped or cross-barred. Unrelated species in Asia and Australia are also called whipsnakes. Length: to 5ft (1.5cm). Family Colubridae; genus *Masticophis*. See also Colubrid.

Coal, a blackish rock composed of petrified vegetable matter, used as a fuel. In the Carboniferous and Tertiary Periods, vegetation subsided in swamp regions to form peat (a low grade fuel) bogs. Sedimentary deposits covered the bog, applying pressure, resulting in various kinds of coal. Coal is classified by fixed carbon content and by petrologic components. Lignite, bituminous coal, and anthracite coal show increasing carbon content; high carbon content results in better fuel. Petrologic components are called macerals, organic counterparts to the minerals in inorganic rock. Cannel coal is derived from microspores and is used in stoves and fireplaces.

Coal Fish. See Pollack.

Coalition, alliance of groups, parties, or states that serves the mutual political interests of its participants. In democratic countries with multiparty systems, coalitions are frequently formed by political parties or groups that seek to govern but alone do not have a majority in the representative assembly.

Coal Mining, the process of removing coal from an excavation, or mine, carried on as a basic worldwide industry. Two principal systems are used: surface (strip) mining, a form of quarrying used when the seam of coal is near the surface; and underground (deep) mining, in which the seam is reached through shafts or tunnels. Power machines have replaced traditional hand tools. Although 3,000,000,000 metric tons are mined annually worldwide there are sufficient reserves to assure the future of the industry.

Coast Guard, US, branch of the armed forces. It is within the department of transportation, but operates as part of the Navy in time of war or when the president directs. Peacetime missions include search and rescue at sea, marine law enforcement, safety and environmental protection, and navigation assistance (buoys, lightships, beacons, etc). The Coast Guard operates over 250 ships, 160 aircraft, and 2,000 small craft with 37,000 military and 6,000 civilian personnel. It was established in 1790 as the Revenue Marine, an agency to enforce maritime law, and was administered by the treasury department. It was later renamed the Revenue Cutter Service and (1915) then became the Coast Guard. In 1939 control of the Lighthouse Service was added and in 1942 it took over functions of the Bureau of Marine Inspection and Navigation. It became a component of the department of transportation in 1967.

Coast Ranges, mountain ranges paralleling the Pacific coast of North America, from S California, N through Oregon and Washington into British Columbia and Alaska; composed of folded and sometimes faulted sedimentary rocks; the faults have caused earthquakes in California. Some S valley areas are cultivated for grapes, fruit, and vegetables; in the N, they are an important source of redwood, spruce, and Douglas fir trees.

Coati, or **Coatimundi,** 3 species of raccoonlike rodents of the SW United States and South America. Most have long, slender brown to black bodies (although some are orange-red) with long tapering snouts and long ringed tails. Coatis forage in groups on the ground or in trees for plant and animal food. Length: 50in (127cm); weight: 25lb (11.3kg). Family Procyonidae.

Coatzacoalcos, city in SE Mexico, on Gulf of Campeche, 134mi (216km) SE of Veracruz. Industries: petroleum, lumber, canning, soap. Pop. 108,818.

Cobalt, metallic element (symbol Co) of the first transition series, discovered about 1735. It is found in cobaltite (CoAsS) and smaltite (arsenide), but the bulk is obtained as a by-product during the processing of other ores. The metal is used in high-temperature steels. It is a ferromagnetic element and a constituent of certain magnetic alloys. Co^{60} (half-life 5.26yr) is an artificial isotope used as a source of gamma rays in radiotherapy, tracer studies, etc. Properties: at. no. 27; at. wt. 58.9332; sp gr 8.9; melt. pt. 2723°F (1495°C); boil. pt. 5198°F (2870°C); most common isotope Co^{59} (100%). See also Transition Elements.

Cobb, Ty(rus Raymond) (1886–1961), US baseball player, b. Narrows, Ga. Cobb played for the Detroit Tigers (1904–26) and the Philadelphia Athletics (1926–30), compiling a record 4191 hits and a record lifetime batting average of .367. He was the first elected member of the Baseball Hall of Fame (1936).

Cobbett, William (1763–1835), British political essayist and reformer. From a poor farming background, Cobbett joined the army and in 1792 was forced to flee to the US after denouncing army injustices. He returned to England and edited the *Political Register* (1802), which from 1804 was the leading voice for social and parliamentary reform despite repressive measures such as the Gagging Acts (1817). He became deeply concerned with the rural effects of industrialization as shown in his *Rural Rides* (1830).

Cobden, Richard (1804–65), English statesman, economist, and businessman. Cofounder of the Anti-Corn Law League (1838), he served in parliament (1841–57, 1859–65) as champion of free trade. He opposed imperialist foreign policies and supported the North in the American Civil War.

Coblenz (Koblenz), city in W West Germany, at confluence of the Rhine and Moselle rivers, 56mi (90km) SE of Cologne. Founded in 9th century BC as a Roman camp, it was later a residence of Frankish kings; from 10th to late 18th century it was held by archbishops of Trier. During WWII, 80% of city was destroyed; site of Church of St Castor (built 836 and rebuilt 1200), and 11th-century fortress of Ehrenbreitsen. Industries: pianos, furniture, textiles. Pop. 118,394.

Cobra, poisonous snake found worldwide. It has immovable, hollow or grooved venom-conducting fangs in the front upper jaw. Included are coral snakes, mambas, kraits, and true cobras. Family Elapidae. Also, several large snakes capable of spreading their neck skin into a hood. The king cobra or hamadryad *(Ophiophagus hannah)* of SE Asia is the largest; length to 18ft (5.5m). Several African and Asian species can spit venom into enemies' eyes.

Cocaine, white crystalline alkaloid extracted from the leaves of the coca plant. It is used in the form of its hydrochloride as a local anesthetic but as a dangerous habit-forming drug it is strictly controlled.

Coccyx, the end of the vertebral column in man, formed by the fusion of four small vertebrae.

Cochin China (Cochinchine), historical region in Vietnam, including greater part of South Vietnam. It is bounded by Cambodia (NW), Annam region of Vietnam (NE), South China Sea (SE), Gulf of Siam (SW). This flat alluvial plain of the Mekong River delta is one of the world's foremost rice-producing areas; fishing is an important industry. Ceded by Annam to France in 1862 by terms of Treaty of Saigon; became part of French Indochina 1887; inc. into Vietnam 1949; became part of South Vietnam 1954. See also Vietnam.

Cochineal, soft-bodied, scale insect found in Mexico and SW United States. Females have red bodies and feed on prickly pear cactus. Until about 1875, crimson dye was produced from the dried female bodies. Length: ⅛in (3mm). Family Dactylopiidae; species *Dactylopius coccus.*

Cochise (c.1815–1874), chief of the Chiricahua Apaches. In 1861 the US Army captured him for a crime he did not commit, killing five of his relatives. He escaped and then led his tribe in war against settlers and the military in Arizona for 11 years. Concurrently, a war of extermination was being raged against his people. Cochise was befriended by Thomas Jeffords and through him made a treaty with Gen. Oliver Otis Howard that created a reservation of the chief's native territory. He lived peacefully on the reservation until his death, after which the treaty was broken and his people were moved from their land.

Cockatoo, large parrot with elongated, erectile crest. Most live in Australia, SW Asia, and nearby islands. They are mostly white, tinged with pink or yellow. They favor treetops, laying white eggs (1–4) in a tree hole nest, and feed on fruit and seeds. Length: 15in (38cm). Family Psittacidae.

Cockburn, (Sir) George (1772–1853), English admiral. After presiding over the capitulation of Martinique to Britain (1809), he was second in command (1813–14) in the War of 1812 and participated in the capture of Washington, D.C. In 1815 he carried out Napoleon's sentence of deportation and was governor of St. Helena (1815–16). He became admiral (1837), senior naval lord (1841), and admiral of the fleet (1851).

Cockcroft, (Sir) John Douglas (1897–1967), English physicist whose research dealt with particle acceleration in an electric field. Working with Ernest Walton, he constructed a voltage multiplier capable of accelerating protons to higher energy levels. The Cockcroft-Walton generator was utilized in the disintegration of lithium atoms by bombarding them with protons. The 1951 Nobel Prize was awarded to both men for their use of particle accelerators to study atomic nuclei. Cockcroft also contributed to the development of the atomic bomb.

Cocker Spaniel, capable gun dog (sporting group) named for proficiency in flushing woodcock. It has a rounded head and broad, square muzzle; the well-feathered ears are long and set at eye level. The sturdy, compact body is set on straight, strongly boned legs; the tail is docked. A well-feathered, flat coat is black, black and tan, parti-colored, or any other solid color. Average size: 14–15in (35.5–38cm) high at shoulder; about 25lb (11.5kg). *See also* Sporting Dog.

Cockfighting, sport, popular in Latin America and Asia, in which two gamecocks are pitted against each other in a fight. The gamecocks—bred for fighting—are placed in a small circular pit. To enhance the action, metal spurs are sometimes attached to the bird's natural spurs. The match goes on until one of the gamecocks refuses to fight or is killed. The sport has its origins in ancient Persia, Greece, and Rome and is still practiced where it is legal in some areas of the United States.

Cockle, bivalve mollusk found in marine waters. Its varicolored, heart-shaped shell has strong, radiating ribs. Many are edible. Length: 2–3in (50.8–76.2mm). Class Pelecypoda; family Cardiidae; species include *Cardium aculeatum.*

Cock-of-the-rock, fruit-eating, brightly colored, parrotlike bird of tropical South America. Its large, erect crest almost hides its bill. After group courtship dances, females lay eggs (2) in a mud-and-stick nest near a cave entrance. The golden cock-of-the-rock is orange-gold with black markings. The Peruvian species is red with black wings and tail. Length: to 12in (30cm). Genus *Rupicola.*

Cockroach, or roach, croton bug, insect with long feelers and flat, soft body found worldwide, though most are tropical. Its head is hidden under a shield (pronotum) and it may be winged or wingless. Living in dark, damp places indoors or outside, some species are serious household pests. Length: ½–2in (13–50mm). Order Blattaria. *See also* Orthoptera.

Coconut Oil, semisolid fat with a characteristic odor, consisting principally of the glyceride of lauric acid ($CH_3(CH_2)_{10}COOH$). It is extracted from pressed boiled coconut meat and used to manufacture soaps, vegetable fats, candles, and cosmetics. Properties: sp gr 0.92; melt. pt. 68–82°F (20–28°C).

Coconut Palm, or copra palm, tall palm native to the seashores of the Indo-Pacific and the Pacific coast of South America; most important commercially of all the palms. To 100ft (30.5m) tall, it has a leaning trunk and a crown of feather-shaped leaves each about 20ft (6.1m) long. Flower clusters have separate male and female flowers; the fruit, the familiar coconut, ripens in 10 to 12 months. The dried meat of the coconut is copra, the valuable commercial product that is the source of coconut oil used in the manufacture of margarine, soap, and cooking oil. Family Palmaceae; species *Cocos nucifera.*

Cocoon, case or wrapping produced by larval forms of animals, such as moths and earthworms, for the resting or pupal stage in their life cycle. Some spiders spin a cocoon that protects their eggs. *See also* Chrysalis; Moth; Pupa.

Cocos Islands, group of 27 small coral islands in Indian Ocean, SW of Java and Sumatra; discovered by Capt. William Keeling 1609; a protectorate of Australia since 1955, the islands were bought by Australia from their owner, John Clunies-Ross, for $7,000,000 in 1978. Exports: copra, coconuts. Area: 5sq mi (13sq km). Pop. 544.

Cocteau, Jean (1889–1963), French writer and painter who worked in ballet, theater, opera, and film. An immensely prolific and versatile artist, Cocteau was influenced by avant-garde movements but never belonged to any group. He is probably best known for his plays, including *Les Enfants terribles* (1929), dramatized from his novel, and for his films, many of which are also adaptations of his novels and plays. They include *Blood of a Poet* (1933), *La Belle et la Bête* (1946), and *Orphée* (1949).

Cod, bottom-dwelling marine fish found in cold to temperate waters, mainly in Northern Hemisphere. A valuable food fish, it is shades of gray, green, brown, or red, with a speckled pattern. Other members of the cod family are haddock, pollock, tomcod, and burbot. Length: to 6ft (182.8cm); Weight: to 211lb (95.8kg); average to 25lb (11.3kg). Family Gadidae; species: 150, including Atlantic *Gadus morhua* and Pacific *Gadus macrocephalus.*

Coddington, William (1601–78), US colonist, b. England. He was one of the commissioners of the Massachusetts Bay Company (1630), but his defense of Anne Hutchinson caused him to move first to Providence, then to what is now Portsmouth (1638). He helped to found Newport (1639). He was governor of Newport (1640) and several times magistrate of the Rhode Island colonies (1674, 1675, 1678).

Code. *See* Cryptography.

Code Civil. *See* Code Napoléon.

Codeine, white crystalline alkaloid extracted from opium by the methylation of morphine. It is used in medicine as an analgesic and in the treatment of coughs. *See also* Opium.

Code Napoléon (1804), French civil code that, with revisions, is still operative. Until the code was enacted, the French were subject to widely diversified laws, based on Roman law, customs, and royal decrees; marriage and family life were controlled almost entirely by the Roman Catholic Church's canon laws. Social breakdowns resulting from the French Revolution necessitated codification. The code was intended to conform only to the dictates of reason. It prohibited social inequalities and freed civilian institutions from the Church's control, permitting freedom of person and contract and upholding the inviolability of private property.

Codling Moth, small, grayish moth whose larva is one of the most destructive insect pests of apples. This brown-headed, pinkish-white caterpillar is the main cause of wormy apples. Species *Carpocapsa pomonella. See also* Moth.

Cod Liver Oil, an oil rich in vitamins A and D obtained from the livers of cod. It is used to prevent rickets in children and for other nutritional purposes.

Cody, William Frederick ("Buffalo Bill") (1846–1917), US frontiersman, scout, and showman, b. Davenport, Iowa. At 14 he rode for the Pony Express and served as scout during the Civil War. Ned Buntline made Cody famous in his semi-fictional dime novels about his exploits, including killing 4280 buffalo in a 17-month period. In 1872, Cody played the lead in his own touring Wild West show. In 1883 he organized the "Wild West" exhibition, with Annie Oakley and Chief Sitting Bull among his star performers.

Coeducation, teaching male and female students in the same classes. In ancient and medieval times, girls were taught separately, if at all. In Europe boys and girls began to attend the same elementary classes after the Reformation. By 1900 most US elementary schools were coeducational but many high schools and colleges were not. The coeducation movement grew in the 20th century as part of the drive for women's rights, and the practice is now widely accepted.

Coefficient, term multiplying a specified unknown in an algebraic expression. Thus, in $5xy$, 5 is the coefficient of xy and $5x$ is the coefficient of y.

Coefficient of Expansion. *See* Expansion, Coefficient of.

Coefficient of Friction. *See* Friction, Coefficient of.

Coelacanth, or latimeria, bony fish, thought to be extinct for over 300,000,000 years, then found in deep marine waters near the Comoro Islands off Africa in 1939. This steel-blue fish has fins at the end of fin stalks; hollow fin spines; heavy bony plates under the throat; and a cartilaginous skeleton. Length: 5ft (1.5m); weight: 127lbs (57.6kg). Order Coelacanthini; species *Latimeria chalumnae.*

Coelenterate, aquatic phylum of animals characterized by having the digestive cavity as the main body cavity. It represents the first animal group to reach the tissue level of organization. They are radially symmetrical, jellylike and have a nerve net and one body opening. Reproduction, which is sexual and asexual, includes polyp and medusa forms in the life cycle; regeneration also occurs. The almost 10,000 known species include jellyfish, sea anemone, coral, comb jellies, and hydroids.

Coenzyme, a nonprotein molecule, usually containing a vitamin and phosphorus. When combined with an apoenzyme, a protein molecule, it activates an enzyme.

Coercion, legal concept involving compulsion and constraint. Coercion is the direct or positive application of physical force to compel a person to act against his will (actual coercion, in legal terms) or where one party is constrained by subjugation to another to do something he would not do if he were not subjugated (implied coercion).

Coffee, tree or shrub native to tropical Africa and Asia and cultivated in tropical South America. They have white or cream flowers and long leaves. The beanlike seeds are ground to make coffee, a drink popular worldwide. Height: to 15ft (4.6m). Family Rubiaceae; genus *Coffea.*

Coggan, Frederick Donald (1909–), archbishop of Canterbury (1974–80). Coggan began as curate in a working-class church in London, and later served in academic positions in London and Toronto. He was made bishop of Bradford in 1956 and archbishop of York in 1961.

Cogito Ergo Sum, (Lat., I think, therefore I am). In his *Meditations* (II), the French philosopher René Descartes attempted to establish his own existence by reference to the act of thinking itself. What thinks must exist in order to think, whatever else may be doubted. Upon this intuitively necessary truth, he wished to devise an entire body of knowledge, newly founded on the certain basis of reason rather than on authority or sense, and therefore free of inherited error. *See also* Cartesian; Descartes, René; Rationalism.

Cognac, town in W France, on Charente River, 23mi (37km) W of Angoulême. Francis I was born here 1494. It was a Huguenot stronghold in 16th century; cognac (brandy) was first manufactured here in the 17th century. Pop. 22,062.

Cognitive Development Theory, theory in developmental psychology concerned with growth in the processes of perceiving, thinking, and knowing. Swiss psychologist Jean Piaget holds that cognitive processes develop through four stages from birth to adult status. During the first stage the child is most concerned with objects around him. Not until the final stage can a person make full use of symbols and logic. Jerome Bruner, an American, believes the course of development is more flexible than Piaget contends. *See also* Intelligence.

Cognitive Psychology, broad area concerned with perceiving, thinking, and knowing—eg, how individuals perceive information by sight or hearing, how they organize and store what they have perceived, how they remember and use information, how they use language and images. *See also* Cognitive Development Theory.

Cohesion, the attraction of molecules of a substance for each other.

Cohn, Ferdinand Julius (1828–98), German botanist. One of the founders of bacteriology as a separate science, his studies of algae and fungi began in 1868, and he published *Contributions to the Biology of Plants* in 1870. He conducted extensive research into lower plants, including bacteria, which he recognized as plants and attempted to classify. *See also* Bacteriology.

Coimbatore, city in S India, on Noyil River; occupies strategic position on E entrance to Palghat Gap, the only break in W coastal mountains for 900mi (1,449km); site of ancient Hindu pagoda of Perur. Industries: cotton, tanneries, coffee, sugar. Pop. 405,592.

Sir John Cockcroft

Buffalo Bill Cody

Colchester, England

Coke, (Sir) Edward (1552–1634), English jurist, As attorney general, he prosecuted the Earl of Essex, Sir Walter Raleigh, and the Gunpowder Plotters (1600–05). A chief justice of Common Pleas (1606), he protected the common law from crown encroachment. He presided over the King's Bench (1613) but was removed by James I (1616). Afterward, he served on both the Privy Council and the Court of the Star Chamber. Elected to Parliament (1620), he became leader of the party that opposed many of the king's policies. He led The Great Protestation (1621), for which he was briefly imprisoned (1621–22). He was the principal author of the *Petition of Right* (1628). His work, *Institutes* (1628–44), includes his famous analysis, *Coke Upon Littleton.*

Coke Processing, the production of a solid residue useful in metallurgy and home heating, from coal. Certain types of bituminous coal are heated to about 2192 °F (1200°C) out of contact with air until most of the volatile constituents have been driven off. What remains is carbon with small amounts of other elements and coal minerals. *See also* Coal.

Col, high, narrow mountain pass that may be the intersection of two cirques or a high point between two mountain valleys. *See also* Cirque.

Colbert, Jean Baptiste (1619–83), French minister of finance to Louis XIV. Having plotted the conviction and imprisonment of finance minister Nicolas Fouquet, Colbert dominated a newly created council of finance. He became controller general (1665), reforming the taille (a major tax) and terminating the financiers' plunder of the treasury. His efforts to increase France's international trade and to reorganize industry helped France to dominate Europe. His powers grew to include control of the navy, and he strongly influenced the country's cultural and intellectual life.

Colchester, city in SE England, on Colne River, 53mi (85km) NE of London; market town for agricultural and horticultural district. The first Roman colony in Britain settled here AD 43. Industries: chemicals, agricultural engineering, footwear. Pop. 132,400.

Colchis, ancient country in the Caucasus on the E side of the Black Sea (now part of the Georgian Republic of the USSR). In Greek legend it was the home of Medea, where Jason and the Argonauts stole the Golden Fleece. It was dominated successively by Persia, Greece, and Rome, and later became the focus of hostility between Byzantium and Persia (AD 6th century).

Cold, Common, very common, mild, contagious viral infection of the upper respiratory tract. More prevalent in cold months, colds usually occur in adults about two or three times a year, but more frequently in children and adults in close contact with children. A cold is caused by a virus, mostly a rhinovirus or enterovirus, with susceptibility perhaps increased by such factors as chilling, and is easily spread from person to person. Symptoms include obstruction and inflammation of the nose, sore throat, cough, hoarseness. The disease is self-limiting, usually disappearing within 10 days. There is no treatment for the common cold. Fever-reducing drugs, pain-relieving drugs, and decongestants may relieve symptoms and bring comfort. Antibiotics have not been found to be effective but may be given in cases where an accompanying bacterial infection is present.

Cold Frame, wood or concrete structure covered with glass or plastic doors and used outdoors to extend the plant growing season. Heated by the sun, it is used to force bulbs, harden off seedlings started indoors, and protect seeds from heavy rains and animals. During winter, the frame can protect perennials, and be used to root shrub seedlings, and cold treat seeds and bulbs.

Cold Sore, also called fever blister, a small sore, often found around the lips, sometimes on the cheeks, ears, or genitals. It first appears as a tiny fluid-filled blister on a red skin patch, sometimes becomes pus-filled, and then dries up, leaving a yellowish or brownish crust for a week or two. Caused by a virus—herpes simplex—it is often associated with a cold, sometimes with other febrile diseases, sunburn, and menstruation.

Cold War, post-World War II political, ideological, and economic confrontation between the Soviet Union and the United States and their respective allies. Serious crises resulted from this situation, including the Berlin blockade (1948–49), and the Korean conflict (1950–53). Each side viewed the other with suspicion and considered world domination the primary goal of its adversary. Mutual distrust and tension characterized the period.

Cole, Thomas (1801–48), US landscape painter, b. England. A founder of the Hudson River school, Cole was fascinated by the American landscape. Early success allowed him to live in Catskill, N.Y., a region that inspired him. His large, romantic, lyric paintings, such as *The Voyage of Life,* are major works. *See also* Hudson River School.

Coleoptera, the largest order of insects (over 250,000 species), comprising the beetles and weevils. All have a front pair of wings not used for flight that are rigid and serve as a protective covering for the delicate flight wings and upper abdomen. Mouthparts are of the chewing type. Larvae are grubs that pass into an inactive pupal stage before maturing. Species vary in size from minute forms that live within spore tubes of fungi to Goliath beetles to 4in (10cm) long. Some are destructive pests of crops, while others (such as the ladybugs) are valuable to man. *See also* Beetle; Weevil.

Coleridge, Samuel Taylor (1772–1834), English Romantic poet and critic. Although he devoted most of his literary life to criticism, political journalism, and philosophy, he is chiefly remembered today as the author of the poems "The Rime of the Ancient Mariner," "Kubla Khan," and "Christabel." His poetry is noted for its rich imagery and exotic settings. In 1798 he and William Wordsworth published *Lyrical Ballads,* a collection of their poems that is generally considered the real beginning of the Romantic movement in English poetry. His greatest critical work, *Biographia Literaria* (1817), documents the critical theories of Romanticism. His criticisms of Shakespeare were highly influential in his day, as were his writings on German metaphysical philosophy.

Colette (Sidonie Gabrielle) (1873–1954), French novelist. Her first works, including the *Claudine* series (1900–04), were published under her first husband's pseudonym, Willy. Her novels, most of which contain strong autobiographical elements, were written in an exuberant style. Among her best-known works are *Chéri* (1920), *The Last of Chéri* (1926), and *Gigi* (1945).

Coleus, genus of bushy house or garden plant native to Africa and Indonesia, with oval, serrated leaves of reddish, green, or yellow combinations. Flowers are inconspicuous. Care: bright light, barely moist soil (equal parts of loam, peat moss, sand). Propagation is by stem cuttings or seeds. Height: to 30in (76cm). Family Labiatae.

Colfax, Schuyler (1823–85), US vice president (1869–73), b. New York City. A Republican party leader in Indiana, he was a US representative (1855–69) before becoming vice president. He was discredited in the Crédit Mobilier scandal.

Colic, spasmodic, cramplike pain in the abdomen usually becoming intense, subsiding, and then recurring. It may occur in the gall bladder (biliary colic), kidney or ureter (renal colic), intestines (intestinal colic), or in some other abdominal organ.

Coligny, Gaspard II de, Seigneur de Châtillon (1519–72), French admiral (1552), Huguenot leader. Announcing his support in 1560, Coligny became the sole leader of the Huguenots (1569) and was responsible for the Peace of Saint-Germain (1570). His suggestion to Charles IX that both sides fight against Spain angered Catherine de Médicis and François de Lorraine, Spanish allies. Catherine ordered Coligny's assassination; unsuccessful, she warned Charles of retaliation. The king demanded the Huguenot leaders' deaths, and Coligny was beaten and decapitated during the St Bartholomew's Day Massacre.

Colima, small state in W central Mexico, on the Pacific Ocean; formed by the foothills of the Sierra Madre Occidental and 70mi (113km) of coastal lowlands; economy based mainly on agriculture, fishing, mining. Colima, capital city, is commercial and agricultural center of state; site of colonial cathedral and state university. Industries: food processing, tanning, tobacco, shoes, leatherware. Founded (city) 1522; (state) 1824. Area: (state) 2,106sq mi (5,455sq km). Pop. (city) 72,074; (state) 317,000.

Colitis, inflammation of the lining of the colon, or large intestine, that produces bowel changes, usually diarrhea and cramplike pains. It may be acute, caused by infection; or chronic, often due to an emotional problem. In severe chronic ulcerative colitis, the colon lining ulcerates and bleeds.

Collage, pictorial technique in which all kinds of objects, chosen for their symbolic value, are pasted onto a painted background. It was begun by Georges Braque (1911) and used by Picasso and Max Ernst. Collage differs from papier collé in which objects are chosen for shape and texture alone.

Collagen, a protein substance that is the main constituent of bones, tendons, cartilage, connective tissue, and skin. It produces gelatin when boiled.

Collagen Diseases, any of several diseases marked by an abnormal change in the makeup of the body's connective tissues. Included in the group are systemic lupus erythematosus (SLE), often called lupus; scleroderma; dermatomyositis; rheumatic fever; and rheumatoid arthritis.

Collar Bone. See Clavicle.

Collared Lizard, big-headed, long-tailed lizard of SW United States and Mexico. Able to run on its hind legs, it is yellowish-green and brown with two black nape bands and light back spots. It eats smaller lizards and insects. Length: to 14in (35.5cm). Family Iguanidae; species *Crotaphytus collaris.*

Collective Bargaining, process through which wages and other conditions of employment are determined in the unionized firm. Representatives of the workers and the owners meet to make offers on a labor agreement that is to remain in force for a specified period. Over the years the process has changed as the issues have grown more complex. An agreement may be several hundred pages in length, cover almost anything, and require the opinions of countless experts on both sides. If an agreement is not reached, a strike or lockout results.

Collective Farms, large agricultural tracts in the USSR that are worked by a community of peasants who share in the profits in proportion to the labor each one contributes. Collectivization of private farms was begun in 1929 and by 1934, 71% of all peasant lands had been collectivized. In 1949 the smaller collectives were consolidated into larger ones. Under Khrushchev, the peasants were given the responsibility for maintaining the farm machinery as well as the land itself.

Collective Security, method by which nations aim at preventing aggression by pledging mutual support in case of attack. Most collective-security agreements are regional in scope (eg, the Organization of American States, the Warsaw Pact), although the founders of the United Nations hoped that it would become a global, collective security arrangement.

Collectivism, political and economic doctrine that advocates public control and ownership of the means of production and distribution. Similar to but more rigorous than classic socialism, it stresses central planning and overall coordination of economic life. Collectivism, to some degree, exists in both socialist and communist countries.

College, in a broad sense, any educational institution above the high school level. The term may also mean: a separate undergraduate school; the undergraduate division of a university; or a professional school, such as a teachers college. *See also* Junior College; Land-Grant College.

Collie, sheepherding dog (working group) bred from Scots shepherd and drover dogs in the mid-19th century. Popular in United States since 1880, it has a lean, wedge-shaped head; small, triangular ears held ¾ erect at alert; almond-shaped eyes; a long, muscular body; straight, medium length legs; and a long tail. The rough-coated variety has a long, straight, harsh coat, except on head and legs, where it is short. The smooth variety has a short, hard coat. Colors are sable and white; black, white, and tan; mottled blue-gray and black with white; and white. Average size: 22–26in (56–66cm) high at shoulder; 50–75lb (23–34kg). *See also* Working Dog.

Collingwood, Robin George (1889–1943), English philosopher and historian. At first an idealist who developed a philosophy of special sciences, he rejected idealism from 1937. In a major early work, *Speculum Mentis* (1924), he developed a system based on five forms of experience and the degree of truth in each, with art as the lowest and philosophy as the only form to yield truth. In *The New Leviathan* (1942), he views all expression as linguistic; the mind-end is consciousness and all acts of consciousness are also linguistic. His other works include *Religion and Philosophy* (1916) and *The Principles of Art* (1938).

Collins, Michael (1890–1922), Irish revolutionary. He fought in the Easter Rising (1916) and helped establish the Irish assembly (1918). He became intelligence director for the Sinn Fein and helped negotiate self-government for southern Ireland (1921). He was killed in the ensuing civil war. *See also* Sinn Fein.

Collins, (William) Wilkie (1824–89), English novelist who made important contributions to the development of the genre of the detective novel in books such as *The Woman in White* (1860) and *The Moonstone* (1868). He collaborated with Charles Dickens in writing many stories, including "The Wreck of the *Golden Mary.*" Collins was a master of intrigue and suspense and a technical innovator of narrative form.

Colloid, substance composed of fine particles which can be readily dispersed in a continuous phase. A solid dispersed in a liquid is termed a sol, a solid or a liquid in a gas an aerosol, a liquid in a liquid an emulsion, and a gas in either a liquid or a solid a foam. Chemists identify three main types: reversible, irreversible, and association colloids. Reversible colloids—including cellulose, proteins, hemoglobin, nylon, polystyrene, and vulcanized rubber—form true solutions, subject to the physical laws of nature, spontaneously formed when a dry colloid and a dispersion medium are brought together. Irreversible colloids—including gelatin, cheese, dough, milk, and clay—cannot be dismantled to their original components and require additional stabilizing compounds, usually adsorbed ions. Sols (dilute suspensions), emulsions, aerosols, foams, and pastes (concentrated suspensions) are irreversible colloidal suspensions. Soaps, detergents, and some dyes are examples of association colloids which have spontaneously aggregated to form stable larger molecules called micelles, which have hydrophobic centers and hydrophilic surfaces.

Colloidal Condensation, preparative technique for irreversible sols similar to precipitation. A supersaturated solution may be carefully condensed so that a large number of small particles are produced rather than a crystallization into large agglomerates. Electrodialysis has been used to agitate and control the deposition.

Colloidal Dispersion, preparative technique for a colloidal system such as an emulsion or a foam. Emulsions are stabilized by an emulsifying agent, such as proteins or clay; foam is stabilized by a foaming agent. Oil-in-water emulsions are used in polishes, cosmetic preparations, and foodstuffs such as margarine and mayonnaise. Meringue and fire-fighting preparations are examples of foams.

Colloidal Particle, a solid or liquid droplet of 10^{-6} to 10^{-2} mm diameter composed of an aggregate of molecules or a single giant molecule. Such particles may be formed by breaking down macroscopic particles by mechanical or chemical (known as peptizing) dissociation or by preparing a supersaturated solution, which then aggregates.

Colobus, or guereza, large, black and white, thumbless monkeys of equatorial Africa. Their long, silky fur was once used to trim women's coats. They are day-active tree dwellers that feed chiefly on leaves. The three species include *Colobus polykomos,* with a bushy white tail and striking white body markings. *See also* Monkey.

Cologne (Köln), city in W West Germany on the Rhine River, 25mi (40km) S of Düsseldorf. Romans est. a fortress here AD 50 and it remained in their control until 5th century. It was made an archbishopric by Charlemagne in 785. It declined toward end of Middle Ages and was ceded to Prussia in 1815; site of Cologne cathedral (started 1248, completed 1880), and Gurzenich, a Renaissance patrician's house; agricultural, commercial, tourist center. Industries: chemicals, textiles, banking, insurance, eau de cologne. Pop. 1,013,771.

Colombia, nation in NW South America. A land of mountains and tropical lowlands, it has vast uninhabited areas. The varying terrain has been partially responsible for regional tensions.

Land and Economy. The Andes, with peaks of nearly 19,000ft (5,795m), cover the NW third of the country and provide coal, platinum, and petroleum. Coffee from the mountains accounts for about 50% of export sales. The E and S slope down to such major rivers as the Orinoco, Putumayo, and Amazon. Between the mountains and equatorial lowlands, grassy plains provide good beef-cattle lands. Sugar cane, cotton, tobacco, and bananas grow well in Colombia.

People. Nearly 70% of Colombians have mixed blood, and many of these mestizos take an active part in public life. Another 20% of the population is of European descent, while Indians and blacks make up the remaining 10%. In the 20th century people have moved to the cities, and about 75% of the population is urbanized. Spanish is the official language, and Roman Catholicism the state religion. About 35% of the people can neither read nor write.

Government. The constitution calls for a president, who cannot succeed himself, a senate, and a chamber of representatives. The Liberal and Conservative parties are the most powerful.

History. Colombia, called New Grenada by the Spanish when they made settlements on the Caribbean coast in the 1520s, took its present name in honor of Christopher Columbus after it gained independence in 1819. Simón Bolívar's Gran Colombia originally included Venezuela and Ecuador, which broke free in 1830, and Panama. Civil war erupted between Liberals and Conservatives (1948-57), but the repressive regime (1953-57) of Rojas Pinella united the two parties under a National Front, in which the presidency would alternate between them. In the open elections of 1974, Liberals won a decisive victory, but the government was unable to control subsequent civil strife, and the Liberal majority in the government was greatly reduced in the 1978 elections. A Conservative was elected president in 1982, and by 1985 there was renewed anti-government guerrilla activity.

PROFILE

Official name: Republic of Colombia
Area: 440,000sq mi (1,139,600sq km)
Population: 26,122,000
Chief cities: Bogotá, capital; Medellín
Government: Republic
Gross national product: $18,400,000,000
Industries (major products): textiles, foodstuffs, iron, steel, petroleum products

Colombo, largest city and capital of Sri Lanka; a port on the Indian Ocean; inhabited by Muslims in the AD 8th century, followed by the Portuguese in 16th century and Dutch in 17th. Taken by the British 1796, it became Sri Lanka's chief port and capital; site of Allied naval base during WWII, several churches, mosques, Buddhist and Hindu temples, the University of Sri Lanka, and several colleges. Industries: ivory carving, gem cutting, tobacco processing, textiles, oil refining. Pop. 562,160.

Colón, city in W central Cuba, 27mi (43km) SE of Cardenas; located on Central Highway; railroad hub; site of polytechnic school. Industries: poultry, cattle, sugar cane, honey, tobacco, fruit. Pop. 84,100.

Colón, largest city and port in E Panama, at Caribbean mouth of Panama Canal; important commercial and free trade center. Founded 1850 as Aspinwall; name changed 1890. Pop. 85,600.

Colon, the large intestine, that part of the digestive tract that extends from the small intestine to the anus. Separated from the small intestine at the colic valve, it begins at a blind pouch, the caecum, and then passes upward (the ascending colon) along the right side of the abdomen, then across (the transverse colon) and then downward (the descending colon) along the left side, at the end of which it makes an S-shaped curve (the sigmoid colon) and opens into the rectum where stiff folds hold the contents until defecation takes place. The colon functions to absorb water from the digested food material and to allow bacterial action for the formation of feces. *See also* Digestive System.

Colonialism, a control by one country over a dependent area or people. Although it is associated with modern political history, the practice is ancient. In Western colonial history, economic, political, military, cultural, and psychological factors all have been involved. In the post–World War II era, the term came to connote exploitation. *See also* Imperialism;

Colonnade, a series of columns at regular intervals. When in front of a building, a colonnade is called a portico. A colonnade surrounding a building or an open court within a building is called a peristyle. The Parthenon at Athens is an example of a peristyle.

Colonna Family, one of the most powerful Roman families. They were descended from the 10th-century counts of Tusculum and took their name from a village in the Alban hills. The first Colonna was Pietro (*c.*1064); by the 13th century they had gained a position of wealth and power. Important members include Pope Martin V, several cardinals, and generals, statesmen, and scholars, including Vittoria (*c.* 1492–1547), a poet who was the center of a group of famous artists including Michelangelo.

Colony, in biology, group of similar animals or plants living together for mutual benefit. Individuals perform like or varied functions and may be structurally separated or united.

Colophon, a method in early printed works by which the printer detailed his role in the creation of the book usually in a paragraph at the end. It has since come to mean a printer's identification or statement of the typestyle used, paper, and possible crafts employed.

Colophony. *See* Rosin.

Color, sensation experienced when light of sufficient brightness and of a particular wavelength strikes the retina of the eye. Normal daylight (white light) is composed of a spectrum of pure colors, each of which has a different wavelength. The colors can be placed in seven bands, red, orange, yellow, green, blue, indigo, and violet, of decreasing wavelength, one band graduating into the next. A pure spectral color is called a hue. If the color is not pure but contains some white it is desaturated and is called a tint. Saturation is the degree to which a color departs from white and approaches a pure hue. A color also has luminosity, or brightness, which determines its shade.

Colors can be mixed to produce other colors. Any color can be obtained by mixing the right proportions of three primary colors. Mixing paints and mixing the same colored lights produce different colors: red and green light mix to produce yellow; red and green paint mix to produce brown. Colored lights combine by an additive process; paints and pigments combine by a subtractive process.

Colorado, state in the W central United States, the highest in the nation, with an average elevation of 6800ft (2074m).

Colombia

Colorado: Great Sand Dunes National Monument

Christopher Columbus

Land and Economy. The N to S ranges of the Rocky Mts, with more than 50 peaks over 14,000ft (4270m), traverse the W half. Their crests form the Continental Divide. The rest of the state is covered by the W portion of the Great Plains, grazing and farming land. Major rivers rise in the state—the Colorado, Rio Grande, Arkansas, North Platte, and South Platte. Colorado's economy has been dominated successively by mining, agriculture, and manufacturing. Huge reserves of petroleum, natural gas, and coal remain. Irrigation made possible the varied agriculture of the plains. Food processing is the state's leading industry. Manufacture of ordnance and other military material in government plants is important. The facilities for year-round recreation make tourism a major aspect of the economy.

People. More than 75% of the population resides in urban areas in a strip N and S of Denver in the center of the state. Less than 5% were born outside the United States, but only approx. 50% were born in Colorado.

Education. There are about 30 institutions of higher education. The US Air Force Academy is near Colorado Springs. The small town of Aspen, once a mining community, has developed as a cultural center, which features a music school and festival each year.

History. The United States acquired the E part of Colorado from France by the Louisiana Purchase of 1803. The remainder was ceded by Mexico in 1848 after the Mexican War. Discovery of gold and silver spurred immigration from other states, and Colorado became a territory in 1861. Building of railroads after 1870 expanded the population rapidly. WWI stimulated agriculture, and WWII shifted the economic emphasis to manufacturing. Another economic boom began during the 1970s with development of energy-related industries.

PROFILE

Admitted to Union: Aug. 1, 1876; rank, 38th
US Congressmen: Senate, 2; House of Representatives, 5
Population: 2,888,834 (1980); rank, 28th
Capital: Denver, 491,396 (1980)
Chief cities: Denver, Colorado Springs, 215,150; Pueblo, 101,686
State Legislature: Senate, 35 members; House of Representatives, 65
Area: 104,247sq mi (270,000sq km); rank, 8th
Elevation: Highest, Mt Elbert, 14,431ft (4401m); Lowest, 3350ft (1022m), Arkansas River on Kansas border
Industries (major products): processed food, machinery, electronics, metals
Agriculture (major products): sugar beets, cattle, sheep, wheat, corn, fruit
Minerals (major): molybdenum, tin, vanadium, tungsten, uranium, lead, zinc, oil shales
State nickname: Centennial State
State motto: Nil Sine Numine (Nothing Without Providence)
State bird: Lark Bunting
State flower: Rocky Mountain Columbine
State tree: Colorado Blue Spruce

Colorado Potato Beetle, or **potato beetle,** potato bug, small, oval beetle that is a major pest of potato plants and other members of the potato family, including the tomato and eggplant. Adults are shaped the same as ladybugs but are twice as long and are yellow with 10 lengthwise, black stripes. Species *Leptinotarsa decemlineata.*

Colorado River, major river of the SW United States; rises in N Colorado, flows generally SW into the Gulf

of California, passing through the Grand Canyon. Length: 1,450mi (2,335km).

Colorado Springs, residential city in E central Colorado, seat of El Paso co, at the foot of Pikes Peak; resort city; location of trade center for Cripple Creek gold field, US Air Force Academy. Founded 1871; inc. 1878. Pop. (1980) 215,150.

Color Blindness, general term for several disorders of color vision. The most common form involves red-green vision, a hereditary defect affecting males almost exclusively, in which the person does not see red or green. A much less common defect, yellow-blue color blindness, is usually the result of disease. Monochromatism is a very rare inherited disorder in which the person sees only black, white, and gray.

Color Vision, ability to discriminate light based upon its wavelength. It is mediated entirely by the three types of cone cells of the retina. Each type of cone cell is maximally sensitive to a particular part of the spectrum. Color is also determined by other factors, such as contrast and adaptation. The rod cells of the periphery do not register color vision. *See also* Vision.

Colosseum, large amphitheater in Rome built AD 72–80 by the Emperor Vespasian and his sons Titus and Domitian. Oval in shape, 620 × 513ft (189 × 156m), 157ft (48m) high, and seating 45,000, it was used for gladiatorial contests. Much of the structure remains, despite partial dismantling during the Renaissance and damage from earthquakes.

Colossians, New Testament epistle written by the apostle Paul during his first captivity in Rome. Addressed to the Christians at Colossae, it warns of the semi-Judaistic and Oriental philosophy that was corrupting their simple faith and questioning the eternalness of Jesus.

Colostrum, the first milk produced by the mammary gland immediately following parturition; it is non-nutritive compared to later milk secretion.

Colt, Samuel (1814–62), American inventor of the Colt revolver, b. Hartford, Conn. A single-barreled firearm with an automatic revolving set of chambers, brought into successive alignment, the Colt was patented in Europe in 1835 and in the United States in 1836. Colt also invented the submarine battery and utilized the first telegraph cable underwater. He established his own plant in Hartford (1847) at the site of the present Colt plant. He developed the first assembly-line procedure.

Colubrid, term for snakes of the family Colubridae. It includes about 80% of the world's snakes. Their habitats vary from terrestial to aquatic to arboreal, with a few species being subterranean. Most are medium to small sized. They all lack any trace of pelvic girdles or hind limbs and have no left lung. The few that are rear-fanged, capable of conducting poison from venom glands, are relatively harmless to man, but some such as the boomslang can cause fatalities. Racers, water, garter and rat snakes are included in the 2,000 species. *See also* Snake.

Columba, Saint (521–97), Irish missionary. He became a priest (*c.* 551) and founded two important monasteries, including Iona (563). From his seat as abbot of Iona, he continued to pursue the conversion of northern Scotland.

Columbia, city in central Missouri, 27mi (43km) N of Jefferson City; site of University of Missouri, Stephens

College; a farm and coal area; medical center. Inc. 1826. Pop. (1980) 62,061.

Columbia, capital and largest city of South Carolina; seat of Richland co. Founded as state capital 1786, it was nearly destroyed in Civil War; childhood home of Woodrow Wilson; site of University of South Carolina (1801), Columbia College (1854), Allen University (1870), Benedict College (1870), Woodrow Wilson Museum, many antebellum houses. Industries: textiles, printing, electronic equipment. Inc. 1854. Pop. (1980) 99,296.

Columbia. *See* Space Shuttle.

Columbia Plateau, region in NW United States, between Cascade and Rocky Mt ranges; extends over Oregon, Idaho, Washington; serves as major source of hydroelectric power, and important agricultural and grazing region. It is underlaid with deposits of lava more than 10,000ft (3,050m) thick, and sedimentary rock; site of Craters of the Moon National Monument, and of Snake River. Area: approx. 100,000sq mi (259,000sq km).

Columbia River, river in SW Canada and NW United States; flows from Columbia Lake in British Columbia through Washington and Oregon, and empties into the Pacific Ocean N of Portland; commands one of the largest drainage basins on the continent. Area: approx. 259,000sq mi (670,810sq km). Length: 1,214mi (1,955km).

Columbine, perennial herbaceous plant native to cool parts of the Northern Hemisphere. It has five-petaled, spurred flowers and notched leaflets. There are 100 species including the North American columbine (*Aquilegia canadensis*) with drooping red bells, found in rocky woods; height: to 2ft (61cm). Family Ranunculaceae.

Columbium. *See* Niobium.

Columbus, Christopher (1451–1506), Italian explorer in the service of Spain, discoverer of America. He was a seaman and in 1476 went into Portuguese service. By about 1480 he had become a master mariner. He became convinced that the Orient could be reached by sailing west. Unable to gain the sponsorship of the Portuguese, he went to Spain about 1484. Finally, Ferdinand and Isabella agreed to sponsor him and, on Aug. 3, 1492, he set out with his three ships, the *Niña,* the *Pinta,* and the *Santa María.*

After more than two months at sea, land was sighted on Oct. 12, 1492; it was one of the Bahamas (probably Watlings Island). Convinced he had found the East Indies, Columbus called the natives Indians. After exploring nearby islands, he returned to Spain in great triumph.

Columbus made a second voyage in 1493 and explored Hispaniola, Cuba, Jamaica, and the Venezuelan coast. He returned to Spain in 1496 to justify his administration (there had been none of the expected "riches of the Orient"). He returned to the colonies in 1498. In 1500, Spain sent a governor to the New World; he had Columbus arrested and returned to Spain in chains. Columbus recouped his fortunes enough, however, to finance one last voyage to America. It was not successful, and he died in 1506 in Spain, neglected and poverty stricken, but still convinced that he had discovered the western route to the East.

Columbus, city in W Georgia, at head of navigation of Chattahoochee River; seat of Muscogee co; 2nd-largest city in Georgia; industrial and shipping center; important Confederate industrial city. Industries: textiles, iron, food processing, lumber, chemicals, furniture, concrete. Settled 1828. Pop. (1980) 169,441.

Columbus, city and capital of Ohio, in the central part of state on the Scioto River, 97mi (156km) NE of Cincinnati; seat of Franklin co. During Civil War, Camp Jackson (now Fort Hayes) served as a recruit collection point, and a Union arsenal was built in 1863; also site of Camp Chase, a Civil War prison. Columbus is the site of Ohio State University (1870), Capital University (1850), Bliss College (1899), Franklin University (1902), Ohio Dominican College (1911), Ohio Technical College (1952), the State Capitol, and the Gallery of Fine Arts (1878). The Battelle Memorial Institute (1929), the largest private research organization of its kind in the world, conducts scientific, technological, and economic research; the Orton Ceramics Foundation, the Chemical Abstracts Service, and Ohio State University research facilities have established this city as a leading research and scientific center. Industries: machinery, fabricated metal, printing, publishing, glassware, refrigerators. Founded as state capital 1812; inc. as city 1834. Pop. (1980) 564,871.

Column, in architecture, a vertical post, supporting part of a building. A column may be free-standing, with a capital, base, and shaft, or it may be partly attached to a wall, in which case it is called an engaged column. A rostral column is a type of triumphal column from which projected the prows of captured ships to commemorate naval victories. Triumphal columns such as the Roman Trajan's Column had narrative reliefs to depict battle victories. Annulated columns, which are clustered together by rings or bands, were popular in medieval England.

Coma, state of unconsciousness caused by a temporary or permanent injury to the brain. It may be caused by a head injury, severe intracranial infection, lack of blood supply to the brain, or other causes.

Coma Berenices, or **Berenice's Hair,** northern constellation situated between Leo and Boötes and north of Virgo. It has few bright stars but numerous galaxies and galaxy clusters. The north galactic pole is located in Coma.

Comalcalco, city in SE Mexico, approx. 26mi (42km) NW of Villahermosa, on Río Seco; agricultural center, produces rice, coffee, fruit, lumber; site of major Mayan ruins. Pop. 71,651.

Comanche, a major Shoshonean-speaking American Indian tribe who apparently separated from the parent Shoshoni in the distant past and migrated from E Wyoming into Kansas. With the attraction of Mexican horses drawing them south, they raided farther and farther, until they became widely known and feared throughout Texas and Mexico. Numbering at most 15,000, they were famous as daring horsemen and for introducing the horse to the Northern Plains tribes. Approximately 3500 Comanche people live on reservations in SW Oklahoma today.

Combine, complex agricultural machine that cuts, threshes, cleans, and gathers cereal crops. Modern combines are self-powered and designed to cut only the top, fruited section, or head, of a cereal stalk, beat the head to release the grain, separate the grain from the chaff, and direct the grain into an attached grain tank.

Combustion, fast chemical reaction emitting heat and light, commonly involving oxygen. In solids and liquids the reaction speed may be controlled both by the rate of oxygen flow to the surface, and by catalysts. Industrial techniques harness this energy in the design of combustion chambers and furnaces. Explosions and detonations are examples of rapid combustion. *See also* Spontaneous Combustion.

COMECON. *See* Council for Mutual Economic Assistance.

Comédie-Française, French national theater, founded in 1680. It is still organized according to a charter granted by Louis XIV and revised by Napoleon. There are two kinds of members: *pensionnaire,* chosen on the basis of audition, and *societaire,* to which the *pensionnaire* can be elevated only upon the death, retirement, or resignation of a *societaire.* Over the years there have been many disputes between actors and management, but the organization continues to produce excellent theater.

Comedy, one of the two types of drama. It differs from tragedy in a lightness of style as opposed to the seriousness of tragedy, by objectivity of perspective rather than the intensely personal viewpoint of tragedy, and usually has a happy ending. It originated in early Greek fertility rites and, in modern usage, refers to any humorous play.

Comedy of Errors, The, (?1592), 5-act farce by William Shakespeare. Written in blank verse, it is an early Shakespeare play, perhaps his first. It is also his shortest. Recent scholars dispute its previously accepted 1592 date of composition, assigning it a much earlier date. Its first known performance was at Grey's Inn (1594). The "Errors" in the title are mistakes in identity, as twin brothers, both named Antipholus, with their twin servants both named Dromio, separated in a shipwreck during their infancy, come together in a plot full of comic confusion.

Comet, small body orbiting the Sun, often in a very elliptical long-period orbit, and probably composed of ice and rocky material. Partial vaporization near the Sun produces a luminous dusty gaseous envelope (coma) and a characteristic luminous tail, up to millions of miles long, that swings around so that it always points away from the Sun. Comets might possibly be ejected, by stellar perturbation, into the solar system from a distant region (Oort's cloud) around the Sun and might finally disintegrate to produce meteors.

Cominform (Communist Information Bureau), organization established in 1947 to provide information to and coordinate the Communist parties of the USSR, Bulgaria, Czechoslovakia, Hungary, Poland, Romania, Yugoslavia, France, and Italy. It replaced the Comintern, which had been abolished in 1943. Due to problems between the USSR and Yugoslavia, the latter was expelled in 1948. The organization was dissolved in 1956.

Comintern. *See* Communist International.

Comitia, assembly of citizens in ancient Rome. The early Comitia Curiata was drawn from the three tribes to elect officials and inaugurate priests. The later Comitia Centuriata, mainly patricians, elected officials, made laws, and declared war. Its lawmaking function was taken over by the Comitia Tribunata in the 3rd century BC. The Comitia ended with the establishment of the empire.

Command Economy, authoritarian socialist economy that uses "commands" flowing from some agency (rather than "dollar votes" flowing from the market) to direct the productive resources to different uses. A requirement for a command economy is that government either owns the means of production or has effective control of them.

Commedia dell' Arte, a style of Italian Renaissance comedy performed on rough stages erected in the streets. The plays were comic and improvised—there were no scripts, but plot outlines or scenarios—and often crude and coarse. An extremely popular form, the Commedia produced several now-familiar stock characters: Harlequin (the clown); The Capitano (a braggart soldier); Pantalone (the deceived father or cuckolded husband); and Colombina (a feisty maid).

Commerce, Department of, a US government department that fosters, serves, and promotes the nation's economic development and technological advancement through activities that encourage and assist states, regions, communities, industries, and firms. Its agencies include the Bureau of the Census, Office of Business Economics, Patent Office, and National Bureau of Standards. Founded 1903 as Department of Commerce and Labor; became separate department 1913.

Commercial Law, body of laws governing business transactions except those relating to carriage of goods (maritime law). An outgrowth of Roman *jus gentium,* it was revived during the Renaissance and administered by special courts in principal trading cities. "Merchant Law," a term applied to the principles of procedure and doctrine, evolved into effective municipal laws. These were incorporated into English common law in the 18th century and then were adopted in the United States. Commercial law influenced the formation of the laws of admiralty, negotiable paper, and of sales. *See also* Roman Law.

Committees of Correspondence, committees formed by towns and villages before and during the American Revolution to coordinate activities against the British. The first committee was formed in Boston (1772).

Commodity Market, market organized by traders in which promises of immediate and future delivery are made. The commodities themselves are not brought to the market place; only contracts for those commodities are sold. Commodity markets deal in items that are subject to sampling and grading, such as grains, sugar, coffee, tea, cotton, wool, rubber, and copper.

Commodus (161–92), Roman emperor (180–192), son of Marcus Aurelius. He amused himself in organizing contests between cripples, fighting as a gladiator, worshiping Mithra, and living in luxury. He raised soldiers' pay 25% and wished to rename Rome after himself. His irresponsible rule helped collapse the western provinces of the empire. He was murdered, and Pertinax followed as ruler. *See also* Mithra.

Common Carrier, any company that undertakes, for hire, the carrying of goods, persons, or messages, treating its entire clientele without individual preference and being responsible for all losses and injuries. The term applies to public utilities, such as trains, buses, motor freight, planes, pipeline operators, and telephone-telegraph agencies.

Common Law, system of legal jurisprudence developed in England and adopted in most English speaking countries. Distinguished from civil law, which is a codified system based on statutes, its chief characteristics are judicial precedents, trial by jury, and the doctrine of the supremacy of law. Named for the king's court, "common to the whole realm," rather than local or manorial courts, it dates back to the Constitutions of Clarendon (1164), which limited jurisdiction of ecclesiastical courts and established supremacy of the king's courts. A basis of the US legal system, rules and principles established before the colonization of America are considered binding, but later English decisions have only "persuasive authority" in the United States. Recently, the courts, unable to keep pace with social developments, especially in areas of commercial, administrative, and criminal law, replaced much of common law with statutes. Equity jurisprudence was devised to ease hardships due to the inflexibility of some rules of common law and are now judged in the same courts as suits of law. *See also* Civil Law; Law; Roman Law.

Common Market. *See* European Economic Community.

Commons, House of, lower elective house of the British Parliament. *See* Parliament, British.

Common Sense, pamphlet written in January 1776 by Thomas Paine. The first clear call for American independence from Britain, it attacked the British monarchy as chiefly responsible for the restrictive acts against the colonists.

Common Stock, or ordinary stock, represents owners' equity in the corporation. Common stock is divided into shares and issued in the form of certificates. Holders of common stock may vote at stockholders' meetings. *See also* Stock.

Commonwealth (1649–60), British republic established after Charles I's execution (1649). It was dominated by Oliver Cromwell and the army, but no stable form of government could be evolved. On Cromwell's death (1658) England fell into chaos and the monarchy was restored (1660).

Commonwealth of Nations, free association of states, consisting of Britain and independent countries once her dependencies. It has developed from the British Empire in the 20th century and stresses cultural and economic cooperation. The British sovereign is head of the Commonwealth, and those members that are dominions, such as Canada, recognize her as their queen. Other members, including India, are republics.

Commune, in social science, a community of people who choose to live together for a shared purpose. In the 19th century many communes were formed to try to put utopian socialist ideals into practice. In the 1960s hippies and others formed communes that were intended to be cooperative, self-supporting, and free of certain values held by the dominant society.

Commune of Paris (1871), Parisian insurrection against the French government. After the collapse of the Second Empire (1870), the royalist National Assembly was elected (1871). Republican Paris, fearing a reinstatement of the monarchy, formed the Commune government in opposition to the Assembly. The Commune was crushed when government troops entered Paris on the first day of *la semaine sanglante* (bloody week), during which 20,000 insurrectionists were slain.

Communism, political and economic system in which the major means of production and distribution are held in common. In purer forms of communism, all property, including housing, is held collectively. Although forms of communism have existed throughout history, in

Commedia dell'arte

Commerce Department: Bureau of the Census

Commodity Market: Soybeans

modern usage the term "Communism" is ordinarily used to describe the economic system advanced by Karl Marx in *Das Kapital* and put into effect in Russia by V.I. Lenin and in China by Mao Tse-tung. As political theory, Communism shares most of the tenets of socialism, and no strict dividing line between the two can be fixed. Both are contrasted to the system of free enterprise and private property known as capitalism.

The origins of communism can be traced to early tribal life. Hunting lands, fishing waters, and early farming plots were looked upon as community assets; such private rights as existed extended only to personal property. Plato's *Republic* (4th century BC) describes a Utopian communist society. Early Jewish sects, such as the Essenes, were communistically organized, as were many early Christian communities; communistic settlements continued to exist among the Christian sects until the 19th century, when such communistic settlements as Oneida, New Harmony, and Amana were founded.

Modern communism, however, is a product of the 19th century. Secret revolutionary societies were founded in Italy, France, and Germany; their purpose was to overthrow the established order and institute a new, propertyless society. Louis Blanc and Louis Auguste Blanqui, both French, were communist theorizers who were also political activists involved in the Revolution of 1848. That year, 1848, also saw the publication of *The Communist Manifesto* by Karl Marx and Friedrich Engels. That work set forth the basic theories of Marxist communism. According to Marxism, a communistic society is historically inevitable; capitalism, because of its emphasis on higher and higher profits, would eventually so reduce the condition of the workers (the individual proletariat) that they would rise up, overthrow the capitalists, and establish a classless society (the dictatorship of the proletariat). Marx's general philosophy of the class struggle, known as dialectical materialism, was fully set forth in his major work *Das Kapital* (1867–85). It is considered the bible of modern Communist parties, and all factions consider themselves the true interpreters of Marx's philosophy.

The history of Communism in the 20th century, despite its foundation on the work of a single man, has been one of incessant infighting and factionalization. In 1903 the Russian Communist party split into two factions, the Mensheviks and the Bolsheviks. The more radical wing, the Bolsheviks, advocated a violent overthrow of the government and the establishment of a socialist state that would transcend national boundaries and eventually become worldwide. Under the leadership of V.I. Lenin, the Bolsheviks were successful in transforming the government that was set up after the Russian Revolution of 1917 into a full fledged Communist state, the first in history. Upon Lenin's death in 1924, the Russian Communist party split between the followers of Joseph Stalin and Leon Trotsky. The Stalinists won and purged the Trotskyites from the party; those who were not executed went into exile, as did Trotsky himself. Stalin remained dictator of Russia for the rest of his life, and Communism both in Russia and in the rest of the world was a reflection of his policies. The Comintern and the Cominform were formed as instruments to coordinate the policies of national Communist parties around the world. Only the schismatic branches of Communism, such as the Trotskyites, remained independent of Moscow. At the end of World War II, the victorious Soviet armies were in occupation in most of E Europe. In each country these occupation forces left behind a fully functioning Communist government, and all the nations of E Europe became in effect puppet governments of the Soviet Union. The old Marxist dream of an international Communist state seemed possible.

In 1948, however, the Communist government of Yugoslavia, under Marshal Tito, broke away from the Soviet Union and pursued an independent course. In 1949 the People's Republic of China was proclaimed, thereby putting the world's most populous country under Communism and creating a potential rival to Soviet hegemony. The Soviet Union and China maintained close relations until the mid-1950s; after that, continual differences and even border clashes in 1969 and 1978 between the two nations made a unified Communism impossible. During the same period, the Communist parties of the West began exhibiting more and more independence and the Communist countries of E Europe, while continuing to be tied to the USSR both militarily and economically, exhibited an independence unheard of in the days of Stalinist monolithic Communism. In 1968, however, Soviet troops invaded Czechoslovakia to depose a liberal reformist government. During the 1970s the Soviet Union developed stronger ties in new areas, including Ethiopia, Angola, Vietnam, and Afghanistan. In W Europe, Communist parties embraced the concept of power through parliamentary means rather than revolution, and Communists joined the cabinet of France's Socialist government in 1981. Perhaps most significant for the development of Communism was the creation in 1980 of Solidarity, an independent labor movement in Poland, the first independent labor movement in the Soviet bloc. *See also* Capitalism; Marx, Karl; Socialism.

Communism, Primitive, a label for the way of life of some small preliterate groups that shared whatever property they had and cooperated closely to survive. This pattern existed long before the development of modern communist ideology.

Communism Peak (Kommunizma, Pik), formerly Stalin Peak or Garmo Peak; peak in SE Tadzhik SSR, USSR, in the Pamirs region; highest peak in USSR. Height: 24,590ft (7,500m).

Communist International, or **Comintern,** also known as the Third International, Communist organization. It was founded by V.I. Lenin in Moscow (1919) because he feared that the Second International might have a resurgence under noncommunist leadership and he wished to claim leadership of the world socialist movement. The Comintern demanded obedience to its decisions and expelled all dissidents, thus alienating potential support among European socialists. In order to placate its allies in World War II, the Soviet Union abolished the Comintern (1943).

Communist Manifesto (1848), work by Karl Marx and Friedrich Engels. Essentially it states that economic factors determine social relations. The authors call upon the workers to substitute communism for the inequitable system of capitalism.

Communist Party, Chinese, political organization established in July 1921 by Li Ta-chao and Ch'en Tu-hsiu. The party was strengthened by its alliance (1924) with Chiang Kai-shek's Kuomintang, but was virtually shattered when the Communists were expelled from Chiang's group in 1927. Mao Tse-tung was the guiding force in revitalizing the party in the early 1930s. Under his leadership, which was solidified during the "Long March" from Kiangsi to Yenan (1934–35), the party revised the Soviet proletariat-based model to fit the peasant-oriented economy of China and achieved total power in China (1949).

Communist Party of America, radical party organized in 1919 to represent the interest of workers, farmers, and the lower middle class. Its program evolved from open revolutionary objectives to so-called "popular front" socialist goals. The party was strongest in 1932 when it polled 102,991 votes in the presidential election. In 1940, following the passage of the Voorhis Act, the party severed its connection with the Communist International and began to lose strength. Subsequently, the Smith Act (1940), the McCarran Act (1950), and the Communist Control Act (1954) drastically reduced its rights and possible influence. *See also* Smith Act.

Communist Party of the Soviet Union, official party of the USSR. It wields all effective political power in the Soviet Union and, as the oldest Communist party in the world, it has considerable influence over the Communist parties in other countries. It has about 15,000,000 members, or less than 5% of the total Soviet population. The party is organized into almost 400,000 local units, called cells, in every part of the Soviet Union. Party organization parallels the hierarchy of the local government administration; it is an organization that assures party control of every level of government. Usually, each party cell consists of a nucleus of full-time, paid cadre and a membership consisting mostly of the government bureaucracy. In addition, there are party cells in all other Soviet institutions, such as the school system and the armed forces; and cells operate in all factories, collective farms, newspapers, and in the entertainment business. Thus the Communist party maintains control over every aspect of life in the Soviet Union. Each party unit has a ruling body called a presidium headed by a first secretary. The local units meet periodically in party congresses. At the national party congress, the central committee is chosen. It, in turn, elects the presidium (formerly politburo), which is the highest ruling body of the Soviet Communist party. The general secretary of the presidium is, in effect, the actual head of the Soviet government.

The Soviet Communist party traces its origins to an organization founded in 1893 by G.V. Plekhanov. In 1903 the party split into the Bolshevik and Menshevik factions. The Bolsheviks, under V.I. Lenin, triumphed after the Russian Revolution of 1917 and became the ruling force in the Soviet Union. After Lenin's death in 1924, the party came under the control of Joseph Stalin. Stalin brought the party under his strict personal control, and the party trials and purges of the 1930s were the methods by which Stalin liquidated all opposition within the party and the nation. Thousands were executed and many more imprisoned or exiled. After Stalin's death in 1953, party membership was broadened and steps taken to assure collective leadership of party affairs. Nikita Khrushchev became the leading figure and led the party in an extensive "destalinization" program. His personal power increased, but in 1964 he was suddenly removed from power. A collective leadership replaced him with Aleksei Kosygin and Leonid Brezhnev occupying the leading positions. They jointly ruled over party and governmental affairs until about 1970, when Brezhnev, as general secretary, emerged as the dominant figure. At Brezhnev's death in 1982, Yuri V. Andropov became general secretary, followed quickly by Konstantin Chernenko in 1984 and Mikhail Gorbachev in 1985. *See also* Communism; Lenin, Vladimir Ilyitch.

Community, in social science, a grouping of people, usually in one place and with a feeling of belonging together. A community is larger than the other basic unit, the family. Examples of communities are hunting and gathering bands of early men, farming villages, and modern cities. Within cities there are many communities in the sense of people with shared jobs or interests or backgrounds, held together by interdependent needs.

Commutative Law, rule of combination in mathematics in which an operation on two terms is independent of the order of the terms. Thus, normal addition and multiplication of numbers is commutative, since $a \times b = b \times a$, and $a + b = b + a$. Vector multiplication, on the other hand, does not obey the commutative law.

Comnenus, Byzantine family of possible Italian origin, it reached its height of importance in the 10th-12th centuries, providing six Byzantine emperors (1057–1185), statesmen, and authors (such as Anna Comnena, 1083–c. 1150, a historian). The family also supplied all the emperors of Trebizond (1204–1461), with the last one, David Comnenus, executed in 1462 by Mohammed II. There were some attempts to link the Bonaparte family with a Corsican branch of the Comnenus family, but no basis was found for such a connection.

Como, city in N Italy, at SW end of Lake Como; capital of Como prov.; defeated by Rome 196 BC; it became a free commune in the 11th century; liberated by Garibaldi 1859; Mussolini was executed here 1945. Landmarks include 14th–18th-century Cathedral of St Maria Maggiore, and Church of St Carpoforo. Industries: silk, tourism. Pop. 97,169.

Como, Lake (Lago di Como), lake in N Italy, fed by Adda River and many other sources; outlet is at Lecco; resort area. Area: 56sq mi (145sq km).

Comoro (Comores) Islands, independent republic off the E coast of Africa, between Mozambique and Madagascar; it is an archipelago in the Indian Ocean at the N entrance to the Mozambique Channel. Four major islands and many small islands, all of volcanic origin, make up the archipelago. The islands are mountainous with fertile soil; the highest point is Mt Karthala, 7,746ft (2,363m), an active volcano on Grand Comoro, the largest island; Anjouan, Mayotte, and Moheli are the other major islands. Moroni, on Grand Comoro, serves as the capital and is the largest city.

The climate is tropical with a dry season from May through October. Agriculture is the chief industry; 35% of land is in plantation ownership, often foreign. Coconuts are grown on rich lowlands, and upland rice in the higher, erosion plagued lands. Vanilla, copra, cocoa, and sisal are major crops and exports; rice, machinery, and petroleum are imported. The people are mainly African with some Arabs and Indians. French and Comoran (a mix of Arabic and Swahili) are both spoken. Most of the people are Muslims.

From 1841 to 1909, France gradually acquired the islands; during WWII they were occupied by British troops. France granted the islands administrative autonomy within the French Union 1946, and in 1958 the territorial assembly voted to remain in the French Republic as an Overseas Territory. In 1968 internal autonomy was achieved; a referendum in December 1974 resulted in 94% of electorate approving independence from France. The island of Mayotte, however, had rejected independence as part of the Comoros. The other islands became independent in 1975, but by the early 1980s the status of Mayotte was still unresolved.

PROFILE

Official name: Comoros Federal Islamic Republic
Area: 838sq mi (2,170sq km)
Population: 343,200
Chief cities: Moroni (capital); Mutsamudu; Fomboni
Religion: Muslim
Language: French, Comoran

Comparative Advantage, in international trade, condition that exists when a country is able to produce a product relatively more cheaply than other products. If one country has a comparative advantage in product A and another country has a comparative advantage in product B, the countries are able to trade good A for B to the advantage of both.

Comparative Psychology, field that compares the behaviors of various animal species. Comparative psychologists study animals to learn more about all species and to aid their understanding of human behavior. *See also* Ethology.

Comparative Statistics, in economics, used to analyze the movement from one equilibrium position to another. This analysis therefore involves no movement of time but simply allows for comparison of two or more time period equilibrium positions. *See also* Market Equilibrium.

Compass, Drawing, instrument used in geometrical constructions to draw circles and mark off equal lengths. Formed of two pointed legs so joined that one may be kept fixed at a point while the other (generally having a pencil point) is turned around it at the desired distance.

Compass, Magnetic, direction-finding instrument consisting of a magnetized needle centrally pivoted so that it rotates in a horizontal plane and is free to align itself

with the earth's magnetic field. It therefore points along the magnetic meridians to the magnetic north pole. The needle moves above a card marked with the points of the compass or the magnet may be attached to the card, which itself rotates.

Compass, Marine, a large magnetic compass used on ships. It consists of parallel magnetic needles attached to the underside of a graduated compass card, which is centrally pivoted in a glass-covered bowl. The bowl, filled with alcohol and water, is supported on gimbals and retains balance despite the ship's rolling.

Competition, in economics, degree of competitiveness or rivalry in a market situation. Competition is advantageous to the consumer since it promotes lower prices and higher output levels. The degree of competition within a particular market is usually strongly related to the number of firms within that market or to the degree of monopoly power held by the firm or firms within the industry.

Compiègne, town in N central France, 45mi (72km) NE of Paris, on the banks of the Oise River; scene of Joan of Arc's capture by the Burgundians May 24, 1430; site of elaborate 15th-century palace and beautiful adjoining forests and parks. Armistice ending WWI was signed Nov. 11, 1918, in a railroad car in the Compiègne forest. Industries: tires, chemicals, glass. Founded as Roman outpost. Pop. 40,720.

Compleat Angler, The (1653), discourse on fishing by Izaak Walton in the form of a dialogue between Piscator (Fisherman), Venator (Hunter), and Auceps (Falconer). A unique literary work, it combines humor, pastoral description, verse, and practical instruction.

Complementary Colors, two spectral colors, such as yellow and blue or red and greenish-blue, that can be mixed to form white light. *See also* Color.

Composite Family, a group (Compositae) of nearly 20,000 different plant species in which the so-called flower is actually a composite flower head made up of a cluster of many, usually tiny, individual flowers. In a typical composite, the daisy, the flower head has a central yellow disk, consisting of a cluster of tiny male and female flowers lacking visible petals. The outer ring of female ray flowers has relatively large white petals. In composites such as the dandelion and endive, the flower head consists entirely of ray flowers. Others, such as thistles, consist entirely of disk flowers. Composites comprise the largest plant family and have great variety of form and size. They are important to man as a source of food, and garden flowers.

Compost, mass of rotted animal and plant matter used as a fertilizer. When properly prepared, with nitrogen added during decomposition, it is crumbly and free of noxious odor and does not compete with plants for nitrogen. Large amounts must be used to compensate for relatively low nutrient content (when compared with artificial fertilizers), but soil structure is greatly improved after several seasons of composting. *See also* Fertilizers.

Compound, substance formed by chemical combinations of two or more elements. Compounds are produced by rearrangement of the electrons orbiting the combining atoms, and usually have quite different properties from those of their constituent elements. Ionic compounds have ionic bonds—they are simply collections of oppositely charged ions in which no distinct molecules exist. Covalent bonding produces two types of compound. In one, covalent compounds, a solid is formed in which the bonds extend throughout the crystal. Such compounds are hard and high-melting: boron nitride is a typical example. More commonly, molecular compounds are formed, in which groups of atoms are bound in distinct molecules. Such compounds tend to be low-melting, volatile, and soluble in nonpolar solvents. *See also* Element; Molecule.

Compound Eye, eye made up of hundreds or thousands of simple eyes, each having light-sensitive cells, nerve fibers, and corneal lens. It is found in insects and most other arthropods.

Compression, Engine, in an internal-combustion engine, the pressure applied to a fuel-air mixture by a rising piston in a cyclinder. Compression is measured as a ratio of piston displacement and combustion-chamber volume. *See also* Diesel Engine.

Compromise of 1850, set of balanced resolutions by Sen. Henry Clay (Ky.) to prevent civil war. The US Congress agreed to admit California as a free state, organize New Mexico and Utah as territories without mention of slavery, provide for a tougher fugitive slave law, abolish the slave trade in Washington, D.C., and assume the Texas national debt.

Compton, Arthur Holly (1892–1962), US physicist, b. Wooster, Ohio. He was appointed head of the physics department at Washington University, later moving to the University of Chicago. He worked in the field of X rays and discovered the scattering process (Compton scattering) for which he was awarded a Nobel Prize in 1927 jointly with C.T.R. Wilson. As head of the early phase of the Manhattan Project, he helped create the first sustained nuclear chain reaction.

Compton, city in S California, 13mi (21km) S of Los Angeles; residential suburb for Los Angeles and Long Beach; site of Compton College (1927). Industries: aircraft, electronics, oil, steel. Inc. 1888. Pop. (1980) 81,286.

Compton-Burnett, (Dame) Ivy (1892–1969), English novelist. Her novels, written mainly in dialogue, take place in upper-middle-class society in Edwardian England. They include *Pastors and Masters* (1925), *A House and its Head* (1935), *The Present and the Past* (1953), and *Mother and Son* (1955).

Compton Effect, or **Scattering,** scattering of electromagnetic radiation (X rays or gamma rays) by electrons, with consequent slight decrease in frequency of the scattered radiation (that is, loss of energy). The effect first described by A.H. Compton can be explained by considering the radiation to be a stream of photons.

Compulsive Personality, personality trait disturbance marked by obsessive concerns and rigid, ritualistic behaviors, making for an inhibited, orderly, stubborn, and relatively unemotional individual. Such people have an inordinate capacity for work and an inability to relax and enjoy life. There is no room for spontaneity; everything is planned and fitted into its proper place.

Computer, Digital, mechanism capable of calculating mathematical problems or manipulating data, usually at high speeds, in accordance with processing instructions and routines either permanently built into or temporarily stored within the computer. In the process of data manipulation or mathematical computation, the computer compares, combines, or otherwise relates facts and figures, producing logical conclusions or recording facts in a prescribed way. Often compared with a human brain because of its decision-making ability, a computer is fundamentally limited to operate in the manner by which it is programmed by a human being. The main elements of a computer are: (1) central processor, (2) data input device, (3) data output device, and (4) facilities for storing instructions and data.

Computer, Electronic, electronic machine that accepts and processes information and supplies results in a desired form. The most widely used and versatile type is the digital computer that manipulates large quantities of information at high speed according to a set of instructions (a program) written in any of various prescribed forms (programming languages). Information fed into the system must be in a discrete form, consisting only of numbers, characters, and symbols, that are converted internally into binary form—combinations of digits comprising only ones and zeros. Both input data and program are stored in the computer memory and can be accessed when required.

The central processing unit of the computer performs operations on the data according to the program instructions. These operations include arithmetical addition, subtraction, multiplication, and division and also logical operations involving decision making on the basis of comparison of input or processed data. The final results are then output in a variety of ways, usually in printed or graphic form or as a display on a screen. Unlike the digital computer, which is basically a counting machine, the analog computer is a measuring device. The hybrid computer is a combination of these two in which the continuously variable input of an analog computer is converted into a set of discrete information for much more rapid and sophisticated digital processing.

Computer Assisted Instruction (CAI), method of instruction featuring interaction of student with computer. Intended to relieve human teachers of routine tasks, it is an economical means of reducing instructional staff. The student is sequentially led by computer through a programmed lesson, including information presentation, testing, evaluation, and, if necessary, a similar repetitive review. A new lesson is begun after mastery of the previous lesson. Data terminals, including visual displays, are the means for student/computer dialog. Some CAI systems allow further dialogs, with students initiating inquiries and computers responding to the limit of the stored data and inherent decision-making process of the program.

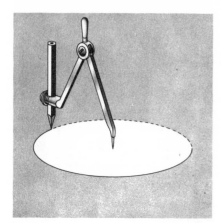

Compass (drawing)

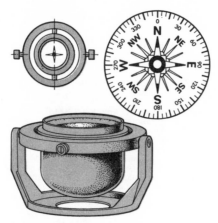

Compass (marine)

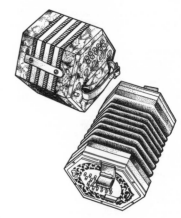

Concertina

Computer Language, a set of words and rules to enable a human being to communicate with a computer. Languages are normally classified into two categories: (1) machine languages having semantics (meaning), which are the specific, detailed computer instructions, and (2) higher level languages, having both semantics and syntax (sentence structure or pattern formation), which are readily understood by the human computer programmer. The latter languages are reduced to machine language by the compiler, assembler, or translator device that serves as an interface device between the programmer and the computer.

The higher level languages can be further classified into: (1) Problem-oriented languages (such as STRESS for structural engineering), in which the programmer need not know much of computer operation or computer solution methods. The problem is described in the specialized language of the user. 2) Procedure-oriented languages, which describe the input, output, and logical functioning of the program. FORTRAN and BASIC are most commonly used. The problem must be described by the input to the translator and the programmer must know the method of computation. (3) Assembly languages or symbolic machine languages used as mechanical aids in writing actual computer instructions and highly dependent on the specific computer used.

Comte, Auguste (1798–1857), French philosopher. The founder of positivism, Comte's basic system is the law of the three stages—theological, metaphysical, and positive—that represent the development of the human race. In the first two stages the human mind is finding causes to explain phenomena, while in the third, explanation of a phenomenon is found in a law. Comte saw philosophy as a coordination of all the sciences with the purpose of improving the human race, and he founded the Religion of Humanity to fulfill this purpose. His philosophy was a major influence on British thinkers, particularly J.S. Mill and Frederic Harrison. His major works include *Positive Philosophy* (1830–42) and *Positive Polity* (1851–54).

Conakry, capital city of Guinea, W Africa, on Toumbo Island, in Atlantic Ocean; site of Polytechnic Institute of Conakry (1963) and international airport; a major port and deep water harbor, it is the administrative, commercial, and economic center of Guinea; terminus of country's only railroad. Exports: ores, agricultural products. Founded 1890. Pop. 525,671.

Concentration Camps, centers where people of certain political, racial, or military persuasions are placed for detainment, punishment, slave labor, or extermination by totalitarian governments, usually without trial or due process of law. Used first by the Spanish during the Cuban rebellion of 1895 and by the British during the Boer War, concentration camps were developed extensively during World War II by Nazi Germany in its systematic genocide against Jews and other minorities. The most infamous of the Nazi "death camps" were Auschwitz and Treblinka in Poland and Buchenwald in Germany. There and at other concentration camps established throughout German-occupied territory, more than 6,000,000 innocent men, women, and children were forcibly enslaved, subjected to cruel medical experiments, or executed barbarically by such means as starvation, gas, beating, and shooting, on the basis of the official racist ideology of the German Reich. Although the Nazis' use of concentration camps is unparalleled for its scale and inhumanity, and has been condemned throughout the world, concentration camps have also been used in the 20th century by the Soviet Union, where they are called Gulags, for the imprisonment of political and religious dissidents. *See also* Gulag.

Concepción, city in S central Chile; capital of Concepción prov. Founded 1550 by Pedro de Valdivia, the conqueror of Chile; destroyed by earthquakes many times and severely damaged in 1960. Industries: glass, textiles, sugar, hides, steel. Pop. 196,000.

Conception, the implantation of the blastocyst in the uterine wall. In humans it occurs 6–7 days following fertilization, which takes place in the fallopian tubes. It marks the start of pregnancy.

Conceptualism, philosophical theory in which the universal is found in the particular. A position between nominalism (which analyzes universals into particulars) and realism (in which universals are real apart from all particulars), conceptualism includes both universals and particulars. Essentially, it holds that the mind is the individual that universalizes by experiencing particulars, finding common factors in them, and then conceptualizing these common factors as universals. One example is the "concrete universal" of Hegelians, in which the mind is the concrete individual capable of grasping the meaning of universals.

Concertina, musical instrument developed *c.* 1830. A compact, hexagonal accordion with studs on both sides, it was preferred in England and was used by 19th-century sailors to accompany sea chanties. The Argentine version is the Bandoneon. *See also* Accordion.

Concerto, musical work for an instrumental soloist accompanied by orchestra and usually designed to show off the performer's technical skill on his instrument. Concertos usually have three parts or movements, the first and last following the form of a sonata. The concertos of such composers as Beethoven, Grieg, Tchaikovsky, and Rachmaninoff are among the most popular of all classical music works.

Conch, gastropod mollusk found worldwide in warm seas. It has a large spiraled shell. Types include true conchs (*Strombus*); spider conchs (*Lambis*), and deep water *Tibia* shells. Length: 4–12in (10.2–30.5cm). Class Gastropoda; family Strombidae.

Conciliation, form of third-party intervention in a dispute, labor or otherwise. The conciliator does not express an opinion about the possible terms of agreement, but acts as a go-between to keep the discussion going. Mediation is a form of conciliation, but the mediator may make suggestions for settlement.

Concord, city in W central California, NNE of Berkeley; center of oil and farming region; manufactures electronic equipment. Settled 1852; inc. 1905. Pop. (1980) 103,251.

Concord, town in E Massachusetts, 19mi (31km) NW of Boston on Concord River; scene of historic Revolutionary War battle of Concord and neighboring Lexington, Apr. 19, 1775. British forces were sent from Boston to destroy ammunition and supplies stockpiled in Concord; the Minute Men courageously checked the British advance at the North Bridge. The battle is commemorated by Daniel C. French's bronze Minute Man statue and the Minute Man National Historic Park (est 1959). Concord developed as a literary center mid-19th century, and the homes of such famous residents as Ralph Waldo Emerson, Henry David Thoreau, Nathaniel Hawthorne, Louisa May and A. Bronson Alcott are preserved as museums; site of Antiquarian Museum, Old Manse (1769) built by Emerson's grandfa-

ther, Walden Pond, and area where Ephraim Bull developed the concord grape. Industries: electronic and wood products, furniture, iron, precision machinery, tourism, fruit, poultry. Settled 1635. Pop. (1980) 16,293.

Concord, capital city of New Hampshire, in S central section, on Merrimack River 15mi (24km) N of Manchester; seat of Merrimack co. Industrial and financial center, it was the scene of New Hampshire's ratification of the Constitution as the ninth and deciding state on June 21, 1788; noted in 19th century for manufacture of Concord stagecoaches; site of St Paul's School, New Hampshire Technical Institute (1961), last home of President Franklin Pierce (1857–60, now a museum); birthplace of Mary Baker Eddy. Quarries N of city produce famous white Concord granite used for building the Library of Congress, Museum of Modern Art in New York City, and the New Hampshire state house (1819). Industries: leather, granite quarrying, electrical equipment, printing. Founded as trading post 1660; settled in 1727; inc. 1733 by Massachusetts as Rumford, by New Hampshire as Concord 1765, as town 1784, as city 1853; designated capital 1808. Pop. (1980) 30,400.

Concordat of 1801, agreement concluded between Napoleon and Pope Pius VII on July 16, 1801. It established the Roman Catholic church as the religion of the majority of French people; the state was to pay the salaries of the bishops and some priests, and France's first consul had the right to nominate bishops to be confirmed by the Pope. Napoleon wanted the concordat to win over the clergy and so disarm the royalists and also to gain the support of Belgium and the Rhineland. The Pope, although he did not want to alienate the royalists, wanted the French army in Rome as protection. Napoleon's publication of the Organic Articles and his claims of the supremacy of the emperor over the Pope made it difficult to implement the agreement. Napoleon regarded the concordat annulled on Feb. 23, 1812, although it remained in force formally in France until Dec. 6, 1905, with passage of the bill separating church and state.

Concordia, in Roman mythology, goddess that personified the union of citizens. She had a temple near the Forum and was represented on coins as holding a cornucopia and olive branch.

Concrete, a hard, strong building material composed of a cementing material, such as Portland cement, and an aggregate of minerals (sand and gravel or broken rock) mixed with water. *See also* Cement.

Concussion, temporary brain malfunction due to a blow to the head. It is manifested by loss of consciousness for a few seconds or minutes, and later by intermittent headache and brief giddiness or difficulty in concentrating. Treatment consists of rest and close observation to ensure that no serious head injuries are present.

Condé, House of (1530–1830), junior branch of the House of Bourbon. Notables of the line included the first prince, **Louis I de Bourbon** (1530–69), a Huguenot leader; he signed the Peace of Longjumeau (1568). His son, **Henry I** (1552–88), was also a Huguenot leader. The third prince was **Henry II** (1588–1646), a Catholic. Arrested for blackmail and sedition (1616), he was later rewarded for loyalty to Louis XIII. **Louis II, the Great Condé** (1621–86), was the last leader of the Fronde uprisings (1648–53). He became one of Louis XIV's greatest generals. **Louis Joseph de Bourbon** (1736–1818) fought in the Seven Years' War and supported the monarchy after the French Revolution.

When his son **Louis Henri Joseph** (1756–1830), the ninth prince and also a royalist, was found hanged, the line ended.

Condensation, deposition of a solid or liquid from its vapor onto a cool surface, occurring when the gaseous vapor pressure exceeds that of its liquid or solid phase. Condensation occurs in pure air that is supersaturated with moisture; in the atmosphere dispersed dust particles can attract moisture when the relative humidity is less than 100%.

Condensation Nucleus, a small solid or liquid particle, like dust, on which water vapor in the atmosphere begins to condense in tiny water droplets or ice crystals with cloud formation.

Condenser. *See* Capacitor.

Conditioned Response, in psychology, any behavior learned through procedures of operant or Pavlovian conditioning. *See also* Operant Conditioning; Pavlovian Conditioning.

Conditioning. *See* Pavlovian Conditioning.

Condor, American vulture that typically soars in search of carrion. The Andean condor *(Vultur gryphus)* of mountainous W South America is glossy black with a reddish head and neck. The almost extinct Californian condor *(Gymnogyps californianus),* gray-brown with an orange head and red neck, is limited to the San Joaquin Valley of California. Length: 3.5–4.5ft (1–1.4m); wingspan: to 12ft (3.7m); weight: to 25lb (11.3kg).

Condorcet, Marie Jean Antoine Nicholas de Caritat, Marquis de (1743–94), French philosopher and mathematician noted for his *Essay on the Calculus of Probabilities* (1785), which systematized that study. He influenced 19th-century thought with his idea of the indefinite progress of man in his *Sketch for a Historical Picture of the Progress of the Human Mind* (1795). Condorcet was president of the legislative assembly (1792), where he promoted a system of educational reforms. Arrested during the Reign of Terror, he died in prison.

Condottieri, leaders of mercenary armies hired to fight numerous wars among 14th- to 16th-century Italian states. Their armies were largely made up of foreigners, and they themselves were often non-Italian. By the late 14th century Italian *condottieri* began conquering principalities for themselves. Famous among *condottieri* were the Englishman John Hawkwood (late 14th century) and Francesco Sforza (who won Milan in 1450).

Conductance, reciprocal of resistance in a direct current circuit; resistance divided by the square of impedance in an alternating current circuit. It is measured in siemens.

Conduction, the transfer of heat from molecule to molecule within a body. If an iron rod is placed in a flame, the heat energy received at one end causes increased vibratory motion of the molecules in that end. By bumping into molecules further along the rod, the increased motion is passed along to them, and finally the end not in the flame grows hot.

Conductivity, Electrolytic, passage of an electric current through an electrolyte. Electrovalent compounds (acids, bases, and salts) in solution break up into positively and negatively charged ions (for example, NaCl'U$Na^{+} + Cl^{-}$); the ions carry the current through the solution. The electrolytic conductivity (κ) is the ratio of the current density to the field strength.

Conductor, substance or body having a relatively low electrical resistance. Metals are the best conductors, as a large number of free electrons are available to provide a current, when they flow in one direction. The resistance of a metallic conductor increases with temperature as the vibrations of lattice atoms increase, hindering the motion of the electrons.

Cone, scaly fruit- or seed-bearing vessel of plants, such as fir, pine, spruce, club mosses, and horsetails. It is made up of scales, varying in number, shape, and size, which separate to release seeds developed at the base. Generally, cones are woody at maturity.

Cone, solid geometric figure swept out by a line (the generator) that joins a point moving in a closed curve in a plane, to a fixed point (the vertex) outside the plane. In a right circular cone the vertex lies above the center of a circle (the base), and the cone's generators join the vertex to points on the circle. Such a cone has a volume $1/3\pi r^2 h$ and a curved surface area πrs, where h is the vertical height, s the slant height, and r the radius of the base.

Cone Shell, gastropod mollusk found in tropical seas, particularly Indo-Pacific. Having heavy, cone-shaped shell with vivid marks and colors, some species can inflict serious or fatal stings. Length: 1–3in (25.4–76.2mm). Family Conidae; 500 species, including rare *Conus dominicanus.*

Confederate States of America (CSA). The government formed in February 1861, by the first 6 states that seceded from the United States. South Carolina was the first state to secede (December, 1860), followed by Mississippi, Florida, Alabama, Georgia, and Louisiana. Texas, Virginia, Arkansas, North Carolina, and Tennessee joined the CSA soon after. There were also Confederate governments in Kentucky and Missouri. Jefferson Davis was elected president, and a constitution recognizing slavery and state sovereignty was adopted. The capital, located originally at Montgomery, was later moved to Richmond. The government dissolved with the war's end in April 1865.

Confederation of Canada, union of Canada after the British North America Act (1867). Under confederation, Canada assumed powers of tariff, taxation, defense, and criminal law. Confederation paved the way for the inclusion in Canada of British Columbia (1871), Prince Edward Island (1873), and Newfoundland (1949). *See also* British North America Act.

Confederation of the Rhine, alliance of German states proposed by Napoleon in January 1806. Agreed to by 16 German princes in July 1806, they renounced their attachment to the Holy Roman Empire, placed themselves under the protection of Napoleon, and pledged 63,000 men to his army. Eventually, the Confederation included Bavaria, Baden, Saxony, Württemberg, Westphalia, Hesse-Darmstadt, and most of the minor states, many of which joined at Napoleon's defeat of the Prussian army on Oct. 14, 1806. A device to control the German princes, the alliance broke apart after Napoleon's defeat in Russia (1812–13).

Configuration, Electron, the particular pattern of electrons occupying the shells and subshells of an atom. The electron configuration is usually written in a notation using 1, 2, 3, etc, for the principal shell and *s, p, d,* and *f* for the subshell. The number of electrons is written as a superscript. For example, the configuration of the helium atom is $1s^2$; that of the chromium atom is $1s^2 2s^2 2p^6 3s^2 3p^6 4s^2 3d^4$.

Conformity, in geology, the undisturbed, continuous layering of sediments in even strata with no evidence of folding, faulting, or intrusion of new materials, or erosion or wind or water change. *See also* Unconformity.

Confucianism, philosophy that dominated China until the early 20th century. In 1970, it had an estimated 370,000,000 followers, mainly in Asia. It is based on the *Analects,* sayings attributed to Confucius (*c.*551–479 BC). At first strictly an ethical system for the proper management of society, it acquired quasi-religious characteristics. In the 1st century AD shrines were erected where sacrifices were offered to Confucius, a practice continuing to the 20th century. After the religions of Taoism and Buddhism eclipsed Confucianism in the 3rd to 7th centuries, neo-Confucianism placed the early precepts on a metaphysical basis. Man is seen as potentially the most perfect form of *li,* the ultimate embodiment of good. Confucianism stresses the responsibility of sovereign to subject, of family members to each other, and of friend to friend. Politically, it acted to preserve the existing order, upholding the status of the mandarins, Confucian literati who ran the Chinese bureaucracy. When the monarchy was overthrown (1911–12) Confucian institutions were ended, but since the Communist revolution in China (1949), many traditional Confucian elements have apparently been incorporated in Maoism.

Confucius (551–479 BC), founder of Confucianism. Born in the Chinese province of Lu of aristocratic ancestry, he was an excellent scholar, athlete, and musician. He opened a school where the sons of wealthy families studied for careers of government service. Tradition holds that he became prime minister of Lu but was framed by dishonest officials and resigned in shame. Wandering throughout China for 30 years, he sought a return to the morality in politics of the early Chou dynasty. He never found real support and returning to Lu in 484 BC, he spent his last years engaged in scholarship. He died disappointed, not realizing the high regard later generations would give his ideas. Although many of his writings were lost, some of his teachings are recorded in the *Analects. See also* Confucianism.

Conger Eel, marine fish found worldwide in shallow warm and temperate waters. Its serpentine body is grayish, sometimes with a reddish tint. A food fish in Europe and Japan, it spawns in deep water. Length: to 8ft (244cm); Weight: 12lb (5.4kg). Family Congridae; species 100, including *Conger oceanicus.*

Conglomerate, in geology, sedimentary rock formed of rounded pebbles bound in a finer matrix. Formerly called "pudding stone," conglomerates are commonly formed along beaches, rivers, or as glacial drift. In glacial tillite the rounded particles may range from pebbles to huge boulders. *See also* Sedimentary Rocks.

Congo, People's Republic of, independent nation in W central Africa. A self-proclaimed scientific socialist state, it gained independence from France in 1960. A developing economy makes it dependent on imports and foreign aid.

Land and economy. Situated on the equator, it is bordered by Gabon, Cameroon, the Central African Republic, Zaire, Cabinda, and the Atlantic Ocean. Topographical regions include the coastal plain, S central Niari valley (the most fertile area), central Bateke Plateau, and the N Congo River basin. The climate is tropical. Subsistence farmers on 2% of the land raise corn, bananas, rice, peanuts, fruits, chickens, and goats. Cash crops are sugar cane, coffee, and tobacco. Potash is the most valuable mineral; oil drilling has begun. Food-processing dominates the industrial sector, and forestry is a major industry.

People: Fifteen ethnic groups divided into 75 tribes comprise most of the population; in addition there are about 12,000 Europeans, mostly French, in the country. French is the official language. Christianity is the dominant religion. Literacy is estimated at 50%.

Government. According to the constitution of 1979, the Congo is a socialist country with one legal political party, the Workers' Party of the Congo (PCT). The president, elected to a five-year term, is chairman of the party. The national assembly is composed of 153 seats.

History. Originally three tribal kingdoms dominated by the slave trade, the region came under French protection in 1883. By 1958 it had become an autonomous member of the French community in Africa, and in 1960 it achieved independence. Abbe Fulbert Youlou, its first president, was deposed in a 1963 coup. Scientific socialism was proclaimed by the next president, Alphonse Massamba Debat. A series of military governments successively took control of the government until 1979, when a government was elected. The country continues to be plagued by ethnic strife and a deteriorating economy.

PROFILE

Official name: People's Republic of the Congo
Area: 132,046sq mi (341,999sq km)
Population: 1,400,000
Density: 10per sq mi (4per sq km)
Chief cities: Brazzaville (capital); Pointe Noire
Government: Socialist republic
Religion: Christian, animist
Language: French
Monetary unit: CFA francs
Gross national product: $950,000,000
Per capita income: $500
Industries: wood products, flour, sugar, brewing, cement, textiles
Agriculture: cocoa, bananas, peanuts, sugar cane, tobacco, forests
Minerals: potash, petroleum, natural gas, oil
Trading partners: France, Federal Republic of Germany, People's Republic of China, USSR

Congo (Zaire), largest river in central Africa, flows from Zambia to the Atlantic Ocean; divided into 4 sections: Upper Congo, the main headstream; Middle Congo, slow-moving and narrow; Lower Congo, beginning at Stanley Pool outlet; and the Estuary, final portion entering the Atlantic Ocean. River forms an excellent system of navigable waterways and hydroelectrical development. Largest drainage basin in Africa: 1,600,000sq mi (4,144,000sq km). Length: 2,900mi (4,669km).

Congo Snake, or **Congo Eel,** blind salamander found in lowland areas of S United States. Its blue-black, elongated body has tiny limbs, a pointed head, and lungs; it has no tongue or gills. It spawns every other year. Length: to 3.3ft (1m). Family Amphiumidae; species: *Amphiuma means, Amphiuma tridactylum, Amphiuma pholeter.*

Congregationalism, Christian church organization in which each local church is autonomous and independent; also called at various times Brownists, Separatists, Independents. Congregationalism is based on the belief that, according to Scripture, Christ is the head of the church and all members are God's priests. Modern Congregationalism began about 1550. Congregation-

Condor

Congo

Jimmy Connors

alists were prominent in Oliver Cromwell's English army and government in the mid-17th century and were a major political force in the American colonies, settling Plymouth Colony in 1620 and establishing Harvard College in 1636. As the modern United Church of Christ with a membership of 2,000,000, Congregationalism occupies a position between Presbyterianism and the Baptists.

Congress of the United States, the legislative branch of the federal government. It was created by Article I, Section 1 of the US Constitution: "All legislative Powers herein granted shall be vested in a Congress of the United States, which shall consist of a Senate and House of Representatives." The first meeting of Congress took place in 1789 in New York City. The Senate is composed of two elected members from each state who serve 6-year terms. One third of the Senate is elected every 2 years. The House of Representatives is comprised of 435 elected members who serve 2-year terms. The number of representatives from each state is determined by population. Both senators and representatives must be residents of the state from which they are chosen. A senator must be at least 30 years old and a citizen for at least 9 years, a representative must be at least 25, and citizen for at least 7 years. A resident commissioner from Puerto Rico (4-year term), and delegates from Guam, the Virgin Islands, and the District of Columbia elected for 2-year terms complete the composition of Congress. The commissioner and delegates do not have voting powers in Congress or in the committees to which they are assigned. The presiding officer in the Senate is the vice president, and the House elects a speaker to preside. The preparation and consideration of legislation is largely accomplished by the 17 standing committees in the Senate and the 21 in the House of Representatives. There are additional commissions and committees, some of which are composed of members from both Houses. Powers of Congress include the right to assess and collect taxes (chief power), regulate commerce, coin money, declare war, propose Constitutional amendments, establish post offices and post roads, establish lower courts, raise and maintain an army and navy, and "to make all Laws which shall be necessary and proper for carrying into execution the foregoing powers, and all other powers vested by this Constitution in the Government of the United States or in any Department or Officer thereof." Legislation must be passed by both Houses and be signed by the president to become law. The House initiates all tax bills and has the power to impeach the president. The Senate can approve treaties and presidential appointments and tries the president if he is impeached. The Constitution requires that Congress meet at least once every year, and the president may call special sessions.

Congreve, William (1670–1729), English dramatist who wrote comedies of manners such as *Love for Love* (1695) and *The Way of the World* (1700). He became manager of the Haymarket Theatre in London in 1707.

Congruence, equivalence of shape and size. Two congruent geometric figures will coincide exactly when superimposed.

Conic, or conic section, curve found by the intersection of a plane with a cone. Depending upon the angle at which the cone is cut, the conic section can be a circle, ellipse, parabola, or hyperbola. A conic may alternatively be defined as the locus of a point that moves so that the ratio of its distances from a fixed point (the focus) and a fixed line (the directrix) is constant. This ratio is called the eccentricity (symbol: e): $e = 1$ gives a parabola, $e > 1$ an hyperbola, $e < 1$ an ellipse. A circle is the limiting case of an ellipse with $e = 0$.

Conifers, cone-bearing trees, usually evergreen, such as pine, fir, hemlock, spruce, redwood, and cedar. They are a major plant resource of North America, furnishing building materials (softwoods), pulpwood, and other products. Classified as gymnosperms, conifers lack showy flowers, but foliage detail, cones, and color give them an ornamental quality. Order Coniferales. Eight families are usually recognized.

Conjugation, in biology, sexual reproduction by fusion of identical gametes. It is characteristic of certain simple animals and lower plants. In spirogyra algae, a temporary conjugation tube is a passageway for the contents of one cell to enter another. Ciliate protozoans adhere to one another and nuclear material is exchanged through a temporary fusion area.

Conjugation, in astronomy, celestial configuration characterized by a coincidence in the longitudes of two celestial objects, usually two planets or a planet and the Sun, as viewed from the Earth. Inferior conjunction occurs when either Mercury or Venus lies between the Earth and the Sun; superior conjunction occurs when they lie on the opposite side of the Sun to the Earth.

Conjunction, logical proposition produced by joining two simple propositions by *and*. An example is the proposition "Bill is boring and Bill is conceited"; it is true only if both parts are separately true. The conjunction of two simple propositions, *P* and *Q*, is written $P \wedge Q$, read "*P* and *Q*."

Conjunctivitis, inflammation of the conjunctiva, the mucous membrane lining of the eyelid. It can be caused by infection, usually bacterial, by exposure to irritants, or by allergy, and produces watery, burning, and itching eyelids. The acute contagious form is known as pink-eye.

Connecticut, state in the NE United States, in the New England region.
  Land and Economy. A narrow plain lies along the shore of Long Island Sound in the S. In the W and E, hill ridges run N and S, with the highest in the NW corner. The Connecticut River Valley between the ridges is fertile farmland. Other major rivers are the Housatonic (W) and the Thames (E). In earlier days, Connecticut was known as a maker of small machines, and manufacturing is the heart of the economy. Defense contracts, including building nuclear submarines, are important. Hartford is the nation's foremost insurance center.
  People. In the 19th century, Connecticut received thousands of immigrants from Europe, creating a mixture of nationalities and races, but by the late 20th century about 90% of its people were born in the United States. More than 75% live in urban areas. Thousands of residents in the SW section commute to jobs in New York City.
  Education. Yale University, founded in 1701, is at New Haven. The University of Connecticut's principal campus is at Storrs. Trinity College, Wesleyan University, and Connecticut College are leading privately-endowed schools. There are about 50 institutions of higher education. The US Coast Guard Academy is at New London.
  History. The first permanent settlements were made in the Connecticut River Valley around Hartford by English from E Massachusetts. Others were established along Long Island Sound, and in 1662 the colony received a charter from Charles II of England. When the American Revolution began, the colony had nearly 200,000 inhabitants. After the war, many migrated to neighboring states or to lands in the Middle West, but later the state's growing light industry drew new residents. In each of the country's major wars, Connecticut

was a prime supplier of arms, munitions, and tools. In 1974, Ella T. Grasso was elected governor, the first woman governor in the United States to be elected governor in her own right. Reelected to a second term in 1978, she resigned in 1980 due to cancer, and died the following year.

PROFILE

Admitted to Union: Jan. 9, 1788; 5th of the 13 original states to ratify the US Constitution
US Congressmen: Senate, 2; House of Representatives, 6
Population: 3,107,576 (1980); rank, 25th
Capital: Hartford, 136,392
Chief cities: Hartford; Bridgeport, 142,546; New Haven, 126,109
State Legislature: Senate, 36; House of Representatives, 151
Area: 5,009sq mi (12,973sq km); rank, 48th
Elevation: Highest, 2,380ft (726m), on Mt Frissell; lowest, sea level
Industries (major products): aircraft engines and parts, helicopters, industrial machinery, household appliances, hardware, silverware
Agriculture (major products): milk, poultry, tobacco
Minerals (major): stone, sand, gravel, clay
State Nickname: Constitution State
State Motto: Qui transtulit, sustinet (He who transplanted, still sustains)
State Bird: American robin
State Flower: Mountain laurel
State tree: White oak

Connecticut Compromise (1787), compromise at Philadelphia Constitutional Convention between large states, which favored representation based on population (Virginia Plan), and small states, which wanted equal representation regardless of size (New Jersey Plan). Proposed by Oliver Ellsworth of Connecticut, the plan was incorporated into the Constitution and included representation by population (House of Representatives) and equal representation for the states (Senate).

Connecticut River, river in New England; rises in Connecticut Lakes, in N New Hampshire; as it flows S, it forms a natural border between New Hampshire and Vermont; continues through W central Massachusetts and central Connecticut to empty into Long Island Sound near Old Saybrook; it has 23 tributaries and is used chiefly in the production of hydroelectricity and irrigation. Discovered 1614 by Adrian Block, Dutch explorer. Length: 407mi (655km).

Connective Tissue, bodily tissue that maintains the body's form and holds it together. Composed of cells, protein fibers, and carbohydrate substance. Bones, ligaments, cartilage, and skin are all connective tissue.

Connors, James Scott "Jimmy" (1952–), US tennis player, b. East St. Louis, Ill. He won the US Open singles championship (1974,1976,1978), the British singles championship (1974, 1982), and the Australian singles championship (1974).

Conodont, any of numerous kinds of toothlike microfossils composed of calcium phosphate and occurring in marine deposits of Paleozoic and early Mesozoic ages. Their origin is uncertain. They have been thought to be polychaete jaw parts, the radular teeth of mollusks, the copulatory structures of nematodes, and even of algal derivation. They have been classified in great detail and are used extensively in stratigraphy.

Conon (died *c.*390 BC), Athenian admiral who used Persian sea power to devastate the Spartan fleet at Cnidos (394 BC).

Conquistador, Spaniard who participated in the conquest of the New World; a professional or semiprofessional soldier, usually from Castile.

Conrad III (1093–1152), first German king (1138–52) of the Hohenstaufen dynasty. He was crowned anti-king to Holy Roman Emperor Lothair II in 1127 and was excommunicated by the pope. He later submitted to Lothair and was crowned German king (emperor-elect) after Lothair's death. His main opposition came from Henry the Proud and then his son Henry the Lion. From this fight arose the two great Italian factions, the Guelphs and the Ghibellines. Conrad was never crowned emperor but was succeeded by his nephew, who ruled as Frederick I. *See also* Hohenstaufen Dynasty; Holy Roman Empire.

Conrad, Joseph (1857–1924), British novelist, b. Teodor Józef Konrad Korzeniowski in Poland. His years as a ship's officer in Asian, African, and Latin American waters suggested the exotic settings of many of his novels. His works include *Almayer's Folly* (1895), *An Outcast of the Islands* (1896), *The Nigger of the 'Narcissus'* (1897), *Lord Jim* (1900), *Typhoon* (1903), *Nostromo* (1904), *The Secret Agent* (1907), *Under Western Eyes* (1911), *Victory* (1915), and the short novel *The Heart of Darkness* (1902). Conrad deals with the psychological conflicts that confront men in extreme situations.

Conscience, the element of a personality that signals "right" or "wrong" about a thought or a deed. In many respects, the psychoanalytic concept of the superego is the same as conscience. *See also* Superego.

Conscientious Objector, person who refuses to serve in the armed forces because of religious, ethical, or philosophical convictions.

Consciousness, an awareness or perception of an inward psychological fact. The concept was defined in 1690 by John Locke. Initially consciousness was considered separate and different from the material substance of the physical world. Behaviorists refer consciousness to awareness and responsiveness as contrasted with their lack during sleep or coma. Today levels of consciousness are correlated with brain waves measured on an electroencephalograph. *See also* Brain Waves.

Consensus, in social science, agreement by a majority on issues, rules, or procedures. It does not mean absence of debate. In a democracy public opinion about parties and candidates changes, but there is consensus on basic policies. Politicians try to manipulate opinion to form a consensus favorable to them. The breakdown of consensus is called "cleavage."

Consent, Popular, fundamental principle of the democratic system, which holds that government is based on the consent of the governed, a concept originated by John Locke. *See also* Locke, John.

Conservation, Laws of, physical laws stating that some property of a closed system is unchanged by changes in the system. The most important are the laws of conservation of matter and of energy. The former states that matter cannot be created or destroyed; the total mass remains constant when chemical changes occur. The total energy of a system also remains the same; energy is simply converted from one form into another. In fact mass and energy are interconvertible according to the equation $E = mc^2$. What is conserved is the total mass and its equivalent in energy. The two classical laws are approximate cases of a law of conservation of mass-energy.

Conservation Law, Nuclear, in a nuclear interaction, the total charge, spin, or other specific quantum number of the interacting particles must equal that of the resulting particles. In strong interactions all quantum numbers are conserved. In weak interactions several of the laws break down, notably that for parity.

Conservatism, political philosophy that favors the preservation of traditional institutions and practices. The conservative, basically distrustful of politics, believes that human attitudes and behavior cannot be improved through legislation. He strongly opposes too much governmental regulation. He believes social change should be gradual and occur within a historical framework. Created as a reaction to the ideas of the Enlightenment, conservatism relies on habit and experience, not pure reason, as the basis for social order.

Conservative Party, Britain's major right-wing political party. Under Sir Robert Peel it developed from the Tory party in the 1830s to protect the interests of both landowners and industry and defend law and order. Disraeli reorganized the party, committing it to democracy and social reform as well as conservatism (1870s). The Liberal decline (1920s) allowed the Conservatives to dominate the interwar years, and the World War II coalition was led by Winston Churchill, the Conservative leader. The postwar party followed moderate policies, although it swung to the right after 1970. Conservative membership is traditionally middle-class and its MPs are mostly businessmen, lawyers, and landowners; nevertheless, it enjoys fairly strong working-class support. The party organization consists of the Parliamentary party, which elects the leader, the National Union of Conservative Associations, and the Central Office.

Constable, John (1776–1837), English painter whose work, together with that of his contemporary, J.W. Turner, was the precursor of the Impressionist movement. Although Constable also painted portraits of considerable interest, his landscapes of the English countryside began the turn toward naturalism and direct observation of nature. Constable studied at the Royal Academy and copied from Claude Lorrain and Ruisdael. He worked at reproducing the effects of clouds and light on water—often using broken color and thick impasto texture. His first success came when *The Hay Wain* (1821) and *View on the Stour* (1822) were shown at the Paris Salon of 1824 and were acclaimed by French romantic artists, especially Delacroix. Constable was neglected in England until 1890 when the small oils on which his large works were based were shown to the public. These are much admired today; most are in the Victoria and Albert Museum. Other museums with major paintings are the National Gallery, London, and the Metropolitan Museum and Frick Collection, New York.

Constance, Council of (1414–18), gathering of Roman Catholic prelates convoked by Antipope John XXIII in 1413 to end the Great Schism between Rome (Pope Gregory XII) and Avignon (Pope Benedict XIII) and to deal with several heresies (notably those of Jan Hus). The council, which was held at the cathedral of Constance in Germany, favored the resignation of all three "popes." Gregory XII resigned, but John XXIII fled and was returned as a prisoner. The council was reconvoked in 1415, and Benedict XIII was deposed in 1417. The election of Martin V in 1417 during the council ended the Great Schism. Jan Hus was condemned and burned as a heretic. *See also* Great Schism; Hus, Jan.

Constance, Lake, lake bordering on Austria, West Germany, and Switzerland; fed and drained by the Rhine River; divides into two arms near the city of Constance; contains remains of prehistoric lake dwellings. Local industries include fruit growing, wine, fishing. Area: 208sq mi (539sq km).

Constant, number or symbol that has a fixed value in an algebraic expression. *See* Variable.

Constanta, chief seaport city in Romania, on the Black Sea; taken by Rome 72 BC; named in 4th century by Constantine; major trade center; site of naval base, marine biology station, many mosques, synagogues, statue of Ovid, Roman and Byzantine ruins, and Orthodox cathedral. Industries: exporting grain, lumber, petroleum. Founded 7th century BC as a Greek colony. Pop. 267,612.

Constantine I, or **Constantine the Great** (280–337), Roman emperor (305–337). In 312 at the Battle of the Milvian Bridge Constantine defeated his rival Maxentius and was declared senior Augustus of the Roman Empire. The victory had religious as well as political implications. Before the battle Constantine had appealed to the God of the Christians for help against the pagan forces of Maxentius; he regarded his victory as the answer to this appeal. Though born and educated a pagan, he was sympathetic to the Christian Church, perhaps seeing in it a means of unifying his people. In 313 Constantine and coemperor Licinius issued the Edict of Milan, which granted Christians freedom of worship and restored properties that had been confiscated from their churches. In 324 he defeated Licinius and became sole Roman emperor. He established a new capital, or a second Rome, at Constantinople in 330. In 325 he convened the First Council of Nicaea to deal with Arianism.

Constantine IV (648–85), Byzantine emperor (*r.*668–85). Under his leadership, the westward advance of the Arabs was decisively halted. The defeat of the Arab forces at Constantinople in 678 saved not only the Byzantine Empire, but also prevented an Arab invasion of Europe.

Constantine V (719–75), Byzantine emperor (*r.*741–75). Slanderously nicknamed Copronymous ("Dung-name"), by his ecclesiastical opponents, this powerful iconoclastic emperor fought the defenders of the images with both theological arguments and political force. He is known especially for repressive measures against the monasteries. Constantine was an effective military commander, and under his leadership Byzantium's Arab and Bulgar enemies were defeated. *See also* Iconoclastic Controversy.

Constantine VII Porphyrogenitus (905–59), Byzantine emperor (*r.*912–59) and scholar. Constantine was a patron of arts and scholarship and was himself the author of two important political works. *On the Administration of the Empire* was a manual of foreign diplomacy intended for the guidance of his son, and *On the Ceremonies of the Byzantine Court* was a handbook written in order to maintain the imperial court ceremonial.

Constantine XI (Palaeologus) (1404–53), Byzantine emperor (*r.*1448–53). Formerly Despot of Morea, Constantine was the last emperor of Byzantium. He was killed fighting against the Turkish forces of Murad II during the seige and ultimate capture of Constantinople.

Constantine I (1868–1923), king of Greece (1913–17; 1920–22). Married to sister of William II of Germany, he was pro-German during World War I. His premier, Eleutherios Venizelos, was pro-Allies, and Constantine left Greece in 1917 when it joined the Allies, but was recalled at his son Alexander's death (1920). There was a military revolt in 1922. He abdicated and died in exile.

Constantine II (1940–), king of Greece. Married to Anne Marie of Denmark, he became king in 1964. In a political crisis of 1965–66 he dismissed the prime minister. After a successful military coup and an unsuccessful counter-coup (1967), Constantine II went into exile. The monarchy was abolished in Greece (1973).

Constantine, ancient Cirta, fortified city in NE Algeria, on Rhumel River; capital of Constantine dept.; founded as Sarim Batim by Carthaginians; was trade center and capital of Numidia and wealthy grain port under Romans; destroyed AD 311 and rebuilt by Constantine. A major inland city, it contains a university and a Muslim school. Industries: agricultural produce, textiles, leather goods, tourism. Pop. 1,682,000.

Constantinople, capital city of the Byzantine Empire. In AD 330 the Roman Emperor Constantine the Great established a "Second Rome" on the site of the old Greek colony of Byzantium. Its location on the Hellespont was strategic, for it lay at the meeting point of Europe and Asia. For over 1000 years, until its capture by the Ottoman Turks in 1453 (and the subsequent change of its name to Istanbul), Constantinople was the hub of the Byzantine world. *See also* Byzantium; Istanbul.

Constantinople, First Council of (381), gathering of Christian bishops and other representatives. It was convoked by Emperor Theodosius I to unite the Eastern Church; there were no Western bishops or Roman legates present. Council decrees granted Constantinople honorary precedence over all churches but Rome, condemned Appolinarianism (the doctrine that Christ had human body but divine spirit), and upheld the doctrine of Christ's humanity. Although it is of a later date, the Nicene Creed is traditionally associated with this council.

Constantinople, Second Council of or Fifth General Council (533), gathering of Christian bishops and other representatives. Convoked by Emperor Justinian and attended almost entirely by Eastern bishops, the council met to decide the controversy of the Three Chapters regarding Nestorianism (the doctrine that two separate persons, one divine and one human, were contained in Christ). The council condemned this doctrine and upheld the position that Christ was one person who was simultaneously both God and Man. Pope Virgilius and the council were not in entire agreement on the matter, but he finally accepted the council version.

Constantinople, Third Council of or Sixth General Council (680), gathering of Christian bishops and other representatives. It was convoked by Emperor Constantine to decide the Eastern Church Monothelite controversy (heresy confessing only one will in Christ). The Rome Synod, convened the same year by Pope Agatho, affirmed the doctrine of two wills—divine and human—in Christ and sent this decision to the council. The council declared the Monotheletics heretical and rejected the physical unity of two wills in Christ. It did, however, admit a moral unity of these wills.

John Dickinson

Rufus King

William Livingston

Constantinople, Fourth Council or Eighth General Council (869–70), gathering of Christian bishops and other representatives. It was convoked to decide the Photian Schism between the Greek and Latin Churches. The controversy began when Ignatius was deposed as patriarch of Constantinople (858) and replaced by Photius. The pope in Rome maintained that Photius was the true patriarch, and his intervention in Eastern Church affairs was resented by Constantinople, which was also in dispute with Rome over the question of authority in Bulgaria. In 867 the Fourth Council confirmed the reinstatement of Ignatius, an action supported by the pope, thus briefly restoring harmony between East and West.

Constantinople, Latin Empire of. On April 13, 1204, the western armies of the Fourth Crusade captured the city of Constantinople and divided the former Byzantine territories among themselves. Western European feudal organizations were imposed upon some of the newly-formed states, and Constantinople was placed under the control of Baldwin, Count of Flanders. The Latin Empire ended when, in 1261, the Greek Empire was restored by Michael Palaeologus.

Constantius I (c.250–306), Roman emperor (305–06). A general, he was appointed caesar (subemperor) in 292 after defeating Carausius. In 296 he put down a rebellion in Britain and in 298 defeated the Alemanni in Gaul. When Diocletian and Maximian abdicated in 305, he became emperor of the West. He was succeeded by his son Constantine I.

Constellation, any of the recognized patterns formed by groupings of conspicuous stars as viewed from earth. Constellations are optical effects caused by perspective, and the mutual proximity of their component stars is essentially illusory. Groupings visible in northern and equatorial regions have long-established names derived by ancient astronomers from animals and mythological figures; southern constellations, however, remained unknown until discovered by European navigators during the 16th and 17th centuries. These latter tend to be named after objects connected with navigation, seafaring, and science.

Constitutional Act of 1791. Instituted by British Prime Minister William Pitt, the act divided French and English Canada, creating a system of government dominated by an appointed executive branch. The elected Legislative Assembly dealt only with local issues. Dissatisfaction with the form of government led to the Rebellion of 1837 and to the Durham Report (1839) reforms. *See also* Durham Report; Rebellion of 1837.

Constitutional Government, government based on a set of principles embodied in a document whose authority stems directly from the consent of those governed. A written constitution was a distinct US departure from the largely unwritten legal code that long had been the foundation for many European governments. The US Constitution created a federalist form of government, with authority shared by the nation and states. The Constitution is a legal instrument, regarded as supreme law, guaranteeing basic civil rights and resources should such rights be violated. It has proved to be highly flexible, adapting to new conditions through interpretation and amendment.

Constitutional Law, as understood in the United States, refers to the body of legal principles arising from interpretation and application of the constitution (federal or state) by courts empowered to judge cases involving the constitutionality of legislative acts. The power of the judiciary to pass on acts of other branches of government is implied from the federal

Constitution, as stated in the opinion of Chief Justice Marshall in *Marbury* v. *Madison* (1803). Constitutional law, in this sense, does not exist in England since there is no written constitution; English courts do not have power over acts of Parliament, for parliamentary supremacy is a fundamental principle of the unwritten English constitution.

Constitutional Types, or somatotypes, classifications of different types of human bodies, and the general theory that there is a relationship between body types and personality traits. Ernest Kretschmer devised the first such theory in the 19th century, but the foremost system is that of William H. Sheldon, who identified three major types of physique: *endomorphy,* characterized by a round, fat, flabby appearance; *mesomorphy,* athletic and muscular; and *ectomorphy,* frail and thin. Though psychologists have not accepted the alleged relationships that these types have to personality, Sheldon's system does provide a convenient way of measuring and classifying body types.

Constitution of the United States, the formal statement of the US system of government. Written in 1787 and ratified in 1788, it replaced the Articles of Confederation and took effect in 1789.

At the end of the Revolutionary War the United States was a weak confederation of 13 states. The divergent interests of the separate states and the unrest on the Western frontier created fear that the Union would not survive. In 1786 at the Annapolis Convention, James Madison and Alexander Hamilton led representatives of five states meeting to settle problems of interstate commerce. Finding that commerce was bound up with many other issues, they called for a meeting of all states to discuss the problems facing the states. The result was the Constitutional Convention, which met in Philadelphia in 1787.

The state legislatures sent their best men to the convention, which met from May 25 to September 17 —George Washington, James Madison, and George Mason came from Virginia; Rufus King and Elbridge Gerry from Massachusetts; Roger Sherman and Oliver Ellsworth from Connecticut; Hamilton from New York; Benjamin Franklin, James Wilson, Gouverneur Morris, and Robert Morris from Pennsylvania; William Paterson from New Jersey; John Rutledge and Charles Pinckney from South Carolina. Only Rhode Island was not represented. The only important men missing were Thomas Jefferson, John Jay, and John Adams, who were representing the United States abroad. George Washington was elected president of the convention, which opened in Independence Hall.

Framing of the Constitution. Madison, the principal architect of the Constitution, was a nationalist, favoring a strong central government of three branches —executive, judiciary, and legislative. He offered the Virginia, or large-state, plan, which provided for legislative-representation based on population, and this was countered by the New Jersey, or small-state, plan which provided for each state to be represented equally. The result was the Connecticut Compromise, keeping the outline of Madison's plan but creating a two-house legislature: the Senate with equal representation of all states and the House of Representatives apportioned according to population. From the New Jersey plan came the key feature that the Constitution should be the supreme law of the land, binding on all states and enforced by all courts. The document adopted by the Constitutional Convention was a short one, laying the ground work for a strong central government with Madison's three branches but not trying to cover every possible eventuality. It is composed of a Preamble, seven articles, and 26 amendments.

Ratification and Amendments. The Constitution had to be ratified by 9 of the 13 states before it could

become law. In some states there was strong opposition, led by anti-Federalists who feared a powerful central government. Among the most prominent was Patrick Henry in Virginia. Only by convincing oratory— particularly by Madison in Virginia and Hamilton in New York—were the wavering states won over and the Constitution ratified.

In 1791 the first 10 amendments, known as the Bill of Rights, were added to provide more protection for individuals. With these and other amendments, the Constitution has served to hold together the large and diverse nation while protecting the rights of the people. The Constitution's preamble states the reasons for adopting a constitution. Article I deals with such matters as the powers of Congress, the composition of the House and Senate and election to them, and restrictions upon the powers of the states. Article II covers the presidency, including election and powers, while Article III outlines the powers and responsibilities of the judiciary. Article IV describes relations between states and the admission of new states. Article V details how amendments to the Constitution shall be made; Article VI states the authority of the Constitution; and Article VII says that nine states will have to ratify the Constitution before it becomes effective.

The first 10 amendments to the Constitution, known as the Bill of Rights, were adopted in 1791. The First Amendment guaranteed freedom of religion, speech, press, and assembly. The Second guaranteed the right to bear arms, while the Third protected citizens against soldiers being quartered in private homes. The Fourth Amendment guarded the public from unreasonable search and seizure, and the Fifth protected accused persons from self-incrimination. The Sixth guaranteed a speedy trial, the Seventh trial by jury, and the Eighth protection from cruel and unusual punishment. The Ninth and Tenth said that the people retained rights not delegated to the federal or state authorities.

The next amendment (XI, 1795) prohibited a citizen of one state from suing another state government. Amendment XII (1804) set up separate ballots for electing the president and vice president. The Civil War Amendments (XIII, 1861; XIV, 1868; XV, 1870) outlawed slavery, declared all people born or naturalized in the United States citizens, and declared that the right to vote could not be denied because of color. Amendment XVI (1913) gave the Congress the right to enact personal income taxes. Popular election of US senators was established by Amendment XVII (1913). Prohibition, enacted by Amendment XVIII (1919), was repealed by Amendment XXI (1933). Women received the right to vote by Amendment XIX (1920). Amendment XXII (1951) limited the length of time a person may be president, and Amendment XXV (1967) set procedures for filling vice-presidential and presidential vacancies. Amendment XXIII (1961) gave District of Columbia residents the right to vote for president. The poll tax was prohibited by Amendment XXIV (1964). The voting age was lowered to age 18 by Amendment XXVI (1971). Amendment XXVII, barring discrimination based on sex, went to the states for ratification in 1972. In 1979, the deadline for ratification was extended to 1982. When the deadline expired, the Amendment was immediately reintroduced as a bill in Congress. *See also* Bill of Rights; Connecticut Compromise; New Jersey Plan; Virginia Plan.

Following is the text of the Constitution of the United States:

THE CONSTITUTION
of the
UNITED STATES OF AMERICA

WE THE PEOPLE of the United States, in Order to form a more perfect Union, establish Justice, insure domestic Tranquility, provide for the common defence, promote the general Welfare, and secure the Blessings of Liberty to ourselves and our Posterity, do ordain and establish this CONSTITUTION for the United States of America.

ARTICLE I.

SECTION 1. All legislative Powers herein granted shall be vested in a Congress of the United States, which shall consist of a Senate and House of Representatives.

SECTION 2. The House of Representatives shall be composed of Members chosen every second Year by the People of the several States, and the Electors in each State shall have the Qualifications requisite for Electors of the most numerous Branch of the State Legislature.

No Person shall be a Representative who shall not have attained to the Age of twenty five Years, and been seven Years a Citizen of the United States, and who shall not, when elected, be an Inhabitant of that State in which he shall be chosen.

Representatives and direct Taxes shall be apportioned among the several States which may be included within this Union, according to their respective Numbers, which shall be determined by adding to the whole Number of free Persons, including those bound to Service for a Term of Years, and excluding Indians not taxed, three fifths of all other Persons. The actual Enumeration shall be made within three Years after the first Meeting of the Congress of the United States, and within every subsequent Term of ten Years, in such Manner as they shall by Law direct. The Number of Representatives shall not exceed one for every thirty Thousand, but each State shall have at Least one Representative; and until such enumeration shall be made, the State of New Hampshire shall be entitled to chuse three, Massachusetts eight, Rhode-Island and Providence Plantations one, Connecticut five, New-York six, New Jersey four, Pennsylvania eight, Delaware one, Maryland six, Virginia ten, North Carolina five, South Carolina five, and Georgia three.

When vacancies happen in the Representation from any State, the Executive Authority thereof shall issue Writs of Election to fill such Vacancies.

The House of Representatives shall chuse their Speaker and other Officers; and shall have the sole Power of Impeachment.

SECTION 3. The Senate of the United States shall be composed of two Senators from each State, chosen by the Legislature thereof, for six Years; and each Senator shall have one Vote.

Immediately after they shall be assembled in Consequence of the first Election, they shall be divided as equally as may be into three Classes. The Seats of the Senators of the first Class shall be vacated at the Expiration of the second Year, of the second Class at the Expiration of the fourth Year, and of the third Class at the Expiration of the sixth Year, so that one third may be chosen every second Year; and if Vacancies happen by Resignation, or otherwise, during the Recess of the Legislature of any State, the Executive thereof may make temporary Appointments until the next Meeting of the Legislature, which shall then fill such Vacancies.

No Person shall be a Senator who shall not have attained to the Age of thirty Years, and been nine Years a Citizen of the United States, and who shall not, when elected, be an Inhabitant of that State for which he shall be chosen.

The Vice President of the United States shall be President of the Senate, but shall have no Vote, unless they be equally divided.

The Senate shall chuse their other Officers, and also a President pro tempore, in the Absence of the Vice President, or when he shall exercise the Office of President of the United States.

The Senate shall have the sole Power to try all Impeachments. When sitting for that Purpose, they shall be on Oath or Affirmation. When the President of the United States is tried, the Chief Justice shall preside: And no Person shall be convicted without the Concurrence of two thirds of the Members present.

Judgment in Cases of Impeachment shall not extend further than to removal from Office, and disqualification to hold and enjoy any Office of honor, Trust or Profit under the United States: but the Party convicted shall nevertheless be liable and subject to Indictment, Trial, Judgment and Punishment, according to Law.

SECTION 4. The Times, Places and Manner of holding Elections for Senators and Representatives, shall be prescribed in each State by the Legislature thereof; but the Congress may at any time by Law make or alter such Regulations, except as to the Places of chusing Senators.

The Congress shall assemble at least once in every Year, and such Meeting shall be on the first Monday in December, unless they shall by Law appoint a different Day.

SECTION 5. Each House shall be the Judge of the Elections, Returns and Qualifications of its own Members, and a Majority of each shall constitute a Quorum to do Business; but a smaller Number may adjourn from day to day, and may be authorized to compel the Attendance of absent Members, in such Manner, and under such Penalties as each House may provide.

Each House may determine the Rules of its Proceedings, punish its Members for disorderly Behaviour, and, with the Concurrence of two thirds, expel a Member.

Each House shall keep a Journal of its Proceedings, and from time to time publish the same, excepting such Parts as may in their Judgment require Secrecy; and the Yeas and Nays of the Members of either House on any question shall, at the Desire of one fifth of those Present, be entered on the Journal.

Neither House, during the Session of Congress, shall, without the Consent of the other, adjourn for more than three days, nor to any other Place than that in which the two Houses shall be sitting.

SECTION 6. The Senators and Representatives shall receive a Compensation for their Services, to be ascertained by Law, and paid out of the Treasury of the United States. They shall in all Cases, except Treason, Felony and Breach of the Peace, be privileged from Arrest during their Attendance at the Session of their respective Houses, and in going to and returning from the same; and for any Speech or Debate in either House, they shall not be questioned in any other Place.

No Senator or Representative shall, during the Time for which he was elected, be appointed to any civil Office under the Authority of the United States, which shall have been created, or the Emoluments whereof shall have been encreased during such time; and no Person holding any Office under the United States, shall be a Member of either House during his Continuance in Office.

SECTION 7. All Bills for raising Revenue shall originate in the House of Representatives; but the Senate may propose or concur with Amendments as on other Bills.

Every Bill which shall have passed the House of Representatives and the Senate, shall, before it become a Law, be presented to the President of the United States; If he approve he shall sign it, but if not he shall return it, with his Objections to that House in which it shall have originated, who shall enter the Objections at large on their Journal, and proceed to reconsider it. If after such Reconsideration two thirds of that House shall agree to pass the Bill, it shall be sent, together with the Objections, to the other House, by which it shall likewise be reconsidered, and if approved by two thirds of that House, it shall become a Law. But in all such Cases the Votes of both Houses shall be determined by Yeas and Nays, and the Names of the Persons voting for and against the Bill shall be entered on the Journal of each House respectively. If any Bill shall not be returned by the President within ten Days (Sundays excepted) after it shall have been presented to him, the Same shall be a Law, in like Manner as if he had signed it, unless the Congress by their Adjournment prevent its Return, in which Case it shall not be a Law.

Every Order, Resolution, or Vote to which the Concurrence of the Senate and House of Representatives may be necessary (except on a question of Adjournment) shall be presented to the President of the United States; and before the Same shall take Effect, shall be approved by him, or being disapproved by him, shall be repassed by two thirds of the Senate and House of Representatives, according to the Rules and Limitations prescribed in the Case of a Bill.

SECTION 8. The Congress shall have Power To lay and collect Taxes, Duties, Imposts and Excises, to pay the Debts and provide for the common Defence and general Welfare of the United States; but all Duties, Imposts and Excises shall be uniform throughout the United States;

To Borrow Money on the Credit of the United States;

To regulate Commerce with foreign Nations, and among the several States, and with the Indian Tribes;

To establish an uniform Rule of Naturalization, and uniform Laws on the subject of Bankruptcies throughout the United States;

To coin Money, regulate the Value thereof, and of foreign Coin, and fix the Standard of Weights and Measures;

To provide for the Punishment of counterfeiting the Securities and current Coin of the United States;

To establish Post Offices and post Roads;

To promote the Progress of Science and useful Arts, by securing for limited Times to Authors and Inventors the exclusive Right to their respective Writings and Discoveries;

To constitute Tribunals inferior to the supreme Court;

To define and punish Piracies and Felonies committed on the high Seas, and Offences against the Law of Nations;

To declare War, grant Letters of Marque and Reprisal, and make Rules concerning Captures on Land and Water;

To raise and support Armies, but no Appropriation of Money to that Use shall be for a longer Term than two Years;

To provide and maintain a Navy;

To make Rules for the Government and Regulation of the land and naval Forces;

To provide for calling forth the Militia to execute the Laws of the Union, suppress Insurrections and repel Invasions;

To provide for organizing, arming, and disciplining the Militia, and for governing such Part of them as may be employed in the Service of the United States, reserving to the States respectively, the Appointment of the Officers, and the Authority of training the Militia according to the discipline prescribed by Congress;

To exercise exclusive Legislation in all Cases whatsoever, over such District (not exceeding ten Miles square) as may, by Cession of particular States, and the Acceptance of Congress, become the Seat of the Government of the United States, and to exercise like Authority over all Places purchased by the Consent of the Legislature of the State in which the Same shall be for the Erection of Forts, Magazines, Arsenals, dock-Yards, and other needful Buildings;—And

To make all Laws which shall be necessary and proper for carrying into Execution the foregoing Powers, and all other Powers vested by this Constitution in the Government of the United States, or in any Department or Officer thereof.

SECTION 9. The Migration or Importation of such Persons as any of the States now existing shall think proper to admit, shall not be prohibited by the Congress prior to the Year one thousand eight hundred and eight, but a Tax or duty may be imposed on such Importation, not exceeding ten dollars for each Person.

The Privilege of the Writ of Habeas Corpus shall not be suspended, unless when in Cases of Rebellion or Invasion the public Safety may require it.

No Bill of Attainder or ex post facto Law shall be passed.

No Capitation, or other direct, Tax shall be laid, unless in Proportion to the Census or Enumeration herein before directed to be taken.

No Tax or Duty shall be laid on Articles exported from any State.

No Preference shall be given by any Regulation of Commerce or Revenue to the Ports of one State over those of another: nor shall Vessels bound to, or from, one State, be obliged to enter, clear, or pay Duties in another.

No Money shall be drawn from the Treasury, but in Consequence of Appropriations made by Law; and a regular Statement and Account of the Receipts and Expenditures of all public Money shall be published from time to time.

No Title of Nobility shall be granted by the United States: And no Person holding any Office of Profit or Trust under them, shall, without the Consent of Congress, accept of any present, Emolument, Office, or Title, of any kind whatever, from any King, Prince, or foreign State.

SECTION 10. No State shall enter into any Treaty, Alliance, or Confederation; grant Letters of Marque and Reprisal; coin Money; emit Bills of Credit; make any Thing but gold and silver Coin a Tender in Payment of Debts; pass any Bill of Attainder, ex post facto Law, or Law impairing the Obligation of Contracts, or grant any Title of Nobility.

No State shall, without the Consent of the Congress, lay any Imposts or Duties on Imports or Exports, except what may be absolutely necessary for executing its inspection Laws: and the net Produce of all Duties and Imposts, laid by any State on Imports or Exports, shall be for the Use of the Treasury of the United States; and all such Laws shall be subject to the Revision and Controul of the Congress.

No State shall, without the Consent of Congress, lay any Duty of Tonnage, keep Troops, or Ships of War in time of Peace, enter into any Agreement or Compact with another State, or with a foreign Power, or engage in War, unless actually invaded, or in such imminent Danger as will not admit of delay.

ARTICLE II.

SECTION 1. The executive Power shall be vested in a President of the United States of America. He shall hold his Office during the Term of four Years, and, together with the Vice President, chosen for the same term, be elected, as follows

Each State shall appoint, in such Manner as the Legislature thereof may direct, a Number of Electors, equal to the whole Number of Senators and Representatives to which the State may be entitled in the Congress: but no Senator or Representative, or Person holding an Office of Trust or Profit under the United States, shall be appointed an Elector.

The Electors shall meet in their respective States, and vote by Ballot for two Persons, of whom one at least shall not be an Inhabitant of the same State with themselves. And they shall make a List of all the Persons voted for, and of the Number of Votes for each; which List they shall sign and certify, and transmit sealed to the Seat of the Government of the United States, directed to the President of the Senate. The President of the Senate shall, in the Presence of the

Constitution of the United States

Gouverneur Morris

Robert Morris

William Paterson

Senate and House of Representatives, open all the Certificates, and the Votes shall then be counted. The Person having the greatest Number of Votes shall be the President, if such Number be a Majority of the whole Number of Electors appointed; and if there be more than one who have such Majority, and have an equal Number of Votes, then the House of Representatives shall immediately chuse by Ballot one of them for President: and if no Person have a Majority, then from the five highest on the List the said House shall in like Manner chuse the President. But in chusing the President, the Votes shall be taken by States, the Representation from each State having one Vote; A quorum for this Purpose shall consist of a Member or Members from two thirds of the States, and a Majority of all the States shall be necessary to a Choice. In every Case, after the Choice of the President, the Person having the greatest Number of Votes of the Electors shall be the Vice President. But if there should remain two or more who have equal Votes, the Senate shall chuse from them by Ballot the Vice President.

The Congress may determine the Time of chusing the Electors, and the Day on which they shall give their Votes; which Day shall be the same throughout the United States.

No Person except a natural born Citizen, or a Citizen of the United States, at the time of the Adoption of this Constitution, shall be eligible to the Office of President; neither shall any Person be eligible to that Office who shall not have attained to the Age of thirty five Years, and been fourteen Years a Resident within the United States.

In Case of the Removal of the President from Office, or of his Death, Resignation, or Inability to discharge the Powers and Duties of the said Office, the Same shall devolve on the Vice President, and the Congress may by Law provide for the Case of Removal, Death, Resignation or Inability, both of the President and Vice President, declaring what Officer shall then act as President, and such Officer shall act accordingly, until the Disability be removed, or a President shall be elected.

The President shall, at stated Times, receive for his Services, a Compensation, which shall neither be encreased nor diminished during the Period for which he shall have been elected, and he shall not receive within that Period any other Emolument from the United States, or any of them.

Before he enter on the Execution of his Office, he shall take the following Oath or Affirmation:—"I do solemnly swear (or affirm) that I will faithfully execute the Office of President of the United States, and will to the best of my Ability, preserve, protect and defend the Constitution of the United States."

Section 2. The President shall be Commander in Chief of the Army and Navy of the United States, and of the Militia of the several States, when called into the actual Service of the United States; he may require the Opinion in writing, of the principal Officer in each of the executive Departments, upon any Subject relating to the Duties of their respective Offices, and he shall have Power to grant Reprieves and Pardons for Offences against the United States, except in Cases of Impeachment.

He shall have Power, by and with the Advice and Consent of the Senate, to make Treaties, provided two thirds of the Senators present concur; and he shall nominate, and by and with the Advice and Consent of the Senate, shall appoint Ambassadors, other public Ministers and Consuls, Judges of the supreme Court, and all other Officers of the United States, whose Appointments are not herein otherwise provided for, and which shall be established by Law: but the Congress may by Law vest the Appointment of such inferior Officers, as they think proper, in the President alone, in the Courts of Law, or in the Heads of Departments.

The President shall have Power to fill up all Vacancies that may happen during the Recess of the Senate, by granting Commissions which shall expire at the End of their next Session.

Section 3. He shall from time to time give to the Congress Information of the State of the Union, and recommend to their Consideration such Measures as he shall judge necessary and expedient; he may, on extraordinary Occasions, convene both Houses, or either of them, and in Case of Disagreement between them, with Respect to the Time of Adjournment, he may adjourn them to such Time as he shall think proper; he shall receive Ambassadors and other public Ministers; he shall take Care that the Laws be faithfully executed, and shall Commission all the Officers of the United States.

Section 4. The President, Vice President and all civil Officers of the United States, shall be removed from Office on Impeachment for, and Conviction of, Treason, Bribery, or other High Crimes and Misdemeanors.

ARTICLE III.

Section 1. The judicial Power of the United States, shall be vested in one supreme Court, and in such inferior Courts as the Congress may from time to time ordain and establish. The Judges, both of the supreme and inferior Courts, shall hold their Offices during good Behaviour, and shall, at stated Times, receive for their Services a Compensation, which shall not be diminished during their Continuance in Office.

Section 2. The judicial Power shall extend to all Cases, in Law and Equity, arising under this Constitution, the Laws of the United States, and Treaties made, or which shall be made, under their Authority;—to all Cases affecting Ambassadors, other public Ministers and Consuls;—to all Cases of admiralty and maritime Jurisdiction;—to Controversies to which the United States shall be a Party;—to Controversies between two or more States;—between a State and Citizens of another State;—between Citizens of different States;—between Citizens of the same State claiming Lands under Grants of different States, and between a State, or the Citizens thereof, and foreign States, Citizens or Subjects.

In all Cases affecting Ambassadors, other public Ministers and Consuls, and those in which a State shall be Party, the supreme Court shall have original Jurisdiction. In all the other Cases before mentioned, the supreme Court shall have appellate Jurisdiction, both as to Law and Fact, with such Exceptions, and under such Regulations as the Congress shall make.

The Trial of all Crimes, except in Cases of Impeachment, shall be by Jury; and such Trial shall be held in the State where the said Crimes shall have been committed; but when not committed within any State, the Trial shall be at such Place or Places as the Congress may by Law have directed.

Section 3. Treason against the United States, shall consist only in levying War against them, or in adhering to their Enemies, giving them Aid and Comfort. No Person shall be convicted of Treason unless on the Testimony of two Witnesses to the same overt Act, or on Confession in open Court.

The Congress shall have Power to declare the Punishment of Treason, but no Attainder of Treason shall work Corruption of Blood, or Forfeiture except during the Life of the Person attainted.

ARTICLE IV.

Section 1. Full Faith and Credit shall be given in each State to the public Acts, Records, and judicial Proceedings of every other State. And the Congress may by general Laws prescribe the Manner in which such Acts, Records and Proceedings shall be proved, and the Effect thereof.

Section 2. The Citizens of each State shall be entitled to all Privileges and Immunities of Citizens in the several States.

A Person charged in any State with Treason, Felony, or other Crime, who shall flee from Justice, and be found in another State, shall on Demand of the executive Authority of the State from which he fled, be delivered up, to be removed to the State having Jurisdiction of the Crime.

No Person held to Service or Labour in one State, under the Laws thereof, escaping into another, shall, in Consequence of any Law or Regulation therein, be discharged from such Service or Labour, but shall be delivered up on Claim of the Party to whom such Service or Labour may be due.

Section 3. New States may be admitted by the Congress into this Union; but no new State shall be formed or erected within the Jurisdiction of any other State; nor any State be formed by the Junction of two or more States, or Parts of States, without the Consent of the Legislatures of the States concerned as well as of the Congress.

The Congress shall have Power to dispose of and make all needful Rules and Regulations respecting the Territory or other Property belonging to the United States; and nothing in this Constitution shall be so construed as to Prejudice any Claims of the United States, or of any particular State.

Section 4. The United States shall guarantee to every State in this Union a Republican Form of Government, and shall protect each of them against Invasion; and on Application of the Legislature, or of the Executive (when the Legislature cannot be convened) against domestic Violence.

ARTICLE V.

The Congress, whenever two thirds of both Houses shall deem it necessary, shall propose Amendments to this Constitution, or, on the Application of the Legislatures of two thirds of the several States, shall call a Convention for proposing Amendments, which, in either Case, shall be valid to all Intents and Purposes, as Part of this Constitution, when ratified by the Legislatures of three fourths of the several States, or by Conventions in three fourths thereof, as the one or the other Mode of Ratification may be proposed by the Congress; Provided that no Amendment which may be made prior to the Year One thousand eight hundred and eight shall in any Manner affect the first and fourth Clauses in the Ninth Section of the first Article; and that no State, without its Consent, shall be deprived of its equal Suffrage in the Senate.

ARTICLE VI.

All Debts contracted and Engagements entered into, before the Adoption of this Constitution, shall be as valid against the United States under this Constitution, as under the Confederation.

This Constitution, and the Laws of the United States which shall be made in Pursuance thereof; and all Treaties made, or which shall be made, under the Authority of the United States, shall be the supreme Law of the Land; and the Judges in every State shall be bound thereby, any Thing in the Constitution or Laws of any State to the Contrary notwithstanding.

The Senators and Representatives before mentioned, and the Members of the several State Legislatures, and all executive and judicial Officers, both of the United States and of the several States, shall be bound by Oath or Affirmation, to support this Constitution; but no religious Test shall ever be required as a Qualification to any Office or public Trust under the United States.

ARTICLE VII.

The Ratification of the Conventions of nine States, shall be sufficient for the Establishment of this Constitution between the States so ratifying the Same.

Constitution of the United States

Done in Convention by the Unanimous Consent of the States present the Seventeenth Day of September in the Year of our Lord one thousand seven hundred and Eighty seven and of the Independence of the United States of America the Twelfth In witness whereof We have hereunto subscribed our Names,

G⁰ Washington—Presidᵗ.
and deputy from Virginia

Attest William Jackson *Secretary*

Delaware
Geo: Read
Gunning Bedford jun
John Dickinson
Richard Bassett
Jaco: Broom
Maryland
James McHenry
Dan ofSt Thos. Jenifer
Danl Carroll
Virginia
John Blair
James Madison Jr.
North Carolina
Wm. Blount
Richd. Dobbs Spaight.
Hu Williamson
South Carolina
J. Rutledge
Charles Cotesworth Pinckney
Charles Pinckney
Pierce Butler.
Georgia
William Few
Abr Baldwin
New Hampshire
John Langdon
Nicholas Gilman
Massachusetts
Nathaniel Gorham
Rufus King
Connecticut
Wm. Saml. Johnson
Roger Sherman
New York
Alexander Hamilton
New Jersey
Wil.: Livingston
David Brearley.
Wm. Paterson.
Jona: Dayton
Pennsylvania
B Franklin
Thomas Mifflin
Robt Morris
Geo. Clymer
Thos. FitzSimons
Jared Ingersoll
James Wilson
Gouv Morris

Amendment I

Congress shall make no law respecting an establishment of religion, or prohibiting the free exercise thereof; or abridging the freedom of speech, or of the press; or the right of the people peaceably to assemble, and to petition the Government for a redress of grievances.

Amendment II

A well regulated Militia, being necessary to the security of a free State, the right of the people to keep and bear Arms, shall not be infringed.

Amendment III

No Soldier shall, in time of peace, be quartered in any house, without the consent of the Owner, nor in time of war, but in a manner to be prescribed by law.

Amendment IV

The right of the people to be secure in their persons, houses, papers, and effects, against unreasonable searches and seizures, shall not be violated, and no Warrants shall issue, but upon probable cause, supported by Oath or affirmation, and particularly describing the place to be searched, and the persons or things to be seized.

Amendment V

No person shall be held to answer for a capital, or otherwise infamous crime, unless on a presentment or indictment of a Grand Jury, except in cases arising in the land or naval forces, or in the Militia, when in actual service in time of War or public danger; nor shall any person be subject for the same offence to be twice put in jeopardy of life or limb; nor shall be compelled in any criminal case to be a witness against himself, nor be deprived of life, liberty, or property, without due process of law; nor shall private property be taken for public use, without just compensation.

Amendment VI

In all criminal prosecutions, the accused shall enjoy the right to a speedy and public trial, by an impartial jury of the State and district wherein the crime shall have been committed, which district shall have been previously ascertained by law, and to be informed of the nature and cause of the accusation; to be confronted with the witnesses against him; to have compulsory process for obtaining witnesses in his favor, and to have the Assistance of Counsel for his defence.

Amendment VII

In Suits at common law, where the value in controversy shall exceed twenty dollars, the right of trial by jury shall be preserved, and no fact tried by a jury, shall be otherwise reexamined in any Court of the United States, than according to the rules of the common law.

Amendment VIII

Excessive bail shall not be required, nor excessive fines imposed, nor cruel and unusual punishments inflicted.

Amendment IX

The enumeration in the Constitution, of certain rights, shall not be construed to deny or disparage others retained by the people.

Amendment X

The powers not delegated to the United States by the Constitution, nor prohibited by it to the States, are reserved to the States respectively, or to the people.

Amendment XI
(Adopted Jan. 8, 1798)

The Judicial power of the United States shall not be construed to extend to any suit in law or equity, commenced or prosecuted against one of the United States by Citizens of another State, or by Citizens or Subjects of any Foreign State.

Amendment XII
(Adopted Sept. 25, 1804)

The Electors shall meet in their respective states and vote by ballot for President and Vice-President, one of whom, at least, shall not be an inhabitant of the same state with themselves; they shall name in their ballots the person voted for as President, and in distinct ballots the person voted for as Vice-President, and they shall make distinct lists of all persons voted for as President, and of all persons voted for as Vice-President, and of the number of votes for each, which lists they shall sign and certify, and transmit sealed to the seat of the government of the United States, directed to the President of the Senate;—The President of the Senate shall, in presence of the Senate and House of Representatives, open all the certificates and the votes shall then be counted;—The person having the greatest number of votes for President, shall be the President, if such number be a majority of the whole number of Electors appointed; and if no person have such majority, then from the persons having the highest numbers not exceeding three on the list of those voted for as President, the House of Representatives shall choose immediately, by ballot, the President. But in choosing the President, the votes shall be taken by states, the representation from each state having one vote; a quorum for this purpose shall consist of a member or members from two-thirds of the states, and a majority of all the states shall be necessary to a choice. And if the House of Representatives shall not choose a President whenever the right of choice shall devolve upon them, before the fourth day of March next following, then the Vice-President shall act as President, as in the case of the death or other constitutional disability of the President.—The person having the greatest number of votes as Vice-President, shall be the Vice-President, if such number be a majority of the whole number of Electors appointed, and if no person have a majority, then from the two highest numbers on the list, the Senate shall choose the Vice-President; a quorum for the purpose shall consist of two-thirds of the whole number of Senators, and a majority of the whole number shall be necessary to a choice. But no person constitutionally ineligible to the office of President shall be eligible to that of Vice-President of the United States.

Amendment XIII
(Adopted Dec. 18, 1865)

Section 1. Neither slavery nor involuntary servitude, except as a punishment for crime whereof the party shall have been duly convicted, shall exist within the United States, or any place subject to their jurisdiction.

Section 2. Congress shall have power to enforce this article by appropriate legislation.

Amendment XIV
(Adopted July 28, 1868)

Section 1. All persons born or naturalized in the United States, and subject to the jurisdiction thereof, are citizens of the United States and of the State wherein they reside. No State shall make or enforce any law which shall abridge the privileges or immunities of citizens of the United States; nor shall any State deprive any person of life, liberty, or property, without due process of law; nor deny to any person within its jurisdiction the equal protection of the laws.

Section 2. Representatives shall be apportioned among the several States according to their respective numbers, counting the whole number of persons in each State, excluding Indians not taxed. But when the right to vote at any election for the choice of electors for President and Vice-President of the United States, Representatives in Congress, the Executive and Judicial officers of a State, or the members of the Legislature thereof, is denied to any of the male inhabitants of such State, being twenty-one years of age, and citizens of the United States, or in any way abridged, except for participation in rebellion, or other crime, the basis of representation therein shall be reduced in the proportion which the number of such male citizens shall bear to the whole number of male citizens twenty-one years of age in such State.

Section 3. No person shall be a Senator or Representative in Congress, or elector of President and Vice-President, or hold any office, civil or military, under the United States, or under any State, who, having previously taken an oath, as a member of Congress, or as an officer of the United States, or as a member of any State legislature, or as an executive or judicial officer of any State, to support the Constitution of the United States, shall have engaged in insurrection or rebellion against the same, or given aid or comfort to the enemies thereof. But Congress may by a vote of two-thirds of each House, remove such disability.

Section 4. The validity of the public debt of the United States, authorized by law, including debts incurred for payment of pensions and bounties for services in suppressing insurrection or rebellion, shall not be questioned. But neither the United States nor any State shall assume or pay any debt or obligation incurred in aid of insurrection or rebellion against the United States, or any claim for the loss or emancipation of any slave; but all such debts, obligations and claims shall be held illegal and void.

Section 5. The Congress shall have power to enforce, by appropriate legislation, the provisions of this article.

Amendment XV
(Adopted March 30, 1870)

Section 1. The right of citizens of the United States to vote shall not be denied or abridged by the United States or by any State on account of race, color, or previous condition of servitude.

Section 2. The Congress shall have power to enforce this article by appropriate legislation.

Amendment XVI
(Adopted Feb. 25, 1913)

The Congress shall have power to lay and collect taxes on incomes, from whatever source derived, without apportionment among the several States, and without regard to any census or enumeration.

Amendment XVII
(Adopted May 31, 1913)

The Senate of the United States shall be composed of two Senators from each State, elected by the people thereof, for six years; and each Senator shall have one vote. The electors in each State shall have the qualifications requisite for electors of the most numerous branch of the State legislatures.

When vacancies happen in the representation of any State in the Senate, the executive authority of such State shall issue writs of election to fill such vacancies: *Provided*, That the legislature of any State may empower the executive thereof to make temporary appointments until the people fill the vacancies by election as the legislature may direct.

This amendment shall not be so construed as to affect the election or term of any Senator chosen before it becomes valid as part of the Constitution.

Amendment XVIII
(Adopted Jan. 29, 1919)

Section 1. After one year from the ratification of this article the manufacture, sale, or transportation of intoxicating liquors within, the importation thereof into, or the exportation thereof from the United States and all territory subject to the jurisdiction thereof for beverage purposes is hereby prohibited.

Section 2. The Congress and the several States shall have concurrent power to enforce this article by appropriate legislation.

Section 3. This article shall be inoperative unless it shall have been ratified as an amendment to the Constitution by the legislatures of the several States, as provided in the Constitution, within seven years from the date of the submission hereof to the States by the Congress.

Charles Cotesworth Pinckney

John Rutledge

Roger Sherman

Amendment XIX
(Adopted Aug. 26, 1920)

The right of citizens of the United States to vote shall not be denied or abridged by the United States or by any State on account of sex.

Congress shall have power to enforce this article by appropriate legislation.

Amendment XX
(Adopted Feb. 6, 1933)

SECTION 1. The terms of the President and Vice President shall end at noon on the 20th day of January, and the terms of Senators and Representatives at noon on the 3d day of January, of the years in which such terms would have ended if this article had not been ratified; and the terms of their successors shall then begin.

SECTION 2. The Congress shall assemble at least once in every year, and such meeting shall begin at noon on the 3d day of January, unless they shall by law appoint a different day.

SECTION 3. If, at the time fixed for the beginning of the term of the President, the President elect shall have died, the Vice President elect shall become President. If a President shall not have been chosen before the time fixed for the beginning of his term, or if the President elect shall have failed to qualify, then the Vice President elect shall act as President until a President shall have qualified; and the Congress may by law provide for the case wherein neither a President elect nor a Vice President elect shall have qualified, declaring who shall then act as President, or the manner in which one who is to act shall be selected, and such person shall act accordingly until a President or Vice President shall have qualified.

SECTION 4. The Congress may by law provide for the case of the death of any of the persons from whom the House of Representatives may choose a President whenever the right of choice shall have devolved upon them, and for the case of the death of any of the persons from whom the Senate may choose a Vice President whenever the right of choice shall have devolved upon them.

SECTION 5. Sections 1 and 2 shall take effect on the 15th day of October following the ratification of this article.

SECTION 6. This article shall be inoperative unless it shall have been ratified as an amendment to the Constitution by the legislatures of three-fourths of the several States within seven years from the date of its submission.

Amendment XXI
(Adopted Dec. 5, 1933)

SECTION 1. The eighteenth article of amendment to the Constitution of the United States is hereby repealed.

SECTION 2. The transportation or importation into any State, Territory, or possession of the United States for delivery or use therein of intoxicating liquors, in violation of the laws thereof, is hereby prohibited.

SECTION 3. This article shall be inoperative unless it shall have been ratified as an amendment to the Constitution by conventions in the several States, as provided in the Constitution, within seven years from the date of the submission hereof to the States by the Congress.

Amendment XXII
(Adopted Feb. 27, 1951)

SECTION 1. No person shall be elected to the office of the President more than twice, and no person who has held the office of President, or acted as President, for more than two years of a term to which some other person was elected President shall be elected to the office of the President more than once. But this Article shall not apply to any person holding the office of President when this Article was proposed by the Congress,

and shall not prevent any person who may be holding the office of President, or acting as President, during the term within which this Article becomes operative from holding the office of President or acting as President during the remainder of such term.

SECTION 2. This article shall be inoperative unless it shall have been ratified as an amendment to the Constitution by the legislatures of three-fourths of the several States within seven years from the date of its submission to the States by the Congress.

Amendment XXIII
(Adopted Mar. 29, 1961)

SECTION 1. The District constituting the seat of Government of the United States shall appoint in such manner as the Congress may direct:

A number of electors of President and Vice President equal to the whole number of Senators and Representatives in Congress to which the District would be entitled if it were a State, but in no event more than the least populous State; they shall be in addition to those appointed by the States, but they shall be considered, for the purposes of the election of President and Vice President, to be electors appointed by a State; and they shall meet in the District and perform such duties as provided by the twelfth article of amendment.

SECTION 2. The Congress shall have power to enforce this article by appropriate legislation.

Amendment XXIV
(Adopted Jan. 23, 1964)

SECTION 1. The right of citizens of the United States to vote in any primary or other election for President or Vice President, for electors for President or Vice President, or for Senator or Representative in Congress, shall not be denied or abridged by the United States or any State by reason of failure to pay any poll tax or other tax.

SECTION 2. The Congress shall have power to enforce this article by appropriate legislation.

Amendment XXV
(Adopted Feb. 10, 1967)

SECTION 1. In case of the removal of the President from office or of his death or resignation, the Vice President shall become President.

SECTION 2. Whenever there is a vacancy in the office of the Vice President, the President shall nominate a Vice President who shall take the office upon confirmation by a majority vote of both houses of Congress.

SECTION 3. Whenever the President transmits to the President pro tempore of the Senate and the Speaker of the House of Representatives his written declaration that he is unable to discharge the powers and duties of his office, and until he transmits to them a written declaration to the contrary, such powers and duties shall be discharged by the Vice President as Acting President.

SECTION 4. Whenever the Vice President and a majority of either the principal officers of the executive departments or of such other body as Congress may by law provide, transmit to the President pro tempore of the Senate and the Speaker of the House of Representatives their written declaration that the President is unable to discharge the powers and duties of his office, the Vice President shall immediately assume the powers and duties of the office as Acting President.

Thereafter, when the President transmits to the President pro tempore of the Senate and the Speaker of the House of Representatives his written declaration that no inability exists, he shall resume the powers and duties of his office unless the Vice President and a majority of either the principal officers of the executive departments or of such other body as Congress may by law provide, transmit within four days to the President pro tempore of the Senate and the Speaker of the

House of Representatives their written declaration that the President is unable to discharge the powers and duties of his office. Thereupon Congress shall decide the issue, assembling within 48 hours for that purpose if not in session. If the Congress, within 21 days after receipt of the latter written declaration, or, if Congress is not in session, within 21 days after Congress is required to assemble, determines by two-thirds vote of both houses that the President is unable to discharge the powers and duties of his office, the Vice President shall continue to discharge the same as Acting President; otherwise, the President shall resume the powers and duties of his office.

Amendment XXVI
(Adopted June 30, 1971)

SECTION 1. The right of citizens of the United States, who are eighteen years of age or older, to vote shall not be denied or abridged by the United States or any state on account of age.

SECTION 2. The Congress shall have the power to enforce this article by appropriate legislation.

Constructivism, abstract movement in sculpture dating from 1913 when Vladimir Taitlin created the first free geometric constructions in space. Antoine Pevsner and Naum Gabo issued the manifesto of the style in 1920, when they published the *Realist Manifesto,* explaining their aesthetic interest in movement in space using materials of the machine age. The constructivist aesthetic influenced modern architecture and sculpture.

Consubstantiation, Christian doctrine stating that after the words of consecration in Communion the substances of bread and wine remain along with the body and blood of Christ. The doctrine is opposed to that of transubstantiation. *See also* Transubstantiation.

Consular Service, corps of government agents stationed abroad concerned with commercial activities and with providing certain essential services for their own nationals living in foreign countries. Consular officials are not diplomatic representatives; their role is established by bilateral treaty and not by international law as is the case for the diplomatic service.

Consulate (1799–1804), name given to the French Republic's government while under Napoleon Bonaparte's control. It consisted of a three-house legislature and a three-consul executive branch, but was actually dominated completely by Bonaparte.

Consuls, two chief magistrates of ancient Rome. Said to have been established in 510 BC, the traditional date for the expulsion of the king, the consuls were elected annually by the Comitia Centuriata to administer civil and military matters. After 367 BC, one consul was a patrician, the other a plebeian. Each had veto power over the other. Under the empire the title was merely honorary.

Consumer Determinism, in economics, the concept that the consumer in a market economy has the ability to control or determine his economic life. The consumer is able to purchase the goods and services available at existing market prices according to his income.

Consumer Equilibrium, in economics, satisfaction level or position from which the consumer would tend not to move. The consumer may be in equilibrium when the combination of goods and services he purchases provides the highest possible utility level.

Consumption Function, foundation of macroeconomic theory, indicates the relationship between consumption and changes in the level of income. When consumers' incomes rise, they will spend a proportion of this new income on consumption goods. In addition, consumption will depend upon such things as interest rates and accumulated wealth.

Contact Dermatitis, acute or chronic inflammation of the skin produced by contact with a certain natural or synthetic substance—for example, wool, poison ivy, detergent—usually appearing as skin redness, swelling, sometimes oozing vesicle formation, accompanied by itching. Treatment consists of removal of the offending agent and application of symptomatically bland compresses and of corticosteroids if necessary. *See also* Allergy.

Contarini, noble Venetian family, dating from at least 7th century, that gave Venice eight doges and many important statesmen and scholars. Domenico was the first Contarini doge (1043–71), and Andrea (r. 1367–82) patriotically donated his wealth to the state. Gasparo (1483–1542) was a humanist scholar, diplomat, theologian, and cardinal. Other Contarini notables were Ambrogio (d. 1499), a great traveler; Giovanni (d. 1603), a painter; and Marco (d. 1689), a patron of music.

Conti Family, younger branch of French royal family in the Bourbon House of Condé. The family began its continuous line with **Armand de Bourbon, Prince de Conti** (1629–66); he took the name from the town of Conti, located near Amiens. The line ended with **Louis François Joseph de Bourbon** (1734–1814), who was exiled after the French Revolution.

Continent, land mass, measured in millions of square miles, that rises to some considerable height above sea level. The continents, which float on plates that make up the earth's crust, do not end at the water line but extend to the limits of the continental shelves. These extensions of the land masses are submerged, continous territories and many offshore islands are highlands whose valleys are under water.

Continental Congress, First (1774), meeting of delegates from all the American colonies except Georgia. It created a unified resistance to the Coercive Acts and the Quebec Act. The Congress issued a Declaration of Rights and Grievances, adopted the Suffolk Resolves, and agreed on economic sanctions against Britain. An association was formed to oversee the commercial boycott of Britain. The delegates agreed to meet again in 1775 if the grievances were not redressed. *See also* Quebec Act.

Continental Congress, Second (1775), convention of colonial delegates principally to plan defense against Britain. It opened on May 10 in Independence Hall in Philadelphia shortly after the battles of Lexington and Concord. The Congress appointed George Washington commander of the Continental Army, tabled a reconciliation plan proposed by Lord North, opened ports in defiance of the Navigation Acts, and sent a diplomatic representative to France. Finally, on July 4, 1776, Congress adopted the Declaration of Independence, severing the colonies from Britain. The Congress continued to meet in different cities as the federal legislature until 1789.

Continental Divide, a line of separation running the length of a continent; determines to which side of the continent waters flow; in United States and Canada it determines whether they drain into the Pacific or Atlantic oceans; the line generally follows the crestline of the Rocky Mts: In South America, it follows the W portion of the Andes Mts.

Continental Drift, a theory which proposes that at one time all present-day land masses were joined in one supercontinent, Pangaea, but that about 200,000,000 years ago it broke up and the resulting land masses, roughly the continents of today, began to move over the earth's surface. The idea was first suggested in 1912 by a German meteorologist Alfred Wegener but the theory lay dormant until 1960 when H.H. Hess, using new evidences—radioactive dating, seafloor spreading, and magnetic field reversal—revived it. The theory explains the existence of similar mountain chains and strata and similar animal orders and plant genera found on different continents, as well as other zoological and geological anomalies. *See also* Plate Tectonics.

Continental Rise, the part of the continental margin that lies between the continental slope and the abyssal plain. It is a gentle incline and consists of sedimentary debris that slumps down from the shelf and slope above.

Continental Shelf, the nearly flat part of the continental margin between the shoreline and the continental slope. The shelves lie at a depth of 200m (656ft) and have an average width of 60km (37mi). Economically important, they produce about 90% of the world's marine food resources, a fifth of the total world production of petroleum and natural gas, and $200,000,000 of sand and gravel.

Continental Slope, the relatively steep slope of the continental margin that lies between the continental shelf and the continental rise and that leads down into deep water. The slope marks the outward edge of the continental crust where it meets the oceanic crust.

Contour Farming, practice of tilling moderately sloping land along lines of equal elevation, to prevent excessive runoff and reduce loss from surface erosion. It also aids in conserving water in the furrows.

Contrabassoon, or double bassoon, woodwind musical instrument pitched one octave below the bassoon. Used in symphony orchestras, it is the largest member of the oboe family. Its tube is 16ft (4.9m) long, doubled on itself four times, with the bell directed downward.

Contraceptives. *See* Birth Control.

Contract, agreement between parties that can be legally enforced. The contract creates rights and obligations, and if the obligations are not satisfied, they can be enforced by a court order. Before an agreement can be a contract, five elements must be present. It must be between competent parties; they must have reached mutual assent; the bargain must be legal; consideration must be involved; and the agreement must be in the proper form.

Contralto, the lowest of the three types of female or boys' voices. The other types are mezzosoprano and soprano. A man singing in this range is called a countertenor.

Control Rocket, small rocket engine used to make fine adjustments to the craft's attitude or orbit. *Attitude control jets* use compressed gas to alter the craft's orientation. *Vernier engines* make adjustments to the craft's speed to change its orbit.

Control Systems, means by which a process is made to conform to prescribed instructions, either by maintaining the values of certain parameters at a constant level or by making them change according to a predetermined plan. Control systems may be mechanical, electromechanical, electronic, fluidic (operated by liquid or gas pressure), or a combination of any of these means. All systems depend on either feed forward (such as a cutting tool that follows the shape of a model) or on feedback (a governor that reduces the input of fuel to an engine when the power exceeds a certain level). Many of the more complex systems used in industry are computer controlled. *See also* Electronic Control Systems.

Convection, transfer of heat by fluid currents, as in the warming of a room by air currents past the radiators. *See also* Heat Transfer.

Convection Cell, an organized circular flow of fluid, such as air or water, based on thermal changes in density and gravitational attraction, with updrafts away from the heat source and subsidence in the cooler outer regions, involved in the formation of clouds in the atmosphere.

Convergence, in mathematics, property of an infinite series (or sequence) of having a finite limiting value. Thus, for the series $1 + \frac{1}{2} + \frac{1}{2^2} + \frac{1}{2^3} \ldots$ the sum of the first two terms is 1.5, the first three 1.75, the first four 1.875, and as more and more terms are taken it approaches the limit 2. Such a series is said to converge. *See also* Divergence.

Convergence Theory, in social science, the theory that capitalist and socialist industrialized societies are tending to become more alike. The theory holds, for example, that technology is the greatest influence on social structure; that many decisions are made by managers, who have similar outlooks whether they work for capitalist or socialist employers; and that features of capitalism such as class distinctions are breaking down.

Convergent Evolution, the tendency of several different species to resemble each other, and to evolve and develop similar characteristics in the effort to adapt to a limited environment.

Convertible Currency, currency that can be exchanged for other currencies for any purpose and without penalty. In order for a currency to be convertible, it must be defined in terms of an accepted standard of value, eg gold, under a pure gold standard. *See also* Exchange Rates.

Convulsion, a bodily malfunction in which violent, involuntary spasms of the voluntary muscles occur, sometimes accompanied by loss of consciousness. May be symptomatic of several diseases.

Cook, James (1728–79), English naval officer and explorer. In 1768–71, Cook led a scientific voyage to Tahiti to observe the transit of Venus. He next surveyed the coast of New Zealand, taking formal possession of parts. He then charted the eastern coast of Australia, naming it New South Wales and claiming it for England. On a second expedition to the South Pacific (1772–75), Cook mapped much of the Southern Hemisphere and sailed farther south than anyone before him. On his last voyage (1776) he discovered the Sandwich (Hawaiian) Islands.

Cook, Thomas (1808–92), English founder of worldwide tourist agency, Thomas Cook & Son. At first a missionary and temperance meeting organizer, he began to arrange group tours for temperance organizations (1841–44). He opened his own firm in 1845, providing his customers with railroad discounts and travel guides. He first offered foreign tours in 1850, the grand tour of Europe in 1856, and the first around-the-world tour in 1872.

Cook, Mount, New Zealand's highest peak, in Southern Alps in Tasman National Park, W central South Island. Height: 12,349ft (3,766m).

Cook Islands, island group in S Pacific Ocean, SE of Samoa; comprised of two major groups, the Northern Cook Islands (Manihiki Islands), and the Lower or Southern Cook Islands; self-governing, with foreign relations conducted through New Zealand. Industries: farming, fishing. Discovered 1773 by Capt. James Cook. Area: 90sq mi (233sq km). Pop. 21,317.

Cooley's Anemia. *See* Thalassemia.

Coolidge, (John) Calvin (1872–1933), 30th President of the United States, b. Plymouth, Vt.; graduate, Amherst College, 1895. In 1905 he married Grace Goodhue; they had two sons. A lawyer who practiced in Northampton, Mass., he became active in Republican politics and was elected to numerous local and state offices. In 1916, he was elected lieutenant governor of Massachusetts; two years later he was elected governor. He gained national attention in 1919 by his strong action against striking policemen in Boston. In 1920 he became the Republican vice-presidential candidate, running with Warren G. Harding. The Harding-Coolidge ticket won an overwhelming victory. Harding died suddenly on Aug. 2, 1923, and Coolidge succeeded him. His first task was cleaning up the scandals of the Harding administration. He fashioned a conservative, business-oriented administration. The country was prosperous, and he was easily elected to a full term in 1924. In foreign affairs, his administration was marked by adroit diplomacy. A laconic man, known as "Silent Cal," he never explained his reasons for not choosing to run for reelection in 1928.

Career: Massachusetts Lieutenant Governor, 1916–19; Massachusetts Governor, 1919–21; Vice President, 1921–23; President, 1923–29.

Coolidge, William David (1873–1975), US physicist, b. Hudson, Mass. He developed a method for drawing tungsten into filaments for light bulbs and radio tubes. He built a tube (Coolidge tube) capable of producing accurate radiation amounts. He also devised portable X-ray units and worked on construction techniques for industrial quality control. He devised the first successful submarine-detection system with Irving Langmuir, and he also did work on the atomic bomb project.

Coon Rapids, city in E Minnesota, on the Mississippi River; suburb of Minneapolis-St Paul; site of Anoka-Ramsey State Junior College (1965). Industries: plastics, metallurgy, aerospace research. Inc. 1952. Pop. (1980) 35,826.

Cooper, James Fenimore (1789–1851), US author, b. Burlington, N.J. Raised in northern New York State, he drew on his background to produce a series of novels about the New York frontier. After a brief stint in the navy, he settled down as a gentleman farmer. In 1820 his first book, *Precaution,* a rather conventional novel of manners, appeared. With the publication of *The Spy* (1821), a novel of the American Revolution, he gained attention. His most successful works were the romantic novels of frontier life known as the Leather-Stocking Tales. *The Pioneers,* the first of these, appeared in 1823. The others were *The Last of the Mohicans* (1826), *The Prairie* (1827), *The Pathfinder* (1840), and *The Deerslayer* (1841). In addition to this series, other novels include *The Pilot* (1823), a story of the

Cook Islands

Calvin Coolidge

James Fenimore Cooper

sea, *The Red Rover* (1828), and the Littlepage trilogy —*Satanstoe* (1845), *The Chainbearer* (1845), and *The Redskins* (1846). A political conservative, Cooper's social criticism included *The American Democrat* (1838). He also wrote *A History of the Navy of the United States* (1839). From 1833 he lived at his home in Cooperstown in upstate New York. *See also* Leather-Stocking Tales, The.

Cooperative Farming, organizing of farmers for improved marketing, purchasing, and credit benefits. Three-quarters of the farmers in the United States belong to cooperatives.

Cooperative Societies, nonprofit, voluntary business groups owned and operated by their membership. Consumers' cooperatives distribute goods directly from producer to consumer. Elimination of the middleman plus large-quantity group purchases reduce costs substantially. Producers' cooperatives serve the marketing needs of farmers and growers.

Cooper's Hawk, North American hawk. It is gray above with a rusty barred chest and tail. The female is much larger than the male. Length: 20in (51cm). Species *Accipiter cooperi. See also* Hawk.

Cooperstown, village in E New York, 59mi (95km) W of Albany; seat of Otsego co. Located at the S end of Lake Otsego, it is the setting for James Fenimore Cooper's "Leather-Stocking Tales"; he refers to the lake as "Glimmerglass." National Baseball Museum and Hall of Fame are here; New York State Historical Association has its headquarters at Fenimore house; also here is Farmers' Museum. A resort community, it was founded by William Cooper (1785), father of James Fenimore Cooper. Inc. 1807. Pop. (1980) 2,342.

Coordinate Geometry. *See* Analytic Geometry.

Coordinate System, reference system used to locate a point in space. A point can be defined by numbers representing distances or angles measured from lines or points of reference. Thus, in a Cartesian coordinate system, a point is defined by distances from intersecting axes. In a polar coordinate system, distance from a fixed point is used together with angular distance from a reference line. In general, two numbers are required to define a position in a plane; three numbers are required in three-dimensional space. In a coordinate system, curves or surfaces can be represented by algebraic functions, thus allowing geometric properties to be studied by algebraic methods. *See also* Cartesian Coordinate System.

Coordination Complex, type of compound in which one or more groups or molecules form coordinate bonds to a central metal atom, usually a transition metal. The complex may involve formation of a complex ion, or may be a neutral molecule as in nickel tetracarbonyl, $Ni(CO)_4$. The coordinating species are known as ligands. Inorganic chemistry is mainly concerned with the study of such compounds; some, such as heme and chlorophyll, have biochemical importance. *See also* Ion, Complex.

Coot, aquatic bird of freshwater marshes. Sluggish, but a strong swimmer and diver, it feeds in or near water and lays buff-colored, brown-spotted eggs (8–12) on floating reed nests. The American coot, or mudhen, is slate gray with white bill and green legs and feet. Length: 13–16in (33–41cm). Species *Fulica.*

Copenhagen (København), capital of Denmark, on E Sjaelland and N Amager islands in the Øresund; a trading and fishing center by early 11th century, a university was founded in 1479; became the capital in 1443; occupied by Germans in WWII; site of Amalienborg Square, enclosed by four 18th-century palaces, which has been royal residence since 1794, 17th-century stock exchange building, Cathedral of Our Lady built *c.* 1209 and rebuilt early 19th century, Tivoli Gardens (1843). Industries: furniture, Copenhagenware, iron foundries, shipyards. Pop. 802,391.

Copernicus, Nicolaus (Mikotaj Kopernik) (1473–1543), Polish cleric and astronomer. His treatise *De Revolutionibus Orbium Caelestium* (1543) expounded the Copernican system and laid the foundations of modern astronomy. By assuming the earth's diurnal rotation and postulating a Sun-centered universe, he challenged both ancient science and religious dogma.

Copland, Aaron (1900–), US composer, b. Brooklyn, N.Y. He is especially known for his works combining American folk elements and melodies with 20th-century symphonic techniques. His popular ballets include *Billy the Kid* (1938), *Rodeo* (1942), and *Appalachian Spring* (1944, Pulitzer Prize, 1945). Less well known has been Copland's experimentation with serial techniques (eg, *Piano Fantasy*, 1957). He also wrote *A Lincoln Portrait* (1942) and *Canticle of Freedom* (1955) and film music.

Copley, John Singleton (1738–1815), US painter of portraits and historical scenes, b. Boston. The finest portrait painter of the colonial period, Copley had little academic training and was a working artist at 15. His extraordinary abilities as a draftsman and colorist made him successful in his 20s. Copley's portraits are marked by realistic detail, such as the use of objects from the sitter's life. Settling in England about 1775, he continued to do portraits and began producing large historical paintings of contemporary events in modern dress. Although these won both critical and popular esteem, Copley's reputation is based on the early American portraits, which are unique in their vigor and immediacy. Many of the finest *(Paul Revere, John Hancock)* are in the Museum of Fine Arts, Boston.

Copper, metallic element (symbol Cu) of the first transition series, known from earliest times. It occurs native and in several ores including cuprite (an oxide), malachite, and chalcopyrite (a sulfide). The metal is extracted by smelting and purified by electrolysis. It is a good thermal and electrical conductor, second only to silver, and is extensively used in boilers, pipes, and electrical equipment. It is also used in alloys such as bronze and brass. The sulfate is an important agricultural poison. Chemically it tarnishes in air, oxidizes at high temperatures, and is attacked only by oxidizing acids. Properties: at. no. 29; at. wt. 63.546; sp gr 8.96; melt. pt. 1981°F (1083°C); boil. pt. 4703°F (2595°C); most common isotope Cu^{63} (69.09%). *See also* Transition Elements.

Copper Age, or chalcolithic age, period in which man discovered how to extract copper by heating its ore with charcoal. This art was known in the Middle East before 3500 BC. A subsequent important development was the alloying of copper with tin to produce bronze. *See also* Bronze Age.

Copperhead, poisonous pit viper, closely related to the water moccasin found in E and Central United States. It likes rocky, wooded areas in the north and swamps in the south. It has a coppery head and chestnut bands on a brown body. It is unaggressive. Length: to 36in (91cm). Family Viperidae; species *Agkistrodon contortrix. See also* Pit-viper.

Coptic Church, the Christian church in Egypt and Ethiopia, claiming St. Mark the Evangelist as its founder. After the Council of Chalcedon in 451, it officially became Monophysite. In the 19th century, it was entitled Coptic Orthodox, to distinguish it from Eastern and Roman rites. Arabic is now used in its services. The church is democratically organized with approximately 22 million members.

Copyright, exclusive right to the publication, sale, or production of a work granted by the government to its creator for a specified time period. Copyrights protect written works, art works, plays, motion pictures, etc., from unauthorized use. Most western nations subscribe to the Universal Copyright Convention, which affords a reciprocal protective arrangement.

Coquina Clam, wedge-shaped clam found in warm seas. Also called butterfly or pompano shell, it varies in color. Length: 0.75in (19.1mm). Class Pelecypoda; family Donacidae; species include *Donax variabilis.*

Coral, colonial coelenterate found in cold to tropical marine waters. Characterized by limestone skeletons secreted by each animal polyp. Reef building corals are found only in waters above 70°F (21.1°C). Soft corals secrete a fleshy material; horny corals (sea fans) secrete fan shaped supports; and stony corals secrete limestone cups. Reef length: 0.25in (6.4mm) to hundreds of miles. Class Anthozoa.

Coral Fish, or reef fish, brilliantly colored, bony tropical fish found among coral reefs and formations. They are usually flat-bodied and round, with a large tail and short fins. Many have poison spines. They can swim in any position. Included are butterfly, angel, cardinal, damsel, and parrot fish.

Coral Gables, residential city in SE Florida, on Biscayne Bay, 5mi (8km) SW of Miami. Superb example of a planned city; site of University of Miami (1925). Inc. 1925. Pop. (1980) 43,241.

Coral Reef, biogenic or organic mass of rock consisting of corals and other calcium carbonate secreting animals. Such reefs grow in warm, shallow marine areas. The growth of reefs is strongly influenced by the prevailing currents and temperatures of the surrounding seawater. The main types of reefs are fringing and barrier. The former is attached to a landmass, which eventually sinks leaving the barrier reef as the only visible land.

Coral Sea, arm of the SW Pacific Ocean, between E coast of Australia, Melanesia (NW), and New Zealand (SW); N part becomes Solomon Sea, S part becomes Tasman Sea; scene of US victory over Japanese 1942.

Coral Snake, American and SE Asian colorfully banded poisonous snake. They have short fangs and potent venom. New World species, gaudily ringed in red, yellow, and black, range from S United States to Argentina and include the eastern coral snake (*Micrurus fulvius*). It is secretive and feeds on snakes, lizards, and frogs. There are numerous snakes that mimic coral snakes. Length: to 24in (61cm). Family Elapidae. *See also* Snake.

Cor Anglais. *See* English Horn.

Corday, Charlotte (1768–93) French patriot. A noblewoman with the full name Marie Anne Charlotte Corday d'Armont, she stabbed the Jacobin Jean Paul Marat to death in his bath on July 13, 1793, and was guillotined on July 17. Influenced by the ideas of "antique heroism" (Plutarch), Voltaire, and the Abbé Ray-

Cordillera Blanca

nal, she supported the principles of the French Revolution but not the Reign of Terror. When Marat decided there should be 200,000 more victims, she decided to kill him rather than Maximilien Robespierre.

Cordillera Blanca, lofty arm of the Andes Mts, in N central Peru. Mostly in Ancash dept., range extends NNW to SSE between the Cordillera Central (E) and the Cordillera Negra (W). Length: approx. 200mi (322km). Highest peak is Nevado Huascarán, 22,205ft (6,772m).

Córdoba, city in central Argentina, 387mi (623km) NW of Buenos Aires; capital of Córdoba district; site of National University of Córdoba (1613). Industries: cement, leather, glass, textiles. Founded by Jerónimo Luis de Cabrera 1573. Pop. 791,000.

Córdoba, city in E Mexico, 55mi (89km) WSW of Veracruz; contains excellent preservations of colonial buildings; scene of Treaty of Córdoba (1821) establishing Mexican independence; important agricultural center. Industries: coffee, tobacco, sugar cane, textiles, tanning, lumber, tobacco. Founded 1618. Pop. 78,495.

Córdoba, city in S Spain, on the Guadalquivir River; capital of Córdoba prov.; ruled by Iberians, Romans, Visigoths, and Moors; flourished under the rule of Caliph Abd er-Rahman III. In 1236 Ferdinand III of Castile captured Córdoba and imposed a new language and Christian culture on the city; site of 8th-century mosque, Roman bridge, and fine art museum. Industries: bronze, copper, chemicals, electrical fittings, fruit. Area: (prov.) 5,297sq mi (13,719sq km). Pop. (city) 235,632; (prov.) 724,116.

Córdoba Caliphate, Muslim monarchy established in Córdoba, Spain, in the 10th century. When the Umayyad caliphate was deposed in Damascus in 750, one member of the family, Abd er-Rahman I, fled to Spain, where he became emir of Córdoba. Abd er-Rahman III assumed the title of caliph. The Umayyads ruled until 1031 as caliphs. *See also* Caliph; Umayyads.

Core (Drilling), a cylindrical rock sample that has been gathered by some sort of drilling device; on land usually by a rotary drill, from the sea often by a metal cylinder with a cutter on the bottom that is driven in by force. The core is used to identify the various layers in the rock or sediment.

Core, Earth, the interior of Earth under the Mohorovicic discontinuity. Information concerning the composition of the core is obtained from seismic measurements. The core may be a plasma, compressed material, in which the electrons have been pushed toward the nuclei of the atoms of the material. Layers exist in the core. The outer one is relatively liquid, the inner is incompressible and probably solid iron with admixture of nickel and some other lighter element still unidentified. *See also* Mantle; Moho.

Coreopsis, a large genus of annual and perennial plants cultivated for their daisylike flower heads. A popular annual is the tall golden coreopsis (*C. grandiflora*), with yellow rays and a reddish-brown center. Height: to 3ft (91cm). Family Compositae.

Corfu (Kérkira), island in NW Greece; 2nd-largest of the Ionian group; with Paxos Island forms a department of Greece; Corfu is the capital; scene of first recorded naval battle 665 BC, with Corinth for possession of Epidamnus; allied with Athens 433 BC against Corinth; held by Romans 229 BC–AD 336, when it fell to the Byzantines; occupied by Venetians 1386–1797; under British protection 1815–64, when it passed to Greece; site of "Pact of Corfu" (1917), uniting Serbia, Croatia, and Slovenia; occupied by Germany during WWII. Industries: olives, olive oil, fruit, livestock, wine, tourism, fishing. Area: 229sq mi (593sq km). Pop. 89,664.

Coriander, a single species, *Coriandrum sativum,* of annual herb native to Europe and Asia Minor and widely cultivated for its aromatic seeds used for food flavoring. It has a hollow stem, divided leaves, and pink or white flowers. Height: to 3ft (91cm). Family Umbelliferae.

Corinth (Korinthos), city in NE Peloponnesus, Greece, at the SW end of the Isthmus of Corinth; 3mi (5km) NE of site of the ancient city of Corinth, destroyed by earthquake (1858); capital of Corinthia dept. Inhabited since Neolithic period (5,500 BC); it was ruled by Bacchiad kings 8th-7th centuries BC; Syracuse and Corcyra 700 BC; prospered as major trade and commercial state 620–500 BC; fought with Sparta during the Peloponnesian War (431–404 BC) and with Athens, Thebes, and Argos against Sparta during Corinthian War (395–387 BC); joined Achaean League 243 BC to fight against Romans, who destroyed city 146 BC. Rebuilt 44 BC by Caesar, Corinth became capital of Achaea; passed from Venetian rule AD 1682–1715 to Turks 1715–1822, and then became part of Greece. Ruins of old Corinth include temple of Apollo, marketplace, amphitheater. Present city is a transportation center. Trading of olives, raisins, wine are important industries. Pop. 15,892.

Corinth, Isthmus of, isthmus in Greece, between the Gulf of Corinth and Saronic Gulf; connects central Greece with the Peloponnesus; crossed by 17th-century Corinth canal; connects the Adriatic and Ionian seas; site of remnants of ancient Isthmian Wall (restored 3rd-6th centuries AD), for the defense of Peloponnesus; sanctuary of Poseidon. Width: approx. 7mi (11km). Length: approx. 20mi (32km).

Corinthian Order, latest and most ornate of the classical orders of architecture, developed by the Greeks in the 4th century BC, but used more extensively in Roman architecture. The shaft is slender, and the capital is elaborately carved. *See also* Orders of Architecture.

Corinthians, two New Testament epistles of St. Paul written to the Christian church in Corinth, a wealthy, vice-ridden city. He discusses the problems of false apostles and immorality. The first letter was written when he was leaving Ephesus, the second from Macedonia.

Corinthian War (395–87 BC), war between Corinth and Sparta. The Corinthian democrats became angry because Sparta, an ally in the Peloponnesian War, refused to destroy the defeated Athens. Corinth then allied with Athens, Argos, and Thebes and declared war on Sparta in midsummer of 395. The indecisive Battle of the Stockade (393) was fought at the Corinthian city walls with dissenting Corinthian aristocrats fighting along with the Spartans. Fighting ended with the Peace of 387, the aristocrats returned to Corinth, and Corinth rejoined the Spartan League.

Coriolanus (1607), 5-act tragedy by William Shakespeare, after Plutarch's *Life of Coriolanus.* Roman hero Coriolanus, a candidate for consulship, is banished by a mob raised by jealous tribunes. He turns for aid to Aufidius, Rome's enemy and his own personal foe, and they march against Rome. The pleas of his mother, Volumnia, dissuade him from his purpose. Rome is saved but Coriolanus is killed by Aufidius.

Coriolis, Gaspard Gustave de (1792–1843), French theoretical physicist who explained the effect of the earth's rotation on objects moving above its surface in terms of the force or effect bearing his name. *See also* Coriolis Force.

Coriolis Force or **Effect,** an apparent force on particles or objects like winds, clouds, or aircraft moving in the atmosphere, due to the rotation of the earth under them, such that the particle's motion is deflected toward the right in the Northern Hemisphere and toward the left in the Southern, but the particle's speed is unaffected. The direction of water whirling around a drain demonstrates this force.

Cork (Corcaigh), seaport in SE Republic of Ireland, at mouth of Lee River; seat of County Cork. Settlement developed around a monastery founded by St Finbar in 7th century. In 9th century Danes occupied city and walled it. Danes were driven out 1172. Oliver Cromwell occupied Cork in 1649 and Duke of Marlborough in 1690. Many public buildings were destroyed in nationalist uprisings in 1920; site of 18th-century St Anne's Church, 19th-century St Patrick's Church, and University College of Cork (1845). Industries: brewing, distilling, tires, fertilizers, woolen goods, motor vehicle assembly, bacon curing. Pop. 128,645.

Cork, protective outer layer of bark on woody plant stems. Cork insulates against severe temperature changes and retards water loss. Commercial cork is obtained from the cork oak (*Quercus suber*), an evergreen native to the Mediterranean area. Grown commercially in Spain, Algeria, and Portugal, the trees are stripped of their corky, thick outer bark every 8–10 years. Height: 60ft (18.3m).

Corm, fleshy, underground stem that produces a plant. Corms have more stem tissue and fewer leaf scales than bulbs. New corms are produced on top of old corms that last one growing season. Examples are gladiolus, tuberous begonia, and crocus.

Cormorant, aquatic, ducklike bird found in coastal and inland waters throughout the world. It has a hooked bill; blackish metallic plumage; long, stiff tail, and webbed feet. Pale blue or green chalky eggs (2–4) are laid in stick-and-seaweed nests on the ground or in trees. Cormorants are used to catch fish in the Orient. Their excrement is the fertilizer guano. Length: 20–40in (51–101cm). Species *Phalacrocoracidae.*

Corn, a single species (*Zea mays*) of tall, annual cereal grass native to the New World and introduced worldwide. It has stout, erect, solid stems with narrow leaves. Male flowers are born in a tassel; pollen from the tassel falls onto elongated silks at ends of ears and germinates. The mature ear bears 1000 seeds on a hard cob. Each ear is enclosed in leaves called husks. Commercial classifications are dent, flint, flour, sweet, and popcorn. Hybridizing has resulted in superior strains. It is used as food for humans and livestock. Manufactured products derived from it are numerous. It is also called maize and Indian corn. Family Gramineae.

Corn, in medicine, an elevated painful thickening of the skin at a point of sustained pressure or pinching, most often occurring on a toe as the result of improperly fitting shoes.

Cornea, part of the sclera, or outer layer of the eye, that forms a transparent protective bulge over the iris.

Corn Earworm, or cotton bollworm, noctuid moth caterpillar that is a serious crop pest in North and South America. It attacks many plants, and is a major pest of cotton and corn. Species *Heliothis zea.*

Corneille, Pierre (1606–84), major French classical dramatist. His plays include the tragedy *Médée* (1635), the epic *Le Cid* (1637), and a comedy *Le Menteur* (1643). He was elected to the French Academy (1647).

Cornet, musical instrument similar to a shortened trumpet. It was used by 19th-century French and Italian composers, by Stravinsky in *Petrouchka* (1911), and in early jazz by King Oliver (*c.*1909). Its tone is more subdued than the trumpet's. *See also* Trumpet.

Cornflower. See Bachelor's Button.

Corn Laws, British laws regulating grain trade in farmers' interests, especially in 18th-19th centuries. The Napoleonic Wars increased grain prices and caused food riots. The Anti-Corn Law League was formed (1838) to promote free trade and cheap food. After the Irish famine, parliament repealed the Corn Laws (1846).

Corn Plant. See Dracaena.

Cornwall, county in SW England, forming a peninsula bounded by Atlantic Ocean, English Channel, and Devonshire, and terminating in Lands End. Terrain consists of rocky indented coast with hills and moors inland; drained by Camel, Fowey, Tamar, and Fal rivers; tourist center with mild climate. Chief towns are Bodmin, Truro, St Austell, Camborne-Redruth. Area: (including Scilly Isles) 1,356sq mi (3,512sq km). Pop. (including Scilly Isles) 397,200.

Cornwallis, Charles Cornwallis, 1st Marquis (1738–1805), English soldier and administrator. At first a successful commander in the American Revolution, he was forced to surrender at Yorktown (1781). As governor-general of India (1786–93, 1805), he reformed the administration, law, and army and suppressed Tipu Sahib's revolt. Cornwallis was viceroy of Ireland (1798–1801), where he defeated the 1798 revolt and French invasion and carried through reforms and parliamentary union with Britain.

Corollary, theorem that follows so obviously from the proof of some other theorem that no, or almost no, proof is necessary. A by-product of another theorem.

Coromandel Coast, rugged coastline of SE India, extending from Point Calimere to Krishna River; the rough seas on coast during monsoon season are a major shipping hazard. Madras, Cuddalore, and Nellore are among the major cities. Length: 450mi (725km).

Corona, city in S California, 12mi (19km) SW of San Bernardino; E of Cleveland National Forest. Industries: processing citrus fruits, plywood, mobile homes. Settled 1898; inc. 1906. Pop. (1980) 37,791.

Corona, outer atmosphere of the sun, visible as a pearly halo during a total eclipse. It extends outward from about 3100m (4991km) above the solar surface (photosphere) and consists chiefly of highly ionized hydrogen, nickel, calcium, and iron atoms at a temperature of 1,000,000°K or more. *See also* Sun.

Corona Borealis, or the Northern Crown, northern constellation situated east of Boötes. It contains several binaries and variables, including the recurrent nova T Coronae Borealis and the irregular variable R Coronae Borealis.

Cordoba, Spain

Cormorant

Cortisone crystals (in polarized light)

Coronado, Francisco Vásquez de (c.1510–54), Spanish explorer. He went to Mexico in 1535, and in 1540 he headed an expedition to locate the seven cities of Cibola, reported to be the repositories of untold wealth. He explored the western coast of Mexico, discovered the Colorado River, the Grand Canyon, followed the route of the Rio Grande eastward, and then headed north through the Texas Panhandle, Oklahoma, and eastern Kansas. His discoveries were impressive, but he found no gold.

Coronal Hole, low-density low-temperature region in the Sun's corona, first observed in 1973, from which X-ray emission is apparently minimal. Such regions appear on X-ray photographs as dark extensive areas, often originating near the Sun's poles. They are associated with disturbances in the solar wind.

Coronary Heart Disease, disease of the coronary blood vessels, particularly the aorta and arteries supplying blood to the heart tissue. The term is also occasionally used to refer to any heart disease.

Coronary Occlusion, blocking of a coronary blood vessel, especially of a coronary artery supplying blood to the heart tissue. The occlusion almost always is caused by a thrombus, or blood clot, in the artery.

Coronary Thrombosis, blood clot in an artery to the heart, preventing blood and with it oxygen and nutrients from reaching that part of the heart supplied by the artery. This phenomenon, known commonly as a "heart attack," may cause injury to the heart tissue or death.

Corot, Jean Baptiste Camille (1796–1875), French painter of landscapes and portraits, one of the most important 19th-century artists. Trained academically, Corot traveled widely, making small oil sketches on the spot and later producing large salon paintings based on them. Critical evaluation of Corot's immense output has varied. His misty landscapes, highly popular in his time, were once considered his best work; later critics prefer the oil sketches and portraits.

Corporate State, concept of government where workers and employers from similar industries are organized into corporations, which, together with other corporations, select representatives who determine national policy. Fascist Italy adopted features of the corporate state, with Benito Mussolini setting himself up as the final arbitrator of differences among the various corporate units.

Corporation, business organization that is legally a separate entity, which gives it limited liability as compared to a proprietorship or partnership. The owners, or stockholders, are not individually responsible for the legal dealings of the corporation, except to the extent of their holdings. The corporation form is most usual in large organizations.

Corpus Christi, port city in S Texas, on Corpus Christi Bay, 200mi (322km) SW of Houston; seat of Nueces co; bay discovered in 16th century by Alonso de Pineda, Spanish explorer, on Corpus Christi Day; more permanent settlement occurred in 1839 when Col. H.L. Kinney est a trading post; population and financial boom came with the discovery of oil in early 20th century. Industries: oil refining, chemicals, fishing, natural gas. Inc. 1852. Pop. (1980) 231,999.

Correggio, real name Antonio Allegri da Correggio (c. 1490–1534), Italian painter born in Correggio. A major Renaissance artist whose works foreshadow the Baroque, Correggio painted mainly in Parma. In frescoes, especially those at the Parma cathedral, he produced brilliant spatial compositions, and daring, though anatomically exact, foreshortening effects. Like the frescoes, his paintings are marked by striking composition and sophisticated play of light and color. Among major works in museums is "Adoration of the Child" in the Uffizi, Florence.

Correggio, town in N central Italy, 8mi (13km) NE of Reggio; former seat of principality of the da Correggio family 12th–17th century; site of 16th-century palace; birthplace of painter Antonio Allegri, called Correggio after the town; agricultural area. Industries: cheese, wine, sausage, pharmaceuticals. Pop. 20,062.

Corregidor, small island at mouth of Manila Bay, Philippines. Known as "the Rock," it was fortified by Spain 18th century; taken by United States in 1898, it became Fort Mills. An Allied stronghold during WWII, it surrendered to Japanese, May 1942; was retaken by US troops February 1945; annexed to Philippines 1947. Area: 2sq mi (5sq km).

Correlation, in geology, relating fossils and structures found in one stratum with those found in an analogous layer in a different locale. *See also* Paleontology.

Correlation, in statistics, a number that summarizes the direction and degree of relationship between two dimensions or variables. Correlations range between 0 (no relationship) and 1.00 (a perfect relationship), and may be positive (as one variable increases, so does the other) or negative (as one variable increases, the other decreases). When two variables are highly correlated, as is IQ with school achievement, one may be used to predict the other. Thus, IQ tests have traditionally been used in American schools to predict likelihood of success in school. *See also* Intelligence Testing; Statistics.

Correspondence, property of two geometric figures in which angles, lines, and points in one bear a similar relationship to angles, lines, and points in another.

Corrigan, Mairead (1944–), Northern Irish peace activist. She received, with Betty Williams, the 1976 Nobel Prize for peace for her attempts to heal religious and national divisions in Northern Ireland. She and Williams, touched by the death of three children in a terrorist incident, organized the Community of Peace People, a peace movement supported by both Protestants and Roman Catholics.

Corrosion, slow gradual chemical attack on the surfaces of solids, especially metals and alloys, by a moist environment. Tarnishing in air is not serious, but electrolytic corrosion underground, where anaerobic bacterial action may occur, and under moist conditions, can produce deep and dangerous structural decay. Materials are protected by plating, painting, or cathodic protection.

Corryvreckan (Corrievreckan), Gulf of, channel off W Scotland, between Jura and Scarba; site of whirlpool around rock that rises to within 15ft (4.5m) of surface.

Corsica (Corse), mountainous island in the Mediterranean Sea, about 105mi (170km) SE of French coast. Until 1768, when France purchased all rights to the island, it was under control of a series of Italian rulers, having been a Roman colony 3rd century BC-AD 5th century; Napoleon was born here 1769. In 1794, Britain took over the island, but Napoleon retrieved it for France; briefly occupied by British (1814 and 1815) and Germans (1942 and 1943). Capital is Ajaccio. Industries: sheep raising, wine and cheese making, tourism. Area: 3,367 square miles (8,721sq km). Pop. 220,000.

Corsini, important Italian family that, from 1244, contributed 56 priors (chief executives) and 8 *gonfalonieri* (supreme magistrates) to the Florentine Republic. Andrea Corsini (1302–73), prior of Florence and bishop of Fiesole, was canonized in 1629. Filippo Corsini (1334–1421) was made count palatinate in 1371 by Emperor Charles IV. Another Corsini, Lorenzo, became Pope Clement XII in 1730, and his nephew Bartolomeo was made prince of Sismano (1731) and a grandee of Spain (1732).

Cortés, Hernando (Hernán Cortez) (1485–1547), central figure in the Spanish conquest and colonization of Mexico, a prominent planter of Cuba who had been in America since 1504. Under the patronage of Diego de Velásquez, Cortés sailed for the mainland with 700 men in 1518. He declared himself independent of Velásquez, gave himself the official standing and legal authority to colonize, and marched inland toward the Aztec capital. Converting many Indians into allies of his cause, Cortés was able to capture Tenochtitlán in 1521. Cortés' personal power, symbolized by his titles and estates, gradually was eroded by the Crown. He died in Spain, but his remains were transferred to Mexico in 1566.

Cortes, the legislature of Spain. Its members are not popularly elected but are named by various agencies of government. The Cortes has little power; it is used chiefly to ratify executive orders. Local cortes (Spanish meaning "courts") were established in Spain in the 12th and 13th centuries as various regions were reconquered from the Moors. Their power waned as the strength of the monarchy grew.

Cortisone, adrenal cortex hormone essential for carbohydrate, protein, and fat metabolism; kidney function; and disease resistance. Synthetic cortisone is used to treat adrenal insufficiency, rheumatoid arthritis, and some other inflammatory diseases. It can cause serious side effects.

Corundum, an oxide mineral, aluminum oxide (Al_2O_3). Found in igneous, pegmatitic, and metamorphic rocks; rhombohedral system pyramidal or prismatic crystals and granular masses. Translucent to transparent in many hues; hardness 9; sp gr 4. Next to diamond, hardest natural substance. Gemstone varieties are sapphire and ruby. Star sapphires reflect light in six-pointed star. Also used in watches and motors.

Corvallis, city in W Oregon on Willamette River, 28mi (45km) SSW of Salem; seat of Benton co; site of forestry research center and headquarters for Siuslaw National Forest; food processing center for fertile agricultural area. Inc. 1857. Pop. 38,502.

Cosecant, ratio of the length of the hypotenuse to the length of the side opposite to an acute angle in a right-angled triangle. The cosecant of angle A is usually abbreviated "cosec A," and is equal to the reciprocal of its sine. *See also* Trigonometric Functions.

Cosenza, city in S Italy; capital of Cosenza prov.; site of many rebellions for Italian independence; town damaged by earthquakes 18th, 19th, 20th centuries; site of restored Romanesque cathedral, Norman castle, and medieval churches. Industries: agriculture, furniture, wool. Pop. 102,475.

Cosgrave, William Thomas (1880–1965), Irish nationalist. He fought in the 1916 rebellion against Britain and helped win independence. Cosgrave was president of the Irish Free State (1922–32) and founded the moderate Fine Gael party.

Cosimo I. *See* Medici, Cosimo I de'.

Cosine, ratio of the length of the side adjacent to an acute angle to the length of the hypotenuse in a right-angled triangle. The cosine of angle A is usually abbreviated "cos A." *See also* Trigonometric Functions.

Cosmic Dust, very fine particles of solid matter in any part of the universe, including meteoric dust and interstellar matter that absorbs starlight and forms nebulae of dark matter in galaxies. Spherical dust particles, about .002in (.05mm) in diameter, found in certain marine sediments, are thought to be the remains of some 5,000 tons of cosmic dust falling on the earth each year.

Cosmic Rays, high-energy particle radiation that consists mainly of protons and also heavier nuclei, neutrinos, and photons and originates in space, possibly from stellar explosions and eruptions. On entering the earth's atmosphere the particles collide and react with oxygen, nitrogen, and other atoms and molecules and large numbers of other elementary particles are produced. These include pions and their decay products (muons, neutrinos, and photons) and also electrons and positrons. These particles can be detected by surface or balloon-borne instruments or by tracks in photographic emulsions.

Cosmology, branch of astronomy concerned with the origin, evolution, and future characteristics of the universe as a whole, its dimensions, structure, and other features. Once considered the province of theology and philosophy, it is now a science based on theoretical physics and mathematics. Experimental data, as in the form of galactic red shifts and the isotropic microwave background radiation, is now available for testing the various cosmological theories including the big-bang theory, with the associated oscillating theory, and the steady-state theory. However, the validity of the laws of physics and the nonvariability of physical constants throughout the unimaginable dimensions and time scale of the universe cannot necessarily be assumed.

Cosmos, a genus of showy late-flowering annual and perennial plants native to tropical America but easily grown in temperate climates. They have fernlike leaves and variously colored ray flowers. The common garden annual *C. bipinnatus,* has single or double flower heads shading from white to red. Height: 4–6ft (1.2–1.8m). Family Compositae.

Cossa, Baldassare (?1370–1419), Antipope John XXIII (1410–15). Elected antipope by the Council of Pisa, he convoked the Council of Constance in 1414 to end the Great Schism. The Council called for his resignation along with the other papal contenders: Gregory XII (Rome) and Benedict XIII (Avignon). He fled the council but was brought back and forced to resign. He was imprisoned until 1418 when he acknowledged Martin V as pope. *See also* Great Schism.

Cossacks, runaway serfs who settled in southern Russia prior to the 16th century. The name is Turkic for "free warriors." The Cossacks held land in common and were governed by village assemblies headed by a hetman, or leader. A militaristic people, they conquered Siberia in the 16th century and took part in the rebellions of Stenka Razin and Pugachev in the 17th and 18th centuries. In the 19th century, their privileges were curtailed by the czar and they were used to suppress revolutions. During the civil war between the Reds and the Whites after the Communist Revolution (1917), they supported the Whites. They strongly resisted collectivization and were suppressed by Stalin.

Costa Brava, coastal strip in NE Spain, near French border, on the Mediterranean; important tourist resort since WWII.

Costa Mesa, city in S California, SSW of Santa Ana; site of Orange Coast College (1947) and Southern California College (1920). Industries: boatbuilding, plastics, electronic equipment. Inc. 1953. Pop. (1980) 82,291.

Costa Rica, nation in S Central America. Second-smallest of the countries between Mexico and South America, it carries influence out of proportion to its size and small population.

Land and Economy. Mountains run the length of the country, with some peaks reaching above 12,000ft (3,660m). They may contain large mineral deposits, but mining is not extensive. Plains exist along the coasts and in the N and NW, the latter region being good for cattle ranches. Farms reach far up mountain slopes, with extensive cultivation of sugar cane, coffee, cocoa, rice, and bananas. Costa Rica is a nation of small landholdings rather than of large estates.

People. Early settlers drove out the Indian peoples and modern Costa Rica, except for blacks in port cities, has a population mainly of Spanish descent. About 90% is literate and 95% belongs to the Roman Catholic church.

Government. A republic, Costa Rica has a president, two vice presidents, and a one-house legislature. All citizens 21 and over have had the vote since 1949. Several political parties exist, but the Communist party has been outlawed.

History. Christopher Columbus reached Costa Rica ("rich coast") in 1502, and during colonial times it was a province of Guatemala. Although it gained independence from Spain in 1821, Costa Rica came under Mexican control for a short period and then belonged to the United Provinces of Central America until that collapsed in 1838. It has generally rejected union with neighboring countries but has participated in supported regional economic cooperation. Costa Rica's government has long been regarded as the most durable democratic system in the region, but during the early 1980s economic difficulties and upheaval in nearby Nicaragua and El Salvador threatened Costa Rica's stability.

PROFILE

Official name: Republic of Costa Rica
Area: 19,650sq mi (50,894sq km)
Population: 2,200,000
Chief cities: San José, the capital; Alajuela
Government: Republic

Cost-Benefit Analysis, in economics, analytical tool used to determine the worthiness of a particular project or to compare various projects. Cost-benefit ratios are computed by first determining the dollar cost of the project and then determining the dollar benefit that will be received by the proposer. If two projects are in competition for the available resources, the one with the lower cost-benefit ratio would be considered more economically feasible.

Costermansville. *See* Bukavu.

Cotangent, ratio of the length of the side adjacent to an acute angle to the length of the side opposite to the angle in a right-angled triangle. The cotangent of angle A is usually abbreviated "cot A," and is equal to the reciprocal of its tangent. *See also* Trigonometric Functions.

Cotinga, mostly brightly colored and bizarrely ornamented tropical birds, such as cock-of-the-rock and umbrella bird. There are some plain and dull-colored species. Family Cotingidae. *See also* Bellbird; Cock-of-the-rock; Umbrella Bird.

Cotonou, city in S Benin (Dahomey), W Africa, approx. 20mi (32km) W of Porto Novo; former capital and largest city in Benin; main port, railroad terminus, shipping center. Pop. 180,000.

Cottian Alps, mountain range N of Maritime Alps, between France and Italy. Highest peak is Mt Viso, 12,602ft (3,844m).

Cotton, perennial and annual shrubby plant native to tropical regions of the world. Although some species can be treelike or ornamental, most cotton is grown for the fibers that develop in the seeds and are made into fabric. The leaves are lobed and flowers are yellow, white, pink, or purple. *Gossypium hirsutum,* or upland cotton, is a tropical American variety grown commercially in the S United States. Cotton needs a long, warm growing season, with ample moisture, except at harvest time. Family Malvaceae.

Cotton Bollworm. *See* Corn Earworm.

Cotton Gin, a machine used for separation of lint from seed. Eli Whitney's invention of 1793, which replaced hand separation, could clean 50lb (22kg) per day and revolutionized the cotton industry.

Cottonmouth. *See* Water Moccasin.

Cottontail, small rabbit with a fluffy white tail. It lives in widely varying habitats from S Canada to Argentina and is brownish with light underparts. Length: 10–17in (25–43cm). Genus Sylvilagus. *See also* Rabbit.

Cottonwood, a tree *Populus deltoides* of the willow family, native to E North America, growing to 90ft (27m). It has heart-shaped quaking leaves. The seeds have a cotton-like coat, from which the name is derived.

Coulomb, Charles Augustin de (1736–1806), French physicist. After serving as a military engineer in the West Indies, he returned to Paris shortly before the Revolution. His invention of the torsion balance led to his experiments in electrostatics and the discovery of the inverse square law that bears his name. The unit of electric charge is named after him. *See also* Coulomb's Law.

Coulomb's Law, the force, F, between two point charges, Q_1 and Q_2, is proportional to the product of the magnitude of the charges and inversely proportional to the square of the distance, d, between them. Usually stated as: $F = Q_1Q_2/4\pi\mathrm{E}d^2$, where E is the absolute permittivity of the intervening space.

Council, Ecumenical, or General Council, formal meeting of Christian bishops and other representatives from throughout the world to define church doctrine and discipline. The last council of all the Christians, before the East-West schism, was in Nicaea (787). Roman Catholic councils must be convened by the pope. Council decrees confirmed by the pope are then considered infallible. There have been 21 Roman Catholic councils, the most recent being Vatican II, convoked in 1962 by John XXIII and concluded by Paul VI.

Council Bluffs, city in SW Iowa, on the bluffs overlooking the Missouri River; site of Union Pacific Railroad E terminus (1863); supply point for California gold rush (1849–50); now a trading center for large agricultural region. Industries: cast iron pipes, grain elevators. Settled by Mormons 1846; inc. 1853. Pop. (1980) 56,449.

Council for Mutual Economic Assistance (COMECON), trade organization formed in 1949 by the USSR and six East European Communist nations in response to the Marshall Plan in Western Europe. Besides the USSR, Bulgaria, Czechoslovakia, Hungary, Poland, Romania, Albania, and E. Germany were the initial members, with Cuba joining in 1972 and Vietnam in 1978. Instead of setting up one large market, the council established a series of bilateral trade agreements but provided for no uniform price system, thus hindering economic development.

Counterpoint, the weaving together of two or more carefully controlled melodic lines. The pitches of the lines must result in harmonic sounds, whether dissonant or consonant, at regular rhythmic points. The melodic lines need not move in the same direction at the same time. There are three main types of counterpoint. The first is the cantus firmus type in which a new melody is added to an already existing tune, as in a descant. The second type is vertible, or double counterpoint, in which two melodies, neither of which is complete in itself, fit together. In this type, the top and bottom melodies may be exchanged. The third type is canon, or imitative counterpoint, in which the same melody is repeated by starting again at various points throughout the work, as in a round.

Counter-Reformation, revival of the spiritual and theological life of the Roman Catholic Church in Europe during the 16th and 17th centuries. It began as a reaction to the Protestant Reformation. Led by humanists, scholasticism was encouraged and a renewed prestige was achieved for the papacy and the church. Bishops' duties were reformed, and new monastic orders appeared, including the Capuchins and Jesuits. Founded by Ignatius Loyola, the Jesuits led the reform movement. Spanish mysticism flourished and encouraged an improved sense of spirituality. The Council of Trent (1545–63) achieved needed reforms in doctrine.

Count of Monte Cristo, The (1844), novel by Alexandre Dumas père. Edmond Dantes, a young sailor, is imprisoned for 14 years in the Château d'If and is befriended by the Abbé Faria who dies leaving Dantes his fortune. Escaping disguised as Faria's corpse, he finds the money and uses it to avenge himself on his enemies.

Couperin, François (1668–1733), French Baroque composer, called "le Grand" to distinguish him from others in his musical family. He composed many pieces for the organ and harpsichord that subsequently influenced J. S. Bach.

Couplet, two consecutive lines of rhyming verse usually the same in length and meter. A closed couplet is one that is complete in logic and grammar. *See also* Heroic Couplet.

Coupling, a mechanical fastening connecting shafts together for power transmission. A flexible coupling is used to compensate for misalignment of shaft axes and mispositioning of shaft centerline; a rigid coupling is used for maximum power transfer with minimum misalignment.

Costa Rica

Gustave Courbet: self-portrait

Bob Cousy

Courbet, Gustave (1819–77), French painter of portraits and landscapes, leader of the 19th-century French school of realists. Largely self-taught by his studies of great works in the Louvre, Courbet rejected traditional theories of subject matter and treatment. A highly-gifted craftsman, he followed his own inclination in art and politics. His monumental treatments of scenes from peasants' lives shocked many but won praise from critics like Baudelaire. His political activity forced him into exile (1873) from France. Major collections of Courbet's work are in the Louvre, Paris, and the Metropolitan, New York.

Court Dances, popular form of social entertainment for the European aristocracy from the Middle Ages through the 19th century. Most of the dances were refined versions of peasant dances. Some of the most frequently performed were the Basse Danse, Gaillard, Gavotte, Gigue, Minuet, and Pavane.

Court Martial, judicial trial proceedings in the US armed forces. In summary courts martial, the court acts as judge, jury, and both trial and defense counsel; in special and general courts martial, juries and counsels are present. Summary courts martial consider minor offenses and sentences are limited to confinement for one month and loss of two-thirds of a month's pay. An accused may object to a summary court martial and request a general or special type. See also Uniform Code of Military Justice.

Courts, tribunals established by governments to decide controversies brought before them in the proper manner and to impose punishment for wrongdoing or to remedy a damage. There are courts at each governmental level, and in the USA all courts are finally subject to the Supreme Court's decisions.

Courtship, period before marriage in which a man woos a woman. In many societies this does not only involve the participants emotionally but includes an exchange of gifts; these are often presented to her parents as well. In many cases where marriage is arranged (as in India) there is no contact between the couple. See also Marriage.

Court Tennis, game, played on an indoor court with four surrounding walls 30 feet (9.1m) high, a ball, and 16-ounce (453-gram) 27-inch (69cm) rackets. The singles court is 78 feet (23.8m) long and 27 feet (8.2m) wide; the doubles court is the same length but 36 feet (11m) wide. A center net is supported by two three-foot (.91m) posts. The object of the game is to place the ball over the net and play the surface of the floor, the walls, and the ceiling in an attempt to put the ball out of the reach of an opponent. The scoring, which is complicated, consists of winning a certain number of sets. Popular with French and English royalty and the forerunner of most modern racket games, court tennis was introduced in the United States in 1876. The most prominent tournament is the World Open.

Cousteau, Jacques Yves (1910–), French oceanographer. Best known as the co-inventor (with Emile Gagnan) of the Aqua-Lung—an independent diving unit permitting divers underwater mobility—he also invented a process of underwater television and conducted a series of undersea living experiments (Conshelf I–III, 1962–65). His famous research ship Calypso made expeditions from 1950, many of which were filmed by Cousteau for television and motion pictures. His books include The Silent World (1953).

Cousy, Robert Joseph "Bob" (1928–), US basketball player, b. New York City. He played for the Boston Celtics (1951–63) and was considered one of the game's finest backcourt men. Elected to the Basketball Hall of Fame in 1970, he was a coach and television commentator after his playing career.

Covalence. See Valence.

Covalent Bond, type of chemical bond in which two atoms share a pair of electrons; both electrons move in the combined field of the two nuclei. Most compounds having covalent bonds have discrete molecules. They tend to be low melting and soluble in nonpolar solvents. See also Chemical Bonds.

Covenanters, 17th-century Scots who entered agreements to defend Presbyterianism. When Charles I attempted to impose Episcopalianism, many Scots subscribed to the National Covenant (1638) and successfully resisted him. By the Solemn League and Covenant (1643) they helped England's parliament against Charles in return for religious concessions. The Covenanters suffered persecution between the Restoration (1660) and the Glorious Revolution (1688).

Covent Garden, leading opera house of England, founded in 1732 in the heart of a produce market in London, located in its present building since 1858. In the late 19th century the opera company achieved world fame as the home of many great singing stars such as Lilli Lehmann, Nellie Melba, and the De-Reszkes. After a decline in the early 20th century, Covent Garden again became one of the world's foremost opera houses under the direction of Rafael Kubelik (1955–58), Georg Solti (1958–69), and Colin Davis (from 1971).

Coventry, city in central England, 16mi (26km) SE of Birmingham. An important weaving center in the Middle Ages, the city was severely damaged in WWII. Industries: cars, bicycles, machinery, electrical equipment, rayon, hosiery. Pop. 337,000.

Coverdale, Miles (1488–1569), English Bible translator. He published the first English translation of the Bible in 1535 and was a principal collaborator in the Great Bible (1539).

Cow. See Cattle.

Coward, (Sir) Noel (Pierce) (1899–1973), English playwright, composer, and performer. In show business from an early age, he first attracted notice as a playwright with his drama The Vortex (1924). He is most noted, however, for his highly polished comedies, including Hay Fever (1925), Fallen Angels (1925), Easy Virtue (1925), Bitter Sweet (1929), Private Lives (1930), Design for Living (1932), Conversation Piece (1934), Tonight at 8:30 (a group of nine one-act plays performed in various groups of three, 1936), Present Laughter (1939), and Blithe Spirit (1942). Other popular works written by him include Cavalcade (1931), a patriotic play; In Which We Serve (1942), a patriotic film; and Brief Encounter (1946), a film. He also composed hundreds of songs, including "Mad Dogs and Englishmen" and "Mad About the Boy," performing many of them in cabaret and revues.

Cowbird, blackbirdlike North and South American bird that follows cattle herds, sometimes picking ticks off the cattle. A nest parasite, the female lays her eggs in the nest of another species, often removing its eggs first. Length: 8in (20cm). Family Icteridae.

Cowpea, or **Black-eyed Pea,** bushy, annual plant native to Asia. It has edible 8–12 in (20–30cm) pods but is grown mainly as a cover crop or for cattle feed. Family Leguminosae; species Vigna sinensis.

Cowper, William (1731–1800), English poet and hymn writer. Subject to intermittent depressive mania, he wrote a variety of prose and poetry, such as the long blank-verse poem The Task (1783), during his lucid periods. His poetry was extremely popular during his lifetime, and some of his hymns have become standards in the Protestant church.

Cowpox, virus-caused contagious disease of cows that produces a skin eruption on the teats and udder. Cowpox pus was used by Edward Jenner to develop a vaccine against smallpox, a serious disease probably caused by the same virus.

Cowrie, or cowry, gastropod mollusk identified by ovoid, polished shell with toothed opening and varied markings. Length: 0.33–3.5in (8.3–88.9mm). Family Cypraeidae; 200 species, including map cowry Cypraea mappa.

Cowslip. See Marsh Marigold.

Coyoacán, federal district in central Mexico, 6mi (10km) S of Mexico City; site of old Cortés palace, first seat of Spanish government. Pop. 338,850.

Coyote, medium-sized wild dog, resembling a small wolf, originally native to W North America. They have moved into many eastern areas formerly inhabited by wolves, including New England. Usually grayish-brown, they have pointed muzzles, big ears, and bushy tails. Their diet consists mainly of rabbits, rodents, and carrion, but they prey occasionally on domestic animals. Species Canis latrans. See also Canidae.

Coypu, large aquatic rodent, also known as nutria, native to South America, that now also lives in North America and Europe, both wild and on fur farms. Coypus have brown outer fur and soft gray underfur that is commercially valuable. Weight: 18lb (8kg). Species Myocastor coypu.

Crab, flattened, triangular, or oval decapod crustacean covered with a hard shell. Primarily marine, some crabs are found in fresh water and a few are terrestrial. Their short abdomen, often called a tail, is bent under. A pair of large foreclaws, a pair of movable eyestalks, and segmented mouth are characteristic. Crabs usually move sideways. Many crabs are edible. Size: pea-sized–12ft (3.7m) from leg tip to opposite leg tip. Some of the 4,500 species are parasitic. Order Decapoda. See also Crustacean; Decapod.

Crab Apple, small sour fruit produced by certain apple trees. The various species grow in North America and Asia. The fruit is used in making preserves and jelly. The name also refers to small, hardy horticultural forms of apple trees. Family Rosaceae; genus Malus.

Crab-eating Monkey. See Macaque.

Crab Grass, weedy annual grass native to Europe and naturalized in the United States. The blades are coarse, hairy, and rough. It bears spreading purple flower spikes and spreads rapidly. Although sometimes cultivated for hay and pasturage, it is considered a noxious weed. It can be eliminated from lawns by uprooting or poisoning. Height: to 3ft (1m). Family Gramineae; genus Digitaria.

Crab Nebula, bright emission nebula in the constellation Taurus, the still expanding remnant of a supernova first observed by Chinese and Japanese astronomers in July 1054. Having a structure characterized by gaseous filaments, the Crab is a powerful radio and X-ray source, with a pulsar located at its center.

Crab Spider, webless spider that moves sideways like a crab and is found worldwide. Red to brown, they hide on flowers and grab their prey as it comes to feed. Length: to 0.8in (20mm). Family Thomisidae. *See also* Spider.

Cracking, treatment of the raw products of the first distillation of oil refining, so as to break up the hydrocarbons into smaller molecules by the controlled use of heat, catalysts, and often pressure. The cracking of petroleum yields heavy oils, gasoline, and such gases as ethane, ethylene, and propylene, which are used in the manufacture of plastics, textiles, detergents, and agricultural chemicals.

Cracow. *See* Krakow.

Craft Unions, organizations formed by the skilled workers in the crafts. Membership is usually limited to those in the trade. Usually conservatively oriented, most craft unions have apprenticeship programs to train new members, which have the additional effect of monitoring entry into the brotherhood.

Craiova, city in S Romania, 112mi (180km) W of Bucharest; capital of Oltenia region, on the Jiul River; site of university (1966) and church of St Demetrius (1652); rich agricultural region with deposits of coal, oil, natural gas. Industries: electrical equipment, food processing. Pop. 175,454.

Cramp, involuntary persistent contraction of a muscle producing sharp pain. It may occur in almost any muscle as a result of overexertion such as can occur in athletics, chronic strain, or from normal physiological causes such as menstruation.

Cranach, or **Kranach, Lucas, the Elder** (1472–1553), German painter and engraver. Court painter to the electors of Saxony and a close friend and follower of Martin Luther, Cranach painted portraits and religious and mythological scenes. Cranach used female nudes in an erotic way new to German art. Among his best-known works are *Eve* (Uffizi, Florence) and *The Judgement of Paris* (Metropolitan, New York).

Cranberry, evergreen shrub or small tree grown mostly in the US. They have oval leaves, pink or whitish flowers, and red, sour fruit. *Vaccinium macrocarpon,* American cranberry, is grown commercially in Massachusetts, New Jersey, and Wisconsin. Family Ericaceae.

Crane, Hart (1899–1932), US poet, b. Harold Hart Crane in Garrettsville, Ohio. Acclaimed as one of the most brilliant and creative 20th-century American poets, he published his first volume, *White Buildings,* in 1926. His major work, *The Bridge* (1930), is a series of related poems in which New York City's Brooklyn Bridge serves as a mystical symbol of the creative power of civilization. After a life plagued by problems, Crane jumped from a ship on a return trip to the United States from Mexico.

Crane, Stephen (1871–1900), US novelist, short story writer, poet, and war correspondent, b. Newark, N.J. He is best known for *The Red Badge of Courage* (1895), a realistic study of the mind of a soldier in the Civil War. Initially a subject of critical controversy, the work has since become an influential classic. *Maggie: A Girl of the Streets* (1893) is a study of urban squalor. His "The Open Boat" (in *The Open Boat and Other Tales of Adventure,* 1898) is considered one of the finest short stories in the English language. Other works include *The Black Rider* (1895) and *War Is Kind* (1899), volumes of verse, *The Monster and Other Stories* (1899), and *Whilomville Stories* (1900).

Crane, large marsh bird found around the world. Long-legged, they have brownish, grayish, or white plumage with bright ornamental heads. They fly with long necks straight and feed on almost anything. After courtship dances, the female lays eggs (2) in a bulky plant-material nest on the ground or above water. Height: 30–60in (76–152cm). Family Gruidae.

Crane Constellation. *See* Grus (the Crane) Constellation.

Crane Fly, long-legged fly resembling the mosquito. This brown to gray insect, ranging from 0.25 to 1.25in (6.35–31.75mm) in length, is found worldwide in damp areas. The larvae are aquatic or semi-aquatic and feed on decaying vegetable matter. Family Tipulidae. *See also* Diptera.

Cranial Nerves, twelve nerves that arise from the brain and are numbered according to the site of origin in the brain. The olfactory nerve (I), is concerned with smell; the optic (II), with vision; the oculomotor, trochlear, and abducens (III, IV, VI), with the movement of certain muscles of the eye; the trigeminal (V), with sensation in parts of the face and with movement of jaw muscles in chewing; the facial (VII), with the sense of taste and with face, scalp, ear, and neck muscle movement, and salivary gland secretion; the auditory (VIII), with hearing and balance; the glossopharyngeal (IX), with taste, touch, and temperature in mouth area organs, pharynx muscle movement, and salivary gland secretion; the vagus (X), known as the "wanderer," with muscle movement in the larynx and pharynx, stimulation of gastric and pancreatic secretion, and movement of autonomic muscles of heart, bronchi, esophagus, stomach, small intestine, and other organs; the accessory (XI), with muscle movement in neck, shoulder, and arm region; and the hypoglossal (XII), with tongue muscle movement.

Cranium, or brain case, dome-shaped, solid, hard bone structure that surrounds and protects the brain. It is made up of eight bones: one frontal, two parietal, two temporal, one occipital, one sphenoid, and one ethmoid.

Cranmer, Thomas (1489–1556), English prelate and reformer. A distinguished theologian, he was appointed Archbishop of Canterbury by King Henry VIII (1533) and divorced Henry from Catherine of Aragon despite papal opposition. Cranmer promoted the English Reformation, encouraging the translation and dissemination of the *Great Bible* (1538) and compiling the first Book of Common Prayer (1548). After Mary's accession (1553), Cranmer was tried, deposed, and burnt at the stake.

Cranston, city in N Rhode Island, on the Pawtuxet River, 5mi (8km) S of Providence; named after colonial Gov. Samuel Cranston. Industries: machinery, chemicals, textiles, beer. Inc. as town 1754, as city 1910. Pop. (1980) 71,992.

Crassus, Marcus Licinius (*c.*115–53 BC), Roman political figure. He commanded part of Sulla's victorious forces in 83 BC and amassed a vast personal fortune in property. Raising a private army, he suppressed the slave rebellion led by Spartacus (71 BC). Crassus served as consul with his rival Pompey, and in 60 BC Julius Caesar formed with them the first triumvirate. After another joint consulship with Pompey (55 BC), Crassus became governor of Syria. He was killed fighting the Parthians at Carrhae.

Crater, Lunar, any of several thousand circular formations on the moon's surface, produced by volcanic activity or, in some cases, by meteoric impact. Craters range in size from tiny depressions to vast walled plains and high ring mountains. Small craters often appear in chains along rills, and many large craters have associated central peaks within them.

Crates, name of four different Greek philosophers: Crates of Thebes (4th century BC), cynic disciple of Diogenes; Crates of Athens (3rd century BC), philosopher, head of the Old Academy; Crates of Mallus (2nd century BC), Stoic philosopher and grammarian; Crates of Tarsus (2nd century BC), Academic philosopher.

Cratinus (*c.*510–422 BC), Greek poet and playwright. Despite his reputation as a great comic poet, he was portrayed as a drunkard in Aristophanes' play *The Knight.* Cratinus retaliated by winning first prize for his play *Wine Flask* (423 BC) in a competition in which Aristophanes' *The Clouds* placed third.

Craxi, Benedetto (Bettino) (1934–), Italian Socialist politician, prime minister (1983–). He left the University of Milan for a political career, becoming a member of the Socialist party's central committee at 22, of the Milan city council in 1960, and of Italy's parliament in 1968. From 1983 he headed a coalition government that moved to curb inflation, cracked down on organized crime, and greatly reduced the role of the Roman Catholic Church in Italian secular affairs.

Crayfish, edible decapod crustaceans found in freshwater rivers and streams of temperate regions, with a few saltwater species. Smaller than lobsters, they burrow into stream banks and feed on animal and vegetable matter. Some cave-dwelling species are blind. Length: to about 6in (15cm). Families Astacidae (Northern Hemisphere), Parastacidae (Southern Hemisphere), Austroastacidae (Australia). *See also* Crustacean; Decapod.

Crazy Horse (died 1877), Indian name, Jashunca-Uitco, Indian chief of the Oglala Sioux. He defeated Gen. George Crook at the Rosebud River (June 17, 1876) and assisted chief Sitting Bull in the massacre of Gen. George Custer's force at the Little Big Horn (June 25). He was shot while resisting imprisonment for allegedly planning a revolt.

Creatine, amino acid found mostly in the muscle tissues of vertebrates (and some invertebrates). It is important to energy production. The alleged anti-cancer agent, Krebiozen, is a creatine.

Crécy (Crécy-en-Ponthieu), village in N France; scene of the first major battle of the Hundred Years War, Aug. 26, 1346. Though greatly outnumbered, King Edward III and the English won the battle through their use of the longbow, firm discipline, and greater mobility. The French were hampered by their use of the crossbow and heavy armor. Victory enabled the English to take Calais.

Credi, Lorenzo Di (*c.*1458–1537), Italian painter and sculptor. A fellow-student with Leonardo da Vinci in the school of Andrea del Verrocchio, Lorenzo painted mostly religious subjects. His best-known work is *The Annunciation* in the Uffizi Gallery, Florence.

Credit, Letter of, document issued by a bank allowing the holder to draw upon an amount of money at some other institution. Liability is assumed by the issuing bank. There are several types of letters of credit; the document itself contains the terms limiting negotiability. Widely used in international commercial transactions, travelers' checks are also a type of letter of credit.

Cree, one of the largest divisions of the Algonquian language family of North American Indians, ranging from James Bay to the Saskatchewan River in Canada. The tribe split into the Plains Cree and the Woodlands Cree, each reflecting the culture of the area. Like the closely related Chippewa, the Cree served as guides and hunters for French and British traders and were a lifeline of the Hudson's Bay Company for decades. At one time numbering over 20,000, at least half that number still survive in Canada, mostly living on reserves in Manitoba.

Creek, a confederation of tribes speaking the Muskhogean tongue, and thus more properly known as Muskhogean Indians. One of the largest tribal groups living in SE United States, they ranged from coastal Georgia into Alabama, Florida, and Mississippi. Following the Creek Wars of 1813–14, they were removed to Oklahoma, where some 15,000 descendants now live; approximately 5000 are scattered throughout the Southeast. These people had a greater effect upon the settlement of the SE Gulf Coast than any other tribe, and their political skills are regarded as second only to those of the Iroquois.

Creeping Jenny. *See* Moneywort.

Cremona, city in N Italy; capital of Cremona prov.; Virgil attended school here; medieval center of learning; site of a Renaissance school of painting; 12th-century cathedral and the Torazzo (13th-century bell tower); violins were made here 16th-18th century by Amati and Stradivari families; agricultural and dairy center. Industries: farming machinery, silk textiles, bricks. Founded 218 BC by Romans. Pop. 82,411.

Creole, pidgin language that eventually becomes the mother tongue of a speech community. Examples are Haitian Creole, based on French, and numerous other French creoles spoken in the Caribbean, Louisiana, Mauritius, and elsewhere. Papiamento, based on Spanish, is spoken in the Netherlands Antilles, while a number of Portuguese creoles are spoken in western Africa.

Cress, various pungent-leaved plants, including rock cress *(Arabis)* with purple or pink flowers; winter cress *(Barbarea)* with yellow flowers; yellow cresses *(Rorippa);* and bitter cresses *(Cardamine).* Family Cruciferae.

Cretaceous Period, the last period of the Mesozoic Era, lasting from 135 to about 65,000,000 years ago. Dinosaurs flourished until the end of this period, when they became extinct. The first true placental and marsupial mammals appeared and modern flowering plants were common. A great continental sea crossed North America from Alaska to the Gulf of Mexico. The Rocky Mountains had their origin. *See also* Geologic Time; Mesozoic Era.

Crete (Kret, Kriti), the largest island of Greece, in E Mediterranean Sea, SSE of the Greek mainland. The chief cities are Canea and Candia. Crete has a mountainous terrain, with rolling country. Sheep and goats are raised in the uplands, making Crete a main producer of wool, hides, cheese, and goat's milk. Mild climate and adequate rainfall support cultivation of cereals, grapes, carob, olives, and oranges. Crete produces olive oil, wine, leather, and handicrafts. Cretans have strong ties with Greece; however, the people possess a unique diction, nomenclature, and physique.

Crane

Crater, Lunar

Crayfish

The people are overwhelmingly Greek Orthodox, under the supervision of the archbishop of Athens.

Crete's impressive history began in the Neolithic period, Early and Middle Bronze Age. Cretan society was far more advanced than any contemporary European civilization. Minoan art and architecture flourished from 1600 BC. Knossos was destroyed along with other leading Crete cities, apparently by some natural disaster. Crete's importance declined, and the Greek mainland became dominant. After 1125 BC the Dorians controlled Crete, setting up a hundred independent political units in which the male Dorians held power and created an oligarchic type of constitution. During the 9th century BC, it was important as a trade route from the Near East; it adopted the Phoenician alphabet and developed the art of finely painted pottery. In the 3rd century BC the island accepted the unstable protection of Macedon and became a notorious pirate center. Crete was conquered by Rome 68–67 BC and later came under Byzantine rule. In AD 826 Arab domination brought slave raiding and piracy by Arab seamen. In 1669, Crete fell to an oppressive Turkish reign; Cretan resentment caused numerous uprisings against the government. In 1898 foreign intervention forced Turkey to evacuate Crete, which became an autonomous state under Turkish sovereignty, governed by a high commission of Britain, France, Russia, and Italy. In 1908, Cretans proclaimed union with Greece; this union was confirmed by the Treaty of London 1913. Area: 3,186sq mi (8,256sq km). Pop. 456,642.

Cretinism, disorder present at birth or beginning in early childhood in which a deficiency of thyroid hormones produces retarded physical and mental development. Symptoms include high birth weight, large tongue, thick skin, potbelly appearance, sleepiness, failure to grow and develop. Treatment consists of administration of thyroid hormones.

Crevasse, deep opening in a glacier. It is the result of stress within the glacier or the movement of the glacier over uneven terrain.

Crew Racing. *See* Rowing.

Cribbage, card game for two players. A standard 52 card deck is used along with a cribbage board (scoring device). Each player receives six cards and discards two into a separate pile called the "crib." Cards in the hand are played alternately, and there are different point values for various combinations. A replacement card is taken from the deck for each card played. Picture cards and 10s count at 10 points, aces as 1 each, and the other cards their face value. The object is to reach 31 points or as close as possible without exceeding the total. After each game, the two other cards, or "crib" are used to add additional points to the score. Generally, 121 points are needed to win the match.

Crib Death. *See* Sudden Infant Death Syndrome.

Crick, Francis H(arry Compton) (1916–   ), English biophysicist. He received (with James Watson and Maurice Wilkins) the 1962 Nobel Prize for medicine or physiology for assisting in the discovery of the molecular structure of deoxyribonucleic acid (DNA).

Cricket, brown to black bug with long antennae and hind legs adapted for jumping; found worldwide. The field and house crickets are the best known of this family. The males produce a chirping sound. Length: 0.3–2in (7.6–51mm). Family Gryllidae. *See also* Mole Cricket.

Cricket, a game popular in Great Britain and other Commonwealth nations, the national summer sport of England, where it originated in the Middle Ages. It is played by 2 teams of 11 persons each on a field about 525 feet by 550 feet (160m × 168m). A game, which may take several days to complete, consists of one or two innings. In an inning all the men of a team bat once in a fixed order; the team scoring the most runs wins. Except for serious injury, no substitutions are allowed. Batsmen and wicketkeepers (catchers) wear gloves, and the fielders are positioned in non-fixed positions around the outlying areas of wickets. The game evolves around two wickets, which are placed near the middle of the field, 66 feet (20.1m) apart. A wicket is made of 3 wooden stumps 28 inches high (71.1cm) with 2 small wooden crosspieces (bails), balanced in grooves in the stumps. At each wicket stands a batsman who uses a cane-handled, paddle-shaped bat. The bowler, who stands at one of the wickets, has six to eight pitches to retire the batsman. Runs are scored each time a batsman exchanges wickets with his partner; on a long hit he may score as many as six runs. The bowler delivers the hard, leather-covered ball, overarm with a stiff arm action, usually on a bounce. If he does not retire the batsman after the alloted pitches, another bowler (a starting fielder) begins the next series of pitches from the opposite wicket. A batter is retired in a number of ways. Some are technical, but the most common are if the bowler breaks the bails of the wicket on the pitch, if the hit ball is caught in the air, or if the fielders retrieve the ball and knock down the bails before the batsman reaches the wicket.

Crime and Punishment (1866), novel by Fydor Dostoevsky. It examines the nature of crime and guilt. Raskolnikov, a penniless St. Petersburg student, kills an old pawnbroker for her money. Surprised in the act by the pawnbroker's sister, he also kills her and flees without the money. Confessing his crimes to Sonia, a girl driven to prostitution, he is overheard and blackmailed. He eventually gives himself up and is exiled to Siberia.

Crimean War (1853–56), war fought by Britain, France, and Turkey against Russia. Russian ambitions in the Middle East aroused British and French fears. When Russia claimed a protectorate over Orthodox Christians in Turkey and occupied Turkish dependencies, Britain and France declared war and sent troops to the Crimean Peninsula (1854). Bad administration and leadership led to the pointless Charge of the Light Brigade and thousands of deaths through disease and lack of supplies. Military efforts centered on Sevastopol, which Russia surrendered in 1855. Peace was reached at the Congress of Paris (1856). An important consequence was the diplomatic isolation of Austria; the war also demonstrated to Britain and Russia the need for military reform.

Criminal Law, branch of law "which defines crimes, treats of their nature, and provides for their punishment." The three elements of criminal law are: an offense must be committed against the public and prosecuted by the state, as distinguished from a tort, or violation of a private right; the act must be a specified crime according to the criminal code; that code must state a definite punishment for the crime charged. Crimes can be classified as *mala in se,* immoral or wrong in themselves, such as murder, rape, arson; or *mala prohibita,* those acts not morally wrong but prohibited by statute for infringing on the rights of others, such as disturbing the peace. They are graded by their gravity as treason, felony, and misdemeanor. In the United States, criminal law consists of statutory and common law, though there is a lessening importance of common law. Each state, as well as the federal government has its own criminal code of law; there are no common law crimes against the US federal government.

Crinoid, primitive class of marine echinoderms, the only class having an upward-directed mouth, which is located with the other main organs in a small central disc. Long feathery arms surround it. It is spineless with tube feet used for respiration. Class Crinoidea. *See also* Feather Star, Sea Lily.

Crinum Lily, tropical bulb plant with long, narrow, evergreen leaves and fragrant flowers that are trumpet or star-shaped. The swamp *Crinum americanum* and grand *Crinum asiaticum* have white flowers and are cultivated in S United States. Family Amaryllidaceae.

Cripps, (Sir Richard) Stafford (1889–1952), British socialist politician. He joined the Labour party as solicitor-general (1930–31) and entered parliament (1931). For cooperating with communists against fascism, he was expelled from the Labour party (1939). Churchill made him ambassador to Russia (1940–42) and minister of aircraft production (1942–45). Readmitted to the Labour party (1945), Cripps held economic appointments. As chancellor of the exchequer (1947–50) he pursued a rigid austerity program.

Critias (450–403 BC), Athenian politician and writer, pupil of Socrates. Exiled during the Peloponnesian Wars for favoring Sparta, he returned to become one of the cruelest of the "30 tyrants" and was killed when the exiled democrats returned.

Critical Mass, minimum mass of fissile material required in a fission bomb to sustain a chain reaction. *See* Fission, Nuclear.

Critical Periods, in psychology, stages of development in which important learning must take place if it is to be effective. For example, dogs will not be suitable as pets unless they get used to people before they are four months old. Some psychologists believe children are particularly prone to develop behavior problems if they do not have close mother attachments in infancy.

Critical Point, the temperature and pressure above which a liquid and its vapor phase can no longer coexist. If a substance is slowly compressed at temperatures and pressures above the critical point it seems to change gradually from gas to liquid, rather than suddenly separating into two phases.

Croaker, or **hardhead,** marine fish found in shallow tropical and temperate waters. A commercial and sporting fish, it is silver with brown bars on its sides. It uses its air bladder and attached muscles to make croaking and drumming sounds. Length: to 20in (50.8cm); weight: 4lb (1.8kg). Family Sciaenidae; species include Atlantic *Micropogon undulatus.*

Croatia (Hrvatska), federal unit and republic in NW Yugoslavia; includes Croatia proper, Slavonia, Dalmatia, and major part of Istria. A former kingdom, Croatia fell under the rule of Hungary 1091; after the fall of Austro-Hungarian Empire in 1918, a kingdom was formed by Serbs, Croats, and Slovenes; political conflicts resulted in the assassination of Stefan Radie, leader of the Croatian Peasant party; his successor formed a separate Croatian state. In 1945, Croatia became a Yugoslav republic. Industries: lumber, coal, petroleum, iron ore, tourism. Pop. 4,426,000.

Croce, Benedetto (1866–1952), Italian philosopher and historian. His *Philosophy of the Spirit* (1902–17) is concerned with aesthetics, logic and linguistics, ethics, and historiography. He was an Italian senator (1910–

20) and minister of education (1920–21). An anti-Fascist, he retired from politics when Mussolini came to power, not returning until 1943 when he became head of the Liberal party. Historical works include *A History of Italy, 1871–1915* (1927) and *History as the Story of Liberty* (1938).

Crockett, David (1786–1836), US frontiersman, b. Green co, Tenn. He served under Andrew Jackson in the Creek Wars (1813–14). He served in the Tennessee legislature (1821–26) and the US Congress (1827–31, 1833–35). A Whig, he opposed the policies of Jackson and the Democrats. He shrewdly cultivated the image of a rough frontiersman. Three books about his life, including *A Narrative of the Life of David Crockett* (1834), supposedly of his authorship were probably not written by him. He moved to Texas in 1835 after not being reelected and died fighting at the Alamo.

Crocodile, flesh-eating, lizardlike reptile found in warm parts of every continent except Europe. Most crocodiles have a longer, more pointed snout than members of the alligator family. All lay hard-shelled eggs in nests. Length: to 23ft (7m). The Asian salt water crocodile *(Crocodylus porosus)* is a man-eater. The American crocodile lives in brackish and salt water around Ecuador, Mexico, the West Indies, and Florida. There are about 15 species including two dwarf species in Africa. Family Crocodylidae. *See also* Reptile.

Crocodile Bird, or Egyptian plover, African bird that feeds on insects, often those infesting crocodiles. It is gray, black, and white, with greenish markings. Dark-speckled, cream eggs (2–3) are buried in the sand. Length: 9in (23cm). Species *Pluvianus aegyptius.*

Crocodile River. *See* Limpopo.

Crocus, hardy perennial flowering plant native to Eurasia and widely cultivated. It is low-growing with a single tubular flower and grasslike leaves arising from an underground corm. It blooms in early spring or fall. Saffron crocus is a popular autumn variety and yellow cloth-of-gold crocus is an early spring favorite. There are 75 species. Family Iridaceae; genus *Crocus.*

Croesus, last King of Lydia (*r.*560–546 BC). Wealthy and friendly to the Greeks, he was overthrown by Cyrus the Great.

Cro-Magnon Man, tall, erect Upper Paleolithic race of man, probably the earliest representatives of *Homo sapiens* in Europe, where they settled between 40,000 and 30,000 years ago. Cultures such as the Aurignacian, for which Cro-Magnon Man was responsible, were distinguished by the manufacture of varied and sophisticated stone tools, as well as bone, horn, and ivory artifacts. Cro-Magnon artists produced the cave paintings of France and northern Spain. *See also* Paleolithic Age.

Cromwell, Oliver (1599–1658), Lord Protector of England, Scotland, and Ireland (1653–58), Puritan soldier and politician. A country landowner, he opposed Charles I in parliament and became a successful parliamentarian officer in the Civil War (1642–48), rising to second-in-command. In the subsequent turmoil he supported the army against parliament and the Presbyterians, and helped bring about the king's execution. He brutally suppressed revolts in Ireland, but showed clemency to the Scottish Covenanters, whom he also defeated (1649–51). More differences between parliament and the army led Cromwell to dissolve parliament and become Lord Protector, head of a military dictatorship (1653). His domestic policy now increased religious toleration and legal and administrative reforms. Backed by a powerful army and navy, his foreign policy supported British trade and colonization. When he died, the government quickly collapsed under his son and successor Richard. *See also* Charles I; Civil War, English; Cromwell, Richard.

Cromwell, Richard (1626–1712), Lord Protector of England (1658–59). Oliver Cromwell's son and successor, Richard was an able officer but an incapable ruler. Ousted from power after eight months, he spent 20 years in exile before returning to live quietly at Cheshunt.

Cromwell, Thomas, Earl of Essex, (1485–1540), English administrator and royal adviser. In Cardinal Wolsey's service Cromwell attracted Henry VIII's attention. His suggestion that the king become head of the church in England (1532) was rewarded with major offices and great wealth. He dissolved the monasteries and directed the Reformation until Henry had him executed for supposed treason.

Cronin, A(rchibald) J(oseph) (1896–1981), Scottish novelist. He was a medical inspector of mines and physician until the success of his first work, *Hatter's Castle* (1931) allowed him to devote all of his time to writing popular, melodramatic novels. Cronin based some of his plots on his own experiences, including *The Citadel* (1937), which dealt with the life of a mining company doctor. Other works included *The Keys of the Kingdom* (1941), *The Judas Tree* (1961), *Pocketful of Rye* (1969), and *Desmonde* (1975).

Cronus, in Greek mythology, the youngest son of Uranus and Gaea. Cronus castrated his father at the instigation of his mother and became head of a new dynasty. By his sister Rhea he was the father of Hades, Poseidon, Zeus, Hestia, Demeter, and Hera.

Crookes, (Sir) William (1832–1919), English scientist. After lecturing in chemistry at Chester College, he inherited a fortune, which enabled him to devote himself to private research. His high-vacuum research led to the invention of the radiometer and the Crookes tube, which led to the discovery of X rays. He was the first to suggest that cathode rays consist of negatively charged particles. He discovered the element thallium and was a well-known spiritualist.

Crop Rotation, practice of growing different crops on the same field, usually in a specified order. A legume sod crop is often included in the sequence. This protects and improves the soil and reduces erosion. Rotated crops generally complement each other, each providing nutrients required by the other.

Croquet, lawn game, popular in Great Britain and the United States, in which wooden balls are hit with wooden mallets through a series of 9 or 10 wire arches. The first player to complete the series and hit the posts placed at each end of the field wins. Croquet was developed in France in the 17th century. The US game, called Roque, was devised in 1899 and uses a different course layout.

Crossbill, forest finch of the N Northern Hemisphere. Varying in color, it has a heavy, curved, scissorlike bill used to pry seeds from evergreen cones. Bluish spotted eggs (4–5) are laid in a twig-and-grass nest. Length: 6in (15cm). Genus *Loxia.*

Crossbreeding, outbreeding, the crossing or mixing of two unlike parents to produce a hybrid, for example, crossing a horse and a donkey to produce a mule.

Crossopterygian, lobefinned fish group extinct for 75 million years except for the coelacanth. It resembles elasmobranchs and terrestrial vertebrates, foreshadowing the latter. Fossil forms show fins in transition to extremities for locomotion, and trunks and tails similar to those of amphibians. The group flourished during the Devonian Period about 400,000,000 years ago and provided the evolutionary stock for land vertebrates. Subclass Choanichthyes.

Cross-pollination, transfer of pollen from the flower of one plant to a flower on another plant. The result of cross pollination is a genetic mix, or hybrid.

Croton, genus of tropical plants native to Australia and islands of the South Pacific. *C. variegatum pictum* is the most popular, with long leaves variegated with green, red, yellow, and white. It grows to 6ft (1.8m).

Croup, respiratory disorder most common in young children caused by an inflammation of the larynx (voice box). Croup can be triggered by bacterial or viral infection, local irritation, or allergy, and is characterized by a harsh, strident-sounding cough. Treatment depends on the cause. Steam inhalation is often helpful.

Crow, large tribe of Siouan-speaking American Indians who early separated from the Hidatsa. They migrated into the Rocky Mountain region from the Missouri River, and today occupy a large reservation area in Montana. They are noted for their physical stature and fine costume; the Crow women are among the most artistic of Plains Indians. The present population of 4500 is divided into the Mountain and River Crow. *See also* Hidatsa.

Crow, large, black birds found in woodlands and farm areas worldwide except in polar regions, South America, and some Pacific islands. The American crow *Corvus brachyrhynchos,* attains a length of 20in (50cm) and a wingspread of 3ft (91cm). Living in large flocks, they feed on plant and animal matter and carrion. They can be crop pests. Considered intelligent, they can sometimes be taught to repeat phrases. Their stick-and-twig nests are built in tall trees for the greenish eggs (3–8). Family Corvidae.

Crowfoot. *see* Buttercup.

Crown Gall, a cancerlike growth that occurs on a wide variety of broadleaved plants, including peaches, apples, roses, raspberries, and sugar beets. The gall, caused by the bacterium *Agrobacterium tumefaciens,* typically forms at the affected plant's crown—the point where the plant emerges from the soil.

Crown of Thorns, spiny, shrubby house plant native to Madagascar with small leaves and clusters of red flowers. Care: bright light, soil (equal parts of potting soil, sand) kept dry between waterings. Propagation is by stem cuttings. Height: to 3ft (91cm). Family Euphorbiaceae; species *Euphorbia splendens.*

Crucible Process, a process for making fine tool and high-speed steel. Carbon steel is melted in fire-clay crucibles in order to make a homogeneous high-quality metal. Coke fires were initially used (1740), but were replaced (1870) by the Siemens regenerative gas furnace that could heat 100 crucibles at a time to temperatures over 3100°F (1700°C). Electric furnaces are now employed.

Crude Oil. *See* Petroleum.

Cruikshank, George (1792–1878), English illustrator and cartoonist. In addition to political and theatrical work, Cruikshank drew illustrations for more than 850 books. The best known are those done for Dickens' *Sketches by Boz* and *Oliver Twist.*

Cruise Missile, or aerodynamic missile, self-propelled missile traveling in the lower atmosphere under constant powered flight. It may be rocket- or jet-powered, eg the German V-1 during World War II. Unlike ballistic missiles, cruise missiles must be aerodynamically designed to minimize atmospheric drag. *See also* Ballistic Missile.

Cruiser, major naval warship displacing 5–10,000 tons, usually serving as a general-purpose combat ship, often taking the place of the more costly battleship. *See also* Battleship.

Crusades (1095–1272), series of military expeditions undertaken by Western European Christians to recover the Holy Land from the Muslims. In 1095 at the Council of Clermont, Pope Urban II urged Christians to go to war to save the Holy Sepulcher, which had been despoiled by the Seljuk Turks who controlled Jerusalem. He promised that the journey would count as full penance. From crosses distributed at the meeting the name Crusade evolved. Peter the Hermit and others spread the message throughout Europe.

Peasants Crusade (1095–96). Even before the first sanctioned crusade could get underway, several thousand French peasants that had set out toward Jerusalem had sacked Belgrade. German peasants turned to attacking Jews and had to be dispersed by the king of Hungary. When the remnants of these two groups reached Constantinople they were quickly shipped across to Jerusalem and easily defeated by the Turks.

First Crusade (1096–99). An organized army under Bishop Ademar and Count Raymond IV of Toulouse captured Nicea (1097), Antioch (1098), and, finally, Jerusalem (1099). Godfrey of Bouillon was elected the first ruler of the Latin Kingdom of Jerusalem.

Second Crusade (1147–49). Preached by Bernard of Clairvaux after the fall of Edessa (1144) to the Turks, it failed in its goal of capturing Damascus.

Third Crusade (1189–91). It followed the fall of Jerusalem (1187) to Saladin. Richard I of England was able to work out a truce with Saladin that allowed Christian access to the Holy Sepulcher.

Fourth Crusade (1202–04). It never reached the Holy Land. Instead it fought with the Venetians against Hungary and in 1204 sacked Constantinople, overthrowing the Byzantine Empire and establishing the Latin Empire of Constantinople.

Children's Crusade (1212). Led by a French peasant boy, Stephen of Cloyes, thousands of children embarked from Marseilles and other ports only to be sold into slavery or to die of hunger or disease.

Fifth Crusade (1218–21). It struck at Egypt with little success.

Sixth Crusade (1228–29). The only nonmilitary Crusade, it was led by Holy Roman Emperor Frederick II. He was able to negotiate a truce with the Muslims that restored some Christian control.

Seventh (1248–50) and **Eighth** (1270) **Crusades.** Both led by Louis IX of France with little success. The Eighth was called off when Louis died in Tunisia.

Ninth Crusade (1271–72). Led by Prince Edward (later Edward I) of England, little was accomplished. The last Latin Kingdom (city state) in the Near East, Acre, fell to the Muslims in 1291.

Crust, Earth, the visible cover or what is sometimes called the silicic phase of Earth. The crust is that part of the planet from the Moho to the outer limit of the core. The silicic rocks are less dense and float on the denser mantle.

David Crockett

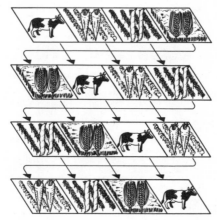

Crop rotation

Cuba

Crustacean, any of a large class (26,000 species) of invertebrate animals in the phylum Arthropoda. Included are the familiar decapods (crabs, lobsters, shrimps, and crayfish), isopods (pill bugs, woodlice), cirripedes (barnacles), and a multitude of other forms, most of which are not distinguished by popular names. The majority of crustaceans are aquatic, either marine or freshwater (although a few are semi-terrestrial). They breathe through gills or the body surface. There are two pairs of antennalike appendages in front of the mouth and at least three pairs of appendages behind the mouth that act as jaws. All have the typical exoskeleton of arthropods. They include some of the largest as well as the smallest arthropods, ranging from the giant Japanese spider crab, 12ft (3.7m) wide with limbs extended, to the water fleas, under 0.01 in (.25mm) in length.

Crux, Crux Australis, or **the Southern Cross,** prominent southern constellation whose four brightest stars, Alpha (Acrux), Beta, Gamma, and Delta, form the famous southward-pointing cross. The constellation contains the Coal Sack, a dark nebula easily discernible against the background of the Milky Way, and the open cluster NGC 4755 or Kappa Crucis (named the Jewel Box by Sir John Herschel).

Cryogenics, the study of physics at very low temperatures. Some materials exhibit highly unusual properties at temperatures within a few degrees of absolute zero: they become super conducting (that is, they can carry an electrical current indefinitely) or "creep" over boundaries, apparently defying the laws of gravity. Such behavior is intensively studied, partly because the low temperatures and small number of energy states involved allow fuller understanding of quantum mechanical principles, and partly for potential applications of immense value.

Cryolite, a halide mineral, sodium-aluminum fluoride (Na_3AlF_6). In pegmatite dikes (Greenland has the only large deposit). Used in aluminum processing. Monoclinic system granular masses or occasional cubic, frequently twinned, crystals. Icy-looking or brown or red; brittle; hardness 2.5; sp gr 3.

Cryosurgery, surgery carried on at a very low temperature in which a freezing probe replaces a cutting edge. It is particularly effective in treating Parkinson's disease and tonsillitis.

Cryptococcosis, serious fungus (*Cryptococcus neoformans*) infection, usually occurring in middle age, more often in men. It affects the central nervous system, including the membranes of the brain, and sometimes the lungs, skin, and other organs.

Cryptography, "hidden writing," also called cryptology. Cryptography involves use of codes and ciphers for safe transmission of secret messages; also involves cryptanalysis, or ways of decoding such messages. The difference between codes and ciphers is primarily technical. In general, ciphers use substitutions for single letters, whereas codes use substitutions (usually 5-letter groups) for whole words, phrases, or sentences. For economy, codes are used commercially with the aid of easily obtainable commercial code books. Modern computers are helpful to the cryptanalyst, but cannot always break code or cipher systems without the aid of human experts.

Crystal, a solid with a repetitive lattice-like structure. Most solids are crystalline, although some, like glass and asphalt, are amorphous. Crystals exhibit many types of atomic symmetries: cubic (table salt), planar (mica), and over two hundred other arrangements.

Macroscopic crystals belong to 32 symmetry classes, which can be grouped into seven crystal systems: triclinic, monoclinic, orthorhombic, trigonal, hexagonal, tetragonal, and isometric. For a given type of crystal, the angles between its planar faces and edges are always the same, no matter how it is broken or reduced. This observation, first made in the 17th century by Nicolaus Steno of Denmark, is the First Law of Crystallography. In all the crystal systems except the isometric, light travels at different velocities along different axes of the crystal because of the differing distances between atoms; thus it will be refracted at different angles and appear to be doubled on leaving the crystal. Such crystals (eg, calcite) are birefringent.

Crystal Lattice, three-dimensional arrangement of atoms, ions, or molecules in a crystalline substance. The term is sometimes used in a more restricted sense to denote the abstraction of the pattern of points on which the atoms, ions, or molecules are located.

Crystallization, process whereby atoms, ions, or molecules aggregate themselves in a regular repeating arrangement, either from the dissolved or pure liquid state, often initiated by supersaturation, to form a solid or oriented liquid crystal with specific physical properties. Crystallization is an important laboratory and industrial technique for purifying (and separating) compounds.

Crystallography, the study of crystal structure by X ray diffraction. Coherent waves will be diffracted, or reinforced in some directions and weakened in others, by striking regularly recurring obstacles of the proper spacing. In crystalline solids this spacing is of the order of a few Ångstroms. Since X rays have wavelengths of comparable size, they are diffracted by the crystals. Knowing the wavelength of the X rays and measuring the angles at which they are strengthened and weakened allows crystallographers to calculate the three-dimensional structures of the crystals. Conversely, a knowledge of the crystal structure allows the wavelengths of unknown X ray sources to be measured. The first great crystallographer, who did his work when both X rays and crystal structure were little understood, was Max von Laue; Sir William Bragg also made important contributions to theory.

Crystal Optics, optical properties of crystals. Transmission of light by crystals differs from transmission by glass in that the refractive index may depend on direction (crystals are not, in general, isotropic). Uniaxial crystals (belonging to the tetragonal, hexagonal, and rhombohedral systems) have two principal refractive indices and display double refraction. Biaxial crystals (orthorhombic, monoclinic, triclinic) have three principal refractive indices. Information on crystal structure can often be obtained by microscopic investigation in polarized light. *See also* Polarization of Light.

Crystal Palace, first building of its size (408×1850ft; 124×564m) made of glass and iron. Designed for the 1851 International Exhibition in London by Sir Joseph Paxton, it was prefabricated and was assembled at the site. Developed by Paxton's work in greenhouse construction, it directly affected train-station design.

Crystal Structure. *See* Crystal.

Cuauhtémoc (*c.*1495–1525), last Aztec ruler of Mexico, unsuccessfully defended Tenochtitlán against Cortés' siege of the capital. Four years later, while on an expedition to Honduras with Cortés, Cuauhtémoc was implicated in a plot to kill the Spaniards and was executed.

Cuba, Republic of, independent nation, on the largest island in the West Indies, 90mi (144km) S of Florida. Since 1959 it has been under the control of Fidel Castro, a left-wing revolutionary. Cuba's economic mainstay is sugar.

Land and economy. Situated entirely in the Tropic Zone, Cuba is in the trade winds belt; its climate is semi-tropical. The island extends 745mi (1,199km) E-W, its width is 22–125m (35–201km). Its 2,500mi (4,025km) coastline includes Havana and Guantanamo harbors, two of the best in the world. About 60% of Cuba is flat to rolling with many fertile valleys. It contains three mountain ranges, the highest being Sierra Maestra. Despite a high level of support and economic investment from the Soviet Union, Cuba's economy has remained essentially stagnant since 1959. It is estimated that from 1959–70, the real per capita GNP declined 9% while other Latin-American countries increased by 24%. Agriculture is the basis of the economy, especially the cultivation and refining of sugar, which accounts for 80% of export earnings. Cuba imports an estimated 40% of its food requirements.

People. Ethnically, the Cuban population is derived from Europe, Africa, Asia, and from the Indians who lived on the island when Christopher Columbus discovered it. Spanish is the official language, and literacy is reported at 95%. Compulsory education was established in 1961. Roman Catholicism is the religion of 85% of the people, although African faiths, Judaism, and Protestant sects are represented.

Government. Cuba, with only one legal party—the Communist party—has been ruled by decree since 1959, although authority is nominally vested in the cabinet.

History. Cuba was discovered and claimed for Spain by Christopher Columbus in 1492; for years Havana served as Spain's crossroad commercial seaport to its colonies. In 1850 Cuban planters started an independence movement, a struggle that precipitated the Ten Years' War (1868) and a general uprising in 1895. The United States supported the revolutionaries after the *USS Maine* was blown up in Havana harbor. In 1898, Spain relinquished its hold on Cuba. An army revolt, led by Gen. Fulgencio Batista in 1933, made him the leading power in the country, and in 1952 he seized the presidency. Opposition to his corrupt regime became apparent, and in 1953 a young lawyer, Fidel Castro, began a guerrilla action against Batista, who quit on Jan. 1, 1959. Castro became premier on Feb. 16, 1959. He nationalized banks and industries and organized state farms under a left-wing government with strong backing from the Soviet Union. In 1961 about 1,400 Cubans, trained in the United States, landed at the Bay of Pigs in a vain effort to regain the island. During the 1970s and early 1980s, Cuba supplied troops and military assistance to Soviet-supported movements, especially in Angola and Ethiopia. At the same time Cuba became a prominent voice in the Third World non-aligned nation movement. Despite some bilateral talks with the United States during the late 1970s, relations between the two nations remain poor. In 1980 Castro lifted emigration restrictions and a flotilla of private vessels brought over 100,000 persons to S Florida. In the mid-1980s the United States criticized Cuba for supporting leftist movements in Nicaragua and elsewhere in Central America. Castro denied U.S. charges that Cuba encouraged terrorism; he did support Nicaragua and suggested that Latin America cancel its U.S. debts.

PROFILE

Official name: Republic of Cuba
Area: 44,218sq mi (114,525sq km)
Population (1975 est): 9,810,781
Density: 222per sq mi (86per sq km)

Chief cities: Havana (capital); Camaguey; Santiago de Cuba
Government: Communist
Religion: Roman Catholic
Language: Spanish
Monetary unit: Peso
Gross national product: $13,920,000,000
Per capita income: $800
Industries (major): sugar products, textiles, chemicals, steel
Agriculture: sugar cane, tobacco, rice, citrus fruits, sweet potatoes
Minerals: iron, copper, salt, manganese, oil, natural gas
Trading partners: Soviet Union (major), Spain, East Germany, Bulgaria, Canada

Cuban Missile Crisis (1962), United States-USSR confrontation over the installation of Soviet rockets in Cuba. US reconnaissance planes first discovered the rockets, which were capable of carrying nuclear warheads to almost anywhere in the Western Hemisphere. This action challenged both the Monroe Doctrine and President Kennedy's warnings to Russia and Cuba against making Cuba an offensive military base. The United States alerted the armed forces and blockaded Cuba. Soviet Premier Khrushchev, after receiving assurances that the United States would not invade the island, dismantled the missile bases.

Cube, result of multiplying a given number together three times. Thus the cube of *a* is $a \times a \times a$, written a^3.

Cube Root, number that must be multiplied together three times to give a specified number. For example, the cube root of 27 is 3, since $3 \times 3 \times 3 = 27$. Cube roots are written in the form $\sqrt[3]{27}$ or $27^{1/3}$.

Cubic Equation, equation of the third degree; that is, one in which the highest power of the unknown is 3. An example is $2x^3 + x^2 + 7 = 0$. Cubic equations have three roots, two of which may be imaginary.

Cubism, innovative movement in 20th-century painting, originating with Pablo Picasso and Georges Braque and joined by Juan Gris, Fernand Léger, Jean Metzinger, Albert Gleizes, and others. Cubism, a term coined by art critic Louis Vauxcelles, was a conscious reaction to the French Romanticism of Ferdinand Delacroix, the sensuous appeal of the Impressionists, and the decorative color of the Fauves, and was a return to the classical tradition of Ingres. Still life was the subject matter, seen as a composition of quasi-geometric forms without atmosphere and light, with restricted colors, verging toward the monochromatic, and without movement. Natural perspective was abandoned, and a new perspective of overlapping, interlocking, semitransparent planes was used in an attempt to present the solidity and volume of the object two-dimensionally, from many different aspects simultaneously. Cubism falls into three phases: the Paul Cézanne phase (1907–09), so-called because of his influence and that of black sculpture and primitive art; the analytical phase (1910–12), which showed an increasing breakdown of form and a use of simultaneity, showing a fragmented object displayed from all angles and open from inside; and the synthetic phase (1913–14), developed by Gris, which discarded imitation completely and sought to recreate the object by means of "emblems" similar to a metaphor in a poem. Gris did not distort the object but painted an analogous construction. Picasso's *Les Demoiselles d'Avignon* is regarded as the source picture of cubism.

Cuckoo, widely distributed forest bird. Common species are the ani, roadrunners, and coucal. True Old World cuckoos are generally brownish with a few species being brightly colored. They feed on small animals. A brood parasite, the female removes one egg of another species and lays her egg—often a match in color—in the nest. Soon after the cuckoo chick has hatched, it throws out the other's eggs and any young that may have hatched. It is then fed by the foster mother. Length: 6–24in (15–61cm). Family Cuclidae.

Cucumber, trailing, annual vine originally from tropical Africa and S Asia. It has yellowish flowers and the fruit is eaten raw or pickled. It needs a warm climate and is sensitive to frost and pests. Family Cucurbitaceae; species *Cucumis sativus.*

Cuenca, city in S central Ecuador; called "marble city" because of many notable buildings. Among richest agricultural areas in Andes, it is also the commercial center of Ecuador. Founded 1557. Pop. 104,470.

Cuernavaca, town in S central Mexico, 37mi (60km) S of Mexico City; site of palace and 1st Mexican sugar refinery, both built by Hernán Cortés (1535), popular resort of Cacahuamilpa Caverns, university (1938). Industries: brewery, tobacco, cement, paper. Pop. 232,355.

Culiacán, city in NW Mexico, 30mi (48km) from Pacific coast; headquarters of Francisco Coronado's expedition up the Gulf of California (1540). Industries: leather, textiles, lumber, mining, corn, tobacco, sugar cane, cotton. Founded 1531 by Nuño Guzmán. Pop. 358,800.

Cullen, Countee (1903–46), US poet, b. New York City. A major figure of the Harlem Renaissance, his poetry includes *Color* (1925) and *The Ballad of the Brown Girl* (1928). *See also* Harlem Renaissance.

Culloden, Battle of (1746), decisive battle of the second Jacobite rising, in which the army of Charles Edward Stuart (Bonnie Prince Charlie) was defeated by forces under the Duke of Cumberland. Culloden ended the Stuart attempts to regain the British throne by force. The battle was followed by a ruthless subjugation of the Scottish Highland clans who had provided most of Prince Charles Edward's army.

Culpeper's Rebellion, in US history, an uprising by North Carolina colonists against the British crown. In 1677 John Culpeper, a surveyor, led the colonists in a protest against British trade policies, which the colonists considered discriminatory. The colonists jailed the British governor and named Culpeper governor. He ruled until 1679, when the British reasserted authority. It is regarded as the first popular uprising in the American colonies.

Cultivator, agricultural implement used to chop or uproot weeds and loosen the soil in fields of crops. Cultivator is a general term applied to a myriad of implements that vary according to the crop, the development of the crop, and the soil.

Cultural Lag, in anthropology, period of delay that occurs when an innovation that produces changes in some aspects of a culture requires adjustments in related areas in that culture. *See also* Culture.

Cultural Relativism, concept in anthropology that holds that the effects of a culture trait are relative to the rest of the culture. Particular practices in one culture fit in with the norms and values of that culture. Wife purchase, for example, may fit in a culture where values and institutions are in accord with it, but it will conflict with the values of other cultures.

Cultural Revolution (1966–69), Chinese Communist movement initiated by Mao Tse-tung to increase revolutionary fervor, promote equality between the masses and the proletariat, and rid China of old ideas, culture, customs, and habits. Higher-ups were purged, especially in the fields of education, culture, and propaganda. The Red Guards, a militant youth organization, was formed to police violations of revolutionary goals. Mao's wife Chiang Ch'ing, a prominent leader of the Revolution and a member of the "Gang of Four," was later arrested (1976) and accused of crimes committed during the Revolution.

Culture, in anthropology, all knowledge that is acquired by man by virtue of his membership in a society. A culture incorporates all the shared knowledge, expectations, and beliefs of a group. Culture in general distinguishes men from animals since only man can pass on accumulated knowledge due to his mastery of language and other symbolic systems. Only man develops and uses culture consistently in the form of tools. *See also* Anthropology, Cultural.

Culver City, city in S California, SW of Los Angeles; center of motion picture industry since 1915. Industries: electronic and aerospace equipment. Inc. 1917. Pop. (1980) 38,139.

Cumae (Cuma), ancient town in SW Italy, W of Naples; thought to be oldest Greek colony in Italy or Sicily, founded about 750 BC; successfully repulsed the Etruscans; defeated by Samnites 5th century BC; under Roman control 338 BC; fortunes declined, and the town disappeared in AD 13th century; site has Greek and Roman ruins as well as cavern where the Cumaean Sibyl pronounced her prophesies.

Cumberland Falls. *See* Great Falls.

Cumberland Gap National Historical Park, region in the Cumberland Gap at junction of Virginia, Kentucky, and Tennessee borders; the Wilderness Road, forged by Daniel Boone, traverses the gap. Area: 20,176acres (8,171hectares). Est. 1940.

Cumbria, county in NW England, formed 1974 from the former counties of Cumberland and Westmorland, and from parts of Lancashire and Yorkshire. It is bounded N by Solway Firth and W by Irish Sea; contains Lake District. Industries: agriculture, dairy farming, tourism. Administrative center is Carlisle. Area: 2,609sq mi (6,757sq km). Pop. 473,800.

Cumbrian Mountains, mountain range in NW England; extends through Cumberland, Westmorland, and N Lancashire; contains highest peak in England, Scafell Pike, 3,210ft (979m).

Cumin, a single species, *Cumin cyminum,* of annual herb native to the Middle East and widely cultivated for its seedlike fruit used as a food flavoring. It has a branching stem and small pink and white flowers. Height: to 6in (15cm). Family Umbelliferae.

cummings, e. e. (1894–1962), US poet, b. Edward Estlin Cummings in Cambridge, Mass. His first work, *The Enormous Room* (1922) was a novel. His poetry, usually exhibiting either sentimental emotion or cynical realism or a combination of both, is characterized by unconventional typography, spelling, and punctuation as well as other innovations. His verse includes *Tulips and Chimneys* (1923), *No Thanks* (1935), and *Poems, 1923–1954* (1954).

Cuneiform, most significant writing system in the ancient Near East. Used in the last three millennia BC, it combined logographic and syllabic forms in wedge shaped pictographs. It also included numbers.

Cunner, small marine food fish found in the North Atlantic. Related to the wrasse, it is brown, olive green, blue, or reddish. Length: to 17in (43cm); weight: 3lb (1.4kg). Family Labridae; species *Tautogolabrus adspersus* (American), *Crenilabrus melops* (English). *See also* Osteichthyes.

Cunobelinus. *See* Cymbeline.

Cupid, in Roman mythology, a winged boy armed with a bow and arrow. He is the equivalent of the Greek god Eros. Although primarily known for shooting arrows of passion, the Romans represented him as the pleasant sleep of death or a beneficent spirit.

Cuprite, or Ruby Copper, a secondary oxide mineral, cuprous oxide (Cu_2O). Found in oxidation zones of copper sulfide veins. Cubic system octahedral, dodecahedral, and cubic crystals and earthy masses. Red to black, brittle, translucent; hardness 3.5–4; sp gr 6.

Curaçao, largest island in Netherland Antilles in Dutch West Indies, in Caribbean Sea; contains natural bay, 18th-century Dutch-style houses, and pontoon bridge across St Anna Bay. Majority of inhabitants are descended from African slaves imported during the 17th and 18th centuries; original Arawak Indians are extinct. Capital is Willemstad. Industries: tourism, cement, tiles, paint, shipbuilding. Length: 36mi (58km). Width: 6mi (10km). Pop. 154,928.

Curare, dark brown resinous poisonous extract obtained from various tropical South American trees of the genera *Chondodendron* and *Strychnos.* It contains many alkaloids, notably D-tubocurarine, which is used as a muscle relaxant. It is used on the poisoned arrows of South American Indians.

Curassow, large, crested, long-tailed, turkeylike game bird of Central and South American tropical forests. It feeds on forest matter and insects. The female lays white eggs (2–3) in a stick-and-leaf nest near the ground. These birds are considered a potential future meat source. Length: 20–40in (50–100cm). Family Cracidae, genera *Crax* and *Mitu.*

Curculio, small weevil with snouts, especially nut weevils and the plum curculio *(Conotrachelus nenuphar),* a pest of plums, cherries, peaches, apricots, and apples. Family Curculionidae. *See also* Weevil.

Curia, political division of ancient Rome. It was composed of patrician and plebeian family units. Military service and electoral function came to be based on the curia. The term later came to refer to public meeting places. In medieval Europe it was used for the court. The modern papal court is still called the Curia.

Curie, Pierre and Marie Sklodowska. Pierre (1859–1906), a French physicist, became a professor at the Sorbonne. His early work concerned the electric and magnetic properties of crystals; he enunciated Curie's law relating magnetism and temperature. After marrying (1895) the Polish Marie Sklodowska (1867–1934), he joined in her work on radioactivity. Together they discovered radium and polonium in 1898 and were awarded a Nobel Prize in 1903 jointly with A.H. Becquerel. After Pierre's death in a road accident, Marie succeeded to his chair and received a second Nobel Prize (for chemistry) in 1911.

Cutting

e.e. cummings

Marie and Pierre Curie

General George Custer

Curie, unit (symbol Ci) used to measure the activity of a radioactive substance, that is, the number of atoms that disintegrate in unit time. One curie is defined as 3.7 × 10¹⁰ disintegrations per second, roughly the activity of one gram of radium.

Curium, radioactive metallic element (symbol Cm) of the actinide group, first made (1940) by Glenn Seaborg and others by alpha-particle bombardment of Pu²³⁹. Properties: at. no. 96; sp gr 13.5 (calc); melt. pt. 2444 °F (1340°C); most stable isotope Cm²⁴⁴ (half-life 1.6 × 10⁷yr). *See also* Transuranium Elements.

Curlew, long-legged shorebird with long down-curved bill and mottled brown plumage. Often migrating long distances, it lives in open areas near water, feeds on small animals, insects, and seeds, and nests on the ground, laying 2–4 eggs. Length: 24in (61cm). Genus *Numenius*.

Curling, game that is the major winter sport of Scotland. It is also popular in Canada and the N United States. It may have originated as early as the 16th century. The game is played by two teams of four persons each on an ice surface 138ft (42m) long by 14ft (4.3m) wide. Each player has two circular stones—dished on bottom and top and having a top handle for the player's grip—which weigh from 40–44 pounds (18–20kg). Players are also provided with a crampit, or spiked metal plate, to get a foothold in the ice, and a broom to sweep the ice in front of the swerving stone. At each end of the ice is a circular target with an area in the center known as the "tee." The ice is sprinkled with water to make it pebbly. While a player sends his stone toward the tee, another player sweeps the surface in front to give the stone a smoother surface on which to ride. Each player delivers two stones, alternately with his opponent. One point is counted for each stone of one side that is closest to the tee. A game is 10 or 12 rounds (16 stones per round).

Curly-Coated Retriever, breed of dog (sporting group) unsurpassed as water retriever and one of the oldest retriever breeds. Brought to the US in 1907, this steady dog has a long head and jaw; small, close ears; short muscular body; long legs; and a short, straight, pointed tail. Its black or liver coat is crisply curled. Average size: 23in (58cm) high at shoulder; 65lb (29kg). *See also* Sporting Dog.

Currant, hardy, primarily deciduous shrub *(Ribes)* of the saxifrage family, native to cooler temperate regions of the Northern Hemisphere and South America. Their red or white fruit is eaten fresh or in preserves. *See also* Gooseberry.

Current, Electric, rate of flow of electric charge through a conductor. Measured in amperes—a flow of some 10¹⁸ electrons per second being equivalent to one ampere. Direct current (D.C.) flows continuously in one direction, whereas alternating current reverses direction periodically. In the United States the power supply has a frequency (number of complete cycles) of 60 cycles per second (hertz), in the United Kingdom it is 50 hertz. The magnitude of an alternating current, *I*, at any instant, *t*, after the start of the cycle is given by: *I* = *I*m sin (2π*ft*), where *f* is the frequency, and *I*m is the maximum current.

Currents, Oceanic, broad slow drifts of water moving in a given direction. Surface currents flow around a gyre, clockwise in the Northern Hemisphere and counterclockwise in the Southern. Waters in a current are warmed at the equator, driven along by the prevailing surface winds, and then rotated partly by deflection at a coastline and partly by the Coriolis force. Oceans

also have deep currents (density currents) caused by temperature and salinity variations. *See also* Coriolis Force; Gyre.

Currier & Ives, 19th-century US firm of lithographers who published hand-colored prints of great commercial popularity and historic interest. Nathaniel Currier (1813–88) founded the business in New York about 1836 and became partners with James Merritt Ives (1824–95) in 1857. The company produced over 7000 lithographs of current events, rural and city scenes, sports, and still lifes.

Cursor Mundi (c.1300), English poem of unknown authorship. Its 24,000 lines, written in a northern English dialect, tell the history of the world from creation to doomsday and are based somewhat on the English poet Caedmon's (died c.680) paraphrase of Genesis. The first four books of the poem cover the events from creation to Solomon's successors; Book 5, the early lives of Mary and Jesus; Book 6, the later life of Jesus and the Apostles; and Book 7, the Last Judgment.

Curtis, Charles (1860–1936), US political leader, b. Kansas Territory near Topeka, Kan. A lawyer, he served as a Republican in the House of Representatives (1893–1907) and Senate (1907–13, 1915–29), where he was party whip in the 1920s. He was vice president under Pres. Herbert Hoover (1929–33).

Curtius, Quintus, early Roman historian, probably living and writing under Claudius. Nothing further is known of this man beyond his principal work, the *History of Alexander the Great*. This book represents the earliest example of Latin prose of non-Roman orientation.

Curvature of the Spine, abnormal deviation in the position of the spine, which normally has four gentle curves. There are three major types: scoliosis, or lateral curvature, which can be due to bad posture or to a prebirth abnormality; lordosis, an accentuation of the inward curve of the neck region or more commonly of the lower back region resulting in a swayback appearance; and kyphosis, an accentuation of the outward curve of the chest region, which in severe form can result in a hunchback appearance. *See also* Lordosis.

Curzon Line, demarcated by the League of Nations in 1919, established the Polish eastern frontier and awarded the city of Vilna to Lithuania and large areas to Russia. Poles invaded the USSR and recovered the territory. The Yalta Conference of 1945 recognized the Curzon line, however.

Curzon of Kedleston, George Nathaniel Curzon, 1st Marquess (1859–1925), English Conservative statesman. He entered parliament (1885) and traveled widely in the East before becoming viceroy of India (1899–1905). There he carried out many reforms before his resignation was engineered. Curzon served in the war cabinet (1915–19) and became foreign secretary (1919–24).

Cush, Kingdom of. *See* Kush, Kingdom of.

Cushing's Syndrome, rare disease characterized by obesity of the body trunk, facial redness, and in women an increase in body hair and menstrual disturbances. The disease is often associated with high blood pressure, diabetes mellitus, brittle bones, and psychological disturbances. It is caused by an excessive amount of adrenal hormones, which can be produced by a tumor or some other cause, and occasionally by the administration of the drug cortisone. Treatment depends on the cause.

Cusk, bottom-dwelling marine fish found on both sides of the North Atlantic. A commercial fish, it is gray, redbrown, or pale yellow and has a long dorsal fin. Length: 3.5ft (106.7cm); weight: 27lb (12.2kg). Family Gadidae; species *Brosme brosme*.

Custard Apple, family of partially evergreen trees native to the Old World and grown in tropical and subtropical America. Leaves are lance-shaped, and yellow flowers produce large, red to brown, heart-shaped fruits with sweet, edible, custard-like pulp. Height: to 30ft (9m). Of the many species *Annona cherimolia*, the cherimoya, is most important. Family Annonaceae. *See also* Papaw.

Custer, George Armstrong (1839–76), US military officer, b. New Rumley, Ohio. He graduated last in his West Point class (1861), but during the Civil War he became a major general in the Union army (1864). He was returned to a lower rank after the war. A striking figure, he went West to fight Indians after the Civil War and was made acting commander of the 7th Cavalry (1866). Court-martialed for disobeying orders, he was suspended from the service for a year (1867). When he returned, he led his men to a decisive victory over the Cheyenne chief Black Kettle at Washita River (1868). In 1876 he was sent to round up hostile Sioux and Cheyenne who were to meet with Sitting Bull. Outmaneuvered by the Indians, he was killed and his command wiped out in the Battle of Little Bighorn.

Custom, in anthropology and sociology, a pattern of habitual behavior characteristic of a particular group of people. For example: eating turkey on the last Thursday of each November is a custom in the United States. Customs are transmitted from generation to generation as the core of a group's culture, but they are not biologically determined and are basically impermanent. Customs tend to be maintained for longer periods in nonindustrial than in industrial societies. When customs are formally established in the religious or moral sphere, they lead to systems of ethics. When formally established as rights or duties, they lead to systems of laws.

Cutaneous Senses. *See* Skin Senses.

Cuthbert (died 760), Archbishop of Canterbury (740–60), whose accomplishments include persuading King Ethelbald to confirm the privilege of the churches of Kent, bringing the conduct of the English church closer to that of the church at Rome, and establishing Christ Church, Canterbury, the burial place of archbishops, and hence the most important church in England.

Cuticle, horny outer layer of skin, popularly the skin around the fingers and toenails. *See also* Epidermis.

Cuttack, city in E India, on Manhanadi delta; capital of Orissa state; under Hindus, Moguls, and Marathas (during 16th and 17th centuries); transportation center with canal network. Industries: steel, glass, paper, flour milling, tobacco. Founded 925. Pop. 194,036.

Cutter, a small, fast-sailing boat with a single mast rigged fore and aft, carrying a mainsail and at least two headsails. Traditionally, the deep and narrow hull has a raking stern, a vertical stem, and a long bowsprit. *See also* Sloop.

Cutting, a piece of a plant used to start a complete new plant of the same kind. Like other methods of vegetative (asexual) propagation, cuttings have the advantage of producing plants that are genetically identical to the parent plants. Cuttings are most commonly taken from young stems, although leaves and pieces

161

of root are used to propagate certain plants. The type of care required depends on the nature of the cutting. Cuttings of woody twigs, including apple and grape, are usually taken during the winter and stored under cool moist conditions until spring, when they are planted in soil to develop the root systems that will enable the cutting to develop into new plants.

Cuttlefish. *See* Squid.

Cutworm, nocturnal moth caterpillar that feeds on plants, often cutting through the stems at ground level. They are dull-colored. Length: to 2in (5cm). Family Noctuidae.

Cuvier, Georges, (Baron de) (1769–1832), French geologist and zoologist, a founder of the disciplines of comparative anatomy and paleontology. His scheme of classification stressed the form of organs and their correlation within the body. He applied this system of classification to fossils and came to reject the theory of the gradual development of the earth and animals, favoring instead a theory of catastrophic changes.

Cuyahoga Falls, city in NE Ohio, on Cuyahoga River, 5mi (8km) N of Akron. Industries: machinery, rubber products, tools, paper products. Inc. 1920. Pop. (1980) 43,710.

Cuza, Alexandru Ioan (1820–73), Romanian ruler, prince of Walachia and Moldavia. After the Russian defeat in the Crimean War, the Turkish sultan recognized Cuza, who was a fairly unknown colonel but had been elected prince in 1859. In 1862 the union of the two principalities was permitted and the resulting entity called Romania. Cuza's domestic reforms included emancipation of the peasantry and establishment of institutions of higher learning. Scandals in Cuza's private life led to his overthrow in 1866.

Cuzco, city in S central Peru, 350mi (564km) SE of Lima; capital of Cuzco dept.; agricultural trade center. Ancient capital of Inca Empire, it is center of archeological research in South America; nearby sites include the fortress of Sacsahuaman, Inca terraces at Pisac, and the Inca city of Machu Picchu. Founded *c.*AD 1100; at height of development (1500) empire extended from Argentina (S) to Colombia (N); fell to Spaniards 1533. Pop. 121,464.

Cyanide, salt or ester of hydrocyanic acid (HCN). They are all intensely poisonous, the most important, sodium cyanide (NaCN), is used in electroplating, the heat treatment of metals, and as an insecticide.

Cybele, in Greek mythology, the goddess of caverns. She personified the earth in its primitive state and was worshiped on the tops of mountains. She exercised dominion over the wild beasts who formed part of her retinue.

Cybernetics, mathematical theory for optimizing control and communication systems originated by the US mathematician Norbert Weiner in 1948. The theory covers a number of disciplines including computers, learning theory, physiology of the nervous system, servomechanisms, automatic control systems, and the theory of communications. It enables comparison to be made between the problems of control, communication, and feedback of information in biological and engineering systems and has been successfully applied to the design of automated factory processes.

Cycad, also called sago-palm, family of primitive, seed-bearing, palmlike shrub and tree; found in tropical and subtropical regions. These plants flourished 125–150 million years ago. Feathery leaves crown a stout, columnar stem. Leaves of most species are poisonous. An edible starch is made from the pith of some. Most of the 90 surviving species are under 20ft (6.1m) tall and include *Dion spinulosum* of the Mexican rain forest and the Cuban corcho *Microcycas calocoma* that produces 2-ft (0.6-m) cones. Family Cycadaceae.

Cyclades (Kikládhes), large island group off S Greece, in S Aegean Sea; dept. of Greece; capital is Hermoupolis. Name was derived from Greek "kyklos," meaning cluster, because the islands encircle island of Delos. During Middle Ages, most of the islands were inc. into the Venetian Duchy of the Archipelago; annexed to Greece 1832. Islands are very mountainous, and rich in mineral deposits. Industries: tourism, mining, agriculture. Area: 993sq mi (2,572sq km). Pop. 86,337.

Cyclamates, white odorless soluble crystalline salts, calcium cyclamate ($(C_6H_{11}NHSO_3)_2(Ca{\cdot}2H_2O)$) and sodium cyclamate ($C_6H_{11}NHSO_3Na$), with a very sweet taste. They have about 30 times the sweetening power of sucrose.

Cyclamen, genus of 20 species of low-growing perennial herbs, native to Central Europe and the Mediterranean region and grown widely by florists. They have tuberous roots, and heart- or kidney-shaped leaves, often marbled or ribbed. The drooping blooms are white, pink, lilac or crimson. Family Primulaceae.

Cycle in electricity, series of changes through which an alternating current passes. Starting from zero it rises through a sine wave to a maximum, declines sinusoidally to zero, declines similarly to a minimum, and climbs back to zero again. The frequency of the current is the number of such cycles in one second. This is measured in hertz (cycles per second).

Cyclone, a system of winds or storm that rotates inward around a center of low atmospheric pressure, counterclockwise in the Northern Hemisphere and clockwise in the Southern Hemisphere, the opposite of anticyclones centered in high-pressure areas. Tropical cyclones, originating near the equator, give rise to hurricanes when strong enough. Although having the same spiral motions, cyclones are distinguished from small-scale systems like tornadoes and waterspouts. *See also* Tornado.

Cyclopropane, colorless gas used as an anesthetic during surgery.

Cyclops, common freshwater predatory copepod crustacean. Transparent and bullet-shaped, it is named for its large median eye. Gravid females carry two large egg sacs. Length: under 1/16in (1.6mm). *See also* Copepod; Crustacean.

Cyclops, various figures in Greek mythology. According to Homer, they were one-eyed cannibal giants in Sicily. In Hesiod, they were Arges, Brontes, and Steropes, the three sons of Heaven and Earth. Cyclops were considered by later authors to be the workmen of Haphaestus, who made the thunderbolt that killed Asclepius.

Cyclostome, or cyclostomata, class of jawless fish including lamprey and hagfish, found in temperate-to-cold waters of Northern and Southern hemispheres at depths of 98.4–3280.8 ft. (30–1000m). These fish have jawless sucking mouths with sharp teeth and no bones, scales, paired fins, or sympathetic nervous systems. Their eellike bodies are supported by cartilage and an unsegmented notochord (skeletal rod). Respiration is through gill pouches. Fertilization is external. There are about 45 species of Cyclostomes.

Cyclotron, earliest field accelerator (1932) in which charged particles describe a spiral path inside two evacuated D-shaped chambers at right angles to a fixed magnetic field. A high-frequency electric field between the chambers accelerates the particles each time they cross the gap, the radius of the path increasing with velocity. The beam is deflected out of the device by a second electric field. Maximum energy is about 25 MeV. *See also* Synchrocyclotron.

Cygnus, the Swan, or the Northern Cross, extensive northern constellation situated between Draco and Pegasus and including five conspicuous stars in the shape of a cross. Cygnus contains the open cluster M39 (NGC 7092) and two important radio sources, Cygnus A and the Cygnus Loop. Brightest star Alpha Cygni (Deneb).

Cygnus Loop, composite bright nebula located in the constellation Cygnus. It is made up of several separately catalogued portions, including the Veil Nebula (NGC 6992/5), and appears as wispy filaments forming roughly circular arcs. The Cygnus Loop is an ancient supernova remnant and a powerful source of radio waves and X rays.

Cylinder, solid figure or surface formed by rotating a rectangle about one side as axis. If the vertical height is h and the radius of the base r, then the volume is $\pi r^2 h$ and the curved surface area $2\pi rh$.

Cylinder, Engine, one of the cylindrical chambers in internal combustion engines. Inside each, a piston is impelled by the pressure of the expansive force of combusting fuel and, in 4-stroke engines, by the recoil of another piston.

Cymbal, saucer-shaped, concave percussion instrument of brass, usually without definite pitch. It is played by clashing together a pair held in both hands, or by striking a suspended cymbal with a beater. Introduced with Turkish martial music (*c.*1750), it is used in symphonic and jazz works.

Cymbeline, or Cunobelinus, (died *c.*AD40), ancient British king. Inheriting the chieftainship of the Catuvellauni from his father, he established his capital at Colchester. Shakespeare used his name but invented his history in *Cymbeline.*

Cymbeline (1610), 5-act play by William Shakespeare. Based on Holinshed's *Chronicles* and Boccaccio's *Decameron,* the play is quasihistorical. King Cymbeline of ancient Britain banishes Posthumus for marrying Cymbeline's daughter Imogen against the king's wishes. Through trickery Posthumus loses a wager on Imogen's fidelity with the crafty Lachimo and sends to have Imogen killed, but she escapes. In the course of Cymbeline's preparations for a war against Rome, the complications of the plot are resolved.

Cymbidium, orchid native to tropical Asia. An epiphyte (grows on other plants), it is generally ivory white or dull purple. There are 70 species and several thousand horticultural hybrids. Among them is *Cymbidium hookerianum,* which has a large green flower with a yellow and purple-spotted large lower petal or lip. Family Orchidaceae.

Cynewulf (*fl.* 800), English poet. Presumed author of *Elene, Fates of the Apostles, The Ascension,* and *Juliana,* because the manuscript of these poems are "signed" *Cynewulf* in runic characters. Internal evidence suggests he was a priest in Mercia or Northumbria in the north of England. Cynewulf's work shows a clarity of narrative unusual in Old English poetry.

Cypress, city in S California, 9mi (14km) NE of Long Beach. Inc. 1956. Pop. (1980) 40,391.

Cypress, evergreen tree native to North America and Eurasia. They have scalelike leaves, roundish cones, a distinctive symmetrical shape, and prefer warmer climates. Height: 20–150ft (6–46m). Family Cupressaceae; genus *Cupressus.*

Cypripedium, or lady's slipper, moccasin flower; orchid found in bogs and swamps of North America, China, and Europe. The lowest petal, or lip, is large, slipperlike, and colored pink, yellow, or white. The leaves are broad and shiny. Species include *Cypripedium acaule,* lady's slipper; *C. reginae,* moccasin flower; and *C. arietinum,* the ram's head. Height: to 3ft (0.9m). Family Orchidaceae.

Cyprus, Republic of, an island nation in the E Mediterranean Sea. The Cypriot population is made up mostly of Greeks (78%) and Turks (18%). The two groups have inhabited the island for centuries, living for the most part under foreign domination. Since independence in 1960, Cyprus has been troubled by internal strife between its Greek and Turkish citizens.

Land and Economy. The Troodos Mts occupy the S and W half of the island. Except for a narrow coastal mountain range in the N, the rest of Cyprus consists of fertile lowlands, sometimes called the Mesaorian Plain. The climate of Cyprus is typical of the Mediterranean area, with mild winters and hot, dry summers. The economy depends for its stability on agriculture, which employs about one-third of the Cypriot work force. Agriculture also supplies raw materials to local industry and accounts for half of all exports. The per capita income of Cyprus is the highest in the E Mediterranean, except for Israel.

People. The Greek Cypriots trace their ancestry back to Mycenaean Greek settlements in the 2nd millennium BC. The ancestors of of the Turkish Cypriots arrived after the Turkish conquest of Cyprus in 1571. Both groups are fiercely exclusive. The Greeks are Christians belonging to the Cyprus Orthodox Church, while the Turks are Muslims. There is no intermarriage and very little socializing between the two groups. Consequently, no sense of national unity or purpose has developed. Many Cypriots speak both Greek and Turkish, and the English language is in widespread use. For both groups, the extended family is the main social unit.

Government. According to the constitution of 1960, power was shared by the Greek and Turkish communities in proportion to their populations. Since 1974, however, each community has maintained a separate government with a president, cabinet, and legislature. Although the Greek government is generally accepted as the legitmate government of all of Cyprus, the separate governments do not recognize each other.

History. For nearly 3,000 years Cyprus has been controlled by the dominant power in the area, from the ancient Phoenicians to the British of modern times. After three centuries of Turkish administration, Cyprus was leased from Turkey by the British in 1878. Great Britain annexed Cyprus at the start of WWI. The Greek Cypriots had for years demanded union with Greece; the campaign increased in violence after WWII. In the 1950s, Greek Cypriot guerrillas carried out attacks on the British military. The governments of Greece and Turkey negotiated a settlement in Zurich in 1959, which was then approved by the British. The republic was est Aug. 16, 1960. Intercommunal fighting broke out

Cyclops

Cyprus

Czechoslovakia

sporadically in the 1960s. UN troops were installed in 1964; however, severe conflicts followed when Greece injected troops of its own in 1967. Tension abated as Greece and Turkey reconciled differences, but Turkey then invaded the island in 1974. The action was condemned internationally, but Turkish forces remained on the island, ostensibly to protect the Turkish minority and a UN peace-keeping force is also on the island. UN-sponsored talks between representatives of both sides have made little progress.

PROFILE

Official name: Republic of Cyprus
Area: 3,572sq mi (9,251sq km)
Population: 650,000
  Density: 182per sq mi (70per sq km)
Chief cities: Nicosia (capital); Limassol; Famagusta
Government: Republic
Religion: Eastern Orthodox, Muslim
Language: Greek and Turkish (both official)
Monetary unit: Cyprus pound
Gross national product: $1,920,000,000
Per capita income (1971): $2600
Industries (major products): cotton, rayon, shoes, soap
Agriculture (major products): wheat, barley, potatoes, citrus fruit
Minerals (major): iron pyrites, asbestos, copper
Trading partners (major): United Kingdom, Greece, Italy

Cyrano de Bergerac, Savinien (1619–55), French writer. He became renowned for his free thinking, humor, and burlesque romances. His works included two prose fantasies, *Journey to the Moon* (1656) and *The Comical Tale of the States and Empires of the Sun* (1662), published posthumously. He was the model for Edmond Rostand's Cyrano.

Cyrano de Bergerac (1897), 5-act drama by Edmond Rostand. First performed in Paris, it remains popular today and has been made into a film (1950) and a TV play (1975). Cyrano, afflicted with an enormous nose, writes love letters to Roxane for his handsome friend Christian, although he loves her himself. When Christian is killed in battle, Roxane enters a convent. She finds out about Cyrano's love for her years later on the day he is killed by an enemy.

Cyrenaica (Barqah), easternmost section of Libya, formerly a province (1951–63); colonized by the Greeks 7th century BC and taken by Rome 96 BC, it formed part of the Ottoman Empire after 16th century; was colonized by Italians in 1930s; scene of many WWII battles. Industries: oil, citrus fruit, sheep and goat raising. Area: 330,258sq mi (855,368sq km). Pop. 350,024.

Cyrenaic School, a school of hedonistic philosophy founded by Aristippus (*fl.* late 4th and early 3rd century BC). Maintaining that happiness lies not in slavery to, but in mastery over, pleasure, this school disappeared before the advance of Epicureanism.

Cyrene, in Greek mythology, queen of Cyrene, mother by Apollo of Aristaeus and Idmon. Apollo fell in love with Cyrene when he saw her wrestle a lion that had attacked her father's flock. She was also the mother by Ares of Diomedes and Thrace.

Cyrene (Shahhat), ancient city in NE Libya, 6mi (10km) from Marsa Susa; founded 630 BC under the Greek dynasty of Battus I as the capital of Cyrenaica; annexed to Persian Empire 525 BC, to Egypt 322 BC, and to Rome 96 BC; conquered by Arabs AD 642. Lib-

yan excavations have uncovered many ruins, notably the temples of Apollo and Zeus. Pop. 6,266.

Cyrillic Alphabet, an alphabet developed in the 9th century for writing Old Church Slavonic and currently used for writing Russian and several other Slavic languages. The modern Cyrillic alphabet uses between 30 and 33 letters, depending on the language. The alphabet is based on the Greek uncial script of the 9th century, reputedly adapted by St. Cyril (d. 869) and St. Methodius (d. 885), "Apostles of the Slavs."

Cyrus the Great, (*c.*600–529 BC), king of Persia, founder of the Achaemenid dynasty and the Persian empire. He took over Media, defeated and captured king Croesus of Lydia (c 546 BC), and captured Babylon (538 BC) and the Greek cities in Asia Minor. He delivered the Jews from their captivity, giving them Palestine to rule. He failed to conquer Egypt under Amasis II. In the Bible, he is called God's appointed servant (Isaiah 40–48). While fighting the Massagets, a tribe northwest of the Caspian, he was defeated and killed. His son, Cambyses, succeeded him.

Cyrus the Younger (*c.*424–401 BC), Persian satrap, son of Darius II. After plotting unsuccessfully to kill his brother Artaxerxes II, king of Persia, he hired Greek mercenaries, who helped him defeat the king at Cunaxa. Cyrus, however, died in battle. The retreat of the Ten Thousand (mercenaries) under Clearchus, Spartan ruler of Byzantium, is told in Xenophon's *Anabasis.*

Cyst, abnormal growth in the form of a sac that contains solid or liquid material produced by the cells in the walls of the sac. It may occur in a glandular organ, such as breast or prostate, or in the skin.

Cysteine, crystalline amino acid (formula $HS \cdot CH_2 \cdot NH_2 \cdot COOH$) that occurs in most proteins. *See* Amino Acid.

Cystic Fibrosis, hereditary disease, first appearing in childhood, in which the body produces abnormally thick mucus that often obstructs the breathing passages, causing chronic lung disease. There is also a deficiency of pancreatic enzymes and an abnormally high salt concentration in the sweat. There is no cure; the disease is treated with antibiotics, salt replacement, and special diet to reduce the need for pancreatic enzymes, but is often fatal in childhood.

Cystitis, acute or chronic infection of the urinary bladder, more common in women, usually caused by bacteria. Symptoms include frequency of urination, burning during and after voiding, difficulty in voiding, low back pain, and slight fever. Treatment consists of antibiotics and increased fluid intake.

Cytology, biological study of living cells, including structure, function, and significance.

Cytoplasm, jellylike, non-particulate matter within a cell membrane, exclusive of the nucleus. *See also* Cell.

Cytosine, a base (nonacid) that is one of the components of deoxyribonucleic and ribonucleic acid (DNA, RNA).

Czartoryski, Adam Jerzy (1770–1861), Polish political figure, the most renowned member of his prominent family. Seeking the restoration of his family's property confiscated in an insurrection against Russia (1794), he became an adviser to the future Czar Alexander I (r.1801–25), with whom he later became disillusioned.

He was deputy foreign minister of Russia (1802–04), foreign minister (1804–06), Polish spokesman at the Congress of Vienna (1815), and member of the executive council (1815–30). He became president of the revolutionary government of Poland during the insurrection of 1830 and went into exile in Paris in 1831 after the suppression of the revolt by the Russians. His residence was the political center of Polish exiles until his death.

Czartoryski, Adam Kazimierz (1734–1823), Polish nobleman. The son of Fryderyk Michal Czartoryski, he became a publisher and minister of education for Poland—the first such minister in the world—and made his palace at Pulawy a center of cultural life. His son was Adam Jerzy Czartoryski.

Czech, language spoken in the western and central two-thirds of Czechoslovakia—the areas known as Bohemia and Moravia—by about 10 million people. A Slavic language, it is closely related to Slovak, spoken in the eastern third of the country.

Czechoslovakia, nation in central Europe, member of the Communist Bloc. The country was formed in 1918 of the former Austro-Hungarian provinces of Bohemia, Moravia, Slovakia, and Ruthenia. The Czechs occupy the W area, Bohemia and Moravia, while the Slovaks inhabit the E. The two ethnic groups, the Czechs and Slovaks, were united with the formation of the Czechoslovak Republic.

Land and Economy. The historic province of Bohemia is a fertile plain nearly encircled by the Ore Mts and the Moravian Hills. Prague lies in the center of this important region. Moravia, also in the W, is a fertile lowland area extending to the Carpathian Mts of Slovakia. The country's industry is well-developed, and employs about 60% of the entire work force. Heavy industry is dominant, as in the production of iron and steel, heavy machinery, and motor vehicles. All industry is nationalized. Prague has an international airport. Bratislava, the capital of Slovakia, has developed as a port on the Danube River. Czechoslovakia is the most prosperous country in E Europe.

People. The population is about 65% Czech and the rest Slovak. The Czech and Slovak languages have separate cultural histories and literatures but are mutually intelligible. The language is Slavonic. More than 80% of the population of the country is Roman Catholic, although the Communist regime confiscated church property in 1949, and subsequently discouraged all church activities. The majority of Czechoslovaks today still live in small communities.

Government. Czechoslovakia is a country composed of two constituent republics, each with separate governments for internal affairs. The national constitution of 1960 provides for a legislature, the National Assembly, elected by the people. The president of the republic is chosen by the assembly, and in turn appoints the premier and his cabinet. The entire government, however, is controlled by the Communist party through its large central committee and 21-member presidium.

History. The Slavs who settled the land in the AD 5th century developed the Moravian empire. Slovakia was conquered AD 900 and ruled by the Magyars (Hungarians) for 1,000 years. Bohemia was a kingdom within the Holy Roman Empire, and later the Austrian Empire. Czech nationalism developed in the 19th century. When Austria-Hungary collapsed in 1918, Czechoslovakia was established as an independent country with T. G. Masaryk as president. In 1938–39, Britain and France permitted Nazi Germany to seize the country. Eduard Beneš returned with his government-in-exile in 1945 when the Allied armies liberated Czechoslovakia. The Communist party gained control in

1948. The government took over all phases of Czech life—farming, business, industry, churches, and schools. Under Alexander Dubček, the government introduced a series of liberal anti-Soviet reforms in 1968. The Soviet Union and its allies—Poland, East Germany, Hungary, and Bulgaria—interfered militarily and ousted Dubček. He was replaced by Gustav Husak, who ended political liberalization, and maintained good relations with the Soviet Union and curbed dissident activity.

PROFILE

Official name: Czechoslovak Socialist Republic
Area: 49,365sq mi (127,855sq km)
Population: 15,238,000
Density: 309per sq mi (119per sq km)
Chief cities: Prague (capital); Brno; Bratislava
Government: Communist
Religion: Roman Catholic 65%; Protestant 35%
Language: Czech, Slovak, Hungarian
Monetary unit: Koruna
Gross national product: $80,530,000,000.
Industries (major products): machinery, chemicals, textiles, military equipment
Agriculture (major products): wheat, barley, potatoes, sugar beets
Minerals (major): coal, iron ore, graphite, copper
Trading partners (major): Soviet Union, East Germany, Poland, West Germany

Czestochowa, city in S Poland, on Warta River, approx. 125mi (201km) SW of Warsaw; site of ancient monastery on Jasna Gosa (Mountain of Light) containing image of the Virgin painted by St Luke (14th century), which was successfully defended against Sweden (1655, 1702) and became a symbol of national strength and unity. City was taken by Germany in WWI and WWII. Industries: iron works, textiles, paper mills. Pop. 200,000.

Czolgosz, Leon (1873–1901), US anarchist, b. Detroit, Mich. He shot and mortally wounded President McKinley (Sept. 6, 1901) at the Pan-American Exposition in Buffalo, N.Y. Czolgosz was immediately apprehended and later executed.

D

Dacca, port city and capital of Bangladesh, 80mi (129km) NE of Khulna, just W of Meghna River; scene of Pakistani surrender to Indian troops in 1971; location of University of Dacca and University of Engineering and Technology. Industries: jute, carpets, boatbuilding, textiles, soap, rubber goods, jewelry. Pop. 1,310,972.

Dace, freshwater fish found in S and E United States. A minnow with a large head and mouth, its sides are marked with a red stripe bordered by two darker stripes. Length: to 11.8in (30cm). Family Cyprinidae; genera include *Phoxinus, Chrosomus,* and *Leuciscus.*

Dachau, town in Bavaria, West Germany, on the Amper River, NNW of Munich. Varied industries and artists' colony; site of concentration camp established by Nazis (1933), infamous for its brutality: liberated by the Allies on April 29, 1945: 32,000 prisoners freed. Memorial chapels and museum opened in 1960s. Pop. 33,100.

Dachshund, German hunting dog (hound group) used to follow badgers to earth; one of the most popular breeds. Its head is tapered and long; rounded, hanging ears are set near the top of the head. The long body is set on short legs; a medium-long tail is carried in line with the back. There are three varieties of coat: short-haired, wire-haired, and long-haired; colors include solid red; black, chocolate, gray, or white with tan marks; and dappled. Average size: 5-9in (13–23cm) high at shoulder; 5–20lb (2–9kg). *See also* Hound.

Dacia, ancient kingdom comprising the heartland of present-day Romania. King Decebalus of Dacia heroically fought off the Romans until defeated by Trajan in 106. Roads, bridges, and a great wall were built by the Romans, who evacuated the province in 270 when faced by barbarian invasions. Latin speech was preserved, however. While the area was under Bulgarian rule, Christianity was introduced during the 9th century.

Dacron, man-made, long-chain polyester fiber made from glycol and terephthalic acid. It has high elastic recovery and low moisture absorption and is not combustible, but melts at about 500°F (260°C). Used extensively in rope and in permanent-press fabrics, *See also* polyester.

Dada or **Dadaism,** movement in literature and the visual arts, which was started in Zurich in 1916 by a group of international artists, including Tristan Tzara, Marcel Janco, Richard Huelsenbeck, Hugo Ball, Jean (Hans) Arp, and others. The group, repelled by war and bored with the prevalent cubist art styles, promulgated complete nihilism, satire, and disgust with and ridicule of civilization. Emphasis was given to the illogical or absurd, and the importance of chance in artistic creation was exaggerated. Adherents of the movement participated in antisocial behavior designed to shock a complacent public. No specific artistic style evolved, but Arp tried to develop the cubist techniques of montage and collage.

Daddy-longlegs. *See* Harvestman.

Daedalus, in Greek mythology, architect and sculptor. In order to escape from King Minos' disfavor, Daedalus made wings of feathers and wax for himself and his son Icarus. Icarus' wings melted when he flew too close to the sun. He fell into the Icarian sea and drowned.

Daffodil. *See* Narcissus.

Daguerre, Louis Jacques Mandé (1787–1851), French painter and inventor of daguerreotypy, an early process whereby a delicate photographic image is produced on a silver-coated copper plate developed with iodine vapor. A painter of stage sets, in 1829 he joined Nicéphore Niepce in photographic experiments. Their process was announced and ceded to the public in 1839 at the same time that William Fox Talbot announced calotypy in England.

Dahlia, genus of popular, late-blooming, tender, tuberous-rooted perennial plants, native to mountainous areas of Mexico and Guatemala. They range from low-growing dwarfs to "trees" more than 20ft (6m) tall. The common or garden dahlia *(D. pinnata)* has been developed into more than 2,000 varieties with a wide range of flower head forms—usually white, yellow, red, purple, or bicolored. Height: 4–5ft (1.2–1.5m). Family Compositae.

Dahomey, nation in W Africa. *See* Benin.

Dairy Cattle, varieties or breeds of domesticated cattle raised mainly for milk production. Cows have large udders and convert most of their food into milk far in excess of that needed for nursing calves. Farmers wean calves a few days after birth; females are raised as replacement stock, most males butchered for meat. Dairy breeds are specialized to produce either a great volume of milk or milk rich in butterfat. The most common dairy breeds are: Holstein, Jersey, Guernsey, Ayrshire, and Brown Swiss. Family Bovidae; species *Bos taurus. See also* Cattle; Dairy Farming.

Dairy Farming, production of milk and its products. Through management of dairy cows and cultivation of feed crops, an efficient kind of farming is carried on, with manure replacing nutrients taken from soil by food crops. Modern dairying with cows fed from silage reduces the seasonal aspects. US dairy breeds include Holstein, Guernsey, Jersey, Ayrshire, Brown Swiss, and Shorthorn.

Daisy, any of several members of the compositae family, especially the oxeye daisy *(Chrysanthemum leucanthemum),* a hardy Eurasian perennial widely naturalized in North America. It has 2in (5cm) flowers with yellow central disks and white ray flowers. Height: 1–3ft (31–92cm).

Dakar, capital and largest city in Senegal, W Africa, on S tip of Cape Vert, on Atlantic coast; grew rapidly after the completion of railroad leading to Senegal River 1855; site of Roman Catholic cathedral and presidential palace; a modern city with excellent educational and medical facilities, including Pasteur Institute. Industries: peanut oil, sugar refining, fertilizers, cement. Founded 1857 as French fort; named capital of Senegal 1958. Pop. 600,000.

Dakota Indians, more commonly known as Sioux, North American Indian tribe now inhabiting the northern plains, mainly North and South Dakota, and eastern Montana, where they migrated from Minnesota, Wisconsin, and Iowa. The tribe has three major divisions: the Santee Dakota, Yankton Dakota, and Teton Dakota. They were noted for their military prowess, and were one of the largest tribes of Indians. Their culture is regarded as the typical "Indian" form in the United States. The present population is approximately 40,000 Sioux living in United States, plus another 5,000 in Canada.

Daladier, Edouard (1884–1970), French statesman, Radical party leader, and minister of war. Prime minister in 1933, 1934, and in 1938–40, he signed the Munich pact in 1938 and declared war on Germany a year later. Impounded by the Vichy government and deported to Germany, he later opposed the Indochina war.

Dalai Lama, ruler of the Yellow Hat sect of Tibetan Buddhism. The Grand Lama of the Yellow Hat monastery at Lhasa was given the title Dalai, meaning "ocean" or "measureless," in the 16th century. The spiritual as well as temporal leader of his people, he was thought to be an incarnation of Avalokita, the Mahayana Bodhista of compassion and mercy. *See also* Lama; Lamaism.

Daley, Richard Joseph (1902–76), US political figure, b. Chicago. He served as mayor of Chicago (1955–76). He figured prominently in national politics in 1960 when he brought Chicago into the Democratic column in a close election and in 1968 when he stamped out protest demonstrations during the presidential convention.

Dalhousie, James Andrew Broun Ramsay, Marquis of (1812–60), British administrator. Also Lord Ramsay upon the death of his brother, he was governor-general of India (1847–56). In addition to acquiring territories such as Punjab, Jhansi, and Nagpur, he expanded the railroad, roads, and telegraph; developed trade and agriculture; and opened irrigation works. As president of the British Board of Trade (1845), he established regulations for the railroad system.

Dali, Salvador (1904–), Spanish artist whose achievements have been attended by enormous personal publicity. His style, a blend of meticulous realism and hallucinatory transformations of form and space, made him an influential Surrealist. His paintings are in major Western museums. Dali has also designed jewelry, fabrics, furniture, and stage decor. He collaborated on *Le Chien Andalou,* a classic film. A noted book illustrator, he has also written two autobiographies.

Dallas, city in NE Texas, the state's second largest city, and the Southwest's leading commercial, financial, and transportation center; seat of Dallas co. Dallas-Fort Worth Regional Airport, opened 1974, is the world's largest commercial airport. City is headquarters of many major US oil firms; three-fourths of all known US oil reserves are located within 500mi (805km) of Dallas. The Big D, as local residents call it, is also noted as a fashion center.

Cotton, cattle, and oil spurred the city's growth since it was first settled in the 1840s. Discovery of the giant East Texas Oil Field in 1930 led to further expansion. While on a visit to Dallas on Nov. 22, 1963, President John F. Kennedy was assassinated. Today the city is one of the fastest growing in the nation. Major schools: Southern Methodist University; University of Dallas; University of Texas, Dallas. Industries: oil refining, women's clothing, aircraft, missile parts, electronic equipment, cotton-processing machinery.

Dallas has several noted museums and cultural institutions, including the Dallas Theater Center, designed by Frank Lloyd Wright. The city boasts professional football, basketball, and baseball teams. Its famed Cotton Bowl stadium features a playoff between two top college football teams each New Year's Day. Inc. 1856 as town, 1871 as city. Pop. (1980) 904,078.

Dalling and Bulwer, William Henry Lytton Earle Bulwer, Baron (1801–72), English author and diplomat. He served in the army, various embassies, and parliament. He was one of the signers of the Clayton-Bulwer treaty (1850), which paved the way for international agreements establishing a Central American canal. This occurred while he was ambassador to the United States. His writings include *An Autumn in Greece* (1826), *France: Social, Literary, and Political* (1834–36), *Historical Characters* (1867), and *Lord Byron* (1835).

Dalmatia, region of Yugoslavia, between Bosnia and Herzegovina and Adriatic Sea. An important Roman province 1st–5th centuries, it became part of Byzantine Empire 6th century; taken by the Hapsburg Empire 1815; after WWII, became part of the federal republic of Croatia under Yugoslav government. Industries: shipbuilding, fishing, textiles, chemicals, wine, olive oil. Area: 4,916sq mi (12,732sq km).

Dalmatian, versatile, ancient breed of dog (nonsporting group) and only coaching dog; best known as firehouse, English coach, or Plum-pudding dog. It has a long, flat-skulled head with long muzzle; dark, golden, or blue eyes; high-set, thin ears close to the head; powerful body; strong legs; and long, tapered, curved tail. Its distinctive short, hard coat has a pure white ground with small black or liver spots. Average size:

Dalmatian

John Dalton

Dandie Dinmont terrier

19–23in (48–58cm) high at shoulder; 35–50lb (16–22.5kg).

Dalton, Hugh, Baron Dalton of Forest and Frith (1887–1962), English statesman. A Labour member of Parliament from 1924, he nationalized the Bank of England while he was chancellor of the exchequer (1945–47). He also was undersecretary in the foreign office (1929–31), minister of economic warfare (1940–42), president of the board of trade (1942–45), and minister of town and country planning (1950). He was the author of *Call Back Yesterday* (1953) and *High Tide and After* (1962).

Dalton, John (1766–1844), English chemist and physicist and one of the fathers of modern physical science. His early interest in meteorology yielded important information on the trade winds, the cause of rain, and the Aurora Borealis. He described color blindness (sometimes called Daltonism) based on his own experiences and those of his brother. His study of gases led to Dalton's law of partial pressures (the sum of the pressure of each gas equals the total pressure of a mixture of these gases), and to his idea that as temperature rises, gases expand. His atomic theory states that each element is made up of indestructible, identical, small particles, and he constructed an atomic weights table.

Dalton's Law, the statement that the pressure exerted by each gas in a mixture of gases does not depend on the pressures of the other gases, provided no chemical reaction occurs.

Daly City, city in W California, suburb of San Francisco; est. 1906 by homeless victims of the San Francisco earthquake. Inc. 1911. Pop. (1980) 78,519.

Dam, Henrik (1895–1976), Danish biologist who shared (with E.H. Doisy) the 1943 Nobel Prize in physiology or medicine for his discovery of vitamin K, the fat-soluble vitamin needed for blood clotting.

Dam, a barrier built across a stream, river, estuary, or section of ocean to confine or check the flow of water for irrigation, flood control or power generation. Dams date back at least as far as the Egyptian civilization of 3500 years ago. Common types are gravity, arch, buttress, and embankment dams. The highest dam is the USSR's Nurek, 1030 ft (314m) high. The Fort Peck Dam in Montana has a record volume of 125,000,000 cu yd (95,000,000 cu m).

Damanhur, city in N Egypt, in Nile River delta, 37mi (59km) ESE of Alexandria; site of ancient city of Hermopolis Parva; communications center and cotton market. Pop. 161,400.

Damascus (Dimasho, or Ash Sham), capital and largest city of Syria, in SW Syria on the Barada River E of the Anti-Lebanon Mts; administrative, financial, and communications center; site of the Citadel (originally Roman, rebuilt 13th century), Umayyad Mosque (8th century), church of St John the Baptist (4th century), several mosques, Syrian University (1923), National Museum. Inhabited since prehistoric times, it is believed to be the oldest continuously occupied city in the world. An ancient Egyptian and Biblical city; became independent Aramaean Kingdom c. 1000 BC; occupied by Babylonians, Persians, Greeks, and Romans; scene of many battles during Crusades; under Ottoman Turks (1516–1918) until occupied by British and taken by French (1920) and made part of French mandate of Syria; made capital of Syria 1961. Industries: textiles (damask fabrics), glass, sugar, cement, furniture. Pop. 936,567.

Damasus I, Roman Catholic pope (366–84), and saint, born in Spain. His election was challenged by the Arian Ursinus who was elected antipope. Both were consecrated by bishops and two factions developed. Eventually Emperor Valentian I expelled Ursinus. Damasus asserted that a pope could be tried by only ecclesiastical courts. Under him, Jerome produced a revised Latin Bible.

Damavand (Demavend), volcanic mountain peak in N Iran, 35mi (56km) NE of Tehran; highest point in Iran, 18,934ft (5,775m); rich in mineral deposits, especially sulfur.

Damocles, in Greek mythology, a courtier of Dionysius of Syracuse (Sicily). His eulogies of Dionysius made him a well-known figure at court. At a banquet, Damocles noticed a sword hanging by a fragile thread above his head. He was thus made to realize that the wealth and power he coveted did not bring happiness and might well be ephemeral.

Damon and Pythias, models of friendship in Roman legend. The legend is based on Pythias' plotting against the tyrant Dionysius of Syracuse (c.430–367 BC). He was condemned to death, but Damon agreed to take his place until the day of his execution so Pythias could return home to settle his affairs. He returned on the day of his execution, and Dionysius was so impressed with the loyalty of the two that he pardoned Pythias.

Dampier, William (1652–1715), English navigator and buccaneer. An adventurous early career included a buccaneering expedition against Spanish America and a trip across the Pacific, after which he was marooned. Sent by England in 1699 to explore the South Seas, he explored the coasts of Australia, discovered New Guinea and gave his name to Dampier Archipelago and Dampier Strait. He later piloted two commercial voyages, one which marooned Alexander Selkirk.

Damping-Off, a fungus disease of seeds or seedling plants. In the most striking form—postemergence damping-off—young seedlings topple over as a result of stem rot at the soil line. Damping-off fungi may also invade a seed before it sprouts (germination failure) or attack a seedling before it reaches the soil surface (preemergence damping-off).

Damselfish, any of 250 species of small marine fishes, found mostly in the tropical waters of the Atlantic and Indo-Pacific oceans. To 6in (15cm) long, brilliantly colored, deep-bodied, usually with a forked tail. Unlike most fish, it has a single nostril on each side. Family Pomacentridae.

Dan, in Genesis, fifth son of Jacob, born to Bilhah. His tribe settled north of Judah near the Mediterranean Sea.

Dana, Richard Henry (1815–82), US author, b. Cambridge, Mass. He shipped as a common sailor on the brig *Pilgrim* (1834) around Cape Horn to California and back. From that experience came *Two Years Before the Mast* (1840), a classic in American literature of the sea. One of the founders of the Free Soil party, he later became active in the Republican party.

Danaë, in Greek mythology, the daughter of Acrisius. She was the mother by Zeus of Perseus, who killed his grandfather and the Gorgon.

Da-nang, formerly Tourane; one of chief cities of Vietnam; contains port on S China Sea; commercial shipping, rail connections, airport, copper, gold, and coal deposits are nearby. First European settlers landed at Da-Nang Bay 1535; it was ceded to France by Annam 1787; site of huge US military base during Vietnam War. Pop. 500,000.

Danbury, city in SW Connecticut, 20mi (32km) NW of Bridgeport, in Fairfield co. Industries: hats, electronics. Settled 1685; inc. 1889. Pop. (1980) 60,470.

Danbury Hatters' Case (Loewe v. Lawlor), brought before the US Supreme Court in 1908 by D.E. Loewe and Co. of Danbury, Ct., who sued the local union of the United Hatters of North America for calling a nationwide boycott. The Supreme Court, citing provisions of the Sherman Anti-Trust Act outlawing secondary boycotts, decided in favor of the plaintiff. Members of the local union were fined $250,000.

Danby, Thomas Osborne, Earl of, (1631–1712), (subsequently Marquess of Carmarthen, Duke of Leeds), English Tory politican. He achieved high office through patronage and financial ability, becoming Charles II's treasurer and chief minister (1673–78). He built up an Anglican court party in Parliament, but was imprisoned (1679–84). Danby organized Tory support for William and Mary; he helped them gain Britain's crown and became their chief minister (1690–95).

Dance, English word derived from Old High German *danson,* to drag or stretch. Dancing is the art of ordered body movements coupled with leaps and measured steps that dates back to the beginning of man. The dancer moves through a predetermined space to the accompaniment of musical instruments or voice. From early man to the present, dance has been a means to communicate emotions, rituals, entertainment, or as a form of popular expression.

Dance of Death, macabre gyrations of the risen dead. In the Middle Ages popular belief had it that the dead rose up at night to dance over their graves to lure the curious and unsuspecting near and to dance them to their death. This superstition was reinforced with stylized dance pageants, paintings, and illustrations depicting the dance and its equalizing nature.

Dandelion, hardy, yellow-flowered, Eurasian perennial plant widely established as a lawn weed in North America. Its deeply notched leaves are sometimes gathered, or specially grown, for salad or cooked greens. The flower heads are occasionally used in making wine. Family Compositae; species *Taraxacum officinale.*

Dandie Dinmont Terrier, Scots hunting dog (terrier group). Purebred since 1700, its name is from a character in Sir Walter Scott's *Guy Mannering* (1815). The Dandie's massive skull is topped by a distinctive topknot. Large eyes are hazel; ears hanging. Its long body has a downward curve in the back; the legs are short; and the 8–10in tail (20.3–25.4cm) is curved up. Its pepper or mustard-colored coat is hard but not wiry and about 2in (5cm) long. Average size: 8–11in (20.3–28cm) high at shoulder; 18–24lb (8–11kg). *See also* Terrier.

Dandolo Family, Venetian family that became rich and powerful by the 11th century, was at its height in the 12th–14th centuries, and held high offices in Venetian government until the fall of the republic. Prominent members included **Enrico** (c.1108–1205), doge of Venice who took Constantinople in 1204; **Giovanni** (doge, 1280–89); **Francesco** (doge, 1328–39); and the last Dandolo doge **Andrea** (doge, 1343–54), who joined the crusade against the Turks (1343–46) and also fought Genoa (1348–54).

Dandruff, dead scalp skin that appears as white or yellowish flakes in the hair. It is made noticeable by oiliness and dense growth of hair, and is sometimes increased by inflammation, commonly seborrheic dermatitis.

Danegeld, land tax levied in medieval England. Originally levied (991) to buy off Danish raiders, the tax was continued until 1162, largely as a source of royal revenue.

Danelaw, areas of northern and eastern England in the early Middle Ages in which Scandinavian customary law prevailed. In the 9th century land between the Thames and Tees rivers was overrun and settled by Danes who had their own legal code, different from Anglo-Saxon law. The Danelaw persisted for several centuries; it had a large free peasantry.

Daniel, biblical prophet and book bearing his name. The book, probably written in the 2nd century BC, relates events in Daniel's life (6th century BC) during Babylonian captivity and his visions. Daniel interprets Nebuchadnezzar's dreams, reads the handwriting on the wall at Belshazzar's feast, and escapes from the lion's den. This book is an early example of apocalyptic literature.

Danish, the official language of Denmark, spoken by virtually all of the country's 5,000,000 inhabitants, and also in Greenland and the Faroe Islands. A Germanic language, it is very similar to Norwegian and is also intelligible to speakers of Swedish.

D'Annunzio, Gabriele (1863–1938), Italian poet, novelist, and playwright. His flamboyant rhetoric greatly influenced Italian poetry of the early 20th century. His poems include *Alcyone* (1904) and his best-known novels are *The Triumph of Death* (1896) and *The Child of Pleasure* (1898). In the novel *The Flame of Life* (1900), he portrayed his mistress, the actress Eleonora Duse. He became a national hero when he seized and ruled Fiume (Trieste) from 1919 to 1921.

Danse Macabre. *See* Dance of Death.

Dante Alighieri (1265–1321), Italian poet famous for the *Divine Comedy,* written in terza rima. Orphaned in adolescence, he married Gemma Donati. He became one of the rulers of the city-state of Florence, and was responsible for the exile of his brother-in-law and that of his best friend, Guido Cavalcanti. Later, Dante was exiled and wrote his inspired and majestic works under the patronage of various nobles until he died in poverty in Ravenna. Other works include *La Vita nuova* (The New Life), Convivio (Banquet), *De monarchia* (On Monarchy), and *De Vulgare eloquentia,* a treatise appealing for the use of the vernacular in literature. *See also* Cavalcanti, Guido; *Divine Comedy; Terza Rima.*

Danton, Georges Jacques (1759–94), French statesman and controversial official of the revolution. He played the role of moderate in the turbulent 1790s, seeking conciliation between the Girondists and Montagnards. Leader of the Jacobins (1793) and a member of the Committee of Public Safety, he was arrested during the Reign of Terror and guillotined, an act that began the fall of the Revolutionary government.

Dantonists, followers of Georges Jacques Danton (1759–94), one of the leaders of the French Revolution. Danton was briefly head of state of the new Republic but came to fear the excesses of the Reign of Terror, during which he was imprisoned and guillotined.

Danube River, second-longest European river; rises in Black Forest of W Germany, flows NE then SE, entering Austria at Passau; continues, forming border between Czechoslovakia and Hungary, flows S into Yugoslavia, then SE and E to form part of Romania-Bulgaria boundary; continues N across SE Romania and E into the Black Sea. It was made an international waterway by Treaty of Versailles (1919), and is presently under control of the Danube Commission, headquartered in Budapest, Hungary. Length: approx. 1,776mi (2,859m).

Danville, city in E Illinois, 120mi (193km) S of Chicago; seat of Vermilion co; former site of a Kickapoo Indian village. Industries: agriculture (corn and soybeans), trading stamps, coal mining. Inc. 1869. Pop. 42,570.

Danville, city in S central Virginia, on Dan River; used as a Confederate military complex during Civil War; site of Sutherlin Mansion; large textile industry. Founded 1793; inc. 1870. Pop. (1980) 45,642.

Daphne, a nymph in Greek mythology. Apollo, struck by one of Eros' gold-tipped arrows, fell in love with Daphne. Daphne, however, shot with one of Eros' leaden-points, scorned all men. To protect her from Apollo, the gods transformed Daphne into a laurel tree. Thereafter, Apollo wore a laurel branch on his head as a symbol of his love and grief.

Daphnia, or water flea, minute, flea-shaped crustacean living in freshwater worldwide. It has four to six pairs of legs and is an important food source for aquatic life. Length: to 0.12in (3mm). Order Branchipoda; group Cladocera.

Daphnis, in Greek mythology, the inventor of pastoral poetry. The son of Hermes (Mercury) and a nymph, Daphnis was taught by Pan to be a minstrel to Apollo. Daphnis pledged his love to the jealous nymph Nomeia, but was seduced by the nymph Chimaera. Nomeia blinded him for his unfaithfulness.

Dardanelles, narrow strait separating NW Turkey and Gallipoli Peninsula. Ancient name was Hellespont; scene of crossing of Xerxes I (480 BC) and Alexander the Great (334 BC); site of Allied campaign WWI (1915). With the Bosporus Strait, Dardanelles creates a water route from the Black Sea through Sea of Marmara to Aegean Sea; it is the only passage to Mediterranean Sea for Russian fleet. Length: 38mi (61km). Width: 1–4mi (2–6km). *See also* Bosporus.

Dardanus, son of Zeus and Electra and ancestor of the Trojans. Dardanus, according to Greek legend, married Bateia, the daughter of Teucer, the first king of Troy. He succeeded Teucer and applied the name Dardania to the entire region. Dardanus placed the Palladium, an image sacred to the goddess Athena, in Troy; Athena, in gratitude, protected the state from its enemies.

Dare, Virginia (1587–?), first English child born in America, in the Roanoke Island Colony. The granddaughter of Roanoke Gov. John White, she disappeared after an Indian attack. Her fate, and that of the rest of the colony, are unknown. *See also* Roanoke Island Colony.

Dar Es Salaam (Daressalam), capital city of Tanzania, in central E Tanzania, on shore of Indian Ocean, S of Zanzibar Channel; major commercial, industrial, and administrative center of Tanzania; site of several colleges. Industries: textiles, clothing, building materials, oil. Exports: agricultural products, diamonds, minerals. Founded 1862 by sultan of Zanzibar. Pop. 430,000.

Darien, the first important Spanish settlement in Central America, founded in 1509. The region, modern Panama, was the principal base for the exploration of the mainland between 1511 and 1519.

Darío, Rubén (1867–1916), Nicaraguan poet. The father of the *Modernista* movement, he exerted a liberating influence on Latin American writers. His poems embraced many subjects, including doubts and loss of faith, the struggle to find harmony in contradictions, and the exotic. His finest book of verse, *Songs of Life and Hope* (1905), is noted for its universality and eloquence. He is regarded by many as the most outstanding poet who ever wrote in Spanish.

Darius I, called "the Great" (c.558–486 BC), Achamenid king of Persia. Troubled by revolts, particularly in Babylon, he restored order by dividing the empire into provinces, allowing some local autonomy and tolerating religious diversity. He also fixed an annual taxation, developed commerce, campaigned to consolidate his frontiers, built roads, and connected the Nile to the Red Sea by canal. His desire to punish the Greeks for their part in the Ionian revolt (499–494) led to his defeat at Marathon in 490.

Dark Adaptation, shift in functional dominance from cone cells to rod cells in the retina as overall illumination is reduced. The complete process takes 35–40 minutes. Thus humans find it difficult to see when they enter a dark room but experience improved vision with time. *See also* Vision.

Dark Ages, term frequently used to describe the period of European history between the fall of Rome (*c.* 395–410) and the Norman Conquest in England (1066) or the reign of Charlemagne in France (*c.*800). The term has become somewhat obsolete as scholars learn more about this period. Although the 4th through the 11th centuries in Europe were characterized by great social and political upheavals, the migrations and conquests of the Germanic tribes made possible the merging of their tribal culture with classical culture, a merger that forms the basis of modern European society. Also significant in this period are the conversion of the West to Christianity, the preservation of classical learning, and the creation of uniquely Christian art and literary forms.

Darling, river in SE Australia; rises in S Queensland and N and W New South Wales; flows SW into Murray River; navigable in rainy seasons. Length: 1,702mi (2,740km).

Darmstadt, city in central West Germany, 12mi (19km) E of Rhine River. Alstadt (Old Town) part of town dates back to Middle Ages. Neustadt (New Town), built in late 18th and early 19th centuries, is well-planned community W of original settlement. City was severely damaged in WWII. Industries: chemicals, steel, machinery. Pop. 136,200.

Darnley, Henry Stuart, or **Stewart, Lord** (1545–67), Scottish noble, second husband of Mary, Queen of Scots. Educated in England, he was a claimant to the English succession. He returned to Scotland (1565) to marry Queen Mary. Weak and vicious, Darnley was involved in the murder of Mary's aide Rizzio (1566). Mary then became party to Darnley's murder at Kirk o'Field, one of her houses.

Darrow, Clarence Seward (1857–1938), US lawyer and labor advocate b. Kinsman, Ohio. He defended Eugene V. Debs (1894) following the Pullman strike. In the Woodworkers case (1898), he won for labor the legal right to strike. He successfully defended William Haywood (1903), accused of assassinating former Idaho Gov. Frank Steunenberg. He achieved further fame in the Loeb-Leopold murder case (1924) and in the Scopes "monkey" trial (1925), successfully opposing William Jennings Bryan. He wrote *Crime, Its Cause and Treatment* (1922).

Darter, freshwater fish of temperate North American waters east of Rocky Mountains. Brilliantly colored, it is bottom-dwelling. Length: 1–9in (2.5–23cm); average 2–2.75in (5–7cm). Family Percidae; species 100, including Johnnydarter *Etheostoma nigrum.*

Dartmoor, moorland region in SW England, in S Devon with isolated granite masses; est. as a national park 1951; source of principal rivers of Devon; site of prison at Princetown built 1806 for French captives; now a convict prison. Area: 365sq mi (945sq km). Highest point is High Willhays, 2,039ft (622m).

Dartmouth, city in S Nova Scotia, Canada; on Halifax harbor opposite Halifax; site of oceanographic institute. Industries: oil refining, electronic equipment, breweries, ship building. Founded 1750. Pop. 65,341.

Dartmouth College v. Woodward (1819), US Supreme Court decision interpreting the contract clause of the Constitution. The Court held that a corporate charter was a contract with which state laws could not interfere. This ruling greatly aided the early growth of capitalism and big business in the United States.

Darts, a game particularly popular in the United States and Great Britain, developed in England in the 15th century. It is played with 3 weighted wooden or metal darts 5–6in (12.7–15.2cm) long. The darts are thrown at a board, 18 inches (45.7cm) in diameter. Indoors, players stand 9ft (2.7m) away. Outdoors, they stand 20–30ft (6.1–9.1m) away. There are several variations of play, as well as types of targets. The object in the 20-point board is to start with a certain score (201, 301, 501, 1001), according to the number of players, and to reach zero by subtracting the amount of points scored from the number indicated.

Daru, Pierre Antoine, Comte (1767–1829), French general, statesman, and historian. As a trusted ally of Napoleon, he became intendant-general of the Grande Armée in 1805 and defeated the Prussian army late that year. After arranging the Prussian indemnity payments, he was minister of state (1811), minister of war (1813), and minister of state during the Hundred Days (1815). He was made a member of the chamber of peers by Louis XVIII (1819). His works include *Histoire de la République de Venise* (1819–21); *Astronomie* (1830).

Darwin, Charles (Robert) (1809–82), English naturalist, b. Shrewsbury. He proposed a biological theory of natural selection as a mechanism of organic change in his monumental *The Origin of Species* (1859). Popularly credited with originating the theory of evolution, Darwin in fact owed much of his theory to the work of others, but utilized fine research ability in merging his own thought with various tentative theories and suggestions already on record.

In 1831 he served as naturalist on the government ship *Beagle,* which surveyed the South American coast, and he returned to the region in 1836 consumed with an interest in animal variations and their causes. He was influenced in his study by the work of a contemporary, Edward Blyth, who suggested that nature selected and preserved the best-adapted species in a

Gabriele D'Annunzio

Clarence Darrow

Charles Darwin

given environment and who recognized the possibility of organic change to be implicit in the theory.

After 20 years of research, the development of several theories by Alfred Russel Wallace spurred Darwin's presentation of his own theories at a meeting of the Linnaean Society in 1858. Publication of *The Origin of Species* followed. It proposed three factors responsible for changes in the plant and animal world: variation (the tendency of each organism to vary in some degree from the parent), a conservative heredity factor that limits the degree of variation, and natural selection, which results in the perpetuation of those organisms best fitted to survive. Darwin elaborated his theory in a number of later works, notably *The Descent of Man* (1871). *See also* Evolution; Natural Selection.

Darwin, seaport in Australia, at the entrance to Port Darwin; headquarters of the Allies in N Australia during WWII; bombed by the Japanese 1942. Cyclone Tracy (December 1974) destroyed 90% of the city; 5-year reconstruction plan includes housing construction that will withstand cyclone-force winds. Its harbor is the major shipping depot for the sparsely populated and undeveloped N region. Founded 1869. Pop. 42,818.

Darwinism, theory of the origin and evolution of the species as developed by Charles Darwin and presented in *The Origin of Species* (1859). Darwin viewed life as a constant competitive struggle in which some members of the species possessed certain advantageous traits. These characteristics were passed down through generations by a process termed "natural selection," strengthening the species and enabling survival of the fittest. *See also* Darwin, Charles Robert.

Darwin's Finches, term applied to the finches of the Galapagos Islands that Charles Darwin carefully observed while on his voyage on the *Beagle*. These observations overthrew Darwin's belief in the immutability of species and were seminal to his development of the theory of evolution. Darwin noted that all the finches on the various islands of the Galapagos group were closely related to a species of finch found on the mainland of South America and were all quite similar to one another—but with some differences from island to island. Studying further, he found that the differences could be correlated with the feeding habits of the different varieties of finches—with, for example, finches with powerful beaks eating large seeds, finches with small beaks eating smaller seeds, finches with fine beaks eating insects—and that the feeding habits were an adaptation to the particular environment of the species. These observations, combined with geological observations and other biological data, led Darwin to formulate a theory of evolution based on the idea of natural selection working on the variability within species to favor the better adapted to the environment. *See also* Adaptive Radiation; Natural Selection.

Data Processing, systematic sequence of operations performed on data, especially by a computer or other electronic or electromechanical device, in order to process new information, revise or update existing information stored in the system, as on magnetic tape, punch cards, or microfiche, or extract information from the system. The data can be in the form of numerical values, scientific or technical facts or measurements, lists of names, places, book titles, etc., with associated relevant information. The main processing operations performed by a computer are arithmetical addition, subtraction, multiplication, and division, and logical operations, which involve decision making on the basis of comparison of data, as in the operation: if condition *a* holds then follow programmed instruction P; if *a* does not hold then follow instruction Q. *See also* Computer, Electronic.

Date Palm, stout-trunked palm *Phoenix dactylifera* native to desert oases of North Africa east to India. One of the most important palms commercially, it is cultivated in the SW United States. It has feather-shaped, gray-green leaves; large flower clusters produce the date fruit of commerce. The wild date palm, *P. sylvestris,* is native to India; its fruits are not edible. Height: to 100ft (30.5m); family Palmaceae.

Dating, Radioactive, any of several methods using the laws of radioactive decay to assess the very considerable ages of archeological remains, fossils, rocks, and of the earth itself. The specimens must contain a very long-lived radioisotope of known half-life, which, together with a measurement of the ratio of radioisotope to a stable isotope (usually the decay product), gives the age. In potassium-argon dating, the ratio of potassium-40 (half-life 1.26×10^{98} yr) to its stable decay product argon-40 gives ages over ten million years. In rubidium-strontium dating the ratio rubidium-87 (5×10^{10} yr) to its stable product strontium-87 gives ages up to several billion years. In radio-carbon dating the proportion of carbon-14 (5730 yr) to stable carbon-12 absorbed into once-living matter (wood, etc) gives ages up to several thousand years.

Daubigny, Charles François (1817–1878), French landscape painter and etcher. A working artist at 17, Daubigny exhibited at the Salon at 21. An open-air painter, often classified as a Barbizon artist, Daubigny had a houseboat studio for over 30 years. His atmospheric oils of the Seine and Oise river areas are in the great museums of the West.

Daugavpils, formerly Dvinsk; city in E Latvian SSR, USSR, on the Dvina River, approx. 85mi (137km) NNE of Vilnius; commercial and industrial center; founded 1274 by Livonian kings; ceded to Russia 1772 by kingdom of Lithuania and Poland. Industries: food and grain processing, textiles, lumber, iron. Pop. 114,000.

Daumier, Honoré (1808–79), French lithographer, painter, and sculptor, one of the great social satirists. He worked for lawyers and booksellers before studying art and contributing lithographs, often lampoons of political figures, to magazines. For many of these he made terra-cotta models. He was jailed for six months in 1832 for a caricature of Louis Phillipe. His output was prodigious—more than 4,000 lithographs and 200 canvases. His work, always focused on humanity, is well represented in museums.

Dauphiné, French province, now occupied by the departments of Drôme Isère, and Haute-Alpes. Created by the Dauphin family's gradual addition of lands to the countship of Viennois, this land and the title dauphin were sold to Charles V of France in 1349 and annexed to France in 1457 as a result of disputes over its independence within the royal family. Revolts in 1789 made Dauphiné one of the birthplaces of the French Revolution.

Davao, seaport and largest city on Mindanao island, Philippines; capital of Davao Del Norte prov.; commercial center; site of university (1965). Exports: abaca, plywood, copra, rice, tobacco. Founded 1849. Pop. 515,520.

Davenport, city in E central Iowa, on the Mississippi River; treaty ending Black Hawk War (1832) signed here; site of first railroad bridge to span Mississippi River (1856); commercial and rail center. Industries: shipping, cereal, aluminum, farm and railroad equipment. Founded 1835; inc. 1836. Pop. (1980) 103,264.

David (*c.* 1040–970 BC), king of Israel (*c.* 1010–970 BC); son of Jesse and father of Solomon; successor of Saul. The Old Testament narrates his conquest of the Philistines, particularly the giant Goliath; his friendship with Jonathan, son of Saul; and the rebellion, reconciliation, and death of his son, Absalom. He unified the Jewish tribes and moved the capital from Hebron to Jerusalem. His descendants held the kingdom until 586 BC. Many Psalms are ascribed to him.

David I (1084–1153), king of Scotland (1124–53). b. Carlisle. His marriage to the countess of Northampton involved him in English politics and he fought for Matilda against King Stephen (1138). He introduced Anglo-Norman feudalism into Scotland, where he reorganized the church and administration and built many castles.

David II (1324–71), king of Scotland (1329–71). Exiled after the defeat by Edward III at Halidon Hill (1333), he fought the English in France and Britain until captured (1346). Released (1357) for a ransom he could not pay, he became dependent on the English king.

David, or **Dewi, Saint** (*c.* 520–600), patron saint of Wales. Traditionally he played an important part in two Welsh synods and founded many churches in South Wales.

David, Gerard or **Gheerardt** (*c.* 1460–1523), Flemish painter whose work was not widely known until the 19th century. Experts disagree on the number of authentic paintings. Though influenced by van Eyck and van der Weyden, David has an austere grace that is distinctive. Among his works are *Madonna Enthroned* (Louvre, Paris) and *Annunciation* (Metropolitan Museum, N.Y.).

David, Jacques-Louis (1748–1825), French painter of historical scenes and portraits. As leader of the neoclassical movement, David had a great effect on art and fashion. Influenced by Poussin and Greek and Roman art, David's work was involved with his Jacobin views and support of Napoleon. Among many major works are *Death of Marat* (Museum of Modern Art, Brussels), *Mme. Récamier* (Louvre, Paris), and *Death of Socrates* (Metropolitan Museum, N.Y.).

David Copperfield (1850), semiautobiographical novel by Charles Dickens that he called his "favorite child." Copperfield retrospectively relates his adventures, misfortunes, and eventual success and happiness. The novel contains many vivid characters, such as Micawber, Uriah Heep, Barkis, and Mrs. Gummidge.

Davies, Arthur Bowen (1862–1928), US painter and lithographer, b. Utica, N.Y. His own work was romantic though he was a member of "the Eight," also called the "ashcan school." President of the Society of Independent Artists, he organized the 1913 Armory Show, which introduced modern art to the United States.

Davis, Bette (1908–), US film actress, b. Ruth Elizabeth Davis in Lowell, Mass. She is well known for her intense roles in such films as *Of Human Bondage* (1934), *Dangerous* (1935), *The Petrified Forest* (1936), *Jezebel* (1938), *The Old Maid* (1939), *The Little Foxes* (1941), and *All About Eve* (1950). She was the first woman to be awarded the American Film Institute's Life Achievement Award (1977).

Davis, David (1815–82), US jurist b. Cecil co, Md. He was instrumental in Abraham Lincoln's presidential nomination and served as Lincoln's campaign manager. An associate justice of the US Supreme Court (1862–77), his opinion in *Ex Parte Milligan* (1866) limited the scope of military courts. He was a US Senator from Illinois (1877–83).

Davis, Jefferson (1808–89), President of the Confederate States of America (1861–65), b. Todd co, Ky. He was elected to the House of Representatives (1845) but resigned to fight in the Mexican War (1846). After the war he entered the Senate (1847–51) and then served as Pres. Franklin Pierce's secretary of war (1853–57). Reelected senator (1857), he resigned when Mississippi seceded from the Union, and became president of the Confederate States of America, a position he held until the end of the Civil War. He served two years in prison and was indicted for treason (1866) but never tried. He refused to seek amnesty after the war.

Davis, or **Davys, John** (1550–1605), Canadian explorer, b. England. He made three voyages in search of a northwest passage (1585–87), and he explored the Davis Strait, Cumberland Gulf, and Baffin Bay. He also fought against the Spanish Armada and invented the Davis quadrant.

Davis, city in central California, 15mi (24km) W of Sacramento; site of University of California at Davis (1908). Industries: canned foods, steel products. Settled 1850; inc. 1917. Pop. (1980) 36,640.

Davitt, Michael (1846–1906), Irish nationalist. Son of an evicted peasant, he became a Fenian and was imprisoned (1870). Released (1877), he founded the Land League to help tenants against absentee landlords (1879). He favored nationalizing land and gradually came to oppose the policies of Charles Parnell.

Davy, (Sir) Humphry (1778–1829), English chemist who isolated potassium, sodium, and the alkaline-earth metals by the application of electrolysis to the decomposition of chemical compounds. He is credited with preparing nitrous oxide, calcium, and boron, discovering chlorine and two chlorine oxides, and providing an explanation for chlorine's bleaching action. He showed that diamonds are a form of carbon and that acidic properties are due to hydrogen, and he invented a safe miners' lamp (the Davy Lamp).

Dawes, Charles Gates (1865–1951), US political leader, b. Marietta, Ohio. He was a lawyer and banker, who served as comptroller of the currency under Republican Pres. William McKinley. His effectiveness as an administrator in France in World War I led to his appointment as the first US budget director (1921). In 1923 he headed the financial commission that drew up the Dawes Plan (1924) to restructure the German economy, for which he received the Nobel Prize (1925). Under Pres. Calvin Coolidge he was vice president (1925–29) and then served in posts under Pres. Herbert Hoover.

Dawes Act (1887), named for Senator Henry L. Dawes (Mass.), ended the Indian reservation system in the United States. Lands held in common by the tribes were surveyed and parcelled out to individual, resident Indians. All Indians were to become citizens of the United States in 1924, at which time they could lawfully sell the property allotted to them.

Dawes Plan (1924), US financial plan developed by Charles G. Dawes to collect and distribute World War I payments. It established a schedule of payments that Germany could bear and arranged for a $200 million gold loan by US bankers to the German government to stabilize German currency.

Dayan, Moshe (1915–81), Israeli army officer and political figure. Growing up in Palestine, he was trained both as a farmer and a soldier. While serving with the British and leading a Palestinian Jewish company against the Vichy French in World War II, he lost his left eye. The black eye patch he wore thereafter became a trademark. He led the successful invasion of the Sinai Peninsula in 1956, and in 1967, as minister of defense, he became a hero of the Six-Day War against Egypt, Jordan, and Syria. He remained active in Israeli policy-making, serving as foreign minister under Menachem Begin (1977–79).

Dayananda Sarasvati (1824–83), Indian religious figure, b. as Mula Sankara. Discontented with the condition of Hinduism in his day, he became the major spokesman for a return to the authority of the Vedas, the earliest and most sacred scriptures of India. He condemned idol worship, child marriage, and the low status of women and advocated remarriage of widows, study of the Vedas by members of all castes, and the founding of charitable and educational institutions. He founded the Arya Samaj (Society of Nobles) in 1875 to propagate his views.

Daydreaming, form of autistic thinking, it is nonobjective and self-directed, unrealistic but gratifying. Daydreaming can be a withdrawal reaction, a psychological defense mechanism that allows the individual to retreat into a fantasy world of gratification that he cannot attain in the real world. Unless carried to extremes, daydreaming is a normal activity and serves an important function in temporarily mastering or dealing with frustration. *See also* Autistic Thinking.

Dayflower, any plant of the genus *Commelina* whose blue or purple flowers wilt after one day. They have jointed, creeping stems, and lance-shaped leaves. Family Commelinaceae.

Day-Lewis, C(ecil) (1904–72), Irish poet and critic. His concern for social justice and left causes is evident in his poetry, particularly that which relates to the Spanish Civil War. His poetry includes *Transitional Poem* (1929), *The Magnetic Mountain* (1933), *Overtures to Death* (1938), and *Selected Poems* (1967). *The Poetic Image* (1947) is his most important critical work. He was England's poet laureate (1968–72).

Day Lily, widely cultivated herbaceous perennial plant native to temperate regions of Central Europe, E Asia, and Japan and found wild on roadsides of E United States. It has long thin leaves and lilylike, yellow to reddish-orange flowers that open for one day. Family Liliaceae; genus *Hemerocallis.*

Dayton, city in W Ohio, on Great Miami River, 45mi (72km) NNE of Cincinnati; seat of Montgomery co; growth came with extension of canals 1830–40 and railroads in 1850s; cash register business began here in 1880; site of University of Dayton (1850), Wright State University (1964), home of Wilbur and Orville Wright, and Wright Patterson Air Force Base. Industries: refrigerators, cash registers, paper, computing scales. Settled 1796; inc. 1805. Pop. (1980) 203,588.

Daytona Beach, resort in E Florida, 92mi (148km) SSE of Jacksonville; noted for hard, white, 25mi (40km) long beach. Settled 1870; inc. 1876; mainland and resort sections consolidated in 1926. Pop. (1980) 54,176.

D-Day (June 6, 1944), the first day of the Allied invasion of Europe in Normandy, France. The Allies commanded by Gen. Dwight D. Eisenhower landed on beaches between Cherbourg and Le Havre. Despite heavy losses, they held their beachheads and pushed the Germans back. Within a year, the war in Europe was over.

DDT, Dichlorodiphenyltrichloroethane, a colorless crystalline organic halogen compound, first used as an insecticide in 1939 against the Colorado potato beetle. It acts as a contact poison, disorganizing the nervous system, and is effective against mosquitoes, fleas, moths, beetles, and other destructive insects. Many species, however, develop resistant populations and birds and fishes, feeding on affected insects, suffer toxic effects. All but essential uses of DDT were banned in the United States in 1971.

Deadfall, kind of primitive trap, especially for large game, constructed so that a heavy weight falls upon the intended victim, either killing it or leaving it disabled and prey to the hunters.

Dead Leaf Butterfly, or Leaf Butterfly, tropical butterfly of S Asia and E Indies. When a dead leaf butterfly rests on a twig, its folded wings look like withered leaves. Genus *Kallima. See also* Butterfly.

Deadly Amanita. *See* Death Cup.

Deadly Nightshade, also belladonna, devil's herb, sleeping nightshade; fatally poisonous, perennial herb native to S Europe and Asia, rare in the United States. Flowers are bell-shaped, purplish, and 1in (2.5cm) long; the fruit is a shiny black berry. The plant has been cultivated for a medicinal supply of the alkaloids scopolamine and atropine, obtained from the roots and leaves. Family Solanaceae; species *Atropa belladonna.*

Dead Reckoning, a navigational position-finding method that determines the position of a ship or aircraft without the help of celestial observation. Calculations are made from the records of the course and distance already covered and provisions are made for estimated drift. Dead reckoning permits the navigator to plot his location and to plan his course and speed.

Dead Sea (Al-Bahr al-Mayyit), salt lake on border between Jordan and Israel; water is supplied by the Jordan River and several smaller streams and springs; historically known by many other names (The Sea, Eastern Sea, Sea of Araba); cities of Sodom and Gomorrah believed to lie under S end; contains large quantities of common salt, potassium, bromine, sodium, chlorine, sulfate, calcium magnesium. Area: 360sq mi (932sq km). Depth: (avg.) 1,000ft (305m).

Dead Sea Scrolls, manuscripts and papyri discovered in 1947 and later in caves and ruins along the Dead Sea, primarily around Qumran. These documents, written in Hebrew or Aramaic, most between 100 BC –50 AD are of importance to scholars, providing valuable information about the relation of early Christianity to Judaism. They include most of the Old Testament, many apocryphal and pseudographical works, Biblical commentaries, and documents that shed light on the history of the time.

Deafness, a lack of the sense of hearing. The *congenitally* deaf are born deaf; the *adventitiously* deaf are born with normal hearing but lose it later in life. There are three major types of deafness: (1) Conductive hearing loss, the most prevalent, in which there is interference with the transmission of sound to sense organs in middle or inner ear, often as a result of childhood infection and high fever or development of bony abnormalities later in life. (2) Sensory-neural hearing loss, usually occurring at birth due to intrauterine infection, Rh incompatibility effects, or other neural damage, or developing in late life as a result of vascular degeneration and advancing age. (3) Central hearing loss or abnormality in the central nervous system, occurring from brain damage or disease or various psychogenic disorders.

The treatment of deafness depends on its cause and ranges from removal of impacted wax and administration of drugs to combat infection to delicate surgical and microsurgical procedures that can, for example, correct some congenital malformations and bony growths. Electronic hearing aids that amplify sound help many hard-of-hearing, and the use of sign language and speech reading or lip reading techniques help the deaf function in normal life. Gallaudet College in Washington, D.C., is the only liberal arts college in the world exclusively for the deaf.

Deak, Ferencz (1803–76), Hungarian political leader. A leader of the Liberal Reform party, he served in the Hungarian legislature (1833–36, 1839–40). He supported the revolution of 1848, drawing up the liberal March Laws, but resigned as Minister of Justice in opposition to Kossuth's more radical programs. After Kossuth's fall in 1849, Deak became the leader of the Hungarian nationalists. In 1867 he was instrumental in drawing up the Ausgleich (compromise) that established the Dual Monarchy.

Deane, Silas (1737–89), US diplomat, *b.* Groton, Conn. During the Revolution, he arranged an alliance with France (1778) and served as a delegate to the Continental Congress (1774–76).

Dearborn, city in SE Michigan, on the River Rouge, adjoining Detroit; home of the Ford Motor Co.; site of Greenfield Village, birthplace of Henry Ford, and his estate, Fair Lane, deeded to the University of Michigan in 1956. Industries: automobiles, bricks, tools, dies, metal products. Settled 1795; inc. 1925. Pop. (1980) 90,660.

Dearborn Heights, city in SE Michigan, 8mi (13km) E of Detroit. Pop. (1980) 67,706.

Death, the end of the body's physical life, a concern of specialists in many fields. Doctors and public health officers study causes of death, death rates, and longevity. Lawyers have to define death in legal terms, not always a simple matter. A current medical-legal-ethical controversy involves the "right to die" for the hopelessly ill. Funeral and burial customs are important parts of social and religious life. Philosophers and theologians discuss life after bodily death. Doctors and psychologists join in a new field called thanatology to study the behavior of the dying and those around them.

Death Cup, also called death cap or deadly amanita, a very poisonous, though rare, mushroom *(Amanita phalloides)* found in wooded areas. Typically it has an olive-green cap, though it may be white or yellow. The distinguishing marks include the remains of the veil in which young death cups are enclosed—an inverted cap under the true cap and a fleshy cup at the bulbous base. The toxin takes at least 8 hours to show an effect, after which time it may cause agonizing pain and severe liver damage often ending in death.

Death in Venice (1911), novella by Thomas Mann, about Gustav von Aschenbach, a great writer, who is unable to survive creatively in a bourgeois environment. This conflict is complicated by his homosexual feelings for a beautiful young boy he meets in Venice. The author used the affinity of genius and disease to symbolize the decay of Western art.

Jefferson Davis

D-day: Dwight D. Eisenhower with troops

Eugene V. Debs

Death of a Salesman (1949), 2-act drama by Arthur Miller. First performed in New York, it won a Pulitzer Prize, Tony Award, and New York Drama Critics' Circle Award. It was also made into a film (1951). Salesman Willy Loman, dedicated to the idea that to be well-liked will bring success, finds instead that it has led to failure for himself and his two sons, while a neighbor boy he had always disliked became successful. Unable to face the breakup of his world, he kills himself so his family can have his insurance money.

Death Rites, rites that accompany the passage of a person from the realm of the living to that of the dead. Though these are often accompanied by mourning this is not always the case, as among certain South American Indians. Symbolic action and speech on burial is a common form of death rite, which can last for a few minutes or for several weeks. *See also* Rites of Passage.

Death's-Head Moth, large European hawk moth that has markings suggestive of a human skull on the upper surface of its thorax. Species *Acherontia atropos. See also* Hawk Moth.

Death Valley, large desert in E California, almost surrounded by high mountains, Panamint Range (W) and Armagosa Range (E); contains the lowest point in the Western Hemisphere, 282ft (86m) below sea level. Named in 1849 by goldseekers who were lost attempting to cross it and survived only by climbing the steep Panamint Mts. Hottest summer temperatures in US occur here, up to 134°F (56.7°C). Gold and silver were mined in 1850s; borax was mined in large quantities in late 19th century and taken out by 20-mule teams. Death Valley National Monument contains the entire valley and is administered by National Park Service. Highest peak is Telescope Peak in Panamints, 11,049ft (3,370m). Area: 1,907,760 acres (772,643hectares).

Deathwatch Beetle, small beetle that tunnels through wood and, especially in old houses, produces a faint ticking sound once thought to presage a death in a family. The sound is actually made by the animal bumping its head against the wood, and is the mating signal of the female beetle. Family Anobiidae; species *Xestobium rufovillosum.*

Debrecen, city in E Hungary, 137mi (220km) E of Budapest; site of Reformed Church serving as the stronghold of Hungarian Protestantism (16th century); city sometimes referred to as "The Calvinist Rome." Louis Kossuth proclaimed Hungary's independence here (1849). Industries: processed food, farm machinery, railroad cars. Pop. 187,103.

Debs, Eugene Victor (1855–1926), US labor organizer, b. Terre Haute, Ind. In 1884 he was elected to the Indiana legislature. He helped establish and was president of American Railway Union (1893–97). He organized the Social Democratic party of America (1898) and was five times its presidential candidate (1900–20). He was one of the founders of the Industrial Workers of the World (IWW). He was imprisoned during the Pullman Strike (1894) and for violation of Espionage Act (1918).

Debussy, Claude Achille (1862–1918), French composer, founder of the Impressionistic movement in music. Contrary to the trends of his time, Debussy wrote highly original music that was delicate, soft, and suggestive rather than emotional and bombastic. He influenced many composers to turn away from the dominant styles of the 19th century to explore new possibilities of orchestral color and form. Many critics

mark Debussy's *Prélude à l'après-midi d'un Faune* (1894) as the beginning of 20th-century music. His orchestral works include *Nocturnes* (1899), *La Mer* (1905), and *Images* (1909). His piano works, among the most important in the piano literature, include the *Suite Bergamasque* (1905, containing the famous "Clair de Lune"), two books of *Images* (1905–07), two books of *Preludes* (1910, 1913), and 12 *Etudes* (1915). His one opera is *Pelléas et Mélisande* (1902).

Decadents, term applied to writers of the late 19th century who believed in art's freedom from social and moral restraints. Influenced by Charles Baudelaire, French decadents included the poets Paul Verlaine, Stéphane Mallarmé, and Arthur Rimbaud, and the novelist Joris Huysman. Verlaine contributed to the review *Le Décadent* (1886–89). English decadents include Oscar Wilde, Ernest Dowson, and Lionel Johnson. Much of the work of the English writers was first published in *The Yellow Book* (1894–97). *See also* individual authors.

Decalogue. *See* Ten Commandments.

Decameron, collection of 100 stories written in 1351–53 by the Italian Giovanni Boccaccio. The stories are set within a frame story about ten young men and women who meet in a church in Florence in 1348 when the Black Death is sweeping the city. Partly to escape the infection and partly for amusement, they flee to a villa in the hills of Fiesole, where they pass the time for ten days telling one another anecdotes, fabliaux, and fairy tales, many of them bawdy. The same type of frame story is later used by Chaucer in the *Canterbury Tales* and is a popular motif in both medieval and modern literature.

Decapod, crustacean order of 8,500 species including shrimp, lobster, and crab. Most are marine, some are found in fresh water. Some crabs are amphibious and some terrestrial. All have eight pairs of legs, the first three pairs modified for feeding, the remaining five are for motion. *See also* Crustacean.

Decathlon, series of 10 different track and field events. It takes place over a two-day period and is considered the most demanding of all athletic events. On the first day the individual must compete in a 100-meter race, long jump, shot put, high jump, and a 400-meter race. The second day includes the 110-meter hurdles, discus, pole vault, javelin, and 1500-meter race. It is an Olympic Games event.

Decatur, Stephen (1779–1820), US naval captain, b. Sinepuxent, Md. Active in the campaigns against pirates in Tripoli (1804) and Algiers (1815), he commanded a fleet against the British in the War of 1812. He was noted for his toast "Our country, right or wrong!"

Decatur, city in central Illinois, on the Sangamon River; seat of Macon co; here in 1860 Lincoln received his first endorsement for the presidency at the state Republican convention; site of Millikin University; major railroad center; agricultural area. Industries: chemicals, electronic components, glass, brass products. Inc. 1839. Pop. (1980) 94,081.

Decay, or **rot,** partial or complete deterioration of a substance caused by natural changes. Plant rot, caused by soil-borne bacteria and fungi, affects any plant part making it spongy, watery, hard, or dry.

Decay, Radioactive. *See* Radioactivity.

Deccan, peninsular plateau region in central India, between Narmada and Krishna rivers; surrounded by many mountain ranges; N Deccan was long a source of conflict between the S Dravidian and N Aryan inhabitants; by 232 BC Aryan culture had reached all of India. N end of the plateau has rich volcanic soil and produces cotton, grains; in the S there are coffee and tea plantations.

December, twelfth month of the year. Its name comes in part from the Latin for "ten" because it was the last month of the old ten-month calendar. It has 31 days. The birthstone is the ruby, turquoise, or zircon.

Decembrists, Russians, including many officers and noblemen, who staged a revolt in December 1825. They were members of the Northern Society, a secret political society demanding representative democracy. On December 14, 3,000 troops led by the Decembrists gathered in Senate Square in St. Petersburg. These troops were not well organized, and Czar Nicholas I quickly suppressed their revolt. Several Decembrists were executed, while others were sent into exile in Siberia.

Decibel (dB), logarithmic unit (one tenth of a bel) for comparing two power levels; frequently used for expressing the intensity of a sound in terms of some reference level. The intensity (I_1) of a sound is expressed in decibels as $10 \log_{10}(I_1/I_2)$, where I_2 is usually the threshold intensity of a note of the same frequency. The perceived noise decibel (PN dB) is the sound pressure in decibels above a datum level of 2×10^{-5} pascal of a band of random noise.

Deciduous Forest, leaf-dropping forest or forest belt found scattered east of the Rocky Mountains in the United States, below Scandinavia throughout Europe, and in most of China and Japan. These forests usually include maple, oak, elm, beech, birch, hickory, ash, and other trees.

Decimal System, commonly used system of writing numbers using a base ten and the Arabic numerals 0–9. It is a positional number system, each position to the left representing an extra power of ten. Thus, 6,741 is $(6 \times 10^3) + (7 \times 10^2) + (4 \times 10^1) + (1 \times 10^0)$. Note that $10^0 = 1$. Decimal fractions are represented by negative powers of ten placed to the right of a decimal point. Thus, 3.145 is $3 + (1 \times 10^{-1}) + (4 \times 10^{-2}) + (5 \times 10^{-3})$, or $3 + 1/10 + 4/100 + 5/1000$.

Decius (Gaius Messius Quintus Trajanus) (201–51), Roman emperor (249–51). Hoping to strengthen the state religion, Decius was responsible for the especially cruel and methodical persecution of Christians in the empire.

Declaration of Independence, historic document adopted by Second Continental Congress (July 4, 1776) in which the 13 American colonies justified their separation from Britain. The Congress adopted a resolution of independence, and a committee of five was appointed to draw up a formal document. Thomas Jefferson, John Adams, and Benjamin Franklin drew up the basic outline for the declaration, and Thomas Jefferson wrote it. It was presented to the Congress on June 28 and adopted on July 4, with a few changes. The formal signing took place on August 2. The Declaration states the necessity of government having the consent of the governed, of government's responsibility to the people. The colonies' grievances against the British crown are outlined. In conclusion, the colonies declared themselves free of Britain and united under a single government. Following is the text of the Declaration of Independence.

IN CONGRESS, JULY 4, 1776
THE UNANIMOUS DECLARATION OF THE THIRTEEN UNITED STATES OF AMERICA,

WHEN in the Course of human events, it becomes necessary for one people to dissolve the political bands which have connected them with another, and to assume among the powers of the earth, the separate and equal station to which the Laws of Nature and of Nature's God entitle them, a decent respect to the opinions of mankind requires that they should declare the causes which impel them to the separation.

We hold these truths to be self-evident, that all men are created equal, that they are endowed by their Creator with certain unalienable Rights, that among these are Life, Liberty and the pursuit of Happiness. That to secure these rights, Governments are instituted among Men, deriving their just powers from the consent of the governed. That whenever any Form of Government becomes destructive of these ends, it is the Right of the People to alter or to abolish it, and to institute new Government, laying its foundation on such principles, and organizing its powers in such form, as to them shall seem most likely to effect their Safety and Happiness. Prudence, indeed, will dictate that Governments long established should not be changed for light and transient causes; and accordingly all experience hath shewn, that mankind are more disposed to suffer, while evils are sufferable, than to right themselves by abolishing the forms to which they are accustomed. But when a long train of abuses and usurpations, pursuing invariably the same Object, evinces a design to reduce them under absolute Despotism, it is their right, it is their duty, to throw off such Government, and to provide new Guards for their future security. Such has been the patient sufferance of these Colonies; and such is now the necessity which constrains them to alter their former Systems of Government. The history of the present King of Great Britain is a history of repeated injuries and usurpations, all having in direct object the establishment of an absolute Tyranny over these States. To prove this, let Facts be submitted to a candid world:

He has refused his Assent to Laws, the most wholesome and necessary for the public good.

He has forbidden his Governors to pass Laws of immediate and pressing importance, unless suspended in their operation till his Assent should be obtained; and when so suspended, he has utterly neglected to attend to them.

He has refused to pass other Laws for the accommodation of large districts of people, unless those people would relinquish the right of Representation in the Legislature, a right inestimable to them and formidable to tyrants only.

He has called together legislative bodies at places unusual, uncomfortable, and distant from the depository of their public Records, for the sole purpose of fatiguing them into compliance with his measures.

He has dissolved Representative Houses repeatedly, for opposing with manly firmness his invasions on the rights of the people.

He has refused for a long time, after such dissolutions, to cause others to be elected; whereby the Legislative powers, incapable of Annihilation, have returned to the People at large for their exercise; the State remaining in the mean time exposed to all the dangers of invasion from without, and convulsions within.

He has endeavoured to prevent the population of these States; for that purpose obstructing the Laws for Naturalization of Foreigners; refusing to pass others to encourage their migrations hither, and raising the conditions of new Appropriations of Lands.

He has obstructed the Administration of Justice, by refusing his Assent to Laws for establishing Judiciary powers.

He has made Judges dependent on his Will alone, for the tenure of their offices, and the amount and payment of their salaries.

He has erected a multitude of New Offices, and sent hither swarms of Officers to harass our people, and eat out their substance.

He has kept among us, in times of peace, Standing Armies, without the Consent of our legislatures.

He has affected to render the Military independent of and superior to the Civil power.

He has combined with others to subject us to a jurisdiction foreign to our constitution, and unacknowledged by our laws; giving his Assent to their Acts of pretended Legislation:

For quartering large bodies of armed troops among us:

For protecting them, by a mock Trial, from punishment for any Murders which they should commit on the Inhabitants of these States:

For cutting off our Trade with all parts of the world:

For imposing Taxes on us without our Consent:

For depriving us in many cases of the benefits of Trial by Jury:

For transporting us beyond Seas to be tried for pretended offences:

For abolishing the free System of English Laws in a neighbouring Province, establishing therein an Arbitrary government, and enlarging its Boundaries so as to render it at once an example and fit instrument for introducing the same absolute rule into these Colonies:

For taking away our Charters, abolishing our most valuable Laws and altering fundamentally the Forms of our Governments:

For suspending our own Legislatures, and declaring themselves invested with power to legislate for us in all cases whatsoever.

He has abdicated Government here by declaring us out of his Protection and waging War against us.

He has plundered our seas, ravaged our Coasts, burnt our towns, and destroyed the lives of our people.

He is at this time transporting large Armies of foreign Mercenaries to compleat the works of death, desolation and tyranny, already begun with circumstances of Cruelty & perfidy scarcely paralleled in the most barbarous ages, and totally unworthy the Head of a civilized nation.

He has constrained our fellow Citizens taken Captive on the high Seas to bear Arms against their Country, to become the executioners of their friends and Brethren, or to fall themselves by their Hands.

He has excited, domestic insurrections amongst us, and has endeavoured to bring on the inhabitants of our frontiers, the merciless Indian Savages, whose known rule of warfare is an undistinguished destruction of all ages, sexes and conditions.

In every stage of these Oppressions We have Petitioned for Redress in the most humble terms. Our repeated Petitions have been answered only by repeated injury. A Prince, whose character is thus marked by every act which may define a Tyrant, is unfit to be the ruler of a free people.

Nor have We been wanting in attentions to our Brittish brethren. We have warned them from time to time of attempts by their legislature to extend an unwarrantable jurisdiction over us. We have reminded them of the circumstances of our emigration and settlement here. We have appealed to their native justice and magnanimity, and we have conjured them by the ties of our common kindred to disavow these usurpations, which would inevitably interrupt our connections and correspondence. They too have been deaf to the voice of justice and of consanguinity. We must, therefore, acquiesce in the necessity, which denounces our Separation, and hold them, as we hold the rest of mankind, Enemies in War, in Peace Friends.

WE, THEREFORE the Representatives of the UNITED STATES OF AMERICA, in General Congress, Assembled, appealing to the Supreme Judge of the world for the rectitude of our intentions, do, in the Name and by Authority of the good People of these Colonies, solemnly publish and declare, That these United Colonies are and of Right ought to be FREE AND INDEPENDENT STATES, that they are Absolved from all Allegiance to the British Crown, and that all political connection between them and the State of Great Britain, is and ought to be totally dissolved; and that as FREE AND INDEPENDENT STATES, they have full Power to levy War, conclude Peace, contract Alliances, establish Commerce, and to do all other Acts and Things which Independent states may of right do. AND for the support of this Declaration, with a firm reliance on the protection of divine Providence, we mutually pledge to each other our Lives, our Fortunes and our sacred Honor.

John Hancock
Button Gwinnett
Lyman Hall
Geo. Walton
Wm. Hooper
Joseph Hewes
John Penn
Edward Rutledge
Thos. Heyward, Jr.
Thomas Lynch, Jr.
Arthur Middleton
Samuel Chase
Wm. Paca
Thos. Stone
Charles Carroll of Carollton
George Wythe
Richard Henry Lee
Th. Jefferson
Benj. Harrison
Thos. Nelson, Jr.
Francis Lightfoot Lee
Carter Braxton
Robt. Morris
Benjamin Rush
Benj. Franklin
John Morton
Jas. Smith
Geo. Taylor
James Wilson
Geo. Ross
Caesar Rodney
Geo. Read
Tho. M:Kean
Wm. Floyd
Phil. Livingston
Frans. Lewis
Lewis Morris
Richd. Stockton
Jno. Witherspoon
Fras. Hopkinson
John Hart
Abra. Clark
Josiah Bartlett
Wm. Whipple
Saml. Adams
John Adams
Robt. Treat Paine
Elbridge Gerry
Step. Hopkins
William Ellery
Roger Sherman
Sam. Huntington
Wm. Williams
Geo. Clymer
Oliver Wolcott
Matthew Thornton

Declaration of the Rights of Man and Citizen (1789), statement of the principles of the French Revolution. It was adopted by the Constituent Assembly on Aug. 26, 1789, accepted by Louis XVI on October 5, and included in the constitution of 1791. Influenced by the US Declaration of Independence and the ideas of Jean Jacques Rousseau, it established the sovereignty of the people and the restrictions for social consideration embodied in "liberty, equality, and fraternity." The Rights of Man was a powerful influence in 19th century democratic and socialist movements.

Declaratory Act, law in which Britain's Parliament, after repeal of the Stamp Act (1766), asserted its right to tax the American colonies.

Declination, angular distance of a celestial body north or south of the celestial equator (north is positive, south is negative), thus measured in degrees along a line passing through the body and the celestial poles. Declination and right ascension form a coordinate system referred to the celestial equator.

Declination, Magnetic, the angle between the magnetic lines of force and the meridians of latitude. Declination is measured in degrees east or west of the magnetic north, which is the spot pointed to by a compass. The lines of equal declination are isogonic lines, the line of zero declination is the agonic line.

Decomposition, natural degradation of organic matter into simpler substances. Organisms of decay are usually bacteria and fungi.

Decorated Style, term used to describe the middle phase of Gothic architecture in England from about 1270 to 1350. Characteristic of the style was the use of vaulted portals and richly designed windows using narrow strips of stone in bar tracery, such as at Exeter Cathedral. Ribs in the vaults of portals became more delicate.

Découpage, form of collage in which surfaces are decorated with paper cutouts or similar material and then permanently preserved by painting or gluing. The technique is simple and has gained popularity as an easily accessible art form.

Deductive Logic, method of inference in which a conclusion follows necessarily from one or more given premises; this is in contrast to induction. Although originally generalized from Aristotle's "syllogism," today a syllogism is only one special case of deduction. *See also* Inductive Logic; Syllogism.

Deed, a signed written document that immediately transfers ownership of land from one existing person, the grantor, to another, the grantee. The transfer is also known as a conveyance, and the terms are used interchangeably.

Deep Scattering Layer (DSL), a "phantom" sound-reflecting layer in the ocean water. Various layers that can be detected during the day by sound-detecting devices disappear at night. Small deep-dwelling fish that feed on the water surface at night may be the cause.

Deep-sea Drilling Project (Project Mohole), a US scientific program sponsored by the National Science Foundation to obtain a core from the mantle of the earth by drilling through the crust, abandoned in 1966. (The moho, or base of the crust, is thinnest under deep oceans.) The core was expected to carry a continuous fossil and sediment record of the earth's history.

Deer, slim, even-toed, long-legged, hoofed, ruminant mammals. There are 17 genera of 53 species distributed in the Americas, Eurasia, NW Africa, Japan, Philippine Islands, and Indonesia. They have been introduced in Australia, New Zealand, New Guinea, and Hawaii. Deer eat grass, bark, twigs, and young shoots. Their habitat is varied and includes forests, arctic tundra, desert, open bush and swamps.

The musk deer is the smallest, the moose the largest. They are mostly brownish and young are often spotted. In some species this spotting is retained into adulthood. Most males bear antlers. During the mating season, males fight fiercely over a harem. Temperate species mate in late fall or winter. The gestation period is 160 days in musk deer and 10 months in the Eurasian roe deer, with usually 1–2 young born. Most deer gather in groups. The family is known to have existed since the Oligocene Epoch. Length:2.5–9.5ft (0.8–3m); weight: 201–1760lb (90–792kg). Family Cervidae. *See also* Artiodactyla; Ruminant.

Deep Sea Drilling Project: core sample

Degas: self portrait in oil

Charles De Gaulle: liberation of Paris, 1945

Deer Fly, or Gadfly, fly, closely related to the horsefly, found worldwide. This 0.28 to 0.4in (7–10mm) fly has a brown or black body with dark wing markings. The female gives a painful bite and is known to transmit anthrax, tularemia, and loa loa. Family Tabanidae, species *Chrysops app.* and *Tabanus spp. See also* Horsefly.

Deerslayer, The (1841), novel by James Fenimore Cooper about Natty Bumppo, a young hunter living among the Delaware Indians in New York State during the French and Indian Wars and his efforts to help the Hutter family against the Iroquois. The book is one of the Leather-Stocking Tales. *See also* Leather-Stocking Tales, The.

Defenestration of Prague (May 1618), an event that marked the beginning of the Thirty Years War. During the Reformation, Catholic Hapsburg supporters persecuted the Protestants. Angry Czechs threw two Hapsburg representatives out of a castle window into a moat.

Defense, Department of (DOD), US, cabinet-level department within the executive branch. It is directed by the secretary of defense who is a cabinet member. The defense department is responsible for all agencies concerned with national security and consists, in addition to secretary of defense, the Joint Chiefs of Staff, the service departments, and the operational military commands. The secretary of defense, with the president, is responsible for all operational military activities, providing civilian control for the Army, Navy, and Air Force. The DOD was originally established as the war department in 1789. In 1947, the National Security Act brought the three branches of the military forces together under the National Military Establishment, which in 1949 was renamed the department of defense. *See also* Joint Chiefs of Staff; Air Force, US; Army, US; Navy, US; and Marine Corps, US.

Defense Mechanism, in psychology, any method that an individual uses (unconsciously) to ward off anxiety caused by unpleasant thoughts or desires. Such mechanisms were first described by Freud in 1894. In their extreme forms, defense mechanisms can be symptomatic of mental disturbance, especially neuroses. However, to some extent all of us use them daily, when we rationalize mistakes, deny faults, or intellectualize unpleasant emotions.

Deficit Finance, government borrowing of funds from future tax revenues in order to finance current purchases of goods and services. This is accomplished through the Treasury Department's sale of government securities. If the government does not have a balanced budget, it must engage in deficit financing. *See also* Balanced Budget.

Deflation, falling prices, the opposite of inflation. Deflation normally occurs during a recession or depression, and it can be measured by the price indexes in the same way that inflation is measured. Excess capacity of the productive facilities within the economy usually is the cause of deflation. Excess capacity leads to an excess supply condition in which suppliers wish to supply more goods at full employment than consumers wish to buy. *See also* Inflation.

Defoe, Daniel (1660?–1731), English journalist and novelist. He joined the Duke of Monmouth's rebellion (1685) and William III's army (1688). He supported the foreign king in the poem *The True-born Englishman* (1701) and was imprisoned for his pamphlet "The Shortest Way with Dissenters" (1702). His works include *Robinson Crusoe* (1719), *Moll Flanders* (1722),

A Journal of the Plague Year (1722), and *Roxana* (1724).

De Forest, Lee (1873–1961), US inventor who developed the audion tube (1907), a device that made live radio broadcasting possible. It remained the key component of radio, television, radar, telephone, and computer systems until the transistor was invented in 1947.

Degas, (Hilaire Germain) Edgar (1834–1917), French painter and sculptor. Classically trained and a lifelong admirer of Ingres, Degas was a perfectionist whose achievement was to combine the discipline of classic art with the immediacy of the modern. His early work reflects his studies of the masters. After meeting Manet and Zola, he showed his work at the Impressionists' exhibitions. Sharing their interest in everyday life, he began painting ballet, cafe, and racing scenes. A brilliant draftsman influenced by Japanese prints and photography, he introduced unusual angles and off-center composition into his carefully planned work. To master movement, he made sculptures of dancers and horses. His use of color and light, always subtle, became concentrated in the late pastels. In his lifetime only one work, *The Cotton Exchange at New Orleans,* was sold to a museum and his rank as one of the greatest French artists was not known until his work was auctioned after his death. His work is in major museums.

De Gasperi, Alcide (1881–1954), Italian politician and prime minister. Born in the region of Trento under Austrian rule, in his early political years he worked for Trentino reunification with Italy. Strongly anti-Fascist, he was imprisoned twice in the 1920s. Active in the resistance during World War II, after the war he was secretary of the Christian Democratic party and prime minister (1945–53).

De Gaulle, Charles André Joseph Marie (1890–1970), French general, president (1959–69), and celebrated patriot. A graduate of the Ecole Spéciale Militaire of Saint-Cyr, he fought in World War I and was wounded and captured in 1916. He later fought against the Bolsheviks in Poland, graduated from the Ecole Supérieur de Guerre in 1924, and served in the occupation of the Rhineland and in Lebanon. A proponent of a mechanized professional army, he was made brigadier general in charge of the 4th Armored Division in 1940. When the Vichy government was created, he went to England as the self-declared head of the French resistance and was sentenced to death by court-martial in France. He was later head of the French Committee of National Liberation in Algiers. After the war, he made two partially successful attempts to reorganize French government (1945–46) and following a period of retirement was elected president of the Fifth Republic in 1958. He settled the Algerian crisis, saw France become a nuclear power, and withdrew from NATO in 1966. He resigned after the refusal of his suggested reforms in 1969.

Degeneration, evolutionary regression. The loss of a function or structure causing a higher form to revert to a lower form.

Degradation, in geology, wearing away or general reduction or erosion of Earth. The carrying off of rocky material by wind, water, or ice are degradative processes. Downcutting of a stream as it cuts its channel is also degradation. Otherwise, the denudation of slopes or the transportation of material is classed as degradation. *See also* Denudation; Erosion.

Degree, unit of angular measure equal to one three hundred and sixtieth of a complete revolution. One

degree is written 1°, and can be divided into 60 parts called minutes ('), which may in turn be divided into 60 parts called seconds ("). 360 degrees are equal to 2 π radians.

Degree Day, a unit of the departure of the average outdoor daily temperature from a standard, such as 65°F (18°C), used in measuring fuel-consumption requirements.

Degree of Arc, angular measure equal to 180th part of the angle subtended by a semicircular arc at the center of the circle. It is measured in degrees, minutes, and seconds, where 60 seconds equal one minute and 60 minutes equal one degree. In astronomy 15 degrees of arc (15°) is equal to one hour of right ascension.

Dehydration, loss of water from a solid, liquid, or gas by physical or chemical means, hastened by the presence of a catalyst, by heat, or by a dehydrating agent, such as sulfuric acid. Dehydration is an old established method of food preservation whereby the growth of predative microorganisms is inhibited. *See also* Food Preservative.

Deimos, smaller of Mars' two satellites, discovered (1877) by Asaph Hall. Diameter 7.5mi (12km); mean distance from planet 14,600mi (23,500km); mean sidereal period 1.26 days.

Deindividuation, in social science, the behavior of those persons in groups who lose their sense of individual identity and responsibility. They may go along with the crowd in failing to help someone in trouble, or they may join in mob violence. *See also* Anonymity.

Deirdre, a tragic figure in Irish mythology. Conchobar, the king of Ulster, kidnapped the beautiful Deirdre with the intention of marrying her, but she fled with Naoise to Scotland. Shortly after returning to Ulster, Naoise and his two brothers were murdered; Deirdre died of grief.

Deism, religious belief or form of theism restricting God's action to an initial act of creation, after which He retired to consider the excellence of his work. Deists held that the natural creation is regulated by law and inscribed with perfect moral principles. Many "philosophes," for example Voltaire and G.E. Lessing, were Deists. *See also* Philosophes.

Déjà Vu (French, literally "already seen"), the experience or feeling that one has encountered the same situation on some previous occasion when, in reality, the situation is a new one. Psychologists explain such experiences by concluding that the situation is probably very similar to some previously experienced situation that can no longer be consciously remembered.

De Kooning, Willem (1904–), US painter, b. Holland; an important abstract expressionist. After studying in Europe, de Kooning went to the United States in 1926. He did free-lance work, including work on a mural under Fernand Léger. He also did murals for the Federal Arts Project. De Kooning began painting abstractions, mainly portraits, in the 1930s but did not have a one-man show until 1948. Though influenced by Picasso and Gorky, de Kooning's paintings are distinctive and original. Marked by organic shapes in harsh colors or white on black, they are done in energetic, almost violent brushwork. His first critical and popular success came in the mid-1950s with the series of paintings called *Woman.* A leader of the New York, or action, school, de Kooning continued to alternate between abstractions and further investigations of the

Woman theme. His work is in private collections and major museums of modern art.

Delacroix, (Ferdinand Victor) Eugène (1798–1863), French painter, a leader of the romantic movement. His masterly composition and brilliant use of color have influenced modern painting since his time. Delacroix considered becoming a writer, and his *Intimate Journals* and *Correspondence* are important descriptions of the life of a painter involved in intellectual life. Classically trained, he also studied the works of the masters. He knew the English painter Constable and admired Byron, Shakespeare, Scott, and Goethe. Delacroix's first success came with large historical paintings such as *The Massacre at Chios* and *The Death of Sardanapalus* (both, Louvre, Paris) that are notable for sensuous and violent subject matter as well as technical excellence. His enormous output included portraits, religious and allegorical studies, and hunting and Oriental scenes. Delacroix also made lithographs and painted major murals for King Louis Phillipe.

De la Mare, Walter (1873–1956), English poet, short story writer, and anthologist. He worked as a clerk for the Standard Oil Company until 1936, when he received a government pension. His poems have great power to suggest mystery and eeriness. His collections of poems include *Songs of Childhood* (1902), *Peacock Pie* (1913), and *Poems for Children* (1930). Of his poetry anthologies, *Come Hither* (1923) is outstanding. His prose includes the novel *Memoirs of a Midget* (1921) and the collection of stories *On the Edge* (1930). He also wrote imaginative stories for children.

Delaunay, Robert (1885–1941), French painter. An artist of the Cubist style, he exhibited with the Munich Blue Rider Group. Central to his work is the use of color to define structure.

Delaware, state in the E United States on the Atlantic Ocean and Delaware Bay, about midway between New York City and Washington, D.C.

Land and Economy. Delaware occupies the N portion of the Delmarva Peninsula between the Atlantic Ocean and Chesapeake Bay; parts of Maryland and Virginia lie to the S. Most of the state is a coastal plain; the higher elevations are in the extreme N. The Delaware River, which carries a great volume of shipping to the port of Philadelphia, forms part of the E boundary. Manufacturing, principally in the Wilmington area, center of the huge E.I. du Pont de Nemours chemical industry, is the mainstay of the economy. Wilmington also contains the home offices of many large corporations. Agricultural production, chiefly poultry raising, is centered in the central and S sections. Shellfishing is important along Delaware Bay.

People. Migration from other states has been significant; only about 3% of the population is foreign-born, but only about 50% was born in the state. A little over 70% resides in urban areas.

Education and Culture. The University of Delaware is at Newark and there are six other institutions of higher education. Notable museums are the Henry Francis du Pont Winterthur Museum near Wilmington, which displays the history of American decorative arts in a number of period rooms, and the Hagley Museum, which emphasizes the history of US industry.

History. The first permanent white settlement was made by Swedes at Fort Christina (Wilmington) in 1638. Called New Sweden, it spread N and S along the Delaware River. In 1655 the Dutch conquered New Sweden and added the land to their colony of New Netherland. The English seized New Netherland in 1664, naming it New York, and the Delaware area remained part of that colony until 1682, when the Duke of York ceded it to William Penn to give his new colony of Pennsylvania a seacoast. In 1704, Penn allowed the three "Lower Counties" to elect an assembly of their own, which functioned as a separate colonial government, although the governor of Pennsylvania was nominally its governor. In the final voting on the Declaration of Independence in July 1776, Caesar Rodney, one of Delaware's three delegates, cast the deciding ballot. Delaware's ratification of the US Constitution came less than three months after the document was finished. The state remained loyal to the Union in the Civil War. Manufacturing development began in 1802 with the establishment of the du Pont gunpowder mill, the first unit of the diversified du Pont industries, whose domination of the state's economy continued into the 20th century.

PROFILE

Admitted to Union: Dec. 7, 1787, first of the 13 original states to ratify the US Constitution
US Congressmen: Senate, 2; House of Representatives, 1
Population: 595,225 (1980); rank, 47th
Capital: Dover, 23,512 (1980)
Chief cities: Wilmington, 70,195; Newark, 25,247
State Legislature: Senate, 21; House of Representatives, 41
Area: 2,057sq mi (5,328sq km); rank, 49th
Elevation: Highest, 442ft (135m), near Centerville; lowest, sea level
Industries (major products): chemicals, processed foods, metal products, machinery, textiles
Agriculture (major products): broiler chickens, cattle, corn, vegetables
Minerals (major): sand, gravel
State nicknames: First State, Diamond State
State motto: Liberty and Independence
State bird: Blue hen chicken
State flower: Peach blossom
State tree: American holly

Delaware Indians, named for Lord De la Warr, this tribe of Algonkin-speaking North American Indians call themselves *Lenni-Lenape,* meaning "real men." The tribe, divided into three major divisions, the Unami, Munsi, and Unalachtigo, lived in New Jersey, Long Island, E Pennsylvania, and N Delaware. Originally numbering about 8,000 persons, most of the Delaware were forced to move in the early 19th century to Indian Territory (now Oklahoma) where about 2,000 live today.

Delaware River, river in New York, New Jersey, and Pennsylvania; rises in the Catskill Mts of SE New York; its East and West branches meet at Hancock, New York; flows SE along New York-Pennsylvania border to Port Jervis then between New Jersey and Pennsylvania S to Delaware Bay. It cuts through Kittatinny Mts forming Delaware Water Gap near Stroudsburg, Pa. At Trenton, New Jersey, it becomes navigable and travels through a highly industrialized area that creates serious pollution problems. Second only to the Mississippi River in annual freight tonnage carried, its upper course furnishes water power through a series of dams and reservoirs that also provide flood control and water to municipalities. River is connected to Chesapeake Bay by the 19mi (30km) Chesapeake and Delaware Canal. Scene of Washington's crossing from Pennsylvania to fight at Battle of Trenton Dec. 25, 1776. Length: 280mi (450km).

De la Warr, Thomas West, Baron (1577–1618), colonial governor of Virginia. A member of Parliament (1597), he was also a soldier, and the first governor of the Jamestown Colony (1610–11). When he arrived the colonists were discouraged and ready to leave, but under his authority the colony was strengthened. A state (Delaware), river, and bay are named after him.

Delbrück, Max (1906–81), US biologist, b. Germany. He shared the 1969 Nobel Prize in physiology or medicine for his discovery that bacterial viruses reproduce sexually, thus showing that genetic recombination occurs.

Delderfield, Ronald Frederick (1912–73), English novelist. He began his career as a playwright and newspaperman. His most famous work was a trilogy dealing with life in the English countryside at the end of the Victorian era: *God Is an Englishman* (1970); *Theirs Was the Kingdom* (1971); *Give Us This Day* (1973). All were best-selling narrative accounts of England's transformation from an agricultural to an industrial society as seen from the perspective of a single family.

Delegated or Enumerated Powers, powers granted to Congress in Article I, Section 8 of the Constitution including the authority to impose and collect taxes, borrow money, regulate commerce at home and abroad, and to declare war. Section 8 also sets forth the implied powers of Congress. *See also* Elastic Clause; Implied Powers.

Delft, city in SW Netherlands; formerly an important commercial center until the 17th century when it was replaced by Rotterdam; center of ceramics industry; site of 13th-century Gothic church, 15th-century Gothic church (Nieuwe Kerk), which contains the tombs of William the Silent and Hugo Grotius, 17th-century town hall, technical university; scene of the assasination of William the Silent (1584). Industries: Delftware (pottery), china, tiles. Founded 11th century. Chartered 1246. Pop. 86,103.

Delhi, capital city of India, on Yamuna River; partitioned into Old Delhi, New Delhi, and Union Territory of Delhi. Old Delhi is the commercial part of the city; New Delhi, planned by English architects, is the administrative center; Old and New Delhi are on sites containing remnants of at least seven cities, some dating back almost 2,000 years. Delhi was held by English 1803–1947; capital of British India 1912, replacing Calcutta; New Delhi became the official capital in 1937 and remained so after the independence of India (1947). Points of interest include Rashtrapate Bhavan, presidential palace; Jami Masjid, India's largest mosque; the marble Red Fort; and National Museum. Most of Delhi's industries are from Old Delhi: cotton textiles, jewelry, clothing, shoes, handicrafts, tourism. Pop. 3,647,023.

Delhi Sultanate (1192–1398), powerful Muslim state in India. Mohammed of Ghor defeated the Hindus at Taraori in 1192, establishing the sultanate, which lasted until the Mogul Empire was established. It included five successive dynasties, the Slave, Khaljis, Tughluqs, Sayyis, and Lodis. Thirty-three different sultans ruled during this time. Under Mohammed ibn Tughluq (1325–51) the sultanate reached its largest area. Tamerlane (Timur) invaded in 1399, and anarchy followed. The Muslims formed separate states, and there was no attempt at forming a unified government, which led to eventual domination by the Mogul empire.

Delian League, confederacy of Greek city-states formed to conduct war on Persia, 478–404 BC. Though League policy theoretically was decided by an assembly in which each member state was considered equal, Athens (which provided the largest fleet) came to dominate the League. By the time peace was concluded with Persia in 449 BC, the League was nothing less than the Athenian empire.

Delilah, biblical Philistine courtesan loved by Samson. She discovered his long hair was the source of his great strength and cut it off, betraying him to the enemy.

Delinquency, Juvenile, crimes committed by youths and all other acts that come under the jurisdiction of juvenile courts. A youth may be defined in widely varying ways, with the lower limit being 7 or 8 and the upper limit, 15, 16, 18, or 21. "Delinquent" acts include those that the law would class as crimes if committed by an adult. Also included are such loosely defined acts as incorrigibility or vagrancy. The original purpose of the special laws and courts for youthful offenders was to spare them the stigma of being processed by criminal courts. Social scientists have sought the causes of juvenile delinquency in personal maladjustments and in society's failures.

Delirium Tremens, serious condition occurring most often when alcohol is abruptly withdrawn from an alcoholic, occasionally as a reaction to barbiturates or other drugs. It produces tremor, loss of appetite, terrifying dreams, various mental and nervous-system disturbances, and if severe, delirium. In some 10% of cases, death occurs.

Delisle, Guillaume (1675–1726), French scientist. The first scientific cartographer and one of the founders of modern geography, he used astronomical observations and accurate measurements to compile the 90 or so maps he published during his lifetime. His first important work—maps of the continents and a globe—was published in 1700. He was premier geographer to the king in 1718 and tutored the young Louis XV. His brother was the French astronomer Joseph Nicholas Delisle.

De Lôme Letter (1898), private correspondence written by Dupuy de Lôme, Spanish minister to the United States, to a Cuban friend. The letter, characterizing Pres. McKinley as weak and two-faced, was stolen and published in the New York *Journal.* This incident increased US sentiment against Spain just before the Spanish-American War.

Delorme, or **de l'Orme, Philibert** (1515?–70), French architect. He studied in Rome and in 1547 was commissioned by Diane de Poitiers to build her chateau at Anet. Under Henry II, he was appointed superintendent of buildings. At Henry's death, he was dismissed by Catherine de Médicis and then wrote two books with illustrations of many of his buildings, which no longer exist. Only parts of the chateau at Anet and the tomb of Francis I at St. Denis survive. A most influential artist, he was known for his introduction of classical forms into French architecture.

Delos (Dhilos), smallest island in Cyclades (Kikladhes) group, Greece, in S Aegean Sea; by Greek legend, considered the center of the islands and birthplace of Apollo and Artemis; appointed treasurer of the Delian League 478–454 BC. Declared a free port by Rome (166 BC), it prospered as an important shipping and slave center; destroyed during Mithridatic Wars (87 BC). French excavations since 1877 have uncovered remains of temples, theaters, commercial buildings.

Delphi, ancient city-state in Greece, 6mi (10km) from Mt Parnassus. The Delphic Oracle, est *c.* 8th century BC, became the most famous oracle and sacred sanctuary in ancient Greece; legend says the priestess Pythia entered the Temple of Apollo from which she

Delphinium

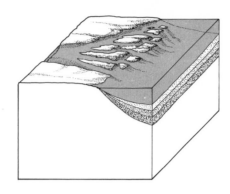

Delta

Cecil B. De Mille

received the prophecy, which was recorded by priests and used to guide important state decisions. The temple was sacked by the Romans; Theodosius I closed the oracle 390 AD with the onset of Christianity; site of the Amphictyonic League, the religious organization of the city-states that established the Pythian Games. French excavations (1892) revealed the artifacts.

Delphinium, or larkspur, any of about 250 species of herbaceous plant native to temperate parts of the Northern Hemisphere. They have buttercuplike leaves and loosely clustered, blue or white, spurred flowers. Spring larkspur *(Delphinium tricorne)* and tall larkspur *(D. exaltatum)* are common wildflowers. Rocket larkspur *(D. ajacis)* has finely cut leaves and is frequently cultivated. Family Ranunculaceae.

Delta, a fan-shaped body of alluvium deposited at the mouth of a river. A delta occurs when a river drops more sediment than waves, tides, or currents can remove. The term was introduced in the 5th century BC by Herodotus to describe the land at the mouth of the Nile River which resembled the Greek letter Δ, delta.

Deluge, The, story of the Great Flood. In one of its earliest pre-Biblical versions, reconstructed from a broken clay tablet from Mesopotamia, some of the gods decide to destroy mankind. But one of them, Enki, thinking this harsh, counsels a mortal, Ziusadra, to build a boat to save the seed of mankind. The flood lasted for seven days; then the sun shone and the earth reappeared. The gods, pleased with his obedience, made Ziusadra immortal. *See also* Noah.

Delusion, false, irrational belief or thought. People suffering from paranoia may have delusions of grandeur, persecution, etc. Those who have delusions of grandeur are convinced that they have an important identity (God, Napoleon, Gandhi) and can be totally out of contact with reality, that is, psychotic. *See also* Paranoiad Personality.

Demand, in economics, the schedule of prices and the quantities that would be purchased by consumers at those prices. For most goods, the normal relationship between price and quantity is inverse, that is, as the price of the good increases, the quantity demanded by consumers declines. The demand for a good is determined by a number of factors, however, including purchaser's income, price of competing goods, and consumer tastes and preferences.

Demand Curve, graphic representation of relationship between prices and quantity demanded. It slopes downward to the right, indicating that consumers will increase the quantity of the good purchased as prices fall.

Demand Shift, in economics, a change in the demand curve at all prices. Thus a different quantity would be purchased at every possible price. Demand shifts may occur because of changes in consumer income, in tastes and preferences, or in the price of substitute goods. *See also* Demand Curve.

Demand Theory, in economics, the body of knowledge and theory relating to consumers' demands for goods and services. Demand theory makes assumptions concerning the logic of consumers' desires and the consumers' preferences for higher utility levels. From these assumptions, economists have developed a theory of behavior. It can be logically shown that the consumer will prefer more of a good at a lower price than at a higher price. It can be shown also that the consumer will react differently to price changes in different goods, depending upon the elasticity of demand.

Demeter, in Greek mythology, the goddess of corn, health, and marriage. She was the daughter of Cronus and Rhea and a sister of Zeus.

Demetrius I (*c.* 336–283 BC), king of Macedonia (294–283 BC). Named Demetrius Poliorcetes ("taker of cities"), this son of Antigonus I ruled Greece (293–289). He freed Athens and Megara in 307, defeated Ptolemy in 306, besieged Rhodes in 305–04, and suffered defeat at Ipsus in 301. He invaded Asia in 287 but was forced to surrender to Seleucus I in 285.

Demetrius II (*c.* 278–229 BC), king of Macedonia (239–229 BC). The son of Antigonus II Gonatus, he was defeated in the Demetrian War against the Achaeans and the Aetolian League. He was the father of Philip V of Macedon.

Demetrius I Soter (187–150 BC), king of Syria (162–150 BC). Sent as a hostage to Rome during the reign of his father, Seleucus III, he saw his kingdom usurped by his uncle Antiochus IV (175 BC), then by his cousin Antiochus V. In 162 BC, aided by the Greek historian Polybius, he escaped from Rome, killed his cousin, and gained the throne. He crushed the revolt of Timarchus in Babylon and attempted to subdue the Maccabees in Jerusalem. He was killed battling against the pretender Alexander Balas.

De Mille, Cecil B(lount) (1881–1959), US film producer and director, b. Ashfield, Mass. He is noted for lavish dramatic spectacles. With his first film, *The Squaw Man* (1913), he established Hollywood as the US film-production capital. He brought stage actors and techniques to film and stabilized the length of feature films. DeMille evinced an unerring assessment of public taste: His Biblical epics—*The Ten Commandments* (two versions, 1923, 1956) and *King of Kings* (1926)—combine a Victorian moral tone with graphic sexuality. Other major films include *Forbidden Fruit* (1921), *Union Pacific* (1939), and *The Greatest Show on Earth* (1953), which won him an Academy Award for best director.

Democracy, political system in which authority is rooted in the consent of the governed. In one form the will of the people is expressed indirectly, through elected representatives. Democracy stresses that all men are endowed with basic civil rights. In the United States, executive, legislative, and judicial branches of government are separated and a system of checks and balances exists to curtail their power. Fixed periodic elections are conducted to insure that government is ultimately responsible to the electorate.

Democratic Party, US political party, the descendant of the Anti-Federalist and Democratic-Republican parties. From Thomas Jefferson's election in 1800 through James Buchanan's election in 1856, the party was strong, gathering its support mainly from farmers, small businessmen, and the professional classes. In this period, Democrats opposed a central bank, protective tariffs, and internal improvements at federal expense. Southern planters in the party promoted expansionism, which led the United States to war with Mexico (1846). Party strength declined after the Civil War until 1932, when Franklin D. Roosevelt was elected. After that, it remained strong until 1952. In 1960, Democratic candidate John F. Kennedy won the presidential election beginning "the New Frontier" era that stressed US world responsibilities for peace and economic growth at home. Lyndon B. Johnson succeeded Kennedy with an ambitious program of domestic legislation. In the 1976 elections, the Democratic candidate, Jimmy Carter, was elected president.

Democratic-Republican Party, US political party, originally called the Anti-Federalist party, or Republicans. Led by Thomas Jefferson, James Madison, and James Monroe, the party opposed strong central government and Alexander Hamilton's economic policies. It supported the French Revolution, advocated an agrarian democracy, strict construction of the Constitution, and other measures to minimize aristocratic control of government.

Democratic-Republicans (Jacksonian), a group within the Democratic-Republican party that supported Andrew Jackson. They were opponents of John Quincy Adams and Henry Clay in the election of 1828. The party had split after Adams' election in 1824. Unlike Thomas Jefferson, who favored minimal government, Jackson believed in the necessity of a strong federal government to curb predatory interests. After Jackson's election this group became known as the Democratic party.

Democritus of Adbera (*c.* 460–*c.* 370 BC), Greek philosopher. Although none of his books survive, he is best remembered for his atomic theory. He suggested that all matter consisted of tiny, indivisible particles; that various atoms differed physically; and that atoms' motions were determined by laws of nature, not the actions of gods. He also stated that the Milky Way consisted of a large mass of tiny stars.

Demographic Transition Theory, or theory of the vital revolution, social theory stating that populations increase and decrease in relation to the degree of social development. In premodern societies, death and birth rates are high. Modernization decreases the death rate, but not the birth rate, causing a temporary acceleration in population growth. With more advanced development, the birth rate also drops and population growth stabilizes.

Demography, term introduced in 1855 by the Frenchman Achille Guillard for the scientific study of human populations, their changes, movements, size, distributions, structures, and developments. The study may be said to have begun with the work of Englishman John Graunt who published the first mortality table (1662). Demographic methods are primarily statistical and quantitative, and they are used by government and business for ascertaining public needs. *See also* Population.

Demonetization, ending the practice whereby the value of a nation's currency is defined by precious metal. Monetary metal, metal coins, and paper money no longer are freely convertible. The reform became widespread after World War I. Demonetization also refers to the withdrawal from circulation of certain kinds of currency, which then cease to be considered legal tender.

Demosthenes (384–322 BC), Athenian orator and statesman. He achieved fame as a public speaker after struggling to overcome physical disabilities. He devoted his life to speaking and fighting on behalf of the Greek states in their resistance to Philip of Macedon. His works include the *Philippics* and *On the Crown*.

Dendrite, that part of a nerve cell, or neuron, that carries impulses to the cell body; for example, impulses from sense organs to the cell body. Dendrites are often short and branching, and there may be more than one per neuron. *See also* Neuron.

Dendrobium, genus of orchid native to SE Asia and popular as a cultivated plant. It has inconspicuous leaves and showy flowers with an unpleasant scent.

The 900 species include *D. nobile* that has white to deep purple flowers with purple centers. Height: to 3ft (91cm). Family Orchidaceae.

Dendrochronology, annual measurement of time by examination of growth rings in trees. This data can be related to wood used in structures, and to the hydrology of the region where it grew, thus fixing points in the climatic history of a particular area. Chronology based on the bristlecomb pine, a particularly long-lived tree, extends back over 7000 years.

Deneb, or **Alpha Cygni,** remote and very luminous white supergiant star in the constellation Cygnus. Characteristics: apparent mag. +1.26; absolute mag. −7.0; spectral type A2; distance 1500 light-years.

Dengue, contagious virus disease transmitted by the *Aedes aegypti* mosquito. Occurring in epidemic form in the tropics and in the warm months in temperate areas, it produces fever, headache, and fatigue, followed by severe back pain, muscle aching, and the appearance of a reddish rash. Recovery usually follows, and second attacks are rare.

Deng Xiaoping. *See* Teng Hsiao-p'ing.

Denikin, Anton Ivanovich (1872–1947), Russian general. After serving in World War I, he became (1918) chief of staff for the Provisional government but was shortly dismissed. He and Gen. Lavr Kornilov staged a revolt against the Provisional government, and he was arrested. He escaped after the Bolsheviks seized power and became commander of the White forces in the Russian Civil War. Defeated by Bolshevik troops in 1920, he left for Constantinople. He lived in France from 1926.

Denis, king of Portugal. *See* Diniz.

Denis, Saint (3rd century? AD), patron saint of France. According tc tradition, he was the first bishop of Paris and was martyred on Montmartre. He is often represented carrying his severed head in his hands. His feast day is October 9.

Denitrification, process that reduces nitrites or nitrates to yield nitrites, nitrogen oxides, ammonia, or free nitrogen. Denitrifying bacteria change the nitrogen of ammonia into free nitrogen that enters the atmosphere or soil. *See also* Nitrogen Cycle.

Denizli, city in SW Turkey, on tributary of Menderes River; capital of Denizli prov.; site of ruins of ancient Greek cities Laodicea ad Lycum and Hierapolis; early Christian center and site of one of "Seven Churches of Asia Minor." Industries: tourism, grain, cotton, tobacco. Founded *c.* 200 BC by Antiochus II. Pop. 83,600.

Denmark, independent kingdom in N Europe situated at the entrance to the Baltic Sea. The country covers most of the Jutland Peninsula and includes the islands of the Danish archipelago. Greenland and the Faeroe Islands are self-governing entities under Danish sovereignty.

Land and Economy. Denmark is a country of low-lying plains consisting mostly of clay and sands deposited in the glacial era. After the Ice Age, the area comprised a continuous land-bridge connecting the Jutland and Scandinavian peninsulas. Subsequent flooding created the present-day fjords and straits. Denmark has a temperate maritime climate, with mild summers and cloudy, humid winters. Although lacking coal, hydroelectric power, and most mineral resources, the economy of Denmark is nonetheless highly industrialized. The industries range from iron, steel, and shipbuilding to a broad range of consumer products. Denmark is also known for its fine porcelains, textiles, and furniture. Only about 8% of the people are engaged in agriculture. Copenhagen is the leading port and manufacturing center.

People. The Danes are a Scandinavian people, closely related to Norwegians and Swedes, and trace their ancestry to Germanic tribes that moved into the area in the early Christian era. The official language is Danish, a Germanic tongue. The people are entitled to complete religious freedom, but the Evangelical Lutheran Church is the official church of Denmark. About 97% of the Danes are members of this church. Nearly 75% of the people live in urban communities.

Government. Denmark is a constitutional monarchy. Succession to the throne is hereditary, and the ruling monarch must be a member of the national church. Executive power lies with the monarch, while legislative power is shared by the monarch and a parliament (Folketing). In executive matters the monarch exercises authority through government ministers. Major international obligations cannot be assumed without the approval of the Folketing, which may also force the resignation of any, or all, of the monarch's ministers. The major political parties are the Social Democrats, Liberals, and Conservatives.

History. Denmark first appears in recorded history with the rise of marauding Danish Vikings in the 8th century AD. King Harold Bluetooth Christianized Denmark in the 10th century. Under Canute II, the Danish kingdom extended over Norway and, for a brief period, all of England. Denmark and Norway were united until the 19th century. As an ally of Napoleonic France, Denmark was forced in 1815 to cede Norway to Sweden. A liberal constitution, approved in 1849, abolished absolute power and created a parliament. Denmark was neutral in WWI, but was invaded and conquered by Nazi Germany in WWII (April 1940). The war caused severe economic difficulties. US financial aid assisted in the post-war industrial recovery. Denmark joined the United Nations in 1945, and later became a member of the North Atlantic Treaty Organization (NATO). Since 1972, it has belonged to the European Economic Community (EEC), although Greenland chose to relinquish membership in 1985. Queen Margrethe II was coronated in 1972. Poul Schlüter of the moderately conservative Socialist People's Party became Danish prime minister in 1982, and the Social Democrats' Atli Dam took office in the Faeroe Islands in 1985. *See also* Faeroe Islands; Greenland.

PROFILE

Official name: Denmark, Kingdom of
Area: 16,629sq mi (43,069sq km)
Population: 5,122,065
Density: 308per sq mi (119per sq km)
Chief cities: Copenhagen (capital); Aarhus; Odense
Government: constitutional monarchy
Religion (major): Evangelical Lutheran Church
Language: Danish (official)
Monetary unit: Krone
Gross national product: $60,800,000,000
Per capita income: $9,663
Industries (major products): food processing, furniture, diesel engines, electrical products
Agriculture (major products): dairy products, hogs, beef, barley
Minerals (major): lignite
Trading partners (major): United Kingdom, Sweden, West Germany, United States

Denominator, Common, number that is a multiple of the denominators of two or more specified fractions. Thus for 2/3 and 1/7, the (least) common denominator is 21, allowing the fractions to be put in the forms 14/21 and 3/21, for addition, etc.

Densitometer, instrument for measuring the optical transmission or reflection (optical density) of a material, such as a photographic film or plate. It can be used in spectroscopy to determine the positions of spectral lines and bands and to measure their relative densities, and thus intensities.

Density, the mass per unit volume of a substance. The density of a solid or liquid is normally constant over a wide range of temperatures and pressures. This fact was used to establish the unit of mass (the gram) in the metric system—the density of water was taken to be one gram per cubic centimeter. The density of a gas, however, depends strongly on both pressure and temperature.

Dentistry, the profession concerned with the care and treatment of the oral cavity, particularly the teeth and their supporting tissue. Besides general practice, dentistry includes such specialties as oral surgery, prosthodontics, periodontics, orthodontics, pedodontics, and public health. Scientific dentistry started in the 16th and 17th centuries in Germany and France when it became recognized as a separate profession; university courses were initiated and dental textbooks were published. Before that time barbers had performed most dental services. Today the practice of dentistry is strictly controlled; there are special educational requirements and licensing procedures in all countries.

Dentition, the type, number and arrangement of teeth. In adult man, there are 32 teeth: in each jaw are 4 incisors; 2 canines; 4 premolars, or bicuspids; 4 back molars; and finally at about 18 years of age, 2 wisdom teeth. Man's teeth cut, grind, and tear food and are not adapted to any particular type of diet. *See also* Tooth.

Denton, city in N central Texas, 38 mi (61km) NW of Dallas; seat of Denton co; named for John B. Denton, lawyer and minister killed by Indians. Industries: processed food, plastics. Founded 1855; inc. 1866. Pop. (1980) 48,063.

D'Entrecasteaux, volcanic island group in SW Pacific Ocean, off SE coast of New Guinea; administered by Papua and New Guinea; group consists of Fergusson (largest), Goodenough, and Normanby islands. Dobu is chief settlement. Named for French navigator Antoine d'Entrecasteaux, who discovered the archipelago 1793. Area: 1,200sq mi (3,118sq km). Pop. 32,336.

Denture, artificial substitute for all the teeth in the upper or lower jaw; usually made of plastic and occasionally reinforced with metal. The retention of such a prosthetic device depends on the firmness of the underlying tissues and the adhesion provided by the saliva of the mouth. When well-fitted and designed, it can improve natural appearance. A partial denture is called a bridge.

Denudation, in geology, all the processes that result in either wearing away or lowering of the Earth's surface. In a narrow sense, denudation may be synonymous with erosion; however, erosion, mass wasting, transportation, are all considered to be processes resulting in denudation. *See also* Erosion.

Denver, capital and largest city of Colorado, in N central Colorado, at foot of Rocky Mts on South Platte River; seat of Denver co. It served as territorial capital 1867; prosperity was greatly spurred with the discovery of gold and silver (1870s and 1880s), and the building of the Denver Pacific Railroad (1870); site of capital building (19th century), many government agencies including the US Mint; Denver Art Museum, Boettcher Botanical Gardens; University of Denver (1864), Loretto Heights College (1891), Regis College (1877), Temple Buell College (1909), Rockmont College (1914); many resort and recreational areas set in the surrounding beautiful scenery; processing, shipping, and distribution center for agricultural area. Industries: aerospace, electronics, rubber goods, luggage, tourism, mining, livestock, meat packing, railroad shops, food processing. Founded 1860 with inc. of Auraria and two other villages, and named in honor of Kansas territorial governor James W. Denver; inc. 1861. Pop. (1980) 491,396.

Deoxyribonucleic Acid (DNA), molecule found in chromosomes and viruses that is resposibile for storing the genetic code. It consists of two long chain polynucleotides shaped like a twisted rope ladder, the sides of which consists of sugar-phosphate chains and the rungs of linked nitrogenous bases. The sugar is 2-deoxy-D-ribose and the four bases are adenine, cytosine, guanine, and thymine. The genetic code is stored by the sequence of the bases, three bases coding for one amino acid. The discovery in the 1970s of restriction enzymes, which cut the DNA molecule at specific sites, made it possible for scientists to insert new genetic material into a DNA molecule. These recombinant DNA, or gene splicing, techniques made possible the manufacture of specific hormones and chemicals by bacteria and will enable correction of genetic mistakes in human DNA. *See also* Nucleic Acids.

Dependence, in psychology, the extent to which an individual needs other people in order to function, as opposed to independence, functioning on one's own. Infants are totally dependent on their parents for satisfying basic survival needs, but most children progress toward some degree of independence as they grow.

Depersonalization, in psychology and psychiatry, a state in which a person feels detached from his own reality or body, and the actions of oneself as well as of others are perceived as dreamlike and unreal. It is a symptom of some serious mental disorders such as the schizophrenic reactions and other psychoses.

Depletion, a special form of depreciation referring to the exhaustion of nonreplaceable natural resources, eg, oil, minerals, or natural gas, as they are exploited for human use. Depletion is usually figured as the percentage of the estimated reserves of the resource that has been used up, ie, mined or pumped.

Deposition, in geology, layering or placing any material in a constructive process. The accumulation of sediment, ore deposits, and organic material by any natural agent that would result in stratification of rock-forming material is deposition.

Depreciation, decline in the value of an asset as it is spread over its economic life. Depreciation covers the decrease in value or usefulness because of use, age, or exposure to the elements but does not cover unexpected losses due to accident or natural disaster. It is a way of measuring an asset's actual cost and actual value to the owner, either a firm or an individual. In the United States deduction for depreciation of an asset may be taken as a business expense in determining taxable income.

Depression, bottom of the business cycle. Depression is associated with high unemployment levels, excess capacity, seriously decreased purchasing power for consumers, and lack of business expansion, encouraged by pessimism. Government influence tends to be

Denmark

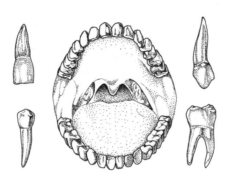

Dentition: (clockwise from lower left) biscuspid. incisor, canine, molar

Denver, Colorado

more effective in curing a depression than in dampening the inflation caused by prosperity. See also Business Cycle.

Depression, emotional state marked by sadness, dejection, feelings of guilt and worthlessness and self-blame. In severe depressions psychomotor retardation can lead to a near stupor. Depressions are often accompanied by physical complaints, including loss of appetite, insomnia, and inertia. Social withdrawal and reality distortion are also usually present.

Depression, Great, in US history, the severe economic crisis that afflicted the country in the 1930s. It was part of a worldwide downturn in economic activity. The Great Depression is generally thought to have begun with the collapse of the stock market in October 1929 and not to have finally ended until about 1940, when increased defense spending strengthened the economy.

Economists differ as to the relative importance of the various causes of the Great Depression, which was both more serious and longer lasting than the usual downturn in the business cycle. Among those causes were the economic dislocations brought about by World War I, the unbridled stock market speculations of the 1920s, the easy credit money that produced more industrial production than consumers were able to purchase, a prosperity that was unequally shared (farmers and workers did not take part in it to the extent that other segments of the economy did), and the protectionist trade policies of a series of conservative Republican administrations that denied foreign markets for US products. The stock market crash of October 1929 was especially wrenching to the economy; it was estimated that $30,000,000,000 was lost in stock values during the crash week. Since a large part of stock speculation was done on margin, or credit, the collapse had a devastating effect on the nation's banking system and, to a lesser extent, on foreign banks that had helped to finance the speculation. Bank failures became commonplace. Whereas 659 banks failed in 1929 (already a high figure, as had been the case throughout the 1920s), 1,352 failed in 1930 and 2,294 in 1931. Virtually any set of statistics proves that the depression was of a much greater magnitude than the ordinary business downturn. Unemployment, which had been at 1,500,000 persons in 1929, jumped to 4,000,000 in 1930 and continued to increase until it reached 13,000,000 in 1932 (almost one-third of the work force). The gross national product fell by almost 50%; from $104,000,000,000 in 1929 to $58,500,000,000 in 1932. Automobile production fell from 5,500,000 cars in 1929 to 1,500,000 in 1932.

Herbert Hoover, who became president only months before the crash, was slow to respond to the downslide. Surrounded by economic conservatives, he tended to a laissez-faire attitude, believing that conditions would right themselves. The Hawley-Smoot Tariff Act, passed by the Republican Congress in 1930 and signed by Hoover, had the effect of helping to spread the US depression worldwide. It brought U.S. tariffs to an all-time high, causing 25 other nations to raise theirs in retaliation. International trade fell alarmingly as a result. Despite his belief in the basic soundness of the economy, Hoover instituted several antidepression measures, including a large public works program and the Reconstruction Finance Corporation. After the Democrats won control of Congress in the 1930 election, there was an upswing of federal programs.

In 1932 the Democrats nominated Franklin D. Roosevelt for president; his campaign promised an active federal program that would bring a "new deal" to the American People. He won an overwhelming victory, and from the date of his inauguration in 1933, the

history of the Great Depression mirrored that of his New Deal, which was designed to end it. In Europe, perhaps the most devastating effect of the depression was the emergence of Adolf Hitler and the Nazi party from the ruins of the German economy. See also New Deal.

Depressive Reaction, a neurotic or psychotic disorder that has as its primary characteristic severe depression. A neurotic depressive reaction is a disorder that occurs when an individual experiences a disturbing event, eg loss of a loved one. He or she typically withdraws, feels helpless and worthless, and may be unable to cope with daily life. Although this disorder responds to treatment with drugs and the support of sympathetic people, it may sometimes develop into a psychotic depressive reaction. Individuals with this severe disorder may lose contact with reality and threaten and attempt suicide. Although such behavior is similar to that of manic-depressives, there is no elated manic stage. Electroshock and psychotherapy are sometimes used to treat psychotic depressive reaction. See also Depression; Manic-Depressive Psychosis.

Depretis, Agostino (1813–87), Italian political leader and a leftist leader of the Risorgimento (the mid-century movement for Italian unification). The head of various national government ministries from 1862, by 1873 he was the leader of the left. He was prime minister 1876–78, 1878–79, 1881–87.

Depth Charge, explosive cannister detonated underwater at predetermined depths and used by naval vessels and aircraft to destroy submerged submarines.

Depth Perception, ability to localize the position of objects in three-dimensional space. Even though the retina is two-dimensional, information about depth is created in the retinal image. These "depth cues" include such factors as linear perspective and relative size. Physiological information, such as ocular convergence, is also important.

DeQuincey, Thomas (1785–1859), English essayist and critic. DeQuincey led an unsettled life after leaving Oxford, where he first took opium. His Confessions of an English Opium Eater (1822) made him famous.

Derain, André (1880–1954), French painter. An artist of the fauvist style, he characterized his prolific landscapes with brilliant color, swift curves, and spontaneous lines. His later style was influenced by Italian masters, and his subjects became precisely drawn in subdued colors. See also Fauvism.

Derby, Edward George Geoffrey Smith Stanley, 14th Earl of (1799–1869), English Conservative statesman and orator. At first a Whig, he gradually became leader of the Protectionists, whom he rallied, and was eventually recognized as Conservative leader (1851). As prime minister (1852, 1858–59, 1866–68) he passed the electoral Reform Act (1867) and ensured Disraeli's succession.

Derby, Thomas Stanley, 1st Earl of (1435–1504), English noble. At Bosworth Field (1485) he commanded a large force which he withheld from aiding Richard III. After the battle he crowned his stepson, the victorious Henry VII, and was made earl.

Derby, city in N central England, on Derwent River, 37mi (60km) NE of Birmingham; important railway junction. England's first silk mill was built here 1719. Industries: railway engineering, aircraft engines, tex-

tiles, electrical equipment, porcelain, paints, hosiery. Pop. 215,200.

Derivative, rate of change of a mathematical function with respect to a change in the independent variable. The derivative is an expression of the instantaneous rate of change of the function: in general it is itself a function of the variable. A common example is in obtaining velocities and accelerations. An object moves a distance x in time t, according to the equation $x = at^2$. In such motion the velocity increases with time (the object accelerates). The expression dx/dt, called the first derivative of distance with respect to time, is equal to the velocity of the object. For the example it equals $2\,at$. The result is obtained by considering a small time interval δt, over which the average velocity is $\delta x/\delta t$, and taking the limit of this as t becomes vanishingly small. The second derivative, written d^2x/dt^2, is equal to the acceleration. Derivatives can similarly be used to find the slope of a curve at a particular point. See also Calculus; Differential Equation; Limit.

Dermatitis, an inflammation of the skin that in acute form produces redness, itching, and blister formation or oozing and in chronic form thickening and darkening of the skin and scales. In contact dermatitis, contact with a particular substance—such as soap or poison ivy—produces the reaction. In atopic dermatitis (often associated with hay fever and asthma) excessive dryness occurs and redness at the neck and elbow and knee bends. In stasis dermatitis, heavy pigmentation and sometimes ulcers develop on the inner sides of lower legs as result of poor circulation. In neurodermatitis, there is no known cause except the patient's repeating rubbing and scratching of the area. The term is also sometimes used for eczema. See also Eczema.

Dermatology, branch of medicine that deals with the diagnosis and treatment of skin diseases and disorders.

Dermis, the inner of the two main layers of the skin. Also known as the true skin, the dermis is made up of connective tissue fibers that give strength and toughness. It is richly supplied with blood vessels and contains many nerve endings, sensory organs of touch, and numerous glands.

Dervish, member of a Muslim religious fraternity, similar to a Christian monk. Central to dervish devotion is the Dhikr or "remembering" of God, often attained through a hypnotic or ecstatic trance.

Descartes, René (1596–1650), French philosopher and mathematician. He received a Jesuit education and saw military service (1612–21). Thereafter he retired to pursue scientific and philosophical inquiries. He founded analytic geometry and contributed to geometrical optics in the treatise that prefaced the Discourse on Method (1637). Here, and in his Meditations, Descartes introduced modern metaphysics, as the work of deduction and intuition. Mind, he held, was essentially separate from matter, which was extended, inert substance. Mind knows matter only through ideas, whose clarity and distinctness, guaranteed by God, confers truth. Descartes died in Sweden, shortly after accepting the invitation of Queen Christina to join her intellecual court. See also Cartesian; Cogito Ergo Sum; Rationalism.

Desegregation, ending laws or customs that separate people on such grounds as sex, age, race, or religion. See also Integration.

Desensitization, process in which a person allergic to a certain substance or substances is subjected to injection of the allergen, or offending substance, in a series of gradually increasing dosages in hope of desensitizing or decreasing the person's sensitivity to the substance. *See also* Allergy.

Desert, arid region of any latitude typified by scant, intermittent rainfall and little vegetation. Since erosion is a great influence, more important in arid as compared to more humid regions, the landforms of any desert are unique. The region can be classified as young, mature, or old, depending on the extent of the remains of the mountain and stream features it once had. *See also* Butte; Degradation.

Desiderius (AD 8th century), last Lombard king (756–74) and father-in-law of Charlemagne. When Desiderius threatened papal territory and his sovereignty, Charlemagne rejected his wife and in 774 captured the Lombard throne.

Desman, aquatic, molelike mammal that eats insects, mollusks, and fish. It has a flexible tubular snout, webbed hind feet, and vertically flattened scaly tail. The Russian *Desmana moschata* has red-brown fur that is commercially valuable. *Galemys pyrenaicus,* found in the Pyrenees, is smaller and lighter in color. Length: body—to 8in (215mm); tail—to 8in (215mm). Family Talpidae.

Desmid, any of a group of tiny single-celled green algae (order Desmidiales) that live in fresh water and are characterized by perforations in their cell walls and highly symmetrical shapes resembling those of diatoms. They differ from diatoms chiefly in their lack of a silica skeleton. Some form colonies. *See also* Green Algae.

Des Moines, capital city of Iowa, in the center of the state near the confluence of the Des Moines and Racoon rivers; site of Iowa State Fair Grounds, Drake University (1881), Grand Valley College (1896), the Des Moines Art Center, Des Moines Symphony. Damaged by severe flooding 1954, the city is now protected by dams and reservoirs. Industries: insurance, publishing, plastics, chemicals, outdoor clothing. Founded as Fort Des Moines 1843; inc. 1851; chartered as city 1857; made capital 1858. Pop. (1980) 191,003.

Desmoulins, Camille (1760–94), pamphleteer and journalist in the French Revolution. His writings and speeches did much to further the revolutionary cause. A critic of the new government, he became alligned with Jacques Danton and was guillotined.

De Soto, Hernando (*c.* 1500–42), Spanish explorer. Commissioned by Emperor Charles V to conquer the North American mainland, De Soto left Spain in 1539 and landed on the Florida coast. He set off by land in search of gold and silver. His travels took him through Georgia, the Carolinas, Tennessee, and Alabama, but he found no riches. A second trip took his expedition to the Mississippi River; they were probably the first white men to see it. He traveled up the Arkansas River into Oklahoma and then returned to the Mississippi, where he died. His men buried him in the river and explored Texas. Eventually they followed the Mississippi to the Gulf of Mexico. Remnants of the group turned up at Veracruz, Mexico, in 1543.

Des Plaines, city in NE Illinois, on Des Plaines River; suburb of Chicago; site of O'Hare International Airport and Glenview Naval Air Station. Industries: radio parts, electrical equipment, greenhouse specialties. Inc. 1925. Pop. (1980) 53,568.

Despotism, absolute or autocratic rule by an individual, without legal sanction or popular consent. The term dates from ancient Greece and has been applied to dictatorial systems under which power was tyrannically and arbitrarily imposed and personal freedoms severely curtailed. The 18th century has been called the "Age of Enlightened Despotism," when a number of rulers exercised absolute power with the rationale that their regimes sought the betterment of the governed.

Dessalines, Jean Jacques (1785–1806), Haitian revolutionary and leader of the independence movement after the capture of Toussaint. Dessalines drove out the French (1803), declared independence (1804) and changed the country's name from St. Domingue to Haiti. He became Emperor Jacques and ruled with nobility (1804–06). A national hero, he is considered the father of Haitian independence.

Destroying Angel, a species of very poisonous mushroom *(Amanita virosa)* common to wooded areas. It is all white with a scaly stem that has a frayed ring under the cap. It, like death cups, is often fatal.

Detective Story, type of narrative fiction that follows this pattern: crime committed (usually murder); clues gathered and interpreted; criminal exposed in a climactic scene. An early example popular in England and the United States was William Goodwin's *Adventures of Caleb Williams* (1794). In the 19th century the police novel evolved, in England based upon the activities of Scotland Yard and in France based on *Memoires* by François Eugène Vidocq. In 1841 Edgar Allan Poe established the genre of the detective story in the United States with *The Murders in the Rue Morgue.*

Detergent, any substance used for cleansing. Strictly speaking, detergents include both soaps and synthetic detergents (syndets), which have molecules that possess a long hydrocarbon chain attached to an ionized group. The hydrocarbon chain attaches to grease and other nonpolar substances; the ionized group has an affinity for water. Substances of this type lower surface tension (that is, they are surface active). The term is often used in the more restricted sense of synthetic detergents, of which there are several types; the commonest are salts of organic sulfonic acids. Domestic detergents often contain additives such as colorants, perfume, bleach, and optical brighteners. *See also* Soap.

Determinant, a square array of numbers associated with a value that is the algebraic sum of all the products that can be formed by using as factors an element from each column in succession (each from a different row). The signs of the products may be positive or negative depending upon whether the number of changes in the rows necessary to restore them to natural order is even or odd. Determinants are used extensively to solve systems of equations.

Determinism, philosophical doctrine that every event can be explained as a result of earlier events. Everything has a cause; no event is purely accidental. What seems to be free choice can be explained if all its antecedents are known. Psychologists recognize a number of determining (if not rigidly controlling) factors in behavior—eg, constitution, health, attitudes, conflicts, and social pressures.

Detonator, a device using sensitive chemicals (initiating explosives) to blast charges of less sensitive compounds (high explosives). The detonating charge is housed in a thin-walled metal or plastic, waterproof capsule. Detonators may be exploded electrically or by igniting a fuse.

Detroit, city and port in SE Michigan, on Detroit River just W of Lake St Clair; seat of Wayne co; most populous city in state. Antoine de la Mothe Cadillac founded French fort and trading post here 1701 named Fort Pontchartrain; captured by British 1760, it was held during a long siege by Pontiac; used as British control center during the American Revolution; it was surrendered to United States by terms of Jay's Treaty 1796. Detroit served as territorial then state capital 1805–1847; it was severely burned in 1805 and rebuilt to resemble Washington D.C. Lost to Britain in War of 1812, it was retaken by US forces under William Henry Harrison in 1813. Detroit contains University of Detroit (1877), Detroit Institute of Technology (1891), Marygrove College (1910), Wayne State University (1933), Mercy College of Detroit (1941), Detroit Bible College (1945), and Michigan Lutheran College (1962). The Ambassador International Bridge (world's longest international suspension bridge) and a vehicular tunnel connect Detroit with Windsor, Ontario; site of Fort Wayne (1841–51), now a military museum; Belle Isle, a park in the Detroit River containing gardens, a conservatory, children's zoo, and an aquarium; the Detroit Institute of Arts; and Renaissance Center, a hotel and office complex dedicated in 1977 and designed to revitalize the city's downtown area.

Detroit is the headquarters of General Motors Corp., Chrysler Corp., Ford Motor Co., and the United Automobile Workers Union, one of the world's largest unions. Detroit is a leading Great Lakes shipping and rail center. Industries: steel, pharmaceuticals, food processing, metal stamping, machine tools, tires, paint, wire goods, automobiles and parts, ball bearings, calculators. Inc. as village 1815, as city 1824. Pop. (1980) 1,203,339.

Deuterium, isotope (symbol D) of hydrogen whose nuclei contain a neutron in addition to a proton. Every million hydrogen atoms in nature contain about 156 deuterium atoms. Deuterium occurs in water as D_2O (heavy water), from which it is obtained by fractional electrolysis. Heavy water is used as a moderator in some fission reactors and it could become a fuel in fusion reactors. Properties: mass no. 2; atomic mass 2.0147.

Deuteron, nucleus of a deuterium atom, consisting of one proton and one neutron. *See* Deuterium.

Deuteronomy, biblical book, fifth and last book of the Pentateuch consisting of discourses delivered by Moses shortly before he died. It explains the laws laid down by the previous books, Genesis, Exodus, Leviticus, and Numbers. *See also* Pentateuch.

Deva, the all-encompassing word for god in the Vedas, the earliest religious texts of India. There were 33 of these gods, 11 for each of the three world categories —sky, air, and earth. Some of the nature gods of Vedic poems appear in present-day Hinduism; they include Surya (the sun) and Varuna (the sky).

De Valera, Eamon (1882–1975), Irish statesman, b. New York City. Active in Ireland's effort toward independence, after the Easter Rebellion of 1916 he was elected president of the Sinn Fein party while imprisoned in England. Opposing W. T. Cosgrave's Free Irish State ministry, he founded the Fianna Fail party in 1924 and succeeded Cosgrave in 1932. He continued as head of Ireland's government with only two brief interruptions until 1959, when he became president of the Republic of Ireland. He retired in 1973.

Devaluation, reduction in value of a country's currency relative to gold. Countries use gold as the international unit of exchange. Devaluation is in effect a decrease in the value of the country's currency relative to all other countries' currencies, which means that a particular country's products become cheaper for other countries to purchase. It also becomes more expensive for the country that has devalued to purchase products from other countries. Thus, with devaluation, imports become more expensive and exports become cheaper. Devaluation is thus often used to rectify a balance of payments deficit.

Developing Countries. *See* Third World.

Developmental Psychology, study of behavior as it changes through all life stages, from the uterus through birth, childhood, adolescence, the middle years, and old age. Behavior is affected by the interaction of physical growth, maturation (eg, changes in the activity of sex glands), and learning. Psychologists study normal growth, change, and self-actualization, as well as life-stage related problems. *See also* Adolescence; Aging; Child Development.

Devi or **Mahadevi,** in Hindu mythology and religion, the great goddess, consort of Siva, daughter of Himavat. In this aspect she is represented as beautiful and adorned with jewels. In her darker aspect as Chandi, Bhairavi, Durga, or Kali, she is frightful with attributes of death, the noose, iron hook, and prayer book. *See also* Durga; Kali.

Deviance, in the social sciences, anything that departs from or conflicts with the standard norm. Deviant behavior is atypical behavior that departs from socially or culturally accepted patterns. In considering both "deviation" and "norm," social scientists take into consideration the group context within which the "deviance" is noted. For instance, members of a teenage gang would consider behavior that showed respect for law "deviant."

Deviated Septum, an abnormality of the muscular wall, or septum, separating the nasal cavities. Such an abnormality can interfere with normal nasal functioning and breathing.

Deviation, in statistics, the difference between any one of a set of numerical values and the mean of the set. If the values are bunched together around the mean, the deviations of the various values will tend to be small. If they are widely dispersed, the deviations will tend to be large.

Devilfish, or manta, devil ray, horned ray, flat-bodied elasmobranch found in tropical and temperate marine waters. A surface feeder, it is a food and game fish in some areas. Its disclike body may be blue, black, or brown and has two slender feeding fins at the head and a poison tail spine. Width: 4–20ft (1.2–6.1m); weight: to 3502lb (1576kg). There are four genera. Family Mobulidae. *See also* Chondrichthyes; Ray.

Devil's Island (Île Du Diable), smallest and southernmost of the Îles de Salut in the Caribbean Sea, off the coast of French Guiana. French penal colony, 1852–1938.

Devolution, War of (1667–68), conflict over the Spanish Netherlands. When Marie Thérèse, daughter of the king of Spain, married Louis XIV of France (1660), she signed away her rights to the Spanish Netherlands in return for a large dowry. The dowry was never paid, and Louis used that as a pretext for invading the territory. French troops won an easy victory, but the United Provinces formed the Triple Alliance with England and

Desman

Admiral George Dewey

Thomas Dewey

Sweden, which in turn forced the return of much of the territory to Spain by the Treaty of Aix-La-Chapelle. *See also* Aix-La-Chapelle, Treaty of; Triple Alliance.

Devon (Devonshire), county in SW England, bounded by English Channel and N by Bristol Channel; hilly in E, NE, S, and Dartmoor; drained by Exe, Tamar, Dart, and Teign rivers. Chief towns are Exeter, Plymouth, and Torbay. Industries: dairy products, cider, tourism, engineering. Area: 2,612sq mi (6,765sq km). Pop. 936,300.

Devon Cattle, dual-purpose breed of horned, dark red domesticated cattle. Originally developed in Devonshire, England, they have been introduced in the United States and Argentina. Yields of milk and meat are fair. *See also* Beef Cattle; Cattle.

Devonian Period, the fourth oldest period of the Paleozoic Era, lasting from 400 to 350 million years ago. It is called the Age of Fishes. Numerous marine and freshwater remains include jawless fishes, placoderms, and forerunners of today's bony and cartilaginous fishes. The first land vertebrate, the amphibian *Ichthyostega,* appeared. Land arthropods included scorpions, mites, spiders, and the first insects. Land plants consisted of tall club mosses, scouring rushes, and ferns. *See also* Geologic Time; Paleozoic Era.

Devonshire, William Cavendish, 1st Duke of (1641–1707), English statesman. He entered parliament in 1661 and played an active and daring role as opponent of the court of Charles II. He withdrew from the post of privy councilor in 1679 in protest against the Roman Catholic interest and aided in the impeachment of royal officials. He opposed James II's rule, and encouraged the accession of the Protestant William of Orange in 1688.

De Vries, Hugo (1848–1935), Dutch botanist. He introduced the concept of mutation into the study of genetics. In 1900 along with Karl Correns and William Bateson, he rediscovered Gregor Mendel's works on heredity. His *Mutation Theorie* (1901–03) influenced later concepts of the role of mutation in evolution.

Dew, water vapor condensed directly on grass and other surfaces near the ground. *See also* Precipitation.

Dewar, (Sir) James (1842–1923), Scottish chemist and physicist who was involved in extremely-low-temperature research. He built a device that produced liquid oxygen. He also constructed Dewar flasks (household varieties are Thermos bottles), which were capable of storing low-temperature liquid oxygen for longer periods than was previously possible. He liquified and solidified hydrogen. The first practical smokeless powder, cordite, was jointly developed by Sir Frederick Abel and Dewar.

Dewey, George (1837–1917), US admiral, Spanish-American War hero, b. Montpelier, Vt. He served in the Civil War and became a commodore in 1896. When the Spanish-American War began (1898) Dewey sailed for the Philippines. On May 1 he entered Manila Bay after midnight and defeated the Spanish fleet at dawn with only 8 US men wounded. He was promoted to Admiral of the Navy (1899), the highest rank ever held by a US naval officer.

Dewey, John (1859–1952), US educator, philosopher, and psychologist, b. Burlington, Vt. While he was a professor at the University of Chicago (1894–1904), he founded (1896) the Laboratory School to experiment with educational methods. He joined the faculty of Columbia University (1904) and taught there until 1930. A chief founder of Functionalism, Dewey strove to make

the social sciences deal with the practical problems of education and mental disturbances. His theories about "learning-by-doing" and individualized instruction had profound impact on US educational practices and the development of applied psychology. His books include *The School and Society* (1899) and *Experience and Education* (1938).

Dewey, Thomas Edmund (1902–71), US lawyer and politician, b. Owosso, Mich. As special investigator of organized crime (1935–37) and district attorney (1937) in New York City, he gained national fame as a racket buster. He became New York governor (1942) and two years later he ran unsuccessfully for president against Franklin Roosevelt. He was reelected governor (1946, 1950). In 1948, he was favored in the presidential race but was edged out by Harry S Truman.

Dewey Decimal System, means of classifying books created by Melvil Dewey in 1876. The system is based on the number 10 used decimally. It is popular because of its subject currency and simplicity. There have been only 18 revisions in the system.

Dew Point, the temperature at which a vapor begins to condense, as water vapor in the air condenses into cloud when the air becomes saturated with the vapor.

Dextran, stable, water-soluble polysaccharide used as a substitute or extender for blood plasma in treatment for shock.

Dharma, sacred law or duty in Hindu tradition. Virtue lies in following one's Dharma, the first of the four man's ends. One's Dharma varies with one's caste and stage in life. In Buddhism the Dharma is the doctrine of Buddha; in Jainism the Dharma is The Good as the principle of motion. *See also* Hinduism.

Dhaulagiri, Mount, seventh-highest peak in the world, in the Himalayan system, N central Nepal; first climbed 1960 by Swiss expedition led by Max Eiselin; the Ganges, Gandak, and Ghagura rivers rise on its slopes. Height: 26,810ft (8,177m).

Dhole, rare, medium-sized, yellowish- to brownish-gray wild dog native to Central and E Asia. It preys chiefly on rodents and other small mammals, but packs are known to attack deer and other large mammals and may even drive tigers from their prey. Length: 30–40in (76–102cm); weight: 30–46lb (14–21kg). Family Canidae; species *Cuon alpinus. See also* Canidae.

Dhow, a sharp-bowed Arab sailing craft, with one or two masts with slanting triangular sails (lateen rigging), used in the Indian Ocean and the Red Sea. In the larger kinds, called baggals, the mainsail is much larger than the mizzensail.

Diabetes Insipidus, a disorder in which there is extreme thirst and excessive output of very dilute urine caused by decreased secretion of the hormone vasopressin (caused by brain tumor or disease, or unknown reason, or occasionally by kidney disease) and which, if untreated—by appropriate medication to decrease urine output—can lead to fall in blood volume, shock, dehydration, and even death.

Diabetes Mellitus, a common metabolic disorder in which the body's inability to obtain and use adequate amounts of the hormone insulin results in disease characterized by inability to handle carbohydrates. It may also affect many other body organs and functions. Susceptibility to diabetes mellitus is inherited but the disease usually develops with obesity, pregnancy, menopause, infection, or severe emotional stress and

is slightly more common in females. A nonhereditary form is produced by cancer of the pancreas. Insulin is normally secreted by islets in the pancreas. In juvenile diabetes, the pancreas is diseased, too little insulin is produced, and severe symptoms result. In maturity, or adult-onset (after 40) diabetes mellitus, the effectiveness and speed of release of insulin from the pancreas is often disturbed, producing minor, or in some cases, almost no, symptoms. In diabetes mellitus, the body cannot handle the sugar end-products of carbohydrate metabolism and convert them to energy compounds. The excess sugar is excreted in urine and signs such as frequent urination, dry mouth, extreme thirst, weakness, weight loss, and blurred vision can result. Diagnosis depends on urine and blood tests as well as special glucose-tolerance tests. The disease cannot be cured but can be treated with carbohydrate-limited diet, exercise, and administration of drugs—either insulin injection or synthetic oral drugs—to lower blood-sugar levels.

Diadochi, generals and administrators who fought over Alexander the Great's empire after his death (323 BC). Perdiccas, supported by Eumenes, lost the regency in battle (321 BC) to Antipater, allied with Antigonus I, Ptolemy I, and Craterus (who was slain). After Antipater's death (319 BC) Antigonus I declared himself king and with his son, Demetrius of Macedon, tried to rebuild the empire but was defeated and slain by Seleucus I and Lysimachus at Ipsus (301 BC). Later Demetrius overthrew Cassander, son of Antipater. After Seleucus I defeated Lysimachus (281 BC) the empire and power were divided among the sons of Ptolemy I, Antigonus I, and Seleucus I.

Diaghilev, Sergei (1872–1929), Russian ballet producer. In 1909 he founded the Ballets Russes in Paris. With Michel Fokine he brought together some of the greatest dancers: Anna Pavlova, Nijinsky; choreographers: Léonide Massine, Bronislava Nijinska, George Balanchine; composers: Stravinsky, Debussy, Richard Strauss; and artists as set and costume designers: Picasso, Chagall, Matisse, to revitalize and reshape ballet choreography and stage production.

Dialect, a regional variety of a language, distinguished from other varieties by features of pronunciation, grammar, and vocabulary. Dialectical differences may be relatively slight (as in the case of dialects of American English), or they may be sufficiently great (as in Italian and Chinese) that mutual comprehension becomes difficult or even impossible.

Dialectical Logic, philosophical concept of G. W. F. Hegel (1770–1831). Hegel argued that ordinary logic, governed by the law of contradiction, is static and lifeless. In the *Science of Logic* (1814–16) he claimed to satisfy the need for a dynamic method, whose three moments of thesis, antithesis, and synthesis, both canceled and preserved the irreconcilable. Logic was to be dialectical, or a process (movement) of resolution by means of conflict of opposing categories; in short, thought was as "living" as organic nature itself. *See also* Dialectical Materialism.

Dialectical Materialism, philosophy according to Karl Marx (1818–83). Marx agreed with Georg Hegel that the course of history was logically dialectical, that is, change occurred in terms of the opposition of thesis, antithesis, and synthesis. Marx believed that Hegel was wrong, however, to define the subject of dialectics as spirit or reason. For Marx, the proper dialectical subject was material, sensuous experience. Mind (soul, reason) was at most derived from material or social realities. *See also* Dialectical Logic; Marx, Karl.

Dialysis, process for separating a colloid from a dissolved substance by virtue of their different rates of diffusion through a semipermeable membrane. In the artificial kidney the unwanted (smaller) molecules diffuse away into the dialysate. Electrodialysis employs a direct electric current to accelerate the process, especially useful for isolating proteins.

Diamond, a native element, carbon (C). Found in volcanic pipes and in alluvial deposits. Cubic system generally octahedral crystals. Brilliant, transparent to transluscent, colorless and many hues, depending on impurities; hardness 10; sp gr 3.5. Hardness, brilliance, and fire make diamonds unsurpassed as gems. Weighted in carats (0–200 gm) and in points (1/100 carat). Largest mines in South Africa and Brazil. About 20% suitable for gem use; others used in industry.

Diamondback Terrapin, brackish water turtle, native to US Atlantic and Gulf coasts. Famous as a food delicacy, it is named for its grooved and ridged carapace plate. Female length: to 9in (23cm); male length: to 5in (13cm). Family Emydidae; species *Malaclemys terrapin. See also* Turtle.

Diamond Necklace Affair, incident at the court of France's Louis XVI in 1785. Deceived by the Comtesse de la Motte, and thinking he could regain Marie Antoinette's favor, Cardinal de Rohan purchased an expensive diamond necklace in the queen's name, which the comtesse stole. The cardinal's unfair treatment before and after his exoneration was held as proof of royal despotism, and indirectly contributed to causes of the French Revolution.

Diana, in Roman mythology, the goddess of woodlands and domestic animals. She was worshipped at her temple on the Aventine as the sister of Apollo. She was a special goddess of women because of her associations as a fertility deity. She was also the protector of slaves. *See also* Artemis.

Diana, Princess of Wales (1961–), consort of Charles, Prince of Wales. Born the Hon. Diana Frances Spencer at Queen Elizabeth's estate of Sandringham, she was a childhood playmate of her future husband's younger brothers. Educated in England and Switzerland, she taught kindergarten before her engagement to Prince Charles. They were married on July 29, 1981 and have two sons, William and Henry. Diana's beauty, charm, and warmth endeared her to the British public.

Diane de Poitiers, Duchesse de Valentinois (1499–1566), mistress and virtual queen of the young Henry II of France. His love for her, as well as her beauty and vivacity, overshadowed the real queen, Catherine de Médicis, witchcraft being one of the rumored means by which Diane maintained her appeal.

Diaphragm, muscular sheet that separates the thoracic, or chest, cavity from the abdominal cavity. It is a characteristic feature of mammals.

Diarrhea, the frequent elimination of more or less loose, watery stools, often accompanied by cramps and gas pains. Diarrhea is a symptom, caused by a functional disorder, such as spastic colitis and its accompanying emotional stress, fatigue, food allergy, or lack of vitamins; by an inflammation; by a generalized body disorder such as kidney disturbance or thyroid gland overfunction; or by infections of the lower bowel caused by bacteria, viruses, or other agents. A mild short attack of diarrhea is not serious and can be treated by bland diet; more severe and longer lasting attacks and those accompanied by fever and other signs should be treated by a physician.

Dias, Bartolomeu (or **Bartholomew Diaz**) (c.1457-1500), Portuguese navigator, the first European to round the Cape of Good Hope. In 1487, under the commission of King John II of Portugal, Dias sailed three ships around the African continent, thereby opening the route to India. He was part of the expedition of Pedro Alvares Cabral (1500) that discovered Brazil, but went down with his ship shortly after leaving Portugal.

Diaspora, the Jewish communities outside Palestine or Israel. Numbers of Jews were sent into exile by the Assyrian conquest (722 BC) and the Babylonian conquest (586 BC). Although Cyrus the Great allowed Jews to return from Babylonia in 538 BC, part of the Jewish exiles remained behind. In the 3rd century BC significant Jewish communities existed in Alexandria, Egypt, and Antioch, Syria. By the period of the destruction of Jerusalem by the Romans (AD 70) and their defeat of Bar Kokba's revolt (AD 135), the Diaspora had spread throughout the Near and Middle East and North Africa and to Rome itself. By then Diaspora Jews far outnumbered those within Palestine, a situation that continues today, but their religious and cultural center remained the Holy Land. The Diaspora gradually extended until it reached from England to China and India, and then, in more recent centuries, throughout the whole world.

Diastole, the time of the cardiac cycle during which the heart muscle is relaxed, and is filling with blood. *See also* Heart.

Diastrophism, an overall term encompassing all the processes of large-scale changes in the earth's crust. Intrusion and metamorphism are considered divisions of diastrophism as are the large movements that produce mountain ranges, ocean basins, and continents. On occasion, diastrophism formerly was used to describe a localized event. It is now reserved to detail large-scale phenomena only.

Diathermy, a form of physical therapy in which heat is generated in tissues by means of high-frequency electric currents of various wavelengths. Three forms are in wide use: shortwave, ultrasound, and microwave. Diathermy can be used to warm (in relief of muscle soreness) or to destroy tissues (as a surgical adjunct).

Diatom, any of a group of tiny to microscopic single-celled algae (class Bacillariophyceae) that are characterized by a shell-like cell wall of silica. The shell, or frustule, consists of two halves that fit together like the top and bottom of a shoe box. Diatom shells occur in a wide variety of highly symmetrical shapes. They live in nearly every environment that has water and is exposed to sunlight, including virtually all bodies of salt and fresh water and even soil, damp rocks, and tree bark.

Diatomaceous Earth, sediment formed from the skeletons of diatoms, microscopic marine plants. The deposits are pure silica and often form large, thick beds on the ocean bottom.

Díaz, Porfirio (1830–1915), president of Mexico (1876–80, 1884–1911). After twice failing to unseat President Juárez, but succeeding against Lerdo in 1876, Díaz retained power for 30 years in a country where political instability and frequent changes of government had marked the first half century of independence. The rural aristocracy, urban middle class, church, intellectuals, and foreign economic interests supported the regime. Growing opposition crystallized under Francisco Madero in 1911; Díaz resigned and sailed for France.

Díaz Ordaz, Gustavo (1911–79), president of Mexico (1964–70), whose term of office was marked by political unrest. The student demonstrations during the 1968 Olympiad were violently suppressed by the army.

Dickens, Charles (John Huffam) (1812–70), English novelist. Immensely popular in his own time, he remains to this day the most widely read novelist in the English language. He created many memorable comic characters in his novels while at the same time attacking social injustices. He spent his childhood in Chatham and London where his father held minor posts in the navy. At the age of 12 he went to work in a shoe-black factory when his father was thrown into debtors' prison. At 17 he became a court stenographer and less than two years later a parliamentary reporter. In 1833 he began contributing sketches on London life, signed Boz, to periodicals. The best of these were collected and published as *Sketches by Boz* (1836). Their favorable reception led to the publication of *Pickwick Papers* (1836–37), which was highly successful. Dickens would continue to write for the rest of his life. Most of his novels first appeared in installments in periodicals. He himself edited two major periodicals: *Household Words* (1850–59) and *All the Year Round* (1858–70). His early novels were *Oliver Twist* (1838), *Nicholas Nickleby* (1839), *The Old Curiosity Shop* (1841), and *Barnaby Rudge* (1841). *Martin Chuzzlewit* (1843) drew upon impressions he received of the United States on a visit in 1842. *A Christmas Carol,* the first and most successful of his holiday stories, appeared in 1843. Between 1844–46 he lived in Italy and Switzerland. *Dombey and Sons* appeared in 1848, followed by *David Copperfield* (1850), his own favorite novel and his most autobiographical work. The 1850s also saw the publication of *Bleak House* (1853), *Hard Times* (1854), *Little Dorrit* (1857), and his only historical novel, *A Tale of Two Cities* (1859). In 1856 he moved to his last permanent home, Gad's Hill Place, Kent. In 1858 he separated from his wife of 22 years, who had bore him 10 children. He was linked romantically with Ellen Ternan, a young actress. *Great Expectations,* considered by many critics to be his finest novel, appeared in 1861. His last completed novel was *Our Mutual Friends* (1865). In 1867–68 he made a triumphant US tour, giving dramatic readings from his works. He died of a stroke in 1870 before completing *The Mystery of Edwin Drood.* He was buried in the Poets Corner of Westminster Abbey.

Dickinson, Emily (1830–86), US poet, b. Amherst, Mass. She is generally considered one of the outstanding poets produced by the United States. Although only a few of her poems were published during her lifetime, more than 1000 were found in her bureau after her death and published over time.

According to her first biographer, she was "a social creature in the highest sense" from age 18 to 23, but at 23 she began to retreat into herself and was a recluse by 1870, the family catching only occasional glimpses of her as she moved quietly about the house. Biographers do not agree on the reasons for her withdrawal, but she did find a world of her own, a world of beauty and suggestion and sometimes of death in simple things—a stone, a glance, a bee, a bobolink. Her poetry employs sharp phrases and rich stanzes with intimated rhyme to display her emotions, her love of nature, and her sense of eternity.

Dickinson, John (1732–1808), US patriot, b. Talbot co, Md. His political writings, collectively known as *Farmers Letters* (1767), influenced the Revolutionary cause while Dickinson himself held to the hope of reconciliation with the Crown. Although he did not sign the Declaration, he fought in the war. Dickinson was executive officer of both Delaware (1781–82) and Pennsylvania (1782–85). At the Constitutional Convention (1787) he championed the small states and signed the Constitution as a representative from Delaware.

Dicotyledons, larger of the two subclasses of flowering plants, angiosperms, characterized by two seed leaves (cotyledons) in the seed embryo. Plant leaves are usually net-veined and flower parts are in fours or fives. The smaller subclass is monocotyledon. This system of angiosperm classification has been used since the late 17th century. The majority of common garden plants are dicotyledons. *See also* Angiosperm, Monoctyledon.

Dictatorship, absolute rule by an individual or group without consent of the governed. Under the Roman republic, a dictator might be appointed for a limited period during an emergency. All power resides in the dictator, with representative assemblies either abolished or existing as showcases. Personal freedoms are severely limited; censorship is enforced; education is tightly controlled; and perhaps most significantly, legal restraints on governmental authority are abolished.

Dictatorship of the Proletariat, stage that Karl Marx felt must precede introduction of pure communism and during which all remaining capitalistic thoughts and attitudes would be weeded out. In this stage the state owns the means of production and directs the production of goods and services. The few capitalistic procedures (eg, wage payment based on productivity) that survive to this stage are dying out.

Diction, the selection of words with awareness of their effectiveness and appropriateness. The manner in which words are used constitutes style. Diction refers to the choice of words. There are four levels of usage —formal, informal, colloquial, and slang. Diction also refers to distinctness of pronunciation.

Dictum, a remark, statement, or observation referring to a case. Gratis dictum is the voluntary offering of information. Simplex dictum is a statement that is made without proof. Obiter dictum is a remark made by a judge in reference to the interpretation and application of the law.

Didactic Literature, creative works primarily intended to instruct their readers or audience in some thesis or doctrine. Such works are distinguished from purely imaginative ones, which are presented as ends in themselves. A didactic work may present direct statements with proofs and examples or use various imaginative devices to translate its points into narratives or dramatic terms. Great didactic works from the ancient world include Hesiod's *Works and Days,* Lucretius' *De rerum natura,* and Vergil's *Georgics.* Most medieval literature, including Dante's *Divine Comedy,* and much Renaissance literature, including Spenser's *Faerie Queene* and Milton's *Paradise Lost,* have strong didactic elements. Didactic writing flourished in the 18th and 19th centuries, with Pope's *Essay on Man* and *Essay on Criticism* being outstanding examples. The "art for art's sake" movement in the 19th and 20th centuries is a reaction against didacticism.

Diderot, Denis (1713–84), French philosopher and man of letters. He assumed direction of the French *Encyclopedia* (1751) soon after incarceration for irreligious writings (1749). *On the Interpretation of Nature* (1754) and *D'Alembert's Dream* (1760) reveal Dide-

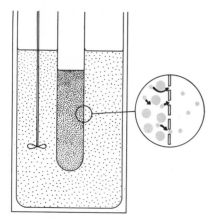

Dialysis

Charles Dickens

Emily Dickinson

rot's scientific materialism, and *Jacques the Fatalist* and *Rameau's Nephew* illustrate his determinism. Also noteworthy were Diderot's contributions to art and literary criticism. He represented a radical phase of the French Enlightenment. *See also* Enlightenment; Materialism.

Dido, in Greek mythology, the founder of Carthage, daughter of the Tyrian king Mutto, sister of Pygmalion, widow of Acerbas. Dido committed suicide to escape marriage to lambas, a local chieftain.

Diefenbaker, John George (1895–1979), Canadian political leader. A homesteader and lawyer in Saskatchewan, he developed a reputation for oratory and foreign affairs expertise. He was elected to the House of Commons (1940) and served as the Progressive-Conservative prime minister (1957–63). He was opposition leader in commons (1963–67) and remained a member until his death.

Dieffenbachia, or dumbcane, erect, evergreen plant native to tropical America. Large, stalked leaves with variegated veins grow near the plant top. Leaf veins are light green, yellow, or white. They are commonly grown as house plants. If the poisonous leaves or fleshy stem are chewed, temporary speechlessness results. Height: to 6ft (1.8m). Family Araceae; genus *Dieffenbachia. See also* Arum.

Diegueño, a confederation of Yuman-speaking North American Indians often commonly termed Mission Indians. The Diegueño proper take their name from Mission San Diego in S California. They were famous for the strong resistance they offered the early Spanish settlers and missionaries. Once numbering perhaps 3,000 persons, today about 700 survivors occupy a small area near San Diego.

Dieldrin, brown solid chlorinated naphthalene derivative ($C_{12}H_8OCl_6$) widely used as a contact insecticide and prepared by the oxidation of aldrin with peracids. It is insoluble in water and used as an emulsion or powder.

Dielectric, insulator, especially one that separates two conductors, as in a capacitor. The permittivity of a dielectric is a measure of the extent to which it can resist the flow of charge. The dielectric strength (usually measured in V/mm) is the maximum field that the dielectric can withstand without breaking down.

Diem, Ngo Dinh (1901–63), prime minister of South Vietnam (1954–63). A nationalist, opposed to both the Communists and the French, he was appointed premier of South Vietnam by Emperor Bao Dai in 1954. The following year the monarchy was abolished and Diem became the sole ruler. At first he received strong US support. Corruption, favoritism of Roman Catholics over the Buddhist majority, and setbacks in the war against the Communists led to growing discontent at home. With covert US support, dissident generals staged a coup in 1963. Diem was murdered during the fighting.

Dien Bien Phu, town in Vietnam, near Laotian border, occupied by the French in 1953 to cut supply lines of the Viet Minh. After a 55-day battle during which the Viet Minh under Gen. Vo Nguyen Giap surrounded the French, the French, under Christian de Castries, finally surrendered. The Vietnamese victory ended a fight begun in 1946 to drive the French from Vietnam. The ensuing peace agreement granted North Vietnam to the Viet Minh and independence to Laos, Cambodia, and South Vietnam.

Diesel Engine, an internal combustion engine in which air is compressed to a temperature sufficiently high to ignite fuel injected directly into the cylinders. There combustion and resulting expansion actuate pistons. Pressure creates the necessary heat to ignite the air-fuel mixture rather than the system found in gasoline engines. *See also* Compression-Ignition Engine.

Diesel Fuel, a petroleum product heavier than kerosene but lighter than heating oil, used to power diesel engines in trucks, buses, trains, and ships. Unlike gasolines, diesel fuels burn unevenly. They are graded against standardized mixtures of hexadecane and alpha methylnaphthalane to establish a cetane number. A cetane number of about 50 is desirable.

Diet, legislative assembly or administrative council, principally important in German history. Charles IV established the diet of the Holy Roman Empire by his Golden Bull of 1356. The diet comprised three estates —the electors (of the Holy Roman Emperor), other lay and church nobility, and representatives of the imperial cities—each of which met separately. Approval by each estate and the consent of the emperor were required on all matters. The most important of the diet's infrequent assemblies were at Nuremburg (1467), Worms (1521), and Augsburg (1530). After the Treaty of Westphalia ended the Thirty Years' War in 1648, the diet lost its legislative character, becoming instead an ambassadorial conference and finally dissolving in 1806 with the breakup of the empire. The term was retained for the legislatures of later German governments and, at times, for those of Austria, Hungary, Poland, Sweden, Denmark, Switzerland, and Japan (which still uses the term).

Dietary Laws, instructions, either secular or religious, which involve what foods may or may not be consumed under certain conditions. Such laws are one of the many ways a social group maintains its identity. Many Hindus, for example, practice vegetarianism, and Muslims undertake ritual fasting. In Judaism, such laws are called *Kashrut.* They prohibit certain foods entirely and indicate that others must be prepared in a certain way. The term *kosher* signifies foods that are "fit."

Differential, small change occurring in the value of a mathematical expression as a result of a small change in a variable. More formally, if $f(x)$ is a function of x, the differential of the function, written df, is given by $df = f'(x)\,dx$, where $f'(x)$ is the derivative of $f'(x)$. The differential of a function is useful in obtaining the results of small changes. For example, if the rate r of a chemical reaction is related to concentration c by the equation $r = 5c^2$, the derivative dr is equal to $10c\,dc$. A small change in the value of c, from 6 to 6.01 say, produces a small change in r, obtained by putting $c = 6$ and $dc = 0.01$; thus $dr = 0.6$.

Differential Equation, equation containing derivatives. For example, the equation $dN/dt = AN$, where N is the number of people in the population, t the time, and A a constant, is a highly simplified equation for population growth. dN/dt, the derivative of population with respect to time, is the rate at which population increases. According to the equation this is proportional to the population: that is, the higher the population, the faster it grows. Differential equations are solved by integration. In this example the result is $N = N_0\,e^{At}$, where N_0 is the initial value. *See also* Calculus; Derivative; Partial Differential Equation.

Diffraction, slight spreading of a light beam into the shadow region when the light travels through a narrow opening or past the edge of an obstacle. It results from the failure of light to travel in straight lines and is a consequence of the wave nature of light. Diffraction patterns can be observed on a screen behind the object: with a circular object or aperture light and dark concentric rings are seen; with a slit, wire, or straight edge there are light and dark bands. Fresnel diffraction occurs with a simple arrangement of light source and diffracting object. In Fraunhofer diffraction a parallel beam of light falls on the object and the diffraction patterns are focused onto the screen by a lens. Fraunhofer diffraction is less mathematically complex than Fresnel diffraction and can provide information on the wavelength of the light.

Other waves, including sound and radio waves and X rays, undergo a similar spreading when traveling through apertures or past obstacles. This accounts for the audibility of sound around corners and the propagation of radio waves over the curved surface of the earth.

Diffraction Grating, optical device for producing spectra by diffraction of light. In one form a light beam is diffracted by passing it through a flat glass plate on which very closely spaced parallel equidistant lines have been ruled. *See also* Diffraction.

Diffusion, spontaneous flow of a substance in a mixture from regions of high concentration to regions of low concentration, resulting from the random motion of individual atoms or molecules. Diffusion apparently ceases when there is no longer a concentration gradient. Its rate increases with temperature. The process occurs quickly in gases, more slowly in liquids, and extremely slowly in solids.

Digby, (Sir) Kenelm (1603–65), English diplomat, scientist, and writer. A Royalist, he defended Charles II in Paris (1641) and was chancellor to his queen (1644). He was exiled in 1643 for his conduct in the Great Rebellion and again in 1649. Among his scientific discoveries was his announcement that oxygen is necessary for plant life (1661); many of his other "discoveries" are not highly regarded now. He was one of the first members of the Royal Society (1663) and friend of Descartes and Sir Thomas Browne.

Digestion, process of breaking down food molecules into forms that can be absorbed by an organism. Digestion occurs by means of physical agents (teeth) and chemical agents (enzymes). This process provides nutrients and energy to keep an organism alive.

Digestive System, that organ system of the body concerned with the digestion of foodstuffs. It is also known as the alimentary system. It begins with the mouth cavity, which includes teeth, tongue, and salivary glands; and continues into the pharynx, which connects with the esophagus, or gullet, that carries food into the stomach. The stomach opens into the small intestine, which then opens into the large intestine, or colon. After food is swallowed it is pushed through the roughly 30ft (9m) of the digestive tract by rhythmic muscle contractions and relaxations known as peristalsis. On its journey the food is transformed into liquid that can be absorbed by the tissues of the body; specifically, the carbohydrates are changed to glucose; the proteins to amino acids; and the fats to fatty acids and glycerol. The indigestible parts are eventually eliminated from the body in a mass (feces) through the rectum, at the end of the colon.

Digit. *See* Numeral.

Digital Computer, computer that accepts input in discrete form, as numbers or characters, rather than in continuously variable form and processes it in the form of digits. *See also* Computer, Electronic.

Digitalis, drug obtained from the leaves of the purple foxglove plant that is used to treat heart disease. It increases contractions of the heart muscles and slows the cardiac rate.

Digital Signal, digits representing zeros and ones, transmitted by radio and translated by computer into dots of various shades to produce pictures similar to half-tone newspaper photographs.

Dijon, city in E France; capital of Côte-d'Or dept. An ancient city, it flourished in the 11th century when rulers of Burgundy made it their royal residence; site of Dijon University (1722), Cathedral of St Bénigne, and 13th-century Church of Notre Dame. Exports: Burgundy wine, mustard, cassis. Pop. 156,787.

Dik-dik, tiny African antelope with soft, yellow-gray to reddish hair and tuft of fur on forehead. Ringed horns are carried only by males. They may live in large groups, families, or singly. The name is derived from its call. Length: to 26in (66cm); height: to 16in (41cm) at shoulder; weight: to 11lb (5kg). Family Bovidae; genus *Madoqua. See also* Antelope.

Dike, an intrusion of igneous rock whose surfaces are very different from those of the adjoining materials. Dikes are usually vertical and the pattern they exhibit is a reflection of the stress fractures of the bedrock that they have intruded. *See also* Igneous Rock; Intrusion.

Dike, in engineering, any barrier or embankment, usually constructed of earth, designed to confine or control water. Dikes are used in reclaiming land from the sea by sedimentation, as practiced in the Netherlands, and are also of value as a control against river flooding (called artificial levees in that case).

Dill, a single species, *Anethum graveolens,* of aromatic annual herb native to Europe and widely cultivated for its small, oval, seedlike fruit and feathery leaves used for flavoring food. Family Umbelliferae.

DiMaggio, Joseph Paul ("Joe"), (1914–), US baseball player, b. Martinez, Calif. A hitter and center fielder for the New York Yankees (1936–42; 1946–51), DiMaggio hit in a record 56 consecutive games in 1941 and had a lifetime .325 batting average. He was elected to the Baseball Hall of Fame in 1955.

Dimetrodon, early mammallike reptile called pelycosaur found in North America during the Early and Middle Permian Period (225–280 million years ago). It was carnivorous, with sharp, differentiated teeth. The "sail fin" on its back, composed of elongated spines from the vertebral column, may have served for temperature regulation. Length: 10ft (3m). *See also* Pelycosaur.

Diminishing Returns, Law of, or the law of increasing costs, states that as more and more of a variable input (eg, labor) is added to the production process, while all other factors are held constant, the addition to total output per unit will begin to decline after some point. While the first unit of labor, for example, might produce ten units of output, the second unit of labor may only produce eight units of output; the third, only six units, etc. While the total output tends to increase, the marginal output (addition to total output) will decline after some point.

Dinaric Alps, SE division of Eastern Alps in Yugoslavia, along E coast of Adriatic Sea; joins Alpine system in the N; extends from Istria to Albania; contains many peaks over 8,000ft (2,400m). Length: 400mi (644km).

Dinaric Subrace, subdivision of the Caucasoid race, characterized by tall stature, swarthy skin, usually black hair and eyes, large straight noses, and flattened occipital regions of the skull. Dinarids form almost the entire Serbian population and predominate in Romania.

Dinesen, Isak (1885–1962), pseud. of Karen, Baroness Blixen-Finecke, Danish writer. Her life on a coffee plantation in Kenya (1914–31) was recounted in *Out of Africa* (1938) later made into a successful film (1985). Her collections of short stories include *Seven Gothic Tales* (1934), *Winter's Tales* (1943), and *Shadows on the Grass* (1961).

Dingo, yellowish-brown, medium-sized wild dog of Australia. It is thought to be a descendant of domestic dogs introduced by aborigines several thousand years ago. It preys mostly on rabbits and other small mammals, but sometimes attacks sheep and cattle. Height: 24in (61cm) high at shoulder. Family Canidae; species *Canis dingo. See also* Canidae.

Diniz, or **Denis** (1261–1325), king of Portugal (1279–1325), son and successor of Alfonso III. A scholar and a poet, Diniz founded the University of Coimbra. As king he encouraged agriculture and commerce and strengthened royal power by checking the wealth of the church and by confiscating the property of the Knights Templar. He was married to St. Elizabeth of Portugal, who mediated the conflicts between Diniz and his son, who succeeded him as Alfonso IV.

Dinocerata, or uintathere, archaic North American mammals of early Tertiary times. Ponderous and short-limbed, many bore short horns and males had powerful tusks. Advanced forms reached rhinoceros proportion.

Dinosaur, extinct reptiles that dominated life on land during Mesozoic era. They first appeared during the Triassic period and became extinct during Cretaceous period. Bipedal carnivores had tearing jaws and sharp teeth; herbivores were usually four-footed and sometimes extremely heavy. No single explanation of their extinction suffices. Many geologic and climatic changes occurred and perhaps these specialized reptiles were unable to adapt. No modern descendents exist. Two orders existed: Saurischia and Ornithischia, both descended from Triassic thecodonts. Length: 2–90ft (0.6–27m).

Diocletian(us Caius Aurelius Valerius) (245–313), Roman emperor (284–305), *b.* Dalmatia. Of humble birth, he rose through the ranks of the army and was proclaimed emperor by his troops. In order to hold the empire together and to administer it more efficiently, he appointed Maximian Augustus (coemperor) in 286 and appointed Constantius I and Galerius as caesars (subemperors) in 293, thus establishing the Tetrarchy. During his reign, Britain was restored to the empire (296) and the Persians were subjugated (298). The Edict of Diocletian (301) attempted to regulate prices and wages but created economic chaos. Diocletian ordered the last major persecution of Christians, beginning in 303. In 305 he retired to his palace in Dalmatia.

Diocletian, Palace of, Roman palace-fortress, built 295–305 at Split, Yugoslavia, by the Emperor Diocletian.

Diode, electronic device with only two electrodes, used mainly as a rectifier. The semiconductor diode, which has largely replaced the electron-tube device, has a single p-n junction. It allows current to flow when, say, a positive voltage is applied with only a very small current flowing in the reverse (negative) voltage direction. *See also* Electron Tube; Semiconductor.

Diogenes (412?–323 BC), Greek Cynic philosopher. Nicknamed the "Dog" by his own contemporaries because of his eccentric public behavior, he is best known as the philosopher who lived in a tub and carried a lantern around Athens at midday searching for an honest man. He went to Athens when young, studied under Antisthenes, and was later captured and sold into slavery at Corinth (his owner freed him). He believed only in practical good as the means to truth; freedom could be achieved by reducing needs to the barest minimum and happiness by returning to nature.

Diogenes of Apollonia (2nd half of 5th century BC), Greek philosopher. A natural philosopher who studied and taught in Athens during a transitional period of Greek thought, he tried to combine ancient ideas with the new biological observations. Influenced by Anaxagoras, he proposed that all things in the world are modifications of air, and further that this common harmony of air was due to an all-encompassing intelligence. He went on to explain perception by using the properties of air. His major works include *On Nature* and the lost treatises *Meteorology, Nature of Man,* and *Against the Sophists.*

Diomede Islands, two islands in the Bering Strait; Big Diomede (Ratmanov) is a possession of USSR; Little Diomede belongs to the United States; between the two islands passes the USSR-US boundary and the international date line. Discovered Aug. 16, 1728 (St Diomede's Day) by Vitus Bering.

Diomedes, two figures in Greek mythology. One the king of the Thracian Bistones owned man-eating horses. Conquered by Hercules, Diomedes was fed to them. The other was the son of Tydeus and a leader in the Trojan War. He founded Arpi in Apulia.

Dionysius the Areopagite (1st century AD), first bishop of Athens, a Catholic saint. As described in Acts 17:15–34, Dionysius was converted to Christianity as he heard Paul preach the sermon of "the unknown God" on the Hill of Mars (Areopagus) in Athens. He was martyred about AD 95. He is often confused with the Pseudo-Dionysius (*c.*500) who forged mystical writings in the name of Dionysius the Areopagite. These writings provided a system of the cosmos and emphasized a union between God and soul and the progressive deification of man. They had an important influence on both the Eastern and Western churches until the 16th century, when their authenticity was contested.

Dionysius the Elder (*c.*430–367 BC), tyrant of Syracuse (405–367). Perhaps the most powerful Greek until Alexander the Great, this despotic and cruel ruler's ambitions were to spread Hellenism beyond the boundaries of the city. To this end, he tried to form an empire in Lower Italy by driving Carthage away (405–404, 398–382, 383–378, 368) and seizing Rhegium (387), Caulonia, and Croton (379). He then displaced the populations within his control to mix the people. A supporter of the arts and an erstwhile playwright, he once sold Plato as a slave.

Dionysius the Younger (*c.*368–*c.*344 BC), tyrant of Syracuse. Son of Dionysius I, he succeeded him in 367 and reigned until 357 when he was driven from Syracuse by Dion. He became tyrant of Locri and then returned to rule Syracuse until 344; he was driven out the second time by Timoleon. Although Dionysius was a cruel and uneducated ruler, Plato wanted to set up the ideal state under him.

Dionysus, in Greek mythology, the god of fruitfulness and wine, the son of Zeus and Semele. He was worshipped by women in orgiastic and secretive rites.

Dior, Christian (1905–57), French fashion designer. In the spring of 1947 he launched the New Look, which swept the fashion world. His was considered the leading fashion design house between 1945 and the mid-1960s.

Diorite, deep-seated igneous rock, similar to granite in its texture, but made up mainly of plagioclase feldspar and hornblende, biotite or augite. It is usually gray or dull green.

Dioscorides Pedanius (*c.*60 AD), Greek botanist, physician, and pharmacologist. He wrote *De materia medica,* the oldest known text on drugs and their use. It included detailed plant descriptions and information on the specific use, dose, and administration of plant-derived drugs.

Dip, in geology, the angle between the maximum slope of a surface and the horizontal. This angle is a measure of the tipping and faulting that disrupts the layers of sedimentary rocks. In geomorphology, dip also means a low place or depression in the land surface.

Diphtheria, an acute, contagious infection, chiefly affecting children, once epidemic throughout the world. The bacteria *Corynebacterium diphtheriae,* often entering through the upper respiratory tract, releases exotoxin that produces symptoms of fever, chills, malaise, mild sore throat, brassy cough, and thick coating of the upper respiratory tract with dead cells and bacteria. The body responds by producing antitoxin and recovery usually follows. Complications, including impaired function of the heart and peripheral nerves, may occur temporarily. Routine immunization of children with diphtheria toxoid confers immunity.

Diplodocus, sauropod dinosaur of North America of the Jurassic period (136–190,000,000 years ago). It was proportionately more slender than other sauropods with an especially long neck and tail. This swamp-dwelling vegetarian was longer than any known dinosaur. Length: to 90ft (27m). *See also* Sauropoda.

Diplomacy, practice of conducting negotiations between nations. Nations maintain agents—diplomats—abroad to represent them in dealings with foreign states. The diplomat also regularly prepares reports for his government on the economic, political, and military affairs of his host country. Major powers generally exchange ambassadors. When an ambassador is not present, a chargé d'affaires will conduct diplomatic relations. Members of the corps advance through the merit system, although ambassadors are appointed. *See also* Embassy; Foreign Service.

Diplomatic Immunity, protection extended to members of the diplomatic corps in the form of exemption from search, arrest, or prosecution in their host country. Visiting diplomats also are further exempt from customs regulations. The embassy or legation building is considered extraterritorial, a status conferring additional protection.

Diplopia, double vision, a disorder of vision that can result from various diseases or from the action of certain drugs on the central nervous system.

Diplodocus

Walt Disney

Benjamin Disraeli

Dipnoi. *See* Lungfish.

Dipole, Molecular, separation of electric charge in a molecule. In a covalent bond between different atoms the electron pair is not equally shared between the two atoms. Thus, in hydrogen chloride, HCl, the electrons are attracted toward the more electronegative chlorine atom, giving it a partial negative charge and leaving an equal positive charge on the hydrogen atom. Such dipoles contribute to the chemical properties of molecules.

Dipper, widely distributed bird found in or near fast-flowing mountain streams where it swims and dives, feeding on aquatic invertebrates and small fish. It has a thin straight bill, short wings and tail, and grayish or brownish plumage. It builds a large, domed, grass-and-moss-lined nest, often behind a waterfall, for its white eggs (4–5). Length: 6.5in (16.5cm). Genus *Cinclus.*

Dipper, Big. *See* Ursa Major.

Diptera, the order of true flies. They are distinguished from other insects by having soft bodies and one pair of wings, with the other pair reduced to knoblike halteres. They have a complete life cycle—egg, larva, pupa, and adult—with the larva being wormlike. This group includes several important pests. Mosquitoes, horseflies, houseflies, black flies, and others either attack man and animals or carry diseases. The Hessian fly, apple maggot, and others attack crops. The bee flies and robber flies, on the other hand, are beneficial, attacking several pest insects.

Dirac, Paul Adrien Maurice (1902–84), English physicist who devised a new version of quantum mechanics. His equation (the Dirac equation) combines relativity and quantum-mechanical descriptions of electron properties, resulting in accurate values and relating them to fundamental principles. He was awarded the Nobel Prize for physics (1933) and the medal of the Royal Society (1952).

Direct Democracy, system, also known as "pure democracy," in which citizens govern themselves directly, not through representatives. Once practiced in ancient Greece, it survives today in the New England town meeting.

Directory, The, (1795–99), set up by the constitution of the year III in revolutionary France, was a governing body including a legislature, judiciary, treasury, and executive, each largely independent of the other, representing the many diverse political viewpoints of France from 1795 to 1799. The five executive directors were able to maintain power only by a careful balancing of countervailing forces and the use, in emergencies, of the military. This large and effective army, greatly successful under the command of Napoleon, was the instrument of a coup in 1797, establishing a dictatorship dependent on the victories of war and setting the stage for Napoleon's rule in 1799.

Disarmament, reduction of weaponry and armies. Efforts to achieve international disarmament have focused on limiting the nuclear arms race between the United States and the Soviet Union. In 1963, nuclear weapons in outer space were banned. A nuclear nonproliferation treaty was signed in 1972, which also marked the start of the Strategic Arms Limitation Talks (SALT).

Disconformity, the hiatus or eroded surface between two layers of rock. The time interval represented by the hiatus is more difficult to estimate than the rate of deposition of a layer. However, it is a necessary factor in determining the age of rock formations. *See also* Unconformity.

Discrimination, prejudicial treatment of an individual or group on the basis of race, religion, ethnic background, sex, or age. In the broader, public sense, discrimination may take the form of housing restrictions, segregated community facilities, and limited employment and educational opportunities.

Disease, an impairment of health or abnormal functioning of an organism, affecting the entire organism or one organ or system of the body. Disease may be acute, producing severe symptoms for a short time; chronic, lasting a long time; or recurrent, with symptoms returning periodically. There are many types and causes of disease: infectious diseases, caused by harmful bacteria, viruses, or other agents; hereditary and metabolic diseases; diseases of growth and development; diseases of the immunological system; neoplastic (tumor-producing) diseases; nutritional diseases; endocrine (hormonal) diseases; diseases due to particular physical agents, for example, lead poisoning; circulatory diseases; and mental diseases.
Treatment depends on the cause and course of the disease, but in general, may be symptomatic, relieving symptoms but not necessarily combating the cause of the disease; or may be specific drug therapy, attempting to cure the underlying cause of the disease. Surgery is also sometimes a method of treatment, as is radiation therapy, physical therapy, and psychotherapy.
Disease prevention involves eradication of disease-producing organisms, vaccines to confer immunity against disease, public health measures, and careful medical care and checkups.

Disjunction, logical proposition produced by joining two simple propositions by the word *or.* An example is the proposition "John is intelligent or John is modest"; it is false if both parts are separately false, otherwise it is true. This is the inclusive disjunction—the type used in mathematics—in which the proposition is true if *both* components are true. In ordinary speech a second type, the exclusive disjunction, is also used expressing an alternative between the two components. The disjunction of two simple propositions, P and Q, is written $P \lor Q$, read "P or Q."

Dismal Swamp, area in SE Virginia and NE North Carolina; extends approx. 40mi (64km) from Suffolk, Va., to Elizabeth City, N.C. Dense forests, undergrowth, and peat bogs attract sportsmen and naturalists; a canal for small pleasure craft from Norfolk to Elizabeth City opened in 1828; in center of swamp is Lake Drummond, 18sq mi (46sq km). George Washington owned and surveyed part of swamp in 1763. Previously covering an area of 2,200sq mi (5,700sq km), it is now approx. 600sq mi (1,554sq km) in size.

Disney, Walt(er Elias) (1901–66), US film animator and studio executive, b. Chicago. His cartoon features, animal, fantasy, and adventure films are internationally renowned. His first success, *Steamboat Willie* (1928), was the first cartoon to use sound. It featured Mickey Mouse, who became the world's most famous cartoon character, rivaled only by another Disney character, Donald Duck. Among his studio's best-loved films are *Snow White and the Seven Dwarfs* (1938), *Fantasia* (1940), *Dumbo* (1941), *Treasure Island* (1950), *The Living Desert* (1953), and *Mary Poppins* (1964). In 1955 the innovative amusement park, Disneyland, opened in Anaheim, Calif.

Displaced Persons, Europeans left homeless after World War II. They at first entered the United States under limited quotas, but later under a President Truman directive, 42,000 persons were admitted. By June 1948, visas were authorized for 205,000, including 3,000 nonquota orphans. The issuance of visas was extended through 1951.

Displacement, in geology, the relative movements of two adjacent groups of rock in relation to each other. Displacement is spoken of in terms of the direction of change and the specific amount of the movement. Lateral displacement is described as strike slip and strike separation whereas vertical displacement is known as dip slip and dip separation. *See also* Faulting; Folding.

Displacement, in physics, replacement of one atom in a compound by an atom of a different element. *See also* Substitution.

Displacement, in psychology, defense mechanism in which there is a psychological shift in meaning, reference, or emotional emphasis from a more to a less disturbing focus. A common form of this mechanism is in the displacement of anger, eg, when a mother, angry at her husband, begins to shout at her child. *See also* Defense Mechanism.

Disraeli, Benjamin, 1st Earl of Beaconsfield (1804–81), English Conservative statesman and writer. He was a novelist before entering Parliament (1837), where he dominated the romantic Young England Tories and helped overthrow Robert Peel after the Corn Laws were repealed (1846). As Conservative leader in the Commons, Disraeli helped Lord Derby reunite the party, was several times chancellor of the exchequer, and piloted an electoral reform act (1867) through Parliament. On Derby's retirement, Disraeli became prime minister (1868). Prime minister for a second time (1874–80) he passed social reform legislation. An imperialist, he secured Britain's half-share in the Suez Canal, and at the Congress of Berlin (1878), he forced Russia to surrender Turkish lands, annexing Cyprus for Britain. His health failing, Disraeli was defeated by his Liberal rival, William Gladstone (1880). *See also* Gladstone, William; Peel, Sir Robert.

Dissenters. *See* Nonconformists.

Dissociation, splitting apart or separating of specific contents of consciousness, or dividing experience into independent regions. In the *dissociative reaction* considerable personality disorganization is reflected in such symptoms as fugue state, depersonalization, amnesia, and sleepwalking. Dissociated states of awareness tend to alternate with one another in consciousness,

Distemper, dangerous contagious disease of young dogs, similar to influenza in humans. Distemper is an airborne viral disease, often complicated by secondary bacterial infections. Symptoms are fever, shivering, discharges, pneumonia, convulsions, spasm, and paralysis. No cures are known, although multiple vaccinations are a preventative. Wild canines, raccoons, and members of the weasel family are also susceptible.

Distillation, evaporation and recondensation process carried out on a liquid at controlled pressures in apparatus comprising a still, a condenser, and a receiver. In destructive distillation the product(s) of decomposition are collected. In fractional distillation various liquid mixtures or fractions are collected depending on their boiling points. In rectification (a type of fractional distillation widely used as a separation procedure in the petroleum industry), where the condenser comprises a series of plates to facilitate liquid–vapor equilibrium, relatively pure products may be collected from a liquid mixture.

Distribution, in economics, portion of the total amount of the goods and services a society produces that each individual or group receives. Sometimes called personal distribution or income distribution in order to distinguish it from the marketing of commodities (physical distribution), it has been an important aspect of economic analysis since Adam Smith focused on the issue in the 18th century.

Distributive Law, rule of combination in mathematics in which a specified operation applied to a combination of terms is equal to the combination of the operation applied to each individual term. Thus, in algebra and arithmetic $3 \times (2 + 1) = (3 \times 2) + (3 \times 1)$; the multiplication is distributed over addition.

Distributor, Engine, an electrical device for distributing the secondary current from the induction coil. This current has to be directed to the various spark plugs of a multicylinder, gasoline internal combustion engine in their proper firing order.

District of Columbia. *See* Washington, D.C..

Dithyramb, irregular poem or chant of a wild or inspired nature. Dithyrambs are primarily identified with ancient Greece. There they originated as improvised choral lyrics sung at banquets in honor of Dionysus, the god of wine. Later other gods were honored, and dithyrambs became important parts of theatrical presentations and great festivals. The dithyramb began to achieve literary distinction with the poet Arion around 600 BC. He developed them for regular choruses with formal presentations. Lasus of Hermione, (*c.*525 BC) was the most famous composer of dithyrambs. Simonides, Pindar, Bacchylides, Philoxenus, and Timotheus also composed them. Dithyrambs gradually used more and more startling linguistic and musical devices. They eventually died out in their classical form in the 2nd century AD. Aristotle maintained that Greek tragedy developed out of the dithyramb. True dithyrambs have been rare since ancient times, but it has been said that Dryden's *Alexander's Feast* (1697) and T.S. Eliott's *The Waste Land* (1922) are among poems containing dithyrambic elements.

Diuretic, drug used to increase the flow of urine and, usually, its salt content. Diuretics are used to treat edema, an over-accumulation of fluid caused by congestive heart failure or other diseases, and abnormal kidney function.

Divergence, property of an infinite series (or sequence) of not having a finite limiting value. Such a series is said to diverge. The harmonic series, $1 + 1/2 + 1/3 + 1/4, \ldots$, is an example of a divergent series. *See also* Convergence.

Diverticulitis, an inflammation of diverticula, small intestinal wall outpouchings, frequently caused by fecal matter obstructing the neck of the pouch. Symptoms include lower left side pain, cramps, nausea, vomiting, sometimes fever, malaise, alternating constipation and diarrhea. If untreated (with antispasmodics, antibiotics, and bland diet) abcess, hemorrhage, and intestinal wall performation can occur, with surgery indicated.

Divination, foretelling the future or discovering what is unknown by understanding various signs. Divination is a form of magic with worldwide distribution. Signs of the future are very often thought to be found in the entrails of animals that are especially sacrificed. Other techniques include casting lots and palmistry. Divination assumes revelation or association between the natural world and human affairs.

Divine Comedy (*c.*1307–21), allegorical, narrative poem by Dante Alighieri. Through this work Dante established Tuscan as the literary language of Italy. It is divided into three parts, *Inferno, Purgatorio,* and *Paradiso* and consists of the author's imaginary tour of Hell, Purgatory, and Heaven. He meets his contemporaries, historical figures, and characters from mythology, the Bible, and classical literature. It is written in terza rima, a complex verse form.

Relying on both pagan and Christian descriptions of the afterlife, Dante divides the three worlds into multiple levels; each soul is carefully placed in his proper level and is punished according to the nature of his sins on earth. Although concerned with his intellectual and religious feelings about man's life on earth and his relationship to God, Dante also uses the allegorical medium to vent his own personal rivalries and political opinions. *See also* Terza Rima.

Divine Right of Kings, political theory, popular in 16th and 17th centuries, that anointed kings derive absolute and irresistible authority directly from God. Law is an instrument of grace, not a contrivance of human wisdom, so that the king is answerable only to God and is above all promulgated laws, including his own.

Diving, water sport in which acrobatic maneuvers are performed off a springboard or highboard. The several types of competition include the 1- and 3-meter springboards and the 5-, 7.5-, and 10-meter firm highboards. The judging, based on points, is complicated and depends not only on the difficulty of the dive but also on the diver's movement at the start, his technique and grace of the flight, and his entry into the water. All world diving is governed by the Fédération Internationale de Natation Amateur, organized in 1908.

Diving Beetle, or predaceous diving beetle, medium-sized, aquatic beetle found in ponds over most of the world. The adult and larva prey on insects, tadpoles, and small fish. Diving beetles have long hind legs adapted for swimming and threadlike antennae. Family Dytiscidae.

Diving Birds, widely differing birds that typically dive —some shallowly, others deeply—for food. Loons are the most adept divers. Others include grebes, albatrosses, diving petrels, tropic birds, pelicans, boobies, cormorants, some ducks and geese, jacana, dippers, and kingfishers. *See also* individual birds.

Division, arithmetical operation signified by $\div$, interpreted as the inverse of multiplication. The quotient of two numbers, $a \div b$, is the number that must be multiplied by b to give a. a is called the dividend and b the divisor. Quotients can also be written as fractions. *See also* Arithmetical Operations.

Divisionism, Italian version of neo-Impressionism which emerged in the late 1880s and 1890s and was practiced by Segantini, Previati, and Pelliza da Valpedo. This movement led to futurism and espoused the technique of juxtaposing small strokes of pure color directly on the canvas and allowing the eye of the viewer to blend them at a distance rather than first mixing the colors on the palette. *See also* Pointillism.

Division of Labor, plan of production in which each individual or group of workers specializes in a single phase of the production process. The performance of one, or a limited number of operations, is characteristic of contemporary mass production in both capitalistic and socialistic economies. The specialization of machines is a closely related aspect.

Divorce, legal dissolution of a valid marriage. Social scientists view divorce as the most constant of all major social problems. Statistics show that the United States has the highest divorce rate of the developed societies; however, the divorce rate of several European countries has actually increased faster in recent years. The US divorce rate steadily increased from the mid-19th century until the end of WWII. Since then it has fluctuated, and the rate of increase has slowed; however, social changes such as improved job opportunities for women, accelerated urbanization, greater mobility, and other factors, indicate the long-term pattern of US divorce rate is upward. The legislative power on divorce is maintained by state rather than the federal government, and state divorce policies are varied.

Dix, Dorothea (Lynde) (1802–87), US pioneer in the treatment of the mentally ill, b. Hampden, Maine. She exposed the inhumane treatment of the insane and inspired legislation resulting in patients being treated in state mental hospitals rather than confined to prisons.

Dixieland, style of jazz music originating in New Orleans in the early 1900s and featuring popular melodies, lively rhythms, and a generally cheerful sound. *See also* Jazz.

Djakarta, capital city of Indonesia, on NW coast of Java; originally a trading post and fort; severely damaged by earthquake 1699; became capital of Indonesia after recognition of its independence by Dutch, Dec. 29, 1949. An administrative, cultural, and educational center, Djakarta is site of University of Indonesia (1950). Industries: iron foundries, printing, sawmills. Exports: rubber, tea, quinine. Founded 1619 by Dutch Jan Pieterszoon Coen. Pop. 4,576,009.

Djibouti, Republic of (formerly French Territory of the Afars and Issas), independent country located at the strategically important Bab el-Mandeb Strait at the entrance to the Red Sea, in the Horn of Africa. The city of Djibouti is the capital and principal port.

About 90% of the land is a stony desert, receiving only about 2–10 in (51–254mm) of yearly precipitation, permitting little agriculture. About half of the inhabitants are nomadic herders, raising sheep, goats,and camels. Most revenue is derived from transshipment at the port of Djibouti, and the country is heavily dependent upon foreign aid.

Almost all inhabitants belong to two major ethnic groups. The Issas, about 50% of the total, are of Somali origin; the Affars (about 40% of total) are of Ethiopian descent. Both groups are Muslim and speak related languages.

France obtained control of the area during the latter half of the 19th century. In 1967 the territory chose to remain a French possession, but it became independent in 1977. At independence a 65-member chamber of deputies and prime minister were elected. Djibouti has been troubled by tension between its two ethnic groups, exacerbated by war between neighboring Ethiopia and Somalia. Refugees, especially from Ethiopia, became a national issue in the mid-1980s. Pop. 325,-000; area: 6,900sq mi (17,870sq km).

Djibouti (Jibuti), capital city of Djibouti (formerly French Territory of Afars and Issas), Africa; on the S shore of the Gulf of Tadjura, S of the Bab el Kandeb Strait; site of Ethiopian railroad terminus; trade center. Founded 1888; named capital 1892, free port 1949. Pop. 62,000.

Djilas, Milovan (1911–), Yugoslav political writer and political leader. A Communist party official and one of Tito's leading cabinet ministers, he was involved in the assertion of independence from the Kremlin in 1948, but his outspoken criticism of Tito's regime especially in the foreign press, ended his political career (1954). *The New Class: An Analysis of the Communist System* was published in 1957, leading to his arrest. He was released in 1966 but subsequently clashed with the government over his views. Other works include *The Unperfect Society* (1969), *Wartime* (1977), and *Tito: The Story from Inside* (1980).

Dmitri (died 1606), pretender to the throne of Russia, b. as Yury Otrepyev. After Tsar Feodor I died in 1598, Otrepyev, then a monk, claimed to be Dmitri, Feodor's son and heir to the throne of Russia. The real Dmitri had died in 1591. Boris Godunov, however, became tsar. In 1603 Otrepyev went to Lithuania, where he obtained support to invade Moscow in 1604. Boris Godunov died in 1605, and Dmitri was proclaimed tsar after bringing about the death of Feodor II, son of Boris. Dmitri's Polish advisers and pro-Polish policies alienated the Russians, and in 1606 Dmitri Vasily Shuysky led a revolt in which Dmitri was murdered.

DNA. *See* Deoxyribonucleic Acid.

Dnepr (Dnieper), river in Ukranian SSR, USSR; rises in Valdai Hills, W of Moscow; flows S through Belorussia, the Ukraine, and cities of Smolensk, Mogilev, Kiev, Cherkassy, Kremenchug, Dnepropetrovsk, Zaporozhye, Nikopol, Kherson, into Black Sea. The 3rd-longest river in Europe, it contains the Dreproges Dam (1932), which made river navigable for entire course; Dnepr is linked by canal to western Bug River; site of hydroelectric stations. Length: 1,430mi (2,300km).

Dneprodzerzhinsk (Dneprodzeržinsk), formerly Kamenskoye; city in Ukrainian SSR, USSR, on Dnepr River. Industries: metallurgy, iron, steel, chemicals, cement, tools. Founded c.1750. Pop. 255,000.

Dnepropetrovsk, city in Ukrainian SSR, USSR, on the Dnepr River; capital of Dnepropetrovsk oblast; site of state university, technical schools, agricultural and teachers' colleges, museums. Industries: iron, steel, food processing, chemicals, heavy machinery. Founded 1787 by G.A. Potemkin for Catherine II; named for Ukrainian Bolshevik, Petrovski (1926). Pop. 1,061,000.

Dnestr (Dniester), river in Ukrainian SSR, USSR; rises in N slopes of Carpathian Mts; flows SE to Black Sea SW of Odessa; part of its course forms Ukrainian-Moldavian republic borders; irregular water levels hamper navigation; site of hydroelectric station; frontier delineation between USSR and Romania 1918–1940. Length: 845mi (1,360km). Basin area: 27,800sq mi (72,000sq km).

Dnieper River. *See* Dnepr.

Dniester River. *See* Dnestr.

Doberman Pinscher, elegant guard and police dog (working group) bred in Germany about 1890. A square-built dog, it has a long, blunt, wedge-shaped head; cropped, erect ears; deep chest; short, firm back and broad loin and hips; straight, medium-length legs; and docked tail. The smooth, hard, short coat is black, red, blue, or fawn—all with rust marks. Average size: 24–28 in (61–71cm) high at shoulder; 60–75lb (27–34kg). *See also* Working Dog.

Dorothea Dix

Djakarta, Indonesia

Dnepr River, USSR

Dobruja (Dobrudja), historic region in SE Romania and NE Bulgaria, located S of Danube River along Black Sea coastline; became part of Romania after second Balkan War (1913). S Dobruja given to Bulgaria by German-imposed treaty of Craiova (1940). Inhabitants include Tatars, Romanians, Turks, and Bulgarians. The region is mainly agricultural; grapes, grains, and sheep are raised. Area: 9,000sq mi (23,310sq km).

Docetism, heresy in Christianity. Docetism (from the Greek "to seem") was the doctrine that Christ did not have a material human body but rather was a phantasmal human and that his birth, death, and other earthly manifestations were merely illusions. This belief, regarded as the first Christian heresy, reached its height with the 2nd century Gnostics. The first to use the name "Docetist" was Serapion, bishop of Antioch (190–203). *See also* Gnosticism.

Dock, any of over 100 species (genus *Rumex*) of flowering plants native to North America and Europe, with oblong or lance-shaped leaves and many small, scaly brown flowers. Most are considered weeds, but some are cultivated for their edible leaves or as ornamentals. Family Polygonaceae.

Doctorow, E(dgar) L(awrence) (1931–), US author, b. New York City. His novels include *Welcome to Hard Times* (1960), *The Book of Daniel* (1971), *Ragtime* (1975), a novel about the United States at the turn of the century, *Loon Lake* (1980), and *World's Fair* (1985). He also wrote short stories, collected in *Lives of the Poets* (1984).

Dodder, leafless, parasitic, twining herb with threadlike stems. Usually straw-colored or orange, with many small yellow flowers, the plant attaches to the stem of a larger plant, releases its contact with the ground, and attaches its roots to the host. Species include *Cuscuta pentagona,* or field dodder. Family Convolvulaceae.

Dodecanese (Dhodhekanisos), island group in Greece, in the SE Aegean Sea, between W Turkey and E Crete; capital is Rhodes; conquered and ruled since 1600 BC by many nations and groups, including Athens, Sparta, Rome, Venice, Crusaders, Knights of St John. Under Turkish control 1500–1912, it was seized by Italy 1912 and passed to Greece 1947.

Dodgson, Charles Lutwidge. *See* Carroll, Lewis.

Dodo, extinct, flightless bird that lived on the Mascarene Islands in the Indian Ocean. The last dodo died about 1800. The true dodo *(Raphus cucullatus)* of Mauritius Island and the similar Réunion solitaire *(Raphus solitarius)* were heavy-bodied with large heads and large hooked bills. Weight: to 50lb (23kg). The Rodriguez or solitaire dodo *(Pezophaps solitaria)* was smaller, with a straight bill and knobbed wings.

Doenitz, Karl (1891–1980), German naval officer. He entered the submarine service in 1916 and in World War II was commander of the submarine fleet until 1943. He then became grand admiral and commander in chief of the German navy until 1945, when Hitler named him as his successor to the Reich. He submitted the German surrender in 1945 and was sentenced to 10 years in prison by the Nuremberg tribunal in 1945.

Doesburg, Theo van (1883–1931), Dutch painter, writer, and critic. He was a founder of the influential art review *de Stijl* in 1917. His art developed from Cubism, and he eventually limited himself to geometric compositions of black and white combined with primary colors. *See also* Cubism.

Dog, mammal closely related to the jackal, wolf, and wild dog. It has a slender, muscular body; long head with slender snout and triangular ears; small paws with five toes on the forefeet and four on the hind; nonretractile claws; and well-developed canine teeth. The dog walks on its toes with the heel, or hock, off the ground. Smell is the dog's most important sense and its hearing is acute. The gestation period is 49–70 days and one or more helpless young are born.

Dogs developed from the tree-dwelling miacis, that lived 40–50 million years ago, through intermediate forms to tomarctus, that lived 15 million years ago. The dog was domesticated 15,000 years ago. There are 400 breeds; the oldest is the Saluki, in existence for 7,000 years. Dog breeds are classified into sporting, hound, terrier, working, toy, and non-sporting groups. Length: body—13.4–53.2in (34–135cm); tail—4.3–21.3in (11–54cm); weight: 3.3–165.31lb (1.5–74kg). Family Canidae; species *Canis familiaris. See also* individual breeds. Following is a list of dog breeds recognized by the American Kennel Club, organized by major groups.

Dog Breeds

Sporting Dogs
Brittany
Pointer
Pointer, German Shorthaired
Pointer, German Wirehaired
Retriever, Chesapeake Bay
Retriever, Curly-Coated
Retriever, Flat-Coated
Retriever, Golden
Retriever, Labrador
Setter, English
Setter, Gordon
Setter, Irish
Spaniel, American Water
Spaniel, Clumber
Spaniel, Cocker
Spaniel, English Cocker
Spaniel, English Springer
Spaniel, Field
Spaniel, Irish Water
Spaniel, Sussex
Spaniel, Welsh Springer
Vizsla
Weimaraner
Wirehaired Pointing Griffon
Hounds
Afghan Hound
Basenji
Basset Hound
Beagle
Black and Tan Coonhound
Bloodhound
Borzoi
Dachshund
Foxhound, American
Foxhound, English
Greyhound
Harrier
Ibizan Hound
Irish Wolfhound
Norwegian Elkhound
Otter Hound
Pharaoh Hound
Rhodesian Ridgeback
Saluki
Scottish Deerhound
Whippet
Working Dogs
Akita
Alaskan Malamute
Bernese Mountain Dog
Boxer

Bullmastiff
Doberman Pinscher
Giant Schnauzer
Great Dane
Great Pyrenees
Komondor
Kuvasz
Mastiff
Newfoundland
Portuguese Water Dog
Rottweiler
St. Bernard
Samoyed
Siberian Husky
Standard Schnauzer
Terriers
Airedale Terrier
American Staffordshire Terrier
Australian Terrier
Bedlington Terrier
Border Terrier
Bull Terrier
Cairn Terrier
Dandie Dinmont Terrier
Fox Terrier
Irish Terrier
Kerry Blue Terrier
Lakeland Terrier
Manchester Terrier
Miniature Schnauzer
Norfolk Terrier
Norwich Terrier
Scottish Terrier
Sealyham Terrier
Skye Terrier
Smooth Fox Terrier
Soft-Coated Wheaten Terrier
Staffordshire Bull Terrier
Welsh Terrier
West Highland White Terrier
Wire Fox Terrier
Toys
Affenpinscher
Brussels Griffon
Chihuahua
English Toy Spaniel
Italian Greyhound
Japanese Chin
Maltese
Manchester Terrier
Miniature Pinscher
Papillon
Pekingese
Pomeranian
Poodle (toy)
Pug
Shih Tzu
Silky Terrier
Yorkshire Terrier
Non-Sporting Dogs
Bichon Frise
Boston Terrier
Bulldog
Chow Chow
Dalmation
French Bulldog
Keeshond
Lhasa Apso
Poodle
Schipperke
Tibetan Spaniel
Tibetan Terrier
Herding Dogs
Australian Cattle Dog
Bearded Collie
Belgian Malinois

Belgian Sheepdog
Belgian Tervuren
Bouvier des Flandres
Briard
Collie
German Shepherd
Old English Sheepdog
Puli
Shetland Sheepdog
Welsh Corgi, Cardigan
Welsh Corgi, Pembroke

Dogbane, N American tall, branched perennial plant with fibrous stems and milky poisonous sap. They bear loose clusters of small, white or pink, bell-shaped flowers. Indian hemp *(Apocynum cannabinum)* was formerly grown for cordage fiber. Family Apocynaceae.

Dogfish, shark found worldwide in marine waters. Generally grayish with white spots, they have no anal fin. They are usually divided into two groups: spiny dogs with a stout, sharp spine in front of each dorsal fin and spineless dogs that lack a spine in front of the second dorsal fin. Length: 4ft (1.2m); weight: 20lb (9kg). The spineless Greenland shark is 21ft (6.4m) long. Suborder Squaloidei. *See also* Chondrichthyes; Sharks.

Doggerel, trivial verse, written for comic or burlesque effect, loosely styled, irregular in meter, often badly written. The word can be used as a term of abuse.

Dogon, Negroid people whose traditional ancestral dwellings are in remote cave-villages in the Hombori Mountains of the Mali Republic. Their patrilineal village society is based on subsistence agriculture, principal foods being millet and sorghum. Their religion is notable for its abstract concepts and a powerful creation myth.

Dogtooth Violet, bulbous perennial plant native to Europe and Asia. The stalked leaves are blotchy and reddish-brown and the flowers are rose to purple. Family Liliaceae; species *Erythronium dens-canis.*

Dogwood, any of several small trees and shrubs in the genus *Cornus* of the dogwood family (Cornaceae). The best known species is the flowering dogwood *(C. florida),* native to E North American forests from S Canada to Florida. In the wild, flowering dogwoods are graceful, sparsely leaved inhabitants of the dimly lit understory of deciduous forests. Their small flowers, enclosed by four large, petallike, white bracts, bloom before the leaves open.

Doldrums, a nautical term for the region over the ocean near the equator characterized by calms, light and variable winds, and squalls, and corresponding approximately with the equatorial trough, a belt of low pressure around the equator.

Dole, Robert Joseph (1923–), US political leader, b. Russell, Kansas. In 1960 he was elected to the US House of Representatives. He served there until 1969, when he entered the US Senate, where he became known as a conservative and highly partisan Republican. He served as Republican national chairman (1971–73) and as Senate majority leader (1985–). In 1976, he was the Republicans'unsuccessful vice-presidential candidate.

Dole, Sanford (1844–1926), US statesman, b. Honolulu, Hawaii, son of missionary parents. He studied law at Williams College and then led demands for democratic government in Hawaii. When a revolutionary group overthrew the queen in 1893, he refused to comply with Pres. Grover Cleveland's demand for her restoration. As first president of the republic (1894–1898) he pressed for US annexation, which came in 1898. Dole was the territory's first governor (1900–03).

Dollar Diplomacy, term used to describe US policy of military and economic interference in Latin American affairs in the early 1900s. A number of Caribbean countries (Dominican Republic, Cuba, Haiti, Honduras, Costa Rica, and Nicaragua) were, at various time, heavily in debt to certain European governments. The United States intervened, citing the threat of European encroachment in the western hemisphere and the need to safeguard US investments in these countries.

Dollfuss, Englebert (1892–1934), Austrian Chancellor (1932–34). A Christian Socialist, he became chancellor at a time when the country was close to economic collapse and threatened by external and internal enemies. In 1932 he obtained a much needed international loan by agreeing not to form a customs union with Germany. In 1933 he dissolved the National Socialist party, which had been calling for union with Nazi Germany. In February 1934 he crushed the Social Democratic party and in April assumed dictatorial powers. He was assassinated on July 25 by Austrian Nazis who were attempting to seize power.

Döllinger, Johann Joseph Ignaz von (1799–1890), German theologian. Professor of church history at the University of Munich (1826–73), he refused to accept the doctrine of the infallibility of the pope promulgated by the Vatican Council in 1870. For his opposition he was excommunicated in 1871. He became a leader in the formation of the Old Catholics, an independent German Catholic church.

Doll's House, A (1879), 4-act drama by Henrik Ibsen. There have been many successful productions of this first important social drama dealing with the problem of women's freedom. Its longest Broadway run was in 1937. It has also been produced on film and for TV. Although Nora escapes the legal consequences of forging her father's name on a check to keep her husband, she is forced to face the realities of her domestic life. Realizing that her husband had been keeping her as a doll, Nora leaves him to establish her own identity.

Dolomite, a sedimentary rock, probably formed by the alteration of limestone by seawater. Also, carbonate mineral, calcium-magnesium carbonate [$CaMg(CO_3)_2$], found in dolomite rocks and metamorphosed rocks. Calcite-like rhombohedral system prismatic crystals, often intergrown, are found in hydrothermal veins. Pearly-white or pink; hardness 3.5–4; sp gr 2.8.

Dolomites (Dolomiti or Dolomiten), part of Italian Alps, in NE Italy; formed of dolomitic limestone and shaped by erosion; first climbed by English in 19th century; landslides caused Vaiont Dam to overflow in 1963 killing 2,000 in nearby Longarone. Highest peak is the Marmolada, 10,964ft (3,342m).

Dolphin, small, toothed whale having distinct beak and slender body. Larger than the porpoise, it is the fastest and most agile and playful of whales. In captivity, the highly intelligent, bottle-nosed dolphin readily learns complicated routines. Length: to 14ft (4.3m). Family Delphinidae; species *Tursiops truncatus.*

Domagk, Gerhard (1895–1964), German chemist. In 1927 he was made director of the research institute of the I.G. Farben industrial works. He is known for his discovery of the drug prontosil, the forerunner of sulfanilamide, the first of the "wonder drugs" used to combat infectious diseases. He was awarded the Nobel Prize in medicine and physiology in 1939 for his discovery.

Domain, set of values possible for the independent variable of a function. Thus for a function $f(x)$ the domain is the set of values of x for which $f(x)$ is real.

Dome, Lunar, any of several broad-based low mountains on the surface of the moon, often characterized by crater pits on their summits.

Domenichino (Zampieri) (1581–1641), Italian painter and architect. In 1602 he worked with Annibale Carraci on the Farnese Palace. Between 1621–23 he was chief Vatican architect. He became a leading painter of the early Baroque style. His landscape paintings, including *The Hunt of Diana* and *Landscape with St. John Baptizing,* had a profound influence on Nicolas Poussin and Claude Lorrain.

Domesday Book, also called Doomsday Book, two-volume census ordered by William the Conqueror and compiled (1085–86) to assess the economic facts of his kingdom so that he might levy a higher Danegeld. Now located in the Record Office, London, it records the ownership and value of all lands at the time of the survey and also at their bestowal and at the time of Edward the Confessor; the value of crops, cattle, etc, is also included along with the social status of the owners. A special edition of the Domesday Book (so-called because no one could escape inclusion) was published in 1783.

Dominance, in genetics, the tendency of one characteristic of a heterozygous pair of alleles to manifest itself over another. For example, if an offspring has one allele each for brown eyes and blue eyes, the brown-eyed allele will dominate and manifest itself over the blue. *See also* Heredity.

Dominance Relationships, or pecking orders, systems of status within social groups in which different individuals are ranked or ordered in terms of status or "dominance." Most such systems in animal societies are based on strength or aggressiveness. In human societies, status depends more on the acquisition of possessions, wealth, or prestige.

Dominic (1170?–1221), Spanish churchman, a Roman Catholic saint, and founder of the Dominicans, b. Domingo de Gúzman. In 1203 Pope Innocent III sent him to S France to preach to the Albigenes. In 1215 he founded the Dominicans, who were pledged to poverty and dedicated to study and preaching.

Dominica, Commonwealth of, largest island of Windward Islands, West Indies, in the Caribbean Sea, between Guadeloupe and Martinique islands; capital and chief port is Roseau; population is largely descended from African slaves; small Carib Indian community remains. Dominica was captured by the French 1778; returned to Great Britain 1783; inc. with Leeward Islands 1833; member of West Indies Federation 1958–62; became self-governing state 1967, received independence in 1978, and became the 151st member of the United Nations. Dominica supported the US invasion of neighboring Grenada in 1983. Crops: copra, bananas, cocoa, coconuts, tobacco, spices. Discovered 1493 by Columbus. Area: 290sq mi (750sq km). Pop. 79,000.

Dominican Republic, independent republic on the E two-thirds of Hispaniola Island, West Indies; it shares the island with the Republic of Haiti (W). The terrain is generally rugged, traversed E-W by the Cordillera Central mountain system, rising to its max. height at Pico Duarte, 10,490ft (3,197m), the highest peak in the West Indies. To both the N and S of this system are smaller, less-elevated ranges. The most fertile area of the country, the Cibao, lies in the NW between two mountain ranges and is drained by the Yuna and Yaque del Norte rivers.

Agriculture dominates the economic activity of the Dominican Republic; sugar, coffee, cacao, and tobacco are the major exported crops. For mainland consumption, tobacco, fruits, vegetables, rice, corn, and tomatoes are cultivated. Dominating the manufactures are textiles, glassware, metal products, paint, and cement. Cattle raising is an important growing industry, as is the mining of bauxite and nickel. In 1973 the Dominican Republic was the world's 15th-largest producer of bauxite and 7th-largest producer of nickel. The majority of the population lives in rural farm areas or urban ghettos. The University of Santo Domingo, the oldest in the Americas, was founded 1538 by the Spanish; there is also the Pedro Henríquez-Urena University and Catholic University. There are many fine examples of colonial architecture in Santo Domingo, among them the cathedral housing Christopher Columbus' remains.

The island was discovered 1492 by Christopher Columbus, who established the first settlement in the New World at Isabella (1493) and by 1496 had founded Santo Domingo as Spain's capital in the West Indies. By 1697, Spain had ceded the W portion of the island, known as Saint Dominque, to France by the Treaty of Ryswick, causing great economic hardship for Santo Domingo. In 1795 the island was once again reunited by the Treaty of Basel and ruled by French-Haitian administration, under Toussaint L'Overture. Haiti declared its independence in 1804 and included Santo Domingo within its borders. The Dominicans revolted against this domination in 1843 and declared the independent nation of the Dominican Republic. Spain regained domination in 1861 but withdrew for the last time in 1865 after political upheavals. The United States gained control of Dominican customs 1905–1941 because of the country's foreign debts. The presence of US Marines was resented by Dominican nationalists, and they were withdrawn in 1924. With the 1930 election came the military dictatorship of Rafael Leonidas Trujillo Molina, who stabilized the economy, but the government grew corrupt. In 1960 he was censured by the Organization of American States (OAS), and a year later was assassinated. The first free election was held in 1962 electing reformist Juan Bosch as president. In 1965, however, civil war broke out between leftist followers of Bosch and the military; after the war was ended by the intervention of 23,000 US troops, in 1966, Conservative Joaquín Balaguer became president (1966–78) and was followed by Silvestre Antonio Guzmán Fernandez (1978–82) and Salvador Jorge Blanco (1982–). During the 1980s austerity measures were instituted to control an economic crisis.

PROFILE

Official name: República Dominicana
Area: 18,703sq mi (48,440sq km)
Population: 5,430,879
Chief cities: Santo Domingo (capital); Santiago; San Francisco de Macorís; San Pedro de Macoris
Religion: Roman Catholic
Language: Spanish
Monetary unit: Peso

Dominicans, Roman Catholic religious order. Known officially as the Order of Friars Preachers and often informally as Black Friars, they were founded by St. Dominic in 1215. They were the first Catholic religious order to have preaching doctrine as their primary task and the first to accept members into the order as a

Dominica

Dominican Republic

John Donne

whole ready to be sent anywhere, rather than into autonomous houses. The order provided houses of study at centers of learning, and under the leadership of Albertus Magnus (died 1280) and Thomas Aquinas (1225–74) rapidly became prominent in the intellectual life of the church. They vigorously propagated Thomism and have often been called on to provide official theologians. They preached against the Albigensians, Moors, and Jews; evangelized from Scandinavia to India and later throughout the world; and were placed in charge of the Inquisition. The order includes both men and women. Their habit is white with a black mantle. They have sought to popularize the saying of the rosary, and they wear rosaries on their belts.

Dominion, self-governing member of the British Commonwealth of Nations. Some dominions recognize the British monarch as titular sovereign while others do not. Dominion status confers trade, technical assistance, and military aid preferences. Dominions are independent nations which freely cooperate. No formal ties, except for a secretariat, exist with Britain.

Dominion Day, national holiday in Canada (July 1). It commemorates the establishment of the Dominion of Canada on July 1, 1867, uniting Nova Scotia, New Brunswick, and Upper and Lower Canada.

Dominoes, game played with rectangular pieces. The standard game uses 28 pieces. Each piece is divided into halves, each half containing from 0 to 6 dots in every combination—0–0, 1–1, 1–0, etc. The dominoes are played one at a time, and must be placed next to a domino that has a corresponding number. Each time a combination of the outer halves totals 5 or multiples of 5, the player receives a similar score.

Domino Theory, tenet of US foreign policy formulated after World War II; often applied to Southeast Asia. It is based on the thesis that if one country falls to Communist rule, its neighbors will inevitably succumb as well. The domino theory was one reason for US involvement in Vietnam and was subscribed to by the successive administrations of Presidents Eisenhower, Kennedy, Johnson, and Nixon.

Domitian (51–96), Roman emperor (81–96), second son of Vespasian. Despite holding no high posts, he succeeded Titus to the throne. Though his rule was at first orderly, he gave way to his cruel, tyrannical nature. He recalled Agricola from Britain, overpowered the Senate, and ruled like an absolute monarch. His repressive politics led to plots against him and a reign of terror. His wife, Domitia, arranged his assassination. The Senate chose Nerva as emperor to show its right to name the emperor.

Don, river in Ukrainian SSR, USSR; rises S of Moscow in mid-Russian Uplands, SE of Tula; flows S then SW to Sea of Azov. Rostov-na-Donu (Rostov-on-Don) is major port city; annual floods are controlled by Tsimlyansk Reservoir. River is navigable for 850mi (1,370km); shipping route for grain, lumber, and coal; fisheries in lower course. Donets River is major tributary; Don Basin lies between Volga River (E) and Dnepr River (W). Area of Basin: 160,000sq mi (414,400sq km). Length: 1,200mi (1,930km).

Donald Bane, Scottish king, the first of a succession of weak kings to rule after the death of Malcolm III (1093). As Malcolm's brother he was supported in his claims to the throne, and he successfully seized Edinburgh Castle. He was unseated by Duncan II, but returned after Duncan's murder, only to be unseated by Edgar in 1097.

Donatello (c.1386–1466), Italian sculptor, b. Donato di Niccolò di Betto Bardi. He worked in Florence, and much of his work shows the influence of the Gothic tradition. For example, his wooden statue "Mary Magdalen" (1455), in the Baptistery, Florence, reflects the expressive and emotional qualities of this style. His "Zuccone" prophet (c.1420), in the Florentine campanile shows his use of realism in its portrayal of an ugly subject. He usually worked in bronze and marble. His realistic style extended from his numerous heroic-type free-standing sculptures to his flat reliefs. In these marble low reliefs, he showed a remarkable mastery of perspective and light and shadow. He received many commissions, among which were the Gates of Paradise doors for the Baptistery in Florence. See also Gothic Art.

Donets (Northern Donets), river in Ukrainian SSR, USSR; rises in mid-Russian uplands, NE of Belgorod, flows SE to the Don River; lower course is navigable; tributaries are Oskol, Aidar, Lugan rivers. Length: 650mi (1,046km).

Donets (Donbas) Basin, major industrial region in Ukranian SSR, USSR, N of Sea of Azov and SW of Donets River; area is primarily in Donetsk and Voroshilovgrad oblasts, extending E into Rostov oblast; supplies up to 50% of USSR's coal and steel. Area: 10,000sq mi (25,900sq km).

Donetsk (Doneck), formerly Yuzovka or Stalino; city in Ukrainian SSR, USSR, on Kalmius River; capital of Donetsk oblast; largest city in Donets Basin; industrial and coal mining area; site of university, mining school, coal research institute, theater; developed after 1870 founding of ironworks by Scottish entrepreneur John Hughes. Industries: iron, steel, chemicals. Pop. 997,-000.

Donizetti, Gaetano (1797–1848), Italian operatic composer. He wrote 67 operas, both comic and serious. His most popular operas, include L'Elisir d'Amore (1832), Lucia di Lammermoor (1835), Roberto Devereux (1837), La Fille du Régiment (1840), and Don Pasquale (1843).

Donkey, or ass, domesticated equine derived from Nubian wild ass of Africa. A hardy saddle and pack animal, it is small and has long ears. Known since 4000 BC, it is also used to produce mules. Height: 3–5ft (1–1.5m) at shoulder. Breeds include Poiton, Spanish Giant, and Savoy. Family Equidae; species Equus asinus asinus.

Donleavy, James Patrick (1926–), US-born Irish author. His first novel The Ginger Man was published in Paris in 1955 but did not reach Britain and the US in unexpurgated form until 1963. It was produced in London as a play in 1959. His other works include A Singular Man (1963), The Onion Eaters (1971), The Destinies of Darcy Dancer, Gentleman (1977), and Schultz (1979).

Donne, John (c.1571–1631), English poet and cleric. Raised a Roman Catholic, but converted to Anglicism, he was ordained in 1615 after years of poverty. In 1621 he became dean of St Paul's Cathedral, London, where his sermons attracted much attention. Although widely known in his lifetime, the poems for which he is now famous were not published until 1633. Noted for their wit, extravagant imagery, and passion, they include love poems, satires, and religious sonnets. See also Metaphysical Poetry.

Donner Party, California-bound group who traveled overland from Illinois using a little-used route south of

the Great Salt Lake (Utah). The party camped at Truckee Lake, Utah, in November 1846 where they were caught in the early snows in the Sierra Nevada Mountains. They escaped starvation by eating the flesh of those who died. Of the 87 members of the party, 47 survived.

Donnybrook, town in E Republic of Ireland; suburb of Dublin; famous for its annual fair, begun in 1204 but condemned in 1855 for unruliness and violence.

Don Quixote de la Mancha (1605, 1615), novel by Miguel De Cervantes, published in two parts, initially intended to be a burlesque of chivalric romances. The author combined tragedy and comedy in his portrayal of the adventures of an elderly country gentleman, Don Quixote, and a peasant, Sancho Panza. Don Quixote is an avid reader of chivalric romances and, like a knight of old, sets out to redress the world's wrong.

Dooley, Thomas Anthony (1927–61), US physician and author who helped focus public attention on problems in Southeast Asia. As a naval officer in Vietnam (1954), he helped to evacuate refugees. In 1958, Dooley helped to found The Medical International Corporation (MEDICO), providing doctors and hospital facilities to underdeveloped nations. His books include Deliver Us from Evil (1956), The Edge of Tomorrow (1958), and The Night They Burned the Mountain (1960).

Doomsday Book. See Domesday Book.

Doppelganger, ghostly counterpart of a person; a double, invisible to others, that haunts him throughout his life.

Doppler, Christian Johann (1803–53), Austrian physicist and mathematician who is remembered as the discoverer of the Doppler effect, which is the change in the observed wave frequency caused by motion of the source and/or receiver of the wave. This effect is utilized in radiolocation, sonar, and astronomy.

Doppler Effect, change in frequency of a wave, usually a sound or light wave, when there is relative motion between wave source and observer; the change depends on the velocities of the wave, source, and observer. With a sound wave the effect is demonstrated by the drop in pitch of a vehicle's siren as the vehicle passes the observer, the velocity of approach suddenly changing to a velocity of recession. With a light wave the source or observer velocity must be very large for an appreciable effect to occur, as when light is received from a rapidly receding galaxy with its spectral lines shifted toward the red end of the spectrum. See also Red Shift.

Dorado, tropical offshore marine fish. A favored sport fish, it has a squarish head, forked tail, and long dorsal fin with 65 rays. Its silvery, blue, and yellow colors change when it is taken from the water. Length: 5ft (152.4cm); Weight: 67lb (30.4kg). Family Coryphaenidae; species common Coryphaena hippurus, pompano dolphin Coryphaena equisetus.

Dorado, or the Swordfish, southern circumpolar constellation. It has no stars brighter than the third magnitude but is easily discerned because it contains most of the Large Magellanic Cloud.

Doradus, S. See Magellanic Clouds.

Dorchester Company, fishing and mercantile company of Dorchester, England. It abandoned its permanent settlement at Cape Ann, Mass. (1626), feeling it was unprofitable. Governor Conant remained and moved to Salem, the original site for Massachusetts Bay Colony (1629).

Dordogne, river in SW France, formed by convergence of Dor and Dogne rivers; famous vineyards along its 293mi (471km) course.

Dordrecht, city in SW Netherlands, 12mi (19km) ESE of Rotterdam, on Meuse River; industrial and shipping center. Founded 1008; chartered 1200. Pop. 101,840.

Doré, Gustave (1833–83), French illustrator, painter, and sculptor. Known best for his engraved book illustrations, he illustrated editions of Dante's *Inferno* (1861), *Don Quixote* (1862), and the Bible (1865). Many of these engravings depict grotesque and bizarre scenes.

Doria, Andrea (1468–1560), Genoese admiral and statesman. In the service of the Hapsburg Emperor Charles V, he freed Genoa (1528) from the French and then became virtually absolute ruler of the city, reforming its constitution, which remained unchanged until 1798. Although he remained active in Genoese affairs, he continued until the end of his life to aid the Emperor against both the French and the Turks.

Dorians, peoples who settled in north Greece *c.*200 BC. About 900 years later they conquered Mycenae, starting a 300-year "dark age" of Greek culture. They were later responsible for developing city-states and dominated classical Greek military achievement.

Doric Order, earliest of the five classical orders of architecture, used originally by the Greeks and imitated by the Romans. The Doric column generally has no base. Its shaft is thick and broadly fluted; its capital is simple and unornamented. *See also* Orders of Architecture.

Dormancy, temporary state of inaction or reduced metabolism. Animals may go dormant by hibernating. Plant seeds cease to grow or develop. An organism can return to a fully active state when conditions, such as temperature, moisture, or day length, change.

Dormouse, mouse size, squirrel-like rodent of Eurasia and Africa that hibernates in winter. Most dormice are active at night and sleep by day. They eat nuts, fruit, seeds, insects, eggs, and tiny animals. Length: 4–8in (10–20cm) excluding tail. Family Gliridae.

Dorr's Rebellion (1841–42), a revolt protesting injustices in the Rhode Island state constitution, which restricted voting privileges to landowners and their oldest sons. Led by Thomas Wilson Dorr, the insurrectionists seized the statehouse and declared Dorr governor. The state militia was brought into action, the rebels dispersed, and Dorr was jailed. A new constitution was adopted (1843).

Dorset, county in SW England, bounded by English Channel(s). It is traversed W to E by North Dorset Downs and by South Dorset Downs near coast; drained by Frome and Stour rivers. Chief towns are Dorchester, Bournemouth, Poole, and Weymouth. Industries: tourism, agriculture, quarrying. Area: 973sq mi (2,520sq km). Pop. 572,900.

Dortmund, city in W West Germany; a port on the Dortmund-Ems Canal; commercially important during Middle Ages; site of the Reinold church (begun in 13th century). Industries: iron smelting, steel, beer. Founded in 9th century. Pop. 627,600.

Dos Passos, John (1896–1970), US novelist, b. Chicago. His work reflects his social conscience. His first novel, *Three Soldiers*, appeared in 1921. Subsequently, he began to develop the innovative techniques that characterize his trilogy, *U.S.A.* (1937). These include stream-of-consciousness writing and the use of contemporary headlines and biographies of prominent Americans in the novels.

Dostoevsky, Fyodor (Mikhailovich) (1821–81), Russian novelist. After writing *Poor Folk* (1846) and *The Double* (1846), he joined a revolutionary group, was arrested, and sentenced to death (1849). Reprieved at the last minute, he was sentenced to four years' hard labor in Siberia. He married (1857) and returned to St. Petersburg, where he edited several journals with his brother Mikhail and wrote *Notes from the Underground* (1864). After *Crime and Punishment* (1866) appeared, he married his secretary, Anna, and left Russia to escape creditors. While abroad, he wrote *The Idiot* (1868–69) and *The Possessed* (1871–72). His last major work was *The Brothers Karamazov* (1879–80).

Dothan, ancient city in central Palestine, in uplands NE of Samaria; ruins have been partially excavated. Here Joseph was sold into slavery by his brothers.

Dothan, city in SE Alabama, 15mi (24km) N of Floridian border; seat of Houston co; scene of annual nationwide peanut festival; site of nuclear power plant, George C. Wallace Junior College (1965); industrial and commercial center. Industries: hosiery, cotton processing, peanut oil, lumber products, farm machinery. Settled and inc. 1885. Pop. (1980) 48,750.

Douai, town in N France, on the Scarpe River, 19mi (30km) S of Lille; became part of France 1713. At its Roman Catholic college, the Old Testament of the Douay Bible was prepared in 1609. Industries: wire, springs, boilers. Pop. 47,570.

Douala (Duala), chief seaport city in Cameroon, W equatorial Africa, on Bight of Biafra; taken from Germans 1914. Industries: brewing, metalworking, textiles. Pop. 340,000.

Douay Bible, first English translation of the Bible authorized by the Roman Catholic Church. Gregory Martin, an Oxford scholar living in exile, was the main translator. The translation is based on the Latin Vulgate. The New Testament was published in Reims in 1582; the Old Testament at Douai in 1609–10. It was revised in 1750 by Richard Challoner.

Double Bass Viol, largest stringed instrument, usually with four strings tuned in fourths (E-A-D-G) and played one octave below the musical notation. Resembling smaller violins but with sloping shoulders, the double bass is held vertically, with the player standing behind, commonly using a bow for classical music, but plucking the strings in jazz where it is primarily a percussion instrument.

Double Galaxy, stellar system consisting of two adjacent galaxies orbiting around a common center, rather like a binary star. The components are often linked by tenuous bridges of intergalactic matter. Multiple galaxies also exist, comprising several component members. *See also* Binary Star.

Double Helix. *See* deoxyribonucleic acid (DNA).

Double Jeopardy, the prosecution of one person for the same offense more than once. A provision of the Fifth Amendment to the US Constitution usually bars such an action.

Double Star, star that appears single when viewed with the naked eye but is in reality two stars seen very close together. Double stars are either gravitationally associated binaries or simply the results of optical effects involving two completely separate objects that happen to lie in or near the same line of sight. *See also* Binary Star.

Double Vision. *See* Diplopia.

Dougga, village in Tunisia, 68mi (109km) SW of Tunis; site of ruins of ancient city of Thugga; includes a Punic Mausoleum (2nd century BC), Roman forum, arches, theater, and a temple built 2nd century AD by Marcus Aurelius in honor of Jupiter, Juno, and Minerva; attracts many tourists.

Douglas, noted Scottish family traceable from the 12th century. The descendants of Sir William de Douglas were powerful landowners based at Douglasdale, Lanarkshire. As earls of Douglas (1358–1488) and earls of Angus (1389–1761), branches of the family played important roles in Scottish affairs, providing bishops and regents.

Douglas, Archibald, 3rd Earl of Douglas (1328?–1400?), Scottish soldier and diplomat. Also called Douglas the Grim, the Black Douglas, Lord of Galloway. The illegitimate son of Sir James Douglas (the Good), he was constable of Edinburgh (1361), ambassador to France for David II of Scotland (1369) and to renew the Franco-Scots alliance (1371). In 1389–91 his diplomatic mission was to gain the inclusion of Scotland in the peace between England and France.

Douglas, Archibald, 4th Earl of Douglas (1369?–1424), Scottish noble. Captured by Hotspur (1402), he joined the victors against Henry IV of England at Shrewsbury (1403) but was again captured. Ransomed, he fought the English in the north and in France. He was created duke of Touraine (1423) but was killed at Verneuil by the duke of Bedford.

Douglas, Archibald, 5th Earl of Douglas (1391?–1439), Scottish noble. He fought against the English in France (1421), and conducted James I back to Scot-

land from his English captivity (1424), later becoming lieutenant-general of Scotland (1437–39).

Douglas, Archibald, 6th Earl of Angus (1489?–1557), Scottish noble. He married Margaret Tudor, sister of Henry VIII of England and mother of James V, boy-king of Scotland, (1514). With Henry's aid Angus ruled Scotland (1526–28), but when James asserted himself, Angus was exiled (1529–42). On James' death, Angus returned and helped repel the English invasions (1547–48).

Douglas, Gavin (c.1475–1522), Scottish poet, instrumental in the emergence of Scots as a language distinct from English or Gaelic. One of the most proficient medieval poets, Douglas completed a rhymed-couplet version of Vergil's *Aeneid* in Scots (1513), the first translation of a classical poem into an English-based language.

Douglas, (Sir) Howard (1776–1861), British military officer. A career soldier, he served in the Peninsular War (1808–12). He was governor of New Brunswick (1823–31), at a time when the border with Maine was in dispute. He prepared the British case when that boundary dispute was submitted to arbitration, wrote on political and military topics, and ended his career as an educator.

Douglas, (Sir) James (1803–77), Canadian fur trader and political leader, b. British Guiana. Working for the Hudson's Bay Company (1821–58), he established Forts Connolly (1827) and Victoria (1842). He served as governor of Vancouver Island (1851–63) and of British Columbia (1858–63). In his term of office, Douglas argued with the elected legislature but maintained a firm rule of law during the Yukon Gold Rush of 1858. He developed Vancouver as a center of western commerce and has been called "the Father of British Columbia."

Douglas, Stephen Arnold (1813–61), US political leader, b. Brandon, Vt. He was secretary of state of Illinois (1840–41) and served in the US House of Representatives (1843–47). Known as the "Little Giant," he was a senator (1847–61). While in Congress, he championed western expansion, popular sovereignty, and sponsored the Kansas-Nebraska Act (1854). He ran for the Senate against Abraham Lincoln (1858), when the Lincoln-Douglas debates took place. In 1860 he again opposed Lincoln, this time as the Democratic nominee for president. *See also* Kansas-Nebraska Act; Lincoln-Douglas Debates.

Douglas, William O(rville) (1898–1980), US Supreme Court member and conservationist, b. Maine, Minn. He was chairman of the Securities and Exchange Commission (1936–39), when he was appointed to the Supreme Court in 1939. Along with Justice Hugo Black, he wrote numerous dissents in the 1940s and 1950s in support of civil liberties, including his eloquent defense of free speech in *Dennis* v. *United States* (1951), an anti-Communist case. He also wrote the majority opinion in *Griswold* v. *Connecticut* (1965), which struck down anti-birth control legislation. He retired in 1975 after serving for the longest period in the court's history and wrote *The Court Years* (1980).

Douglas Fir, evergreen tree native to NW United States and Canada. It is an important timber pine, and is also grown in the E United States as an ornamental. Height: to 300ft (91m). Family Pinaceae; species *Pseudotsuga taxifolia.*

Douglas-Home, Sir Alec (1903–), British Conservative politician. Entering Parliament (1931), he became Neville Chamberlain's parliamentary private secretary (1937–39) and subsequently held ministerial posts. Although a lord (14th Earl of Home, from 1951), he became foreign secretary (1960–63), but had to renounce his peerage to become prime minister (1963–64). He was created a life peer (Baron Home of the Hirsel) in 1974.

Douglass, Frederick (1817–95), US abolitionist and social reformer, b. Tuckahoe, Md. An escaped slave, he became a popular lecturer for the Massachusetts Anti-Slavery Society and earned enough money to purchase his freedom. He began (1847) publication of an abolitionist paper, *North Star*. He helped recruit black soldiers during the Civil War, and after the war he held several government posts, including minister to Haiti (1889–91).

Doum Palm, also doom palm, branched-trunk palm native to upper Egypt and the Sudan. Sacred to ancient Egyptians, it has fan-shaped leaves borne in clusters at the end of each branch. Fruits are edible and have a gingerbread flavor. Height: to 30ft (9.1m); family Palmaceae; species *Hyphaene theobaica.*

Fyodor Dostoevsky

Stephen A. Douglas

William O. Douglas

Douris (active *c.*500 BC), Athenian vase painter. His many extant works show great draftsmanship and often dramatic tales. Examples are at the Louvre, Paris, and the Metropolitan Museum of Art, New York City.

Douro (Duero), river in Spain and Portugal; rises in mountainous N central Spain; flows W across Spain to form part of NE border of Portugal (W central border of Spain); continues through Portugal to its mouth on the Atlantic, 2mi (3km) S of Porto; supports hydroelectric power plants along Portuguese stretch of the river. Length: 556mi (895km).

Douroucouli, or night monkey, gray, squirrel-sized monkey found from Nicaragua to NE Argentina. It is a night-active tree dweller and eats fruit and insects. Species *Aotus trivirgatus. See also* Monkey.

Dove, cooing, plump-bodied bird found worldwide except in polar and subpolar areas and on some isolated islands. These pigeon-related birds have small heads, short legs, and dense, variously colored plumage. They feed mostly on vegetable matter and build flimsy stick platform nests in a tree or on the ground for the pale white eggs (1–2). Both parents incubate the eggs and feed the young. A special substance, ''pigeon's milk,'' is produced in the parents' crops during incubation and fed to the fledglings. Length: 6–30in (15–76cm). Family Columbidae.

Dover, town in SE England, on Strait of Dover (strait connecting English Channel and North Sea). One of the Cinque Ports (confederation of SE coastal towns 11th–14th centuries organized to protect England before Navy was created) and important seaport. Pop. 101,700.

Dover, capital city of Delaware, on the St Jones River, 45mi (72km) S of Wilmington; shipping and canning center for the surrounding farm and fruitgrowing region; site of Dover Air Force Base; contains fine examples of Georgian architecture. Industries: gelatin food products, synthetic polymers, adhesives, latex, resins, chemicals. City laid out 1717; made state capital 1777; inc. 1929. Pop. (1980) 23,512.

Downey, city in S California, SE of Los Angeles; suburban community for the Los Angeles and Long Beach areas. Industries: metallurgy, rubber, aerospace, chemicals. Inc. 1957. Pop. (1980) 82,602.

Downpatrick, town in E Northern Ireland, approx. 15mi (24km) SE of Belfast; St Patrick is thought to have founded a church here *c.* 440, and Ireland's three great saints (Patrick, Columba, and Bridget) were long thought to be buried here; other early religious structures remain. Industries: textiles, grains, sheep. Pop. 8,401.

Downs, North and South, two chalk hill ranges in SE England, running parallel and separated by The Weald, a valley approx. 30mi (48km) wide; the North Downs extend SE approx. 100mi (160km) from S outskirts of London, to Kent near the coast; the South Downs extend approx. 65mi (105km) from E Hampshire through W Sussex to E Sussex, near Brighton. The ranges, especially the South, are noted sheep pasturing areas.

Down's Syndrome. *See* Mongolism.

Doyle, (Sir) Arthur Conan (1859–1930), British novelist. He was a physician before writing the detective novel *A Study in Scarlet* (1887), featuring character Sherlock Holmes. Other Sherlock Holmes stories are collected as *Adventures of Sherlock Holmes* (1891)

and *The Memoirs of Sherlock Holmes* (1893). Holmes was revived by popular demand in *The Return of Sherlock Holmes* (1904). Among his other works were *The Lost World* (1912), featuring the eccentric scientific explorer Professor Challenger, and *The White Company* (1890). In later life he became interested in spiritualism.

D'Oyly Carte, Richard (1844–1901), English impresario associated with the operas of Sir William S. Gilbert and Sir Arthur Sullivan. He founded the Savoy Theatre in London (1881)—the first to be lighted electrically—for the purpose of producing Gilbert and Sullivan's works. The company is still in existence.

DPT Injection, vaccination against diphtheria, pertussis, and tetanus routinely given all children.

Dracaena, or dragon tree, corn plant, genus of house plant with stalklike trunk and long, arching leaves of green streaked with white, red, or gold. In its native Africa it grows to 60ft (18.3m). There are also shrubby varieties. Care: bright indirect light, soil (equal parts loam, peat moss, sand) kept moist. Propagation is by stem cuttings and sections or air layering. Height: to 8ft (2.5m). Family Agavaceae.

Drachenfels, peak in the Siebenbirge range, W West Germany, on the E bank of Rhine River. According to legend it is site of Siegfried's slaying of the dragon; the Drachenburg, a fortress now in ruins, was built here in 1117 by Archbishop Frederick I of Cologne. Drachenfels is German for ''dragon's rock.'' Height: 1,053ft (321m).

Draco, or the Dragon, northern circumpolar constellation situated north of Cygnus and surrounding Ursa Minor. Brightest star Gamma Draconis (Etamin).

Dracon, one of six men elected by the archons of Athens to pass laws. In 621 BC he drew up laws famous for their severity and for allowing the city to settle intra-family disputes. Death was specified even for minor crimes. Most of his laws, except those for homicide and differentiating premeditated and involuntary crime, were repealed by Solon.

Draft Riots, outbreaks against conscription in the Civil War. Both the Confederacy (in 1862) and the Union (in 1863) passed laws to draft men into their armies. Riots against such laws occurred in the North, the worst in July 1863 in New York City, where over 1,000 were killed or injured.

Dragger, any fishing boat equipped to operate a dragnet, that is, an open conical net designed to be drawn along the bottom.

Dragon Tree. *See* Dracaena.

Drainage System, collective description of the streams, lakes, and other surface manifestations of water and its removal from a particular region. Another term for the region that contributes water to a stream and its tributary waters is a drainage region. Two adjacent regions are separated by a divide. *See also* Hydrology.

Drake, (Sir) Francis (1540–96), English sailor and adventurer. A brilliant seaman, he won fame and fortune raiding Spanish shipping and colonies in the Caribbean (1570–73). In the *Golden Hind* Drake sailed west around the world (1577–80), plundering Spanish ports and ships in the Pacific. Queen Elizabeth I knighted him (1581) and he became mayor of Plymouth (1582). Further raids against Spain and her colonies increased his

wealth and fame (1585–87). Drake's seamanship and daring contributed greatly to the defeat of the Spanish Armada (1588). His last expedition was less successful and he died of dysentery in the West Indies.

Drava River, river in Austria and Yugoslavia; rises in Carnic Alps; flows E through Austria into Yugoslavia; empties into the Danube; forms part of Yugoslav-Hungarian border. Length: approx. 450mi (725km).

Dravidian Languages, family of languages spoken in the southern third of India by nearly 150,000,000 people. The four major Dravidian languages are Telugu, Tamil, Kannada (Kanarese), and Malayalam. Tamil is also spoken in Sri Lanka. Another Dravidian language, Brahui, is spoken in Pakistan. The Dravidian languages were probably spoken throughout most of India until its speakers were driven south by the invading Indo-Europeans about 1000 BC.

Dravidian Literature. The cultural center of Dravidian literature was the ancient city of Madura. During the first three centuries of the Christian era, Tamil literature attained its golden age. *Kural* of the weaver Tiru-valluvar, an allegory about wisdom, wealth and pleasure, was one of the most popular works in Tamil. The *Tiruvāchegam* of Mānikkar Vāchager was also famous, and its aphorisms were widely quoted. The works of the 12 Ālvārs, or saints, of whom the best known are Tiru-mangai and the female saint, Andāl (*c.* AD 800) helped to make Dravidian literature unique.

Drawing, trace left by chalk, crayon, charcoal, pen, or pencil on a surface; specifically in art history, representations or patterns sketched on paper. In ancient Egypt sketches were drawn with a brush on potsherds. During the Middle Ages drawing as an autonomous technique was mainly restricted to the pattern book used in workshops. In the 14th century the first independent drawings on paper appeared, and the techniques then used in modeling by hatching and highlighting with white were described by Cennino. Pisanello (Antonio Pisano) drew from nature for the purpose of study.

Drawing achieved independence as a means of artistic expression with Leonardo da Vinci. He considered his sketches like the rough drafts of poems; his unfinished drawings were used to suggest fresh ideas for major works. Raphael was influenced by him and was considered a great natural draftsman. Michelangelo's drawing technique of close-hatching resembled the chisel. He supposedly destroyed most of his sketches, not wanting the public to view the evidence of his labors.

At this time Giorgio Vasari collected drawings to keep a record of the various styles of the artists. In the Academy of the Carraccis drawing was systematically cultivated. Among north Italians, Jacopo da Pontormo and Tintoretto produced great drawings. In northern Europe, Albrecht Dürer was known for his vast and varied drawings and Pieter Brueghel for his studies of Genre figures and landscapes. Rembrandt, John Ruskin and the Pre-Raphaelites, Vincent van Gogh, Henri Matisse, Paul Klee, and Pablo Picasso were all interested in the art of drawing, as were the sculptors François Rodin and Aristide Maillol.

Dreadnought, H.M.S., one of the first of a new class of British battleships launched in 1906, larger and faster than its predecessors, with turbine engines and a main armament of large-caliber guns. These changes enabled battleships to direct fire over long ranges and reduce the danger of torpedo attack. *See also* Battleship.

Dreams. *See* Sleep and Dreams.

Dredger, any fishing vessel fitted with dredges (usually attached to outriggers) that rake up mollusks, crustaceans, or other catch from the sea-bottom. Simple dredges used in shallow water are long, pronged sticks with attached collecting bags. Deep-sea dredges are operated by research vessels at depths of up to 3,300ft (1000m).

Dredging, a method of surface mining employing a floating barge with a boom at one or both ends and usually a concentrating plant in the hull. The dredge is sunk into the bottom and bucket-lines continuously excavate materials which are screened and washed to obtain heavy minerals. *See also* Placer Mining.

Dreiser, Theodore (Herman Albert) (1871–1945), US author, b. Terre Haute, Ind. After working on various newspapers in the Midwest, he moved (1894) to New York City, where he made his living as a writer and editor on magazines before turning to creative writing fulltime in 1911. He became one of the foremost exponents of naturalism in American writing. His long, brooding but compassionate novels depicted man as the victim of biology, economics, society, and chance and probed the nature of modern urban, industrialized society in America.

His first novel, *Sister Carrie* (1900), was given only limited circulation by its publisher because of its alleged immorality. Dreiser had frequent clashes with censorship in his career. His second novel, *Jennie Gerhardt* (1911), like *Sister Carrie,* explores the life of a "fallen woman." His Cowperwood Trilogy, *The Financier* (1912), *The Titan* (1914), and *The Stoic* (1947), explores the life of a business magnate. *The Genius* (1915) and its sequel, *The Bulwark* (1946), explore the life of an artist. His greatest work, the novel *An American Tragedy* (1925), depicts a poor young man driven to murder by the dream of success.

Dresden, city in SE East Germany, on the Elbe River, 100mi (161km) SE of Berlin; capital of Dresden district. It was almost destroyed in WWII. Dresden china has been famous since the 18th century. Industries: optical instruments, chemicals, clothing. Settled by Germans 13th century. Pop. 509,331.

Dresden, Battle of (Aug. 26–27, 1813), Napoleon's last significant victory. This defeat of Prussian, Russian, and Austrian forces was accomplished in part by the French troops and artillery's exceptional mobility.

Dreyfus Affair. The affair began with the court martial of Alfred Dreyfus, a French army officer and a Jew, for treason in 1894. Convicted under scanty evidence of sending military information to the Germans, Captain Dreyfus was deported for life. His case became the focus of ardent anti-Semitism and nationalism on one side and a growing anti-military revisionist movement by his supporters. Demands to reopen the case by such Dreyfus supporters as Emile Zola increased, especially as evidence incriminating a Major Esterhazy was suppressed and covered up. Finally Colonel Henry, an accomplice, confessed to the forgeries and committed suicide. Dreyfus was given clemency (1899), but it was not until 1906 that he was fully cleared. The affair stifled French anti-Semitism but opened political and social divisions that troubled France for decades.

Drift, in geology, gradual change in the landmass, related to creep. In oceanography it indicates the slow oceanic circulation, and sedimentary drift is a general description of surface debris, which is either river or glacier-carried. It may also indicate an accumulation such as a snowdrift or sanddrift. Continental drift is the movement of continents (tectonics).

Drill, large, gregarious, ground-foraging monkey found in rain forests of C W Africa. It has a doglike muzzle and huge teeth. Length: 32in (82cm). Species *Mandrillus leucophaeus. See also* Baboon; Mandrill.

Drina River, river in Yugoslavia, formed at the confluence of the Tara and Piva rivers, 8mi (13km) NE of Maglic Peak; receives Cotina and Lim rivers; supports hydroelectric plant at Zvornick; navigable for 206mi (331km). Length: 285mi (459km).

Drive, basic biological need of an organism that motivates it to achieve satisfaction, eg, hunger "drives" an organism to find food. Drive is a fundamental concept in the psychology of motivation and an important principle in learning theory and psychoanalytic theory.

Drive-Reduction Theory, in psychology, assumption that satisfying a basic biological need or drive is necessary for learning to occur. The theory's foremost advocate was Clark Hull during the 1930s and 1940s. Applied primarily to the behavior of animals, it was gradually superseded by more diverse and complex learning theories. *See also* Drive.

Drogheda (Droichead Atha), town in NE Republic of Ireland, in S Louth, 4mi (6km) from mouth of Boyne River. Danes controlled town in 10th century; in 1394, Irish princes surrendered to Richard II. Oliver Cromwell stormed Drogheda in 1649 and killed most of the inhabitants. Battle of Boyne was fought near here in 1690, and town surrendered to William III. Industries: textiles, brewing, engineering, cement, fertilizers, cattle export. Pop. 19,744.

Dropsy. *See* Edema.

Drought, a condition that occurs when evaporation and transpiration exceed precipitation for considerable periods. Four kinds are recognized: permanent, typical of arid and semi-arid regions; seasonal, in climates with a well-defined dry and rainy season; unpredictable, an abnormal failure of expected rainfall; and invisible, when even frequent showers do not restore sufficient moisture lost to evaporation.

Drowning, one of the leading causes of accidental death, suffocation caused by water or other liquid in the lungs, depriving the body of needed oxygen. At first, breathing rate and depth increases, heartbeat increases, and neck veins become prominent as the body fights for oxygen. If submersion continues, however, within short time—5 minutes—breathing ceases and death can result unless prompt first aid, including artificial respiration, is given. Drowning usually occurs in deep water but can occur in few inches of water, even in a bathtub.

Drug, a chemical agent used therapeutically to cure a disease or correct a disorder. Drugs may be obtained from plant, animal, or mineral sources, but most today are synthetic. Some drugs are chemotherapeutic agents, fighting infection by acting on disease-causing organisms, either killing or immobilizing them. Included in this group are the antibiotics, the sulfa drugs, and the antimalarial, antituberculosis, antiviral, and antifungal agents. Other drugs are pharmacodynamic, affecting various systems of the body. Digitalis, a common example of such an agent, increases heart muscle contraction. Other drugs may be used in diagnosis, prevention, or other ways. Drugs are commonly administered orally, topically, or by injection. Dosage, effectiveness, speed of action, possible toxicity vary with the particular drug and the individual being treated. *See also* Pharmacology.

Drug Abuse and Addiction, habitual or compulsive use of a mood-altering substance to the extent that physiological or psychological dependence is established. The addicting agents can be alcohol, opiates (as morphine and heroin), cocaine, barbiturates, sedatives, hypnotics, stimulants, and other psychoactive drugs. Evidence of physiological dependence is demonstrated by the occurrence of withdrawal symptoms such as hallucinations, tremors, and convulsions when the addicting agent is withdrawn from use. Drug abuse leads to mental and physical deterioration and is the source of serious social problems. Death resulting from an overdose of one or a combination of drugs is not uncommon. A number of programs have been established to treat abuse and addiction with varying degrees of success.

Druids, pre-Christian Celtic priests in ancient Britain, Ireland, and Gaul, suppressed by Rome. The earliest Druidic records date from the 3rd century BC, but the Druids probably existed far earlier. They conducted a strongly ritualistic religion and were also a powerful political influence.

Drum, primitive, universal, percussion instrument, generally a hollow cylinder or vessel with skins stretched across openings, and struck with hands or beaters. Brought from Asia by the Crusaders, drums appeared in European orchestras with Turkish band instruments about 1750. Symphony orchestras use the snare (side or military) drum, a shallow cylinder with two skin heads, the lower crossed by strings (snares); the tenor (field) drum, a deeper tube with two heads; the larger bass drum, beaten with padded mallets; the timpani (kettledrum), with a single, tunable head; and the tambourine, a shallow, single-headed drum with metal jingles set loosely around the rim. Jazz bands use drums extensively, often for solos. *See also* Timpani.

Drumfish, or croaker, tropical and temperate marine fish found in brackish or fresh water. It uses its air bladder and attached muscles to make drumming sounds. The American freshwater drum, or Thunder-pumper *(Aplodinotus grunniens)* is found in lakes and streams from Canada to Guatemala. The marine black drum *(Pogonias cromis)* grows to 4ft (121.9cm), weights up to 146lb (65.7kg). Family Sciaenidae.

Drumlin, hill created by a glacier out of either debris or bedrock. Drumlins usually occur in groups. They are ellipsoidal in shape and the long axis is parallel to the movement of the parent glacier. The head end points toward the retreating glacier and is steeper and higher than the tapering tail. *See also* Deposition.

Drupe, or **stone fruit,** any fruit with a thin skin, fleshy pulp, and hard stone or pit enclosing a single seed. Drupes are usually produced by flowers with petals attached beneath the ovary (superior ovary). Examples are plum, cherry, peach, olive, almond, and coconut.

Drury Lane Theatre, London's oldest theater still in use. It was built in 1663 and known as the Theatre Royal, on Bridges St. Rebuilt in 1674 by Christopher Wren after being completely destroyed by fire, it is the most famous playhouse in London.

Druses, or **Druzes,** religious sect of the Near East. An offspring of the Ismaili Muslims, it includes elements of belief from other religions. The Druses originated in the reign of Caliph al-Hakim (996–1021). Al-Hakim claimed to be divine, and a cult grew up about him. The Druses are a continuation of this cult. Their name comes from al-Darazi, the first to proclaim the cult publicly. The man who gave form to the Druse faith was Hamza Ibn Ali. Stressing pure monotheism, he maintained that al-Hakim would live in hiding until he came for the Last Judgment but also emphasized the possibilities of direct communication with divinity as a living presence. The Druses are secretive about their beliefs and rituals. They allow no conversion or intermarriage and divide members of the faith itself into two groups, those fully initiated into its tenets (less than 10% of the total) and those not so initiated. Persecuted in Egypt, the Druse community was able to sustain itself only in the mountains of what is now Syria, Lebanon, Jordan, and Israel. They number about 370,000.

Drusus, 90 BC.

Dryads, in Greek mythology, forest nymphs who guarded trees. They carried axes to punish those who harmed the trees they protected.

Dry Cell, zinc casing filled with chemical paste surrounding a carbon rod. The rod is a positive electrode, the zinc casing a negative. Chemical reaction provides the source of electricity that flows whenever the carbon-zinc circuit is closed. A flashlight switch, for instance, closes the circuit and produces current for the light.

Dryden, John (1631–1700), English poet and playwright. He produced his *Heroic Stanzas* on Cromwell's death in 1659, followed by *Astraea Redux,* praising Charles II, in 1660. As Poet Laureate (1668–88) Dryden wrote numerous fine plays, poems, and essays. After embracing Catholicism (1687), he lost his post. His poems include *Annus Mirabilis* (1667), *Absalom and Achitophel* (1681), *Mac Flecknoe* (1682), *The Hind and the Panther* (1687), and *Alexander's Feast* (1697). His most noted plays are *All for Love* (1678) and *Marriage à la mode* (1673).

Dry Dock, any structure in dock areas that can be closed off and pumped free of water. Ships are floated in and left resting on props at the bottom of the dry dock. Repairs or maintenance can proceed on otherwise unapproachable parts of the vessel.

Dry Farming, production of crops in semiarid areas without irrigation. Wheat, sorghum, and beans are successful dry crops, highly dependent upon soil management for availability of moisture and supply of nutrients. It is made possible by the fallow system, in which land is plowed and tilled but left unseeded for one growing season.

Dryopithecus, several species of extinct apelike primates, representative of the dryopithecines, the group believed to be the basal stock of both modern apes and men. Widespread in Europe, Africa, and Asia during late Miocene and Pliocene times. *Dryopithecus* itself is thought to be ancestral to chimpanzees and gorillas. Another drypithecine, *Ramapithecus* (of 12,-000,000 years ago) is believed to be at the base of hominid evolution.

Dry Tortugas, group of seven islands in SW Florida, at entrance to Gulf of Mexico; site of Fort Jefferson National Monument (est. 1935), federal bird sanctuary (est. 1908); virtually uninhabited due to nonexistence of fresh water (hence its name). Discovered 1513 by Ponce de León; annexed to United States with Florida 1819. Area: 75sq mi (194sq km).

Dualism, doctrine in philosophy and metaphysics that recognizes two basic and mutually independent principles, such as mind and matter, body and soul, or good and evil. Characterized by precise definition of con-

Theodore Dreiser

W.E.B. Du Bois

Duck: Mallards

cepts, dualism contrasts with monism, in which reality has a single ultimate nature. Both Plato and Descartes were dualists, but more modern philosophers, influenced by the discoveries of modern science, have tended more toward monism.

Duarte (Fuentes), José Napoleón (1926–   ), El Salvador political leader, president 1980–   . He received an engineering degree from Notre Dame University in the US in 1948, then held various nonpolitical jobs until 1960, when he helped found the Christian Democratic party. He was mayor of San Salvador from 1964–70 and ran for president in 1972. He may have won the election, but the government declared him the loser, and he went into exile in Venezuela until 1979, then returned and was named president by the ruling military junta. With limited popular support and with El Salvador embroiled in civil war, he had difficulty in carrying out programs of land redistribution and tax reform.

Dubai (Dubayy), one of the seven constituent states of the United Arab Emirates, in E Arabia, on the Persian Gulf. A dependency of Abu Dhabi until 1833, it became a British protectorate in the 19th century; it was at war with Abu Dhabi from 1945–48; oil was discovered in the early 1960s. Chief industry is oil production, and it serves as the principal port of the UAE. Capital is Dubai. Area: approx. 1,500sq mi (3,888sq km). Pop. 206,861. *See also* United Arab Emirates.

Du Barry, Marie Jeanne Bécu, Comtesse (1743–93), French adventuress. She was mistress of, among others, Jean du Barry, who facilitated her rise under the false title of comtesse du Barry, eventually engineering, through a marriage to his brother, her acceptance as last mistress of Louis XV of France. A great patron of the arts and normally politically inactive, she was executed by the Revolutionary tribunal for associations with the British and her aid to the émigrés.

Du Bellay, Guillaume, Seigneur de Langey (1491–1543), French diplomat and writer. Important as one of Francis I's most competent diplomats and antagonist of Emperor Charles V, he executed the Treaty of Cambrai. He went to England (1529–30) and helped Henry VIII obtain his divorce; from 1532–36 he worked to unite the German princes in opposition to Emperor Charles V. He was governor of Turin (1537–39) and of Piedmont (1539–42). A friend of prominent writers of the time, including Rabelais, he wrote *Ogdoades* and *Epitome de l'Antiquité des Gaules et de France* (1556).

Dublin, capital of Republic of Ireland, at mouth of Liffey River on Dublin Bay; seat of County Dublin; commercial center and seaport. A Danish town until 1014 when defeated by Brian Boru, it returned to Danish control but in 1170 Richard Strongbow took Dublin for the English, and it became center of English authority in Ireland. Ravaged by religious wars 1640–90, improvement in city's fortunes occurred in 18th century. Strikes beginning in 1913 finally ended in Easter Rebellion of 1916; site of Christ Church Cathedral (1053), St Patrick's Cathedral (1192), St Audoen's Arch (1215, gate from town's walls), Trinity College (1591), University College (1908), and Abbey Theatre (1904); birthplace of Oscar Wilde (1854), George Bernard Shaw (1856), James Joyce (1882). Jonathan Swift served as dean of St Patrick's for 30 years and is buried there. Industries: brewing, distilling, clothing, footwear, textiles, fertilizers. Pop. 566,034.

Du Bois, W.E.B. (1868–1963), educator, author, and black leader, b. William Edward Burghardt Du Bois in Great Barrington, Mass. He taught economics and history at Atlanta University (1896–1910), and founded

the Niagara movement (1909) that later became the National Association for Advancement of Colored People. He was the editor of the group's magazine, *Crisis* (1910–32). He urged liberation of African colonies at several Pan African conferences (1900–27), and was co-chairman, with Kwame Nkrumah, of the fifth Pan African congress (1945). He became a communist (1961) and emigrated to Ghana (1962) where he died. His writings include *The Souls of Black Folk* (1903) and *Color and Democracy* (1945).

Dubrovnik, seaport town in Yugoslavia, in Dalmatia, on the Adriatic Sea; built by Greek refugees, became part of Byzantine Empire 867; site of 14th-century mint, cloisters, Franciscan and Dominican monasteries; sponsors an annual music festival; tourist center. Products: wood, grapes, cheese, olives. Pop. 58,920.

Dubuffet, Jean (1901–85), French painter and sculptor. After several years in business, Dubuffet began his art career in 1942. Among his best-known works are assemblages of glass, sand, rope, and other junk arranged into crude shapes, which he called *pâtes*. He also collected the work of psychotics and others who were untrained and called it *art brut* (raw art).

Dubuque, city in NE Iowa, on the Mississippi River opposite Wisconsin-Illinois state line; seat of Dubuque co; named for Julien Dubuque, lead miner (1788); growth was rapid after Black Hawk War (1832); site of University of Dubuque (1852), Clarke College (1843); a rich farming area and trading center. Industries: meat packing, metal and woodworking. Settled 1833 (oldest Iowa city); inc. 1841. Pop. (1980) 62,321.

Duccio di Buoninsegna (c.1255–1319), Italian painter. Duccio was the first great painter of the Sienese School. In his works he added naturalness and lyricism to rigid Byzantine figures. His two major surviving works are the *Rucellai Madonna* (commissioned 1285, Uffizi Gallery, Florence) and the *Maestà* altarpiece done for Siena Cathedral (1308–11), panels of which can be seen at several museums in Europe and the United States.

Duchamp, Marcel (1887–1968), French painter. Influenced by Paul Cézanne, he later turned to the Cubist and Futurist styles, causing a sensation at the 1913 New York Armory Show with his *Nude Descending a Staircase*. After World War I he became a founder of the Dada movement in New York. He was also the inventor of "ready-made" art, treating commonplace objects as works of art; and he constructed many nonfunctional machines. *See also* Dada.

Duck, worldwide waterfowl valued as game and domesticated for their eggs and meat, rich in iron and B vitamins. They nest in cool areas and migrate to warm areas over winter. All have long necks, short legs, webbed feet, varied color, and dense plumage underlaid by down, and waterproof feathers. Males, or drakes, are usually much brighter.

Dabbling ducks feed from the water surface; others dive for food. All strain seeds, aquatic insects, crustaceans, and mollusks from the water with their flat bills. Most engage in complex courtship, lay a large clutch, and are flightless during a post-breeding molt. Ducks are divided into eight tribes: whistling, or tree, duck; sheldrake; dabbling river duck; perching duck; diving pochard; sea duck; stiff-tailed duck; and torrent duck. Length: 1–2ft (30–60cm); weight: to 16lb (7.2kg). Family Anatidae.

Duckweed, a family (Lemnaceae) of 4 genera and 40 species of tiny, aquatic, monocotyledonous, rootless flowering plants. The flowers are almost invisible; there

are no leaves. The Watermeal *(Walffia arrhiza)* is the smallest of all flowering plants.

Ductless Gland. *See* Endocrine System.

Dudley, city in W central England, 10mi (16km) NW of Birmingham. Industries: coal mining, wrought iron products, boilers, chains, tiles, bricks. Pop. 300,700.

Duel, prearranged armed contest between two persons with deadly weapons. Believed to have originated during battles among medieval Germanic tribes, the duel became a judicial practice. This declined in the 16th century when duels became associated with knighthood and chivalry. The purpose was usually not to kill, but to draw blood. The 19th century saw a revival of duels especially in Germany among university students. In the United States, Alexander Hamilton was killed in the famous duel with Aaron Burr (1804). Adverse public opinion has made dueling illegal in most countries.

Duffy, (Sir) Charles Gavan (1816–1903), Irish-Australian statesman and writer. He helped found and edit the *Nation* (1842), the organ of the Young Ireland movement; served in Parliament (1852–55); and was tried for his political activities. He emigrated to Australia and in Victoria became minister of public works (1857), minister of lands (1858, 1862), prime minister (1871–73), and speaker of the legislative assembly (1877). He returned to Europe (1880) and in 1891 became the first president of the Irish Literary Society. He wrote *Ballad Poetry of Ireland* (1845), *Young Ireland—1840–50* (1880–83), and *Conversations with Thomas Carlyle* (1892).

Dufy, Raoul (1877–1953), French painter. An Impressionist, Dufy converted to the Fauvist style early in his career about 1905 under the influence of Henri Matisse. His style changed again about 1909 while he was with Georges Braque at L'Estaque. He developed a bright, decorative, calligraphic style well suited to his subjects, such as racing and boating scenes. He also did textile designs and book illustrations. *See also* Fauvism.

Dugong, or sea cow, large plant-eating aquatic mammal found in shallow coastal waters of Africa, Asia, and Australia. Gray and hairless, they have no hind legs and their forelegs have been modified into weak flippers. Length: 12ft (3.6m); weight: 600lb (270kg). Species *Dugong dugon.*

Du Guesclin, Bertrand (c.1320–80), French soldier and constable. France's leading soldier of the time, he reorganized the French army to use sieges and guerrilla tactics to defeat the English. Twice taken prisoner by the English, and twice ransomed, he defeated Peter the Cruel in Spain and put the crown of Castile on Henry of Trastamara (1369). Under Charles V, he freed southern and western France from the English (1370–79).

Duiker, or duikerbok, small sub-Saharan African antelope usually found in scrubland. The female is larger than the male and occasionally carries stunted horns: male horns are short and spiky. It is gray to reddish yellow. Height: to 26in (66cm) at shoulder; weight: to 37lb (17kg). Family Bovidae; species *Sylvicapra grimmia.*

Duisburg, city in W West Germany, at confluence of Rhine and Ruhr rivers. Center of German armaments industry, it suffered extensive damage in WWII. Industries: textiles, chemicals, metal products. Founded 9th century. Pop. 587,000.

Duke of York Islands, group of 13 coral islands in SW Pacific, in the Bismarck Archipelago, between NE New Britain Island and SW New Ireland Island; part of Papua New Guinea. Largest island is Duke of York. Area: 23sq mi (60sq km). Pop. 5,870.

Dulcimer, medieval stringed instrument originally Persian, with a flat, triangular sounding board and 10 or more strings struck with hand-held hammers. It is the prototype of the pantaleon and cimbalon. In early America the zither was called a dulcimer.

Dulles, John Foster (1888–1959), US political leader, b. Washington, D.C. He held diplomatic posts under Presidents Woodrow Wilson, Franklin D. Roosevelt, and Harry Truman. He helped to form the United Nations at the San Francisco Conference (1945) and was US delegate there (1945–49). He served as Pres. Dwight D. Eisenhower's secretary of state (1953–59), favoring a policy of "containing" Communism.

Dulong, Pierre-Louis (1785–1838), French chemist and physicist. After training in medicine he became assistant to Berthollet, finally being appointed professor at the École Polytechnique. He discovered the explosive nitrogen trichloride, and in 1819 he helped formulate Dulong and Petit's law of specific heats, which aided in the determination of atomic weights. His other studies involved the refracting power and the specific heat of gases.

Dulse, any of a group of fairly large red seaweeds (genus *Rhodymenia*, especially *R. palmata*), that are used as a food condiment. Dulses grow chiefly in cold northern seas. *See also* Red Algae.

Duluth, Daniel Greysolon, Sieur (1636–1710), Canadian explorer. A soldier, he emigrated from France to Canada in 1675 and worked as a fur trader. He explored Lake Superior (1678), founded Fort St Joseph (1686), and was commandant of Fort Frontenac (1690–96). He established trading relations with the Sioux and wrote an account of his travels. He gave his name to the city of Duluth, which he founded as a fort in 1679.

Duluth, city in NE Minnesota, at W edge of Lake Superior, 140mi (225km) NE of Minneapolis; seat of St. Louis co. Area visited by Sieur Duluth, a French voyager (1679); the W terminus of the St Lawrence Seaway, it is near rich iron ore ranges and wheat fields; tourist center. Industries: meat packing, publishing, electronics manufacturing. Trading post est 1792. City founded 1856; inc. 1870. Pop. (1980) 92,811.

Dumas, Alexandre (1802–70), French novelist and dramatist. His success began with his numerous romantic historical plays, such as *La Tour de Nesle* (1832). He is best remembered now for the swashbuckling historical novels *The Three Musketeers* (1844) and *The Count of Monte Cristo* (1845).

Dumas, Alexandre (1824–95), French dramatist and novelist. The illegitimate son *(fils)* of Alexandre Dumas *père,* his first great success was *La Dame aux Camélias* (1852), a realistic view of the demi-monde milieu of Paris. His didactic later plays, such as *Les Idées de Madame Aubray* (1867), provoked changes in French social laws.

Dumbarton Oaks Conference (1944), meeting held near Washington, D.C., by representatives of the United States, Great Britain, USSR, and China. The six-week meeting resulted in a plan for an international coalition to preserve world peace after World War II. The organizational structure, agreed upon at that meeting, became the basis for the United Nations charter adopted the next year.

Dumfries, town in S Scotland, on the Nith River; amalgamated with Maxwelltown 1929; seat of Dumfriesshire. Robert Burns died and was buried here 1796; his house is now a museum. Industries: knitwear, hosiery, chemicals. Pop. 88,215.

Dumont D'Urville, Jules Sébastien César (1790–1842), French explorer. After making coastal surveys of Australia (1826–29), he sailed to Antarctica (1837–40) where he discovered Joinville Island and Adélie Land. An admiral in the French navy, he led two expeditions around the world in the ships *Astrolabe* (1826–29) and *Zélée* (1837–40). He described his voyages and supplied maps in a 49-volume work.

Dumuzi, ancient Mesopotamian king of the city of Erech who was worshiped as a fertility god after his death. A ritual reenactment of the marriage of Dumuzi and Inanna, the patron deity of Erech, was held each New Year's day. As late as the 6th century BC Jews knew him as Tammuz and recounted the story of his descent into the underworld, identifying this with the annual withering of vegetation.

Dunant, Jean Henri (1828–1910), Swiss philanthropist. A founder of the Red Cross and recipient of the first Nobel Peace prize (1901) with Frédéric Passy, he donated his entire fortune to a campaign to secure relief for wartime wounded. He was responsible for the Geneva Convention of 1864, which set down wartime rules and established the International Red Cross.

Duncan I (died 1040), king of the Scots, son of Cronan, lay abbot of Dunkeld, and grandson of Malcolm II. He was killed in 1040 by Macbeth for reasons unclear to historians. Two of his sons, Malcolm III Canmore and Donald Bane, were later kings of the Scots.

Duncan II (died 1094), king of Scotland, eldest son of Malcolm III. His father gave him as a hostage to William the Conquerer, and Duncan was knighted in Normandy in 1087. When his father died and his uncle Donald Bane was elected king, Duncan led a force of English and Normans and captured the throne. His followers were driven out, however, and he was killed the following year.

Duncan, Isadora (1878–1927), US dancer, b. San Francisco, who achieved fame first in Europe with her dances based on Greek classical art. She was one of the greatest influences on modern dance chiefly because of her innovative and pioneering expressions of feeling. She was noted for her Greek costumes with many scarves draped about her neck. She died in a tragic accident when a scarf she was wearing caught in a wheel of a car in which she was riding and strangled her. Her autobiography is *My Life* (1926–27).

Dundalk, city in NE Maryland, on the Patapsco River. City was in path of British march on Washington in War of 1812. Industries: steel; radio, electronic, and automotive parts; yachts. Inc. 1946. Pop. (1980) 71,293.

Dundee, city in E Scotland, on N shore of the Firth of Tay; important port and university town. Industries: jute, linen, heavy engineering, lumber, shipbuilding. Pop. 194,732.

Dune, hill or ridge of windblown particles, most often sand. Dunes are found wherever wind flow is obstructed and sandy particles that it carried are deposited. Dunes occur in a variety of shapes depending on the direction of the wind, whether or not it is constant, and the surrounding landforms, which affect direction and velocity.

Dunedin, city and port in New Zealand, on SE coast of South Island at head of Otago Harbor; site of first university in New Zealand, University of Otago (1869). Industries: iron, brass, clothing, shoes. Founded 1848 as a Free Church of Scotland settlement. Pop. 120,426.

Dunes, Battle of the (June 4, 1658), fought on the dunes of Dunkerque (Dunkirk) between French troops under the Vicomte de Turenne aided by English Cromwellian troops and Spanish troops led by Don John of Austria allied with English royalists under the Duke of York. The Spanish army was defeated according to the plan of French Prime Minister Mazarin, who wanted to force Spain into the "grand marriage" alliance of Louis XIV and the Spanish Infanta.

Dung Beetle, or tumblebug, small to medium-sized scarab beetle that feeds on dung. Some species form balls of dung as food for their larvae. The balls may be tumbled, or rolled, some distance before being buried in the ground. Family Scarabaeidae. *See also* Scarab Beetle.

Dunkirk (Dunkerque), city in N France, on Strait of Dover, 44mi (71km) NW of Lille. Evacuation of Allied troops from here May 29–June 2, 1940, was caused by German breakthrough to the English Channel. It is a leading French port and one of the major iron and steel areas of W Europe. Founded in 7th century; came under French rule 1662. Pop. 83,759.

Dunkirk Evacuation (1940), evacuation of 338,000 British, French, and other Allied troops from Dunkirk, France, to England after the initial German breakthrough in World War II. These forces, trapped against the English Channel, abandoned their equipment, and were transported in 220 naval and over 660 other vessels, many of them civilian (May 29–June 2).

Dunmore, John Murray, Earl of, (1732–1809), British colonial governor. He was governor of New York (1770) and Virginia (1771–75). He led the Indian campaign (1774) known as Lord Dunmore's War in the Ohio region. Expelled as Virginia governor at the start of the Revolution, he served as governor of the Bahamas (1787–96).

Duns Scotus, John (1265–1308). Scottish theologian and scholastic philosopher. A member of the Franciscan order, he was ordained in 1291 and subsequently lectured at Cambridge, Oxford, and Paris. His principal works were his commentaries on the works of Peter Lombard. His philosophy came to be called Scotism. *See also* Lombard, Peter; Scholasticism.

Dunstan, Saint (910–88), English monk who became counsellor to King Edmund of Wessex, and made important religious reforms as abbot of Glastonbury. He was driven into exile in Flanders under Edwig, but when Edgar became king he was made archbishop of Canterbury (959–88). He is important for his reforms of monasticism, rebuilding churches, and furthering education.

Duodenum, first section of the small intestine shaped like a horseshoe. The pyloric sphincter separates it from the stomach. Alkaline bile and pancreatic juices enter the duodenum and mix with intestinal secretions to aid in digestion.

Du Pont de Nemours, Eleuthère Irénée (1771–1834), US industrialist, b. France. He was the founder of the huge, diversified chemical company, and family empire. With his father **Pierre Samuel Du Pont de Nemours** (1739–1817), he came to the United States (1799). They started a business backed by French government capital, producing high-quality gunpowder near Wilmington, Del. (1804). Du Pont prospered during the War of 1812 and made a fortune. He was director of the Second Bank of the United States in Philadelphia. The company, E. I. Du Pont de Nemours and Co., continued under his sons and grandsons.

Dura (Europus), ancient city of Syria, on the Euphrates River. Founded *c.* 300 BC, it was abandoned *c.* AD 257; site has yielded many valuable archaeological remains of Mesopotamia from Hellenistic to Roman times. Present village of Salihiye is here.

Durand, Asher Brown (1796–1886), US engraver and painter, b. Jefferson Village, N.J. Famous for his engravings of John Trumbull's "The Signing of the Declaration of Independence," he was also prominent in the Hudson River School of landscape painters. *See also* Hudson River School.

Durango (Victoria de Durango), state in NW Mexico, in the fertile valley of the Nazas River; highly developed agriculturally; vast plains in middle region provide excellent pastures and mountainous N regions are rich in minerals. Durango, the capital city, is major commercial center for the state; noted for 18th-century cathedral and government palace. Industries: lumber, mining, grain, cotton, sugar cane, tobacco, tanneries, foundries, textiles. Area: (state) 46,196sq mi (119,648sq km). Founded (city) 1556; (state) 1824. Pop. (city) 209,000; (state) 1,122,000.

Durban, formerly Port Natal; chief port of South Africa, on N shore of Natal Bay, 300mi (483km) SE of Johannesburg; scene of 1908–09 national convention, initiating the 1910 Union of South Africa; site of University of Durban (1960), University of Natal (1949), and Durban Museum; busiest port of South Africa, and important industrial center. Exports: sugar, oranges, pineapples, wool, coal, maize. Industries: petroleum, textiles, automobiles, paint, sugar refining. Settled 1824. Pop. 851,000.

Dürer, Albrecht (1471–1528), German engraver, designer of woodcuts, and painter. Son of a goldsmith, Dürer at the age of 15 was apprenticed to Nuremberg painter and book illustrator Michael Wolgemuth. After traveling throughout Germany and to Italy in the early 1490s, he returned to live permanently in Nuremberg.

In his workshop he produced paintings, engravings, and woodcuts, forms in which he had acquired immense technical skill. He was influenced by the engravings of Martin Schongauer and the art of Mantegna. He spent much of 1505 and 1506 in Venice, seeing the High Renaissance there firsthand. By this time he had become well established and received several commissions for altarpieces. For the Emperor Maximilian he designed a huge woodcut, *Triumphal Arch.* A convert to Protestantism, he had deep and often troubled feelings about religion that are frequently apparent in his art. His studies of the ideal proportions of the human body and of perspective are also evident in his works. In 1526 he presented Nuremberg with *Four Apostles* that reflects his religious and theoretical thinking, His other well-known works include *Self-Portrait* (1493) and *Knight, Death, and Devil* (1513).

John Foster Dulles

Alexandre Dumas (fils)

Eleanora Duse

Durga, in the Hindu pantheon, the wife of Siva. Depicted as a 10-armed goddess, she is both destructive and beneficent but is worshiped today as a warrior against evil. Her festival, which occurs in September or October is the occasion for family reunions.

Durgapur, city in E central India, on the Damodar River. Dams on river furnish hydroelectric power to area. Industries: iron, steel, coal. Pop. 206,638.

Durham, city in N central North Carolina in Piedmont area; seat of Durham co. After the Civil War James B. Duke and other tobacco industrialists developed the area; Duke University was founded here 1838. In 1959 the 5,000-acre (2,025-hectare) Research Triangle Park opened. Industries: textiles, hosiery, cigarettes. Settled 1750; inc. 1869, Pop. (1980) 100,831.

Durkheim, Emile (1858–1917), French sociologist, one of the founders of modern sociology. Educated in Germany and France, he taught at the University of Bordeaux and at the Sorbonne in Paris. Influenced by the positivism of Comte, Durkheim is credited with laying the framework for the analysis of social systems. His main works are *The Division of Labor in Society* (1893), *The Rules of the Sociological Method* (1894), *Suicide* (1897), and *The Elementary Forms of Religious Life* (1912).

Durrell, Lawrence (George) (1912–), British author, b. India. After attending a number of schools in India and England and working at odd jobs, he began to travel widely. The novel *The Black Book,* expressing an atmosphere of moral decadence, was published in 1938. From 1941 to 1958 he held various British official and diplomatic posts. The short story collections *Esprit de Corps* (1958) and *Stiff Upper Lip* (1959) spoof diplomatic life and describe places where he lived. His masterpiece is *The Alexandria Quartet,* a novel published in four parts—*Justine* (1957), *Balthazar* (1958), *Mountolive* (1958), and *Clea* (1960). Other novels include *Tunc* (1968), *Numquam* (1970), *Monsieur* (1975). He also wrote several volumes of poetry.

Durrës (Durazzo), city in W Albania, on coast of Adriatic Sea; capital of Durrës prov. Albania's major port. Exports: grain, olive oil, tobacco. Founded 625 BC as a joint colony of Corcyra and Corinth; population is largely Muslim. Pop. 53,800.

Duse, Eleanora (1859–1924), Italian actress. She made her debut at the age of four in *Les Miserables;* at 14 she played Juliet. Known for her beautiful use of her hands and her scorn for the use of make-up and corsets, she played all over the world in such plays as *Théodora, La Locandiera,* and *La Dame aux Camélias.* She introduced several plays of Gabriele d'Annunzio, and also gave notable performances in works of Ibsen *(Ghosts, Lady from the Sea)* and James Huneker *(Iconoclasts).* Her health forced her retirement before World War I, but she later gave special matinees in London (1923) and eight performances at the Metropolitan Opera House in New York City. She died in Pittsburgh while on tour.

Dushanbe (Dušanbe), formerly Stalinabad; city and capital of Tadzhik SSR, USSR, at the foot of the Gissar Mts; industrial, trade and transport center; site of Tadzhik University and Academy of Sciences (1951). Industries: cotton milling, leather goods, food processing. Founded 1925. Pop. 493,000.

Düsseldorf, city in W West Germany, at confluence of Rhine and Düssel rivers; a cultural center. In 14th-16th centuries it was capital and residence of dukes of Berg; became part of Prussia in 1815; occupied by France

1921–25. Industries: chemicals, textiles, iron, steel. Founded in 13th century. Pop. 664,336.

Dust, Galactic, dust found in the outer arms of spiral galaxies. It seems to be made up of minute particles, perhaps of graphite and ice. *See also* Interstellar Matter; Nebula; Star.

Dust Bowl, name applied to an area of about 100,000,000 acres (40,500,000 hectares) of the Great Plains in the United States, where there has been much wind erosion damage. Due to drought, overplanting, and mismanagement, much of the topsoil was blown away in the 1930s. Subsequent government soil conservation programs, such as crop rotation, terracing and strip planting, reduced damage.

Dust Devil, a brief, small-scale whirlwind containing sand or dust and ranging from 10 to 100ft (3 to 30m) in diameter.

Dust Storm, or **duster,** a violent storm laden with fine dust picked up by high winds sweeping a drought or arid region. *See also* Sandstorm.

Dusty Miller, plants with stems and leaves covered with fine, whitish hairs. *Senecio cineraria* is a 2–2½ft (61–76cm) perennial with flat-topped clusters of cream or yellow flowers, grown mainly for its woolly-white foliage. Family Compositae.

Dutch, the official language of the Netherlands, spoken by virtually all of the country's 13 million inhabitants, and also in the Netherlands Antilles and in Surinam (the former Dutch Guiana). Dutch is a Germanic language and thus belongs to the Indo-European family.

Dutch, History of. *See* Netherlands.

Dutch East India Company (1602–1798), trading company chartered by the Dutch government. It was given extensive political and military authority to protect and control trade in Asia. It was one of the world's first joint-stock companies. One of the most successful of the many European trading companies, at one time it had a monopoly on all Dutch trade from Africa east to South America. Driving out British and Portuguese traders, it monopolized the rich Spice Islands trade. It established Batavia (Djakarta), Indonesia (1619) as its heaquarters and founded a colony at the Cape of Good Hope in southern Africa (1652). The company was nationalized in 1798.

Dutch Elm Disease, a serious fungus disease that has caused the destruction of many thousands of American elms. The disease-causing fungus *(Ceratocystis ulmi)* plugs water-conducting tissues, causing wilting of leaves and usually the eventual death of the tree. The fungus is transmitted from tree to tree by bark beetles and underground through the root systems of adjacent trees. The disease can be controlled by strict sanitation procedures, including prompt removal of seriously infected trees, spraying to kill the bark beetles, and fungicide treatment.

Dutchman's-breeches, perennial wildflower native from Nova Scotia to Kansas. It has clusters of yellow-tipped white flowers with widely separated spurs (breeches). Height: to 10in (25cm). Family Fumariacea; species *Dicentra cucullaria.*

Dutchman's-Pipe, woody, perennial vine found in woods of NE North America. The leaves are heart-shaped, and purple and white flowers are are U-

shaped with flaring mouths. Length: 30ft(9m). Family Aristolochiaceae; species *Aristolochia durior.*

Dutch Wars, three 17th-century Anglo-Dutch naval conflicts arising from commercial rivalry. The first war (1652–54) stemmed from efforts to exclude the Dutch from England's trade. England, although more successful in the fighting, was exhausted, and the peace treaty was inconclusive. The second war (1664–67) followed England's seizure of New Amsterdam (New York). The Dutch inflicted heavy losses and England had to modify her trade laws, but by the Treaty of Breda (1667) both sides kept their colonial conquests. The third war (1672–78) arose from French ambitions in the Low Countries. France invaded the Netherlands with English support but the Dutch were victorious at sea and stemmed the French advance on land. England made peace (1674) and the war ended with French territorial gains in the Spanish Netherlands and Dutch trade gains.

Dutch West India Company (1621–1791), trading company chartered by the Dutch government to control trade on Atlantic coasts of America and Africa. The company's original activities involved slave trading and harassing the Spanish fleet as much as normal trade. Although unable to wrest Brazil from the Portuguese (it ceased its efforts in 1661), the company did found settlements in the Caribbean and establish New Netherland (now New York and New Jersey), which was lost to England in the 1660s. Afterward the company confined itself mainly to the African slave trade.

Duvalier, François (1907–71), president of Haiti (1957–71), whose prominence as a public health specialist was a springboard to politics. Elected, he declared himself president-for-life and used voodoo worship and the feared Tontons Macoutes (an extralegal vigilante group) to cement the dictatorship. He died of a stroke and was succeeded by his son **Jean Claude** (1951–) in 1971. Known as "Baby Doc," he was somewhat more liberal than his father but was ousted from office and forced to leave the country in 1986 as accusations of human rights abuses and protests against his government grew. He fled to France.

Dvina, Northern, river in N Russian SFSR, USSR, formed at confluence of Sukhona and Yug rivers; flows. N, turns NE into Dvina Bay of White Sea near Archangel'sk where delta is formed, connects with Volga-Baltic Waterway by Sukhona River and Northern Dvina canal. Length: 465mi (750km).

Dvina (Daugava), Western, river in Ukrainian SSR, USSR; rises in Valdai Hills, flows S and W through Belorussia and Latvia republics to delta at Gulf of Riga of Baltic Sea. Riga is main port. River is navigable in lower course; two dams are at Latvia; supports hydroelectric stations; connects by canal with Berezina and Dnepr rivers. Length: 635mi (1,022km).

Dvořak, Antonín (1841–1904), Czech Romantic composer. Dvorak adapted the spirit of Czech nationalism and folk music to a classically oriented style influenced by Brahms and Wagner. He composed in every form, but is especially known for his orchestral works, which include nine symphonies, two sets of *Slavonic Dances,* and a number of overtures and symphonic poems. His *Cello Concerto* (1895) is regarded as one of the supreme achievements in that form. He lived in the United States (1892–94), a stay that inspired his most popular work, the *Symphony No. 9* ("From the New World") (1893) and his "American" *String Quartet No. 6. See also* Romanticism in Music.

191

Dwarfism, condition in which a person is much below normal size and lacks the ability for normal growth. Dwarfism is associated with several inherited disorders including mongolism, Turner's syndrome, and achondroplasia, a condition in which there is normal mentality, normal trunk and short arms and legs; and can also be acquired as a result of chronic kidney disease, cystic fibrosis, and potentially treatable pituitary gland malfunction in which too little growth hormone is secreted.

Dwarf Pea. *See* Chick-pea.

Dwarf Star, low-magnitude star appearing in the main sequence of the Hertzsprung-Russell diagram. Dwarfs belong to the spectral classes G, K, and M, and are characterized by small diameter and very high density in comparison to giant stars of the same spectral types. They are also about 10 magnitudes fainter.

Dye, substance used to impart color to textiles, hair, wood, etc. Dyes are classified according to the way they are applied, which in turn depends on the fiber to be colored. Direct dyes can be applied directly to the fabric; they are acidic or basic compounds that bind to fibers such as wool and silk. Indirect dyes, used for cotton, need a mordant (a compound such as aluminum hydroxide or tannic acid), which is first applied to the cloth and forms a colored precipitate with the dyestuff. Vat dyes are insoluble substances that are first reduced to a colorless soluble form that is reoxidized in the fiber. Ingrain dyes are made on the fibers by chemical reaction. *See also* Aniline Dyes; Mauve Dye.

Dynamics, in economics, change or changes occurring in economic conditions over a period of time. Dynamics is often used in equilibrium analysis in order to see the movement of the economic situation over time. Dynamics is also important in simulation models where changes affect the relationship through the movement over time.

Dynamite, a solid, blasting explosive that contains nitroglycerin incorporated in an absorbant base, such as charcoal. Shock-resistant, but easily detonated by heat or percussion, it is used in mining, quarrying, and engineering. Invented in the 19th century by Alfred Nobel.

Dynamometer, an electrical rotating device used to measure the output torque of rotating machinery; acting as an electric brake, generator, or motor, depending on the device under test. Direct readings are obtainable from an attached scale.

Dyne, the unit of force in the metric centimeter-gram-second (cgs) system of units. One dyne is the force that gives a mass of one gram an acceleration of one centimeter per second per second. One newton equals 100,000 dynes.

Dysentery, an infectious disease characterized by frequent loose stools, intestinal bleeding, and in severe cases, intestinal ulceration. Spread by fecal-contaminated food and water, it often occurs in epidemic form in crowded areas with poor sanitation and in particular in tropical areas. One type, caused by bacteria (usually *Shigella*), is usually treated with antibiotics. The other type, caused by ameba *(Endamoeba histolytica),* is harder to treat; the ameba sometimes occurs in cyst form and produces chronic dysentery, characterized by intermittent diarrhea and other often mild symptoms.

Dysfunction, distinction in the highly refined sociological theory of structural functionalism that means any function, or consequence of a social system, that lessens the system's adaptation to its setting, thereby reducing its ability to survive. *See also* Structural Functionalism.

Dyslexia, a term variously defined but generally used to mean marked difficulty in learning to read. Often used for persons who habitually reverse the letters of words (reading "was" for "saw"), letters themselves ("b" for "d"), or perceive letters upside down. The causes—brain damage, other neurological problems, environmental factors—are disputed, as are modes of treatment.

Dysmenorrhea, painful menstruation, distinct from normal functional menstrual discomfort or premenstrual tension. It can occur shortly after menarche (primary) or later in life (secondary), and is characterized by cramplike pain in the lower abdomen, sometimes radiating to the back and thighs.

Dysprosium, metallic element (symbol Dy) of the Lanthide group, first identified in 1886 by Lecoq de Boisbaudran. Chief ores are monazite (phosphate) and bastnasite (fluorocarbonate). The element has few commercial uses. Properties: at. no. 66; at. wt. 162.5; sp. gr. 8.56 (25°C); melt. pt. 2565°F (1407°C); boil. pt. 4235°F (2335°C); most common isotope Dy^{164} (28.-18%). *See also* Lanthanide Elements.

Dzerzhinsk (Dzerzinsk), formerly Chernorech, then Rastyapino; city in Russian SFSR, USSR, on Oka River; industrial center named (1929) for Soviet secret service founder Felix Dzerzhinsky. Industries: textiles, chemicals, engineering works. Pop. 257,000.

Dzhambul (Dzambul), formerly Aulie Ata; city in SE Kazakh SSR, USSR, on Talas River; capital of Dzhambul oblast. Founded in 7th century, city was ruled by Arabs and became capital of Karakhan State 10th–12th centuries; annexed to Russia 1864. Industries: sugar refining, fruit canning, chemicals, metal and leather products. Pop. 264,000.

Dzungaria (Zhuangaerpendi), arid region in NW China, between Tien Shan and Altai mts; ruled by Dzungars, a Mongol tribe, in the 17th century; overtaken by Chinese in 1850s; 35% of the population is nomadic; oil discovered in 1955 brought railway transportation and further development of the area. Pop. 1,500,000.

E

Eadmer or **Edmer of Canterbury** (*c.* 1055–1124), English monk in Canterbury. An Anglo-Saxon by birth, Eadmer is known as friend and confidant of Anselm of Canterbury, and as a writer on historical and religious subjects. His most important writings were a history of Britain from the time of the Norman Conquest to 1120 *(Historia novorum),* biographies of Anselm and other English saints, and a tract on the conception of the Virgin Mary.

Eagle, widespread strong, flesh-eating, diurnal birds of prey. Sea and fishing eagles, including the bald and stellar eagles, are large birds, frequenting seacoasts where they dive for fish and feed on other small animals and carrion. Old World serpent eagles, including harriers, are stocky reptile-eating birds. The large harpy eagles inhabit tropical forests and the booted eagles with feathered legs, including true eagles *(Aquila),* are open country predators. They have long hooked bills, broad wings, and powerful toes with long curved claws, and are usually brownish, black, or gray with light or white markings. They nest high on seacoasts or island mountains, building massive grass-and-leaf-lined stick nests, called aeries. These nests are often used for many years. Light brown eggs (1–2) are laid. Several species are endangered as a result of hunting, pesticide poisoning, and a low reproduction rate. Length: 16–40in (41–102cm). Family Falconidae. *See also* Falcon.

Eakins, Thomas (1844–1916), US painter, b. Philadelphia. After studying art and anatomy in Philadelphia, Eakins went to Paris (1866–70) where he developed his precise, realistic style. On his return to Philadelphia he taught at the Pennsylvania Academy of Fine Arts (1870–86). He had to resign from this position because of his insistence on using live nude models.

Most famous for his portraits, he insisted on portraying reality, so that many of them are not flattering, although they are often penetrating. He was also a photographer and sculptor. Among his many famous works are "The Gross Clinic" (1875), which created a scandal because of its realism; "The Chess Players" (1876), both at the Metropolitan Museum of Art, New York City; and "The Biglon Brothers" (1873), National Gallery, Washington, D.C.

Ear, specialized sense organ of hearing. It converts sound waves to nerve impulses that are carried to the brain and also maintains a sense of orientation and equilibrium. In most mammals the ear consists of the outer ear, middle ear, and inner ear. The visible outer ear contains the ear canal that carries sound waves to the eardrum, a flexible, thin membrane separating the outer and middle ears. The middle ear is an air-filled passage connected to the pharynx by the Eustachian tube, and to the inner ear by three tiny bones, the hammer (maleus), anvil (incus), and stirrup (stapes). These bones conduct sound vibrations to the oval window, a thin membrane leading to the inner ear. The inner ear, or labyrinth, contains the spiral-shaped cochlea and organ of Corti, the essential hearing organ. Sound vibrates a membrane lining the cochlea, causing thousands of feathery hairs in the organ of Corti to bend. These vibrations merge into the acoustic nerve that transmits nerve impulses to the brain. The inner ear also contains three semicircular canals and the utricle and saccule sacs that function to maintain orientation and equilibrium.

Earache, pain in the ear that can be caused by wax accumulation, a foreign body in the ear, referred pain from teeth, mouth, or jaw, but is most often produced by infection of the middle ear or of the auditory canal. Treatment depends on the cause.

Earhart, Amelia (1898–1937), US aviator, b. Atchison, Kan. The first woman to cross the Atlantic as a passenger in 1928, she became the first woman pilot to make solo flights across the Atlantic (1932) and from Honolulu to Oakland, Calif. (1935). In an attempt to fly around the world, she disappeared between New Guinea and Howland Island in the Pacific (1937).

Earp, Wyatt (Berry Stapp) (1848–1929), US law enforcement officer, b. Monmouth, Ill. Raised in Iowa, he was a sheriff, stagecoach driver, surveyor, and railroad construction worker. In 1879 he went to the silver mining camp at Tombstone, Ariz., as the deputy sheriff. In 1881 he and his two brothers took part in the famous gunfight at the O.K. Corral. He also served as US marshal in Dodge City and Wichita, Kansas.

Earth, third planet from the sun, with one natural satellite, the moon. The Earth has outer radiation belts, an oxygen-rich atmosphere, and a lithosphere, or solid crust, beneath which is the mantle and the outer and inner core. Mean distance from the sun, 92,900,000mi (149,569,000km); mass, 5.976×10^{27}g; volume, 1.083×10^{27}cu cm; equatorial radius, 3,963,221mi (6,378,188km); polar radius, 3,949,921mi (6,380,785km); rotation period, 23hr 56min; period of sidereal revolution, 1.00004 years; composition in order of abundance, oxygen, silicon, aluminum, iron, magnesium, calcium, sodium and potassium, titanium, phosphorous, hydrogen. *See also* Solar System.

Earthenware, vessels and other utensils or ornaments made of clay, fired at relatively low temperatures, resulting in porous, opaque, non-ringing pieces.

Earthquake, a number of rapid, consecutive, elastic waves in Earth. A major quake is usually preceded by a few foreshocks (small quakes) and followed by many minor aftershocks. The source of a quake may be shallow or up to 430mi (692km) deep. The shallow quakes are thought to be the rapid release of slowly accumulated strain along fault lines extending over a wide region. The rupture of a fault and the friction between faulting rock surfaces produces the elastic waves. The origin of the slowly accumulated strain is not known. However, areas of weakness may be placed under stress by continental drift. Scientists are accumulating data for successful prediction of earthquakes, including changes in local magnetism in rocks and water level change in deep wells, the occurrence of foreshocks or a lull in small-scale tremors, and changes in animal behavior. *See also* Seismology.

Earthshine, or earthlight, phenomenon observed during the crescent phase of the Moon, whereby the darkened portion of the lunar disk is illuminated by an ashen light reflected onto it by the Earth.

Earthside, Lunar, face of the moon that is permanently turned toward the earth. Gravitational effects of the earth on the moon slowed down and ultimately captured the moon's axial rotation. The lunar earthside exhibits numerous and varied surface features, including several large maria. *See also* Farside, Lunar; Mare.

Earthworm, terrestrial and semi-terrestrial annelids having cylindrical, segmented bodies covered with tiny bristles. Most are a uniform red, pink, or brown. They are mainly subterranean in moist soil. Their burrowing loosens and aerates soil, making it fertile. Most are hermaphroditic. Worms are eaten by many animals. Tropical species are largest. Length: 2in–11ft (5cm–33m). The four families include several hundred species. Class Oligochaeta. *See also* Annelida.

Earwig, slender, brownish-black insect found in dark, damp areas. Some have a pair of forceps on the end of the abdomen. Two suborders, found in Malaya and South Africa, are ectoparasites of bats and rodents. Order Dermaptera.

East Anglia, E England, centered on counties of Norfolk and Suffolk, formerly an Anglo-Saxon kingdom, founded *c.* 600 AD It was usually dependent on other kingdoms until the Danish invasion (9th century). After 917 East Anglia became an earldom of Anglo-Saxon England.

East Bengal, region on Bay of Bengal; included in East Pakistan (1947); became part of Bangladesh (1971).

Amelia Earhart

Easter Island carving

George Eastman

The population is mainly Muslim. Area: 44,514sq mi (115,291sq km).

Eastbourne, city in S England, on English Channel at foot of S Downs, 3mi (5km) SW of Beachy Head; vacation resort. Pop. 72,700.

East Chicago, city in NW Indiana, on Lake Michigan, 18mi (29km) SE of Chicago. Industries: oil refining, steel, chemicals. Inc. 1889. Pop. (1980) 39,786.

East China Sea, N branch of the China Sea, bordered by Korea and Japan (N), E China (W), Taiwan (S), and the Ryukyu Islands (E). Area: approx. 482,300sq mi (1,249,157sq km). Depth (max.): approx. 15,000ft (4,575m).

East Cleveland, city in NE Ohio; site of General Electric lamp factory and electrical research laboratories. Inc. 1911. Pop. (1980) 36,957.

East Detroit, city in SE Michigan, 10mi (16km) NE of Detroit. Industries: structural steel, tools. Inc. 1925 as Halfway Village; renamed and inc. as city 1929. Pop. (1980) 38,280.

Easter, the central Christian feast, celebrating the resurrection of Christ on the third day after his crucifixion. In the West it is celebrated between March 22–April 25, on whichever Sunday follows the first full moon on or after March 21 (the vernal equinox).

Easter Island (Pascua, Isla de), island in S Pacific Ocean, about 2,000mi (3,220km) off W coast of Chile, to which it was annexed 1888. Inhabited mostly by Polynesian farmers, the island is famous for its hieroglyphs and formidable statues carved in stone standing up to 40ft (12m) tall. Chile has named the island an historic monument. Discovered Easter Day, 1722, by Dutch seaman Jakob Roggeven. Area: 46sq mi (119sq km). Pop. 1,135.

Easterlies, any broad currents or persistent patterns of winds from the east, such as the tropical easterlies or trade winds and the equatorial and polar easterlies. The trade winds occur in the northern and southern margins of the tropics during the summer and cover most of the tropics during winter. *See also* Westerlies.

Easter Lily, bulbous house plant native to Formosa with large, white, trumpet-shaped, fragrant flowers and narrow, arching leaves. Care: bright indirect light, moist soil. Propagation is by offsets or seeds. Height: to 3ft (92cm). Family Liliaceae; species *Lilium longiflorum.*

Eastern Orthodox Church, a community of over 125,-000,000 Christians, located primarily in the Soviet Union, Eastern Europe, and the Middle East. They share the same form of worship and episcopal organization, but each Orthodox church has its own national head. Iconography is prominent, as well as elaborate ritual. The clergy may be married prior to ordination. There is no central governing body, and they reject the jurisdiction of the Roman pope, the principal point dividing the Eastern Orthodox from the Roman Catholics. When Constantine, the emperor who first made Christianity lawful throughout the Roman Empire, moved his capital to Byzantium (later Constantinople, now Istanbul) in 330, a culture separate from Rome developed. Conflicts grew between the Eastern patriarchs and the bishop in Rome. The schism that developed in the 11th century was made irreparable when Crusaders invaded Constantinople (1204). Attempts at reconciliation in 1274 and 1439 failed. In 1962 several Orthodox observers attended the second Council of the Vatican.

The following year the Eastern Orthodox churches agreed to open a dialogue with Rome.

Eastern Rite, teachings of those Eastern churches that have maintained a link with the Roman Catholic Church. The Eastern rite differs in liturgical practices from the Latin rite. These churches, divided into national groups, are under the jurisdiction of the Holy See in Rome. *See also* Latin Rite.

Eastern Roman Empire. *See* Byzantine Empire.

East Goths. *See* Ostrogoths.

East Hartford, town in E central Connecticut, opposite Hartford on Connecticut River. A colonial manufacturing center, it was site of first US powder mill (1775). Industries: airplane engines, steel fabrication, paper, bottling works. Settled 1639; inc. 1783. Pop. (1980) 52,563.

East India Company (1600–1874), British trading company and political organization in India. Founded for the East Indian spice trade, it was forced by Dutch competition to concentrate on India, where it gradually won a monopoly and political supremacy. The British government assumed its political direction (1773, 1784). When the company lost its monopoly (1813–33), it served as an administrative agency until abolished.

East India Company, French, a government-controlled business founded in 1664 under Louis XIV for trade with the Eastern world. Growing, but never financially sound, the company became involved in Indian political intrigue and conflicts with the British and, defeated by the British under Robert Clive, dissolved by the time of the French Revolution.

East Lansing, city in S central Michigan, on Red Cedar River, 5mi (8km) E of Lansing; site of Michigan State University (1855), first US state agricultural college. Surrounding farm area produces sugar beets, grain, livestock. Settled 1849; inc. 1907. Pop. (1980) 43,309.

East Lothian, co in SE Scotland, E of Edinburgh, between the Firth of Forth and Lammermuir Hills; co seat is Haddington; chief river is Tyne. Area's S uplands are pasture and woodlands; coastal plains are farmed; site of castles of Dirleton, Tantallon, and Hailes. Oliver Cromwell defeated Scots at Dunbar 1650. Area: 267sq mi (692sq km).

Eastman, George (1854–1932), US photographic inventor and manufacturer, b. Waterville, N.Y. He introduced machine-coated plates (1879), paper roll film (1884), celluloid roll film and the Kodak camera (1888), and daylight-loading film (1891), thereby creating the basic materials for still and motion picture photography. He founded the Eastman Kodak Co. in 1892.

East Meadow, residential city in SE New York, on W Long Island, 23mi (37km) E of New York City. Pop. 46,352.

East Orange, city in NE New Jersey, adjacent to Newark, it is also suburb of New York City; site of Upsala College (1893). Industries: hydrants, waterworks supplies, insurance. Settled 1678, city was part of Orange until 1863; chartered as city 1899. Pop. (1980) 77,025.

East Paterson, borough in NE corner of New Jersey, 2mi (3km) SE of Paterson. Industries: television receiving communications equipment. Inc. 1916. Pop. (1980) 77,025.

East Providence, city in E Rhode Island, on Providence and Seekonk rivers. Originally part of Massachusetts, it was annexed to Rhode Island 1862; site of Bradley Hospital, one of world's first children's neuropsychiatric facilities. Industries: metal products, chemicals, jewelry, oil storage. Inc. 1958. Pop. (1980) 50,980.

East Prussia, former province of Prussia, in NE Germany. Bordered by Poland and Lithuania (S and E), it extended to Memel and Baltic Sea (N and NE); low-lying, heavily-wooded area; controlled by Teutonic Knights and Poland 13th-17th centuries; in 1701 Frederik III of Brandenburg was crowned King of Prussia, uniting E Prussia with Prussia. Since 1945 East Prussia has been divided between Soviet Union (N) and Poland (S). Industries: lumbering, shipbuilding, fishing, stock raising. Area: 14,283sq mi (36,993sq km). Pop. 2,500,000.

East River, strait in New York City, SE New York; connects Long Island Sound (N) with New York Bay (S). Manhattan Island forms W shore and borough of Queens and the Bronx on Long Island forms the E shore. Length: 16mi (26km). Width: 600–4,000ft (183–1,220m).

East Saint Louis, city in SW Illinois, on the Mississippi River, opposite St Louis, Missouri, to which it is connected by four bridges; site of Cahokia Courthouse (1837), oldest courthouse W of Allegheny Mts. Industries: brick, tile, machinery, gasoline. Founded 1795 as Illinoistown; inc. 1865. Pop. (1980) 55,200.

Eau Claire, city in W central Wisconsin, at confluence of Eau Claire and Chippewa rivers; seat of Eau Claire co; developed around sawmills built on Eau Claire River (1800s). Industries: paper, dairying, tires, defense products. Inc. 1872. Pop. (1980) 51,509.

Eban, Abba (Solomon) (1915–), Israeli diplomat, b. Aubrey Solomon Eban in South Africa. Raised in England, he served in the British army in the Middle East during World War II. Working for the Jewish Agency for Palestine after the war, he helped maintain relations with the British in the period before the founding (1948) of the state of Israel. In 1947 he began his diplomatic career as a liaison officer of the US Special Committee on Palestine. He was Israel's first permanent UN representative (1949–59) and during that time also served as ambassador to the United States. After being elected a Mapai (Labor party) member of the Israeli parliament in 1959, he served as minister of education and culture (1960–63), deputy prime minister (1963–65), and foreign minister (1966–74). He wrote *Abba Eban: An Autobiography* (1977).

Ebbinghaus, Hermann (1850–1909), German psychologist whose work *On Memory* (1885) founded the scientific study of memory. Using himself as a subject for his research, he described in detail the process of learning, remembering, and forgetting of verbal materials. He also founded the first German psychology journal in 1890.

Ebionites, literally, "poor men," a sect of ascetic Jewish Christians who flourished from the 2nd to 4th centuries east of the Jordan River. Outside the mainstream of Christianity, they held property in common, believed poverty basic to Christianity, stressed Christ's humanity rather than divinity, emphasized Mosaic law, and used only the Gospel of St. Matthew as scripture. There were two divisions: the Pharisaic Ebionites, who stressed Mosaic law, and the Essenic Ebionites, who tended more toward Gnosticism.

Ebony, hard, fine-grained, dark heartwood of various Asian and African trees of the genus *Diospyros* in the ebony family (Ebenaceae). The major commercial source of ebony is the macassar ebony *(D. ebenum)* of S India and Malaysia. Ebony is prized for woodcarving and cabinet work.

Ebro, river in NE Spain; rises in Cantabrian Mts; flows SE into the Mediterranean Sea, below Tortosa; scene of Spanish Civil War battle (1938) fought along banks. Supplies energy for 50% of Spain's hydroelectricity. Length: approx. 575mi (926km).

Eccentricity (symbol *e*), number defining the form of a conic section: *e* less than 1 is an ellipse; $e = 0$ is a circle; $e = 1$ is a parabola; *e* greater than 1 is a hyperbola. For an ellipse it is the ratio of the distance between the foci to the length of the major axis. It is one of the elements determining the orbit of a celestial body.

Ecclesiastes, biblical book of aphorisms written by one called "the Preacher," thought to be Solomon. The author dwells on vanity in all things and expresses skepticism about the state of the world: "One generation passeth away, and another generation cometh: but the earth abideth forever." He exhorts his readers to "Fear God, and keep his commandments: for that is the whole duty of man."

Ecclesiasticus, book of the Apocrypha. The work of Jesus ben Sira, a teacher in Jerusalem, *c.* 190 BC, it follows the tradition of Jewish wisdom literature.

Echidna, or **spiny anteater,** any of two species of egg-laying, burrowing, nocturnal mammals that compose the family Tachyglossidae (order Monotremata) found in New Guinea, Australia, and Tasmania. It is stocky, to 30in (76cm) long, with spines as well as hair on the upper parts, and has a small mouth and an extensible tongue. The female lays a single egg and transfers it to a pouch. *See also* Anteater.

Echinoderm, phylum of spiny-skinned marine invertebrate animals related to same evolutionary stock that produced Chordates. They are radially symmetrical with five axes and have calcareous skeletal plates in their skin. Their hollow body cavity (coelom) includes a water vascular system and tube feet. Reproduction is sexual, and a bilaterally symmetrical larva resembling that of Chordates is produced; regeneration also occurs. The 5,700 species include sea urchins, sea cucumbers, and starfish.

Echo, in Greek mythology, an Oread or mountain nymph. She was deprived of speech except to repeat the last words of others as a punishment for helping Zeus to deceive his wife Hera. Echo faded to just a voice, when Narcissus spurned her love.

Echo, sound reflected from a surface so that it returns to the source and is heard after a silent interval of 0.1 seconds or more. This minimum time for differentiating the echo from the original sound implies a path difference of about 32 yards (30m). High notes provide a better echo than low notes. Echoes are useful in echo-sounding devices but are objectionable in auditoriums, where they are eliminated by using absorbent material on the walls and avoiding curved surfaces that can focus echoes like a mirror. *See also* Anechoic Chamber; Underwater Sound.

Echolocation, system of orientation in some animals, such as whales and bats. They emit high frequency sound waves and determine position by the returning echoes. *See also* Echo Sounding Sonar.

Echo Sounder, device that sends sound pulses through water to the sea bottom where they are reflected back to a ship's hull or platform and detected. Continuous recordings provide a profile of the bottom by translating the time needed for the echo to return to the detector. *See also* Echolocation.

ECHO Viruses, a group of viruses found in the feces of apparently healthy individuals, resulting in the inappropriate name Enteric Cytopathogenic Human Orphan. There are 28 types of these RNA-containing viruses. They are known to cause diseases such as aseptic meningitis, skin rashes, enteritis, and diarrhea. ECHO 28 is the common cold virus.

Eclampsia, a rare disorder occurring in the last 10 weeks of pregnancy, characterized by high blood pressure, swelling, excessive weight gain, convulsions, and albumin in the urine. The cause is unknown. Treatment includes various drugs to control the symptoms. Delivery may be hastened or caesarean section performed.

Eclecticism, in philosophy, the combination of elements from different systems of thought without resolving conflicts among the systems. The method was favored by Roman philosophers, including Cicero; some Renaissance thinkers; and 19th century philosophers led by Victor Cousin, who coined the term.

Eclipse, temporary concealment of one celestial body by another. The term usually signifies the obscuration of the Sun (solar eclipse) or Moon (lunar eclipse), as viewed from the Earth. Both lunar and solar eclipses may be either total or partial but solar eclipses may also be annular. An annular, or ring, eclipse occurs when the new Moon is too far away from the Earth to mask the Sun's disk completely.

Eclipsing Variable, or binary, regular variable star in which the light variations are due to the fact that the star is a binary having a bright component associated with a darker companion. The two stars regularly pass in front of each other and are at maximum brightness only when they are seen shining together. The prototype of the best-known class of eclipsing variables is Beta Persei (Algol).

Ecliptic, great circle on the celestial sphere, inclined at 23½° to the celestial equator, that is the yearly path of the Sun as seen from Earth or the Earth's orbit as seen from the Sun. The ecliptic plane thus passes through the centers of both Earth and Sun. The planets are always located near the ecliptic.

Eclogues, or "Selections," sometimes called *Bucolics* or "Pastoral Poems," ten poems written by 1st-century BC poet Virgil, modeled on the *Idylls* of Greek poet Theocritus. As in Virgil's other works, there is a great sympathy for suffering.

Ecology, or environmental biology, bionomics, biological study of relationships between living things and their environments. It is also involved with interactions of organism groups to each other and their surroundings.

Econometrics, quantitative branch of economics, involves the application of statistics to economic problems. Ordinarily, econometrics involves using computer programs to seek solutions to real-world economic problems.

Economics, study of how individuals in a particular society choose to allocate scarce resources in order to produce goods that are demanded by that society. It involves the study of the methods used in producing the goods in order to obtain maximum efficiency in the use of the scarce resources. Economics also involves the process of deciding how goods are distributed to various individuals and groups within a society as well as dealing with the study of economic growth within the society. The society must somehow provide for future wants as well as for present needs and must allocate goods in such a way that future needs will be met.

Economic Systems, elements in a society that answer these questions: What should be produced? How is it to be produced? and For whom is it to be produced? Economists distinguish between systems that are characterized by private ownership of producer goods and market control over the system and those that are characterized by some authoritarian structure where economic decisions are made by planning agencies. The USA is often cited as an example of the free enterprise, market (capitalistic) system, while the USSR is often called a command (communistic) system, where producer goods are owned by the government, or by some agency of the government. *See also* Capitalism; Communism; Socialism.

Economies of Scale, decreasing unit costs as plants expand operations, usually resulting from the increased efficiency associated with producing more output. The expanded firm may now be able to take advantage of technological conditions that were impossible at the smaller scale of operation or it may be able to hire more specialized workers. Economies of scale do not always occur as the firm expands. The firm may reach a size beyond which expansion is no longer desirable.

Ecosystem, or ecological system, community of living things and its environment. It is self-sustaining only if it recycles elements, has a constant energy source, and can incorporate energy into organic compounds and pass it from organism to organism.

Ecuador, Republic of, independent nation on the NW coast of South America. It is governed by an army junta. Fish and oil (found in 1972) are its chief exports.

Land and economy. The Andes Mts divide the country into three areas: costa, hot, humid lowlands; Sierra, temperate highlands, and Oriente, tropical lowlands. In addition to coffee, fish, and bananas, oil exports were started in 1972, and nationalization of the oil industry began in 1974. Forestry is an important industry. Deposits of copper, iron, lead, and coal are still largely untapped.

People. Population is made up of 40% Indians, 40% mixed descent (mestizo), 10% Spanish descendants, and 10% blacks. The majority are subsistence farmers. Most of the people are Roman Catholic. Primary education is compulsory, and the literacy rate is 60%.

Government. According to the constitution of 1979, the government is led by the president, who is popularly elected to a five-year term. The unicameral chamber of representatives has 69 seats. One of Ecuador's main foreign policy problems is the defense of its 200mi (322km) of fisheries jurisdiction off the Pacific coast. Ecuador is a member of the United Nations, Organization of American States, and Andean Common Market.

History. Spanish conquistadores subjugated the Inca Empire in 1532 and incorporated it into the viceroyalty of New Granada until 1822, when Simon Bolivar led a successful fight for independence. Instability characterized political life from independence until after WWII. Galo Plaza Lasso, elected president in 1948, was the first president since 1925 to finish his term (1948–52). José Velasco Ibarra was president three times from 1952. In 1972 he was ousted by Gen. Guillermo Rodriguez Lara. A three-person military junta subsequently ruled, overseeing elections (1978) to return the government to civilian government in which Jaime Roldós Aguilera was elected. With his death in 1981, Vice-President Osvaldo Hurtado Larrea assumed the post (1981–84) followed by León Febres-Cordero (1984–).

PROFILE

Official name: Republic of Ecuador
Area: 109,483sq mi (283,561sq km)
Population: 8,078,000
Density: 74 per sq mi (29 per sq km)
Chief cities: Quito (capital); Guayaquil
Government: Military Junta
Religion: Roman Catholic
Language: Spanish
Monetary unit: Sucre
Gross national product: $8,460,000,000
Per capita income: $371
Industries (major): processed foods, textiles, cement, petroleum products
Agriculture: bananas, coffee, cacao, rice, sugar cane, cotton
Trading partners: United States, Japan, Federal Republic of Germany

Ecumenism, movement toward unity among different churches. With Vatican Council II (1962–65), the term became widely known. Churches are all to recognize the universal aspects of religion and to assume a more noticeable role in the modern world. Through discussions and joint projects, a common ground is sought amid the diversity of denominations.

Eczema, form of chronic dermatitis characterized by redness, oozing, blisters, itching. It can be caused by contact with a substance to which the skin has been sensitized, such as poison ivy or detergent. More generalized eczema may occur with no identifiable cause, usually in persons with histories of allergies. Treatment is with local medication. *See also* Allergy; Dermatitis.

Eddy, Mary Baker (1821–1910), founder of the Christian Science Church, b. Bow, N.H. Subject to convulsions, she sought a cure through both physical and mental healing. She discovered the spiritual and philosophical system of Christian Science in 1866 while reading the Bible after a serious fall. Her book *Science and Health* (1875) explains the Christian Science system. The Church of Christ, Scientist was chartered in 1879. Mary Baker Eddy also founded the *Christian Science Journal* (1883), The Christian Science Publishing Society (1898), and the *Christian Science Monitor* (1908). *See also* Christian Science.

Eddy Current, current induced in a conductor when subjected to a varying magnetic field. Eddy currents cause a loss of energy in a.c. generators and motors; the reaction between the eddy currents in a moving conductor and the field in which it moves retards the motion of the conductor.

Ede, city in E Netherlands, in Gelderland prov. Industries: yarn, pianos, metallurgy. Pop. 79,897.

Edelweiss, small perennial plant native to the Alps and other high Eurasian mountains. It has white, downy leaves and its small yellow flower heads are enclosed in whitish bracts. Family Compositae; species *Leontopodium alpinum.*

Edema, or dropsy, abnormal accumulation of fluid in spaces between cells of body tissues. It is frequently

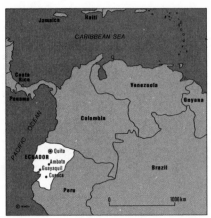

Ecuador

Mary Baker Eddy

Thomas A. Edison

associated with liver or kidney disturbance, pregnancy, and heart failure.

Eden, (Sir) Anthony, Earl of Avon (1897–1977), English Conservative politician. He resigned as foreign secretary (1938) in protest against appeasement but re-entered the cabinet during World War II and served again as foreign secretary (1939–45, 1951–55). He promoted the Anglo-Soviet war alliance, the establishment of the United Nations, and France's withdrawal from Indochina. As prime minister (1955–57) he ordered British troops into Suez; the resulting crisis led to his resignation.

Eden, in the Bible, garden created by God as the home of Adam and Eve, until they were banished for eating the forbidden fruit from the tree of knowledge.

Edentate, small group of mammals (order Edentata) found from Kansas to Patagonia. The roughly 30 species include the armadillos, sloths, and anteaters. Although "edentate" means "toothless," only the anteaters truly fit this description.

Ederle, Gertrude (Caroline) (1907–   ), US swimmer, b. New York City. She shared a gold medal as a member of the US women's relay swimming team in the 1924 Olympics. In 1926 she was the first woman to swim the English Channel.

Edina, town in SE central Minnesota. Area has 60 lakes and large amount of park land. Industries: electronic and computer equipment. Inc. 1888; village of Morningside was annexed 1966. Pop. (1980) 46,073.

Edinburgh, (Prince) Philip (Mountbatten), Duke of (1921–   ), husband of Queen Elizabeth II of Great Britain and Ireland, b. Corfu, Greece. He served as a British naval officer (1939–52), rising to the rank of commander before his wife ascended the throne and he became prince consort.

Edinburgh, capital city and port of Scotland, on S shore of Firth of Forth, 40mi (64km) E of Glasgow on both banks of the Clyde River; Capital of Scotland since 14th century. Leith serves as its seaport; birthplace of Sir Walter Scott (1771). John Knox lived here; his home (1556) still stands; site of University of Edinburgh (1582), Heriot-Watt University (1966), Royal Scottish Museum, and National Museum of Antiquities. At Edinburgh Castle the annual tattoo is held. Holyrood Abbey (1128) and Holyrood Palace (built *c.* 1500 by James IV) are here. Mary Queen of Scots lived in Holyrood Palace 1561–67; here she married Lord Darnley, saw her secretary David Rizzio murdered, and finally married the Earl of Bothwell; statue to Sir Walter Scott stands in the East Princes Street Gardens. His death in 1832 marked the end of Edinburgh's golden age that began in the middle of the 18th century. Industries: brewing, distilling, printing, electronics, rubber, tourism. Pop. 470,085.

Edirne (Adrianople), fortified city in NW Turkey, 130mi (209km) NW of Istanbul, at the confluence of Maritsa and Tundzha rivers; capital of Edirne prov.; regional agricultural market and manufacturing center; site of mosque of Selim II (1574), and palace ruins. Founded by Hadrian *c.* AD 125, city fell to Visigoths 378; passed to Turks 1361; taken by Russia 1829–79; restored to Turkey 1923. Industries: cotton, silk, cheese, grain, fruit, tobacco, leather, soap, cattle. Pop. 54,885.

Edison, Thomas Alva (1847–1931), US inventor, b. Milan, Ohio. The most productive inventor of his time, he received over 1,000 patents for practical applications of scientific principles. Self-educated, he spent

most of his childhood in Port Huron, Mich., and became a railroad newsboy at 12 and a telegraph operator at 16. He patented his first invention, an electronic vote recorder, in 1869. With money made from an improved stock-ticker system, he set up his own plant in 1871 in Newark, N.J., where besides manufacturing he developed automatic telegraph transmitters and receivers and (1874) a quadruplex telegraphic transmittal system. In 1876 he discontinued manufacturing to set up in Menlo Park, N.J., the first US industrial research laboratory. There he developed the carbon telephone transmitter (1877–78); the phonograph (1877–78); and the first commercially successful incandescent lamp (1879), for which he developed a complete distribution system—from dynamos to household sockets. He moved his laboratory to large, modern quarters in West Orange, N.J., in 1887. There he developed the mimeograph, dictating machines, the fluoroscope, early motion picture cameras and projectors, and an iron-alkaline storage battery. In 1883 he discovered the Edison effect, which would later form the basis of the electron tube. In 1889 he formed the Edison Electric Light Company, which through mergers became General Electric in 1892. During World War I he headed the US Navy consulting board on ship defenses and helped to develop the manufacture of previously imported chemicals, including carbolic acid. Late in life he attempted to develop a practical rubber substitute.

Edmer of Canterbury. *See* Eadmer of Canterbury.

Edmonton, capital city of Alberta, Canada, on the North Saskatchewan River; trade center for the surrounding agricultural area; site of Edmonton House, 19th-century trading post, University of Alberta (1906); petrochemical center since the 1947 discovery of oil. Industries: oil refining, meat packing. Est 1795 as a Hudson's Bay Co. trading post. Pop. 491,359.

Edmund (921?–46), English king. Succeeding his half-brother Athelstan as king (939), he reconquered northern England from the Vikings. During his reign a monastic revival began. He was murdered by a banished robber.

Edmund Ironside (981?–1016), English king. On the death of his father, Ethelred the Unready, Edmund was proclaimed king (1016). Edmund won several victories over the rival claimant, the Dane Canute, before Canute defeated him. The two divided England, and Edmund ruled Wessex until his death. *See also* Canute.

Edmund Rich, Saint (1175?–1240), English ecclesiastic and scholar. Renowned as a teacher at Oxford, he preached the Sixth Crusade in England (1227) and became Archbishop of Canterbury (1234–40). He opposed King Henry III's favoritism toward foreign counselors and eventually withdrew to France to become a monk. He was canonized *c.*1249.

Edred, or **Eadred,** (died 955), English king. Crowned in 946 he strove successfully to keep Northumbria in England and supported the monastic revival.

Education, the ways a society informs and instructs its members. Before the first formal schools, family and group members taught children basic survival skills as well as cultural traditions. Modern formal education is an enormous enterprise, yet the early influences of the family and the informal education of the mass media are also crucial parts of learning.

Education, Department of, US department, formed from part of the Department of Health, Education and Welfare (HEW). It was created in 1979 and con-

solidated 170 educational programs from various agencies, including the Office of Education from HEW. The department establishes policy and administers and coordinates federal assistance to education.

Educational Psychology, branch of psychology focusing on learners and learning. Educational psychologists study child development, the learning process, teacher-student relationships, and ways of measuring abilities and achievement.

Edward I (1239–1307), king of England. He won influence and fame suppressing the baronial revolt (1263–65) against his father, Henry III, and crusading (1270–72). Succeeding his father (1272), he carried out important administrative, judicial, and financial reforms, which increased royal power and weakened feudalism. By summoning frequent parliaments and including commoners in them, he contributed greatly to Parliament's development. Edward conquered Wales and incorporated it into England (1275–95). Although he also conquered Scotland in 1296, the remainder of his reign was occupied with Scottish revolts.

Edward II (1284–1327), king of England. As king (from 1307), Edward's general inability and reliance on favorites alienated his barons, who increasingly took control of England, especially after the Scots decisively defeated him at Bannockburn (1314). He regained control (1322) only to rely on new favorites and alienate his queen, Isabella, who became mistress of an exiled baron. These two invaded England (1326) and deposed and murdered Edward. *See also* Isabella; Mortimer, Roger de.

Edward III (1312–77), king of England. Succeeding Edward II in 1327, he unsuccessfully tried to conquer Scotland. His claim to the French throne (1340) led to the Hundred Years' War. Despite brilliant military successes at Crécy (1346), Calais (1347), and Poitiers (1356), Edward was forced to renounce his claims at the Treaty of Bretigny (1360). During his reign, much important anti-papal and commercial legislation was enacted, the role of Parliament increased, and the Black Death caused considerable economic and social changes. Edward's later years were overshadowed by his sons' quarrels and territorial losses. *See also* Bretigny, Treaty of; Edward the Black Prince.

Edward IV (1442–83), king of England. Heir of the House of York, he defeated the rival Lancastrians, supporters of Henry VI, and became king (1461). Initially his ally, the Earl of Warwick, ruled England, but Edward gradually assumed more authority. Warwick deposed Edward and reinstated Henry (1470), but Edward obtained help from Burgundy and crushed his enemies (1471). He re-established order and began important administrative reforms.

Edward V (1470–83), king of England. He succeeded his father, Edward IV, in April 1483, with his uncle Richard as regent. Richard imprisoned Edward and his younger brother and, proclaiming them illegitimate, made himself king as Richard III. The two boys were murdered, probably in August 1483. *See also* Richard III.

Edward VI (1537–53), king of England and Ireland, and only legitimate son of Henry VIII. An intelligent boy, he was a gifted student and a fanatical Protestant. During his reign (1547–53) leading Protestants came to England and his regents continued the English Reformation. His uncle, the duke of Somerset, ruled initially as lord protector but he was overthrown by the duke of Northumberland (1549) and executed (1552). Northumberland persuaded Edward to appoint Lady Jane

Grey (Northumberland's daughter-in-law) heiress to the throne.

Edward VII (1841–1910), king of Great Britain and Ireland. The eldest son of Queen Victoria, he was excluded from government affairs by his mother, but was allowed to pay official visits and perform minor functions. He turned his energies to social life, travel, and sport, and was involved in several scandals. As king (1901–10) he restored court pageantry and became very popular. He attempted to maintain European peace through personal contacts between rulers and contributed noticeably to the growth of the Anglo-French alliance.

Edward VIII (1894–1972), king of Great Britain and Ireland, subsequently duke of Windsor. In World War I he served on the army staff. He was a popular royal heir, but becoming king in 1936 he decided to marry an American divorcee, and had to abdicate. During World War II he was governor of the Bahamas.

Edward, Prince Antony Richard Louis (1964–), third son and fourth child of Queen Elizabeth II of Britain. He is fifth in line of succession to the British throne.

Edward the Black Prince (1330–76), outstanding English general, eldest son of Edward III. He distinguished himself in France at Crécy (1346) and led the English to victory at Poitiers (1356). As his father's viceroy in Aquitaine (1363–71), he proved an incapable ruler, despite further military success in Spain (1367) and brutal measures at Limoges (1370).

Edward the Confessor (1003?–1066), English king. The Anglo-Saxon heir, he was made king (1042) by Earl Godwin of Wessex, who dominated England. Godwin's power was weakened by Edward's Norman favorites, and Godwin's family was exiled (1051). Returning (1053), Godwin and his son Harold became the effective rulers, and Edward devoted himself to religion.

Edward the Elder (died 924), king of Wessex (899–924). He was the son of Alfred the Great and is supposed to have ruled jointly with his father. His reign saw the power and territory of Wessex extended at the expense of the Danes and other English kingdoms.

Edward the Martyr (died 978), king of England (c.963–78). He was popularly regarded as a saint after his murder, which may have been the responsibility of his stepmother Aelfrida.

Edwin (d. 633), king of Northumbria (616–33). He became a Christian in 627, and his reign was important for the spread of Christianity. He died defeated in battle by a Welsh king Cadwallon and the heathen King Penda of Mercia.

Edwy (died 959), king of Wessex (955–59). His reign is noted for his quarrel with Dunstan, who was subsequently exiled. He was succeeded by his younger brother Edgar.

Eel, marine and freshwater fish found worldwide in shallow temperate and tropical waters. They have snakelike bodies, no scales, dorsal and anal fins continuous with the tail, and an air bladder connected to throat. All spawn and die in the sea; American and European eels in the Sargassum Sea. Eggs develop into ribbonlike larva, the leptocephalus; then into the elver or glass eel; and finally into the adult. Length: to 10ft (305cm). Families include Freshwater, Spaghetti or Moray, Conger, and Snake eels. Order Anguilliformes.

Eel Grass, flowering plant that grows under water. It has long, grasslike leaves and spikes of inconspicuous flowers. Family Potamogetonacae; species *Zostera marina.*

Effectors, or motor neurons, specialized output cells that activate the voluntary muscles of the body. Effector impulses originate in the brain and result in the often complex and delicate muscle activity called behavior.

Egbert or **Ecgberht** (died 839), king of Wessex (802–39) and ruler over all the other English kingdoms in the course of his reign. In 828 he defeated Beornwulf of Mercia, and he or his son Ethelwulf conquered other kingdoms thereafter. He also made a perpetual alliance with the church of Canterbury.

Egg, or **ovum,** reproductive cell of female animals surrounded by protective jelly, albumen, shell, chorion, egg case, or membrane depending upon species. Egg functions are: supply food reserve in the form of a yolk for embryo; supply nucleus containing half the chromosomes of future embryo; supply almost all the cytoplasm upon union with the sperm. The amount of yolk in an egg depends on when the embryo actively begins to feed. Bird and insect eggs have a large yolk, mammalian eggs a much smaller one. The lifespan of a mature human egg is 12–24 hours, sea urchin eggs—40 hours, most invertebrates, amphibians, and fish—minutes.

Eggplant, shrublike plant of the nightshade family, native to Africa or India; until the 20th century grown mainly as an ornamental. The leaves are large and the 2in (5.1cm)-wide violet flowers produce a berry fruit ranging from a small egg-shape to a large pear-shape. Height: 2–3ft (61–92cm). Species: cultivated *Solanum melongena;* wild *S. incanum.*

Ego, in psychoanalysis, the conscious level of personality that deals with the real world. According to Sigmund Freud, the child is first driven by the impulses of the id. The ego develops as he learns to live with others and balance the demands of the id and of the superego (which sets standards and ideals). *See also* Id; Superego.

Egret, white heron of temperate and tropical wetlands known for its plumes, once popular for decorating hats. They are long-legged, long-necked, slender-bodied wading birds with daggerlike bills. They feed on small animals, nest in rookeries, and lay pale bluish eggs (3–6) in a platform nest on the ground or in a tree. Height: 20–40in (51–102cm). Genus *Egretta.*

Egypt (Misr), an independent nation in the Middle East. The ancient land of the Pharaohs, it is now a republic with limited economic resources.

Land and economy. Mostly a rainless, arid desert, Egypt is located in the NE corner of Africa bordered on the N by the Mediterranean Sea, W by Libya, S by the Sudan, and E by the Red Sea, Gulf of Suez, and Israel. Geographically, it is divided into four regions. The Nile Valley and delta provide the cultivated land—less than 3% of the total; the Aswan Dam increased fertile land by about 30%. The W and S deserts and the E desert, along the Red Sea and the Nile, are high plateaus of rugged hills and mountain peaks. Its climate is temperate. The highest peak is Mt Catherine in the Sinai 8,652ft (2,639m) above sea level; the lowest is the Qattara Depression, 400ft (120m) below sea level, in the W desert. The economy is basically agricultural, with half the labor force engaged in land production; maximum land holding is limited to 100acres (40hectares) per family. Cotton is the principal crop for cash. Oil, major industries, and public utilities have been nationalized. Alexandria is the chief port. The Suez Canal, a major source of income before its closure (1967–75), has never regained its preeminence because it does not accommodate supertankers. With yearly imports almost double the value of exports, the country is heavily dependent on foreign aid.

People. The most heavily-populated country in the Arab world, 99% of the people live in the Nile Valley and delta, which have a population density of 2,500per sq mi (965per sq km). In the rural regions, the farmers (fellahin) are descended from Arab settlers who mixed with the indigenous pre-Islamic tribes after the Muslim invasion. The cosmopolitan cities of Cairo and Alexandria are attracting more rural dwellers as industrial jobs become available. Sunni Islam is the principal religion (90%). Arabic is the official language; literacy is 44%. With disease under control, life expectancy has risen to 53 years and the growing population is one of Egypt's major problems.

Government. The 1971 constitution set up a strong presidential-type government with authority in the elected president. When the elected unicameral People's Assembly grants emergency powers, the president may rule by decree.

History. Egypt fell under Roman domination in 58 BC when the Ptolemies (Cleopatra) used Julius Caeser and Marc Antony to regain domination of their dynasty. Rome annexed Egypt and killed the last Ptolomy. In succeeding years Egypt came under Persian rule (616–28), followed by the Arabs (639–42), who introduced the Islam religion. In the 10th century the ruling Fatamids founded Cairo (969). In 1250 militant Mamelukes seized control; they were unseated by the Ottoman Turks in 1517. The modern state of Egypt began with the 1805 rule of Muhammed Ali, a political, social, and economic reformer. In 1856, Suez Canal building costs plunged Egypt into debt and opened the door to British intervention, occupation of Cairo, and protectorate status in WWI. Nationalism grew, and in 1922 a parliamentary kingdom under British domination was established. The final struggle between the Wafd nationalists and the king, Farouk, came in 1952 when Gen. Muhammed Naguib led an uprising and became premier. Farouk abdicated, and Egypt was declared a republic on June 18, 1953. Strong man of the revolt, Gen. Gamal Abdal Nasser deposed Naguib and became president. Opposition to the existence of Israel was the rallying cry for Egyptians, and in October 1956 Nasser barred Israel from use of the nationalized Suez Canal. Israeli forces invaded the Sinai peninsula, Britain and France bombed the canal, and the war was over on November 7. In 1967, Egypt took over the Gaza Strip and closed the Gulf of Aqaba to Israeli shipping. In the Six-Day War that followed, Israel captured Gaza and the E bank of the Suez. A UN ceasefire ended hostilities; a peace-keeping force was placed in the area. Following his death in 1970, Nasser was succeeded by Vice-president Anwar al-Sadat, whose nationalistic policies were partly responsible for the 1973 Arab-Israeli War.In 1979, however, Israel and Egypt signed a peace treaty, and Israel began a phased withdrawal, which was completed in 1982, from the Sinai. Subsequent talks between the two countries stalled over the issue of Palestinian autonomy. As a result of the peace treaty Egypt was ostracized by other Arab countries and suspended from the Arab League. Now isolated, Egypt became heavily dependent on the United States for economic and military assistance. Sadat faced internal dissent from leftists and Islamic fundamentalists, and was assassinated in 1981. Vice-president Hosni Mubarak succeeded to the presidency. During 1982, a ten-year-trial confederation was begun with Sudan and, by the mid-1980s, Egypt had resumed relations with most of the Arab countries. *See also* Arab-Israeli Wars; Aswan High Dam; Egypt, Ancient; Suez Canal.

PROFILE

Official name: Arab Republic of Egypt
Area: 386,660sq mi (1,001,449sq km)
Population: 39,640,000
Density: 106per sq mi (41per sq km)
Chief cities: Cairo (capital); Alexandria; Giza; Suez
Government: Republic (one-party system)
Religion: Islam
Language: Arabic (official)
Monetary unit: Egyptian pound
Gross national product: $18,600,000,000
Per capita income: $259
Industries: chemicals, steel, cement, fertilizer, petroleum products, electrical instruments, textiles
Agriculture: sugar cane, maize, rice, wheat, citrus fruits
Minerals: petroleum, phosphate, salt, iron, manganese, gold, gypsum, titanium
Trading partners: United States, West Germany, Italy, Japan, Romania

Egypt, Ancient, civilization that flourished along the Nile River in NW Africa from before 3400 BC until 30 BC, when the last Egyptian king, Ptolemy XIV, was put to death by order of Octavian (later Roman Emperor Augustus), and Egypt was annexed to Rome. As a result of the extensive scholarship of Egyptologists of the 19th and 20th centuries, a considerable body of information exists on Egyptian history, even from the earliest periods. Traditionally, Egyptian history is separated into five periods: the Old Kingdom (or Old Empire); the First Intermediate Period; the Middle Kingdom (or Middle Empire): the Second Intermediate Period; and the New Kingdom (or New Empire). The individual dynasties are numbered, generally in Roman numerals, from I through XXX.

The kingdoms of Upper Egypt and Lower Egypt were united in about 3100 BC by Menes, King of Upper Egypt, and he founded the first Egyptian dynasty. From the beginning, a form of theocracy is believed to have existed, with the king, or pharaoh, regarded as divine. Elaborate burial rites and tombs, from which so much modern knowledge of Egypt derives, also developed early. By the beginning of the II dynasty, about 2890 BC, considerable trade existed between Egypt and the Sinai; the Egyptians possibly traded as far north as the Black Sea. The Old Kingdom began in the III dynasty, during 2686 BC. Khufu (or Cheops), founder of the IV dynasty, ruled *c.*2600, built the great pyramid at Gizeh (al Jizah). His successors Kahfre (who is believed to be represented as the face of the Sphinx) and Menkaure built the other pyramids at Gizeh. Pepi II of the VI dynasty, who ruled from *c.*2294–*c.*2188, organized the caravan trade with Nubia, the Sudan, and Punt. The capital probably was at Memphis. During the VI dynasty, priests and local governors, whose office became hereditary, achieved great power at the expense of the king. The Old Kingdom disintegrated in about 2181 BC. Complete power passed to the provinces. No central records were kept, resulting in a period of historical obscurity.

During the first Intermediate Period, the capital was moved to Heracleopolis, where the weak rulers of the IX and X dynasties resided. Some central authority was restored when Intef, a Theban noble, proclaimed himself king in 2134 and founded the XI dynasty. The capital was moved to Thebes, center for the worship of the god Amon.

The Middle Kingdom (c.2050–1786 BC) The great rulers of the XII dynasty brought the Egyptian kingdom

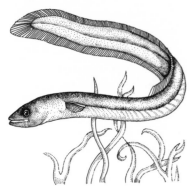

Eel

Egret

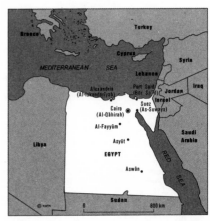

Egypt

to its highest flowering. Amenemhat I, founder of the dynasty in about 1891, centralized power at Thebes by reducing the long powerful nobles to a feudal status. He and his successors reestablished the old trade routes, reopened mines, and extended the Egyptian border to the Second Cataract of the Nile. They irrigated al Fayyum, thereby greatly increasing the amount of arable land. They built forts along the Nile and constructed a canal that bypassed the First Cataract. Great building projects were carried out; among the most impressive was the great temple of Amon at Karnak. A uniform writing system was adopted, and Egyptian literature reached its peak.

The XII dynasty—and the Middle Kingdom—came to an end in 1786, when the country was invaded and conquered by the Hyksos. The Hyksos were a Semitic people from Syria. Their weapons, new to Egypt, included the horse-drawn war chariot, the bronze sword, and the composite bow (made of wood, sinew, and horn). The Hyksos ruled Egypt during the Second Intermediate Period and founded the XIII–XVII dynasties. They adapted themselves readily to Egyptian culture but introduced Oriental deities into the Egyptian religion; artifacts of the period also show Oriental influence.

The New Kingdom. Began about 1570 BC when the Hyksos were expelled by an Egyptian general who assumed the throne as Amasis I and founded the XVIII dynasty. His son and successor was Amenhotep I, who continued his father's military victories by reconquering Nubia, which had been allied with the Hyksos. He also invaded Syria. Thutmose I, who became king *c.*1504, extended Egypt's border to the Third Cataract and subdued Syria as far as the Euphrates River. Thutmose III, who assumed sole power in 1468 BC, brought the empire of the New Kingdom to its zenith by conquering territories east of the Euphrates and by extending Egyptian power below the Third Cataract. The conquests of the kings of the XVIII, XIX, and XX dynasties brought unprecedented wealth into Egypt, including thousands of slaves. Great tombs and temples were built, the most spectacular of which were located in the Valley of the Kings, across the Nile from Thebes. The tomb of Tutankhamen, a king of the XVIII dynasty, was discovered in 1922 and has been a source of much information about Egypt of the New Kingdom.

Amenhotep IV, who ruled *c.*1375–58, changed his name to Ikhnaton in honor of the sun god Aton. He attempted to institute a monotheism with Aton as the sole god, established a new capital at Akhetaton in honor of Aton, and directed all royal artists and architects to works honoring the sun god. His lack of interest in non-religious affairs was costly; Nubia and Syria were lost during his reign. His successors ruled over a greatly weakened and reduced empire. Even his religious reforms did not survive him; a conservative priesthood restored the old polytheism at his death. Ramesses I founded the XIX dynasty in about 1320 and his successors gradually rebuilt the empire until it reached the splendor of Ramesses II. Some of the greatest wonders of Egypt were built under his reign, including Abu Simbel, the Ramesseum, and temples at Luxor and Karnak. He also carried on a long war against the Hittites, a war that only ended when he married (1267) a Hittite princess.

The wars with the Hittites weakened Egypt and a series of ineffectual rulers followed Ramesses II, who ruled with his wife, Queen Tiy. After them, the New Kingdom declined, and foreign influence was increasingly felt in the country. The capital was moved to Tanis in 1085, marking the end of the New Kingdom. The Tanite (or XXI) dynasty was replaced by the Libyan dynasty, which ruled from Bubastis. It was replaced by Nubian conquerors, who founded the XXII dynasty. The capital was moved to Saïs in 712, and the country fell under Assyrian domination. In 525 the Persians took

control until 405, when the Egyptians revolted, and the last native dynasties appeared. Unable to reestablish Egypt's former grandeur, the new ruling class fell to the armies of Alexander the Great in 332. Alexander founded the great port city of Alexandria and moved the Egyptian capital there. After Alexander's death his empire was divided among his generals and Ptolemy became the ruler of Egypt as Ptolemy I. Under him and his successors, known as the Ptolemies, Alexandria became the greatest city in the Hellenistic world. It was a great center of learning and its library was a legendary repository of ancient and modern manuscripts. The Ptolemies maintained a powerful empire for two centuries, and Egypt under them was the greatest of the Hellenistic nations. Roman power was on the ascendancy, however, and when Ptolemy XI asked Pompey and his Roman army for aid in 58, it marked the end of Egyptian independence; Pompey restored him to the throne but he became a Roman puppet. His daughter Cleopatra tried to assert her independence by her celebrated machinations with Julius Caesar and Marc Antony, but she was defeated and committed suicide. Her son Ptolemy XIV (whose father probably was Julius Caesar) was the last Ptolemy to rule; he was put to death at the age of 13 by Octavian (later Emperor Augustus). From that time, Egypt became a province of Rome and was ruled directly from there.

Egyptian Architecture, architecture developed before 3000 BC and characterized by post and lintel construction, massive walls covered with hieroglyphic and pictorial carving, flat roofs, and such structures as the pyramid, mastaba, obelisk, and steeply battered pylon. Houses were built of clay or baked bricks. Tombs and temples reproduced features of domestic architecture but on a massive scale using permanent materials. A prominent example of Old Kingdom (2680–2258 BC) architecture is the funeral complex at Saqqara built by Imhotep for King Zoser, which consists of a 200-foot-high stepped pyramid surrounded by a columned processional hall and niched limestone wall. Middle Kingdom tombs at Bani Hasan (1991–1786 BC) were carved from the rock cliffs on the banks of the Nile. Examples of New Kingdom architecture are the massive mortuary temple of Queen Hatsheput at Deir el Bahari (1480 BC) and the temple of Amon at Karnac (1570–1085 BC).

Egyptian Art, the artistic and architectural works of ancient Egypt, usually classified according to the ancient dynasties as follows: In the Old Kingdom period (*c.*2686–2181 BC) works were chiefly relief sculpture and painting characterized by front and side views of the human figure, flat color tones, symmetry in sculpture, and minimal suggested movement (static figures). Relief decorated private tombs and temples and portrayed the daily life of the subjects. Statues were realistic. A great architect of this period was Imhotep. Painting was subordinate to sculpture. In the Middle Kingdom period (2050–1786 BC) art became increasingly formalized and less realistic. There was little relief sculpture and more painting, jewelry work, and figurines. The New Kingdom (*c.* 1570–1085 BC) saw greater boldness of design. Art and technique reached its peak in this period in the realistic portrayal of the family life of the pharoah Ikhnaton and his family, including the famous bust of Queen Nefertiti in Berlin. Art of the Saite period (8th century BC) returned to the simpler modes of the earlier Old Kingdom.

Ancient Egyptian architecture was characterized by massively thick walls, flat stone roofs, and relatively few columns. Belief in life after death led to the construction of huge, permanent temples and tombs. With the decline of Egyptian power during the Ptolemaic dynasty, the distinctive Egyptian art styles declined

and gave way to dominance by Greek and Roman forms.

Egyptian Mythology. The polytheistic mythology associated with Egypt developed when small agricultural communities, each with its own local deities, were united under the pharaohs. In the melding, some gods and their stories were identified with others and some joined into families to form the vast pantheon, producing a multiplicity of myths that explained the same phenomenon. Each religious center, meaning virtually every city, had its own creation myth justifying itself as the center of existence. Although there is an account of the Flood there is no Eden in the myths, no past Golden Age or prediction of the end of the world to come, reflecting the relatively stable society that existed under the pharaohs.

Ehrlich, Paul (1854–1915), German bacteriologist. He shared the 1908 Nobel Prize in physiology or medicine for his work on immunity, which included diphtheria antitoxin studies and the development of basic standards and methods for studying toxins and antitoxins. His subsequent search for a "magic bullet" against disease and his discovery of salvarsan, a chemical effective against syphilis microorganisms, introduced the modern era of chemotherapy (a term he coined).

Eichmann, Adolf (1906–62), Austrian Nazi, head of the Gestapo's Jewish section in World War II. He supervised the Nazi policies of deportation, slave labor, torture, medical experimentation, and mass murder in the concentration camps, which led to the death of some 6,000,000 Jews during the war. Escaping to Argentina (1945), he was abducted by Israelis (1960) and executed in Israel for his crimes against humanity.

Eider Duck, large sea duck found in northern areas of Europe, Asia, and North America. Its down is used for pillows and quilts. Genus *Somateria. See also* Duck.

Eidetic Imagery, or photographic memory, capacity to obtain purely mental images that are so vivid that the person having them can describe them in detail. Few people have the ability to form eidetic images.

Eiffel, Alexandre Gustave (1832–1923), French engineer who established metal as an architectural material. His Eiffel Tower, built for the 1889 Paris Exhibition, was the world's tallest structure until 1930. He also designed the Bon Marché store in Paris and was the engineer for the frame of the Statue of Liberty.

Eiger, mountain peak in S central Switzerland, in the Bernese Alps. Height: 13,025ft (3,973m).

Eight, The, group of American painters formed in 1907. *See also* Ashcan School.

Eight Masters of T'ang and Sung, the term traditionally used in Chinese schools for eight outstanding prose writers during the T'ang (618–906) and Sung (960–1279) dynasties. During the T'ang, Han Yü (768–824) and Liu Tsung-Yüan (773–819) instituted a return to the simpler style of several centuries earlier. Six other masters furthered this reform during the Sung. They were: Ou-yang Hsiu, Wang An-shih, Su Shih, Su Hsün, Su Chê, and Tsêng Kung.

Eijkman, Christiaan (1858–1930), Dutch medical researcher and physician. He shared the 1929 Nobel Prize in physiology or medicine "for his discovery of the antineuritic vitamin." Eijkman was the first to recognize a dietary deficiency disease, demonstrating that beriberi was produced by a lack of a certain dietary substance, later identified as vitamin B_1.

Einaudi, Luigi (1874–1961), Italian economist and statesman, was president of Italy (1948–1955). In the years immediately after World War II he was governor of the Bank of Italy and designer of Italy's postwar program of monetary stabilization. In 1948 he became Italy's first elected president.

Eindhoven, industrial city in S Netherlands, approx. 55mi (89km) SE of Rotterdam. Industries: electrical equipment, textiles, steel. Founded 1232. Pop. 192,562.

Einstein, Albert (1879–1955), German-American physicist, b. Ulm, Germany. He published three important theoretical papers: the first concerned the application of quantum theory to photoelectricity (for which he was awarded a Nobel Prize in 1921), the second contained a mathematical analysis of the Brownian motion, and the third contained the first publication of the special theory of relativity—a paper that completely revolutionized physics and led to the atomic bomb, through its equation of mass and energy. In 1915 Einstein produced his general theory of relativity, which has far-reaching implications in astronomy. Being a Jew, he left Germany when Hitler came to power, spending the rest of his life in the United States, becoming a US citizen in 1940. He wrote to President Roosevelt in 1939 advocating research on the atom bomb, but after the war he worked devotedly for peace. Element 99 (einsteinium) is named after him. *See also* Quantum Theory; Relativity Theory.

Einsteinium, radioactive metallic element (symbol Es) of the actinide group, first identified in 1952 as a decay product of U^{235} produced in the first large hydrogen-bomb explosion. Properties: at. no. 99; most stable isotope Es^{254} (half-life 276 days). *See also* Transuranium Elements.

Eire. *See* Ireland, Republic of.

Eisenhower, Dwight David (1890–1969), 34th president of the United States, b. Denison, Texas, graduate, West Point, 1915. In 1916 he married Mamie Doud; they had two sons. A professional soldier whose career spanned World Wars I and II, he rose slowly in rank in the peace-time army between those wars. By the beginning of World War II, he had reached the rank of colonel. He gained the attention of Gen. George C. Marshall and was given increasingly important assignments. He commanded the invasion of North Africa in 1942, where he showed a mastery of military planning and logistics. More importantly, he displayed a great gift for getting the various Allied military commanders to work together. In 1944, he assumed command of the entire Allied military operation in Europe. He planned Operation Overlord, the invasion of France, which began on D Day, June 6, 1944, when the largest military force ever assembled in history landed on the beaches of Normandy. By the time Germany surrendered on May 7, 1944, Eisenhower—by now a five-star general—was the most famous hero of the war.

He returned to the United States as army chief of staff. He was approached by both political parties to run for president; instead, he became president of Columbia University (1948). In 1950, at President Truman's request, he returned to Europe as NATO commander. He resigned that position in 1952 to run for the Republican presidential nomination.

After a close fight with Senator Robert A. Taft, he won the nomination. He chose Richard M. Nixon as his running mate. He easily defeated his Democratic opponent, Adlai E. Stevenson, Jr., and soon fulfilled his campaign pledge of ending the Korean War. He continued Truman's internationalist policies but adopted a more conservative, pro-business domestic program. He suffered a major heart attack in 1955 but recovered and ran for re-election in 1956, again against Stevenson. He and Nixon won by an even greater landslide than in 1952.

His second term was plagued by both domestic and foreign problems. In 1957, he used federal troops to force school integration in Little Rock, Ark., and in 1958, he sent US Marines to Lebanon. In 1959 a summit meeting with the Soviet Union was cancelled after a US spy plane was shot down over Russia. In 1961 relations with Cuba were broken. Despite all those setbacks, he left office in 1961 still one of the most popular presidents in US history.

Career: US Army, 1915–52; Columbia University president, 1948–52; president, 1953–61.

El. For other cities beginning with "el," see second part of name.

El Alamein. *See* Al-Alamein.

Eland, largest, oxlike African antelope. Giant or Derby eland of Central Africa has more massive horns than common eland of Central and S Africa. Common eland is uniformly gray; Derby is tan with black neck with white band at base. Both sexes carry heavy, spiralled horns. Gregarious and slow-moving, they are good jumpers. They have been trained to harness, but now are greatly reduced in number. Length: to 117in (3m); height: to 70in (1.8m) at shoulder; weight: to 1980lb (900kg). Family Bovidae; species giant or derby *Taurotragus derbianus,* common *Taurotragus oryx. See also* Antelope.

Elasticity, the study of the changes in shape or volume of solids, liquids, or gases subjected to external forces. The ratio of the forces to the cross-sectional area of the body is called stress; the body's change in shape is called strain; and the ratio of the stress to the strain is called an elastic modulus of the material. *See also* Strain; Stress.

Elasticity of Demand, measure of the responsiveness of consumers to price change. It is found by dividing the percentage *change in quantity* demanded by the percentage change in price. If there were a 10% price increase in the good and the quantity demanded of the good decreased by 10%, the elasticity would be unitary. If the percentage change in quantity demanded exceeded 10%, the good could be said to have an *elastic demand,* that is, a fairly small change in price elicited a relatively large change in demand. If the percentage change in quantity is less than 10%, the good could be said to have an *inelastic demand.*

Elastomer, any of a variety of plastic, rubberlike substances with the physical properties of natural rubber, used in tires and other products. Important are copolymers in which the main molecular chain is composed of carbon atoms, usually based on petroleum derivatives (Buna S, Buna N, butyl rubber). Polysulfide rubbers (thiokols) and silicones are other elastomers.

Elba (Isola d'Elba), Italian island in Tyrrhenian Sea; largest of Tuscan Archipelago; chief port and town is Portoferraio, on N coast. Island is mountainous, and is a major supplier of Italy's iron ore, mined since Etruscan and Roman times; site of exile of Napoleon I (1814–15); his villa still remains. Industries: fisheries, wine, iron ore, tourism. Area: 86sq mi (223sq km). Pop. 26,830.

Elbe River, river in central Europe; rises in Krknoše Mts of NW Czechoslovakia, flows across Czechoslovakia into East Germany, NW through central East Germany, across West Germany and into the North Sea at Cuxhaven, West Germany. In 1945 river was made part of demarcation line between East and West Germany. It is navigable for 525mi (845km). Length: 725mi (1,167km).

Elbert, Mount, mountain peak in central Colorado, in Sawatch Range of the Rocky Mt system; highest peak in the state and the US Rocky Mts, 14,433ft (4,402m).

Elbrus (Elborus), Mount (Gora El'Brus), two peaks in the Caucasus Mts, Russian SFSR, USSR; formed by two extinct volcanoes; W peak is highest in Europe, 18,481ft (5,637m). E peak is 18,356ft (5,599m) high.

Elburz Mountains (Alborz, Reshteh-ye Kūhhā-ye), narrow mountain group in N Iran, along SW and S coasts of the Caspian Sea; divides the dry inland plateau from the agriculturally rich lowlands; contains Mt Damāvand, highest peak in Iran, 18,934ft (5,774m). Length: 600mi (966km).

El Cajon, city in S California, E of San Diego; site of Grossmont College (1961). Industries: electronic equipment, missile parts, metal products. Inc. 1912. Pop. (1980) 73,892.

Elche, city in SE Spain; scene of annual mystery play; site of Greek, Roman, and Arabic ruins. Industries: leather, dates, soap, palm oil. Pop. 122,663.

Elder, shrub and small tree found worldwide in temperate and subtropical areas. They have divided leaves and clusters of tiny white flowers. Their small berries are important to wildlife and used in making wine, jellies, and medicine. The common elderberry shrub *(Sambucus canadensis)* has coarse-toothed leaflets, white flower clusters, and purple berries; height: to 13ft (4m). There are 40 species. Family Caprifoliaceae.

El Dorado, mythical city of fabulous wealth, located in the interior of South America, which spurred many expeditions particularly in the 16th century. Departing from Peru, Ecuador, Venezuela and Brazil, the conquistadores' searches through the Amazon valley extended geographical knowledge of the continent, but did not result in large-scale colonization, given the harsh climate and living conditions encountered. The first official expedition, led by Felipe de Hutten, left the Venezuelan coast in 1541.

Eleanor of Aquitaine (1122?–1204), queen consort of France, and later of England, and duchess of Aquitaine. She married Louis VII of France, accompanying him on the Second Crusade (1147–49). Divorcing in 1152, she married Henry (later Henry II of England) and had three sons, Richard, Geoffrey, and John. Eleanor supported her sons' revolt against Henry (1173), helped collect Richard's ransom (1193), and supported John on his accession (1199).

Eleanor of Castile (1230?–1290), queen consort of England, married Edward I (1254), and gave him her father's claim to Gascony. She is chiefly remembered for the crosses her husband had made to mark her funeral procession from Lincoln to London and her fine tomb at Westminster Abbey.

Eleanor of Provence (1220?–1291), queen consort of England, married Henry III in 1236. Her French relatives and courtiers were unpopular at the English court. A loyal wife, she raised troops for her husband during the Barons Wars (1264–65).

Eleaticism, teachings of the Eleatic school of Greek philosophy. Founded in the 6th century BC by Parmenides and including Xeno among others, the school taught that absolute reality is immobile, immutable, and indivisible. Change in the world, which is perceived by the senses, is only apparent; reason alone knows the real essence. *See also* Parmenides.

Elecampane, large-leaved, Old World perennial plant naturalized as a weed in NE United States and E Canada. A hairy plant, it has yellow, daisylike flowers. Height: to 5ft (1.5m). Family Compositae; species *Inula helenium.*

Elections, selection of candidates for public office through voting. In modern times, the electoral process, with its choice of competing candidates, popular enfranchisement, and use of the secret ballot has become an integral part of democracy. The electoral tradition dates back to the Greek city-states of the 5th and 6th centuries BC. The US Constitution granted the right to hold elections, delegating to the states responsibility for establishing methods. Though the right to vote was originally a function of owning property, a requirement often accompanied by age, sex, and sometimes religious restrictions, enfranchisement has been gradually extended to the general populace through passage of constitutional amendments. Nondemocratic societies utilize elections as a rubber stamp for their policies without offering voters any true choice among alternative candidates.

Electoral College, method outlined by the US Constitution for the indirect selection of the president and vice-president. The Electoral College is composed of representatives from the states. Each state has the same number of electors as it has US representatives and senators, and each slate of electors is pledged to a presidential and vice presidential candidate. Voters in each state select the slate of electors that represents the candidate of their choice. Each state's chosen slate then votes for the president and vice president. In modern practice, the candidate with a plurality of votes in each state receives all that state's electoral votes. If one party's candidates have not received a majority of the elector's votes, the election is decided in the House of Representatives.

Electra (*c.* 418–414 BC), tragedy by Sophocles. The heroine, Electra, helps her brother Orestes avenge their father Agamemnon's death by plotting to kill their mother Clytemnestra and stepfather Aegisthus. There is controversy as to the accuracy and originality of this play. Euripides wrote a similar play with the same title in 413 BC.

Electra Complex. *See* Oedipus Complex.

Electrical Capacity. *See* Capacitance.

Electrical Circuit, the path provided for an electrical current, composed of conductors and conducting devices and including a source of electromotive force that drives the current around the circuit. Current flows according to several definite laws of which the most important is Ohm's Law. *See also* Ohm's Law.

Electrical Stimulation of the Brain, research technique in which a minute electrical current is applied to a small area of the brain via ultrafine electrodes which may be permanently implanted in an animal's skull. If stimulation of a portion of the brain causes a particular behavior, it is assumed that that portion helps control this behavior.

Electric Eel, freshwater tropical fish found in South America. Not a true eel, its ribbonlike body is dark brown to black and bordered by an anal fin extending

Dwight D. Eisenhower

Eland

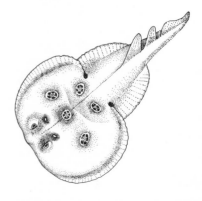

Electric fish

along its underside. It breathes air at water surface. Electric organs make up 80% of its body and produce charges up to 650 volts. Length: 9.5ft (2.9m). Family Electrophoridae (also called Gymnotidae); species *Electrophorus electricus.*

Electric Field, or electrostatic field, region surrounding an electric charge in which a force would be experienced by another charged particle. The force is attractive if the charges differ in polarity and repulsive if they are the same. The strength of the field *(E)* upon unit charge at a distance *r* from a charge *Q* is equal to $Q/4\pi r^2 E$, where E is the permittivity.

Electric Fish, freshwater tropical fish with electric organs for generating high voltages. The knifefish found in N South America are long, thin, and have a long rippling anal fin. Family: Gymnotidae; species include banded *Gymnotus carapo.* The electric catfish native to tropical Africa is pinkish with black spots. Length: to 4ft (1.2m); weight: 50lb (22.5kg). Family Malapteruridae; species *Malapterurus electricus. See also* Electric Eel.

Electric Flux, quantity of electricity displaced across an area in a dielectric medium, expressed as the product of the area and the component of the electric vector at right angles to the area.

Electric Furnace, enclosure heated by electric current. Electric furnaces are used for melting and producing metals, alloy steels, and refractory materials. Three main methods of heating are used: striking an arc between electrodes in the furnace; inducing eddy currents in the material to be melted by an alternating magnetic field; and by passing a high current through the material, heat being produced by the resistance.

Electricity, the form of energy associated with static or moving electric charges. No explanation can be given of the nature of an electric charge, the study of electricity being concerned with the properties of matter that is so charged. Charge exists in two forms, called for convenience positive and negative. The basic unit of negative electric charge is the electron; the proton and the positron are positively charged to an equal but opposite extent. The electron and the proton are the charged components of atoms, so that an atom containing equal numbers of electrons and protons is electrically neutral, whereas an excess of either will cause the atom concerned to be charged—negatively if the electrons are in excess and positively if the protons are in excess.

Electrostatics is concerned with the properties of charges at rest, largely with the forces that exist between charges. It is an observed fact, for which there is no explanation, that like charges repel each other, whereas there is a force of attraction between unlike charges. The region surrounding a charge, within which these forces act, is called an electric field. Electric charges are also acted upon by forces when they move in a magnetic field and a flow of charged particles creates its own magnetic field. Electricity and magnetism are, in fact, different aspects of the same phenomenon, known as electromagnetism.

Current electricity is the form of electricity that is supplied by power stations, consists of a flow of charged particles. In metal atoms the outer electrons are not tightly bound to the rest of the atom; they are therefore free to flow through a metal wire when acted upon by an electromotive force. A current of one ampere consists of a flow in one direction of some six million million million electrons in one second.

Electric Motor, an electric rotating machine that converts electrical energy into mechanical energy by the interaction of a magnetic field with an electric field. Electric motors are convenient, economical, safe, free from smoke and odor, comparatively quiet, and have replaced most other motive power in industry, farms, and homes when there is a convenient source of electricity. Electric motors may be alternating current (induction, synchronous, and repulsion) or direct current (self-exciting, compound, and shunt series, and universal).

Electric Process, or **Arc Furnace Process,** in steel production, a method for producing steel using electricity as the source of heat. This produces very high temperatures necessary for melting. Carbon electrodes produce electric arcs that strike into the metal bath. The use of three arcs to produce heat in three phases is in general use.

Electrocardiogram (EKG), a graphic tracing of the electric current generated by the heart muscle during a heartbeat, used to determine abnormality. It is made by applying electrodes to various parts of the body to lead off the heart current to the recording instrument. After electrodes are in place, a millivolt from an outside source is introduced. Computerized electrocardiograms are now in use in most large hospitals.

Electrochemical Equivalent, number of grams of a given element liberated or deposited from ions in electrolysis by passage of one coulomb of electricity.

Electrochemical Series. *See* Electromotive Series.

Electrochemistry, branch of physical chemistry concerned with electrolytes. It includes such topics as the ionization of acids and bases, the properties and reactions of ions in solution, the conductivity of electrolytes, and the study of the processes occurring in electrochemical cells and electrolysis.

Electroconvulsive Therapy (ECT), electrical stimulation of the brain leading to convulsions; used primarily in treating some emotional disturbances. When current is applied, the individual immediately loses consciousness, his body becomes rigid, and his breathing stops for a few seconds. Then a brief period of muscular convulsions occurs. After treatment, the individual has a temporary memory loss and may be confused. Three to eight treatments are often sufficient to break through a severe depression.

Electrodynamics, a branch of physics concerned with the motion of electrically charged particles and their effects upon each other.

Electroencephalography, study of the electrical activity of the brain by means of an electroencephalograph (EEG). This consists of a number of electrodes, which can be attached to the scalp to pick up the tiny oscillating currents produced by brain activity; a high-gain amplifier; and a means of recording the brain waves detected as a continuous trace on a paper strip. Interpretation of these waves, which have frequencies between about 8 and 25 hertz, requires great skill. The instrument is used in brain research and in the diagnosis of epilepsy and some other brain diseases.

Electrolysis, chemical reaction caused by passing an electric current through a conducting liquid (electrolyte). The reaction is the result of transfer of electrons at the electrode surfaces. For instance, in electrolysis of dilute acids, hydrogen ions gain electrodes at the cathode: $H^+ + e'U H$; $2H'U H_2$. At the anode hydroxide ions lose electrons: $OH - e'U OH$; $20H'U H_2O + O$; $2O - O_2$. The acid becomes more concentrated, the overall reaction being $2H_2O'U 2H_2 + O_2$. The type of electron-transfer reaction occurring depends on the electrode potentials of ions present, and the electrode material may play a part in the reaction. For example, in electrolysis of copper salts with a copper anode, atoms of the electrode ionize and enter into solution: $Cu'UCu^{2+} + 2e$. Electrolysis is an important method of obtaining chemicals, particularly extracting reactive elements such as sodium, potassium, magnesium, aluminum, and chlorine.

Electrolyte, liquid that can conduct electricity. In electrolytes the current is carried by positive and negative ions rather than by electrons. These are present in fused ionic compounds, in solutions of ionic compounds, or in solutions of acids and bases, which dissociate into ions.

Electrolytic Solution, solution that is an electrolyte, that is, a conductor of electricity. Water itself is a relatively poor conductor but its conductivity is increased by adding ionic compounds. Thus, a solution of sodium chloride contains sodium ions (Na^+) and chloride ions (Cl^-), which transport the current. Covalent acids and bases also form electrolytic solutions in water by dissociating into ions: for example, $HCl'UH^+ + Cl^-$.

Electromagnet. *See* Magnetism.

Electromagnetic Induction. *See* Induction.

Electromagnetic Spectrum, distribution of different types of electromagnetic waves with regard to frequency or wavelength, ranging from low-frequency (high-wavelength) radio waves, through infrared (heat) waves, light, ultraviolet waves, X rays, to very-high-frequency (very-low-wave-length) gamma rays. *See also* Electromagnetic Wave.

Electromagnetic Wave, wave of energy composed of electric and magnetic fields vibrating sinusoidally at right angles to each other and to the direction of motion; it is thus a transverse wave. The waves travel in free space at a constant speed of 186,282 mi (299,-792.5 kilometers) per second (speed of light), which is reduced when traveling through a more dense medium, such as air or glass. The properties of the waves depend on their frequency, the electromagnetic spectrum extending from low-frequency radio waves, through infrared waves, light, ultraviolet waves, X rays, and high-frequency gamma rays. All these waves are produced, basically, by the acceleration of charged particles. The higher-frequency waves result from transitions between energy levels in the nucleus (gamma rays) or atom (X rays, ultraviolet, light, infrared). Radio waves are produced by the acceleration of free electrons. Electromagnetic waves can undergo reflection, refraction, interference, diffraction, and polarization. Other phenomena, such as the absorption or emission of light, can only be explained by assuming the radiation to be comprised of quanta of energy rather than waves. *See also* Quantum Theory; Radio.

Electrometallurgy, a branch of metallurgy dealing with the application of electric current for the extraction or refining of metals. The raw ore is subjected to an electric current that causes the metal to be deposited at the positive pole in a process known as electrowinning. Some ores require leaching with aqueous solution before being electrolyzed; others do not. Electroplating is a process in which metals are deposited on a base of less valuable metal, as in silver plating. The operation of the electric furnace in the manufacture of steel and the refining of other metals is also called electrometallurgy.

Electromotive Force (e.m.f.), the sum of the potential differences in a circuit. It is equal to the energy liberated when unit charge passes completely around the circuit in the direction of the resultant e.m.f. *See also* Voltage.

Electromotive Series, series of chemical elements arranged vertically in decreasing order of their electrode potential. The series illustrates the relative tendencies of metals to form positive ions in solution, the more electropositive metals being higher up the series. For example, metals higher than hydrogen displace hydrogen from acids by reactions of the type $Ca + 2H^{+} \rightarrow Ca^{2+} + H_2$. The series is also called the electrochemical series, especially in the context of relative abilities of elements to form ions in chemical reactions.

Electron, stable lightest elementary particle (symbol e) with negative charge, mass 9×10^{-31} kg (1/1836 that of the proton), and spin ½. Discovered by J. J. Thomson (1897), electrons are constituents of matter, moving around the nucleus in complex orbits. Their total charge balances that of the protons in the nucleus of a neutral atom. Removal or addition of an atomic electron produces a charged ion. Chemical bonds are formed by the transfer or sharing of electrons between atoms. When not bound to an atom they are responsible for electrical conduction. Beams of electrons are used in several electronic devices, such as TV tubes. High-energy beams, from particle accelerators, are used in nuclear research. *See also* Beta Rays; Current, Electric; Electron Emission; Lepton.

Electron Emission, liberation of electrons from the surface of a substance. It can occur as a result of the effect on the substance of heat (thermionic emission), light (photoelectric emission), high electric field (field emission), bombardment by ions or other electrons (secondary emission), or it may result from radioactive decay. In all cases, the electrons must acquire energy from the outside source in excess of the work function of the substance. Most electron and cathode-ray tubes depend on thermionic emission, while photoelectric cells rely on photoelectric emission. Field emission is important in the field-emission microscope and secondary emission is the principle behind electron multipliers and storage tubes. *See also* Radioactivity.

Electronic Circuits, numbers of electronic components wired together to form a unit capable of performing some function, such as detection or amplification of a signal or acting as a gate in a logic circuit. The components commonly used in electronic circuits are resistors, capacitors, inductors, and transformers in conjunction with electron tubes or semiconductor devices. For most purposes semiconductor devices have replaced electron tubes and wiring between components is largely by printed circuits in which the components are soldered to a board on which connections are made by a copper conducting film; a photographic mask is used to coat the part of the film required for interconnections, the unprotected metal being removed by etching. Double-sided printed circuits are in common use, in which both sides of the board have a circuit printed on them. *See also* Integrated Circuits.

Electronic Control Systems, a control system based on an electronic circuit. Complex control systems rely upon computers, the control functions are then carried out by logic circuits. These circuits consist of gates, which give a high output current when the input currents conform to a predetermined pattern. For example, an AND gate gives a high output when all the inputs are simultaneously high. *See also* Control Systems.

Electronic Data Processing (EDP), a method of selecting and sorting a wide range of information through the use of punched cards or an electronic digital computer. The computer is far faster than cards, but requires human instruction, called programming.

Electronic Music, music produced by electronic devices rather than by traditional instruments. Such music may simply reflect the fact that a musical performer is playing an instrument that uses electronic resonators to produce the sound (as in an electric organ), or may be an entire composition artificially produced on tape or by a computer. A number of new electronic instruments have been invented in the 20th century including the Ondes Martenot, the Theremin, and the Moog Synthesizer. Some composers who have composed new works entirely out of electronically-produced sounds include Karkheinz Stockhausen, Morton Subotnick, and Vladimir Ussachevsky.

Electronics, study and use of circuits based on the conduction of electricity through electron tubes and semiconducting devices. The science began with the discovery in 1887 by Heinrich Hertz (1857–94) of radio waves, but was unable to progress far until J. J. Thomson (1856–1940) discovered the electron in 1897. This enabled John Fleming (1849–1945) to invent the diode electron tube, which was modified into the triode by Lee De Forest (1873–1961) in 1907. These devices, with further modifications and improvements, provided the basic components for all the electronics of radio, TV, and radar until the end of World War II.

A major revolution occurred in 1948 when a team at Bell Telephone Laboratories, led by William Shockley, produced the first semiconducting transistor. Semiconductor devices are much lighter, smaller, and reliable than vacuum tubes; moreover they do not require a high operating voltage and they lend themselves to microminiaturization in the form of integrated circuits. These characteristics have enabled electronic computers and automatic control devices to change the face of both industry and scientific research; they have also enabled man to walk on the moon.

The idea of a computer was first proposed by the 19th-century British mathematician, Charles Babbage (1792–1871). The first large electronic computer (ENIAC) was built at the University of Pennsylvania, during World War II, using 18,000 electron tubes. Modern computers contain up to 80,000 transistors and are considerably smaller than ENIAC.

Electron Microscope, type of microscope that uses a beam of electrons instead of light to illuminate the object. The electron beam is produced by electron emission using an electron gun and is focused by a magnetic or electrostatic lens. It is directed onto the sample, the emerging electrons being focused by a second magnetic lens onto a fluorescent screen, which can be photographed. By accelerating the electrons to 100 keV a resolution of about half a millionth of a millimeter can be obtained. The transmission microscope produces a two-dimensional image and requires a very thin sample; the scanning microscope can produce a three-dimensional image.

Electron Tube, electronic device consisting of a system of electrodes arranged within an evacuated glass tube; for special purposes a gas at low pressure may be introduced into the tube. The diode, used for rectification, consists of a negative cathode, which emits electrons when heated (either directly or indirectly by a separate heater filament), and a positive anode or plate. The triode, used for amplification, has a perforated control grid situated between the cathode and the anode; a signal fed to the grid will provide an amplified signal at the anode. A tetrode has an extra electrode (screen grid) and a pentode has a fifth electrode (suppressor) between the grid and the anode. Electron tubes have been largely replaced by transistors and other semiconductor devices.

Electron Volt, unit of energy (symbol ev) equal to the energy acquired by an electron in falling freely through a potential difference of one volt. It is equal to 1.602×10^{-19} joule.

Electrophoresis, movement of electrically charged particles in a fluid under the influence of an applied electric field. Positive sols, such as metallic oxides or hydroxides, migrate to the cathode, and negative sols (metals, metallic sulfides) to the anode. Bacteria, viruses, and especially proteins may be separated, analyzed, and purified by electrophoresis.

Electroplating, deposition of a coating of one metal on another by making the object to be coated the cathode in an electrolytic cell. Positive ions in the electrolyte are discharged at the cathode and deposited as metal ($M^{+} + e \rightarrow M$). Electroplating is used to produce a decorative or corrosion-resistant layer, as in silver-plated tableware, chromium-plated automobile parts, and nickel-plated steel.

Electroscope, instrument for detecting the presence of an electric charge. The commonest device is the gold-leaf electroscope in which two gold leaves hang from an insulating support. A charge applied to the support causes the leaves to separate.

Electrostatic Generator. *See* Van de Graaff Generator.

Element, substance that cannot be split into simpler substances. All atoms of a given element have the same atomic number, and thus the same number of electrons—the factor determining chemical behavior. The atoms can have different mass numbers and, in general, a natural sample of an element is a mixture of isotopes. At present the known elements range from hydrogen (at. no. 1) to the highly unstable, element 106. They have a striking variation in distribution. Hydrogen and helium are the most common elements in the universe; oxygen and silicon are most common in the earth's crust. Technetium, astatine, promethium, and all elements of atomic number greater than 93 are not found in the earth's crust at all, being radioactive elements made artificially. *See also* Periodic Table.

Element 104, element with atomic number 104, first claimed in 1964 by a Soviet team at the Joint Institute for Nuclear Research at Dubna. They obtained the isotope of mass number 260 (half-life 1.5 seconds) by bombarding plutonium with neon ions. The element was named Kurchatorium after Igor Vasilevich Kurchatov, the former head of Soviet nuclear research. Later, in 1969, Albert Ghiorso and a team at Berkeley, California, obtained the isotope with mass number 257 (half-life 4–5 seconds) by bombarding californium with carbon nuclei. They proposed the name Rutherfordium after the New Zealand physicist, Ernest Rutherford.

Element 105, element with mass number 105, first reported by a Soviet team at the Joint Institute for Nuclear Research at Dubna. They claimed the isotopes of mass numbers 260 and 261, as a result of bombarding americium with neon ions. In 1970 the team at Berkeley, California, led by Albert Ghiorso, reported the isotope 260 (half-life 1.6 seconds) obtained by bombarding californium with nitrogen nuclei. The Soviet team has suggested the name Nielsbohrium, after Niels Bohr, and the Americans have suggested Hahnium, after Otto Hahn.

Elementary Particles and Antiparticles, bodies of matter that cannot be or have not been subdivided and are thus the basic constituents of matter. They are distinguished from each other by their mass (usually expressed in equivalent energy units) and a set of quantum numbers, including charge and spin. Except for the photon, they can be classified by their nuclear interactions into hadrons (mesons and baryons), which are subject to the strong interaction, and leptons, which are subject to the weak interaction. Charged particles also experience electromagnetic interaction. Each elementary particle has an associated antiparticle, which has the same mass and a charge, baryon number, and strangeness equal in magnitude but opposite in sign. Of the large number of particles known, most of which have been discovered in the last 25 years, only the proton, electron, neutrino, photon, neutron (when in a nucleus), and their antiparticles are stable. The others break up (decay) after a characteristic time (lifetime) to form stable particles. When an elementary particle collides with its own antiparticle, mutual annihilation occurs with the production of radiant energy and, at high energies, particle-antiparticle pairs. Particles are studied by their high-energy reactions produced in particle accelerators and by cosmic rays. *See also* Quark.

Elementary Subparticles. *See* Subparticles, Elementary.

Elephant, largest land animal, found in Africa and India. They are herbivorous mammals distinguished by their long tusks and trunk. The tusks are elongated upper incisors, sometimes over 11ft (3.4m) long. The flexible, grasping trunk is an elongated muscular nose and upper lip; at the tip are nostrils and one or two fingerlike extremities for picking up small objects. Elephants have poor vision and fair hearing, but their senses of smell, touch, and balance are acute. Intelligent animals with complex emotions and definite personalities, they are gregarious, show concern for fellow herd members, and are easily trained to perform complex tasks. Adults have no enemies besides man. Average lifespan in captivity is 60 years. The largest is the African bush elephant *(Loxodonta africana)*. The African forest *(L. cyclotis)* is the smallest and the Indian or Asian *(Elephas maximus* or *E. indicus)* is intermediate. Elephants are only living members of mammal order Proboscidea; extinct members are mammoths and mastodons. Height: to 13ft (4m) at shoulder; weight: over 6ton.

Elephant Bird, large, flightless bird of Madagascar that became extinct 1,000,000 years ago. Ostrichlike, it had large legs but small vestigial wings. Its eggs—the largest single cells known—measured up to 13×9.5in (33×24cm). Height: to 10ft (3m); weight: to 1,000lb (450kg). Family: Aepyornithidae.

Elephantiasis, disease caused by parasitic invasion of lymph channels, with swelling of legs, and external genitals, and thickening and fissuring of skin.

Elephantine, island in S Egypt, in Nile River below Aswan Dam; site of many ancient ruins, most notable are the Elephantine papyri, describing a Jewish colony (*c.* 5th century BC), and the Nilometer, dating from Ptolemic era, used to measure depth of the Nile.

Elephant Seal, largest seal, breeds on S California coast and in sub Antarctic regions. Named for its large size and elephantlike trunk. N species *Mirounga angustirostris;* more numerous S species *Mirounga leonina.*

Elephant seal

T. S. Eliot

Elizabeth II

Elephant's-foot, or Hottentot's bread, tropical climbing vine native to S Africa. Its tuberous roots are edible. Length: 10ft (3m). Family Dioscoreaceae; species *Dioscorea elephantipes.*

Elephant Shrew, any of about 20 species of small insect-eating African mammals. They have long, pointy snouts, long tails, and powerful hind legs. Length: 3.5–12.5in (89–318mm). Family Macroscelididae. *See also* Insectivore.

Eleusinian Mysteries, religious rites performed at Eleusis, Attica, in ancient Greece to honor the myth of Demeter (goddess of harvest) and Persephone. Based on the cyclical changes of the seasons, hopes for fruitful harvest, and the promise of salvation, the lesser mysteries were held around February and the greater at the end of September or beginning of October to coincide with the sowing of the harvest—the symbolic reunion of the corn-mother (Demeter) and the corn-maiden (Persephone) after Persephone's stay in the underworld with Pluto (which coincided with the storage of the harvest underground). The ceremony concluded with the showing of an ear of corn. At first only citizens of Attica were allowed to be initiates, or "seers;" later all Greeks and Romans, except criminals, could participate. The mysteries were finally ended by Roman Emperor Theodosius in the 4th century AD.

Eleuthera Island, central Bahama Islands, E of New Providence Island; site of US missile tracking station. Industries: tomatoes, pineapples, dairy products. Colonized by British 1647. Area: 164sq mi (425sq km). Pop. 6,247.

Elevator, a car or platform used for vertical transportation of passengers or freight to different levels of a building. The car or platform travels in vertical guides in a shaft or hoistway. Powered mechanisms regulate hoisting and lowering. Modern elevators in large buildings utilize computers for scheduling and traffic problems, making operation completely automatic. Some elevators can travel 1800ft (550m) per minute. In 1853 Elisha G. Otis exhibited what is considered the first modern elevator in the Crystal Palace at the New York World's Fair. A mechanical elevator, it featured automatic braking in the event that the hoisting mechanism failed. The first successful electric elevator appeared in 1889.

Elf Owl, smallest owl, found only in the SW United States and Mexico. It and its slightly larger European counterpart, the little owl *(Athene noctua),* feed mainly on insects. Length: about 6in (15cm). Species *Micrathene whitneyi. See also* Owl.

Elgar, Edward (1857–1934), English romantic composer. His *Pomp and Circumstance Marches* (1902–07) brought him fame. He composed a great deal of orchestral music, including two symphonies and the *Enigma Variations* (1899).

Elgin, city in NE Illinois, on the Fox River, 38mi (61km) WNW of Chicago. Elgin watches were first made here in the 19th century; site of Judson College and Elgin Community College (1949). Industries: tools, machinery, chemicals, dairy products. Founded 1835; inc. 1854. Pop. (1980) 63,798.

Elgin Marbles (5th century BC), group of classical Greek sculptures, including large portions of the friezes and the pediments of the Parthenon and one of the caryatids of the Erechtheum, both on the Acropolis in Athens. Collected by Lord Elgin, British ambassador to Turkey, they were sold to the British government in

1816 and are now on display in the British Museum, London. As the largest surviving group of classical Greek sculptures, they show the level of artistry of Greek sculptors and are essential to a stylistic understanding of the Parthenon.

El Giza (Al-Jizah) city in Egypt, on W bank of Nile; suburb of Cairo, close to pyramids and Sphinx. Industries: cotton, textiles, footwear, beer, motion pictures. Pop. 345,261.

Eli, biblical high priest at Shiloh who tutored young Samuel in service to God. The news of his sons' deaths and the capture of the Ark of the Covenant by the Philistines caused his death, passing the high priesthood back to the family of Eleazar.

Elijah, biblical Tishbite prophet and teacher of Elisha bent on destroying idolatry. He lived in poverty, performing miracles (eg raising the widow's son from the dead). He was fed by ravens in the wilderness and departed from earth in a whirlwind.

Eliot, George (1819–80), English novelist whose real name was Marian Evans. Her romantic union with G.H. Lewes, whose wife was still living, created a major scandal. In 1851 she joined the editorial staff of the *Westminster Review.* Early and well known novels, all realistic works about the problems of middle class people, include *Adam Bede* (1859), *The Mill on the Floss* (1860), and *Silas Marner* (1861). *Middlemarch* (1872) is often considered her best work.

Eliot, T(homas) S(tearns) (1888–1965), British poet and critic, b. St. Louis, Mo. He moved to England in 1914 and became a British citizen in 1927, the same year he converted to Anglo-Catholicism. He found early encouragement for his poetry in fellow expatriate Ezra Pound. After the publication of his first poem, *The Love Song of J. Alfred Prufrock* (1915), he devoted the rest of his life to literature as a poet, playwright, critic, and editor. *The Waste Land* (1922) created a literary sensation with its unique, complex language utilizing literary allusions and mythical and religious symbolism to descry the emptiness of contemporary life. Later poems, notably *Ash Wednesday* (1930) and the *Four Quartets* (1935–42) held out hope through religious faith. Of his five plays in verse, *Murder in the Cathedral* (1935), his first, was the most successful. His critical works, including *The Sacred Wood* (1920), *The Use of Poetry and the Use of Criticism* (1933), and *Elizabethan Essays* (1934), did much to revive interest in earlier poetry and to raise the scholarly standards of 20th century criticism. In 1948 he was awarded the Nobel Prize for literature.

Elisha, biblical prophet of Israel. A disciple of Elijah, he annointed Jehu king over Israel, fulfilling the curse on Ahab.

Elizabeth, in the New Testament, wife of Zacharias and mother of John the Baptist. She was related to Mary, mother of Jesus.

Elizabeth (1709–62), czarina of Russia (1741–62). She was the daughter of Peter the Great and was herself a great patron of the arts. The University of Moscow and the Academy of Fine Arts were founded in her reign and a number of baroque churches and palaces were built. She conducted a war against Sweden (1741–43) and annexed the southern portion of Finland (1743). She never married and was succeeded by her nephew, Peter III.

Elizabeth, in full, Elizabeth Amalie Eugenie (1837–98), Bavarian-born empress of Austria, also queen of Hun-

gary from 1867. Married to the young emperor Francis Joseph I of Austria in 1854, she was very popular with her subjects but led an uneasy private life. She was stunned by her son's suicide in 1889 and was murdered in Genoa by an Italian anarchist nine years later.

Elizabeth I (1533–1603), queen of England (1558–1603). the daughter of Henry VIII and Anne Boleyn, On her accession she reestablished Protestantism by the Acts of Supremacy and Uniformity (1559); Despite their relatively tolerant administration, Roman Catholic discontent led to the Rising of the Northern Earls (1569–70), the Ridolfi Plot (1571), and to subsequent plots in favor of Mary, Queen of Scots, the Roman Catholic claimant to the succession. As a threat to Elizabeth, Mary was eventually executed (1587). Refusing to marry, Elizabeth directed her foreign policy towards weakening the main Roman Catholic powers, France and Spain, without provoking war. But in 1587 war with Spain broke out and despite the defeat of the Armada in 1588 continued throughout her reign. Her last years were marked by financial difficulties and by the rebellion of the Earl of Essex. In addition to her own shrewdness and strength of character, Elizabeth had competent counselors, such as William Cecil, Lord Burghley, and her reign saw the rise of England as a major European naval power. Commerce and industry grew, and colonization began. The arts also flourished, particularly the theater, poetry, and architecture.

Elizabeth (1900–), queen consort of George VI of Great Britain. She was Lady Elizabeth Bowes-Lyon until her marriage (1923). Her children were Elizabeth, Queen of England, and Margaret, Countess of Snowdon.

Elizabeth II (1926–), queen of Great Britain, Northern Ireland, and the Commonwealth (1952–), daughter of George VI. She married (1947) Philip Mountbatten, Duke of Edinburgh, and they had four children, Charles, Anne, Andrew, and Edward. In World War II, she was a skilled truck driver and mechanic. She was crowned in 1953. She traveled extensively, particularly in the Commonwealth countries, and remained popular in Great Britain despite criticism of the institution of monarchy. In 1977 she celebrated the silver jubilee of her accession.

Elizabeth, city in NE New Jersey, on Newark Bay, 5mi (8km) S of Newark; seat of Union co; scene of many Revolutionary War battles, including Battle of Elizabethtown (1780) in which much of city was burned; site of Nathaniel Bonnell House (1682), and the 18th-century Boudinot House and Belcher mansion. Industries: sewing machines, chemicals, swimming pool equipment, biscuits. Settled 1664 on land purchased from Delaware Indians. Inc. 1855. Pop. (1980) 106,201.

Elizabethan Style, art style prevalent during Elizabeth I's reign in England (1558–1603). During this golden age of English prosperity and colonial expansion, the art produced reflected fierce patriotic love of all things English. Influenced by Netherlandish art rather than Italian, the style was vigorous, highly colored, naive in expression, stiff, direct, and lacking in grace.

Elizabethan Theater, drama that took place in England during the reign of Elizabeth I (1558–1603). Most often associated with William Shakespeare, Elizabethan drama combines two movements in Western art and thought: classical and medieval. Also drawing on native forms of folk drama, Elizabethan drama is characterized by a spiritual vitality and a belief, sometimes wavering, that the universe is benevolent, harmonious, and hierarchically ordered. Masters of the period are

William Shakespeare (1564–1616) and Ben Jonson (*c.*1572–1637).

Elizabethville. *See* Lubumbashi.

Elk. *See* Red Deer.

Elkhart, city in N Indiana, at the confluence of Elkhart and St Joseph's rivers. Industries: musical instruments, electrical equipment, mobile homes. Settled 1824; inc. 1877. Pop. (1980) 41,305.

Ellery, William (1727–1820), American patriot and a signer of the Declaration of Independence, b. Newport, R. I. He attended the Continental Congress (1776–81; 1783–85) and later served as Rhode Island's chief justice in 1785.

Ellesmere Island, ice-capped island of Canada, in Arctic Ocean, W of NW Greenland; 2nd largest and northernmost island of the Arctic Archipelago. The island's vegetation supports herds of musk oxen; site of many geological, glaciological, and geographical expeditions; Eskimo settlements. First sighted 1616 by William Baffin; not explored until late 19th century. Area: 82,119sq mi (212,688sq km).

Ellice Islands, former name of Tuvalu. *See* Tuvalu.

Ellington, (Edward) Duke (1899–1974), US jazz bandleader, pianist, and composer, b. Edward Ellington in Washington, D.C. One of the great figures of jazz history, he organized his first band in 1918 and continued as a great jazz bandleader through the 1970s, with many other great jazz musicians playing in his bands. He toured the world, made many recordings, and appeared in films. His many compositions include piano suites, classic jazz band arrangements, and many songs such as "Mood Indigo" (1930), "Caravan" (1937), and "I Got It Bad" (1941).

Ellipse, conic formed by cutting a right circular cone with a plane inclined at such an angle that the plane does not intersect the base of the cone. When the intersecting plane is parallel to the base, the ellipse becomes a circle. An ellipse is a conic with an eccentricity less than 1. In rectangular Cartesian coordinates its standard equation is $x^2/a^2 + y^2/b^2 = 1$. Two lines of symmetry can be drawn through the ellipse: the longer one is the major axis (length $2a$); the shorter is the minor axis (length $2b$). The area of an ellipse is πab. The ellipse has two foci on the major axis and one of its properties is that the sum of the distances from a point on the ellipse to the two foci is constant.

Elliptical Galaxy, type of regular galaxy having either a globular or lenticular structure and characterized by the absence of spiral arms. Graded EO to E7 according to increasing ellipticity, elliptical galaxies consists of old stars free of gas and dust. *See also* Galaxy; Spiral Galaxy.

Ellis, (Henry) Havelock (1859–1939), English psychologist and author. His seven-volume *Studies in the Psychology of Sex* (1897–1928) promoted the scientific study of sex. He was also a pioneer in the study of dreams and hallucinogenic drugs.

Ellis, Ruth (1926–55), last woman to be hanged in Britain before the suspension of capital punishment as the penalty for murder in 1965. A model, she was convicted of the murder of 25-year-old racing-driver David Blakely.

Ellis Island, island in New York harbor that served as chief US immigration station (1892–1943). Officials recorded arrivals here, often Americanizing names or giving immigrants entirely new names. Abandoned in 1954, it was proclaimed a National Historic Site (1965).

Ellsworth, Lincoln (1880–1951), US polar explorer, b. Chicago. He financed the Norwegian explorer Roald Amundsen, the first person to reach the South Pole (1911) and made a successful dirigible flight with Amundsen from Spitzbergen over the North Pole to Alaska (1926). He explored vast regions of the Arctic Ocean (1931) and made the first flight over Antarctica (1935).

Ellsworth, Oliver (1745–1807), chief justice of the US Supreme Court (1796–99), b. Windsor, Conn. He served as a delegate to the Continental Congress (1777–84), on the Connecticut Governor's Council (1780–84), and as superior court judge (1785–89). He was prominent at the Constitutional Convention (1787) where he and Roger Sherman introduced the Connecticut Compromise, settling the controversy between large and small states over representation. He was also responsible for the term "United States" being used in the Constitution. He served as senator from Connecticut (1789–96), chaired the committee forming the federal judiciary. After serving as chief justice, he became commissioner to France (1799–1800). He served on the Connecticut Governor's Council (1803) and died before taking office of first chief justice of the new state supreme court.

Elm, hardy, deciduous trees of north-temperate zones, popular as shade trees. Suitable varieties include the American elm *(Ulmus americana),* English elm *(U. procera),* and Scotch elm *(U. glabra).* All are susceptible to the deadly Dutch elm disease. Height: over 100ft (30m). The smaller Chinese elm *(U. parvifolia)* and Siberian elm *(U. pumila)* are resistant to the disease. Family Ulmaceae. *See also* Dutch Elm Disease.

Elmhurst, city in NE Illinois, 17mi (27km) W of Chicago's center; site of Elmhurst College (1871), and a large industrial park housing about 100 light industries. Settled 1843; inc. 1910. Pop. (1980) 44,251.

Elmira, city in S central New York, on Chemung River; seat of Chemung co; scene of signing of Treaty of Painted Post (1791); site of Confederate prison camp 1864–65, Elmira College (1853); home and burial place of Mark Twain. Industries: fire engines, iron, steel, food. Settled 1788; inc. 1864. Pop. (1980) 35,327.

El Monte, city in S California, 12mi (19km) E of Los Angeles; founded in 1852 by Santa Fe Trail pioneers. Industries: aerospace, electronic equipment, plastics. Inc. 1912. Pop. (1980) 79,494.

El Paso, city and port of entry in extreme W Texas, across Rio Grande River from Ciudad Juárez, Mexico; seat of El Paso co. First visited in 1536 by Cabeza de Vaca; permanent settlement built by Juan María Ponce de León; site of University of Texas at El Paso (1913), scene of annual Sunbowl football game featured during the Sun Carnival (est 1901), Fort Bliss (founded 1848) headquarters of Army Air Defense Center. Industries: tourism, meat packing, clothing, copper refining and smelting, oil refining, food processing. Settled 1827; inc. 1873. Pop. (1980) 425,259.

El Salvador, Republic of, nation in Central America, on the Pacific Ocean and bordered by Guatemala (W) and Honduras (N and E). The people are mixed Indian and Caucasian and mostly Roman Catholic.

Land and Economy. Two mountain ranges running E-W traverse the country creating valuable fertile upland plains. The climate is tropical, but the heat is modified by the elevation. The economy is primarily agricultural, relying especially on the coffee and sugar cane grown on the mountain slope plantations. Industrialization is progressing with many cotton textiles produced for export. The civil war of the early 1980s, however, disrupted much of the economy.

People. About 85% of the population is of mixed Indian and Caucasian stock with the majority employed in agriculture. Land ownership is concentrated in the hands of a small number of wealthy families, and most of the rural population consists of landless peasants, accounting for much of El Salvador's political instability. Education is free, and literacy is about 50%.

Government. According to the constitution of 1962 (partially suspended in 1979), El Salvador is a republic, with a president, elected every five years and ineligible for immediate reelection; a unicameral legislature, the National Assembly of Deputies, elected for two-year terms by popular vote; and a Supreme Court and lesser courts. There is universal suffrage at 18 years of age.

History. Spain took the country from the Indians in 1524 and established the first permanent settlement. El Salvador won its independence from Spain in 1821. Under Mexican control until 1823, when it became a member of the United Provinces of Central America, El Salvador regained its autonomy in 1839. Since that time political instability has been the keynote with frequent coups and revolutions and a rapid succession of presidents. Attempts to reunite the Central American nations were unsuccessful, although cooperation improved through the Organization of Central American States (1951) and a Central American common market (1959). By 1979, Pres. Carlos Humberto Romero was unable to control mounting violence between leftist guerrillas and rightist paramilitary groups. He was overthrown and replaced by a five-person military-civilian junta. In 1980 the junta pledged its support to a land reform program but continued to support the right indirectly through the army. The junta was disbanded, and moderate José Napoléon Duarte became president, but fighting continued, resulting in thousands of civilian deaths and worldwide accusations of human rights violations. In 1982, the land reform program was considered a failure, and Alvaro Magaña Borjo succeeded Duarte as president. In 1984, however, Duarte was elected to the presidency again. The continuing civil war received international attention throughout the 1980s.

PROFILE

Official name: Republic of El Salvador
Area: 8,260sq mi (21,393sq km)
Population: 4,670,000
Density: 565per sq mi (218per sq km)
Chief cities: San Salvador (capital); Santa Ana
Government: Republic
Religion: Roman Catholic
Language: Spanish (official)
Monetary unit: Colon
Gross national product: $3,100,000,000
Per capita income: $650
Industries (major products): cotton textiles and yarn, footwear, cement
Agriculture (major products): coffee, sugar cane
Trading partners (major): United States, West Germany, Guatemala

Elyria, city in N Ohio, 23mi (37km) W of Cleveland, on the Black River; seat of Lorain co; site of first secondary school W of Allegheny Mts (1830); International Society for Crippled Children founded here 1915. Industries: fittings, electric motors, chemicals, aircraft parts. Founded 1817; inc. 1892. Pop. (1980) 57,504.

Emancipation, Edict of (1861), declaration by Czar Alexander II of Russia that the serfs in that country were free and that serfdom was abolished. Under the edict the serfs were granted land in return for redemption payments to be paid by them to the former landowners over the next 49 years. In many ways the emancipation was unsuccessful. Often the amount of land the serfs received was insufficient to support them. Also, the commune in which they lived maintained control over a major portion of their lives.

Emancipation Proclamation, (1863) declaration by President Lincoln. In the early days of the Civil War, President Lincoln was urged by abolitionists to issue a law ending slavery. Lincoln, more anxious to save the Union than end slavery, waited until Union forces repelled the Confederates at Antietam, Md., in September 1862 before issuing the Emancipation Proclamation. It stated that, after Jan. 1, 1863, all slaves in the rebel states would be free.

Embargo Act (1807), act passed under President Jefferson to force England and France to remove restrictions on US trade. It prohibited ships from leaving the United States bound for any foreign ports but was a failure.

Embassy, headquarters of a diplomatic mission in a foreign country. It is the site where diplomatic business is conducted and also serves as an information center and usually the ambassadorial residence. *See also* Diplomatic Service; Extraterritoriality.

Embolism, blocking of a blood vessel usually by a clot, but also by a foreign body, gas bubble, or fat globule. Symptoms include coldness, numbness, tingling, severe pain. Anticoagulants and surgery are treatments. *See also* Arteriosclerosis.

Embroidery, art of ornamenting textiles, fabrics, and other materials with needlework. Embroidery is not woven into a fabric but is sewn on an already finished cloth. About 300 different embroidery stitches exist, occurring in four categories: flat, looped, chained, and knotted stitches. From the time when needles were invented, whether a sharp fish bone, a thorn, a pointed stick, or a metal wire, the natural instinct seems to have been for man to decorate his utilitarian garments. The Bayeux Tapestry (11th century) is one of the most famous embroideries executed. Today crewel work (wool embroidery), needlepoint, and bargello are popular forms of embroidery.

Embryology, biological study of the origin, development, and activities of an embryo. This science, in tracing the progression of events leading from an egg to an adult, follows the zygote through cleavage, morula stage, blastula stage, and gastrula stage when two and then three germ layers, precursors of body organs, appear.

Emerald, variety of beryl, varying in color from light to deep green; highly valued as gemstone. Color due to small amounts of aluminum; stone may lose color when heated. Mined in Upper Egypt in 1650 BC; now found mainly in Colombia. Used as charm by ancients. *See also* Beryl.

Emergency Powers of the President, inherent authority of the US president to act in times of national emergency. The definition and declaration of a national emergency is left to the president's discretion, although periods of foreign danger and economic depression are understood to fall into this category.

Duke Ellington

El Salvador

Emu

Emerson, Ralph Waldo (1803–82), US essayist and poet, a key figure in American thought and literature, b. Boston. After graduating from Harvard University (1821), he taught school, attended Harvard Divinity School (1825–26), and was a Unitarian minister in Boston (1829–32). Rejecting the formal structure of the church, he resigned his pastorate and went to Europe. There he met Thomas Carlyle, Samuel Taylor Coleridge, and William Wordsworth and became acquainted with German Romanticism. On his return to the United States he began giving lectures; many of these were published or were incorporated into his essays.

In 1835 he settled in Concord, Mass., becoming friends with Henry David Thoreau, Bronson Alcott, Margaret Fuller, and others of the Transcendentalist movement. Emerson's book *Nature* (1836) expressed the fundamental principles of Transcendental thought. Subsequent works included two series of *Essays* (1841, 1844); *Poems* (1846); *Representative Men* (1850), biographical essays; *English Traits* (1856), lectures given in England in 1847. *The Conduct of Life* (1860); *May-Day and Other Pieces* (1867), poetry; and *Society and Solitude* (1870). In these works Emerson preached his philosophy: belief in the soul; the unity of God with man and nature; self-reliance; and hope. *See also* Transcendentalism.

Emery, impure form of the mineral corundum, aluminum oxide, that occurs as dark granules with magnetite in them. An unusually hard mineral, it is used as an abrasive.

Emigration, leaving one's homeland to settle elsewhere. The 19th and early 20th centuries saw a great emigration to the United States. Fears and prejudice resulting from this movement led to passage of a quota system (1921). This was followed by the National Origins Act (1924), excluding Asians. The act was not reversed until 1965.

Emilia-Romagna, region in N central Italy, bordering on Adriatic Sea; capital is Bologna; named for the ancient Aemilian Way (187 BC); contains good hydroelectric and transportation systems. Products: cereals, rice, vegetables, dairying. Industries: processed foods, tourism, motor vehicles, refined petroleum, chemicals. Area: 8,542sq mi (22,124sq km). Pop. 3,948,135.

Emmanuel. For monarchs so named, *see* Manuel.

Emmet, Robert (1778–1803), Irish nationalist leader. In July 1803 he led an attack upon Dublin Castle, which was intended as a prelude to a French invasion to help his movement. He hoped to destroy the Act of Union (1801), which placed Ireland under the British Parliament. His plot failed, and he was arrested, tried, and executed. His speech upon sentencing, with the words "Let no man write my epitaph," inspired later Irish nationalists.

Emotion, human feeling involving complex mental and physical reactions. Emotions are associated with predictable physiological changes such as increased heart and breathing rates, sweating, dryness of the mouth, and trembling. Physiological studies have implicated the reticular formation in the brain as important for emotional changes: greater emotional intensity involves greater nervous activity in that part of the brain. Basic expressions of emotions, such as facial patterns of crying and smiling, appear to be unlearned. Other expressions are acquired from one's culture; eg, Americans register surprise by raising eyebrows and widening their eyes, while the Chinese register surprise by sticking out their tongues.

Emphysema, accumulation of air in tissues, most often occurring in the lungs (pulmonary emphysema). Causes are unknown but air pollution and heavy smoking exacerbate the symptoms which include wheezing, cough, and shortness of breath. Treatment can include antibiotics, relief of spasms and secretion with inhalators, and ventilation exercises.

Empiricism, from the Greek *empeiria* "experience," philosophical doctrine that experience is the only source of knowledge. Epicurus (341–270 BC) was one of the first empiricists. *See also* British Empiricism.

Empyema, infection of the pleural cavity yielding large amounts of pus, usually secondary to a lung infection. Treatment includes antibiotics and drainage of the cavity.

Ems Dispatch (1870), final cause of the Franco-Prussian War in 1870. Alarmed at the candidacy for the Spanish throne of Prince Leopold, a relative of King William of Prussia, the French requested assurance of the permanence of Leopold's refusal. William declined, informing his prime minister, Otto von Bismarck, of the conversation, who in turn published an insulting version of the telegram and inflamed the French to war.

Ems River, river in West Germany; rises in Teutoburger Wald, NW West Germany and flows NW into North Sea near Emden. It is connected with Ruhr region by the Dortmund-Ems canal system. Length: 208mi (335km).

Emu, large, dark-plumed, flightless Australian bird. A strong runner with powerful legs, it lives in groups and feeds mostly on plant matter. Large greenish eggs (8–10) are incubated by the male in a scraped–ground nest. Height: 5ft (1.5m); weight: to 20lb (9kg). Species *Dromaius novaehollandiae*.

Emulsion, a mixture of liquids in which one is present in droplets of microscopic size. Emulsions may be formed spontaneously or by mechanical means if the liquids have no mutual solubility and they are stabilized by emulsifying agents. A familiar emulsion is milk (droplets of fat in an aqueous solution).

Enamel, paint that consists of zinc oxide and lithopone, brown linseed oil, and high-grade varnish. The finish is hard, glossy and highly durable. The term enamel paint is derived from its resemblance when dry to the finish found on glass-enamel products. It is not water soluble and must be thinned with turpentine or other spirit.

Enamels, objects decorated with a vitreous glaze or combination of glazes, usually opaque, fused to a metallic, glass, or ceramic surface. The base of enamel is a clear, vitreous compound called flux, which is composed of silica, minium, and potash. The flux is colored by the addition of oxides of metals. The amount of acid in it regulates the density or opacity of the enamel. Pulverized enamel is carefully and evenly spread over those parts of the metal designed to receive it. The piece is then dried in front of a furnace, placed gently on a fireclay, and introduced carefully into the furnace. When the enamel shines all over it is withdrawn, a process that takes a few minutes. There are several different modes of enameling: champlevé, cloisonné, basse-taille, plique-à-jour, painted enamel, encrusted, and miniature-painted. These processes were used at different times in history. *See also* Cloisonné.

Encaustic Painting, painting technique in the ancient world and early Christian era, using pigments mixed with hot wax. The Mummy portraits from Fayoum (1st century BC to 3rd century AD) demonstrate the lively

coloring, sculptural modeling, and excellent survival qualities of this art.

Enceladus, satellite of Saturn.

Encephalitis, virus-caused disease of the brain and spinal cord usually epidemic, transferred from animal to man by insects. Similar to meningitis (bacterial infection), symptoms include fever, headache, vomiting, stiff neck and back, increasing to convulsions, hallucinations, and possible paralysis. Accurate diagnosis by analysis of spinal fluid is crucial to differentiate encephalitis from forms of meningitis treatable by antibiotics. Complete and spontaneous recovery is frequent; otherwise the symptoms are treated. *See also* Equine Encephalitis; Meningitis.

Encke, Johann Franz (1791–1865), German astronomer noted for his study and calculations of the movements of comets, including one which bears his name. Encke's comet has the smallest known orbit, passing close to the sun approximately every 3½ years. Encke was director of the Berlin observatory (1825–63).

Enclosure, land policy, dating from the 12th century, involving subdivision and fencing of the common lands and large open fields of the medieval English agrarian economy. The practice led to problems in the 16th and 17th centuries when landlords expelled tenant farmers without adequate reason or compensation in order to enclose the land to serve their own interests. The practice peaked in the late 17th century, waning in the early 18th century. The process of enclosure began in places by private agreements but became chiefly associated with the policy of Parliamentary Enclosure Acts for individual parishes, mainly from 1750 onward.

Encyclical, letter sent to all churches of a particular area, originally by any bishop, but now by the Pope. It usually deals with doctrinal matters, but is not held to be infallible. Well-known encyclicals sent in modern times include Pope Paul's 1968 letter condemning birth control; Pius XI's 1931 letter against Italian Fascism and 1937 letter against the Nazis; and Pius X's letter condemning modernism in 1907. The term is also applied to letters issued by Anglican bishops at the conclusion of the Lambeth conferences.

Encyclopedists, French philosophes who presented their rationalist, humanitarian, and deist views through the publication of the *Encyclopédie, ou Dictionnaire raisonné des sciences, des arts, et des métiers* in the latter half of the 18th century. Encountering severe opposition from the religious and political establishment, the primary editor, Denis Diderot and such prominent authors as Voltaire, Rousseau, and Montesquieu helped prepare the philosophical basis of the French Revolution.

Endangered Species, plants and animals in imminent danger of extinction due to a variety of causes, including destruction of their habitats, loss of their natural food sources, extermination by humans, or the end of the evolutionary line. Since the 17th century, 130 species of birds and mammals have become extinct and 240 are now considered endangered. By the year 2000, it is estimated that 50,000–100,000 plant and animal species will become extinct. Species in danger of extinction are listed by the International Union for Conservation of Nature and Natural (Wildlife) Resources (IUCN) in the *Red Data Book.*

Endive, leafy Old World annual or biennial plant widely cultivated for its sharp-flavored leaves used cooked or in salads. It resembles leaf lettuce, but has more substantial leaves. There are two types: curly endive with slender, wavy-edged leaves and escarole with broad flat leaves. Family Compositae; species *Cichorium endivia. See also* Chicory.

Endocarditis, inflammation of the lining of the heart. Often bacteria-caused, it is also associated with rheumatic fever.

Endocrine System, body system made up of all the endocrine, or ductless, glands that secrete chemical substances known as hormones directly into the blood stream where they act to control body functions. The endocrine system, together with the nervous system, controls and regulates all body functions; the endocrine system is occasionally considered the chemical control or the "liquid nervous system." The endocrine system differs from other body systems in that its member parts—the ductless glands—are not structurally linked or connected to one another. The chief endocrine glands are (1) the pituitary gland, located at the base of the brain, often called the master gland. It secretes more than 15 hormones that act on other endocrine glands and in many areas of the body, regulating growth, development, and other body functions. (2) The thyroid gland, located in the throat, which secretes thyroxine to regulate growth and metabolism. (3) The parathyroid glands, also located in the throat, which regulate calcium metabolism. (4) The adrenal glands, situated atop the kidneys, which secrete adrenaline, the "stress" hormone, and various steroids that regulate salt and water balance in the body. (5) The islands of Langerhans in the pancreas, which secrete insulin for carbohydrate metabolism. (6) The sex glands, or gonads—in males, the testes, which secrete testosterone; in females, the ovaries, which secrete estrogens and progesterones. *See also* articles on specific endocrine glands.

Endoderm, or entoderm, innermost cell layer of embryos of higher animals. It forms the liver, pancreas, digestive tract, and respiratory system. It also is the inner cell layer of a simple animal body.

Endodontics, dental specialty that deals with the treatment and prevention of diseases of the soft tissue in the center of the tooth called the dental pulp. Diseased pulp is removed but the tooth can be maintained in the jaw as long as the blood supply to the anchoring fibers is preserved or restored. This is often preferable to replacement with an artificial tooth.

Endogamy, set of institutionalized precepts that define the boundaries within which marriage is enjoined in a society. These vary from mere tendencies to strictly enforced laws deciding the group from which the spouse is taken. *See also* Exogamy.

Endometrium, highly vascularized tissue lining the uterus. upon conception it forms part of the placenta to maintain the developing fetus during pregnancy.

Endosperm, tissue surrounding the developing embryo of a seed. It provides food for growth.

Endothermic Reaction, chemical reaction in which heat is absorbed, thus causing a fall in temperature. *See also* Chemical Reaction.

Energy, one of the great unifying concepts of physics. Energy has many forms: mechanical, atomic, heat, chemical, and others. It undergoes transformations: thermonuclear reactions in the sun release solar energy; photosynthesis in plants stores this energy in chemical form; ingestion of the plant by animals allows muscles to transform this energy yet again into physical action. The concept of energy came into being with Galileo, Newton, and Leibniz. Its conservation through all its transformations was established almost simultaneously by Joule, Rumford, and Kelvin in the mid-19th century. The relationship between energy, momentum, and mass of a particle was established in 1905 by Einstein, who recognized that energy and mass could be transformed into each other according to the relation $E = mc^2$.

Energy, Department of(DOE), US cabinet department, established 1977. DOE is responsible for administering a comprehensive national energy plan, including research and development, regulatory functions, and promoting energy conservation, competitive energy industries, and the nuclear weapons program. The department is a consolidation of several organizations including Energy Research & Development Administration (ERDA), Federal Energy Administration (FEA), and Federal Power Commission (FPC).

Energy Crisis, the social hardships and economic dislocations caused by the shortage or high cost of petroleum and other fuels. About 65% of the energy used in the world comes from petroleum and natural gas. Since the early 1970s petroleum prices have skyrocketed, and several periods of acute petroleum shortage have occurred. To combat this energy crisis, nations have increased use of non-petroleum energy sources. Another fuel, coal, is being increasingly utilized in countries that have large reserves, such as the United States. The use of nuclear fission to produce energy has been plagued with engineering and operational problems. Hydroelectric power also produces problems, such as the loss of vast amounts of water by evaporation from reservoirs. Other sources, including solar energy, wind power, tidal water movement, and geothermal energy, cannot currently meet more than a small portion of the world's energy demands. Conservation is another important method of dealing with the energy crisis.

Energy Efficiency. *See* Thermodynamics.

Eneuresis, bed-wetting, or involuntary urination while sleeping, considered a disturbance only if it lingers long into childhood. It could indicate emotional difficulties or stress in the home. Behavior therapy may be an effective treatment.

Engelbrektsson, Engelbrekt (1390–1436), Swedish national hero. He led a revolt against Eric of Pomerania, king of Denmark, Sweden, and Norway. A mine owner, Engelbrektsson in 1434 became leader of a peasants' and miners' uprising against the tyrannical king. The rebellion soon gained support from the clergy and the nobility. Engelbrekt seized castles throughout eastern and southern Sweden until the diet of 1435 accepted his demands and made him regent. He was murdered shortly thereafter.

Engels, Friedrich (1820–95), German political writer and Socialist. He was a disciple of Karl Marx, with whom he collaborated in formulating the theory of dialectical materialism. As agent in England of his father's textile business (1842–44) he took an interest in the workers' conditions and, under the influence of the Chartist movement, wrote *The Condition of the Working Classes in England* (1845). This brought him into touch with Marx, then an exile in England, and together they wrote the *Communist Manifesto* (1848). While Marx was doing research and writing in London, Engels supported him, and from 1870 until Marx's death (1883) he helped Marx with his writings. He completed *Das Kapital* (1894), which Marx left unfinished.

Engels, formerly Pokrovsk; port city in Russian SFSR, USSR, across Volga River from Saratov; served as capital of German Volga Autonomous SSR 1923–41; renamed 1932 to honor Friedrich Engels. Industries: bricks, food processing, chemicals, machinery. Settled 1747 by Ukrainians. Pop. 167,000.

England, largest part of Great Britain, bounded E by the North Sea, S by the English Channel, W by the Atlantic Ocean, Wales, and the Irish Sea, and N by Scotland.

Land and Economy. England is mainly lowland with low hills and downs in the SE, Cotswold hills in the NW, and a granite and sandstone plateau on the SW peninsula rising to over 2,000ft (610m) on Dartmoor. The Pennine range of hills extends S-N centrally, with moorland in the NE and SW and the Cumbrian Mts in the NW. The highest point is Scafell Pike, 3,210ft (979m). The principal islands are Isle of Man, off the Welsh coast, the Isle of Wight, off the S coast, and the Scilly Isles, off the SW coast. The principal lakes are situated in the Lake District and include Windermere (largest), Derwentwater, and Ullswater. The main rivers are the Thames, Ouse, Humber, Trent, Mersey, and Severn. Over 50% of the agricultural land is arable, and about 35% is permanent pasture; sheep are grazed on rough uplands. Main products are cereals, vegetables, beef, sheep, fruit in the S, dairy farming in the W. Fishing, especially herring and cod, is centered on the E coast. Mineral resources include coal (particularly in Northamptonshire, Derbyshire, Yorkshire, and Leicester), offshore petroleum (mainly in the North Sea), building stone, clay, and iron. Heavy industry, including iron and steel, shipbuilding, motor vehicles, textiles, railroad rolling stock, and engineering, is concentrated in the Midlands and N. Other industries include refining, pottery, aircraft, glass, electrical goods, agricultural machinery, and pharmaceuticals.

People. The people are of mixed ethnic origin, including Celt, Roman, Anglo-Saxon, and Norman. The main religious group is the Church of England.

History. Before the Roman invasion in AD 43, the Celts occupied England. The Romans remained until the 5th century but had been harassed by German tribes (Angles, Saxons, Jutes) from the 3rd century. Christianity arrived in the 6th century. By the 7th century Saxon kingdoms such as Sussex, Wessex, Kent, and Mercia were identifiable. The Danes and other Scandinavians invaded in the 9th century but their advance was halted by Alfred the Great (878). The struggles between the Danes and the English for control continued into the 11th century.

Edward the Confessor of Wessex took the throne in 1042, but when he died (1066) without heirs, William of Normandy invaded, conquered England, and became William I of England. William's dynasty was succeeded by the Plantagenets in 1154. Henry II, the first Plantagenet, was followed by less successful rulers, and in 1215 rebellious barons forced John to grant the Magna Carta. The barons' increased strength in the early 14th century led to the murder of Edward II (1327).

English rulers continued to press their claims to lands in France, which led to involvement in the Hundred Years War. In the mid-15th century, rival claims to the English throne triggered the Wars of the Roses, which ended with the victory of Henry VII and the establishment of the Tudor dynasty (1485). The Act of Union (1536) completed the unification of Wales and England. Under Henry VIII Protestantism became stronger as a result of Henry's struggles with the Roman Catholic Church. The Tudors continued on the throne through the reign of the childless Elizabeth I, who was succeeded in 1603 by James I (James VI of Scotland), the first Stuart monarch. For the subsequent history of England, *see* Great Britain.

PROFILE

Official name: England
Area: 50,333sq mi (130,362sq km)
Population: 46,019,000
Density: 911per sq mi (351per sq km)
Chief cities: London (capital); Birmingham; Liverpool

England, Church of, developed in Great Britain as a result of the conflict between the papal authority and that of monarchs. This tension reached its peak in the 16th century as religious dissatisfaction mounted. Henry VIII's divorce led to the break with Rome (1534), and the destruction of shrines. The Church of England's stand against Roman Catholics and Puritans eventually gave way to religious tolerance. *See also* Anglicanism.

English, the most universal of the world's languages, the mother tongue of about 300 million people in the United States, Canada, Great Britain, Ireland, Australia, New Zealand, most of the Caribbean islands, and as a second language by many millions more throughout the world. A Germanic language, it may be said to have come into existence with the arrival of the Anglo-Saxons in Great Britain in the 5th century AD.

English Channel, arm of the Atlantic Ocean, between France and Great Britain; connected with North Sea at E end by Strait of Dover. Train-ferry service between Dover, England and Dunkirk, France was started in 1936. Width: 20–150mi (32–242km). Length: 350mi (564km).

English Cocker Spaniel, small hunting dog (sporting group); one of the oldest land spaniels. A responsive and faithful dog, it has a well-developed head and square muzzle; low-set, lobular ears hang close to the head. A short, compact body is set on strong legs; the tail is short. The coat, which may be white and a color, roan, or black and tan, is short on the head and flat and longer on the body; chest, belly, and legs are feathered. Average size: 16–17in (40.5–43cm) high at shoulder; 28–34lb (12.5–15.5kg). *See also* Sporting Dog.

English Foxhound, hunting dog (hound group) used for riding to hounds; stouter than American foxhound. It has a large head with pronounced brow and long nose; low-set ears carried close to cheeks; a large-chested, muscular body; straight, strong legs with round feet; and tapering tail carried up. The short, dense, hard coat is black, white, and tan. Average size: 21–25in (53.5–63.5cm) high at shoulder; 60–70lb (27–32kg). *See also* Hound.

English Horn, woodwind musical instrument similar to the oboe, but 6in (15cm) longer and pitched one fifth lower, with curved double-reed mouthpiece and pear-shaped bell. It is used in solo passages in Franck's *D Minor Symphony* and Rossini's *William Tell. See also* Oboe.

English Renaissance Architecture, architecture of Elizabethan and Jacobean England (1558–1625), between the Perpendicular style of the late Gothic and the Palladian classicism of Inigo Jones. It was primarily secular architecture and achieved its fullest expression in great country houses such as Longleat, Burghley House, and Wollaton Hall. These houses, often of an E or H shape, looked outward through large windows and were typically set with towers, gables, and parapets.

English Setter, bird dog (sporting group) bred 400 years ago in England. An aristocratic outdoor dog, its long, lean head has a square muzzle and hanging lips;

Endive

English springer spaniel

Enna, Sicily

rounded ears hang close to the head. The medium-length body and legs are graceful, and a straight, feathered tail tapers to a point. The long, straight flat coat can be black; white and tan; black, lemon, orange, or liver with white; or solid white. Average size: 25in (63.5cm) high at shoulder; 60lb (27kg). *See also* Sporting Dog.

English Springer Spaniel, hunting dog (sporting group); specialist for finding game. It has a broad head and square, lean jaw; long, wide, hanging ears set at eye level; and a neat, compact body set on muscular legs. The docked tail is carried horizontally. A flat or wavy coat is feathered on ears, chest, legs and belly; colors are liver or black with white or tan markings; blue or liver roan; white with tan, black, or liver markings. Average size: 18–20in (46–51cm) high at shoulder; 45–55lb (21–25kg). *See also* Sporting Dog.

English Toy Spaniel, small dog (toy group) known in England since the 16th century; probably originated in Japan or China. It has a well-domed head; square, deep muzzle; and short nose turned up between large, dark eyes. Low-set ears hang almost to the ground. The body is small and compact; legs are short and stout; tail is docked and carried level with the back. The long, silky, wavy coat may be black and tan (King Charles variety), chestnut red (ruby), red and white (Blenheim), or white, black, and tan (Prince Charles). Average size: 10in (25cm) high at shoulder; 9–12lb (4–5.5kg). *See also* Toy Dog.

Engraving, intaglio (incised) printing process. Tools called burins are used to cut out lines drawn on a copper plate or on an end-grain block of wood. There are many different kinds of burins to cut different size lines. When magnified, the engraved line has a pointed end. After a proof of the print is made on an etching press, corrections may be made on the plate or woodblock with such tools as a scraper and burnisher. In modern engraving, different intaglio processes such as etching, aquatint, and engraving are frequently combined in a single plate.

Enid, city in N Oklahoma, 65mi (105km) NNW of Oklahoma City; seat of Garfield co; site of Phillips University (1907) and Vance Air Force Base. Industries: oil refining, grain elevators, meat packing. Founded 1893 on site of US land office in Cherokee Strip. Inc. 1894. Pop. (1980) 50,363.

Eniwetok, uninhabited coral atoll in W central Pacific Ocean; part of the Ralik Chain, Marshall Islands; approx. 40 islands encircle a lagoon with a circumference of 50mi (81km); taken from Japan by United States during WWII; scene of US atomic and thermonuclear weapons tests (1950s).

Enlightenment, or **Age of Reason,** vast revolution of western thought in the 18th century. It was based on an ultimate reliance in the perfectibility of man through reason in his relations with himself, his fellows, and the universe. Extending to all the branches of the western intellectual world, this school of thought included Rousseau, Hume, Voltaire, Mendelssohn, Addison, Kant, Montesquieu, Franklin, Jefferson, and many others, and made possible such dramatic events as the French and American revolutions. Supported by the rising bourgeoisie and opposed by church and nobility, the Enlightenment fostered a new humanism. It raised the individual to the position of ultimate importance, placed a new faith in the progress of man, with the state as its natural agent; and espoused a belief in natural religion (Deism), law, and universal order. Some vocal proponents were the Masons and the Encyclopedists.

Enlil, chief god of the Sumerian pantheon and later of Babylon and Assyria. He was guardian of the city of Nippur, the political and religious center of southern Mesopotamia. As the god of air Enlil shared his dominion with three supreme deities, Anu, god of heaven, Ea, god of water, and Ninhursag, goddess of Earth, but he alone was responsible for bringing the Me, or laws governing all existence.

Enna, town in Sicily, Italy, 64mi (103km) SE of Palermo; capital of Enna prov; scene of Sicilian slave revolt 134–32 BC; site of octagonal towers and castle of Frederick II; mythical birthplace of Ceres, and scene of rape of Proserpina by Pluto; agricultural center and summer resort area. Pop. 28,653.

Enoch, several biblical figures, including Cain's eldest son whose name was given to the city built by Cain. Also, the son of Jared and father of Methuselah.

Enschede, city in E Netherlands, on Twente Canal; devastated by fire (1862); site of university (1961) and natural history museum; customs station. Industries: pharmaceuticals, textiles, paper, dairy products, beer. Founded 1118. Pop. 141,597.

Ensenada, seaport city in NW Mexico, on Pacific Ocean. Industries: fishing, fish processing, wine, agriculture, mining. Pop. 113,320.

Enteritis, chronic or acute inflammation of the lining of the intestine. Causes include emotional distress, allergy, or infectious disease. Mild to extreme diarrhea and abdominal pain are symptoms. Treatment usually includes a bland diet. *See also* Gastroenteritis.

Enterokinase, an enzyme released by the intestine during digestion. It activates the digestive enzyme trypsin. *See also* Trypsin.

Entomology, scientific study of insects. *See also* Insect.

Entropy, a quantity related to the number of accessible quantum states available to a system. If the number of such states is N, then the entropy S of the system is given by $S = k \ln N$, where k is the Stefan-Boltzmann constant. Since an isolated system will always tend to its most probable states (largest value of N) its entropy tends to increase. This is the Second Law of Thermodynamics. For example, in a system of 10 atoms that have two directions of spin, the number of different combinations of states N is 2^{10} for sufficiently high temperatures; thus the entropy of this system is $10 \, k \ln 2$. But at low temperatures, all spins become aligned, the total number of possible states drops to one, and the entropy goes to zero. This is the Third Law of Thermodynamics. *See also* Statistical Mechanics; Thermodynamics.

Enugu, city in S Nigeria; capital of East-Central state; trade and coal mining center; site of technical college (1955). Pop. 172,000.

Environment, aggregate of conditions, substances, and other organisms affecting existence of an organism. Physical factors of the environment include water, temperature, and soil.

Enzymes, group of proteins that function as catalysts in biological chemical reactions. As they are not used up in these reactions, they are effective in tiny quantities and as they are highly specific, enormous numbers of them occur in nature. Many enzymes require the presence of accessory substances (coenzymes) in order to function effectively. Enzymes are essential for the replication of DNA and RNA molecules and for the manufacture of protein in the cell. They are important experimental markers of specific gene activity. The names of enzymes end in the letters *-ase* except for a few, such as pepsin, that retain older names.

Eocene, the second oldest of the five major epochs of the Tertiary period, extending from the end of the Paleocene to the beginning of the Oligocene. During the Eocene all the major orders of modern mammals and many modern bird orders appeared.

Eohippus, or dawn horse, extinct progenitor of the horse that lived during Eocene epoch (58 million years ago) in swampy areas of North America. It had a small head with large eyes set mid-face, short neck, and arched back. Each forefoot had four toes, the hind feet three. Teeth were simple and suitable for browsing on soft vegetation. Height: 17.7–23.6in (45–60cm).

Eolian (or Aeolian) Formation, one that was created by wind transported material. This may be a dune on a riverbank or ripple marks in sand on a beach or desert, or the growth phase of dune building. It also can be used to describe shapes carved in rock by the wearing away of softer materials. *See also* Butte; Desert; Dune.

Eolithic Age, or "Dawn Stone" Age, name given to the period between approximately 2,500,000 and 500,000 years ago in which man, or near-man, used fractured stone tools. Eoliths are so primitive that the untrained eye cannot always distinguish them from naturally broken stones. *See also* Paleolithic Age.

Eos, Greek mythological figure. Eos was the dawn-goddess, daughter of Hyperion and Thea, who drove through the sky in a chariot drawn by a pair of horses. Homer and other poets described her in colors evocative of the morning sky: "rosy-fingered" and "saffron-robed." Eos was often involved in romantic adventures.

Eosinophil, white blood cell with an affinity for the red dye eosin. It increases in number in certain diseases.

Epeirogeny, in geology that form of diastrophism that results in the formation of large features of the earth's crust such as continents, and oceans and the creation of large areas within those features, such as plateaus and basins. This leaves the formation of mountains as the distinct preserve of orogeny. The movements that constitute epeirogeny are primarily vertical ones. In some processes that result in the formation (or deformation) of mountain topography, epeirogeny and orogeny interact and overlap, making distinctions difficult. *See also* Deformation; Orogeny; Tectonics.

Ephedrine, a widely used drug, chemically similar to epinephrine (adrenalin), that stimulates the central nervous system and is used to counter the effects of depressants, to treat bronchial asthma by dilating bronchioles, to dilate pupils of the eyes, as a nasal decongestant, and to treat low blood pressure.

Ephemeris (pl. Ephemerides), list of tables providing the positions of a planet or comet for a given selection of dates, as derived from orbital data. The term also signifies an annual publication supplying such tables along with information concerning the Sun, eclipse and occultation data, data for certain stars, astronomical constants, etc. One of the most important of such publications is *The American Ephemeris and Nautical Almanac*, which, since 1960, has been merged with the (British) *Astronomical Ephemeris*.

Ephemeris Time (ET), system of time reckoning normally employed in the compilation of astronomical data for almanacs and Ephemerides. It takes no account of irregularities in the Earth's rotation and is calculated on the basis of the tropical year. It is slightly in advance of Universal Time.

Ephesians, New Testament epistle written by Paul during his first captivity in Rome. Addressed to the Christian church at Ephesus, it stresses unity for all through Christ.

Ephesus, ancient Ionian city of W Asia Minor, site of a noted temple of Artemis (Diana). Trade made it a rich seaport under the Greeks and Romans. Croesus, king of Lydia, captured it (*c.*550 BC), Cyrus the Great (*c.*546 BC), Alexander the Great (334 BC), and the Romans (133 BC) later held it. It was sacked by the Goths (AD 262). The important church Council of Ephesus was held there in 431.

Epic, long narrative poem in grandiose style in which heroes perform superhuman tasks of strength. The earliest known form of Greek literature, epics were originally used to transmit history orally. Using the literary device of repetition, they often involved gods, men, and legendary battles. Homer is the author of the two most famous epics, the *Iliad* and the *Odyssey.* Later examples include *Beowulf,* Vergil's *Aeneid,* John Milton's *Paradise Lost,* and Edmund Spenser's *Faerie Queene. See also* Gilgamesh Epic.

Epicanthic Fold, or Mongolian eyefold, downward and inward fold of the upper eyelid over the inner corner of the eye, producing the so-called "slant" eye characteristic of numerous peoples of Asiatic origin, some American Indians, and the Khoisan groups of Southern Africa.

Epicenter, the spot on Earth's surface directly above the focus of an earthquake. Depending on the character of the focus, the epicenter may be a small circle or a line. *See also* Focus, Earthquake.

Epictetus (*c.* 50– *c.* 138), Greek Stoic philosopher. His teachings were recorded in *Discourses* and *Enchiridion* by his disciple, Arrian. An admirer of Socrates and Diogenes, he stressed the brotherhood of man, influencing Christian thought.

Epicureanism, school of Greek philosophy founded by Epicurus in the late 4th century BC. Opposing the idealistic and skeptical mood of the times, Epicurus wanted to provide security in an unsure world. He grounded his system on the uncontestability of sense experience; pleasure and pain are the ultimate good and evil. Intelligent choice is necessary for the good life. Under the Roman Empire, Epicureans chose to withdraw from view and the last known member of the school was Diogenes of Oenoanda (*fl.* 200 AD).

Epicurus (341–270 BC), Greek philosopher, founder of the Epicurean school. Although only fragments of his works remain, his loyal disciples passed on his doctrines of friendship, peace of mind, and spiritual enjoyment as goals of the good life. *See also* Epicureanism.

Epidemic, uncontained and rapid spread of a disease through a general population. The study of epidemics concerns itself with causes and patterns of contagion and methods of containing disease. Black plague, smallpox, and typhoid have been causes of historic epidemics; hepatitis, influenza, venereal disease are present concerns of epidemiologists.

Epidermis, outer layer of skin that contains no blood vessels. It is made up of two cell layers, including the outer, horny *stratum corneum* that protects the delicate underlayers from injury and infection and the inner *stratum germinativum* containing cells to replace sloughed off outer cells and the pigments responsible for skin color. A boundary membrane separates the epidermis from the dermis.

Epigram, A Greek word meaning "inscription." In classical literature, the term refers to a brief Greek or Latin poem expressing, in a pointed or witty fashion, one single thought.

Epilepsy, cerebral disorder characterized by disturbances in consciousness, motor and sensory functions, often accompanied by convulsions. Causes of epilepsy are not clearly understood but are believed by some to be related to minute brain lesions. Seizures usually first manifest themselves in children between 3 and 15 years old, slightly more often in males. They are divided into several categories, the most familiar being grand mal, petit mal, and pyschomotor. Grand mal seizures, up to five minutes long, may anticipate their onset with so-called auras, and may involve calling out, loss of consciousness, loss of muscular control. Petit mal attacks are shorter, up to 30 seconds duration, and milder, although there may be an almost unnoticeable loss of consciousness. Psychomotor attacks last up to two minutes, with confusion of motor and sensory abilities evident. Treatment calls for minimizing brain trauma if possible, anti-convulsant drugs, and education of the patient to lead as normal a life as possible. *See also* Aura.

Epinephrine, or adrenaline, hormone produced by the medulla of the adrenal glands. It is chemically a catecholamine, $C_6H_3(OH_2)CHOHCH_2NHCH_3$ and is secreted under conditions of stress to prepare the body for "flight or fight" by stimulating the blood flow and increasing the blood sugar level. Synthetic ephinephine, made from pyrocatechol, and the extract obtained from the adrenal glands of sheep and cattle are used in medicine.

Epiphany, Christian feast, celebrated on January 6th. It commemorates Christ's baptism, his presentation to the Magi, and his first miracle at the marriage feast at Cana.

Epiphyte, or air plant, plant that grows on another plant but is not a parasite. They usually have aerial roots and produce their own food by photosynthesis. Epiphytes are common in tropical forests. Examples are certain ferns, orchids, and Spanish moss.

Epirus (Epirusipeiros), province on mainland of NW Greece, bounded by Pindus Mts (E), Albania (N and W), Ionian Sea (S); Arta is the administrative center. This province occupies the S portion of a region known in ancient times as the home of the oracle of Dodona; united under Pyrrhus (3rd century BC); made a republic *c.* 200 BC and sided with Macedonia against Rome; plundered by Aemilius Paullus (AD 167) and subsequently occupied by Serbs, Albanians, Venetians, and Turks (1430); semi-independent state controlled by Ali Pasha of Albania (1788–1820); S Epirus passed to Greece 1881; N Epirus remains part of Albania. Industries: cattle, sheep, dairy products, olives, citrus fruit, rice. Pop. 310,344.

Episcia, genus of perennial plants native to South America, with trailing stems, hairy leaves and single flowers of red, purple, or white. There are about 30 species, many grown as houseplants. Family Gesneriaceae.

Epistemology, branch of philosophy that critically examines the nature, limits, and validity of knowledge or belief, at one time contrasted with metaphysics and logic. Beginning with the work of Descartes, in the 17th century it was recognized that many previously "philosophical" questions would be better studied scientifically, and what remained of metaphysics was absorbed into epistemology. *See also* Descartes; Logic; Metaphysics.

Epistles, 21 writings forming a section of the New Testament; more than half are attributed to Paul. The Epistle to the Romans contains the single most complete formulation of Paul's teachings. Written in response to problems facing the first Christian congregations, some contained instructions to specific communities, others were directed to all Christians.

Epithalamium, nuptial poem, usually lengthy and serious in tone, written to honor a bride and bridegroom and pray for their prosperity. The form was perfected by the classical poets Sappho, Anacreon, Pindar, Theocritus, and Catullus. The most famous examples in English literature are Edmund Spenser's "Epithalamion" and "Prothalamion."

Epithelium, the protective membrane that covers every surface of the body that might come into contact with foreign matter. Thus, epithelium covers not only the skin, but various internal organs and surfaces such as the intestines, nasal passages, and mouth. There are various types of epithelial cells, including ciliated, columnar and squamous or flattened. Membranes may be one cell layer thick or many layers such as on the skin. Epithelial cells may also produce protective modifications such as hair and nails, or secrete substances such as fat.

Epoch. *See* Geologic Time.

Epodes, collection of 17 poems of varying length, written by the Roman poet Horace and appearing in 30 BC. Modeled to some extent on the poems of Archilochus, *Epodes* also reflects the influence of Catullus. These poems contain Horace's first attempts at impassioned political commentary.

Epoxy, any of a group of thermosetting polymers with outstanding mechanical and electrical properties, stability, heat and chemical resistance, and adhesive qualities. Used in casting and protective coatings. Popular epoxy glues are sold in two separate components, a viscous resin and an amine or anhydride hardener, which are mixed just before use.

Epsom Salts, hydrated forms of magnesium sulfate found in nature in the mineral epsomite and in mineral waters and used in medicine as a cathartic.

Epstein, (Sir) Jacob (1880–1959), English sculptor, b. New York City. After studying in Paris, he went to England where he became a citizen in 1907. His works include controversial monumental sculptures and bronze portraits. Among his famous works are "Rima" (1925; London, Hyde Park) and an alabaster "Adam" (1939; Blackpool).

Equal Rights Amendment (ERA), proposed amendment to the US Constitution, passed by Congress in 1972. It must be ratified by 38 states to become the 27th amendment. The amendment states first that "equality of rights under the law shall not be denied or abridged by the United States or by any State on account of sex" and secondly, "Congress shall have the power to enforce, by appropriate legislation, the provisions of this article." The proposed amendment provoked great controversy between pro- and anti-ERA groups in the United States and was not ratified by its June 30,1982, deadline. The amendment was reintroduced in Congress that same year.

Equation, mathematical statement that two expressions are identical. An equation of the form $x^2 = 8 - 2x$ is true only for certain values of x ($x = 2$ or $x = -4$). These values are the solutions of the equation. This type of equation is contrasted with an *identity,* such as $(x + 2)^2 = x^2 + 4x + 4$, which is true for all values of x. Equations are classified in various ways: the highest power of the variable (2 in the case above) is the degree of the equation. Equations are said to be linear, quadratic, cubic, quartic, etc. according to whether their degree is 1, 2, 3, 4, etc. *See also* Differential Equation; Simultaneous Equations.

Equator, imaginary circle on the Earth's surface that lies midway between the North and South poles and is the zero line of terrestrial latitude. It divides the Earth into the Northern and Southern hemispheres.

Equatorial Currents, the parts of the North and South Atlantic and Pacific gyres that flow near the equator. As they move west, their waters warm and begin to deflect either north or south in a clockwise or counterclockwise direction. Nearer the equator is the Equatorial Countercurrent, which flows east between the North and South Equatorial Currents.

Equatorial Guinea, Republic of, nation in W Africa. The people are Negroid and mostly Roman Catholic. As one of the emerging African nations, it is striving to stabilize its place in the world economic picture.

Land and Economy. The country consists of Bioko (formerly Fernando Pó) in the Gulf of Guinea, Rio Muni prov. on the mainland facing the Gulf, and Pagalu Island (Annabon), less than 7sq mi (18sq km) in area and located 370mi (596km) SW in the Atlantic. The hot, humid climate supports an agricultural economy; the main products are coffee, cacao, and timber. Libreville on Bioko and Port Gentil on the coast of Rio Muni are the major ports.

People. There are two principal ethnic groups: Bubis, who occupy Bioko and Fangs, who occupy Rio Muni. Most of the people are Roman Catholic although a large number still practice animism. Spanish is the official language, but a large number of African languages are also spoken.

Government. The constitution of 1973 was suspended in 1979, when the military seized control of the government. The Supreme Military Council, led by Lt. Col. Teodoro Obiang Mbasogo ruled by decree until 1982 when a new constitution set Mbasogo's term at 7 years and allowed Assembly elections in 1983.

History. Originally a Spanish colony, the country began a movement toward independence in 1960 with local elections. Greater autonomy was achieved in 1964, followed by complete independence in 1968. In 1969 most of the Spanish left the area to avoid confrontation with the indigenous inhabitants. Equatorial Guinea is a member of the Organization of African Unity and the United Nations. Francisco Macias Nguema seized emergency powers in 1969, declaring himself president for life in 1972. Under his increasingly brutal regime, thousands fled the country. He was deposed in a military coup in 1979 and subsequently executed.

PROFILE

Official name: Republic of Equatorial Guinea
Area: 10,831sq mi (28,005sq km)
Population: 354,000
Density: 33per sq mi (13per sq km)

Episcia

Jacob Epstein's St Michael

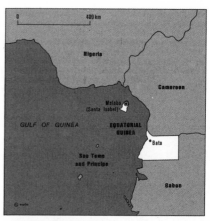

Equatorial Guinea

Chief city: Malabo (capital)
Government: Republic
Religion: Roman Catholic
Language: Spanish (official)
Monetary unit: Peseta
Gross national product: $70,000,000
Per capita income: $240
Industries (major products): negligible
Agriculture (major products): cacao, coffee, timber, palm oil, bananas
Trading partners (major): Spain

Equidae, horse family including one genus, *Equus,* with five subgenera—true zebra, Grevy's zebra, Asiatic wild ass, African wild (and domestic) ass, and wild (and domestic) horse. Class Mammalia; order Perrissodactyla. *See also* Horse.

Equigravitational Point, the point between two celestial bodies, such as Earth and Moon, at which the sum of the two gravitational forces is zero. A space vehicle reaching this point will begin to be accelerated toward the body it is approaching.

Equilateral Triangle, triangle having all three of its sides equal in length; the three interior angles will also be equal and each of magnitude 60°. *See also* Triangle.

Equilibrium, in economics, position that it is natural to move toward and that, if all things remain equal, there is no tendency to move from. In economics, an equilibrium for the economy as a whole is a position at which the total demand for goods and services equals the total supply of those goods and services. At this position there tends to be neither inflationary pressures nor recessionary tendencies. An equilibrium of supply and demand is a position where market price is set such that the quantity that producers are willing to produce equals the quantity that consumers are willing to buy.

Equilibrium Constant, constant characterizing the chemical equilibrium of a particular reversible reaction at a specified temperature. *See also* Chemical Equilibrium.

Equilibrium of the Firm, in the economics theory of the firm, position at which the firm maximizes its profit position. A business firm maximizes profit by equating marginal revenue and marginal cost. When the firm produces that output at which the addition to revenue for the last unit produced is equal to the addition to cost for the last unit produced, the firm is in an equilibrium position. The firm has no tendency to move from this equilibrium, and it will always expand output to reach this position or contract output to reach this position. *See also* Firm, Theory of.

Equilibrium Price. *See* Market Equilibrium.

Equilibrium Sense, or vestibular sense, human ability to remain upright in relation to gravity and to detect changes in position and momentum. The principal organs of equilibrium are contained in the inner ear—the utricle, which transmits orientation information, and the semicircular canals, which are concerned with acceleration and deceleration. These systems help humans locate their bodies in space.

Equine Encephalitis, a virus-caused disease associated with a similar disease in horses, in the United States divided into Eastern and Western equine encephalitis. Both seem to attack the very young (under one year) more than other age groups, with the Eastern variety also affecting the very old. Symptoms include headache, drowsiness, vomiting, and, later, muscular twitching and convulsions. Treatment is usually symptomatic.

Equinox, one of the points at which the ecliptic intersects the equator, called the vernal equinox as the sun crosses the equator moving north (on or about March 21) and the autumnal equinox as the sun moves south (on or about September 21).

Equity, in economics, the value of an item less any amount owed on it. Equity normally refers to the difference between a firm's assets and its liabilities. As the asset value increases relative to liabilities, the equity is greater.

Equity, in law, a field of jurisdiction that involves the application of morals to the interpretation of the law. It is a sense of fairness and justness applied to the court's decision.

Equivalence Principle, principle that energy and mass are equivalent according to the equation $E = mc^2$ (c is the velocity of light). *See also* Relativity Theory.

Equivalent, Electrochemical. *See* Electrochemical Equivalent.

Era. *See* Geologic Time.

Erasistratus (*c.*300–250 BC), Greek physician. He made important discoveries concerning the heart and brain, among which were his description of the heart valves, his idea of the heart as a pump, and his detailed studies of the brain and the linking of brain convolutions with increasing complexity in the brain.

Erasmus, Desiderius (*c.*1466–1536), Dutch scholar, considered the greatest of the Renaissance humanists. The illegitimate son of a priest named Gerard, he himself was ordained a Catholic priest (1492). He traveled much, including six visits to England, where he became a friend of Thomas More. The first edition of his *Adages* (1500) brought him fame. In 1501 he published his version of Cicero's *De officiis,* the first of many classical works he edited. His *Enchiridion militis (Manual of the Christian Knight)* (1503) emphasized simple piety as an ideal of Christianity and called for reform of the church. *The Praise of Folly* (1509) is a satire on human nature. Beginning in 1514 he worked with the publisher Johann Froben in Basel, publishing *Novum Instrumentum* (1516), his important Latin translation of the Greek New Testament, and a number of editions of the Christian Church Fathers, notably Jerome (1516). His *Colloquies,* satirizing church and society, appeared in 1518. His works had an early influence on Luther and other Protestant reformers, but he himself sought change from within the Catholic church and found the course of the Reformation at least as upsetting as the faults of the Catholic church that he had criticized. In *On Free Will* (1524) he openly clashed with Luther. *See also* Humanism.

Erbium, metallic element (symbol Er) of the lanthanide group, first isolated in 1843 by C.G. Mosander. Chief ores are monazite (a phosphate) and bastnasite (fluorocarbonates). The element is used in some specialized alloys and erbium salts are used as pink colorants for glasses. Properties: at. no. 68; at. wt. 167.26; melt. pt. 2,772°F (1,522°C); sp gr 9.045 (25°C); boil. pt. 4,550°F (2,510°C); most common isotope Er[166] (33.-41%). *See also* Lanthanide Elements.

Erfurt, city in East Germany, on Gera River; capital of Erfurt district. One of Germany's oldest cities, first mentioned by St Boniface in 8th century. Martin Luther lived here as Augustinian Monk 1505–1508; scene of Congress of Erfurt (1808); site of Krämerbrücke (Merchants' Bridge, 1325) across Gera River, 15th-century cathedral, Governor's palace. Industries: commercial flower growing, optical instruments, precision tools. Pop. 203,974.

Erg, the unit of energy in the metric centimeter-gram-second (cgs) system of units. One erg is the work done by a force of one dyne acting through a distance of one centimeter. One joule equals 10,000,000 ergs.

Ergonomics, the application of psychological principles to man-machine systems. Ergonomics involves the design of machines, tools, and work areas to better fit human physiological and psychological limitations.

Ergot, fungus (*Claviceps*) disease of rye plants and other small grasses. Part of the fungal body contains alkaloids that are generally poisonous to man but when purified and in appropriate doses can be used medicinally—ergotamine to treat migraine headaches, ergonovine to induce uterine contractions to eject the afterbirth.

Erhard, Ludwig (1897–1977), German statesman and economist, largely responsible for West German economic recovery after World War II. Succeeding Konrad Adenauer as chancellor (1963–66), he resigned because of economic and administrative troubles and was made honorary chairman of the Christian Democrats.

Eric IX Jedvarsson (died 1160), king of Sweden, patron saint of Sweden. He led a crusade against pagan Finland (1157). He was killed by a Danish prince while attending mass. His feast day is May 18.

Ericson, Leif (*fl.* 1000), Norse explorer, son of Eric the Red. According to Norse sagas, he discovered and wintered in Vinland on the North American continent (*c.*1000). He was on a voyage from Norway to bring Christianity to Greenland and was blown off course. The lack of archeological evidence casts doubt on Vinland's location, but a probable site is Newfoundland. *See also* Vinland.

Ericsson, John (1803–89), US inventor, b. Sweden. He came to the United States in 1839 to build ships for the navy. During the Civil War, he constructed a new type of ironclad ship, the *Monitor.* The battle between the *Monitor* and the Confederate ironclad ship *Merrimack* made him a Union hero.

Eric the Red (950?–1000?), Norse explorer and discoverer of Greenland. Exiled from Norway and Iceland for manslaughter, Eric, on voyage of discovery, found Greenland (982). After three years there, he was able to bring colonists from Iceland to establish permanent settlements (986).

Eridu, ancient Sumerian city and modern site of Abu Shahrein, S Iraq. Iraqi excavations (1946–49) indicated that Eridu dates from 5000 BC, making it the oldest settlement in S Mesopotamia; site of temples ornately adorned in silver, and lapis lazuli and painted pottery dating from 3500 BC.

Erie, city in NW Pennsylvania, on Lake Erie; seat of Erie co. Site was first occupied by French in 1753 as Fort Presque Isle; occupied by British 1760; Commodore Perry launched fleet here for Battle of Lake Erie (1813); site of restoration of Perry's flagship *Niagara,* and Presque Isle State Park. Pennsylvania's only port on Great Lakes. Exports: lumber, coal, iron ore, petroleum, grain, fish. Industries: meters, boilers, plastics, paper. Inc. 1851. Pop. (1980) 119,123.

Erie, Lake, one of the Great Lakes, bordered W by Ontario, Canada, E by New York, S by Ohio and Pennsylvania, SW by Michigan; part Great Lakes-St Lawrence Seaway system. It is the shallowest and second smallest of the Great Lakes. Industrial centers on its shores have seriously polluted the lake, but government regulation has stimulated its recovery somewhat. Discovered in 1669 by the French explorer Louis Jolliet; British and French fought for its possession and then British and US forces. In the battle of Lake Erie during War of 1812, Oliver Perry led a successful naval engagement against the British. Area: 9,910sq mi (25,667sq km). Depth (max.): 210ft (64m).

Erie Canal, historic waterway in New York state, now part of the New York State Barge Canal. It provides an inland water route from the Hudson River (at Albany) westward to Lake Erie (at Buffalo), following generally the Mohawk River Valley. The need for a water route connecting the eastern seaboard with the Great Lakes was recognized in the 18th century, and the Mohawk Valley was seen as a logical route. After efforts to get federal financing failed, the New York State legislature in 1817 agreed to finance the canal's building, and work was begun. De Witt Clinton, who became governor that year, was its chief promoter. A great engineering feat of its day, the canal made use of numerous locks and aqueducts in the course of its 363-mi (584-km) length. It was finally completed in 1825 and was an immediate success. The Erie Canal formed the chief route for the migration of settlers to the Middle West and was the route by which agricultural products were shipped E and manufactured products were shipped W. It was widened and deepened several times. The canal brought an economic boom to all of New York state, and its success caused a spate of canal building in other parts of the country. With the coming of the railroads around 1850, the importance of the Erie Canal lessened, and it fell into disrepair. In 1903, however, it was incorporated into the New York State Barge Canal system. It was repaired and modernized, and once again took its place as an important commercial route.

Erie Indians, also known as the Cat Nation, a sedentary tribe of Iroquoian-speaking North American Indians once occupying N Ohio, W New York, and NW Pennsylvania. Once numbering 15,000 persons, they were almost wiped out in a bloody war with the Iroquois in 1653–56; the few hundred survivors were incorporated into the Seneca tribe, mostly living in Oklahoma today.

Erikson, Erik H(omburger) (1902–), US psychoanalyst, b. Germany. He extended Freudian theory into adolescence and adulthood, coining the term *identity crisis.* He emphasizes social relationships, however, rather than sexual needs, as the key to growing up. He also has done much to encourage the psychoanalytic study of historical personages in such works as *Young Man Luther* (1958), *Gandhi's Truth* (1969, Pulitzer Prize 1970), and *Toys and Reasons* (1977).

Eritrea, province in N Ethiopia, on Red Sea; capital is Asmara; chief ports are Assab and Massawa; under control of Ethiopia until taken by Ottoman Empire 16th century; during 19th century Ethiopia fought Egypt and Italy for control of Eritrea, but Italy claimed it after 1890, using it as base for capturing Ethiopia 1935. Since 1962 Eritrea has been part of Ethiopia. Eritrean separatists did not accept the union, and fighting between Eritrean nationalists and Ethiopian troops became particularly savage in the mid-1970s. Area: 48,000sq mi (124,320sq km). Pop. 1,947,600.

Ermine, small, slender-bodied mammal called a stoat in Eurasia and short-tailed weasel in North America. Ermines have short black-tipped tails and a brown coat that turns white in winter. The dense, silky winter coat has lost some of its commercial popularity. Length: 9 in (230mm); weight: to 10 oz (280g). Family Mustelidae; species *Mustela erminea. See also* Weasel.

Ernakulam, city in S India, on Malabar coast; site of numerous colleges, and Jewish community reputedly founded 2nd-3rd centuries. Industries: fishing, kerosene, lumber, perfume, soap. Pop. 213,811.

Ernst, Max (1891–1976), German painter and sculptor. Founder of a Dada group in Cologne (1919), he later became prominent in the surrealist movement. He used paintings and collages and developed the form known as frottage, in which rubbings are made on paper held over various textured surfaces, to express his often fantastic visions. His most outstanding sculptures are bronzes done since the early 1940s.

Eros, in Greek mythology, the god of love. A winged child, he was the youngest of the gods and the son of Aphrodite. He was known for the pranks he played on both men and the gods.

Eros, asteroid discovered in 1898 by C. G. Witt. It has an irregular shape. In 1931 and 1975 it approached to within 14,000,000 mi (23,000,000 km) of the Earth. Mean diameter 17mi (29km); mean distance from Sun 144,000,000mi (232,000,000km); mean sidereal period 1.76 yr.

Erosion, in geology, the degradative alteration of landforms by the transportation of the debris of the earth via wind, water, glacial movement, gravity, and living organisms. Economically, erosion may have disastrous results as in the blowing away of topsoil or the weathering of man-made structures, or the alteration of water systems. *See also* Denudation.

Eruption, the appearance of volcanic materials on the earth's surface either on land or under sea. Any volcanic material constitutes an eruption, whether it is violent or simply leaking of laval material from volcanic fissures. Any constructive process resulting in the appearance of new material is also eruptive.

Erysipelas, contagious skin infection caused by a streptococcus organism. Symptoms include chills and fever, followed by well-delineated, elevated areas of the skin, which become red, shiny, and appear swollen.

Erythema, redness of skin caused by congestion of the capillaries, sometimes as a result of infection. Redness appears first on the face, usually lasts a week.

Erythrocyte, the yellowish, usually disk-shaped, nonnucleated vertebrate red blood cell containing the pigment hemoglobin that carries oxygen to the tissues and gives the blood its red color. Normal human blood contains about 5,000,000 such cells per cubic millimeter of blood on the average, but the number is somewhat higher in men and somewhat lower in women.

Erythromycin, generic name of an antibiotic used to treat infections caused by streptococci, staphylococci, pneumococci and other gram-positive bacteria.

Erzgebirge (Krusnehory or **Ore Mountains),** range extending about 95mi (153km) along the Czechoslovakian-East German border. Uranium, lead, zinc, wolframite, tin, copper, bismuth, antimony, arsenic are the chief ores mined. Highest peak is Klínovec, 4,080ft (1,244m).

Erzurum, city in NE Turkey, near source of the Kara Su River, on Turkish-Russian rail line; capital of Erzurum prov.; site of strategic military station, First Nationalist Congress (July 1919), Atatürk University; trade and agricultural center. Founded 5th century as Theodosiopolis; captured 1071 by Seljuks, 1515 by Turks, and 1828, 1878, and 1916 by Russians. Industries: processed food, cement, metal works. Pop. 162,925.

Esarhaddon, King of Assyria (*c.*681–669 BC), son of Sennacherib. He crushed revolts and defeated the Chaldaeans, who ruled Babylon. He conquered Egypt (675–669 BC) and overpowered Elam. His son Ashurbanipal succeeded him.

Esau, or **Edom,** son of Isaac and Rebecca, who sold his birthright to his twin brother Jacob. Isaac was then tricked into giving the blessing he meant for Esau to Jacob. Esau settled on Mt Seir and became the leader of the Edomites, a tribe in constant conflict with the Jews.

Escalator, a moving staircase, electrically powered, driven by chain and sprocket, and held in the correct plane by two tracks. Usually inclined at 30° and limited to rise to 60ft(18m). As the tracks approach the landing, they pass through a protective comb device. It is used as transportation between floors in mass pedestrian areas such as department stores, office buildings, and subways. The Otis Elevator Company exhibited the first escalator in 1900 at the Paris Exhibition.

Escape Velocity, Rocket, velocity required to free a rocket of the gravitational field of a celestial body or stellar system. Escape velocities for the Earth (7 miles per second); Moon (1.5mps); and solar system (25mps at the position of the Earth's orbit) can be calculated from the formula $v = (2GM/R)^{1/2}$, where G is the gravitational constant, M the mass of the planet or system, and R the distance of the rocket from the center of mass of the system.

Escarpment, or scarp, steep slope of a continuous cliff face or a plateau. Loosening of less-resistant rock by wind or water produces spectacular cliff faces such as the Grand Canyon. Escarpments are produced by faulting and differential erosion. *See also* Faulting.

Eschatology, branch of systematic theology, the study of final, last things. The term was first used in the 19th century with the critical analysis of the New Testament. It deals not only with the study of the kingdom of God, but also with the final destiny of mankind.

Escobedo v. Illinois (1964), landmark US Supreme Court decision. It overturned the conviction of a man who had been denied assistance of his attorney during police interrogation and who subsequently confessed to murder. The court held that an accused must be permitted to consult with his attorney "when the process shifts from investigatory to accusatory." This case and *Miranda v. Arizona* (1966) were indicative of Chief Justice Warren's concern for police abuse and his faith in the adversary system of justice. *See also* Miranda v. Arizona (1966).

Escondido, city in S California, 28mi (45km) N of San Diego. Industries: avocado processing, textiles. Inc. 1888. Pop. (1980) 62,480.

Escorial, Museums of, Spanish art museums, 30mi (48.3km) NW of Madrid. The enormous San Lorenzo del Real monastery was begun in 1563 by Philip II as a church, monastery, and royal burial chamber and houses many works of Spanish art. Its church contains a huge high altar and 42 smaller altars as well as sculpture and paintings by Spanish and Italian artists of Philip's era. Decorations of later periods reflect the Mannerist and Baroque styles. The complex contains such items as manuscripts, enamels, goldwork, ivories, and tapestries.

Esdras, two books of the Bible, the first being the beginning of the Apocryphal books. Esdras I includes parts of Chronicles II, Ezra, and Nehemiah. Esdras II, also known as the Ezra Apocalypse, is the product of Jewish and Christian apocalyptic thought and uses the typical imagery of apocalyptic literature. *See also* Apocrypha.

Eshkol, Levi (1895–1969), prime minister of Israel (1963–69), b. as Levi Shkolnik in Ukraine. He went to Palestine as a Zionist and established one of the first kibbutzim (cooperative farms). After Israel's independence (1948) he became minister of finance (1952–53), succeeded David Ben-Gurion as prime minister, and created the Israel Labor party.

Esker, sand and gravel ridge of fairly gentle slope. It is the result of debris carried by streams that run under or through an old, almost stationary glacier or a retreating one. *See also* Erosion; Faulting.

Eskimo, from Abnaki *Eskimantsic,* and Ojibwa *Askkimey,* meaning "eaters of raw flesh." Inhabitants of arctic and subarctic regions, these Mongoloid latecomers into North America are not regarded by anthropologists as actually American Indians, due to the cultural and linguistic differences they have developed. Their language is distinct from all other aboriginal Americans, and is related only to the Aleut. Today some 25,000 live in Alaska, 15,000 in Canada, and about 40,000 in Greenland. These people have adapted themselves particularly well to the harsh climate of the Far North, and are famous for their marine and mechanical skills. *See also* Aleut.

Eskisehir, city in NW central Turkey; capital of Eskisehir prov.; site of ancient Phrygian city of Dorylaeum. Industries: farm and railroad equipment, refined sugar, cement. Pop. 258,266.

Esophagus, a part of the digestive system, a muscular tube that connects the pharynx to the stomach. A series of involuntary muscular contractions (peristalsis) of the walls of the esophagus move food along from the pharynx to the stomach. Secretions of the mucous lining of the esophagus provide lubrication.

ESP. *See* Extrasensory Perception.

Espalier, a tree or shrub trained to grow flat against a wall, fence, or other support. Espaliered trees are often grown in closely planted rows to form attractive symmetrical patterns. In North America, espaliers are grown chiefly for ornament, but in Europe it was long customary to espalier entire orchards for high yields per acre.

Esparto, or needlegrass, coarse grass with sharply pointed grains and long bristles, used in Mediterranean region for ropes, cord, and paper. Height: to 3ft (0.9m). There are about 150 species. Family Gramineae; genera *Stipa* and *Lygeum.*

Erie Canal

Max Ernst: sculpture

Eskimo

Esperanto, artificial language devised in 1887 by the Polish linguist L.L. Zamenhof in the hope that it would eventually become the language of all of mankind. Its spelling and grammar are completely consistent, while its vocabulary is based mainly on that of Western European languages.

Espionage, theft of state secrets considered crucial to national security. Espionage is understood to be internationally practiced, although spying is classified as high treason by most governments. Military data is of the highest value, but political information also is important. While earlier espionage activities were generally conducted by individuals or small groups, modern espionage usually involves large spy networks utilizing advanced technological methods.

Esquirol, Jean (Etienne Dominique) (1772–1840), French pioneer in the humane treatment of the mentally disturbed. He drafted the law (1838) that established humane treatment in France, founded the first instructional clinic in psychiatry (1817), and wrote the first modern work on clinical psychology, *Les Maladies Mentales* (1838).

Essay, short, prose nonfictional composition on a particular subject, written from a limited, personal point of view. The essay form originated with the French writer Montaigne in the 16th century. Famous English essayists include Abraham Cowley, Francis Bacon (17th century); Addison and Steele, Henry Fielding, Dr. Samuel Johnson, Oliver Goldsmith (18th century); Charles Lamb (19th century). Noted US essayists include Ralph Waldo Emerson, Henry David Thoreau, Oliver Wendell Holmes (19th century). Noted essayists of the 20th century include Clarence Day, James Thurber, George Santayana, Agnes Repplier, Christopher Morley, and E. B. White.

Essen, city in W West Germany, on the Ruhr River, 18mi (29km) NNE of Düsseldorf; grew up around a 9th-century Benedictine convent; from 13th-18th centuries it was a small, imperial state ruled by abbess of convent. Prussia annexed it 1802; site of 11th-century cathedral. Industries: steel, glass, textiles, chemicals. Founded 9th century; chartered as city 10th century. Pop. 674,000.

Essenes, Jewish religious sect, which existed in Palestine from the 2nd century BC to the end of the 1st century AD. The members of the sect lived in communal groups, isolated from the rest of society. Sharing all possessions in common, they stressed ritual purity and were stricter than the Pharisees in their observance. A secrecy developed about the sect, and they shunned public life as well as temple worship. The Dead Sea Scrolls were probably their work.

Essequibo, longest river in Guyana, South America; rises in Serra Uaçari on E Brazil-W Guyana boundary; flows N to Atlantic Ocean, N of Georgetown; navigable for most of 630mi (1,014km).

Essex, Robert Devereux, 2nd earl of (1566–1601), English courtier and soldier. A dashing figure, he reached his peak of favor with Elizabeth I in 1596 after a successful attack on Cadiz. He was made earl marshall (1597) and was sent to Ireland as lord lieutenant (1599). His signing of an unauthorized truce with the Irish rebels provoked the queen's anger and his fall from favor. Unable to regain her affection, he led a rebellion (1601), which failed, and he was subsequently executed.

Essex, one of the seven kingdoms (the Heptarchy) of Anglo-Saxon England. It included modern London,

Middlesex, Essex, and much of Hertfordshire. In the 7th century it was merged with Mercia and came under Danelaw jurisdiction during the 8th and 9th centuries. *See also* Heptarchy.

Essex, county in SE England (reorganized 1974), bounded by North Sea and Thames; flat indented coastline with resorts, including Southend-on-Sea, and ports, including Harwich. Inland N is mainly agricultural, producing cereals and vegetables; some dairy farming in S. Towns in SW are part of Greater London. Other towns include Chelmsford and Colchester. Area: 1,528sq mi (3,958sq km). Pop. 1,410,900.

Estates-General, national assembly composed of separate divisions, or "estates", each representing, historically, a different social class. In France, the assembly was divided into three estates—clergy, nobility, and commoners—representing the three major divisions of European society before the French Revolution. From its establishment in 1302, the upper classes in the French assembly traditionally allied against the Third Estate. In 1789, however, the three estates united in their refusal to dissolve the assembly at the command of Louis XIV, thus precipitating the French Revolution. The Dutch parliament still retains the name States (Estates)-General. *See also* French Revolution.

Este, Italian aristocratic family that ruled in Ferrara (13th–16th centuries) and in Modena and Reggio (15th–18th centuries). An important Guelf family in support of the papacy through the Middle Ages, the Este decisively established their rule over Ferrara in 1240. With the rule of Niccolo III came control over much of Emilia. **Ercole I** (reigned 1471–1505) and his son, **Cardinal Ippolito I** (died 1520), were both patrons of the poet Ludovico Ariosto, who dedicated his *Orlando Furioso* to the cardinal. **Alfonso II** (reigned 1559–97) was the patron of the poet Torquato Tasso.

Ester, any of a class of organic compounds formed, along with water, by reaction between an alcohol and an acid. The commonest type, those formed by carboxylic acids, have the general formula RCO.OR'. Simple esters are fragrant volatile compounds, used as flavorings. Fats are esters of glycerin and long-chain carboxylic acids. *See also* Fat.

Esterházy Family, Magyar clan whose many prominent members since the 16th century contributed greatly to the histories of Austria and Hungary. Instrumental in freeing Hungary from the Turks, the Esterházys were noted for their military and political ability, as well as their generous patronage of such artists as Joseph Haydn.

Esther, biblical book that describes measures taken by Esther to avert the mass killing of her people, the Jews. It was Haman the Agagite who advised the Persian King that Jews were a pernicious race and received permission to undertake their annihilation. The feast of Purim, a Jewish holiday, usually in March, celebrates Haman's overthrow. This book is supposedly written by Mordecai, Esther's cousin and guardian.

Estivation, ability of certain organisms, including snails and some rodents, to spend the summer in a dormant state. It serves, in desert areas, as a survival mechanism during water and food shortages.

Estonia (Estonskaja), constituent republic of the USSR. It is a low plateau covered with glacial deposits and many lakes and has a mild climate. It is bordered W by the Baltic Sea, SW and N by Gulfs of Riga and Finland, S by Latvia, and E by the USSR. It extracts considerable amounts of shale oil and gas and has a

productive fertilizer industry. Pig-raising, fishing, and dairy-farming are major occupations in an economy that has been collectivized and integrated into the USSR since the late 1940s.

People and History. Members of the Finno-Ugrian family of peoples, Estonians reached the area in the beginning of the Christian era from the Volga region and intermarried with German settlers. Their culture is influenced both by the Germans and the Finns. Over 55% of the population is urban and about 35% belongs to the Lutheran Church. The Russian minority is over 20%. Pagan Estonian tribes were conquered in the 13th century by Danes and Germans. Christianity was introduced, and Estonian peasants came under the economic subjugation by Hanseatic merchants (1561). By 1629, Sweden held all of Estonia, which was conquered by Russia in 1710. By the mid-19th century nationalist rebellions started, were repressed, and heavy emigration to the United States followed. Russia's defeat in WWI led to the formation of an independent republic in 1918, an independence recognized by the USSR in 1920. A dictatorship established in 1934 gave Estonia more political stability, but the Nazi-Soviet Pact of 1939 placed the Baltic countries under USSR rule. The country was occupied by the Germans in WWII and retaken by Soviet forces in 1944.

PROFILE

Official name: Estonia Soviet Socialist Republic
Area: 17,431sq mi (45,100sq km)
Population: 1,357,000
Chief cities: Tallinn (capital); Tartu
Government: Constituent republic of USSR
Religion: Lutheran (major)
Language: Estonian
Industries: paper, plywood, textiles, fertilizers, electrical and radio apparatus, glass, leather goods, concrete, bricks, processed fish
Agriculture: fishing, timber, dairy cattle, hogs, flax, potatoes, sugar beets
Minerals: shale oil, natural gas, peat, limestone, dolomite, marl, clay, phosphorite

Estremadura (Extremadura), historic region in W central Spain, on the Portuguese border; crossed by Tagus and Guadiana rivers; includes provinces of Cáceres and Badajoz; battlefield during Spanish-Portuguese wars; birthplace of Francisco Pizarro and Hernán Cortéz. Industries: sheep and pig raising, lumber, silver, coal, copper, wine, oil, cereals. Pop. 1,145,376.

Estrogens, the female sex hormones, including estrone, ertradiol, and estriol. They control the menstrual cycle, prepare for fertilization and nourishment of the embryo, and determine the female secondary sex characteristics. Estrogens are produced in the ovaries, cortex of the adrenal glands, and testes and are also made synthetically. They are used in oral contraceptives and to treat the symptoms of menopause, threatened abortion, and many other conditions. Evidence suggests that long-term administration of estrogens, as well as increased levels of estrogens metabolized in the body, increase the risk of uterine and breast cancer.

Estrone, steroid hormone (formula $C_{18}H_{22}O_2$) formed from estradiol and found in pregnancy urine. It is one of the three estrogens but has less activity than estradiol. It is used in the treatment of menopausal symptoms. *See also* Hormones; Steroid.

Estrus Cycle, physiological changes occurring during the female reproductive cycle of most placental mammals. Controlled by hormones, it is evident among mammals other than man. Cycles of different animals vary in frequency and length. Typically, ovulation is associated with the estrus (heat) period.

Estuary, coastal region in which a river mouth opens into the ocean and greatly changes the salinity of the seawater. Estuaries are typified by the ratio of inflow to loss of fresh water or by shape. To some extent, an estuary is a drowned river mouth, or one whose access to open sea is partially blocked by offshore bars, spits, or sand islands.

Eta Meson, uncharged elementary particle (symbol η) that is a meson with zero spin. *See also* Hadron.

Etching, method of intaglio (incised) printing used especially for reproducing black and white designs. In this process, acid, which bites into a metal plate, is used to eat away the outlines of the design. When magnified, the etched line has almost square ends. The etching process allows a more freely drawn figure than does the engraving process.

First, the artist covers the metal plate, usually copper, with an acid-proof ground made of a mixture containing asphaltum. Next, the design is drawn onto the grounded plate with an etching needle so that the lines penetrate the ground. The plate is then placed in an acid that eats away the exposed line. To create shading, the etcher places an acid resist over the desired areas and once again immerses the plate to allow the acid to wear away the still exposed lines. When the plate is finished, it is rolled with ink and placed in an etching press to be printed. Corrections and changes can be made by covering the plate with a new ground and reworking it.

Ethanol, or ethyl alcohol, colorless volatile liquid (C_2H_5OH) produced by the fermentation of molasses, grains, etc, or by the catalytic hydrogenation of ethylene. Its many uses include beverages, cleaning solutions, rocket fuels, cosmetics, and pharmaceuticals. Properties: sp gr 0.789; melt. pt. -179.1°F (-117.3°C); boil. pt. 173.3°F(78.5°C).

Ethelbert (died 616), king of Kent, who came to power in 560. Although his attempt to extend his kingdom westward was thwarted in 568 by the West Saxons, by the late 6th century he was the strongest ruler in England south of the Humber River. The first Christian king in Anglo-Saxon England, he allowed Augustine and his monks to settle and preach in Canterbury and founded the see of Rochester.

Ethelred II (968–1016), king of England (978–1016), called the Unready (fr. OE without *rede* or counsel). He ascended the throne on the murder of his half brother, Edward the Martyr (978), and was soon beseiged by Danish plunderers. In 994 he began to pay off the raiders with money raised by the Danegeld, but the Danes returned nonetheless in 997. A massacre of Danes in 1001 brought only severe retaliation from the Danish king Sweyn and his successor, Canute.

Ether, colorless volatile flammable liquid ($C_2H_5OC_2H_5$) prepared by the action of sulfuric acid on ethanol followed by distillation. It is used as an anesthetic, industrial solvent, fuel additive, and refrigerant. This compound (diethyl ether) is a typical member of the ethers with the general formula ROR. Properties: melt. pt. -177.2°F (-116.2°C), boil. pt. 94.1°F (34.5°C).

Ether, the hypothetical medium that was supposed to fill all space, even inside matter, and to offer no resistance to motion. Postulated as a medium to support the propagation of electromagnetic radiations, it is now regarded as an unnecessary assumption.

Ethical Culture, Society for, association founded in the United States by Felix Adler in 1876. Adler broke with Judaism and Christianity, and developed a moral system that does not have to rely on a religious basis, the essential ethical rule being to live so as to evoke the best in others, and therefore in oneself.

Ethics, the study of human conduct in the light of moral principles; also called moral philosophy. Moral principles may be postulated on religious, political, or individual criteria. They may be thought to be innate or to evolve from experiential discrimination.

Ethiopia (Yaitopya), independent nation in E Africa. Ruled by Haile Selassie for 44 years until a coup deposed him in 1974, it is on the coast of E central Africa. Coptic Christians make up the largest religious group. The first known coffee plant was grown here.

Land and Economy: An inland country until federation with Eritrea in 1952, it is bounded by the Red Sea, Djibouti, Kenya, and Sudan. A high central plateau, 8,000ft (3,200m) above sea level, is cut by the Blue Nile and Rift Valley, dropping off to lowlands of Sudan (W) and Somali plains (SE). The climate ranges from temperate to humid, with a June-September rainy season. With 90% of the population in farming, the country is self-sufficient in food. The major export is coffee. Development of potash reserves is expected, and copper mining is underway. Development programs have been financed by foreign countries and international agencies.

People: Ethiopians are descended from two African tribes, the Hamite (Cushite) and Semite, and from Negroes dating from the 8th century BC. Amharic is the official language, but English is widely spoken. Literacy is estimated at 5%.

Government: Ruled since Haile Selassie's removal as a one-party socialist state, Ethiopia is ruled by a military government. Since 1976, Lt.-Col. Mengistu Haile Mariam has served as chairman of the provisional military administrative council.

History: The Old Testament records a visit to Ethiopia by the Queen of Sheba. Its ruling house is said to have descended from King Solomon's son. Modern history dates back to Menelik (reigned 1889–1913), whose line of succession led to Emperor Haile Selassie, crowned in 1930. His reign was interrupted by the 1936 Italian invasion. British troops freed the country in 1941. Selassie was deposed by a military junta in 1974; the new socialist government vowed to abolish the feudal land system, nationalize financial institutions, abolish the monarchy, and offer religious freedom. The government has been unable to unify the country. A secessionist guerrilla movement in the province of Eritrea escalated during the mid-1970s; by 1977 the rebels controlled most of the province but were brutally crushed by government forces the following year. In the early 1980s, however, sporadic fighting continued there and also in Tigre province. In the Ogaden region war erupted between the area's ethnic Somalis supported by Somali national troops and the Ethiopian army who with aid from Cuban troops were largely victorious. Drought, resulting in famine, struck in the 1980s. Worldwide attention brought aid and by the end of 1985 some rains had fallen, but hundreds of thousands had died and more than a million had fled the country.

PROFILE

Official name: Ethiopia
Area: 471,777sq mi (1,221,902sq km)
Population: 29,710,000
Density: 67per sq mi (26per sq km)
Chief cities: Addis Ababa (capital); Asmara
Government: Military junta
Religion: Coptic Christian
Language: Amharic
Monetary unit: Ethiopian dollar
Gross national product: $3,980,000,000
Per capita income: $88
Industries: food processing, cement, shoes, textiles, brick
Agriculture: coffee, wheat, barley, millet, tobacco, sugar cane, cattle, sheep, civet
Minerals: platinum, gold, silver, manganese, tin, asbestos, potash, sulphur, salt, coal, iron
Trading partners: United States, West Germany, Japan, Italy

Ethnocentrism, intense identification with one's own culture as the best. All human groups have a conscious and an unconscious tendency to assume the superiority of their own culture while devaluing other cultures and the unfamiliar. Ethnocentrism is an automatic, emotional response, not a rational one. *See also* Discrimination; Prejudice.

Ethnography, study of the culture of a single tribe or society. Ethnographers gather anthropological data by direct observation during a period of residential fieldwork. Techniques used include participation in the group's economic and social life, linguistic fluency, and interviews with informants. *See also* Anthropology; Ethnology.

Ethnology, the comparative study of cultures. Using ethnographic material from two or more societies, ethnology can attempt to cover their whole cultural range or concentrate on a single cultural trait. Originally a term covering the whole of anthropology, toward the end of the 19th century historical ethnology was developed in an attempt to trace cultural diffusion. Now ethnologists concentrate on cross-cultural studies, using statistical methods of analysis. *See also* Anthropology, Cultural; Ethnography.

Ethology, study of animal behavior, first outlined in the 1920s by Konrad Lorenz of Austria and Niko Tinbergen of the Netherlands. Ethologists study natural processes that range across all animal groups, such as the release and inhibition of innate behavior patterns. Field, rather than laboratory, observation is emphasized, but experimental models are used. Evolutionary and neuroanatomical studies are included.

Ethyl Alcohol. *See* Ethanol.

Etna, Mount (Mongibello), active volcano on E coast of Sicily, Italy; highest active volcano in Europe and highest mountain in Italy. Pindar and Aeschylus described the first known eruption (475 BC); major eruptions occurred in 1169, 1669, 1971; lower slopes are used for agriculture. Height: 10,958ft. (3,342m).

Etruria, ancient region in Italy, bounded by the Tiber River, Apennines, and Tyrrhenian Sea. Inhabitants migrated from Asia Minor *c.* 900 BC and divided into several city-states; Etruscan civilization peaked *c.* 500 BC; it was gradually taken over by Rome. Site of kingdom created by Napoleon AD 1801; inc. by French Empire 1808; commercially and agriculturally prosperous; celebrated for its art.

Etruscans, earliest inhabitants of Etruria NW of the Tiber (modern Tuscany) who came to prominence and dominated an extensive empire in central Italy by 500 BC, before the rise of Rome. The Etruscans formed a religious confederation of independent city-states with its center at Volsinii. Their origins remain obscure. They developed a vital culture, material artifacts of which show distinct characteristics that were derived from E Mediterranean and Greek sources. But much of their sophisticated metalwork, naturalistic sculpture (including the Capitoline wolf, bronze portrait busts, and painted terracotta sarcophagi), and funerary frescoes depicting everyday scenes and festivals reveal an energetic, individual style not directly based on any other tradition. Their language was entirely unlike those of the other early Italian peoples. Herodotus maintained that the Etruscans emigrated from Lydia in the 12th century BC. Modern scholarly opinion is divided as to their early development but it is certain that their civilization had attained cultural unity by the 7th century BC.

By 500 BC the Etruscans were at the zenith of their power, controlling Umbria, much of Latium, and colonies in the major islands of the Mediterranean and in coastal Spain. Rich in iron ore and clay, they exploited these materials to the fullest in their arts and carried on an extensive trade with the East. Their influence in the Mediterranean conflicted with Greek interests and diminished by the late 5th century BC. At the same time the Celts halted their northern expansion and the Samnites forced them from Campagna. The Romans, two of whose kings, Tarquinius Priscus and Tarquinius Superbus, were Etruscan, adopted many features of Etruscan art, religion, politics, and technology before they began in the 4th century to spread over Italy and vanquish Etruscan cities. Veii fell in *c.*396 BC, and Etruscan independence ended entirely in 88 BC, when the last families allied with Roman general Sulla against Marius.

Etymology, the branch of philology dealing with the history and derivation of words. The term also refers to the derivation of a given word. The etymology of the word *telephone,* for example, is that it is a combination of the Greek *tele* ("distant") and *phone* ("sound"). The word *coach,* by contrast, is derived from the city of Kocs, in Hungary, where coaches were invented and first used.

Euboea (Evvoia) mountainous island in SE central Greece, in Aegean Sea, separated from mainland by Euripos channel; 2nd-largest island in Greece, after Crete; Chalcis is the administrative center. Under Athenian domination 506–411 BC, taken by Philip II of Macedon 350–194 BC; after the fall of Rome, it was held successively by Byzantines, Venetians, and Turks (1470–1821); it was inc. into Greece after independence was declared (1830). Industries: livestock, grapes, timber, grains, marble quarries, lignite and magnesite mining. Area: 1,467sq mi (3,800sq km). Pop. 165,369.

Eucalyptus, group of trees native mainly to Australia and Tasmania and cultivated in warm and temperate regions. They are a valuable source of hardwood and oils. Generally, they have tall, slender trunks, sometimes covered with exuded gum; bluish or whitish leaves; petalless flowers with abundant nectar; and woody fruits. Height: to 300ft (91m). The 500 species include the Australian mountain ash *Eucalyptus dalryurpleana;* the Tasmanian blue gum *E. globulus;* and the coolabah tree *E. coolabah.* Family Myrtaceae.

Eucharist, Christian sacrament, the central rite of the mass or church service. It reenacts the Last Supper: Christ gave his disciples bread, saying, "This is my body," and wine, saying, "This is my blood."

Euchre, card game usually played by two sets of partners using a 32 card deck, from seven to ace in each suit. Each player receives five cards, and trump is then established by using a card from the deck or a trump nominated by a player. There are five tricks in each game, which count toward points. The team that establishes trump must win all five tricks to score two

Ethanol: rectification

Mount Etna: night eruption

Euonymus

points. Scoring three or four tricks counts as 1 point. If they fail to make three tricks, their opponents receive two points. It takes five points to make a game.

Euclid (330?–275 BC), Ancient Greek mathematician, about whom very little is known, except that he taught at Alexandria during the reign of Ptolemy. He is remembered for his text books on geometry, especially the *Elements,* which was first printed in 1482 in a Latin translation of the Arabic. Other works include *Data* (on geometry) and *Phaenomena* (on astronomy) and several books that have been lost.

Euclid, city in NE Ohio, on Lake Erie, adjacent to Cleveland; site of National American Shrine of Our Lady of Lourdes. Industries: multigraphing equipment, road machinery, airplane parts, castings. Settled 1798; inc. 1848. Pop. (1980) 59,999.

Euclidean Geometry, geometry based on similar assumptions to those used by Euclid (*c.*300 BC) in his book *Elements.* Euclid's geometry is a prime example of an axiomatic system of reasoning, although his original postulates have since been extended. He used a number of simple "definitions" of point, line, etc, together with a set of axioms, which he called "common notions." These concerned basic ideas about equality, of the type "the whole is greater than the part." Finally, he proposed five postulates on geometrical properties, including the famous fifth postulate on parallel lines. On these foundations, he built a vast structure of theorems on the properties of plane and solid figures. Euclid's geometry is the geometry that fits normal measurements made on Earth. *See also* Axiomatic Method; Non-Euclidean Geometry.

Eudoxia (1669–1731), Russian tsarina, was married to the warlike Tsar Peter I the Great in 1689. The marriage was unsuccessful, and she was sent to a monastery in 1698, which she secretly left. She was imprisoned and her lover tortured to death in 1718, but regained her freedom in 1727 after her grandson became tsar as Peter II.

Eugene, city in W Oregon, on Willamette River, 62mi (100km) S of Salem; seat of Lane co; headquarters of Willamette National Forest; site of University of Oregon (1872). Industries: meat packing, timber, fruit and vegetable canning. Settled 1851; inc. 1864. Pop. (1980) 105,624.

Eugene of Savoy (1663–1736), French prince and general in the service of the Holy Roman Empire. He entered Austrian service in 1683 and won distinction fighting the Turks at Vienna (1683), Belgrade (1688), and Zenta (1697). In the War of the Spanish Succession (1701–14), his victories over the French included Blenheim (1704), Oudenarde (1708), and Malplaquet (1709), all won with the English Duke of Marlborough. In 1714, Eugene negotiated the Peace of Rastatt. He again defeated the Turks in the war of 1714–18.

Eugene Onegin (1823–31), Romantic novel in verse by Aleksandr Pushkin. Composed in 14-line stanzas, the poem develops the character of Onegin as a prime example of the "superfluous man"—detached, arrogant, and cynical. Alternately bored and disgusted by high society, he is nevertheless unable to escape its restrictions.

Eugenics, movement founded in the 19th century by Francis Galton that proposed controlled improvement of the human race through selective breeding, ie, encouraging people with the best qualities to mate with each other while preventing criminals, the retarded, and the insane from mating. Galton concluded that

"geniuses" ran in families and were largely the products of superior heredity. Modern scientists, however, recognize that variations in environment are just as important in influencing differences as are variations in heredity.

Eugénie (1826–1920), consort of Napoleon III and French empress. Born of a Spanish father and American mother, she became the wife of Louis Napoleon shortly after he declared the second empire in 1853. Regent in her husband's absences (1859,1865,1870), her influence as a Catholic and conservative was often felt in French affairs. When the empire fell in 1870 she fled to England, where she became friends with Queen Victoria after her husband's death in 1873. Her only child, a son, was killed in 1879 in the Zulu War.

Euglena, flagellate protozoa found in fresh water. It has an elongated body that appears green because of the 15 or so chloroplasts in it; there is a characteristic "eyespot" and a single flagellum. It moves by beating the flagellum and by alternately elongating and contracting the body to produce a squirming motion. Length: 3/2500–4/250in (.03–.4mm). Most common is *Euglena gracilis.* Class Mastigophora.

Eulachon, or candlefish, marine smelt of inshore temperate waters or cold seas of Northern Hemisphere. It has oily flesh and was used by Indians to make torches. Length: 12in (30.5cm). Family Osmeridae; species *Thaleichthyes pacificus.*

Eulalia, tall perennial grass native to SE Asia and widely cultivated for lawn or border ornamentals. It has white, plumelike flower clusters and striped leaves. Species *Miscanthus sinensis.* Or, perennial grass of Australia and SE Asia important as forage. Genus *Eulalia.* Family Gramineae.

Euler Diagram, simple diagram used in logic to illustrate syllogisms. Classes of objects are represented by circles so that, for example, a premise of the type "some *a* is *b*" can be represented by overlap of these circles. *See also* Venn Diagram.

Eumenides, in Greek mythology, earth and fertility goddesses. They also had moral and social functions.

Eunuchoidism, a deficiency of testicular function which, before puberty, retards development of genitals, and of secondary sex characteristics (facial hair, deepening voice). It can also occur after puberty with milder effect.

Euonymus, genus of deciduous or evergreen shrubs and woody vines found in North America, Central America, Europe, and Asia. They have square twigs, short, narrow leaves and inconspicuous flowers. The fruits are orange-red. Height: 2–12ft (0.6–3.7m) Among 120 species are strawberry bush *Euonymus americanus,* burning bush *E. atropurpureus,* European spindle tree *E. europaeus,* and evergreen, climbing *E. fortuneii.* Family Celastraceae.

Euphrates (Firat, or **Al-Furat),** river formed by the confluence of the Murat Nehri (E) and the Kara Su (W), it flows from E Turkey across Syria into central Iraq where it joins the Tigris River. Mesopotamia, along the lower Euphrates, was the birthplace of the ancient civilizations of Babylonia and Assyria, and site of the ancient cities Sippar, Babylon, Erech, Larsa, Ur. Length: 2,235mi (3.598km).

Euripides, (*c.*484–406 BC), Greek playwright. Considered one of three great writers of Greek tragedy, with Aeschylus and Sophocles, he was a close friend of

Socrates, who may have influenced his writing. His plots were complicated; his ideas sometimes controversial and offensive; but his language was simple. His heroes, whether gods or mortals, are portrayed with sceptical candor. His contemporaries saw him as a morose misogynist. Only 18 of his 92 plays survive. His reputation grew after his death.

Europa, in Greek mythology, wife of Asterius, mother by Zeus of King Minos of Crete. She was carried off to Crete by Zeus, who was disguised as a white bull.

Europa, satellite of Jupiter; one of the Galilean satellites. Diameter 1,800mi (2,900km); mean distance from planet 414,000mi (670,600km); mean sidereal period 3.55 days.

Europe, western fifth of the Eurasian land mass, considered a separate continent. Of the continents only Australia is smaller.

    Land. Mainland Europe is a roughly triangular peninsula of Eurasia, wide where the Ural Mts form much of the E boundary and growing narrow as it reaches W to the Iberian Peninsula. The Caucasus Mts also help separate the continent from Asia and provide its highest peak, Elbrus (18,481ft; 5,637m). Other major ranges are the Apennines of Italy, the Pyrenees between France and Spain, the Kjølens of Scandinavia, and the Alps of W central Europe. Plains reach from W France across N Germany and Poland and over much of the USSR. Major islands of Europe include the British Isles, Sicily, Sardinia, Corsica, and Iceland. The Caspian and Black seas help to separate Europe from Asia. The Caspian is the world's largest lake, with an area of about 144,000sq mi (372,960sq km). Because of wide channels leading to the Mediterranean, the Black ranks as a sea rather than a lake. Europe's longest river, the Volga, drains into the Caspian Sea. Other important waterways are the Danube of central Europe and the Rhine and Rhône farther W.

    Lying mostly in the N temperate zone and being nearly surrounded by seas, such as the Mediterranean, North, Baltic, Norwegian, and Barents, Europe has a mild climate. The far N, the E, and parts of Spain suffer from little rainfall; but about 75% of the land supports pine, cedar, oak, and other forests. The far N consists of tundra. Wolves and bears are now scarce, but rabbits remain plentiful and deer survive in many places. Important for furs are fox, mink, and weasel. Birds include finches, thrushes, and grouse, but storks are becoming scarce. Eggs of the Caspian Sea sturgeon are world-famous as caviar.

    People. Southern Europeans are often short and dark; short, lighter people live in the central areas, and taller, fair ones occupy the N. People of the SE are often Greek Orthodox. Those of the S central and W, except for scattered examples, are Roman Catholic, and many of those N of France and Italy are Protestant. Major languages include Germanic tongues in the N, Slavic in the central and E, and Latin (Romance) in the W central and S.

    Economy. Many European farms are relatively small, raising a variety of crops—from beets and potatoes to wheat and rice. Grapes, olives, and citrus fruits flourish in the S. Scandinavia and the Low Countries are noted for dairy products. A few countries, especially the USSR, have petroleum, and iron ore is fairly common. Lead, zinc, manganese, and nickel are also found. European industry is highly developed, although the Mediterranean nations are somewhat less diversified.

    History. About 500 years before the Christian era, Greece had an advanced civilization, but by Christ's time the Romans flourished. After the fall of the Roman Empire in AD 476, warlike tribes fought for power. Crusades to take the Holy Land from the Muslims brought

Europeans in contact with Arabic medicine and culture, and late in the 13th century Christians ceased mounting Crusades and gradually launched a new age of learning and artistic achievement, the Renaissance. The development of printing from movable type in the 1450s increased the spread of information, which continued as Christopher Columbus and Vasco da Gama explored the seas and Martin Luther questioned Roman Catholic practices. In E Europe the Ottoman Turks built an empire, German Catholics held central Europe in the Holy Roman Empire, and in the W the English gained power, especially after defeating the Spanish Armada in 1588. The French Revolution at the end of the 18th century caused monarchs to worry about holding their thrones, a concern that continued as Napoleon Bonaparte undertook the conquest of Europe. After his defeat in 1815, European nations concentratedon empire building around the globe. Germany's growing strength helped lead to World War I (1914–18), and during that period of turmoil Communist revolutionaries overthrew the Russian monarchy. Aggressive dictators came to power in Germany and Italy, leading to World War II (1939–45), which revealed the USSR as a major power and left Europe divided between Communist and non-Communist ideologies. The free nations of W and S Europe have sought closer economic and political links through such organizations as the European Communities, which includes the European Economic Community. The Soviet-bloc countries have developed similar ties, although the establishment of an independent labor movement in Poland (1980) created some tensions in the region. Contacts between the two blocs have become more frequent and closer. In W Europe, Socialist and Communist politics have gained wider acceptance, and a Socialist-led government was elected in France in 1981. In Central and N Europe the commitment to neutralism remains strong.

PROFILE

Area: 3,700,000sq mi (9,583,000sq km)
Largest nations: USSR, European (1,940,000sq mi; 5,000,000sq km); France (211,207sq mi; 549,000sq km); Spain (194,897sq mi; 504,800sq km)
Population: 725,000,000
Density: 196per sq mi (75per sq km). Most populous nations: USSR, European, 241,700,000; Germany, West, 61,439,000; Italy, 56,160,000
Chief cities: Paris; Moscow; London
Manufacturing (major products): steel, automobiles, chemicals, airplanes, textiles
Agriculture (major products): wheat, oats, barley, sugar beets, grapes, dairy products
Minerals (major): petroleum, iron ore, lead, zinc, nickle, manganese, magnesium

European Atomic Energy Community (Euratom), since 1958 an organization of European countries to control and develop the nuclear energy capabilities of its member nations. Treating this energy as a resource of the entire European community, Euratom has facilitated international coordination of both manpower and materials.

European Deer. *See* Fallow Deer.

European Economic Community (EEC), the principal economic organization of the European Communities, devoted to regional integration of W and S Europe. The EEC, established in 1957, originally consisted of six members: Belgium, France, West Germany, Italy, Luxembourg, and the Netherlands; Denmark, Ireland, and the United Kingdom joined in 1973; Greece joined in 1981; and Spain and Portugal have applied for membership. The original purpose of the EEC was to eliminate tariffs between members and erect a common tariff barrier against non-members. The second stage saw the facilitation of free movement of goods, services, labor, and capital in a common market between members; in 1979 a common currency for exchange transactions was instituted. Members employ a common taxation system, the value-added tax. The Common Agricultural Policy (CAP) has consistently been the subject of greatest conflict within the community. Many other countries have associate status with the EEC.

European Free Trade Association (EFTA), organization of European countries established to facilitate free trade among its members. In 1981 the membership consisted of Austria, Iceland, Norway, Portugal, Sweden, and Switzerland; Finland was an associate member and Portugal had applied for membership in the European EconomicCommunity (EEC). EFTA was established in 1960. Its aims are similar to those of the larger EEC after which EFTA was modeled, although EFTA aims for a lesser degree of economic integration among members. In 1966 all tariff restrictions between members were lifted; by 1977 full tariff-free trade between EFTA and EEC members took place.

European Parliament, body consisting of 436 members representing the constituent nations of Belgium, Denmark, France, West Germany, Ireland, Italy, Luxembourg, the Netherlands, the United Kingdom, and Greece. The Parliament forms part of the permanent structure of the European Communities, along with a Council of Ministers, a Commission, and a Court of Justice. It meets in Luxembourg and Strasbourg, France.

European Water Snake. *See* Grass Snake.

Europium, metallic element (symbol Eu) of the lanthanide group, first isolated as the oxide 1901 by Eugène Demarçay. Chief ores are monazite (phosphate) and bastänite (fluorocarbonate). The metal is used in pyrophoric alloys and as a neutron absorber in reactors. Properties: at. no. 63; at. wt. 151.96; sp. gr. 5.25 (25° C); melt. pt. 1519°F (826°C); boil. pt. 2622°F (1439°C); most common isotope Eu^{153} (52.18%). *See also* Lanthanide Elements.

Eurydice, in Greek mythology, the wife of Orpheus. In fleeing from Aristaeus she was mortally bitten by a snake. Orpheus pursued her to the Underworld and persuaded Hades to release Eurydice. They made a bargain that Orpheus broke when he turned to look at his wife before emerging to earth. Eurydice was whisked back to Hades forever.

Eustachian Tube, a mucous-lined tube that connects the middle ear and the nasopharynx and functions to equalize internal and external pressure. It sometimes carries infection from the throat to the middle ear.

Euthanasia, the action of inducing the painless death of a person for reasons assumed to be merciful.

Eutrophication, the process by which a lake or stream becomes rich in inorganic nutrients by natural or artificial means. Compounds of nitrogen, phosphorus, iron, sulfur, and potassium are vital for plant growth, but in excess, the growth of algae and other aquatic weeds is overstimulated and the waterway becomes choked with algal growth or bloom. Since all living things need oxygen, the use of it by the aquatic weeds deprives other biota and results in a net decrease of oxygen affecting all the plant and animal life in that water. Turbulence aerates water, increasing oxygen content.

Evangelicalism, popular movement within Protestantism, emphasizing the God-given directive to preach the Word. Scripture is central to faith and gives direction to men's lives. Evangelists stress the basic evil nature of man. Influenced by Martin Luther, they believe that justification is through faith alone.

Evans, (Sir) Arthur John (1851–1941), English archeologist who excavated the ruins of the city of Knossos in Crete, and found evidence of a Bronze Age civilization which he named the Minoan Age. He authored *The Palace of Minos* (4 vols., 1921–35).

Evans, Dame Edith (1888–1976), British stage and screen actress. While with the Old Vic (1925–26; 1936) she played a variety of roles, including Katharina in *The Taming of the Shrew* and the Nurse in *Romeo and Juliet*. Some of her best remembered roles were Mrs Millamant in Congreve's *Way of the World* and Lady Bracknell in Wilde's *The Importance of Being Ernest*. She received great acclaim for her role in Enid Bagnold's *The Chalk Garden*, and was awarded the New York Film Critics' Award for her performance in *The Whisperers* in 1967. Her last stage appearance was a lively one-woman show in 1974.

Evans, Walker (1903–75), US photographer, b. St. Louis. He is famed for his portrait images of the poverty-stricken rural South of the 1930s, many published in *Let Us Now Praise Famous Men* (coauthored by James Agee, 1941). His works also include stark studies of Victorian architecture and building interiors. *See also* Agee, James.

Evanston, city in NE Illinois, on Lake Michigan 15mi (24km) N of Chicago; site of Grosse Point Lighthouse (1860), Northwestern University (1851), National College of Education (1886), Kendall College (1934); national headquarters for Rotary, National Merit Scholarship Corporation, and National Women's Christian Temperance Union. Industries: textbooks, foodstuffs, hospital and dairy supplies. Settled 1826; inc. 1892. Pop. (1980) 73,706.

Evansville, port city in extreme SW Indiana, on the Ohio River; seat of Vandenburgh co; shipping and commercial center; site of University of Evansville (1854), Indian mound village state memorial. Industries: aluminum, refrigeration equipment, pharmaceuticals, fabricated plastics. Founded 1812; inc. 1819. Pop. (1980) 103,496.

Evaporation, in chemistry, removing liquid as vapor in order to concentrate solutions or to form crystals, usually performed at the solution's boiling point. The rate of evaporation is affected by heat input, liquid agitation, and speed of vapor passing over the liquid's surface.

Eve, in Genesis, first woman, created by God from Adam's rib to be his companion and wife. Tempted into eating the forbidden fruit, Eve made Adam eat it, causing God to drive them from the Garden of Eden.

Evening Primrose, any of various annual, biennial, and perennial plants of genus *Oenothera* native to the Western Hemisphere, with four-petalled yellow, pink, or white flowers that open in the evening. The North American common evening primrose *(O. biennis)* is now widely naturalized in Europe. Height: to 6ft (1.8m). Family Onagraceae.

Evening Star, not a star but a planet visible near the horizon in the early evening, appearing as a brightly shining object that does not twinkle. Although Mars, Jupiter, and Saturn occasionally appear as evening stars, the term most often refers to Venus, which shines so brightly as to be sometimes visible during daylight.

Everest, (Sir) George (1790–1866), a British surveyor-or-geographer for whom Mt. Everest is named. He went to India when he was only 16 and began his career of exploration and surveying in that country. The survey and boundaries of India today are in great part based on his work. His career also included surveys of the Himalayas. He returned to England in 1843.

Everest, Mount, highest mountain in the world, in central Himalayas between Tibet and Nepal, Asia. First successful attempt to reach the top was accomplished on May 29, 1953 by a British expedition led by Edmund Hillary and Tenzing Norkay of Nepal. Named after George Everest, the 1st surveyor-general of India; Tibetan name is Chomo-Lungma, or Mother Goddess of the World. Height: 29,028ft (8,854m).

Everett, port city in NW Washington, on Puget Sound, 28mi (45km) N of Seattle; seat of Snohomish co, Capt. George Vancouver first landed in the area 1792. Industries: aircraft, lumber, paper products, tourism, fishing, salmon canning, agriculture, dairying. Settled 1862; inc. 1893. Pop. (1980) 54,413.

Evergreen, plants that retain their green foliage for a year or more. Deciduous plants lose their leaves every autumn. Evergreens are divided into two groups: narrow-leaved or conifers and broad-leaved. Conifers include fir, spruce, pine, hemlock, and juniper. Among the broad-leaved evergreens are English holly, southern magnolia, box, mountain laurel, heath, and rhododendrons. All conifers are not evergreen, such as the deciduous larches. Evergreens are used extensively in landscape architecture, especially in northern gardens. *See also* Conifers.

Everlasting, or **immortelle,** type of flower that keeps its color and shape when dried. Best known is the *Helichrysum,* with daisylike yellow, brown, purple, or white blooms. Other popular plants include globe amaranth *(gomphrena globosa), Statice, Lunaria,* and *Xeranthemum.* For drying, flowers are cut when just starting to open and hung upside down in bunches to dry in a well-ventilated room.

Evert, Christine. *See* Lloyd, Christine Evert.

Everyman (first printed *c.*1529), author unknown (Dutch origin), one of the oldest morality plays in the English language. Everyman, summoned by Death to appear before God for judgment, calls on his friends for help: Strength, Beauty, Knowledge, Good Deeds, and Fellowship. Only Good Deeds will accompany him to the judgment seat.

Évian-les-Bains, town in E France, on S shore of Lake of Geneva; fashionable health spa. Industries: liqueurs, precision instruments. Pop. 6,052.

Evidence, facts or proof provided by testimony during legal process. Lawyers produce evidence that is considered by the judge and jury in a trial.

Evolution, theory that organisms originate from simpler forms of another organism and that a new species is the end of gradual development and change from the simpler forms. Early work with evolutionary theory was initiated by Jean Lamarck during the early 1800s, but it was not until Charles Darwin wrote *The Origin of Species* during the mid-1800s that the theory was considered worthy of argument.

Mount Everest

Evergreen: cedar

Exeter, England

Present-day evolutionary theory is derived from Darwin's work and maintains that in any population of a gene pool, there are random mutations in genetic forms and characteristics. Mutated forms are of no value to the survival of an organism. Most species reproduce in greater quantities than their environment can support, and so only those members best adapted to the environment survive. When mutated characteristics provide survival advantages, mutants survive to pass on these new characteristics. In this way a species effects gradual changes to adapt and survive in a competitive, and often changing, environment.

Evolution also occurs over a geographical area. A species tends to be widely distributed over a range of conditions and small groups of the population develop in specialized ways to better adapt to their particular conditions. The resulting subspecies do not differ greatly from their near neighbors, but there may be a complete species change from one end of the spectrum to the other. *See also* Darwinism; Natural Selection.

Evolutionary Socialism is based on the assumption that movement from capitalism to socialism can be made through the ballot (i.e., the government can be an instrument of reform), and that revolution is not necessary. *See also* Socialism.

Excalibur, in medieval legend, the name of King Arthur's sword. According to Sir Thomas Malory, who recounted the Arthurian legend in the 15th century, the name means "cut-steel." Malory described two versions of its origin. In the first, the boy Arthur miraculously pulled the sword out of a stone; in the second, he was given the sword by the Lady of the Lake.

Exchange Rate, rate at which one country's currency can be converted to another country's currency. The exchange rate will vary according to the demand for and supply of the countries' goods and services. The overall state of the country's balance of payments determines whether the rate will change. *See also* Balance of Payments.

Excise Tax, tax paid by the manufacturer of consumer goods, usually luxury goods such as jewelry, perfume, tobacco, and alcohol. The excise tax is normally a percentage of retail selling price.

Excited State, state of an atom, ion, molecule, when its energy level is higher than that of the ground state. An atom, for example, can be in an excited state as a result of absorption of a photon, causing one of the electrons to occupy an orbital of higher energy.

Exclusion Principle, Pauli, basic law of quantum mechanics, proposed by Wolfgang Pauli (1925), stating that no two electrons in an atom can possess the same energy and spin. More precisely, the set of four quantum numbers characterizing an elementary particle must be unique. In atoms, these numbers specify an electron's spin direction and the energy state in which it resides or would reside in a magnetic field.

Exclusive Powers, rights delegated by the US Constitution to the national and state governments. Certain powers are granted specifically to the federal government, others to the states. Still others are concurrent and may be exercised by both. The states may employ powers not explicitly granted to the federal government or denied to the states.

Excretory System. *See* Urogenital System.

Executive Privilege, right invoked by the US President to justify withholding information from Congress or the courts. Presidents have cited the need for confidentiality, endangerment of national security, and the public interest to defend their actions. The precedent was established by President Washington in 1796 when he refused to supply Congress with certain documents. During the 1973 Watergate controversy, President Nixon claimed executive privilege when he refused to surrender the White House tapes.

Exeter, city in SW England, on Exe River, 37mi (60km) NE of Plymouth; episcopal seat, famous for cathedral (1270–1369) and Guildhall (1160), probably the oldest municipal building in England; railroad, industrial, commercial, and tourist center for area. Industries: agricultural machinery, metal and leather products, pharmaceutical goods. Pop. 94,100.

Exeter Book, manuscript copied *c.*975, containing the largest extant collection of Old English poetry. The manuscript, probably copied from an earlier book, was given to Exeter Cathedral by Bishop Leofric. It contains both religious and secular verse, as well as 95 riddles.

Existentialism, philosophical movement arising in Germany shortly after World War I, later spreading to France and Italy, and discussed after World War II in the popular press. Not a philosophical "school" as such, few doctrines are shared by all its exponents. Developing the ideas in Sören Kierkegaard's writings on "existence," Karl Jaspers expounded the themes that have since been remolded by such writers as Martin Heidegger, Jean-Paul Sartre, Nikolai Berdyaev, and Albert Camus into a liberal philosophy with no hope for man's perfectability.

Exobiology, study of environmental conditions and possible biochemical and evolutionary pathways to life beyond Earth. It is concerned with such experiments as creation of amino acids from electrical discharges in methane-ammonia atmosphere (eg primeval Earth or present Jupiter) or survival of bacteria or mosses under Martian conditions. The Viking lander (1976) tested the Martian soil for gaseous byproducts of metabolic activity, but the test results were inconclusive.

Exodus, biblical book, second book of the Pentateuch, named by Greek translators for its account of the Israelites' flight from Egypt after God freed them from bondage. The narrative is divided into two sections, the first historical and the second legislative.

Exogamy, set of rules defining the inner social circle in which marriage (or in some cases all sexual relations) is forbidden. An example is the nuclear family in Western society. *See also* Endogamy; Incest Taboo.

Exophthalmos, abnormal protrusion of the eyeball caused by edema, aneurysm, or endocrine disorder. Onset may be sudden or gradual depending on the cause.

Exorcism, ritual expulsion of evil spirits from a person, place, or thing, usually performed by a religious leader, such as a priest, witch doctor, or sorcerer. Exorcism is a practice common to a great many religions. It is performed with verbal incantations, whippings, or sacrifices.

Exothermic Reaction, chemical reaction in which heat is evolved, thus causing a rise in temperature. *See also* Chemical Reaction.

Expansion, phase of the business cycle that occurs as economic conditions improve and move toward prosperity. Expansion is normally associated with increases in employment and increases in purchasing power. *See also* Business Cycles.

Expansion, mathematical process of replacing an expression by a sum of individual terms or by an infinite series. Thus, the expression $(x + 1)(x + 3)$ can be expanded to $x^2 + 4x + 4$: the function $\sin x$ can be expanded into the converging series $x = x - x^3/3! + x^5/5! - x^7/7! \ldots$

Expansion, Coefficient of, the number indicating the rate of change of volume of a given substance as the temperature or pressure on that substance changes. For a gas, the coefficient of expansion is usually large; for a solid, it is much smaller.

Expansion Chamber. *See* Cloud Chamber.

Ex Parte McCardle (1869), important US Supreme Court decision recognizing that the jurisdiction of the court to hear appeals is controlled by Congress. This decision raised the possibility of Congress entirely abolishing the appellate jurisdiction of the Supreme Court, leaving it a very limited role in the judicial system, but no efforts toward this end have ever been successful.

Ex Parte Milligan (1866), US Supreme Court decision overruling President Lincoln's Civil War proclamation subjecting civilians to trials for treason by military courts. The court declared such a practice unconstitutional and asserted that Lincoln had exceeded his authority.

Expatriation, voluntary renunciation of citizenship in favor of that of another state. An individual's right of expatriation was confirmed by the US Congress (1865). Grounds for expatriation include willingness to swear allegiance to a foreign state, serving in a foreign army without US government consent, or voting in a foreign election.

Experimental Psychology, use of scientific experimental design in psychological investigations. Close observation, careful recording, and other components of the scientific method are easiest to carry out in a laboratory, but psychologists also use them in clinics, schools, or the community at large.

Explosives, chemical compounds that, on ignition by heat, friction, impact, or detonation, undergo rapid decomposition or burning, producing large amounts of gas or heat and exerting tremendous pressure as they expand.

Exponent, superscript number placed to the right of a symbol indicating its power; for example, in $a^4 (= a \times a \times a \times a)$, 4 is the exponent. Certain laws of exponents apply in mathematical operations. For example: $3^2 \times 3^3 = 3^{(3+2)} = 3^5; 3^4 \div 3^3 = 3^{(4-3)} = 3^1; (3^2)^3 = 3^{(2 \times 3)} = 3^6; 3^{-5} = 1/3^5$. *See also* Power.

Exponential Function, in general a function of x of the form a^x, where a is a constant. More specifically, the exponential function is e^x, where e is the base of natural logarithms, 2˙7182818.... It can be represented by a power series $1 + x + x^2/2! + \ldots$.

Ex Post Facto Law, a law of retrospective effect that punishes a person for an offense that was not punishable at the time it occured. It is illegal to do so in the United States.

Expressionism, movement in early 20th-century art that had two main outlets of creativity—Die Brücke, founded in Dresden in 1905, and the Blue Rider, a

Munich group dating from 1911. Die Brücke reacted to the current academic style of painting and sought a more emotional and freer style of expression. Its main members were Ernst Kirchner, Karl Schmidt-Rottluff, and Erick Heckel. These artists painted in rapid brushstrokes, often using broken lines, rough textures, intense colors, and angular forms charged with emotion. They made woodcuts as well as paintings and were somewhat influenced by van Gogh, Ensor, and Munch. The Blue Rider group was especially influenced by cubism and was headed by Kandinsky, whose abstract expressionist style had great influence over later abstract painters. Among the active members of this group were Alex von Jawlensky, Paul Klee, Franz Marc, and August Macke. World War I brought an end to both of these groups.

Expressionist Theater, a theatrical style originating in Germany and popular in Europe and America throughout the 1920s. A reaction against theatrical realism, its beginnings are in August Strindberg's later works, especially *The Ghost Sonata* (1907). It attempted to present emotional rather than apparent reality and used symbols and bold psychological interpretations of people and events. Two important Expressionists are Frank Wedekind (German, 1864–1918), and Elmer Rice (American, 1892–1967).

Extinction, in experimental psychology, the pattern an organism follows when it stops performing a given behavior. Basically, a behavior will gradually extinguish (stop occurring) if it is not followed by any reward (reinforcement).

Extrapolation, process of estimating the value of a function beyond the range of its known values. One method is simply to extend a curve on a graph beyond the region for which known values exist. Various mathematical approximation techniques also exist. *See also* Interpolation.

Extrasensory Perception (ESP or psi), a hypothesized ability to respond to events in the external world without using sensory information or any process of rational inference. ESP includes clairvoyance, precognition, and telepathy, and is one of the concerns of parapsychology. A typical ESP study might require subjects to try to guess stimuli (for example, playing cards) that are presented in a random order. When subjects can consistently name the cards at rates exceeding chance guessing, there is said to be evidence for ESP. Though parapsychologists such as J. B. Rhine have succeeded in objectifying and controlling the study of ESP phenomena to some extent, this area of psychology remains controversial in the eyes of many scientists. The chief difficulty for investigators of ESP phenomena is to find ESP effects that are consistent and reproducible—hallmarks of scientific objectivity. On the other hand, scientists will also be the first to admit that there are events and phenomena that are as yet unexplainable by modern science. *See also* Parapsychology.

Extraterritoriality, state of legal immunity granted to members of the diplomatic corps, their families, and the premises they occupy. Immunity takes the form of exemption from arrest or prosecution and from search or seizure.

Extrinsic Factor, or Vitamin B_{12}, provides cobalt, a trace element needed in erythrocyte formation; deficiency results in pernicious anemia. *See also* Intrinsic Factor.

Extrusion, in geology, the breaking out of igneous material onto the earth's surface. Any volcanic product reaching the surface becomes extrusive material whether it is ejected through a volcano's cone or through pipelike channels or fissures in the crust. Extrusive material varies in size and composition from light, volcanic ash to huge ejections of plutonic material from deep beneath crustal rock. *See also* Igneous Rock; Volcano.

Extrusion, operation of forcing copper, aluminum, magnesium, their alloys, or plastics at the optimum temperature through a die to manufacture specific shapes such as rods, tubes, and various hollow or solid sections. Plastic extrusion can produce composite sheets, and coat film and wire.

Eye, the special sense organ of vision. It converts light energy to nerve impulses that are transmitted to the visual center of the brain. Each eye lies in a bony socket, called the orbital cavity, which also includes muscles and other tissues to hold and move the eye, and protective structures, such as the lacrimal apparatus that produces tears. The eyeball itself is spherical and composed of three layers: the sclera, the choroid, and the retina. The *sclera* is a tough fibrous membrane—seen as the white of the eye—that helps retain the eye shape; it contains a "window," the transparent *cornea* that protects the iris. The *choroid,* or middle layer, contains blood vessels to provide food and oxygen to the eye. It contains the *iris,* the pigmented part of the eye, in the center of which is a hole, the *pupil,* through which light passes to the *crystalline lens* where the light rays are bent to make an image on the *retina.* The retina, the innermost layer of the eye, contains the nerve cells—*rods and cones*—responsible for converting the image into a nerve impulse that in turn is transmitted along the *optic nerve* to visual centers of the brain. A watery fluid, the *aqueous humor,* is present between the cornea and iris; a jellylike substance, the *vitreous humor,* behind the lens; both help maintain shape of the eye. *See also* Vision.

Eyebright, small annual and perennial plants widely distributed in northern and southern temperate and subarctic regions. They have terminal spikes of white, yellow, or purple tubular flowers. European eyebright (*Euphrasia officinalis)* was formerly used to treat eye diseases. Family Scrophulariaceae.

Eyre, Lake, salt lake in Australia, in NE South Australia state; lowest point on continent, 39ft (12m) below sea level; largest lake in Australia. Area: 3,430sq mi (8,884sq km). Depth (max.): 4ft (1m).

Ezekiel, Book of, book of the Old Testament, third of the major prophet books. It is a record of the life of the priest and prophet Ezekiel, who preached to the Jews in Exile. It records his visions and prophecies of the destruction of Jerusalem (582 BC) and his judgment of Israel's eventual redemption and restoration.

Ezra, in the Bible, a continuation of Chronicles I and II. It records the priest Ezra's journey from Babylon to Jerusalem to spread the law of Moses. It also includes an account of the rebuilding of the Temple, part of the city's restoration after it was destroyed by Nebuchadnezzar, and a census of Ezra's companions on his trip to the Holy City.

F

Fabian, Saint, Roman Catholic pope (236–50). He reorganized the church, dividing Rome into seven areas, and provided for churches to be governed by presbyters and deacons under his review. He began a registry for the deeds of martyrs; he was martyred during the persecution of Christians by the Emperor Decius.

Fabian Society, a non-Marxist organization of British socialists who believed that socialism would be attained through gradual political change. Including George Bernard Shaw and Beatrice and Sidney Webb, the society gained widespread recognition and led to the formation of the Labour party (1900).

Fabius Maximus Verrucosus, Quintus, called Cunctator (Lat. "delayer") (died 203 BC), Roman consul, dictator, and priest. A conservative military genius, he is famed for his strategy of avoiding pitched battle while conducting harassing raids during the Second Punic War, a tactic that wore Hannibal's forces to exhaustion. The Romans became bored with his methods, removed him from office, and were defeated at Cannae. Reinstated in 214, he served with honor until his death. The term *Fabian* came to mean a policy of delay.

Fable, a literary genre in the form of a short allegorical tale which is intended to convey a moral. The characters are often animals, whose words and deeds are used to satirize those of human beings. The oldest extant fables are the Greek tales of Aesop and the Indian stories of the *Panchatantra.* Other collections of fables were made by Jean de La Fontaine, John Gay, and Ivan Krylov.

Factor Analysis, in statistics and psychometrics, a complex mathematical method for reducing a large number of measures or tests to a smaller number of "factors" that can completely account for the results obtained on all the tests, as well as for the correlations between them. *See also* Intelligence Testing.

Faculae, very bright areas seen on the Sun's surface just before the appearance of a sunspot or sunspot group in the same region, and persisting for some time after its decay. *See also* Sun.

Faeroe Islands, group of 22 volcanic islands in N Atlantic Ocean between Iceland and Shetland Islands; possession of Denmark since 1380. Seventeen of the islands, which are high and rugged with little vegetation, are inhabited. Since 1947 the people have had home rule and send two representatives to Danish parliament. Industries: fishing, whaling, fowling, sheep raising, farming. Settled by Norsemen in 11th century. Area: 540sq mi (1,339sq km). Pop. 41,211.

Fahd Ibn (Abdul Aziz) al-Saud (1922–), King of Saudi Arabia. A son of King Ibn Saud, he was raised and educated in the Saudi royal court. He was appointed the country's first minister of education in 1953 and directed the establishment of a public school system. In 1962, he became interior minister and in 1968 deputy prime minister. Known as one of the more progressive Saudi princes, he advocated cooperation with the United States and opposed the Arab oil boycott in 1973. After the assassination of King Faisal in 1975, he was named crown prince to the ailing King Khalid and conducted the day-to-day affairs of the Saudi kingdom. In 1982, he succeeded Khalid as king.

Fahrenheit, Gabriel Daniel (1686–1736), German physicist and instrument maker. He invented the alcohol thermometer (1709), the first mercury thermometer (1714), and devised the temperature scale that bears his name. He also showed that atmospheric pressure causes variations in the boiling point of liquids, and that water, below its freezing point, can remain in a liquid state. *See also* Thermometer.

Faïence, earthenware covered with a decorative layer of white opaque glaze made of lead and tin. The clay used is of a fine quality so that it can be thinly shaped and can withstand being fired at a high temperature. Faïence is often called delftware because Delft was a center of production in the 17th century. Faïence was also produced in Rouen during this period.

Fainting, or **syncope,** temporary impairment of consciousness accompanied by general weakness of muscles. An attack may be preceded by giddiness, sensory distortions, nausea, pallor, profuse cold sweat. Causes may include a deficient flow of blood to the brain, a change in the blood contents, or emotional disturbances.

Fairbanks, Charles Warren (1852–1918), US political leader, b. Union co, Ohio. The last of the "log cabin statesmen," he was a Republican senator (1897–1905). He was vice president under Pres. Theodore Roosevelt (1905–09).

Fairbanks, Douglas (1883–1939), US silent film star, b. Douglas Ullman in Denver. He was a co-founder of United Artists Films (1919). His swashbuckling acrobatics and breezy charm enhanced many costume adventures, including *The Mark of Zorro* (1920), *The Three Musketeers* (1921), *Robin Hood* (1922), *The Black Pirate* (1926), and *The Private Life of Don Juan* (1934).

Fairbanks, city in central Alaska, on the Tanana and Chena rivers, 400mi (644km) N of Anchorage and 100mi (161km) S of the Arctic Circle. Severe temperatures range from −66°F (−54°C) to 96°F (36°C); snowfall averages 60 inches (1,524mm). University of Alaska was founded here 1922; Eielson Air Force Base and Fort Wainwright are nearby. Construction of Alaskan oil pipeline in 1970s accelerated growth. Industries: industrial chemicals, fur goods, gold, silver, and coal mining. Founded in 1902 when gold was discovered. Pop. (1980) 22,645.

Fairfax of Cameron, Thomas, 3rd Baron (1612–71), English soldier. He was commander in chief of the Parliamentary Army (1645–50) in the Civil War. A popular commander, he won a decisive victory at Naseby (1645) but played a limited role in politics.

Fairfield, city in W California, 40mi (64km) SW of Sacramento. Industries: sleeping bags, aluminum cans. Founded 1859; inc. 1903. Pop. (1980) 58,099.

Fairfield, town in SW Connecticut, in Fairfield co, on Long Island Sound; summer resort. Settled 1639. Pop. (1980) 54,849.

Fairy Ring, a circle or ring of mushrooms, usually *Marasmius oreades,* that appears seasonally in lawns or meadows. It is usually marked by richer, greener growth. In folklore the area enclosed was said to be the dancing ground of fairies.

Fairy Shrimp, branchiopod crustacean found in temporary pools and small ponds. It has an elongated trunk of 20 or more segments and anterior paddlelike limbs with gills for feeding and respiration. It has no carapace and its eyes are on stalks. Length: ⅜–5⅛in (1–13cm). Order Anostraca. *See also* Crustacean.

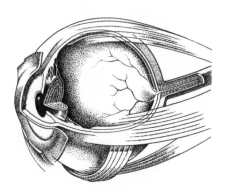

Eye

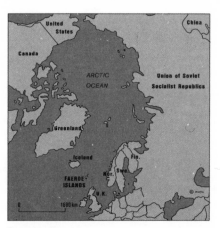

Faeroe Islands

Douglas Fairbanks

Fairy Tales and **Folktales** spring from an ancient world-wide oral tradition which, like language itself, obeys universal laws and structures. That there are many versions of the same tale in different parts of the world is not merely coincidence, but a function of a universal need for the same social utopia and the subsequent collective oral creation of a tale that satisfies a specific aspect of that need. Some tales, like those of Hans Christian Andersen, are largely of literary origin, while others, like those of Charles Perrault *(Mother Goose Tales)*, are reworkings of older oral tales. *See also* Andersen, Hans Christian; Perrault, Charles.

Faisal I (1885–1933), king of Syria (1920) and Iraq (1921–33). He became a member of the Turkish parliament in Constantinople (1913) and later directed the Arabs in a desert campaign under the British against the Turks until the capture of Damascus (1918). After the French ousted him as king of Syria (1920), he secured the throne of Iraq and formed the state of Iraq (1921). His son, Ghazi, and grandson, Faisal II, successively succeeded him.

Faisal Ibn al-Saud (1906–75), king of Saudi Arabia (1964–75); son of King Ibn Saud; brother of King Saud. He was viceroy of Hejaz (1926), became crown prince and foreign minister of Saudi Arabia (1953), and king after Saud was deposed (1964). He began educational and economic programs and joined other Arab states in the Six Day War against Israel (1967). He was assassinated by a nephew.

Faisal II (1935–58), third king of Iraq (1939–58), grandson of Faisal I. After the death of Ghazi, his father, he became king, with Abdul Illah as regent. Both were assassinated in a coup d'etat led by Abdul Karim Kassem; Iraq became a republic.

Faith Healing, the supplication to a divine being or power for cures. It can be traced to the miraculous works of Jesus Christ and his apostles as recorded in the New Testament. Such prayers and rituals may be traced throughout the history of man. Christian Science is structured around belief in faith healing.

Fakir, Muslim or Hindu monk or wandering mendicant. Fakirs are thought to possess special powers, to be able to perform magic and incredible feats of endurance, such as walking on fire.

Falaise, town in N France, 19mi (31km) SE of Caen; birthplace of William the Conqueror; important during the Normandy campaign of WWII; site of château (12th–13th century), and annual livestock and wool fair held since 11th century; agricultural market. Pop. 6,711.

Falange, Spanish political party. It was founded in 1933 by José António Primo de Rivera, son of the dictator. Closely fashioned after the Fascist party in Italy and the Nazi party in Germany, it became the sole legal political party after the forces of Francisco Franco triumphed in the Spanish Civil War. Its power declined in the 1960s and 1970s, although it remained the only legal political party. *See also* Civil War, Spanish.

Falashas, ethnic group in Ethiopia, probably descendants of early converts to Judaism. Once a large group, they now number about 30,000. Their form of Judaism relies solely on observance of the Old Testament. They speak local dialects, attend services led by priests, and celebrate only biblical feasts.

Falcon, widely distributed, bold, hawklike bird of prey, sometimes trained by man to hunt game. They have

keen eyesight, short hooked bills, long pointed wings, streamlined bodies, strong legs with hooked claws, longish tails, and gray or brownish plumage with lighter markings. They hunt during the day, feeding on insects, birds on the wing, rodents, and other small animals on the ground. They lay brown-spotted white eggs (2–6) in a tree-hole nest. Length: 6–25in (15–64cm). Family Falconidae.

Falconry, sport in which birds and small animals are hunted, using falcons. The falcon, a bird of prey closely related to the hawk, is taken when young to be trained. The falconer wears a glove upon which the hooded falcon sits. When the hood is taken off, the falcon heads straight for the quarry, leaving the prey untouched after the kill. The falcon then returns to the falconer's wrist. Falconry attained its greatest popularity in late medieval and early modern Europe, and was one of the chief pastimes of royalty before declining after the 17th century. Although still used for hunting in certain parts of the world, it has never regained the favor it once enjoyed.

Falkland Islands (Islas Malvinas), group of islands SE of Argentina in S Atlantic Ocean. A British crown colony, group includes 2 large islands, East and West Falkland, and 200 small islands; discovered by English navigator John Davis in 1592. Capital is Stanley; main industry is sheep farming. Exports: wool, skins, tallow, guano. Area: 4,618sq mi (11,961sq km). Pop. 1,852.

Falklands War, military conflict fought between Great Britain and Argentina (April–June 1982) over the question of sovereignty over the Falklands (Sp: Malvinas) Islands, located c. 250 mi. (400 km) off the Argentine coast. On April 2, after the breakdown of deadlocked negotiations, Argentine forces invaded and occupied the Falklands, South Georgia, and South Sandwich Islands, which had been administered and occupied by Great Britain since the 19th century. Despite attempts by the United Nations and the United States to negotiate a settlement, the Argentine government refused to withdraw its troops. The British dispatched a naval task force to the South Atlantic and after establishing a blockade of the islands and staging an amphibious landing at Port San Carlos, the British eventually surrounded the Argentine troops at the capital, Port Stanley, and forced them to surrender on June 14. Losses on both sides of the conflict were heavy. Although the British resumed their administration of the islands, the basic issue of sovereignty remained unresolved.

Falla, Manuel de (1876–1946), Spanish composer who developed Spanish nationalism in music by using Spanish folk songs as the basis for many of his compositions. Among his popular works are the opera *La Vida Breve* (1905), *Nights in the Gardens of Spain* (1915) for piano and orchestra, and the music for the ballets *El Amor Brujo* (1915) and *The Three-Cornered Hat* (1919).

Falling Bodies, Law of, theory propounded by Galileo, disproving Aristotle's contention that bodies of different weights fall at different speeds. Galileo's law proved that falling bodies obey the law of uniformly accelerated motion. He performed experiments showing that the gravity of the Earth produced constant downward acceleration and that this acceleration was independent of size, weight or composition of the falling bodies. *See also* Gravitation.

Fallopian Tube, or oviduct, either of two narrow ducts leading from the upper part of the uterus into the pelvic cavity and ending near each ovary. After ovulation, the ovum enters and travels through the Fallopian tube where fertilization can occur. The fertilized ovum, or

embryo, continues into the uterus where it becomes implanted. If the fertilized ovum remains in the tube, an ectopic (or tubal) pregnancy occurs. If fertilization does not occur, the ovum is shed along with uterine lining at menstruation. Conception can be prevented by surgical ligation or cauterization of the tubes to prevent passage of the ovum. Infection can also effect closure of the tubes.

Fallout, Atomic, radioactive contamination in the atmosphere following a leakage or accident at a nuclear reactor or a nuclear bomb explosion. Large wind-borne particles fall to Earth after a few hours, no more than 300mi (483km) from the source. Lighter particles entering the troposphere are detected after a longer period at about the same latitude as the source. Any particles entering the stratosphere eventually fall over the whole Earth's surface, often many years later.

Fallow Deer, European deer, introduced in the United States and commonly kept in parks. The Middle Eastern species may be extinct. It is fawn-colored with white spots. Antlers are flattened and palmate with numerous points. Length: to 4.5ft (1.4m); height: to 3ft (1m); weight: to 160 lb (72kg). Family Cervidae; species *Dama dama. See also* Deer.

Fall River, city and port in SE Massachusetts, on Mt Hope Bay, at mouth of Taunton River; seat of Bristol co; scene of Revolutionary War skirmish, and of trial of Lizzie Borden (1892). Battleship *Massachusetts* (WWII) is berthed here as war memorial. Industries: paper boxes, women's clothing, textile machinery, luggage. Settled 1656 as Freeman's Purchase; inc. 1803; chartered as city 1854. Pop. (1980) 92,574.

False Decretals, also called **Pseudo-Isidorian Decretals,** collection of purported Church documents published in France about 847–52 and compiled by Isidore Mercator. They were identified with St. Isidore of Seville (died 636) and believed to be genuine until 1558. Included were false documents—58 papal decrees, 1 canon, and forged papal letters—intermixed with genuine documents—early papal letters, canons of 54 councils, and papal writings. They were assembled to support claims of papal supremacy and to support the bishops against secular interference. Throughout the Middle Ages the canons in the Decretals were one of the main sources of canon law; by the early 19th century the genuine parts had been distinguished from the forgeries.

False Pregnancy, signs of pregnancy, such as the absence of menstruation, without the presence of an embryo. It can be caused by psychological factors, by an endocrine disturbance, or by a tumor.

Famagusta (Ammókhostos), port city on E coast of island of Cyprus, on Famagusta Bay. During 15th and 16th centuries it was seat of Venetian governors of Cyprus; site of medieval governor's palace and Cathedral of St Nicholas; British naval base during WWII. Before 1975 war, city's population was about 67% Greek, 33% Turkish. Chief industry is citrus fruits. Founded 3rd century BC. Pop. 38,960.

Familiar Spirit, supernatural spirit closely associated with a magician or religious leader. The familiar spirit is a widespread concept. He is usually the servant of a magician and can take the shape of an animal.

Family, institutionalized bio-social group made up of adults and children. It forms a unit that deals with both economic and affective needs and provides a sociocultural context for the procreation, care, and socialization of offspring. It can consist of a nuclear or extended network. *See also* Kinship.

Famine, extreme prolonged shortage of food available to a population, produced by both natural and man-made causes and resulting typically in widespread starvation and death. Periods of social upheaval, such as the peasant uprisings in medieval Europe, the Irish emigrations of 1845–47, and the French and Russian revolutions are often associated with acute famines. Drought, excessive rainfall, drastic alterations in the weather pattern of an area, and warfare can produce the destruction of crops and livestock during famine. Rapid population growth is increasingly a factor in the occurrence of famines, especially in underdeveloped areas.

Fan, in geology, a spread of fine and coarse materials resulting from the rapid deposition of both dissolved and suspended materials carried downstream by a river. The alluvial deposits appear at river outlets on desert floors when the velocity of the river water drops very suddenly.

Faneuil, Peter (1700–43), American merchant, b. New Rochelle, N.Y. He settled in Boston as a young man, and by the late 1730s his own thriving business and a large inheritance made him one of Boston's wealthiest citizens. Eager to provide the city with a public market place, he built Faneuil Hall. This landmark building, completed in 1742, was badly damaged by fire in 1761 but was rebuilt in 1763. Put to frequent use as a meeting place by patriots during the Revolution, it acquired the name "Cradle of American Liberty." The building was enlarged to its present size in 1805 by Charles Bulfinch. It is now a focal point in the redevelopment of downtown Boston.

Fang, a long pointed tooth, particularly a hollow grooved tooth used by a snake to inject its venom, or, loosely, a tooth that a carnivorous animal uses to seize and tear prey.

Fang-Bulu, a pair of Bantu languages of the Niger-Kordofanian family of African languages, found in Gabon and Cameroon. Together with Yaoundé they are understood by about 1,000,000 speakers.

Fan-si-pan, mountain peak in NW Vietnam, between Red and Black rivers. Highest point in the country, 10,306ft (3,143m).

Fanti, black African people of Ghana. An Akan people numbering about 250,000, they follow a matrilineal system of political succession and material inheritance and a patrilineal system of military succession. They traded between the African interior and Europe and became embroiled in conflicts with the Ashanti. They were first aided and later dominated by the British.

Fantin-Latour, Ignace Henri Jean Théodore (1836–1904), French painter. Noted for his realistic group portraits, including "Hommage à Eugène Delacroix" (1864; Paris, Louvre), he also did still lifes and lithographs illustrating the music of Wagner and others.

Farad, unit of capacitance (symbol F) equal to the capacitance of a capacitor that acquires a charge of one coulomb when a potential difference of one volt is applied across the plates.

Faraday, Michael (1791–1867), English physicist, chemist, and experimentalist. He liquefied chlorine, discovered benzene and two chlorides of carbon, and enunciated the laws of electrolysis. Moving from chemistry to electricity, he discovered electromagnetic induction, made the first generator, built a primitive electric motor, and studied nonconducting materials (dielectrics). The unit of capacitance (the farad) is named after him.

Faraday's Laws, (1) the mass of substance liberated from an electrolyte is proportional to the current passing and the time for which it passes; (2) when the magnetic flux through a circuit changes an electromotive force is induced in the circuit proportional to the rate of decrease of magnetic flux.

Farce, a type of comic drama characterized by its unrealistic characterizations, its improbable plot lines, and an emphasis on physical humor. Modern farce is a 19th-century invention and was developed by Arthur Wing Pinero in England and Eugène Marin Labiche and Georges Feydeau in France.

Farming. *See* Agribusiness; Agriculture; Collective Farms; Cooperative Farming.

Farm Machinery, equipment used for growing and harvesting crops. Implements have evolved from sticks to self-powered or tractor-drawn machines that, in some cases, have cut labor twentyfold. Soil preparation, planting, cultivating, and spraying can now be done in multi-foot swaths instead of single rows. Harvesters combine multiple farming operations into a single, self-powered machine.

Farnese, celebrated Italian family. Through the skill of **Ranuccio Farnese** (died *c.*1460), who militarily defended the Papal States and won the gratitude of Pope Eugenius IV (1431–47), the family began to increase its wealth and establish itself among the Roman aristocracy. Ranuccio's son Alessandro became **Pope Paul III** (1534–49), and his illegitimate son **Pier Luigi** (1503–47) was first duke of Parma and of Piacenza (from 1545). Pier Luigi's grandson **Alessandro** (1545–92), also duke of Parma and Piacenza, served Philip II of Spain as regent of the Netherlands (from 1577). The line ended with the death of **Antonio** in 1731.

Farnese, Alessandro (1468–1549). *See* Paul III, Roman Catholic pope.

Farnese Bull, large sculpture group originally done by Greek artists in Rhodes. A Roman copy of the group, depicting the punishment of Dirce by binding her to the horns of a bull, was found in the Caracalla baths and can now be seen in the National Archeological Museum, Naples.

Farnese Palace, a noted palace in Rome, designed by Antonio da Sangallo for Cardinal Alessandro Farnese in the 16th century. Michelangelo worked on it and it was completed by Giacomo della Porta. It is now the site of the French Embassy in Rome.

Farquhar Islands, group of islands in Indian Ocean, NE of Madagascar; British-owned and part of British Indian Ocean Territory. Area: 3sq mi (8sq km).

Farside, Lunar, side of the moon permanently turned away from the earth, owing to the satellite's captured rotation. Some 9% of the farside may be viewed from Earth because of lunar libration. Compared with the earthside, the farside has far fewer maria, but many craters. It was first photographed by the Russian probe Luna 3 in 1959. *See also* Libration; Mare.

Farsightedness, or hyperopia, correctible optical defect in which the rays of light entering the eye are focused behind the lens, causing distortion and making close vision difficult. Causes are a too-short eyeball or ineffective refraction.

Fasces, emblem adopted by the Italian Fascist party in 1919. The fasces, depicting an ax surrounded by rods, was the symbol of state power in ancient Rome. *See also* Fascism.

Fascism, nationalist, anti-Communist movement founded in Italy by Benito Mussolini in 1919 as a reaction to the revolutionary movements that swept Europe after World War I. Glorification of the state and complete individual subordination to its authority were basic to Fascist dogma, as was preservation of a rigid class structure and law and order. The Fascist party was organized in military fashion with its black-shirted members using the ancient Roman salute. As the head of the party, Mussolini was seen as the embodiment of Italy's highest ideals and its salvation from the threats of anarchy and Communism. The Fascists ruled Italy from 1922 until the war's end in 1945. *See also* Fasces; Mussolini, Benito; World War II.

Fashoda Incident (1898), largely diplomatic struggle between France and Great Britain for control of Egypt's Upper Nile. Britain desired continuous territory from Egypt to South Africa, and France wanted a path from the Atlantic Ocean to the Red Sea. Their respective expeditions, led by Britain's Lord Kitchener and Maj. J.B. Marchand, met at Fashoda. France backed down after a British threat of war.

Fastolf, Sir John (1378?–1459), English soldier and administrator. He fought at Agincourt (1415) and again in France (1417–40). He was a counselor to Richard, Duke of York, and invested his large war profits in English estates. Shakespeare's Falstaff was modeled on Sir John.

Fat, substance used by animals to store energy and shield them from the cold. Fats are esters of glycerin with carboxlic acids such as palmitic, lauric, and stearic acid, which have 16 or 18 carbon atoms. Vegetable oils are similar to fats, but are viscous liquids rather than semisolids, and have double chemical bonds in the acid molecules, that is, they are unsaturated.

Fates, also called Parcae, corresponding to the Greek Moerae. There were three, the daughters of Night. Clotho, the spinner, personified the thread of life. Lachesis was chance, the element of luck that a man had a right to expect. Atropos was inescapable fate, against which there was no appeal.

Fathom, a unit used in measuring the depth of water. One fathom equals 6ft (1.83m). Originally it was the span of a man's arms.

Fatima (606–632), daughter of the prophet Mohammed, wife of Ali. Fatima and Ali felt deprived of their rightful inheritance by Abu Bakr, first Muslim Caliph after Mohammed's death. Their disappointed followers, the Shi'a sect of Islam, honor Ali as the rightful successor to Mohammed and offer devotion to Fatima, similar to that offered the Virgin Mary in Roman Catholicism. Her symbol, the "hand of Fatima," is often displayed in Shiite processions, and she is accorded a place of honor in heaven. *See also* Abu Bakr; Shi'a.

Fátima, village in W central Portugal; site of shrine of Our Lady of the Rosary of Fátima, Roman Catholic pilgrimage site, visited 1967 by Pope Paul VI.

Fatimid, or **Fatimite,** dynasty of North African caliphs (909–1171) claiming descent from Fatima, related to the Shiites (a Muslim sect). Exploiting social friction, Ubaydullah aroused the Berbers to become the first Fatimid caliph (in Tunisia). He captured the Abbassid holdings of Cyrenaica, Libya, and Alexandria (914). The third caliph, al-Mansur, seized Sicily (946). The fourth, al-Aziz, took Egypt (969), made Cairo the capital, and built the great mosque, Al-Azhar. The Fatimid realm eventually encompassed all of North Africa, Sicily, Egypt, Syria, and western Arabia, including Baghdad. The Normans, Turks, Venetians, and Crusaders took territory in the 11th through 13th centuries. The viziers and generals then took control, until Nureddin and Saladin of Syria liquidated the Fatimid caliphate in Egypt in 1171.

Fats and Oils, natural substances of animal or plant origin (or synthetic compounds). Usually fats are solid and oils liquid at room temperature; both are greasy in texture. Fats and oils are one of the principal foods.

Fatty Acid. *See* Lipid.

Faulkner, (Arthur) Brian (Deane) (1921–77), politician of Northern Ireland. A member of the Unionist party, he became a member of the Northern Ireland Parliament in 1949 and was minister of home affairs (1959–63), commerce (1963–69), and development (1969–71). He was prime minister of Northern Ireland (1971–72) and continued as leader of his party until 1974. He was chief executive of the Northern Ireland administration (1974) and a member of the Constitutional Convention (1975). In these capacities he showed a willingness to accept power sharing with Roman Catholics.

Faulkner, William (1897–1962), US author, b. New Albany, Miss. He was raised in Oxford, Miss., where he later made his home. He joined the Royal Air Force in Canada in 1918, briefly attended the University of Mississippi after World War I, and lived for a short time in the early 1920s in New York City, New Orleans, and Europe. His first book was a collection of poems, *The Marble Faun* (1924). *Soldier's Pay,* a novel, appeared in 1926 and another novel, *Mosquitoes,* in 1927. With *Sartoris* (1929), his third novel, Faulkner created Yoknapatawpha County, the setting of most of his future works.

Drawing on his own background and on the people he knew best, he wrote a series of novels and stories that depict the South through the 19th and 20th centuries. The primary themes of the so-called Yoknapatawpha Saga include the relationship of the past to the present and the effects of the disintegration of traditional Southern society. An innovative stylist, he often used the stream-of-consciousness technique and complex time sequences. He was awarded the Nobel Prize in literature for 1949. His works include *The Sound and the Fury* (1929), *As I Lay Dying* (1930), *Sanctuary* (1931), *Light in August* (1932), *Absalom, Absalom!* (1936), *The Unvanquished* (1938), *The Hamlet* (1940), *Go Down, Moses and Other Stories* (1942), *Requiem for a Nun* (1951), *A Fable* (1954), *The Town* (1957), *The Mansion* (1959), and *The Reivers* (1962). He received Pulitzer Prizes for the latter two works.

Fault Block, in geology, crustal region bounded partly or completely by faults, which acts as a single unit during block faulting or any similar tectonic event. The Sierra Nevada mountains (California) are a prime example. *See also* Tectonics.

Faulting, in geology, that process of fracture and displacement of materials that produces a fault. A fault is a distinct break in rock structures, and this break may extend for either a few centimeters or hundreds of miles. Faults are classified by the inclination of the fault

Henri Fantin-Latour: self-portrait

Michael Faraday

William Faulkner

surfaces and direction of the relative movement of the resulting fault blocks.

Faunus, in Roman mythology, a fertility god. Mainly a woodland deity, his female counterpart was Fauna.

Faure, François Félix (1841–99), French merchant and politician, 6th president of the Republic after the resignation of Jean-Paul Casimir-Périer in 1895. In this position he helped bring about the Franco-Russian alliance and took an unfortunate conservative stance on the Dreyfus Affair. He died in office.

Fauré, Gabriel (1845–1924), French Romantic composer. His numerous works were characterized by a soft, refined, intimate quality and the prominence of melody. He composed chamber music, solo piano pieces, operas, many songs, and a highly regarded *Requiem* (1887). One of his most popular works is the *Elegie* for cello and orchestra (1883). *See also* Romanticism in Music.

Faust (1808–1831), drama by Johann Wolfgang von Goethe based on the legend of Dr. Johann Faustus (1480–1540). There is also a drama by Christopher Marlowe and an opera by Gounod on this theme. The Goethe play is in two parts with a prologue. In the first part, Faust promises to forfeit his soul to Mephistopheles in exchange for one moment of perfect contentment. Mephistopheles tries various means to please Faust, which end in Faust's seduction of Margaret, an innocent young girl; this affair ends in tragedy as Margaret becomes insane and finally dies. In Part II Helen of Troy is recalled from Hades. She and Faust have a child, Euphorion, representing the spirit of poetry. After Helen and Euphorion disappear into the air, Faust and Mephistopheles establish an abode for contented people. Realizing that contentment lies in helping others, Faust pronounces himself perfectly contented and dies. Although he has lost his wager, his soul is taken into heaven.

Fauvism, first major avant-garde movement in 20th-century painting. It was characterized by intense use of pure, brilliant color, often rapid brushwork, and somewhat flatly painted surfaces. The subject matter tended to be landscapes, still lifes, and figure compositions, sometimes portraits. The movement came about as a reaction to the academic style and was influenced by the work of Gauguin and Van Gogh. The group contained many artists who had studied under Gustave Moreau. Among its members were Henri Matisse, Albert Marquet, Georges Rouault, Maurice de Vlaminck, André Derain, A.C. Friesz, Georges Braque, Raoul Dufy, and Kees van Dongen. These artists exhibited together in the Salon d'Automne of 1905, at which they were dubbed "fauves," meaning "wild beasts," because of their use of brilliant color, and in the Salon des Indépendants of 1906. After this period, many of the artists evolved different styles, including Cubism, and their painting no longer shared the common traits of fauvism.

Fawkes, Guy (1570–1606), English conspirator in the Gunpowder Plot, who was discovered with barrels of gunpowder in the Houses of Parliament on the night of Nov. 4–5, 1605, for which he was tried and executed in 1606. He was a Roman Catholic who fought in the Spanish Netherlands from 1593 to 1604.

Fayetteville, city in S central North Carolina, on Cape Fear, 50mi (81km) S of Raleigh; seat of Cumberland co. A Tory center during American Revolution, town was renamed (1783) for Marquis de Lafayette; served as state capital (1789–93) and was scene of state convention that ratified US Constitution (1789). Industries:

textiles, lumber, power tools. Inc. 1783. Pop. (1980) 59,507.

Fealty, in feudalism, the loyalty and obligations due to a king or lord by his vassal, or the specific oath of loyalty and consent taken by the vassal. In about the 9th century, fealty meant refraining from participation in any action that endangered the lord's life or property. By the 11th century, the positive duties of a vassal to his lord were established, including personal military service, financial obligations, and other forms of personal service. The oath of fealty was followed by an act of homage, and in the case where the granting of a fief was involved, by the rite of investiture.

Fear, intense emotional state aroused by anticipation of pain or injury from some event. Some capacity for fear is desirable and adaptive because it can lead to avoidance of or escape from harmful events. Abnormally strong or inappropriate fears, however, can become phobias. *See also* Phobia.

Feather, growth comprising the skin covering of birds. It is composed of keratin, a fibrous protein. Body contour feathers grow in demarcated skin tracts separated by bare areas. Short, fluffy down feathers serve for insulation and long, quill-like contour feathers constitute wing and tail surfaces. Contour feathers have a central shaft with paired, interlocking branches. These are shed and replaced (molted) at least once a year. *See also* Bird.

Feather Star, crinoid echinoderm found in shallow marine waters clinging to underwater debris. Ten arms with feathery branches radiate from the tiny central disc. Reproduction is sexual. Class Crinoidea; species include rosy feather star *Antedon*.

February, second month of the year. Its name is derived from the Roman god Februus. February has 28 days except in leap years, when it has 29. The birthstone is the amethyst.

February Revolution, insurrection of the French working class in 1848, causing the rapid downfall of the government of King Louis Philippe. The result of a poor economy and increasingly reactionary king, this revolution saw the creation of a troubled constitutional republic, with the election in December of Louis Napoleon (later Emperor Napoleon III) as its president. Paralleled by similar rebellions throughout Europe, the republican movement was largely unsuccessful.

Fechner, Gustav Theodore (1801–87), German physician and psychologist who helped found experimental psychology by using objective, precise methods to study psychophysics—the relationships of physical stimuli to sensation and perception. "Fechner's law" is that the relationship between the strength of a stimulus and the perceived intensity of a sensation is a constant.

Federal Bureau of Investigation (FBI), agency of the Department of Justice. It is charged with investigating all violation of federal laws, with the exception of those assigned to other agencies. The FBI's wide range of responsibilities includes jurisdiction in criminal, civil, and security fields. Among these are subversive activities such as espionage and sabotage, interstate gambling and interstate transportation of stolen property, and assault on or killing of the president. The FBI achieved great prominence under its long-time director, J. Edgar Hoover. During the 1970s and early 1980s its activities came under critical public scrutiny and were investigated. The tactics used by the agency in its "Abscam" operation—that of undercover FBI agents

attempting to bribe public officials and members of Congress—were considered questionable. Est. 1908.

Federalism, division of political power between US federal and state governments. The powers of the federal government are delegated by the Constitution; other "residual" powers are reserved to the states, guaranteeing them a considerable degree of autonomy. The federal government has supreme authority; the states cannot nullify federal law nor can they withdraw from the union. An increasing centralization of power has been a feature of American federalism since the New Deal programs of the 1930s.

Federalist Papers, The, a series of 85 essays on political theory published from 1787–88. Written by Alexander Hamilton, James Madison, and John Jay, the Federalist papers strongly showed support for the Federalist Constitution. All but the last eight essays appeared in the New York papers, and were widely read as they were published. Although the essays were not significantly influential at the ratification convention, they are widely accepted as a classical work on political theory. They were published in a two-volume edition in 1788.

Federalists, US political party led by George Washington, Alexander Hamilton, John Adams, and John Jay. It was formed in 1787 to promote ratification of the Constitution. The Federalists represented mainly planters, merchants, bankers, and manufacturers. The Federalist Papers were essays written by Hamilton, James Madison (who later became an anti-Federalist), and Jay expressing the Federalists' support for sound money, government banking, and strong federal powers. The Federalists were opposed to the states' rights, agrarian philosophy of the Republicans led by Thomas Jefferson.

Federal Republic of Germany. *See* Germany, West.

Federal Reserve System, central banking authority of the United States, established by the Federal Reserve Act of 1913 and strengthened by the Banking Acts of 1933 and 1935. Twelve regional banks are supervised by a Federal Reserve Board of Governors, with each of seven members appointed by the US president for 14 years. All national banks are members as are many state and commercial banks. More than three-fourths of all US commercial bank deposits are in member banks. Each member bank owns stocks in its district bank and must maintain reserves on deposit there. The purpose of the Federal Reserve System is to maintain sound monetary and credit conditions in the United States. It attempts to do so by regulating the flow of money through its Federal Reserve Notes, the US legal tender, and by regulating credit through varying its discount rate on loans to member banks and by varying the percentage of total deposits member banks must keep in reserve.

Federal Style, US architectural style between c.1780 and c.1820, based on English neoclassicism and influenced by the designs of Robert and James Adam. Buildings in this style were usually made of brick with windows and doors that were often framed by shallow wall arches. Other elements of the style included slender proportions and delicate decoration. Outstanding architects using this style were New Englanders Charles Bulfinch and Samuel McIntire.

Federated States of Micronesia. *See* Pacific Islands, Trust Territory of the.

Feedback, process of returning a part of the output energy of a device to the input. In negative feedback the output energy is arranged to cause a decrease in the input energy. A governor is a negative feedback device, the output being coupled to the input so that constant speed is obtained, irrespective of load. In positive feedback, the output energy reinforces the input energy. This occurs when a loudspeaker feeds into a microphone coupled to the same amplifier. In this case the amplifier will oscillate.

Feeds, term applied to the diet of farm animals provided by man. Feeds include such grains as wheat, corn, rye, soy beans, seeds, and some nonvegetative matter, such as fish meal. Many feeds are prepared commercially after extensive nutritional research.

Feininger, Lyonel (1871–1956), US painter, b. New York City. On the faculty of the Bauhaus (1919–33), he worked mostly in watercolors and graphic media. His style was strongly influenced by the cubists. In 1937 he returned to the United States where his style reached its maturation in such watercolors as "Dawn" (1938; Museum of Modern Art, New York City).

Feira de Santana, city in E Brazil, 60mi (97km) NNW of Salvador; noted site of cattle fairs; railway, livestock, and shipping center. Exports: cotton, tobacco, beans. Pop. 136,000.

Feldspars, group of common aluminum silicate minerals; principal constituents of igneous rocks. Orthoclase and microcline are potassium feldspars of monoclinic and triclinic system, respectively. Members of the plagioclase series (sodium and calcium feldspars) have physical properties similar to microcline, but with crystals frequently twinned. Several are cut as gems: amazonite, a green form of microcline; moonstone, white with a bluish stain, is a plagioclase variety as is labradorite, an iridescent red, blue, or green, and sunstone, a spangled variety, frequently reddish. Hardness 6; sp gr 2.55.

Felidae, cat family containing 3 genera *(Felis, Pantheon, Acinouyx)* and 36 species of carnivores, ranging from the housecat to the tiger. Order Carnivora. *See also* Cat.

Feminism, women's movement to obtain equal opportunity in politics, education, and employment. In the 18th century, when Mary Wollstonecraft's *Vindication of the Rights of Women* (1792) appeared, law and theology had long treated women as inferior to men. Women in the French and American revolutions had pressed without success for the inclusion of women's emancipation in the new constitutions. Women could not control property, the disposal of their children, or their own persons. In 1848 at the Seneca Falls Convention in New York, feminists, referred to as suffragettes because of their emphasis on gaining the right to vote, issued a declaration of independence for women. The movement, led by Susan B. Anthony and Elizabeth Cady Stanton, spread through the United States and Europe. Emmeline Goulden Pankhurst used militant means and hunger strikes to attempt to win suffrage in Britain, founding the Women's Social and Political Union in 1903. After marching, demonstrating, and being jailed, women won further entrance into higher education, trades and professions, and property rights. In the United States the woman-suffrage advocate Susan B. Anthony had been dead for 14 years when women finally won the right to vote in 1920. Margaret Sanger pressed for legalized birth control, winning it in the 1930s; a UN Commission on the Status of Women was established in 1946; but the Women's Liberation Movement, as it came to be known, had an upsurge of strength in the 1960s. The National Organization for Women (NOW), formed in 1966, and other women's groups tried to remove remaining legal and social barriers to equality for women by encouraging legalized abortion, federally supported child-care centers, and equal pay for women. The Equal Rights Amendment, passed in 1972 by Congress after pressure from Bella Abzug, Shirley Chisholm, and others in the National Women's Political Caucus, met opposition as it was submitted for ratification by the states. *See also* Seneca Falls Convention; Woman Suffrage; Women's Liberation Movement.

Femur, upper leg bone, extending from the pelvis to the knee. It is the longest and strongest bone of the skeleton. Its rounded smooth head articulates with the pelvis at the acetabulum, or hip socket; its large flattened lower end—felt on both sides of the knee—articulates with the tibia, the larger of the lower leg bones.

Fence Lizard, or spiny lizard, any of North and Central American lizards. Rough-scaled, its body is short and broad and grayish-brown, green, or blue. Most males have prominent blue patches on each side of belly. They are insectivorous. Length: 4–15in (10–38cm). There are 50 species; 15 are native to the United States. Family Iguanidae; genus *Sceloporus. See also* Lizard.

Fencing, the sport of dueling with foil, épée, and saber. It is conducted among individuals and teams, on a strip 40ft (12.2m) long and 6ft (1.8m) wide, which is marked off by 2 parallel warning lines 10ft (3m) from each end, beyond which the fencers may not step. Fencers wear wire-mesh masks, heavy canvas jackets, and gloves. The tip of the weapon is blunted and points are scored by touching the opponent. In épée matches, the whole body is included in the target area; with foils, the torso is the target area. With both weapons, touches are made with the point. In saber matches, the target area is any part of the body above the waist. Winning touches are five in foil or saber, and three in épée. The scoring is done electrically. Fencing was first included in the Olympic Games in 1896. In the United States the sport is regulated by The Amateur Fencers League of America (formed 1891).

Feng Yü-hsiang (1882–1948), one of the colorful warlords of 20th-century China. He built up in N China a large, personally devoted army that remained a significant force in modern Chinese politics until 1930. Feng's conversion to Christianity earned him the title of Christian General. His wife, Li Tehch'uan, remained active in the government of the Chinese People's Republic.

Fenian Cycle (Finn Cycle), group of Irish sagas dealing with the semi-divine hero Finn and his sons Oisin and Diarmaid. Written in Gaelic *c.*1200, the stories have an older oral tradition and feature incidents of heroic prowess and magical intervention upon which some of the incidents in Arthurian literature are based. The longest story in the cycle is *The Old Men's Conversation,* which is actually a collection of Finn stories.

Fenian Movement, 19th-century Irish nationalist organization. Formed in 1858, the Fenians sought independence from Britain by revolution. Following the arrests of their leaders in 1866 and the lack of response to their activities in Ireland, Irish immigrants in the United States took up their cause. Under John O'Neill the American Fenians planned several invasions of Canada, which were thwarted by United States and Canadian authorities (1866–70). A Fenian campaign in England (1866) also failed.

Fennel, aromatic herb native to Europe and Asia Minor and widely cultivated for food flavoring. Its shoots are eaten as a vegetable. It has divided leaves, yellow flowers, and small, oblong seedlike fruits. Height: to 3ft (0.9m). Family Umbelliferae; species *Foeniculum vulgare.*

Fenugreek, annual plant native to S Europe and Asia. It has white flowers and long, beaked pods. It is used as forage and a potherb. Height: to 2ft (61cm). Family Leguminosae; species *Trigonella foenumgraecum.*

Fer-de-lance, widely distributed Central and South American lance-headed pit viper that hunts rats. It has black-edged, light diamond markings on brown ground color. Terrestrial, its venomous bite is often fatal to human beings. Up to 70 live young are born at one time. Length: to 8ft (2.5m). Family Viperidae; genus *Bothrops. See also* Pit Viper; Snake.

Ferdinand I (1793–1875), emperor of Austria (1835–48), king of Hungary (1830–48). This weak sovereign let Prince Metternich govern for him. Faced with revolutions in Hungary, Italy, and Vienna, he was forced to abdicate and flee in 1848. His nephew Francis Joseph succeeded him as emperor of Austria in 1849.

Ferdinand I (1503–64), Holy Roman emperor (1556–64), king of Bohemia and of Hungary (1526–64). He succeeded to the thrones of Bohemia and Hungary on the death of his brother-in-law Louis II. He never really controlled Hungary; he had to pay tribute to Sultan Suleiman I to retain his title. He had a strong hold on Bohemia, where he suppressed the Protestants. His elder brother, Holy Roman Emperor Charles V, gave him considerable control over Germany. Ferdinand warred against the German Protestants with varying success, ending in the religious truce of the Treaty of Augsburg (1555). In 1558 Charles V abdicated in his favor.

Ferdinand (1861–1948), prince (1887–1908) and tsar of Bulgaria (1908–18). A prince of Saxe-Coburg, he was chosen to succeed Alexander as ruler of Bulgaria. Russia opposed his selection, so he was not recognized by the major powers until 1896. In 1908 he declared Bulgaria independent of the Ottoman Empire and himself the tsar. With Russian backing he allied Bulgaria with Serbia, Greece, and Montenegro in the first Balkan War (1912–13), which ended Turkish dominance in the Balkans. But in the second Balkan War (1913), Greece and Serbia joined with Romania and Turkey in defeating Bulgaria. Most of Macedonia was lost to Greece and Serbia. Bulgaria joined the Central Powers in World War I. After defeat in the war, Ferdinand abdicated in favor of his son Boris III.

Ferdinand I (Ferdinand the Great) (died 1065), Spanish king of Castile (1033–65) and León (1037–65). He succeeded his father, Sancho III of Navarre, in Castile, conquered León, and took parts of Navarre from his brother. He successfully fought the Moors, making vassals of the rulers of Seville, Toledo, Zaragoza, and Badajoz. His kingdoms were divided at his death among his sons.

Ferdinand I (1379?–1416), Spanish king of Aragón and Sicily and count of Barcelona (1412–16). A prince of Castile, he acted as regent for his nephew John II. In 1410 his uncle, Martin, died, leaving vacant the thrones of Aragon and Sicily and the county of Barcelona. After defeating his rivals, Ferdinand succeeded to his uncle's offices. He was succeeded by his son Alfonso V.

Ferdinand II (Ferdinand the Catholic) (1452–1516), Spanish king of Aragon (1479–1516), of Castile and León (as Ferdinand V, 1474–1504), of Sicily (1468–1516), and of Naples (1504–16). He became joint king of Castile and León after marrying Isabella I in 1469 and inherited Aragon from his father, John II, in 1479. After he and Isabella conquered the Moorish kingdom of Granada in 1492, they ruled over a united Spain. In 1492 they sponsored the voyage of Christopher Columbus to the New World, expelled the Jews from Spain, and initiated the Spanish Inquisition.

Under Ferdinand, Spain became involved in the Italian wars against France. The result was an almost united Italy under Spanish control. After Isabella's death in 1504, Ferdinand acted as regent in Castile for their insane daughter Joanna and later for her son Charles I (who succeeded Ferdinand and ruled most of Europe as Holy Roman Emperor Charles V). In 1506 Ferdinand married Germaine de Foix and used her rights in Navarre as pretext for conquering that kingdom.

Ferdinand III (1199–1252), Spanish king of Castile (1217–52) and León (1230–52). He was the son of Alfonso IX of León and Barengaria of Castile. His mother renounced her rights to Castile in his favor in 1217, and when he inherited León from his father in 1230, he permanently united the two kingdoms. He spent most of his reign successfully fighting the Moors. He expelled them from Córdoba, Jaén, Seville, and Murcia. Thus, at his death all of Spain except for the kingdom of Granada had been Christianized. His son Alfonso X succeeded him. Ferdinand was canonized in 1671.

Ferdinand VII (1784–1833), king of Spain (1808–33), son of Charles IV and María Luisa. As crown prince he was involved in court intrigues, made overtures to Napoleon I, and was arrested (1807) by his father. An uprising in 1808 forced his father's abdication, but the French forced Ferdinand himself off the throne and installed Joseph Bonaparte. Ferdinand was imprisoned by the French during the Peninsular War but was restored in 1814. Thereafter his reign was increasingly reactionary. All mainland colonies in the Western Hemisphere were lost during his reign. He altered the Spanish constitution so his daughter Isabella II could succeed him, which set off the Carlist wars. *See also* Carlists.

Ferdinand I (1345–83), king of Portugal (1367–83), son and successor of Peter I. His overwhelming ambition for the throne of Castile kept Portugal in almost continuous war with that country. Finally, in 1382 he married his daughter and heiress to King John I of Castile; upon Ferdinand's death, however, his illegitimate half brother, John I, was elected king.

Ferdinand I (1865–1927), king of Romania (1914–27). Named heir in 1889, he became king when his uncle Carol I died in 1914. Ferdinand kept Romania neutral in World War I until 1916 when Romanian armies invaded Transylvania. Although the Romanians were crushed by the armies of the Central Powers, Ferdinand had won the loyalty of his people and he returned in triumph in 1918. His coronation took place in 1922. By the terms of the peace treaties, Romania more than doubled its territory, although many of the settlements were disputed. Ferdinand's land reform efforts failed.

Ferdinand I (1751–1825), king of the Two Sicilies (1816–25) and of Naples (as Ferdinand IV). Son of Don Carlos de Bourbon (later Charles III of Spain), his reign in Naples from 1759–1825 was interrupted from 1806–1815 by the French occupation. His 1768 marriage to Marie Caroline, sister of French queen Marie An-

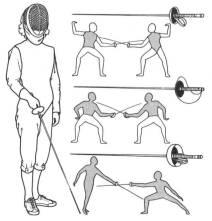

Fencing

Enrico Fermi

Ferret

toinette, marked the beginning of his reactionary policies. In 1816 he united his kingdoms of Naples and Sicily into the Kingdom of the Two Sicilies. The constitutionalist uprising of 1820 forced him to grant a constitution, but with the aid of Austria he regained his hold in 1821.

Ferdinand II (1810–59), king of the Two Sicilies (1830–59), son of Francis I. Originally considered a liberal, he came to be noted for his despotic rule; in 1849 he quelled a popular revolution begun in 1848, the first of many uprisings to sweep Europe that year. Ultimately, his authoritarian rule weakened the kingdom and led to its collapse and incorporation into a united Italy in 1860 after his death.

Ferdinand I de' Medici (1549–1609), grand duke of Tuscany. The younger son of Cosimo the Great, he resigned his cardinal's hat to succeed his brother Francesco (1541–87) as grand duke in 1587. By marrying Christine of Lorraine (granddaughter of Catherine de' Medici, herself a Florentine and then French queen) in 1589, he provided a French counterbalance to Spanish influence in Italy.

Ferdinand II de' Medici (1610–70), grand duke of Tuscany (from 1620). Son of Cosimo II (1590–1620) and father of Cosimo III (1642–1723), he was a pupil of Galileo. In 1657 he established the Academia del Cimento, said to be the first academic institution in Europe devoted to the natural sciences. His weak rule in the midst of Medici extravagence is held responsible for depletion of family fortunes.

Ferdinand III (1769–1824), grand duke of Tuscany and archduke of Austria. Succeeding as grand duke in 1790 when his father, Leopold II, became Holy Roman emperor, his reign was interrupted by the French occupation (1799–1814). Noted for his enlightened and liberal rule, he managed to avoid the reactionary violence typical of Italian restorations after Napoleon's defeat as well as overwhelming dependence on Austria.

Fergana (Ferghana), formerly Skobelev, city in E Uzbek SSR, USSR; capital of Fergana oblast; site of teachers' college. Industries: cotton, silk, clothing. Founded 1876 by Russians as Novy Margelan. Pop. 135,000.

Ferlinghetti, Lawrence (1920–), US author, b. Yonkers, N.Y. A major voice of the Beat Generation movement, he was a founder of City Lights Bookshop in San Francisco. Through City Lights Publishing House, he published the works of many modern poets and writers. Ferlinghetti's collections of poetry include *Pictures of the Gone World* (1955), *A Coney Island of the Mind* (1958), *The Secret Meaning of Things* (1969), *Open Eye, Open Heart* (1973), and *Who Are We Now?* (1976). He has also written a novel, *Her* (1960), and several plays.

Fermentation, energy-yielding pathway by which sugar and starch molecules, catalyzed by enzymes or micro-organisms such as yeast, are broken down anaerobically. Old-established uses, where the major products are carbon dioxide and ethanol, include bread making, wine and beer brewing, cheese maturing, and drug manufacture. Fermentation is a major metabolic degrading pathway where the products may differ due to different enzymes directing the last stages.

Fermi, Enrico (1901–54), Italian physicist who worked mainly in the fields of atomic behavior and structure, and the quantum theory. He showed that transmutations may be caused by neutron bombardment of elements, synthesized transuranium, and constructed the

first atomic pile. He was honored with the 1938 Nobel Prize and by having the element fermium named after him.

Fermium, radioactive metallic element (symbol Fm) of the actinide group, first identified (1953) as a decay product of U^{235} produced in the first large hydrogen-bomb explosion (1952). Properties: at. no. 100; most stable isotope Fm^{257} (half-life 80 days). *See also* Transuranium Elements.

Fern, tracheophyte, or nonflowering plant, that produces spores rather than seeds. Some are vines, some trees, and some float on ponds. Many grow on trees. Most grow in warm, moist areas. The best known genus, *Pteridium* (bracken), grows in old fields. They are characterized by two perennial generations: the conspicuous sporophyte that possesses leafy fronds, stems, and roots, and reproduces by minute spores usually clustered on the leaves; and the inconspicuous gametophyte that resembles tiny moss and produces sperm and ova. Ferns usually have flat leaves on a stalk. Fronds unroll from curled fiddleheads and are divided into leaflets. Ferns were represented during Devonian times. Class Filicinae.

Fernández de Córdoba, Gonzalo (1453–1515), Spanish general, known as the Great Captain. He negotiated the surrender of the Moors in Granada in 1492. He was commander of the troops of Ferdinand and Isabella in the Italian wars and was successful in removing French influence from Naples and Sicily. He became the first viceroy of Naples after the Spanish victory.

Fernando Pó. *See* Bioko Island.

Ferrara, city in N Italy, 57mi (92km) SW of Venice; capital of Ferrara prov. An independent commune in 10th century, city was ruled by House of Este 1240; prosperity declined under papal rule 1598; ceded to France 1797; restored to pope 1815; birthplace of Girolamo Savonarola, reformer and martyr of the Roman Catholic church (1452); site of Este Castle (1385–1570), Cathedral of St Giórgio (1185), university (1391). Industries: agriculture, chemicals, sugar, alcohol, shoes. Pop. 154,876.

Ferrarese School, northern school of painting of the Italian Renaissance. Among the artists of this school in the 15th century were Cosimo Tura and Ercole de' Roberti. During the 16th century, this school was led by Dosso and his brother Battista del Dosso, and was influenced by Venetian and Roman artists of the period.

Ferraro, Geraldine Anne (1935–), US politician, b. Newburgh, N.Y. Educated at Marymount Manhattan College, Hunter College, and Fordham University law school, she married in 1960 and raised three children. She became an assistant district attorney in 1974 and then served in Congress as a Democrat (1978–83). In 1984 she was nominated as the first woman candidate for US vice president. Although defeated in the election she remains active in Democratic party politics.

Ferret, small, carnivorous weasel-like animal. They are agile killers, with long necks, slender bodies, long tails, short legs, pink eyes, and yellow fur. The wild black-footed *Mustela nigripes* of North America is rare, and may be almost extinct. The domesticated *Mustela putorius caro*, related to the European polecat, is used by hunters to kill rats and flush rabbits from their burrows. Length: 19in(48cm); weight: 1lb(.45kg). Family Mustelidae. *See also* Polecat; Weasel.

Ferric Compounds, those compounds in which the element iron has a higher valance (usually three) than in ferrous compounds.

Ferrol (El Ferrol del Caudillo), port city in NW Spain; site of a major Spanish naval station; birthplace of Gen. Francisco Franco. Industries: shipbuilding, iron works. Founded 1726. Pop. 87,736.

Ferromagnetism, form of magnetism exhibited by substances, such as iron, cobalt, and nickel, with high magnetic permeabilities. *See also* Magnetism.

Ferry, Jules François Camille (1832–93), French republican statesman, opposed the empire of Napoleon III, holding several political offices after its fall. Twice premier (1880–81; 1883–85), he accomplished extensive educational reform, arousing clerical enmity, and oversaw the establishment of a French colonial empire in Africa and Indochina. He was assassinated.

Fertile Crescent, historic region in the Middle East. It curves across the N section of the Syrian desert, including parts of Jordan, Iraq, Israel, Syria, Lebanon; is watered by Tigris and Euphrates rivers; site of many violent invasions from the Arabian peninsula; location of man's earliest cultures; artifacts have been found dating from 8,000 BC. *See* Tigris-euphrates Region.

Fertility Drug, a drug used to induce ovulation. Some drugs used are Clomiphene, a weak estrogen that is thought to stimulate pituitary gland gonadotropin secretion, and Perganol, which contains human pituitary gonadotropin. Both can induce ovulation, but both must be used carefully and often result in multiple pregnancy.

Fertilization, impregnation of an egg nucleus by a sperm nucleus to form a zygote. Stages of fertilization are: penetration—sperm clumps on egg surface; activation—completion of egg meiosis; and fusion of egg and sperm nuclei—restores diploid number of chromosomes. It is external (fish, amphibians) or internal (reptiles, birds, mammals). *See also* Reproduction, Sexual.

Fertilizer, substance (natural or artificial) added to soil, containing chemicals to improve plant growth by increasing soil fertility. Manure and compost were the first fertilizers. Other natural substances, such as bonemeal, ashes, guano, and fish, have been used for centuries. Modern chemical fertilizers, composed of nitrogen, phosphorus, and potassium in powdered, liquid, or gaseous forms, are now widely used. Specialized fertilizers also contain essential trace elements.

Fès (Fez), city in N central Morocco, approx. 150mi (242km) ENE of Casablanca; a sacred city of Islam containing over 100 mosques. Industries: agriculture, leather goods, metal works. Founded 790. Pop. 325,327.

Fescue, grass native to Northern Hemisphere and cultivated widely for pasture and fodder. Some species, such as red fescue *(Festuca rubra),* are also used in lawn mixtures. The short, five-leaved sheep fescue *(F. ovina)* grows in dense tufts on mountains and forms turf in sandy soil. Blue fescue has smooth, silvery leaves in clumps and is cultivated for ornamental borders. There are about 100 species. Family Gramineae.

Fetish, object possessing supernatural powers. The power of the fetish derives from a deity or consecration or is inherent. Claws or amulets may be fetishes. They are often carried around, especially by witch doctors, as sources of magical power. *See also* Amulet; Totem; Witch Doctor.

Fetishism, sexual dysfunction in which a particular object or body part becomes an essential aspect of sexual arousal and gratification. In religious fetishism, a particular object is imbued with inordinate religious importance that is not consistent with the usual norms of the culture.

Feudalism, the social system that prevailed in most of Western Europe during the 10th through the 13th centuries, consisting of a body of social institutions based on the contract of vassalage and the distribution of fiefs.

Geographical distribution. Feudalism dominated during this period in France, Germany, Burgundy-Arles, Italy, England, the Christian kingdoms of Spain, and some former Roman territories of the Near East. Occasionally the term is applied to other areas of the world during other periods, but these feudal-type societies are not part of the same political and social development.

Characteristics. Feudalism was characterized by decentralization of government, with many small kingdoms existing in each present-day nation. It was based upon the loyalties and obligations between individuals of different social classes, particularly between the lord and his vassals. The rights to real property were divided; the owner of the property retained certain rights to the land, while the vassal had others. Political powers normally assigned to the state were likewise apportioned, including defense, administration of justice, and taxation. The church participated in feudal relationships, churchmen being vassals of secular lords and in turn having secular vassals.

Development. Feudalism arose in the 7th century Frankish kingdom of the Merovingians in France. By the Carolingian period in the 8th century, it was well established there and spread to the rest of Western Europe, coming to England with the Norman Conquest (1066). During a period of political and social instability, it provided a means of mutual protection, of reclaiming war-ravaged land for agriculture, and of institutionalizing legal and moral obligations.

Fever, elevation of the body temperature above normal, caused by infection, numerous other disorders. Fever can be reduced medically or mechanically, but the cause should be determined first.

Feverfew, bushy Eurasian perennial plant widely naturalized in E North America. It has fine-lobed aromatic leaves and small, white flower heads borne in open clusters. Height: to 3ft (91cm). Family Compositae; species *Chrysanthemum parthenium.*

Fez. *See* Fès.

Fianna Fáil, "Warriors of Eyre," a political party formed in Ireland in 1926 to oppose the 1921 treaty that created the Irish Free State. The party controlled Irish politics almost continuously from the 1930s to 1973, and has taken a stance of absolute Irish independence, revitalization of the Gaelic language, and Irish economic improvement.

Fiat Money, money that has a value only because it is issued by a government and has the confidence of the population; ie, it cannot be redeemed for any commodity that is intrinsically valuable. The most common example is paper currency.

Fiber, Natural, naturally occurring fibrous material that can be made into yarn, textiles, carpets, rope, felt, etc. Natural fibers are made up of long narrow cells. Animal products are based on protein molecules; they include wool, silk, mohair, angora, and horsehair. Vegetable fibers are mainly cellulose; they include cotton, linen, flax, jute, sisal, and kapok. Asbestos is a natural inorganic fiber. A class of fibers, including rayon and acetate, is obtained from natural products modified chemically.

Fiber, Synthetic, fiber made from a synthetic resin by forcing it through a fine nozzle (spinneret). The resin is melted and extruded through the spinneret, or first dissolved in a solvent which is removed, either by hot air or by a liquid-coagulating bath. The result is a monofilament which can be woven into textiles, made into rope, etc. For many textiles, particularly in clothing, staple yarn is used, consisting of short fibers twisted together. Synthetic fibers are polymeric materials having long-chain molecules. Many types, with various properties, exist, including nylon and other polyamides, polyesters, and acrylics.

Fiber Optics, branch of optics employing the phenomenon that light entering a glass fiber is conducted by reflection from one end of the fiber to the other without loss of energy. Images may be magnified, distorted, or scrambled, depending on the configuration of the fiber bundles. Fiber optics is used in medicine to observe organs internally (endoscopy), and in photography and spectroscopy. Fiber optics have widespread use in telecommunications, providing high-speed data links and wide-band width connections and ultimately replacing metal cable systems.

Fibrillation, small involuntary contraction of muscle, most often associated with heart disorders. Symptoms of the more common atrial fibrillation include fainting and nausea; ventricular fibrillation can be fatal.

Fibrin, fibrous protein that polymerizes during the clotting process to form the basic meshwork of the blood clot. *See also* Blood Clotting.

Fibrinogen, precursor protein of fibrin, synthesized by the liver and released into the blood stream. It is converted to fibrin by thrombin during the clotting process. *See also* Blood Clotting.

Fibroma, tumor, usually benign although tending to ulcerate, composed mainly of fibrous or connective tissue. It can occur in the mouth, uterus, or gastrointestinal tract.

Fibula, smaller of the two lower leg bones. It extends from the knee region to the ankle, ending in the projection that may be felt on the outer side of the ankle. *See also* Tibia.

Fichte, Johann Gottlieb (1762–1814), German philosopher. He turned Kantian influence in the direction of subjective idealism in *System of Morality* (1800) and embraced romantic nationalism in his *Addresses to the German Nation* (1807–08). His philosophic system is pivoted on the so-called "ego," which becomes aware of its own freedom and its unity with the absolute.

Ficino, Marsilio (1433–99), Italian philosopher. A Greek scholar and head of the Florentine Academy, he promoted the study of Plato and philosophy generally. Although a humanist, he had inclinations toward mysticism. His *De Religione Christiana,* a synthesis of Greek mysticism and Christianity, was the standard Latin text on the subject for 100 years. *See also* Humanism.

Fiddler Crab, amphibious crab found worldwide that burrows in sandy beaches and drier parts of salt marshes. It is named for the male's huge claw that is used in courtship signaling and mating season battles. Width: under 1in (25mm). Family Ocypodidae; genus *Uca. See also* Crab.

Fief, in feudalism, a unit of property granted by a lord to his vassal as a reward for past services or in exchange for future service, loyalty and mutual protection. The lord maintained the ultimate rights to the land, while the vassal had its use and most of the profits from it.

Field, Cyrus West (1819–92), US financier and promotor of the first trans-Atlantic telegraph cable, b. Stockbridge, Mass. Field conceived the idea after his retirement from business, and after two unsuccessful attempts the cable was laid by the steamship *The Great Eastern* in July 1866. Field also developed the Wabash Railroad with Jay Gould.

Field, Stephen Johnson (1816–99), US jurist and public official, b. Haddam, Conn. A California state representative (1849), state supreme court justice (1859–63), and associate justice of the US Supreme Court (1863–97), he championed due process of law and opposed judicial interference in governmental affairs.

Field Artillery, light and medium artillery pieces, either drawn by trucks or self-propelled and capable of deploying rapidly into field positions. *See also* Artillery; Howitzer.

Field Emission. *See* Electron Emission.

Field Hockey, a sport that uses many of the elements found in ice hockey, soccer, and basketball. It is played by 2 teams of 11 persons each, 5 forwards, 3 halfbacks, 2 fullbacks, and a goal-keeper, on a field 100 yards long (91.5m) and 55–60 yards wide (50–55m). At each end of the field is a goal 7ft (2.1m) high and 12 feet wide (3.7m). In front of the goal is a 16-yard (14.6m) striking zone (15-yard, 13.7m for women). A goal, which may be scored from the striking zone, counts as one point. Each match consists of two 35-minute halves (30 for women). Players carry a stick approximately 36 inches in length (91.4cm) with a canelike curve to the striking edge. The plastic ball (about the size of a baseball) is advanced by throwing, catching, or striking. Penalties vary according to team and individual, technical and personal, whether they are made by the attacking team or defending team, and whether they are made inside or outside the striking circle. Field hockey was developed in England in mid-19th century.

Fielding, Henry (1707–54), English novelist. He wrote comedies, such as *Historical Register for the Year 1736,* and later took up political journalism. His novels include *Joseph Andrews* (1742) and *Tom Jones* (1749).

Field Mouse, any of the many small, mostly herbivorous, mostly nocturnal rodents that forage in the wild all over the world. They live on the ground in grassy nests and feed on seeds and grass. Genus *Microtus.*

Field of the Cloth of Gold (1520), conference between Henry VIII of England and Francis I of France held near Calais, France. Richly dressed, handsomely attended, and with lavish surroundings, the two kings failed to make the hoped-for alliance against the Holy Roman Emperor Charles V.

Field Spaniel, hunting dog (sporting group) introduced to US in 1880s; has good scenting powers and can retrieve. A beautiful dog, its well-developed head has a long, lean muzzle; long, wide ears hang in folds. The medium-length body has a straight or slightly arched back; legs are long; the tail is carried low. Colored black, liver, golden liver, mahogany, or roan, the flat coat is silky and abundantly feathered on chest, belly, and legs. Average size: 18in (45.5cm) high at shoulder; 35–50lb (16–22.5kg). *See also* Sporting Dog.

Field Trials, a competition for hunting dogs. Trials are divided into five categories: beagle trials, hound trials, pointing dog trials, retriever trials, and spaniel trials. In each of these categories, the animal, on land and/or in water, must perform one or more maneuvers in the sighting, retrieving, and returning of the game. Field trials originated in England in the 17th century, and the first public trials in the United States were conducted in 1874 near Memphis, Tenn. Over 7,000 field trials are held annually in the United States.

Fieschi, noble Genoese family of the Middle Ages. Their Guelf (pro-papal and anti-imperial) politics and alliances with Angevin kings of Sicily dated from mid-13th century, when Sinibaldo Fieschi became Pope Innocent IV, and were to shape the family destiny until Andrea Doria decisively put Genoa into imperial hands in 1528 and the line ended. Ottobono Fieschi also became pope, as Adrian V (1276), and Caterina Fieschi (1447–1510) was later canonized as St Catherine of Genoa.

Fife, county in E Scotland, between firths of Tay and Forth; capital is Cupar. Former Pictish kingdom, it officially became a region 1975; ecclesiastical capital of Scotland until the Reformation; one of Scotland's most prosperous counties with fertile soil and rich coal fields; site of St Andrews, Scotland's oldest university. Products: sugar beets, livestock, wheat, oats, barley, turnips. Industries: quarrying, coal mining, fisheries, shipbuilding, engineering works, weaving, brewing. Area: 505sq mi (1,308sq km). Pop. 336,339.

Fife, shrill-toned musical instrument similar to flute, but with a smaller barrel and six to eight finger holes, sometimes with keys like the piccolo's. It has been used with drums by infantry since the Crusades. *See also* Flute.

Fifth Column, saboteurs, spies, and other non-uniformed para-military elements operating behind the battle area, conducting guerrilla warfare or other operations designed to confuse or disorient the opposing force. *See also* Guerrilla Warfare.

Fifty-Four, Forty or Fight, expression used by Americans in their struggle with England over ownership of the Oregon territory. Settlers extended land rights to latitude 54° 40′N. It was a Democratic campaign slogan in 1844.

Fig, mainly evergreen trees found in warm regions, especially Polynesia, Indo-Malaysia, and Asia Minor. Among the hundreds of species is the common orchard fig, *Ficus carica,* native to the Mediterranean. Its tiny flowers have no petals and are found on the inside of fleshy receptacles that become the thick outer covering holding the seeds, the true fruit of the fig tree. Height: to 30ft (9.1m). Other fig species include banyan *(F. benghalensis),* sycamore *(F. sycomorus),* and rubber tree *(F. elastica).* Family Moraceae.

Fighting Fish, betta, or Siamese fighting fish, freshwater tropical fish of Indochina and Malay Peninsula. Popular with home aquarists, this aggressive fish is short-finned and drab in its natural form. Selective breeding has produced brilliantly colored specimens with long, flowing fins. Males will fight until exhausted or injured. Length: 2–3in (5.1–7.6cm). Family Anabantidae; species *Betta splendens.*

Cyrus W. Field

Millard Fillmore

Finland

Figure-Drawing Test, in psychology, a projective technique used to assess personality. The subject is asked to draw a person and then a person of the opposite sex. The technique has been useful in the diagnosis of mental disorders and reveals information about the subject's self-concept, spontaneity, sexual identity, and other personality dimensions. *See also* Projective Techniques.

Figure Skating, sport, created by Jackson Haines, a US ballet master, in Austria in 1864 after the introduction of steel blades to skates in 1850 by E. W. Bushnell of Philadelphia. Although the first figure skating organization was founded in Canada in 1878, it was not until Sonja Henie's performance in the 1936 winter Olympic Games that the sport reached international prominence.

Figures of Speech, figurative language; that is, linguistic constructions in which words or thoughts are employed in unusual combinations to heighten effect or establish unusual connections or oppositions. They are sometimes divided into two types: the trope, meaning "turn," in which the literal meaning of the words changes; and those figures in which not the words, but the thought expressed undergoes an inventive twist. For example, puns and metaphors are tropes, while apostrophes and antitheses are not. *See also* Metaphor; Pun.

Figwort, perennial Northern Hemisphere plants with a strong smell and loose, terminal clusters of yellow, greenish, or purple flowers, The figwort family (Scrophulariaceae) consists mostly of herbs and small shrubs. Some members are saprophytes or parasites, some lacking chlorophyll.

Fiji, independent nation in SW Pacific Ocean. It is an archipelago, consisting of the islands of Vitu Levu, Vanua Levu and about 800 much smaller islets. The main islands are of volcanic origin, Mt Tomaniivi rising to 4,341ft (1,323m) on Viti Levu, whereas the smaller islands are low-lying coral reefs. The climate is generally hot and wet. Main products are copra, sugar, rice, bananas, hardwood, gold, and manganese. Industry apart from handcrafts is limited to sugar and copra processing. Indigenous Fijians are of Melanesian stock, with Polynesians, mainly Tongans, forming a minority group. Both groups are outnumbered by Asian Indians, descendants of laborers taken there to work the sugar plantations. Government is based upon the British system, with representation proportional to ethnic groups. Discovered in 1643 by Tasman; visited by Captain Cook in 1774; ceded to Britain in 1874 after tribal wars and exploitation by Europeans. Fiji retained some self-government, which was expanded after WW II. In 1970 it became an independent nation with dominion status within the Commonwealth of Nations.

PROFILE

Official name: Fiji
Area: 7,053sq mi (18,272sq km)
Population: 612,046
Density: 87 per sq mi (33 per sq km)
Chief city: Suva (capital), 66,018
Government: Parliamentary democracy
Religions (major): Methodist and Hindu
Gross national product: $540,770,000
Trading partners (major): Great Britain, Australia, United States, Japan

Filarete (Antonio Averlino) (*c.*1400–*c.*1465), Italian sculptor and architect. Best known as the sculptor of the bronze doors of St. Peter's, Rome (completed 1445), he also designed the Ospedale Maggiore in Milan and wrote *Il trattato d'architettura.*

Filariasis, group of disorders caused by infection with a nematode worm, usually in the tropics. Lymph involvement is typical, with chills, headache, nausea, and muscle pain preceding lymphatic inflammation. Treatment with drugs reduces symptoms. *See also* Elephantiasis.

Filbert, trees and shrubs native to the Northern Hemisphere. They have yellow male catkins and small red-centered female flowers that bear edible brown nuts sometimes called hazelnuts. Height: 3–35ft (0.9–11m). There are about 15 species. Family Betulaceae; genus *Corylus.*

Fillmore, Millard (1800–74), 13th president of the United States, b. Locke, N.Y. He married twice: Abigail Powers in 1826 and Caroline Mcintosh in 1858. A lawyer in New York state, he was an early leader in the Anti-Masonic party. After serving in the state legislature, he was elected to the US House of Representatives (1832). In 1835, he changed his affiliation to the new Whig party and remained in the House until 1843, rising to become Ways and Means Committee chairman. In 1848, he became comptroller of New York and later that year, he was a successful vice-presidential candidate, running with Zachary Taylor. As vice-president he presided over the Senate during the bitter slavery debates of 1850. When Taylor died on July 9, 1850, Fillmore became president. As president he attempted to avoid a national crisis by mediating between the proslavery, antislavery forces. He encouraged and signed the Compromise of 1850, which included the Fugitive Slave Law. His enforcement of that law embittered the Whig abolitionists and helped bring into being the new Republican party. He—and the Whig party itself—were victims of the great slavery dispute; he was not nominated in 1852.
Career: New York State Assembly, 1829–31; US House of Representatives, 1833–43; comptroller, state of New York, 1848–49; vice-president, 1849–50; president, 1850–53.

Filtration, process of removing solids from liquids by passage through a suitable medium such as filter paper, glass wool, or sand.

Finback Whale, or common rorqual, one of the fastest and largest whales, it may swim 30mph (48kmph) when pursued. Length: to 79ft (24m); weight: over 50 tons. Species *Balaenoptera physalus. See also* Rorqual.

Finch, any of a family (Fringillidae) of small or medium-sized birds, including sparrows, cardinals, canaries, buntings, and grosbeaks, found over most of the world, except Australia, New Zealand, and the Pacific islands. Some are drab, a few brightly colored, and most have a cone-shaped bill and feed on seeds, with some eating berries, other fruit, and insects. Most finches lay 2 to 6 eggs in open cup-shaped nests.

Finger Lakes, series of 11 long, narrow, glacial lakes in central New York, including Canandaigua, Cayuga, Keuka, Owasco, Seneca, and Skaneateles. Cayuga and Seneca are longest, approx. 35mi (56km). New York State's wine industry is here. City of Hammondsport at end of Keuka Lake is its commercial center; site of Wells College and Cornell University on Cayuga Lake; Keuka College on Keuka Lake. Skaneateles Lake supplies Syracuse with part of its water supply. Many resorts and tourist attractions are in the Finger Lakes region.

Finisterre, cape in NW Spain, on coast of Galicia in Atlantic Ocean; has an irregular coast with sandy beaches, inlets, and rocky headlands.

Finland, Gulf of, E arm of Baltic Sea, between Finland and USSR; chief ports are Leningrad and Tallinn, USSR and Helsinki, Finland. Width: 10–75mi (16–121km). Length: 285mi (459km).

Finland, Republic of, an independent country of N Europe. Historically, Finland has been dominated by Russia or Sweden. The Finns are a hardy, prosperous people who have excelled in commerce and the arts.
  Land and economy. Geologically, Finland lies on the Fenno-Scandian shield, one of the most ancient portions of the earth's crust. It was covered with glaciers in the Ice Age; hence, its relative flatness, its low, rounded hills, and multitude of lakes, rivers, and bogs. The Finnish population lives primarily in the fertile coastal areas. The central plateau contains a wealth of forestlands. Farther N lies Lapland and the treeless tundra of the Arctic Circle. Finland's economy has traditionally centered on its vast timber resources. Since WWII, however, new industries, such as shipbuilding and metalworking, have developed. Helsinki, the capital, is the manufacturing center. Most business is in private hands, and the majority of Finland's farms are small. About 60% of the country's total export income is derived from forest products.
  People. The origins of the Finns are uncertain. The Finnish language is related to Hungarian and Estonian and more remotely to Turkish. It is not an Indo-European tongue. The Finno-Ugrian peoples arrived in Europe prior to the Slavs. More than 90% of Finland's population speaks Finnish, while about 7% speaks Swedish. The state church of Finland is the Evangelical Lutheran Church, to which 90% of all Finns belong. The rapid industrialization of the post-war period caused an exodus from rural to urban areas.
  Government. The constitution provides a parliamentary form of government in combination with a strong presidency. The chief executive is the president, elected to a six-year term; he appoints the prime minister and his cabinet, directs foreign policy, and serves as commander-in-chief of the armed forces. The Finnish parliament is a single chamber comprising 200 members elected to 4-year terms. The prime minister and his cabinet deal with daily functions of government. The large number of political parties results in an unstable parliament. Each of Finland's 12 provinces has its own elected officials.
  History. The Finno-Ugrian peoples, who were nomadic hunters, reached the Baltic area more than 2,000 years ago. In the Middle Ages, Sweden conquered and Christianized the Finns. For more than 400 years, until 1809, Finland was an integral part of Sweden. Russia controlled Finland in the 19th century. A growing nationalism led to an independence movement; the country became a republic in 1919. After the outbreak of WWII, the Soviet Union invaded Finland (1939) and took control of strategic territories. The Finns later allied themselves with Germany, but signed an armistice with the Soviet Union and Great Britain in 1944. After the war Finland established sound economic relations with the Soviet Union and the nations of the West. As president for 25 years (1956–81), Urho Kekkonen skillfully guided his country in its sometimes difficult neutral stance, balancing ties with both Western Europe and the Soviet Union. Mauno Koivisto, his successor (1982–   ), pledged friendly ties with the Soviet Union.

PROFILE

Official name: Finland, Republic of
Area: 130,120sq mi (337,009sq km)
Population: 4,757,000
Density: 36per sq mi (14per sq km)
Chief cities: Helsinki (capital); Tampere; Turku
Government: Democratic republic
Religion: Evangelical Lutheran Church (official)

Language: Finnish, Swedish (both official)
Monetary unit: Markka
Gross national product: $31,800,000,000
Per capita income: $5,149
Industries (major products): paper, machinery, metalworking, furniture, electrical products
Agriculture (major products): forest products, dairy products, wheat, sugar beets
Minerals (major): copper, zinc
Trading partners: Sweden, West Germany, Great Britain

Finlay River, river in N British Columbia, Canada; important tributary of the Peace River; rises in the Stikine Mts; flows 210mi (338km) SE to the Parsnip River at Finlay Forks. Length: 240mi (386km).

Finno-Ugric Languages, group of languages spoken by about 20,000,000 people in parts of NE Europe and Siberia. The Finnic branch includes Finnish, Estonian, Lappish, and, in the Soviet Union, Mordvinian, Udmurt, Mari, and Komi. The Ugric branch consists of Hungarian plus two minor languages of Siberia: Khanty (Ostyak) and Mansi (Vogul). Together with the remote Samoyed languages the Finno-Ugric languages form the Uralic family.

Finsteraarhorn, mountain peak in S central Switzerland, on boundary of Valais and Bern cantons; first climbed 1812. Highest of Bernese Alps, 14,019ft (4,276m).

Fiord, or **fjord,** narrow, steep-walled bay with mountainous, glaciated coasts, or a very narrow drowned estuary. Fiords are almost always perpendicular to the coastline that they are part of and they appear to have been formed from narrow fingers of glacier. *See also* Glaciology.

Fir, evergreen trees native to cooler, temperate regions of the world. They are pyramid-shaped and have flat needles and erect cones. Included are the silver and balsam firs. Height: 50–300ft (15–91m). Family Pinacea; genus *Abies. See also* Conifers.

Fire Ant, reddish black ant, 0.12 to 0.24in (3–6mm) long, native to South America and introduced into southern parts of the United States. It is a mound builder that feeds on young plants and seeds. It has a very painful sting. Family Formicidae, species *Solenopsis saevissima richteri. See also* Ant; Hymenoptera.

Fire Blight, a highly infectious and destructive disease of apples, pears, and related fruit trees that causes a blackened, scorched appearance of leaves and twigs, as if seared by fire. Other symptoms of the disease, caused by the bacterium *Erwinia amylovora,* include cankers on stems and discolored flowers and fruit. Control of the disease is difficult. Some tree varieties are resistant to the disease.

Fireclay, clay that will withstand high temperatures without deforming. Fireclay is used for firebrick, crucibles, and many refractory shapes. Fireclay approaches kaolin in composition, better grades containing at least 35% alumina when fired.

Firefly, light-emitting beetle found in moist places in temperate and tropical regions. Adults are soft-bodied and slender. Light-emitting organs on the abdomen underside give off flashes of light in a species-characteristic rhythm. The flashing is believed to be a sexual attractant. The luminous larvae and wingless females of some species are called glowworms. Length: to 0.5in (13mm). There are 2,000 species. Family Lampyridae.

Fire Island, long, narrow stretch of land off S central Long Island; separates Great South Bay from the Atlantic Ocean. Fire Island National Seashore occupies part of the island; includes beaches, wooded areas, and marshland. Popular summer resort area. Length: 32mi (52km).

Firm, Theory of the, in economics, that part of price theory devoted to analysis of the individual business firm. The analysis includes the computation of total cost, average cost, and marginal cost, as well as total and marginal revenue. Theory of the firm concentrates on an analysis of the method of maximizing the firm's profit. Profit maximization differs depending upon whether the business firm is a monopoly, an oligopoly, an imperfectly competitive firm, or a purely competitive firm. *See also* Price Theory.

Firn, mountain snow that has been converted to granular ice in a mountain glacier and, with an accumulation of broken rock materials at its base, digs out round basins called cirques.

First Amendment, addition to the United States Constitution mandating the freedoms of speech, the press, religion, and peaceful assembly. It is included within the Bill of Rights, and has been increasingly enforced by the US Supreme Court. Chief Justice Earl Warren increased the assurance of the First Amendment in the *New York Times v. Sullivan* (1964), which concerned the protection of the press from libel, and in *NAACP v. Alabama* (1958), which protected any peaceful demonstration from harassment by a state agency.

First World War. *See* World War I.

Fiscal Policy, government spending and tax policies, used to achieve a particular economic goal. Fiscal policy may be used to dampen inflationary pressures or to stimulate expansion within the economy. When the economy is suffering from inflation, the traditional fiscal policy is to decrease government spending and increase taxes, thus easing demand pressures by diminishing the money in consumers' pocketbooks. The traditional fiscal policy during a recession is to increase government spending and cut taxes, thus stimulating the economy by increasing demand for goods and services.

Fish, Hamilton (1808–93), US political leader, b. New York City. A lawyer, he served in Congress (1843–45) as a Whig. He later served as lieutenant governor (1847–48) and as governor (1849–50) of New York. He was a US Senator (1851–57). As secretary of state under Pres. Ulysses S. Grant (1869–77), Fish successfully handled the *Alabama* claims dispute. *See also* Alabama Claims.

Fish, aquatic vertebrate characterized by fins; respiration through gills; streamlined fusiform body; scale, bony plate, or scaleless body covering; and two-chambered heart. Fish are the most ancient form of vertebrate life, dating from Silurian period (450,000,000 years ago). Fish reproduce bisexually; fertilization is external or internal, and eggs develop in the water or inside the female, according to species. There are 25,000 species, representing 40% of all living vertebrates, divided into 37 orders and 289 families. The classification of fish varies. Generally they are divided into two superclasses: Agnatha, jawless fish including hagfish and lamprey, and Pisces. Pisces is divided into two main classes: Chondrichthyes (cartilaginous fish) including subclasses Elasmobranchii (shark and ray) and Holocephali (chimeras); Osteichthyes (bony fish) including the lungfish and lobefin and the higher bony fish. Length: 0.5in–over 40ft (1.3cm–12m).

Fish Culture, or aquaculture, breeding and raising fish under controlled conditions. The goal is high-level production for food or for stocking lakes, ponds, and streams for sportsmen. The most widely bred fish in the world are carp, rainbow trout, and Mozambique cichlid. Fish culture for food supply is practiced on a large scale only in Asia.

Fisher, Saint John (*c.* 1459–1535), English Roman Catholic prelate. Fisher held several posts at Cambridge, and preached moral austerity before opposing Henry VIII's proposed divorce (1529). Created cardinal (1535), he was tried and executed for denying that Henry was supreme head of the church under the Act of Supremacy. He was canonized in 1935.

Fisher, large, long-tailed carnivorous marten of North America that has commercially valuable fur. They have brown to black fur with white-tipped outer hairs. Females are smaller than males and their fur is more valuable. Good climbers, they are the only known predators of porcupines. Length: 3.5ft (1m); weight: to 18lb (8kg). Family Mustelidae; species *Martes pennanti. See also* Marten; Sable.

Fishery, or **Commercial Fishing,** harvesting large amounts of fish from the seas, large inland lakes, and rivers for food and other commercial uses. Fishing boats and fleets employ several methods for catching fish, including pole and line, harpoon, purse seine, and trawling. About 70% of the commercial fish catch is taken in the Northern Hemisphere; the greatest catches are taken in the area between the Philippines and Japan. Other fishing areas include the North Atlantic, the North Pacific, and the North Sea. The most significant Southern Hemisphere areas are the Pacific coast of Peru and the South African coast. Herrings, sardines, and anchovies make up the largest percentage of the total catch. Others caught in large commercial quantities are cod, haddock, hake, redfish, sea bream, mackerel, tuna, salmon, and flatfish. Major fishing nations include the United States, Soviet Union, Japan, Spain, Peru, Iceland, and the Scandinavian countries.

Fishing, a water sport popular in both fresh and salt water. The two basic types of freshwater fishing include fly casting and bait casting, and the technique is to "play" the fish rather than reel it in by force. To this extent, the equipment used for fly rods and reels is light. The bait used is either live (worms, insects, and minnows) or artificial (flies and lures). Bait casting requires a sturdier rod and reel, and the bait can either be live or artificial. Some of the various techniques include trolling from a moving boat, bottom fishing, or casting and pulling in. Saltwater fishing generally requires heavier rods and reels, and includes trolling and casting from the surf, and trolling and bottom fishing at sea. Popular freshwater game fish include bass, pike, muskellunge, salmon, and trout. Ocean game fish include bonefish, marlin, sailfish, tarpon, and tuna. Numerous tournaments are held for the number and size of fish caught and for accuracy and distance in casting.

Fish Louse, common parasitic crustacean found on the skin or in the gill cavity of freshwater or marine fish. It has a top-to-bottom flattened body, one pair of compound eyes, and a shieldlike carapace. Large claws on antennae and two suckers on the jaws are used for attachment to the host. Subclass Branchiura. *See also* Crustacean.

Fission, form of asexual reproduction. The parent cell divides into 2 or more daughter cells. Binary fission produces 2 equal daughter cells (bacteria, blue-green algae, protozoa). Multiple fission produces 4, 8, or 16 daughter cells, each developing into a new organism.

Fission, Nuclear, form of nuclear reaction in which a heavy atomic nucleus, such as uranium, splits into two parts at the same time emitting two or three neutrons and releasing a large quantity of energy—3×10^{-11} joules per fission or 7.5×10^{13} joules per kg (compared to 4×10^{7} joules per kg for coal). Every 100,000 atoms of natural uranium contains six atoms of the isotope U-234 and 720 atoms of U-235; the rest is U-238. U-235 is fissioned by neutrons traveling at all speeds, whereas U-238 absorbs all but the fast neutrons (traveling at over 17×10^{6} m/s), forming the fissile plutonium-239 isotope. As most neutrons released in the fission process are fast, a chain reaction cannot be sustained in natural uranium, as most neutron collisions will be with the plentiful U-238. In a thermal reactor, a moderator is used to slow down the neutrons released in the fission so that enough neutrons are released in the process to sustain a chain reaction. In a fast reactor, no moderator is used, but the natural uranium is enriched with U-235 or Pu-239. In the atom bomb, pure U-235 or Pu-239 is used and the chain reaction is uncontrolled. However, these isotopes can be safely stored in quantities below the critical mass, as so many neutrons escape from the surface that the chain reaction cannot be sustained. *See also* Binding Energy; Fission Reactor.

Fission Reactor, device for producing energy from nuclear fission. There are two main types: thermal and fast reactors. Thermal reactors use thin natural-uranium fuel rods embedded or immersed in a moderator so that neutrons escaping from one rod are slowed down before entering another. The heat of the reaction is collected by a coolant, which may be a gas or a liquid. In advanced gas-cooled reactors carbon dioxide is the coolant. In the boiling-water reactor the coolant water is allowed to boil in contact with the fuel elements. In the pressurized-water reactor boiling is prevented by increased pressure. In both cases the water acts as moderator. The heated coolant is used to raise steam in a heat exchanger in order to drive a turbine and generator, as in a conventional power station. In a fast reactor natural uranium enriched with U-235 or Pu-239 is used without a moderator. Owing to the high core temperature (7,500°C), liquid sodium is used as the coolant. In a breeder reactor the core of a fast reactor is surrounded with a blanket of natural uranium, some of the escaping neutrons being captured by U-238 to form more Pu-239 than is needed to enrich the core. *See also* Fission, Nuclear.

Fistula, abnormal opening between two internal organs such as lung and heart, or from an organ to the body surface.

Fitzgerald, (Lord) Edward (1763–98), Irish nationalist, served for a time in the British army in America during the Revolution and was severely wounded at Eutaw Springs (1781). He was discharged for his sympathies with the French Revolution. He later joined the revolutionary United Irishmen and helped form the uprising of 1798. He was betrayed and died of wounds received during his capture before the unsuccessful rebellion took place.

FitzGerald, Edward (1809–83), English author and translator. His most noted achievement was his free translation from the Persian of the *Rubáiyát of Omar Khayyám* (1859). He also translated Calderon (1853)

Hamilton Fish

F. Scott Fitzgerald

Flanders lace

and Aeschylus (1865). *See also* Rubáiyát of Omar Khayyám.

Fitzgerald, F(rancis) Scott (Key) (1896–1940), US author, b. St. Paul, Minn. He began his first novel, *This Side of Paradise* (1920), while in the army, which he entered in 1917. He drew on his own experiences, as he generally did, and the book, along with *The Beautiful and the Damned* (1922), established him as a chronicler of the "Jazz Age," the frenetic period after World War I. In 1920 Fitzgerald married Zelda Sayre, also a writer. To finance their expensive and hectic life, he wrote popular short stories for magazines.

During most of the 1920s he lived in Europe, mingling with wealthy and sophisticated expatriates. His masterpiece, *The Great Gatsby,* was published in 1925. Frequently in debt, Fitzgerald was also plagued by his wife's growing insanity and his own bouts of alcoholism and loss of popularity in the 1930s, during which time he became a scriptwriter in Hollywood. His last novels were *Tender Is the Night* (1934) and the unfinished *The Last Tycoon* (1941).

FitzGerald, Garret (1926–), Irish political leader, prime minister 1981– . Educated at Belvedere College and University College in Dublin, he then studied law at Kings Inn. He worked for Aer Lingus, the Irish airlines, wrote, and taught until 1965 and served in the Senate until 1969, when he was elected to the Dail (house of representatives). He became minister of foreign affairs in 1973, leader of the Fine Gael party in 1977, and prime minister in 1981. His goals were to achieve stability in Northern Ireland and deal with Ireland's financial problems. He risked his political future in 1985 by signing an accord with Prime Minister Thatcher giving Ireland a role in administering the North while recognizing British sovereignty.

Fitzgerald, George Francis (1851–1901), Irish physicist who worked with electrolysis and electric waves and who is noted for his electromagnetic theory of radiation. As an explanation of the Michelson-Morley experiment, he suggested the theory that objects change shape (the Lorentz-Fitzgerald contraction) due to their movement through the ether. *See also* Michelson-Morley Experiment; Relativity Theory.

Fitzwilliam, (Sir) William (1526–99), English political figure. Lord deputy of Ireland (1572–75, 1588–94), he suppressed Irish rebellions arising from the "plantation" scheme of settling Scots and English in Ireland. He was governor of Fotheringhay Castle when Mary, Queen of Scots, was executed there (1587).

Fiume. *See* Rijeka.

Five, The, or "The Russian Five," a group of five prominent Russian composers (Rimski-Korsakov, Borodin, Mussorgski, Balakirev, and César Cui) who banded together to promote Russian nationalism in music in the late 19th century.

Five Dynasties Period (907–60), period of contention and division in China following the collapse of the great Tang era. It takes its name from the five abortive attempts to reestablish imperial unity and control until this was achieved by the Sung Dynasty. During this period nine classics were first printed from wood blocks.

Five-Year Plan, series of national economic plans for the Soviet Union. Introduced by Stalin in 1928 to develop the country as quickly as possible, an agriculturally and industrially self-sufficient nation was the ultimate goal. Certain quotas of manufactured goods and

agricultural products were to be met, and bonuses were given when quotas were reached ahead of time.

Flag, North American flowering plant with sword-shaped leaves and a large asymmetrical flower. Included are sweet flag *(Acorus calamus)*—Family Araceae; cattail flag *(Typha latifolia)*—Family Typhaceae; and blue flag *(Iris versicolor)*—Family Iridaceae.

Flagellate, any of numerous protists (single-celled organisms) placed in the superclass Mastigophora. They all possess, at some point in their life cycles, one to several whiplike structures called flagella for locomotion and sensation. Most have a single nucleus and many are covered with a thin, firm outer covering (pellicle) or coated with a jellylike substance, cellulose, or chitin. Reproduction is by fission (asexual splitting) or sexual (involving the production of gametes). They are divided into two major groups: the phytoflagellates, resembling plants, and the zooflagellates, resembling animals. Phytoflagellates contain chlorophyll and produce their food photosynthetically (such as *Euglena* and all dinoflagellates). Zooflagellates are colorless and take in food independently or live as symbionts or parasites (such as *Trypanosoma*). Flagellates may be solitary or colonial (*Volvox,* for example).

Flagstad, Kirsten (1895–1962), Norwegian soprano. She first performed in 1913 but was relatively unknown outside Scandinavia until her debut at the Metropolitan Opera in New York in 1935. She was one of the great 20th-century Wagnerian sopranos, singing leads in Wagner's operas at the Metropolitan and the Bayreuth Festivals. She was the first director of the Royal Norwegian Opera (1958–60).

Flagstaff, city in N Arizona, 63mi (101km) NE of Prescott; seat of Coconino co. Elevation: 6,907ft (2,107m) above sea level. Noted as a health resort; location of Northern Arizona University (1899). Industry: lumber. Settled 1876; inc. 1928. Pop. (1980) 34,641.

Flagstone, any hard, evenly stratified stone, such as shale or slate, that splits into flat pieces. Used for paving in outdoor paths, terrace floors, etc.

Flamboyant Style, final phase of French Gothic architecture (14th–16th century). The name comes from the flamelike forms of the elaborately ornate tracery used in cathedrals, as on the west facade of the Cathedral at Rouen (1370).

Flamen, in ancient Rome, a priest devoted to the worship of one deity. Flamens were chosen from the patrician class and offered daily sacrifices to the deity. They were identified by the apex (a conical cap).

Flamenco, dance and dance music of Spanish gypsies. It is characterized by stamping of the feet (zapateado), hand clapping (palmada), the skillful use of castanets, colorful costumes, and erotic movements. The dancing is often accompanied by florid, sad songs *(cante flamenco* or *cante hondo)* and guitar. Famous flamenco dancers have included Vincente Escudero and José Greco.

Flame Test, testing for the presence of metallic atoms, whose main spectral emission lines give characteristic colors in a Bunsen flame, performed on a platinum wire dipped in hydrochloric acid. Lithium and calcium produce a red color, sodium yellow, potassium lilac, strontium crimson, barium apple-green, copper blue-green, and lead, arsenic, antimony, and tin blue-gray.

Flamingo, long-necked, long-legged wading bird of tropical and subtropical lagoons and brackish lakes.

They are pinkish or reddish and have large wings and webbed feet. They invert their specialized bills to filter small organisms from the water. They nest in huge colonies, laying a single chalky white egg in a cone-shaped mud nest. Height: to 5ft (1.5m). Family Phoenicopteridae.

Flanders (Vlaanderen, or Flandre), former county in W Belgium and France, encompassing modern boundaries of East and West Flanders provs., Belgium, and a portion of France's Nord dept. The area flourished in 13th and 14th centuries with Flemish cloth industry; part incorporated into Spanish Netherlands in 1584, after some of it was given to France; Louis XIV annexed portions in 1668; part of the region was ceded to France (1797), but was later awarded to the Netherlands.

Flanders Field, near Waregem, Belgium, a cemetery in which the US Army buried 368 casualties of World War I. The field was made famous in a poem, "In Flanders Fields," by the Canadian John McCrae, a medical officer later killed in the war.

Flare, Solar, intense localized eruption of high-energy radiation occurring in the sun's chromosphere above an associated sunspot group on the photosphere. Flares are accompanied by ejection of high-energy particles that cause radio and magnetic disturbances on earth. *See also* Sunspot.

Flat-Coated Retriever, powerful water dog (sporting dog group) developed in England from the Labrador retriever and the Newfoundland. Not particularly popular in the United States, this retriever has a long head, large nose, and long jaw capable of carrying hare or pheasant. Small ears are close to the head. The body has a short, square back, and the short, straight tail is carried up. A black or liver-colored coat is dense and flat. Average size: 23in (58cm) high at shoulder; 60–70lb (27–32kg). *See also* Newfoundland; Retriever; Sporting Dog.

Flatfish, bottom-dwelling, mainly marine fish found in all but coldest seas. Includes some of the world's most valuable food fishes—halibut, flounder, plaice, turbot, and sole. Flatfish have a flat body, both eyes on same side, and a white underside. Length: to 10ft (305cm); weight: to 700lb (315kg). Order Pleuronectiformes; 600 species.

Flathead, river in W Canada and N Montana, rises in SE British Columbia, flows S through Flathead Lake, Montana, to Clark Fork River near Paradise. Length: 245mi (394km).

Flathead Indians, term applied to many North American Indian tribes, from their custom of deforming heads of infants to develop an elongated skull as a socially desirable shape. The usage applies most specifically to the Chinook. Ironically, the inhabitants of the Flathead Reservation in Montana never followed this practice; early travelers may have seen flat-headed slaves among the people.

Flatworms. *See* Platyhelminthes.

Flaubert, Gustave (1821–80), French novelist. He spent most of his life in Rouen among the provincial bourgeoisie featured in many of his works. A Realist, his novels include *Madame Bovary* (1857), *Salammbô* (1862), *Sentimental Education* (1869), and *The Temptation of St Anthony* (1874).

Flax, slender and erect plant with dainty flowers that last only one day. Species include: blue, perennial

Linum perenne, with small leaves, branching stems, and blue flowers; crimson *Linum grandiflorium,* a 1-ft (30-cm) annual; yellow *Linum virginianum,* native to America; and *Linum usitatissimum,* cultivated for linen fiber and linseed oil. Family Linaceae. *See also* Linseed Oil.

Flea, wingless, flat jumping insect found worldwide. They feed on the blood of birds and mammals and live a year or more. They may carry bubonic plague, endemic typhus, and tapeworm. Length: 0.1in (2.5mm). Order Siphonaptera.

Fleabane, small annual, biennial, and perennial plants found wild worldwide. Most have lance-shaped leaves and daisylike flowers with yellow disks and white, rose, or purplish rays. Hybrids are cultivated in gardens. Height: 4–40in (10–102cm). Family Compositae; genus *Erigeron.*

Fleahopper, green to shiny-black jumping leaf bug found worldwide. It sucks plant juices and may be a pest on cultivated plants. There are several generations a year. Length: to 0.08in (2mm). Family Miridae.

Fleming, (Sir) Alexander (1881–1955), Scottish bacteriologist. He shared the 1945 Nobel Prize in physiology or medicine for his part in the discovery of penicillin and its therapeutic effect. In 1928 Fleming noticed that a mold, identified as *Penicillium notatum,* liberated a substance that inhibited the growth of some bacteria. He named it penicillin. However, the importance of this discovery was not recognized until further work by Howard Florey and Ernst Chain.

Fleming's Rules, memory devices to relate the directions of the current, field, and mechanical rotation in electric motors and generators. In the *left hand rule* the forefinger represents flux, the second finger the electric motive force, and the thumb motion; when extended at right angles to each other the appropriate directions are indicated. The *right hand rule* applies the same principle to generators.

Flemish, one of the two official languages of Belgium, the other being French. It is spoken in the northern half of the country by about 5½ million people. Flemish is actually the same language as Dutch, but for historical and cultural reasons it is called Flemish in Belgium and Dutch in the Netherlands.

Flemish Gothic Architecture, Belgian architectural style significant in Flanders in the 14th and 15th centuries when the wool trade made the cities of Ghent, Bruges, and Ypres prosperous. Secular architecture, like the Cloth Hall at Ypres, was particularly important. Cathedrals, like that at Antwerp, had very high and ornate towers.

Flemish Renaissance Architecture, Belgian architectural style of the 16th century centered in Antwerp. It was influenced by the Italian Renaissance through visiting architects and through the translations of Alberti and Serlio. The Town Hall of Antwerp (1561–66), designed by Cornelius Floris, is a characteristic structure, with its dominating gable, large windows, and free ornamentation. Strapwork decoration was common and influenced English Renaissance architecture.

Fletcher v. Peck (1810), first US Supreme Court case interpreting the contract clause of the Constitution. Chief Justice John Marshall expanded the meaning of the term "contract" to include land grants from states.

Fleury, André Hercule de (1653–1743), French cardinal, received his position and the powers of first minister through his tutelage (1715) of the young Louis, later King Louis XV of France. Named a cardinal and first minister in 1726, he set the financial affairs of France in order, compensating for the excesses of Louis XIV. Under his guidance France enjoyed a brief period of peace, but became involved in two successional wars in the decade before his death.

Flicker, North American woodpecker with brownish to yellowish plumage and red, black, and white spots and bars. Unlike other woodpeckers, they do not drill into wood for food but use their slender, curved bills to hunt for ants on the ground. They do cut nest holes in trees. Genus *Colaptes. See also* Woodpecker.

Flight, Bird, propulsion through air by flat wing surfaces extended and moved by powerful muscles anchored to the breastbone. A bird's wing acts both as wing (providing lift) and propeller (providing thrust). The downstroke provides most of the power. Flight is partially controlled by the flight feathers being manipulated so air is always exerting the greatest pressure on the lower surface for maximum lift. The position of the wing feathers, especially near the tips, also determines altitude and speed. Tail feathers are important for balance and steering. A bird's hollow bones and streamlined trunk also aid in flight. Their legs are capable of exerting a powerful thrust for takeoff and absorbing the shock of landing. Though birds specialize in soaring, gliding, long-distance flight, or short bursts of speed, many can vary performance depending on need. *See also* Bird.

Flightless Birds, large, non-flying birds often having weak or poorly developed wings but strong legs, webbed feet, or other adaptations for walking, running, or swimming. They include the ostrich, rhea, cassowary, emu, kiwi, and penguin. Others, such as the New Zealand wren and some rails, often live on islands and fly with great difficulty.

Flint, city in S Michigan, on Flint River, 58mi (93km) NNW of Detroit; seat of Genesee co; one of world's leading auto production centers; site of branch of University of Michigan, and junior college. Industries: paints, varnishes, airplane engines, automobiles, automobile accessories. Founded 1819 as fur trading post; chartered 1855. Pop. (1980) 159,611.

Flint Clay, a hard, flinty fireclay. Flint clay is a kaolinite, usually found at greater depths than most clays. It is used almost exclusively in the production of firebrick and crucibles.

Flocculi, or plages, cloudy markings on the solar disk, visible on spectroheliograms. They appear to be chromospheric phenomena—clouds of calcium or hydrogen associated with faculae. *See also* Faculae.

Flood, the rising of some water in a stream, lake, or behind a dam to such a level that regions normally never underwater are submerged. The height of the water between normal level and the crest of the flood is the flood wave. When a stream overflows its banks (the channel it has cut) it inundates the flat adjoining ground or floodplain. Rivers without deep channels in flat regions have well-established floodplains and floods occur in such areas whenever more than normal amounts of water enter the drainage system. *See also* Drainage System; Hydrology.

Floodplain, a flat portion of a river valley consisting of alluvium deposited by the river; normally found at the river's lower or middle course. The plain is nearly at the high water level of the river and is covered with water when the river overflows its banks at flood stage. *See also* Alluvium.

Florence (Firenze), city in central Italy, on the Arno River; capital of Firenze prov. and Tuscany region; site of Roman military colony; 12th-century trade and industrial center; scene of Guelph-Ghibellines power struggle (13th century); under Medici rule 1434–1527, when it was restored to dukes of Florence. City was the cultural and artistic center of W Europe 14th–16th centuries; suffered major flood damage in 1966. Notable buildings include 13th-century Cathedral of Santa Maria del Fiore and Church of Santa Croce, the Campanile, Strozzi palace, the Medici-Riccardi palace, the Uffizi gallery. Industries: ornamental glass and pottery, furniture, tourism. Pop. 464,425.

Florence, industrial city in NW Alabama, on the Tennessee River; seat of Lauderdale co. Industries: cotton, minerals, textiles, steel fabrication. Settled 1818; inc. 1826. Pop. (1980) 37,029.

Florey, (Sir) Howard Walter (1898–1968), British pathologist, b. Australia. He shared the 1945 Nobel Prize in physiology or medicine for his part in the discovery of penicillin. Florey isolated the antibacterial agent from the mold discovered by Alexander Fleming, work that made the large-scale preparation of penicillin possible.

Florida, state in the extreme SE United States, which extends farther S than any continental state.

Land and Economy. Florida is a peninsula about 500mi (805km) long with an average width of 120mi (193km) between the Atlantic Ocean and the Gulf of Mexico. At its S end the Florida Keys, a chain of small islands, stretch W. The land is mostly level, with thousands of lakes and vast swamplands, of which the Everglades in the S are most notable. The St Johns in the NE and the Apalachicola in the W are the largest of the many rivers. The subtropical climate favors two major elements in the economy—agriculture and tourism. Florida is a leader in the production of fruit and vegetables. It is a year-round resort area that offers varied facilities for recreation. The John F. Kennedy Space Center at Cape Canaveral is the nucleus of an electronics and research industry.

People. One of the fastest-growing states, Florida increased its population two and one half times between 1950 and 1970 and by almost half between 1970 and 1980. The influx came mainly from states of the North and the Middle West and included many retired persons, who tended to settle in cities and towns. More than 80% of the people reside in urban areas. Jacksonville, which covers most of Duval County, is one of the largest US cities in area. St Augustine, settled by the Spanish in 1565, is the oldest community of European origin in the United States. A huge Cuban community established in southern Florida beginning in 1959 after Castro assumed power has transformed Miami into a center of Latin American culture and trade.

Education. There are more than 60 institutions of higher education.

History. The Spanish explorer Ponce de Leon landed on the E coast in 1513 and claimed the land for Spain. The first permanent settlement at St Augustine became the center of East Florida. Pensacola, founded in 1698, was the center of West Florida. Both Floridas were ceded to Great Britain in 1763 after the Seven Years' War, but were returned to Spain in 1783 after the American Revolution. All Florida was purchased by the United States in 1819 for $5 million and became a territory in 1821. Between 1835 and 1842 most of the native Seminole Indians were exterminated in war. Florida seceded from the Union in January 1861 to join the Confederacy, but was little affected by the Civil War and the Reconstruction period. After 1880, building of railroads, clearing of forests, and draining of swamps signaled an era of growth. Space exploration from Cape Canaveral began in the 1950s, and it was the site of most of the US space launches, including the manned moon landing mission in 1969 and the space shuttle in the 1980s. In 1980 a sudden influx of over 100,000 new Cuban arrivals placed severe strains on Florida's resources.

PROFILE

Admitted to Union: March 3, 1845; rank, 27th
US Congressmen: Senate, 2; House of Representatives, 15
Population: 9,739,992 (1980); rank, 7th
Capital: Tallahassee, 81,548 (1980)
Chief cities: Jacksonville, 540,898; Miami, 346,931; Tampa, 271,523
State Legislature: Senate, 40; House of Representatives, 120
Area: 58,560sq mi (151,670sq km); rank, 22d
Elevation: Highest, 345ft (105m), in Walton co. near Alabama border. Lowest, sea level
Industries (major products): processed foods, chemicals, electrical equipment, transportation equipment, paper
Agriculture (major products): citrus fruits, vegetables, cotton, poultry, cattle
Minerals (major): phosphate rock, titanium
State nickname: Sunshine State
State motto: "In God We Trust"
State bird: Mockingbird
State flower: Orange blossom
State tree: Sabal Palm

Florida Keys, chain of small coral and limestone islands, extending in an arc off the S tip of Florida in a curve to the SW. The more significant islands are Key West, Key Largo, Long Key, Vaca Key, and Big Pine Key; resort area, with commercial fishing. Length: approx. 150mi (242km).

Flotation, separation process whereby certain particles are carried out of suspension by a foam, used in the concentration of copper, lead, and zinc ores. An aqueous suspension of powdered ores, dosed with chemicals to affect their surface tensions, is aerated and a specific mineralized froth skimmed off.

Flounder, or fluke, sanddab, turbot, and (incorrectly) sole, marine flatfish found in shallow and deep waters of Atlantic and Pacific. An important food fish, it is gray, brown, or green on the eye side. Length: to 46in (116.8cm); weight: to 26lb (11.7kg). Families: right-eye Pleuronectidae, left-eye Bethidae; species include summer *Paralichthys dentatus. See also* Flatfish.

Flow Charts or **Diagrams,** used in scheduling programs. Various tasks or activities are listed within circles interconnected by directional time-sequence (flow) lines. A "critical path," commanding priority attention from management, can be determined as establishing minimum program time. Flow charts must be updated as variations in predictions occur.

Flower, reproductive structure of a flowering plant. Set on a shortened stem, it has four sets of organs arranged in whorls, or rings: sepals, leaf-like structures that protect the buds; petals, often brightly colored; stamens, stalks bearing anthers and pollen; and pistil, with ovary, style, and stigma. Reproduction occurs when pollen is transferred from the anthers to the stigma. A pollen tube grows down to the ovary where fertilization occurs and a seed is produced. The ovary

Florence, Italy

Florida: citrus groves

Flying dragon

bearing the seed ripens into a fruit and other flower parts wilt and fall. Flowers are bisexual, containing stamens and pistils, or unisexual, containing stamens or pistils.

Floyd, William, (1734–1821), American legislator and a signer of the Declaration of Independence, b. Brookhaven, L.I. After serving as New York's delegate to the Continental Congress (1774–77; 1778–83), he was elected to the first US House of Representatives in 1789.

Flugelhorn, brasswind musical instrument similar to the cornet, but with a wider bore and bell. It has a mellow tone like a French horn. *See also* Cornet.

Fluid Flow, the behavior of a moving fluid, determined by its velocity, pressure, and density. These three independent quantities are related by three basic equations: the equation of continuity, which relates the amount of fluid flowing into a volume with the amount flowing out of that volume; Euler's equation of motion, which shows how the velocity of the fluid changes with time at a given point in space; and the adiabatic equation, which describes the exchange of heat between different parts of the fluid. In incompressible fluid flow, which applies to most liquids, these equations take on a particularly simple form. Compressible flow equations are necessary for high-speed aerodynamic calculations. Often a fluid is treated as "ideal," meaning that no internal friction, or viscosity, is supposed. The equations for realistic fluids are so complicated that complete solutions to most problems do not exist; numerical solutions must be attempted by computer techniques.

Fluidics, use of fluids—gases or liquids—in controlling and actuating devices, to carry out switching and amplifying operations more familiarly associated with electronic circuits. Fluidic circuits were developed in the United States in the 1960s for use in rocket and aircraft guidance.

Fluid Mechanics, the study of the behavior of liquids and gases. Fluid *statics* includes the study of pressure, density, and the principles of Pascal and Archimedes. Fluid *dynamics* includes the study of streamlines, Bernoulli's equation, and the propagation of waves. Engineers use fluid mechanics in designing bridges, dams, and ships. Physicists use fluid mechanics in studying the structure of the nucleus. Astronomers have used fluid mechanics to explain the spiral structure of the galaxies.

Fluke, or trematoda, a parasitic flatworm. Infection results from ingestion of uncooked fish containing encysted worms or by entry through the skin of larvae present in infected waters. The worms may then enter various tissues such as the liver, lungs, and intestines, causing edema and decreased organ function, or they may stay in the bloodstream. Once contracted, treatment is difficult. Prevalent in Asian countries, these flukes are not common in the more developed parts of the world.

Fluorescence, emission of radiation, usually light, from a substance the atoms of which have acquired energy from a bombarding source of radiation, usually ultraviolet waves or electrons. When the source of energy is removed the fluorescence ceases. With phosphorescence, which is produced by a similar process, the emission persists for a short time.

Fluorine, gaseous nonmetallic element (symbol F) of the halogen group, isolated 1886 by Henri Moissan. Chief sources are fluorspar and cryolite. The element, obtained by electrolysis, is the most electronegative of all elements and attacks many compounds. It is used in making fluorocarbons and in extracting uranium. Properties: at. no. 9; at. wt. 18.9984; density 1.696 g dm^{-3}; melt. pt. $-363.3°F$ ($-219.62°C$); boil. pt. $-306.65°F$ ($-188.14°C$); most common isotope F^{19} (100%). *See also* Halogen Elements.

Fluorite, a halide mineral, calcium fluoride (CaF_2) found in sedimentary rocks and pegmatites. Cubic system crystals and granular and fibrous masses. Brittle, glassy, and colorless when pure. Hardness 4; sp gr 3.1. Chinese make carvings called "green quartz."

Fluorocarbon Plastics, plastics made from a class of chemically inert compounds, composed entirely of carbon and fluorine. The best known is the resin polytetrafluoroethylene, or Teflon. They are valued for their nonflammability, low chemical activity, and low toxicity.

Fluorocarbons, technically chlorofluoromethanes, used as propellants in aerosol spray cans and as refrigerants. These are highly volatile and inert gases, yet in the stratosphere they are broken down by sunlight to release chlorine atoms reacting with ozone to reduce the ozone layer that protects organisms from dangerous quantities of solar ultraviolet rays.

Flute, woodwind musical instrument, now usually made of silver alloy. Air is blown across a mouth hole near the end of a straight tube held horizontally; holes covered by keys arranged in the Boehm system provide a range of 3 octaves, permitting rapid scales and trills. Tones are mellow in the lower register and brighter in the higher.

Fly, any of various large, stout-bodied, two-winged insects belonging to the order Diptera. Most have spherical heads, large compound eyes, and a pair of long, movable antennae on the head. All have mouths that take in food by suction. A second pair of wings is vestigal, forming knobs called halteres used for balance. The housefly *(Musca domestica)* comprises 90% of all flies occurring in human habitations. It is a hazard to public health wherever decomposing organic waste and garbage accumulate. Adult houseflies are gray with yellow areas on the abdomen. On their feet they carry millions of disease-causing microorganisms. Tiny glandular pads on the feet enable flies to walk on vertical planes or hang from ceilings. Their white larvae are called maggots. *See also* Diptera; Housefly.

Fly Agaric or **Fly Amanita,** a species of poisonous but rarely fatal mushroom *(Amanita muscaria)* common to open woods and pastures. It has a broad yellow, orange-red, or scarlet cap with prominent white warts, a ring high on the stem and concentric rings above the bulb. Said to be hallucinogenic, it produces delirium, convulsions, and digestive upsets.

Flycatcher, various small birds that catch insects in mid-flight. New World flycatchers, commonly known as tyrant flycatchers, include phoebes, peewees, and kingbirds, and inhabit most of the Western Hemisphere but are chiefly found in the tropics. Fierce defenders of their nesting territories, they lay white to olive, often spotted, eggs (2–4) in cup-shaped nests. Old World flycatchers live in Eurasia, Africa, parts of Asia, Australia and nearby regions. Some are brightly colored. They lay their eggs (2–6) in cup-shaped branch nests, holes in trees, or gravel pits. Family Muscicapidae.

Flying Dragon, gliding lizard native to SE Asia and Indonesia. It has a dewlap and wattles on the sides of its neck and 5–6 elongated ribs support extensible skin folds that are spread for gliding flight from branch to branch. Length: 8–12in (20–30cm). Family Agamidae; genus *Draco. See also* Lizard.

Flying Fish, marine fish found worldwide in tropical seas. Dark blue and silver, it uses its enlarged spineless pectoral and pelvic fins to glide above water surface for as long as 13 seconds. Length: to 18in (45.7cm). Family Exocoetidae; species 50, including *Exocoetus volitans* and Atlantic *Cypselurus heterurus.*

Flying Fox, fruit-eating bat with a foxlike head, found in the tropics from Madagascar to the SW Pacific. Flying foxes sometimes cause substantial damage to fruit crops. They are usually grayish brown or black. Wingspan: 5.5ft (1.7m), weight: to 2lb (0.9kg). Genus *Pteropus. See also* Fruit Bat.

Flying Lemur, or **Colugo,** nocturnal gliding mammal of SE Asia resembling a large flying squirrel. "Wingspans" to 3ft (91cm); weight: to 4lb (1.8kg). The two species (genus *Cynocephalus*) are the only members of the order Dermoptera.

Flying Squirrel, gliding rodent of the squirrel family that lives in forested areas of Eurasia and North and South America. They glide by means of furry membranes on both sides of the body that stretch out flat and taut when the legs are extended. Except for some Indian species that weigh over 4lb (1.8kg), most flying squirrels are small.

FM. *See* Frequency Modulation.

Focal Length, distance from the midpoint of a mirror or the center of a thin lens to the focal point of the system. For a spherical surface it is half the radius of curvature. For converging systems it is given a positive value, for diverging systems, a negative value.

Foch, Ferdinand (1851–1929), French marshal. He was instructor and then director (1903–11) of the Ecole de Guerre. In World War I he was a commander in the battle of the Marne (1914), the first battle of Ypres (1915), and on the Somme (1916). In March 1918, Foch became supreme allied commander, shaping the final victory over the Germans. *See also* World War I.

Focus, either of two points on the major axis of an ellipse such that the distance from one focus to any point on the ellipse and back to the other focus is constant. When the distance between the foci is zero the figure is a circle. For an orbiting celestial body, such as a planet, the center of gravitational attraction lies at one focus, the primary focus, of an ellipse. The other focus is the secondary focus.

Focus, Earthquake, region in earth from which a quake originates. Quakes are classified by the depth of occurrence. Most quakes are shallow-focus. Shallow-focus ranges from 37–186mi (60–300km). Deep-focus is 186–435mi (300–700km) into earth's interior. *See also* Earthquake.

Foehn, a warm, dry wind on the lee or downwind side of mountains, tending to produce aridity. *See also* Winds.

Fog, water vapor in the atmosphere condensed at or near the ground, as opposed to water vapor condensed in the air in clouds. *See also* Precipitation.

Foggia, city in Italy, 162mi (261km) ESE of Rome, in center of Great Apulian Plain; capital of Foggia province. Frederick II held parliament here 1240; heavily damaged during WWII; military airfields were captured by British 1943; remains include ruins of castle of Frederick II; agricultural region and wool market. Industries: olives, grapes, tobacco, cellulose, paper. Pop. 153,-736.

Folding, in geology, pronounced bending in the layer of rock. Folds are defined according to the axes of the folds. Thus, an upfold, which is an arch, is an anticline; a downfold, a syncline. The fold system may be symmetrical (in neat waves), asymmetrical, overturned, or recumbent (the axis of the fold is parallel to the horizon). A single folding is known as a monocline.

Folic Acid, yellow crystalline derivative of glutamic acid (formula $C_{19}H_{19}N_7O_6$) forming part of the vitamin B complex and used in the treatment of anemia. *See also* Vitamin.

Folk Art, term used to describe the art of folk cultures, especially those of isolated rural communities with traditions that have continued for generations. It also applies to the art of ethnic groups, such as Hassidic Jews and Pennsylvania Mennonites. Folk art usually involves the decoration of useful, everyday objects within a community, such as cradles, plows, ox yokes, weather vanes, and quilts. Much care is given to the decoration of objects to be used at special occasions, such as community festivals and marriages. Often, the same motifs, which are usually simple in design, are handed down from generation to generation to be used in surface decoration.

Folklore, the lore of the common people, or the traditions, customs, and beliefs of the people as expressed through nonliterary tales, songs, and sayings. In contrast to "art literature," which is transmitted through the printed page, "folk literature" has an oral source, and is transmitted primarily through memory and practice. The best-known study of folklore is Sir James Frazer's *The Golden Bough* (1890–1915).

Folk Music, music associated with communities, nationalities, and peoples rather than composed by individuals; often handed down orally from generation to generation. American folk music includes ballads, gospels, spirituals, and work songs among other forms.

Folk Theater, a type of drama or entertainment that uses folklore, traditional and regional material, and nonprofessional actors. It is generally performed by natives of rural areas and is often impromptu. Elements of folk drama—music, dance, or themes—are often incorporated into more professional pieces of drama. In some ways, medieval drama, which combined religion with superstitions and agricultural themes, was folk theater.

Folkways, shared patterns of behavior and beliefs common to a particular group of people. The term was first used by W.G. Sumner in 1906. Folkways are not the result of individual adjustment, but instead are learned directly from other members of the group. Unlike mores, they are usually not verbalized as law.

Follicle-stimulating Hormone (FSH), hormone produced by the anterior pituitary. It regulates ovulation by stimulating the ovary to secrete estrogens, thus promoting development of the egg. It stimulates spermatogenesis in the male.

Folsom Culture, early North American culture characterized by the use of fluted stone spear points. The first "Folsom point" to be found was in 1926 at Folsom, N.M. Folsom people lived around 9000 to 7000 BC, hunted a now extinct form of bison on the Great Plains, and gathered food.

Fomalhaut, or **Alpha Piscis Austrini,** white main-sequence star in the constellation Piscis Austrinus. Characteristics: apparent mag. +1.16; absolute mag. +1.8; spectral type A3; distance 23 light-years.

Fon, Kwa-speaking people of S Benin (Dahomey) and Nigeria. Their polygynous, patrilineal society is based on subsistence agriculture, with a market system using cowrie shells as money. Hunters form a class with special social and religious status, while ancestor worship plays an important part in their religion.

Fond du Lac, city in E Wisconsin, at S end of Lake Winnebago; seat of Fond du Lac co; farming and manufacturing center; popular resort area. Industries: dairy products and equipment, tools, leather goods. Settled 1836; inc. 1852. Pop. (1980) 35,863.

Fontaine, Jean de la (1621–95), French poet and fabulist. Elected to the Académie Française in 1683, he drifted from one patron to another. He was best known for his *Books of Fables* (1668–94), a delightful collection of animal tales based on Aesop's and other fables, in which he passed judgment on society.

Fontainebleau, town in N France, near W bank of the Seine, 37mi (60km) S of Paris; surrounded by forest of Fontainebleau; site of French Renaissance palace built by Francis I, now serves as the summer residence of France's president; US art school, military college, school of engineering. Industries: tourism, cabinetmaking, grape shipping. Pop. 19,595.

Fontainebleau, French palace built 1528–40 for King Francis I. Begun by the master mason Gilles Le Breton and completed by the Italian architects Primaticcio and Serlio, it is irregular in plan. The appeal of its exterior depends on lakes, formal gardens, and vistas. Its interiors, decorated by Primaticcio, Rosso, and others, are of more architectural interest.

Fontanel, soft space at the junction of the cranial bones of an infant. The fontanels close as the cranial bones grow toward each other, and do not exist in older children or adults.

Fontenoy, town in SW Belgium, 5mi (8km) SE of Tournai; scene of 1745 battle during which French, under Marshal Saxe, defeated British and allies, led by Duke of Cumberland. Pop. 665.

Foochow (Fuzhou, or **Fu-chou),** formerly Minhow; port city in SE China, on Min River, 25mi (40km) from the coast of the East China Sea; capital of Fukien prov. Dates from the T'ang dynasty (618–906); visited by Marco Polo (13th century). One of the first treaty ports open to foreign trade (1842), it flourished as the major port in China (1850) and world's largest tea-exporter but declined (early 20th century) with the lessened demand for tea and silting of Min River. In 1949, after Communist takeover, port was blockaded by Nationalist Chinese. A large thoroughfare connects the old walled city to the riverside commercial section. Industries: chemicals, textiles, food processing, paper, bamboo, tea, plastics, machine shops. Pop. 900,000.

Food, material containing essential nutrients (proteins, fats, vitamins, minerals, carbohydrates) taken into an organism to maintain life and growth. Foods of plant origin are cereals, tubers, legumes, nuts, vegetables, fruits, oils, and sugars; those of animal origin are meat, eggs, fish, shellfish, milk, and fat.

Food Additive, any of various substances added to food. They include flavors, flavor enhancers, antioxidants and other preservatives, coloring matter, sweeteners, and vitamins and essential mineral salts.

Food and Agricultural Organization (FAO), specialized agency of the United Nations. It serves as coordinator for worldwide food production, distribution, and consumption. Its member countries have no enforcement powers. It has field technicians and provides fellowships for studies of underdeveloped countries. Organized in 1943, it joined the United Nations in 1945. Its headquarters are in Rome.

Food Chain, transfer of food energy through a series of organisms with each organism eating the member below it. Its sequence is green plants (producers), herbivores (primary consumers), and carnivores (secondary consumers). Decomposers act at each stage and at the end of the chain.

Food Poisoning, or ptomaine poisoning, can be caused by a number of organisms, most common being *Salmonella.* Such organisms are most frequently ingested from animals or animal products such as meat, most often fowl, and eggs. Symptoms include colicky abdominal pain, watery diarrhea, nausea, and fever. Vomiting may occur. Symptoms usually appear within 8–48 hours after infected food has been ingested and will usually subside within two to five days although the diarrhea may persist longer. In severe cases, dehydration is a complication. Treatment includes bed rest, fluids to prevent dehydration, no food until cramps and vomiting subside.

Food Preservative, substance used to preserve food in an edible condition, by making it or its environment unfavorable to the growth of microorganisms, and to ensure that it retains its original quality. Traditional methods used to prevent spoilage are dehydration, exclusion of air, smoking, salting, pickling, and immersing in wine. Quality is preserved by the use of ascorbic acid to prevent discoloration, of sulfur dioxide and benzoic acid as firming and bleaching agents, and of glutamates to preserve the flavor of meat.

Fools' Gold. *See* Iron Sulfide.

Foot, in poetry, unit of verse meter. Each foot is composed of a group of two or three syllables, one of which is stressed. Most commonly used feet are anapest, dactyl, iamb, trochee. *See also* Meter.

Foot-and-Mouth Disease, or hoof-and-mouth disease, aphthous fever, contagious viral disease of cattle, swine, sheep, goats, horses, and deer. Its symptoms—fever, blisters of the mouth and hoofs, drooling, and weight loss—can result in death. An effective vaccine for the disease has been produced using recombinant DNA techniques. The disease rarely occurs in man. Effective inspections, quarantines, slaughter of diseased animals, and sanitation have kept the disease under control in the United States.

Football, contact sport played in the United States. It is second in popularity only to baseball. It is played by 2 teams of 11 persons each—a fullback, two halfbacks, a quarterback, a center, two guards, two tackles, and two ends—on a field 100 yards (91.5m) long by 53 yards (48.5m) wide. The field is marked off by latitudinal stripes every 5 yards (4.6m) and is flanked on each end by an area (end zone) 10 yards (9.1m) long. At each end of the end zone are H-shaped goal posts. An inflated leather, speroid ball is used, with the object of moving the ball—by the ground or air—across the opponent's goal line. The defending team must stop the ball carrier by pushing him out of bounds or by bringing him to the ground (tackling). A game consists of two halves, each having two 15-minute quarters. At the end of each half, the teams exchange goals. The scoring can occur in four ways: a touchdown is six points (crossing the opponent's goal line), a conversion is one point (kicking the ball through the uprights of the goal post following a touchdown), a field goal is three points (kicking the ball through the uprights of the goal posts), and a safety is two points (downing the ball carrier behind his own goal line). In other than professional football, the conversion can count as two points if the ball is run or passed into the end zone following the touchdown. Except for certain instances in professional ball, games can end in a tie. Each half starts with a kickoff, and after the receiving team has run back the ball, it must advance 10 yards in 4 attempts (downs) or turn the ball over to the opponents. The ball is usually turned over by punting (kicking) on the last down or attempting a field goal. If a player fumbles and loses possession of the ball during the series of downs, the opposing team takes over the ball. Substitutions are freely allowed.

History. Football has its roots in England in the Middle Ages and has similarities to rugby and soccer. The US version of the game was adopted after 1875. College football began in 1869 and has since flourished with a host of post-season contests, the most prominent being the Rose Bowl, an annual event since 1916. Professional football also began in the 19th century, and the National Football League (NFL), first formed in 1920 as the American Professional Football League, has enjoyed the greatest success. The American Football League, formed in 1960, merged with the NFL in 1969. The United States Football League (USFL) began play in 1983.

Football, Association. *See* Soccer.

Foot Binding, the practice of compressing girls' feet with tight bandages to prevent growth of the feet. In China this was common up to the 19th century among the middle and upper classes. Foot binding rendered women's feet useless and suggested that their men were sufficiently prosperous to support them.

Foot-pound, the unit of energy in the English foot-slug-second system of units. One foot-pound is the work done by a force of one pound acting through a distance of one foot.

Foraminifera, marine, planktonic, ameboid protozoans characterized by multichambered lime shells. Accumulations form the white cliffs of Dover and chalk beds of Mississippi and Georgia. The size of a pinhead, shells may be spiral-shaped, straight, or clustered. Filaments of protoplasm extend from the perforations in the shell and form a covering web. Examples are *Globigerina, Polystomella, Nodosaria.*

Forbidden City, a walled area in N Peking, China, in the Inner or Tatar City; site of Imperial Palace, T'ien an Men Square, Great Hall of the People, the Museum of History and Revolution, and the Temple of Heaven; so named because it was formerly closed to the public. Area: 0.3sq mi (0.8sq km).

Forbidden City, western name for Lhasa, capital of Tibet; name derives from its remoteness and the hostility of the Tibetan clergy toward foreign visitors. *See also* Lhasa.

Force, loosely speaking, a push or pull. A force acting on a body may (1) balance an equal but opposite force or combination of forces to maintain the body in equilibrium, (2) change the state of motion of the body (in magnitude or direction), or (3) change the shape or state of the body. There are four basic forces in nature.

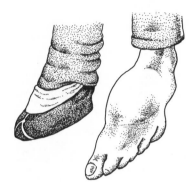
Foot-binding

Gerald R. Ford

Henry Ford

The most familiar, and the weakest, is the gravitational force, an attractive force which varies inversely as the square of the distance between any two masses. Much stronger is the electromagnetic force, which also follows the inverse-square law and may be attractive or repulsive. Two other forces are recognized, both operating only on the subatomic level. The weak nuclear force associated with the decay of particles is intermediate in strength between the gravitational and electromagnetic force, while the strong nuclear force associated with the "glue" holding nuclei together is the strongest force known in nature.

Forcing, in horticulture, speeding up the development of a plant or part of a plant, usually by providing heat and moisture. Forcing was formerly widely used in northern regions to produce leaf vegetables during winter. It is still often used to accelerate the blooming of bulbs and cut stems of flowering shrubs such as forsythia or dogwood.

Ford, Ford Madox (1873–1939), English novelist, poet, and critic; b. Ford Madox Hueffer. He is best known for his influence on such writers as Ezra Pound, Joseph Conrad, and D. H. Lawrence and for his editorship of *English Review,* a literary magazine. His chief work is the tetralogy *Parade's End* (1924–28).

Ford, Gerald Rudolph (1913–   ), 38th president of the United States (1974–77), b. Omaha, Nebraska. He was originally named Leslie King, Jr., but assumed his stepfather's name when his mother remarried. He graduated from the University of Michigan and the Yale University law school and was admitted to the Michigan bar in 1941. In 1948 he married Elizabeth Bloomer; they had four children. After service in the Navy in World War II, he was elected (1948) as a Republican to the US House of Representatives. A conservative and a loyal party supporter, he rose in Republican ranks, and in 1964 he was named House minority leader. In 1973, when Vice President Spiro T. Agnew was forced to resign, President Nixon nominated Ford to replace him. He became vice president on Dec. 6, 1973, the first to come into office under the 25th Amendment to the Constitution.

By the time Ford became vice president, the Nixon administration was deeply involved in the Watergate affair. Ford repeatedly expressed his confidence that Nixon was not involved in the scandals. Nixon was forced to resign, however, on Aug. 9, 1974, and Ford became president. Ford retained most of the Nixon cabinet and advisers, and, a month after he assumed office, pardoned Nixon for all crimes he might have committed while president. He was widely criticized for the pardon. Ford continued the Nixon policy of easing tensions with both the Soviet Union and China. In domestic affairs, he opposed Democratic programs aimed at countering the recession, maintaining that their great costs would add to inflation, and vetoed a number of such bills. In 1976, Ford announced his intention to run for a full term. He entered the Republican primaries, where he was opposed by Ronald Reagan, the former governor of California. Ford received the Republican nomination but was defeated by Democrat Jimmy Carter.

Career: US House of Representatives, 1949–73; vice president, 1973–74; president, 1974–77.

Ford, Henry (1863–1947), US automobile maker and industrialist, b. Dearborn, Mich. He developed a working gasoline automobile (1892), and later founded Ford Motors (1903). He brought out the economical Model T in 1908. He initiated the conveyorbelt assembly line (1913) and introduced the 8-hour day with a $5 minimum wage, while opposing unionization. Ford established a closely controlled organization whose indus-

trial and transport holdings made Ford Motors materially self-reliant. He established the Ford Foundation (1936) which he and his son Edsel endowed and contributed over $40,000,000 to charitable causes (1908–47).

Foreign Aid, money or credit extended to less developed nations to help them in their development programs. Technology may also be provided. Often the more developed nations set conditions for receiving aid, including adherence to certain policies; spending all or most of the aid money on goods or services of the granting nation; or using the grantor country's ships to transport goods. Foreign aid is a relatively recent phenomenon.

Foreign Legion, skilled professional military group of mixed national origin, created in 1831 to control French colonies around the world. After fighting in two world wars and later French colonial struggles, the Legion moved its headquarters from Algeria to S France.

Foreign Service, corps of agents who serve as their country's diplomatic representatives abroad. The Rogers Act (1924) combined the US diplomatic and consular services into one agency under the jurisdiction of the State Department. It also provided for promotion on the basis of merit, although ambassadors remain political appointees. Members of the foreign service are trained to staff embassies, legations, and consulates, and to conduct negotiations with representatives of their host nations.

Forensic Medicine, branch of science dealing with the relations and applications of medical facts to legal matters. Forensic medicine would, for example, concern itself with the definition of death or with the timing of death if foul play is suspected.

Forest Fires, burning of woodland vegetation, caused by natural means, such as lightning, or by accident or arson. Ground fires burn the humus layer of the forest floor; surface fires burn undergrowth and surface litter; stand fires burn tree trunks, but not foliage; crown fires burn all vegetation. Control of forest fires has three main aspects: prevention, spotting, and fire fighting. Prevention is largely a matter of public relations, as most fires are started by people rather than by nature. Spotting is a system of locating fires in their early stages, usually by lookouts in high towers or airplanes. Fire fighting varies with type of fire and degree of severity.

Forestry, the science of managing wooded areas with their associated waters and wastelands. The chief objective is usually the raising of timber, but conservation of soil, water, and wildlife is also a consideration. Systematic management had its beginnings in German states in the 16th century, where forests were divided into sections for timber felling and regeneration, to sustain annual yield. Education in technical forestry began in western Europe in the 19th century. Now many universities throughout the world offer forestry curricula. Modern forestry includes silviculture, dendrology, forest protection, engineering, utilization, and management. Many operations are included, with emphasis on cycles of cutting and replenishment, selection and breeding, insect control, and limitation of forest fires.

Forests, Types of. There are a number of systems for classifying forest types. One system includes the following eight categories: (1) temperate region deciduous forests, made up of summer-green trees of North America, Europe, temperate Asia, and South America; (2) deciduous monsoon forests of Asia with heavy rainfall; (3) tropical deciduous forests blending with grass-

lands; (4) temperate coniferous forests dominated by pines and firs; (5) tropical rain forests, typified by those of central Africa and South America, with profuse, diverse growth; (6) coastal rain forests where warm ocean currents influence the climate; (7) temperate rain forests with broadleaved evergreen trees; (8) tropical scrub forests in dry areas.

Forget-me-not, perennial plant native to Eurasia and North America that is one of the spring's first flowers. The pink, flaring, five-lobed flowers change to blue as they mature. They are a popular garden flower. Water forget-me-nots grow in marshlands and have shorter, weaker stems. There are 50 species. Family Boraginaceae; genus *Myosotis.*

Forgetting, inability to bring memories to consciousness. A traditional theory attributes forgetting to the decay of memory information with time, but modern psychology tends to regard interference from other memories as critical. Forgetting is viewed as an inability to retrieve stored information because other information "gets in the way." *See also* Memory.

Forging, the shaping of metal articles by hammering or pressing metal blanks between pairs of forging dies. The upper die is attached to the ram of a forging hammer or press so that it can be raised and dropped (with or without additional pressure) against the rigidly supported lower die. Most metals are forged hot, but cold forging is an important technique.

Forli, city in Italy, SE of Bologna; capital of Forli prov. Founded by Rome 2nd century, city was scene of struggle between Guelph and Ghibelline factions during 13th century; Caterina Sforza, widow of Gerolamo Riario, ruled city 1488–1500, when she surrendered to Cesare Borgia; city was part of Papal States 1504–1859; site of 12th-century Abbey of S. Mercuriale, 15th-century citadel, 14th-century Palazzo Communale. Industries: textiles, shoes, chemicals, appliances. Pop. 109,758.

Formaldehyde, colorless suffocating and poisonous gas (HCHO) prepared by the catalytic oxidation of methane or methanol. It is used in the manufacture of plastics, as a germicide, preservative, and reducing agent, and as a corrosion inhibitor. Properties: melt. pt. −133.6°F (−92°C); boil. pt. −6°F (−21°C).

Formic Acid, colorless fuming liquid (HCOOH) prepared by treating sodium formate with sulfuric acid and distilling or by acid hydrolysis of methyl formate. It is used in the manufacture of paper, textiles, insecticides, and refrigerants. Properties: sp gr 1.22; melt. pt. 46.9°F(8.3°C); boil. pt. 213.5°F(100.8°C).

Formosa Strait, branch of the Pacific Ocean, between Fukien prov., China, and Taiwan; it links the East China and South China seas. Width: 115mi (185km).

Formosus (816?–96), Roman Catholic pope (891–96). Made a cardinal bishop in 864, he was excommunicated by Pope John VIII, but was absolved by Marinus I in 883. After his death, Formosus' body was placed on trial for having received two bishoprics. Found guilty, the body was thrown into the Tiber River. His papal decrees were declared invalid but later reinstated.

Formstecher, Solomon (1808–89), German Jewish philosopher, a great force in the reform movement within Judaism, which he analyzed and justified in his literary works. As a rabbi, he stressed the dynamics of religion and the progressive nature of Judaism.

Formula, in mathematics, general rule or relationship expressed in mathematical symbols. Examples are the formula $V = 4/3\pi r^3$, for the volume of a sphere, and the cosine formula (or rule) $c^2 = a^2 + b^2 - 2ab \cos C$, for the sides of a triangle.

Forster, E(dward) M(organ) (1878–1970), English author. His novels deal with the individual's blind acceptance of social convention, denying the free and spontaneous in life. They include *Where Angels Fear to Tread* (1905), *The Longest Journey* (1907), *A Room with a View* (1908), *Howards End* (1910), and, his most famous work, *A Passage to India* (1924). His short stories were collected in *The Celestial Omnibus* (1911) and *The Eternal Moment* (1928). *The Art of the Novel* (1927) is an important collection of lectures in literary criticism. *Abinger Harvest* (1936) and *Two Cheers for Democracy* (1951) are collections of essays on literature, society, and politics. Forster also, with Eric Crozier, wrote the libretto for Benjamin Britten's opera version of Melville's *Billy Budd* (1951). Though Forster's novels are conventional in structure, the excellence of his style places him among the foremost fiction writers of his time.

Forsythia, or golden bells, ornamental shrub that flowers in April with bright yellow, bell-shaped flowers; the leaves, which may have marginal teeth, appear afterward. Height: 4–8ft (1.2–2.4m). Species include the showy *Forsythia spectabilis; F. obovata,* grown in northern areas; and *F. suspensa.* Family Oleaceae.

Fort, a strong, armed place surrounded by protective works and garrisoned with armed troops. Throughout history different materials from earth and stone to timber and concrete have been used to construct the defensive works. Designs of forts have varied from simple rectangles and squares to more elaborate forms such as lunettes or star shapes. "Fort" can also refer to an unfortified place where troops are stationed.

Fortaleza (Ceará), port city in NE Brazil, 270mi (435km) NW of Natal; capital of Ceará state. Industries: sugar refining, textiles, soap, shipping. Founded 1609. Pop. 520,175.

Fortas, Abe (1910–82), US jurist, lawyer, and public official, b. Memphis, Tenn. He was appointed by Pres. Lyndon Johnson to be an associate justice of the US Supreme Court in 1965. In 1968 he was nominated to be chief justice. When the nomination was blocked by a Senate filibuster, he asked that his name be withdrawn. In 1969 he resigned under pressure when his financial association with a former client convicted of stock manipulation was made public.

Fort Collins, residential and industrial city in W Colorado, 40mi (64km) NNE of Boulder; seat of Larimer co. Industries: plastics, timber, sugar, canned goods. Settled 1864; inc. 1879. Pop. (1980) 64,632.

Fort-de-France, port city and capital of Martinique, French West Indies, on Fort-de-France Bay; tourist resort; Napoleon's wife, Empress Josephine, was born nearby. Settled 1762 by French. Pop. 97,000.

Forth, Firth of, sunken estuary of the Forth River, Scotland, running W to E between Alloa and the North Sea. Edinborough is on the S shore. Length: 51mi (82km).

Fort-Lamy (N'Djamena), capital of Chad, N central Africa, on the Chari river; it is a transportation center and major regional market for livestock, salt, dates, grains. Pop. 135,502.

Fort Lauderdale, city, SE Florida, 25mi (40km) N of Miami; seat of Broward co. Est. by Maj. William Lauderdale as military post in 1838. Over 270mi (435km) of natural and artificial waterways within the city. Inc. 1911. Pop. (1980) 153,256.

Fort Myers, coastal city, SW Florida, seat of Lee co. Settled 1835 as Fort Harvie in Seminole War; used as Union base in Civil War; site of Thomas Edison's winter estate. Inc. 1905. Pop. (1980) 36,638.

Fort Smith, city, W Arkansas, on Oklahoma border; seat of Sebastian co. Industries: sheet metal, auto bodies, optical equipment, glass. Settled 1817; inc. 1842. Pop. (1980) 71,384.

Fort Sumter, in Charleston Harbor, S.C. In April 1861, the Civil War began here when Confederate cannon fired on the Union garrison commanded by Maj. Robert Anderson. Although 4,000 shells were fired, no one on either side was killed. After two days, Anderson surrendered to Confederate Gen. P.G.T. Beauregard.

Fort Wayne, city in NE Indiana, at confluence of St Joseph and St Marys rivers; seat of Allen co; 2nd-largest city in Indiana. French built trading post here *c.* 1680; it was captured by British during French and Indian War and held by Indians (1763) during Pontiac's Rebellion; the Miami Indians were subdued by Anthony Wayne (1794). Development was spurred by Wabash and Erie canals, and railroad in the mid-1800s. City contains burial place of John Chapman (Johnny Appleseed); site of Concordia Senior College (1839), St Francis College (1890), Indiana Institute of Technology (1930). Industries: heavy trucks, copper wire, stainless steel, mining machinery, pumps, tanks. Inc. 1840. Pop. (1980) 172,196.

Fort William. *See* Thunder Bay.

Fort Worth, city in N central Texas, 30mi (48km) W of Dallas; seat of Tarrant co. Developed mid-19th century by US cavalry as a fortress for westward-bound settlers, by 1870 the city was supply center for cattlemen on the Chisholm Trail. In early 20th century, Fort Worth was packinghouse and oil refining center; since WWII, industrial development has increased rapidly; site of Texas Christian University (1873), Texas Wesleyan College (1890), Amon Carter Museum of Western Art, annual Southwestern Exposition and Fat Stock show, Carswell Air Force Base. Industries: aviation, automobiles, food processing, brewing, machinery. Settled 1843; inc. 1873. Pop. (1980) 385,141.

Forum, Roman, chief market and public gathering place of ancient Rome from the 6th century BC, when the swampy area it occupies was drained. Set in a valley from the Capitoline hill along the Quirinal, Oppian, and Palatine hills, it held many civic buildings including basilicas and temples, the curia (senate), treasury, rostra (speaker's platform), and the arches of Septimius Severus and Titus. The emperors built additional forums when it became inadequate for their needs.

Fossa, catlike carnivorous animal of the civet family native to Madagascar. They have short legs and redbrown fur. Nocturnal forest-dwellers, they eat small wild animals and are thought to be predators of farm animals. Length: body—28in (71cm); tail—28in (71cm). Family Viverridae; species *Cryptoprocta ferox.*

Fossil, any direct evidence of the existence of an organism more than 10,000 years old. Fossils mostly consist of original structures, such as bones or shells, or wood, often altered through mineralization or preserved as molds and casts. Imprints such as tracks and footprints are also fossils. Leaves are often preserved as a carbonized film outlining their form. Occasionally organisms are totally preserved in frozen soil (mammoths), peat bogs and asphalts lakes (woolly rhinoceroses), or trapped in hardened resin (insects in amber). Fossil excrement, called caprolites, frequently contains undigested and recognizable hard parts. Very few animals and plants that die become fossilized. Since fossils reveal evolutionary changes through time, they are essential clues for geologic dating. *See also* Geologic Time; Index Fossil.

Foster, Stephen C(ollins) (1826–64), US composer of songs, b. Lawrenceville, Pa. He gained knowledge of black spirituals by writing for ministrel shows. Though his songs were very popular, he had little business sense and died in poverty. Many of his songs are now American classics. They include *Oh! Susanna* (1848), *Camptown Races* (1850), *Old Folks at Home* (1851), *My Old Kentucky Home* (1853), *Jeanie with the Light Brown Hair* (1854), and *Old Black Joe* (1860).

Foucault, Jean Bernard Léon (1819–68), French physician and physicist. In addition to proving that the Earth spins on its axis, he worked on a method to measure the absolute velocity of light, and by 1850 he showed that it is slower in water than in air. Also credited with pointing out the occurrence of eddy currents (Foucault currents) and devising an improved reflecting telescope mirror.

Fouché, Joseph, Duc d'Otrante (1763–1820), French master of political intrigue who retained power as minister of police (1799–1802, 1804–10; 1815) throughout the turbulent political times of Napoleon and the Revolution. Girondist and then Jacobin, he was an anti-Christian and proponent of regicide in the early 1790s, later changing in preparation for Napoleon, in whose governments he managed to secure a place of prominence. Exiled (1816), he died a very rich man.

Foundry, a workshop in which metals are processed by melting and casting in molds. Modern foundries are highly automated both in mixing of the sand and clay used for molds and in the molding process itself. Pattern-making is a skilled operation. Sand or clay is packed over the pattern, which is then removed, forming a cavity in which the casting is made. The mold is made in halves, each enclosed in its own mold box. The halves are joined with pins and bushings before pouring. *See also* Mold, Metal.

Fountain Valley, city in S California, 28mi (45km) SE of Los Angeles; site of marine helicopter facility. Industries: mobile homes, aerospace, electronic parts. Inc. 1957. Pop. (1980) 55,080.

Fouquet (Foucquet), Jean (*c.*1420–c.1480), French painter. The most prominent French painter of the 15th century, he was court painter to Charles VII and Louis XI and protégé of Etienne Chevalier, for whom he illuminated a book of hours. Influenced by a trip to Italy and by the rich sculpture of French churches, he painted portraits and historical and religious scenes.

Fouquet, Nicolas (1615–80), member of the French moneyed aristocracy, held a number of financial offices, finally becoming minister of finance in 1653 under Louis XIV, with the aid of the diplomat Mazarin. Constant warfare and corruption made a chaos of government financial records, and when Mazarin died Louis XIV had Fouquet arrested in 1661 for embezzlement. He was banished after a four-year, illegal trial. The king changed his sentence to life imprisonment.

Fouquier-Tinville, Antoine Quentin (1746–1795), ruthless French Revolutionary, served as prosecutor for the Revolutionary Tribunal which accounted for the execution by guillotine of thousands during the Reign of Terror. After Robespierre's loss of power, Fouquier-Tinville was himself guillotined.

Four Horsemen of the Apocalypse, allegorical figures described in the Biblical Book of Revelations (6:1–8) as one of the visions appearing when seals of the book are opened. The riders are: (1) on a white horse, rider with a bow and crown of conquest; (2) on a red horse, a rider with power and a sword to take peace from the earth; (3) on a black horse, a rider with a pair of balances; and (4) on a pale horse, Death as the rider. The four are given the power to kill with the sword, with hunger, with death, and with the beasts of the earth.

Fourier, François Marie Charles (1772–1837), French utopian socialist. He supported cooperativism and set forth detailed plans for the organization of the communities (called phalanxes). Unlike most socialist writers, Fourier suggested that capital for the enterprise come from the capitalist, and he provided for payment to capital in his division of output. *See also* Utopian Socialism.

Fourier Series, series of sine and cosine functions used to represent other periodic functions. Any single-valued periodic function can be analyzed as a sum of simple harmonic components, thus:

$$f(x) = \frac{a_0}{2} + (a_1 \cos x + b_1 \sin x) + (a_2 \cos 2x + b_2 \sin 2x) + \ldots.$$

In this series the nth coefficients a_n and b_n are given by

$$a_n = \frac{1}{\pi} \int_{-n}^{n} f(x) \cos nx \, dx.$$

$$b_n = \frac{1}{\pi} \int_{-n}^{n} f(x) \cos nx \, dx.$$

Fourier analysis, named after the French physicist Jean Baptiste Fourier, is an invaluable tool in handling complex periodically changing quantities in many branches of science.

Four-o'clock, bushy, tuberous plant with flowers that open in the late afternoon. Perennial in the tropics, it is treated as an annual in cold climates. The trumpet-shaped flowers are pink, red, lavender, yellow, or white, often on the same plant. Height: 1.5–3ft (46–91cm). Species include common *Mirabilis jalapa.* Family Nyctaginaceae. *See also* Bougainville.

Fourteen Points (1918), Pres. Woodrow Wilson's unsuccessful plan to achieve a liberal peace after World War I. It called for an end to secret agreements; navigational and economic freedom; reduction of armaments; impartial adjustment of colonial claims; evacuation of Russian, Belgian, and French territories; readjustment of Italian frontiers; autonomy for the nationalities in Austria-Hungary; restoration of occupied Romanian, Serbian, Montenegran territories; autonomy for nations under Turkish rule; Polish independence; and the formation of an association of nations. Although not adopted as a group at the Versailles peace treaty, several points were included in the treaty, and Wilson's dream of a League of Nations was realized. *See also* League of Nations; Versailles, Treaty of.

E. M. Forster

Stephen Foster

France

Fourth Dimension, time considered as an additional dimension, together with the three dimensions of space, in a full description of the motion of a particle. *See also* Relativity Theory.

Fovea. *See* Blind Spot; Optic Nerve.

Fowl, various domestic or game birds raised or hunted for food. *See* Game Bird; Poultry.

Fowler, Henry Watson (1858–1933), English lexicographer. He is known for *A Dictionary of Modern English Usage* (1926; rev. ed. 1965 by Sir Ernest Gowers) and other writings on English usage and style.

Fowles, John (1926–   ), British writer whose novels make strong comments on English ethical and social mores. *The Collector* (1963) and *The Magus* (1966) have both been made into films; *The French Lieutenant's Woman* (1969), *Daniel Martin* (1977), and *A Maggot* (1985) have also been bestsellers.

Fox, Charles James (1749–1806), British Whig politician who entered Parliament in 1768. In 1770–72 he was a lord of the Admiralty and in 1773–74 a lord of the Treasury. In 1782 he became foreign secretary in Rockingham's government and in 1783 formed a coalition government with Lord North. Thereafter he led the small Whig opposition to the long government of William Pitt returning to office as foreign secretary briefly in 1806.

Fox, George (1624–91), English religious leader, founder of the Society of Friends (Quakers). He embarked upon his evangelical calling in 1646 in response to an "inner light." He was imprisoned eight times between 1649–75. In 1671–72 he traveled to America to visit Quaker colonists there. His *Journal,* amended by William Penn, appeared in 1694.

Fox, small, wild animal native to all continents except Australia and Antarctica. Foxes are generally sharp-muzzled, big-eared, and bushy-tailed. The typical North American red fox *(Vulpes fulva)* is about the size of a small dog. It is usually yellowish-red or reddish-brown above and white or grayish below. Other color phases may occur in the same litter. Omnivorous, its diet includes small mammals, insects, eggs, fruit, and grass. The Old World red fox *(Vulpes vulpes)* is similar but slightly larger. Height: 16in (41cm) at shoulder; length: 23in (58cm) without tail. Family Canidae; genera *Vulpes, Urocyon. See also* Canidae.

Foxe, John (1516–87), English Anglican clergyman and historian. He was a Protestant who went into exile to avoid Mary I's persecution, returning in Elizabeth I's reign to complete his monumental *Actes and Monuments of these latter and perilous Dayes,* commonly called *Foxe's Book of Martyrs* (1563). A graphic description of religious persecutions from John Wycliffe to Thomas Cranmer, the book aroused widespread bitter hostility in England to Roman Catholicism, yet Foxe was a tolerant man and opposed the execution of Jesuits in 1581.

Foxglove, any of a genus *(Digitalis)* of hardy Eurasian biennial and perennial plants with long, spiky clusters of two-lipped, tubular flowers. The common biennial foxglove *(D. purpurea),* source of the heart-stimulant digitalis, is widely grown for its showy white, rose, purple, or blue flowers. Family Scrophulariaceae.

Fox Indians, more accurately known as Mesquakie, from *Meshwakuhug,* "the Red Earth People"; the name comes from a French error in translation. An Algonquian-speaking tribe of North American Indians

inhabiting Wisconsin. Always warlike, they allied themselves with the Sauk. Today most of the approximately 550 Mesquakie live in and around Tama, Iowa.

Fox River, river in SE central Wisconsin; rises in Columbia co, flows S near Wisconsin River (the two rivers are connected by a canal here); turns NE into Lake Winnebago, and drains from N end of lake, continuing to its mouth at the head of Green Bay; forms waterway between Wisconsin River and Lake Michigan. Length: approx. 175mi (282km).

Fox Terrier, a popular hunting dog (terrier group) recognized in two varieties since the 1880s—the smooth and the wire. The fox terrier has a narrow, tapered head; V-shaped, drooping ears; a short, straight-backed body; straight legs; and a high-set tail carried up. The predominately white coat is smooth, flat, and hard in the smooth variety and broken, hard, and wiry in the wire. Average size: 15.5in (39.5cm) high at shoulder; 15–19lb (7–8.5kg). *See also* Terrier.

Fraction, quotient of the form a/b; a is called the numerator and b the denominator. If a and b are whole numbers the quotient is a simple fraction. *See also* Fraction, Algebraic; Fraction, Complex.

Fraction, Algebraic, fraction in which the denominator or both numerator and denominator are algebraic expressions. For example, $\dfrac{x}{(x^2+2)}$ is an algebraic fraction.

Fraction, Complex, fraction in which both numerator and denominator are themselves fractions.

Fractional Distillation. *See* Distillation.

Fracture, break in a bone. The amount of stress that a bone can sustain without fracture apparently depends on both the size and the age of the bone. A compound fracture is one in which the bone has broken through the skin.

Fragonard, Jean Honoré (1732–1806), French painter. A student of Jean Chardin and François Boucher, he also studied the Italians and the northern landscape painters of the 17th century. Using many different styles during his career, he is best known for the lighthearted spontanaity of his amorous scenes, rustic landscapes, and decorative panels.

Frame of Reference, mathematical coordinate system for describing events in space and time with respect to a given observer. In the theory of relativity, this frame of reference is four-dimensional, and the description of events in other frames of reference depends on the relative speeds of those frames with respect to the frame of reference of the observer.

France, Anatole (1844–1924), pseud. of Jacques Anatole François Thibault, French author. After writing poems and short stories he achieved recognition with the novels *The Crime of Sylvester Bonnard* (1881) and *Thais* (1890). He supported Zola in the Dreyfus affair, and his writing became increasingly political as in the novels *Contemporary History* (1896–1901) and *Penguin Island* (1908). He was elected to the French Academy (1896) and awarded the Nobel Prize for literature (1921).

France, the largest nation in W Europe. For centuries, France has been at the center of Western culture, both as a major political power and as a leader in the arts and sciences. Its capital, Paris, is one of the world's most beautiful and famed cities.

Land and Economy. The geography of France may be divided into three principal regions; Alpine mountains, ancient uplands, and low-lying plains. The Pyrenees (SW) and the Alps (SE) are the tallest and most recent mountains geologically. The best farmlands are in the Paris Basin, which extends from the English Channel to the plateau region of the Massif Central, and in the Aquitane Basin in W and SW France. The major river systems are the Seine, Rhône, Loire, and Garonne. About three-fifths of the land-area of the country is under cultivation. France is one of the world's leading producers of wheat, dairy products, and wine. French industry ranks fifth in the world. Iron and steel, aircraft, motor vehicles, chemicals, textiles, and foodstuffs are among France's most valuable manufactured products. The country's major import is oil.

People. France has been inhabited since prehistoric times. The chief ethnic strains are Celtic (Gauls), Germanic, and Latin. The French language is descended from the Latin tongue brought to Gaul by the conquering Romans. French is spoken in all parts of France and often serves internationally as a language of diplomacy. The majority of modern French people are urban dwellers. In religion, most are Roman Catholics. No country can boast greater achievements in the fine arts than those of the French. As in many countries, the traditional extended family is giving place to the nuclear family.

Government. The constitution of the Fifth French Republic was approved by the French people in 1958. This constitution, under the sponsorship of Charles de Gaulle, shifted much power from parliament to the president of the republic. The president is elected to a seven-year term, has the right to dissolve parliament and call new elections, and may present bills to popular referendum. Parliament consists of two houses, the National Assembly and Senate. France has many political parties, including Socialists, Gaullists, Radicals, Communists, and Independent Republicans.

History. The area of France was ruled by the Romans from 51 BC until the 5th century. The Merovingian dynasty established the Franks, and in the late 8th century Charlemagne came to power, firmly entrenching the Carolingian dynasty. Royal authority subsequently weakened and was not revived until the Capetians came to the throne in the late 10th century. During the Middle Ages the monarchs were able to increase their authority gradually at the expense of the nobility and to extend their dominions over what is now modern France. Struggles with England, as in the Hundred Years War, and the Holy Roman Empire were frequent.

France emerged from the Middle Ages as the leading nation-state of Europe. The boundaries of France have changed very little since the reign of Francis I (r.1515–47). French power and influence expanded under Cardinal Richelieu, minister to Louis XIII (r.1610–43). The reign of Louis XIV was the golden era in the history of the French monarchy. The French Revolution (1789) destroyed the monarchy; the First Republic was est. in 1792. Napoleon was crowned emperor in 1804, and France dominated European politics in the Napoleonic era. After Napoleon's defeat (1815), a restoration of the monarchy was followed by the Second Republic (1848–52) and then the Second Empire (1852–70). During the 19th century France contended with Great Britain in establishing a colonial empire, while contending with an awakening Germany for power on the continent. Germany's victory in the Franco-Prussian War (1870) was humiliating to France. In 1907 France allied herself with Russia and England in the Triple Entente. Although a victor in World War I, France suffered great human and economic loss. In World War II, France was unprepared for Germany's air and armored attacks. The country fell in June 1940, and political instability marked the post-war years. France was instrumental in forming the European Economic Community. Charles de Gaulle became premier in 1958, establishing the Fifth Republic. The Gaullist party controlled French politics until 1974, when Valéry Giscard d'Estaing, an Independent Republican, was elected president. In 1981 the leader of the Socialist party, François Mitterrand, defeated Giscard d'Estaing in the presidential elections, and Socialists won by a wide margin in parliamentary elections. With the first Socialist government of the Fifth Republic, Mitterrand announced a major new program of nationalization of several industries and—reversing a trend begun under Napoleon—decentralization of government administration. The 1986 legislative elections resulted in a majority for the conservatives.

Following is a list of the rulers of France.

RULERS OF FRANCE

Pepin III (the Short)	751–68
Carloman	768–71
Charlemagne	768–81
Louis I (the Pious)	814–40
Charles II (the Bald)	840–77
Louis II	877–79
Louis III	879–82
Carloman	879–84
Charles the Fat	885–87
Odo (Eudes)	888–98
Charles III (the Simple)	893–923
Robert I	922–23
Rudolf	923–36
Louis IV	936–54
Lothair	954–86
Louis V	986–87
Hugh Capet	987–96
Robert II	996–1031
Henry I	1031–60
Philip I	1060–1108
Louis VI	1108–37
Louis VII	1137–80
Philip II Augustus	1180–1223
Louis VIII	1223–26
Louis IX (St Louis)	1226–70
Philip III	1270–85
Philip IV (the Fair)	1285–1314
Louis X	1314–16
John I	did not rule
Philip V	1316–22
Charles IV	1322–28
Philip VI	1328–50
John II (the Good)	1350–64
Charles V	1364–80
Charles VI	1380–1422
Charles VII	1422–61
Louis XI	1461–83
Charles VIII	1483–98
Louis XII	1498–1515
Francis I	1515–47
Henry II	1547–59
Francis II	1559–60
Charles IX	1560–74
Henry III	1574–89
Henry IV	1589–1610
Louis XIII	1610–43
Louis XIV	1643–1715
Louis XV	1715–74
Louis XVI	1774–92
Louis XVII	did not rule
National Convention	1792–95
Directory	1795–99
Consulate	1799–1804
Napoleon I	1804–14
Napoleon II	did not rule
Louis XVIII	1814–24
Charles X	1824–30
Louis Philippe	1830–48
Louis Napoléon	1848–52
Napoleon III	1852–70
Adolphe Thiers	1871–73
Marshal Patrice de MacMahon	1873–79
Jules Grévy	1879–87
Sadi Carnot	1887–94
Jean Casimir-Périer	1894–95
Félix Faure	1895–99
Émile Loubet	1899–1906
Armand Fallières	1906–13
Raymond Poincaré	1913–20
Paul Deschanel	1920
Alexandre Millerand	1920–24
Gaston Doumergue	1924–31
Paul Doumer	1931–32
Albert Lebrun	1932–40
Marshal Philippe Pétain	1940–44
Charles de Gaulle	1944–46
Félix Gouin	1946
Georges Bidault	1946
Léon Blum	1946
Vincent Auriol	1947–54
René Coty	1954–59
Charles de Gaulle	1959–69
Georges Pompidou	1969–74
Valéry Giscard d'Estaing	1974–81
François Mitterrand	1981–

PROFILE

Official name: French Republic
Area: 211,207sq mi (547,026sq km)
Population: 53,446,000
Density: 253per sq mi (98per sq km)
Chief cities: Paris, the capital; Marseilles; Lyon; Toulouse
Government: Democratic republic
Religion (major): Roman Catholic
Language: French (official)
Monetary unit: Franc
Gross national product: $531,330,000,000
Per capita income: $7,150
Manufacturing (major products): automobiles, aircraft, electronics, steel, chemicals, aluminum, textiles, clothing, perfume
Agriculture (major products): livestock, wheat, potatoes, sugar beets, wines, fruits
Minerals (major): iron, coal, petroleum, bauxite, uranium, gypsum, potash
Trading partners (major): West Germany, Great Britain, United States, Italy

Franche-Comté, historic territory in E France. Peopled by the Celtic Sequani, this land came under the rule of the Romans in 52 BC and was then variously under Burgundian, Frankish, independent, German, Holy Roman, Austrian, Spanish, and French rule in the centuries that followed. Its final assumption into France came about in 1678, and it was broken up into *départements* after the Revolution.

Francis (1554–84), duke of Alençon and Anjou, youngest son of Henry II of France and Catherine de Médicis. He opposed his mother, a Catholic extremist, and brother in the Catholic-Huguenot Wars and later led two invasions of the Spanish-controlled Netherlands. Although very homely, he was twice considered for marriage to Queen Elizabeth I.

Francis I (1708–65), Holy Roman emperor (1745–65), duke of Lorraine (1729–35) and Tuscany (1737–65). In 1736 he married the Hapsburg heiress Maria Theresa. Her accession (1740) precipitated the War of the Austrian Succession. In 1745 Francis succeeded Charles VIII as emperor, but the real ruler was his wife. *See also* Austrian Succession, War of the; Maria Theresa of Austria.

Francis II (1768–1835), Holy Roman emperor (1792–1806), emperor of Austria as Francis I (1804–35). Repeatedly defeated by France, in 1806 he was forced by Napoleon to dissolve the Holy Roman Empire but had already proclaimed himself Austrian emperor. In 1810 his daughter, Marie Louise, married Napoleon, but in 1813 Austria rejoined the anti-French coalition. From 1809 Austrian affairs were run by Prince Metternich.

Francis I (1494–1547), king of France (1515–47). A leader of the Renaissance, he was best remembered for his contributions to the humanities, which include establishment of the *Lecteurs royaux* (a teaching group) and support of the arts. He was a man of valor and action unsuited for subtle political complexities. Repression of religious reform, centralization of monarchical power, and foolish financial policies earned the dissatisfaction of his people. Excluding the Marignano expedition to Italy of 1515, his foreign policy met with little success, embroiling him in a long and costly struggle with the Emperor Charles V over the imperial crown. After a severe defeat at Pavia in 1525, Francis was imprisoned and forced to give up Burgundy as a condition of the Treaty of Madrid (1526). An ensuing war with Charles (1527–29) led to the loss of Italy, but campaigns in the 1540s were more successful. He was succeeded by his son, Henry II.

Francis I (1777–1830), king of the Two Sicilies, son of Ferdinand I and Marie Caroline (sister of Marie Antoinette). Early in his career, as regent for his father, he had liberal sympathies towards the Carbonari uprising of 1820 and opposed the reactionary Austrian troop intervention in Naples. However, after his accession to the throne in 1825, he became an extreme reactionary, requesting a greater Austrian presence.

Francis II (1836–94), king of the Two Sicilies (1859–60). The son of Ferdinand II and the last Bourbon king of Naples, he was driven from his throne by Giuseppe Garibaldi and deposed by the plebiscite of October 1861. His dominions were then annexed by Victor Emmanuel II in 1861.

Franciscans, the Order of Friars Minor, religious order founded by St Francis of Assisi in 1209. The original Rule of St Francis, reformulated in 1223, stressed not only individual but corporate poverty. There have been many disputes over the question of poverty. The Capuchin order resulted from a 16th-century reform.

Francis de Sales, Saint (1567–1622), French religious leader, a Roman Catholic saint. A renowned preacher, he was a leader of the Counter-Reformation in France. He was instrumental in the conversion of Chablais from Calvinism. In 1602 he was appointed bishop (in exile) of Geneva. With Jeanne de Chantal he founded the Visitation Nuns. His *Introduction to the Devout Life* (1609) teaches the perfection of spiritual life. The patron of writers, his feast day is January 29.

Francis Ferdinand (1863–1914), archduke of Austria, heir apparent and nephew of Francis Joseph, emperor of Austria. He married Countess Sophie Chotek (1900) but publicly renounced all claims to the throne for their children because she was only from a minor Czech noble family. He and his wife were assassinated by the Serbian nationalist Gavrilo Princip in Sarajevo, Bosnia, on June 28, 1914. The ensuing Austrian ultimatum to Serbia precipitated World War I.

Francis Joseph (1830–1916), emperor of Austria (1848–1916), king of Hungary (1867–1916). He succeeded his uncle Ferdinand who abdicated amidst the turmoil of the revolution of 1848. He quickly brought the revolution under control, defeating the Hungarians under Kossuth and the Italians under Victor Emmanuel II of Sardinia, both in 1849. But in the Italian War of 1859 he lost Lombardy to Sardinia and in the Austro-Prussian War (1866) he lost Venetia to Italy and, more importantly, lost Austria's prestige among the German states. In 1867 he was forced to grant Hungary coequal status with Austria in the Dual Monarchy. His long reign was beset by nationalist strife, court intrigue, and personal tragedy. His brother Maximilian, Emperor of Mexico, was executed by Mexican nationalists (1867); his son, Crown Prince Rudolf, committed suicide (1889); his wife, Empress Elizabeth, was assassinated (1898) as was his nephew, the heir apparent Archduke Francis Ferdinand (1914). Francis Joseph died in the midst of World War I, two years before the complete collapse of his empire.

Francis of Assisi (1182?–1226), founder of the Franciscans, Roman Catholic saint, b. Giovanni de Bernardone. In 1205 he renounced his worldly life for one of poverty and prayer. In 1209 he received permission from Pope Innocent III to begin a monastic order. The Franciscans were vowed to humility, poverty, and devotion to aiding mankind. In 1212 he established an order for women, the Poor Clares, and in 1221, a lay fraternity. He traveled to France, Spain, and to the Holy Land in 1219–20. In 1221 he gave up leadership of his order to retire to his birthplace, Assisi, Italy. In 1224 he received the stigmata, the appearance of the crucifixion wounds on his own body. His feast day is October 4.

Francium, radioactive metallic element (symbol Fr), discovered (1839) by Marguerite Perey. It occurs naturally in uranium ores and is a decay product of actinium. Properties: at. no. 87; most stable isotope Fr^{223} (half-life 22 min). *See also* Alkali Elements.

Franck, César (1822–90), French Romantic composer, b. Belgium. His organ music is considered among the best after J.S. Bach. He also composed chamber music, *Symphonic Variations* for piano and orchestra (1885), and the popular *Symphony in D Minor* (1888).

Franco, Francisco (1892–1975), Spanish general and caudillo (dictator) of Spain (1939–75). A professional soldier, he was from early in his career associated with right-wing politics. He joined the 1936 military uprising that set off the Spanish Civil War and quickly became the Nationalist leader. He assumed leadership of the Falange party, and by 1939, with the aid of Nazi Germany and Fascist Italy, he successfully brought the war to an end and became Spain's dictator. Despite his association with Germany and Italy, he kept Spain neutral in World War II.

After World War II, Franco presided over Spain's impressive economic development and kept firm control over its politics. He declared Spain a monarchy in 1947 with himself as regent. In 1969 he designated Juan Carlos, grandson of the last king of Spain, as heir to the throne, and Juan Carlos became king upon Franco's death. *See also* Civil War, Spanish; Falange.

Franconia, historic region of Germany around the Main River. A duchy of the East Frankish kingdom, it was later divided among several ecclesiastical princes, of whom the bishop of Würzburg was the most powerful. Bavaria still has districts of Upper, Middle, and Lower Franconia.

Franco-Prussian War, also called the **Franco-German War,** 10-month conflict in 1870–71 between

Francisco Franco

Felix Frankfurter

Fraser River: Canada

French emperor Napoleon III and the combined forces of Germany. Bismarck, wishing to bring the south German states into a national union, encouraged the growing rift between France and Prussia in the late 1860s. When the throne of Spain was offered to a prince from the ruling house of Prussia, the French protested vigorously, demanding assurance from King William I of Prussia that the offer would never be accepted. He refused to give it, and Bismarck inflamed the French to declare war by publishing the Ems Dispatch. As Bismarck had hoped the south German states, seeing France as the aggressor, joined the North German Confederation. They were led by General von Moltke, who after a successful series of battles began a siege of Paris that ended three months later with the city's collapse. This French disaster led to the unification of Prussia and southern Germany, their annexation of Alsace-Lorraine, dissolution of French controls on Russian agression, the indirect unification of Italy, the formation of the Paris Commune and a new French republican government, and a European tension that precipitated two world wars. *See also* Ems Dispatch.

Frangipani, shrubs and small trees native to Central America and the West Indies and now grown in other warm regions. They have fragrant white, yellow, pink, or red flowers and a milky sap. Family Apocynaceae: genus *Plumeria.*

Frankenstein (1818), novel by Mary Wollstonecraft Shelley that deals with a monster created from inanimate matter. Unloved because of its revolting appearance, the monster takes revenge on its creator, Dr. Frankenstein. The 1931 film version, starring Boris Karloff and directed by James Whale, was a great success and spawned countless sequels and imitations.

Frankfort, capital city of Kentucky, on Kentucky River, 52mi (84km) E of Louisville; seat of Franklin co; site of Kentucky State College (1886), "Liberty Hall" (1796) reportedly designed by Thomas Jefferson, the Old Capitol (1827–30), Frankfort Cemetery where Daniel and Rebecca Boone are buried. Industries: tobacco, whiskey-distilling, shoes, furniture. Settled 1779; named capital 1792. Pop. (1980) 25,973.

Frankfurter, Felix (1882–1965), US jurist and educator, b. Austria. An assistant US attorney (1906–11) and law officer in the War Department (1911–14), he helped found the American Civil Liberties Union (1920). He was a New Deal "brain trust" advisor to Pres. Franklin Roosevelt, who appointed him an associate justice of the US Supreme Court (1939–62). One of the most scholarly justices, he advocated judicial restraint and pursued a middle-of-the-road course on the area of civil liberties.

Frankfurt-on-Main (Frankfurt-am-Main), city and port in central West Germany, on the Main River, 17mi (27km) N of Darmstadt. In 8th century it became one of Charlemagne's royal residences; made a free imperial city 1372; annexed by Prussia 1871; site of 13th–15th-century Gothic church of St Bartholomew, house in which Goethe was born (1749), Städel Art Museum (1816), and university (1914). Industries: chemicals, clothing, machinery, electrical equipment. Founded 1st century AD by Romans. Pop. 631,000.

Frankfurt-on-Oder, city in E Germany, on Oder River, 50mi (81km) ESE of Berlin; capital of Frankfurt district. During Middle Ages city was river crossing on trade route from Germany to Poland. City was under siege during Thirty Years' War (1631), Seven Years' War (1759), Napoleonic Wars (1806–08, 1812–13), and in WWII when 70% of city was destroyed before Soviet

capture March 18, 1945. Industries: machinery, textiles, shoes, soap. Chartered 1253. Pop. 62,000.

Frankincense, or olibanum, gum resin extracted from bark of various trees *(Boswellia)* found in Africa and Asia. It is burned as incense and the spicy oil, extracted from the resin, is used in perfumes.

Franklin, Benjamin (1706–90), US inventor, diplomat, and statesman, b. Boston. As a young man, he worked in Philadelphia as a printer, where he published the witty *Poor Richard's Almanac* (1732–57). He made a number of inventions, such as the Franklin stove, and experimented with electricity. He also initiated a great many civil improvements in Philadelphia, including a library, a fire company, and a university. He represented Philadelphia at the Albany Congress (1754), where he proposed that the colonies unite under an elected council and a president with veto power. The idea was rejected at that time but was to come to fruition later on when the Constitution was written. He spent 16 years in England prior to the American Revolution (1757–62, 1766–75), attempting to reconcile the differences between Britain and the colonies. Returning to the colonies he was a delegate to the Second Continental Congress. There he helped draft and signed the Declaration of Independence and organized a postal system, serving as postmaster general (1775–76). Sent to France (1776–85), he helped bring that country into the Revolution on the colonists' side. He was one of the signers of the peace treaty in Paris (1783) that ended the Revolution. Franklin also attended the Constitutional Convention (1787).

Franklin, (Sir) John (1786–1847), English rear admiral and arctic explorer. He served England in the Battle of Copenhagen (1801) and the Battle of Trafalgar (1805). He later commanded two explorations of the North American coast (1819–22 and 1825–27), for which he was knighted. In 1845 he led an ill-fated arctic exploration in search of a northwest passage. When no word was heard from him, a series of expeditions was organized to learn his fate. Finally, in 1859, a search party sent by his wife found that he and all of his crew had been lost.

Franklin, district and northernmost region in Canada; encompasses islands N of Canadian mainland (almost coextensive with Arctic Archipelago), and Boothia and Melville peninsulas; with districts of Mackenzie and Kewatin, it comprises Canada's Northwest Territories; inhabited by Eskimos; oil reserves. Founded 1895; boundaries est. 1920. Area: 549,253sq mi (1,422,565sq km).

Franks, Germanic people who settled along the Rhine in the 3rd century AD. Under Clovis (reigned 481–511) they overthrew Roman rule in Gaul and established the Merovingian empire. The empire was later divided into the kingdoms of Austrasia, Neustria, and Burgundy, but it was reunited by the Carolingian dynasty, notably Charlemagne. The partition of Charlemagne's empire produced the East and West Frankish kingdoms, which became respectively Germany and France. *See also* Austrasia; Burgundy; Carolingians; Merovingians; Neustria.

Franz Josef Land (Zeml'a Franca–Iosifa), archipelago in the Arctic Ocean; part of Archangel'sk Oblast, USSR; a group of approx. 85 islands including Aleksandra Land, George Land, Wilczek Land, Graham Bell Island, Hooker Island, and Rudolf Island; generally ice-covered; most northerly land in E hemisphere; site of meteorological station (est. 1929 by USSR). Discovered 1873 by Australian expedition under Karl Weyprecht and Julius Von Payer; claimed

1926 as a Russian national territory. Area: 8,000sq mi (20,720sq km).

Frasch Process, named after German-born chemist Herman Frasch, a method for mining sulfur from the earth by pumping superheated water to the sulfur deposits, melting the mineral, and forcing it to the surface. The process was first put to practical use in Louisiana and by 1902 had made the United States independent of imported sulfur.

Fraser, Simon (1776–1862), Canadian explorer and fur trader. Fraser moved to Canada from the United States in 1784 and joined the Northwest Company in 1792. He extended their trade routes west to British Columbia (1805–08) and founded a string of trading posts. His exploration of the Fraser River and Red River did not prevent personal bankruptcy.

Fraser, river in S British Columbia, Canada; rises in the Rocky Mts and flows NW then S around the Cariboo Mts and into the Strait of Georgia. Discovered 1793 by Alexander Mackenzie and explored 1808 by Simon Fraser. Length: 850mi (1,369km).

Fraunhofer, Joseph von (1787–1826), German physicist and optical instrument maker. His studies of the dark lines (Fraunhofer lines) in the solar spectrum were instrumental in establishing spectroscopy. Although he mapped the positions of these lines, he was unable to explain them. He also invented a diffraction grating device. *See also* Diffraction.

Frazer, (Sir) James George (1854–1941), Scottish anthropologist, folklorist, and classical scholar. He gained recognition with the publication of *The Golden Bough: a Study in Magic and Religion* (1890) which held that the history of thought is a logical progression from the magical to the religious to the scientific. Although much of his theory has been discredited, he was influential in breaking ground in research of primitive customs. Other works include *Folk-Lore in the Old Testament* (1918).

Frederick I (c. 1123–90), Holy Roman emperor (1152–90) and German king (1152–90), called Frederick Barbarossa. A Hohenstaufen, he succeeded his uncle, Conrad III. He planned to absorb Lombardy into a personal kingdom, but the Italian cities, encouraged by Pope Alexander III, formed the Lombard League against him. He set up an antipope, but after his defeat at Legnano (1176) he was reconciled with Alexander and made peace (1183) with the Lombards. He asserted his authority in Germany, at first conciliating but later (1180) overthrowing the Guelph, Henry the Lion. He drowned in Cilicia en route to join the Third Crusade. *See also* Hohenstaufen Dynasty; Lombard League.

Frederick II (1194–1250), Holy Roman emperor (1215–50), German king (1215–50), and king of Sicily (1198–1250), b. Italy. Son of Emperor Henry VI and Constance of Sicily, he devoted himself to Italian affairs. When elected German king at the instigation of Pope Innocent III, he promised to make his son, Henry, king of Sicily. Instead he gave Germany to Henry (1220), although he later deposed him (1235) and made another son, Conrad IV, German king. In Sicily, Frederick set up a centralized royal administration. Attempting to extend his rule to Lombardy, he was met by a revival of the Lombard League and papal opposition. He went on crusade and was crowned (1229) king of Jerusalem, but this failed to appease the pope. In 1245, Innocent IV deposed him, and civil war ensued in both Germany and Italy. *See also* Lombard League.

Frederick III (1415–93), Holy Roman emperor (1440–93) and German king (1440–93). He succeeded his cousin Albert II. After the death in 1458 of his ward Ladislas V of Bohemia and Hungary, he attempted to win those thrones. Instead he lost Austria, Carinthia, Carniola, and Styria to Matthias Corvinus of Hungary, only recovering them on Matthias' death in 1490. By marrying in 1477 his son Maximilian to Mary, heiress of Burgundy, he acquired an enormous inheritance for the Hapsburgs.

Frederick II (1712–86), king of Prussia (1740–86), called Frederick the Great. Succeeding his father, Frederick William I, he adopted an aggressive policy toward Austria and made Prussia a major European force. In the War of the Austrian Succession (1740–48) he won Silesia from Austria. During the Seven Years War (1756–63), Austro-Russian forces reached Berlin (1760), but Russia's withdrawal from the war enabled Frederick to recover and make a peace confirming the status quo. Later he gained Polish Prussia in the first partition of Poland (1772) and waged another war against Austria (the War of the Bavarian Succession, 1778–79). Frederick carried out some internal reforms, but his administration was autocratic and overcentralized. A patron of Voltaire, among others, he wrote extensively in French and was a gifted musician. *See also* Austrian Succession, War of the.

Frederick III (1463–1525), elector of Saxony (1486–1525), called the Wise. Although he remained a Roman Catholic, he protected Martin Luther, bringing the latter's case before the Diet of Worms (1521) and giving him refuge afterward at Wartburg.

Frederick Augustus I (1750–1827), elector (1768–1806) and king (1806–27) of Saxony. He entered the war against France, but after the Prussian defeat at Jena (1806), he made a separate peace with Napoleon, who approved the title king of Saxony and made him (1807) grand duke of Warsaw. He was captured by the Prussians in the Battle of Leipzig (1813) and lost much of his kingdom to Prussia at the Congress of Vienna (1815).

Frederick Augustus II (1797–1854), king of Saxony (1836–54). Coregent with his uncle King Anton from 1830, he instituted the 1831 constitution. As king he resisted further change. His refusal to accept the Frankfurt Parliament's plan for a united Germany in 1848 led to a revolt in 1849, which was repressed with Prussian aid.

Frederick Louis (1707–1751), prince of Wales, father of George III of England. The alienated eldest son of George II, he led opposition to his father's government after a bitter quarrel over Frederick's allowance. He managed to topple prime minister Robert Walpole and later settled the grievances with his father.

Frederick Henry (1584–1647), prince of Orange-Nassau. Son of William the Silent, he succeeded his brother Maurice in 1625 as stadtholder of the Dutch Republic. In 1631 the stadtholdership was granted to the House of Orange on a hereditary basis. Frederick Henry established an alliance (1635) with France and Sweden against the Hapsburgs in the Thirty Years War and successfully campaigned against Spanish outposts in the Netherlands. One year after his death the independence of the Netherlands was recognized by the Peace of Westphalia.

Frederick William (1620–88), elector of Brandenburg (1640–88), called the Great Elector. At the Peace of Westphalia (1648), which ended the Thirty Years War, he received Eastern Pomerania, and by intervention in the war (1655–60) between Poland and Sweden, he won recognition of his sovereignty over Prussia, formerly a Polish fief. In addition to these acquisitions, he built up the army, curtailed the privileges of the nobility, and fostered trade.

Frederick William I (1688–1740), king of Prussia (1713–40). Succeeding his father, Frederick I, he devoted himself to building up the strictly disciplined army and further centralizing the government. He intervened briefly in the Great Northern War and won part of Western Pomerania. He despised the arts and was brutal to his son, Frederick II.

Frederick William II (1744–97), king of Prussia (1786–97). He succeeded his uncle, Frederick II. He joined (1792) the alliance against France but made peace in 1795 in order to consolidate his acquisitions in the east as a result of the second (1793) and third (1795) partitions of Poland. He kept an extravagant court and left the country virtually bankrupt.

Frederick William III (1770–1840), king of Prussia (1797–1840). Son and successor of Frederick William II, he declared war on France in 1806 and suffered a disastrous defeat at Jena. After the Peace of Tilsit (1807), major reforms were carried out by his ministers, Barons Stein and Hardenberg. Later, allied with Russia, Prussia took part in the final defeat of Napoleon. After 1815 the king joined the Holy Alliance and refused to grant a promised constitution.

Frederick William IV (1795–1861), king of Prussia (1840–61). He succeeded his father, Frederick William III. He gave way at first to the 1848 revolution, calling a constituent assembly, but he later dissolved the assembly and issued a conservative constitution. When the Frankfurt Parliament offered him the German crown (1849) he refused it because it came from an elected body. His own plan for a German confederation excluding Austria was abandoned (1850) because of Austrian opposition. His brother William became regent in 1858 when Frederick William could no longer govern.

Fredericton, capital city of New Brunswick, Canada, at the head of St John River; seat of York co; location of the University of New Brunswick (1859); major trade and rail center; lumber is the major industry. Settled 1740 by French; made provincial capital 1785. Pop. 45,248.

Free Association, psychoanalytic (Freudian) technique to recover repressed memories or discover unconscious associations. The patient is instructed to relax and let his thoughts run freely and then to give an uncensored report of his stream of consciousness. Unconscious material presumably reveals itself as it guides the "free" associations.

Free Church. *See* Congregational Church.

Free City, designation used during the Middle Ages for important European cities that were recognized as autonomous states, exempt from duties and taxes and under imperial protection. Hamburg, Bremen, and Lübeck held this status in Germany until 1937. Danzig (Poland) and Fiume (Yugoslavia) were, for a time, free cities under the League of Nations.

Freedmen's Bureau, US government agency established in 1865 at the end of the Civil War to aid newly freed blacks. Administered by the War Department, the agency provided relief work and educational services, as well as legal protection for blacks in the South. The bureau also acted as a political machine, recruiting black voters for the Republican party.

Freedom of the Seas, fundamental principle of international law affirming that no state has sovereignty over the seas beyond its territorial waters and guaranteeing the right to fish and sail on the high seas, to fly over them, and to lay cables and pipelines.

Free Enterprise, system in which the market concept is supreme, that is, the market decides what goods will be produced and who will consume them. Individual firms may combine resources as they wish in the production process, and individual consumers may purchase whatever goods they wish, limited only by their means. Significant government control of the economic process is absent.

Free Fall, state of motion of an unsupported body in a gravitational field. *See* Gravity.

Free French, a group formed by Charles de Gaulle upon the creation of the Vichy government in 1940 for the continuance of the war against Germany. Operating outside France, these men were soon aligned with internal resistance groups, and though considered traitors by the Vichy administration, they managed to gain the increasing support of the French people. The Free French aided the Allies throughout the war, forming a provisional government after the D-Day invasion in 1944.

Freemasonry, secret fraternal order begun in England in the 17th century. Members are commonly called "Masons." The name stems from the fact the order uses secret rituals used by real stonemasons in the Middle Ages. Those craftsmen called themselves "free and accepted masons" when seeking work. The group's name was taken from that title.

Freeport, major town on SW coast of Grand Bahama Island, Bahama Islands, in West Indies. Tourism is main industry. Pop. 25,859.

Free Port, area in which goods may be landed and reshipped without customs intervention. Free ports aid in quicker movement of ships and goods. When the goods are moved to the consumer, they then become subject to customs duties. Free ports include Copenhagen, Singapore, Stockholm, and New York City.

Free Silver, in US history, coinage of silver at a ratio of 16 to 1 with gold. Proponents in the 1870–1890s included inflationists, who favored increasing the amount of money in circulation, and mine operators. With the repeal (1893) of the Sherman Silver Purchase Act (1890), free silver became a campaign issue in 1896.

Freetown, seaport and capital city of Sierra Leone, West Africa; capital of British West Africa 1808–74; site of Njala University (1963), Fourah Bay College (1827), University of Sierra Leone (1967), and a technical institute; excellent harbor. Exports: diamonds, iron ore. Industries: food, beverages, cigarettes, petroleum refining, shoes, beer. Area settled 1787; Freetown founded 1792 by freed slaves from England. Pop. 214,000.

Free Trade, economic policy favoring the elimination of tariffs or duties in international trade. Protectionists oppose free trade, advocating import duties and restrictive quotas to safeguard domestic industry from foreign competition.

Free Verse, verse with no regular meter and no apparent form. The unsystematized rhythm is close to that of prose. Dylan Thomas was one of the many modern poets who employ free verse.

Free Will, in philosophy, is the power of an individual to determine his own behavior. The controversy between affirmation and denial of free will has been persistent in Western thought and has influenced philosophy, law, theology, ethics, and psychology. Theologists have struggled to make the concept of God's omnipotence and omniscience compatible with man's responsibility for his own salvation. Forensic law tries to define the point at which individuals become legally responsible for their behavior. Progress in the physical and biological sciences have narrowed the realm of free will to the point that most psychologists are determinists. This is problematical for those who see moral decisions and artistic creation diminished when viewed as merely a series of causally determined events. Advocates of free will have argued that the human will, unlike inanimate objects, can initiate its own action. Others, like Spinoza, have found freedom through determinism by identifying free will with the affirmation of a reality. Existentialists, like Sartre, believe men to be totally free and entirely responsible, a state which is the source of dread. Those arguing against free will use the concept of the unconscious to provide the unseen motive for apparently existential behavior. In common practice persons believe they determine their actions and hold each other accountable. The practical result of this is that members of a society behave more ethically. Thus the concept is useful, if misnamed, since individuals perhaps possess neither freedom nor unfettered will.

Freezing Point, the temperature at which a substance changes phase from liquid to solid. The freezing point for most substances increases somewhat as pressure increases.

Frege, Gottlob (1848–1925), German logician. He was a professor of mathematics at Jena (1879–1918), and, along with George Boole, one of the founders of symbolic logic and the creator of a logistic system in which the notion of a propositional calculus appears in modern dress. Frege attempted to derive arithmetic from a set of logical axioms in his *Foundations of Arithmetic* (1884).

Freiburg im Breisgau (Freiburg), city in SW West Germany, at edge of Black Forest. Hapsburgs took possession of city 1368 and it was held by Austrians until 1805, except for two short periods of French possession; site of University (1457), and 13th-century Gothic cathedral. Industries: textiles, optical goods, paper, chemicals. Pop. 174,000.

Freighter, a ship designed to carry dry cargo or freight, as distinct from oil tankers and bulk carriers of ore or grain. Most modern of the cargo ships are the container ship, which carries prepacked, truck-delivered, steel containers, and the LASH (Lighter Aboard Ship) vessel, which carries steel lighters or barges, each about 60ft (18m) long and 30ft (9m) wide and carrying 500 tons of cargo. The superstructure of the LASH hull is dominated by a large traveling crane supported by legs from each side of the stern ship. Tracks for the crane extend well aft of the stern deck, so that barges may be lowered directly into the water or picked up from the water and placed in their storage position.

Frémont, John C(harles) (1813–90), US explorer and general, b. Savannah, Ga. He made a number of important expeditions but was best known for his exploration and mapping of the Oregon Trail (1842). Frémont was sent to serve the army in California during the

Frederick II of Prussia

John C. Fremont

French bulldog

Mexican War. He disobeyed Gen. Stephen Kearny, was court-martialed in 1848, and resigned his commission. He served as senator from California (1853–54) and was the first presidential candidate of the Republican party. Campaigning on an anti-slavery platform he lost to James Buchanan. After serving in the Civil War, he was territorial governor of Arizona (1878–83).

Fremont, city in W California, SSE of Oakland; site of a General Motors complex, and Mission San Jose de Guadalupe (1797), which is now restored as a museum. Inc. 1956. Pop. (1980) 131,945.

French, Daniel Chester (1850–1931), US sculptor, b. Exeter, N.H. In addition to "Minute Man" (1875; Concord, Mass.), which commemorates the American Revolution, he did the seated figure of Lincoln in the Lincoln Memorial (1919; Washington, D.C.).

French, major world language, spoken in France and parts of Belgium, Switzerland, Canada, Haiti, and a number of other countries. Descended from Latin, it is one of the Romance languages and is thus part of the Indo-European family. It was one of the two official languages of the League of Nations and is one of the six official languages of the United Nations.

French and Indian Wars (1754–63), a series of wars in colonial North America. A part of a larger conflict, the Seven Years War (1756–73), it pitted Britain and American colonists against French Canadian colonists and Indians. The fighting began (1754) when Virginia troops under George Washington attempted to evict French Canadians who had built Fort Duquesne on land Virginia claimed and were defeated. Initial British efforts to capture the French forts in the West and then cities on the Canadian rivers were unsuccessful. They were defeated badly at the Battle of the Wilderness (1755) by superior Indian and French land forces. By 1757, Prime Minister William Pitt had improved British resources as they took the fortresses at Louisburg, Duquesne (1758), but were repelled at Ticonderoga. Ticonderoga fell in 1759. On the plains of Abraham the British under Gen. James Wolfe decisively defeated the French under the Marquis de Montcalm (1759) and gained Quebec. Both leaders were killed. Montreal surrendered to Britain's Gen. Jeffrey Amhurst (1760). The Treaty of Paris (1763) gave almost all of French Canada to Britain, as well as French Louisiana east of the Mississippi River and part of Florida. The war ended French military and political power in North America.

French Bulldog, sweet-tempered dog (nonsporting group) bred from toy English bulldogs in France in 1860s. It has a large, square bulldog face with short nose; prominent lower jaw; and thick, hanging lips. Its broad-based, erect, bat-type ears distinguish it from the larger bulldog. The body is short; legs stout and muscular; and short tail straight or screw-shaped. Soft, loose skin is wrinkled on head and shoulders; a short coat is all brindle, fawn, or white; or brindle and white. Average size: 12in (30.5cm) at shoulder; 19–28lb (8.5–12.6kg).

French Canadians. The French founded the first settlements in Canada in 1604. Immigration declined after 1675, but today they represent 31% of the Canadian population. Dominated by the Jesuits and European commercial interests, the French settled into a paternalistic, authoritarian society unable to prevent British encroachment. After 1760 French Canadians followed a course of opposition to confederation, defending their language and culture with success. The Riel Rebellions (1869 and 1885), opposition to World War I, and urban industrialization after World War II further weak-

ened their influence. Only in Quebec have they succeeded in preserving social autonomy.

French Community, association composed of France, her overseas territories, and her former African colonies, established in 1958 as the successor to the French Union. The constitutionally created Community handled the foreign policy and the military, cultural, judicial, and economic affairs of its member states. With the achievement of independence by the African nations by the end of 1960, Community was replaced by bilateral and multilateral agreements.

French Equatorial Africa, former French federation in W central Africa, consisting of Chad, Gabon, Middle Congo (now Congo) and Ubangi-Shari (now Central African Republic). Territories colonized by French in late 19th century; became autonomous republics 1958; gained independence 1960.

French Guiana (Guyane Française), Department of, a French overseas department on the NE coast of South America. It was the site of the infamous Devil's Island penal colony. A dense tropical forest covers about 90% of the land, rendering most of the area uninhabitable. The small population lives mostly along the coast, 75% in Cayenne and vicinity. The country's economy is dependent upon France, since agricultural output does not meet local demands, and the fishing industry provides the only real export surplus. However, huge undeveloped bauxite deposits appear promising. Aside from a few Indians and blacks, the population is composed mostly of Creoles and Europeans. The vast majority lives in urban areas along the coast. Most of the people are Roman Catholics. French Guiana operates as a regular department of France, electing one deputy each to the national assembly and senate in Paris. The country itself is administered by a perfect and an elected 16-member council-general. Explored by the Spanish about 1500, the country was settled by the French in 1604. The colony, controlled at various times by the Dutch, English, and Portuguese, came into permanent French possession in 1817. The people have had full French citizenship since 1848 and have sent deputies to Paris since 1870. French Guiana became a French Department in 1947.

PROFILE

Official name: Department of French Guiana
Area: 34,749sq mi (90,000sq km)
Population: 60,000
 Density: 1.4per sq mi (0.5per sq km)
Chief city: Cayenne (capital)
Government: Overseas Department of France
Religion: no official
Language: French (official)
Monetary unit: franc
Gross national product: $40,000,000
Per capita income: $940
Industries: negligible
Agriculture (major products): timber, cocoa, bananas, shrimp
Minerals (major): bauxite
Trading partners (major): France, United States

French Horn, brass wind musical instrument. The principal symphony orchestra horn, it has a flared bell, long conical tube coiled in a circle, three valves, and funnel-shaped mouthpiece. Versatile, but difficult to play, its romantic mellow tones, blending with either brass or woodwinds, were favored by Wagner, Brahms, and Richard Strauss.

French Revolution, popular uprising in France that began in 1789, resulting in the overthrow of the monarchy of Louis XVI and the establishment of a shortlived

republic. The revolutionary era ended with the establishment of the empire in 1804. The revolution was begun by the meeting of the States General—a legislative body representing in three parts the clergy, the nobility, and the common people—in 1789, but the events which led to this meeting can be traced to the reign of Louis XIV. The "Sun King" had incurred an enormous debt in financing his long wars, and the debt was a part of the inheritance of Louis XVI. Since France did not levy realistic taxes on its nobility, which had become divorced from any real function, or the church, there were exceedingly heavy taxes on the working classes, who further experienced a bitter famine in the winter of 1788. In addition, the unwieldy government set up by Louis XIV had become outdated and had lost all semblance of effective popular representation. This paralleled the rise of a wealthy and well-educated bourgeoisie inflamed with the principles of the Enlightenment. Pressured from all sides, the French king was compelled to call the States General for the first time in 175 years.

Well-intentioned but vacillating, Louis allowed control of the new assembly to fall to the bourgeoisie by a series of reversed decisions that won him no allies. Meanwhile, Parisian rebels had armed themselves and gained munitions and concessions in storming (July 14, 1789) the Bastille, a nearly empty but symbolic prison. The power of the new National Assembly established, the representatives wrote the beginnings of the constitution of 1791, ensuring basic human rights; the demise of feudal monopoly, inequality, and privilege; and the restriction of royal power. The king, however, lacked ambition to form a coherent constitutional monarchy, and a worsening economic picture aroused urban workers. In an effort to survive financially, the assembly claimed the property and income of the French church, adding the papacy to its list of enemies. Attempting escape to royalist forces, King Louis was captured and, shortly before the Jacobin coup over the more moderate Girondists, was finally executed in 1793. During this time the Paris commune had forced several reforms, a republic had been created under the National Convention of 1792, and France had declared war on Austria and Britain. Internal rebellion met with mass executions, and the guillotine dealt with political enemies by the thousands. This period, called the Reign of Terror, was administered by the fanatic idealist Maximilien Robespierre, himself guillotined in the popular Thermidorian Reaction of 1794. His death lessened the power of the Paris commune, and of the Jacobins, who were slaughtered throughout France. After internal struggles had somewhat subsided, the National Convention was dissolved in favor of the Constitution of the year III, setting off a riot that was effectively suppressed by the cannon fire of the young Napoleon Bonaparte. The new constitution established the government of the Directory in 1795, which was composed of a distinct executive (the five directors), legislature, treasury, and judiciary. Its main fault was the lack of central organizing power in a wildly unstable France.

Meanwhile, France was at war with half of Europe. The enlistment by law of all men between the ages of 18 and 25 had given it an army that, separated from civilian politics and often commanded by men risen from the ranks, was efficient, dedicated, and increasingly resentful of civilian disloyalty and inadequate supplies. With this army, Napoleon performed magnificently in Italy and Austria. When threatened by a royalist resurgence in 1797, three of the directors used the power of this new hero to establish a dictatorship-dependent for survival on the victories of French armies. Faced with a military crisis, strongly in need of some sort of stability, France was ripe for the establishment of Napoleon Bonaparte as first consul of a new government in 1779. Effectively ending the bloody and temporarily unsuccessful attempt for democracy, Napoleon's government soon became a military dictatorship. He was made emperor of the French in 1804 and was followed by a constitutional monarchy in 1814. *See also* Bastille; Directory; Girondists; Jacobins; Napoleon I; Reign of Terror.

French Somaliland. *See* Djibouti, Republic of.

French Territory of Afars and Issas, Africa. *See* Djibouti, Republic of.

French West Africa, former federation of eight French overseas territories, including modern republics of Dahomey, Guinea, Ivory Coast, Mauritania, Niger, Mali, Upper Volta, Senegal; federation abolished 1959.

Freons, trademark for a group of fluorocarbons used as refrigerants, aerosol propellants, cleaning fluids, and solvents. They are all clear, stable, and inert liquids. Examples are Freon-11, CCl_3F; Freon-12, CCl_2F_2; and Freon-14, CF_4.

Frequency, Sound. *See* Wave Frequency.

Frequency Modulation (FM), variation of the frequency of a transmitted radio carrier wave by the signal being broadcast. The technique gives radio reception fairly free from static interference.

Fresco Painting, method of painting on freshly spread plaster while it is still wet. In true fresco, or *buon fresco,* the paint combines chemically with the moist plaster so that, when dry, the painted surface does not peel. Dry fresco, or *fresco secco,* involves the application of paint in a water and glue medium to a dry plaster wall. It does not last as well as true fresco.

Fresnel, Augustin Jean (1788–1827), French physicist whose pioneer work in optics helped to establish and to remove several objections to the wave theory of light. His work involved light-aberration studies, production of devices to create interference fringes, and obtaining circularly polarized light. *See also* Diffraction.

Fresnel Lens, a type of theatrical spotlight consisting of a piece of heat-resistant glass cast with concentric portions of lenses of different diameters and approximately the same focal length. The Fresnel lens is two or three times more efficient than a plano-convex lens.

Fresno, city in S central California, 155mi (250km) SE of San Francisco; seat of Fresno co; site of oldest junior college in California, Fresno City College (1910), and California State University-Fresno (1911). Industries: agriculture, wines, prefabricated structures. Founded 1872; inc. 1885. Pop. (1980) 218,202.

Freud, Anna (1895–1982), English psychoanalyst, b. Austria, youngest of Sigmund Freud's six children. She applied psychoanalysis to the development of children, was an early user of play therapy, and wrote a number of books including *Normality and Pathology in Childhood* (1965).

Freud, Sigmund (1856–1939), Austrian psychiatrist and founder of the psychoanalytic movement, b. Freiberg, Moravia. Working with Josef Breuer, Freud developed new methods for treating mental disorders—free association and dream interpretation (summarized in *The Interpretation of Dreams,* 1900). He developed theories of the neuroses involving childhood relationships to one's parents and stressed the importance of sexuality in both normal and abnormal development. These controversial aspects of his theories were not well-received by his contemporaries, but gradually his ideas became widely discussed and gained acceptance. Later Freud extended psychoanalysis to a wide variety of cultural and social-psychological phenomena.

The impact of Freud's writings (such as *The Psychopathology of Everyday Life,* 1904; *The Ego and the Id,* 1923; and *Civilization and Its Discontents,* 1930) on modern thought is incalculable. The influences on medicine, psychotherapy, and psychology are obvious, but they also are considerable for literature, religion, education, and child care. Freud brought sex out into the open as a topic fit for discussion. He caused psychologists to realize that human motivations could be unconscious and made them look very closely at child-parent relations as a source for both healthy and sick development. No individual has influenced the development of modern psychiatry and psychology more than Freud.

Frey, in Norse mythology, the son of the fertility god Njord, and himself ruler of peace, fertility, rain, and sunshine. He was one of the Aesir, and Gerd, daughter of the giant Gymir, was his wife. The boar was sacred to him.

Freycinet, Louis Claude de Saulces de (1779–1842), French explorer, sailed with Captain Baudin in exploration of the southern Australian coast (1800–1805). He made maps and wrote a report of this expedition, and in 1817 commanded another on the *Uranie,* gaining valuable additions to natural history, published in *Voyage Around the World* (13 vols., beginning 1824). He helped found the Paris Geographical Society in 1821.

Friar, title given to a brother or member of one of the mendicant orders established during the Middle Ages. Often distinguished by the color of their mantles, the four chief mendicant orders are the Dominicans, Franciscans, Carmelites, and Augustinians.

Fribourg, town in W Switzerland, 17mi (27km) SW of Bern on the Sarine River; capital of Fribourg canton; ruled by Kyburgs 1218, Hapsburgs 1277, Savoy 1452; became member of the Swiss Confederation 1481; site of a university (1889), and Cathedral of St Nicholas (13th century). Products: chocolate, cheese. Industries: food processing, metal working, chemicals. Founded 1178. Pop. 40,200.

Friction, resistance encountered when surfaces in contact slide or roll against each other or when a fluid flows along a surface. Sliding friction is caused by the momentary interlocking of irregularities in the surfaces, rolling friction by deformation of the surface, and both are directly proportional to the force pressing the surfaces together and the surface roughness. Fluid-viscous friction is velocity dependent as well as material affected.

Friction, Coefficient of, a number associated with any two materials characterizing the force necessary to push one material along the surface of the other. If one body has a weight N and the coefficient of friction is a/b, then the force f necessary to move the body without acceleration along a level surface is $f = a/b$ N. The coefficient of *static* friction determines the force necessary to *initiate* movement; the coefficient of *kinetic* friction determines the (lesser) force necessary to *maintain* movement.

Friedman, Milton (1912–), US economist, b. Brooklyn, N.Y. An important member of the Chicago school of economics, he supports monetary policy as the best means of controlling the economy. Extremely influential, he has published extensively. His works include *A Monetary History of the United States 1867–1960* (1963), written with Anna Schwartz, a seminal book in monetary economics; *A Theory of the Consumption Function* (1957); *Essays in Positive Economics* (1953), which suggests economic decisions should not consider normative judgments; *Capitalism and Freedom* (1962), which argues for a guaranteed income; *Free to Choose* (with Rose Friedman) (1980), and *Bright Promises, Dismal Performance* (1983). He was awarded the 1976 Nobel Prize in economics.

Friedrich, Caspar David (1774–1840), German painter. One of the greatest German Romantic painters, he created eerie, symbolic landscapes, such as "Monk at the Seashore" (1808; Berlin) and "Men Observing the Moon" (1819; Dresden).

Friends, The Religious Society of, also known as Quakers. This religious movement was started in 1647 by George Fox in England. The Friends believe in the inward nature of religion and object to established churches and ministries. Coming to America in 1656, they established religious communities in Rhode Island, and in 1682 William Penn settled a religious colony in Pennsylvania. The Quakers are known for their simple style of living and pacifist ideals. Worldwide membership is about 200,000. *See also* Quakers.

Friesland, province in N Netherlands; includes part of West Frisian Islands in North Sea, and extends W to shore of Ijsselmeer; Frisians, a Germanic group, in the area, still speak a strong dialect, hardly recognizable as Dutch; association with the United Provinces was not formalized until 1748. Capital is Leeuwarden. Industries: dairy and cattle farming. Area: approx. 1,325sq mi (3,432sq km). Pop. 560,614.

Frieze, in architecture, (1) the middle section of an entablature, between the architrave and the cornice; (2) the relief carving on such a middle section; or (3) the space between a picture-rail (or panel top) and the ceiling or cornice of a room.

Frigate, small warship of 1,000–3,000 tons providing antisubmarine protection to fleet and merchant ships. Frigates are normally slower, less well-armed and less costly than destroyers. In the 18th century the frigate was a three-masted sailing ship with 32 to 48 cannon, employed like a modern cruiser. *See also* Cruiser.

Frigate Bird, rapidly flying, powerful seabird that soars over tropical oceans, stealing food from other birds. It has a small, dark body; short, fragile legs; scissorlike tail; and tremendous saillike wings. One chalky white egg is laid in a nest on a bush or rock on an oceanic island. Length: 3ft (91cm). Family Fregatidae.

Frigg, in Norse mythology, the wife of Odin and the mother of Balder. She was known as Frija and Frea to Germanic people. The word Friday is derived from her name.

Frigidity, female inability to perform sexually, the result of organic or psychogenic factors. It may vary in severity from diminished sexual feeling to an inability to achieve sexual arousal in any form. Reality factors (such as fear of pregnancy or disease) are somewhat more important in explaining female frigidity than male impotence. *See also* Impotence.

Frilled Lizard, dull-colored, Australian lizard with a fold of skin that spreads into a ruff when the mouth is opened in aggressive display. The cartilaginous frill has serrated edges, red, blue, and brown spots and is 8in (20cm) wide. It is arboreal and frequently runs on its hind legs. Length: to 36in (91cm). Family Agamidae; species *Chlamydosaurus kingi. See also* Lizard.

Frisch, Karl von (1886–), Austrian ethologist who shared the 1973 Nobel Prize in physiology and medicine for his pioneering work in the new field of ethology. He deciphered the "language of bees" by studying their "dance recruitment" in which one bee tells others in the hive the direction and distance of a food source.

Frisian Islands, chain of islands in North Sea, off the coast of W Europe; owned by Netherlands, West Germany, and Denmark. The Danish North Frisians are primarily resorts; the German North Frisians are mainly dunes and mud flats where cattle and sheep are raised; the German East Frisians also have resorts; the West Frisians (Netherlands) follow N coastline of country and are primarily sand flats and dunes, with some cattle grazing and small resorts.

Fritillary, strong-flying moth that usually feeds at night and prefers violet leaves. Most have brown or orange wings marked with black or silvery spots and zigzag lines. Family Nymphalidae. *See also* Moth.

Friuli, historic region of NE Italy, bordering N and E on Austria and Yugoslavia, S on the Adriatic Sea, and W on the Veneto region. The SE portion includes the former Free Territory of Trieste. From the 2nd century BC it was under Roman rule until it became a Lombard duchy in the 6th century AD. Later passing to the Franks and the Holy Roman Empire, it was acquired by Venice in 1420 and Austria in 1797. In 1866 and 1919 Italy received those portions of the territory it now holds.

Friuli-Venezia Giulia, autonomous district in NE Italy; Trieste is the capital: Founded after WWII, it encompasses Udine and Pardenone provinces; granted limited autonomy 1963. Industries: shipyards, dairying, textiles, ceramics. Area: 3,028sq mi (7,843sq km). Pop. 1,242,987.

Frobisher, (Sir) Martin (*c.*1535–94), English navigator. In 1576, searching for a northwest passage to India, he reached the Canadian inlet since named Frobisher Bay. His crew returned with samples of black earth, starting rumors of gold. He was sent to the same area in 1577 in a vain search for gold, and made a third trip for colonization in 1578. Frobisher later served under Sir Francis Drake (1585); was sent to Spain by Sir Walter Raleigh (1592); and was knighted for his part in destroying the Spanish Armada (1588).

Frog, tailless amphibian, found worldwide, characterized by long hind limbs, webbed feet, and external eardrums behind the eyes. Most frogs begin life as fishlike larvae (tadpoles) after hatching from gelatinous eggs usually laid in water. Some frogs remain aquatic, some are terrestrial, some live in trees, and some burrow underground. Most have teeth in the upper jaw and all have long sticky tongues, attached at mouth front, to capture live food. Male frogs frequently have vocal sacs in the throat region.

Frogs of the family Ranidae are found worldwide and are the only amphibians correctly called frogs. True frogs are streamlined and smooth-skinned with bullet-shaped bodies, pointed heads, large eardrums, and long, webbed toes. Toads have rough, bumpy skin and are toothless. Bullfrogs, leopard frogs, and green frogs are well-known US representatives. Length: 1–12in (2.5–30cm). Subclass Salientia (or Anura) is divided into 16 families. *See also* Amphibia; Toad.

Frog Hopper. *See* Spittle Bug.

Sigmund Freud

Frilled lizard

Robert Frost

Frogs, Greek comedy by Aristophanes (405 BC). A satire about the resurrection of the dead, the play takes its title from a chorus of frogs. Aeschylus and Euripides, both dead, compete when Dionysus travels to Hades to bring back to life the better writer.

Fronde (1648–53), a number of civil reactions against the growing power of the French throne. The Fronde of the Parlement (1648–49) started when Anne of Austria, acting as regent for Louis XIV, proposed to cut the salaries of high court officials. The Parlement rejected this plan and, after a series of armed conflicts, was able to force some restrictions on royal authority. The Fronde of the Princes (1650–53) was a rebellion led by nobles desirous of greater political power. The Great Condé, a powerful military leader, inspired riots and war against the King but was defeated, losing his bourgeois and aristocratic support. The crown's victory established a monarchy whose authority was unchecked until 1789.

Front, Weather, the interface or transition zone between two air masses of different density as well as different temperature, since this usually regulates density. Thus a polar front separates cold and warm air masses that have originated respectively in polar and tropical regions and often creates cyclonic disturbances that dominate the weather. Fronts of different kinds are often depicted on weather maps. With stationary fronts, air masses remain in the same areas and weather changes little. Cold fronts occur as a relatively cold and dense air mass moves under warmer air. With warm fronts, the warmer air is pushing over colder air and replacing it. An occluded front, on the other hand, is a composite of two fronts. When a cold front overtakes a warm or a stationary front, occlusion occurs and a wave cyclone often develops, with cyclonic weather changes. *See also* Air mass; Cyclone.

Frontenac, Louis de Buade, compte de Palluau et de (1620–98), governor of New France (1672–82, 1689–98), Frontenac rose to brigadier in the French army (1639–89). He founded Fort Frontenac (1673), appeased the Iroquois, and favored fur traders over farmers. His autocratic rule led to recall in 1682. In his second term, Frontenac repulsed an English attack (1690) and briefly attempted an attack on New York. He encouraged LaSalle's explorations and extended French domain to Lake Winnipeg and the Gulf of Mexico.

Fronton Games, a variety of games played with a ball off of walled surfaces, either by hand or with rackets, a bat, or wicker baskets. Included in the various games are *Frontennis,* played with tennis-like rackets and a hard rubber ball; *Pelota de goma,* played with hardwood bats and a rubber ball; *Pelota de cuero,* played with a hardwood bat and a leather ball; *Fronton a mano,* played by hand with a hard leather ball; and *Jai Alai,* played with curved wicker baskets. In all games, of which *Jai Alai* is most popular, the general idea is to return the ball—after it has caromed off of one or more walls—before the second bounce. *See also* Jai Alai.

Frost, Robert (Lee) (1874–1963), US poet, b. San Francisco. After his father's death (1885), his Scottish-born mother brought her family to New England. Frost dropped out of Dartmouth College to work in a cotton mill and as a cobbler. He then attended Harvard for two years but dropped out because of ill health. He farmed (1899–1906) then taught school (1906–12). He wrote poetry, but few poems were published. In 1912 he took his family to England. His lyric poems *A Boy's Will* (1913) and narrative poems *North of Boston* (1914) were enthusiastically received in England, establishing his reputation as a poet. In 1915 he returned

to the United States and purchased a farm in Franconia, N.H. From 1916 he taught in a number of universities and colleges including Amherst, Harvard, and the University of Michigan. He published many volumes of poetry and received the Pulitzer Prize for poetry in 1924, 1931, 1937, and 1943. In 1961 he recited his poem "The Gift Outright" at the inauguration of John F. Kennedy. He used simple forms and colloquial speech in his poems depicting the landscape and people of New England often to make profound statements about life and death. Among his many well known poems are "Birches," "The Death of the Hired Hand," "Mending Wall," "The Road Not Taken," and "Stopping by Woods on a Snowy Evening."

Frostbite, freezing of the body tissues, either superficially or penetrating beneath surface cells. Symptoms are hard, white areas of skin. First-aid treatment includes rapid rewarming of the affected area in water of about 100°F (38°C).

Frothingham v. Mellon (1923), US Supreme Court case in which a citizen was denied the right to challenge a congressional spending bill. The court held that her status as a taxpayer was not, by itself, sufficient indication of an interest or possible injury to sustain her as a proper party to sue the government. The decision was modified in *Flast v. Cohen* (1968). *See also* Flast v. Cohen.

Fructose, white crystalline sugar ($C_6H_{12}O_6$) that occurs in fruit and honey. It is made commercially by the hydrolysis of beet sugar and is used in foods and medicine.

Fruit, mature ovary of a flowering plant. It serves to reproduce and spread the plant and is important to humans and animals as food. Fruits are classified as simple, aggregate, or multiple. Simple fruits, dry or fleshy, are produced by one ripened ovary of one pistil and include legumes, nuts, apples, pears and citrus fruits. Aggregate fruits develop from several simple pistils; examples are raspberry and blackberry. Multiple fruits develop from a flower cluster; each flower produces a fruit with all merging into a single mass at maturity; examples are pineapple and fig.

Fruit Bat, large Old World bat that feeds chiefly on fruit and flowers. Larger species are gregarious and roost in large groups. Family Pteropodidae. *See also* Flying Fox.

Fruit Fly, or pomace fly, yellowish fly, 0.12 to 0.16in (3–4mm) long, found worldwide. Primarily found around decaying fruit; a few are parasitic on insects. Several species in this group are used in heredity studies. Family Drosophilidae. *See also* Diptera.

Frunze, city and capital of Kirgiz SSR, USSR, on Chu River; birthplace of General Mikhail V. Frunze; site of university, medical and teachers' colleges, theater, museum, botanical gardens. Industries: textiles, food processing, machinery. Founded 1862 as Pishpek, a Russian fortress. Pop. 522,000.

Frustration, the prevention of the satisfaction of an aroused physiological, psychological, or social need. Frustration may be imposed from the outside or it may also originate from within an individual, as in setting goals beyond one's ability. Frustrations may lead to increased effort, to anger, and to aggressive behavior. *See also* Aggression.

Fry, Elizabeth (1780–1845), English social worker and prison reformer. The daughter of John Gurney, a rich Quaker banker, she married Joseph Fry (a London

merchant) in 1820. She agitated for more humane treatment of women prisoners and of convicts sentenced to transportation to Australia and later became active in other fields of reform, notably improving standards for nurses and facilities for women's education. In 1838 she was requested by King Louis Philippe of France to inspect French prisons, which led to penal reforms in France.

Fuad I (1868–1936), sultan of Egypt (1917–22); first king of modern Egypt (1922–36); son of the deposed Khedive, Ismail Pasha. He founded the University of Cairo (1906); succeeded his brother, Hussein Kamil, as sultan; and opposed the Wafd party, which forbade him to rule without parliament. He suspended (1928) and restored (1935) the constitution. His son, Farouk I, succeeded him.

Fuchs, (Sir) Vivian Ernest (1908–   ), British geologist and explorer who made the first land crossing of the Antarctic. He led the Falkland Island Dependencies Survey in the Antarctic (1947–50). In 1957 he headed the British section of the Commonwealth Transarctic expedition and made the hazardous 2,250 mi (3,620km) journey across the Antarctic, which earned him knighthood.

Fuchsia, or lady's-eardrop, shrubby plant found mainly in temperate America and New Zealand. It has crisp, oval leaves, trailing stems, and trumpet-shaped, waxy flowers. The 80 species include the crimson-purple *Fuchsia procumbens* and cultivated *Fuchsia speciosa*. Family Onagraceae.

Fuel Cell, electrochemical cell for direct conversion of the energy of oxidation of a fuel to electrical energy. Suitably designed electrodes are immersed in an electrolyte, and the fuel (eg, hydrogen) is supplied to one and the oxidizer (eg, oxygen) to the other. Electrode reactions occur, leading to oxidation of the fuel, with production of current. Fuel cells are used in space vehicles.

Fuel Injection, method of introducing fuel into the cylinders of an internal combustion engine, utilizing a pump rather than piston-created suction. It distributes fuel more evenly for greater power with less tendency for engine knock or vapor lock.

Fugitive Slave Laws, laws passed in 1793 and 1850 to ensure that escaped slaves were returned to their owners. When slavery was abolished in Northern states, the Underground Railroad and laws helped Southern slaves obtain freedom. The Compromise of 1850 had a tougher fugitive slave law than the 1793 statute, with heavy penalties. According to the 1850 laws, fugitive slaves were denied legal rights. Abolitionists fought against the new law.

Fugitives, The, Southern writers who championed regionalism and agrarianism in the 1920s. They published (1922–25) *The Fugitive* magazine. They included John Crowe Ransom, Allen Tate, and Robert Penn Warren.

Fugue, in music, a composition of several simultaneous parts or voices where one melody is used successively in each voice. In other words, the accompaniment for a melody in one voice is the same melody in other voices. Fugue writing was a popular form in music of the Baroque period and reached its peak in the music of J. S. Bach. Composers of the 20th century have also given it much attention.

Fuji, city in S central Japan, 20mi (32km) NE of Shizuoka; commercial and market center. Paper milling is the main industry. Pop. 180,639.

Fujisawa, city in Japan, on Sagami Bay, 11mi (18km) SW of Yokohama; site of 14th-century Buddhist temple. Pop. 260,950.

Fujiwara, a strong and wealthy Japanese family since the 7th century, after whom the Fujiwara (late Heian) period of history (857–1160) was named. Influencing the imperial family through marriage of Fujiwara women to it, they exerted control of the government as "advisors" to the emperor. Although their power reached its zenith under Michinaga Fujiwara (966–1027), their influence continued to be felt into the 20th century.

Fujiyama (Fuji-san), highest and most sacred mountain in Japan, in Fuji-Hakone Izu National Park, 70mi (113km) WSW of Tokyo. A dormant volcano, it is noted for symmetrical cone; site of summer and winter sports, mountain climbing. Height: 12,389ft (3,779km).

Fukien (Fujian), province in SE China, on Formosa Strait opposite Taiwan. Foochow is the capital. The climate is warm and moist; inhabitants are of mixed Asian stock, speaking over 100 dialects. An important overseas port in T'ang dynasty (618–906), it flourished as a center of Chinese culture during Sung dynasty (960–1279). Because of its strategic location near Taiwan, Fukien has maintained a large military complex since 1950. Industries: fishing, shipbuilding, rice, tea, sweet potatoes, maize, sugar cane, fruit, lumber, sugar refining, paper, food processing. Area: 46,000sq mi (119,140sq km). Pop. 16,760,000.

Fukui, city in Honshu, Japan, 70mi (113km) NNW of Nagoya; capital of Fukui prefecture; former seat of a feudal daimyo landholder; site of heavy bombing 1945, 1948 earthquake, university (1949). Industries: rayon, habutai, paper, leather, woodworking, soy sauce, textiles. Pop. 200,509.

Fukuoka, city in N Kyushu, Japan, on SE shore of Hakata Bay and Naha River; capital of Fukuoka prefecture; one of three ancient Japanese ports; battle site of Mongol invasions led by Kublai Khan (1274 and 1281); foreign trade began in 1899; site of Kyushu Imperial University (1910), 16th-century Shinto Temple. Industries: Hakata (china) dolls, textiles, herbs, fish, rice pottery, chemicals. Pop. 1,002,000.

Fukushima, city in N central Japan, on Abukuma River, 150mi (242km) N of Tokyo; capital of Fukushima prefecture; site of feudal castle, railroad junction; seat of Fukushima University and Fukushima medical college. Industries: tea, silk, rice, tobacco, fishing, lumber, horse breeding. Pop. 243,083.

Fukuyama, city in SW Honshu, Japan, on Inland Sea; important commercial and industrial center. Industries: rice, soybeans, silk, electronic equipment. Pop. 293,334.

Fulani, Fulah, or **Fulbe,** African people of mixed Negro and Berber origins, living scattered through W Africa. Their language belongs to the West Atlantic group of the Niger-Congo family. Originally a pastoral people, they helped spread Islam throughout W Africa from the 16th century and were politically ascendant until defeated by the French and British in the 19th century.

Fulcrum, the point about which a lever rotates. Its importance was recognized by Archimedes, who said: "Give me a lever long enough and a fulcrum strong enough and I will move the world." *See also* Lever.

Fu Literature, prose poems popular during China's Han dynasty (202 BC–AD 220). *Fu* were elaborately descriptive and about such subjects as the capital cities. They glorified the dynasty. Ssu-ma Hsiang-ju (179–117 BC) was the best practitioner.

Fuller, Melville Weston (1833–1910), chief justice of the US Supreme Court (1888–1910), b. Augusta, Me. He was appointed chief justice by President Cleveland. A strict constructionist, his most important cases included *Plessy* v. *Ferguson* (1896), which upheld "separate but equal" laws of segregation and *Lochner* v. *New York* (1905), a "due process" clause interpreted so the state could not set a 10-hour day for bakers. He was known as an authority on international law, helped to settle a boundary dispute between Venezuela and Great Britain (1899), and was a member af the Hague Tribunal (1900–10).

Fuller, R(ichard) Buckminster (1895–1983), US architect and engineer, b. Milton, Mass. Believing that only technological design can solve modern world problems, he popularized several revolutionary designs. The best known is the geodesic dome, a spherical structure composed of light, strong, triangular parts. His largest dome, 384ft (117m) in diameter, is the Union Tank Car Co. maintenance shop in Baton Rouge, La. (1958). He is also the author of several unorthodox books, including *Operating Manual for Spaceship Earth* (1969) and *Earth Inc.* (1973). Other works include *Grunch of Giants* (1983).

Fuller's Earth, claylike substance that contains more than half silica. Originally used to remove oil and grease from wool, it is now used to decolor petroleum and vegetable oils. *See also* Silica.

Fullerton, city in S California, 17mi (27km) NE of Long Beach. Industries: aerospace, food processing, electronics. Founded 1887; inc. 1904. Pop. (1980) 102,034.

Full Faith and Credit Clause, Article 4 of the US Constitution, declaring that each state must accept the statutes, public acts, and judicial (noncriminal) proceedings of other states.

Fulmar, or shearwater, scavenging oceanic bird of Arctic and Antarctica. Heavily built with dull coloring, it has a large head; hooked bill; short neck; throat pouch; long, broad wings; and short tail. A single white egg is laid on bare rock. Length: 12–25in (30–63cm). Family Procellariidae.

Fulton, Robert (1765–1815), US inventor and engineer, b. Little Britain, Pa. He began as a painter, but soon became involved in inventions and engineering projects. He obtained many patents in Britain and in the United States, including some for torpedoes and other tools of naval warfare. His main interest was in navigation and, as early as 1796, he was urging the United States to build canals. His great triumph was the steamboat *Clermont,* launched in 1807, whose voyage between New York City and Albany pioneered the use of the steamboat for carrying passengers and freight.

Fumarole, a vent, usually volcanic, but without lava, ash, or other rock debris surrounding it, from which gases and vapors are emitted. The fumarole is sometimes described by the composition of its gases, such as a chlorine fumarole. The term is also applied to a spring or geyser that emits steam.

Fumigant, substance used for killing bacteria, molds, vermin, and such, by exposure to vapors. Common fumigants are sulfur dioxide, produced by burning sulfur, and formaldehyde and hydrocyanic acid.

Fumitory, any of a genus *(Fumaria)* of annual or biennial plants with finely dissected leaves and clusters of small, single-spurred flowers, including *F. officinalis* once grown as an antiscurvy medicine. Family Fumariaceae.

Funabashi, city in Honshu, Japan, on Tokyo Bay. Industries: tobacco, rice, wheat, horsebreeding. Pop. 325,426.

Function, mathematical relationship or correspondence between two sets of numbers or other entities. For example, associated with a set of numbers x there is another set of numbers y such that each value of x has a corresponding value of y equal to x^3 ($x = 1$ corresponds to $y = 1$, $x = 2$ corresponds to $y = 8$, etc.). Here, y is said to be a function of x, expressed by $y = x^3$; x is called the independent variable and y the dependent variable. The set of values of x is the domain of the function and the set of values of y is the range.

A function is often referred to as a mapping; that is, a rule associating objects in one set with objects in another. It defines a relationship (functional relationship) between number, quantities, etc. For example, the area of a circle is a function of its radius ($A = \pi r^2$), the logarithm of a number is a function of the number (log x), etc. A general notation for a function of x is $f(x)$ or $F(x)$. *See also* Graph.

Functional Disorders, mental disorders that cannot be accounted for by an organic disturbance. They include schizophrenia, depression, manic depressive psychosis, and paranoia. Though their precise nature is unknown, functional disorders are presumably caused by psychological factors.

Functionalism, important sociological theory devised by Emile Durkheim (1858–1917). Functionalism says that man's customs, collective sentiments, and institutions are not present in isolated individuals but rather emerge only as a result of human interaction. It also suggests that these aspects of society form a cohesive whole that is exterior to the individual and exerts control over his actions. This causal relationship—from society to man—marked the beginnings of the study of sociology.

Fundamentalism, movement within US Protestantism attempting to maintain what it believes to be traditional interpretations of the Christian faith. It emerged in reaction to liberal, or modernist, trends within Protestantism in the later 19th century. Conservatives began to establish schools and conferences emphasizing literal interpretations of the Bible. It took its name from *The Fundamentals* (1910–12), a series of widely distributed small books produced by conservative scholars. The doctrines most emphasized by fundamentalists are: the divinely inspired and infallible nature of the Bible; the Trinity; immediate creation by the command of God; Man's fall into depravity; the necessity for salvation of being "born again" by faith in Christ; Christ's deity, virgin birth, miracle-working power, and substitutionary atonement for man and his physical resurrection, ascension, and imminent premillennial Second Coming; and the physical resurrection of man for Heaven or Hell. Fundamentalism also stresses domestic and foreign evangelism and strong opposition to evolution, Communism, and ecumenism.

Fundy, Bay of, inlet of the Atlantic Ocean separating New Brunswick, Canada, and Nova Scotia, Canada. Industries: shipping, fishing, tourism. Length: 170mi (273km). Width: 58mi (93km).

Fungicide, in agriculture and gardening, a chemical that kills fungi, used to prevent or reduce crop losses from fungus diseases. The most important group of fungicides—including a majority of copper, sulfur, and organic compounds—is used to protect healthy but susceptible plants from fungus infections. The other main group of fungicides—including dinitro compounds, lime sulfur, and organic mercury compounds—is used to eradicate fungus infections already established in plant tissues.

Fungus, any of a wide variety of plants that cannot make their own food by photosynthesis, including mushrooms, truffles, molds, smuts, and yeasts. Fungi range in size from single-celled yeasts, visible only under a microscope, to giant puffballs about 5ft (1.5m) in diameter. They have relatively simple structures, with no roots, stems, or leaves. The main body, or thallus, of a typical multicellular fungus consists of a usually inconspicuous network of very fine filaments, called a mycelium. The mycelia occasionally develop spore-producing, often conspicuous, fruiting bodies, such as mushrooms and puffballs.

Fungi are divided into three ecological groups on the basis of their food sources. Fungal parasites depend on living animals or plants; saprophytes utilize the materials of dead plants and animals; and symbionts obtain food in exchange for a variety of "services" performed for other plants. All three groups are of great importance to man. The parasites are responsible for many destructive plant diseases and for a few but sometimes serious diseases of man and other animals. The saprophytes are important in decay processes that recycle dead organisms into materials for living ones. The symbionts include a group of fungi (mycorrhizae) that play key roles in the nourishment of many higher plants and in the decomposition of rocks into soil. *See also* Mold; Mushroom.

Fungus Infection, or **mycosis,** broad category of disorders, which may or may not be contagious. Diseases caused by fungi range from superficial disorders, such as athlete's foot or other ringworms, to serious pulmonary and central-nervous-system infections. Symptoms such as fever, loss of weight, and malaise may be mild and the disease may go undiagnosed since symptoms frequently resemble bacterial disease. Fungicidal drugs are useful in the treatment.

Funk, Casimir (1884–1967), US biochemist, b. Poland. Working in France, Germany, England, and the US, his idea that deficiency diseases such as beriberi, scurvy, and rickets were caused by the lack of a specific chemical substance established the "vitamin hypothesis." He was responsible for isolating nicotinic acid (later found to be an antipellagra factor) and for early studies of cancer and sex hormones.

Furneaux Islands, group of islands off NE coast of Tasmania, Australia, at E end of Bass Strait, separated from Tasmania by the Banks Strait; includes Flinders Island (largest), Cape Barren Island, Clark Island, and many smaller islands. Discovered 1773 by British navigator Tobias Furneaux. Industries: dairy products, sheep, tin. Area: approx. 900 sq mi (2,331sq km). Pop. 1,240.

Furze, or gorse, prickly, evergreen shrub native to European wastelands. It has dark green spines and fragrant, yellow flowers. Height: to 4ft (1.2m). Family Leguminosae; species *Ulex europaeus.*

Fuse, in electrical engineering, a safety device protecting against overloading. Fuses are commonly a strip of

Melville Weston Fuller

Robert Fulton

Gabon

easily fusible metal placed in an electrical circuit such that when overloaded, the fuse will melt, interrupting the circuit and preventing damage to the rest of the system.

Fushun, city in NE China, on Hun River; site of one of the world's largest opencut coal mines. Industries: mining, oil refining, aluminum reduction, chemicals, heavy machinery. Developed by Russia as mining center 1902; under Japanese control from 1905 until after WWII, when it was regained by China. Pop. 1,700,000.

Fusin (Fuxinshi, or Fou-hsin), city in NE China, 25mi (40km) NE of Mukden. Developed by Russians as an agricultural and mining region about 1900; mines were controlled by Japan 1905–end of WWII, when they were restored to China. Industries: coal mining, synthetic fuel oil, carbon black, heavy machinery, chemicals, firebrick, aluminum. Pop. 188,600.

Fusion, Nuclear, or thermonuclear reaction, reaction between light atomic nuclei in which a heavier nucleus is formed with the release of energy. This process, which is the basis of the energy produced in the interior of stars, has only occurred on earth in hydrogen bomb explosions. In order for a thermonuclear reaction to occur, the electrostatic repulsive forces between the interacting nuclei have to be overcome: this involves temperatures in excess of 40×10^6 °C. In the case of the hydrogen bomb the heat is provided by an atom bomb surrounded by a layer of hydrogenous material. Controlled fusion reactions are the subject of much contemporary research. The problem is to contain a highly ionized gas (plasma) within a magnetic field long enough to allow a thermonuclear reaction to occur. The temperature above which this will occur is called the ignition temperature. *See also* Fusion Reactor.

Fusion Reactor, device in which nuclear physics fusion takes place. Contemporary research is concentrating on devising methods of containing a plasma (highly ionized gas) so that it yields more energy than is required to raise it to its ignition temperature (minimum temperature for a fusion reaction to occur). The Lawson criterion (worked out in 1957 by J. D. Lawson) shows that for the deuterium-tritium reaction at its ignition temperature, the product of the plasma density (particles per cm^3) and the containment time (seconds) must exceed 10^{14} for energy breakeven. The most promising devices consist of a toroidal (tire-shaped) vessel through which high current pulses are passed to create the plasma and raise its temperature. The current pulse also creates a strong magnetic field, which makes the charged particles travel along helical paths and thus contract away from the walls of the tube. This pinch effect helps toward solving the problem of containment, but unfortunately the plasma develops kinks due to plasma instabilities. Devices of this type include the U.S. Stellarators and the Russian Tokamaks. The latter are now regarded as the most promising and several are in operation outside the U.S.S.R. Other devices using linear magnetic bottles, stoppered at the ends by magnetic mirrors, and laser beams to raise the temperature of pellets of hydrogenous substances have been tried unsuccessfully. *See also* Fusion, Nuclear.

Futurism, early modern movement in painting and sculpture; began in Italy in 1909. Its aim was to glorify the modern machine, such as the automobile and the locomotive, rather than to attempt to depict nature and figures realistically. Many futurists, such as Marcel Duchamp, showed the simultaneous movements of persons. Some were influenced by cubism. Leading futurists included the painters Carlo Carrà and Gino Severini and the sculptor Umberto Boccioni.

Fyodor I (1557–98), tsar of Russia (1584–98). The son of Ivan the Terrible and Anastasia Romanova, he was the last of the Rurik dynasty. During his reign, the autonomy of the Russian Orthodox Church was established with the creation of the Patriarchate of Moscow in 1589. Russia's influence over Siberia and the Caucasus was extended. He was succeeded by his brother-in-law Boris Godunov, who had actually controlled the government.

G

g, a unit of acceleration based on the acceleration of falling bodies near the earth's surface: one $g = 32$ ft/sec² (9.8m/sec²). *See also* Gravity.

G, the universal constant of gravitation, equal to 6.67 $\times$ 10⁻¹¹ newton-meter²/kg².

Gabbro, intrusive igneous rock, dark in color, granitelike in texture, and made up primarily of plagioclase feldspar and pyroxene. A very strong traprock, it is used for crushed stone. *See also* Igneous Rocks; Plagioclase.

Gabon Republic, nation in W Africa, on the equator. The people are chiefly Bantus and Pygmies. Recent discoveries of mineral deposits —especially petroleum —have stimulated the country's economy.

Land and Economy. The tropical climate creates heavily forested areas throughout the country. Mountains and plateaus dominate the inland portion, falling away to coastal lowlands along the Atlantic. The economy is thriving; newly discovered deposits of manganese, uranium, and crude oil—now accounting for two-thirds of export earnings—have added to the already immense timber profits. Export values far exceed import costs, and rail lines have further aided development.

People. The majority of the people are Bantu, but there are a considerable number of Fangs and Pygmies. French is the official language, but a large number of native languages and dialects are in common use. About half the people are Roman Catholic, and the remainder practice traditional religions. Education is mandatory from 6 to 16 years of age.

Government. The republic consists of a president, a 47-member unicameral National Assembly, and an independent Supreme Court.

History. After discovery by the Portuguese in the 15th century, Gabon became an important slave-trade center. In 1839 the French incorporated the area into the French Congo and reestablished it as a separate colony in 1910. It became an overseas territory of the French Union in 1946 and an autonomous member of the French Commonwealth in 1958. Gabon proclaimed its independence in 1960 and joined the United Nations the same year. Omar Bongo, upon assuming the presidency in 1973, declared Gabon a one-party state. Under pressure to liberalize the government, Bongo allowed independent candidates to run in the 1980 municipal elections.

PROFILE

Official name: Gabonese Republic
Area: 103,346sq mi (267,666sq km)
Population: 585,000
  Density: 5.6 per sq mi (2.2 per sq km)
Chief cities: Libreville (capital); Port Gentil

Government: Republic
Religion: Islam, Roman Catholicism, tribal religions
Language: French (official)
Monetary unit: franc
Gross national product: $310,000,000
Per capita income: $630
Industries (major products): forestry, petroleum products, food processing
Agriculture (major products): palm oil, coffee, cocoa, bananas, cassava
Minerals (major): petroleum, manganese, uranium
Trading partners (major): France, United States, West Germany

Gaboon Viper, nonaggressive viper native to Central African forests and closely related to the puff adder. The stocky body supports a head twice as wide as the neck. Its fangs are 1.5in (4cm) long and a brilliant geometric pattern of yellow, blue, pale purple, and brown serves as camouflage. It has enlarged, hornlike scales between its nostrils. Length: to 6ft (1.8m). Family Viperidae; species *Bitis gabonica. See also* Puff Adder; Viper.

Gaborone, capital of Botswana, 150mi (240km) NW of Pretoria, South Africa; served as administrative headquarters of former Bechuanaland Protectorate (1965); remained capital after protectorate's independence as Botswana (1966). Pop. 30,000.

Gabriel, biblical archangel, who is also mentioned in the New Testament. He, with the archangels Michael, Raphael, and Uriel, stood next to God. He destroyed Sodom and interpreted prophetic visions. The word Gabriel is a Hebrew description of the angelic office, but religious tradition has made it a proper name.

Gadolinium, metallic element (symbol Gd) of the lanthanide group, first isolated as the oxide in 1880. Chief ores are monazite (phosphate) and bastänite (fluorcarbonate). The element has some specialized uses including neutron absorption and the manufacture of certain ferrites. Properties: at. no. 64; at. wt. 157.25; sp gr 7.898 at 25°C; melt. pt. 2,394°F (1,312°C); boil. pt. 5,-432°F (3,000°C); most common isotope Gd¹⁵⁸ (24.-87%). *See also* Lanthanide Elements.

Gadsden, city in NE Alabama, on Coosa River; seat of Etowah co; site of a junior college. Industries: steel, textiles, tires, rubber products. Settled 1840; inc. 1871. Pop. (1980) 47,565.

Gadsden Purchase (1853–54), the acquisition of 45,000 square miles (116,550 sq km) of land in southern New Mexico and Arizona, south of the Rio Grande River, from Mexico. Following the Treaty of Guadalupe Hidalgo (1848), ending the Mexican War, the United States-Mexico border was only vaguely described, and Pres. Franklin Pierce wanted to purchase this strip that was considered the best route for a railroad to the Pacific. The sale was negotiated by James Gadsden, Minister to Mexico, for $10,000,000.

Gadwall, temperate N Hemisphere surface-feeding dabbling, or river, duck with a drab, broad body and flat bill; long neck; short legs; and webbed feet. After courtship rituals, the female lays cream-colored eggs (8–12) in a marsh depression. Length: 20in (50cm). Species *Anas strepera.*

Gaea, in Greek mythology, the goddess of earth. She was the mother and wife of Uranus and the mother of Cyclopes and the Erinyes.

Gaelic, language spoken in scattered parts of Ireland and Scotland. The variety spoken in Ireland is also referred to as Irish and sometimes Erse. It is one of the official languages of Ireland and is taught in all schools but the number of speakers continues to diminish. In Scotland it has no official status and is gradually dying out. Gaelic is one of the Celtic languages.

Gagarin, Yuri Alekseyevich (1934–68), Russian cosmonaut and national hero, the first man to orbit the earth. His historic flight took place on April 12, 1961, in the 5-ton spacecraft Vostok ("East"). Attaining a height of 188mi (303km), Gagarin made his single orbit in 1 hr. 48 min. and landed safely in the Soviet Union. He died seven years later in a plane crash.

Gage, Thomas (1721–87), English general in North America. He fought in the French and Indian War with Gen. Edward Braddock, taking part in the unsuccessful march on Fort Duquesne (1755). Later governor of Montreal (1760), he succeeded General Jeffrey Amherst as head of the British forces in North America (1763) and became governor of Massachusetts (1774). His soldiers fought the patriots at Lexington (April 1775), the battle that began the American Revolution. He resigned in October of the same year.

Gaillardia, or blanketflower, genus of showy annual and perennial plants mostly native to W North America. The garden perennial *G. aristata* has striking 4in (10cm) daisylike flowers with reddish disks and yellow or red rays. Height: 3ft (91cm). Family Compositae.

Gainesville, city in N central Florida, 65mi (104km) SW of Jacksonville, seat of Alachua co; home of University of Florida. Industries: wood products, electronic equipment. Founded 1854; inc. 1869. Pop. (1980) 81,371.

Gainsborough, Thomas (1727–88), English painter. In 1740 he became a pupil in London of the French engraver Hubert Gravelot. Throughout his life he preferred painting idyllic landscapes but turned to portraits to earn a living. In 1759 he settled in Bath, where he painted many of his friends in the theater, including David Garrick and Mrs. Siddons. His elegant, refined, and vividly colored portraits were influenced by Anthony Van Dyck. In 1768 he became an original member of the Royal Academy. He moved to London in 1774 and won the favor of George III, becoming the rival of Sir Joshua Reynolds. In his last years he painted "fancy pictures"—life-sized idealized portraits of rustics. Well-known works include *The Blue Boy, Perdita,* and *Lady Innes.*

Gal (from Galileo), measure of acceleration equal to 1 centimeter per second per second.

Galactic Cluster. *See* Cluster, Stellar.

Galactosemia, a genetic inability to convert galactose (in milk) to usable glucose. Symptoms, appearing in infants within a few days of birth, include vomiting, possible edema, and feeding difficulty. It is controlled by eliminating milk and milk products from the diet.

Galahad, in Arthurian legend, son of Lancelot and Elaine. He qualified as the best knight by passing the test of the Perilous Seat and drawing a sword from a floating stone, so replacing Percival as the seeker of the Holy Grail. Galahad is successful in the quest because he is a pure knight.

Galápagos Islands, archipelago owned by Ecuador in Pacific Ocean, 650mi (1,047km) W of Ecuador, on the Equator. Group consists of 13 large and many smaller islands, mainly barren lava piles; there is vegetation on upper slopes of high, volcanic mountains. Islands are known for unusual range of wildlife; named for huge almost-extinct land tortoises; visited by Charles Darwin 1835. Discovered 1535 by Tomás de Bertanga, Spanish navigator; Ecuador claimed the archipelago in 1832. Area: 3,029sq mi (7,845sq km). Pop. 3,000.

Galápagos Tortoise, nearly extinct turtle found on the Galápagos Islands. Each island has at least one isolated population. They are strictly herbivorous. Height: to 67.5in (1.7m); weight: to 500lb (225kg). Family Testudinidae; species *Geochelone elephantopus.*

Galati, port city in Romania, on the Danube River; capital of Galati co; in ancient times an important Roman port; seat of International Danube Commission (1856–1945). Exports: grain, timber. Industries: iron, steel, shipbuilding, grain, chemicals, textiles. Pop. 179,189.

Galatia, region of Asia Minor near modern Ankara in Turkey. The Gauls held the area from the 3rd century BC but their expansion was halted by Attalus I in 230 BC. Galatia was conquered by the Romans in 189 BC and its name given to a large Roman province in 25 BC.

Galatians, New Testament collection of letters by Paul, written in indignation at the increase in false teachings, arguing against Judaizing teachers and stressing apostolic authority.

Galaxy, any of the innumerable vast collections of stars distributed throughout the enormous void of the universe, of which the Milky Way galaxy is a typical example. Formerly called extragalactic nebulae, galaxies are gravitationally bound rotating systems, each comprising billions of stars and having either irregular or, far more commonly, regular structures. Regular galaxies are differentiated into elliptical and spiral systems, the latter being further subdivided into normal and barred spirals. Although they tend to be grouped into clusters, galaxies are apparently retreating from each other at enormous speeds, as demonstrated by red shifts in their spectra. The more distant galaxies, which are observed at an earlier period in the life of the universe, seem to be retreating at greater velocities—evidence supporting big-bang theories of cosmology. *See also* Andromeda Galaxy.

Galaxy Cluster, system of associated galaxies often comprised of hundreds or thousands of separate members all moving together through space. Several thousand clusters are known, one of the most notable being the Virgo-Coma cluster, a gigantic concentration of about 10,000 galaxies located near the north galactic pole.

Galen (*c.* AD 130–200), Greek physician. His work and writings provided much of the foundation for the development of medicine. He tried to synthesize all that was known of medical practice and to develop a theoretical framework for an explanation of the body and its diseases. He made numerous anatomical and physiological discoveries, including ones concerning heart-muscle action, kidney secretion, respiration, and nervous-system function. He was among the first to study physiology through the use of detailed and ingenious animal experimentation. Galen's theories influenced medical practice for centuries. William Harvey's 17th-century discovery of the circulation of the blood was one of the first major steps away from Galenian medicine.

Galena, a sulfide mineral, lead sulfide (PbS). A major ore of lead in igneous and sedimentary rock. Cubic system, granular masses, cubic and octahedral crystals common, sometimes fibrous. Lead-gray, metallic, brittle. Hardness 2.5–2.7; sp gr 7.5.

Galicia, region in SE Poland (Western Galicia) and W Ukraine (Eastern Galicia), bordered by Czechoslovakia (S) and Carpathian Mountains (N); part of Poland from 14th century until the partitions of Poland (1772, 1795, and 1815) when Austria took possession; in 1918 Poland took W Galicia and was awarded E Galicia in 1921. The 1939 partition of Poland gave E Galicia to Ukraine; agricultural area with some mineral wealth, especially oil. Products: rye, wheat, corn, potatoes, flax, tobacco, hops. Area: 32,332sq mi (83,740sq km).

Galicia, region in NW Spain; bounded by Atlantic Ocean (N and W), Portugal (S), Asturias and León provs. (E); includes provinces of Lugo, Orense, Pontevedra, La Coruña; scene of 19th-century literary and cultural revival; site of Shrine of Santiago de Compostela; pilgrimage center; naval base. Industries: fishing, livestock, mining, dairying, chemicals, textiles. Area: 11,256sq mi (29,153sq km). Pop. 2,583,674.

Galilee, region in N Israel, bounded by Jordan River and Sea of Galilee (E) and Plain of Esdraelon (S); it was ruled from 8th century BC by Babylonia, Persia, Egypt, Syria; came under Roman dominance in 63 BC. It was the home and ministry of Jesus Christ; his disciples were area fishermen; center of Judaism and Talmudic studies after the fall of Jerusalem AD 70. Nazareth is a major urban center in the region. Industries: olives, grains, fishing.

Galilee, Sea of (Kinneret, Lake), fresh-water lake in N Israel, on W Syrian-E Israeli border; approx. 75% of its water is fed and drained by the Jordan River. Israel's major reservoir, it is industrially important as a fishing center and source of irrigation for the Negev Desert. In biblical times, it was site of nine prosperous fishing towns on its shores, including Magdala, Capernaum, Tabigha, and Tiberias (the only one still remaining); site of numerous archeological excavations. Area: 64sq mi (166sq km).

Galileo (1564–1642), Italian scientist, professor at Pisa, later moving to Padua and then to Florence. While studying medicine he deduced the formula for the swing of a pendulum from the oscillation of a hanging lamp in Pisa Cathedral. He later studied the laws of falling bodies, disproving Aristotle's view that the rate of fall is proportional to the weight. His work on the three laws of motion was important, although it was Newton who formulated them mathematically. He also discovered the parabolic flight path of projectiles. His work on astronomy followed his invention of the telescope, which enabled him to discover sunspots, lunar craters, Jupiter's satellites, and the phases of Mercury. In *Sidereus Nuncius* (1610) he announced his support for the Copernican view of the universe, with the earth moving around the sun. This was declared a heresy by Pope Pius V. In *Dialogo Sopra i Due Massimi Sistemi del Mondo* (1632) he defied the pope by making his views even more explicit; as a result he was brought before the Inquisition at the age of 70. While publicly recanting, he is said to have muttered: "Eppur si muove" (meaning "Even so the earth *does* move"). For his remaining years he was silenced by the Church.

Gall, an abnormal swelling or protuberance of plant tissue stimulated by an invasion of any of a wide variety of parasitic or symbiotic organisms, including bacteria, fungi, insects, and nematodes. Most gall organisms stunt but do not kill the affected plants.

Galla, Hamitic people who make up 40% of the population of Ethiopia, living mainly in the south. Characteristically tall and dark-skinned, they are predominantly nomadic pastoralists. In the 16th century they invaded their present homelands from the south and east. Their religions include Christianity, Islam, and paganism.

Gallatin River, river in Wyoming and Montana; rises in the Gallatin Range in NW Wyoming, NW corner of Yellowstone National Park, flows N to Montana, unites with Jefferson and Madison rivers to form the Missouri River. Length: 125mi (201km).

Gall Bladder, pear-shaped organ, located under the large right lobe of the liver, that stores bile secreted by the liver. When bile is needed for digestion the gall bladder is stimulated to contract, expelling the stored bile through the cystic duct, into the common bile duct, then into the small intestine. Gallstones sometimes form in the gall bladder, impairing its function.

Galleon, general-purpose wooden sailing ship appearing in the 16th century, larger than the earlier carrack and caravel. The galleon featured a larger front and rear deck structure (forecastle and quarterdeck), and was rigged with a front spritsail, two main masts with several square sails each, and one or two lateen masts at the rear. *See also* Carrack.

Galley, oared Mediterranean ship, much larger and wider than the ancient trireme, and used by the Italian, French, and Turkish navies in the 15th and 16th centuries. More maneuverable than fully-rigged sailing ships, galleys were less effective in the more turbulent Atlantic due to their low freeboard.

Gallic Wars, the campaigns of 58–51 BC whereby Caesar conquered the Gauls. His intervention was requested against the Helvetii and the invading Germans. By 57 he had subdued SW and N Gaul and extended Roman influence to the Rhine and N France and Belgium. In 56 he conquered the Veneti, leaders of anti-Roman Confederacy, and in 55–54 marched into Germany and Britain. He put down occasional revolts in N Gaul and then faced a united Gallic force under Vercingetorix, defeating it with quick, bold strategy (51). His classic commentary *The Gallic Wars* describes the campaigns.

Gallinaceous Bird, bird living and nesting on or near the ground. They include the peacock, partridge, quail, curassow, grouse, turkey, chicken, and other species found throughout most of the world. Their strong, usually spurred legs are well-adapted for walking and running and the feet, equipped with three toes in front and one behind, are used to scratch for seeds, grains, and fruit. These game birds often have soft, abundant plumage, brighter colored in the male. They usually nest in a simple ground depression. Order Galliformes.

Gallinule, weak-flying marsh bird that lives in and near temperate and tropical ponds and lakes. Narrow-bodied, they have bright forehead shields; short, bright beaks; long necks, legs, and toes; and short tails. Length: 1ft (30cm). Family Rallidae.

Gallipoli Peninsula, narrow cape of W Turkey, extends between Aegean Sea (W) and Dardanelles (E); site of Gelibolu port on NE coast; scene of 1915 WWI Gallipoli Campaign which was an Allied expedition to gain control of the Dardanelles and Bosporus straits and Constantinople, thus opening Black Sea supply route to Russia; although Australia, New Zealand, and France sent reinforcements, Allied troops withdrew by January 1916 without gaining hold, and suffering heavy losses. Length: approx. 50mi (81km).

Galápagos Islands

Galileo

Gambia

Gallium, metallic element (symbol Ga) of group IIIA of the periodic table, predicted by Mendeleev (as ekaaluminum) and discovered spectroscopically in 1875 by Lecoq de Boisbaudran. Chief sources are as a by-product from bauxite and some zinc ores. The metal is used in high-temperature thermometers and in semiconductors. Properties: at. no. 31; at. wt. 6972; sp gr 5.91 at 29.6°C; melt. pt. 85.6°F (29.78°C); boil. pt. 4,357°F (2,403°C); most common isotope Ga^{69} (60.4%).

Gallstones, or cholelithiasis, stonelike formations, usually containing cholesterol, found in the gall bladder. Affecting three times as many women as men, gallstone cause is not known positively but may be related to liver dysfunction. Symptoms range from none to excruciating pain.

Gall Wasp, small black wasp found worldwide. The female lays eggs in plant tissue and a gall develops as the larvae hatch and mature. They are usually found on oak trees and roses. Length: 0.16–0.32in (4–8mm). Family Cynipidae.

Galsworthy, John (1867–1933), English novelist and playwright. His novels deal with the English upper middle class. The most noted of his novels are those about the Forsyte family, grouped in three trilogies: *The Forsyte Saga* (1906–22), *A Modern Comedy* (1924–28), and *End of the Chapter* (1931–33). His plays, such as *Justice* (1910), deal with social issues and were quite popular.

Galton, (Sir) Francis (1822–1911), English anthropologist, explorer, and eugenicist, who conducted important studies on human intelligence. He believed heredity to be more important than environment in human development, and was a proponent of selective parenthood. He was influential in the development of standard statistical techniques, such as curves of normal distribution, correlation of coefficients, and percentile grading. Works include the important *Natural Inheritance* (1889).

Galvani, Luigi or **Aloisio** (1737–98), Italian physician and physicist who became professor of anatomy at Bologna and did pioneer studies in electrophysiology. His experiments with frogs' legs indicated a connection between muscular contraction and electricity, although the correct explanation was given by Volta. Nevertheless, Galvani's name is commemorated in the galvanometer, galvanic currents, and galvanized iron.

Galvanizing, the coating of iron or steel articles with zinc, either applied directly in a hot zinc bath or electrodeposited from cold sulfate solutions. Ash cans, nails, pails, and wire netting may be thus protected from atmospheric carbonic acid due to preferential attack on zinc rather than iron.

Galvanometer, instrument for detecting, comparing, or measuring electric currents, usually by the reaction between the magnetic field created by the current and a magnet. The main types are the moving-coil galvanometer and the moving-magnet instrument.

Galveston, city in E central Texas; port of entry on Galveston Island in Gulf of Mexico; seat of Galveston co. Originally part of Mexico and occupied by pirate Jean Laffite, it was annexed to Republic of Texas 1839; served as Confederate naval center during Civil War; first US city to adopt commission plan of municipal government. Industries: oil refining, shipbuilding, tourism. Exports: grain, cotton, flour, sulfur, chemicals, fertilizer. Settled 1830s; inc. 1839. Pop. (1980) 61,902.

Gama, Vasco da (c.1469–1525), Portuguese navigator and discoverer of the sea route to India. In 1497 he led the historic expedition in search of a maritime route to the Indies. He reached South Africa, sailed around the Cape and across the Indian Ocean to Calicut, India. He thus established the route still used by ships today, opening up the resources of Asia to Western European powers. In 1524, he went to India as viceroy, becoming head of the first European enclave in Asia. He died there only months later.

Gambia, Republic of The, nation in W Africa. The people are Negroid and mostly Muslim. It is the smallest state in Africa, with an economy dependent upon one product—the peanut.

Land and Economy. The country includes the island of Banjul at the mouth of the Gambia River and an approximately 10-mi (16-km) wide strip of land on each side of the river for about 290mi (467km) inland. It is one of the poorest countries in Africa; rice and other foods are grown but only for local consumption. In recent years tourism has been promoted by the government as part of its program of economic diversification.

People. Five major tribes make up the country; the Mandinkas are the largest. English is the official language; however, a number of native languages and dialects are in use. There is no official religion but 85% of the people are Muslim; most of the rest practice animism. About 90% of the people farm.

Government. A republic, the Gambia has chosen to remain within the British Commonwealth. The president is leader of the majority party in the 43-member parliament. Sir Dawda Jawara has been the country's leader since 1970.

History. Inhabited since ancient times, the country includes the famous Stone Circles, ironstone pillars in groups, which probably represent burial grounds, dating from about 400 BC. Early Portuguese settlements in the 1450s did not survive; the British arrived in 1588 and finally took control in 1765. It became a British Crown Colony in 1888. The Gambia achieved independence in 1965, but in a 1970 referendum chose to join the Commonwealth. The Gambia maintains very close ties with Senegal, which surrounds it on three sides, and in 1981, Senegalese troops supported Jawara against an attempted coup. He announced that his country had merged with Senegal (1982) in a confederation called Senegambia.

PROFILE

Official name: Republic of The Gambia
Area: 4,361mi (11,295sq km)
Population: 584,510
  Density: 134 per sq mi (52 per sq km)
Chief cities: Banjul (capital); Georgetown
Government: Republic
Religion: Islam
Language: English (official)
Monetary unit: dalasi
Gross national product: $150,000,000
Per capita income: $270-$280
Industries (major products): negligible
Agriculture (major products): peanuts, rice, peanut oil
Trading partners (major): Great Britain, Japan, Netherlands

Gambia River, river and major trade artery in W Africa; rises in Fouta Djallon Mts, Guinea; flows NW through Senegal and W into Atlantic Ocean at Banjul. Lower 200mi (322km) of river, all in Republic of The Gambia, are navigable year-round. Length: 700mi (1127km).

Game Bird, any bird hunted by humans for food, especially members of the two major bird orders Galliforme

and Anseriforme. Galliformes include the chicken, turkey, quail, pheasant, partridge, guan, and currasow. Typically, they are ground birds with strong legs adapted for walking and running and strong toes to scratch the ground for fruits and seeds. They often have abundant plumage and elevated tails and make simple ground-depression nests. Anseriformes, including the duck, goose, and swan, are waterfowl, with rounded, open nostrils, dense undercoats of down, and special glands to waterproof their plumage.

Gamete, haploid reproductive cell that joins with another cell to form a new organism. Female gametes (ova) are motionless; male gametes (sperm) are motile.

Game Theory, branch of mathematics concerned with the analysis of problems involving conflict. Game theory can be applied to "true" games such as poker and chess, but its application is much wider, including problems in business management, sociology, economics, and military strategy. They involve situations in which there is a conflict of interest, incomplete information, and an element of chance. Game theory is concerned with analyzing the basic features of these problems and devising methods of finding the best strategy, that is, the one with the highest probability of obtaining a successful result. It was first introduced by Emil Borel and developed by John von Neumann in 1928.

Gametophyte, generation of plants that bears the female and male gametes (sexual reproductive cells). In flowering plants these are the germinated pollen grains (male) and ovules containing the embryo sac (female). *See also* Alternation of Generations; Fern; Moss.

Gamma Globulin, one of the protein components of the blood serum. It contains approximately 85% of the circulating antibodies of the blood, and is thus the major serum immunoglobulin. *See also* Antibody.

Gamma Rays, highly energetic electromagnetic radiation emitted spontaneously by certain radioactive substances when the nucleus makes a transition to a lower energy state. They usually accompany the emission of alpha or beta rays. Their energies are characteristic of the emitting isotope, the rays being very penetrating, and lie at the extreme end of the electromagnetic spectrum, beyond the X ray region, with a wavelength range of about 10^{-11} to 5×10^{-13} meters. *See also* Annihilation.

Gamow, George (1904–68), US nuclear physicist and cosmologist, b. Russia. Educated in Leningrad, he worked in various European universities before going to the United States in 1934. He was a proponent of the "big-bang" theory of the creation of the universe, and he contributed to the deciphering of the genetic code. He also proposed the quantum theory of radioactivity and the liquid-drop model of atomic nuclei. With Edward Teller, he established the Gamow-Teller theory of beta decay and the internal structure of red giant stars.

Gandhara, historic area in modern NW Pakistan, on middle Indus River. Originally a Persian colony (6th century BC), it passed to Maurya empire of India 324–185 BC; under Asoka, Gandhara flourished as a cultural and Buddhist center; its greatest prosperity came with the leadership of Kanishka during the Kushan dynasty (AD 1st-3rd centuries), who developed the Gandhara School of art, noted for statues of Buddha and Buddhist reliefs: in 5th century, the entire area was besieged by the Huns.

Gandhi, Indira Nehru (1918–84), Indian political figure, the first woman elected (1966) prime minister of India. The daughter of Jawaharlal Nehru, she served as president of the Indian National Congress party in 1959–60. In 1975, after nine years as prime minister, she was found guilty of using illegal practices in the election of 1971. She refused to resign, invoked emergency powers, and arrested many of her opponents. Defeated in 1977, Gandhi faced charges of corruption before making a political comeback. In 1980, her party was victorious, and she was again prime minister. Gandhi was assassinated in 1984 by two Sikhs , members of her own security force. She was succeeded by her son, Rajiv.

Gandhi, Mohandas (Karamchand) (1869–1948), Indian leader. Known as the Mahatma ("Great Lord"), he is considered the father of India because of his leadership of the country's nationalist movement from 1919 to 1947, when independence was granted. His method, called *Satyagraha* ("soul force"), included all forms of non-violent resistance to British rule, such as strikes, refusal to pay taxes, refusal to respect courts. Gandhi's beliefs included: the importance of simple, moral lifestyles over other accomplishments; tolerance and respect for all men (in contrast to the prevalent system); the dignity of labor; a self-sufficient, self-governed India. His experiences in South Africa, where he spent 21 years trying to end oppression of the Indians and the massacre of a mob at Amritsar by the British in 1919 led him to believe that freedom could not be taken by force. In 1920 he instituted a hand-spinning and weaving program. In 1930 he led thousands on a dramatic 200-mile (322km) protest march to the sea. His methods succeeded, and he came to be considered an exemplar of the moral life. He was assassinated by a Hindu Brahmin who objected to his religious tolerance.

Gandhi, Rajiv (1944–), Indian political figure, prime minister 1984– . The older son of Indira Gandhi and grandson of Jawaharlal Nehru, he was raised in the prime minister's residence in New Delhi. After attending Cambridge University in England, he became a commercial pilot and entered politics only on the death of his younger brother, Sanjay, who had been his mother's heir apparent. By 1983 he was general secretary of the Congress party and was known as "Mr. Clean." His brief political career culminated in his swearing in as prime minister on the day his mother was assassinated. As prime minister, he won high marks for maintaining an honest administration but had difficulty in resolving the issue of Sikh separatism.

Gandolfi, family of, Italian artists in Bologna. **Gaetano** (1734–1802), influenced by Tiepolo, was a church painter and decorator; his brother **Ubalde** (1728–81) was a decorator and sculptor; and Gaetano's son **Mauro** (1764–1834) was an engraver and portrait painter.

Ganges, sacred river in India; rises in the Himalayan Mts, and is formed by the confluence of two headstreams, Bhagirathi and Alaknanda; it flows S then SE, receiving tributaries, and empties into the Bay of Bengal through the combined Brahmaputra-Ganges delta. In Hindu religion and legend, the Ganges is the earthly personification of the Goddess, Ganga; pilgrims travel to bathe in its waters for purification. Plains of Ganges are extremely fertile and support one of the world's most densely populated areas; dams divert water to the dry lands for irrigation; also used for hydroelectric power. Length: 1,560mi (2,496km).

Ganglion, any identifiable, relatively large concentration of neurons or cell bodies in the nervous system. Ganglia are found both inside and outside of the central nervous system; e.g., the basal ganglia are located within the cerebral cortex.

Gangrene, death of body tissues associated with loss of blood supply and bacterial infection; also seen as a result of diabetes or of an embolism or thrombosis. Symptoms include inflammation and ulceration of the organ or skin.

Gannet, fast-diving marine bird of cooler offshore waters, related to tropical boobies. Heavy-bodied with a tapered bill, long pointed wings, short legs, and webbed feet, it is white with a yellowish head and black wing tips. It feeds on fish and nests in huge colonies on rocky islands. One chick is reared although 1-3 bluish eggs are laid. Length: 25–35in (63–89cm). Family Sulidae.

Ganoid Fish, primitive bony fish with hard scales of bone overlaid with layers of enamellike substance. Although most are extinct, modern examples are bowfin, gar, paddlefin, and sturgeon.

Ganymede, in Greek mythology, the son of Tros, king of Troy. Zeus, charmed by his unusual beauty, sent an eagle to carry Ganymede to Olympus. There he became the cup bearer of the gods.

Ganymede, largest of Jupiter's satellites; one of the Galilean satellites. Ganymede is larger than Mercury. Diameter approx. 3,100mi (5,000km): mean distance from planet 621,000mi (1,000,000km): mean sidereal period 7.15 days.

Gar, primitive freshwater bony fish found in shallow weedy waters of North America, east of Rocky Mountains. Its long cylindrical body is covered with bony diamond-shaped flat plates. It has a long snout studded with teeth and vertebrae resembling those of reptiles. Length: to 10ft (305cm); Weight: to 302lb (136kg). Family Lepisosteidae; species 8, including alligator gar *Lepisosteus spatula* and longnose *Lepisosteus osseus.*

Garbanzo. *See* Chick-pea.

Garbo, Greta (1905–), Swedish film actress, b. Greta Gustaffson. She is famous for her aura of mystery and legendary romantic beauty. Her silent films included *Torment* (1926) and *Flesh and the Devil* (1927), but her greatest successes were the sound films *Anna Christie* (1930), *Grand Hotel* (1932), *Queen Christina* (1933), *Anna Karenina* (1935), *Camille* (1936), and the comedy *Ninotchka* (1939). She retired in 1941.

García Lorca, Federico (1898–1936), Spanish poet and dramatist. Lorca's poetry, from *Book of Poems* (1921) to *Poet in New York* (1940), was internationally acclaimed. His plays include *The Shoemaker's Prodigious Wife* (1930) and *Blood Wedding* (1933), performed in the United States (1935) as *Bitter Oleander.* He was killed by Fascist soldiers at the outbreak of the Spanish Civil War.

García Márquez, Gabriel (1928–), Colombian novelist. His novel *One Hundred Years of Solitude* (1967) has become one of the most popular books ever in the Spanish-speaking world. It focuses on the remote town of Macondo, which was also the setting of his previous novels. The events are sometimes nonrealistic but the town's up-and-down history has been interpreted as symbolic of Latin America's. Macondo's feuding, eccentric citizens are both funny and tragic. *Withered Leaves* (1955) began the saga. His other works include *The Autumn of the Patriarch* (1976) and *Chronicle of a Death Foretold* (1983). In 1978, he formed Habeas, a human rights organization. He fled to Mexico in 1981. In 1982, he was awarded the Nobel Prize in literature.

Garda, Lake (Lago di Garda), lake in N Italy; largest of Italian lakes; fed by the Sarca River; drained through Mincio River into the Po; resort area. Area: 143sq mi (370sq km).

Gardena, city in SW California; suburb of Los Angeles; site of Japanese cultural exhibit; population is 25% Oriental. Industries: aerospace, electronic components, textiles. Inc. 1930. Pop. (1980) 45,165.

Garden City, city in SE Michigan, 15mi (24km) W of Detroit. Industries: wire cloth, aluminum extrusions, golf balls. Inc. as village 1927, city 1934. Pop. (1980) 35,640.

Garden Grove, city in S California, S of Anaheim; suburb of Los Angeles and Long Beach, where a majority of residents are employed in aerospace and defense industries. Founded 1877; inc. 1956. Pop. (1980) 123,351.

Gardenia, genus of evergreen shrubs and small trees native to tropical Asia and Africa; they have white or yellow fragrant, waxy flowers. Height: to 18ft (5.5m). Family Rubiaceae.

Garfield, James Abram (1831–81), 20th President of the United States, b. Orange, Ohio, attended Williams College. In 1858 he married Lucretia Rudolph; they had six children. A lay preacher in the Disciples of Christ church, he was admitted to the bar and elected to the Ohio senate in 1859. He served in the Civil War until 1863, when he was elected to the US House of Representatives. A loyal party man, he rose in power in the House and by 1876, was Republican leader there. He supported the Radical Republicans and was a hard-money advocate.

The 1880 Republican convention deadlocked and he was finally—on the 36th ballot—nominated as the compromise candidate. Chester Alan Arthur was chosen as his running mate.

His four-month administration was characterized by party squabbles for federal jobs and political patronage. On July 2, 1881, a disappointed job seeker, Charles J. Guiteau, shot and mortally wounded the president. He died on September 19 and was succeeded by Arthur.

Career: Ohio State Senate, 1860–61; US House of Representatives, 1863–80; president, 1881.

Garfish, or gar pike, billfish, silver gar, marine needlefish found in all tropical and temperate waters, also in bays and coastal rivers. Its long garlike body is green and silver with a dark-green back stripe; jaws are elongated with sharp teeth. Length: to 4ft (122cm). Family Belonidae; species 26 including Atlantic *Tylosaurus marinus* and *Belone bellone.*

Gargantua, La vie tres horrificque du grand (1534), satirical book by François Rabelais. Chronologically preceding *Pantagruel* (1532), the story focuses on the educational and martial adventures of Gargantua, Pantagruel's father. The author mocks educational and religious traditions and celebrates an ideal of self-disciplined freedom.

Garibaldi, Giuseppe (1807–82), guerrilla general in the mid-19th century movement for Italian independence and unification. A political exile, influenced by the liberal thought of Giuseppe Mazzini, in 1834 he went to Latin America, where he led Italian forces for Uruguay against Argentina. During 1848–49 his confrontation at Milan with the Austrians, symbol of European reactionary forces, and in central Italy with the French elevated him to the stature of a national hero symbolizing Italian unity. In 1860, Garibaldi successfully led his guerrilla army against Sicily and Naples, uniting Italy under King Victor Emmanuel II of Sardinia-Piedmont. He attacked Rome in 1862 and 1867 but was defeated. He commanded a French army in the Franco-Prussian War (1870–71) and sat in the Italian Parliament from 1874.

Garland, Judy (1922–69), US singer and film actress, b. Frances Gumm in Grand Rapids, Minn. Beginning her film career at 13, she gained popularity in the Andy Hardy films and *The Wizard of Oz* (1939). "Over the Rainbow" from *The Wizard of Oz* became her trademark song. Her other major films included *Meet Me in St. Louis* (1944), *Easter Parade* (1948), and *A Star is Born* (1954). Her later life was marked by great personal unhappiness, but she made a successful comeback on the international concert circuit, breaking box-office records in the 1960s.

Garland, city in NE Texas, 14mi (23km) NE of Dallas; agricultural area. Industries: electronic equipment, oil, aircraft, food products, varnish, clothing. Inc. 1891. Pop. (1980) 138,857.

Garlic, bulbous herb native to S Europe and central Asia. It has onionlike foliage and a strong-smelling bulb made up of sections called cloves that are used for flavoring. Family Liliaceae; species *Allium sativum. See also* Allium.

Garner, John Nance (1868–1967), US political figure and Vice-president (1933–41), b. Blossom Prairie, Tex. He was a Texas legislator (1898–1902) and US Congressman (1903–33), serving as speaker of the House (1931–33). Vice-president under President Roosevelt, he helped obtain passage of New Deal legislation. He retired in 1941.

Garnet, two series of common orthosilicate minerals: the pyralspite series (pyrope, almandite, and spessartite); and the ugradite series (uvarovite, grossularite, and andradite). Found in metamorphic rocks and pegmatites. Cubic system dodecahedral and trapezohedral crystals and rounded grains and granular masses. Brittle, glassy, of many hues; hardness 6–7.5. sp gr 4. Some varieties important as gemstones.

Garonne River, river in SW France; rises on slopes of Pyrenees, in Spain; flows NW to join the Dordogne River N of Bordeaux and form the Gironde Estuary, which empties into the Atlantic Ocean. Length: 357mi (575km).

Garrick, David (1717–79), English actor. He is credited with replacing the formal declamatory style of acting with easy, natural speech. His success in his formal acting debut as Richard III resulted in his being hired by the Drury Lane Theatre (1742), where he remained until his retirement in 1776, becoming its manager in 1747. He traveled on the Continent with his wife (1763–65), returning to play successfully until his final performance in *The Wonder, a Woman Keeps a Secret* (1776). The Garrick Club and the Garrick Theater, both in London, were named in his honor.

Garrison, William Lloyd (1805–79), US abolitionist, who exerted great influence on the anti-slavery movement, b. Newburyport, Mass. In 1831 he started the *Liberator* in Boston, which held considerable sway until

Indira Gandhi

Greta Garbo

William Lloyd Garrison

Garrison closed it down in 1865, after it published the amendment to the Constitution abolishing slavery in the United States. In 1831 he founded the New England Anti-Slavery Society, influential until 1840. After the Civil War he concentrated on other reform programs, including temperance and women's suffrage.

Garter Snake, harmless snake, usually striped, ranging from S Canada through Central America. Twelve species live in the United States, including the slender ribbon snake and stouter true garter snake. Their ground color is usually olive-brown with yellow, orange, red, or blue stripes often checkered or spotted with black. They often live near water, are good swimmers, and feed on frogs, fish, and earthworms. Length: to 2ft (61cm). Family Colubridae; genus *Thamnophis*. *See also* Snake.

Garvey, Marcus (1887–1940), US black nationalist leader, b. Jamaica, British West Indies. While an editor in Jamaica, he organized the Universal Negro Improvement Association (UNIA), based on the theory that blacks and whites could not live together while blacks were a minority. Favoring a back-to-Africa movement, Garvey brought his plan to New York in 1916 where he attempted to find investors for his Black Star Line, a fleet of ships to carry blacks back to Africa. In 1922 the Black Star Line failed and the UNIA collapsed, and in 1923 Garvey was convicted of mail fraud. In 1927 he was pardoned by Pres. Calvin Coolidge.

Gary, city in NW Indiana, on S tip of Lake Michigan, 35mi (56km) SE of Chicago; one of world's largest steel centers. Dunes National Lakeshore Park is nearby; serviced by Burn Harbor to the E. Industries: steel, hardware, springs, windshield wipers, clothing, bedding, steel bridges. Founded 1905 by US Steel Corp.; inc. 1906. Pop. (1980) 151,953.

Gas, state of matter in which a substance has no fixed shape or volume, flowing freely and expanding to fill any container. The interactions between the atoms or molecules are low compared with thermal energies and the particles have random motion. The viscosity of gases increases with temperature. *See also* Liquid; Solid.

Gas, Natural, a naturally occurring, combustible, gaseous mixture of hydrocarbons used as a fuel and in the production of plastics, drugs, antifreeze and dyes. Natural gas is the gaseous element of petroleum and is extracted as casehead gas from oil wells. Certain wells, however, yield only natural gas. Before natural gas may be used as a fuel, the heavier hydrocarbons of butane and propane are extracted and as liquids are forced into containers as bottled gas. The remaining gas, called "dry gas," is piped to consumers for use as fuel. Dry gas is composed of the light hydrocarbons methane and ethane. *See also* Petroleum.

Gascony (Gascogne), historic region and province in SW France, bounded by Bay of Biscay (W), Pyrenees (S), and Garonne River (N and E). Settled 6th century by Basques; Franks established duchy of Gascony 632; captured and held mid-12th–15th centuries by English; became part of France 1453 at end of Hundred Years' War. The region was divided into three departments and made part of four others in 1790.

Gasoline, fuel used in internal-combustion engines. Gasoline is a colorless volatile highly flammable mixture of alkane hydrocarbons with 6–9 carbon atoms, obtained by distillation of petroleum. Commercial gasoline contains additives such as antioxidants and antiknock agents. Its quality is specified by its octane rat-

ing, obtained by comparison of performance with a standard mixture of hydrocarbons.

Gaspé Peninsula, peninsula in SE Quebec, Canada, S of St Lawrence River, N of New Brunswick; contains several lakes and rivers, thick forests; good hunting and fishing. Length: approx. 150mi (242km).

Gastonia, city in SW North Carolina; seat of Gaston co. Named for William Gaston, North Carolina Supreme Court judge; textile center. King's Mountain National Military Park is nearby. Inc. 1877. Pop. (1980) 47,333.

Gastric Juice, a mixture of substances secreted into the stomach; they break down complex proteins and carbohydrates into simpler units during digestion. They include hydrochloric acid, the enzyme pepsin, and mucus.

Gastritis, inflammation of the lining of the stomach, chronic or acute. It may be caused by chemicals, food, or disease.

Gastroenteritis, inflammation of the lining of the stomach and intestine. It may be caused by viruses, bacteria, chemicals, or allergy. *See also* Gastritis.

Gastroenterology, branch of medicine that deals with the diagnosis and treatment of diseases and disorders of the gastrointestinal tract, including the stomach and small and large intestines.

Gastropod, mollusk usually identified by coiled shell and body, found in marine and fresh waters and on land. This univalve class includes snails, slugs, sea hares, limpets, whelks, and periwinkles. The body consists of a head with tentacles and a foot, both forming the base for movement, and asymmetrical vascera and mantle, which secrete the coiled shell. Land types (pulmonate gastropods) have modified mantle and mantle cavity used for breathing air. Sea hares and slugs are symmetrical and do not have a visible shell; limpets have a tent-shaped shell. Class Gastropoda.

Gastrotricha, phylum of microscopic, many celled animals similar to rotifers. Structurally similar to simple worms, they have bristles covering the entire body. Reproduction is hermaphroditic and parthenogenetic (egg develops without fertilization).

Gates, (Sir) Thomas (died c.1621), member of the London Company, which organized the first settlement of Virginia. He was separated from the other colonists en route from England (1609) and, shipwrecked, was unable to rejoin them until late spring of 1610. Only a handful of the original 500 had survived, and he was dissuaded, with others, from a return to England only by the arrival of Governor De La Warr. After De La Warr left for England to bring aid to the colony, Gates was governor (1611–14). He left the colony in 1614 and died before he could return.

Gatun, town in Panama Canal Zone, Central America; site of man-made Gatun Lake, formed by the Gatun Dam across the Chagres River, and the two sets of Gatun Locks, which raise and lower vessels from the lake. Area of lake: 166sq mi (430sq km).

Gaucho, colorful cowboy of Argentine history and legend, an important political force in the 18th and 19th centuries. At first free-wheeling nomads of the Argentine pampas, the mixed-blood gauchos became farmhands and horse soldiers as civilization advanced, and fenced their lands. They became the subject of a distinctive South American literature.

Gaudi, Antoni (1852–1926), Spanish architect. He created a modern style of architecture distinctively Mediterranean in character, combining Gothic elements with Art Nouveau. His designs, which combine sculptural and pictorial elements, include, in Barcelona, the Church of the Sagrada Family, Güell Park, and dwellings for factory workers.

Gauguin, (Eugène Henri) Paul (1848–1903), French painter. A leader of the anti-naturalist-symbolist movement in art, he gave up a career as a stockbroker to devote all his energies to painting. He exhibited in the first four postimpressionist shows (1879–86) and in 1891 left his family in France to go to Tahiti. In the South Seas he executed his most famous paintings—primitive, exotic, aggressive glorifications of the Noble Savage, using abstract patterns and flat, strong colors in depictions of native figures and landscapes. He also produced woodcuts and painted wood-reliefs in the same primitive style. Gauguin's life was dogged by illness, poverty, and harassment from the French colonial government for his protests against social injustice on the various South Seas islands where he lived for short periods. A friend of Vincent van Gogh, he had a large following in symbolist circles in Paris.

Gauls, ancient Celtic peoples who settled Gaul, the area S and W of the Rhine, N of the Pyrenees, and W of the Alps, in the 4th and 3rd centuries BC. The Romans under Caesar conquered Gaul (58–51 BC) and thereafter the Gauls were thoroughly Romanized. The successful Gallo-Roman culture survived until the German invasions of the 5th and 6th centuries AD, which gradually created a number of independent kingdoms. *See also* Gallic Wars.

Gaur, ancient ruined city in NE India, 8mi (13km) S of English Bazar; Hindu capital of Bengal, captured by Muslims, it served as center of Muslim government and culture (1200–late 16th century); site of Kadam Rasul Mosque (1530), Golden Mosque, Bara Sona Mosjid.

Gaur, or **seladang,** large wild ox formerly in hilly forests from India to Malay Peninsula, now much reduced in range. Black to brown with white stockings, it has a saddlelike hump on its back and flattened, curved horns. Height: to 7ft (2.1m) at shoulder; weight: 2000lb (900kg). Family Bovidae; species *Bos gaurus*. *See also* Ox.

Gauss, Karl Friedrich (1777–1855), German mathematician. As a child prodigy from a poor family his education was sponsored by the duke of Brunswick. In 1807 he became director of Göttingen Observatory, where he remained until his death. He contributed to the study of electricity and magnetism and made significant advances in such branches of mathematics as number theory and the theory of series. The unit of magnetic flux density is named after him.

Gauss's Law, the total electric flux of a closed surface in an electric field is the magnitude of the charge within that surface divided by the electric constant. The law also applies to surfaces drawn in a magnetic field and similar statements can be made for a gravitation field.

Gavelkind, system of inheritance common in Britain before the Norman Conquest. As compared with primogeniture, by which the firstborn son inherited his father's estate or tenement, the custom of gavelkind entitled all sons to share equally in the estate.

Gavial, crocodilian living in India and Burma. Characterized by a long, narrow, rodlike snout, it is harmless to man, feeding almost exclusively on fish. Length: to

21ft (6.4m). Family Gavialidae; species *Gavialis gangeticus*. *See also* Crocodile.

Gavle (Gefle), seaport city in E Sweden; seat of Gävleborg co; site of Viking burial ground, 16th-century castle, 17th-century church. Exports: iron ore, wood pulp. Industries: shipyards, lumber, textiles, chemicals. Chartered 1446. Pop. 86,911.

Gavotte, originally a peasant dance of the 14th century. It was popularized by Marie Antoinette and became a fashionable 18th-century court dance. Similar to, but livelier than, the minuet, it has a 4/4 rhythm.

Gay, John (1685–1732), English poet and dramatist. His best-known work is the ballad-opera *The Beggar's Opera* (1728), a political satire burlesquing Italian opera style. *The Threepenny Opera* (1928) by Bertolt Brecht and Kurt Weill is based on *The Beggar's Opera.*

Gaya, holy city in NE India, on Phalgu River; sacred pilgrimage center administered by Hindus and Buddhists; nearby, Lord Buddha received enlightenment and God Vishnu sacrificed demon of Gaya; seat of Magadha University (founded by Buddhists 1962). Pop. 179,826.

Gay-Lussac, Joseph Louis (1778–1850), French chemist and physicist who did pioneer research on the behavior of gases. He discovered the law of combining gas volumes (Gay-Lussac's law) and the law of gas expansion often also attributed to J.A.C. Charles (who discovered it earlier but did not publish his results). In the field of chemistry, he prepared (with Louis-Jacques Thenard) the elements potassium and boron; investigated fermentation and hydrocyanic acid; and invented a hydrometer. *See also* Charles' Law.

Gaza (Ghazzah), seaport city in W Israel, on Gaza Strip, on SE Mediterranean Sea coast. One of five city-kingdoms of Philistines, it was under frequent attack because of its strategic position between Palestine and Egypt; became a Muslim holy city after capture by Arabs AD 634; part of British Palestine mandate 1917–48; under Egyptian rule 1948–67, when it was occupied by Israel; largest city and administrative center of the Gaza Strip. Pop. 118,300. *See also* Gaza Strip.

Gaza Strip, small region in W Israel, on SE Mediterranean Sea; part of Britain's Palestine Mandate after WWI; by 1947 Britain intended to give up the area; the peace talks of Arab-Israeli War (1948–49) made it an Egyptian possession; it was occupied by Israel after 1967 war. Since WWII, it has served as a Palestine Arab refugee center. Area: 140sq mi (363sq km). Pop. 365,000.

Gazelle, dozen species of fast, graceful, small-to-medium antelopes native to Africa and Asia, frequently inhabiting plains and treeless areas. The lyre-shaped horns, common to both sexes in African species, are generally lacking in females of Asiatic species. All are light brown with white rump. Bedouins hunt gazelles with falcons and dogs.

Dorcas gazelle of N Africa is a typical small representative. Two Asiatic gazelles, Mongolian and Tibetan (genus *Procapra*), are somewhat goatlike in appearance and inhabit mountainous plateaus. The gerenuk *(Litocranius walleri)* and the dibatag or Clarke's gazelle *(Ammodorcas clarkei)* are sometimes considered gazelles. Length: 39–49in (1–1.2m); height: 20–25in (51–64cm) at shoulder. They can run 40mph (64kmph) for over 15 minutes. Family Bovidae; genus *Gazella. See also* Antelope.

Gazetteer, a geographical index or dictionary containing, generally in alphabetical order, a list of names and descriptions of places. The first such gazetteer was edited in 1693 by the English historian Laurence Echard *(The Gazetteer's: or, Newsman's Interpreter: Being a Geographical Index).*

Gaziantep, formerly Aintab; city in SW Turkey, between the Taurus Mts and Euphrates River; capital of Gaziantep prov.; agricultural and trade center. Ancient Hittite city, it was taken by Saladin 1183; conquered by Ottomans 1516; resisted French occupation 1920–21; returned to Turkey 1921. Exports: pistachio nuts, grapes. Pop. 294,950.

Gdańsk (Danzig), seaport city in N Poland, on Gulf of Danzig; capital of Gdańsk prov.; settled by Slavs in 10th century; taken over by Poland 15th century; made part of Prussia 1793; Treaty of Versailles (1919) est. it as a free city, serving as port for Poland; inc. into Germany 1939; returned to Poland 1945. Industries: shipbuilding, metallurgy, machinery, chemicals, food processing, lumber. Pop. 364,300.

Gdynia, seaport city in N Poland, on Gulf of Danzig, Baltic Sea; major port and naval base. Industries: shipbuilding, metallurgy, machinery, food processing. Inc. 1926. Pop. 190,100.

Gear, a toothed wheel, usually attached to a rotating shaft. Operating in pairs, the teeth of one gear engage those of the other, to transmit and modify rotary motion and torque. The smaller member of a gear pair is called a pinion. If the pinion is on the driving shaft, speed is reduced and torque amplified; if the gear is on the shaft, speed is increased and torque reduced. A screw-type gear, called a worm, may have only one tooth; a pinion must have at least five.

Geb, in Egyptian mythology, the earth god, son of Shu and Tefnut, husband of Nut and father of Osiris. He is depicted as a goose, or as a man with a goose on his head. In the Egyptian myth of creation, the air separates Geb, the earth, from Nut, the sky.

Gecko, any of about 65 species of small to medium, mostly arboreal lizards wide-spread in warm areas worldwide. Their remarkable climbing ability is due to microscopic suction cups on their feet. They make chirping or barking calls. Length: 1–6in (3–15cm). Family Gekkonidae. *See also* Lizard.

Gegenschein, or counterglow, faint luminous patch visible at a point along the ecliptic, that is diametrically opposite to the sun. Best seen in tropical regions it is a phenomenon allied to the zodiacal light, and often appears as an extension of it.

Geiger Counter, or **Geiger-Müller Counter,** type of ionization chamber in which a high voltage is applied across the electrodes. Radiation or particles entering the chamber ionize gas atoms and the resulting ions, gaining energy from the electric field between the electrodes, can produce many more ions. The resulting current quickly subsides so that a pulse of current is produced for each particle. Each pulse activates a counting circuit enabling several thousand particles per second to be counted. *See also* Ionization Chamber.

Geisel, Theodor Seuss. *See* Seuss, Dr.

Gel, coherent mass consisting of a liquid comprising minute particles dispersed or arranged in a fine network throughout the mass. Their appearance may be notably elastic or jellylike (as in gelatin or fruit jelly) or quite rigid and solid (as in silica gel, a material resembling coarse white sand used as a dehumidifier, and vulcanized rubber).

Gelatin, colorless or yellowish protein obtained from collagen in animal cartilages and bones by boiling in water. It is used in photographic film, sizing, capsules for medical drugs, explosives, and as a culture medium for bacteria.

Geldof, Bob (Robert Frederick Xenon) (1951–), Irish rock performer and fundraiser. After leaving school, he held various jobs before organizing a "new wave" rock group called the Boomtown Rats in 1975. By the late 1970s the group enjoyed considerable success in London, and Geldof also appeared in films. In 1984 television reports of famine in Ethiopia inspired him to establish the Band Aid charity to raise funds for famine relief. July 1985 concerts in London and Philadelphia were extremely successful, prompting Geldof's nomination for the Nobel Peace Prize.

Gelsenkirchen, city and port in W West Germany, on the Rhine-Herne Canal; site of 16th–18th-century moated castle. Industries: coal, glass, clothing, oil refining. Pop. 320,100.

Gem, any of about 100 minerals, either opaque, transparent, or translucent, valued for their beauty, rarity, and durability. The most highly valued stones are transparent ones, such as the diamond, ruby, emerald, and sapphire. Pearl, amber, and coral are gems of organic origin. Gemstones are cut to bring out their color and brilliance and are often set in jewelry. Gems with a design cut into the stone are intaglios; with a design in relief, cameos.

In ancient Babylon, intaglios were used for rings and amulets. Intaglios and cameos were used in Greek and Roman jewelry. Antique classical gems often carried engraved pictures of notable contemporary statues and paintings that have since been destroyed and are evidence of the existence of these lost works of art. During the Byzantine period, Constantinople became the center of gem-cutting. Especially during the Middle Ages, many gems were thought to have magical powers. During the Renaissance, northern Italy became the center of skillful gem engraving, using classical gems as models. The art of cutting and polishing gemstones was developed in the 15th century probably beginning in France and the Netherlands. *See also* Lapidary.

Gem, Artificial, imitations of natural gemstones made of various substances. The first appeared in prehistoric times. Glass is frequently used; the best quality being made of material containing lead oxide and cut and polished. Plastics have replaced glass in some instances. Pearls are simulated by coating glass beads with pearl essence, a derivative of fish scales. Imitation diamonds are made of strontium titanate or rutile. Ruby and sapphire, emerald and spinel are also made synthetically. *See also* Gem.

Gemeinschaft, in sociology, ideal-type concept formulated by Ferdinand Toennies in 1887, denoting social systems based on spontaneous, small-group, face-to-face relationships. The family and "primitive" societies are often called Gemeinschaft-like. *See also* Gesellschaft.

Gemini, or **the Twins,** northern constellation, situated on the ecliptic between Taurus and Cancer and lying northeast of Orion; the third sign of the zodiac. It contains the star cluster M 35 (NGC 2168) and the planetary nebula NGC 2392. Brightest star: Beta Geminorum (Pollux). The astrological sign for the period May 21–June 21.

Gemini Space Program, the US manned-flight space program that followed Mercury, preceded Apollo. The Gemini was a two-person craft first manned by Maj. Virgil Grissom and Lt. Cmdr. John Young on March 23, 1965; they made three earth orbits. Subsequent flights and experiments through Gemini 12 (Nov. 11–15, 1966) demonstrated space walks, space docking maneuvers, and tests of longevity including a 14-day flight by Lt. Col. Frank Borman and Cmdr. James Lovell, Jr., in December 1965. All were preparatory to the moon landing.

Geminorum Stars. *See* Dwarf Star.

Gemsbok. *See* Oryx.

Gender, the classification of nouns and pronouns according to sex. Personal pronouns and some nouns have a different word for masculine, feminine, neuter, or common gender. "I" and "you" have assumed gender.

Genealogy, the study of family origins and history. The genealogist compiles lists of ancestors and then arranges them in pedigree charts. Genealogy began with early oral traditions and advanced to written pedigrees, and began to develop in its present form in the early 16th century.

General Agreement on Tariffs and Trade (GATT), international trade agreements, based on the most-favored nation principle, that involve most noncommunist countries. Any tariff reduction one nation gives to another member of the group must be extended to all members. GATT is designed to prevent "tariff wars." The agreement has been periodically renegotiated since 1948. *See also* Most-Favored Nation Clause.

General Council. *See* Council, Ecumenical.

General Equilibrium, in economics, an equilibrium in the production sector, in the consumption sector, and in the resources sector of the economy as a whole. This analysis attempts to account for interrelationships by showing the effect of a change in the price of one good or resource on all other sectors of the economy.

General Paresis, chronic brain disorder associated with a syphilitic infection of the central nervous system; also known as paresis and general paralysis. It involves general mental deterioration and paralysis and is ultimately fatal. This last or fourth stage of neurosyphilis is rarely seen today because of the effectiveness of antibiotic therapy. *See also* Syphilis.

General Theory of Relativity, part of Einstein's theory of relativity that applies to observers whose relative motion is not constant. *See also* Relativity Theory.

Generator, Electric, a device for producing electrical energy. Most frequently it refers to a device that converts the mechanical energy of a turbine or internal combustion engine into electrical energy by employing electromagnetic induction. The term is also used for other sources such as chemical batteries, fuel cells, and solar cells.

Genes, biochemical substances in the chromosomes that encode the hereditary information that determines an individual's characteristics. The building block of genes is DNA (deoxyribonucleic acid), a chemically complex substance that is the basis of genetic organi-

Gazelle

Genet

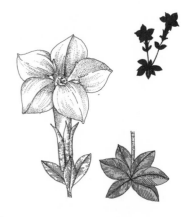

Gentian

zation in both plants and animals. Using recombinant DNA techniques, scientists can insert a gene from one species of bacteria, plants, or animals into the DNA of another species, enabling it to produce the protein encoded by that gene. The technique will eventually enable correction of defective genes. *See also* Chromosomes; Heredity.

Genesee River, river in N Pennsylvania; rises in the Allegheny Mts; flows through W New York, through Letchworth State Park (noted for its picturesque gorge and waterfalls), to Lake Ontario at Rochester; supplies hydroelectricity to Rochester. Length: 158mi (254km).

Genesis, first book of the Old Testament and Pentateuch. It is comprised of three sections. The first relates the history of the universe and God's relation to it; the second is an account of man before Abraham; and the third recounts Israelite history until the descent into Egypt.

Genêt, Jean (1910–86), French dramatist and novelist. The hardships of his childhood quickly led him into delinquency and crime. It is in his books such as *Our Lady of the Flowers* (1944) and *Thief's Journal* (1949) that he records his experiences of Europe's bars, brothels, and prisons. His plays, among the best known of which are *The Maids* (1947) and *The Balcony* (1956), are concerned with an equivocal world of illusions, masks, and mirrors. A collection of his poems, *Treasures of the Night*, was published in 1980.

Genet, catlike carnivore of the civet family native to W Europe and S and E Africa. Solitary and nocturnal, genets have long slender bodies, short legs, gray to brown fur with black or brown spots, and banded tails. Length: body—19in (48cm); tail—19in(48cm); weight to 4.5lb (2kg). Family Viverridae; genus *Genetta. See also* Civet Cat.

Genetic Engineering, also called gene splicing and recombinant DNA technology, the construction of a DNA (deoxyribonucleic acid) molecule consisting of a desired gene segment and a vector DNA, which is then introduced into a bacterial, plant, or mammalian cell. The desired gene is expressed in that cell. The technique has been used successfully to introduce the gene for human growth hormone into bacteria; the bacteria then produce the hormone. Other substances produced by bacteria in this manner include insulin, urokinase, and beta-endorphin. Gene splicing may also be used to isolate genes and determine their structure. Recombinant DNA technology was developed in the 1970s at Stanford University and the University of California, which have patented the technique because of its potential commercial value. The ethics of genetic engineering, given the possibility that scientists may one day be able to alter the genetic structure of humans, has been challenged by theologians. *See also* Deoxyribonucleic Acid.

Genetics, biological science and study of heredity, mutation, and development in similar or related plants and animals. Geneticists study molecular structures involved in heredity and evolution and the genes involved in the structure or alteration of a population. They also study the effects of heredity or environment on character and how these two factors interact. Related areas of study involve various inherited diseases and defects. Heredity is also examined relative to behavior, learning ability, and physiology. The application of genetics has provided improved plant and animal stocks for human use.

Geneva (Genève), city in SW Switzerland, on Rhone River, at S end of Lake Geneva; capital of Geneva canton. Former seat of Burgundian kingdom, it was conquered by Franks in 6th century; passed to Holy Roman Empire in 12th century; accepted the Reformation 1536 and became center of Protestantism under John Calvin 1541; became part of Swiss Confederation 1815; scene of Geneva Convention 1864, an international agreement on the wartime treatment of soldiers; headquarters of the League of Nations 1920–46; European center for United Nations; site of University of Geneva, founded by Calvin 1559, 10th-12th-century Gothic cathedral. Industries: banking, watches, jewelry, enamelware, iron goods, tourism. Pop. 155,800.

Geneva Conventions, series of rules outlining the treatment of wounded soldiers and prisoners during war. The first Geneva Convention was in 1864. The rules are also known as the Red Cross treaties.

Geneva (Leman or Genève) Lake, crescent-shaped lake in SW Switzerland; S section extends into E France; it is crossed E to W by the Rhone River. Surrounded by mountains, it is noted for clear blue water and great beauty; site of several lakeside resorts. Length: 45mi (72km). Width: approx. 9mi (14km). Area: 224sq mi (580sq km).

Genghis Khan (1167?–1227), original name Timujin, conqueror and emperor of the Mongol empire stretching across central Asia from the Caspian Sea to the Sea of Japan. He united the Mongol tribes and demonstrated military genius and ruthlessness as he captured Peking (1227), took over Iran, and invaded Russia as far as Moscow. He established law codes, tolerated ethnic and religious minorities, and increased contact between East and West. His empire was divided and expanded by his sons and grandsons.

Genoa (Genova), seaport city in NW Italy, on the Gulf of Genoa; capital of Genoa prov. and region of Liguria. An important commercial center in the Middle Ages, its fortunes declined in the 15th century and it came under foreign control; occupied by Napoleon 1796; inc. by France 1805; passed to Sardinia 1815; birthplace of Christopher Columbus (*c.* 1451); site of Cathedral of San Lorenzo, Ducal palace, Church of San Donato, university (1471), Academy of Fine Arts (1751). Exports: rice, wine, olive oil, silk, coral, marble, macaroni. Industries: iron, steel, textiles, shipbuilding, chemicals. Pop. 798,892.

Genocide, deliberate governmental policy aimed at destroying a racial, religious, or ethnic group. The word has become synonymous with the Nazi extermination of Jews during World War II, although the practice existed for centuries. The UN General Assembly has defined genocide as an international crime, but no court with international criminal jurisdiction exists.

Genotype, genetic or hereditary makeup of an individual that may or may not be manifested in observable traits or behaviors; contrasted with phenotype, the observable characteristics. *See also* Phenotype.

Genre Painting, art term usually referring to realistic portrayals of scenes of daily life. This type of painting was quite prevalent among Dutch and Flemish masters of the 17th century.

Gens, in Roman history, a clan, or a group of families, claiming descent from a common ancestor and sharing a common name. Other requirements for membership in any particular gens included purity of blood, personal liberty, and descent from free-born parents. In anthro-

pology, the term is used to identify a patrilineal descent group.

Gentian, perennial plant in temperate regions; many species are alpine plants. It has heart-shaped leaves and usually blue, tubular flowers. Among 300 species are the dark blue *Gentiana clusii*, fringed *Gentiana crinita*, and yellow *Gentiana lutea*, whose bitter root is used as a gastrointestinal tonic. Family Gentianaceae.

Gentian Violet, a purple dye used in biology as a bacterial stain and in medicine as a bactericide to kill certain bacterial strains.

Gentileschi, Orazio (1563–1647), Italian painter. A follower of Caravaggio, he is known for his portraits and historical paintings. In 1626 he went to England as the court painter to King Charles I, where he introduced the style of Caravaggio.

Genus, group of closely related plant or animal species with common characteristics. The genus name is usually a Latin or Greek noun. Example: genus *Quercus* denotes oak trees and *Felis* denotes all cats. A genus contains from one to several species.

Geochemistry, study of the chemical composition of the earth and the changes that have resulted from chemical and physical processes.

Geode, small, hollow rock nodule with inner walls lined with crystals, generally quartz or calcite. Formed by gelatinous silica and mineral-bearing water within a cavity, the beautiful crystals are prized by collectors.

Geodesic Dome, in modern architecture, a dome or vault made of light, straight structural elements arranged to form a hemispheric surface. Originally patented by R. Buckminster Fuller, such a dome provides economy by means of lightness of materials and lack of supporting columns. At the same time structural stresses are spread out evenly over the entire dome rather than focused at one or a few points.

Geodesy, a branch of geophysics that includes determination of the size and shape of the earth, its gravitational field, and the location of fixed points.

Geoffrey of Monmouth (*c.*1100–1154), English chronicler best known for his *Historia Regum Britanniae (History of the Kings of Britain)*. Based on Latin manuscripts, Welsh genealogies, and oral tradition, it is primarily a fictional account but was accepted as an historical document until the 16th century. During the Middle Ages, the *Historia* was translated into French, Middle English, Welsh, Spanish, and Old Norse. Included were the tales of King Arthur and his court, which became the basis for medieval Arthurian romance.

Geography, science that studies the relationship between the earth and mankind. It includes the size and distribution of land masses, seas and resources, climatic zones, and plant and animal life. Because it seeks to relate all the earth's features to man's existence, geography differs from other earth sciences such as geology, meteorology, and oceanography, which study this planet's features as specific phenomena.

Geoid, the theoretical surface of Earth. The roughly elliptical Earth is bulged out at the Equator and flattened at the poles. *See also* Geodesy.

Geologic Time, the time scale of the history of the earth divided into periods ranging into millions of years.

Until recently, only methods of relative dating were possible. These include the world-side study, a comparison and correlation of sequences of rock formations and the fossils they contain. The gathered data are used to distinguish earlier from later deposits, to estimate periods of passed time, and to reconstruct geologic and climatic events by assuming that geological processes in the past were the same as today. Measurement of the disintegration of certain radioactive elements in rocks (called absolute dating) has provided previously unattainable accuracy. The largest divisions of geologic time are called eras, each of which is broken down into periods. Periods, in turn, are subdivided into series or epochs. *See also* Historical Geology.

Geology, study of the materials of the earth, their origin, arrangement, classification, change, and history. Geology is divided into several categories: geophysics, the study of physical properties of earth; geochemistry, the chemical makeup of earth; mineralogy, arrangements of minerals; petrology, rocks and their combination of minerals; stratigraphy, arrangement and succession of rocks in layers; paleontology, study of fossilized plant and animal remains; geomorphology, study of landforms; structural geology, classification of rock structures and the forces that produced them; hydrology, study of surface and subsurface waters; economic geology, study of materials of practical use to man; engineering geology, study of the land in terms of construction on it; environmental geology, geological study applied to the best use of the environment by man; oceanography, combination of several fields as they relate to the total study of oceans. *See also* Historical Geology.

Geomagnetic Storm. *See* Magnetic Storm.

Geometric Isomer. *See* Isomers.

Geometric Mean, square root of the product of two numbers. For example, the geometric mean of 8 and 2 is $\sqrt{8\times2} = 4$. The geometric mean of *n* numbers is the *n*th root of their product $\sqrt[n]{a\cdot b\cdot c\cdot \ldots}$. *See also* Arithmetic Mean.

Geometric Progression, sequence of numbers in which the ratio of each term to the preceding term is a constant (called the common ratio). It has the form $a, ar, ar^2, ar^3, \ldots$ The sum of these terms, $a + ar + ar^2 \ldots$, is a geometric series. If there are *n* terms the sum equals $a(1-r^n)/(1-r)$. Infinite geometric series converge to $a/(1-r)$ if *r* lies between -1 and $+1$.

Geometry, branch of mathematics concerned broadly with studies of shape and size. To most people geometry is the Euclidean geometry of simple plane and solid figures. Geometry is, however, a much wider and more abstract field with many subdivisions. Analytic geometry, introduced in 1637 by Descartes, applies algebra to geometry and allows the study of more complex curves than those of Euclidean geometry. Projective geometry is, in its simplest form, concerned with projection of shapes—operations of the type involved in drawing maps and in perspective painting—and with properties that are independent of such changes. It was introduced by Jean-Victor Poncelet in 1822. Even more abstraction occurred in the early 19th century with formulations of non-Euclidean geometry by Farkas Bolyai and N.I. Lobachevski. Differential geometry—based on the application of calculus and ideas such as the curvature and lengths of curves in space—was also developed during this period. Geometric reasoning was also applied to spaces with more than three dimensions. Topology is a very general form of geometry, concerned with properties that are independent of any continuous deformation of shape. *See also* Euclidean Geometry, Non-Euclidean Geometry, Topology.

Geomorphology, a science dealing with the land and submarine relief features of the earth's surface and the physical, chemical, and biological processes that act upon them. It seeks to interpret these features through the use of the principles of physiography and of dynamic and structural geology.

Geophysics, earth science that deals with the physics of earth. The areas that are called geophysical are geodesy, geothermometry, seismology, tectometry, hydrology, oceanography, atmospheric and meteorologic studies, the related fields of geomagnetism and geoelectricity, geochronology and geocosmogony, and geophysical exploration and prospecting.

Geopolitics, study of the relationship between geography and political life. Three basic environmental factors are believed to have an impact on the political development of nations: actual physical configurations; climatic variables; and wealth of natural resources. Geopolitics fell into disrepute because of its identification with Nazi propaganda of the 1920s.

George, Saint, early Christian martyr who became patron saint of England. According to tradition he was born in Palestine and martyred at Nicomedia sometime before 323. Many stories grew up about St George, including the 12th-century tale of his killing a dragon to save a maiden. Scholars now class all these as legendary.

George I (1660–1727), king of Great Britain and Ireland (1714–27); elector of Hanover (1698–1727). A great-grandson of James I of England and a Protestant, he succeeded Queen Anne under the provisions of the Act of Settlement (1701), thus becoming the first Hanoverian king of England. He favored the Whigs over the Tories, suspecting the latter of Jacobite sympathies. In 1715 and 1719 he put down Jacobite uprisings. In 1718 he formed the Quadruple Alliance with Holland, France, and Germany that guaranteed Hanoverian succession. He was disliked in England because he did not speak English and spent much of his time in Hanover.

George II (1683–1760), king of Great Britain and Ireland (1727–1760); elector of Hanover (1727–1760). Influenced by Robert Walpole, he supported the Whigs. He brought Britain into the War of the Austrian Succession (1740–49) to protect Hanover, personally commanding victorious forces at Dettingen (1743). He suppressed the last Jacobite rebellion (1745–46). His reign also saw imperial acquisitions in Canada and India.

George III (1738–1820), king of Great Britain and Ireland (1760–1820); elector and then king of Hanover (1760–1820); grandson of George II. He initially sought an active role in government during the ministries of Bute, Grenville, Pitt, Grafton, and North (1760–82), influencing the disastrous colonial policy that led to American independence (1776) but effectively suppressing the anti-Catholic Gordon Riots (1780). He consolidated Tory power by calling the "Younger Pitt" to office (1783–1801, 1804–05), though opposing and defeating Pitt's plans for Catholic emancipation (1801). Suffering increasingly from bouts of insanity after 1765, he became blind (1805) and completely insane (1811). Under the Regency Act (1811) his son (later George IV) acted as regent (1811–20).

George IV (1762–1830), king of Great Britain and Ireland (1820–30). He served as regent during the periods of George III's madness (1788–89; 1811–20). In 1785 he secretly married Maria Fitzherbert, but she was Roman Catholic and the marriage was not recognized. In 1795 he married Caroline of Brunswick in order to obtain parliamentary settlement of his debts. They separated within a year. In 1812 he decided to retain his father's Tory advisers instead of replacing them with the Whigs, whom he had supported earlier. A patron of the arts, he was, however, disliked for his extravagances and dissolute habits. He was succeeded by his brother William IV.

George V (1865–1936), king of Great Britain and Northern Ireland and emperor of India (1910–36). He became heir apparent after his elder brother, Albert, Duke of Clarence, died (1892). He married Princess Victoria Mary of Teck (1893). Of the house of Saxe-Coburg-Gotha, he adopted the surname Windsor (1917).

George VI (1895–1952), king of Great Britain and Northern Ireland (1936–52) and emperor of India (1936–48). He was proclaimed king when his brother, Edward VIII, abdicated. George married Lady Elizabeth Bowes-Lyon (1923). He visited Canada and the United States (1939) and South Africa (1947). He was succeeded by Elizabeth II.

George, Lake, glacial lake in E New York, N of Albany; outlet N to Lake Champlain. Discovered by Isaac Jogues, a French Jesuit, in 1646; scene of many battles during French and Indian Wars and American Revolution. Center of a large tourist area and largest lake within Adirondack State Park. Area: 33mi (53km) long, 1–3mi (1.6–5km) wide.

Georgetown, largest city and capital of Guyana, South America, on mouth of Demerara River. During Dutch occupation (1784), it was called Stabroek, and was the capital of united colonies of Essequibo and Demerara; renamed Georgetown 1812. Principal port of country, it is site of outstanding tropical botanical gardens and a university (1963). Exports: sugar, rice, timber, bauxite, diamonds, gold. Industries: sawmills, shipbuilding, food processing, brewing, rum distilling, woodworking. Founded 1781. Pop. 182,000.

Georgia, state in the SE United States, on the Atlantic Ocean N of Florida. In the Civil War, it was one of the six original states of the Confederacy.

Land and Economy. A coastal plain in the E and S occupies about half the state. To the N is the Piedmont, a region of rolling hills and farmland. In the extreme N, the Blue Ridge Mts run from E to W. Of the many rivers that flow SE, the Savannah, the Ogeechee, and the Altamaha are the largest. The products of Georgia's forests and farms, which formed its economic base from earliest times, are still important, but manufacturing development during WWII moved the main emphasis to industry. Manufacture of aircraft, automobile and truck bodies, and boats has become a major enterprise. Atlanta is the financial center of a multi-state region.

People. Almost all Georgia's people were born in the United States. Business expansion has attracted thousands of residents from the N states. Urban growth came late and slowly, but in 1980 about half of the population lived in metropolitan areas.

Education. There are more than 60 institutions of higher education.

History. In 1732, George II of Great Britain gave Gen. James E. Oglethorpe a large land grant in the area. Oglethorpe founded a settlement on the Savannah River the next year. At the Battle of Bloody Marsh in 1742, he defeated the Spaniards, who threatened the colony from Florida. Georgia became a royal province in 1754. Its delegates to the Continental Congress in 1776 supported national independence, and Georgia was among the earliest to ratify the US Constitution. In 1792, Eli Whitney of Savannah invented the cotton gin that simplified the processing of cotton, bringing prosperity to all Southern planters. The state was ravaged in 1864 by the Union armies of Gen. William T. Sherman. It was readmitted to the Union in 1870, but its economy and society were slow in recovering from the effects of the war. In 1976 a native son, Gov. Jimmy Carter, was elected 39th president of the United States.

PROFILE

Admitted to Union: Jan. 2, 1788, 4th of the 13 original states to ratify the US Constitution
US Congressmen: Senate, 2; House of Representatives 10
Population: 5,464,265 (1980); rank, 13th
Capital: Atlanta, 425,022 (1980)
Chief cities: Atlanta; Columbus, 169,441; Macon, 116,860; Savannah, 141,634.
State legislature: Senate, 56; House of Representatives, 180
Area: 58,876sq mi (152,489sq km); rank, 21st
Elevation: Highest, Brasstown Bald, 4,784ft (1,459m). Lowest, sea level
Industries (major products): textiles, paper, naval stores (turpentine, resin, gums), lumber, transportation equipment, processed foods, chemicals
Agriculture (major products): peanuts, nuts, poultry, hogs, peaches
Minerals (major): clays, marble, bauxite
State nicknames: Empire State of the South, Peach State
State motto: "Wisdom, Justice, and Moderation"
State bird: brown thrasher
State flower: cherokee rose
State tree: live oak

Georgian Architecture, style of English architecture that flourished between the accession of George I to the throne in 1714 and the death of George IV in 1830. Early Georgian architecture was strongly influenced by the Palladian revival, led by Colin Campbell and Lord Burlington. A more historical neoclassicism, developed by Robert Adam and John Soane, led to the later Greek revival phase. In the United States, the Royall House, Medford, Mass. (*c.*1747), and Independence Hall, Philadelphia, are good examples of the Georgian style, while the White House, Washington, D.C., is a fine example of the neoclassical trend.

Georgian Bay, inlet of Lake Huron in SE Ontario, Canada; contains many islands, 40 of which are included in Georgian Bay Islands National Park. Length: approx. 125mi (201km), width: 50mi (81km).

Georgian SSR (Socialist Republic Gruzinskaja), one of 15 union republics in USSR, bounded by Azerbaijan SSR (SE), Armenian SSR and Turkey (S), Black Sea (W), Caucasus Mts (N and NE); Tbilisi is the capital. Region was conquered by Pompey for Rome 65 BC; Christianized by St Nino *c.* 330; ravaged by Mongol invasions 13th century but rebuilt under rule of Erekle II (1744–98) who est. Russian protection by treaty with Catherine the Great. Tsar Alexander I annexed Georgia to Russia 1801, causing war with Persia (1804–13). Area regained independence after Russian Revolution (1917), but was inc. into USSR 1921 by Joseph Stalin; became constituent republic 1936. The Georgian language (dating from *c.* 325 BC) is the most important of the Caucasian languages and the only one

George III

Savannah, Georgia

East Germany

to be used in ancient as well as modern literature. Industries: wine, brandy, tea, tobacco, fruit, grain, hydroelectricity, maganese mining, steel, pig iron, textiles, lumber, coke; oil and kerosene pipeline terminus. Area: 26,911sq mi (69,699sq km). Pop. 5,030,000.

Geosyncline, a great basin or trough where deposits of sediment and volcanic rock, thousands of meters thick, have accumulated during slow subsidence through long geologic periods. The term was proposed by the 19th-century scientist James D. Dana to describe the formation basin of the Appalachian Mountains. The different kinds of marine fossils in the strata indicate that the Appalachians were formed from an uplifted shallow-water basin and the Alps from a deepwater one. *See also* Syncline.

Geothermal Energy, energy from deep within the earth's crust. This energy can be tapped to heat buildings or to generate electricity. Water can seep downward to great depths, as well as travel horizontally, within the crust. A geothermal reservoir exists where a layer of impermeable rock traps the superheated water underneath it. This water can be tapped with a well, and in some locations it rises naturally through geological faults. Because of the decrease in pressure as it rises, the water usually turns into steam. Very hot steam can be used efficiently to turn turbines to generate electricity. In this way the energy can be sent over long distances. Low-temperature steam and hot water from geothermal wells usually are used for local heating only. Although it currently accounts for a very small percentage of the world's total energy production, geothermal energy may be more widely used in the future.

Geotropism, responses of plant growth to the stimulus of gravity. In general, plant stems are negatively geotropic and grow up; roots are positively geotropic and grow down. Growth curvature is caused by accumulation of auxin on the lower side of the stem, increasing growth and bending it up. Growth response may also be at right angles to gravitational force (horizontal rhizomes) or any other angle (branches of main roots). *See also* Auxin.

Gera, city in S East Germany, capital of Gera district, 47mi (76km) ESE of Erfurt; rail and road junction. Industries: textiles, metals, tobacco products, food processing. Chartered early 13th century. Pop. 115,238.

Geranium, house and garden plant native to S Africa. Shrubby or trailing, it is densely branched with hairy, fan- or ivy-shaped leaves that emit a spicy aroma. Red, pink, or white flower clusters are borne on stalks above the leaves. Care: full sun, soil (3 parts loam, 1 part peat moss, 2 parts sand) kept dry between waterings. Propagation is by stem cuttings. Height: 1–3ft (30–91cm). Family Geraniaceae; genus *Pelargonium.*

Gerbil, small rodent native to dry areas of Asia and Africa, often domesticated as a pet. It has big eyes and ears, long hind legs, and long tail. Its fur may be buff, gray, brown or red. Mostly nocturnal, plant-eating burrow-dwellers, gerbils often hoard food but require little water. Females bear litters of 1–8 young three weeks after breeding. Length: 3–5in (7–12cm). Family Cricetidae.

Geriatrics, branch of medicine that deals with the diseases and other medical problems of the elderly, who are subject to degeneration and aging of certain tissues and other disorders not common in younger people.

Géricault, (Jean Louis André) Théodore (1791–1824), French painter. A forerunner of the Romantic

movement, he began as a painter of battle scenes and then became a copyist of the Italian masters. He later associated himself with the Romantic cry for revolution. His most famous painting, "Raft of the Medusa" (1819), took for its subject a shipwreck that was a political scandal. He wrote numerous pamphlets attacking government activities. On a visit to London he drew many sketches depicting poverty in the streets, as well as realistic sketches of horses and horse races.

German, language spoken by about 120,000,000 people in West and East Germany, Austria, Switzerland, and by German communities in many other countries. High German (*Hochdeutsch*), of the south, is the standard dialect, but Low German (*Plattdeutsch*) is generally spoken in the north. Like the other Germanic languages, German belongs to the Indo-European family.

German Confederation (1815–66), loose federation of German states under Austrian presidency, created by the Congress of Vienna to replace the Holy Roman Empire. It collapsed with the 1848 revolutions, was restored in 1850, and was finally destroyed by the Prussian defeat of Austria in 1866.

German East Africa, German protectorate in East Africa from 1885 until World War I, when it became three League of Nations mandates under the British, Portuguese, and Belgians. The former colony is now included in the independent nations of Tanzania, Ruanda, and Burundi.

Germanic and Scandinavian Mythology. Qualities that are singularly Teutonic are difficult to isolate in the mythology of the north countries. What does make Germanic folklore somewhat unique, however, is the mass of recorded literature, written and collected by monks, antiquarians, and ethnologists. One of the collections is known as the *Elder Edda,* short poems composed in the 8th to 11th centuries in Norway, Iceland, and Greenland, including the story of Siegfried and the Nibelungenlied. The *Younger Edda* is a collection of the early 13th century; a 9th-century collection of myths and heroic stories is the *Old Norse Scaldic Verse.*

Germanic Languages, group of languages forming a subdivision of the Indo-European family. One branch includes English, German, Yiddish, Dutch, Flemish, Frisian, and Afrikaans; another includes Swedish, Danish, Norwegian, Icelandic, and Faroese. Gothic, the language of the ancient Goths but long extinct, constituted a third branch.

Germanium, metalloid element (symbol Ge) of group IVA of the periodic table, predicted (as ekasilicon) by Mendeleev and discovered in 1886. Chief source is as a by-product from smelting zinc ores or from the combustion of certain coals. The element is important in transistors, rectifiers, and similar semiconductor devices. Properties: at. no. 32; at. wt. 72.59; sp gr 5.3 at 25°C; melt. pt. 1,719°F (937.4°C); boil. pt. 5,126°F (2,830°C); most common isotope Ge[74] (36.54%).

German Measles, or rubella, a virus-caused contagious disease characterized by a light pink rash beginning on the face and spreading down. The disease is mild, requiring only symptomatic relief, usually of itching. Young children are frequently immunized against rubella to prevent contagion to women in child-bearing years since rubella can cause serious damage to a fetus. *See also* Rubella.

German Shepherd, dog used for sheepherding, police work, and guiding the blind; (working group) bred from old breeds of German herd and farm dogs. An aloof

and self-confident dog, it has an arched forehead; long, strong muzzle; pointed, erect ears; a long, solid body; medium-length, straight, oval-boned legs; and bushy, curved tail. The medium-length double coat is straight and harsh; kennel clubs accept most colors except white. Average size: 24–26in (61–66cm) high at shoulder; 60–85lb (27–38kg). *See also* Working Dog.

German Shorthaired Pointer, breed of dog that is an all-purpose pointer, night trailer, and retriever (sporting group). This intelligent dog has a clean-cut head with broad skull, squarish muzzle, and large nose; the broad ears lie flat. The body is short-backed and powerful, legs well-muscled, feet webbed, and tail docked. Coat is short, thick, and hard, and colored solid liver or liver and white spotted. Average size: 23–25in (58–63.5cm) high at shoulder; 55–70lb (25–32kg). *See also* Sporting Dog.

German Wirehaired Pointer, all-purpose hunting dog (sporting group) bred in Germany and brought to United States in 1920. Popular in the Midwest, this dog has a long head and muzzle with beard and whiskers; rounded, hanging ears; brown eyes set under bushy eyebrows; muscular legs with webbed feet; and docked tail. The 2in (5cm) long water-resistant coat is straight and wiry; color is liver and white. Average size: 24–26in (61–66cm) high at shoulder; 60lb (27kg). *See also* Sporting Dog.

Germany, a nation in central Europe divided since 1945 into two independent countries, West Germany and East Germany. For centuries the German peoples have occupied the strategic central region of Europe. A unified German nation existed from 1871 to 1945. Twice in the 20th century this German nation initiated and was defeated in world wars. The history of Germany since 1945 is covered in the separate articles on East Germany and West Germany that follow this article.

The Germans enter recorded history in the time of Julius Caesar's Gallic campaigns. The Goths, Allemani, Teutons, and Franks were among the more notable early Germanic tribes. The history of the German nation begins with Charlemagne (AD 800) who extended Frankish power over much of W Europe. In the medieval period German power, which was paramount in Europe, was focused in the Holy Roman Empire and in the Hapsburg dynasty. The Reformation was begun in Germany (1517) by Martin Luther. The Protestant movement spread rapidly, but left the German states as disunited as before. The Thirty Years War (1618–48) ended with Germany reduced to hundreds of tiny states and petty kingdoms. Unification began with the rise of Prussia under the Hohenzollerns in the 17th century. Its center was Berlin, capital of the Brandenburg state. Prussia allied itself with Russia and Britain in defeating Napoleon (1815) and subsequently gained the Rhineland, part of Poland, Westphalia, and most of Saxony. German nationalism became apparent after 1830 in widespread revolts and calls for a national constitution and parliament. Under Chancellor Otto von Bismarck Prussia organized all German states N of the Main River; the S states joined Prussia in the Franco-Prussian War (1870–71), creating a unified German empire. Germany allied itself with Austria-Hungary (1879) and Italy (1882), and under Kaiser Wilhelm II sharply increased its military and naval strength. In World War I, Germany fought France, Great Britain, Russia, and the United States. Harsh terms were imposed on Germany by the victors. The world-wide economic collapse after 1929 led to severe political dislocations in Germany. Adolf Hitler and the National Socialist party gained power in 1933, and Hitler soon installed himself as dictator. The German economy recovered strongly. Germany rearmed; in

1936 alliances were made with Italy and Japan. Germany began the war with the invasion of Poland (1939). By 1941, Germany was at war with Great Britain, the Soviet Union, and the United States. Defeat came in 1945. *See also* Holy Roman Empire.

Following is a list of the rulers of Germany until 1945.

RULERS OF GERMANY

Frederick I	1701–13
Frederick William I	1713–40
Frederick II the Great	1740–86
Frederick William II	1786–97
Frederick William III	1797–1840
Frederick William IV	1840–61
William I	1861–88
Frederick III	1888
William II (Kaiser Wilhelm)	1888–1918
Friedrich Ebert	1919–25
Paul von Hindenburg	1925–34
Adolf Hitler	1934–45

Germany, East, officially the German Democratic Republic, a Communist nation in central Europe. After World War II, Germany was divided into four occupation zones. The Soviet zone became East Germany in 1949. Berlin, which lies in East Germany, is divided into E and W sectors. East Berlin is the capital of East Germany.

Land and Economy. East Germany lies on the North German Plain. It is bordered by the Baltic Sea (N), Poland (E), and by Czechoslovakia and West Germany (S) and (W). The country is drained by the Elbe River, a major commercial waterway. Except for extensive deposits of a soft, brown coal called lignite, the country is poor in mineral resources. The Communist government owns nearly all farmland, which has been organized into cooperative and state farms. Manufacturing is the fastest growing segment of the East German economy, led by the chemical and metallurgical industries. The economy ranks second only to the Soviet Union in total output of E European nations.

People. In East Germany the dominant ethnic type is Nordic, or Teutonic. There is also more Slavic influence apparent here than among other Germans, as in physical types, names, and style of settlement. Most East Germans are Protestants, although the Communist regime discourages religious practice. Between 1945 and 1960, more than 3,000,000 East Germans migrated to West Germany; to halt this outflow of workers, the Communist government built the Berlin Wall (1961). German is the official language throughout the country, but several dialects are spoken. About 75% of the population live in cities. The living standard in East Germany is below that of West Germany, but is the highest standard of any of the Communist-bloc countries of E Europe.

Government. The East German republic is governed by the Communist party, called the Socialist Unity Party. The constitution provides a bicameral legislature, parliamentary executive, council of ministers, and council of state. The constitution also specifies the country's formal alignment with the Soviet Union. The nation is divided into 15 administrative districts. The courts are controlled by the ministry of justice and the prosecutors.

History. At the end of World War II the Soviet Union stripped its German occupation zone of much of its industrial capacity. During the Cold War, Berlin became the focus of East-West tension. In 1948, the Communists blockaded West Berlin by shutting off all entry routes; for nearly a year all supplies from the West were airlifted to the city. The German Democratic Republic was established under Soviet auspices in 1949. A revolt by East German workers in 1953 was quelled by Soviet troops. The East German economy recovered strongly in the 1960s; the country became one of the world's ten leading industrial powers. In 1970, East and West Germany signed a basic treaty recognizing each government; since then relations between the two countries have improved and economic ties have developed. In the mid-1980s, although still closely allied with the Soviet Union, East Germany attempted to establish some political and economic ties with other western countries.

PROFILE

Official name: German Democratic Republic
Area: 41,768sq mi (108,179sq km)
Population: 16,850,000
Density: 403per sq mi (156per sq km)
Chief cities: East Berlin (capital); Leipzig; Dresden
Government: Communist
Religion (major): Protestantism
Language: German (official)
Monetary unit: Deutsche mark
Gross national product: $107,610,000,000
Per capita income: $4,360
Manufacturing (major products): chemicals, clothing, electrical equipment, iron and steel, heavy machinery, optical products, processed foods
Agriculture (major products): dairy products, potatoes, barley, oats, livestock, rye
Minerals (major): iron ore, copper, lignite, tin, potash
Trading partners (major): Soviet Union, Czechoslovakia, Poland, West Germany

Germany, West, officially the Federal Republic of Germany, a nation in central Europe. West Germany is the fourth-ranking industrial power in the world; it is also the most populous European nation outside the USSR. The area of West Germany is more than twice that of East Germany and has nearly four times the population. West Germany is closely allied with the nations of the West, both politically and economically. Its capital is Bonn.

Land and Economy. West Germany reaches from the Alps (S) to the North Sea. The Bavarian Alps, with many peaks reaching above 6,000ft (1,830m), are drained by the Danube. The South German Hills contain some of the country's most fertile farmlands and are drained by the Main and Neckar rivers. The major land region is the North German Plain, a broad low-lying area that is traversed by the Rhine, Ems, Weser, and Elbe rivers. West German agriculture provides about two-thirds of the nation's food requirements; food imports are substantial. The country is overwhelmingly industrial. The Ruhr Valley is the chief manufacturing region. The industrial establishment is especially notable for its vast steel works, automobile, electronics, chemical, and textile industries.

People. The West German population includes a variety of ethnic strains, but the two principal groups are the Nordic, or Teutonic, Germans of the N; and the Alpine type of the S. A wide variety of dialects are still in use throughout the country; the universal literary language is Middle High German. About half of all West Germans are Protestants, and nearly half are Roman Catholics. West Germans have one of the highest living standards in the world; over 80% of the population lives in urban communities.

Government. West Germany is a constitutional democracy. Parliament consists of two houses, the Bundestag (Federal Diet) and the Bundesrat (Federal Council). The Bundestag is the law-making body; its 496 members are elected by secret ballot to 4-year terms. This house also elects the chief executive of government, the chancellor. The Bundesrat, whose members are appointed by the 10 states, approves or rejects legislation passed by the Bundestag. The leading political parties in West Germany are the Christian Democratic Union, the Social Democratic party, and the Free Democratic party. West Germans 18 years old and older are entitled to vote.

History. Germany lay in ruins at the end of World War II, its cities devastated, its economic life brought to a halt. The invading Soviet, US, and British forces sought to eradicate Nazism; the country was divided into occupation zones, as was the city of Berlin. War criminals were tried at Nuremburg. The Cold War began with the Soviet blockade of Berlin (1948). The British, French, and US zones were united to form the West German nation (1949). For 10 years the economy had a 10% annual growth rate. West Germany rearmed and joined the North Atlantic Treaty Organization (NATO) in 1955. Konrad Adenauer was the country's first chancellor. Willy Brandt, who served as chancellor from 1969 to 1974 spearheading closer relations with East Germany under the policy of Ostpolitik, resigned over an espionage scandal. He was succeeded by Helmut Schmidt, who served until 1982, and faced problems resulting from a downturn in the economy, increased inflation, and a vocal anti-nuclear movement. He was replaced by Helmut Kohl, a Christian Democrat, under whom the economy began a slow recovery. US Pres. Reagan, amidst much controversy, attended ceremonies at a military cemetery in Bitburg, West Germany, to commemorate the 40th anniversary of the end of WWII.

PROFILE

Official name: Federal Republic of Germany
Area: 95,790sq mi (248,096sq km)
Population: 61,439,000
Density: 643per sq mi (248per sq km)
Chief cities: Bonn (capital); West Berlin, Hamburg, Munich, Cologne
Government: federal republic
Religion: Lutherans (over 50%); Roman Catholics (45%)
Language: German (official)
Monetary unit: Deutsche mark
Gross national product: $638,000,000,000
Per capita income: $11,000
Manufacturing (major products): iron and steel, chemicals, automobiles, electrical goods, tools, processed foods, cameras, scientific instruments
Agriculture (major products): livestock, grains, sugar beets, wines, fruits, vegetables
Minerals (major): coal, iron ore, potash
Trading partners (major): France, Italy, Great Britain, United States

Germicide, any substance for destroying disease-causing microorganisms. Germicides include antiseptics, disinfectants, and antibiotics.

Germination, growth of the plant embryo after the seed ripens and falls from parent. It may occur immediately or after a dormant period. To germinate, a seed or spore needs favorable temperatures and light conditions, moisture, and oxygen. The process begins with the rehydration of embryo protoplasm and production of amino acids and energy that produce embryo growth. Germination is completed when the root appears outside the seed coat.

Germiston, city in NE Republic of South Africa; site of world's largest gold refinery. Industries: chemicals, textiles, engineering. Pop. 132,273.

Gerona, city in NE Spain; capital of Gerona prov.; site of 14th-century Gothic cathedral, Romanesque cloister, 13th-century church. Industries: textiles, chemicals, electronic equipment, soap. Area: (prov.) 2,273sq mi (5,887sq km). Pop. (city) 50,338; (prov.) 414,397.

Geronimo (1829–1909), chief of the Chiricahua Apaches. He led his tribe in war against white settlers in Arizona for more than 10 years. The Apaches hid in the Sierra Madre Mountains between raids. In 1886 he surrendered his tribe to General Miles, and they were taken by way of Florida and Alabama to Ft. Sill, Okla., where they lived until 1913, when they were freed.

Gerry, Elbridge (1744–1814), US political figure and vice president (1813–14), b. Marblehead, Mass. Elected to the Massachusetts General Court (1772), he obtained supplies during the American Revolution and signed the Declaration of Independence and the Articles of Confederation. He refused to sign the Constitution until the Bill of Rights was added. Special envoy to France during the XYZ Affair (1797–98), he was governor of Massachusetts (1810–11) but gerrymandering led to his defeat in 1812. Elected vice president under James Madison, he died in office.

Gerrymandering, US political practice that permits the majority party in a state legislature to rearrange electoral districts for its own political advantage. Strong party districts are combined with weaker ones in such a way as to ensure the party a permanent majority. This political maneuver was named after Elbridge Gerry by his political opponents in 1811. During his second term as governor of Massachusetts his party rearranged the election districts in its favor in order to retain control of the state.

Gershom, in the Bible, eldest son of Moses and Zipporah. While traveling to Egypt, Zipporah circumcised Gershom to avert God's threat on Moses' life.

Gershwin, George (1898–1937), US composer, b. Brooklyn, N.Y. His popular songs and orchestral works contain elements of jazz and popular music. His best known orchestral works are *Rhapsody in Blue* (1923) for piano and orchestra, *An American in Paris* (1928), and *Piano Concerto in F* (1925). His masterpiece is the folk opera *Porgy and Bess* (1935). He also composed for films and Broadway shows. His *Of Thee I Sing* (1931) was the first musical comedy to win a Pulitzer Prize. His brother Ira Gershwin (1896–) won fame as his lyricist.

Gerson, Jean Charlier de (1363–1429), French theologian. He became chancellor of the University of Paris in 1395, but his greatest work was his effort to end the Great Western Schism (1378–1417) during which two, and later three, men claimed the title of pope. At the Council of Constance (1415) Gerson advocated the doctrine called *conciliarism:* the church in council has authority superior to the pope as an individual. The council arranged the end of the schism. *See also* Constance, Council of.

Gesellschaft, in sociology, ideal-type concept formulated by Ferdinand Toennies in 1887, denoting social systems based on large groups and indirect, impersonal relationships. Modern industrial societies and bureaucracies are often called Gesellschaft-like. *See also* Gemeinschaft.

Gesneria, mostly herbaceous, perennial plants of the family Gesneriaceae, native to tropical South America. Most species found today were first cultivated in greenhouses. These plants are tuberous and have ornamental, showy flowers that make them popular houseplants. Woody gesneriads also originated in South America and have showy flowers. *See also* African Violet; Episcia; Gloxinia.

Gestalt Psychology, viewpoint in psychology that stresses the importance of patterns or whole configurations in experience. Gestalt theory is most often ap-

West Germany

Geronimo

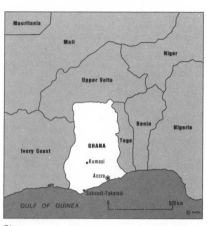

Ghana

plied to perception. People can "see" a complete picture even if certain fragments are missing. A melody has a total configuration to the human ear that is more than the sum of individual notes. Gestalt theory opposes studying behavior processes by analyzing their parts individually.

Gestapo, secret state police of Nazi Germany. Originally founded (1933) by Hermann Goering in Prussia, it soon became a national organization. It was taken over by Heinrich Himmler (1936–45) and became in effect a unit of the SS. With virtually unlimited powers, the Gestapo ran the Nazi concentration and extermination camps. *See also* Himmler, Heinrich.

Gestation, period of carrying young in uterus between fertilization and birth. Gestation periods are specific to species and range from 12 days (Virginia opossum) to 22 months (Indian elephant).

Gethsemane, in the New Testament, the garden where Jesus met with his disciples on the eve of his crucifixion. It was here Jesus was betrayed by Judas and arrested by the Romans. The Gospel of Luke locates it at the foot of Mount Olivet, east of Jerusalem. The exact spot has not been determined.

Gettysburg, borough in S Pennsylvania; seat of Adams co; scene of historic Civil War battle, the Gettysburg Campaign (1863), where Robert E. Lee and his Confederate troops were defeated by Union Army under George Meade; site of Gettysburg Address made by President Lincoln (Nov. 19, 1863), Gettysburg National Cemetery for Civil War victims, Gettysburg National Military Park, and farm of President Dwight D. Eisenhower. Industries: tourism, electrical equipment, shoes. Settled *c.* 1780; inc. 1806. Pop. (1980) 7,194.

Gettysburg Address (Nov. 19, 1863), Pres. Abraham Lincoln's speech at the dedication of the national cemetery on the Civil War battlefield site at Gettysburg, Penn. One of the most quoted of modern speeches, it is famous for its eloquence and brevity. The final sentence contains a phrase that has become a definition of democracy: "government of the people, by the people, for the people."
Following is the text of the Gettysburg Address.

THE GETTYSBURG ADDRESS

Fourscore and seven years ago our fathers brought forth on this continent a new nation, conceived in liberty, and dedicated to the proposition that all men are created equal.

Now we are engaged in a great civil war, testing whether that nation, or any nation so conceived and so dedicated, can long endure. We are met on a great battlefield of that war. We have come to dedicate a portion of that field as a final resting place for those who here gave their lives that that nation might live. It is altogether fitting and proper that we should do this.

But, in a larger sense, we cannot dedicate—we cannot consecrate—we cannot hallow—this ground. The brave men, living and dead, who struggled here, have consecrated it far above our poor power to add or detract. The world will little note, nor long remember what we say here, but it can never forget what they did here. It is for us the living, rather, to be dedicated here to the unfinished work which they who fought here have thus far so nobly advanced. It is rather for us to be here dedicated to the great task remaining before us—that from these honored dead we take increased devotion to that cause for which they gave the last full measure of devotion—that we here highly resolve that these dead shall not have died in vain—that this nation, under God, shall have a new birth of freedom—and that gov-

ernment of the people, by the people, for the people, shall not perish from the earth.

Geum, genus of perennial plants grown in Europe, Asia, and North America. They have orange, yellow, or red semidouble or double roselike flowers and pinnately divided leaves. The leaflet at the leaf tip is larger than the others. Height: 1.5–2ft (46–61cm). Family Rosaceae.

Geyser, a hot spring that erupts intermittently, ejecting superheated water and steam; the water occupies a natural crooked tube reaching deep into the earth. When the water at the bottom boils, the resulting steam pushes up, causing the rest to boil vigorously and fountain into the air. Most geysers occur in Iceland, New Zealand, and Yellowstone National Park.

Ghaghara (Gogra), navigable river, rises in Tibet, China, flows SE through Nepal meeting Ganges River in E India. Length: 570mi (918km).

Ghana, West African empire from the 4th to 13th centuries. It conducted an extensive gold and salt trade and exacted tribute from surrounding states. Its decline began with the Muslim invasions in the 11th century.

Ghana, Republic of, independent African nation, formerly the British Gold Coast colony. Ghana's 334-mi (538-km) coast was a 15th-century trading post for Europeans.
Land and economy. Ghana is located on the W coast of Africa just N of the equator, bounded on the N by Upper Volta, on the W by the Ivory Coast, on the E by Togo. Its lengthy coastline backs onto plains whose rivers and streams are passable only by canoe. Along the Ivory Coast frontier is a band of tropical forests (Ashanti) producing minerals and timber. Ghana's chief crop is cacao beans (70% of its exports). Industrial diamonds, bauxite, manganese are its chief minerals. With the completion of the mainly US-financed Akosombo hydroelectric project on the Volta River, Ghana has started its first heavy industry, an aluminum reduction plant.
People. Fifty languages still spoken today are derived from the tribes (Adansi, Akwamu, and Ga) who migrated down the Volta River in the 13th century. English is the official tongue. About 30% of the population is literate. About 45% of Ghanians are animists, followed by Christians (43%), and Muslims (12%).
Government. By the constitution of 1979 executive power is vested in the president, who is popularly elected to a four-year term. The parliament is composed of 140 seats for which elections are held every five years.
History. Named for a West African empire, Ghana's first contact with Europe came in 1482 when the Portuguese landed and built a trading base. An English trading company, formed about 1672, was taken over by the British government, which ruled until 1951, when a constitution was adopted, and Kwame Nkrumah was elected prime minister. In 1956, UN action ended Britain's trusteeship over Togoland. It merged with Ghana and on March 6, 1957, became a completely independent state within the commonwealth. Nkrumah was given dictatorial powers in 1964 and declared Ghana a socialist state with one legal party. In 1966 a coup ousted his regime, calling it corrupt and oppressive. Free elections were held in 1969; however, a 1972 bloodless coup put army Col. Ignatius K. Acheampong in power. Acheampong was ousted in a bloodless coup in 1978 by Lt. Gen. Frederick Akuffo, who was in turn removed the following year by Flight Lt. Jerry Rawlings. Acheampong and Akuffo were executed, and Rawlings oversaw previously scheduled elections to return the country to civilian rule, in which Dr. Hilla Li-

mann was elected. After Limann was ousted in 1981, a council of seven, headed by Rawlings, was established (1982). Several attempts were made to oust Rawlings, but he remained in control of the government.

PROFILE

Official name: Republic of Ghana
Area: 92,099sq mi (238,280sq km)
Population: 11,300,000
   Density: 123 per sq mi (47 per sq km)
Chief cities: Accra (capital); Kumasi
Government: Republic
Religion: animist (major), Christian, Muslim
Language: English (official)
Monetary unit: new cedi
Gross national product: $10,100,000,000
Per capita income: $380
Industries (major products): wood products, cement, rubber
Agriculture (major products): cacao, corn, cassava, nuts, sweet potatoes, wood
Minerals (major): bauxite, industrial diamonds, gold, manganese
Trading partners (major): United Kingdom, United States, Japan, European Common Market

Ghats, two mountain systems in S India; the Western Ghats extends from the Tapti River to Cape Comorin and forms the W edge of Deccan Plateau; the Eastern Ghats extends from the Mahanadi River to the Nilgiri Hills and forms the E edge of Deccan Plateau. Length: (Western) 1,000mi (1,610km); (Eastern) 900mi (1,450km). Height: (Western) 3,000–5,000ft (915–1525m); (Eastern) 2,000ft (610m). Highest peak is Anai Mundi: 8,841 ft (2,697m).

Ghent (Gent or Gand), city in NW central Belgium, 31mi (50km) NW of Brussels; capital of East Flanders prov.; major cloth center in 13th century; site of signing of treaties of Pacification of Ghent (1576) and, in 1814, to end War of 1812 and establish freedom of the seas; besieged and occupied by Germans in WWI and WWII. Industries: flower seeds, bulbs, metallurgy. Pop. 142,-551.

Ghent, Treaty of (1814), treaty between the United States and Great Britain that ended the War of 1812. With neither side making major concessions, the Belgian document was essentially an agreement to end hostilities and to restore prewar boundaries.

Ghetto, section of a city inhabited almost exclusively by one ethnic group. The term originated in Europe, designating a separate area of a city for Jews. The first compulsory ghettos were in Spain and Portugal in the late 14th century. Characterized by homogeneity, cultural cohesion, shared economic conditions, and exclusivity, ghettos are often founded in religious, racial, or cultural heritages. Ghettos also may generate alternate life styles that deviate from those of the larger society.

Ghibellines, pro-imperial political faction in Italy during the Middle Ages, opposed to the pro-papal Guelphs. The name Ghibelline derived from a castle, Waiblingen, belonging to the Holy Roman imperial family, the Hohenstaufens; but, during the struggles that occurred in north and central Italy between Emperor Frederick II and the popes (mid-13th century), the term came to designate those in the imperial camp.

Ghiberti, Lorenzo (1378–1455), Italian sculptor, goldsmith, architect, painter, and writer. He made two of the three huge, richly gilded bronze doors for the Baptistry in Florence, known as the Doors of Paradise. On the first (1403–24) he depicted 28 New Testament scenes. For the second (1425–47) he was allowed to use his own judgment and created his masterpiece; he chose 10 scenes from the Old Testament, each one appearing like a picture in a frame, with the plane of the background as the sky or ground. A major transitional figure between the late Gothic and Renaissance worlds, he also designed the stained-glass windows for the Duomo in Florence and wrote the first artist's autobiography.

Ghirlandaio, Domenico (1449–94), Italian painter. One of the most prolific Italian fresco painters in 15th-century Florence, he epitomized the trend toward realism of figures, settings, landscapes, and detail. He worked on the Sistine Chapel with Botticelli and others, his major contribution being the *Calling of the First Apostles.* Michelangelo was an apprentice in his large workshop.

Ghost Crab, or sand crab, amphibious crab found worldwide. They live on sandy beaches and mud flats and are relatively independent of water when mature. Their compact body is protectively colored and fast moving. Width: to 2in (5cm). Family Ocypodidae; genus *Ocypode. See also* Crab; Crustacean.

Ghost Flower. *See* Indian Pipe.

Ghost Shark. *See* Chimaera.

Giacometti, Alberto (1901–66), Swiss sculptor and painter. During the 1930s he produced surrealist sculpture and during the 40s and 50s he produced his greatest works—emaciated, dreamlike figures, built of plaster of Paris on a wire foundation. His paintings and drawings are more representational, but their gray coloring and agitated brushwork give them the same visionary quality. *See also* Surrealism.

Giant Grouper. *See* Jewfish.

Giant Panda, large bearlike mammal of China, a member of the raccoon family. Covered with thick, woolly, white fur, it has a black nose, and brownish-black eyepatches, ears, legs, and shoulder band. Primarily vegetarians, they may eat fish or small rodents. A popular though rare zoo animal, it bears cubs in January but is hard to breed in captivity. Height: 4–5ft (1.2–1.5m) at shoulder; weight: 250lb (114kg). Family Procyonidae; species *Ailuropoda melanoleuca. See also* Panda.

Giant's Causeway, promontory in Northern Ireland, on N coast of Antrim; formed by columnar basalt. It consists of several thousand pillars, mainly hexagonal, of varying height.

Giant Schnauzer, cattle dog (working group) bred in Württemberg and Bavaria in Germany. A loyal, reliable dog used for police work in Germany, it has a rectangular, elongated head; high-set, V-shaped ears that can be cropped; a strong, compact body; long, muscular legs; and high-set, docked tail. The hard, wiry coat, which is either solid black or pepper and salt, features a coarse topknot, beard, and eyebrows. Average size: 21.5–25.5in (54.5–65cm) high at shoulder; 65–78lb (29–35kg). *See also* Working Dog.

Giant Star, star belonging to a luminosity class midway between main-sequence stars and supergiants. They lie directly above the main sequence on the Hertzsprung-Russell diagram and are characterized by large dimensions, high luminosity, and low density. Giants are found throughout the entire surface-temperature range. Those of spectral type G-M (the red giants) contrast with corresponding dwarfs of the main sequence.

Giap, Vo Nguyen (1912–), Vietnamese general and minister of defense. A successful practitioner of modern guerrilla warfare, he led the Viet Minh forces that drove the Japanese out of Vietnam in 1945 and decisively defeated the French at Dien Bien Phu (1954). He later commanded North Vietnamese forces in the Vietnam War of the 1960s and 1970s, during which he organized the 1968 Tet offensive. When Vietnam was unified, he served as defense minister (1976–80) and was a member of the Politburo.

Gibberellin, organic compound that stimulates stem elongation, fruit and flower formation, dormancy, and plant response to light and temperature. Originally isolated from the fungus *Gibberella fujikuroi,* it may interact with some auxins.

Gibbon, Edward (1737–94), English historian. Author of one of the great classics of history, *The History of the Decline and Fall of the Roman Empire* (6 vols., 1776–88); he displayed such a sense of the sweep and continuity of history that his first volume achieved immediate success. The succeeding five volumes, adding to his acclaim, carried the history to its natural conclusion, the fall of Constantinople in 1453. Of independent means, Gibbon traveled widely during his lifetime. He decided to write his great history in 1764 while visiting the Forum in Rome.

Gibbon, small, slender, long-limbed arboreal ape living in SE Asian and East Indies forests. They have shaggy brown, black, or silvery gray coats. Most agile of all tree-living mammals, they travel by swinging from branch to branch with their arms. Height: to 3ft (91.5cm); weight: 11–28lb (5–13kg). Species include the siamang *Hylobates syndactalus.*

Gibbons v. Ogden (1824), first US Supreme Court decision dealing with the commerce clause of the Constitution. The Court's broad definition of the word "commerce" is primarily responsible for the extensive power of the federal government to regulate interstate activity.

Gibraltar, town at NW end of Rock of Gibraltar, between Mediterranean Sea and Atlantic Ocean; a British crown colony. One of the Pillars of Hercules, the colony is a free port and military fortress. Taken from Spain by British 1704, it was formally ceded to Britain by Treaty of Utrecht (1713); Spain has made many attempts to reclaim it; in a 1967 UN-supervised referendum, residents reaffirmed allegiance to Britain. During WWI and WWII it served as a key naval station; economy depends on military installations, port dues, and tourism. Communications with mainland Spain, severed in 1969, were restored in 1981. Area: 2.5sq mi (6.5sq km). Pop. 29,934.

Gibson, Charles Dana (1867–1944), US illustrator, b. Roxbury, Mass. Noted for his illustrations of the Gibson Girl. His books of illustration include *The Education of Mr. Pipp* (1899), *The Americans* (1900), *The Social Ladder* (1902), and *The Gibson Book* (1906).

Gide, André (1869–1951), French novelist, playwright, and critic. He rejected his Protestant upbringing and was regarded as a disturbing influence on youth because of his controversial views. His works *The Immoralist* (1902) and *The Counterfeiters* (1926) show a parallel search for spiritual truth and liberation of the individual. *The Journals of André Gide* (4 vols., 1947–51) was an autobiographical work. He was an editor of the *Nouvelle Revue française* and was awarded the Nobel Prize for literature in 1947.

Gideon, biblical judge, Israelite hero, and father of Abimelech. Called by an angel of God, he destroyed the altar of Baal. After a victorious attack on the Midianite camp, with only 300 soldiers, he refused to be made king.

Gideon v. Wainwright (1963), landmark US Supreme Court decision overruling *Betts v. Brady* (1942). The court held that representation by an attorney is a constitutional necessity in all criminal trials. This decision led to the establishment of legal aid programs for indigents and formed the foundation for the Escobedo and Miranda decisions. *See also* Escobedo v. Illinois (1964).

Gielgud, Sir Arthur John (1904–), British stage actor whose consistently excellent performances in both modern and classical roles after 1921 established him as one of the century's finest actors. He played almost every major Shakespearian role and his outstanding Hamlet, first performed in 1929, delighted audiences on more than 500 occasions. Other major appearances were made in *The Importance of Being Earnest* (1939), *The Lady's Not For Burning* (1948), and *The Cherry Orchard* (1954).

Gifu, city in Honshu, Japan, on Kiso River; capital of Gifu prefecture; former medieval castle town, taken in 1564 by Oda Nobunaga; center of civil struggles in 17th century; site of Institute of Nawa Entomology (1896). Industries: tourism, chemicals, automobiles, textiles, paper, sake, lead, woodworking, cutlery. Pop. 409,000.

Gigantism, or giantism, generalized over-growth of an individual, believed to be caused by pituitary disturbance or by pre-pubescent overproduction of the growth hormone. The body may remain in proportion or have distorted extremities and head. *See also* Acromegaly.

Gijón, seaport city in N Spain, on the Bay of Biscay; of Roman origin, it was recaptured from Moors by Christians in early 8th century; refuge port for defeated Spanish Armanda (1588); site of ancient Roman baths, 15th-century church; summer resort. Industries: glass, food, tobacco, steel, iron, chemicals. Pop. 187,612.

Gila Monster, sluggish, poisonous lizard found in deserts, near water, of SW United States and N Mexico. It has a stout body, massive head, fat tail, and beadlike scales of orange-pink, yellow, and black. Nocturnal, it eats small mammals and eggs. Length: to 24in (61cm). Family Helodermatidae; species *Heloderma suspectum. See also* Lizard.

Gila River, river in W New Mexico; flows W across Arizona to the Colorado River at Yuma. Length: 630mi (1,014km).

Gilbert, (Sir) Humphrey (1539?–83), Canadian explorer. A brilliant navigator, Gilbert wrote a "Discourse" on the Northwest Passage (1576) and sailed to Canada from his native England in 1578 and 1583. He established the first British colony in North America at St. John's, Newfoundland (1583). Gilbert used his private means in searching for a passage to the Pacific.

Gilbert, William (1544–1603), English physicist and physician to Queen Elizabeth I. Considered the "father of electricity," his *De Magnete, Magneticisque Corporibus* (1600) laid the foundation for the scientific study of magnetism. He was the first to recognize terrestrial magnetism and concluded that a type of magnetism keeps the planets in their orbits. He coined the terms electricity, magnetic pole, electric attraction, and electric force. The C.G.S. unit of magnetomotive force is named the gilbert in his honor.

Gilbert, (Sir) William Schwenck (1836–1911), English librettist and playwright. He collaborated with Sir Arthur Sullivan on an immensely successful series of 14 comic operas frequently performed by D'Oyly Carte's company. His lyrics reveal an exuberant, often macabre humor and a talent for inventive rhymes. Gilbert and Sullivan works include *H.M.S. Pinafore* (1878), *The Pirates of Penzance* (1879), *The Mikado* (1885), and *The Yeomen of the Guard* (1888).

Gilbert Islands, former name of Kiribati. *See* Kiribati.

Gilbert of Sempringham, Saint (*c.*1083–1189), English Roman Catholic priest who founded the Gilbertines, the only monastic order of exclusively English origin. He was born in Lincolnshire, the son of a Norman knight. He began the order for women only, but it grew to have double monasteries, with houses for monks and nuns.

Gil Blas (1715–35), picaresque novel in four volumes by Alain René Le Sage. Gil Blas, the innocent hero, seeks his fortune and is corrupted by the people and adventures he encounters. Finally, his good intentions triumph. The speed and wit of the narrative make it Le Sage's masterpiece.

Gilboa, Mount, mountain ridge in NE Israel, on Esdraelon plain; scene of battle in which King Saul was defeated by Philistines and killed himself. Length: 10mi (16km). Height: 1,630ft (497m).

Gilded Age, period after the Civil War when wealth and political power received increased public attention. The period also was characterized by a good deal of corruption and speculation. The term came from the novel *The Gilded Age* (1873) by Mark Twain and Charles Dudley Warner.

Gilead, mountainous region in Jordan, on Jordan River, between Dead Sea and Sea of Galilee; traditional reconciliation place of Jacob and Laban, birthplace of the prophet Elijah, and place where Jephthah was made a judge of Israel.

Gilgamesh Epic, an anonymous Babylonian epic based on early Sumerian sources. It appeared in two versions: the first written *c.*1800 BC; the second, *c.*1200 BC. The epic recounts the struggles of Gilgamesh, mythic king of Uruk, against his enemies. It deals with such themes as the transitory nature of human existence, the value of friendship, and the importance of heroes.

Gills, the breathing organs of aquatic animals through which the animals obtain oxygen from the water. Gills contain many small blood vessels called gill capillaries. As water flows over the gills, the oxygen diffuses into the capillaries and is carried to larger blood vessels. Waste products carried back to the gills by the blood diffuse out through the gills into the water. Gills are found in echinoderms, mollusks, aquatic arthropods, fishes, and larval forms of amphibians. *See also* Gill Slits.

Ginger, herbaceous, perennial plant native to tropical E Asia and Indonesia and grown commercially in Florida. It has fat, tuberous roots and yellow-green flowers with purple edges spotted with yellow. The

André Gide

Ginseng

Giorgione: painting in oil

kitchen spice is made from the tubers of *Zingiber officinale*. Family Zingiberaceae. *See also* Cardamom.

Gingivitis, inflammatory disease of the gums that makes them tender and swollen and leads to their bleeding easily. In severe cases ulceration and fever may develop. It is believed that poor diet, bad tooth alignment, and faulty dentures predispose to infections.

Ginkgo, or gingko, maidenhair tree, oldest extant species of tree, native to temperate regions of China, Korea, and Japan. Dating from the Triassic Period most species were destroyed during the Ice Age. A good city tree, it was introduced in the United States in 1784. It has fan-shaped leaves and small, foul-smelling fruit with edible, nutlike seeds. Height: to 120ft (37m). Family Ginkgoaceae; species *Ginkgo biloba*.

Gin Rummy, two-handed card game with a standard deck. This game evolved from rummy and differs only in the scoring and the number of cards dealt each player (10). In knock rummy, a player may elect to go out if the unmatched cards in his hand total 10 points or less. Whichever player has the fewest number of points wins the hand. *See also* Rummy.

Ginsberg, Allen (1926–), US author, b. Newark. The major writer of the Beat Generation, his work is influenced by his interest in Zen Buddhism and meditation and by the use of drugs. His most famous poems are "Howl" (1956), a condemnation of American society, and "Kaddish for Naomi Ginsberg (1894–1956)" (1961), a lament for his mother, who became insane. *See also* Beat Generation.

Ginseng, two perennial plants from North America and E Asia. Both have yellow-green flowers and 6–9 in (15–41 cm) leaves. The dried tuberous roots are valued for use in Chinese traditional medicine. Height: to 18in (46cm). Family Araliaceae; species Chinese *Panax schinseng* and North American *Panax quinquefolius*.

Giorgione, Il (*c*.1475–1511), Italian painter, b. Giorgio Barbarelli. One of the major painters of the Venetian High Renaissance, he was a pupil of Bellini. He broke away from his teacher's style and evolved his own mysterious, romantic one creating a unity of figures and landscape. His "Tempest" (*c*.1507, Academy, Venice), puzzling to his contemporaries, is the first landscape of mood. Only a small number of the paintings attributed to him (among them the Castelfranco "Madonna" and "Laura") are universally accepted as his, and many of the works he undoubtedly began were finished by Titian and Sebastiano del Piombo, whom he influenced greatly.

Giotto (*c*.1266–1337), Italian painter. The father of all modern painting, he was the first artist to create visually and psychologically convincing human forms, and the first since the Greeks to represent three dimensional form and space. He revolutionized art completely, arranging his dramatic, individualized figures realistically in relation both to each other and to their setting. His knowledge of anatomy and perspective was inaccurate, but through the use of light and shadow he gave his figures depth that cut into the space around them. His greatest achievement was the fresco cycle in the Arena Chapel at Padua (*c*.1305), a serenely dramatic, simple rendering of 38 scenes from the life of Joachim and Anna, the Virgin Mary, and Christ. He was also the architect of the Campanile (belltower) of the Duomo in Florence; just begun at his death, its 26 bas-relief scenes begin with the creation

of man and end with the depiction of his most advanced achievements.

Giovanni di Paolo (1403–83), Italian painter. He was one of the most influential and prolific Sienese painters of the 15th century. His style is distinctive for the languid grace of the figures, who often have wistful, even ugly faces; in his later work the forms are heavier and distorted, and the colors darker.

Giraffe, even-toed, hoofed, cud-chewing mammal inhabiting African savannas. The tallest existing mammal, it has a long neck, long legs and blotched coloring. Like other mammals, it has only seven neck vertebrae. The unique horns of both sexes are two to four bony knobs covered with skin; sometimes a fifth knob is present between the eyes. Though shy, they live in large herds. They mate in summer. The gestation period is 15 months and a single calf is born. Able to outrun a horse, its maximum speed is 28mph (45kmph). Height: to 18ft (5.5m); weight: to 1.5ton (1,350kg). Family Giraffidae; species *Giraffa camelopardalis*. *See also* Artiodactyla; Ruminant.

Girl Scouts, an organization for girls. Its purpose is to inspire girls to develop personal values and to share planned activities. There are a wide variety of projects in social action, environmental action, youth leadership, career exploration, and community service. It was founded in Savannah, Ga., by Juliette Gordon Low in 1912 and was modeled after the Boy Scouts and Britain's Girl Guides. Its publications include *American Girl*, *Brownie Reader*, and *Girl Scout Leader*. Membership: about 3,000,000.

Girondists, also **Girondins,** political organization of the French Revolution that began with legislators from Gironde. The bourgeois Girondists advocated a mild republicanism and tried to prevent the execution of Louis XVI. They managed to start a war with Austria, for the inspiration of national unity, but conflicted increasingly with the Jacobins and lost their leaders to the guillotine in a Parisian revolt in 1793.

Giscard d'Estaing, Valéry (1926–), president of France (1974–81). Giscard first entered the ministry of finance in 1949. In 1956 he was elected to parliament. He served as minister of finance in the cabinets of Debré and Pompidou (1962–66). His parliamentary group represented the right wing of the Gaullist majority. In the 1974 presidential elections, he narrowly defeated a coalition of the Communist and Socialist parties. He was defeated in 1981 by François Mitterrand.

Gitlow v. New York (1925), US Supreme Court case in which the court, upholding a conviction for publication of a Communist pamphlet, held that the First Amendment's freedom of speech provisions were protected against incursions by the individual states.

Giza (Al-Jizah), city in N Egypt, on W bank of Nile River; suburb of Cairo; capital of Giza governorate; Great Sphinx and pyramid of Khufu (Cheops) are nearby; site of University of Cairo (1908). Industries: motion pictures, textiles, cigarettes, footwear, tourism. Pop. 345,261.

Glacier, a large mass of ice, consisting mainly of recrystallized snow, which moves slowly by creeping downslope or outward in all directions due to the stress of its own weight; it survives from year to year. Glaciers terminate where the rate of loss of ice by melting and ablation is equal to the forward advance of the glacier. There are three main types: mountain or valley glaciers, piedmont glaciers, and ice sheets and ice caps.

Glacier National Park, park in NW Montana along the continental divide in the Rocky Mts; adjoins Waterton Lakes National Park in SW Alberta, Canada; together they form the Waterton-Glacier International Peace Park. Est. 1932. It is characterized by many glaciers, glacier-fed lakes, mountains, forests, and waterfalls. A variety of animal and plant life are found in this pristine wilderness. Area: 1,013,100acres (410,306hectares). Est. 1910. *See also* Waterton Lakes National Park.

Glaciology, study of glaciers. A glacier is a moving ice mass made up of snow and ice. They may be classified by climate into polar and temperate, both built up by snowfall and decreased by melting. The movement of the ice-river creates strains both within itself and on the terrain it moves over. Variation of glaciation at different historic periods is a subdivision of glaciology. *See also* Glacier; Historical Geology.

Gladiators. Perhaps originally an Etrurian custom, gladiatorial combats were first recorded at Rome in 264 BC. Gladiators were generally prisoners of war, slaves, or condemned prisoners, who were trained to fight one another or wild beasts in public arenas. The gladiator who lost a battle was usually killed, though onlookers sometimes waved their handkerchiefs as a signal that they wished his life to be spared. Abolished by Constantine I in AD 325, the combats persisted into the 5th century.

Gladiolus, genus of 300 species of flowering plants native to Europe and Africa and widely cultivated. They grow from a corm that may be planted in early spring to a flowering spike of funnel-shaped flowers and tall, swordlike leaves. Cultivated hybrid species are various colors. Height: to 3ft (0.9m). Family Iridaceae. *See also* Iris.

Gladstone, William E(wart) (1809–98), English political figure. He entered Parliament as a Tory in 1832 and served as president of the Board of Trade in Sir Robert Peel's cabinet (1843–45). Thereafter he held several cabinet posts, serving most impressively as chancellor of the exchequer. He joined the Liberal party in 1859 and became its leader in 1867. He was prime minister four times (1868–74, 1880–85, 1886, 1892–94). A social reformer and Christian moralist, his programs included disestablishment of the Church of Ireland (1869) so that Irish Catholics would no longer have to support a church to which they did not belong, the Irish Land Act (1870), which gave the Irish tenant farmers some security, the Elementary Education Act (1870), introduction of the secret ballot, and reorganization of the judiciary. He denounced the Turkish atrocities in Bulgaria (1875) and achieved a third parliamentary Reform Act (1884). His attempts to reform Irish government included the Land Bill of 1881 and the advocacy of the Irish Home Rule Bill (defeated in 1886 and 1893), which led to his government's defeat in 1886 and 1894 and shattered the Liberal party.

Gland. *See* Endocrine System; Hormones.

Glanders, or equinia, farcy, contagious disease of horses, donkeys, and mules attacking the mucous membranes and lymphatic systems. The organism *Malleomyces mallei* enters the digestive tract, gets into the blood, traveling to the lungs and skin, resulting in sticky nasal emissions, fever, vomiting, and ulcers. It is cured by antibiotics. Infection to humans and premises can occur from exposure to broken skin of affected animals.

Glasgow, city in SW central Scotland; largest city in Scotland. Situated on both banks of the Clyde River, 20mi (32km) from its mouth, it is a major port accessible to ocean-going ships; site of University of Glasgow (1451), Royal College of Science and Technology (1796 as Anderson's Institution), Art Gallery and Museum (1901), cathedral (1197–1457), and Provand's Lordship, a museum that is oldest house in Glasgow (1470). Industries: shipbuilding, heavy engineering, flour milling, brewing, distilling, textiles, tobacco, chemicals, printing. Pop. 880,617.

Glass and Glassware, an amorphous substance made by melting together silica and smaller proportions of alkali with a base, such as lime or lead oxide, which hardens the mixture and lowers its temperature, resulting in its fusion without crystallization. Glass melts slowly and can be worked only while it remains warm and supple. It must be cooled gradually to prevent breakage. Fused silica is the simplest glass and is used when stability through changing temperatures is needed. Soda-lime glass is used in the manufacture of bottles and drinking glasses. Flint glass, which is heavy and refracts light well, is used in lenses and prisms.

Glass objects, especially jewelry and small containers, were found in Egypt as early as 2500 BC. Glass figurines and vessels were common in the Middle East during the 8th and 7th centuries BC and also in Greece. Probably around the 1st century AD in Syria, the blowing pipe was discovered and revolutionized the glassmaking industry by allowing glassware to be mass produced in a variety of thinness and size. The 12th through the 14th centuries saw a highly developed industry producing enamel Islamic mosque lamps in Syria and Egypt. During the 13th century Venice rose to prominence as a glassmaking center of delicate, thin, colored glass. Crystal glass, which was strong enough to be engraved, was produced in Bohemia. In the late 17th century heavy, lead glass was developed in England. During the 19th century, cut glass and pressed glass were fashionable in the United States. Scandinavia has been a leader in the glassmaking industry in the 20th century, both in industrial and decorative design.

Glass Blowing, handcraft. A hollow iron blowpipe, 4–5 feet (1.2–1.5 meters) long, is dipped into molten glass to form a bubble from which any variety of objects are formed by squeezing, stretching, twirling, reheating, or cutting. When the final design is achieved, it is broken from the pipe. The glass can also be blown into iron molds. In the commercial production of glass-blown products, a machine is used.

Glass Fish, formerly called ambassid, freshwater fish found in shallow waters of N India. A favorite aquarium fish, it has a translucent body. Length: to 2in (5.1cm). Family Centropomidae; species includes *Chanda ranga.*

Glass Harmonica, antique musical instrument improved by Benjamin Franklin (1763) and used by Mozart (1791) and Beethoven (1814). Delicate sounds are produced by fingertips touching glass saucers in graduated rank, revolving in water on a horizontal, pedal-operated spindle.

Glass Snake, or glass lizard, legless lizard found in North America, Eurasia, and Africa. It is cylindrical with a groove along each side and is chiefly brown or green, though some are striped. It has moveable eyelids. Length: 24–48in (61–122cm). Family Anguinidae; genus *Ophisaurus. See also* Lizard.

Glasswort, fleshy plant found in salt marshes throughout temperate regions of the Northern Hemisphere. It has succulent stems, and inconspicuous leaves and flowers. Family Chenopodiaceae; genera *Salicornia* and *Salsola.*

Glastonbury, market town in SW England, on Brue River, 22mi (35km) SW of Bath. According to legend, it was site of first Christian church in England, founded by Joseph of Arimathea, and burial place of King Arthur. Industries: tanning, footwear. Pop. 6,571.

Glauber, Johann Rudolf (1604–68), German chemist and physician. He was the first to realize that an acid reacts with a base to form a salt. He prepared hydrochloric acid, sodium sulfate (known as Glauber's salt), and tartar emetic.

Glaucoma, group of eye diseases characterized by increasing pressure of fluid within the eye leading to progressive loss of vision. Causes are unknown although heredity seems to be a factor. It occurs most frequently in patients over 40 and is accompanied by need for frequent changes in corrective lenses, mild headache, and impaired ability to adapt to the dark.

Glaucus, the name of several figures in Greek mythology. Pontius Glaucus was a sea divinity. Once a fisherman, he was changed into a god and endowed with the gift of prophecy. Glaucus of Potniae was the son of the king of Thebes (Sisyphus) by Merope, and father of the Trojan war hero Bellerophon.

Gleizes, Albert (Léon) (1881–1953), French painter and writer. Through his writings, he was the chief disseminator of cubist ideas. In 1911 he exhibited with the first cubist group. In 1912 he and Jean Metzinger published the influential *On Cubism.* By 1919 his paintings had become religious in tone, combining Catholic themes with cubist ideas. *See also* Cubism.

Glencoe, Massacre of, in Scotland the killing of the MacDonalds on Feb. 13, 1692, for a technical failure to declare allegiance to the new British king, William III. About 40 died in the surprise attack by Campbell soldiers under orders of Sir John Dalrymple, the king's secretary of state.

Glendale, town in SW central Arizona, 8mi (13km) NW of Phoenix. Industries: agriculture, lettuce, melons, truck crops. Founded 1892; inc. 1910. Pop. (1980) 96,988.

Glendale, city in S California, 6mi (10km) N of Los Angeles; first land grant from Spain in California (1784). Industries: defense and aerospace plants; motion pictures. Inc. 1906. Pop. (1980) 139,060.

Glendower, Owen. *See* Owen Glendower.

Glenn, John Herschel, Jr. (1921–), US astronaut, b. Cambridge, Ohio. He piloted the first US orbiting spacecraft, Friendship 7, on Feb. 20, 1962 (3 orbits). He co-authored *We Seven* (1962) and wrote *P.S., I Listened to Your Heartbeat.* He was elected to the US Senate from Ohio (1972).

Glider, a winged aircraft with no power source of its own, which sustains flight through the controlled loss of altitude. A glider gains altitude only by descending in upward-moving air, such as thermal updrafts, that is, rising faster than the glider's rate of descent. It is capable of virtually all the maneuvers of a powered aircraft.

Glinka, Mikhail (1803–57), Russian composer, important as the founder of nationalism in Russian opera and the first Russian composer to receive acclaim outside his own country. His two operas, *A Life for the Tsar* (1836) and *Russlan and Ludmilla* (1842), inspired the composers who called themselves the "Russian Five." Late in his life he lived in Italy and Spain and wrote songs and orchestral music including the *Jota Aragonesa.*

Gliwice, city in SW Poland, 14mi (23km) W of Katowice. Chartered 1276, city became part of Prussia 1742, and part of Poland by Potsdam Conference 1945. Industries: coal mining, smelting, chemicals. Pop. 197,000.

Globeflower, perennial flowering plant native to colder parts of the Northern Hemisphere. The yellow sepals form large blossoms and buttercuplike leaves surround the stem. The European globeflower *(Trollius europaeus)* is cultivated in the United States and has yellow or orange globular blooms. There are about 15 species. Family Ranunculaceae.

Globe Theatre, Elizabethan public theater most closely associated with Shakespeare's career. Built in 1598 and patterned after the 16th-century playhouses, it had polygonal walls with a roof over the stage and galleries. It was built by the Chamberlain Company of which Shakespeare was an original shareholder. Destroyed by fire in 1613, it was rebuilt in 1614 but was permanently closed down by the Puritans in 1644.

Globigerina, one-celled genus of marine protozoa whose empty shells are an important component of ocean floor ooze. Its shell is spiralled into a lumpy sphere with needlelike extensions. *See also* Foraminfera.

Globular Cluster. *See* Cluster, Stellar.

Globulins, a complex mixture of globular proteins found in the blood serum, some of which serve as carriers of lipids, hormones, and inorganic ions. The immunoglobulins are included in this general category.

Glochidium, bivalve larva of freshwater clam. It develops from fertilized eggs in the gills of the female and is expelled into the water where it must become parasitic on fish to survive. When it develops into a young clam, it drops to the bottom and grows to adult size.

Glockenspiel, musical percussion instrument with set of steel bars on horizontal frame, tuned to chromatic scale, and played with two hammers. It is called a celeste when played from a keyboard, as in Mozart's *The Magic Flute* (1791). The bell-lyra is a portable glockenspiel for marching bands.

Glomerulonephritis, kidney disease apparently related to streptococcal infection. Chronic forms may be fatal.

Glorious Revolution (1688–89), events resulting in the deposition of James II of England (1685–88). The birth (1688) of a son to James, a Catholic convert, led to fears in England of a Catholic heir to the throne. Tories and Whigs united in inviting William of Orange, Dutch Protestant husband of Mary, daughter of James, to remove James. William landed (1688), and James fled to France. In 1689 Parliament invited William and Mary to rule England jointly. The Declaration of Rights and Bill of Rights (1689) barred Catholic succession to the throne and demonstrated Parliament's supremacy over the crown.

Glottis, aperture between the vocal cords at the lower end of the pharynx. It opens into the trachea.

Gloucester, Gilbert de Clare, 8th Earl of (1243–95), English noble. He joined Simon de Montfort (1263), then siding with Prince Edward, he defeated de Montfort at Gresham (1265). He fought the Welsh (1276–83), and married Edward I's daughter, Joan (1290).

Gloucester, Humphrey, Duke of (1391–1447), English noble and literary patron, youngest son of Henry IV. He fought at Agincourt (1415) and was regent of England (1420–21). He became protector (1422–29) under his brother Bedford during Henry VI's minority. His marriage (1422) to Jacqueline of Hainault was annulled (1428) and her lands lost to Burgundy. He quarreled with his uncle, Henry Beaufort, refusing to recognize him as papal legate and opposing his policy of peace with the French. Arrested for high treason (1447), he died in custody.

Gloucester, Richard de Clare, 7th Earl of (1222–62), English noble. He was sent as envoy to Scotland (1255) and Germany (1256). Defeated by the Welsh (1257), he joined Simon de Montfort, but quarreled with him (1259), and with Prince Edward (1261).

Gloucester, Robert, Earl of (died 1147), illegitimate son of Henry I of England. He joined his half-sister Matilda in invading England (1139) and captured Stephen of England (1141), but failed in his claims for the English throne.

Gloucester, Thomas of Woodstock, Duke of (1355–97), English noble, youngest son of Edward III, brother of John of Gaunt. After unsuccessful campaigns in Brittany and Essex (1380–81), he led the lords appellant against his nephew Richard II in 1386, but was arrested in 1397, and probably murdered.

Gloucester, city in England, on the Severn River; river port and market town; seat of Gloucestershire. Industries: timber, grain, matches, toys, aircraft components. Pop. 90,700.

Glowworm, luminous firefly larva or a wingless adult female firefly. *See also* Firefly.

Gloxinia, herbaceous plant with tuberous roots and short stems, native to South America. *Sinningia speciosa* (common gloxinia) has elongated, bell-shaped flowers ranging from purple to violet, sometimes with red or white variations. Family Gesneriaceae. *See also* Gesneria.

Glubb, (Sir) John Bagot (1897–1986), British commander of Jordan's Arab Legion, known as Glubb Pasha. After World War I he helped the British oversee Palestine and Trans-Jordan but resigned to join the Arab Legion, which kept order among the tribes. In 1948 he created a Palestinian force against Israel. Hussein I of Jordan dismissed him (1956) because of anti-British feeling in the Middle East. Among his books are *Story of the Arab Legion* (1948) and *Syria, Lebanon, and Jordan* (1967).

Glucagon, protein hormone secreted by the alpha cells of the endocrine pancreas. It helps regulate blood sugar by raising blood glucose levels. *See also* Insulin.

Gluck, Christoph Willibald von (1714–87), German operatic composer who studied in Italy and Vienna. After composing his early operas in the Italian tradition, Gluck became dissatisfied with the pomp and mannerisms of older operas and set out to reform them, putting text and music into a more meaningful, coherent whole. Consequently, the art of opera was reformed, operas became more realistic and effective, and Gluck's ideas influenced Mozart, who composed several operas. Gluck's finest operas were *Orfeo ed Euri-*

Glasgow, Scotland

Mıkhail Glinka

Gnu

dice (1762), Alceste (1767), and Iphigénie en Tauride (1779).

Glucose, colorless crystalline sugar ($C_6H_{12}O_6$) that occurs in fruit and honey. Other carbohydrates in the bodies of animals are converted to glucose before being utilized as an energy source. It is prepared commercially by the hydrolysis of starch using hydrochloric acid and is used in confectionary, tanning, treating tobacco, and pharmaceuticals.

Glucoside, a carbohydrate-containing compound that yields a glucose and a nonsugar component when decomposed by the process of hydrolysis.

Gluon, a particle that can be thought of as the "glue" that holds quarks together. Quarks are the fundamental particles that combine to form elementary particles such as protons and neutrons. The gluon is the energy quantum in strong nuclear interactions. It is analogous to the photon, which is the energy quantum in electromagnetic interactions.

Glutamic Acid, colorless crystalline amino acid used in the form of its sodium salt (sodium glutamate) as a food flavoring. See also Amino Acid.

Glycerin, or **glycerol,** thick syrupy sweet liquid ($CH_2OH \cdot CHOH \cdot CH_2OH$) obtained by the saponification of fats and oils in the manufacture of soap or from propylene or acrolein. It is used in the manufacture of plastics, explosives, cosmetics, foods, antifreeze, paper coating, etc. Properties: sp gr 1.26; melt. pt. 64.4 °F (18°C); boil. pt. 554°F (290°C).

Glycine, colorless soluble cystalline amino acid; the principal amino acid in sugarcane. See also Amino Acid.

Glycols, or diols, class of alcohols containing two hydroxyl groups. The simplest is ethylene glycol, or ethane diol, $C_2H_4(OH)_2$, a viscous liquid used in plastics and antifreeze.

Glycosuria, excretion of an abnormally large amount of sugar in urine. It is found with disease such as diabetes.

Gnat, a common name for many species of small, biting dipterous flies. In the United States, black flies, buffalo gnats, sand flies, midges, fungus gnats and fruit flies are all termed gnats. In Great Britain, mosquitoes are commonly called gnats. See also Diptera.

Gnatcatcher, warbler ranging from N United States to Argentina and named for its habit of searching crevices and leaves for insects. It is grayish with a slender, depressed bill. The blue-gray gnatcatcher (Polioptila caerulea) has a beautiful song and builds a lichen-covered nest high in a tree. Other species nest in low bushes. Pale bluish-speckled eggs (3–5) are laid. Length: 5in (12.5cm). Family Sylviidae; subfamily Polioptilinae.

Gneiss, general term that describes a coarse-grained rock laminated with minerals and largely recrystallized, but which lacks the breaking pattern of schist. They derive by metamorphic process from igneous or sedimentary rocks. See also Metamorphic Rocks.

Gnosticism, religious movement including numerous sects, widespread by the 2d century AD. All Gnostics promised salvation through a special knowledge of God revealed to them alone. These sects incorporated many tenets of Christianity, and Gnosticism was a seri-

ous competitor of early Christianity, which condemned it as heresy.

Gnu, or wildebeest, large, oxlike antelope. The white-tailed gnu (Connochaetes gnou) is almost extinct, except for a few protected herds in S Africa. The brindled gnu (Connochaetes taurinus) lives in E and S Africa. They have a massive, buffalo-like head, horns, and slender body. Both sexes bear horns. The brindled gnu is silver with brownish bands and black neck, face, and shoulder mane. Its beard is black or white. The horse-like tail is used to brush away flies. Length: to 78in (2m); height: to 51in (1.3m); weight: to 605lb (272kg). Family Bovidae. See also Ruminant.

Go, board game of Oriental origin for two players. On a board consisting of 361 intersections, black and white stones are alternately placed one at a time with the object of encircling the opponent's pieces and territory. The more skillful player generally uses the white stones.

Goa, city in S India, on Arabian Sea; made a Portuguese colony when captured 1510 from the sultan of Bijapur; in 1961, Goa was inc. with Daman and Diu to form a self-governing union territory. Industries: rice, cashews, spices, salt, oil, fishing, lumber, coir, coconuts, manganese mining. Pop. 857,180.

Goat, horned ruminant raised mainly for milk, meat, leather, and hair. Closely related to sheep, goats are brown or gray, have a bearded chin, pronounced odor in males, and bulging forehead in both sexes. The horns of males sweep up and backward. The male is a buck or billy, the female a doe or nanny, and the young a kid. Wild species are generally nomadic in rugged mountains. The gestation period is five months and usually two young are born. Five species include the ibex (Capra ibex), markhor (Capra falconeri), and wild goat or besang (Capra hircus), which is thought to be a forerunner of many domestic breeds. Length: to 55in (1.4m); height: to 33in (85cm). Family Bovidae; genus Capra. See also Ruminant.

Goatfish, or surmullet, marine fish found in tropical and temperate inshore and shallow waters. It is an elongated, brilliantly colored fish, with a forked tail and long fleshy whiskers. Length: to 24in (61cm). Family Mullidae; species, 55 including Atlantic spotted Pseudopeneus maculatus.

Goatsucker, large-mouthed, nocturnal bird widely distributed in warm areas, including the whippoorwill, nighthawk, and nightjar. Their plumage helps them blend with their surroundings. Some species have elongated, ornate tails and wing feathers. They fly with their mouth, surrounded by bristles, open to catch insects. They lay scrawled eggs (2) on bare ground or leaves. Length: 7–12in (17.5–30cm). Family Caprimulgidae.

Gobelins, site of a French workshop that produced famous large wall hangings during the 17th century. The Gobelins workshop of Flemish artists was organized by Charles Le Brun, painter to King Louis XIV.

Gobi (Mandarin Shamoh), desert in central Asia; one of the world's largest deserts; extends E and W from Kinghan Mts to Tien Shan; fierce sandstorms, harsh winters, hot summers and erratic cloudbursts make it uninhabitable; scattered, nomadic Mongolian sheep and goat herding tribes live along grassy periphery of desert. Elevation: 3,000–5,000ft (915–1,525m). Area: approx. 500,000sq mi (1,295,000sq km).

Goby, marine tropical fish found inshore or around coral reefs. Popular with aquarists, it is brightly colored. Suction area, formed from fused pelvic fins, is on front of body and is used to hang onto underwater surfaces. Length: 0.5–4in (1.2–10.2cm). Family Gobiidae; species 400, including neon goby Elactinus oceanops and the tiny Pandaka pygmaea.

God, the name given in many religions to the creator and mover of the universe, in others to a variety of supernatural beings. Judaism, Christianity, and Islam are monotheistic, holding that there is one God. In Hinduism, Brahma is considered the soul of the world, but there are lesser gods. In polytheistic religions such as those of ancient Greece and Rome there is a heavenful of gods and goddesses. Skeptics deny the existence of any god (atheism). See also Agnosticism; Allah; Atheism; Brahma; Buddhism; Christianity; Deism; Greek Mythology; Hinduism; Islam; Jehovah; Judaism; Zeus. See also Yahweh.

Godavari, river in central India rises in Western Ghats Mts; flows SE across Deccan Plateau to Bay of Bengal, NW of Rajahmundry; navigable in lower course; densely populated delta; source of the Rampadasagur hydroelectric-irrigation project. Sacred to the Hindus, there are many pilgrimage centers along its banks. Length: 900mi (1,450km).

Godfrey of Bouillon (c.1061–1100), first Latin ruler of Jerusalem (1099–1100). For service in his army, Holy Roman Emperor Henry IV rewarded Godfrey with the duchy of Lower Lorraine (c.1082). In 1096 he set out on the First Crusade. After the capture of Jerusalem (1099) he refused the title king, but became ruler as the defender of the Holy Sepulchre. His brother succeeded him as Baldwin I.

Godiva, Lady (died 1080), English benefactress, wife of Leofric, earl of Mercia. According to tradition she rode naked through the streets of Coventry (1040) to obtain the people's relief from taxation by her husband. She founded endowed monasteries at Coventry and Stow.

Godolphin, Sidney Godolphin, 1st Earl of (1645–1712), English political figure. Secretary of state (1684) under James II, he regained office under William III (1688–96) but maintained secret contact with James. A Tory, as lord treasurer under Anne (1702–10), he helped finance the military campaigns of his ally the duke of Marlborough.

Godoy, Manuel de (1767–1851), Spanish statesman. He became the lover of Queen Maria Luisa and rose rapidly in the court of King Charles IV. He became chief minister in 1792. He allied Spain with France against Great Britain during the Napoleonic upheavals, an alliance that resulted in the defeat of Trafalgar (1805). Opposition to him increased after France overran Spain in the Peninsular War. He was captured by a mob at Aranjuez but was rescued by the French. They gave him refuge, and he died in France.

Godunov, Boris (1551–1605), tsar of Russia (1598–1605). When his brother-in-law Tsar Fyodor died, Boris was chosen tsar. His persecution of the boyars and his inability to deal with a famine made him unpopular. Therefore, when a pretender to the throne claiming to be Prince Dmitri (Fyodor's son), who had actually been killed as a child, invaded in 1604, he was able to gain popular support. Boris died suddenly, and his own son was overthrown as tsar by the pretender.

Godwin, William (1756–1836), English political philosopher, husband of Mary Wollstonecraft and father of

Mary Shelley. A dissenting minister (1778–83), he became an atheist and anarchist. His belief in the power of man's reason is expressed in *Enquiry Concerning Political Justice* (1793) and in the novels *Caleb Williams* (1794) and *St Leon* (1799). *See also* Shelley, Mary; Wollstonecraft, Mary.

Godwin-Austen (Dapsang or **K2),** mountain in Pakistan in Karakoram Range, S central Asia; second highest peak in the world; discovered 1856 in survey of India and named for topographer Henry Godwin-Austen, surveyor of the region. The summit was first reached in 1954 by Ardito Desio. Height: 28,250ft (8,616m).

Godwit, seacoast-wintering sandpiper with long, upcurved bill. Nesting on grassland or tundra, it breeds noisily and lays 4 greenish eggs. Length: 1ft (30cm). Genus *Limosa.*

Goebbels, Joseph (1897–1945), German Nazi leader. He joined the Nazi party in 1924 and worked with Gregor Strasser, leader of the left wing of the party. Switching loyalty to Hitler in 1926, Goebbels founded the paper *Der Angriff* and became the leading Nazi propagandist. He was elected to the Reichstag in 1928, and when the Nazis came to power (1933), became minister of propaganda. As such he ruled much of Germany's cultural life. He was a brilliant orator and a masterful propagandist. He committed suicide with his entire family in April 1945.

Goering, Hermann Wilhelm (1893–1946), German Nazi leader. A World War I flying ace, he early joined the Nazi party and took part in the abortive Munich putsch in 1923. Elected to the Reichstag in 1928, he became its president in 1932. When the Nazis came to power in 1933, Goering became minister of air and prime minister of Prussia, where he founded the Gestapo. In 1936 he became director of the four-year economic plan. As virtual creator of the German air force, he enjoyed great prestige at the beginning of World War II, but defeat in the Battle of Britain and the Allied air raids on Germany discredited him. Sentenced to death at Nuremberg, he committed suicide.

Goethe, Johann Wolfgang von (1749–1832), German poet. One of the greatest German writers and thinkers, his range is vast: from simple love poems to profound philosophical poems or scientific theories. In his long life he was lawyer, botanist, politician and civil servant, physicist, zoologist, painter, and theater manager. Johann Gottfried von Herder taught him to appreciate Shakespeare, and this influenced his *Götz von Berlichingen* (1773). His major works include *The Sorrows of Young Werther* (1774), a novel *Italian Journey* (1816), the classical drama *Iphigenie auf Tauris* (1787), *Torquato Tasso* (1789), *Egmont* (1788), *Wilhelm Meisters Lehrjahre* (1795–96), *Elective Affinities* (1809), and his most famous work, *Faust* (1808, 1832). *See also* Faust.

Gog and Magog, according to the Bible two hostile forces that will appear on earth before the end of the world. In Celtic mythology, Gogmagog was a chieftain in Western England who was slain by Corineus. In the Guildhall, London, they are two wooden statues representing a race of giants conquered by Trojan Brutus, legendary founder of Britain.

Gogol, Nikolai (1809–52), Russian novelist and dramatist whose work marks the transition from pure Romanticism to early realism. He made his reputation with folk tales, such as *Taras Bulba* (1835), the stories *Diary of a Madman* (1835) and *The Nose* (1836), and the drama *The Inspector General* (1836), which show the early development of his characteristically grotesque satirical style. Dismayed by reactionary criticism, he turned to religion for spiritual support and lived mostly in Rome from 1836 to 1848. Here he completed the first and only published part of his major work *Dead Souls* (1842) and the short story *The Overcoat* (1842). He spent the last ten years of his life working on the second part of *Dead Souls* but this was destroyed before publication.

Goiânia, city in SE central Brazil; capital of Goiás state; site of Catholic University (1959), and federal University (1964). Principal industry is livestock. Pop. 362,152.

Goiter, enlargement of the thyroid gland accompanied by swelling at the front of the neck. Caused most frequently by iodine deficiency, it is occasionally accompanied by hypothyroidism or, in areas where goiter is endemic, by cretinism in children. Usual treatment is to increase intake of iodides; hormone therapy or surgery is more rare.

Golan Heights (Ha Golan, Ramot), disputed region in SW Syria. During the seven-day Arab-Israeli War (1967), Israel occupied the area and later colonized it; Syria subsequently rejected the UN peace plan (November 1967) and broke off diplomatic ties with Britain and United States. Conflicts continued between Syria and Israel.

Golconda, ruined town and fortress in SE India; a Bahmani kingdom 1364–1512, capital of a Muslim sultanate and famous for diamonds, 1512–1687; conquered by Aurangzeb 1687–88 and annexed to Delhi empire.

Gold, metallic element (symbol Au) of the third transition series, known from earliest times. The metal occurs native: some gold is also obtained as a by-product in the electrolytic refining of copper. It is used in jewelry and as a monetary standard. Gold leaf can be made as thin as 0.0001 mm. Colloidal gold is sometimes used in coloring glass. The radioisotope Au^{198} (half-life 2.7 days) is used in radiotherapy. The metal is unreactive, being unaffected by oxygen and common acids. It dissolves in aqua regia. Properties: at. no. 79, at. wt. 196.-9665; sp gr 19.32; melt. pt. 1,945°F (1,063°C); boil. pt. 4820°F (2,662°C); most common isotope Au^{197} (100%). *See also* Transition Elements.

Goldberg, Arthur Joseph (1911–), US public official and jurist, b. Chicago. Appointed general counsel for the Congress of Industrial Organizations (CIO) and the United Steelworkers of America (1948), he was instrumental in both the AFL-CIO merger (1955) and the passage of the Ethical Practices Act (1957). Named US secretary of labor by President Kennedy (1961–62), he was later appointed an associate justice of the US Supreme Court (1962–65), where he defended civil rights, personal liberties, and due process. In 1965, he was appointed by Lyndon Johnson to be US ambassador to the United Nations (1965–68).

Golden Algae, a group of mostly microscopic primarily freshwater plants (division Chysophyta). The best-known members of the group are the tiny single-celled diatoms, common among both salt- and freshwater plankton. Many single-celled golden algae form colonies. The multicelled types are usually threadlike in form. All members of the group contain characteristic yellow-brown pigments that in many cases mask the algae's green chlorophyll.

Golden Ass, The, or **Metamorphoses** (2nd century AD), prose work by Lucius Apuleius. In 11 books it recounts the adventures of Lucius of Corinth, who in Book III is transformed into an ass by the magic of Pamphile and her maid Fotis. It is the only Roman novel to survive intact.

Golden Bull (1222), Hungarian "Magna Carta" issued by Andrew II (1175–1235), under pressure from the lower nobility. This document extended certain rights to the nobility, including tax exemption, freedom to dispose of their property, prohibition of arbitrary imprisonment, and guarantee of annual assembly.

Golden Bull (1356), edict promulgated by Holy Roman Emperor Charles IV defining the procedures for electing the Holy Roman emperor. It provided for election by majority vote of seven princely electors. The procedures remained in effect until the dissolution of the empire in 1806.

Golden Eagle, Northern Hemisphere eagle with brown plumage and gold feathering on the head and neck. An excellent hunter, it flies over open country, preying on birds and small mammals. Sometimes small groups attack large animals. Species *Aquila chrysaetos. See also* Eagle.

Goldeneye, diving duck of cool temperate regions. It has yellow eyes, short black bill, rounded head, and black and white plumage. Species *Bucephala clangula. See also* Duck.

Golden Fleece, in Greek mythology, the magic fleece of a ram given by Hermes to Nephele, the wife of Athamas. When Athamas's second wife, Ino, out of jealousy planned death for Nephele's children, Phrixus and Helle, the ram carried them away. When Phrixus arrived at Colchis he sacrificed the ram and hung the fleece in a wood guarded by a dragon. The quest of Jason and the Argonauts was for the Golden Fleece, a task put on him by Aetes.

Golden Moles, blind burrowing mammals found in Africa south of the Sahara. They have two picklike claws on each front paw and a leathery padded snout for pushing through soil. They feed on worms and other small invertebrates. Length: 3–7in (8–18cm). Family Chrysochloridae.

Golden Plover, arctic-breeding, migratory, meadow-living shorebird that is black below and brown above with gold spots. Genus *Pluvialis. See also* Plover.

Golden Retriever, hunting dog (sporting group) bred in Scotland in the 19th century for water and land bird retrieving. Ruggedly built, it has a broad head and rectangular muzzle; short, rounded ears hanging flat; shortish body; medium-length legs; and a curved tail. The flat coat can be straight or wavy with a ruff at the neck and feathering on the legs and tail; color is golden. Average size: 23–24in (58.5–60cm) high at shoulder; 65–75lb (29.5–34kg). *See also* Sporting Dog.

Goldenrod, North American perennial plant that grows almost everywhere. It has small yellow (sometimes white) flowers in one-sided clusters and blooms in late summer. Height: 1–8ft (0.3–2.4m). *Solidago luteus,* hybrid of goldenrod and aster, is cultivated in gardens. Family Compositae.

Golden Section, mathematical principle of proportions considered pleasing to the eye, used in antiquity and revived for architecture during the Italian Renaissance. It was based on the ratio 3:5, in which the smaller part of the building is to the size of the greater part approximately as the greater is to the whole.

Golden Wattle, shrub or small tree native to Australia. Its yellow flowers grow in clusters. Height: to 30ft (9m). Family Leguminosae; species *Acacia longifolia.*

Goldfinch, small (to 4.5in, or 11.4cm) seed-eating, sparrowlike bird that frequents woods and cultivated areas in North America and Europe. They often live in flocks and lay bluish-white eggs (3–6) in a cup-shaped nest. The yellow American goldfinch *(Spinus tristis)* has a black crown and tail and black and white wings. The red-faced European goldfinch *(Carduelis carduelis)* has a brownish body with yellow and black wings. Family Fringillidae.

Goldfish, freshwater carp originally found in China. Probably the most popular aquarium fish, it was domesticated by the Chinese about 1000 years ago. The wild form of this hardy, adaptable fish is plain and brownish. Selective breeding has produced gold and variegated red, yellow, white, and black forms with flowing fins, including the fantail, blackmoor, lionhead, comet, celestial, eggfish, and shubunkin. Family Cyprinidae; species *Carassius auratus.*

Golding, William (1911–), English novelist. His novels are concerned with the nature of humankind. They include *Lord of the Flies* (1954), *The Inheritors* (1955), *Pincher Martin* (1956), *Free Fall* (1959), *The Spire* (1964), *The Scorpion God* (1971), *Darkness Visible* (1979), *Rites of Passage* (1980), *A Moving Target* (1982), and *The Paper Man* (1984). He was awarded the Nobel Prize in literature in 1983 for his novels.

Goldsmith, Oliver (1728–74), Irish poet, novelist, essayist, and dramatist. His works include the essay *The Citizen of the World* (1762), the poems "The Traveller" (1764) and "The Deserted Village" (1770), a novel *The Vicar of Wakefield* (1766), and the play *She Stoops to Conquer* (1773). Goldsmith hated the literary pedantry of his day and sought to achieve a naturalness in his own work.

Gold Standard, monetary situation under which the amount of currency within an economy is tied to the quantity of gold backing within that economy. Under the gold standard the money supply cannot expand faster than the quantity of gold stock does.

Golf, sport played with a small hard ball and a series of clubs over a course. The course is usually more than 6,000 yards (5,460m) long and is divided into 18 consecutive numbered holes varying in length from 100 to 650 yards (91m to 595m) from tee to green. Competition may be at 18, 36, 54, or 72 holes, and the winner may be decided by the lowest stroke total (medal play) or by the amount of holes won from an opponent (match play). Play begins off the tee with the object of getting the ball into the cup or hole on the green. The hole is 4.25in (11cm) in diameter and 4in (10.2cm) deep. The area between the tee and the green is the fairway, which may contain such hazards as water, sand traps, tall grass, and trees. Players use a set of golf clubs for the various drives, approach shots, and putting. For the long drives, there are four woods standardized with the numbers from 1 to 4. For shorter shots, irons, standardized 1 through 10, are used. Once on the green, a putter is used. Other specialized clubs are sometimes substituted for the standard clubs. Players either compete individually, or with partners, where one ball is used for each pair of partners, who play their ball on alternate shots.

Golf has its origins in Scotland in the 15th century. In 1754 the Royal and Ancient Golf Club of St Andrews, Scotland—where the basic rules of golf were established—was founded. The game is now enjoyed worldwide with international tournaments for amateurs (Walker and Americas Cups) and professionals (Curtis

Johann Goethe

Samuel Gompers

Charles Goodyear

and Ryder Cups). Other famous tournaments include those in the United States (the Masters, Open, and the PGA), and Great Britain (Open). There is competition for both men and women and an annual professional tour in the United States (sanctioned by the Professional Golf Association), Europe, and Asia.

Golgotha, site outside Jerusalem, also called Calvary, where Jesus and two others were crucified under the rule of Roman procurator Pontius Pilate. Two places, the Church of the Holy Sepulchre and a hill near Damascus Gate, have each been proposed as the site.

Goliath, biblical Philistine giant slain by David who accepted Goliath's challenge and felled him with a stone from a slingshot. This encouraged the Israelites, who had been held at bay by Goliath, to defeat the Philistines.

Gomel', city in Belorussian SSR, USSR, 140mi (225km) N of Kiev on Sozh River; capital of Gomel' oblast. City was acquired 1772 by Russia from Poland; Jews accounted for 40% of population until WWII when city was taken by Germans, and Jews were executed (1941–43). Industries: farm machinery, ship repair, fertilizer, tugboats, glass, plywood, paper; trades in wool, flax, lumber. Pop. 360,000.

Gómez, Juan Vicente (1857–1935), president of Venezuela (1908–15, 1922–29, 1931–35). A financial backer and adviser to President Cipriano Castro, Gómez took complete control of the government when Castro left on a trip to Europe. During his 27-year tenure, Venezuela became a major producer and exporter of petroleum; the revenues were used to cancel the country's debts and to initiate an impressive public works program.

Gómez Palacio, city in N Mexico 3 miles (4.8km) across the Nazas River from Torreón. Industries: textiles, tanning, iron, steel, explosives, chemicals, liquor, sugar, tobacco. Pop. 139,743.

Gomillion v. Lightfoot (1960), US Supreme Court civil rights decision. The court found that it had jurisdiction to hear a case involving statutory redistricting that eliminated almost all of the black voters from the electoral districts of Tuskegee, Ala. Declaring this law unconstitutional, the court weakened the non-intervention stance it had taken in *Colegrove* v. *Green*.

Gompers, Samuel (1850–1924), US labor leader, b. England. He emigrated with his parents to New York City in 1863 and went to work as a cigar maker, joining the local union in 1864. He served as its president (1877–81). In 1881 he helped to found the Federation of Organized Trades and Labor Unions. When it was reorganized as the American Federation of Labor in 1886 Gompers became its first president, serving until his death except for the year 1895. Gompers successfully competed with the older Knights of Labor and later with the more radical Industrial Workers of the World. He stressed basic issues—higher wages and shorter hours—not social upheaval. During World War I he organized and headed the War Commission on Labor and served on the Advisory Commission to the Council of National Defense.

Gomulka, Wladyslaw (1905–82), Polish Communist political leader. Active in the defense of Warsaw in 1939, he had been imprisoned for anti-Fascism during the 1930s. A leader of the Polish Workers' party and a member of the National Council of Poland after World War II, he was dismissed in 1949 and imprisoned from 1951–54 for ideological impurity. Reinstated as a member of the central committee of the Communist

party in 1956, he became first secretary and denounced the Russian terror tactics. He also pressed for and achieved greater freedom for Poland within the Marxist framework. Gomulka did, however, remain a supporter of the Soviets in their foreign policy (eg, 1968 invasion of Czechoslovakia). He was forced to resign during the food riots of 1970.

Gonadotropins, general name for the two pituitary hormones, follicle-stimulating hormone and luteinizing hormone; present in both males and females, where they stimulate development and function of the sex organs, the ovary and testis.

Gonads, primary sex glands. In males they are the testes; in females, the ovaries. Gonads produce several hormones, including testosterone (males) and estrogen (females). Gonadal hormones are crucial in the development of physical sexual characteristics such as the enlargement of breasts and growth of pubic hair and may be related to sexual behavior. In humans, however, these hormones have more to do with the development of sexual behavior than with the precise form it takes. *See also* Ovaries; Testes.

Goncourt, Edmond de (1822–96), French novelist and social historian. He wrote in collaboration with his brother Jules until his death (1870). Novels of which he was the sole author include *La Fille Élisa* (1877) and *Les Frères Zemganno* (1879). The Prix Goncourt, one of France's top literary awards, was provided for in his will.

Gondwanaland, the name given to the southern continent which began to break away from the single land mass Pangaea about 200,000,000 years ago. The name comes from Gondwana, a geological province in east central India that is a key to the theory that South America, Africa, and India were once a single continent.

Goniometer, instrument used mainly by mineral collectors to help in the identification of crystal forms by measuring the critical angles of related sets of crystal faces. These angles are characteristic for certain minerals.

Gonorrhea, most common venereal disease, caused by a gonococcus and transmitted usually through sexual activity. Sometimes carriers of the disease, particularly females, show no symptoms. In males, symptoms usually occur between two and eight days after exposure and include a profuse, purulent discharge from the urethra; homosexual men may also have anal or pharyngeal infections. Females may show increased or painful urination, vaginal discharge, or signs of rectal infection. Complications include systemic infection, endocarditis, meningitis. Infants of infected parents may be infected at birth. Treatment is a course of antibiotics.

Gonzaga, Italian dynasty that ruled Mantua (1328–1708) and Montferrat (1536–1708). The family's power in Mantua was established by **Luigi Gonzaga** (1267–1360), a supporter of the Holy Roman Emperor. **Giovanni Francesco** (1395–1444), a general in imperial service, was a patron of the humanist Vittorino da Feltre. **Giovanni Francesco II** (1466–1519) was a leader of Italian defense against Charles VIII's French invasion (1494) and wed Isabella d'Este, a great Renaissance art patron.

Goodman, Benjamin David ("Benny") (1909–), US jazz clarinetist and bandleader, b. Chicago. He formed his own band in 1934 and became famous in 1939 as the "King of Swing" with his theme songs

"Let's Dance" and "Goodbye." His Carnegie Hall appearance in 1938 was the first performance there by any jazz musician. After 1944 he continued to play with many other great jazz performers, made many best-selling recordings, appeared on television and in films, and toured worldwide. Widely acclaimed as a jazz clarinetist, he also played classical music.

Good Neighbor Policy, US policy of nonintervention in the affairs of Latin America. President Hoover in 1928 urged a new approach to offset hostility bred by previous US armed intervention in the Caribbean. President Roosevelt introduced the Good Neighbor Policy in his inaugural speech (1933) and declared his opposition to military interference. The Organization of American States, an extension of this policy, was founded (1945) to foster hemispheric solidarity. In 1961, President Kennedy introduced the Alliance for Progress, an updated version of Roosevelt's policy.

Good Samaritan, subject of a New Testament parable found in Luke's gospel. The compassion of the Samaritan towards a beaten man is contrasted with the negligence of Israel's leaders who are preoccupied with ceremonial law.

Goodyear, Charles (1800–60), US industrial inventor, b. New Haven, Conn. Despite early business failures that sent him to debtor's prison, he patented an acid and metal coating (1837) and discovered and patented vulcanized rubber (1844). Financial difficulties forced him to sell his rights for a fraction of their worth and allowed others to reap profits from his work.

Goose, widely distributed waterfowl, related to ducks and swans, valued as game and raised commercially for their dark, protein-rich meat, feathers used in pillows, and the delicacy *pâté de foie gras*. Heavier than ducks, they have blunt bills, long necks, shortish legs, webbed feet, and, in the wild, a combination of gray, brown, black, and white dense plumage underlaid by down. They live near fresh or brackish water but spend time on land, grazing on meadow grasses. They fly with flocks in V-shaped formations making long, noisy migrations. Wild geese breed in colonies, mate for life, and build grass-and-twig, down-lined nests for 4–7 eggs. Weight: 3–16lb (1.3–7.2kg). Family Anatidae.

Gooseberry, very hardy shrub (*Ribes grossularia*) of the saxifrage family, native to cool or temperate regions of Europe and North America. Fruit may be red, white, amber, or green.

Goosefoot, or pigweed, many species of herbs and sub-shrubs, with mealy, often lobed, leaves that look like goose feet. The 550 widely distributed species, mostly weeds, also include spinach and beets. Family Chenopodiaceae.

Gopher, small, stout, burrowing rodent of North and Central America that has fur-lined, external cheek pouches and long incisor teeth outside the lips. Black to almost white, they live mostly underground, digging shallow tunnels to get roots and tubers and deep ones for shelter and food storage. Length: 5–17in (127–432mm). Family Geomyidae. *See also* Ground Squirrel.

Gopher Tortoise, true tortoise native to SE and SW United States and Mexico. Vegetarian, it has a brownish-tan, high-domed shell, stumpy legs, and powerful forelimbs for digging burrows. Length: 15in (38cm). Family Testudinae; genus *Gopherus*. *See also* Turtle.

Goral, shaggy, mountain-dwelling, goatlike ruminant found in Central Asia, China, Korea, and Burma. Its brownish fur blends with rocks. It has short, conical horns and lives in small family groups. Length: to 51in (1.3m). Family Bovidae; genus *Naemorhedus.*

Gorbachev, Mikhail Sergeyevich (1931–), Soviet political leader, Communist party general secretary (1985–). A law graduate of Moscow University, he joined the Communist Party in 1952 and rose rapidly. He was elected to the party's Central Committee in 1971 and became secretary for agriculture in 1978, a candidate member of the Politburo in 1979, and a full member in 1980. He succeeded Konstantin Chernenko as general secretary in 1985. Representative of a younger generation of Soviet leaders, he projected a practical image in relations with the US, including a summit conference with Pres. Reagan in late 1985.

Gordian Knot, a knot tied by king Gordius which bound the yoke of his chariot to a tree. The ends of the knot could not be seen. It was said it could only be untied by the conqueror of Asia. Alexander the Great cut the knot with his sword.

Gordon, Charles George (1833–85), English soldier and administrator, known as Chinese Gordon. He first distinguished himself in the Crimean War (1853–56). In 1860 he took part in the China expedition that captured Peking. He was personally responsible for the burning of the Summer Palace. He commanded the British-Chinese forces in the Taiping Rebellion (1863–64). In 1873 he was appointed governor of Equatoria (S Sudan) by the khedive of Egypt. Between 1877–79 he was governor of the Sudan, where he attempted to suppress the slave trade. In 1884 he returned to the Sudan and attempted to put down the Mahdi Rebellion. For 10 months in 1885 he was trapped and besieged at Khartoum. He was killed two days before a relief force from England arrived.

Gordon Setter, superior bird and gun dog (sporting group) dating from 1620 in Scotland. An eager worker, its finely chiseled head is heavy, with a long muzzle and broad nose. Low-set ears are folded close to the head; the strong body is deep-chested; legs are big-boned. The feathered tail is carried horizontally and flags constantly as the dog moves. The soft, straight or slightly waved coat is long on ears, chest, belly, and legs; colors are black with tan marks. Average size: 24–27in (61–68.6cm) high at shoulder; 55–80lb (25–36kg). *See also* Sporting Dog.

Gorgas, William Crawford (1854–1920), US surgeon whose successful mosquito-control program in Panama wiped out malaria and yellow fever there and made possible the building of the Panama Canal.

Gorges, (Sir) Ferdinando (1566?–1647), English colonizer. He was a founder of the Virginia Company of Plymouth (1606), which acquired charter rights to New England. Gorges transferred charter to Council for New England (1620), which granted patents to the Plymouth and Massachusetts Bay colonies. Gorges received full rights to Maine (1639).

Gorgias, dialogue of Plato, on the philosophy of rhetoric as it relates to ethics. Consisting of a discussion between Gorgias, Socrates, and Callicles, Socrates (presenting Plato's viewpoint) argues that the techniques of rhetoric should serve the ends of justice.

Gorgon, monster figures in Greek mythology. According to Hesiod, they were Stheno, Euryale, and Medusa, the daughters of Phorcus and Cero. *See also* Medusa.

Gorgonian. *See* Sea Fan.

Gorilla, gregarious great ape living in African rain forests. The largest primate, they are mostly brown or black and are powerfully built, with long arms and short legs. They walk on all fours and live mostly on the ground, searching for fruits and other vegetarian foods. Gorillas are generally shy and peaceful. Unless provoked, they rarely attack humans. Height: to 70in (178cm); weight: 600lb (270kg). Species *Gorilla gorilla. See also* Primates.

Gorki (Gor'kij), formerly Nizhni Novgorod; city in Russian SFSR, USSR, 250mi (403km) NE of Moscow, at confluence of Volga and Oka rivers; capital of Gorki oblast. City united with Moscow state 1417; trade and cultural center 18th-19th centuries; renamed in 1932 for Russian writer; site of 14th-century kremlin, Archangel Cathedral (1631), state university (1918), convents, palace. Industries: automobiles, aircraft, plastics, textiles, clothing, shipyards, woodworking, food processing, oil refining, glass, chemicals. Founded 1221. Pop. 1,332,000.

Gorky, Maxim (1868–1936), Russian dramatist and writer, b. Aleksei Maksimovich Peshkov. Gorky championed the worker and peasant in *Sketches and Stories* (1898); in the play *The Lower Depths* (1902), produced by the Moscow Art Theatre with Anton Chekhov's support; and in the novel *Mother* (1907). He also wrote autobiographical volumes (1913–24) and other plays, including *Yegor Bulichev* (1932) and *The Enemies* (1935). He has been called the father of social realism.

Gorlovka, city in Ukrainian SSR, USSR, in Donets Basin; industrial center; site of mining school. Industries: coal and mercury mining, coke, fertilizer, steel, chemicals, machinery. Founded 1867. Pop. 343,000.

Gorse. *See* Furze.

Goshawk, swift hawk with gray or brownish plumage and a long, rounded tail. It feeds on small mammals, including rabbits and squirrels, and birds. Length: 20in (51cm); wingspan: 4ft (122cm). Species *Accipiter gentilis. See also* Hawk.

Gospel, four histories of the life of Christ in the New Testament: Matthew, Mark, Luke, and John. The name is from Middle English "godspel," meaning "good tale."

Gospel Songs, informal and emotional religious spirituals or hymns that developed from slave songs, Protestant hymns, and the call and response singing in slave churches. Gospel style usually involves choral singing with a lead singer or singers. Originally performed at revivals or religious celebrations during the early 20th century, it had a strong influence on black rock music beginning in the 1950s. *See also* Spirituals.

Gosplan, state planning committee of the Soviet Union, one of the more important units in the economic decision-making process. Responsible directly to the council of ministers, Gosplan creates and administers plans in all sectors of the economy.

Gossaert, Jan (Mabuse) (*c.*1478–1533), Flemish painter. He is largely responsible for introducing the Italian Renaissance style to the Low Countries. He traveled widely in Italy and absorbed diverse Italian influences into his many religious paintings and portraits.

Göta Canal, waterway in S Sweden; connects Göteborg (W) with Stockholm (E); consists of a series of rivers, lakes, coastal waterways, and canals. The canal was built 1810–32 by Baron Baltzar von Platen and Scottish engineer Thomas Telford, from the 16th-century plan of Bishop Hans Brask, and serves several industrial towns in S Sweden. Total length: 360mi (580km).

Göteborg (Gothenburg), city in SW Sweden, at confluence of Göta and Kattegat rivers; seat of Goteborgoch Bohus co, chief seaport and 2nd-largest city in Sweden. Settled by Dutch merchants, it became important port after mid-18th century as the center of British trade with Europe; its system of liquor regulation (1865) became basis of Swedish liquor laws; made a free port 1921; site of Dutch-style canals, several museums, university (1891), oceanographic institute, technical college (1829). Industries: shipyards, automobiles, food processing, textiles, ball bearings, timber, brewing, fishing. Founded 1619 by King Gustavas Adolphus. Pop. 444,651.

Gotha, city in SW East Germany. Since 1785 city has been center of geographical research and publishing; *Almanach de Gotha,* authoritative reference work on nobility and royalty, has been published here since 1836; site of 15th-century church of St Margaret, 17th-century castle. Industries: publishing, rubber products, precision instruments. Founded 1189. Pop. 57,328.

Gothic Architecture, architecture of medieval Europe from the 12th to the 16th century. Characterized by the pointed arch and ribbed vault, Gothic architecture is religious in inspiration and ecclesiastical in nature. Its greatest and most characteristic expression is the cathedral, a structure of soaring spaces, lightness, and multiple articulation of forms. The introduction of a system of flying buttresses was a technical advance that made the light walls and large windows possible. An early prototype is the Abbey Church of St Denis (1140–44). Ever higher and lighter structures with increasingly intricate vaulting and tracery followed. The Gothic style was succeeded by the Renaissance style, which originated in Italy in the 15th century.

Gothic Art, originally an architectural style that began in the middle of the 12th century in north-central France and spread to other forms of art, especially sculpture and stained glass, and to England, Spain, Italy, Germany, and even as far as Sweden. From it evolved the International Gothic style and, in the 15th century, the Renaissance style. The Gothic style was first used in ecclesiastical architecture to solve technical problems created by the Romanesque style. In rebuilding the church of St Denis (1140–44), Abbot Suger used the first Gothic arches. Soon the rib vault and broad stained-glass windows became standard architectural practice.

The High Gothic phase is apparent at Chartres, where the cathedral was rebuilt after the fire of 1194. The building contains numerous large stained-glass windows and has flying buttresses for support, as well as rib vaults and pointed arches. Other High Gothic cathedrals include those of Bourges, Rheims, and Amiens. The next phase, the Rayonnant, involved refinements of the High Gothic style, such as in Sainte-Chapelle, built around 1240 for Louis IX. The outbreak of the Hundred Years War interrupted the further development of the Gothic style in France. However, by then it had spread to the rest of Europe. In England, Canterbury Cathedral is early Gothic, and Salisbury and Lincoln cathedrals are High Gothic. The Decorated style in England from 1290 to 1350 involved such elements as star vaults and the ogee arch.

Eventually the Gothic style spread beyond ecclesiastical architecture to that of private estates and municipal buildings. Gothic sculpture usually involved that done for the exterior doors of cathedrals, such as the Royal Portal at Chartres. The realism of the High Gothic style is exemplified by the west facade of Notre Dame in Paris. In the Late Gothic, sculptured figures were carved in affected poses with vacant expressions. In the 15th century the decline was checked and the figures became stronger, as in the "Entombment of Christ" at Solesmes, France. Gothic painting is known essentially from panel paintings for altarpieces and from illuminated manuscripts such as the 13th-century Psalter of Isabelle de France, with its jewel-like miniatures; the 14th-century Belleville Breviary by Jean Pucelle; and the *Book of Hours* made for Jean, duc de Berry, by the Limburg brothers in the 15th century.

Gothic Novel, type of novel particularly popular in 18th-century England and 19th-century England and the United States, containing strong elements of the supernatural. The emphasis is on setting and story rather than characterization. Mary Wollstonecraft Shelley's *Frankenstein* (1818) is an outstanding example. Gothic novels were important influences on the poetry of the Romantic period, the short stories of Poe, and later novels. *See also* Novel.

Gothic Revival, revival of Gothic decorative themes and architectural motifs. The movement began with Horace Walpole's Gothic-style English mansion "Strawberry Hill" (1770). Many landowners went so far as to place Gothic "ruins" on their estates. The style was used in private homes in 18th century England, the United States, and France and was extended to public buildings and churches in the 19th century. Trinity Church, New York City (1839–46), is a prime example.

Goths, Germanic people, who by the 3rd century AD lived N of the Black Sea. They split into two groups, the Ostrogoths and the Visigoths. Conquered (*c.*370) by the Huns and later allies of the Eastern Roman Empire, the Ostrogoths conquered Italy (489) under Theodoric and ruled there until ousted by Emperor Justinian in the mid-6th century. The Visigoths settled in Lower Moesia at the end of 4th century. Under Alaric they sacked Rome in 410. Moving into Gaul and northern Spain, they reached the height of their power under Euric (reigned 466–84). They were expelled from Gaul by the Franks (507), but their Spanish kingdom survived until the Moorish conquest (711). The Goths were Arian Christians. *See also* Alaric; Theodoric the Great.

Gotland, island off SE coast of Sweden, in Baltic Sea; capital is Visby. Island belonged to Sweden 13th century; became part of Denmark 1570; was returned to Sweden by Treaty of Brömsebro 1645. Industries: sugar-beet processing, barley, rye, cement, fisheries, sheep, tourism. Area: 1,225sq mi (3,173sq km). Pop. 54,400.

Gottfried von Strassburg, (*fl.*1200–1220), Middle High German romance poet. Little is known of his life, but he was apparently well educated in literature and theology. He was a rival of Wolfram von Eschenbach and an admirer of Walther von der Vogelweide. The subject matter of his Arthurian stories, such as *Tristan und Isolt,* is largely borrowed from French and British sources, but his treatment of characters is often more profound and perceptive than the originals. *See also* Arthurian Romance.

Göttingen, city in E West Germany, on the Leine River, 55mi (89km) SSW of Brunswick; site of 14th-century town hall and wall, University of Göttingen (1737). Industries: optical and precision instruments, textiles, aluminum. Founded 953. Pop. 123,600.

Gordon setter

Maxim Gorky

Evangelicalism: Billy Graham

Gouache Painting, painting method using opaque watercolor. The paint is mixed to a thick consistency. Upon drying, the colors lighten and are similar to pastels in appearance.

Goujon, Jean (c.1510–68), French Renaissance sculptor and architect known for his decorations in low relief for buildings. He was associated with Pierre Lescot, the architect of the Louvre, where a number of Goujon's works are found today.

Gounod, Charles (1818–93), French composer. He composed church and choral music but is chiefly known for his operas, the most successful of which were *Faust* (1859), *Mireille* (1864), and *Roméo et Juliette* (1867).

Gourami, or kissing gourami, white tropical fish of Malay Peninsula, Thailand, and Sunda Islands. Popular with aquarists, it has a protrusible, suckerlike mouth; two fishes often join mouths for unknown reasons. Length: to 10in (25.4cm). Family Anabantidae; species include *Helestoma temmincki.*

Gourd, annual vine grown in North America for ornamental rather than eating purposes. Fruit shapes range from round to irregular. Its smooth or warty rind may be green, yellow, orange, white, or red. The 750 species are mainly from tropical and subtropical regions. Family Cucurbitaceae. *See also* Melon; Pumpkin.

Gout, possibly hereditary form of arthritis associated with an excess of uric acid. Adult males are primary victims. Symptoms usually affect one joint, often the big toe, with intense pain that may last several weeks.

Goya, Francisco José de (1746–1828), Spanish painter. The leading artist of the neo-Baroque style, he sympathized with the Enlightenment and the French Revolution but was still esteemed at the Spanish Court, where he painted a portrait, "The Family of Charles IV," shocking in its almost grotesque revelation of the corrupt inner life of its subjects. Among Goya's most vivid, expressive works are his portraits and nude studies of his mistress, the Duchess of Alba. When Napoleon's occupation of Spain failed to bring reforms, Goya's bitter disillusionment was reflected in such brilliantly colored, dramatic works as "The 3rd of May, 1808," commemorating the execution of a group of Madrid citizens. Although continuing to paint vigorously in his old age, partly spent in self-chosen exile, his paintings and several series of etchings ("The Disasters of War" and "The Disparates") seem a powerful reflection of private despair.

Gozzoli, Benozzo (c.1421–97), Italian painter, b. as Benozzo di Lese di Sandro. His numerous frescoes, such as that of the Medici Family as the Magi in the Chapel of the Medici Palace, Florence, faithfully depict 15th-century Italian life. He began as an assistant to Fra Angelico, but his work is entirely secular in mood and outlook.

Graben, an elongated, trenchlike, down-dropped segment of the Earth's crust enclosed by two or more similarly trending normal faults. The Basin and Range province in Utah and Nevada consists of grabens and horsts that form sedimentary basins and mountain ranges. *See also* Horst.

Gracchus, Gaius Sempronius (153–121 BC), Roman statesman. He swore to avenge the murder of his brother Tiberius. As tribune (123–21) he organized the radical social reforms planned by his brother Tiberius (died 133 BC) and sought to check the power of the senate by uniting the plebeians and the equites and by

reforming agrarian laws to benefit the poor. He granted seats in the judiciary (formerly controlled by the senate) to the equites. His visionary progressive measures were short-lived; he was defeated in the election of 121, his measures attacked, and he was killed during the riots that followed.

Gracchus, Tiberius Sempronius (163–133 BC), Roman statesman and reformer. An aristocrat appalled by the grossly unequal distribution of wealth, he declared his intention to reform agrarian law in favor of the poor. He was elected tribune in 133 and proposed the Sempronian Law to reapportion public lands. The law was passed but before it could be implemented another election was scheduled. The senate, wary of Tiberius' power, postponed the voting. Tiberius was murdered during a riot involving senators and their followers. His brother Gaius sought to avenge his death and carry out his reforms.

Grackle, New World blackbird with a long, creased, keel-shaped tail and jaw modifications to allow it to open nuts that, along with insects and eggs, are its favorite food. The common purple grackle (*Quiscalus quiscula*) of E North America is iridescent; length: 11in (28cm). The larger boat-tailed grackle or jackdaw (*Cassidix mexicanus*) of SW North America and SE United States marshlands builds a twig, stick, and mud nest for its blotched greenish, bluish, or brownish eggs (3–6). Family Icteridae.

Graft, Tissue, a portion of skin, bone, or other tissue removed from its original site and transferred elsewhere in the body to repair a defect. The tissue may be taken from the individual requiring the repair (autograft), from another individual of the same species (homograft or allograft), or from an individual of another species (heterograft).

Grafting, a method of plant propagation in which, typically, a twig of one variety (the scion) is forced to grow on the roots of another variety (the rootstock or stock). Most fruit trees are propagated by a grafting process called budding, in which the graft scion is a single bud. Grafting is an efficient way to produce new plants that are genetically identical with the parent plant from which the scions are cut. Grafting onto special rootstocks is widely used to produce dwarf fruit trees that have normal-size fruit.

Graham, "Billy" (William Franklin) (1918–), US evangelist, b. Charlotte; N. C. Although ordained as a Southern Baptist, he became the "first evangelist" (1944) of Youth for Christ. The Billy Graham Evangelistic Association serves as a base for worldwide crusades. He has a weekly syndicated column, delivers radio broadcasts, and founded the magazine *Decision* (1960). *Peace With God* (1952), *World Aflame* (1965), and *Angels* (1975) were successful books, and he also has great facility with mass audiences and mass media.

Graham, Martha (1894–), US modern dancer and choreographer, b. Pittsburgh. After studying with Ruth St Denis and Ted Shawn, she founded her own company and created a new dance technique, which is taught at her school in New York City. Her company is one of the longest-lived and most widely traveled of all modern dance groups. She believes dance should be realistically expressive, rather than romantic, and that it should portray universal, rather than personal, experience. In 1981, she created a new ballet, *Acts of Light.*

Grahame, Kenneth (1859–1932), British author of children's books. He created Mole, Rat, Badger, and Mr Toad in the classic *Wind in the Willows* (1908).

Earlier books included *The Golden Age* (1895) and its sequel *Dream Days* (1898). A. A. Milne based the play *Toad of Toad Hall* (1930) on Grahame's book.

Graian Alps (Alpes Graies or **Alpi Graie),** mountain range of France and Italy; forms an arc from Cottian Alps (SE France) to Little St Bernard Pass (French-Italian border) to Dora Baltea Valley (NW Italy). Highest peak is Gran Paradiso, 13,323ft (4,064m).

Grail, Holy, object of quest of the knights of Arthurian romance. The cup supposedly was used by Christ at the Last Supper, and possibly by Joseph of Arimathea to catch the blood flowing from Christ's wounds. The quest of the grail became a search for mystical union with God.

Gram, unit of mass (symbol g) defined as one thousandth of a kilogram. *See also* Physical Units.

Gram Atom, the quantity of an element whose mass in grams is equal to its atomic weight. It has been replaced by the SI unit, the mole. *See also* Mole.

Grammar, the branch of the science of linguistics that deals with a language's inflections, its phonetic system (phonology), and with the arrangement of words in sentences (syntax). The rules for the English language were developed on the basis of Latin grammar that is inflectional (use based on form), even though English was more of a syntactical language (use based on word order). New approaches are being advanced, and grammar is evolving as the language evolves.

Gram Molecular Volume, the volume occupied by a mass of gas equal to its molecular weight in grams (2 grams of hydrogen, 32 grams of oxygen, etc.). At a given temperature and pressure it has approximately the same value for all gases. It is 22.415 liters for a perfect gas at 760 millimeters of mercury pressure and 0°C.

Grampus, or Risso's dolphin, beakless blunt-snouted dolphin found in all oceans. It is dark above and light below. Length: 13ft (4m). Species *Grampus griseus. See also* Dolphin.

Gram's Method, method of staining bacteria for classification. A bacterial smear is stained with gentian violet, washed with Gram's solution, and counter-stained with safranine. The violet stain is retained by Gram-positive bacteria and lost by Gram-negative bacteria.

Granada, city in SW Nicaragua, on NW shore of Lake Nicaragua; capital of Granada dept. The oldest city in Nicaragua, it is a trade center in an agricultural region; historical residence of conservative Nicaraguan landholding aristocracy. Industries: sugar, coffee, animal skins. Founded 1523. Pop. 51,363.

Granada, city in S Spain, 80mi (129km) SE of Córdoba at junction of Darro and Genil rivers; capital of Granada prov. Important as Moorish fortress and stronghold 8th-15th centuries, its surrender in 1492 to the Christian armies of Ferdinand and Isabella marked the end of Moorish control in Spain. The city, renowned for its Moorish art and architecture, is site of Alhambra Palace (1248–1354), the 11th-century Alcazaba Moorish citadel, 16th-century cathedral containing tombs of Ferdinand and Isabella, Carthusian monastery of Cartuja (1516), University of Granada (1531). Industries: tourism, textiles, soap, liqueurs. Area: (prov.) 4,838sq mi (12,530sq km). Pop. (city) 190,429; (prov.) 733,375.

Grand Alliance, War of the (1688–97), war between France and the Grand Alliance. Louis XIV of France invaded the Palatinate while the Holy Roman Emperor Leopold I was fighting the Turks. Leopold formed an alliance (the Grand Alliance) with the Netherlands, Spain, and England. There were notable French victories at Namur (1692, 1695) and an English naval victory at La Hogue (1692). Peace was concluded at the Treaty of Ryswick (1696).

Grand Banks, underwater plateau in the Atlantic Ocean off the coast of Newfoundland. Growth of abundant marine life is encouraged by flow of Gulf Stream along its E edge; one of world's most important fishing grounds.

Grand Canal, inland waterway in NE China; extends from Peking (N) to Hangchow (S); one of the world's oldest and longest waterways. Construction began in 6th century BC and continued for 2,000 years; the major building (605–18) was done under Sui dynasty; it was reconstructed and lengthened (1265–89) to Peking under Yuan dynasty and Kublai Khan. Modern canal is mainly used for industrial purposes. Length: 1,000mi (1,610km). Width: 100–200ft (31–61m). Depth: 2–15ft (.6–5m).

Grand Canal, main waterway in Venice, Italy; crossed by three bridges, including the Rialto Bridge; with smaller canals it forms major Venetian transportation system. Length: approx. 2mi (3km). Width: 100–200ft (31–61m).

Grand Canyon National Park, park in NW Arizona. It spans the great gorge of the Colorado River, along the most spectacular parts. There is vast exposure of rocks representing eons of geological time. The canyon is 217mi (349km) long and 4–18mi (6–29km) wide. Area: 673,575acres (272,798hectares). Est. 1908.

Grand Cayman, largest island of Cayman Islands, British West Indies, in NW Caribbean Sea; capital is Georgetown. Exports: fruit, rope, hardwoods. Area: 76sq mi (198sq km). Pop. 8,932.

Grand Coulee Dam, the world's largest concrete dam, in N central Washington, on Columbia River. Constructed 1933–42 under auspices of Columbia Basin Project, it is used for irrigation, flood control, and navigation; and is largest US source of hydroelectricity; Franklin D. Roosevelt Lake, a leading US reservoir, was created by the dam and extends 151mi (243km) to the Canadian border. Height: 550ft (168m). Length: 4,173ft (1,273m).

Grand Forks, city in E North Dakota, on Red River; seat of Grand Forks co; site of University of North Dakota (1883), and US Bureau of Mines research laboratory. Industries: meat packing, beet-sugar refining, flour milling. Settled 1871; inc. 1881. Pop. (1980) 43,765.

Grand Jury, a group of varying size, that is a part of a court and investigates in secret the acts of a crime within its jurisdiction. It also determines which person(s) should stand trial for the crimes under its investigation.

Grand Mal, type of epileptic attack characterized by loss of consciousness and muscle contractions, lasting up to five minutes. *See also* Epilepsy.

Grand Prairie, city in NE Texas, 13mi (21km) W of Dallas. Industries: aircraft, steel products, tanks, bottling. Pop. (1980) 71,462.

Grand Rapids, city in W Michigan, on Grand River, 61mi (98km) WNW of Lansing; seat of Kent co; site of an Indian village; site of Calvin College (1876), Aquinas College (1886), Grand Rapids Junior College (1914), Reformed Bible Institute (1940), and Grace Bible Institute (1946). Industries: furniture, business machinery, auto parts, chemicals. Founded 1826 as trading post; chartered as city 1850. Pop. (1980) 181,843.

Grand River, river in N South Dakota, formed by the confluence of North and South Forks; empties into the Missouri River near Mobridge. Shadehill Dam was built on river in 1951 for flood control and irrigation; part of Missouri River Basin project. Length: approx. 200mi (322km).

Grand Teton National Park, park in NW Wyoming. It has a series of peaks embracing the most spectacular part of the Teton Range. The area was a landmark of Indians and "Mountain Men." It includes part of Jackson Hole, winter feeding ground for elk. Area: 310,442acres (125,729hectares). Est. 1929.

Granger Movement, US agrarian movement that began in the 1860s. Organized on a local basis, individual granges established cooperative grain elevators, mills, and stores. Together, grangers brought pressure on state legislatures to regulate railroads and grain elevator costs.

Granite, igneous rock from deep within the earth, composed chiefly of potash, feldspar, and quartz, with some mica or hornblende. Its texture is grainy and even, and its color is usually light gray, though feldspar may redden it. Its durability makes it a valuable construction material. *See also* Igneous Rocks.

Grant, Ulysses Simpson (1822–85), commander of the Union forces in the Civil War and 18th president of the United States (1869–77), b. Point Pleasant, Ohio (original Christian name: Hiram Ulysses), graduate, West Point, 1843. In 1848 he married Julia Dent; they had four children. Grant served with distinction in the Mexican War but in 1854 he was forced out of the army for alcoholism. He remained in private life until the Civil War began; in 1861 the governor of Illinois named him commander of a volunteer regiment.

Grant rose swiftly in rank and assignments and won the first major Union victory at Fort Donelson (Feb. 16, 1862). He barely escaped defeat at the battle of Shiloh but the Vicksburg Campaign (1862–63) was one of his greatest triumphs. In October 1863 he became commander of the West. In March 1864, President Lincoln, after a long search, named him commander in chief of the Union forces. Grant personally took command of the forces in the Wilderness campaign (May-June, 1864), which was supposed to destroy the Confederate forces of General Robert E. Lee. It was the bloodiest campaign of the war but failed to defeat Lee. Grant next confronted Lee at the siege of Petersburg (June 1864–April 1865); its fall, on April 3, resulted in Lee's surrender to Grant and the end of the war.

Still in charge of the army after the war, Grant was responsible for administering the Reconstruction policies of the government toward the South. At first a moderate, he tended to side with President Andrew Johnson against the Radical Republicans. In 1867, Johnson named Grant as secretary of war. The incumbent secretary, Edwin M. Stanton, with the backing of other Radicals, refused to vacate the office, and instituted impeachment proceedings against Johnson. Grant eventually became secretary, but by that time he had joined the Radicals, and his relations with Johnson had deteriorated.

Grant's popularity as a war hero made him attractive as a political figure. In 1868 the Republican party, under the control of the Radicals, nominated Grant unanimously for president. He was easily elected over his Democratic rival, Horatio Seymour.

Grant was almost totally lacking in political ability and judgment; from the beginning, his administration was a failure. With the exception of Secretary of State Hamilton Fish, his cabinet and staff consisted of old friends, political hacks, and wealthy contributors to the party. Graft and corruption, none of which immediately touched the president, were rife. Grant, with the backing of the Radicals, entered on a punitive Reconstruction policy toward the South.

Grant was easily renominated and reelected in 1872. His second four years were no better than the first; numerous members of his administration were involved in the scandals. He retired from office totally discredited as a politician. He retained his renown as a great general, however, and enjoyed the esteem of the public.

Career: US Army, 1843–54, 1861–68; secretary of war, 1867–68; president, 1869–77. *See also* Civil War, American; Reconstruction.

Grant's Gazelle, a heavily built gazelle of the East African plains, noted for its long, graceful, diverging, ringed horns. Height to 35in (89cm); weight to 175lbs (79kg); body fawn with inconspicuous lateral band; reddish and white markings on head; white patch on rump. Family Bovidae; species *Gazella granti*. *See also* Gazelle.

Granuloma, growth or nodule of connective tissue and capillaries usually associated with a disease such as tuberculosis, syphilis, or a nonorganic foreign body.

Granuloma Inguinale, mildly contagious venereal disease characterized by granuloma, then by ulcerations of the skin in the genital-anal area. Antibiotics are effective.

Granville, John Carteret, 1st Earl of (1690–1763), English statesman. Secretary of state (1721–24) in Walpole's administration, he used his position to gain influence with the king and intrigue against Walpole. He was lord-lieutenant of Ireland (1724–30), and lord president of the council (1751–63). An expert in foreign affairs he never succeeded, however, in forming his own administration.

Grape, deciduous vine found in mild to temperate regions of North America, Europe, and China. Grapes have long been cultivated for making wine and eating. Both cultivated and wild species have small, greenish flowers and small, purple, red, or green clustered fruits. Cultivated grapes are also dried to make raisins. Family Vitaceae; genus *Vitis*. The grape family includes 600 species of vines and shrubs.

Grapefruit, important citrus fruit *(Citrus paridisi)* of the rue family, similar to the shaddock, a West Indies fruit, from which it was developed. Grown in Florida, Texas, and California, it is a subtropical evergreen tree yielding a sour fruit with a thick yellow rind, and a yellow juicy pulp. Many seedless or pink-fleshed varieties have been developed.

Grape Hyacinth, perennial, bulbous plant native to the Mediterranean region. They have long, narrow leaves and bell-shaped flower clusters that are blue, white, or pink. Family Liliaceae; genus *Muscari*.

Grape Ivy, climbing, evergreen house plant with rambling stems and glossy, toothed leaves, native to N South America. Care: bright indirect light, soil (equal parts loam, peat moss, sand) kept slightly dry between waterings. Propagation is by stem cuttings. Family Vitaceae; species *Cissus rhombifolia*. *See also* Houseplant.

Graph, diagram representing a functional relationship between numbers or quantities using Cartesian coordinates. Two scales (axes) are drawn at right angles. The point of intersection (origin) has the value zero and the scales have positive values to the right and above the origin and negative values to the left and below the origin. Distances along the horizontal axis (abscissa) represent values of the independent variable (x); those along the vertical axis (ordinate) give values of the dependent variable (y). Thus a point on the graph represents a pair of numbers and a curve represents all possible pairs of numbers belonging to the function. Graphs are used for representing experimental results, by plotting a number of points and drawing a smooth curve through them, showing the relationship between the variables.

Graphite, gray and soft crystalline allotrope of carbon that occurs naturally in deposits of varying purity and is made synthetically by heating petroleum coke. It is used in pencil leads, lubricants, electrodes, electrical brushes, rocket nozzles, and as a moderator in nuclear reactors. Properties: sp gr 2.0-2.25.

Graptolite, any of an extinct group of colonial invertebrate animals of doubtful relationships; sometimes considered a separate phylum but also thought to be related to the chordates. They are found most frequently as flattened fibers of carbon resembling pencil marks in black shales of Ordovician and Silurian age. Uncompressed graptolite skeletons etched out of limestone show that they were composed of many small tubes regularly arranged along branches, which are presumed to have been attached to a common bladder-like float. The skeletal covering of the tubes is made of a chitin-like material. They are valuable as index fossils.

Grass, Günter (1927–), German novelist, poet, and playwright. His prose narrative combines evocative description with historical documentation in the Mannerist style. Powerful techniques were employed to effect grotesque comedy in *Cat and Mouse* (1961) and *The Tin Drum* (1959) and to satirize the Nazi era, the war, and its aftermath, as in *Dog Years* (1963). Other works include *From the Diary of a Snail* (1972), *Inmarypraise* (1974), *The Flounder* (1978), *The Meeting at Telgte* (1981), and *Headbirths Or The Germans are Dying Out* (1982).

Grass, nonwoody plants found worldwide. Long, narrow leaves sheathe the hollow, jointed stems. Stems may be upright or bent and may lie on the ground or grow underground. The small flowers, lacking petals and sepals, are arranged in spikelets between two bracts. Since grass grows from the base, removal of the tips does not inhibit growth, making it suitable for lawns and pastures. Kentucky bluegrass is favored for lawns in cool areas; buffalo grass and Bermuda grass in warm areas. Branched fibrous roots prevent soil erosion.

The seedlike fruits of grass store oil and protein and are called grains. Economically, the grasses are the most important plant family. Cereal grasses such as rice, millet, corn, and wheat are cultivated for seed. Others are grown as forage for domestic grazing animals and for erosion control and ornamentation. Furniture is made of some grasses, such as bamboo. Height: 1in–100ft (2.5cm–30m). There are 5,000–10,000 species. Family Gramineae. *See also* Monocotyledon.

Grasse, town in SE France, 17mi (27km) W of Nice. In 12th century it was an independent republic; became

Ulysses S. Grant

Thomas Gray

Great Britain

part of countship of Provence 1227. Chief industry is manufacture of perfumes. Pop. 135,330.

Grasshopper, plant-eating insect found worldwide. They have hind legs enlarged for jumping. The forewings are leatherlike and hind wings are membranous and fan-shaped. When at rest, the wings are folded over the back. Length: 0.5–4in (12.7–102mm). Order Orthoptera; families Acrididae and Tettigoniidae. *See also* Locust; Mormon Cricket; Orthoptera.

Grass of Parnassus, about 30 species of perennial herb *Parnassia* of the saxifrage family, growing to 18in (46cm) and native to damp, cold to temperate or mountainous regions of North America and Eurasia. They have a graceful, showy appearance.

Grass Pink, or swamp pink, orchid found in wet areas in NE and SE United States. Each plant has a cluster of 2 to 10 pink flowers with purple, cream, or rust-red hairs covering the large lower petal. Leaves are narrow and pointed. Family Orchidaceae; species *Calopogon pulchellus.*

Grass Snake, or ringed snake, a single species of egg-laying Old World snake *(Natrix natrix)* belonging to the same genus as American water snakes. Variable in color, it is usually brown with a yellow collar. Length: to 6ft (1.8m). Family Colubridae.

Gratian(us), Flavius (359–83), Western Roman emperor (375–83). Coemperor first with his father, Valentinian I, he later ruled with his brother Valentinian II. Advised by St Ambrose, he tried to stamp out paganism in the empire. He was assassinated by supporters of Maximus.

Grattan, Henry (1746–1820), Irish statesman. Trained as a lawyer, he entered the Irish parliament (1775) and through his oratory quickly became a leader of the party supporting Ireland's independence from the British parliament, a goal achieved in 1782. Always a supporter of parliamentary reform, he spent his later years striving for Roman Catholic emancipation.

Graves, Robert (1895–1985), British poet, novelist, and critic. After publishing his autobiography, *Goodbye to All That* (1929), he emigrated to Spain. Other works include *I, Claudius* (1934), *Claudius the God* (1934), *The White Goddess* (1947), *The Crowning Privilege* (1955), and *They Hanged My Saintly Billy* (1980).

Gravireceptors, nerve endings and organs located in skeletal muscles, joints, and inner ear that are sensitive to bodily equilibrium and gravitational field direction and strength. They have been found to be temporarily affected by prolonged weightlessness.

Gravitation, one of the four forces known (the others being electromagnetism and the weak and strong nuclear forces). Immensely weak compared to the other forces, gravitation is nonetheless obvious to man because of the great mass of the earth. The gravitational force F between two masses m_1 and m_2 a distance r apart was found by Isaac Newton to be $F = Gm_1m_2/r^2$, where G is a constant of proportionality called the universal constant of gravitation. A more powerful treatment of gravitation was developed by Albert Einstein, who showed in his general theory of relativity how to understand gravitation as a manifestation of the underlying structure of space-time. Only recently have attempts been made to detect the *gravitational waves* predicted in Einstein's theory.

Gravitational Waves, waves of energy, similar to electromagnetic waves, postulated by Einstein's gen-

eral theory of relativity as being emitted from a massive accelerating body, such as an exploding or collapsing star, and as traveling at the speed of light. Experimental results put forward as evidence for such waves have not yet been generally accepted.

Graviton, hypothetical elementary particle of zero mass thought to be continuously exchanged between bodies of mass and thus to be the carrier of the gravitational force.

Gravity, the gravitational force field of a planet or other celestial body at its surface. The earth's gravity produces an acceleration of 32ft/sec² (9.8m/sec²) for any unsupported body. If the mass M and radius R of a planet are known, the acceleration due to gravity (g) at its surface can be determined from $g = GM/R^2$, where G is the universal constant of gravitation.

Gravity, Artificial, a force mimicking that of gravity but produced kinematically (ie, by acceleration or rotation). It could be maintained on space stations or on long space voyages to provide more nearly earthlike environment.

Gravity Anomaly, deviation in gravity from the expected value. Gravity measurements over deep ocean trenches are lower than average, those in mountainous regions are higher than average.

Gray, Thomas (1716–71), English poet. His "Elegy Written in a Country Churchyard" (1751) brought him fame. Other poems include "Ode on the Death of a Favourite Cat Drowned in a Tub of Gold Fishes" (1747) and "The Descent of Odin" (1768). His letters are important for their witty observations of contemporary life.

Graylag, common gray wild goose of Europe thought to be the ancestor of the domestic goose. Species *Anser anser. See also* Goose.

Grayling, fresh water food and sport fish found in N North America and Eurasia, characterized by a long, flaglike dorsal fin and small mouth. Length: 12–16in (30.5–40.6cm). Family Salmonidae; species includes *Thymallus arcticus.*

Graywocke, any of a variety of sandstones that consist of a heterogeneous mixture of rock fragments, feldspar, and quartz of sand size strongly bonded together in a mud matrix. Graywockes are thought to have originated in deep sea water through the action of currents. *See also* Sandstone.

Graz, formerly Gratz; city in Austria, on Mur River, 87mi (140km) SSW of Vienna, in Styrean Alps; home of astronomer, Johannes Kepler (1594–1600); site of 17th-century arsenal, university (1585), and technical university (1811). Industries: steel, machinery, paper, glass, leather, textiles. Pop. 248,500.

Great Awakening, series of loosely related 18th-century religious revivals in the American colonies. The revivals started with the preachings of Jonathan Edwards in New England (1734), William Tennent in New Jersey, Samuel Davies in Virginia, and were united by the forceful tour of George Whitefield (1739–41). Baptist revivals occurred in 1760 and Methodism evolved in the pre-Revolutionary period. The revivalism, although initially fostering intolerance, eventually led to the formation of many churches, and a general spirit of religious freedom. Colleges and universities such as Princeton, Brown, Rutgers, Dartmouth, and Pennsylvania started as seminaries during the Great Awakening.

Great Barrier Reef, coral reef off NE coast of Queensland, Australia; tourist area; contains the largest deposit of coral in the world. Length: 1,250mi (2,013km). Area: more than 80,000sq mi (207,200sq km).

Great Basin, desert area in W United States; comprises most of Nevada, parts of Utah, Idaho, California, Wyoming, and Oregon; area of interior drainage to Great Salt Lake; includes Mojave Desert, Death Valley, and Carson Sink; complex topographical basin.

Great Bear, The. *See* Ursa Major.

Great Bear Lake, lake in NW Territories, Canada; drains into the Mackenzie River; the lake is icebound eight months a year; explored 1825 by John Franklin. In 1929 radium ore was discovered on the E shore. Length: 192mi (309km). Depth: 1,356ft (414m).

Great Britain, kingdom in NW Europe, officially called United Kingdom of Great Britain and Northern Ireland. It consists of England, Wales, Scotland, Northern Ireland (Ulster), the Channel Islands, and the Isle of Man. For a description of the land, economy, and people of the constitutent parts of Great Britain, see separate articles on England, Northern Ireland, Scotland, and Wales.

Great Britain is a constitutional monarchy. The Parliament, the supreme legislative power, has two houses: the House of Lords, with about 1,000 members drawn from the hereditary peerage, life peers, and the episcopate, and the House of Commons, with 635 members elected for a maximum of 5 years. Wales was united with England in 1536, and Scotland in 1707; both send representatives to Parliament. Devolution measures were defeated by Scottish and Welsh voters in 1979, but the devolution movement still commands popular support, especially in Wales. Northern Ireland, represented in the House of Commons by 12 members, also had its own parliament at Stormont (Belfast) from 1921 to 1972, when all powers were assumed by Parliament because of sectarian violence in Ulster. The Channel Islands and the Isle of Man are crown dependencies with their own legislatures. The Channel Islands, as part of the old Duchy of Normandy, came under the control of the English crown in 1066. The Isle of Man became subject to England in 1346.

History. The kingdoms of England and Scotland were under one rule from 1603, when James VI of Scotland ascended the English throne as James I. Although the realms were not formally united until 1707, the history of Great Britain begins with James' accession. For the history of England prior to 1603, *see* England.

The relations of James I and his son Charles I with Parliament were stormy, as Parliament's control of taxation thwarted many of the crown's plans. The struggle led to the first Civil War (1642–46) and then the second Civil War (1648), which was followed by the execution of Charles I and the proclamation of the Commonwealth (1649), headed by Oliver Cromwell. The Restoration in 1660 brought Charles II to the throne. His brother James II acceded in 1685 and was opposed for his Roman Catholicism, particularly after the birth of a male heir. William of Orange, husband of James' Protestant daughter Mary, invaded in 1688 in the Glorious Revolution, and as William III, he and Mary ascended the throne in 1689. After William's death, their daughter Anne took the crown, and by the Act of Settlement, the crown passed to the house of Hanover in 1714.

The early years of the Hanoverians were devoted to consolidation domestically, while Britain was becoming a great colonial and maritime power abroad. The loss of the American colonies in the Revolutionary War was balanced by gains in India. Demands for political reform were stimulated by the American and French revolutions but the governing class resisted attempts at reform. Rebellion in Ireland in 1798 was followed in 1800 by the union of Ireland and Britain. Political changes received new impetus with the extension of the franchise in the Reform Act of 1832.

The 19th century was a time of development for Britain as the nation continued its rapid industrialization and became the world's foremost power, with a huge overseas empire. Politically, the long reign of Queen Victoria was marked by the emergence of national political parties. The Liberal party was long headed by William Gladstone, while the Conservatives were led by Benjamin Disraeli and Randolph Churchill. Further extensions of the franchise, the growth of trade unions, and reforms in Ireland were major domestic issues. In the early 20th century, the Liberals' influence declined and the new Labour party increased its power in Parliament.

The great events of the 20th century all had major effects on Britain. The Irish Free State was established in 1926. The nation was slow to recover from World Wars I and II and was severely hit by the Depression of the 1930s. After World War II, its colonies achieved independence, and Britain's position as a world power eroded. Domestically, the country was split by Ireland's demands for independence and was shocked by the abdication of Edward VIII in 1936. Although the monarchy remained popular, Elizabeth II had no real power. Neither Conservative nor Labour governments were able to solve Britain's economic problems. The country's entry into the European Community in 1973 did not improve economic conditions and under Conservative Margaret Thatcher—Britain's first female prime minister—the economy deteriorated even further. High unemployment was partly responsible for civil riots in 1981. A year-long miners' strike (1984–85) added to high unemployment through the 1980s. Argentina's invasion (1982) of the Falkland Islands, a British possession, precipitated a war with Britain. By midyear, the British had recaptured the islands, and peace settlement talks were in progress. The government has been unable to curb continuing violence between Catholics and Protestants in Northern Ireland and terrorism increased throughout Great Britain during the mid-1980s.

Following are lists of the rulers and prime ministers of England and Great Britain.

RULERS OF ENGLAND AND GREAT BRITAIN

Egbert (Ecgberht)	829–39
Ethelwulf	839–58
Ethelbald	858–60
Ethelbert	860–66
Ethelred I	866–71
Alfred the Great	871–99
Edward the Elder	899–924
Athelstan	924–40
Edmund I	940–46
Edred	946–55
Edwy	955–59
Edgar	959–75
Edward the Martyr	975–78
Aethelred II (the Unready)	978–1016
Edmund II (Ironside)	1016
Canute (Cnut)	1016–35
Harold I (Harefoot)	1035–40
Hardecanute	1040–42
Edward the Confessor	1042–66
Harold II	1066
William I (the Conqueror)	1066–87
William II (Rufus)	1087–1100
Henry I (Beauclerc)	1100–35
Stephen	1135–54
Henry II	1154–89
Richard I (Coeur de Lion)	1189–99
John (Lackland)	1199–1216
Henry III	1216–72
Edward I (Longshanks)	1272–1307
Edward II	1307–27
Edward III	1327–77
Richard II	1377–99
Henry IV	1399–1413
Henry V	1413–22
Henry VI	1422–61
Edward IV	1461–83
Edward V	1483
Richard III	1483–85
Henry VII	1485–1509
Henry VIII	1509–47
Edward VI	1547–53
Mary I	1553–58
Elizabeth I	1558–1603
James I	1603–25
Charles I	1625–49
Commonwealth	1649–60
Charles II	1660–85
James II	1685–88
William III and Mary II	1689–94
William III	1694–1702
Anne	1702–14
George I	1714–27
George II	1727–60
George III	1760–1820
George IV	1820–30
William IV	1830–37
Victoria	1837–1901
Edward VII	1901–10
George V	1910–36
Edward VIII	1936
George VI	1936–52
Elizabeth II	1952–

PRIME MINISTERS

Sir Robert Walpole	1721–42
Earl of Wilmington	1742–43
Henry Pelham	1743–54
Duke of Newcastle	1754–56
Duke of Devonshire	1756–57
Duke of Newcastle	1757–62
Earl of Bute	1762–63
George Grenville	1763–65
Marquess of Rockingham	1765–66
William Pitt the Elder (Earl of Chatham)	1766–68
Duke of Grafton	1768–70
Frederick North (Lord North)	1770–82
Marquess of Rockingham	1782
Earl of Shelburne	1782–83
Duke of Portland	1783
William Pitt the Younger	1783–1801
Henry Addington	1801–04
William Pitt the Younger	1804–06
William Wyndham Grenville, Baron Grenville	1806–07
Duke of Portland	1807–09
Spencer Perceval	1809–12
Earl of Liverpool	1812–27
George Canning	1827
Viscount Goderich	1827–28
Duke of Wellington	1828–30
Earl Grey	1830–34
Viscount Melbourne	1834
Sir Robert Peel	1834–35
Viscount Melbourne	1835–41
Sir Robert Peel	1841–46
Lord John Russell (later Earl)	1846–52
Earl of Derby	1852
Earl of Aberdeen	1852–55
Viscount Palmerston	1855–58
Earl of Derby	1858–59
Viscount Palmerston	1859–65
Earl Russell	1865–66
Earl of Derby	1866–68
Benjamin Disraeli	1868
William E. Gladstone	1868–74
Benjamin Disraeli	1874–80
William E. Gladstone	1880–85
Marquess of Salisbury	1885–86
William E. Gladstone	1886
Marquess of Salisbury	1886–92
William E. Gladstone	1892–94
Earl of Rosebery	1894–95
Marquess of Salisbury	1895–1902
Arthur J. Balfour	1902–05
Sir Henry Campbell-Bannerman	1905–08
Herbert H. Asquith	1908–15
Herbert H. Asquith	1915–16
David Lloyd George	1916–22
Andrew Bonar Law	1922–23
Stanley Baldwin	1923–24
James Ramsay MacDonald	1924
Stanley Baldwin	1924–29
James Ramsay MacDonald	1929–31
James Ramsay MacDonald	1931–35
Stanley Baldwin	1935–37
Neville Chamberlain	1937–40
Winston Churchill	1940–45
Winston Churchill	1945
Clement Attlee	1945–51
Sir Winston Churchill	1951–55
Sir Anthony Eden	1955–57
Harold Macmillan	1957–63
Sir Alex Douglas-Home	1963–64
Harold Wilson	1964–70
Edward Heath	1970–74
Harold Wilson	1974–76
James Callaghan	1976–79
Margaret Thatcher	1979–

PROFILE

Official name: United Kingdom of Great Britain and Northern Ireland
Area: 94,226sq mi (244,045sq km)
Population: 55,883,100
Density: 593per sq mi (229per sq km)
Chief cities: London (capital); Birmingham; Glasgow
Government: monarchy and parliament
Religion: Anglicanism (England), Presbyterianism (Scotland)
Language: English
Monetary unit: pound sterling
Gross national product: $353,630,000,000
Per capita income: $3,380
Industries (major products): motor vehicles, machinery, textiles, iron, steel
Agriculture (major products): cereals, potatoes, sheep, cattle
Minerals (major): coal, iron ore, petroleum
Trading partners (major): United States, West Germany, Netherlands, France

Great Circle, circle on a spherical surface whose center is coincident with the center of the sphere. Thus lines of longitude lie on great circles; lines of latitude, with the exception of the equator, do not.

Great Dane, giant hunting and fighting dog (working group) bred in Germany over 400 years ago for bear hunting. Also called German mastiff, it has a narrow, long head with large, blunted muzzle; high-set, medium-length ears that droop forward, or if cropped are erect; broad, deep chest; short back; long, strong legs; and straight, slender tail. The short, smooth coat is brindle, fawn, blue, black, or harlequin. Average size: 30in (76cm) minimum height at shoulder; to 150lb (68kg). *See also* Working Dogs.

Greater Antilles, largest of three major island groups of West Indies, between Atlantic Ocean (NE) and Caribbean Sea (S and SW), and Gulf of Mexico (NW). Group includes Cuba, Haiti, Dominican Republic, Jamaica, Puerto Rico; Puerto Rico is a commonwealth associated with United States; remaining four islands are independent.

Greater Sunda Islands, larger of 2 island groups comprising Sunda Isles, Indonesia; located in W Malay Archipelago, between South China Sea and Indian Ocean; includes Java, Sumatra, Borneo, Celebes, and adjacent small islands. Pop. 112,138,626.

Great Falls, city in central Montana, on Missouri River; seat of Cascade co. Nearby is Giant Springs; site of College of Great Falls (1932), and log cabin of cowboy artist Charles Russell. Industries: oil and copper refining, flour. Inc. 1888. Pop. (1980) 56,725.

Great Lakes, chain of five freshwater lakes in central North America, between Canada and the United States; includes lakes Superior, Michigan, Huron, Erie, Ontario; they are connected by straits, small rivers, and canals. Formed at the end of the Ice Age, they are drained by the St Lawrence River. First of lakes to be discovered was Huron, visited by Samuel de Champlain in 1615; French traders and explorers continued developing and exploring the land for France until 1763 when Canada was ceded to Great Britain. War of 1812 saw conflict between US and Britain over lakes Ontario and Erie. Opening of New York state's Erie Canal 1825 connected this area with Hudson River and Atlantic (now accomplished by Barge Canal). Deepening of St Lawrence for seaway opening in 1959 connected Great Lakes with world shipping; Illinois Waterway connects it with Mississippi River; steel, iron ore, coal, petroleum, and grains are shipped from April until December. Industrialization and population increases have created pollution problems especially in lakes Erie, Ontario, and Michigan. Major cities on the lakes include Chicago, Detroit, Buffalo, Cleveland, Milwaukee. Combined surface area of lakes is 95,000sq mi (246,050sq km). *See also* articles on each lake.

Great Leap Forward, government policy inaugurated by Mao Tse-tung in China in 1958 to try to catch up with and surpass Western powers in economy in record time. Peasants were organized into communes, and tens of millions were mobilized to smelt iron in primitive handmade furnaces. The resulting chaos and decline in agrarian and industrial production led to its abandonment by 1960–61.

Great Nebula. See Orion Nebula.

Great Plains, high, grassy slope of central North American continent, reaching from central Canada down the central plains states to Texas; W border is the Rocky Mts. Somewhat sparse in population, the principal economic activities are farming, cattle, and sheep raising; wheat is dominant crop.

Great Pyrenees, bearlike guard and mountain dog (working group) that originated in Asia and appeared in Europe 1800–1000BC. A favorite of royalty and peasant alike, it has a wedge-shaped head with rounded crown; medium-sized, V-shaped ears carried close to the head; a straight, broad body; shortish, sturdy legs; and a long tail curled over the back. The white double coat is long, flat, and thick. Average size: 25–32in (63.5–81.3cm) high at shoulder; 90–125lb (40–56kg). *See also* Working Dog.

Great Dane

Great Smoky Mountains

Greece

Great Saint Bernard Pass, Alpine pass on the Italian-Swiss border that links Valais canton, Switzerland, and Valle d'Aosta, Italy. Altitude: 8,110ft (2,474m).

Great Salt Lake, large, shallow lake of salt water in NW Utah; fed by the Bear, Weber, and Jordan rivers, it is a descendant of prehistoric Lake Bonneville that covered much of the Great Basin. Area: approx. 2,000sq mi (5,180sq km). Depth: 35ft (11m).

Great Schism (1378–1417), rift between the Roman popes and the king of France. It began when Pope Gregory XI died in 1378 and was succeeded by an Italian, Urban VI. The French cardinals dissented, declared the election invalid, and elected an anti-pope, Clement VII (and his successor Benedict XIII), who stayed at Avignon. The Roman pope was supported by the Holy Roman Empire, England, Hungary, Poland, and other northern European countries, the anti-pope was backed by France, Scotland, Spain, Portugal, and some German princes. Reconciliation took place at the Council of Constance.

Great Slave Lake, lake in Northwest Territories, Canada; the 5th-largest lake in North America. Discovered 1771. Length: 298mi (480km). Depth: 2,015ft (615m).

Great Smoky Mountains, part of the Appalachian Mt system, on the North Carolina-Tennessee border. One of the oldest ranges on earth, it is rich in hardwood and holds the largest virgin forest of red spruce. Named for the smoky haze that envelops them, they were first settled in early 19th century in lower valleys. Artifacts of these early pioneers have been preserved by the National Park Service. Log cabins, barns, farm implements, and a great mill powered by a water wheel are on display. Highest point is Clingmans Dome, 6,643ft (2,026m). In 1926 it was set aside as Great Smoky Mts National Park. Area: 516,626acres (209,079hectares).

Great Trek, migration of Boer farmers and pastoralists from the Cape Colony (South Africa) in the late 1830s and 1840s to escape British domination. Defeating the Xhosa peoples in their new lands, these "Voortrekkers" formed the Transvaal and the Orange Free State and maintained independence for most of the time preceding the Boer War (1899–1902).

Great Wall, fortified wall in N China, extending from Shanhaikuan to Chiayükuan; originally built as a series of many walls, it was unified under the Ch'un dynasty (204 BC). The Ming dynasty (1368–1644) is responsible for the modern form of the wall; constructed of stone, earth, and brick, its purpose was to ward off northern invaders; guard stations and watch towers are spaced at regular intervals. Length: 1,500mi (2,415km). Width: 15–30ft (5–9m) at the base, 12ft (4m) at the top. Height: 20–50ft (6–15m).

Grebe, brownish, grayish, or blackish freshwater diving bird found worldwide that flies laboriously, with legs set so far back it cannot walk on land. White, bluish, or greenish chalky eggs (2–8) are laid in a soggy aquatic weed nest after special courtship rituals. Length: 9–14in (23–36cm). Family Podicipedidae.

Greco, El (1541?–1614?), Spanish painter, b. Domenikos Theotokopoulos in Crete. He was trained by Greek monks as an icon painter. In 1577 he settled in Toledo and tried to win favor at the Spanish Court but never really succeeded. The intensely personal vision reflected in his works is ecstatically mystical and passionate, with elongated, distorted figures; disturbing color schemes; eerie, supernatural lighting; and a disregard for normal rules of perspective. His early style was influenced by Michelangelo and other Italian mas-

ters, his later style by Byzantine art, but through all phases of his career his art remained uniquely individual. His first major commission in Spain was the enormous Altar of San Domingo el Antiguo in Toledo; some of his later paintings, such as "Burial of Count Orgasz," "Agony in the Garden," and "Resurrection" depict an increasingly rapturous vision of suffering. In his final years he painted many portraits and one famous landscape, "View of Toledo."

Greece, a small nation on the Balkan Peninsula in the E Mediterranean Sea. A magnificent civilization flourished there in the 1st millennium BC, and splendid ruins stand throughout Greece, attesting to that golden age. Modern Greece is a small country with a developing economy, which has undergone considerable political turmoil in the 20th century.

Land and Economy. Greece has a diverse geography. The mainland territory is very mountainous, and is enclosed by the sea on three sides. The soil is generally poor, except in the scattered plains of central and N Greece. Nearly half of all Greeks are farmers; important crops include fruits and vegetables, tobacco, olives, and wheat. Tobacco is the country's major export crop. Greece is historically a maritime country; nearly one-fifth of its territory consists of 437 islands, and fishing and shipping are of special economic importance. The Greek merchant fleet is the seventh largest in the world. In the late 1970s manufacturing surpassed agriculture in the value of output for the first time. Tourism provides a major contribution to the national income.

People. The Greeks call themselves "Hellenes." The Greek language is spoken by nearly all Greeks, making Greece one of the most homogeneous of all nations. Modern Greek differs sharply from the Greek tongue of ancient times. The official religion of Greece is the Greek Orthodox Church, with 97% of all Greeks as members. Since World War II, the population has been moving steadily from the poorest farming villages to the cities. The family is the dominant social unit; a Greek's primary loyalty is to his kinsmen. The living standard has been rising steadily.

Government. Greece became a democratic republic in 1974 after Greeks rejected a return to monarchy in a referendum. According to the constitution of 1975, the head of state is the president, elected by the parliament. Members of parliament are elected to four-year terms. The prime minister is head of the majority party in the parliament. The country is divided into 52 administrative districts, each directed by a governor. Cities and towns are governed by elected officials.

History. Greece was ruled by the Ottoman Turks for more than 500 years, until the 1820s when France, England, and Russia recognized Greek independence. The constitutional monarchy was est. in 1844. For many decades Greece sought to acquire foreign territories inhabited by Greeks. By the end of World War I, Greece had added Thrace, Crete, a portion of Macedonia, S Epirus, and many islands. In World War II, Greece repelled an assault by Italy (1940), and was attacked and occupied by German forces (1941). Following liberation by the Allies, Communists attempted to seize power in a bloody civil war, ending only in 1949 when the monarchy was reinstated with US assistance. The Greek army seized power in 1967, and King Constantine fled the country. Col. George Papadopoulos became prime minister. This military government resigned in 1974 and was replaced by a civilian government led by Constantine Karamanlis. In 1980, Karamanlis became president, and George Rallis was elected prime minister. He was defeated in 1981 elections, and the new Socialist prime minister, Andreas Papandreou, opposed Greece's membership in NATO and the EEC, which Greece had joined the same year. During the first year of his term, economic pressures

forced Papandreou to ignore his campaign promises to leave these organizations. *See also* Greece, Ancient.

PROFILE

Official name: Hellenic Republic
Area: 50,944sq mi (131,944sq km)
Population: 9,405,000
  Density: 185per sq mi (71per sq km)
Chief cities: Athens (capital); Salonika; Piraeus
Government: republic
Religion: Eastern Orthodox
Language: Greek (official)
Monetary unit: drachma
Gross national product: $36,710,000,000
Per capita income: $2,885
Manufacturing (major products): textiles, clothing, cigarettes, shoes, processed foods, chemicals
Agriculture (major products): wheat, olives, tobacco, citrus fruits
Minerals (major): iron, lignite, bauxite, magnesite, chromite
Trading partners (major): West Germany, Great Britain, France, Japan, Italy

Greece, Ancient, civilization that flourished on the Greek peninsula, in Asia Minor (modern Turkey), on the N coast of Africa, and in the western Mediterranean from about 3000 BC until 146 BC, when the weakened Greek cities fell before the power of the Roman Empire. The civilization of the ancient Greeks has had a profound influence on the modern Western world; in virtually every field of the arts, sciences, and philosophy the ancient Greeks laid the groundwork for the modern discipline. Democracy was introduced by the Greeks and was practiced in its purest form in the Greek city-states. The philosophies of Socrates, Plato, and Aristotle continue to influence Western thought.

In the 3rd millennium BC, a culture known today as the Aegean civilization developed centered on the island of Crete (the Minoan civilization) and in the Peloponnesus on the mainland (the Mycenaean civilization). The Minoans made primitive use of bronze and developed a pictograph script (known to modern archaeologists as Linear A). They built great palaces and developed the rudiments of a maritime trade. The culture of the Mycenaeans roughly paralleled that of the Minoans (their pictograph writing is known as Linear B) and is believed to have been largely borrowed from the Minoans. This Bronze Age of Greek history is the period celebrated in the epic poems of Homer. By about 1400 the Minoan civilization on Crete had deteriorated, but the Mycenaeans on the mainland continued to prosper until the 12th century. About that time they were conquered by the Dorians, who invaded from the north. Beginning about 1400, various Greek-speaking peoples had begun migrating into southern Greece, including, in addition to the Dorians, the Achaeans, Aeolians, and Ionians. As they settled into agricultural communities, they developed the self-contained political, economic, and social unit known as the city-state. As populations grew and agricultural land became scarce, colonies were planted on the Greek islands, in Asia Minor, in North Africa, and in Italy, France, and Spain. Eventually, these colonies became themselves city-states, virtually independent of the sponsoring cities. Thus the groundwork laid for a great Greek empire.

The Greek city-states developed separately and were often at war with each other. Nevertheless, they shared certain common traits. They all spoke Greek, and they shared similar religious traditions. Politically, they typically evolved from a monarchy to an aristocracy to a tyranny and, finally, either to a democracy or an oligarchy or military dictatorship. Except for cooperating in such religious ventures as the Olympic Games and in maintaining such shrines as the Delphic Oracle, the Greek city-states were basically independent of each other until the beginning of the Persian Wars in 512 BC. That long conflict began when the Greek colonies in Asia Minor revolted against their Persian overlords and were given aid by Athens, the largest and richest of the Greek cities. Persia retaliated by attacking the Greek mainland. In order to counter the great Persian army, Athens organized the Delian League in 478. All the important Greek cities, including Sparta, were members. The great Greek victories at Marathon (490), Salamis (480), and Plataea (479) ended the Persian threat to Greece, but the Delian League continued to fight the war until its successful conclusion in 449. The success of the Delian League in the war encouraged Athens to continue it afterwards, and it became, in effect, the instrument of the Athenian empire. At its height it comprised almost 150 Greek cities. Athens, under the leadership of Pericles, now entered into its Golden Age. Art, architecture, literature, and philosophy flourished. Pericles successfully put down (448) an attempt by Euboea to break away from the Delian League. In 445, Athens and Sparta signed a truce that gave each of the great Greek cities 15 years of peace. In 431, however, the increasing rivalry of the two cities erupted into the Peloponnesian War. In time the strength of the Athenian navy was overwhelmed by the great Spartan army, and Athens was destroyed as a power. Sparta was the most powerful Greek city for the next 30 years.

Continuing rivalries weakened the Greek cities, however, and they were unable to defend themselves against the growing power of Macedon, a country in northeastern Greece. Under Philip II, who ruled from 359–336, Macedon conquered Upper Macedon, Thrace, and Chalcidice. More important, Philip created the greatest army the world had seen. His son, Alexander the Great, who ruled from 336–323, used that army to conquer the entire Greek world and place it under his Macedonian Empire. Under Alexander, Greek civilization was spread throughout the known Western world and as far east as India. His empire did not survive his death, however, and was divided among his generals. As Macedonian influence declined, the Greek cities revived their rivalries. Alliances were formed, such as the Aetolian and Achaean leagues, to forge some kind of unity, but they were mostly unsuccessful. Warfare was almost incessant. In the meantime, Rome was growing in power. In 146 what was left of the Greek cities fell under Roman control, and the ancient Greek world came to an end. Hellenism, as Greek culture had come to be called, retained its strength, however, and became the basis for the civilization of the Roman Empire. *See also* Alexander the Great; Delian League; Peloponnesian War; Persian Wars; Sparta.

Greek, one of the two great classical languages of antiquity. Its descendant, Modern Greek, is spoken by about 10,000,000 people in Greece and 500,000 more on Cyprus. Greek has profoundly influenced the vocabulary of many languages. The word *photograph,* for example, is a combination of the Greek words for *light* and *write.* Like English, Greek is an Indo-European language.

Greek Architecture, the Hellenic architecture of the Dorians, who succeeded the Myceneans in Greece. The major works were produced between 700 and 146 BC and followed a definite system of construction based on rules of form and proportion. The greatest structures are temples of post-and-lintel construction. These vary from the simplicity of the Doric order to the greater elegance and decoration of the Ionic and Corinthian orders. The best example of the Doric is the Parthenon. The Ionic was more common on the coast of Asia Minor, as in the temples of Miletus, and the Corinthian was only used extensively after the masterpieces of the Athenian empire had been built.

Greek Mythology. The Greek imagination was anthropomorphic, creating the Olympian pantheon in man's image, with all his faults and virtues. In the myths, the gods are capable of great pettiness or vindictiveness, revenge and favoritism. Even the creation of the universe takes place without magic as a series of procreations. The Greek myths were generally explanatory, offering answers to questions of human nature and the universe, clarifying abstract ideas, or explaining religious matters in a more or less rational manner bordering on the scientific. Because of this rationalism the myths never gained importance in the religion of the people.

Greek Revival Architecture, architectural style of the late 18th and early 19th centuries occasioned by the discovery of Greek architecture. Its first example was James Stuart's garden temple at Hagley, England, but the style became even more influential in US public buildings. Benjamin Latrobe's Bank of Pennsylvania, Philadelphia (1799), the first example of Greek revival in the United States, is an imitation of a Greek Ionic temple.

Greek War of Independence (1821–29), the rebellion of Greece against Turkish rule that led to the independence of modern Greece. In 1820 Prince Ypsilanti led a premature raid against the Turks. He was defeated but other groups staged isolated raids all over Greece, and the Turks made brutal reprisals. From 1822–24 there were two civil wars in Greece between the various factions. In 1824, Mehemet Ali of Egypt joined the Turks; Athens fell in 1826. Britain, France, and Russia intervened in 1827, the year the Turkish fleet was crushed at Navarino. By the Treaty of Adrianople (1829), Greek autonomy was established, followed in 1832 by independence. *See also* Greece.

Greeley, Horace (1811–72), US journalist whose editorial policies helped to rouse northern popular opinion against slavery, b. near Amherst, N.H. His liberal views gained him the editorship of the *Jeffersonian* (1838) and the *Log Cabin* in the presidential campaign (1840). In 1841, he founded and edited the New York *Tribune,* where his progressive ideals of socio-economic reform and his powerful antislavery editorials were highly influential. His homilies included "Go West Young Man." He helped to organize the Republican party in the 1850s and supported Abraham Lincoln in his presidential campaign (1860). Greeley fruitlessly sought office, broke with the Republican party and finally became the unsuccessful presidential candidate for the dissenting Liberal Republicans in 1872.

Green Algae, a large group of marine and freshwater algae (division Chlorophyta). Green algae range in size from microscopic single-cell types to large complex plants. Some of the single-cell types form colonies. Others live in a symbiotic relationship with fungi, forming the plant known as a lichen; and others live in symbiotic associations with certain marine invertebrates. The larger types take a variety of forms, including tubes, threads, and leaflike sheets such as sea lettuce. The chlorophyll in these green algae is not obscured by other pigments. *See also* Lichen.

Greenaway, Kate (1846–1901), English author and illustrator of books for children. Her illustrations of a joyous world of children are executed with charm and delicacy, but without sentimentality. Her first major success was *Under the Window* (1879). Other titles include *Marigold Garden* (1885) and *A Apple Pie* (1886). The Kate Greenaway Medal is the English counterpart of the Caldecott Medal in the United States.

Green Bay, city and port of entry in E Wisconsin, 112mi (180km) N of Milwaukee, on S end of Green Bay and at mouth of Fox River; seat of Brown co; home of Green Bay Packers professional football team; site of Tank Cottage (1776), and National Railroad Museum. Industries: cheese processing, fisheries, shipyards, paper, iron, steel. Trading post est. by Jean Nicolet 1634; settled 1701; inc. 1854. Pop. (1980) 87,899.

Greenbrier, or cat brier, climbing, woody vine native to North America, Europe, Asia, and Bolivia. It has prickly stems, small flowers that are green, yellow, or white, and black berries. The extract sarsaparilla is obtained from the dried roots of some species. Family Liliaceae; genus *Smilax.*

Greene, (Henry) Graham (1904–), English novelist and dramatist. His novels, written from a Roman Catholic viewpoint, include *Brighton Rock* (1938), *The Power and the Glory* (1940), *The Quiet American* (1955), *Our Man in Havana* (1958), *Travels with My Aunt* (1969), *The Honorary Consul* (1973), *The Human Factor*(1978), *Dr.Fischer of Geneva or the Bomb Party* (1980), *Ways of Escape* (1981), and *Monsignor Quixote* (1982), His plays include *The Living Room* (1953) and *The Potting Shed* (1957).

Green Flash, the greenish or bluish hue of the upper rim of the Sun just as it is about to disappear with setting or appears with rising, due to atmospheric effects on the sun's light.

Greenhouse, or hothouse, glass- or plastic-paned structure with a wood or metal frame. Temperature and humidity can be controlled for growing plants out of season. Earliest greenhouses date from ancient Rome; Pliny described mica-glazed pits used to grow plants and vegetables for Tiberius Caesar. Greenhouses range in size from small lean-tos and window greenhouses for the home to huge public and commercial greenhouses.

Greenhouse Effect, the heating effect on the earth caused by the absorption by the atmosphere of long-wave (infrared) radiation emitted from the earth's surface and its counter radiation back to the surface, as opposed to short-wave (ultraviolet) radiation transmitted rather freely from earth through atmosphere to space. *See also* Radiation.

Greenland, Danish island-territory in the NW Atlantic. The people are predominately Eskimo and mostly Lutheran. The largest island in the world, 1,660mi (2,673km) long and 800mi (1,288km) wide at its widest, over 85% of Greenland is ice-capped and uninhabitable. The economy is based almost entirely upon fishing, and seal-hunting has traditionally been important. Most of the inhabitants are Greenlanders—a mixture of Eskimos and those of European descent—and live almost exclusively on the SW coastal fringes. Both Greenlandic (a mixture of Eskimo dialects) and Danish serve as official languages. Greenlanders have Danish nationality and send two representatives to the Danish parliament. Eric the Red, who discovered the island in 982, purposely misnamed it to attract colonists. By the 12th century there was a colony of about 10,000, but by 1400 the settlements had disappeared. Colonization was reinstituted in 1721 under Hans Egede of Norway, "the Apostle of Greenland," and Godthåb was founded in 1727. The island was under direct Danish control from 1729 until 1979, when home rule was instituted. Negotiations regarding withdrawal from the EEC—the major point of contention being fishing rights—began in 1982.

PROFILE

Official name: Greenland
Area: 840,000sq mi (2,175,600sq km)
Population: 44,465
Chief cities: Godthåb (capital); Holsteinsborg; Sukkertoppen
Government: Parliamentary self-rule under Danish sovereignty
Gross national product: $80,000,000
Per capita income: $1,730
Agriculture (major products): fish and fish products
Minerals (major): quartz, mica, feldspar, cryolite, chiolite.

Green Mountains, northern branch of Appalachian Mts, extends S to N from W Massachusetts, through Vermont and into SE Canada; heavily wooded and scenic area; range is famous for its granite quarries, especially in Barre, Vermont area. Highest peak is Mt Mansfield, 4,393ft (1,340m).

Green River, longest tributary of the Colorado; flows from W Wyoming S to SE Utah. Length: 730mi (1,175km).

Greensboro, city in N North Carolina, 26mi (42km) E of Winston-Salem; seat of Guilford co; birthplace of O. Henry; site of Greensboro College (1838), Guilford College (1834), Bennett College (1873), University of North Carolina at Greensboro (1891), North Carolina Agricultural and Technical State University (1891). Nearby is national military park commemorating Revolutionary War battle of Guilford Courthouse. Industries: cellophane products, chemicals, textiles. Settled 1749; inc. 1829. Pop. (1980) 155,642.

Green Snake, or grass snake, slender North American and Asian snake. The rough green snake *(Opheodrys aestivus)* of North America has keeled scales; the smaller, smooth green snake *(O. vernalis)* is unkeeled. Both are solid green with pale bellies. Length: to 30in (76cm). Family Colubridae. *See also* Colubrid; Reptile; Snake.

Green Turtle, edible marine turtle found in tropical waters of Atlantic and Pacific. In danger of extinction, with a head too large to fit inside the shell. Its forelegs are powerful flippers. Length: to 4ft (1.2m); weight: to 500lb (225kg). Family Cheloniidae; species *Chelonia mydas. See also* Turtle.

Greenville, city in NW South Carolina, on Reedy River; seat of Greenville co; site of Furman University (1825), Bob Jones University (1927). Industries: textiles, clothing, chemicals, machinery, electronic equipment. Settled 1797; inc. 1907. Pop. (1980) 58,242.

Greenwich, borough of Greater London, SE England, on S bank of the Thames River; site of the Royal Observatory (1675–1958), royal palace (1433) housing the Royal Naval College, and Greenwich Hospital. The Greenwich meridian serves as basis for standard time and nautical calculation throughout the world, accepted by Washington Meridian Conference (1884). Pop. 207,200. *See also* Greenwich Time.

Greenwich, residential town in SW Connecticut, on Long Island Sound, on New York border. Industries: publishing, printing. Settled as part of New York 1640; annexed by Connecticut 1656. Pop. (1980) 59,578.

Grimm, Jacob Ludwig Karl

Horace Greeley

Greenland

Grenada

Greenwich Time, Greenwich Mean Time (GMT), or **Greenwich Civil Time (GCT),** system of time reckoning based on mean solar time as measured on the Greenwich (0°) meridian. Calculated from 0 hours to 24 hours, it is equivalent to Universal Time.

Gregorian Chant, religious music of the Roman Catholic Church, named for Pope Gregory I (590–604) but believed to have originated after Gregory. The music is sung by choir and soloists, with simple melodies and no accompaniment, steady rhythms, and religious text.

Gregory I, Roman Catholic pope (590–604) and saint. A Benedictine monk, he was concerned for the poor. When consecrated, he maintained his belief in monasticism as a new life for the church. He removed lay officials from the Vatican, warned against fanaticism, and initiated the conversion of Anglo-Saxons through the Benedictine order, earning the title "The Great."

Gregory VII, Roman Catholic pope (1073–85) and saint, b. Hildebrand. His pontificate was filled with conflict and an unsuccessful plot was made on his life because of his relation with King Henry IV, who was later excommunicated. A reformer, he opposed simony, increased the papacy's temporal power, and tried to free the clergy from family and civil ties.

Gregory IX, Roman Catholic pope (1227–41), b. Ugolino di Segni (c.1143). Made cardinal deacon by his uncle, Pope Innocent III, he served as a papal legate to Germany. He ordered the 1233 Inquisition and placed the Dominicans in charge of it. In 1234, he formed the Decretals, a code of canon law still used in the 20th century.

Gregory XI, Roman Catholic pope (1370–78), b. Pierre Roger de Beaufort (1331) in France. The last of the Avignon popes, he was advised by Catherine of Sienna to move back to Rome in 1377. His concern for recovering lands of the papal states led to war. He issued the first condemnation of John Wycliffe's teachings.

Gregory XIII, Roman Catholic pope (1572–85), b. Ugo Buoncompagni (1502). He served as a papal legate to France and Belgium. Concerned with education, he supported schools, training the clergy, and missionary work, giving special support to the work of the Jesuits. He restored the Catholic Church in Poland.

Gregory of Nazianzus, Saint (c.330–c.390), Roman Catholic bishop, theologian, and Doctor of the Church. He was born in Cappadocia (now in Turkey) and became a friend of St Basil the Great, who made him a bishop. For a time Gregory was patriarch of Constantinople, upholding the Nicene Creed against the Arian heresy, but retired to lead a monastic life and write. During his career he produced more than 680 poems, letters, and orations. His most important contribution was his exposition of the Trinity: God the Father, God the Son, and God the Holy Spirit.

Gregory of Tours, Saint (c.538–593), bishop and historian of Gaul. After he became bishop of Tours in 573 he used his influence to end political feuds. He is most important, however, for his writings. His *History of the Franks* consists of two books on current affairs which are major sources on his times. He also wrote on miracles, martyrs, and church fathers.

Grenada, State of, island republic in SE Caribbean Sea 90mi (145km) N of Venezuela. The country consists of Grenada, the southernmost of the Windward Islands, and the smaller islands of Carriacou and Petit Martinique, part of the Grenadine Islands. The main

island, covered with forested, volcanic mountains, is 21mi (34km) long and 12mi (19km) wide. The economy is almost entirely agricultural, and spices are the leading export. Over 50% of the population is of African descent and another 40% is mixed African and East Indian. There are a few Carib Indians (the original inhabitants) and a few whites. Christianity predominates. About 93% of the people are literate. Discovered by Christopher Columbus in 1498, the island was colonized by the French in 1650. Ceded to the British in 1763, it remained a British colony until 1974 when it became an independent nation within the Commonwealth. It has been a UN member since 1974. Following a coup in 1979, the parliament was dissolved. A coup in 1983 and US fears about Cuban influence there led in October to a US invasion of Grenada and the establishment of a pro-US government.

PROFILE

Official name: State of Grenada
Area: 120sq mi (310sq km)
Population: 110,394
 Density: 883per sq mi (342per sq km)
Chief city: Saint George's (capital)
Government: associated state of Great Britain
Language: English (official)
Monetary unit: East Caribbean dollar
Gross national product: $30,000,000
Per capita income: $300
Agriculture (major products): bananas, coconut, nutmeg
Trading partners (major): Great Britain

Grenadine Islands, archipelago in S Windward Islands, at E end of Caribbean Sea; extends over 60mi (97km) between Grenada and Saint Vincent in West Indies; includes approx. 600 small islands; S Grenadines are included in independent nation of Grenada. N Grenadines are part of independent country, St. Vincent and the Grenadines. Industries: cotton, limes, livestock, tourism. Pop. 13,247. *See also* Grenada; St. Vincent and the Grenadines.

Grendel, half-human monster, adversary of Beowulf in the great Old English epic of about the 8th century. Grendel was one of Cain's descendants and the personification of evil. He threatened and murdered the Danes of Hrothgar's Hall until the hero, Beowulf, a young warrior of the Geats, destroyed him by tearing off his arm.

Grenoble, city in SE France, on Isère River; surrounded by French Alps; capital of Isère dept.; capital of Dauphiné until 1349 when lands passed to the crown; site of University of Grenoble (1339), nuclear research center (1959), 13th-century cathedral, winter Olympics (1968). Industries: chemicals, plastics, kid gloves, sports equipment. Pop. 169,740.

Grenville, George (1712–70), English statesman; member of Parliament from 1741; navy treasurer (1756–62), first lord of the admiralty (1762–63), and prime minister (1763–65). He was responsible for the Stamp Act, which provoked violent reactions in the colonies and eventually caused the downfall of his ministry. *See also* Stamp Act.

Grenville, William Wyndham, Baron (1759–1834), English prime minister. A longtime friend of the younger William Pitt and a supporter of Roman Catholic emancipation, he formed the "ministry of all the talents" (1806–07) after Pitt's death. *See also* Pitt, William.

Grey, (Lady) Jane (1537–54), Queen of England. A cousin of Edward VI, she was married to Guilford Dudley, son of the duke of Northumberland, as part of the

duke's scheme to oust the Tudor dynasty. On Edward VI's death in 1553, she was proclaimed queen, but Princess Mary's claim quickly was established and Lady Jane was executed in February 1554. *See also* Mary I.

Greyhound, a coursing dog (hound group) known 2700 BC in ancient Egypt and favored by royalty over the centuries. Traditionally used to hunt hare, it is also used for racing. A graceful dog, it has a long, tapered head and muzzle; small ears thrown back and folded; dark, bright eyes; broad, muscular back; well-arched loin; long legs; and a long, fine, tapered tail. The short, smooth coat can be any color. Average size: 26in (66cm) high at shoulder; 65lb (29kg). *See also* Hounds.

Grieg, Edvard (1843–1907), Norwegian composer. Called the "Chopin of the North," he used Norwegian folk themes in his music, much of which is for the piano or voice. Among his best-known works are the song "I Love Thee," the two *Peer Gynt* suites for orchestra, and the immensely popular *Piano Concerto in A minor.*

Griffith, Arthur (1872–1922), politician and a founder of the Irish Free State. He edited "The United Irishman" (1899–1906), which proclaimed the Sinn Fein policy of national self-reliance. He was president of the Sinn Fein party (1910) and of Dail Eireann (1922).

Griffith, D(avid) W(ark) (1875–1948), US filmmaker, b. La Grange, Ky. He directed the first of his 500 short films for the Biograph Company in 1908. For these films he greatly advanced the expressive range of cinematic techniques. His feeling for realistic narrative and characterization and his sense of varied composition, lighting, and dramatic editing (montage) established the art of film in the United States. His principal feature films include *Enoch Arden* (1911); *The Birth of a Nation* (1915); *Intolerance,* a complex masterpiece that failed commercially (1916); *Broken Blossoms* (1918); *Way Down East* (1920); *Orphans of the Storm* (1922); and *Isn't Life Wonderful* (1924). *See also* Birth of a Nation, The; Montage.

Griffon, or griffon vulture, carrion-eating bird of prey of Eurasia and N Africa. It has gold or sandy-brown plumage. Gregarious, large flocks nest in caves or on cliffs. A single white, often flecked, egg is laid. Length: 40in (102cm). Species *Gyps fulvus.*

Grimaldi, Genoese Guelph (pro-papal) family of Middle Ages, and lords of Monaco from 15th century. With the Fieschi, the Grimaldi were leaders in Genoa's mid-13th-century pro-Angevin struggle against Emperor Frederick II, which began a long period of ties to the house of Anjou. In 1419 a branch of the family took possession of Monaco and in 1659 assumed the title of prince, now held by Prince Rainier III (reigned 1949–).

Grimké, Sarah (1792–1873) and **Angelina** (1805–79), US abolitionists and feminists, b. Charleston, S.C. Sisters in a wealthy Southern family, the two women went North and joined the Society of Friends. They soon became involved in the antislavery movement, writing abolitionist appeals to Southerners (1836). Opposition to their speaking against slavery in public places led to their demand for women's rights.

Grimm, Jacob Ludwig Karl (1785–1863) and **Wilhelm Karl** (1786–1859), eminent German philologists. They are best remembered for their collections of folklore. Jacob collected the tales from German peasants, and Wilhelm arranged them. The first volume of the tales was published in 1812, the second in 1815, and a volume of historical notes in 1822. Some of the best-known tales are "Snow-White," "Rumplestiltskin,"

"Tom Thumb," "The Golden Goose," "Hansel and Gretel," and "Rapunzel."

Grimm's Law. A landmark in the history of the scientific study of language, the law of consonantal mutations was first developed in Jacob Grimm's *Deutsche Grammatik* (1822). Grimm discovered significant correlations among German and other Indo-European languages, demonstrating that sound changes are not random, but a regular process. The importance of the finding lay in its successful application of the genetic method to philology, and in its rejection of the speculative approach to the history of language.

Grimsby, seaport in E central England, near mouth of Humber River estuary, Humberside; one of world's leading fishing ports; trades in fish, grain, coal, timber. Industries: frozen and processed foods, chemicals. Pop. 93,800.

Gris, Juan (1887–1927), Spanish painter and writer. He settled in Paris in 1906 and, with Picasso and Braque, became a leading cubist artist. His later works included collages, architectonic paintings, richly colored still lifes, and stage sets and costumes for Diaghilev. *See also* Cubism.

Grisaille, a painting executed entirely in shades of gray. It may be the first stage of an oil painting, the model for an engraver to work from, or a work in its own right.

Grissom, Virgil (1926–67), US astronaut, b. Mitchell, Ind. He was a member of the first US space team (Mercury program) and was the second American in space (1961). He was killed in a flash fire while training for a moon flight.

Griswold v. Connecticut (1965), landmark US Supreme Court decision in which Justice William O. Douglas developed the "penumbra theory" of the right to privacy as protected by the First Amendment. The Court invalidated a state anti-contraceptive law.

Grivas, George (1898–1974), a Greek general who led the Greeks of Cyprus in rebellion against Great Britain from 1955–1959. He formed the EOKA force to fight for *enosis* (union with Greece) but clashed with Archbishop Makarios and retired. He returned in 1964 but could not achieve his goal.

Grizzly Bear, large omnivorous brown bear once widespread in W North America, now rare except in W Canada, Alaska, and Yellowstone and Glacier parks. Length: to 8ft (2.4m); weight: 790lb (356kg). Species *Ursus horribilis.*

Grodno, city in Belorussian SSR, USSR; 150mi (242km) W of Minsk, on Neman River, near Poland and Lithuanian boundaries; capital of Grodno oblast. City was taken by Lithuanian forces 14th century; part of 1569 Polish-Lithuanian union; annexed to Russia with partition of Poland 1795; occupied by Germany in WWI and WWII; became part of the Soviet Union July 16, 1944; site of 12th-century ruins of Borisoglebsk Church, castle built by King Stephen of Poland (1586), 16th–17th-century baroque churches. Industries: wool, leather, tobacco, furniture, glass, electrical equipment, automobile parts, bicycles, appliances, chemicals. Pop. 182,000.

Groin, an artificial dam of rocks or wooden pilings that juts out from a beach face, causing sand to accumulate against the updrift side. Groins are now considered a less effective and more expensive way of maintaining beaches than a beach-nourishment program.

Groningen, city in NE Netherlands; capital of Groningen prov.; fine medieval buildings; trade center for regional agricultural products. Industries: textiles, machinery, printing. Pop. 163,357.

Gropius, Walter (1883–1969), German-born architect and director of Bauhaus (1919–28). He pioneered the functional design that became known as the International Style. Its principles are embodied in his Fagus Factory at Alfeld (1911) and in the US embassy at Athens (1957–61). He joined the Harvard University architecture school in 1937. *See also* Bauhaus; International Style.

Grosbeak, finches with large, seed-cracking beaks that frequent wooded areas throughout much of the world, feeding on seeds, grain, fruits, and tree buds. The males are bright red, yellow, or blue; the females are duller, often brownish. Brown-spotted, blue or greenish eggs (2–5) are laid in cup-shaped, rootlet-lined nests built in trees or bushes. Length: 6–10in (15–25cm). Family Fringillidae.

Grossglockner, peak in S Austria, in the Hohe Tauern range in the Tirol Alps. Highest point in Austria, 12,460ft (3,800m).

Gros Ventres, an Algonquian-speaking tribe of North American Indians occupying the Milk and Missouri rivers, Montana, and nearby Saskatchewan. They are a division of the Arapaho who separated in early days and formed a distinct group. They number approximately 1,000 persons today, living on the Fort Belknap Reservation in Montana. *See also* Hidatsa.

Grosz, George (1893–1959), German illustrator and painter. He savagely satirized corruption in Germany in books of pen drawings and caricatures, such as *Ecce Homo* (1920). He had to flee Germany and came to the United States in 1932, where he continued to satirize bourgeois materialism. His paintings, however, are lyrical and romantic.

Grotius, or **De Groot, Hugo** (1583–1645), Dutch jurist and statesman. He is considered a founder of international law. He held the chief political office of Rotterdam from 1613 until 1618, when he was ousted by political foes. He was sentenced to life imprisonment but escaped in 1621 and lived in Paris. His most famous work was *De Jure Belli et Pacis* (The Law of War and Peace, 1625).

Ground Beetle, predatory beetle found worldwide and often seen running on the ground or hiding under rocks or logs. Length: 1/8–3 1/3in (3–85mm). Family Carabidae.

Groundhog. *See* Woodchuck.

Ground Pine, any of several club mosses with creeping stems and erect branches whose foliage somewhat resembles pine needles. *See also* Club Moss.

Groundsel, large worldwide genus of herbaceous annual and perennial plants and woody shrubs and small trees. Perennial golden groundsel or ragwort *(Senecio aureus)* of E North America has flat-topped clusters of yellow, daisy-like flowers. Height: 2ft (61cm). Family Compositae. *See also* Ragwort.

Ground Squirrel, small, terrestrial squirrel of Eurasia, Africa, and North America. Active by day, they find shelter in burrows or crevices and eat plants, seeds, insects, and sometimes eggs and small animals. Most have grayish-red to brown fur; some are striped or spotted. Length, excluding tail: 4.5–13.5in. (11.4–34cm.); weight: 0.25–1.75lbs. (113–793g). Genus *Citellus.*

Ground State, lowest possible energy level of an atom, ion, molecule. *See also* Excited State.

Ground Water, water that lies in a zone beneath the surface of the earth. The water comes chiefly from the atmosphere, although some is of volcanic or sedimentary origin. Ground water moves through rocks and soil and can be tapped by wells.

Group Dynamics, area of social psychology concerned with the ways members of groups interact with each other and come to decisions or otherwise achieve the group's purpose. The term was originated by Kurt Lewin in the 1930s. Studies of group dynamics are concerned with such matters as how individual group members influence each other, how problems can be solved collectively, how individuals are affected by group (conformity) pressures, and how effective the group finds different styles of leadership. Findings from such studies have many practical implications—constructing groups for maximum effectiveness, developing management techniques, etc.

Grouper, tropical marine fish found from Florida to South America and in Indo-Pacific oceans. It has a large mouth, sharp teeth, mottled pattern, and ability to change color. Length: to 12ft (3.6m); weight: 50–1,000lbs. (23–450kg). Family Serranidae; species giant, *Epinephelus itajara* and Queensland, *Epinephelus lanceolatus.*

Group Theory, branch of abstract algebra applicable to symmetry properties. A group is a collection of entities, with associated operations, obeying a specific set of rules (associative law, existence of an inverse, etc). The theory is concerned with the properties of such groups. It was developed mainly by the French mathematician Evariste Galois during the early 19th century in his study of the solutions of equations and has many applications in mathematics and physical science. The symmetry elements of an object, for example—operations, such as rotations, that bring an object back to its original position—form a group. Group theory is particularly useful in quantum mechanics, spectroscopy, and theories of elementary particles.

Group Therapy, psychotherapy practiced in a group situation, in which the group itself usually becomes an integral part of the treatment. Though the amount of time the therapist spends with any individual patient in group therapy is minimal, this form of therapy offers several distinct advantages. Group influence is a very powerful aid to therapeutic suggestion, and the group generates an atmosphere of mutual helping, support, and constructive criticism, which in turn builds these interpersonal skills in the group members. In family therapy the group members are members of the same family. Groups are frequently organized on the basis of problems that the members have in common, eg, smoking, obesity, sexual difficulties, aging.

Grouse, plump game bird of N Northern Hemisphere. Hen-to-turkey-sized, they are fowllike but have feathered tarsi and toes enabling them to walk on snow, feathered nostrils, and often distensible, brightly colored air sacs on their neck. Some species, such as the ptarmigan, are seasonally monogamous, with males helping rear the young; others, including the sage grouse, are polygamous and the males do not help with the young. Family Tetraonidae. *See also* Capercaillie; Prairie Chicken; Ptarmigan; Sage Grouse.

Growth, irreversible process in an organism that increases its size, weight, or protein content. This process involves cell division or enlargement, or the addition of outside material.

Growth Curve, graphic plotting of growth measurements as they vary with time. Growth results from cell division or enlargement and is evident by an increase in size, weight, or amount of outside materials absorbed. As time progresses, the resulting curve may be linear, S-shaped, or irregular.

Growth Factor, substance required by an organism for its growth but which it is unable to synthesize and must therefore obtain from its diet. *See also* Vitamin.

Growth Hormone, or **Somatotropin,** protein hormone produced by the anterior pituitary; it effects general growth of the body. Over-secretion results in acromegaly in the adult, and giantism in the young; under-secretion results in "pituitary dwarfism."Growth hormone can now be produced by recombinant DNA techniques in adequate quantities for use in medical treatment.

Growth Ring. *See* Annual Ring.

Grozny (Groznyj), city in Russian SFSR, USSR, in Caucasus Mts; capital of Checheno-Ingush ASSR. An oil-producing center since 1893, city has pipeline terminus to Black Sea and Donets Basin. Industries: oil, petrochemicals, food processing, machinery, sawmills, wood products. Founded 1818 as a fort on Russian frontier. Pop. 392,000.

Grünewald, Matthias (*c.*1475–1528), German painter, b. Mathis Gothart Neithart. Although a contemporary of Dürer, he was almost untouched by the Renaissance, except in his use of perspective and his feeling for light and color. He used Renaissance techniques only to heighten the emotional impact of his late Gothic imagery. His greatest work was the folding altarpiece for Isenheim Monastery in Alsace (1513–15), a majestic sequence of religious scenes with great variations in mood and level of intensity; the facial expressions are exalted and passionate.

Grunion, also smelt, marine silverfish found in shallow tropical and temperate waters, particularly along Baja and S California coast. It spawns en masse high on the beach at the highest tide; eggs hatch at the next high tide. Family Atherinidae; species *Leuresthes tennis.*

Grunt, marine fish found in shallow tropical waters of W Atlantic and Pacific. A deep-bodied fish with large mouth, it produces sounds by grinding pharyngeal teeth. Family Pomadasyidae; species includes bluestripe *Haemulon sciurus.*

Guacharo. *See* Oilbird.

Guadalajara, city in SW Mexico, near Santiago River; capital of Jalisco state; site of 16th–17th-century cathedral, governor's palace (1643), university, theater, state museum, baroque churches, direct railroad line to United States; noted for scenic beauty and mild climate. Industries: wheat, corn, peanuts, fruit, textiles, brewing, metal goods, tourism. Founded 1531; est. 1542. Pop. 2,000,000.

Guadalajara, town in central Spain, 34mi (55km) NE of Madrid; capital of Guadalajara prov.; ruled by Moors 8th-11th centuries; captured by Christians 1085; site of the Infantado Palace (1461), Roman bridge. Crops: cereals, vegetables, olives, grapes, fruit. Industries:

Guadeloupe

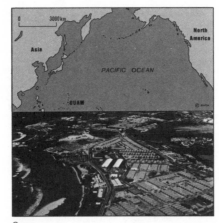

Guam

Guatemala

woolens, leather, soap. Area: (prov.) 4,707sq mi (12,191sq km). Pop. (city) 31,917; (prov.) 147,732.

Guadalcanal, tropical island in W central Pacific Ocean, approx. 600mi (966km) E of New Guinea; largest island of British Solomon Island Protectorate. Inhabitants are mostly Melanesians. Port of Honiara is government center, and site of an international airport; scene of heavy fighting between Japanese and US forces in WWII. Crops: coconuts and lumber. Discovered 1788 by English. Area: 2,510sq mi (6,501sq km). Pop. 23,922.

Guadalquivir, river in S Spain; rises in the Sierra de Cazorla; flows W and SW, empties into Gulf of Cadiz; serves as source of irrigation for near Sierra Morena; site of several hydroelectric plants. Length: 408mi (657km).

Guadalupe-Hidalgo, Treaty of (1848), signed by the United States and Mexico to end the Mexican War. Long negotiations between Nicholas Trist and Santa Anna were stalled until Mexico City finally fell. The United States acquired the present states of Texas, California, Nevada, Utah, New Mexico, and Arizona plus parts of Wyoming and Colorado. The United States agreed to pay $15,000,000 and to pay Mexican debts owed to Americans.

Guadeloupe, overseas French department in E West Indies, in Leeward Islands; comprised of islands of Basse-Terre (Guadeloupe proper) (W), Grande Terre (E), and several lesser dependencies. Basse Terre (city) is capital and Pointe-à-Pitre is chief port and trade center. Discovered 1493 by Christopher Columbus; settled 1635 by French; dept. est. 1946. Exports: rum, pineapples, sugar, bananas, coffee. Tourism is main industry. Area: 683sq mi (1,769sq km). Pop. 334,-900.

Guadiana, river in S central Spain; rises in La Mancha Plateau; flows W then S to form part of the Spanish-Portuguese border; empties into the Gulf of Cádiz; used for irrigation in the Merida region of Spain; source of hydroelectric power and transportation. Length: 510mi (821km).

Guam, southernmost and largest of the Mariana Islands, in W Pacific Ocean; an unincorporated US territory. Approx. half the inhabitants are Chamorros, a Micronesian people; site of US Navy base and large carved stones that may have been erected by an ancient culture previous to the immigration of the Chamorro. The economy is dominated by US military installations and tourism. Discovered by Ferdinand Magellan in 1521, Guam came under US control in 1917. It was the first US territory to be occupied (1941) by Japan during WWII and was only recaptured by US forces after heavy fighting in 1944. Since 1973, Guam has sent a non-voting delegate to the US House of Representatives. Area: approx. 209sq mi (541sq km). Pop.: 105,816. Capital: Agaña.

Guan, medium-sized game bird found in Central and South American tropical forests, feeding mainly on fruit. They are greenish, brownish, or grayish with brownish-red or coppery markings. Family Cracidae.

Guanay, white-breasted Peruvian cormorant; a bird that feeds on anchovies in the Humboldt Current area. It is the main source of the fertilizer guano. Length: 20–40in (51–102cm). Species *Phalacrocorax bougainvilli.*

Guano, dried excrement of sea birds and bats. It contains phosphorous, nitrogen, and potassium and is a

natural fertilizer. It is found mainly on certain coastal islands off South America and Africa.

Guantánamo, city in E Cuba, 10mi (16km) N of Guantánamo Bay; trade and agricultural center; served by port of Caimanera on Guantánamo Bay; site of US naval station and airport. Pop. 129,005.

Guaraní Indians, concentrated in S Brazil and in Paraguay. The Guaraní who remained independent and not collected in Jesuit missions are distinguished from the Christianized Guaraní by the name "Cainguá." The Guaraní language still is spoken by mestizos and acculturated Indians of the area; it is the second official language of Paraguay.

Guarneri, a family of violin makers who worked in Cremona, Italy, beginning with **Andrea Guarneri** (*c.* 1626–1698). His grandnephew **Giuseppi Antonio Guarneri** (1683–1745) was the greatest craftsman of the family.

Guasave, city in W Mexico, on Sinaloa River. Industries: fishing, livestock, wheat, cotton. Founded 1595 by Spanish as a Guasave Indian mission. Pop. 148,475.

Guatemala, Republic of, nation in Central America, on the Atlantic (NE), Pacific (S) oceans and bordered by Mexico (W and N), Belize (E), Honduras (E), and El Salvador (E). The country is one of the world's leading coffee producers.
   Land and Economy. The Sierra Madre Mts, many of volcanic origin, parallel the Pacific Ocean in the S, branching off into four principal ranges in the N. A mountain plain approx. 30mi (48km) wide extends along the Pacific side for approx. 200mi (322km) from Mexico to El Salvador. The climate is tropical but moderated by the elevation. Although the economy is basically agricultural (coffee and bananas are the chief exports), mining has become increasingly significant, and petroleum was discovered in 1974. The principal ports, Puerto Barrios on the Atlantic and San Jose on the Pacific, are connected with the capital of Guatemala City by a transcontinental railroad.
   People. Over 50% of the people are of Indian origin; the remainder are mostly Ladinos (mixed Spanish and Indian). The majority of the people are Roman Catholic and Spanish speaking. Elementary education is free and compulsory.
   Government. A republic, the government is invested in three departments: executive, with a president elected for 6 years and ineligible for reelection for another 12 years; legislative, with a unicameral National Congress, elected every 4 years; judicial, with a Supreme Court and lesser courts. There is universal suffrage at 18 years of age.
   History. The home of the Mayan Empire for 1000 years, Guatemala was occupied by the Spanish from 1524–1821. Under Mexican control until 1823, when it became a member of the United Provinces of Central America, it re-established its independence in 1839. Throughout its history, Guatemala has been characterized by political upheaval and revolution. Justo Rufino Barrios attempted to form a regional union in the late 19th century and although he failed became the national hero. Communists and anti-Communists battled for control after World War II, and the United Fruit Company, a US firm, played a major role in domestic affairs. In the 1970s, Guatemala pressed its claims to Belize, a British colony, and nearly went to war in 1975. In 1976 the nation was rocked by a severe earthquake that left about 25,000 dead and almost 20% of the population homeless. Dislocation accompanying the earthquake and subsequent civil wars in nearby Nicaragua and El Salvador contributed to escalating instability, deterioration of human rights, and fighting

between Guatemalan leftists and rightists during the late 1970s and 1980s. A 1982 coup put the military in power, but by 1985 elections were held and in 1986 Marco Vinicio Cerezo Arevalo became Guatemala's first civilian president since 1970.

PROFILE

Official name: Republic of Guatemala
Area: 42,042sq mi (108,889sq km)
Population: 7,262,000
   Density: 172per sq mi (67per sq km)
Chief cities: Guatemala City (capital); San Pedro Carcha
Government: republic
Religion: Roman Catholic
Language: Spanish (official)
Monetary unit: quetzal
Gross national product: $6,930,000,000
Per capita income: $846
Industries (major products): food, beverages, tobacco
Agriculture (major products): coffee, cotton, bananas
Minerals (major): zinc, lead
Trading partners (major): United States, El Salvador, West Germany

Guatemala City, capital city of Guatemala, 50mi (81km) N of the Pacific Ocean, on a plateau in the Sierra Madre; largest city in Central America. Est. 1776 as capital to replace Antigua (which had been destroyed by earthquakes) as the colonial capital of Spanish Central America; city became the capital of the Central American Federation 1823–38; destroyed by earthquakes 1917–18, 1976; political, cultural, commercial, transportation, and educational center; site of the national and presidential palaces, a cathedral (1782–1815), San Carlos University (1676). Exports: coffee, minerals, gold, copper, silver, lead. Industries: mining, furniture, textiles, clothing, food processing, handcrafts. Founded 1527. Pop. (municipal) 717,322.

Guava, trees and shrubs native to tropical America and the West Indies and the source of fruits of the same name. The large white flowers produce a 4in(10cm) berry-like fruit, usually yellow with white, pink, or yellow flesh. The 140 species include the common *Psidium guajava* and the strawberry guava *(P. cattleyanum),* with purplish-red fruits. Family Myrtaceae.

Guayaquil, city and port in W Ecuador, on the Guayas River, 40mi (64km) inland from Pacific coast; capital of Guayas prov, it is largest city of Ecuador. In 17th and 18th centuries city was frequently attacked and burned by buccaneers. Industries: textiles, leather goods, soap, alcohol. Founded 1535 by Sebastián de Benalcázar of Spain. Pop. 823,730.

Guaymas, port city in NW Mexico, on Gulf of California, near Yaqui River; noted for excellent fishing; resort area. Exports: gold and silver ores, cotton, pearls, tobacco. Industries: shipping, lumber, shark liver oil extracting, tourism. Est. in early 18th century by Jesuit missionaries. Pop. 84,730.

Guayule, shrub native to desert regions of N Mexico and Texas. The latex extracted from it is a commercial source of rubber. Height: 2–3ft (61–91cm). Family Compositae; species *Parthenium argentatum.*

Guchkov, Aleksandr (1862–1936), Russian political figure. He was the founder of the Octobrist party (1905), supporting a constitutional monarchy. In World War I he was head of the Russian Red Cross and chairman of the Central War Industries Committee. He was president of the third Duma and was sent to receive the abdication of Czar Nicholas II. From March to May 1917 he was minister of war in the provisional government but resigned. He left Russia after the Bolshevik Revolution (November 1917).

Gudgeon, freshwater carp found in rivers from England to Central China. It has a small mouth, fleshy whiskers on the upper lip, elongated body, and variable color. Length: to 15.7in (40cm). Family Cyprinidae; species includes common *Gobio gobio.*

Gudrun, a heroine in old Norse legends, the wife of Sigurd and the sister of Gunnar. She is depicted in several poems as a suffering wife and sister.

Guelph, city in SE Ontario, Canada, 15mi (24km) ENE of Kitchener on the Speed River; site of Ontario Reformatory and University of Guelph (1964). Industries: tobacco warehouses, textiles, electrical appliances, rubber, iron, steel. Founded by novelist John Galt 1827. Pop. 58,364.

Guelphs, Italian pro-papal political faction of Middle Ages, opposed to pro-imperial Ghibellines. "Guelph" derives from "Welf," the name of the German family contending with the Hohenstaufens for the imperial crown in the 12th and 13th centuries, but came to cover the Italian opponents of Hohenstaufen Emperor Frederick II. As each Italian city-state took sides and the Hohenstaufen line died out in 1268, Guelphism came to designate pro-Angevin, pro-papal sympathy into the 15th century.

Guenon, long-tailed, slender, medium-sized monkey of sub-Saharan Africa. They are day-active tree dwellers living in small troops dominated by an old male. Their omnivorous diet consists mainly of fruit, leaves, and roots. They make good pets while young but often turn savage as they grow older. Genus Cercopithecus. *See also* Monkey.

Guereza, Ethiopian name applied to any of several African monkeys of the genus *Colobus* (especially *C. guereza*) that have long white hair along the sides of the body and tail contrasting sharply with the black or reddish ground color. *See also* Colobus.

Guernica, town in N Spain; center of Basque nationalism; site of old oak tree under which medieval Vizcaya parliament met. The severe bombing by Germans during Spanish Civil War (1937) was protested in Pablo Picasso's "Guernica." Industries: food processing, furniture, metallurgy. Pop. 14,678.

Guernsey, second-largest of Channel Islands of United Kingdom, NW of Jersey; constitutes a bailiwick with several smaller islands, including Alderney and Sark. Guernsey breed of dairy cattle was developed here. Capital is St Peter Port. Industries: farming, dairying, tourism, horticulture. Area: 24sq mi (62sq km). Pop. 51,138.

Guernsey, common breed of dairy cattle originally from English Channel Isle of Guernsey. Well-known in the United States, it gives rich, yellow milk, second only to the Jersey breed in butterfat content, but greater in overall volume. Larger than Jerseys, Guernseys are brown and white. Weight: 1,700lb (765kg). *See also* Dairy Cattle.

Guerrilla Warfare, small-scale ground combat operations designed to harass rather than destroy an opponent. Such tactics are often employed by insurgents or irregular soldiers lacking powerful weapons. By conducting limited forays against supply lines and small installations, they are often able to avoid open engagements with conventional military units and tie down a disproportionate share of their adversaries' military strength. Although practiced effectively by such diverse groups as the American revolutionaries of the 18th century and the Viet Cong troops in Southeast Asia, guerrilla warfare is normally not decisive by itself and is generally complemented by conventional combat.

Guevara, Ernesto "Che" (1928–67), revolutionary leader and theorist, a key-figure in Fidel Castro's Cuba. A physician born in Argentina, Guevara became associated with Castro in Mexico and returned with him to Cuba in 1956 to carry out the guerrilla activities directed against the regime of Fulgencio Batista. When Castro came to power, Guevara was placed in charge of economic planning. Guevara disappeared in 1965; two years later he was captured and killed in Bolivia.

Guiana Highlands (Guiana Massif), mountainous tableland in N South America, extends from Venezuela to French Guiana; includes forested plateau, mountains of crystalline rocks, sandstone, lava caps, and waterfalls, notably Angel Falls, the world's highest waterfall, 3,212ft (979m). Products: cedar, mahogany, vanilla, rubber, medicinal plants, gold, diamonds. Length: approx 1,200mi (1,932km). Width: 200–600mi (322–966km).

Guidance System, Spacecraft, system of gyroscopes, detectors, radar antennae, receivers, computers, vernier engines, and other elements necessary to stabilize, correct, and control a space vehicle path. Gyroscopes define the coordinate axes of the body, and detectors measure differences between these directions and the planned ones. Servomechanisms operate vernier engines or swing gimbaled nozzles to correct errors. Tracking radar dishes follow the craft. Balloons or aircraft give meteorological data to central computers, which determine adjustments necessary to correct for atmospheric conditions.

Guided Missile, missile capable of being controlled during the major part of its flight, either by ground crew or by onboard systems reacting to perceived conditions. Initial guidance is concerned with flight stability on lift-off and is usually handled from the ground. Midcourse guidance places the missile roughly on target. Final guidance makes fine adjustments to the flight path, possibly using information obtained from the target itself.

Guide Fossil. *See* Index Fossil.

Guild, one of many organizations formed by special interest or skilled groups during the Middle Ages, from about the 10th to the 15th centuries. In the period of feudalism, guilds were formed for self-protection, social life, and profit by those outside the rural manorial system. In 10th-century England, the London peace-guild was formed to protect city land owners. In the 12th and 13th centuries, craftsmen in towns throughout Europe organized guilds to maintain price and quality levels of goods, to protect their interests, and to supervise the training of apprentices. By the 14th and 15th centuries, there were also religious guilds, burial guilds, merchant and money-lender guilds. At first self-governing, guilds in the later Middle Ages were subject to municipalities and became politically influential. The longest-lasting guilds were those made up of teachers and students; these were primarily responsible for the forming of the university system.

Guildford, city in Surrey, SE England, on Wey River 26mi (42km) SW of London. A market center and seat of University of Surrey (1966), it has many historic buildings. Industries: engineering, plastics, knitwear. Pop. 56,887.

Guild Socialism, type of British socialism that advocated government control of the means of production and the contracting of workers through national guilds. Based more on the control of industry than direct political involvement, the Guild Socialist movement was prominent from 1906–25, when disorganization and financial troubles caused its effective demise.

Guillaume de Lorris (*c.* 1210–37), French romance writer. He began the *Roman de la Rose* (*c.* 1230), an allegory in which a courtly lover becomes enamored of a rosebud whose reflection he sees during a dream. Before the poem was completed, Guillaume died, and Jean de Meung composed the second half. *See also* Jean de Meung; Roman de la Rose.

Guillemot, small, usually black and white seabird of cold Northern Hemisphere coastlines. They dive for ocean-bottom food. Nesting in colonies, they lay oval eggs (2) on rocky coasts. Length: 13in (33cm). Genera *Cepphus* and *Uria.*

Guinea, Gulf of, inlet of the Atlantic Ocean, off W Africa, formed by great curve in coastline extending from the Ivory Coast to the Gabon estuary; E section includes Bight of Biafra.

Guinea (Guinée), Republic of, nation of W Africa on the Atlantic coast. The country is traditionally divided into four regions: Lower Guinea, the narrow coastal area; Foutah Djallon, a highland area rising sharply from the coast; Upper Guinea, with plains sloping NE to the Sahara; and the Forest Region, an isolated hill area in the SE. The Niger, Senegal, and Gambia rivers all have their source in the Foutah Djallon. The agricultural economy relies heavily on coffee and banana crops. The mineral wealth—huge reserves of high-grade bauxite, large deposits of iron ore, gold, and diamonds—holds great potential for the future.

People. There are three main ethnic groups: the Foulahs (or Peuls), the Malinkes, and the Soussou. French is the official language, but seven other languages are in common use. The majority of the people are Muslim. The literacy rate is about 10%, which impedes economic progress.

Government. Guinea is a one-party socialist state. The president serves as head of state and secretary-general of the party, the Democratic Party of Guinea (PDG). The regime of Sekou Touré (1958–84) was cited for human rights violations.

History. Visited by the Portuguese in the early 1500s, Guinea, through the slave trade, became a center of European interest during the next 300 years. The French gained control in the early 1800s, establishing the colony of French Guinea in 1891. It became a territory in 1946, and chose independence through a referendum vote in 1958. Under Pres. Sekou Touré, Guinea had close ties with the Soviet Union. During the late 1970s and 1980s he improved relations with the West; ties with neighboring African countries remain troubled. Touré's successor, Lansana Conté, who ousted the interim president in a coup, pledged to correct the wrongs in the government.

PROFILE

Official name: Popular and Revolutionary Republic of Guinea
Area: 94,926sq mi (245,858sq km)
Population: 4,762,000
Density: 56per sq mi (22per sq km)
Chief city: Conakry (capital)
Government: republic
Language: French (official)
Monetary unit: syli
Gross national product: $1,470,000,000
Per capita income: $140
Agriculture (major products): coffee, bananas
Minerals (major): aluminum, bauxite, diamonds

Guinea-Bissau, Republic of, nation of W Africa, on the Atlantic coast. Formerly known as Portuguese Guinea, the nation gained its independence in 1974.

Land, Economy, and People. The heavily forested coastal area, hot, humid and swampy, rises gradually to inland grassy plains. The many rivers are the main source of transportation as the country has no railroads and few paved roads. The government is striving to diversify the economy, which is based almost entirely on agriculture. Rice is the principal staple crop, and peanuts, coconuts, and palm kernels are produced for export. More than 30 tribes and subtribes make up the almost entirely black population. About 65% of the inhabitants practice traditional tribal religions, followed by Islam, claiming about 30%.

Government and History. A republic, the country is governed by the National Popular Assembly, made up of 120 deputies elected to three-year terms. Fifteen members are chosen to form the State Council, whose leader serves as the nation's president. Explored by the Portuguese in the 15th century, the area became an important slave trade center in the 17th and 18th centuries. Colonization began in the 19th century. In the 1960s local patriots conducted guerrilla warfare until the Portuguese granted independence in 1974, with Luis Cabral serving as president. His party called for the eventual unification with the Cape Verde Islands. In 1980, Cabral altered the constitution, giving himself greatly increased powers, but was deposed in a coup, jailed, and, upon release in 1982, exiled to Cuba. The government was dissolved and replaced by a Council of Revolution that opposed unification with Cape Verde, although negotiations for the restoration of government relations were begun in 1982.

PROFILE

Official name: Republic of Guinea-Bissau
Area: 13,948sq mi (36,125sq km)
Population: 777,214
Density: 56per sq mi (22per sq km)
Chief city: Bissau (capital)
Government: republic
Religion: Traditional, Islam
Language: Portuguese (official)
Monetary unit: Portuguese Escudo
Gross national product: $140,000,000
Per capita income: $275
Agriculture (major products): peanuts, rice, millet, coconuts, palm oil
Trading partners (major): Portugal

Guinea Fowl, pheasantlike African and Madagascan game bird typified by the common domestic guinea hen *(Numida meleagris).* It is bluish, grayish, or blackish with white spots and an ornamental crest. Other species have spurs; some have feather tufts on the head; and one has a long, ornamental tail. They travel in large flocks, often running, in open forest or brushland, feeding on vegetable matter and small invertebrates. They lay pitted, buff eggs (6–15) in a shallow grass-lined ground nest. Length: 20in (51cm). Family Numididae.

Guinea Pig, domesticated form of South American rodent, now a laboratory animal and pet. Large-headed and short-legged, guinea pigs have no tails and come in many colors and textures. Bred as food by the Incas, guinea pigs grow rapidly and produce up to 5 litters yearly. Vegetarians, they make good pets, being

Guinea

Guinea-Bissau

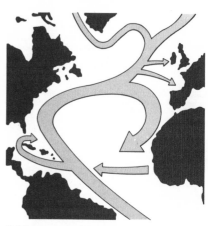

Gulf Stream

clean, healthy, and gentle. Length: to 10in (254mm); Weight: to 2lb (907g). Species *Cavia porcellus. See also* Cavy.

Guinevere, in Arthurian legend, Arthur's queen and Lancelot's love. In Thomas Malory's *Le Morte d'Arthur* she betrayed the king and was sentenced to die at the stake, was rescued by Lancelot and later restored to Arthur. Toward her life's end she took the veil and then was buried with her king.

Guinness, Sir Alec (1914–), British actor. His first major role was in *Twelfth Night* at London's Old Vic (1936–37). He became world-famous after WWII playing the English eccentric in such films as *Kind Hearts and Coronets, The Lavender Hill Mob,* and *The Ladykillers.* He also appeared in *Vicious Circle* (1946); *The Cocktail Party* (1950, 1968); *Exit the King* (1963); *Wise Child* (1967); *Time Out of Mind* (1970). He played in such films as *Bridge on the River Kwai,* for which he won an Academy Award (1957); *Doctor Zhivago* (1966), *The Comedians* (1970), and *Star Wars* (1977). In 1986, his autobiography *Blessings in Disguise* was published.

Guiscard, Robert (*c.*1015–85), Norman soldier who drove the Byzantines out of southern Italy and established Norman power in Sicily. Guiscard allied himself with the papacy and delivered Pope Gregory VII from the siege of Emperor Henry IV. He had hoped to conquer the Byzantine Empire but died in Cephalonia during a campaign.

Guise, House of, ducal house of Lorraine, most influential family in 16th-century France. **Claude, duke of Lorraine** (1496–1550) founded the house. His son **François** (1519–63) supervised the massacre of a congregation of Huguenots at Vassy in 1562, which precipitated the Wars of Religion. His brother **Charles** (1524–74), cardinal of Guise, played an important role at the Council of Trent. François' son Henri fought in the 3rd and 4th religious wars and helped organize the St. Bartholomew's Day Massacre in 1572. He led the Holy League, which opposed any toleration of Protestantism. The Guise family's power declined when the Huguenot Henry IV converted to Catholicism in 1593.

Guitar, stringed musical instrument with fretted neck and flat body, played by plucking or strumming its four to seven strings, sometimes 12, tuned in pairs. Of Oriental origin, it was brought to Spain in the 12th century and replaced the lute in 17th-century Europe in accompanying folk songs. Spanish concert virtuosos, especially Andrés Segovia, developed music for classical guitar. Jazz and rock instrumentalists use an electrically amplified modification.

Guitar Fish, elasmobranch found worldwide in tropical and temperate marine waters. A bottom-feeding ray that travels in schools, its elongated body is flattened along the side of the head and trunk. It is usually brown with spots, and its young are born alive. Length: 5–6ft (1.5–1.8m). There are nine genera and 45 species including *Rhinobatos productus.* Family Rhinebatidae.

Gujarat, state in W India, on Arabian Sea; capital is Ahmedabad. Est. 1960 when former state of Bombay was separated into Marathi- and Gujarati-speaking areas. Industries: agriculture, dairy products, mining, textiles, oil refining, machine tools. Area: 72,000sq mi (186,480sq km). Pop. 30,930,000.

Gujranwala, city in Punjab, NE Pakistan; capital of Gujranwala district; market center for cotton and grains. Industries: iron safes, brassware, textiles, pottery, ivory bangles. Pop. 366,000.

Gula, in Babylonian mythology, the goddess of healing, daughter of Anu, associated with Shamash. She is depicted as a healer and destroyer, able to control disease and death. Her festival was held in late April.

Gulag (acronym in Russian for Chief Administration of Corrective Labor Camps), a network of detention centers and forced labor prisons within the Soviet Union for the punishment of political crimes. Prisoners, frequently incarcerated without trial, live under brutal conditions, and many die before completing their sentences. Established in 1918, this secret concentration camp system has been used to silence political and religious dissidents within the Soviet Union and was described in detail by Aleksandr Solzhenitsyn in *The Gulag Archipelago.* Utilized extensively to enforce the ideological policies of the Stalinist regime, Gulags remain an important tool used to stifle dissent.

Gulf Stream, the relatively swift-moving western boundary current of the North Atlantic gyre which flows from the equator north along the North American east coast. Though long considered to be one huge wide mass of water, research indicates it is many interacting thin streams which cause the local variations in water temperature. Its warm waters affect the coastal climate.

Gulfweed, any of a group of large brown seaweeds of the genus *Sargassum.* The best known gulfweed, *S. bacciferum,* floats by means of berry-shaped air bladders and is common in tropical American seas. *See also* Brown Algae.

Gull, or sea gull, graceful seabird found soaring and gliding along most coastlines. Gregarious, particularly during feeding, they eat carrion, rubbish, fish, shellfish, eggs, and young birds. Generally gray and white with black markings, they have hooked bills, pointed wings, rounded tails, and webbed feet. They lay smudged brownish eggs (2–3) in a seaweed-and-grass ground nest. Length: 11–32in (28–81cm). Family Laridae.

Gullet. *See* Esophagus.

Gulliver's Travels (1726), satirical fable in four parts by Jonathan Swift. The author uses Gulliver as a vehicle to satirize man. Lemuel Gulliver, a surgeon, visits Lilliput, Brobdingnag, Laputa, and the land of the Houyhnhnms and Yahoos. The inhabitants of the first are tiny and of the second are immense; the wise men in the third engage in ridiculous enterprises; in Houyhnhnm land horses have reason and beasts take the form of men.

Gum Arabic, or acacia gum, soluble yellowish gum obtained from certain species of acacia trees and consisting of a complex carbohydrate polymer. It is used in foods, cosmetics, pharmaceuticals, and adhesives.

Gums, secretions of plants that swell or are soluble in water. Gums are chemically complex, consisting mainly of various saccharides bound to organic acids by glycoside linkages. Common examples are gum arabic, agar, and tragacarth. *See also* Resin.

Gun. *See* Machine Gun; Naval Guns.

Gun Cotton. *See* Nitrocellulose.

Gunpowder, mixture of saltpeter (potassium nitrate), charcoal, and sulfur. When ignited in a confined space, it expands rapidly and produces a propellant force. Used extensively in firearms to about 1900, it was replaced by other chemicals.

Gunpowder Plot (1605), Roman Catholic conspiracy to blow up England's James I and the houses of Parliament and to establish Roman Catholicism in Britain. The plotters, led by Robert Catesby, took gunpowder into the cellars beneath Parliament and a man named Guy Fawkes was to ignite it. The authorities, however, were alerted and Fawkes was arrested and executed along with his fellow conspirators. The plot increased antagonism between Roman Catholics and Protestants.

Guntur, city in SE India, 220mi (354km) N of Madras; ceded to Great Britain 1823; important market for textiles and tobacco. Pop. 269,991.

Guppy, or millions fish, live-bearing topminnow found in fresh waters of West Indies, Venezuela, Guianas, and N Brazil. The wild guppy is gray with bright-colored spots; selective breeding has produced lyretail, swordtail, and veiltail varieties. A popular aquarium fish. Length: to 2.5in (6.4cm). Family Poecilidae; species *Poecilia* or *Lebistes reticulatis.*

Gupta (*fl.c.* 320–480AD), ruling dynasty of the Maurya Empire covering most of northern India. Their state was the prototype of Indian empires to follow. The Guptas conquered territory and collected tribute from defeated rulers but allowed them to remain on their thrones and continue to rule. The Guptas were considered benevolent, and art and literature flourished under their rule.

Gurkha, or Gorkha, Hindu ruling caste of Nepal since 1768. They speak a Sanskritic language. Their racial characteristics are a mixture of Mongoloid and Caucasoid. The name often denotes a Nepalese soldier in the British or Indian army.

Gurnard, also flying gurnard, tropical marine bottom-dwelling fish. It has a large bony head and enlarged pectoral fins used to glide above the water surface. Length: to 18in (45.7cm). Order Dactylopteriformes; species include *Dactylopterus volitans.*

Guru, a Sanskrit term for a teacher and spiritual master. In traditional Hindu education, boys lived in the home of a guru, who was their guide in studying the sacred books (Vedas) and saw to their physical health and ethical training. In many Hindu sects the guru is responsible for initiating novices. In Sikhism the guru was the leader of the community until the guruship was terminated in 1708.

Gustavus I Vasa (?1496–1560), king of Sweden, son of Erik Johansson who supported the Sture party. He led a victorious rebellion against the invading Danes in 1520. In 1523 he was elected king and the Kalmar Union was destroyed. During his reign Sweden became independent of Denmark, the Protestant church was established, and the Bible was translated into Swedish. Founder of the Vasa dynasty, he established hereditary monarchy in 1544.

Gustavus II Adolphus (1594–1632), king of Sweden, succeeded his father Charles IX (1611) during a constitutional crisis. Aided by Chancellor Axel Oxenstierna, Gustav's reign was distinguished by sweeping legal, administrative, and educational reforms. He established secondary schools, reformed the Riksdag, 1617, and established uniform judicial procedures. He ended war with Denmark (1613) and Russia (1617). Hoping to increase Sweden's control of the Baltic and to support Protestantism, he entered the Thirty Years' War in Germany and died in battle. His daughter Christina succeeded him.

Gustavus III (1746–92), king of Sweden, succeeded his father Adolf Frederik in 1771 during a period of civil strife. His new constitution strengthened sovereign power. During his reign, known as Gustavian Enlightenment, he instituted financial reforms, religious toleration, a free press, and a strong navy. A gifted writer and patron of the arts, he founded the Swedish Academy. An aristocratic conspiracy led J. Anckarström to assassinate him.

Gustavus VI (1882–1973), king of Sweden, succeeded Gustavus V in 1950, the last Swedish king to hold political power. He was a fine athlete, archeologist, and an authority on Chinese ceramics. His grandson Carl Gustavus succeeded him.

Gutenberg, Johann (1400?–?68), German goldsmith and printer. He is credited with the invention of printing from movable type. Gutenberg was experimenting with printing in the 1430s, and the process he developed was based on techniques used for making playing cards and mass-produced woodblock prints. He went into a partnership with Johann Fust, and when the association was dissolved, Gutenberg gave up claims to his invention. He printed the first Bible, known as the Gutenberg Bible (*c.*1455).

Gutta-percha, or **palaquium,** evergreen tree found in Malaya, Sumatra, and Borneo. It is the source of gutta-percha, a rubberlike gum used in electric insulation, golf balls, and dentistry. This flat-topped tree has long, oval leaves that are green above and copper with silky hairs below. Height: to 100ft (30.5m). Family Sapotaceae; species *Palaquium gutta.*

Guyana, Republic of, nation in NE South America, on the Atlantic Ocean. Once known as British Guiana, Guyana proclaimed its independence in 1970 after 152 years as a British colony.

Land, Economy, and People. A flat coastal area roughly 50mi (81km) in width contains about 90% of the population. Most of the rest of the country is covered by dense tropical forest, making access to the rich inland bauxite difficult. The economy, improving through the exploitation of mineral resources—especially bauxite, the leading export—remains heavily agricultural, relying principally upon sugar and rice. About half the people are of East Indian descent, having been imported by the British as laborers. About 33% are of African descent; most of the rest are American Indian or of mixed lineage. The principal religious groups are Christian, Hindu, and Muslim.

Government and History. The constitution provides for a unicameral 53-member national assembly. Members are elected for five years under a system of proportional representation. The president leads the majority party in the assembly and appoints the cabinet. The major political forces are the People's National Congress and the People's Progressive party. Since independence the country has suffered from considerable political instability.

Explored by the Spanish in 1499, the area was settled by the Dutch in 1620, who ceded it to the British in 1814. The British brought in African slaves and large numbers of indentured East Indians to work the plantations. Guyana achieved self-government as a British Commonwealth nation in 1966 and gained full independence in 1970. In a step to bolster the economy bauxite mining was nationalized in 1975. In 1978, Guyana received worldwide attention as the site of the mass suicide of members of a US cult, the Peoples' Temple, led by Rev. Jim Jones, who had been living in Guyana. A border dispute, in which Venezuela claimed Guyana territory, dominated the 1980s.

PROFILE

Official name: Republic of Guyana
Area: 83,000sq mi (214,970sq km)
Population: 850,000
Density: 10per sq mi (4per sq km)
Chief city: Georgetown (capital)
Government: republic
Language: English (official)
Monetary unit: Guyana dollar
Gross national product: $480,000,000
Per capita income: $380
Industries (major products): food processing, including rum
Agriculture (major products): sugar cane, coconuts, rice, corn
Minerals (major): bauxite, gold
Trading partners (major): United States, Great Britain, Caribbean countries

Guyenne, also Guienne, province of SW France, part of Aquitaine. Guyenne passed to the English in the 12th century. After the Treaty of Paris in 1259, Henry III of England held the province as a vassal of France's Louis IX. By the close of the Hundred Years' War, France had reconquered Guyenne. Many bitter struggles of the 16th century Wars of Religion and the Fronde in the 17th century were fought in Guyenne.

Guyot, a flat-topped seamount whose top is thousands of meters below sea level. It is thought that the flat top was caused by wave action at sea level, thus their present depth is important proof for the lowering of the ocean floor.

Gwalior, city in N central India, 65mi (105km) SSE of Agra, S of Chambal River; overlooked by the Gwalior fort, a Hindu stronghold on the Rock of Gwalior, which houses elaborate shrines, temples, and palace of Man Singh; 15th-century Jain figures are sculpted out of the cliffs of the hill; was the capital of the former princely state of Gwalior (dissolved 1956). Industries: cotton, flour, oilseed processing, textiles, porcelain, plastics. Pop. 406,755.

Gwinnett, Button (1735?–77), American patriot and a signer of the Declaration of Independence, b. England. He represented Georgia at the Continental Congress in 1776 and 1777. He was later killed in a duel with Gen. Lachlan McIntosh after a Georgian expedition failed in a campaign against the British.

Gwyn, or **Gwynne, Nell** (1650–87), English actress. She made her first stage appearance at 15 in *The Indian Emperor.* Much in demand as a speaker of prologues and epilogues, she attracted the attention of King Charles II while reciting the epilogue to Dryden's *Tyrannic Love* (1669), later becoming his mistress and bearing him two sons. Her last stage role was in *Conquest of Granada* (1670).

Gymnastics, sport that involves the performance of various athletic feats on a horizontal bar, long and side horse, flying rings, parallel bar, and balance beam, in addition to rope climbing, club swinging, trampolining, and tumbling. Except for rope climbing, which is scored on speed, events are scored on the basis of form, difficulty of optional exercises, and execution. Men and women compete separately in individual and team competition. The all-around individual champions are determined by excellence in six or more events; team competitions are scored on the basis of total points for all events. Gymnastics was brought to the United States in the 1800s and became part of the modern Olympic Games in 1896. Although ancient Greece used gymnastics as a method of training for the Olympics, it was Frederick Jahn, a German, who introduced the side bar with pommels, the horizontal and parallel bars, the balance beam, and jumping standards in the late 1700s. Two gymnasts, Olga Korbut (USSR) and Nadia Comaneci (Romania), took honors at the 1972 and 1976 Olympic games respectively. They sparked a new interest in the sport.

Gymnosperm, seed plants having seeds borne on open scales, usually in cones. Most trees commonly referred to as evergreens are gymnosperms. All living seed-bearing plants are divided into two main groups: gymnosperms and angiosperms, that have seeds enclosed in an ovary. Gymnosperms are abundant in nature and widely cultivated. They include cycads, ginkgo, pines, spruces, cedars, and ephedras. *See also* Angiosperm; Conifers.

Gynecology, branch of medicine that deals with diseases and disorders of the female reproductive tract. Most gynecologists are also obstetricians. *See also* Obstetrics.

Györ, port city in NW Hungary, at the confluence of the Råba and Danube rivers; seat of Györ-Sopron co; 12th-century cathedral. Industries: steel, textiles, flour milling, distilling. Settled by Romans. Pop. 119,000.

Gypsies, nomadic people, probably originating from N India, now inhabiting Europe, Asia, Siberia, America, Africa, and Australia. Speaking the distinctive Romany language and traditionally living in decorated horse-drawn carriages, gypsies have been distrusted and persecuted in Europe since their first appearance in the 13th century. They were originally believed to have come from Egypt, hence their name. They are known for their resourcefulness in leading a nomadic life in urban societies.

Gypsophila, genus of the pink family containing annual or perennial plants commonly known as baby's breath, native to Europe, Asia, and North Africa. Growing 6in to 3ft (15–91cm), they have narrow leaves and pink or white flowers in single or double blossoms. They are grown in gardens or for cut flowers.

Gypsum, the commonest sulfate mineral and source of plaster of Paris. Hydrous calcium sulfate ($CaSO_4 \cdot 2H_2O$). Huge beds in sedimentary rocks. Monoclinic system prismatic or bladed crystals. Varieties are alabaster, massive; selenite, transparent and foliated; satinspar, silky and fibrous. Clear, white, and tinted. Hardness 2; sp gr 2.3.

Gypsy Moth, small tussock moth whose caterpillar feeds on the leaves of more than 500 species of shrubs and trees. The caterpillar is covered with tufts of stiff hairs. When young, the larva is pale brown. As an adult, it has five pairs of blue and six pairs of red tufted spots on its back. Length: 2in (5cm). Species *Porthetria dispar. See also* Tussock Moth.

Gyre, a large circular flow of ocean water with a calm center region called an eddy. There are three gyres in both the Atlantic and Pacific and one in the Indian Ocean. They are narrowest and swiftest on their western sides.

Gyrfalcon, bird of prey found in Arctic tundra and nearby mountains. It has a hooked beak, long pointed wings, and long tail. It is gray-brown or a mixture of dark and whitish coloring. It feeds on birds and mammals and lays spotted buff-colored eggs in a stick nest on a cliff. Length: 20–25in (51–63.5cm). Species *Falco rusticolus.*

Gyrocompass, a compass that consists of a continuously driven gyroscope, used where a magnetic compass would be unreliable owing to large masses of iron or steel nearby. The heavy base of the gyroscope confines the spinning axis to a horizontal plane so that the rotation of the earth causes it to assume a position parallel to the axis of the earth. Thus, it always points to true north.

Gyropilot, an automatic pilot consisting of devices for detecting and correcting changes in the attitude of an airplane. The gyropilot makes the correction by moving the appropriate control (rudder for azimuth and sudden change in heading, aileron for roll, and elevator for pitch).

Gyroscope, a symmetrical but nonspherical body, usually mounted in gimbals allowing unrestricted motion. If the body is set spinning, a change in the orientation of the outer gimbals will not change the orientation of the spinning body; thus one can determine changes in direction aboard a vessel without external references. A torque applied to a fast-spinning gyroscope, such as can be applied by leaning it out of the vertical, will result in a phenomenon known as precession: the gyroscope will not fall but will rotate about its fixed point, with the axis of spin describing a cone around the vertical.

H

Haarlem, city in W Netherlands, near North Sea, on Spaarne River; capital of North Holland prov.; center of 16th–17th-century Dutch painting. City has many fine museums and monuments. Industries: flowers, tulip bulbs, ships, textiles, electronic equipment. Chartered 1245. Pop. 164,672.

Habakkuk, biblical author and eighth of the 12 minor prophets. His short book bemoans the condition of Judah and the success of God's enemies.

Habeas Corpus, legal term from Latin for "You have the body." The most common legal form (habeas corpus ad subjectiendum) is a writ issued to a person detaining another. In it he is ordered to appear with reasons for detention before a judge or court. Consideration and decisions are then arrived at as to whether the prisoner is justly detained.

Haber, Fritz (1868–1934), German physical chemist whose early work involved electrochemistry and thermodynamic gas reactions. With Karl Bosch (1908–09), he invented the process (Haber process) for converting atmospheric nitrogen into ammonia. He was awarded the 1918 Nobel Prize for this work. He also devised the means of manufacturing large amounts of ammonia for use in nitrogen fertilizers.

Habsburg. *See* Hapsburg.

Hachinohe, port city in N Honshu, Japan, on the Oirase River; Industries: fisheries, cement, textiles, food processing, chemicals. Pop. 208,801.

Guyana

Gypsy moth

Haile Selassie

Hachioji, city in SE central Honshu, Japan, 27mi (43km) W of Tokyo. Industries: weaving, silk, poultry, wood. Pop. 253,527.

Hackberry, any of about 80 species of shrubs and trees, making up the genus *Celtis* of the elm family. The common hackberry *(C. occidentalis)* of E North America usually grows to 40–60ft (12–18m) and has an edible, cherrylike fruit.

Hackney, light horse breed for heavy harness and carriage use. An English breed developed during the early 18th century from the Norfolk Trotter and Thoroughbred, it has short legs and robust build. Colors are chestnut, bay, or brown, with white marks. Its tail is docked and its mane pulled for show. Small Hackneys qualify as ponies. Height: 48–56in (122–142cm) at shoulder; weight: 800–1,200lb (360–540kg).

Hadar. See Beta Centauri.

Haddock, marine food and commercial fish found in cold and temperate waters, primarily in Northern Hemisphere. Dark gray and silver, it has a large, dark blotch near the pectoral fins. Length: to 44in (111.8cm); weight: to 36lb (16.3kg). Family Gadidae; species *Melanogrammus aeglefinus*.

Hades, in Greek mythology, the son of Cronus and Rhea and brother of Zeus and Poseidon. Hades ruled as master of the Underworld, or Hades. He was also known as Pluto.

Hadley Cell, an atmospheric circulation cell, named for British scientist George Hadley, who proposed it (1735) to explain the trade winds, in which winds rise and flow poleward from the equator and then descend and flow equatorward, transferring heat convectively. *See also* Easterlies.

Hadrian, Publius Aelius (76–138), Roman emperor (117–138). He was adopted by Emperor Trajan who named him his successor. As emperor, Hadrian pacified Moesia (118), withdrew the Eastern army to the Euphrates, and suppressed Bar Cocheba's revolt in Jerusalem (132). He continued to persecute the Jews, destroying the Temple of Jerusalem and building a Roman temple in its place. He traveled extensively throughout the empire and had defensive walls built in Germany and in Britain. He promoted major building programs, including the Arch of Hadrian in Athens, the Pantheon in Rome, and his villa at Tibur. After the drowning of his male lover Antinoüs, he encouraged his deification. He enlarged and reformed the civil service and provided alms and circuses for the poor of Rome.

Hadrian's Villa, seaside country palace built for the Emperor Hadrian *c.*135 AD at Tivoli, Italy. Because it covered 7sq mi (18.13sq km), it cannot be considered a typical Roman villa. Instead, it was a royal city, which contained many extravagant and sophisticated buildings.

Hadrian's Wall, northern boundary wall of Roman Britain erected by Emperor Hadrian 122–126 AD and extending 73.5mi (118km) from Wallsend-on-Tyne to Bowness-on-Solway. About 7.5ft (2.3m) thick and 6–15ft (1.8–4.6m) high, it supported many stone forts along its length. The Romans held it until 400. An extensive ruin survives.

Hadron, member of a class of elementary particles that are subject to strong interaction. The group can be divided into baryons, such as the neutron and proton, and mesons, such as the pion, kaon, and eta meson. Over 150 hadrons have been discovered, mostly since

about 1950, and with the exception of the proton and antiproton they are all unstable. Unlike leptons, they have a measurable size; experiment indicates a substructure postulated to consist of quarks. *See also* Lepton; Multiplet; Quark; Strange Particles.

Haerbin. See Harbin.

Hafnium, metallic element (symbol Hf) of the third transition series, first discovered in 1923. Chief source is as a by-product in obtaining zirconium. It is used as a neutron absorber in reactor control rods. Properties: at. no 72; at. wt. 178.49; sp gr 13.31; melt. pt. 4041°F (2229°C); boil pt. 8316°F (4606°C); most common isotope Hf^{180} (35.24%). *See also* Transition Elements.

Hagen, city in W West Germany, on the Ennepe River. Industries: iron, steel, chemicals, machinery, paper. Chartered 1746. Pop. 201,512.

Hagfish, or slime eel, eellike, jawless fish found in temperate-to-cold marine waters. It has underdeveloped eyes, slightly rounded tail and 4–6 fleshy whiskers around its suctorial mouth. Feeding by drilling into fish and eating interior parts, it secretes a slimy mucous from pores along its sides. Length: under 30in (76cm). Family Myxinidae; species, 21 including the common North Atlantic *Myxine glutinosa*. *See also* Cyclostome.

Haggadah, Passover, the story of the Exodus and the redemption of the people of Israel by God, read during Passover services. Developed over a period of centuries, it includes excerpts from the Bible, rabbinical writings, psalms, stories, and prayers.

Haggai, biblical author and 10th of the 12 minor prophets. After the Captivity, he encouraged the people in rebuilding the Temple in Jerusalem.

Haggard, Henry Rider (1856–1925), English novelist. He was in the colonial service in the Transvaal 1875–79, and Africa provides the background for his romantic adventure novels, including *King Solomon's Mines* (1885), *She* (1887), and *Allan Quatermain* (1887).

Hagia Sophia (532–37), a masterpiece of Byzantine architecture designed by Anthemius of Tralles and Isidorus of Miletus for Emperor Justinian. Originally a Christian church, it was converted to a mosque (1453) and then in the 20th century restored as a museum. The central dome, flanked by half domes and semidomes, is supported on pendentives. The interior is lavishly decorated with colored marble and gold-touched mosaic.

Hagiographa, third and final part of the Jewish Scripture (Christian Old Testament). It contains poetic and historical sacred writings, consisting of Psalms, Proverbs, Job, Song of Songs, Ruth, Lamentations, Ecclesiastes, Esther, Daniel, Ezra, Nehemiah, and Chronicles I and II.

Hague, The ('s Gravenhage or **Den Haag),** city and seat of government of the Netherlands, in W Netherlands on shore of North Sea; capital of South Holland prov. 's Gravenhage translates as "the count's wood," referring to the 13th-century hunting lodge of the counts of Holland around which the city grew; city became an important European intellectual and political center by 17th century. Many medieval structures remain, including the Binnenhof, the Hall of Knights, and the Mauritshuis, which contains works by Rembrandt and Vermeer; site of International Court of Justice. Much of The Hague's economy depends upon diplo-

matic and administrative activities. Industries: textiles, metals, chemicals, processed foods. Pop. 479,369.

Hague Peace Conferences, meetings hailed because they inaugurated arms arbitration and enabled neutrals to arbitrate between warring nations. They also allowed any party to call for an impartial investigation and arranged for an international court at The Hague (1899). The second conference (1907) developed rules for "civilized warfare" that later were disregarded.

Hahn, Otto (1879–1968), German chemist. He became director of the Kaiser-Wilhelm Institute in 1928. With Lise Meitner he discovered protoactinium and several nuclear isomers; he was later a co-discoverer of nuclear fission, for which he won a Nobel Prize in 1944. During World War II he remained in Germany but was in disfavor. After the war he was appointed president of the Max Planck Institute.

Hahnium. See Element 105.

Haida, tribe of North American Indians speaking the Skidegattan branch of the Na-Dené language; closely related to the Tlingit and the Tsimshian. They inhabit the Queen Charlotte Islands in British Columbia; a small group that moved to Alaska in the 19th century is now known as the Kaigani. The Haida are regarded as the typical totem pole Indians, and are famed for their wood sculpture. Today approximately 1,500 occupy the area.

Haifa (Hefa), principal seaport city in N Israel, on Mediterranean Sea; 2nd-largest city in Israel; urban, transportation, and industrial center; site of Haifa University (1963) and technical institute (1924); world center of Bahaism. Industries: shipping, oil refining, chemicals, textiles, automobiles, cement, fishing, shipbuilding and repair. Pop. 227,200.

Haiku, a Japanese poetry form consisting of 17 syllables in a five-seven-five pattern, it came into prominence through its mastery by Matsuo Bashō (1644–94), still regarded as the finest practitioner. He was adept at both cheerful and sad *haiku*. The form remains extremely popular in Japan. Despite its brevity, its best authors have adapted it to modern conditions.

Hail, pellets of concentric ice layers, like an onion, formed in clouds and falling to earth's surface. *See also* Precipitation.

Haile Selassie (1891–1975), emperor of Ethiopia (1930–74) b. as Lij Tafari Makonnen. Through his relative Emperor Menelik II, he rose rapidly to a position of power. By 1916 he gained control of Ethiopia as imperial regent. After Empress Zauditu, Menelik's daughter, died (1930), Tafari became Emperor Haile Selassie ("Might of the Trinity"). After Italy invaded Ethiopia in 1935, he was forced into exile (1936) although he appealed to the League of Nations to support his cause. He and the British drove out the Italians in 1941. He consolidated his rule after his return and subsequently became a leader among independent African nations, helping to found the Organization of African Unity in 1963. Unrest at lack of reforms increased in the late 1960s and early 1970s, and he was deposed by the military in 1974.

Hainan, island off SE China, in South China Sea, separated from mainland by Hainan Strait; second-largest Chinese island; under Chinese control since AD 1st century and long a place of political exile. Occupied by Japanese during WWII; taken 1950 by Chinese Communists. Industries: rubber, coffee, rice, sugar cane, fruit, lumber; tin, copper, maganese, lead, silver, coal, graphite, and antimony mining. Area: 13,000sq mi (34,000sq km). Pop. 2,800,000.

Haiphong (Hai-phong), seaport city in N Vietnam, 10mi (16km) from Gulf of Tonkin on narrow connecting channel on branch of Red River Delta; manufacture, trade, and food processing center. Developed by French, city became chief naval base of French Indochina; occupied during WWII by Japanese; bombed by French 1946 in French-Indochina war; included in new state of N Vietnam 1954; heavily bombed by United States in Vietnam War (1965–68 and 1972). Industries: cement, glass, chemicals, cotton. Est. 1874. Pop. 1,-190,900.

Hair, an appendage of the skin that has protective and sensory functions. Hair is made up of three layers: outer flat scalelike cuticle layer, middle keratinized cortex layer that contains the pigment, and inner medulla layer. Hair grows in a follicle, a tubular structure extending down through the epidermis to the upper dermis. The hair follicle ends in a papilla, a highly vascularized point that supplies nourishment for hair growth.

Hair Worm. *See* Horsehair Worm.

Haiti, Republic of, independent nation occupying W third of Caribbean island of Hispaniola. The people are descended from slaves and French settlers; it is the world's oldest black republic. The economy depends on the export of coffee and bauxite. Haiti is the poorest country in Latin America.

Land and Economy. Two-thirds of the country is rough, mountainous terrain unsuitable for cultivation; 2,200,000acres (891,000hectares) are arable. The temperature in the main population areas ranges from 70° to 90°F (21°–32.2°C) with humidity high along the coast. Coffee is its chief export product; bauxite and copper its main minerals. Haiti is one of the most densely populated countries in the world; 90% of the people live on farms too small for family subsistence.

People. About 90% of the people are of African descent, the rest of European or Levantine stock or mulattoes. The official language is French, but the majority speaks creole, a dialect derived from Norman, French, Spanish, African, and Arawak Indian words. Roman Catholicism is the state religion; voodoo is widely practiced. Haiti's literacy rate is 10%, the lowest in Latin America.

Government. The current law is the 1964 constitution with a lifetime term for the president. No political parties are recognized.

History: Discovered by Christopher Columbus in 1492, Hispaniola was divided in 1672 when Spain ceded a portion to France. Slaves, brought from Africa to work the plantations, gained independence in 1804 and renamed the area Haiti. In 1822 Haiti conquered the Spanish-speaking part of the island (Dominican Republic), which broke away in 1844. From 1843 to 1915 Haiti had 22 dictatorships. Dr. Francis (Papa Doc) Duvalier was elected president in 1957; a 1964 constitution awarded him a lifetime term. Following his death in 1971, he was succeeded by his son, Jean Claude Duvalier. Political repression, combined with extreme poverty and famine in 1977 and 1980, resulted in thousands of Haitians fleeing the country for southern Florida, often in unseaworthy boats. US immigration authorities classified them as economic rather than political refugees, and in 1981 the US Coast Guard began turning vessels back to Haiti. Demonstrations against the government led to Jean Claude (Baby Doc) Duvalier's fall and exile in 1986, when a junta took control of the country.

PROFILE

Official name: Republic of Haiti
Area: 10,714sq mi (27,749sq km)
Population: 5,740,000
Density: 536per sq mi (207per sq km)
Chief cities: Port-au-Prince (capital); Cap Haitien
Government: president, Jean Claude Duvalier
Religion: Roman Catholic (state religion)
Language: French (official)
Monetary unit: gourde
Gross national product: $1,300,000,000
Annual per capita income: $260
Industries (major products): cigars, molasses, rum
Agriculture (major products): coffee, sugar cane, bananas, tobacco, rice
Minerals: bauxite, copper
Trading partners (major): United States (60% of total exports), EEC countries

Hake, marine food and commercial fish found in cold and temperate waters. Its elongated, streamlined body is silvery with brown. Length: to 4ft (121.9cm); weight: to 40lb (18.1kg). Family Gadidae or Merluccidae; species include Atlantic silver *Merluccius bilinearis* and Pacific *Merluccius productus.*

Hakodate, major port city on SW Hokkaido Island, N Japan, on the Tsugaru-Kaikyo (strait); formerly capital of Hokkaido prefecture; opened to US ships 1854. Industries: shipbuilding and repair, iron works, fishing. Pop. 307,000.

Halakah, the legal aspects of Judaism. It consists of practices, rites, and the very conduct of Jews, and is contrasted with Haggadah, or nonlegal materials. It is traced to Moses on Mt Sinai, but has been developed throughout time.

Halcyon, Greek mythological figure. The daughter of Aeolus, best known as the beloved wife of Ceyx, king of Thessaly. When Ceyx was drowned in a shipwreck, Halcyon ran to the seashore to find his body. The gods, feeling sorry for the couple, changed them into kingfishers. There are seven days each winter when the sea is calm ("halcyon weather"), for then Ceyx and Halcyon make their nest on the water and care for their children.

Hale, George Ellery (1868–1938), US astronomer, b. Chicago. Hale organized Chicago's Kenwood observatory in 1888, the Yerkes (Wis.) observatory in 1895, the Mt Wilson, Calif., observatory in 1904 and initiated work on the Mt Palomar, Calif., observatory, whose 200-inch (508-cm) telescope bears his name. He invented an instrument, the spectroheliograph, for photographing the Sun and later developed the spectrohelioscope for observation of the Sun. He was widely honored for his work in solar studies, particularly the discovery of the Sun's magnetic field.

Hale, Nathan (1755–76), American Revolutionary War captain and hero. He was hanged by the British as a spy. A Yale graduate, he taught school before joining the Continental Army in 1775. Having volunteered to go behind British lines on Long Island to gain military secrets, he was captured on Sept. 21, 1776, and hanged the next day. His last words are said to be, "I regret that I have but one life to lose for my country."

Halfbeak, marine and freshwater fish of E Pacific and Atlantic. Silver with a crimson jaw, it has a long, needlelike lower jaw and uses its short pectoral fins in attempts to glide like flying fish. Length: 12–18in (30.5–45.7cm). Family Exocoetidae; species, 60, including *Hyphorhamphus unifasciatus.*

Half-life, the time taken for one-half of the atoms present in a given amount of radioactive isotope to undergo one disintegration. *See also* Radioactivity.

Halibut, flatfish found in deep cold to temperate seas worldwide. An important commercial fish, it is brownish on the eye side; white below. Prolific, producing 2,-000,000 eggs at one spawning, they live up to 40 years. Length: to 9ft (274.3cm); weight: to 700lb (315kg). Family Pleuronectidae; species Atlantic *Hippoglossus hippoglossus* and giant Pacific *Hippoglossus stenolepsis.*

Halide, salt of a halogen, or an organic compound containing a halogen. The halide salts, fluorides, chlorides, bromides, and iodides, contain negative ions. The alkyl halides are organic compounds such as methyl chloride (CH_3Cl), containing an alkane radical bound to a halogen atom.

Halifax, Charles Montagu, Earl of (1661–1715), English statesman whose political success was a result of his great financial skills. He became lord of the treasury and in 1692 established the borrowing system of the national debt. He founded the Bank of England and was chancellor of the exchequer in 1694; he became first lord of the treasury in 1697 and was prime minister (1714–15). Twice impeached (1701, 1703) but never convicted, he was also a successful minor poet.

Halifax, port city and capital of Nova Scotia, Canada, on Atlantic Ocean; seat of Halifax co; important embarkation port during WWII; site of naval base since 1910, Saint Mary's University, Dalhousie University, Nova Scotia Technical College. Industries: oil refining, breweries, iron, fishing. Founded 1749. Pop. 117,882.

Halite, the most abundant halide mineral of the halite group, sodium chloride (NaCl). Found in sedimentary rocks, salt domes, and dried lakes. Cubic system interlocking cubic crystals; also granular and massive. Colorless, white, or gray with glassy luster. Hardness 2.0; sp gr 2.2. Important as table salt and source of chlorine. *See also* Sodium Chloride.

Hall, Asaph (1829–1907), US astronomer, b. Goshen, Conn. He was professor of mathematics at the US Naval Observatory, Washington D.C. (1862–91) and professor of astronomy at Harvard (1896–1901). In 1877 he discovered Phobos and Deimos, the two moons of Mars.

Hall, Charles Francis (1821–71), US arctic explorer, b. Rochester, N.H. His first expedition (1860–62), along the SE coast of Baffin Island, discovered traces of the Eskimos' attack on Martin Frobisher who was searching for the Northwest Passage (1576–78). Hall's second expedition (1864–69) found remnants of John Franklin's expedition lost in 1845. He died while leading a government party to the North Pole (1871).

Hall, G(ranville) Stanley (1846–1924), seminal figure in US psychology, b. Ashfield, Mass. He is credited with many firsts; eg, founding one of the first US psychology laboratories, the first US psychology journal (1887), and the American Psychological Association (1892). His books *The Contents of Children's Minds* (1883) and *Adolescence* (1904) contributed powerfully to the development of the child-study movement. In 1909 he brought Freud and Jung to Clark University, of which he was president (1889–1920), thus introducing psychoanalysis to the United States. His many successful students included John Dewey and James M. Cattell.

Hall, Lyman (1724–90), American patriot and a signer of the Declaration of Independence, b. Wallingford, Conn. A physician in Georgia, he was sent by that state to the Continental Congress (1775–80). He later served for one year (1783) as the governor of Georgia.

Halle, city in S central East Germany, on Saale River; capital of Halle district; site of University of Halle (1694) which combined with University of Wittenberg (1817), medieval town hall, 15th-century tower; birthplace of George Handel (1685). Industries: coal mining, food processing, machinery. Founded 9th century. Pop. 237,349.

Haller, Albrecht von (1708–77), Swiss biologist, physician, and poet. Well known as a botanist for his descriptions of alpine flora and as a poet for his glorification of the mountains (*Die Alpen,* 1729), he was appointed professor of anatomy, medicine, and botany at the University of Göttingen in 1736. There he did research on the contractility of muscle tissue, and his resulting treatise (1752) laid the foundations of modern neurology. He returned to his native Bern in 1753, maintaining a private medical practice. His anatomy summary, *Elementa physiologiae corporis humani* (8 vols., 1757–66), became the first standard physiology text.

Halley, Edmund (1656–1742), British scientist who accurately predicted the return in 1758 of the comet bearing his name, and who first published a map of the winds (1686).

Halloween, in medieval times a holy evening. It took place on Oct. 31, the eve of All Saints' Day. The souls of the dead were to visit their former homes on this day.

Hallstatt, town in W Austria, on Hallstätter Lake; archeological excavations (1846–99) unearthed cultural relics dating from *c.* 900 BC, known as the Hallstatt era of the Iron Age. Industries: tourism, salt mines, wood carving. Pop. 1,340.

Hallucination, perceptual experience without appropriate sensory (receptor) stimulation, which can be viewed as a falsification of reality. Though they may occur in any sense (hearing, sight, touch, taste, or smell), auditory hallucinations appear to be the most common. Though usually symptomatic of psychotic disorders, hallucinations may also occur during altered states of consciousness.

Hallucinogen, drug that causes hallucinations, that is, unusual perceptions without external cause. Hallucinogenic drugs, such as marijuana, mescaline, and lysergic acid diethylamide (LSD), have been used in primitive religous ceremony and have an extensive illicit use. Some are employed in experimental investigation and treatment of mental illness.

Halogen Elements, elements fluorine, chlorine, bromine, iodine, and astatine belonging to group VII of the periodic table. They react with most other elements and with organic compounds; reactivity decreases down the group. The halogens are strongly electronegative and produce crystalline salts containing negative ions of the type F^-, Cl^-, etc. The name halogen means "salt-producer."

Hals, Frans (1580–1666), Dutch painter. He was unique in his ability to capture fleeting expressions in his paintings of robust, vital figures, such as the *Laughing Cavalier.* He also created many group portraits of drinkers, governors of charitable institutions, and children and musicians. His later works, more subdued in color and mood, have a dignity and strength approaching his contemporary, Rembrandt.

Haiti

Alexander Hamilton

Dag Hammarskjöld

Hälsingborg, port city in SW Sweden, on the Øresund opposite Helsingør, Denmark; site of 13th-century church, 12th-century castle. Industries: shipbuilding, sugar refining, copper, clay, brewing, rubber, coal. Pop. 101,685.

Ham, in Genesis, second of Noah's three sons. After the Flood, his irreverence resulted in a curse by Noah, who predicted that Ham's descendants would be subservient to those of his brothers, Shem and Japheth.

Hamadan, city in W Iran, at foot of Mt Alvand; capital of Hamadan governorate. Ancient city of Ecbatana, it was capital of Media 6th century BC; passed to Arabs AD 645; chief trade center of W Iran. Industries: agriculture, rugs, leather, wood products. Pop. 124,379.

Hamadryas, or sacred baboon, small baboon living in the plains and rocky hills of NE Africa and Arabia. Adults and males have a rufflike mane around the neck. It was sacred to ancient Egyptians. Weight: to 40lb (18kg). Species *Comopithecus hamadryas. See also* Baboon.

Hamamatsu, city on S central Honshu, Japan, near the Pacific coast approx. 55mi (89km) SE of Nagoya; site of daimyo castle; suffered Allied bombings May-June 1945. Industries: textiles, tea, musical instruments. Pop. 469,000.

Haman, biblical prime minister of Ahasuerus, king of Persia. An enemy of the Jews, he was hanged on gallows erected for Mordecai, cousin to Ahasuerus' wife Esther, who was to die for refusing to bow before Haman.

Hamburg, city that is also a constituent state of West Germany, on the Elbe River near its mouth on the North Sea; capital of the state. A successful medieval trading port, by 1510 it was an imperial free city. Present urban area was created 1937 by incorporating towns of Harburg, Wandsbek, and Altona into city structure; site of 19th-century Renaissance town hall, 18th-century Renaissance-style church, University of Hamburg (1919); birthplace of Johannes Brahms and Felix Mendelssohn. Industries: food products, chemicals, metal goods, fishing, publishing. Founded AD 808 by Charlemagne. Pop. 1,714,400.

Hamden, town in S Connecticut; N residential suburb of New Haven; site of Quinnipiac College (1929), Mount Sacred Heart College (1954), South Central Community College (1967), and many pre-Revolutionary War and Civil War houses. Industries: firearms, machinery, electronics, rolled steel, aircraft, handbags. Settled 1638; inc. 1786. Pop. (1980) 51,071.

Hamilcar Barca (died 228 BC), military commander of Carthage, father of Hannibal and Hasdrubal. He fought with distinction in Sicily and during the First Punic War and withdrew without surrender. After quelling a revolt of mercenaries led by Spendius and Matho (241–38), he conquered S and E Spain. He was drowned at Helice during a siege.

Hamilton, Alexander (1755–1804), US political figure, b. Nevis, West Indies. During the first years of the republic he was the leading proponent of a strong national government. He came to the North American mainland in 1772 and studied at King's College (now Columbia) in New York City in 1773–74. He joined the Continental Army in 1776 as a captain, and in 1777 General Washington appointed him his aide-de-camp and secretary. In 1780 he married into the influential Schuyler family of New York. After the war he became a lawyer in New York and a member of the Continental

Congress. At the Annapolis Convention (1786), he proposed the Philadelphia Constitutional Convention of 1787. Hamilton served as a delegate to the Constitutional Convention. He was the principal contributor to *The Federalist Papers,* advocating the new constitution, and led the fight in New York State for ratification. As the first secretary of the treasury (1789–95) he established the national currency and the Bank of the United States (1791) and proposed the assumption of all state war debts by the national government, numerous excise taxes and import tarrifs, and the encouragement of manufacturing and industry. Although he resigned from the cabinet in 1795, he remained politically active. A leading spokesman for the Federalists, he opposed Thomas Jefferson and his Democratic-Republicans. He advocated strong measures against revolutionary France and strong ties with England, the country's leading trading power. He alienated many of his fellow Federalists by first working against President John Adams, then by throwing his support to Thomas Jefferson rather than to his own Federalist rival in New York, Aaron Burr, when the 1800 election resulted in an electoral tie. In 1804 he thwarted Burr's campaign for governor of New York. Burr challenged him to a duel and killed him.

Hamilton, Emma, (Lady) (1761?–1815), wife of ambassador and archeologist Sir William Hamilton and, from 1798, mistress to Lord Horatio Nelson, by whom she had a daughter, Horatia (b.1801). *See also* Nelson, Horatio.

Hamilton, capital and chief seaport of Bermuda Island, at the head of Great Sound. Founded 1790 and settled by English; inc. 1793; made capital 1815; made a free port 1956. Tourism is the major industry. Pop. 3,000.

Hamilton, city in SE Ontario, Canada, approx. 40mi (64km) SW of Toronto on Lake Ontario; seat of Wentworth co; site of Royal Botanical Gardens, airport, harbor, railroad. Industries: textiles, iron, steel. Settled 1813. Pop. 312,003.

Hamilton, city in New Zealand, on central North Island, on Waikato River; commercial center of dairy farming and sheep raising region; site of University of Waikato (1964). Founded 1864. Pop. 157,900.

Hamilton, city in SW Ohio, on Great Miami River, 27mi (43km) N of Cincinnati; seat of Butler co; site of branch of University of Miami (1968). Industries: automobile bodies, safes, pumps, motors. Founded in early 19th century on site of abandoned Fort Hamilton; inc. 1857. Pop. (1980) 63,189.

Hamilton River. *See* Churchill River.

Hamite Subrace, former subdivision of the Caucasoid race. Designation of the pale-skinned pastoralists of black Africa (such as Berbers) as Hamites has been discredited by linguistic investigations showing their languages to be of diverse origins.

Hamlet (*c.*1601), 5-act tragedy by William Shakespeare. Written in blank verse, it was probably based on the *Ur-Hamlet* (original *Hamlet*) by Thomas Kyd. At its first performance (*c.*1601) the part of Hamlet was doubtless played by Richard Burbage, the star of Shakespeare's company. Tradition credits Shakespeare himself with originating the part of the Ghost. Hamlet, prince of Denmark, is told by his father's ghost that Claudius, the late king's brother and new husband of the widowed queen Gertrude, poisoned the late king. Hamlet promises the Ghost to avenge his father's death. Weeks pass, and still Hamlet delays. He writes passionate letters to Ophelia, daughter of Claudius'

counsellor Polonius. A company of players arrives at the castle and Hamlet arranges for them to act out a tragedy similar to the alleged murder of his father. As the player poisons his victim Hamlet watches his uncle and sees signs of guilt, but fails to act on an opportunity to kill Claudius while the king is at prayer. He denounces his mother and accidentally stabs Polonius. Convinced he is mad, the king and queen have Hamlet banished to England. When he returns, Ophelia has gone mad and drowned. Hamlet and Ophelia's brother Laertes fight over the right to be her chief mourner. The king takes advantage of their antagonism to urge them to fight a duel with a poisoned sword, and also poisons a cup of wine intended for Hamlet. The Queen drinks the poisoned wine and dies; Hamlet and Laertes wound each other with the poisoned sword and Laertes dies asking Hamlet's forgiveness. Hamlet stabs the king, then dies himself, saying "The rest is silence."

Hamlin, Hannibal (1809–91), US political leader, b. Paris Hill, Maine. He was a lawyer, and served in the House of Representatives (1843–47), Senate (1848–57), and as Republican governor of Maine (1857). Opposed to slavery, he became vice president under President Abraham Lincoln (1861–65) and was his close advisor. He returned to the Senate for two terms (1869–81).

Hammarskjöld, Dag (1905–61), Swedish diplomat, succeeded Trygve Lie as secretary general of the United Nations (1953). His "quiet diplomacy" secured release in 1955 of 11 US airmen held prisoner in China. In 1956 he helped resolve the Suez Canal crisis. In 1960 he sent a UN force to keep peace in the Congo. En route to Katanga for peace talks his plane crashed. He was awarded a posthumous Nobel Prize in 1961. His book *Markings* (1964) is a spiritual diary.

Hammerhead Shark, aggressive, man-eating fish found in all tropical marine waters and warmer temperate zones. Recognized by its unusual head that is extended laterally in two hammerlike lobes with an eye and nostril located at the tip of each lobe. It is grayish above and whitish below. Length: to 15ft (4.6m); width: 36in (0.9m); weight: to 1,500lb (675kg). Species, several including the common *Sphyrna zygaena.* Family Sphyrnidae; *See also* Chondrichthyes; Sharks.

Hammer v. Dagenhart (1918), US Supreme Court decision that declared unconstitutional a federal law prohibiting the interstate shipment of goods produced in factories employing children under age 14 for long hours. This case represents the old restrictive view of the powers of the federal government and was overruled in *United States v. Darby* (1941).

Hammond, city in NW Indiana, on Illinois border; connected to Calumet Harbor on Lake Michigan, Ill. and Indiana Harbor, Ind. by a ship canal; named for George Hammond, founder of meat packing plant (1868); site of the Calumet branch of Purdue University. Industries: books, soap, margarine, steel forgings. Settled 1851; inc. 1884. Pop. (1980) 93,714.

Hammond Organ, electrophonic keyboard instrument producing amplified music with discs rotating in an electromagnetic field. Invented by Laurens Hammond in 1934 to replace pipe organs in small churches, it was later used in jazz and popular music.

Hammurabi (*fl.*1792–50 BC), king of Babylonia in the first dynasty. He extended his rule over Mesopotamia, organized the empire, built canals and wheat granaries, and classified the law (the Code of Hammurabi).

Hammurabi, Code of, ancient code of law compiled under Hammurabi, king of Babylonia (*fl.* 1792–50 BC). Found carved on a diorite column by J. de Morgan in Sousa in 1901, it is now in the Louvre. Composed of 3,600 lines of cuneiform, it illustrates Babylonian social structure, economic conditions, industries, law, and family life.

Hamnam (Hamhung, Hungnam), port city in North Korea, on the Sea of Japan; formed by merger of Hamhung and Hungnam; birthplace of Gen. Yi Song-gye, founder of Yi dynasty that ruled Korea 1392–1910. Hungnam was annexed to Korea 1910. Industries: pig iron, carbonates, bricks, cement, acid, calcium. Pop. 143,600.

Hampton, seaport city in SE Virginia, on James River, 7mi (11km) N of Newport News; site of many US government installations; oldest continuous English settlement in America. Industries: defense, tourism, seafood packing, fertilizer, building materials. Founded 1610; inc. 1908; consolidated with Elizabeth City co 1952. Pop. (1980) 122,617.

Hampton Roads, a partly sheltered harbor in SE Virginia, through which the James, Nansemond, and Elizabeth rivers flow to the Chesapeake Bay; since colonial times, it has been an important harbor and one of the busiest US ports, serving Newport News and Hampton (N shore), Norfolk and Portsmouth (S shore); site of Civil War naval battle between the *Monitor* and *Merrimack*. Length: 4mi (6km). Depth: 40ft (12m).

Hamster, small, nocturnal, burrowing rodent native to Eurasia and Africa with internal cheek pouches for carrying food. Golden hamsters, popular pets and lab animals, are descendants of one nest discovered in Syria in 1930. Smaller and lighter than wild species, golden hamsters reproduce frequently with up to 15 per litter, offering a useful supply for research. Disease-resistant and almost odorless, golden hamsters are—unlike wild ones—easy to handle. They eat fruit, greens, seeds, nuts, and meat. Length: to 6in (15cm). Family Cricetidae; Species *Mesocricetus auratus*.

Han, either of two rivers in China. In E central China, rises in Nancheng, flows SE to Yangtze River at Hankow. Length: 750mi (1,208km). In SE China, rises on border of Fukien-Kiangsi provs., flows S to South China Sea at Swatow. Length: 100mi (161km).

Hanau, city in central West Germany, on Main River 10mi (16km) E of Frankfurt. Old town, chartered 1303, grew around medieval castle of counts of Hanau; new town was founded in early 17th century by Protestant Dutch refugees; they were united 1833; site of St Mary's church (14th century), Philippsruhe and Wilhelmsruhe palaces (18th century), Dutch-Walloon church (1600–08); much of old town's notable buildings were destroyed during WWII bombings; birthplace of Brothers Grimm. Industries: metal and mineral processing, engineering, rubber goods, chemicals, jewelry. Pop. 54,868.

Han Chinese, or **Han-Jen,** Mongoloid people constituting about 94% of the Chinese population and inhabiting the densely populated eastern half of China. They consist of various groups sharing the same culture, traditions, and written language, although within the Han Chinese language there are several mutually unintelligible dialects. Their ancient hierarchical society, based on Taoist, Confucian, and Buddhist tenets, has been reorganized under communism and the traditional agricultural economy is being modernized.

Hancock, John (1737–93), US statesman and revolutionary, b. Braintree, Mass. He was chosen to represent Massachusetts at the Continental Congress (1775–80, 1785, 1786), serving as president (1775–77). His was the first signature on the Declaration of Independence (1776). He helped to draw up the constitution of Massachusetts (1780) and became that state's first governor (1780–85). He was reelected governor in 1789 and served until his death.

Handball, a ball game played between two or three individuals or between two two-player teams with a black hard rubber ball. It is most popular in the United States. It is played on a court, indoors or out, of one wall (20 × 34 ft; 6 × 10m), or three or four walls (20 × 40ft; 6 × 12m). In the single-wall game, the wall is 16 feet (4.9m) high. In the three- and four-wall game, three walls are 20 feet high (6.1m), and the back wall is 12 feet high (3.7m). In all games, the object is to keep the ball out of the opponent's reach, and points are scored when the non-server cannot return the ball. The first player or team to score 21 points wins. The serve changes hands when the server cannot return the ball. Play begins by bouncing the ball once and hitting it off one or more of the walls; the ball must then be returned before a second bounce. In order to protect the hands,

special gloves are used. Handball—the four-wall variation—was played in Ireland in the Middle Ages. One-wall handball was introduced in Brooklyn, N.Y., in the 1880s. Intercollegiate and national championships are held annually.

Handel, George Frideric (1685–1759), German composer who lived in England after 1712, b. Georg Friedrich Handel in Halle. With J. S. Bach, Handel is regarded as the greatest composer of the Baroque period. He composed a great many operas (eg, *Atalanta, Serse, Berenice*), oratorios (eg, *Samson, Esther, Judas Maccabeus*), organ music, chamber concertos, sonatas, and songs. Among his most popular works are the *Water Music* (1715–17) and the *Royal Fireworks Music* (1749), both composed for outings and holidays promoted by the English royal court. Handel's best known work is the oratorio *The Messiah* (1741), famous for its "Hallelujah Chorus." Handel was greatly honored in his own day, especially in England. He is buried in Westminster Abbey. *See also* Baroque Music.

Handy, W(illiam) C(hristopher) (1873–1958), US composer and musician known as the "father of the blues," b. Florence, Ala. He led his own band in 1903 and was particularly popular after composing several hits including "Memphis Blues" (1912), and "St. Louis Blues" (1914). After 1923 he devoted his time exclusively to composing and publishing many other classic blues songs.

Han Dynasty (202 BC–AD 220), Chinese dynasty. It was founded by Kuang Wu-ti and was ruled by his family for more than four centuries. It is considered by the Chinese to be one of their greatest periods of rule. Han rulers laid the administrative and ideological basis for more than 2,000 years of stability and greatness for the Chinese empire. Under the Han the Confucian state cult was formalized through the examination system, bureaucratic patterns for rule were fashioned, literary and art traditions established, and imperial expansion spread Chinese influence throughout E Asia.

Hangchow (Hangzhou), port city in E China, on Hangchow Bay; capital of Chekiang prov.; S terminus of the Grand Canal; capital of Wu-Yüeh kings (907–960) and Southern Sung dynasty (1132–1276); visited and written about by Marco Polo (13th century); sacked by Taiping forces (1861); fell under Communist control (1949); site of monasteries and shrines dating from 10th century; seat of Chekiang and Hangchow universities. Industries: silk, pig iron, steel, chemicals, food processing, tools, electronic equipment, rubber, cement, paper. Pop. 1,100,000.

Hankow. *See* Wuhan.

Hannibal (247–183 BC), Carthaginian general, one of the foremost military commanders in history, son of Hamilcar Barca and brother of Hasdrubal. He took command of Carthaginian forces in Spain (221 BC), conquered much of the land, and besieged and broke Saguntum, an ally of Rome. With 35,000 select troops and elephants he crossed the Alps into Italy and with forces reduced by the difficult march won brilliant victories at Ticinus and Trebia (218). He then crossed the Apennines, pillaged Etruria, destroyed two Roman legions, and, unable to draw Fabius Cunctator into battle, halted at Apulia for the winter. At Cannae in 216 he wiped out Roman forces in his greatest triumph, but, deprived of support from Carthage, was unable to take Rome. He was gradually forced south, his gains fading from want of reinforcements. In 203 he was ordered to Carthage and, after 16 years of battle in Roman territory, was finally defeated at Zama in 202 by Scipio Africanus Major. He governed Carthage and sought constitutional reforms until his enemies forced him to flee to Syria where he was defeated in a naval battle against the Rhodian fleet. He went to Bithynia where he committed suicide to thwart extradition to Rome. *See also* Punic Wars.

Hanoi (Ha-noi), city in NE Vietnam, on Red River, approx. 50mi (81km) from its port at Haiphong; capital of Vietnam 1954–1976; transportation, manufacture, and trade center. City was 7th-century seat of Chinese rule; taken by French 1883, it became capital of Tonkin; 1887–1945 capital of Indochina; liberated 1945 by the Viet Minh (the Communist-dominated Vietnam Independence League), it was recaptured by French 1946–1954; bombed by United States during Vietnam War; site of university (1956), Institute of Oriental Medicine, polytechnical college, Pagoda of Great Buddha. Industries: rice milling, textiles. Pop. 1,443,500.

Hanover, House of, royal family of Great Britain from 1714 to 1901. In 1692, Augustus of Hanover married Sophia, of the Palatinate, granddaughter of James I of England. By the terms of the English Act of Settlement (1701) their son succeeded in England as George I

(1714). His successors were George II, George III, George IV, William IV, and Victoria. Salic law forbade Victoria's accession in Hanover, so her uncle Ernest Augustus, Duke of Cumberland, became king there in 1837. Victoria was succeeded (1901) by her son Edward VII, who took his father's family name, Saxe-Coburg.

Hanover (German, **Hannover**), former kingdom and province of Germany. Most of the area was part of the duchy of Brunswick-Lüneburg held by the Guelph family. In 1692, Duke Ernest Augustus was created elector of Hanover, and his lands were known thereafter as Hanover. His son George succeeded to the British throne in 1714; the personal union with Britain lasted until 1837, when, on the accession of Victoria in Britain, Hanover went to her uncle Ernest Augustus. Divided during the Napoleonic era, Hanover was reconstituted as a kingdom in 1815. It allied itself with Austria in the Austro-Prussian War of 1866 and, after Austria's defeat, was annexed by Prussia. After World War II it was incorporated into the state of Lower Saxony.

Hanover (Hannover), city in N West Germany, on Leine River, 35mi (56km) WNW of Brunswick; capital of Lower Saxony. In 1636 city became residence of dukes of Calenberg-Göttingen (predecessors of House of Hanover who ruled Britain 1714–1901); site of 15th-century Gothic city hall, 14th-century Marktkirche (market church), Leineschloss (17th-century chateau) that houses parliament of Lower Saxony, university (1880), and medical school (1963). Industries: steel, rubber, machinery textiles, chemicals. Founded 12th century; chartered 1241. Pop. 549,100.

Hanseatic League, German commercial union of the Middle Ages which grew from smaller local unions, or Hansas. Containing several German cities, the League functioned as protector of the merchants of its member towns and worked to establish favorable trade conditions in foreign lands. Pressured by the Dutch and English, and by increasing German political organization, the League had lost its effectiveness by the mid-17th century.

Hanukkah, or **Chanukah,** meaning "consecration" or "dedication," an 8-day festival celebrated in Judaism. it is also known as the Feast of Lights. It is a major ceremony, involving services at home and in synagogue, which commemorates the rededication of the Temple in 165 BC and the miracle of a one-day supply of oil lasting for eight days. Gifts are given and games played.

Hanuman, or entellus langur, leaf-eating monkey of S Asia that has bristly hairs on top and sides of its head. Species *Presbytis entellus*. *See also* Langur.

Hapsburg, name of a royal Austrian family, one of the principal houses of Europe in the 15th through 20th centuries. The name derives from Habichtsburg (hawk's nest), the family castle in Switzerland.

Beginning with Otto, the first count of Hapsburg, in the 11th century, there was a direct male line until 1740 when the Pragmatic Sanction allowed a daughter, Maria Theresa, to succeed, an event that changed the name of the house to Hapsburg-Lorraine.

Frederick V, the Hapsburg king of Germany, was crowned Holy Roman Emperor in 1452, and the title remained in the family until the empire was dissolved in 1806. His son Maximilian married (1477) Mary, daughter of Charles the Bold of Burgundy, which allowed the family to acquire the Netherlands, Luxembourg, and Burgundy. Maximilian's descendants gained control of Spain, Naples, Sicily, and Sardinia. The peak of Hapsburg power was reached under Charles I, king of Spain (HRE Charles V) in the 16th century. His vast realm proved too unwieldy, however, and the family split into two branches, the Spanish Hapsburgs and the Austrian Hapsburgs. The Spanish Hapsburgs died out in 1700. The last ruling Austrian Hapsburg, Charles I, abdicated in 1918.

Well-known Hapsburgs include Marie Antoinette, queen of France, Marie Louise, second wife of Napoleon I, Maximilian, emperor of Mexico, and Emperor Francis Joseph of Austria-Hungary.

Hara-kiri, or more properly, "seppuku," Japanese form of ritualized suicide by disembowelment. Seppuku originated with samurai in the middle ages. Although it was generally voluntarily performed to avoid becoming an enemy prisoner, to prove loyalty, or to protest the actions of a superior, leaders often ordered subordinates to commit seppuku following an insubordination. It is still practiced today, most often as a form of protest.

Harare (formerly **Salisbury**), capital city of Zimbabwe, in NE part of the country; commercial, industrial, transportation center. As Salisbury the city served as capital of Federation of Rhodesia and Nyasaland 1953–63

John Hancock

W.C. Handy

Warren G. Harding

and Rhodesia 1965–79; site of University of Rhodesia (1957), two cathedrals, national museum, library, Rhodes National Gallery. Products: maize, cotton, tobacco, citrus fruits. Industries: gold mining, textiles, steel, processed foods, clothing, tobacco, chemicals, furniture. Founded 1890 as fort by the Pioneer Column. Pop. 513,000.

Harbin (Haerbin), port city in Manchuria, China, on Sungari River; capital of Heilungkiang prov. A Russian concession 1896–1924, it was under Japanese rule 1932–45; fell to Communist control 1950. Industries: oil, coal, machinery, aircraft, sugar refining, tractors, meat packing, food processing, railroad shops. Pop. 2,000,000.

Harbor Seal, also called common seal or spotted seal *(Phoca vitulina),* North American seal usually found in coastal waters of Canada and Alaska. Adults have a spotted grey or black coat, pups are born white or gray. They feed on fish and crustaceans, come ashore frequently, and congregate in herds when they are on land. Size is about 5ft (1.5m), 150lbs (68kg), but they can grow larger. Although they are not hunted commercially, they are useful to man for clothing and food.

Hardecanute (*c.*1019–42), king of Denmark (1035–42), king of England (1040–42). Son of Canute of England and Emma of Normandy. His claim to the English throne after Canute's death was opposed by his half brother Harold Harefoot, who was elected king in 1037. Hardecanute attacked England in 1040. Harold died in 1040, and Hardecanute became king. Cruel and oppressive, he avoided dynastic struggle by indicating Edward the Confessor, Emma's son by Aethelred, as his successor.

Harding, Warren Gamaliel (1865–1923), 29th president of the United States (1921–23), b. Blooming Grove (now Corsica), Ohio, attended Ohio Central College. In 1891 he married a wealthy widow, Florence Kling De Wolfe, who urged him into a political career. He bought and published a newspaper in Marion, Ohio. He served in the Ohio state senate as a Republican and in 1904 he served a term as lieutenant governor. He unsuccessfully ran for governor in 1910, and in 1914 he was elected to the US Senate.

After the 1920 Republican convention deadlocked, Harding was chosen as presidential candidate by a clique of party leaders in a "smoke-filled room." He ran on a platform of returning the country to "normalcy," a word of his own coinage. He easily defeated his Democratic rival, James M. Cox.

An unambitious, easygoing man, Harding displayed almost no talent or taste for the presidency. He left control of the administration to his advisors, who became known as the "Ohio gang." Soon reports of large-scale corruption and graft circulated—the most important example was the Teapot Dome scandal—and congressional investigations were begun. Harding became ill and died before most of the scandals, among the worst in US history, were uncovered. He was succeeded by Vice President Calvin Coolidge. Among Harding's staff who were prosecuted after his death were Albert B. Fall, his secretary of the interior, and Harry M. Daughtery, his attorney general.
Career: Ohio State Senate, 1899–1903; Ohio lieutenant governor, 1904–05; US Senate, 1915–21; president, 1921–23. *See also* Teapot Dome Scandal.

Hardness Scale, a scale used to furnish a rough estimate of a mineral's resistance to scratching by testing it against a predetermined series of minerals (or test objects) graded from 1 through 10. A flat surface of the mineral to be tested is scratched by a sharp edge of

the test object. Anything scratchable by talc is valued at 1, by diamond at 10.

Hardpan. *See* Laterite.

Hardy, Thomas (1840–1928), English novelist and poet. His novels, most of them tragic works set in the region of Wessex, include *Far From the Madding Crowd* (1874), *The Return of the Native* (1878), *The Mayor of Casterbridge* (1886), *Tess of the d'Urbervilles* (1891), and *Jude the Obscure* (1895). Hardy later concentrated on poetry, in volumes such as *Wessex Poems* (1898). Noted poems by him include "The Darkling Thrush" (1900), "Channel Firing" (1914), and "The Convergence of the Twain" (1914). Between 1903 and 1908 he published *The Dynasts,* an epic-drama.

Hare, large member of the herbivorous rabbit family (Leoporidae) widely distributed around the world, with long ears and large hind feet. In contrast to rabbits, true hares (genus *Lepus*) move by leaping as well as running and their young are born with open eyes and a full coat of fur. Length 15–30in (38–76cm); weight: 3–15lb (1.3–7kg). Hares include jackrabbits, snowshoe rabbits, and European hares. *See also* Rabbit.

Harebell, or Scottish bluebell, slender-stemmed perennial bellflower native to Eurasia and North America. It bears nodding blue, bell-like flowers. Many North American wildflowers are also called harebells. Height: to 2ft (61cm). Family Campanulaceae; genus *Campanusla rotundifolia. See also* Bellflower.

Harelip, congenital cleft in the upper lip caused by the failure of the two parts of the palate to unite. Heredity may be a factor, as may metabolic disorders or diseases of mother or infant. Corrective surgery usually is postponed until an affected child is 18 months old.

Harem, a man's wives, concubines, and female servants. It is especially associated with Islam, which requires the strict segregation of women. The most famous harem was that of the Turkish sultans, which often had several hundred women, guarded by eunuchs, before its abolition in 1909. *See also* Concubinage.

Harlan, John Marshall (1833–1911), US jurist and lawyer, b. Boyle co, Ky. A county judge (1858), and Kentucky state attorney general (1863), he was appointed an associate justice of the US Supreme Court (1877–1911) where he was noted for his advocacy of civil rights, best revealed in his eloquent dissent in *Plessy v. Ferguson* (1896), the case that established the "separate but equal" racial segregation doctrine, which stood as law until 1954.

Harlan, John Marshall (1899–1971), US jurist and lawyer, b. Chicago, the grandson of Supreme Court Justice Harlan (1833–1911). He received the Legion of Merit Award in World War II and later served as chief counsel for the New York State Crime Commission (1951–53). Appointed to the US court of appeals in February 1954, he was made an associate justice of the US Supreme Court in November 1954. An advocate of judicial restraint in matters concerning social and economic legislation, he defended the expansion of civil rights and liberties.

Harlem, community of Manhattan borough, New York City. A fashionable 19th-century community, an influx of blacks *c.* 1905–1920 made it one of the largest black settlements in the United States and a political and cultural center for blacks. Founded 1658 by Dutch; annexed to New York City 1731.

Harlem Renaissance, period of creativity, particularly in literature, among US blacks in the 1920s. Centered in Harlem, the black ghetto in New York City (not all the writers were New Yorkers, however), the Renaissance produced such writers as Countee Cullen, Langston Hughes, and Claude McKay. *See also* Harlem.

Harlequin Bug, or fire bug, calico bug, collard bug, orange and black bug that is a vegetable garden pest in S United States. They suck juices from plants. Length: .35in (8.9mm). Family Pentatomidae; species *Murgantia histrionica. See also* Stink Bug.

Harlequin Duck, small sea duck with a short bill and distinctively patterned plumage. Species *Histrionicus histrionicus. See also* Duck.

Harley, Robert, 1st Earl of Oxford (1661–1724), English statesman. He gradually assumed leadership of the Tory party, supplanting both Marlborough and Godolphin in Queen Anne's confidence. As chancellor of the exchequer (1710), he promoted peace with France and the formation of the South Sea Company. He survived impeachment in 1715 for conduct relating to the treaty of Utrecht (1713) and for his Jacobite leanings.

Harmonic, oscillation of a periodic quantity, such as a musical note, whose frequency is a whole-number multiple of the fundamental frequency. *See also* Timbre.

Harmonica, or mouth organ, simplest reed instrument. It is a box in various sizes holding free metal reeds in diatonic scale, which are vibrated when the player blows or inhales through openings while moving the harmonica across his lips. Of European origin (*c.*1820), it is considered an amateur or novelty instrument, except when played in bands or by expert soloists.

Harmonic Motion, repeated motion as of a pendulum, atomic vibrations, or an oscillating electrical circuit. Simple harmonic motion is governed by a restoring force proportional to the displacement of the particle: $F = Kx$, where K, called the spring constant, determines the strength of the restoring force. The above equation pervades all branches of physics.

Harmonic Progression, sequence of the form $1/a$, $1/b$, $1/c$, ... , where a, b, c, etc., form an arithmetic progression. The simplest is formed by the reciprocals of the positive integers: 1, 1/2, 1/3, 1/4, ... Strings with lengths proportional to these terms (and with identical diameter and tension) vibrate with harmonic musical tones.

Harmonium, keyboard instrument producing music when air propelled by a pedal-operated bellows vibrates metal reeds. It is equipped with stops to vary tone colors. Developed in France (*c.*1840), it became popular in the United States in modified form as a small parlor organ.

Harold I Harefoot (died 1040), English king of Danish origins, succeeded his father Canute in 1035. Despite Hardecanute's rival claim, he became ruler of all England (1037). *See also* Canute.

Harold II (1022?–1066), king of England (1066). Second son of Godwin, earl of Wessex, as a young man he was appointed to the earldom of East Anglia. His succession in 1053 to the earldom of Wessex thus made him the most influential figure in England except the king. Upon the death of Edward the Confessor, the council, following the dying king's request, named Harold king. William of Normandy at once gathered an army of 15,000 men to enforce his rival claim. Tostig,

Harold's disenfranchised brother, joined forces with Harold III of Norway to attack from the north. Harold soundly defeated this force at Stamford Bridge (Sept. 25, 1066), but had to march south immediately to meet William's army at Hastings. In this battle Harold was defeated and killed.

Harold III (1015–66), called "Hard-Ruler," king of Norway, son of Sigurd Sow. A great warrior, he served the Byzantines. Shared throne with Magnus I until Magnus's death in 1047. From 1047 to 1064 he tried to conquer Denmark, and he died while helping Earl Tostig in the effort to conquer England in 1066.

Harold Bluetooth (c. 910–c.985), king of Denmark beginning c.935. On a runic stone at Jelling he wrote that he "had united all Denmark and Norway under himself and made the Danes Christians." Unable to maintain his hold on Norway, he was killed by the forces of his son Sweyn.

Haroun al-Raschid (c.764–809), fifth Abbasid caliph (786–809); son of al-Mahdi; successor of his brother, al-Hadi. He successfully invaded Asia Minor, reaching the Bosporus in 782; concluded a treaty with the Byzantine empress Irene; and subdued northern part of Africa. He had diplomatic relations with Charlemagne and China; killed or imprisoned the Barmecides, a rich, generous Persian family in 798; crushed uprisings; patronized the arts; and encouraged canals, mosques, and public works. He captured Heraclea (S Italy) and Tyana (S Turkey) in 806 and imposed a tax on the Byzantine emperor Nicephorus I. Al-Amin succeeded him.

Harp, ancient musical instrument with strings plucked by hand. Used in symphony orchestras, it came from Egypt (c.3000 BC) and later Ireland (c.800). A large triangular frame supported vertically carries 46 strings tuned diatonically, C strings colored red and F strings blue; seven pedals raise the pitch by halftones. The double-pedal harp was invented by Sebastian Erard in Paris (1810).

Harpies, in Greek mythology, wind spirits. They were associated with the underworld.

Harpoon, a weapon, usually a barbed spear, used in hunting fish and whales. It has a flat triangular, sharpened head, detachable from the shaft and attached to a strong line. The harpoon may be thrown by hand or shot from a gun. The head of a modern whaling harpoon carries an explosive charge.

Harp Seal, North American seal (*Pagophilus groenlandicus*) that ranges widely over the Arctic seas, with the largest herds found off the W coast of Greenland and the E Arctic Ocean. To whelp, they migrate to Labrador and the Gulf of St Lawrence. Adults are silver with black harp-shaped marks on their backs; pups are pure white. Large scale commercial hunting of the seals, desirable for their pelts, blubber, and meat, has decreased the population despite quotas set by the Canadian government and has caused much controversy.

Harpsichord, sensitive keyboard musical instrument resembling a small, often ornately decorated grand piano. Its metal strings are mechanically plucked by quills (not struck by hammers), producing thin, tinkling tones blending well with the flute and violin. Traditionally associated with Baroque music (16th–18th centuries), it was later replaced by the piano. It was revived in this century by Wanda Landowska and Rosalyn Tureck.

Harpy Eagle, broad-winged, long-tailed eagle of tropical rain forests in New Guinea, the Philippines, and South America. Included are the monkey-eating eagle (*Pithecophaga jefferyi*) of the Philippines and the harpy (*Harpia harpyja*) of South America that feeds on Capuchin monkeys. There are four species. *See also* Eagle.

Harrier, diurnal bird of prey with owllike face that frequents pastures and grasslands where it pounces on small animals. They have small bills, long wings, legs, and tails, and may be gray, black, or brown with a white rump. Bluish-white eggs (3–8) are laid in a ground nest. Length: 15–20in (38–51cm). Genus *Circus*.

Harrier, pack hunting dog (hound group); first English pack dates from 1260. Used for hare hunting and can be followed on foot. A smaller version of the foxhound, it has a medium-sized head with a pronounced forehead; flat, thin, ears carried close to the head; a level, muscular body; straight, well-boned legs; and a long, high-set tail. The short coat is black, tan, and white. Standard size: 19–21in (48.26–53.5cm) high at shoulder; 40–50lb (18–22.5kg). *See also* Hound.

Harrisburg, capital city in SE Pennsylvania, 100mi (161km) W of Philadelphia, on Susquehanna River; seat of Dauphin co. John Harris built a trading post and ferry here 1718; by 1785 the town of Harris' Ferry was appointed co seat and known as Harrisburg; scene of Harrisburg Conventions of 1788 and 1828, which proposed 12 amendments to the federal constitution; became state capital 1812. It is site of the capitol (1906), John Harris Mansion (1766), Rockville Bridge (1899), Sunken Gardens, Harrisburg Area Community College (1965). Industries: steel, food processing, textiles, clothing, metal products, aircraft parts. Settled 1717; inc. 1860. Pop. (1980) 53,264.

Harrison, Benjamin (1833–1901), 23rd president of the United States (1889–93), b. North Bend, Ohio, graduate, Miami University (Ohio), 1852. He was the grandson of William Henry Harrison. In 1853 he married Caroline Scott; they had two children. In 1896, after his wife's death, he married her niece, Mary Dimmick; they had one child. A highly successful corporation lawyer in Indiana, Harrison became a leader in the new Republican party. He served with distinction in the Union army during the Civil War. After the war, he returned to his law practice in Indiana and increased his involvement in Republican politics.
  In 1881 he was sent to the US Senate. He was defeated for reelection in 1887, but the following year the Republicans nominated Harrison to run for the presidency against the incumbent, Grover Cleveland. After a notably corrupt campaign, Harrison won the election with a majority of the electoral votes, although President Cleveland polled the most popular votes. As President, Harrison signed into law the Sherman Antitrust Act, the Sherman Silver Purchase Act, and the McKinley Tariff Act. He ran for re-election in 1892 but was defeated by Cleveland.
  Career: US Army, 1862–65; US Senate, 1881–87; president, 1889–93.

Harrison, William Henry (1773–1841), soldier and 9th president of the United States (March 4–April 4, 1841), b. Charles City co, Va. He attended Hampden-Sydney College and the University of Pennsylvania medical school. He was the son of Benjamin Harrison, a signer of the Declaration of Independence.
  Harrison was a professional soldier who won fame in the Northwest Territory as an Indian fighter in the battles of Fallen Timbers (1794) and Tippecanoe (1811). He was governor of the Indiana Territory (1800–13), and during the War of 1812 he commanded US troops in the Indiana and Illinois country.
  In 1814, Harrison settled in North Bend, Ohio. His fame as a soldier made him an attractive political figure to the Ohio Whigs. He served in both the US House of Representatives and Senate and was briefly (1829) US minister to Colombia. In 1836 he was nominated by one faction of Whigs for the presidency but was defeated.
  The Whigs nominated Harrison for president in 1839 and chose John Tyler as his running mate. Thus was born the campaign slogan "Tippecanoe—and Tyler, Too." Despite Harrison's aristocratic Virginia background, he was pictured as a plain western farmer living in a log cabin. It was the most spectacular campaign in US history, and the old soldier won by a landslide. Harrison was inaugurated and began assembling his cabinet. He contracted pneumonia, however, and died only a month after taking office.
  Career: US Army, 1791–98, 1812–14; US House of Representatives, 1816–19; US Senate, 1825–28; US minister to Colombia, 1829; president, 1841.

Harrow, borough of NW Greater London, England: mainly residential; some light industry; site of Harrow School (1571), whose graduates include Byron, Galsworthy, Peel, Palmerston, and Churchill; St Mary's church (11th century). Pop. 201,300.

Harrow, agricultural implement used to smooth and pulverize plowed land, to cover seeds and fertilizers, to cut up crop residues before plowing, and to root out weeds after sowing.

Hart, John (1711–79), American legislator and a signer of the Declaration of Independence, b. Stonington, Conn. After serving as a delegate from New Jersey to the Continental Congress (1776), he became chairman of the New Jersey council of safety (1777–78).

Hartebeest, large antelope native to African grasslands south of Sahara Desert. Light to dark brown, both sexes have lyre-shaped horns united at the base and rising sharply from the forehead. Its shoulders are higher than the rump, causing a clumsy gait, but it can run 40mph (64kmph). Lichtenstein's hartebeest (*Alcelaphus lichtensteini*) is a common game animal. Length: to 78in (2m); height: to 59in (1.5m); weight: to 400lb (180kg). Family Bovidae. *See also* Ruminant.

Hartford, capital city and port of entry in central Connecticut, on the Connecticut River; largest city of Connecticut. First settlers came from New Town, Mass. (1635–36), led by Thomas Hooker and Samuel Stone; they formed Connecticut Colony (1639) and adopted Fundamental Orders. Hartford was joint capital with New Haven (1701–1875), when it was appointed sole capital; scene of Hartford Convention (1814). Known as the insurance capital of the world, it has approx. 35 insurance company headquarters; site of old State House (1796), Wadsworth Atheneum (1842), Harriet Beecher Stowe House (1871), Mark Twain Memorial (1873), capitol (1878), Trinity College (1823), University of Hartford (1957), American School for the Deaf (1817); birthplace of Noah Webster, John Fiske, J.P. Morgan. Industries: typewriters, precision instruments, computers, electrical equipment, tobacco processing. Inc. 1784. Pop. (1980) 136,392.

Hartford Fern. *See* Climbing Fern.

Harunobu, Suzuki (1718–70), Japanese ukiyo-e (color) printmaker. His elegant, poetic prints usually depicted genteel young ladies in houses or gardens, often with bands of clouds above or streams flowing in the background. He perfected a technique of printing in more than 10 colors.

Harvestman, or daddy-longlegs, spiderlike animal, found worldwide, with legs that may be several times the body length. The head and abdomen are broadly joined. It feeds on living or dead insects and plant juices. Body length: 0.1–0.5in (2.5–12.7mm). Order Phalangida.

Harvest Mite. *See* Chigger.

Harvey, William (1578–1657), English physician and anatomist. In 1628 he discovered the circulation of the blood. This finding, a landmark in medical history, marked the beginning of modern physiology. Harvey, a careful experimenter, was one of the first to use quantitative methods in biological research, and his view of the heart as a pump helped establish a mechanistic way of thinking that subsequently pervaded much of science. His findings on blood circulation, published in *De Motu Cordis et Sanguinis (On the Motions of the Heart and Blood)*, were ridiculed at first and only later were generally accepted. Harvey also made important studies in embryology.

Harz Mountain, mountain range on border of East and West Germany, extending about 60mi (97km) between Elbe and Leine rivers; resort and mining area. Highest peak is Brocken, 3,747ft (1,143m).

Hasa, Al, oasis region in E Saudi Arabia, on W coast of Persian Gulf; controlled by Turks 1875 to 1914 when captured by Ibn Saud. The largest oasis in Saudi Arabia, it is fed by numerous artesian springs. Industries: oil, dates, wheat, rice. Area: 41,200sq mi (106,708sq km). Pop. 500,000.

Hasdrubal, name of two Carthaginian generals. The elder (died 221 BC) was the son-in-law of Hamilcar Barca and succeeded his command in Spain where he expanded Carthaginian power and founded Cartagena. The younger (died 207 BC) was Hamilcar Barca's son and the brother of Hannibal. He took command in Spain when Hannibal marched into Italy. Defeated by Publius Cornelius Scipio (215), he crossed the Alps to join Hannibal but was forced to withdraw to the Metaurus valley (207) where his army was defeated and his head sent to Hannibal's camp. *See also* Punic Wars.

Hashemite, a branch of Koreish, including Mohammed the Prophet, and a modern Arab dynasty of his descendents founded by Husayn ibn-Ali, king of the Hejaz (1916–24). His first son, Ali, succeeded him for a year. His second son, Abdullah, became king of Trans-Jordan (1921–51), succeeded by his grandson, Husein ibn-Jalal. And his third son, Faisal, became king of Iraq (1921–33). Faisal's branch of the Hashemite dynasty was destroyed in the 1958 revolution in Iraq.

Hasidism, a popular pietist movement within Judaism founded by Israel Baal Shem Tov (1699–1761). It taught the ability of all men to reach God, and followers became known for tolerance and glorification of the founder. The movement, centered in E Europe until World War II, strongly supported Orthodox Judaism. Main centers are now in Israel and the United States.

Hassam, (Frederick) Childe (1859–1935), US painter and illustrator, b. Boston, Mass. His use of brushstroke and color shows the influence of Impressionism. Many of his early paintings were of street scenes and women; later he did landscapes, especially of the shore.

Benjamin Harrison

William Harrison

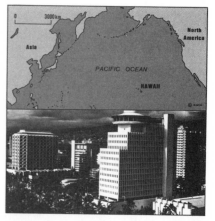

Hawaii

Hassan II (1929–   ), king of Morocco (1961–   ), son and successor of Mohammed V. He dissolved the National Assembly in 1965, assumed all executive and legislative powers, and in 1970 provided a new constitution by referendum. He survived attempted coups (1971, 1972), eliminated foreign ownership of business (1973), and seized much of the Spanish Sahara (1976) after organizing a march of hundreds of thousands of his subjects across the border of that colony (1975).

Hastings, seaside resort in S England, in East Sussex; famous for Battle of Hastings (1066) and as chief of Cinque Ports. Pop. 74,600.

Hastings, Battle of (1066), battle fought near Hastings, Sussex, England, between King Harold of England and a rival claimant to his throne, William, duke of Normandy. Harold's defeat and death in battle led to the establishment of the Norman dynasty by William the Conqueror. See also William I.

Hastings, Warren (1732–1818), British colonial administrator, the first governor general of India (1772–84). He fought at the battle of Plassey with Clive (1757), served on the Calcutta Council, and was governor of Fort William. He reorganized the revenue collection system and closed the British East India Company stores. Pitt's India Act of 1784 brought Hastings home for impeachment proceedings for corruption in his Indian administration. He was impeached (1788), but in 1795 he was acquitted.

Hatchet Fish, marine fish found in deep temperate and tropical seas. Only fish that flies by moving its pectoral fins, it is silvery and has light organs along the underside of its deep, muscular abdomen. Length: to 3.5in (8.9cm). Family Sternoptychidae (or Characidae); species: 21, including Carnegiella marthae.

Hathor, ancient Egyptian goddess of love and happiness, music, and dance, depicted with the horns of a cow or as a cow. She was thought to appear at the bedside of a newborn child to determine his fate.

Hatshepsut (died c.1469 BC), queen of Egypt (c.1490–1469 BC), daughter of Thutmose I. She married her half brother, Thutmose III, ruled as "king" with him, revived mining in the Sinai, and built obelisks at Karnak.

Hatteras, Cape, SE part of Hatteras Island off the E coast of North Carolina; notable for its beaches, migratory wildlife, fishing, and violent storms. Area: 28,500acres (11,543hectares).

Hattiesburg, city in SE Mississippi, on Leaf River; seat of Forrest co; site of University of Southern Mississippi (1911); trade center for agricultural region. Industries: lumber products, explosives, chemicals. Founded 1881; inc. 1884. Pop. (1980) 40,829.

Hausa, Negroid people of Islamic culture, inhabiting N Nigeria and S Niger. Hausa society is feudal and based on patrilineal descent. Their language is a member of the Chad group of Afro-Asiatic languages; it is the official language of N Nigeria and a major trade language of W Africa. Hausa crafts, especially weaving, leatherwork, and silver, are the basis of an extensive trade.

Hausa States, the loosely connected predominantly Hausa communities of N Nigeria. Frequently conquered by neighbors, they came under British administration in the early 20th century and became a part of Nigeria. They were converted to Islam in the 14th–16th centuries.

Havana (La Habana), capital city of Cuba, on NW coast, 90mi (145km) SSW of Key West, Florida; excellent harbor; site of El Morro Castle (1597), cathedral (1704), University of Havana (1728), international airport; center of Cuban politics and commerce. City was a major Spanish naval station in New World; taken by English 1762; restored to Spain 1763; scene of sinking of US battleship Maine, Feb. 15, 1898, which precipitated the Spanish-American War. Industries: textiles, chemicals. Exports: sugar, tobacco, coffee. Founded 1519; capital of Cuba since 1898. Pop. 1,800,000.

Havana Brown Cat, domestic short-haired cat breed developed from black Shorthair and chocolate-point Siamese breeds. It has a long head, large ears, oval chartreuse eyes, and medium-sized body. The tobacco brown coat is smooth and of medium length.

Hawaii, state of the United States, situated in the Pacific Ocean about 2,400mi (3,864km) SW of California.
   Land and Economy. Hawaii is an archipelago of 8 large and 124 small islands, many of them uninhabited, stretching over 2,000mi (3,220km) SE to NW. Of volcanic origin, the islands are mountainous; volcanic activity occurs at intervals. Valleys support rich agriculture. Federal government operations, particularly defense establishments, and an extensive tourist business are major aspects of the economy. Hawaii's geographic isolation conditions its economic life in many ways.
   People. The population displays a mixture of origins, reflecting the 19th- and 20th-century immigrations from Asia, the United States, and Europe. Intermarriage has complicated the pattern, and no racial strain is in the majority. The 1970 census showed about 40% of Caucasian blood, 26% Japanese, with smaller elements of Chinese, Hawaiians (descendants of the original Polynesian settlers), Koreans, Filipinos, and others. More than 80% of the people reside in urban areas, mostly in and around Honolulu on the island of Oahu.
   Education. There are 13 institutions of higher education. The state-supported University of Hawaii, centered in Honolulu, has several other campuses.
   History. Voyagers from Polynesian islands to the S reached the Hawaiian Islands as early as AD 800 and over the next five centuries created a society. The first white visitor was Britain's Capt. James Cook in 1778. The islands became a supply center for merchant ships, and in 1820 US missionaries arrived, followed by businessmen who started the sugar industry. US influence grew, and in 1893 a group of US citizens deposed Queen Liliuokalani, last in the line of monarchs who had ruled Hawaii, and set up a republic with Sanford Dole as president. In August 1898, the United States formally annexed the islands, and they became a territory in 1900. Their development as a defense bastion proceeded; the base at Pearl Harbor on Oahu was the site of the Japanese attack in December 1941 that took the United States into WWII. Tourism, always important to Hawaii, accelerated during the 1970s and 1980s.

PROFILE

Admitted to Union: Aug. 21, 1959; rank, 50th
US Congressmen: Senate, 2; House of Representatives, 2
Population: 965,000 (1980); rank, 39th
Capital: Honolulu, 365,048 (1980)
Chief cities: Honolulu; Hilo, 37,017
State Legislature: Senate, 25; House of Representatives, 52
Area: 6,450sq mi (16,706sq km); rank, 47th
Elevation: Highest, Mauna Kea (on island of Hawaii), 13,796ft (4,208m). Lowest, sea level

Industries (major products): processed foods, concrete, electronic components
Agriculture (major products): sugar, pineapples, vegetables, cattle
Minerals (major): sand, gravel
State nickname: Aloha State
State motto: Ua mau ke ea o ka aina i ka pono ("The life of the land is perpetuated in righteousness")
State bird: Nene (Hawaiian goose)
State flower: Hibiscus
State tree: Kukui (candlenut tree)

Hawaiian Goose. See Ne-ne.

Hawaiian Honeycreeper, medium-sized, brightly colored songbirds found in the Hawaiian Islands. Their beak shapes and sizes vary but most have tubular, brush-tipped tongues and feed on nectar. The green honeycreepers, or parrotbills, have dense, fluffy plumage. Thick-skinned honeycreepers have leathery skin and bright plumage. Most build cup-shaped nests for their spotted eggs (2–3). Family Drepanididae.

Hawk, temperate and tropical diurnal birds of prey with short, hooked bills for tearing meat and strong claws for killing and carrying their prey. Females are larger than males. They have red, brown, gray, or white plumage with streaks and bars on the wings. They lay eggs (3–5) in a sturdy twig-and-stick nest high in a tree. The downy young, or hawklets, are blind and helpless and fed by the parents for six weeks. Length: 1–2ft (30.5–61cm). Order Falconiformes; genera Accipiter and Buteo.

Hawke, Robert (1929–   ), Australian prime minister (1983–   ) and labor leader. A graduate of the University of Western Australia and Oxford University, he was appointed research officer of the Australian Council of Trade Unions in 1958 and became its president in 1970. In 1973 he rose to the presidency of the Australian Labour Party. Elected to Parliament for the first time in 1980, in 1983 he led the Labour party to victory in the national elections, replacing Malcolm Fraser as prime minister.

Hawkins, or **Hawkyns, (Sir) John** (1532–95), English naval commander. With Queen Elizabeth I's support, he led two lucrative expeditions to Africa and the West Indies (1562–63, 1564–65). On his third expedition (1567–69) the Spaniards destroyed most of his ships. He was prominent in plans to improve the navy and in the battle against the Spanish Armada (1588).

Hawk Moth, or **Sphinx Moth, Hummingbird Moth,** medium-to-large moth characterized by narrow wings, spindle-shaped body, and long sucking tube coiled beneath its head. Strong fliers, they usually feed at dusk, hovering over flowers like hummingbirds and sucking nectar through the extended tube. The large, smooth-skinned caterpillar is called a hornworm because of a hornlike protrusion on its posterior segment. Family Sphingidae. See also Moth.

Hawksbill, or tortoise-shell turtle, carnivorous marine turtle found in tropical seas. Characterized by a mid-dorsal keel on its carapace, it is prized for its brown and yellow horny plates. Length: to 33in (84cm). Family Cheloniidae; species Eretmochelys imbricata. See also Turtle.

Hawthorn, or haw, thorn, thorn apple, shrub or small tree grown in North America and Europe. They have white, pink, or red flowers in spring, bone-hard thorns, and small red fruit eaten by some birds and used for jelly or jam. Height: to 30ft (9.1m). Family Rosaceae; genus Crataegus.

Hawthorne, Nathaniel (1804–64), US novelist and short-story writer, b. Salem, Mass. After graduating from Bowdoin College (1825), he returned to Salem, where he began to write tales and historical sketches. Like Edgar Allan Poe, he was a leader in the development of the short story as a particularly American fictional form. His *Twice-Told Tales* appeared in 1837. Unable to make a living as a writer, however, he worked as a clerk in the Boston Customs House during 1839–41. While living in Concord, Mass., he wrote *Mosses from an Old Manse* (1846). Subsequently, he worked at the Salem Customs House (1846–49) and wrote his first novel, *The Scarlet Letter* (1850). The following year *The House of Seven Gables*, a novel, and *The Snow Image and Other Twice-Told Tales* were published.

In 1853 he was appointed US consul in Liverpool, England. He lived in England until 1858 and then in Italy (1858–59). Other works include the novels *The Blithedale Romance* (1852) and *The Marble Faun* (1860). *See also* individual works.

Hawthorne, city in S California, 12mi (19km) SW of Los Angeles. Industries: toys, cash registers, defense products. Inc. 1922. Pop. (1980) 56,447.

Hay-Bunau-Varilla Convention (1903), US agreement with Panama in which the United States was given sovereignty over a 10-mile (16-km) wide strip of land across Panama, to be used for a transoceanic canal, in return for a guarantee of Panamanian independence, and an immediate payment of $10,000,000 and $250,000 annually in perpetuity. The agreement was reached after the United States had helped Panama achieve its independence from Colombia.

Haydn, Franz Joseph (1732–1809), Austrian composer, b. Rohrau. One of the greatest composers of the Classical period, from 1761 to 1790 he served as musical director for the wealthy Esterházy family and composed many of his best works. Later he made two trips to England, composing the last 12 of his 104 symphonies for concerts there. Haydn brought the sonata form to masterful fruition in these symphonies, many of which have popular names, including "Military," "Clock," and "London"—all composed in the early 1790s.

His works influenced his friend Mozart, who in turn influenced him. One of the most prolific of all composers, Haydn also composed many songs, string quartets, masses, chamber music pieces, concertos, and two oratorios late in his life, *The Creation* (1798) and *The Seasons* (1801). *See also* Classical Music; Oratorio.

Hayes, Rutherford Birchard (1822–93), 19th president of the United States (1877–81), b. Delaware, Ohio, graduate, Kenyon College (1843), Harvard law school (1845). In 1852 he married Lucy Webb; they had eight children. Originally a Whig, Hayes was an early supporter of the new Republican party. He served in the US House of Representatives (1865–67), where he supported the Radical Reconstruction program. He was elected governor of Ohio three times (1867, 1869, 1875). In 1876 he won the Republican nomination for president. His Democratic opponent was Gov. Samuel J. Tilden of New York.

The Hayes-Tilden election was extremely close, with electoral votes of four states in dispute. An electoral commission, in an openly political decision, awarded all disputed votes to Hayes, who thus won by one electoral vote, even though Tilden had polled more popular votes.

Despite the cloud under which he came into office, Hayes, once president, was a courageous and honest administrator. He ended the era of Reconstruction by removing federal troops from the last two southern states (Louisiana and South Carolina). He made important reforms in the civil service, which were unpopular with important segments of the Republican party, and he was not renominated in 1880.

Career: US Army, 1861–65; US House of Representatives, 1865–67; Ohio governor, 1868–72, 1876–77; president, 1877–81.

Hay Fever, seasonal allergy induced by pollens, which may vary from season to season. Symptoms include itching of the nose, pharynx, and eyes, which can develop abruptly, followed by tearing, sneezing, clear nasal discharge. Headache, depression, and insomnia may also accompany attacks. Control of symptoms with medication is possible; desensitization is often effective.

Haymarket Massacre (May 4, 1886), riot in Haymarket Square, Chicago. In the incident seven policemen were killed and scores injured by a bomb explosion that occurred during a protest meeting being held by anarchists. Although the bomb thrower was never found, eight anarchists were arrested, tried, and convicted. Seven were sentenced to death and one to life imprisonment. Four of the condemned men were actually executed. One committed suicide, and the three others were pardoned in 1893 by Gov. John Altgeld. The incident turned public opinion against the labor movement, and membership in organizations such as the Knights of Labor declined.

Hay-Pauncefote Treaty (1901), promised equal rates through the Panama Canal to all nations and the opening of the canal without discrimination to all vessels, commercial or military. It was negotiated by US Secretary of State John Hay, and Lord Pauncefote, British ambassador to the United States.

Hayward, city in W California, on San Francisco Bay; site of California State College at Hayward (1957), Chabot Community College (1961). Industries: steel, food processing, school buses, carnations and roses, chemicals, building materials. Settled 1854; inc. 1876. Pop. (1980) 94,167.

Hazelnut. *See* Filbert.

Hazlitt, William (1778–1830), English essayist and critic. Hazlitt abandoned his education for the ministry, met Charles Lamb in London, and wrote for various periodicals from 1812 onward. His miscellaneous essays include the famous *Characters of Shakespeare's Plays* (1817–18) and *The Spirit of the Age* (1825).

Headache, one of the most frequent discomforts suffered by humans. It may be caused by or accompany disease, and may also be caused by emotional disorder or distress, pressure on cranial nerves, or by the dilation or contraction of certain blood vessels. The most frequent causes of minor short-lived headaches are daily tensions and fatigue. Chronic long-lasting headaches with no apparent medical basis are classified as cluster, tension, or migraine headaches, the last often accompanied by a family history. Diagnosis of the cause of chronic headaches may often be lengthy. Mild pain may be relieved by analgesics; other treatment depends on diagnosis. *See also* Migraine.

Head Deformation, changing the shape of the head in infancy. Boards or bandages are bound tightly to the infant's soft head; thus the forehead or back of the head is flattened or the crown lengthened. The practice existed in the Pacific Northwest, Borneo, the New Hebrides, and elsewhere.

Headhunting, taking and sometimes preserving the heads of enemies. Once a widespread custom, it is still found in New Guinea and was reported in Europe after 1900. Captured heads are believed to give victors their victims' powers, to prove courage, or to be necessary for fertility.

Health and Human Services, Department of, US cabinet department, formed from parts of the Department of Health, Education and Welfare (HEW). It was renamed in 1979 after the establishment of a separate Department of Education. It began operating in 1980 and consolidated the services of several programs including Medicare and Medicaid, Social Security, and the Federal Drug Administration.

Hearing, or audition, process by which sound waves are transformed into the experience of hearing. Sound waves are systematic compressions and decompressions of the air. The physical mechanism of hearing begins when sound waves strike the outer ear (the auricle); they next strike the eardrum, and the vibration continues along three small bones, the ossicles, which are attached to the cochlea, the organ of audition. Within the cochlea are receptors called hair cells, which transmit via the auditory nerve to the brain. Many of the distinctions humans make among sounds are psychological; for example, the difference between noise and music is learned in part, although physical factors do play a role.

Hearne, Samuel (1745–92), Canadian fur trader and explorer, b. England. Hearne navigated for the Hudson's Bay Company (1768–70). In 1770 he made the first overland voyage to the Arctic Ocean. He founded Cumberland House in 1774, the first inland trading post of the Hudson's Bay Company. Captured by the French (1782) when Fort Prince of Wales was taken, he commanded Fort Churchill (1783–87). Hearne was an early advocate of western expansion.

Hearst, William Randolph (1863–1951), US publisher, b. San Francisco. He built a publishing empire that included 18 newspapers, nine magazines, a syndicated weekly supplement, news services, and radio stations. Along with his rival, Joseph Pulitzer, he practiced sensational journalism and prompted war fever for Spanish-American War (1898). He served as a congressman from New York (1903–07).

Heart, a chambered muscular organ that contracts rhythmically due to its unique cardiac muscle tissue. Through its contraction it pumps blood throughout the body. In man, the heart is located behind the sternum (breastbone) between the lower parts of the lungs. It lies in a double-walled sac, the pericardium, the outer fibrous layer of which is separated from the inner serous layer by pericardial fluid that serves to protect the heart. The heart itself is divided into halves by a muscular wall, the septum. The right side contains only deoxygenated blood; the left side, only oxygenated blood. Each side is divided into two chambers: an upper thin-walled atrium, or auricle, and a lower thick-walled ventricle. The opening between atrial and ventricular chambers is guarded by atrioventricular valves—the tricuspid on the right side, the mitral, or bicuspid, on the left side.

The heart contracts rhythmically; the average heart beat for an adult is 70 to 72 beats per minute. The beat is controlled mainly by the heart's own "pacemaker," the sinoatrial node, a bundle of muscle cells, blood vessels, and nerves located where the superior vena cava opens into the right auricle. An electrical impulse originates in the sinoatrial node and travels through the two atria to the ventricles, causing contraction. The rhythmic series of contractions pumps blood through the body.

Heart Attack, or myocardial infarction, the diminishing or failure of blood supply to the heart, generally though not always the result of coronary occlusion or thrombosis. The pain of a heart attack is typically persistent, described as constricting or oppressive; shortness of breath is common. Vomiting, nausea, and pale, cold, moist skin may occur. If the victim survives, immediate hospitalization is necessary. Treatment in specialized coronary care units makes the prognosis good. *See also* Angina Pectoris; Coronary Thrombosis.

Heartburn, or pyrosis, burning sensation along the esophagus occurring soon after eating, especially overeating. It is caused by gastric contents spreading back to esophagus and throat. It may be relieved by standing, drinking fluids, or by antacids.

Heart Defects, Congenital, anomalies of the circulatory system caused during embryonic development. Most common is a hole in the membrane separating the two ventricles of the heart. Symptoms may include murmurs and pulmonary artery hypertension. Surgery is common but not always necessary, or in the cases of infants may be postponed. *See also* Heart Murmur.

Heart Failure, disorder in which an abnormality in the circulatory system prevents the heart from pumping blood at the rate necessary to supply body tissues. Symptoms include respiratory distress, in later stages even in bed, edema, fatigue. Treatment is with bed rest, avoidance of stress, and medication.

Heart-Lung Machine, a device that supplies and distributes oxygen to the body when the natural circulation is interrupted during open-heart surgery. It consists of an oxygenator, which substitutes for the lungs, and a pump, which performs the circulatory functions of the heart.

Heart Murmur, a rumbling sound produced by the heart in addition to the sounds normally produced during heartbeat. It can be heard through a stethoscope. A murmur may be a result of heart disease, but some normal hearts—especially in children—also produce murmurs. Murmurs may be produced by vibration of heart valves, backward leakage of blood through a valve, and other conditions.

Heart of Atlanta Motel v. United States (1964), US Supreme Court civil rights decision. The court decided to uphold the ban on racial discrimination in public accommodations of the Civil Rights Act of 1964 as a valid Congressional exercise of the commerce power.

Hearts, card game played by two to eight players using a standard 52-card deck. After all the cards have been distributed, the player to the left of the dealer leads. Suits must be followed if possible. The object is to avoid taking tricks that contain hearts, or to capture all the cards in the heart suit. In a variation of the game, called Black Lady, the queen of spades counts as 13 "hearts." All other hearts count as one point each.

Heart Transplant. *See* Organ Transplant.

Heat, a form of energy related to atomic and molecular energy states. Historically, heat was felt to be a material substance (called caloric) that was contained in bodies and could flow from one to another. (Indeed, an earlier version of this theory postulated *two* fluids, caloric and frigoric, that carried heat or cold between substances.) Under this theory, boring a cannon pro-

Nathaniel Hawthorne

Rutherford B. Hayes

William Randolph Hearst

duced heat because the cannon material was broken up and released some of its (finite) store of caloric. But if that were so, continued boring would at last produce no further heat. Count Rumford of Bavaria (Benjamin Thompson) showed that he could produce unlimited amounts of heat by boring cannon with a blunt tool, and postulated that heat might be related to motion. James Joule then determined the mechanical energy needed to produce a given amount of heat energy (by rotating paddles in water and measuring the temperature increase). Thus the caloric theory was supplanted by the kinetic theory of heat.

Heat Balance, or heat budget, the equilibrium between the solar radiation received by the Earth and its atmosphere, and the radiation that they, in turn, emit. About one-third of the solar radiation is reflected, mostly from clouds, and scattered back into space, whereas the rest is absorbed by clouds, atmosphere, and Earth. The heat absorbed powers the circulation of the atmosphere, oceans, and water cycle. Eventually the heat is reradiated into space, maintaining the Earth's heat equilibrium. *See also* Circulation, Atmospheric.

Heat Content. *See* Heat of Reaction.

Heath, Edward Richard George (1916–), British politician. After a term in civil service and in merchant banking, he became a Conservative member of Parliament (1950). Subsequent parliamentary appointments include government chief whip (1955–59); minister of labor (1959–60); lord privy seal with foreign office responsibilities (1960–63); leader of the opposition (1965–70); and prime minister (1970–74). He successfully concluded negotiations for Britain's entry into the European Economic Community (1973), but was defeated by Harold Wilson's Labour party (1974) and lost the leadership of the Conservatives to Margaret Thatcher. In 1977, he became a member of the Independent Commission of International Development Issues (Brandt Commission).

Heath, genus *(Erica)* of evergreen shrubs and trees native to Africa, the Mediterranean region, and Britain. They have small, thick or needlelike leaves and small bell-like flowers. The fruit is usually a small berry. The heath family (Ericaceae) includes 500 species of herbs, shrubs, and small trees.

Heather, small, evergreen shrub native to Europe and Asia Minor. It has scalelike leaves and small bell-shaped flowers of pink, lavender, or white. It is common on the moors of Great Britain. Family Ericaceae; species *Calluna vulgaris.*

Heat of Formation. *See* Heat of Reaction.

Heat of Fusion, the amount of heat energy absorbed by a liquid at its freezing point in changing to a solid. Heats of fusion vary from about one calorie per gram (helium) to 80 cal/g (water). These quantities of heat are also released by the substances as they melt.

Heat of Neutralization, heat evolved by the complete neutralization of one mole of an acid or base. For all strong acids or bases its value is approximately 13,700 calories per mole (57,500 joules per mole).

Heat of Reaction, heat released or absorbed when substances react together. Usually it is measured for complete reaction between stoichiometric numbers of moles at constant pressure, in which case it is the change in heat content (or enthalpy). Conventionally, it is taken to be negative for exothermic reactions and positive for endothermic ones. The heat of formation of

a compound is the heat of reaction to form one mole of the compound from its elements (in their standard states).

Heat of Sublimation, the heat to supply to a substance at constant temperature necessary to transform it directly from solid to vapor, without passing through the liquid phase.

Heat of Vaporization, the heat absorbed by a liquid at its boiling point as it changes to a gas. Values range from 5 cal/gram (helium) to 1,211 cal/gram (copper).

Heat Pump, year-round air conditioning system based on the principle of refrigeration. Cooling is obtained by placing the evaporator in the conditioned air space. Heating is done by having the condenser in the conditioned space. As in normal refrigeration systems, a source of external power, such as electricity, is required in the condensing portion of the cycle.

Heatstroke, or sunstroke, occurs in conditions of high heat and humidity to persons predisposed. Symptoms are cessation of sweating and loss of consciousness.

Heat Transfer, the passage of heat—the total quantity of energy in a given quantity of matter—to other things, moving from warmer heat sources to cooler heat sinks. The heat may be conceived as the energy of the random motions of the molecules or atoms of which matter is composed, transferred to other things by means of one or more of the processes of conduction, convection, or radiation. Conduction involves the direct transfer of energy by means of the elastic impact of the internal particles or molecules of a substance, like the passage of heat from a hot cup to the hand holding it. Convection involves transfer by fluid motion, like heating of a hand in the air from a car heater. Radiation involves the transfer by electromagnetic waves, like heating of a hand in the sun by its long infrared rays. All three transfer processes are intimately intermingled in the heating and cooling of the land, sea, and air of the earth.

Heat Treatment, the subjecting of a metal or alloy to a cycle of heating and cooling to alter its physical properties. In a process called annealing, metal is heated to a predetermined temperature, held for a time, then cooled to room temperature. This improves ductility and reduces brittleness. Annealing is intermittently carried out during the working of a piece of metal, when ductility is lost through hammering. Annealing temperatures vary, but must not be in a range that allows crystal growth.

Heavy Water, or **Deuterium Oxide,** water in which the hydrogen atoms are replaced by deuterium atoms; used as a moderator in some nuclear reactors. Molecular weight 20. *See* Deuterium.

Hebe, in Greek mythology, goddess of youth, daughter of Zeus and Hera. She performed domestic duties on Olympus and served as cupbearer to the gods.

Hébert, Jacques René (1757–94), French Revolutionary journalist. He gained political power through his newspaper by arousing the Parisian working class. This popular influence helped cause the Reign of Terror and the deposition of the Girondists in 1793, and later pressure by the Jacobins resulted in plans for a popular rebellion. Hébert was seized and guillotined in 1794.

Hebrew, the language of the Jews and Judaism, a Semitic language. As a result of the influence of the Babylonians, it was submerged by Aramaic. After the

destruction of the 2nd Temple in AD 70, its use almost totally ceased. With the use of Hebrew by poets, and rabbinic usage, it became a literary and even holy language used in synagogue services. In the 18th century, Hebrew was revived and became used in secular circles. In 1948, when the state of Israel was founded, Hebrew was declared the official national language.

Hebrews, New Testament epistle. The authorship is uncertain and it has been attributed to Paul, Luke, Barnabas, and Apollos. A discussion of Christianity's superiority over Judaism, it stresses that Christ is more worthy than Moses.

Hebrides (Western Isles), islands off the W coast of Scotland in the Atlantic; divided into the Inner Hebrides (principal islands: Skye, Rhum, Eigg, Islay, and Mull) and Outer (principal islands: Lewis with Harris, North and South Uist). Occupations are fishing, farming. Pop. 29,615.

Hebron (Al Khalil), town in W Jordan; traditionally one of the oldest cities in the world; taken by Judas Maccabeus in 2nd century BC, by the Edomites 586 BC, by Arabs AD 636, by crusaders 1099; 16th-century Hebron became part of Ottoman Empire; part of League of Nations mandate 1922–48; joined Jordan in 1948. Town is the traditional burial place of Sarah and Abraham; site of 12th-century crusader church and wall built by Herod. Industries: tanning, manufacturing of blue hand-blown glass. Pop. 38,348.

Hecate, Greek goddess who presided over magic and spells. Daughter of Perses and Asteria, she had power over heaven, earth, and the sea. She bestowed wealth and all the blessings of daily life. Hecate was represented clad in a long robe and holding burning torches.

Hecatoncheires, in Greek mythology, 100-armed, 50-headed sons of the deities Uranus and Gaea. The most famous was Briareus. He and his brothers successfully aided Zeus against the attack by the Titans. They may have represented the forces of nature that appeared in earthquakes and tidal waves.

Hector, in Greek mythology, the son of Priam and Hecuba, the husband of Andromache. He was killed by Achilles in the Trojan War.

Hecuba, in Greek mythology, the wife of Priam, king of Troy, mother of Hector. She was taken prisoner when Troy was captured by the Greeks.

Hedgehog, spiny nocturnal Eurasian mammals of the family Erinaceidae. The European hedgehog *(Erinaceus europaeus)* is about 9in (23cm) long, brownish above and lighter below, and has a pointed snout. It feeds on insects and other small animals and defends itself by rolling into a prickly ball.

Hedgehog Cactus, cactus native to North America that forms clumps with unbranched, cylindrical stems, and bright pink flowers. Its fleshy fruit is edible. Height: to 1.5ft (46cm). Family Cactaceae; genus *Echinocereus. See also* Cactus.

Hedonism, from the Greek *hedone* or "pleasure," may be of three types: pleasure of the moment, as taught by Aristippus; careful discrimination of pleasure sought, as taught by Epicureans; or emphasis on complete and lasting happiness as found in eudemonism. Basically, hedonism springs from the premise that man seeks pleasure in all he does.

Hegel, Georg Wilhelm Friedrich (1770–1831), German philosopher. He studied at Tübingen (1788–93) and taught at Jena (1805). He was director of the gymnasium (high school) at Nürnberg until 1816, and professor of philosophy at Heidelberg, then Berlin, where he became famous for a romantic, metaphysical system that traced the self-realization of spirit by so-called dialectical "moments" to perfection. First in the *Phenomenology of Spirit* (1807) and then, in *Science of Logic* (1812–16), Hegel claimed to express the course of universal reason with his metaphysical dynamism. His lectures on the history of philosophy, aesthetics, and philosophy of history were published posthumously. *See also* Dialectical Logic.

Hegira, the emigration of Mohammed from Mecca to Medina in 622. Islamic dating begins with this year, as indicated by the letters A.H. (Anno Hegirae). Thus AD 622 is 1 AH. *See also* Mohammed.

Heidegger, Martin (1889–1976), German philosopher. Influenced by Edmund Husserl, he has had a major influence on 20th-century existentialism. Publishing his principle work, *Being and Time,* in 1927, he sought the "meaning of being" in terms of the individual human situation. *See also* Existentialism.

Heidelberg, city in SW West Germany, on Neckar River; University of Heidelberg (1386) became one of 19th century's leading universities; site of city hall (1701–03); Philosophenweg (Philosophers' Way), path overlooking city. Industries: printing presses, precision instruments, textiles, leather goods. Founded 12th century. Pop. 129,700.

Heidelberg Man, species of man contemporary with Pithecanthropus, known from a jawbone discovered near Heidelberg, Germany, in 1907. The massive teeth are human in arrangement, but the chin is undeveloped. *See also* Pithecanthropus.

Heilungkiang, province in NE China, bordered by USSR; capital is Harbin; present-day boundaries were fixed in 1949; mining, lumber, and agricultural center. Area: 272,000sq mi (704,480sq km). Pop. 21,390,000.

Heimlich Maneuver,a first-aid measure for relieving choking, named after its developer, Dr. Henry J. Heimlich. Standing behind the choking victim, the rescuer wraps his arms around the victim and places one fist against the victim's body between the rib cage and the navel. The other hand is placed over the first. The fist is quickly and forcefully pressed into the victim, causing the diaphragm to react convulsively to drive out the choking food or other object from the victim's throat.

Heine, Heinrich (1797–1856), German poet and prose writer. Heine felt himself an outsider, as seen in the early *Book of Songs* (1827). In 1826 he published his satirical, descriptive *Pictures of Travel,* and in 1831 he settled in Paris, writing on German life and letters. The pain and terror suffered in the last eight years of his life from a paralytic illness are recorded in *Poems 1853 & 1854* and *Romanzero* (1851). Most of his memoirs were destroyed by relatives.

Heisenberg, Werner Karl (1901–76), German physicist and philosopher. He became professor at Leipzig and later in Berlin. He is best known for his discovery of the uncertainty, or indeterminancy, principle (1927), which holds that it is impossible to precisely measure both the velocity and position of an object at the same time. He was awarded the 1932 Nobel Prize for his work on quantum mechanics. *See also* Quantum Theory; Uncertainty Principle.

Hejaz (Al-Hijaz) province in Saudi Arabia, along Red Sea coast. Center of Islam, it contains the Muslim holy cities of Mecca (birthplace of Mohammed) and Medina (first Islamic capital). A former independent kingdom under Hussein Ibn Ali (1916), it was taken by Ibn Saud in 1924 and has been part of Saudi Arabia since 1932. Products: dates, wheat, millet, livestock. Area: 150,000sq mi (388,500sq km). Pop. 2,000,000.

Helen, in Greek mythology, the immortal daughter of Leda and Zeus, sister of Pollux, and half-sister of Castor. She married Menelaus, king of Sparta, but after three years she was carried off by a prince of Troy. Since all of her many suitors had pledged to aid the man she would marry, her abduction provided the immediate cause of the Trojan War.

Helena, Saint (*c.*255–330), mother of Roman Emperor Constantine I (Constantine the Great). She was the concubine of Constantius Chlorus. He married another woman when he became emperor as Constantius I, but Helena's son was named emperor in 306, and she became a Christian. Early church historians relate that Helena inspired the building of the Church of the Nativity in Bethlehem. Later tradition says that she found the true cross on which Christ died.

Helena, capital city of Montana, in W central part of state; seat of Lewis and Clark co. City was first settled by prospectors in 1864 as Last Chance Gulch; by 1868 population was 7,500 and $16 million worth of gold had been mined. In 1875 it was named capital of Montana territory, remaining as such when state was formed 1889; site of Carroll College (1910). Industries: mineral smelting, bakery equipment, ceramics, paints. Chartered as city 1881. Pop. (1980) 23,938.

Helgoland (Heligoland), island of West Germany, in North Sea. Under German control since 1890 (except for 1945–52); it played a strategic role in WWI and WWII with installation of German fortifications; now a resort and fishing area. Area: 150acres (61hectares). Pop. 2,312.

Helicopter, aircraft whose support is derived from lift provided by power-driven propellers or rotors revolving around a vertical axis. It is capable of vertical takeoff and landing; hovering; and forward, backward, and lateral flight. Military applications include rescue, reconnaissance, and combat. In civil aviation short-haul transport, crop dusting, power and pipeline patrol are common uses.

Heligoland. *See* Helgoland.

Heliopolis (Misr al-Jadidah), ruined ancient holy city in N Lower Egypt, in the Nile delta, 6mi (10km) N of Cairo; noted center of sun worship for god Ra, from *c.*1580–1090 BC. Formerly seat of viceroy of N Egypt, it was site of Cleopatra's Needles (obelisks, assembled here, now displayed in London and New York City) and temple containing historical records.

Heliotrope, herbaceous plant found worldwide. It has fragrant, five-lobed flowers in curled sprays. Seaside heliotrope *(Heliotropium curassavicum)* grows on beaches and swamps in the United States. Garden heliotrope *(H. arborescens)* is shrublike with purple or white flowers. There are 250 species. Family Boraginaceae.

Heliotropism. *See* Phototropism.

Heliozoa, or **sun animal,** order of freshwater, amebоid protozoa characterized by a spherical body surrounded by needlelike extensions of protoplasm. Many secrete a gelatinous capsule or a perforated silica skeleton. Length: 1/625–0.04in (1/25–1mm). Common examples are *Actinophrys sol* and *Actinosphaerium.*

Helium, gaseous nonmetallic element (symbol He) of the noble-gas group, discovered in 1868 by Pierre Janssen, who noticed its lines in the Sun's spectrum. It is the second most common element in the universe. The element was first obtained in 1895 from the mineral clevite. The chief source is from natural gas. Helium is also found in some radioactive minerals and in the earth's atmosphere (0.0005% by volume). It is used in balloons, in divers' air supplies to protect against the "bends," and in welding, semiconductor preparation, metallurgy, and other applications requiring an inert atmosphere. It has the lowest melting point of any element and is extensively used in low-temperature research. The element forms no chemical compounds. Properties: at. no. 2; at. wt. 4.0026; sp gr 0.1785 g dm^{-3}; melt. pt. −457.96°F (−272.4°C) (26 atm); boil. pt. −452.07°F (−269.14°C); most common isotope He^4 (100%). *See also* Noble Gases.

Helix, a curve generated when a point moves over the surface of a cylinder in such a way that the curve is inclined at a constant angle to the axis of the cylinder, as in the thread of a bolt.

Hellbender, large aquatic salamander of E and Central United States. Because metamorphosis is not complete, adults lose gills but lack eyelids and retain larval teeth. It has gray or brown loose, wrinkled skin. Length: to 30in (76cm). Family Cryptobranchidae; species *Cryptobranchus alleganiensis. See also* Salamander.

Hellebore, or bear's foot, winter-blooming herbaceous plant native to Eurasia. Most familiar is the Christmas rose *(Helleborus niger)* that bears large white flowers in midwinter to early spring. There are about 20 species. Family Ranunculaceae. *See also* Buttercup.

Hellen, the eponymous ancestor of the Hellenes, or the Greek people. According to an early ethnological theory (which was cast in the traditional mythological form of a genealogy), the Dorian, Ionian, and Aeolian tribes were descended from a common ancestor. He was identified as Hellen, son or brother of Deucalion, and father of Dorus, Xuthus, and Aeolus. The name Hellenes was generally acknowledged as that of the Greek people by the 7th century BC.

Hellenica, Xenophon's history of the Greeks from the close of Thucydides' account of the Peloponnesian Wars (411 BC) to the battle of Mantinea (362). Its style is erratic, and its contents often sketchy.

Hellenism, the culture of classical Greece, most particularly that of Athens during the 5th century BC. Art and architecture saw the expansion and embellishment of the Acropolis, most outstandingly the building of the Parthenon. Tragedy was perfected in the plays of Aeschylus, Sophocles, and Euripides, and comedy in those of Aristophanes. Herodotus and Thucydides excelled in the writing of history and Socrates, then Plato, established standards for philosophy.

Hellenistic Age, era from 323 to *c.*30 BC in E Mediterranean and Near East between the death of Alexander and the ascension of Augustus. Greek dynasties (the Ptolemies and Seleucids) were established in Egypt, Syria, and Persia. Alexandria and Pergamum became major cultural and trading centers, adding unique elements to, while also preserving, much of Greek culture. Major literary figures were the poets Callimachus and Theocritus and the prose writer Lucian. Numerous Stoic and Epicurean philosophers flourished. Important works of art included the sculptures the "Venus de Milo" and the "Dying Gaul." Hellenistic city planning influenced the Romans, who eventually dominated and overshadowed Hellenistic culture.

Hellespont. *See* Dardanelles.

Hellgrammite, or **Dobson,** aquatic larva of the dobsonfly found worldwide. These larvae have chewing mouthparts and are an important fish food. The adult has sickle-shaped jaws and clear, 2in (51mm) wings. Length: 1in (25mm). Order Megaloptera; Family Corydalidae.

Hellman, Lillian (1905–84), US playwright and author, b. New Orleans. Her plays deal with psychological weakness and contemporary social issues. In *The Children's Hour* (1934) a child accuses two teachers of an abnormal relationship, ruining their lives. *The Little Foxes* (1939) shows the violent passions within a Southern family. *Watch on the Rhine* (1941) deals with the difficult decision of a gentle man to act against a Nazi. Some of her later works are *The Autumn Garden* (1951), *Toys in the Attic* (1960), and an adaptation of the Burt Blechman novel *My Mother, My Father, and Me* (1963). Her nontheatrical writing includes the autobiographical volumes *An Unfinished Woman* (1969), *Pentimento* (1973), *Scoundrel Time* (1976), and *Maybe* (1980).

Helmholtz, Hermann-Ludwig Ferdinand von (1821–94), German anatomist, physicist, and physiologist. He made great contributions in acoustics and optics, expanding Thomas Young's three-color theory of vision and inventing an ophthalmoscope and an ophthalmometer. His experiments on the speed of nerve impulses led to a study of animal heat, which in turn led to work on the principle of conservation of energy and the introduction of the concept of free energy.

Helots, class of probably indigenous Greeks between free men and slaves. In Sparta they outnumbered Spartans. Often used in agriculture and as domestics, they were owned by the state, which used them as soldiers after the Persian Wars. They were freed in 369 BC.

Helsinki (Helsingfors), seaport city in Finland, on Gulf of Finland; capital of Finland and of Uusimaa prov.; site of University of Helsinki (1640), national art gallery, sports stadium; scene of 1952 Olympic games and the initial US–USSR Strategic Arms Limitation Talks (SALT) (1969). Founded 1550 by Gustavus I of Sweden; rebuilt after fire of 1808; became capital 1812. Industries: food processing, textiles, china, chemicals. Pop. 496,872.

Helvetii, ancient Celtic people that inhabited S Germany and migrated in the 2nd century BC to the western part of modern Switzerland. In 58 BC they invaded SW Gaul and were defeated by Caesar. They lived thereafter in Belgian Gaul and upper Germany under Roman control until AD 260 when they were attacked and later subjugated by the Alamanni.

Hematite, an oxide mineral, ferric oxide (Fe_2O_3). A common substance of altered sedimentary deposits. Rhombohedral system tabular crystals, flat scales, radiating masses (sometimes kidney-shaped). Earthy or metallic, red or black; hardness 5–6; sp gr 5.3. Most important iron ore. Sometimes polished as gem.

Helicopter

Ernest Hemingway

Queen Henrietta

Hematoma, localized mass of usually clotted blood collected in an organ or tissue because of a break in a blood vessel. Treatment depends on location and size.

Hemichordata, a subphylum of the phylum Chordata, which includes two orders of primitive marine animals, the Enteropneusta or Balanoglossida and the Pterobranchia. Most of the animals do not have common names. Characteristics include a short notochord, or backbone; a partially or completely solid dorsal nerve chord, which is close to the surface; and optional gill slits. The most commonly observed is Balanoglossus, a wormlike organism living in mud or sand on the ocean floor.

Hemingway, Ernest (Miller) (1899–1961), US author, b. Oak Park, Ill. After graduating from high school in 1917 he worked as a newspaper reporter. In World War I he served as an ambulance driver in France, then joined the Italian infantry and was wounded. After the war he became a correspondent in Paris for the Toronto *Star*. He met Gertrude Stein, who strongly influenced his direct, terse prose. He published *Three Stories and Ten Poems* (1923), the short stories *In Our Time* (1924), and the novel *The Torrents of Spring* (1926), but it was with the novel *The Sun Also Rises* (1926) that he established his reputation as a writer. This novel about expatriates also established Hemingway as the spokesman for the Lost Generation. He maintained his reputation with *A Farewell to Arms* (1929) and such short stories as "The Killers" and "The Snows of Kilimanjaro." *To Have and Have Not* (1937) was not as well received as his two previous novels, but *For Whom the Bell Tolls* (1940), which drew on his experience as a correspondent in the Spanish Civil War, was a critical and popular success. Hemingway's nonfiction as much as his fiction concerned itself with people leading dangerous or especially virile lives and facing the consequences with stoic courage. *Death in the Afternoon* (1932) is about bullfighting; *Green Hills of Africa* (1935), about big-game hunting. The novel *The Old Man and the Sea* appeared in 1952. Hemingway received the Nobel Prize for literature in 1954. He committed suicide in 1961. Several works were published after his death: *A Moveable Feast* (1964), memoirs of Paris in the 1920s; *Islands in the Stream* (1970), a novel; *The Nick Adams Stories* (1972), *The Dangerous Summer* (1985), about bullfighting; and *The Garden of Eden* (1986), a novel.

Hemiplegia, paralysis of one side of the body. It can be caused by brain injury, and may be accompanied by spasticity.

Hemiptera, or Heteroptera, order of insects, including lice and water bugs, found worldwide. They may be winged or wingless and have three life stages: egg, nymph, and adult. The piercing and sucking mouthparts are on the front of the head and extend along the underbody. Length: 0.25–4in (5.6–102mm). *See also* Assassin Bug; Bedbug.

Hemlock, evergreen trees native to North America and Asia. The needles are linear and flat, with two white bands beneath. The small cones are pendulous and the branches droop. They are sensitive to dust, smoke, and wind. Height: 50–250ft (15–76m). Family Pinaceae; genus *Tsuga*.

Hemlock, poisonous herb found worldwide as a weed. Resembling the wild carrot, it has a taproot, lacy foliage, and umbels of white flowers. Its leaf stalks have conspicuous purple spots. Family Umbelliferae; species *Conium maculatum*.

Hemoglobin, iron-containing protein of red blood cells. It can bind oxygen or carbon dioxide, thus endowing the red cell with the ability to carry oxygen from the lungs to body tissues and exchange it for carbon dioxide.

Hemolysis, the destruction or breakdown of red blood cells at an abnormally high level, usually caused by hereditary defects, toxins, chemicals or by Rh incompatibility in infants, the last called *Erythroblastosis fetalis*.

Hemolytic Streptococci, types of streptococcal bacteria that release an enzyme that destroys red blood cells and liberates hemoglobin, causing disease in men and animals. Best known is *Streptococcus pyongens*, which causes scarlet fever.

Hemophilia, or bleeder's disease, hereditary disease characterized by failure of the blood to coagulate. Transmitted genetically as a sex-linked recessive trait, males only are affected. Spontaneous subcutaneous and intramuscular hemorrhaging occurs, as does hemorrhaging at slight injury. Replacement with normal blood is the usual treatment, although coagulation factors have been isolated and are available on a limited basis.

Hemorrhaging, or bleeding, loss of blood from a broken blood vessel, usually caused by injury. Massive hemorrhaging may cause faintness, sweating, rapid pulse and breathing. It may be internal or external. Treatment calls for stopping bleeding; replacing blood.

Hemorrhoids, or piles, varicosities of the veins underlying the mucous lining of the anus and rectum. Extremely common, they manifest externally as small rounded lumps, which may enlarge under strain. Internally, the lumps are softer, more thinly covered, and bleed more easily. The most common complaint is itching. In extreme cases surgery may be indicated; usually heat and a topical or systemic analgesic are recommended.

Hemp, annual herb native to Asia and cultivated throughout Eurasia, North America, and parts of South America. It has compound palmate leaves. Small, spikelike clusters of seed-producing flowers grow on female plants; male plants have branching clusters of pollen-producing flowers. The slender stems are hollow with fibrous inner bark, also called hemp and used widely for ropes and cloth. Its seeds are fed to birds and oil from the seeds is used in soap and paint. The flowers, leaves, and resinous juice are used to produce marihuana and hashish. Height: to 16ft (5m). Family Cannabinaceae; species *Cannabis sativa*.

Henbane, annual or biennial plant native to the Mediterranean. The entire plant is fatally toxic. Leaves are coarsely toothed, stems hairy, and the plant has a bad odor. Bell-shaped yellow flowers with purple veins produce black seeds which are the source of the alkaloid hyoscyamine. Height: 1–2.5ft (30.5–76.2cm). The 12 to 15 species include black henbane *Hyoscyamus niger*, white henbane *H. albus,* and Egyptian henbane *H. muticus*. Family Solanaceae.

Hen Harrier. *See* Marsh Hawk.

Henley, William Ernest (1849–1903), English poet and editor. His most famous poems are "Invictus" (1875), which ends with the line "I am the master of my fate, I am the captain of my soul," and "England, My England" (1892). As an editor he introduced the works of Kipling, H.G. Wells, and Yeats to a wider audience.

Henna, or Egyptian privet, Jamaica mignonette, small shrub found in Middle East and N Africa and cultivated in Egypt. Since ancient times, a red dye has been extracted from the leaves and used as a hair color and cosmetic. Family Lythraceae; species *Lawsonia inermis*.

Henrietta Maria (1609–69), queen consort of Charles I of England. After the Duke of Buckingham's death (1628), her influence over the king's foreign policy was paramount. Her subjects distrusted her because of her Roman Catholicism.

Henry II (973–1024), Holy Roman emperor (1002–24) and German king (1002–24). He succeeded his cousin Otto III. He maintained order in Germany, went to Italy three times (1004, 1013–14, and 1021–22) to subdue the Lombards, and fought constantly with the Poles. He was canonized in 1146.

Henry III (1017–56), Holy Roman emperor (1039–56) and German king (1039–56). He succeeded his father, Conrad II. Imperial power reached its zenith in Henry's reign. He made the duke of Bohemia and, for a time, the king of Hungary vassals of the empire and contained revolts in Germany. Supporting the Cluniac reform movement, in 1046 he deposed two rival popes and effected the election of Clement II. He later appointed three more popes in succession.

Henry IV (1050–1106), Holy Roman emperor (1056–1106) and German king (1056–1106). Embroiled in controversy with the popes over the lay investiture of clerics, he deposed Pope Gregory VII and was in turn deposed by the pope (1076). Rebellion in Germany made Henry seek papal absolution at Canossa (1077), but thereafter he continued the struggle, setting up the antipope Clement III. In 1104 his son Henry joined the German rebellion and deposed him. *See also* Gregory VII.

Henry V (1081–1125), Holy Roman emperor (1106–25) and German king (1106–25). Having deposed his father, Henry IV, he inherited the quarrel with the papacy over investiture. After a prolonged and violent struggle, he reached a compromise with Pope Calixtus II in the Concordat of Worms of 1122. *See also* Worms, Concordat of.

Henry VI (1165–97), Holy Roman emperor (1190–97) and German king (1190–97). The son of Frederick I, he married (1186) Constance, heiress of Sicily, and much of his reign was devoted to securing that inheritance; he was finally crowned king of Sicily in 1194. A rebellion in Germany was quelled when the rebels' ally Richard I of England came into his custody. He failed to get the consent of the German princes to make the empire hereditary in the Hohenstaufen family, although he was succeeded by his son Frederick II.

Henry VII (*c.*1275–1313), Holy Roman emperor (1308–13) and German king (1308–13). A Luxembourg, he succeeded the Hapsburg Albert I. He acquired Bohemia for his family by marrying his son to Elizabeth of Bohemia (1310). Henry revived imperial ambitions in Italy but, although crowned king of the Lombards (1311), could not maintain authority there.

Henry I (1068–1135), king of England, younger son of William I. On William II's death, he was crowned king (1100). His elder brother Robert, duke of Normandy, claimed his throne, but Henry defeated him and captured all his lands at Tinchebrai (1106). Henry married an Englishwoman and reformed the judicial and fiscal administration, but his reign was troubled by unruly barons, wars with the French and Welsh, and the death (1120) of his heir, William.

Henry II (1133–89), king of England, son of Geoffrey Plantagenet and Matilda, daughter of Henry I. He inherited the Angevin lands, obtained Aquitaine by marrying Eleanor (1152), and succeeded to the throne (1154). He reformed the judicial, monetary, and military systems, but his attempt to bring church courts under secular control through the Constitutions of Clarendon (1164) failed. By the Treaty of Montmirail (1169), Henry secured France's sanction for his sons' succession to his territories and Prince Henry was crowned heir (1170). After the murder of Thomas à Becket (1170), Henry's life was beset by trouble with the Roman Catholic Church, revolts in Ireland and Normandy, and strife with his own sons.

Henry III (1207–72), king of England, son of John, whom he succeeded when a minor in 1216. He married Eleanor of Provence (1236). His favoritism to foreigners led to resentment among his barons, who revolted against him and refused to finance his overseas campaigns. Forced to make substantial constitutional concessions by the so-called "Mad Parliament" (1258), he enlisted French and papal aid but the barons, under Simon de Montfort, defeated him at Lewes (1264). His son Edward's victory at Evesham (1265) enabled him to retain executive power while granting many reforms.

Henry IV (1367–1413), king of England, son of John of Gaunt and cousin of Richard II. Banished by Richard (1398), he returned to claim his father's estates (1399) and, finding Richard deserted by his supporters, induced him to resign his crown. Henry's reign was disturbed by Welsh and Scottish wars, assassination attempts, and rebellions, chiefly fomented by the Percy family.

Henry V (1387–1422), king of England, eldest son of Henry IV. After fighting on his father's behalf at Shrewsbury (1403), in Wales, and in Scotland, he succeeded him (1413) and immediately demanded the restoration of territories formerly ceded to France. Invading France, he captured Harfleur and won a great victory at Agincourt (1415). Further military and diplomatic success led to his adoption as the French king's heir by the Treaty of Troyes (1420).

Henry VI (1421–71), king of England, succeeded his father, Henry V, in 1422. After he came of age (1442), his reign was characterized by military and diplomatic disasters in France. At home, his feebleness permitted the Yorkist and Lancastrian factions to instigate the Wars of the Roses. Deposed by the Yorkists (1461), he was temporarily restored (1470) but was again deposed and murdered.

Henry VII (1457–1509), king of England, founder of the Tudor dynasty. Having killed Richard III at Bosworth (1485), Henry united the warring factions by marrying the Yorkist heiress, Elizabeth. His financial acumen restored England's fortunes after the devastations of civil war. He concluded various advantageous foreign treaties, such as the treaty of Etaples (1492), and took effective action against pretenders to his throne.

Henry VIII (1491–1547), king of England, succeeded his father, Henry VII, in 1509. In 1513, victories over the Scots (at Flodden) and French reestablished England as a European power, a position maintained by Cardinal Wolsey's diplomacy. Henry's decision to divorce Catherine of Aragon, who could not bear a male heir, in favor of Anne Boleyn, led to a confrontation with the papacy. Dismissing Wolsey (1529), he appointed Thomas Cranmer his advisor. He compelled the clergy to acknowledge him supreme head of the church, and he was excommunicated (1533–35). Under Thomas Cromwell's direction, he initiated other anti-ecclesiastical moves in the 1530s, including transferring church revenues to the crown, appropriating monastic property, and executing those who, like Sir Thomas More, objected. This reorganization of church government broke papal power in England. Successful campaigns against the Scots, and heresy and treason trials at home occupied his later years. From his controversial six marriages (Catherine of Aragon, Anne Boleyn, Jane Seymour, Anne of Cleves, Catherine Howard, Catherine Parr), he had only one son and two daughters.

Henry I (1008–60), king of France (1031–60). His reign was characterized by struggles with rebellious vassals. Although Henry was crowned by his father, Robert II, his younger brother Robert claimed the throne and was supported by their mother, Constance of Provence. In the ensuing civil war, Henry was forced to cede Burgundy to Robert. Henry at first supported (1035–47) and then fought unsuccessfully against (1054, 1058) William, duke of Normandy. He was succeeded by his son Philip I.

Henry II (1519–59), king of France (1547–59). The second son of Francis I, Henry and his older brother were held hostage in Spain from 1526 until the Peace of Cambrai (1530). Upon his brother's death, Henry became heir to the throne. He married Catherine de Médicis. As king, Henry continued his father's policies of strengthening the monarchy and effecting administrative reform. The struggles with Emperor Charles V also continued. A militant Catholic, he initiated harsh, systematic repression of Protestants. Defeated in Italy and faced with national bankruptcy, Henry signed the Peace of Cateau-Cambrésis (1559) with the Hapsburgs, giving up France's claims in Italy. He died after he was accidentally wounded in a tournament.

Henry III (1551–89), king of France (1574–89), last of the Valois dynasty. As duke of Anjou he defeated the Huguenots (1569) in the Wars of Religion. With his mother, Catherine de Médicis, he instigated the Massacre of Saint Bartholomew's Day (1572). Elected king of Poland in 1573, he returned to France to assume the throne on the death of his brother Charles IX (1574). He made peace with the Huguenots (1576), but when his younger brother Francis died in 1584 and the Protestant Henry of Navarre became heir to the throne, he renewed the wars. His troops were defeated at Coutras (1587). Henry de Guise, leader of the Catholic League, seized Paris and expelled Henry (1588). The king felt compelled to ally himself with Henry of Navarre. He was assassinated by a Catholic fanatic, Jacques Clément, during the siege of Paris.

Henry IV or **Henry of Navarre** (1553–1610), king of Navarre (as Henry III, 1572–1610), first Bourbon king of France (1589–1610). Raised as a Protestant, he nevertheless married (1572) Margaret of Valois, sister of the French king Charles IX. Henry escaped the Massacre of Saint Bartholomew's Day (1572) by renouncing his Protestantism. He was kept as a virtual prisoner at the French court until his escape in 1576 when he joined the Protestants. He became heir to the French throne in 1584 on the death of the younger brother of King Henry III. King Henry was persuaded by Henry de Guise, leader of the Catholic League, to deny Henry of Navarre his right. The War of the Three Henrys resulted. Henry defeated the king's forces in 1587 and was reconciled with him after the Catholic League expelled the king from Paris (1588). Henry III was assassinated in 1589, but Henry of Navarre did not gain Paris until after he renounced his Protestantism in 1594. With the Edict of Nantes (1598) he gave the Huguenots political rights and religious freedom. He encouraged economic growth and Canadian exploration after more than three decades of chaotic religious war. He was assassinated by a religious fanatic. His second wife was Marie de Medici, mother of the future Louis XIII.

Henry I (876?–936), king of Germany (919–36), called Henry the Fowler. Duke of Saxony, he was elected to succeed Conrad I as king. He asserted his authority over the German princes and reconquered Lotharingia (Lorraine, 925). He bought off (926) the Magyar raiders but in 933 defeated them on the Unstrut River. He was succeeded by his son, Otto I, first Holy Roman emperor.

Henry II (1335?–1379), Spanish king of Castile and León (1369–79). He was the illegitimate son of Alfonso XI and revolted against the rule of his half brother, Peter the Cruel. Henry defeated Peter in 1366, but Peter, with the aid of England in the person of Edward the Black Prince, maintained the throne. In 1369, however, after the departure of the English, Henry again defeated Peter and killed him in a duel. He was succeeded by his son, John I.

Henry III (1379–1406), Spanish king of Castile and León (1390–1406), son and successor of John I. His marriage to Catherine of Castile ended a long dynastic struggle; her father, John of Gaunt, renounced his claims to Castile in her favor. Henry was succeeded by his son, John II.

Henry IV (1425–74), Spanish king of Castile and León (1454–74), son and successor of John II. He was a weak ruler, and the nobles refused to accept as heiress to the throne his daughter, Juana La Beltraneja. He finally accepted his half sister Isabella but reneged after her marriage in 1469 to Ferdinand of Aragón. Upon Henry's death, civil war erupted between the forces of Isabella and those of Juana. Isabella won and succeeded to the throne.

Henry of Navarre. *See* Henry IV (1553–1610).

Henry the Cardinal (1512–80), king of Portugal (1578–80), son of Manuel I and successor of Sebastian. He was created a cardinal in 1545 and acted (1562–68) as regent to his nephew, Sebastian. After Sebastian was killed in battle in North Africa, Henry assumed the crown. Henry's death marked the end of the Aviz dynasty, and, after Philip II of Spain asserted his rights in Portugal, the beginning of 60 years of Spanish rule.

Henry the Lion (1129–95), duke of Saxony (1142–80) and Bavaria (1156–80). The son of Henry the Proud, he only gradually recovered his father's lands. Both he and Emperor Frederick I sought to end the feud between their families, the Guelphs and Hohenstaufens. But Henry's power in Saxony, which he extended by conquest of the Wends, finally alienated Frederick, who confiscated his lands (1180), and forced him to flee to England. He was reconciled with Emperor Henry VI, Frederick's son, in 1195.

Henry the Navigator (1394–1460), Portuguese prince and patron of explorers. He was the third son of John I, the brother of Duarte, and the uncle of Alfonso V. In 1416 he established at Sagres (near Lagos) an observatory and a school for the study of geography and navigation. Although he made no journeys himself, he sponsored numerous Portuguese navigators who, in turn, made many important discoveries. They formed the basis for the great Portuguese empire of the 16th century. Among their discoveries were the Madeira Islands, and they explored the West African coast as far south as Sierra Leone.

Henry the Proud (1108?–39), duke of Saxony (1137–38) and Bavaria (1126–38). A Guelph, he inherited Bavaria from his father and was made duke of Saxony by Emperor Lothair II, whose daughter he married. Lothair designated him heir to the throne, but he was defeated in the election by the Hohenstaufen Conrad III, who deprived him of his duchies.

Henry, Joseph (1797–1878), US physicist, b. Albany, N.Y. His improvements in electromagnetics were essential for the development of the commercial telegraph. His work with the induced current principle led to the development of the transformer. He introduced (1850) a system of using the telegraph for sending weather reports, making possible the US Weather Bureau. He became (1846) the first secretary of the Smithsonian Institution and was an organizer of the American Association for the Advancement of Science and its first president (1849).

Henry, O. (1862–1910), pseud. of William Sydney Porter, popular US short-story writer, b. Greensboro, N.C. His typical surprise ending gave rise to the term the "O. Henry ending." After editing and publishing the humor magazine *The Rolling Stone,* Henry served three years in prison on a charge of embezzlement. While in prison he published the first of his short stories signed "O. Henry" ("Whistling Dick's Christmas Stocking," 1899).

After his release, Henry moved to New York City, the scene of much of his fiction. Henry's first book, *Cabbages and Kings* (1904), was a collection of stories of revolution and adventure in Latin America. This work was followed by many more collections, including *The Four Million* (1906), *Heart of the West* (1907), *The Gentle Grafter* (1908), *Roads of Destiny* (1909), and *Strictly Business* (1910). In 1918 the O. Henry Memorial Awards, given to the best stories published each year in American magazines, were established.

Henry, Patrick (1736–99), US patriot, orator, and lawyer, b. Hanover co, Va. Elected to the Virginia House of Burgesses (1765–75), he denounced the Stamp Act. He was a member of the Continental Congress (1774–76), and became convinced that war with Britain was inevitable. It was then he delivered his "Give me liberty or give me death" speech and made his reputation as a gifted orator. He helped draw up the Virginia Convention and from 1776–79 and from 1784–86 he was governor of Virginia. He opposed Virginia's ratification of the Constitution as adverse to state's rights although he was a leader in the movement for the Bill of Rights.

Henry, unit of inductance equal to the inductance of a closed loop that gives rise to a magnetic flux of one weber for each ampere of current that flows.

Henry IV, parts I (1598) and II (1600), 5-act historical dramas by William Shakespeare, based on Raphael Holinshed's *Chronicles* and an epic by Samuel Daniel. Part I takes up English history at exactly the point where Shakespeare ended his *Richard II.* King Henry believes that the wild behavior of his son Prince Hal is heaven's vengeance for Henry's sin in having deposed Richard II. Hal promises at his father's deathbed to reform, and upon becoming king he professes not to know his old tavern companion Falstaff and has his former cronies hustled off to prison.

Henry V (*c.*1600), 5-act historical drama by William Shakespeare, based on Raphael Holinshed's *Chroni-*

King Henry V of England

Patrick Henry

Katharine Hepburn

cles, a history by Edward Halle, and Robert Fabyan's *New Chronicles*. A nationalistic play, it dramatizes the enthusiasm of the people of Great Britain for fighting a foreign war. King Henry V's patriotism often becomes chauvinism. The wild Prince Hal protrayed in *Henry IV* has totally reformed, becoming a "mirror of all Christian kings." He leads his troops to victory over the French at Agincourt and woos the French king's daughter Katharine. The play was made into a film (1945), in which Laurence Olivier's performance as Henry won him the New York Film Critics Circle Award (1946).

Henry VI, Parts I, II, III (c.1590–92), historical dramas by William Shakespeare, based on Raphael Holinshed's *Chronicles* and material by Edward Halle. Shakespeare altered the chronology to suit his dramatic purpose, however, keeping Joan of Arc alive to take part in a battle that actually occurred 20 years after her death. The death of Henry V while his son is still a boy sets off rivalry and dissension among nobles contending for power. England loses its French possessions despite the valiant leadership of Lord Talbot. *Henry VI*, parts I, II, and III, are part of a tetralogy, with *Richard III*, dramatizing the Wars of the Roses.

Henry VIII (1613), historical play by William Shakespeare, probably in collaboration with John Fletcher, based on Raphael Holinshed's *Chronicles* and material by Edward Halle. It begins with a description of the splendor of the "Field of the Cloth of Gold" (1520) and ends with the christening of Princess Elizabeth (1533). During the first performance of the play a cannon used for a royal salute in Act I set fire to the Globe theater and it burned to the ground.

Henry's Law, principle in physical chemistry which states that the weight of a gas dissolved in a fixed quantity of a liquid is directly proportional to the pressure of the gas on the liquid, at constant temperature. Thus, the more a gas is compressed, the more will be absorbed in a liquid.

Hens and Chicks, also houseleek, sempervivum; a succulent perennial plant native to dry sunny regions of Europe, popular in rock gardens. The grayish, or bluish, tongue-shaped leaves grow in basal rosettes and are marked with red. The pink or rose daisylike flowers grow in clusters. Species include *Sempervivium tectorum*, with leaf rosettes 3–4in (7.6–10.2cm) in diameter, and *S. arachnoideum*, the cobweb houseleek, in which the 1in (2.5cm) leaf rosettes are covered with cobwebby, white fibers. Family Crassulaceae.

Henson, Matthew Alexander (1866–1955), US explorer. He accompanied Robert Peary in his discovery of the North Pole (1909). He recounted these experiences in *A Negro Explorer at the North Pole* (1912).

Heparin, a polysaccharide sulfuric acid ester occurring in the liver and lungs of animals that prolongs the clotting time of blood by preventing the formation of fibrin. It is used in vascular surgery and in treatment of postoperative thrombosis and embolism.

Hepatica, or liverleaf, genus of 10 species of small, herbaceous perennial plants native to wooded regions of North America and Eurasia. The three-lobed leaves stay green during winter and the flowers are blue, pink, or white. Family Ranunculaceae.

Hepatitis, inflammation of the liver, in its most common form caused by two viruses differentiated as infectious hepatitis or serum hepatitis. Infectious hepatitis is usually spread through fecal contamination, serum hepatitis by blood transfusion or poorly steril-

ized injections. Symptoms include lethargy, nausea, fever, perhaps jaundice. Recovery is usually spontaneous although hospitalizing is usual to forestall complications and to provide symptomatic relief. Hepatitis B has been linked with liver cancer; an effective vaccine has been developed against this form of hepatitis.

Hepburn, Katharine (1909–), US stage and film actress, b. Hartford, Conn. She is famed for her intelligence, wit, and patrician looks. Among her sophisticated film comedies are *Holiday* (1938) and *The Philadelphia Story* (1940); she made nine films with Spencer Tracy, including *Adam's Rib* (1949) and *Pat and Mike* (1952). Her dramatic films include *Morning Glory* (1933), *Alice Adams* (1935), *The African Queen*, (1951), *Long Day's Journey into Night* (1962), *Guess Who's Coming to Dinner* (1967), *The Lion in Winter* (1968), *A Delicate Balance* (1973), and *On Golden Pond* (1981), for which she won an Academy Award (1982).

Hephaestus, ancient Greek god of fire and crafts. Son of Zeus and Hera, he is equivalent to the Roman Vulcan. Blacksmith and armorer to the Olympian gods, with a forge under Etna (or Stromboli), he is depicted as crippled and uncouth but clever and able enough to create Pandora, the first woman, and to wed Aphrodite.

Hepplewhite, George (?–1786), English furniture designer and cabinetmaker. Light in scale, usually with tapered legs, his furniture combined pale woods with mahogany. There was often inlay or painted decoration present. Hepplewhite was best known for his shield-back chairs.

Heptaméron (1558), collection of 72 tales by Marguerite de Navarre, modeled on Boccaccio's *Decameron*. The stories, related by 10 travelers, provided scope for the author's moral and religious opinions on love and contemporary customs.

Heptarchy, generally recognized term for the seven Anglo-Saxon kingdoms from the 5th century to the Danish invasions in the 9th. Including Mercia, Northumbria, Sussex, Kent, East Anglia, Essex, and Wessex, the heptarchy represents a simplified historical version of the complex political makeup of England at that time.

Hera, in Greek mythology, the daughter of Cornus and Rhea, queen of the Olympian gods, sister and wife of Zeus. Depicted with crown and scepter, she was worshiped as patron of Argos and Samos. In myths she appears as a jealous scold who persecuted her rivals but aided heroes of her choice such as Jason and Achilles.

Heraclitus (536–470 BC), important pre-Socratic philosopher. He held that all things are constantly changing, even the universe as a whole. Since only change is real, the orderliness of successive changes, or the world's destiny, is all that remains the same.

Heraclius (575?–641), Byzantine emperor (r.610–41). One of Byzantine's greatest rulers, Heraclius came to power in difficult times. The government of the empire had come to a standstill; recurrent financial crises had eroded its economic, political, and military might. Byzantium's enemies had overrun vast territories: Slavs and Avars were settling in the Balkans, and the Persians were invading Asia Minor. Under Heraclius, far-reaching reforms in the army and administration led to an improvement in the internal situation. From 622 to 628, Heraclius fought and defeated the Persians. The Perso-Byzantine war is sometimes considered the

first medieval crusade, since it restored the Holy Land and the Holy Cross to the empire.

Heraldry, historic system in which personal and inherited symbols are granted for the practice of bearing and displaying armorial ensigns. During the Middle Ages heraldic symbols were displayed on the shield and helm. The herald, frequently a tournament official, became an expert at identifying men and families by their insignia; his function evolved into one of designing and granting armorial bearings. Although heraldry is almost as old as civilization, its immediate origin dates to 12-century Germany; the practice soon spread to France, Spain, and Italy, and was brought to England by the Normans. Today, in England, the Court of Chivalry, officiated by the earl marshal and kings-of-arms, still awards arms to individuals and corporations, as well as honorary arms to approved American citizens of British descent.

Herb, seed plant with a soft rather than woody stem that withers away after one growing season. Most herbaceous plants are flowering plants, or angiosperms. Also, any plant used as a flavoring, seasoning, or medicine, such as thyme, sage, and mint.

Herbert, Edward, Lord Herbert of Cherbury (1583–1648), English philosopher. Called "the father of deism," he is remembered for *On the Truth* (Lat. *De Veritate*, 1624) and for his *Autobiography* (publ. 1764). *See also* Deism.

Herbert, Henry Howard Molyneux, 4th Earl of Carnarvon (1831–90), English statesman. A Conservative, he put forth several liberal plans as undersecretary for the colonies (1858–59) and colonial secretary (1866–67, 1874–78); he submitted the bill (1867) for federation of the Canadian provinces, leading to Canadian independence; a bill to abolish Gold Coast slavery (1874); and a plan for federation in South Africa (1877). After resigning in protest over the British entry into the Russo-Turkish conflict, he served as lord lieutenant of Ireland (1885–86), where he opposed Gladstone's policy of home rule.

Herbicide, chemical preparation used for killing vegetation, usually weeds. Some are selective, and kill only certain species of plants. Others kill all plant life. Some organic herbicides have been discovered to be carcinogens, and their use has been banned. Others, such as Agent Orange, which was used to destroy ground cover during the Vietnam War, have apparent but undetermined health effects.

Herculaneum (Erolano) ancient city in Italy, on site of modern Resina and Portici at foot of Mt Vesuvius; devastated AD 63 by earthquake; buried AD 79 with Pompeii by eruption of Mt Vesuvius; archeological excavations begun 1709 have unearthed Villa of the Papyri, a basilica, and theater.

Hercules, legendary Greek hero of great strength and courage, generally depicted with a club and wearing a lion skin. His 12 labors justify his fame. Hercules killed the lion of Nemea and the nine-headed Hydra, captured the Erymanthean boar and golden-antlered Cerynean stag. He destroyed the Stymphalian birds; then cleaned the Augean stables by diverting two rivers through them. Hercules captured the Cretan bull and the man-eating horses of Thrace, stole the Amazon Queen's girdle, the cattle of Eurstheus, and the golden apples of the Hesperides, and finally brought Cerberus out of Hades.

Hercules Beetle, tropical American scarab beetle. The male has two horns—a long one on the head and a shorter one on the thorax. Length: to 7.5in (19cm) including horn. Species *Dynastes hercules.*

Herder, Johann Gottfried (1744–1803), Prussian philosopher and cultural historian. Herder understood human society to be an organic and secular totality that developed as the result of an historical process. His claim that the nation and its language defined an essential cultural unity anticipated "nationalist" sentiment. Herder was also a founder of German Romanticism and an opponent of Immanuel Kant. He wrote *Ideas and the Philosophy of History of Humanity* (1784–91), which applies the concept of history to all areas of human culture.

Herdsman Constellation. *See* Boötes.

Heredity, transmission of physical and other characteristics from parent to offspring by means of genes in the chromosomes. Study of heredity began with the work of Gregor Mendel in the 19th century. Though physical traits are often determined directly by the laws of heredity (eg, eye and hair color), complex traits such as intelligence are influenced by environmental factors.

Hereford, widespread breed of beef cattle. Originally from Herefordshire, England, there are numerous herds in the United States and Argentina. They gain weight quickly on minimal feed and adapt to semiarid conditions. Red with white faces, they are usually horned. *See also* Beef Cattle.

Herero, Negroid people of Namibia (South-West Africa). By tradition, the Herero are nomadic pastoralists, practicing ancestor worship, although European influence and Christianity are now evident. Both matrilineal and patrilineal descent exist in a society governed by localized autonomous political units. Large numbers of the Herero died during a revolt against German rule (1903–07).

Heresy, a persistent deviation from dogma, considered dangerous by orthodox members of a faith. The early Christian Church struggled over beliefs such as Arianism. In later times such outstanding rebels as Joan of Arc and Jan Hus were condemned as heretics. In modern times heresy charges are rare. *See also* Arianism; Gnosticism; Inquisition; Nestorianism.

Hermaphrodite, organism with both male and female sexual organs. Most are invertebrates (planarian, earthworm, snail), sessile, or slow moving. They reproduce by two individuals mating and exchanging sperm or one individual's ovum and sperm uniting. Hermaphroditic plants are termed monoecious.

Hermes, Greek god equivalent to the Roman Mercury, represented with winged hat and sandals and carrying a wand twined with snakes. Hermes was the messenger of the gods and patron of travelers, gamblers, thieves, and commerce. He conducted the souls of the dead to Hades. Arcadia, Athens, Sparta, Argos, and Boeotia were centers of his worship.

Hermitage, Russian art museum, Leningrad. The largest public art collection in the Soviet Union was first housed in Rastrelli's Winter Palace. When this building was damaged by fire, the collection was moved to the New Hermitage museum, built by a Munich architect (1840–49). Catherine the Great was responsible for the size and quality of the collection. She was able to acquire several important private collections that came onto the world art market while she was empress. The Hermitage has excellent examples of European painting, expecially of the French Impressionist school. It also has numerous examples of Russian art throughout history.

Hermit Crab, small, common crablike crustacean found in tidal pools and shallow water worldwide. It uses sea snail shells for protection of its soft abdomen, using larger shells as it grows to adult size. Some forms are terrestrial and do not use shells as adults. Family Paguridae. *See also* Crustacean.

Hermit Thrush, North American songbird that is brownish with a spotted breast and reddish-brown tail. A fine singer, it grows to 7in (18cm). Family Turdidae; species *Hylocichla guttata.*

Hermon, Mount (Jabal ash-Shaykh), snow-capped mountain on Syria-Lebanon border, in Anti-Lebanon mountain range, 28mi (45km) WSW of Damascus; a sacred mountain of ancient Palestine; traditional scene of the Transfiguration. Height: 9,232ft (2,816m).

Hermopolis, ancient Egyptian center of worship of Thoth, the god of learning, and also of the Heliopolitan Ennead. Located 160mi (258km) S of Cairo, the modern site is called El Ashmunen. The Greeks associated the god Hermes with Thoth and renamed the site for him.

Herne, city and port in W West Germany, on Rhine-Herne Canal; site of Renaissance castle with Gothic chapel. Industries: textiles, radios, television sets. Chartered as city 1897. Pop. 189,400.

Hernia, protrusion of an organ, or part of an organ, through its enclosing wall or through connective tissue. Common types of hernias are protrusion of an intestinal loop through the umbilicus (umbilical hernia) or inguinal canal of the groin (inguinal hernia), or protrusion of part of the stomach or esophagus into the chest cavity through the opening (hiatus) of the esophagus into the diaphragm (hiatus hernia).

Herniated Disc. *See* Slipped Disc.

Hero and Leander, fictional lovers of classical antiquity. Each night Leander swam the Hellespont from Abydos to Sestos to court Hero until he drowned one stormy night. Hero drowned herself in sorrow. Christopher Marlowe's poem recounting the tale is the best known celebration of their love.

Herod Antipas (21 BC–AD 39), tetrarch of Galilee and Petraea (4 BC–AD 39), son of Herod the Great. He had John the Baptist beheaded at the instigation of his wife Herodias and his step-daughter Salome. He refused to intervene in the trial of Jesus, leaving his fate up to the Roman procurator Pontius Pilate. The emperor Caligula banished him to Gaul in AD 39.

Herodotus (*c.*484–425 BC), Greek historian and geographer. Little is known of him. He made lengthy journeys through the ancient world (Asia Minor, Mesopotamia, Babylon, and perhaps Egypt), spent long periods in Athens, and helped colonize Thurii in S Italy. He is most known for his lengthy, vivid, frequently anecdotal history of the Persian Wars. Considered the beginning of Western history writing, his work contains diverse information and is rich in anecdotes. *See also* Thucydides.

Heroic Couplet, two consecutive lines of iambic pentameter rhyming verse used in epic or "heroic" poetry. It was mastered by John Dryden and perfected by Alexander Pope. In modern poetry the heroic couplet is associated with light verse or satire.

Heroin, synthetic derivative of morphine, requiring a smaller dose to produce similar but faster effects, including reduction of pain, euphoria, and depressed respiration. Nausea and vomiting are side effects. It produces dependence or addiction. Illegal in the United States, its abuse has been widely publicized.

Heron, wading bird with long, daggerlike bill found in lakes, streams, and swamps. White, bluish, grayish, or brownish, they have long thin necks, long broad wings, thin legs, and short tails. They crumble their well-developed powder down feathers to absorb body slime. Feeding mainly on fish, they nest in groups and lay 3–6 light-colored eggs. Height: 1–6ft (0.3–1.8m). Family Ardeidae.

Herophilus (*fl.* 300 BC), Greek anatomist who practiced at Alexandria and was one of the first to experiment with post-mortem examinations. He identified various parts of the head and brain including the retina and also studied various glands and internal organs.

Herpes Simplex, acute herpes virus disease of the skin or mucous membrane in which clusters of fluid-containing blisters are seen, particularly on the lip borders, nostrils, or genitals. When accompanying a cold or fever, they are called cold sores or fever blisters.

Herpes Zoster. *See* Shingles.

Herpetology, zoological study of amphibians and reptiles. Areas of study include taxonomy (classification), life history, and geographical distribution. *See also* Zoology.

Herrara, José Joaquin (1792–1854), Mexican military and political leader. He served as second-in-command under General Santa Anna in the war with the United States (1846–47) and succeeded him as president (1848–51). As president, he attempted to reorganize the government along federalist lines and established the country's international credit, but military and political disorders impeded any progress.

Herring, marine schooling fish found worldwide. One of the most important food fish, it is canned as sardine and sold as fresh or pickled herring. It has laterally compressed body, deeply forked tail fin, and large mouth. Length: 3–18in (7.6–45.7cm). Family Clupeidae; species 190, including *Clupea harengus.*

Herschel, (Sir) William (1738–1822), English astronomer. Born in Hanover, Germany, he fled to Britain during the Seven Years War. A renowned maker of telescopes, he made many discoveries, including the planet Uranus (1781), and mapped numerous galactic nebulae.

Hertz, Heinrich Rudolph (1857–94), German physicist who became assistant to Hermann Helmholtz and held professorships at Karlsruhe and later at Bonn. He discovered, broadcasted, and received the radio waves predicted by James Maxwell. He also demonstrated the phenomenon of electromagnetic or electric waves ("hertzian waves"), and showed that their velocity and length could be measured and that heat and light are electromagnetic waves. The establishment of wireless telegraphy was dependent on his discoveries.

Hertz, Si unit of frequency (symbol H_z) equal to the frequency of a periodic phenomenon that has a period of one second. This unit replaces the cycle per second.

Hertzsprung-Russell Diagram, or **H-R diagram,** graph of the relationship between a star's luminosity (usually indicated by increasing absolute magnitude on the Y axis) and its surface temperature (shown by spectral types or color indexes in descending order on the X axis). The graph, independently devised by Ejnar Hertzsprung and Henry Norris Russell, illustrates the fact that stars fall into very well defined classes, and indicates patterns of stellar evolution.

Herzl, Theodor (1860–1904), Jewish leader and the founder of political Zionism. He was born in Austria-Hungary and worked as a lawyer and a journalist. He decided that the only solution to discrimination against Jews was to found a Jewish state. In 1897 he became president of the Zionist Organization, which worked throughout Europe to establish a Jewish national home in Palestine. Herzl wrote of himself as the founder of the Jewish state, and in 1949 his body was reburied in the newly established state of Israel. *See also* Zionism.

Herzog, Chaim (1918–), Israeli military leader and statesman, b. Northern Ireland. He emigrated in 1935 to Palestine, where he was active in Zionist affairs before serving in the British Army during World War II. After the establishment of Israel in 1948, he became director of intelligence. Later appointed to various diplomatic posts, he became well-known as an author and lecturer. After the 1967 Arab-Israeli war, he was named governor of the occupied West Bank. From 1975 to 1978, he was Israel's UN representative. In 1983, he was elected President of Israel.

Hesiod (8th century BC), Greek poet. The first major poet after Homer, he was the first to reveal his personality through his poetry. Troubles with his brother about their inheritances moved him to compose his best known work *Works and Days.* In *Theogony* he traced the mythological history of the gods. He was considered a great classical poet, but his writings were not as acclaimed as Homer's.

Hesperides, Greek mythological characters who figured in the "Twelve Labors of Hercules." The Hesperides were the daughters of Atlas and Hesperis. They had been entrusted by Juno with the guardianship of her precious golden apples, and were assisted in this task by a watchful dragon. As the last and most difficult of his labors, Hercules was told to steal the golden apples from the Hesperides. He sought the help of their father Atlas. Atlas, who had been condemned to bear the weight of the sky upon his shoulders, agreed to fetch the apples if Hercules would take his place in the meanwhile. But when Atlas returned with the prize, he was unwilling to resume his burden. Hercules tricked him, and carried off the apples of the Hesperides.

Hess, Rudolf (1894–), German Nazi leader. He joined the Nazis in 1921 and took part in the abortive Munich putsch (1923). Although Adolf Hitler's deputy from 1933, he lacked influence. In 1941, he flew alone to Scotland, hoping to make peace with the British. Imprisoned for the rest of the war, he was afterward sentenced to life imprisonment in Spandau Prison, Berlin.

Hess, Victor Francis (1883–1964), US physicist, b. Austria. As a result of his investigations of the ionization of air, he suggested that a radiation similar to X rays came from space; these were later named cosmic rays. He shared the 1936 Nobel Prize for physics with Carl David Anderson. Soon after receiving the prize, Hess emigrated to the United States; he became a citizen after World War II.

Johann Herder

Heinrich Hertz

Wild Bill Hickok

Hesse, Hermann (1877–1962), German novelist and poet. He ran away from a theological school in Maulbronn and spent much of his life studying Indian mysticism and Jungian psychology, as expressed in the novels *Demian* (1919), *Siddhartha* (1922), *Steppenwolf* (1927), *Narziss und Goldmund* (1930), and *The Glass Bead Game* (1943). He received the 1946 Nobel Prize for literature.

Hesse (Hessen), state in central West Germany, bounded by Baden-Württemburg and Bavaria (S), Rhineland-Palatinate (W), North Rhine-Westphalia and Lower Saxony (N) and East Germany (E); capital is Wiesbaden. Hilly, agricultural area with some heavy forests, it contains some of Germany's oldest cities (Frankfurt, Mainz, Worms). Industries: wine making, chemicals, machinery, mining. Area: 8,150sq mi (21,109sq km). Pop. 5,549,800.

Hessian Fly, brown to black, 0.16 to 0.24in (4–6mm) long fly found north of the Tropic of Cancer and in New Zealand. It is a serious pest of wheat and other grains. Family Cecidomyiidae, species *Mayetiola destructor.* *See also* Diptera.

Hestia, Greek goddess of the burning hearth. In the myths, she is the unmarried daughter of Cronus and Rhea who scorned the attentions of Apollo and Poseidon and who was installed in Olympus by Zeus. She was revered as the oldest of the Olympian gods. In Greece a flame burned continuously at her state shrine. In Rome, six virgins tended the fire at her temple, where she was worshiped as Vesta. *See also* Vestal Virgins.

Heterozygote, an organism possessing a different characteristic on each allele of a chromosome pair. *See also* Homozygote.

Heuchera, or alum root, herbaceous perennials of the saxifrage family. Growing to 28in (71cm), they are native to cool to temperate regions of North America, mostly near the Rockies. Their flowers may be white, greenish, red, or purple.

Hevelius, Johannes (1611–87), astronomer born in Danzig, where he used his home observatory to chart the lunar surface, catalog more than 1,500 stars, and discover four comets. His lunar atlas *Selenographia* charted features of the moon, many of which today bear the names he gave them.

Hevesy, Georg von (1885–1966), Hungarian chemist, winner of the 1943 Nobel Prize for chemistry. Codiscoverer of the element hafnium (1922), Havesy was also an early researcher into the uses of radioactive isotopes, including their use as "tracers" in living tissue. He fled Germany, where he had been teaching, in the early 1940s, to live in Sweden. He also worked with Niels Bohr in Copenhagen and Ernest Rutherford in England.

Hewes, Joseph (1730–79), American patriot and one of the signers of the Declaration of Independence, b. Kingston, N.J. A prosperous businessman and shipowner, he was a member of the Continental Congress (1774–77; 1779).

Hexagon, six-sided plane figure. Its interior angles add up to 720°. For a regular hexagon, one whose sides and interior angles are all equal, each interior angle will be 120°.

Hexameter, verse line of six metrical feet. Dactylic hexameter, the oldest form of Greek verse, characterizes the epic poetry of Homer. Examples of English-language hexameter poems are Henry Wadsworth Longfellow's *Evangeline* and Arthur Hugh Clough's *Bothie. See also* Meter.

Hexapla, Old Testament edition compiled in six columns by the Alexandrian Origen (c.185–c.254) about 231–245. Each page has six versions of text: Hebrew, Greek translation of the Hebrew, and the four Greek versions—Aquila, Symmachus, Septuagint, and Theodotion. Some sections have three additional Greek versions, or a total of nine columns. Manuscript copies of several parts of this work have survived.

Heydrich, Reinhard (1904–42), Nazi official, deputy chief of the Gestapo. A protégé of Heinrich Himmler, he participated in the Röhm purge in 1934 and in 1935 was appointed second-in-command to Himmler. After ruthless action against resistance in Norway and the Netherlands, Heydrich was made Deputy-Protector of Bohemia and Moravia in 1941. He was assassinated by Czech patriots in Prague in 1942, in reprisal for which the village of Lidice was razed to the ground and all its inhabitants murdered or deported.

Heyerdahl, Thor (1914–), Norwegian ethnologist whose "drift voyages" in primitive craft showed how ancient peoples may have crossed the oceans. With five companions, Heyerdahl drifted on the single-sailed balsa raft, *Kon Tiki,* 4,300mi (6,923km) across the Pacific from Peru to Polynesia (1947) in an attempt to prove that the Polynesians came from South America and not from SE Asia. Pursuing his theory, Heyerdahl led archeological expeditions to the Galápagos Islands (1953) and to Bolivia, Peru, and Colombia (1954). In 1970, Heyerdahl sailed from Africa to America in the papyrus boat *Ra II.* He wrote numerous books about his activities, including *Tigris Expedition* (1981) about his 1977 expedition.

Heyward, Thomas, Jr. (1746–1809), American patriot and a signer of the Declaration of Independence, b. St. Luke's Parish, S.C. A circuit judge in South Carolina (1779–89), he was that state's delegate to the Second Continental Congress (1776–78) and later served in the Revolutionary War.

Hialeah, industrial city, SE Florida, 5mi (8km) NW of Miami, Dade co. Settled 1921 on banks of Miami Canal. Site of Hialeah Park race track. Industries: aluminum, chemicals, electronic products. Inc. 1925; pop. (1980) 145,254.

Hiawatha, The Song of (1855), long narrative poem by Henry Wadsworth Longfellow based on American Indian folklore. It recounts the often fantastic adventures of Hiawatha, an Ojibwa Indian who becomes the leader of his people. The idea of the poem is derived from the Finnish epic *Kalevala,* and the meter is the same.

Hibernation, dormant condition adopted by certain mammals to spend the winter in a confined area. The mammal's adaptive mechanisms to avoid lack of food, desiccation, and extreme temperatures, include decreased blood pressure, heartbeat, respiration rate, and endocrine gland activity.

Hibiscus, or mallow, rose mallow, genus of plants, shrubs, and small trees native to tropical and temperate regions of the Eastern and Western hemispheres. Most species have large white, yellow, or red flowers with darker or variegated centers. Valued as ornamentals, the hibiscus is also used in making perfume. Some species are considered weeds. Family Malvaceae.

Hickok, James Butler ("Wild Bill") (1837–76), US law enforcement officer, b. Troy Grove, Ill. He was a teamster, stagecoach driver, and marksman. He served in the Union Army during the Civil War as a guerrilla fighter and was a scout for George Custer in his wars against the Indians. He served as US marshal in Kansas (1869–71). In 1872–73 he toured the country with Buffalo Bill as a sharpshooter and trick rider. He was shot to death in a saloon in Deadwood, S.D., while playing poker.

Hickory, deciduous tree native to E North America. They are grown for ornament, timber, and nut production. Height: 130ft (40m). Family Juglandaceae; genus *Carya. See also* Pecan.

Hicks, Elias (1748–1830), US Quaker preacher and abolitionist, b. Hempstead, N.Y. A farmer, he made preaching tours through the United States and Canada. His strong unitarian beliefs caused a schism of the Society of Friends, resulting in two divisions, the Hicksite and the Orthodox friends. His antislavery views were published in *Observations on Slavery* (1811).

Hicksville, city in SE New York, on W Long Island, NE of Mineola. Industries: electronic devices, photographic equipment, paper products. Settled 1648. Pop. 48,075.

Hidalgo y Costilla, Miguel (1753–1811), Mexican priest and revolutionary, the leader of the independence movement in its earliest phase. The Hidalgo revolt (1810–11) mushroomed quickly; within a few months, he had an "army" of 80,000 Indians and mestizos. Guanajuato and Valladolid were taken, but Hidalgo did not attack Mexico City. Defeated by the royalists at Calderón bridge, Hidalgo took flight, but soon was captured, tried, shot, and decapitated.

Hidatsa, a sedentary, Siouan-speaking Indian tribe occupying the Milk, Heart, and upper Missouri River area in Montana. In late prehistoric times, the Hidatsa separated from the Crow tribe to form a unit of their own. Almost entirely wiped out by a smallpox epidemic in 1837, they moved in with the Mandan, taking on many of the traits of that people. Today, approximately 1,000 Hidatsa live on Fort Berthold Reservation in North Dakota.

Hierapolis, name of two ancient cities; it means Holy City in Greek. The city in Phrygia in W Asia Minor was located 7mi (11.3km) N of Laodicea. It was devoted to the worship of Leto. The Romans enlarged it, building baths around the hot springs that still exist. It was an early center of Christianity. The city in Syria, originally called Mabbog, was located 50mi (80.5km) NE of Alepo. A center of worship of the nature goddess Atargatis, it was a chief stop on the road between Antioch and Seleucia-on-Tigris.

Hierarchy, in sociology, a ranked system in which the comparative position of an individual or a group is determined according to his or its social proximity to power. The terms "upper class" and "lower class" come from those groups' positions on a hierarchical scale.

Hieroglyphics, form of writing with picture characters. The Egyptians used hieroglyphs as an integral part of their designs in painting, sculpture, and carving. The pharaoh's name, written in symbols and surrounded by an oval line (called a cartouche), appeared frequently in Egyptian art. In painting, hieroglyphs were painstakingly drawn and painted with brilliant colors. Beginning with the Ptolemaic period in Egypt, knowledge of hieroglyphs became limited to members of the priesthood.

Around the 4th century AD, Christianity marked the end of the use of hieroglyphs in Egypt. It was not until the discovery of the Rosetta Stone in 1799 that the Egyptian hieroglyphs could be deciphered.

Hierro, island, formerly known as Ferro, westernmost of Canary Islands, Santa Cruz de Tenerife prov., Spain. Volcanic soil is unfertile. Industries: wine, brandies, figs. Area: 107sq mi (277sq km). Pop. 5,503.

Higashiosaka (Fuse), city in Honshu, Japan; formed by the union of Kasaka and Kusume, 1937. Industries: engineering works, chemicals, pottery, rubber. Pop. 500,173.

High, in meteorology, an area of high pressure, often shown on weather maps, associated in the Northern Hemisphere with clockwise, outward, anticyclonic atmospheric circulation. *See also* Low; Weather Maps.

High Blood Pressure, elevation of maximal (systolic) or minimal (diastolic) arterial blood pressure above normal levels, generally considered to be 140 millimeters of mercury (mm Hg) for systolic pressure and 90 mm Hg for diastolic pressure. Persistence of high blood pressure, called hypertension, may be of unknown cause (essential, or primary, hypertension) or may be secondary to a variety of conditions, including kidney, cardiovascular, or central nervous system disease, adrenal gland tumors, and toxemia of pregnancy. Treatment of high blood pressure is by weight reduction, salt restriction, and antihypertensive drugs. Hypertension shortens life and, if untreated, leads ultimately to damage of vital organs.

High-fidelity Sound, sound that has been reproduced without distortion. In hi-fi phonographs, the pick-up and amplifier must give a combined response that falls with increasing frequency to compensate for the pre-emphasis of high frequencies introduced during recording to reduce high-frequency noise. Hi-fi systems should be capable of reproducing all audible frequencies, the ratio of the loudest to the quietest sounds being up to 55 decibels. Frequencies up to at least 12,000 hertz should be distortion-free.

High Point, city in N North Carolina, 14mi (23km) SW of Greensboro. In 1850 railroad survey's highest point of new N-S route intersected with E-W highway on which town was established, hence name High Point. Southern Furniture Market is held four times a year here at exhibit complex; site of High Point College (1924). Industries: furniture, hosiery. Founded 18th century by Quakers; inc. 1859. Pop. (1980) 64,107.

High School, secondary level of education, traditionally grades 9 through 12. However, in some systems, senior high schools only include 10th through 12th grades, while junior high schools include 7th through 9th. High school seeks to prepare students for a field of work or for college entrance.

High-temperature Physics, production and analysis of the effects of temperatures above 4,000°C. At such temperatures, atoms begin to be stripped of their electrons, and a fourth state of matter, called a plasma, is achieved. Normal stars are plasmas; so is the region around an exploding hydrogen bomb. To make controlled thermonuclear fusion a reality, physicists must find a way to confine a plasma at temperatures of over a million degrees.

Hillary, (Sir) Edmund Percival (1919–), New Zealand explorer and mountain climber who was first to climb Mt Everest. He participated in the New Zealand and British expeditions to the Himalayas (1951 and 1952). In 1953, he and his Sherpa guide, Tenzing Norkay, reached the summit of Mt Everest, the world's highest mountain. In 1955, he led the New Zealand section of the Commonwealth Transantarctic expedition.

Hillman, Sidney (1887–1946), US labor leader, b. Lithuania. After leading a successful strike against Hart, Schaffner & Marx, a clothing firm in Chicago (1910), he rose in union ranks to become first president of the Amalgamated Clothing Workers (1915). He quit the American Federation of Labor to help found the Congress of Industrial Organizations (1935), headed the CIO's Political Action Committee (1943–46), and rallied labor support for President Roosevelt's New Deal. He established the American Labor party and helped form the World Federation of Trade Unions (1945).

Hilo, city on E coast of Hawaii on Hilo Bay; seat of Hawaii co; 2nd-largest city of Hawaii; tourist center; port of entry; site of Hilo College, Lyman House Museum, Hawaii Volcanoes National Park; severely damaged by tidal waves 1949 and 1960. Industries: sugar, rice, coffee, papaya, orchids. Settled 1820 by New England missionaries. Inc. 1911. Pop. (1980) 37,017.

Himalayan Cat, longhaired domestic cat breed developed recently from Persian and Siamese breeds. It has a Persianlike body, round head, small ears, short tail, and long thick coat. The eyes are Siamese blue and coat color is cream or white with seal, lilac, blue, or chocolate points.

Himalayas, great system of mountains in S Asia, extending N-S approx. 1,500mi (2,415km) in a long arc between Tibet and India-Pakistan and between the Indus River (E) and the Brahmaputra River (W); divided into 3 ranges: the Greater Himalayas (N), which include Mt Everest; the Lesser Himilayas, running parallel to the Greater; and the Outer Himalayas (S). The range marks the beginning of the high Tibetan plateau; its geological formation took place during the Tertiary Period.

Himmler, Heinrich (1900–45), German Nazi leader. He took part in the abortive Munich putsch (1923) and in 1929 became head of the SS. After the Nazis came to power (1933), he assumed control of the entire German police system. A fanatic racist, he controlled the Jewish extermination program. He became minister of interior (1943) and head of the army's home organization (1944). In April 1945 he tried secretly to negotiate peace with the Allies and was expelled from the party. Captured by the British, he killed himself.

Hims. *See* Homs.

Hinayana Buddhism, "Small Vehicle," pejorative name for the older, more conservative schools of Buddhism; Hinayana claims to stand in direct succession from Buddha; its center is the brotherhood of Buddhist monks. Homage is paid to Buddha, but he is not worshiped. Each person must seek his own salvation, unaided by the meritorious Bodhistas. The goal of Hinayana is that of all Buddhism—the attainment of Nirvana. Also known as Theravada, "Way of the Elders," this is the Buddhism of Ceylon and SE Asia. *See also* Nirvana.

Hindemith, Paul (1895–1963), German composer who emigrated to the United States in 1933, then returned to his native Germany late in his life. A major 20th-century composer, Hindemith experimented with dissonance and atonality early in his career, but eventually his works became more melodic and tonal in character. He was a master of counterpoint in music, and many of his compositions are Neoclassic and contrapuntal in style. He composed prolifically in all forms. Among his works are the song cycle *Das Marienleben* (1924); symphonies; concertos, such as the viola concerto *Der Schwanendreher* (1935); ballets; chamber music; operas; and sonatas for every instrument. His best-known work is the symphony he derived from his opera *Mathis der Maler* (1934). *See also* Neoclassic Music.

Hindenburg, Paul von (1847–1934), German general and president (1925–34). Commanding the army on the eastern front in World War I, he defeated the Russians in the Battle of Tannenberg (August 1914). In 1916 he became supreme commander and, with his chief of staff, Erich Ludendorff, directed the entire war effort, civilians as well as military, until the end of the war. Elected president in 1925, he presided over the collapse of the Weimar Republic.

Hindi, the most widespread language in India, spoken principally in the north-central part of the country by about 180,000,000 people. It shares with English the title of official language. Like the other languages of northern India, Hindi is descended from Sanskrit and thus belongs to the Indo-European family.

Hinduism, religion recognizing the *Veda* as authoritative. From 500 BC to AD 500 many conditions shaped the emerging faith; the result is a complex mixture of beliefs within a common social structure. Preeminent among the many popular Hindu gods is the Trimurti, or Trinity, consisting of Brahma, the Creator; Shiva, the Destroyer; and Vishnu, the Preserver. These gods compose the threefold manifestation of "Absolute Reality," or Brahman. The chief end of life in Hinduism is Moksa, liberation from suffering and rebirth. Three other goals: duty (dharma), material success (artha), and love (karma) were also formulated as part of the Hindu teaching. The four goals may be sought by following one or more of the three ways, or "yogas." These ways are the paths of personal devotion, works, and knowledge. Having about 470,000,000 followers worldwide, more than 85% of India's population is Hindu.

Hindu Kush, principal Asian mountain range; extends WSW 500–600mi (805–966km) from NE Afghanistan; site of Baroghil Pass; sparsely populated. Highest peak is Tirich Mir in N Pakistan, approx. 25,260ft (7,704m).

Hindu Sacred Literature. The sacred oral traditions and written texts of Hinduism are the basis of Indian society. They are divided into *Sruti,* the primary revelation, and *Smrti,* which is everything else. The Vedas, hymns extolling the gods and containing the liturgy for ritual sacrifices, are the most sacred texts. The great epic poems contain important sacred material. The *Bhagavadgita,* part of the epic *Mahābhārata,* is the most influential Hindu text. It emphasizes devotion. The spells and rituals of the *Tantras* typify Hinduism on a popular level. *See also* Brahmanas; Mahābhārata; Ramayana; Sanskrit Literature.

Hipparchus (*fl.*150 BC), Greek astronomer who worked on the island of Rhodes. He estimated the distance of the moon from the earth, drew the first accurate star map with more than 1,000 stars, divided stars into orders of magnitude based on their brightness (a system fundamentally in use today), and developed an organization of the universe which, while it still had the earth at the center, provided for accurate prediction of the positions of the planets.

Hippias (5th century BC), Greek Sophist. Since none of his own writings survive, we know him only through the writings of Plato. Because of Hippias' claim to have mastered all the fields of learning of his time, Plato regarded him, and all Sophists, as superficial. *See also* Sophists.

Hippocrates (*c.*460–377 BC), Greek physician often called "the father of medicine." Little is known about Hippocrates, and the writings known as the Hippocratic Collection probably represent the works of several people. Nonetheless, Hippocrates exerted a tremendous influence on medicine, freeing it from superstition, emphasizing bedside or clinical observation, and providing guidelines for surgery and for the treatment of fevers. Most importantly he is credited with providing an ideal of ethics and professional conduct for physicians through the Hippocratic Oath, the most famous Hippocratic document.

Hippocratic Oath, an oath taken by physicians. It is based on the ideals and principles of the ancient Greek physician Hippocrates. Various abridged versions of the original oath are administered today.

Hippopotamus, large, water-loving, plant-eating mammal related to the pig, native to Africa. *Hippopotamus amphibius* has a massive gray or brown body with a big head, short legs, and short tail. Males weigh up to 5tons; females are slightly smaller than males. These hippos usually live in groups, spending much time in water. They can close their nostrils underwater but usually rise to breathe at frequent intervals. Pigmy hippopotamuses, *Choeropsis liberiensis,* are much smaller, solitary, and spend more time on land. They weigh about 400lb (180kg). Both are hunted as food and for their hides and teeth. Family Hippopotamidae.

Hirabayashi v. United States (1943), US Supreme Court decision unanimously upholding curfew and registration requirements placed on all persons of Japanese ancestry early in World War II. The court called it a justified temporary emergency war measure.

Hirohito (1901–), emperor of Japan (1926–). His visit to Europe in 1921 made him the first crown prince to travel abroad. Although he has generally exercised little political power during his reign, he did persuade the Japanese government to surrender to the Allies in 1945, announcing that surrender himself on the radio on August 15. Under the constitution drawn up by the occupation forces he lost much of his power, becoming mostly an imperial figurehead. He is a recognized authority on marine biology.

Hirosaki, city in N Honshu, Japan, 21mi (34km) SW of Aomori; site of 17th-century Buddhist temple, ruins of feudal castle, university (1949); center for silk culture and fruit growing. Industries: textiles, soybeans, brewing, sake. Pop. 157,603.

Hiroshige, Ando (1797–1858), Japanese ukiyo-e (color) printmaker. He first did portraits of women and actors and then turned to poetic landscapes. The most famous are 53 wood-block prints depicting his trip from Edo to Kyoto by the Tokaido Highway.

Hiroshima, city in SW Honshu, Japan, at W end of Inland Sea; capital of Hiroshima prefecture; consists of 6 islands connected by 81 bridges; site of military headquarters for Sino-Japanese war 1894–95, Russo-Japanese war 1904–05, and regional headquarters in WWII. First atomic bomb was dropped here Aug. 6, 1945, killing approx. 130,000 people, and destroying 90% of the city. Designated as "Peace City" by the Japanese government, memorials include Peace Park, Peace Tower, and a hospital specializing in treating survivors suffering from the effects of radiation expo-

Hispaniola

Alfred Hitchcock

Adolf Hitler

sure; site of annual conference on atomic bombs, Hiroshima University (1949). Industries: sake, canneries, paper, machinery, automobiles. Founded 1594. Pop. 541,998.

Hirsch, Samuel (1815–89), a rabbi and philosopher of Judaism, born in Prussia, best known for his work for the Reform movement in Judaism in both Germany and the United States. He served in Philadelphia as rabbi of a reform congregation. In 1869 he was appointed president of the first Conference of American Reform Rabbis. His philosophical system was based on the understanding of religion as dynamic rather than static.

Hispaniola, second-largest island in West Indies, between Cuba (E) and Puerto Rico (W), in N central Caribbean Sea. Haiti occupies W third of island and Dominican Republic remaining (E) portion; mountainous, agricultural region with subtropical climate. Discovered 1492 by Christopher Columbus who est. Española, first Spanish colony in New World; part became French colony of Santo Domingo; island declared independent Republic of Haiti 1804, later formed Dominican Republic (1844). Industries: bauxite mining, coffee, cocoa, sugar cane. Area: 29,530sq mi (76,483sq km). Pop. (combined) 8,600,000. *See also* Dominican Republic; Greater Antilles; Haiti.

Hiss-Chambers Case (1949–50), legal case involving Alger Hiss, a former State Department employee, who was accused of passing secret documents to Whittaker Chambers, a Communist agent. Hiss was convicted of perjury (1950) for denying that he passed the documents to Chambers, who testified against him. Hiss served a prison sentence.

Histamine, a substance derived from the amino acid histidine, occurring naturally in many plants and in animal tissues. Its several functions in the body include dilation of the capillaries. It is implicated in allergic reactions.

Histidine, colorless soluble crystalline amino acid, which is the precursor of histamine. *See also* Amino Acid.

Histoplasmosis, infection of the lymph nodes or reticuloendothelial system by the fungus *Histoplasma capsulatum,* usually by inhalation. Especially common in the US midwest, the infection itself is generally asymptomatic but causes severe symptoms such as pneumonia, anemia, and liver and spleen enlargement in a few cases.

Historia Augusta or **Augustan History,** important collection of biographies of the Roman emperors from Hadrian to Numerian, of unknown authorship and date. The original title of the manuscript is uncertain and the work itself has become garbled, with its original ordering uncertain. Nevertheless, it is an important document on Roman history.

Historical Geology, study of sedimentary rocks, which record in stone series of events in the history of the earth. The different layers contain plant and animal remains that give clues to the living systems and to water and temperature conditions that prevailed when a particular stratum was deposited. The injection of igneous material into a sedimentary layer is a record of the volcanic activity of a particular time and region. The composition of the rocks and the fossils in them give a record of the time and evolution of plants and animals.

Historicism, the view that an adequate account of any subject capable of description in time must be histori-

cal. All things must be explained in terms of their origins and comprehended in their development from inception to maturity, for example, the chicken from the egg. The term has been associated with the philosophy of F. Hegel and Karl Marx. Historicism often connotes deterministic expectation. *See also* Determinism.

Hitachi, port city on Pacific coast of Honshu, Japan, 83mi (133km) NE of Tokyo; most important mining and manufacturing center of Joban-Hitachi industrial district. Pop. 193,210.

Hitchcock, (Sir) Alfred (1899–1980), English film director, in Hollywood since 1940. He created droll, sophisticated, and suspenseful thrillers, including *The Thirty-nine Steps* (1935), *Suspicion* (1941), *Notorious* (1946), *Dial M for Murder* (1954), *Rear Window* (1954), *Vertigo* (1958), *Psycho* (1960), and *Frenzy* (1972). He was knighted by Queen Elizabeth II in 1980.

Hitler, Adolf (1889–1945), Nazi dictator of Germany, b. Austria. Brought up in Austria, he did not graduate from high school and for a time made his living painting postcards in Vienna. Moving to Munich in 1913, he served in the German army in World War I, became a corporal, and was decorated for bravery. After the war he returned to Munich and soon became leader (1921) of the small National Socialist German Workers' or Nazi party. Already an impressive demagogue, in November 1923 he attempted to seize the Bavarian government, but his Beer Hall Putsch was a fiasco. Imprisoned for nine months, he set out his extreme racist and nationalist views in *Mein Kampf.* After his release, Hitler worked to revive the Nazi party, which gathered strength dramatically with economic depression in 1929. As parliamentary government floundered and street violence (largely fomented by the Nazis) grew, President Hindenburg appointed Hitler chancellor in a coalition on Jan. 30, 1933. Within a month the Reichstag Fire gave him the excuse for establishing a one-party regime; and the process was completed by a purge (June 30, 1934) in which he liquidated possible rivals in both the party and the state. On Hindenburg's death (Aug. 2, 1934), Hitler proclaimed himself head of state. In the following years he consolidated his dictatorship and rearmed Germany for expansion. The remilitarization of the Rhineland (1936) was followed by the occupation of Austria (March 1938) and Czechoslovakia (October 1938 and March 1939) and the attack on Poland (September 1939). The last precipitated World War II. Initially successful in the west, the German armies began to meet setbacks after the invasion of Russia in 1941 and the entry of the United States into the war. An assassination attempt against Hitler (July 1944) led to further tightening of the brutal dictatorship at home; systematic extermination of about 6,000,000 Jews was carried out throughout the war (the Holocaust). As the war ended, Hitler married his mistress Eva Braun and committed suicide in Berlin (April 30, 1945).

Hittites, ancient people who built a powerful empire in Asia Minor and N Syria (*c.*2000–1200 BC). Primarily of Indo-European stock, they invaded Babylonia (*c.*2000 BC), seized Cappadocia, and conquered Syria and Palestine. Ramses II of Egypt checked them near Kanesh on the Orontes River (*c.*1290) and made a treaty. Boghazkeui and Carchemish were their great cities. After 1200 BC the Thracians, Phrygians, and Assyrians invaded the Hittite lands, and their loose empire broke up.

Hives, popular term for the transient, itchy, reddish or pale raised skin patches of urticaria. Hives may be caused by allergy to certain foods or drugs, by irritants

such as sunlight or animal danders, or by emotional stress.

Hoatzin, shaggy crested, awkward-flying bird of N South American river valleys. It has a large crop for storing vegetable matter. The hatchlings have claws on their wings and are able to climb trees. Resembling a long slender crow, the brownish adult has rounded wings and a long tail. The female lays 2 to 5 oval spotted white eggs in a tree nest near a river. Species *Opisthocomus hoazin.*

Hoban, James (*c.*1762–1831), US architect, b. Ireland. He designed the State Capitol in Columbia, S.C., in 1791 and the White House in Washington, D.C., in 1792.

Hobart, city in Tasmania, SE Australia, on the Derwent River; site of the University of Tasmania (1890); excellent deepwater port. Exports: wool, newsprint, food products, meat. Industries: cement, leather, metal ore, tourism. Founded 1804; inc. 1842. Pop. 164,010.

Hobbes, Thomas (1588–1679), English philosopher. After serving as a tutor, Hobbes traveled extensively in Europe. Fleeing England (1642), he remained a royalist in exile until the restoration of Charles II (1660). In *De Corpore* (On Bodies), *De Homine* (On Man), and *De Cive* (On the State), he presented his view that matter and its motion comprise the valid subject matter of philosophy. Organic and inorganic matter obey similar laws of self-assertion and collision respectively. Nature, including the human, is a theater of necessary causes and determined effects. Hobbes' materialism is projected on the political plane in *Leviathan* (1651). *See also* Leviathan; Materialism.

Ho Chi Minh (1890–1969), Vietnamese political figure, b. as Nguyen That Thanh. In 1911 he left Vietnam as a seaman on a freighter. For part of World War I he lived in the United States. Between 1917–23 he lived in France. In 1919 he unsuccessfully petitioned the Versailles Peace Conference to recognize the right of self-determination of the Vietnamese people. In 1920 he joined the French Communist party. Returning to Vietnam after 1927, he presided over the founding of the Vietnamese Communist party in 1930. Threatened with arrest, he fled to Moscow in 1932, then moved to China in 1938. In 1941 he returned to Vietnam and founded the Viet Minh to fight the Japanese. With the Japanese driven out, in 1945 he declared Vietnam an independent nation and was himself appointed president. The French returned and contested Ho's authority until their defeat in 1954. The 1954 Geneva Conference recognized Ho as president of the Democratic Republic of Vietnam (North Vietnam). When the government of the South backed by the United States refused to hold elections in 1956 as had been agreed upon, Ho organized the National Liberation Front (Viet Cong) to attempt to gain control of the South. Vietnam was still divided at his death.

Ho Chi Minh City. *See* Saigon.

Hockey, Ice. *See* Ice Hockey.

Hockney, David (1937–), British painter, who made his name during the Pop Art movement with witty, often deliberately naïve, paintings, such as *Flight into Italy-Swiss Landscape* (1962). In the late 1960s and the 1970s he developed a more realistic, classical style. Typical of this style are his portrait of Celia Birtwell and Ossie Clark (1970) and *A Bigger Splash* (1967). His graphic work, executed with an economical but powerful sense of line, includes many fine portraits and his series of etchings, *A Rake's Progress* (1961–63).

Hodeida (Al-Hudaydah), major seaport city in W Yemen Arab Republic, on the Red Sea; developed mid-19th century by Turks; main port of entry for Yemen. Exports: coffee, hides, dates. Pop. 100,000.

Hodgkin, Dorothy Mary Crowfoot (1910–), English chemist. After teaching at both Oxford and Cambridge she spent some time at the University of Ghana before becoming professor at Oxford. In 1964 she was awarded the Nobel Prize for her determination of the structure of vitamin B_{12} by X-ray crystallography. She also determined the structure of penicillin and several other macromolecules by the same process.

Hodgkin's Disease, condition characterized by painless enlargement of the lymph glands, lymphatic tissue, and spleen, with spread to other areas. Fever is a common symptom, and weight loss, anemia, loss of appetite, and night sweats may occur. The condition is twice as common in males as in females. Treatment varies with the stage of the disease but in general consists of radiotherapy, combinations of drugs, or both. Cure or long-term survival is achieved in most cases but depends on the extent of involvement at diagnosis.

Hoe, Richard March (1812–86), US inventor of the rotary printing press (1846), b. New York City. His press printed at far higher speeds than the traditional "flat-bed" press. Later developments by William Bullock and Hoe further increased the pace by printing on a roll or "web" of paper, rather than on single sheets. The rotary press and the web feed are the foundations of the newspaper industry.

Hofei (Hefei or Ho-fei), formerly Luchow; city in E China; capital of Anhwei prov. Industries: textiles, chemicals, food processing. Founded during Han dynasty (202 BC–AD 220). Pop. 400,000.

Hoff, Jacobus Hendricus van't (1852–1911), Dutch physical chemist, professor at Amsterdam, Leipzig, and Berlin. His research involved advanced investigations of the carbon atom; the theory that gas laws are also applicable to dissolved substances; and the chemical application of thermodynamics. He was awarded the first chemistry Nobel Prize in 1901 for his studies on chemical equilibrium, reaction rates, and osmotic pressure.

Hoffa, James Riddle (1913–75?), US labor leader, b. Brazil, Ind. Hoffa worked his way up in the International Brotherhood of Teamsters beginning in 1932. He served as Teamsters' vice president (1952–57) under Dave Beck, succeeding Beck as president (1957–71). Hoffa organized the Teamsters into a powerful union with a membership of 1,600,000 in 1967, when he began an 8-yr. jail term for jury tampering, with 5 yrs. added for mail fraud and mishandling of union funds. His sentence was commuted in 1971 by Pres. Richard Nixon. Hoffa was reported missing, apparently abducted, in 1975 and is presumed dead.

Hoffmann, E(rnst) T(heodor) A(madeus) (1776–1822), German novelist and composer. His works include an unfinished novel, studies of Beethoven and Mozart, and an opera, but he is famous for his Romantic tales, *The Golden Pot* (1813), *The Legacy* (1817), and *Mlle de Scudéry* (1818).

Hofmann, Melchior (1495–1543), German Anabaptist leader. He was a mystic, believed that Christ would soon return to earth for the judgment day, and urged his followers to be saintly. He spread Anabaptist beliefs in Holland, where his followers were called Melchiorites. Later he was imprisoned in Strasbourg and died after 10 years in prison.

Hofmannsthal, Hugo von (1874–1929), Austrian dramatist, poet, and essayist. He wrote *The Play of Everyman* (1911), a verse drama regularly staged at the Salzburg Festival, of which Hofmannsthal was a founder. He was one of Richard Strauss's librettists and collaborated with him on *Der Rosenkavalier* (1911) and other operas. The importance of language to Hofmannsthal is clearly expressed in the *Chandos Letters* (1902).

Hofuf (Al-Hufuf), city in E Saudi Arabia, in the Hasa oasis, on caravan route from Riyadh to United Arab Emirate; important market center for dates, fruit, and wheat. Industries: brass and copper wires, textiles. Pop. 100,000.

Hog, medium-sized mammal native to the Old World, including various domesticated pigs, wild boars, and wart hogs. They have long pointed heads, stocky bodies, short legs with cloven hoofs, and small tails. Usually they have short bristly hair. In the wild, groups live in wooded areas, digging with their snouts for plant or animal food. Rapid runners and good swimmers, they wallow in mud to protect their light skin from sunburn. They are clean, intelligent animals that do not overeat. Wild hogs are hunted for sport or food. Most domestic pigs are derived from the wild hog, *Sus scrofa.* Length: 2–6ft (61–183cm); weight: to 600lb (270kg). Family Suidae.

Hogan, traditional Navaho dwelling. The hogan is a conical, hexagonal, or octagonal building with a domed roof. Traditionally built of logs and sticks covered with mud, sod, or adobe, it presented a very earthlike appearance. More modern hogans are of stone construction.

Hogarth, David George (1862–1927), English archeologist, writer, and diplomat. Between 1887–1907 he participated in several important excavations including those at Knossos, Crete, and Carchemish, Syria. From 1909 until his death he was director of the Ashmolean Museum at Oxford. In 1915 he was sent by the British government to Egypt to organize an Arab revolt against Turkey. In this endeavor he worked with Lawrence of Arabia. He was British commissioner on the Middle East Commission of the Paris Peace Conference (1919). His *A Wandering Scholar in the Levant* (1896) is a fascinating travel book. Important scholarly works include *The Ancient East* (1914), *The Archaic Artemis of Ephesus* (1909), and *Kings of the Hittites* (1926).

Hogarth, William (1697–1764), English painter, engraver, and printmaker. His early works were portraits. He did some historical painting but is most famous for his narrative prints, executed in a decorative Rococo style. In a series of engravings including "A Harlot's Progress," "The Rake's Progress," and "Marriage à la Mode," he satirized British social institutions.

Hog Cholera, or hog plague, a virus-caused communicable disease of swine. Symptoms include fever, loss of weight, diarrhea, sores on the under portion of the body.

Hogg, James (1770–1835), Scottish poet known as "The Ettrick Shepherd." He combined farming and literary work after publishing *The Mountain Bard* in 1807 on Walter Scott's recommendation, but made his reputation by *The Queen's Wake* (1813).

Hognose Snake, harmless North American snake ranging throughout the United States. It is stocky with an upturned snout. Variable in color, it is mostly spotted brown, gray, yellow, or orange. When alarmed it will hiss, spread its neck, then play dead. Length: to 33in (84cm). Family Colubridae; genus *Heterodon. See also* Puff Adder; Snake.

Hohenstaufen Dynasty, German princely family, several of whose members were Holy Roman emperors and German kings. Frederick married (1079) the daughter of Emperor Henry IV and was created duke of Swabia. His son was elected German king as Conrad III in 1138. Conrad was followed by Frederick I, Henry VI, Philip of Swabia, Frederick II, and Conrad IV. The family's power in Germany was challenged by the Guelphs, and in Italy they were in constant conflict with the Lombard cities and the papacy. Frederick II shifted the family's main interests to Italy, and the rapid decline of the family began with his death (1250).

Hohenzollern Dynasty, German princely family that ruled Brandenburg, Prussia, and Germany. Burgraves of Nuremberg from 1191, the Franconian line of the family received Brandenburg in 1415 (*see* Frederick I, elector of Brandenburg). Prussia, acquired by a junior branch of the family, was added to Brandenburg in 1618. Frederick William the Great Elector further expanded and consolidated their territories, and his son Frederick I adopted the title "king in Prussia." Frederick William I built up the famous Prussian army, and Frederick II used it to great effect against the Hapsburgs. Finally Germany was united in 1871 under the Hohenzollern emperor, William I. His grandson William II abdicated at the end of World War I (1918).

Hohokam Culture, farming culture of the southern Arizona desert, arising in the last centuries BC and surviving until about AD 1400. Sophisticated irrigation systems were the basis of Hohokam prosperity, and sizable settlements were founded; other remains include engraved and sculptured shells, pottery, and temple mounds, all showing Mexican influence.

Hōjó, Japanese family. Installing themselves as advisors to the young Kamakura Shoguns (military leaders), the Hōjó family effectively controlled the government of Japan 1200–1333.

Hokkaido, formerly Yezo; second-largest of the four main islands of Japan, and largest prefecture in Japan; capital is Sapporo; site of several national parks, major winter resort area, 1972 Winter Olympics. Crops: rice, corn, potatoes, barley, wheat. Industries: dairying, fishing, lumber, coal, paper, brewing, tourism. Became part of Japan 1604. Area: 30,313sq mi (78,511sq km). Pop. 5,184,287.

Hokusai, Katsushika (1760–1849), Japanese ukiyo-e (color) printmaker. His early work included portraits of women and actors. He also did illustrations of flowers, birds, and city scenes, but his landscape art was his greatest work. Known for his use of design and color, he showed man's relationship to nature, often portraying nature as the dominant force.

Holbein, Hans, the Younger (1497–1543), German painter, decorative artist, and woodcutter. In the field of decorative arts, he designed bookbindings, armor, silverware, and the like. His best-known woodcuts were his 51 prints of the "Dance of Death." The Italian influence is evident in his use of ornament and rich color in his portraits. In Basel, he painted portraits of the wealthy and became a close friend of Erasmus. Eventually he settled in London, where he did his greatest portraits of German merchants residing there and of the royal British court of Henry VIII. His carefully drawn portraits of Henry and his third wife Jane Seymour are famous examples of his realistic and decorative style. He died in London of the plague.

Holguín, city in SE Cuba, 19mi (31km) SW of Gibara, its port on the Atlantic Ocean. Located in fertile plateau area, known as "Cuba's granary," it is site of nationalist insurgency during Ten Years' War (1868–78), and Spanish Revolution (1895–98). Exports: tobacco, cattle products. Industries: tobacco, sugar cane, livestock, coffee, lumber, food processing, furniture. Founded *c.* 1720, and named for Garcia Holguín, Mexican conquistador of 16th century. Pop. 131,656.

Holland, name popularly given to the entire Netherlands, properly refers only to one of the country's provinces. A medieval county in the Holy Roman empire in the 10th century after it gained independence from Lorraine, it was seized by the county of Hainaut in 1299 and passed to Burgundy (1433) and Austria (1482). In 1490 Maximilian of Austria put down a Dutch rebellion. In the next 200 years Holland became a sea power and led the United Netherlands in its long battle for independence from Spain.

Hollerith Code, a computer code consisting of 12 levels, or bits per character, which defines the relation between an alpha-numeric character and the punched holes in an 80-column computer data card.

Holley, Robert W(illiam) (1922–), US biochemist, b. Urbana, Ill. He shared the 1968 Nobel Prize in physiology or medicine for his part in discoveries of how genes determine the function of cells. Holley described the first full sequence of subunits in nucleic acid, the genetic material of a cell. This was an important step to understanding gene action.

Holly, any of 300 species of shrubs and trees found worldwide. They have alternate, simple leaves and small flowers. Male and female flowers are usually on separate plants. There is no nectar-secreting disk in the flowers. The one-seeded fruit is usually red. The English holly tree *(Ilex aquifolium)* has spiny evergreen leaves. Height: to 50ft (15m). American holly *(I. opaca)* has duller, smoother leaves and is taller. Both are widely cultivated as ornamentals. Family Aquifoliaceae.

Hollyhock, biennial plant native to temperate Europe and China and now naturalized in the United States. They have leafy stems and showy flowers of red, white, rose, yellow, or orange. Height: 3–9ft (0.9–2.7m). Family Malvaceae; species *Althea rosea.*

Hollywood, city in SE Florida, 18mi (29km) N of Miami. Originally Hollywood-by-the-Sea; settled as port and resort. Industries: electronic equipment, building products,cement.Inc.1925:Pop.(1980)117,188.

Holmes, Oliver Wendell (1809–94), US author and physician, b. Cambridge, Mass. A graduate of Harvard University, he studied medicine in Boston and Paris, receiving his medical degree in 1836. Meanwhile, he began to write poetry, gaining fame with "Old Ironsides" (1830). After practicing medicine for several years, he became professor of anatomy and physiology at Dartmouth College (1838–40) and later at Harvard (1847–82). He wrote a controversial study of childbed fever that emphasized its transmission through lack of personal hygiene by doctors. Combining literature with medicine, he wrote three novels dealing with abnormal psychology—*Elsie Venner* (1861), *The Guardian Angel* (1867), and *A Mortal Antipathy* (1885).

A noted wit, he began writing the "breakfast-table"

E.T.A. Hoffmann

Holly

Oliver Wendell Holmes, Jr.

series in 1857. In these conversations around a breakfast table, Holmes discusses a variety of topics. The series includes *The Autocrat of the Breakfast Table* (1858), *The Professor at the Breakfast Table* (1860), *The Poet at the Breakfast Table* (1872), and *Over the Teacups* (1891). His son, Oliver Wendell Holmes, Jr., was a Supreme Court justice.

Holmes, Oliver Wendell, Jr. (1841–1935), US jurist and legal scholar, b. Boston. He was the son of the physician and author, Oliver Wendell Holmes (1809–94). After serving in the Civil War, he then practiced law (1867–82). He co-edited the *American Law Review* (1870–73), *Kent's Commentaries* (1873), and wrote *The Common Law* (1881). He was a justice of the Massachusetts Supreme Court (1882–99), and served as its chief justice (1899–1902). He then became (1902) an associate justice of the US Supreme Court, serving until 1932. Known as "The Great Dissenter," he wrote eloquent dissents that showed his support of laws protecting child labor and in favor of wages and hours acts. Generally a champion of civil liberties, he expressed the "clear and present danger" standard in *Schenck* v. *United States* (1919) to prevent abuses of these liberties.

Holmium, metallic element (symbol Ho) of the lanthanide group, first identified spectroscopically in 1878. Chief ore is monazite (phosphate). The element has few commercial uses. Properties: at. no. 67; at. wt. 164.9304; sp gr 8.795 (25°C); melt. pt. 2685°F (1474°C); boil. pt. 4883°F (2695°C); most common isotope Ho^{165} (100%). *See also* Lanthanide Elements.

Holocaust, the program of persecution and planned extermination of European Jews and others carried out by the German Nazis, beginning with Adolf Hitler's rise to power in 1933 and ending in 1945 with Germany's surrender in World War II. Designated "the final solution to the Jewish question," the program was effected in many notorious concentration camps ("death camps") established throughout German-occupied Europe, such as Treblinka, Auschwitz, Dachau, and Bergen-Belsen. In Poland alone about 3,350,000 citizens of Jewish descent were interned in ghettos, deported to extermination camps, and slaughtered. In all, more than 6,000,000 persons were executed or died of mistreatment, disease, or starvation under this program. Nearly two decades had passed before a substantial attempt was made to understand the place of the Holocaust in the experience of our time. In commemoration, Holocaust Day (Yom Ha-Qaddish) is observed annually in Israel on the 27 of Nisan.

Holocene Epoch. *See* Quaternary Period.

Holofernes, biblical Assyrian general enlisted by King Nebuchadnezzar to subdue Judea. He was slain by Judith, a Jewish widow, as he slept.

Holography, so-called three-dimensional photography in which laser light is used to store light wave patterns on a photographic plate. When light from a similar source is reflected against the plate, the three-dimensional image appears. Although the concept of holography was appreciated in the 1940s, experiments could not proceed until the development of a sufficiently coherent light source—the laser.

Holon, city in W central Israel, in Tel Aviv–Jaffa metropolitan area. Industries: textiles, metal products, food processing, glassware. Became a city 1941. Pop. 88,500.

Holstein, S part of the West German state of Schleswig-Holstein. Part of the German duchy of Saxony *c.*

800; Holstein passed to Denmark in the 15th century, to Austria in 1864, and to Schleswig-Holstein in 1866. *See also* Schleswig-Holstein.

Holstein, or Holstein-Friesian, widespread breed of dairy cattle, originally developed in Holland, constituting the major proportion of milk producers in the United States. Their milk is low in butterfat, only 3-5%. Originally black and white, red and white strains have been developed. In 1951 one Holstein gave a record 21,402 quarts of milk. Weight: 1,500lb (675kg). *See also* Dairy Cattle.

Holtzman Inkblot Technique, in psychology, a projective technique used to assess personality characteristics and to aid in the diagnosis of mental disorders. The individual must interpret a series of 90 ambiguous inkblots. Responses are interpreted in relation to those responses commonly given by disturbed and normal people. *See also* Projective Techniques.

Holy Alliance. In 1815 Czar Alexander I of Russia organized an alliance of the rulers of Russia, Prussia, and Austria at the Congress of Vienna. The members were supposed to live according to Christian principles and promote peace, but many regarded the alliance as useless and ineffective. Alexander was under the influence of mystical trends in Russia at the time, and the alliance was one of the results of this influence.

Holy Communion. *See* Eucharist.

Holy League, name for a number of European alliances in the 15th to 17th centuries. The various purposes of these varying leagues included papal checks on French power, Spanish checks on Holy Roman imperial power, French Catholic assertions against French protestants, and European reactions to invasions by the Turks.

Holyoke, city in W Massachusetts, on Connecticut River. Named for Elizur Holyoke, pioneer settler, it was part of West Springfield until 1850. Mt Tom ski area and Mt Holyoke College are nearby. Industries: textiles, paper, metals. Chartered 1873. Pop. (1980) 44,678.

Holy Orders, in the Roman Catholic, Eastern Orthodox, and Anglican churches, the sacrament by which a person becomes a minister of the Gospel, a priest distinguished from the lay members of the church. The orders of bishop, priest, and deacon were instituted by Christ. The authority of bishops extends in succession from the Apostles. Only bishops can ordain new ministers. Other churches ordain ministers but do not believe in the Apostolic Succession.

Holy Roman Empire, a European empire founded in 962, when the German king Otto I was crowned in Rome, and surviving until 1806. Some historians date it to Charlemagne's coronation in 800. The emperors claimed to be the temporal sovereigns of Christendom, ruling in cooperation with the spiritual sovereign, the pope. However, the empire never encompassed even all of western Christendom (its basic areas were Germany, Austria, Bohemia and Moravia, northern Italy, and the Low Countries), and its relationship with the papacy was extremely stormy. The emperorship was based on the German kingship. Once elected by the German princes, the German king sought papal election as emperor. He did not always receive it; and from Maximilian I (reigned 1493–1519) the title emperor was assumed without papal coronation. By that time, although the office remained technically elective, the emperorship had become hereditary in house of Hapsburg, which held the office from 1438. Earlier dynasties

who held the title included the Salians and Hohenstaufens. Under these rulers in the 11th, 12th, and 13th centuries the empire was at the height of its power. Under the Hapsburgs it became an increasingly nominal entity, its rulers concentrating on their dynastic interests in Austria while the other German princes pursued their own ends. The fiction was finally dissolved by Napoleon I, who forced the abdication of Emperor Francis II in 1806.

Holy See, centralized jurisdiction of the Roman Catholic Church. It includes the pope, with his authoritative powers as the visible head of the church. It is the seat of church government in Rome with powers over churches throughout the world. *See also* Papacy.

Homage, Medieval. *See* Feudalism.

Homeopathy, method of medical treatment based on the idea that "like cures like," or, in other words, that a disease should be treated by using drugs and other agents that produce the symptoms of the disease in a healthy person. Homeopathy was popularized by the 18th-century German physician C.F.S. Hahnemann and is now mainly of historical interest.

Homeostasis, tendency of a physical or biological system to try to maintain a balance or constancy. The term is most often applied to the way the human nervous system regulates such things as body temperature, water balance, and blood pressure.

Homeothermic Animal, warm-blooded organism with a relatively constant body temperature, independent of environmental temperature.

Homer (*c.* 9th century BC), Greek epic poet. No definite facts are known about him: by tradition he was blind; by tradition he wrote the *Iliad* and the *Odyssey*. Seven cities claim to be his birthplace. His style was serious, realistic, and descriptive. Aristotle admired his beautiful writing; Vergil imitated it. His epics were used as texts by schoolchildren, and the Greeks regarded him as a genius. Other works have been ascribed to him, although it is unlikely that he wrote them. Later scholars have even questioned his existence. *See also* Homeric Hymns; Iliad; Odyssey.

Homer, Winslow (1836–1910), US painter, b. Boston. He began as an illustrator for *Harper's Weekly* and usually drew naturalistic outdoor scenes. He painted several realistic oils of Civil War subjects in 1862. His best-known works are his paintings of the Maine coast, showing the moods of the sea and man pitted against them. Above all, Homer's careful handling of color and light and shadow in both oil and watercolor contributed to the realism of his work.

Homeric Hymns, a collection of hymns that were sung as invocations to the gods. Authorship is unknown, although some have been wrongly attributed to Homer. Of the surviving hymns, the most famous are Hymn to the Delian Apollo and Hymn to the Pythian Apollo.

Home Rule, movement to secure autonomy for Ireland within the British Empire. Isaac Butt's Home Government Association (founded 1870) was succeeded by the more militant Home Rule Association, led by Charles Parnell. William Gladstone introduced two Home Rule bills (1886, 1893), but both were defeated. Moderate reforms (1898–1903) failed to pacify the demands for self-government. The Third Home Rule Bill was passed in 1912, but its implementation was delayed by the outbreak of World War I. It failed to satisfy either the growing Irish republican feeling or the Ulster Unionists.

Homestead Act (1862), US legislation enacted during the Civil War to encourage Westward expansion. The government granted 160 acres (65 hectares) of government land to anyone who would live on it and improve it for 5 years. Along with the Morrill Act for education, and with subsidies for the railroads, the Homestead Act opened the West to widespread settlement.

Homestead Massacre (July 6, 1892), violent labor incident. Striking workers at the Carnegie Steel Plant in Homestead, Penn., fired at 300 Pinkerton detectives hired by a company official, Henry C. Frick, who sought to break the union. During the battle 10 persons were killed and many others injured. The state militia was sent in on July 9, remaining for three months, and strike breakers worked in the plant, weakening the power of the steelworkers union.

Homogenization, a process that reduces a substance contained in a fluid to very small particles and redistributes the particles evenly through the fluid. For example, the fat in milk is broken down so thoroughly that particles do not recombine and cream will not rise.

Homology, similarity in form, function, or evolution of living things based on a common genetic heritage. For example, a man's arm and a seal's flipper are homologues, having developed from a common ancestor; the wing of a bird and of a bat are not because they evolved independently. *See also* Evolution.

Homophony, music characterized by a single melodic line accompanied by chords and other subordinate musical material, as opposed to monophony (melody without accompaniment) and polyphony (music with several simultaneous melodies). Of these three general styles, homophonic style is the one most familiar to modern listeners and is generally characteristic of most music since the time of Haydn. *See also* Polyphony.

Homoptera, order of insects, including scales and lantern flies, found worldwide. Most are terrestial plant feeders with sucking mouthparts on the back of the head; some adults lack mouthparts. They may be winged or wingless and have three life stages; egg, nymph, and adult. Length: to 6in (152mm). *See also* Aphid; Cicada; Leafhopper; Scale.

Homo sapiens, modern humans, who first appeared about a quarter of a million years ago. Scattered fossil remains of that age, or somewhat younger, include those of Steinheim Man and Swanscombe Man, both of whom had skull capacities within the modern range. Also, they both predated Neanderthal Man who appears to have arisen contemporaneously with later, indisputably *Homo sapiens* types. For this reason Neanderthal Man is now often regarded as a variety of *Homo sapiens.* In Europe, Neanderthal Man was abruptly replaced by Cro Magnon Man about 30,000 years ago.

Homosexuality, sexual attraction to and preference for relations with persons of one's own sex. The term is now often used in reference to attraction between males, as distinguished from Lesbianism. No truly reliable figures have been gathered on the number of homosexual persons in the population, many homosexuals being reluctant to identify themselves as such, but an estimate of 10% of the U.S. population is sometimes given as a rough gauge. Homosexuality is recorded as an ancient and universal form of sexual behavior. It was an accepted or tolerated form of sexual expression in ancient Greece and Rome. Largely because of Biblical injunction, homosexuality was suppressed and punished, sometimes by imprisonment and death, in many parts of the Judeo-Christian world. The Soviet Union maintains severe strictures on all homosexual behavior, but Communist China, many Western nations, and some states of the United States no longer prosecute acts performed in private by consenting adults and not involving minors, coercion, or intimidation. In 1975 the American Psychiatric Association removed homosexuality from the category of mental disorder, and gay rights groups have actively sought government protection of homosexuals' civil rights. *See also* Lesbianism.

Homozygote, an organism possessing identical alleles on a chromosome pair. This is a purebred organism and will always produce the same kind of gamete. *See also* Heterozygote.

Homs (Hims), city in Syria, on Orentes River; capital of Hims governorate; site of Arab mosque (1908). Industries: refined petroleum, processed foods, flour, cotton, silk. Pop. 215,526.

Homunculus, according to some 16th- and 17th-century biologists, was a completely formed miniature human being, found in the sperm head. Part of the preformation theory, specifically the belief hel by a group of preformationists, called spermists.

Honan (Henan), province in NE China; capital is Chengchou. An ancient center of Chinese civilization (from 2000 BC), remains have been found of two capital cities of the Shang dynasty (1523–1027 BC); site of San Men Dam (1960s) and People's Victory Canal. Products: wheat, tobacco, sesame, cotton, peanuts, soybeans. Industries: coal and iron mining, aluminum, textiles. Area: 65,000sq mi (168,350sq km). Pop. 50,320,-000.

Honduras, British. *See* Belize.

Honduras, Republic of, independent nation in Central America, bounded by Nicaragua, Guatemala, El Salvador, the Caribbean, and the Pacific; its agricultural economy is largely dependent on bananas—an industry long dominated by U.S. companies—and coffee.

Land and economy. Two major mountain ranges bisect the country, with tropical lowlands along the coasts and fertile valleys between the mountain branches. The dry season, from November-May, seriously affects the growing season. The economy is agricultural, based on bananas, forestry, and fishing. Beef exports have increased in the 1970s. Timber is an important resource, along with mineral deposits and offshore oil.

People. About 90% of the population is a mixture of Caucasian and Indian (mestizo) with small minorities of Indians and blacks. Education is secular and free from ages 7–15. The literacy rate is 50%. Most Hondurans are Roman Catholic, and freedom for all creeds is guaranteed by the constitution. The annual population growth is estimated at 3.4%. Spanish is the official language, although English is spoken in the N coastal banana-growing areas.

History and Government. W Honduras was the site of the Mayan Empire for centuries. It was claimed for Spain by Christopher Columbus in 1502, joined the Central American Federation in 1821, and gained independence in 1838. Unstable regimes have marked its history; an army coup in 1972 occurred over charges that the United Fruit Co. had bribed Honduran officials. The military continued to rule until 1980 when Gen. Policarpo Paz Garcia handed the government over to a newly-elected constitutional assembly, which was to draft a new constitution and organize direct presidential elections; Gen Paz remained as provisional president. In 1982, Dr. Robert Suazo Cordova became president, and military rule ceased. Long-standing animosities with neighboring El Salvador resulted in a border conflict, the so-called "soccer war" (1969–80). Pres. José Azcona Hoyo, inaugurated in 1986, pledged to pursue peace negotiations with Nicaragua although relations were tense between the two countries due to the presence of Nicaraguan "contras" in Honduras.

PROFILE

Official name: Republic of Honduras
Area: 43,277sq mi (112,088sq km)
Population: 3,565,000
Density: 82per sq mi (32per sq km)
Chief cities: Tegucigalpa (capital); San Pedro Sula
Government: Constitutional Republic
Religion: Roman Catholic
Language: Spanish
Monetary unit: Lempira
Gross national product: $1,900,000,000
Per capita income: $528
Industries (major): textiles, chemicals, food products
Agriculture (major): bananas, beef, coffee, corn, timber
Minerals (major): gold, silver, copper, zinc
Trading partners: United States, El Salvador

H I and H II Regions, interstellar regions made up of neutral (H I) or ionized (H II) hydrogen. H I regions produce characteristic emissions of radio waves at the frequency of 21cm. H II regions, having been excited by nearby hot stars, shine optically as emission nebulae.

Honey, a thick sweet liquid, comprised primarily of the sugars levulose and dextrose, plus minerals and about 17% water. It is manufactured by honeybees, which collect nectar and partially digest it. It is then deposited in the hive cells, where the water is evaporated. It is an excellent food. *See also* Honeybee.

Honey Ant, any of several genera of ants, found worldwide, in which "repletes" are found in the caste system. The replete ant serves as a storage vessel for plant nectar and honeydew, which it later feeds back to the workers. *See also* Ant; Hymenoptera.

Honey Badger. *See* Ratel.

Honeybee. The most common honeybee is *Apis mellifera,* which has been domesticated for the production of honey. It is found worldwide and is yellow and black in color and about 0.5in (12.5mm) long. It constructs its brood and honey storage cells from wax. Family Apidae, tribe Apini. *See also* Bee; Honey.

Honey Guide, small, drab bird of Africa and S Asia that leads humans and animals to bees' nests and shares in eating the honey, a food it otherwise would not be able to obtain because of its small beak. They also obtain nourishment from beeswax. Nest parasites, the female lays her egg in the nest of another species. The young, equipped with a sharp beak tip, kills his nest mates and then eats the food provided by the foster parents. The beak tip falls off and the young honey guide develops the typical gray to green to yellowish-green adult plumage with brown and white on its tail. Length: 8in (20cm). Family Indicatoridae.

Honey Mesquite. *See* Mesquite.

Honeysuckle, woody shrubs and vines found in temperate areas worldwide. It has opposite leaves, bell-shaped, fragrant flowers, and berries eaten by birds. The North American trumpet honeysuckle *(Lonicera sempervirens)* is a woodland vine with long, tubular flowers, red outside and yellow inside. There are 200 species. Family Caprifoliaceae.

Hong Kong, British colony in S China, 90mi (145km) SE of Canton; capital is Victoria; comprised of Hong Kong Island, Kowloon Peninsula, the New Territories on the mainland, and approx. 235 islets in the South China Sea. Ceded to Britain after Chinese defeat during Opium War by terms of Treaty of Nanking (1842); peninsula was acquired 1860 and New Territories 1898. Since the est. of Communist regime in China (1950), over 3,000,000 people have immigrated to Hong Kong and live within a 40sq mi (104sq km) area. It is a major center of world commerce in the Far East due to the good harbor, administration, and absence of custom duties. Industries: agriculture, fishing, mining, tourism, textiles, plastics, electrical equipment, shipping, rope, paint, shipbuilding, tobacco, engineering, printing, publishing. Area: (total colony) 404sq mi (1,061sq km). Pop. 5,000,000.

Honolulu, capital city of Hawaii, on SE Oahu Island; seat of Honolulu co. Center of Hawaiian royalty and foreign consuls, it became the permanent capital of the kingdom of Hawaii 1845; remained capital after 1898 annexation of islands by the United States and after 1959 declaration of Hawaii as 50th state. On Dec. 7, 1941, the US naval base at Pearl Harbor was bombed by Japanese, precipitating US entry into WWII; during the war it served as strategic base and staging point for US Pacific forces. Paramount in Honolulu's development has been the rise in tourism, peacetime defense activity, expansion of harbor, diversification of industry, and construction of international airport; site of University of Hawaii (1907), Jackson College (1949), Kawaiahao Church (1841), Iolani Palace, Waikiki Beach, Punchbowl volcano, and Diamond Head crater. Industries: sugar processing, pineapple canning, tourism, defense. Pop. (1980) 365,048.

Honorius I, Roman Catholic pope (625–38). A disciple of Pope Gregory I, he continued his missionary work in England, established St Peter's Treasury, and restored many buildings in Rome. His concessions to the Byzantine Empire aligned him with the Monotheletes in the belief that Christ has only one will, as well as one nature. He was condemned a heretic, posthumously, causing controversy over the doctrine of infallibility.

Honshu, largest of four main islands in Japan, between Sea of Japan and the Pacific Ocean. Considered mainland of Japan, it produces 90% of Japan's industrial output; location of six of Japan's largest cities, including Tokyo. Industries: textiles, oil refining, rice, tea, machinery, electronics, chemicals, metals, shipbuilding, printing, publishing. Area: 89,000sq mi (230,510sq km). Pop. 82,569,581.

Hood, Mount, inactive volcano in the Cascade Range of NW Oregon; mountain climbing and skiing area; highest point in state, 11,235ft (3,427m).

Hoof-and-Mouth Disease. See Foot-and-Mouth Disease.

Hoofed Mammals. *See* Ungulate.

Hooghly, tributary of the Ganges River, in NE India; formed at the confluence of the Bhagirathi, Jalangi, and Matabhanga rivers; flows S to Bay of Bengal near Sagar Island; commercially important trade route, almost entirely navigable. Length: 160mi (258km).

Honduras

Herbert Hoover

J. Edgar Hoover

Hooke, Robert (1635–1703), English philosopher and experimental physicist. Active in astronomy, he determined the center of gravity of the moon and earth; implied that Jupiter rotated; indicated the 5th star in Orion; and built a Gregorian telescope. In other fields he described the nature of combustion, was the first to use the word "cell," made a compound microscope, and utilized balance springs in watches. His law of elasticity bears his name.

Hooker, Thomas (1586–1647), English colonist and Puritan clergyman. He left England for Holland and then New England (1633), seeking religious freedom. Pastor of first church of Cambridge, Mass., he was discontented with conditions there and led colonists to found and settle Hartford, Conn. (1636). He helped cause the adoption of the "Fundamental Orders of Connecticut" (1639), considered to be the first constitution in America. He also was an organizer of the New England Confederation. *See also* New England Confederation.

Hooke's Law, the proportionality between the force *F* applied to a spring and the distance *x* that it stretches: $F = kx$, where k is a constant describing the strength of the spring. *See also* Elasticity; Hooke, Robert.

Hookworm, roundworm common in warmer areas of the world, parasitic in man. Usually contracted when the larva penetrates the host's skin, it then migrates to the intestine where it causes anemia, laziness, and lack of physical and mental energy. Phylum Nematoda; species *Necator americanus* (tropical) and *Ancylostoma duodenale* (Europe and Asia).

Hooper, William (1742–90), American patriot and a signer of the Declaration of Independence, b. Boston, Mass. He was a member of the North Carolina state assembly (1773) and later served in the Continental Congress (1774–77).

Hoopoe, zebra-striped, fawn-colored bird that lives in open areas, city parks, and lawns throughout Old World warmer areas. It has a fanlike crest and long, curved bill. It utters a "hoo-hoo-hoo" call and feeds on small invertebrates. Nesting in a tree cavity or under a stone, the female defends herself and her brood—pale blue or whitish eggs (4–8)—by emitting a foul-smelling, blackish-brown liquid from a tail gland. Length: 1ft (30cm). Family Upupidae; species *Upupa epops*.

Hoop Snake. *See* Mud Snake.

Hoover, Herbert Clark (1874–1964), 31st president of the United States, b. West Branch, Iowa; graduate, Stanford University, 1895. In 1899 he married Lou Henry; they had two sons. Hoover was a highly successful mining engineer and operated as an international mining consultant in many parts of the world. During World War I and in the postwar period, he was widely acclaimed for his humanitarian work in relief for war refugees. He headed numerous relief organizations and was US Food Administrator.

Hoover served as secretary of commerce in the administrations of both Presidents Harding and Coolidge. He won the Republican nomination for president in 1928 and easily defeated Democrat Alfred E. Smith. Hoover's presidency began only months before the Great Depression, which was triggered by the stock market crash of October 1929. As a conservative who believed the economy to be in basic good health, he opposed massive government intervention, although he did establish the Reconstruction Finance Corporation. As the economy worsened, Hoover's popularity decreased.

In 1932 about 15,000 veterans, known as the Bonus Marchers, converged in protest against Washington, and Hoover used federal troops to disperse them. He ran for reelection in 1932 but was soundly defeated by Franklin Delano Roosevelt.
Career: chairman, Commission for Relief in Belgium, 1915–19; US Food Administrator, 1917–18; American Relief Administrator, 1919–23; secretary of commerce, 1921–29; president, 1929–33.

Hoover, J(ohn) Edgar (1895–1972), director of the Federal Bureau of Investigation (1924–72), b. Washington, D.C. He worked as a file reviewer for the Department of Justice (1917) and became assistant director of the Bureau of Investigation in 1921. He reorganized the bureau, compiling a vast fingerprint file and building a crime laboratory and training academy. Capture of notorious criminals in the 1930s brought fame and glamour to Hoover's FBI. After the bureau became the Federal Bureau of Investigation (1935), he concentrated on fighting Communism and investigating threats to internal security. He continued in office, by special presidential dispensation, beyond retirement age. He wrote *Masters of Deceit* (1958) and *J. Edgar Hoover on Communism* (1962).

Hoover Dam, one of the world's largest dams, on the Colorado River between Arizona and Nevada. Built by US Bureau of Reclamation, it opened in 1936; irrigates 650,000acres (263,250hectares) in S California and Arizona. Height: 726ft (221m). Length: 1,244ft (379m).

Hop, rough, twining vine native to North America, South America, and Eurasia. It has rough stems, heart-shaped leaves, and small male and female flowers borne on separate plants. The female catkins are covered with lupulin, a yellow powder used as a sedative. The dried female flowers of *Humulus lupulus* are used for flavoring beer. Family Moraceae.

Hopeh (Hopei, or **Hebei),** province in NE China, on the Gulf of Chihli in Yellow Sea; capital is Shih-chia-chuang; remains of Peking man found here indicate Hopeh has been inhabited for at least 500,000 years. After the 14th century there was much agricultural development, due to the introduction of cotton cultivation and extended irrigation works; industrial development was aided after WWI by British and Japanese funding. In 1928 the Chinese Nationalists added parts of Chahar and Jehol provs. to Hopeh. Crops: cotton, wheat, soybeans, corn, millet, sweet potatoes, fruits, nuts, rice, oilseeds. Industries: chemicals, steel, machines, textiles. Area: 75,000sq mi (194,250sq km). Pop. 41,-410,000.

Hopewell Culture, culture centered in Ohio and Illinois, and reaching its peak in the last centuries BC and the first four centuries AD. Hopewell people were efficient farmers, built complex earthworks, such as the serpent mounds of Ohio, for ceremonial and business purposes, and traded extensively. *See also* Cahokia Mounds.

Hop Hornbeam, slow-growing, ornamental tree native to North America and Eurasia. It has scaly bark, translucent leaves, and green hoplike cones. The American hop hornbeam *(Ostrya virginiana)* is also called ironwood, because of its hard, heavy wood used for fence posts. Height: to 70ft (21m). There are seven species. Family Betulaceae.

Hopi, from Hópitu, meaning "the peaceful people," a Shoshonean-speaking tribe of North American Indians, the only such group to take on a Pueblo culture. They are famous for having retained the purest form of pre-Columbian life to survive in the United States today.

About 6,000 Hopi people inhabit 11 villages in Coconino co, Arizona, on three mesas north of Winslow. In 1981, 1.8 million acres (725,000 hectares) in Arizona were partitioned equally between the Hopi and Navaho Indians. Some relocation of both tribes was necessary.

Hopkins, Stephen (1707–85), American legislator and a signer of the Declaration of Independence, b. Providence, R.I. Governor of Rhode Island (1755–67), he later took part in the formation of the Navy and attended the general congress in Philadelphia (1774–76).

Hopkinson, Francis (1737–91), US political figure, poet, musician, and signer of the Declaration of Independence, b. Philadelphia. He composed the first secular song by a native Amerian, "My Days Have Been So Wondrous Free" (1759), and his satirical poem, "The Battle of the Kegs" (1778), was popular during the American Revolution. He represented New Jersey in the Continental Congress (1776), was judge of the admiralty in Pennsylvania (1779–89) and US district court judge (1789–91), and urged adoption of the Constitution. One of his final musical scores was *Seven Songs for the Harpsichord* (1788).

Hopper, Edward (1882–1967), US painter, b. Nyack, N.Y. A pupil of Robert Henri and greatly influenced by the Ashcan School, he was a realistic painter of the American scene. Hopper often placed lonely figures in his carefully drawn settings. Many scenes were of New York City and New England. *See also* Ashcan School.

Horace (65–8 BC), Roman poet, b. as Quintus Horatius Flaccus. Although he fought at Philippi (42 BC) with Brutus, he won favor in Augustan Rome. His friend Vergil introduced him to Maecenas, who as his patron provided him with an income and a farm. Horace's first *Satires* appeared in 35 BC, followed by *Epodes* (30 BC), *Odes* (c.24 BC), *Epistles* (c.20 BC), and *Ars Poetica* (c.13 BC). His simple, direct Latin lyrics provided a vivid picture of the Augustan age.

Horehound, or hoarhound, common name for *Marrubium vulgare,* an aromatic herb of the mint family found in Eurasia and as a roadside weed in North America. Its woolly white leaves are used for flavoring cough lozenges and candies.

Horizon, in geology, a term used in two ways; first, a continuous horizontal surface or time-plane between two strata that has no thickness, and second, a horizontal layer from a few inches to a foot in thickness that is characterized either by a distinct fossilized flora or fauna or by a particular mineral.

Horizon, Celestial, great circle on the celestial sphere, the plane of which contains the line through an observer's position at right angles to the vertical. It lies midway between the observer's zenith and nadir and cuts the observer's meridian at the north and south points.

Horizon, Soil. *See* Soil Profile.

Hormones, chemical substances, secreted by the endocrine, or ductless, glands of the body directly into the bloodstream. Hormones exercise chemical control of body functions, regulating virtually all body functions—growth, development, sexual maturity and functioning, metabolism, emotional balance (in part), and so on. Hormones circulate in the body in very small amounts and often exert their effects (on target organs, for example) at great distances from their point of secretion. They are somewhat slow to take effect, exert widespread action, and are also somewhat slow to disappear from the system. The secretion and activity of the various hormones are closely interdependent, with one stimulating or inhibiting secretion of another, with two or more acting together to produce a certain effect—in general maintaining an extremely delicate equilibrium that is important to health and well being. Too much or too little of any particular hormone, caused by disease or malfunction of the secreting endocrine gland, usually produces body abnormality or disease. In many cases this can be treated by administration of hormone or by correcting the endocrine gland disorder. There are numerous hormones. Some of the best known are thyroxin, adrenalin, insulin, estrogen, progesterone, testosterone. *See also* Endocrine System and separate articles on the various endocrine glands; on specific hormones; on hormonal diseases.

Hormuz (Ormuz), Strait of, strait between N end of Oman, SE Arabian Peninsula and S coast of Iran; connects the Persian Gulf with the Gulf of Oman.

Horn, a defensive or offensive structure—generally elongated and pointed—growing from the head region of some mammals. Considered a skin appendage, a typical horn is made up of a central bony core that is covered by a sheath of the skin protein keratin; in the rhinoceros, the entire horn is made of keratin. Horns typically grow during the entire life of the animal. *See also* Antler.

Hornbeam, small, hardy tree found throughout the Northern Hemisphere. It has smooth bark, a short trunk, spreading branches, and clusters of green nuts. The American hornbeam *(Carpinus caroliniana)* is sometimes known as blue beech. Family Betulaceae.

Hornbill, tropical African and Australasian brownish and black-and-white bird, named for its swollen, brightly-colored bill, often having folds and a horny hood. They also have long eyelashes. The female lays eggs (1–4) in a high tree trunk cavity and then uses droppings, mud, and regurgitated food to erect a barricade, imprisoning herself and her eggs for 6–16 weeks. The male feeds her through a tiny slit in the barricade wall. Length: 15–60in (38–152cm). Family Bucerotidae.

Hornbook, children's primer of the late 16th to late 18th centuries. The hornbook consisted of a sheet of paper mounted on a wooden frame shaped like a paddle and held by a handle. The paper contained the alphabet in small and large letters and, often, the vowels and consonants, the Lord's Prayer, and Roman numerals.

Horned Owl, owl with hornlike feather tufts on its head, yellow eyes, and a frightening call. Fierce and strong, they feed on rodents, hares, and other small mammals. The eagle owl *(Bubo bubo)* is the largest European owl; the great horned owl *(Bubo virginianus)* is a typical North American species. Length: over 2ft (61cm). *See also* Owl.

Horned Rattlesnake. *See* Sidewinder.

Horned Ray. *See* Devilfish.

Horned Toad, or horned lizard, insect-eating lizard found in dry, open areas in W North America. It is sand-colored and has spines on head and body and a stumpy tail. Despite its formidable appearance it is harmless and makes a good pet. Length: 3–5in (7.6–12.8cm). There are 14 species. Family Iguanidae; genus *Phrynosoma. See also* Lizard.

Horned Viper, or horned asp, poisonous snake native to deserts of N Africa and Arabia. It is stocky, brown with black markings, and has a sharp, pointed scale over each eye. It sinks vertically into the sand. Length: to 2ft (61cm). Family Viperidae; species *Cerastes cerastes. See also* Viper.

Hornet. *See* Wasp.

Horns, family of wind musical instruments of ancient, universal origin, first used for signaling and ceremonies. Once made from animal horns and later from tractable metals, they have usually been made of brass since the Renaissance. They appeared in the opera orchestras of 17th-century Europe. The horn is the ancestor of the trumpet, trombone, tuba, baritone horn, which are instruments developed in the early 19th century by Adolphe Sax of Brussels. Sax added pistons and slides for playing chromatics to the traditional tubes with flaring bells and cupped or funnel-shaped mouthpieces.

Horse, hoofed mammal that evolved in North America but became extinct during late Pleistocene Epoch. Early horse forms crossed the Bering land bridge, radiated throughout Asia, Europe, and Africa and produced the modern horse family. The only surviving true wild horse is Przewalski's wild horse. Hunted by Paleolithic man for food, the horse was first domesticated about 5,000 years ago in Central Asia. Horses returned to the New World with the Spanish conquistadors in the 1500s.

Horses are characterized by one large functional toe and two side toes reduced to splints, molars with crowns joined by ridges for grazing, elongated skull, and simple stomach. Fast runners, they usually live in herds and walk, canter, trot, or gallop. Gestation is 11–12 months; one colt is born and it can walk at birth. Modern horse breeds are divided into two groups: *light* horse, for riding, racing, and driving, and *draft* horse, massive work animal. All species in the family can interbreed. The true horse is distinguished from other equines (zebras and asses) by its short ears, small head, and chestnuts (horny, wartlike growths on the inside hind legs), large hooves, and hair-covered tail. Family Equidae; species *Equus caballus.*

Horse Chestnut, or buckeye, tree native to temperate and tropical regions. The 15 deciduous *Aesculus* species include the common horse chestnut *Aesculus hippocastanum* that has large, palmate leaves, long, showy flower spikes, and large, spiny nuts containing two inedible kernels. They tolerate urban pollution and salt spray of seaside areas. Height: to 100ft (30.5m). The two *Billia* species are evergreen and native from S Mexico to Colombia. Family Hippocastanaceae.

Horsefly, black fly, 0.8 to 1.2in (20 to 30mm) long, a pest of man and other animals; found worldwide. The female has bladelike mouthparts and gives a painful bite. Family Tabanidae, species *Tabanus spp. See also* Deer Fly.

Horsehair Worm, hair worm or thread worm, long, thin worms with featureless body, usually black or brown. The young are parasitic in insects and the adults are free-living in soil or fresh water. Length: to 31.5in (800mm). Phylum Nematomorpha.

Horsehead Nebula, dark nebula forming part of the Orion Nebula (M42) and obscuring some of its light. The dark matter strikingly resembles a horse's head.

Horse Mackerel, commercial marine food fish found in the Atlantic from the North Sea to Africa. Blue-green and silver with a white belly, it travels in schools. Family Carangidae (jack, scad, and pompano); species *Trachurus trachurus.* See also Osteichthyes.

Horsepower, a unit indicating the rate at which work is done, adapted by James Watt in the 18th century. He defined it as the weight (550lb) a horse could raise 1ft in 1 second, or 550ft-lb per second. At the output shaft of an engine or motor, it is termed "brake horsepower," or "shaft horsepower." In large reciprocating engines, it is termed "indicating horsepower" and is determined from pressure in the cylinders. The electrical equivalent of one horsepower is 746 watts.

Horse Racing, sport that consists of speed trials between two or more horses over an oval circuit. Most popular is thoroughbred racing, where the rider sits in a saddle atop the horse. The types of races include flat racing (on dirt), turf racing (on grass), and steeplechase racing (over an obstacled course with hurdles and water holes). Distances vary from three furlongs (for two-year-olds) and upward, and include a variety of races, by either age, sex, or weight (handicap). In the United States the horses start from a closed chute. Wagering is allowed via a parimutuel betting system, which pays off on first- second- and third-place finishers, as well as in other combinations of play (picking the first, second finishers, etc).

History. Horse racing began in Egypt around 1500 BC. Organized racing was popular in England among royalty in the 12th century. The oldest race is the Epsom Derby, which originated in England in 1780, and the most famous race is the Grand National Steeplechase, held annually at Liverpool, England, since 1939. In the United States, most popular is the Triple Crown for three-year-olds. which includes the Kentucky Derby, Preakness, and Belmont Stakes.

Horseradish, plant native to Europe and cultivated for its pungent, fleshy root used as a seasoning. It has escaped cultivation and is widespread as a weed. A coarse plant with lance-shaped, toothed leaves, it has white flower clusters at the plant top and egg-shaped seedpods. Height: to 3ft (91cm). Family Cruciferae; species *Armoracia lapathifolia.*

Horseshoe Crab, marine arthropod found on Atlantic and Gulf of Mexico coasts of United States and Asian coasts from Japan to Philippine Islands. Its horseshoe-shaped carapace is jointed to a spiny abdomen and ends in a long, stout spine. It has five pairs of walking legs and can swim upside down. Length: to 24in (61cm). Class Merostomata, genus *Limulus. See also* Arthropod.

Horseshoe Pitching, a game played by two or more persons using horseshoes on an outdoor court. The court is usually 50ft (15.2m) long and 10ft (3m) wide. The actual pitching distance is 40 feet (12.2m) for men and 30 feet (9.1m) for women. The object is to encircle an iron peg 1ft (0.3m) high that is set into the ground at either end of the court. A game consists of 50 points. Encircling the peg (ringer) is three points, leaning against the peg is two points, and each horseshoe closer to the peg (within 6in; 15.2cm) than that of an opponent's is one point. The game originated with Greek and Roman soldiers. The National Horseshoe Pitchers of the United States (formed 1914) oversees the professional aspect of the sport. Amateur competition is governed by the Amateur Athletic Union. *See also* Quoits.

Horsetail, or scouring rush, any of about 25 species of small, flowerless, rushlike plants (genus *Equisetum*) that occur on all continents except Australia. The hollow, round-jointed stems have a whorl of tiny leaves at each joint. Because of their high silica content, horsetails are very abrasive and were formerly used for polishing wood and scouring pots. Horsetails have existed for more than 300,000,000 years, and their fossils are found in coal from the Carboniferous period.

Horthy, Miklós von Nagybánya (1868–1957), Hungarian admiral and statesman, commander of the Austro-Hungarian fleet in World War I, regent of Hungary, 1920–44. At the end of World War I Horthy returned to Hungary to organize a counterrevolution against Béla Kun's Bolshevik government. As regent and head of state, he suppressed all political opposition and resisted the return of Charles I, deposed Austro-Hungarian emperor. Through his efforts, Hungary joined the Axis Powers in 1941. When Hungary was occupied by German troops in 1944, Horthy was deposed.

Horticulture, the cultivation of garden, orchard, and nursery crops. It includes fruit growing (pomology), the production of vegetables (olericulture), production of flowers (floriculture), and ornamental horticulture (landscape gardening). Horticulture became a major industry in 17th-century Europe, when the growth of large urban areas made it impractical for individuals to produce necessary garden crops on their own land.

Horus, falcon-headed god of ancient Egypt, son of Isis and Osiris. In the myths, he came to rule earth after avenging the murder of his father. Horus is closely identified with all the pharaohs of Egypt, who used his name as the first of their titles and were thought to rule as him on earth, and after death, as his father Osiris in the underworld.

Hosea, biblical author and first of the 12 minor prophets. He condemned Israel for worshiping false gods and promised mercy to the faithful.

Hospice, an organization designed to help people who are dying. A typical hospice team consists of nurses, social workers, members of the clergy, and others who can give medical, psychological, and other kinds of help to the dying person and his or her family. Some patients receive hospice care while staying at home. In other cases, patients may stay at a hospice, or at the hospice unit of a hospital.

Hospitalet, city in NE Spain; suburb of Barcelona; site of agricultural institute. Industries: steel, textiles, chemicals. Pop. 241,978.

Hospitallers. *See* Knights Hospitallers.

Hosta, or plantain lily, funkia, perennial plant native to E Asia and Japan. They have veined leaves and lilylike flowers ranging from white to blue to lilac. Family Liliaceae; genus *Hosta.*

Hot Bed, or hot frame, heated, wood or concrete, outdoor ground frame covered with glass or plastic doors used by gardeners to extend the growing season. Heat is supplied by an underground heating cable, steam, hot water, or fermenting manure covered with fine soil. Temperature can be as high as 90°F (32°C) in this structure and seedlings can be grown throughout the year.

Hot Springs, city in W central Arkansas, 47mi (76km) WSW of Little Rock; seat of Garland co., in Ouachita Mts; site of health resort with 47 thermal springs; national park, 1921. Settled 1807; inc. 1851. Pop. (1980) 35,166.

Hottentot, or Khoikhoi, Khoisan-speaking people of southern Africa, now almost extinct; characteristically of short stature, with a dark yellowish skin, probably of

Hornbill

Hottentot fig

Sam Houston

mixed Bushman and Negro origin. Traditionally they were nomadic pastoralists. Many of them were displaced or exterminated by the early Dutch settlers; their surviving descendants have mostly been absorbed into the Cape colored population.

Hottentot Bread. *See* Elephant's-foot.

Hottentot Fig, succulent vine found on deserts and seashores in warm regions and cultivated as a ground cover. Not a true fig, it has woody stems with succulent leaves and large, daisylike, yellow or rose-purple flowers. The fig-shaped fruits are edible but not tasty. Family Aizoaceae; species *Carpobrotus edulis*.

Houdini (1874–1926), US magician, b. Erich Weiss in Appleton, Wisc. No packing case or set of handcuffs could contain this escape artist, who also specialized in exposing fraudulent mediums in print. Author of *The Unmasking of Robert-Houdin* (1908), he had an extensive library on magic now in the Library of Congress.

Houdon, Jean-Antoine (1741–1828), French sculptor. He was a leading portrait sculptor, best known for his busts, including many of American Revolutionary leaders. They were executed in a classical style and reflected an individualistic treatment of character.

Hounds, dogs that hunt by sight or by ground scent. Sight-hunters are coursing hounds; they chase quarry at great speed and overtake and kill or capture it. Probably man's oldest hunting companions, they are tall, have long legs, deep chests, and long heads. Large enough to take down elk and deer, they include the Saluki, Afghan, Irish wolfhound, and greyhound. Ground-scenters, or tailing hounds, follow game by ground scent and flush it. They have large noses, long ears, shorter legs, and are usually black, tan, red, and white. Examples are the bloodhound, beagle, and basenji.

Hour Angle, angle measured westward along the celestial equator from the observer's meridian to the line passing through a celestial body and the celestial poles (hour circle of the body). It is given in hours, minutes, and seconds and ranges from 0 to 24 hours.

Hour Glass Sea. *See* Syrtis Major.

Housatonic, river in W Massachusetts; rises near Pittsfield in the Berkshire Mts; flows S through W Connecticut to Long Island Sound at Stratford. Length: 130mi (209km).

Housefly, black and gray fly, 0.24 to 0.28in (6–7mm) long, that breeds in animal waste and decaying vegetable matter. This species, with several closely related species, is found worldwide. Because of their breeding habits, and because they also feed on human food, they transmit several diseases, including typhoid, yaws, tuberculosis, and various intestinal protozoa. Family Muscidae, species *Musca domestica. See also* Blowfly; Diptera.

Household Equilibrium, or consumer equilibrium, in economics, condition that occurs when the consumer allocates his income between the purchase of various goods and services in such a way that he obtains the highest level of satisfaction (utility). While he may choose between alternative goods, substituting one for another, the consumer's total bundle of goods is limited by his total income or budget, ie, the budget constraint.

Houseleek. *See* Hens and Chicks.

House of Commons, lower house of the bicameral British parliament and the repository of virtually all legislative authority. The power of the House of Commons is rooted in its control of financial matters. The Commons has 635 members—516 from England, 36 from Wales, 71 from Scotland, and 12 from Northern Ireland. Members are elected either at large or as representatives of specific districts and serve terms of no more than five years. A general election may be called before that time if the prime minister (the leader of the majority party in the Commons) cannot secure a majority on important issues. Although the Commons originated in the 13th century, it did not achieve complete legislative supremacy until the Parliamentary Act of 1911 removed from the House of Lords its veto power over money bills. *See also* House of Lords; Parliament, British.

House of Lords, upper house of the British parliament, having both legislative and judicial functions. In its legislative capacity the Lords have been completely subordinate to the House of Commons since the Parliament acts of 1911 and 1949 checked virtually all its power except the delay passage of a bill for a year. It has no absolute veto over Commons legislation. All bills except for appropriation may be initiated by the Lords. Life peers, whose titles may not be inherited, and hereditary peers sit in the House. Hereditary peers may resign their titles to run for election to the Commons. There are special "law lords" who act as judges when the house acts as Great Britain's highest court. *See also* House of Commons; Parliament, British.

House of Representatives, one of the two chambers of the US Congress and part of the legislative branch of the federal government. The House was intended to represent the popular will and its members are directly elected. Total membership is fixed at 435, with representatives serving two-year terms. A representative must be at least 25, a US citizen for 7 years, and a resident of the state from which he or she is elected. Certain exclusive powers are delegated to the House by the Constitution. The primary ones are the authority to originate revenue bills, the right to initiate impeachment proceedings, and the power to elect the president in case of a tie or lack of majority in the electoral college. The presiding speaker is a leader of the majority party. Each party has a floor leader who manages party programs. The committee system is a dominant feature of the House and has the power to control proposed bills. Bills passed by the House are sent to the Senate for consideration. *See also* Congress of the United States; Senate of the United States.

House-Tree-Person Technique, in psychology, a projective technique devised by J.N. Buck and used to assess personality characteristics. The subject is asked to draw, in turn, pictures of a house, tree, and person. Interpretations of the drawings are assumed to reveal the subject's attitudes toward his home (house), his unconscious self (tree), and his ideal self (person). The technique is used in the diagnosis of mental disorders in both adults and children. *See also* Projective Techniques.

Housing and Urban Development, Department of (HUD), US federal cabinet-level department within the executive branch. It was created in 1965. The purpose of HUD is to assist in the growth and development of urban communities and metropolitan areas, so that they provide decent housing, a suitable living environment, and expanding economic opportunities. HUD's programs include Community Planning Development, Housing Production and Mortgage Credit, Federal Di-

saster Assistance, and Federal Insurance. It is directed by the secretary of Housing and Urban Development.

Housman, A(lfred) E(dward) (1859–1935), English poet and classical scholar. Although he devoted his life to scholarship, he is best known as the author of two small volumes of poetry, *A Shropshire Lad* (1896) and *Last Poems* (1922).

Houston, Samuel (1793–1863), US soldier and statesman, b. Lexington, Va. He lived with the Cherokee Indians for three years, and later took an Indian wife. In the War of 1812, he fought with Andrew Jackson against the Creeks. He was a congressman from Tennessee (1823–27) and governor (1827–29). Moving to Texas, he became commander-in-chief of the Texas army (1835). The successful battle at San Jacinto (1836) against Santa Anna's Mexican army assured his reputation. He was the first president of Texas, serving 1836–38 and 1841–44. When Texas became a state (1845) he was its first senator (1846–59). His pro-Union stance isolated him and when Texas voted to secede (1861), he was removed from office and retired.

Houston, industrial city and port of entry in SE Texas, 25mi (40km) NW of Galveston Bay, connected to the Gulf of Mexico by Houston Ship Canal; seat of Harris co. The largest city in Texas, it served as capital of Republic of Texas 1837–39, 1842–45; ship canal was completed 1914 and city developed as a deepwater port. Coastal oil fields, natural gas, sulfur, salt, limestone for chemical production, demand for shipbuilding in WWII, and est. of NASA's Manned Space Center led to Houston's tremendous growth. It is the site of World Trade Center (1962), Houston International Airport (1969), Manned Space Center (1961), Astrodome (1965), Rice University (1891), Texas Southern University (1927), University of Houston (1934), University of St Thomas (1947), Sam Houston Historical Park. Exports: petroleum products, cotton, rice, lumber. Industries: oil and oil refining, natural gas, synthetic rubber, meat packing, printing, publishing, sugar and rice processing, agriculture, chemicals, steel, electronic equipment, oil well machinery. Founded 1836 and named for Sam Houston; inc. and made co. seat 1837. Pop. (1980) 1,594,086.

Hovercraft. *See* Air-Cushion Vehicle.

Howard, prominent English family, particularly in the Tudor era; dukes of Norfolk and earls of Surrey. John Howard was named 1st duke of Norfolk by Richard III (1483). He was killed at Bosworth (1485). His son (1443–1524) and grandson (1473–1554), both called Thomas, conquered the Scots at Flodden (1513). Thomas II's son, Henry, Earl of Surrey, was executed on trumped-up treason charges (1542). The fourth duke (1536–72) also was executed for treason. Catherine Howard married Henry VIII.

Howard, Catherine (1520?–42), fifth queen of Henry VIII, granddaughter of Thomas, 2nd duke of Norfolk. Henry married her in July 1540, but evidence of premarital unchastity was produced against her (November 1541). She was beheaded in February 1542.

Howard, Charles. *See* Carlisle, Charles Howard, Earl of.

Howard, Charles, 1st Earl of Nottingham. *See* Nottingham, Charles Howard, 1st Earl of.

Howard, Frederick, 5th Earl of Carlisle (1748–1825), English politician and writer. One of the commissioners sent to America by Lord North in 1778, he tried to reconcile the Colonies with England. He was viceroy of Ireland (1780–82) and guardian of Lord Byron (1798). In addition to writing political tracts, he also was the author of a group of poems and two tragedies.

Howard, Oliver Otis (1830–1909), US military leader, b. Leeds, Maine. He fought in the battles of Bull Run, Fair Oaks (where he lost his right arm), Antietam, Fredericksburg, Chancellorsville (where he was defeated by Stonewall Jackson), and Gettysburg. As commander of the Army of the Tennessee, he accompanied Sherman's troops through Georgia. At the war's close, he headed the Freemen's Bureau during Reconstruction, that helped and protected Southern blacks. He was a founder and president (1869–73) of Howard University, superintendent of the US Military Academy at West Point (1881–82), and directed campaigns against the Indians.

Howe, Elias (1819–67), US inventor, b. Spencer, Mass. Trained as a machinist, he invented the sewing machine. His first patent was in 1846, but it was 1854 before he cleared his titles legally and became wealthy from his invention. In the Civil War, he served as a private and used his own money to support the regiment.

Howe, Julia Ward (1819–1910), US author, lecturer, and suffragist, b. New York City. She is best known as author of the "Battle Hymn of the Republic," which first appeared in the *Atlantic Monthly* during the Civil War. In 1843 she married the Boston educator Samuel Gridley Howe. She was an active campaigner for women's rights, and also wrote books, stories, and poems.

Howe, Richard Howe, Earl (1726–99), British admiral. After notable service in the Rochefort expedition (1757) and at Quiberon Bay (1759), he commanded the British navy in North America early in the American Revolution, supporting his brother, Gen. William Howe. He won the famous First of June naval victory (1794) against the French and was appointed admiral of the fleet in 1796.

Howe, Samuel Gridley (1801–76), US educator of the blind, b. Boston. He first received blind students as pupils in his father's house on Pleasant Street in Boston. This was the beginning of the now famous Perkins School for the Blind, of which he was first director (1832–76). He also took an interest in the treatment of mentally defective children and campaigned for prison reform and abolition of slavery. His wife was Julia Ward Howe, author of "The Battle Hymn of the Republic" and active in the woman suffrage movement and in movements for international peace.

Howe, William Howe, Fifth Viscount (1729–1814), British general. Despite his disagreement with the British policy in North America, he was sent to Boston (1775) and fought in the Battle of Bunker Hill. From 1775 to 1778 he commanded British forces in North America, scoring some successes. Lack of support from Britain led him to resign (May 1778).

Howells, William Dean (1837–1920), US novelist and critic, pioneer of American literary realism, b. Martins Ferry, Ohio. As assistant editor (1866–71) and editor (1871–81) of *The Atlantic Monthly,* Howells promoted the works of Henry James, Mark Twain, and others. *Their Wedding Journey* (1872) and *A Chance Acquaintance* (1873), two of the first realistic novels of ordinary middle-class life in the United States, brought little critical reaction, but *The Rise of Silas Lapham* (1885), his best known work, brought national recognition. In the "Editor's Study" (1886–91) and the "Easy Chair" (1900–20) of *Harper's* magazine, his essays and criticisms continued to promote European and American realist writers.

Some of Howells' novels that depict American life include *A Modern Instance* (1882), *Indian Summer* (1886), *A Hazard of New Fortunes* (1890), and *The Quality of Mercy* (1892). His socialist sympathies are reflected in the novels *A Traveler from Altruia* (1894) and *Through the Eye of the Needle* (1907). At the time of his departure from *The Atlantic Monthly* in 1881, Howells was one of the most influential figures in American literary life, but long before his death he was considered out of fashion, his realism genteel, and his optimism unjustified. *See also* Realism.

Howitzer, a projectile-firing artillery piece that, because of its low muzzle velocity, is capable of curved fire and hence may reach targets hidden to high-velocity guns. Howitzers were first used in the late 16th century.

Howler Monkey, Central and South American monkey noted for the loud penetrating call of the male. The largest New World monkeys, they are gregarious tree dwellers and feed chiefly on leaves. Height: to 36in (91cm); weight: to 20lb (9kg). Genus *Alouatta. See also* Monkey.

Howrah, city in E India, on Hooghly River opposite Calcutta; seat of Howrah district. Industries: iron, steel, food processing, textiles, jute. Pop. 599,740.

Hoxha, Enver (1908–85), Albanian Communist leader. Educated in French schools, he taught French until his articles criticizing the Albanian government led to his dismissal from his post in 1934. Hoxha led the underground resistance movement to the 1939 Italian invasion and occupation and in 1941 established the National Liberation Front. In 1946, when Albania became a people's republic, he became premier. Hoxha resigned the premiership in 1954 to become first secretary of the central committee. In 1960 Hoxha quarreled with Russia and led his country into a close relationship with the People's Republic of China. Relations with China were strained from 1976 and closer ties were attained with Yugoslavia, Italy, and Greece by the early 1980s.

Hoyle, Edmond (1672–1769), English writer on card games. His works became widely accepted as the highest authority on the games. His *A Short Treatise on the Game of Whist* (1742) and his treatises on backgammon and chess are still used. His name in the expression "according to Hoyle" is also still used to convey a sense of authority.

Hoyle, (Sir) Fred (1915–   ), British astronomer and cosmologist. He worked with Thomas Gold and Hermann Bondi on the development of the steady-state theory at Cambridge, subsequently (1966) becoming director of the Institute of Theoretical Astronomy. He held academic posts in the United States and also wrote several books, including science-fiction novels. *See also* Steady-State Theory.

Hradec Králové, city in N Czechoslovakia, 60mi (97km) E of Prague, on Elbe River; capital of Východo český district. Prosperous area during Middle Ages, it suffered during the Hussite and Thirty Years wars; made a bishopric 1653; scene of the nearby Battle of Königgrätz (1866). It is the site of two medieval marketplaces, 14th-century town hall and cathedral, 17th-century palace, medical school (1946). Industries: photographic equipment, musical instruments, chemicals, machinery. Founded 10th century. Pop. 66,744.

H-R Diagram. *See* Hertzsprung-Russell Diagram.

Hsi (Si or West River), river in S China; rises in Yunnan prov. at confluence of the Hungshui and Yu (Siang) rivers; flows generally E through Kwangsi and Kwangtung provs. to South China Sea at Canton, forming a vast delta with the Chu (Pearl) River. The delta is a rich agricultural and densely populated area. River is navigable for most of its 1,250mi (2,013km).

Hsia Dynasty (2205?–1766? BC), the legendary earliest period of dynastic rule in China.

Hsian (Xi'an), city in central China, 80mi (129km) N of the confluence of the Wei and Yellow rivers; capital of Shensi prov. Formerly called Hsien-yang, capital of China under Shih Hwang Ti (247–210 BC); it was called Changan under the Western Han dynasty (202 BC–AD 9), and Siking under the Tiang dynasty (618–907). It was the first seat of Buddhism, Judaism, Islam, and Nestorian Christianity in China; Empress Dowager and Emperor Kuang Hsü fled to Hsian after the Boxer Rebellion (1900–02). Chiang Kai-shek kidnapped here (1936), resulting in agreement for united front with the Communists. It is the site of Northwestern University (1937), Northwestern Institute of Technology (1960); within city walls (1368–1644), there are many notable palaces, temples, and historical ruins. Industries: textiles, iron, steel, thermoelectricity, cotton, chemicals, cement. Pop. 1,600,000.

Hsiang (Xiang), navigable river in SE central China; rises in NE Kwangsi Chuang, flows N into Tung-t'ing Hu Lake; a N-S trade route; highly developed agricultural valley. Mineral resources include coal, antimony, and lead. Length: 715mi (1,151km).

Hsiangt'an (Xiangtan), port city in SE China, 20mi (32km) SSW of Ch'angsha, on Xiang River; Mao Tsetung was born nearby. Industries: tea processing, rice, cotton, herbs, coal mining. Pop. 300,000.

Hsinchu, city in NW Taiwan, Republic of China, 40mi (64km) SW of T'aipei; commercial center. Industries: oil refining, fertilizers, textiles, agriculture. Founded early 18th century by Chinese settlers from mainland. Pop. 201,678.

Hsining (Xining), city in W China, approx. 100mi (161km) NW of Lanchow on Hsining River; capital of Tsinghai prov. Industrial growth was spurred by completion of highway to rich Tsaidam basin, and by the completion of railroad system 1959; distribution center for agricultural produce. Industries: chemicals, machinery, flour milling, meat packing, textiles, coal mining. Pop. 250,000.

Hsüan Tsung (685–762), Chinese emperor (reigned 713–56) of the T'ang dynasty. Also known as Ming Huang ("The Enlightened Emperor"), he provided the empire with one of its most important periods of wealth, grandeur, and cultural brilliance. His rule is known as the golden age of Chinese poetry. He abdicated when confronted by revolts.

Hsüchou (Xüzhou), city in E central China, 175mi (282km) W of Yellow Sea; transportation center. Industries: iron and coal mining, steel, tools, food processing. Pop. 1,500,000.

Hsü Shên (AD 55?–149), author of the first Chinese dictionary. Although he employed a complicated system of character arrangement, he ended the chaos created by the absence of a dictionary. His work also helped Chinese writers to understand their language heritage.

Huai (Hwai), river in E China; rises in the Tungpeh Mts; flows into the Yellow River; irrigates a rich agricultural region. Length: 350mi (564km).

Huainan, city in E China, approx. 110mi (177km) NW of Nanking; China's major coal mining center. Founded 1949. Pop. 350,000.

Hua Kuo-feng (Hua Guofeng) (*c.*1918–   ), Chinese political leader; premier, chairman of the Military Commission, and chairman of the Communist party of the People's Republic of China (1976–81). When Teng Hsiao-ping was ousted as prime minister in early 1976, he was replaced by Hua, a party functionary then almost unknown in the West. After the death of Mao Tse-tung later that year, it became known that Hua had also been named chairman of the party, thereby making him, in effect, the successor to both Mao and Chou En-lai. His resignation, offered in 1980, was officially accepted in 1981 amid criticism of his regime. In 1982, he was ousted from the central committee.

Huálapai, Yuman-speaking tribe of North American Indians living along the upper Colorado River east to Peach Springs, Ariz. They are closely related to the Yávapai and Havasupai. Never more than 1,000 persons, today they are mainly stock raisers, with a population of approximately 700 living on the Huálapai Reservation.

Huancayo, city in S central Peru, 125mi (201km) E of Lima; capital of Junín dept.; agricultural center; predominantly Indian population; site of church (1617) and many examples of colonial architecture. Industries: silver, copper, and coal mining; potatoes, wheat, maize, Indian textiles. Pop. 91,200.

Huangshih, city in China, on Yangtze River. Industries: iron, steel, cement, building materials, textiles, food processing. Founded 1950. Pop. 200,000.

Huari, also **Wari,** an important prehistoric cultural period in Peru, named for a major archeological site in the Mantaro Basin. The Huari Empire lasted from about AD 600–1000, and exerted considerable influence throughout the Peruvian region.

Huáscar (*c.*1495–1533), son of Huayna Capac, who became emperor at his father's death. He controlled northern Peru at the time of Pizarro's arrival but shared the empire with his younger half brother Atahualpa who rebelled against him and had him murdered.

Huayna Capac (died 1525), last of the great Inca rulers (1493–1525), restored order to an empire torn by civil war (1511–12). He died on the eve of the Spanish conquest; his realm was divided between his two sons, Atahualpa and Huáscar.

Hubble, Edwin Powell (1889–1953), US astronomer, b. Marshfield, Mo. Educated at Chicago and Oxford universities, he worked at Mount Wilson Observatory from 1919. The first to state formally that galactic nebulae were galaxies outside the Milky Way, he also detected and studied their recession.

Hubble Constant, ratio of the velocity of recession of a galaxy to its distance. All galaxies beyond the Local Group are receding from us and from each other, as indicated by their red shifts, the velocity increasing with distance. The limit of the observable universe should thus occur when the recessional velocity equals the velocity of light. Assuming that the Hubble constant holds at very large distances this limit is about 10 billion

Julia Ward Howe

Howard Hughes

Langston Hughes

(10¹⁰) light-years. If the rate of expansion of the universe has always been constant the Hubble constant gives the age of the universe as about 10¹⁰ years.

Hubris, in Greek mythology and literature, the wanton arrogance or presumptuousness of spirit that led to insolent disregard of moral laws and restraints. The wrath of the gods, personified by Nemesis, would inevitably descend upon the guilty.

Huckleberry, shrub native to North America with oval leaves, bell-shaped flowers, and dark-blue berries. Family Ericaceae; genus *Gaylussacia.*

Huckleberry Finn, The Adventures of (1884), novel by Mark Twain, a more serious and accomplished sequel to *Tom Sawyer,* which combines adventure with social comment on pre-Civil War Mississippi Valley life and the moral problems that confront a young boy. The novel, considered to be Twain's most characteristic in character, plot, and style, and his finest, is regarded by some critics as the greatest American novel. The story is narrated by Huck Finn, who flees his drunken father and his confining life with Widow Douglas and Miss Watson.

Huck meets Miss Watson's runaway slave, Jim, and together they travel down the Mississippi River on a raft, encountering numerous adventures and giving shelter to two confidence men, one of whom sells Jim. Huck and Tom Sawyer attempt to rescue Jim, but it develops that Miss Watson has meanwhile died, freeing Jim in her will. Huck's father has also died, leaving intact his son's fortune, but Huck plans to leave again, lest Aunt Sally attempt to "sivilize" him. *See also* Tom Sawyer, The Adventures of.

Huddersfield, city in N central England, in West Yorkshire. Industries: wool, textiles. Pop. 130,060.

Hudson, Henry (died 1611), English navigator and explorer. During his last four years he led several expeditions in search of a passage to China. On his first trip he reached Newland (Spitsbergen), opening up fisheries there to England. On a third trip (1609) he reached the American coast, sailed up the river that bears his name, opening up the area for later trade. On a fourth trip, he passed through the strait which bears his name and entered the inland sea (Hudson Bay). In 1611 he was set adrift by an angry crew and never heard from again.

Hudson Bay, inland bay in E Northwest Territories, Canada; bound on E by Quebec, S by Ontario, SW by Manitoba. Part of Northwest Territories, the bay contains Southampton, Mansel, and Coats islands; many rivers drain into the bay, including Churchill and Nelson; navigable July–October. Explored by Henry Hudson in 1610. Length: 850mi (1,369km). Width: 650mi (1,047km).

Hudson River, river in E New York state; rises near Mt Marcy in the Adirondacks and flows S to New York Bay at New York City. Discovered 1524 by Giovanni da Verrazano and explored 1609 by Henry Hudson, it has become one of the most important waterways of the world. Ocean vessels can navigate to Albany. Divisions of the New York State Barge Canal connect the Hudson with Lake Champlain, the Great Lakes, and the St Lawrence River. The lower end of the river is flanked on the W by the Catskill Mts, passing such points of interest as West Point, Hyde Park, and Bear Mt. Length: approx. 315mi (507km).

Hudson River School, group of US landscape artists active between 1825 and 1875. They were so named because many painted romantic scenes of the Hudson

River Valley. Among the most famous of this group were Thomas Cole, John Kensett, George Inness, and Asher Brown Durand.

Hudson's Bay Company, corporation chartered in 1670 by Charles II of England to promote trade and settlement in the Hudson Bay region of North America and to seek a northwest passage to the Orient. The company concentrated on the fur trade, establishing coastal forts, such as Fort Albany (1678) and Fort Churchill (1717), for this purpose. Intense French competition ended after Canada was awarded to Britain in 1763, but the new North West Company based in Montreal proved a formidable adversary. Both companies opposed the Earl of Selkirk's plan to settle the Red River area and were involved in the fighting in that area between 1812–16. The two companies were forced to merge in 1821 under the older name. Until 1856 the company monopolized western Canada. A government investigation of the company in 1857 led to its reorganization and refinancing in 1863. In 1869 it lost its right to govern territories and much of its land to the newly created government of Canada. The sale of land to settlers and the railroads allowed the company to expand into many diverse businesses and industries. In 1930 the huge conglomeration was forced to split up and divest. The fur company remained centered in London. The stores and other businesses still retained were incorporated in Canada. It remains one of the chief business firms in Canada.

Hudson Strait, strait in NE Canada, between S Baffin Island and N Quebec; connects Hudson Bay with Atlantic Ocean and Foxe Channel; passageway to the Arctic Ocean. Length: 450mi (724km).

Hué, city on E coast of Vietnam, on Hué River; former capital of Annam; market and rice trade center with rail connections; site of University of Hué (1957), airport, and nearby naval station. Founded *c.* 3rd century, the city was occupied by Chams and Annamese; it was a dynastic seat after 16th century. First Vietnamese king was crowned here 1802; city was taken by French 1883 and occupied WWII by Japanese; scene of postwar struggle for independence from French. Much of the city was destroyed during long and heavy fighting (esp. Tet offensive 1968) during Vietnam War, but is being reconstructed. Pop. 200,000.

Huelva, city in SW Spain, 53mi (85km) WSW of Seville on the Odiel River; capital of Huelva prov.; site of Roman aqueduct, and monastery where Christopher Columbus lived before crossing the Atlantic (1492). Exports: cork, sulfur, copper. Industries: fishing, petrochemicals, tourism. Area: (prov.) 3,894sq mi (10,085sq km). Pop. (city) 96,689; (prov.) 397,683.

Huerta, Victoriano (1854–1916), Mexican general and president (1913–14). Instructed by President Francisco Madero to suppress the revolt led by Félix Díaz, Huerta instead joined forces with the rebels. Madero was arrested and killed; Huerta became president. Defeated by the Constitutionalists led by Carranza, Huerta fled to the United States.

Huggins, Charles Brenton (1901–), US physician, b. Halifax, Nova Scotia. He shared the 1966 Nobel Prize in physiology or medicine with F.P. Rous for his pioneering work in cancer chemotherapy and his development of ways of investigating and treating cancers through the use of hormones.

Hugh Capet (*c.*938–96), king of France (987–96), founder of the Capetian dynasty. Hugh inherited the title of duke of the Franks from his father Hugh the Great in 956. He allied himself (978–86) with the Ger-

man emperors against the Carolingian king of France, Lothair. In 987 he was elected king of France on the death of Lothair's son Louis V, the last Carolingian king of France. Although his election was disputed by Charles I of Lower Lorraine, he was able to fix the succession on his son, who became Robert II.

Hughes, Charles Evans (1862–1948), US secretary of state and chief justice of the US Supreme Court (1930–41), b. Glen Falls, N.Y. He achieved national prominence as counsel for the state committees investigating abuses in New York gas utilities and insurance companies (1905–06). Twice governor of New York (1907–10), he was appointed by President Taft as associate justice of the Supreme Court (1910–16). He was the Republican presidential candidate (1916) but lost to Woodrow Wilson. He served as secretary of state under Presidents Harding and Coolidge (1921–25). He organized the Washington Conference on Armaments and negotiated over 50 treaties with foreign nations. He was a member of the Permanent Court of Arbitration (1926–30) and judge of the Permanent Court of International Justice (1928–30). Appointed chief justice by President Hoover, he was a moderate conservative. He upheld constitutional liberties and freedom of the press, but restrained judicial power over administrative agencies. His rulings against the National Recovery Administration and other New Deal agencies prompted President Roosevelt to try and increase the number of justices (1937).

Hughes, Howard Robard (1905–76), U.S. industrialist, aviator, and motion picture producer, b. Houston. He inherited (1925) an industrial corporation from his father who had invented a widely used cone-shaped oil drill. In 1935 he set the world speed record of 352 mph (566 kph) in an airplane of his own design. Subsequently he became one of the richest men in America, heading the Summa Corp. (formerly the Hughes Tool Co.), the Hughes Aircraft Co., and other companies. In the 1930s and 40s he occasionally produced motion pictures. The last 20 years of his life were lived in almost total seclusion.

Hughes, Langston (1902–67), US author, b. Joplin, Mo. He gained notice during the Harlem Renaissance, his first book of poems, *The Weary Blues,* appearing in 1926. A prolific poet, short-story writer, playwright, and novelist, his works deal with black life in America and combine racial pride and protest. In addition to 10 books of poetry, he is noted for the "Simple" stories, sketches concerning a black Everyman. *See also* Harlem Renaissance.

Hughes, Ted (1930–), British poet and short story writer whose major works include *Hawk in the Rain* (1957), *Lupercal* (1960), *Wodwo* (1967), *Gaudette* (1977), and *River* (1983). In these works he explores the theme of man's identity in a hostile universe and uses material from the animal world, mythology, and folklore. He was named Britain's poet laureate in 1984.

Hugh the Great (died 956), duke of the Franks, son of Robert, Count of Paris. Hugh held vast lands between the Seine and Loire rivers and was suzerain of Normandy and Burgundy. He helped to elect the Carolingian Louis IV king, but fought him when Louis tried to assert his independence. He was the father of Hugh Capet, who became the first Capetian king of France.

Hugo, Victor (1802–85), French poet, dramatist, and novelist. He received a pension from Louis XVIII for his first collection of *Odes* (1822) and presented his manifesto of Romanticism in the *Préface de Cromwell* (1827). Later works include the plays *Hernani* (1830) and *Ruy Blas* (1838) and the novels *Notre Dame de*

Paris (1831) and *Les Misérables* (1862). He led the Romantic and later the Humanitarian movement until the death of his daughter in 1843 caused a 10-year cessation of writing, and political convictions sent him to voluntary exile in the Channel Islands (1852–70). Returning to Paris on the fall of the Second Empire, he became a senator and received widespread recognition and respect.

Huguenots, French Protestants of the 16th–18th centuries. The Reformation began in France shortly after it did in Germany (1517). Persecution of Protestants then started, and many, including John Calvin, fled France. Although persecuted in France, Protestantism spread and gained supporters among the aristocracy. In 1560, Protestant nobles led by Louis I de Bourbon, prince de Condé, attempted to seize power, but many of the rebels were killed. In 1562 tension between the Roman Catholics and Protestants touched off the Wars of Religion, which lasted until 1598 and included the St Bartholomew's Day Massacre of Protestants (1572). When the Protestant Henry IV ascended to the throne (1589), he found that he could pacify his kingdom only by converting to Catholicism (1593) and promulgating the Edict of Nantes (1598). The edict recognized Catholicism as the official religion but gave Protestants considerable rights.

Under Louis XIII (*r.*1610–43) Protestant rights were gradually reduced, and civil wars broke out again. Louis XIV (*r.*1643–1715) reaffirmed the remaining Protestant rights in 1643 but later began to withdraw them, and persecution resumed. He revoked the Edict of Nantes in 1685. With their religion once more illegal, hundreds of thousands of Protestants, including many skilled artisans and members of the bourgeoisie, fled France. In the 18th century French public opinion began to turn against persecution of Protestants. In 1789 their full civil rights were restored, and religious equality was guaranteed by the Napoleonic Code of 1802.

Hu Han-min (1879–1936), modern Chinese revolutionary leader and close associate of Sun Yat-sen. An early top figure in the ruling Kuomintang, Hu was elected president of the Legislative Yuan in 1928. His arrest by Chiang Kai-shek in 1931 caused a major crisis in the Kuomintang, which led to his eventual release.

Huhehot (Huhehaote), city in N China; capital of Inner Mongolia Autonomous Region. Connected by rail to Peking, it is an important trade and distribution center for NW China. Industries: chemicals, textiles, farm machinery, flour milling, food processing. Pop. 700,000.

Hui Tsung (1082–1135), Chinese emperor (reigned 1101–25). The last emperor of the Northern Sung dynasty, he spent his last decade in captivity. He founded the first imperial Chinese academy of painting, established imperial porcelain kilns, and was an accomplished painter.

Huk (Hukbalahap), peasant revolutionary movement in the Philippines. Originally formed to resist the Japanese in World War II, they soon became Communist oriented. After the war they fought for reforms against the Philippine government. The guerrilla group won much popular support because of the repressive tactics used against them, but they were undermined and largely defeated by the reforms of President Ramón Magsaysay and the surrender and imprisonment of their leader, Luis Taruc, in 1954. The movement revived briefly in 1969–70.

Hull, Cordell (1871–1955), US secretary of state under Franklin D. Roosevelt (1933–44), b. Overton co, Tenn. A strong spokesman against totalitarianism, he advocated maximum aid to the Allies. Considered the "Father of the United Nations," he received the Nobel Peace prize (1945). He was member of House of Representatives (1907–21, 1923–31) and authored the first federal income tax law (1913).

Hull, city in SW Quebec, Canada, on the Ottawa River; seat of Hull co; site of a hydroelectric station. Industries: lumber, iron, steel. Pop. 61,039.

Hull (Kingston-upon-Hull), city in NE England, in Humberside, at mouth of Hull River on Humber estuary; a major seaport and industrial town, among world's leading fishing ports; exports industrial products of Midlands and North; seat of University of Hull. Chartered 1299. Pop. 279,700.

Human Anatomy. *See* Anatomy.

Humanism, a philosophical viewpoint that stresses human reason as a source of authority and strives for human good in the present world. Humanist ideas can be found from ancient to modern times, but the flowering of humanism came during the Renaissance. Italian scholars of the 14th century began a fresh study of Greek and Latin authors, called the "new learning." Medieval scholars studied the classics to bolster Christian theology. Renaissance men like Petrarch and Vittorini da Feltre studied the classics for their own sake and saw them as means to educate people for their own improvement. The movement spread northward from Italy to include such scholars as Sir Thomas More, Michel de Montaigne, John Calvin, and Desiderius Erasmus. These men were typically skeptical of the authority of the Roman Catholic Church but did not abandon religion. Calvin broke with the Church, but Erasmus remained in it as a reformer. Since the Renaissance a wide variety of thinkers have called themselves humanists. In the 20th century, the New Humanist literary critics reacted against naturalism. Some Christian humanists reject traditional views of God and the church as getting in the way of the well-being of humankind.

Human Rights, powers, conditions of existence, and possessions to which an individual has a claim or title by virtue of being human. The concept of the inalienable rights of the human being has traditionally been linked to the idea of the higher or natural law. Important commentaries on that idea in earlier times appear in the works of several of the Greek dramatists, the Greek and Roman stoics, early Christian thinkers, Aquinas, medieval English legal scholars, Grotius, Milton, and Locke. The concept of human rights was most notably formulated, however, in the 18th century with the United States Declaration of Independence (1776) and Constitution (1789), with its Bill of Rights (1791), and in the French Declaration of the Rights of Man and of the Citizen (1789). These documents gave new expression and scope to rights proclaimed earlier in such compacts between monarchs and nobles as the English Magna Carta (1215), Petition of Right (1628), and Bill of Rights (1689). Important also in the development of the concept of human rights were the various international agreements during the 19th and 20th centuries aimed at abolishing slavery and the traffic in women and children, alleviating labor conditions, and establishing the laws of war. During its existence the League of Nations (1919–46) attempted to promote the fulfillment of such agreements. Reaction against the horrors of World War II led to such important developments in the field of human rights as the Atlantic Charter (1941), Declaration of the United Nations (1942), and the Charter of the United Nations (1945). The Commission of Human Rights of the UN Economic and Social Council proposed an International Bill of Rights of which the first part, the Universal Declaration of Human Rights, was proclaimed by the UN in 1948.

Humbert I and II, kings of Italy. *See* Umberto I; Umberto II.

Humboldt, (Baron) (Friedrich Heinrich) Alexander von (1769–1859), German scientist and explorer. He made scientific trips in Europe and Central and South America; established the use of isotherms; studied volcanoes, the origins of tropical storms, and the increase in magnetic intensity from the equator toward the poles. His *Cosmos* (5 vols., 1845–62) is a classic scientific work.

Humboldt Current, a cold ocean current of the South Pacific that flows north along the northern coast of Chile and Peru to southern Ecuador with a width of 550 miles (885 km). It is slow and shallow, transporting 525,000,000 cu ft (14,857,000 cu meters) of water per second. There is rich plankton growth, making this among the world's greatest fishing grounds for anchovies and tuna.

Hume, David (1711–76), philosopher, historian, and man of letters, b. Edinburgh, Scotland. Hume left Scotland in 1734 and lived thereafter in London and Paris. His remarkably original *A Treatise of Human Nature* (1739–40) initially was a literary failure. More successful were his *History of England* (1754–62) and various essays and philosophical "inquiries." He also held a succession of minor official posts and traveled extensively. Widely known for his humanitarianism and skepticism, Hume held a form of empiricism that affirmed the contingency of all phenomenal events. The posthumous *Dialogues Concerning Natural Religion* (1779) indicates the extent of his atheism.

Humectant, substance such as glycerol, which has an affinity for water, added to stabilize moisture content. Humectants are used in cosmetic moisturizing creams, and in products such as tobacco, in which a certain moisture content has to be maintained.

Humerus, upper arm bone, extending from the scapula, or shoulder blade, to the elbow. The rounded head of the humerus joins with the scapula at the glenoid cavity. A notch, or depression, called the olecranon cavity, on the posterior roughened lower end of the humerus provides the point of articulation for the ulna, one of the forearm bones.

Humidity, or relative humidity, a measure of the water-vapor content of air, the ratio of the actual vapor pressure to the saturation vapor pressure, at which water normally condenses, usually expressed in percentage and measured by a hygrometer. *See also* Hygrometer.

Hummingbird, brightly colored New World birds that are the smallest of all birds. Mostly tropical, their almost invisible, rapid wing beats create a humming noise. They have narrow heads, short weak legs, long slender bills, and long, bushy-tipped protractile tongues with two tubes for sucking nectar from flowers. Unmatched by any bird in flying ability, they can fly slowly or quickly, up or down, back and forth, or hover. During courtship, males perform spectacular aerial displays. The female builds a delicate cup nest of plant down, moss, and saliva for her eggs (2). Length: 2.25in (6cm)–8.5in (21.6cm). Family Trochilidae.

Hummingbird Moth. *See* Hawk Moth.

Humpback Whale, whale found worldwide in distribution. Long knobby flippers and rounded back characterize this humpback whale. Height: 40ft (12m); weight: 32tons. Genus *Megaptera.*

Humperdinck, Engelbert (1854–1921), German music teacher and composer. He is chiefly remembered for his first opera, *Hansel and Gretel* (1893), based on Grimm's *Fairy Tales,* a phenomenal success in its day. His only other successful opera was *Die Königskinder,* which was introduced at the Metropolitan Opera in New York City in 1910.

Humphrey, Hubert H(oratio) (1911–78), US vice president and senator, b. Wallace, S.D. He served as mayor of Minneapolis, Minn. (1945–49). With Democrat and Farmer-Labor party support, he then entered the US Senate. He was elected vice president in 1964 on a ticket with President Lyndon B. Johnson. When Johnson decided not to run for reelection in 1968, he won the Democratic presidential nomination despite opposition from those who were upset by his participation in the escalation of the Vietnam War. He lost the election to Richard Nixon. In 1970 and 1976, he was reelected to the Senate. He was an unsuccessful contender for the Democratic presidential nomination in 1972.

Hunan, province in SE central China, S of Tung Ting Lake; capital is Changsha; birthplace of Mao Tse-tung. Industries: coal, tungsten, antimony and zinc mining; rice, tea, oilseed, wheat, beans, cement, electrical equipment, tools. Area: 80,000sq mi (207,200sq km). Pop. 37,810,000.

Hundred Days (March 4–June 16, 1933), first days of the New Deal. During this period following his inauguration, Pres. Franklin D. Roosevelt proposed and Congress approved many of the New Deal bills designed to bring economic relief and recovery from the Depression. Banks and businesses were regulated, aid was given to farmers and homeowners, and programs were initiated to provide work for the unemployed. *See also* New Deal.

Hundred Schools, term referring to the classical period of Chinese philosophy (551–233 BC). The primary concern of the many philosophical schools of the late Chou period was ethics. Of the reputed "hundred schools," six were to prove historically significant, and of these, only Confucianism has had central importance in Chinese history. *See also* Confucianism.

Hundred Years War, hostilities between France and England pursued, with some interruptions, between 1337 (French seizure of English-held Guyenne) and 1453 (English defeat at Castillon). The refusal of Edward III of England to pay feudal homage for his French territories began the war, the first phase of which saw English successes at Crécy (1346) and Calais (1347). As ransom for the French king, captured in 1356, England forced considerable territorial concessions (1360). Richard II desired peace, but French determination to eject the English gradually won them back their ceded territories. Henry V temporarily arrested this trend at Agincourt (1415) and with the Treaty of Troyes (1420). Subsequent English failure at the siege of Orléans (1428–29) and the Battle of Patay (1429), through Joan of Arc's intervention, ensured their ultimate expulsion from French soil.

Hungary, independent nation of central Europe. It is a member of the Communist bloc but has historical ties to W European culture.

Land and Economy. Its landlocked frontiers were marked after WWI, and Hungary is bordered NE by the

Alexander Humboldt

Hubert Humphrey

Hungary

USSR, N by Czechoslovakia and the Danube River, E by Romania, W by Austria and Yugoslavia. Mostly a flat plain, the Alfold (Great Plain), the country is divided by a highland running NE to W. Hungary had a predominantly agricultural economy before WWII; it was subsequently heavily industrialized. The farm labor force has fallen from 50% in 1950 to 30%; the country is self-sufficient in agriculture. Hungary is dependent on imports for raw materials, mostly from the USSR. Major enterprises are either state-owned or cooperatives. An economic reform program aimed at greater efficiency and production of more consumer goods and export products was introduced in 1968, rejected in 1975, but reinstituted in 1978.

People. Ancestors of modern Hungarians came from the Russian steppes between the Volga and the Urals, displacing the Huns and Avar peoples. Culturally and physically Hungarians are a mixture of Magyar (major), Slovak, Ruthene, Romanian, Serb, Croat, and Turk. About 65% of the population is Roman Catholic with Protestant and Greek Orthodox minorities. The large Jewish population, once 6% of the total, was largely eliminated during the WWII German occupation. Literacy is estimated at 98%.

Government. A unicameral elected National Assembly elects the Presidential Council. Candidates for assembly seats and legislation originate in the Hungarian Socialist Workers (Communist) party.

History. The Magyars, founders of Hungary, came from the region between the Volga and the Urals. Driven N early in the Christian era, they lived as vassals in the 5th–9th centuries at the mouth of the Don River. Organized into tribes, they moved W to the mouth of the Danube, and adopted Christianity. With the exception of a short period after WWI, Hungary was a monarchy for 1,000 years. Its brief Communist dictatorship in 1919 was followed by a 25-year regency under Adm. Nicholas Horthy, a regime purged by German occupation in WWII. The Nazis were driven out by the Soviets, and the USSR supported a dictatorship by Communist leader Matyas Rakosi (1947). The violent Hungarian uprising of 1956 erupted against his repressive regime. Moderate Imre Nagy replaced Rakosi; however, Soviet forces crushed the national uprising, Nagy was executed by the Russians, and Janos Kadar became first secretary of the Hungarian Communist party. Under Kadar, Hungary has been strongly allied with the Soviet Union on foreign affairs, but some liberalization has occurred domestically, and the country has increased economic ties with the West.

PROFILE

Official name: Hungarian People's Republic
Area: 35,919sq mi (93,030sq km)
Population: 10,672,000
  Density: 297per sq mi (115per sq km)
Chief cities: Budapest (capital), Györ, Miskolc, Debrecen
Government: People's republic
Religion: Roman Catholic (major)
Language: Hungarian (official)
Monetary unit: Forint
Gross national product: $41,830,000,000
Per capita income: $3,000
Industries: iron, steel, machines, tools, chemicals, motor vehicles, communication equipment, milling, distilling, pharmaceuticals
Agriculture: corn, wheat, potatoes, grapes
Minerals: bauxite, coal, natural gas
Trading partners: USSR, E Europe

Hung-shui (Hongshui), river in S China. Rising in Kweichow-Yunnan border region, it joins Yü River at Kweihsien to form the West River. Length: 900mi (1,449km).

Huns, nomadic Mongol people, probably of Turkish, Tataric, or Ugrian stock, who spread from the Caspian steppes (present-day Soviet Union) to wage a series of wars on the Roman Empire. Lacking the cultural development attributed to more sedentary peoples, they were very skilled in the arts of war, particularly military horsemanship. During the first half of the 4th century, they conquered the Ostrogoths and the Visigoths, coming west to the Danube River. About 432, the Huns were collecting an annual tribute from Rome. Attila moved still further westward to Italy and Gaul, but after his death in 454, the power of the Huns was broken. Many took service in the Roman armies. The rest settled on the lower Danube.

Hunting-gathering Societies, small-scale societies where the members subsist mainly by hunting and by collecting plants rather than by cultivation. There is a very low subsistence ratio of people to land so the groups are always small bands. Although their technology is extremely simple they have very sophisticated kinship and ritualistic systems. Hunting-gathering societies are most numerous in lowland South America and some parts of Africa.

Huntington, Samuel (1731–96), American jurist and a signer of the Declaration of Independence, b. Windham, Conn. Before becoming governor of Connecticut (1786), he served as chief justice of the state's superior court (1784) and as president of the Continental Congress (1779–81).

Huntington, port and largest city in W West Virginia, 48mi (77km) W of Charleston, on Ohio River; seat of Cabell co; transportation, shipping, commercial center for tobacco and fruit. Industries: chemicals, coal, electrical products, handblown glassware. Founded 1871. Pop. (1980) 63,684.

Huntington Beach, city in S California, 14mi (23km) SE of Long Beach; noted for its beaches. Industries: oil refineries, communications, metallurgy, truck farming, food packing. Inc. 1909. Pop. (1980) 170,505.

Huntsville, city in N Alabama, 23mi (37km) NE of Decatur, seat of Madison co. First settlement in Alabama to receive charter (1811); temporary capital and site of Alabama constitutional convention (1819); burned by Union troops 1862. Industries: sheet metal goods, farm implements, natural gas wells. Settled 1805. Pop. (1980) 142,513.

Hunyàdi, János (1387–1456), Hungarian soldier and national hero. Voivode (governor) of Transylvania (1440); regent for Ladislas V (1446–52). This brilliant general took part in the Hussite Wars and defeated the Turks in several battles. Although many nobles had deserted his army, in 1456 he defeated the Turkish fleet on the Danube River and broke the siege of Belgrade, his greatest achievement.

Hupeh (Hupei, or **Hubei),** province in central China; capital is Wuhan. Industries: agriculture, iron, steel, silk, cattle, coal, paper. Area: 72,000sq mi (186,480sq km). Pop. 33,710,000.

Hurling, a game similar to field hockey, the national sport of Ireland. It is played outdoors by 2 teams of 15 people each on a field 80 by 140 yards (73 by 127m) with goal posts 16 feet (4.9m) high and 21 feet (6.4m) wide, with a crossbar 8 feet (2.4m) above the ground. Each player carries a 3-foot (0.9-m) field hockey–type stick; the ball used is rubber covered with horsehide, and about 10 inches (25.4cm) in circumference. The object is for the player to catch the ball on the stick, run with it and hurl it toward a teammate or toward the goal

he is attacking. The ball may not be picked up or thrown by hand. Three points are scored by getting the ball into the net under the crossbar, one point by hitting it over the crossbar. The sport is governed by the Gaelic Athletic Association, formed in 1884. *See also* Field Hockey.

Huron, small confederation of Iroquoian-speaking tribes of North American Indians who once occupied the St Lawrence Valley from Ontario to Georgian Bay. Almost completely annihilated in wars for control of the fur trade with the Iroquois (1650–56) when their population was reduced from 15,000 to about 500 persons, they wandered widely throughout the east, settling finally in Ohio, where they became known as the Wyandot. Others fled to the Great Lakes area, and eventually settled in Kansas. Today, some 1,250 live on reservations in those states and in Ontario, Canada.

Huron, Lake, second-largest of the Great Lakes; forms a boundary between the United States and Canada. Michigan borders its S and W shores; its many islands, attractive shoreline, and clean water make it a popular recreational area. Lake Huron drains Lake Superior and feeds Lake Erie; part of the Great Lakes–St Lawrence Seaway system, carries ocean-going vessels and is subject to violent storms. Étienne Brulé, French explorer, is believed to be the discoverer (1612) of Georgian Bay of Lake Huron; Samuel de Champlain visited Lake Huron in 1615. Area: 23,010sq mi (59,596sq km). Depth: max. 750ft (229m).

Hurricane, an intense and devastating tropical cyclone with winds ranging from 75 to 136 mi (121 to 219 km) per hour and up, known also as a typhoon in the Pacific. Arising over oceans 10 to 20 degrees from the equator, hurricanes have a calm central hole, or eye, surrounded by inward spiraling winds and cumulonimbus clouds, with barometric pressure falling to 28.5 in (72.4 cm) or lower. Storm winds and waves of hurricanes take many lives and cause extensive shipping and coastal damage, but weather satellites usually provide adequate warning of their approach. *See also* Weather Modification.

Husayn ibn-Ali (1856–1931), Arabian leader. After 1908 he reigned over Mecca and the Hejaz (a kingdom in NW Arabia), then controlled by Turkey. He revolted successfully against the Turks (1916) and made himself king of Arabia, but Ibn-Saud, ruler of Nejd, defeated him and forced him to abdicate in 1924. After exile in Cyprus (1924–30), he died in Amman, Jordan, the capital of his son, Abdullah. His other son, Faisal I, was king of Iraq.

Husein or **Husayn** (*c.*626–80), Muslim leader. He was the second son of Ali and Fatima (Muhammed's daughter). When his older brother Hasan was forced to abdicate as the fifth caliph, Husein was unable to restore his family's claim. Husein and his followers were massacred on Oct. 10, 680, by the Umayyads. The day of his defeat is celebrated as a holy day by the Shiite sect of Muslims, who consider Husein to be a saint and the rightful heir of Muhammad.

Hu Shih (1891–1962), Chinese philosopher, educator, and diplomat. He studied at Columbia University under John Dewey and became an influential teacher at Peking University. From 1938 to 1942 he was ambassador to the United States and from 1946 to 1948 chancellor of Peking University.

Huss, or **Hus, Jan** or **John** (1369?–1415), Bohemian (Czech) religious reformer. A teacher and priest at Prague, he became leader of a reform movement and was influenced by the beliefs of the English reformer

John Wycliffe. Huss got into conflict with the pope and other church authorities and was excommunicated. He was treacherously arrested at Constance in 1414 and burned as a heretic the next year.

Hussein I (1935–), king of Jordan (1953–). Educated in England, he succeeded his father who was declared insane. Pro-Western, he was attacked by other Arab leaders, especially President Nasser of Egypt. Political pressure kept Jordan out of the Central Treaty Organization (1955) and forced the dismissal (1956) of Gen. John Bagot Glubb, British commander of the Arab Legion (Jordanian Army). Hussein imposed martial law in 1957. In 1967 he led his country into the Arab-Israeli War and lost all of Jordan west of the Jordan River to Israel. In 1970 he defeated a Palestinian-led civil war, but at the 1974 Arab summit meeting he was forced to relinquish Jordan's claim to west bank Jordan to the Palestinian Liberation Organization. In 1978, he married American Elizabeth Halaby, who became Queen Noor al-Hussein.

Husserl, Edmund (1859–1938), German philosopher, known as the founder of the phenomenological movement. He studied man's consciousness as it related to objects and the structure of experience. His work influenced many later philosophers and sociologists. Among his important books are *Ideas: General Introduction to Pure Phenomenology* (1913) and *Cartesian Meditations* (1931).

Hussitism, religious reform and nationalist movement in Bohemia led by John Huss (1369?–1415). A disciple of the English theologian, John Wycliffe, Huss preached in Czech rather than in Latin and opposed the authority of the pope, which led to his excommunication in 1409. Emperor Sigismund urged Huss to attend the Council of Constance in Geneva in 1414 to attempt a conciliation. There he was tried for heresy and burned at the stake. A revolt followed in Bohemia, as much to oppose the prosperous German Catholics and the wealth of the Church as to further religious reform. These Hussite wars (1420–33) strengthened the country's nationalism.

Hutcheson, Francis (1694–1746), Scottish philosopher. In his best known book, *Inquiry into the Origin of Our Ideas of Beauty and Virtue,* Hutcheson referred to an innate "sense" or "feeling," which distinguished the beautiful and the good. The phrase "the greatest good for the greatest number" utilized by Jeremy Bentham was of his coinage. *See also* Utilitarianism.

Hutchinson, Anne Marbury (1591?–1643), English colonist and religious leader. After settling the Massachusetts Bay Colony (1634) with her family, her ideas of personal apprehension of God's grace conflicted with the Puritan "covenant of works" established by the church and state. Banished by Gov. John Winthrop after a sedition trial (1637), she settled Portsmouth, R.I., with her followers until her husband's death (1642). She then moved to Long Island and then to the Pelham area of New York City where she was killed by Indians.

Hutter, Jacob (d.1536), Austrian Anabaptist and founder of the Hutterites. When Anabaptists in the Tyrol were persecuted, Hutter led three groups into Moravia and established communal styles of living. He was charged with heresy for his beliefs and was burned at the stake at Innsbruck.

Hutterites, German-speaking Anabaptists practicing communal living. The sect originated in Moravia in the 16th century, moved to the Russian Ukraine, and in 1874 to the W United States. Some also live in western Canada. Communities are governed by bishops and preachers. All things are held in common ownership. Family life, simple ways, and pacifism are stressed.

Hutton, James (1726–97), Scottish geologist. At a time when the science of geology did not exist, he sought to formulate theories of the origin of the earth and of atmospheric changes. He concluded that the earth's history could be explained only by observing current forces at work within it and thus laid the foundations of modern geological science. His great work is *Theory of the Earth* (2 vols., 1785, 1795).

Huxley, Aldous (Leonard) (1894–1963), English novelist. He abandoned his medical studies, became a journalist and began to satirize the hedonism of the 1920s in novels such as *Crome Yellow* (1921), *Antic Hay* (1923), and *Point Counter Point* (1928). *Brave New World* (1932) presents a nightmarish utopia of the future. Later novels include *Eyeless in Gaza* (1936), *The Devils of Loudun* (1952), and *Island* (1962). *Brave New World Revisited* (1958) is a collection of essays. *See also* Brave New World.

Huxley, Andrew Fielding (1917–), English physiologist. He made significant contributions to an understanding of how a nerve impulse is conducted along a fiber. He shared the 1963 Nobel Prize in physiology or medicine with John C. Eccles and Alan L. Hodgkin for this work.

Huxley, (Sir) Julian Sorell (1887–1975), English biologist, the son of Leonard and brother of Aldous Huxley. Julian's writings and lectures promoted modern evolutionary theory and helped to revive the study of evolution. He served as secretary of the Zoological Society of London (1935–42) and as the director general of UNESCO (1946–48). He is the author of *The Individual in the Animal Kingdom* (1911) and *Heredity, East and West* (1949).

Huxley, Thomas (Henry) (1825–95), English biologist and educator. He was the nineteenth century's leading proponent of Darwinism and agnosticism. Unable to afford a university education, he served in the Royal Medical Service (1846–50). As assistant surgeon on the exploratory ship *HMS Rattlesnake,* he conducted important studies of marine life. For these studies he was elected to the Royal Society in 1851, of which he was president 1883–85. In 1854 he became a lecturer at the Royal School of Mines, with which he would be affiliated until 1885, and was instrumental in its evolving into the Royal College of Science. In an 1860 debate at Oxford University he brilliantly defended Darwinism against an attack led by Bishop Samuel Wilberforce. In the 1870s he was instrumental in reforming the British educational system. His most famous work is *Evolution and Ethics* (1893). He was the grandfather of three noted Huxleys: Andrew (physiologist), Aldous (novelist), Julian (biologist).

Huygens, or **Huyghens, Christian,** name often Latinized as Hugenius (1629–95), Dutch physicist and astronomer. He made numerous contributions to science, notably the first statement of the wave theory of light, the recognition of Saturn's rings, and the use of the pendulum in clocks.

Hwang-Ho. *See* Yellow (Hwang-Ho).

Hyacinth, bulbous plant native to the Mediterranean region and Africa. It has long, thin leaves and spikes of flower clusters. The small flowers may be white, yellow, red, blue, or purple. Family Liliaceae; genus *Hyacinthus.*

Hyades, in Greek mythology, the daughters of Atlas, nymphs placed by Zeus among the stars as reward for the care given the infant Dionysus after the death of his mother Semele. Another story has them mourning for their dead brother Hyas until they are made a constellation.

Hyaline Membrane Disease, disease of newborns, usually premature, in which a glassy membrane lines the alveoli (air cells), alveolar ducts, and bronchioles of the lungs.

Hyaluronidase, protein enzyme that participates in the breakdown of some complex muco-polysaccharides of connective tissue, such as hyaluronic acid. Present in most cells, it is also a constituent of some insect and snake venoms.

Hybrid, the offspring of two true-breeding parents of different gene composition; the cross result of the combination of homozygous parents.

Hyde, Douglas (1860–1949), Irish nationalist leader and author. A major force in reviving Irish literature through the Gaelic League, of which he was first president (1893–1915), he was chosen first president of Eire (1938–45).

Hyderabad, city in S India, in Musi River valley; capital of Andhra Pradesh state; capital of former state of Hyderabad (1724–1948); site of ancient ruins, Char Minar (1591), and Old Bridge (1593); seat of Osmania University (1918). Industries: tobacco, textiles, machine tools, food processing, furniture. Founded 1589 as capital of Golconda kingdom. Pop. 1,796,339.

Hyderabad, city in Sind, Pakistan, on Indus River; site of university (1947). Industries: gold and silver embroidery, jewelry, pottery, and textiles. Founded 1768 by Ghulam Shah Kalhora. Pop. 624,000.

Hydra (Idhra or **Ydra),** Greek island in the Aegean Sea, off E coast of Peloponnesus; mostly rocky terrain; played important role in Greek War of Independence (1812–29). Chief town is Hydra on N coast. Industries: sponge fishing, trading. Pop. (island) 2,766; (town) 2,546.

Hydra, freshwater coelenterate with cylindrical body and six tentacles around its mouth opening. Possessing thread cells that shoot poisonous thread capsules (nematocysts) at prey, they move by gliding or somersaulting. Length: 0.5in (13mm). Reproduction is either sexual or by asexual budding or regeneration. Class Hydrosoa; order Hydroida; species include *Hydra littoralis.*

Hydra, or the Water Monster, extensive equatorial constellation, the largest star group in the sky, situated south of Cancer and Leo to the west and Virgo and Libra to the east. It contains the open cluster M48 (NGC 2548). Brightest star Alpha Hydrae (Alphard).

Hydrangea, primarily deciduous woody shrubs and vines of the saxifrage family, native to the Western Hemisphere and Asia. They are grown for their showy clusters of flowers, which may be white, pink, or blue. Some will change color if iron or alum is fed to the roots.

Hydration, assimilation of water onto an ion, electron, or compound either by weak bonds, as in hydrate formation, or by chemical combination with an unsaturated compound. Gypsum is the hydrate of calcium sulfate, zeolite of feldspar. Ethylene can be hydrated industrially to produce ethanol.

Hydraulic Mining, methods of surface mining that involve the breaking down of earth or rock by high-pressure jets of water delivered by large nozzles (called hydraulic giants). It is sometimes used in mining terrace placer deposits. Large quantities of water transport loosened materials to sluices where the valuable minerals are recovered in riffles. Also used for removing overburden from iron ore deposits and in alluvial tin mines.

Hydraulics, the physical science and technology of the behavior of fluids (usually water or oil) in both static and dynamic states. It deals with practical applications of fluid in motion, such as the flow through pipes, and the design of storage dams, pumps, and water turbines, and devices for utilization and control (nozzles, valves, jets, and flow meters). *See also* Fluid Mechanics; Hydrodynamics.

Hydrazine, fuming corrosive liquid ($H_2N{\cdot}NH_2$) obtained by the reaction of sodium hydroxide, chlorine, and ammonia or by the oxidation of urea. It is used as a jet and rocket fuel, in explosives, and as a corrosion inhibitor. Properties: sp gr 1.004, melt. pt. 35.6°F (2.0 °C), boil. pt. 236.3°F (113.5°C).

Hydride, chemical compound of hydrogen with another element, especially a more electropositive element. The hydrides of the electropositive metals, such as lithium hydride (LiH), and sodium hydride (NaH), are saltlike ionic compounds containing the negative ion H^-. They are useful reagents for hydrogenation reactions.

Hydrocarbon, organic compound containing only carbon and hydrogen. Many thousands of different hydrocarbons exist; they fall into two main classes, aliphatic and aromatic hydrocarbons. The aliphatic hydrocarbons are mainly open-chain compounds, including such groups as the alkanes (paraffins), the alkenes (olefins), the alkynes (acetylenes), and terpenes. Aromatic hydrocarbons have properties similar to benzene; most contain benzene rings as in naphthalene and anthracene.

Hydrocephalus, accumulation of abnormal amounts of fluid in the cranium, usually because of obstruction or excess production, resulting in reduction of brain size and mental deterioration.

Hydrochloric Acid, or **muriatic acid,** solution of the pungent colorless gas hydrogen chloride (HCl) in water obtained by the action of sulfuric acid on salt, as a by-product of the chlorination of hydrocarbons, or by the electrolysis of brine. It is widely used in the chemical, food, and metallurgical industries. The concentrated commercial acid contains 38% HCl and has sp gr 1.19. Its boiling point is 227.4°F (108.6°C).

Hydrodynamics, a branch of fluid mechanics dealing with the motion of fluids and the forces acting on solid bodies immersed in fluids. Practical applications were introduced by Archimedes, but the basic theory was not understood until the 17th century. Later, Leonhard Euler, who recognized that dynamical laws for fluids can be expressed in simple form only if the fluid is assumed to be incompressible, derived the basic equations for a frictionless fluid. Principles are important in nozzle design, flow measurements, and predictions of wing lift in flight. Recent theories have made possible the development of modern aircraft wings, the design

Sir Julian Huxley

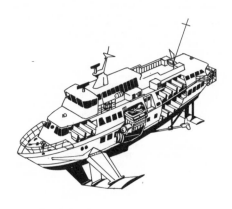

Hydrofoil

Hyena

of gas turbines and compressors, and the development of rockets.

Hydroelectric Power Plant, a center in which the mechanical energy of falling water is converted into electrical energy. The typical hydroelectric facility includes a dam, behind which is a reservoir; hydraulic turbines, through which controlled dam overflow falls; power generators situated directly above the turbines that drive them; and an electrical transmission system.

Hydrofluoric Acid, colorless corrosive fuming liquid consisting of a solution of the gas hydrogen fluoride (HF) in water, prepared by distilling a mixture of sulfuric acid and fluorspar. It is used in frosting and etching glass, pickling metals, and cleaning stone and brick.

Hydrofoil, a flat or curved plane surface designed to obtain reaction from the water through which it moves. Also, an underwater fin, attached by struts to a seaplane or speedboat for lifting the hull as speed is increased. Hydrofoil ships are capable of speeds up to 80 knots.

Hydrogen, gaseous nonmetallic element (symbol H), first identified as a separate element by Henry Cavendish (1766). It is usually classified along with the alkali metals in group 1A of the periodic table. Hydrogen is the most abundant element in the universe (75% by mass) and the lightest of all. Properties: at. no. 1; at. wt. 1.0079; density 0.08988 g dm⁻³; melt. pt. −434.45 °F (−259.14°C); boil. pt. −421.91°F (−252.87°C); most common isotope H¹ (99.985%). Research has shown that it can be solidified. *See also* Deuterium; Tritium.

Hydrogenation, chemical reaction between molecular hydrogen and an element or compound, sometimes under pressure, usually in the presence of a metal catalyst such as nickel, platinum, or palladium. An unsaturated compound, such as benzene, may accommodate the extra hydrogen, but a saturated species will break up (destructive hydrogenation).

Hydrogen Bomb. *See* Nuclear Weapon.

Hydrogen Bond, type of chemical bond formed between certain hydrogen-containing molecules. The hydrogen atom must be bound to an electronegative (electron-withdrawing) atom, the bond being formed between the positive charge on hydrogen and the negative charge on an atom in an adjacent molecule. Hydrogen-bonding occurs in water, and in many biological systems.

Hydrogen Peroxide, syrupy liquid (H_2O_2), usually sold in aqueous solution, prepared by electrolytic oxidation of sulfuric acid or discharge through a mixture of oxygen and hydrogen in the presence of water. It is used in bleaching, as a disinfectant, and as a rocket fuel oxidizer. Properties (anhydrous): sp gr 1.46; melt. pt. 28.4°F (−2°C); boil. pt. 317.4°F (158°C).

Hydrogen Sulfide, colorless poisonous gas with the smell of bad eggs (H_2S) prepared by the action of sulfuric acid on iron sulfide. It is used in chemical analysis. Properties: melt. pt. −118.8°F (−83.8°C); boil. pt. −76.3°F (−60.2°C).

Hydrographic Chart, or nautical chart, a map of the physical features of oceans and adjoining coastal areas. They also contain tide and current information. The most detailed ones exist for coastal areas because more information has been collected, but new sonar devices are enabling the mapping of deep-water parts of the ocean.

Hydrography, the science of charting the water-covered areas of the earth. Navigational charts have been made since the 13th century, but these were accurate only for seacoasts. Interest in the charting of oceanic areas away from seacoasts only developed in the 19th century. The US Coast Survey, established in 1807, produced its first official nautical charts in 1845. Now, detailed bathymetric surveys are available for geological studies. Hydrographic offices are run by governments of maritime nations to furnish their mariners with nautical charts.

Hydrology, study of the earth's waters; their occurrence, circulation, distribution, chemical and physical composition. The hydrologic cycle describes the evaporation of water from various bodies, atmospheric water and its movement, and its return to land. The continental water systems, both surface and underground, are studied by hydrologists. *See also* Limnology; Oceanography.

Hydrolysis, reversible chemical reaction of water with a substance, often assisted by catalysts. Hydrolysis proceeds by a double decomposition mechanism, exemplified by the reaction $AB + HOH \rightleftharpoons AH + BOH$, where A and B are different molecular entities. In digestion enzymes catalyze the hydrolysis of carbohydrates, proteins, and fats into forms that the body can assimilate.

Hydrometer, instrument for measuring density or specific gravity of a liquid. It consists of a long-necked, sealed glass bulb that is weighted. The neck is calibrated to read specific gravity. When immersed in the liquid to be measured, its depth gives liquid density. Hydrometers are used to check concentrations of liquids in storage batteries, freezing points of radiator solutions, "proof" of alcohol.

Hydrophobia. *See* Rabies.

Hydrophyte, or aquatic plant, plant growing only in water or damp places. The waterlily is considered the most important water garden plant. Among the oxygen-producing plants used in home aquariums are anacharis and cabomba. Others that float are azola, water fern, and water hyacinth.

Hydroponics, or soilless agriculture or tank farming, growing of plants in solution or a moist inert medium containing necessary nutrients instead of soil. This technique was developed during the 1850s. It requires special apparatus including tank, solution reservoir, pump, and timer installed in a greenhouse. Added nutrients include potassium nitrate, ammonium sulfate, calcium sulfate, and monocalcium phosphate. Although developed for use in areas where soil and growing conditions are inadequate, the technique is not used on a large scale. Crops that do well under hydroponic methods include tomatoes, lettuce, kale, spinach, and cucumbers. Houseplants may be grown hydroponically in ceramic or glass containers filled with water and feed biweekly with diluted plant food. Suitable plants include African violet, fuchsia, coleus, philodendron, and geranium.

Hydrosphere, the aqueous vapor of the entire atmosphere and the envelope of the earth, including oceans, lakes, streams, and underground water. The water at the earth's surface measures 350,000,000 cu mi (1,465,000,000cu km), 99% of which is contained in the oceanic water layer.

Hydrostatics, a branch of fluid mechanics dealing with the charateristics of liquids at rest and with the pressure in a liquid, especially that exerted on an immersed body. Practical applications of laws have resulted in development of parabolic telescope mirrors and submarines. *See also* Fluid Mechanics; Hydrodynamics.

Hydrotherapy, the use of water within or on the surface of the body to treat disease.

Hydrotropism, plant growth in response to water stimulus. It is not a strong tropism and plant responses to higher oxygen and water content, such as the growth of willow roots through riverbanks, are often confused with it.

Hydroxide Ion, the ion OH⁻, produced in solutions of bases. *See also* Base.

Hyena, predatory and scavenging carnivore native to Africa and S Asia. The spotted or laughing hyena (*Crocuta crocuta*) of the sub-Sahara is the largest and has sparse gray fur with dark round spots. The brown hyena *(Hyaena brunnea)* of S Africa is smaller and has dark brown bands around its legs and feet. The striped hyena *(Hyaena hyaena)* of N Africa, India, and the Near East is the smallest and has yellow-gray fur with black stripes. Weight: 75–175lb (34–79kg). Family Hyaenidae.

Hygrometer, instrument used to measure the water-vapor content, or humidity, of the atmosphere. One type, the psychrometer, compares the wet and dry bulb temperatures of the air, whereas other types measure absorption or condensation of moisture from the air or chemical or electrical changes caused by that moisture.

Hygroscopic, term designating a substance that, on standing, reacts with or absorbs water vapor from the air. Magnesium and calcium chlorides are typical examples. Some hygroscopic solids, said to be deliquescent, absorb sufficient water to dissolve, yielding a concentrated solution.

Hyksos, Semitic people who established a dynasty of Egyptian kings ruling from Memphis in Egypt. About 1685 BC they invaded Egypt from Canaan in the east, using horsedrawn chariots; seized the kingship from the Pharaohs; and ruled a great empire on the lower Nile. In 1550 BC Amasis I, with the help of Nubian mercenaries, drove them out and set up the XVIII dynasty.

Hymenoptera, insect order of sawflies, ants, wasps, hornets, and bees. All have a complete life cycle, with egg, larva, pupa, and adult. They have two pair of membranous wings, which move together in flight. They are found worldwide, living solitarily or in social groups. The larvae are grublike or caterpillarlike, and feed on plants or are parasitic or predaceous.

Hyperbaric Chamber, a sealed chamber in which pressures higher than normal atmospheric pressure are employed in the treatment of diseases. Because of increased oxygen level, some bacteria (especially those causing tetanus and gangrene) are retarded. Babies born with heart defects receive more oxygen from the chamber during operations. Carbon-monoxide poisoning and pressure-related diseases such as decompression sickness are also successfully treated with hyperbaric chambers.

Hyperbola, plane curve traced out by a point that moves so that its distance from a fixed point, the focus, always bears a constant ratio (the eccentricity) greater than one to its distance from a fixed straight line (the directrix). The curve has two branches and is a conic section. Its standard equation in Cartesian coordinates is $x^2/a^2-y^2/b^2=1$.

Hyperglycemia, abnormal amount of sugar in the blood, one of the symptoms of diabetes mellitus. *See also* Diabetes Mellitus.

Hyperides (389–322 BC), a leading Greek orator and public prosecutor. An early supporter of Demosthenes, he supported the Lamian war. After Athens was defeated, Hyperides was condemned to death.

Hyperinflation, or galloping inflation, or runaway inflation, condition in which inflation breeds more inflation because it affects the expectations of consumers. If consumers feel that prices are going to rise very rapidly and they therefore attempt to spend money before its purchasing power declines, hyperinflation results. Hyperinflation has generally been associated with wartime or postwar conditions.

Hyperinsulinism, overproduction of insulin, which may result from tumors in the pancreas or from other organic disturbances such as pituitary dysfunction, or from functional causes such as overexertion or poor nutrition. Hyperinsulinism produces symptoms of hypoglycemia, or low blood sugar, such as sweating, dizziness, headaches.

Hyperion, in Greek mythology, a Titan, son of Uranus and Gaea and the father of Helios, the Sun; Selene, the Moon; and Eos, the dawn. Hyperion drove his chariot across the sky each day and returned each night by the River Oceanus.

Hyperkinetic Children, children with a disorder marked by excessive and apparently pointless activity, difficulty in concentrating, and impulsiveness. The causes of this hyperactivity are unknown. Drug treatment has reduced the symptoms of many patients.

Hyperon, member of a class of elementary particles with an anomolously long lifetime. The group includes the lambda particle (symbol λ), sigma particles (Σ^+, Σ°, Σ^-), xi particles (Ξ°, Ξ^-), and omega particle (Ω^-). A lambda can replace a neutron in a nucleus to form a hypernucleus. *See also* Baryon; Strange Particles.

Hyperplasia, an increase in the normal number of cells in an organ or tissue, as opposed to an increase in the size of the cells (hypertrophy).

Hypersensitivity, a condition wherein an individual reacts to a stimulus such as light, Sun, or a chemical to an uncommon degree. Most hypersensitive reactions are treated as synonymous with allergies. Most common are hay fever, asthma, infantile eczema, and some food reactions. Some individuals become sensitized to drugs, such as penicillin, or to chemicals after initial contact. Sensitivity to light and sun increases as pigmentation in the skin decreases. *See also* Allergy.

Hypertension. *See* High Blood Pressure.

Hyperthyroidism, excessive production of thyroid hormone, with enlargement of the thyroid gland (goiter). Enlargement may be diffuse and accompanied by protrusion of the eyeballs (exophthalmic goiter, or Graves' disease) or may be due to nodules or tumors, which are usually benign. Symptoms include rapid heart rate, high blood pressure, high metabolism, and weight loss. *See also* Goiter.

Hypertrophy, enlargement of an organ, such as the heart, caused in part by an increase in the size of its cells, as opposed to an increase in the number of cells (hyperplasia).

Hyperventilation, prolonged deep and rapid breathing, or any condition in which excessive amounts of air enter the alveoli (air cells) of the lungs, reducing carbon dioxide in the blood to undesirably low levels.

Hypnosis, state of heightened suggestibility that resembles sleep. Very little has been learned about hypnosis since it was first described two centuries ago. Since the time of F. A. Mesmer (1733–1815), it has provoked far more emotional and superstitious concern than serious research. It is, however, fairly well established that hypnosis is physiologically close to a state of relaxed wakefulness; there is increased suggestibility; there can be a slight improvement in recall; in some cases of deep hypnosis it is possible to produce hypnoanesthetic effects; and hypnosis can relieve symptoms in hysterical (conversion) reactions.

Hypnotic, any drug that induces sleep. *See also* Drug.

Hypochondria, exaggerated chronic concern with illness, infection, or pain, without appropriate justification. Hypochondriacs constantly complain of aches and pains, weakness, and fatigue and seek out doctor after doctor in hope of cure. They respond well to placebo treatment.

Hypoglycemia, abnormally low amount of sugar in the blood, which may result from fasting, excess insulin, and various metabolic and glandular diseases. Symptoms are dizziness, headache, cold sweats, and, in severe cases, odd behavior, hallucinations, and convulsions.

Hypomanic Personality, personality pattern disturbance showing a mixture of elevated mood state and restless agitation. It is distinguished from the *hypomanic reaction* in which there is a sudden appearance of manic-like behavior, which though not psychotic may represent the early stage of a true manic reaction.

Hypotension, abnormally low blood pressure, seen in severe hemorrhage or circulatory disturbances (circulatory shock). It may occur on change of position in persons with certain kidney or adrenal gland diseases (postural hypotension), or it may follow the administration of certain drugs.

Hypotenuse, side opposite the right angle in a right-angled triangle. It is the longest side of the triangle. *See also* Triangle.

Hypothalamus, principal forebrain structure, often described as the primary sensory sending structure. Along with other neural areas, it regulates several motivational stages, including the initiation of hunger, thirst, and sexual behavior.

Hypothesis, an assumption made to account for or relate known facts. The formulation of an hypothesis is basic in everyday experience as well as in scientific investigations, where it is stated as a formal proposition. Consequences inferred from an hypothesis are put to further inquiry, thus enabling the assumption to be tested in a particular situation. In science, hypotheses are held provisionally. Even the great unifying concepts of modern science are merely working hypotheses, open to modification or rejection in the face of new facts.

Hypothyroidism, deficiency of thyroid hormone, most common in women and resulting in low metabolism, fatigue, menstrual disorders, and, if severe, anemia and mental deterioration. If severe in children, mental retardation and short stature, a condition called cretinism results. *See also* Cretinism.

Hyrax, gregarious plant-eating mammal native to Africa and SW Asia. Tree climbers, they resemble short-eared rabbits. Length: to 24in (61cm). They are the only members of the order Hyracoidea. Family Procaviidae.

Hyssop, common name for *Hyssopus officinalis,* an aromatic herb of the mint family. A hardy perennial native to Eurasia, it is used in seasoning food and in medicine. It is also cultivated as an ornamental subshrub.

Hysterectomy, an operation in which all or part of the uterus and its surrounding structures are removed. Hysterectomy may be subtotal, with removal of the body of the uterus only; total, with removal of the cervix; or radical, with removal of the entire uterus and its surrounding connective tissue.

Hysteresis, phenomenon occurring in the magnetic and elastic behavior of substances in which the strain for a given stress is greater when the stress is decreasing than when it is increasing. When the stress is removed a residual strain remains. The phenomenon is particularly important in ferromagnetic materials, in which the magnetization lags behind the magnetizing force.

Hysteria, psychoneurosis characterized by emotional instability, suggestibility, dissociation, and psychogenic functional disorders. Conversion hysteria has symptoms that are the same as organic diseases. Dissociative hysterias alter conscious awareness and are manifest as amnesia, sleepwalking. Leading researchers in hysteria have included J.M. Charcot, Pierre Janet, and Sigmund Freud. Freud believed hysteria was caused by frustrated sexual needs and could be relieved by a "catharsis reactivation" of the memory.

I

Iamb, metrical foot consisting of an unstressed followed by a stressed syllable, or a short followed by a long, as in the word *amaze.* The meter is called iambic. Iambic trimeter is characteristic of Greek drama; iambic pentameter is predominant in English-language verse. *See also* Meter.

Iasi, city in NE Romania, 10mi (16km) from frontier between Romania and USSR; capital of Iasi co; capital of Romania until 1861 when it was moved to Bucharest; scene of signing of Treaty of Iasi (1792) ending Russo-Turkish War (1787–92); site of University of Iasi (1860), 15th–19th-century monasteries, 15th-century Church of St Nicholas. Industries: furniture, textiles, pharmaceuticals, chemicals. Pop. 183,776.

Ibadan, city of SW Nigeria, W Africa, approx. 90mi (145km) NNE of Lagos; capital of Western state; industrial and commercial center, handles regional cacao and cotton trade; site of University of Ibadan (1962). Industries: plastics, soap, chemicals, cigarettes, wood and metal products, processed foods. Founded 1830 as a military base in Yoruba civil war. Pop. 1,800,000.

Ibagué, city in W central Colombia, 60mi (97km) W of Bogotá, on the E slope of the Andes Mts; capital of Tolima dept. Industries: gold mining, coffee, rice, sugar cane. Founded 1550. Pop. 200,000.

Ibaraki, city in S Honshu, Japan, 13mi (21km) NNE of Osaka; agricultural area. Pop. 163,903.

Ibarra, Francisco de (*c.*1539–75), Spanish conquistador, explored an area N of Zacatecas, Mexico, that became the audiencia of Nueva Vizcaya. Ibarra was named governor and captain-general of the area in 1562; the appointment was re-confirmed in 1573.

Iberia, ancient region S of Caucasus Mts, USSR; it approximates E part of Georgian SSR. Founded as independent kingdom between 6th–4th centuries BC, it became a vassal of the Roman Empire after defeat by Roman general Pompey (65 BC). Inc. 8th century as part of Georgia.

Iberian Peninsula, peninsula in SW Europe, occupied by Spain and Portugal, separated from Africa by Strait of Gibraltar and from the rest of Europe by Pyrenees Mts; bordered by Atlantic Ocean (N and W) and Mediterranean Sea (S and E). Area: 230,400sq mi (596,736sq km).

Iberians, the prehistoric people of S and E Spain in pre-Roman and early Roman times. Their culture was distinct from that of Celtic-dominated N and central Spain. The best known group of tribes was the Tartessians. Both Greek and Carthaginian influences can be detected in their alphabet and art forms. Their economy was based on agriculture, mining, and metalworking.

Iberville, Pierre Le Moyne, Sieur d' (1661–1706), Canadian naval officer and explorer. Scion of a great Canadian family, he engaged in diplomatic missions and in 1685 helped seize Rupert House, Albany, and Moose Factory from the Hudson's Bay Company. In 1688–89, he led an expedition to the Mississippi delta and established Fort Maurepas (now Biloxi), which was the first French settlement on the Gulf coast. Iberville fought the British on land and sea in the 1690s with great success. He was governor of Louisiana from 1703 until his death.

Ibex, several species of wild Old World goats. Long, backward curving horns measure up to 5ft (1.5m) on the male. All have great climbing ability and long, yellow-brown hair. Height: 3ft (0.9m) at shoulder; weight: 240lb (108kg). The Alpine ibex *(Capra ibex),* once common, is now almost extinct. *See also* Goat.

Ibis, tropical lagoon and marsh wading bird with long, down-curved bill, long neck, and lanky legs. Closely related to the spoonbill they may be black, whitish, or brightly colored. Feeding on small animals, they nest in colonies, laying 2–5 light colored eggs. Length: 2–3ft (61–91cm). Subfamily Threskiornthinae.

Ibiza, island of Spain, 80mi (129km) off E coast, in W Mediterranean SW of Majorca; part of Balearic group. Noted for Roman, Carthaginian, and Phoenician artifacts, the mild climate and beautiful scenery have made Ibiza a major tourist center. Industries: tourism,

Ibis

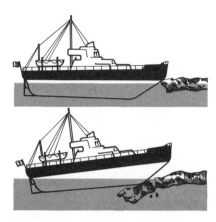

Icebreaker

Iceland

fishing, salt works, almonds, figs, olives. Area: 221sq mi (572sq km). Pop. 45,075.

Ibizan Hound, coursing breed of dog. Believed to be the sacred dog of ancient Egypt. Brought to United States in 1956. This graceful dog has a long, slender head and muzzle; prick ears; long, arched neck; deep chest; straight back; and low-set, sickle-shaped tail. The short, solid color coat can be white, red, and lion; white and red; or white and lion. Average size: 22–28in (56–71cm) high at shoulder; 42–50lb (19–23kg).

Ibn-Saud (*c.*1880–1953), founder and first king of Saudi Arabia (1932–53). He lived in exile with his family in Kuwait until 1900 when he captured Ar Riyadh, the chief city of his family, in Nejd (N central Arabia). By 1912 he had recaptured all of Nejd. In 1924–25 he defeated Husein Ibn Ali, his rival for control of Arabia, thus securing Hejaz (the region with Mecca and Medina). In 1932 he constituted his domain as Saudi Arabia with himself as king. He granted oil-drilling concessions to US companies in the 1930s. Although anti-Zionist, he played only a minor role in the Arab-Israeli War of 1948. He was succeeded by his oldest son, Prince Saud.

Ibn Sina. *See* Avicenna.

Ibo, or **Igbo,** Kwa-speaking people of eastern Nigeria. Originally their patrilineal society consisted of politically and socially autonomous village units, but during the 20th century an ethnic unity developed in reaction to British colonial rule, and they now form the bulk of the Nigerian urban middle class.

Ibsen, Henrik (1828–1906), Norwegian playwright. He profoundly influenced world theater with tense, skillful dramas of complex individuals in conflict with bourgeois institutions. His widely translated works include *Brand* (1866), *Peer Gynt* (1867), *A Doll's House* (1879), *Ghosts* (1881), *An Enemy of the People* (1882), *The Wild Duck* (1884), *Hedda Gabler* (1890), *The Master Builder* (1892), and *When We Dead Awaken* (1899).

Icarus, mythological Greek character who was imprisoned with his father Daedalus by King Minos of Crete. Daedalus, architect of the Labyrinth, made wings of feathers and wax in order to escape Minos. Daedalus was successful, but Icarus, despite a warning, flew too near the sun, melted his wings, and fell into the sea. The Icarian Sea bears his name.

ICBM. *See* Intercontinental Ballistic Missile.

Ice, or **Snow, Crystals,** usually taking the form of six-sided crystals, platelets, or columns, made when water vapor condenses below the freezing point and composing high cirrus clouds but also often present in gray portions of other clouds. Clumps of numerous ice crystals form snowflakes. *See also* Cloud; Precipitation.

Iceberg, a large drifting piece of ice, broken off from a fresh-water glacier. In the Northern Hemisphere the main source of icebergs is the SW coast of Greenland. In the south, the glacial flow from Antarctica releases huge tabular icebergs, some over 60mi (97km) long. Icebergs can be dangerous to shipping, since only a small portion is visible above the water. *See also* Glacier.

Ice Boating, a winter sport, also known as ice yachting. The boats are stiletto-shaped craft with three ski-like runners and a raked mast. The most popular craft used is the bow-steered Skeeter class, which is 22ft

(6.7m) long, weighs about 300lb (135kg), and is limited to 75sq ft (7sq m) of sail. Competition crafts are classified according to sail area and can hold one or two persons. The sport originated in the 18th century in Scandinavia and became popular in the United States and Canada in the 1860s. The most prominent competition is the Ice Yacht Challenge Pennant of America, begun in 1881.

Icebreaker, a ship with a heavy bow and armored sides, designed to make a passage through ice. Powerful engines enable the ship to plow through the ice. For breaking thick ice, the bow is designed to climb partly up on the ice, permitting the ship to break the ice with its weight. Propellers forward and aft allow great maneuverability. Iceboats are used regularly to clear channels in the Great Lakes and in the Baltic Sea, and they are also used in Arctic and Antarctic explorations and to clear Artic shipping lanes. In 1977 a Soviet nuclear-powered (Arktika) icebreaker became the first surface ship to reach the North Pole and return through Arctic ice.

Ice Hockey, a fast-action sport, most popular in the United States and Canada. It is played by two teams of six persons each on a rink usually 200 feet long and 85 feet wide (61m by 25.9m), surrounded by walls 3.5 to 4 feet (1.1–1.2m) high. Ten feet (3m) from each end of the rink is a goal net 4 feet (1.2m) high and 6 feet (1.8m) wide. The rink is evenly divided by colored lines into three zones—attacking, neutral, and defending—each 60 feet (18.3m) long. A vulcanized rubber puck 1 inch (2.5cm) thick and 3 inches (7.6cm) in circumference is used. Each player wears ice skates, carries a wooden stick that is angled at one end, and wears protective equipment; the goalie has leather leg guards and usually wears a face mask. Besides the goalie, the other five players are made up of two defensemen, two forwards, and a center. Play begins at center ice; the object is to advance the puck into the opponent's goal. Each goal counts as one point and regulation games (three 20–minute periods) may end in a tie, or in sudden-death following the end of regulation time. Substitutions are freely allowed, and the game is officiated by two linesmen and a referee. Only the referee may call penalties, which are for such violations as high-sticking, roughing, or tripping. A penalty results in one or more players leaving the ice and going to the penalty box for two or more minutes. Depending upon the penalties, teams may play short-handed.

History. Ice hockey originated in Canada in the 1870s and later came to the United States. Amateur hockey has been an event in the winter Olympic Games since 1920. There are two professional major leagues, the National Hockey League (formed 1917) and the World Hockey Association (formed 1972). The NHL has 18 teams divided into 4 divisions and plays an 80-game schedule. The WHA has 14 teams divided into 3 divisions and plays a 78-game schedule. Following the end of scheduled play in both leagues are playoffs. Most famous is the NHL playoff for the Stanley Cup, which is awarded to the winner in the NHL. In the WHA the playoff prize is the Avco Cup.

Iceland (Island), independent island nation in the North Atlantic Ocean. Its economy is dominated by fishing, which Iceland feels is threatened by foreign fishing trawlers.

Land and economy. Situated E of Greenland and just S of the Arctic Circle, Iceland is 75% volcanic in origin with a 6,590ft (2,010m) above sea level lava desert, glaciers, and lakes. The rest is either grazing land or under cultivation. Damp, cool summers characterize a climate tempered by the Gulf Stream. Winter temperatures average 30°F (−1°C) with high winds. Fishing is the economic mainstay, with 14% of the pop-

ulation dependent on it; 14% depends on agriculture, and 30% on manufacturing and construction. Fish products account for 70% of exports. Its per capita income is higher than the European average.

People. Icelanders are descended from Norwegian settlers and Celts from the British Isles; the Icelandic language has remained almost unchanged since the 12th century and remains closest to Old Norse. Literacy is rated at 99.9%, the highest in the world. Religious freedom is complete. About 97% of the population belongs to the Evangelical Lutheran Church, with other Protestant and Roman Catholic minorities.

Government. Iceland is a constitutional republic with an elected president, who serves as head of state, and a parliament (*Althing*). Real executive power is vested in the prime minister, leader of the majority party in the parliament.

History. Settled by Norwegians in the 9th and 10th centuries, ruling chiefs established a republic, the *Althing,* said to be the oldest parliament in the world. In 1262, Norway took control of the island, and it passed to Denmark in the 14th century. In the early 19th century the rise of nationalism brought demands for independence, and home rule and sovereignty were granted under the Danish crown. During WWII Iceland depended on the United States for defense, until a plebiscite in 1944 established it as an independent republic. Iceland is a member of NATO and, according to a 1951 treaty, allows US military forces on the island. In the mid-1970s the presence of foreign fishing fleets near Iceland led to clashes, particularly with British ships. In 1975, Iceland unilaterally extended its fishing limit to 200 nautical mi (370km), resulting in the most serious "cod war" between the two countries and a temporary break in diplomatic relations; by the end of 1976 British trawlers no longer entered Iceland's waters. During the early 1980s, Iceland was plagued by very high inflation rates.

PROFILE

Official name: Republic of Iceland
Area: 39,768sq mi (103,000sq km)
Population: 224,384
Chief city: Reykjavik (capital)
Government: Constitutional republic
Religion: Evangelical Lutheran
Language: Icelandic
Monetary unit: Krona
Gross national product: $2,400,000,000
Per capita income: $9,000
Industries: processed fish (canning and freezing), aluminum smelting, cement, ammonium nitrate, diatomite, clothing, shoes, chemicals, fertilizers, hydroelectric power
Agriculture: potatoes, turnips, hay, fish, cattle, sheep
Minerals: natural hot water, skeletal algae, perlite
Trading partners: United States, United Kingdom, West Germany

Icelandic Literature. Early Icelandic literature emerged in the 13th century from the oral tradition of Eadic and skaldic poetry, both of which were based on ancient Icelandic mythology. Other early writings (14th–16th centuries) include sagas of Norse monarchs, translations of foreign romances, and religious works. From the 14th–19th centuries the rímur, a narrative verse poem, was popular. The 19th century was probably the most important period in the development of Icelandic literature. Romantic lyric poets such as Bjarni Thorarensen and Jónas Hallgrímsson were influential in stimulating literary activity. Other figures were Jón Thóroddsen, who published the first novel in Icelandic, and Matthías Jochumsson, the founder of modern Icelandic drama. The late 19th century saw the development of Icelandic realism. Important 20th-century writers include Gunnar Gunnarsson and Halldor Laxness.

Iceland Moss, a flattened, branched, partially erect lichen that grows in arctic and high cold mountainous regions. Especially in Scandinavia, Iceland moss has been used as a medicine and as food for livestock and people.

Iceland Spar, a transparent form of calcite that has the property of bending light two ways so that an image seen through it appears double. It is used in polarizing prisms, in polarizing microscopes, and other optical instruments. *See also* Calcite.

Ice Skating, a winter sport, believed to have originated in Scandinavia in the 2nd century AD. The first completely iron skates were introduced in the 17th century. Previously, ice skates were made of bone and then wood. In the 1850s steel skates, with straps and clamps to fasten them to the shoes, were introduced. This was soon followed by the permanent skate, where the skate and the shoe formed a single unit. The first US skating club was organized in Philadelphia in 1849. The first artificial rink in US opened in New York City in 1879.

I-ch'ang (Yichang, or Ichang), city in E central China, on Yangtze River; terminus for ocean-going steamers from Shanghai; site of airport; opened to foreign trade 1876. Crops: rice, tea, beans. Pop. 160,000.

Ichikawa, city in central Honshu, Japan, 10mi (16km) E of Tokyo. Pop. 295,603.

I Ching, meaning "Book of Changes," a Chinese work that is one of Confucianism's Five Classics. Along with the Four Books, they make up the canon of Confucianism. *I Ching* contains material for divination, plus philosophical writings. According to legend the former were written in about the 11th century BC and the latter by Confucius around the 6th century BC. *I Ching* tries to explain human existence and natural occurrences.

Ichinomiya, city in SE Honshu, Japan; site of 7th-century Shinto shrine; textile center. Pop. 238,000.

Ichneumon Wasp, parasitic wasp that attacks other insects and spiders. The female's ovipositor is as long as its body or longer. Found worldwide, the largest representative found in the United States is 1.5in (38.1mm) or more in length and its ovipositor is several times the length of its body. Family Ichneumonidae. *See also* Hymenoptera.

Ichthyology, zoological study of fish. Although true fish are in the Class Osteichthyes, it also includes lamprey, shark, ray, and skate, and sometimes whale and porpoise (mammals).

Ichthyornis, extinct ternlike North American bird of the Cretaceous period. Although it had a keeled breastbone and well-developed wings like modern birds, it had teeth in individual sockets, a characteristic of earlier birds.

Ichthyosaur, extinct fish-shaped, marine reptile of from 65–225,000,000 years ago. These fish eaters had limbs reduced to paddles, a fleshy back fin, and a fishlike tail. Fossils indicate they bore live young. Length: to 30ft (9m).

Ichthyosis (fish-skin disease), characterized by harshness, dryness, and scaliness of the skin, caused by excessive growth of the horny layer. The disease is usually hereditary.

Iconoclastic Controversy, a dispute in the Byzantine Empire over devotion to sacred images. Between 726 and 843, six emperors ordered icons to be taken out of churches and persecuted orthodox Christians for venerating them. The Second Council of Nicaea decided that Christians could venerate, but not worship, images. This stand was reaffirmed by a synod in 843, and the controversy ended.

Iconography, in religion, symbolic and pictorial representation of religious concepts and personages, central in the worship of the Eastern churches. Early Christian art was basically symbolic, and grew mystical. *See also* Iconoclastic Controversy.

Ictinus (5th century BC), Greek architect. After designing the Parthenon with Callicrates (447–432 BC), he worked on rebuilding and enlarging the Temple of the Mysteries at Eleusis. He also designed the Temple of Apollo Epicurius at Bassae (*c.*430 BC), most of whose columns still stand.

Id, in psychoanalytic theory, the deepest level of the personality, which includes primitive drives (eg, hunger, anger, sex) that demand instant gratification. Even after the ego and the superego develop and limit these instinctual impulses, the id is a source of energy and often of unconscious conflicts. *See also* Ego; Superego.

Ida, Mount (Kaz Daği), mountain in Ida mountain range, NW Turkey, SE of site of ancient Troy. According to Homeric legend, mountain was dedicated to Cybele, goddess of fertility and mother goddess of Anatolia.

Idaho, state in the NW United States, bordered on the N by the province of British Columbia, Canada.

Land and Economy. Much of the state is mountainous and forested, with many lakes. The Snake River, along the W boundary, flows for 40mi (64km) through Hells Canyon, which is more than 1mi (2km) deep. Hydroelectric dams have been built in this part of the river. In the S, irrigation projects have created agricultural areas, especially along the upper valley of the Snake, where crop and livestock production and processing are centered. Year-round resorts and wilderness hunting and fishing have made tourism a major source of income.

People. Idaho is among the states lowest in population density. More than 66% of its people live in or near the Snake River valley in the S, and more than half inhabit areas classified as urban. About 98% were born in the United States, but only about 50% are native to the state. Immigration has been chiefly from other W and N states.

Education and Research. There are nine institutions of higher education. The National Reactor Testing Station in the E Snake River valley is an important nuclear research center.

History. In 1805, the US explorers Meriwether Lewis and William Clark traversed the region. In a few years fur trappers were active and trading posts were established; missionaries moved among the Indians. The Oregon Trail, leading to the new Pacific Coast settlements, crossed S Idaho. Discovery of gold in 1860 brought a rush of immigrants, and Idaho Territory was created in 1863. Intermittent war with the Indians ended in 1877 with the surrender of Chief Joseph of the Nez Perce tribe. After Idaho's admission to the Union, labor disputes marked by violence racked the state. By 1900 the steady development of the state's resources was under way. The signing of the Central Idaho Wilderness Act (1980) placed more than 2,300,000 acres (930,000 hectares) of undeveloped land under protection.

PROFILE

Admitted to Union: July 3, 1890; rank, 43rd
US Congressmen: Senate, 2; House of Representatives, 2
Population: 943,935 (1980); rank, 41st
Capital: Boise, 102,451 (1980)
Chief cities: Boise; Pocatello, 46,340; Idaho Falls, 39,590
State Legislature: Senate, 35; House of Representatives, 70
Area: 83,557sq mi (216,413sq km); rank, 13th
Elevation: Highest, Borah Peak, 12,662ft (3,862m); Lowest, Snake River, 710ft (217m)
Industries (major products): processed foods, lumber, paper, chemicals
Agriculture (major products): potatoes, sugar beets, wheat, sheep, cattle
Minerals (major): silver, lead, zinc, phosphate rock
State nickname: Gem State
State motto: Esto perpetua (Let It Be Forever)
State bird: Mountain bluebird
State flower: Syringa
State tree: Western white pine

Ideal Gas Law, the law relating pressure, temperature, and volume of a gas: $pV = NkT$, where N is the number of molecules of the gas and k is a constant of proportionality. From this law, one can see that at constant temperature, the product of pressure and volume *(pV)* is constant (Boyle's Law); and at constant pressure, the volume is proportional to the temperature (Charles' Law). *See also* Boyle's Law; Charles' Law.

Idealism, doctrine or view that asserts the ideal as fundamental. The doctrine gives preference to mind (spirit, soul) negatively, as opposed to materialism; that which pertains to "ideas" or "ideals," as alternatives to objects, entities, and "reals." Idealism stresses supraspatial and temporal categories and content, rather than experiential or tactile entities. Idealism can be qualified in many ways, eg, subjective, epistemological, or aesthetic idealism, Platonic or Hegelian idealism.

Ideograph, system of using pictures to represent ideas or emotions, such as a picture of the sun to present the idea of "day" or "warmth" or a picture of a man pointing to his mouth to show hunger. It is often found with pictographs. *See also* Pictography.

Idomeneus, in Greek mythology, Cretan king. He led the Cretans at the siege of Troy. On his way home during a stormy sea voyage, he pledged to sacrifice to the gods the first living thing he met, if he returned home safely. Idomeneus' son greeted him and he offered the boy as a sacrifice. A plague ensued and the Cretans banished Idomeneus.

Idrisids, ruling Islamic family of what is now Morocco (788–974). Idris I (died 793), a descendant of the Prophet Mohammed, founded the state and its capital city, Fez, with support from the local Berber tribesmen. The dynasty later became less unified and suffered from attacks by Berbers. It fell in the 10th century to the Fatimids, a succeeding dynasty led by Ubaydulla.

Idylls of the King (1842–1885), series of poems by Alfred Tennyson based on the Arthurian legend. It includes *Morte d'Arthur* (1842), *Guinevere* (1859), *The Holy Grail* (1871), and *Balin and Balan* (1885). The works romanticize the legend with its story of the triumph of sin over virtue.

Ieyasu Tokugawa (1542–1616), Japanese shogun. Building on the work of Nobunaga and Hideyoshi, Ieyasu completed the unification of Japan and was made shogun, military ruler of the country, in 1603. Acting as regent for Hideyoshi's heir, Hideyori, Ieyasu defeated his last opponents at Sekigahara in 1600 but later turned against Hideyori in 1615, destroying his forces on trumped-up charges and becoming unchallenged supreme leader. He ensured his line's continuity by retiring early in favor of his son, who in turn did the same. The Tokugawa shogunate (1603–1867) remained in power through a tightly controlled coalition of daimyo (feudal lords) and strategic land and mine possessions until 1867.

Ife, city in SW Nigeria, W Africa, approx. 50mi (81km) ENE of Ibadan; trade center in agricultural region; oldest Yoruba town (*c.* 1300); site of many fine artworks dating from 12th century, Ife Museum, and University of Ife. Pop. 176,000.

Ife, Kingdom of, SW Nigeria from about the 11th century to its defeat by other tribes in the 1880s. Its capital, Ife, became the spiritual center of the Yoruba and now handles considerable agricultural trade.

Ifni, region of SW Morocco, on Atlantic Ocean; former Spanish overseas territory, controlled by Spain 1860–1969; ceded to Morocco 1969, after border fighting between Spanish and Moroccan forces. Area: 580sq mi (1,502sq km).

Igloo, Eskimo dwelling, especially snow house of eastern Eskimos built of snow blocks stacked into a low dome and welded together by frozen water. Igloos are constructed as temporary dwellings in the winter and provide excellent defense against the cold.

Ignatius, Saint.. *See* Loyola, Saint Ignatius of.

Ignatius of Antioch, Saint, 1st-century bishop of Antioch and martyr. On his way to Rome under sentence of death, he wrote seven letters to Christian communities *(Epistles)*. These letters are valuable sources on the early church. Ignatius was put to death in Rome during the reign of Trajan.

Ignatius of Constantinople, Saint, called Nicetas (799–878), patriarch of Constantinople. He was the son of Emperor Michael I of the Byzantine Empire. He became a monk, then an abbot, and finally was elected patriarch of Constantinople (846), the leading center of the church in the Eastern Empire. Ignatius became involved in disputes, was deposed (858) and replaced by Photius, but was restored (867) to his position.

Igneous Rocks, the broad class of rocks produced by the cooling and solidifying of the molten magmas deep within the earth. They may take intrusive or extrusive forms. Intrusive rocks, such as granite, are those formed beneath the earth's surface by the gradual cooling of molten material; extrusive rocks, such as basalt, are formed by the rapid cooling of molten material upon the earth's surface.

Ignition, Engine, the process or means of igniting fuel in an engine. Air and gas vapor are mixed in the carburetor, then delivered to the cylinder, where the mixture is compressed. The heat of compression and the higher pressure favor ready ignition and quick combustion. The charge is then ignited by a spark produced by the spark plug. The main type of ignition in common use is the battery-and-coil system. *See also* Spark Plug, Engine.

Iconography: representations of the Sun

Iguacu Falls, Brazil

Chicago, Illinois

Igor (died 945), duke of Kiev (912–45). According to the medieval Russian *Primary Chronicle,* he was the son of Rurik, the semilegendary founder of the first Russian dynasty. Igor unsuccessfully led (941) an expedition against Constantinople; he later signed a commercial treaty with the Byzantines. He died while attempting to collect tribute from Slavic tribesmen.

Igorot, several ethnic groups of northern Luzon in the Philippines. Medium-sized with brown skin and straight hair, they are believed to be a mixture of early Indonesian and later Malayan stocks. Two main subdivisions are the wet-rice, terrace-cultivating, highland Igorot and the dry-rice, seasonal-garden Igorot of the lower rain forests. All work brass and iron and do weaving.

Iguaçu (Iguassu) Falls, waterfalls in Brazil, on Iguaçu River, 14mi (23km) above its confluence with the Paraná River. Two main sections are composed of hundreds of waterfalls separated by rocky islands; drops approx. 210ft (64m) into a narrow gorge. Argentina and Brazil national parks are on either side; first mapped 1892.

Iguana, lizard found in the New World, and in Madagascar and the Fiji Islands. Its teeth are attached to the inner edges of the jaw. There are 400 terrestrial, arboreal, burrowing, semi-aquatic, and semi-marine species, or large iguana of tropical America. It is greenish with a serrated dewlap on throat and crest along back. Length: to 6ft (1.8m). Family Iguanidae; genus *Iguana. See also* Lizard.

Iguanodon, primitive, bipedal ornithopod dinosaur living in Europe during late Jurassic and early Cretaceous times. It had a spiked thumb that may have served as a defense weapon. Its jaws and teeth, like those of later ornithischian dinosaurs, were specialized for grinding food plants. Length: 30ft (9m). *See also* Ornithopoda.

IJsselmeer, large freshwater lake in NW Netherlands, formed in 1932 by dike which divided the Zuider Zee into the saline Wadden Zee and the freshwater IJsselmeer. Large land areas have been reclaimed by control of water level in the shallow lake. Dike supports a roadway. Length of dike: 19mi (31km).

Ikhnaton. *See* Amenhotep IV.

Île-de-France, historical region and province of N central France, bounded by Picardy (N), Champagne (E), Orléannis (S), and Normandy (W). Hugh Capet est. in 987 the first French crown lands that were to encompass this region, whose capital was Paris; site of many Gothic cathedrals and châteaus, including Fontainebleau and Versailles.

Île de la Cité, island in Seine River in Paris, France; site of Notre Dame Cathedral and Palais de Justice; original settlement of Paris. *See also* Paris.

Ileitis, inflammation of the ileum, part of the small intestine. Symptoms of acute ileitis resemble those of acute appendicitis.

Ilesha, city in SW Nigeria, W Africa; shipping center for regional agricultural products. Crops: nuts, yams, cacao. Pop. 224,000.

Ilex. *See* Holly.

Ilhéus (Ilhéos), city in E Brazil, on the Atlantic, at mouth of Cachoeira River. Exports: cacao, coffee,

sugar, tobacco, lumber. Settled 16th century; inc. into Bahia state 18th century. Pop. 100,687.

Ili (I-li), river in China and USSR; formed by union of K'ung-chi-ssu and T'e-k'o-ssu rivers in N ranges of the Tien Shan; flows through a fertile valley in W China; empties into Lake Balkhash in the USSR. Length: 800mi (1,288km).

Iliad, historic Greek epic poem of the late 8th century BC, attributed to Homer; with the *Odyssey,* a rich source for understanding the religion and people of the period. The *Iliad* describes the activities of the gods and mortals in the last weeks of the 10-year siege of Troy, when after a quarrel with Agamemnon, Achilles refused to continue the battle. After Achilles' friend, Patroclus, was killed by Hector, prince of Troy, Achilles led the invasion and killed Hector, returning Hector's body to King Priam for a hero's funeral.

Ilium. *See* Troy.

Illinois, state in the N central United States, on the E bank of the Mississippi River; one of the richest states in production and trade.

Land and Economy. Except for rolling hills in the NW, the land is virtually level. The Illinois is the largest of many rivers flowing SW into the Mississippi. The black loam soil is enormously productive; Illinois is among the top producers in many types of agriculture. The state has a well-developed industrial sector dominated by heavy industry, including steel and machine tool production. Reserves of bituminous coal are extensive and there is some oil; mining and drilling are mostly in the S. Illinois products are widely distributed through the country and overseas. Chicago is the focus of many railroads and highways. Its port on Lake Michigan handles domestic waterborne commerce through the Great Lakes and the Illinois Waterway leading to the Mississippi and, since the St Lawrence Seaway was opened in 1959, has received large oceangoing vessels.

People. Farmlands and factories have attracted immigrants from other states and from foreign nations since the early 19th century. Many residents are of German, Scandinavian, Russian, Irish, and Italian descent. About 35% of Chicago's population is black; more than 80% of the people reside in urban areas.

Education and Research. There are about 140 institutions of higher education. The state-supported University of Illinois at Urbana has many branches. Notable privately endowed institutions include the University of Chicago and Northwestern University. A large concentration of medical facilities is in Chicago. The Argonne National Laboratory and the University of Chicago carry on extensive research. A large atom-smasher is at Batavia.

History. Father Jacques Marquette and Louis Jolliet, French explorers, sailed up the Illinois River in 1673, and a few French settlements were made in the next century. In 1763 the land was ceded to Great Britain; it was occupied by American troops in the Revolution. Illinois Territory was organized in 1809; it became a state nine years later. Illinois became a power in national politics with the emergence of Abraham Lincoln as a voice of the pro-Union, antislavery policies that brought him election as president. In 1942 the atomic age was inaugurated at the University of Chicago when researchers set off the first self-sustaining atomic chain reaction. During his tenure as mayor of Chicago from 1955 until his death in 1976, Richard J. Daley dominated Illinois politics. Many of the state's industries experienced a downturn during the 1970s and early 1980s.

PROFILE

Admitted to Union: Dec. 3, 1818; rank, 21st
US Congressmen: Senate, 2; House of Representatives, 24
Population: 11,418,461 (1980); rank, 5th
Capital: Springfield, 99,637 (1980)
Chief cities: Chicago, 3,005,072; Rockford, 139,712; Peoria, 124,160; Springfield
State Legislature: Senate, 59; House of Representatives, 177
Area: 56,400sq mi (146,076sq mi); rank, 24th
Elevation: Highest, Charles Mound (in extreme NW), 1,235ft (377m); Lowest, Mississippi River (in extreme SW), 279ft (85m)
Industries (major products): steel, farm and construction machinery, communications equipment, electronic components, appliances, transportation equipment, processed foods.
Agriculture (major products): corn, soybeans, hogs, cattle
Minerals (major): coal, petroleum, fluorspar, stone
State nickname: Prairie State
State motto: "State Sovereignty-National Union"
State bird: Eastern cardinal
State flower: Meadow violet
State tree: Oak

Illinois Indians, confederation of Algonquian-speaking North American Indians who occupied Illinois, Wisconsin, Iowa, and Missouri in prehistoric times. They built Cahokia Mound near St Louis, one of the largest man-made structures in North America. Following the murder of Pontiac in 1769, the Ottawa warred on the Illinois, reducing the population from 8,000 to 225. Today, about 500 of their descendants live in Oklahoma, with a few in Kansas and neighboring states.

Illinois River, river in NE Illinois, formed by confluence of Des Plaines and Kankakee rivers; flows SW across Illinois to Mississippi River at Grafton; forms major part of Illinois Waterway, connecting Great Lakes and Mississippi. Length: 273mi (440km).

Illuminated Manuscripts, illustrations of the Gospels and other religious books, dating from about the 5th century on. Early medieval illuminations were made primarily by monks in monasteries. Later, illumination became a widespread style of illustration, and many different schools developed, such as the Hiberno-Saxon, the Carolingian, and the Winchester schools. During the Gothic period, illumination was used for both religious and secular book illustrations. Illumination was at its height during the 14th and 15th centuries, when the International Gothic style was in use by such French and Flemish artists as Jean Pucelle, the Limbourg brothers, and Jean Fouquet.

Illusion, lack of correspondence between the physical measurement of an object and the perception of that object. Best known are the so-called optical (geometric) illusions, eg, the Müller-Lyer illusion in which two lines of equal length appear unequal because of the diagonal lines that are attached to their ends in different ways. There is no single explanation of geometric illusions; their effect occurs primarily in the brain. Other visual illusions center on the perception of color, brightness, motion, and depth. Explanations of the way they operate vary. Analogous phenomena occur in the other senses; there are touch illusions that resemble geometric illusions and several auditory illusions as well.

Illyria, ancient region on the N and E shores of the Adriatic inhabited by the Dalmatians and the Pannonians, fierce piratical tribes of Indo-European origin.

They remained free of Greek and Macedonian domination but were defeated by the Romans in 168 BC and their land was annexed as Illyricum and about AD 9 was divided as the imperial provinces of Dalmatia and Pannonia. Modern Illyria is N of central Albania.

Iloilo, city in Philippines, on SE Panay Island, on Iloilo Strait; capital of Iloilo prov. Region first settled by Malay chiefs; became commercial center about 1688; declared foreign trade port 1855; site of three universities. Exports: sugar, rice, copra, hemp, canned fish, piña cloth. Pop. 213,000.

Ilorin, city of SW Nigeria, W Africa; marketing and processing center for large agricultural region. Industries: cattle, poultry, cigarettes, palm products, handcrafts, pottery, wood carving, metal working. Pop. 247,956.

Image, Optical, points to which light rays from an object converge (real image) or from which they appear to diverge (virtual image) after reflection or refraction. A real image of an object can be projected onto a screen and can form an image in a photographic emulsion; this is not the case for a virtual image, such as that produced by a plane mirror. *See also* Aberration; Lens; Mirror.

Imaginary Number. *See* Number, Complex.

Imagism, movement in poetry in the period 1909–17 whose credo summed up briefly was: use the language of common speech, create new rhythms, allow absolute freedom in choice of subject, present an image, produce poetry that is hard and clear, use concentration—the very essence of poetry. Amy Lowell was the principal exponent of the movement and brought out three anthologies called *Some Imagist Poets* (1915, 1916, 1917). *See also* Lowell, Amy.

Imamis, or **Twelvers,** a subgroup of the Shi'a sect of Islam. Forming the main body of the Shi'as, the Imamis assert that the 12th imam, or head of the Shi'a party, is still on earth, although hidden, and will return at some future time. About 1500, Twelver Shi'ism became the official religion of Iran. *See also* Islam.

Imhotep, vizier to Pharaoh Zoser of Egypt in the 3rd dynasty of the Old Kingdom (2663–2645 BC), and architect of the first great stone pyramid at Sakkarah. He is also credited with being a physician and writer. Imhotep was deified as the patron of scribes and son of Ptah, the builder-god of Memphis, during the time of the New Kingdom (1554–1075 BC), an honor that came to few men of common birth.

Immanuel. *See* Manuel.

Immigration (US), movement of people to the United States, involving more than 40,000,000 people. Before 1890 immigrants were primarily Anglo-Saxon Protestants from the British Isles, Germany, and Scandinavia. Immigration after 1890 involved mainly Roman Catholics and Jews from eastern and southern Europe, forced to leave because of famine, lack of social and economic opportunities, political notability, or religious persecution. Once a particular group of immigrants settled in an area, they urged others from their homeland to join them. The Homestead Act of 1862 encouraged potential emigrants; the steamship lines vied for their patronage; Northern Pacific Railroad agents touted land bargains; and young American industries sent out a call for workers. The rate of immigration corresponded to economic cycles in the United States; increasing when prosperity was high. Attitudes of native Americans toward immigrants ranged from eagerness to exploit them and fear that they would denigrate the quality of life in the United States, to pride in the strength the country had derived from its ethnic mix. Earlier settlers were often racially biased against those who followed. There were many who blamed immigrants for rising crime rates, labor unrest, and the deterioration of cities. Chinese immigration was restricted in 1882 and Japanese in 1908; mechanisms to control immigration included restrictions on naturalization and denial of elective office to foreign-born. Restrictive policies won out with the passage of the Johnson Act (1924), which established a national origins quota favoring northwestern Europeans. The quota system, reaffirmed (1952) in the Immigration and Nationality Act, was abolished in 1965. The polyglot of subcultures that immigration brought to the United States offers to the mainstream a variety of life styles and values, encouraging cultural borrowing. The strong ethnicity of some immigrants has resisted the melting pot. *See also* Chinese Exclusion.

Immunization, a process or procedure that confers immunity against a disease, usually by stimulating the production of antibodies that combat the disease. In a common type of immunization, weakened forms of infecting organisms are injected into the bloodstream, causing only a very mild form of the disease but sufficient to stimulate antibody production that will provide lasting immunity. Vaccines can also be manufactured using recombinant DNA techniques to produce only the immunoreaction portion of the virus.

Immunoglobulin. *See* Antibody.

Immunology, study of immunity, autoimmunity, and allergy. It is concerned with the provision of active immunity (vaccination, etc) as a means of preventing disease, passive immunity (injections of antitoxins) to treat infection, and diagnosis by a variety of laboratory animals. Autoimmunity is an abnormal injurious reaction as a result of an overactive immune response to the body's own tissues. Allergic reactions result from an overactive response to harmless foreign substances such as dust, rather than to infective organisms.

Immunosuppressive Drug, any chemical used to prevent or weaken the body's immune response, that is, its ability to form antigens. Such drugs are used so that a beneficial antigen (such as a tissue graft) may be retained or an allergic reaction may be prevented. *See also* Antibody.

Impala, or **Pala,** long-legged, medium-sized African antelope. Having sleek, glossy brown fur with black markings on its rump. it is gregarious. Long, lyrate horns are found only on males. It leaps up to 30ft (9m). Length: to 5ft (1.5m); height: to 39in (1m) at shoulder. Family Bovidae; species *Aepyceros melampus.*

Impatiens, genus of more than 100 species of succulent annual plants native to damp areas of Indonesia. They have white, red, or yellow spurred flowers and seedpods that, when ripe, pop and scatter their seeds, giving the plants the name touch-me-not. Tropical Old World species are frequently cultivated as houseplants and bloom throughout the year. Family Balsaminaceae.

Impeachment, method of removing public officials from office. Nationally, the House of Representatives is constitutionally empowered to initiate impeachment proceedings. The Senate is empowered to try the accused, with a two-thirds vote necessary for conviction. Conviction by the Senate can lead to a criminal trial on the same charges. Twelve impeachments have been brought by the House, including that of President Andrew Johnson, who was acquitted (1868). The presidential pardon does not extend to individuals who have been impeached.

Imperialism, domination of one people or country by another. Such domination can be economic, cultural, political, and religious as well as physical. The building of trading empires by major European powers in the 16th century marked the beginning of modern imperialism. Overseas colonies were established to serve as a source for raw materials and to provide a market for manufactured goods. Exploitation of native populations over the centuries led eventually to the national liberation movements of the 20th century.

Imperial Moth, large, stout-bodied yellow moth of E North America. Wingspread: 4–6in (10–15cm). The hairy caterpillar is green, brown, or blackish, with yellow spines on its two front segments. It eats tree leaves. Length: 3–4in (7.5–10cm); species *Eacles imperialis. See also* Moth.

Imperial Valley, valley in SE California, extending S into NW Mexico; most of it is below sea level and was desert until irrigated by All-American Canal that brings water from Colorado River. Has a growing season of 300 days and supports 2 crops per year. Crops: winter fruits and vegetables, dates, grain, cotton. Brawley, Calexico, and El Centro are main cities of valley.

Impetigo, skin disease caused by streptococcal or staphylococcal infection and characterized by multiple, spreading lesions with yellowish-brown crusts appearing primarily on the face and extremities.

Implication, logical proposition of the type "if *P* then *Q*," connecting two simple propositions—*P* (the antecedent) and *Q* (the consequent). In the form used in mathematical logic the two simple propositions need not be connected. This is called *material implication*—an example is "if the earth is flat then gold is a metal." A material implication is false only when the antecedent is true and the consequent false, otherwise it is true (the example given is a true implication). In normal discourse *formal implication* is used, in which the simple propositions are related in meaning; for example "if I am not given more money then I will leave this job." An implication is written as *P*'U*Q*, read "*P* implies *Q*."

Impotence, male inability to perform sexually, the result of organic or psychogenic factors. Impotence may be temporary (eg, when brought about by anxiety regarding performance with a new sexual partner) or a more or less permanent condition in which almost no form of sexual arousal is possible. The term is used loosely to describe various sorts of sexual failure, including lack of erection, loss of pleasure, and inability to reach orgasm. *See also* Frigidity.

Impressionism, French school of painting during the late 19th century. Its main concern was with the use of color, especially to reflect light and atmosphere. Rapid brushstrokes were often used to reduce form to areas of broken color. Much Impressionist painting was done out-of-doors, and typical scenes were landscapes. Much attention was given to painting a subject as it appeared in sunlight. Claude Monet was a key figure in the Impressionist school. Other major painters of this group were Renoir, Degas, Pissarro, Sisley, Morisot, Bazille, and Manet. The first Impressionist exhibition took place in the spring of 1874 in the studio of the Parisian photographer Nadar.

Impressionism in Music, a movement in the history of music, roughly 1890 to 1930. The movement is represented chiefly in the works of Claude Debussy who, against his Romantic contemporaries, composed music that is subtle, soft, atmospheric, and refined rather than overtly emotional, with an emphasis on tone color rather than form. Debussy's first full-blown Impressionistic piece was the *Prelude to the Afternoon of a Faun* (1892), called by some musicologists the beginning of 20th-century music. Many other modern composers were subsequently influenced by Debussy's style and methods, including Ravel, Roussel, Delius, Respighi, Falla, Griffes, Scriabin, and Stravinsky and Schoenberg in their early works. *See also* Romanticism in Music.

Imprinting, a special form of learning that occurs within a critical period in very young animals. The first object encountered becomes the one that is followed thereafter. In nature, this is usually a parent; in experiments, humans, other animals, and even inanimate objects may become substitutes. Imprinting has been studied seriously only in birds, especially ducklings, but it also seems to occur in the young of some mammals and fish.

Inbreeding, breeding of two related offspring, either by mating brother and sister or by self-pollination. This technique results in the refining or strengthening of certain characteristics, and is used to produce uniform strains.

Inca, Indian group that migrated from the Peruvian highlands into the Cuzco area about AD1250. Expansion and consolidation occurred at a slow but steady rate until the reigns of Pachacuti (*c.*1438) and his son, Topa Inca (died 1493), when Inca influence dramatically increased to include the area between Ecuador in the north and Chile to the south. The Inca empire was bureaucratic and militaristic: local administrators and leaders were moved to other areas and co-opted into Inca society; roads facilitated communication and the collection of tribute. The last of the emperors of a united realm, Huayna Capac, was dead only a short time when civil war broke out between his two sons. Pizarro used the internal conflict to advantage, completing the downfall of an already weakened empire.

Incense Cedar, widely distributed genus *(Libocedrus)* of evergreen trees native to Chile, North America, New Zealand, and China. They may be pyramid-shaped or spreading and have flat, scalelike leaves. The cones are oblong. The aromatic wood is used for interior work and furniture, especially cedar chests. Height: 50–100ft (15–30m). Family Taxodiaceae.

Incest Taboo, taboo (prohibition accompanied by intense horror) on sexual relations within an exogamous kin group, which may be biological, classificatory, or affinal. It defines both impossible and possible sexual relations. *See also* Endogamy; Exogamy.

Inchon (Inch'ŏn), port city in NW South Korea, on Yellow Sea; port opened for foreign trade 1883; site of arrival of UN forces in Korean War, 1950. Exports: rice, dried fish, soy beans. Industries: steel, iron, textiles, matches, flour, chemicals, lumber. Pop. 799,982.

Inchworm. *See* Measuring Worm.

Incisor, one of the front teeth in mammals, generally used for cutting, holding, or plucking. There are many variations: rodents have curved, continuously growing incisors for gnawing and carnivores have small points that help hold prey. The tusks of elephants are enlarged upper incisors. Man has two incisors in each half of each jaw, eight in all.

Immigration (US): Ellis Island

India

Ganges River, India

Inclination, Magnetic, or dip, the angle made by a free-floating magnet with the magnetic lines of force. At the north magnetic pole the inclination is zero; at the magnetic equator it is 90°. *See also* Declination, Magnetic.

Inclined Plane, plane inclined to a horizontal reference plane. The angle of the plane is the angle between two lines, one in each plane, both at right angles to their line of intersection.

Income Tax, tax levied against the income of individuals or businesses. In the United States, the income tax is a progressive tax, ie, higher-income groups pay a higher percentage of their income in taxes. Although it is thus presumably based on the ability-to-pay principle, individuals in middle-income groups actually bear the major part of the burden. Corporations may be able to shift part of their income-tax burden to the consumer in the form of higher prices. The US government derives most of its revenue from the income tax.

Income Tax Amendment (1913), the 16th Amendment, allowing Congress to levy and collect taxes. During World War I, heavy taxes were placed on luxuries, high incomes, and excessive profits on war earnings. In the 1920s, Andrew Mellon helped engineer tax reductions for the wealthy, shifting a substantial part of the tax burden to middle-income groups and enabling the wealthy to feed the stock market speculation that led to the crash of 1929.

Incunabula, term meaning those books printed from the time of the invention of typography (in the 1450s) to the end of the 15th century. The known number of such works totals about 35,000. Georg Wolfgang Panzer produced the first catalog of those editions in 5 volumes 1793–97.

Indépendants, Salon des, society of artists founded in Paris in 1884 by Seurat, Signac, and others, which allowed any artist who so wished to display his works in its exhibitions. The artist was asked to pay a fee but was not required to have his work judged by a selection committee. Many artists whose works were considered avant-garde exhibited with this group.

Independence, city in W Missouri, 9mi (14km) E of Kansas City; seat of Jackson co; site of Mormon Colony 1831–33; world headquarters of Reorganized Church of Jesus Christ of Latter-Day Saints; home of Harry S. Truman and site of Harry S. Truman Library (1957). Industries: printing, publishing, oil refining, chemicals. Founded 1827; inc. 1849. Pop. (1980) 111,806.

Independent Variable. *See* Variable.

Index Fossil, any fossil of limited time distribution that clearly marks certain beds or strata of rocks. Its occurrence in rocks located miles apart proves that these deposits were formed at the same time. These fossils are important in mapping rock formations and in locating valuable resources. *See also* Fossil.

Index of Refraction. *See* Refraction.

India, an independent nation on the Indian subcontinent of S Asia. India has produced two major religions—Buddhism and Hinduism—and more recently Mahatma Gandhi's nonviolent resistance movement. An imbalanced economy is a persistent problem. The world's second-most populous country (after the People's Republic of China), India proudly regards itself as the world's largest democracy.

Land and economy. The Indian subcontinent is bordered by the Bay of Bengal, Bangladesh, and Burma (E), the People's Republic of China, Nepal, Bhutan and Sikkim (N), Pakistan and the Arabian Sea (W), and the island nation of Sri Lanka on the (S). A land with three seasons—cool, hot and dry, and rainy—it is divided into three regions. The N mountains (Himalayas) are the least populated. S of this is the flat, broad river plain (Gangetic plain) including the Ganges River—this is the most populous and prosperous portion. Below this is the hilly, dry plateau (Deccan plateau). Starting from primitive farming, India has made forward strides in agriculture since 1947; 70% of the population raises crops. Industry has been dominated by jute and cotton with steel and chemicals in recent production; India now has the world's eighth-highest industrial output. Oil exploration is taking place in the Bay of Bengal. In 1965, India undertook a plan to achieve self-sufficiency in food; despite a soaring birth rate (12,000,000 Indians are born annually), the program was largely successful by the late 1970s, and India stopped importing grains.

People. Ethnically, Indians are divided into two main groups, Aryans (N) and Dravidians (S). Eighty percent of the population is Hindu and practices a religion based on reincarnation and the caste system, a strict division of people into 4 major social classes with a total of 1,000 subdivisions. Outlawed now by the constitution, the caste system is breaking down. India has about 60,000,000 Muslims and minorities of Sikhs, Jains, Buddhists, and Parsis. Freedom of religion is guaranteed. There are more than 200 separate languages spoken in India; Hindi (spoken by 50%) and English are the official languages; 14 others have also received official recognition. Free compulsory education through age 14 is assured.

Government. India is a democratic republic; power resides in the prime minister, who represents the majority party of the bicameral parliament. The prime minister heads the Council of Ministers (Cabinet) which is responsible to the lower house of parliament.

History. Indus Valley ruins reveal an Indian civilization dating from 2500 BC. In 1500 BC migrating shepherds (Aryans) from central Asia came down through the Himalayan passes, pushing the merchant Dravidians S. They perfected Sanskrit and initiated the caste system. Buddhism's founder, Siddhartha Gautama, lived from 563–483. The Golden Age of India under the Gupta dynasty (AD 320–500) was followed by Hun, Muslim, Tartar, and Mogul invasions. Vasco da Gama established Portuguese trading posts after 1498. By 1600 the British East India Company, with Mogul permission to trade in spices and textiles, controlled much of India. It was not until after the 1919 Amritsar Massacre of Indians that Mohandas Gandhi (1869–1948) emerged as a prominent nationalist leader. Under the banner of the mainly Hindu Indian National Congress he led the people against colonial rule with a mass movement based on nonviolent disobedience. In 1934, Muslims demanded that a separate state of Pakistan be carved out of India. After 40 years of India's struggle for freedom, Britain withdrew in 1947, and India attained self-government within the British Commonwealth. The same year partition gave Pakistan to the Muslims, and Kashmir became an Indian state. Since partition, India and Pakistan have fought three wars, the first (1947–49) resulting in the partition of Kashmir between India and Pakistan. A 1950 constitution made India a democratic republic. Gandhi was assassinated in 1948. Jawaharlal Nehru was India's first prime minister. His daughter, Indira Gandhi, became prime minister in 1966. In 1975, after Gandhi had been accused of election fraud, and in the face of growing economic problems and political unrest, a state of emergency was declared, and thousands of political opponents were arrested. After the state of emergency was lifted in 1977, national elections were held, and Gandhi's

Congress party was defeated. In the elections of 1980, however, she was returned to office. Gandhi, assassinated in 1984 by Sikhs who were members of her security guard, was succeeded by her son Rajiv Gandhi. Sikh extremists continued to use terrorist tactics in their quest to control the state of Punjab.

PROFILE

Official name: Republic of India
Area: 1,266,598sq mi (3,280,488sq km)
Population: 658,337,000
 Density: 520per sq mi (201per sq km)
Chief cities: New Delhi (capital); Bombay; Calcutta; Madras; Poona
Government: Republic (with parliament)
Religion: Hindu (83%)
Language: Hindi (official)
Monetary unit: Rupee
Gross national product: $125,990,000
Per capita income: $143
Industries: cotton fabrics, iron, steel products, machinery, chemicals, processed foods, fertilizer, wool and silk, tanned hides, sewing machines, typewriters
Agriculture: tea, sugar, rice, wheat, nuts, barley, corn, rubber, cotton, tobacco
Minerals: coal, mica, manganese, salt, iron ore, bauxite, gypsum
Trading partners: United States, United Kingdom, Japan, USSR

Indiana, state in the N central United States, in the country's richest farming region.

Land and Economy. The land slopes gradually to the W and S, and many rivers, of which the Wabash is the largest, flow in this direction. There are numerous lakes, especially in the N. The original forest was cleared by the first settlers for farming, which remains a major sector of the economy; the state ranks high in agricultural production. Development of varied manufacturing, particularly in heavy industry complexes in the NW along Lake Michigan, has placed Indiana among the nation's leaders in this category. Access to the lake and to the Ohio River in the S, with an extensive highway and railroad system, ensures efficient distribution of Indiana's farm and manufactured products.

People. Early settlement was made largely by people from states to the E and SE; their descendants form the bulk of the population. About 95% were born in the United States and about 75% in Indiana. About 65% reside in areas classified as urban, mostly in many small communities.

Education. There are nearly 50 institutions of higher education. Indiana University, a state-supported institution at Bloomington, has several branch campuses. The University of Notre Dame, a Roman Catholic institution near South Bend, is nationally known.

History. The French explored the land and in the early 18th century founded several forts to protect their fur trade. France ceded it to Great Britain in 1763. During the American Revolution, US troops occupied the territory; it passed to the United States at the war's end. Indiana Territory was created in 1800. Severe fighting that lasted at least until 1811 was needed to subdue the Indians. After achieving statehood in 1816, Indiana remained a rural area until late in the 19th century, when the pace of industrialization quickened, continuing into the 20th century.

PROFILE

Admitted to Union: Dec. 11, 1816; rank, 19th
US Congressmen: Senate, 2; House of Representatives, 11
Population: 5,490,179 (1980); rank, 12th
Capital: Indianapolis; 700,807 (1980)

Chief cities: Indianapolis; Fort Wayne, 172,196; Gary, 151,953; Evansville, 130,496
State Legislature: Senate, 50; House of Representatives, 100
Area: 36,291sq mi (93,994sq km); rank, 38th
Elevation: Highest, 1,257ft (383m), NE corner, Wayne County, near E boundary. Lowest, Ohio River, 320ft (98m)
Industries (major products): steel, electrical machinery, aircraft, automobile parts, farm machinery, processed foods
Agriculture (major products): hogs, corn, soybeans, cattle
Minerals (major): coal, petroleum, limestone
State nickname: Hoosier State
State motto: "The Crossroads of America"
State bird: Cardinal
State flower: Peony
State tree: Tulip Tree

Indian Affairs, Bureau of (BIA), division within the US Department of the Interior. Originally established in 1824, the BIA's major responsibilities are the Indian and Alaskan peoples who live on reservations. The bureau works to train native peoples to manage their own affairs under a trust relationship with the federal government and to develop their resources. The BIA became an object of protest for Indian rights organizations, beginning in the late 1960s; the organizations charged the BIA with insensitivity toward Indians.

Indianapolis, capital and largest city of Indiana, in central Indiana, 150mi (242km) SE of Chicago at confluence of Falls Creek and White River; seat of Marion co. Selected as site of capital 1820, Indianapolis was made capital 1825; development was spurred in 19th century by the coming of National Road, introduction of Madison Railroad (1847), discovery of natural gas, development of trolley system, and beginning automobile industry. The annual 500-mi (805km) auto race at Indianapolis Motor Speedway is held in nearby suburb; site of War Memorial (1901), state capitol (1878), Butler University (1850), Indiana Central College (1902), Marian College (1937). Industries: chemicals, electrical machinery, transportation equipment, flour, meat packing, pharmaceuticals. Settled 1820; inc. 1847. Pop. (1980) 700,807.

Indian Architecture falls into three phases. Buddhist, Hindu, and Jain architecture, from the 2nd century BC, consists of religious structures—stupas, rock-cut cave temples, and the elaborately carved chaitya temples. Following the Mogul conquest in the 16th century a modified Islamic architecture was introduced: mosques, with minarets and elaborate grillwork, palaces surrounded by pools and gardens, and grandiose tombs, like the famous Taj Mahal. After the British conquest in the 18th century a variety of European classical styles were used in churches, administration buildings, and town houses.

Indian Languages, North American. There are more than 100 North American Indian languages, falling into many different families: Algonkian, Athapascan, Siouan, Iroquoian, Muskogean, among others, in the United States and Canada; Uto-Aztecan, in the United States and Mexico; Oto-Manguean, in Mexico; and Mayan, in Mexico and Guatemala. Nahuatl, the language of the Aztecs, is the most widely spoken of these languages; Navajo ranks first among those spoken in the United States.

Indian Languages, South American. There are more than 1,000 South American Indian languages, with approximately 10–12,000,000 speakers. Among the more important families are Chibchan, Arawakan, and Tupian. Widely spoken languages are Quechua (the language of the Incas) and Aymara, of both Peru and Bolivia, and constituting the Quechuamaran family. Another important language is Guarani, of Paraguay, belonging to the Tupian family. Most of the rest are spoken by only a few hundred or a few thousand people.

Indian Mutiny or **Sepoy Mutiny** (1857–58), uprising of the native soldiers in the British forces in India. The revolt occurred when Governor General Canning continued policies of Westernization in India, disregarding traditions of Hindus and Muslims alike. The immediate cause of the mutiny was the use of a mixture of pigs' and cows' lard in the cartridges that sepoys (the native soldiers) had to bite in order to use in their rifles. Hindus and Muslims were offended by the substance. Those who complied with orders to use the cartridges were shunned by their compatriots, and those who refused were imprisoned by the British. The rebels gained a focus when they took Delhi, and the Mogul Emperor Bahadur Shah II reluctantly took their side. Canning ordered British troops to retake Delhi. Sir Henry Lawrence held the loyalty of the sepoys in the Punjab, and Colin Campbell did the same in the Deccan. It was these forces that retook Delhi and Lucknow and gave the British the victory. After the suppression of the revolt, the British government took away the right of the British East India Company to rule India.

Indian Mythology, The characters of the Indian myths inhabit a wondrous land where the real and the miraculous are inseparable. The favorite stories deal with fairies and ogres and genii, objects that change their size and animals or people that change their shape. The earliest records of Indian mythology are in the Vedas and the explanatory texts appended to them, the Brahmanas, dating from the first and second centuries BC. The best loved tales are found in the Bhagavadgita and the Ramayana, or tales of Rama, of the late 16th century. *See also* Brahmana; Rig Veda.

Indian Ocean, world's 3rd-largest ocean, bounded approx. by S Asia (N), Antarctica (S), E Africa (W), SE Australia (E); chief arms are Arabian Sea, Bay of Bengal, Andaman Sea; seasonal monsoons control most of the currents. The first ocean to be extensively navigated, it was crossed by Vasco da Gama on the first voyage from Europe to India (1497), and traversed E-W by Juan Sebastián del Cano, first to circumnavigate the globe (1521); scene of large-scale oceanographic exploration during 19th and 20th centuries. Area (including numerous branches): 28,920,000sq mi (74,902,800sq km).

Indian Pipe, or ghost flower, parasitic plant found in forests of Northern Hemisphere. It feeds on decaying organic matter. This plant has a translucent, white or pinkish, waxy stem with a nodding flower and no leaves. Height: 4–10in (10–25cm). Family Pyrolaceae; species *Monotropa uniflora.*

Indian Removal, Policy of, US program restricting eastern Indians to certain areas. This forcible removal action, originated by Sec. of War John C. Calhoun in 1823 and continuing until the policy of "reserving land" began in 1853, fixed a permanent Indian frontier and thereby encouraged white settlement. The Indians were removed to parts of Arkansas, Missouri, Nebraska, Kansas, and Oklahoma. It was designed to remove the danger of hostile Indians in sections settled by whites.

Indians, North American, the aboriginal people of North America, believed to be of generalized Mongoloid stock and to have crossed from Asia via the Bering Strait or the Aleutian Islands about 20,000 BC or earlier. These people spread throughout North, Central, and South America and developed into many distinct regional varieties with hundreds of different languages. The Indians of the United States, Canada, and Mexico may be divided into eight distinct cultural and geographic groups: the Arctic area (Aleut, Eskimo); the Northeastern-Mackenzie area (mainly Eastern Woodland tribes); the Northwest Coast area (Tlingit, Haida, Kwakiutl); the Southwestern area (Five Civilized Tribes, Tuscarora, Powhatan Confederacy); the Plains area (Blackfoot, Crow, Comanche, Dakota); the California-Intermountain area (Paiute, Shoshoni, Nez Percé); the Southwestern area (Pueblos, Navaho, Apache); and the Mesoamerican area (Maya, Toltec, Aztec).

Indians, South American, the aboriginal populations of South America, derived from North American groups that had migrated southward. Three main culture groups inhabiting distinct geographic areas are recognized. (1) Indians of the Andean area developed the highest cultures of the continent. After AD 1300 the Quechua culture dominated almost the entire region. The Incas encountered by the Spaniards were a Quechua branch. (2) The Indians of the Amazon Basin are mainly isolated primitive agricultural communities of many localized tribes. Some were cannibalistic. The use of blowgun and poisoned arrows is widespread. (3) The Indians of the pampas, including warlike nomadic tribes and the southern Araucanians. They successfully resisted Inca and Spaniard alike. In the southernmost portion of the continent live the Tierra del Fuegans who hunt and fish and have only rude temporary shelters.

Indian Territory, area set aside for Indians by the US government. The Indian Removal Act of 1830 gave the president authority to designate specific Western lands for settlement by Indians removed from their native lands. In 1834 the Indian Intercourse Act set aside Kansas, Nebraska, and Oklahoma N and E of the Red River as the Indian Territory. In 1854 Kansas and Nebraska were redesignated territories open to white settlement. W Oklahoma was opened to white settlement in 1889. In 1907 the last of the Indian Territory was dissolved when Oklahoma became a state.

India-Pakistan Wars, series of conflicts between India and Pakistan. War first broke out in 1947, when the two countries became independent of Britain. There were serious conflicts in 1947–48, 1965, and 1971. The genesis of the hostilities lay in the antipathy between Hindus and Muslims. Early in the 20th century the two groups worked together in the Indian National Congress to oppose Britain, but the Muslims gravitated to the Muslim League. During World War II, Muslim support made Britain more sympathetic to Muslim demands for a separate state. After independence (1947) religious rioting led to casualties of perhaps 1,000,000. Hindus (*c.*10,000,000) left Pakistan for India, and Muslims (over 7,000,000) fled from India to Pakistan. In Kashmir, in NW India, the Hindu ruler wanted his state to become part of India, while his Muslim subjects were oriented toward Pakistan. There were also disputes in Bengal and the Punjab. India consolidated its position in these areas, while Pakistan opposed India. The war in Kashmir continued until 1949, when the United Nations arranged a truce. India-Pakistan negotiations continued to 1954 without resolution of problems in Kashmir. In 1965 fighting erupted on India's frontier with W Pakistan in the desolate Rann of Kutch region. Fighting soon became widespread, with each nation launching troop and air assaults. With international intervention threatened, Pakistan and India agreed to another truce. An agreement on negotiations and a cease-fire was signed in 1966. An era of peace began to fall apart in early 1971 after civil war erupted between W and E Pakistan. India sided with the E, which called itself Bangladesh. The war climaxed with India's invasion of Bangladesh in December 1971. Fighting also started with Pakistan in the W. Pakistan was soon defeated; it lost E Pakistan, had about 100,000 troops captured; and suffered hardship. The force of world opinion led to a cease-fire in December. An accord signed in 1972 lessened tension, further reduced by Pakistan's recognition of Bangladesh in 1974. Mujibur Rahman, Bangladesh's leader in the fight for independence, led the new country until his overthrow and death in 1975. Relations continued to improve following Rahman's death.

Indicator, in chemistry, substance applied in minute quantities which, by a change of color, fluorescence, or by precipitate formation, allows the course of a chemical reaction to be followed. Indicators can detect endpoints in reactions involving a change of pH or an oxidation-reduction reaction. Universal indicator is a liquid that undergoes a spectral range of color changes from pH 1 to 13.

Indic Languages, subdivision of the Indo-European family. Spoken mainly in the N two-thirds of India, but also in Pakistan, Sri Lanka, and Nepal, the major Indic languages are Sanskrit (the progenitor of all the others), Hindi, Urdu, Bengali, Punjabi, Marathi, Gujarati, Oriya, Assamese, Sinhalese, Sindhi, and Nepali. Romany, the language of the gypsies, is also an Indic language.

Indifference Curve, or iso-utility curve, graphical representation of various combinations of two goods that would hold the consumer at a particular utility level.

Indigestion, incomplete digestion or lack of digestion by the stomach or intestine, causing abdominal distress. It may result from excessive secretion of acid by the stomach, inability to absorb fats, or from an underlying disease such as gallstones or appendicitis. It is sometimes a manifestation of emotional stress.

Indigo Bunting, small finch of North and South America. The male has deep blue plumage; the female is brown. Length: 5–6in (12.7–15.2cm). Family Fringillidae; species *Passerina cyanea.*

Indigo Snake, harmless, dark blue snake ranging from SE United States to Argentina. It hisses and vibrates its tail when disturbed. Length: to 110in (2.8m). Family Colubridae; species *Drymarchon corais. See also* Snake.

Indium, metallic element (symbol In) of group IIIA of the periodic table. Chief source is as a by-product from zinc ores. The element is used in certain low-melting alloys and in semiconductors. Properties: at. no. 49; at. wt. 114.82; sp gr 7.31; melt. pt. 313.9°F (156.61°C); boil. pt. 3776°F (2080°C); most common isotope is In^{115} (95.72%).

Indochina, SE peninsula of Asia, including Burma, Thailand, Cambodia, Vietnam, West Malaysia, Laos. Name refers to former federation of states of Vietnam, Laos, and Cambodia associated with France within the French Union (1945–54). European penetration of the area began in 16th century; by the 19th century France controlled Cochin China, Cambodia, Annam, and Tonkin, which formed into a union of Indochina 1887; Laos was added 1893. By the end of WWII France had an-

Indigo snake

Indonesian children

Indus River

nounced plans for a federation within the French Union, allowing more self-government for the states. Cambodia and Laos accepted the federation, but fighting broke out between French troops and Annamese nationalists, who wanted independence for Annam, Tonkin, and Cochin China as Vietnam. The war resulted in a breakup of French control of the area, officially by the Geneva convention of 1954. The region again became a battleground in the 1960s and 1970s. *See also* Vietnam War.

Indo-European Languages, the world's largest language family, extending over all of Europe, the Western Hemisphere, and a part of Asia. It includes the Germanic, Romance, Celtic, Slavic, Baltic, Iranian, and Indic subgroups, thus embracing such disparate languages as English, Spanish, Russian, Greek, Icelandic, Welsh, Albanian, Lithuanian, Armenian, Persian, Sanskrit, and Hindi. About half the world's population speaks one or another Indo-European language.

Indonesia, independent nation between W Pacific Ocean and NE India Ocean. The site of ancient cultures and the unreached goal of Columbus in 1492. It is now the world's largest Muslim nation. A SW Asian archipelago of more than 13,500 islands, tropical Indonesia extends 3,000mi (4,800km) across the equator between Asia and Australia, forming a natural barrier between the Indian and Pacific oceans. Formerly the Netherlands East Indies, its major islands are Sumatra, Java, Sulawesi, and S Kalimantan (Borneo). Malaysia is to the N and W, the Philippines to the N, and Australia to the SE. Divided between shallow seas and volcanic mountains, Indonesia has frequent earthquakes and more than 20 typhoons each year. Average temperature is 80°F (27°C) and annual rainfall averages 80in (203cm). In spite of excellent volcanic soil and superior natural resources, especially oil, Indonesia's development has been stymied by a lack of education and training. In 1966, the government undertook a foreign-aid plan to improve food and industrial production. Oil, rubber, and timber are its major exports.

People. Indonesians are primarily of Malay descent, probably coming from China's Yunnan prov. (2500 BC). A later influx of Indian traders who intermarried and spread the Buddhist-Hindu religion still influences the distinctive island of Bali. About 90% of Indonesians are Muslim. Freedom of religion is guaranteed by the constitution, and the literacy rate is 60%. Indonesian is the spoken and written language.

Government. A 1945 constitution provides for a centralized state and a Consultative Assembly divided between elected and appointed members who in turn elect the president. In fact, the military and its political party maintain tight control over the government.

History. Indonesia's Spice Islands were the destination of Columbus in 1492. By then Java and Sumatra had achieved two major empires of high civilization (12th and 14th centuries); some temples and examples of ancient art remain from this period. Western infiltration began in 16th century with the Portuguese, followed by the Dutch, who came in 1602 and ruled the rich colonial possession for 300 years. Movement for independence started between the two world wars. In August 1945, Sukarno, leader of a freedom crusade, declared a republic, and full independence was granted in 1949. Many short-lived administrations followed. In 1960, Sukarno imposed an authoritarian regime allied to Asian Communist states and the Indonesian Communist party (PKI). Fighting erupted between the Communists and the anti-Communist army. Sukarno's power was transferred to politically moderate General Suharto, who was elected president in 1973. His military government, however, has been ac-

cused of corruption, particularly in nationalized industries, and repression. In 1976, Portugal relinquished its claim to East Timor, and Indonesia, fighting against independence guerrilla forces, annexed the territory that same year. During the 1980s famine and human rights violations in this area received international attention.

PROFILE

Official name: Republic of Indonesia
Area: 735,269sq mi (1,904,347sq km)
Population: 138,891,000
  Density: 189per mi (73per sq km)
Chief cities: Djakarta (capital); Bandung
Government: Republic
Religion: Islam
Language: Bahasa Indonesian
Monetary unit: Rupiah
Gross national product: $52,200,000,000
Per capita income: $240
Industries: petroleum products, processed foods, cotton, textiles, tires, cement
Agriculture: timber, rubber, rice, sweet potatoes, tobacco, coffee, peanuts, soybeans, tea, spices, palm oil
Minerals: oil, tin, coal, bauxite, manganese, copper, nickle, gold, silver
Trading partners: Australia, France, Japan, United States, United Kingdom

Indore, city in W central India, on the Saraswati and Khan rivers; capital of former Indore state; site of the maharajas of Indore palace, Glass Temple, and monuments of the Holkar dynasty (1733–1818). Industries: textiles, iron, steel, chemicals. Pop. 572,622.

Indra, in Vedic mythology, ruler of heaven, great god of storms, thunder and lightening, worshiped as rainmaker and bringer of fertility to the fields. In the creation myth he slew the Vritra, dragon of drought, to give water, the Sun, and dawn to the Earth.

Induction, process by which an electromagnetic force (emf) is generated in a circuit when the magnetic flux through the circuit changes. The direction of the induced current is such that its magnetic field tends to keep constant the number of lines linked with the circuit. The magnitude of the current is proportional to the rate of change of flux. In a transformer the changing magnetic field created by the alternating current in the primary coil induces a current in the secondary coil. A generator consists of a constant magnetic field created by a permanent magnet or a current-carrying coil within which a conducting coil is rotated. This coil is thus subjected to a changing magnetic field and consequently an emf is generated within it.

Induction, Magnetic, or magnetic flux density, the magnetic flux passing through a unit area of a magnetic field in a direction at right angles to the magnetic force. It is measured in teslas.

Inductive Logic, method of reasoning by which a general proposition is supported through consideration of particular cases that fall under it; often contrasted to deductive logic. Aristotle referred to induction as "a passage from individuals to universals." *See also* Deductive Logic; Logic.

Indus River, river of India and Pakistan; rises in Kailas mountain range of Tibet, China; flows WNW through Jammu and Kashmir regions of India, then SW through Pakistan and into the Arabian Sea. Semi-navigable along shallow lower part, the river is used chiefly for irrigation and hydroelectric power. A 1960 treaty gave joint rights of use to India and Pakistan. The Indus

Valley is the most densely populated and chief agricultural region of Pakistan; scene of prehistoric Indus civilization. Length: approx. 1,900mi (3,059km).

Industrial Health, branch of medicine concerned with the health problems associated with a person's occupation and in particular with diseases that may result from occupational exposure to health hazards, e.g., the black lung disease of coal miners.

Industrialization. *See* Industrial Revolution.

Industrial Revolution, term traditionally applied to the widespread economic changes that took place in Great Britain, Western Europe, and the United States in the 18th and 19th centuries. It describes the process by which the economies of the countries were so transformed that the societies were changed from those in which most of the population made livings as farmers, merchants, and craftsmen to those based on modern industrialized economies. The term is also used more generally to describe a similar process in other parts of the world. Japan, for example, went through its industrial revolution in the first half of the 20th century, and in much of the Third World the industrial revolution was just beginning to develop in the last quarter of the 20th century. The conditions needed to bring about an industrial revolution include adequate supplies of labor, raw materials, and fuel; an efficient transportation system; enough capital, or wealth, to finance the building of the mills and factories in which the goods are produced; and a market in which to sell the goods. All these conditions were met in England in the 18th century. It was the first country to go through such an upheaval and its transformation is generally considered the classic example of an industrial revolution.

The population of Great Britain had doubled during the 17th century, creating more people than the agricultural, artisan, mercantile society could effectively use. The Bank of England, founded in 1694, was an instrument capable of providing the capital necessary for industrialization. Britain's expanding colonial empire offered both a source of raw materials (eg, cotton from the American colonies) and a market for its manufactured goods. Finally, Britain had large deposits of coal and iron ore. Textile making, a cottage industry in the 18th century, was the first to feel the effects of the revolution. The fly shuttle was invented in 1733, the spinning jenny in 1770, and the power loom in 1783. Large factories employing hundreds of persons were built. An international trade was established and great fortunes made.

In 1709 a process had been perfected for the production of pig iron by the use of coal. It allowed the making of the heavy machinery needed to convert Britain to an industrial economy. The revolution in metallurgy was climaxed in 1855 by the invention of the Bessemer process for making steel. The single most important invention, however, was the steam engine. James Watt, a Scot, patented an improved steam engine in 1769, and it was quickly adapted to many uses. Important among them were the steam railroad and the steamship, which together revolutionized transportation.

Along with the great wealth it produced, the industrial revolution brought serious social upheavals. The mechanization of agriculture (eg, the reaper) threw thousands out of work. Most of the displaced workers gravitated to the industrial cities, where mills and factories needed vast numbers of unskilled workers. Wages and living conditions were abominable; salaries were so low that women and children were forced into the labor market to augment family income. Vast amounts of coal were needed to fuel industry and transportation, and nowhere were the working conditions so bad as in the coal mines. There were virtually no social welfare programs in the laissez-faire atmosphere of the newly industrialized society. The sick, the injured, and the elderly could look only to woefully inadequate private charity for help.

In the United States, the industrial revolution was later than in England and developed along regional lines. The NE became industrialized quite early; the mill towns of New England developed only a generation or so after their English counterparts.Some of the newly settled western lands—notably Ohio and the coal-bearing areas of W Pennsylvania—were industrialized in the first half of the 19th century. The South, on the other hand, remained primarily agricultural until after the Civil War. Except for pockets of industry such as Birmingham, Ala., the South did not experience its industrial revolution until well into the 20th century.

Industrial Workers of the World (IWW), labor union; also known as the "Wobblies." This group was formed (1905) in Chicago by Daniel DeLeon, Eugene V. Debs, and William D. Haywood. It was designed to combine both skilled and unskilled labor in one organization. It was effective among lumbermen, migratory workers, and miners in the Northwest. The group, which advocated a socialistic society and employed militant tactics, supported strikes by textile workers (1912) and silk weavers (1919) in the East. The IWW split up after World War I.

Industry Equilibrium, in economics, condition in which there is no tendency for more firms to enter a particular industry nor is there a tendency for existing firms to leave it. This equilibrium position is expected to exist when normal profits are being earned by firms within the industry and may be disturbed if cost conditions change or if the industry is subjected to outside interference.

Indus Valley Civilization (*fl.c.*2500–*c.*1500 BC), ancient civilization of the Indus River Valley of present-day Pakistan. First rediscovered by British archaeologist John Marshall in 1921, it is the earliest known urban culture of the Indian subcontinent. Three major cities—Mohenjo-daro, Harappo, and Chanhu-daro—have been extensively excavated. All followed the same plan: a grid plan city with wide streets laid out before a hill citadel. Each city contained large granaries and an elaborate community bath. Agriculture was highly organized and trade was carried on with Mesopotamia. The pictographic script was deciphered in 1969 and found to be related to Dravidian. It is believed that the cities were overrun by Aryan invaders.

Inequality, mathematical statement that one expression is less, or greater, than another. The symbols $>$, for "is greater than," and $<$, for "is less than," are used: for example, $2x + 4 > 12$, which is equivalent to $12 < 2x + 4$. Inequalities of this type may be handled in a somewhat similar way to equations: thus, in the case above, $x > 4$. The symbols $\geq$ and $\leq$ are also used, for "greater than or equal to" or "less than or equal to," respectively.

Inert Gases. *See* Noble Gases.

Inertia, the quality possessed by bodies that requires force to be applied to change their states of motion. Newton's First Law of Motion is sometimes called the Law of Inertia. Frames of reference in which Newton's First Law holds are called inertial frames; Einstein's Special Theory of Relativity applies to all such frames.

Inertial Guidance, system of controlling missiles or spacecraft whose orbits are largely above the earth's atmosphere. Main components include gyroscopes for stability, sensors for detecting changes in orientation, motors or jets for correcting differences between planned and actual flight path, and accelerometers for determining velocity and position. It can be supplemented by radar observations and control to correct gyro drift. *See also* Guidance System, Spacecraft.

Infarction, localized cell damage caused by interruption of the blood supply, usually by a clot. A clot in one of the coronary arteries supplying the heart muscle (myocardium) is a cause of heart attacks (myocardial infarction). *See also* Coronary Thrombosis.

Infection, invasion of the body by microorganisms that multiply in the tissues and cause damage to cells, or the disease state caused by the invasion.

Infectious Mononucleosis, an infectious disease occurring primarily in adolescence and the twenties and thought to be associated with a herpes virus. Among its symptoms are enlargement of the spleen and lymph glands, liver dysfunction, fever, sore throat, and abnormal white blood cells. Although it is a benign disease, with low mortality, it poses the risk of rupture of the spleen.

Inferiority Complex, personality pattern marked by chronic feelings of unworthiness and a tendency toward setting excessively high standards and making unrealistic comparisons with others.

Infinite Set, mathematical set of objects, as of all the whole numbers, that contains an unlimited infinite number of members. A finite set, as of the letters of the Roman alphabet, contains a specific finite number of members. *See also* Sets.

Inflammation, protective reaction of body tissue to destruction or injury, with resulting pain, heat, swelling, redness, distention of small blood vessels, and migration of white blood cells into the affected area.

Inflation, continual upward movement of prices. Though normally associated with periods of prosperity, inflation may also occur during recessions. Inflation usually occurs when there is relatively full employment. Under *cost-push inflation,* prices rise because the producers' costs increase. Under *demand-pull inflation,* prices increase because there is excess consumer demand for goods.

Many economists feel that money supply is a major factor in determining the rate of inflation. They contend that the rate of increase of the money supply ultimately controls the consumers' ability to demand goods. If the money supply is increased, then consumers' demands for goods increase relative to productive capabilities of the economy, which leads to increases in prices and to rationing the scarce goods. Therefore, the government often uses fiscal and monetary policy to control inflation.

Inflection, in linguistics, a change in word form which distinguishes tense, person, number, gender, voice, or case. In English, this is usually achieved by adding endings to the word stem ("house, houses"; "jump, jumped"). Another type of inflection sees the word stem change ("bring, brought"). Although the system is relatively simple for some languages, it is far more complex for languages such as Latin, German, and French.

Inflorescence, flower or flower cluster. Inflorescences are classified according to branching characteristics. Racemose inflorescence has a main axis and lateral flowering branches, with flowers opening from the bottom up or from the outer edge in. Types include panicle, raceme, spike, and umbel. Cymose inflorescence has a composite axis with the main stem ending in a flower and lateral branches bearing additional later-flowering branches.

Influenza, a highly contagious respiratory infection of viral origin and of varying severity. There are three general types of influenza viruses, with each type having many variations. Symptoms include headache, inflammation of the nose and throat, and muscle pain, often generalized. Influenza may occur in isolated cases, may affect many persons in a city, state, or region (epidemic), or may be worldwide, as in 1917 (pandemic). Mortality has been reduced by the availability of influenza vaccines and by the advent of antibiotics, giving protection against pneumonia, influenza's most serious complication.

Information Theory, mathematical analysis of the laws controlling systems designed to communicate or manipulate information. Largely originated by Claude E. Shannon in 1948, the theory sets out to quantify both information itself and the ability of various systems to transmit, store, and process it. One of the basic postulates of information theory is that information can be treated like a measurable physical quantity, such as density or mass. The theory has been widely applied by communication engineers and some of its concepts have found application in psychology and linguistics.

Infrared Radiation, long-wave, thermal radiation in the electromagnetic spectrum, between light and microwaves in frequency. *See also* Radiation.

Inglewood, city in S California, 8mi (13km) SW of Los Angeles; location of Hollywood Park Racetrack and Northrop Institute of Technology (1942). Industries: electronics, aerospace, truck farming, machinery, Founded 1873; inc. 1908. Pop. (1980) 94,245.

Ingolstadt, city in S West Germany, on the Danube River. City was besieged in 1632 by Gustavus II of Sweden in Thirty Years' War, and destroyed by French in 1800. University built here in 1472 was stronghold of Catholic Reformation; site of Gothic Liebfrauen-münster (15th–16th century), and ruins of Jesuit college (1555). Industries: oil refining, textiles, automobiles. Founded AD 806. Pop. 70,841.

Ingres, Jean Auguste Dominique (1780–1867), French painter. Painting in a classical style with emphasis on the careful drawing of figures, he was best known for his portraits, including one of the comtesse di Haussonville now in the Frick Museum, New York City, and his sensual pictures of bathers, including "Bather of Valpinçon" in the Louvre. He also executed large ceiling paintings.

Inherent Powers, powers that a nation uses to defend its sovereignty. Such powers are exclusive and not shared with the states.

Inhibitor, any compound that stops or substantially reduces the rate of a chemical reaction. Inhibitors are as specific in their action as catalysts and are widely used to prevent corrosion, oxidation, or polymerization. *See also* Antioxidant.

Initiative and Referendum, two methods of direct legislation. *Initiative* involves putting a proposition on a ballot for voter approval by securing the required number of voters' signatures. *Referendum* involves allowing the voters to approve a law previously approved by the legislature. If the law is defeated by the voters, it becomes null and void.

Injection, introduction of a fluid or gas into body tissues through a needle or catheter to treat, diagnose, or prevent disease. Injections are usually either intravenous (into a vein), intramuscular (into a muscle), or intrathecal (into the spinal cord).

Ink, colored fluid or viscous solid used for writing, drawing, or printing. Color may be imparted by a suspended pigment or a soluble dye. Soluble dyes, often based on aniline, are suitable for ball-point pens. Printing inks usually contain finely divided carbon black suspended in a drying oil, often with added synthetic resins. Some inks dry by evaporation of a volatile solvent rather than by hardening of a drying oil.

Inky Cap, any of the common terrestrial mushrooms (genus *Coprinus*) that have conical caps on thin stems and gills that dissolve into a fluid at maturity. *C. comatus* (shaggy mane or lawyer's wig) is considered choice. *C. atramentarius* contains an Antabuse-like substance and should not be eaten with alcohol.

Inland Sea (Seto-naikai), arm of the Pacific Ocean between Japanese islands of Honshu (N), and Shikoku and Kyushu (S); connected to Pacific by Straits of Akashi (NE), Naruto (SE), Bungo (SW), and Shimonoseki (W); divided into Iyo Sea (SW), Sue Sea (W), Harima Sea (E), Hiuchi Sea (central); includes numerous islands and islets; site of Inland Sea National Park, est. 1934. Area: approx. 3,670sq mi (9,505sq km).

Inn (En), river in central Europe; rises in SE Switzerland, flows NE through Engadine Valley, through W Austria, to SE West Germany and into Danube River at Passau; source of more than 20 hydroelectric plants. Length: 317mi (510km).

Innate Ideas, Platonic theory revived by the Rationalists, that certain "ideas," such as number, contradiction, and identity, are present in the mind at birth rather than being produced by subsequent experience. *See also* Rationalism.

Inner Mongolia (Neimenggu, or **Neimengku),** autonomous region in N China, on N and NE rim of China bordering Outer Mongolia and USSR; capital is Huhehot. Separated from Outer Mongolia after 1911 revolution, it was made autonomous region in 1947. The terrain is mostly high plateau although the W is dominated by the Gobi Desert. Industries: agriculture, coal, iron, steel mills, grazing. In 1970, during the Cultural Revolution, Inner Mongolia's size was cut by about half, but in 1980 its former borders were restored, giving it an area of 460,000sq mi (1,200,000 sq km).

Inness, George (1825–94), US landscape painter, b. near Newburgh, N.Y. His early works showed the influence of the Barbizon School, while his later landscapes became more delicate in color and detail. *See also* Barbizon School.

Innocent I, Roman Catholic pope (401–17) and saint. He developed the role of the papacy in religious controversies and condemned Pelagianism by excommunicating Pelagius in 417. He could not prevent the sacking of Rome by the Visigoths in 410, but stolen church treasures were returned. *See also* Pelagianism.

Innocent II, Roman Catholic pope (1130–43), b. Gregorio Papareschi. In 1122, he helped draft the Concordat of Worms and served as a papal legate to France. Antipope Anacletus II, elected in opposition to Innocent, led Rome until his death in 1138. Bernard of Clairvaux, supporting Innocent, helped end the schism. *See also* Worms, Concordat of.

George Inness: June 1882

Innsbruck, Austria

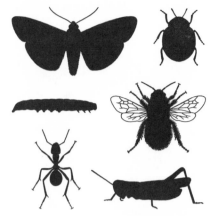

Insect

Innocent III, Roman Catholic pope (1198–1216), b. Lotario di Segni (c.1161). He stressed moderation; increased papal control over civil matters; and established the courts of Inquisition in his quest to be political, as well as religious, ruler of Western Europe. During his papacy, the term "transubstantiation" became part of Communion dogma. He allowed the Franciscan and Dominican orders to form and backed the fourth and fifth crusades. See also Inquisition; Transubstantiation.

Innsbruck, resort city in W Austria, on Inn River, 85mi (137km) SW of Salzburg; former residence of collateral line of Hapsburgs; capital of the Tirol since 1420; site of Winter Olympics 1964, 1976. Industries: chemicals, boats, metalworking, textiles. Pop. 115,197.

Inns of Court, four legal societies in London (Lincoln's Inn, Inner Temple, Middle Temple, Gray's Inn), dating from the 14th century, that have the exclusive right to admit persons to practice as barristers (lawyers) in England. The three grades of membership are benchers (senior members), barristers, and students.

İnönü, İsmet (1884–1973), Turkish army officer and statesman, closely associated with Mustafa Kemal (later called Atatürk) in the formation of the Turkish republic, and succeeding him as president (1938–50). He maintained Turkish neutrality in World War II. İnönü was premier 1923–37, 1961–65.

Inorganic Chemistry, one of the main branches of chemistry. It is concerned with the study of the atomic structure and properties of the elements, the relationships and reactions between them, and the preparation and properties of their compounds. It includes the study of elemental carbon, its oxides, metal carbonates, and sulfides, but all other carbon compounds belong to the study of organic chemistry. See also Organic Chemistry.

Input-Output Model, a matrix illustrating the flow of intermediate as well as final goods between the various sectors of the economy. The columns of the matrix may represent the input into each of the sectors and the rows may be used to represent the output of the sectors. An individual cell in the input-output matrix thus represents the input from one sector that results in output of another sector. The total of any one column thus represents the total of the input that is used and the total of any one row represents the total of the output that is produced. See also Models, Econometric.

Inquisition, a court set up by the Roman Catholic Church in the Middle Ages to seek out and punish heresy. The inquisitor held power direct from the pope to take testimony, question witnesses and those accused of heresy, and decide guilt or innocence. The accused had none of the rights expected in a democratic system of law and sometimes were questioned under torture. Punishments for the guilty ranged from penances and fines to banishment, imprisonment, and death by fire. Kings and nobles supported what amounted to organized persecution of Jews, Protestants, and others considered enemies of church and state, including those charged with witchcraft. The medieval Inquisition was active in Europe (except England and the Scandinavian countries) from the 12th to 15th centuries. A later tribunal, the Spanish Inquisition, was instituted in 1480 at the request of the rulers of Spain and was not finally and formally abolished until 1834. The Roman and Universal Inquisition, or Holy Office, was active in Europe in the 16th and 17th centuries. See also Spanish Inquisition.

In re Gault (1967), landmark US Supreme Court decision that extended various due process rights including the right to counsel and to remain silent to proceedings in a juvenile court.

Insect, small invertebrate animals, including beetles, bugs, butterflies, ants, and bees. There are nearly 1,000,000 known species of insects—more than all other animal and plant species combined. They are common everywhere except seas and polar regions. Adult insects have three pairs of jointed legs, usually two pairs of wings, and a segmented body with a horny outer covering, or exoskeleton. The head has three pairs of mouthparts, a pair of compound eyes, three pairs of simple eyes, and a pair of antennae.

Most insects are plant eaters, many being serious farm and garden pests. Some prey on small animals, especially other insects, and a few are scavengers. Reproduction is usually sexual. Most insects have two active life stages, the larva (caterpillars and grubs) and the adult (butterflies and beetles). The larva is transformed into the adult by complete metamorphosis during the pupal stage. Young grasshoppers and some other insects, called nymphs, resemble wingless miniatures of adult insects. The nymphs develop during a series of molts, incomplete metamorphosis, and become adults with functional wings at the last molt. Silverfish and a few other primitive wingless insects do not undergo metamorphosis. The newly hatched silverfish is a tiny, sexually immature replica of the adult. Phylum Arthropoda; class Insecta. See also Arthropod.

Insect Control, any of various methods employed to reduce the population of insects harmful to man as disease carriers or as destroyers of valuable crops. The most common method has been the use of chemical sprays, mostly hydrocarbon derivatives. Since many of these have been found to be harmful to other organisms, however, biological controls such as introduced predators and sterilization techniques are considered more desirable. Engineering techniques used to combat disease-carrying insects include swamp drainage and spraying oil on bodies of water containing larvae.

Insecticides, substances used to destroy or control insect pests. They may be stomach poisons, such as lead arsenate or sodium fluoride; contact poisons, such as DDT and organophosphates; and systemic poisons, such as octamethylpyrophosphoramide, which are more toxic to insects after absorption into the plant leaves on which they feed. Organophosphates are preferred to chlorinated hydrocarbons (such as DDT) because they break down into nontoxic substances and cause less ecological damage.

Insectivore, small order of nocturnal mammals (Insectivora), many of which eat insects. Nearly worldwide in distribution, some species live underground, some on the ground, and some in streams and ponds. Most insectivores have narrow snouts, long skulls, and five-clawed feet. Length: mostly smaller than 18in (46cm); weight: mostly less than 1lb (0.5kg). Only three families are always placed in the order: Erinaceidae (moon rats, gymnures, hedgehogs), Talpidae (moles, shrew moles, desmans), and Soricidae (shrews). However, five other families—including tree shrews, tenrecs, and solenodons—are often included in the order.

Insectivorous Plant, or carnivorous plant, plants with mechanisms for trapping insects. The insects are digested with protease and other enzymes outside the plant body. These plants have poorly developed root systems and are often found in nitrogen-deficient sandy or boggy soils. The 500 species are classified in 6 unrelated families and range in size from microscopic fungi to the pitcher fungus of Borneo that contains 7pt (3.31liters) of insect-trapping liquid. Some plants are active insect trappers, such as the Venus flytrap (Dionaea muscipula) with hinged leaves that close on the insect; sundew (Drosera intermedia), that traps insects with a sticky substance and then encloses them in leaves; and bladderwort (Utricularia) that sucks insects into its underwater bladders. Other plants have pitcher-shaped leaves, such as the pitcher plant (Sarracena flava) and tropical liana (Nepenthes).

Insolation, a contraction of "incoming solar radiation" reaching the earth, measured in the solar constant and consisting of a broad range of electromagnetic radiation from infrared to X- and gamma rays, including visible light. See also Solar Constant.

Instinct, traditional concept in the biological and social sciences referring to behaviors that are unlearned and innately determined, as opposed to behaviors that are learned from experience. In the 19th century instincts were often cited to explain behavior, but the term fell into disrepute with the advent of behaviorism. The term has recently been revived in the work of ethologists such as Konrad Lorenz. The behavior of many lower organisms, such as courting behaviors of birds and aggressive patterns in fish, is, beyond doubt, instinctive. However, it is much more difficult to apply the term accurately to the behavior of higher animals and humans.

Instrument Landing System, Aircraft, a combination of three radio systems that guide the pilot to a landing when visibility is poor. A glide slope beam sent from the runway indicates the proper angle of descent, as the localizer beam indicates its direction. The outer marker beam, set about 5mi (8km) from the runway, and the middle marker, at about 0.5mi (0.8km), show distance.

Instruments, Aircraft, measuring devices used to control the profile and direction of the flight path and gauges that indicate the condition of aircraft systems. Instruments associated with the flight profile or altitude are the altimeter, air speed indicator, and vertical speed indicator. Direction is observed with the directional gyro and the turn-and-bank indicator. The artificial horizon displays both kinds of information. Systems instrumentation may include engine condition gauges, radio navigation instruments, fuel-flow meters, and cabin pressurization and oxygen gauges along with displays for radar and electrical systems.

Insulation, the prevention or the slowing down of the flow of heat, electricity, sound, or other forms of energy from one region to another. Materials used to achieve these ends are also called insulation, or insulators.

Heat or thermal insulation for houses typically consists of a stable, porous material, such as foam, glass wool, or rock wool, that traps pockets of air. Air is an excellent thermal insulator, but loses its effectiveness if it moves. For example, if the space between the inner and outer walls of a frame house is filled with air only, in winter the layer of air touching the inner wall will be warmed by conduction through the wall and will rise. The layer of air touching the outer wall, cooled by conduction, will sink. This sets up a circulation pattern that serves as a mechanism for transporting heat from the inside to the outside. The use of the porous insulator prevents such circulation. Insulation can also be achieved by the use of solid materials that are poor conductors of heat. An adobe house, for example, uses the principle that earth is a good insulator. Many good thermal insulators are also good sound insulators. Good electric insulators include air, glass, rubber,

305

and various plastics and ceramics. Metals are good conductors (poor insulators) of heat, electricity, and sound.

Insulation, Electrical, material of high resistance used to confine electricity within conductors. The type of material used varies with many parameters such as voltage, frequency, strength, flexibility, ease of removal, water resistance, temperature range, and chemical environment. Common materials include polyethelene, mylar, PVC, teflon, rubber compounds, paper, asbestos, mica, glass, porcelain.

Insulation, Heat, materials used for retarding the flow of heat, classified into reflective and bulk materials. Aluminum foil is the most common reflective material, although there is some industrial use of coated steel and refractory materials. Typical bulk materials include fiberglass wool, mineral wool, vegetable fibers and organic papers, foamed plastics, and fire brick.

Insulin, a hormone secreted by the pancreas and responsible for regulation of amino acid, lipid, and carbohydrate metabolism. Sugar unmetabolized because of lack of insulin accumulates in excess amounts in blood and urine, resulting in diabetes mellitus, in which protein and lipid metabolism is also affected. *See also* Diabetes Mellitus.

Insurance, formal social device wherein one party (the insured) transfers the financial consequences of risk of loss to another (the insurer) for a consideration (the premium). Insurance is practical because of the loss-sharing principle and the law of large numbers. Each insured contributes to a common fund, and the losses of the unfortunate few are reimbursed from this fund.

Intaglio Printing, type of printmaking in which a design is cut into a plate by such techniques as engraving, etching, soft ground, or aquatint. *See also* Printmaking.

Intarsia, the art of decorating furniture by use of inlay, with pieces of wood, ivory, mother of pearl, or tortoise shell. Used in antiquity and during the Renaissance, intarsia reached its peak during the 17th century. The rococo phase of intarsia that followed was called marquetry.

Integer, any of the numbers . . . −3, −2, −1, 0, 1, 2, 3, . . ., of which there is a limitless (infinite) number. The positive integers are the natural numbers. The negative integers and zero allow any two numbers to be subtracted. The theory of numbers is concerned with the properties of integers.

Integral, mathematical function used in calculus. For a graph of a function of a variable *x*, the integral is the area enclosed between the curve and the *x* axis. It is written in the form $\int f(x)dx$.

The symbol for an integral is an elongated "S," standing for "sum": the operation of finding an integral (integration of the function) is equivalent to dividing the area into a number of small rectangles parallel to the *y* axis, and taking the limit of the sum of their area as the number increases (and each elementary rectangle becomes thinner). A definite integral is the area between given values of *x;* if these are unspecified the integral is indefinite. The derivative of the indefinite integral of a function is the original function: thus, integration is the inverse of differentiation.

Integral Calculus. *See* Calculus.

Integrated Circuit (IC), complete electronic circuit incorporating semiconductor devices manufactured in one tiny unit. Hybrid integrated circuits have separate components attached to a ceramic base with interconnections by wire bonds or a conducting film. Monolithic integrated circuits have all the components manufactured into or on top of a single chip of silicon, interconnections between components being by conducting film. Miniaturization of such circuits has produced chips as small as a few millimeters square and containing hundreds of thousands of components.*See also* Electronic Circuit.

Integration, in social science, drawing together groups to make a whole. The term is often applied to efforts to create harmony between blacks and whites in the United States. Desegregation—ending laws and customs that kept the groups separate—is easier than full integration. *See also* Assimilation.

Integumentary System, the covering of the body—in man, the skin. *See also* Skin.

Intelligence, general ability to learn and to deal with problems, new situations, and abstract concepts. No one definition suffices since intelligence can be manifested in so many different ways (eg, adaptability, memory, reasoning, cleverness). Psychologists operationally define intelligence as a score on a test that samples some of the important components of intelligence, especially those related to performance in school. *See also* Intelligence Testing.

Intelligence Quotient (IQ), number summarizing an individual's relative standing in general intelligence as measured by a test. For the most common tests, the average score is defined as 100, with about 95% of all people falling between 70 and 130. *See also* Intelligence Testing.

Intelligence Testing, began with the work of Alfred Binet, who in 1905 devised the first successful test, the Binet-Simon Scale, to aid in identifying mentally deficient pupils in Parisian schools. Subsequent developments included the intelligence quotient (IQ), group tests first used to screen army recruits in World War I, and sophisticated tests such as the Wechsler Intelligence Scales. Modern tests are used for many purposes including predicting success in school, counseling job applicants, identifying exceptional children, and diagnosing the mentally disturbed. *See also* Intelligence; Intelligence Quotient; Stanford-Binet Scales.

Intendant, agent of the French king in the provinces. Primarily tax collectors in the 16th century, their power was greatly increased by Louis XIV, who made them his representatives at the local level, dealing with administrative, judicial, financial, and police matters. Their power was increasingly contested and the office was abolished during the French Revolution.

Intensity, Earthquake, effect of an earthquake on man and his works or on Earth's visible surface. Thus, intensity of an undersea quake is zero, that of a minor quake on a poorly constructed town is great. Earthquake intensity can be reduced by sound construction and proper location of cities. The modified Mercalli scale measures intensity from I (not felt except by a few people in special spots) to XII (extensive damage). *See also* Earthquake; Seismology.

Interaction, Nuclear, interaction in which elementary particles can take part and by which they may be classified. Hadrons (protons, neutrons, etc.) are subject to the strong interaction. This involves the strong force, which acts over a tiny range (10^{-13} cm, proton diameter). Two hadrons inside this range interact, in about 10^{-23} second, by producing other particles or being deflected. Leptons (electrons, etc.) are subject not to the strong but to the weak interaction, involving a much weaker force and a much lower probability of interaction. *See also* Elementary Particles.

Intercontinental Ballistic Missile (ICBM), long-range (5,000 miles plus) missile for military purposes. Installed in scattered well-protected underground sites (silos), they can deliver thermonuclear warheads across oceans in 30 minutes to a one-mile-wide error ellipse. Guided by self-contained inertial systems to eliminate jamming, capable of directing multiple warheads to targets hundreds of miles apart, and equipped with decoys, they are considered to have no effective counterweapon. *See also* Ballistic Missile; Inertial Guidance.

Interferometer, instrument in which a wave, especially a light wave, is split into component waves that travel an unequal distance so that on recombination they form interference patterns. The patterns are used for accurate measurement of wavelength, length, index of refraction, etc, for testing the quality of lenses and prisms, and other purposes. The Michelson interferometer was used in ether-measurement experiments from which Einstein's special theory of relativity developed. The stellar interferometer is used to measure the diameters of giant stars.

Interferon, an antiviral agent produced by most cells of the body when infected with certain viruses. It has prospects for therapeutic use, but is still experimental.

Interglacial Age, the interval between ice ages; the period of glacial retreat.

Interior, United States Department of, federal cabinet-level department under the executive branch; directed by the secretary of the Interior. The department's responsibilities include the administration of approximately 500,000,000acres (202,500,000hectares) of federal land and 50,000,000acres (20,250,000hectares) of trust land, mostly the conservation of mineral and water resources, fish, and wildlife, the preservation of scenic and historical areas, and the promotion of mine safety. The department is also charged with the social and economic development of the US territories, and it administers service programs to Indians and Alaska native people. It was established in 1849 as the Home Department.

Intermediate Range Ballistic Missile (IRBM), missile capable of traveling distances between several hundred and 1,500 miles. Military advantages include extremely short warning time (about 5 minutes) and compatibility with mobile launchers (nuclear submarines). *See also* Ballistic Missile.

Internal Combustion Engine, an engine in which fuel is burned within the engine rather than in a separate chamber. Piston and rotary-type gasoline and diesel engines are all internal combustion types.

Internalization, in social science, the process of taking into oneself society's attitudes, values, and ways of behaving. From parents, teachers, and others children learn roles and absorb normative standards. Taking in these norms is a major factor in the development of personality. Observing some standards for roles is necessary for social control of behavior. *See also* Role; Socialization.

Internal Medicine, branch of medicine that deals with the diagnosis and treatment of diseases and disorders of adults that may be treated by medical means rather than by surgical or other techniques.

Internal Revenue Service (IRS), division of the US Treasury Department. The main purpose of the IRS is to administer and enforce the internal revenue laws. Individual income tax, social insurance, retirement taxes, corporation income, excise, estate and gift taxes are the main revenues collected by the IRS. It was established in 1862.

International Bank for Reconstruction and Development (World Bank) (IBRD), organization established in 1944 under an agreement drawn at the Bretton Woods Conference. Its role is to make loans to member governments to enable them to pursue developmental projects. Loans have been granted in such areas as agriculture, education, electric power, engineering, postwar reconstruction, telecommunications, and transportation. The major part of the bank's resources is derived from the world's capital markets. *See also* Bretton Woods Conference.

International Court of Justice, The (ICJ), United Nations judicial organ. Its predecessor was the Permanent Court of International Justice (PCIJ), in the League of Nations. The court consists of 15 judges from various areas of the world. Disputes between nations are heard and judgments are rendered. Its headquarters is in The Hague Peace Palace, the Netherlands.

International Date Line, an imaginary line extending between the North Pole and the South Pole (approximately corresponding along most of its length to the 180th meridian of longitude) that arbitrarily marks off one calendar day from the next. This line is a consequence of the various time zones that exist as one moves eastward or westward so that noon approximately corresponds to the time at which the sun crosses the local meridian.

International Geophysical Year (IGY) (July 1957–Dec. 1958), vast program to study the earth and its cosmic environment by scientists of 66 nations. Achievements included launching of space satellites, which led to discovery of the Van Allen radiation belts; evidence of seismically active rifts in a chain of submarine mountains; and approximate measurement of continental area of Antarctica. As one result of IGY, Antarctica was declared a nonmilitary area to be used only for scientific study.

International Labor Organization (ILO), specialized branch of the United Nations, consisting of about 120 nations, established in 1919 as an associate agency of the League of Nations. It seeks, internationally, the improvement of working conditions, the raising of labor standards, and the promotion of economic and social stability. ILO Headquarters is in Geneva, Switzerland. The ILO was awarded the Nobel Peace Prize in 1969.

International Law, formerly called Law of Nations, deals with the body of rules deemed legally binding resulting from treaties, agreement, and customs between national states. Its sources are also international statute laws enacted by agencies, conferences, or commissions of international organizations, such as the League of Nations or United Nations; by decisions of international tribunals, and as the arbitration tribunals of the World Court under the League of Nations and the UN; by instructions and manuals to diplomatic agents; and by decisions of international law by national courts, such as prize courts; and are influenced by the opinions of expert jurists and publicists. Sanctions for failure to comply with these rules include force of public opinion, self-help, intervention by third parties,

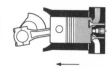

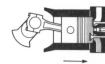

Intercontinental ballistic missile: launching

Internal combustion engine: 4-stroke

Intracoastal waterway: Miami, Florida

confirmation by such international organizations as the UN, and finally retaliation or war.

International Monetary Fund (IMF), agency seeking to stabilize the currencies of over 100 participating nations. It promotes consultations on currency-related problems, stimulates international trade, and promotes the establishment of stable currency exchange rates among members. Organized at the Bretton Woods Conference (1944) and founded in 1945, its headquarters are in Washington, D.C.

International Monetary System, structure of world monetary relationships. When countries exchange goods and services with other countries, it is not uncommon for exports to exceed imports or imports to exceed exports, thus creating a balance of payments deficit or surplus. When a deficit exists, a country must pay the other country the difference. This payment may involve exchange of gold or some mutually acceptable monetary unit (usually a so-called hard currency, eg, the dollar).

International Phonetic Alphabet, a series of symbols compiled to represent all of the sounds in all languages. In English it uses a different symbol for the "th" in "with" and the one in "them." The phonetic symbols are especially useful for distinguishing the different vowel sounds.

Interoceptive Sense, or deep sense, conveys information about stimuli occurring within the internal organs and tissues of the body. The receptors are so-called free nerve endings within the organs, and they convey information about the deformation of the organs, such as the expansion of the lungs. The same receptors also probably convey information about internally caused pain, eg, heart attack.

Interpol (International Criminal Police Organization), organization composed of police forces from more than 100 countries, including most of the countries of the western world and Yugoslavia (the only Communist member), established in 1923. Its headquarters are in Paris. Interpol's principal functions are to provide member nations with information concerning international criminals and to assist in their apprehension.

Interpolation, mathematical procedure for finding intermediate unknown values of a function lying between two known values. A common method is to assume that the three values lie on a straight line. *See also* Extrapolation.

Interposition, doctrine espousing the right of states to block enforcement of federal law. It was invoked in the South during the Civil War and, more recently, after the Supreme Court's desegregation rulings.

Interrupted Fern, large North American fern of rocky, dry areas with tall, erect fronds having small, fertile pinnae midway. When ripe, the pinnae drop off, leaving gaps in the frond. Its fiddleheads are woolly. It is a popular greenhouse plant. Height: to 4ft (122cm). Family Osmundaceae; species *Osmunda claytoniana*.

Intersection, point, or locus of points, common to two or more geometrical figures. Two nonparallel lines meet in a point; two nonparallel planes meet in a line.

Interstellar Matter, gas molecules and dust grains distributed at very low densities throughout the space between the stars of the galaxy. The matter consists mainly of cold neutral hydrogen, although small amounts of other elements such as carbon and helium

have been found, as well as minimal quantities of simple compounds such as water, ammonia, cyanogen. The dust grains are mainly ice or perhaps ice-covered graphite particles. *See also* H I and H II Regions; Nebula.

Intestinal Obstruction, impediment to passage of the feces through the intestine. Obstruction may occur when the intestine fails to contract, most commonly because of inflammation of the membrane covering the abdominal organs (peritonitis). It may also result from adhesions, hernias, tumors, foreign bodies such as gallstones, or other mechanical causes, or from constant contraction of the intestine. The symptoms are colicky pain and, depending on the site of the obstruction, nausea and vomiting or abdominal distention or both.

Intestine, part of the digestive system, either the small intestine or the large intestine, or colon. *See also* Colon; Small Intestine.

Intolerable Acts (1774), British legislation designed to punish the colonists after the Boston Tea Party. Also known as the Coercive Acts, they closed the Boston port and moved the customs house to Salem. (Boston Port Bill). British officials who were accused of capital offenses would be tried in England (Administration of Justice Act); another law (the Massachusetts Government Act) had the effect of annulling the Massachusetts Charter, giving the governor power to control and limit town meetings and making the council and judiciary appointive instead of elective. The colonists' opposition to the acts resulted in the calling of the First Continental Congress.

Intoxication. *See* Alcoholism.

Intracoastal Waterway, water passage, partly natural, partly man-made; extends from Boston down the Atlantic coast to Miami, then up the W coast of Florida across the Gulf of Mexico to Brownsville, Tex.; provides partly sheltered route for commercial and pleasure craft.

Intrauterine Device (IUD), a device inserted into the uterus to prevent pregnancy. IUDs are made of metal or plastic and are of various shapes, including a loop, coil, T, and triangle.

Intrinsic Factor, a mucoprotein present in gastric juice, involved in absorption of vitamin B_{12} by the intestine. *See also* Extrinsic Factor.

Intrusion, an emplacement of rock material that either was forced or flowed into spaces among other rocks. An igneous intrusion, called a pluton, consists of magma that never reached the earth's surface but filled cracks and faults, then cooled and hardened. A sedimentary intrusion consists of clay, chalk, salt, or other plastic sediment forced upward under pressure. *See also* Dike.

Inuit, collective name for the native Eskimo people of Alaska, Greenland, and the Northwest Territories, Arctic Quebec, and northern Labrador areas of Canada. Many Inuit still live by the traditional skills of fishing, trapping, and hunting in their remote communities. In 1980, an Inuit Circumpolar Conference was held to promote the rights, interests, cultural unity, and civilization of the inhabitants of the Arctic polar region.

Inversion, an atmospheric condition in which a property of the air, like moisture or temperature, increases with altitude. In a temperature inversion, the air temperature rises with altitude and a cap of hot air encloses

the cooler air below. With little wind or turbulence to break up the condition, pollution builds up in the enclosed air, often to dangerous degrees.

Invertebrate, animal with no spinal column, or backbone. Included are 20 phyla, the two largest being Arthropoda and Mollusca. *See also* Animal.

Investiture, the installation into an office by a superior authority. The right to invest bishops and abbots in their positions became a matter of intense struggle between medieval popes and emperors. Gregory VII forbade lay investiture and Holy Roman Emperor Henry IV then sought to overthrow the pope. A compromise—secular selection and spiritual investiture—was reached in the Concordat of Worms (1122).

Invisible Hand, as described by Adam Smith, theory that individuals, acting in their own self-interest, will do what they should for the good of the entire society, as if led by an invisible hand. It is another expression of the doctrine of laissez faire. *See also* Laissez Faire.

Io, in Greek mythology, a mistress of Zeus, whom he turned into a heifer in order to prevent her discovery by his wife, Hera. Suspicious Hera had the hundred-eyed Argus guard Io. With the aid of Hermes, who put Argus to sleep, Io escaped, swam the Ionian Sea, and was restored by Zeus.

Io, satellite of Jupiter; one of the Galilean satellites. Recent research has confirmed that Io has an atmosphere. Diameter 2,272mi (3,658km); mean distance from planet 262,000mi (421,820km); mean sidereal period 1.77 days.

Iodine, nonmetallic element (symbol I) of the halogen group, discovered (1811) by Bernard Courtois. Iodides are found in sea water. The black volatile solid gives a violet vapor. Chemically it resembles chlorine, but is less reactive. It is used as a medical antiseptic and potassium iodide is used in photography. The isotope I^{131} (half-life 8 days) is used in treatment of thyroid-gland disorders. Properties: at. no. 53; at. wt. 126.-9045; sp gr 4.93; melt. pt. 236°F (113.5°C); boil. pt. 363.83°F (184.35°C); most stable isotope I^{127} (100%). *See also* Halogen Elements.

Io Moth, large yellowish, stout-bodied moth of North America with large eyespots on its hind wings. The caterpillar is green with a white-bordered, reddish stripe on each side of its body. Its venomous spines can sting tender skin. Length: 2in (5cm). Species *Automeris io*. *See also* Moth.

Ion, particle of atomic size with a positive or negative charge. Simple ions can be formed by atoms gaining or losing electrons. More complex ions are charged groups of atoms held together by covalent bonds. Positive ions are called cations (they are drawn to a cathode); negative ions are called anions (drawn to an anode). Many crystalline solids are composed of arrays of ions of opposite charge. Ions are also responsible for the conduction of electricity by liquids and gases. *See also* Ion, Complex; Ionic Bond; Ionization.

Iona, island off W Scotland, in Inner Hebrides, separated from the Isle of Mull by the Sound of Iona; landing place (AD 563) of St Colomba. Area: 2,264acres (917hectares).

Ionian Islands (Iónio Nísoi), island group off SW Greece, in Ionian Sea; consists of seven main islands, Corfu, Paxos, Leukas, Ithaca, Cephalonia, Zante, and Cerigo, and several smaller ones. Unified as a province under Byzantine Empire AD 890, it was captured by

Venetians 1500–1797; ceded to France under Treaty of Campo Formio (1797); made a British protectorate 1815 called "United States of the Ionian Islands"; ceded to Greece 1864. Industries: shipping, timber, fruit, livestock, fishing, soap, shipbuilding, wine, grains. Area: 890sq mi (2,305sq km). Pop. 183,633.

Ionians, original Greek peoples. They were largely responsible for Classical Greek culture including Homeric epic, elegy, iambic poetry, architecture and sculpture, and the rational thought that dominated the 6th century BC.

Ionian Sea, branch of the Mediterranean Sea, between W Greece and SW Italian Peninsula and E Sicily; connected to the Adriatic Sea by Strait of Otranto, and to the Tyrrhenian Sea by Strait of Messina; forms the gulfs of Squillace and Taranto. Ionian Islands lie in the E waters; chief ports are Catania and Syracuse (Sicily), Corfu and Patras (Greece), Taranto (Italy). Depth: 10,000ft (3,050m).

Ionic Bond, or electrovalent bond, type of chemical bond in which ions of opposite charge are held together by electrostatic attraction. *See also* Chemical Bonds.

Ionic Equilibrium, equilibrium state existing in solutions of electrolytes. Strong acids and bases are completely dissociated into ions when in aqueous solution, but weak acids or bases are only partly dissociated. Electrolyte, AB, when placed in solution, may partly dissociate into A^+ and B^-. $[A^+]\,[B^-]/[AB]$, where [] indicates activities, is a constant, termed the equilibrium constant.

Ionic Order, one of the five orders of classical architecture. It developed in the Greek colonies of Asia Minor in the 6th century BC and became known in Greece in the 5th century BC. It is characterized by slender columns with 24 flutes and prominent volutes, or spiral scrolls, on the capitals. The best example of the Ionic order is the Erechtheum on the Acropolis.

Ionic Transport. *See* Transport.

Ionization, process in which neutral atoms or molecules are converted into ions. Positive ions can be formed by supplying energy to detach electrons from the atom, as by the action of X rays, ultraviolet radiation, or high-energy particles. The minimum energy to form an ion is the ionization energy (or potential). The opposite process—electron capture by a neutral species to yield a negative ion—is much less probable. Both types of ion can also be produced by breaking bonds, which can be induced by photons, particles, etc, or may occur spontaneously, as in the ionization of acids when dissolved in water.

Ionization Chamber, instrument for measuring the intensity of ionizing particles or radiation, such as X-rays. The gas-filled chamber contains two electrodes across which a voltage is applied. Passage of radiation through the chamber ionizes the gas and the ions formed move towards the charged electrodes. The current thus produced in an associated circuit is proportional to the radiation intensity. *See also* Geiger Counter.

Ionosphere, the deep region of ions or charged particles in the atmosphere. *See also* Atmosphere.

Ion Propulsion, method of propelling rockets by heating metals such as cesium to produce ions and electrons. The ions are accelerated through a potential difference to provide power. Presently in development, ion propulsion offers advantages of longer acceleration periods, high mass efficiency, and increased lifetimes for satellite control systems.

Iowa, also Ioway, Siouan-speaking tribe, closely related to the Oto and Missouri, who lived in various areas of Iowa for centuries. They apparently separated from the Winnebago in early times to form a separate tribe. Never a large group (1000–1200 people), they now number 250, occupying their own land in Iowa and Oklahoma.

Iowa, state in the N central United States, on the W bank of the Mississippi River.

Land and Economy. Level or slightly rolling, the land rises gradually to the W and N. Iowa was originally prairie, covered with high grass that was plowed to create farmland. Timber is found primarily along the rivers. The state is bounded on the E by the Mississippi and on most of the W by the Missouri; the principal river in the state is the Des Moines. As an income source, agriculture maintains a fair balance with industry, which has grown steadily. Farm-related manufacturing is important, but the state's industrial production is broadly diversified.

People. The first settlers came in the 1830s from the E and S states. Later, farmers from Europe, notably Germans, Scandinavians, Scots, Irish, and Dutch, came to work the soil. About 80% of Iowa's people were born in the state, and fewer than 60% live in urban areas.

Education and Research. There are nearly 60 institutions of higher education. The University of Iowa and Iowa State University are both state-supported. Agricultural research at these and other institutions has contributed largely to the state's development and use of the land.

History. As part of the Mississippi valley, Iowa was included in the Sieur de la Salle's claim to the region for France in 1682. French hunters and trappers explored the region until it was sold to the United States in the Louisiana Purchase of 1803. Indians still occupied the land, and it was not legally opened for settlement until after the Black Hawk War in 1832. In 1838 Congress created the Territory of Iowa. After admission to the Union in 1846, Iowa grew rapidly as a farming area. Industrial development was intensive after WWII.

PROFILE

Admitted to Union: Dec. 29, 1846; rank, 29th
US Congressmen: Senate, 2; House of Representatives, 6
Population: 2,913,387 (1980); rank 27th
Capital: Des Moines, 191,003 (1980)
Chief cities: Des Moines, Cedar Rapids, 110,243; Davenport, 103,264
State Legislature: Senate, 50; House of Representatives, 100
Area: 56,290sq mi (145,791sq km); rank, 25th
Elevation: Highest, 1,675ft (510m), in Osceola co, NW part of state. Lowest, 480ft (146m), Mississippi River
Industries (major products): processed foods, farm and construction machinery, electrical machinery
Agriculture (major products): hogs, cattle, corn, soybeans, alfalfa
Minerals (major): cement components, limestone, sand, gravel
State nickname: Hawkeye State
State motto: "Our liberties we prize and our rights we will maintain"
State bird: Goldfinch
State flower: Wild rose
State tree: Oak

Iowa City, city in E Iowa, on Iowa River; seat of Johnson co; seat of University of Iowa (1847). Industries: sheet metal, pharmaceuticals, creameries, hatcheries. Founded 1839; inc. 1853. Pop. (1980) 50,508.

Iphigenia, in Greek literature, daughter of Agamemnon and Clytemnestra, sister of Electra, Chrysothemis, and Orestes. Iphigenia was demanded in sacrifice to Artemis after her father killed a hind sacred to the goddess. Relenting at the last moment, Artemis carried her off to install Iphigenia as priestess of her temple at Aulis. The dramatist Euripides told her story in *Iphigenia at Aulis.*

I-pin, formerly Suchow; city in S central China, at junction of Min and Yangtze rivers. Pop. 275,000.

Ipoh, city in Malaysia, on Kinta River; capital of Perak state; captured by Japanese 1941; site of Chinese rock temples; commercial center for Kinta valley region. Industries: tin mining, rubber. Pop. 247,969.

Ipswich, city in Suffolk, E England, on Orwell estuary; manufactures agricultural machinery. Pop. 122,600.

Iqbal, Muhammad (1876–1938), Indian Muslim poet, philosopher, and political leader. In 1930 he became president of the Muslim League. He advocated the establishment of an independent Muslim state on the Indian subcontinent. For this he is considered to be the father of Pakistan. He wrote poetry and philosophical essays in both Urdu and Persian. His most significant book of poetry is *The Secrets of the Self* (1915).

Iráklion (Candia), largest city and seaport on island of Crete, S Greece, in Sea of Crete; capital of Crete governorate and Iráklion prefecture. Founded AD 832 by Muslim Saracens, it was conquered by Byzantines (961), Venetians (1204), Turks (1669); became part of Greece 1913; site of ancient ruins of Cnossus. Exports: wine, olive oil, raisins, almonds. Pop. 77,783.

Iran, independent nation in the Middle East. Known as Persia until 1935, it is a mountainous W Asian major oil producer. Under the monarchy, oil revenues provided the impetus for rapid westernization and modernization until the 1979 fundamentalist Islamic revolution reversed the trend.

Land and economy. The world's 4th-largest oil producer in 1978, Iran is bordered on the N by the USSR and the Caspian Sea, S by the Persian Gulf and the Gulf of Oman, W by Turkey and Iraq, and E by Afghanistan and Pakistan. It is enclosed by rugged mountains guarding the entrance from Turkey and the USSR. Zagros Mountains (NW) are an area of volcanic cones and intense extremes of heat and cold. Fertile valleys mark its central portion with oil in the foothills. The N highlands (Elburz range), forming an arc around the Caspian Sea's S shore, have heavy rains and a volcano (Demavend). Rice, cotton, silk, and tea are grown in the plains. The E uplands are barren and largely uninhabited. Annual rainfall ranges from about 40in (102cm) along the Caspian to 8in (20cm) inland. Major industries include iron and steel, oil refining and petrochemicals, and transportation equipment. Traditional exports include Persian carpets and caviar.

People. About two-thirds of Iranians are descended from Aryan tribes who migrated from the Asian steppes c.2000 BC. Among this group are many of Iran's tribal minorities, mostly nomads living in the mountain fringes, including Kurds, Baluchis, Bakhtiaris, and Lurs. Non-Aryan minorities include Arabs, Turks, Armenians, and Jews. Many of the minority groups are strongly separatist. Literacy is estimated at 30%. Over 90% of Iranians belong to the Shiite sect of Islam, and it is the state religion.

Government. According to the constitution of 1979, Iran is an Islamic republic. The president is popularly elected to a four-year term, as are the 270 members of the *Majlis* (parliament). The president selects the prime minister. Effective power, however, rests with the Ayatollah Ruhollah Khomeini.

History. According to Babylonian inscriptions, a Persian state was in existence in 1500 BC. During the next 1,500 years succeeding waves of Indo-Europeans swept across the land. In 480 BC, the Persians were defeated by the Greeks; in 331 BC Alexander the Great added Persia to his empire. By AD 641, conversion to Islam was complete. From 1500–1700, Persia was ruled by a dynasty of Iranian rulers (Safawids) before Ottoman Turks deposed them. A 1906 revolt by the masses hastened approval of a constitution with parliamentary provisions under a shah. In 1925, Riza Khan Pahlevi instituted a new dynasty. He was forced to resign by the Western powers in 1941 and was succeeded by his son, Mohammed Riza Pahlevi. After WWII the Teheran conference guaranteed Iran's independence. During the early 1950s, the Shah was forced to leave the country during a governmental crisis precipitated by an unsuccessful attempt to nationalize the oil industry. The Shah returned, however, with strong backing from the United States and other Western powers, subsequently embarking on a program of rapid modernization, including land reform. His programs and increasingly repressive rule brought opposition that erupted into civil strife in 1977–78. In an attempt to restore order, the Shah imposed military rule, but unrest continued, and he fled the country in 1979. The militant Islamic fundamentalist leader, Ayatollah Ruhollah Khomeini, returned to Iran from exile in Paris and assumed leadership. When the Shah was admitted to the United States, the US embassy in Teheran was seized by student militants, and most of its staff was held hostage for 14 months with the Ayatollah's support. In 1980 a new government was elected, with moderate Abolhassan Bani-Sadr as president. Bani-Sadr, however, soon found himself in conflict with the fundamentalist-dominated *Majlis* and was forced out of office in 1981. The government, now with little moderate representation, faced growing unrest, especially from the leftist People's Mujahadeen, and resorted to execution of political opponents. The economy suffered from dislocation stemming from the revolution; a border war with Iraq, begun in 1980; and falling world oil prices in the mid-1980s.

PROFILE

Official name: Islamic Republic of Iran
Area: 636,294sq mi (1,648,001sq km)
Population: 36,869,000
Density: 58per sq mi (22per sq km)
Chief cities: Teheran (capital); Isfahan; Meshed; Tabriz
Government: Republic
Religion: Islam (Shi'a sect)
Language: Persian (Farsi)
Monetary unit: Rial
Gross domestic product: $66,777,000,000
Per capita income: $1,600
Industries: petroleum products, iron, steel, textiles, carpets, wool, food products
Agriculture: wheat, rice, barley, cotton, tobacco, fish (caviar), silk, sheep, nuts, fruit
Minerals: oil, iron, copper, lead, chromite, zinc, coal, emeralds, turquoise, sulfur, coal, manganese
Trading Partners: France, West Germany, United Kingdom, Japan

Iranian Languages, subdivision of the Indo-European family. The major Iranian languages are Persian, Pashto, Kurdish, Mazanderani, Gilaki (of Iran), Baluchi

Iran

Ireland

(of Iran and Pakistan), and Tadzhik and Ossetian, spoken in the Soviet Union.

Iraq (Al-'Iraq), independent nation in the Middle East. Once the ancient land of Mesopotamia, it was formed after WWI. Petroleum is its economic base in a one-party political system based on Arab nationalism.

Land and economy. Land of the Tigris and Euphrates rivers, it is bordered by Turkey (N), Kuwait (S), Iran (E), Syria (NW), Jordan (W), Saudi Arabia (SW), and the Persian Gulf (SE). The land drops from 10,000ft (3,000m) above sea level, along the Turkish and Iranian boundary, to the Shatt al-Arab, formed by the junction of the Tigris and Euphrates, and the Persian Gulf marshes; 68% is desert, waste, or urban; 18% agriculture; 10% grazing lands; and 4% forests. Temperatures can reach 120°F (49°C) in July with an average annual rainfall of 4–7in (102–178mm). More than 60% of revenue is derived from the nationalized petroleum industry. Iraq is the world's 5th-largest oil producer. It leads the world in date production. Exports include hides, skins, wool, and cement. Imports are wheat, rice, machinery, tea, and sugar. Basra is the leading port.

People. Iraqis are mainly of Arab descent. Muslims compose 95% of the population and include Arabs, Kurds (15%–20%), Turks, Persians, and Indians. Non-Muslims include Assyrians, Yezidis, Sabians, Chaldeans, Armenians, and Jews. The mountain-dwelling Kurds are the most distinctive group in language and customs. Their desire for autonomy led to guerrilla war 1974–75 and to repression since then. Literacy is estimated at 20%–40%. Arabic is the official language.

Government. A 1970 constitution provides for a 14-member Revolutionary Command Council (RCC) as the governing body. The chief of state is elected by the RCC. In 1980 elections were held for a 250-seat national assembly.

History. Home of the Babylonians, Parthians, and Sumerians and a center of arts and learning before the 7th-century Muslim conquest, Iraq became an outpost of the Ottoman empire in the 19th and early 20th centuries. Misrule and neglect fired Arab nationalism. Although hampered by isolation, lack of education, and religious antagonisms, an Arab movement gained momentum before WWI. The three Turkish provinces of Basra, Baghdad, and Mosul were formed into a British-mandated territory after WWI and in 1932 became a sovereign state under pro-Western Hashemite rule. An army revolution in 1958 led to a pro-communist regime, and in 1968 the Arab Socialist Ba'ath party, now the only legal party, took power. In 1970, Ba'athists also seized power in Syria, but relations between Iraq and Syria have been strained, although some economic cooperation began in 1979. In 1980 a border war in the Shatt al-Arab region erupted between Iraq and Iran, quickly becoming an on-going stalemate.

PROFILE

Official name: Republic of Iraq
Area: 167,924sq mi (434,924 sq km)
Population: 11,505,000 (1975)
  Density: 69per sq mi (26per sq km)
Chief cities: Baghdad (capital); Basra; Mosul
Government: Socialist republic
Religion: Islam
Language: Arabic (official)
Monetary unit: Dinar
Gross national product: $30,430,000,000
Per capita income: $1,550
Industries: petroleum products, processed foods, textiles, cigarettes, cement, skins
Agriculture: wheat, barley, rice, dates, millet, cotton, tobacco, sheep
Minerals: oil

Trading partners: USSR, United States, France, Italy, United Kingdom, Netherlands, Spain

Irbid, city in N Jordan, 42mi (68km) N of Amman; agricultural and marketing center; garrison town in conflicts between Israel and Jordan. Pop. 125,000.

Irbil (Erbil), city in NE Iraq, between Great and Little Zab rivers; capital of Irbil prov.; site of ancient city of Urbillum (Arbela), an important shipping center to Baghdad; modern transportation and commercial center. Industries: grain, tobacco. Pop. 90,320.

Ireland, Northern, part of the United Kingdom of Great Britain and Northern Ireland, occupying the NE of Ireland, bounded S and W by the Republic of Ireland and N and E by the Irish Sea. The region is divided into six counties, collectively called Ulster.

Land and economy. Northern Ireland is a mainly volcanic plateau with the Sperrin Mountains rising to 2,241ft (684m) in the W and the Mourne Mountains rising to 2,795ft (852m) in SE from lowlands of Armagh and Down. It has many lakes, mainly in Fermanagh, with largest lake in the United Kingdom, Lough Neagh. The principal rivers are the Foyle, Lagan, and the Upper and Lower Bann. It is primarily an agricultural region; industry is centered in Belfast and Londonderry and includes textiles (especially linen), textile machinery, shipbuilding, and engineering.

Government. Formerly, Northern Ireland had its own parliament (Stormont) in addition to representatives at Westminster. From 1974 it was under the direct rule of the British Parliament.

History. The political problems of Northern Ireland date from extensive settlement of Scottish and English Protestants in the reign of James I. In 1690, at the Battle of the Boyne, Irish Roman Catholics supported James II, whereas the Protestants followed William III. Ireland was partitioned in 1921 into the Irish Free State (a dominion of the British Empire), with six counties of Ulster remaining in the United Kingdom. Thus the political problems of the province arise from religious conflict between the Protestant majority and the Catholic minority, a political and economic underclass also. The Protestant majority favors continued union with Great Britain, whereas Catholics generally support unification with the Republic of Ireland.

In the 1960s civil strife developed as a result of protests by the Catholic minority against discrimination. Troops were sent in 1969 to restore order. However acts of terrorism continued as a result of the activities of the Provisional Irish Republican Army (IRA) and the extreme Protestant Ulster Defence Association. In 1972 the Ulster Parliament at Stormont was suspended and direct rule assumed from London. In 1973 a new assembly was introduced, with proportional representation. Government was by an executive formed 1974 from representatives of the major political parties. This attempt at "power sharing" collapsed in May 1974, when the Protestant Ulster Workers Association called a successful general strike. Direct rule from Britain was resumed. Violence, which had gradually decreased after imposition of direct rule and arrival of British troops, increased again during the late 1970s and 1980s. In 1981, a 7-month hunger strike conducted by IRA prisoners resulted in the death of ten strikers. Increased tensions throughout the province made a return to home rule in the near future unlikely. The 1985 Anglo-Irish treaty, giving the Republic of Ireland a formal role in how the North is administered, was bitterly opposed by Protestants.

PROFILE

Official name: Northern Ireland
Area: 5,452sq mi (14,121sq km)

Population: 1,538,800
  Density: 282per sq mi (109per sq km)
Chief cities: Belfast (capital); Londonderry

Ireland (Eire), Republic of, country in NW Europe in the British Isles between the Atlantic and the Irish Sea, occupying the NW and S parts of the island of Ireland.

Land and Economy. The Irish Republic consists of a central fertile plain, with scattered glacial deposits (including the extensive Bog of Allen), surrounded by broken upland masses including the Donegal Mts (NW), Wicklow Mts (SE), and Kerry Mts (SW). Carrantuohill is the highest point, 3,414ft (1,041m). It has numerous lakes, including the famous Lakes of Killarney in the SW, extensive sea inlets, bays, and many small islands, especially along the rugged W coast. Shannon is the major river, and is the longest in the British Isles. Settlement is very dispersed and agriculture, especially livestock raising, is the main industry; others are mainly agriculture-based. There are also textile, brewing, and engineering industries. Most of Ireland's trade is with the United Kingdom.

People. The people are predominantly Roman Catholic (over 95%). Irish (Irish Gaelic) is the first official language and is taught in schools and widely understood. English is the second official language.

Government. Ireland is a republic having parliamentary democracy with a written constitution. The president is elected every seven years. There are two houses of the Irish legislature—the Dail (House of Representatives) and the Seanad (Senate). Bills passed by the Dail may be amended or delayed by the Seanad. The country is partitioned into 26 counties, grouped in 4 provinces (Ulster, Munster, Leinster, and Connaught).

History. The early inhabitants of Ireland were relatively free from the invasions of the rest of the British Isles until the 8th-century incursions of Norsemen. At that time the people were organized in tribes under provincial kings of Ulster, Munster, Leinster, Connaught, and Meath. Brian Boru became king of all Ireland in 1002 and finally defeated the Norsemen in 1014, freeing the country from foreign interference. The country was conquered by the English under Henry II in 1171, thus initiating the strife with England that continued to modern times. Up to 1782 the Irish parliament (introduced 13th century) was not independent of Britain; even with the repeal of Poyning's Law, Roman Catholics could not hold political office. William Pitt achieved legislative union in 1800 and Catholic Emancipation in 1829. The country suffered from the Great Potato Famine 1845–49, which killed hundreds of thousands, and from emigration, especially to the United States. An act to grant Home Rule was passed in 1914, but it was suspended during WWI. In 1920, Ireland was partitioned. The southern portion received dominion status as the Irish Free State in 1922, and civil war erupted between the Irish Republic Army (IRA), opposed to partition, and supporters of the treaty with Britain. Full independence was achieved in 1937. Since then the problem of Northern Ireland has continued to be a major political issue in Ireland, and both major political parties—the Fine Gael and Fianna Fáil—now favor eventual unification, with some autonomy for Northern Ireland. An agreement (1985) with Great Britain, giving Ireland the role of advisor to the government of Northern Ireland was intended to stabilize conditions. Despite Ireland's entrance into the European Economic Community in 1973, the country still suffers from high unemployment and lack of regional development. *See also* Ireland, Northern.

PROFILE

Official name: Republic of Ireland
Area: 27,136sq mi (70,282sq km)

Population: 3,368,217
Density: 124per sq mi (48per sq km)
Chief cities: Dublin (capital); Cork; Limerick
Government: Parliamentary democracy
Religion: Roman Catholicism
Languages: Irish, English
Monetary unit: Irish pound
Gross national product: $9,500,000,000
Per capita income: $3,000
Industries (major products): processed food, tobacco, beer, machinery
Agriculture (major products): meat, dairy produce, corn, root crops
Trading partners (major): Great Britain, United States, West Germany, France

Iridium, metallic element (symbol Ir) of the third transition series, discovered (1803) by Smithson Tennant. It occurs associated with platinum; chief source is as a by-product from smelting nickel. The element is used alloyed with platinium in pen tips, electrical contacts, and similar applications. Properties: at. no. 77; at. wt. 192.22; sp gr 22.42 (17°C); melt. pt. 4370°F (2410°C); boil. pt. 7466°F (4130°C); most common isotope Ir^{193} (62.6%). *See also* Transition Elements.

Iris, the colored part of the eye. It controls the amount of light that enters the pupil in the center of the eye by increasing or decreasing the size of the pupil. The iris is part of the choroid, the middle layer of the wall of the eye.

Iris, genus of about 300 species of flowering plants widely distributed, mostly in temperate areas. They may be bulbous or rhizomatous. The showy flowers have three erect inner petals, called standards, three drooping outer sepals, called falls, and flat, swordlike leaves. Bearded garden irises are rhizomatous hybrids; height: to 3ft (90cm). The fragrant orrisroot comes from the dried rhizomes of fleur-de-lis *(Iris florentina). See also* Crocus; Gladiolus.

Iris, in Greek mythology, a minor deity representing the rainbow. She is a messenger of the gods and is depicted as swift-footed, golden-winged, and robed in many colors. She appears in the *Iliad* and, in her role as messenger, is prominent in the myth of Ceyx and Halcyone.

Irish Literary Renaissance, period of exceptional literary creativity in Ireland in the late 19th and early 20th centuries. An outgrowth of the movement for self-government, it emphasized the revival of an Irish literature. Under the leadership of the Irish National Theatre Society, which founded the Abbey Theatre Company, Irish drama was fostered. Among those involved in the movement were William B. Yeats, Lady Augusta Gregory, AE, J. M. Synge, and Sean O'Casey.

Irish Moss, or carrageen, a small dark purple seaweed *(Chondrus crispus)* with tufted fronds, common on North Atlantic coasts. Commercial Irish moss, which consists of dried carrageen or another similar purple seaweed *(Gigartina mamillosa),* is used as an agent for thickening or emulsifying foods and drugs. *See also* Red Algae.

Irish Rebellion of 1798, uprising against British rule by the United Irishmen, that attempted to establish a republic with French support. Wolfe Tone headed the expeditionary force sent from France. The leaders were arrested, and the revolt in the north was crushed at Ballinahinch. An uprising by Wexford's Catholic peasantry was defeated at Vinegar Hill (1798).

Irish Republican Army (IRA), semi-military, primarily Roman Catholic organization dedicated to establishing a united Irish republic. Formed in 1919, the IRA waged guerrilla warfare against British rule. Some members ("Irregulars") rejected the Anglo-Irish settlement (1921), fighting a civil war until 1923. Periodically active since that time, in 1969 the "provisional" wing ("Provos"), committed to armed struggle, split from the "official" IRA, which emphasized political activities. Thereafter, the Provos became prominent in the violence among Roman Catholics, Protestants, and British troops in Northern Ireland. Guerrilla violence and unrest continued into the 1980s. In an effort to achieve recognition as political prisoners, several convicted Provo members of the IRA went on hunger strikes in 1980 and 1981 but they were denied political recognition even though their leader, Bobby Sands, and others died as a result. Violence continued through the 1980s despite an Anglo-Irish accord (1985) designed in part to diminish the IRA's influence.

Irish Sea, arm of Atlantic Ocean, between Ireland and Great Britain; connected with Atlantic by North Channel (N) and by St George's Channel (S). Scotland, Wales, and England are on its E shore and Ireland on W. Chief ports are Dublin, Liverpool, Barrow-in-Furness. Isle of Man, Anglesey, and Holyhead are largest islands. Area: 40,000sq mi (103,600sq km).

Irish Setter, bird and gun dog (sporting group) bred in Ireland as red and white dog from early 18th century and as the popular solid red from 19th. A beautiful dog, it has a long, lean head with deep muzzle and low-set, hanging ears. The body and neck are long and the legs sturdy. A tapered tail is carried straight. The fine, flat mahogany or chestnut red coat is longer on ears, legs, chest, belly, and tail. Average size: 26–27in (66–69cm) high at shoulder; 50–70lb (23–32kg).

Irish Terrier, an all-round working dog (terrier group) bred in Ireland for vermin control and brought to US about 1873. Lithe, yet animated, it has a long, flat head, squared off by chin whiskers. The small, V-shaped ears droop forward. Legs and body are moderately long. The tail, docked to ¾ length, is set high. Its dense, wiry coat is whole-colored in bright red, red wheaten, or golden red. Average size: 18in (45.5cm) high at shoulder; 27lb (12kg). *See also* Terrier.

Irish Water Spaniel, water dog (sporting group) developed in Ireland of ancient lineage. Its large, domed head with square muzzle has a curly topknot and long, lobular ears. The medium-long body is higher at hindquarters. Legs are medium-long with large feet. A long, characteristic "rat tail" tapers to a fine point. A solid liver coat is in tight ringlets on the body and longer and wavy on the legs and belly. Average size: 22–24in (56–61cm) high at shoulder; 45–65lb (20–29kg). *See also* Sporting Dog.

Irish Wolfhound, large Celtic hunting dog (hound group) dating from 273 BC and used by royalty to hunt Irish wolf and elk. A commanding dog, it has a long head with long, pointed muzzle; small, thrown-back ears; deep and wide-chested body with long back and drawn-up belly; long, straight legs; and long, slightly curved tail. The coat is rough on body, legs, and head; wiry and long over eyes and under chin. Colors are gray, brindle, red, black, white, and fawn. Average size: 34in (86cm) high at shoulder; 140lb (63kg). *See also* Hound.

Iritis, inflammation of the iris, the colored part of the eye, which forms the contractile pupil. Usually the disease also involves the muscular ciliary body at the base of the iris. Pain, redness, and mistiness of vision are the symptoms, caused by trauma, infection, or systemic disease.

Irkutsk, city in Russian SFSR, USSR, 45mi (72km) from Lake Baikal, on Angara River; capital of Irkutsk oblast; largest city in E Siberia; growth spurred from trade with China and Amur Valley, Lena goldfields; cultural and educational center. Industries: lumber, machine tools, electrical equipment, mica processing, hydroelectricity. Founded 1652. Pop. 543,000.

Iron, common metallic element (symbol Fe) of the first transition series, known from earliest times. Chief ores are hematite (Fe_2O_3), magnetite (Fe_3O_4), and iron pyrites (FeS_2). It is obtained in a blast furnace by reducing the oxide with coke (carbon), using limestone to form a slag. The pure metal—a reactive soft element—is rare: most iron is used alloyed with carbon and other elements in the various forms of steel. The element has four allotropic forms, one of which is ferromagnetic. Properties: at. no. 26; at. wt. 55.84; sp gr 7.874; melt. pt. 2795°F (1535°C); boil. pt. 4982°F (2750°C); most common isotope Fe^{56} (91.66%). *See also* Steel Transition Elements.

Iron Age, period succeeding the Bronze Age in which man learned to smelt iron. The Hittites probably developed the first important iron industry in Armenia soon after 2000 BC. Iron's superior strength and the widespread availability of its ore caused it gradually to supersede bronze. *See also* Bronze Age.

Iron Curtain, term coined in 1946 by Winston Churchill in a speech at Westminster, Mo., to describe the division between Communist Eastern Europe and the West. Soviet policy restricts travel, communications, and exchange of ideas across this boundary.

Iron Law of Oligarchy, social theory devised by Robert Michels that suggests that a certain amount of oligarchy—government by the few—is inevitable when control is needed as a result of conflict in society. Even in a democracy, Michels said, elitism follows from leadership.

Iron Lung, a term popularly used for the Drinker respirator, which is a device that provides long-term artificial respiration. It consists of a metal tank in which the patient's body is enclosed but with his head outside. By alternating negative and positive pressure in the tank, breathing is maintained.

Irony, figure of speech in which what is said is the opposite or different from what is meant. Irony can also refer to a situation or event, as when, intending good, evil is done. Often found in epigrams, it hides deep passion under a cloak of indifference, eg, Oscar Wilde's "A thing is not necessarily true because a man dies for it." *See also* Epigram.

Iroquois Confederacy or **Iroquois League,** North American Indian confederation of five (later six) tribes living in upper New York State. The confederacy, including the Mohawk, Oneida, Onondaga, Cayuga, and Seneca tribes, joined with the Tuscarora tribe in 1722, to become known as the Six Nations. The confederacy was marked by good organization and effective leadership. Voting in the federated council was conducted by tribe, and war could be waged only after a unanimous decision, although some intertribal conflict occurred.

Irrawaddy (Irawadi), river in central Burma, formed by union of Mali and Nmai rivers; flows S, traversing length of Burma, and serves as economic and communications route for Myitkyina, Bhamo, Mandalay, Pakokku, Pye, Henzada; forms a vast delta extending S 180mi (290km) to Andaman Sea; beginning in S Burma, between Bassein River (W) and the Irrawaddy River, it is one of world's greatest rice-producing regions. With the Chindwin River, its chief tributary, the Irrawaddy is one of the major rivers of Asia. River length: approx. 1,000mi (1,610km).

Irredentists, Italian party of late 19th and early 20th centuries that sought annexation of nearby territories, such as Trentino and Trieste, containing large numbers of Italians. After Italy's unification (1860–70), they aimed to gain Italian-inhabited areas controlled by Austria and worked to keep Italy out of the Triple Alliance, which included Austria. They also influenced Italy's decision to enter World War I with the Allies (again against Austria).

Irrigation, artificial watering of land to supply necessary moisture for growing crops. It occurs worldwide in regions with inadequate precipitation and dates to 2000 BC in Egypt. Primitive forms, such as buckets and water wheels, are still used in remote areas. Surface water in streams, rivers, and lakes or subsurface water from wells is used, depending on locality. Dikes, sprinklers, surface gravity, or underground pipes transport the water to desired locations. Suitable drainage systems are imperative when irrigating because concentrations of dissolved salts are injurious to plants and salt-saturated soil is agriculturally worthless.

Irtysh (Irtyš), river in NE Kazakh SSR and W Siberia, USSR, and central Asia; rises in W Mongolian Altai Mts, China; flows W into Lake Zaisan, then NW in Kazakh and Siberia to join Ob River near Khanty-Mansiysk; largest tributary of the Ob River; navigable for complete length of 2,760mi (4,444km).

Irving, Washington (1783–1859), US author, b. New York City. The first American to achieve international fame as a writer, he began his career writing satirical pieces for newspapers and was a participant in the *Salmagundi Papers* (1807–8). Under the name Diedrich Knickerbocker, he wrote *A History of New York* (1809), a social satire that gained him acclaim. In 1815 he went to England, where he lived for many years. While there, *The Sketch Book of Geoffrey Crayon, Gent.* (1820) appeared. Many of the stories in *The Sketch Book* drew on scenes and legends from his childhood in New York State. The most famous stories are "The Legend of Sleepy Hollow" and "Rip Van Winkle."

In 1826 he went to Madrid, where he did research for his four books about Spanish life and history. These included *A Chronicle of the Conquest of Granada* (1829), *The Legends of the Alhambra* (1832), and two books on Columbus (1828, 1831). After returning to the United States in 1832, he traveled briefly in the West, which provided the background for *Astoria* (1836) and *The Adventures of Captain Bonneville, U.S.A.* (1837). Except for an interlude (1842–46) as US minister to Spain, he spent the rest of his life at his home in Tarrytown, N.Y.

Irving, city in NE Texas; NW suburb of Dallas; site of Texas Stadium (home of Dallas Cowboys, professional football team), Dallas–Fort Worth Airport (1974), site of the University of Dallas at Irving. Industries: building supplies, insecticides, cleaning materials, electronic equipment, tools, food processing, oil distribution. Inc. 1914. Pop. (1980) 109,943.

Irvington, town in NE New Jersey, adjoining Newark. Founded 1692 as Camptown, it was renamed 1852 for Washington Irving. Industries: model electric trains (since 1900), cutlery, metal castings. Inc. 1898. Pop. (1980) 61,493.

Irish terrier

Washington Irving

Isfahan, Iran

Isaac, in the Bible, only son of Abraham and Sarah, born when Abraham was 100 and Sarah in her 90s. God, who commanded Abraham to sacrifice Isaac in an act of faith, rescinded the order just before the killing. Isaac married Rebecca and they had two sons, Jacob and Esau.

Isabella (1292–1358), queen of England (1308–27), wife of Edward II, daughter of Philip IV of France. Neglected by her husband, she formed a liaison with Roger de Mortimer. They raised armies, deposed Edward II, and proclaimed her eldest son, Edward III, king (1327). She virtually ruled England until 1330 when Edward III had Mortimer executed. *See also* Mortimer, Roger de.

Isabella I, or **Isabella the Catholic** (1451–1504), Spanish queen of Castile and León (1474–1504). She was the daughter of John II. When her half brother Henry IV died, Isabella contested the right of Henry's daughter, Juana of Portugal, to succeed. A long struggle resulted, but Isabella won and was crowned in 1479. She married Ferdinand II of Aragon, and they ruled their two kingdoms jointly, thereby forming the basis for a unified Spain. The reign of Isabella and Ferdinand was one of the most important in Spanish history. The last Moorish stronghold on the peninsula, the kingdom of Granada, was rechristianized under the rule of the Catholic kings, as Ferdinand and Isabella were known. Christopher Columbus, under their sponsorship, discovered the New World, thereby opening the way for the great Spanish empire of the 16th century. The Jews were expelled from Spain, the Spanish Inquisition was inaugurated, and a policy of forcible conversion of the Moors was begun. All these took place in the momentous year of 1492. Upon Isabella's death, she was succeeded in Castile by her daughter Joanna. *See also* Spanish Inquisition.

Isabella II (1830–1904), queen of Spain (1833–68). She was the daughter of Ferdinand VII and Maria Christina. Her father changed Spanish law so that she could succeed. Her uncle, Don Carlos, contested her right to the crown, and the first of the Carlist wars began. Until she came of age, Isabella's reign was under the regency first of her mother and then Baldomero Espartero. Her reign was beset by constant conflict and in 1868 she abdicated. In 1870 she renounced her claims in favor of her son, Alfonso XII. *See also* Carlists.

Isabel of Bavaria (1371–1435), daughter of the duke of Bavaria and queen consort of Charles VI of France. The insanity of her husband occasioned her meddling in state affairs, most conspicuously the treaty of Troyes (1420) in which she disinherited her son, the future Charles VII, in favor of Henry V of England.

Isaiah, biblical prophet during the reigns of Judah's kings, Uzziah, Jotham, Ahaz, and Hezekiah. The Book of Isaiah, thought to be written by several persons over a long span of years, describes Messianic blessings and announces the birth of Immanuel as a sign that Judah will not perish.

Ischia, island off S Italy in the Tyrrhenian Sea, between Gulf of Gaeta and Bay of Naples. Known as Emerald Isle, it is a health resort and tourist center; suffered last volcanic eruptions 1301; earthquakes are common. Chief town is Ischia, containing remains from 5th-century BC Greek construction. Area: 18sq mi (47sq km). Settled in 8th century BC. Pop. 14,076.

Isfahan (Esfahān), city in central Iran, on Zayandeh River; capital of Esfahān prov. The ancient city of Aspadana, it was Arab capital 7th century. Seljuk Turks (1051) and Shah Abbas I (1598) adorned the city with beautiful and ornate buildings, including the Shaykh Lutfullah Mosque, Masjid-i-Shah (imperial mosque), and the Ali Qapu (gateway to the royal palace). The city was besieged by Afghans 1723, and most of the population was massacred. Considerable restoration has been done; site of University of Esfahan (1966). Industries: steel, textiles, carpets, metalwork, handcrafts. Pop. 424,045.

Isherwood, Christopher William Bradshaw (1904–86), English writer who collaborated with W.H. Auden on experimental verse dramas: *The Dog Beneath the Skin* (1935) and *The Ascent of F6* (1936). Isherwood wrote novels on international politics. *All the Conspirators* (1928) was his first; he then went to Germany for 4 years and developed material for *The Last of Mr. Norris* (1935) and *Goodbye to Berlin* (1939). These formed the basis for John Van Druten's play *I am a Camera* (1951) and the musical *Cabaret* (1966). He emigrated to the United States in 1939. Later he withdrew into Hindu mysticism. He co-authored the play *A Meeting By the River* (1979) with Don Bacharey and wrote the book *My Guru and His Disciple* (1981).

Ishihara Test, a method of detecting the presence of color blindness by showing the subject plates that contain dots of various sizes and colors. *See also* Color Blindness.

Ishii, Kikujiro (1866–1945), Japanese diplomat. In 1907–08 he negotiated the Gentleman's Agreement with the United States that excluded the immigration of Japanese laborers into the United States. He was ambassador to France (1912–14), foreign minister (1915–16), and ambassador to the United States (1918–19). In 1917 he negotiated the Lansing-Ishii Agreement with the United States that recognized Japanese interests in China.

Ishmael, several biblical figures, most notably Abraham's son by Hagar and half brother to Isaac. He married an Egyptian and fathered 12 sons and one daughter, who married Esau, Isaac's son.

Ishtar, principal goddess of the Assyro-Babylonian pantheon. In ancient mythology she is the daughter of Anu, the sky god, and Sin, the moon god. Through the centuries, as she absorbed local deities and her power grew, she came to exhibit diverse attributes, those of a compassionate mother goddess and of a lustful goddess of sex and war. Ishtar is identified with the Sumerian Inanna, Phoenician Astarte, and the biblical Ashtoreth. Because of her confusion with other gods her name became synonymous with goddess.

Isis, in Egyptian mythology, the wife of Osiris and mother of Horus, worshiped as the protector of children. After the murder of Osiris by his brother Seth, Isis searched for and retrieved the dismembered parts of Osiris' body and magically revived him. The epitome of faithfulness and maternal devotion, her fame was spread throughout the ancient world by the Ptolemies and the Romans.

Iskenderun, formerly Alexandretta; port city in S Turkey, 60mi (97km) SE of Adana, on Gulf of Iskenderun. City was taken by Arabs 7th century; occupied by Turkey 1515; became part of French-mandated Syria after WWI; regained by Turkey 1939. By mid-20th century it was the main Turkish port on the Mediterranean. Exports: cotton, grain, fruit, wool, hides. Founded after 333 BC by Alexander the Great to commemorate his victory over the Persians at Issus. Pop. 79,291.

Islam, monotheistic religion founded by Mohammed in Arabia in the 7th century. Members of this faith are called Muslims. The Koran (sacred book) and the Hadiths (oral reports of Mohammed's words, or comments on his words) are the primary Muslim sources. The central themes of Islamic doctrine are belief in the unity of God or Allah, in Mohammed's prophetic mission, and in the universal Judgment Day to come. Islam is strictly monotheistic, hence *shirk* or idolatry is an unforgivable sin. Allah's mercy is shown by the fact that he sent 28 prophets to mankind, including Moses and Jesus, the last being Mohammed. Muslims are expected to observe the Sharia, the law defining the path in which God wants them to walk. A Muslim's duty is further set by the Five Pillars of Islam: confession of faith, customarily through reciting the *shahada*, "There is no God but Allah, and Mohammed is his prophet"; prayer five times daily; fasting during the sacred month of Ramadan; almsgiving; and making at least one pilgrimage to the shrine at Mecca.

During Mohammed's lifetime, his followers were all in Arabia. After his death in 632, Muslim armies quickly conquered an empire three times the size of Rome's and stretching from Spain to the Indus valley. The great Islamic empires were broken up, but there are currently over 500,000,000 Muslims spread over the world. There are heavy concentrations in the Middle East, North Africa, Afghanistan, Pakistan, and Indonesia and smaller but still substantial numbers in central and southern Africa, India, China, SE Asia, the Philippines, and parts of the USSR. There are 800,000 Muslims in the Western world. *See also* Koran; Mohammed; Shi'a; Sunnis.

Islamabad, city in NE Pakistan, 9mi (14km) NE of Rawalpindi; capital of Pakistan. Construction of the city began in 1960, to replace Karachi as capital; site of National University (1965), Grand National Mosque; nearby are ruins of Taxila. The economy of Islamabad is based mainly on government activity. Pop. 235,000.

Islamic Architecture, architectural style developed by the followers of Mohammed. Because the earliest (7th century) Muslims were nomadic, their first mosques were captured Christian churches whose spires served as minarets. Later, liturgical needs dictated architectural form: minarets from which the faithful could be summoned; a courtyard with a central fountain for ritual washing, surrounded by colonnaded walks for protection from the sun; a praying chamber surmounted by a dome and horseshoe arches to lend magnificence; and rich surface decorations of mosaic, carved stone, and paint. A notable early example is the Mosque of Damascus (715). Later mosques that exemplify the style are those at Tabriz, Persia (1204), Cairo (1384), and Isfahan, Persia (1585).

Islamic Art, the arts produced by peoples who, beginning with the 7th century, adopted the Islamic faith. During Mohammed's time, the Arabs had little art of their own; they adopted the art of countries they conquered, such as Syria, Egypt, Mesopotamia, and Persia. The mosque, with its *mihrab*, or prayer niche, and *mimbar*, or prayer pulpit, was highly decorated, as was the Koran, the sacred book of the Muslims. Calligraphy and illumination were major forms of decoration. Religious art was highly geometric, often using the arabesque, because the Muslim religion forbade use of human or animal forms in religious decoration. Humans and animals appear frequently in secular paintings, such as in frescoes and mosaics. Islamic art included highly ornamented metalwork, often inlaid with red copper. The most famous center of metalwork was 13th-century Mosul, in N Mesopotamia. Islamic art also included highly developed pottery and ceramics, with excellent glazes and decoration, such as those produced during the 12th and 13th centuries in Persia and during the 13th and 14th centuries in the city of Kashan.

The Islamic *minai,* or enamel, technique reached its zenith in the 16th century in Isfahan, where entire walls were decorated in faience. Perhaps the best known art of the Islamic world is the highly developed one of rug making. Some of the finest carpets in the world date from the 16th and 17th centuries and were made from wool and silk under the rule of the Safavids.

Islamic Law, or **Sharia,** practical ordinances of the Islamic religion. Found in the Koran, it is believed to be the revelations by God to Mohammed, the traditional sayings of Mohammed, the consensus of the community in the past, and analogical reasoning. The Sharia is divided into two sections of equal importance: Ibadet, duties owed to God by way of worship, and Muamalet, practical duties toward men and society. There are four schools of law, often called Four Rites of Muslim Law, in the different areas of the Muslim world, differing only slightly in interpretation. Muslims once were expected to submit totally to the laws of one of the schools, but modern Muslim states have adopted legal codes limiting the dominance of the Sharia, and attempts are being made to adapt it to modern times.

Island Arc, the chain of volcanoes that occur along one side of a deep ocean trench. They rest on the plate of lithosphere that is not moving down into the deep earth. Their andesitic lavas may be formed from the partially melted material of the descending plate. Northern Japan and the Aleutian Islands are examples of island arcs.

Isle of Wight, island off the S coast of England; separated from the mainland by the Solént and Spithead; independent administrative county. The island's mild climate and attractive scenery have made it a popular tourist resort. Area: 147sq mi (382sq km).

Isleta, or Tuei, Tanoan-speaking tribe of Pueblo Indians living along the Rio Grande Valley in New Mexico. The largest Southwestern pueblo in size, it has a population of approximately 2,500.

Ismail (1486–1524), shah of Persia (1502–24), founder of the Safavid dynasty. He reestablished Persian independence after centuries of Arab control and established Shiite Islam as the state religion of Persia. He warred successfully against the Uzbek Turks (1510) but was defeated by the Ottoman sultan Selim I (1514).

Ismailia (Al-Isma'iliyah), city in NE Egypt, on Lake Timsah; capital of Ismailia governorate; seat of Suez Canal administration; rail and commercial center. Founded 1863 by Ferdinand de Lesseps as base of operations for construction of Suez Canal. Pop. 187,000.

Isma'ilis, or **Seveners,** the smaller of two subgroups of the Shia sect of Islam. All the Shiites believe in the authority of a succession of imams, spiritual guides, going back to Mohammed's son-in-law, Ali. A dispute arose about the successor to the sixth imam. Those who chose Isma'il, and on his death his son Mohammad, are called Isma'ilis. They are also called Seveners, because they believe that Mohammad was the seventh and last imam. They look for his return on Judgment Day. *See also* Imamis; Shi'a.

Ismail Pasha (1830–95), ruler of Egypt (1863–79). In 1867 he received the title khedive. The high price received for Egyptian cotton because of the US Civil War and its aftermath swelled the treasury. Ismail built schools, palaces, irrigation projects, and the Suez Canal. But much of the money was squandered and in 1875 Egypt was forced to sell its interests in the canal to Britain. In 1876, Egypt's finances were put in the control of a Franco-British debt commission. The Ottoman sultan replaced Ismail Pasha with his son Tewfik Pasha in 1879.

Isobar, a line of equal and constant pressure at the earth's surface or at a constant height above it on a weather or other map. The patterns of isobars depict how the atmospheric pressure varies, showing "highs" and "lows" across the area of the map. *See also* High; Low.

Isocrates (436–338 BC), Athenian rhetorician. He wrote speeches for others, as well as numerous tracts on politics and education, but was himself shy of public speaking. He founded a school in Athens and was an influential teacher and prose stylist *(Panegyricus).*

Isogamy, in biology, the fusion of reproductive cells that act like sex cells but that are similar in size and structure. It is found in algae, some protozoans, and primitive plants and is unlike anisogamy, where male and female sex cells differ in appearance.

Isolationism, US policy advocating noninvolvement in European foreign wars and alliances. It was first enunciated by President Washington and, with the exception of the War of 1812, followed by all presidential administrations to the beginning of the 20th century. After World War I, its spirit was reaffirmed by the Senate's refusal to join the League of Nations. A series of neutrality acts in the 1930s were designed to keep the United States out of the impending European war. After World War II, a new internationalist spirit was evident, but the aftermath of the Vietnam War rekindled a degree of isolationism.

Isomers, two or more chemical compounds having the same molecular formula but different properties as a result of having a different arrangement of atoms within the molecule. Structural isomers have different structural formulae, for example, urea ($CO[NH_2]_2$) and ammonium cynate (NH_4CNO) have the same molecular formula (CH_4N_2O). Geometric isomers differ in their symmetry about a double bond; the cis- form of a compound has certain atoms or groups on the same side of a plane, whereas the trans- form has them on opposite sides. For example, maleic acid is the cis- form of fumaric acid. Optical isomers are mirror images of each other and differ only in the direction they rotate the plane of polarized light and the angle of their crystal form.

Isoniazid, a drug used to treat tuberculosis.

Isopod, any of about 4,000 species of crustaceans, including seven aquatic and one terrestrial suborder, characterized by flattened, oval bodies with all the hard-plated segments more or less alike. The land forms are the familiar sow bugs and pill bugs. Marine species include wood-borers (gribbles) and specialized fish parasites.

Isostasy, the maintenance of an equilibrium in the earth's crust and its crustal movement. There exists a balance between the land masses and the continental plates on which they float so that the plates rise and sink on the surface of Earth's mantle in such a fashion that the relative constancy of the system as a whole is maintained. The spread of the continental plates by the upwelling of material from deep within Earth's crust is balanced by the subduction or submergence of the opposite edges of the plates. *See also* Continental Drift; Tectonics.

Isotherm, a line of equal and constant temperature on a weather or other map. The patterns of isotherms depict how the temperature changes across the area of the map.

Isotonic Solution, solution in which cells can be immersed without taking up water, or with the same osmotic pressure as another solution with which it is compared.

Isotope, any of the atoms of an element with the same number of electrons or protons (same atomic number) but a different number of neutrons in the nucleus, so that both mass number and mass of the nucleus vary between isotopes. The atomic weight of an element is an average of the isotope masses. The isotopes of an element all have similar chemical properties, since these depend on the number of electrons orbiting the atom; physical properties, however, do vary. Most elements have two or more naturally occurring isotopes, some of which are radioactive (radioisotopes). Many radioisotopes can be produced artificially by bombarding elements with high-energy particles, such as alpha particles. Radioisotopes are used in medicine, research, and industry. *See also* Dating, Radioactive; Radioactivity.

Iso-utility Curve. *See* Indifference Curve.

Israel, an independent nation in the Middle East. Predominantly a Jewish state, Israel is on the edge of the Mediterranean. Its main problems are peace with its Arab neighbors and an economy drained by efforts to maintain its sovereignty.

Land and economy. At the E end of the Mediterranean Sea, Israel is bordered by Lebanon (N), Syria and Jordan (E), Egypt (SW), and the Mediterranean (W). It is divided into four regions: the coastal plain along the sea, the Jordan Rift Valley (including the Jordan River, Sea of Galilee, and the Dead Sea), the central mountains, and the Negev Desert, which constitutes half of the total area. Highest point is Mt Meron, 3,963ft (1,209m) above sea level. The Dead Sea, 1,302ft (397m) below sea level, is the lowest point on the earth's continental surface. Present area includes all land assigned under the 1947 UN partition resolution, plus the land occupied after the 1967 Israel-Arab war (the West Bank of the Jordan River, including East Jerusalem, and the Gaza Strip). Parts of the Sinai were returned in 1974–75. Principal privately owned export products are citrus fruits, polished diamonds, machinery, plastics, chemicals, pharmaceuticals, and clothing. Government-owned enterprises include mining, chemicals, petroleum refining, and railways. Israel produces 80% of its own food needs; 20% of the land is under cultivation; out of 1,058,000acres (428,490hectares), 448,000acres (181,440hectares) are irrigated. Its three seaports are Haifa, Ashdod, and Elat. The international airport is at Lod.

People. Since independence, immigration has quadrupled Israel's Jewish population (the majority coming from Arab countries); non-Jewish minorities include Muslims, Christians, and Druses. An estimated 45% of the Jewish population was born in Israel, 28% in Europe or the Western Hemisphere, 27% in Asia or Africa. Hebrew and Arabic are official languages. The school system provides ten years of free, compulsory classes. The country has 7 universities; literacy is estimated at 88% of Israeli Jews and 48% of Israeli Arabs. Military service is compulsory for men and unmarried women.

Government. Israel is a republic with power in the hands of the prime minister. Legislative power lies in the Knesset, a unicameral body elected by direct secret ballot.

History. Once the land of Canaan, then Israel, then Palestine, the modern state of Israel was born on May 14, 1948, after 2,000 years of Jewish statelessness and half a century of efforts by Zionists. In 1917, Britain's Balfour Declaration supported the idea of a Jewish state and assumed a Palestine mandate. Nazi persecution increased immigration in the 1930s and 1940s, and in 1947 a UN partition plan divided Palestine into two states, one Arab and one Jewish, with Jerusalem an international city. Neither side agreed, and civil war broke out; when Britain gave up the mandate in 1948, Israel was declared a state. Arab armies crossed the frontier and were defeated. A 1949 armistice brought no peace; terrorism continued on both sides. Proclaiming an imminent Arab attack, Israel invaded the Sinai in 1956. A UN cease-fire ended the hostilities. In 1967 Egyptian armies recaptured the Gaza Strip and closed the Gulf of Aqaba. In the Six-Day War that followed, Israel occupied more territory, including East Jerusalem and the entrance to the Suez Canal. In 1973, Egypt and Syria, aided by the USSR, launched another war which was settled by a UN cease-fire and disengagement agreement. In 1979, Israel and Egypt signed a peace treaty, and Israel began a phased withdrawal, which was completed in 1982, from the Sinai, returning the territory to Egypt. Subsequent talks between the two countries stalled over the issue of Palestinian autonomy on the West Bank. Israel has allowed religious extremists to establish new West Bank settlements and in 1981 announced that cabinet offices would be moved to East Jerusalem. In 1978, Israel invaded S Lebanon, where Palestinian guerrillas were based, and captured a narrow strip of territory. It was subsequently turned over to a UN peace-keeping force and Israeli-backed Lebanese Christian Militia. Sporadic fighting continued, however, intensifying in 1981, the same year Israeli jets bombed a nuclear site in Baghdad, where they alleged that Iraq was producing a nuclear bomb for use against Israel. In 1982, Israel attacked Lebanon in retaliation for what Israel considered increased activity by the PLO. Peace negotiations called for complete evacuation of the PLO from Beirut. Israeli troops remained in Lebanon until mid-1985 when withdrawal was completed. *See also* Palestine.

PROFILE

Official name: State of Israel
Area: 7,993sq mi (20,702sq km)
Population: 3,689,000
Density: 462per sq mi (178per sq km)
Chief cities: Tel Aviv-Jaffa; Jerusalem (capital); Haifa
Government: Republic
Religion: Hebrew
Languages: Hebrew and Arabic
Monetary unit: shekel
Gross national product: $15,710,000,000
Per capita income: $3,666
Industries: polished diamonds, processed food, chemicals, tires, petroleum products, aircraft, electronics, textiles, clothing, plastics, pharmaceuticals
Agriculture: citrus fruits, vegetables, cotton, durra, wheat, barley, olives, bananas, melons, figs
Minerals: gypsum, limestone, copper, iron, phosphates, magnesium, manganese, clay, rock salt, sulphur, potash
Trading partners: United States, European Common Market.

Israel, name with many biblical connotations, including the people dwelling in Palestine; the name given the North Kingdom; the name given Jacob after he wrestled with the angel; and the name taken by the returning exiles after the Babylonian captivity.

Israel

Istanbul, Turkey: Blue Mosque

Italy

Istanbul, city and seaport in NW Turkey, on both sides of Bosporus at entrance to Sea of Marmara; capital of Istanbul prov. Known as Byzantium until Constantine chose it as site for new capital of his Eastern Roman or Byzantine empire (AD 330), renamed Constantinople. It was patterned after Rome, set out on seven hills; some of the ancient moats and walls remain. The Hagia Sophia (built AD 360, converted from a church to a mosque and later to a museum) survives and is one of world's great architectural creations. Captured by Ottoman Turks 1453 the city was the capital until 1922; with the establishment of the new Turkish Republic after WWI the capital was moved to Ankara; site of Istanbul University (1453), a technical university (1944). Mosques of Beyazid II, Sulayyman I, and Ahmed I have been built since 1508, when an earthquake destroyed much of city. Industries: shipbuilding, cement, textiles, glass, shoes, pottery, tourism. Founded 660 BC by Greeks. Name was changed 1930. Pop. 2,312,751. *See also* Byzantium; Constantinople.

Italian Art. Roman art was modeled after Greek art. By the 6th century, trade with the Byzantine empire had brought a Byzantine influence to Italian art, which lasted through the 11th century. The chief centers of the Italo-Byzantine style were Venice, Tuscany, Rome, and the deep south. Mosaics and stylized, geometric forms became standard. Icon panels were the main type of paintings during the 11th through the 13th centuries, with major schools in Siena, Lucca, and Pisa. Many painted crucifixes and altarpieces date from this period, with Giotto and Duccio as outstanding masters. By the time of the Renaissance, the emphasis was on balance and harmony, with such masters as Ghiberti, Donatello, Botticelli, and Michelangelo.

Italian Greyhound, delicate breed of dog (toy group) 2,000 years old. A favorite in ancient Pompeii; brought to England in early 17th century. This elegant dog has a long, narrow head; small, thrown-back, and folded ears; long, slender neck and body with curved back; long, straight legs; and a slender, curved tail carried low. The short, glossy coat may be any color. Average size: 6–10in (15–25.5cm) high at shoulder; 7–10lb (3–4.5kg). *See also* Toy Dog.

Italian Literature. Italian vernacular literature emerged in the 13th century with the work of the Sicilian poets at the court of Frederick II; they developed the sonnet, a form that spread throughout Europe. Religious poetry also flourished. Major figures of the 14th century were Dante (early 14th century), whose *Divine Comedy* ranks as a masterpiece of world literature, Petrarch, and Boccaccio. Their writings established Tuscan as the vernacular literary language, although the humanists in the 15th century wrote in Latin. The Renaissance produced outstanding poetry and philosophy, especially in the work of Tasso, Ariosto, and Machiavelli. The 19th-century political movement for Italian unification and independence inspired a literary flowering. The major figure to emerge was Gabriele d'Annunzio. Important 20th-century writers include Alberto Moravia, Cesare Pavese, Eugenio Montale, and Umberto Saba, among others.

Italo-Ethiopian War (1935–36), conflict between Italy and Ethiopia. The war had its roots in the Italian defeat by the Ethiopians at Aduwa in 1896, which preserved Ethiopian independence. Partly in revenge and partly to create a larger empire, the Italian dictator Benito Mussolini followed a small conflict with full-scale war in 1935. The modernized Italian army won easily over the poorly-equipped Ethiopians, and Ethiopian Emperor Haile Selassie was forced into exile. Ethiopia then became part of Italian East Africa until Haile Selassie was

reinstated in 1941 by South African, Free French, and British forces.

Italy (Italia), independent nation in S Europe. A land of widely divergent customs, dialects, and character, it has been a democracy since the end of WWII.

Land and economy. A 700-mi (1,127-km) long peninsula shaped like a boot, Italy extends into the Mediterranean and includes the islands of Sardinia, Sicily, Pantelleria, and the Lipari group. It is bordered N by Austria, Switzerland, and France, and W by Yugoslavia. Except for the fertile Po valley in the heel of the boot and small coastal areas, the terrain is mainly rugged and mountainous and subject to earthquakes. The climate is generally Mediterranean and mild except in the Alps and Dolomite ranges. High levels of industrial investment brought impressive growth in the 1954–1963 period. Following a brief recession, growth gathered momentum again until slowed by strikes, higher labor costs, and recessions in the 1970s and early 1980s. Essentially a private enterprise system, the government controls some major industries and commercial enterprises, electricity, transportation, radio, and television. Mountains and unfavorable climate make it largely unsuited for agriculture and there are few mineral deposits, with the exception of natural gas. Living standards and productivity in the S, with high density and lower population, continue to be below the N. About 40% of the gross national product comes from industry and construction; agriculture accounts for 10% and services for 49%. Tourism is a major economic factor.

People. Italy is marked by a great divergence among its people. In the industrial N and the central portion, habits and culture are close to W European countries. The poverty-stricken and often primitive S is closer to North Africa and still shows signs of Moorish and Spanish occupation, particularly in regard to the closely circumscribed position of women. Minority units are small, the largest being German-speaking people of Bolzano prov. and the Slovenes near Trieste. There are also ancient communities of Albanian, Greek, Ladino, and French peoples. About 99% of the population is Roman Catholic, the state religion. Literacy is estimated at 93%. Education is compulsory between the ages of 6 and 14. In 1974, Italians voted to retain a law permitting divorce, a statute opposed by the church.

Government. A 1948 constitution established Italy as a highly centralized democratic republic with a bicameral elected parliament. The president is elected by parliament. The Christian Democrats have dominated most governments during the post-war period.

History. The unification of Italy as a constitutional monarchy under King Victor Emmanuel in 1870 marked the start of modern Italy. Before that it had been divided and torn apart since the fall of the Roman Empire. A monarchy with an elected parliament, Italy joined the Allies in WWI. In 1922, Benito Mussolini came to power; he eliminated political parties, reduced personal liberties, and installed a fascist dictatorship. In WWII, Italy joined with Germany until 1943, when Sicily was invaded by the Allies. A strong Italian resistance movement drove out the Germans in 1945. Under the 1947 peace treaty, some border adjustments were made with France and Yugoslavia, and Italy gave up its overseas possessions. Italy's position with the Roman Catholic Church has been governed by a series of accords, the most recent being the Lateran Pact of 1929, which recognized the sovereignty of Vatican City. Throughout the post-war period Italy has been plagued by unstable politics, with 40 governments between 1946 and 1980. During the late 1970s urban terrorism, by such leftist groups as the Red Brigade, increased. The Communist Party, allowed to partici-

pate in governments since 1977, is one of Italy's largest parties, controlling many local governments. An assassination attempt on the life of Pope John Paul II took place in 1982.

PROFILE

Official name: Italy
Area: 116,303sq mi (301,225sq km)
Population: 56,160,000
  Density: 483per sq mi (186per sq km)
Chief cities: Rome (capital); Milan; Naples; Turin; Genoa
Government: Democratic republic
Religion: Roman Catholic
Language: Italian
Monetary unit: Lira
Gross national product: $298,200,000,000
Per capita income: $3,040
Industries: industrial and electrical machinery, motor vehicles, steel products, typewriters, shoes, textiles, machine tools, synthetic fabrics, chemicals, oil refining, processed foods
Agriculture: grapes, olives, tobacco, cattle, sheep, fish, citrus fruits, wheat, rye, rice, tomatoes, nuts
Minerals: coal, zinc, lead, copper, marble, natural gas
Trading partners: Federal Republic of Germany, France, United States

Ithaca (Itháki), island of Ionian archipelago, SW central Greece, at entrance of Gulf of Corinth; legendary home of Homer's Odysseus. Industries: olives, vineyards, currants. Area: 37sq mi (96sq mi). Pop. 4,156.

Ito, Prince Hirobumi (1841–1909), Japanese statesman. Ito became a major promotor of westernization following study in England (1863). He played a major part in the Meiji Restoration and served as interpreter for the emperor (1868) and governor of Hyogo. Part of the Iwakura Mission to the United States and England, he was the chief architect of the constitution (1889) and was foreign minister, president of the house of peers, president of the privy council, negotiator of the treaty of Shimonoseki (1895), and four times prime minister. He was assassinated by a Korean patriot.

Iturbide, Agustin de (1783–1824), helped Mexico achieve independence (1821) and was named emperor (1822–23). Iturbide joined forces with Vicente Guerrero and issued the Plan of Iguala (1821), a call for the union of colonists under an independent monarchy. Iturbide was crowned, but his reign was a short one. Dissent crystallized when Santa Anna and Guadalupe Victoria issued the Plan of Casa Mata, calling for the end of the empire and the creation of a republic. Iturbide abdicated and was exiled. Early in 1824, he returned to Mexico, was arrested and shot.

Itzá, Toltec Indian group that migrated to northeastern Yucatán (Mexico) between AD 975 and 1200. The ceremonial center of Chichén was transformed into a city by the Itzá; the Itzá themselves were absorbed into Maya society.

IUD. See Intrauterine Device.

Ivan III (1440–1505), grand duke of Russia, known as Ivan the Great. He brought Yaroslav, Rostov, and Novgorod under Moscow's control and in 1480 freed Russia from the Mongols. He began the long struggle with Poland for control of Belorussia, the Ukraine, and Lithuania. His marriage to Zoë, niece of the last Byzantine emperor, led to his claim that Moscow was a "third Rome," the direct heir of Byzantium. Important buildings in the Kremlin were constructed during his reign.

Ivan IV, or **Ivan the Terrible** (1530–84), tsar of Russia (1533–84). He won control of the Volga by taking over Kazan and Astrakhan and expanded control over Siberia. His conflict with the boyars led to his formation of the *Oprichnina,* a group of soldiers who killed and took away the land of the boyars. In 1547 he was crowned first tsar of all Russia. He attempted to gain free access to the Baltic in wars with Poland and Sweden (1558–82) but failed. He was known for his cruelty; in a fit of rage, he killed his eldest son. He had seven wives.

Ivanhoe (1819), novel by Sir Walter Scott, based on the enmity Scott supposed to have existed between Saxon and Norman in England under Richard I. Wilfred of Ivanhoe returns from Richard's crusade and after various adventures, including a tournament and captivity in a Norman castle, is reunited with the lady Rowena.

Ivanovo, formerly Ivanovo Vozinesensk, city in Russian SFSR, USSR; capital of Ivanovo oblast. Industries: textiles, textile machinery, leather, dyes. Founded 1871 by inc. of two villages. Pop. 465,000.

Ives, Charles (1874–1954), US composer, b. Danbury, Conn. A successful insurance executive, he is recognized as a pioneer in 20th-century music, predating many other composers in his use of dissonance and unusual effects. His works often contain American folk music as a thematic basis, such as the *Variations on "America"* for organ (1891) and the *Symphony No. 2* (1902). He composed songs, symphonies, and chamber and piano music. His *Symphony No. 3,* though composed in 1904, won a Pulitzer Prize in 1947.

Ivory, hard, yellowish-white dentine, comprising the bulk of an elephant's tusk, or a similar substance obtained from tusks or teeth of other mammals.

Ivory Coast (Côte d'Ivoire), Republic of, nation in W Africa, on the Atlantic coast. The country is one of the world's leading producers of tropical wood, coffee, and cocoa, and has one of Africa's most promising developing economies.

Land and economy. A mountainous plateau rising gradually from a coastal plain, the Ivory Coast is heavily forested with valuable tropical hardwoods. Mountainous regions dominate the W and NW areas. The climate is tropical with heavy rainfall in the inland forest regions. The economy is agricultural, relying heavily on the coffee, cocoa, and timber industries. The Ivory Coast is first in Africa and second in the world in the production of tropical hardwood; however, coffee is its most valuable export. Rubber plantations were introduced in the 1960s. In 1977, off-shore oil deposits were discovered.

People. There are more than 60 tribes within the country. Tribal villages abound, with many local chiefs. Abidjan presents a strong contrast to the rest of the country for it is highly Europeanized. Animistic religions dominate, but about 25% of the people are Muslim.

Government. A republic, the government consists of a president elected every 5 years; a unicameral legislature (national assembly) with 147 members elected every 5 years; and a judicial branch with all judges appointed by the president. The sole legal political party is the Democratic Party of the Ivory Coast.

History. The French began ivory trade in the area in the 15th century and obtained rights to the territory in 1842, but did not actually occupy the area until 1882. It was part of the French Territory of West Africa from 1904 until granted its independence in 1960. It signed an agreement with France in 1961 retaining their close ties. From 1960 the nation was led by Pres. Felix Houphouët-Boigny, who was elected to his sixth term in 1985.

PROFILE

Official name: Republic of Ivory Coast
Area: 124,503sq mi (322,463sq km)
Population: 8,200,000
Density: 66per sq mi (25per sq km)
Chief city: Abidjan (capital)
Government: Republic
Language: French (official)
Monetary unit: CFA Franc
Gross national product: $8,560,000,000
Per capita income: $1,293
Industries: textiles, chemicals, plastics, processed foods
Agriculture (major products): coffee, cocoa, timber
Minerals (major): diamonds
Trading partners (major): France, United States, West Germany

Ivy, woody, evergreen vine native to Europe and Asia. Its long, climbing stems cling to upright surfaces by aerial roots. The leaves are leathery. The common English ivy (*Hedera helix*) is propagated by cuttings and grows outdoors in moist shady or sunny areas. It is an outdoor ornamental in all but the coldest areas of the United States. Family Araliaceae.

Ivy Arum, a single species of climbing plant *(Scindapsus aureas)* of the arum family, native to the Solomon Islands, with large leathery leaves, spotted and lined with yellow. It climbs by aerial rootlets arising from nodes. Commonly kept as a houseplant, it needs warmth, moisture, and considerable light.

Iwaki (Taira), city in NE Honshu, Japan, on Iwaki River; transportation center. Industries: coal mining, chemicals, machinery. Pop. 334,508.

Iwo, city in SW Nigeria, W Africa; regional trade center for cacao, farm products; coffee milling. Pop. 183,907.

Iwo Jima, formerly Sulphur Island; largest of the Japanese Volcano Islands in W Pacific Ocean; scene of successful US campaign to take island from Japanese 1945; it was returned to Japan 1968. Industries: sugar refining, sulfur mining. Area: 8sq mi (21sq km).

Iwo Jima, Battle of (February–March 1945), US assault during World War II on a Japanese-held island. US Marines suffered 20,000 casualties in this desperate battle. The flag-raising on Mt Suribachi at the end of the battle is remembered as a symbol of courage.

Ixtacalco, city in S central Mexico, adjacent to Mexico City; site of Floating Gardens; industrial area. Pop. 474,700.

Ixtacihuatl (Iztaccíhuatl), dormant snow-capped volcano in central Mexico, on Puebla-Mexico state border, 35mi (56km) SE of Mexico City; named by the Aztecs, means "white woman"; contains three summits; last erupted 1868. Height: 17,342ft (5,289m).

Ixtapalapa, city in S central Mexico, 5mi (8km) SE of Mexico City; on site of pre-Columbian Indian village. Pop. 533,569.

Izhevsk (Izevsk), city in Russian SFSR, USSR, on Iz River, in Ural Mts; capital of Udmurt ASSR; major Russian arms manufacturing center (19th century); forms industrial complex with Votkinsk, 30mi (48km) NE; railway, industrial, and cultural center. Industries: armaments, steel, tools, furniture, construction machinery, paper milling equipment, sawmills, breweries, motor vehicles. Founded 1760 around an old ironworks in the Urals. Pop. 549,000.

İzmir, formerly Smyrna; port city in Turkey, on Gulf of İzmir; capital of İzmir prov. City was ruled by Ottoman Empire 1424–1919, when it was tentatively assigned to Greece; it passed to Turkey by terms of Treaty of Lausanne, Oct. 11, 1922. City has been seat of SE headquarters of NATO since 1952; 2nd-largest port in Turkey. Exports: fruit, tobacco, cereal, silk, carpets, cotton. Settled by Aeolians and Ionians in 11th century BC. Pop. 636,078.

J

Jabalpur, city in central India, 150mi (242km) NNE of Nagpur; capital of Jabalpur district; site of Jabalpur University (1957) and military post; transportation and distribution center. Industries: cement, pottery, cloth, weapons, ammunitions, brassworks, cigarettes. Pop. 533,751.

Jabiru, largest stork of Western Hemisphere, found from Mexico to Argentina. It is black and white with reddish-orange lower neck. It typically nests in top of palm trees. Height: to 55in (140cm). Species *Jabiru mycteria. See also* Stork.

Jacana, long-toed water bird of tropical lakes with a slender body, narrow bill, wrist spurs, and tapered claws. It is black or reddish-brown, sometimes with a bright frontal shield. Known as "lily-trotter," it runs over floating vegetation, feeding on aquatic plants and small animals. Buff or brown, black-splotched, waxy eggs (4) are laid in a floating nest after noisy breeding. Length: 10–13in (25–33cm). Family Jacanidae.

Jacaranda, tree native to tropical America and cultivated in greenhouses worldwide. The ornamental *Jacarunda mimosifolia* and *J. cuspidifolia* have showy blue flowers. There are 50 species. Family Bignoniacea.

Jack, or crevalle jack, bony food and game fish found in warm waters of the American Pacific and Atlantic coasts. It has a high body profile with massive head and snub nose. Colors are green and silver with yellow blotches. Length: 2.5ft (76.2cm); weight: 20lb (9.1kg). Family Carangidae; species *Caranx bartho.*

Jackal, big-eared, Old World wild dog that resembles a coyote in habits, size, and general appearance. They prey on small animals, ranging from newborn antelopes to insects, and eat carrion, fruit, and seeds. The golden or Asiatic jackal *(Canis aureus)* ranges from Turkistan in Asia to Tanzania in Africa. The black-backed and side-striped jackals *(Canis mesomelas* and *Canis adustus)* inhabit savannas of E and S Africa. Length: 2ft (0.6m); weight: 20lb (9kg). Family Canidae. *See also* Canidae.

Jackdaw, gregarious black bird of Eurasia and N Africa. It is smaller than a crow and has a gray neck and whitish eyes. Colonies breed in holes in buildings with both parents building the nest and feeding the young. The female incubates the eggs (2–8). Species *Corvus monedula. See also* Crow.

Jack-in-the-pulpit, North American perennial, woodland plant with a green or brown hoodlike covering over the flower spike. Male and female flowers are often on separate plants. The one or two long, stalked leaves have three ovate leaflets. Its fruit is a cluster of red berries. Sometimes called Indian turnip, its tuberous roots were used by Indians as food. Height: to 3ft (0.9m). Family Araceae; genus *Arisaema triphyllum.*

Jackrabbit, big, slender, long-eared hare of W North America. Jackrabbits rely on their great speed, powerful leaps, and evasive moves to escape coyotes and other predators. Most are gray with white underparts, but the common northern white-tailed jackrabbit has a lighter winter coat. *See also* Hare.

Jackson, Andrew (1767–1845), 7th president of the United States (1829–37). He was born in the Waxhaw settlement on the border between North and South Carolina. His long military career began in the American Revolution, when he was captured by the British at the age of 13. Orphaned about that time, he wandered to western North Carolina (now Tennessee), where he was admitted to the bar. He settled (1788) in Nashville, where he married Rachel Donelson Robards. He was a delegate to the Tennessee constitutional convention in 1796 and served briefly as US representative and senator from the new state. He was also a judge in the Tennessee superior court.

In the War of 1812, Jackson defeated the Creek at the Battle of Horseshoe Bend (1814). His brilliant generalship against the British in the Battle of New Orleans (1815) made him the great hero of the war. In 1818 he was sent to fight the Seminoles on the Georgia border. He pursued them into Spanish Florida, where he caught and executed two British subjects and captured Pensacola. His actions enraged both the Spanish and the British, but it only made him a greater hero in the eyes of the US public. He served briefly as territorial governor of Florida.

Jackson soon emerged as the leader of one faction of the old Jeffersonian Republican party. To many, particularly westerners, he became the symbol of a new democratic, eqalitarian society. Jackson ran for president in 1824 against John Quincy Adams, Henry Clay, and William H. Crawford. Jackson won the most votes, but the election was decided by the House of Representatives. In what the Jacksonians called a "corrupt bargain," Clay threw his support to Adams, who was elected.

Jackson won the 1828 election easily. His presidency shifted the balance of power from the landed gentry and urban commercial interests of the East to the farmers and small businessmen of the West and the working classes of the East. He greatly increased the power of his party—now known as the Democratic party—by the introduction of the spoils system. He defended the Union against the rising states rights and nullification tendencies of the South.

Jackson won a landslide victory in 1832. In his second term, Jackson's fight with eastern commercial interests was centered on his long, ultimately successful, opposition to the Second Bank of the United States.

Career: US House of Representatives, 1796–97; US Senate, 1798; US Army, 1812–18; governor, Florida territory, 1821; president, 1829–37. *See also* Democratic Party; War of 1812.

Jackson, Robert Houghwout (1892–1954), US jurist and lawyer, b. Spring Creek, Pa. An assistant US attorney general (1936), US solicitor general (1938), and US attorney general (1940), he was appointed an associate justice of the US Supreme Court (1941–54). His opinion in *Youngstown v. Sawyer* (1952) declared Pres. Truman's steel mill seizures unconstitutional.

Andrew Jackson

François Jacob

Jai Alai

From 1945 to 1946 he was chief US prosecutor at the Nuremburg war crimes trials.

Jackson, Thomas ("Stonewall") (1824–63), Confederate Civil War general, b. Clarksburg, Va. His stand at the First Battle of Bull Run (1861) gained him his nickname, "Stonewall," and he pushed his troops so hard that they were called "Jackson's Foot Cavalry." Known as Robert E. Lee's best general, he won victories in the Shenandoah Valley (1862) and at Chancellorsville, where he was killed in May 1863.

Jackson, city in SW central Mississippi, on Pearl River; capital and largest city of Mississippi; seat of Hinds co. Originally a trading post est. 1700s and known as Le Fleur's Bluff, it was chosen as site of state capital 1821; scene of race riots in 1960s and again in 1970 at Jackson State College. It is site of Millsaps College (1890), Belhaven College (1894), old capitol (1839), governor's mansion (1839). Industries: textiles, glass, electrical equipment, meat products, lumber, oil, natural gas. Inc. 1833. Pop. (1980) 202,895.

Jackson, city in W Tennessee, 85mi (137km) ENE of Memphis, on Forked Deer River; named for Pres. Andrew Jackson. Home of John "Casey" Jones is preserved as museum; site of Union University (1834), Lane College (1882), Lambuth College (1924), Jackson State Community College (1965). Industries: textiles, lumber, furniture, livestock, tile, power tools, store fixtures, aluminum foil. Settled 1819; inc. 1823 as town, 1845 as city. Pop. (1980) 49,131.

Jackson Hole, valley in NW Wyoming, E of Teton Range; N section is in Grand Teton National Park; remainder is in Teton National Forest and Jackson Hole Wildlife Park. The region was first visited by trapper David Jackson (1828–29). Area: approx. 384sq mi (995sq km).

Jacksonville, seaport city in NE Florida, on St John's River; seat of Duval co and largest city in Florida; served as Confederate base during Civil War; developed into a deepwater port during 19th century; devastated by fire 1901; site of Confederate Monument (1898), Fort Caroline National Monument, Edward Waters College (1866), Jones College (1918), Jacksonville University (1934), Gator Bowl. Industries: cigars, fertilizers, concrete, food processing, tourism, lumber, phosphate, paper, chemicals. Settled 1816 by Lewis Hogan; inc. 1832. Pop. (1980) 540,898.

Jack the Ripper (*fl.* 1888), murderer of at least seven prostitutes in the East End of London in late 1888. The name given the murderer came from his mutilation of his victims. Despite public outcry at police inefficiency, he has never been definitely identified.

Jacob, in the Bible, son of Isaac and Rebekah and younger twin brother of Esau. While fleeing after tricking Esau out of Isaac's blessing, he wrestled with an angel to obtain God's blessing. He married Leah and Rachel; the descendants of his son Joseph became the 12 tribes of Israel.

Jacob, François (1920–), French biologist. With Jacques Monod he discovered that a substance that they named *messenger RNA* carried hereditary information from the cell nucleus to the sites for protein synthesis and that certain genes, called operator genes, control the activity of other genes. They shared the 1965 Nobel Prize in physiology or medicine with another French biologist, André Lwoff.

Jacobins, French political radicals belonging to a club that played an important role during the French Revo-

lution. The club met in a former Dominican monastery in the Rue St Jacques. Begun in 1789 by some deputies to protect the revolution from a reaction by the aristocrats, the club split in 1791 when the moderates left it. Thereafter more democratic and more popular in orientation, the Jacobin movement developed a network of clubs throughout France where leaders conferred and public discussions were held. In 1793–94, the club was an instrument of Maximilien Robespierre and, as the greatest power in the country, became part of the government's administrative machinery. It ceased to exist after Robespierre's downfall in 1794. Political radicals or sympathizers with the French Revolution are also called Jacobins.

Jacobites, name given to supporters of James II and his Stuart descendants, who attempted to regain the English throne after the Glorious Revolution of 1688 deposed James II. With unofficial French encouragement, Jacobites were found among Scots (the homeland of the Stuarts), Irish (James II was Catholic), and disgruntled Tories (Whigs dominated the government). In 1715 the "Old Pretender," called James III by his supporters, attempted insurrection and failed; in 1745 the "Young Pretender," called Charles III, did the same. By the late 18th century, the claims of the "king over the water," as the Jacobite pretenders were termed, had only occasional sentimental appeal.

Jacob's Ladder, or Greek valerian, charity, perennial plant native to Europe. It has feathery leaves and small, cup-shaped, blue flowers in clusters. Height: to 3ft (91cm). Family Polemoniaceae; species *Polemonium caeruleum.*

Jacquerie, violent insurrection of the lower classes against the nobility in NE France in 1358 during the Hundred Years' War. Enraged by the increased war taxes and the pillaging of the English invaders and the French nobility, the peasants and some townspeople revolted. They destroyed numerous castles and killed the inhabitants. The revolt, which spread throughout the region, was defeated by the nobles, who executed the leader Guillaume Carle and massacred thousands of peasants.

Jade, a semiprecious mineral of two major types—jadeite, which is often translucent, and nephrite, which has a waxy quality. Both types are extremely hard and durable. Jade is found mainly in Burma and Turkestan and comes in many colors, most commonly green and white. Jade carving is usually done with diamond drills and lapidary wheels. The earliest Oriental jade carving was done in China in the late Neolithic period, when ceremonial objects and items of personal adornment were made. By the Chou dynasty (*c.*1027–256 BC), jade carving was a highly developed art. During the Ming dynasty (1368–1644), the dragon motif was introduced into jade carving. During the Ch'ing dynasty (1644–1912), jade carving reached its peak in such creations as enormous jade "mountains" and screens. Jade was also used extensively for decorative objects and tools in Central America and Mexico, especially in the Mayan culture of Yucatán.

Jade Plant, succulent, treelike houseplant native to S Africa and Asia. It has smooth, fleshy, rounded leaves, thick stems, and small white flowers. Care: bright light, soil (equal parts loam, peat moss, sand) kept dry between waterings. Propagation is by stem and leaf cuttings. Height: to 30in (76cm). Family Crassulaceae; species *Crassula argentea.*

Jaeger, gull-like predatory, fast-flying seabird that breeds in the Arctic and winters in the subtropics. It has a dark, stocky body with pointed wings and long tail

feathers. It feeds on small land animals and seabirds. Olive brown, black-spotted eggs (2–3) are laid in a shallow depression of tundra moss. Length: 13–20in (33–51cm). Genus: *Stercorarius.*

Jaén, city in S Spain, 178mi (287km) S of Madrid; capital of Jaen prov.; site of Moorish citadel and 16th-century church. Industries: linen, olive oil, alcohol. Area: (prov.) 5,212sq mi (13,499sq km). Pop. (city) 78,156; (prov.) 661,146.

Jagatai, or **Chagatai** (d.1242), Mongol ruler. A son of Genghis Khan, he led armies in his father's conquests. Upon his father's death (1227) he was awarded Turkistan and Afghanistan as his khanite. In the early 14th century his descendants, the Jagatids, divided the khanite, with Samarkand the capital of the west and Kashgar the capital of the east. Tamerlane reunited the khanite *c.*1369. The Jagatid dynasty was swept away by the conquering Uzbek Mongols *c.*1500.

Jagger, Mick (Michael Philip) (1944–), British rock singer. He helped organize the Rolling Stones rock group while a student at the London School of Economics in 1962 and became its lead vocalist. By 1963 the group was popular in Britain and from 1964 made hugely successful tours of the US and Europe. Their recordings regularly sold by the millions. Jagger's flamboyant, hard-driving, sensual style characterized his delivery. He was also the group's lyricist and appeared in films.

Jaguar, spotted big cat found in woody and grassy areas from S Texas and New Mexico to Argentina. It has a chunky body, rounded ears, and yellowish coat with black rosettes. This fierce cat eats large mammals, turtles, and fish. The gestation period is 99–105 days and 2–4 young are born. Length: body, 44–84in (112–213cm); tail, 21–26in (53–66cm); weight: 150–225lb (68–101kg). Family Felidae; species *Panthera onca. See also* Cat.

Jaguarundi, small, ground-dwelling cat found in Central and South America. Weasellike, it has a long, slender body, short legs, long tail, small head, and is black, brown, gray, or fox red with no spots. Types, according to color, include colcollo, jaguarundi, and eyra. Length: 36–52in (91–132cm); weight: 10–20lb (4.5–9kg). Family Felidae; species *Felis vagouaroundi.*

Jai Alai, a fast-action game, the most popular of the fronton games. It is played on a court about 176 feet (53.6m) long and 95 feet (29m) wide, bounded on the front, back, and one side by walls 44 feet (13.4m) high. The fourth wall has a wire netting, behind which the audience sits. Each player has a curved wicker basket (a *cesta*) attached to his arm. A hard-rubber ball is used. The object is to hurl the ball so that after it bounces off one of the side walls it cannot be returned to the front wall. Depending upon the number of players (two, four, six), 6 to 40 points are needed to win. Jai alai originated about the 17th century in the Spanish Basque regions and is now also popular in Latin America and the United States, where parimutuel betting is allowed. *See also* Fronton Games.

Jainism, ancient monastic religion of India. Its roots are traced back through a series of teachers, the last being Parshva in the 8th century BC and Mahavira in the 6th century BC. Jains do not accept Hindu scriptures, rituals, or priesthood, but they do believe that people go through cycles of rebirth. Monks can attain release from the cycle by ascetic living and meditation. Jains are extremely careful to observe the rule of not injuring any living creature *(ahimsa)*. There are about 2,000,-000 Jains today.

Jaipur

Jaipur, city in NW India, 140mi (225km) W of Agra; capital of Rajasthan state and former Jaipur state; site of Rajasthan University (1947), maharajah's palace, and 20-ft (6-m) crenellated wall that surrounds the city; transportation and commercial center. Industries: banking, jewelry, enamels, muslins, glass, ivory, marble carvings. Founded 1727 by Marharajah Jai Singh II. Pop. 613,144.

Jakarta. *See* Djakarta.

Jalapa Enriquez, city in E central Mexico, on the slopes of the Sierra Madre Oriental; conquered by Hernán Cortes 1519; served as military base *c.* 18th century; site of Mt Orisaba, Indian villages, local museum containing archaeological collection, university. Industries: coffee, tobacco, tourism. Pop. 183,216.

Jalisco, state in W central Mexico, bordered by the Pacific Ocean (W); conquered 1529 by Nuno de Guzman; occupied by French during the wars of intervention; retaken 1866. Terrain is mountainous (S), with tropical plains along the coast; site of two universities, technological institute. Products: wheat, maize, rice, grains, lumber, cinnabar, iron, tin, silver, gold, livestock. Industries: processed foods, textiles. Area: 30,941sq mi (80,137sq km). Pop. 4,157,000.

Jamaica, island nation in the Caribbean, 90mi (145km) S of Cuba; economy depends on agriculture, bauxite, mining, and tourism. The majority of population is of African descent. It is an independent member of the British Commonwealth.

Land and economy: Mountains cover 80% of the land, which has a tropical maritime climate in the path of the tradewinds. The economy depends on tourism, mining, light manufacturing, construction, and agriculture; Jamaica is the world's second-largest producer of alumina and bauxite, the chief export products. Principal crops are sugar cane for rum and molasses, bananas, coconuts, and citrus fruits. Manufactured goods include tires, chemicals, cement, and food products. Tourism attracts more than 500,000 visitors a year. Unskilled rural migrants moving to the cities have raised the unemployment rate to about 30% in 1980.

People: More than 90% of the inhabitants are of African origin, together with large groups of East Indians and Chinese. English is the official language, but many speak a Jamaican Creole. Primary education is free, and literacy is estimated at 85%. The Anglican Church is predominant.

Government: The Jamaica Constitution, signed in 1962, set up a British-style parliamentary system of government. The British crown appoints governor-general, but executive power resides in the prime minister, who is leader of the majority party in the popularly-elected parliament and who appoints the cabinet. Local parish government is headed by elected council members.

History. Jamaica was discovered by Christopher Columbus in 1494 and was held by the Spanish until 1655 when British forces occupied the island. Sugar and slavery made it an important possession. After a long period of colonial rule, Jamaica started on the road to independence in the 1930s. Self-government was granted in 1959, and Jamaica achieved full independence in 1962. Michael Manley, son of a prominent politician, became prime minister in 1972 with a platform of democratic socialism. His policies, however, resulted in virtual bankruptcy, and he was unable to control violence in Kingston. In the national campaign of 1980—marked by killings—Manley's party was defeated, and moderate Edward Seaga became prime minister. He advocated close ties with the United States and a return to free enterprise.

PROFILE

Official name: Jamaica
Area: 4,411sq mi (11,424sq km)
Population: 2,587,000
   Density: 587per sq mi (226per sq km)
Chief city: Kingston (capital)
Government: Parliamentary system in British Commonwealth
Religion (major): Anglican
Language (major): English
Monetary unit: Jamaican dollar
Gross national product: $2,540,000,000
Per capita income: $1,143
Industries (major products): tires, chemicals, clothing, food products
Minerals: bauxite, alumina
Trading partners: Great Britain, United States, and Canada

James I (1566–1625), king of England, son of Mary, Queen of Scots. Crowned James VI of Scotland on his mother's abdication (1567), James passed his minority mainly under the control of the Presbyterians, who wished to protect him against Roman Catholic influence. Forced to choose between France and England as allies for Scotland, James opted for Protestant England (1586). On Elizabeth I's death, he became king of England (1603). He concluded peace with Spain (1604), but at home his failure to conciliate either the Puritans or the Catholics caused discontent. His reliance upon favorites and his troubled relationship with the House of Commons weakened his effectiveness as a ruler.

James II (1633–1701), king of England, Scotland, and Ireland, second son of Charles I. After the Restoration (1660), James, then duke of York, was prominent in national affairs and won a naval victory over the Dutch at Southwold Bay (1672). As a Roman Catholic, he was forced to resign the admiralty by the Test Act (1673). Despite the rival claim of the duke of Monmouth, James succeeded his brother Charles II (1685), but his support of Roman Catholicism alienated his subjects. Compelled to flee (1689), he lived his last 12 years in exile.

James I (1394–1437), king of Scotland (1406–37). His father, Robert III, decided to send him to France to keep him safe from the duke of Albany, next in line to the throne. On his way to France he was captured (1406) and detained by the English. Though he technically succeeded to the throne on his father's death (1406), neither the regent Albany nor Albany's son, who succeeded him as regent (1420–24), ransomed James until pressured by the nobles to do so in 1424. Upon his return James became an energetic and decisive monarch, taking measures to break the power of the nobles and Highland lords, restore law and order, and improve commerce and the army. He had many of his enemies arrested or slain and confiscated their estates. He acted against corruption and brought the chief financial officers of the kingdom under his personal supervision. His attempts to retain church revenues embroiled him with the papacy. He improved the system of justice for common people and sought to have the Scottish parliament meet annually and to include burghers as members. He was assassinated by a group of conspirators led by the earl of Atholl. James is generally believed to be the author of *The Kingis Quair* (*c.*1423), a long love-dream allegory in vernacular Scots about his captivity and romance with his future wife Joan. This work, in the tradition of Chaucer, marks the beginning of the golden age of Scottish literature.

James II (1430–60), king of Scotland (1437–60). Only six years old when his father, James I, was assassinated, for years he was under the domination of vying clans, particularly the Douglases. In 1452 he killed the current earl of Douglas and destroyed the clan's power by 1455. He improved the courts and regulated the coinage. He was killed while in England aiding the Lancastrians in the Wars of the Roses.

James III (1451–88), king of Scotland, son of James II, whom he succeeded in 1460. Unable to control his nobles, James was challenged by his brother Albany, whom Edward IV of England recognized as king in 1482. Peace was arranged with Albany, but a fresh rebellion resulted in James' defeat at Sauchieburn and his subsequent murder.

James IV (1473–1513), king of Scotland, nominal leader of the rebels who killed his father, James III, in 1488. A strong and energetic monarch, James maintained his authority throughout Scotland. Peace with England (concluded 1497) was promoted by his marriage to Henry VII's daughter, Margaret (1503), but in 1513 he led an invasion of England and was killed at Flodden.

James V (1512–42), king of Scotland, succeeded his father, James IV (1513). Efforts to retain control of his nobles and independence from his uncle, Henry VIII of England, occupied most of James' reign. His death followed the English rout of his forces at Solway Moss. He was succeeded to the throne by his infant daughter Mary.

James, three persons in the New Testament: **James the Greater** (died *c.*43), one of the Twelve Disciples of Jesus, brother of the disciple John. He was beheaded on orders of Herod Agrippa I. **James the Less,** also one of the twelve Disciples, son of Alphaeus and one of the three Marys at the cross and tomb. **James the Brother of Jesus** (died *c.*62), a witness to the Resurrection and a leader, perhaps first bishop, of the church in Jerusalem. He was either stoned to death or thrown from a tower. He is usually identified as the writer of the epistle of that name. The Roman Catholic Church claims he is a cousin, not a brother, of Jesus and that he is the same person as James the Less.

James, Henry, Jr. (1843–1916), US novelist, short-story writer, and critic, b. New York City. The son of Henry James, Sr., and brother of William James, he received his early education abroad but went to Harvard Law School for a law degree. Encouraged by William Dean Howells, he entered upon a literary career and published his first novel *Watch and Ward* in 1871. In 1876 he established residence in England, and in 1915 became a British subject.

James, the master of a complex prose style, had a keen insight into values of character. He felt strongly that a writer should "never allow anything to enter a novel which was not represented as a perception or experience of one of the characters." Usually the central figure in his works was an American involved in one of the arts, either wealthy himself or moving in wealthy or influential circles. In many of these novels the principal theme lies in the contrast of American and European traits. Among his many works are the novels *Roderick Hudson* (1876), *Daisy Miller* (1879), *The Portrait of a Lady* (1881), *The Bostonians* (1886), *The Wings of the Dove* (1902), and *The Ambassadors* (1903).

James, Jesse (Woodson) (1847–82), US outlaw, b. Clay co, Mo. He and his brother Frank fought for the Confederacy during the Civil War. In 1866 they formed an outlaw band and terrorized the frontier, robbing banks and trains in Missouri and nearby states. In 1882, while living under the assumed name Tom Howard in St Joseph, Mo., he was shot by Robert Ford, one of the members of his own gang, for a large reward.

James, William (1842–1910), US philosopher and psychologist, b. New York City. Regarded by many as the greatest of American psychologists and an outstanding philosopher, he pioneered research in many areas, including emotions, consciousness, attention, and the laboratory study of human functions. A precursor of the functionalist school, he also did much to establish psychology as relevant to practical problems. His masterpiece, *Principles of Psychology* (1890), is one of the great achievements in psychology. Other noted works include *The Varieties of Religious Experience* (1902) and *Pragmatism* (1907). *See also* James-Lange Theory; Pragmatism.

James River, river in Virginia, formed by the confluence of the Jackson and Cowpasture rivers in central Virginia; flows E into Chesapeake Bay at Hampton Roads. First permanent English settlement in North America was made on lower river at Jamestown (1607). Union forces used river in their unsuccessful attempts to take Richmond. River is navigable to Richmond for about 100mi (161km) of its 340mi (548km).

Jamestown Settlement, first successful English colony in America (1607). Despite able leadership of John Smith, the Virginia Company colony nearly failed because of malaria, hunger, and Indian attacks. New settlers and supplies (1610), marriage of John Rolfe to Pocahontas, and commercial development of tobacco by Rolfe (1614) enabled the colony to grow. The House of Burgesses first met and slavery was initiated in 1619. Jamestown was placed under direct royal rule in 1624. *See also* Pocahontas; Powhatan; Rolfe, John; Smith, John.

Jammu and Kashmir, once the largest princely state of India, possession of its 54,000sq mi (139,860sq km) and legendary Vale of Kashmir is now divided between India and Pakistan. Bordered by India and Pakistan, the Himalayas stand above heavily populated valleys of the Indus and Jhelum rivers. Basic economy includes rice cultivation, animal husbandry, a few silk factories, rice and flour mills, and tourism. The population of the Indian State is 4,615,176, and the capital is Srinagar. Muslims constitute the largest religious group, with some Buddhists, Dogras, and Sikhs; Kashmeri is the language; several monasteries are served by lamas; education is free. After early Buddhist and Hindu rule, it became part of the Mogul empire in 1587 and came under British domination in 1846. When India was partitioned in 1947, the battle for Kashmir started. After years of fighting, the UN decision of 1972 set cease fire lines.

Jamshedpur, city in NE India, at junction of Subarnareka and Karkhai rivers. It was founded early 20th century as a steel mill area of the Tata Iron and Steel Works; first mill opened 1911. Industries: blast furnaces, coke ovens, chemicals, wire, agricultural equipment, iron, steel. Pop. 465,200.

Janesville, city in S central Wisconsin, 32mi (52km) SE of Madison on Rock River; seat of Rock co; site of Tallman House and Underground Railroad station; trade center in dairying, grain, and tobacco region. Industries: fountain pens, electrical equipment, automobiles. Founded 1835; inc. 1853. Pop. (1980) 51,071.

Japanese Literature

Henry James

Jesse James

Japan

Janissaries, elite, disciplined soldiers of the Ottoman army. Established in the 14th century by the sultan Orkhan, they were originally recruited from Christian youths and other war captives who had been converted to Islam. They eventually made and unmade sultans, became ungovernable, and were massacred in their barracks by the sultan Mahmud II (1826).

Jansen, Cornelis (1585–1638), Dutch theologian. At the University of Louvain he studied problems raised for Catholics by Lutheran and Calvinist doctrine. He also became involved in a conflict between the university and the Jesuits over teaching theology. In his writings he argued for a return to St Augustine's views on grace and salvation. Jansen was bishop of Ypres at the time of his death. His *Augustinus,* which was the basis for the doctrine called Jansenism, was declared heretical after his death. *See also* Jansenism.

Jansenism, a reform movement in the Roman Catholic Church in the 17th and 18th centuries. The name comes from the Dutch theologian Cornelis Jansen (1585–1638), but the movement grew strongest in France, led by Antoine Arnauld (1612–94) and others and centered at the abbey of Port-Royal. Some Jansenist ideas, such as doctrines of predestination, resembled Protestant beliefs, but the Jansenists advocated reforming rather than leaving the church. Still, their ideas were condemned in four papal bulls. Controversy between Jansenists and the church authorities who opposed them flared up at intervals until the movement was virtually broken up during the reign of Louis XIV.

January, first month of the year. It was named after the god Janus and has 31 days. The birthstone is the garnet.

Janus, in Roman mythology, god of all doorways. He was also the god of all beginnings and presided over daybreak. The month of January is named after him.

Japan (Nihon, Nippon), independent nation in E Asia. Since WWII, its economic development has made it one of the world's financial powers.
  Land and economy. The Japanese archipelago, off the E coast of Asia, is made up of four main mountainous islands—Hokkaido, Honshu, Shikoku, and Kyushu —and some 3,000 smaller islands. About 80% of the country is hills and mountains with active and nonactive volcanoes and frequent earthquakes. The climate ranges from subtropical on S Honshu to cold on Hokkaido. Tropical storms in the early fall carry torrential rain and typhoons. Although only 19% of the land is arable, persistence and skill result in high per-acre yields; farms produce 80% of the food needed, including rice. Fish is a major source of food and income, and Japan has been a world leader in its total catch. Natural resources are few, and hydroelectric power provides less than half the supply needed; thermal power has also been developed. Japan must import petroleum and many minerals needed for heavy industry. It ranks second to the United States in motor vehicle production, and steel and electronics are also leading industries. Japan leads the world in large ship building, and its merchant fleet is among the world's largest. Production is oriented toward exports, which earn more than 10% of the gross national product.
  People. The Japanese are a Mongoloid people originally from mainland Asia. There has been little mixture for the past 1,000 years. Buddhism, the dominant religion, influences philosophy, institutions, and the arts. Shintoism, a belief based on myths and legends, was the state religion in the 19th century and was used by the government to support the Emperor's divinity. After WWII, its official status was removed.

Christians number about 750,000. Schooling is free through junior high school. Very competitive exams regulate the entrance to higher education. Literacy is almost 100%.
  Government. Japan is a constitutional monarchy, with the Emperor as symbol of state. The bicameral Diet, main body of power, is elected by universal adult suffrage. Executive power rests in the cabinet and the prime minister (a Diet member). Conservative pro-Western governments have dominated since WWII, including the Liberal Democratic Party, which has led every government since it was established in 1955.
  History. According to tradition, Japan was founded 660 BC by the Emperor Jimmu, descendant of the Sun Goddess and ancestor of the present royal family. Two changes in AD 405 brought a social revolution: the use of Chinese script and the introduction of Buddhism; these innovations started the adoption of Chinese culture. First contact with the West came in 1552 when a Portuguese navigator was blown off his course and landed; traders and missionaries followed. Fearing eventual conquest, Japan expelled all foreigners in 1638. Japan was isolated until 1854, when US Commodore Matthew Perry opened it up to trade. Japan won Taiwan (Formosa) from China in 1894; Korea was annexed in 1910; the German Pacific islands became Japan's mandate after WWI, and Manchuria fell to Japan in 1931. In 1933, Japan resigned from the League of Nations. The military's influence on government increased, and Japan attacked China in 1937 and bombed the US base at Pearl Harbor, Hawaii, on Dec. 7, 1941, precipitating the US entrance into WWII. After almost four years of war, Japan was defeated, losing all its non-Japanese possessions; government was placed under Allied control. Reforms gradually introduced a self-governing democracy. Japan's remarkable postwar economic recovery was matched by increased participation in international affairs and agencies. In the late 1970s and early 1980s, Japan experienced some economic difficulties. The higher cost of imported oil, which fuels the economy, resulted in inflation and deficits, and Japan's major trading partners, including the United States and West Germany, pressured Japan to reduce exports to their countries.

PROFILE

Official name: Japan
Area: 143,689sq mi (372,155sq km)
Population: 117,000,000
  Density: 814per sq mi (314per sq km)
Chief cities: Tokyo (capital); Osaka; Yokohama; Kyoto; Nagoya
Government: Constitutional monarchy
Religion: Buddhism
Language: Japanese
Monetary unit: Yen
Gross national product: $990,000,000,000
Per capita income: $8,460
Industries: motor vehicles, ships, electronics, precision instruments, iron, steel, chemicals, fertilizer, textiles, ceramics, wood products, food products, optics, television, toys
Agriculture: rice, wheat, barley, tobacco, potatoes, tea, beans, fruits, fish, forests
Minerals: coal, gold, silver, copper, lead, zinc, salt, petroleum
Trading partners: (major) United States, West Germany, Saudi Arabia

Japan, Sea of, branch of W Pacific Ocean, lying between Japan (E), the Korean peninsula (SE), and the coast of the USSR (W). Area: 389,100sq mi (1,007,769sq km).

Japan Current. *See* Kuroshio Current.

Japanese, the national language of Japan, spoken by virtually all of the country's 111,000,000 people. It belongs to no linguistic family, though in grammatical structure it resembles Korean and may actually be related to it. Written Japanese uses both Chinese ideographs, known as *kanji,* and syllabic characters, known as *kana.* The latter, of which there are two types—*hiragana* and *katakana*—each consisting of 50 characters can in theory represent any word in the language. But because of the large number of homonyms in Japanese there would be too many ambiguities and thus most Japanese words are spelled with a combination of the ideographs and syllabic characters.

Japanese Architecture, architectural style derived from Chinese religious structures in the 6th century. The Buddhist temple is constructed of gracefully curved wooden columns supporting the wide overhanging roof and thin exterior walls of woodwork and plaster. The gateway, drum tower, and pagoda are also built of wood, and the group is usually set on a picturesque wooded hillside. One-story domestic structures are traditionally built according to modules whose basic unit is a mat, 6 feet by 3 feet. Interior wooden posts support the roof. The outer walls are movable panels of wood or rice paper that slide in grooves. The interior is flexibly subdivided by screens and decorated with simplicity and delicacy.

Japanese Art. Originally was strongly influenced by China. From the **Asuka period** (593–710) come primitive tomb and wall paintings as well as Buddhist scrolls. During the **Nara period** (710–784), figures in painting became less angular and more lifelike and robust. The **Heian period** (780–1180) saw Japanese painting come into its own, in screens, hand scrolls, book illustrations, and landscapes. During the **Kamakura period** (1185–1338), many scroll paintings were produced. There was a trend toward realism in both scrolls and portraits, and the new ink brushstroke technique was introduced. During the **Muromachi period** (1338–1573), cultural activity centered around the Zen monasteries. Masanobu (c.1453–1540) and his son Motonobu (c.1476–1559) founded the Kanō school. The following **Momoyama period** produced large numbers of wall paintings such as decorative frescoes for the castles of warriors. During the **Edo period** (1615–1867), the Nanga painting school reacted to the academicism of the Kanō school. Outstanding print-makers made *ukiyo-e* prints of Kabuki actors, women, and landscapes. After the fall of the Tokugawa shogunate (1868), many Japanese artists attempted to assimilate Western painting styles, while others clung to the traditional Japanese style.

Japanese Beetle, beetle native to E Asia and accidentally introduced in North America about 1916. Adults are greenish-bronze and coppery brown and feed on fruits and leaves of many plants. The cream-colored to brown, lin (25mm) larvae feed primarily on grass roots and soil humus. Length: 0.5in (13mm). Species *Popillia japonica.*

Japanese Exclusion, attempt to deny immigration rights to Asians. Between 1891–1910, about 25,000 Japanese had immigrated to the United States, particularly to the Western states. Since many of these immigrants were laborers, US workers felt threatened. The Gentlemen's Agreement (1907) between Japan and President Theodore Roosevelt sought to limit Japanese entry. Some states passed legislation that restricted the rights of Japanese in America. The Immigration Bill (1924) excluded Japanese as aliens ineligible for US citizenship.

Japanese Literature, the body of creative writing of Japan. Japanese literature is one of the oldest and richest in the world. The earliest extant works are the *Kojiki* (712) and the *Nihongi* (720), both histories written in Chinese characters used phonetically. The earliest recorded Japanese poetry is in the *Manyoshu* (760), which contains poems dating to the 4th century.

Heian Period: 794–1185. The invention of the Kana syllabaries (*c.*800) encouraged writing. The *Kokinshu* (905), an anthology of poetry commissioned by the emperor, provided a pattern for *tanka* (short poems). Classical prose developed during this period. *Taketori Monogatari (Tale of the Bamboo Cutter)* is the oldest surviving work. Diaries and accounts of court life also flourished, such as Sei Shonagon's *Makura no Soshi* (*Pillow Book, c.*1000). By far the most significant work was Murasaki Shikibu's *Genji Monogatari* (*The Tale of Genji, c.*1010), the first true novel and one of the world's classics.

Middle Ages: 1185–1603. The *Shinkokinshu* (1206) was an influential collection of poems that are dark in tone and are similar to the *renga* (linked verse) that developed during this period. The No theater was refined by Kanami Kiyotsugu (1333–84) and his son Zeami Motokiyo (1363–1443). Although the "war tales" genre appeared in this period, typified by *Heike Monogatari (Tale of the Heike)*, Buddhism colored much of the prose. Notable works are: *Hojoki* (*Account of My Hut, c.*1212) and *Tsurezuregusa* (*Essays in Idleness, c.*1333).

Tokugawa Period: 1603–1868. During this period literature, once the preserve of the aristocracy, became the field of the commoners. Although *tanka* were still written, *haiku* became popular, and Matsuo Basho (1644–94) was the greatest poet of this form. There were developments in the puppet theater and Kabuki, which benefited from the work of the great dramatist Chikamatsu Monzaemon (1653–1725). Perhaps the most famous prose writer of the period was Saikaku Ihara (1642–93).

Modern Period: With the increase in foreign contacts, Western literature had a major influence. Poetry flourished, and major figures such as Yosano Akiko (1878–1942), Ishikawa Takuboku (1885–1912), and Hagiwara Sakutaro (1886–1942) found new means of expression through contact with Western poetry. Writers of modern fiction have earned a reputation abroad as well as at home. They include such figures as Natsume Soseki, Tanizaki Junichiro, Mishima Yukio, Abe Kobo, and Nobel Prize–winner Kawabata Yasunari.

Japanese Music. The music of Japan owes its heritage to Chinese music. Japanese sacred music is divided into *gagaku,* which is orchestral music first introduced into Japan from China around AD 600, and *kangura,* which originated in the 13th century and is used in modern worship. The latter centers around a few notes and is played on the koto (zither) and flutes. Japanese music also includes traditional, ceremonial Nogaku, or No, drama, involving singers accompanied by flutes and drums. Secular music includes vocal music, such as opera, and especially chamber music. In general, the scale most frequently used in Japanese music is the semitonic penta-scale. Rhythm is usually double time. Japanese music tends to be monophonic rather than polyphonic.

Japanese Mythology. The oldest recorded myths of the Japanese appear in the *Kojiki,* a Shinto text of AD 712. In it is described the creation of the world when the gods Izanagi and Izanami made Earth out of muddy water. When Buddhism was introduced from Korea in the 5th and 6th centuries it brought countless new figures to the country's mythology, and the old gods were declared to be reincarnations of Buddhist deities.

Japanese Spaniel, Asian dog (toy group) also called Japanese Chin. Probably originated in ancient China; brought to West by Comm. Perry in 1850. It has a large, rounded head with short muzzle and wide nose between the prominent dark eyes; square, compact body; small, slender legs; and tail twisted over the back. The profuse, long, straight coat is black and white or red and white. Average size: 9in (23cm) high at shoulder; 7lb (3kg). *See also* Toy Dog.

Japanese Theater, descended from ritual dances, assumed three major forms: No, puppet theater, and Kabuki. In addition to the traditional forms, newer styles of drama, influenced by the West, have developed out of the desire to portray modern events and ideas realistically. *See also* Kabuki Theater.

Japanning, the use of colored varnish to produce a hard, brilliant coating imitative of Japanese lacquer.

Japheth, in Genesis, Noah's son who, with his brothers Shem and Ham, survived the Flood aboard the ark.

Japurá, river in NW South America; rises at the confluence of the Caquetá and Apaporis rivers, SW Colombia; flows SE to unite with the Amazon River near Tefé, Brazil. Length: approx. 1,750mi (2,818km).

Jasmine, climbing shrub known in the Mediterranean since ancient times and grown as an ornamental. It produces fragrant yellow, red, or white flowers, and the oil is used in perfumes. Species include *Jasminum sambac* and the white *J. officinale,* which is hardy into temperate zones. Height: 15–20ft (4.6–6m); family Oleaceae.

Jason, hero of Greek mythology. Sent on a quest for the Golden Fleece by his uncle King Pelias to prevent him from claiming his throne. Jason sailed aboard the *Argo* with heroes including Heracles, Theseus, Orpheus, Castor, and Pollux and had adventures with Harpies and Amazons. He found the fleece in Colchis and fled with the sorceress Medea, daughter of the king. Later, tragedies left him a wanderer who died under the prow of the old *Argo. See also* Medea.

Jasperware, unglazed stoneware first made in England by Josiah Wedgwood in 1775. White in its natural state, jasperware is then stained, most commonly pale blue, but also dark blue, lilac, green, black, and yellow. White decorations in the neoclassical style are molded separately and then applied to the piece of jasperware. Jasperware objects include vases, plaques, cameos, tableware, and portrait medallions.

Jaundice, yellowing of the skin and other tissues, prominently the whites of the eyes, by an excess of bile pigment in the blood, with subsequent accumulation in the tissues. It may occur in the newborn as a result of faulty metabolism of bile pigment or secondary to other causes; if severe in the premature infant, it may produce widespread destruction in the brain. In adults, jaundice may occur when the flow of bile from liver to intestine is blocked by an obstruction such as a gallstone, or in diseases of the liver such as cirrhosis or hepatitis. In addition to the yellowing of tissues, the symptoms of jaundice include itching, dark urine, and pale stools. *See also* Cirrhosis; Hepatitis.

Java (Djawa), island in Indonesia; member of the Greater Sunda Islands, bounded by Sumatra (SE), Malay Peninsula (E), and lying between the Java Sea and Indian Ocean; Djakarta is the capital. It is the 4th-largest island of Indonesia, constituting three provinces, two autonomous districts, and more than 65% of the country's total population, making Java one of the most densely populated areas of the world, 2,200 people per sq mi (850 per sq km). A mountainous area, it is crossed by numerous volcanic formations, some of which are still active; the climate is warm and humid, with moderate rainfall; extensive irrigation systems make it a fertile agricultural area. Long before recorded history, Java was a center of civilization, as indicated by the 1891 discovery of the Java man and other fossilized human remains. From the 4th–15th centuries it served as the seat of a highly developed Hindu-Buddhist civilization, whose center was the powerful Majapahit state; its rule over much of Indonesia and the Malay Peninsula was halted 1518 by Muslim conquest; European settlement began 1596 and continued with est. of Dutch East India Co. post at Batavia 1619. Island was occupied 1811–16 by Britain under Thomas S. Raffles; retaken and held by Dutch until Japanese occupation of WWII; scene of Dutch-Indonesian conflicts 1945–46 ending in Linggadjati Agreement and independent Indonesia (1947); site of Bandung Technical Institute (1959), University of Indonesia (1950), National University (1949), University of Padjadjaran (1957), Airlangga University (1954), Diponegoro University (1960), Gadjah Mada University (1949); cultural, political, economic center. Crops: sugar, kapok, rubber, tea, coffee, tobacco, cacao, cassava, peanuts, maize, cinchona, rice, sweet potatoes, bananas, fruit trees, soybeans. Industries: teak wood, textiles, agriculture, fishing, handcrafts. Area: 48,842sq mi (126,501sq km). Pop. 76,100,000.

Java Man, or *Pithecanthropus erectus,* extinct race of hominid whose skeletal remains were found at Trinil, Java, in 1891. His skull was apelike, but his limb structure was akin to modern man's. *See also* Pithecanthropus.

Java Sea (Djawa, Laut), shallow extension of the Pacific Ocean in SE Asia; bordered by Java (S), Borneo (N), Flores Sea and Makassar Strait (E), Sumatra (W); scene of WWII Allied defeat by Japanese naval forces (1942), leaving Java vulnerable to Japanese invasion. Depth (max.): 300ft (92m). Area: 120,000sq mi (310,800sq km).

Javelin, in field events, wooden or metallic spear with a metal tip weighing a minimum of 1lb, 12.218oz (800g). It has an overall length that varies from 8ft, 6.362in to 8ft, 10.299in (260–270cm).

Jawara, (Sir) Dauda Kairaba (1924–), Gambian political figure. He served as minister of education and prime minister (1960–70) of Gambia when it was a British colony and became its president when it became a republic in 1970. After defeating an attempt to overthrow him in 1981, Jawara announced the merger of his country with neighboring Senegal.

Jay, John (1745–1829), first chief justice of the US Supreme Court (1789–95), b. New York City. He was an influential member of the Whig party, and during the American Revolution he served as a delegate to the Continental Congress (1774–77, 1778–79), becoming its president during the second period. He was chairman of the committee that drafted the first state constitution of New York (1777) and was appointed the first chief justice of New York (1777–89). He also served as minister to Spain (1779–82) and then went to join Benjamin Franklin in Paris to negotiate a peace with Great Britain. He was secretary for foreign affairs under the Articles of Confederation (1784–89). Together with Alexander Hamilton and James Madison he wrote the *Federalist Papers* (1787–88), explaining and urging ratification of the US Constitution. As a member of the New York Constitutional Convention, he helped secure ratification (1787) by that state. While US chief justice, he ruled on *Chisholm* v. *Georgia* (1793) which was reversed with the adoption of the 11th Amendment, stipulating that a state could not be sued by an individual (1795). In 1794 he was sent to Britain as a peace negotiator and concluded the controversial Jay's Treaty. When he returned, he was governor of New York (1795–1801). *See also* Federalist Papers, The; Jay's Treaty.

Jay, any of several harsh-voiced, often brightly colored, birds related to magpies and crows (family Corvidae). About 1ft (30cm) long, they have strong, cone-shaped bills, eating almost anything in their open forest and brushland homes. They usually lay 3 to 7 pale green or white spotted eggs in an open nest in a tree. *See also* Blue Jay.

Jayawardene, J(unius) R(ichard) (1906–), president of Sri Lanka (1978–). One of the founders of the United National Party in 1946, he remained actively involved in its leadership. Jayawardene introduced (1978) a new form of government modeled after the French. Elected prime minister in 1977, he became Sri Lanka's first president the next year and was reelected to a six-year term in 1982.

Jay's Treaty (1794), agreement between the United States (represented by John Jay) and Britain (represented by Lord Grenville) principally to settle points of dispute outstanding between them since the Revolutionary War. Its provisions regarding trade helped establish American commerce. The United States agreed not to aid privateers hostile to Britain, and Britain withdrew from the Northwest Territory.

Jazz, musical style that evolved in the United States in the late 19th century out of African and European folk music, popular songs, and American vaudeville. Jazz is characterized by a steady rhythm, usually four beats to the bar, with accents on the second and fourth beats; prominence of melody, often with elements derived from the blues; and improvisation and spontaneous creation by the performer. Early jazz was developed in New Orleans in the form of blues, Dixieland, and ragtime music. In the 1920s jazz spread to Chicago and New York City and became known across the world as a unique musical style indigenous to America. Subsequent developments included the big "swing" bands in the 1930s and the "bebop" (now called "bop") style of the 1940s. Jazz elements influenced serious composers such as Maurice Ravel and Darius Milhaud and also became a part of other popular musical styles such as rock-and-roll. Among the greatest of jazz musicians were Louis Armstrong, Duke Ellington, W. C. Handy, Scott Joplin, Benny Goodman, and Art Tatum.

Jean de Meun or **Meung,** real name Jean Clopinel (*c.*1250–*c.*1305), French poet and scholar. He continued the *Romance of the Rose* by Guillaume de Lorris. Under Jean de Meun, the work, originally a romantic allegory, became a satire on women, royalty, and the church. Meun also translated the *Life and Letters of Abélard and Héloïse.*

Jefferson, Thomas (1743–1826), 3rd president of the United States (1801–09), b. Goochland (now in Albermarle) co, Va., graduate, William and Mary College. In 1772 he married Martha Wayles Skelton; they had six children.

Jefferson received the education and upbringing of an 18th-century landed aristocrat. He was a talented architect and musician, an inventor, and a respected amateur botanist. His political writings, based on John Locke and Jean Jacques Rousseau, made him the foremost advocate of democracy of his day. He was admitted to the Virginia bar in 1767.

In the Virginia House of Burgesses, Jefferson led the

John Jay

Thomas Jefferson

Edward Jenner

patriot faction, and his writings spread his influence throughout the colonies. He was a delegate (1775) to the First Virginia Convention. At the Second Continental Congress in 1775–76, he was asked to draft the Declaration of Independence, his most famous work. He became governor of Virginia in 1779, but he was not an effective administrator. He served in the Second Continental Congress, which sent him (1785) as minister to France. While there, he witnessed the early stages of the French Revolution and sympathized with the revolutionary movement.

In 1790, President Washington named Jefferson secretary of state. A factional rivalry soon developed in the cabinet between Alexander Hamilton and Jefferson. Hamilton's faction represented the urban, commercial interest and favored alliance with Britain, while the Jeffersonians were agrarians and favored France. The factions gradually formed into political parties: the Hamiltonians became Federalists and the Jeffersonians became Republicans (later Democrats).

In 1796, Jefferson ran against John Adams, and when Adams won, Jefferson became vice president. Jefferson was elected president in 1801 after a deadlock in the House of Representatives. He set about ridding the presidency of its royalist trappings and sought to reduce the overall influence of the federal government. He pushed through the Louisiana Purchase and sent the Lewis and Clark Expedition to explore the West. In his second term, he sponsored the ill-fated Embargo Act of 1807. After his retirement, he founded the University of Virginia.

Career: member, Virginia House of Burgesses, 1769–75; delegate, Second Continental Congress, 1775–76; governor of Virginia, 1779–81; minister to France, 1785–89; secretary of state, 1790–93; vice president, 1797–1801; president, 1801–09. *See also* Declaration of Independence; Louisiana Purchase.

Jefferson City, capital city of Missouri, located in central part of state on Missouri River; seat of Cole co; occupied by Union troops during Civil War June 1861; site of 1917 Italian Renaissance capitol of Carthage marble, housing paintings by Thomas Hart Benton and N. C. Wyeth; Missouri state museum; and Lincoln University (1866). Industries: shoes, clothes, electrical appliances, bookbinding. Chosen as state capital 1821; legislature moved there 1826. Inc. as town 1825, as city 1839. Pop. (1980) 33,619.

Jeffreys, (Sir) Harold (1891–   ), English astronomer and geophysicist. He ascertained that the four outer planets are very cold, constructed models of them, and investigated the origin of the solar system. Studying the thermal history of the Earth, he was the first to hypothesize that its core is liquid. He co-authored the standard tables of earthquake-wave travel times and explained the origin and function of monsoons, sea breezes, and cyclones.

Jehad. *See* Jihad.

Jehoshaphat, in the Bible, son of Asa and king of Judah. He and Ahab, king of Israel, signed an alliance, the first between the two countries.

Jehovah, a variant form of the name of the God of Judaism. It developed from YHWH (or JHVH, YHVH; a Hebrew tribal name for God) and the vowel symbols of the word *Adonai* ("My Lord") during the Middle Ages. It came to be used synonymously for the ineffable name *Yahweh*. Christians quickly assumed this transliterated form. In the 19th and 20th centuries, scholars began the return to *Yahweh*.

Jehovah's Witnesses, Christian group taking its name from a passage in the Old Testament: "Ye are

my witnesses, saith Jehovah" (Isaiah 43:10). They are active in preaching and door-to-door missionary work and distribute millions of Bibles and tracts. Centered in the United States, they have also held international conferences. The Watch Tower Bible and Tract Society, incorporated in 1884, acts as the legal agency for the witnesses.

Jellyfish, marine coelenterate found in coastal waters and characterized by tentacles with stinging cells. The adult form is the medusa. It has a bell-shaped body with a thick layer of jellylike substance between two body cell layers, many tentacles, and four mouth lobes surrounding the gut opening. The common *Aurelia* is transparent with four violet circles near its center. Diameter: 3in–12in (76.2–304.8mm). Class Scyphozoa.

Jena, city in S East Germany, on the Saale River; scene of 1806 Prussian defeat by Napoleon; site of University of Jena (1557–58). Industries: glass, optical and precision instruments, pharmaceuticals. Founded 9th century; chartered 13th century. Pop. 88,346.

Jenkins, Roy (Harris) (1920–   ), British political figure and president of the Commission of the European Community (1977–81). A journalist and author, he was a member of Parliament for 28 years (from 1948) and a Labour cabinet member for 8. A proponent of European unity, he established the European Monetary System while president of the Commission of the European Community. He was responsible for two important law reforms concerning libel and obscenity. He helped form the new Social Democratic Party (SDP) (which formed an alliance with the Liberal Party in 1982) in Britain, in 1981, was elected to Parliament in 1982, and served as leader of the SDP (1982-1983). His works include *The Labour Case* (1959) and *Asquith* (1964).

Jenkins' Ear, War of (1739–41), war between England and Spain arising out of long-term mercantile and maritime grievances, most notorious of which was the boarding of Robert Jenkins' ship at Havana in 1731 by a Spanish official who cut off one of the English captain's ears.

Jenner, Edward (1749–1823), English physician. He developed vaccination as a means of preventing smallpox. Aware that a cowpox infection seemed to protect people from a subsequent smallpox infection, Jenner inoculated a healthy boy with cowpox. The boy developed that mild disease but months later when inoculated with smallpox did not develop that dreaded disease; he had been vaccinated against it. This finding established the principle of vaccination as an invaluable tool in medicine.

Jerboa, jumping, burrowing rodent of Eurasian and African deserts with hindlegs four times longer than front legs. Nocturnal, it has a satiny, sand-colored body and an extremely long tail. Herbivorous, it does not drink water. Length: 2–8in (51–203mm). Family Dipodidae.

Jeremiah (*c.*650–585 BC), Hebrew prophet whose life and teachings are recorded in the Old Testament Book of Jeremiah, the 24th book of the Bible. He fearlessly denounced social injustice and false worship in the Kingdom of Judah. When Babylonia invaded Judah, captured Jerusalem, and took many Jews into exile, Jeremiah saw this as a punishment from God. He urged the people to make peace and to believe in God, teaching that they could preserve their worship even in disaster and exile. His ideas were influential in later Old Testament writings and in the New Testament.

Jerez de la Frontera, city in SW Spain, 13mi (21km) NE of Cadiz, N of Guadalete River. An ancient Roman colony, it was taken by Moors 711, reconquered 1264 by Alfonso X. Site of 15th-century church of Santiago; Gothic church of San Miguel (1462); Carthusian Monastery (1477), now a national museum. Industries: lumber, citrus fruits, livestock, vegetables, cork, olives, grain, bottles, barrels, sherry. Pop. 149,867.

Jericho, ancient city of Palestine, in Jordan valley, N of Dead Sea; modern Ariha is near ancient city. Captured by Joshua from Canaanites (1,400 BC), city was later destroyed by Herod (1st century BC) and rebuilt S of old site; destroyed several times after this. In 1950 excavations revealed a Hellenic fortress from the 2nd century and site of Herod's city.

Jerome, Saint (*c.*347–420), Bible scholar and father of the Roman Catholic Church. His original name was Eusebius Hieronymus. After a thorough literary education he spent four years of intense study in a monastic type of community in the Syrian desert. Later he went to Rome and became secretary to Pope Damasus I. The pope commissioned Jerome to prepare a standard text of the Gospels for use by Latin-speaking Christians. Jerome revised the Gospels from the Old Latin and later made a new translation of the Psalms and the Old Testament from Greek and Hebrew sources. His work was the basis for what later became known as the Vulgate, or authorized Latin text of the Bible.

Jersey, largest island in Channel Islands of United Kingdom; constitutes a bailiwick; capital is St Helier. Official language is French, although English is spoken everywhere. Main occupations: farming, horticulture, tourism. Area: 45sq mi (117sq km). Pop. 79,342.

Jersey, widespread breed of small dairy cattle of French descent, developed on the Isle of Jersey. The butterfat content of their milk, 5.3%, is the richest of all dairy cattle, but relatively low in volume. Usually fawn or brown, some American varieties have white markings. *See also* Dairy Cattle.

Jersey City, port city in NE New Jersey, on Hudson River and Upper New York Bay, across from New York City; seat of Hudson co; 2nd-largest city in state. Originally a Dutch settlement, it came under British control in 1664; in 1779 "Light-Horse Harry" Lee, under George Washington, captured it; site of St Peter's College (1872), Jersey City State College (1929), New Jersey College of Dentistry and Medicine (1955). Industries: oil refining, chemicals, paper products, locomotives, clothing. Founded 1630; inc. 1838 as Jersey City. Pop. (1980) 223,532.

Jerusalem (Yerushalayim, or **Al-Quds),** city on Israeli-Jordanian border, 35mi (56km) SE of Tel Aviv; capital of Israel and Jerusalem district; sacred city of the Christian, Jewish, and Muslim religions. City contains many educational institutions, including Hebrew University (1925), and many churches, synagogues, and shrines. Industries: tourism, diamond processing, plastics, shoes, construction. Originally a Jebusite stronghold (2000–1500 BC), city was captured by King David after 1000 BC and known as "city of David"; it developed into religious center of country. Destroyed by Nebuchadnezzar of Babylon *c.* 586 BC, it was rebuilt by Herod *c.* 35 AD, but again destroyed by Titus AD 70. The Roman colony of Aelia Capitolina was established, and Jews were forbidden within city limits (135–mid-5th century). Christian control was granted by Persians *c.* 614. City was conquered 1077 by Muslim Seljuks, whose mistreatment of Christians precipitated the Crusades, as a result of which was formed the kingdom of Jerusalem 1094–1187. It was held by Turks from

1244–1917, when it became the British mandated territory of Palestine; it was divided in 1949 between Jordan and Israel, in 1950 it was designated capital of the new state of Israel, although most countries did not recognize it as Israel's capital. During the Six Day War (1967), Israeli troops took East Jerusalem, uniting the Arab section with the Israeli city. Since then the status of Jerusalem has continued to be controversial. Talks between Israel and Egypt after their peace treaty (1980) stalled, partly over Israel's refusal to relinquish East Jerusalem. In 1981, Israel announced that its cabinet offices would be moved to East Jerusalem. Palestinians—with the support of most Arab nations—have called for the creation of an independent Palestinian West Bank nation with Jerusalem as its capital. Some countries outside the region favor granting international status to the city. Pop. 420,000.

Jerusalem, Latin Kingdom of, feudal state created in Palestine and Syria by the Crusaders. After Jerusalem fell in the First Crusade (1099), Godfrey of Bouillon ruled it. He refused to be king, but his brother, Baldwin I, took the title, as did many successors, such as Baldwin II, the Angevins Fulk and Baldwin V, Guy of Lusignan, Amalric II, and Emperor Frederick II. The kings, who were elected, ostensibly oversaw the Latin counties of Antioch, Edessa, Tripoli, and Jerusalem, but the feudal lords fought among themselves. The kingdom warred with the Mamelukes of Egypt, the Seljuk Turks, and the Byzantine emperors. The royal authority was undermined by the military orders (eg the Knights Templars), and the Seljuks seized Edessa (1144). Saladin captured Jerusalem in 1187, and the kingdom essentially ended when the Christians were defeated at Gaza (1244). Acre, the capital after Jerusalem fell, was captured in 1291.

Jerusalem Artichoke, North American perennial sunflower with edible (potatolike) tubers used as food for man and livestock. It is not a true artichoke. Height: to 12ft (3.6m). Family Compositae; species *Helianthus tuberosus.*

Jesuits, officially the Society of Jesus, a Roman Catholic order of religious men founded by Ignatius Loyola in 1540. The order played a significant role in the Counter-Reformation. They often were the first Christian missionaries in the New World, Asian, and African areas. Because they gave allegiance only to their general in Rome and the pope, they came to antagonize many European rulers. In 1773 Pope Clement XIV, pressured by the kings of France, Spain, and Portugal, abolished the order. They continued to exist in Prussia and Russia. The order was reestablished in 1814. The largest male order, today there are over 33,000 members. It takes as long as 15 years to gain full membership in the order. Jesuits have distinguished themselves in education, scholarship, and missionary work.

Jesus, Society of. *See* Jesuits.

Jesus Christ (*c.*4BC–*c.*AD30), the founder of Christianity. His name combines a well known Hebrew name, Jesus (originally Joshua, "God is salvation"), with Christ, which comes from a Greek translation of a Hebrew word for messiah, anointed one, a long-expected king and deliverer of Israel. What is known of Jesus' life comes from study of the Gospels of Matthew, Mark, Luke, and John, the first books of the New Testament. He was born about 4 BC, near the end of the reign of Herod the Great. (A 6th-century error put the first year of the Christian calendar several years after Christ's birth date.) Jesus' mother, Mary, and her husband, Joseph, lived in Nazareth in Galilee, but they had to journey to Bethlehem in Judea for a census and Jesus was born there in a stable. He probably grew up in Galilee. About AD 26 or 27, John the son of Zachariah began a preaching and baptizing ministry in Galilee, and Jesus was one of the many who went to John and were baptized in the Jordan River. Thereafter, Jesus began his own ministry, preaching to growing numbers and gathering 12 disciples around him. He told people to love God and to love their neighbor—who is anyone, even a foreigner or an enemy. He taught that salvation depends on true devotion to God's will rather than on following the letter of the religious law.

In about 29 or 30 Jesus and his disciples went to Jerusalem just before the Jewish feast of the Passover. The city gave him a triumphal welcome, but he knew that the end of his earthly ministry was near. A small group in the priestly hierarchy in the Temple in Jerusalem feared Jesus was a source of trouble. A few days after the entry into Jerusalem, Jesus gathered his disciples for a Last Supper, at which he instituted the sacrament of Holy Communion. That same night he was arrested by agents of the priests and denounced before Pontius Pilate, the Roman governor, on the charge that he claimed to be king of the Jews. Roman soldiers crucified Jesus on a hill outside the city wall; he died after suffering for three hours and was buried. On the third day his tomb was found empty. On 9 occasions he appeared to his disciples, and 40 days after his Resurrection he ascended into heaven. His followers then began their own ministry to take his word to all people.

Christians worship Christ as the Son of God, who lived as a man to bring God's message to the world. They also believe he is one with God; he is at once truly human and truly divine. By his preaching and the sacrifice of his death and his Resurrection, he showed humankind how to live rightly and how to find eternal life. *See also* Apostle.

Jet, a dense variety of lignite coal formed from driftwood buried on the sea floor; often polished as jewelry.

Jet Engine, Aircraft. *See* Turbojet Engine.

Jet Propulsion, the movement of a body by way of thrust provided by the rearward discharge of a jet of gas (or fluid), as in jet engines or rockets. In jet engines the ejected gas consists of a mixture of air taken from outside and gases resulting from internal combustion. *See also* Rocket.

Jet Stream, a narrow, swiftly moving wind between slower currents at altitudes of 6 to 10mi (10 to 16km) in the upper troposphere or lower stratosphere, principally in the zone of prevailing westerlies. High-flying aircraft may be helped or hindered by the jet stream and the rapid wind variations around it. *See also* Circulation, Atmospheric.

Jetty, an engineered structure designed to direct and confine a current or tide. They are often built in pairs on either side of a harbor entrance or at the mouth of a river. Groins, breakwaters, seawalls, and small piers are examples of jetties.

Jewelweed, North American succulent plant found in marshes, swamps, and damp woods. Pale jewelweed, or touch-me-not *(Impatiens pallida),* has pendant, pale yellow blossoms; height: to 5ft (1.5m). The spotted jewelweed *(Impatiens biflora)* has orange flowers with purple spots. When crushed, the stems and leaves exude a juice that is a remedy for the itching caused by poison ivy. Family Balsaminaceae.

Jewfish, also giant grouper, marine fish found in tropical and temperate waters of the Atlantic and Pacific. It is spotted and mottled. Length: to 8ft (2.5m); weight: to 750lbs (340kg). Family Serranidae; species include *Epinephelus itajara* and *Premicrops lanceolata.*

Jews, a people who have maintained an identity over thousands of years in spite of dispersion and persecution. The Jews originated in the ancient Middle East, and for centuries they lived in kingdoms in Palestine. Then they were dispersed over the world, sometimes living as ghetto minorities, sometimes as citizens. In the 20th century Jews established the national state of Israel. Millions more live in other countries—6,000,000, for example, are US citizens. Jews differ among themselves in physical appearance, language, and to some extent in customs, so there is no simple definition of Jewishness. The sense of identity is found in religious beliefs and traditions going back through the Hebrew prophets to the time of Moses and Abraham. *See also* Judaism.

Jew's Harp, primitive musical instrument. Probably first called "Jaw's Harp," it is an iron frame held in the player's teeth, with a flexible metal strip vibrated by his finger. The player changes tone and pitch by shaping his mouth.

Jezebel, in the Bible, Phoenician wife of Ahab, king of Israel. She supported worship of Baal and, clashing with Elijah, drove him out of Israel. Her death was caused by Jehu, usurper of her son Jeram's throne. Ahaziah, her daughter, was queen of Judah.

Jhansi, walled city in N central India; capital of Jhansi district of Uttar Pradesh state; served as capital of Maratha principality 1770–1853; scene of European massacre (1857) during India Mutiny; its fortress, built by Bundela Rajputs, dates from 1613. Industries: railroad workshops, rolling mills, brassware, rugs, silk. Founded 1732. Pop. 198,101.

Jidda (Juddah), port city in Saudi Arabia, on the Red Sea 46mi (74km) W of Mecca; under Turkish rule until 1916, when it joined independent Hejaz; taken 1925 by Ibn Saud; site of several government ministries, traditional tomb of Eve; serves Mecca as port for pilgrims. Pop. 561,000.

Jig, a dance, originating in England, that reached its popularity during the 16th century. Jigs were frequently named for the clown characters who danced them in English comedy, and "Nobody's Jig" was among the most popular. In the United States, jigs were the forerunners of dances in minstrel shows. Most jigs are couple dances in 6/8 time. The Irish jig and English Morris jig are complicated solo dances.

Jihad, or **Jehad,** religious war of Muslims against nonbelievers. Established in the Koran as a divine institution, such warfare is a sacred religious duty undertaken especially for the purpose of advancing Islam and protecting Muslims from evil. There are four ways in which Muslims may fulfill their Jihad duty: by the heart, by the tongue, by the hand, and by the sword.

Jim Crow Laws, measures enacted in the US South from 1877 to the 1950s to legalize racial segregation in public facilities, including theaters, schools, parks, and restaurants. The term "Jim Crow" was derived from the name of a minstrel act and came to mean segregation. The laws began to be challenged after the 1954 Supreme Court ruling *(Brown* v. *Board of Education of Topeka, Kansas)* which stated that segregated schools were unlawful.

Jimson Weed, also thorn apple; poisonous bad-smelling weed originally native to Asia. All parts of the plant are toxic and can cause death. Leaves are wavy-toothed, and the trumpet-shaped flowers, to 4in (10.2cm), are white or purplish. Alkaloids present are atropine, hyoscyamine, and scopolamine. Height: 4ft (1.2m); family Solanaceae; species *Datura stramonium.*

Jingoism, term used to describe a posture of chauvinism or aggressive nationalism. It originated in the Russo-Turkish War (1877–78) when British supporters of the war came to be called jingos, after a line of a popular song of the day: "We don't want to fight, yet by jingo, if we do/We've got the ships, we've got the men/And got the money, too!"

Jinnah, Muhammad Ali (1876–1948), founder of Pakistan. He obtained his law degree in England and returned to practice in India. In 1906 he joined the Indian National Congress where he became an advocate of Hindu-Muslem unity. Between 1910–19 he was a member of the legislative council of the viceroy. In 1913 he joined the Muslim League and became its president in 1916. In 1920 he resigned from the Indian National Congress although he still hoped Hindus and Muslims could work together. But in 1940 he called for a completely separate Muslim nation on the Indian subcontinent. With the creation of Pakistan in 1947, Jinnah became governor general and president of the constituent assembly.

Jinzhou (Chinchou), city in NE China, on main line of Peking-Mukden railroad; noted transportation center. Industries: textiles, paper, oil refining, chemicals. Pop. 400,000.

Jívaro, or **Shuara,** a tribe of Indians of the E Andean region of Ecuador and Peru, famed for their manufacture and use of the *tsantsa,* the shrunken heads of their victims. They once numbered over 30,000 people; today, 20,000 inhabit the lowland Andean Montaña region.

Joab, in the Bible, David's nephew and general of David's army. Failing to reconcile David and his son Absalom, Joab killed Absalom. Backing Adonijah's claim to the throne, Joab was killed by Solomon.

Joan of Arc (Fr. Jeanne d'Arc) (1412–31), the national heroine of France and a Roman Catholic saint; also known as Joan of Lorraine and the Maid of Orléans; b. Domremy-la-Purcelle. A deeply religious peasant girl, she claimed to hear heavenly voices and see visions of saints urging her to save France, which was then in the midst of the Hundred Years War (1337–1453), ravaged by the English and their Burgundian allies, while the dauphin Charles VII remained uncrowned because Reims, the traditional place of investiture, was held by his enemies. In early 1429, wearing men's clothes, Joan went to the dauphin, recognizing him immediately though he had hidden himself among his courtiers, and persuaded him to give her troops. She then went to Orléans and, inspiring the French forces, broke the long English siege of that city. She next drove the English from the Loire towns and defeated them at Patay. After this victory she persuaded the indecisive dauphin to proceed to Reims and be crowned with herself standing near him. She then attempted to liberate Paris but was unsuccessful.

In early 1430 she was captured by the Burgundians and turned over to Bishop Pierre Cauchon, who had taken the English side, to be tried at Rouen for witchcraft and heresy. The proceedings against her occupied the winter and spring of 1431. Under great pressure she resolutely maintained her innocence, except for a few days during which she signed an abjuration of heresy. After being sentenced to imprisonment, she withdrew her abjuration and reaffirmed her innocence,

Jerusalem, Israel

Jewelweed

Pope John XXIII

was turned over to secular authorities, and burned at the stake. In 1456, after the English had been driven out of France, new proceedings annulled the 1431 trial and verdict. In 1920 she was canonized a saint and the French government declared an annual national holiday in her honor for her role in awakening national consciousness in France.

Job, biblical patriarch and book that describes Job's life and raises the question: Is Job's goodness, wealth, and rank a form of selfishness? Satan asks if Job fears God for naught and, if the blessings were removed, would he curse God to his face? Receiving permission, the Devil destroys Job's property and his children and inflicts him with a terrible disease, causing his wife's breakdown. Job's reply to all this suffering, "Shall we not receive good at the hand of the Lord, and shall we not receive evil?" answers Satan's question. Later, Job curses the day he was born when three men of wisdom come to console him. Jehovah appears and eloquently reproves Job, rebukes his opponents, and vindicates the patriarch's integrity.

Jobs, Steven (Paul) (1955–   ), US entrepreneur. An orphan, he was adopted by the Jobs family. Known as a "loner," he studied electronics after school and worked summers at Hewlett-Packard, where he met Stephen Wozniak, an engineering wizard. After Jobs dropped out of college he designed video games, traveled, and returned to California, where he and Wozniak designed, built, and marketed a compact home computer known as the Apple. When their company went public in 1980, its sales exceeded $130 million. In 1985 Jobs left Apple, announcing plans to form a new computer firm.

Jodhpur (Marwar), walled city in NW India; site of old fortress housing gem collection of the maharaja; riding breeches named after city. Industries: textiles, ivory carvings, lacquerware, glassware, bicycles. Founded 1459 by Rao Jodha. Pop. 318,894.

Joel, biblical author and second of the 12 minor prophets. The first prophet to Judah, he reflects on the country's ruin and despair, later detailed by other prophets.

Joe-Pye Weed, perennial plant of E North America. It has leaves in whorls and terminal clusters of pink or purple flower heads. Height: 3–12ft (0.9–3.6m). Family Compositae; genus *Eupatorium.*

Joffre, Joseph Jacques Césaire (1852–1931), French military figure. He began his military career as an engineer in the colonies. In 1911 he was appointed commander in chief of the French army. Underestimating German strength at the outbreak of World War I, he at least led an orderly retreat and made a successful counterattack at the Battle of the Marne (1914). After the Germans nearly captured Verdun (1916), he was relieved of his command and served as chief military adviser to the government, then as chairman of the Allied War Council.

Jogjakarta, city in S Java, Indonesia, 175mi (282km) WSW of Surabaja, at foot of Mt Merapi; capital of Jogjakarta autonomous district; served as capital of Dutch-controlled sultanate 1755; scene of native uprising led by Prince Dipo Negoro protesting Dutch forced-labor practices and exploitation (1825–30); Javanese stronghold during Indonesian independence movement (1940s); temporary capital of Indonesia 1945–49; site of palace of Jogjakarta sultans (1757), housing Gadjah Mada University (1949), Java University (1921), Sono Budojo Museum, and 11th-century Hindu temples. Industries: cigars and cigarettes, railroad shops, sugar, silvercraft, wood carving, leather goods,

batik cloth. Founded 1749 by Sultan Hamengku Buwono I. Pop. 342,267.

Johannesburg, city in NE Republic of South Africa; became a municipality in 1896; occupied by British forces 1900; in 1903 an elected council assumed local government. Johannesburg is the country's largest and leading industrial city, producing 20% of South Africa's annual output and containing the world's richest gold deposits; site of University of Witwatersrand (1922), Rand Afrikaans University (1966), Union Observatory (1903), art gallery, theaters, zoo. Industries: gold mining, chemicals, leather products, textiles, engineering. Founded 1886 as gold mining camp; chartered 1928. Pop. 1,441,000.

John XXIII, Roman Catholic pope (1958–63), b. Angelo Guiseppe Roncalli (1881). Before his election, he served as director of the Society for Propagation of the Faith, a diplomat in Bulgaria, and papal nuncio in France. He convened the Second Vatican Council to deal with renewal of the church and unity of all Christians in 1962. In his concern for the care of souls, he made many ecumenical advances.

John II Comnenus (1088–1143), Byzantine emperor (r. 1118–43). Known to his contemporaries as Calojohn ("John the Good," or "John the Handsome"), he was the greatest ruler of the Comnenian dynasty. John gained important military successes in the Balkans and in Asia Minor.

John (1167?–1216), king of England, youngest son of Henry II. In Richard I's absence, he had himself declared heir (1191) and succeeded Richard in 1199. His probable murder of his nephew Arthur (1203), territorial losses in France (1204–05), and aggressive acts against the church made him extremely unpopular. Excommunicated in 1212, he was forced to submit and enlist the pope's support against his enemies (1213). At Runnymede (1215) he was compelled to accede to his barons' demands in the Magna Carta. Thereupon John attacked his opponents. Civil war ensued, during which John died, possibly poisoned. *See also* Magna Carta.

John II, called the Good (1319–64), king of France (1350–64). He succeeded his father Philip VI. He appointed dishonest, unpopular advisers. He was forced to debase the coinage and impose harsh taxes in order to pursue the Hundred Years War. In 1356 he was captured by the British at the Battle of Poitiers. While he was in captivity in England his son (later Charles V) put down the Jacquerie rebellion. With the signing of the Treaty of Brétigny (1360), John was released in exchange for a huge ransom and other hostages. When one of the hostages escaped, John returned to England, where he died.

John III Sobieski (1624–96), king of Poland (1674–96), commander of the Polish army (1665). Plotted against Poland (1669–72). He allied himself with Charles of Lorraine and successfully relieved the Turks' siege of Vienna in 1683. By decisively defeating the Turkish armies, three times the size of his own, he saved Europe from Muslim conquest and was acclaimed the hero of Christendom. He was a patron of the arts and letters but the remaining years of his rule were marked by a decline in his prestige as a result of the country's political stagnation. His death marked the virtual end of Polish independence; thereafter, foreigners occupied the Polish throne for 70 years.

John I or **John the Great** (1357–1433), king of Portugal (1385–1433). He was the illegitimate son of Peter I and grand master of the powerful Knights of Aviz.

After the death of his half brother Ferdinand I, he resisted the plan for a regency for Ferdinand's daughter, Beatrice, and her husband, the king of Castile. After an ill-fated invasion from Castile, John was elected king in 1385 and ushered in one of the great periods of Portuguese history. He was succeeded by his son Duarte. Another son was Henry the Navigator.

John II (1455–95), king of Portugal (1481–95). He was the son and successor of Alfonso V. He was a great patron of navigators and explorers (although he turned down Christopher Columbus), and Portugal's great empire had its beginnings in his reign. He was succeeded by a cousin, Manuel I, who was also his brother-in-law.

John III (1502–57), king of Portugal (1521–57), son and successor of Manuel I. The Portuguese empire reached its height during his reign but had already begun to decline by its end. Brazil was colonized during his reign. He introduced the Inquisition into the country in 1536 and generally favored clerical, particularly Jesuit, interests. He was succeeded by his grandson, Sebastian.

John IV (1605–56), king of Portugal (1640–56). As duke of Braganza he freed Portugal from the Spanish rule of Philip IV. He became king in 1640, thereby founding the Braganza dynasty, and increased the power of Portugal during his reign. He was succeeded by his son, Alfonso VI; his daughter, Catherine of Braganza, married Charles I of England.

John V (1689–1750), king of Portugal (1706–50). The son of Peter II, he came to the throne during the War of the Spanish Succession and kept Portugal's part in that conflict small. He generally allied himself with England. Rich from gold from Brazil, he beautified Lisbon and kept a luxurious court. He favored clerical interests and reduced the power of the Cortes. He was succeeded by his son Joseph.

John VI (1769–1826), king of Portugal (1816–26). The son of Maria I and Peter III, he took over when his mother became insane in 1792 and was named regent in 1799. During the upheavals of the Napoleonic Wars, he was forced to flee (1807) to Brazil. He was named king at his mother's death in 1816 and returned to Portugal in 1821. Attempting to rule constitutionally, he put down a revolt led by his wife, Queen Carlotta, and his son, Dom Miguel. His son, Dom Pedro I, left behind in Brazil as regent, declared Brazil independent in 1822 and became its first emperor. At his death, John VI was briefly succeeded by Dom Pedro (as Peter IV) and then by his granddaughter, Maria II.

John, one of the Twelve Disciples of Jesus. The brother of the disciple James the Greater, together they were called Boanerges ("Sons of Thunder") by Jesus for their militant devotion. John is the author of the fourth Gospel, three epistles, and the Revelation. He witnessed the Transfiguration and accompanied Jesus to Gethsemane. Jesus left the care of his mother to John. He is reputed to have once visited Rome and miraculously escaped martyrdom and to have died at an old age at Ephesus.

John, Augustus (Edwin) (1878–1961), British portrait and landscape painter and etcher. His portraits depict mainly gypsies, beggars, and tramps. His works include "Lyric Phantasy" (1911) and "Galway" (1916). Also noted for portraits of famous people, including "George Bernard Shaw" (1914).

John, First, Second, and Third Epistles, part of the New Testament, the first letter was authored by the

Apostle John. The second and third are often attributed to him but there is evidence they were written by another John. These epistles tell of faith through Jesus Christ, warn against false teachers, and call for unity.

John, Gospel of, one of the New Testament's four gospels, it was written by the Apostle John and supplements the first three gospels that were devoted to Jesus' life in Galilee. It differs noticeably from the other gospels, because it uses no parables, stresses the kingly nature of Christ, and puts a unique emphasis on the Holy Spirit.

John Dory, also **Dory,** marine food fish found along E Atlantic coast of Europe. Its disk-shaped body is yellow to olive. Length: to 27.6in (70cm); weight: to 44lb (20kg). Family Zeidae; species include *Zeus faber.*

John Henry, hero of American folk ballad celebrating the black railroad worker who outdrove a steam drill with his hammer while working on the Big Bend tunnel of the Chesapeake and Ohio Railroad. The story originated during the actual drilling in the West Virginia hills in 1873. John Henry's legend traveled through America's work camps gathering details until he became as famous as Paul Bunyan and Pecos Bill.

John of Austria, called **Don John** (1547–78), Spanish military leader and statesman. He was the illegitimate son of Holy Roman Emperor Charles V and half brother of Philip II of Spain. He suppressed the Morisco rebels in Granada (1569). In 1571 as admiral of the Holy League formed by Pope Pius V, Spain, and Venice he defeated the Turks in the naval Battle of Lepanto. He took Tunis from the Turks in 1573. Appointed governor general of the Netherlands (1576), he had to contend with William the Silent's rebellion.

John of Austria, the younger, called **Don John** (1629–79), Spanish general and statesman. The illegitimate son of Philip IV, he suppressed Masaniello's revolt in Naples (1647) and the rebels in Catalonia (1651–52). He was viceroy of Sicily (1648–51). During the war between Spain and France, he was sent to the Netherlands as governor general (1656). After defeat by the French and English under Turenne in the Battle of the Dunes (1658), he was recalled to Spain. He failed (1661–64) to reconquer Portugal. With other nobles, he gained control of the government of the young king Charles II (1677) and exercised power until his death in 1679.

John of Brienne (*c.*1148–1237), king of Jerusalem (1210–25), emperor of Constantinople (1228–37). A minor French noble, he married Mary of Montferrat, queen of Jerusalem (1210). He became regent for their daughter Yolande in 1212. He captured Damietta in Egypt (1219) during the Fifth Crusade. In 1225 he married his daughter to Holy Roman Emperor Frederick II, who then claimed the title king of Jerusalem. In 1228 John was elected regent of Constantinople, then ruled as coemperor with Baldwin II after 1231. In 1236 he successfully defended Constantinople against Bulgaria and Nicaea.

John of Gaunt, Duke of Lancaster (1340–99), fourth son of Edward III and brother of Edward, the Black Prince. English nobleman and statesman, he was a dominant administrator and peace-maker between factions during Edward III's senility and the minority of his nephew Richard II. His first marriage made him duke of Lancaster (his oldest son, Henry Bolingbroke, became Henry IV); his second gave him claims to Castile, which he failed to make good; his third marriage legitimatized four children, henceforth known as the Beauforts.

John of Salisbury (*c.*1115–80), English churchman. He studied theology in France (1136) but returned to England (1150) to become secretary to the archbishop of Canterbury. The *Policraticus* (1159) and the *Metalogicus* (1159) reveal the urbanity and humanism of the author, who supported Thomas à Becket in his controversies with King Henry II. After Becket's murder, John became bishop of Chartres (1176).

John O'Groats, point in Scotland, at NE tip of mainland, on Pentland Firth. Dutchman John de Groot settled here in 16th century; it is supposedly the northernmost point of Scotland; however, that distinction actually belongs to Dunnet Head, several miles away. Expression from "Land's End to John O'Groats" is used to denote longest land distance in Britain, 876mi (1,410km).

John Paul I (1912–78), Roman Catholic pope (1978), b. Albino Luciani. He was made archbishop of Venice in 1969 and cardinal in 1973. On becoming the 263rd pope of the Roman Catholic Church after the death of Paul VI, he also became the first pope in history to assume a double name. A modest but gregarious man, he endeared himself to the world despite the brevity of his reign—34 days—the shortest in modern history.

John Paul II (1920–), Roman Catholic pope (1978–), b. Karol Wojtyla. Born in Wadowice, Poland, he studied literature, wrote poetry, and was a member of an acting group as a student. He was ordained a priest in 1946 and was sent to Rome for study. He became auxiliary bishop of Krakow, Poland, in 1958 and archbishop in 1964. In 1967, he was appointed cardinal. An influential and popular figure at the Vatican, he was elected pope in 1978, on the death of John Paul I, the first non-Italian pope in 455 years. A charismatic personality and tireless traveler, he survived an assassination attempt in Rome in 1981 and visited Britain in 1982, the first pope to do so.

Johns, Jasper (1930–), US painter, b. Augusta, Ga. His early work was in the abstract expressionist style, which he abandoned to begin painting canvases covered with images (flags, targets, and numbers). Examples of works of this period are "Three Flags" (1958) and "Target with Four Faces" (1955). After 1961 he began to attach real objects to the canvas. Common objects found in the street or studio appeared against painted fields ("False Start," 1959). He also executed numerous lithographs and drawings that show the influence of collage and imprint technique.

Johnson, Andrew (1808–75), 17th president of the United States (1865–69), b. Raleigh, N.C. In 1827 he married Eliza McCardle; they had five children. Johnson came from an extremely poor family who apprenticed him as a young boy to a tailor. He had no formal education; his wife taught him to write.

Johnson was an early supporter of Andrew Jackson and between 1828 and 1843 he served in a variety of local and state offices. In 1843 he entered the US House of Representatives; he served there until 1853, when he became governor of Tennessee. In 1857 he went to the US Senate. By that time, Johnson had won a wide reputation as a Jacksonian Democrat. He was a strong advocate of homestead laws, and his views on slavery, while basically southern, were mild. He was a Unionist and refused to leave the Senate when Tennessee seceded from the Union. He became a leader of the War Democrats, and in 1862 President Lincoln named him military governor of Tennessee. Johnson's status as a southerner and a War Democrat caused him to be chosen—on a National Union ticket —as Lincoln's running mate in the 1864 election. Johnson assumed the presidency when Lincoln was assassinated only a month after inauguration.

Johnson assumed office immediately after the end of the Civil War. He favored a moderate Reconstruction policy toward the South; the Radical Republicans, who controlled Congress, advocated a harsher policy. The result was unprecedented dissension between the executive and legislative branches of government. Congress passed the constitutionally questionable Tenure of Office Act, the president deliberately defied it, and the House of Representatives impeached him—Johnson was the first president to be impeached. The Senate, by a small margin, refused to remove him from office. Johnson's political effectiveness was at an end, however, and he did not run for reelection 1868. He went to the Senate again in 1875 but died shortly after taking office.

Career: alderman, Greeneville, Tenn., 1828–30; mayor, Greenville 1830–33; state representative 1835–37, 1839–41; Tennessee state senator, 1841–43; US House of Representatives, 1843–53; governor of Tennessee, 1853–57; US Senate, 1857–62; military governor of Tennessee, 1863–64; vice president, 1865; president, 1865–69; US Senate, 1875. *See also* Impeachment; Reconstruction; Tenure of Office Act.

Johnson, James Weldon (1871–1938), US author and black leader, b. Jacksonville, Fla. He wrote successful songs and light operas with his brother, John Rosamond Johnson (1873–1954), but is best known for his poetry—especially *God's Trombones* (1927), seven sermons in verse—and the novel *The Autobiography of an Ex-Coloured Man* (1912). He served as US consul in Venezuela and Nicaragua and helped found the NAACP.

Johnson, Lyndon Baines (1908–73), 36th president of the United States (1963–69), b. Stonewall, Tex., graduate South West Texas Teachers College, 1930. In 1934 he married Claudia Alta (Lady Bird) Taylor; they had two daughters. In 1935, Johnson became state director for the National Youth Administration, a New Deal agency. He was elected to the US House of Representatives in 1937 as a New Deal Democrat. He served there (except for a brief period in the Navy in World War II) until elected to the Senate in 1948.

Johnson rose quickly in the Senate hierarchy, and in 1954 he became majority leader. He proved to be one of the most effective leaders in Senate history. He suffered a heart attack in 1955 but recovered and was back to work within a year.

After losing the presidential nomination to John F. Kennedy in 1960, Johnson became Kennedy's running mate. Kennedy gave Johnson extensive duties as vice president; in particular, Johnson was placed in charge of the space program. After Kennedy was assassinated on Nov. 22, 1963, Johnson was sworn in as president within minutes.

Johnson immediately embarked upon the most ambitious legislative program since the New Deal. Within the next few years, Congress passed into law a medical program for the elderly (Medicare); a series of strong civil rights acts; various antipoverty and urban renewal projects; and federal aid to education, science, medicine, and the arts. Johnson was elected by a landslide in 1964 and continued his domestic programs, which he named the Great Society.

Johnson's successful domestic record was not matched in foreign affairs. He greatly expanded the Vietnam War after securing the approval of the Senate in the Gulf of Tonkin Resolution. The war became costlier, both in manpower and in money; it grew increasingly unpopular, and a strong antiwar faction arose. Senators Eugene McCarthy and Robert F. Kennedy entered primary contests to oppose Johnson for the 1968 nomination. In March 1968, however, Johnson announced that he would retire. At the same time he announced a partial halt to the bombing in Vietnam, with the view toward opening peace talks. *See also* Vietnam War.

Career: US House of Representatives, 1937–48; US Senate, 1949–61; vice president, 1961–63; president, 1963–69.

Johnson, Samuel (1709–84), English lexicographer, poet, and critic. He settled in London in 1737 and began writing pieces for *Gentleman's Magazine.* A prolific writer, Johnson's works include the satire *The Vanity of Human Wishes* (1749), *Rasselas* (1759), the 10-volume *Lives of the Poets* (1779–81), the periodical *The Rambler* (1750–52), the *Dictionary of the English Language* (1755), which established his reputation, and the essays comprising *The Idler* (1758–60). He was a founder (1764) of The Club, later known as The Literary Club, which included David Garrick, James Boswell, Edmund Burke, and Oliver Goldsmith. Boswell wrote a noted biography of Johnson.

Johnson, Walter Perry (1887–1946), US baseball player. One of the greatest pitchers of all time, he won 416 games, 110 of them shutouts, and struck out 3,508 batters in his career with the Washington Senators (1907–27). He was elected to the Baseball Hall of Fame in 1936.

John the Baptist, in the New Testament, Nazarite prophet and son of Zacharias and Elisabeth. He was born in Judah six months before the birth of Jesus. He spent 30 years in the desert preparing for his priestly duties and later preaching the word of God. He baptized Jesus at Betharba. He was executed by Herod Antipas, whose wife Herodias demanded John's head after his disapproval of her marriage.

Joint Chiefs of Staff (JCS), the principal military advisors to the president, the National Security Council, and the secretary of defense. Its responsibilities include planning the strategic direction of the armed forces. The JCS consists of a chairman and the chiefs of staff of the Army, Air Force, and Navy. The commandant of the Marine Corps participates equally when matters under discussion involve the Marine Corps.

Joint Committee, a Congressional committee composed of members from both the House of Representatives and the Senate. Upon referral of a bill, the committee decides favorably or unfavorably, recommends amendments, or allows proposed legislation to die in committee without action. Joint committees may be either permanent or temporary, and the composition is controlled by the political party in power.

Joist, a support used in ceilings and floors, usually small timbers or metal beams placed parallel to each other from wall to wall.

Joliet, Louis (1646–1700), French-Canadian explorer who, with Jacques Marquette, was the first white man to travel the Mississippi River from its confluence with the Wisconsin River to the mouth of the Arkansas River. His expedition was commissioned in 1672 by the governor of New France, who hoped to prove that the Mississippi emptied into the Pacific Ocean.

Joliet, city in NE Illinois, on Des Plaines River 30mi (48km) SW of Chicago; seat of Will co; named for Louis Joliet, French explorer who first visited area with Jacques Marquette in 1673; site of St Francis College (1874), Joliet Junior College (1902), Pilcher Park Arboretum, and Bird Haven (sanctuary for hundreds of

Andrew Johnson

Lyndon B. Johnson

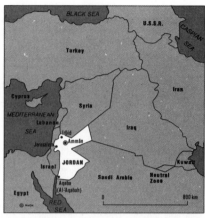

Jordan

bird species). Industries: chemicals, wire, earth-moving equipment, wallpaper. Settled 1831; inc. as city 1852. Pop. (1980) 77,956.

Joliot-Curie, Irène (1897–1956) **and Frédéric** (1900–58), French physicists. Irène, the daughter of Pierre and Marie Curie, met Frédéric Joliot when they were both working as assistants to the Curies. She worked on the physical, and he the chemical aspects of radioactivity. Their discovery of artificial radioisotopes was rewarded by a Nobel Prize in 1935. Active in the resistance during World War II, they became Communists. Although Frédéric was responsible for France's first nuclear reactor he was removed from his official position for political reasons.

Jonah, fifth of the 12 minor prophets and subject of the Book of Jonah in the Old Testament. After the fall of Jerusalem, he was sent to Nineveh as a prophet but, feeling it hostile, attempted an escape during which he was swallowed by a fish. Miraculously saved, he went to Nineveh and was instrumental in saving it from God's threatened judgment.

Jonathan, several biblical figures, including Saul's son and David's loyal friend who was killed in the battle of Mt Gilboa. Also, a priest descended from Gershom and Moses; the son of the priest Abiathar; and an uncle and a brother of David.

Jones, (Alfred) Ernest (1879–1958), British psychiatrist. He introduced psychoanalysis into Britain (1910) and founded the London Clinic for Psychoanalysis (1925). He helped to bring Sigmund Freud to safety in England after the Nazi invasion of Austria. His best known writing is *The Life and Work of Sigmund Freud* in three volumes (1953–57).

Jones, Inigo (1573–1652), English architect. He designed elaborate machinery and settings for court masques and in 1615 became the king's surveyor of the works. As a result of his architectural studies in Italy he imported the style of Palladio to England. He designed the Palladian Queen's House, Greenwich, and the Royal Banqueting Hall in Whitehall, London. The latter, with its solidity and perfect proportions, is generally considered his masterpiece. He continued designing through the Civil War period and influenced the Palladian revival of the 18th century.

Jones, John Paul (1747–92), American Revolutionary War naval officer, b. John Paul in Scotland. He joined the Continental navy in 1775, and proved successful at capturing supplies and enemy vessels. With his flagship *Bonhomme Richard* he engaged the British ship *Serapis* in an epic battle off the coast of England (1779). He boarded and captured the *Serapis* while his ship burned and then sank. He was awarded a Congressional gold medal (1787). Jones served in the Russian navy (1788–89).

Jones, Robert Tyre, Jr. ("Bobby") (1902–71), US golfer, b. Atlanta. Although never turning pro, he won four US Opens (1923, 1926, 1929, 1930), three British Opens (1926, 1927, 1930), and crowned his reputation in 1930 by winning golf's amateur "grand slam," which included the US and British opens and the US and British amateurs. He also helped to conceive and design (1934) the Augusta National Golf Course, home of the Masters Tournament.

Jones Act (1916), legislation reinforcing the US commitment to Philippine independence. The United States promised to withdraw from the island when a stable government was formed. The act also provided for a governor to be appointed by the US president, granted the governor veto power (with presidential approval) and appointive authority (with confirmation by the Philippine Senate). The Senate was to be elected by male suffrage. Free trade between the United States and the Philippines was also included.

Jönköping, city in Sweden, on S end of Lake Vättern; border treaty was signed here 1809 between Sweden and Denmark. Industries: airplanes, machinery, paper, matches. Chartered 1284. Pop. 108,500.

Jonson, Ben (1572–1637), English dramatist, lyric poet, and actor. A friend of Shakespeare, he was popular and influential in Elizabethan and Stuart drama. His comedies include *Everyman in His Humour* (1598), *Everyman Out of His Humour* (1599), *Volpone* (1607), *Epicoene* (1609), *The Alchemist* (1610), and *Bartholomew Fair* (1614). He also wrote the neoclassic tragedies *Sejanus* and *Catiline* and several court masques. His poems include the famous "Drink to me only with thine eyes."

Jordaens, Jacob (1593–1678), Flemish painter. He is known for his religious, mythological, and realistic works and for his portraits. He was considered to be Flanders' main painter after the death of Rubens. His works include "The Ferry at Antwerp" and "The King Drinks!"

Jordan (Al-Urdunn), independent nation in the Middle East. A constitutional monarchy, its economy was damaged by Middle East wars, but has recovered with financial aid from foreign countries.

Land and economy. An arid rocky desert with few natural resources, Jordan is bordered by Israel (W), Saudi Arabia (S), Syria (N), and Iraq (E). It is landlocked except for a 16-mi (26-km) strip along the Gulf of Aqaba that provides access to the Red Sea. A N-S geological depression forming the Jordan River, Lake Tiberias, and the Dead Sea is its outstanding topographical feature. The river now separates Jordan from the Israeli-occupied West Bank. The rainy season extends from November to March; the rest of the year is dry. The economy—heavily dependent upon foreign aid from the United States, Kuwait, and Saudi Arabia —has been hindered by low agricultural production, lack of tourists, and a large refugee population, after the loss of the West Bank in the 1967 war with Israel. Irrigation of the Jordan Valley added vegetables, wheat, olives, and barley to crops grown by small landowners. Phosphate is its chief export (30%), along with tobacco, distilling, flour milling, soap, and textiles.

People. Dating back to nomadic tribes in the Bronze Age, Jordan's population today is of Arab stock with small groups of Circassians, Chechens, Turkomans, Armenians, and Druzes. 50% are rural dwellers, 44% urban, and 6% nomads. Since 1948 about 750,000 Palestinian Arabs and 500,000 refugees have entered the country, and thousands more refugees live in UN-administered camps in the West Bank region. Sunni Islam is the principal religion (97%) with the remainder Christian. Literacy is about 55%.

Government. Jordan is a constitutional monarchy with power vested in the king, who signs all laws and holds veto power over both houses of the National Assembly.

History. A part of the Ottoman Empire from the 16th century to WWI, the present countries of Israel and Jordan were given to Great Britain as the mandate for Palestine and Transjordan. In 1922, Britain divided the mandate into the Emirate of Transjordan, with the Hashemite Prince Abdullah as ruler; it continued the Palestine mandate. In 1946 the Transjordan mandate came to an end, and the area became the independent Hashemite Kingdom of Transjordan. Jordan's W boundary was changed in a 1949 agreement. Jordan,

fighting with the Arab states in the 1967 Six-Day War with Israel, lost W lands as far as the Jordan River and old Jerusalem. Civil war erupted (1970–71) between the Jordanian army and Palestinian guerrillas, who were subsequently expelled from the country. Jordan was ostracized by most of the Arab world until 1974, when King Hussein recognized the Palestinian Liberation Organization (PLO) as the legitimate representatives of the West Bank Palestinians, thus indirectly supporting the creation of an independent Palestinian state. In 1984, he resumed ties, severed in 1979, with Egypt and, by 1985, had agreed to a Jordanian-Palestinian delegation to participate in peace negotiations with Israel.

PROFILE

Official name: Hashemite Kingdom of Jordan
Area: 37,738sq mi (97,741sq km)
Population: 2,800,000
   Density: 74per sq mi (29per sq km)
Chief cities: Amman (capital); Zarqa
Government: Constitutional monarchy
Religion: Islam
Language: Arabic
Monetary unit: Dinar
Gross national product: $1,000,000,000
Per capita income: $523
Industries: tobacco products, flour milling, distilling, building materials, olive oil, textiles, mother of pearl, plastic, cement, steel, leather goods
Agriculture: vegetables, wheat, barley, olives, fruits
Minerals: potash, phosphate
Trading partners: United Kingdom, Federal Republic of Germany, Syria, Kuwait, Lebanon, Japan, Yugoslovia

Jordan (Nahr Al-Urdunn, or **HaYarden),** river in the Middle East; rises in the Anti-Lebanon Mts at the confluence of the Hisban, Dan, and Banias rivers; flows S through Jordan, Israel, and the Sea of Galilee and empties into the Dead Sea. Frequently mentioned in the Bible, it is the traditional site of Christ's baptism. Length: 200mi (322km).

Joseph I (1678–1711), king of Hungary (1687–1711) and Germany (1690–1711) and Holy Roman emperor (1705–11). He was involved through most of his reign with the War of the Spanish Succession, allied with England and Holland against France, attempting to gain the throne of Spain for his brother, the future Emperor Charles VI.

Joseph II (1741–90), king of Germany (1764–90) and Holy Roman emperor (1765–90). He was dominated by his mother and co-ruler Maria Theresa until her death (1780), but then initiated radical social reforms in place of her policy of slow progress. His beliefs were formed by reading Voltaire and the French *encyclopédistes*, but his instrument was an all-powerful state for which he was the sole spokesman. His measures to allow religious toleration, end the nobility's stranglehold on local government, and to promote unity by compulsory use of the German language were not popular. The clergy and nobles opposed them, and even the peasants rebelled in many of his states. The schemes typical of Joseph's "enlightened despotism" were largely reversed by his brother Leopold II, who succeeded him.

Joseph, in Genesis, eldest son of Jacob and Rachel. After receiving a coat of many colors from Jacob, he was sold into slavery by his jealous brothers. In Egypt, he lived with Potiphar. During the great famine, his stores from the seven good years fed all of Egypt and his father and brothers. In the New Testament, Joseph is the name of several men including the husband of

Mary, mother of Jesus. He was of the house of David, and settled as a carpenter in Nazareth. To escape Herod, he fled with his family to safety in Egypt. He died before Jesus was crucified.

Joseph, Chief (1840?–1904), American Indian, b. Oregon. He was chief of the Nez Percé tribe of the Wallowa Valley, succeeding his father (1873). He is best known for his brilliant tactics during his attempt (1877) to lead 800 of his people through Idaho, Washington, and Montana to Canada while fighting off the US Army. He was finally forced to surrender to Colonel Miles, 40mi (64km) from the Canadian border after a five-day battle.

Josephine (1763–1814), consort of Napoleon I and empress of the French. She was born Marie Joséphine Tascher de la Pagerie, and her first marriage, to Vicomte Alexandre de Beauharnais, ended with his death (1794) in the Reign of Terror. She married Napoleon (1796) as the young officer rose to spectacular military fame. He forgave her indiscretions and infidelity, and she was coronated with Napoleon in 1804. Her inability to bear him a son caused him to seek and obtain annulment of their marriage (1809). He remained, however, generous and devoted to her.

Joseph of Arimathea, in the New Testament, a prosperous Israelite and member of the Sanhedrim who was converted to Christianity by Jesus. He begged for and received Jesus' body from Pilate for burial.

Josephus, Flavius (*c.*37–*c.*100), Jewish leader and historian, b. Joseph ben Matthias in Jerusalem. A member of the Pharisees, who sought cooperation with the Romans, he was sent to Rome in 64 to obtain the release of Jewish prisoners. Returning to Jerusalem, he was reluctantly drawn into the revolt against Rome (66–70). Appointed military governor of Galilee, he defended the city as best he could, then fled (67) to a cave with 40 diehards. All but Josephus and one other died rather than surrender. Josephus ingratiated himself to the Roman commander, Vespasian. When Vespasian became emperor in 69, Josephus took his family name, Flavius, as his own. In 70 Josephus went to Rome where he obtained citizenship and remained for the rest of his life. Between 75–79 he wrote his *History of the Jewish War,* the only detailed account of the revolt. In *The Antiquities of the Jews* he traced their history from the Creation up to the outbreak of the revolt. His *Against Aplon* is a defense of Judaism.

Joshua, biblical book named for Joshua, the son of Nun, who became leader of the Israelites after Moses' death. The book, divided into three sections, deals with the conquest of Canaan, its apportionment, and the farewell and death of Joshua, emphasizing that divine action was responsible for Israel's conquest of Canaan.

Joshua Tree, grotesque desert tree found in the United States from California to Utah. It has dagger-shaped, spine-tipped leaves and greenish-white flowers in long clusters. Height: to 40ft (12m). Family Agavaceae; species *Yucca brevifolia.*

Josiah, in the Bible, son and successor of Amon as king of Judah, he ascended to the throne at the age of eight after his father was murdered. During his reign a copy of the Deuteronomic Code was discovered and, guided by its precepts, he vowed to remove all forms of idolatry.

Joule, James Prescott (1818–89), English physicist. He established a reliable value for the mechanical equivalent of heat, laying the foundation for the law of conservation of energy. Joule's law (1840) states how to measure the rate of heat production in a part of an electric circuit. The joule, a unit of work, is named in his honor.

Joule, the unit of energy in the metric meter-kilogram-second (mks) system of units. One joule is the work done by a force of one newton acting through a distance of one meter. One joule is about ¾ of a foot-pound. *See also* Erg.

Joust, in the Middle Ages in Western Europe, one of the main attractions at a tournament of knights. In the 11th century, the joust was single combat on horseback with lance and sword, ending in the death or injury of one of the knights. The church continually condemned jousts, and by the 15th century they were reduced simply to the unhorsing of the heavily armed adversary.

Joyce, James (1882–1941), Irish novelist. He was educated by Jesuits but renounced Catholicism and left Ireland in 1904 to live and work in Europe. Joyce revolutionized the form and structure of the novel. In his novels action and thought are abandoned because they can be located in time, which ceases to be a positive factor, and consciousness itself is presented. The stream-of-consciousness technique is increasingly apparent in Joyce's work, which includes *Dubliners* (1914), *A Portrait of the Artist as a Young Man* (1916), *Ulysses* (1922), and *Finnegans Wake* (1939), all set in Dublin. *See also* Stream-of-Consciousness Novel.

J Particles. *See* Quark.

Juan Carlos I (1938–), king of Spain (1975–). The grandson of Alfonso XIII, he was designated as heir to the throne by Francisco Franco in 1969. He became king when Franco died in 1975. Empowered to command the armed forces, nominate the prime minister, convene and dissolve parliament, approve laws, and grant pardons, Juan Carlos proved himself a forceful king. He was active in negotiations for autonomy for Catalonia and the Basque region.

Juan de Fuca Strait, strait between S Vancouver Island, SW Canada, and the N shore of W Washington; N arm of strait is called Haros Strait. Discovered 1592 by Spaniard Juan de Fuca. Length: approx. 100mi (161km); width: 10–20mi (16–32km).

Juan Fernández Islands, volcanic island group in S Pacific Ocean, approx. 400mi (644km) off the coast of Chile. The three main islands comprising the group (Más a Tierra, Más Afuera, and Santa Clara) are under jurisdiction of Chile. Alexander Selkirk, the model for Daniel Defoe's *Robinson Crusoe,* spent five years on Más a Tierra in the early 1700s. Area: 70sq mi (181sq km).

Juárez, Benito (1806–72), president of Mexico (1858–72). With the triumph of the liberal Juan Alvarez, Juárez was appointed minister of justice and wrote the law limiting church and military prerogatives that bore his name. Elected chief justice of the supreme court (1857) he automatically became chief of state in 1858 in accordance with the constitution of 1857. From 1858 until 1867, Juárez presided over a government in flight: in Veracruz hiding from the rival Comonfort administration; in the north during the period of Maximilian's empire. From 1867 until his death, Juárez governed from Mexico City.

Juárez. *See* Ciudad Juárez.

Juba, river in E Africa; rises in the mountains of S Ethiopia at the confluence of the Dava and Ganale rivers; flows S and empties into the Indian Ocean near Kismayu, Somali; used for irrigation. Length: 1,000mi (1,610km).

Judaea, ancient name for S end of Palestine when it was under Persian, Greek, and Roman rule, before it became kingdom of Judah; bounded by Samaria (N), Jordon and Dead Sea (E), Sinai Peninsula (S), Mediterranean Sea (W).

Judah, in the Bible, fourth son of Jacob and Leah and forefather of one of the most important tribes of ancient Israel. Also, the southern kingdom when, after Solomon's death, only the tribes of Judah and Benjamin followed the house of David. There were wars between the kings of Judah and Israel for 60 years.

Judaism, often defined as the religion and civilization of Jews, involves all aspects of life. Difficult to define, it is primarily an historical religion, which concentrates on the works of God throughout the past, present and future. It is a monotheistic religion stressing man's relationship with God. The foundations are the Old Testament and the Talmud which show religion as part of everyday living. They cover civil laws as well as religious ones. The religion and the community are interwoven. Through faith, good living and conduct, salvation may be attained. Modern Judaism is split into three large groups—Orthodox, Conservative, and Reform Judaism. They mainly differ in the practice of ritual observances and the use of Hebrew in services. Some beliefs are formulated differently in each group. Judaism as a religion today continues to encompass an awareness of a common historical development, a rich literature, and the sense of national identity. *See also* Talmud; Torah.

Judas Iscariot, in the New Testament, the son of Simon and one of the 12 apostles, always enumerated last. He betrayed Jesus to the Romans with a kiss, usual greeting of the disciples, for 30 pieces of silver. His name connotes treachery and evil.

Judas Maccabeus (died 161 BC), Jewish warrior who led a revolt against Syria, starting in 167 BC. When edicts of King Antiochus IV threatened to end Jewish religious practices, a revolt broke out, and Judas took command. Using guerrilla tactics, he defeated Syrian armies and later recaptured the Temple in Jerusalem. The festival of Hanukkah celebrates his retaking of the Temple. Judas was killed in battle, but his brothers continued the fight and made Judea independent.

Judas Tree, or redbud, small tree native to S Europe and W Asia. It has round leaves and purplish-rose flowers in clusters. Height: to 40ft (12m). Family Leguminosae; species *Cercis siliquastrum.*

Jude, Epistle of, a book of the New Testament of the Bible, a letter in one chapter. The letter exhorts all Christians to keep the faith and live righteously. The author calls himself the brother of James, probably the one mentioned in Mark 6:3. The letter may have been written about AD 70–80, but some authorities argue for another author and a date in the 2nd century.

Judges, biblical book that originally contained the Book of Ruth. It is an account of events from Joshua to Samson and is considered a valuable early history of the Israelites in Palestine.

Judicature, Supreme Court of, system resulting from the reorganization of the Higher Courts of Great Britain by act of Parliament (1971). The Supreme Court of Judicature is made up of the Appeal Court, which hears civil and criminal appeals from High Court of Justice and the Crown Court; the High Court of Justice, having civil jurisdiction; and the Crown Court, which deals with higher levels of criminal work than are handled by magistrate courts and with important and difficult criminal and civil cases. The Appeal Court, in cases of major legal importance, can submit a case for final appeal to the judges of the House of Lords.

Judiciary Acts, a series of legislation that established the structure of the US judicial system. The first (1789) set up the Supreme Court, with a chief justice and 5 associates, 13 district courts, and 3 circuit courts and created the office of attorney general. The second act (1801), reducing the number of justices to 5, creating 16 circuit courts and adding marshals, clerks, and attorneys, was repealed in 1802. Later that year, a new act restored the number of Supreme Court justices to six and established six circuit courts.

Judith, book included in the Roman Catholic Bible but considered apocryphal by Protestants and Jews. It recounts the story of Judith, a Jewish widow, who delivered the city of Bethulia from the Assyrian siege. She advised the Assyrian general Holofernes to expect victory and then beheaded him as he slept.

Judo, a form of jujitsu and one of the most popular of the Japanese martial arts. It is a system of weaponless self-defense that was developed in 1882 by Jigoro Kano, a Japanese jujitsu expert. Kano modified many of the holds he considered too dangerous to be used in sport, and also developed the system of belts—a ranking method used to determine the proficiency of judo practitioners. A white belt indicates a novice and a black an expert. There is a wide range of colors in between as well as other colors beyond the black belt awarded to those who are considered "masters." Kano's methods, which placed more of an emphasis on physical fitness and mental discipline than on self-defense, depend greatly upon the skill of using an opponent's weight and strength against him. Such a technique makes it possible for a physically inferior individual to overcome a physically superior one. Judo matches begin with a ceremonial bow, after which each contestant grabs the other by the collar and sleeve of his jacket. The techniques used include holds, trips, strangles, and falls, with the end of the match signaled by one of the contestants slapping the mat two times to acknowledge defeat. A point system is also employed. International competition is held every two years.

Jugurtha (*c.* 156–104 BC), king of Numidia (108–106 BC). On the death of his father (118 BC) he had one of his brothers murdered. With Rome's approval, he divided Numidia with another brother. In 112 BC he attacked and seized Cirta, his brother's capital; a number of Romans were killed. In retaliation Rome invaded Numidia (111 BC), beginning the Jugurthine War. Jugurtha quickly made peace and was ordered to Rome to explain his actions. While in Rome, he had a potential rival murdered. War broke out again. Jugurtha defeated a Roman force in 110 BC with the aid of his father-in-law Bocchus of Mauretania, but in 106 BC Bocchus turned Jugurtha over to the Romans. He died in a Roman prison.

Jujitsu, a weaponless system of self-defense, used in hand-to-hand combat; involves such techniques as striking, kneeing, holding, throwing, choking, and joint locking. The methods used in jujitsu are varied and include as many as 50 different systems, including judo, karate, and aikido, that have been developed

James Joule

James Joyce

Benito Juárez

over a period of 2,000 years by Buddhist monks in Japan, China, and Tibet. The origins of jujitsu can be traced to 16th-century Japan, where Japanese warriors devised a secondary combat system to complement the tactics of their swordsmen. By the early 19th century—when the samurai were forbidden to carry weapons—jujitsu became a highly specialized form of self-defense. *See also* Judo.

Julian Alps, forested mountain range of NE Italy and NW Yugoslavia, between Carnic Alps and Dinaric Alps. Highest peak is Triglav, 9,396ft (2,866m).

Julian Day or **Julian Date (JD),** day specified according to a dating system introduced by Joseph Scaliger (1582) and named for his father Julius Caesar Scaliger. Julian days, which commence at noon (1200 hrs), are calculated from Jan. 1, 4713 BC, independent of months and years. Julian dating is used in astronomy principally in studying long-period phenomena, such as variable stars.

Julianus, Flavius Claudius, or Julian the Apostate (331–63), Roman emperor (360–63). Leader of an attempt to revive classical paganism, he opposed Christianity. His efforts on behalf of the pagan cults were futile, however, because Christianity had already become firmly established throughout the Roman Empire.

Julius I, Roman Catholic pope (337–52) and saint. He played a major role in increasing Roman and papal authority and in condemning Eastern Arianism. His attempt to unite the West in opposing Arian heresy failed. *See also* Arianism.

Julius II, Roman Catholic pope (1503–13), b. Guiliano della Rovere (1443). The nephew of Pope Sixtus IV, he tried to recover papal lands and, in 1506, established the Swiss Guard to protect the pope and Rome. He built up the treasury through the sale of benefices and began St Peter's basilica.

Julius Caesar (c.1598), 5-act tragedy by William Shakespeare, based on Plutarch's lives of Caesar, Antony, and Brutus. Presented countless times worldwide, it was filmed eight times, notably in the 1952 US production. Brutus, a noble Roman patriot, reluctantly conspires with Cassius to assassinate Caesar. In turn the conspirators are outwitted and defeated at the hands of the triumvirate Octavius, Antony, and Lepidus.

July, seventh month of the year. It was named after Julius Caesar and has 31 days. The birthstone is the ruby or onyx.

July Revolution (1830), insurrection in France against the reactionary government of King Charles X. The immediate cause was the July Ordinances that dissolved the newly elected chamber of deputies, reduced the electorate, and imposed rigid press censorship. Street fighting broke out in Paris. Charles was forced to flee. He abdicated and named his grandson Henri his heir, but he was rejected in favor of the duc d'Orléans who was proclaimed King Louis Philippe. It was a triumph of the upper middle class over both the reactionaries and the more revolutionary forces favoring a republic.

Jumping Hare, or springhaas or springhare, a nocturnal burrowing rodent native to dry areas of Africa. It has short front legs for digging and long hind legs and tail for jumping. Gray to brown in color, it eats plants and roots. Length: 14–16in (35–40cm.); weight: 9lb (4kg). Species *Pedetes capensis.*

Jumping Mouse, mouse-size nocturnal rodent of North America, N Europe, and Asia having long hind legs and a tail that is longer than its body. Plant-eaters, they travel by leaping or jumping, and they hibernate underground. Family Zapodidae.

Jumping Spider, worldwide spider that leaps on its prey trailing a strand of silk so it can climb back. Most are brightly colored and active during the day. Length: to 0.7in (18mm). Family Salticidae. *See also* Spider.

Junco, or snowbird, hardy North American finch frequently observed when the first snow falls. The typical eastern junco *(Junco hyemalis)* is slate-colored with a white belly and outer tail feathers. Females and other species are reddish-brown. They lay their eggs (4–5) in a ground nest. Length: 6in (15cm). Family Fringillidae.

June, sixth month of the year. It was named for the goddess Juno and has 30 days. The birthstone is the pearl or moonstone.

Juneau, seaport city and capital of Alaska, on Gastineau Channel, 90mi (144km) NE of Sitka, bordering British Columbia; transportation center connecting with Seattle, Wash., and Vancouver, B.C. Industries: mining, lumbering, salmon canning. Founded 1880, administration seat transferred from Sitka 1906; made state capital 1959; pop. (1980) 19,528.

June Beetle, large green beetle that is a serious farm and garden pest. Adults eat leaves and fruit of many plants. The stout, dirty-white larvae injure roots of grasses, garden vegetables, and ornamentals. Species *Cotinus nitida.*

June Bug. *See* May Beetle.

Jung, Carl Gustav (1875–1961), Swiss psychiatrist. After working with Sigmund Freud (1906–1914), Jung broke with him to found his own school, analytic psychology. For many years Jung investigated and wrote extensively about the human personality, especially its spiritual and unconscious aspects, including the archetypes of the collective unconscious. He identified introversion and extroversion as basic personality types and stressed the importance of personal transformations and self-discovery for the development of a healthy personality. Though his writings are sometimes regarded as obscure, Jung's insights and scholarship rank him among the foremost theorists in psychology. Among his noted works are *Wandlungen und Symbole der Libido* (1912, tr. as *Psychology of the Unconscious;* 1952 rev. ed., tr. as *Symbols of Transformation)* and *Modern Man in Search of a Soul* (1933).

Jungfrau, mountain peak in S central Switzerland, in Bernese Alps; site of Jungfraujoch pass and alpine research station. First climbed in 1811. Height: 13,642ft (4,161m).

Jungle Cat. *See* Chaus.

Jungle Fowl, often known as red jungle fowl *(Gallus gallus),* the ancestor of all domestic poultry, long domesticated by man and bred into many varieties. The jungle fowl is native to Southeast Asia where noisy flocks frequent deep woods and forest edges. Chicken-like, they have high arched tails, double-wattled throats and combs. *See also* Chicken.

Juniper, genus of evergreen shrubs and trees native to temperate regions of the Northern Hemisphere. They have needlelike or scalelike leaves and may be tall and upright or low and spreading. These shapes-

make them popular as ornamentals. The aromatic timber is used for making pencils, and the berrylike cones for flavoring gin. Family Taxodiaceae.

Junkers, in German history, the landed aristocracy of Prussia. They formed the officer class of the Prussian, later German, army and dominated the civil service. Otto von Bismarck was a Junker.

Juno, in Roman mythology, chief goddess, the sister and wife of Jupiter. She was the goddess of childbirth and therefore was worshipped mainly by women. She later became the female deity of the state. *See also* Uni.

Juno, asteroid discovered (1804) by Karl Ludwig Harding. Diameter 150mi (240km); mean distance from Sun 247,000,000mi (398,700,000km); mean sidereal period 4.36yr.

Jupiter, in Roman mythology, the supreme deity. He presided over the sky. He was depicted holding a sceptre, a symbol of his authority. Juno was his wife.

Jupiter, largest of the planets and fifth from the Sun. Jupiter has at least 16 satellites, the four largest having diameters greater than 1,900mi (3,060km). It has a gaseous surface with outer clouds of frozen ammonia crystals. The temperature under the clouds is estimated to between 0°F (-18°C) and 100°F (38°C). The planet is encircled by a ring of rocky debris that is 18mi (29km) thick and 5,000mi (8,000km) wide. Mean distance from the Sun, 483,000,000mi (778,000,000km); mass and volume, 318 and 1300 times that of Earth, respectively; equatorial diameter, 88,700mi (143,000km); polar diameter, 84,000mi (135,000km); rotation period, 9hr 50–56min; period of sidereal revolution, 11.86 years; composition, mainly hydrogen, which may be squeezed into a metallic state near the core where pressures and temperatures are high. *See also* Solar System.

Jura Mountains, mountain range in E France and NW Switzerland; extends from Rhine River at Basel, to Rhône River, SW of Geneva. Region contains pine forests, good pasture lands, rivers producing hydroelectric power. Highest peak is Crêt de la Niege in France, 5,652ft (1,724m).

Jurassic Period, the middle division of the Mesozoic Era. It lasted from 195,000,000 to 135,000,000 years ago. There were large saurischian dinosaurs such as *Atlantosaurus* and *Allosaurus* and ornithischian dinosaurs such as *Camptosaurus* and *Stegosaurus.* Plesiosaurs and pterosaurs appeared. The first known bird, *Archaeopteryx,* dates from this period. Cycads were dominant plants. Primitive mammals were present, among them the group ancestral to the later marsupials and placentals. *See also* Geologic time; Mesozoic Era.

Justice, Department of, federal cabinet level department within executive branch. It is responsible for the enforcement of federal laws, furnishing legal counsel in federal cases, and construing the laws under which other departments act. It conducts all suits in which the United States is concerned in the Supreme Court, supervises federal penal institutions, and upon request gives legal advice and opinions to the president and other heads of the executive department. It is directed by the attorney general, who also supervises and directs the activities of the US attorneys and marshals in the various judicial districts. The Justice Department was established in 1870, but the office of attorney general existed from 1789.

Justinian I (the Great) (*c.*482–565), Byzantine Emperor (*r.*527–565). Born the son of a Balkan peasant, Justinian became one of the most cultured men of his time, and one of the greatest rulers of the Byzantine Empire. Under Justinian, the generals Belisarius and Narses reconquered for Byzantium large parts of the old Roman Empire in North Africa, Italy, and Spain. Together with his forceful wife Theodora, he embarked upon vast building programs; the Church of St Sophia in Constantinople was erected during his reign. Justinian's most lasting achievement was his legislative work, in particular his revision of Roman law.

Justinian Code, monument of Byzantine law, and the greatest contribution of the Emperor Justinian to posterity, the Code was prepared in the 6th century by a commission headed by the legal scholar Tribonian. To the revision of Roman law, Justinian added other legislative works, now known collectively as the "Corpus of Civil Law."

Jute, natural fiber obtained from *Corchorus capsularis* and *Corchorus olitorius,* both native to India. Grown as a crop in India and Bangladesh, the plants mature in three months from seed and grow to 15ft (4.6m). The fiber is obtained from the bark by soaking and thrashing. Jute is used to make burlap, twine, and rope.

Jutes, one of the three Germanic-speaking tribes that invaded England in the 5th century after the decline of Roman rule. They settled around Kent and the Isle of Wight. Bede called them *Iutae,* and some believed they came from the western fiords of Jutland. But their social system was Frankish in character, differing from the other two tribes, the Saxons and Angles. Modern scholars believe the Jutes may have come from the Rhine delta region.

Jutland (Jylland), peninsula in N Europe, containing Denmark and N Schleswig-Holstein state of West Germany. It is bounded by Skagerrak (N), North Sea (W), Kattegat and Little Belt (E), and Eider River (S). Largest naval battle of WWI took place between British and German fleets off W coast of Jutland. Land along E coast is fertile, supporting dairying and livestock; W coast is sandy and marshy. There are many lakes on peninsula. Highest point is Denmark's Yding Skovhøj, 568ft (173m). Iron, marble, and limestone are mined. Politically, Jutland refers only to Danish part of peninsula; its area (including offshore islands) is 11,441sq mi (29,632sq km) and pop. is 2,109,370.

Juvenal(is), Decimus Junius (*c.*55–*c.*140), Roman poet. His harsh, bitter, and direct satires denounced the affectations and immorality of the empire.

K

Kaaba, or **Ka'ba,** central shrine of Islam, in the Great Mosque in Mecca. A cube of stone and marble, in one corner sits the Black Stone, by tradition given to Adam on his fall. The object of pilgrimage, each Muslim circles it seven times, touching the Black Stone for forgiveness.

Kabuki Theater, a stylish mixture of dance and music, mime and naturalism, a major form of entertainment in Japan since the late 16th century. In contrast to the No theater, which had its origins with the nobility, Kabuki was the theater of the common people. It has always emphasized visual delights and acting skills, but it also draws morals by presenting tragic conflicts. Character traits are accentuated by symbolic makeup colors and costume changes. Steeped in Kabuki tradition, one family often performs for many generations. The color and grace of Kabuki have been a strong influence on many Japanese and Western film makers.

Kabul, city and capital of Afghanistan and Kabul prov.; easternmost city on Kabul River; largest city in Afghanistan. Included in Muslim empire of Delhi 1526–1738; occupied by British 1842 (First Afghan War) and 1879; modernized by the emir Abd-er-Rahman Khan. Old streets and bazaars mingle with modern business center; site of university (1931), tomb of Timur Shah, Kabul Museum. Industries: food processing, textiles, leather goods. Pop. 377,715.

Kaesong, city in S North Korea, 35mi (56km) NW of Seoul, on the North-South Korean boundary; because of its strategic position during Korean War (1950–53), it was passed between communist and UN possession many times; scene of war's first peace conference in 1951; remained in North Korean territory by Panmunjom armistice in 1953; trade center. Pop. 140,000.

Kaffir Cat, or African wild cat, Caffre cat, Egyptian cat, small buff and dark-striped cat found throughout Africa and Syria. Worshipped by ancient Egyptians, it is thought to be an ancestor of the domestic cat. Length: body—24 in (61cm); tail—12in (30.5cm). Family Felidae; species *Felis lybica. See also* Abyssinian Cat; Cat.

Kafirs, or **Nuristanis,** people speaking a Dardic language and living in the Hindu Kush mountains of Nuristan in Afghanistan, and near Chitral in W Pakistan. Kafir women cultivate grain; men herd cattle and goats, and hunt. Despite fierce opposition, Islam has been introduced into their traditionally polytheistic society.

Kafka, Franz (1883–1924), Austrian novelist, b. Prague. Son of a successful Jewish businessman, Kafka suffered under his father's dominance. Little known in his lifetime, he became famous in 1945 with the English translation of his novels, such as *The Trial* (1925), *The Castle* (1926), *America* (1927), and *Metamorphosis* (1915). His work recorded modern man's fate of having been caught in an incomprehensible nightmare world. The heroes persisted in hope, but their endeavors were absurd. His collections of autobiographically oriented short stories foreshadowed his novels.

Kagoshima, prefecture and city, its capital, on S Kyushu, S Japan. City is a port lying on Kagoshima Bay; originally the seat of the Satsuma daimyo; St Francis Xavier landed here 1549; besieged by British 1863; suffered destruction from fire 1877 and volcano (Ontake) 1914; bombed by Allies June–August 1945. Industries: lumber, mining, Satsuma ware, shipbuilding. Pop. (city) 457,000.

Kagu, nearly extinct, almost flightless, heron-sized New Caledonian bird. It has a large head with back-pointing crest, large black-and-white barred wings, and orange-red legs. It feeds on insects and worms and emits sharp calls, chiefly at night. Aggressive males help build a twig-and-leaf nest for a single brown-splotched, rust-colored egg. Length: 22in (56cm). Species *Rhinochetus jubatus.*

K'ai-feng, historic city in E central China; served as capital of China during the Five Dynasty period (907–60) and under Northern Sung dynasty (960–1127) as Pienching; site of a Jewish settlement that flourished from 1163 until lost under Muslim influences (15th century). Industries: silk, flour. Pop. 330,000.

Kaiserslautern, city in W West Germany, on Lauter River; devastated during Thirty Years War (1635) and French Revolution (1793); seat of provincial government 1889; site of University of Trier and Kaiserslautern (1970) and remains of Charlemagne's 9th-century castle. Industries: ironworks, textiles, furniture, machinery, beer. Chartered 1276. Pop. 100,300.

Kala-azar, an insect-borne disease carrying a high mortality and caused by infection with the parasite *Leishmania donovani,* apparently transmitted by the sandfly. The liver and spleen are particularly affected and become enlarged. Additional symptoms include fever, anemia, fluid retention, and wasting. The disease occurs worldwide but primarily along the Mediterranean coast, in southern Russia and Asia, and in South and Central America and Mexico.

Kalahari, desert in Namibia, Botswana, and South Africa; between Orange and Zambezi rivers; inhabited by San and Khoikhoi, nomadic hunters and farmers. Area: 100,000sq mi (259,000sq km).

Kalamazoo, city in SW Michigan, 47mi (76km) S of Grand Rapids, on Kalamazoo River; seat of Kalamazoo co; site of Kalamazoo College (1833), Western Michigan University (1903), Nazareth College (1897), and Kalamazoo Valley Community College (1966). Industries: paper, drugs, musical instruments, gas heaters, machine tools. First settled 1829; inc. as city 1884. Pop. (1980) 79,722.

Kalanchoe, genus of succulent, perennial plants native to Old World tropics. It has oval, waxy leaves and scarlet flower clusters. Often grown as a houseplant, varieties include *K. pinnata* with feathery leaves and the cigarette plant *(K. verticilata)* with cylindrical leaves and clusters of plantlets growing at the leaf tips. Height: 7in (17.8cm). Family Crassulaceae.

Kale, cabbage-related plant grown as a cool weather crop. A short-stemmed, loose plant, it has large, bluish-green, curly-edged leaves that are eaten as a vegetable. It matures in 60–65 days. Height: 12–16in (30.5–40.6cm); width: 24–36in (61–91cm). Family Cruciferae; species *Brassica oleraceae acephala.*

Kali, a goddess in Hindu mythology. Often destructive, she also protects humanity from disease. She is usually depicted as black, with blood on her hands and parts of her face. As a destroyer she is adorned with a skull or skulls, which show her predilection for blood sacrifices, and frequently with snakes. When she acts charitably she is often called "Blessed Dark One." In India she has many shrines.

Kalinin, Mikhail Ivanovich (1875–1946), Soviet political figure, first president of the Soviet Union (1923–46). Popular with the peasants, he was elected to the Communist party Central Committee in 1919 and to the Politburo in 1925.

Kalinin, city in Russian SFSR, USSR, 100mi (161km) NW of Moscow on Volga River; capital of Kalinin oblast. A rival of Moscow, it was annexed to Moscow by Ivan III 1485; site of 14th-century monastery and castle. Industries: iron products, textiles, railroad cars, rubber. Founded 1180 as a fort. Pop. 408,000.

Kaliningrad (Königsberg), city and seaport in W European USSR, on the Pregolya River; capital of Kaliningrad oblast. A member of the Hanseatic League in 1340, it became residence of dukes of Prussia in 1525; made coronation city of kings of Prussia in 1701; occupied by Russia 1945 after a long siege; site of University of Königsberg (1544), 14th-century Gothic cathedral and 17th-century citadel; birthplace of Immanuel Kant (1724) who taught at the university. Industries: shipbuilding, food processing, automobile parts, textiles. Founded 1255 as Königsberg; name changed in 1946 when Potsdam Conference awarded it to USSR. Pop. 359,000.

Kalmar Union (1397–1523), union of Denmark, Norway, and Sweden. It began with the crowning of Eric of Pomerania, grand-nephew of Queen Margaret of Norway and Denmark, which was held in the city of Kalmar (1397). Queen Margaret had appointed Eric heir after her son Olav IV's death. The constitution she presented for the union is regarded as a draft since it was written on paper, not parchment, and the seals are damaged. The union established a common defense system but did little to disturb the countries' domestic systems. It lasted until the coronation of Gustav I (1523).

Kalmia, evergreen shrub native to North America with long leaves and bell-shaped flowers of pink, purple, or white. Height: 2–10ft (0.6–3m). Family Ericaceae; genus *Kalmia.*

Kamakura, city in Honshu, Japan, on Sagami Sea near mouth of Toyko Bay; site of bronze statue of Buddha, Museum of Modern Art, and Museum of National Treasures. An important ancient city of Japan, it was seat of Yoritomo shogunate 1192–1333, and Ashicaga shogunate 1333–1573; suffered earthquake 1923; now mainly a residential and resort area; fishing industry. Pop. 163,117.

Kamchatka Peninsula, peninsula in NE Russia SFSR, USSR; separates the Sea of Okhotsk (W) from Bering Sea and Pacific Ocean (E); terminates (S) at Cape Lopatka. A fishing, timbering, and fur trapping area with some farming and cattle raising in S, it was first visited by Russians 1696; they completed conquest in 1732. Area: 104,200sq mi (269,878sq km). Pop. 275,000.

Kamehameha, five kings of Hawaii. **Kamehameha I** (*c.* 1758–1819) united all of the Hawaiian Islands under the Kamehameha dynasty by 1810. He instituted harsh laws and punishment for transgression, but modernized his kingdom by doing away with human sacrifice and by offering the peasants protection from landlords. **Kamehameha II** or **Liholiho** (1797–1824) was responsible for admitting the first US missionaries. **Kamehameha III** or **Kauikeaouli** (1813–1854) was the brother of Kamehameha II. He came to the throne so young that Kaahumanu, Kamehameha I's favorite queen, acted as regent until 1832. Kamehameha III was a liberal ruler who adopted constitutions in 1840 and 1852 and secured his country's independent recognition. **Kamehameha IV** or **Alexander Liholiho** (1834–63) made social and economic reforms, and opposed annexation to the United States. His brother, **Kamehameha V** (1830–1872), the last in the dynasty, was less democratic.

Kamikaze ("Divine Wind"), suicide tactic employed by Japanese pilots in late World War II entailed crashing explosive-laden planes onto US ships. First employed in late 1944, this tactic inflicted serious losses on the US Navy at Okinawa.

Kabul, Afghanistan

Kaffir cat

Kagu

Kampala, capital and largest city of Uganda, in E Africa, 21mi (34km) NNE of Entebbe. A well-planned modern city, it has mosques, Hindu temples, Anglican and Roman Catholic cathedrals; site of Makerere University College (1963); a commercial center and livestock and agricultural market. Industries: textiles, food processing. Made capital 1962. Pop. 331,900.

Kampuchea. See Cambodia.

Kananga, formerly Luluabourg; city in S central Zaire, on the Lulua River; capital of Kasai-Occidental prov. In 1895 troops of Independent State of Congo revolted; they were not defeated until 1901; since 1960, when Zaire became independent, there have been many clashes between rival tribes. Industries: cotton, food processing. Founded 1884. Pop. 595,954.

Kanazawa, city on central Honshu, Japan, on the Sea of Japan; capital of Ishikawa prefecture; prominent as the seat of the Maeda daimyo (16th–19th centuries); site of Kenokuran Park, with a famous No theater. Industries: textiles, machinery. Pop. 395,000.

Kanchenjunga (Kinchinjunga or **Kangchenjunga),** mountain in E Himalayas, between Nepal and Sikkim; the central peak of the Himalayan range; third-highest mountain in the world; has 5 peaks, the tallest of which is 28,168ft (8,591m).

Kandahar, city and provincial capital in S Afghanistan, approx. 285mi (459km) SW of Kabul. Leading trade center; 2nd-largest city in Afghanistan. Wall encircles old section of city; sacked by Genghis Khan 1222; captured by Mongul empire 16th century and by Persians 1625; revolted for independence 1706–08; became first Afghan capital 1709; site of tomb of Ahmed Shah Durani. Industries: textiles, fruit, sheep. Pop. 115,000.

Kandinsky, Wassily (1866–1944), Russian painter, theorist, and writer on art. His discoveries and experimentation with abstract painting resulted in truly innovative and revolutionary contributions. His early academic style evolved into a semi-abstract method in 1908 ("The Street in Murrau"). His first completely abstract work was "Composition I" (1910). Among his noted works of this period are "Small Pleasures" and "Black Lines" (1913). After 1921 his works became more geometric in form ("Black Relation," 1924).

Kandy, city in Sri Lanka, on the Kandy Plateau; former capital of ancient kings of Ceylon (1592); occupied by Portuguese 16th century, Dutch 18th century; captured by the British 1815; site of Dalada Maligawa, noted Buddist temple, which contains what is traditionally believed to be one of Buddha's teeth, brought to Ceylon (Sri Lanka) in 4th century; a palace, art museum, oriental library, University of Sri Lanka (1942); market center for region producing tea, rice, rubber, cocao. Chief industry is tourism. Pop. 93,602.

Kanesian. See Hittite.

Kangaroo, any of about 47 species of herbivorous, leaping marsupial mammals of the family Macropodidae, native to Australia, Tasmania, New Guinea, and adjacent islands. Size ranges from 9in (23cm) to 8ft (2.4 m). All have long, powerful hind legs and long tails used for balancing. Short forelimbs function as arms, but the digits of the hand bear sharp claws and the thumb is not opposable. The head is small, the ears large and rounded, the coat soft and woolly. Young kangaroos, called joeys, are only partially developed at birth and attach themselves to the mother's teats within a pouch for months. See also Marsupial.

Kangaroo Rat, tiny, desert-dwelling rodent that carries seeds in its cheek pouches. They have long hind legs and tail and they are hoppers. They dry and store seeds and seldom drink water. Family Heteromyidae; genus *Dipodomys.*

K'ang-hsi (1654–1722), Chinese emperor (as Shêng-tsu, 1662–1722). He campaigned deep in Mongolia, added three provinces in the north (1662–1705), made a treaty with Russia on the northern border (1689), conquered Yunnan and Formosa (1681–83), and won control of Tibet (1705–21). While he ruled as a conqueror, keeping the peace with strategically placed garrisons, he adopted Chinese culture, encouraging the arts and sponsoring collections of Chinese literary classics and major works of reference, notably a 5,000-volume encyclopedia. He tolerated the Christians and for a time actively encouraged the Jesuit scholar-missionaries, but in 1717 he issued an anti-Christian decree.

Kano, city in N central Nigeria; capital of state of Kano; commercial center for agricultural region producing nuts, cotton, cattle. City dates from before the 10th century, when it was part of the Hausa empire; it was a Muslim posession 16th century; conquered by the Fulani in early 19th century; taken by British 1903. Industries: textiles. Pop. 300,000.

Kano School, school of Japanese painting originating in the 15th century. The style, based on Chinese ink painting, was usually simple and restrained, but occasionally elaborate, as in decorative screen painting. Masanobu (c. 1453–1540) founded the school. The official painter to the shogun, he received important commissions from many lords and government officials. His son Motonobu (c. 1476–1559) continued this tradition. Other artists of the Kano School included Eitoku, Sanraku, Tanyu, Naonobu, Sansetsu, and Tsunenobu, all of whom painted during the 17th and 18th centuries. During the 17th century part of the school moved to Edo and was henceforth called the Edo Kano. Kano artists remaining in Kyoto became known as the Kyoto Kano.

Kanpur, city in India; major industrial center and railroad junction; site of Indian Institute of Technology since 1960. Industries: leather, textiles, sugar. Pop. 1,275,242.

Kansas, state in the central United States. The geographical center of the 48 coterminous states is in Smith co near the N boundary.

Land and economy. The land rises gradually from E to W, marked by some level areas and hill ranges. The highest portions are a high plateau. Important rivers are the Kansas and the Arkansas. The only lakes are man-made. In much of the state the soil is especially suitable for wheat-growing, and in all sections pasturage is plentiful for raising beef and dairy cattle. Manufacturing is centered in the cities of the E and S. Oil is drilled and refined in the SE, and large natural gas deposits occur in the SE and SW.

People. Pioneers from the E and S states flocked to Kansas when settlement began in 1854. They were followed by German, Swedish, Czech, and Russian farmers. Only about 2% of the present population is foreign-born. About 65% live in urban areas.

Education. There are more than 50 institutions of higher education.

History. The Spanish explorer Coronado traversed the region in 1541 and French hunters and traders were present through the 18th century, but when the land passed from France to the United States in the Louisiana Purchase of 1803, it was still Indian country. The tribes were moved to other lands, and in 1854 the

Territory of Kansas was created and opened for settlement. Immigrants came from the then slave states of the South and the anti-slavery states of the East. Violence between the factions marked the struggle for Kansas' future. It was admitted to the Union as a free state in 1861, just before the Civil War began. After the war, Kansas was an assembly and supply area for thousands of immigrants bound for the Far West. The state's own population grew from 364,000 in 1870 to over 1,400,000 in 1890 as its agricultural potential was realized. Industrial development occurred during the 20th century, with aircraft manufacturing important since mid-century.

PROFILE

Admitted to Union: Jan. 29, 1861; rank, 34th
US Congressmen: Senate, 2; House of Representatives, 5
Population: 2,363,208 (1980); rank, 32nd
Capital: Topeka, 115,266 (1980)
Chief cities: Wichita, 279,272; Kansas City, 161,087; Topeka
State legislature: Senate, 40; House of Representatives, 125
Area: 82,264sq mi (213,064sq km); rank, 14th
Elevation: Highest, 4,135ft (1,261m), Wallace co, extreme NW. Lowest, 700ft (214m), Verdigris River, SE corner
Industries (major products): aircraft, other transportation equipment, processed foods, machinery, chemicals
Agriculture (major products): wheat, cattle, sorghum
Minerals (major): petroleum, natural gas, coal
State nickname: Sunflower State
State motto: Ad Astra per aspera ("To the Stars Through Difficulties")
State bird: western meadowlark
State flower: sunflower
State tree: cottonwood

Kansas City, city in NE Kansas, at confluence of Kansas and Missouri rivers, across Missouri-Kansas border from its sister city, Kansas City, Mo.; seat of Wyandotte co; 2nd-largest city in Kansas. Part of an Indian reservation 1818, it was acquired by Wyandotte Indians 1843, who called it Wyandotte City; sold to federal government 1855. Modern city was formed 1886 with inc. of many adjoining communities. It is site of Kansas City Kansas Community College (1923), Donnelley College (1949). Industries: livestock, packing houses, grain storage, soap, flour, automobiles, paper products, chemicals. Pop. (1980) 161,087.

Kansas City, city in W Missouri, on Missouri River, across Missouri-Kansas line from its sister city, Kansas City, Kan. The 2nd-largest city in Missouri, it was est. 1821 as trading post by François Chouteau; industrial development started c. 1865–80 with introduction of railroad and expansion into cattle trade center. It is the site of Avila College (1866), Rockhurst College (1910), University of Missouri at Kansas City (1929). Industries: food processing, aerospace equipment, chemicals, petroleum products, livestock, packing houses, hay, grain. Inc. 1846 as Town of Kansas, 1853 as City of Kansas, 1889 as Kansas City. Pop. (1980) 448,159.

Kansas-Nebraska Act (May 30, 1854), US Congressional measure, sponsored by Sen. Stephen A. Douglas, which allowed US territories to decide for themselves such domestic matters as whether to allow slavery. The act did away with the earlier policy of congressional mandate for the territories. The act was written to solve the growing slavery controversy, but actually caused the problem to become worse since neither pro- nor anti-slavery forces were satisfied with the measure.

Kant, Immanuel (1724–1804), German philosopher. From 1740–46 he studied at Königsberg, then supported himself as a private tutor. In 1755 he returned to the university and was made a professor in 1770. The order, regularity, and modesty of his life was undisturbed by the notoriety caused by the publication of his "critical philosophy;" particularly *The Critique of Pure Reason* (1781), *Critique of Practical Reason* (1788), and *Critic of Judgment* (1790). In addition to his technical treatises, Kant produced several topical essays in support of religious liberalism and enlightenment. *See also* Enlightenment.

Kaohsiung (Kachsiung), port city in S Taiwan; site of naval base. Industries: fertilizer, shipbuilding, paper products, wood, cement, aluminum, textiles, fisheries, petrochemicals. Pop. 1,000,000.

Kaoliang, several grain sorghums native to China and Manchuria. They have slender, dry, pithy stalks; open, erect panicles; and small, white or brown seeds. They are used for human food, alcoholic liquor, thatching, and fuel. *See also* Sorghum.

Kaolin. *See* China Clay.

Kaon, or **K meson,** elementary particle that is a positively charged or neutral meson with zero spin. *See also* Hadron.

Kapital, Das (3 vols., 1867, 1885, 1895), major work of economic analysis by Karl Marx in which he presents his theory of capitalism. Marx believed that capitalism was dependent upon the exploitation of labor. Volumes 2 and 3, edited by Friedrich Engels, were published after the death of Marx.

Kapok, tropical tree grown commercially in Java, Sri Lanka, the Philippines, and Africa. A horizontally branching tree, it has palmate leaves and white or pink flowers. Its pods burst to release silky fibers, the commercial kapok used for flotation devices. Height: to 120ft (37m). Family Bombacaceae; species *Ceiba pentandra. See also* Balsa; Baobab.

Karachi, largest city in Pakistan, on the Arabian Sea, NW of the Indus River delta, in SE Pakistan. Former capital of Pakistan (1947–59); early Hindu settlement; passed to British 1843, and developed into a major port. It now serves as chief trade center for inland agricultural products, as well as Pakistan military headquarters; site of major airport. Industries: shipping, automobile assembly, oil refining, steel, food processing, textiles, chemicals. Pop. 3,469,000.

Karaganda, city in Kazakh SSR, USSR, 135mi (217km) SSE of Tselinograd; capital of Karaganda oblast; central core of approx. 50 mining settlements that surround it. Industries: coal mining, iron and steel foundries, flour milling, cement mining equipment, footwear. Founded 1857 as a copper mining settlement; old city was est. early 1930s, new city developed after WWII. Pop. 580,000.

Karageorge (Karadjordje), or **George Petrovic,** (1762–1817), Serbian national hero. He led an insurrection against the Turks, enjoying victories at Ivankovac, Misar, and Belgrade, and freeing the whole province of Belgrade from Ottoman rule by 1806. He began to lay the foundations for administrative and government institutions, making an internationally recognized alliance with Russia in 1812, but Turkey reneged on her agreements, and Karageorge was forced to flee to Austria in 1813.

Karakoram Range, mountain range in India and Pakistan; includes Godwin Austen, 28,250ft (8,616m), which is the second highest peak in the world.

Karakul, breed of sheep from central Asia with curled, glossy fur on adults and wiry, coarse hair on young. Tightly curled, black or gray pelts derived from young lambs are called "Persian lamb." "Broadtail" pelts are obtained from still- or new-born lambs. This short, uncurled, glistening hair forms a pattern called moiré. *See also* Sheep.

Kara-Kum (Kara Kumy) Desert, desert area in S Central Asia USSR; extends from the Caspian Sea (W) to the Amudarja River (E) including most of Turkmen republic. The Kara Kum canal carries irrigation water 500mi (805km) from Kelif to Ashkhabad. Desert extends 600mi (966km) E to W, and 250mi (403km) N to S. Area: 115,000sq mi (297,850sq km).

Karate, martial art considered one of the most lethal methods of unarmed combat in the world. The technique, which involves a formal method of physical and mental training, includes a variety of blows using the hands, legs, elbows, and head. As a competitive sport, contestants are only allowed to use a few of the techniques so as to avoid serious injuries and all punches, blows, strikes, or kicks are minimized.

Karelian Autonomous Soviet Socialist Republic (ASSR) (Karelia), autonomous region in NW European USSR, bounded by Murmansk oblast (N), White Sea and Arkhangelsk oblast (E), Vologda and Leningrad oblasts, and Finland (W); capital is Petrozavodsk. First est. 1923 as an autonomous republic, it absorbed 14,000sq mi (36,260sq km) of Finnish land after 1939–40 war between USSR and Finland, and was raised to a constituent republic in 1940 (Karelo-Finnish SSR), but returned to present status in 1956. Agriculture is carried on in S; fishing and lumbering are chief industries; area contains valuable mineral deposits. Area: 66,540sq mi (172,339sq km). Pop. 742,000.

Karl-Marx-Stadt, formerly Chemnitz; city in S East Germany, 40mi (64km) SW of Dresden, on Chemnitz River; capital of Karl-Marx-Stadt district. Devastated during Thirty Years War (1618–1648), it recovered at end of 17th century with introduction of cotton industry; site of 15th-century church of St Jacob, 12th-century palace church, and early 12th-century palace that was formerly a Benedictine abbey founded by Emperor Lothair. Industries: carpets, hosiery, machinery, machine tools. Founded 1143 and awarded a linen-weaving monopoly. Pop. 305,113.

Karlsruhe, city in SW West Germany, on Rhine river, 37mi (60km) S of Mannheim; capital of duchy (1771) and of former state of Baden 1919; severely damaged in WWII; site of university (1865), technical college (1825), school of fine arts, and school of music; center for atomic research since 1956. Industries: textiles, jewelry, chemicals, brewing, pharmaceuticals, oil refining. Founded 1715 by margrave of Baden-Durlach. Pop. 278,200.

Karma, Vedic concept related to belief in reincarnation. According to Karmic law, the acts in past incarnations explain present circumstances, just as acts in this life can affect future lives. Salvation involves canceling the effects of past evil deeds by virtuous actions in this life. *See also* Hinduism; Reincarnation; Veda.

Karnak, village in central Egypt, on the Nile River, 1mi (1.6km) E of Luxor, with which it shares site of ancient city of Thebes. Many ruins of the pharaohs' architecture remain, including Great Temple of Amon from XVIII dynasty (1570–*c.*1342 BC); its half is a court and hypostyle (structure resting on pillars) hall, 388ft × 170ft (118m × 52m), containing 134 pillars in 16 rows; E half contains many halls and shrines.

Karst Topography, a limestone plateau characterized by irregular protuberant rocks, sinkholes, caves, disappearing streams, and underground drainage. Such topography is named after its most typical site in the Karst region of Yugoslavia.

Kasai (Cassai), river in SW Africa; rises in central Angola, flows E, then N and NW through W Zaire to the Congo River; forms part of Angola-Zaire boundary. Navigable for 475mi (765km) of its 1,338mi (2,154km) length.

Kashmir. *See* Jammu and Kashmir.

Kashmir or **Cashmere Goat,** small wool goat native to the Himalaya Mountains of India and Tibet. It has a thick white coat with long guard hairs and silky underwool used in textiles.

Kasparov, Garry (1963–), Soviet chess champion. Born Garry Weinstein, he adopted a Russianized version of his mother's name after his father's death. He won the world junior championship (1980) and the Soviet title (1981) and then qualified to challenge world champion Anatoly Karpov. After a first match was cancelled midway by chess authorities when Karpov's game collapsed, Kasparov captured the world title from Karpov in a rematch (1985) to become at 22 the youngest world chess champion.

Kassel, city in West Germany, on the Fulda River, 71mi (114km) WNW of Erfurt; transportation and manufacturing center; site of 14th-century church. Pop. 203,500.

Kassites or **Cassites,** an ancient people, possibly of Persian origin, who penetrated Mesopotamia in the 3rd millennium BC. By the middle of the 18th century BC they had conquered Babylonia. They introduced the horse and had a system of government dominated by a small feudal aristocracy. In the 1st millennium BC the Elamites forced the Kassites to withdraw to the Zagros Mountains in Iran, where they were known until about the beginning of the Christian era.

Katmandu, capital of Nepal, in central Nepal at N foot of Mahābhārat mountain range, S Himalaya Mts; Political, commercial, and educational hub of Nepal; site of university (1958). Founded in AD 723; made capital 1768. Pop. 150,000.

Katowice, city in S Poland, 45mi (72km) WNW of Krakow; occupied by Germans 1939–1945; important railroad, educational, and cultural center. Industries: coal mining, metal working, iron, zinc. Founded 16th century. Pop. 344,000.

Katydid, green to brown leaflike insect found worldwide. Its wings are arched over its back and it has long antennae. Most species produce a call sounding like "katy-did." Tropical species are the largest. Length: over 5in (127mm). Family Tettigoniidae. *See also* Orthoptera.

Kauai Island, one of the Hawaiian Islands; geologically the oldest, containing extinct volcanoes. It is extremely wet in parts; one of its mountains, Wailaleale, receives an annual rainfall of 450in (1,143cm). Industries: tourism, agriculture. Area: 549sq mi (1,422sq km).

Kaunas, city and port in W European USSR, in Lithuania on Neman River; became part of Russia 1795 during the third partition of Poland; taken by Germans WWI; became capital of Lithuania 1918–1940; again taken by Germans in WWII; site of Lithuanian Gothic church of Vytautas (15th century), university (1922), polytechnic institute (1950), and a medical institute (1951). Industries: iron, steel, chemicals, plastics, textiles. Founded late 10th century. Pop. 359,000.

Kaunda, Kenneth (1924–), president of Zambia from 1964. He became involved in nationalist politics in 1949, and by 1960 was the leader of the United National Independence party. He served as a legislator and became president upon Zambia's independence from Britain. He nationalized copper mines and in 1972 outlawed all but his own political party.

Kauri Pine, evergreen tree native to New Zealand. It has flaky bark, bronze-green leaves, and round cones. It is valued for its strong timber and kauri resin used in varnishes and adhesives. Height: to 100ft (30m). Family Pinaceae; species *Agathis australis.*

Kawaguchi, city in central Honshu, Japan, on Ajikawa and Kizagawa rivers; NW suburb of Tokyo; industrial area. Pop. 346,000.

Kawasaki, industrial city on central Honshu, Japan, on Tokyo Bay between Tokyo and Yokohama; suffered extensive damage from Allied bombings WWII; site of 12th-century temple. Industries: machines, automobiles, petrochemicals, ships. Pop. 1,015,000.

Kayak, canoe of Eskimo origin, traditionally built of sealskins stretched on a wooden framework. It is decked, apart from the cockpit, and propelled by a single double-bladed oar. Silent and maneuverable, it is still favored for hunting. *See also* Canoe.

Kayseri, city in central Turkey, at foot of Mt Erciyas; capital of Kayseri prov. City became part of Ottoman Empire 1515 after being captured by Crusaders 1097, the Mongols 1243, and Mamelukes of Egypt 1419; site of many historical remains. Industries: textiles, sugar, cement. Pop. 207,039.

Kazakh, Turkic-speaking people who inhabit the Kazakh Soviet Socialist Republic and the adjacent Sinkiang area of China. Traditionally nomadic pastoralists, herding horses and sheep, they have undergone stabilization in this century within the Soviet collective farm system.

Kazakh (Kazachskaja) Soviet Socialist Republic, constituent republic of S USSR, bordered by Siberia (N), China (E), Kirghiz, Uzbek, and Turkmen republics (S), and Caspian Sea (W); capital is Alma-Ata. Gradually taken by Russia 1730–1856, it became an autonomous republic 1920 and a constituent republic 1936. Central part of region is steppe with desert; mountains are in S and E, and lowlands in N and W; much of the USSR wheat and cattle are raised here; region contains large iron ore deposits and coal mines as well as copper, lead, zinc, nickel, chromium, silver. Industries: synthetic rubber, textiles, medicine, fertilizers. Area: 1,050,00sq mi (2,719,500sq km). Pop. 12,850,000.

Kazan, port and city in E European USSR, on the Volga River, 200mi (322km) E of Gorkij; capital of Tatar ASSR. An 18th-century outpost of Russian colonization, in 1773 city was burned by Emelian Pugachev, peasant leader; rebuilt by Catherine II; site of University of Kazan (1804) where Lenin and Tolstoy studied. Industries: electrical equipment, building

John Keats

Helen Keller

John Kennedy

materials, food products, chemicals, explosives, furs. Founded 1437. Pop. 980,000.

Kazantzakis, Nikos (1885–1957), Greek politician and writer who studied law at Athens and Paris universities and directed the Greek ministry of public welfare (1919–27). He is best known for his novel *Zorba the Greek* (1946), but he also wrote poetry and analyses of the works of Bergson and Nietzsche.

Kea, New Zealand parrot that is olive-colored with red and yellow wings and a brush-tipped tongue for feeding on nectar. During winter it frequents sheep-raising areas, feeding on carcasses. Species *Nestor notabilis.*

Keats, John (1795–1821), English romantic poet, b. London. He gave up medical studies to devote himself to writing poetry. Becoming a member of the Leigh Hunt circle, he wrote his first important poem, "On First Looking into Chapman's Homer," in 1816. Other poems include "Endymion" (1817), "The Eve of St Agnes" (1819), "Lamia" (1820), "The Fall of Hyperion" (1818–19), "To a Nightingale" (1819), and "Ode on a Grecian Urn" (1819). Keats had an unhappy love affair with Fanny Brawne and died of tuberculosis in Rome.

Keble, John (1792–1866), English clergyman and poet. At Oriel College, Oxford, Keble's sermon "National Apostasy" (1833) launched the Oxford, or Tractarian, Movement, which began as a High Church endeavor to revive the independence and power of the Anglican Establishment. The *Christian Year* (1827) and *Lyra Innocentium* (1846) were examples of his considerable poetical gifts. *See also* Oxford Movement.

Keeshond, Dutch dog of Arctic origin (nonsporting group); national dog of Holland during late 18th-century civil strife. It has a foxlike face, characteristic spectacles markings; small, triangular, erect ears; compact body; straight legs; and high-set, curved tail. A mixture of gray and black with gray or cream undercoat, the long, harsh coat stands out, except on legs and head, where it is short and smooth. Standard size: 18in (46cm) high at shoulder; 32–40lb (14–18kg). *See also* Nonsporting Dog.

Kekkonen, Urho (1900–), president of Finland (1956–81). A lawyer, writer, sportsman, and life-long public servant, he maintained good relations with the USSR. Called the "builder of neutrality," he concluded the Finnish-Soviet Treaty in 1948, extended in 1970, which guarantees that Finnish territory cannot be used to launch an attack on the USSR. Poor health forced him to resign in 1981.

Keller, Helen Adams (1880–1968), US author and social worker, b. near Tuscumbia, Ala. She overcame the loss of sight, hearing, and speech, yet achieved distinction as a lecturer and scholar. Illness rendered her blind and deaf at the age of nineteen months, and later she became dumb. Her teacher, Anne Sullivan, helped her to speak at the age of seven and remained with her 1887–1936. Keller obtained a degree cum laude from Radcliffe College in 1904 and mastered several languages. She lectured throughout the world and worked extensively for the relief of the handicapped. Her books include *The Story of My Life* (1902), *The World I Live In* (1908), and *The Open Door* (1957).

Kellogg, Frank Billings (1856–1937), US diplomat and political leader, b. Potsdam, N.Y. A lawyer, he was prosecutor of the Standard Oil trust case (1911). He was a Republican senator from Minnesota (1917–23) and was a delegate to the Pan American Conference

in Chile (1923). He was ambassador to Great Britain (1924–25). As Pres. Calvin Coolidge's secretary of state (1925–29), he is best known for his part in negotiating the Kellogg-Briand Peace Pact (1928). After receiving the Nobel Peace Prize (1929), he became a judge on the Court of International Justice.

Kellogg-Briand Pact (ratified 1929), originally between the United States and France and later ratified by the European powers, it renounced war as a solution to controversies. It marked the beginning of US acceptance of international cooperation. Contemporary discussion centered around interpretation, especially of self-defense, and the pact's practicality.

Kells, Book of (8th century), a finely illuminated copy of the Gospels in Latin, containing local records. It was discovered in what is now Meath County, Ireland, and is now at Trinity College, Dublin.

Kelp, any of various large brown seaweeds common on Atlantic and Pacific coasts. Kelps typically consist mainly of rootlike holdfasts, stemlike stipes, and leaflike blades. Giant kelp *(Macrocystis)* exceeds 150ft (46m) in length. Formerly a principal source of iodine and potassium compounds, kelp is now used chiefly as a fertilizer. *See also* Brown Algae.

Kelvin, William Thomson, 1st Baron (1824–1907), Irish physicist and mathematician who developed James Joule's convertibility ideas of heat and work. He devised the absolute, or Kelvin, scale of temperature and provided theoretical knowledge for the laying of the first transatlantic cable. Among his inventions are the galvanometer, electrometer, and tide predictor. His work laid the foundation for thermodynamics and for the theory of electric oscillation.

Kelvin, the temperature scale developed by Lord Kelvin with a zero point at absolute zero and a degree the same size as the degree Celsius. The freezing point of water occurs at 273 °K (or kelvins) and the boiling point at 373 kelvins. *See also* Temperature Scales.

Kemerovo, city in central Siberian USSR, on the Tom River, 125 mi (201km) E of Novosibirsk; capital of Kemerovo oblast; major coal mining center of Kuznetsk Basin. Industries: coke, chemicals, fertilizers, mining machinery, plastics. Founded 1720 as Shcheglova; name changed 1863. Pop. 464,000.

Kendo, martial art, the traditional Japanese form of stick fighting. The two contestants wear protective armor and fight with sticks, usually made of bamboo. The footwork is vital, with short, fast, gliding steps the preferred technique to overcome an opponent.

Kenitra, port city in NW Morocco, 10mi (16km) from the Atlantic Ocean, on the Sebou River; US forces landed November 1942. Exports: mineral ores, agricultural products. Industries: food processing, oil refining, fertilizer, spinning. Pop. 135,960.

Kennedy, Edward Moore (1932–), US Senator, b. Brookline, Mass. Youngest of three brothers who were US senators, he was elected to finish his brother John's term as senator from Massachusetts (1962). He was assistant Democratic whip (1969–71) and worked for liberal legislation, particularly in health and welfare. After his brothers John and Robert were assassinated, he was frequently mentioned as a presidential candidate. He campaigned unsuccessfully for the 1980 Democratic presidential nomination but in 1982 announced that he would not be a candidate in 1984 and concentrated on his Senate duties.

Kennedy, John Fitzgerald (1917–63), 35th president of the United States (1961–63), b. Brookline, Mass.; graduate, Harvard, 1940. In 1953 he married Jacqueline Bouvier; two children survive. He was the son of Joseph P. Kennedy and the brother of Edward M. Kennedy and Robert F. Kennedy. After distinguished service in the Navy in World War II, Kennedy was elected to the House of Representatives as a Democrat in 1946. He served there until he entered the Senate in 1953.

In 1956, Kennedy made an unsuccessful bid for the vice-presidential nomination and then immediately began preparations for the 1960 presidential nomination. He won seven primaries in 1960 and was nominated on the first ballot. He chose Lyndon B. Johnson as his running mate.

Kennedy, who defeated Richard M. Nixon by a small margin, was the first Roman Catholic president and, at 43, the second youngest president. Kennedy's domestic program, named the New Frontier, called for increased federal involvement in civil rights, education, medicine, urban renewal, and medical insurance.

It was foreign affairs, however, that occupied most of Kennedy's attention. The ill-fated Bay of Pigs invasion of Cuba took place shortly after his inauguration. In June 1961 he met in Vienna with Nikita Khrushchev of the Soviet Union; the meeting was not productive and Kennedy stepped up the US involvement in Vietnam partly as a result of the failure of that meeting. Kennedy established the Peace Corps and a new Latin American policy, known as the Alliance for Progress. His most spectacular success in foreign affairs occurred in October 1962, when, during the Cuban Missile Crisis, he forced the Soviet Union to remove its missiles from Cuba.

In November 1963, Kennedy embarked on a political trip through Texas. While riding through the streets of Dallas in a motorcade on November 22nd, he was shot and killed. The Warren Commission later decided that he had been assassinated by Lee Harvey Oswald.

Career: US House of Representatives, 1947–53; US Senate, 1953–61; president, 1961–63. *See also* Cuban Missile Crisis; Peace Corps; Vietnam War; Warren Commission.

Kennedy, Robert Francis (1925–68), US lawyer and political leader, b. Brookline, Mass. He served as counsel to the Senate Permanent Subcommittee on Investigations, presided over by Sen. Joseph McCarthy. After managing the successful 1960 presidential campaign of his brother John, he became US attorney general (1961–64), a post in which he vigorously enforced civil rights laws and investigated corruption in organized labor. After his brother's assassination, he left the cabinet and was elected (1964) senator from New York. While a candidate for the Democratic presidential nomination, he was assassinated after a speech in Los Angeles in June 1968.

Kennelly, Arthur Edwin (1861–1939), US electrical engineer, b. England. In 1902, after Guglielmo Marconi's experiments with radio waves, Kennelly noticed that the waves could reach beyond the Earth's horizon. He suggested that they did this by bouncing off a layer of ions high in the atmosphere. Physicist Oliver Heaviside made a similar proposition, and the layers are called Kennelly-Heaviside layers.

Kenner, city in SE Louisiana, on Mississippi River; site of New Orleans International Airport. Industries: lumbering, woodworking, sheet metal. Founded 1855; inc. 1952. Pop. (1980) 66,382.

Kenny, (Sister) Elizabeth (1886–1952), Australian nurse. She became famous for her then unorthodox method of stimulating and reeducating muscles affected by infantile paralysis (polio), a method at first disapproved of by most physicians, but by the 1940s largely accepted, with nurses and physiotherapists being trained in her methods.

Kenosha, city and port of entry in SE Wisconsin, 35mi (56km) S of Milwaukee, on Lake Michigan; seat of Kenosha co; site of Wisconsin's first public school (1849), Carthage College (1846), and University of Wisconsin extension center. Industries: automobiles, clothing, brass and copper products, truck farming, electronic equipment, tourism. Settled 1835; inc. 1850. Pop. (1980) 77,685.

Kent, county in extreme SE England, S of the Thames estuary and NW of the Straits of Dover; capital is Maidstone. Romans landed here 1st century BC; it was the first kingdom of Anglo-Saxon Heptarchy; converted to Roman Christianity by Augustine, Archbishop of Canterbury, 597; remained a subkingdom until 9th century. The Medway and Stour rivers drain Kent; apart from the North Downs, the county is low-lying, with Romney Marsh (renowned for sheep) in the SE; site of numerous castles, notably the 15th-century Dover castle, 11th–15th-century Canterbury Cathedral, 11th-century Rochester Cathedral, chapel (c. AD 350, reputedly the earliest place of Christian worship in England), 7th-century King's School. Crops: hops, fruits, vegetables, cereals. Industries: paper, pottery, iron, shipbuilding, brewing. Area: 1,443sq mi (3,737sq km).

Kent, Kingdom of, SE division of Anglo-Saxon Britain, settled by the Jutes under Hengist (c.450). Culturally distinct from its Saxon and Mercian neighbors, Kent remained a separate kingdom until the West Saxon conquest (825).

Kentucky, state in the E central United States. A border State between North and South, Kentucky remained neutral in the Civil War.
   Land and Economy. The land is generally rolling except in the SE, where the Pine and Cumberland mts dominate a rugged plateau. The Ohio River forms the N boundary and the Mississippi the W. The Kentucky and Tennessee rivers are the largest in the state. About 40% of the land is forested. The rich agricultural region is mostly in the center. Grasslands provide pasturage for cattle and for horses, for which Kentucky is famous. Manufacturing, expanding since WWII, is in the larger towns. Mining and oil drilling are concentrated in the SE.
   People. Kentucky was first settled by English, Scots, Irish, and German immigrants from Virginia, North and South Carolina, and Pennsylvania; as large plantations developed, slaves were brought in. All these elements are present in the population, which has retained a rural character to a large degree. Slightly more than 50% reside in urban areas.
   Education. There are about 40 institutions of higher education.
   History. The region was the first W of the Allegheny Mts to be colonized. In the 1770s, the frontiersman Daniel Boone blazed the Wilderness Road from Virginia and North Carolina through Cumberland Gap in the SE corner of Kentucky. Thousands of settlers followed this route, while others came down the Ohio River. After a period of war with the Indians and dispute over land rights, Kentucky was admitted to the Union in 1792. At the outbreak of the Civil War, the state's loyalties were divided. Kentuckians fought in both Union and Confederate armies, and the state was invaded by both. After the war, Kentucky prospered; industry gradually became important in its economy. Because of the increase in the price of imported oil to the United States beginning in the 1970s, coal mining in Kentucky experienced an upsurge.

PROFILE

Admitted to Union: June 1, 1792; rank, 15th
US Congressmen: Senate, 2; House of Representatives, 7
Population: 3,661,433 (1980); rank, 23d
Capital: Frankfort, 25,973 (1980)
Chief cities: Louisville, 298,451; Lexington, 204,165; Covington, 49,013
State legislature: Senate, 38; House of Representatives, 100
Area: 40,395sq mi (104,623sq km); rank, 37th
Elevation: Highest, 4,150ft (1,266m), Big Black Mt, Harlan Co. Lowest, 540ft (165m), Ohio River
Industries (major products): processed foods; tobacco products, machinery, chemicals
Agriculture (major products): tobacco, corn, soybeans, dairy cattle, hogs, fruit
Minerals (major): coal, petroleum, natural gas, fluorspar, stone, sand, gravel
State nickname: Blue Grass State
State motto: "United We Stand, Divided We Fall"
State bird: Kentucky cardinal
State flower: goldenrod
State tree: tulip tree

Kentucky and Virginia Resolutions (1798 and 1799), first important declarations of states' rights. Written by Thomas Jefferson (Kentucky Resolutions) and James Madison (Virginia Resolutions), they expressed opposition to the Alien and Sedition Acts. These resolutions stated that the federal government had no right to exercise powers not granted it by the Constitution and that states had the right to judge the constitutionality of any federal acts.

Kentucky River, river in Kentucky; formed in N central Kentucky by joining of North and Middle forks, flows NW to Ohio River at Carrollton; navigable by use of locks. During pioneering days was main means of entry into region. Boonesboro on the river is built on site of fort built by Daniel Boone (1775). Frankfort, state capital, is also on river. Length: 259mi (417km).

Kenya, independent nation in E Africa. The largest tea producer in Africa, it includes the city of Nairobi, the E African commercial center.
   Land and economy. Located on the E coast of Africa, Kenya is bordered by Ethiopia and Sudan (N), Tanzania (S), Uganda and Lake Victoria (W), and Somalia and the Indian Ocean (E). The N 60% of the country is arid. The Great Rift Valley, 30–40mi (48–64km) wide, includes Mt Kenya, 17,040ft (5,197m), and the high plateaus, 3,000–10,000ft (915–3,050m) above sea level, containing some of Africa's most fertile land. About 85% of the population lives in the S 40% of Kenya. A program of resettlement has been moving subsistence African farmers from tribal reserves onto lands purchased from Europeans. The largest producer of tea in Africa, 90% of its exports is agricultural. Nairobi is the commercial center for East Africa. Tourism (safaris) is important to the economy.
   People. Kenya's ethnic origins are divided between Kikuyu (20%), Luo (14%), Baluhya (13%), Kamba (11%), Kisli (6%), and Meru (5%). Among non-Africans 31% are Asians, Europeans, and Arabs. Religious estimates include Protestants (37%), Roman Catholics (22%), Muslims (3%). Africans are mainly subsistence farmers, Asians are in commerce, and the Europeans are large farmers, businessmen, and professionals. Overall literacy is estimated at 25%.
   Government. The president, who leads the country, is popularly elected, although Kenya has been a de facto one-party state since 1969 and officially since 1982. Members of the National Assembly are also popularly elected.
   History. Movements from the coast inland brought groups of African, Cushite, Bantu, and Nilotic-speaking people into what is now Kenya. Britain and Germany divided its trade and territory until 1920, when it became a protectorate of the United Kingdom. The first African participation in government came in 1957 with a restricted direct vote. From 1952–59 terrorist Mau Mau rebellions against Britain wracked the country. Independence within the Commonwealth of Nations came on Dec. 12, 1963, when the Kenya African National Union party formed a government headed by Jomo Kenyatta. Protests against Kenyatta's increasingly autocratic rule were repressed in the mid-1970s. Following his death in 1978, he was succeeded by Daniel arap Moi. Relations between neighboring Uganda and Tanzania have been strained, and a period of dramatic economic growth following independence had ended by the late 1970s, when Kenya was plagued by inflation and trade deficits and began importing food.

PROFILE

Official name: Republic of Kenya
Area: 224,960sq mi (582,646sq km)
Population: 15,820,000
   Density: 70per sq mi (27per sq km)
Chief cities: Nairobi (capital); Mombasa, 401,000
Government: Elected National Assembly elects chief of state
Religion: Animist, Christian
Language: English (official), Swahili (national)
Monetary unit: Kenya shilling
Gross national product: $2,500,000,000
Per capita income: $337
Industries: bark extracts, hides, dairy products, construction materials, petroleum products
Agriculture: coffee, tea, cereals, cotton, sisal, cattle, forests, corn, fruits

Kenyatta, Jomo (1893?–1978), president of Kenya (1964–78). He entered politics in defense of his own Kikuyu tribe and of black African rights. He was imprisoned (1953) for Mau Mau terrorism and exiled but was then elected president of the Kenya African National Union (1960). He helped gain Kenya's independence from Britain in 1963, and became president in 1964. He suppressed opposition and outlawed opposition political parties (1969).

Kepler, Johannes (1571–1630), German astronomer. He became Tycho Brahe's assistant (1600) and, after

Tycho's death, used his master's extremely accurate observational data to deduce three laws of planetary motion, especially the statement that planets move in elliptical orbits around the sun. Kepler's work was a vindication of Copernicus and a foundation for Isaac Newton's work.

Keratin, a fibrous protein present in large amounts in the superficial cells of the skin where it serves as a protective layer; also in hair, wool, and horns.

Kerensky, Aleksandr F(eodorovich) (1881–1970), Russian political figure, head of the provisional government (July–November 1917). Elected to the Duma (legislature) as a moderate socialist in 1912, he became prime minister in July 1917, shortly after the overthrow of the tsar (March 1917). He suppressed Kornilov's uprising but had to flee after the Bolshevik Revolution (November 1917). He wrote several accounts of this period.

Kerosene, a distilled petroleum product heavier than gasoline and lighter than diesel fuel. Kerosene, known historically as an illuminant, is now used in camping stoves, tractor fuels, and turbine fuels for jet and turbo-prop aircraft.

Kerry Blue Terrier, all-round working dog (terrier group) bred in Co. Kerry, Ireland, as Irish blue terrier. A long-lived breed, the Kerry blue has a long head with face whiskers; V-shaped, folded ears; a short, straight back; powerful, long legs; and a long tail. The soft, dense coat is wavy and trimmed for show; color is any shade of blue-gray or gray-blue. Standard size: 17–19.5in (43–50cm) high at shoulder; 30–40lb (13.5–18kg). *See also* Terrier.

Kestrel, or windhover, small falcon of Europe, Asia, North America, and Africa that hovers over its prey—usually rodents, insects, or small birds—before attacking. Length: 12in (30cm). Species *Falco tinnunculus*.

Ketone, group of organic substances containing a carbonyl group (C:O) and having the general formula R′.C:O.R″, where R′ and R″ are univalent hydrocarbon radicals. The simplest member of the group is acetone, dimethyl ketone (CH_3COCH_3).

Ketone Bodies, the three chemical compounds acetoacetic acid, hydroxybutyric acid, and acetone. When present in the blood in high concentrations, they lead to lowered pH. Occurs in starvation, diabetes mellitus, and low-carbohydrate, high-fat diet.

Kettering, city in SW Ohio, S of Dayton; site of Kettering College of Medical Arts (1967). Industries: electric motors, precision tools, building materials. Founded 1796. Inc. as Van Buren township 1841; inc. as village and renamed 1952; inc. as city 1955. Pop. (1980) 61,186.

Kettledrums. *See* Timpani.

Key, Francis Scott (1779–1843), US poet, b. Carrol co, Md. He wrote the US national anthem, "The Star Spangled Banner," while watching the shelling of Ft McHenry (1814) as a prisoner on a British ship in Chesapeake Bay. The anthem first appeared anonymously as a poem, "In Defense of Fort M'Henry." It was adopted as the national anthem by Congress in 1931.

Keynes, John Maynard (1883–1946), English economist. He first came to prominence with *Economic Consequences of the Peace* (1919), which criticized the inequitable, unworkable economic provisions of the Versailles Treaty. *Treatise on Money* (1930) presented the theory of return on capital and the theory of the demand for money and analyzed the relationship between saving and investment. *The General Theory of Employment, Interest, and Money* (1936) was profoundly influenced by the Great Depression. In it, Keynes established the foundation of modern macroeconomics. He advocated governmental economic planning and the active intervention of government in the economy to stimulate employment and prosperity.

Key West, southernmost city of the continental United States, in SW corner of Florida, on Key West Island, seat of Monroe co. Less than 4mi (6km) long and 2mi (3km) wide; site of US Navy station. Industries: commercial fishing, cigar making, tourism. Est. 1822; inc. 1828. Pop. (1980) 24,292.

KGB, committee of state security of the USSR; regulates both the secret and regular police force and the detention (labor) camps in the Soviet Union. Although the KGB and its antecedents (NKVD, NKGB) had a history of almost autonomous control through systematic terrorism over the state security apparatus, the KGB has, since the late 1950s, been subordinate to

Kentucky Derby

Kenya

Francis Scott Key

Communist party control and concerns itself mainly with internal intelligence.

Khabarovsk (Chabarovsk), city in southeastern USSR, on Amur River; capital of Khabarovsk Kraj, served as capital of Soviet Far East 1926–38. Industries: oil refining, shipbuilding, trucks, aircraft, machine tools. Founded 1858 as a tsarist fortress. Pop. 536,000.

Khalid ibn Abd al-Aziz al-Saud (1912–82), king of Saudi Arabia (1975–82). In 1962 he was appointed first deputy prime minister and was crown prince (1965–75). On March 25, 1975, a few hours after his half brother King Faisal's assassination, he was chosen king of Saudi Arabia. Although king, he retained his duties as prime minister. Extremely popular with the people, he continued most of Faisal's policies.

Khalkas, people who constitute 75% of the population of the Mongolian Peoples Republic. Traditionally nomadic pastoralists, they have to some extent been settled by the Soviet attempts to develop collective farms.

Khania (Canea), port town in NW Crete, Greece, on Gulf of Khania; taken by Ottoman Empire 1646; served as capital of Crete from 1841 to mid-20th century; heavily damaged during German invasion 1941. Exports: wines, citrus fruits, olives. Pop. 40,564.

Kharkov (Char 'Kov), city in Ukrainian republic, USSR, 400mi (644km) SW of Moscow, at the confluence of the Kharkov, Lopan, and Udy rivers; capital of Kharkov oblast. In 17th century city served as stronghold of Ukrainian Cossacks in defending Russia's S border; served as capital of Ukraine 1921–34; site of Cathedral of Protectoress (1686), Cathedral of the Assumption (1771), and a university (1805). Industries: food and tobacco processing, chemicals, printing. Founded 1656. Pop. 1,428,000.

Khartoum (Al-Khurtum), capital of Sudan, at junction of the Blue Nile and White Nile rivers; capital of Khartoum prov.; commercial and transportation center. City was founded 1820s by Mohammed Ali; besieged by Mahdists in 1885; occupied and rebuilt by British Gen. Horatio Kitchener 1898; named seat of government in 1956 when Sudan became independent; site of governor-general's palace, several churches and cathedrals, Kitchener School of Medicine (1924), University of Khartoum (1956), Gordon Memorial College (1903). Industries: cement, gum arabic, chemicals, cotton textiles. Pop. 400,000.

Khazars, Turkic people who first appeared in the lower Volga River region around the 2nd century AD. They allied themselves with the Byzantine Empire in fighting the Persians (610–41). Between the 8th and 10th centuries their empire extended from north of the Black Sea to the Urals and from west of the Caspian Sea to the Dnieper River. From 737 their capital was Itil. They conquered the Volga Bulgars, taxed the eastern Slavs, and fought against the Arabs, Persians, and Armenians. In the 8th century, their ruling class was converted to Judaism by exiles from Constantinople. In 965 their empire was destroyed by the army of Sviatoslav, duke of Kiev. Some scholars believe that they are the progenitors of many Eastern European Jews.

Kherson (Cherson), seaport city in Ukrainian SSR, USSR, on Dnieper River near its mouth on Black Sea; capital of Kherson oblast. Founded 1778 by Grigori Potemkin as a naval station, shipbuilding center, and fortress (still standing), it is site of 18th-century cathedral containing Potemkin's tomb. Industries: cotton textiles, shipbuilding, food processing. Pop. 331,000.

Khmer Rouge, name given to the Communist National United Front of Cambodia, which seized control of the government in 1975. After the overthrow in 1970 of the neutralist Sihanouk government, in which the Communist's had participated, the Khmer Rouge turned to armed conflict in its ultimately successful bid for power. In April 1976 Khieu Samphan was named chief of state and Tol Saut premier. By 1979, however, internal opposition to this brutal regime had mounted, and rebel forces aided by invading troops from the Communist government of Vietnam seized control. Since then the Khmer Rouge has been engaged in guerrilla warfare against the Vietnamese-backed government.

Khmers, or Cambodians, people of mixed Mongoloid/ Australoid racial background who constitute 90% of the population of Cambodia; they also live in Thailand and the Mekong delta region of Vietnam. Traditionally agriculturalists cultivating rice and practicing weaving and metalwork, the Khmers are mainly Theravada Buddhists.

Khoisan, a group of Afro-African languages of South Africa. Hottentots (Khoi, in their tongue) and Bushmen (San) are the two largest groups of native speakers. Sandawe and Hatsa of Tanzania are also Khoisan. All are characteristically click-languages.

Khomeini, Ayatollah Ruholla Mussavi(1900?–   ), Iranian religious leader. An Islamic scholar with great influence over his Shi'ite students, he published an outspoken attack on Riza Shah Pahlevi in 1941 and remained an active opponent of his son, Mohammed Riza Shah Pahlevi. Exiled in 1964, he sent tape-recorded lectures back to his students in Iran. With the fall of the Shah in 1979, he returned to Iran in triumph. He assumed power over military and public affairs, imposing rigid Islamic standards of manners and morals. Approving the seizure of the American Embassy and hostages by Iranian students in 1979, His rule was characterized by strict religious orthodoxy, ruthless elimination of political opposition, economic turmoil, and war with Iraq.

Khorana, Gobind (c. 1922–   ), US biochemist, b. India. He shared the 1968 Nobel Prize in physiology or medicine for his part in discoveries about how genes determine cell function. Khorana established how the genetic code should be read—in nonoverlapping triplets in sequence with no gaps. In 1976, a technique developed by Khorana led to the construction of a bacterial gene.

Khrushchev, Nikita Sergeevich (1894–1971), Soviet political figure, first secretary of the Communist party (1953–64) and head of the Soviet government (1958–64). He joined the party in 1918 and was elected to the central committee in 1934. Noted for economic success and ruthless suppression of opposition in the Ukraine, where he was secretary of the Communist party, he was elected to the Politburo in 1939. He denounced Stalin (died 1953) in a spectacular speech to the Twentieth Party Congress, expelled his staunchest backers from the central committee, and became premier in 1958. Favoring détente with the West, he yielded to US President Kennedy in the Cuban missile crisis (1962). This development, economic setbacks, and trouble with China led to his ouster by Brezhnev and Kosygin in 1964. He was noted for his folksy and irascible qualities.

Khufu or **Cheops,** ancient Egyptian king (c. 2900–2877 BC), founder of the IV dynasty. He built temples and the Great Pyramid of Khufu at Giza near Cairo.

Khyber Pass, major pass from central Asia to Pakistan, through Safed Koh mountain range; used for centuries by invaders, merchants, migrating peoples; connects the Kabul River Valley in Afghanistan (W) with Peshawar, Pakistan (E). A modern strategic military road, it was scene of intense fighting during Afghan Wars 1839–42 and 1878–80; site of two former British outposts, Ali Masjid and Landi Kotal. Elevation: 3,500ft (1,068m). Length: approx. 30mi (49km).

Kiang, wild Asian ass found in mountains of Tibet and Sikkim up to 18,000ft (5490m). The most numerous wild ass, it is red and white in summer and dun colored in winter. Height: 59in (150cm) at shoulder. Family Equidae; species *Equus hemionus kiang. See also* Ass.

Kiangsi (Jiangxi), province in SE China; capital is Nan-ch'ang; mostly mountainous terrain; fertile regions are drained by the Kan River. Originally known as Kan, under Chou dynasty (772–481 BC), ruled by dynasties of Western Chin, Southern Sung, and T'ang, until passed to Manchu rule 1650. Products: rice, wheat, beans, sweet potatoes, citrus fruits, tobacco, sugarcane, cotton, peanuts. Industries: lumbering, fishing, porcelain, silk, mining of tungsten, coal, uranium. Exports: bamboo, varnish, turpentine, fish. Area: approx. 66,000sq mi (170,940sq km). Pop. 21,070,000.

Kiangsu, province in E China; capital is Nanking; one of China's smallest and densely populated regions; extremely fertile region, it contains the Yangtze River delta and is also highly industrialized; site of Shanghai, chief manufacturing city of China. Under Ming dynasty (1368–1644) became a separate province 1667; taken by Japan 1937; freed by Chinese Nationalists 1945; and taken by Communists 1949. Products: rice, cotton, wheat, barley, soybean, peanuts, tea, sugar cane. Industries: silk, fertilizer, textiles, food processing, cement. Area: approx. 41,000sq mi (106,190sq km). Pop. 47,000,000.

Kickapoo, major tribe of North American Indians of Algonquian linguistic stock, originally occupying southcentral Wisconsin. They are closely related to Fox and Sauk. In 1852 part of the tribe went to Texas, and on into Mexico, where many of their descendants still inhabit a reservation area in Chihuahua. Eventually most of the Kickapoo moved to Oklahoma, where some 1,500 now live.

Kidd, William (c.1645–1701), pirate, also known as "Captain Kidd." A sea captain, he began his career as a privateer for the British against the French and pirates in the West Indies. Sailing to London, he was commissioned in 1695 to continue these actions in the Madagascar area. However, when he reached Madagascar he turned pirate himself, prompted in part by the lack of French booty. He eventually abandoned ship and went to New England to exonerate himself. He was sent to England, tried for murder and piracy, and hanged.

Kidney, either of a pair of excretory organs that extract water and waste from the blood, producing the secretion urine that is discharged from the body. Lying in the small of the back, the kidneys are fist-sized and bean-shaped. Each kidney is made up of about 1,-000,000 highly specialized tubules, known as nephrons. The upper end of each nephron is saclike (Bowman's capsule) and contains numerous specialized capillaries, the glomeruli, that filter the blood entering through tiny branches of the renal artery. The filtered fluid passes through other portions of the convoluted and straight tubule, where further action takes place. Eventually the "cleaned" blood reenters the circulatory system through the renal vein. The waste-containing fluid, urine, is passed into the ureter, which carries it to the bladder. The amount of fluid passing through the glomerulus filter daily is some 190 quarts (180 liters), but much of the fluid is reabsorbed before urine is formed.

Kidney, Artificial, a device used therapeutically to remove waste products from the blood in cases of kidney malfunction. The blood is shunted through this mechanism, which, by way of a series of semipermeable membranes, substitutes for the normal kidney in filtering the blood. The process is called artificial dialysis. *See also* Dialysis; Kidney.

Kidney Stones (renal calculi), small, hard, pebblelike masses composed largely of mineral salts and formed in the kidney. Passage of a stone through the tube leading from the kidney to the bladder causes excruciating pain.

Kidney Transplant. *See* Organ Transplant.

Kidron, valley in Jordan, occupied by Israel, from 1967; source of Kidron Brook, which flows E to separate Jerusalem from the Mount of Olives and empties into the Dead Sea; the biblical reference to the valley of Jehoshaphat, traditionally located in the N section of Kidron Valley, is said to have been a place of judgment (Joel: 3).

Kiel, seaport city in West Germany, 40mi (64km) NW of Lubeck on Kiel Bay; capital of Schleswig-Holstein state; joined Hanseatic League 1284; ceded to Denmark 1773, to Prussia 1866; scene of sailors' mutiny that began German revolution (1918); site of university (1665), dairying research institute, 13th-century castle where Tsar Peter III was born. Industries: shipyards, textiles, processed food, printed materials. Chartered 1242. Pop. 260,900.

Kiel Canal (Nord-Ostsee Kanal), man-made waterway in N West Germany, connecting North Sea with Baltic Sea. Built to facilitate movement of German Fleet 1887–95, in 1905–14 it was widened and deepened for use by ocean-going vessels; declared an international waterway by Treaty of Versailles (1919), an act that was repudiated by Adolf Hitler; it was restored for international traffic following WWII. Length: 61mi (98km).

Kierkegaard, Sören (1813–55), Danish philosopher. His writings fall into three periods, the aesthetic, the ethical, and the religious. The founder of Christian existentialism, he believed that his God is known only by a "leap of faith," which also is a leap into the eternal and the irrational. Only the immediacy of personal experience confers reality. His fierce independence and defiance of authority made his life painful and lonely. His main works are *Either/Or* (1843), *Fear and Trembling* (1843), *Stages on Life's Way* (1845), and *Concluding Unscientific Postscript* (1846). *See also* Existentialism.

Kiev, city and port in Ukrainian SSR, USSR, on E bank of Dnieper River, 470mi (757km) SW of Moscow; capital of Ukrainian SSR and Kiev oblast; 3rd-largest city of USSR. City was part of Lithuania 14th century, Poland 16th century, taken by Russia 1686; served as capital of independent Ukrainian Republic 1918–19; taken by Bolsheviks 1920. In 1934 capital of Ukrainian SSR was moved from Kharkov to Kiev; site of cathedral of St Sophia (1037, USSR's oldest), monastery of St Michael (1108), Church of St Andrew (1753), university (1834). Industries: beet sugar, flour, footwear, furniture, shipbuilding, machine tools. Founded before 5th century. Pop. 2,133,000.

Kigali, city in Rwanda, E of Lake Kivu; capital of Rwanda since 1962, when Rwanda gained its independence; the government began intensive economic expansion with hopes of attracting private industry; chief administrative and economic center; site of international airport, technical school. Industries: iron, tin, cotton, textiles. Pop. 40,000.

Kikuyu, Negroid people forming the dominant group in Kenya. Traditionally, they live by intensive cultivation; crops include millet and sorghum, with coffee and corn as cash crops. Their patrilineal, egalitarian society is based around the village community, organized into age groups with initiation ceremonies as each individual qualifies for a new group. The Mau Mau rebellion against British rule in 1952–56 was organized by the Kikuyu.

Kilimanjaro, Mount, mountain in NE Tanzania; highest mountain in Africa, near the Kenya border; site of peaks Kibo, 19,340ft (5,899m) and Mawenzi 16,896ft (5,153m), joined by a broad saddle. Well-developed S slope produces coffee and sisal. Kibo was first climbed in 1889, Mawenzi in 1912.

Killdeer, noisy, ploverlike shore bird of North American meadows known for its *kill-dee* alarm call and distraction displays. It is white with a double black breast ring and chestnut rump and tail. It lays marked eggs (4) in a scrape nest. Species *Charadrius vociferus.*

Killer Whale, toothed whale inhabiting all oceans, especially those in colder regions. A fierce predator of large animals, it is black above and white below and distinguished by a white patch above each eye and a long erect dorsal fin. Length: 30ft (9m). Species *Orcinus orca.*

Killifish, or **Killie,** freshwater fish also found in brackish coastal marshes of America. A hardy topminnow popular with aquarists, it is used to control mosquitoes. Length: 1.5–6in (3.8–15.2cm). Family Cyprinodontidae; species: 300, including common *Fundulus heteroclitus.*

Kiln, in ceramics, an oven for firing ware. Early kilns were holes in the ground into which the ware was placed. A wood pyre was built over it. Later, special wood and coal oven-type kilns were built. Today, most kilns are electrically or gas fueled. Commercial kilns are continuous, the most successful being tunnel kilns. Here, ware is conveyed slowly from a comparatively cool region at the entrance to the full heat in the center. As it nears the exit, it cools gradually.

Kilogram, unit of mass (symbol kg) defined as the mass of the international prototype cylinder of platinum-iridium kept in Paris. 1 kilogram is equal to 2.-20462 pounds. *See also* Physical Units.

Kilowatt Hour, unit of electrical energy equal to the energy used when a power of one kilowatt (1000 watts) is expended for one hour. It is the unit for which domestic and industrial users of electricity are charged.

Kimberley, city in Republic of South Africa, 60mi (97km) ENE of Nelson; Cecil Rhodes took control of Kimberley diamond fields 1888; it was besieged for four months during Boer War 1899. The world's diamond center, the land is marked by deep pits, the result of extensive diamond mining. Industries: diamond mining, cutting, polishing; processing of lime, gypsum, iron, manganese, asbestos. Pop. 107,104.

Kim Il Sung (1912–), chief of state of the Democratic People's Republic of Korea (North Korea) and chairman of its Korean Workers' party from 1948, b. Kim Sung Chu. He joined the Korean Communist party in 1931. He led guerrilla fighting against the occupying Japanese in the 1930s and a Korean unit in the Soviet army in World War II. In 1950 he led a North Korean invasion of South Korea that precipitated the Korean War (1950–53).

Kinesthetic Sense, or proprioception, internal sense that conveys information from the muscles and tendons of the body. Specialized receptors connect to a nervous system tract that provides information about the contraction and expansion of muscles. This sense is also called the position sense because it allows humans to know the position of their limbs without reference to vision, giving them a sense of "feeling."

Kinetic Art, term used to describe art, especially sculpture, in which an element of motion is present. Early kinetic art included mobile sculpture by Duchamp, Calder, and Gabo, as well as Moholy-Nagy's light machine of 1930. Sometimes kinetic sculpture is designed so that the parts can be completely rearranged, as in Kobashi's art. Ultvedt's sculptures are driven by electric motors with gears, cranks, and levers, and Tinguely's sculptures are often driven by water. Kinetic painting includes op art.

Kinetic Energy, energy of motion. A body of mass m and speed v has a kinetic energy of $\frac{1}{2}mv^2$. *See also* Energy; Potential Energy.

Kinetic Theory. In the kinetic theory, temperature is a measure of the number of energy states available to the atoms of a system. Heat is a measure of the amount of energy that the system gains or loses as a result of a temperature change. Two materials at the same temperature may be very different potential sources of heat; this difference is measured by a characteristic called heat capacity, or specific heat. *See also* Thermodynamics.

King, Martin Luther, Jr. (1929–68), US clergyman and civil rights leader, b. Atlanta, Ga. Pastor of a Baptist church in Montgomery, Ala., in 1955 he led the black boycott of Montgomery's segregated transport system; when it was successful, he and the passive resistance tactics he advocated attracted national attention. Thereafter he founded and worked through the Southern Christian Leadership Conference to further desegregation nationally. He organized the massive March on Washington in 1963, opposed the Vietnam War, and had begun a national campaign against poverty when he was assassinated in Memphis, Tenn., April 4, 1968. In 1964 he was awarded the Nobel Peace Prize. Attempts to have his birthday declared a national holiday have failed, but several states have made Jan. 15 a legal holiday.

King, Rufus (1755–1827), US statesman, b. Scarborough, Maine. As a member of the Continental Congress (1784–87), he introduced legislation calling for a constitution and prohibiting slavery in the Northwest Territory. He then helped to draft and pass the federal Constitution. He moved to New York in 1788. He served as a US Senator (1789–96; 1813–25) and as ambassador to Great Britain (1796–1803; 1825–26). He was an unsuccessful presidential candidate (1816).

King, William Lyon Mackenzie (1874–1950), prime minister of Canada (1921–30; 1935–48). A lawyer and social worker, King was a successful labor mediator before entering politics. His career was marked by the drive for national unity, concessions to the Progressives, and support of French-Canadian rights. Trained by Sir Wilfred Laurier, King led the Liberals (1919–48). He was more interested in foreign policy than social legislation and a firm supporter of free enterprise.

Kingbird, or tyrant flycatcher, aggressive New World flycatcher, centered in tropical America, that dives at intruders and snaps up insects. The eastern kingbird *(Tyrannus tyrannus)* is black with a white belly, white-tipped tail, and red crest. It lays brown-flecked, white eggs (4–5) in a cup-shaped nest. It grows to 6.8in (17cm).

Kingfish, or whiting, marine food fish found in Atlantic, it is metallic silver with dark bar markings. Length: to 17in (43.1cm); weight: 2–3lb (0.9–1.4kg). Family Sciaenidae; species include Atlantic Northern *Menticirrhus saxatilis.*

Kingfisher, compact, highly colored birds that have straight sharp bills and dive for fish along the rivers, streams, and lakes where they live. They swallow the fish head first when back on their perch. They nest in a deep, horizontal hole in a soil bank, laying white eggs in a filthy nest. The young form a circle and rotate to receive food brought by the parent. Wood kingfishers have flattened, hook-tipped bills and live in forests feeding on land animals, large invertebrates, small frogs, and snakes. They drill a nest in a tree or soil bank. Length: 5–18in (13–46cm). Family Alcedinidae.

King George's War (1744–48), inconclusive struggle between France and Britain for control over North America. Both sides enlisted Indian aid in fighting over disputed boundaries in Nova Scotia, New England, and the Ohio Valley. By the Peace of Aix-la-Chapelle (1748) conquered territory was restored by mutual agreement.

King James Bible, the translation of the Bible ordered by King James I of England in 1604 and completed in 1611, also called the Authorized Version. Whether or not it was specifically authorized by the king for use in churches, the King James Version became the standard Bible in Anglican communion. Considered a masterpiece of translation, this Bible has had great influence on English literature. Several revisions of the King James text have been published, the Revised Version in the late 19th century and the Revised Standard Version (1946–57). *See also* Bible.

King John (*c.*1596), 5-act tragedy by William Shakespeare, based on an older drama from Raphael Holinshed's *Chronicles.* John, having seized the throne from Prince Arthur, prepares to defend himself against France and Austria, supporters of Arthur, but the marriage of his niece and the French dauphin brings a peaceful settlement. Excommunicated by the pope for disobedience, John is suspected of murdering Prince Arthur. His lords turn against him and join the dauphin and John is poisoned by monks. The dauphin and his army return to France and peace is restored.

King Lear (*c.*1605), 5-act tragedy by William Shakespeare based on an older anonymous play *King Leir* and Raphael Holinshed's *Chronicles.* Lear, king of Britain, divides his realm between his flattering daughters Goneril and Regan, leaving his youngest daughter Cordelia, who loves him, with nothing. When his older daughters turn him out, Cordelia joins him in exile. When Cordelia is killed, Lear dies of grief. Goneril poisons Regan and kills herself; her husband, the duke of Albany, succeeds to the throne.

Kinglet, fearless, active songbird that breeds in cool areas of North America and Eurasia. They have a small

Mount Kilimanjaro

Martin Luther King

Kingfisher

crest that reveals a brightly colored spot when expanded; short, straight bill; and downlike plumage. They feed on insects. Both parents build a bulky, hanging nest for small white or buff spotted eggs (5–10) laid in tiny chambers. The female incubates the eggs and both parents feed the young. Length: 3–4in (7.6–10cm). Genus *Regulus*.

King Philip's War (1675–76), Indian war in New England. The Indian chief Philip (Metacomet) of the Wampanoags, who was friendly to the Plymouth Colony, believed increased colonization meant the destruction of the Indians. The war started over the murder of an Indian; 12 towns in central Massachusetts were destroyed in the conflict. The war ended when troops of the New England Confederation defeated the Narragansett Indians (1675) and the Nipmucks (1676) and killed Philip in Rhode Island (1676). *See also* New England Confederation.

King Snake, harmless, shiny snake found from central and S United States to Central America. Its color varies, being mostly black with white or yellow markings. It feeds on other snakes, including poisonous species. Length: to 50in (1.3m). Family Colubridae, genus *Lampropeltis. See also* Snake.

Kings I and II, biblical books, called Third and Fourth Kingdoms in the Greek Septuagint. These books recount the histories of Judah and Israel from the beginning of Solomon's reign (970 BC) through the fall of Judah and destruction of Jerusalem (586 BC). Having reference to previous historical accounts, the unknown author presents this material to suit his purpose, as a revelation of God's presence in the history of Israel.

Kingston, city in Ontario, Canada, on Lake Ontario; Canada's capital 1841–44; site of Fort Frontenac and Fort Henry, built during War of 1812; Queen's University, Royal Military College, Roman Catholic bishoprics, cathedrals. Industries: textiles, aluminum products, synthetic yarns, ceramics, locomotive manufacture. Founded 1783 by United Empire Loyalists. Pop. 56,032.

Kingston, seaport city on SE coast of Jamaica, West Indies, in the Caribbean Sea; capital and commercial center of Jamaica with excellent harbor; site of University College of West Indies (1946), Royal Botanical Gardens, handcrafts market, Institute of Jamaica and museum. Founded 1692 after earthquake destroyed Port Royal, it became permanent capital 1872; was severely damaged in 1907 earthquake. Industries: tourism, food processing, oil refining, clothes, shoes. Exports: sugar, rum, molassas, bananas. Pop. 600,000.

Kingston-upon-Hull. *See* Hull.

Kingstown, capital and seaport in St Vincent, Windward Islands, in the West Indies, on SW coast at head of Kingstown Bay; site of botanical garden (1763); port of entry and tourist center. Exports: cotton, sugar cane, molasses, cacao, fruit. Pop. 17,258.

King William's War (1689–97), North American part of the war between England and France. Frontenac, French governor of Canada, sent expeditions against the New York, New Hampshire, and Maine frontiers. The English, under Sir William Phipps (of Massachusetts), sailed up the St Lawrence River to take Quebec, but failed (1690). Bloody border conflicts with the Indians also occurred. Port Royal, Nova Scotia, was captured and then lost by the English (1690–91).

Kinkajou, nocturnal foraging mammal of the raccoon family found in forests of Central and South America. Slender-bodied, it has a small round head and long tongue. Primarily a fruit and insect eater, it lives almost entirely in trees, aided by a long prehensile tail. The soft woolly fur is tawny-yellow to brown. Length: to 22.5in (572mm); weight: to 5.5lb (2.5kg). Family Procyonidae; species *Potos flavus*.

Kinnock, Neil Gordon (1942–), British politician and Labour party leader. Educated at University College in Cardiff, Wales, he gained a seat in the House of Commons by the age of 28. He became a member of the party's national executive committee (1978) and earned a reputation as an eloquent public speaker. During the first term of Prime Minister Thatcher's government, Kinnock was the opposition spokesman on education. He became the Labour party leader (1983) without ever having held a government office.

Kinshasa, formerly **Léopoldville,** capital and largest city of Zaire, on border of Zaire and Republic of Congo; port on Stanley Pool of Congo River; transportation hub. In 1926 it replaced Boma as the capital of the Belgian Congo; when Zaire gained its independence (1960), it continued as the capital of the new country; in 1966 name was changed from Leopoldville. Industries: food processing, brewing, tanning, chemicals, textiles. Founded 1881 by Henry Stanley and named Leopoldville for his sponsor, Belgian King Leopold II. Pop. 1,990,717.

Kinship, system standing for a complex of rules in a society governing descent, succession, inheritance, marriage, residence, and sexual relations. Kinship terms do not stand for blood relations but are culture-specific: two people are kinsmen if they are consanguinally related, although kinship is often extended to cover relations of affinity as well. *See also* Clan; Endogamy; Exogamy; Family; Incest Taboo; Nuclear Family.

Kiowa, major tribe of Tanoan-speaking North American Indians who moved from their earlier Yellowstone–Missouri River homeland into the southern Plains region, where they eventually allied with the Comanche and Arapaho. With these tribes they became one of the widest-ranging peoples of the western United States, raiding as far south as northern Mexico. Today about 330 Kiowa live in the Anadarko area of Oklahoma.

Kiowa Apache, North American Indian tribe that split from the parent Apache group several centuries ago, migrating south onto the Plains from the British Columbia-Montana region. They integrated thoroughly with the Kiowa and only their Athapascan language distinguishes them from that tribe. About 450 survive today in Oklahoma, living intermixed with the host group.

Kipling, (Joseph) Rudyard (1865–1936), British author, b. India. He achieved recognition with his stories about India, including *Plain Tales from the Hills* (1887), and with his novel *The Light That Failed* (1891). *His Barrack Room Ballads and Other Verses* (1892), including the poem "If," underlined his imperialist views. He wrote many children's adventures and animal stories, including *The Jungle Book* (1894), *Captain's Courageous* (1897), and *Kim* (1901), and the schoolboy stories *Stalky and Co.* (1899). His post–World War I stories, such as *Debits and Credits* (1926), show a more profound artistry.

Kirchhoff, Gustav Robert (1824–87), German physicist, professor at Heidelberg and later in Berlin. He worked with Robert Bunsen, and developed the spec-

troscope and used it to discover the elements cesium and rubidium (1860). He also examined the solar spectrum, worked on black-body radiation, and enunciated several laws (Kirchhoff's laws) relating to electric circuits. *See also* Blackbody.

Kirchhoff's Laws, two rules about multiple-loop electric circuits that are based on the laws of the conservation of charge and energy. Essentially they state that (1) charge does not accumulate at one point and thin out at another, and (2) around each loop the sum of the electromotive forces equals the sum of the potential voltage across each of the resistances.

Kirghiz, central Asiatic, Turko-Mongolian people, who inhabit the Kirghiz Soviet Socialist Republic. A Muslim people, whose language with its rich oral tradition belongs to the Turkic group, they are nomadic pastoralists who were colonized by Russia in the 19th century. The process of settlement and industrialization has recently accelerated.

Kirghiz (Kirgizskaja) Soviet Socialist Republic, constituent republic of Central Asian USSR; borders on China (SE) and Kazakh republic (N), Uzbek (W), and Tadzhik republics (SW) SSRs; capital is Frunze. Russia annexed this region between 1865–76 when it conquered central Asia. The people fought Bolshevik control 1917–21. In 1924 it became an antonnous oblast within Russian republic and a constituent republic in 1936. Region is mostly mountainous; highest peak is Pobedy Peak, 24,409ft (7,445m), on Chinese border. Industries: irrigated farming, livestock, farm machinery, textiles, sugar refining, building materials. Area: 76,600sq mi (198,394sq km). Pop. 3,511,000.

Kiribati(formerly Gilbert Islands), independent island nation composed of about 33 islands straddling the Equator over a vast area in W Pacific. British navigators began discovering the islands during the late 18th century, and they became a British protectorate in 1892, subsequently administered jointly with the nearby Ellice Islands (now Tuvalu). Full independence within the Commonwealth of Nations was granted to Kiribati in 1979. The people are mostly Micronesian, although there are Polynesian and European minorities, and Christianity predominates. The mining of phosphates dominated Kiribati's economy until 1980, when production ended because of diminishing resources. Agriculture is now the major economic activity, and copra is the principal export. Capital: Tarawa; area: 264sq mi (684sq km); pop. 57,000.

Kirin (Jilin, or **Chi-lin),** city in NE China, on the Sungari River; capital of Kirin prov. 1750–1954. Early junk-building and lumber center (17–18th centuries), a seat of military government 1750–1911; industrial growth came with introduction of the railroad in 1912. Industries: chemicals, lumber, paper, matches, food processing, tobacco, plastics. Founded 1673. Pop. 1,200,-000.

Kirkuk, city in NE Iraq; headquarters of Iraq Petroleum Co.; oil pipeline terminus to ports on Mediterranean Sea. Industries: oil, textiles, cotton, grains, sheep. Pop. 167,413.

Kirov, city and riverport in Russian SFSR, USSR, on W bank of Vyatka River; capital of Kirov oblast. It became capital of an independent republic that was annexed by Ivan III in 1489; site of 17th-century cathedral. Industries: metal products, meat processing, lumber, leather, furs. Founded 1181. Pop. 384,000.

Kirovabad, city in W Azerbaijan SSR, USSR, S of Kura River, 110mi (178km) SE of Tbilisi; under Persian control from 17th century until it was taken by Russia in 1804; birthplace of Persian poet Nizami Gandzhevi (1141); site of 17th-century mosque. Industries: building materials, carpets, wine, cotton textiles, agricultural implements. Founded AD 1139 after earthquake had destroyed original city (6th century) 4mi (6km) E. Pop. 216,000.

Kirovograd, city in Ukrainian SSR, USSR, on E bank of Ingul River, 155mi (250km) SE of Kiev; capital of Kirovograd oblast. Between 1881 and 1919 it was scene of several pogroms. Industries: agricultural machinery, food processing, building materials. Founded as fortress 1754 and named for Empress Elizabeth (Elisavetgrad); name changed to Kirovograd 1935. Pop. 233,000.

Kisangani, formerly Stanleyville; city and port in N central Zaire, on the Congo River; a transportation center of NE Zaire. In the 1950s it was a stronghold of Patrice Lumumba until his assassination in 1961; site of university (1963). Industries: metal goods, beer, textiles. Founded 1883 by Henry M. Stanley as Stanleyville. Pop. 297,829.

Kish, ancient city of Mesopotamia. It was located in the Euphrates River Valley east of Babylon. In the 4th millennium BC it was a rich, strong Sumerian city. Excavations since 1922 have revealed that Sargon, king of Akkad, built a palace (c.2800 BC) and Nebuchadnezzar and Nabonidus, kings of Babylon, erected temples (6th cent. BC.)

Kishinev (Kišsin'ov), city in Moldavian SSR, USSR, 90mi (145km) NW of Odessa on the Byk River; capital of Moldavian SSR. Town was captured by Turks in 16th century, and by Russians 1812; Romania held city 1918–40; Axis powers controlled it 1941–44, and USSR seized it Aug. 24, 1944; site of university (1945). Industries: building materials, food processing, plastics, rubber, textiles. Founded early 15th century. Pop. 492,000.

Kissing Bug, or conenose, brown to black bug found in South and Central America, Mexico, and Texas. It bites humans and rodents, usually about the mouth, and is a carrier of Chagas' disease. Length: 1–11/3in (25–33mm). Family Reduviidae; genera *Triatoma* and *Rhodinus. See also* Assassin Bug.

Kissinger, Henry Alfred (1923–), US political scientist and secretary of state, b. Germany. While a professor at Harvard, he wrote several books on political science and served as advisor to various government agencies. He became Pres. Richard Nixon's assistant for national security (1969) and became the chief advisor on foreign policy. Nixon named him secretary of state (1973) and he continued in that post (until 1977) under Pres. Gerald Ford. In 1973 he shared the Nobel Peace Prize with Le Duc Tho for arranging a cease-fire in the Vietnam War, even though actual fighting continued to 1975. He arranged summit meetings for Nixon in China and Russia for détente. He also mediated the Middle East problems. His *White House Years* (1979) won the American Book Award for history in 1980. He also wrote *Years of Upheaval* (1982), an account of foreign affairs during Pres. Richard M. Nixon's second term.

Kitakyushu, port city in N Kyushu, Japan, on Shimonoseki Strait, site of technical institute (1921); important commercial center. Industries: shipbuilding, fishing, iron, steel, textiles, chemicals, machinery, glass, cement. Formed 1963 with inc. of Kokura, Moji, Tobata, Wakamatsu, Yawata. Pop. 1,042,321.

Kitasato, Shibasaburo (1852–1931), Japanese bacteriologist famous for the isolation of the bacilli that cause tetanus, anthrax (1889), and dysentery (1898). In 1890 he prepared a diphtheria antitoxin. He also discovered the infectious organism that causes bubonic plague. He studied under Robert Koch in Germany.

Kitchener, Horatio Herbert (Earl), (1850–1916), English military leader and colonial administrator. He crushed the Mahdi's revolt at Omdurman (1898) and subsequently blocked French expansionism in the Sudan. He was British commander in chief (1900–02) in the Boer War and then in India (1902–09), where his quarrel with Lord Curzon, the viceroy, caused the latter's resignation. Proconsul of Egypt (1911–14), he then became secretary of state for war, brilliantly but autocratically organizing the British army at the start of World War I. He was drowned when his ship was sunk by German submarines while on a mission to Russia.

Kitchener, formerly Berlin, city in SE Ontario, Canada, in the Grand River Valley; site of Woodside National Park; renamed in 1916 in honor of Lord Kitchener. Industries: rubber products, metal products, packaged meats. Settled by Mennonites from Pennsylvania 1806. Pop. 131,870.

Kitchen Midden, or **Shell Mound,** prehistoric refuse heaps composed chiefly of the discarded remains of edible shellfish mixed with evidence of human artifacts. Most of these middens were established in Europe and North Africa (from about 4,000 to 2,000 BC) after the disappearance of the large game animals hunted by early man during the Ice Age. Middens are also known from North, Central and South America.

Kite, diurnal bird of prey found in tropical and subtropical areas worldwide. They have hooked bills, narrow wings, long, sometimes forked tails, and long, curved claws. Hawklike, they circle, soar, and glide. Most European and Asian species are scavengers; American species generally feed on small live animals. They lay their eggs (2–5) in a bulky tree nest. Length: 18–24in (46–61cm). Family Accipitridae.

Kittiwake, whitish arctic gull with a greenish-yellow bill, black wing tips, and short dark legs that flies low over open seas. To 14in (36cm) long, with a wingspan of 3ft (.91m), it lays spotted pale eggs (1–3) in a cup-shaped nest in sea cliffs. Family Laridae; species *Rissa tridactyla.*

Kitwe, city in N central Zambia, S Central Africa, 180mi (288km) N of Lusaka; site of Zambia Institute of Technology. Industries: copper mining, food processing, clothing, plastics. Founded 1936. Pop. 160,000.

Kiva, underground ceremonial chamber of Pueblo Indians. Each religious society has its own kiva, and many of its rites are performed here. Kivas are rectangular or circular and are highly decorated.

Kiwi, chicken-sized, flightless, fast-running, forest and scrub land bird of New Zealand. It has hairlike feathers and a long, flexible bill used to probe for food along the ground, usually at night. Large white or greenish eggs (1–2) are laid in a leaf-lined scrape or burrow. The male incubates the eggs. Species *Apteryx australis.*

Klamath, tribe of about 1,000 Shapwailutan-speaking North American Indians, closely related to the Modoc, who inhabit the Klamath Lake area in Oregon.

Klee, Paul (1879–1940), Swiss painter. He was an influential genius of the abstract art movement. Influenced by cubism and fascinated by hieroglyphics, primitive art, and children's drawings, he developed his own pictorial language. His great technical skill in various media allowed him to combine subtle coloring with this new language, resulting in witty, inspiring works that convey great meaning through simple compositions. He studied art in Munich (1900), traveled in Italy and France (1905), and earned a meager living doing exhibitions and illustrations after returning to Munich (1906). By the end of World War I, Klee had established himself as a master. He taught painting at the Bauhaus until his final return to Switzerland in 1933 after his art was confiscated by the Nazis for being "degenerate." His most famous work is *Twittering Machine* (1922).

Klipspringer, small antelope, native to rocky areas of Africa below the Sahara Desert. Short, spiked horns are usually only on the male. It has a thick coat of grizzled, bristly hair and tiny, cylindrical hooves that permit leaps onto small footholds. Height: to 23in (0.6m) at shoulder; weight: to 35lb (16kg). Family Bovidae; species *Oreotragus oreotragus. See also* Antelope.

Klondike Gold Rush (1896–1904). The discovery of gold by George Carmack at Bonanza Creek (1896) in the Klondike region of the Yukon territory of Canada began an onrush of prospectors sailing up the Lynn Canal to Dyea and Skagway. By 1899 most claims had been staked, and the population of Dawson had grown to 25,000. Access to the Yukon caused the Alaska Boundary dispute, and $100,000,000 of gold was mined before the lodes were exhausted in 1904.

Klystron, an electron tube that is velocity modulated and makes use of the controlled speed of a stream of electrons. They are used in ultra-high frequency circuits, where they can produce oscillations up to 400,000 megacycles per second.

K-Meson. *See* Kaon.

Knickerbocker School, name given to a group of writers associated with New York City in the first half of the 19th century. Besides individual publication, their work appeared in New York newspapers and in *Knickerbocker* magazine. Among the writers were William Cullen Bryant, Lydia M. Child, James Fenimore Cooper, Joseph R. Drake, Fitz-Greene Halleck, Washington Irving, Clement Moore, George P. Morris, James K. Paulding, Nathaniel Willis, and Samuel Woodworth.

Knight, in the Middle Ages in Western Europe, a fully equipped mounted warrior, provided with a helmet and chain mail before the 14th century and with a complete suit of steel armor by the 15th century. Under the feudal system, a knight was one of the armed retainers of a lord or king, and was bound to the lord as a vassal. Knight service, or the equivalent in monetary donations, was due the lord by most vassals. Originally, the knight was a practical warrior, but by the 12th century he was a romantic figure and idealized as the symbol of manhood and virtue. Less and less often associated with actual warfare, some knights made their living entirely by the ransoms earned in tournaments.

Knights Hospitallers or **Knights of Saint John of Jerusalem,** military religious order established early in the 11th century. They cared for Christian pilgrims who fell ill in Jerusalem, where they had a hospital and hostel. During the Crusades the Hospitallers policed routes to Jerusalem, together with their bitter rivals, the Knights Templars. After the fall of Jerusalem they sought to protect the Mediterranean from the Turks. Today there remain a Catholic charitable order and an Anglican one, which still maintains a hospital in Jerusalem.

Knights of Labor, workers' group formed in Philadelphia (1869). It was organized by Uriah S. Stephens, a tailor, and became a national organization in 1878. Skilled and unskilled workers, regardless of race, sex, or color, were eligible to join the local assemblies, which together formed one union. It reached peak membership of over 700,000 in 1886. The union declined after the Haymarket Square incident in May 1886, and several strike failures. The organization was dissolved in 1913. *See also* Haymarket Massacre.

Knights Templars, military religious order established in 1118 with its headquarters in the supposed Temple of Solomon in Jerusalem. With the Knights Hospitallers the Templars protected routes to Jerusalem for Christians during the Crusades and amassed a great fortune for their order. Fighting between the two orders contributed to the failure of the Crusades. The possessions of the Templars in France attracted King Philip IV, who urged Pope Clement V to abolish the order in 1312. Their property was confiscated and many were tortured and executed.

Knossos (Cnossus), ancient city in Greece, on the N coast of Crete, 4mi (6km) SE of Candia. Occupied prior to 3000 BC, it was center of Bronze Age culture; early Minoan culture was destroyed 1500 BC; rebuilt and destroyed again c. 1400 BC ending Minoan civilization. Knossos prospered as a Greek city; it was traditional capital of King Minos; site of great palace c. 2000 BC, including a labyrinth, a chamber built, according to Greek myth, by Daedalus to house the Minotaur.

Knot, sandpiper that nests in Siberia and winters in temperate coastal areas. It is generally chestnut and brown with black markings and feeds on small animals. Spotted greenish to buff eggs (4) are laid in a tundra scrape. Length: 10in (25cm). Species *Calidris canutus.*

Knot, a unit of measurement equal to one nautical mile per hour. Ship and airplane speed is measured in knots as is that of wind and currents.

Knotweed, or doorweed, wire grass, widespread flowering annual weed plant. It has small, lancelike leaves and brown flowers and grows prostrate with the wiry branches forming dense mats. Family Polygonaceae; genus *Polygonum.*

Know-Nothing Party ("American Party," "Native American Party"), third-party political movement active in the 1850s. Party members, when asked about their motives, purposes, and program, would reply, "I know nothing." In fact, however, Know-Nothings were fanatically patriotic and strongly opposed to Roman Catholics, particularly Irish Catholics who immigrated to the United States in the 1850s. By 1856 the party was more a conservative Unionist movement than the nativist organization it had been earlier. After the 1856 presidential campaign, the party disintegrated.

Knox, Henry (1750–1806), American Revolutionary War military officer, b. Boston. As commander of the Continental Army artillery he hauled the guns captured at Fort Ticonderoga to Boston. He took part in every major battle of the war and was close adviser to George Washington, becoming a brigadier general in 1776. He founded the Society of the Cincinnati (1783). He was the first secretary of war (1785–94).

Knox, John (c.1515–72), leader of the Protestant Reformation in Scotland. He was ordained a Roman Cath-

Henry Kissinger

Knossos, Crete

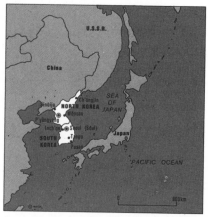

Korea

olic priest but took up the cause of the Reformation. He was imprisoned in France and later lived for a time in exile in England and after Mary I came to the throne (1553) went to Geneva, where he was influenced by John Calvin. Knox continued to promote the Protestant cause in Scotland. After a struggle with Scotland's new Catholic ruler, Mary Queen of Scots, from 1561 his side prevailed by the late 1560s. He is one of the great leaders of Presbyterianism. *See also* Presbyterianism.

Knoxville, city in E Tennessee, 105mi (169km) NE of Chattanooga on Tennessee River; seat of Knox co. City was a supply center for westward-bound wagon trains (1792); Tennessee's first capital 1697–1812, 1817–19; headquarters of Confederate armies in E Tennessee 1861; taken by Union troops at Battle of Fort Sanders 1863; site of Tennessee Valley Authority, University of Tennessee (1794), Knoxville College (1863). Industries: livestock, farming, tobacco, marble quarrying, ore processing, textiles, furniture, cement, steel products, glass, chemicals, plastics, railroad shops, tourism, lumber. Settled 1786; inc. 1815. Pop. (1980) 183,139.

Koa, Hawaiian tree valued for its wood, used in cabinetmaking. It has clustered flowers and 6-in (15-cm) pods. Height: to 60ft (18m). Family Leguminosae; species *Acacia koa.*

Kobe, port city on SW Honshu, Japan, on N shore of Osaka Bay; capital of Hyogo prefecture. In 1878 Kobe absorbed Hyogo, an important fishing port since 9th century; since the late 1800s it has become a major port of Japan; cultural center; site of several early Buddhist structures, Kobe University of Economics (1948), and Kobe University (1949); suffered Allied bombings in WWII. Industries: shipping, shipbuilding, rubber, steel, textiles, printing. Pop. 1,361,000.

Koch, Robert (1843–1910), German bacteriologist. He was awarded the 1905 Nobel Prize in physiology or medicine for his discovery of the bacillus that causes tuberculosis. This work laid the foundation for methods of determining the causative agent of a disease.

Kochi, seaport on S coast of Shikoku, Japan, on Tosa Bay; capital of Kochi prefecture. Industries: agriculture, fishing, machinery, silk, paper. Pop. 289,000.

Kodály, Zoltán (1882–1967), Hungarian composer who, with Bartók, collected Hungarian folk tunes and used them in his compositions, which include the *Psalmus Hungaricus* (1923) and the *Peacock Variations* (1939) for orchestra, and a popular suite from his opera *Háry János* (1926).

Kodiak Bear. *See* Alaskan Brown Bear.

Kodiak Island, island in the Gulf of Alaska, SE of the Alaska Peninsula. Chief industry is fishing, especially salmon; Kodiak bear and Kodiak king crab are native. Island was covered with ash 1912 when Mt Katmai erupted on mainland; site of US Navy base. Area: 5,363sq mi (13,890sq km).

Koestler, Arthur (1905–83), Hungarian writer. While working as a journalist during the Spanish Civil War, he was captured by Franco's forces and imprisoned until 1937. He then went to France to work and was interned in a concentration camp after the German invasion, escaping in 1940. He joined the British army and later settled in England. His novels include *Darkness at Noon* (1941), *Thieves in the Night* (1946), and *The Call Girls* (1972). His later philosophical works explore the nature of art, science, and man and include *The Sleepwalkers* (1959), *The Ghost in the Machine* (1967), *The*

Case of the Midwife Toad (1971), and *The Thirteenth Tribe: The Khazar Empire and its Heritage* (1976).

Kohl, Helmut (1930–), West German political leader. He was elected to the legislature of Rhineland-Palatinate in 1959 and rose through the ranks of the Christian Democratic Union party, eventually becoming premier of his home state in 1969. In 1982, he succeeded Helmut Schmidt as chancellor of West Germany. His conservative political philosophy advocated strong support for the western military alliance and a return to the traditional values of the West German state.

Kohlrabi, garden vegetable with lobed leaves borne on a bulblike, above-ground stem. The edible, turnip-like bulb is greenish-white or purplish. It matures in 55–60 days. Family Cruciferae; species *Brassica oleracea gongylodes.*

Kolyma, river in Russian SFSR, USSR; rises in Kolyma Mts, flows N and E into Arctic Ocean. From June to October it is navigable for approx. 1,000mi (1,610km) of its 1,500mi (2,415km).

Komodo Dragon, giant monitor lizard found in SE Asian jungles. It is solid brown and feeds on carrion, also killing young deer and wild pigs. Its dwindling populations are strictly protected. Length: to 10ft (3m); weight: to 300lb (135kg). Family Varanidae; species *Varanus komodoensis. See also* Lizard; Monitor Lizard.

Komsomolsk-on-Amur (Komsomolsk), city in Russian SFSR, USSR, on W bank of Amur River. Industries: steel, oil refining, wood products. Founded 1932 by Young Communist League. Pop. 259,000.

Kondratieff Cycles, long-term business cycles that last 50–60 years. Named for Russian economist N. D. Kondratieff, these cycles involve long movements of trade, output, and price changes and may be associated with major technological changes. *See also* Business Cycles.

Kongo, or **Bakongo,** Negroid people of the Atlantic coast of W Africa, living in the Congo Republic, Zaire, and Angola. Once they had a powerful empire, and their culture is still rich in sculpture and music. Their traditional livelihood is based on sedentary agriculture, staple crops including cassava and manioc, with coffee as a cash crop. Ancestor worship and fetish cults dominate their religion.

Kongo, Kingdom of the, African state from the 14th century to about 1700. In the area now included in Zaire and Angola, it was ruled by a king, or *manikongo.* The kingdom began trade with Portugal in 1482. The Portuguese brought Christianity, which Manikongo Afonso I tried to spread. Afonso was, however, hampered by the greed of the Portuguese, who carried on a brisk slave trade. Under continued depredations by the Portuguese and repeated attacks from interior tribes, the kingdom collapsed, and Portugal took control.

Konstanz (Constance), port city in S West Germany, on Lake Constance, 75mi (121km) S of Stuttgart; became a free imperial city in 1183; scene of Council of Constance (1414–18) which ended Great Schism by disposing of three popes and electing a new pope, Martin V. City passed to Austria 1548, to Baden 1805; site of 11th-century cathedral, Kaufhaus (1388 council meeting place), university (1966); birthplace of Count Graf von Zeppelin (1838), soldier and aviator. Indus-

tries: textiles, chemicals, electrical equipment. Founded as Roman fort AD 4th century. Pop. 60,821.

Konya, city in S central Turkey, 145mi (233km) S of Ankara. It was capital of Seljuk sultans of Rum, 1073–1472, when it became part of Ottoman Empire; served as religious center of whirling dervishes, founded here in 13th century; site of teacher training college (1962). Industries: sugar, flax, fruit, cotton goods, leather. Pop. 246,381.

Kookaburra, or laughing jackass, large, heavy kingfisher of Australia and Tasmania known for its loud, fiendish screams. Groups often scream in unison at dawn, midday, and dusk. A wood kingfisher, it feeds on rodents, lizards, and other land animals. Species *Dacelo gigas. See also* Kingfisher.

Kootenay (Kootenai), river in Canada; rises in Rocky Mts, SE British Columbia; flows S through NW Montana and NW Idaho, then N through Kootenay Lake in Canada; unites with the Columbia River at Castlegar; explored by David Thompson 1807; used to generate hydroelectricity. Length: 407mi (655km).

Koran, the sacred scriptures of Islam. The book was written in Arabic, and the Arabic title is Qur'an. According to Muslim belief, the Koran contains the actual word of God as revealed to the Prophet Mohammed in the 7th century. Its 114 chapters, or *suras,* are the source of Islamic belief and a guide for the whole life of the community, making known to men the correct way to live. The message of the Koran holds true eternally, and wherever the Muslim religion has spread the book has been dutifully studied. *See also* Islam; Mohammed.

Korea, Democratic People's Republic of, independent nation in NE Asia, known as North Korea. Established after WWII, its communist government operates N of the 38th parallel.

Land and economy. North Korea, a country where 16% of the land is arable and cultivated, is located in NE Asia with the Soviet Union (N) and South Korea (S) as its neighbors. Moderately high mountain ranges and hills separate the valleys and small plains. Warm in the summer, it is cold in the winter with some snow. Its mineral resources are highly developed and it ranks among the world leaders in yield of tungsten, graphite, and magnesite. It produces sufficient coal for its own needs. With assistance from the Soviet Union and China, Korea has developed its economy, especially nationalized heavy industry. Agriculture is collectivized, with rice and corn the main crops. Individuals are allowed to grow small plots for household use.

People. North Koreans' background is essentially the same as that of South Koreans. Racial origins are Tungusic (Mongol and Chinese). Between 1925 and 1940, many South Koreans worked in the industrial sections of the N. They returned S after 1945 when the peninsula was divided between US and Soviet spheres. Korean is the official language. There are two writing styles, one phonetic and the other based on Chinese characters. Confucianism was the dominant religion until 1945. Literacy is 90%.

Government. North Korea is controlled by the Communist Labor party (KLP) headed by a premier and a Supreme People's Assembly.

History. Korea was a semi-independent state with Chinese ties until conquered by Japan in 1910. After the defeat of Japan in WWII, Korea was separated along the 38th parallel into US and Soviet zones; the USSR occupation was N of the parallel. Numerous efforts to unite the countries failed, and observed elections to determine choice of government were allowed only in the S. On Aug. 15, 1948, the S portion became the Republic of Korea. The Soviets established the

Democratic Republic of Korea in the N. In 1950 North Korean forces invaded South Korea. The United States aided the Republic, while Communist countries assisted the N. The war ended in a stalemate in July 1953. From 1953, North Korea continued, under Premier Kim Il Sung, its criticism and harassment of South Korea while developing its economy and taking a gradually fuller role in world affairs. In 1980, however, talks between North and South Korea were held to discuss closer ties. The same year Kim Chong Il, son of Kim Il Sung and his apparent political heir, was appointed to the Politburo and by 1985 was influential in several areas of government. Although contacts with the S improved by the mid-1980s, relations remained strained.

PROFILE

Official name: Democratic People's Republic of Korea
Area: 46,540 sq mi (120,539 sq km)
Population: 19,000,000
Density: 408 per sq mi (158 per sq km)
Chief cities: Pyong Yang (capital); Hamhung
Government: Communist People's Assembly
Religion: none
Language: Korean
Monetary unit: Won
Gross national product: $10,400,000,000
Industries:' cement, coke, iron, ferro alloys, textiles
Agriculture: rice, barley, wheat, soybeans, cattle, fish, sweet potatoes, yams
Minerals: tungsten, magnesite, lead, zinc, pyrite, cement, iron ore, copper, gold, phosphate, salt, coal
Trading partners: USSR, People's Republic of China

Korea, Republic of, independent nation in NE Asia, known as South Korea. It occupies the S portion of the Korean peninsula. It is a racially mixed society; its main crop is rice.

Land and economy. Located on the peninsula projecting SE from China, South Korea is a 600-mi (966-km) long by 135-mi (217-km) wide mountainous area below the 38th parallel, with harbors on its W and S coast. Seoul, the Republic of Korea's capital, sits in the NW central part of the country. The climate is hot and humid in the summer, dry in the winter. Poor in natural resources, lacking skilled workers, and densely populated, Korea still suffers from the after-effects of the Korean War. Economic growth was impeded by 1974–75 oil price increases, which caused inflation. About 25% of the gross national product comes from agriculture, fishing, and forestry; about 20% of the land is arable; and 80% is devoted to grain, especially rice. Coal provides Korea's fuel requirements and is also exported. Since 1960 production of textiles, footwear, and electronics for export has increased dramatically. About 25% of South Korea's budget is allocated to defense expenditures. The United States has supported Korea with military and civilian aid.

People. High in population density, Korea is an ethnically homogenous society. Descended from the Tungasics (Mongols with Chinese mixture), the people are concentrated in the fertile valleys of the S and the urban Seoul section. More than 600,000 Koreans live in Japan. Korean is the national language, with English developing as the 2nd tongue. Literacy is rated at 85%. About 16% of the population practices Buddhism and Shamanism; Confucianism is a cultural influence. There are about 2,000,000 Christians.

Government. Authority is vested in the president, who is elected by direct secret ballot. The constitution provides for an elected unicameral National Assembly.

History. Legend has it that Korea's founder was of divine origin; Korea's calendar starts with the founding date of 2333 BC. When it was unified in AD 7th century, it had been a semi-independent state much influenced by China. In 1910, Japan annexed Korea. After WWII, the 1945 Potsdam Conference divided Korea into Soviet and US occupation zones. Unification efforts failed, and on June 25, 1950, North Korean forces invaded the South. The United States helped South Korea, and Chinese Communists aided the North. The war ended in a stalemate on July 27, 1953. Syngman Rhee was Korea's first president (1948–60); riots caused by allegations of election irregularities deposed him. In a 1961 military coup, Maj. Gen. Park Chung Hee took power. He consolidated his power and was elected to three terms as president. During the late 1970s opposition to his increasingly repressive regime grew, and he was assassinated by the head of the Korean Central Intelligence Agency in 1979. The military assumed control and soon faced popular opposition and civil rioting. In 1981 martial law was lifted and Chun Doo Hwan, who had held power since 1979, was elected president. Although his cabinet was plagued by scandal and corruption, he stressed moral purity and integrity. The choice of Seoul for the 1988 Summer Olympics was resented by North Korea, with which overall relations were somewhat eased. Opposition to the authoritarian government of Chun Doo Hwan sparked increased demonstrations during 1985 and 1986.

PROFILE

Official name: Republic of Korea
Area: 38,031sq mi (98,500sq km)
Population: 37,000,000
Density: 973 per sq mi (376 per sq km)
Chief cities: Seoul (capital); Pusan; Inchon
Government: Republic
Religion: Buddhism, Shamanism, Christianity
Language: Korean
Monetary unit: Won
Gross national product: $16,800,000,000
Industries: rubber products, glass products, electronics, petrochemicals, clothing, plywood, processed food, furniture, ships, fertilizers
Agriculture: rice, barley, wheat, tobacco, soybeans, fish, forests, yams
Minerals: tungsten, coal, iron ore, bismuth, graphite, cement
Trading partners: United States, Japan

Korean War (1950–53), conflict primarily between the United States and the Republic of Korea (South Korea) on one side and the Democratic People's Republic of Korea (North Korea) and the People's Republic of China on the other side. When Japanese occupation of Korea ended at the close of World War II, the country was divided along the 38th parallel. The north came under the influence of the Soviet Union and the south under the influence of the United States. On June 25, 1950, troops from North Korea invaded the south. President Harry S. Truman reacted swiftly by committing US ground, sea, and air power to the defense of South Korea. The United Nations also condemned North Korea's action and placed token forces of 15 other nations under US command. President Truman named General Douglas MacArthur as supreme commander.

After initial victories by the North Korean forces, the UN forces counterattacked, staged an amphibious landing at Inchon, and drove the Communist forces from the south. The UN forces pursued the Communists into the north, captured Pyongyang, the capital, on October 19, and by the middle of November had driven the forces almost to the Yalu River, which separates Korea and China. That incursion into North Korean territory had been made with the intention of unifying the two Koreas, despite a warning from China that it would not countenance such a move. In November 1950 a Communist counteroffensive was launched, this time with hundreds of thousands of Chinese troops, who streamed across the border. In the bloodiest fighting of the war, the tide again changed, and the UN forces were driven back into the south and Seoul, the South Korean capital, was retaken by the Communists. After months of fierce fighting, the battle lines were drawn more or less along the 38th parallel, where they remained until the end of the war.

General MacArthur was opposed to Truman's policy of containing the war so as to avoid a major land war in China. After MacArthur made public statements in favor of carrying the war into China, Truman fired him for insubordination on April 10, 1951, and replaced him with Gen. Matthew B. Ridgway. On July 10, 1951, General Ridgway began truce talks with North Korea. By now the goal of unifying Korea had been discarded, and the United States aimed at keeping the 38th parallel as the border. The talks dragged on, with sporadic fighting alternating with cease-fires, until July 27, 1953, when an armistice was finally signed. The two Koreas remained independent of each other with a 2.5mi (4km) demilitarized zone carved out between them. Casualties in the war were high. The United States suffered 54,000 men killed and 100,000 wounded. The losses of the two Koreas and China were several times that figure.

Korematsu v. United States (1944), US Supreme Court decision that upheld the constitutionality of the Japanese evacuation and encampment program ordered by Pres. Franklin Roosevelt early in World War II to combat a "potentially grave danger to public safety." The court justified the incarceration of US citizens without the rudiments of due process protections as "an emergency war measure," but many commentators criticized the court for succumbing to mass hysteria generated by the war, and the decision was overturned in 1983.

Koriyama, city in N central Honshu, Japan, on Abukuma River. Scene of heavy damage during WWII. Industries: machinery, textiles, chemicals. Pop. 241,673.

Kornberg, Arthur (1918–), US biochemist, b. Brooklyn, N.Y. He shared the 1959 Nobel Prize in physiology or medicine for his work on the synthesis of deoxyribonucleic acid (DNA), the hereditary material of most cells, and ribonucleic acid (RNA), the hereditary material of some viruses. In 1982, he and a team of scientists successfully reproduced DNA.

Koryaks, Paleo-asiatic people who inhabit the Koryak National Okrug in the Soviet Far East. Linguistically related to the Chukchi, the Koryaks are nomadic fishermen and reindeer herders who have undergone some Soviet collectivization.

Kosciusko, Thaddeus (1746–1817), Polish patriot and soldier. Championing the ideals of French liberal philosophy, he came to America in 1776 to fight with the Revolutionary army. He became an aide to Gen. Washington and was granted American citizenship. Returning to Poland in 1784, he was a major general in the army (1789). After the second partition of Poland in 1793, he led a revolutionary movement to regain Polish independence. Initially successful (he became the dictator of Poland), the invading armies of Russia and Prussia proved too strong. Kosciusko was imprisoned (1794–96) and exiled. He believed in the equality of men and liberated his serfs. He contributed the property granted him by the US Congress for the education of black Americans. Kosciusko worked for Polish independence from his various places of exile until his death.

Kosciusko, Mount, peak in Australian Alps; winter sport resort. Highest peak in Australia, 7,316ft (2,231m).

Kosice, city in E Czechoslovakia, on Hernád River, 135mi (217km) NE of Budapest; formerly part of Hungary, it became part of Czechoslovakia 1920 by Treaty of Trianon; site of 14th–15th-century Gothic Cathedral of St Elizabeth, and 14th-century Franciscan monastery. Industries: iron, steel, petroleum refining. Chartered 1241. Pop. 136,397.

Kossuth, Lajos (1802–94), Hungarian leader. He entered the National Diet in 1830 and quickly made a name for himself as a fiery, eloquent advocate of autonomy for Hungary, within or independent from the Austrian Empire. He was imprisoned for his political activities between 1837–40. After a successful campaign for a separate constitution for Hungary, he was named finance minister in 1848 in the new government. He led the insurrection of July 1848 and was appointed virtual dictator of Hungary. In 1849 he was named president of an independent Hungary, but his army was crushed by the Austrians with Russian help. He was forced to flee to Turkey. He traveled to the United States where he was hailed as a liberator. He lived in England and Italy, refusing amnesty as late as 1890. After his death his body was returned to Budapest and buried in state.

Kostroma, city in Russian SFSR, USSR, on W bank of Volga River at the mouth of the Kostroma River; annexed by Moscow 1364; scene of election of Michael Romanov as tsar in 1613; site of 16th-century Ipatyev Monastery and the Uspenky Cathedral (1250). Industries: linen, metallurgy, ship repairing, plywood, footwear. Founded 1152. Pop. 251,000.

Kosygin, Aleksei N(ikoloevich) (1904–80), Soviet political figure, premier (1964–80). Elected to the Communist party Central Committee (1939) and Politburo (1948), he was removed in 1953 but regained his seat in 1960. After Khrushchev's fall (1964), he became premier and second in command to Leonid Brezhnev. He was considered mainly an economic administrator.

Krafft-Ebing, Richard von (1840–1902), German psychiatarist. His *Psychopathia Sexualis* (1886) described sexual pathologies and did much to bring discussions of the sex drive into the open. He also was one of the first physicians to conclude that general paresis was caused by syphilis.

Krait, SE Asian snake of the cobra family, with potent venom. The blue krait and black-and-yellow banded krait are common. Length: to 4ft (1.2m). Family Elapidae; genus *Bungarus*. *See also* Cobra.

Krakatoa (Rakata), small volcanic island in center of Sunda Strait, Indonesia, between Java and Sumatra. Violent eruption, and ensuing 50ft (15m) tidal wave, killed 36,000 people in 1883 and produced atmospheric effects experienced around the world for months afterward. During 1960s it was again active.

Krakow (Crakow), city in S Poland, on the Vistula River; capital of Krakow prov. City was made a bishopric *c.* 1000; Polish royal residency 1300–1600; taken by Sweden in 1655 and by Austria in 1795; made independent state in 1815; retaken by Austria in 1846; made part of independent Poland after WWI; site of Polish Academy of Sciences, University of Krakow (1364), Jagiellonian University, several museums and galleries containing Rennaissance art. Industries: steel mills, metals, chemicals, electrical equipment, rail equipment. Founded *c.*700. Pop. 583,000.

Kraków, Poland: Wawel Castle

Kremlin, Moscow

Kudu

Krasnodar, city and port in Russian SFSR, USSR, on E bank of Kuban River, 160mi (258km) S of Rostov-na-Donu; capital of Krasnodar Krai; site of Worker's Scientific Institute. Industries: food processing, oil refining, machine tools, textiles, metalworking. Founded 1794 by Catherine II. Pop. 560,000.

Krasnoyarsk (Krasnojarsk), city and riverport in S Central USSR, on W bank of upper Yenisei River; capital of Krasnoyarsk Krai. Founded 1628 by the Cossacks as a fort, it was frequently attacked in later 17th century by Tartars and other tribes; became capital of Yeniseisk government 1822; site of Siberian Institute of Forestry. Industries: shipbuilding, heavy machinery, cement, lumber, flour milling. Pop. 781,000.

Krebs, (Sir) Hans Adolf (1900–81), British biochemist, b. Germany. He shared with F. A. Lipmann the 1953 Nobel Prize in physiology and medicine for his discovery of the citric acid cycle, the process that results in the production of energy in living organisms. He was knighted in 1958.

Krebs' Cycle, or **Citric Acid Cycle,** final stage in the oxidation of food to produce energy, occurring in the mitochondria of living cells. Acetyl coenzyme A is converted to hydrogen atoms and carbon dioxide by a cyclic sequence of enzyme-catalyzed reactions. The hydrogen atoms undergo further oxidation in the electron transport (respiratory) chain, during which energy in the form of ATP is produced and water is formed.

Krefeld, city in W West Germany, on Rhine River, 19mi (31km) WSW of Essen. An important linen-weaving center until it passed to Prussia in 1702, it developed into center of silk industry when given monopoly by Frederick II. Industries: textiles, steel, dyes, machinery. Chartered 1373; inc. neighboring Verdingen 1929. Pop. 227,100.

Kreisky, Bruno (1911–), Austrian chancellor (1970–83). A socialist who escaped to Sweden after the German annexation of Austria in 1938, he returned to his homeland in 1951, becoming secretary of state in the foreign ministry in 1953. He was foreign minister (1959–66), before becoming chancellor of Austria in 1970. Under his leadership, Austria gained prosperity and social stability. His invitation to PLO leader Yasir Arafat for meetings in Vienna in 1979 was a diplomatic attempt to reach a settlement in the Middle East.

Kremlin, The, the historic nucleus of Moscow; a 90-acre (36.5-hectare) site bounded by the Moscow River and Kremlin Quay (S), Red Square and Lenin's tomb (E), Moscow Historical Museum and St Basil's Cathedral (W), and old Alexander Gardens (S). The term "kremlin" is a medieval expression meaning the walled central section of any town; several other old cities retain theirs, but Moscow's is the most famous. Its walls were completed between 1485–95 and are adorned with 20 different towers. Within the walls several cathedrals face onto a central square. Along the walls are palaces and museums. The largest building, the Great Kremlin Palace (1838–49), was the tsar's Moscow residence. It now houses the Supreme Soviet (parliament) of USSR and Communist party conventions. In 1955 the Kremlin was opened to the public.

Krill, shrimp-like marine crustaceans ranging in size from a fraction of an inch to several inches. They live in the open ocean, from the surface down to a depth of more than 1 mile (2 km). Krill feed on microplankton and diatoms. They in turn are a chief food of baleen whales and fish.

Krishna, most celebrated hero of Hindu mythology, who in his youth performed labors similar to those of Heracles. He slew the king of the Hayas and demons of Putana and Dhenuka, carried off a princess and conquered Saubha, with trickery and deceit typical of folk heroes. He is generally depicted in a bejeweled sari and conical crown carrying a flute.

Krivoy Rog (Krivoj Rog), city in SE central Ukrainian republic USSR, 80mi (129km) SW of Dnepropetrovsk on the Ingulec and Saksagan rivers; rich iron producing region. Burial mounds (8th–4th century BC) indicate Scythians inhabited area and made use of iron ore. Germans occupied area 1941–44 and destroyed most of mining installations. Industries: foundries, coal mining, steel, chemicals, cement, coke. Founded 17th century. Pop. 573,000.

Kropotkin, Pëtr A(lekseevich) (Prince) (1842–1921), Russian anarchist. Jailed for seditious propaganda in St Petersburg in 1874, he escaped into exile in 1876. Again jailed in France in 1883–86 for anarchist activities, he lived in London after 1886, returning to Russia after the March 1917 revolution. Supporting Kerensky and the war against Germany, he denounced Bolshevik centralism and forcible suppression of opposition. A prolific author, he wrote *Memoirs of a Revolutionist* (1899).

Kruger, (Stephanus Johannes) Paulus (1825–1904), Boer political figure also known as Oom Paul. He helped settle the Transvaal, and after its annexation by the British (1877), he worked for independence and served as president (1883–1900). He organized continuing resistance to British rule and defeated the Jameson Raid of 1895, designed to capture Transvaal. During the Boer War (1899–1902) he represented the Boers in Europe, where he died.

Krugersdorp, city in NE Republic of South Africa, 20mi (32km) W of Johannesburg; site of Pardekraal monument (1838), an annual pilgrimage center, technical college, Sterkfontein Caves; important gold mining center for Witwatersrand. Named in honor of Stephanus Johannes Paulus Kruger. Industries: gold, uranium, manganese, asbestos, lime. Founded 1887. Pop. 91,202.

Krupp Family, German industrial family, particularly prominent in steel and arms manufacturing. **Alfred Krupp** (1812–87) expanded his father's small iron foundry into a giant industry. He was the first steelmaker to install the Bessemer process and was one of the leaders in the industrial development of the Ruhr valley. His son **Friedrich Alfred Krupp** (1854–1902) expanded into shipbuilding and the manufacture of chrome and nickel steel alloys and armor plate. Krupp had the monopoly of German arms manufacture during World War I. Among its products was Big Bertha, a monstrous but inaccurate train-borne gun that shelled the Paris area from a distance of 70 mi (113km). Under Friedrich's son-in-law, **Gustav von Bohlen und Halbach** (1870–1950), who assumed the Krupp name, the Krupp works were a mainstay of the Nazi war effort. His son **Alfried Krupp** (1907–67) was imprisoned for his war activities and required to sell a portion of his Krupp interests. Alfried's son Arndt decided not to enter the business, and it passed from family control.

Krypton, gaseous nonmetallic element (symbol Kr) of the noble-gas group, first discovered 1898. Krypton is present in the Earth's atmosphere (0.00015% by volume) and is obtained by the fractionation of liquid air. It is used in fluorescent lamps. The meter is defined by the wavelength of an emission line in the krypton spectrum. Chemically it is extremely inert but it does have

a well-defined difluoride. Properties: at. no. 36; at. wt. 83.8; density 3.733 g dm^{-3}; melt. pt. −249.88°F (−156.6°C); boil. pt. −242.14°F (−152.3°C); most common isotope Kr^{84} (56.9%). *See also* Noble Gases.

K2. *See* Godwin-Austen.

Kuala Lumpur, city in S Malay Peninsula, Malaysia, 200mi (322km) NW of Singapore; capital of Malaysia, Selangor state, and largest city of the Malay Peninsula. Made capital of the Federated Malay States (British protectorate 1895), Federation of Malaya 1948, and Federation of Malaysia 1963, it is site of University of Malaya (1949) and 4,000-acre (1,628-hectare) industrial estate. Industries: tin, rubber. Founded 1857 as a tin mining camp. Pop. 500,000.

Kublai Khan (1216–1294), Mogul emperor (1260–94). Grandson of Genghis Khan, in 1279 he completed the conquest of China, deposing the Sung dynasty and founding the Yuan dynasty that would rule until 1368. His attempt to conquer Japan failed (1281) when his fleet was destroyed by a typhoon. He respected and encouraged Chinese scholarship and art. He brought economic prosperity through vast public works projects and the encouragement of trade. Marco Polo visited his court at Peking.

Kudu, Nyala, Sitatunga, and **Bushbuck,** several species of striped antelopes native to Africa south of the Sahara. All females are hornless. Greater kudu, the largest, stands 51in (130cm) at shoulders, with wide, spiraling horns and long fringe of hair from chest to neck. Lesser kudu is smaller without a neck fringe. There are two species of nyala—one in SE Africa, one in the Ethiopian mountains. The former has a conspicuous black belly fringe. The secretive bushbuck is smaller, with short horns and habits similar to the North American white-tailed deer. Sitatunga is a large swamp-dweller, feeding on aquatic vegetation. Family Bovidae; genus *Tragelaphus*. *See also* Antelope.

Kuei-yang (Kweiyang, Guiyang), city in SW China, 220mi (354km) S of Chungking; capital of Kweichow prov. Rail center; site of Kweichow University. Industries: cement, paper, textiles, chemicals, petroleum products. Pop. 1,500,000.

Kuhn, Richard (1900–67), Austrian-German chemist. He became professor at Heidelberg and was awarded a Nobel prize in 1938 for his work on the synthesis of vitamins A and B$_2$. He was forced by the Nazis to decline the prize and had to await the end of the war to receive the honor.

Kuibyshev (Kuybyshev, or **Kujby'šev),** city and river port in SE Russian SFSR, USSR, on left bank of Volga River at mouth of Samara River; capital of Kuibyshev oblast; scene of Pugachev's rebellion against Catherine II (1773–74); seat of anti-Bolshevik provincial government and Russian constituent assembly; during WWII, when Moscow was threatened by German army, Kuibyshev became temporary capital; site of university (1919). Industries: automobiles, aircraft, ballbearings, flour milling, oil refining. Founded 1586. Pop. 1,047,-000.

Kuiper, Gerard Peter (1905–73), Dutch-born US astronomer, b. Harenkarspel, Netherlands. He emigrated in 1933. One of the most influential authorities on the solar system, he has made important discoveries about the outer planets and advanced the condensation theory of planetary genesis.

Kukai (774–835), real name Kobo Daishi, founder of the Shingon school of Japanese Buddhism. He renounced Confucianism, studied in China, and in the *Ten Stages of Consciousness* (830) showed a systematic grasp of major Oriental religions. His monastery at Mt Koya is the base for Shingon sects with followers numbering about 8,000,000.

Ku Klux Klan, secret white supremacy organization. First founded (1866) in Pulaski, Tenn., after the Civil War, it used intimidation and terror in an attempt to establish white supremacy in the South and to prevent newly enfranchised blacks from voting. Its trademark was the white hood and robe that its members wore. The chief executive of the Klan is the Grand Wizard (Nathan Bedford Forrest is believed to have been the first). It was formally disbanded (1869) and in 1870–71 the Ku Klux Klan Acts were passed to aid enforcement of the 14th and 15th Amendments. The Klan was revived in Georgia (1915) by William J. Simmons. It was anti-immigrant, anti-Catholic, and anti-Jewish, as well as white supremacist. It was prominent in the 1920s when membership reached 5,000,000. After a series of newspaper exposés, membership declined until it was about 9,000 in 1930. After World War II, Samuel Green again revived the Klan. The Klan continued operations in the 1970s but had no national importance. *See also* Force Acts.

Kumamoto, city in W central Kyushu, Japan, approx. 75mi (121km) S of Kitakyushu; capital of Kumamoto prefecture. An important castle town under Hosokawa daimyo 1632–1868, it became trade center for agricultural products; site of Buddhist temple, Kumamoto Medical University. Industries: food processing, marketing, textiles, chemicals. Pop. 488,000.

Kumasi, city in central Ghana, approx. 115mi (186km) NW of Accra; capital of Ashanti Region; 2nd-largest city in Ghana. Flourished as capital of Ashanti kingdom from 18th century; besieged by British 1874, 1896, and 1900; annexed by Britain 1901, after violent native uprising; industrial development spurred by construction of railroad *c.*1901 to major ports on Gulf of Guinea; seat of Kumasi College of Technology (1951). Industries: cacao, handcrafts, lumbering. Pop. 275,000.

Kumquat, hardy evergreen tree or shrub *(Fortunella)* of the rue family. Growing to 15ft (4.6m), they yield a small citrus fruit, orange when ripe. The shrubs are often grown for ornament and the fruit is used to make jelly or marmalade.

Kun, Béla (1885–1937), Hungarian Communist political leader. An associate of Lenin and a Bolshevik from his youth, he received training in Moscow after his release from a Siberian prisoner-of-war camp. In 1919, after replacing Mihály Károlyi as premier, he changed the newly formed republic into the Hungarian Soviet Republic, introducing radical changes in the government. Defeated with the help of the Romanians, he fled to Vienna and later to the Soviet Union in 1920.

Kung, Hans (1928–), Swiss Roman Catholic theologian. He was ordained in 1954 and became professor of theology at West Germany's Tübingen University in 1960. He served as advisor to the Second Vatican Council (1962–65) and became the first important Roman Catholic theologian to question the doctrine of papal infallibility, the divinity of Christ, and the dogma of the Virgin Mary, for which he was censured by the Vatican (1979) and forbidden to teach Catholic theology. Tübingen at first sought to remove him from the faculty in 1980 but then agreed to a compromise settlement.

Kung Fu, a martial art, a generic term referring to the many styles of Chinese infighting. Although it was developed in Canton, China, as *gung fu,* its acceptance as an Oriental concept of self-defense is questionable.

Kunlun, central Asian mountain system lying between the Himalaya and the Tien Shan ranges; forms natural boundary between N Tibet and Torim basin of Sinkiang; sparsely settled by nomads. Highest peak is 25,348ft (7,731m). Length: 1,000mi (1,610km).

Kunming (K'un-ming), city in S China, 380mi (612km) SW of Chungking, on N shore of Lake Tien, on Burma Road; capital of Yunnan prov.; on railroad line to Hanoi and N Vietnam. A strategic area during WWII, it was used as US air base, and Chinese military headquarters; seat of university (1934). Exports: fur, tea, precious stones, tin. Industries: iron, copper smelting, textiles, chemicals, machinery, electrical equipment, food processing. Pop. approx. 1,100,000.

Kuomintang or **Nationalist Party,** the ruling political force in China from 1928 until 1949 and subsequently in Taiwan. Initially a secret revolutionary alliance against Manchu rule in China, it became an open political party in 1912 and was reorganized with Leninist structure and discipline by Sun Yat-sen in 1924 with the aid of Soviet advisers. Sun provided the Kuomintang with the program and doctrine that remain the basic program of the Nationalists in Taiwan. Sun was later succeeded by Chiang Kai-shek as head (1938–75) and by Chiang Ching-Kuo (1976–).

Kurchatovium, *See* Element 104.

Kurdistan region of SW Asia, including parts of E Turkey, NE Iraq, NW Iran, and small sections of NE Syria and Soviet Armenia. It extends N to S from the Aras River and Turkish border with Armenian republic, SSR, USSR, to Diyala Tributary of Tigris River in Iraq, and E to W from mountains of Iran W of Hamadán to Tigris River. In the 7th century the Kurds were converted to Islam by the conquering Arabs. They were under the control of Seljuk Turks in 11th century, Mongols from 13th–15th centuries, and then became part of the Ottoman Empire. When this empire was liquidated by Treaty of Sèvres in 1920, Kurdistan was to become autonomous, but Kurdish demands were not met. The people are nomadic herders, with some farming in the valleys of the high mountains. Area: 74,000sq mi (191,668sq km). Pop. 2,750,000.

Kurds, people who inhabit Kurdistan, a geographical region consisting of the adjacent mountain areas of Turkey, Iraq, and Iran. They are seminomadic pastoralists as well as sedentary farmers cultivating wheat and cotton. Although the latter have lost many tribal characteristics, Kurdish national feeling remains strong.

Kurgan, city in Russian SFSR, USSR, on Tobol River, 140mi (225km) E of Chelyabinsk; capital of Kurgan oblast; site of Neolithic burial mounds (*c.* 6,000 BC); trading center for farm products. Industries: agricultural machinery, electrical equipment, machine tools, food processing. Founded 17th century. Pop. 310,000.

Kuril (Kuril'skije) or **Kurile Islands,** chain of 30 large and many smaller islands extending 750mi (1,208km) from S Kamchatka Peninsula to NE Hokkaido, Japan, separating Sea of Okhotsk from Pacific Ocean. Of volcanic origin, the islands have active volcanoes and many earthquakes. Islands were discovered 1634 by Martin de Vries, Dutch navigator; Russian fishermen occupied N islands; Japanese fishermen occupied S islands. In 1875, Russia withdrew from islands in exchange for Japan's surrender of Sakhalin. Since end of WWII, dispute over ownership of islands has been major reason for failure of Japan and USSR to sign peace treaty. Industries: whaling, vegetables. Highest peak is Atlasova volcano, 7,674ft (2,341m) on Atlasova Island. Area: 6,020sq mi (15,592sq km). Pop. 15,000.

Kuroshio Current, also called the Japan current. It is the western boundary current of the North Pacific gyre and flows along the east coast of the Japanese islands. It is comparable to the Gulf Stream along the east coast of North America.

Kursk, city in Russian SFSR, USSR, at confluence of Tuskoc and Seim rivers. An old city, it was destroyed by Mongols 1240 and rebuilt as a frontier post 1586. Important WWII victory for USSR occurred nearby (1943). Industries: chemicals, synthetic fibers, shoes, electrical equipment. Founded 1095. Pop. 382,000.

Kush or **Cush, Kingdom of,** former state in Nubia. Lasting roughly 1100 BC to AD 350, it conquered Egypt in the 7th–8th centuries BC. It was thereafter defeated by the Assyrians and moved its capital to Meroë in the Sudan. After Roman and Arab attacks in the north, Meroë was captured by the Axumites around AD 350, and the Kushites are thought to have fled west, possibly to the Lake Chad area.

Kutch, Rann of, large salt marsh, W India; site of battles between India and Pakistan in 1965 and 1971.

Kutuzov, Mikhail I(larionovich) (1745–1813), Russian general. Supreme commander against Napoleon, he met and withstood the enemy at Borodino (1812). Then, after abandoning Moscow, he forced the French to retreat in winter through desolate territory, harrying them by guerrilla warfare. A brilliant leader, he became a field marshal in 1812.

Kuvasz, guard and herding dog (working group) brought to eastern Europe from Tibet in the 15th century. It has an elongated head with straight muzzle; V-shaped ears held close to the head; medium-length body, quite broad across the back; medium-length legs; and long tail carried low. The white, medium-length double coat covers slate gray or black skin. There is a mane on the neck and chest; feathering on legs; and short smooth hair on head, ears, and paws. Average size: 28–30in (71–76cm) high at shoulder; 100–115lb (45–52kg). *See also* Working Dogs.

Kuwait (Al-Kuwait), State of, independent Arab state in NE corner of the Arabian peninsula on the Persian Gulf. A leading oil producer, its people enjoy the world's highest per capita GNP.

Land and economy. Except for Al-Jahrah Oasis and a few fertile sections in the SE and coastal areas, the country is almost entirely desert. The vast majority of the population is concentrated in the cities. Kuwait has about 15% of the world's petroleum reserves, and oil dominates the economy. The sharp increases in oil prices in 1974 sent the country's economy skyrocketing. The government has utilized its huge financial resources to create a welfare state with no taxes and free medical care, education, and social security.

People. The people are predominantly Arab, and Arabic is the official language. Islam is the official religion. More than half of the people are literate and with expanded free educational facilities, the literacy rate is rapidly increasing. Almost half of the people are non-Kuwaiti workers from Iran, Pakistan, and other Middle Eastern countries.

Government and history. A constitutional monarchy, the country is governed by an emir and a 50-member National Assembly. Founded in 1756 by members of the al-Sabah dynasty, Kuwait is still ruled by the family today. In 1899 a treaty was drawn up in which Great Britain administered foreign relations and protected the territorial rights. Kuwait became independent in 1961, and shortly thereafter Iraq lay claim to the country. Through a protection agreement with the United Kingdom, Kuwait requested and received British troops to forestall the Iraqis. Since then, relations between Kuwait and Iraq have improved, and Kuwait supported Iraq in the war against Iran in the 1980s. Kuwait joined the United Nations in 1963. Since 1967, Kuwait has granted considerable economic aid to developing Arab nations. The oil industry was completely nationalized in 1975. Kuwait's refusal to release Shiite terrorist prisoners held for embassy bombings (1983) provoked violence, including an assassination attempt on Emir Jabir al-Ahmad Al Sabah in 1985.

PROFILE

Official name: State of Kuwait
Area: 6,200sq mi (16,058sq km)
Population: 1,266,000
Density: 204 per sq mi (79 per sq km)
Chief city: Kuwait (capital)
Government: constitutional monarchy (emirate)
Religion: Islam (official)
Language: Arabic (official)
Monetary unit: Kuwaiti dinar
Gross national product: $21,870,000,000
Per capita income: $15,970
Industries (major products): light and heavy petroleum and petroleum products
Minerals (major): crude petroleum, natural gas
Trading partners (major): Japan, United States, Great Britain, West Germany, Saudi Arabia, Iran

Kuznets, Simon (1901–), US economist, b. Russia. He developed the national income accounting system in the 1930s. The Kuznets cycle, an intermediatebusiness cycle of about 20 years duration, was discovered by and named after Kuznets. He received the 1971 Nobel Prize in economics for his research on the economic growth of nations.

Kuznetz (Kuzneck) Basin, basin of W Siberia, USSR, between Kuznetz Ala-Tau range and Salair Ridge, often called Kuzbas. Rich coal and iron ore deposits discovered 17th and 18th centuries have made it a major industrial region. Area: 10,000sq mi (25,900sq km).

Kwakiutl, major tribe of North American Indians speaking the Wakashan tongue, and closely related to the Bellabella. From a total population of 3,500 in 1600, they presently number some 2,500, occupying Queen Charlotte and northern Vancouver islands in British Columbia. They are the classic "potlatch" people, whose wooden sculpture and totem poles are world famous.

Kwangju, formerly Koshu; city in SW Korea; capital of South Cholla prov.; railroad and educational center. Industries: textiles, rice milling, rayon, beer. Pop. 502,753.

Kwangtung (Guangdong), southernmost prov. in China, on South China Sea; Canton is the capital. Prov. has an 800-mi (1,280-km) coastline with approx. 730 islands, Hainan being the largest. The British community of Hong Kong and Portuguese colony of Macao lie on the coastal Pearl River estuary. After 211 BC, Kwangtung came under Chinese suzerainty; it was an important center for China's early trade and foreign contacts, mainly through Canton, which had seen Arab, Hindu, and Parsi trade for centuries, and after

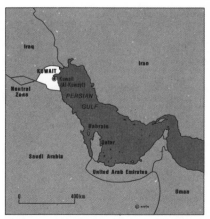

Kuwait

Kyoto: Silver Pavilion

Labor Movement: AFL-CIO

L

*c.*1650 European contacts through Portuguese traders. Prov. was scene of unrest during Chinese Revolution (1911); city was occupied by Japanese (1938–45) during Sino-Japanese War. Area: 89,344sq mi (231,401sq km). Pop. approx. 42,800,000.

Kwashiorkor, meaning "displaced child," is a disease of infants and young children occurring primarily in the tropics or subtropics and caused by a diet deficient in high-quality protein and calories. Children with the disease show retarded growth, mental apathy, anemia, fatty liver, digestive and skin disorders, and changes in skin pigment, with thick patches that may become pinkish and virtually raw.

Kweichow (Guizhou), prov. in S China, bounded by provinces of Szechwan (N), Hunan (E), Yunnan (W),and by Kwangsi Chuang autonomous region (S); capital is Kweiyang. In the rural area the population includes mostly Miao aboriginal tribesmen, who were cast out of other provinces because of their unwillingness to accept Chinese customs; they are noted for their embroideries. Kweichow came under Chinese suzerainty 10th century; during WWII it served as military base for Chinese and Allied forces. Area: approx. 67,181sq mi (173,999sq km). Pop. approx. 17,140,000.

Kyd (Kid), Thomas, 1558–94, English playwright, friend of Christopher Marlowe. His play *The Spanish Tragedy* (*c.* 1585) was the first "blood and revenge" drama, similar to Shakespeare's *Hamlet.* It was later revised by Ben Jonson. Kyd may have written a lost play suggesting *The Taming of the Shrew.*

Kyoto, city in W central Honshu, Japan, approx. 26mi (42km) NE of Osaka; capital of Kyoto prefecture; early center of silk industry; site of the imperial residence for over 1,000 years, containing palaces, shrines, and other early structures. Modern city is site of Kyoto University (1897), Doshisha University, Kyoto University of Industrial Arts and Textiles (1949). Industries: lacquerware, porcelain, embroidery, precision tools and machines, food processing, metals. Pop. 1,461,000.

Kyprianou, Spyros (1932–), president of Cyprus. He became foreign minister of Cyprus in 1960, when Archbishop Makarios became president of the new republic, resigning in 1972 under pressure from Greece's military government. In 1976, he became speaker of the House of Representatives and served in that post until Makarios' death (1977). He then served as acting president until he was elected president in 1978 and again in 1983.

Kyushu, island of S Japan, 3rd-largest and southernmost of four principal Japanese islands. Terrain is mountainous, with irregular coast forming many natural harbors; the Chikugo River, longest on Kyushu, irrigates the NW rice growing region. Most densely populated of the Japanese islands, its industrial cities include Kitakyushu, Kumamoto, Kurume, Fukuoka; chief port is Nagasaki, first to be opened to Western trade. Crops: rice, tea, tobacco, fruits, soybeans. Industries: mining, textiles (silk), porcelain, metals, machinery. Area: approx. 16,205sq mi (41,971sq km). Pop. 12,072,179.

Kyzyl (Kizil) Kum Desert, desert in Uzbek and Kazakh SSR, USSR, between Amu Darya and Syr Darya rivers. Irrigated agriculture is carried on in river valleys; semi-nomadic tribesmen raise caracul sheep in sparsely vegetated desert. Area: 115,000sq mi (297,858sq km).

Labor, in childbirth, the normal delivery of the fetus at the end of pregnancy. The first stage, lasting 2 to 10 hours, is measured from the onset of contractions that occur at 5-minute intervals lasting at least 30 seconds each. During this stage the cervix dilates up to 4in (10cm). Transition follows as the cervix is almost fully dilated, leading to the second stage when dilation is full. This stage may last from 30 minutes to 2 hours, at the end of which the infant is born. The third stage takes about 5–10 minutes, and is the period from birth to delivery of the placenta.

Labor, Department of, US federal cabinet level department within the executive branch. The Labor Department administers and enforces statutes benefiting wage earners, improving their working conditions, and providing opportunities for employment. The department is headed by the secretary of labor. It was established in 1884 as the Bureau of Labor in the Department of the Interior. In 1903 it was part of the Department of Commerce and Labor; in 1913 it became a separate department.

Labor Force, all members of the population who are working, looking for work, or have a job (even if they are currently not at work because they are on vacation, sick, on strike, etc). In the United States, labor force statistics are gathered by the Department of Labor, Bureau of Labor Statistics.

The absolute size of the labor force varies with the time of the year and with economic conditions. Normally the labor force expands in the summer as schools close and contracts in the fall as schools open. In recessions, when employment opportunities are limited, many people leave the labor force (ie, they stop looking for work) and return to it when jobs are available. The size of the labor force is an important measure of the health of the economy.

Labor Movement in the United States, historic attempt of working people to improve working conditions and their economic position. Unlike their European counterparts, which have often worked for a change in the governmental system to socialism or Communism, US labor unions and their members have generally accepted capitalism. Members of craft unions, organized on a trade or occupational basis in the late 18th century, could be fined or imprisoned when employers, using English common law, accused them of criminal conspiracy. The Supreme Court restricted use of this doctrine in 1842, and thereafter the legality of unions depended on the means they employed to gain better worker conditions. The National Labor Union, formed in 1866, and the Knights of Labor (1869) included trade unions, suffragettes, farmers' organizations, and other reform groups of diverse goals; each soon foundered. Samuel Gompers, learning from their mistakes, organized the American Federation of Labor (AFL) in 1886; membership was restricted to skilled laborers only and the AFL had the pragmatic goals of raising wages, improving work conditions, honoring contracts, and instigating collective bargaining.

The struggle between management and labor often erupted into violence, as when police and labor protestors were killed in the Haymarket Massacre (1886) in Chicago. The federal government did not remain neutral, and federal troops were used against strikers when violence broke out in response to the govern-

ment's use of the Sherman Antitrust Act against the American Railway Union. Opposed by the federally backed employers on one side and the more radical Industrial Workers of the World (IWW) on the other, the AFL nonetheless grew to include 4,000,000 workers by 1920. Another 1,000,000 belonged to unaffiliated unions, including the railroad brotherhoods. The influence of the federal government over labor-management relationships enhanced labor's prestige during World War I, but during the prosperity of the 1920s union membership decreased. Under President Franklin D. Roosevelt's New Deal policies in the 1930s, a series of laws, including the National Labor Relations (Wagner) Act (1935), made organizing easier. The right to join a union and the duty of employers to bargain with workers were ensured. This stimulated organization on an industry-wide basis, including workers formerly excluded from the craft unions. When the automobile, steel, and other mass-production industrial unions were expelled from the AFL, they created the Congress of Industrial Organizations (CIO) in 1938.

Rivalry between the CIO and AFL and labor's increased power during World War II stimulated union growth until 14,000,000 workers were organized by 1945. George Meany, president of the AFL, and Walter Reuther, president of the CIO, negotiated a merger in 1955, and by then 17,500,000 workers were in unions. Because of apathy at the local union level, power often became concentrated in the hands of a few national leaders. Amid charges of corruption, union power was curbed by the Taft-Hartley Act of 1947 and the Landrum-Griffin Act of 1959. Membership in the AFL-CIO declined, partly due to the expulsion of allegedly corrupt unions such as the International Brotherhood of Teamsters, and partly due to the growing percentage of the white collar workers (traditionally difficult to organize) in the work force. Young workers in the 1960s saw the unions as unsympathetic to their concerns with civil rights, war, and pollution. Future growth will depend on organized labor's ability to adapt to the needs of white-collar, female, minority, and young workers. Labor has shown some success in these areas, and there has been increased unionization among teachers, government employees, and health and farm workers. Economic downturns in the late 1970s and early 1980s weakened the bargaining power of unions.

Labour Party, British socialist political party with financial and institutional links with trade unionism. Established under this name in 1906, the Labour party rapidly gained strength, joining World War I coalition governments and subsequently becoming the official opposition, eclipsing the Liberal party. Ramsay MacDonald formed the first, short-lived Labour administration (1924). In power (1929–31) with Liberal support, and as part of Churchill's World War II administration (1940–45), Labour took office alone in 1945 under Clement Atlee with an extensive program of reconstruction, nationalization, and expanded social welfare services. Thirteen years in opposition (1951–64) adjusted Labour's policies to postwar affluence and gained support outside its traditional working-class base. The party returned to power under Harold Wilson (1964–70, 1974–76) and James Callaghan (1976–79).

Labrador, region in Newfoundland, E Canada; bordered by NE Quebec (W and S) and Labrador Sea (E); the coastal region is indented with fjords, the mountains becoming increasingly higher toward N; the inland plateau is heavily forested, with innumerable lakes and rivers, notably the Churchill River, which drains into Lake Melville. The coast was known to the Norsemen *c.* 10th century, and was visited by John Cabot (1498) and Corte-Real (1500); came under Great Britain by Treaty of Paris 1763; boundaries between Newfound-

Labrador Current (Arctic Current or Arctic Stream)

land and Quebec under dispute 1809–1927 when matter was settled by British Privy Council; became part of Canada 1949. Industries: lumbering, fishing, mining. Area: 112,826sq mi (292,219sq km). *See also* Newfoundland.

Labrador Current (Arctic Current or Arctic Stream), current of N Atlantic Ocean, flows S from Baffin Bay along coast of Labrador, E Canada, to meet the Gulf Stream in the Grand Banks area of NW Atlantic Ocean; the meeting of the cold water and ice flow from Labrador current with the warm waters of the Gulf Stream causes dense fogs in this area.

Labrador Retriever, water dog (sporting group) developed in Newfoundland around 1822. Strongly built, it has a wide head; long, powerful jaws; a wide nose; low-set, hanging ears; short, wide body; and medium-length legs. The distinctive tail, thick at the base and tapered to a point, is carried up. The hard, dense coat is short; colors are black, yellow, or chocolate. Average size: 22.5–24.5in (57–62cm) high at shoulder; 60–75lb (27–34kg). *See also* Sporting Dog.

Lac, a secretion of the lac insect, *Laccifer lacca,* deposited on tree twigs. Sticky and resinous, it is harvested in Asia mainly for use in shellac and red lac dye. From 17,000 to 90,000 insects are needed to produce 1lb (454g) of shellac. Lac products have been used in India since 1200 BC.

Lacaille, Nicholas Louis de (1713–62), French astronomer noted for mapping the constellations visible from the Southern Hemisphere and naming many of them. In 1750 he led an expedition to the Cape of Good Hope. There, over a period of two years, he mapped the position of 10,000 stars, giving them all catalog numbers. His *Star Catalog of the Southern Sky,* still in use, was published in 1763.

Laccolith, an intrusive igneous rock body that forms a dome over the strata which it has penetrated. The base is typically horizontal while the upper surface is convex. Generally under 10mi (16km) in diameter with thicknesses of 100–3,000ft (30–915m), they contain more acidic than basic rocks. The Henry Mountains of Utah have a well-known laccolith.

Lacewing, or aphid lion, delicate green insect found worldwide. It is found on grass and weeds, feeding on aphids. Length: 0.5–1in (13–25mm). Order Neuroptera; family Chrysopidae. *See also* Neuroptera.

Lac Insect, scale insect found in tropical and subtropical areas. The Indian *Laccifer lacca* is found in SE Asia and India and is the major source of lac for the production of shellac and varnishes. The female scale lives in a resinlike cell and is capable of producing a layer of lac 0.5in (13mm) thick. Length: to ⅛in (3mm). Family Lacciferdae. *See also* Scale Insect.

La Coruña, seaport city in Spain, on Atlantic Ocean; capital of La Coruña prov. Captured 1370 by Portugal, it was launching point of Spanish Armada 1588; destroyed by Sir Francis Drake 1589; taken by French 1823, and by Carlists 1836. Industries: wine, linen, hams, sardines, leather. Area: (prov.) 3,041sq mi (7,876sq km). Pop. (city) 189,654; (prov.) 1,004,188.

Lacquer, paint that forms a film by loss of solvent by evaporation. The film is usually composed of a cellulose ester (such as nitrocellulose) in combination with an alkyd resin and the solvent may be a ketone (such as methylbutyl ketone), an alcohol, or some other cellulose solvent.

Lacquerware, objects such as furniture and utensils painted with lacquer, which is the painting medium derived from the resin of the *Rhus vernicifera,* a tree common in Japan and China. Lacquer is applied in several layers. When dry, the durable surface is hard and impervious to water.

Lacrimal Gland, protective accessory organ of the eye that produces tears. Located in the orbital cavity in a slight depression, the gland produces, under autonomic nervous control, slightly germicidal tears that flow through ducts to the surface of the eye to lubricate it.

La Crosse, city in W Wisconsin, at confluence of Mississippi, Black, and La Crosse rivers; seat of La Crosse co; site of Wisconsin State University (1909), Viterbo College (1931), Western Wisconsin Technical Institute. Industries: dairying, farm equipment, air conditioning units, beer, rubber, truck trailers. Founded late 18th century as French fur trading post; inc. 1856. Pop. (1980) 48,347.

Lacrosse, a fast-action ball game, popular in the United States and in Canada, where it is the national

game. It is played by two teams of 10 persons each on a field 110yd (100m) long and 60–70yd (55–64m) wide. In Canada there are 12 players on a side; in box lacrosse, 6 on a side. Each team defends a goal 6ft wide and high (1.8m) at one end of the field and scores points by putting the ball in the opponent's goal (1 point). A game consists of four 15-minute periods, plus two 5-minute overtime periods if a regulation game ends in a tie. Each player carries a stick, or crosse, with an adjustable meshwork head. The hard rubber ball, at least 7.75in (19.7cm) in circumference, is kept in play by being carried, passed, or hit with the stick, or rolled, or kicked. Only the goalkeeper may touch the ball with his hands. Besides the goalkeeper, each team has three attack players, near the opponent's goal; three midfielders, who play on both attack and defense; and three defensemen, near their own goal. Players wear protective pads and masks. Defensive play consists of impeding attacking players by body checking or taking the ball away. Rule infractions for various kinds of rough play result in personal fouls, for which the player must leave the game for 1–3 minutes, and expulsion fouls, for which the player is suspended for the game. Minor infractions are technical fouls, resulting in the ball's loss or the player's suspension for 30 seconds.
Lacrosse was developed by Canadian Indians as baggataway; each side sometimes had as many as 1,000 men. French Canadians adopted the sport, calling it *la crosse* for the netted stick's resemblance to a bishop's crosier. The game's modern rules were framed in the 1860s by William G. Beers, who promoted it vigorously. Long played primarily in eastern colleges, the game's US popularity grew rapidly from the 1960s. *See also* Box Lacrosse.

Lactation, the act of secreting and producing milk to feed young. After hormonal-induced breast enlargement during pregnancy, a pituitary hormone (prolactin) stimulates breast cells to begin secreting milk. The milk "comes in" the breast's lactiferous ducts leading to the nipple in from 1 to 3 days after delivery and then is stimulated by suckling, which, in turn, triggers neural and hormonal changes that control and maintain lactation. *See also* Breast.

Lactic Acid, colorless optically active syrupy liquid (formula $CH_3CHOHCOOH$) formed from lactose in milk by the action of bacteria; used in foods and beverages, in tanning, dyeing, and adhesive manufacture. Properties: sp gr 1.2; melt. pt. 64.4°F (18°C); boil. pt. 251.6°F (122°C).

Lactogenic Hormone, or prolactin, polypeptide hormone produced by the pituitary gland. It stimulates secretion of milk by the mammary gland following delivery of the baby.

Ladino, a dialect of Spanish spoken by the descendants of Jews who were exiled from Spain in 1492. Prior to World War II it was spoken by Jews in a number of countries in E and S Europe, the N coast of Africa, and the Western Hemisphere. Today most Ladino speakers live in either Turkey or Israel.

Ladislas I (1040?–95), king of Hungary (1077–95), son of Bela I. Heroic and beloved, he reestablished internal order after dealing with barbarian and German invasions and a recurrence of paganism. Known for his wise laws, he also subjugated Bosnia, Croatia, and part of Transylvania. He was canonized by the Roman Catholic Church in 1192.

Ladislas I (or IV) Lokietek (1260–1333), king of Poland (1320–33). He became duke of Poland as Ladislas IV in 1296 and worked to unite Poland. After wars lasting from 1305–12, he united Great and Little Poland. Crowned in 1320, he introduced legal reforms. As an ally of the Teutonic Knights, he saved Danzig from Brandenburg, but later warred with the Knights from 1327 to 1333.

Ladislas II (or V) Jagello (1350–1434), grand duke of Lithuania (1377–86) and king of Poland (1386–1434). As grand duke he opposed the Teutonic Order (1377–86) and then married Jadwiga, queen of Poland, which led to his election as king and his acceptance of Roman Catholicism. His lands stretched from the Baltic to the Black Sea and almost to Moscow. With Lithuanians, he defeated the Teutonic Knights at Tannenberg (1410). Poland became a great power during his reign.

Ladoga (Ladožskoje), lake in NW European USSR; largest lake in Europe. Formerly divided between Finland and USSR, since 1947 it has been entirely within USSR. It is drained by Neva River which empties into Gulf of Finland; canals along S part of lake connect Leningrad with Caspian Sea. During WWII, the lake's frozen surface was a lifeline for supplying Leningrad during winter months (1941–43). Island of Valaam (one of many) in lake is site of 12th-century Russian monastery. Area: 7,000sq mi (18,130sq km).

Ladybird Beetle, or ladybug, lady beetle, beetle that typically preys on aphids, scale insects, and other plant pests. They are about the size and shape of a small split pea, and are tan, red, or black with red, black, yellow, or white markings. Because they have big appetites and reproduce rapidly, they are a beneficial insect. Family Coccinellidae.

Lady Fern, feathery fern found in temperate areas of the world in moist, shady places. The 30in (76cm) leaves are 10in (25cm) wide and grow in circular clusters. Height: to 36in (91cm). Family Aspliniaceae; species *Athyrium filix-femina. See also* Fern.

Laertes, in Greek mythology, king of Ithaca and father of Odysseus. It was on his funeral canopy that Penelope worked to delay her selection of a suitor in the *Odyssey.*

Laetrile, a highly controversial drug claimed by some to be effective in arresting cancerous growth or in bringing symptomatic relief to cancer patients. The chief component of laetrile is amygdalin, a substance found in the pits of apricots, bitter almonds, and related fruits. The US Food and Drug Administration has found no evidence that laetrile is effective in cancer treatment.

Lafayette, Marie Joseph Paul Yves Roch Gilbert du Motier, Marquis de (1757–1834), French officer, statesman, and hero of the American Revolution. Sympathetic to the American cause, he arrived in Philadelphia in 1777 and was commissioned a major general. He was wounded at Brandywine and wintered at Valley Forge (1777–78) with Washington. In 1778–80 he was in France negotiating for financial and military aid. In 1781 he distinguished himself in the Yorktown campaign that led to Cornwallis' surrender. He returned to France in 1781, but made a visit to the United States in 1784. In 1789 he first became a member of the States-General, then the National Assembly. After the fall of the Bastille in that year he was appointed commander of the militia. He lost his popular support when in 1791 he ordered his troops to fire on a crowd petitioning for the abolition of the monarchy. In 1792 he led an army in the Austrian campaign, but was relieved of his command after the overthrow of the monarchy. He fled France and was imprisoned by the Austrians until released on Napoleon's demand in 1797. He lived in retirement until the Restoration (1814) when he became a member of the Chamber of Deputies. He made a triumphant visit to the United States in 1824–25. In 1830 he played a major role in the July Revolution, supporting the moderates and favoring Louis Philippe's ascendancy.

Lafayette, city in S Louisiana, 55mi (89km) WSW of Baton Rouge; seat of Lafayette parish; site of University of Southwestern Louisiana (1900) and Heyman Oil Center, headquarters for numerous oil companies. Industries: lumber, oil, natural gas, sashes, doors, concrete pipes, sugar refining, packing plants. Founded 1770s by Acadians fleeing Nova Scotia; inc. as town 1836, as city 1914. Pop. (1980) 81,961.

Lago di Como. See Como, Lake.

Lagoon, the shallow stretch of seawater protected from waves and tides of the ocean by energy-absorbing sand or coral barriers. Lagoons lie roughly parallel to the coast and are often stagnant. They receive sediment from both streams and the ocean which forms thick muddy deposits. Thus they support abundant plant and animal life.

Lagos, capital city of Nigeria, in SW Nigeria, on Atlantic coast approx. 75mi (121km) SW of Ibadan, occupying Lagos Island and mainland areas; capital of Lagos state. City grew as Yoruba settlement 17th through 19th centuries, coming under British control 1861 after years of Portuguese exploitation through slave trade; became capital of independent Nigeria 1960. Modern city has undergone an industrial-commercial boom, attracting a young population and creating housing and sanitation problems; has an excellent harbor; site of international airport, National Museum. Industries: brewing, ship repair, food processing, textiles, rubber products. Pop. 1,060,848.

Lagrange, Joseph Louis (1736–1813), French mathematician. Educated at Turin, Lagrange became professor of mathematics there before his appointment as head of the Berlin Academy on Leonhard Euler's recommendation. Later appointments and honors were numerous. He created the calculus of variations, devised a mathematical analysis of perturbations in gravity, and made contributions in many other areas, including the mathematics of sound and mechanics.

Lagrangian Points, or positions, points in space where a small body, influenced by the gravitational

Marquis de Lafayette

Battle of Lake Erie: Oliver Perry

Jean Baptiste Lamarck

attraction of two larger ones, will tend to remain at rest relative to them. In such a three-body system, the most stable of these positions, originally postulated (1772) by J. L. Lagrange, are the two points where the small body occupies one vertex of an equilateral triangle with the larger ones at the other two.

Lahore, city in E Pakistan, on the Ravi River near Indian border; capital of Punjab prov.; commercial and industrial center. Lahore was settled in ancient times; important city during Ghazni and Ghuri sultanates (11th–12th centuries); increased in importance as part of the Sikh kingdom (1767); passed to Britain 1849; site of the Shalamar Gardens, several impressive tombs and a mosque, University of Punjab (1882), and a military cantonment. Industries: iron, steel, textiles, rubber, gold and silver jewelry. Pop. 2,148,000.

Lahti, lakeport city in S central Finland, on the Päyänne lake system; site of 1912 city hall designed by Eliel Saarinen. Industries: beer, clothing, furniture. Chartered as city 1905. Pop. 89,360.

Laing, R(onald) D(avid) (1927–), Scottish psychiatrist. His unusual views about mental illness have gained him international attention as the "philosopher of madness." Laing holds that the mentally ill are not necessarily abnormal, that a psychosis may be a reasonable reaction to the stresses of the world. His books include *The Divided Self* (1965), *Politics of the Family* (1971), and *The Voice of Experience* (1982).

Laissez Faire, policy advocating governmental noninterference in the economic sphere. A reaction to the tight controls of mercantilism, laissez faire was described by Adam Smith in *Wealth of Nations* (1776). He envisioned a free enterprise system based on private ownership that, if guided by individual initiative and unhindered by bureaucracy, would develop a "natural" and beneficial economic order. Unprecedented industrial growth in the late 19th century led to a concentration of economic power and to demands that big business be subject to governmental regulation. *See also* Mercantilism.

Lake, an inland body of water, generally of considerable size and too deep to have rooted vegetation completely covering the surface. Lake water has a low concentration of dissolved materials and it freezes at 0° C rather than having the indefinite freezing properties of sea water. The expanded part of a river and a reservoir behind a dam are also termed lakes.

Lake Charles, port of entry and city in SW Louisiana, on Lake Charles; connected with Gulf of Mexico by a 30mi (48km) channel; seat of Calcasieu parish; site of McNeese State College (1939) and Sowela Technical Institute; shipping center for oil, lumber, rice, cotton. Industries: oil refining, chemicals, rubber, concrete pipe. Settled 1852; inc. 1867; chartered as city 1886. Pop. (1980) 75,051.

Lake District, region of NW England, in Cumbria, containing the principal English lakes. Its spectacular mountain and lakeland scenery and its associations with William Wordsworth and Samuel Coleridge make it a major tourist attraction. Highest point is Scafell Pikes, 3,210ft (979m). Among its 15 lakes are Derwentwater, Grasmere, Hawes Water, Buttermere, Windermere. Interesting ruins in district are Druids Circle at Keswick, ancient castles and churches, remains of Roman occupation. Lake District National Park was est. 1951. Area: 80,000acres (32,370hectares).

Lake Dwellings, the remains of prehistoric settlements built on piles found within the margins of lakes

in Germany, Switzerland, Italy, and France. A lacework of tree trunks across the piles formed the platform on which were erected huts with clay floors. Cattle and sheep were also raised on the platform. Archeologists have established a culture sequence (from the Neolithic into the Iron Age) for Central Europe based on sequences of lake dwellings one upon the other.

Lake Erie, Battle of (1813), War of 1812 battle in which the US fleet under Cmmdr. Oliver H. Perry defeated British Capt. Robert Barclay's fleet near Put-In-Bay, Ohio. The victory gave the United States control of Lake Erie cutting off supplies to British troops in the area. Perry's report, "We have met the enemy and they are ours," made him a national hero.

Lakeland Terrier, hunting dog (terrier group) bred in England's Lake District. The Lakeland's narrow build is suited to its purpose—squirming through rocky dens after game. The head is rectangular; ears V-shaped and folded; body narrow; legs long, to run with hounds; and docked tail carried straight up. The hard, wiry coat is fairly long with furnishings on muzzle and tail; colors include blue, black, liver, red grizzle, and wheaten. Average size: 14.5in (37cm) high at shoulder; 17lb (7.6kg). *See also* Terrier.

Lake of the Woods, lake in Canada, SE of Montreal, and W of Ontario; receives Rainy River, and is drained by the Winnipeg River. Length: 70mi (113km). Width: 60mi (97km).

Lake Poets, term first occurring in the *Edinburgh Review* of 1807, referring to English poets Samuel Taylor Coleridge, Robert Southey, and William Wordsworth. They spent much time together in the Lake District; however, only Wordsworth was deeply influenced by the locality, having been born there.

Lakewood, suburban city in S California, NE of Long Beach. Inc. 1954. Pop. (1980) 74,654.

Lakewood, residential town in N central Colorado, in Jefferson co; suburb of Denver. Pop. (1980) 112,848.

Lakewood, city in NE Ohio, 5mi (8km) W of Cleveland on Lake Erie. Industries: bolts, screws, conveying equipment. Settled as East Rockport; renamed in 1889; inc. as city 1911. Pop. (1980) 61,963.

Lakshmi, or Lakshmi-Sri or Padma, in Hindu mythology, the lotus goddess, wife of Vishnu, who existed at the beginning of creation floating on the rolling ocean, borne by a lotus leaf. Lakshmi was worshiped as a fertility goddess of the soil and the family. She is depicted sitting or standing on the lotus, holding a lotus, or symbolically as the lotus.

Lamaism, Western term for the religion of Tibet. It is a mixture of Mahayana Buddhism and Tibet's pre-Buddhist Bonism. King Srong-tsen Gampo (*c.* 620–50) sent to China and India for Buddhist teachers. The Bon priests opposed the new ways, but Buddhism was reintroduced into Tibet in the 8th century by the Indian scholar Padmasambhava. There are now two sects, Red Hat and Yellow Hat. The Dalai Lama, a member of the Yellow Hat, became revered as the "Living Buddha" and the spiritual and temporal ruler of Tibet. Each new Lama is considered a reincarnation of the one before him. In 1950 the Chinese occupied Tibet. In 1959 the Tibetans tried a revolt that failed, and the 14th Dalai Lama fled. In 1979, the Chinese invited him to return if he would guarantee cooperation with them. He refused.

Lamarck, Jean Baptiste Pierre Antoine de Monet, Chevalier de (1744–1829), French biologist. He promoted theories of biological transformation, asserting that acquired characteristics are heritable. His theory, known as Lamarckism, influenced evolutionary thought throughout most of the 19th century. Proposed in 1809 in *Philosophie zoologique,* Lamarckism maintains that new biological needs of an organism promote a change in habits from which develop new structures that are then transmitted to offspring as permanent characteristics. The giraffe, for example, would develop a long neck in order to reach needed food in the form of leaves high on a tree. The theory caused much debate and was eventually rejected, although followers of Michurin and Lysenko in the Soviet Union held similar theories until recently.

Lamartine, Alphonse-Marie Louis de (1790–1869), French Romantic poet. His *Méditations poétiques* (1820), containing psalms, odes, and moving elegies, won him fame and patronage in a diplomatic career. Later poems, collected in *Récueillements poétiques,* echoed his liberal political position, which culminated in his becoming a hero of the 1848 Revolution with his oratory and his *Histoire des Girondins.*

Lamb, Charles (1775–1834), English essayist and poet. He collaborated with his sister Mary Ann (1764–1847) in *Tales from Shakespeare* (1807). He contributed regularly to the *London Magazine* (1820–23), in which his *Essays of Elia* first appeared.

Lambda Particle. *See* Hyperon.

Lame Duck, term used to describe an officeholder between the time he is defeated for reelection and the time his successor takes over. Before ratification of the 20th Amendment (also known as the "Lame Duck Amendment") in 1933, Congress and the president held office until the March following a November election. Newly elected officials now assume office in January.

Lamentations, biblical book by the prophet Jeremiah discussing Israel's desperate situation and the beginning of the exile.

La Mesa, city in S California, 8mi (13km) NE of San Diego; trade center for surrounding farm areas. Inc. 1912. Pop. (1980) 50,342.

Laminar Flow, fluid flow without turbulence. In laminar flow, the fluid flows in layers in a predictable way. As the velocity increases, or as the viscosity of the fluid decreases, a point is reached at which laminar flow breaks up into turbulent flow, marked by the existence of eddies. For a given fluid this point occurs at a certain value of the Reynolds number.

Lamprey, also sea lamprey, lamprey eel, eel-like, jawless fish found in marine waters on both sides of the Atlantic and in the Great Lakes. Adults spawn in fresh water and are brown, green, red, or blue above and whitish below. Lampreys live in salt water and attach themselves by mouth to other fish, sucking their blood. Length: to 3ft (91cm); weight: to 2.25lb (1kg). There are 8 genera and 25 species including sea lamprey *Petromyzon marinus.* Family Petromyzondiae. *See also* Cyclostome.

Lanai, island in central Hawaii, W of Maui; it was purchased in 1922 by a pineapple company and developed as a pineapple growing center. Highest point is Mt Lanaihale, 3,370ft (1,028m). Area: 141sq mi (365sq km).

Lancashire, county in NW England, bordered by Irish Sea (W), Cumbria (N), North and West Yorkshire (E), Greater Manchester and Merseyside (S); drained by the Lune and Ribble rivers. Lancaster is co seat; Blackpool and Blackburn are the major towns. It lost much of its area and the majority of its pop. with the co reorganization in 1974. Area: 1,175sq mi (3,043sq km). Pop. 1,369,250.

Lancaster, House of, English royal line. The dynasty was founded by Edmund "Crouchback," earl of Lancaster (1245–96), the second son of Henry III. On the death of Edmund's son Henry, 1st duke of Lancaster (1361), the Lancastrian titles and lands passed to his daughter, Blanche, and her husband, John of Gaunt. Their son, Henry Bolingbroke, became Henry IV (1399) on deposing Richard II. He was the first of England's three Lancastrian kings. Bolingbroke's son, Henry V, died (1422), leaving his heir, Henry VI, a child. Dissensions during the regency (1422–42) and Henry VI's feebleness as king weakened the Lancastrians, encouraging Yorkist claims to the throne and leading to the Wars of the Roses (1455–85).

Lancaster, city in SE Pennsylvania, on the Conestoga River; seat of Lancaster co. A rich agricultural area in Pennsylvania Dutch country, it served as state capital 1799–1812; site of Wheatland, home of Pres. James Buchanan (built 1828 and a national shrine since 1962), Franklin and Marshall College (1787), Lancaster School of the Bible (1933), Evangelical Lutheran Church of the Holy Trinity (*c.* 1760), and Old City Hall (1795). Industries: linoleum, watches, radio tubes, cigars, razors, tools. Settled by German Mennonites 1709; inc. as borough 1742, as city 1818. Pop. (1980) 54,725.

Lancelet. *See* Amphioxus.

Lan-chow (Lanzhou, or Lan-chou), city in NW China, on S Yellow River, near Great Wall; capital of Kansu prov.; nearly destroyed by earthquake 1920, since rebuilt; under Chinese Communist control 1949. A major transportation center, it is beginning of Silk Road that leads to central Asia; served by many railroads; seat of university (1946), teachers' colleges. Industries: food processing, cement, textiles, leather goods, fruits, tobacco, livestock, dairy products, oil refineries, chemicals. Pop. approx. 1,450,000.

Landau, Lev Davidovitch (1908–68), Soviet physicist. His many contributions included the basic theories describing ferromagnetism and liquid helium. In the 1930s he calculated the way in which the atoms in small regions (called domains) of a substance like iron line up in a magnetic field, creating the strong effect known as ferromagnetism. In the 1940s and 1950s he created the theory that underlies the superfluid behavior of liquid helium. He received the Nobel Prize in physics in 1962.

Land Crab, crab found in tropical America, W Africa, and Indo-Pacific with gills placed in carapace cavities to breathe air. A forest floor scavenger, it migrates to water to breed. Size: to 12in (30cm) across back. Family Gecarcinidae. *See also* Crab.

Land Dyak, or Dayak, indigenous people of SW and C Borneo. Based on subsistence agriculture, hunting, and fishing, their society is remarkably classless, with both matrilineal and patrilineal descent. The inhabitants of whole villages live in a single communal long house. A complex, animistic, polytheistic religion is practiced and Western influence so far has been slight.

Land-Grant College, one of many US institutions that were financed by the Morrill Act of 1862 or later federal laws. The 1862 act allowed states to sell federal land to fund colleges that were to teach "agriculture and the mechanic arts." Later acts provided more federal aid. The land-grant colleges pioneered in providing low-cost higher education and in establishing research and public service as functions of colleges. Many developed into major state universities.

Land-Grant Railroads, railroads financed and built by sale of public lands to encourage railroad construction. Beginning with the first grant made in 1850, over 155,000,000 acres (63,000,000 hectares) were granted. In return, the railroads agreed to transport US property and troops without charge. This was later adjusted to a 50% reduction of commercial rates and discontinued in 1946.

Landscape Painting, the artistic painting of natural outdoor scenes. In the West it began in approximately the 14th century with the frescoes at the pope's palace in Avignon (*c.*1343). In the East landscape art had been perfected by the 8th century. Landscapes held a major place in Flemish and Italian art of the Renaissance, culminating in the works of Rembrandt and Leonardo da Vinci. The 19th century also saw great English landscape painters such as Turner and Constable, the Impressionists in France, and the Hudson River School in the United States. In the 20th century general interest in landscape painting has declined, although a number of artists have continued to make it their main concern (eg, the American John Marin).

Land's End, extreme W point of England in SW Cornwall; the Longships lighthouse is just offshore. The peninsula's scenery is a tourist attraction.

Landslide or **Landslip,** noticeable slip or fall of a mass of earth or rock. The phenomena are classed according to the angle of the slide and the type of material that is descending and whether or not it is wet. Landslides are frequently the indirect result of man's activities such as road or dam construction, both of which undercut rock formations and their support structures. *See also* Avalanche.

Landsteiner, Karl (1868–1943), US pathologist, b. Austria. He distinguished four different blood types, later labeled A, B, AB, and O, and paved the way for scientific blood transfusion. He showed that blood of some groups is incompatible with that of others and that if incompatible bloods are mixed they will form clotlike lumps. His findings explained why some transfusions of blood in the past had been beneficial, while others had been fatal. He won the Nobel Prize in physiology or medicine (1930) and later helped to identify the RH factor.

Lanfranc (*c.*1005–89), archbishop of Canterbury. A Benedictine in 1041, he became head of the celebrated monastery school of Bec, France, in 1045. He was a trusted counsellor of William the Conqueror and *c.* 1063 became abbot of St Stephen's, Caen. After his consecration at Canterbury (1070), he made his diocese dominant over the others and replaced Saxon prelates with Normans, bringing the English Church closer to the reforms of Pope Gregory VII.

Lange, Christian Louis (1869–1938), Norwegian peace maker. He worked for the Nobel Committee (1900–09) and the International Parliamentary Union (1909–33) and represented Norway in the League of Nations. An advocate of disarmament, he received the Nobel Peace Prize in 1921 (with Karl Branting).

Lange, David Russell (1942–), New Zealand political leader, prime minister 1984– . After earning a law degree from the University of Auckland he worked in London before returning to practice law in Auckland. He lost a bid for a seat in Parliament (1976) but ran successfully in 1977, becoming deputy party leader (1979) and Labour party president (1983). He became New Zealand's youngest prime minister of the century (1984), promising to work to reduce the country's deficit, halt the rise in unemployment, and refuse New Zealand's port facilities to nuclear-armed ships.

Langmuir, Irving (1881–1957), US chemist, b. Brooklyn, N.Y. With the General Electric Company, he pioneered the development of gas-filled tungsten light bulbs, invented the atomic blowtorch, and made extensive studies in surface chemistry. He was awarded a Nobel Prize in 1932, being the first US chemist to be so honored.

Language, the sum total of sounds and signs (written alphabet, hieroglyphs, ideographs) by which human beings communicate facts, ideas, feelings. All human languages consist of words and rules for their use and combination. Linguistics studies the structure and history of languages and has distinguished from 2,500 to 5,000 different languages. A language, in this sense, is the particular form that verbal communication has among a geographically and culturally distinct people.

Langur, or leaf monkey, 15 species of medium to large monkeys of S Asia and East Indies that feed mainly on leaves. They are slender and have long hands and tails. Gregarious, day-active tree dwellers, they are found from sea level to snowy Himalayan slopes at an elevation of 13,000ft (4,000m). Length: 16–31in (41–79cm). Family Cercopithecidae; genus *Presbytis*. *See also* Monkey.

Lanier, Sidney (1842–81), US musician and poet, b. Macon, Ga., whose verse reflects Southern social change and the rhythms and thematic development of music. In 1867 Lanier published his first novel, *Tiger-Lilies*. Publication in 1875 of "Corn" and "Symphony," poems dealing with agricultural conditions in the South and industrial conditions in the North, respectively, brought him national recognition. Subsequent important poems include "The Song of the Chattahoochee" (1877), "The Marshes of Glyn" (1878), and "The Revenge of Hamish" (1878). Series of lectures were later published as *The Science of English Verse* (1880), *The English Novel* (1883), and *Shakespeare and His Forerunners* (1902). He was a flutist in Baltimore's Peabody Orchestra and a teacher of English literature at Johns Hopkins University.

Lanolin, a purified fatlike substance derived from sheep's wool and used with water as a base for ointments and cosmetics.

Lansing, capital city of Michigan, 50mi (81km) WSW of Flint on Grand River; site of original Michigan State University (1850), now in East Lansing, Lansing Community College (1957). Industries: automotive parts, trucks, tractors, tents, awnings. Settled by 1840 by New Yorkers; made state capital 1847; inc. 1859. Pop. (1980) 130,414.

Lantern Fish, marine fish found in Atlantic and Mediterranean. Identified by light organs along sides, it is found in deep water during the day and near the surface at night. Length: 1–6in (2.5–15.2cm). Family Myctophidae; species 150, including *Myctophum punctatum*.

Lantern Fly, tropical and subtropical plant hopper with a wingspread often exceeding 6in (152mm). Its long head has a hollow part, formerly thought to emit light. Family Fulgoridae. *See also* Homoptera.

Lanthanide Elements, or **Rare Earths,** series of rare metallic elements with atomic numbers between 57 and 71. They are: lanthanum, cerium, praseodymium, neodymium, promethium, samarium, europium, gadolinium, terbium, dysprosium, holmium, erbium, thulium, ytterbium, and lutetium. Their properties are similar and resemble those of lanthanum from which the series takes its name. They occur in monazite and other rare minerals and are placed in group IIIb of the periodic table. All form trivalent compounds (some also form divalent and quadrivalent compounds). *See also* Periodic Table.

Lanthanum, metallic element (symbol La) of the Lanthanide group, first identified in 1839. Chief ores are monazite (phosphate) and bastnasite (fluorocarbonate). The metal is used in lighter flints. Properties: at.no. 57; at. wt. 138.9055; sp gr 6.15 (25°C); melt. pt. 1688°F (920°C); boil. pt. (6,249°F) (3,454°C); most common isotope La^{139} (99.91%). *See also* Lanthanide Elements.

Lanugo, soft woolly hair that covers the human fetus and that of other mammals during development. It is shed and virtually disappears at birth.

Lanús, city in E Argentina, 6mi (10km) S of Buenos Aires; administrative center; site of technical school. Industries: textiles, paper, chemicals, rubber products, tanneries. Pop. 375,428.

Laocoön (*c.* 2nd century BC), marble sculpture group. It illustrates the myth of the Trojan priest who objected to his people's bringing the wooden horse within the city walls and so angered the gods who sent two large serpents to kill him and his two sons. The sculpture was discovered on the Esquiline hill in Rome in 1506 and is now in the Vatican Museum.

Laos (Lao), independent nation in SE Asia. Its development has been hampered by geography and a low-level economy. For six centuries a monarchy, it fell to the Pathet Lao Communist forces in 1975.

Land and economy. Located in the very center of the SE Asian peninsula, Laos borders on five nations: China (N), Vietnam (E), Cambodia (S), Thailand (S and W), including 500mi (805km) along the Mekong River, and Burma (NW). Covered with jungles and mountains, Laos has no access to the sea. Its three-season climate is monsoonal. With natural resources largely unexplored, 85% of the population is engaged in subsistence farming. Exports are primarily tin, timber, and coffee. Almost all manufactured products are imported.

People. Laos' sparse population is concentrated along the Mekong River valley. The Lao majority is descended from a SW Chinese people, the Tai, who migrated in the 13th century. Mountain tribes without a common language or tradition inhabit the central and S regions. Theravada Buddhism is the principal religion, while the mountain tribes are animist. Lao is the dominant language. French is the language used in schools, and many tribes speak dialects never recorded. Literacy is about 25%.

Government. Laos has been ruled as a Communist people's republic since 1975. The king and other former regime leaders remained as advisors until 1977.

History. United in the 14th century under King Fa Ngum, Laos was the object of centuries-long invasions by neighboring countries. Siam ruled in the 19th century, France beginning in 1883, Japan in WWII, and France again in 1946. In 1949, Laos received full sove-

Irving Langmuir

Sidney Lanier

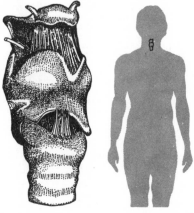

Larynx

reignty within the French Union and, in 1953, complete independence. Conflicts among the conservative Royalists, Communists (Pathet Lao), and neutralists kept the country at war. In 1962 a coalition government named neutralist Prince Souvanna Phouma as premier. In 1964 the Communist forces, with aid from Communist North Vietnamese troops, seized Laotian territory, and in 1971 the United States bombed their supply line through Laos (Ho Chi Minh Trail). In 1973 a coalition government with the Pathet Lao was formed. In 1975 the coalition was dismantled, and the monarchy was succeeded by the Communist Pathet Lao regime. Since then, although relations with the US have improved, Laos has retained close ties with Vietnam and has been affected by Vietnam's involvement in the turmoil of SE Asia.

PROFILE

Official name: People's Democratic Republic of Laos
Area: 91,428sq mi (236,799sq km)
Population: 3,427,000
 Density: 37 per sq mi (15 per sq km)
Chief city: Vientiane (capital)
Government: Communist people's republic
Religion: Theravada Buddhism
Language: Lao (dominant), French
Monetary unit: Liberation Kip
Gross national product: $220,000,000
Per capita income: $100
Industries: opium, cigarettes, textiles
Agriculture: coffee, rice, maize, tobacco, cotton, poppies, citrus fruits, teak, cardamon
Minerals: tin
Trading partners: Malaysia, Singapore, Thailand, Japan

Lao Tzu (c.604–c.531 BC), Chinese philosopher. According to Chinese legend he founded Taoism, a religion which became a mystical reaction to the moral-political concerns of Confucianism (Buddhism now embraces both). Although there is uncertainty about his identity, he is believed to have been the author of *Tao Te Ching*, Taoism's main scriptural book. *Tao* is the "Way"; *te* is its "virtue." Its emphasis on perseverance, nature, and the cyclical has greatly influenced Chinese culture. *See also* Taoism.

La Paz, largest city and administrative capital of Bolivia in W Bolivia; former location of Inca village; one of the centers of revolt during war of independence; scene of revolutions and civil disorders intermittently into the 1960s. Industries: tanning, flour milling, brewing, distilling, manufacturing clothing, furniture, metal products. Altitude: 12,000ft (3,660m). Pop. 660,700.

Lapidary, the art of cutting and polishing gemstones. Originally all gems were cut *en cabochon* (smooth, polished surface, convex) or in flat plates. Tiny cuts, producing facets, were then added. Soft gemstones are sometimes tumbled to polish; most are shaped by grinding on abrasive wheels. Numerous facets with three or four sides bring out light and color. Most common faceted forms are brilliant cut, rose cut, and drop cut. *See also* Gems.

Lapis Lazuli, or **Lazurite,** a semiprecious gemstone, silicate mineral, found in metamorphosed limestones. Cubic system rare dodecahedral crystals, more often granular masses. Glassy, deep blue; hardness 5–5.5; sp gr 2.4.

Lapland, vast region in N Europe, almost entirely within the Arctic Circle, contains N and NE part of Norway, northernmost parts of Finland and Sweden, and the Kola Peninsula of Russia. Land is mountainous in Norwegian and Swedish sections; tundra predomi-

nates over the NE, and the Norwegian coast offers excellent hunting and fishing. Lapland is rich in high grade mineral deposits, and supports large reindeer herds. There is a great variety in temperatures; the extreme cold of winter is moderated on the W fringes of Norway where the harbors are open all year. The midnight sun in the summer months causes rapid growth of vegetation. Area: 150,000sq mi (388,500sq km). Pop. 36,500.

La Plata, city in E Argentina, 35mi (56km) ESE of Buenos Aires; capital of Buenos Aires prov.; well-planned city laid out in 3mi (5km) square centered on Plaza Moreno, site of cathedral. Parks surrounding it contain gardens, museums, and observatories. Industries: meat packing, oil refining, electrical equipment. Founded 1882. Pop. 506,287.

Lapps, people inhabiting N Scandinavia and the Kola Peninsula of the Soviet Union. The mountain Lapps are nomadic herders of reindeer, while those of the forest and coast are seminomadic and live by hunting, trapping, and fishing. Their racial origins are uncertain, although they are linguistically related to the Finno-Ugrian people.

Lapwing, slow-flying, crested plover found in the Eastern Hemisphere and South America. It is usually black, white, and sand-colored. Pear-shaped, blotched eggs (4) are laid near water. Family Charadriidae; species *Vanellus vanellus.*

Larch, genus *(Larix)* of deciduous trees native to cold and mountainous regions of the Northern Hemisphere. They have cones and needlelike leaves that are shed annually. The wood is valued for its toughness. Family Pinaceae.

Lardner, Ring(gold) W(ilmer) (1885–1933), US short-story writer and humorist, b. Niles, Mich. He spent 15 years as a reporter for Chicago newspapers and served for a time as editor of a baseball weekly. In 1915 he published *You Know Me, Al,* a collection of short stories about baseball players. His great talent lay in re-creating the language of the common people and delineating their lives satirically. Among his best known stories are "Haircut," "Champion," and "The Love Nest."

Laredo, city in S Texas, across Rio Grande from Nuevo Laredo, Mexico; seat of Webb co. Occupied by Texas Rangers 1846 and Texas Volunteers 1847; port of entry handling imports and exports between United States and Mexico. Industries: agriculture, coal, natural gas, oil refining, railroad shops, tiles, brooms, clothing, tourism. Founded 1755 by Spanish settlers; inc. 1852. Pop. (1980) 91,449.

Lares, in Roman mythology, gods of the cultivated fields. The Latins, Sabines, and Etruscans worshiped the Lares at the point where two fields came together. The household Lar was invoked for important family occasions (marriages, funerals).

Large Intestine. *See* Colon.

Lark, small, inconspicuous Old World birds found in open areas, chiefly in Africa. Known for their beautiful songs, they grow to about 6in (15cm), have crested heads; cone-shaped bills; long, pointed wings; and a straight claw on their rear toes. They feed on insects, larvae, crustaceans, and berries. Buff or whitish eggs (2–7) are laid in a grass cup-shaped nest on the ground. The male defends the nest, often using the broken-wing ruse. Family Alaudidae.

Larkin, Philip Arthur (1922–85), distinguished British poet. His first book *The North Ship* (1945) and later volumes, *XX Poems* (1951), *Less Deceived* (1955), *The Whitsun Wedding* (1964), and *High Windows* (1974), show a reaction against symbolist and romanticist poetry and a deeply felt interest in the importance of the unspectacular. A compilation of his newspaper columns on jazz, *All That Jazz,* was published in 1970. Larkin edited the *Oxford Book of Twentieth Century Verse* (1973).

Larkspur. *See* Delphinium.

La Rochefoucauld, François, duc de (1613–80), French classical writer and moralist. His *Maxims* (1665) reflect the wave of pessimism at that time and his belief that self-interest is at the root of all human behavior.

La Rochelle, port city in W France, on Bay of Biscay 75mi (121km) SSE of Nantes; capital of Charente Maritime dept. A Huguenot stronghold during the 16th century the city fell to Cardinal Richelieu 1627–28, site of Renaissance town hall and old fishing port. Industries: chemicals, tourism, fishing, naval and aircraft construction, automobiles. Chartered 12th century. Pop. 77,494.

Larva, a developmental stage in many animals, occuring between birth and maturity, in which the immature animal is structurally different from its parents. The larva has a well-developed alimentary system and stores food so that transformation to the adult stage can occur. Time of larval stage varies with species. Some larvae are: the planula (cnidaria); the pilidium (ribbonworm); the trochophore (annelid); the nauplius (crustacean); caterpillars, grubs, maggots, and nymphs (insects); the tadpole (frog).

Laryngitis, inflammation of the larynx (organ of speech) usually occurring during a respiratory-tract infection and accompanied by dryness, soreness, and hoarseness.

Larynx, or voice box, triangular-shaped box located between the trachea and the root of the tongue. Folds in the lining of the larynx form the vocal cords, thin bands of elastic tissue that vibrate when outgoing air passes over them, setting up sound waves that are changed into sound by the action of throat muscles and the tongue.

La Salle, René Robert Cavelier, Sieur de (1643–87), French explorer in North America. In 1668 he sailed for Canada to make his fortune in the fur trade. He explored the Great Lakes area and was commandant of Fort Frontenac on Lake Ontario (1674). His greatest achievement was exploring the Mississippi River to its mouth (1682) and claiming it for the king of France. He named the adjacent lands Louisiana after Louis XIV. His later efforts to colonize the area were unsuccessful.

LaSalle, city in S Quebec, Canada, on the St Lawrence River; suburb of Montreal on S shore of Montreal Island. Inc. 1912. Pop. 76,713.

Lascaux, Cave Paintings of, prehistoric paintings in a cave in the Department of Dordogne, southwestern France. Discovered in 1940, the caves consist of the Great Hall, with a ceiling covered with Paleolithic animal paintings, including four huge bulls; the Painted Gallery, with red and black bovine animals and horses; the Lateral Passage, with damaged paintings; and the Chamber of Engravings, with engraved figures and animals. The Main Gallery has friezes of animals, the

343

Chamber of Felines is decorated with cats, and the Shaft of the Dead Man contains a painting of a man between a rhinoceros and a bison.

Laser, a device that provides light amplification by stimulated emission of radiation. A natural development of the maser, it operates by the same principle of "pumping" atoms up to high-energy states and then passing radiation of a certain frequency through them to stimulate them to emit similar radiation. The intense coherent beam of light emitted by lasers has been used to measure the distance from the Earth to the Moon, "weld" retinas to chosen points in an eye, and measure amounts of pollution in the atmosphere. *See also* Maser.

Lashkar, city in N central India, adjoining city of Gwalior (S). It served as capital of former Gwalior state, abolished in 1956 and inc. as part of Madhya Pradesh state; site of Victoria College and the palace of the maharaja of Gwalior; trade and commercial center. Founded *c.* 1800, just S of Gwailor. Pop. (met. Gwalior-Lashkar) 406,160.

Laski, Harold Joseph (1893–1950), English political scientist, educator and socialist. He was chairman of the Labour party (1945–46). Through teachings, writings, and lectures, he advocated socialism in England and the United States. He wrote *Democracy in Crisis* (1933), *The American Presidency* (1940), and *Reflections on the Revolution of Our Time* (1943).

Las Palmas (Las Palmas de Gran Canaria), seaport city in Spain, on NE Grand Canary Island; capital of Las Palmas prov.; chief port and largest city of Canary Islands; site of governor's palace, 18th-century cathedral. Exports: sugar, tomatoes, almonds, bananas. Industries: fishing, tourism. Founded 1478. Area: (prov.) 1,569sq mi (4,064sq km). Pop. (prov.) 579,710; (city) 287,038.

La Spezia, city in Italy, on Gulf of Spezia; capital of La Spezia prov.; site of medieval Castel Saint Giorgio, and rebuilt 15th-century cathedral; major naval base of Italy since 1861. Industries: shipbuilding, iron foundries, oil refining. Pop. 120,717.

Lassa Fever, a little-understood, mysterious viral infection, first recognized as a disease in Africa in 1969. The infection can produce wide-ranging symptoms, including very high fever, mouth ulcers, heart damage, muscle aches, and kidney failure, and affect almost every part of the body. The disease occurs sporadically and is often fatal.

Last Supper, or **Lord's Supper,** in the New Testament, St Paul's designation for the sacred meal instituted by Jesus on the eve of his crucifixion. The 12 disciples were present to eat the Passover meal and take communion.

Las Vegas, city in S Nevada, 25mi (40km) WNW of Hoover Dam; seat of Clark co, largest city in Nevada. It was settled by Mormons 1855, in an unsuccessful attempt at lead mining; abandoned 1857. Growth was spurred 1905 with completion of railroad; area experienced a rapid population growth in 1950s and 1960s. It is famous for numerous nightclubs, casinos, and hotels; site of University of Nevada at Las Vegas (1957). Industries: tourism, ranching, mining, dairy products. Inc. 1911. Pop. (1980) 164,674.

Latakia (Al-Ladiqiyah), city in W Syria, on the Mediterranean Sea; capital of Latakia governorate. Originally the ancient Phoenician city of Ramitha, it was captured by Saladin 1188; part of the Ottoman Empire from 16th century to WWI. While Syria was a French League of Nations mandate, Latakia served as capital 1920–42 of Alawites territory; became part of Syria 1946; in 1959 a deepwater port was completed. Exports: asphalt, cotton, fruit, bitumen, cereals. Industries: tobacco, sponge fishing, cotton ginning, vegetable oil milling. Pop. 121,570.

Latent Heat, the heat absorbed by a substance as it changes its phase, that is, goes from solid to liquid or liquid to gas. When ice melts, its temperature remains the same until it has been completely transformed into water; the heat necessary to do this is called the heat of fusion. Similarly the heat necessary to transform water into steam at constant temperature is called the heat of vaporization.

Lateran Councils, five general councils of the Roman Catholic Church, named for the Basilica of St John Lateran in Rome, where they were held. The first council was held in 1123. Available sources show that it condemned simony and confirmed the Concordat of Worms. The second, in 1139, produced 30 decrees dealing with such matters as simony and marriage of clerics. The third, in 1179, decreed that the pope was to be elected by the College of Cardinals alone. The fourth council, in 1215, showed the power of Pope Innocent III. Of 70 decrees, some of the most important were those condemning the Albigensians and Waldensians and proclaiming a new Crusade. The fifth, in 1512–17, condemned what were considered false opinions and established many regulations for the conduct of the Church. The work of this council was carried further by the Council of Trent. *See also* Worms, Concordat of.

Lateran Treaty (Feb. 11, 1929), concordat between Italy and the state of Vatican City. By its terms (confirmed by the Italian constitution of 1948), Italy recognized the Vatican as an independent and sovereign state with the pope as its temporal head. Roman Catholicism was affirmed as Italy's official state religion, and the Vatican recognized Italy's claims to the papal states and Rome as well as the Italian state itself.

Laterite, a reddish soil found in humid tropical regions. It is produced by the sub-aerial decay of rocks. It contains aluminum and/or iron hydroxides and may be used as an ore of either metal if concentrations are sufficiently high.

Latex, milky fluid produced by certain plants, the most important being that produced by rubber trees, which contains about 60% water, 35% rubber, and 5% proteins, carbohydrates, and lipids. It is used in paints, special papers, and adhesives and to make sponge rubbers. Synthetic rubber latexes are also produced.

Lathe, a machine tool that performs turning operations that remove unwanted material from a workpiece (either wood or metal), which is rotated against a cutting tool. Several types of lathes are used: the speed lathe has a cutting tool supported on a rest and is hand-manipulated; an engine lathe's cutting tool is clamped onto a power-driven slide; screw-cutting lathes have a lead screw that drives the carriage on which the cutting tool is mounted; a turret lathe has a pivoted holder for cutting tools.

Latimer, Hugh (*c.*1485–1555), English clergyman and Protestant martyr. He lived in a time of struggle between Roman Catholic and Protestant forces in church and state, and he passed in and out of favor. During the reign of Edward VI he was free to preach, and his plain-spoken sermons helped establish Protestant ideas in England. When Mary Tudor, a Catholic, became queen, Latimer was charged with heresy and burned at the stake with Bishop Nicholas Ridley. Latimer's last words were: "We shall this day light such a candle, by God's grace, in England as I trust shall never be put out."

Latin, one of the two classical languages of antiquity, the language of the Roman Empire, the official language of the Roman Catholic Church, and the forerunner of the modern Romance languages. In the Middle Ages Latin was the language of science and philosophy in all Western countries and a knowledge of Latin was essential to any liberal education until well into this century. The Latin (or Roman) alphabet is used to write more than 100 languages (including English) today. And Latin words form a large part of the vocabulary of all, but especially Western, languages. *See also* Alphabet, Latin.

Latin American Conferences, series of meetings in the 1930s to revise and improve US policy in Latin America. It marked the beginning of Pres. Franklin D. Roosevelt's Good Neighbor Policy. The Montevideo Conference (1933), attended by Sec. of State Cordell Hull, denied any state the right to intervene in the affairs of any other state. In 1936, at the Buenos Aires Conference, which President Roosevelt himself attended, the Western Hemisphere states agreed to consultation when war was threatened. At the Lima Conference (1938), attended by Hull, the Declaration of Lima was adopted. This document reaffirmed the sovereignty of American states as well as a policy of resistance to intervention by foreign powers. *See also* Good Neighbor Policy.

Latin American Integration Association (formerly Latin American Free Trade Association), organization of 11 countries to increase regional trade and economic integration. The member states—Argentina, Brazil, Chile, Mexico, Paraguay, Peru, Uruguay, Bolivia, Colombia, Ecuador, and Venezuela—pledged themselves (1960) to eliminate tariffs and other restrictions on imports. In 1980, however, the organization gave up attempts at tariff reductions, deciding instead to develop less ambitious bilateral trade agreements.

Latin League, name of several confederations of the Latins (Latini) first formed for religious and later for political purposes. The league of Ferentina was the political hub of Latium from the 6th to the 4th centuries BC. Representatives of individual states met at the shrine of Diana to choose officers and determine policy. The only documented league was that led by the ancient city of Alba Longa, which was destroyed by the Romans *c.* 600 BC. Rome and the league signed a defensive pact in 493 BC against invading tribes. By 338 BC Rome had absorbed or colonized the separate Latin states and subsequently drew from them manpower and wealth.

Latin Rite, organization and liturgical practices of the churches belonging to Western Catholicism, or the Roman Catholic Church, as distinguished from the Eastern Rite. *See also* Eastern Rite.

Latins (Latini), ancient inhabitants of Latium in W Italy, nomadic invaders of diverse stock of whom the S Villanovans are thought to have introduced the Latin tongue. These tribes drew together to form communities *(populi)* and later larger political states that began in the 4th century BC to be dominated by Rome. The Latins evolved a political structure of equal representation of states that was retained even after their colonization by Rome. Loyal to Rome, they were granted Roman citizenship in the 1st century BC. *See also* Latin League.

Latium (Lazio), autonomous region in central Italy; comprised of provs. of Roma, Frosinone, Latina, Rieti, and Viterbo; bordered by the Tyrrhenian Sea (W), Apennines (E), Tuscany (N), and Campania (S). Capital is Rome; Civitavecchia is the major port. Products: wheat, vegetables, fruit, meat, olives, grapes. Industries: fashion, motion pictures (Rome), chemicals, pharmaceuticals, food, fishing, tourism. Est. 1948; received autonomy 1970. Area: 6,642sq mi (17,203sq km). Pop. 4,565,448.

La Tour, Georges de (1593–1652), French painter, known for his religious and genre scenes. His early style was Manneristic, but his mature style was naturalistic, after the Baroque manner of Caravaggio. His early works include "The Cheat" and "St. Jerome." His mature works include "Christ and St Joseph in the Carpenter's Shop" (*c.*1645).

Latter Day Saints, Church of Jesus Christ of. *See* Mormons.

Latter Day Saints, Reorganized Church of Jesus Christ of, a Mormon group that rejected Brigham Young's leadership after the death of the first leader, Joseph Smith. There are more than 150,000 members, with headquarters in Independence, Mo. *See also* Mormons.

Latvia (Latvijskaja Sovetskaja Socialisticeskaja Republika), constituent republic of the USSR. It is a large fertile lowland located in NE Europe, bordered by Estonian (N) and Lithuanian (S) republics, Baltic Sea (W), and Russian republic (SE). One-fifth of the country is less than 130ft (40m) above sea level; it has 2,980 lakes. Forests cover 26% of the country. The climate is damp, and the largest waterway is the Western Dvina River. Collectivization of agriculture has reduced the number of private farms to about 1,500. Nationalized industrial production has increased, with machinery, metals and textiles the leading products.

People and history. The majority of the people are Letts and Latgolians, Baltic groups akin to the Slavs. About 25% are Russians, with minorities of Belorussians, Lithuanians, Poles, and Jews. Lutherans and Roman Catholics were the dominant religious groups before the USSR discouraged organized religion. Conquered and Christianized in the 13th century by Germans, the Letts subsequently came under Polish, then Swedish rule. Through the Russian victories over the Swedes and the 18th-century partitions of Poland, Latvia passed to Russia. German merchants and landowners continued their domination, making serfs of the Letts until the mid-19th century. After the collapse of Russia in WWI, a democratic republic was declared in 1918. By 1936 political weakness permitted a dictatorship. The USSR was granted military bases in 1939 and in 1940 occupied the country. Latvia was occupied by Germany in WWII from 1941–44, when it was retaken by the USSR.

PROFILE

Official name: Latvia Soviet Socialist Republic
Area: 24,595sq mi (63,701sq km)
Population: 2,529,000
Chief city: Riga (capital)
Government: Constituent republic of USSR
Religion: Lutheran and Roman Catholic
Language: Latvian
Industries: textiles, machinery, electrical equipment, shipbuilding, distilling, food and dairy processing
Agriculture: stock raising, dairy farming, forests

Las Vegas, Nevada

Laurel and Hardy (left and center)

Lausanne, Switzerland

Laud, William (1573–1645), English clergyman. He became predominant in the Anglican church after Charles I's accession (1625), supporting the king against Parliament. Appointed chancellor of Oxford University (1629) and archbishop of Canterbury (1633), he tried, with disastrous results, to insist on uniformity of action and observance within the national church. Parliament impeached him for high treason (1640), and he was tried (1644) and cleared by the House of Lords but was executed under a bill of attainder.

Laudanum, alcoholic tincture of opium, prepared from granulated opium and formerly used medicinally to treat diarrhea. In the early 19th century, opium addicts frequently used laudanum. The name was originally given by Paracelsus in the 16th century to a preparation made of gold and pearls mixed with opium.

Laughing Gas, or nitrous oxide, colorless nonflammable gas (formula N_2O) obtained by the decomposition of ammonium nitrate or from nitrites and used as an anesthetic. Properties: melt. pt. $-131.4°F$ ($-90.8°C$); boil pt. $-127.3°F$ ($-88.5°C$).

Launcelot, Sir, legendary knight of King Arthur's Round Table, the subject of numerous medieval and later romances. As the lover of Queen Guinevere, he caused dissension among Arthur's knights that resulted in the breakup of their fellowship.

Laurasia, the name for the northern continent containing North America and Eurasia that formed when a northern rift, the Tethyan trench, split apart Pangaea from east to west along a line slightly north of the equator. The name is a combination of Laurentian, a geologic period in North America, and Eurasia. See also Continental Drift.

Laurel, evergreen shrubs and trees native to S Europe and cultivated in United States. Included is the noble or bay laurel (Laurus nobilis) with stiff, leathery, oval leaves, tiny yellowish flowers, and purple berries; height: 60–70ft (18–21m). The foliage was used by ancient Greeks to crown their victors. Family Lauraceae.

Laurel and Hardy, comedy team of the thin **Stan Laurel** (1890–1965) (Arthur Stanley Jefferson) and the fat **Oliver Hardy** (1892–1957). Their best films include From Soup to Nuts (1929) and The Music Box (1932).

Laurens, Henry (1724–92), US Revolutionary War leader, b. Charleston, S.C. An opponent of Britain before the Revolution, he served in the Continental Congress (1777–79) and was its president (1777–78).

Laurier, (Sir) Wilfrid (1841–1919), prime minister of Canada (1896–1911). A lawyer, Laurier was the first French Canadian to lead a federal party (Liberals, 1888–1919). Throughout his career, Laurier propounded religious reconciliation and national unity. Entering commons in 1874, he was pro-tariff and opposed to clerical politics. He opposed the Riel Rebellions and African War (1899) and supported Canada's entry into World War I, despite opposing the draft.

Lausanne, city in W Switzerland, on Lake Geneva, on S slope of Mt Jorat. Originally a Celtic settlement, it was destroyed c. 379; episcopal see since 6th century; adopted Reformation 1536; became capital of Vaud canton 1803; scene of Lausanne Conference 1922; site of Gothic cathedral (1275), 13th-century bishop's palace, 13th-century castle, university (1890). Industries: radios, leather, clothes, beer, chemicals, wine, woodworking. Pop. 134,300.

Lausanne, Treaty of (1923), agreement signed at Lausanne, Switzerland, that abrogated the harsh Treaty of Sèvres (1920) imposed after World War I on the collapsing Ottoman Empire and ended the war between Greece and Turkey. Turkey obtained full sovereignty over mainland Turkey and renounced claims to Greek islands in the Aegean. Britain obtained Cyprus, and Italy received Rhodes and the Dodecanese Islands.

Lava, molten rock or magma that reaches the earth's surface and flows out through a volcanic vent in streams or sheets. There are three main types of lavas: vesicular, like pumice; glassy, like obsidian; and even-grained. Chemically lavas range from acidic to ultrabasic, though 90% of all lavas are basic. Basic lavas have a low viscosity and flow easily covering large areas. Acid lavas are highly viscous and rarely spread far.

Laval-des-Rapides (Laval), city in S Canada, NW of Montréal on Ile Jésus in the St Lawrence River. Formed by merger of island communities in 1965; 2nd-largest city in Quebec. Industries: chemicals, paper, iron. Pop. 246,243.

Lavender, common name for aromatic herbs or shrubs of the genus Lavandula of the mint family. L. spica, erroneously known as L. vera or L. officinalis, is a Mediterranean woody perennial ornamental subshrub. Its fragrant flowers when dried are used for sachets and to perfume linens and clothing. Oil from the leaves is used in perfume and both flowers and leaves are used in making lavender water and aromatic vinegar.

Laver, any of various edible purple gelatinous seaweeds of the genus Porphyra. In Japan, laver (called amanori or nori) is pressed and dried for use in cooking. In Europe, red laver (chiefly P. laciniata and P. vulgaris) is stewed or pickled. See also Red Algae.

Laveran, Charles Louis Alphonse (1845–1922), French physician. He contributed greatly to tropical medicine and parasitology, winning the 1907 Nobel Prize in physiology and medicine for his work on the role played by protozoa in causing diseases. Laveran discovered the parasite responsible for malaria and studied trypanosomiasis and leishmaniasis.

Lavoisier, Antoine Laurent (1743–94), French chemist, The father of modern chemistry, he was an advocate and practitioner of accurate measurement. His careful experiments enabled him to demolish the phlogiston theory by demonstrating the function of oxygen in combustion. He named both oxygen and hydrogen and showed how they combined to form water. In collaboration with Berthollet and others he published Methods of Chemical Nomenclature (1787), which laid down the modern method of naming substances. His Elementary Treatise on Chemistry (1789) was the first textbook of chemistry. He was guillotined after the Revolution, having been arrested for his former activities as a tax-farmer (a tax collector empowered to make a personal profit, which Lavoisier used to finance his research).

Law, (Andrew) Bonar (1858–1923), British statesman, b. Canada. A member of Parliament from 1900, he led the Unionists in the British Parliament (1911–21), was chancellor of the exchequer (1916–18), and prime minister (1922–23).

Law, system of rules governing human conduct imposed by politically organized society and enforced by threat of punishment. Custom is probably the prime source of law. Religious and ethical systems usually developed a legal order, as exemplified by the early law codes of Hammurabi (Babylonia), the law of Manu (India), Islamic law (Arabia), and Mosaic law (Palestine). Ancient Greek laws, together with the law of twelve tables, formed Roman Law, which was codified in the Corpus Juris Civilis of Justinian, and greatly affected the growth of Western law. German law temporarily replaced Roman law after the collapse of the Roman Empire. This later blended with Roman law and during the Renaissance and the revival of trade it spread through the world as modern civil law. The law of nature, a simplified restatement of Roman law, especially incorporating those laws of contract and property, prepared the way for the codifications of continental Europe, most famous of which is the Napoleonic Code. In England, common law developed as the outgrowth of Germanic customary law and was based on judicial precedents. US law, founded on English common law, has the unique feature of the coexistance of federal and state law. Modern law reflects the complexity of modern society, with an ever-widening range to regulate many different branches of human conduct. See also Hammurabi.

Lawn Bowling, an outdoor game, most popular in England and Canada, is played on a smooth grass plot about 120 feet square (36.6m square), which is divided into 6 alleys 120 feet long and 20 feet (6.1m) wide. After one of the players throws a small white ball (jack) at some spot not less than 75 feet (22.9m) down the alley, each player in turn rolls a ball toward the jack. A point is given for each ball nearer the jack than that of an opponent's ball. Usually, 21 wins. In a singles match, each player rolls four balls. In a team match, each player rolls two balls. Lawn bowling originated in Great Britain about the 13th century.

Lawrence, D(avid) H(erbert) (1885–1930), English author. The son of a coal miner, he became a school teacher. In 1909 he had some poems published in the English Review and in 1911 his first novel The White Peacock appeared. In 1912 he went to Europe with Frieda von Richthofen, whom he married in 1914. During World War I, because of his pacifism and her being German, many people suspected them of being spies. In 1919 they left England to travel and live in Europe, Ceylon, Australia, New Mexico, and Mexico. Lawrence believed that modern Western society was dehumanizing, that people were losing contact with their basic physical and sexual selves. The semiautobiographical novel Sons and Lovers had appeared in 1913. The Rainbow (1915) and Women in Love (1921) traced a family's history through several generations, concentrating on two women of the last generation. In the 1920s Lawrence wrote novels such as The Plumed Serpent (1926) with Nietzschean heroes. Lady Chatterley's Lover (1928) was long banned in England and the United States because of its explicit description and discussion of sex. Among his best known short stories are "The Prussian Officer" and "The Rocking-Horse Winner." Etruscan Places (1932) is his most important travel book. Studies in Classic American Literature (1916) is a provocative work of criticism. Lawrence died of tuberculosis at age 45.

Lawrence, Ernest Orlando (1901–58), US physicist, b. Canton, S.D. He became professor at the University of California where he built the first cyclotron, a subatomic particle accelerator. His invention earned him the 1939 Nobel Prize. With the cyclotron he researched atomic structure, produced radioactive phosphorus, iodine, and other medicinal isotopes, and caused various elements to exhibit transmutation. In his honor, the element lawrencium was named.

Lawrence, T(homas) E(dward) (1888–1935), British author and soldier, known popularly as Lawrence of Arabia. He worked in the Middle East as an archaeologist. In World War I he worked for British intelligence, organizing a revolt of Arab tribesmen against the Turks and acquiring a legendary reputation. His *The Seven Pillars of Wisdom* (1926) is an account of this campaign. Discontented with British policy in the Middle East, he sought obscurity in the Royal Air Force, joining under the name "Ross." He died in a motorcycle accident.

Lawrence, city in NE Kansas, on Kansas River 28mi (45km) E of Topeka; seat of Douglas co; center of free state abolitionists; scene of attack Aug. 21, 1863 by William Quantrill's pro-slavery group in which 150 people were killed; site of University of Kansas (1863) and Haskell Institute (1884), largest Indian school in country. Industries: farm chemicals, corrugated boxes, greeting cards, food processing. Founded 1854 by members of New England Emigrant Aid Society and named for society's treasurer, Amos A. Lawrence; inc. 1858. Pop. (1980) 52,738.

Lawrence, city in NE Massachusetts, on Merrimack River; seat of Essex co. Industries: textiles, textile machinery, leather goods, clothes. Founded 1655 as part of Methuen and Andover, to 1847; inc. as city 1853. Pop. (1980) 63,175.

Lawrencium, radioactive metallic element (symbol Lr) of the actinide group, first made (1961) by bombarding californium with boron nuclei. The element has been made only in trace amounts and has not been identified chemically. Properties: at. no. 103; most stable isotope Lr^{256} (half-life 8s). *See also* Transuranium Elements.

Laws of Motion, three laws proposed by Sir Isaac Newton in his *Principia* (1687) that form the basis of the classical study of motion and force. According to the First Law, a body resists changes in its state of motion —a body at rest tends to remain at rest unless acted on by an external force, and a body in motion tends to remain in motion at the same speed and in the same direction unless acted on by an external force. According to the Second Law, the change in motion of a body as a result of a force is directly proportional to the force and inversely proportional to the mass of the body; that is, if the change in motion, or acceleration, is a, the force is F, and the mass is m, then $a = F/m$. According to the Third Law, to every action there is an equal and opposite reaction. This law may be expressed mathematically in the relation between the impetus acting on a body, Ft (force multiplied by time) and the change in momentum, mv (mass multiplied by velocity); according to the Third Law, $Ft = mv$. *See also* Acceleration; Force; Momentum.

Lawton, city in SW Oklahoma, 80mi (129km) SW of Oklahoma City; seat of Comanche co; site of Cameron College (1907) and Fort Sill, US field artillery center. Industries: mobile homes, cotton, cement products, bedding. Inc. 1901. Pop. (1980) 80,054.

Layering, a method of plant propagation that induces root formation on a stem or branch while it is still attached to the parent plant. In simple stem layering the stem or branch is fastened down and covered with soil until a root system develops, when the stem or branch is cut from its parent and grown as a separate individual. In air layering a ball of moistened rooting-soil mixture is placed on the branch or stem to be layered, held in place by a plastic wrap, and left until a root system develops. Root formation is accelerated by slashing the bark in the layering region.

Lazarus, the name of two men in the New Testament. In chapters 11–12 of the Gospel of John, Lazarus is the brother of Mary and Martha of Bethany. He died and four days later Jesus miraculously restored him to life. In Luke 16:19–31 Lazarus is the poor man in Christ's parable about a beggar and a rich man.

Lazurite. *See* Lapis Lazuli.

Lead, metallic element (symbol Pb) of group IVA of the periodic series, known from ancient times. Chief ore is galena (sulfide), from which it is obtained by roasting. It is used in pipes, batteries, cable sheaths, and alloys such as solder and type metal. The element is also used in making the gasoline additive tetraethyl lead. It is also used as a shield for X rays and other radiation. Chemically, it is unreactive and resists corrosion. Properties: at. no. 82; at. wt. 207.19; sp gr 11.3; melt. pt. 617.5°F (325.3°C); boil. pt. (3,182°F) (1,750°C); most common isotope Pb^{208} (52.3%).

Lead Poisoning, condition caused by absorption of lead from the digestive tract, lungs, or skin. It occurs among children who eat chips of lead-containing paint in deteriorating buildings and among workers in lead-using industries. Its first symptoms, such as mild diarrhea, anemia, and irritability often go unnoticed until serious effects such as convulsions occur. If untreated it can be fatal. In 1978 the Department of Labor issued stricter safety standards for workers exposed to lead.

Leaf, thin and flat plant organ that is involved with photosynthesis and transpiration. Leaves are simple or compound (divided into leaflets), have parallel or net-like veins for transporting water and nutrients and small openings (stomata) for exchanging gases. Growing laterally from the stem or twig, a leaf consists of a blade and a stalk, or petiole, attaching it to the branch or stem. It has limited growth, maturing for one or more seasons and then dropping off. Modified leaves include: succulent leaves with thick, fleshy water storage tissue; tendrils that coil around supports; and spines that become hard, slender, and conical (thorns are modified branches).

Leaf Beetle, small, oval beetle that feeds on leaves. Many, including the Colorado potato beetle and striped cucumber beetle, are yellow with black markings. Family Chrysomelidae.

Leaf-cutting Ant, or parasol ant, large ant that cuts and transports bits of leaves to its nest. These beds of macerated leaves are used to grow the fungi that leaf-cutters eat. They live in large colonies in sometimes enormous underground nests. Genus *Atta.*

Leafhopper, brightly colored insect found worldwide. These insects suck juices from trees and plants, some sucking enough juice to remove the chlorophyll. Others carry plant diseases. Length: to 0.5in (13mm). Family Cicadellidae. *See also* Homoptera.

Leaf Insect, leaf-mimicking insect found in the tropics. They are related to walking sticks but have broad bodies, wings, and legs. Length: 3–6in (76–152mm). Family Phasmatidae. *See also* Orthoptera; Walking Stick.

Leaf Mold, compost or humus composed chiefly of rotted vegetable matter, such as fallen leaves. *See also* Compost.

Leaf Monkey. *See* Langur.

Leaf-nosed Bat, any of a large variety of small insect-eating bats living in the tropics and subtropics worldwide. They have fleshy leaflike organs on the end of their snouts that probably aid them in detecting echoes. Families Hipposideridae and Phyllostomatidae.

Leaf Roller, insect larva that nests in a rolled leaf. Leaf rollers include some moth caterpillars of the Tortricidae family and some skippers—bean skipper *Urbanus proteus* and canna skipper *Calpodes ethlius.*

League of Nations, international organization (1919–46), forerunner of the United Nations. Created as part of the Treaty of Versailles ending World War I, it required that members respect the territorial independence of all members, excluding acts of aggression. The refusal of the United States to participate impaired the league's efficiency and, although some achievements were accomplished, it could not prevent World War II. Dissolved in 1946, it did provide the groundwork for establishing the United Nations.

Leah, in the Bible, daughter of Laban and sister of Rachel. She was made the bride of Jacob after he worked seven years to win Rachel's hand, because their father felt the eldest should marry first. Leah was the mother of Reuben, Simeon, Levi, Judah, Issachar, Zebulun, and Dinah.

Leakey, Louis S. Bazett (1903–72), English archeologist and anthropologist who discovered fossils in East Africa that proved man to be older than had been thought. In 1931 he began to research Olduvai Gorge in Tanzania. Working with his wife, Mary Douglas Leakey (1913–), he found there animal fossils and tools. Leakey authored numerous books, including *Adam's Ancestors* (1934) and *Stone-Age Africa* (1936). Mary Leakey continued working in East Africa, often in conjunction with her son, Richard (1944–), who became director of the National Museums of Kenya.

Lear, Edward (1812–88), English artist and writer, traveled in Europe and Asia. His nonsense verse, including *The Book of Nonsense* (1846) and *Laughable Lyrics* (1876), portrays a world of fantasy, often tinged with melancholy. A popularizer of the limerick, he illustrated his books with line drawings. *See also* Limerick.

Least Bittern, small bird of temperate and tropical Americas. It is secretive, lives on swamp floors, and lays bluish or greenish white eggs (3–6) in a canopied grass nest on the ground. Length: 1–1.5ft. (30–46cm). Species *Ixobrychus exilis. See also* Bittern.

Leather, animal hides cured by tanning to prevent decay and increase flexibility; often finished by glazing, enameling, or lacquering and colored by staining or dyeing. Suede is produced by raising a nap on the flesh side by buffing with emery. Artificial leathers were formerly a strong fabric coated with pyroxylin but are now usually vinyl polymers. *See also* Tanning.

Leatherback Turtle, sea turtle found in all tropical oceans. The largest of all turtles, it has a smooth, black, leathery skin with seven ridges running lengthwise, and no external plates. Its forelegs are enormous flippers. It feeds on jellyfish. Length: to 7ft (2.1m); weight: 1,200lb (540kg). Family Dermochelyidae; species *Dermochelys coriacea. See also* Turtle.

Leather-Stocking Tales, The, five novels by James Fenimore Cooper about Natty Bumppo, an American frontier scout. The title is derived from Natty's nickname, Leather-Stocking, which refers to his deerskin leggings. The novels are *The Pioneers* (1823), *The Last of the Mohicans* (1826), *The Prairie* (1827), *The Pathfinder* (1840), and *The Deerslayer* (1841). The narrative of Natty's life follows a different sequence, however: *Deerslayer, Mohicans, Pathfinder, Pioneers, Prairie.* The novels trace the adventures of Natty and his Indian friend, Chingachgook, during the French and Indian wars and in the post-revolutionary United States.

Leaves of Grass (1855), collection of poems by Walt Whitman, revised and augmented until 1892. The first edition contained 12 poems, the first and longest of which was later titled "Song of Myself." Scholars agree that the crucial edition is the third (1860), which contains many new poems, including the famous "Out of the Cradle Endlessly Rocking," and regroupings of previous ones.

Lebanon (Al-Lubnan), independent nation in the Middle East. The historic home of the Phoenicians, it was engulfed by civil war between its religious divisions in the mid-1970s, and strife has continued since then.

Land and economy. Situated on the E end of the Mediterranean Sea with a coast of 120mi (193km), it is bordered by Syria (N and E) and Israel (S). Topographically, it is dominated by a narrow coastal plain. Behind this plain are the Lebanese Mts, the fertile Beqaa Valley, and the Anti-Lebanon range leading to Syria. About 65% of the land is desert, waste, or urban; 27% agricultural, and 8% forests. The main rivers are the Litani and the Orontes. Before the civil war, Lebanon served as the banking, financial, and trade center of the Middle East. Although much of the transshipment traffic has begun again, and oil is exported from Iraqi and Saudi Arabian pipelines ending in Lebanon, Beirut has lost its preeminence as a financial center, and the tourist industry has not recovered.

People. With its population almost evenly divided between Arabs and Christians (Maronites), Lebanon also includes Armenians and Greek Orthodox. Muslims are divided into three sects—Sunni, Shiite, and Druse. The official language is Arabic. Agriculture provides a living for the majority, and the cities of Beirut and Tripoli are commercial centers. Lebanon has the highest percentage of skilled workers in the Middle East. Literacy is 86%, highest in the Arab world.

Government. A parliamentary republic provides for division of public positions among all religions. A unicameral legislature and president are both elected. The president, customarily a Christian, appoints the prime minister, a Muslim.

History. Driven by orthodox Byzantine persecution, Lebanon was colonized in the 6th century by the Monothelites (now Maronites) and was often a refuge for heretics. It was then fragmented politically and ruled by various factions for centuries. Lebanon was governed by a Christian military governor, assisted by a council representing all other sects, from 1864 until the end of WWI, when it became a French mandate. In 1944 the country became fully independent. After the establishment of Israel (1948), Lebanon accepted thousands of Palestinian refugees, many of whom settled in the S and ultimately upset the country's delicate balance between religious groups. Turmoil marked its presidential administrations and, in 1958, the United States sent Marines to quell a revolt. Lebanon has been the seat of Palestinian commando raids into Israel, bringing Israeli raids in reprisal. Demands by Muslims for a greater voice in government escalated in the 1970s. In 1975 civil war erupted between Muslims and Maronite Christians. After savage battles that ultimately wrecked the economy and left thousands dead, a cease-fire was called in 1976 and enforced by the Arab Deterrent Force, consisting mainly of Syrian

Lebanon

Robert E. Lee

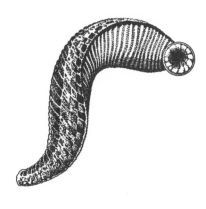

Leech

troops. In 1978 fighting was renewed when Israeli troops invaded the S in retaliation for Palestinian attacks into Israel launched from the area. The Israelis retreated only with the arrival of a UN peace-keeping force and after handing over most territory to the Israeli-backed Christian militia. In Beirut renewed fighting occurred between the Syrians and the Christian militia. In 1981, Israel again invaded because of Palestinian activity; when Syrian missiles were discovered in Lebanon, tensions between Israel and Syria were lessened by US diplomacy. Another invasion (1982) by Israel resulted in the evacuation of the PLO from Beirut. After the assassination (1982) of President Bashir Gemayel, a massacre—allegedly by those loyal to Gemayel with some involvement by Israel—of hundreds of Palestinian refugees in West Beirut took place. Gemayel's brother, Amin Gemayel, became president that same year. By 1984 multinational forces (including US, France, and Saudi Arabia) had been forced to withdraw, and by 1985 Israeli troops had withdrawn to S Lebanon, leaving Syria with firmer control over the country. Terrorism continued to occur in and originate from Lebanon.

PROFILE

Official name: Republic of Lebanon
Area: 4,015sq mi (10,632sq km)
Population: 3,100,000
   Density: 772 per sq mi (298 per sq km)
Chief cities: Beirut (capital); Tripoli
Government: Parliamentary republic
Religion: Christian (Maronites) and Islam
Language: Arabic (official)
Monetary unit: Lebanese pound
Industries: food products, textiles, leather goods, cement, publishing
Agriculture: apples, citrus fruits, olives, tobacco, grapes, cereals, wheat
Trading partners: France, Middle East countries

Lebedev, Pyotr Nikolayevich (1866–1911), Russian physicist noted for demonstrating that light exerts minute pressure on solid bodies. He was a professor at the University of Moscow and also worked on the origin of the Earth's magnetism. A physical research institute in Moscow was named in his honor.

Le Bel, Joseph Achille (1847–1930), French chemist who proposed that the chemical bonds from a carbon atom are arranged in space as if they pointed towards the corners of a regular tetrahedron. This theory allowed chemists to work out the molecular structures of organic compounds. He is regarded as the cofounder of stereochemistry, in collaboration with J. H. van't Hoff.

Le Brun, Charles (1619–90), French painter. He painted religious, mythological, and historical subjects, as well as portraits. He was also a draftsman and decorator. He achieved great prestige in his time and helped Paris succeed Rome as the new capital of the arts. His notable works include *Portrait of Jabach and His Family* and *Chancellor Séguier.*

Le Carré, John (1931–), pseud. of David Cornwell, English novelist. He writes well-crafted thrillers. His best known book is *The Spy Who Came in from the Cold* (1963), a realistic treatment of spies and their world that draws on his own experience in British Intelligence. Later novels include *The Looking-Glass War* (1965), *A Small Town in Germany* (1968), *Tinker, Tailor, Soldier, Spy* (1974), *The Honourable Schoolboy* (1977), *Smiley's People* (1980), *The Little Drummer Girl* (1983), and *A Perfect Spy* (1986).

Le Châtelier's Principle, a principle announced by the French chemist Henry-Louis Le Châtelier (1850–1936) in 1888. It states that if a system (usually of chemically interacting substances) in a state of equilibrium is disturbed (by heat, for example) the system will tend to neutralize the disturbance and restore equilibrium. This applies not only to reversible chemical reactions but also to reversible physical processes such as the evaporation or crystallization of a liquid.

Lecithin, substances containing fatty acids and choline and found in many animal tissues, especially in nerves, semen, and the liver.

Le Corbusier (1887–1969), French architect, b. Charles Édouard Jeanneret in Switzerland. He promoted the International modern style but eventually developed his own style. His prolific ideas and experiments with modern construction methods resulted in unique designs for both individual houses and entire cities. Often inspired by industrial designs he used strong cubist forms, usually of white concrete, and often placed his buildings on pillars. After 1940 he developed a complex modular system of harmonious but differing proportions, represented in his chapel at Ronchamp near Belfort (1954). He also designed the main glass wall and windowless end walls of the UN Secretariat, New York City (1947) and the Visual Arts Center, Harvard University (Cambridge, Mass., 1961–62).

Ledum, small, evergreen, bog shrub found in damp, acid soils of cold northern climates. It has small, white flowers. Family Ericaceae; genus *Ledum.*

Lee, Ann (1736–84), English mystic. Known as the founder of the United Society of Believers in Christ's Second Appearing, popularly called the Shakers, she was imprisoned many times in England for her beliefs before emigrating to America in 1774. She founded a colony at Niskeyuna (near Albany, N.Y.) in 1776 and gained many converts. She was followed as the anointed successor of Christ, and her beliefs in community of goods, withdrawal from the world and its sins, and celibacy were the basis of Shaker communities. She did not escape persecution in America, and the frequent beatings and jailings she suffered probably contributed to her early death.

Lee, Francis Lightfoot (1734–97), American patriot and a signer of the Declaration of Independence, b. Stratford, Va. After serving in the Continental Congress (1775–79) and helping prepare the Articles of Confederation, he briefly served in the Virginia senate. *See also* Declaration of Independence.

Lee, Henry ("Light-Horse Harry") (1756–1818), US Revolutionary soldier and father of Robert E. Lee, b. Prince William co, Va. His excellent service during the Revolution earned him the nickname Light-Horse Harry Lee. He served as governor of Virginia (1792–95) and as a Federalist congressman (1799–1801). On the occasion of George Washington's death (1799), Lee described him as being "first in war, first in peace, and first in the hearts of his countrymen."

Lee, Laurie (1914–), British writer. His poetry, as in *The Sun My Monument* (1944), *The Bloom of Candles* (1947), and *My Many-Coated Man* (1955), is attractively simple. His best-selling autobiography *Cider with Rosie* describes with immense charm his childhood in a remote Cotswold village. He is the author of *As I Walked Out One Midsummer Morning* (1969) and *A Rose for Winter* (1955), accounts of his travels in Spain and Cyprus, and of a verse play, *The Voyage of Magellan* (1948).

Lee, Robert Edward (1807–70), commander of Confederate forces in the Civil War, b. Stratford, Va. Son of a hero of the Revolution and the governor of Virginia, he was a graduate of the US Military Academy at West Point (1829). Although Lee regarded slavery as evil and saw advantages of the Union, he believed even more in state's rights. His loyalty to his native Virginia was paramount. Declining Lincoln's offer to head Union troops, he became advisor to Jefferson Davis, the Confederate president (1861). After Gen. J. E. Johnston was wounded, Lee became a commander of the Confederate forces (1862). In 1862 he led the successful defense of Richmond and won at the Second Battle of Bull Run. He lost the 1862 battle at Antietam but gave the Union its worst defeats at Fredericksburg (1862) and Chancellorsville (1863). His attempt to penetrate the North ended in the defeat at Gettysburg in July 1863. He surrendered to Ulysses S. Grant at Appomattox Court House on April 9, 1865. Lee's skill in analyzing military situations and use of field defenses are still studied. After the war Lee attempted to ameliorate the war wounds. He became president of what is now Washington and Lee University (1865).

Lee, Tsung-dao (1926–), US physicist, b. China. He showed that among sub-atomic particles, the law of conservation of parity (that nature, in effect, makes no distinction between right- and left-handedness) does not always hold. Working with Chen Ning Yang, Lee suggested that in certain types of sub-atomic reactions, parity is not conserved, and this was subsequently verified by experiment. He was awarded the 1957 Nobel Prize in physics.

Leech, freshwater, marine, and terrestrial annelid found worldwide in tropical and temperate regions. Its tapered, ringed body is equipped with a sucking disc at each end. Most leeches are found in ponds where they live on the blood of invertebrates, fish, amphibians, and turtles. Length: 0.5–2in (13–51mm). There are over 300 species. Class Hirudinea. *See also* Annelida.

Leeds, city in N England; university and cultural center; important agricultural markets. Headingley cricket ground and large residential estates lie N of the modern city center. Industries: woolens, clothing, engineering, paper, textiles, printing. Pop. 749,000.

Leek, onionlike biennial garden vegetable originating in Europe and Asia. It has white or pinkish flowers and a small bulb that is cooked along with the broad, flat, folded leaves. Height: 2–3ft (61–92cm). Family Amaryllidaceae; species *Allium porrum.*

Leeuwenhoek, Anton van (1632–1723), Dutch maker of microscopes and naturalist. He ground lenses and built microscopes that magnified up to 270 times. The first to describe protozoa (1674) and bacteria (1676), Leeuwenhoek was elected to the Royal Society of England in 1680 for his contributions to science. He discovered red blood cells in a classic study of capillary circulation. His wide-ranging microscopic examinations included studies in anatomy, histology, physiology, embryology, botany, chemistry, and physics and helped to refute the then widespread belief that living things could evolve from lifeless matter.

Leeward Islands, N group of Lesser Antilles in E West Indies, extending SE from Puerto Rico to Windward Islands, between Atlantic Ocean (E) and Caribbean Sea (W). The islands are primarily of volcanic origin; now an agricultural and winter resort center; group includes the US Virgin Islands, Guadeloupe and dependencies (French), St Eustatius and Saba (Dutch), St Martin (a divided Dutch-French dependency), British Leewards (St Kitts-Nevis, Montserrat), British Virgin

Islands, and Antigua, a former British dependency that became independent in 1981. Settlement was begun by British in the 17th century; conflict ensued shortly after with French settlements; possession was further contested by Spanish, who were later forced out. Islands were Anglo-French pawns for nearly two centuries, until end of Napoleonic Wars (1815). A severe earthquake shook Leewards Oct. 8, 1975. Industries: limes, coconuts, tobacco, vegetables, dairy products, tourism.

Legendre, Adrien Marie (1752–1833), French mathematician. His work on number theory and elliptic integrals was not properly appreciated until the end of his life. In his study of quadratic residues, Legendre discovered the law of reciprocity much praised and used by C. F. Gauss. He introduced the method of least squares, to calculate the paths of comets. His most influential work was *Elements of Geometry* (1794).

Léger, Fernand (1881–1955), French painter. His work was important to the development of the cubist style. His works include *The Mechanic* (1920) and *Three Women* (1921). He also designed sets and costumes for ballets and operas.

Leghorn (Livorno), industrial town in Italy, on the Tyrrhenian Sea; capital of Livorno prov. Fortified in the 14th century by the Pisans, it prospered under Medici rule; it was the first free port on the Mediterranean (1590); site of 16th-century cathedral, remains of 17th-century city walls; seat of Italian naval academy. Exports: wine, marble, textiles, olive oil. Industries: shipbuilding, oil refining, iron, steel, distilling, chemicals. Pop. 177,526.

Leghorn, chicken breed, the most important variety being the White Leghorn. *See also* White Leghorn.

Legionnaire's Disease, a bacterial infection that struck during a convention of the Pennsylvania American Legion in Philadelphia in 1976, causing almost 200 people to become ill, of whom 29 died. Symptoms include headache, fatigue, fever, chills, abdominal pain, and gastrointestinal disorders. Chest X-rays may show evidence of pneumonia. The bacillus bacterium responsible for the disease was identified in 1977. The disease can be treated with the antibiotic erythromycin.

Legislative Processes, procedures followed by the legislature in enacting laws. Bills are introduced by a sponsoring legislator, often in response to pressure from constituents or private interest groups. In the United States, they are then sent for study and amendment to committee, where the majority of bills are shelved. If passed out of committee, a bill then goes to the floor for a vote. The procedure takes place in both the House and Senate before the bill is sent to the president for his signature.

Legislature, representative assembly whose primary function is the enactment of laws. In the United States it is a bicameral body, composed of two chambers, the Senate and the House of Representatives, all of whose members are popularly elected. The legislature is empowered to levy taxes and appropriate public funds and to provide a check on the executive branch. It is also designed to reflect the interests and desires of its various constituents and to act as a forum for debate.

Legnica, city in SW Poland, on the Kaczawa River approx. 38mi (61km) WNW of Wroclaw; commercial and industrial center in farming region. Town was officially est. 1252 and contains medieval structures; scene of Battle of Legnica (1241), in which Poles stopped Tartar invasion; passed to Bohemia 14th century, and Prussia 1742; returned to Poland by Potsdam Conference 1945. Industries: textiles, food processing and marketing, metals. Pop. 75,800.

Legume (Leguminosae), family of many plants, shrubs, and trees including beans, clover, and acacia. Many have nitrogen-fixing roots and are planted for forage and cover crops. A legume can be the fruit, a seed-bearing pod, or the entire plant.

Le Havre, commercial seaport city in N France, at mouth of Seine River on English Channel. Primarily a fishing and naval port until 1815, the city is now the principal export center for Paris and a transatlantic passenger port; site of a major Allied base during WWI; severely damaged during WWII; site of St Joseph church, a memorial to war victims, and Romanesque Church of St Honorine. Industries: chemicals, fertilizers, lumber, food processing, oil refining, shipbuilding. Founded 1516 as Le Havre-de-Grâce. Pop. 219,583.

Lehua, a showy hardwood tree common to many Pacific islands with bright red flowers borne in flat-topped clusters. The blossoms are used for decorative purposes. Species *Metrosideros villosa*.

Leibniz, Gottfried Wilhelm (1646–1716), German philosopher. He was educated at Leipzig, Jena, and Altdorf, studied jurisprudence (1667), and formulated ideas of a universal "characteristic" or logic. He went to Paris (1672) on a diplomatic mission and studied mathematics under Christian Huygens. He shared with Isaac Newton discovery of the calculus (1684). He contributed to the science of dynamics and forged a remarkable metaphysical system, based on the universality of centers of force and consciousness, known as "monads." Historiographer for the House of Hanover, courtier, and inventor, he was a truly encyclopedic genius, but published few complete works; *New Essays* (pub. 1765), *Theodicy* (1710), and many essays. *See also* Monad; Pre-established Harmony.

Leicester, Robert Dudley, Earl of (1532–88), English nobleman, favorite of Queen Elizabeth I. The mysterious death (1560) of his wife apparently cleared the way for Leicester to marry Elizabeth. The queen, however, soon realized the impracticability of the match. Though the marriage never took place, Leicester remained influential despite his feud with William Cecil, his remarriage (1578), and support for the Puritans. As governor of the United Provinces (the Netherlands) (1586), he involved England in Protestant Europe's struggle against Spain.

Leicester, city in central England, 90mi (145km) NW of London; country seat of Leicestershire. In 9th century it was one of five boroughs of region conquered by Danes. During the War of the Roses, Richard III stayed in Leicester the night before he was killed; his body was brought back here for burial, Aug. 22, 1485; site of 14th-century church of St Martin, 15th-century Guild Hall, and University of Leicester (1957). Knitting frame was first installed here in 1680, and hosiery has been an important industry ever since. Industries: boots, shoes, textiles, textile and woodworking machinery. Founded by Romans as Ratae Coritanorum; there are many remains of Roman origin. Pop. 290,600.

Leiden, city in W Netherlands, on the Oude Rijn River; site of University of Leiden (1575); birthplace of artists Rembrandt, Lucas van Leyden, and others whose works are displayed in the municipal museum. Industries: metal working, printing, rugs and blankets, food processing. Pop. 99,891.

Leipzig, city in S central East Germany, at the confluence of the Pleisse, White Elster, and Parthe rivers. Founded as a Slavic settlement in 11th century, it became commercial center at intersection of important trade routes; scene of 1813 Battle of Nations, which ended Napoleon's power in Germany. Printing industry, founded 1480, is still important; site of Karl Marx University (founded 1409 as University of Leipzig), 16th-century church of St Thomas, 13th-century Pauline Church, old stock exchange (1682); birthplace of Richard Wagner is preserved. Industries: textiles, machinery, toys, chemicals. Chartered end of 12th century. Pop. 566,630.

Leishmania, animallike, flagellate protozoan that is parasitic in the human liver and spleen. A small, ovate cell with no flagellum when in a human, it is carried by a sand flea in which it is elongate and has a flagellum. It causes the diseases leishmania and kala azar. Class Mastigophora; species *Leishmania donovani*.

Lemaître, Georges Édouard, (1894–1966), Belgian astronomer and cosmologist responsible for the "big bang" theory of the origin of the universe. In this theory the universe is thought to have begun suddenly and cataclysmically with the explosion of a primeval super-atom. He studied at Cambridge and at the Massachusetts Institute of Technology. In 1927 he became professor of astrophysics at the University of Louvain where he proposed his theory, which explained the recession of the galaxies in terms of Albert Einstein's theory of general relativity.

Le Mans, city in NW France, on Sarthe River 117mi. (188km) from Paris; capital of Sarthe dept.; besieged during Hundred Years' War (1337–1453); devastated by Huguenots 1562; scene of French defeat by Prussia 1870–71; birthplace of Henry II of England and John II of France; site of annual auto races, and Cathedral of St Julien du Mans (11th–13th centuries). Industries: food processing, textiles, machinery, automobile components. Founded by Romans 3rd century. Pop. 155,245.

Lemming, plump mouse-size rodent living near the Arctic. It has long, soft, brownish fur, small ears, and a tiny tail. Prolific plant-eaters, lemmings often emigrate in search of food. Emigrating hordes of Norway lemming, famous for population explosions, sometimes drown attempting to cross wide bodies of water. Family Cricetidae.

Lemnos (Limnos), volcanic island of Greece, in N Aegean Sea, off Turkey; mountainous terrain, soil is fertile; capital is Kastron; sacred to ancient Greece, became colony of Athens *c.* 500 BC; passed to Venice 1464, taken by Ottoman Turks 1479 and ceded to Greece 1913; source of Lemnian earth (a medicinal soil). Industries: fruit, wine, silk, fish. Area: 186sq mi (482sq km). Pop. 20,000.

Lemon, an evergreen tree *(Citrus limonia)* of the rue family growing to 12ft (3.7m), probably native to subtropical Asia. It yields the familiar sour yellow citrus fruit. It is grown primarily in California in the United States, and is cultivated in subtropical regions elsewhere.

Lemonwood, or wild coffee, tropical evergreen shrub native to South Africa and grown in S Florida. It has small, fragrant yellow flowers and shiny black fruit. Family Rubiaceae; species *Psycotria capensis*.

Lemur, primitive, mostly arboreal and nocturnal primate found in wooded areas of Madagascar and the Comoro Islands. They look like big-eyed squirrels with grasping, monkeylike hands and feet. Some are herbivorous, some feed mainly on insects, and others are omnivorous. Lemurs have changed little in 50,000,000 years and are believed to closely resemble the early ancestors of man and other primates. Length: 8in–4ft (20–122cm). Family Lemuridae. *See also* Primates.

Lena, river in E central Russian SFSR, USSR; rises on W slopes of Baikal Mts, W of Lake Baikal, flows NE and N along E side of central Siberian uplands into Laptev Sea through a delta 250mi (403km) wide; its tributaries number about 1,000. Yakutsk is only town on its course. River was first reached by Russians 1630. Navigable for 2,135mi (3,437km) of its 2,670mi (4,300km).

Lend-Lease, US program authorized by Congress in 1941 to give war aid to Great Britain. Aid was given on terms "the President deems satisfactory" and was soon extended to the USSR and China. Eventually, nearly all US war allies were recipients. When the program ended in 1945, over $50,000,000,000 had been expended.

L'Enfant, Pierre Charles (1754–1825), US architect and engineer, b. France. He went to America (1777) and served in the Continental army. At George Washington's invitation he planned the national capital (1791), but the high cost of construction caused his dismissal. More than a century later the development of Washington, D.C., was pursued according to his plans.

Lenin, Vladimir Ilyich (1870–1924), sometimes N. Lenin, founder and leader of the Russian Communist party and the Soviet state, b. as Vladimir Ilyich Ulyanov. After his brother's execution for an anti-tsarist plot (1887), he joined Plekhanov's Marxists and became a professional revolutionary. Arrested in 1895, he was exiled to Siberia (1897–1900). In 1900 he started the revolutionary newspaper *Iskra (The Spark)* abroad, and in 1903 formed the Bolshevik party. He was in Russia for the 1905 uprising but abroad again 1907–17, consolidating a tight, loyal group. Entering Russia after the March 1917 revolution, with the help of the Germans, who permitted him to cross Germany by train, he and Leon Trotsky organized the Bolshevik Revolution (November 1917). As premier, he was responsible for the creation of the Cheka (secret police), the dissolution of the Constituent Assembly, the Treaty of Brest-Litovsk, nationalization of industry, and the New Economic Policy. From 1918–21 he led the fight against anti-Bolshevik forces in Russia. Ascetic, disciplined, energetic, and totally political, he founded a utilitarian kind of Marxism based on the implementation of theory in action adapted to circumstances. His vast output includes *What Is To Be Done?* (1902), *Imperialism: The Highest Stage of Capitalism* (1917), and *State and Revolution* (1917). *See also* Russian Revolution.

Leninabad, town in NW Tadzhik SSR, USSR, on the Syr Darya River, 90mi (145km) S of Tashkent; capital of former Leninabad oblast. City was captured 329 BC by Alexander the Great; fell to the Russians 1866; called Khodzhent until 1936. It has a teachers' college and theater. Industries: textiles, clothing, shoes, food canning, automobile repair. Pop. 123,000.

Leninakan, city in NW Armenian SSR, USSR, on a tributary of the Araks River, 55mi (89km) NW of Yerevan, near the Turkish border. Originating as a fortress, Aleksandropol, on the site of the old village of Gumri, it was renamed 1924 and destroyed by an earthquake in 1926. Industries: cotton and knitwear, lumber, bicycles, meat processing, penicillin. Exports: silk, cloth, rugs. Est. 1837. Pop. 192,000.

Le Mans, France

Lemming

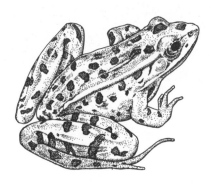

Leopard frog

Leningrad (Leningrado), second-largest city of the USSR; major Baltic seaport at the E end of the Gulf of Finland, built on the Neva delta; capital of Leningrad oblast. Founded as St Petersburg (1703) by Peter the Great, it was capital of Russia 1712–1918; scene of the 1825 Decembrist revolt and the Red Sunday incident in the 1905 revolution; the original center of the Russian revolution of 1917; renamed Petrograd in 1914 and Leningrad in 1924; suffered extensive damage in WWII; rebuilt since 1945; major cultural center; site of A. A. Zhdanov University (1819), the Saltykov-Shchedrin public library, numerous other libraries and educational institutions, Academy of Sciences, Winter Palace (1754–62), adjoined by the Hermitage Art Museum (orig. 1764), Palace of Art, St Isaac's cathedral (1819–58). Industries: shipbuilding, heavy engineering, brewing, publishing, printing, food processing, textiles, electronics, chemicals. Est. 1703. Pop. 4,480,000.

Leningrad, Siege of (August 1941–January 1944), military struggle of World War II. Invading Germans surrounded and besieged the Soviet city for 900 days, causing widespread famine and the death of almost 1,000,000 of its 3,000,000 inhabitants. Supply lines across the ice of Lake Ladoga enabled the city to survive until an army was marshaled strong enough to break the siege.

Lenin Peak, formerly Kaufmann Peak; mountain in Trans Alai Range between Kirgiz SSR and the Gorno Badakhshan Autonomous oblast, NE Tadzhik SSR, USSR; 2nd-highest peak in USSR. Height: 23,405ft (7,139m).

Lenni-Lenape, or Delaware Indians, a major Algonquian-speaking tribe of Eastern Woodlands Indians occupying New Jersey, E Pennsylvania, N Delaware, and Staten Island, Manhattan Island, and Long Island, New York. They are divided into three groups: the Unami, Unalachtigo, and Munsee. Some 10,000 originally occupied the eastern region, but were removed following the Revolution; today, about 1,000 of their descendants live in Oklahoma, and about 300 are in Ontario. Initially hostile to whites, they later served as excellent scouts, interpreters, and warriors during the American Revolution.

Lens, piece of transparent glass, plastic, quartz, etc, bounded by two surfaces, usually both spherical, that changes the direction of a light beam by refraction and hence can produce an image. A converging lens is convex in form (bulging at the center) and bends light rays toward the lens axis. A diverging lens is concave (thinnest at the center) and bends rays away from the axis. The image may be right-way-up or inverted, real or virtual depending on the relative positions of object and focal point of the lens; it may also be magnified or reduced in size. Lens images suffer from various aberrations so that they may be blurred and have false colors. An achromatic lens—a concave-convex lens combination of different indices of refraction—reduces chromatic aberration. *See also* Aberration; Image, Optical; Refraction; Wave Dispersion.

Lent, in the Christian year, a period of 40 days beginning with Ash Wednesday and ending with Easter. It is a period in which fasting and penitence have long been observed in preparation for the remembrance of the crucifixion and resurrection of Jesus Christ.

Lentil, annual plant long grown in the Mediterranean region, SW Asia, and N Africa. It has featherlike leaves and is cultivated for its nutritious seeds, used as food, forage, and a source of flour. Height: to 18 in (46cm). Family Leguminosae; species *Lens culinaris.*

Lenz's Law, an electromagnetic law deduced in 1834 by Russian physicist Heinrich F. E. Lenz. It states that an induced electric current always flows in the direction that will oppose the charge that produced the current. For example, this law will indicate the direction of the current induced by a permanent bar magnet pushed and withdrawn through a coil of wire.

Leo, or the Lion, equatorial constellation situated on the ecliptic between Cancer and Virgo; the fifth sign of the zodiac. Four galaxies lie in this constellation: M 65 (NGC 3623), M66 (NGC 3627), M95 (NGC 3358), and M96 (NGC 3358). Brightest star: Alpha Leonis (Regulus). The astrological sign for the period July 23–Aug. 22.

Leo I, Saint (*c.*390–461), also called Leo the Great, pope (440–61). As a leader of the early Christian Church, he consolidated the authority of the Roman see, producing a central church government for the Western church. He also claimed Rome's jurisdiction over Spain, Gaul, and Africa. His support for doctrinal matters was considered important to the Eastern Church; he read the Dogmatic Letter, accepted as the "Voice of Peter" at the Council of Chalcedon.

Leo III, Roman Catholic pope (795–816) and saint. Unrest in Rome resulted in a brutal, physical attack on him during a harvest procession in 799. He sought Charlemagne's assistance and, in 800, crowned Charlemagne emperor. During his papacy, Latin became the empire's official language.

Leo IX, Roman Catholic pope (1049–54) and saint, b. Bruno of Toul in Alsace. Elected in the court of Emperor Henry III in Worms rather than Rome, he insisted on approval by the clergy and people of Rome. He developed a source of funds for preserving St Peter's and reformed the College of Cardinals by developing a papal cabinet that became the Curia. He traveled extensively, seeking out corruption.

Leo III (680?–741), Byzantine emperor (*r.*717–741). Born of peasant parents in North Syria, Leo began his rise to power in the service of Justinian II. Anastasius II appointed Leo military leader of one of Byzantium's largest provinces. He became emperor after a revolt against Theodosius III, and thereupon established the Syrian dynasty. In 717–718, he successfully defended Constantinople against an Arab siege, and later expelled the Muslims from Asia Minor. Leo also developed a new system of provincial administration. The *Ecloga,* a legal manual published by Leo in 740, marked an important legislative advance. Leo opposed the veneration of icons, and thereby initiated a crisis in the Greek state that would last for over a century. *See also* Iconoclastic Controversy.

León, city in central Mexico, 32mi (512km) WNW of Guanajuato; site of railroad connecting El Paso, Tex., with Mexico City. Industries: iron goods, knives, shoes, silver, lead, copper, tin. Founded 1576; inc. 1836. Pop. 453,976.

León, city in W Nicaragua, near Pacific coast NW of Managua; capital of León dept.; 2nd-largest city in Nicaragua. Founded 1524 near Lake Managua by Fernández de Córdoba, city was moved to present site after earthquake 1609; historically a center of liberals rivaling Granada, the conservative center. Industries: cigars, cotton gins, leather goods. Pop. 90,897.

León, city in NW Spain, 82mi (132km) NW of Valladolid; capital of León prov. Occupied by Moors in 8th century, it was recaptured 882 by Alfonso III of Asturias; capital of medieval León kingdom until 1230 when Castile and León united; site of Romanesque church of San Isidoro (1149), 16th-century palace (now city hall), 13th–15th-century Gothic cathedral containing fine collection of Gothic stained glass, Renaissance-style monastery of San Marcos (1533–1541). Industries: leather, cotton, textiles, cigars, tourism. Area: (prov.) 5,972sq mi (15,467sq km). Pop. (city) 105,235, (prov.) 648,721.

Leonardo da Vinci (1452–1519), Florentine painter, sculptor, architect, engineer, and scientist. Apprenticed to Andrea del Verrocchio (1466–72), he remained at Verrocchio's studio probably until 1476. He was the founder of the Classic style of painting of the High Renaissance and was among the first to use the chiaroscuro technique. His early works include the unfinished "St. Jerome" (*c.*1480) and a portrait of Ginevia de' Benci. He moved to Milan (1482) to act as civil and military engineer to Duke Lodovico Sforza, where he executed "Madonna of the Rocks," "Portrait of a Musician," and numerous other works, including the "Last Supper" (1495–98). He made many architectural plans and designed and directed court festivals. Here he also began his scientific work and wrote his *Treatise on Painting.* Returning to Florence (1500), he executed the "Mona Lisa" and began "St Anne with the Madonna and Child." One of his last known paintings is "St John the Baptist." In 1517 he became chief painter, architect, and engineer to Francis I at Amboise, France, where he died. *See also* Chiaroscuro; Renaissance Art.

Leonidas (died 480 BC), heroic king of Sparta (490?–480 BC) during the Persian king Xerxes' invasion of Greece. Stationed at the strategic pass of Thermopylae, Leonidas was either deserted by the majority of his outnumbered Greek forces, or commanded their retreat, and was left with only a few hundred Spartans and Thespians against the overwhelming Persian army. Not a man retreated in their two-day battle to the death.

Leonine Rhyme, rhyme occurring within the verse line; usually the rhyming of the last syllable of the line with the middle one, which precedes the caesura. It was named after the 12th-century cleric, Leo of St Victor, who used it in his Latin verses. *See also* Caesura.

Leontief, Wassily (1906–), US economist, b. Russia. He developed the input-output table, which relates the empirical data of general equilibrium. An input-output table clearly illustrates the inter-industry relationships of an economy or a subcomponent of the economy, the sources of the input, and the destinations of the output. The table is an essential tool in the development of rational government economic planning. For this work, he received the Nobel Prize in economics in 1973. His report on world resources (1976) concluded that a greater population and life style can be sustained without environmental damage.

Leopard, athletic, spotted big cat found throughout Africa and S Asia. A round-headed cat with a short nose and long, thin tail, its dark-spotted coat is yellow. A good tree climber and swimmer, it feeds on birds, monkeys, antelope, and cattle. The gestation period is three months and 2–3 young are born. Length: body—37.4–59in (95–150cm); tail—23.6–37in (60–94cm); weight: to 200lb (90.7kg). There are 24 subspecies. Family Felidae; species *Panthera pardus. See also* Cat.

Leopard Frog, true frog native to United States, found in meadows or near ponds. Most are metallic bronze or green with dark, oval spots on their slender bodies and powerful legs. The southern leopard frog is considered a separate species, *Rana spenocephala.* Length: 5in (13cm). Family Ranidae; Species *Rana pipiens.* See also Frog.

Leopold I (1640–1705), Holy Roman emperor (1658–1705), king of Hungary (1655–1705), king of Bohemia (1656–1705). His reign saw almost constant warfare with either the Ottoman Turks or the French under Louis XIV. In 1664 the Turks gained control of Transylvania. In 1683 they besieged Vienna before being repulsed. In 1697 the Turks were defeated at Zenta, and Leopold gained most of Hungary. His armies fought against France in the Third Dutch War (1672–78). In 1686 Leopold formed the League of Augsburg against France. In 1688 France invaded the Palatinate, beginning the War of the Grand Alliance (1688–97). In 1701 the War of the Spanish Succession broke out. Leopold died before it ended.

Leopold I (1790–1865), first king of independent Belgium (1831–65). Son of the duke of Saxe-Coburg-Saalfield, he rose to corps command in the Russian army, serving 1805–14. In 1816 he married Princess Charlotte, daughter of the English prince who later became George IV. He refused the throne of Greece in 1830, but in 1831 was elected king of Belgium when it separated from Holland. His powers were limited under the new constitution, but he ably maintained the independence and unity of the nation and introduced important political and financial reforms.

Leopold II (1835–1909), king of Belgium (1865–1909). Succeeding his father, Leopold I, he initiated a period of colonial and commercial expansion. After financing Henry Stanley's Congo explorations (1879–84), Leopold persuaded the powers at the Berlin Conference (1884–85) to give him personal control over the Congo Free State. International protest, however, forced him to relinquish control to the Belgian government in 1908.

Lepanto, Battle of (1571), naval clash between forces of the Ottoman Empire and various Christian powers. When the Ottoman Turks attempted to take Cyprus from Venice in 1571, Greece, Austria, Spain, and Venice stopped them in this battle. Pope Pius V and King Philip II of Spain had assembled their forces with those of the Venetians at Messina, Sicily. The Turkish navy lay in the Gulf of Patras off the coast of Lepanto, Greece. Two hundred ships under Don John of Austria formed four squadrons and attacked them. The allied Christians then defeated the Turks.

Lepidodendron, a genus of extinct treelike club mosses of the order Lepidodendrales (class Lycopsida). Common during the Upper Carboniferous, it reached 100ft (30m) in height.

Lepidoptera, order of insects, including moths, butterflies, and skippers, widely distributed on every continent except Antarctica. They are characterized by four membranous wings covered with overlapping scales. Lepidoptera undergo complete metamorphosis. The larvae (caterpillars) have 5–8 pairs of legs and chewing mouthparts for feeding on plant tissues. Adults have sucking mouthparts for feeding on nectar and plant juices. Larvae of many species are farm and garden pests, but many adults are valuable plant pollinators. All species serve as food for many other small animals. There are about 17 superfamilies of Lepidoptera, including one of butterflies and one of skippers. They range in size from tiny moths only ⅛in (3.2mm) long to giant forms with wingspreads up to 11in (28cm). *See also* Insect.

Lepidus, distinguished Roman family. **Marcus Aemilius Lepidus** (died 152 BC) was censor, curile aedile, praetor in Sicily, consul, and triumvir. An able senator, he is known for his extensive building programs. His descendant **M.A. Lepidus** (died 77 BC) was a tribune and as consul led an army against the senate leader Catulus, who defeated him. His younger son, **M.A. Lepidus** (died 13 BC), served as consul with Caesar, then as triumvir with Antony and Octavian, and again as consul, governing Rome and Italy during the Philippi campaign. He then governed Africa and fought in Sicily until Octavian forced him to retire.

Leprosy (Hansen's disease), a communicable disease caused by the microorganism *Mycobacterium leprae* in which granular nodules develop on the skin, mucous membranes, and peripheral nerves. The spread and enlargement of the skin nodules produce the leonine appearance of the face and the other well-known and dreaded deformities of the disease. In tuberculoid leprosy, one of the two main types, damage to the nerves occurs early in the disease, so that the skin nodules (leprids) may not be felt. In this form, the nodules contain very few microorganisms. In lepromatous leprosy, the nodules (lepromas) contain many *Mycobacterium leprae* organisms and thus are a source of spread of the infection to others. The disease can be arrested by drug administration, but nerve damage is irreversible.

Lepton, member of a class of elementary particles that are not subject to the strong interaction. The group consists of the electron, muon, and the two neutrinos together with their antiparticles. The neutrinos react solely through the weak interaction; the electron and muon, being charged, are also subject to the electromagnetic force. Leptons, which all have half-integral spin, are thought to have no quark substructure but to be truly elementary. *See also* Hadron.

Leptospirosis, or Weil's Disease, infection with the spirochete *Leptospira.* It is passed to many by contact with infected rats. Symptoms include fever, jaundice, hemorrhagic tendencies, and muscle pain.

Lérida, city in NE Spain, on the Segre River; capital of Lérida prov. Scene of Julius Caesar's victory over Pompey's generals, 49 BC; captured 1149 by Raymond Berenguer IV; site of medieval university. Industries: wine, leather, livestock, arms, chemicals, fruit. Area: (prov.) 4,644sq mi (12,028sq km). Pop. (city) 90,884; (prov.) 347,015.

Lerma, Francisco Gómez de Sandoval y Rojas, Duque de (1552–1625), Spanish statesman. As chief minister to Philip III, he was virtual ruler of Spain from 1598. Intent on stopping Spain's costly wars, he eased relations with James I of England and signed a truce with the Netherlands. He drove the Moriscos from Spain in 1609. He became a cardinal in 1618; that same year he was driven from office by his son.

Lesbianism, homosexuality between women. The practice derives its name from the band in ancient Greece of reputedly homosexual women presided over by the poet Sappho on the island of Lesbos. Lesbianism has historically been less censured by society than male homosexuality. In the 19th century, long-standing sexual relationships between two women—so-called "Boston marriages"—were viewed with considerable tolerance. In the 1960s and 1970s many homosexual women became more assertive in identifying themselves, aligning themselves with both the gay rights and the women's liberation movements. *See also* Homosexuality.

Lesbos (Lesvos), island in E Greece, off NW Turkey in Aegean Sea; with Lemnos and Hagios Evstrátios forms department of Greece; Mytilene is the capital. An important cultural center 7th–6th centuries BC; home of Sappho, Alcaeus, Aristotle, and Epicurus; held by Macedonia, Rome, Byzantinum, and finally Ottoman Turks, who occupied the island 1462–1913, when it passed to Greece. Exports: olives. Industries: fishing, livestock, wine, wheat, citrus fruits, marble, soap. Settled *c.*1000 BC by Aeolians. Area: approx. 630sq mi (1,632sq km). Pop. 117,371.

Lesotho, formerly Basutoland; small kingdom in S Africa, completely surrounded by the Republic of South Africa. King Moshoeshoe II serves as head of state, and Prime Minister Leabua Jonathan is head of government.

Lesotho is dominated in E by Drakensburg Mts; the remainder is hilly tableland with a generally dry climate. Subsistence farming is carried on in W; main crops are maize, sorghum, and wheat. South Africa is a major factor in Lesotho's economic survival, as Sothos work in its mines, providing an important source of income. Lesotho is developing light industries, livestock grazing, and diamond exploitation. Over 97% of the population is of Basotho heritage, and a majority is Christian. Lesotho has one of the highest literacy rates in Africa (70%); the University of Botswana, Lesotho, and Swaziland is located in Roma.

Between the 16th–19th centuries, a Basotho tribal group emerged as a result of an influx of various displaced refugees from tribal wars. Chief Moshoeshoe I, ruling 1820–70, created the homogeneous and united tribe needed for defense against repeated Boer and Zulu attacks. He placed Basutoland under British protection 1868; when the protectorate was annexed to Cape Colony 1871 without Sotho approval, civil strife ensued until it was placed under direct control of Britain 1884–1959. It was governed by a British high commissioner in South Africa who worked through a resident commissioner of Maseru, until Oct. 4, 1966, when Basutoland became the independent Kingdom of Lesotho. During the late 1970s, Lesotho began a program designed to reduce its economic dependence on South Africa.

PROFILE

Official name: Kingdom of Lesotho
Area: 11,720sq mi (30,355 sq km)
Population: 1,498,000
Density: 129 per sq mi (49 per sq km)
Chief city: Maseru (capital)
Religion: Christianity
Language: English, Sesotho
Monetary unit: maloti

Less Developed Countries (LDCs), those nations, found primarily in Africa, Asia, and Latin America, that are unable to produce an adequate income to provide for the needs of their population, with resulting widespread poverty. These nations generally exhibit high rates of population growth, low rates of saving and investment, and low rates of economic growth.

Lesseps, Ferdinand Marie, Vicomte de (1805–94), French diplomat and promoter of the Suez Canal. He first had the idea of a canal to link the Red Sea and the Mediterranean in 1832, but he did not gain the initial concession until 1854. Digging began in 1859, using 30,000 Egyptian laborers, who were withdrawn in 1863. The work was finished with mechanical equipment from Europe. The canal was opened by the Empress Eugénie in November 1869, In 1879, de Lesseps headed a French company that began work on the Panama Canal, which he had to abandon nine years later, owing to political and financial troubles.

Lesser Antilles, one of three major island groups in West Indies archipelago, between Atlantic Ocean (E) and Caribbean Sea, stretching in an arc from Puerto Rico (N) to N coast of Venezuela, South America. The group includes Virgin Islands, Leeward Islands, Windward Islands, Barbados, Trinidad and Tobago, Netherland Antilles, and Venezuelan islands off NE Venezuela coast. Pop. 2,749,000.

Lessing, Doris (May) (1919–), Rhodesian novelist and playwright. Her books are strongly autobiographical, reflecting her membership of the Communist Party, her two failed marriages and her southern African background. This is especially so of the Martha Quest series—*Martha Quest* (1952), *A Proper Marriage* (1954), *A Ripple from the Storm* (1958), *Landlocked* (1965), and *The Four Gated City* (1969). Her later works included the *Canopus in Argos: Archives* science fiction series (*Shikasta,* 1979; *Marriages Between Zones Three, Four and Five,* 1980; *The Sirian Experiment,* 1981; *The Making of the Representative for Planet 8,* 1982; and *The Good Terrorist* (1985).

Lettuce, annual salad plant widely cultivated. Varieties of *Lactuca sativa* are cool weather crops; hot weather causes them to bolt, or go to seed prematurely. The large leaves form a compact head or loose rosette. They mature in 45–90 days. Wild species include the compass plant *(Silphium laciniatum),* a prickly lettuce-like plant believed to be the ancestor of cultivated forms. It has thin deeply lobed leaves and yellow flower heads; height: 3–5ft (0.9–1.5m). Blue lettuce *(L. floridana)* has lyre-shaped leaves and blue flowers; height: 3–6ft (0.9–1.8m). Family Compositae.

Leucine, white soluble essential amino acid found in proteins. *See also* Amino Acid.

Leucippus (5th century BC), Greek philosopher. He is believed to have been a native of Miletus in Asia Minor. He first stated the atomic theory of matter, which was developed by Democritus. *See also* Democritus.

Leukemia, an acute or chronic malignant disease characterized by abnormal numbers or types of white blood cells (leukocytes) in blood, bone marrow, and other tissues. Besides its division into acute and chronic forms, leukemia is also classified by the type of leukocyte involved (lymphocytes, lymphoblasts, and others). The acute lymphoblastic form is the most common malignant disease of childhood. Improved methods of treatment have reduced the death rate per 100,000 in children ages 0–14 from 3.8 in the 1940s to 2.9 in the 1970s. Increased rates of leukemia incidence have been associated with radioactive fallout from atomic bomb explosions. Some forms of leukemia have also been associated with exposure to petrochemical and rubber industry chemicals. The precise cause has not yet been determined.

Leukocyte (white blood cell), a colorless, amebalike structure containing a nucleus and cytoplasm and found in the blood. Leukocytes are either granular (granulocytes) or nongranular (agranulocytes), depending on the presence or absence of granules in the cytoplasm. Granulocytes are subdivided into neutrophils, eosinophils, and basophils; agranulocytes are either lymphocytes or monocytes. Normal blood contains 5,000 to 10,000 leukocytes per cubic millimeter of blood. Excessive numbers of leukocytes, or immature forms, are seen in such diseases as leukemia. Leukocytes have a phagocytic action (destroy harmful cells) and multiply when infection is present in the body.

Lepidoptera

John L. Lewis

Sinclair Lewis

Leukocytosis, an increase in the number of white blood cells above the normal maximum. Infection and inflammation are among the causes.

Leukopenia, reduction of number of white blood cells to below a normal level.

Leukoplakia, whitish patches on the gums, tongue, vulva, or mucous membrane of the cheeks, often seen in smokers and sometimes becoming malignant.

Levant, collective term for lands lining the E coast of the Mediterranean Sea, extending from Egypt to Turkey; still used when referring to Syria and Lebanon, known as the Levant States at the time of the French mandates.

Levee, broad low ridges of fine sediment deposited along the sides of rivers during floods. A levee may also be built artificially along the bank of a river or an arm of the sea to protect the land from flooding.

Levelers (*fl.* 1645–49), Puritan political and religious movement in England. The name alludes derisively to their demands for equality. Their leader was John Lilburne, and their program, which found extensive support in Cromwell's army, demanded complete constitutional reform, with abolition of the monarchy, proportional representation, and one supreme representative legislature elected by universal adult male suffrage. Cromwell opposed and finally crushed the movement.

Lever, a simple machine used to multiply the force or velocity applied to a body. A lever consists of a rod and a fulcrum, or point about which the rod rotates. In a lever of the first kind (a crowbar, for example), the applied force and the body to be moved are on opposite sides of the fulcrum, with the point of application farther from it. This lever multiplies the force applied by the ratio of the two distances. In a lever of the second kind, (as in a catapult) these relative distances are reversed, and the result is a multiplication of the speed.

Leverrier, Urbain Jean Joseph (1811–77), French astronomer, joint discoverer (with John Couch Adams) of the planet Neptune. Like Adams, he realized that anomalies in the orbit of Uranus could be due only to the gravitational influence of a hitherto undiscovered planet, but he was luckier than Adams in that notice was taken of his theory, which was proved correct by the Berlin Observatory in 1846.

Levi, in Genesis, third son of Leah and Jacob. He and his brother Simeon avenged Shechem's rape of their sister, Dinah, by killing all the males in Shechem's city. For this deed, Jacob prophesied the scattering of the two brothers' people over Israel.

Levites, in Judaism, the assistants to the Temple priests as assigned by the Bible to the tribe of Levi. From the age of 20–50, they served in the sanctuary as musicians, gatekeepers, teachers, scribes, and caretakers. The Levite tradition is still handed down from generation to generation, and a Levite is called up to read the Torah after a kohen (priest) in the synagogue service.

Leviticus, biblical book, third book of the Pentateuch, dealing with the indescribable holiness of God. Primarily a manual to instruct priests on ritual technicalities, it also exhorts reverent use of the proper rituals in worshiping God. Many of the laws in Leviticus, traditionally ascribed to Moses, are repeated in Deuteronomy in less detailed form.

Lewis, C(live) S(taples) (1898–1963), British scholar, critic, and author. He was best known for his novels on religious and moral themes, including *The Screwtape Letters* (1942). He also wrote children's books and critical works, and was professor of medieval and Renaissance English at Cambridge University (1954–63).

Lewis, Francis, (1713–1802), American patriot and a signer of the Declaration of Independence, b. Wales. A successful merchant, he was a delegate from New York to the Stamp Act Congress (1765) and attended the Continental Congress (1774–79).

Lewis, John L(lewellyn) (1880–1969), US labor leader, b. Lucas co, Iowa. A coal miner, he became active in union affairs and was elected president of the United Mine Workers Union (UMWU) (1920–60). After splitting with President William Green over unionization of mass-production industries, Lewis formed the Congress of Industrial Organization (CIO) and was its president (1935–40). He withdrew the UMWU from the CIO (1942). Lewis' strike actions during World War II led to the restrictive labor legislation of the Smith-Connally Act (1943) and Taft-Hartley Act (1947).

Lewis, (Harry) Sinclair (1885–1951), US author, b. Sauk Centre, Minn. The son of a country doctor, he attended Yale University, becoming involved in socialist activities. After graduation (1908), he held a variety of newspaper and editorial jobs. He began writing short stories, and his first novel appeared in 1914. It was not until the publication of the novel *Main Street* in 1920, however, that he gained acclaim. A satirist, he poked fun at American middle-class life. Among his targets were conformity and hypocrisy in business, medicine, and religion.

Lewis' early work, specifically *Babbitt* (1922) and *Arrowsmith* (1925), is generally considered his best. Other novels include *Elmer Gantry* (1927), *Dodsworth* (1929), *Ann Vickers* (1933), *It Can't Happen Here* (1935), and *Cass Timberlane* (1945). Awarded the Nobel Prize for literature in 1930, he was the first American to receive that honor.

Lewis, Sir W(illiam) Arthur (1915–), British economist, b. St. Lucia, B.W.I. He earned his doctorate at the London School of Economics (1940), before becoming a lecturer at the University of London. He was associated with many universities in England and the United States, served as UN advisor to the prime minister of Ghana, and was a founder of the Caribbean Development Bank. His *The Theory of Economic Growth* (1955) was an influential economics text. He shared the 1979 Nobel Prize for economics with Theodore Schultz of the United States.

Lewis, (Percy) Wyndham (1884–1957), English novelist, painter, and critic; founder of the Vorticist movement. The clarity of style displayed in his paintings is sustained in his fiction, such as *Tarr* (1918), *The Apes of God* (1930), and *Self-Condemned* (1954), which deals uncompromisingly with the weaknesses of human nature.

Lewis and Clark Expedition (1804–06), exploration of the Louisiana Purchase and the country beyond as far as the Pacific by two army officers, Meriwether Lewis and William Clark. The purpose of the successful expedition, backed by President Jefferson and Congress in 1803, was to find a land route to the Pacific, strengthen US claims to Oregon Territory, and to gather information about the Indians.

Lexington, city in NE central Kentucky, 75mi (121km) E of Louisville, in bluegrass region; seat of Fayette co. A famous breeding center of thoroughbred horses, the city's first race track was constructed 1795; named by a group of hunters after the Revolutionary War battle of Lexington (1775). It contains homes of Henry Clay, John Hunt Morgan, and Mary Todd Lincoln; site of University of Kentucky (1865), Transylvania College (1780). Exports: oil, coal, farm and quarry products. Industries: tobacco, horses, automobile parts, electrical machinery, distilling, bluegrass seed, typewriters, paper products. Founded 1779; inc. 1832. Pop. (1980) 204,165.

Lexington and Concord, Battle of (April 19, 1775), first major battle of the Revolutionary War. Warned by Paul Revere and William Dawes that 700 British troops under Lt. Col. Francis Smith were marching from Boston to Concord to seize militia stores, 70 Minutemen under Capt. John Parker met them at the Lexington Green. A skirmish followed that left 8 Americans dead. The British reached Concord and destroyed the supplies, but were attacked by a larger force of American militia at Concord's North Bridge. The colonists harassed Smith's men all the way back to Boston, beginning a siege there that was to last nearly a year.

Leyden, Lucas van (*c.*1494–1533), real name Lucas Hugensz, Dutch painter and engraver. "The Raising of Lazarus" (1508) is one of his best early works. A year later he executed a famous series of nine prints, "The Circular Passion." "Milkmaid" is one of the earliest genre engravings. His largest work is "Ecce Homo," influenced by Albrecht Dürer.

Leyden Jar, the earliest and simplest device for storing static electricity and the prototype electrical condenser, developed in 1745. It consists of a foil-lined glass jar partially filled with water and closed with a cork through which protrudes a knobbed brass rod that is wired to the foil. To charge the jar, friction is applied to the tip of the rod. A charge can be demonstrated by touching the rod and receiving a mild shock. The Leyden jar is used for classroom demonstrations.

Leyte, island in E central Philippines, SW of Samar Island and separated from it by the narrow San Juanico Strait. Island is irregularly shaped and mountainous, with many natural harbors; population is centered around Tacloban, a major oil port to the NE. Discovered 1521 by Ferdinand Magellan, it was governed by Spain until home rule was established by the United States 1901. Leyte Gulf (on E shore) was the scene of decisive US victory over Japanese air and naval forces Oct. 1944. Products: copper, asphalt, manganese, iron, sugar, corn, cotton, hemp. Area: 2,785sq mi (7,213sq km). Pop. (Leyte and Southern Leyte provs.) 1,091,887.

Lhasa (Lasa, or **La-sa),** city in SW China, on the Lasa River; capital of Tibet autonomous region; site of the great palace of the Dalai Lama, as well as many temples, monasteries, and convents. Many monastic institutions were closed or destroyed after Tibetan revolt from Chinese rule 1959. Called "Forbidden City" because of historical hostility of lamas to foreigners, it was first visited by Europeans in 1904. Pop. 175,000.

Lhasa Apso, Tibetan dog (nonsporting group) used to guard lamaseries. It has a narrow head with medium-long muzzle, large nose, and hanging ears. The long body is set on shortish legs; the tail is carried in a screw-shape over the back. Kennel clubs' preferred color for heavy, long, straight coat is golden. Average size: 11in (28cm) high at shoulder; 13–15lb (6–7kg).

Libby, Willard Frank (1908–80), US chemist, b. Grand Valley, Colo. He became a professor at Chicago and later at the University of California. During 1941–45 he worked on the separation of isotopes for the atom bomb. This led to an interest in nuclear physics and to the invention of carbon-14 dating of archeological objects, for which he was awarded a Nobel prize in 1960.

Liberalism, political and social philosophy that stresses protection of individual liberties and civil rights. The liberal doctrines, which evolved in the late 18th century, were an outgrowth of John Locke's theories, reflecting his faith in man's rational nature and urging limits upon governmental power. By contrast, contemporary liberals favor greater governmental control, believing that social and economic reforms can best be accomplished through legislation.

Liberal Party, British political party developed from the former Whigs after the 1832 Reform Bill. Its program of free trade, religious liberty, anti-imperialism, and low budgets appealed to the newly enfranchised industrial middle class, and the Liberals were in office almost continually for nearly thirty years (1846–74). After a Third Reform Bill (1884) Liberal prime minister Gladstone promoted Irish home rule, a course that weakened and split the party. With increased reliance upon minority groups, the Liberals were victorious in the elections of 1892, 1906, and 1908, but since World War I have lost much of their vote to the Labour party. Although nearly 20% of the British electorate voted Liberal in recent elections (which motivated the party's campaign for proportional representation), the party has managed to retain few parliamentary seats. In an attempt to increase its political influence, the party formed an electoral alliance with Britain's New Social Democratic Party in 1981.

Liberal Party, Canadian political party. In 1854 more radical elements of the Reformers united to form the Liberal party. Their first administration (1873–78) under Alexander Mackenzie was anti-railway and advocated free trade. Under the leadership of Wilfrid Laurier (1896–1911) the Liberals supported ethnic conciliation, independence, and immigration. The party opposed conscription in World War II, finding support among the French and the western Progressives. Lester Pearson (1963–68) and Pierre Trudeau (1968–79; 1980–84) have led their most recent governments.

Liberator, The (1831–65), militant abolitionist newspaper founded by William Lloyd Garrison, an outspoken foe of slavery.

Liberia, an independent republic in W Africa, bordered by Guinea (N), Ivory Coast (E), Atlantic Ocean (S), and Sierra Leone (NW). Liberia can be viewed as two geographical regions: a coastal plain extending approx. 50mi (81km) inland and a plateau region covered by a thick tropical rain forest, and broken by the Bomi Hills, Bong, and other mountains.

Economy. The economy is based on agriculture, mining, and industry. Liberia's most valuable cash crop is rubber; cacao, palm kernels, coffee, citrus fruits, kola nuts, and rice are also grown. The discovery of high-grade iron ore in the Bomi Hills has contributed greatly to Liberia's economic growth and provides its number one export. Other industries include rubber processing, oil refining, fish canning, and brewing. The economy relies heavily on US technical assistance, investments, and exports. Liberia's lenient tax and inspection policies encourage world trade, and the registration of a huge merchant vessel fleet.

People and government. Most of the people of Liberia belong to the more than 20 tribes, and speak numerous dialects, although English is the official language. The descendants of black US settlers, known as Americo-Liberians, have enjoyed higher economic status and provide most of the political and social leadership. Most of the tribal people inhabit small villages in the rain forest, while the Americo-Liberians live along the coast, mainly in Monrovia. The differences between the groups is lessening through intermarriage and education, although Liberia still has one of the lowest literacy rates in Africa.

From 1947 until 1980, Liberia had a form of government based on that of the United States, with a strong president, bicameral legislature, and a judicial branch with a supreme court. In 1980, however, the constitution was suspended and the country placed under martial law. The People's Redemption Council was granted full legislative and executive powers.

History. The coast of Liberia was inhabited by various seafaring tribes when Portuguese traders arrived in 15th century; the Portuguese monopolized trade until the 16th century, when Dutch, English, French, and German competitors established themselves. In 1817 the American Colonization Society began a project for resettlement of freed black slaves. The first settlement was at Cape Masurado (now Monrovia) in 1822. In 1847 the Independent Republic of Liberia was created, but suffered much from internal disorder and went bankrupt in the early 1900s. Since then, the country has relied heavily on economic assistance from the United States. The True Whig Party dominated the country's government until 1980, when amid accusations of corruption and political unrest, the military assassinated the president and assumed control. The new regime received international condemnation for its continued execution of political foes. Promises of civilian rule remained unfulfilled, and troubles within the country and with neighboring Sierra Leone continued through the mid-1980s.

PROFILE

Official name: Republic of Liberia
Area: 43,000sq mi (11,370sq km)
Population: 1,733,000
Chief cities: Monrovia (capital); Harper; Buchanan
Religion: Protestantism, Roman Catholicism, animism, Islam
Language: English
Monetary unit: Liberian dollar

Liberty Island (formerly Bedloe's), island in SE New York, in New York Bay, SW of Manhattan Island; part of Statue of Liberty National Monument; connected to Manhattan by ferry. In 18th century island served as a quarantine station; in 1841 Fort Wood was built and the Statue of Liberty was placed on it in 1885. Although island is in New Jersey waters, it was agreed in 1834 to keep it part of New York geographically. Name changed from Bedloe's Island to Liberty Island 1956. Area: 10acres (4hectares).

Libra, or the Scales, southern constellation situated on the ecliptic between Virgo and Scorpius. As the seventh sign of the Zodiac, it formerly contained the First Point of Libra, the intersection of the ecliptic and the equator marking the autumnal equinox. Owing to precession this point has shifted westward into Virgo. Brightest star Beta Librae. The astrological sign for the period Sept. 23–Oct. 23.

Library Classification. *See* Classification, Library.

Library of Congress, US national library located in Washington, D.C. It is supported mainly by congressional appropriations. The library was originally established (1800) to serve as a research facility for members of Congress. Since its founding its responsibilities have been expanded to include copyrighting, interlibrary loans, and the publication of cumulative catalogs. Its collection includes over 60,000,000 items. The library is directed by a librarian appointed by the president and confirmed by Congress.

Libration, slight oscillatory motion of the Moon through which small portions of its far side become temporarily visible on Earth. It results from a combination of factors: namely, irregularities in the Moon's rotation caused by the effect of Earth's gravity; lack of uniformity in the Moon's orbital velocity compared with its axial rotation; and the inclination of the Moon's axis to its orbital plane, which produces a seasonlike latitudinal motion.

Libreville, capital city of Gabon, W Africa, at mouth of Gabon River on the Gulf of Guinea; administrative and educational center; formerly the leading port, trade has been dispersed to other harbors of Gabon; lumber is chief industry and export. Founded 1843 by French traders, and named Libreville ("Freetown") 1848. Pop. 60,000.

Libya (Libiya), independent nation in N Africa. An invasion route for centuries, it gained independence through UN action. Oil is its chief commodity, and its government is a military dictatorship.

Land and economy. A country of 95% desert or semidesert, Libya, located on the N central coast of Africa, is bounded by 1,100mi (1,771km) of the Mediterranean Sea (N), Egypt (E), Sudan (SE), Tunisia and Algeria (W), and Niger and Chad (S). The highest point is 10,335ft (3,152m) in the S mountain area. Cultivation is possible only along the narrow coast, the slopes of two N hill areas, and a few oases. Libya has no permanent rivers; only 2% of the land is arable; 4% is used for grazing. The "ghibli," a hot, dust-filled wind from the S, occurs in the spring. Oil is Libya's main product and earns more than 95% of export revenues. Limited by meager rainfall, Libya is not self-sufficient in foodstuffs although subterranean sources of water are being tapped. Most of the skilled and industrial workers are foreigners. Gradual restructuring of the economy along socialist lines began in 1977.

People. Libya's topographical features result in 90% of the people living on less than 10% of the land, primarily the coastal regions; 20% live in the largest cities, Tripoli and Benghazi. The population is a mixture of Arab and Berber; nomadic or semi-nomadic tribes, Tebou and Touareg, live in the S. Sunnite Islam is the state religion; Arabic is the official language. Literacy is 30%–35%.

Government. According to the constitution of 1977, the government is operated by a 12-man Revolutionary Command Council (RCC). The chairman of the RCC is the chief of state.

History. Occupied in ancient times by the Phoenicians, Carthaginians, Greeks, Romans, Vandals, and Byzantines, Libya spent centuries under foreign rule. It was an Italian colony from 1911 until WWII. In 1947, King Idris I combined with the Allies and liberated the country. On Nov. 21, 1949, a UN General Assembly resolution approved Libyan independence, making it the first country to achieve independence through UN action. On Dec. 24, 1951, it declared itself a constitutional monarchy under King Idris. A military coup overthrew his regime in 1969 and the new leader, Col. Muammar el-Qaddafi abolished the monarchy and announced the Libyan Arab Republic. Its goal of confederation with other Arab states has not been realized despite attempts with Egypt (1972); Tunisia (1974); Syria (1980); and Chad, where Libyan troops invaded (1980) in support of the government, but were forced to leave in 1981 after Chad rejected unification. In 1982, planning for a merger with Syria was resumed. Qaddafi has been a fervent opponent of Israel, lending considerable support to Palestinian guerrilla groups. Worldwide terrorist attacks, alleged to be encouraged and initiated by Qaddafi, led the US to bomb centers of terrorist activity in Libya in 1986. A prominent member of the Organization of Petroleum Exporting Countries, Libya has consistently urged higher prices for crude oil.

PROFILE

Official name: Socialist People's Libyan Arab Jamahiriya
Area: 679,216sq mi (1,759,540sq km)
Population: 2,850,000
Density: 4.2 per sq mi (1.6 per sq km)
Chief cities: Tripoli (capital); Benghazi
Government: Military dictatorship
Religion: Islam
Language: Arabic
Monetary unit: Libyan dinar
Gross national product: $23,390,000,000
Per capita income: $10,000
Industries: petroleum products, processed foods, leather goods, embroidered fabrics
Agriculture: wheat, barley, fruits, dates, olives, peanuts, tobacco
Minerals: oil, natural gas
Trading partners: West Germany, Italy, United States

Libyan Desert (As-Sahra' al-Libiyah), desert region in NE Africa, extending over SW Egypt, E Libya, NW Sudan; region consists of sand dunes, rocky plateaus; few inhabitants.

Lichen, a composite plant consisting of a fungus in which microscopic, usually single-cell, algae are embedded. The fungus and its algae form a symbiotic association in which the fungus contributes support, water, and minerals, while the algae contribute food produced by photosynthesis. Lichens can grow on almost any surface—rock, tree trunk, or soil—exposed to light. They are extremely slow-growing, often long-lived plants that are typically small, less than 1ft (30cm) in diameter. More than 15,000 species occur in most terrestrial habitats from the Arctic and Antarctic to the tropics.

Li Ch'ing-chao (1081–after 1141), Chinese poet. She is regarded as one of China's greatest poets. A writer of *tz'u*, poems of irregular length most popular in the Sung dynasty (960–1279), her eloquence made the commonplace seem special. She often used objects from nature to symbolize a sense of loneliness and loss. Also a poetry critic, her comments on her contemporaries were perceptive.

Lichtenstein, Roy (1923–), US painter, b. New York City; a major exponent of the pop art movement. His works are typically large comic-strip sequences, complete with all the photo-reproduction techniques in evidence. The copies, which include the balloon with words, demonstrate the uniformity and rigidity of comic-strip art.

Licinius, Valerius Licinianus (?270–325), Roman emperor (311–23). In 313 Licinius, together with Constantine the Great, issued the "Edict of Milan," legislation that favored the Christians in the empire. A few years later, however, Licinius reversed his position and resumed attacks on the Christians.

Licorice, perennial plant native to the Mediterranean region and grown in California. It has spikes of blue flowers. The dried roots are used to make candy, tobacco, beverages, and cough medicine. Height: to 3ft (91cm). Family Leguminosae; species *Glycyrrhiza glabra.*

Liberia

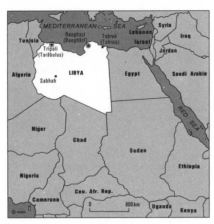

Libya

Liechtenstein

Lie, Trygve (1896–1968), Norwegian diplomat, first secretary-general of the United Nations (1946–53). A lawyer and Labor party leader, he held ministerial posts beginning in 1935; he was foreign minister (1941–46). He headed Norway's delegation to the 1945 San Francisco conference that created the United Nations. In the Korean War, he supported UN action. Soviet hostility to his actions caused him to resign.

Liebig, Justus, Baron von (1803–73), German chemist. After training as an apothecary, he studied in Paris under Joseph Gay-Lussac and later became professor at Giessen and then at Munich. He was the first to realize that animals derive their energy from the combustion of food and to divide foods into carbohydrates, fats, and proteins. He introduced synthetic fertilizers into agriculture and showed that plants derive their minerals from the soil. He showed that fermentation was a chemical process and invented the chemical condenser that bears his name. He was made a baron in 1845.

Liebknecht, Karl (1871–1919), German lawyer and anti-war Socialist, son of Wilhelm Liebknecht. Imprisoned for treason, he was elected a legislator (1908). His resistance to German entry into World War I earned him another jail term. With Rosa Luxemburg, he was a leader of the extreme left, or Spartacist group, of Socialists, who favored a communist regime. Liebknecht and Luxemburg were both killed while under arrest (Jan. 15, 1919) during the Spartacist revolt in Berlin.

Liebknecht, Wilhelm (1826–1900), German revolutionary, journalist, and companion of Karl Marx, formed the short-lived revolutionary republic of Baden (in Germany) in 1848. After an association with Marx in London, he returned to Germany in 1864 to organize labor according to Marxian principles. He served as a legislator and was imprisoned for opposition to the Franco-Prussian War.

Liechtenstein, independent principality on the E shore of the Rhine River between NE Switzerland and W Austria. Liechtenstein is an alpine country with terraced slopes, suited for fruit trees, vines, and dairy farming; the fertile Rhine plain yields corn and vegetables. Prior to WWII, the economy depended primarily on agriculture; it now prospers with modern industries including machinery, textiles, processed foods, furniture, pottery, pharmaceuticals, wine, tourism, and postage stamps.

The native inhabitants of Liechtenstein are descendants of the Alamanni, a German tribe. By the early 1970s, due to increased economic development and the need for labor, 33% of the population consisted of foreigners. The state religion is Roman Catholicism, and German is the national language.

Liechenstein is a constitutional monarchy with a democratic and parliamentary base. The constitution (1921, amended in 1972), requires a parliament made up of 21 members. Parliament-approved proposals to grant women suffrage had been defeated several times, making Liechtenstein the only W European country to deny women the vote. By 1980, however, local referendums had granted the franchise to women in two cantons (local political divisions). Switzerland maintains the country's postal, telephone, and telegraph services, and handles diplomatic relations with other states. Social legislation is modeled after that of Switzerland, and education is required through the secondary school level. Liechtenstein has no army; Swiss frontier guards are stationed at the border in accordance with customs treaty.

History. Liechtenstein was part of the Roman province of Rhaetia, which passed in mid-5th century to a Germanic tribe. In 1396 the county of Vadus was placed under the suzerainty of the Holy Roman emperor; in 1699 the lordship was sold to Austrian Prince Johann Adam von Liechtenstein, and in 1719 the territories were given the title Imperial Principality of Liechtenstein. Liechtenstein was a member of Napoleon's Confederation 1806–14, and the German Confederation 1815–66, until it achieved independence. Liechtenstein was closely aligned with Austria and then Switzerland; the customs treaty was signed between Switzerland and Liechtenstein in 1923. Franz Josef II became prince in 1938. Liechtenstein's well-developed economy consistently provides its people with one of the world's highest per capita incomes.

PROFILE

Official name: Principality of Liechtenstein
Area: 62sq mi (161sq km)
Population: 25,808
Chief cities: Vaduz (capital); Schaan; Balzers
Religion: Roman Catholic
Language: German
Monetary unit: Swiss franc

Liège, city in E Belgium, 58mi (93km) ESE of Brussels; capital of Liège prov.; famous educational center during Middle Ages; won for France by Napoleon (1794–1815); Congress of Vienna (1815) gave the area to the Netherlands. Industries: foundries, firearms, machinery. Settled 558; est. as bishopric 8th century. Pop. 139,333.

Liepaja (Lepaya), second-largest city of the Latvian Republic, USSR, on the Baltic Sea, 120mi (193km) WSW of Riga. Founded by Teutonic Knights, it came under the rule of Lithuania 1418, Prussia 1560, Sweden 1701, and Russia 1795. It was a German naval base in both world wars. This ice-free port is a noted health resort known for its baths; site of city theater. Industries: steel, agricultural machinery, explosives, paints, wire, linoleum, cork and leather goods, shipbuilding, food processing, fish canning, timber. Exports: timber, steel products, linoleum, matches. Est. 1263. Pop. 104,000.

Life-Support System, in aerospace technology, system supplying food, water, and oxygen to astronauts. Eleven pounds of water and two pounds of oxygen must be recycled per person each day. Food cannot yet be recycled and must be stored in dehydrated form. Liquid body wastes, used wash water, and water vapor in the cabin can be drawn through wicks, evaporated, and condensed again as pure water. Carbon dioxide can be vented or absorbed by plants.

Ligament, band of tough stringy connective tissue that joins bone to bone and reinforces joints. In the wrist and ankle joints, for example, they surround the bones like firm elastic bandages. Ligaments, which contain a gluelike organic substance known as collagen, form part of the supporting tissues of the body.

Light, type of electromagnetic wave that on striking the retina of the eye causes a visual sensation. The wavelength range is very narrow being approximately 750–400 nanometers (10^{-9}m), different wavelengths producing different color sensations. Sources of light include incandescent (strongly heated), flourescent, and phosphorescent substances. Incandescent sources can be heated by an electric current, as in a light bulb, by combustion, as in a match, by nuclear fusion reactions, as in the Sun, or by other means. Many properties of light, such as reflection, refraction, interference, diffraction, and polarization, can be ex-

plained in terms of waves. Other phenomena, including the photoelectric effect and the emission and absorption of light, necessitate the assumption that light consists of a stream of photons. Both waves and photons travel in free space at the speed of light, about 186,000mi (300,000km) per second. *See also* Color; Fluorescence.

Light, Speed of, universal constant giving the speed of propagation of electromagnetic waves, including light, in free space and equal to 186,281.7mi (299,-792.5 km) per second. Symbol: c. *See also* Light.

Light Adaptation, shift in functional dominance from rod cells to cone cells within the retina as overall illumination increases. Unlike dark adaptation, this process is nearly instantaneous. Thus humans can discern color and form soon after emerging from prolonged darkness.

Lightning, the visible flash of light accompanying an electrical discharge between clouds or between Earth and clouds, produced by a thunderstorm. A typical discharge consists of several lightning strokes, initiated by leaders that follow an irregular path of least resistance, the lightning channel. Intense heating by the discharge expands the channel very rapidly to a diameter of 5 to 10in (13 to 25cm), creating the sound waves of thunder.

Light Waves. *See* Light.

Light-Year, unit of astronomical distance equal to the distance traveled in free space by light in one year. One light-year is equal to 5.88×10^{12}mi (9.46×10^{12}km) or to 0.307 parsec.

Lignin, celluloselike organic compound that adds stiffness to plant cell walls. It fills spaces between cellulose fibers in wood and certain plants. Wood is 25–30% lignin. It is used to manufacture synthetic rubber and pigments.

Lignite. *See* Coal.

Lignum Vitae, tropical, New World evergreen tree. It is the source of a hard, dense wood used in bearings, pulleys, etc. A short-trunked tree, its flowers are blue or purple. Height: to 30ft (9.1m). Family Zygophyllaceae; species *Guaiacum officinale*.

Liguria, region in NW Italy, on the Ligurian Sea between France and Tuscany; comprised of Genoa, Imperia, La Spezia, and Savona provs.; Genoa is the capital. Region is geographically divided into narrow coastal strip, the Italian Riviera (world-famous winter resort area), and mountainous inland region. It was conquered by Romans 2nd century BC, ruled by Genoa 16th century–1815, when it was annexed to Sardinia; it was active in movement for Italian independence. Products: vegetables, flowers, olives, fruits, wine grapes. Industries: shipbuilding, tourism, chemicals, lumber, textiles, fishing. Area: 2,098sq mi (5,434sq km). Pop. 1,881,982.

Lilac, ornamental shrub brought to America before the 18th century. It blooms in early May, bearing panicles (pointed clusters) of tiny white to purple flowers. Height: to 8ft (2.4m) with French hybrids to 15 ft (4.6m). Species include the common *Syringa vulgaris*, Persian *S. persica*, and the 3–4ft (0.9–1.2m) dwarf Korean *S. velutina*. Family Oleaceae.

Lilburne, John (?1614–57), English political figure, leader of the Levelers. After imprisonment (1638–40) for anti-episcopal writings, he fought for the Parliamentarians (1642–45) and resigned from army. His pamphleteering against the army leaders led to his arrest (1649) for treason. Freed and acquitted, he nonetheless continued under suspicion. *See also* Levelers.

Liliuokalani, Lydia Kamekeha (1838–1917), last monarch of Hawaii (1891–93), b. Honolulu. A dedicated Hawaiian nationalist, Liliuokalani denounced American dominance and tried to restore lost power to the crown by changing the constitution. The plan alarmed resident Americans, who staged a rebellion aided by US troops (1893). The queen formally abdicated in 1895. The islands were annexed by the United States in 1898.

Lille, city in N France, 130mi (224km) NNE of Paris; capital of Nord dept. During 16th century dukes of Burgundy had official residence here; after 1668 it served as capital of French Flanders; birthplace of Charles de Gaulle (1890); site of 17th-century Flemish Vielle Bourse (old stock exchange), 17th-century gateways, and elaborate citadel (1667–1673). University of Douai moved here in 1808 (now University of Lille). Industries: textiles, machinery. Pop. 177,218.

Lily, genus (*Lilium*) of perennial, bulbous plants grown in warm Northern Hemisphere regions. They are native to temperate and tropical regions worldwide. They have erect stems and various leaf shapes. The showy flowers are solitary or clustered in combinations of colors including white, red, orange, yellow, green, purple, and pink. Most lilies prefer well-drained, moist soil and a sunny location. Exact cultivation requirements vary according to species. Height: 3–9ft (0.9–2.7m). Family Liliaceae. The lily family includes over 2,000 species.

Lily of the Valley, perennial plant native to Europe, Asia, and E United States. It has broad, elongated leaves and tiny, white, bell-shaped fragrant flowers on a stalk. Family Liliaceae; species *Convallaria majalis*.

Lima, capital city of Peru, on central Pacific coast, just SE of port of Callao; capital of Lima dept.; commercial, administrative, and cultural center of Peru. Founded 1535 by Francisco Pizarro, and called the "City of Kings," it was seat of Spanish viceroyalty; occupied by Chilean forces 1881–83 (War of the Pacific); site of University of San Marcos (1551), cathedral (16th century), National Library (1821); suffered earthquakes 1687 and 1746. Products: cotton, vegetables, grain, sugar, fruit. Industries: textiles, leather goods, oil refining, furniture, food processing, foundries, cement, pharmaceuticals. Pop. 3,317,648.

Lima Bean, perennial plant native to tropical America. Cultivated as an annual, it is a climber with oval leaves and yellowish-white flowers. Its broad, flat seeds are a popular vegetable. Family Leguminosae; species *Phaseolus limensis*.

Limbic System, the brain's cortical and subcortical structures and their interconnections, all of which are involved in motivation and emotion. Destruction of limbic tissue usually results in deterioration in patterns of behavior.

Lime, small tropical tree (*Citrus aurantifolia*) of the rue family, probably native to Asia. The trees grow to 8–15ft (2.4–4.6m) and yield the familiar small green acid fruit used for flavoring and juice. 317, 338, 594.

Lime, calcium oxide (quicklime) or calcium hydroxide (slaked lime). Calcium oxide, CaO, consists of whitish lumps obtained by roasting limestone (calcium carbonate) until all the carbon dioxide has been driven off. It is used as a refractory, a flux, and in glass making, water treatment, food processing, and as a cheap alkali. Calcium hydroxide, Ca(OH)$_2$, is a white crystalline powder obtained by the action of water on calcium oxide. It is used in mortar, plaster, cements, and in agriculture.

Limerick, short humorous verse, usually taking the form of five anapestic lines with the rhyme scheme *a a b b a*. First recorded in 1820, the form was popularized by Edward Lear in his *The Book of Nonsense* (1846). Subsequently it was employed to express a variety of subjects or thoughts in an epigrammatic manner. *See also* Lear, Edward.

Limestone, sedimentary rock composed primarily of calcium carbonate. Generally formed from deposits of the skeletons of marine invertebrates, it is used to make cement, as a source of commercial lime, and as a building material. *See also* Sedimentary Rocks.

Limit, value approached by a mathematical function as the independent variable approaches some specified value. For example, the function $1/(x^2 + 1)$ has values $\frac{1}{2}, \frac{1}{5}, \frac{1}{10}, \frac{1}{17}$, etc., as x takes values of 1, 2, 3, 4, etc. As x increases indefinitely the functional value ap-

proaches zero: one says that the function tends to zero as x approaches infinity. The limit of a sequence is the value approached by the terms as the number of terms increases. Similarly, the limit of a series is the value approached by the sum as more and more terms are included. The concept of limits is fundamental to differential and integral calculus. *See also* Calculus; Series.

Limnology, science of freshwater lakes, ponds, and streams. These bodies of water are explored in terms of chemistry, physics, and biology. The plants, animals, and environment are quantitatively examined in light of food cycles, chains, habitat, and zonation of organisms. Freshwater bodies are subject to greater extremes of temperature and are therefore more fragile ecosystems and more specialized than those in marine environments. *See also* Hydrology.

Limoges, city in W central France, on Vienne River; capital of Haute-Vienne dept. Porcelain industry began 1771 (producing world-famous Limoges china); makes use of kaolin found in abundance nearby; site of cathedral (13th-16th centuries), ceramics museum, and museum containing many paintings by Renoir (born here 1841). Industries: china, shoes, textiles, clothing. Pop. 147,406.

Limpet, simple gastropod mollusk found clinging to rocks along marine shores. It has a caplike, rather than coiled, shell and large muscular foot. Length: to 5in (127mm). Families Acmaeidae and Fissurellidae; species include keyhole limpet *Megathura*.

Limpkin, long-legged wading bird found from SE United States to South America and famous for its wailful cry. Related to crane and rail, it is brownish with whitish streaks. It uses its long bill for digging snails and lays brown-spotted pale eggs (6–7) in a large grass-and-rush platform nest over water. Length: 27in (69cm). Species *Aramus guarauna*.

Limpopo (Crocodile), river in SE Africa; its headstreams rise in the high country of central Republic of South Africa; it flows NE and E along N border of Transvaal prov. and turns SE as it enters Mozambique, continuing SE to Indian Ocean. Length: approx. 1,100 mi (1,771km).

Lincoln, Abraham (1809–65), 16th president of the United States (1861–65), b. Hardin co (now Larue co), Ky. In 1842 he married Mary Todd; Robert Todd Lincoln was their son. Lincoln was born into a very poor frontier family, and had little formal education. The family moved to Indiana in 1816 and to Illinois in 1830. In 1831, he settled in New Salem, Ill., where he worked in a store, ran a mill, and began reading law. He became a Whig and in 1834 was elected to the Illinois legislature. In 1836 he was admitted to the bar and began to practice in Springfield, and in 1846 he was elected to the US House of Representatives for one term.

Lincoln's opposition to slavery was slow in developing; it was the Kansas-Nebraska Act (1854)—considered pro-slavery—that finally crystallized his views. The author of that bill was Sen. Stephen A. Douglas of Illinois. In 1858, Lincoln, by now a Republican, was chosen to run for the Senate against Douglas. The race was the occasion for the Lincoln-Douglas debates on the Kansas-Nebraska Act and on slavery itself. Douglas won the election, but Lincoln won national fame. As a result, he became a leading candidate for the 1860 Republican presidential nomination, which he won on the third ballot. He went on to win the election over the badly divided Democrats.

Lincoln was inaugurated on March 4, 1861, after the southern states had seceded; on April 12, Fort Sumter was fired on and the Civil War began. After a somewhat slow start, Lincoln conducted the war with vigor and efficiency. He called up the militia, blockaded southern ports, and increased executive powers. He had early difficulties with his military commanders but after he chose Gen. Ulysses S. Grant his commander in chief, the war went well.

On Sept. 22, 1862, Lincoln issued the Emancipation Proclamation, which freed the slaves (but only in rebellious areas), and on Nov. 19, 1863, he delivered the Gettysburg Address. Lincoln won reelection in 1864, this time running on the National Union ticket with Andrew Johnson. He saw the war brought to a successful close but died before the South could be readmitted to the Union. On Apr. 14, 1865, while attending Ford's Theater, he was shot by John Wilkes Booth, a disaffected southerner. He died the next day.

Career: Illinois State Legislature, 1834–41; US House of Representatives, 1847–49; president, 1861–65. *See also* Civil War, American; Emancipation Proclamation; Gettysburg Address; Kansas-Nebraska Act.

Lincoln, market town in E England; county seat of Lincolnshire; site of Lincoln Cathedral (built 1075–1501, restored 1922–32) and Lincoln castle (built by

William the Conqueror, 1068). Industries: agricultural and metal products, machinery. Pop. 73,200.

Lincoln, capital city of Nebraska, located in SE part of state, 52mi (84km) SW of Omaha; seat of Lancaster co; site of University of Nebraska (1867), Nebraska Wesleyan University (1887), Union College (1891), and modern city hall with 400-ft (122-m) tower designed by Bertram Goodhue with sculptures by Lee Lawrie; home of William Jennings Bryan is preserved. Industries: rubber products, meat processing, railroad cars, flour milling. Founded 1864 as Lancaster; when Nebraska was admitted to Union 1867, name was changed in honor of Abraham Lincoln, and city was made capital; inc. as town 1869, as city 1887. Pop. (1980) 171,932.

Lincoln-Douglas Debates, series of seven 1858 debates between Sen. Stephen Douglas and Abraham Lincoln. Douglas was the incumbent Democrat running for the US Senate seat from Illinois. Lincoln was the Republican candidate. The issue was slavery and its political, legal, and moral implications. Lincoln was eloquent in his defense of the Union and democratic ideals. Although Lincoln lost the election, his view of slavery as a "moral, social, and political wrong" enhanced his standing as a national figure. Douglas' stance on slavery, expressed in his Freeport speech, evaded the moral issue. *See also* Freeport Doctrine.

Lind, James (1716–94), Scottish physician famed for eradicating scurvy from the British navy with his recommendation to include fresh citrus fruit and lemon juice in the daily diet of seamen. Prior to his intervention, more British sailors died from scurvy than from combat wounds. He also made recommendations for combating typhus, for distillation of seawater for drinking, and for creating hospital ships.

Lind, Johanna Maria (Jenny) (1820–87), Swedish soprano. Known as the "Swedish Nightingale," she made her debut in 1838 and gave many triumphant operatic performances in Europe and recitals in the United States which were managed by P.T. Barnum. She was Sweden's most famous singer and one of the most glamorous and celebrated coloratura sopranos of the 19th century.

Lindbergh, Anne Morrow (1907–), US author, b. Englewood, N.J. Married (1929) to the aviator Charles Lindbergh, she accompanied him on many flights and wrote *North to the Orient* (1935) and *Listen! The Wind* (1938) recording her experiences. Other works include *Gift from the Sea* (1955), essays on the problems of women; *The Unicorn* (1956), poems; and *Dearly Beloved* (1962), a novel. Several volumes of her diaries and letters have also been published, including *War Within and Without* (1980).

Lindbergh, Charles Augustus (1902–74), US aviator, known as "Lucky Lindy" and "The Lone Eagle," b. Detroit, Mich. He became an international hero when he landed his plane *The Spirit of St Louis* outside Paris on May 21, 1927, completing first nonstop transatlantic solo flight. He married Anne Morrow (1929), and their two-year old son was kidnapped and murdered in 1932. The resulting publicity forced the Lindberghs to live in England (1935–39). An isolationist, he was active in the America First Committee and was accused of pro-Nazi sentiments. He resigned his Air Corps Reserve commission but accompanied combat missions during World War II as consultant to aircraft manufacturers. In 1954 he was made brigadier general in the Air Force Reserve. He was awarded the Pulitzer Prize for his book, *The Spirit of St Louis* (1953).

Linden, or basswood, tree found in tropical to temperate zones. A common shade or honey tree and source of commercial lumber, it has heart-shaped, finely toothed leaves and white or yellow, nectar-filled flowers. Height: to 120ft (37m). Among 80 species is American *Tilia americana*. Family Tiliaceae.

Line, set of points extending in two directions without end. The term can be synonymous with curve, or can be taken to mean a straight line—the shortest distance between two points. In a rectangular Cartesian coordinate system a straight line has the equation $y = mx + c$, where m is the gradient and c the intercept on the y-axis.

Linear A, script written on tablets found on Crete and the Greek mainland. It is a syllabic form of writing, but it is still not deciphered. It has been dated from 1450 to 1200 BC.

Linear Accelerator, or linac, particle accelerator in which electrons or other charged particles travel through a straight vacuum chamber. Electrostatic accelerators are simple linear accelerators. In other types energy is gained in regions of high-frequency

Queen Liliuokalani

Abraham Lincoln

Charles Lindbergh

electric field, produced between cylindrical electrodes. Higher energies can be achieved by carrying the particles along a waveguide with a microwave field. Final energies depend on the length of the chamber, and can reach several GeV.

Linear B, Mycenaean Greek writing deciphered (1952) by Michael Ventris on tablets dating from 1500–1200 BC. It used a syllabic form of writing with the consonants simplified. The discovery showed that Mycenaeans on the Greek mainland were using a Greek language.

Linear Function, mathematical function the value of which is given by a polynomial involving no powers of its variables, as in f $(x) = 7x + 3$. The graph of a simple linear function is a straight line.

Linear Programming, mathematical procedure in which a multi-variable linear function is analyzed to find maximum and minimum values. It is useful in business planning and industrial engineering to produce optimal control conditions, as in inventory control, where costs must be minimized in terms of storage time, warehouse space, customer delivery schedules, reorder times, and transportation expenses. *See also* Inventory Control.

Line Islands, island group in central Pacific, S of Hawaiian islands, extending across the equator from Kingman Reef to Flint Island. US territories are Kingman Reef, Jarvis, and Palmyra islands; British territories are Washington, Fannin, and Christmas islands. Area S of the equator is claimed by both Britain and United States. Area: 158sq mi (409sq km). Pop. 1,180.

Ling, also red hake, squirrel hake, commercial food fish found in Atlantic from Newfoundland to Virginia. Brown and silver, it has long dorsal and ventral fins. Length: 2.5ft (76.2cm); weight: 8lb (3.6kg). Family Gadidae; species include *Urophycis chuss* and *Molva molva.*

Lingua Franca, a language that serves as a means of communication between people who normally do not speak the same language. A lingua franca may be a hybrid language such as Pidgin English, used among the hundreds of tribes in E New Guinea, or it may be a full-fledged language such as Swahili, which is spoken mainly as a second language by millions of people in East Africa.

Linguistic Analysis, or philosophical linguistics, is the philosophy of language. Of concern to philosophers of language are such matters as a priori and a posteriori sentences. Kant divided the category of a priori sentences into analytic and synthetic, but this subdivision remains open to question. Issues of syntax and linguistic usage are important areas of interest to present-day philosophers. The works of Rudolph Carnap and Ludwig Wittgenstein of the Vienna Circle of logical positivists are fundamental texts. *See also* Logical Positivism.

Linguistics, the science of a language system. Synchronic (structural) linguistics is the study of the language as it is actually spoken and the rules that govern its structure. Diachronic (comparative) linguistics is the study of the history and formation of the language or group of languages. It includes comparing languages, etymology, and the study of the culture of the people. *See also* Grammar; Phonetics; Syntax.

Linkage Groups, a group of inherited characteristics or genes that occur on the same chromosome and that remain connected in such a way that they assort and are inherited together through successive generations.

Linköping, city in SE Sweden, near Lake Roxen; capital of Österjötland co. Prospered in the Middle Ages as a religious and intellectual center; site of 13th-century castle, library, university, 12th-century Romanesque cathedral, containing 344-ft (105-m) spire; an episcopal see since 1120. Industries: motor vehicles, airplanes, processed food, electrical appliances. Pop. 109,236.

Linnaea, or twinflower, perennial trailing evergreen vine found in cool, moist areas worldwide. It has glossy leaves and fragrant, pink, bell-shaped flowers growing in pairs. Family Caprifoliaceae; species *Linnaea borealis.*

Linnaeus, Carolus (1707–78), Swedish botanist and explorer. He was the first scientist to outline the principles for defining the genera and species of organisms. He formalized binomial nomenclature, giving Latin names for the genus and the species to each organism, making consistent use of specific names, and including all known organisms in a single classification. This approach was the foundation of the modern science of taxonomy. Linnaeus published his first nomenclatorial system, *Systema naturae,* in 1735, followed by *Genera plantarum* (1737) and *Species plantarum* (1753). *See also* Taxonomy.

Linnet, small Old World songbird with brownish plumage that feeds on flax seed. Family Fringillidae; species *Carduelis cannabina.*

Lin Piao (Lin Biao) (1908–71), Chinese Communist military leader. He won fame as commander of the Fourth Field Army, which helped insure victory over Nationalist forces in 1949 and entered Korean War against United Nations forces in 1950. Lin was designated Mao Tse-tung's heir apparent while helping to lead the 1965–69 Cultural Revolution in China. He was later accused of plotting revolt and was said to have perished in a plane accident.

Linseed Oil, oil pressed from seeds of cultivated flax (*Linum usitatissimum*). Because of its drying qualities, it is an important ingredient of oil paints and printing inks. See also Flax.

Lin Yutang (1895–1976), Chinese writer. After studying philology at Harvard (1919–21) and Leipzig (1922–23), he was a professor at Peking University (1923–26). He edited a number of periodicals, the most notable of which were *Lunyü* (Analects fortnightly), which he founded in 1932, and *Jenchienshih* (This human world), a literary journal. In 1936 he emigrated to the United States. He subsequently wrote books on China, including *My Country and My People* (1935) and *Moment in Peking* (1939).

Linz, city in Austria, 95mi (153km) W of Vienna on the Danube River. Railroad junction and river port. Industries: steel, nitrate, machinery, electrical equipment, tobacco products; site of Roman camp (Lentia) AD 1st century. Pop. 202,874.

Lion, tawny, large cat, found in prides on African savannahs south of the Sahara and in SW Asia. It is yellow to buff with light spots under the eyes. The male has a long neck mane that darkens with age. A night hunter, it feeds on antelope, zebra, and bush pigs. The gestation period is three months and 2–6 young are born. Length: 8–11ft (2.4–3.3m); weight: 400–600lb (180–270.2kg). Varieties include Senegal, Masai, Somali, and Indian. Family Felidae; species *Panthera leo. See also* Cat.

Lionfish, or zebra, turkey, dragon, cobra fish, marine tropical fish found in shallow waters of Indian and W Pacific. A rust-red and white striped fish with numerous long spines and rays, it carries 13 venomous spines in its dorsal fin that can inflict painful and, in rare cases, even fatal wounds. Length: up to 12 in (30cm). Family Scorpaenidae; species *Pterios volitans.*

Lions, Gulf of, arm of Mediterranean Sea, extending from Hyères, France (E), to Cape Creus, Spain (W). Chief port is Marseilles.

Lipari Islands (Isole Eolie), volcanic group of small islands off the N coast of Sicily, Italy, in the Tyrrhenian Sea; includes islands of Stromboli, Vulcano, Salina, and Lipari. Exports: wine, raisins, fish, pumice. Industries: agriculture, livestock, fishing, lobstering. Area: 44sq mi (114sq km). Settled late 6th century BC. Pop. 10,043.

Lipchitz, Jacques (1891–1973), sculptor, b. Lithuania. He was one of the finest of the early cubist sculptors. His early works include "Bather" and "Man with a Guitar" (1916). His later work was of a larger scale and included his most important "Figure" (1926–30). Subsequent works stressed sensuality and volume: "Benediction" (1942) and "Harpist."

Lipetsk (Lipeck), city in Russian SFSR, USSR, 65mi (105km) N of Voronezh, on Voronezh River; capital of Lipetsk oblast; founded as an iron milling center by Peter the Great. Industries: iron pipe and castings, tractors, chemicals, cement, food processing. Est. 1707. Pop. 387,000.

Lipid, one of a large group of organic compounds in living organisms that are insoluble in water but soluble in alcohol and ether. Lipids are a major food source for animals. They form an important food store and energy source of plant and animal cells and a structural component of cell membranes. The class includes animal fats, vegetable oils, and natural waxes; the basic components are fatty acids. Storage fat is composed chiefly of triglycerides, which consist of three molecules of fatty acids linked to the alcohol glycerol.

Lipmann, Fritz Albert (1899–   ), US biochemist, b. Germany. He was awarded the 1953 Nobel Prize in physiology or medicine "for his discovery of coenzyme A and its importance for intermediary metabolism." Coenzyme A plays an essential intermediary role in the body's metabolism of carbohydrates, fats, and proteins and thus in the transfer of energy in the body.

Li Po (c.701–62), Chinese poet. He and Tu Fu are considered the two greatest poets of the T'ang dynasty (618–906), China's golden age of literature. He was known for his wandering and drinking, and his verse is said to have an airy, intoxicating quality. Unlike many of his contemporaries, he was not concerned with such matters as patriotism and heroism but rather with physical pleasure. "The Song of Wine" is one of his most famous poems.

Lippi, Filippino (1457?–1504), Italian painter. The son of Filippo, he followed the style of Botticelli in his early work; his mature style influenced the Florentine Mannerists in the 16th century. "Apparition of the Virgin to St Bernard" (c. 1488) is in his mature style. A later work, "Adoration of the Magi" (1496), precurses the Florentine Mannerists. *See also* Mannerism.

Lippi, Fra Filippo (1406?–69), Italian painter. One of the major forces in Florentine painting, he was influenced by Masaccio and Fra Angelico and in turn influenced Botticelli and others. His works include the

Barbadori altarpiece (*c.*1437), "Coronation of the Virgin" (c.1441–47), "Annunciation" (*c.*1438), and "Adoration of the Child" (*c.*1459).

Lippizaners, a breed of horse that is of small stature, having a long back, thick neck, and powerful conformation. They have the ability to perform the intricate and delicate movements of *haute école,* often seen in the circus.

Liqueur, a flavored distilled liquor, with an alcohol content from 48 to 120 proof (24–60%); made by combining fruits or herbs with a base and spirit and sweetening with sugar syrup. Fruit, when used, is steeped in the spirit; herb liqueurs may be produced by distillation or percolation. Liqueurs were first produced by monks and alchemists and have been called balms, cremes, elixirs, and oils. They are popular after-dinner drinks and are also used as flavorings in desserts.

Liquid, state of matter, intermediate between a gas and a solid, in which a substance has a relatively fixed volume but flows to take the shape of its container. Liquids have higher viscosity than gases, and their viscosity decreases with temperature. *See also* Gas; Solid.

Liquid Crystal, any substance that flows like a liquid yet has the kind of ordered molecular structure characteristic of crystals. There are many organic crystalline substances that can be brought to a liquid crystal state when heated. They are classified according to the kind of molecular arrangement that obtains. Liquid crystals have unique properties that have been applied to optical displays and temperature-variation detection systems.

Liquid Oxygen, oxygen in the liquid state (at one atmosphere pressure, oxygen liquefies at −183°C.) It is widely used in rocket engines as an oxidizer reacting with various liquid fuels to produce high-velocity gases.

Lisbon (Lisboa), port city and capital of Portugal, on SW coast of Portugal, at the mouth of the Tagus River on Atlantic Ocean. An ancient settlement, the city was occupied by Phoenicians and Carthaginians before Moorish occupation 716; taken by Portuguese 1147, under King Alfonso I; after 14th century it became a leading European port, until Spanish occupation 1580–1640. With its fine harbor, it has again become a major port and handles most of Portugal's international trade; site of Moorish mosque, aqueduct, many medieval buildings, University of Lisbon (1911), Technical University of Lisbon (1930). Pop. 760,150.

Lister, Joseph, Lord (1827–1912), English surgeon. His acceptance of the germ theory and consequent introduction of antisepsis to surgical practice ushered in the era of modern surgery. Lister used phenol to kill germs and succeeded in lowering dramatically the rate of post-surgical infection.

Liszt, Franz (1811–86), Hungarian composer and pianist. He invented the solo recital and startled his contemporaries with his piano virtuosity and showmanship. He was patron and friend to many of the great artists of his day, such as Chopin and Grieg, and his music influenced subsequent composers, including Wagner, Richard Strauss, and Ravel. He composed two popular piano concertos, 19 Hungarian rhapsodies, études, numerous piano pieces, and many transcriptions for piano of other composers' music. His symphonic poems (eg, *Les Préludes*) were among the first successful efforts in this form.

Litchi, or lichee, evergreen tree native to China and the Philippines. It has dense foliage of glossy, leathery leaves. The red, globular fruit, litchi nut, is edible dried or preserved. Height: to 40ft(12m). Family Sapindaceae; species *Litchi chinensis.*

Liter, in the metric system, a unit of capacity equal to the volume occupied by one kilogram of water at 4°C and at standard atmospheric pressure. It is equivalent to one cubic decimeter. One liter equals 1.057 liquid quarts. *See also* Weights and Measures.

Literature. *See* Individual Countries.

Lithium, common metallic element (symbol Li) of the alkali-metal group, first isolated in 1817. Ores include lepidolite and spodumene. The element, which is the lightest of all metals, is used in alloys and as a heat-transfer medium. Chemically it is similar to sodium, although it does have some resemblance to the alkaline-earth metals. Properties at. no 3; at. wt. 6.941; sp gr 0.534; melt. pt. 354.2°F (179.0°C); boil. pt. 2,402°F (1,317°C); most stable isotope Li^7 (92.58%). *See also* Alkali Elements.

Lithography, in art, planographic (surface) method of graphic reproduction developed in the late 18th century and based on the inability of grease to mix with water. First, a design is made on a stone or metal plate. Usually, blue-gray Bavarian limestone is used. The design is drawn with a greasy substance such as lithographic crayons or pencils, rubbing ink, or asphaltum. The drawing is then etched with a syrupy solution of gum arabic and nitric acid. Next, the stone is washed with water. Eventually, lithographic ink is rolled onto the stone, and it is run through a press.

Lithosphere, that part of the Earth that is rock as opposed to hydrosphere, biosphere, and atmosphere. *See also* Earth.

Lithuania (Litovskeja Sovetskaja Socialisticeskaja Respublika), a constituent republic of the USSR. It is bounded W by Baltic Sea, N by Latvia, E by Belorussian republic, S by Poland, and SW by Kaliningrad oblast. Covered with glacial deposits, it is low and flat, is drained by the Neman River, and has nearly 2,000 lakes. Almost 50% of the land is arable; forests cover 17% of the area, and meadows and pastures 25%. The economy is largely agricultural (dairy farming and stock raising), but industry has been developed since 1940. There are no major mineral resources.

People and History. A predominantly Roman Catholic agricultural people, the Lithuanians work on some 1,800 collective farms. The population was depleted by huge emigration before WWI (mainly to the United States and Canada) and by the extermination of the Jewish minority during WWII. About 80% of the population is Lithuanian, with increasing minorities of Russians and Belorussians, and Letts. Settled by pagan Liths along the Neman River about 1500 BC, Lithuania was conquered by the Teutonic Knights in the 13th century and later emerged as a powerful duchy, one of the most extensive medieval states. Grand Duke Jagiello married the Polish queen Jadiwiga in 1386. The two states were allied until 1569 when they were formally joined. Through the 18th-century partitions of Poland, Lithuania passed to Russia. The collapse of Russia in WWI permitted Lithuanian nationalists to assert themselves, and an independent republic was proclaimed in 1918. Instability brought dictatorships, a fascist constitution in 1938, and Soviet occupation in 1940. During WWII Germany held the country from 1941 until it was regained by the Soviets in 1944.

PROFILE

Official name: Lithuanian Soviet Socialist Republic
Area: 25,174sq mi (65,201sq km)
Population: 3,366,000.
Chief city: Vilnius (capital)
Government: Constituent republic of USSR
Religion: Roman Catholic
Language: Lithuanian
Industries: food processing, shipbuilding, textiles, machinery, metal products, chemicals, electrical equipment
Agriculture: dairy farming, hogs, flax, sugar beets, potatoes

Litmus, in chemistry, natural coloring matter used as an indicator. It is red in the acidic state, but changes to blue at pH 6.8. *See also* Indicator.

Little America, region in Antarctica, S of Bay of Whales, on outer edge of Ross Ice Shelf. Explored 1928–30 by Adm. R. E. Byrd's expedition; used as a headquarters for his 2nd expedition (1933–35), the US Antarctic Service Expedition (1939–1941), and the US Naval Operation High Jump expedition (1946–47).

Little Bear Constellation. *See* Ursa Minor.

Little Bighorn, Battle of the (June 25, 1876), engagement between Indians, under Sioux chiefs Sitting Bull, Crazy Horse, and Gall, and the 7th US cavalry detachment led by Col. George Custer. Custer's attempted surprise attack on the much larger Indian force was unsuccessful. The 2,500 Indians wiped out Custer's 266 officers and men near the Little Bighorn River in the Montana Territory.

Little Entente, an alliance between Romania, Yugoslavia, and Czechoslovakia after World War I to maintain post-war boundaries. Through political and economic unity, and the support of France and Poland, the alliance managed to prevent *Anschluss* (the uniting of Germany and Austria) and departure from the treaties of World War I until the rise of Hitler in the late 1930s.

Little Rock, Arkansas city and state capital, seat of Pulaski co. Made territorial capital 1821; state capital 1836; occupied by Union forces in Civil War, Sept. 1863. School desegregation began 1957. Industries: lumber, furniture, paper products, electrical equipment, plastic, bauxite and marble mining, cotton and grain farming, cottonseed products. Founded 1819; inc. 1835. Pop. (1980) 158,461.

Littoral Zone, strictly used, the beach area between high and low tides. However, the term also refers to the benthic zone between high tide and a depth of 656ft. (200m). The larger zone is divided into the eulittoral—from high tide to a 164ft (50m) depth and the sublittoral—from 164–656ft (50m to 200m). The lower edge of the eulittoral is the lowest limit at which abundant attached plants can grow.

Litvinov, Maksim Maksimovich (1876–1951), Soviet diplomat. Involved in Russian revolutionary activity from 1898, he became Soviet ambassador to Britain after the Bolshevik Revolution (1917). As Soviet representative to the League of Nations, he was an eloquent advocate of disarmament and cooperation with the United States where he later served as ambassador (1941–43).

Liu Pang, Chinese emperor (reigned 206–194 BC). Known as Han Kao Tsu or the "High Progenitor," he was the first emperor of the Han Dynasty in China and a hero in Chinese history. A rough and ready general, he united the country for one of its most famous periods of rule.

Liu Shao-ch'i (Liu Shaoqi) (1900–69), a leader of the Chinese Communist movement. Trained in Moscow 1920–22, he became one of the chief theorists of the Chinese Communist party and second in rank from 1954 until purged by Mao Tse-tung during the Cultural Revolution of 1965–69. He lived in disgrace until his death, but was rehabilitated and memorialized in 1980.

Liutprand, or **Luitprand** (died 744), Lombard king (712–44). He unified and expanded Lombardy and brought it to the height of its power. His conquest of Roman lands was halted only by personal appeals to his Catholic conscience by popes Gregory II and Zacharias. He instituted several reforms of the Lombard penal code.

Live-forever, or stonecrop, succulent perennial plant native to Europe. It has smooth, thick, oval, grey-green leaves and clusters of tiny reddish-purple flowers. Height: to 2ft (61cm); family Crassulaceae; species *Sedum telephium.*

Live Oak, North American red oak trees. The spreading evergreen oak *(Quercus virginiana)* grows in SE United States. Its leathery leaves have rolled, unlobed edges. It is a valuable timber tree. In poor soil, it may be shrubby. Height: to 50ft (15m). Family Fagaceae. *See also* Oak.

Liver, the largest gland in the body, a soft, reddish-brown organ lying mostly in the upper right quadrant of the abdominal region. It has many functions, including formation of bile, carbohydrate storage, regulation in part of carbohydrate metabolism, breakdown of hormones, detoxification of drugs and other substances, destruction of worn-out red blood cells, and an important role in fat metabolism. It produces and secretes bile, which empties from hepatic ducts into the cystic duct leading to the gall bladder, where the bile is stored until needed. The bile empties into the common bile duct and then into the small intestine, where it functions in metabolism, primarily fat metabolism, acting to emulsify fats, make them water-soluble, and to activate other digestive enzymes.

Liverpool, city in NW England, in Merseyside, on Mersey estuary; a leading port since mid-18th century, it is country's 2nd-largest seaport; site of University of Liverpool (1903), 1754 town hall, Bluecoat Chambers of 1716–17, an art gallery; birthplace of William Gladstone (1809). Industries: food processing, electrical equipment, chemicals, rubber. Settled late 8th century by Norsemen; chartered 1207 by King John. Pop. 548,800.

Liverwort, any of about 10,000 species of tiny, simple, nonflowering green plants, which, like the related mosses, lack specialized tissues for transporting water, food, and minerals within the plant body. Liverworts are found in almost all nondesert land habitats, especially in the damp tropics; a few species even occur in Antarctica. Liverworts make up two classes (Hepaticae and Anthocerotae) of the plant division Bryophyta. *See also* Bryophyte.

Livingston, Robert R. (1746–1813), US Revolutionary war patriot and diplomat, b. New York City. He served in the Continental Congress (1775–76, 1779–81, 1784–85) and helped draw up the Declaration of Independence, although he thought the decision to separate from England was unnecessary. Under Pres. Thomas Jefferson, he and James Monroe went to France and successfully negotiated the Louisiana Pur-

Franz Liszt

Little America: Admiral Byrd

Robert Livingston

chase (1803) for $15 million. He also financed the first US steamship, Robert Fulton's *Clermont* (1807).

Livingstone, David (1813–73), Scottish clergyman and explorer in Africa. He first entered Africa as missionary in 1841. He discovered the Zambezi River (1851) and attempted to end the slave trade by introducing Christian ways. After crossing from the east to west African coasts, he was commissioned to explore the Zambezi (discovering Victoria Falls in 1855) and later the upper Nile (1866). Following considerable speculation on his well-being, Henry M. Stanley was sent to find him. The two met in 1871 on Lake Tanganyika. Livingstone could not be persuaded to leave and died in Africa, having published various accounts of his travels. His remains were buried in Westminster Abbey.

Livius Andronicus, Lucius (*c.*284–204 BC), the originator of Roman epic poetry and drama. A Greek born in Tarentum, he was taken as a slave by a member of the Livian family when Tarentum surrendered. A teacher of Greek and Latin, his principal work, the *Odusia,* a translation of Homer's *Odyssey,* may have been intended as a schoolbook. He produced the first dramatic presentation ever given in Rome. Of his comedies and tragedies based on Greek works, only fragments remain.

Livonia, city in SE Michigan, W of Detroit; site of Madonna College (1937) and Schoolcraft College (1961). Industries: automobile parts, tools and dies, paints. Founded 1835; inc. 1950. Pop. (1980) 104,814.

Livonian Brothers of the Sword, a group of knights who brought what is now Latvia and Estonia to Christianity by violent conquest. Founded with the pope's sanction in the early 13th century, the knights carried out several brutal campaigns and were finally crushed themselves by Lithuanian forces in 1236. The church then reorganized the band, which ruled for another three centuries.

Livy (59 BC–AD 17), Roman historian, b. Titus Livius. With Tacitus and Sallust he is regarded as one of the three greatest Roman historians. He began his *History of Rome* around 29 BC. It covers Roman history from Aeneas' arrival in Italy, 753 BC to 9 BC. Livy used the best sources available at the time. His descriptions are vivid and he frequently draws moral conclusions. Thirty-five of the original 142 books are intact and fragments of all but two of the remaining books exist.

Lizard, reptile found on every continent. They have scales, paired copulatory organs, and flexible skulls. Typical lizards have cylindrical bodies with four legs, long tails, and movable eyelids. The majority are 12in (30.5cm) long. Chiefly terrestrial, many live in deserts. There are also semiaquatic and tree-dwelling forms, including the flying dragon. Burrowing species frequently have reduced limbs or are legless. There are two venomous species. Length: 2in–10ft (5cm–3m). There are 20 families of 3,000 species. Order Squamata; suborder Sauria.

Lizard Fish, reptilelike fish (genus *Synodus*) found in shallow waters of the Atlantic and Pacific. A cylindrical fish with silver and olive-brown coloration, it uses its pectoral fins to prop itself up on the sandy bottom. Length: 12in (30.5cm). There are 36 species. Family Synodontidae.

Ljubljana, city in NW Yugoslavia, on the Ljubljanica River, 75mi (120km) NW of Zagreb; capital of republic of Slovenia; transportation, commercial, and industrial center. Location of the ancient Roman city of Emona

(founded 1st century BC); destroyed by Huns AD 5th century; restored by Slavs, made part of Carinthia 12th century, under the Hapsburgs 1277; seat of Illyrian Provinces 1809–93; scene of Congress of Laibach 1821; under Austrian control until it was made part of Yugoslavia 1918. It is the site of medieval fortress, Tivoli Park, museum, art gallery, university (1595). Industries: textiles, paper, machinery, leather, tobacco, chemicals. Pop. 173,530.

Llama, or guanaco, alpaca, South American even-toed, ruminant mammal related to the camel. The guanaco is found in the wild; the llama and the alpaca are known only in domesticated form. They have been used as beasts of burden by the Indians for over 1,000 years. They have long, woolly coats and slender limbs and neck. The llama is structurally similar to the guanaco. The smaller alpaca is bred for its superb wool. Family Camelidae; genus *Lama.*

Llanos, vast plains in N South America, in SW Venezuela and E Colombia; drained by the Orinoco River; sparsely populated; some cattle raising. Area: (Venezuela) approx. 125,000sq mi (323,750sq km); (Colombia) approx. 100,000sq mi (259,000sq km).

Llewelyn ab Gruffydd (died 1282), Welsh prince. Despite paying homage to Henry III of England (1247), he rebelled successfully (1256–63) but was later compelled to acknowledge Wales subject to England (1267). Refusing homage to Edward I, Henry's successor (1272), he again rebelled but was forced to submit at Conway (1277).

Llewelyn ab Iorwerth or **Llewelyn the Great** (died 1240), Welsh prince. Master of most of Wales by 1202, Llewelyn exploited King John of England's political weakness to liberate Wales from English rule (1212–15). Between 1218 and 1238 Llewelyn consolidated his power by dynastic alliances.

Lloyd George, David (1863–1945), Welsh political figure. A member of Parliament (1890–1944), he was the leading Liberal politician in the Britain of his time. Appointed chancellor of the exchequer (1908), he introduced the "People's Budget" (1909), financing social welfare through higher taxation of the wealthy, and the National Insurance Act (1911). An effective minister of munitions (1915) but critical of the conduct of the war, he became prime minister (1916) and was influential at the Versailles peace conference (1919). His handling of the Irish situation (1921) and party finance caused criticism, and he resigned (1922). Although still widely respected, he never again wielded power.

Lloyd Webber, Andrew (1948–), British composer. He composed the musical theater work *Joseph and the Amazing Technicolor Dreamcoat* (1967) while still a student at the Royal College of Music. His lyricist, Timothy Rice, was also his collaborator on the popular and controversial rock opera *Jesus Christ Superstar* and on *Evita,* a musical based on the life of Eva Perón. *Cats,* combining Lloyd Webber's music with verse by T. S. Eliot, was a long-running hit in both Britain and the United States.

Lobachevski, Nikolai Ivanovich, (1793–1856), Russian mathematician. Educated at Kazan University he was appointed professor there in 1814. His outstanding achievement was the creation of one of the first comprehensive non-Euclidean systems of geometry, which denies Euclid's axiom of parallels.

Lobby, group or individual representing special interests and attempting to influence legislation and government decisions. Lobbyists exert pressure through

public relations, campaign contributions, personal contacts with public officials, and congressional testimony. Lobbyists are required to register annually with the House and Senate and to submit quarterly reports of their activities.

Lobelia, trailing or bedding plant found worldwide. Many are grown as ornamentals. Flowers are red, white, or blue and irregularly shaped. Leaves are simple. Species include the blue-flowered, annual *Lobelia erinus;* the red, perennial *Lobelia cardinalis,* native to E North America; and the poisonous Indian tobacco *Lobelia inflata.* Family Lobeliaceae.

Lobengula (1833–94), Matabele king from 1870 in what is now part of Rhodesia. The initial instability of his rule caused him to invite British support in return for certain land and mineral concessions. This unfortunate policy allowed the formation of Cecil Rhodes' British South Africa Company (1889) and in 1893 the British destroyed the Matabele government and assumed effective rule.

Lobito, port city in W central Angola, on Lobito Bay, 240mi (386km) S of Luanda; an important W African port and trade link with interior; agricultural exports. Founded 1843. Pop. 65,000.

Lobotomy, or **Leucotomy,** a form of brain surgery consisting of cutting into the skull and severing nerve fibers that connect the thalamus with the frontal lobes of the brain. It was used for treating certain mental disorders, but modern tranquilizing drugs have replaced this operation except in rare instances.

Lobster, large, long-tailed marine decapod crustacean, important commercially in North America and Europe. The true lobster possesses an enlarged, bulbous pair of pincers. The American lobster (*Homarus americanus*) reaches an average length of 10in (25cm) and weight of 3.5lb (1.6kg). The record is 45lb (20.3kg). The spiny lobster, lacking claws, wards off enemies with whiplike motions of stiffened antennae. *See also* Decapod, Crustacean.

Local Color, literary form emphasizing customs, dialect, and other characteristics that have escaped standardizing cultural influences. The American form, influenced by English and French traditions, was popular in the late 19th century and had its greatest impact on the short story. Bret Harte's "The Luck of Roaring Camp" (1868) is often considered the first American example. Other local colorists include George Washington Cable, Mary E. Wilkins Freeman, Joel Chandler Harris, E. W. Howe, Sarah Orne Jewett, and Joaquin Miller.

Local Group of Galaxies, small galaxy cluster to which the Milky Way Galaxy belongs. The Local Group contains about 18 or 20 galaxies, including the Andromeda Galaxy (M 31) and its satellites. The system is about 2,000,000 light years across, with the Milky Way Galaxy at one end. *See also* Galaxy Cluster.

Locarno Pact, agreement made between Belgium, Italy, Great Britain, Poland, France, Czechoslovakia, and Germany in 1925 that demonstrated a resumption of normal European international relations and strengthened the member nations' commitment to the Treaty of Versailles. Gaining Germany's admission to the League of Nations, the pact was directed toward an age of peace, but was quickly abandoned by Hitler in 1936.

Locke, John (1632–1704), English philosopher. He studied at Oxford and served as physician to the Earl

Lockyer, (Sir) Joseph Norman

of Shaftesbury (until 1682). He went into exile in Holland (1683), but returned after the Glorious Revolution, when his *Essay Concerning Human Understanding* (1690), the first great work of British Empiricism, appeared. At the same time, his *Essays on Civil Government* (1690), establishing his version of the contract of government, was published. Locke advocated a concept of limited sovereignty, implying a right to restore liberty where threatened. In religion, he was a rationalist.

Lockyer, (Sir) Joseph Norman (1836–1920), British astronomer who discovered the element helium. He was a pioneer of the study of the Sun's spectrum. In 1868 he developed a technique for examining prominences at the edge of the Sun and attributed a portion of the spectrum to a new element which he named helium, 40 years before helium was discovered on Earth.

Locomotive, any separate unit of a railroad that generates the power needed to pull freight and passenger cars. There are three main sources of power in use today—steam, oil, and electricity. Steam locomotives were in general use until the 1940s, when they were superseded by diesel and electric types. Electric locomotives are dependent on overhead trolley wires, a third (electrified) rail, or turbine-powered generators.

Locoweed, perennial plant native to the North American plains. It has clustered rosy or bluish-purple flowers and is poisonous to sheep, cattle, and horses. Height: to 18in (46cm). Family Leguminosae; species *Oxytropis lambertii.*

Locus, in geometry, the path traced by a specified point when it moves to satisfy certain conditions. For example, a circle is the locus of a point in a plane moving in such a way that its distance from a fixed point (the center) is constant.

Locust, any grasshopper that migrates en masse is considered a migratory locust. They are found where bodies of water or large humid areas meet arid areas. When a large population develops, the nymphs constantly irritate each other and finally they move en masse on foot. As they feed and develop, they emerge as adults and take to the air. The plant consumption of a swarm equals the daily food consumption of 1,500,-000 people. Length: 0.5–4in (12.7–102mm). Order Orthoptera. *See also* Cicada; Grasshopper; Orthoptera.

Locust Tree, deciduous trees and shrubs native to United States, Mexico, and Central America. The featherlike leaves are oblong and fragrant, flower clusters are white, pink, or purple. Family Leguminosae; genus *Robinia.*

Lod (Lydda), town in central Israel, 11mi (18km) SE of Tel Aviv. An ancient site, it was occupied by Samarians 4th century BC; devastated by fire AD 66 by Celestius Gallus during Jewish-Roman War, and AD 68 by Vespasian; later rebuilt by Hadrian; served as temporary seat of Jewish teachers after destruction of the Second Temple (70); made an episcopal see 5th century; destroyed by Saladin 1191, later rebuilt by Richard I of England; mentioned in Bible as site of Peter's healing of the paralytic; railway and airport center. Industries: telephone equipment, chemicals, oil products, cigarettes. Pop. 29,300.

Lode, an ore formation consisting of a closely spaced series of veins, usually in stratified layers. The veins are in tabular deposits in fissures and cracks of a body of rock from which they differ in composition. They are the result of the gradual precipitation of minerals carried by underground water or gases after the formation of the embedding rock (country rock). *See also* Ore.

Lodi, industrial town in N Italy, on the Adda River approx. 20mi (32km) SE of Milan; built 1158, near ruins of ancient city (sacked by Milanese in 1111); site of Romanesque cathedral and Renaissance church; scene of Napoleon's victory over Austrians May 10, 1796. Industries: machinery, electrical equipment, dairying, ceramics, wrought iron. Pop. 28,691.

Lódź, second-largest city in Poland, approx. 75mi (121km) SW of Warsaw; capital of Lód prov. Before 19th century, town was a small regional market center; growth began when it came under Russian rule 1815, attracting many textile manufacturers; became part of Poland 1918, after which privately owned textile companies were taken over by government; site of university and technical university (1945). Pop. 798,000.

Loess, buff-colored deposit of fine silt or clay, generally unstratified and sometimes exposed in bluffs. The loess in the Mississippi Valley is believed to be of glacial origin, while that in the Mongolian desert seems to have been formed by the wind.

Lofoten Islands, Norwegian island group off NW coast of Norway, in Norwegian Sea; extends ESE from coast; SW of sister group, the Vesterålen. Chief islands are Moskenesoya, Aust Vagoya, and Vest Vagoya. Main industry is fishing. Area: approx. 475sq mi (1,230sq km).

Logan, Mount, peak in SW Yukon, Canada, in St Elias Mts. Highest peak in Canada, 2nd highest in North America; 1st ascent 1925. Height: 19,850ft (6,054m).

Loganberry, or **Logan Blackberry,** biennial bramble hybrid developed by Judge J. H. Logan in his California garden in 1881. A blackberry-red raspberry cross, it is disease prone and grown only on the Pacific coast. The canes produce large, red berries eaten fresh or preserved. Family Rosaceae; species *Rubus ursinus loganobaccus. See also* Blackberry.

Logarithmic Function, mathematical function the value of which depends on the logarithm, to a particular base, b, of the independent variable, x, and is thus given by $f(x) = \log_b x$. For natural logarithms, where the base is exponential e, the logarithmic function is the inverse of the exponential function.

Logarithms, computation aid, devised by John Napier (1614) and developed by the English mathematician Henry Briggs (1556–1630). Numbers are converted to their logarithms, found from tables, and their multiplication, division, square root, cube root, etc, are determined by addition, subtraction, and division, respectively, of the logarithms involved. The resulting number is then checked in tables for its antilogarithm, that is, the inverse function of the logarithm, which gives the answer. A number's logarithm is the number, x, indicating the power to which a fixed number, b, must be raised to yield the specified number, n; that is, if $b^x = n$, then $\log_b n = x$. The number b is the logarithmic base: common logarithms have base 10; natural logarithms have base e (2.71828 . . .). A logarithm is written as the sum of an integer (the characteristic) and a decimal fraction (the mantissa). The characteristic indicates the location of the decimal point in the number, being positive for numbers greater than one and negative for those less than one. The mantissa is the logarithm of the digits in the number, regardless of decimal place.

Loggerhead Turtle, carnivorous sea turtle found in warm waters of the Atlantic and Pacific. Characterized by a large head, it has oarlike flippers and is red-brown. Length; 3ft (91cm); weight: 300lb (135kg). Family Cheloniidae; species *Caretta caretta. See also* Turtle.

Logic, branch of philosophy dealing with the systematic study of the structure of propositions and the criteria of valid inference. In abstracting from the content of propositions in order to examine their logical form, logic evaluates soundness or validity rather than truth *per se.* The history of logic begins with Aristotle, proceeding through Arabian and European logic in the Middle Ages and various post-Renaissance scholars, and resulting in the mathematical elaborations of the 19th and 20th centuries. *See also* Symbolic Logic.

Logical Positivism, also called scientific empiricism and logical empiricism, school of philosophy that evolved out of the Vienna Circle of the 1920s and 1930s. Beginning as a continuation of 19th-century Viennese empiricism, it resulted in a philosophical attitude based on logic. It rejected metaphysics as logically meaningless and advocated a thorough analysis of philosophical and scientific terminology.

Logos, in philosophy, means intellect or reason, or in a larger sense the rational principle that orders the universe. The Stoics thought of this principle as the soul of the world. In theology, there have been debates about the meaning of the Greek word *logos* as used in the Gospel of John. The term was translated as *Word:* "In the beginning was the Word and the Word was with God, and the Word was God. The same was in the beginning with God." *Word* can be taken to mean God or something else such as wisdom.

Logwood, or bloodwood, spiny evergreen tree native to Central America, West Indies, and Colombia. The small, fragrant flowers are yellow. Its dark red heartwood yields a dye used in biological stains. Height: to 40ft (12m). Family Leguminosae; species *Haematoxylon campechianum.*

Lohengrin, in Teutonic mythology, a knight, son of Parcival, associated with legends of the Holy Grail. In one story, Lohengrin arrives in Antwerp asleep in a boat drawn by a swan. He awakens to save a princess from an annoying suitor, then marries her. When the princess asks him his name, defying his wish, the swan boat appears and Lohengrin departs.

Loire River, longest river in France; rises in Cévennes Mts in SE France, flows N through central and W France to Atlantic Ocean at Saint-Nazaire. It is connected by canals to Rhône and Seine river systems. Length: 630mi (1,014km).

Loki, in Norse mythology, a mischievous demon. Although friends with Odin and Thor, he was known for his pranks. He was regarded as an enemy of the gods.

Lollards, followers of the 14th-century English religious reformer John Wycliffe. They challenged both doctrines and practices of the church, including transubstantiation and the need for confession. They rejected the sole authority of the pope, and they denounced the wealth of the church and church involvement in civil affairs. Lollards went out as "poor preachers," teaching that the Bible was the source of belief. They won support from some nobles as well as many common people, but after they were declared heretics the movement lost force. However, Lollard ideas helped prepare the way for the Protestant Reformation. *See also* Wycliffe, John.

Lomas de Zamora, city in E Argentina, 9 mi (14km) SSW of Buenos Aires. Industries: chemicals, electrical equipment, cement, Pop. 272,116.

Lombard, Peter (c. 1100–60) Italian theologian. He is best known for his *Sentences,* a series of four books on the Trinity, Creation and Sin, the Incarnation and Virtues, and the Sacraments and Four Last Things. This work became the source of Catholic theology until replaced by Aquinas' *Summa Theologica.*

Lombard League, 12th- and 13th-century alliance of cities of Lombardy in northern Italy (including Milan, Venice, Brescia, Bergamo, Mantua, Verona). Founded in 1167 to resist the Holy Roman Emperor Frederick Barbarossa, by the Peace of Constance (1183) the league acknowledged fealty to Frederick, but the cities were granted local liberties and jurisdiction. The league was formed again in 1226 against Frederick II and ended with his death in 1250.

Lombards, Germanic people thought to have migrated from Gotland. They inhabited the area east of the lower Elbe until driven west by the Romans in AD9. They were allied with Arminius in 175 and invaded N Italy in 568 under Alboin. They conquered much of Italy from their center Pavia and later adopted Catholicism and Latin customs. Their kingdom attained its zenith under Liutprand (died 744). They were defeated by the Franks under Charlemagne (774) and declined thereafter.

Lombardy (Lombardia), industrial region in N Italy; comprised of provinces of Bergamo, Brescia, Como, Cremona, Mantua, Milano, Pavia, Sondrio, and Varese; Milan is capital city. Geographically the region is marked by mountains, glaciers, and numerous lakes; it was center of powerful Lombard kingdom 569–774; defeated by Charlemagne 774. Products: cereals, sugar beets, vegetables, fruits, olives, livestock. Industries: automobiles, steel, chemicals, textiles. Area: 9,200sq mi (23,830sq km). Pop. 8,882,366.

Lomé, seaport city and capital of Republic of Togo, W Africa, on Gulf of Guinea. An administrative, commercial, and industrial center, it is site of University of Benin (1970), rail line, airport. Industries: coffee, cocoa, palm nuts, copra. Pop. 135,000.

Lomonosov, Mikhail Vasilievich (1711–65), Russian scientist and poet. He helped found the University of Moscow (1755) and was one of the first Russian scientists to suggest the law of conservation of mass, atomic theory, and a kinetic theory of heat. He formulated Russian classical literary theory in his *Letter on the Rules of Russian Versification.* His poetry includes the odes *Evening Meditations* (1748) and *Morning Meditations* (1751).

Lomonosov Ridge, a submarine ridge that stretches from the Asian continental shelf, past the North Pole to the edge of the North American continental shelf near Ellesmere Island. Discovered in 1948–49 by Soviet polar explorers, it has aided in determining ocean water circulation, the pattern of ice drift, and major life provinces in the Arctic.

London, Jack (1876–1916), pseud. of John Griffith, US novelist and short-story writer, b. San Francisco. His works concentrate on the brute-in-man concept. His early years were spent along the San Francisco waterfront, which he describes in his autobiographical novels *Martin Eden* (1909) and *John Barleycorn* (1913). He spent three years as a sailor and traveled widely. During 1899–1903 he wrote essays, poems, over 100 short stories, and eight novels. *Call of the Wild* (1903), his most popular work, was written during

London, England: Tower Bridge

Henry Wadsworth Longfellow

Longhorn

this period. He espoused socialism and was influenced by Marx and Nietzsche.

London, city in SE Ontario, Canada, on the Thames River; location of six colleges and universities. Industries: paper, textiles, refrigerators, diesel locomotives. Founded 1826; inc. as village 1840, town 1848, city 1855. Pop. 240,392.

London, capital city of the United Kingdom, located on both sides of Thames River, about 40mi (64km) from its mouth in SE England. A Roman town from AD 43–409, it was attacked by Danes 851; Alfred the Great freed London from their control in 886; city was political capital of England by 14th century. In 16th century Elizabeth I introduced social reforms and added to city's wealth and power. Almost destroyed by a plague in 1665 and fire in 1666, city went on to become a world leader in trade, culture, and politics by time Queen Victoria reigned (1837–1901).

In 19th century people began moving from city's center to outer rings of boroughs; the Industrial Revolution brought about working-class suburbs. WWI caused little damage to city, but WWII bombing killed 30,000 residents and destroyed 100,000 houses; site of Westminister Abbey (with a few remnants from original 1065 building), St Paul's Cathedral (rebuilt by Sir Christopher Wren 1668), Houses of Parliament (1840–60), Tower of London (1078), National Gallery (1838), Buckingham Palace (1705), Westminster Hall (1099), University of London (1836); Kensington, Hyde, Green, and St James parks.

International trade, although declining, is still one of London's major economic activities. Heathrow Airport (W of city), Gatwick Airport (S), and Foulnes (E) have greatly increased air freight shipments, while shipping from its docks has lessened. Famous London fogs have decreased considerably since passage of Clean Air Act of 1956; tourism continues to be an important industry. Industries: brewing, tanning, clothing, furniture, paper, printing, engineering. City is also center of banking and investment business. Its many theaters, museums, galleries, opera and concert halls also make it a cultural center. The City of London and its 32 boroughs make up Greater London. Pop. 7,111,500.

Londonderry (Derry), borough in Northern Ireland, at the mouth of the Foyle River on Lough Foyle; capital of Londonderry co; hilly farming and cattle-raising region. It grew around abbey founded by St Columba (546); destroyed by the Danes in 812; name changed from Derry to Londonderry when town passed to corporations of the City of London (1613); besieged by James II for 105 days (1689); site of many early structures including Roman Catholic and Protestant cathedrals, and a triumphal arch commemorating the 1689 siege; the modern city is important as a maritime center, with a naval base. Industries: shipping and shipbuilding, linens, fishing, tanning, brewing, and marketing of regional agricultural products. Area of borough; 814sq mi (2,108sq km). Pop. (city) 54,000; (borough) 130,889.

London Economic Conference (1933), international financial meeting, also known as World Monetary and Economic Conference. The United States met with the League of Nations members in London to work for international economic stability in the midst of the Depression. The meeting ended without accomplishment after the United States rejected the plan of returning to the gold standard.

Long, Crawford Williamson (1815–78), US physician, b. Danielsville, Ga. In 1842 he began using ether as an anesthesia for surgery but did not publish or publicize his work until years later, after William Morton

and others had been given credit. *See also* Morton, William.

Long, Huey Pierce (1893–1935), US political leader, b. near Winnfield, La. Elected governor of Louisiana in 1928 by appealing to rural voters on a tax-the-rich program, he was impeached for bribery and misconduct in 1929 but was not convicted and served until 1931. He then built a powerful machine that controlled Louisiana politics for decades. He served in the US Senate (1931–35). He began (1933) the "Share Our Wealth" movement and proposed legislation against the wealthy, gaining wide popularity. He was feared by President Roosevelt and liberals as a potential dictator. His presidential bid, however, ended with his assassination.

Long Beach, city in S California, 20mi (32km) S of Los Angeles; oil discovered in 1921; site of four man-made oil islands in its harbor; the Queen Mary has been berthed here since 1967 and used as a tourist center, museum, and hotel. Industries: oil, automobile parts, canning, chemicals. Inc. 1888. Pop. (1980) 361,334.

Longfellow, Henry Wadsworth (1807–82), US poet, b. Portland, Me. After graduating from Bowdoin College (1825), he studied modern languages in Europe and then taught at Bowdoin (1829–35) and Harvard University (1835–54), until he resigned to devote himself solely to writing. His first book of poetry, *Voices of the Night,* appeared in 1839. In 1841 *Ballads and Other Poems* was published. It contained two of his most popular shorter poems, "The Wreck of the Hesperus" and "The Village Blacksmith." Perhaps Longfellow is best-remembered for his narrative poems dramatizing American history and legend. These include *Evangeline* (1847), *The Song of Hiawatha* (1855), *The Courtship of Miles Standish* (1858), and *Paul Revere's Ride* (1861). In them, Longfellow combines the epic form and some of the techniques of European literature with his own simple and sentimental style.

Longhorn, almost extinct breed of beef cattle, originally from Mexico, descended from European cattle introduced by Spanish conquistadors. Once the mainstay of Western herds, they are now used only as rodeo and show animals. *See also* Beef Cattle; Cattle.

Long-horned Beetle, or long-horned borer, woodboring beetle found worldwide. It has long antennae, long legs, and cylindrical white or yellow body. Length: 0.12–6in (2–152mm). Family Cerambycidae.

Long Island, fourth-largest island in the United States, in SE New York, separated from Manhattan by the East River; W end of island contains New York City boroughs of Queens and Brooklyn; E end counties of Nassau and Suffolk. Long Island Sound separates it from Connecticut (N); Atlantic Ocean is on its S. Originally inhabited by Algonquin Indians; Massachusetts Bay Colony and Dutch West India Company claimed it in 17th century. Treaty of Hartford (1650) divided it between them. Farming, fishing, and whaling were carried on in 18th and 19th centuries; many farms still on island. Easy access to New York City has caused rapid growth of industry and population. Glacial deposits provide sand, gravel; there are many wooded areas, beaches, bays, and inlets. Commercial and sport fishing are on S and E coasts. Limited natural water supply forces strict conservation measures. Tourism and recreation are supported on the E and S parts of the island. Length: 118mi (190km). Width: 12–20mi (19–32km).

Longitude, a measurement of location, east or west of the prime meridian (the imaginary north-south line

passing through both poles and Greenwich, England). Longitude is measured in degrees, minutes, and seconds and is 180° both east and west of the prime meridian.

Longitudinal Wave, type of wave, such as a sound wave, in which the particles of the transmitting medium are displaced along the direction of energy propagation, that is, in the direction of wave motion. *See also* Wave.

Long March, a remarkable feat by Chinese Communist forces. They broke out of Nationalist encirclement in 1934 and for more than a year traveled 6,000 miles (9,600km) under the leadership of Chu Teh and Mao Tse-tung from Kiangsi Province through western China to Shensi Province. There, new Communist headquarters were established at Yenan.

Long Parliament (1640–1660), English Parliament summoned by Charles I and not formally dissolved until 1660. It impeached Charles' ministers and censured him in the Grand Remonstrance (1641). Its refusal to cooperate with Charles or be dissolved was a major victory for representative government over the crown. The Parliament was reduced by Pride's Purge (1648) and the remaining legislators, known as the Rump Parliament, condemned Charles I (1649). The Long Parliament thereafter had little authority and was dissolved at the Restoration (1660). *See also* Pride's Purge.

Longview, city in E Texas, 120mi (193km) E of Dallas; seat of Gregg co; site of Le Tourneau College (1946). Industries: petrochemicals, aircraft parts, steel, chemicals, plastic, paper, lumber, machinery. Inc. 1872. Pop. (1980) 62,762.

Loon, diving bird of Northern Hemisphere known for harsh and eerie, often nocturnal, call. It has black, white, and gray plumage. An excellent swimmer, it often stays submerged while fishing. It runs on water and flaps its wings to take flight; it splashes down on its chest later. It lays olive eggs (2) in a grass-and-reed nest near water. Length: 30in (76cm). Family Gaviidae.

Lope de Vega Carpio, Félix (1562–1635), Spanish dramatic poet, contemporary of Cervantes. He wrote nearly 2,000 plays of which 431 texts survive, dominating the Spanish theater for 50 years. He invented the "comedia" form, freeing drama from classical and medieval restraints. His *Fuente Ovejuna,* portraying peasants united against injustice, is considered the first major drama of class conflict.

López Portillo (y Pachecho), José (1920–), president of Mexico (1976–82). A professor at Mexico's National University during the 1950s, he took a post with the Ministry of National Patrimony in 1959; in 1965 he was named director general of legal affairs under Pres. Gustavo Díaz Ordaz and three years later became undersecretary in charge of planning. While engaged with his administrative posts, he also produced scholarly writings and two novels, *Quetzalcóatl* (1965) and *Don Q* (1969). His administration was characterized by rapid economic growth, spurred by high petroleum revenues and followed by recession as oil prices fell, and by better relations with other Central American countries, the United States, and Spain.

Loquat, evergreen shrub or small tree native to China and Japan and naturalized in subtropical climates worldwide. Used for shade and hedges, they have white flowers and yellow, plumlike fruit prized as a dessert or flavoring. Height: to 20ft (6.1m). Family Rosaceae; species *Eriobotrya japonica.*

Lorain, city and lakeport in N Ohio, on Lake Erie at mouth of Black River, 25mi (40km) W of Cleveland; important ore shipping port. Industries: shipbuilding, iron, steel, automobile assembling. Founded 1807; inc. 1834 as Charleston; renamed 1876. Pop. (1980) 75,416.

LORAN, navigational aid used to guide ships and airplanes to their destinations. The name LORAN stands for LOng-RAnge Navigation. It consists of two ground stations that emit electronic pulses, which the ships and planes can use to guide their course. The stations have a day range of 800mi (1,288km) and a night range of 1,600mi. (2,576km) and are accurate to within 1mi (1.6km) of their location.

Lord Dunmore's War (1774), dispute involving colonial settlers and Indians in a conflict over land. Virginia's royal governor, John Murray, Earl of Dunmore, took control of western Pennsylvania. Then settlers began moving into Kentucky. These two infringements into lands that the Indians considered theirs provoked the Shawnee and Ottawa tribes into war. Col. Andrew Lewis led his troops to victory over Chief Cornstalk at the Battle of Point Pleasant. The war ended with the Treaty of Camp Charlotte, by which the Indians relinquished hunting rights in Kentucky.

Lorentz, Hendrik Anton (1853–1928), Dutch physicist and professor at Leyden. His early work was concerned with James Maxwell's theory of electromagnetic radiation. This led him to the Lorentz transformation and the prediction of the Lorentz-Fitzgerald contraction, both of which were essential steps in the discovery of special relativity. He was responsible for the idea of local time. Some of his work was concerned with thermodynamics and the Zeeman effect, for which he was awarded a Nobel Prize in 1902 (jointly with Pieter Zeeman). *See also* Lorentz-Fitzgerald Length Contraction; Lorentz Transformation.

Lorentz-Fitzgerald Length Contraction, theory, put forward independently by H. A. Lorentz (1895) and George Fitzgerald (1893) to explain the result of the Michelson-Morley experiment, that a body moving with high velocity through the ether experiences a contraction in length in the direction of the motion. *See also* Relativity Theory.

Lorentz Transformations, relations (for H.A. Lorentz) connecting the space and time coordinates of an event as observed from two frames of reference, especially at relativistic velocities. Shown by Einstein (1905) to be a consequence of the theory of special relativity. *See also* Relativity Theory.

Lorenz, Konrad (1903–), pioneer Austrian ethologist. Lorenz did classic studies of imprinting in birds and aggression in other animals. He wrote the controversial *On Aggression* (1966) in which he argued that human aggression is instinctual. He received a Nobel Prize in 1973.

Lorenzo the Magnificent. *See* Medici, Lorenzo de.

Loris, primitive tailless, tree-dwelling nocturnal primate of S Asian and East Indies forests. They have soft, thick fur and big eyes, and feed mainly on insects. Length: 8–16in (20–41cm). Species slender *Loris tardigradus,* slow *Nycticebus coucang* and *N. pygmaeus. See also* Primates.

Lorrain, Claude (1600–82), professional name of Claude Gellée, French landscape painter, draftsman, and etcher. With Nicolas Poussin, he was the finest artist of the classical Baroque style. His mature works include "Embarkation of St Ursula" (1641) and "Ermini and the Shepherds" (1666). His later works anticipated in many ways the Impressionists and Romantics ("Perseus and Medusa").

Lorraine, historic region and former province in NE France, now comprised of Moselle, Meurthe-et-Moselle, Meuse, and Vosges depts.; part of medieval Austrasia, and kingdom of Lotharingia 9th century; passed to house of Lorraine 1048–1738; united as an official province of France 1766; E part was ceded to Germany 1871, passed back to France after WWI, again annexed to Germany during WWII, after which the region was returned to France. Chief cities are Nancy, Metz, Thionville, and Verdun-sur-Meuse. Products: hops, grapes, wine, beer, iron ore, coal, coke, dairy products.

Lory, brightly colored parrot, native to Australia, with a brush-tipped tongue for feeding on nectar and fruit. The typical Papuan lory *(Charmosyna papou)* of New Guinea is crimson with black cap and pants; green wings, back, and tail; and glossy blue nape. The smaller lorikeet *(Trichoglossus)* is also found, often in large groups, in Malaya.

Los Angeles, city in SW California, near shore of Pacific Ocean; the largest city in California, and 3rd-largest in the United States. Originally a cattle farming center known as El Pueblo de Nuestra Señora La Reina de los Angeles, it was taken from Mexico by the United States 1846; city grew as railroads arrived (Southern Pacific, 1876, and Santa Fe, 1885). The discovery of oil deposits (1894), improvements of harbor facilities (1912), and the developing motion picture industry at Hollywood (early 20th century) attracted settlers; as the city expanded, it attracted more diverse industries, and was chosen as host of the Summer Olympic Games in 1932 and 1984. Major problems of the city's growth have been its water shortage (a 300-mi/483-km pipe from the Colorado River supplies the city with most of its water) and air pollution. The metropolitan area of Los Angeles comprises approx. 34,000sq mi (88,060sq km), enveloping the separate cities of Beverly Hills, Santa Monica, and San Fernando. It is the site of Los Angeles County Museum of Art, Los Angeles County Museum of Natural History, Southwest Museum, Municipal Art Gallery; institutes of higher education include the University of California at Los Angeles (1881), University of Southern California (1879), California Institute of Technology, Loyola University of Los Angeles (1865); tourist attractions include Griffith Park, the Hollywood Bowl, the Plaza district of the old city, and the many Pacific seaside resorts; it is also the home of several professional sports teams. Industries: aircraft, heavy machinery, wood products, textiles, tires, chemicals, oil refining, food processing and canning, printing, publishing, plastics, clay, furniture, fine instruments, shipping, electronic equipment, entertainment, tourism. Founded 1781; inc. 1850. Pop. (1980) 2,966,763.

Lost Generation, designation for disillusioned American intellectuals, writers, and artists after World War I. The term is attributed to a remark made by Gertrude Stein, the author and art patron, to Ernest Hemingway. Her words, "You are all of a lost generation," appear in the preface of Hemingway's book, *The Sun Also Rises* (1926), a novel about a fun-seeking group of American and English expatriates. Other writers of the Lost Generation also expressed their loss of idealism, which had resulted from the war, in their work. Like Hemingway, many of the Lost Generation were expatriates in Paris. Other Lost Generation writers include F. Scott Fitzgerald, Ezra Pound, and John Dos Passos.

Lot, in the Bible, son of Haran and nephew of Abraham. He accompanied Abraham to Canaan, choosing to settle the fertile Jordan valley. When God destroyed Sodom and Gomorrah, Lot, his wife, and two daughters were allowed to escape, but his wife, disobeying God's orders, looked back and became a pillar of salt.

Lothair II (or **III**), called "the Saxon" (1070?–1137), king of Germany and Holy Roman emperor (1125–37). He secured the throne and defeated the rival Hohenstaufens (1128–35), the family of the former Holy Roman emperor, Henry V. He fought in support of Pope Innocent II and expanded German rule. Invaded Italy (1136–37).

Lotharingia, the part of Charlemagne's empire inherited by his descendant Lothair II (855–69) for whom it is named. The Treaty of Verdun (843) divided the Carolingian empire among Charlemagne's three grandsons, the middle part going to Lothair I. Another split in 855 gave the northern part of Lothair's kingdom to his son Lothair II. Roughly, Lotharingia included modern Lorraine (the name is a later form of Lotharingia), Alsace, NW Germany, all of Luxembourg, Belgium, and The Netherlands.

Lotto, Lorenzo (*c.* 1480–*c.* 1556), Venetian painter. He was one of the finest artists of the High Renaissance. "The Assumption" is an early work. His mature work, marked by softer tones, includes "Christ Taking Leave of His Mother" and "Bridal Couple with Cupid." *See also* Renaissance Art.

Lotus, water lily native to Africa and Asia. Flowers are blue, white, or pink. The white lotus *(Nymphaea lotus)* was once considered sacred. Family Nymphaeaceae.

Loudness, magnitude of the sensation produced when the human ear responds to a sound. There is no simple relationship between loudness and the intensity of the sound; the response of the ear also depends to a certain extent on the frequency.

Loudspeaker, device for converting oscillating electric currents into sound. The most common type has a moving coil attached to a stiff paper cone (often elliptical) suspended in a strong magnetic field. The oscillating currents in the speech coil cause the cone to vibrate at the frequency of the currents, thus creating sound waves. A modern loudspeaker gives uniform response between 80 and 10,000 hertz. For higher efficiency a small diaphragm is used at the apex of an exponential horn.

Louis I (1786–1868), king of Bavaria (1825–48), member of Wittelsbach family, succeeded his father, Maximilian I. He was best known for his generous patronage of the arts, which made Munich a vibrant cultural center. He quickly changed from liberal to conservative and became so unpopular that he had to abdicate at the time of the 1848 revolution in favor of his son Maximilian II. Louis' affair with Lola Montez caused a national scandal.

Louis I, called **the Pious** (778–840), king of France and of Germany (814–840), emperor of the West, succeeded his father, Charlemagne (814–40). Sincerely religious, he was troubled by rebellious sons and their territorial squabbles, which they pursued to the neglect of all else and hastened the end of the Carolingian Empire. He divided his empire among his sons (817) to take effect after his death, but the final disposition took place only after his sons made war on each other. His son Lothair I succeeded him as emperor.

Louis III (863?–882), king of France (879–82). He and his brother Carloman divided their father's West Frankish kingdom and warded off rival claims by Louis the Younger, who based his opposition on their father's divorce of their mother. During Louis' reign Scandinavian maurauders, the Normans, posed a serious threat. In 881 Louis won a decisive victory that temporarily stopped the Norman invasions in northern France.

Louis IV or **Louis d'Outremer** (?921–954), king of France (936–954). Called d'Outremer (from overseas) because he was raised in England. He attempted to reestablish his father's claim to Lorraine (938) but was subverted by his vassal, Hugh the Great, working in collusion with Otto I of Germany. Louis allied himself with Otto, had Hugh excommunicated (948), and forced Hugh to make peace (951).

Louis V or **Louis le Fainéant** (967?–87), king of France. The last Carolingian ruler, he was crowned in 979 while his father, Lothair, was still ruling. He became sole king in 986 but was overshadowed by Hugh Capet, Duke of the Franks, who succeeded Louis to the throne. His nickname Fainéant means "do nothing."

Louis VI or **Louis the Fat** (1081–1137), king of France (1108–37). Working to build the power of the crown over independent local nobles, he notably increased the importance of the royal courts. With Abbot Suger of St Denis as his advisor, he worked closely with the church. He began a war (1104) against King Henry I of England, duke of Normandy, a struggle that was to continue intermittently for centuries. Before his death he arranged the marriage of his son, Louis VII, and Eleanor, daughter of the duke of Aquitaine.

Louis VII or **Louis the Young** (1120?–80), king of France (1137–80). His marriage to Eleanor of Aquitaine extended the French crown's lands to the Pyrenees Mountains. As king he consolidated royal power by cultivating the church and the emerging towns. In 1147 he went on the Second Crusade. On his return he claimed that his wife had been unfaithful and had their marriage annulled (1152). She then married his archrival, Henry II of England, whose holdings thereby became greater than those of Louis. A long war between France and England ensued.

Louis VIII (1187–1226), king of France (1223–26). He invaded England (1216) at the invitation of barons opposing King John but was defeated at Lincoln (1217) and returned to France. He then successfully launched a crusade against the Albigensians and broke their power in Avignon. *See also* Albigenses.

Louis IX or **Saint Louis** (1214–70), king of France (1226–70), canonized in 1297. Louis was guided throughout much of his career by his mother, Blanche of Castile, who served as his regent during his youth (1226–36) and during his first absence from France (1248–52). Recovery from a serious illness prompted Louis to go on the Sixth Crusade in 1248–54. Unsuccessful, captured, and ransomed, he returned after six years' absence. In 1270 he undertook another crusade and died of fever at Tunis.

Throughout his reign Louis worked for peace among Christian nations. In the Treaty of Paris (1259) he improved relations with England when he recognized Henry III as duke of Aquitaine. An exemplary medieval Christian, pious and chivalric, he supported the pope and arbitrated international disputes. Early in his reign he successfully defended his throne from usurpations of power by feudal lords. In order to discourage private warfare among his nobles, he reformed the administration of justice. The court of judicial officers met as a

Louisiana

Lorenzo Lotto: Adoration of the Shepherds (detail)

Louis XIV

New Orleans, Louisiana: French quarter

separate body, the Parliament of Paris, to consider feudal and royal rights and obligations. Subjects were allowed to appeal decisions of their lords to this royal body.

Louis X or **Louis the Stubborn** (1289–1316), king of France (1314–16). Son of Philip IV and Joan of Navarre, he dismissed his father's unpopular financial advisors and tried to raise money for a proposed campaign in Flanders by selling charters of privileges to clergy and dissident nobles. In 1315–16 he held the first representative assemblies in France, summoning them to approve royal taxes.

Louis XI (1423–83), king of France (1461–83), noted for enlarging its borders. He was involved in a nobles' plot to overthrow his father, Charles VII; confined (1447–56) to Dauphiné in southern France; and exiled to The Netherlands in 1456. In 1461 he took the throne and vigorously suppressed, as had his father, the rebellions of the nobles. He devoted most of his reign to struggles against Charles the Bold of Burgundy. These struggles were complicated by his nobles' frequent cooperation with Charles. Louis pursued a flexible policy aimed at peace with England, war with Burgundy, and the consolidation of his power at home. In 1482 he defeated Charles the Bold's daughter Mary of Burgundy, and the Treaty of Arras gave Burgundy to France. During his reign southern provinces also were added to France. He thus left his nation larger and more powerful.

Louis XII (1462–1515), king of France (1498–1515). He was a popular but inept ruler. During the reign of his cousin Charles VIII (1483–98), Louis led an unsuccessful noblemen's revolt. He was imprisoned and later restored to favor and fought for Charles in Italy (1494). He had his first marriage annulled so as to marry (1499) Anne of Britanny (Charles' widow) and thereby keep Britanny a part of France. His foreign wars were unsuccessful. Only briefly did he make good his claim to the duchy of Milan. Successful in dividing Naples with Ferdinand of Aragon, he lost it in a subsequent war (1503) with him. His subjects approved his administration of justice, low taxes, and support of the lower classes. His third wife (1514) was Mary Tudor, sister of Henry VIII of England.

Louis XIII (1601–43), king of France (1601–43), son of Henry IV and Marie de Médicis. He forcibly ended his mother's regency, had her Italian lover murdered, and exiled her to Blois. Increasingly however, he came to rely on her advisor, Cardinal de Richelieu. Both Louis and Richelieu favored strong royal authority, opposition to the Spanish and Austrian Hapsburgs, and strategic alliance with Protestant opponents of the Spanish, both in and out of France.

When Marie de Médicis attempted to oust Richelieu, Louis refused and exiled his mother. In 1635 he declared war on Spain and showed great courage in defending Paris against attack. His wife, Anne of Austria, whom he disdained, unexpectedly bore his child, the future Louis XIV, in 1638 after 20 years of childless marriage.

Louis XIV (1638–1715), king of France, (1643–1715) known as the "Sun King" and celebrated as an absolute monarch. So unexpected was his birth, his parents having been childless for 20 years, that he was called "the gift of God." His father, Louis XIII, died when he was four. During his minority Cardinal Jules Mazarin was minister of state, dealing with such matters as the revolt of the Fronde (1648–53). In 1661 Louis assumed the throne, determined to rule and overcome any weaknesses in French central authority. He entrusted finances and the elaboration of mercantile economic

policy to Jean Colbert. More to his personal interest was the army, which François Michel Le Tellier had all but created afresh for Louis' purposes.

In 1667 and 1672 Louis warred in The Netherlands for added territory; during 1683–84 he was laying new claims in The Netherlands, Alsace, and Genoa. The War of the League of Augsburg (1688–97) created German enmity and little gain. His enemies—England, The Netherlands, the Holy Roman Empire—in the War of the Spanish Succession (1701–14) forced him to separate the crowns of France and Spain for his future heirs.

Louis XV (1710–74), king of France (1715–74). He became king at the age of five, succeeding his great-grandfather, Louis XIV. Cardinal Fleury served as his educator and advisor for almost 20 years and Guillaume Dubois was France's administrator during Louis' minority (1715–23). When Fleury died (1743), Louis XV took personal charge, with unfortunate consequences. Bored by the court life he inherited from Louis XIV, he was equally bored by the daily details of government administration. Court intrigues, unpopular and offensive to the clergy, usually involved his many mistresses, notably the duchess of Chateauroux, Mme. de Pompadour, and Mme. du Barry.

The Seven Years War (1756–63) brought France the loss of much of her colonial empire and virtual bankruptcy. Louis attempted to reform the parlements (1771) in order to tax the aristocracy. The new Maupeou parlements, named for his chancellor, represented his attempt to diminish aristocratic privilege, but Louis XVI restored the old parlements. In general, his reign was marked by disasters—financial, military, and political.

Louis XVI (1754–93), king of France (1774–92). He inherited a crown already unpopular with major elements of France and urgently in need of money. A series of ministers, Turgot, Jacques Necker, Charles de Calonne, unsuccessfully attempted to force the aristocracy to pay its share of taxes. The need for money became acute after French participation in the American Revolution (1778–1783).

When Louis summoned the Estates General (1789), he reverted to a method of raising taxes used infrequently since Louis X, and one that admitted others besides the king to share his power. The aristocrats quickly lost control to the Third Estate, middle-class members who constituted themselves as the National Assembly. Louis increasingly isolated himself from their reforming spirit, especially as events became more violent. After the fall of the Bastille (July 1789), a Paris mob brought Louis back to Paris from Versailles (October 1789). In 1791 he attempted to flee France with his wife, Marie Antoinette, and family. Brought back by the army, he agreed to support the Constitution of 1791 but intrigued with aristocrats, émigrés, and Austria against the new government. War fever and suspicion of his treason led to his imprisonment, abolition of the monarchy and establishment of a republic (1792). He was guillotined in 1793. *See also* Estates General; French Revolution.

Louis XVII (1785–95), second son of King Louis XVI of France and Marie Antoinette. Upon the guillotining of his father (1793), Young Louis was considered by royalist émigrés the next king of France. (His elder brother had died in 1789.) He was first confined with his family but was later separated from them, and, according to accounts, put into solitary confinement and harshly treated. He died in prison.

Louis XVIII (1755–1824), Bourbon king of France (1814–24) restored to the throne after the end of Napoleon's empire. The younger brother of Louis XVI, he

spent the years 1791–1814 in exile wherever the fortunes of Napoleonic wars allowed him: England, Verona, Sweden, Belgium. Restored to the throne by the Charter of 1814, he reluctantly accepted constitutional limitations of his power. He was deeply conservative and supported government censorship and clerical control of education.

Louis II, called **the German** (804?–876), king of Germany (843–876); one of the rebellious sons of Emperor Louis I. His brother Lothair became emperor (an empty title), and Louis and another brother, Charles, forced him to divide the empire three ways. Louis received the lands extending from the Rhine to the eastern frontier of the empire, essentially those that later formed Germany. Regarded as the founder of the German kingdom.

Louis I (1326–82), king of Hungary (1342–82) and Poland (1370–82), called "the Great." The son of Charles I, Louis was appointed king of Poland by Casimir III. Though the union of the two countries was not a success (Louis ruled Poland through regents), Louis, after a successful struggle with Venice for the Adriatic coast, had control of one of the largest realms in Europe, and Hungarian might was acknowledged throughout the Balkans. He encouraged commerce, industry, and science. In Hungary, he introduced administrative reforms that curbed the power of the nobility, but in Poland he granted the nobles a charter that gave them extensive privileges.

Louis II (1506–26), king of Hungary (1516–26), son and dissolute successor of Ladislas II. In 1521 the Turks captured Belgrade; in 1526 they crushed the Hungarians at the Battle of Mohács in which Louis and 20,000 perished. The Protestant Reformation expanded significantly during his reign.

Louis II (822?–875), king of Italy (844); emperor of the West (855–875); king of Lorraine (872–875); succeeded his father, Emperor Lothair I. He defended his kingdom from the Arabs and enlarged his possessions considerably at the expense of his two brothers, Lothair II and Charles of Provence. He had no male heirs.

Louis, Joe (1914–81), US boxer, b. Joseph Louis Barrow, Lafayette, Ala. He won the world's heavyweight title from James J. Braddock (1937) in Chicago, Ill, and retired undefeated (1949). He attempted to regain his title in 1950 but lost to Ezzard Charles in New York City. Louis held the title longer than any other heavyweight.

Louisiana, state in the S central United States, on the Gulf of Mexico at the mouth of the Mississippi River.

Land and economy. The state is a level coastal plain. The Mississippi River bisects its S half; the Red and Ouachita rivers are other major rivers. Vast marshes lie along the S coast. Agricultural production is widespread. Commercial fishing in the Gulf of Mexico is important. Major manufacturing is in the S, associated with the extraction of mineral resources. Much of Louisiana's oil is obtained from offshore wells. Water transportation has aided commerce; the Mississippi has long been a route for products of states to the N. New Orleans is one of the nation's leading ports.

People. Louisiana displays a broader range of national influences than most states. The French began settling about 1700, and were followed by Germans. A number of Acadian French deported by the British from Nova Scotia arrived in the 1750s, and Spanish joined the colony a few years later. Americans from other S and E states settled in the N. Slaves were imported for cotton and sugar plantations. French and Spanish influ-

361

ences are strongest in the S. New Orleans is notably cosmopolitan. About 65% of the population lives in urban areas.

Education. There are nearly 30 institutions of higher education. Louisiana State University is supported by the state, which also administers 10 other institutions. Tulane University is the best known of the privately endowed institutions.

History. The Sieur de La Salle claimed the area for France in 1682. By secret treaty, in 1762, France ceded it to Spain, which ceded it back in 1800. France sold it to the United States in the Louisiana Purchase in 1803. The next year the Territory of Orleans, comprising the present state, was organized. On its admission to the Union, it was renamed Louisiana. The Battle of New Orleans, last engagement of the War of 1812, was won by the Americans on Jan. 8, 1815. The state joined the Confederacy in January 1861, and Union troops took New Orleans in 1862 and controlled the Mississippi a year later. Louisiana's economy was wrecked by the Civil War, and postwar reconstruction proceeded more slowly than in much of the South. Industrial growth did not come until the 20th century. For most of the 20th century, the Longs, a Democratic political family, have dominated Louisiana politics. Drilling of Louisiana's offshore oil resources, begun on a large scale after WWII, has transformed the state's economy.

PROFILE

Admitted to Union: April 30, 1812; rank, 18th
US Congressmen: Senate, 2; House of Representatives, 8
Population: 4,203,972 (1980); rank, 19th
Capital: Baton Rouge, 219,486 (1980)
Chief cities: New Orleans, 557,482; Shreveport, 205,815; Baton Rouge
State legislature: Senate, 39; House of Representatives, 105
Area: 48,523sq mi (125,675sq km); rank, 31st
Elevation: Highest, Driskill Mountain, 535ft (163m). Lowest, 5ft (2m) below sea level, at New Orleans
Industries (major products): chemicals, processed foods, petroleum products, paper products, wood products
Agriculture (major products): rice, sugarcane, cattle, sweet potatoes, soybeans, cotton
Minerals (major): petroleum, natural gas, sulfur, salt
State nickname: Pelican State
State motto: "Union, Justice, Confidence"
State bird: brown pelican
State flower: magnolia blossom
State tree: bald cypress

Louisiana Purchase (1803), a transaction involving a large area of land purchased from France by the United States. The 825,000sq mi (2,100,000sq km) of territory, from the Mississippi River to the Rocky Mountains, was bought for $15,000,000. With national security and the control of the Mississippi in mind, President Thomas Jefferson sent James Monroe to France to join Robert Livingston, US minister. The two men negotiated the purchase from Napoleon, who had lost interest in a colonial empire in the New World. The Louisiana Purchase doubled the area of the United States, and 13 states were admitted from the territory.

Louis Napoleon. *See* Napoleon III.

Louis of Nassau (1538–74), count of Nassau-Dietz, Netherlands leader. He was the brother of William the Silent and led the revolt against Spanish rule. When the duke of Alva arrived in 1564, Louis and William left the Netherlands to raise a fighting force. Defeated in several battles with the Spaniards, Louis was killed at Mookerheide.

Louis Philippe (1773–1850), king of France (1830–48). The revolution that brought him to power in 1830 was a bourgeois reaction to the aristocratic restoration of the Bourbons, Louis XVIII and Charles X. The revolution that ended his reign in 1848 was a proletarian and middle-class reaction to his own conservatism. He had, for example, refused to extend the right to vote to members of the lower classes. For much of his reign, however, he was a liberal, supporting constitutional restraint on the monarchy and becoming known as the "Citizen King." His chosen title, "Louis Philippe, King of the French," rather than "Philippe VII, King of France," was meant to convey the idea of a limited monarchy.

Louisville, industrial city and port of entry in NW Kentucky, on the Ohio River; seat of Jefferson co; largest city in Kentucky; est. as military base 1778 by George Rogers Clark, the Virginia legislature officially chartered it 1780 and named it for Louis XVI of France; city developed into an important shipping center by mid-19th century; first major southern city to adopt ordinance against racial housing discrimination (1967). It is host to the famous Kentucky Derby, horse race held annually since 1875 at Churchill Downs; site of Locust Grove Mansion (1790), University of Louisville (1798), Spalding College (1829), Bellarmine College (1950). Industries: whiskey, appliances, synthetic rubber, cigarettes, trucks, trailers, paint. Inc. 1780. Pop. (1980) 298,451.

Lourdes, town in SW France, at foot of Pyrenees on Gave de Pau River; site of Roman Catholic shrine commemorating the appearances of Our Lady of Lourdes to St Bernadette in 1858; pilgrimage center. Pop. 18,096.

Louse, Chewing, louse, ranging from white to reddish-brown to black, found worldwide. It has chewing mouthparts and feeds on feathers, hair, scales, and fatty matter. They do not attack humans. Length: 0.02–0.4in. (0.5–10mm). Order Mallophaga.

Louse, Sucking, flat, white to brown louse found worldwide. It sucks blood from mammals, including humans. Head lice *(Pediculus humanus capitis)* and body lice *(Pediculus humanus corporis)* carry epidemic typhus and transmit skin diseases. Length: 0.08–0.2in (2–5mm). Order Anoplura.

Lousewort. *See* Wood Betony.

Louvre, French art museum, Paris. France's enormous national collection contains art from most ages and countries and is housed in the Louvre Palace, which was built as a 16th-century chateau for Francis I. Francis I began the Louvre collection by commissioning the Italian artists Primaticcio and Andrea del Sarto to make bronze reproductions of famous statues of antiquity. Under Louis XIV, several important art collections, especially of Italian works, were acquired. During this period, French artists were given royal patronage and so produced many paintings for the Louvre collection. In 1848 the collection became the property of the state.

Lovebird, small parrot of the Old World, mainly Africa and Madagascar. Often kept in cages, the mates maintain a close relationship. The rosy-faced lovebird *(Agapornis rosericollis)* of S Africa inserts grass under his rump feathers and carries it to the nest.

Lovelace, Richard (1618–58), English cavalier poet, best known for his lyrics to "Lucasta." A handsome and courageous man, he supported King Charles I in Parliament (1642); was imprisoned, fled to France, and fought as a mercenary (1643–46); returned home and was again imprisoned (1648–49); and died in poverty.

Love's Labour's Lost (*c.* 1588), 5-act comedy by William Shakespeare. One of his earliest plays, it is a satire on literary affectations. Ferdinand, king of Navarre, and his 3 attendants decide to form a monastic academy of study. When the princess of France and her 3 ladies arrive he will not let them in the palace but has pavilions placed for them in the park. At a masque, the ladies exchange tokens and costumes so the lords woo the wrong ladies. When the lords ask for the ladies in marriage, the ladies impose a year's penance on them, after which the marriages can take place. The gentlemen grudgingly agree—for the present "love's labour's lost." The first recorded performance was at Queen Elizabeth's court in 1597.

Low, or depression, an area of low pressure, often shown on weather maps, associated in the Northern Hemisphere with counterclockwise, inward, cyclonic atmospheric circulation. *See also* High; Weather Maps.

Lowell, Amy (1874–1925), US poet and critic, b. Brookline, Mass. A member of the prominent Lowell family, which included several poets, she decided at the age of 28 to become a poet herself and spent the next eight years studying form and technique. She originated polyphonic prose, a prose form that makes use of poetic technique. She assumed leadership of the Imagist movement in the 1910s. Her ability to recreate physical perception in her poems was probably her outstanding quality. Her volumes of poetry include *Men, Women, and Ghosts* (1916) and *What's O'Clock?* (1925; Pulitzer Prize 1926). *See also* Imagism.

Lowell, James Russell (1819–91), US poet, author, and editor, b. Cambridge, Mass. Under the influence of his first wife, Maria White, he wrote some of his best poetry, and also became involved in the abolitionist movement. He gained acclaim for *Poems* (1844), *A Fable for Critics* (1848), the first series of *Biglow Papers* (1848), and *The Vision of Sir Launfal* (1848). In 1855 he succeeded Henry Wadsworth Longfellow as professor of modern languages at Harvard, where he taught until 1876. Much of his later work was literary criticism. He was the first editor of *Atlantic Monthly* (1857–61) and from 1864–72 was editor of *North American Review.* During 1877–80 he served as US minister to Spain and during 1880–85 was minister to England.

Lowell, Percival (1855–1916), US astronomer, b. Boston, famous for his prediction of the existence of the planet Pluto and his initiation of the search that ended in its discovery 14 years after his death. He founded Lowell Observatory at Flagstaff, Ariz., with his own money to study the "canals" of Mars, which he thought to be the traces of a once flourishing civilization. In 1905 he organized a systematic search for Planet X, an unseen planet beyond Neptune, now called Pluto. His astronomical works include *Mars and Its Canals* (1906), *The Evolution of Worlds* (1909), and *The Genesis of the Planets* (1916).

Lowell, Robert (1917–77), US poet, b. Boston. A member of the prominent Lowell family, his works are very personal. Among his volumes are *Land of Unlikeness* (1944), *Lord Weary's Castle* (1946; Pulitzer Prize, 1947), *The Mills of the Kavanaughs* (1951), *For the Union Dead* (1964), *Notebook 1967–68* (1969), and *The Dolphin* (1973; Pulitzer Prize, 1974). *Life Studies* (1959), which won a National Book Award, includes both prose and poetry about his family life. A conscientious objector in World War II, he was jailed for his beliefs.

Lowell, city in NE Massachusetts, at confluence of Merrimack and Concord rivers, 28mi (45km) NW of Boston; seat of Middlesex co; site of huge textile mills (built 1820 at Pawtucket Falls) to utilize power loom designed by Francis Cabot Lowell, and Lowell Technological Institute (1895); birthplace of artist James Whistler (1834), whose home is a museum. Industries: plastics, chemicals, rubber products, electronic equipment. Founded 1653 as part of Chelmsford; inc. as city 1836. Pop. (1980) 92,418.

Lowry, Lawrence Stanley (1887–1976), British painter best known for the highly personal way in which he portrayed, almost primitively, industrial landscapes of Salford (Manchester), with naively drawn buildings, factories and crowds of dark simple figures. Although his early work received some attention, his first one-man exhibition in London was not until 1939. He was regarded as an eccentric of 20th-century painting, although his work recalls the complex crowd scenes of Peter Bruegel.

Low Temperature Physics. *See* Cryogenics.

Loyalists, colonists remaining loyal to England during the Revolutionary War, also called Tories. They were mostly landholders, clergy (Anglicans), and office holders under British authority. The largest concentration of loyalists were in New York, Pennsylvania, the Carolinas, and Georgia. Many were eventually forced from the United States and returned to England or settled in Canada.

Loyalists, in the Spanish Civil War, the faction that supported the Second Republic; they were also known as republicans. They were opposed—and eventually defeated—by the Nationalists, or insurgents.

Loyang (Luoyang, or Lo-yang), city in E central China, on Lo River; temporary capital of China in 1932; nearby are the Lungmen Caves, containing Buddhist sculpture from T'ang period (618–906). Industries: tractors, mining machinery, coal mining, food processing, textiles. Pop. 750,000.

Loyola, Saint Ignatius of (1491–1556), Spanish religious leader who founded the Jesuits. An aristocrat, he was a warrior in his youth. While recovering from war wounds, he determined to be a knight in the service of God. His *Spiritual Exercises* (1522) gave ways to train body and soul for spiritual combat. After seven years study at the University of Paris, Ignatius and six companions went to Rome and asked permission from Pope Paul III to found an order to carry on spiritual and charitable works. The pope approved this plan, and in 1541 Ignatius became head of the Society of Jesus, or Jesuits. *See also* Jesuits.

LPG (Liquefied Petroleum Gas), a liquefied gas of light hydrocarbons, principally propane and butane, produced in the distillation of crude oil and the refining of natural gas. It is used as a fuel and raw material in chemical industries and as bottled gas for home heating and cooking.

LSD (lysergic acid diethylamide, or lysergide), a very potent synthetic hallucinogenic drug derived from lysergic acid. It has had limited use in the study and treatment of psychiatric disorders. Besides producing hallucinations and bizarre behavior, it has been reported to cause psychosis and chromosomal damage.

Amy Lowell

Robert Lowell

Lucerne, Switzerland

Luanda (Sao Paulo de Luanda), seaport city in NW Angola, on Baja do Bengo; capital of Angola, and Luanda district. Economy of city was historically based on slave trade with the New World, under which it prospered until the abolition of slavery in the 19th century. Luanda became an important modern manufacturing and trade center. Industries: textiles, building materials, machinery, oil products, agricultural products. Founded 1576 by Portuguese. Pop. 475,328.

Lubbock, city in NW Texas, 250mi (403km) W of Fort Worth; seat of Lubbock co; site of Texas Technological College (1923), and Lubbock Christian University (1957); major cotton market. Industries: farm equipment, mobile homes, pumps, cottonseed oil. Founded 1891; inc. as city 1907. Pop. (1980) 173,979.

Lübeck, seaport city in NE West Germany, on Trave River near its mouth on Baltic Sea. A free imperial city 1226, it was captured by French 1806; autonomy restored 1815 when it joined the North German Confederation; made part of Schleswig-Holstein 1937; site of 13th–15th-century city hall, 14th-century churches of St Jacob and St Catherine, Hospital and Church of Holy Ghost (13th century); all restored after suffering heavy damage in WWII. Industries: foundries, textiles, machine shops, shipyards. Founded 12th century; burned in 1138; reest. 1143. Pop. 231,205.

Lublin, city in SE Poland, approx. 95mi (153km) SE of Warsaw; capital of Lublin prov.; city grew around a 12th-century fortification built for protection against Tartar invaders, and developed as a trade center along SE route to Ukraine; site of German WWII concentration camp, Majdanek; state university, Roman Catholic university. Industries: heavy machinery, food processing, tobacco products. Pop. 272,000.

Lubricant, oil, grease, graphite, or other substances introduced between moving parts to reduce friction and dissipate heat. Vegetable oils and animal fats and oils have been used from ancient times but most lubricants are now derived from petroleum. Solid lubricants are usually graphite or molybdenum disulfide and synthetic silicones are used where high temperatures are involved.

Lubumbashi, formerly Elisabethville, city in SE Zaïre, near Zambia border; capital of Shaba prov.; 2nd-largest city in Zaïre; capital of independent state of Katanga (now Shaba) 1960–63; site of a university (1955). Industries: copper smelting, textiles, food products, beverages, bricks. Founded 1910. Pop. 401,612.

Lucan(us), Marcus Annaeus (39–65), Roman poet. A nephew of the younger Seneca, he was born in Spain. His *Bellum Civile* or *Pharsalia* is an epic on the civil war between Caesar and Pompey. It is admired more for its rhetoric than for its poetry. He was forced to kill himself after being implicated in a plot against Nero.

Lucca, city in N central Italy, 10mi (16km) NE of Pisa; capital of Lucca prov. Ancient town was settled prior 180 BC; it was a major Tuscan town when it was sold to Florence 1341; made independent republic 15th century until 1805, when it was given to Napoleon; made part of Tuscany 1847, and Italy 1860; site of cathedral of San Martino (11th–14th centuries), church of San Frediano (begun 6th century), Roman remains. Industries: textiles, paper, food products. Pop. 91,656.

Lucerne (Luzern), city in central Switzerland, 25mi (40km) SSW of Zurich on Lake of Lucerne; capital of Lucerne canton; joined Swiss Confederation 1332; site of several covered bridges decorated with paintings,

monument for Lion of Lucerne, Glacier Garden, 15th-century town hall, 17th-century historical museum, 17th-century Baroque Jesuit church, 8th-century monastery. Industries: sewing machines, electrical apparatus, beer, metal products, aluminumware, elevators, printing. Pop. 65,300.

Lucerne (Luzern), lake in central Switzerland, bordering on Lucerne, Uri, Schwyz, Unterwalden cantons. The lake is surrounded by mountains crossed by Reuss River. Depth: 702ft (214m). Length: 23mi (37km). Width: .5–2mi (.8–3km).

Lucian (*c.* AD 120–*c.* 200), Greek satirist, born in Samosata on the Upper Euphrates. Lucian is best known as the contributor of the satiric dialogue to Greek literature. He made use of this unique form of dialogue in some 80 works. His writing was witty, and drew attention to the foibles of contemporary life and manners. Religion and philosophy were among Lucian's favorite targets.

Lucilius, Gaius (*c.* 180–102 BC), earliest Latin satirist. Of good family and education, he was the friend of scholarly Greeks and knew Scipio well. Living mostly in Rome, his works were posthumously collected in an edition of 30 books. Only fragments survive. *See also* Satire, Roman.

Lucknow, city in N India, on the Gomati River; capital of Uttar Pradesh state. It served as the capital of kingdom of Oudh 1775–1856, then of Oudh prov. 1856–77, and the United Provinces 1877; during one of the Sepoy Mutiny conflicts, the British were forced to abandon their fortress after a long siege (June-November 1857); it was retaken by British 1858; served as a center for the independent Pakistan movement (1942–47); site of many ancient buildings, notably the Pearl Palace, Imambara mausoleum, unfinished mosque and mausoleum of Mohammed Ali Shah; university (1921). Industries: railroad shops, paper, metal, distilling, printing, handcrafts. Pop. 826,246.

Lucretius, or Titus Lucretius Carus, (early half of 1st century BC), Latin poet and philosopher. According to Jerome, Lucretius was born in 94 BC, was sometimes mad and when lucid wrote books that were later corrected by Cicero, and killed himself in 51 or 50 BC. Little else is known of him apart from his one poem, *De Rerum Natura*, or *On the Nature of Things*, a rendering of the atomic theory of Lucretius' master, Epicurus.

Lucullus, Lucius Licinius (*c.* 115–56 BC), Roman military commander, served in various campaigns under Sulla before he became consul in 74. He then gained control of Roman lands in Asia, where he defeated Mithridates (74–71) and took Armenia (69). For his skillful economic reforms in his territories, which curtailed certain Romans' profits, he earned powerful enemies, and he was replaced by Pompey in 66.

Luddites, English textile workers who resisted mechanization of their industry (1811–16). Taking their name from a probably mythical Ned Ludd, they systematically wrecked machinery, to which they attributed low wages and unemployment. They were severely repressed.

Ludlow, Roger (1590–1664?), one of the founders of Connecticut, b. England. He was an Oxford lawyer and assistant of the Massachusetts Bay Company. He helped found Dorchester, Mass., and served (1634) as deputy governor of Massachusetts. He presided (1636) at Windsor over the first Connecticut court and also finished the state's first codification of laws, known

as Ludlow's Code or the Code of 1650. He returned to England in 1654.

Lugano, town in SE central Switzerland, on N shore of Lake Lugano, at mouth of Cassarate River. Town was taken from duke of Milan by Swiss Confederation 1512; site of 19th-century town hall, 13th-century church of San Lorenzo, 15th-century church of Santa Maria; health resort, episcopal see. Industries: banking, chocolate, leather, metal, printing, flour, tourism. Pop. 22,280.

Lugano, Lake of, lake in S Switzerland and N Italy, between lakes Maggiore and Como; narrow irregular shape; drained by Tresa River. Area: 19sq mi (49sq km). Depth: 945ft (288m).

Lugansk (Voroshilovgrad), city in the Ukrainian republic, USSR, in the Donets Basin, on Lugan River, 420mi (676km) ESE of Kiev; capital of Voroshilovgrad oblast; occupied by Germans in WWII; site of agricultural and teachers' colleges and a metalworking school. Industries: steel-pipe rolling, coal mining machinery, enameling, meat packing, food, textiles. Est. *c.* 1795. Pop. 382,000.

Lu Hsun (1881–1936), pseud. of Chow Shu-jen, Chinese writer. A major figure in 20th-century Chinese literature and a great influence on succeeding generations of China's writers, he came to be regarded as a model of Socialist Realism in the People's Republic of China, although his writings were proscribed in Taiwan. Among his works are the *Early Outline History of Chinese Literature,* the story "Diary of a Madman" (1918), *The True Story of Ah Q* (1921), *Hesitation* (1926), and numerous prose essays.

Luke, apostle of Jesus. He was the author of one of the four gospels and the *Acts of the Apostles* of the New Testament. Luke, a physician and companion of the apostle Paul, wrote as an eyewitness of the life of Jesus and, when necessary, drew on other references then current. His gospel stresses the human and divine natures of Jesus and the concept of Christianity as a universal brotherhood.

Lully, Jean Baptiste (1632–87), French composer and court conductor for Louis XIV, b. Italy. His music is mainly ballets and operas. His operas, the style of which dominated French opera until the late 18th century, include *Alceste* (1674), *Amadis de Gaule* (1684), and *Armide et Renaud* (1686).

Lumbago, pain in the lower back (lumbar region).

Lumber, timber or logs after being prepared for market. Logs are transported from the forest, stored in water or a storage yard. Each log then enters the sawmill on a chain conveyor and is brought to a head saw (a bank saw, gang saw, or circular saw). Logs are then broken down (turned into boards of various thicknesses); resawed (cut into thinner boards); ripped (the bark removed from edges of the boards); and crosscut (the ends squared and defects removed). After production, lumber may be dipped into a chemical preservative, measured and graded, and piled to dry in open air or in kilns. Lumber of large dimension, suitable for heavy construction, is called timber.

Lumen, unit of luminous flux in the SI system of units, defined as the amount of light emitted per second in a solid angle of one steradian from a small source of intensity equal to one candela.

Luminosity, in astronomy, the amount of radiation emitted by a star or other celestial body. Magnitude is the measure of luminosity. The brighter the object the lower the magnitude number assigned. In modern usage one magnitude is defined as a difference in brightness of 2.512 times. Thus, a difference of five magnitudes corresponds to a ratio of 100 to 1. The sun's apparent magnitude is -26.7; the faintest stars visible through the largest telescopes are of apparent magnitude 20.

Lumpfish, bony cold water marine fish found on Atlantic coasts. A bottom-dwelling fish, it has a globose body and a modified sucking disk formed by pelvic fins under and behind the head. Length: 2ft (61cm); weight: 20lb (9.lkg). Family Cyclopteridae; species *Cyclopterus lumpus. See also* Osteichthyes.

Luna Moth, large North American moth of the giant silkworm family. Its 4in (10cm) wings are bright green with a purplish-brown band on the leading edge of the front wings and a large dark spot near the center of each hind wing. Species *Actias luna. See also* Moth.

Lunar Eclipse. *See* Eclipse, Lunar.

Lund, city in SW Sweden; became Roman Catholic archepiscopal see for Scandinavia 1103–04; site of University of Lund (1668), museum of folk customs, Romanesque cathedral. Industries: clothing, paper, printing, packaging materials, textiles. Pop. 54,410.

Lunda, a central African Bantu people who developed two powerful kingdoms through trade and conquest in the centuries before European domination. They follow complex and varying systems of inheritance and political structure.

Lungfish, or dipnoi, long, eellike bony fish found in shallow freshwater in Africa, South America, and Australia. A living fossil of a group dominant 300,000,000 years ago, it has air bladders and gulps air at the water surface. During the dry season, it curls up in mud cocoon and breathes air (except for Australian species). Family Lepidesirendiae; Family Ceratodontidae; Australian *Neoceratodus forsteri;* species African *Protopterus aethipicus,* South American *Lepidosiren paradoxa. See also* Choanichthyes; Osteichthyes.

Lungs, organs of the respiratory system in which the exchange of gases between air and blood takes place. The lungs are located on either side of the heart and are covered by a double-layer sheet of connective tissue called pleura. Between the layers is the fluid-containing pleural cavity that cushions the lungs and prevents friction. The lungs themselves are filled with air sacs from the walls of which protrude alveoli. Alveoli are one cell thick and contain networks of fine capillaries. Gaseous exchange takes place between the blood-containing capillaries and the oxygen-containing alveoli walls. The freshly oxygenated blood then carries oxygen to all parts of the body. *See also* Respiratory System.

Luoyang. *See* Loyang.

Lupine, annual and perennial plants and subshrubs native to the Mediterranean region, North America, and South America. They have oblong leaves, showy flowers of white, rose, yellow, or blue, and pods containing beanlike seeds. Height: to 8ft (2.4m). Family Leguminosae; genus *Lupinus.*

Lupus Erythematosus, an inflammatory disease of unknown cause involving the skin or generalized to the connective tissue of the body (systemic form). The skin lesions are red patches covered with scales, often on the cheeks and nose and forming a butterfly pattern. The systemic form varies in severity, is four times more common in women than in men, and may involve one or more organs in addition to the skin. Symptoms depend on the organ involved, but arthritis, weight loss, fatigue, fever, and anemia are common. Remissions and flareups are characteristic.

Lupus Vulgaris, tuberculosis of the skin, in which brownish nodules and ulcers are formed, and scarring is severe.

Luria, Salvador E(dward) (1912–), US molecular biologist, b. Italy. He shared the 1969 Nobel Prize in physiology or medicine for contributing to the knowledge of the growth, replication, and mutation of bacterial viruses.

Luristan (Lorestan), governorate in W Iran, in region of Zagros Mts; capital is Khorramabad; mountainous petroleum-producing region; noted for the Luristan bronzes, metal works found in 1930s, thought to have been made by Scythian, Cimerian, or Median craftsmen as early as 8th century BC. Products: oil, wool, cattle. Area: 12,116sq mi (31,380sq km). Pop. 686,307.

Lusaka, capital city of Zambia, S central Africa; site of the University of Zambia (1965) and Hodgson Technical College. Industries: foodstuffs, beverages, clothing, cement. Founded by Europeans 1905. Pop. 415,000.

Lusitania, Roman province on the Iberian peninsula, comprising modern Portugal and parts of western Spain. It took its name from the Lusitani, a warlike tribe that bitterly fought Roman conquest of their lands. Their great leader was Viriatus, who showed great military and diplomatic talents in opposing the Romans until he was assassinated, probably with Roman collusion, in 139 BC. Traditionally, the Portuguese have looked upon themselves as descendents of the Lusitani.

Lu-ta (Lüda), municipality in China comprising Port Arthur (Lüshun) and Dairen (Dalien), on Liaotung peninsula; site of many naval facilities, including Port Arthur Naval Base District; commercial, industrial and shipping center. Pop. 7,000,000.

Lute, stringed musical instrument with fretted fingerboard, pear-shaped back, and head with pegs for tuning. It was popular in 16th-century Europe for solos and ensembles. Early lute compositions survive today in Baroque revival, also in some by Bach and Handel.

Luteotropic Hormone. *See* Prolactin.

Lutetium or **Lutecium,** metallic element (symbol Lu) of the Lanthanide group, first isolated in 1907 from element ytterbium. Chief ore is monazite (phosphate). The element has no commercial uses. Properties: at. no. 71; at. wt. 174.97; sp gr 9.835 (25°C); melt. pt. 3,013°F (1656°C); boil. pt. 5999°F (3315°C); most common isotope Lu^{175} (97.41%). *See also* Lanthanide Elements.

Luther, Martin (1483–1546), German leader of the Protestant Reformation and founder of Lutheranism. He left the study of law in 1505 to become an Augustinian monk and later became a priest and a professor of theology. He agonized over the problem of salvation, finally deciding that it was won not by good works but was a free gift of God's grace. Luther's beliefs made him object to the sale of indulgences (which remitted penalties for sin) by the Roman Catholic Church, and in 1517 he posted his 95 Theses in Wittenberg. This started a quarrel between Luther and church leaders, including the pope. Luther decided that the Bible was the true source of authority and renounced obedience to Rome. He maintained his stand in debates with Johann Eck and at the Diet of Worms (1521). For this he was excommunicated, but strong German princes supported him, and he gained followers among churchmen and the people. Thus the Protestant Reformation began in Germany. Luther wrote hymns, catechisms, and numerous theological treatises and translated the New Testament into German. He married a former nun, Katharina von Bora, in 1525 and had six children. *See also* Lutheranism.

Lutheranism, the doctrines and the church that grew out of the teaching of Martin Luther. Luther hoped to reform the church rather than start a new one, but his doctrines led him to a complete break with the Roman Catholic Church. He believed that the Bible was the sole authority in religion and rejected the supremacy of the pope and the powers of the hierarchy of bishops. He held that grace cannot be conferred by the church but is the free gift of God's love. He objected to the Catholic doctrine of transsubstantiation—that, in the Eucharist, the bread and wine are actually transformed into the body and blood of Christ. Instead, Luther believed in the real presence of Christ "in, with, and under" the bread and wine. These and other essentials of Lutheran doctrine were set down in the Augsburg Confessions drawn up by Philipp Melanchthon in 1530. The confessions have ever since been basic documents of the Lutherans. From its start in Germany, Lutheranism spread to Scandinavia and other parts of Europe and around the world. Today the Lutheran Church is the largest Protestant denomination, enrolling about one third of all Protestants. There are large numbers of Lutherans in Germany, the United States, and Scandinavia. The church has no central governing body, and churches in each country have developed their own traditions. In 1947 the Lutheran World Council was formed as a coordinating body. *See also* Luther, Martin.

Luthuli, Albert John Mvumbi (1898–1967), South African civil rights leader. He moved from teaching to politics in response to South African racism. A Zulu chief, he was president (1952–60) of the African National Congress and was repeatedly harassed by the government for his nonviolent protest. He received the Nobel Peace prize in 1960. Although forced underground that same year, he continued to lead nonviolent resistance until his death. He wrote *Let My People Go* (1962).

Luxembourg, independent grand duchy in W Europe, bordered by West Germany (E), France (S), Belgium (N and W). It is ruled by a hereditary sovereign as the head of state and a premier as head of government who is responsible to a unicameral legislature (Chamber of Deputies).

Luxembourg is divided into two topographical sections, the heavily forested and elevated Ardennes plateau (N), and the fertile Bon Pays (S). The SW is part of the rich Luxembourg-Lorraine iron mining area, which makes Luxembourg a major iron and steel producer. The people, strongly Roman Catholic, enjoy one of the highest per capita incomes. Along with iron and steel production, the country's industries include chemicals, cement, tanning, textiles, agriculture, wine, slate, tourism, and banking.

Jean, ascending as grand duke in 1964, is the hereditary sovereign and chief of state. The government runs as a democratic parliament; the Council of Government headed by the premier is responsible to the Chamber of Deputies. All laws and decrees are brought before a 21-member Council of State, advisors appointed by the grand duke for life.

Founded 963 as a fief of the Holy Roman Empire, it was made a duchy by John of Luxembourg, king of Bohemia, in 1354. After occupation by France (1684–97), Spain (1697), and Austria (1714), it was formally ceded to France by the Treaty of Campo Formio (1797). It was made a grand duchy (1815), and at the same time it joined the German Confederation (with its fortress garrisoned by Prussians). Luxembourg's neutrality was confirmed by London Conference 1867; during WWI and WWII, its neutrality was violated by German occupation forcing Grand Duchess Charlotte to establish a government-in-exile in London in WWII. When liberated by Allied troops, its policy of neutrality was abolished, and military service was initiated (abolished 1967). Luxembourg became a member of the United Nations (1946) and NATO (1948). Luxembourg signed a treaty with Belgium and Netherlands for full economic union, and the Benelux Economic Union became effective 1960. Luxembourg was also an original member of the European Economic Community (EEC), and in 1981 former premier Gaston Thorn became president of the EEC. In the late 1970s and early 1980s, with the steel industry experiencing a serious downturn, international banking assumed much greater importance in Luxembourg's economy.

PROFILE

Official name: Grand Duchy of Luxembourg
Area: 999sq mi (2,587sq km)
Population: 354,000
Chief cities: Luxembourg (capital); Esch-sur-Alzette; Dudelange
Religion: Roman Catholic
Language: Letzeburgisch, French, German
Monetary unit: Luxembourg franc
Gross national product: $1,900,000,000

Luxembourg, city in S Luxembourg, 25mi (40km) NE of Esch-sur-Alzette at the confluence of the Alzette and Pétrusse rivers; capital of the Grand Duchy of Luxembourg. The walled town developed around a 10th-century castle and grew to be one of Europe's strongest fortifications; the town was demilitarized and the fort dismantled by the Treaty of London (1867); held by Germany during both world wars. It is the site of Cathedral of Notre Dame (16th century), town hall (19th century), ducal palace (16th century); commercial, administrative, and cultural center. Industries: iron and steel, furniture, leather products, machinery, textiles, beer, tourism, food processing. Founded 10th century as Lützelburg. Pop. 78,400.

Luxemburg, Rosa (1870–1919), German socialist leader, b. Poland. She became a German citizen through marriage and after 1898 was a leader of the Social Democratic party. With Karl Liebknecht she founded the Spartacus (later Communist) party during World War I. She was arrested for her part in the Spartacist uprising in Berlin (January 1919) and was murdered while being taken to prison.

Luxor (Al Uqsor), city in Egypt, on E bank of Nile River: Partially occupies site of the ancient city of Thebes; site of Temple of Luxor, built by Amenhotep III, Temple of Karnak, and royal cemeteries. A major winter resort area, tourism is main industry. Pop. 84,600.

Luzon, largest island of the Philippines, occupying the N part of the group. Island is irregularly shaped with many natural harbors, and the principal land mass to N has three mountain ranges, all running N to S: Sierra Madre (E), Cordillera Central, and the Zambales Mts (W). Manila, largest city of the Philippines, Quezon City, the capital, and Malabon are grouped together on Manila Bay, just NW of the Philippines' largest lake,

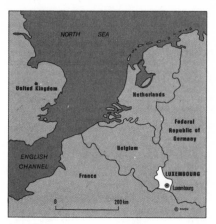

Luxembourg

Luxor, Egypt: Colossus of Memnon

Lyrebird

Laguna de Bay. The Cagayan is Luzon's longest river, flowing 200mi (322km) N from central Luzon to the Philippine Sea. As well as the most populous of the islands, it is the chief producer of agricultural and industrial products, including rice, coconuts, sugar, coffee, tobacco, abacá, fish, ships, lumber, textiles, chemicals, gold, copper, and chromite. Area: 40,420sq mi (104,688sq km). Highest peak is Mt Pulog, 9,606ft (2,930m). Pop. 16,669,724.

Lvov, (Prince) Georgi Yevgenievich (1861–1925), Russian political figure, premier of the provisional government (March-July 1917). A Constitutional Democrat, he was authorized by the Duma to form a new government upon Tsar Nicholas II's abdication. After concessions to the left, he lost support and resigned as premier in favor of Kerensky. He settled in Paris.

Lvov (L'vov), commercial city of Ukrainian SSR, USSR, 115mi (184km) SW of Lutsk, between the Raztoche and Gologary Mts. on a tributary of the Bug River; capital of Lvov oblast. Founded 1250 by Galician prince Lev, it was ceded to Poland and chartered 1340; included in Austrian province of Galicia 1772; scene of WWI battles; became capital of the independent Ukrainian Republic 1918; reverted to Poland 1919; ceded to the USSR 1945. A cultural center, Lvov is the site of a university (1661), 14th-century Roman and Armenian Catholic cathedrals, 16th-century palace, 18th-century cathedral and many old churches and monuments. Industries: metalworking, leather, textiles, radio and telegraph equipment, glass, chemicals, woodworking, food processing, petroleum refining, automobile assembling, paint, agricultural machinery. Pop. 655,000.

Lyallpur, city in E Pakistan, approx. 75mi (121km) W of Lahore, in the Punjab region; important textile center, also a marketing and processing place for regional agricultural products. Founded 1892. Pop. 820,000.

Lycia, region in SW Asia Minor inhabited in ancient times by the Lycians who are thought to have migrated from Crete via Miletus. They fought with Priam at Troy and are mentioned in the *Iliad*. Defeated by the Persians (546 BC) and then by Alexander, the area was held by the Ptolemies until granted to Rhodes by the Romans (189 BC). It was freed from Rhodian rule in 169 BC.

Lydia, a territory in west Asia Minor. Under the Mermnad dynasty (*c.* 700–550 BC), it was a powerful kingdom until it fell to the Persians and became their stronghold in the West. It was later taken by Alexander. It was the first realm to coin money and was famous for its musical innovations.

Lye. *See* Sodium Hydroxide.

Lyell, (Sir) Charles (1797–1875), Scottish geologist. Immensely influential in shaping 19th-century ideas about science, he wrote *Principles of Geology* (3 vols., 1830–33), which went into 12 editions in his lifetime. His geological ideas are based on uniformism. His other works include *Elements of Geology* (1838) and *The Geological Evidences of the Antiquity of Man* (1863). Lyell also first divided the Tertiary period into Eocene, Miocene, and Pliocene epochs.

Lymph, a clear, slightly yellowish, fluid derived from the blood. It contains white blood cells that function in immunity and in combating infection. Lymph flows through a series of vessels that make up the lymphatic system.

Lymphatic System, system of connecting vessels and organs that transport lymph through the body. Lymph flows into tiny and delicate lymph capillaries and from them into lymph vessels, or lymphatics. These extend throughout the body and join to form larger vessels that join at lymph nodes that collect lymph, storing some of the white blood cells. Lymph nodes empty into large vessels that link up into lymph ducts that empty back into the circulatory system.

Lymph Node, a cavity of the lymphatic system into which lymph vessels empty. The nodes contain numerous lymph-carried white blood cells that act to destroy bacteria and other foreign invaders of the body. Lymph nodes are located throughout the body and often become swollen in presence of infection. *See also* Lymphatic System.

Lymphogranuloma Venereum, a venereal disease resulting from infection by a parasitic microorganism of the genus *Chlamydia* in which ulcers appear on the genitals with subsequent enlargement of lymph nodes in certain regions.

Lynchburg, city in S central Virginia, 48mi (77km) ENE of Roanoke; served as Confederate supply base during Civil War; site of Virginia Seminary and College (1888), Randolph-Macon Women's College (1891), Lynchburg College (1903), Lynchburg Baptist College, Central Virginia Community College. Industries: tobacco, textiles, footwear, steel, medical supplies, electronic equipment. Founded 1757 by Quakers; inc. 1852. Pop. (1980) 66,743.

Lynn, city in NE Massachusetts, on Massachusetts Bay, 11mi (18km) NE of Boston; site of first colonial ironworks (1643), first Christian Science Church (1875) and home of founder Mary Baker Eddy, and first turbojet engine (designed and built 1942). Industries: electrical equipment, jet engines, marine turbines. Founded 1629 as Saugus; inc. 1631; namechanged 1637; inc. as city 1850. Pop. (1980) 78,471.

Lynx, small cat found in forests of C and N Europe, along the French-Spanish border, and in North America. Ranging in color from yellow-gray to reddish-brown, it can be spotted or unspotted and its underparts are white. It has long legs, large feet, tufted ears, and beardlike hair on its cheeks. The gestation period is 67–74 days and 2–4 young are born. Length: body —33.5–43.4in (85–110cm); tail—4.7–6.7in (12–17cm). There are two species: *Lynx lynx* with several subspecies and *Lynx rufus*. Family Felidae. *See also* Bobcat; Canada Lynx.

Lyons (Lyon), city in E central France, at confluence of Rhône and Saône rivers; capital of Rhône dept. City became part of French crown lands 1307; developed as trading center on important route to Italy by 16th century; devastated 1793 by French Revolutionary troops; center of French resistance movement in WWII; site of oldest stock exchange in France (1506), university (1808), 12th–14th-century Cathedral of St John, annual international trade fairs; noted gastronomical center. Industries: silk, rayon, chemicals, clothing, metal. Founded 43 BC as Roman colony. Pop. 462,841.

Lyra, a small constellation (the Lyre) in the Northern Hemisphere between Hercules and Cygnus. It contains Vega, a star of the first magnitude, and two stars of the third magnitude.

Lyre (Lyra), stringed musical instrument resembling a small kithara played with a plectrum. Its sound box is sometimes made of turtle shell. Used solo or to accompany singers, it originated in prehistoric Asia Minor and

was used by Hebrews, Greeks, and Romans. *See also* Kithara.

Lyrebird, two Australian songbirds: superb lyrebird (*Menura novaehollandiae*) and Albert's lyrebird (*M. alberti*). These large, perching birds have lyre-shaped tails displayed during elaborate courtship performances. The female builds a large, dome-shaped nest with a side entrance for the single grayish-purple egg.

Lysander (died 395 BC), Spartan general and statesman who restored the Peloponnesian fleet, winning great victories at Notium and Aegospotami, which were instrumental in Athens' eventual defeat.

Lysenko, Trofim Denisovich (1898–1976), Russian agronomist and geneticist. He expanded Lamarckism, the theory of the inheritability of acquired characteristics, to include his own ideas of plant genetics. Lysenko, who promised the Soviet Union vast increases in crop yield and type through the application of his theories, enjoyed official sanction under Stalin, but in the 1950s his influence waned.

Lysergic Acid Diethylamide. *See* LSD.

Lysine, crystalline soluble essential amino acid found in proteins. *See* Amino Acid.

Lysippus (*fl.* 2nd half of the 4th century BC), Greek sculptor. His work was influential and innovative in proportion, composition, and detail. His style directed much of later Hellenistic sculpture. One of his best-known works is "Apoxyomenos" ("Youth Scraping Himself"), of which a Roman copy is in the Vatican Museum, Rome.

Lysistrata, Greek comedy by Aristophanes (411 BC). The Athenian Lysistrata encourages the other women to entice and then ignore their husbands until the men end the war with Sparta. Its high-spirited broad humor and its treatment of the battle between the sexes have made it a classic.

M

Maastricht, city in S Netherlands, near Belgian border, approx. 15mi (24km) N of Liège, Belgium, on Meuse River; capital of Limburg prov. Built on site of Roman settlement, it contains 6th- and 12th-century churches. Town was frequently besieged by Spaniards 14th-18th centuries; occupied by Germans during WWII. Industries: steel, glass, cement, grain, dairy products. Pop. 111,044.

Macadamia, two species of trees of the family Proteaceae, native to Australia. Both have stiff, oblong, lance-like leaves, but the leaves of *Macadamia ternifolia* have serrated margins and those of *M. integrifolia* have smooth margins. Macadamia trees may reach 60ft (18m) in height. The edible seeds of the tree are round, hard-shelled nuts, covered by thick husks that split when ripe.

Macao (Macau), Portuguese overseas province in SE China, on South China Sea, 40mi (64km) W of Hong Kong. Colony consists of Macao Peninsula and two islands, Taipa and Colôane. The city of Macao, approx. coextensive with the peninsula, was settled 1557 by

Portuguese; it enjoyed great prosperity in 18th and 19th centuries as one of two Chinese ports (with Canton) open to foreign trade; declared a free port and independent by Portugal 1849; not recognized by China as Portuguese territory until 1887; Portuguese administration faced opposition from Communist Chinese. Industries: fishing, textiles, tourism. Area: approx. 6sq mi (16sq km). Pop. 260,000.

Macaque, diverse group of omnivorous medium-to-large monkeys found from NW Africa to Japan and Korea. Most are yellowish-brown forest dwellers—agile on ground and in trees—and are good swimmers. Weight: to 29lb (13kg). Genus *Macaca. See also* Monkey.

MacArthur, Douglas (1880–1964), US general, b. Little Rock, Ark. Son of Lt. Gen. Arthur MacArthur, he spent his entire life in military service. He led a brigade in World War I, and participated in all the important US offensives. He was made superintendent of West Point (1919–22) and later, US Army chief of staff (1930–35). He retired from the army (1937) to work in the Philippines, where he was when World War II began. He was recalled to active duty (1941). Escaping the Japanese invasion, he mounted the island-hopping assault that led to the Japanese defeat. He received the Japanese surrender and directed the occupation there after the war. He took command of the UN troops when the North Koreans attacked South Korea. President Truman relieved him of command following a policy disagreement (1951). *See also* Korean War.

Macaulay, Thomas Babington (1800–59), English historian, poet, and statesman. After serving two terms in Parliament as a Liberal, he was appointed a member of the supreme council of India, where he drew up a penal code used well into the 20th century. He returned to Parliament (1839–47) and in 1847 began to write *History of England from the Accession of James the Second* (5 vols., 1848–61).

Macaw, tropical American harsh-voiced parrot often seen in zoos. They have partially bare faces, sword-shaped tails, and large powerful bills to eat nutmeats. Some smaller species have protective green plumage, but larger species are brightly colored, such as the scarlet macaw *(Ara macao)* that has a red tail and yellow wings with bright blue on its back and wings.

Macbeth (died 1057), king of Scotland, hero of Shakespeare's tragedy named after him. He killed Duncan I, whose armies he commanded, seizing the kingdom (1040). Macbeth survived Siward of Northumbria's attempt to dethrone him (1046) but was later defeated by him (1054) and then killed by Malcolm III.

Macbeth (*c.*1606), 5-act tragedy by William Shakespeare, based on Raphael Holinshed's *Chronicles.* Moved by his own ambition and that of his unscrupulous wife, Macbeth murders Duncan, king of Scotland, and takes the crown, fulfilling a witches' prophecy. One murder leads to another, Lady Macbeth goes mad and dies, and the rest of the witches' prophecy comes true when Macduff leads an army from ambush and Macbeth is killed.

MacBride, Sean (1904–), Irish political figure, the son of Irish patriots Maud Gonne and John MacBride. Sean served in the Irish Republican Army and then founded the Clann na Poblachta (1946) political party and was in the Irish parliament (1947–58), and represented Ireland at the Council of Europe (1954–63). Active in international peace causes, he was UN commissioner for Namibia (1974–76). He won the Nobel Peace prize (1974).

Maccabees, prominent Jewish family that ruled Judea from 164–63 BC. In 168 BC the Seleucid ruler Antiochus IV invaded Jerusalem and in the following year rededicated the Temple to Zeus and outlawed Jewish religious practices. Mattathias, a high priest, and his five sons fled to the mountains and organized a guerrilla army. After Mattathias' death in 166 BC his son Judas Maccabaeus took command and recaptured Jerusalem in 164 BC. This event is celebrated as Hanukkah, the Festival of Lights. Judas Maccabaeus was succeeded as ruler of Judea by his brother Jonathan (*r.*160–143). The family maintained control of Judea until 63 BC when Pompey conquered the nation for Rome. Further attempts by members of the Maccabee family to regain control failed.

Maccabees, Books of, four historical books bearing a common title; I and II are part of the Apocrypha of the Old Testament. I Maccabees discusses the Maccabean leaders; II Maccabees glorifies the temple. Book III is a Greek document lauding the Jews saved from the elephants of Ptolemy IV. Book IV, also in Greek, deals with martyrdom.

McCarthy, Joseph Raymond (1908–57), U.S. Senator, b. Grand Chute, Wis. A circuit judge before beginning his career in the Senate (1947–57), he achieved national attention by claiming, in a 1950 speech, that the State Department had been infiltrated by Communists. He continued to make accusations against organizations and public officials, exploiting the public's concern over the spread of Communism in Asia and Europe. He was appointed chairman of the Senate's Permanent Subcommittee on Investigations (1953), conducting controversial inquiries, including the nationally televised Army-McCarthy hearings (1954). His charges were not substantiated, and he was charged with using improper means. The Senate censured him (1954) and his popularity declined.

McClintock, Barbara (1902–), plant geneticist, b. Hartford, Conn. A graduate of Cornell University, where she also earned her PhD (1927), she began working at Cold Spring Harbor Laboratory in 1942. Her theory that genes can be mobile, "jumping" from place to place on a chromosome or from one chromosome to another, received little attention when reported (1951) but gained her the Nobel Prize in Physiology or Medicine (1983) as the significance of the phenomenon became apparent in genetic research.

McCormick, Cyrus Hall (1809–84), US inventor, b. Rockbridge co, Va. He invented the reaper in 1831. A large scale manufacturing operation and widespread advertising, with his inventions of the twine binder and side-rake, brought him financial success and revolutionized harvesting.

McCullers, Carson (1917–67), US author, b. Columbus, Ga. Her first novel, *The Heart Is a Lonely Hunter,* appeared in 1940 and is about a deaf mute in a Southern town. Like her subsequent novels, it is a compassionate and sensitive work. Perhaps her most popular book is *The Member of the Wedding* (1946), which deals with a lonely twelve-year-old girl. The book was successfully dramatized in 1950. Other works include *Reflections in a Golden Eye* (1941) and *The Ballad of the Sad Cafe* (1951; dramatized 1963).

McCulloch v. Maryland (1819), landmark US Supreme Court case in which the court reinforced the federal government's supremacy over the states by denying a state the right to tax a US Bank.

Macdonald, (Sir) John Alexander (1815–91), first prime minister of the Dominion of Canada (1867–73; and again 1878–91). Macdonald became a lawyer in 1836 and then a power in Conservative politics after 1844. He supported responsible government after 1849 and served as prime minister of Upper Canada (1857–62). Macdonald encouraged western settlement, took over the Hudson's Bay Company lands (1869), and furthered railway interests before being implicated in the Pacific Scandal of 1873. He supported trade with England and favored high tariffs as part of his protectionist national policy.

MacDonald, (James) Ramsay (1866–1937), British political figure. Surmounting the problems of his illegitimate birth and poverty, he became a leader of the Independent Labour party (later the Labour party), and its treasurer (1912–24). A member of Parliament (1906–18) his opposition to Britain's role in World War I aroused furious opposition, and he was defeated in the 1918 elections. Returned to Parliament (1922–29), he became Britain's first Labour prime minister (1924). Prime minister again (1929–35), he was forced to seek Liberal and Conservative support for his financial policies (1931) and became increasingly distrusted by Labour. He lost power in 1935.

Macedonia, region in SE Europe, on Balkan Peninsula; its boundaries are included in NE Greece, SE Yugoslavia, and SW Bulgaria. Ancient Macedonian Empire (338–168 BC) was made a Roman province 148 BC; it was included in Bulgarian and Serbian empires when they fell in the 14th century to Ottoman Turks, who held it until 1912. Its independence from Turkey, and claims of Greece, Yugoslavia, and Bulgaria to the region, precipitated the Balkan Wars 1912–13. Territorial boundaries, with Bulgarian exclusion, were determined 1919; Bulgarian claim came after Greek-Bulgarian conflicts and settlement by League of Nations 1926. Industries: tobacco, grains, cotton, livestock, iron, copper, lead, chromite mining. Area: approx. 25,700sq mi (66,563sq km).

Macedonian Wars. Under Philip V, Macedon began to wage war with Rome. In the First Macedonian War (215–205 BC), Philip was victorious but he was defeated and humiliated and forced to relinquish his navy and pay heavy tribute to Rome as a result of the Second Macedonian War (200–197). His indemnity was decreased when he cooperated with Rome. His powerful son Perseus consolidated Macedon, extended its influence, and threatened Pergamum, thus bringing about the Third Macedonian War (171–168). Perseus lost his entire kingdom to Rome. Macedon was divided into four republics and later annexed as the first of the Roman provinces (146), thereafter declining. *See also* Philip V.

McGuffey, William Holmes (1800–73), US educator, b. Washington co, Pa. Professor of languages at several universities and president of Cincinnati College (1836–39) and Ohio University (1839–43), he was the creator and author of the McGuffey readers, spellers, and primers, which taught grade school students good English and moral lessons. A major influence on the minds of 19th-century Americans, the McGuffey series sold 122,000,000 copies from 1836–1920.

Mach, Ernst (1838–1916), Austrian physicist and philosopher. He was interested in the physiology and psychology of the senses and in problems of epistemology. In physics, his name is associated with the Mach number. He believed that physical phenomena should only be explained by data perceived by the senses and he developed the main principles of scientific positivism.

Machiavelli, Niccolò (1469–1527), Florentine statesman and political theorist, an outstanding figure of the Italian Renaissance. He served from 1498 to 1512 as an official and diplomat of Piero Soderini's republican government of Florence. Machiavelli lost his post when the Medici returned to power; he devoted the remainder of his life to writing a number of important literary, political, and historical works. His *Discourses on the First Ten Books of Livy* (1513–17) argued that the experience of the past could provide solutions for the present. A pamphlet, *The Prince,* written in 1513, made Machiavelli famous. Advocating the need of the ruler to preserve and enhance his own power and that of the state by whatever means necessary, *The Prince* became a guidebook to power politics and made Machiavelli's name synonymous with cunning, ruthlessness, and political immorality.

Machine Gun, a weapon that fires automatically and is capable of sustained rapid fire. The firing mechanism is operated by recoil or by gas from fired ammunition. The gun may be water- or air-cooled, and is often fired from a tripod. The ammunition is of .60 caliber or 15.24mm or under. The first widely used machine gun was invented by the American Hiram Maxim in 1883. The Maxim gun was first employed by the British in 1893 against tribal warriors in the Transvaal.

Mach Number, ratio of the speed of a moving body to the speed of sound in air, expressed as a decimal equivalent, 0.8 being subsonic and 1.2 supersonic. It takes its name from the Austrian investigator of supersonic speeds and shock waves, Ernst Mach (1838–1916).

Machu Picchu, ancient Inca city in S central Peru, in the Andes Mts approx. 50mi (81km) NW of Cuzco. The ruins sit on a high rock between two mountain peaks, and terraced gardens and stonework leading to a citadel extend over about 5sq mi (13sq km). Discovered 1911 by Hiram Bingham.

McKean, Thomas (1734–1817), American jurist and a signer of the Declaration of Independence, b. in Chester co, Pa. After representing Delaware as a delegate to the Continental Congress (1774–83), he later served as governor of Pennsylvania (1799–1808).

Mackenzie, (Sir) Alexander (1764–1820), Canadian fur trader and explorer. Mackenzie moved to Montreal in 1778 from Scotland and joined a consortium of fur traders. In 1787 he became a partner in the North West Company after extensive trading in Detroit and the Great Lakes. In 1789, he journeyed from Fort Chipewyan along the Slave and Mackenzie rivers to the Arctic Ocean. In 1793, his journey to the Pacific via the Peace and Fraser rivers proved the impossibility of a sea passage to the west. It was the first crossing of North America north of Mexico. He quit the North West Company in 1799, published descriptions of his journeys, *Voyages. . . to the Frozen and Pacific Oceans* (1801), and sat in the Legislative Assembly (1805–08).

Mackenzie, Alexander (1822–92), prime minister of Canada (1873–78). Mackenzie edited the Reform newspaper *Lambton Shield* (1852–54) while working as a building contractor in Ontario. He presided over the first Liberal administration of Canada on a platform of trade with the United States and opposition to railroad interests.

Mackenzie, William Lyon (1795–1861), Canadian political leader and rebel. A shopkeeper in York (1820), he attacked the Family Compacts in the *Colonial Advocate* (1824). Between 1828 and 1836 he was six times

Douglas MacArthur

Machu Picchu, Peru

William McKinley

elected and ejected from the Legislative Assembly for his espousal of independence. With Louis Papineau, he led the Rebellion of 1837 and was in exile in the United States until 1849. He fought against business interests and banks and encouraged free education and universal suffrage. His writings and speeches advanced the cause of confederation. *See also* Rebellion of 1837.

Mackenzie, river in W Mackenzie district, Northwest Territories, Canada; rises in the Great Slave Lake and flows NW into the Arctic Ocean. The entire system, including all of the headstreams, forms the largest river in Canada. It is of great economic importance for goods shipped N. Old fur-trading posts still remain along the river. Discovered 1789 by Alexander Mackenzie. Navigable for most of its 2,635mi (4,242km).

Mackenzie Mountains, mountain range in Northwest Territories, Canada, extending from E Yukon Territory through W Mackenzie district; forms watershed of the tributaries of the Mackenzie and Yukon rivers. Highest point is Keele Peak, 9,750ft (2,974m).

Mackerel, marine schooling fish of the N Atlantic. An important commercial fish closely related to the tunas, it is silvery blue with dark side bars. Length: 12in–5ft (30.5–152.5cm); weight: 1–100lb (0.5–45kg). Family Scombridae. Species of mackerel include the Atlantic *Scomber scombrus,* the king mackerel *Scomberomorus cavalla,* and the Spanish mackerel *Scomberomorus maculatus.*

McKinley, William (1843–1901), 25th president of the United States (1897–1901), b. Niles, Ohio. He attended Allegheny College and in 1871 he married Ida Saxton. After serving in the Union Army, McKinley was admitted to the bar and practiced in Canton. In 1876 he was elected as a Republican to the US House of Representatives, and in 1889 he became chairman of the Ways and Means Committee. He wrote the protectionist McKinley Tariff Act (1890), which was unpopular with the public but highly regarded by Ohio industrialists, one of whom, Marcus A. Hanna, became McKinley's political manager.

McKinley was elected governor of Ohio in 1891 and reelected in 1893. In 1895, Hanna began a successful campaign to win the 1896 presidential nomination for McKinley. McKinley won the election over William Jennings Bryan, who ran on a platform of free trade and free silver coinage.

As president, McKinley fulfilled his conservative Republican platform. He became involved somewhat reluctantly in the Spanish-American War but saw it quickly ended. He was easily reelected in 1900, this time with war hero Theodore Roosevelt as his running mate. On Sept. 6, 1901, while in Buffalo, N.Y., McKinley was shot by Leon Czolgosz, an anarchist. He died on September 14 and was succeeded by Roosevelt.

Career: US House of Representatives, 1876–82, 1884–91; governor of Ohio, 1892–96; president, 1897–1901.

McKinley, Mount, peak in S central Alaska, in the Alaska Range; highest peak in North America. Permanent snowfields cover more than half of the mountain; wildlife is abundant, especially caribou and white Alaska mountain sheep. First scaled 1913 by Hudson Stuck, it was named for President McKinley; included in Mount McKinley National Park (1917). Height: 20,320ft (6,198m).

MacLeish, Archibald (1892–1982), US author, b. Glencoe, Ill. A poet and playwright, his works include *Conquistador* (1932; Pulitzer Prize 1933), an epic

poem; *Collected Poems 1917–1952* (1952; Pulitzer Prize 1953); *New and Collected Poems 1917–1976* (1976), *J.B.* (1958; Pulitzer Prize 1959), a play; and *Six Plays* (1980). Noted short poems by him include "Ars Poetica," "The End of the World," "You, Andrew Marvell," and "Immortal Autumn."

Macleod, John James Rickard (1876–1935), Scottish physiologist. He shared the 1923 Nobel Prize in physiology or medicine with Frederick Grant Banting for the discovery of insulin. The actual discovery was made by Banting and Charles Best working in Macleod's University of Toronto laboratory.

MacMahon, Marie Edmé Patrice de (1808–93), French military and political figure. He gained fame in the Crimean War for his assault on the Malakoff Tower, which led to the fall of Sevastopol (1855). In the war against Austria (1859) he won an important victory at Magenta, for which he was made a marshal of France and duke of Magenta. Governor-general of Algeria 1864–70, he was called to serve in the Franco-Prussian War but was overwhelmed at the Battle of Worth. He put down the Paris Commune in 1871. In 1873 he was elected president of the Third Republic. A monarchist, he objected to but accepted the republican constitution of 1875. In 1877 he forced the resignation of the republican premier, dissolved the chamber of deputies, and called for new elections. But the new chamber was even more republican and MacMahon was forced to accept a republican ministry. He resigned in 1879 before his seven year term was up.

McMillan, Edwin Mattison (1907–), US chemist and physicist, b. Redondo Beach, Calif. He became professor of physics at the University of California and was awarded the Nobel Prize for chemistry in 1951 for his discovery of several transuranic elements. While working with E. O. Lawrence on the cyclotron he developed the synchrocyclotron for which he was awarded a share in the 1963 Atoms for Peace prize.

Macmillan, (Maurice) Harold (Earl of Stockton) (1894–), English political figure. As a member of Parliament (1924–29, 1931–64), he held a number of cabinet posts, including minister of housing and local government (1951–54) and chancellor of the exchequer (1955–57). He succeeded Anthony Eden as Conservative prime minister (1957–63), improving Anglo-American relations after the Suez crisis and trying unsuccessfully to obtain Britain's entry into the European Economic Community.

McMurdo Sound, Antarctica, SW inlet of Ross Sea between Ross Island and coast of Victoria Land; site of major US research and exploration base.

MacMurrough, Dermot (died 1171), Irish king. King of Leinster, it was his request for help that brought the Anglo-Normans to Ireland. He succeeded his brother in 1126 and secured his claim by 1141 after blinding or killing 17 rivals. He abducted the wife of another Irish king and was driven from the country in 1166. He was responsible for compiling the *Book of Leinster,* a collection of Gaelic traditions.

MacNeice, Louis (1907–63), British poet, b. Belfast, N. Ireland. An important poet of the 1930s, he was less overtly political than his friends W.H. Auden and Stephen Spender. His poems include *Autumn Journal* (1939), *Autumn Sequel* (1954), *Visitations* (1954), and *Solstices* (1961). He worked for the British Broadcasting Corporation, for which he wrote several radio plays. *See also* Auden, W.H.; Spender, Stephen.

Mâcon, town in E France, capital of Saône-et-Loire dept.; Huguenot possession in 16th century; railroad center. Industries: wine, printing, copper founding. Pop. 40,490.

Macon, city in central Georgia, 78mi (126km) SE of Atlanta, seat of Bibb co; agricultural region and distributing center for grain, cotton, fruit, nuts, drugs; site of natural clay and limestone deposits, Mercer University (1833), Wesleyan College (1836), Macon Junior College (1968), Robins Air Force Base. Settled 1821; chartered 1832. Pop. (1980) 116,860.

Macroeconomics, study of the economic system as a unit, rather than its individual components as in microeconomics, including the fundamental decisions that an economic system must make, the determination of national aggregates (GNP, national income, personal income), the study of the monetary sector of the economy (the banking system), and the economic relationships among countries (international trade). Keynesian economics is typically closely identified with macroeconomics. *See also* Microeconomics.

Madagascar, Republic of (formerly Malagasy Republic), nation in Indian Ocean about 250mi (400km) E of Africa, The people, a mixture of Asian and African descent, rely almost entirely on agriculture as the basis of their economy.

Land and Economy. Madagascar, the 4th-largest island in the world, stretches about 980mi (1,580km) N to S with a maximum width of 360mi (580km). Dominated by a central mountainous area that slopes gently to a coastal plain on the W but drops abruptly to the Indian Ocean on the E, the island provides fertile, usable land except for a small semi-arid section in the S. Eighty percent of the population are farmers owning cattle, sheep, pigs, and goats. Rice is the chief food crop and coffee the most valuable export. Madagascar is the world's largest producer of vanilla and is also one of the leading producers of graphite. The principal seaports are Tamatave and Majunga.

People. Physically the people of Madagascar resemble Africans, but their language is akin to Indonesian. Indonesians settled Madagascar over 2,000 years ago, but the influx of African peoples caused an amalgamation of races. About half of the population practices traditional animist religions, and about 40% are Christian. Conflicts between the country's two principal ethnic groups, the Merina of the inland highlands, and the more French-influenced Cotiers of the coasts, account for most of the country's instability. About 50% of the people are literate.

Government. According to the constitution of 1975, the president is popularly elected to a seven-year term and serves as the chairman of the Supreme Revolutionary Council. In fact, there is one legal political party, controlled by the military. Commander Didier Ratsiraka was named president by referendum in 1975.

History. Although there was some Arab contact from 900, and Portuguese discovery in 1500, the island was finally colonized by the French in the mid-1600s. In the 1780s the Merinas, a central highlands people, brought about unification. In 1885, France was granted protectorate rights by the British for ceding certain territorial rights to them. In 1958, it became an autonomous republic known as the Malagasy Republic, and in 1960 gained full independence, with Philibert Tsiranana elected the first president. In 1972, however, he handed the government over to the military, and a series of military regimes has since governed the country. The name was changed back to Madagascar in 1975. The banning of martial arts (1984), directed at a Kung fu sect, sparked violence throughout the mid-1980s.

PROFILE

Official name: Democratic Republic of Madagascar
Area: 226,657sq mi (587,042sq km)
Population: 9,112,000
Density: 40 per sq mi (16 per sq km)
Chief cities: Antananarivo (capital); Tamatave
Government: Republic
Religion: Traditional beliefs, Christianity
Language: Malagasy (official), French
Monetary unit: Malagasy franc
Gross national product: $2,490,000,000
Per capital income: $130
Industries: cigarettes, sugar
Agriculture(major products): rice, sugar cane, cassava, coffee, vanilla
Minerals(major): graphite, salt, chromium ore
Trading partners (major): France, United States, West Germany

Madame Bovary (1857), naturalistic novel by Gustave Flaubert, who was prosecuted for the novel's alleged immorality. Set in provincial Normandy, it relates the story of Emma Bovary, whose dreams of romance are not realized by her husband, a country doctor, or her lovers. She falls into debt and eventually commits suicide.

Madame Butterfly (1904), 3-act opera by Giacomo Puccini, Italian libretto by Giuseppe Giacosa and Luigi Illica, after David Belasco's play. First performed at La Scala, Milan, it was a fiasco, but was successfully revised three months later at Brescia under Arturo Toscanini. Pinkerton (tenor), a US Navy officer visiting Nagasaki, "marries" Madame Butterfly, Cio-Cio-San (soprano); when he returns three years later with an American wife, Butterfly kills herself. Other roles are Suzuki (mezzo-soprano) and Sharpless (baritone).

Madder, perennial vine native to S Europe and Asia with whorled leaves and greenish-yellow flower clusters. A red dye is produced from the roots. Height: to 4ft (1.2m). Family Rubiaceae; species *Rubia tinctorum.* The madder family includes primarily tropical plants, shrubs, and trees, such as the coffee and gardenia.

Madeira, river in W Brazil, formed by union of the Mamoré and Beni at the Brazil-Bolivia border; most important tributary of the Amazon. Length: 2,100mi (3,381km).

Madeira Islands, group of islands in Atlantic Ocean off coast of Morocco, N of Canary Islands; coextensive with Funchal district of Portugal. The group consists of two inhabited islands, Madeira and Porto Santo, and two uninhabited groups, Desertas and the Selvagens. Capital is Funchal on Madeira Island. Islands were discovered mid-14th century; year-round resort area. Industries: sugar cane, Madeira wine, embroidering, reed furniture. Area: 308sq mi (798sq km). Pop. 268,700.

Madison, Dolley (1768–1849), wife of President James Madison, b. Guilford co, N.C. Born Dolley Payne, the daughter of a Quaker family, she married in 1790 John Todd, who died three years later. In 1794 she left the Quakers to marry James Madison. During her time as first lady (1809–17) and as hostess for President Thomas Jefferson, a widower, she became known for her charm, grace, and talent for entertaining.

Madison, James (1751–1836), 4th president of the United States (1809–17), b. Port Conway, Va. He graduated from the College of New Jersey (now Princeton University) in 1771, and in 1794 he married Dolley Payne Todd.

Madison's first experience at statecraft was at the convention (1776) that drafted the Virginia constitution. He has been called the "father of the US Constitution"; he served at both the Annapolis Convention and at the Federal Constitutional Convention (1787). At the latter meeting, he played a major role in the final forming of the US Constitution. Along with John Jay and Alexander Hamilton he wrote the Federalist Papers in support of ratifying of the Constitution.

Madison served in the House of Representatives from 1789 to 1797. It was a period when the political party system was solidifying, and Madison quickly became a leader of the Jeffersonian faction. When Thomas Jefferson became President, he chose Madison as secretary of state, an office Madison held throughout Jefferson's two terms. He was Jefferson's personal choice to succeed him as president.

Madison's two terms as president were marked by deteriorating relations with Great Britain, culminating in the War of 1812. Highly unpopular, particularly in New England, it became known to his Federalist opponents as "Mr. Madison's War." The war went badly, and in 1814–15, the Hartford Convention was called by New England Federalists. It considered seceding from the Union, but the Treaty of Ghent, which ended the war in a stalemate, was signed before the convention could achieve any of its aims. Madison retired to "Montpelier," his plantation in Virginia.

Career: member, Continental Congress, 1780–83, 1787; delegate, Annapolis Convention, 1786; delegate, Federal Constitutional Convention, 1787; US House of Representatives, 1789–97; secretary of state, 1801–09; president, 1809–17. *See also* Annapolis Convention; Federalist Papers, The; War of 1812.

Madison, capital city of Wisconsin, on isthmus between Lake Mendota (N) and Lake Monona (S), 83mi (134km) W of Milwaukee; seat of Dane co; named for President James Madison; site of University of Wisconsin (1836), Edgewood College of the Sacred Heart (1927), Madison College, St Raphael's church (1854), Grace Episcopal church (1858), a Unitarian church designed by Frank Lloyd Wright; trading and manufacturing center. Industries: meat and dairy products, medical equipment, automobile parts. Est. as capital of Territory of Wisconsin 1836; inc. 1846 as village, 1856 as city. Pop. (1980) 170,616.

Madras, seaport city in SE India, on the Bay of Bengal; capital of Tamil Nadu state. The city grew around Fort St George, a British post (1640), and developed as a trading center; it was besieged and occupied by French 1746, but returned to British by the Treaty of Aix-la-Chapelle (1748); harbor was constructed 1862–1901; site of Madras University (1857); nearby is Mt St Thomas, legendary site of the martyrdom of Thomas the Apostle (AD 68); he is supposedly buried in Madras. Exports: hides, skins, oilseeds, cotton, chrome, magnesite. Industries: textiles, railroad stock, bicycles, printing, automobiles, motorcycles, motion pictures. Founded 1639. Pop. 3,169,930.

Madrid, capital city of Spain, and Madrid prov., on Manzanares River, 34mi (55km) WSW of Guadalajara. Taken from Moors 932 by Ramiro II of León again taken from Moors by Alfonso VI of Castile 1083; in 1561, Philip II made Madrid his official residence and capital of Spain. It was beautified in 18th century during Bourbon rule; occupied by French during Peninsular War (1808–14); the city developed tremendously during Isabella's reign (1833–68). Madrid remained loyal to the Republican government until entrance of Francisco Franco in 1939, during the Spanish Civil War; site of the Royal Palace (1737–64), now a museum, Ministerio de Hacienda national library, University of Madrid (1499), technical school, numerous museums (notably the Museo del Prado), several parks and plazas. Industries: plastics, wine, beer, publishing, motion pictures, optical instruments, electrical appliances, radio and telephone equipment, jewelry, leather goods. Area: (prov.) 3,087sq mi (7,995 sq km). Pop. (city) 3,500,000; (prov.) 3,792,561.

Madrid Hurtado, Miguel de la (1934–), president of Mexico (1982–). Educated at the National University of Mexico and Harvard University, he was appointed director of credit in the finance ministry in 1972, working closely with José Lopez Portillo. In 1976, Madrid Hurtado became deputy finance minister and in 1979, minister of planning and budget. In that position, he formulated Mexico's global development plan. In 1982, as the candidate of the Institutional Revolutionary Party, he was elected president, succeeding Lopez Portillo. The early part of his term was devoted to trying to end Mexico's severe recession.

Madrigal, form of vocal music originating in Italy in the 14th century. Early madrigals feature two or three vocal parts and a highly ornamented upper voice. Later forms in the 16th century featured love lyrics, no set form, and four or five voices. The "classical" period of the madrigal (*c.* 1540–80) was dominated by Italian (Gabrieli, Palestrina) and Flemish composers (Lasso, Rore, Willaert). The "late" period (*c.* 1580–1620) featured the Italians (Marenzio, Gesualdo, Monteverdi) and English composers (Byrd, Morley, Weelkes, and Wilbye).

Madroño, or laurelwood, broad-leafed, evergreen tree native to British Columbia and N United States west of the Rocky Mountains. It has small, white flowers and orange-red fruit. Height: 50–100ft (15–31m). Family Ericaceae; species *Arbutus menziesii.*

Madurai, city in S India, 270mi (435km) SSW of Madras, on the Vaigai River; served as capital of Pandya dynasty (5th century BC-AD 11th century), and Nayak kingdom (*c.* 1550–1736); passed to British 1801 by the Carnatic Nawabs. Famous as the "city of festivals and temples," it contains the massive Meenakshi temple adorned with colonnades and gate towers enclosing the "Tank of the Golden Lilies" quadrangle; university (1966). Industries: weaving, dyeing of silk and muslin, brassware, wood carving, tourism. Pop. 548,298.

Maenad, from Gr. *mainomai* "to rage," female follower of Dionysus, the Greek god of wine and revelry. She is depicted carrying a staff entwined with ivy and surmounted by a pine cone while dancing orgiastic revels.

Maeterlinck, Maurice (1862–1949), Belgian playwright, essayist, poet, and mystic philosopher who wrote in French. A symbolist despite the realism of his time, his most popular plays are *Pelléas and Mélisande* (1892), a favorite of Sarah Bernhardt, made into an opera by Claude Debussy (1902), and *The Blue Bird* (1909), an allegorical fable. He won the Nobel Prize for literature 1911.

Magdeburg, port city in W East Germany, on Elbe River, 82mi (132km) WSW of Berlin; capital of Magdeburg district. In the 13th century city was granted a charter by archbishop of Magdeburg (prince of Holy Roman Empire) that served as model for hundreds of medieval towns in Germany. During Thirty Years' War (1618–1648) the city was burned and 85% of population perished; site of 11th-century Romanesque church and 13th-century cathedral; birthplace of physicist Otto von Guericke and Baron von Steuben. Industries: steel, paper, textiles, chemicals, machines. Founded 805. Pop. 277,656.

Magellan, Ferdinand (*c.*1480–1521), Portuguese and Spanish explorer. He commanded the first expedition to circumnavigate the globe. Twice wounded while exploring the East Indies for Portugal, he found vast trade potential in the Spice Islands. After fighting against the Moors, he fell out of favor with the Portuguese King Manuel and, renouncing his citizenship, went to Spain. There, he organized an expedition to reach the Spice Islands by sailing west. Leaving Spain with five ships in 1519, he reached Brazil and sailed south, seeking a westward passage. In November 1520 he sailed through the strait later named for him and reached the Philippines in March 1521. Although he was killed by natives in the Philippines, one of his ships did return to Spain, establishing a new route between Europe and Asia.

Magellan, Strait of, strait in S South America, between S Chile and the Tierra del Fuego island group; connects the Atlantic and Pacific oceans; especially important in colonial times for ships rounding South America. Discovered by Ferdinand Magellan 1520. Length: 350mi (564km).

Magellanic Clouds, two small satellite galaxies of the Milky Way Galaxy, visible in south circumpolar skies as misty stellar concentrations. The Small Cloud (Nubecula Minor), located in the constellation Tucana, is irregular: the Large Cloud (Nubecula Major), mostly in Dorado, is vaguely spiral. Distance about 150,000 light years. *See also* Galaxy.

Maggiore, Lake, lake in N Italy and S Switzerland; 2nd-largest in Italy; crossed N to S by Ticino River and fed by the Maggia, Toce, and Tresa rivers; Borromean Islands are off the W shore; bordered by the Swiss Alps; resort area. Area: 82sq mi (212sq km).

Maggot, the name given to many legless Diptera larvae. It is primarily used to describe those larvae that infest food and waste material. *See also* Diptera.

Magic, Primitive, manipulation of supposed supernatural powers to achieve a desired effect. Delineation of the boundary between magic and primitive religion is generally impossible, but magic tends to be used for some limited practical end either benign or malevolent, while religion has a more philosophical role. In primitive societies, the dangerous force of magic is usually mediated by a particular person with special powers to control it. *See also* Religion, Primitive; Sorcery.

Magic Square, any square matrix divided into cells and filled with numbers or letters in ways once thought to have special magical significance. The most familiar lettered square is the SATOR square, composed of the words SATOR, AREPO, TENET, OPERA, and ROTAS. Arranged both vertically and horizontally the words read the same and form a cross through the middle that reads TENET. In arithmetical magical squares the numbers are generally arranged so that each column, every row, and the two main diagonals produce the same constant sum.

Maginot Line, series of fortifications constructed by France on its northeastern border with Germany. The purpose of the line was to prevent a quick German attack on France's vital frontier industries, but the defensive works also fostered a false sense of security. It was named after André Maginot, French minister of war (1929–32), who directed its construction and was still not complete at the outbreak of World War II

James Madison

Madras, India

Madrid, Spain

(1939). The line was flanked by the Germans, and France fell in 1940.

Magma, molten material that produces all igneous rocks. The term refers to this material while it is still under the earth's crust. In addition to its complex silicate solution, magma contains gases and water vapor. It is believed to exist in separate chambers beneath the surface of the earth.

Magna Carta (1215), "great charter" of English civil liberties. It was issued by King John, under compulsion from his barons, at Runnymede, on June 15, 1215. John's financial exactions had united clergy and laity in demands for guarantees of civil rights. The 63 clauses into which Magna Carta is traditionally divided protected the rights of the church, the feudal lords, the lords' subtenants, and the merchants and regulated royal privileges, the administration of justice, and the behavior of royal officials. For subsequent generations Magna Carta became the basis and epitome of the subject's rights, protecting him against his sovereign's impositions.

Magna Graecia, area of southern Italy heavily colonized by Greece starting about the 8th century BC and continuing until the 2nd century BC. Of the colonial cities, Cumae was the most important. Others were Neapolis, Paestum, Elea, Croton, Sybaris, Heraclea, and Locri. Internecine struggles and the Punic Wars led to Roman dominance of the colonies.

Magnesium, common metallic element (symbol Mg) of the alkaline-earth group, first isolated (1808) by Sir Humphry Davy. Chief sources are magnesite, dolomite, and other minerals. Magnesium burns in air with an intense white flame and is used in flashbulbs, pyrotechnics, and incendiaries. Magnesium alloys are used in aircraft for their lightness. Chemically, the element is similar to calcium. Properties: at. no. 12; at. wt. 24.305; sp gr 1.738; melt. pt. 1199.8°F (648.8°C); boil. pt. 1994°F (1090°C); most common isotope Mg^{24} (78.-7%). *See also* Alkaline-Earth Elements.

Magnetic Anomaly, small variations in the Earth's magnetic field caused by iron objects or deposits. *See also* Anomaly.

Magnetic Bottle, configuration of magnetic fields used to contain the plasma in a fusion reactor or experimental device, especially a linear configuration in which the ends are stoppered with magnetic mirrors. *See also* Fusion Reactor.

Magnetic Field, region surrounding a magnetic pole, or a conductor through which a current is flowing, in which there is a magnetic flux. A magnetic field can be represented by a set of lines of force emanating from the poles of a permanent magnet or running around a current-carrying conductor. These lines of force can be seen if iron filings are sprinkled onto a sheet of paper below which a permanent magnet is placed. The filings align themselves with the lines of force, the density of the lines being greatest where the field is strongest.

Magnetic Field, Earth, the composite of all the lines of force surrounding the dipole magnet that is the Earth. If the line between the magnetic poles (magnetic axis) is thought of as a bar magnet, the magnetic lines of force represent the paths of alignment of tiny magnets if they were free to move in space.

Magnetic Field Reversal, the reversing of polarity whereby the north pole becomes the south and vice versa. Analyses of the magnetic direction of land and ocean basaltic lavas and sea-floor sediments have

shown that the earth's main magnetic field has undergone frequent and rapid reversals. The field has changed 9 times in the last 4 million years. *See also* Sea-floor Spreading.

Magnetic Flux, measure of the size of a magnetic field expressed as the component of the magnetic field strength at right angles to a given area multiplied by the area. It is measured in maxwells (cgs units) or webers (SI units).

Magnetic Poles, two regions in which the magnetism of a magnet appears to be concentrated. If a bar magnet is suspended to swing freely in the horizontal plane one pole will point north; this is called the north-seeking or north pole. The other pole, the south-seeking or south pole, will point south. Unlike poles attract each other, like poles repel each other.

Magnetic Poles, Earth, the ends of the bar magnet that is Earth. The north magnetic pole is at about 76° N latitude and 102°W longitude. The south magnetic pole is at about 68°S latitude and 145°E longitude. The magnetic axis does not pass through Earth's center. *See also* Magnetic Field, Earth; Polar Wander.

Magnetic Recording, formation of a record of sounds on a wire or tape by means of a pattern of magnetization. In a tape recorder, plastic tape impregnated with iron oxide is fed past an electromagnet, which is energized by the amplified currents produced by a microphone. The variations in magnetization retained by the particles of iron oxide on the tape represent the oscillating current produced by the sound. For playing back, the tape is fed past a similar electromagnet, which feeds an amplifier and loudspeaker.

Magnetic Resonance, the phenomenon of absorption of radio and microwave frequencies by atoms placed in a magnetic field. Devices called electron-spin resonance (ESR) spectrometers use microwaves for the investigation of atoms and molecules. Nuclear-magnetic resonance (NMR) spectrometers use radio frequencies for research in nuclear physics.

Magnetic Storm, or geomagnetic storm, a disturbance in Earth's magnetic field. Since it encompasses all of Earth, the effects of such a storm are global. Auroras are seen, both in areas where such displays are normal and in others as well. Radio signals are disturbed. There is a regularly reappearing cycle of such magnetic storms as well as irregular ones. *See also* Aurora; Magnetosphere.

Magnetism, properties of matter and of electric currents associated with a field of force (magnetic field) and with a north-south polarity (magnetic poles). All substances possess these properties to some degree as orbiting electrons in their atoms produce a magnetic field in the same way as an electric current produces a magnetic field; similarly, an external magnetic field will affect the electron orbits. All substances possess weak magnetic (diamagnetic) properties and will tend to align themselves with the field but in some cases this weak magnetism is masked by the stronger forms of magnetism: paramagnetism and ferromagnetism.

Paramagnetism is caused by electron spin and occurs in substances having unpaired electrons in their atoms or molecules. The most important form of magnetism, ferromagnetism, occurs in substances such as iron and nickel, which are capable of being magnetized by even a weak field due to the formation of tiny regions, called domains, that behave like miniature magnets and align themselves with an external field. These domains are formed as a result of strong interatomic forces caused by the spin of electrons in unfilled inner

electron shells of the atoms. Permanent magnets, which retain their magnetization after the magnetizing field has been removed, are ferromagnetic. Electromagnets have a ferromagnetic core around which a coil is wound. The passage of a current through the coil magnetizes the core.

Magnetism, Terrestrial, magnetic field associated with the Earth. It is similar to that which would be produced by a powerful bar magnet, pointing north-south, situated at its center. The present positions of the Earth's magnetic poles are: N = 76°N lat, 102°W long; S = 68°S lat, 145°E long. The magnetic field at any point on the Earth's surface is defined by three magnetic quantities: the horizontal component of the magnetic flux density; the angle of dip (or inclination), that is, the angle through which a magnetic needle will dip from the horizontal when suspended in a vertical plane; and the angle of declination (or magnetic variation), that is, the angle between the geographic and magnetic meridians. The cause of the Earth's magnetism is not known.

Magnetite, an oxide mineral, ferrous and ferric iron oxide ($FeFe_2O_4$). Most magnetic mineral, valuable iron ore. Found in igneous and metamorphic rocks. Cubic system octahedral and dodecahedral crystals, granular masses common. Black, metallic, and brittle. Hardness 6; sp gr 5.2. Permanently magnetized deposits are called lodestone.

Magnetochemistry, branch of chemistry concerned with investigating the magnetic properties of compounds. In particular, magnetic measurements made on transition-metal complexes, which are often paramagnetic due to unpaired electrons, give information on their structure and electron configuration. *See also* Magnetism.

Magnetohydrodynamics (MHD), study of conducting fluids under the influence of magnetic fields. A MHD generator is a source of electrical power consisting of a flame or plasma flowing between the poles of a strong magnet. The free electrons in the flame or plasma constitute a current when they flow, under the influence of the magnetic field, between electrodes inserted into the flame or plasma. The concentration of free electrons in a flame can be increased by adding to it elements, such as sodium and potassium, of low ionization potential.

Magnetometer, instrument for comparing magnetic field strengths or magnetic moments. It usually consists of a short bar magnet with a long nonmagnetic pointer attached to its center so that it is at right angles to the axis of the magnet. The magnet is pivoted, like a compass needle, at its center and the pointer travels over a calibrated scale. Field strengths of magnets are compared by measuring the deflections of the pointer.

Magnetosphere, that region in space around the Earth in which the magnetic field of Earth has an important part in controlling the physical activity observed. The magnetosphere is a two-part region; the lobe closer to the Sun is larger and blunt, the other lobe, an elongated tail extending several hundred times the radius of Earth into space. The shape of the magnetosphere is determined by the stress exerted on the magnetopause (outermost edge) by the solar wind.

Magnetron, a vacuum tube containing an anode and a heated cathode. The flow of electrons from cathode to anode is controlled by an externally applied magnetic field. When attached to a resonant line, it can act as an oscillator. It is capable of generating high frequencies and high power in short bursts and is used in radar systems and microwave ovens.

Magnitogorsk, city in Russian SFSR, USSR, on the SW slope of Magnitnaya Mt, on the dammed upper Ural River, 160mi (258km) SSW of Chelyabinsk. An old village, in the early 18th century it was named Magnitnaya when magnetized iron was discovered in two nearby mountains; in 1930 the Soviet government began to develop the area; by 1933 it was a large city with US-built plants; it is now the leading USSR metallurgical center; site of teachers' and metallurgical colleges. Industries: military equipment, machinery, nitrate fertilizers, cement, clothing, shoes, foodstuffs, glass. Pop. 402,000.

Magnitude, in astronomy, numerical value expressing the brightness of a celestial object on a logarithmic scale. Apparent magnitude is the magnitude as seen from Earth, determined by eye, photographically, or photometrically, and ranges from positive through zero to negative values, the brightness increasing rapidly as the magnitude decreases. A difference of over 2.5, first magnitude being exactly 100 times brighter than sixth magnitude (just visible to the naked eye). Absolute magnitude indicates intrinsic luminosity and is defined as the apparent magnitude of an object at a distance of 10 parsecs.

Magnitude, Earthquake, a measure based on the movement of the ground as recorded by seismographs. It is a logarithmic expression and the jump from one number to the next represents a factor of 30. On the Richter scale of earthquake magnitude, a small quake may be less than zero, a major (very infrequent) quake might register 7 or 8. *See also* Seismic Waves.

Magnolia, trees and shrubs native to North America, Central America, Asia, and the Himalayas. Valued for their showy flowers of white, yellow, purple, and pink, they are mostly deciduous; some are evergreen and can stand cooler temperatures. Height: to 100ft (31m). Family Magnoliaceae. The magnolia family includes 10 genera of shrubs, trees, and vines native to North America and Asia.

Magpie, widely distributed chattering birds closely related to jays. The typical Northern Hemisphere black-billed magpie (*Pica pica*) is blackish with a long greenish-black tail, and white on its shoulders, wing linings, and belly. Both parents build a domed, stick and mud nest, lined with hair and feathers, for pale spotted eggs (6–9) incubated by the female. The male helps feed the young. Length: 20in (51cm). Family Corvidae.

Magritte, René (1898–1967), Belgian painter. A leading surrealist, he was at first influenced by cubism and futurism; later, he evolved a realistic style. His early works include "La Statue volante" (1927) and "La Belle captive" (1931). His mature works, marked by brighter color and juxtaposition of objects, include "The Liberator" and "L'Empire des Lumières" (1954).

Magyars, the people associated with the state of Hungary, descendants of Finno-Ugric and Turkish tribes who mingled with Avars and Slavs in the 9th century. Although incorporated into the Austro-Hungarian Empire, the fiercely independent Magyars demanded special minority rights to preserve their language and culture, finally achieving first the Dual Monarchy in 1867 and independence in 1918.

Mahabharata, meaning "Great Epic of the Bharata Dynasty," poem consisting of almost 100,000 couplets. It is considered one of India's two major epics, along with the *Ramayana*. The verse is important both as literature and Hindu religious instruction. The plot revolves around a power struggle between two related families. It was written *c.*400 BC–*c.*AD 200 and compiled into its present form by *c.*AD 400.

Mahayana Buddhism, one of the main schools of Buddhism. Emerging in India somewhere between the 1st century BC and the 1st century AD, the Mahayana school stressed compassion as well as wisdom as necessary for salvation, and claimed to be more universal in its appeal than the older, more conservative Hinayana school. The Bodhista, or "being destined for enlightenment," is seen as the ideal of human life. Various schools sprang from the Mahayana sect and spread to Tibet, China, Korea, and Japan. *See also* Buddhism.

Mah Jongg, a widely played game, believed to have originated in China. The equipment consists of 144 decorative rectangular tiles, made of wood, ivory, or plastic. There are 108 suit tiles, 28 honor tiles, and 8 flower or season tiles. The three suits are bamboo or sticks, circles or dots, and character or cracks. The

game itself is complicated, but the basic object is to accumulate sets.

Mahler, Gustav (1860–1911), Austrian composer and conductor. Famous in his own lifetime as a conductor, Mahler was relatively ignored until the 1960s when his nine symphonies became recognized as important achievements of the Romantic period and bridges to 20th-century music. Many of his works combine orchestral with vocal and choral parts, require massive orchestras, and contain novel instrumental effects. *See also* Romanticism in Music.

Mahogany, tropical deciduous tree with wood valued for furniture making. It has leaves composed of smaller leaflets, large clusters of flowers, and winged seeds. Among 1,400 species is the familiar New World Honduran *Swietenia macrophylla* found from S Mexico to N South America; height to 60ft(18m). *Swietenia mahogonii* has a short, swollen trunk and is native to the West Indies and S Florida. Family Meliaceae.

Maidenhair Fern, dainty North American fern found in limestone areas. The wedge-shaped leaves are borne on slender, shiny black, erect stalks. Leaves of most unfold pink, then turn pea green. Height: 10–20in (25–51cm). Family Adiantaceae; species *Adiantum capillus-veneris. See also* Fern.

Maidstone, county town of Kent, SE England, on Medway River, 30mi (48km) SE of London. Industries: paper, brewing. Pop. 125,300.

Maidu, a Penutian-speaking tribe of North American Indians occupying the Feather River and American River area of N California. From a population of 9,000 their numbers were decimated by Gold Rush miners to approximately 1,100 today. They are excellent basket makers.

Mailer, Norman (1923–), US author, b. Long Branch, N.J. After serving with the US army in the Pacific in World War II, he wrote his first novel, *The Naked and the Dead* (1948). In 1969 he won both a Pulitzer Prize and a National Book Award for his nonfiction work, *The Armies of the Night* (1968), a personal chronicle about the antiwar march on the Pentagon in Washington, D.C., in October 1967. Other works include the novels *The Deer Park* (1955), *An American Dream* (1965), *Ancient Evenings* (1983), and *Tough Guys Don't Dance* (1984), and *Miami and the Siege of Chicago* (1969), *Executioner's Song* (1979; Pulitzer Prize 1980), *Of Women and Their Elegance* (1980), and *Pieces and Pontifications* (1982), all nonfiction.

Maillol, Aristide (1861–1944), French sculptor, tapestry designer, painter, and draftsman. In 1893 he exhibited a tapestry at the National Society Salon; from 1894–98 he worked on woodcuts. His major works of sculpture include "Mediterranean," and "Action in Chains and Desire" (1905). His work, marked by subtlety and clear surface, brought him international fame.

Maimonides, or **Moses ben Maimon** (1135–1204), Jewish physician and philosopher. He was born in Spain but left to avoid persecution after a Muslim invasion and settled in Cairo. There he became doctor to the court of Sultan Saladin and also treated hundreds of private patients. He became even more noted for his scholarly works on Judaic law and on philosophy. He tried to reconcile Aristotle's thinking with Hebrew theology. Maimonides' works influenced such thinkers as Thomas Aquinas.

Maine, state in the extreme NE United States, on the Atlantic Ocean and bordered on the W, N, and E by the provinces of Quebec and New Brunswick, Canada.

Land and Economy. The coastline is broken by bays and inlets; hundreds of islands lie offshore. The land is generally rolling; the highest mountains are in the central part. Principal rivers are the Penobscot, Kennebec, and Androscoggin, which flow into the Atlantic. Thousands of lakes are in the interior. More than 75% of the state is forested. Maine's natural resources are the foundation of the economy. Coastal fisheries, chiefly lobsters, clams, and herring, and the great supply of timber are major income producers. Potatoes are a major crop. Recreational opportunities draw visitors all year, and tourism is an important source of revenue.

People. The population has grown slowly. Most of the residents are descended from English, Scots, Irish, and French settlers. Only about 50% resides in areas classified as urban.

Education. There are about 25 institutions of higher education.

History. Scattered English settlements were made along the coast soon after 1600, when the name "Maine" was applied to the mainland as distinct from the islands. The province was organized on a charter

from Charles I of England in 1639. Its capital, Gorgeana (1642), later reincorporated as the town of York, was the first incorporated city in the American colonies. Under a new charter in 1691, the land became part of the colony of Massachusetts Bay. It remained part of the state of Massachusetts until admitted to the Union in its own right in 1820. Industrial development was gradual in the 19th century. WWII, which spurred shipbuilding and brought military and naval establishments to the state, was an economic stimulus.

PROFILE

Admitted to Union: March 15, 1820; rank, 23d
US Congressmen: Senate, 2; House of Representatives, 2
Population: 1,124,660 (1980); rank, 38th
Capital: Augusta, 21,819 (1980)
Chief cities: Portland, 61,572; Lewiston, 40,481; Bangor, 31,643
State legislature: Senate, 33; House of Representatives, 151
Area: 33,215sq mi (86,027sq km); rank, 39th
Elevation: Highest, 5,268ft (1,607m), Mt Katahdin; lowest, sea level
Industries (major products): wood products, lumber, paper, textiles, processed foods, shoes
Agriculture (major products): poultry, potatoes, blueberries, apples, vegetables
Minerals (major): granite, cement, feldspar
State nickname: Pine Tree State
State motto: Dirigo ("I Direct")
State bird: chickadee
State flower: pine cone and tassel
State tree: eastern white pine

Main River, river in E West Germany, formed by confluence of Roter Main and Weisser Main at Kulmbach; flows W through West Germany to Rhine River at Mainz; connected to Danube River by canal; navigable for about 240mi (386km). Length: 310mi (499km).

Main Sequence Stars, stars found along or near a diagonal distribution line on the Hertzsprung-Russell diagram. This line, known as the main sequence, runs from top left (hot bright blue stars) to bottom right (cool dim red stars) and represents the distribution class to which 90 percent of all the known stars, including the sun, belong. It also serves to trace the evolutionary pattern that most stars seem to follow for part of their existence, the stages at which they join or leave the main sequence being governed by their mass and energy output.

Mainz, city in W central West Germany, on W bank of Rhine River, 20mi (32km) WSW of Frankfurt am Main; capital of Rhineland-Palatinate state; seat of first German archbishop (St Boniface, 746); became a free city 1118; archbishop made an imperial elector 1356. City passed to France 1797; made a fortress of German Confederation by Congress of Vienna (1815); birthplace of Johann Gutenberg, who made Mainz first printing center of Europe in 15th century; site of six-towered Romanesque cathedral (1009), 18th-century church of St Peter, Johann Gutenberg University, (founded as University of Mainz 1477, closed 1816, reinstituted 1946). Industries: wine, chemicals, motor vehicles, cement, optical instruments, machinery. Founded 1st century BC as Roman camp. Pop. 172,195.

Maitland, William (?1528–73), Scottish nobleman, known as "Secretary Lethington." Made Mary Queen of Scots' secretary of state (1561), he resisted church domination of government affairs and tried to unite Scotland and England by ensuring Mary's right of succession to Elizabeth I. He died in prison after holding Edinburgh Castle (1571–73) against James VI's supporters.

Majolica (Maiolica), tin-glazed earthenware painted in blue, green, manganese purple, yellow, or orange and made in Italy from the 14th to the 18th century. The term originally referred to luster painted ceramics from Majorca that were shipped to Italy.

Majorca (Mallorca), island of Spain, largest of the Balearic Islands, in W Mediterranean, approx. 115mi (185km) from the Spanish coast; capital is Palma. Held at different times by the Romans, Vandals, and Byzantines, it was taken 797 by the Moors, captured and made kingdom of Majorca 1276 by James I, king of Aragon; scene of peasant uprising 1521–23, and romance between composer Frederic Chopin and author George Sand; served as Italian base opposing Loyalists during Spanish Civil War (1936–39); scene of annual dance festivals celebrating the harvest; site of Caves of the Dragon containing underground lakes, and 13th-century Franciscan school. The island offers beautiful scenery and mild climate. Industries: tourism, fishing, lead, iron and coal mining, wine, jewelry, handicrafts, limestone and marble quarrying, olives, figs,

Norman Mailer

Majolica pitcher

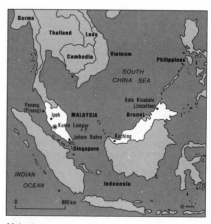

Malaysia

oranges, lemons, almonds. Area: 1,405sq mi (3,639sq km). Pop. 460,030.

Makarios III (1913–77), Cypriot clergyman and political figure, b. as Mikhail Khristodoulou Mouskos. Archbishop of the Orthodox Church of Cyprus (1950-77) and leader of the *enosis* (union of Cyprus with Greece) movement, he was president of Cyprus (1960–77), from its independence from Britain. He later abandoned *enosis* because it inflamed Turkish Cypriots. In 1974 he was forced to leave the country for several months as Greece and Turkey interfered with the nation's internal affairs, but later resumed his duties as archbishop and president.

Mako, also called mackerel shark, found worldwide in tropical marine waters. Deep cobalt to blue-gray above and pure white below, it is a strong swimmer and known to attack man. Length: to 13ft (3.9m); weight: 1,000lb (450kg). Family Isuridae (also called Lamnidae); species long fin *Isurus paucus,* short fin *Isurus xyrhinchus. See also* Chondrichthyes; Shark.

Malabar Coast, SW coast of India, between the Western Ghats (E) and Arabian Sea (W); Cochin and Calicut are the chief ports; traditional site where the Apostle Thomas started his missionary work (AD 52); Portuguese-based trading posts were est. here 1498–1503; area experienced an influx of Dutch 1656, French 1720s; by late 18th century, British had occupied the area. Industries: fishing, coconuts, rice, spices, rubber. Length: 550mi (886km).

Malabo, seaport town and capital of Equatorial Guinea, on Fernando Po Island in Gulf of Guinea. Industries: fish processing, cacao, coffee. Founded 1827 as British base to suppress slave trade. Pop. 20,000.

Malabsorption Syndromes, a group of diseases in which the common feature is either failure to digest certain nutrients or disruption of the process whereby the compounds produced by digestion are carried through the intestinal wall and into the blood for distribution to the tissues. Malabsorption has a variety of causes, among which are lesions of the small intestine, as in celiac disease or tropical sprue, abnormal bacterial growth in the intestine, disease of the intestinal lymph glands, or intolerance to certain substances such as sucrose. Ability to absorb fats, proteins, carbohydrates, vitamins, iron, calcium, sodium, potassium, and magnesium may be impaired, with the symptoms depending on the substance involved. Emaciation is a common manifestation. Treatment is mainly regulation of diet and replacement of deficiencies.

Malachi, biblical author and last of the 12 minor prophets. His book of prophecies closes the Old Testament with the promise of Elijah's return to help Israel.

Malachite, a carbonate mineral, basic copper carbonate (CU_2CO_3 $(OH)_2$), found in weathered copper ore deposits. Monoclinic system, silky green; hardness 3.5–4; sp gr 4. Sometimes used as a gem.

Málaga, seaport city in S Spain, on the Mediterranean Sea; capital of Málaga prov. Taken from Visigoths by Moors 711 it remained under Moorish rule until 1487, when it was captured by Ferdinand and Isabella. During the Spanish Civil War (1936–39), city was taken from loyalists by Francisco Franco; site of 8th-century fortress, 14th-century Moorish citadel, and several scenic parks. Industries: wine, olive oil, shoes, candy, flour, tourism. Founded *c.* 1100 BC by Phoenicians. Area: (prov.) 2,809sq mi (7,275sq km). Pop. (city) 374,452; (prov.) 867,330.

Malagasy Republic. *See* Madagascar, Republic of.

Malamud, Bernard (1914–86), US author, b. New York City. A short story writer and novelist, his works generally deal with Jewish characters. His books include *The Assistant* (1957); *A New Life* (1961); and *The Fixer* (1966), a novel about a Jew accused of ritual murder; *Dubin's Lives* (1979), and *God's Grace* (1982). In 1967 Malamud won both a Pulitzer Prize and a National Book Award for *The Fixer.* A short-story collection, *The Magic Barrel,* also won a National Book Award (1959), and *The Natural* (1952) later became a popular movie. *The Stories of Bernard Malamud* appeared in 1983.

Malaria, an insect-borne, often chronic disease resulting from infection with one of four species of the parasitic microorganism *Plasmodium,* acquired through the bite of the *Anopheles* mosquito and affecting the red blood corpuscles. *Plasmodium falciparum* malaria is the most serious form, with severe complications that may lead to death. Attacks of fever, chills, and sweating typify the disease and occur as new generations of parasites develop in the blood, with the frequency of attacks related to the species involved. The disease is treated with antimalarial drugs.

Malawi, independent republic in E central Africa; bounded by Tanzania (N and NE), Zambia (W), Mozambique (E, S, and SW). The president is the head of state and government and is answerable to a unicameral National Assembly. More than 20% of the land is covered by Lake Malawi, drained (S) by Shire River, its only outlet; much of the remaining area is plateau. The economy is overwhelmingly agricultural, with 25% of the land being arable. Chief crops are tea, tobacco, sugar cane, grain, and potatoes. Malawi's economy heavily depends on almost 30% of the populace working in industries in Zimbabwe, South Africa, and Zambia. From 1950, Malawi began to develop its own light industries, and tourism is of growing importance. Almost 99% of the population is Bantu-speaking black African, the majority being Christian or Muslim. Housing, education, health, and economic standards are relatively poor.

History. From 15th-18th centuries, Malawi grew with immigration of Bantu-speaking tribes from N and W. Visited by David Livingstone in 1859, who focused on the need for European intervention against slave trading. The British Central African Protectorate (Nyasaland) was est. 1891 and slave trade was ended. Against strong opposition from black Africans fearing white-oriented policies, the Federation of Rhodesia and Nyasaland was formed 1953. It survived until 1963; Nyasaland became independent as Malawi on July 6, 1964. In the same year, Malawi joined the United Nations; it became a republic 1966, and in 1971 Hastings Kamuzu Bandu, in office since 1966, was named president-for-life. Despite close ties with South Africa, Malawi remains neutral in international affairs. *See also* Tumbuka.

PROFILE

Official name: Republic of Malawi
Area: 45,193sq mi (117,050sq km)
Population: 5,800,000
 Density: 128per sq mi (49.5per sq km)
Chief cities: Lilongwe (capital); Blantyre; Zomba
Religion: Christianity, Islam
Language: English, Cinyanja, Citumbuka (all official)
Monetary unit: Kwacha

Malay, the official language of Malaysia, spoken by about half the country's population, or some 6,000,000 people. It is also one of the official languages of Singapore. Malay is for all practical purposes the same

language as Indonesian, both belonging to the Austronesian family.

Malayalam, language spoken on the W coast of extreme S India, principally in the state of Kerala. It belongs to the Dravidian family of languages. There are about 20 million speakers. It is one of the 15 constitutional languages of India.

Malay Archipelago, island group in SE Asia, between the Indian Ocean and the E central Pacific Ocean, N of Australia. The world's largest archipelago, it includes major islands of Luzon, Mindanao, New Guinea, Celebes, Java, Sumatra, and Borneo. Malay Archipelago is a purely geographic label, as the islands have been claimed and reclaimed in various groups by different foreign powers since 1st century BC. Since WWII they have divided into three main autonomous groups: The Philippines (1946), Indonesia (1949), and Federation of Malaya (1957, now Malaysia). W half of New Guinea Island (Irian Barat) is Indonesian territory; E half is Papua New Guinea.

Malayo-Polynesian Languages, another name for the Austronesian languages. *See* Austronesian Languages.

Malay Peninsula, promontory in SE Asia, between Strait of Malacca and South China Sea; comprises SW Thailand and West Malaysia. A mountain range, culminating in Mt Gunong Tahan, 7,186ft (2,192m), extends along its entire length; it is one of world's richest tin and rubber areas. Length: 700mi (1,127km). Area: 70,000sq mi (181,300sq km).

Malaysia, Federation of, nation in SE Asia. Lying in the extreme SE tip of Asia, it occupies the S half of the Malay Peninsula and most of N Borneo. The people are principally Malay and Chinese. Malaysia is the world's leading producer of tin and contributes about 35% of the world's rubber supply.

Land and Economy. The country divides into two distinct sections: W Malaysia or Malaya, which consists of 11 states lying on the S half of the Malay Peninsula, and E Malaysia, which consists of two states, Sabah and Sarawak, 400mi (644km) across the South China Sea on the N shores of Borneo. A mountain range runs N–S through the heart of Malaya, sloping off to a coastal lowland plain to the W where the majority of the people live. Both Sabah and Sarawak have swampy, alluvial coastal plains with tropical rain forests dominating most of the land. The hot and humid climate of Malaysia is ideal for the rubber industry, the country's main source of income. Malaysia is the world's leading producer of tin, and the largest producer of iron ore in the Far East. Although most natives are farmers, industry has developed rapidly, and Malaysia now processes many of its own resources. The country has good highway and rail services, plus excellent coastal shipping facilities.

People. About 85% of the population lives in Malaya; more than 35% is of Malay origin, with almost as many Chinese. Malay is the official language, but English and Chinese are widely spoken.

Government. A federal constitutional monarchy provides for a House of Representatives including 144 members elected by the people, and a Senate composed of 48 members, two from each of the 13 states and 22 appointed by the central government. From the nine states governed by hereditary rulers, a supreme head of state is chosen each five years to represent the country at ceremonial functions. Each of the 13 states has its own executive and legislature.

History: Although the country contained settled communities 2,000 years ago, the first real kingdom was est. by Buddhists from Sumatra about 800. During the 13th century Singapore was settled, and Arab traders brought Islam to the area. The Portuguese, the first Europeans to arrive (1509), had been expelled by the Dutch by 1641. In the late 18th century, the British made their appearance and by 1826 had formed the Straits Settlement, a colony made up of Panang, Malacca, and Singapore. The opening of the Suez Canal in 1869 and the introduction of rubber trees from Brazil in 1877 made the area even more prosperous. When the Japanese withdrew after WWII, everything was left in a state of disrepair. The Communists attempted a take-over, but by declaring a state of emergency that lasted until 1960, the government was successful in allaying the threat. Accusing the British of neo-colonialism, Indonesia sent guerrilla fighters into Malaysia in 1963, but the problem was resolved by a 1966 treaty. Malaya achieved independence in 1957, and the federation was formed in 1963. Singapore, originally a member, withdrew in 1965 because of internal problems. A separatist movement in Sabah and Communist guerrillas remained as problems in the mid 1970s. Civil unrest and opposition to the government resulted in the imposition of a state of emergency in 1977, but by 1979 unrest had declined, although tensions among the country's ethnic and political groups remained throughout the 1980s.

PROFILE

Official name: Federation of Malaysia
Area: 127,316sq mi (329,748sq km)
Population: 13,250,000
Density: 104per sq mi (40per sq km)
Chief cities: Kuala Lumpur (capital); Penang; Ipoh
Government: Federal constitutional monarchy
Religion: Islam
Language: Malay
Monetary unit: Malaysian dollar
Gross nationalproduct: $17,960,000,000
Per capita income: $529
Industries (major products): petroleum products, refined sugar, rubber goods, steel, lumber
Agriculture (major products): rubber, rice, palm oil, tea, pepper, coconuts, spices
Minerals (major): tin, iron
Trading partners (major): Japan, United States, European Economic Community

Malcolm II Mackenneth (died 1034), king of Scotland (1005–34) who in 1018 defeated the Northumbrians at Carham and secured the Anglo-Saxon district of Lothian permanently for Scotland. In the same year he gained control over Strathclyde, and thus completed the political unification of northern Britain. In 1031 he paid nominal homage to Canute, although the Danish ruler never interfered with his rule.

Malcolm III, or **Malcolm Canmore** (1031?–93), king of Scotland (1059–93). He succeeded his father, Duncan I, by slaying the usurper, Macbeth. Despite paying homage to William I (1072), he repeatedly raided England.

Malcolm X (Malcolm Little) (1925–65), US militant black leader, b. Omaha, Nebr. While serving a prison sentence, he joined the Black Muslims, a black separatist group. He then became a Black Muslim minister on his release in 1952. He later came into conflict with the group's leader Elijah Muhammad and formed a rival group, the Muslim Mosque, in 1963. In 1964 he converted to Islam. He was assassinated in February 1965.

Malden, city in E Massachusetts, on Malden River. Industries: processed foods, aluminum products, tools. Founded 1640; chartered 1881. Pop. (1980) 53,386.

Maldives, Republic of, independent island nation in the Indian Ocean 400mi (644km) SW of Sri Lanka. The country consists of some 2,000 coral islands in 12 distinct clusters. The islands, lying in a hot, humid climate, are covered with coconut palms. The economy is based almost entirely on the fishing industry with bonita the main export. In a move to bolster the economy, the government has encouraged tourism. The people are mostly of Arab, Indian, and Sri Lankan descent living at subsistence level in a one-crop economy. Virtually the entire population is Muslim. Divehi, a dialect of Sinhalese, is the principal language; Arabic is also spoken. Most of the people are illiterate.

Government and History. A republic, the government consists of a president, elected every four years; the Majlis (House of Representatives), consisting of 54 members elected every five years; and a Supreme Court and lesser courts. The entire system directly reflects Islamic influence.

The Portuguese, the first Europeans to arrive, controlled the area from 1558–73. The Dutch gained control in the 17th century, only to be ousted by the British, who controlled the island from 1887 until 1965. Independence was achieved in 1965, and the republic was declared in 1968. The economy has suffered from the 1975 closure of a British air base. Maldives became a member of the Commonwealth of Nations in 1982.

PROFILE

Official name: Republic of Maldives
Area: 115sq mi (298sq km)
Population: 143,046
Density: 1,244per sq mi (480per sq km)
Chief city: Male (capital)
Government: Republic
Religion: Muslim (official)
Language: Divehi (official)
Monetary unit: Rupee
Per capita income: est. less than $100
Industries (major products): fishing, food processing
Agriculture (major products): coconuts, taro
Trading partners (major): Sri Lanka

Malevich, Kasimir (1878–1935), Russian painter. He founded suprematism, a form of geometric abstractionism, in 1913. Malevich's manifesto, published in 1915, stated that the combination of geometric figures expressed "pure emotion." The epitome of the style is his *Suprematist Composition: White on White* (1919).

Malherbe, François de (1555–1628), French poet and critic, dictator of early 17th-century French literary style. He became a court writer in 1610 and severely criticized the emotional, decorative style of his contemporaries while pursuing simplicity and rationality in his own work.

Mali, independent republic in W Africa, surrounded by Algeria (N and NE), Upper Volta and Ivory Coast (S), Niger (E and SE), and Guinea, Senegal, and Mauritania (W). The flat lowlands of Mali are bisected W and E by the Niger River, dividing the Sahara Desert (N) from fertile agricultural region (S). The area produces sorghum, rice, millet, cotton, peanuts. Mali has various light industries including canning, cotton ginning, peanut oil extraction, bricks, textiles, and cigarettes; large mineral resources are largely unexploited. More than 83% of the population are black tribesmen; 65% of these are Muslim with an extremely low literacy rate.

According to the constitution of 1979, the government is led by a popularly elected president and an 82-member national assembly. There is only one legal political party. Moussa Traoré took control of the government in a military coup in 1968 and was elected president the following year.

Mali's importance peaked in the 14th century under the Mandingo Empire, which was a center for Muslim learning. By the early 15th century, the area was engulfed by civil strife that continued into the 18th century and was complicated by repeated invasions. French advancement began in the late 19th century and by 1898 Mali was almost totally occupied by the French and became French Sudan. The country voted in 1958 to join the French Community as the autonomous Sudanese Republic; it became the independent Republic of Mali in 1960. A devastating drought incapacitated the country from 1969–74 and again from 1979–85 causing famine, disease, poverty, and a mass exodus by many tribes. Border disputes with Algeria and Upper Volta (Burkina Faso) continued well into the 1980s.

PROFILE

Official name: Republic of Mali
Area: 478,764sq mi (1,240,000sq km)
Population: 6,469,999
Chief cities: Bamako (capital); Mopti; Ségou; Kayes
Religion: Islam
Language: French, tribal languages
Monetary unit: Franc

Mali, a powerful West African trading empire of the Middle Ages (*c.*1000–*c.*1500), noted for its exports of gold. A Muslim state, it developed major cultural centers and reached its peak under Mansa Musa in the 14th century.

Malinowski, Bronislaw (1884–1942) Polish-English anthropologist, considered the founder of social anthropology. His work with the peoples of New Guinea and the Trobriand Islands helped him to formulate his functional theory, which held that every aspect or norm of a society is a function vital to its existence. He taught at the University of London and Yale.

Mallard, river duck that is the ancestor of most domestic ducks. Males have a green head and neck and engage in complex courtship displays to attract females. It dabbles, or feeds from the surface. Species *Anas platyrhynchos. See also* Duck.

Mallarmé, Stéphane (1842–98), French poet. A leader of the symbolist movement, he was influenced by Baudelaire and Verlaine. Through his poetry he sought to evoke an intuitive ideal world. His works include *Hérodiade* (1869), *L'Après-midi d'un faune* (1876), and *Un Coup de dés jamais n'abolira le hasard* (1897). His style is complex.

Mallow, annual and perennial plants native to temperate regions of North America, S Europe, and Asia. The flowers are pink and white. Many are considered weeds. Family Malvaceae; genus *Malva.* The mallow family includes over 900 species of plants native to temperate and tropical regions. Some are valued for their showy flowers and others for food or fiber.

Malmö, seaport city in SW Sweden, on the Øresund; major trade and shipping center during Hanseatic period; mostly ruled by the Danish, passed to Sweden 1658; now a naval and commercial port; site of Malmöhus castle (1434), city hall (1546), 14th-century St Peter's Church. Exports: grain, sugar, clay, cement. Industries: shipping, processed foods, cement, textiles, clothing, metal goods, shipbuilding, railway cars. Pop. 243,591.

Malnutrition, inadequate dietary intake, which does not allow for optimum health. Common causes are economic deprivation, in which inadequate quantities of protein or calories are consumed; unavailability of foods containing necessary vitamins and minerals; poor eating habits; or metabolic defects involving the digestive tract, liver, kidneys, and red blood cells.

Malocclusion, the misalignment of the row of teeth in the upper jaw with those in the lower jaw, resulting in improper contact between the biting surfaces of the teeth. If untreated, it can lead to deformities of the jaws or difficulties in chewing. Malocclusion may be hereditary in origin or due to early loss of teeth due to decay. *See also* Orthodontics.

Malory, (Sir) Thomas (*fl.*1469), English prose writer, author of *Le Morte d'Arthur.* His identity is obscure, but he was probably the Thomas Malory from Warwickshire who fought in the Wars of the Roses, became a member of parliament in 1456, and served several prison sentences between 1450 and 1470.

Malpighi, Marcello (1628–94), Italian physiologist. He was the founder of microscopic anatomy, demonstrating how blood reaches the tissues through tiny vessels (capillaries) that are too small to be seen with the naked eye. Harvey had inferred that there must be capillaries, but had never seen them; Malpighi used the microscope to study the fine structure of plant and animal tissues and was able to pinpoint and explain the network of tiny veins he could see on the lung surface. He extended the use of the microscope into many fields, including the study of gland cells and of the brain, and also ventured into the field of embryology.

Malraux, André (1901–76), French novelist and politician. An archeologist who became involved in revolutionary activities in China, his early novels examine the heroism of individuals who, engaged in social revolution, are seen to transcend the human condition—*The Conquerors* (1928), *Man's Fate* (1933), and *Man's Hope* (1937). *The Psychology of Art* (1947–1950) examines art as a search for transcendental achievement. In 1959 he was appointed minister of cultural affairs by Charles de Gaulle.

Malt, grain product, usually derived from barley, used in beverages and foods. The grain is softened in water, allowed to germinate, and kiln-dried. This activates enzymes that convert the starch to malt sugar. Most malt is used in the manufacture of beer. *See also* Barley.

Malta, an independent island country in the Mediterranean Sea, approx. 60mi (96km) S of Sicily; comprises Malta, Gozo, and Comino islands. The topography is flat, with a limestone top layer; the climate is temperate and hot in the summers. There are no rivers in Malta, and rainfall is barely sufficient for growing vegetables; terracing is practiced on a large scale. Agriculture supports approx. 25% of the population; crops are potatoes, wheat, onions, beans, oranges, cotton, grapes, and cumin seeds; livestock is also important. Malta's location is favorable for shipping routes, and it is noted for good harbors. Industries include manufacture of lace, buttons, gloves, hosiery, textiles, and skilled ship and dock repairing; the economy is also highly dependent on tourism. The population consists of elements of all the peoples who have inhabited the islands, including the Phoenicians. The islands are overpopulated, with severe unemployment; majority of the people is Roman Catholic.

Malta became a fully independent country in 1964. A republic was proclaimed in 1974 but Malta remained within the Commonwealth of Nations. According to the constitution of 1974, the unicameral house of representatives is composed of 65 members. The prime minister, the head of government, is leader of the majority party or coalition in the house. Formerly a Carthaginian and Phoenician colony, it was taken by Ro-

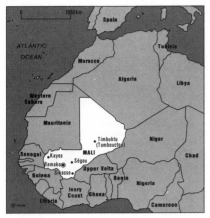

Mali

Malta

Mammoth

mans 218 BC; in 1530 it was given to the Knights of St John by Emperor Charles V. It was held by Napoleon 1798–1800, when it was taken by the British. In the 19th century, Malta prospered as powerful British naval base, but in the 1970s it experienced a great economic decline as a result of Britain's withdrawal from naval facilities, completed in 1979.

PROFILE

Official name: Republic of Malta
Area: 122sq mi (316sq km)
Population: 315,262
Chief cities: Valletta (capital); Sliema; Mdina; Victoria
Government: Republic
Religion: Roman Catholic
Language: Maltese, English, Italian

Maltese, aristocratic breed of spaniel dog (toy group) that has existed for 2,800 years as a pet of royalty and the wealthy. It has a medium-length head and fine, tapered muzzle; low-set drop ears; dark, round eyes, compact body; fine-boned legs; and long tail curved over the back. The long, flat, silky coat flows almost to the ground and is pure white. Average size: 5in (13cm) high at shoulder; 2–7lb (1–3kg). *See also* Spaniel; Toy Dog.

Malthus, Thomas (1766–1834), English economist and minister famous for his *Essay on the Principle of Population* (1798). According to Malthus, population increases geometrically, that is, in the order of 2, 4, 8, 16, 32, and so on. However, the food supply can only be increased arithmetically, that is, in the order of 1, 2, 3, 4, 5, and so on. Accordingly, population would eventually outdistance a nation's food supply, with famine, war, and disease as the inevitable consequences.

Mamba, poisonous African tree snake of the cobra family. It has long venom fangs in its upper jaw and large front teeth in its lower jaw. The black mamba is largest. Others are green or green and black. Length: to 14ft (4.3m). Family Elapidae; genus *Dendroaspis*. *See also* Cobra.

Mamelukes, ruling dynasty of Egypt (1250–1811). Originally they were Turkish and Circassian prisoners of Genghis Khan who were sold as slaves to the sultan of Egypt, who trained them as soldiers. They fought for Egypt but then seized power. In 1250, Bahri founded the first Mameluke dynasty. It was a time of great cultural advancement with monuments and military conquests but internal political chaos. Ottoman sultan Selim I took control for a time, but the Mamelukes did not really lose power until Mohammed Ali Pasha ordered them all killed in 1811, leaving only the province of Baghdad under Mameluke control.

Mammal, class (Mammalia) of vertebrate animals numerous on all major land masses and in oceans. Characterized by full, partial, or vestigial hair covering and—in the female—by mammary glands. Mammals have an effective temperature-regulating system and a four-chambered heart, with circulation to the lungs separate from that to the rest of the body. The air-pumping ability of mammal lungs is increased by action of the muscular abdominal diaphragm. As a group, mammals are active, alert, and intelligent. They range in size from shrews weighing a fraction of an ounce to the largest of all animals, the up-to-150-ton blue whale. Mammals generally bear fewer young and give them better care than do most other animals.

Mammals include 17 orders of placentals, one marsupial order—all live-bearing—and an order of egg-laying monotremes. Mammals probably evolved about 180,000,000 years ago from a group of warm-blooded reptiles. They became the dominant land animals after

the extinction of the dinosaurs about 70,000,000 years ago. *See also* Chordate; Marsupial; Monotreme; Placental Mammals; Vertebrate.

Mammary Glands, glands that secrete milk to feed the young, a characteristic mammalian feature. *See* Breast; Lactation.

Mammography, examination of breast tissue by X ray, often to detect the presence of a malignant tumor in an early stage of development.

Mammoth, extinct, Pleistocene elephant. Its tusks were downwardly directed and often greatly curved. The most prominent types were the southern mammoth of Europe and Asia, the imperial mammoth of North America, and the woolly mammoth of N Eurasia and North America. The latter is known from frozen complete cadavers as well as bones. Many cave paintings by early man exist. Genus *Mammuthus*.

Man, Isle of, island off the NW coast of England, in the Irish Sea. Occupied by Vikings *c.* 600, it was a dependency of Norway until 1266; belonged to earls of Derby 14th century until 1735; part of the British crown since 1765. Tourism and agriculture are important; sheep and cattle thrive on the hills. Products: grain, root crops, fruit, flowers, vegetables. Industries: dairying, fishing, quarrying. Man has its own government. Capital is Douglas. Area: 221sq mi (572sq km). Pop. 58,773.

Man, Prehistoric, any of the evolutionary stages of early man preceding recorded history. Included are all the members of the family Hominidae and australopithecines, which developed alongside the *Homo* line. The australopithecines were followed by the pithecanthropines and, ultimately, *Homo sapiens,* our own species. The australopithecines may have been derived from *Ramapithecus* of 13,000,000 years ago. *Australopithecus* itself existed from about 3,000,000 to 1,000,000 years ago and includes fossils formerly called *Zinjanthropus* and *Paranthropus*. The material is mostly from E and S Africa. The *Homo* line, which branched off from the australopithecine line, about 2.8–2 million years ago, includes *Homo habilis* (2–1.5 million yrs ago), *Homo erectus* (1.5–1 million yrs ago), and *Homo sapiens,* our species (less than .5 million yrs ago). *Homo sapiens* is believed to have developed in two directions, one leading to Neanderthal Man and similar types in Asia and Africa, and the other to the modern races of man represented in Europe by Cro-Magnon Man of 30,000 years ago.

Managua, capital city of Nicaragua, in W central Nicaragua on S shore of Lake Managua; economic, industrial, and commercial hub of Nicaragua; suffered damage from earthquake 1931, after which much of the city was rebuilt, and another Dec. 23, 1972, that killed over 10,000 people and necessitated further reconstruction. City was made capital 1855, being neutral ground between bitterly opposed political factions in León and Granada. Pop. 556,470.

Manama (Al-Manamah), city in N Bahrain, SW Asia, in the Persian Gulf; capital, principal port, and commercial center of Bahrain. It was made a free port 1958; deepwater harbor was built 1962. Industries: oil refining, pearl fishing, boatbuilding, cloth. Pop. 94,697.

Manatee, large plant-eating aquatic mammal found in shallow coastal waters and large rivers of subtropical and tropical North and South America and W Africa. Length: 7–12ft (2.1–3.6m); weight: 500lb (225kg). Family Trichechidae; genus *Trichechus. See also* Sirenia.

Manchester, city in NW England, in Greater Manchester; a major British city and commercial hub; in England's densest metropolitan region. Manchester Ship Canal (1887–94) made it a major port; center of liberalism and of Anti-Corn Law League in 19th century; home of University of Manchester and Hallé Orchestra. Industries: textiles, printing, publishing. Pop. 506,300.

Manchester, city in S New Hampshire, on Merrimack River; state's largest city; one of seats of Hillsborough co; many textile mills moved S (1935) and city's economy suffered; site of St Anselm's College (1889), New Hampshire College of Accounting and Commerce (1932), Notre Dame College (1950), John Stark home, and Stark Park, a memorial to Gen. John Stark, hero of French and Indian and Revolutionary wars. Industries: textiles, rubber, automobile accessories. Settled 1722; inc. 1751 as Derryfield; renamed 1810; chartered as city 1846. Pop. (1980) 90,936.

Manchester Terrier, sport dog (terrier group) also known as black and tan terrier, bred in the Manchester area of England, and now registered in toy and standard varieties. Originally used for rat killing and rabbit coursing, this sleek dog has a long head. Ears are pointed and erect in the toy and erect or folded in the standard. The moderately short body is slightly arched; legs are long; and the tail is short and pointed. The smooth, short coat has well-defined zones of jet black and mahogany tan. Standard size: toy—5–12lb (2–5.4kg), 7in (18cm); standard—16lb (7kg), 14–16in (36–41cm). *See also* Terrier.

Manchu, a Tungusic tribal people related to the Jurchens who had ruled China as the Chin dynasty. The Manchu people grew in power and numbers in the 16th century and finally under their great leader Nurhachi created the military structure by which they were able to defeat Ming dynasty China and establish their own rule under the name Ch'ing Dynasty.

Manchukuo, former country in E Asia; founded 1932 by Japanese from conquered Manchuria and Jehol prov., China; Changchun served as the capital, later renamed Hsinking; ruled by Henry Pu Yi as a Japanese puppet state and developed industrially as a war base; dissolved 1945 at the close of WWII.

Manchuria, industrial region in NE China, bordered by Soviet Union (N and NE), Korea (SE), Yellow Sea (S), Inner Mongolia (W); Mukden is the chief city. The N, E, and W borders are lined with Khingan highlands and Ch'angpai Shan Mts; its central area is the alluvial Liao-Sungari lowland; the population is 90% Chinese. Ruled by lesser Chinese dynasties until *c.* 1125, region was ruled by the Nu-chen (later known as Manchus) 1125–1234, when they were dispersed by the Mongols; the Manchus reunited and conquered all of China 1606, ruling until 1912. Russian influence was dominant 1898–1904; Japan defeated Russian forces during Russo-Japanese War (1904–05). S Manchuria and Port Arthur developed rapidly with the introduction of the South Manchurian Railroad. Jehol prov. was annexed 1928; by 1931–32, Japanese troops had occupied Manchuria and Jehol prov. and created the puppet state of Manchukuo (1932–45); Russian takeover of Manchuria and China (1945–46) caused the dismantling and removal of more than 50% of the industrial plants; Nationalist regime was overthrown by Communists 1949. In 1954, Manchuria was divided into three provinces: Liaoning, Kirin, Heilungkiang; all are under control of Peking. Industries: iron, steel, mining, agriculture, chemicals, oil refining, textiles, ceramics, ships, lumber, livestock, food processing, aluminum, aircraft, locomotives. Area: 600,000sq mi (1,554,000sq km).

Manchurian Incident

Manchurian Incident. On Sept. 18, 1931, Japanese forces seized Mukden and quickly extended their control over all of Northeast China, known as Manchuria. The Chinese regard this as the real start of World War II and their war with Japan. The United States and the League of Nations denounced Japanese actions. Japanese military leaders in Manchuria claimed they moved to maintain internal peace and security for Manchuria.

Mandalay, city in central Burma, on Irrawaddy River; capital of Mandalay division and district; largest city and trade center of Upper Burma. City contains Fort Dufferin, a moated citadel; the Seven Hundred and Thirty Pagodas (Kuthodaw), Arakan Pagoda, many bazaars, a university (1958), palace of King Thebaw. Founded 1857 by King Mindon, Mandalay was last capital (1860–85) of Burmese Kingdom. It was occupied by Japanese 1942–45 and 85% destroyed. Industries: textiles, jade. Pop. 417,266.

Mandan, the Dakota name for a Siouan tribe of North American Indians inhabiting the upper Missouri River area between the Heart River and the Missouri River, in W North Dakota. From an early population of 3,600, disease epidemics introduced by white travelers decimated the tribe; today, about 350 live on the Fort Berthold Reservation in North Dakota.

Mandarin, the major dialect of Chinese, spoken by about three-fourths of the population of China, or some 600,000,000 people. It was the language of the imperial court and Peking and is spoken in all but the western and extreme southern provinces and the populous southeastern coastal strip.

Mandarin, Asian perching duck that typically lives in forest trees and nests in holes well above ground. Species *Aix galericulata. See also* Duck.

Mandela, Nelson Rolihlahla (1918–), South African anti-apartheid leader. After studying law at the University of the Witwatersrand he became a law partner of Oliver Tambo, with whom he cofounded the Youth League (1944) of the African National Congress (ANC), South Africa's oldest black nationalist organization. The ANC was banned by the white government (1960), and Mandela was imprisoned (1962) for subversive activity and for leaving the country illegally to seek international support for the movement. While in prison he was tried and given a life sentence (1964). He has refused to accept his freedom conditional on his renouncing armed struggle for black rights and has become a folk hero to black South Africans. His wife **Winnie Nomzamo Mandela** often publicized her husband's cause during the 1980s and by mid-decade had emerged herself as one of the foremost leaders of South Africa's blacks.

Mandolin, soprano stringed musical instrument of the lute family. Four to six pairs of wire strings tuned in fifths are played in sustained tremolo by a vibrating plectrum. A serenading instrument in 18th-century Italy, it was later a fad in America (1920s) and was used for novel effects in operas and symphonies. *See also* Lute.

Mandrake, herb native to the Mediterranean and used since ancient times as a medicine. The plant has narcotic properties and contains the alkaloids hyoscyamine, scopolamine, and mandragorine. Leaves are borne at the plant base, and the spindle-shaped and branched root is often thought to represent the human figure. Large greenish-yellow or purple flowers produce a many-seeded berry. Height: 1ft (30.5cm); family Solanaceae; species *Mandragora officinarum.*

Mandrill, colorful baboon living in dense rain forests of Central W Africa. They live in small troops and forage for their omnivorous diet on the forest floor. The bright colored male has a red-tipped, pale blue nose, yellow-bearded cheeks, and a naked reddish rump. Weight: to 120lb (54kg). Species *Mandrillus sphinx. See also* Baboon; Drill; Monkey.

Manet, Édouard (1832–83), French painter. Associated with the Impressionist movement, his later work approaches abstraction in its emphasis on pattern. Manet's first work submitted to the Paris Salon of 1859, "Absinthe Drinker," was rejected; his "Spanish Guitar Player" received an honorable mention in 1861. "La Déjeuner sur l'herbe" was rejected by the 1863 Salon and prompted public and critical outcry when shown at the Salon des Refusés. "Olympia," shown two years later, elicited a similar response. Manet's erotic subject matter, harsh colors, and detached, impersonal style rendered these works controversial. In 1867 he exhibited at the Paris World's Fair and helped with the first Impressionist exhibition in 1874. Although he did not exhibit then, his work was closely aligned with that group. His colors had lightened, and his sub-

ject matter was more conventional, involving landscapes, beach scenes, and the like. A work of this period, "Bar at the Folies-Bergere," was well received by the public and the critics alike. *See also* Impressionism.

Mangabey, large, silky gray monkeys that live in dense central African forests. Mangabeys associate in small troops and feed chiefly on fruit. Tree dwellers, they are generally silent and apparently communicate by expressive grimaces. Length: 15–35in (38–89cm); weight: to 13lb (6kg). Family Cercopithecidae; genus *Cercocebus. See also* Monkey.

Manganese, metallic element (symbol Mn) of the first transition series, first isolated in 1774. Chief ores are pyrolusite (dioxide) and rhodochrosite (carbonate). The metal is used in alloy steels and certain ferromagnetic alloys. Properties: at. no. 25; at. wt. 54.938; sp gr 7.21–7.44; melt. pt. 2271°F (1244°C); boil. pt. 3807°F (2097°C); most common isotope Mn^{55} (100%). *See also* Transition Elements.

Mange, animal skin disease caused by parasitic mites imbedded in the skin that lay eggs and die. The new generation matures and spreads the itchy lesions, causing loss of hair or fur. Secondary bacterial infections of the inflamed skin can be fatal.

Mango, evergreen tree native to SE Asia and grown widely in the tropics for its fruit. It has oblong leaves, pinkish-white clustered flowers, and yellow-red fruit that is eaten ripe or preserved when green. Height: to 90ft (27m). Family Anacardiaceae; species *Mangifera indica.*

Mangrove, tropical, evergreen tree and shrub found in swampy areas. Its stiltlike aerial roots cause thick undergrowth, making this tree important in building new land along tropical coasts. Seeds germinate while still on the tree. Among 120 species are the red *Rhizophora mangle* found from S Florida to South America and in W Africa; height: to 100ft (30m). *Rhizophora mucronata* grows in E Africa and tropical Asia. Family Rhizophoraceae.

Manhattan, borough of New York City in SE New York; coextensive with New York co; bounded by Hudson River (W), New York Bay (S), East River (E), and Harlem River (E and N). In 1626, Manhattan Indians sold the island to Peter Minuit of Dutch West India Co. for about $24 worth of trinkets. Town of New Amsterdam was built at tip of island; it served as capital of New Netherlands during Dutch control; English captured colony 1664 and renamed it New York. In 1898, Manhattan became one of five boroughs est. by Greater New York charter. A cultural, commercial, and financial center, it is site of Columbia University (1754), New York University (1831), City University of New York (1848), Manhattan College (1853), Barnard College (1889), Cooper Union (1859), Juilliard School of Music (1926), Metropolitan Museum of Art, Museum of Modern Art, Museum of the City of New York, Rockefeller Center, Lincoln Center for the Performing Arts, St Patrick's Cathedral, United Nations. Industries: electrical, chemical, fabricated metal products, publishing, broadcasting, stock exchange, port facilities, entertainment, tourism. Pop. (1980) 1,427,533.

Manhattan Project, code name given to the US atomic bomb project during World War II. Work on the bomb, suggested by Albert Einstein and other scientists, was carried on in great secrecy under Gen. Leslie Groves at several locations in the United States. The first test was at Alamogordo, N.M., in 1945.

Manic-Depressive Psychosis, an affective psychotic reaction marked by severe mood swings ranging from exaggerated feelings of elation and optimism to deep depression. Manic and depressive symptoms may alternate in a cyclical pattern, be mixed, or be separated by periods of remission. Although disturbances of thought and judgment may be present, they are considered secondary to the disturbances of mood. *See also* Depression.

Manichaeanism, heretic belief founded by the Persian sage Mani (*c.*215–77) and based on asceticism and the battle between light and darkness. Mani preached that he, along with Jesus, Buddha, and the prophets, was sent to this world to release the particles of light stolen by Satan and trapped in the brains of men. The Manichaean sect spread to Egypt by the end of the 3rd century and to Rome and Africa in the 4th century; it survived until the 13th century in Chinese Turkestan. *See also* Zoroastrianism.

Manifest Destiny, slogan to justify the US westward and southward expansion movement in the 19th century. Coined by a Democratic editor, John L. O'Sullivan (1845), it was exploited by Pres. James K. Polk when

the United States annexed Texas and won lands from Mexico. Later the theory of manifest destiny contributed to the acquisition of Alaska, Hawaii, and territory taken in the Spanish-American War.

Manila, largest city of the Republic of the Philippines, on Manila Bay, W Luzon island; capital of Republic of Philippines until Quezon City replaced it in 1948. The chief industrial, financial, and cultural center of the Philippines, the city has long been an important port, hosting Spanish galleons from the 16th century. Spanish traders built the old walled city (Intramuros) on the site of a Muslim settlement. Following the Spanish-American War (1898), development expanded beyond the old city, much of which was destroyed in WWII. The port receives the vast majority of imports to the Philippines, and is the site of the University of Manila, the University of Santo Tomás, the University of the Philippines, Far Eastern University, and Manila Central University, as well as the National Museum and Malacañan Palace. Industries: shipbuilding, textiles, tobacco, chemicals, lumber, food processing, shipping. Pop. 1,438,252.

Manila Hemp, or abaca, plant native to the Philippines and introduced into SE Asia and Central America. The fibers obtained from leafstalks of the mature plant are used for cloth, matting, and cordage. Fiber length: to 15ft (4.6m) Family Musaceae; species *Musa textilis.*

Manitoba, province in S central Canada, in the plains region. It is bordered by Ontario (E), the states of Minnesota and North Dakota (S), Saskatchewan (W), and Northwest Territories and Hudson Bay (N).

Land and Economy. In the S the land is chiefly prairie; rolling country and low hills lie to the N. Three great lakes—Winnipeg, Winnipegosis, and Manitoba—lie in the central portion. The Red River of the North, the Saskatchewan, Nelson, Winnipeg, and Assiniboine are the major rivers. More than one third of the land is forested, but the rich farmlands of the S and center support the agriculture that has been a mainstay of the economy.

People. Most of the population is of British origin, but there are strong elements of French, Ukrainians, Germans, and Scandinavians. The S is the most heavily populated area.

Education. The University of Manitoba, the University of Winnipeg, and Brandon University are the institutions of higher education.

History. French and English fur traders entered the region in the 1600s, and in 1670, Charles II of England granted the land to the Hudson's Bay Co., a fur enterprise. The first settlers were Scots in 1811. The Canadian government bought the rights of the Hudson's Bay Co. in 1870, and Manitoba joined the Confederation. Railroad building in the 1880s accelerated the development of the economy. After new discoveries (1915), a mining boom began, to be followed by another in the 1960s. The socialist New Democratic Party controlled the government for most of the period from World War II to 1977 and again beginning in 1981.

PROFILE

Admitted to Confederation: July 15, 1870; rank, 5th
National Parliament representatives: Senate, 6; House of Commons, 13
Population: 1,005,953
Capital: Winnipeg
Chief cities: Winnipeg; St James-Assiniboia, St Boniface
Provincial legislature: Legislative Assembly; 57 members
Area: 251,000sq mi (650,090sq km); rank, 6th
Elevation: Highest: 2,800ft (854m), Duck and Riding mts; lowest, 400ft (122m)
Industries (major products): meat, apparel, railroad equipment
Agriculture (major products): wheat, barley, oats, cattle, dairy products, poultry
Minerals (major): copper, gold, zinc, silver, nickel, petroleum
Floral emblem: pasqueflower

Manitou, a North American Indian (Algonquin) term for the spiritual power common to all things in nature. It was also used for any of numerous personified nature deities at whose head stood the Great Manitou or Kitchi-Manitou.

Manizales, city in Colombia, 110mi (177km) NW of Bogotá; capital of Caldas dept. Founded 1847 by gold prospectors, it was destroyed by earthquake (1878) and fire (1925); 45mi (72km) aerial tramway connects it with Mariquita; major coffee center. Industries: gold, silver, mercury mining. Pop. 199,904.

Man-made Elements. *See* Element 104; Element 105.

Mann, Horace (1796–1859), US educator, b. Franklin, Mass. He was elected to both the Massachusetts

Manhattan, New York City

Thomas Mann

Mao Tse-tung

House and Senate (1827–37), where he worked for passage of a new state education bill. While secretary of the Massachusetts board of education (1837–48), he established teacher-training schools, increased teachers' salaries, and improved teaching practices. In 1848 he went to Congress as an anti-slavery Whig and in 1853 he became the first president of Antioch College.

Mann, Thomas (1875–1955), German novelist and essayist. He modeled his concepts of the "burger" from his wealthy merchant father and of the exotic artistic temperament from his mother. These two elements he later represented as the polarity inherent in human life. His most powerful works, in which he apologized for the conservative traditions in Germany, came from WWI. His opposition to fascism grew from WWII. His novels include *Buddenbrooks* (1901), *Tonio Kröger* (1903), *Death in Venice* (1912), *The Magic Mountain* (1924), *Joseph and His Brothers* (1933–43), *Doctor Faustus* (1947), and *Confessions of Felix Krull, Confidence Man* (1954). Leaving Germany in 1933, he took US citizenship in 1944 and settled in Zurich in 1952. He was awarded the Nobel Prize in literature in 1929 and the Goethe Prize in 1949.

Manna, or flowering ash, tree native to S Europe and Asia Minor. Its leaves, composed of 7 leaflets each, have rust-colored hairs underneath. Flowers are white and showy with large petals. Size to 60ft (18.3m). A sugary exudate, manna, is collected from cuts in the bark and used medicinally. Height: to 60ft (18m). Family Oleaceae; species *Fraxinus ornus.*

Mannerheim, Carl Gustaf Emil von (1867–1951), president of Finland. A baron, he served in the Russian army, rising to major general in World War I, before withdrawing at the Bolshevik Revolution (1917). He returned to Finland and was regent 1918–19. In 1920 he founded the Mannerheim League for Child Welfare. He was head of the defense council from 1931, was made a field marshal (1933), and commanded the Finnish forces 1939–44. He planned the Mannerheim Line for defense against Russia. He was president of Finland, 1944–46.

Mannerism, Italian style of painting, sculpture, and architecture that developed *c.*1520–80 in opposition to the classicism of the High Renaissance. Characteristics of this style were distortions of the proportions of human figures and other forms; canvases were often crowded. In architecture, decorative motifs that often had no structural function were incorporated into designs. Active Mannerist artists were Pontormo and Rosso Fiorentino in Florence and Parmigianino in Rome.

Mannheim, city in central West Germany, on E bank of Rhine River at mouth of Neckar River, across from Lüdwigshafen; major port of upper Rhine River. Originally a fishing village, it was fortified in 1606 and destroyed during Thirty Years' War (1622). Rebuilt in 1699, it was seat of Rhine Palatinate 1719–77; passed to Baden 1803; site of 18th-century palace, university (1967). Industries: automobiles, chemicals, cellulose, tobacco, paper, textiles, steel. Founded 766; chartered 1607. Pop. 311,200.

Manometer, a device for measuring pressure. It consists of a U-shaped tube containing a liquid, one end open to the atmosphere and the other end attached to the vessel whose pressure is to be measured. If the pressure in the vessel is greater than atmospheric, it will force the liquid down on one side and up on the other. The difference in height of the liquid is used to determine the difference in pressure.

Manorial System, agriculture and land distribution system existing in the corn-raising areas of England, Northern France, Germany, and Denmark during the period of feudalism. Typical of the system were the English manor and the German *mark,* villages surrounded by arable fields and wasteland. A lord presided over the manor, which he held either outright or in fief from a greater lord or king. The villagers, or *villeins,* worked the land in common, with each villein family being directly responsible for one *virgate* or strip, which rotated from year to year. In exchange for the use of the land, the villein owed labor services in the lord's fields, payment of chickens, livestock, and an irregularly demanded money levy called *tallage.* Thus the labor of the villagers supported the lord, the knightly and clerical classes, and one another. The custom, or law, of the manor fixed the duties and payments of the villein, who might be considered a serf or a freeman. Justice was meted out and custom determined in the manorial court, often presided over by the lord and attended by the villagers as nominal and sometimes actual advisers. *See also* Feudalism.

Mansa Musa (d. 1337), Muslim emperor of Mali (1312–37). He brought his domain to the peak of its power and renown. He led an impressive pilgrimage to Mecca (1324–25) and gained international recognition by giving away vast quantities of gold.

Mansfield, Katherine (1888–1923), British short-story writer, *b.* New Zealand. Her works, all collections of short stories, include *In a German Pension* (1911), *Bliss* (1920), *The Garden Party* (1922), and *The Dove's Nest* (1923). She was a writer of subtlety and warmth, who created atmosphere with the lightest of touches.

Mansfield, city in N central Ohio, 54mi (87km) WSW of Akron; seat of Richland co; site of reconstructed blockhouse from War of 1812, French provincial mansion (pre-Civil War), and writer Louis Bromfield's house, now an ecological center and experimental farm. Industries: rubber products, electrical industries, sheet steel, plumbing fixtures. Settled 1808; inc. as village 1828, as city 1857. Pop. (1980) 53,927.

Mantegna, Andrea (1431–1506), Italian painter. His work influenced northern Italian painting for 50 years. One of his early fine works is the altarpiece in S. Zeno, Verona (1456–59). In 1459 he went to Mantua as a court painter to the Gonzaga family. He remained there for the rest of his life. His works include the innovative "St Sebastian" and "Dead Christ," which modernized formal compositions, and "Madonna of Victory" (1495).

Mantinea, city in ancient S Greece, near Argolis border in E Peloponnesus; scene of Peloponnesian War battle during which Agis defeated the Argives and Mantineans (418 BC); Theban victory over Sparta resulting in death of Epaminondas (362 BC).

Mantis, or praying mantis, insect found worldwide. It has powerful front legs used to catch its insect prey. Colors range from brown and green to bright pinks, enabling each species to blend with the foliage or flowers it hides on. Length: 1–6in (25–152mm). Family Mantidae.

Mantle, layer of Earth between core and crust. This is a solid layer since it transmits both P and S seismic waves. The mantle itself is not homogeneous, becoming denser with increasing depth. The shadow zones, or areas of deflected P and S waves, are part of the mantle, which is otherwise a good conductor of seismic waves since it is dense rock (usually olivine) in its lower layers. *See also* Moho.

Mantua (Mantova), city in N Italy, on Mincio River, 22mi (35km) SSW of Verona; capital of Mantova prov. An ancient Etruscan settlement, it became independent 1115; prospered politically and culturally under the Gonzagas 14th-18th centuries; passed to Austria 1708; taken by Napoleon 1796–97; ceded to Italy 1805, to Austria 1814, returned to Italy 1866; site of church of San Andrea (begun 1472), cathedral (rebuilt 16th century), Vergilian Academy of Sciences and Fine Arts. Industries: shipping, machinery, furniture, tourism. Pop. 65,390.

Manuel I or **Emmanuel I** (1469–1521), king of Portugal (1495–1521). He was the cousin of John II, whom he succeeded. He was king during what is known as Portugal's Golden Age. Portuguese explorers and navigators covered the globe, and Portugal's great empire in the East was developed. Enormous wealth poured into the country from that empire. In 1497, Manuel expelled the Jews and Moors from Portugal. His son, John III, succeeded him.

Manumission, the legal granting of freedom to slaves. US slave owners sometimes freed their slaves in their wills, and many opponents of slavery hoped such manumission would bring a gradual end to the system. The Emancipation Proclamation (1862) and finally the 13th Amendment (1865) ended slavery.

Manx, language formerly spoken on the Isle of Man. Closely related to Scottish Gaelic, it was spoken by all the native inhabitants of the island until about 1700, when English began to be introduced. By 1900 there were only a few thousand speakers left and the last of these were gone by 1950.

Manx Cat, tailless, short-haired domestic cat bred on Isle of Man in Irish Sea. An intelligent and devoted pet, it has a round head, prominent ears, short back, and hindquarters higher than the shoulders. The luxurious double coat can be any color. Because of frequent back deformity, Manx have a tendency to hop. They are difficult to breed.

Manzanita, or bearberry, shrub with broad, oval leaves, white or pink flower clusters, and reddish-brown fruit. Height: 8–12ft (2.4–3.7m). Family Rubiaceae; species *Arctostaphylos manzanita.*

MAO Inhibitors. See Monoamine Oxidase Inhibitors.

Maori, or **Maui,** Polynesian people who have inhabited New Zealand for at least 600 years. Noted for artistic skills such as woodcarving and singing, the Maoris experienced a loss of cultural identity following their uprising against and subsequent defeat by British colonists in 1860. They are fully integrated into Western-oriented New Zealand society, and most Maoris have adopted Christianity.

Mao Tse-tung (Mao Zedong) (1893–1976), Chinese Communist leader. One of the original founders of the Chinese Communist party in 1921, Mao eliminated competitors for leadership and became chairman in 1935 and one of the foremost leaders in the world Communist movement. A leading theoretician on guerrilla warfare, Mao held that the path to power in China lay through the mobilization of the peasantry. He helped in the founding of the Kiangsi Soviet Republic in China in 1931, led the famous Long March (1934–35), and built his reputation as a theorist and military leader in Yenan from 1936 until the end of World War II when he launched his successful drive for rule over all China. In 1949, Mao created the Chinese People's Republic and remained its chief decision maker through remaining decades during which he eliminated competitors and sought to transform China's traditional culture into a revolutionary Communist society. Although he fell into disfavor posthumously in 1978, Mao's accomplishments were ultimately judged to outweigh his mistakes, and his policies continued to influence the party.

Map, any graphic representation of various geographical, geologic, political, ecological, physiographic, or meteorological variables on the earth's surface. There are many different techniques for plotting and showing the distribution of these features. Maps can be flat, or three dimensional, or plotted on a spherical surface called a globe. *See also* Map Projection.

Maple, deciduous trees native to temperate and cool regions of Europe, Asia, and North America. They have unisexual, yellowish or greenish flowers and winglike seeds. They are grown for ornament, shade, or timber depending on species, while the sugar maple is also tapped for its sap. Most species have brilliant foliage in autumn. Height: 15–120ft (4.6–37m). Family Aceraceae; genus *Acer.*

Mapping. *See* Cartography.

Map Projection, any systematic method of drawing the earth's meridians and parallels on a flat surface. Only on a globe can areas and shapes be represented with any fidelity. On flat maps of large areas distortions are inevitable. Projections are either geometrical derivations (cylindrical, conical, or azimuthal) or networks and grids derived mathematically in the transposition from globe to flat surface.

Mapp v. Ohio (1961), landmark US Supreme Court case overruling previous decisions and strengthening the interpretation of the Fourth Amendment's ban on illegal searches. The court declared that evidence obtained in such a search was inadmissible in subsequent criminal prosecutions.

Map Turtle, or sawback, lake and river turtle of N and central United States. Flat-shelled, many have ridged dorsal keels. Their limbs, head, and shell are marked with numerous whorls and lines. Females are often larger than males. They eat mollusks. Length: to 11in(28cm). Family Emydidae; genus *Graptemys. See also* Turtle.

Maputo, formerly Lourenço Marques, capital city of the state of Mozambique, SE Africa; first visited by Antonio do Campo (1502); explored by Portuguese trader Lourenço Marques, whose name it took while Mozambique was a Portuguese possession; linked by rail to South Africa, Swaziland, and Zimbabwe; site of university. Industries: coal, footwear, rubber. Inc. 1887. Pop. 500,000.

Marabou. *See* Adjutant Stork.

Maracaibo, port city in NW Venezuela, between Lake Maracaibo and Gulf of Venezuela; capital of Zulia state; Venezuela's 2nd-largest city; site of cathedral, colonial edifices, university (1891). Founded 1571 by a German adventurer-explorer, it was seized 1669 by Henry Morgan; expanded after discovery of oil 1917. Industries: coffee, cacao, sugar, dairy products, beer, lumber. Pop. 786,389.

Maracaibo, Lake, Lake in NW Venezuela, S arm of Gulf of Venezuela; major transport route; fed by Catatumbo River (SW); rich oil field region. Discovered 1499 by Alonso de Ojeda. Area: 5,217sq mi (13,512sq km).

Maracay, city in N Venezuela, on Pan American Highway, 50mi (81km) WSW of Caracas; capital of Aragua state; capital of Venezuela 1908–35; site of agricultural school, national airport, military aviation school. Industries: textiles, coffee, cacao, sugar, tobacco, timber, cattle, paper, soap. Pop. 255,134.

Marat, Jean Paul (1743–93), French political figure, b. Switzerland. A noted physician in London and Paris, his *Philosophical Essay on Man* (1773) was attacked by Voltaire for its extreme materialism. At the outbreak of the French Revolution (1789) he founded the inflamatory journal *L'Ami du Peuple.* He was forced to flee to London (1790, 91) and to hide in the Paris sewers. Backed by Robespierre and Danton, he came out of hiding and was elected to the National Convention where he worked for the Jacobins. He was stabbed to death in his bath by Charlotte Corday, a Girondist sympathizer.

Marathi, language spoken in W India, principally in the state of Maharashtra. It is one of the Indic languages and thus part of the Indo-European family. Speakers of Marathi number about 45,000,000. It is one of the 15 constitutional languages of India.

Marathon, a plain on the E coast of Greece connected to Athens by a main road, and the scene of the Persian invasion Sept. 490 BC. Here an Athenian force under Miltiades defeated a numerically superior army led by Datis and Artaphernes and freed Attica from the threat of Persian invasion. *See also* Persian Wars.

Marathon Racing, one of the most demanding of track and field events. The standard marathon race is 26 miles, 385 yards (42.2km). The race duplicates the length run by Pheidippides to announce the Greek victory at Marathon in 490 BC. Usually, the race starts and ends on a stadium track, with the bulk of the race run through a marked course in city streets. Marathon racing was first included in the modern Olympic Games of 1896. The most famous distance race is the Boston Marathon, held annually in Boston since 1897.

Marble, metamorphic rock composed largely of recrystallized limestones and dolomites. The term is more loosely used to refer to any crystalline calcium carbonate rock that has good pattern and color when cut and polished. The color is normally white, but when tinted by serpentine, iron oxide, or carbon, can vary to shades of yellow, green, brown, or black. *See also* Metamorphic Rocks.

Marbury v. Madison (1803), US Supreme Court case that established the supremacy of the Constitution over congressional legislation and the court's role as interpreter of the Constitution. It also established the court's power to overturn unconstitutional legislation.

Marceau, Marcel (1923–), French actor, the greatest mime of his time. In 1947 he founded a company to reawaken interest in the art of mime. Since that time his character, "Bip," became widely known and imitated. He and his mime company have toured extensively and appeared on television numerous times.

March, third month of the year. It was named for the Roman god Mars and has 31 days. The birthstone is the aquamarine or bloodstone.

Marches, autonomous region in E central Italy, on the Adriatic Sea; comprised of the provinces of Ancona, Ascoli Piceno, Macerata, and Pesaro e Urbino; capital city is Ancona. Region has mountains and hills with many rivers; part of the Papal States 16th century–1860, when it was united with Italy. Industries: agriculture, textiles, chemicals. fertilizer, fishing, refined petroleum. Area: 3,742sq mi (9,692sq km). Est. 1948; received autonomy 1970. Pop. 1,397,892.

Marcion (died c.160), heretic sect leader. A wealthy shipowner native to Sinope, he was excommunicated in 140 and 144 for immorality. He then organized a sect that believed in a Christian gospel of love (as exemplified by Jesus in the New Testament), rejecting the Old Testament as a gospel of the God of Law. Marcion believed that only St Paul understood this distinction, and he wrote prologues to the Pauline epistles. The Marcionites were absorbed by the Manichaeists at the end of the 3rd century.

Marcomanni, ancient west German tribe first mentioned by Caesar. Driven from Saxony and Thuringia by the Teutones and Cimbri, they migrated to the upper Main, then to Gaul and Bohemia (c.8 BC). A strong people, they fought against Roman campaigns led by Domitian, Nerva, and Marcus Aurelius. After AD 500 they moved from Bohemia to Bavaria.

Marconi, (Marchese) Guglielmo (1874–1937), Italian electrical engineer and inventor. He began experimenting with wireless telegraphy in 1894, forming the Marconi Wireless Telegraph Co., Ltd., in England in 1897 to encourage commercial applications. He improved inventions of others and originated a magnetic detector (1902), a directional aerial (1905), and a continuous wave generating system (1912), steadily increasing transmission distance. He attracted worldwide attention by making transatlantic contact between Poldhu, England, and St John's, Newfoundland, in 1901. Marconi and Karl F. Braun shared the 1909 Nobel Prize for physics for work in wireless telegraphy. A US court upheld the basic Marconi patents in 1914, bringing him fame as the creator of the wireless. After World War I he worked on short waves, then microwaves, living to see the advent of commercial radio.

Marcos, Ferdinand Edralin (1917–), Filipino political figure, president of the Philippines (1965–86). After serving as a congressman from 1949 with the Liberal party, he moved to the Nationalist party in 1964. Elected president in 1965, he was reelected in 1969, becoming the first president of the Philippines to serve a second term. His presidency was marked by student unrest and guerrilla activity. In 1971 and 1972 he declared martial law and in 1973 he established a new

and authoritarian constitution. In 1978, Marcos assumed the position of first premier. Martial law was lifted in 1981, and he was reelected to a six-year term but was forced fo flee to the US, amidst charges of election fraud, in 1986. He was succeeded by Corazon Aquino.

Marcus Aurelius (Antoninus) (121–180), Roman emperor (161–180) and philosopher, b. as Marcus Annius Verus. With his stepbrother Lucius Verus as coemperor, he succeeded his adoptive father Antoninus Pius as emperor in 161. After the death of Lucius Verus in 169, he reigned as sole emperor. His reign was troubled by numerous revolts and invasions. In 161 he repelled a Parthian invasion of Syria. In 167–68, he drove the Marcomanni, a Germanic tribe, out of Italy. There were also revolts in Egypt, Spain, and Britain. He lowered the taxes of the poor and was lenient to political prisoners, but persecuted Christians. His *Meditations* is an important work of Stoic philosophy.

Marcy, Mount, peak in the Adirondack Mts, NE New York. Lake on S slope is source of the Hudson River. State's highest peak. Height: 5,344ft (1,630m).

Marduk, the supreme deity in the Babylonian pantheon of gods. Originally an earth deity who personified water's fertilizing quality, he acquired the attributes of local deities as the power of Babylon grew. Marduk became not only the grain producer, but the bringer of light and justice and the creator of all things. His attributes are the spade and the sword.

Mare (plural, maria), any of the dark expanses on the moon's surface. Originally thought to be seas (hence the Latin term), they are in fact huge circular or irregular plains, much smoother than the surrounding areas, perhaps of a basaltic material.

Margaret I (1353–1412), queen of Denmark, Norway, and Sweden. She was the daughter of Waldemar IV of Denmark and the wife of Haakon VI of Norway. In 1376 her son Olaf, age 5, became Danish king under his parents' regency. At Haakon's death in 1380, Olaf became King Olaf V of Norway. After Olaf's death in 1387 Margaret ruled Denmark and Norway. She defeated Sweden's King Albert of Mecklenburg in 1389. In 1397 her nephew Eric of Pomerania was crowned king of Denmark, Norway, and Sweden.

Margaret of Austria (Savoy) (1480–1530), daughter of Hapsburg emperor Maximilian I, regent of Netherlands (1507–30) for her nephew Charles (later emperor Charles V). Born at Brussels, Belgium, in 1497 she wed the Spanish infante John and in 1501, Philibert II of Savoy. In 1529, with Louise of Savoy (mother of Francis I of France) she negotiated the Peace of Cambrai, sometimes called La Paix des Dames.

Margaret of Austria (Parma) (1522–86), illegitimate daughter of Hapsburg emperor Charles V (Charles I of Spain), Duchess of Parma. Married to the duke of Florence, Alessandro de' Medici, from 1531 until his death in 1537, in 1538 she wed Ottavio Farnese, duke of Parma (from 1547) and was regent of the Netherlands (1559–67) for Philip II of Spain, her half-brother. At first sympathetic to Netherlandish nationalists, then repressive, finally she resigned as regent when the harsh duke of Alva was brought in.

Margaret Rose (1930–), princess of Great Britain; the daughter of King George VI, and sister of Queen Elizabeth II. The wife (1960–78) of Antony Armstrong-Jones, earl of Snowdon, she had two children, David Albert Charles, Viscount Linley (b. 1961), and Sarah Frances Elizabeth (b. 1964).

Margaret Tudor (1489–1541), queen of Scotland, daughter of Henry VII of England. She married Scotland's James IV (1503) and at his death (1513) became regent for their son, James V. Ousted from power (1515), she manipulated both the pro-French and pro-English factions, thereby maintaining considerable influence. She was able to end regency of James V (1524) and became his chief adviser (1528–34).

Margarine, a food made from vegetable fats with aqueous milk products, salt, flavoring, food coloring, emulsifier, and vitamins A and D blended in. Used for cooking and as a spread. Corn or safflower oil is the most popular modern fat ingredient due to interest in polyunsaturated fats in relation to health.

Margay, small cat found in forests from Mexico to S Brazil. A cat with a good disposition, it is sometimes kept as an unusual pet. Its coat is cream yellow with black spots. Length: body—17.7–27.6in (45–70cm); tail—13.8–19.7in (35–50cm). Family Felidae; species *Felis wiedii.*

Guglielmo Marconi

Marcus Aurelius: statue in Rome

Francis Marion

Marginal Analysis, significant concept in economics that refers to basing decisions on the final units under consideration, a much more meaningful tool of analysis than comparison of totals. A primary application of marginal analysis is to the theory of the firm. The firm assumed to be interested in maximizing profits. It has been shown that it can maximize profits through equating the additional cost per unit of output to the additional revenue per unit of output. Marginal analysis is also useful in analyzing consumer decisions.

Marginalism, economic analysis simultaneously introduced in 1878 by economists William Jevons and Léon Walras. Marginal analysis involved the concept of the extra utility, eg the additional satisfaction someone gets from receiving an extra unit of some commodity. Previously, economists had difficulty explaining why water, which is so important to life, sold for a much lower price than such a seemingly superfluous good as diamonds. Marginalism made it clear that the last or extra unit of abundant water contains less satisfaction than the last or extra unit of relatively scarce diamonds.

Marginal Utility, in economics, the addition to total utility that occurs from obtaining one more unit of a good. For most goods, the marginal utility would be expected to be positive, implying that the consumer receives an addition to his total utility by obtaining increasing amounts of the good.

Margrethe II (1940–), queen of Denmark, daughter of Frederik IX. In 1972, she became the first queen regent since the Middle Ages and the first democratically appointed sovereign in Denmark's history. Married in 1967 to the French Count Henri Laborde Monpezat, he became Prince Henrik of Denmark on their wedding day. They have two sons. The queen is well-educated, artistic, and speaks several languages.

Marguerite, or Paris daisy, perennial plant native to the Canary Islands. It has mounded foliage and white or lemon-yellow flower heads about 2in (5cm) across. Height: to 3ft (91cm). Family Compositae; species *Chrysanthemum frutescens.*

Maria II (1819–53), queen of Portugal (1826–53). She was the daughter of Peter I, who abdicated in her favor when he became emperor of Brazil (as Pedro I). She was betrothed to her uncle, Dom Miguel, but he attempted to usurp the crown, thereby setting off the Miguelist Wars. Maria's forces, led by her father and supported by English sea power, defeated Miguel in 1834. Her reign, however, was marked by continual political unrest. She was succeeded by her son, Peter V.

Maria Christina (1806–78), queen of Spain, consort of Ferdinand VII. At her behest Ferdinand named their daughter Isabella II as heir. She was regent to Isabella after Ferdinand's death and marshalled Isabella's forces against the Carlists, the supporters of Don Carlos, the late king's brother and pretender to the throne. Forced from the regency in 1840, she returned in 1843 and thereafter played a major role in the political intrigues and dissensions that marked Isabella's reign. *See also* Carlists.

Mariana Islands, volcanic and coral island chain in W Pacific Ocean, approx. 1,500mi (2,415km) E of the Philippines and N of the Caroline Islands; extends N to S approx. 500mi (800km) along the Marianas Ridge. Group includes Guam, Saipan, Tinian, Rota, Pagan, and ten other islands; most are mountainous volcanic formations. Discovered by Ferdinand Magellan 1521, and named Islas de los Ladrones (Islands of Thieves)

the islands were named Marianas Islands in 1668. The Northern Marianas (all of the group except Guam) were sold by Spain to Germany in 1898, and Japan received a mandate for them in 1917. Guam came under US control in 1898, although it was taken by Japan in 1941. In 1944, US forces recaptured Guam after heavy fighting, and the Northern Marianas were incorporated in the US Trust Territory of the Pacific Islands. In 1975 voters in the Northern Marianas approved separate status from the rest of the Trust Territory, becoming a commonwealth of the United States in 1976, with Guam remaining an unincorporated US territory. The inhabitants of the island, excluding US personnel, are Micronesians, Chamorros, and Japanese. Agaña, Guam, Garapan, and Saipan are chief centers; site of ancient stone structures, notably on Guam, which have attracted archeological interest. Main occupation is subsistence farming, although government employment, including the large naval base on Guam, is a major source of income. Exports: sugar cane, coconuts, coffee. Area: approx. 400sq mi (1,036sq km). Pop. 98,000 (concentrated in Guam).

Marianao, city in NW Cuba; suburb of Havana; city developed rapidly in late 19th century during sugar boom. Industries: chemicals, textiles, beer. Founded 1719. Pop. 350,260.

Maria Theresa of Austria (1717–80), empress of the Holy Roman Empire, archduchess of Austria, queen of Hungary and Bohemia. Daughter of Emperor Charles VI, her disputed succession to the Hapsburg lands led to the War of the Austrian Succession (1740–48). She married (1736) Francis Stephen of Lorraine, who became Emperor Francis I (1745). She made politically advantageous marriages for many of her children, including Marie Antoinette. *See also* Austrian Succession, War of the.

Marie Antoinette (1755–93), queen of France, daughter of Francis I and Maria Theresa of Austria. Married (1770) to the French dauphin, later Louis XVI, her extravagant and frivolous conduct caused her great unpopularity at court and made her hated by the populace. At the outbreak of the French Revolution (1789), a mob attacked the palace at Versailles. The removal of the royal family to Paris soon followed. Foiled at Varennes in an attempt to escape (1791), Louis and Marie were afterward viewed as traitors. They were guillotined two years later.

Marie de Médicis (1573–1642), queen of France. Daughter of the grand duke of Tuscany, she was married in 1600 to Henry IV of France, with whom she frequently quarrelled. He was assassinated the day after he crowned her queen in 1610. She was then regent for seven years, favoring Spain and the Catholic Church. Her ambitious and stubborn nature, however, led to disagreement with her son, Louis XIII. Cardinal Richelieu healed the breach, but Marie showed little gratitude and plotted against him. Despite her denunciation of Richelieu, Louis remained loyal to him. Marie was forced in 1631 to flee to Brussels, never again to see France.

Marigold, scented mostly annual plants native from New Mexico to Argentina. Those most commonly cultivated are the French marigold *(Tagetes patula),* height: to 1.5ft (45cm) and the African or Aztec marigold *(Tagetes erecta),* height: to 3ft (91cm). They have showy yellow, orange, or red flower heads. Organic gardeners often plant marigolds to repel insects and nematode worms. Family Compositae.

Marihuana, a hallucinogenic drug prepared from the dried flowering spikes of the hemp plant *Cannabis*

sativa and smoked in cigarettes. Of the two types, Indian and American, the former is the more potent. Marihuana produces feelings of elation, intensifies experiences, particularly sensations (possibly excepting touch), and distorts the time sense; large doses produce intoxication. The heightening of unpleasant experiences appears to have caused psychological disturbances in some unstable persons. In 1976 the FDA approved the use of marihuana to treat severe glaucoma. In 1981 the FDA recommended the use of tetrahydrocannabinol (THC), the active ingredient in marihuana, in conjunction with chemotherapy for cancer patients, and several states permitted prescriptions of marihuana for cancer and glaucoma patients.

Marimba, percussion instrument with tuned wooden bars ranging 5 to 6 octaves, set in a frame over resonators and struck with mallets. Brought from Malaysia via African Bantus to Guatemala, it is now used in marimba bands throughout Latin America. Darius Milhaud and Paul Creston wrote modern concertos for the marimba.

Marine Biology, science and study of life in the sea, including organisms that live in the water and along shores. Marine biologists explore how these organisms fit into the human environment as well as their own.

Marine Corps, United States, branch of the armed forces that is a service within the department of the Navy. It consists of approximately 196,000 personnel, and it conducts the land operations connected with naval operations. The commandant of the Marine Corps is a member of the Joint Chiefs of Staff and participates on an equal basis when Marine Corps matters are under consideration. He is also responsible for Marine training and doctrine and for providing troops and equipment to the Fleet Marine Forces. The operational forces consist of three divisions, three aircraft wings, and supporting troops, and are organized into task forces to conduct amphibious operations. The US Marines officially began in 1798 as part of the Navy, although there had been a continental Marine Corps during the Revolutionary War. The Marine Corps has been involved in US military operations from the War of 1812 through the Vietnam conflict. *See also* Joint Chiefs of Staff; Navy, United States.

Marine Engineering, branch of engineering that deals with the construction, maintenance, and operation of the power plant and other mechanical equipment of seagoing vessels, docks, and harbor installations.

Marion, Francis (1732–95), American Revolutionary War officer, known as the "Swamp Fox," b. Berkley co, S.C. He commanded the South Carolina militia in guerrilla-type raids on the British. He participated in the defense of Charleston.

Maritime Alps, S division of W Alps along French-Italian border; extends 120mi (193km) from Ligurian Apennines (Cadibono Pass) ESE to Cottian Alps (Maddalena Pass) WNW. Highest peak is Punta Argentera, 10,817ft (3,299m).

Maritime Law, or admiralty law, deals with laws relating to commerce and navigation, thus to all marine matters including questions of contracts, torts, injuries, piracy, and of prize. A branch of commercial law controlled by national courts and influenced by municipal law, it is composed of national laws and rules of their admiralty courts and international treaties and conventions. Its bases are customs and usages dating from ancient times—those of 8th or 9th-century Rhodes are the earliest known—and influenced by Roman civil law; they were codified during the Middle Ages. In England maritime law was once under the jurisdiction of separate courts of admiralty, but these cases are now assigned to the high court of justice. The US Constitution grants authority over maritime law to federal courts.

Marius, Gaius (*c.*157–86 BC), Roman general. Of equestrian family rank, he served in Numantia and later as proconsul in Spain. He married the patrician Julia (later Caesar's aunt) and served as Metellus' legate in Numidia, where he distinguished himself in the Jugurthine War. He was elected consul seven times and became the bitter enemy of Sulla. Marius created a new army of the proletariat with improved organization and training. When Sulla took command of the Roman forces in the East, Marius fled. He allied himself with Cinna, seized Rome, and slaughtered his enemies. Granted the eastern command, he died before assuming it. Sulla was victorious in the ensuing civil war.

Marjoram, or sweet marjoram, common name for *Majorana hortensis,* an herb of the mint family with aromatic leaves used for flavoring meats and dressings. It is not to be confused with pot marjoram *(Origanum vulgare).*

Mark, apostle of Jesus. He was the author, with Peter's assistance, of one of the four gospels of the New Testament, written about 30 years after Jesus' death. This gospel was written for Gentiles, stressing Jesus's activities and nature as the Son of God, and does not refer to the Old Testament.

Market Equilibrium, market position from which there is no tendency to move; the position at which both buyer and seller are satisfied. This equilibrium occurs when the quantity supplied equals the quantity demanded at a particular market price, called the *equilibrium price.* The quantity is called the *equilibrium quantity.* Market equilibrium occurs when the supply and demand curves are equal and the market exactly clears at this market price.

Marketing, that portion of the production-distribution-consumption continuum dealing with the transfer of goods and services from one owner to another. The marketing function can occur at all levels, and one can examine the marketing practices at the wholesale or retail enterprise. Recent estimates suggest that approximately 50% of the consumers' expenditures pay for marketing activities, broadly defined, and that almost one third of the US labor force is engaged in commodity distribution. Marketing activities are expanding, and now include some responsibility for product development, design, packaging, pricing, and advertising.

Market Mechanism, in economics, the interaction of supply and demand that determines a market price and market output level. The market mechanism is based on the demand schedule, which is a schedule of prices and the quantities that would be demanded by consumers at these prices, as well as the supply schedule, which is a schedule of prices and the quantities that would be supplied by producers at these prices. As prices increase, consumers will demand less and producers will be willing to produce more. As prices decline, consumers will demand more and producers will be willing to produce less. Through the interaction of the two forces, an equilibrium price is reached.

Market Structure. A market economy may include many different market structures, ranging from purely competitive (many firms producing a homogeneous product, with free entry) to monopolistic (only one seller). Generally, as the market becomes less and less competitive, prices of goods tend to be higher and the output levels of the industry tend to be lower. As the degree of monopoly power increases, the market mechanism is less and less able to operate because more market control is placed in the hands of fewer firms.

Market System, the system of decision-making within a free enterprise, price-oriented economy. It determines, through response to consumer demands, what goods will be produced; through the individual firm's decision-making process, how these goods will be produced; and through the interaction of supply and demand, how these goods will be allocated. The market system basically involves the interaction of supply provided by the firms and demand provided by consumers in determining the quantity of the good.

Markhor, largest wild goat; it inhabits mountains of Afghanistan and W Himalaya Mountains. Males have long, corkscrew horns, and shaggy beards. Height: 40in (102cm) at shoulder; weight: 200lb (90kg). Family Bovidae; species *Capra falconeri. See also* Goat.

Marlborough, John Churchill, 1st Duke of (1650–1722), English general and political figure. He was a supporter of William of Orange in the Glorious Revolution (1688). Queen Anne created him duke of Marlborough (1702), and he led the English and allied armies against Louis XIV in the War of the Spanish Succession, gaining great victories at Blenheim (1704), Ramillies (1706), Oudenaarde (1708), and Malplaquet (1709). On the ascendancy of his political enemies, he was dismissed from all his offices (1711). He was restored to military command in 1714.

Marlborough, Sarah Jennings Churchill, Duchess of (1660–1744), favorite of England's Queen Anne. She married John Churchill, later duke of Marlborough (1678), and her influence with the future queen assisted his career. Through her Whig sympathies, she lost favor after 1707. She supervised the building of Blenheim Palace.

Marlin, popular marine sport billfish found in the warm waters of the Atlantic and Pacific. Not abundant in any area, it is dark blue with a coppery tint and violet-blue side bars. The long bill is rounded in cross-section. Length: to 26ft (7.9m); weight: 1,400lb (635kg). Species include the blue marlin *Makaira nigricans* and the Pacific striped *Tetrapturus audax.* Family Istiophoridae.

Marlowe, Christopher (1564–93), English poet and playwright. From *Tamburlaine the Great* (1587) until his death six years later, he wrote six tragedies (one unfinished) and the heroic poem *Hero and Leander.* Noted for his supreme mastery of language, he used blank verse in his dramas and began the development of heroic tragedy by restoring to it the grandeur of the early Greek tragedians. His plays, which were the first ever written for the public theater, are *The Tragical History of Doctor Faustus* (1589), *The Jew of Malta* (1589), *Edward II* (*c.*1590), *The Massacre of Paris* (1590), and *Dido, Queen of Carthage* (completed by Thomas Nash).

Marmara, Sea of, sea in NW Turkey, between Europe (N) and Asia (S). It is connected with Black Sea (E) by the Bosporus, and with the Aegean Sea through the Dardanelles. Its largest island is Marmara, famous for alabaster and marble quarries. Istanbul is located at entrance of Bosporus on Sea of Marmara. Sea is easily navigable due to lack of strong currents and negligible tidal range. Area: 4,430sq mi (11,474sq km).

Marmoset, tiny day-active, tree-dwelling monkey of tropical America. The size of small squirrels, they have soft dense fur varying in color. Marmosets of certain genera are often called tamarins, Family Callithricidae; genera *Saguinus, Leontideus. See also* Monkey.

Marmot, stocky, ground-living rodent of the squirrel family native to North America and Eurasia. Most have brown to gray fur; short, powerful legs; and furred tails. Plant-eaters by day, they find shelter and hibernate in grass-lined burrows. They mate in spring and have 2–8 young in early summer. Length, excluding tail: 15–28in (38–71cm); weight: 7–17lbs (3–8kg). Family Sciuridae.

Marne River, river in NE France; rises in Langres plateau, flows NW to Seine River near Paris. Marne Rhine Canal and Marne-Saône Canal connect it with Aisne, Meuse, Moselle, and Saône rivers. In 1914 and 1918 bitter battles were fought on its banks; US forces reached river August 1944. Navigable for 220mi (354km) of its 325mi (523km).

Maronites, Christian sect founded, according to claims, by St Maro in the 5th century and based on Monotheletic beliefs (only the divine will present in Christ). Probably dating from 7th century Syria, with present colonies also in Lebanon, Israel, Cyprus, and the United States, the sect was excommunicated in 680 at the Council of Constantinople. It was taken back into the Church in 1181, and in 1584 Pope Gregory XIII founded the Maronite College at Rome. The Maronites are a uniat body—an eastern church in union with Rome—and retain their own language (Syriac), canon law, and ceremonies.

Marquand, J(ohn) P(hillips) (1893–1960), US author, b. Wilmington, Del. A novelist, he is noted for his books about wealthy New Englanders. Among these are *The Late George Apley* (1937; Pulitzer Prize 1938), *Wickford Point* (1939), and *H. M. Pulham, Esq.* (1941). He also wrote a number of detective stories and novels about a Japanese detective, Mr. Moto.

Marquesas Islands, volcanic island group, part of French Polynesia, in E central Pacific Ocean, S of the equator and N of Tuamotu; the group of twelve includes Fatu Hiva, Hiva Oa, and Nuku Hiva. Capital is Hakapehi on Nuku Hiva. French took possession and settled islands in 1842, bringing with them European diseases that decimated the native Polynesians. Islands are mountainous, with fertile valleys and several good harbors; scene of Herman Melville's *Typee.* Exports: tobacco, vanilla, copra, cotton. Discovered 1595 by Alvaro de Medaña, Spanish navigator. Area: 480sq mi (1,243 sq km). Pop. 5,593.

Marquette, Father Jacques (1637–75), French Jesuit missionary and explorer in America. In 1666, Marquette arrived in Quebec as a missionary priest. After two years, he moved deeper into the wilderness to preach among Indians around the Great Lakes. Chosen (1672) by the Canadian government to explore, he, Louis Joliet, and five others were the first white men on the upper Mississippi, exploring it as far as the mouth of the Arkansas River. He was the first white man to live on the site of Chicago.

Marrakesh (Marrakech), city in W central Morocco, at NW foot of Atlas Mts; one of the cities of Islam and site of many medieval structures, notably the Koutoubya mosque; seat of Université Ben Youssef. Industries: tourism, leather goods. Founded 1062 by Yusuf ibn Tashfin. Pop. 332,741.

Marriage, state in which two individuals are joined together by a number of bonds, which include the economic, the religious, and the sexual. One major reason for marriage is the procreation and upbringing of children. Marriage is distinguishable from a sexual union accompanied by co-residence in that it involves rites that establish it officially in a society. *See also* Courtship; Polyandry; Polygamy.

Marriage of Figaro, The (1786), 4-act opera by Wolfgang Amadeus Mozart, Italian libretto by Lorenzo Da Ponte, after Pierre Beaumarchais' comedy. Its Vienna premiere was conducted by Mozart. Although one of the oldest operas performed continuously in Western repertoires, it is musically and politically revolutionary. The story is of servants mocking aristocratic masters, challenging the feudal practice of "droit du seigneur." Principal roles are Figaro and the Count (baritones), Susanna and the Countess (sopranos), Cherubino (mezzo-soprano).

Marrow, soft tissue, containing blood vessels, found in the hollow cavities of bones. The marrow found in many bones, including the long bones, is somewhat yellowish and functions for fat deposition. The marrow in the flattish bones, including the ribs, sternum, cranial bones, parts of the pelvis, and the ends of the long bones, is reddish and contains reticular cells that give rise to myeloblasts. The myeloblasts give rise eventually to the red blood cells as well as to most of the white blood cells and the platelets.

Mars, fourth planet from Sun, with 2 satellites (Phobos and Deimos) and the only planet other than Earth that might support life. Its thin atmosphere is mainly carbon dioxide with traces of water vapor; Temperature, −100°F (−73°C) to over 60°F (16°C); mean distance from Sun, 141,320,000mi (227,940,000km); mass, 0.11 of Earth; diameter, 4,210mi (6,762km); rotation period, 24hr 37min; period of sidereal revolution, 687 days. *See also* Solar System.

Mars, in Roman mythology, god of war. Although second in importance only to Jupiter, there is little known of his early character. He was the father of Romulus and Remus.

Marsala, ancient Lilybaeum, seaport city in W Sicily, Italy, approx. 18mi (29km) S of Trapani on Cape Boeo; site of 16th-century cathedral and city walls; Garibaldi's forces landed here 1860 in conquest of Sicily. Exports: wines (famous white Marsala), salt, grain. Pop. 84,280.

Marseilles, seaport city in SE France, on Gulf of Lions; capital of Bouches-du-Rhône dept. Second-largest and oldest city in France, it is connected with Rhône River by an underground canal; during Crusades (11th-14th century) it was commercial center and shipping port for Holy Land. The 19th-century conquest of Algeria by France and opening of Suez Canal brought prosperity to the city. In the harbor is Chateau D'If, a prison built 1524 on small rocky isle; site of 13th-14th-century St Victor's Abbey Church, 17th-century city hall, and Chapelle de la Charité. Industries: flour, soap, vegetable oil, cement, sugar. Founded 600 BC by Phocaean Greeks from Asia Minor. Pop. 914,356.

Marsh, shallow lake whose waters are stagnant or feebly flowing and which is filled with vegetation, rushes, reeds, and types of trees whose roots like the muddy soil. A marsh may also be a piece of low land that at times dries enough to be tilled. Marsh areas may occur high in mountains or adjacent to the sea.

Markhor

John Marshall

Thurgood Marshall

Marshall, Alfred (1842–1924), English Neoclassical economist, one of the greatest modern economists. His *Principles of Economics* (1890) was a landmark work. Prior to its publication, economists had argued about whether demand or supply played a more important role in determining a product's price. Marshall, however, showed that supply and demand were like the blades of a pair of scissors. Both blades are equally needed if the scissors are to work properly. Many of Marshall's other concepts—elasticity; the short run, with variable and fixed cost; and the long run—were also important contributions to economics, and his microeconomic theory provided part of the foundation of modern economics.

Marshall, George Catlett (1880–1959), US army officer and public official, b. Uniontown, Pa. As army chief of staff during World War II, he helped formulate Allied strategy. After the war, he was secretary of state (1947–49) and of defense (1950–51). He won the 1953 Nobel Peace prize for the European Recovery Program (Marshall Plan), which provided economic aid to postwar Europe. *See also* Marshall Plan.

Marshall, John (1755–1835), chief justice of the US Supreme Court (1801–35), b. Fauquier co, Va. He served as an officer in the Continental Army throughout the Revolutionary War. His only formal education was the study of law for several months under George Wythe at the College of William and Mary. He was a member of the Virginia House of Burgesses 1782–88. He gained national prominence as a member of the Virginia constitutional ratification convention (1788), when he argued successfully for the Constitution against Patrick Henry; and for his defense of Jay's Treaty during the ratification controversy. He accepted a post (1797) offered by President John Adams as minister to France and returned to the United States in great favor after negotiations with Charles Maurice de Talleyrand in the XYZ Affair. He refused the post as associate justice and became a Federalist member of the House of Representatives from Virginia (1799–1800). He served as secretary of state (1800–01) until his appointment as chief justice. Marshall raised the Supreme Court to great prestige and established basic precepts for constitutional interpretation. Important cases he presided over include *Marbury* v. *Madison* (1803), which set a doctrine of judicial review; *Fletcher* v. *Peck* (1810) and *Dartmouth College* v. *Woodward* (1819), establishing doctrines of sanctity of contracts; *McCulloch* v. *Maryland* (1819), which expanded congressional power through implied power; *Gibbons* v. *Ogden* (1824), which designated national power over commerce; and *Cohens* v. *Virginia* (1821), which established the supremacy of the Supreme Court over state legislatures. He also wrote *Life of George Washington* (5 vols., 1804–07).

Marshall, Thurgood (1908–), US jurist and lawyer, b. Baltimore, Md. A civil rights advocate opposed to civil disobedience, he was the special counsel and later chief counsel for the NAACP (1938–62). He played a key role in obtaining US Supreme Court desegregation decisions, including *Brown* v. *Board of Education of Topeka* (1954, 1955). A US Appeals Court judge (1961–65), he was appointed solicitor general in 1965. In 1967 he became the first black to be appointed an associate justice of the US Supreme Court. On the court, he consistently championed civil rights and civil liberties.

Marshall Islands, group of atolls and reefs in W Pacific Ocean, E of the Caroline Islands. Administered as part of the US Trust Territory of the Pacific Islands, it is comprised of two great chains, Ralik (W) and Ratak (E), which run almost parallel NW to SE, covering an ocean area of 4,500sq mi (11,655sq km). Native inhabitants are Micronesian; Kwajalein in Ralik Chain, and Majoru in Ratak Chain are government centers. Annexed to Germany 1885, the group was taken by Japan 1914; Japan received a mandate for islands from the League of Nations 1920; taken by US forces in WWII (1944). The residents of Bikini and Eniwetok were evacuated, and the United States conducted atomic bomb tests on the two islands from 1946–54. In the 1970s inhabitants returned to the islands, but in 1978 Bikinians were evacuated again because of high levels of radioactivity in their bodies. In 1979 the Marshalls became self-governing and the Trust Territory was scheduled for termination in the early 1980s. Exports: copra, sugar, coffee. Industries: coconuts, fishing, subsistence farming. Total land area: approx. 70sq mi (181sq km). Pop. 20,206. *See also:* Pacific Islands, Trust Territory of the.

Marshall Plan, a program of economic aid to Europe proposed by Sec. of State George C. Marshall in 1947. The European Recovery Act (1948) authorized the plan. The United States spent about $14,000,000,000 in 5 years to help the European nations recover from the destruction of World War II. The plan was considered a great economic, social, and political success.

Marsh Birds, birds with toes adapted for walking on marshy vegetation. Some, such as the coot, are aquatic. Many, including crane, limpkin, and seriema, are long-legged; others, including some rails, are tiny and live secretively on the forest floor. Order Gruiformes.

Marsh Deer, or **Swamp Deer,** deer of E South American wetlands. It is reddish-brown with black legs and doubly forked antlers. Height: to 3ft (.91m); weight: to 200lb (91kg). Family Cervidae; species *Blastocerus dichotomus.*

Marsh Gas. *See* Methane.

Marsh Hawk, or hen harrier, Northern Hemisphere hawk with gray or brownish plumage, sometimes with white spots. Length: 20in (51cm). Species *Circus cyaneus.*

Marsh Mallow, perennial plant native to E Europe and naturalized in salt marshes of the E United States. It has pink flowers. Height: 3–4ft (0.9–1.2m). Family Malvaceae; species *Althea officinalis.*

Marsh Marigold, or cowslip, perennial herbaceous plant native to cold and temperate swamps of the Northern Hemisphere. It has hollow stems, kidney-shaped leaves, and large pink, white, or yellow flowers. There are about 20 species. Family Ranunculaceae; genus *Caltha.*

Marsilius of Padua (c.1275–1342), Italian political theorist, also known as Marsiglio dei Mainardini. He studied medicine in Paris (1311–20) and wrote the *Defensor Pacis* (1324), an antipapist landmark in political philosophy. This work refuted the pope's claims to "plenitude of power" even over secular matters, and instead said that the church should be subordinate to the state. He described the state as the great unifying power of society, with its power derived from the people through a popularly elected government. In 1326 he fled to Emperor Louis of Bavaria, where he spent the rest of his life.

Marston Moor, battle site 7 mi (11km) west of York, England. It was the scene of the decisive defeat of royalist forces under Prince Rupert by the Parliamentarians under Fairfax (July 2, 1644) in the English Civil War.

Marsupial, any mammal of the order Marsupialia, which consists of the kangaroos, wombats, bandicoots, opossums, and others, native to the New World and Australia. Most develop no placenta; females have a pouch (marsupium) on the abdomen containing the teats and serving to carry the young. Marsupials usually have numerous teeth; some over 44. Young are almost embryonic at birth.

Marsupial Frog, South American tree frog. Females carry fertilized eggs in a pouch on their backs. The young may hatch as tadpoles or remain in the pouch until metamorphosed, depending on species. *Gastrotheca marsupiata* is green with dark spots on its back and has striped legs; length: to 3in (7.6cm). *See also* Tree Frog.

Marten, carnivorous mammal of the weasel family found in forested areas in Eurasia and North and South America. Long-bodied and short-legged, they are hunted for their fur. The dark brown skins of the Siberian *Martes zibellina* are the most valuable but the skins of the lighter stone or beech *Martes foina* are also prized. Family Mustelidae.

Martha's Vineyard, island in Atlantic Ocean off SW coast of Cape Cod, SE Massachusetts; named by explorer Bartholomew Gosnold for his daughter and the grapevines he found when he visited the island in 1602; site of Duke's County Historical Society museum housed in 1765 home. Connected to mainland by ferry, it is a summer tourist center. First settled by English 1642. Area: 108sq mi (280sq km).

Martí, José (1853–95), Cuban poet and essayist. Known as the "apostle" of Cuban independence, he was idealistic and visionary. His verse reflected his belief that poetry and politics were inseparable. He was forced into exile and lived in New York before returning to Cuba, where he died fighting the Spanish. Latin Americans have been strongly influenced by his works and career. *Ismaelillo* (1882), *Versos libres* (published posthumously), and *Versos sencillos* (1891) contain his best poems. *The America of José Martí* (1953) is a collection of essays.

Martial(is), Marcus Valerius (c.40–c.104), Roman poet. He lived in Rome from about AD 64 enjoying the patronage of the emperors Domitian and Titus and the friendship of Juvenal and Quintilian. He wrote witty epigrammatic poems in new meters and forms. These were collected in 15 books. In AD 98 he retired to his native Spain.

Martial Law, the suspension of internal civil judicial procedures, and their replacement by direct military rule by the executive branch of government. In the United States, martial law has been used only infrequently, such as in the border states during the Civil War and in San Francisco following the 1906 earthquake.

Martin, Saint (died c. 397), often called St Martin of Tours. He was born in what is now Hungary but moved to Italy and then France. In 371 the people of Tours chose him their bishop. He preached to spread the faith and to combat the Arian heresy. One of many tales about this popular French saint is that he divided his cloak with a beggar.

Martin I, Roman Catholic pope (649–55) and saint. He stressed papal authority over all and refused to obey the emperor's edict forbidding religious discussions.

He was arrested, publicly degraded, and exiled. He died shortly thereafter, being the last pope to be martyred.

Martin. *See* Purple Martin; Swallow.

Martinique, island in Windward Islands, West Indies; an overseas French dept.; volcanic island is largest of Lesser Antilles. Fort de France is capital and chief trade center; Mt Pelée volcano (N) is highest peak, 4,429ft (1,351m). Island has rain forests (N), which slope to plains and coastal valleys where agriculture is centered. French is the official language; site of technical colleges, Institut Henri Vizioz; birthplace of Empress Josephine. Discovered 1502 by Christopher Columbus, it was inhabited by Caribs until displaced by French settlers from 1635; attacked 17th century by Dutch and British, it was officially French after Napoleonic Wars; became overseas dept. 1946. Exports: sugar, rum, fruits, cocoa, tobacco, vanilla, vegetables. Agriculture and tourism are major industries: Area: 425sq mi (1,101sq km). Pop. 342,000.

Martin v. Hunter's Lessee (1816), landmark US Supreme Court case in which Chief Justice Marshall upheld the court's right to reverse state court decisions that conflicted with rights granted under the Constitution.

Martynia, or unicorn plant, rank-growing, annual wild flower of S and central United States. Leaves and stems are covered with sticky hairs. Flowers are white, yellow, or violet and seed pods resemble unicorn's horn. Height: to 18in (46cm). Family Martyniaceae; species *Martynia proboscidea.*

Marvell, Andrew (1621–78), English poet and satirist. Though a Puritan and a friend of Milton, he genuinely admired both Cromwell and Charles I and was member of parliament for Hull during the Commonwealth and the Restoration. His poetry, combining intellectual wit and passion, includes "The Garden" (*c.*1653), "Bermudas" (*c.*1653), and "To His Coy Mistress" (published 1681).

Marx, Karl (1818–83), German social philosopher and political activist, founder (with Friedrich Engels) of the world Communist movement. He studied history, philosophy, and law and received a doctorate from the University of Jena in 1841. He rejected the philosophical idealism of G.W.F. Hegel but accepted his dialectical method and combined it with the philosophical materialism of Ludwig Feuerbach and Moses Hess to produce his own approach of dialectical materialism. In Paris after 1843 he met Friedrich Engels, with whom he was to share a lifelong collaboration. His association with such French radicals as P.J. Proudhon, Louis Blanc, and the followers of Saint-Simon and Fourier deepened his socialist commitments.

In Paris he wrote *Toward the Critique of the Hegelian Philosophy of Right* (1844), which proclaimed that "religion was the opium of the people." He also wrote, with Engels, *The German Ideology* (1845–46), describing inevitable laws of history. Expelled from France, he went to Brussels, published a newspaper, and joined the Communist League, an international workers' society, for which he and Engels wrote their epochal *Communist Manifesto* (1848). From 1848, Marx was to devote his life to scholarly and political activity aimed at analyzing and overthrowing capitalism. Expelled from Belgium (1848), he participated in the revolutionary movements in France and Germany. Expelled from both those countries, he finally went to London (1849), where he was to live until his death.

Although Engels assisted him financially, Marx's London years were largely spent under conditions of poverty, illness, and family tragedy as he toiled on research in the British Museum and produced a stream of writings, including *The Class Struggles in France, 1848–1850* (1950) and *Das Kapital* (3 vols., 1867, 1885, 1894), whose last two volumes were edited by Engels. The monumental *Kapital,* systematically criticizing what Marx saw as capitalism's exploitative and self-destructive tendencies, became the "bible of the working class." In 1864 he became one of the founders of the International Workingmen's Association (the "First International"), an association of labor, reform, and radical movements. His defense of the Paris Commune (1871) in speeches and *The Civil War in France* (1871) gave him an international reputation, and he became the leading spirit of the International. He denounced both the nonrevolutionary reformism of British labor leaders and the anarchism advocated by Mikhail Bakunin. Split into factions, the International dissolved in 1874. Marx, however, continued to be consulted by many as a kind of socialist prophet. During this period he generally, as in *Critique of the Gotha Programme* (1875), advocated a hard line and less collaboration with bourgeois elements. Since his death the ideas of Marx have continued to have immense influence. *See also* Communist Manifesto.

Marx Brothers, US vaudeville and film comedians. They were **Chico (Leonard)** (1891–1961), piano player with a broad Italian accent; **Harpo (Arthur)** (1893–1964), mute harp player; **Groucho (Julius)** (1895–1977), moustached wisecracker; and **Gummo (Milton)** (1897–1977) and **Zeppo (Herbert)** (1901–79), who both left the team early. Their films included *Animal Crackers* (1930), *Duck Soup* (1933), and *A Night at the Opera* (1935). In 1947, Groucho became the host of "You Bet Your Life," one of TV's first quiz shows.

Marxism, school of socialism that arose in 19th-century Europe as a response to the growth of industrial capitalism, named for Karl Marx. Marx articulated an economic interpretation of history; all changes in social structure were determined by changes in productive activity. Increased productivity created more complex and oppressive forms of social organization and an increase in the numbers of the proletariat. The misery necessarily induced by capitalism would also produce an inevitable working-class revolution that would destroy capitalist society. Marxism, both a general theory and a scientific method of investigating the nature of economic systems, became a party ideology in the 1860s.

Mary, Saint, the mother of Jesus Christ, often called the Blessed Virgin Mary. The Gospels tell of events in her life. The angel Gabriel appeared to her (the Annunciation) to tell her that she would conceive a child, by the power of the Holy Spirit, who would be called the Son of God. Thus she was a virgin at the time of the birth. The Gospels also tell of the birth of Jesus and of his mother's presence at his Crucifixion. Over the centuries beliefs developed about Mary in the Roman Catholic Church. The doctrine of the Assumption holds that Mary "at the conclusion of her life on earth was assumed body and soul into heavenly glory." The dogma of the Immaculate Conception holds that Mary from her conception was free of original sin. The Virgin Mary (Madonna) has been a favorite subject of painters and sculptors.

Mary, Queen of Scots (1542–87), daughter of James V of Scotland, whom she succeeded (1542). She married Francis II of France (1558), but after his death (1560) she returned to Scotland, determined to restore Roman Catholicism there. Her marriage to Henry, Lord Darnley (1565), strengthened her claim to the English throne. Darnley's implication in the murder of David Rizzio, her favorite (1566), occasioned her connivance at Darnley's death (1567). She then married the earl of Bothwell, her nobles revolted, and she abdicated (1567). Escaping from Lochleven (1568), she fled to England, where Elizabeth I imprisoned her. Her repeated intrigues in the Ridolfi Plot (1572) and the Babington Plot (1586) led Elizabeth to consent reluctantly to her execution.

Mary I, or **Mary Tudor** (1516–58), queen of England. The daughter of Henry VIII and Catherine of Aragon, she was known as "Bloody Mary." Her courageous backing of Catherine (1532–33) caused Henry's severe displeasure, but she was later reconciled with him and declared capable of inheriting the crown. On Edward VI's death she overcame Lady Jane Grey's challenge for the throne and became queen (1553). Her determination to reintroduce Roman Catholicism in England occasioned the major errors of her reign: her marriage to Philip of Spain (1554) and persecution of her Protestant subjects. News of the loss of Calais to the French (1558) hastened her death.

Mary II (1662–94), Queen of England, Scotland, and Ireland, wife of William III. Although her father, James II, was a Roman Catholic, Mary was a Protestant. She married the Dutch noble William of Orange in 1677, and her support enabled them to become joint sovereigns in 1689 following the Glorious Revolution that deposed James. She died from smallpox, and William then ruled alone.

Maryland, state in the E United States, on the Atlantic Ocean, just N of Virginia.

Land and Economy. Maryland is divided nearly in half by Chesapeake Bay, a 200-mile (320-km)-long arm of the Atlantic. E of the bay lies a coastal plain, a center of agriculture. To the W the land is rolling; the Blue Ridge Mts cross the W tip of the state. The Potomac River forms the irregular W boundary of most of Maryland. Baltimore, on the W shore of Chesapeake Bay, is the heart of the state's industry and one of the nation's leading ports. Shellfishing in Chesapeake Bay, although once important, has declined because of pollution.

People. Maryland's first settlers were largely English, and their descendants predominated in the E. The industrialized Baltimore area drew immigrants of varied stock, but about 80% of the people were born in the United States. Nearly that percentage resides in urban areas. Baltimore is only about 30mi (48km) NE of Washington, D.C., and their metropolitan areas virtually merge to form a continuous urbanized zone.

Education and Research. There are about 50 institutions of higher education. The University of Maryland is state-controlled. Best-known of the private institutions is Johns Hopkins University in Baltimore; its medical school is world-famous; the US Naval Academy is at Annapolis. Many scientific establishments doing research for the armed services and other agencies of the US government are in Maryland, close to Washington.

History. A charter for a large territory that included the present Maryland was granted by Charles I of England to Cecilius Calvert, 2nd Lord Baltimore, in 1632. His brother Leonard led the expedition that made the first settlements in 1634. Other communities sprang up in the late 17th century, and black slaves were imported to work tobacco plantations. Despite loyalist sentiment in some rural counties, Maryland was active in the drive for US independence. In the Revolution its troops were ranked among the best in the Continental army. In 1791, Maryland ceded a section of land on the Potomac River to create the District of Columbia, site of the national capital of Washington, D.C. In the Civil War, Maryland was one of the border states that did not secede from the Union, but its citizens served in both armies. The Battle of Antietam, one of the war's fiercest, was fought in W Maryland on Sept. 17, 1862. After the war, industry developed rapidly around Baltimore. In both world wars, the city was a major center of war matériel production. During the 1970s, Vice-Pres. Spiro Agnew, a former governor of Maryland, and Marvin Mandel were both found guilty of criminal activities while serving as governor.

PROFILE

Admitted to Union: April 28, 1788; 7th of the 13 original states to ratify the US Constitution
US Congressmen: Senate, 2; House of Representatives, 8
Population: 4,216,446 (1980); rank, 18th
Capital: Annapolis, 31,740 (1980)
Chief cities: Baltimore, 786,775; Dundalk, 85,577; Towson, 77,809
State legislature: Senate, 43; House of Delegates, 142
Area: 10,577sq mi (27,394sq km); rank, 42d
Elevation: Highest, 3,360ft (1,024m), Backbone Mt; lowest, sea level
Industries (major products): steel, copper, metal products, aircraft, ships and boats, processed foods, chemicals, apparel
Agriculture (major products): tobacco, corn, soybeans, apples, poultry
Minerals (major): stone, cement
State nickname: Old Line State, Free State
State motto: fatti maschii, parole femine ("Manly Deeds, Womanly Words")
State bird: Baltimore oriole
State flower: black-eyed Susan
State tree: white oak

Mary Magdalene, an early follower of Jesus Christ, from the village of Magdala on the W bank of the Sea of Galilee. According to the Gospels, Christ freed her of seven demons; she accompanied Christ on his preaching in Galilee, witnessed the Crucifixion and burial, and was the first person to see Christ resurrected. She has been confused with Mary of Bethany (sister of Lazarus) and a repentant prostitute who anointed Christ's feet. A Roman Catholic saint, her feast day is July 22.

Masaccio, real name Tommaso Cassai or Tommaso di Ser Giovanni di Mone (1401–28), Italian painter. He worked in Florence. His classically balanced compositions show careful modeling of figures through use of light and shadow. He was influenced by Brunelleschi in his use of space and perspective, as shown in his fresco "The Trinity with Donors." With Masolino, he worked on the "Madonna with St. Anne" frescoes. Other famous works include the altarpieces for San Maria del Carmine in Pisa and the frescoes in the Brancacci Chapel in Florence.

Masai, Nilotic African people of Kenya and Tanzania, consisting of several subgroups. They are characteristically tall and slender. Their patrilineal, egalitarian society is based on nomadic pastoralism, cattle being equated with wealth. The traditional Masai kraal is a group of mud houses surrounded by a thorn fence. They have a system of age groups whereby individuals move together through a hierarchy consisting of junior and senior warriors followed by junior and senior elders.

Masaryk, Jan (1886–1948), Czechoslovak diplomat, son of Tomáš. Foreign minister under Eduard Beneš, he assumed the same role in the government-in-exile in London. He was also vice-premier. After the Allied

Marx Brothers

Mt. Vernon Place, Baltimore, Maryland

Boston, Massachusetts

victory, he returned to head the foreign ministry once again, attempting to resist increasing Communist domination. His fatal fall from his office window in 1948 was ruled a suicide by the government.

Masaryk, Tomáš (1850–1937), Czechoslovak statesman, first president of Czechoslovakia (1918–35). This noted writer devoted his life to gaining independence for Czechoslovakia. His Czechoslovak National Council was recognized by the Allies in 1918 as the provisional government of the future state. In 1918, Masaryk was elected president by acclamation. Minority problems and the fragmentation of political life were the two major problems during his tenure.

Mascarene Islands, group of islands in Indian Ocean, E of Madagascar. Discovered 16th century by Portuguese, comprised of islands of Mauritius and Rodriguez (part of the island country of Mauritius), and Réunion (belongs to France).

Mascon, any of several high-density regions of the moon's surface that produce stronger gravitational effects than the surrounding areas, causing noticeable perturbations in the orbits of spacecraft. The word is derived from the term "mass concentration" and the phenomenon seems to indicate that the lunar interior is not uniform.

Masefield, John (1878–1967), English poet and novelist. A writer of inventive and rhythmical verse, he was Poet Laureate from 1930 until his death. His long narrative poems include *The Everlasting Mercy* (1911), innovative in its use of colloquialism, and *Reynard the Fox* (1919). His most famous poem is "Sea Fever." He also wrote verse dramas and adventure novels.

Maser, a device using "inverted" populations of atoms (that is, atoms artificially kept in states of higher energy than normal) to provide amplification of radio signals. The term is an acronym for "microwave amplification by stimulated emission of radiation." The principle of the maser was first discovered by Charles Townes of Columbia University, who later received the Nobel Prize for his work. The first maser used electrostatic plates to separate high-energy ammonium atoms from low-energy ones. Radiation of a certain frequency would then stimulate the high-energy ammonium atoms to emit similar radiation and strengthen the signal. The very narrow frequency emitted made the ammonium maser one of the most accurate "atomic clocks" known. *See also* Laser.

Maseru, town in W Lesotho, S Africa, on the Caledon River; since 1966, it has served as the capital of the independent kingdom of Lesotho. Originally an obscure trading town, it flourished when made capital of British Basutoland protectorate 1869–71, 1884–1966; trade, transportation, and administrative center. Industries: candles, retreaded tires, carpets. Pop. 29,000.

Mashhad, city in NE Iran; capital of Khorasan prov. City served as capital of Persia under Nadir Shah (18th century); strategically important in 19th and 20th centuries because of proximity to Russian and Afghan borders. Name (meaning "shrine") is derived from Shiite shrine located here; it has tombs of Caliph Harun and Imam Reza, two ancient Shiite holy people; site of university (1947); important trade center and junction on caravan route. Industries: carpets, textiles, pharmaceuticals, food processing. Pop. 425,000.

Masinissa (c. 238–149 BC), Numidian king, fought against the Romans in Spain in the second Punic War, but changed sides in 206 and helped bring about the downfall of Carthage. He was supported in his North

African kingdom by the Romans and gradually annexed Carthaginian lands. His reign greatly organized and settled the Numidian people.

Masochism, taking pleasure in being hurt or abused physically or psychologically. Masochism is often, though not always, linked with sexual arousal and gratification, and may take the form of a desire to be dominated or mistreated in one's relations with others.

Mason, George (1725–92), US Revolutionary patriot, b. Fairfax co, Va. He was elected to the Virginia House of Burgesses (1759). A strong defender of liberty and a constitutional philosopher, he wrote the Fairfax Resolves (1774), describing the colonial position in relation to the crown, and the Virginia Bill of Rights (1776), which Thomas Jefferson used as a model to the preamble of the Declaration of Independence. Mason served in the Virginia House of Delegates (1776–88). He was a delegate to the 1787 Constitutional Convention, but objected to the centralization of powers concept and refused to sign the document.

Mason-Dixon Line, boundary between Pennsylvania and Maryland, surveyed by Charles Mason and Jeremiah Dixon (1763–67). It is the traditional line between the North and South.

Masque, allegorical dramatic presentations given in England during the late 16th and early 17th century. They consisted of verse, comedy with plot, and, as an essential feature, an entrance for a group of masked dancers. Noted for their decor, famous masques include *The Masque of Blackness* (1605) and *The Masque of Beauty* (1608).

Mass, central act of worship in the Roman Catholic Church. It involves a number of prayers, rituals, and the Eucharistic service. In the Church of England, high churchmen celebrate the Eucharist, or the Mass. *See also* Eucharist.

Mass, measure of the quantity of matter in a body. Mass may be defined in two ways. The gravitational mass of a body is determined by its mutual attraction to another, reference body, such as the Earth, as expressed in Newton's law of gravitation. Spring scales and platform balances provide a measure of gravitational mass. The inertial mass of a body is determined by its resistance to a change in its state of motion, as expressed in the second law of motion. Inertia balances provide a measure of inertial mass. According to Einstein's principle of equivalence, upon which his general theory of relativity is based, the inertial mass and the gravitational mass of a given body are equivalent.

Massachusetts, state in the NE United States, on the Atlantic Ocean, in the New England region.

Land and Economy. The coastline is indented by bays and inlets, creating many small harbors. Fishhook-shaped Cape Cod in the SE is a distinctive feature. To the W the land is rolling. The broad valley of the Connecticut River traverses the state from N to S. The Berkshire Hills are in the W. Besides the Connecticut, the principal rivers are the Housatonic (W) and the Merrimack (NE). Many smaller streams supply abundant water power to generate electricity. The Connecticut Valley is a notable farming area.

People. Massachusetts is one of the most densely populated states in the country, with about 85% living in the urban areas, principally in the greater Boston area and the Connecticut Valley. Some are descended from the first English settlers, but in the 19th century many overseas immigrants, largely Irish, Poles, and Italians, were drawn to employment in the factories.

About 85% of the population was born in the United States.

Education. A pioneer in public education, Massachusetts has many universities and colleges. Harvard University at Cambridge (1636) is the oldest US university. The Massachusetts Institute of Technology, also at Cambridge, is a major center of scientific training and research. The University of Massachusetts, with its central campus at Amherst, is the state university.

History. The first settlement was made in 1620 at Plymouth on Massachusetts Bay by the Pilgrims, a group of English settlers seeking religious freedom. Boston was founded by English Puritans in 1630 and became the center of the colony of Massachusetts Bay. Through the years several wars were waged against Indians who ravaged frontier towns. Massachusetts strongly resisted the policies of the British crown that led to the Revolution. The first fight of the war was at Lexington on April 19, 1775; Bunker Hill (June 17, 1775) was the last battle in the colony. After achieving statehood, Massachusetts prospered. Its fishing and whaling fleets were famous, and large vessels from Massachusetts carried on a lucrative worldwide trade. Manufacturing flourished, especially in textiles and shoes. The 19th century was a time of intellectual ferment, marked by the work of writers such as Ralph Waldo Emerson, Henry David Thoreau, and Nathaniel Hawthorne; educators like Horace Mann; and abolitionists. In the Civil War, Massachusetts was a foremost supporter of the Union with men, money, and supplies. During the 1920s traditional industries such as textiles declined, but later in the century the economy was revitalized through the aerospace and electronics industries. The Kennedys, a nationally prominent political family, are from Massachusetts.

PROFILE

Admitted to Union: Feb. 6, 1788; 6th of 13 original states to ratify the US Constitution
US Congressmen: Senate, 2; House of Representatives, 12
Population: 5,737,037 (1980); rank, 11th
Capital: Boston, 562,994 (1980)
Chief cities: Boston, Worcester, 161,799; Springfield, 152,319; New Bedford, 98,478
State legislature: Senate, 40; House of Representatives, 240
Area: 8,257sq mi (21,386sq km); rank, 45th
Elevation: Highest, 3,491ft (1,065m), Mt Greylock; lowest, sea level
Industries (major products): electrical machinery, metal products, communications equipment, shoes, apparel, processed foods
Agriculture (major products): cranberries, dairy products, poultry, cigar-wrapper tobacco
Minerals (major): stone, sand, gravel
State nickname: Bay State
State motto: Ense petit placidam sub libertate quietem ("By the sword she seeks quiet peace under liberty")
State bird: chickadee
State flower: mayflower
State tree: American elm

Massachusetts Bay Colony, one of the earliest settlements in North America. It was founded as a trading company at Salem (1629). The charter brought to the colony by Puritan Governor John Winthrop (1630) encouraged a large migration of Puritans seeking religious and economic opportunities. This colony was not administered from England, since all the officers lived in the colony. There was an assembly, called a General Court, with representatives from the town meeting. The colony spread to Boston, Charlestown, and parts of Connecticut. Religious dissidents Roger Smith and

Anne Hutchinson were expelled from the colony and settled in Rhode Island. The British crown sought to end self-government for the colony, the charter was cancelled (1684), and the area was put under direct English rule. It merged with Plymouth and Maine in 1691. *See also* Puritanism.

Massachusetts Government Act (1774), one of Britain's Intolerable Acts. Britain virtually annulled the Massachusetts charter by appointing officials who had formerly been elected, limiting public meetings, and naming judges. In reaction, the colony adopted the Suffolk Resolves, and except for Boston, which was under the crown, acted as an independent state. *See also* Intolerable Acts;

Mass Action, Law of, principle that a chemical reaction rate is proportional to the product of the concentrations of each reactant.

Massasauga, North American rattlesnake found in central and SW United States. It has large black blotches down its back and spots along sides. Length: to 30in (76cm). Family Viperidae; species *Sistrurus catenatus*. *See also* Rattlesnake.

Massasoit (1580?–1661), American Indian. He was chief of the Wampanoag tribe of Massachusetts and in Rhode Island. In 1621 he made a treaty with John Carver of Plymouth Colony that the Indians would not harm the Pilgrims if the Pilgrims respected the lands and rights of the Indians. He and his braves shared the first Thanksgiving with the Pilgrims. There were no wars between whites and Wampanoags as long as Massasoit was alive, and the Indians helped the Pilgrims to survive in their new country.

Mass Defect, the difference in mass between the total rest mass of protons and neutrons from which a particular nucleus is formed and the slightly lower mass of the nucleus itself. The mass defect is converted into energy so that the particles can be bound tightly together to form the nucleus. *See also* Binding Energy.

Massenet, Jules (1842–1912), French composer who dominated French lyric opera of the late 19th century. He composed many operas including *Le Cid* (1885), *Werther* (1892), and *Thérèse*. His two masterpieces are considered to be *Manon* (1894) and *Thaïs* (1894).

Massif Central, extensive mountainous plateau region in S central France; core is Auvergne Mts, which extend to Cévennes (SE) and Causses (SW). Hydroelectric power is produced along W edge, agriculture is carried on in valleys, grazing on mountain slopes; large deposits of coal and kaolin (for china) are mined. Highest peak is Puy de Sancy, 6,187ft (1,887m). Area: 33,000sq mi (85,470sq km), about 16% of France's area.

Massive, Mount, mountain in Sawatch Range of the Rocky Mts, in central Colorado. It is 2nd-highest of US Rockies, 14,421ft (4,398m).

Mass Production, manufacture of goods in large quantities by standardizing and assembly-line methods. In the United States, it began in the cotton mills after Eli Whitney's revolutionary invention of the cotton gin (1793). The factory system, using unskilled labor (often women and children) to tend large machines, replaced the skilled worker using hand tools and helped to create industrial cities. Many of the methods were brought from England, but US inventors like Samuel Colt used interchangeable parts and precision measurements in the firearms industry. The proving ground for the assembly line, with parts on a conveyor belt moving past stationary workers, was Henry Ford's Highland Park plant (1913). Later, machines took over more and more of the repetitious labor. More recent developments include automated controlling devices, computers, and electronic sensors.

Mass Spectrograph, instrument for separating ions according to their mass (or more precisely, according to their charge-to-mass ratio). In the simplest types, the ions are first accelerated by an electric field and then deflected by a strong magnetic field; the lighter the ions the greater the deflection. By varying the field, ions of different mass can be focused in sequence onto a photographic plate and a record of charge-to-mass ratios obtained. In a mass spectrometer the ions are detected electrically. The apparatus is used to measure atomic and molecular mass, identify isotopes, determine chemical structure.

Mastai-Ferretti, Giovanni. *See* Pius IX.

Mastectomy, removal of the breast by surgical operation, usually because of the presence of a malignant tumor. The radical mastectomy involves removal of adjacent tissue, chest muscle, and underarm and chest-wall lymph nodes. In the modified radical mastectomy, the pectoral muscles are preserved. Another alternative is the quadrantectomy or removal of that quarter of the breast containing the tumor.

Masters, Edgar Lee (1869–1950), US author, b. Garnett, Kan. As a child, he lived near the Spoon River in Illinois. From this experience came his most notable work, *Spoon River Anthology* (1915), a series of free-verse epitaphs in the form of monologues. Never so successful in poetry again as in that work, he spent many of his later years writing biographies.

Mastiff, massive watch and fighting dog (working group) bred in England over 2000 years ago. Properly called Old English mastiff, it has a broad, rounded head with dark-colored, blunt, square muzzle; small, V-shaped ears lying close to the cheeks; a deep-chested body; wide-set legs with large feet; and a high-set, long tail. The short, coarse, double coat is apricot, silver fawn, dark fawn, or brindle—all with dark muzzle, ears, and nose. Average size: 27–33in (69–84cm) high at shoulder; 165–185lb (74–83kg). *See also* Working Dog.

Mastodon, extinct Mastodontidae, family of proboscideans existing from Oligocene through Pleistocene times. Differing from elephants in construction and placement of teeth, they had lower as well as upper tusks. The rusty-haired American mastodon was hunted by early man. Height: 9ft (2.7m).

Mastoiditis, inflammation of the cavity of the mastoid process (bone lying behind the ear) or of its cells.

Masurian Lakes, low-lying area in NE Poland, covered by over 2,700 lakes; scene of heavy fighting early in WWI; assigned to Poland at Potsdam Conference, 1945.

Matabele, also called Ndebele, Bantu people of southern Africa, formed from Nguni (a Bantu subdivision) outcasts of South Africa in the 1820s and 1830s. Under the Zulu general Mzilikazi, they increased their numbers and migrated north, where they later conflicted with British settlers. Defeated in 1896, they settled into an agricultural and pastoral existence.

Mata Hari (1876–1917), Dutch courtesan and double agent, b. Gertrud Margarete Zelle. She was the wife of a Dutch colonial officer, with whom she lived in Java until 1901. She deserted him and traveled to Europe, calling herself Mata Hari and claiming to be a former temple dancer of Javanese birth. She became well known in Paris, and was in the pay of both French and German intelligence services. She was executed by the French as a spy during World War I.

Matamata, side-necked turtle found in South America. It is a mass of bumps, warts, and fringes of skin. The large head is flat and triangular with a long proboscis. Length: to 16in (41cm). Family Chelidae; species *Chelys fimbriata*. *See also* Turtle.

Matamoros, city in NE Mexico, near the Rio Grande estuary, opposite Brownsville, Tex.; formerly called San Juan de los Esteros, it was renamed 1851 in honor of Mexican independence leader Marino Matamoros; fell 1846 to Zachary Taylor's forces during the Mexican War; site of highway linking Mexico with the United States. Industries: trade, fishing. Pop. 187,000.

Maté, or yerba maté, South American evergreen shrub or tree. In the wild, it is a tree; cultivated, it is a small shrub. The dried leaves are used to make a stimulating beverage called Paraguay tea. Height: to 20ft (6m). Family Aquifoliaceae; species *Ilex paraguayensis*.

Materialism, the philosophical contention that only matter, or physical entities, are real or existent. Everything real is explicable in terms of material constituents and their motions, interactions, and relationships. Materialism may or may not involve specific claims about the nature of history as it did with Karl Marx, or about values, as it did with the Epicureans. Many scientists are also materialists. *See also* Marx, Karl.

Mathematical Model, any set of formulae or equations that describe the behavior of a physical system in purely mathematical terms. Model theory, in mathematics, is concerned with the study of axiomatic systems in terms of objects, called models of the systems, that are constructed on the assumption that all the axioms in the system are true to them.

Mathematics, study concerned originally with the properties of numbers and space; now more generally concerned with deductions made from assumptions about abstract entities. Mathematics is often divided into applied mathematics, which involves the use of mathematical reasoning in engineering, physics, chemistry, economics, etc, and pure mathematics, which is purely abstract reasoning based on axioms. However, the two fields are not totally independent—the subjects of pure mathematics are often chosen for their application to specific problems and the abstract results of pure mathematics, such as group theory and differential geometry, often find practical uses. The main divisions of pure mathematics are into geometry and algebra. Often analysis, reasoning using the concept of limits, is distinguished from algebra; it includes the differential and integral calculus. *See also* Algebra; Arithmetic; Calculus; Geometry; Set theory; Trigonometry.

Mather, Cotton (1663–1728), American Puritan minister, b. Boston. The son of Increase Mather, he had a great influence on Massachusetts religious and political life. He wrote a manifesto (1689) in defense of the colonial imprisonment of royal Gov. Edmund Andros and, during the Salem witchcraft trials (1629–93), he supported the belief in demoniac possession as demonstrated in his *Wonders of the Invisible World* (1693). Works published during his life numbered over 400, including *The Ecclesiastical History of New England* (1702). He was one of the founders of Yale University, and was elected to the British Royal Society (1713).

Mather, Increase (1639–1723), American Puritan minister, b. Dorchester, Mass. He was minister of Boston's Second (North) Church (1664–1723). From the pulpit Mather and his son Cotton influenced both political and religious life in the colonies. During the revolts of 1688–89, when Massachusetts lost its charter, he represented the colony's interests in England and obtained a new colonial charter (1691). His writings include *Cases of Conscience* (1693), which helped to end the Salem witchcraft trials. He served as president of Harvard College (1685–1701).

Matilda, or **Maude,** (1102–1167), empress of Germany, daughter of Henry I of England, mother of Henry II. She married Henry V of Germany (1114). Although she was recognized as Henry I's successor, Stephen became king (1135). Landing in England (1139), Matilda gained general acceptance (1141), but Stephen besieged her in Oxford (1142) and forced her to leave England.

Matisse, Henri (Émile) (1869–1954), French painter and sculptor. His early painting included naturalistic compositions in neutral tones. He was greatly influenced by Paul Cézanne's cubism and by fauvism, and he developed a style of painting that was highly colored, with well-defined subject matter. Throughout his work, there is an emphasis on design and pattern, as in his large movement painting "The Dance." He made numerous collages using bright colors and designs cut from construction paper, as well as many church decorations in stained glass. As a sculptor, he worked briefly in terra cotta and bronze and treated his figures in a simple and rhythmic manner.

Matriarchy, hypothetical form of society that is not only matrilineal (transmission of group membership by the female line) but in which women are household heads and govern the group. *See also* Patriarchy.

Matrix (pl. matrices), array of numbers in rows and columns. The number of rows need not equal the number of columns. Matrices do not have single quantitative values in the same way that determinants do. They are more general mathematical entities that can be combined (added and multiplied) according to certain rules. They are useful in the study of transformations of coordinate systems and in solving sets of simultaneous equations.

Matsu (Ma tsu), island off SE China, 100mi (161km) NW of Taiwan, in East China Sea. After Communist takeover of China's mainland 1949, Matsu remained a Nationalist-held outpost and has since been the target of propaganda and artillery from the mainland.

Matsuyama, city in NW Shikoku, Japan, on the Inland Sea; capital of Ehime prefecture; site of daimyo castle, museum. Industries: textiles, paper, chemicals, machinery, mining, cattle. Pop. 367,000.

Matter, the substance of the universe. Ordinary matter is made up of electrons, protons, and neutrons. (The neutron is an unstable particle that splits into an electron and proton within about 1,000 seconds if left to itself.) These three particles are combined into elements, an ordered series of atoms having between one and about 106 protons in their nuclei. (Many other subatomic particles can be produced at high energies and live for short periods of time.) The elements other than hydrogen and helium were built up by thermonuclear reactions in stars; we are literally made up of stardust. Four forces are known to be associated with matter. At large distances, all unchanged matter exerts

Cotton Mather

François Mauriac

Mauritania

an attractive force; this is called gravitation. Changed particles exert an attractive or repulsive electromagnetic force. This force accounts for nearly all everyday phenomena—the sense of touch, for example, is dependent on the repulsion of molecules at close range. Two other forces hold the protons in the nucleus together; these are called the weak and strong nuclear forces.

Matter, States of, a classification of matter according to its structural characteristics. Four states of matter are generally recognized: solid, liquid, gas, and plasma. Any one element or compound may exist sequentially or simultaneously in two or more of these states: for example, water, ice, and water vapor can all exist at one temperature and pressure. Solids may be crystalline (have a regularly repeated molecular structure), as in salt or steel; or amorphous, as in tar or glass. Liquids have molecules that can flow past one another but which remain almost as close as in a solid. In a gas, molecules are so far from one another that they travel in relatively straight lines until they collide. In a plasma, such as a star, temperatures are so high that atoms are torn apart into electrons and nuclei.

Matterhorn, mountain peak in Switzerland, in the Pennine Alps, on Swiss-Italo border 6mi (10km) SE of Zermatt; noted for sheer cliffs, which have challenged climbers; first climbed 1865 by Edward Whymper. Height: 14,700ft (4,484m).

Matthew, apostle of Jesus. He was the author of the first of the four gospels in the New Testament. Matthew wrote for Jewish converts to Christianity, assuring them that Jesus of Nazareth is the Messiah expected in the Old Testament.

Matthias Corvinus (1440–90), king of Hungary (1458–90), the son of János Hunyadi. This enlightened despot was a patron of arts and letters. While protecting the peasants, he reformed the administration, strengthened the army, promoted commerce, and founded a new university at Buda and a famous library, the Bibliotheca Corvina. A brilliant soldier, he nearly fulfilled his dream of uniting central Europe under his rule. He took Bohemia from the Turks (proclaimed king of Bohemia, 1469) as well as Styria, Austria, and Corinthia. When Matthias died, Hungary was the most powerful state in central Europe.

Maugham, W(illiam) Somerset (1874–1965), English novelist, short-story writer, and essayist; influenced by Maupassant. He traveled widely in Asia and the United States. His novels, including *Of Human Bondage* (1915), *The Moon and Sixpence* (1919), and *The Razor's Edge* (1944), deal with the unpredictable and passionate aspects of human nature.

Maui Island, island of S central state of Hawaii; 2nd-largest of the Hawaiian islands. Highest point is Haleakala Volcano in Haleakala National Park, 10,023ft (3,057m). Main commerce is sugar cane and pineapples. Chief town is Wailuku. Area: 728sq mi (1,886sq km). Pop. 38,691.

Mauna Loa, volcanic mountain on the S central island of Hawaii, in Hawaii Volcanoes National Park; contains Kilauea and Mokuaweoweo, two of the world's largest active craters; lava flows from its eruptions (1881, 1942, 1949) have reached the sea in recent years. Height: 13,680ft (4,172m).

Maupassant, Guy de (1850–93), French short-story writer and novelist. He was encouraged to write by Gustave Flaubert and, influenced by the Naturalists, produced the short story *Boule-de-suif* for their collec-

tion *Les Soirées de Médan* (1880). His other short stories include *La Maison Tellier* (1881), *Contes de la Bécasse* (1883), and *L'Inutile Beauté* (1890). *Pierre et Jean* (1888) is his finest novel; others include *Bel-Ami* (1885).

Maupertuis, Pierre Louis Moreau de (1698–1759), French astronomer, mathematician, and philosopher. Responsible for the first precise measurements of the meridian in Lapland (1737) and the "principle of least action" in physics. Maupertuis was also a pioneer in genetics and an early evolutionist, as well as a director (1740) of the Berlin Academy of Science.

Mauriac, François (1885–1970), French novelist and playwright. Mauriac was preoccupied with sin and salvation, and his novels, *A Kiss for the Leper* (1922), *Genitrix* (1923), and *The Desert of Love* (1925), portray the futility of pursuing fulfillment in materialism and secular love. His three-volume *Mémoires* (1959–67) stress his reactions to contemporary moral values. He also wrote a study of Charles de Gaulle (1964). He was awarded the Nobel Prize for literature in 1952.

Mauritania (Mauritanie), an independent republic in W Africa, bordered by Western Sahara (N and NW), Algeria (N), Mali (E and S), Senegal (SW), the Atlantic Ocean (W). Along the S Senegal River, rich alluvial soil is irrigated by river flooding and rainfall, providing pasture for cattle and sheep; two-thirds of the country is covered by the Sahara desert region. In the mountainous regions, occasional rainfall is stored for the cultivation of large palm groves. The economy is traditionally based on agriculture; in the 1960s mining began adding to the nation's progress. Iron ore mining (begun 1963) was Mauritania's first heavy industry; its production financed an improved harbor and railroad. Some agriculture still exists in the Senegal valley where rice, wheat, peanuts, dates, and potatoes are grown, and sheep, goats, cattle, and camels are raised. The economy was severely affected by drought in the mid-1970s. About 80% of the inhabitants are Moors of Arab-Berber origin. Although most were nomads, the majority gave this up and moved to urban areas because of the drought. Approx. 20% are black African villagers living in the S. Most of the inhabitants are Muslim and speak Arabic, which is one of the national languages, with French. Formal education, although increasing, is difficult to adapt to nomadic life style; some traveling schools have been established.

A 1980 draft constitution calls for a popularly elected national assembly whose members serve four-year terms, with executive power vested in the prime minister.

Mauritania was settled by the Moors; by the 15th century, Portuguese, Dutch, and French traders had visited the area. In 1817 a treaty signed on the banks of the Senegal River confirmed French influence; Mauritania became a French protectorate in 1903, a French colony in 1920, and a territory in 1946. In 1958 a new capital at Nouakchott was created, and Mauritania was granted internal autonomy; complete independence was attained and a new republic formed in 1960. In 1975, Spain withdrew from its former colony of Western Sahara, dividing it between Morocco and Mauritania, both of which subsequently began fighting with the region's guerrilla independence movement, the Polisario Front. By 1978, Mauritania was virtually bankrupt from the combined impact of the war and drought, and the president was deposed in a military coup. The following year Mauritania renounced its claims to the Western Sahara, signing a peace treaty with the Polisarios. In 1980 the country was returned to civilian rule, but was back under military rule by 1981. Drought, a weak economy, and military coups continued through the mid-1980s.

PROFILE

Official name: Islamic Republic of Mauritania
Area: approx. 419,230sq mi (1,085,806sq km)
Population: 1,589,000
Chief cities: Nouakchott (capital), Atar, Kaedi
Religion: Islam
Language: French, Arabic
Monetary unit: Ouguiya

Mauritius, independent island nation, member of the Commonwealth of Nations, in the Indian Ocean approx. 500mi (805km) E of Madagascar. Sugar, the principal commodity, accounts for about 90% of the export trade.

Land, Economy, and People. The country consists of the main island, 38mi (61km) long and 29mi (47km) wide; Rodrigues Island, 334mi (554km) E; St Brandon Rocks, 250mi (403km) NE; and the Agalega Islands, 580mi (934km) N. Mauritius is a volcanic island fringed by coral reefs. The climate is maritime sub-tropical. The economy is dominated by the sugar industry; tea is a secondary crop. Favorably located in the Indian Ocean, it is a natural link for air and sea transport. Tourism is a growing factor in the economy. There are four important ethnic groups: Indian, Creoles (mixed African and European descent), European and Malagasy, and Chinese. Hindus and Muslims predominate, with a fairly large group of Christians. About 60% of the population is literate.

Government and History. Queen Elizabeth II, the head of the Commonwealth, is represented by a governor-general. There is a Legislative Assembly consisting of a speaker, 62 elected members, 8 additional appointed members to assure balanced representation, and an attorney-general. Elections are held every five years; there is universal adult suffrage. Visited by the Portuguese in 1510 and abortively settled twice by the Dutch, the island was permanently settled by the French in 1721. The British captured the island in 1810 and controlled it until 1968, when it gained its independence.

PROFILE

Official name: Mauritius
Area: 720sq mi (1,865sq km)
Population: 830,700
 Density: 1153.8per sq mi (445.4per sq km)
Chief city: Port Louis (capital)
Government: parliamentary democracy
Language: English (official)
Monetary unit: Mauritius rupee
Gross national product: $200,000,000
Per capita income: $240
Industries (major products): sugar, molasses
Agriculture (major products): sugar cane
Trading partners (major): United Kingdom, United States, France, South Africa

Maurois, André (1885–1967), French biographer, historian, and novelist. He wrote popular histories of England, France, and the United States, wartime reminiscences (*The Silence of Colonel Bramble*, 1918), and novels, such as *Atmosphere of Love* (1928). But he remains best known for his numerous biographies, including those of Percy Shelley (1923), Benjamin Disraeli (1927), Marcel Proust (1949), and Victor Hugo (1954). He was elected to the Académie Française in 1938.

Maury, Matthew Fontaine (1806–73), US naval officer and one of the founders of oceanography, b. near Fredericksburg, Va. He was superintendent of the US Naval Observatory and Hydrographic Office (1842–61) and produced charts showing winds and currents for the Atlantic, Pacific, and Indian oceans. By mapping a profile of the sea bed, he showed that a transatlantic cable would be feasible. In 1868 he became professor of meteorology at Virginia Military Institute. His text *The Physical Geography of the Sea* (1855) introduced modern oceanography.

Mawrya, Indian dynasty. *See* Gupta.

Maxentius, Marcus Aurelius Valerius (died 312), Roman emperor from 306, whose father, Emperor Maximian, abdicated in 305. He managed to gain the imperial throne with his father's help but was plagued by the rivalries of Lucius Domitius Alexander in Africa and Constantine in Spain. Constantine finally killed him in the Battle of Milvian Bridge.

Maximian (Marcus Aurelius Valerius Maximianus) (died 310), Roman emperor (286–305, 306–08). Named by Diocletian first as caesar, then as augustus, he was responsible for governing Italy and the West. He abdicated with Diocletian (305); was recalled to aid his son Maxentius, now emperor; and was again emperor (306–08) until deposed by Maxentius.

Maximilian I (1459–1519), Holy Roman emperor (1493–1519) and German king (1486–1519). Son and successor of Holy Roman Emperor Frederick III, he inherited the Low Countries by his marriage to Mary of Burgundy (1477). He was almost constantly at war with France, first to secure Mary's lands, and then to protect his possessions in Italy.

Maximilian II (1527–76), Holy Roman emperor (1564–76), king of Bohemia (1562–76), and king of Hungary (1563–76). He was the son and successor of Holy Roman Emperor Ferdinand I. A Protestant sympathizer, he was tolerant to Protestants in his domain. He ended a war with the Ottoman Turks (1568) by a truce with Sultan Selim II in which he agreed to continue paying tribute for his lands in Hungary.

Maximilian (1832–67), emperor of Mexico (1864–67), archduke and younger brother of Emperor Franz Josef of Austria. Maximilian courted the liberals and alienated the conservative supporters of the French-dominated regime; he refused to return Church properties confiscated during the preceding administrations. When Napoleon III withdrew from the Mexican venture, Maximilian was easily defeated by forces led by Porfirio Díaz and Juan Álvarez.

Maximilian I (1756–1825), king (1806–25) and elector (1799–1806) of Bavaria. He was made king by the peace of Pressburg (1805) after allying himself with Napoleon I. He later joined (1813) the anti-Napoleon coalition. At the Congress of Vienna (1815) he strongly opposed the consolidation of Germany, protecting Bavarian independence. He granted a liberal constitution to Bavaria in 1818.

Maximilian II (1811–64), king of Bavaria (1848–64). He was the son of King Louis I. At his accession he attempted unsuccessfully to form a coalition of small German states against the large powers, Prussia and Austria. He later supported Austria in order to stem Prussian power. He was a great patron of art and literature.

Maximilian I (1573–1651), duke (1597–1651) and elector (1623–51) of Bavaria. Head of the Catholic League, he fought against the Protestants in the Thirty Years War. After his army defeated (1620) Elector Frederick V of the Palatinate at White Mountain, Holy Roman Emperor Ferdinand II awarded Maximilian Frederick's electoral vote. This award was confirmed by the Treaty of Westphalia (1648).

Maximus, Saint (1) (*c.*380–479), bishop of Turin whose discourses record northern Italian liturgy and the survival of paganism. (2) (*c.*480–662), also called the Confessor, Greek theologian. An ascetic who opposed Monotheletism (belief in only the divine will in Jesus), he believed man brought evil into the world because of his desire for pleasure and that Christ was sent to restore the balance of reason over sense and so redeem the world.

Maxwell, James Clerk (1831–79), Scottish mathematician and physicist. He became professor at Aberdeen, then Kings College (London), and finally Cambridge, where he organized the Cavendish Laboratory. He mathematically showed that Saturn's rings must consist of small solid particles. He also investigated the motion of molecules in gases, developing with Ludwig Boltzmann the equations for the kinetic theory of gases. His greatest achievements were in the fields of electricity and magnetism and were published in his *Treatise on Electricity and Magnetism* (1873). He provided the equation underlying the electromagnetic theory and demonstrated that light and electricity exhibit similar properties and that light is an electromagnetic wave.

Maxwell's Equations, a series of classical equations, proposed by James Clerk Maxwell (1831–79) in 1864, which linked light with electromagnetic waves. The equations connect the magnetic field strength, the electric displacement, the current density, the magnetic flux density, and the electric field strength. From these equations, which were a breakthrough in electromagnetic theory, Maxwell showed that each vector obeys a wave equation and it was this realization that led him to understand that light is propagated as electromagnetic waves.

May, fifth month of the year. The origin of the name May is unknown, although some believe it was derived from the Greek goddess Maia. It has 31 days. The birthstone is the emerald or agate.

Maya, one of the most important tribes of Central American Indians. They occupied Yucatán, Chiapas, and Tabasco in Mexico; all of British Honduras and Guatemala, and a part of Honduras. Speaking the Maya-Quiché language, in prehistoric times they were famous for their magnificent architecture, as well as their astronomical and mathematical knowledge, and sheer aesthetic excellence.

Mayagüez, seaport city in W Puerto Rico, on Mona Passage; severely damaged by 1918 earthquake and tidal wave; site of airport, college of the University of Puerto Rico (1763), US government agricultural research station. Products: sugar cane, coffee, tobacco, tropical fruits. Industries: shipping, needlework, beverages, canned foods, electronic components. Pop. 106,500.

Mayakovski, Vladimir (1893–1930), Soviet poet and dramatist. Leader of the futurist movement, he was founder (1923) and editor of the journal *Left Arts Front.* His work developed from the intensely personal to the socially conscious and propagandistic and includes the poems *The Cloud in Trousers* (1915) and *150 Million* (1920) and the plays *Mystery Bouffe* (1918), *The Bedbug* (1928), and *The Bathhouse* (1929). The major poet of the Soviet revolution, he died a suicide.

Mayan, family of languages spoken on the Yucatán Peninsula of Mexico and in Guatemala by the Maya Indians, whose ancestors built the great Maya Empire of a thousand years ago. There are several dozen of these languages, the most important being Yucatec, of Mexico, and Quiché, Cakchiquel, Mam, and Kekchi, of Guatemala. The ancient Mayas had a hieroglyphic writing system, which has still not been fully deciphered.

Mayan Architecture, architecture of the Mayan people, in Central America and later in the Yucatán peninsula. The classic Maya period is AD 300–900. The greatest monuments are palaces and temples, the latter built on pyramidal platforms, with rich stone carving as ornament.

May Apple, also mandrake, perennial wildflower found in woodlands of E North America and E Asia. Each plant has two umbrella-shaped leaves and a waxy, ill-scented, white, nodding flower. The lemon-like fruit is edible; the poisonous root was used as a medicinal cathartic. Height: 12–18in (31–46cm). Family Berberidaceae; species *Podophyllum peltatum.*

May Beetle, or June bug, medium-sized, stout, brownish scarab beetle that feeds on tree foliage. The white grubs that eat roots of various crops are one of the most destructive soil pests. Genus *Phyllophaga.*

Mayflower, or trailing arbutus, evergreen wildflower found in temperate woodlands. It has clusters of white or pink, spicy-smelling flowers and oval, leathery leaves. Family Ericaceae; species *Epigaea repens.*

Mayflower, ship that brought the Pilgrims from England to New England in 1620. Under Capt. Christopher Jones, the *Mayflower* set sail on September 16, and on November 19 the passengers sighted land. Before the Pilgrims disembarked on December 26 at Plymouth, Mass., they composed the famous Mayflower Compact, an agreement for the temporary government of the colony based on the will of the majority. The original *Mayflower* is lost, but a replica sailed by a British crew from England to Massachusetts in 1957 is on permanent exhibit at Plymouth, Mass.

Mayflower Compact, agreement to establish a preliminary government for the Pilgrims. It was signed by the 41 adult, male passengers of the *Mayflower* on Nov. 21, 1620, at sea off the New England coast. The compact bound signers to majority-rule government in the Pilgrim colony, pending receipt of a royal charter. The compact is significant as a first step in the development of democracy in America. *See also* Pilgrims; Plymouth Colony.

Mayfly, soft-bodied insect found worldwide. The adult lives only a few days and the aquatic larvae may live several years. Adults have fanlike front wings and vestigial mouthparts and often emerge from streams and rivers in swarms. Nymphs are brown with leaflike gills; length: 0.4–1in (10–25mm). Order Ephemeroptera.

Mazarin, Jules (1602–61), Italian papal nuncio who became cardinal and statesman in France. Chosen by Cardinal Richelieu to be his successor (1642), Mazarin derived great support from the young Louis XIV's regent, his mother, Anne of Austria. This situation made his power impregnable until his death, except for the period of the Fronde uprising (1648–53), when he controlled state matters in secret from abroad. His negotiations and treaties established a peace in Europe that favored France. The Peace of Westphalia in 1648 and the Peace of the Pyrenees in 1659 gained much new territory for France and the marriage contract with the Spanish infanta gave France's Louis XIV claims on Spain's inheritance.

Mazarin Bible or **Gutenberg Bible,** first Bible to be printed and first large book to be printed from movable metal type. It was probably printed about 1455 at Mainz by Johann Gutenberg, by whose name it is also known. It has 42 lines per page and is sometimes described as the 42-line Bible. The name Mazarin Bible is derived from the Mazarin Library in Paris, where a copy of the Bible was found in the late 18th century.

Mazatlán, seaport city in W Mexico, on the Pacific coast; major industrial and commercial center in W Mexico; terminus of railway connecting United States with Mexico City; resort. Exports: tobacco, metal ores, istle, shrimp, hides, oregano, fish, woods. Industries: trade, tourism. Pop. 169,500.

Mazzini, Giuseppe (1805–72), Italian patriot and political thinker of the Risorgimento (Italian unification movement). A member of the *Carbonari,* the Italian republican underground from 1830, in 1831 he founded the "Young Italy" movement, dedicated to republican unification of Italy. He fought in the Italian revolutionary movement of 1848, ruled in Rome in 1849 upon ouster of the pope, but then was exiled. Although he was active in revolutionary activities during the 1850s, he played a minor role toward the 1861 establishment of a unified Italian kingdom; having favored a unified republican state, he refused allegiance to the monarchy.

Mbabane, town in NW Swaziland, SE Africa, in the Mdimba Mts; capital and administrative center of the country; commercial center for surrounding agricultural region; tin and iron are mined nearby. Pop. 24,000.

Mbuji-Mayi, formerly Bakwanga; city in S central Zaire, Equatorial Africa; capital of Kasai-Oriental region; commercial center on Sankura River; site of trade schools, hospital. City grew rapidly after Zaire's independence (1960); noted for diamond mining. Pop. 336,654.

Mbundu, or Ovimbundu, a Bantu people of western Angola once noted for extensive trade. They were defeated by the Portuguese in the 17th century. The Mbundu followed a mixed system of inheritance and were organized into several chiefdoms. This agricultural people numbers over 1,000,000.

Mead, Margaret (1901–78), US anthropologist, b. Philadelphia. She did classic field work in the cultures of the Pacific islands, New Guinea, and Samoa, summarized in such books as *Coming of Age in Samoa* (1928) and *Growing Up in New Guinea* (1930). She helped develop the national-character approach to studying complex societies, showing how the development of the individual is affected by the culture he lives in. More recently she has been concerned with modern societies and sex roles. Among her later works were *Male and Female* (1949), *Childhood in Contemporary Societies* (1955), and *Culture and Commitment* (1970). From 1926 to 1969, she served as curator of Ethnology at the American Museum of Natural History. Her autobiography, *Blackberry Winter,* was published in 1972. In recent years, although the importance of her work is still highly regarded, some of her early conclusions about Samoan society were criticized for shortcomings in perspective and sampling technique.

Mead, Lake, reservoir on the Nevada-Arizona border, in Lake Mead National Recreational Area; formed from impounding the Colorado River by the Hoover Dam. One of the largest reservoirs in the world; 247sq mi (640sq km). Depth: 589ft (180m).

Vladimir Mayakovski

Mayfly

Medea

Meadowlark, either of two species—the eastern meadowlark (*Sturnella magna*) and the western meadowlark (*S. neglecta*)—of blackbird-related birds of North America, sometimes considered game birds. They are mottled brown with yellow breast and black bib. They feed on the ground and lay 4 to 6 bluish or greenish tinted spotted eggs.

Mealybug, fluffy, waxy scale insect found worldwide. It sucks sap from trees and other plants. Length: 0.2in (5mm). Family Pseudococcidae.

Mean, or arithmetic mean, the average; found by adding a group of numbers and dividing by the number of items in the group. The mean is the most common measure of central tendency and also usually the most meaningful, because it includes every number in the data set in its computation.

Meander, a naturally occurring looplike bend of a river or stream channel. They form on a flood plain where there is little resistance in the alluvium. They lengthen the river, thus reducing its gradient and velocity. Meanders migrate slowly downstream, depositing sediment on one bank while eroding the opposite. Sometimes meanders make complete loops, which when cut off form oxbow lakes. *See also* Oxbow.

Mean Sea Level, average height of the sea calculated from readings taken hourly and over a 19-year cycle at certain points on the open coast. Used as a standard or fixed geodetic point. *See also* Geodesy.

Measles (rubeola), an extremely contagious virus disease of the respiratory tract and reticuloendothelial system. Symptoms appear about two weeks after exposure and include cough, conjunctivitis, and typical spots on the oral mucous membranes. Three or four days later, a rash erupts behind the ears or on the face, then spreads over the body. Intolerance of light is characteristic. Complications such as pneumonia and encephalitis may occur, and middle-ear infection is a hazard of the disease. Death may result from complications or from severe disease. Vaccination or one attack usually produces immunity to measles.

Measure for Measure (1604), 5-act comedy by William Shakespeare, based on George Whetstone's play taken from a story by Giovanni Battista Giraldi (called Cynthio). Different in method and spirit from Shakespeare's other plays, its moods are partly satire and partly religious exaltation. In the absence of Vincentio, duke of Vienna, his deputy Angelo imprisons Claudio, but offers to release him if Claudio's sister Isabella will keep a rendezvous with him. She agrees but sends Mariana. Angelo tells Isabella he has executed her brother; at this point the duke returns and sentences Angelo to death, but releases him when Isabella pleads for mercy. Claudio is produced unharmed and Angelo is betrothed to Mariana.

Measurement. *See* Weights and Measures.

Measuring Worm, or inchworm, looper, spanworm, moth caterpillar that crawls with characteristic looping movements, suggestive of measurement. Family Geometridae.

Mecca (Makkah), city in W Saudi Arabia; capital of Hejaz prov.; birthplace of Mohammed; holiest city of the Islamic faith; site of the Great Mosque (the Haram), which encloses Kaaba, holding the sacred black stone, and Zamzam, the holy well. City was ancient caravan station and market center and an Arab shrine before the time of Mohammed; the flight (hegira) of Mohammed from Mecca 622 began Muslim era. Egypt

controlled city during 13th century; Ottoman Turks held it 1517–1916, when Husein ibn-Ali secured Arabian independence. Mecca fell in 1924 to Ibn-Saud, who later founded Saudi Arabian kingdom. Much of Mecca's commerce depends on the pilgrims; oil revenues began to add income after WWII. Pop. 185,000.

Mechanical Engineering, field of engineering concerned with the economical design, construction, and operation of power plants, engines, and machinery, and with research and testing in search of new developments. Technical areas involving the mechanical engineer are mechanisms and kinematics, materials and materials testing, thermodynamics, heat production and distribution, manufacturing processes, drafting, fluid control. Some fields of specialization in mechanical engineering are power generation, heating and refrigeration, transportation.

Mechanics, branch of physics concerned with the behavior of matter under the influence of forces. It may be divided into statics—the study of matter at rest—and dynamics—the study of matter in motion, and into solid mechanics and fluid mechanics. Dynamics may be further divided into kinematics—the description of motion without regard to cause—and kinetics—the study of motion and force. In statics, the forces on a body are balanced and the body is said to be in equilibrium; static equilibrium may be stable, unstable, or neutral. Classical dynamics rests primarily on the three laws of motion formulated by Sir Isaac Newton in his *Principia* (1687). Modern physics has shown these laws to be special cases approximating more general laws. Relativistic mechanics deals with the behavior of matter at very high speeds, approaching that of light, while quantum mechanics deals with the behavior of matter at the level of atoms and molecules. *See also* Laws of Motion; Quantum Theory; Relativity.

Medan, city in NE Sumatra island, Indonesia, on Deli River; capital of North Sumatra prov.; largest city on the island; site of Islamic University of North Sumatra (1952), University of North Sumatra (1957); shipping and commercial center. Exports: rubber, tobacco, coffee, sisal. Industries: machinery, tile, automobiles, tourism. Pop. 635,562.

Medawar, (Sir) Peter Brian (1915–   ), English biologist. He shared the 1960 Nobel Prize for physiology and medicine with Frank Macfarlane Burnet for the discovery of acquired immune tolerance. Medawar confirmed Burnet's theory that an organism can acquire the ability to recognize foreign tissue during embryonic development, and if that tissue is introduced in the embryonic stage it may then be reintroduced later without inducing an immune reaction. In 1978 his experiments indicated that women who had pregnancies before age 20 were known to be less likely to develop breast cancer.

Medea, in classical mythology and literature, the daughter of Aestes, king of Colchis, granddaughter of Asteria, the starry heavens, and wife of the hero Jason. In some descriptions she is the daughter of Hecate. She helped Jason steal the Golden Fleece and escape. When he remarried, Medea killed Jason's bride and her own children and fled in a chariot drawn by dragons.

Medellín, city in NW central Colombia, approx. 150mi (242km) NW of Bogotá; capital of Antioquia dept. and 2nd-largest city of Colombia; in wealthy coffee-producing area; site of several 17th-century churches, gold mint. Industries: steelworks, sugar refineries, chemicals. Founded 1675. Pop. 1,070,924.

Medford, city in E Massachusetts, on Mystic River; site of Craddock House (1634), Tufts University (1852), and examples of pre-Revolutionary War architecture. Industries: waxes, chemicals, publishing, printing. Settled 1630; inc. as city 1892. Pop. (1980) 58,076.

Median, in statistics, a measure of central tendency found by ranking the data from smallest to largest and locating the middle item, which is then called the median. If there is an even number of items, the average of the two middle items is taken as the median. The median is a "better" measure of central tendency than the mean when the distribution of the data is skewed.

Medici, Italian family that ruled Florence and, later, Tuscany from the 15th to 18th centuries, produced three popes, married into royal families throughout Europe, and provided magnificent patronage to the arts. A banking fortune provided the financial basis for the unofficial, Republican rule (from 1434) of **Cosimo the Elder** (1389–1464). His grandson **Lorenzo** ruled Florence and was an arts patron. In 1531, **Alessandro** became first duke of Florence. In 1569, **Cosimo** was named grand duke of Tuscany by the pope, and his successor **Francesco** I had the title confirmed by the Holy Roman emperor in 1575. Medici popes were **Giovanni** (Leo X, 1513–21), **Giulio** (Clement VII, 1523–34), and **Alessandro** (Leo XI, 1605). The line ended at Gastone de' Medici's death in 1737. *See also* individual biographies.

Medici, Alessandro de' (1510–37), first duke of Florence, illegitimate son of Lorenzo de' Medici (1492–1519). Appointed (1523) by his uncle, Pope Clement VII, to rule Republican Florence with his cousin Ippolito, he was expelled by a popular revolt (1527). He was restored (1531) as the first hereditary duke of Florence by his father-in-law, Emperor Charles V.

Medici, Cosimo de', the Elder (1389–1464), de facto ruler of Florence from 1434, patron of literature. With the Medici banking fortune he led the oligarchy that was expelled from Florence in 1433 but returned to rule permanently the next year. He was an early Renaissance patron of Greek scholars exiled by the fall of Constantinople in 1453 and of the artists Brunelleschi, Michelozzo, Lorenzo Ghiberti, Donatello, Andrea del Castagno, Fra Angelico, and Benozzo Gozzoli.

Medici, Cosimo I de' (1519–74), grand duke of Tuscany. Son of Giovanni de' Medici (1498–1526), he came from secondary branch of the Medici (descended from Lorenzo, 1395–1440) and became duke of Florence when the primary branch ended with death of Duke Alessandro (1537). Having conquered Siena and unified Tuscany, he was given title of grand duke of Tuscany in 1569 by Pope Pius V. He was patron of artists Ammanati, Vasari, Pontormo, and Bronzino.

Medici, Giovanni de' (1475–1521), original name of Pope Leo X (1513–21). *See* Leo X.

Medici, Lorenzo de' (1449–92), called Lorenzo the Magnificent, Florentine merchant prince, grandson of Cosimo the Elder, and successor to his father Piero (died 1469) as virtual ruler of Florence. Having survived attempted assassination in the Pazzi conspiracy (1478), like his predecessors he governed the Florentine Republic not with any official title, but by an elaborate system of political patronage. Himself a notable poet, he was a great Renaissance patron, having assembled the Florentine Platonic Academy and supported Marsilio Ficino, Pico della Mirandola, Politian (Angelo Poliziano), Guiliano da Sangallo, Botticelli, Verrocchio, Leonardo da Vinci, and Michelangelo.

Medicine, the science concerned with the cure and prevention of disease and the preservation of health. To judge from ancient pictographs showing medical procedures and from ancient skulls and skeletons, the practice of medicine goes back to prehistoric man. Egyptian medicine included magico-religious elements along with empirical therapies for many ailments. Hebrew medicine placed a marked emphasis on hygiene. Greek medicine had become thoroughly secular by the 6th century BC and there existed several medical schools. The Romans and then the Arabs carried on and developed further the Greek medical tradition. During the Renaissance this knowledge was brought back to Europe. The dawn of modern medicine coincided with accurate anatomical and physiological observations first made in the 17th century. By the 19th century practical diagnostic procedures for many diseases had been developed; bacteria had been discovered and immunizing serums were developed. The great developments of the 20th century include chemotherapy, or the treatment of various diseases with specific chemical agents, new surgical procedures, and sophisticated diagnostic devices such as radioactive tracers.

Medieval Music, music produced in Europe during the Middle Ages, roughly 1100 to 1400. Music during this period was dominated by Christian liturgical vocal choruses called chants, which were sung in polyphonic style, i.e., several different parts were sung simultaneously by different sections of the chorus. Perhaps the most significant composer of the period was the Frenchman Guillaume de Machaut (1300–77) who developed the form of the motet that other composers used for several hundred years. Secular songs were transmitted orally by traveling Saxon, French, and German troubadors. In the 14th and 15th centuries, guilds of professional musicians were formed, and musical notation began to become more sophisticated, enabling composers to transmit whole works to later generations. *See also* Gregorian Chant; Motet; Musical Notation; Polyphony.

Medina (Al-Madinah), city in Saudi Arabia, 210mi (338km) N of Mecca, 120mi (193km) from Red Sea coast. Originally called Yathrib, the city was renamed Medinat an Nabi, "the Prophet's city," after Mohammed fled there 622, making it his capital; in 661 the caliphs moved their capital to Damascus. Medina was under Turkish rule 1517–1916, when the independent Arab kingdom of Hejaz was formed; in 1932 it was inc. into Saudi Arabia; site of Great Mosque containing tomb of Mohammed (a Muslim pilgrimage site), Islamic University (1962), 12th-century wall, radio station. Lying in a prosperous oasis, the city is a noted pottery center. Crops: fruits, vegetables, grains. Pop. 150,000.

Medina-Sedonia, Alonso Peréze de Guzmán, Duque de (1550–1615),commander in chief of the ill-fated Spanish Armada of 1588. He accepted this post through loyalty to the king, although his lack of naval experience and the difficulty of his assignment caused him considerable doubt. His defeat by the English and by the Irish Sea, therefore, did not halt his career and he was retained by the Spanish king as admiral of the ocean. In 1596 he lost Cádiz to the English and his squadron was defeated at Gibraltar (1606).

Mediterranean Fruit Fly, yellow, spotted-winged fly, 0.16 to 0.2in (4–5mm) long, a serious pest in most fruit-growing areas of the world. An exhaustive effort is being made to keep it out of US citrus-growing areas, where it became a serious threat, especially in Southern California and Florida in 1981. Family Tephritidae, species *Ceratitis capitata. See also* Diptera.

Mediterranean Sea, largest inland sea in the world; an arm of the Atlantic Ocean, between Africa and Europe; extends from the Strait of Gibraltar to the SW Asia coast; receives several tributaries, including the Nile, Rhône, Ebro, Tiber, Po, and Vardar rivers. In ancient times the Mediterranean was dominated by Roman and Byzantine maritime power; it was controlled by Venice and Genoa in the Middle Ages. In 1500 the discovery of the route around Cape of Good Hope to India gave trade power to the French, English, and Spanish ports. In 1869 the opening of the Suez Canal resulted in the Mediterranean becoming one of the world's busiest shipping waters. The salinity of the Mediterranean is approx. 10% as a consequence of rapid evaporation rate; the fish life is less impressive than in other oceans; however, the sea is a source of tuna, sponge, coral, sardines, and anchovies. Area: approx. 965,000sq mi (2,499,350sq km).

Mediterranean Subrace, subdivision of the Caucasoid race, characterized by rather swarthy skin, dark often curly hair, brown eyes, short slender stature. Their habitat is Europe and the Mediterranean littoral, extending east to Arabia.

Medulla Oblongata, principal hindbrain structure, the portion of the brain that joins the spinal cord. Medulla functions are necessary to maintain life, for example, they control respiration and heartbeat. The medulla also contains part of the reticular formation, an anatomically distinct tract of neurons that plays a role in arousal states: consciousness, wakefulness, and attention. General anesthetics, such as ether, probably work by depressing medulla activity.

Medusa, monster figure of Greek mythology. She was one of the Gorgons, three monstrous sisters. According to mythology, Athena turned her hair to serpents and her face turned the viewer to stone. She was slain by Perseus, who used her head to destroy his enemies.

Meer, van der, family of Dutch painters. Jan van der Meer II (Jan Vermeer II, 1628–91) was a landscape painter and the father of Jan van der Meer III (Jan Vermeer III, 1656–1705), who painted landscapes and animal subjects, and still-life painter Barent van der Meer (Barend Vermeer, 1659–1702). *See also* Vermeer, Jan.

Meerschaum or **Sepiolite,** a clay silicate mineral, hydrated magnesium silicate, found mainly in Asia Minor. Opaque white, fibrous; hardness 2–2.5; sp gr 2. Used chiefly for tobacco pipes.

Meerut, city in N India, 40mi (64km) NE of Delhi; capital of Meerut district. City dates to 3rd century BC; taken by Muslims 1191, Tamerlane 1398; ceded to British 1803 who est. military fort; first outbreak of Sepoy Mutiny began here May 10, 1857. Industries: textiles, chemicals, paint, sugar, steel smelting and refining, hosiery, soap. Pop. 250,126.

Megalithic Monuments, large structures generally built of undressed stone during the Neolithic and early Bronze Age. Megalithic building ranges N through Spain, up the coast of W Europe and into Scandinavia. The most ancient types were stone tombs, of which the basic unit was the dolmen, made of several upright supports and flat roofing slabs. Another type were the menhirs, simple uprights usually unconnected with any grave sites and often decorated with magical symbols. They were frequently arranged in parallel rows (as at Carnac, France) or in circles, half-circles, and ellipses (as at Stonehenge and Avebury, England).

Megapode, or mound bird, Australian game bird with short, rounded wings, strong legs, and clawed feet. One group, typified by the hen-sized, crested scrub fowl *(Megapodius),* rakes debris into a large compost pile. In this mound, the female excavates a deep hole for each large oval egg (5–8). There is a long incubation period. Other megapodes, such as the turkey-sized, blackish maleo, often migrate to special areas to build their incubators in black sand warmed by the sun or in areas heated by underground volcanic action. Family Megapodiidae.

Mégara, seaport town in E central Greece, on Saronic Gulf. In ancient Greece it served as the capital of Mégaris; flourished under the Dorians as a center of maritime trade, and est. colonies of Chalcedon and Byzantium; economic ruin came with the Peloponnesian War; birthplace of Euclid, mathematician who founded the Megarian school of philosophy and logic. Industries: wine, flour, olive oil. Pop. 15,450.

Megatherium, a genus of extinct ground sloth, about 20ft (6.1m) long and very massive. During Pleistocene times, it ranged from South America into S United States. The front feet bore huge claws, and it had plant-grinding teeth along the sides of its jaws.

Mehmed II. *See* Mohammed II.

Meiji Restoration (1868), shift of power in Japan from the Tokugawa shogunate (1603–1867) to the emperor and his supporters. Spurred by foreign contact (such as Admiral Perry's visit in 1853) and a weakened central government, a group of young samurai allied against the Tokugawa shogunate, forcing an "imperial restoration" of power to Emperor Meiji, age 14 at the time. The samurai leaders engineered an abrupt change in the government, trading feudal isolationism for foreign trade, advanced technology, a more democratic government, and overall modernization of the Japanese state and society. *See also* Tokugawa.

Mein Kampf (My Struggle) (1924–26), two-volume work by Adolf Hitler, considered the "bible" of the Nazi movement. Hitler dictated the first volume, basically an autobiography, when he was imprisoned in Bavaria after the unsuccessful Munich putsch of 1923. The second volume was devoted to the policies of National Socialism and the propaganda methods Hitler was to use later in his rise to power.

Meiosis, process of two consecutive nuclear divisions to form germ cells, reducing the chromosome number from diploid to haploid. Mature gametes are produced by the first meiotic division that reduces the chromosome number to half; the second division forms four haploid reproductive cells. Spermatogenesis yields four functional sperm and oogenesis yields one mature ovum, and three polar bodies that will degenerate.

Meir, Golda (1898–1978), Israeli political figure, b. as Goldie Mabovitch in the Ukraine. In 1906 she emigrated to Milwaukee, Wis., with her family. She became a schoolteacher and active in the Zionist movement. She and her husband Morris Meyerson (hebraized to Meir in 1956) moved to Palestine in 1921 to live on a kibbutz. She became active in the Palestine labor movement, serving as the executive secretary of the Women's Labor Council (1928–32) and as its spokesperson in the United States (1932–36). In 1936 she was named head of the political department of Histadrut (General Federation of Jewish Labor). Between 1946–48 she often acted as de facto leader of the Jews in Palestine seeking an independent state because so many of the other leaders were imprisoned. After independence she served at the same time as ambassador to Russia and as minister of labor (1949–56). Between 1956–66 she served as foreign minister. She became secretary-general of the Mapai (later Labor) party in 1966. In 1969 she became prime minister. She resigned in 1974 after criticism over lack of preparedness at the outbreak of the 1973 Arab-Israeli War. She continued to be a leading voice in the Labor party until her death.

Meistersingers, German lyric poets of the 14th–16th centuries who were moralistic and followed a strict religious code, often forming private lodges in the south German towns. Strict rules, derived from the 12 old masters, such as Walther von der Vogelweide, were followed. The first meistersinger is thought to have been Heinrich von Meissen; Hans Sachs, the writer of over 4000 songs, is the best known.

Meitner, Lise (1878–1968), Austrian physicist. Together with Otto Hahn, she discovered protactinium and the fission of uranium, and investigated beta decay and nuclear isomerism. She worked with Fritz Strassmann on the products resulting from neutron bombardment of uranium. She is also noted for her research on disintegration products of actinium, thorium, and radium.

Meknès, city in N central Morocco, approx. 35mi (56km) WSW of Fès; prospered under Sultan Ismail who built an extravagant palace here 1672, part of which still exists. Industries: textiles, cement, metals, oil distilling, food processing and canning. Founded 10th century. Pop. 244,520.

Mekong (Lan-ts'ang Chiang), river in SE Asia; rises (as the Dza Chu) in Tibet, China; rushes S through Yunnan prov., forms Burma-Laos border, and part of Laos-Thailand border; flows S through Cambodia and South Vietnam into South China Sea, creating a vast river delta that is one of the foremost rice-producing regions in Asia. Length: approx. 2,600mi (4,186km).

Melanchthon, Philipp (1497–1560), German educator, theologian, and leader of the Reformation. A humanist scholar, he wrote textbooks for study of Greek and Latin, and he helped found and reform universities in Germany. At Wittenberg he became a friend of Martin Luther and a leader in Luther's reform movement. In 1530, Melanchthon drafted the Augsburg Confession, which became a basic statement of Lutheranism. *See also* Lutheranism.

Melanesian People, inhabitants of the central Pacific, N and E of Australia and New Guinea. Most Melanesians live by fishing and subsistence agriculture, and there is considerable cultural diversity. Religious beliefs include totemism, animism, ancestor worship, and cargo cults.

Melanin, a dark pigment found in the skin, hair, and parts of the eye. Melanin, carotene, and hemoglobin are mainly responsible for skin color.

Melanocyte Stimulating Hormone (MSH), produced by the pituitary gland; stimulates certain cells in the skin to synthesize melanin, a brown skin pigment. *See also* Melanin.

Melba, (Dame) Nellie (1861–1931), Australian coloratura soprano. She made her debut in Paris in 1887 and subsequently appeared in Brussels (1887), London (1888), Paris (1889–91), and New York (1893–96; 1907–20). She became director of the Melbourne Conservatory in 1927.

Golda Meir

Nellie Melba

Herman Melville

Melbourne, William Lamb, 2nd Viscount (1779–1848), British statesman. He became a Whig member of Parliament (1806), but lost his seat (1812) for supporting Roman Catholic emancipation. Returned to Parliament (1816), he later became Irish secretary (1827) and home secretary (1830–34). As prime minister (1835–41) he was the young Queen Victoria's political mentor, encouraging moderate reforms but resisting further parliamentary liberalization.

Melbourne, capital city of Victoria state, Australia, on the Yarra River at the N end of Port Phillip Bay, major center of finance, commerce, and transportation; site of the University of Melbourne (1853), Conservatorium of Music (1910), and Royal Melbourne Technical College (1887). Exports: wool, flour, meat, fruit, dairy products. Industries: automotive, aircraft, textiles, agricultural machines, chemicals, tobacco. Founded 1835 by Tasmania settlers; inc. 1842; became capital 1851. Pop. 76,900.

Melchites, originally the Christians of Egypt and Syria who accepted the decrees of the 451 Council of Chalcedon and remained in communion with Constantinople, calling themselves "Emperor's men." Today the term is applied to Eastern Orthodox Christians and Orthodox Christians of Egypt and Syria that have reunited with Rome. Led by the patriarch of Antioch, they follow a Byzantine rite in Arabic.

Meleager, in Greek mythology, a prince of Calydon and member of the *Argo* expedition. The Fates decreed at his birth that his life was linked to the life of a certain firebrand upon the hearth. When Meleager killed his uncles in an argument after the successful hunt of the Calydonian boar, his mother Althaea, in her grief and anger, took the brand that she had carefully preserved and threw it on the fire. Meleager burned and died.

Meletius, Saint (died 381), bishop of Antioch (360–81). Banished from his see by the emperor in 360, he was one faction in the Meletian Schism of Antioch (362–81). The supporters of Eustathius, bishop of Antioch (324–30), had Paulinius consecrated in 362 because they found Meletius' theology suspect. Although banished (365–66 and 371–78), Meletius was restored in 378 and presided at the Council of Constantinople (381). His feast day is February 12.

Melodrama, form of drama, originally French, relying on exaggerated acting style and strongly emotional situations rather than character development. Music is often provided to heighten the emotional effect. Melodramatic playwrights include Jean Jacques Rousseau (Pygmalion, 1770), Victor Hugo, Joseph Bouchardy, and Thomas Holcroft.

Melon, annual vine. The cantaloupe, or muskmelon, *(Cucumis melo reticulatus)* is from S Asia and Central America. It has a musky odor and netlike veins on its surface. The winter or casaba melon *(Cimelo inodorus)* is from S Asia and is grown in S United States. It has a ridged or smooth rind, like the honeydew, and is without a musky smell. Family Cucurbitaceae. *See also* Cantaloupe; Gourd.

Melos (Milos), island in SE Greece, belonging to Cyclades Islands. Melos is the major town; 1820 excavations unearthed the famous statue of Venus de Milo. Industries: grain, cotton, olive oil, fruits, mining. Area: 58sq mi (150sq km). Pop. 4,499.

Melville, Herman (1819–91), US author, b. New York City. After his bankrupt father's death in 1832, Melville worked at various jobs until 1839 when he signed aboard a trading ship bound for England. In 1841 he signed on the whaler *Acushnet.* He jumped ship in the Marquesas Islands, where he spent a month among the natives of the Typee Valley. This experience became the subject of his first book, the novel *Typee* (1846). Shortly after publication of his second novel, *Omoo* (1847), he married Elizabeth Shaw, daughter of the chief justice of Massachusetts. The novels *Mardi* and *Redburn* followed in 1849.

After a visit to Europe in 1849, the Melvilles moved to a farm in western Massachusetts, where he wrote his greatest work, *Moby-Dick* (1851), several other novels *(White-Jacket, Pierre, Israel, Potter, The Confidence Man),* and some distinguished short fiction (collected in *The Piazza Tales).* He moved to New York in 1863 and worked as a customs inspector (1866–85).

After his death, the manuscript of *Billy Budd* was discovered along with a number of previously unpublished poems. A relatively neglected writer during his own lifetime, Melville is generally regarded today as one of America's greatest writers, not only as a symbolist, but also as a philosopher and social critic.

Memling, Hans (*c.*1435–1494), Flemish painter, b. Germany. He probably studied in Brussels under Rogier van der Weyden. He was the head of a prolific workshop and painted chiefly religious works. His balanced compositions gave realistic attention to details, such as the color and texture of a fabric.

Memory, capacity to learn and remember information and experience. Modern psychologists often divide memory into two phases, short-term (STM) and long-term (LTM). An item in STM (eg, a phone number dialed once) lasts for several seconds after an experience, but fades unless it is rehearsed (practiced). An item enters LTM (relatively permanent storage) if it stays in STM long enough (depending on other factors such as its meaningfulness and importance). Many psychologists believe that items in LTM are never really lost. They view forgetting as an inability to get the items out of storage and into consciousness; eg, a person may often easily identify information that he or she cannot recall directly.

Memory, Computer, part of a computer that stores information in words or bytes, each of which has an identification number (address) assigned to it for immediate use by the central processing unit. It may consist of magnetic cores or it may be a solid-state memory in which bits of information are stored as one of two states in bistable multivibrators. The latter form is smaller and faster than core memory but the stored information is lost if the supply voltage is cut.

Memphis, ancient city of Egypt, 14mi (23km) S of Cairo, part of which is now occupied by village of Mit Ra-hina. Huge statues of Ramses II, temples of Ptah, Ra, and Isis have been unearthed. City was important from its founding 3110 BC (by Menes, Egypt's first king), until 4th century BC when Alexandria began to develop. In the 7th century AD much of its ruins were used by Arabs in building Cairo.

Memphis, commercial city and river port in SW Tennessee, on Chickasaw Bluff above Mississippi River; seat of Shelby co; largest city in Tennessee. Location of French (1698), Spanish (1794), and US (1797) forts; first permanent settlement est. (1819) by Andrew Jackson, Marcus Winchester, and John Overton. Plagued with epidemics of yellow fever late 19th century. It is site of Memphis State University (1909), Southwestern University (1848), Riverside and deSoto parks, Liberty Bowl, and many antebellum houses. The assassination of Martin Luther King there (1968) caused rioting. Industries: lumber, automobiles, food products, pharmaceuticals, paints, toiletries. Inc. 1826 as town; 1849 as city. Pop. (1980) 646,356.

Menander (342–292 BC), Greek comic playwright. Composer of 108 comedies in 30 years, he was a quiet, dedicated artist. His favorite theme was unhappy love; his style was amusing and perceptive rather than broadly humorous. With Philemon, he was one of the leaders of New Comedy. Mostly fragments remain, but an entire play, *The Peevish Man,* was discovered in 1957.

Menarche, the first menstrual period at puberty. Age of onset varies from 10 to 15 years in the human female. *See also* Menstrual Cycle.

Mencius, or **Meng-ko** (371–289 BC), "Second Sage" of Confucianism. A disciple of Confucius' grandson, Mencius spent most of his life searching for a feudal lord who would put his teachings into practice. He failed to win their support for his doctrines and, like Confucius, achieved his greatest success as a teacher. He actively refuted the rival doctrines of Mo Tzu and Yang Chu. His sayings are recorded in the *Book of Mencius. See also* Confucianism.

Mende, Negroid people of Liberia and SE Sierra Leone. Their traditional livelihood is by shifting agriculture, rice being the staple crop with cocoa and ginger as cash crops. Their patrilineal society is noted for the *poro,* a secret society that holds ritual power over educational, moral, and military issues as well as religious beliefs.

Mendel, Gregor Johann (1822–84), Austrian naturalist. He discovered the laws of heredity and in so doing laid the foundation for the modern science of genetics. Mendel joined the monastery at Brno in 1824 and was ordained in 1847; his plant experiments began in 1856 in the monastery gardens. His experimental breeding of the garden pea led him to formulate three laws: the principle of segregation, the purity of gametes, and the mathematical ratio of possible combinations. His discoveries published in "Experiments with Plant Hybrids" (1866), were virtually ignored until 1900, when his work was rediscovered and recognized.

Mendeleev, or **Mendeleyev, Dimitri Ivanovich** (1834–1907), Russian chemist. He studied at St Petersburg, where he later became professor. Having heard lectures of the Italian chemist Stanislao Cannizzaro he developed an interest in the relationship between the 63 elements then known, devising the periodic law and the modern form of the periodic table at about the same time as the German Lothar Meyer. His table enabled him to predict the existence of several elements, including gallium and scandium. His work, published in Russian in 1869, was quickly translated into German and brought him worldwide acclaim. His textbook *Principles of Chemistry* (1869, trans. 1905) became a standard.

Mendelevium, radioactive metallic element (symbol Md) of the actinide group, first made in 1955 by alpha-particle bombardment of Es^{253}. Properties: at. no. 101; most stable isotope Md^{258} (half-life 2 months). *See also* Actinide Elements.

Mendelssohn, Felix (1809–47), in full Jakob Ludwig Felix Mendelssohn-Bartholdy, German composer and conductor. A child prodigy, he composed the famous suite for *A Midsummer Night's Dream* at the age of 17. His *Violin Concerto* (1844) is a standard in the repertory. Among his other significant works are five symphonies (including the "Scotch" and "Italian" symphonies), many piano pieces called *Songs Without Words*

(1830–45), and chamber music. His two oratorios, *St Paul* (1836) and *Elijah* (1846), are probably the greatest oratorios of the 19th century. Mendelssohn was also recognized as the foremost conductor of his day. *See also* Oratorio.

Menelaus, in Homer's classic epic, the *Illiad,* the king of Sparta, husband of Helen and brother of the commander of the Greek forces at the siege of Troy, Agamemnon. The rulers of Greece came to the aid of Menelaus after Helen's abduction by the Trojan prince, Paris. During the war Menelaus met Paris in a duel, but Paris escaped. Helen and Menelaus were reunited after the success of the Greek siege.

Menelik II (1844–1913), emperor of Ethiopia (1889–1913). He became emperor with Italian support, succeeding John IV. He defeated an Italian invasion in 1896, effectively securing Ethiopian independence. Having proved himself an able and aggressive king, he greatly expanded and modernized his empire, establishing a capital at Addis Ababa, increasing imperial power, and constructing a railroad.

Mene, mene, tekel, upharsin, from the Aramaic, "numbered, numbered, weighed, divided," the handwriting on the wall that appeared before Belshazzar, king of the Chaldeans, at a feast (Book of Daniel 5:25). Daniel was called to read and interpret it and he predicted that God had weighed Belshazzar and his kingdom and found them wanting because Belshazzar did not follow the ways of God; the kingdom would be divided and given to the Medes and Persians. That night Belshazzar was killed and the Mede, Darius, took his kingdom.

Menes (*fl.*3150 BC), Egyptian king credited with unification of upper and lower Egypt. He may have also used the names Aha, Narmer, and Scorpion. He is possibly the first Egyptian king of historical mention and is said to have founded his capital at Memphis.

Menger, Karl (1840–1912), German economist, member of the Austrian School. He is best known for his capital theory and for his theory of imputation. He pointed out that capital was a scarce productive resource, and consequently entitled to remuneration, just like labor. According to Menger's imputation theory, value is "imputed" to goods; they do not have any "intrinsic" value.

Menhaden, schooling, herringlike, marine fish found in the temperate Atlantic. An important industrial fish used for meal and oil, it is green or blue and silver. Length: to 20in (50.8cm). Family Clupeidae; species *Brevoortia tyrannus.*

Menhir. *See* Megalithic Monuments.

Menière's Disease, a disease of the labyrinth of the inner ear in which the symptoms are deafness, vertigo, and ringing in the ears.

Meninges, three membranes that cover the brain and spinal cord. The outermost membrane, the dura mater, is a tough protective covering. Within it is the second membrane, the arachnoid, whose blood vessels supply the nervous system with nourishment. The inner membrane, the pia mater, is a delicate layer on the surface of the brain and spinal cord. Between the arachnoid and the pia mater is the subarachnoid space, which contains cerebrospinal fluid.

Meningitis, inflammation of the membranes (meninges) covering the brain and spinal cord, resulting from infection with meningococci or other microorganisms. Several vaccines to combat meningitis have been developed in recent years.

Meniscus, curved upper surface of a liquid in a container, due to surface tension. The surface of water in an air-water-glass system is concave, whereas in an air-mercury-glass system the mercury surface is convex.

Mennonites, Christian denomination named after Menno Simons (1496–1561). It is a development from the 16th-century Anabaptists. Strict discipline, separation from the world, and conformity to Scripture are essential. The churches are congregational in structure, with a lay clergy. *See also* Anabaptists.

Menominee, river in NE Wisconsin; rises at confluence of Michigamme and Brule rivers; flows SE forming a natural Wisconsin-Michigan border, empties into Green Bay near Menominee; used for hydroelectricity. Length: 125mi (201km).

Menominee, or **Menomini,** an Algonquian-speaking tribe of North American Indians once occupying the Menominee River, Wis., to the area around Michilimackinac. In 1975 the population was approximately 3,500, inhabiting the Menomini Reservation in NE Wisconsin.

Menopause, in humans, the time at which the menses or menstrual cycles disappear; this generally occurs between the ages of 45 and 55 years.

Menorca (Minorca), island of Spain; 2nd-largest of the Balearic Islands, in the Mediterranean Sea, approx. 25mi (40km) NE of Majorca; capital is Mahon; S coast is known as its Riviera. Occupied at different times by Carthaginians, Romans, Vandals, Moors, in 13th century it was conquered by James I of Aragon; captured by British 1709; taken by France 1756; returned to Spain by treaty 1783; site of 14th-century cathedral, fine churches and palaces, air and naval base. Industries: shoes, cheese, textiles, soap, wine, tourism, marble, slate, lime, hemp, flax, fishing, citrus fruits, potatoes, olives, cereal, grapes. Area: 264sq mi (684sq km). Pop. 50,217.

Menotti, Gian-Carlo (1911–), US composer, b. Italy, known chiefly for his many operas. *The Medium* (1946) and *The Saint of Bleecker Street* (1954) both won Pulitzer Prizes. His *Amahl and the Night Visitors* (1951) was the first opera composed expressly for television. *The Most Important Man* (1971) is considered by Menotti one of his best works. His first symphony was *Halcyon* (1976). *La Loca* (1979) was written for Beverly Sills, who sang the title role in her farewell operatic appearances.

Mensheviks, moderate faction of the Russian Social Democratic Labor party that broke with Lenin's Bolsheviks at the 1903 party congress because of his insistence on a centralized party of professional revolutionaries. After the Bolshevik seizure of power in November 1917, many Mensheviks capitulated to the Bolsheviks. The Mensheviks were suppressed in 1922.

Menshikov, Aleksandr Danilovich (1672–1729), Russian statesman. Raised from stableboy to second in command of the Russian Empire by Peter the Great, he became field marshal in 1708, fighting valiantly at the battle of Poltava (1709). He virtually ruled Russia under Catherine II, but was exiled to Siberia by her successor, Peter II, in 1727.

Menstrual Cycle, in humans and primates, the period during which the ovum matures and is released, and the endometrium (uterine lining) proliferates. The average cycle is 28 days divided into four phases: menstrual, starting at the onset of menses, lasting 3–5 days; proliferative, during which the ovum matures and the endometrium is replaced; ovulation, time when the egg is released, ready for fertilization, occurring at midcycle (day 14–15); and progestational, during which the endometrium is maintained ready for implantation should fertilization take place. During the latter phase, the site from which the egg is released becomes the corpus luteum and secretes progesterone. In the absence of fertilization, the corpus luteum degenerates, progesterone secretion drops, and menses begins, initiating a new cycle. In the event of conception, the corpus luteum remains, and maintains the endometrium with progesterone until the placenta is formed, which then starts to secrete progesterone. The menstrual cycle normally begins at puberty (10–15 years) and ceases with menopause (45–55 years).

Mental Health, absence of disease or the normal state, an application of the medical (disease) model to the psychological (mental) sphere. Although this extension has only limited usefulness in practice, "mental health" has come to represent, rather vaguely, all aspects of psychological disturbance, treatment, control, prediction, prevention, and causes.

Mental Retardation, intellectual deficiency, defined as subaverage general intellectual functioning originating in the developmental period (to age 16). Mental retardation can be described as mild, moderate, or severe. Mild (IQ 70–85) impairment permits a limited but more or less independent existence; moderate impairment (IQ 50–70) seriously limits the individual although special training may allow him to function minimally; severe impairment (IQ below 50) requires nearly total care and these individuals benefit very little from training.

Menzies, (Sir) Robert Gordon (1894–1978), Australian prime minister (1939–41, 1949–66). He served as attorney general (1934–39). As leader of the United Australia party, he was elected prime minister in 1939. Forced by the Labor party to resign in 1941, he was reelected in 1949. He supported ANZUS (1951) and SEATO (1954).

Meperidine. *See* Demerol.

Mercantilism, 16th–18th-century trade policy advocating state intervention in economic affairs; basically, state regulation of the economy to maximize exports. Foreign trade was to be publicly controlled so as to produce the maximum possible surplus in the nation's trade balance, thus increasing the country's store of gold and silver, which constitute the "nation's wealth."

Mercator, Gerhardus (1512–94), Flemish geographer, cartographer. He developed the first modern type of map projection. He worked as cartographer to the Emperor Charles V and as cosmographer to the Duke of Jülich and Cleves (from 1559). In 1568 he produced the first nautical chart to use the Mercator projection (of which he was not the inventor). Mercator also popularized the name *atlas* for a bound collection of maps, by prefacing his collection (1595) with an illustration of the Titan Atlas supporting a globe.

Merchant Adventurers, English trading company, chartered in 1407. Its principal trade was exporting English woolen cloth to the Netherlands, but by 1550 its officers controlled almost three-quarters of England's overseas trade. Attacked as a monopoly in the 17th century, they lost many privileges, and their charter was abrogated (1689).

Merchant of Venice, The (*c.*1597), 5-act comedy by William Shakespeare. The "pound of flesh" plot comes from *Il Pecorone* by Giovanni Fiorentino (1558), and the casket story from Giovanni Boccaccio's *Decameron.* Antonio arranges a loan from Shylock to help his friend Bassanio win the hand of Portia. Bassanio's suit is successful but Antonio is unable to repay the money and Shylock claims a pound of flesh in forfeit. Portia, disguised as a lawyer, appears at the trial and saves Antonio's life by saying that Shylock may have the pound of flesh but not a drop of blood. Still in disguise, Portia tricks Bassanio, then reveals herself and chides him but eventually forgives him.

Mercia, kingdom of Anglo-Saxon England, covering at its greatest extent the area between Wales, the Thames and Humber rivers, and East Anglia. Settled by the Angles (*c.*500), Mercia pursued expansionist policies until Offa, king of Mercia (757–96), ruled over virtually all England. Its power declined with the late 9th-century Danish attacks and the ascendancy of Wessex.

Mercury, the smallest planet and the one closest to the Sun. It has a very thin atmosphere and is visible only after sunset or before sunrise. It has no satellites. Mean distance from the Sun, 36,000,000mi (58,000,000km); mass and volume, .055 and .037 times that of Earth, respectively; diameter, 3000mi (4800km); rotation period, 58.7 days; period of sidereal revolution, 88 days; temperature, daylight up to 800°F (426°C), nights down to 32°F (0°C). *See also* Solar System.

Mercury, liquid metallic element (symbol Hg) of group IIB of the periodic table, known from earliest times. Chief ore is cinnabar (sulfide), from which it is extracted by roasting. The element is a dangerous cumulative poison. It is extensively used in barometers, thermometers, and laboratory apparatus, and in mercury-vapor lamps and mercury cells. Properties: at. no. 80; at. wt. 200.59; sp gr 13.55; melt. pt. −37.97°F (−38.87°C); boil. pt. 673.84°F (356.58°C); most common isotope Hg^{202} (29.8%).

Mercury, in Roman mythology, god of merchants. His feast day was May 15. He was usually depicted holding a purse in his hand.

Mercury Poisoning, condition caused by ingestion, breathing, or absorption through the skin of mercury compounds. Mercury poisoning by inhalation has always been a problem in mercury-using industries but poisoning from ingestion of foods, chiefly fish and birds, containing mercury is a recent and serious problem. Mercury poisoning produces common symptoms, including uncoordination, loss of balance, sensory disturbances, and loss of peripheral vision, often causing a delay in proper treatment.

Meredith, George (1828–1909), English novelist and poet. His novels and poems brought him little financial success, and he supplemented his income by journalism. His novels include *The Ordeal of Richard Feverel* (1859), *Beauchamp's Career* (1876), and *The Egoist* (1879), in which Meredith analyzes the moment of self-discovery with great psychological subtlety. His poetry, such as *Modern Love* (1862), is vigorous and inventive.

Felix Mendelssohn

Prosper Mérimée

Merlin

Merganser, sea duck with slim, hooked bill that typically dives for fish. The American merganser *(Mergus merganser)* is also known as the goosander.

Mérida, city in SE Mexico; capital, major cultural, commercial, and communications center of Yucatán state; site of numerous examples of Spanish colonial architecture, notably 16th-century cathedral; university. Exports: hides, chicle, sisal, agricultural equipment. Industries: tourism, handicrafts, henequen. Founded 1542 by Francisco de Montejo. Pop. 253,800.

Mérimée, Prosper (1803–70), French novelist and short-story writer. He translated from the Russian and wrote historical novels and short stories, combining passion and objectivity. His works include the collections of short stories *Mosaïque* (1833) and *Colomba* (1840). He also wrote *Carmen* (1845), on which Georges Bizet based his 1875 opera.

Merino, important fine-wool sheep breed originated in Spain and introduced in the United States and Australia. Many local varieties have heavy white wool and soft, pliable under wool. They have short, woolly heads, folds of neck fat, and tightly spiralled horns on the male. *See also* Sheep; Wool.

Merlin, small European falcon related to the American pigeon hawk. Length: 12in (30cm). Species *Falco columbarius.*

Merovingians (*c.*448–751), dynasty of Frankish kings whose territory roughly coincided with modern France. Clovis I (*r.*481–511), the first of the line, established his authority by conquest and assassination. His conversion to Christianity solidified the bond between him and his subjects. The policy of equal inheritance rights for each son, however, led to the frequent division of the kingdom and savage battles for supremacy ensued. After the death of the last strong ruler, Dagobert I in 639, the separate regions were mainly ruled by powerful mayors of the palaces, who used the Merovingian kings as puppets. One of these mayors, Pepin the Short, ultimately deposed Childeric III in 751 to found the Carolingian dynasty.

Merry Wives of Windsor, The (*c.*1597), 5-act comedy by William Shakespeare. According to tradition the play was written at the command of Queen Elizabeth, who after seeing *Henry IV* and being captivated by the character of Falstaff, wanted to see a play about Sir John in love. The action concerns Falstaff's advances to Mistress Ford and Mistress Page and their ridicule of his efforts, using Mistress Quickly as a go-between. Ford's daughter Anne is wooed by Slender, Sir Hugh Evans, Dr. Caius, and Fenton, who eventually wins her.

Mersey River, river in England; formed by the junction of the Goyt and Etherow rivers, flows W through NW England, draining S Greater Manchester and N Cheshire; entering the Irish Sea through a wide estuary on which Liverpool stands. Length: 70mi (113km).

Merton, Thomas (1915–68), US poet and religious writer, b. France. While studying at Cambridge and Columbia universities he converted to Roman Catholicism, in 1941 became a Trappist monk, and was later ordained a priest. He is best known for his autobiography, *The Seven Storey Mountain* (1948) and wrote more than 15 volumes of poetry, meditation, and philosophy including *Figures for an Apocalypse* (1947).

Mesa, city in SW central Arizona, 15mi (24km) E of Phoenix, in Maricopa co. Shipping center for citrus fruits; winter resort. Industries: electronic components, aircraft parts. Founded by Mormons 1878; inc. 1883. Pop. (1980) 152,453.

Mesa, a large, broad, flat-topped hill or mountain of moderate height with steep clifflike sides. A mesa is capped with layers of resistant horizontal rocks, usually lavas. Buttes are smaller, more eroded mesas. Both occur commonly in arid areas of the Southwest.

Mesabi Range, hills in NE Minnesota that are rich in high-grade iron ore and talconite. Open-pit iron mines have been in operation since 1892.

Mescalero, a division of the Apache, once inhabiting the region between the Rio Grande and Pecos rivers in New Mexico. Approximately 2000 live on reservation lands in New Mexico today.

Mescaline, substance obtained from the dried tops of the Peyote cactus *Lophophora williamsii.* It produces visual hallucinations and other unusual psychological effects.

Meshach, in the Bible, Daniel's companion who, with Shadrach and Abednego, was miraculously saved from the fiery furnace, punishment for eschewing idolatry.

Mesmer, Franz (or **Friedrich**) **Anton** (1734–1815), German physician. He developed the treatment of "animal magnetism" in Vienna and Paris. Animal magnetism was later called "mesmerism," now hypnosis. Though branded as a quack in his own lifetime, Mesmer's work was important because it aroused further interest in new treatments and the possible uses of hypnosis. *See also* Hypnosis.

Mesohippus, fossil horse descended from Eohippus. Existing during Oligocene epoch (38,000,000 years ago), it had longer legs and straighter back than Eohippus. Each foot had three toes, with the middle being longest. Teeth were low-crowned. Height: 24in (61cm). *See also* Eohippus.

Mesolithic Age, or Middle Stone Age, period in man's evolution following the Paleolithic, usually reckoned to begin about 10,000 BC in Europe. The first food-producing economies evolved, and boats and sleds were invented. Microliths, tiny flint scrapers for dressing skins, were a characteristic artifact. *See also* Paleolithic Age; Neolithic Age.

Meson, member of a subgroup of hadrons, all of which have zero or integral spin. They include the pions, kaons, and eta mesons. There is no restriction on the numbers of mesons produced or destroyed in a nuclear reaction or present in a particular energy state. *See also* Baryon; Hadron; Quark.

Mesophyte, plant that grows under average moisture conditions, thriving where there is a good balance of water and evaporation. These plants have well developed root and leaf systems. *See also* Hydrophyte; Xerophyte.

Mesopotamia, ancient region in SW Asia, between Tigris (E) and Euphrates (W) rivers, and extending between mountains of Armenia (N) and Persian Gulf (S); generally corresponds to modern central Iraq, NE Syria, and S Armenia. Historically, it was the site of one of the first permanent settlements (*c.* 5000 BC) as shown through excavations of Jarmo, which have also unearthed the earliest known pottery. Sumerians, occupying S, used stone as building material, developed written communication (*c.* 3000 BC), and a canal system. Semites initiated their dominance of the S *c.* 2350

BC. In N, Kingdom of Mitanni was dominant until 12th century BC, when Assyria reigned supreme. Assyria was superseded by Babylonia 612 BC; the area was under Persian control 539 BC–331 BC, when it fell to Alexander the Great and Seleucid Dynasty; it was successively ruled by Parthians (141 BC–AD22), Sassanians (226–628), Caliph at Mecca (641–750), Abbasid caliphate (750–1258), Mongols (1258–1410), Turks (1638–*c.* 1850s); occupied by Britain during WWI and became a British mandate 1920, and kingdom of Iraq 1921.

Mesozoa, phylum of tiny, multicellular animals parasitic in invertebrates. Since they do not have well defined cell layers of ectoderm and endoderm, they are not included in the subkingdom Metazoa and may represent a separate line of evolution. Reproduction is complex and includes free swimming ciliated larva. A typical Mesozoan is composed of about 25 elongated cells. Length: 0.3in (7mm).

Mesozoic Era, the second of the three major divisions of geologic time. It is divided into three periods: the Triassic, Jurassic, and Cretaceous. Called the Age of Reptiles, dinosaurs dominated the land, ichthyosaurs and plesiosaurs the seas, and pterosaurs the skies. Mammals, birds, and flowering plants had their beginnings. For most of the era, the continents are believed to have been conjoined into one huge land mass (Pangea). *See also* Geologic Time.

Mesquite, city in NE Texas; suburb of Dallas; site of a junior college. Industries: telephone equipment, pharmaceuticals, paint, rock quarrying. Inc. 1887. Pop. (1980) 67,053.

Mesquite, or **Honey Mesquite,** deciduous tree common in SW United States and Mexico. It has a 50-ft (15-m) taproot that allows it to grow in deserts, small leaflets, and 2-in (5-cm) spines. Bees make honey from the flower nectar and the pods are used as forage. Height: 9–20ft (2.7–6.lm). Family Leguminosae; species *Prosopis juliflora.*

Messerschmitt, Wilhelm (1898–1978), German aircraft designer and builder. He organized his own aircraft manufacturing company in 1923. His aircraft were the main support of the German Luftwaffe in World War II. In 1937 he became a member of Hitler's War Council. He produced the Me-262, a twin-jet, and a swept-wing jet fighter that the Russians used as a model for their MIG.

Messiah, a long-awaited king who, people hope, will bring an age of peace and righteousness. The term comes from a Hebrew word meaning anointed, that is, consecrated for office. In Old Testament times the Jews looked for a ruler to give them religious and political liberty. Jesus was falsely accused of claiming to be such a king. Early Christians sometimes called Christ the Messiah, and the name is still current in the titles of works such as Handel's oratorio, *Messiah.*

Messier Catalog, a list of 109 star clusters, nebulae, and galaxies compiled by Charles Messier (1730–1817) in 1784. Messier's purpose was to make comet-hunting easier by listing all of the permanent celestial bodies. The catalog numbers are in common use.

Messina, seaport city in Sicily, Italy, on the Strait of Messina; capital of Messina prov. A free city of Rome 241 BC, it was conquered by Saracens 9th century; prospered under Normans 1061; taken by Crusaders 1190; ruled by Spain 1282–1714; liberated by Giuseppe Garibaldi 1860; severely damaged by earthquakes 1783, 1908; site of Norman-Romanesque cathedral (rebuilt 12th century), university (1548), biological marine institute (1806). Exports: wine, citrus fruit, olive oil, chemicals. Industries: chemicals, pharmaceuticals, processed foods. Founded *c.* 730 BC by Greeks. Pop. 265,918.

Metabolism, chemical and physical processes and changes continuously occurring in a living organism. They involve the breakdown of organic matter, resulting in energy release, and the addition of organic components to store energy. These processes produce, maintain, and destroy protoplasm, releasing energy for vital functions. *See also* Anabolism.

Metabolite, any chemical substance that is involved in the metabolic processes of cells in organisms. These substances function in the various biological energy exchanges necessary for growth, maintenance, and reproduction. *See also* Metabolism.

Metal Fatigue, the progressive fracture of metals subjected to repeated cycles of stress. Metals will fail (break, tear, or otherwise deform permanently) under repeated or reversed loads at stress levels much lower than for a single loading. This phenomenon is of particular significance in the design of safe aircraft.

Metalloid, element intermediate in properties between those of a metal and a nonmetal. In moving from left to right across the periodic table and moving down the groups, there is a transition from metallic to nonmetallic properties. Metalloid elements occur as borderline cases in groups III–VI; examples are germanium and arsenic. They are often semiconductors and have amphoteric hydroxides and oxides.

Metals, chemical elements that are typically lustrous solids, often malleable and ductile, that are good conductors of heat and electricity. The physical properties of metals can be modified by mixing with other metals or small amounts of a nonmetal, such as carbon, to form alloys. Chemically, metals are electropositive elements; that is, they lose electrons to form positive ions. Their oxides and hydroxides are bases and a metal, or its oxide, will react with an acid to form a metal salt.

Metamorphic Rocks, broad class of rocks that have been changed by heat or pressure from their original nature—sedimentary, igneous, or older metamorphic. The changes characteristically involve new crystalline structure, the creation of new minerals, or a radical change of texture. Thus the metamorphic slate made from sedimentary shale, the metamorphic gneiss from igneous granite. A special kind of metamorphism is the invasion of a rock by igneous material.

Metamorphosis, change of form, structure, or substance during development of various animals, such as when a caterpillar changes into a moth. Sometimes this change is gradual (grasshopper) and is incomplete metamorphosis. Complete metamorphosis involves a change in habit or environment, as crawling maggots becoming flies capable of reproducing and flying.

Metaphor, figure of speech that draws a comparison. It differs from ordinary comparisons in its inventiveness and from a simile in the complexity of the idea expressed. "Fleece as white as snow," is a simile, whereas "His political life was a constant swimming against the tide," is a metaphor. *See also* Simile.

Metaphysical Poetry, 17th-century English literary form, characterized by complexity of thought, wit, elliptical syntax, and sometimes violent rhythms. The term, first applied by Dryden to Abraham Cowley, was popularized by Samuel Johnson. Contemporaries called such verse "strong-lined." Chief among the metaphysical poets was John Donne. Others include George Herbert, Richard Crashaw, Henry King, Andrew Marvell, and Henry Vaughan.

Metaphysics, the branch of philosophy that deals with the first principles of reality, with the nature of the universe. The term comes from the Greek *meta ta physika,* "after the things of natures." In Aristotle's works, the First Philosophy came after the Physics. Metaphysics is divided into ontology, the study of the essence of being, and cosmology, the study of the structure and laws of the universe. Great philosophers from Plato and Aristotle to Kant and Whitehead have written on metaphysics. Skeptics, however, have charged that speculation that cannot be verified by objective evidence is useless.

Metastasis, transfer of cells or microorganisms beyond their original sites, especially characteristic of malignant tumors and spreading infections such as tuberculosis.

Metazoa, subkingdom of animals whose bodies originate from a single cell and are composed of numerous differentiated cells; from coelenterates through the mammals. It does not include sponges (subkingdom Parazoa) or protozoa (subkingdom Protozoa).

Metchnikoff, Élie (1845–1916), Russian bacteriologist. He shared the 1908 Nobel Prize in physiology or medicine with Paul Ehrlich for work on the mechanism of immunity, which included the discovery that white blood cells were important in the body's resistance to infection and disease. He was also noted for his theories of longevity.

Meteor, the luminescent phenomenon produced by small, stony or metallic bodies from interplanetary space entering the earth's atmosphere, as well as the solid body itself (more properly called a meteoroid). Brilliant meteors are called fireballs and consist of a large luminous head followed by a sparkling cometlike wake or train. Some, called bolides, explode with a sound like thunder. Most meteors disintegrate to dust before they reach the surface of the earth. *See also* Meteorite; Meteor Shower.

Meteorite, a particle or body from space (meteoroid) that has survived passage through the atmosphere and come to rest on Earth. Meteorites generally have a pitted surface and fused charred crust. There are three main types: iron meteorites (siderites); stony meteorites (aerolites); and mixed iron and stone meteorites. Some are tiny particles; others weigh up to 60 tons. Meteorites have been dated to about the same time as the origin of the Earth—about 5000 million years ago.

Meteorology, the study by scientists (meteorologists) of atmospheric and weather phenomena with the goals of the understanding, accurate prediction, and artificial control or modification of these phenomena, particularly as human and other life on Earth is affected. *See also* Climatology.

Meteor Shower, the appearance of a swarm of hundreds of meteors occurring simultaneously and traveling in parallel paths although they appear to emanate from a single point, called the radiant. Radiant positions frequently rise together with various constellations and such commonly predictable showers are therefore named Leonid, Perseid, Geminid, etc. Other showers occur infrequently at varying intervals. It is thought that shower meteoroids are fragments of steadily disintegrating comets.

Meter, pattern that occurs when the rhythm of a poem becomes regular enough to be measured. Meter imposes a regular recurrence of stresses that divides a line into equal units called metrical feet. Most commonly used feet are anapest, dactyl, iamb, trochee. The meter of a poem is described according to the kind and number of metrical feet per line. For example, iambic pentameter has five iambs per line.

Meter, unit of length (symbol m) defined as 1,650,763.73 wavelengths of radiation corresponding to a line in the spectrum of krypton-86. 1 meter is equal to 39.3701 inches.

Methane, or marsh gas, colorless, odorless, flammable gas (formula CH_4), the first member of the alkane series of hydrocarbons. It is the chief constituent of natural gas, from which it is obtained; used in the form of natural gas as a fuel and in the pure form as a starting material for the manufacture of many chemicals. Properties: melt. pt. −296.5°F (−182.5°C); boil. pt. −263.2°F (−164°C).

Methanol, or methyl alcohol, colorless poisonous flammable liquid (formula CH_3OH) obtained synthetically from carbon monoxide and hydrogen, by the oxidation of natural gas, or by the destructive distillation of wood. It is used as a solvent, rocket fuel, denaturant for ethanol, and in chemical synthesis. Properties: melt. pt. −144°F (−97.8°C), boil. pt. 148.1°F (64.5°C).

Methodist Church, originally not planned as a new sect, started in England as a trend within Protestantism. With an emphasis on life rather than creed, Anglican theology was continued. John Wesley, an Anglican priest, founder of Methodism, stressed God's mercy. In 1784, the Methodist Episcopal Church in America was founded. The Bible is studied as a continuing form of inspired revelation. *See also* Wesley, John.

Methuselah, in the Bible, son of Enoch and sixth in line from Seth, son of Adam and Eve. He died at the age of 969 and is said to be the oldest person who ever lived. He was the father of many, including Lamech, the father of Noah.

Metric System, a decimal system of weights and measures based on the meter, which was originally defined in terms of the earth's circumference and is now defined in terms of a wavelength of light. Conversions between larger and smaller units are made by use of powers of ten. This system is used internationally by scientists and is in general usage in many countries. Used first in France (1799) its spread has been slow with a few countries still using other systems today. *See also* Weights and Measures.

Metronome, an instrument designed to indicate the exact rhythm of a musical composition, invented by J. N. Mälzel in 1816. It consists of a ticking pendulum that moves back and forth at a rate controlled by an adjustable weight sliding up and down the pendulum. Modern metronomes are often electric clocks. Metronomes help the musical performer to know the general pace of a work and the composer's intentions.

Metropolitan Museum of Art, US art museum, New York City. Founded in 1870, this museum has art from nearly every country and period. The original museum building, designed by Richard Morris Hunt, was completed in 1880 and is now part of the present building. Several wings designed by McKim, Mead, and White were added later. The section added in 1975, designed by Kevin Roche, houses the Lehman collection. The museum's collection includes numerous Egyptian, Greek, and Roman works. The medieval collection has art from the early Christian to the Gothic era, much of it housed in a separate building called The Cloisters. In addition to European sculpture, there are more than 4,600 European paintings ranging from the 15th century to the present, as well as some 1,300 US paintings and 350 US sculptures. The Altman collection of Chinese porcelains is part of the 30,000 pieces of Oriental art in the museum. The American Wing houses paintings, sculpture, furniture, and decorative arts.

Metternich, (Prince) Klemens Wenzel Nepomuk Lothar von (1773–1859), Austrian statesman. As a student in Strasburg during the French Revolution, he saw and came to loathe revolutionary excesses. In 1795 he married the granddaughter of the distinguished Austrian chancellor Wenzel von Kaunitz. He entered the Austrian foreign service in 1797. He was appointed ambassador to Saxony (1801), Prussia (1803), and France (1806) before becoming foreign minister (1809). Between 1809–13 he followed a policy of conciliation toward Napoleon, arranging the marriage of Archduchess Marie Louise of Austria to Napoleon in 1810. But in 1813 he formed the Quadruple Alliance with England, Prussia, and Russia to defeat Napoleon. He reached the zenith of his influence at the Congress of Vienna (1814–15), which, after the defeat of Napoleon, restored Europe to a grouping of stable, antidemocratic states. This period between 1815–48 has been called the Age of Metternich. He was finally driven from power by the Revolution of 1848.

Metz, city in NE France, on Moselle River; capital of Moselle dept. One of Roman Gaul's chief cities, it was burned by Vandals 406 and Huns 451. After 8th century, bishops of Metz ruled a vast empire; made a free imperial city in 12th century; taken by French 1552. In 1871, Germany took it in Franco-Prussian War; Treaty of Versailles (1919) restored it to France; site of Gallo-Roman ruins, Cathedral of St Étienne (1221–1516), Place Sainte Croix (13th–15th century). Industries: metals, machinery, tobacco, clothing. Pop. 117,199.

Meuse (Maas), river that flows into Netherlands from NE France, joins Waal River and enters the North Sea; forms border between Belgium and Holland; scene of heavy fighting during WWI, including the Battle of Verdun. Length: 560mi (902km).

Meuse-Argonne Offensive (September-November 1918), World War I campaign in which US troops cut the Sedan-Mezieres railroad, the main supply line for the sector's German forces. Coupled with British and French successes, this action helped end the war.

Mexicali, city in NW Mexico, bordering Calexico, Calif.; capital of Baja California state; seat of episcopal see. Products: cotton, cereal. Chief industry is tourism. Pop. 390,400.

Mexican Bean Beetle, brown or yellow ladybird beetle with 16 black spots on its wing covers. One of the few harmful ladybird beetles, it is a serious pest of beans. Species *Epilachna varivestis.*

Mexican Border Campaign (1916–17), punitive military expedition. Mexican revolutionary Pancho Villa's raids in New Mexico had resulted in the loss of US lives. In retaliation, a US force of 15,000 men under Gen. John J. Pershing entered Mexico on March 15,

Prince Metternich

Mexico

Mexico City: library, National University

1916. The expedition's forces grew and penetrated 300 miles (480km) into Mexico, arousing anti-American feeling there. US withdrawal (Jan. 27, 1917) averted war. Mexican Gen. Venustiano Carranza was soon able to establish a constitutional government.

Mexican Stone Pine. *See* Piñon.

Mexican War, (1846–48), conflict between Mexico and the United States. Mexican insistence on the Nueces River as the southwestern border of Texas clashed with the Texans' claim to the Rio Grande as the southern frontier. When US Gen. Zachary Taylor moved his troops into the disputed area, hostilities commenced. The US blockade of Mexican ports on the Gulf and Pacific coasts and the march inland from Veracruz to Mexico City and into northern and central Mexico from Texas forced Mexico to sue for peace. By the Treaty of Guadalupe Hidalgo, Mexico relinquished all claims to Texas above the Rio Grande and ceded New Mexico and California to the United States in return for $15,000,000. The final territorial adjustment was made with the Gadsden Purchase of 1853.

Mexico, a federal republic, located immediately S of the United States, that lifted itself into the modern world during the 20th century. Its people, descended from the Spanish and Indians, comprise the most populous Spanish-speaking nation in the world.
   Land and Economy: Topographically, the country ranges from low desert plains and jungle coastal areas to high plateaus and mountains. Beginning in S Mexico, the Sierra Madres spreads into two arms, the Occidental running near the W coast, and the Oriental, a continuation of the Rockies, extending along the Gulf of Mexico as far S as Vera Cruz. Between the ranges lies the central plateau with temperate climate and vegetation. The coastal lowlands are tropical, becoming subtropical with altitude. Starting in 1950, the economic growth has been steady, with emphasis on production for export. Agrarian reform, started in the 1920s, is nearly completed. Dominance by foreign investors, except under special conditions, has been curtailed. The oil industry was nationalized in 1938. New oil and gas reserves were found in 1975, giving Mexico the world's second-largest proven oil reserves (after Saudi Arabia) and making it an important oil and gas exporter. Tourism attracts about 2,200,000 visitors and brings about $1,000,000,000 into the country.
   People: About 65% of the Mexicans are mestizos of mixed Spanish and Indian blood, with the Indian predominant. Spanish is the official language, and about 77% of the people are literate. Education is secular, free, and compulsory until the age of 15, and vocational education is encouraged. Although most of the people are Roman Catholic, all church real estate is vested in the nation. Care of church buildings is the responsibility of the clergy. Programs for housing, health, and industry have increased life expectancy from 39 years in 1941 to 60 years.
   Government: Under the constitution of 1917, Mexico is a federal republic of 31 states with power separated into the executive, legislative, and judicial branches. The president is elected by universal adult suffrage. Each state is headed by an elected governor with state powers limited.
   History: The major Indian civilizations of the Olmec, Maya, Toltec, and Aztec existed in Mexico when Hernán Cortés crushed Mexico in 1519–21 and founded a Spanish colony that lasted 300 years. Father Miguel Hidalgo declared independence in 1810, and the republic was est. in 1822. Political leaders were Gen. Guadalupe Victoria, who became the first president of Mexico, and Gen. Antonio Lopez de Santa Ana who controlled politics from 1833–55. Santa Ana was the leader in 1836 when Texas declared itself independent

of Mexico. Benito Juarez served from 1858–71. He deposed Austrian Archduke Maximilian (1864–67) who was supported as Mexican emperor by Napoleon III. Gen. Porfirio Diaz, president from 1877–80 and 1884–1911, became a dictator. Mexico's social and economic problems came to a head in 1910 when Pancho Villa and Emiliano Zapata led a revolt. Under various names, the revolutionary party continues to dominate Mexican politics. In 1976, inflation, balance-of-payment deficits, and other economic problems came to a head. The peso was sharply devalued, and the government instituted an austerity program. The economy improved in 1977, partly because of new-found oil wealth, which will help balance the economy against the high unemployment and birth rate. The decrease in international oil prices in 1981 again brought economic problems. During the 1980s, relations with the United States were strained because of conflicts over offshore fishing rights, petroleum prices, and illegal Mexican aliens seeking employment in the United States.

PROFILE

Official name: Estados Unidos Mexicanos (United Mexican States)
Area: 761,602sq mi (1,972,549sq km).
Population: 69,000,000.
Chief cities: Mexico City (capital), Guadalajara
Government: Federal Republic
   President: Miguel de la Madrid Hurtado
Religion: Roman Catholic
Language: (official) Spanish
Monetary unit: Peso
Gross national product: $59,000,000,000
Per capita income: $870
Industries (major): petroleum products, iron, steel, chemicals, aluminum, pharmaceuticals, cement
Agriculture: cotton, coffee, sugar cane, cattle, fruits, corn, fish, wheat
Minerals: silver, gold, copper, zinc, coal, petroleum
Trading partners: United States (major)

Mexico, state in cental Mexico; terrain is mountainous (E), contains the Valley of Mexico (N), volcanic belt (S and W); chief river is Lerma; Toluca is capital. Area: 8,286sq mi (21,461sq km). Pop. 6,245,000.

Mexico, Gulf of, gulf on SE coast of the United States and E coast of Mexico; Cuba is at the Gulf's entrance; connects with Atlantic Ocean through straits of Florida, and with the Caribbean Sea through Strait of Yucatán. The Mississippi and Rio Grande rivers empty into the gulf; source of shrimp and petroleum. Depth (max.): 12,714ft (3,878m). Area: approx. 700,000sq mi (1,813,000sq km).

Mexico City, capital and largest city in Mexico, near the S edge of the great central plateau. The former capital of Aztec civilization, it was taken by Hernán Cortés 1521; seat of the viceroyalty of Spanish colonies 1521–1821; captured by Mexican revolutionaries 1821; taken 1847 in Mexican War; site of Summer Olympic Games 1968, canal (1900), National Palace, Palace of Fine Arts, University of Mexico (1551). Industries: chemicals, tourism, cement, tobacco, petroleum, textiles, glassware. Pop. 8,906,000.

Mezzotint, method of engraving by scraping a design into a copper plate with a rocker, a tool with a serrated edge. The roughened surface produced, called a burr, results in light and dark tones in the print.

MHD. *See* Magnetohydrodynamics.

Miami, resort city in SE Florida, 70mi (112km) SW of West Palm Beach on Biscayne Bay; seat of Dade co and 2nd-largest city in Florida. Originally a small Indian

and agricultural community, it quickly developed (1895) when Henry M. Flagler extended Florida East Coast Railroad, dredged the harbor, and initiated the construction of recreational facilities; it experienced 1920s land boom; was devastated by hurricane 1926. It is site of Barry College (1940), Miami-Dade Junior College (1960), Orange Bowl and Miami stadiums, many sporting and recreational facilities, and luxury hotels. Industries: tourism, clothing, concrete, metal, meat products, fishing, printing, publishing. Inc. 1896. Pop. (1980) 346,931.

Miami Beach, island city, in SE Florida, across Biscayne Bay from Miami on Atlantic Ocean. Dade co. Popular resort and tourist community; connected by four causeways to Miami; famous for hotels and palatial estates, winter entertainment. Inc. 1915. Pop. (1980) 96,298.

Miami River, formerly Great Miami; river in W Ohio; rises in Indian Lake, flows S into Ohio River at the Indiana line. Length: 160mi (258km).

Miao, or **Meo,** people inhabiting the mountains of China, Vietnam, Laos, and Thailand. Consisting of numerous groups, they are a predominantly agricultural people cultivating maize, rice, and the opium poppy. They traditionally practice spirit and ancestor worship.

Mica, a group of common rock-forming minerals of the sheet silicate (SiO_4) type. All contain aluminum, potassium, sodium, or calcium, and water in the form of OH ions. All have perfect basal cleavage. Common members are muscovite, biotite, phlogopite, and lepidolite.

Micah, biblical author and sixth of the 12 minor prophets. A contemporary of Amos, Hosea, and Isaiah, he anticipated the destruction of Jerusalem, but incorporated elements of apocalyptic hope.

Michael, biblical archangel along with Gabriel, Raphael, and Uriel. A messenger of God, he appears as the defender of the Jewish people and is considered highest of the archangels. In the New Testament, he destroys the dragon (Satan).

Michael VIII Palaeologus (1234–82), Byzantine emperor (r.1259–82), and founder of the Palaeologan dynasty. A brilliant military commander and a consummate diplomat, Michael led the Greeks to a victory in their struggle against Latin rule. On June 25, 1261, his troops recaptured Constantinople, and Michael became the restorer of the Byzantine Empire.

Michael (1596–1645), tsar of Russia (1613–45), founder of the Romanov dynasty. His election as czar ended the chaotic period known as the Times of Trouble that had existed since the death of Feodor I in 1598. Between 1619–33 he had to share his rule with his father, Feodor Nikitich Romanov, who was also patriarch of Russia. Michael made peace with Sweden (1617) and Poland (1618). During his reign some Western influences were introduced but the peasants were further reduced to serfdom. He was succeeded by his son Alexis.

Michael, Princess (Marie-Christine von Reibnitz) (1945–), British noblewoman, wife of Prince Michael of Kent. Princess Michael, a Roman Catholic, had been married and divorced before her 1978 marriage to Prince Michael, so their marriage caused controversy as he is distantly in line for the British throne. Her father, an Austrian baron who for a time during World War II held a post in the Nazi SS, and her mother were divorced in 1950. Publicity about her father's past associations involved her in controversy again in the mid-

1980s. The princess runs an interior design business as well as carrying out various charitable and other public duties.

Michelangelo Buonarroti (1475–1564), Italian sculptor, painter, and architect. Raised in Florence, he was apprenticed (1488) to the painter Domenico Ghirlandaio, and later became a student under the patronage of Lorenzo de' Medici. In 1496 he moved to Rome to begin work on the "Pietà." He spent all of his productive years in Florence and Rome, working on commissions. Noted for his temper and impatience, he was often in conflict with his patrons and associates. Despite these difficulties, patrons vied with one another for Michelangelo's favor. He considered himself primarily a sculptor and created realistic, three-dimensional heroic figures, endowed with an inner personality and pent-up energy, such as his "David." Among his early sculptures were his tender "Pietà" for St Peter's, his majestic "Moses," and his "Dying Slave" and "Rebellious Slave" for the tomb of Julius II.

Michelangelo's greatest painting achievement was his fresco work on the ceiling in the Sistine Chapel, which he completed in only four years. His figures have a sculptured roundness to their bodies. The enormous area is unified by theological themes such as the creation of the world and man, as in "The Creation of Adam," and the end of the world, as in "The Last Judgment." He used garland-bearing nude youths to link together the Genesis scenes, thereby unifying the whole.

As an architect, Michelangelo was commissioned by the Medici family to build the New Sacristy in Florence to house the tombs of members of the family. This project took 14 years to complete and included the allegorical figures of "Day" and "Night" in Giuliano's tomb. He also built the Laurentian Library for the Medicis, in which his recessed columns and other features differed from the current architectural practices. His most successful and influential building projects were his designs for the Campidoglio square civic center and for St Peter's interior.

Michelozzo (Michelozzi) (1396–1472), Italian sculptor and architect. He received many commissions in Florence from the Medici family. With Lorenzo Ghiberti, he worked on such projects as the north doors for the Baptistery in Florence. He worked with Donatello on many tombs. His most important work was the Medici-Riccardi Palace, Florence.

Michelson, Albert Abraham (1852–1931), US physicist, b. Germany. In 1887 he conducted an experiment with Edward Morley to determine the velocity of the Earth through the ether, using an interferometer of his own design. The negative result acted as the starting point for the development of the theory of relativity. He was able to determine quite accurately the speed of light, and was awarded a Nobel Prize in 1907. *See also* Relativity Theory.

Michelson-Morley Experiment, famous experiment performed in 1887 by US physicist A.A. Michelson and E.W. Morley to detect the velocity of the Earth with respect to a hypothetical medium in space called ether, which was supposed to carry light waves. The negative results seriously discredited the ether theory and led to Albert Einstein's proposal in 1905 that the speed of light is a universal constant.

Michigan, state in the N central United States that borders on four of the five Great Lakes—Superior, Michigan, Huron, and Erie.

Land and Economy. Michigan comprises two peninsulas separated by the narrow Straits of Mackinac, which connect lakes Michigan and Huron. The Upper Peninsula to the N lies between lakes Superior and Michigan; to the S, the Lower Peninsula is between Lake Michigan and lakes Huron, St Clair, and Erie. The Lower Peninsula is level or rolling; it contains most of the population. The highest ground is in the Upper Peninsula. Manufacturing is largely concentrated in the cities in the S; the motor vehicle industry centers in Detroit and Flint. Mineral deposits and mining are located in the Upper Peninsula.

People. Michigan was settled by pioneers from the E states, but the economy attracted thousands of immigrants. Swedes, Norwegians, Finns, and Canadians came in the 19th century as lumbermen and miners. Before WWI, the motor industry was drawing numbers from Italy and E Europe. During WWII, an influx of blacks joined the labor force. Nearly 75% of Michigan's people lives in urban areas.

Education. There are nearly 90 institutions of higher education. The University of Michigan is the principal state-supported institution.

History. Beginning with a settlement at Sault-Ste-Marie between lakes Superior and Huron in 1641, the French built forts and settlements through the area, but lost its control to Great Britain by the 1763 treaty that ended the Seven Years' War. After the Revolution, the British did not evacuate the region until 1796, when they were compelled to by terms of the Jay Treaty (1794). Michigan became a US territory on July 1, 1805. In the War of 1812, the British captured Detroit, and their Indian allies terrorized the settlements. The opening of the Erie Canal in New York in 1825 aided Michigan's growth by linking it with the Atlantic through the lakes. After joining the Union, the state rapidly developed its timber and mining resources, which were superseded as the prime strength of the economy by the industrial boom, led by the motor vehicle sector, beginning about 1914. The auto industry switched to wartime production during WWII, experiencing tremendous growth, but fell into serious decline during the late 1970s and early 1980s. Gerald Ford, a congressman from Michigan, served as US president (1974–77).

PROFILE

Admitted to Union: Jan. 26, 1837; rank, 26th
US Congressmen: Senate, 2; House of Representatives, 19
Population: 9,258,344 (1980); rank, 8th
Capital: Lansing, 130,414 (1980)
Chief cities: Detroit, 1,203,339; Grand Rapids, 181,843; Flint, 159,611
State legislature: Senate, 38; House of Representatives, 110
Area: 58,216sq mi (150,779sq km); rank, 23d
Elevation: Highest, 1,980ft (604m), Mt Curwood; lowest, 572ft (174m), Lake Erie
Industries (major products): motor vehicles and parts, machinery, machine tools, hardware, furniture
Agriculture (major products): dairy products, cherries, apples, pears, sugar beets
Minerals (major): iron ore, salt, gypsum, limestone
State nickname: Great Lake State, Wolverine State
State motto: Si quaeris peninsulam amoenam, circumspice ("If you seek a pleasant peninsula, look about you.")
State bird: robin
State flower: apple blossom
State tree: white pine

Michigan, Lake, 3rd largest of the Great Lakes, bounded by Michigan (N and E), Wisconson (W), and Illinois and Indiana (S); at the N end it is connected with Lake Huron by the Straits of Mackinac. Lake was discovered in 1634 by Jean Nicolet, French explorer. Passed to Britain 1763 and United States 1796. Area was relatively unsettled until 1830s due to transportation difficulties. The St Lawrence Seaway has opened lake to international trade. Indiana Dunes National Lakeshore is on S shore; many islands in N part of lake. Chicago is on its SW shore. Only one of the Great Lakes entirely within the United States. Area: 22,178sq mi (57,441sq km).

Michoacán, mountainous state in SW Mexico; extends NE to central plateau. Hydroelectric power plants aid development of Michoacán's coastal region; site of training center for Latin American rural teachers, sponsored by the Organization of American States. Products: sugar cane, tobacco, coffee, cereals, livestock, lumber. Industries: mining, tourism, oil. Area: 23,202sq mi (60,093sq km). Pop. 2,805,000.

Micmac, an Algonquian-speaking tribe of North American Indians once inhabiting Nova Scotia, Cape Breton Is., Prince Edward Is., and Newfoundland. They were probably the first Indians to meet the early white explorers from Europe, *c.* AD 100. About 4,000 still live in the northeastern area today.

Microbiology, biological study of microorganisms, their structure, function, and significance. Types of microorganisms include viruses, bacteria, protozoa, and microscopic unicellular algae and fungi. Aspects of this study involve disease organisms and useful organisms, such as bacteria to fight disease or yeasts to promote fermentation. Microbiology began during the 17th century with the invention of the microscope, enabling scholars to view microorganisms for the first time. Pioneers in the field include Robert Hooke, Anton Van Leeuwenhoek, and Louis Pasteur.

Microcephaly, the condition of having a very small head. It is usually accompanied by severe mental retardation and is thought to be caused by either genetic factors, infections during the mother's pregnancy, or radiation during pregnancy. *See also* Mental Retardation.

Microeconomics, one of the two major subdivisions of economics, the study of individual components of the economic system. Microeconomics involves the basic market process and the operation of supply and demand factors in determining market price and output as well as the study of the individual firm and how the firm makes decisions to maximize its profit situation. Microeconomics also typically involves analysis of the market conditions for the factors of production. *See also* Macroeconomics.

Micronesia, collective term for a large area of island groups in W Pacific Ocean, generally those S of Japan, W of the International Date Line, N of Melanesia, and E of the Philippines; comprises a subdivision of Oceania, as do Polynesia and Melanesia. The indigenous Micronesian peoples speak a variety of languages. The area includes the independent island nations of Tuvalu and Kiribati; the US territory of Guam and US Commonwealth of the Northern Mariana Islands; and the Marshall and Caroline Islands, both part of the US Trust Territory of the Pacific Islands. *See also*: Pacific Islands, US Trust Territory of the.

Microphone, device for converting sound into oscillating electric currents of the same frequency. Main types are: the carbon microphone, in which the sound pressure causes a variation in the electrical resistance of carbon granules held between a diaphragm and a carbon block; the crystal microphone, in which the sound impinges upon a crystal, creating an oscillating current by the piezoelectric effect; the moving coil microphone, in which a coil attached to a diaphragm oscillates in a stationary magnetic field.

Microscope, optical instrument for producing an enlarged image of a very small object. The compound microscope consists basically of two converging lens systems, the objective and the eyepiece, of short focal length. The object to be studied is placed close to the objective and is illuminated by a strong source of light. The light enters the objective, which produces a magnified image of the object. This image is further magnified by the eyepiece to produce the final image seen by the eye through the eyepiece. There are usually three objective lenses on a microscope giving a choice of low, medium, and high magnification. The highest magnification can be over 1,000 times so that details much smaller than one thousandth of a millimeter can be resolved.

Microsurgery, delicate surgery performed under a binocular microscope using specialized instruments, microneedles as small as 2 mm long, and sutures 20 micrometers in diameter. It is used to repair nerves and blood vessels, for eye surgery, to reattach severed limbs, to transplant body organs, in brain surgery, for correcting spinal bifida, and for treatment of stroke. Microsurgery was first used by the Swedish surgeon G. Holmgren in the 1920s for ear operations, and by the 1940s it was used for corneal transplants. During the 1950s, techniques were developed to suture tiny blood vessels and nerves in such a way to retain their function, making possible the first successful limb reimplantation by microsurgery in 1962.

Microwave, any electromagnetic radiation that has a wavelength that ranges between one millimeter and one meter. This range is between infrared and shortwave radio wavelengths. These waves, which travel in straight lines, are used in radar, in moderate distance communication, and for such specific applications as microwave ovens.

Midas, as described by the Roman, Ovid, a king rewarded by Bacchus for rendering a service to the god's teacher, Silenus. Midas asked that anything he touched should become gold. Bacchus agreed, with the result that Midas was unable to eat or drink because his food was immediately transmuted to the precious metal.

Middle Ages, period of European history between the Greco-Roman period and modern times. Dates used by historians to delineate the Middle Ages vary, but the period is generally considered to have begun with the sack of Rome by Alaric (410) or with the death of the last Roman emperor, Romulus Augustus, in 476. Dates for the close of the Middle Ages show even more discrepancy, as they depend less upon actual events and more upon the gradual transition to the period known as the Renaissance. In Italy, the Renaissance is said to have begun with the writing of Dante, Boccaccio, and Petrarch and the artistic works of Giotto and others in the late 12th and early 13th centuries. In England Chaucer (died 1400) is one of the primary literary landmarks for the close of the Middle Ages, and in Germany the printing of the Gutenberg Bible (*c.* 1455) may be considered a sign that the Renaissance was underway. Outside dates for the period are, therefore, the 5th to the 15th centuries.

Religion. The Middle Ages marked the rise of Christianity in the West, the emergence of a strong papacy, and the rise of monastic orders. It is the period of liturgical development, doctrinal disputes, church-state struggles, and the Crusades.

Society and Politics. The beginning of the Middle Ages in the West was characterized by barbarian invasions, the decentralization of power, and the rise of

Michelangelo's Pietà *(Florence, detail)*

Albert Michelson

Milan, Italy

feudalism. In the East the cultural and political center was Constantinople, capital of the Byzantine Empire.

Art, Literature, and Learning. Although once considered a period void of learning and creativity, the Middle Ages produced an extension of literacy to greater numbers of people, the rise of vernacular literatures, the beginnings of universities, and its own unique form of art and architecture, such as the Romanesque and Gothic styles. Philosophy developed throughout the latter half of the period, reaching its peak in the 13th century. Much of our modern thought, music, and political structure has roots in this stormy and fascinating period.

Middle East, term for the region comprising the lands of SW Asia and NE Africa; includes Turkey, Cyprus, Syria, Israel, Jordan, Iraq, Iran, Lebanon, Saudi Arabia, Yemen, P.D.R. Yemen, Oman, United Arab Emirates, Qatar, State of, Bahrain, Kuwait, Egypt, The Sudan, Libya. *See also* individual countries.

Middlesbrough, city in NE England; port on Tees estuary. Industries: iron, steel, chemicals, engineering, shipbuilding. Pop. 153,300.

Middle Stone Age. *See* Mesolithic Age.

Middleton, Arthur (1742–87), American patriot and a signer of the Declaration of Independence, b. Charleston, S. C. A South Carolina delegate to the Continental Congress (1776–78; 1781–83), he was captured (1780) and later released by the British. He was elected to the state senate after the close of the Revolutionary War.

Middleton, municipal borough in NW England, 6mi (10km) NNE of Manchester on Irk River; site of 12th–16th century church of St Leonard. Industries: chemicals, engineering, soap, plastics. Pop. 53,419.

Midge, punkie, or no-see-um, brown to black fly resembling the black fly; 0.025 to 0.2in (0.6–5.0mm) long. The female bites animals and other insects. Found worldwide, they breed in fresh, brackish, or salt water or moist earth. Family Ceratopogonidae. *See also* Diptera.

Midland, city in W Texas, 20mi (32km) N of Odessa; seat of Midland co. Originally a small cow town, oil strike in 1921 brought economic and population boom. Industries: oil, cattle, chemicals, agriculture, natural gas. Founded 1884; inc. 1906. Pop. (1980) 70,525.

Mid-Ocean Ridge, the great median ridge of the sea bottom where new lithosphere is being formed. The ridges, consisting of two parallel crests with a deep valley between, are the spreading edges of the plates that cover the earth and are also known as the margins of tension. They form a world-encircling system that extends, with several side branches, along the Mid-Atlantic Ridge, up, around, and down through the Indian Ocean (the Mid-Indian Ridge), and across the Pacific (the Pacific-Antarctic Ridge). The system also extends into the continents in a few places, such as the Great Rift in Africa and along the Gulf of California. *See also* Sea-floor Spreading.

Midrash, in Hebrew literature, rabbinical interpretation and exposition of the text of the Old Testament, written from about the 4th to 11th centuries. These writings are divided into *halakah,* which deals with legal sections of the Bible, and *haggadah,* which deals with biblical legends. A large part of the Talmud is Midrashic writing.

Midsummer Night's Dream, A (*c.* 1595), 5-act comedy by William Shakespeare. Since its first US per-

formance in New York (1826) it has been revived many times, in New York, on tour, and at the Connecticut Stratford Festival. In early Athens, Lysander and Demetrius love Hermia, Helena loves Lysander. Puck, servant to the fairy king Oberon, gives Lysander a love potion, mistaking him for Demetrius. Oberon gives the same potion to his philandering Queen Titania, causing her to fall in love with Bottom, one of a traveling troup of players. By morning, all the spells wear off and all the lovers are reconciled.

Midway Islands, coral atoll in central Pacific Ocean, 1,300mi (2,080km) WNW of Honolulu; US unincorporated territory comprised of two islands, Eastern and Sand, which are administered by the Navy. Islands were annexed to the United States 1867; received cable station 1903; came under authority of US Navy Department, and was made a civilian air base 1935; scene of Battle of Midway, an important WWII Allied victory over Japanese naval and air forces, June 3–6, 1942. Area: 2sq mi (5sq km). Pop. 2,256.

Midwife Toad, European tailless amphibian that is brown with green and red spots. The mute male acts as caretaker of the eggs, keeping the strings wrapped around his legs until larvae hatch. Length: to 2in (5cm). Family Discoglossidae; species *Alytes obstetricans. See also* Frog.

Mies Van Der Rohe, Ludwig (1886–1969), German-born architect who in the United States (1938–1969) perfected the elegant, unornamented skyscraper. He was a member and director (1930–33) of the Bauhaus. In 1938 he joined the Armour Institute (now Illinois Institute of Technology) and opened his own firm in Chicago. In all his works, such as Farnsworth House in Plano, Ill. (1950), Chicago's Lake Shore Drive Apartments (1951), the Seagram Building in New York (1958), his great concern with quality of materials and their handling is evident. *See also* Bauhaus; Skyscraper.

Mieszko I, of the Piast dynasty, first historical king of Poland (*c.*960–92). In 963 he united several principalities so that his realm stretched from the Vistula to the Oder River, and in 966 he was converted to Christianity by Bohemian missionaries. Thus Poland was brought into the Western cultural sphere of influence.

Migdal, ancient fortified town in N Israel, approx. 30mi (48km) E of modern Haifa, on W shore of Sea of Galilee; thought to be the biblical Magdala, home of Mary Magdalene; site of many archeological excavations.

Mignonette, plant native to N Africa. It has small flowers clustered in a terminal spike, thick stems, and coarse, lance-shaped leaves. Among 70 species is the annual *Reseda odorata* with strongly scented flowers; height: to 18in(46cm). Family Resedaceae.

Migraine, periodic attacks of headache, usually beginning on one side, in which constriction of the cranial blood vessels is a feature. Attacks are often accompanied by gastrointestinal and visual disturbances.

Migration, Animal, periodic movements of organisms, usually in groups, from one area to another, to find food, breeding areas or better climates. Thousands of lemmings die during migrations, improving the survival rate for those remaining by reducing competition for food. Birds usually migrate along established routes (flyways). Fish migrate between fresh and salt waters or from one part of the ocean to another. Mammals migrate, usually seasonally, in search of adequate food. Some invertebrates also migrate.

Migration, Human, geographical movement of people either as individuals or as a group. Emigration is movement out of one nation to settle in another; immigration is movement into a country. Sociologists study migration for several reasons: to analyze the effects it has on pre-existing social structures; and to locate and predict migration trends.

Miguel (1802–66), Portuguese prince and pretender to the throne, younger brother of Peter IV. When Peter abdicated (1826) in favor of his infant daughter, Maria II, he made an agreement with Dom Miguel whereby Miguel would marry Maria and act as her regent in a constitutional monarchy. Miguel, however, with the aid of absolutists, tried to usurp the throne, thereby beginning the Miguelist Wars. In 1833, Maria's forces, under the leadership of her father, were finally able to defeat Miguel. He went into exile and renounced his claims to the throne, but his followers continued to make trouble during Maria's reign.

Mikado, ancient title of the emperor of Japan meaning "exalted gate." According to Shinto myth, the Mikado was directly descended from the nature gods.

Mikoyan, Anastas I(vanovich) (1895–1978), Soviet political leader. He joined the Communist party central committee (1923) and the Politburo (1935–66). After 1926 his specialty was trade, and he was commissar for foreign trade (1938). He was the first to denounce Joseph Stalin after his death (1953) and supported Nikita Khrushchev. He was first deputy premier (1955–57, 1958–64). He became Soviet president in 1964 but resigned the next year.

Milan (Milano), industrial city in N Italy, 76mi (122km) NE of Genoa; capital of Lombardy region and Milano prov. An important city of Western Roman Empire, it was a free commune by 12th century; powerful Italian state under Sforza family 1447–1535, when it was taken by Spanish; ceded to Austria 1713; ruled by Napoleon 1796–1814; made capital of Cisalpine 1804; part of Italy 1860. Milan is the site of white marble cathedral (1387–1858), Ambrosian library, Ospedale Maggiore (1456), La Scala theater, University of Milan (1924). Industries: machinery, textiles, chemicals, automotive. Pop. 1,710,263.

Milan, Edict of (313), legislation by which Constantine I (the Great) decreed religious tolerance throughout the Roman Empire. Thus the long and terrible persocution of the Christians by the emperors of Rome was ended, and the Christian church leaders were able to assume a powerful position in civil administration, wedding church to state.

Milan Decree (1807), statement of Napoleon's naval policy during Napoleonic Wars with Britain. It was in retaliation for Britain's prohibition of neutrals' trade with European ports that excluded British ships, unless the vessels first passed through a British port and paid duties there. The Milan Decree declared that any ship that complied with British regulations would be considered British property and could be seized. Napoleon's action further limited neutral trade.

Mildew, a name applied to various moldlike fungi, especially to two groups of serious plant pests: downy mildews and powdery mildews. The downy mildews (order Peronosporales) are parasites of higher plants that sometimes cause severe damage to crops. They form velvety gray patches of spores on leaves. One species, *Phytophthora infestans,* which causes late blight of potatoes, was responsible for the Irish famine of 1845–48. Powdery mildews (order Erysiphales) are a small but widespread group of plant parasites that form a characteristic powdery white coating on infected leaves. They are generally less destructive than downy mildews.

Miletus, ancient, ruined Greek city in SW Turkey; one of the greatest cities in Asia Minor before 500 BC, it was known for its colonization, commercial, and cultural importance. It was taken by Persia late 6th century BC; conquered by Alexander 344 BC; experienced a brief revival under Romans. By AD 6th century all significance had diminished and site was abandoned.

Milhaud, Darius (1892–1974), a leading 20th-century French composer. He experimented with polytonality and included American jazz elements in works, such as *La Création du Monde* (1923) for orchestra. A prolific composer, he produced many operas, symphonies, concertos, chamber music pieces, ballets, and religious compositions.

Military Law, system of rules governing military personnel. Each nation's legislature usually sets its military code, including the establishing of tribunals and defining offenses and appropriate penalties. The US military law, based on the English code, is called the Uniform Code of Military Justice. The Constitution gives to the president, as commander in chief, and to Congress the ability to make military law. Civil law is superior to military law, but during war times it may be suspended and military laws extended to civil crime.

Milk, river in NW Montana, rises in Rocky Mts; flows NE across the Canadian border, turning E and SE into Montana, empties into Missouri River near Fort Peck Dam; used for irrigation and hydroelectricity. Length: 625mi (1,006km).

Milkfish, valuable food fish found in tropical waters of the Atlantic and Pacific. Cultivated on fish farms in the Philippines, this silvery fish has a deeply-forked tail. It spawns in brackish water. Length: to 5ft (152.5cm). Family Chanidae; species *Chanos chanos.*

Milk Snake, shiny patterned snake ranging from Canada to Ecuador. Closely related to the king snake, it is usually tricolored with brown (or red), black, and yellowish transverse rings or blotches. It feeds mostly on mice. Length: to 3ft (91.4cm). Family Colubridae; species *Lampropeltis doliata. See also* King Snake; Snake.

Milkweed, perennial plants with a milky sap native to North and South America. The seeds have silky plumes and flowers are greenish, orange, rose, or purple. Height: 2–5ft (0.6–1.5m). Family Asclepiadaceae; genus *Asclepias.* The milkweed family includes milky plants, shrubs, woody vines, and some succulent desert plants, mostly native to tropical Africa.

Milky Way Galaxy, barred spiral galaxy containing the solar system. Often called the Galaxy or the Milky Way system, it is a lens-shaped structure 100,000 light years across with a dense nucleus and halo of stars surrounded by spiraling star and dust streams. The broad band of innumerable stars visible from Earth—the Milky Way proper—represents the Galaxy's outer edge; the central region, however, is optically obscured by dust and gas in the spiral arms. Our own Sun is situated on one of the spiral arms, about 32,000 light years from the center of the galaxy. *See also* Andromeda Galaxy; Galaxy.

Mill, James (1773–1836), British historian and economist. A divinity graduate from Edinburgh University, he proved too intellectual for his parishioners and thus he turned to a literary career. His monumental *History of India* (1818) gained him a position with India House in 1819. He published *Elements of Political Economics* (1821), the first English textbook on economics. He was the father of John Stuart Mill.

Mill, John Stuart (1806–73). English philosopher. He received an extraordinary education from his father, James Mill, recounted in his *Autobiography* (1873). He served in the East India Company, edited several periodicals, and was a member of Parliament (Westminster, 1865). He advocated a form of utilitarianism, in a book by that name (1861). *On Liberty* (1859) became famous for its defense of civil liberties. In *System of Logic* (1843) he attempted to provide a rigorous account of inductive reasoning. His epistemology was empiricist. *See also* Mill, James; Utilitarianism.

Millais, (Sir) John Everett (1829–96), English painter. He was a member of the Pre-Raphaelite Brotherhood. His carefully detailed landscape paintings are known for their accurate portrayal of nature. He also did portraits and historical works. *See also* Pre-Raphaelite Brotherhood.

Millay, Edna St. Vincent (1892–1950), US poet, b. Rockland, Me. A popular poet, her bohemian lifestyle personified the 1920s image of "flaming youth." She first attracted critical attention with her poem "Renascence" (1912) and later acquired a large following with such volumes as *A Few Figs from Thistles* (1920), *Second April* (1921), and *The Harp-Weaver and Other Poems* (1923), which won a Pulitzer Prize. She was also a political activist, supporting such causes as that of Sacco and Vanzetti.

Miller, Arthur (Asher) (1915–), US playwright, b. New York City. After his first play *The Man Who Had All the Luck* (1944), he wrote a novel *Focus* (1945), then a play *All My Sons* (1947), which won the Critics' Circle Award. *Death of a Salesman* (1949) won a Pulitzer Prize as well as the Critics' Circle Award. Other notable plays include *The Crucible* (1953), *A View from the Bridge* (1955), *After the Fall* (1963), and *The Price* (1968). He also wrote the screenplay for the film *The Misfits* (1961) and the television drama *Playing for Time* (1980). More recent works include volume two of *Arthur Miller's Collected Plays* (1981) and the play *The American Clock* (1980).

Miller, Henry (Valentine) (1891–1980), US author, b. New York City. Most of his novels, which are fictionalized autobiography, were first published in Paris, where he lived during 1930–39. His work was banned in the United States until 1961 for its explicit treatment of sex. His books include *Tropic of Cancer* (1934) and *Tropic of Capricorn* (1938), novels, and *The Air-Conditioned Nightmare* (1945), nonfiction. Later works include *Gliding into the Everglades and other Essays* (1977), *Sextet* (1977), *What To Do About Alf* (1978), and, in admiration of D.H. Lawrence, *The World of Lawrence* (1980).

Miller's Thumb, freshwater fish found in fast-flowing streams of Europe. One of the sculpins, it has a large bony head and tapered body. Length: to 4in (10.2cm). Family Cottidae; species *Cottus gobio.*

Millet, Jean François (1814–75), French painter. Somewhat influenced by the Barbizon school, he is best known for his landscapes showing groups of hard-working peasants, such as in "The Gleaners" (1857) and the "Angelus" (1859), both in the Louvre.

Millet, cereal grass that produces small, edible seeds, found worldwide. The stalks have flower spikes and the hulled seeds are white. In the Soviet Union, W Africa, and Asia it is an important food staple. In the United States and W Europe it is used mainly for pasture or hay. Pearl millet *(Pennisetum glaucum)* grows in poor soils and is used as food in India and Africa. Proso *(Panicum miliaceum)* is used as birdseed and livestock feed in the United States. Height: 1–10ft (30cm–3m). Family Gramineae.

Millikan, Robert Andrews (1868–1953), US physicist, b. Morrison, Ill., professor at Chicago and later at the California Institute of Technology. His oil-drop experiment, in which he measured the charge on an electron, provided final proof that electricity exists in the form of particles. He also verified Einstein's photoelectric equation, did some preliminary cosmic-ray studies, and determined a value for Planck's constant. He was awarded a Nobel Prize in 1923 for his research on electronic charge and the photoelectric effect.

Millipede, or thousand-legger, invertebrate animal found worldwide. It has a flattened body, one pair of antennae, two pairs of legs per segment and is orange, brown, or black. They avoid light and feed on plant tissues. Some tropical species squirt a repellent or poisonous secretion from pores in body segments. Length: 0.2–11in (5–279mm). Class Diplopoda. *See also* Myriapoda.

Milne, A(lan) A(lexander) (1882–1956), English essayist, dramatist, and author of books for children. For his young son Christopher Robin he wrote the verses in *When We Were Very Young* (1924) and *Now We Are Six* (1927) and the stories in *Winnie-the-Pooh* (1926) and *The House at Pooh Corner* (1928).

Milo, or **Milon** (6th century BC), legendary Greek athlete, a spectacular wrestler who inspired numerous improbable legends. One of these states that he carried an ox on his shoulders through the Olympic stadium, killed it with one punch, and ate it that day. He was also known as a soldier and defender of his native Croton, a Greek colony in S Italy.

Miloš Obrenovich (1780–1860), Serbian ruler. It was largely due to his diplomatic skill that Serbia attained a measure of independence from the Turks in 1830, with himself recognized as hereditary prince. His autocratic methods brought such unpopularity that he had to abdicate in 1839, but he was reinstated in 1858.

Milosz, Czeslaw (1911–), Polish poet and writer. Born in Vilna, Lithuania, he published his first book of verse, *Poems of the Frozen Times,* in 1932, at the age of 21. After World War II, he served as Polish cultural attaché in Washington, D.C., and as first secretary for cultural affairs in Paris. In 1951 he sought political asylum in France and in 1960 came to the US where he taught at the University of California at Berkeley. A prolific author of poetry, fiction, essays, autobiography, and criticism, his work was circulated clandestinely in Poland and scantily translated into English. He was awarded the Nobel Prize for literature in 1980. His works include the poetry volumes, *Selected Poems* (1973), *Bells in Winter* (1978), a novel, *The Usurpers* (1955), and his autobiography, *Native Realm* (1981).

Miltiades (c.550–489 BC), Athenian nobleman and father of Cimon, he is credited with the plan to meet the Persians in the field at Marathon (490 BC). He led an ineffective naval expedition at Paros (489 BC), where he was wounded.

Milton, John (1608–74), English poet and prose writer. Born in London, educated at Cambridge University, he traveled in Europe (1638–39), and served as Latin secretary to the Commonwealth government (1649–60). In 1652 he became blind. His work is characterized by Latinized language and grandeur of imagery. A Puritan, he nevertheless questioned Christian orthodoxy. His greatest works are *L'Allegro* and *Il Penseroso* (both 1632), *Comus* (1634), *Lycidas* (1637), *Areopagitica* (1644), *Paradise Lost* (1667), *Paradise Regained* (1671), and *Samson Agonistes* (1671).

Milwaukee, city and port of entry in SE Wisconsin, on W shore of Lake Michigan; seat of Milwaukee co. The North West Co. est. a fur trading post here 1795; by 1838, the village of Milwaukee was founded; great influx of German refugees 1848–1900 influenced and stimulated political, social, and economic growth; it was scene of racial disorder 1960s. It is site of Marquette University (1881), Alverno College (1857), University of Wisconsin at Milwaukee (1908). Industries: machinery, diesel and gas engines, construction and electrical equipment, beer. Inc. 1839 as village, 1846 as city. Pop. (1980) 636,212.

Mimicry, form of protection, including shape or coloration, developed by an organism to resemble its environment. For example, the viceroy butterfly mimics the coloration of the inedible monarch butterfly. *See also* Camouflage; Protective Coloration.

Mimosa, plants, shrubs, and small trees native to tropical North and South America. They have showy featherlike leaves and heads or spikes of white, pink, or yellow flowers. Family Leguminosae; genus *Mimosa. See* Beta Crucis.

Mindanao, second largest island of the Philippines, in S part of archipelago, NE of Borneo. The terrain is mostly mountainous, heavily indented with gulfs and bays. There is a large Muslim population as evidenced by several mosques. Products: corn, rice, coconuts, timber, coffee, abaca. Area: 36,537sq mi (94,631sq km). Pop. 7,292,691.

Mindoro, island in N central Philippines, S of Luzon and at N extreme of the Sulu Sea; with neighboring islands it constitutes the province of Mindoro. The island has several good harbors, and a mountain range divides it N-S; many streams and rivers drain the mountain region and irrigate fertile central plains (E and W). Farming and mining occupy most of the inhabitants, who are chiefly Visayan and Tagalog. Visited by Spaniards 1570 and besieged by Moros in the 17th and 18th centuries, the island was occupied in WWII by Japan until US forces attacked. Capital is Calapan on N coast. Highest peak is Mt. Halcon, 8,487ft (2,580m). Products: coal, sulfur, gold, coconuts, abaca, rice, fruits, corn. Area: 3,758sq mi (9,733sq km). Pop. 473,-940.

Mindszenty, Jozsef Cardinal (1892–1975), Hungarian Roman Catholic prelate and cardinal. An outspoken opponent of totalitarianism, he spent much of his life in jail or self-imposed confinement: he was jailed in 1919 for opposition to Béla Kun's Bolshevik regime; in 1944, for opposing the German-controlled government. In 1948, after his celebrated trial, he was incarcerated by the Communist government. He was released briefly during the 1956 Hungarian revolution but with the return of the Communist power he sought asylum in the US legation in Budapest. In 1971, he left the legation for the first time in 15 years after agreeing to leave Hungary and live in Rome. He became a cardinal in 1946.

Mineralogy, investigation of naturally occurring inorganic substances found on earth and elsewhere in the solar system. Major subdivisions are crystallography,

Darius Milhaud

John Milton

Mink

composition and atomic arrangement in minerals; paragenetic mineralogy, associations and order of crystallization of minerals; descriptive mineralogy, physical properties used in identification of minerals; and taxonomic mineralogy, classification of minerals by chemical and crystal type. *See also* Geochemistry; Petrology.

Minerals, natural, homogeneous and, with a few exceptions, solid and crystalline materials that form the Earth and make up its rocks. They have a definite chemical composition or range of compositions and are mostly formed through inorganic processes. More than 3,000 minerals have been identified. They are classified on the basis of chemical makeup, crystal structure (which is a reflection of the internal arrangement), and physical properties such as hardness, specific gravity, cleavage, color, and luster. Aggregates of minerals form rocks except in the few cases where a rock is composed of a single mineral. Minerals are economically important as ores (eg, those rich in valuable metals), as gems (eg, diamonds, rubies), as structural materials (eg, calcite and gypsum), in ceramics (feldspars), as chemicals, fertilizers, and as natural pigments.

Minerva, in Roman religion, the goddess of handicrafts, the professions, the arts, and, later, war. Commonly identified with the Greek Athena, Minerva was honored in association with Mars in the "Quinquatrus," which lasted five days during the spring. She was venerated throughout the empire. Particular homage was paid by corporations of artisans, flute players, and doctors.

Ming Dynasty (1368–1644), the last of the great Chinese dynasties before the conquest of China by the Manchus. The Ming brought a period of cultural and philosophical advance during which China influenced many adjacent areas, including Japan. Great seagoing expeditions were launched to the S and W, reaching the E coast of Africa. Peking was laid out in its present form, and the traditional bureaucracy was reinforced.

Miniature Bull Terrier, smaller version of the bull terrier; evolved from small bull terriers and the old toy bull terrier. Average size: up to 14in high (35.5cm) at shoulder; to 20lb (9kg). *See also* Bull Terrier.

Miniature Pinscher, small, deerlike dog (toy group) bred in Germany several centuries ago. It has a flat skull and tapering muzzle; erect ears cropped to a point; compact, wedge-shaped body; straight legs; and high-set, erect, docked tail. The smooth, hard, short coat may be red, black with tan and rust red, or solid brown with rust or yellow. Average size: 10–12in (25.5–30.5cm) high at shoulder; 8–10lb (3.5–4.5kg). *See also* Toy Dogs.

Miniature Schnauzer, German-bred dog classified in terrier group in US, but not in Germany or England. Breed dates from 1899 and was brought to US in 1923, where it has become one of the most popular of all breeds. Its rectangular head has abundant whiskers. Ears are either cropped with pointed tips or uncropped and folded. The short, deep body is set on strong legs. The docked tail is carried erect. Average size: 12–14in (30.5–35.5cm) high at shoulder; 15lb (7kg). *See also* Terrier.

Mining, the process of obtaining valuable metallic and nonmetallic materials from the Earth's crust. Included are underground, surface, and underwater methods. Mostly mining involves the physical removal of rock and earth. Petroleum, gas, and some sulfur are extracted by techniques not called mining. Any mining

operation comprises four stages: prospecting, exploration, development, and exploitation. Once a valuable deposit has been found and delimited, decisions are made on modes of entry, subsidiary developments and removal techniques. In underground mining, shafts or cross-cut tunnels are dug. Surface mining involves both open-cut and open-pit methods. Underwater mining is accomplished by dredging.

Mink, small semiaquatic mammal of the weasel family with soft, durable, water-repellent hair of high commercial value. Old World minks (*Mustela lutreola*) resemble American minks (*Mustela vison*) but do not have such valuable fur. They have long, slender bodies, short legs, and long, bushy tails. In the wild, mink have dark brown fur with long black outer hair. Ranch mink have been bred to produce skins of silver, pastels, and variations of natural shades. They eat fish, rodents, and birds. Length: 2ft. (61cm); weight: 21lb (1kg). Family Mustelidae.

Minkowski, Hermann (1864–1909), Russian-German mathematician, b. Alexota. Graduating from Königsberg, he held professorships successively there, at Zurich, and at Göttingen. He was deeply interested in the work on relativity of Einstein, a former pupil, and contributed to its mathematical foundations. It was he who first saw the necessity of treating time mathematically as a fourth dimension (Minkowski space-time).

Minneapolis, city and port of entry in SE Minnesota, just SE of St Paul, its twin city, at Falls of Saint Anthony; seat of Hennepin co; largest city in Minnesota. In 1683, Louis Hennepin, a French explorer, visited the falls; Fort Snelling military reservation was est. 1819; Minneapolis was settled 1847; St Anthony was annexed by Minneapolis 1872; the town developed into a lumber center and flour milling area. Minneapolis is the site of University of Minnesota (1851), Augsburg College (1869), Stevens House (1849), and Fort Snelling State Park; processing, distribution, trade, railroad, and grain market center. Industries: milling, farm machinery, food processing, electronic equipment, publishing, printing, fabricated metals, textiles. Inc. 1856. Pop. (1980) 370,951.

Minnesinger, name given to the poet-musicians of medieval Germany. Most of the poems, usually about chivalric love, were sung. Some minnesongs are preserved in medieval manuscripts, such as the Heidelberg collection. Among the best known of the Minnesinger were Walther von der Vogelweide (*c.* 1170–1230) and Oswald von Wolkenstein (*c.* 1377–1445). Minnesinger poems have been sources for many modern operas, novels, and plays.

Minnesota, state in the N central United States, bordered on the N by the provinces of Manitoba and Ontario, Canada.

Land and Economy. The land is level or rolling except in the rugged hills of the NE. Much of it is richly fertile. The N is forested. There are more than 10,000 lakes, some of which are sources of the central branch of the Mississippi River. In the NE, Minnesota borders on Lake Superior. Through the lake port of Duluth pass shipments of iron ore, which is found in the Mesabi Range N of the lake. Taconite, a rock containing low-grade iron, is mined as the higher-grade ores are depleted.

People. In the late 19th century, thousands of immigrants from Europe, chiefly Germans, Swedes, Norwegians, and Finns, came to work the state's forests, farms, and mines. Their descendants comprise a sizable element of the population. About 66% of the people resides in urban areas. The metropolitan area of Minneapolis-St Paul holds about half the population.

Education and Research. There are nearly 60 institutions of higher education. The state-supported University of Minnesota has several campuses. The Mayo Clinic at Rochester, one of the world's greatest medical centers, is a focus of research.

History. French fur traders entered the region in the 17th century and controlled it until 1763, when the part E of the Mississippi River passed to Great Britain by the Treaty ending the Seven Years' War. After the Revolution, this area was ceded to the United States, which acquired the lands W of the river from France by the Louisiana Purchase in 1803. Fort Anthony, now Fort Snelling, was built in 1820 at the junction of the Minnesota and Mississippi rivers; other tracts of land were bought from the Indians, and settlement began. Minnesota Territory was organized in 1849. Minnesota was the first state to respond to President Lincoln's call for troops in the Civil War. The state grew rapidly after the war; its population, which numbered 172,000 in 1860, was 1,310,000 in 1890. During the 20th century, mining and manufacturing began to dominate Minnesota's economy, although during the 1970s the dumping of iron industry wastes into Lake Superior was a controversial issue.

PROFILE

Admitted to Union: May 11, 1858; rank, 32d
US Congressmen: Senate, 2; House of Representatives, 8
Population: 4,077,148 (1980); rank, 21st
Capital: St Paul, 270,230 (1980)
Chief cities: Minneapolis, 370,951; St Paul; Duluth, 92,811
State legislature: Senate, 67; House of Representatives, 134
Area: 84,068sq mi (217,736sq km); rank, 12th
Elevation: Highest, 2,301ft (702m), Eagle Mt; lowest, 602ft (184m), Lake Superior
Industries: (major products): processed foods, machinery, electrical equipment, chemicals, paper
Agriculture: (major products): dairy products, oats, corn, soybeans, poultry
Minerals (major): iron ore, taconite, sand, gravel
State nickname: Gopher State, North Star State
State motto: L'Etoile du Nord (Star of the North)
State bird: common loon
State flower: pink and white lady's-slipper
State tree: red (Norway) pine

Minnesota, river in S Minnesota; rises in Big Stone Lake on E South Dakota-W Minnesota line; flows SE then NE to Mississippi River at Mendota. Length: 332mi (535km).

Minnow, subfamily of freshwater fish found in temperate and tropical areas; includes shiners, dace, chubs, tench, and bream. More specifically, the term includes small fish of the genera *Phoxinus* and *Leuciscus*. Length: 1.5–18in (3.8–45.7cm). Family Cyprinidae.

Minoan Architecture, architectural style represented by the elaborate palaces at Knossos and Phaestos in Crete, built *c.* 2200 BC and rebuilt after an earthquake *c.* 1700 BC. The Palace of Minos at Knossos was composed of many small, brightly painted rooms and corridors that led to larger pillared halls, courtyards surrounded by colonnaded walks, and the grand throne room.

Minoan Civilization (*fl. c.*3000–1200 BC), ancient culture of Crete, named for the legendary King Minos. Its capital was Knossus, an impressive city with large palaces. The Minoans traded throughout the Mediterranean region as evidenced by their distinctive "bull-motif" pottery found throughout the area. They were skilled metalworkers. Knossus was destroyed several times by earthquakes and rebuilt. Invasions by Mycenaean Greeks beginning around 1400 led to the gradual disintegration of the Minoan civilization.

Minoan Script. *See* Linear B.

Minos, two characters in Greek mythology. One, son of Europa and Zeus, a famous law-giver, king of Crete and later consigned to Hades as a judge of human souls. The other, Minos II, his grandson, who exacted annual tribute from Greece in the form of human victims for the man-eating Minotaur that Minos kept in the labyrinth. *See also* Theseus.

Minsk, capital city of the Belorussian SSR; USSR, also a capital of the Minsk oblast, on Svislach River, 400mi (644km) WSW of Moscow. Known as early as 1067, it was ravaged by Tartars in 1505; annexed by Russia in 1793; partially destroyed by Napoleon 1812; occupied by Germans 1918 and Poles 1919; seized by Germans 1941; retaken by Soviet forces 1944; site of Belorussian State University (1921), Belorussian Academy of Sciences, polytechnic, lumber trade, medical, and teachers' colleges, swamp research institute, modern civic center, state museum, opera and ballet theaters, 17th-century cathedral. Industries: furniture, prefabricated houses, food processing, railroad shops, cement, automobiles, tractors, bicycles, lathes, instruments, machine tools, radios, phonographs, linen, cotton goods, shoes, mirrors, porcelain, leather goods. Pop. 1,273,000.

Mint, or *Mentha,* a widely distributed group of plants of the Labiatae family including such aromatic herbs as rosemary, lavender, sage and thyme, and such garden flowers as salvia. They are characterized by four-sided stems and opposite, aromatic leaves. The flowers, usually small and clustered at leaf joints or into spikes, always have an upper and lower lip. Mints are grown for ornament, for flavor and aroma, and for use in medicine.

Minuit, Peter (1580–1638), first governor of New Netherland, b. Netherlands. He bought Manhattan Island (1620) for Dutch West India Co. from Indians for $24 worth of trinkets. He was recalled as governor (1631). He returned (1638) as leader of New Sweden on the Delaware River, founding colonies at Trenton, N.J., and Wilmington, Del.

Miocene Epoch. *See* Tertiary Period.

Miohippus, fossil horse that lived during the Miocene Epoch (28,000,000 years ago). A slim, graceful animal the size of a Shetland Pony, it had three toes on each foot, but only the middle toe touched the ground. Teeth were low-crowned for browsing.

Mira, a variable star of the southern constellation Cetus. Mira is a binary, with a red giant primary, spectral type M6, and a faint B-type companion. Brightness varies over a cycle of about 330 days.

Miranda, satellite of Uranus.

Miranda v. Arizona (1966), landmark US Supreme Court decision illustrative of the liberal stance of the court regarding criminal matters during the term of Chief Justice Earl Warren. The court declared that detention by police was inherently coercive and that confessions obtained after police questioning were highly suspect. Expanding the doctrine of *Escobedo* v. *Illinois,* the court set out a stiff code of police conduct that required that an accused be fully informed of his rights and be allowed to contact counsel before questioning. *See also* Escobedo v. Illinois (1964).

Miriam, in the Bible, sister of Moses and Aaron. A prophet, she watched over the baby Moses until he was found in the bullrushes by the Pharaoh's daughter. For criticizing the marriage of Moses to a Cushite woman, she became leprous but was later healed.

Miró, Joan (1893–1983), Spanish painter and graphic artist. He also designed ceramics and stage sets. His early works were realistic landscapes and portraits that showed fauvist and cubist influences. Later his style became abstract and surrealistic. He is especially known for his imaginative use of highly colored freeforms. He was commissioned to paint for the new East Building of the National Gallery of Art in Washington, D.C. where his work was displayed in 1978. In 1981 three separate exhibitions honored his 87th birthday.

Mirror, highly polished reflecting surface, usually glass, coated on back or front with silver or aluminum, that is usually plane, spherical, or paraboloid. Image production follows the laws of reflection. Plane mirrors produce a laterally inverted virtual unmagnified image. Spherical mirrors (portions of a spherical surface) are concave (caving inward) or convex (bulging out). A

concave mirror converges a narrow beam of light; a convex mirror causes divergence. The image can be right-way-up or inverted, real or virtual depending on the relative position of object and focal point of the spherical mirror; it may also be magnified or reduced in size. A spherical mirror suffers spherical aberration, which is absent in the concave paraboloid mirror, such as used in reflecting telescopes. This shape thus produces a much sharper image. *See also* Aberration; Focal Length; Image, Optical; Reflection.

Mishima, Yukio (1925–70), Japanese author, b. as Kimitake Hiraoka. His novels, short stories, plays, and essays reveal a conflict between his obsessions with beauty and violence. His early novel *Confessions of a Mask* (1949) is a partially autobiographical study of homosexuality. *The Temple of the Golden Pavilion* (1956) concerns a psychopathic monk who burns down his temple because of its beauty. *The Sailor Who Fell from Grace with the Sea* (1963) is a horror tale. His final work, the tetralogy *The Sea of Fertility* (1970), is an epic of modern Japan. In 1970, with members of Tatenokai ("The Shield Society"), his own army, he seized the commanding general's office of Tokyo's military headquarters and committed ritual suicide.

Mishna, collection of Jewish legal traditions and moral precepts that form the basis of the Talmud. The Mishna was compiled about AD 200 under Rabbi Judah I. It is divided into six parts: laws pertaining to agriculture; laws concerning sabbaths, fasts, and festivals; family laws; civil and criminal laws; laws regarding sacrifices; and laws concerning ceremonial regulations.

Miskolc, city in NE Hungary, on Sajó River; site of 13th-century Gothic church. Industries: iron, steel, vehicles, textiles, furniture, paper, wine, flour, lignite mining, shoes. Pop. 199,000.

Missile, self-propelled flying weapon, powered by rocket, ramjet, or turbojet. *Ballistic* missiles travel in the outer atmosphere and can only be powered by rockets. *Cruise* missiles travel in the lower atmosphere and can utilize jet engines. *Guided* missiles carry self-contained guidance systems or can be controlled by radio from the ground. *Unguided* missiles are freeflying with no control other than initial aim and amount of fuel.

Mission Indians, a general term applied to those North American Indians who lived adjacent to the Spanish Catholic missions of coastal California about 1769–1823. Numbering about 40,000 persons, they were required to live in and around the missions and perform various labors. The term is unfortunate, since many unrelated peoples were involved; the major tribes included the Chumash, Costanoan, Diegueño, Fernandeño, Gabrielino, Juaneño, and Luiseño.

Mission Style, a style of architecture loosely associated with Spanish colonial missions built in North America from the 16th century. Typical buildings are the *presidio,* military stronghold; *hacendado,* large house of a wealthy landowner; and churches.

Mississauga, city in Ontario, Canada; on W side of Lake Ontario; SW suburb of Toronto. Pop. 250,017.

Mississippi, state in the S central United States, bordered on the S by the Gulf of Mexico and on the W by the Mississippi River. It was one of the six original states of the Confederacy in the Civil War.
    Land and Economy. The land slopes from the hills in the NE. Much of it is suitable for agriculture. An E-W strip across the center, known as the Black Prairie, has exceptionally rich soil. Pine forests are widespread. The prinicpal rivers in the state are the Yazoo and its tributaries and the Peral. Mississippi's soils and its warm climate have made agriculture and forestry the mainstays of the economy. Commercial fisheries operate on the Gulf Coast. Since the mid-20th century, efforts to attract and encourage industry have been successful. The extraction and refining of petroleum, found chiefly in the S, is important.
    People. The early settlers were English, Scots, and Irish from states along the Atlantic coast. Thousands of blacks were imported to work the cotton plantations; more than 35% of the population now is black. About 45% lives in urban areas.
    Education. There are more than 40 institutions of higher education. The University of Mississippi is the principal state-supported establishment.
    History. The Sieur de la Salle, voyaging down the Mississippi River, claimed the region for France in 1682, and a French settlement was made on the Gulf coast in 1699. Great Britain received the area in 1763 by the treaty ending the Seven Years' War, but during the American Revolution the Spanish gained actual control and refused to recognize the transfer of the land to the United States by treaty after the war. Spain finally yielded in 1795 and the Territory of Mississippi was organized in 1798. Mississippi seceded from the

Union on Jan. 9, 1861, and Jefferson Davis, a US senator from the state, became president of the Confederate States of America. The state was a battleground in the Civil War. Jackson and Meridian were burned by Union forces, and Vicksburg, on the Mississippi, fell on July 4, 1863, after a long siege. It took years to repair the ravages of war and the political turmoil of the Reconstruction era. William Faulkner, Nobel Prize-winning novelist, won his fame writing of life in his native state. Mississippi was a focus of the civil rights movement of the 1960s.

PROFILE

Admitted to Union: Dec. 10, 1817; rank, 20th
US Congressmen: Senate, 2; House of Representatives, 5
Population: 2,520,638 (1980); rank, 31st
Capital: Jackson, 202,895 (1980)
Chief cities: Jackson; Biloxi, 49,311; Meridian, 46,577
State legislature: Senate, 52; House of Representatives, 122
Area: 47,716sq mi (123,584sq km); rank, 32d
Elevation: Highest, 806ft (246m), Woodall Mt; lowest, sea level
Industries (major products): lumber, wood products, paper, furniture, apparel, chemicals
Agriculture (major products): soybeans, cotton, dairy products, cattle, poultry
Minerals (major): petroleum, natural gas
State nickname: Magnolia State
State motto: Virtute et armis (By valor and arms)
State bird: mockingbird
State flower: magnolia
State tree: magnolia

Mississippi, river in central United States; rises in NW Minnesota, flows SE, forming many state borders, into the Mississippi river delta and the Gulf of Mexico; together with the Missouri River, it forms the longest river system in the world after the Nile and the Amazon. Chief tributaries are the Ohio, Missouri, Arkansas, Tennessee, Wabash, Cumberland, Platte, and Yellowstone. Major economic navigable waterway, it connects with the Great Lakes-St Lawrence Seaway (N) and the Intracoastal Waterway (S); discovered by Hernán DeSoto 1541; explored by Fathers Marquette and Joliet 1673. In 1803 the United States gained possession of river by terms of Louisiana Purchase; a major outlet for mid-continent development in 19th century; Union forces made use of it for many engagements, especially taking of New Orleans (1862) and Vicksburg (1863). Steamboats first traveled on river in 1811. Mark Twain, who served as a riverboat pilot, wrote *Life on the Mississippi* in 1883. By this time the railroads were giving river transportation strong competition. Since 1950s many improvements have been made to river's channels and traffic has increased, especially in moving bulkier freight (petroleum, limestone, chemicals). Springtime flooding as the tributaries bring melting snows and heavy rains to the Mississippi has had disastrous effects in some years. Despite dams on the upper river and floodways and levels at critical points, a year of especially heavy rains such as 1973 can still be ruinous. In the delta area sugar cane is raised, shrimp fisheries are maintained, and sulfur, natural gas, and oil are available in large quantities. Cotton growing is important in the lower valley and freshwater fish are plentiful upstream. From December to mid-March the upper course is frozen over; thick fogs also occur during warm spells of this period. Length: approx. 2,350mi (3,784km).

Mississippian Period. *See* Carboniferous Period.

Mississippi Bubble (October 1720), economic disaster in France caused by the collapse of the Compagnie des Indes (Mississippi Company). In 1717, the Scotsman John Law, backed by Philippe I, regent of France, gained a monopoly over commercial exploitation and colonization of Louisiana. Law claimed that Louisiana was rich in gold and silver; people rushed to invest. By 1719 Law controlled almost all French colonies and the royal bank. By 1720 doubts set in and the speculative bubble burst. Law fled France and his financial empire collapsed. France was left with an enormous national debt. In spite of the financial failure, the scheme had brought many settlers to Louisiana and had resulted in the founding of New Orleans in 1718.

Missouri, state in the central United States on the W bank of the Mississippi River.
    Land and Economy. In the N and W the land is prairie and rolling hills. In the S, the low ridges of the Ozark Mts run NE-SW. The Missouri River flows W to E across the state to its junction with the Mississippi. The two great rivers have been major influences on the history of the state as lines of travel and transportation. Much of the farming lies N of the Missouri. A major portion of the industry is in the areas of St Louis on the Mississippi in the E and Kansas City on the Missouri in the W. The Ozark region is the center of most mining.

Mississippi River: Baton Rouge, Louisiana

Jefferson City, Missouri, state capitol

Billy Mitchell

People. Missouri's early settlers came mostly from Kentucky, Tennessee, Virginia, and North Carolina. Germans, Irish, and English moved into the St Louis area in the mid-19th century. More than 90% of the present population was born in the United States. About 70% lives in urban areas.

Education. There are seven institutions of higher education. The first school of journalism in the United States was founded at the state-supported University of Missouri in 1908.

History. The first settlements were made by the French in the mid-18th century. The United States acquired the region from France in the Louisiana Purchase of 1803, and it became a territory in 1812. In the following decades Missouri was the main corridor of the westward migrations. St Louis became a supply center. Wagon trails to Oregon, California, and the Southwest began at St Joseph and Independence. Vivid pictures of these years in Missouri, a border state between the Northern and Southern cultures, appear in the writings of Mark Twain, a native of Hannibal. Missouri had been admitted to the Union without restrictions on slavery, but when the Civil War began sympathies were bitterly divided between the Union and the Confederacy. Guerrilla fighting and several pitched battles ensued before the state was kept in the Union. After the war and into the 20th century the state's development was steady. The two world wars, especially, stimulated growth of St Louis and Kansas City as industrial and distribution centers, although subsequently St. Louis declined in population and industrial importance.

PROFILE

Admitted to Union: Aug. 10, 1821; rank, 24th
US Congressmen: Senate, 2; House of Representatives, 10
Population: 4,917,444 (1980); rank, 15th
Capital: Jefferson City, 33,619 (1980)
Chief cities: St Louis, 453,085; Kansas City, 448,159; Springfield, 133,116
State legislature: Senate, 34; House of Representatives, 163
Area: 69,686sq mi (180,487sq km); rank, 19th
Elevation: Highest, 1,772ft (540m), Taum Sauk Mt; lowest, 230ft (70m), St Francis River, Dunklin county
Industries (major products): transportation equipment (space capsules, rocket engines, aircraft, automobiles), processed foods, chemicals
Agriculture (major products): hogs, cattle, poultry, soybeans, corn, winter wheat
Minerals (major): lead, barite, limestone
State nickname: "Show Me" State
State motto: Salus populi suprema lex esto ("The welfare of the people shall be the supreme law")
State bird: eastern bluebird
State flower: hawthorn
State tree: dogwood

Missouri, river in central and NW central United States, rises at the confluence of the Jefferson, Madison, and Gallatin rivers in S Montana, flows E to central North Dakota, S across South Dakota, E across Missouri and joins the Mississippi River just N of St Louis. Chief tributary of the Mississippi, and the longest river in the US, third longest in the world after the Nile and the Amazon. Fathers Marquette and Louis Joliet first saw the river in 1673; Meriwether Lewis and William Clark explored parts of it 1804–06. Used by traders, gold seekers, and pioneers as a way to the Northwest. Known as the "Big Muddy" for its great erosion of farm lands along its banks. Flooding is also a serious problem, especially in the spring. Sioux City, Iowa, is head of navigation for river, due to dams upstream. Freezing of river December to March and resulting low water levels interrupt navigation; summer problem of low

water is controlled by releasing water from Gavin Point Dam. Length: 2,565mi (4,130km).

Missouri Compromise (1820), US agreement to settle disputes between the states over slavery. With 11 free and 11 slave states, there was a balance in the Senate. When Missouri applied for admission as a slave state (1817), the balance was threatened. Heated disagreements over slavery broke out in Congress (1819). Henry Clay did much to ensure the passage of the agreement, which combined the admission of Maine as a free state with Missouri as a slave state and prohibited slavery in the Louisiana Purchase north of the 36° 30′ line.

Mistletoe, tropical, evergreen plant semiparasitic on the branches of broad-leaved trees. It has small, thick, yellowish-green leaves. The small, yellowish flowers produce waxy, white, poisonous berries. Among 1,000 species are *Viscum album* found throughout Europe and Asia and common mistletoe *Phoradendron flavescens* of E United States, usually found on oaks. Family Loranthaceae.

Mitchell, Maria (1818–89), US astronomer, educator, b. Nantucket Island, Mass. While conducting a special study of sunspots and nebula, she discovered a new comet in 1847. She was the first woman elected to American Academy of Arts and Sciences (1848) and was the first professor of astronomy at Vassar College (1865–88).

Mitchell, William ("Billy") (1879–1936), US military officer, b. France. He helped form the American Expeditionary Force aviation program in World War I and was court-martialed in 1925 for his attacks on the navy's vulnerability.

Mitchell, Mount, peak in W North Carolina, in Black Mts; highest peak E of Mississippi River, 6,684ft (2,039m).

Mite, variously colored arthropod found worldwide as a parasite on plants and animals. The larva has three pairs of legs; the adult has four pairs and the head and abdomen are fused. Length: 0.02–0.1in (0.5–3mm). Class Arachnida; order Acarina. *See also* Chigger; Red Spider.

Mithra, or **Mitra,** god of India and Persia from ancient times, and the chief religious figure of Persia after the 6th century BC. A god of both Sun and Sun, who had created life by spilling the blood of the sacred bull, Mithra came to represent all that was good in a cult that spread throughout Europe. Mithraism was gradually replaced by Christianity after the 3rd century AD.

Mithridates VI Eupator Dionysus (c.131–63 BC), last of the six kings of Pontus called Mithridates. As a youth he fled from his mother and seized Sinope. He imprisoned his mother, murdered his brother, wed his sister and extended his kingdom. A brave and clever leader, he occupied Lesser Armenia, Colchis, E Pontus, and much of Greece, engaging in the Mithradatic Wars against Rome. Finally defeated, he fled to Colchis and the Crimea, tried to raise another army and suffered a revolt led by his son Pharnaces. He ordered himself killed by a guard.

Mithridatic Wars, campaigns of expansion led by Mithridates VI, king of Pontus, against the Romans. The First Mithridatic War was brought on by Micomedes' attempts to invade Pontus (88–84 BC). As a result Mithridates took control of most of Asia Minor and much of Greece. Sulla defeated him in Greece and during the Second Mithridatic War (83–81) he repulsed Sulla's

attempts to raid the Pontic coast. In the Third Mithridatic War (74–63), he was defeated by Lucullus, expelled from Pontus, and driven into the Crimea by Pompey.

Mitla, a Central American archeological site, probably 13th-century, near Oaxaca City, Mexico, famous for the unmatched mosaic work displayed on several buildings. Stone bands and panels of striking geometric patterns in high and low relief were precision-set into the rubble mass of the walls. Mitla succeeded Monte Albán as the Zapotec capital; by the time of the Spanish conquest, Mixtec influence predominated. The buildings were arranged in quadrangles. Tombs complemented the visible architecture.

Mitochondrion, small body found in the cytoplasm of most cells, containing enzymes and other agents necessary for metabolism. The "powerhouses," or energy producers of the cell, mitochondria have their own genetic material.

Mitosis, nuclear division of a cell resulting in two identical cells. This division includes five phases: interphase —DNA and chromosomes self-duplicate; prophase— chromosomes coil, centrioles start separating, and astral rays and spindles form; metaphase—doubled chromosomes are along cell's equatorial plate, centrioles move to opposite sides, and nuclear membrane disappears; anaphase—doubled chromosomes separate and move apart and cytoplasmic division starts; telophase—chromosomes uncoil, nuclear membrane forms, spindle and astral rays disappear, and cytoplasmic division is completed, resulting in two new cells identical to the original cell.

Mitterrand, François (Maurice) (1916–), president of France. A lawyer, he served in various government posts after 1944, including minister of state, minister of the interior, and minister of justice. He was elected to the National Assembly in 1946. Although defeated by Charles de Gaulle in the presidential election of 1965, he did surprisingly well at the polls. In 1974, he ran as the Socialist presidential candidate, losing to Valéry Giscard d'Estaing. In 1981, he defeated Giscard d'Estaing to become the Fifth Republic's first left-wing French president.

Mixtec, Indian civilization centered in the province of Oaxaca, Mexico. At the time of the Spanish conquest, the Mixtec invasion and conquest of the Zapotec was underway. The Mixtec numbered 275,000 at the beginning of the 16th century; epidemics and forced migrations drastically reduced their number.

Mixture, in chemistry, any material that is made up of several components each of which retains its specific identity no matter in what proportion or how closely the components are mixed. *See also* Solution.

Mnemonic Device, an aid to memory. Strategies designed to improve memory include rhymes, peg-word systems, and visual imagery. For example, if a list of items is to be memorized, rhymed associations with the items will aid memory; eg, one is a bun, two is a shoe, three is a tree, etc. The numbers are peg words (previously memorized) that easily suggest the other words. A third set of items may be attached by visualizing an image of the first item in a bun, the second in a shoe, etc. *See also* Memory.

Moa, extinct flightless ostrichlike bird of New Zealand thought to have been hunted out by the Maori tribe for food. They had small heads, variously colored downy feathers, and strong legs. Feeding on roots and shoots, they nested on ground. Height: to 12ft (3.6m). Order: Dinornithiformes.

Mobile, commercial and seaport city in SW Alabama, at the mouth of Mobile River, seat of Mobile co; site of US Air Force base; only seaport in state. Exports: cotton, coal, agricultural and forest products. Industries: textiles, paper, lumber, aluminum, shipbuilding. Settled 1711 by France, occupied 1813 by United States; inc. 1819. Pop. (1980) 200,452.

Mobile, a form of sculpture developed by Alexander Calder in the early 1930s and named by Marcel Duchamps. A mobile consists of a series of shapes (representational or abstract) cut from metal, wood, or plastic and connected by wires so that the parts and whole revolve freely when suspended in space. This form moves from the traditional ideas of sculpture as static toward objects in motion.

Mobutu Sese Seko (1930–), president of Zaire and military commander, b. Joseph-Désiré Mobutu. He worked for Congolese (Zairean) independence with Patrice Lumumba, whom he later imprisoned and killed (1960–61) when he assumed control of the army. He became chief of state after toppling Joseph Kasavubu in 1965. His domestic policies included Africanization and economic development; in foreign affairs he sought to make Zaire a leader of black African nations. Despite serious economic and military crises in 1977–78, Mobuto was reelected in 1977 and 1984 under a one-party system.

Moby-Dick (1851), novel by Herman Melville. Now considered Melville's masterpiece, it was largely ignored until 70 years after its publication. Narrated by Ishmael, a wanderer, the plot line is deceptively simple. In the 1840s, Ahab, the one-legged captain of the whaling ship *Pequod,* sails from New Bedford across the Pacific to search out and destroy the white whale, Moby-Dick, which had maimed him. After cutting himself off from normal human contacts and establishing his power over the crew by various dramatic means, he finds Moby-Dick, but the whale destroys the *Pequod* with its captain and all the crew, except Ishmael, who survives floating on a coffin to be rescued by the *Rachel.* Melville's rich, ripe, rolling, rhetorical style, jammed with factual detail about whaling and sailing, and his complex development of symbolism, charges the massive novel with metaphysical and sociological overtones and undertones and gives it epic grandeur.

Mochica, a prehistoric cultural period of northern Peru, *c.*200 BC–AD 600, sometimes called "Early Chimú." Named for their home area in the Moche Valley, these people were famous for their magnificent pottery, large quantities of which have survived.

Mock Epic, or mock heroic, literary work that burlesques or satirizes the grand epic style. Famous examples are *The Rape of the Lock* (1714) by Alexander Pope, in which trivial events are described in highly exalted language; *Dunciad* (1728–43), also by Pope, a more serious satirical poem; and "Ode on the Death of a Favourite Cat" (1747) by Thomas Gray.

Mockingbird, any of a group of New World songbirds, known for their beautiful song. The common mockingbird *(Mimus polyglottos)* of the United States is typical of the group—about 10.5in (27cm) long, ashy above with brownish wings and tail marked with white. Perched high, it spreads its wings and tail and utters up to 20 songs. Males help build bulky, open, cup-shaped nests of grass and twigs for pale greenish-blue, brown-spotted eggs. An isolated group (genus *Nesomimus*) occurs on the Galapagos Islands.

Mode, in statistics, a measure of central tendency that is computed by determining the item that occurs most frequently in a data set. It is a quick measure of central tendency, but is not as commonly used as the median or mean.

Models, Econometric, are composed of a number of mathematical equations (estimated, based on previous economic data), each representing a particular sector or subsector of the economy. Econometric models are used to simulate the operation of the economic system. Econometric models, unlike input-output models, are dynamic in nature. They allow time movements to occur and provide for interaction between the various sectors of the economy. *See also* Input-Output Model.

Modena, city in N Italy, 207mi (333km) NNW of Rome; capital of Modena prov. A Roman colony 183 BC; it passed to House of Este 1288; made a duchy 1452; conquered by France 1796; joined kingdom of Italy 1860; site of 11th-century Romanesque cathedral, 17th-century ducal palace, 14th-century campanile, Palazzo dei Musei, university (1175). Industries: automobiles, machine tools, metalworking. Pop. 178,959.

Modern Dance, dance style that began to develop in the early part of the 20th century as a protest against classical ballet and the overly personal interpretive dance of Isadora Duncan. In Europe and the United States, such innovators as Rudolph van Laban, Ruth St Denis, and Ted Shawn attempted to make dance a viable contemporary art form. Rather than merely to entertain, their aim was to communicate with their audience and to heighten their viewers' awareness of life's experience.

Modernism, movement in the Roman Catholic church during the late 19th and early 20th centuries to adapt Catholic beliefs to developments in modern science, philosophy, and history. At first tolerated by Pope Leo XIII, the movement wanted the church to view the Bible more critically according to limitations of Biblical authors and to adopt a philosophy of action rather than doctrine. The modernists, however, who were centered at the Institut Catholique, Paris, were condemned by Pius X in 1907; all suspect clerics were required to take an anti-modernist oath.

Modesto, city in central California, 24mi (39km) SE of Stockton; seat of Stanislaus co; site of one of the world's largest wineries and canneries. Industries: food processing, paper products, fruit and nut orchards. Inc. 1884. Pop. (1980) 106,105.

Modigliani, Amedeo (1884–1920), Italian painter and sculptor. A few of his early works were landscapes, but the majority of his paintings deal with female portraits and nudes. Showing the influence of the Cubist style, his females usually have elongated limbs, small mouths, and eyes with overly large pupils. As a sculptor, he did numerous heads that show the influence of primitive African art in their vertically elongated style. *See also* Cubism.

Modoc, North American Indian tribe closely related to the Klamath. They inhabited N California. From an early population of 500, they declined to 334 members living on the Klamath Reservation in Oregon. They are noted for their defense against the US Army during the Lava Beds War of 1872–73.

Modulation, process of varying the characteristics of one wave system in accordance with the characteristics of another wave system. In amplitude modulation, the amplitude of a high-frequency (radio) carrier wave is varied in accordance with the frequency of a current generated by a sound wave. This enables the sound wave to be broadcast and, in fact, all forms of broadcasting rely on modulation. For static-free short-range broadcasting, frequency modulation is used. In this it is the frequency of the carrier wave that is modulated.

Mogadisho, capital city and chief port of Somalia, E Africa, on the Indian Ocean, along Benadir coast. Taken 1871 by sultan of Zanzibar, it was leased (1892), then sold (1905) to Italy; occupied by the British 1941; commercial center connected to Gulf of Aden by road; site of 13th-century mosques, native fort restored 1933–34, museum, airfield. Industries: oilseed pressing, lumbering. Pop. 400,000.

Mogul, or **Mughal, Empire** (1526–1857), Indian domain founded by Babur, a Muslim descendant of both Tamerlane and Genghis Khan, in 1526 when he conquered Delhi and Agra. Under **Akbar** (*r.*1556–1605), Babur's grandson, the empire was at its height, extending from Afghanistan to the Bay of Bengal, from Gujarat in the south to northern Deccan. Akbar's grandson **Shah Jahan** (*r.*1629–58) built many splendid buildings, including the Taj Mahal. Under **Aurungzeb** (*r.*1658–1707), a Muslim fanatic, there were many Hindu revolts that weakened the empire. The empire began to break up under **Muhammed Shah** (*r.*1719–48). After 1803 the Mogul emperors were merely puppets of the British. In 1857 the last emperor, Bahadur Shah, was forced to abdicate because of his part in the Indian Mutiny.

Mohair, a fiber similar to wool, obtained from the angora goat and used for knitting yarns. Produced only in Asia Minor for thousands of years, mohair became important in European textile manufacture in the 19th century. Angora goats are now raised in the United States and S Africa.

Mohammed (*c.*570–632), Arab founder of Islam. Muslims believe him to have been the last and most perfect messenger of God, following Adam, Abraham, Moses, and Jesus. He was a wealthy merchant in Mecca. At the age of 40 he had a vision in a cave of Mt Hira near Mecca that commanded him to preach. His subsequent visions and teachings are recorded in the Koran, the holy scripture of Islam. His new religion alienated the leaders of Mecca. In 622 to escape an assassination attempt he fled to Yathrib (subsequently renamed Medina, "City of the Prophet"). Muslims date their years from this flight, the Hegira. Mohammed ruled Medina as a theocratic state. He defeated an attack from Mecca in 624 and conquered Mecca in 630. At the time of his death, his religion controlled Arabia and was making inroads in Syria and Iraq. *See also* Islam.

Mohammed II (1429–81), Ottoman sultan (1451–81), also known as Mohammed the Conqueror. In 1453 he captured Constantinople, ending the Byzantine Empire and firmly establishing the Ottoman Empire. He moved his capital from Adrianople to Constantinople and made it a cosmopolitan city by repopulating it with Muslims, Christians, and Jews from conquered territories. He conquered most of the Balkans (1456–58), but was stopped at Belgrade.

Mohammedanism, an archaic name for Islam, the religion founded by Mohammed in the 7th century. Muslims rejected the term Mohammedanism because it might suggest that Mohammed is deified. *See also* Islam.

Mohammed Riza Pahlevi (1919–80), shah of Iran (1941–79). He succeeded his father, who was deposed by the British and Soviets because of his pro-German leanings. In 1953 he fled Iran after a clash with the then powerful premier Mohammed Mussadegh. He was quickly restored to power with US assistance. He remained under foreign domination until the early 1960s when steadily increasing oil revenues allowed him to plot an independent course. In 1963 he announced his "White Revolution" program of land redistribution, educational improvement, and female emancipation. He attempted to build up Iran as the most important military power of the Near East, independent of US, Soviet, or Arab domination. The Iranian people experienced considerable material improvement but the shah allowed little political liberalization. Growing unrest eventually led to military rule (1978). When rioting occurred, the shah was driven into exile (1979) by followers of the Ayatollah Khomeini. Illness brought him for medical treatment to the United States, where unfavorable political pressures caused him to go to Panama. After Iran requested his extradition, the shah took asylum in Egypt, where he died in a military hospital in Cairo. *See also* Pahlevi Dynasty.

Mohave, or **Mojave,** a Yuman-speaking tribe of North American Indians once numbering about 3,000 persons living along both sides of the middle Colorado River. Today about 850 occupy the Colorado River Reservation in Arizona.

Mohawk, one of the major divisions of the League of the Iroquois. Most of the 1,500 Mohawk today live on the Grand River Reserve near the east end of Lake Ontario, Canada.

Mohegan, an important tribe of North American Indians of the Algonkin language family formerly occupying the Thames River area of Connecticut. They were the major tribe of the region following the end of King Philip's War; their most famous chief was Uncas. Once numbering 2,200, about 20 Mohegan people live with the Pequot near Norwich, Conn., today.

Mohenjo Daro, one of the main city centers of the Indus Valley civilization (about 2500 to 1500 BC). Its remains (in modern Pakistan) show that its inhabitants built large granaries, employed a system of writing, used standard weights and measures, traded extensively, constructed carts and boats, and were competent plumbers and metalworkers.

Mohican, or **Mahican,** an Algonkin-speaking tribe of North American Indians formerly inhabiting the upper Hudson River in New York, east to the Housatonic River in Connecticut. Once numbering about 3,000 persons, they joined the Stockbridge in 1736, and the surviving 525 today occupy the Stockbridge-Munsee reservation in Wisconsin. They have become well known from J.F. Cooper's *The Last of the Mohicans.*

Moho, the seismic discontinuity layer at the base of Earth's crust. The layer was discovered by Yugoslavian geophysicist Andrija in 1909 when the velocity of seismic waves was measured and found to be different in a number of sites at varying distances from an earthquake epicenter. The moho layer is about 6mi (10km) from the surface in ocean regions and 20mi (32km) from the surface under land masses. The moho is explained by a difference in density of rocks as they change from crust to mantle and therefore act as deflectors of seismic waves. *See also* Core, Earth; Seismology.

Moi, Daniel (Torotich) Arap (1924–), president of Kenya (1978–). Moi, who became the British-appointed representative to the Kenya Legislative Council in 1958, served Kenya in several ministerial posts before his appointment by Pres. Kenyatta as

Amedeo Modigliani: portrait in oil

Mohammed Riza Pahlevi

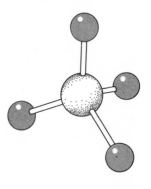

Molecule

Kenya's vice-president (1967). He was elected president of Kenya in 1978, succeeding Kenyatta. The pro-Western Moi quickly solidified his position as Kenya's second president. He was elected president of the Organization of African Unity (1981).

Moism, school of Chinese philosophy of Mo tzu and his followers (*fl.* 5th century BC). With representatives in all parts of China, the Moists were the only one of the "hundred schools" to have had group organization and regular meetings. Adhering to utilitarian doctrines, Moism advocated promotion of the general welfare and universal love. After the 1st century BC, there are no longer any references in Chinese literature to Moism as an existent body of opinion. *See also* Hundred Schools; Mo tzu.

Mojave Desert, arid region with low, barren mountains in S California; surrounded by mountain ranges (N and W), borders the Colorado Desert (SE); formed by volcanic eruptions and deposits from the Colorado River; site of Death Valley National Monument; many mineral deposits and small streams. Area: approx. 15,000sq mi (38,850sq km).

Molal Solution, solution containing one gram molecular weight of the desired species in one kilogram of solvent. When applied to electrolytes in solution, this measure refers to the concentration of undissociated substances, and has given rise to the concentration concept of molality.

Molar, one of the back teeth of mammals, adapted for grinding and chewing food. Several cusps—the points or ridges on the top surface—occlude with counterparts on the opposing molar. Herbivores have sharp cusps arranged in triangular shearing patterns for slicing. In man there are 3 permanent molars on each side of each jaw, a total of 12. *See also* Tooth.

Molarity, measure of concentration of a particular component in a solution, usually designated M. There are 6.02×10^{23} (Avogadro's number) molecules in a mole. Concentration may either be expressed as, for example, 1.2×10^{23} molecules per liter or, more conveniently, 0.2 moles per liter of solution. The concentration of such a solution is 0.2 M.

Molasses Act, or **Sugar Act** (1733), law passed by Parliament that charged a prohibitory duty on foreign molasses and sugar entering the English colonies. The act protected British West Indies sugar growers and was resented by American colonists.

Mold, any of a wide variety of tiny fungi that forms furry growths on food, leather, textiles, and other organic materials in moist environments. Some molds, including *Asperigillum* and *Penicillium,* are important in cheese-making or as sources of antibiotics and some organic chemicals. Like other fungi, molds cannot make their own food by photosynthesis. They are generally saprophytes that obtain their food by assisting in the decay of the organic materials on which they grow. The "body" of a mold, called the mycelium, consists of a network of fine filaments through which nutrients are absorbed. Molds reproduce by means of spores produced in sporecases or other reproductive structures that give molds their characteristic black, blue, green, orange, or red colors. Most familiar molds are members of the orders Mucorales and Eurotiales.

Mold, Metal, mold for casting metal, usually made of sand or clay. This is packed over the face of the pattern that forms the cavity for the casting. The mold must be strong, resisting pressure of the hot, liquid metal, and permeable to allow gases to escape the cavity. It must

also resist fusion with the metal that is poured in through special channels. *See also* Foundry.

Moldavia, historic region in E Romania, N of E Wallachia, E of Transylvania; included Bessarabia and Bukovina; conquered by Greeks, Romans, and Bulgars, under Mongol rule during 13th century; became a dominion of the Ottoman Empire 1504. A former Danubian principality founded 14th century, it merged with Wallachia 1861 to create Romania. At present the largest part is the Moldavian Soviet Socialist Republic, a constituent of USSR. Products: grain, livestock, grapes. Industries: lumbering, petroleum extraction. Area: approx. 14,690sq mi (38,047sq km).

Moldavia (Moldavian Soviet Socialist Republic or **Moldavskaja Sovetskaja Socialistideskaja Respublika),** constituent republic of the USSR, bounded N, E, and S by Ukrainian republic and W by Romania; occupies the central portion of former Bessarabia. After 1940 Soviet annexation of Bessarabia, the Moldavian autonomous republic, except for its predominantly Ukrainian districts, joined central Bessarabia to form Moldavian republic. It was held by Germans and Romanians 1941–44. The main cities are Kishinev (capital), Belicy, Bendery, Tiraspol. The main navigable river is the Dniester. Industries: canning (Tiraspol), wine, distilling, flour milling, sugar refining, tobacco processing. Exports: grapes, wine, fruit, nuts, hides, wheat, canned goods. Area: 13,012sq mi (33,701sq km). Pop. 3,914,000.

Mole, burrowing short-furred mammal of Eurasia and North America. About the size of a small rat, most moles have short tails and spadelike forefeet adapted for digging. Both the common European mole and the common eastern mole of North America live mostly underground and feed largely on earthworms and insects. Family Talpidae.

Mole, unit of substance (symbol mol) defined as the amount of substance containing the same number of entities (atoms, ions, etc) as there are atoms in 0.012 kilogram of carbon-12. The mass of 1 mole of a compound is its gram molecular weight. *See also* Physical Units.

Mole Cricket, brown insect found worldwide. It has broad, spade-shaped front legs for burrowing in moist places. Although it spends most of its life underground, it is a strong flier. Length: over 1in (25mm). Family Gryllidae.

Molecular Biology, biological study of the chemical and physical makeup of molecules comprising living organisms. A major area of study is genes and their components and functions in heredity, evolution, and the makeup of living organisms, particularly humans.

Molecular Model, a simple type of molecular model is made by joining small colored balls, representing atoms, by stiff metal springs, representing single bonds. The balls have holes, into which the springs fit, arranged to give possible spatial dispositions of bonds. More sophisticated models include different sizes of atom and allow scale models of molecules to be built. Molecular models are invaluable aids, not only in visualizing shapes of molecules but also in indicating "strain" in bonds and possible conformations that the molecule may adopt in reaction.

Molecular Weight, or relative molecular mass, sum of the atomic weights of all the atoms in a molecule. It is thus the average mass per molecule of a specified isotopic composition of a substance to 1/12 of the

mass of an atom of carbon-12. The molecular weights of the reactants must be known in order to make quantitative calculations about a chemical reaction.

Molecule, smallest particle of a substance capable of independent existence and of exhibiting the characteristic properties of that substance. Molecules consist of two or more atoms held together by chemical bonds. For example, water molecules consist of two atoms of hydrogen bonded to one atom of oxygen (H_2O).

Molière (1622–73), pseud. of Jean Baptiste Poquelin, French playwright. Trained as a lawyer, he abandoned the law and joined an amateur dramatic group. His first important work was *L'Étourdi (The Blunderer),* performed at Lyons in 1655. An accurate observer of contemporary manners and types, he is remembered principally for his comedies of character, such as *The School for Wives* (1622), *Tartuffe* (1664), *The Misanthrope* (1666), and *The Imaginary Invalid* (1673). He wrote other kinds of plays as well: farce, as *The Imaginary Cuckold* (1660); comedy ballet, such as *The Bores* (1661); and spectacular "machine plays," eg, *Amphitryon* (1668) and *Psyche* (1671). Some of the plays are in verse, others in prose. He directed his own plays and often played the leading role himself. Although his plays ridiculed customs and character types, it was done without bitterness.

Molina, Luis de (1535–1600), Spanish theologian. After joining the Jesuits (1553), Molina taught at Evora, Portugal. His *Free Will as Gratuitous Gift* (1588) taught, in effect, that God bestows grace on those whose supplication is sincere. His notion that God is able to foresee just who will make good use of free will gave rise to the "Molinist Controversy."

Mollusk, any of a large group of invertebrate animals of some 100,000 living species in the phylum Mollusca. Included are the familiar snails, clams, and squids, and a host of less well-known forms. Originally marine, the group now has representation in the oceans, fresh water, and on land. There are six classes: the primitive gastroverms, chitons, univalves (snails), bivalves (clams, etc), tusk shells, and cephalopods (squids, etc). The mollusk body is divided into three regions: the head, the foot, and the visceral mass. Associated with the body is a thin sheet of tissue called the mantle, which secretes the limy shell typical of most mollusks. The head is well developed only in snails and in the cephalopods, which have eyes, tentacles, and a well-formed mouth. The foot is used for crawling in univalves and for digging in bivalves. The visceral mass contains the internal organs of circulation (blood vessels and heart), respiration (gills), excretion (kidney), digestion (stomach and intestine), and reproduction (gonads). The sexes are usually separate but there are many hermaphroditic species. In most, the fertilized egg goes through several larval stages before attaining the adult form. *See also* Bivalves; Cephalopods; Gastropods.

Molting, shedding and replacement of the outer covering, such as feathers, exoskeleton, skin, and hair. It occurs in birds, reptiles, and insects to replace old coverings or allow for growth.

Moltke, Helmuth Karl Bernhard, Graf von (1800–91), Prussian field marshal. He entered the Prussian army in 1822 and joined the general staff in 1833. From 1858 until he resigned in 1888, he was head of the general staff. He reorganized the army and was the strategist of Prussia's war against Denmark (1864), the Austro-Prussian War (1866), and the Franco-Prussian War (1870–71).

Moluccas (Spice Islands, Maluku), island group in E Indonesia; constitutes a province of Indonesia; Ambon is the capital; includes larger islands of Halmahera, Ceram, Buru; island groups of Sula, Batjan, Obi, Kai, Aru, Tanimbar, Banda, Babar, Leti; smaller islands of Ambon, Ternate, Tidore. Originally explored by Magellan (early 16th century), later settled by Portuguese; taken by Dutch *c.* 1605–21 to monopolize spice trade; occupied by British 1810–14 but returned to Dutch control. Industries: spices, copra, forest products, sago. Area: 32,307sq mi (83,675sq km). Pop. 995,000.

Molybdenite, a sulfide mineral, molybdenum sulfide (MoS_2). Major ore of molybdenum, found in pegmatites, igneous and metamorphic rocks. Hexagonal system tabular prisms, flakes, and fine granules. Lead-gray, metallic luster with layers flexible. Hardness 1–1.5; sp gr 4.7.

Molybdenum, metallic element (symbol Mo) of the second transition series, first identified and isolated in 1778. Chief ores are molybdenite (sulfide) and wulfenite (lead molybdate). It is used in alloy steels and molybdenum compounds are used as catalysts and lubricants. It is an essential trace element for plant growth. Properties: at. no. 42; at. wt. 95.94; sp gr 10.22; melt. pt. 4,730°F (2,610°C); boil pt. 10,040°F (5.560°C); most stable isotope Mo^{98} (23.78%). *See also* Transition Elements.

Mombasa, port and capital city of Mombasa Island in Kenya, in the Indian Ocean; includes portions of mainland, to which it is connected by a causeway; import, commercial, and industrial center. A center for Arab trade in slaves and ivory 8th–16th centuries, the city was burned several times by Portuguese; passed from Portuguese to Arabs 1698; taken by Zanzibar in the 19th century; passed 1887 to Great Britain; site of remains of Portuguese Fort Jesus (1593–94). Exports: coffee, fruit, grains. Industries: glass, processed foods, cement, soap, aluminum products, lime. Pop. 320,000.

Momentum, the product of the mass and velocity of a body. The principle that the total momentum of any system of bodies is conserved (remains constant) at all times, even during collisions, is one of the great fundamental laws of physics, holding an equivalent position to the law of the conservation of mass-energy. *See also* Angular Momentum.

Monaco, sovereign principality in Europe, on the Mediterranean Sea (S), bounded on all other sides by France; near Italy. Major geographical regions are Monaco-Ville, the capital, a high rocky promontory that extends into the sea; La Condamine, the port area; Monte Carlo, the residential and resort area, with its casino district; and Fontvieille, the light manufacturing district. Gambling contributes directly only about 4% of the nation's income, but it attracts tourists whose spending amounts to 55%. Industry is responsible for 25%–30% of the nation's income. There are no personal or corporate income taxes; the government is supported by excise taxes, stamp sales, and taxes on alcohol and tobacco. There is a customs union with France. Native Monegasques are outnumbered eight to one by other nationalities, chiefly French, who comprise approx. 50% of the population. Originally settled by the Phoenicians, it later fell under Roman rule and was Christianized about AD 100. It passed through several rulers before coming under the Grimaldi family of Genoa in the 13th century. It is now ruled by descendants of a French branch of the family that assumed the name Grimaldi. France assumed protection of Monaco in 1860 and should the male Grimaldi line die out, Monaco would become an autonomous state under France. Monaco adopted a constitution in 1911 establishing a ruling princedom and an appointed council, which is now elected. The marriage of Prince Rainier to US movie actress Grace Kelly (1956) received worldwide attention. Princess Grace died in a car accident in 1982.

PROFILE

Official name: Principality of Monaco
Area: 0.7sq mi (1.8sq km)
Population: 25,000
Chief cities: Monaco-Ville (capital); Monte Carlo
Government: Hereditary monarch with elected National Assembly
Religion: Roman Catholic
Language: French
Monetary unit: Franc

Monad, in Greek usage, the number one; extended in philosophy to apply to any unit. The 17th-century German philosopher Gottfried Leibniz applied the term to autonomous centers of force that, he felt, comprise the fundamental metaphysical reality of which the universe is composed. These monads, or souls, do not interact, but are organized to correspond in a "pre-established harmony." They are also indestructible, indivisible, and eternal. *See also* Pre-established Harmony.

Monarch Butterfly, or milkweed butterfly, a large butterfly that has brownish-orange wings with black veins and borders. Its larva feeds on milkweed, giving it a taste disliked by birds. The viceroy butterfly mimics coloration of the monarch. Species *Danaus plexippus*. *See also* Viceroy.

Monarchianism, 2nd–3rd century heretical movement in the Christian church. It safeguarded the Divine Unity (or monarchia) of the Godhead by not distinguishing the divine persons of the Trinity. In destroying the idea of the Trinity, monarchianism did not support the independent existence of Christ. This heresy is said to have originated with Noetus (*c.* AD 250) and was carried on by his disciples Epigonus and Cleomenes.

Monarchy, form of government in which one individual, whose power is usually hereditary, represents the state. Monarchs with absolute power are nearly extinct; those states that remain monarchies are generally constitutional, with the royalty performing ceremonial functions.

Monasticism, a religious way of life, typically an ascetic life apart from the rest of the world. Such a way of striving toward perfection has been found in Hinduism, Buddhism, Islam, and Christianity. St Anthony, in the 3rd and 4th centuries, is considered the founder of Christian monasticism. In the 5th century St Benedict set down rules for a monastery at Monte Cassino in Italy, and his laws were widely followed. The Benedictines, Cistercians, and other orders built great abbeys such as Clairvaux in France, and these often were centers of agriculture and of art and learning. Monks and nuns worked as well as devoting hours to prayer.

Monck, or **Monk, George, 1st Duke of Albemarle** (1608–70), English soldier. In the English Civil War, he fought initially for Charles I (1643–44). Joining the Parliamentarians, he commanded unsuccessfully in Ireland (1647–49) and successfully in Scotland (1650, 1654) and defeated the Dutch at sea (1652). He engineered the Stuart Restoration (1660) and fought in the second Anglo-Dutch war (1666–67).

Moncton, city in New Brunswick, Canada, on the Petitcodiac River; educational and cultural center for French Canadian sector of New Brunswick; site of three colleges, one seminary, and one university; major center of transportation. Founded 1763 as The Bend by German settlers; name changed in 1855 to honor the British General Robert Monckton. Pop. 55,934.

Mondale, Walter Frederick (1928–), vice president of the United States (1977–81), b. Ceylon, Minn. In 1955 he married Joan Adams; they had two sons and a daughter. As a young lawyer in Minnesota, he became active in the state Democratic-Farmer-Labor party. He served as state attorney general (1960–64), and when Hubert H. Humphrey became vice president (1965), Mondale was appointed to complete Humphrey's term in the US Senate. Mondale was elected to a full term in 1966 and again in 1972. He became identified with the more liberal wing of the Democratic party in the Senate; that fact was instrumental in his being chosen as the Democratic running mate of Jimmy Carter in 1976. After defeat in the 1980 election, he went into private law practice, but emerged in 1984 as the Democratic nominee for president, losing the election to Ronald Reagan.

Mondrian, Piet (1872–1944), Dutch painter. His early works were naturalistic landscapes painted in neutral colors. He was later influenced by the fauvist and cubist styles. His fame rests on his balanced, geometric, abstract style, in which he used black lines in a gridlike pattern to outline rectangular shapes of white and primary colors.

Monera, a large biological grouping comprising the bacteria and blue-green algae. Sometimes considered distinct enough from other protists to be called a separate kingdom. The main difference is in the organization of the genetic materials. Monerans, also called procaryotes, do not have their genetic material packed into a distinct nucleus and lack mitochondria and chloroplasts. Those protists with a distinct nucleus containing several chromosomes are called eucaryotes.

Monet, Claude (1840–1926), French painter. Painting almost entirely out-of-doors, he included many seascapes and city scenes among his early works. In the 1870s, he began to use the loose, broken-color brushstroke of Impressionism to create in his works an atmosphere of pattern, light, and color. He painted numerous views of the Seine and many series of the same subject, such as his haystack and Rouen Cathedral facade series, showing the effects of sunlight on the subject at different hours of the day. He also painted enormous waterlily panels.

Money Supply, in a general sense, that portion of the public's purchasing power that is readily available. Defined in the narrow economic sense, the money supply consists only of currency and demand deposits. A broader definition includes time deposits as well.

Moneywort, or creeping Jenny, creeping perennial plant native to Europe and naturalized in North America. It has pairs of penny-shaped, nearly evergreen leaves and yellow flowers and spreads rapidly by rooting runners to form a mat. Family Primulaceae; species *Lysymachia nummularia.*

Mongolia (Mongol Ard, Uls), landlocked nation in central Asia lying between China and the USSR. A vast plateau with extensive grasslands embraces the heartland of the country; part of the Gobi Desert occupies the S. An agricultural economy relies primarily on herd animals with more than 80% of the total land area devoted to pastureland. Herdsmen make up the majority of the labor force and have been organized into collectives. Crops are grown on large-scale state farms. More than 90% of the people are indigenous Mongolians; 75% Khalkha Mongols. The church was suppressed in the 1930s; at that time Tibetan Buddhist Lamaism was predominant. Only one active monastery remains.

Governmental power is vested in the People's Great Khural of Deputies, elected every three years by universal suffrage. From this body is chosen a nine-member Presidium to exercise state affairs. Under Genghis Khan in the 13th century, Mongolia conquered most of Asia and much of Europe. In the 14th century the empire collapsed and came under Chinese rule. During the 1911 Chinese Revolution, Mongolia, with Russian backing, declared its independence; a republic was formed in 1924. Officially recognized by China in 1946, Mongolia became a member of the United Nations in 1961. In 1966 a Mongolian-Soviet assistance pact reinforced their anti-Chinese position. Since then Mongolia has developed closer ties with the USSR; relations with China have been strained, resulting in sporadic border incidents.

PROFILE

Official name: Mongolian People's Republic
Area: 604,247sq mi (1,565,000sq km)
Population: 1,561,000
Density: 2.5 per sq mi (1 per sq km)
Chief cities: Ulan Bator, capital; Darhan; Choybalsan
Government: People's Republic
Language: Khalkha Mongolian (official)
Monetary unit: Tugrik
Gross national product: $1,270,000,000
Per capita income: $460
Agriculture (major products): livestock
Minerals (major): coal, tungsten, copper, gold, tin, molybdenum
Trading partners (major): COMECON member countries

Mongolian Eyefold. *See* Epicanthic Fold.

Mongolian Wild Horse. *See* Przewalski's Horse.

Mongolism (Down's syndrome), a condition that is usually caused by the presence of an extra chromosome 21 (three instead of the usual two), in which the typical features are mental retardation, flattened skull and nose bridge, shortened digits, and a vertical fold on the inner side of the eye, resulting in a slant-eyed appearance.

Mongoloid Race, one of the major human racial groupings. Mongoloid physical characteristics include: medium skin pigmentation; rather flat face; epicanthic fold; straight black hair; little facial or body hair. Mongoloids make up most of the population of Asia and the indigenous peoples of the Americas.

Mongols, a nomadic people of Mongolia, Manchuria, and Siberia. They live in felt tents; eat meat and milk; and raise horses, sheep, and goats. Expert archers and horsemen, they were once savage conquerers and rulers of the largest territory in history. Under Genghis Khan (1167–1227) they built an empire that in part survived until the 16th century. They were poor administrators, however, and their empire was never really under their governmental control.

Mongoose, small, agile, carnivorous mammal of the civet family, native to Africa, S Europe, and Asia. They have slender, thickly furred bodies and long, bushy tails. Active hunters by day and night, they eat rodents, insects, eggs, birds, and snakes. The Indian mongoose *(Herpestes edwardsi)* is famous for killing cobras. Some species may be domesticated but their destruc-

Monaco

Monkey: Chimpanzee

James Monroe

tiveness is so great that they are not allowed in the United States, even in zoos. Length: 1.5–4ft (46–122cm). Family Viverridae. *See also* Meerkat.

Monitor and Merrimack, Civil War naval battle off Hampton Roads, Va., March 9, 1862. The *Merrimack*, a scuttled vessel, was raised and made into an ironclad by the Confederates. It was used to sink wooden Union ships. The *Monitor,* a new flat-top ironclad, battled the *Merrimack* and heavily damaged it, helping to maintain the Union blockade.

Monitor Lizard, powerful lizard native to Africa, S Asia, Indonesia, and Australia. It has a long, forked, snakelike tongue and a powerful tail. The majority are dull-colored with yellow markings. Many are semi-aquatic. Length: 8in–10ft (20cm–2m). There are 30 species. Family Varanidae; genus *Varanus. See also* Komodo Dragon.

Monkey, wide variety of mostly tree-dwelling, day-active, omnivorous primates inhabiting the tropics and subtropics. Most monkeys have high intelligence, flat manlike faces, grasping hands, and other characteristics of advanced, anthropoid primates. They fall into two broad groups—Old World monkeys (superfamily Cercopithecoidea) and New World monkeys (superfamily Ceboidea). The 60 Old World species, sometimes called true monkeys, include macaques, baboons, barbary apes, langurs, and colobuses. Some, such as baboons, are primarily ground dwellers, but all are excellent climbers. Most have short or long but always nongrasping tails. They range from Japan and N China through S Asia and nondesert Africa. The 70 species of New World monkeys include howlers, capuchins, spider monkeys, and marmosets. They are all tree dwellers, and most have grasping tails. Most have no thumbs, and the nostrils are usually separated more widely than in Old World monkeys. They live in tropical Central and South America. *See also* Primates.

Monkey Puzzle Tree, evergreen tree native to mountainous regions of Chile and Brazil. It has tangled branches, sharp, flat leaves, and edible nuts. It is grown mainly as an ornamental, but its timber is sometimes used in carpentry. Height: to 100ft (30m). Family Pinacae; species *Araucaria araucana.*

Monmouth, James Scott, Duke of (1649–85), English soldier, illegitimate son of Charles II, b. The Hague. He became a successful general and the hope of the Protestants opposing the succession of the Catholic duke of York. Exiled (1679), he plotted his father's murder (1683). In 1685 he returned to England and was proclaimed king. Following his defeat at Sedgemoor, he was executed.

Monnet, Jean (1888–1979), French economist. Active in government since World War I, he served as a member of the British Supply Council, helping organize the Allied war effort. His Monnet Plan (1947) instituted the modernization of French industry. He presided (1952–55) over the European Coal and Steel Community, which he established. It laid the groundwork for the European Economic Community. In 1955 he formed the Action Committee for a United States of Europe serving as its president (1955–75).

Monoceros, or the Unicorn, faint equatorial constellation situated south of Gemini and east of Orion. The Milky Way passes through this group, which also contains several bright and dark nebulae, including the Rosette Nebula (NGC 2237), and some star clusters, such as NGC 2244.

Monocotyledon, subclass of flowering plants, angiosperms, characterized by one seed leaf (cotyledon) in the seed embryo. Plant leaves are usually parallel-veined and flower in threes. Lilies, orchids, palms and grasses are monocotyledons. The larger subclass is dicotyledon. This system of angiosperm classification has been used since the last half of the 17th century. *See also* Angiosperms; Dicotyledons.

Monod, Jacques (1910–76), French biologist who, with François Jacob, developed the idea that messenger RNA carries hereditary information from the cell nucleus to the cellular sites of protein synthesis and also the concept of the operator gene controlling the activity of other genes. He and Jacob, together with André Lwoff, were awarded the 1965 Nobel Prize in physiology or medicine.

Monomer, chemical compound composed of single molecules as opposed to a polymer, which consists of molecules built up from repeated monomer units. For example, propylene is the monomer from which polypropylene is made, similarly methyl methacrylate is the monomer for polymethyl menthacrylate, which is sold as Lucite, Plexiglas, and Perspex.

Monomotapa, former SE African empire, also known as Mwanamutapa, of the Shona, a Bantu people, from the 15th century. Noted for its remarkable stone architecture and rich gold mines, the empire crumbled under pressure by the Portuguese by the 17th century.

Mononucleosis. *See* Infectious Mononucleosis.

Monopoly, an industry containing a single firm, a situation of imperfect competition. The demand for the product class is the demand curve the monopoly firm faces. A monopoly has complete market power and may therefore determine either its level of output or its price. Normally, a monopolistic industry will charge higher prices and produce smaller output than more competitive industries. For this reason, antitrust laws attempt to prevent monopoly power. In a situation where the existence of a monopoly is deemed necessary, the government attempts to regulate its price structure to allow only a "fair" rate of return.

Monosaccharide, a sweet-tasting carbohydrate that cannot be broken down by hydrolysis; a simple sugar. *See also* Glucose.

Monotheism, belief in the existence of a single God in the universe. This God is envisioned as the creator of all and is both personal and transcendent. Judaism, Christianity, and Islam are the three major monotheistic religions.

Monotheletism, or **Monothelitism,** 7th-century heresy in the Christian church asserting the existence of only one will (divine) in Jesus rather than the orthodox belief in the existence of human and divine wills. This position, which was politically motivated to gain the support of Monophysites and so stave off the Persian and Muslim invasions, was drawn up in the Ecthesis of 638 and in the Typos of 648. The heresy was condemned at the Lateran Council of 649 and the Council of Constantinople in 680.

Monotreme, any of the egg-laying mammals of the order Monotremata, native to Australia and New Guinea. The platypus and the echidna are the only living representatives. *See also* Echidna.

Monroe, James (1758–1831), 5th president of the United States (1817–25), *b.* Westmoreland co, Va. He attended William and Mary College and studied law

(1780–83) under Thomas Jefferson, whose lifelong friend and political supporter he became. In 1786 he married Elizabeth Kortright; they had three children.

Monroe was wounded in the American Revolution, during which he achieved the rank of lieutenant colonel. He served in Congress under the Articles of Confederation and opposed the adoption of the US Constitution. He served as a diplomat, as governor of Virginia, and in the US Senate.

When Jefferson became president (1801) he sent Monroe on various special missions to Europe. Monroe and Robert Livingston negotiated the Louisiana Purchase (1803). He was secretary of state under President Madison and also served briefly as secretary of war. Chosen by the Jeffersonians to succeed Madison, he was easily elected.

Monroe's administration is remembered as the "era of good feelings." Relations improved with Britain, France, Spain, and Canada. His most impressive achievement was the Monroe Doctrine. The Missouri Compromise (1820) settled the slavery issue for three decades. Monroe encouraged the settling of Liberia, whose capital, Monrovia, was named after him.

Career: delegate, Continental Congress, 1783–86; US Senate, 1790–94; minister to France, 1794–96; governor of Virginia, 1799–1802, 1811; special envoy to France, Great Britain, and Spain, 1803–07; secretary of state, 1811–17; secretary of war, 1814–15; president, 1817–25. *See also* Louisiana Purchase; Missouri Compromise; Monroe Doctrine.

Monroe, city in NE Louisiana, on Ouachita River; seat of Ouachita parish; site of one of the largest natural gas fields in United States (1916), Northeast Louisiana State College (1931), and antebellum houses. Industries: carbon black, chemicals, paper, paper bags. Founded 1785 as Miro; renamed 1819. Inc. 1900. Pop. (1980), 57,597.

Monroe Doctrine (1823), US foreign policy statement formulated by John Quincy Adams and presented to Congress on Dec. 2, 1823, by Pres. James Monroe. The doctrine attempted to prevent European intervention in Latin America's new republics by asserting flatly that the Americas were no longer open to European colonization. The United States promised not to interfere in European affairs and discouraged European attempts to force colonial status on new Latin American nations. The doctrine was viewed with suspicion by some Latin Americans who saw it as justification for US intervention.

Monrovia, seaport city and capital of Liberia, at the estuary of the St. Paul River; largest city in Liberia; seat of Monserrado co; site of University of Liberia (1862), several church missions, modern airport, government hospital, submarine base, modern harbor. Exports: iron ores (from the Bomi Hills), forest products, rubber, gold, palm oil and kernels, cassava. Industries: paint, fish processing, cement, bricks, oil refining, pharmaceuticals. Settled 1822 by freed US slaves on site chosen by the American Colonization Society; named in honor of US President James Monroe. Pop. 204,000.

Mons, town in SW Belgium, 32mi (52km) SW of Brussels; Charlemagne declared it capital of Hainaut prov. in the 9th century; 14th-century center of the lace and cloth trade; scene of the British Expeditionary Force's first battle (1914); site of a technical college (1837) and State University Center (1965). Industries: mining, textiles, sugar. Pop. 61,732.

Monsoon, a seasonal wind produced by variations in air temperatures and pressures between continents and oceans. *See also* Winds.

Monstera, climbing plant of tropical America with deeply incised leaves. It bears edible fruits. The *Monstera deliciosa* is a popular house plant. It is commonly and incorrectly called a split-leaved philodendron. It rarely blooms indoors. The erect stem needs support for the leathery leaves that can grow 4ft (1.2m) long. Family Araceae.

Montagnards (The Mountain), far left members of the French Revolutionary government. They rose to power over the Girondists in 1793 and began the infamous Reign of Terror, when thousands were guillotined for often slight political differences. Allied with the Parisian Jacobins under Robespierre, the Montagnards gradually lost public support and were effectively ousted by the Thermidorean Reaction (1794).

Montaigne, Michel Eyquem, (Seigneur de) (1553–92), French essayist. Originally a magistrate, he retired from public life to his private lands in 1571 to compose his *Essais* (1580). Written in a style that alternated between high eloquence and racy colloquialism, the *Essais* constituted an intellectual autobiography that moved from stoicism through skepticism to a mature acceptance of all that life offered. A new edition of the *Essais*, with additions, was published in 1588, and he continued to work on them until his death.

Montale, Eugenio (1896–1981), Italian poet and critic. He worked as a librarian in Florence and as literary editor of *Corriere della Sera*. A hermetic poet, his work is influenced by T.S. Eliot, and includes *Ossi di seppia* (1925), *Le occassioni* (1940), *Xenia Poems* (translated 1970), *New Poems* (1976), *Quaderno di quattro anni* (1977, a collection of over 100 new poems), and *It Depends* (1980). He was awarded the 1975 Nobel Prize for literature.

Montana, state in the NW United States bordered on the N by the Canadian provinces of British Columbia, Alberta, and Saskatchewan.

Land and Economy. The W 40% is mountainous. The Rocky Mts run from S to N, with many subsidiary ranges. The remainder of the state is largely high plains, where grazing and farming produce a major part of the state's income. The Missouri River flows from W to E across the state and is dammed to create the huge Fort Peck storage reservoir. Falls on the river generate electric power. Other large rivers are the Milk and the Yellowstone. Forests and mines, which are economically important, are situated in the mountains. Tourism is an important source of revenue.

People. Montana is one of the most sparsely populated states, with a density of only 4.8 persons per square mile (12.4 per sq km). A little more than half resides in urban areas. Almost all inhabitants are natives of the United States.

Education. There are 12 institutions of higher education.

History. French and Spanish fur traders and prospectors were active before 1800, but when the United States acquired the region from France by the Louisiana Purchase in 1803, it was little known. Reports by the Lewis and Clark expedition of 1804–06 led to the development of the fur trade and the establishment of settlements, army posts, and missions. Discovery of gold brought a rush of immigrants after 1852, and Montana Territory was organized in 1864. Military action over many years subdued hostile Indians. The opening of the Northern Pacific Railroad in 1883 was an enormous stimulus to the state's growth, especially in farming and mining. During the early 1980s copper mining slumped, but the strip mining of coal underwent expansion.

PROFILE

Admitted to Union: Nov. 8, 1889; rank, 41st
US Congressmen: Senate, 2; House of Representatives, 2
Population: 786,690 (1980); rank, 44th
Capital: Helena, 23,938 (1980)
Chief cities: Billings, 66,798; Great Falls, 56,725; Missoula, 33,388
State legislature: Senate, 50; House of Representatives, 100
Area: 147,138sq mi (381,087sq km); rank, 4th
Elevation: Highest, 12,799ft (3,904m), Granite Peak; lowest, 1,800ft (549m), Kootenai River
Industry (major products): lumber, wood products, processed primary metals, processed foods
Agriculture (major products): wheat, barley, potatoes, sheep, cattle
Minerals (major): copper, zinc, phosphate rock, petroleum, natural gas, coal
State nickname: Treasure State
State motto: Oro y plata (gold and silver)
State bird: western meadowlark
State flower: bitterroot
State tree: ponderosa pine

Montane Biome. *See* Biome.

Montcalm, Louis Joseph de, Marquis de Saint-Véran (1712–59), French general in North America. Commander-in-chief of French army in Canada (1756–59), he won several victories in the colonial wars against the British, including Fort Ontario (1756), Fort William Henry (1757), Fort Carillon (Ticonderoga, 1758), and Montmorency (1759). Lacking support from France, he was defeated by Gen. James Wolfe at Quebec, where he was mortally wounded.

Monte Albán (*c.* 400 BC–*c.* AD 900), ancient Zapotec religious center located southwest of Oaxaca, Mexico. Monte Albán was built on a level hilltop and along the adjacent valleys; stepped platforms supported the religious monuments.

Monte Carlo, town in N Monaco, on the French Riviera and Mediterranean Sea; famous resort, tourist center with world's oldest casino; noted for scenery, mild climate, luxurious hotels, and annual car rally and Monaco Grand Prix. Founded 1856 by Prince Charles III of Monaco in agreement with a joint stock company that wished to build and operate the casino. Pop. 10,000.

Monte Carlo Method, method of solving certain types of physical problems by statistical experiments based on the application of mathematical operations to random numbers. It is based on the work of William Sealy Gossett (pseudonym Student) and takes its name from the famous casino in Monaco.

Montego Bay, seaport city in NW Jamaica, West Indies; commercial center with good harbor and rail connections; site of St James church, dome tower airport, remains of Arawak Indian settlement (visited by Christopher Columbus 1494) before European development. Industries: tourism, sugar cane, bananas, coffee, ginger, rum, fruit export. Pop. 50,000.

Montenegro (Crna Gora), constituent republic in SW Yugoslavia, at S end of Dinaric Alps, bordered by Albania (SE), Adriatic Sea (SW); Titograd is capital, and Kotor is major port. Region is mountainous and isolated; divided into Brda region and Montenegro proper (W) by Zeta River; population is largely Serbian. Region was independent principality of Zeta within Serbian Empire until 14th century, when defeated by Turks; formal recognition of independence occurred 1878 at Congress of Berlin; became one of six Yugoslavian autonomous republics 1946. Industries: sheep and goats, mining, corn, wheat, tobacco, iron, steel. Area: 5,332sq mi (13,810sq km). Pop. 530,000.

Monterey, city in W California, at S end of Monterey Bay; capital of Spanish prov. of California 1774–1822; site of California's first theater (1844) and first newspaper (1846). Founded 1770 by Franciscans; inc. 1859. Pop. (1980) 27,558.

Monterey Park, city in S California, 8mi (13km) E of Los Angeles; site of 2 Industrial parks. Inc. 1916. Pop. (1980) 54,338.

Monterey Pine, evergreen tree native to S California. It has heavy, irregular branches and bright green 6 in (15cm) needles. It is grown as an ornamental. Height: to 100ft (30m). Family Pinaceae; species *Pinus radiata*.

Monterrey, city in NE Mexico, 150mi (242km) S of Laredo, Texas; capital of Nuevo León state. Captured 1846 by US forces under Zachary Taylor; site of university (1937), Obispado chapel, 18th-century cathedral, Topo Chico hot springs. Industries: mining, petroleum, glass, textiles, furniture, processed foods, plastics, beverages, electrical equipment, flour, paper. Founded 1579. Pop. 1,500,000.

Montesquieu, Charles-Louis de Secondat, Baron de (1689–1755), French social philosopher, magistrate in Bordeaux. He launched his criticism of contemporary society in the *Persian Letters* (1721). His *Spirit of Laws* (1748) attempted to explain the evolution of societies in terms of environmental features: climate, geography, demography. Judicial laws, he held, had their seat in nature as surely as those of physical science. His method, however, was not entirely empirical, nor was his infant "sociology" free of abstraction.

Monteverdi, Claudio (1567–1643), Italian composer, the first great opera composer and a pioneer in modern orchestration. He advanced violin technique by trying out new effects in orchestral playing. His many operas include *L'Orfeo* (1606), *Il Ballo delle Ingrate* (1608), and *L'Incoronazione di Poppea* (1642). He also composed religious music and many madrigals.

Montevideo, capital city and port of Uruguay, in S part of country on the Rio de La Plata, 135mi (217km) E of Buenos Aires, Argentina; largest city in Uruguay and one of South America's major ports. Originally a Portuguese fort (1717), captured by Spanish 1724; became capital of Uruguay 1828; suffered from civil wars 1843–1851; site of University of the Republic (1849), the Prado (a park), with botanical gardens and a promenade, and the legislative palace. Industries: textiles, dairy products, wines, packaged meats, tourism. Pop. 1,229,748.

Montez, Lola (1818?–61), born Maria Dolores Eliza Rosanna Gilbert. Irish-American adventuress, styled herself as a Spanish dancer but became famous rather for her great beauty and extravagant social life. She became the mistress of Louis I of Bavaria in 1846, but her involvement in politics caused her exile and Louis' abdication two years later. She moved to America, married a San Francisco journalist, and toured Australia as a dancer.

Montezuma, name of two Aztec emperors. **Montezuma I** (*c.* 1390–1464) increased the geographical scope of the empire through a series of wars. **Montezuma II** (1480–1520) allowed the Spaniards under Cortés to enter central Mexico unhindered. Montezuma II was imprisoned by the Spaniards, and killed by his own subjects when they rose up against the intruders.

Montfort, Simon de, Earl of Leicester (1208–65), English baron. He married Henry III's sister (1238) and became adviser to the king. Complaints about his ruthless enforcement of English authority in Gascony (1248–52) caused his recall. Quarreling with Henry, he joined the barons at Oxford (1258). Henry's repudiation of his agreements occasioned the Barons' War (1263–65). De Montfort defeated him at Lewes (1264) and as virtual ruler of England under the Provisions of Oxford summoned a parliament, but was killed in renewed fighting at Evesham. *See also* Barons' War.

Montgolfier, Joseph Michael (1740–1810) and **Jacques Étienne** (1745–99), French pioneer balloonists. In 1783 they carried out their initial experiments with a model hot air balloon and gave their first public demonstration of manned balloon flight in June 1783.

Montgomery, Bernard Law, 1st Viscount Montgomery of Alamein (1887–1976), British general. As commander of the British Eighth Army, he stopped the German offensive in North Africa at Alamein (1942) and led the invasion of Sicily and Italy (1943). He helped plan the Normandy landings (1944), leading his troops into Germany, and commanding the British occupation forces there (1945–46). Made field marshal (1944) and viscount (1946), he was deputy supreme allied commander, Europe (1951–58). His abrasive personality caused conflict with other Allied commanders, notably General Eisenhower, but his total commitment to victory won universal admiration.

Montgomery, commercial city in SE central Alabama, 85mi (137km) SSE of Birmingham, seat of Montgomery co. Location of US Air Force Special Staff School; state capital in 1847; first capital of the Confederacy in 1861. Industries: livestock, cotton, lumber, meat-packing, fertilizer. Settled 1818; inc. 1837. Pop. (1980) 178,157.

Montmorillonite, a general name for a group of clay minerals, hydrous calcium-sodium aluminum-magnesium-iron silicate. Moisture sensitive clays weathered out of igneous rocks. Common constituent of soil. Used in paper industry for "carbon-less" paper. White, yellowish, or gray. Hardness 1–2; sp gr 2.5.

Montpelier, capital city of Vermont in N central Vermont, 37mi (60km) SW of Burlington at confluence of Winooski and North Branch rivers; seat of Washington co; location of land grant 1780; settled 1787; made state capital 1805. It is the site of Vermont College (1834), Wood Art Gallery (1899), Dewey House; birthplace of Adm. George Dewey. Industries: tourism, sawmill and granite machinery, granite, clothespins, maple sugar and syrup, plastics. Inc. 1855. Pop. (1980) 8,241.

Montpellier, city in S France, 6mi (10km) N of Mediterranean Sea; capital of Hérault dept. City was center of fief under counts of Toulouse until 13th century when it passed to kings of Majorca; in 1349 it was purchased by Philip VI of France; site of University (1289), botanical garden (1593); birthplace of philosopher August Comte (1798). Industries: cottons, candles, soaps, chemicals. Founded 8th century. Pop. 195,603.

Montreal, city on Montreal Island, Quebec, Canada, on N bank of St Lawrence River. The largest city in Canada, it is also the world's largest inland seaport. City was under French control until 1760 when British took over; occupied by Americans November 1775–June 1776; British and French clashed in Montréal 1837–38; served as seat of Canadian government

Mordovinian (Mordovskaja) Autonomous Soviet Socialist Republic

Eugenio Montale

Glacier National Park, Montana

Alberto Moravia

1844–49. Population is mostly Roman Catholic of French extraction. A major cultural and educational center, it is the site of many churches and cathedrals, museums, parks and recreational facilities; home of baseball's National League Montreal Expos, National Hockey League's Montreal Canadiens; location of the 1976 Summer Olympics, McGill University (1829), and the University of Montréal (1876); focal point of transportation, finance and industry in E Canada. Major industries: aircraft, electrical equipment, railroad rolling stock, textiles, metal wares, food processing, chemicals. Originally the Indian village of Hochelaga; visited 1535 by Jacques Cartier; settled 1642 by French. Pop. 1,080,546.

Mont-Saint-Michel, rocky isle 1mi (1.6km) off NW France, in Gulf of Saint-Målo (arm of English Channel); site of Benedictine abbey built 708 by St Aubert, destroyed 1203 and rebuilt. Base of the island is circled with ramparts, towers, and bastions rising three storeys to support the abbey and church. The church spire holds a statue of St Michael, 456ft (138m) above the bay. Nave of the church is 12th-century Romanesque style; the choir is 14th-century Gothic; the facade was added in 18th century.

Montserrat, island in Leeward Islands, British West Indies, between Atlantic Ocean (E) and Caribbean Sea (W). Plymouth is capital and chief port. The island is mountainous, volcanic, intensively cultivated; Soufrière is highest peak, 3,000ft (914m); site of severe earthquake Oct. 8, 1975. Discovered 1493 by Christopher Columbus, it was colonized 1632 by English; held briefly by French; returned to Great Britain 1783; member of former Leeward Islands colony and former member of Federation of West Indies; currently part of Caribbean Common Market; rejected self-government 1966. Shipping of agricultural produce, especially cotton, is main industry. Area: 38sq mi (98sq km). Pop. 12,162.

Montserrat, volcanic mountain in NE Spain; terrain is jagged and eroded; site of 9th-century Benedictine monastery, containing 13 hermitages, carving of Virgin Mary; here Ignatius Loyola conceived the idea of founding the Society of Jesus (Jesuits); traditional site of castle of Holy Grail. Approx. height: 4,054ft (1,236m).

Monza, city of N Italy, 10mi (16km) NE of Milan; scene of assassination of King Umberto I of Italy 1900; site of 6th-century cathedral (founded by Lombard queen Theodelinda), 13th-century town hall. Industries: felt hats, carpets, textiles. Pop. 121,155.

Moog Synthesizer, computer tool for composing music by translating ideas into synthetic sounds, electronically produced. Wave forms generated by programmed or manipulated circuitry and modified by altering intensity, frequency, duration, etc, are combined to create complex signal patterns. Output is obtained from selected mixtures preserved on magnetic tape.

Moon, natural satellite of the planet Earth and about the same age (4.5–5 billion years). The Moon has no light of its own and reflects less than 10% of the light that falls on it. The different phases of the Moon occur as it revolves around the earth and are determined by its position in relation to both the Earth and the Sun. When the shadow of the Moon covers part of the Earth's surface a solar eclipse occurs. When the Earth's shadow falls onto the Moon a lunar eclipse occurs. The tides of the Earth's oceans are a result of the gravitational influence of the Moon. With an escape velocity of 1.5mi (2.4km) per second there is no atmo-

sphere as such. Mean distance from the Earth, 239,000mi (384,790km); mass and volume, .012 and .02 times that of the earth, respectively; diameter, 2,160mi (3,478km); rotation period and period of sidereal revolution, 27.32 days; surface temperature, from below −247°F (−155°C) to above 212°F (100°C).

Moonfish, or **Opah,** marine fish found in all seas and important as a food fish in Japan. Its oval-shaped body is laterally compressed; colors are blue and rose with white spots. Length: to 6ft (182.9cm); weight: to 600lb (270kg). Family Lampridae; species *Lamprius regius.*

Moonflower, twining herb similar to morning glory; it produces large, pure white flowers in early evening. A perennial in warm areas, it grows to 15ft (4.6m). Family Convolvulaceae; genus *Calonyction.*

Moon Illusion, illusion in which the Moon on the horizon appears larger than the Moon in the overhead (zenith) position. It is best attributed to misperception of distance, ie, the horizon sky appears farther away than the zenith sky.

Moore, George Edward (1873–1958), British ethical theorist, epistemologist, and metaphysician. While studying at Cambridge University, he published *Principia Ethica* (1903). This work, along with some papers, was a major factor in the declining influence of Hegelianism and Kantianism in British philosophy. He also published *Ethics* (1912), *Philosophical Studies* (1922), and *Some Main Problems of Philosophy* (1953) during his lifetime. *Philosophical Papers* (1959) and *Commonplace Book* (1962) were published posthumously. He held that "good in itself" could not be analyzed as a concept.

Moore, Henry (1898–), English sculptor and painter. As a draftsman, he is best known for his drawings of people seeking shelter in the London Underground during World War II. His artistic fame, however, has resulted chiefly from his sculpture. In the 1920s Moore did many sculptures of reclining women. During the next decade his figures became increasingly abstract, with holes used to help define space and form. His later works often include family groups.

Moore, Marianne (1887–1972), US poet, b. St Louis. Her verse covers a wide range of topics and is stylistically complex while emphasizing precise observation. Her works include *Observations* (1924) and *Collected Poems* (1951; Pulitzer Prize 1952).

Moors, nomadic people of North Africa of Berber and Arabic stock. Early converts to Islam, the Moors crossed over to Spain and Portugal in 711 and very quickly conquered most of the peninsula. Abd ar-Rahman I, the last survivor of the Umayyad dynasty from Damascus, established the emirate (later caliphate) of Córdoba in 756. That city and Toledo, Seville, and Granada became the great centers of Moorish commerce and culture. Generally hospitable to Jews and Christians, the Moorish rulers were great patrons of art and architecture, science, and philosophy. Throughout their rule, the Moors were systematically opposed by the Christian rulers of northern Spain, who gradually extended their power south. At the same time, dissension grew within the Moorish ranks. The puritanical Almoravids came across from North Africa in 1086 and conquered the more worldly Spanish Moors. They in turn were replaced by the even more puritanical Almohads.

By that time Christian power was striking at the very heart of Moorish power. Toledo fell to the Christians in 1085, Córdoba in 1236, and Seville in 1248. By 1250 all of Portugal had been taken from the Moors. Only

the kingdom of Granada remained Moorish; it survived until 1492, when it fell to Ferdinand and Isabella. As Spain and Portugal became re-Christianized, most of the Moors were expelled; a few converted to Christianity, but they generally suffered from the Spanish Inquisition. Today, the populations of Algeria, Mauretania, Morocco, and Tunisia are of basically Moorish stock. *See also* Almohads; Almoravids; Granada; Spanish Inquisition; Umayyads.

Moose, largest species of deer, found in Alaska, Canada, NW United States, Norway, Sweden, Siberia, Manchuria, and Mongolia in moist, wooded areas. It is dark brown with a broad muzzle, heavy mane, and large dewlap. The massive antlers grow to 78in (198cm). Once heavily hunted, moose are now protected. It is called an elk in Europe. Length: to 9ft (3m); height: to 5.5ft (1.7m) at shoulder; weight: to 1,800lb (810kg). Family Cervidae; species *Alces alces. See also* Deer; Elk.

Moraine, a general term indicating a mound, ridge, or other visible accumulation of unsorted glacial drift, predominantly till. End, or terminal, moraines are formed when a glacier is neither advancing nor retreating and the rock material is dumped at the glacier's edge. Ground, or frontal, moraines are sheets of debris left after a steady retreat of the glacier. *See also* Till.

Moravia, Alberto (1907–), pseud. of Alberto Pincherle, Italian novelist. His early novels, including *The Time of Indifference* (1929) and *The Fancy Dress Party* (1941), were increasingly critical of Fascism, and Moravia was forced into hiding until 1944. Later works, examining hypocrisy and alienation, include *The Woman of Rome* (1947), *The Conformist* (1951), *Two Women* (1957), and *1934* (1983). An essay collection, *Man as an End,* appeared in 1966.

Moravia, fertile region and former province of Czechoslovakia; bordered by Bohemia (W), White and Carpathian Mts (E), and Sudetes Mts (N); European textile center; horse breeding region. Made part of new Czechoslovakia 1918; occupied by Germans in WWII. Split into 19 administrative regions after Communist takeover in 1948.

Moravian Gate (Gap), strategic N-S mountain pass and ancient trade route of central Europe between SE Sudetes and W Carpathian Mts, where Silesia (formerly in Germany), Poland and Czechoslovakia meet.

Moray Eel, vicious marine fish found in rocks and reefs of tropical and temperate waters. It is eaten in parts of the world, but some species are poisonous. Its long, serpentine body is without pectoral fins. Colors are blue, brown, and slate, sometimes in a banded or spotted pattern. Length: 4–5ft (121.9–152.4cm). Among the 80 species are the Atlantic *Gymnothorax funebris* and the spotted *Gymnothorax moringa.* Family Muraenidae. *See also* Eel.

Mordecai, biblical cousin and foster father of Esther. With Esther, he thwarted Haman's efforts to destroy the Jews.

Mordovinian (Mordovskaja) Autonomous Soviet Socialist Republic, autonomous republic in W central USSR; capital is Saransk. Annexed by Russia 13th century; made an autonomous oblast 1930, and an ASSR 1934. Products: rye, wheat, oats, beans, potatoes, corn, tobacco, livestock. Industries: beekeeping, lumber, automotive, food processing. Area: approx. 10,000sq mi (25,900sq km). Pop. 976,000.

More, (Sir) Thomas (*c.* 1478–1535), English statesman and author, a Roman Catholic saint. A leading humanist, he was a friend of Erasmus. His *Utopia* (1516) imagined an ideal state founded on reason. Shakespeare's play *Richard III* is based on More's history. During the 1520s he wrote several important treatises against Lutheranism.

In 1518 he entered in the service of Henry VIII. He was knighted in 1521 and became Henry's trusted friend and adviser and succeeded Cardinal Wolsey as lord chancellor (1529), although he had disapproved of Henry's divorce from Catherine of Aragon. He resigned in 1532 claiming poor health but probably as much over his growing disagreements with the king. In 1533 he enraged Henry by refusing to attend Anne Boleyn's crowning. Henry had him arrested and placed in the Tower of London (1534). More refused to subscribe to the Act of Supremacy that made Henry the head of the Church of England. He was beheaded on a charge of treason for this insubordination. *See also* Utopia.

Morel, any of a genus of terrestrial mushrooms *(Morchella)* that have conic caps resembling pine cones and hollow stems, especially M. esculenta, one of the most prized edible fungi. Growing only in the wild, it can be found only in spring. Some "false morels" that resemble true ones are toxic.

Morelia, city in SW Mexico; capital of Michoacán state; site of Colegeo de San Nicolas (1540), the oldest institution of higher learning in Mexico, 17th-century baroque cathedral, 18th-century aqueduct. Founded 1541 as Valladohid, name was changed 1828 in honor of revolutionary hero Morelos y Pavón. Industries: lumber, handicrafts, agriculture. Pop. 209,014.

Morelos, state in S central Mexico; named in honor of Morelos y Pavón who led historic defense against Spain 1812; terrain is mountainous with semi-arid valleys. Products: sugar cane, tropical fruits, cereals, vegetables, rum, sugar. Area: 1,917sq mi (4,965sq km). Pop. 866,000.

Morgan, John Pierpont (1837–1913), US financier, b. Hartford, Conn. Beginning as a member of his father's banking firm, he played an important role in the consolidation of eastern railroads and the organization of US Steel Co. He established J. P. Morgan and Co., a finance house that engaged in gold speculation during the Civil War. Morgan was also a leading US art collector.

Morgan, Thomas Hunt (1866–1945), US geneticist, b. Lexington, Ky. He was one of the most important founders of the science of genetics. In 1907 Morgan made an important advance—the use of the Mediterranean fruit fly *Drosophila* as a tool for genetic research. He then went on to discover that chromosomes were the carriers of hereditary material. He was awarded the 1933 Nobel Prize in physiology and medicine.

Morgan, light horse breed developed in New England by Justin Morgan from a versatile horse of same name foaled in 1789. A superior saddle, driving, racing, and farm horse with stamina and docility, it has a high-held head, round and deep short-backed body, and wide-set thin legs. Height: 58–64in (147–163cm) at shoulder; weight: 800–1,200lb (360–540kg).

Morgan Le Fay, a fairy enchantress of Arthurian legend and romance linked with various personages in Celtic mythology. She was skilled in the arts of healing and of changing shape. She was once described as Arthur's sister, and on another occasion accused of stirring up trouble between Arthur and Guinevere, but finally emerged as a beneficent figure, carrying Arthur to Avalon, her marvelous island.

Moriscos, Christianized Moors of Spain. As Moorish Spain was reconquered by Christian rulers from the north, they generally established a policy of voluntary conversion of the Moors; later it was decreed that all Moors either convert or be expelled from Spain. Many Moors ostensibly became Christians but were secretly still Muslims, or were suspected of being. The Spanish kings regarded them as a threat, and they were persecuted by the Spanish Inquisition. In 1568 they revolted and were put down three years later. In 1609, Philip III ordered all Moriscos expelled.

Morison, Samuel Eliot (1887–1976), US historian, b. Boston. Educated at Harvard, he was a member of the faculty there during most of his long teaching career. He was named official US navy historian for World War II (1942), and retired from the navy as a rear admiral (1951). He directed the Harvard Columbus Expedition, which traced Columbus' routes across the Atlantic, and the ensuing *Admiral of the Ocean Sea* (2 vols., 1942) won him the Pulitzer Prize. He won a second Pulitzer Prize for *John Paul Jones* (1959). Among his other works are *The Growth of the American Republic* (with Henry Steele Commager, 1930), *The Oxford History of the American People* (1965), and *The European Discovery of America* (2 vols., 1971–74).

Morley, Edward William (1838–1923), US chemist, b. Newark, N.J. He worked with A.A. Michelson on the famous experiment (1887) that demonstrated the absence in the universe of a stationary hypothetical substance called ether that was supposed to carry light waves. *See also* Michelson-Morley Experiment.

Mormon, The Book of, one of the scriptures of The Church of Jesus Christ of Latter-day Saints, or Mormons. Joseph Smith, founder of the Mormon Church, told that in 1827 he was led by a heavenly messenger, Moroni, to discover a set of inscribed gold plates. These plates held the record, as told by a prophet named Mormon, of a migration from Jerusalem to the Americas beginning in 600 BC. *See also* Mormons.

Mormon Cricket, wingless grasshopper found in W United States. It feeds on range grasses, wheat, and alfalfa. When weather conditions are favorable for a number of years, they multiply rapidly, migrate, and do serious crop damage. Length: 1–2in (25–51mm). Family Tettigoniidae; species *Anabrus simplex. See also* Grasshopper.

Mormons, members of the Mormon Church. The new title is The Church of Jesus Christ of Latter-day Saints. The church was established in upstate New York in 1830 by Joseph Smith. He reported that an angel directed him to discover *The Book of Mormon,* the source of Mormon doctrine. Believing that they were to found Zion, or a New Jerusalem, Smith and his followers moved west. They tried to settle in Ohio, Missouri, and Illinois but were driven out. Other settlers resented and attacked Mormons for a number of reasons, one being the Mormon belief that a man could take several wives. Joseph Smith was shot to death in Illinois in 1844. Brigham Young then rose to leadership and took the Mormons to Utah Territory (1847) where they established Salt Lake City. Opposition to the Mormons continued, but they prospered through hard work. The Mormon president renounced polygamy in 1890, and Utah became a state in 1896. In 1978, Pres. Spencer W. Kimball announced a revelation that permits blacks to become priests.

The Mormon Church has more than 6,000,000 members. Headquarters remains in Salt Lake City, but the church has spread to other states and abroad. Many young members undertake missionary trips. All "worthy" males are considered members of the priesthood. The church is governed by a hierarchy headed by the president and a Council of Twelve Apostles. *See also* Mormon, The Book of; Smith, Joseph.

Morning Glory, family of twining and trailing vines native to tropical South America. Blue, purple, pink, or white flowers are funnel-shaped with 5 shallow lobes or a flaring disk; they bloom in summer and early autumn. Species of morning glory include the small-flowering *Ipomoea lacunosa; I. purpurea,* with heart-shaped leaves; and *I. pandurata,* or man-of-the-earth, which has a white flower with purple center and large underground tubers. Family Convolvulaceae.

Moro, Muslim peoples of the S Philippines, comprising nine separate groups speaking distinct languages. From the first Spanish settlements in the area in 1571 to their suppression by US forces under General John J. Pershing in 1913, the Moro lived by piracy and raiding their Christian neighbors to the north, as well as by fishing and trading.

Morocco (Al-Magreb), independent nation in N Africa. It is a constitutional monarchy with both modern and traditional elements.

Land and Economy. Situated on the NW corner of Africa with 1,200mi (1,932km) of coastline on the Atlantic Ocean and Mediterranean Sea, Morocco is bordered by Western Sahara and Algeria (S and E). The Atlas Mts run inland, parallel to the Atlantic, with ranges rising 13,600ft (4,080m) above sea level. Climate on the Atlantic side of the Atlas is semi-tropical; on the Mediterranean coast the climate is mild. The rugged Rif Mts face Gilbraltar. In the W and central portions of the country are rich plains and cultivated plateaus. About 70% of the Moroccans derive their income from agriculture. Morocco ranks first in world phosphate exports. Foreign-owned farm lands were nationalized in 1973. Tourism attracts over 1,000,000 people yearly to Morocco's ruins, beaches, oases, and legendary cities.

People. Moroccan population is made up of three main divisions: the indigenous Berbers and descendants of 8th- and 11th-century Arab invaders. The slave trade brought many Sudanese to the S section. Foreign residents are mostly French and Spanish. Languages include Arabic, French, and Spanish. Berber is spoken in the rural areas. Islam is the established state religion. Literacy is estimated at 15%.

Government. Final civil and religious authority rests with the king. The unicameral parliament is elected by universal adult suffrage. The king may dissolve parliament and in emergency conditions may rule by decree.

History. The earliest records about this area were in Hanno's *Periplus,* which mentions Carthaginian coastal colonies. Islamic Arabs invaded in the 8th century, and the present Alaouite dynasty, rulers of Morocco since 1649, claims to be descended from the prophet Mohammed. European powers vied for Moroccan resources, and in 1912 it became a protectorate of France by terms of the Treaty of Fez. Nationalist uprisings continued for two decades, and nationalists organized for independence in 1944 under the Istiqlal Party. Political independence from France came on March 2, 1956. Later agreements with Spain restored Spanish zones of influence to Morocco. Mohammed V, sultan since 1927, was succeeded by his son, King Hassan II, and Morocco became a constitutional monarchy in 1962. Army revolts and several attempts to assassinate the King failed. Hassan dramatically asserted Moroccan claims to the Spanish Sahara in 1975 by leading a march into the area. In 1975, Spain agreed to cede its territory of Western Sahara to Morocco and Mauritania, both of which subsequently annexed their portions of the territory and began fighting against the Polisario Front, the region's guerrilla independence movement. In 1979, Mauritania renounced its claim, but Morocco continued fighting although the Organization of African Unity recognized (1980) the region as a sovereign state. In 1981, Morocco announced it would accept a cease-fire while a referendum on independence was held, but fighting continued through the early 1980s. By the mid-1980s, Morocco still claimed ⅔ of Western Sahara.

PROFILE

Official name: Kingdom of Morocco
Area: 172,413sq mi (446,550sq km)
Population: 19,531,000
Density: 113per sq mi (44per sq km)
Chief cities: Rabat (capital), Casablanca, Marrakech, Tangier
Government: Monarchy
Religion: Islam (state)
Language: Arabic
Monetary unit: Dirham
Gross national product: $14,460,000,000
Per capita income: $520
Industries: carpets, leather goods, clothing, textiles, processed food, wine, chemicals, pharmaceuticals
Agriculture: cereals, barley, wheat, corn, citrus fruits, sugar beets, sheep, dates, grapes, almonds
Minerals: phosphate, cobalt, antimony, lead, manganese, zinc, oil, coal
Trading partners: France, United States, West Germany, USSR

Morpheme, the smallest meaningful unit of speech. It may be an entire word—"work"—or a part of one—"re" in "rework". An inflectional (paradigmatic) morpheme is the added "s, es, ed, ing." A derivational morpheme is the "hood" in "motherhood." The root of the word is a separate morpheme.

Morpheus, in Greek mythology, the god of dreams, supposedly expert in imitating the forms of men. He was the son of Hypnos, the god of sleep.

Morphine, the principal alkaloid of opium, used to dull sensation and relieve pain. *See* Opium.

Morpho Butterfly, large, tropical American butterfly noted for brilliant blue metallic luster of upper surfaces of its wings. Family Morphoidae.

Morris, Gouverneur (1752–1816), US statesman and diplomat, b. Morrisania, N.Y. Morris served his state in both legislative and executive capacities during the American Revolution. As a delegate to the Continental Congress (1777–78) and to the Constitutional Convention of 1787, Morris took an active part in establishing the bases for the new government. He later served as minister to France and England (1789–94) and in the US Senate (1800–03).

Morris, Robert (1734–1806), American banker, financier of the Revolution and a signer of the Declaration of Independence, b. England. Arriving in Maryland in 1774, he soon became vice-president of the Pennsylvania Committee of Safety (1775–76) and was a member of the Continental Congress (1776–78). US superintendent of finance (1781–84), he established the first US commercial bank and chartered the Bank of North America (1781).

Morris, William (1834–96), English poet and craftsman. With his friends Burne-Jones and Dante Gabriel

J. Pierpont Morgan

Morocco

Samuel F. B. Morse

Rossetti, he started a firm of decorators known as Morris and Company, which designed wallpaper, furniture, and tapestries. Also a poet, his most notable works are *The Defence of Guenevere and Other Poems* (1858), and *The Life and Death of Jason* (1867), and *The Earthly Paradise* (3 vol. 1868–70). One of his most important ventures was the Kelmscott Press, established in 1890. There he designed the type, page borders, and bindings of fine books.

Morse, Samuel F(inley) B(reese) (1791–1872), US inventor and artist, b. Charlestown, Mass. As a portrait painter, Morse helped to found the National Academy of Design in 1826. Beginning in 1832, Morse experimented for 12 years on a practical system of using electricity to send messages by telegraphy. He developed the Morse Code to simplify the system. In 1844 he sent the message "What hath God wrought?" from Washington to Baltimore. He collaborated with Cyrus Field (1857–58) in laying the first transatlantic cable. Morse was also one of the founders of Vassar College (1861).

Morse Code, the code used for radiotelegraphy. It consists of dots and dashes created by the interrupting of a continuous radio wave. The dashes are three times the length of the dots. Characters vary in length from a single dot or dash to five dots or dashes or a combination thereof. The code is named for its American inventor, Samuel F. B. Morse.

Morte D'Arthur, Le (*c*. 1469), Arthurian prose romance by Thomas Malory. Its 21 books deal principally with the quest for the Holy Grail, the death of King Arthur, and the disintegration of the fellowship of the Round Table. Malory borrowed much of his material from earlier French romances, but skillfully recast these diffuse originals into a continuous and dramatic narrative. His austere prose style further underlines the tragedy implicit in the downfall of Arthur. *See also* Arthurian Romance.

Mortimer, Roger de, 8th Baron Wigmore, 1st Earl of March (1287–1330), English nobleman. Having secured his position in Ireland against the Lacy family, he opposed the Despensers in Wales and was imprisoned (1322). Escaping to France, he returned to England (1326) as the paramour of Queen Isabella, and, after Edward II's deposition and death, virtually ruled England until executed by Edward III.

Mortmain, a term meaning the ownership of land by a perpetual corporation. Originally referring to tenure by a religious organization, it now includes ownership by charitable and business corporations. A French word meaning "dead hand," mortmain had a troubled history throughout the Middle Ages when the Roman Catholic Church acquired large properties that were exempt from taxation. In many countries tax-exempt church properties are now restricted to essential buildings and properties.

Morton, James Douglas, 4th Earl of (*c*.1516–81), Scottish statesman. As Mary Stuart's lord chancellor (appointed 1563), he supported unenthusiastically her marriage to Lord Darnley, and subsequently approved Darnley's murder (1567), opposing Mary thereafter. Succeeding as regent (1572), he administered Scotland efficiently but was criticized for his pro-English policy. French influence at court finally caused his downfall and execution for complicity in Darnley's death.

Morton, John (1420?–1500), English statesman and prelate. After taking a degree in law at Oxford he practiced in the ecclesiastical courts of London and re-

ceived substantial ecclesiastical preferment from the Lancastrians. Following their defeat in 1461 he lived in exile, returning only in 1470. In the tumultuous times that followed, Morton made himself useful as prelate and statesman to Edward II. When Richard III ascended Morton worked in the interests of the earl of Richmond, who, when he became Henry VII in 1485, appointed Morton archbishop of Canterbury (1486), lord chancellor (1487) and cardinal (1493).

Morton, William Thomas Green (1819–68), US dentist who pioneered in the use of ether as an anesthesia in 1846, b. Charlton, Mass. He publicized his work and generally received credit for the discovery, although ether had been used earlier by Crawford W. Long. *See also* Anesthesia.

Mosaic, type of surface decoration using designs made of small pieces of material, such as stone, tile, or glass, closely set together in some adhesive material, such as wet mortar. Mosaics were often used in floor and wall decorations as early as the 4th millennium BC in Mesopotamia. In the Near East, mosaics were made of natural pebbles, and by the 5th century BC, the technique in Greece had developed to the degree where delicate designs with much detail were common. By the 3rd century BC, pebbles were replaced by cut marble cubes, or tesserae, in Hellenistic mosaics. During Roman times, floor mosaics, usually featuring a center design surrounded by a decorative, geometric border, were made. In the early Christian era, the floor mosaic was replaced by the wall mosaic, which was used to decorate church interiors. The marble cubes were replaced by brightly colored glass cubes, sometimes of golden color, especially during the Byzantine era. Mosaic art reached its height in the 6th century in such buildings as San Vitale in Ravenna, and again in the 11th and 12th centuries in Hagia Sophia in Istanbul.

Mosaic, any of several virus diseases that results in mottling of leaves with light green or yellow blotches. Some mosaics also cause curling and puckering of leaves and stunting of plants. They are serious diseases of many crops, including apples, peaches, beans, cucumbers, and tobacco.

Moscow (Moskva), capital and largest city of USSR, and of Moscow oblast, in Russian SFSR, on the Moskva River E of its junction with the Moscow Canal, 400mi (640km) SE of Leningrad. Archeological remains indicate site has been inhabited since Neolithic times; Russian documents do not mention it until 1147 (as a village). It became a separate principality by end of 13th century and in 1367 the first stone walls of Kremlin were built. In 1341 it took principality of Vladimir and from 1462–1505 Grand Duke Ivan III (first to take the title of tsar) led successful campaign to annex principality of Novgorod; he defeated Tartars and invaded Lithuania. Polish troops occupied Moscow in 1610, but were driven out in 1612. Moscow was capital of grand duchy of Russia 1547–1712, when it was moved to St Petersburg (now Leningrad). In 1812 the city, which was built almost entirely of wood, burned to the ground; Napoleon and French troops were occupying city and fire forced them out. In 1918 it became capital of USSR. German siege of Moscow during WWII was broken by Russians, giving Germany its first major defeat of the war. The Kremlin is the center of the city, and the administrative center of the USSR; it includes palaces, churches, and government buildings within its 40-ft (12-m) walls. Adjoining it are Red Square, Lenin Mausoleum, the 16th-century cathedral of Basil the Beatified (now an anti-religious museum). City is also site of University of Moscow (1755), Tretyakov Gallery (1880), Bolshoi Theater, about 90 other

institutes of higher education, and 450 scientific institutes. Industries: metalworking, oil refining, automobiles, film making, precision instruments, chemicals, wood and paper products, tourism. Pop. 7,911,000.

Moscow (or **Muscovy**), **Grand Duchy of,** 15th–18th century state. **Ivan I** (1301–40) began a consolidation of territories much increased by **Ivan II** (1440–1505), who absorbed Novgorod in 1478. **Ivan the Terrible** (1530–84) gathered together all the Russian lands under his rule and in 1547 became Tsar of all Russia. This consolidation was followed by a period of anarchy known as the Time of Troubles (1598–1613) that lasted until the Romanov dynasty was established. Conquests in Siberia and the Ukraine, despite Polish rivalry, further strengthened Moscow. Under **Peter the Great** (1672–1725) the kingdom of Russia became an empire. The cradle of Russian culture, Moscow was an autocracy ruled by a boyars' Duma and a national assembly.

Moscow (Moskva), river in W central USSR; rises W of Uvarovka in Smolensk-Moscow Upland, flows NW, then E past Moajsk and Zvenigorod, and SE past Moscow and Bronnicy to the Oka River below Kolomna. It receives the Severka and Pachra rivers from the right and the Ruza and Istra from the left. Below the mouth of the Moscow Canal, the river has a lock system and forms the Pererva Reservoir at L'ublino. It is navigable below the Moscow Canal April-November. Length: 315mi (507km).

Moseley, Henry Gwyn-Jeffreys (1887–1915), English physicist. His initial studies involved radioactivity; later he discovered a relationship between the X-ray spectra of the elements and their atomic numbers. His investigations showed that the atomic number of an element and not its atomic weight determines its major properties.

Moselle (Mosel), river in France and Germany; rises in Vosges Mts, NE France, flows NW past Remiremont, Épinal, and Toul; turns N to flow past Metz and Thionville, and NE to leave France and form Luxembourg-German boundary; flows through Germany to empty into Rhine at Koblenz; connected to Rhine, Meuse, and Seine rivers by canals. Along its steep slopes between Trier and Koblenz Riesling grapes are grown from which Moselle wines are made. Length: 320mi (515km).

Moses (*c*. 13th century BC), in the Bible, prophet and leader of the Jewish people. A Levite born in Egypt, he was found as a baby by the pharaoh's daughter and raised at court. Answering God's call, he led the Hebrew tribes from Egypt to Canaan and gave them the Ten Commandments. He did not enter the Promised Land but God allowed him to see it from Mt Pisgah just before he died.

Moses, Grandma (1860–1961), b. Anna Mary Robertson in Greenwich, N.Y. At age 76 she gave up embroidery because of arthritis and began to paint. Having lived on farms her entire life, she painted landscapes in a primitive style, showing people involved in various farm activities.

Mosque, the Muslim place of worship. Usually decorated with abstract and geometric designs, the building's parts include the *mihrab,* or prayer niche, which shows the direction of Mecca; the *minaret,* or tower, from which the meuzzin calls prayers; the *courtyard* for washing before prayer; and the *madrasa,* or school. The first domed mosque, the Dome of the Rock, Jerusalem, was built in 691. Other famous mosques include the Mosque of the Prophet, Medina, containing

Mohammed's tomb; the Mosque at Mecca, containing the Kaaba; and the 3-domed Pearl Mosque, Agra.

Mosquito, fragile, tan to black insect, 0.12 to 0.36in (3–9mm) long, of great economic importance; found worldwide. The adult female sucks blood from warm-blooded animals, including man. It transmits several diseases of man including malaria, yellow fever, dengue fever, viral encephalitis, and filariasis. The larvae are aquatic and are found in lakes, rivers, and salt marshes, and in other areas that retain water. Family Culicidae. *See also* Diptera.

Mosquito Fish, freshwater fish of the SE United States known for its ability to eat large amounts of mosquito larvae. Colors are brown and gray with bluish shimmer. Length: 2.25in (5.7cm). Family Poecilidae; species *Gambusia affinis.*

Moss, any of about 15,000 species of small simple nonflowering green plants that typically grow in colonies, often forming dense carpets. Mosses are primitive plants that do not have specialized tissues for transporting water, food, and minerals, although they do have parts resembling stems, leaves, and roots of the higher (flowering) plants. They grow on soil, rocks, and tree trunks in a wide variety of land habitats, from the tropics to circumpolar regions. They favor shady damp places and some species live in freshwater lakes and streams. Because carpets of moss can absorb large amounts of water, they help reduce soil erosion. The peat mosses, which are especially water-absorbent, are widely used as a substitute for natural humus to improve soil quality. *See also* Bryophyte.

Mössbauer, Rudolph Ludwig (1929–), German physicist. He is credited with discovering the Mössbauer effect (also called the recoil-free gamma-ray resonance absorption), which states that in certain cases gamma-ray energy may be emitted or absorbed by some excited nuclei without the nucleus exhibiting a recoil. This effect has been used to verify the theory of relativity and to study solid material properties. For his work he shared with R. Hofstadter the Nobel Prize in physics in 1961. *See also* Relativity Theory.

Mossi, Negroid people inhabiting Upper Volta and found in small numbers elsewhere in West Africa. Their traditional livelihood is a form of sedentary agriculture, staple crops including millet and sorghum. The Mossi feudal kingdom traditionally worshiped ancestors and practiced an earth cult; Christianity and Islam now prevail.

Moss Pink, creeping, evergreen, perennial plant with crowded leaves on numerous stems that form a mat on the ground. The flowers are purple, pink, rose, white, or lavender, often with darker centers. Family Polemoniaceae; species *Phlox subulata.*

Most Favored Nation Clause, provision in trade treaties whereby nations grant to each other the most favorable commercial benefits, such as tariff reductions, which, individually, each nation may accord to a third nation.

Mosul (Al-Mawsil), city in N Iraq, 200mi (322km) NNW of Baghdad, on Tigris River; capital of Ninawa prov. An ancient city, it was taken by Muslims 636; major Mesopotamian center 8th–13th centuries; occupied by Ottomans 1534–1918; under British occupation and mandate 1918–32; awarded to Iraq by League of Nations 1926 after a dispute for its possession between Iraq and Turkey. Nearby are ruins of ancient Nineveh; seat of Mosul University (1967). Industries: oil, cement, sugar, livestock, agricultural produce. Pop. 243,311.

Motet, musical form important in the development of polyphonic music from about AD 1200 to 1600. The Medieval motet (13th and 14th centuries) consisted of three voice parts sung in Latin. The Flemish or Renaissance motet (15th and 16th centuries) consisted of four or five voice parts sung by chorus. Around 1600 the motet began to develop new features, such as instrumental accompaniment, solo singers, and use of languages other than Latin. These features developed mainly in Germany, as in the six motets of J. S. Bach. *See also* Polyphony.

Moth, chiefly nocturnal insects distinguished from butterflies and skippers by stout bodies and threadlike or featherlike antennae. At rest, a moth's wings are spread horizontally, held rooflike over its body, or wrapped around its body. Order Lepidoptera. *See also* Lepidoptera.

Mother Goose, traditionally in France a figure who told folktales. The phrase *Les Contes de Ma Mère l'Oye* (Tales of Mother Goose) appeared on Charles Perrault's 1697 collection of tales. The name first appeared in England on a collection of 50 traditional folk rhymes and 16 songs from Shakespeare compiled by John Newbery in 1760. He called the collection *Mother Goose's Melody or Sonnets for the Cradle.*

Mother-of-Pearl, shiny substance lining many mollusk shells. It is composed of calcium carbonate deposited in layers interspersed with some organic material. Diffraction of light causes iridescent play of colors. It is used in making buttons and jewelry. *See also* Mollusk.

Motherwell, Robert (1915–), US painter, b. Aberdeen, Wash. Associated with the school of action painters, he is best known for his abstract expressionistic works.

Motion. *See* Laws of Motion.

Motion, Stellar, change in position of a star due to both proper motion and to radial motion along the line of sight.

Motmot, Mexican and Central and South American bird that has a green body, turquoise head, and serrated bill for crushing insects. The ornamental, graduated tail often has a central naked rectrix decorated with a racket-shaped tip. They drill a tunnel into an earthen bank and excavate a cavity for the dull white eggs (3–4) that both parents incubate. Length: 7–18in (18–46cm). Family Motmotidae.

Motorcycle, a two-wheeled automotive vehicle, that combines the principles of a bicycle and the internal combustion engine. First designed in 1884 by Gottlieb Daimler, it did not become popular until about 1910. Most have four-stroke engines. Transmission is through chain or gearing between engine and gearbox. Usually controls on handbars govern the throttle, clutch, and front brake.

Motor Neurons. *See* Effectors.

Mott, Lucretia Coffin (1793–1880), US social reformer, b. Nantucket, Mass. A Quaker, she championed intellectual freedom and was an outspoken opponent of slavery. She became a Quaker minister (1821) and traveled lecturing on social reform and religion. One of the founders of the American Anti-Slavery Society (1833), she also helped establish the Philadelphia Female Anti-Slavery Society. Because she was refused a seat as delegate to the World's Anti-Slavery Convention in London (1840), she turned some of her attention to feminism. With Elizabeth Cady Stanton, she organized the first women's rights convention at Seneca Falls, N.Y. (1848).

Mo tzu, or **Mo ti** or **Micius** (470–391 BC), founder of the Moist school of Chinese philosophy. Both a high government official and the founder of a school for government service, his belief in universal love clashed with the prevailing Confucian views. *See also* Confucianism.

Mouflon, or European mouflon, wild sheep of Sardinia and Corsica, introduced widely in Europe at various times. Smaller than argali and bighorn sheep, they bear woolly underfur and are considered an ancestor of domestic sheep. Family Bovidae; species *Ovis musimon. See also* Sheep.

Moulmein (Maulmain), port city in S Burma, at mouth of Salween River, on E shore of Gulf of Martaban; division and district seat; communications center with railroad and airport. Exports: rice, teak. Pop. 171,767.

Mound Builders, name given to the North American Indians responsible for groups of earthen mounds found in the Ohio and Mississippi river valleys. The mounds, sometimes with a hut-like structure inside, are either sacrificial or mortuary. They contain skeletons or ashes with buried ceremonial objects.

Mountain, a part of the earth's surface that rises conspicuously higher, at least 1,000 ft (305m), than the surrounding area. Mountains have a restricted summit area, comparatively steep sides, and considerable bare rock surface. They are identified geologically by their most characteristic feature, for example, fold, volcanic, or fault-block mountains. Mountains occur as single isolated masses, as ranges, and in systems or chains.

Mountain Ash, small tree or shrub grown in Europe and the United States. The rowan tree *(Sorbus aucuparia)* of Europe is grown as an ornamental in the United States; height: to 50ft (15.2m). The North American *S. americana* grows to 30ft (9.1m) and *S. scopulina* has larger fruit. Family Rosaceae.

Mountain Goat, ruminant native to Rocky Mountains from Alaska to Montana and introduced in Black Hills of South Dakota. Classified as a goat-antelope, rather than a goat, its thick, shaggy fur is white to yellow and its shoulders are humped. It is a sure-footed climber and jumper although less graceful than the bighorn sheep. It is probably monogamous. Length: to 62in (1.6m); weight: to 200lb (90kg). Family Bovidae; species *Oreamnos americanus.*

Mountain Laurel, broad-leaved evergreen shrub native to E North America. It has pink or white flowers. The leaves are poisonous. Height: 4–25ft (1.2–7.6m). Family Ericaceae; species *Kalmia latifolia.*

Mountain Lion. *See* Puma.

Mountain View, city in W California, 11mi (18km) NW of San Jose; site of Moffet Naval Air Station and Ames Laboratory of the National Aeronautics and Space Administration. Industries: shipping, publishing, printing, research. Settled 1852; inc. 1902. Pop. (1980) 58,655.

Mountbatten of Burma, Louis Francis Albert Victor Nicholas Mountbatten, 1st Earl (1900–79), British naval commander and statesman. A grandson of Queen Victoria, he saw distinguished naval service during World War II, ousting the Japanese from Burma. In 1947 he became India's last viceroy and first governor-general (1947–48). He served as first sea lord and chief of naval staff (1955–59). He was assassinated by IRA terrorists.

Mount Desert, island off SE coast of Maine, partly in Acadia National Park; Bar Harbor is the chief city; resort area. Settled 1762. Area: 100sq mi (259sq km).

Mount McKinley National Park, park in central Alaska, the second largest national park. Mt McKinley, 20,320ft (6,198m), is the highest peak in North America. There are large glaciers, caribou, Dall sheep, timber wolves, grizzly bears, and other wildlife. Area: 1,939,493acres (785,495hectares). Est. 1917.

Mount Rainier National Park, park in W central Washington. It is the greatest single-peak glacial system in the United States. Glaciers radiate from the summit and slopes of this ancient volcano. There are dense forests and subalpine flowered meadows. Area: 241,781acres (97,921hectares). Est. 1899.

Mount Rushmore National Memorial, memorial in SW South Dakota, in Black Hills, containing huge sculptured busts of US presidents George Washington, Thomas Jefferson, Abraham Lincoln, and Theodore Roosevelt carved out of granite into face of Mt Rushmore; designed by Gutzon Borglum, the work took 14 years to complete; visible for a distance of 60mi (97km). Area: 1,278acres (518hectares). Est. 1925; dedicated 1927; completed 1941.

Mount St. Helens, a volcano in southwestern Washington that erupted cataclysmically on May 18, 1980. Landslides and volcanic flows dramatically altered the nearby topography. Ash expelled by the blast reached a height of 10 miles (16 km) and covered vast areas. Mount St. Helens is part of a chain of volcanic mountains that extends from Lassen Peak in northern California to Mount Garibaldi in British Columbia, Canada. Its previous eruption occurred in the mid-1800s.

Mount Vernon, city in SE New York, on Bronx River adjacent to New York City; site of Old St Paul's Church seized by Hessian soldiers during Revolutionary War; scene of journalist John Peter Zenger's arrest (1734) in classic freedom of press case. Industries: truck bodies, cosmetics, electronic components. First settled 1664 as Hutchinson's; inc. 1851 by Home Industrial Association of New York, as community of homes for New York City workers; chartered as city 1892. Pop. (1980) 66,713.

Mourning Cloak Butterfly, common, medium-sized butterfly with purple-brown wings bordered with yellow. Its larvae feed on leaves or willows, elms, poplars, and hackberries. Species *Nymphalis antiopa.*

Mourning Dove, small, grayish dove common in North America, known for its plaintive, mournful cry. Species *Zenaidura macroura. See also* Dove.

Mouse, name for small rodents with pointed snouts and long tails, mostly members of the families Muridae and Cricetidae. The big-eared and short-legged gray or brown house mouse *(Mus musculus)* is probably best known. Prolific nest-builders, house mice may live in human habitations or in the wild. They are omnivorous and often destructive, and may carry human diseases. Domesticated as laboratory mice or pets, they are often albino or multicolored. Length: about 3in (76mm), excluding tails; weight: to 1oz (30g).

Mousebird, or coly, small, crested, long-tailed, fruit-eating bird found in warm parts of Africa south of the

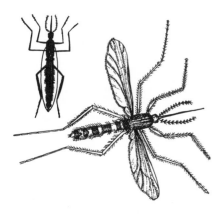

Mosquito

Lucretia Mott

Mudpuppy

Mule

Sahara. It is sometimes considered a pest. Mouselike, they are grayish with bright markings and scamper along branches. White or creamy eggs (2–6) are laid in a cup-shaped nest in a tree or bush. Family Coliidae.

Movement. *See* Laws of Motion.

Mozambique (Moçambique), independent nation in E Africa, formerly called Portuguese East Africa. It gained its independence in 1975. Its chief export crop is cashew nuts.

Land and Economy. Located on the SE coast of Africa with neighbors Tanzania (N), Malawi, Zambia, and Zimbabwe (W), the Republic of South Africa and Swaziland (S), and the Indian Ocean (E), it is divided into lowlands (44% of country) and uplands, with mountains along the W border. The Zambezi River bisects the country. Droughts and floods are common in the S section. Although subsistence farming engages most of the population, Mozambique has been developing cash crops and is the world's leading exporter of cashew nuts. A portion of foreign earnings comes from migrant laborers working in South African and Zimbabwean gold mines. Inexpensive power, irrigation, and commercial fishing are benefits from the new Cabora Bassa dam on the Zambezi River.

People. With Portuguese as the unifying language, Mozambique consists of numerous tribal groups: Tsonga and Changones in the S, Sena and Manica in the center, Nianja in the NW, Macuas in the N, and Makondes in the NE. Isolated N tribes are mainly animists or fetishists with some Islam practiced. S tribes have been affected by Catholic and Protestant missionaries.

Government. According to the constitution of 1975, the revolutionary Communist coalition party, Frelimo, is the country's directing power. Executive power is vested in the president, who also heads Frelimo.

History. Portuguese rule of Mozambique started with Vasco da Gama's exploration in 1498. Traders, missionaries, and prospectors followed. Mozambique was given to Portugal at the Berlin West Africa Congress (1884–85), and in 1952 it was designated as an overseas province of Portugal. The 1974 revolution in Portugal paved the way for some reforms. After 10 years of anti-colonial agitation, an independence movement (Front for the Liberation of Mozambique) took power in September 1974. When most of the Europeans departed and the economy was nationalized, considerable economic disruption resulted. Mozambique is one of the militant 'front-line states' opposed to white minority rule in South Africa. During the 1980s, Mozambique often accused South Africa of aiding the rebellious Mozambique National Resistance (MNR) forces.

PROFILE

Official name: People's Republic of Mozambique
Area: 302,328sq mi (783,030sq km)
Population: 9,200,000
  Density: 30.4per sq mi (11.7per sq km)
Chief cities: Maputo (capital); Nampula
Government: people's republic
Religion: Tribal, Islam, Catholic
Language: Portuguese
Gross national product: $2,000,000,000
Per capita income: $334
Industries: cement, alcohol, textiles, food products
Agriculture: cashews, cotton, sugar, copra, tea, cassava, maize
Minerals: coal, diamonds, bauxite
Trading partners: West Germany, Portugal, South Africa, United States, USSR

Mozart, Wolfgang Amadeus (1756–91), Austrian composer and musical genius, b. Salzburg. Playing

and composing from early childhood, Mozart completed a total of 626 works before dying in poverty at the age of 35. Composing in the dominant Classical-Rococo styles of his time, he brought these forms to perfection. His operas *The Marriage of Figaro* (1786), *Don Giovanni* (1787), and *The Magic Flute* (1791) are ranked among the finest ever written. His 27 piano concertos set the form for concertos for decades to come. His 40 symphonies, piano sonatas, chamber music, sets of variations, vocal music, masses and other religious compositions all contain supreme achievements of the Classical period. *See also* Classical Music.

MSH. *See* Melanocyte Stimulating Hormone.

Much Ado About Nothing (c.1598), 5-act comedy by William Shakespeare. The main plot, augmented by several characters of Shakespeare's own creation, is based on a work by Matteo Bandello. Claudio, persuaded by Don John that his fiancée Hero has been unfaithful to him with Borachio, denounces her as they are about to be married. Claudio has really seen Margaret, whom he mistakes for Hero, talking to Borachio. Hero faints and has it given out that she is dead. When Don John's villainy is revealed Claudio agrees to marry Hero's cousin to atone for Hero's death. At the altar the "cousin" is revealed to be Hero.

Mucopolysaccharide, any of the complex carbohydrates that are the chief constituents of the ground substance filling the spaces between cells and fibers of connective tissues. There exists a whole range of inherited disorders (mucopolysaccharidoses) that are marked by abnormal production, storage, and excretion of any of these substances. Symptoms include skeletal deformities, mental deficiency, heart defects, and deafness.

Mucous Membrane, membrane lining all body channels that communicate with the air, such as the respiratory tract, the digestive tract, and the glands secreting mucus.

Mucus, a slippery, viscous fluid containing mucin produced by mucous linings of the body. It serves for lubrication and protection: nasal mucus traps airborne particles; mucus of the stomach protects the lining from irritation by secreted hydrochloric acid during digestion.

Mud Dauber Wasp, black wasp with yellow markings, 0.75 to 1in (19–25mm) in length; found worldwide. It constructs its nests in the form of 1in (25mm) long mud tubes attached to building walls and ceilings. Its larva feed on spiders. Family Sphecidae, genera *Sceliphron* and *Chalybion. See also* Hymenoptera; Wasp.

Mudpuppy, aquatic salamander of streams and rivers in S Canada and United States. It has dark red gills at the sides of the neck and brown-spotted skin. Fertilization is internal. Length: to 15in(38cm). Family Necturidae; species *Necturus maculosus. See also* Salamander.

Mudskipper, amphibianlike fish of Africa, Asia, and Australia. It gulps air and carries water in its gill cavities to survive out of water when the tide recedes. It hops on mud with its large pectoral fins. Length: 8in (20cm). Family Periophthalmidae, Species include *Periophthalmus barbarus.*

Mud Snake, or hoop snake, snake found in swamps and lowlands of SE United States. A shiny, iridescent black with red sides, it has a stiffened, blunt tail tip. Eats

aquatic salamanders. Length: 5ft (1.5m). Family Colubridae; species *Farancia abacura.*

Mud Turtle, freshwater, bottom-crawling turtle ranging from New England to Argentina. It has a short tail, fleshy chin barbels, and hinges across its undershell. There are 12 species. Length: 6in(15cm). Family Kinosternidae; genus *Kinosternon. See also* Musk Turtle; Turtle.

Mugabe, Robert (Gabriel) (1924–), Zimbabwe political leader. He received part of his education in South Africa and taught in Ghana (1956–60). Returning home, he joined Joshua Nkomo in the African nationalist movement. He was arrested in 1962, 1963, and 1964 and was held in detention until 1974. He went into exile in Mozambique after 1974, cooperating with Nkomo until the end of the Rhodesian war. In 1980, he was elected prime minister of the new Republic of Zimbabwe; as prime minister he initially displayed a conciliatory attitude toward both his black and white opponents. Later, he worked to discredit rivals such as Nkomo.

Mukden (Shenyang, or **Shen-yang),** city in Manchuria, NE China, on Hun River, 100mi (161km) N of Yellow Sea; capital of Liaoning prov. City consists of three major divisions: old Chinese walled area containing former imperial palace and arsenal district; new Japanese-built city with administrative offices; Teihsi district, housing vast industrial complexes and residential areas. An early center for Chinese colonization in S Manchuria, city was captured by Manchus 16th century who made it their capital (1625) and gave it the present name. Mukden was made center of railroad system *c.*1900; scene of important Japanese victory during Russo-Japanese War (1905), as a result of which Mukden and S Manchuria fell under Japanese control; seat of Chang Tso-lin and other Manchurian warlords; fell to Communist control November 1948; site of Manchurian Polytechnic Institute, Chinese Medical Institute, and Manchurian branch of Chinese Academy of Sciences; industrial and cultural center. Industries: coal, oil-shale, steel, machinery, chemicals, electrical equipment, agriculture, wire and cable. Pop. 3,000,000.

Mulberry, family *(Moraceae)* of trees and shrubs found in temperate regions and containing a milky latex. The family also includes two herbaceous plants, the hop and hemp plants. Other characteristics are simple leaves, unisexual flowers, and the production of fibers or edible fruits. Among the 1,400 varieties are 10 species of *Morus,* deciduous trees with fleshy, edible fruits, including the white mulberry *M. albas,* to 45ft (13.7m), of China, and the red mulberry *M. rubra,* to 70ft (21.3m), of E and central United States.

Mulch, layer of loose material placed over soil and around growing plants. Mulches, including leaves, straw, pine needles, woodchips, stones, newspaper, and synthetics (fiberglass, plastic) are used to stabilize soil temperature, keep weeds down, nourish plants, and conserve moisture. During winter, mulches also protect herbaceous perennials, produce humus, prevent soil heaving, and keep roots from freezing. Nature's mulches include fallen leaves, grasses, and snow.

Mule, hybrid cross between horse and ass. Known since ancient times and popularized in the United States by George Washington, it is compact and muscular with long ears. Almost always sterile, types include draft, sugar, farm, cotton, pack, and mining. Height: 48–70in (122–178cm) at shoulder; weight: 600–1,600lb (271–720kg).

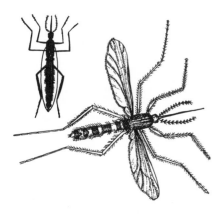

Mule Deer, long-eared deer found from W Canada to N Mexico. A solitary animal, its antlers branch into two equal parts and it has a black tail. It is a popular game animal. Height: to 3.5ft (1.1m) at shoulder. Family Cervidae; species *Odocoileus Hemionus*. *See also* Deer.

Mulhouse, city in E France, on Ill River and Rhône-Rhine canal, 18mi (29km) NW of Basel, Switzerland. A free imperial city of 13th century, it joined a Swiss confederation in 1515. In 1586 it became a neutral republic until 1798 when it voted to unite with France; Germany held it 1871–1918; site of 16th-century town hall. Industries: cotton, wool, chemicals, automobile parts. Founded 717. Pop. 119,326.

Mullein, hardy biennial plant *(Verbascum)*, including common mullein *(V. thapsus)* that has 1-ft (30-m) leaves and long, dense, yellow flower spikes; height: to 6ft (1.8m). Family Scrophulariaceae.

Muller, Hermann Joseph (1890–1967), US geneticist, b. New York City. He was awarded the 1946 Nobel Prize in physiology or medicine for his discovery of the production of mutations by means of X-ray irradiation. Muller worked with geneticist Thomas Hunt Morgan, studied the rate and nature of mutations, and determined that X-rays could produce mutations. He warned against needless X-ray use and of the dangers of radioactive fallout.

Muller, Paul (1899–1965), Swiss chemist. He received the 1948 Nobel Prize in physiology and medicine for his discovery of the effectiveness of DDT as a contact poison against several insects, a discovery that at that time led to the control of many fly-borne diseases and to greater agricultural output.

Mullet, also called gray mullet, a schooling marine fish found worldwide in shallow tropical and temperate waters. Caught commercially, its torpedo-shaped body is green or blue and silver. Length: to 3ft (91.4cm); weight: to 15lb (6.8kg). Among the 100 species is the widely distributed striped *Mugil cephalus.* Family Mugilidae.

Mulliken, Robert Sanderson (1896–), US chemist, b. Newburyport, Mass. After studying at M.I.T. he moved to Chicago, where he became professor. In 1966 he was awarded a Nobel Prize for his fundamental work on chemical bonds and molecular orbitals.

Mulroney, Brian (1939–), Canadian political leader, prime minister 1984– . A graduate of St. Francis Xavier University in Nova Scotia and Laval University law school in Quebec City, he became a labor lawyer then head of a mining company while building a political base in Quebec. His first elective office was the leadership of the Progressive Conservative party (1983), and he became prime minister a year later in a landslide Conservative victory, promising to improve Canadian-US relations and to reduce unemployment and Canada's deficit.

Multan, city in E central Pakistan, in the Chenab River valley approx. 200mi (322km). SW of Lahore; industrial and commercial center. Ancient settlement was taken by Mahmud of Ghazni 1006 and by Tamerlane 1398; held by British 1848–1947; site of ancient Muslim tombs and Hindu temple. Industries: textiles, foundries, glassware, food processing, pottery, crafts. Pop. 544,000.

Multi-Party System, prevailing political system in most democratic societies where voting is on the basis of proportional representation. This entitles smaller parties to representation in the legislature along with major parties, which are often unable to muster majorities. The parties then ally to form temporary coalitions that support a leader and a program. Such alliances are tenuous and can lead to instability in government and frequent shifts in political rule.

Multiple Myeloma, malignant tumor of the bone marrow. It occurs mostly in middle age. Mild cases may be cured by surgery or irradiation.

Multiple Sclerosis (MS), a disease of the nervous system, usually of the white matter (which conducts nerve impulses), in which there is degeneration of the sheath covering the nerve fibers (myelin sheath), resulting in weakness, lack of coordination, and speech and visual disturbances. Affected persons typically have relapses and remissions over many years. Its cause is unknown, but recent theories about the causes of the disease have included a possible viral origin, demonstrated by a virus detected in the blood of MS victims, as well as a possible hereditary factor, a brain protein, present in those afflicted.

Multiple Stars, stellar systems consisting of three or more stars orbiting around a common center of gravity. One typical example is the Mizar-Alcor system in Ursa Major. The main star Mizar is triple while the fainter Alcor is a spectroscopic binary. *See also* Binary Star.

Multiplet, group of elementary particles, all hadrons, with about the same mass, identical in all other properties except electric charge, and having up to four members. The nucleons and pions form multiplets. In strong interactions, members of a multiplet are all equivalent. A supermultiplet is a larger, more sophisticated and symmetrical grouping of hadrons involving eight quantum numbers, all members having identical spin.

Multiplication, arithmetical operation signified by $\times$, interpreted as repeated addition. Thus $a \times b$ is $a + a + \ldots + a$, in which b terms are added. In $a \times b$ ("a multiplied by b"), a is the multiplicant, b the multiplier, and the result is the product. *See also* Arithmetical Operations.

Mummy, a body treated for burial with preservatives. Mummification was most commonly practiced in ancient Egypt, where the internal organs were first removed, the body soaked in resin and other substances and then wrapped in linen bandage. The Incas of South America, the original inhabitants of the Canary Islands, and several other peoples also practiced mummification. Naturally preserved mummies have been discovered in Scandinavian peat bogs.

Mumps, a contagious disease, most common in children and caused by a myxovirus (one of a large group of viruses that includes the influenza virus). It has an incubation period of 18 to 22 days, after which fever and painful inflammation of the salivary glands begin, with marked swelling, especially in the parotid glands below and in front of the ears. Meningitis develops in about 10% of cases, and the infection may involve other organs such as the pancreas. In males past puberty, inflammation of the testes with subsequent sterility in some cases may occur. An attack of mumps results in persistent immunity.

Munch, Edvard (1863–1944), Norwegian painter and printmaker. As a printmaker, he made lithographs and woodcuts, often using many colors. He painted portraits and murals, but his best-known works are his highly expressionistic paintings that show basic human emotions, such as fear. For example, in "The Cry," the background is distorted to echo the circular shape of the cry from the figure's mouth. *See also* Expressionism.

Muncie, city in E Indiana, on White River, 50mi (81km) ENE of Indianapolis; seat of Delaware co; site of Ball State University (1918). City is subject of studies by sociologists Robert and Helen Lynd, "Middletown" and "Middletown in Transition." Industries: machine tools, wire, metal goods, glass. Settled 1818; inc. as town 1854, as city 1865. Pop. (1980) 77,216.

Munich (München), city in S West Germany, on Isar River near Bavarian Alps; capital of Bavaria; major cultural and trade center. In 1255 city was chosen as site of residence for Wittelsbach family, and became capital of dukedom 1506; made capital of kingdom of Bavaria 1806; scene of "Beer Hall Putsch" (Nov. 8–9, 1923), Hitler's unsuccessful revolt against Bavarian government; site of University of Munich (founded 1472, transferred here 1826); Church of Our Lady (1468–88), Renaissance-style St Michael's Church (1583–97), Propyläen (1846–62), a monumental neoclassic gate; scene of world-famous annual beer festival, Oktoberfest. City hosted 1972 summer Olympics in which Palestinian guerrillas attacked Israeli living quarters. Industries: chemicals, brewing, pharmaceuticals, automobiles, processed food, tobacco, optical instruments, tourism. Founded 1158 by Henry the Lion, Duke of Saxony. Pop. 1,311,300.

Munich Agreement (1938), pact signed by representatives of Britain, France, Germany, and Italy. In it Neville Chamberlain for England and Edouard Daladier for France acceded to Adolf Hitler's demands for German occupation of the Sudeten area of Czechoslovakia. Although the agreement averted war temporarily and was hailed by many in Britain and France, it became a symbol of the Western nations' policy of appeasement toward Hitler. *See also* Sudetenland.

Munro, Hector Hugh (1870–1916), English author, pseud. Saki. A journalist, he wrote short stories that combine fantasy and wit. Among his works are *Not So Stories* (1902), *Reginald* (1904), *Reginald in Russia* (1910), and *Beasts and Super-Beasts* (1914). He was killed in France during World War I.

Münster, port city in W West Germany, on Dortmund-Ems Canal. Founded as Carolingian episcopal see *c.* AD 800, its bishops ruled much of Westphalia as princes of Holy Roman Empire from 12th century to 1803; became part of Prussia in 1816 and capital of province; site of 13th-century cathedral, 14th–15th-century Lambertikirche (Church of St Lambert), 14th-century Gothic city hall, university (1902), and Westphalian state museum. Industries: textiles, beer, metal products. Pop. 264,200.

Munsterberg, Hugo (1863–1916), US psychologist, b. Germany. He is often described as the founder of applied psychology because of his pioneering efforts to bring psychology into education, law, and business. His publications include *Psychology and Industrial Efficiencies* (1913) and *Psychology and Social Sanity* (1914).

Muntjac, or **Barking Deer,** small S Asian deer. It is brown with cream markings and has tusklike canine teeth and short, two-tined antlers. It is generally found in pairs, and barks when agitated. Height: to 23in(580mm) at shoulder; weight: to 40lb(18kg). Family Cervidae; genus *Muntiacus. See also* Deer.

Muon, negatively charged elementary particle (symbol), originally thought to be a meson but now classified as a lepton. It has spin ½, a mass about 212 times that of the electron, and decays rapidly into an electron, neutrino, and antineutrino. *See also* Lepton; Neutrino.

Murasaki Shikibu (978?–1026?), Japanese diarist and novelist. As a lady at the court of the Empress Akiko, she kept a diary from 1007–1010, showing glimpses of court life in the capital. She is better known for her immense novel, *The Tale of Genji* (1001–1005), which is considered to be the oldest full novel in the world. Despite the lack of powerful action, her character delineation of Prince Genji and his lovers is superb.

Murat, Joachim (1767–1815), French military figure and king of Naples (1808–15). He helped bring Napoleon to power (1799) and was rewarded with the hand of Napoleon's sister Caroline (1800). His brilliance as a leader of the cavalry ensured many major victories, including Marengo (1800), Austerlitz (1805), and Jena (1806). He succeeded Joseph Napoleon to the crown of Naples in 1808. A popular and constructive monarch, he attempted to retain his crown after the French defeat at Leipzig (1813) by first negotiating with Austria. He then rejoined Napoleon during the Hundred Days. After defeat by the Austrians, he tried once more to regain his crown, but was captured and executed.

Murcia (Morcia), city in SE Spain, on Segura River 47mi (76km) SW of Alicante; capital of Murcia prov.; suffered destruction during Spanish Civil War (1936–39); site of 14th-century Gothic-Romanesque cathedral, with a 310-ft (95-m) tower, university (1915) 18th-century episcopal palace. Industries: vegetable canning, textiles, citrus fruits, gunpowder, aluminum. Settled by Romans; traditionally founded 825 by Moorish emperor Abder-Rahman II. Area: (prov.) 4,369sq mi (11,316sq km). Pop. (city) 243,759; (prov.) 832,313.

Murdoch, (Jean) Iris (1919–), British novelist and philosopher, *b.* Dublin. Her novels, complex and puzzling, include *Under the Net* (1954), *The Sandcastle* (1957), *A Severed Head* (1961), *A Fairly Honourable Defeat* (1970), *A Word Child* (1975), *Henry and Cato* (1976), *The Sea, The Sea* (1978), *The Philosopher's Pupil* (1983), and *The Good Apprentices* (1986). Apart from her novels, she has written a critique, *Sarte, Romantic Rationalist* (1953).

Muriatic Acid. *See* Hydrochloric Acid.

Murillo, Bartolome Esteban (1617–82), Spanish painter. He painted in Seville and was especially known for his religious pictures and for his sympathetic paintings of poor people, particularly of beggar boys. His later work included many paintings for the Cathedral of Seville and other public buildings. His careful draftsmanship and brushwork and his naturalistic style showed the influence of the Italian and Flemish masters.

Murmansk, city in Russian SFSR, USSR; capital of Murmansk oblast; ice-free port on the E shore of the Kola Gulf of Barents Sea, on NW Kola Peninsula, 625mi (1,006km) N of Leningrad; largest city in the world N of the Arctic Circle. Founded 1916 as a supply port, it was occupied by US, British, and French forces 1918; it was a major WWII port for Anglo-American convoys; site of a polar research station. Industries: fishing, shipbuilding, fish canning, metal and woodworking, nets, barrels. Exports: fish, lumber, apatite. Pop. 382,000.

Muromachi. *See* Ashikaga.

Murphy, Frank (1890–1949), US jurist and statesman, b. Harbor Beach, Mich. He was assistant US attorney (1919–20) and mayor of Detroit (1930–33). He served as governor general and later US high commissioner

Hermann Muller

Frank Murphy

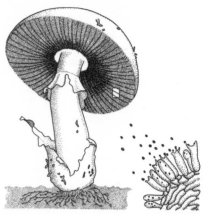

Mushroom

of the Philippines (1933–36). He was attorney general (1939–40) in Pres. Franklin D. Roosevelt's cabinet. In 1940, Roosevelt appointed him associate justice of the US Supreme Court and he served until his death. He was a champion of civil rights, dissenting, in *Korematsu* v. *United States* (1944), which concerned the internment of Japanese-Americans.

Murray River, major river in Australia, in states of New South Wales, Victoria, and South Australia; flows W then S through Lake Alexandrina into Encounter Bay and empties into the Indian Ocean. Navigable for small vessels during the rainy season; used for irrigation. First explored 1824. Length: 1,609mi (2,590km).

Murre, two species of black and white sea birds, native to the Arctic Circle and northern oceans south to Portugal and Korea. Brünnich's murre *(Uria lomvia)* has a heavier beak and nests further north than the common murre *(U. aalge),* which in some populations has a ring around the eye at breeding season. Length: to 16in (41cm). Family Alcidae. *See also* Auk.

Muscat (Masqat or Muskat), port town and capital of Oman on the SE Arabian Peninsula; fine harbor on the S coast of the Gulf of Oman makes it trade center for Oman. Exports: dried fish, dates, mother of pearl. Pop. 7,000.

Muscle, a type of tissue that has the ability to contract and can be excited to contract electrically, mechanically, or chemically. There are three basic types of muscle tissue: skeletal muscle, smooth muscle, and cardiac muscle. Skeletal muscle, or striated muscle, makes up the largest single tissue part of the human body, comprising about 40% of body weight. It is attached to the skeleton and is characterized by cross-markings, known as striations. It typically contains many nuclei per cell. Most skeletal muscles require conscious effort for contraction, and therefore are also known as voluntary muscles.

Smooth muscle lines the digestive tract, the blood vessels, and many other organs. Smooth muscle is not striated and typically has only one nucleus per cell. It is not under conscious control and is therefore also known as involuntary muscle. Cardiac muscle is found only in the heart and differs from the other types of muscle in that it beats rhythmically and does not need stimulation by a nerve impulse to contract. Cardiac muscle has some striations, but not so many as in skeletal muscle, is more regularly arranged, and has one nucleus per cell.

Muscle Tone, or tonus, the continuous state of partial contraction of certain muscles of the body, which helps to maintain erect posture.

Muscovy, former principality in W central Russia. Founded *c.* 1280 by Alexander Nevski's son, Daniel, with the fortified village of Moscow at its center, it was united with the principality of Vladimir in the 15th century. *See* Moscow.

Muscovy Duck, tropical American perching duck with greenish black plumage and heavy red wattles. It has been domesticated worldwide and is raised for its succulent flesh. Species *Cairina moschata.*

Muscular Dystrophy, any of a group of disorders in which the characteristic feature is progressive painless degeneration and atrophy of the muscles with no nervous system involvement. Of the three main types, the most common is pseudohypertrophic muscular dystrophy, in which the symptoms of muscular degeneration begin in childhood and consist of increasing weakness, a peculiar swaying gait, and an initial apparent increase

in muscle size (pseudohypertrophy), with subsequent atrophy. Those affected rarely reach maturity, since the heart and respiratory muscles become involved. This form of muscular dystrophy is sex-linked and affects males primarily.

Muses, in classical mythology, nine daughters of the Titan Mnemosyne (memory) and Zeus. Each muse presided over a branch of literature, art, or science. Calliope was the muse of epic poetry, Clio of history, Erato of love poetry, Euterpe of lyric poetry, Polyhymnia of sacred poetry, Melpomene of tragedy, Terpsichore of choral dance and song, Thalia of comedy, and Urania of astronomy.

Museum of Modern Art, US art museum, New York City, founded in 1929 and moved in 1939 to its present quarters, designed by Philip Goodwin and Edward D. Stone and later expanded by Philip Johnson. The collection represents mostly European or US artists. Among the Impressionists and post-Impressionists represented are Monet, Cézanne, Gauguin, van Gogh, Toulouse-Lautrec, Redon, and Rousseau. There are numerous examples by Picasso. Other European artists include Matisse, Braque, Rouault, Duchamp, Kirchner, Klee, Chagall, Mondrian, and Dali. Some of the US painters represented are Hopper, Shahn, Wyeth, and Pollock. The large sculpture collection, some of which is displayed in a garden, includes such artists as Rodin, Maillol, and Moore.

Mushroom, any of a variety of relatively large fleshy fungi, many of which are gathered for food. The term is applied especially to stalked fungi with umbrella-shaped caps, such as the common edible meadow mushroom *(Agaricus campestris)* or the deadly amanita *(Amanita phalloides).* Inedible mushrooms are sometimes called toadstools. Other fungi commonly called mushrooms include bracket fungi, puffballs, and morels. A typical mushroom fungus consists of two parts: an extensive underground cobwebby network of fine filaments—the mycelium—which is the main body of the fungus, and a short-lived fruiting body—the familiar visible mushroom—which may spring up overnight. Since many mushrooms are poisonous, wild mushrooms should be eaten only after they have been exactly identified as edible species. All simple tests of edibility, such as indications that a mushroom is eaten safely by insects, result every year in deaths or severe illness among mushroom gatherers. *See also* Fungus.

Music, the production of sound in rhythmic, harmonic, and melodic patterns for the sake of artistic expression and the pleasure the sounds give the listener. Music is found in every culture, ancient and modern, but ancient music has survived only through oral traditions since notational systems for recording music are relatively recent inventions. *See also* Musical Notation. For articles on the history of music, *see* the names of individual composers, musicians, conductors, and orchestras; Medieval Music; Renaissance Music; Baroque Music; Classical Music; Romanticism in Music; Impressionism in Music; Neoclassical Music; Electronic Music.

For articles on music theory, *see* Musicology; Polyphony; Rhythm.

For articles on musical instruments, *see* Orchestra; Organ; Percussion Instruments; Piano; Stringed Musical Instruments; Woodwind Instruments.

For articles on the forms of musical composition, *see* Ballet; Concerto; Fugue; Jazz; Musical Comedy; Opera; Symphony.

Musical Notation, systematic methods for transcribing musical sounds and compositions to a written form so that composers can transmit their musical ideas to other composers and performers. The system used

today (5-line staffs, keynotes, bar lines, notes on and between the lines, etc) developed in the 1600s from an earlier system called "mensural" notation which was less precise and incapable of representing the complex musical patterns of music since the Baroque Period. *See also* Musicology.

Musicology, the study of music, including the historical and the theoretical analysis of musical performance and composition as well as the acoustic analysis of music as sound. One of the first great achievements of musicologists was the rediscovery and publication of the complete works of J. S. Bach in the 19th century. Because of this work Bach is now recognized as one of the greatest of all composers.

Musk, strong-smelling, semi-liquid substance obtained from pods under the belly skin of the male musk deer. It is used in the perfume industry because of its long-lasting and fixative qualities. Or, any penetrating, odoriferous substance secreted by many animals, such as civets, muskrats, and musk turtles. *See also* Musk Deer;

Musk Deer, small, timid forest and brushland deer of central and NE Asian highlands. They have long, thick, bristly, brown hair. The male has tusks instead of antlers and secretes musk, used in perfume and soap. Height: to 24in(610mm) at shoulder; weight: to 241lb(109kg). Family Cervidae; species *Moschus moschiferus.*

Muskellunge, freshwater fish found in the Great Lakes. A pike, it has a shovellike bill, sharp teeth, and elongated body. It eats fish, amphibians, birds, and small mammals. Length: to 5.5ft (167.6cm); weight: 110lb (49.9kg). Family Esocidae; species *Esox masquinongy.*

Muskmelon. See Cantaloupe.

Muskogean, family of American Indian languages spoken originally in Florida, Georgia, Alabama, and Mississippi, but now mainly in Oklahoma. The major Muskogean languages are Choctaw, Chickasaw, Creek, and Seminole.

Musk Ox, large, wild, shaggy ruminant, related to oxen and goats, native to N Canada and Greenland. In Europe and Siberia, it was exterminated in prehistoric times. Its deep brown fur reaches almost to the ground. Down-directed, recurved horns form a helmet over the forehead. Herd forms defensive circle for protection of calves. Length: to 7ft (2.1m); weight: to 902lb (410kg). Family Bovidae; species *Ovibos moschatus. See also* Ruminant.

Muskrat, large, aquatic rodent native to North America. An expert swimmer having partially webbed hind feet and a long, scaly tail, its commercially valuable fur is glossy brown, durable, and waterproof. It lives in a tunnel or nests by a lake or stream. Length: to 14in (36cm); Weight: to 3lb (1.3kg). Family Cricetidae.

Musk Turtle, small aquatic turtle native to United States. Abundant in sluggish streams, it has a high-domed carapace, and its reduced plastron is hinged. Musky secretion gives it nickname "stinkpot." Family Kinosternidae; genus *Sternotherus. See also* Turtle.

Muslim League, political organization of the Indian subcontinent, founded in 1906 by Aga Khan III to protect and promote the political rights of Muslims in India. At first it cooperated with the Indian National Congress, but fearing Hindu domination it turned to independent action. Under the leadership of Muhammed Ali Jinnah it called in 1940 for the establishment of a separate Muslim state. During World War II the League supported the British war effort in contrast to the Congress stance. It became the dominant part of independent Pakistan (1947), but by 1953 it had to contend with several competing parties. During the martial law imposed by Ayub Khan (1958–63) it was officially banned. In 1962 it split into two factions: the Convention Muslim League supporting Ayub Khan and the Council Muslim League in opposition to him. With Ayub's resignation (1969), the Convention faction fell apart. The Council faction fared poorly in 1970 elections and ceased to be a major political force in Pakistan.

Mussel, bivalve mollusk having thin, pear-shaped shells of equal size with iridescent interiors. Most marine species, found worldwide, occur in dense colonies on wharf pilings on rocky shores. A clump of threads called a byssus is used for attachment. Freshwater mussels, found in northern continents only, produce pearls and the shells are used for buttons. Families Mytilidae (marine), Unionidae (freshwater). *See also* Bivalve; Mollusk.

Mussolini, Benito (1883–1945), Italian dictator, founder of Europe's first Fascist party, called Il Duce. An active socialist in his youth, amid post-war chaos he abandoned socialism and embraced ultra-nationalism and violent anti-leftism, organizing the Fascist party between 1919 and 1921. His Fascist militia's March on Rome (1922), unopposed by King Victor Emmanuel III, weakened liberal resistance and precipitated Mussolini's appointments as prime minister and head of government. Opposition was suppressed by assassination, the police, the Fascist militia, press control, and suspension of parliamentary government (1928). Possible conflict between the Roman Catholic Church and the state was obviated by the Lateran Treaty (1929). The 1930s saw Mussolini's imperialist attack on Ethiopia (1935) and close ties with Germany's Adolf Hitler (Rome-Berlin Axis). Il Duce waited until France fell before bringing Italy into World War II in 1940. Military failure caused his fall from power in 1943, but after his arrest he was freed by the Germans and set up in a puppet government until the German defeat (1945), when he was captured, tried, and executed by Italian Partisans. *See also* Lateran Treaty; World War II.

Mussorgsky or **Moussorgsky, Modest** (1839–81), Russian Romantic composer, one of the "Russian Five" who promoted nationalism in Russian music. He composed relatively few works, several of which are quite popular, including *Night on Bald Mountain* (1867) and *Pictures at an Exhibition* (1874), and the opera *Boris Godunov* (1874).

Mustang, feral horse of North American Great Plains descended from escaped Spanish horses. It has short ears, low-set tail, round leg bones and can be any horse color. During the 17th century there were 2–4,000,000 mustangs; today 20,000 survive in SW United States.

Mustard, annual and perennial plants, including radish, cabbage, turnip, alyssum, and stock, native to the north temperate zone. These plants have pungent flavored leaves, cross-shaped, four-petaled flowers, and pointed pods. There are 2,500 species, including black mustard *(Brassica nigra)* whose seeds are ground to produce the condiment mustard, and white mustard *(B. alba)* with seeds that produce a hotter mustard. Both have coarse leafy stems and loose clusters of yellow flowers; height: 6–10ft (1.8–3m). Family Cruciferae.

Mustard Gas, a poisonous gas first used in 1917 during World War I by the Germans. It is a blistering agent, one of the thioethers, compounded from carbon, hydrogen, sulfur, and chlorine. By 1918 both sides were using this gas. It inflicted many casualties but relatively few fatalities and was eventually banned.

Mutation, sudden variation in an inherited characteristic of an individual organism that makes it different from the parent organisms. This change, because it occurs in the genes, can be passed on to a mutant's offspring. Natural mutations are rare, occur randomly, and usually produce an organism unable to survive in its environment. Occasionally, the mutant is better adapted and, through natural selection, may become the next evolutional generation. The mutation rate can be increased by exposing genetic material to X rays, other ionizing radiation, or a mutagenic chemical substance, such as mustard gas. Molecular bases of mutation include changes in bases in the DNA molecule (point mutation), insertion or deletion of a base to restore the replication reading frame to the correct position (frameshift mutation), replacement of an amino acid (misserie mutation), and termination of protein synthesis (nonsense mutation).

Mutualism, relationship with mutual benefits for the two or more organisms involved. It is *obligative* if one species is incapable of surviving without the other and *facultative* if the organisms can survive independently.

Myasthenia Gravis, disease that causes weakness of the muscles. Generally affecting the facial muscles first, it may spread to include muscles of the neck, trunk, and limbs. Although there is a 10% death rate, the condition can be stabilized by drug treatment. The disease is an autoimmune one; i.e., antibodies produced by the patient destroy acetylcholine receptors at the nerve-muscle synapse and thus interfere with neuromuscular transmission. Eventual identification of these antibodies will make possible specific immune therapy.

Mycenae (Mikínai), ancient ruined city in NE Peloponnesus, Greece, approx. 7mi (11km) N of modern Árgos in Argolis dept. Founded 2900 BC, it grew to be a major center during the Bronze Age; its civilization became known as the Mycenaean era (*c.* 1600–1100 BC). Mycenae controlled the road from Peloponnesus to Corinth and a majority of the Aegean area. It declined *c.* 1100–470 BC with invasions of the Dorians and Argives; it fell to ruins *c.* 2nd century BC. Traditionally the residence and capital of King Agamemnon, it is the scene of dramatic tragedies portrayed by Aeschylus in the *Oresteia.* Famous archeological excavations by Heinrich Schliemann in 1874 and 1876 unearthed such notable ruins as the Treasury of Atreus, Lion Gate, beehive, and shaft grave tombs, an acropolis, palace, city walls, and numerous golden ornaments and weapons.

Mycenean Architecture flourished 1400–1200 BC on Crete and the Greek mainland after the destruction of Knossos. The Myceneans adopted certain Cretan structures like the beehive tomb, as in the Treasury of Atreus at Mycenae, but also developed unique features, like the fortified acropolis at the center of a city and the monumental planning of buildings along a single axis.

Mycorrhiza, or fungus root, symbiotic relationship between certain fungi and the root cells of some vascular plants. The soil fungus invades the roots, causing them to swell and then it grows a covering of threads around them. Water and minerals enter the roots through these threads. Sometimes the fungus digests organic material for the plant. Common hosts are orchid and pine tree roots.

Mycosis. *See* Fungus Infection.

Myelin, protective sheath around peripheral nerve fibers; it insulates the fiber to prevent loss of electrical impulse during nerve conduction.

Myna, or mynah, tropical bird of SE Asia, related to the starling. They mimic other birds and are popular pets because they can sometimes be taught to talk. Wild mynas feed mainly on fruit but will eat almost anything. Bluish eggs (3–4) are laid in a tree cavity. Genera *Gracula* and *Acridotheres. See also* Starling.

Myoglobin, a protein found in animals. In vertebrates it is the pigment responsible for the red color of muscle tissue. Like hemoglobin, myoglobin combines readily with oxygen for use in rapidly contracting muscles. Myoglobin has been used extensively in protein-structure research. In 1962 John C. Kendrew was awarded a Nobel Prize for his construction of a three-dimensional crystalline model of sperm whale myoglobin.

Myosin, thick filimentous protein present in muscle cells; associated with actin in the contractile process.

Myrdal, Alva Reimer (1902–86), Swedish educator and diplomat, wife of Gunnar Myrdal, with whom she coauthored *The Crisis in the Population Question* (1934). After World War II, she worked for UN social organizations before becoming Swedish ambassador to India (1955). In 1962, she was elected to parliament; her work on behalf of international disarmament began with her appointment as special assistant to the foreign minister (1961) and as Swedish disarmament negotiator (1962). From 1966 until her retirement in 1973, she served as a cabinet minister in charge of disarmament and church affairs. Among the many awards she received are the Albert Einstein Peace Prize (1980) and the Nobel Peace Prize (1982).

Myrdal, (Karl) Gunnar (1898–), Swedish economist. A professor of political and international economy at the University of Stockholm (1933–50, 1960–), Myrdal also served as executive secretary of the UN Economic Commission for Europe (1947–57). He is well known for *Political Element in the Development of Economic Theory* (1930) and for his massive study of US race relations, *An American Dilemma* (1944). In 1974 he was awarded the Nobel Prize for economics.

Myriapoda, class of arthropods with bodies made up of many similar segments. Each segment bears one or more pairs of legs. *See also* Centipede; Millipede.

Myron (*fl. c.*480–450 BC), Greek sculptor. Often worked in bronze, his sculpture was in keeping with the classical tradition of idealized form and balanced, harmonious composition. Most of his works have been lost, but two that are identified through Roman copies are *Discobolus* and *Athena and the Satyr Marsyas.*

Myrrh, fragrant gum resin exuded from small trees and shrubs found in E Africa and Arabia. The brown resin is used in making incense and perfumes.

Myrtle, family (Myrtaceae) of trees and shrubs found in tropical and subtropical regions, especially in Australia and South America. Main characteristics are simple leaves, often marked with transparent dots; bisexual white, pink, or yellow flowers; and a berry fruit. The 100 genera and 3,000 species range in size from creepers to 300ft (91.4m) tall. The largest genus is *Eucalyptus.* The typical genus is *Myrtus,* trees and shrubs with glossy leaves and dark berries.

Mysore, city in S India, 85mi (137km) SW of Bangalore; headquarters of Mysore division and Mysore district. City served as capital of Mysore dynasty 1799–1956, when princely states were disbanded; site of University of Mysore (1916), Chamundi Hill (housing a park and Hindu temple), maharaja's palace (1897), Jaganmohan and Lalitha Mahal palaces. Industries: textiles, rice, sandalwood oil, chemicals, leather goods, coffee, cigarettes. Pop. 355,636.

Mythology, a body of myths, or traditional stories, dealing with gods and legendary heroes. The mythology of a people serves to present their world view, their explanations of natural phenomena, their religious and other beliefs. Mythological literature includes the Greek *Iliad* and *Odyssey,* the Scandinavian *Edda,* the Indian *Ramayana,* and the Babylonian *Gilgamesh,* among others. Various interpretations of mythology have been made by anthropologists such as Sir James Frazer and Claude Lévi-Strauss. In literature, myth has been used as the basis for poetry, stories, plays, and other writings.

Myxedema, disease caused by insufficiency of thyroid hormone resulting in fatigue, a tendency toward weight gain, and poor tolerance to cold. Treatment involves administration of thyroid extracts.

N

Nabis, group of French painters organized by Paul Sérusier in 1892 and who patterned their works after Gauguin's colorful and decorative paintings. Associated with the group were Denis, Bonnard, Vuillard, Roussel, Vallotton, Toulouse-Lautrec, and Maillol. The Nabis exhibited together in 1892 and 1899, before dissolving as a group.

Nablus (Nabulus, or **Shechem),** town in W Jordan, 30mi (48km) N of Jerusalem. As ancient city of Shechem it was important in Biblical times; Samaritans made it their capital 9th century BC; there is still a small community of Samaritans here. Destroyed 129 BC,it was rebuilt and named Neapolis by Hadrian. After Arab-Israeli War of 1967 it was occupied by the Israelis. Industries: soap, olive oil, shepherd's coats. Pop. 44,223.

Nabokov, Vladimir (1899–1977), US author, b. Russia. He lived in Western Europe before going to the United States in 1940. Many of his novels were written in Russian and later translated into English. His works include *Laughter in the Dark* (1938), *Bend Sinister* (1947), *Lolita* (1955), and *Ada* (1969). He also wrote short stories and poetry.

Nader, Ralph (1934–), US consumer affairs activist and lobbyist, b. Winsted, Conn. Nader's book *Unsafe at Any Speed* (1965), a call for improved automobile design, led to the enactment of the National Traffic and Motor Vehicle Safety Act of 1966. Nader subsequently expanded his range of interests: health hazards in mining; the use of nuclear power; meat processing methods; and investigations of the Internal Revenue Service, the Federal Trade Commission, the US Congress, and the airlines industry. He heads a public

Mycenae, Greece

Myna

Mysore palace, India

interest law firm staffed with specialists in consumer affairs.

Naga, people inhabiting the Naga Hills of Assam and the upper Chindwin river region of upper Burma. A farming people, cultivating rice, they were formerly notorious head-hunters. The Indian state of Nagaland was formed in 1961.

Nagano, city in Japan, on branch of Shinano River in central Honshu, 110mi (177km) NW of Tokyo; capital of Nagano prefecture; site of Buddhist Zenkoji Temple. Pop. 307,000.

Nagasaki, seaport in W Kyushu, Japan; capital of Nagasaki prefecture. It was the first Japanese port to receive Western ships (Portuguese and Spanish, mid-16th century); became a center of European and Christian influence in Japan; port was closed to foreigners 1641–1858, reopened 1859. The inner city was destroyed by second US atomic bomb dropped on Japan Aug. 9, 1945; it is now a shipbuilding, fishing, and silk center. Pop. 450,000.

Nagoya, port city in central Honshu, Japan, at head of Ise Bay (Pacific Ocean); capital of Aichi prefecture; grew around daimyo castle (1610); site of various Buddhist and shinto monuments, including a 2nd-century shrine; city suffered extensive bombing WWII; site of university (1939), technical institute (1949). Industries: automobiles, aircraft, machinery, textiles, chemicals, porcelain, lumber. Pop. 2,080,000.

Nagpur, city in W central India, 265mi (427km) N of Hyderabad; capital of Nagpur district and Nagpur division. City served as capital of kingdom of Nagpur (from 1743), Central Provinces (from 1861), Central Provinces and Berar (from 1903), Madhya Pradesh state (1947–56); site of Nagpur University (1923). Industries: cigarettes, textiles, pottery, glass, leather, pharmaceuticals, brassware, hand weaving. Founded 18th century by Gond prince. Pop. 866,144.

Nagy, Imre (1895–1958), Hungarian statesman, premier 1953–55 and 1956. Expelled from the Communist party in 1955 for alleged anti-Soviet nationalism, he was recalled to the premiership in 1956 in the wake of the anti-Soviet uprising of Oct. 24. He promised free elections, economic reforms, and abolition of the one-party dictatorship. He also demanded the withdrawal of Soviet troops and freed Cardinal Mindszenty from prison. Although the Soviets promised concessions, demonstrations continued and on Nov. 4, Soviet troops and tanks moved in to suppress the insurgents. Nagy and three of his associates were executed in 1958.

Naha (Nafa or **Nawa),** seaport city at S tip of Okinawa, Japan; capital of Okinawa prefecture. Industries: pottery, textiles, sugar, Panama hats, lacquerware. Pop. 306,446.

Nahua, the most important tribal group and language of central Mexico. The Aztec were the major division of the Náhuatl peoples. Today about 800,000 Indians still speak the language, primarily occupying the states of Mexico, Michoacán, Puebla, and Guerrero, with scattered remnants in Veracruz, and sections of Central America.

Nahum, biblical author and seventh of the 12 minor prophets. He predicted the eventual fall of Nineveh.

Nails, metallic fasteners, varying in size, pointed at one end and flattened to a head at the other; used for fastening wood. The main types are common wire nails, for rough work; box nails, similar to common but

lighter in weight; finishing nails, including small brads, with narrow heads that can be set below the work surface; and casing nails, for moldings and trim. Nails of an inch or more in length are sold by the penny (d) size: 6d common nails, for example, are 2in (5.1cm) long and weigh about 175 to the pound; 6d finishing nails weigh 300 to the pound. Nails under an inch in length (brads or tacks) are specified by length.

Nairobi, capital and largest city of Kenya, in S central part of country; communications, administrative, and industrial center. It replaced Mombasa as capital of British East Africa Protectorate 1905; in the 1950s Nairobi was a Mau Mau rebellion center; scene of the first All Africa Trade Fair; site of airport, Nairobi National Park (1948), National University, several institutions of higher learning, Caryndon Memorial Museum, Sorsbie art gallery. Industries: beverages, cigarettes, textiles, chemicals, livestock, food processing, coffee, furniture, glass, building materials. Founded 1899 on site of Masai watering hole; made municipality 1919; inc. as city 1950. Pop. 650,000.

Nakasone, Yasuhiro (1918–), Japanese prime minister. After graduation from law school, he served as a naval lieutenant in the Pacific during World War II. In 1947, he began a career in politics with election to parliament as a representative of the Liberal Democratic party. Serving in several cabinet posts and becoming secretary general of his party, he advocated economic cooperation with the United States and reform of the Japanese constitution. In 1982, he became prime minister.

Namibia (formerly South West Africa), territory whose status is disputed by the United Nations and South Africa; its principal export item is diamonds.
   Land and Economy. In a region of sparse population, the international territory in SW Africa is bordered by Angola and Zambia (N), Botswana (E), Republic of South Africa (S), and the Atlantic Ocean (W). Most of the area is a high plateau with an uninhabited desert coastal strip. About 30% of the land is arable. Diamonds are the principal resource, accounting for 60% of all mineral exports. Exports bring $250 million into Namibia's treasury annually.
   People. Namibia (88% non-white) is divided N and S by tribal and regional differences; the N section is the most westernized. Control of farming, mining, and industry is in the hands of the white minority (12%).
   Government. The government consists of an assembly, elected by white voters, and administrators appointed by South Africa, which has final authority in all matters.
   History. First settled by the Bushmen, it was a German protectorate from 1884, then under South African rule from 1915. In 1920, South Africa received a League of Nations mandate for Namibia but no trusteeship agreement was reached with the United Nations in 1946, and the area's status has been disputed since then. In 1966, South Africa instituted its apartheid laws there, and the South West Africa People's Organization (SWAPO), favoring independence and black majority rule, began a guerrilla war against South Africa. Fighting between SWAPO and South African troops escalated in 1980, and South Africa launched attacks into Angola, where SWAPO bases were located. In 1981 a UN-sponsored conference in Geneva to negotiate a ceasefire failed, making any quick resolution to Namibia's status unlikely.

PROFILE

Official name: Namibia
Area: 318,827sq mi (825,761sq km)

Population: 908,800
   Density: 2.9per sq mi (1.1per sq km)
Chief cities: Windhoek (capital); Tsumeb
Government: UN international territory; administered by South Africa; assembly
Religion: Animist and Christian
Language: Afrikaans and English (both official)
Monetary unit: Rand
Industries: diamonds, sheep pelts (major)
Agriculture: cattle, sheep
Minerals: diamonds, copper, lead, zinc, tin, vanadium, iron ore, silver, phosphate, manganese, cadmium, fluorspar
Trading partners: Republic of South Africa

Nan-ch'ang, (Nan-ch'ang-hsien), city in SE China, on S Kan Kiang River; capital of Kiangsi prov. A walled city dating from 12th century, the fortifications were torn down for area reconstruction. Army Day, celebrated each year on August 1, commemorates Communist revolt against Nationalist forces under Chiang Kai-shek (1927). Industries: rice, tea, cotton, hemp, farm tools, paper, food processing. Pop. 675,000.

Nancy, city in NE France, on Meurthe River, 178mi (287km) E of Paris; capital of Meurthe-et-Moselle dept. City developed around castle of dukes of Lorraine; made duchy capital in 12th century; ruled by Stanislaus I, ex-king of Poland and duke of Lorraine, 1738–66; passed to French crown 1766. City contains outstanding examples of 18th-century architecture; site of Place Stanislas (1752–56), 15th-century Church of the Cordelien, Church of Notre Dame (1740), containing tomb of Stanislaus and his queen, and University of Nancy (1854). Industries: foundries, salt, glass, machine tools, textiles. Pop. 111,493.

Nanking (Nanjing), city in E China, 150mi (274km) W of Shanghai, on Yangtze River; capital of Kiangsu prov.; served as capital of China until end of 14th century, then 1928–37 and 1946–49. Treaty of Nanking (1842) ended Opium War with Britain and opened five ports to foreign trade; Nanking was declared a treaty port 1858 but not opened until 1899; served as seat of Sun Yat-sen's provisional presidency (1912) during Chinese Revolution; capital of Kuomintang 1928; fell to Japan (December 1937) during Sino-Japanese War, causing mass destruction, called the "rape of Nanking." Nationalist capital, moved to Chungking 1937, returned to Nanking, 1946; under communist control April 1949. City is site of 26-mi (42-km) wall surrounding most of city and suburbs, tomb of Sun Yat-sen, Nanking University (1902), Ginling College (1915); it is the literary center of China; noted for porcelain and textiles, especially nankeen cloth. Pop. 1,750,000.

Nansen, Fridtjof (1861–1930), Norwegian explorer, statesman, scientist, author, and humanitarian. A vigorous outdoorsman in his youth, he took up zoology and obtained his doctorate for tissue studies. He crossed the Greenland icecap on foot (1888), gaining material for two books, *Across Greenland* (1891) and *Eskimo Life* (1891). For his next expedition he constructed a ship, *Fram*, to be frozen in the Arctic ice, allowing him to drift to 84°N. Leaving the *Fram*, he and F.H. Johansen pushed to 86°14′N (1895), the farthest north man had gone. Nansen then settled to more formal scientific pursuits, and assumed an increasing role in government. As a Norwegian delegate to the League of Nations he repatriated half a million refugees and later worked to help the world's starving. He was awarded the Nobel Peace Prize in 1922. Other books include *Norway and the Union with Sweden* (1905), *Through Siberia* (1914), and *Armenia and the Near East* (1928).

Nanterre, city in N central France; WNW suburb of Paris. Industries: automobiles, perfume. Pop. 96,004.

Nantes, city in NW France, on Loire River, 107mi (172km) W of Tours; capital of Loire-Atlantique dept. An ancient Gallic capital prior to Roman conquest (58–51 BC), it was residence of dukes of Brittany late 10th century until 1525, when it became part of France; Henry IV issued Edict of Nantes here (1598) guaranteeing Protestants religious freedom; site of University of Nantes (1460), and ducal castle of 9th or 10th century. Industries: metals, dyes, clothing, biscuits, bicycles. Pop. 263,689.

Nantes, Edict of (1598), law granting considerable religious freedom to French Protestants, called Huguenots, promulgated by Henry IV at Nantes in Brittany. It guaranteed freedom of conscience, social and political equality, and established a special court, composed of both Catholics and Protestants, to hear disputes arising from the edict. Protestant worship was limited, however, to areas they already held (about 100 fortified towns) and was not permitted, in particular, within five leagues of Paris. Secret agreements promised the crown's financial support of the armies garrisoned in the 100 towns. Although it only recognized the status quo and disallowed Protestant expansion, Catholics (including Pope Clement VII) resented the edict. Louis XIII, acting on Richelieu's advice, withdrew the political and military provisions of the edict (1629). Louis XV revoked it entirely in 1685.

Nantucket, island in SE Massachusetts, 25mi (40km) S of Cape Cod in Atlantic Ocean; with Muskeget and Tuckernuck islands comprises Nantucket co, coextensive with town of Nantucket, the co seat. Formerly a large whaling port, now a tourist and artist center; annexed to Massachusetts from New York 1692; site of whaling museum, 18th-century windmill. Settled 1659. Area: 57sq mi (92sq km).

Napa, city in W California, 10mi (16km) N of San Pablo Bay; seat of Napa co; famous for its wine and vineyards. Industries: steel products, concrete, leather. Settled 1847; inc. 1872. Pop. (1980) 50,879.

Naphtha, any of several volatile liquid hydrocarbon mixtures. In the first century AD, "naptha" was mentioned by Pliny the Elder. Alchemists used the word for various liquids of low boiling point. Several types of products are now called naphtha (ie coal-tar naphtha, shale naphtha, petroleum naphtha). Petroleum naphtha contains aliphatic hydrocarbons, boils at higher temperatures than gasoline and lower temperatures than kerosene.

Naphthalene, an important hydrocarbon ($C_{10}H_8$) composed of two benzene rings sharing two adjacent carbon atoms. Naphthalene is soluble in ether and hot alcohol and is highly volatile. It is used in moth balls, dyes, and synthetic resins, in coal tar and in the high-temperature cracking process of petroleum. It crystallizes in white plates, melting at 176°F (80°C) and boiling at 424°F (218°C).

Napier, or **Neper, John** (1550–1617), Scottish mathematician. As the laird of Marchiston he treated mathematics as a hobby but nevertheless invented logarithms and the present form of the decimal notation. Napier's bones were calculating devices invented by him in an attempt to simplify logarithmic calculations.

Naples (Napoli), seaport and industrial city in Italy, 117mi (188km) SE of Rome, on Bay of Naples; capital of Campania and Naples provs. Founded on ancient Parthenope *c.* 600 BC, it was under Roman rule 4th century BC; under Byzantine rule AD 6th century; capital of kingdom of Naples 13th–19th centuries; ceded to Austria 1713; joined kingdom of Italy 1860. Notable buildings include church of Holy Apostles (founded by Constantine), church of St Paul (1817–31), university (1224), Virgil's tomb, 13th-century Gothic cathedral, medieval castles. Industries: textiles, steel, shipbuilding, tourism, aircraft, food processing. Pop. 1,223,342.

Napoleon I, full name Napoleon Bonaparte (1769–1821), famous general and emperor of France, military and organizational genius. Born in Corsica, he spoke French with an Italian accent and was an indifferent student at the military academy at Brienne. The hero of the French liberation of Toulon from the English (1793), he there made an important ally in Vicomte Paul de Barras. The fall of Maximilien Robespierre (1794) occasioned counter-revolutionary upheavals and monarchist plots. Increasingly the army became the key to control. Napoleon saved the National Convention at Barras's request; his reward was command of the Army of Italy. His victories there against Austria, he later said, "made me conceive the ambition of performing great things." His Egyptian campaign (1798) went badly, and during his absence the Coalition (England, Austria, Russia, and Turkey) regained most of Italy. In Paris, the government's control was deteriorating. Abbé Sieyès, one of the directors, believed only military dictatorship could prevent the return of the monarchists. Napoleon returned from Egypt and carried out the coup d'état of the 18th Brumaire. He thus became one of three consuls, with Sieyès another. By 1799 he was first consul. In 1800 he wrested victory at Marengo from the Austrians and made a precarious peace with England. He then turned to the establishment of order at home. He centralized the administration of local departments and the collection of taxes. He established the Bank of France and set the value of the franc. His Napoleonic Code established legal freedoms won in the Revolution, and the Concordat (1801) made peace with the Roman Catholic Church.

To end forever the threat from his monarchist rivals, Napoleon crowned himself emperor (1804), with Pope Pius VII presiding. European wars involved him thereafter, and he achieved his greatest victory at Austerlitz over Russia and Austria (1805). He was never able to overcome English superiority at sea, however, and his invasion of Russia (1812) was a disaster. With his French subjects increasingly weary of war and his enemies closing in upon him, Napoleon was forced to abdicate (1814). Confined to the island of Elba, Napoleon escaped and, for 100 days, seemed triumphant. But his foreign enemies confronted him, and he was defeated conclusively at Waterloo (1815). He sought the protection of the English and was exiled once more, on St Helena, where he died, perhaps, as he claimed, of slow arsenic poisoning. In 1796 he married Josephine de Beauharnais, from whom he was divorced. He then married Marie Louise of Austria (1810), and they had one son, styled Napoleon II.

Napoleon II (1811–32), only son of Napoleon I and Marie-Louise. His full name was François Charles Joseph Bonaparte. His father's empire collapsed when he was three, and he was then taken by his mother to her father's court in Austria. In 1818 his grandfather, Francis I, created him duc de Reichstadt. Too ill to take advantage of the possibilities the 1830 revolution presented to Napoleon's direct heir, he died of tuberculosis in 1832.

Napoleon III (1808–73), also known as **Louis Napoleon,** emperor of France (1852–71). Nephew of Napoleon I and heir to the Napoleonic title and mystique when Napoleon II died (1832). Exiled because he was a Bonaparte, he twice attempted a military coup, then confidently awaited events to bring him to power. In 1848, under a new constitution providing popular election of the president, he won an overwhelming victory. He involved France in an unpopular war supporting Pope Pius IX against Italian republicans. Ensuing leftist uprisings caused parliament to disenfranchise 3,000,000 electors. He then dismissed the parliament, which was already wary of his lust for power, arrested his enemies, and became emperor (1852). Plebiscites gave his reign a semblance of legitimacy. Under Napoleon III, France enjoyed a period of economic vitality and a gradual relaxation of political authoritarianism. He tried to restore French importance by seeking peace. By supporting emerging nations—Poland, Italy, Germany, Romania, and Mexico—he cultivated new allies. He was unprepared for the rapid rise of Prussia, whose crushing defeat of France in the Franco-Prussian War (1870–71) ended his reign. Already in ill health, he died two years later. *See also* Franco-Prussian War; Second Empire.

Napoleonic Code. *See* Code Napoléon.

Nara, city in S central Honshu, Japan, approx. 25mi (40km) E of Osaka; capital of Nara prefecture; resort, and cultural-historical center. It was the first capital of Japan, under Emperor Jimmu (710–84), site of first Buddhist temple, Horyuji (7th century), 8th-century bronze image of Buddha at the temple Todai-ji, Imperial Museum containing treasures from the 8th century, university (1949). Pop. 247,082.

Narayanganj (Narainganj), port city in Bangladesh, on Meghna River 12mi (19km) E of Dacca. Industries: jute, textiles, leather. Pop. 186,769.

Narbonne, town in S France, 31mi (50km) E of Carcassonne. Capital of Gallia Narbonensis *c.* AD 309, it was prosperous industrial town in 12th and 13th centuries; site of St Just Cathedral (13th–14th centuries), and 13th-century archepiscopal palace, now the town hall and museum. Industries: sulfur, copper, clothing. Founded 118 BC as Roman colony. Pop. 40,543.

Narcissus, in Greek mythology, a beautiful youth who fell in love with his own reflection. According to legend, he rejected the love of the nymph Echo, and she induced him to fall in love with his own image. He pined away and was turned into a flower.

Narcissus, numerous species of Old World bulb plants cultivated in gardens throughout the world. They bloom in early spring. The long, pointed leaves surround yellow, orange, or white trumpetlike flowers. Favorite species are the yellowish daffodil *(Narcissus pseudonarcissus)* and jonquil *(N. jonquilla).* Family Amaryllidaceae.

Narcotics, drugs used to reduce pain, diminish sensation, and induce sleep but which lead to addiction and to profound stupor, coma, or convulsions when given in excessive doses. Morphine, codeine, and meperidine (Demerol) are among the narcotics commonly used in medicine.

Narragansett, a major Algonquian-speaking tribe of North American Indians related to the Niantic, who occupied Rhode Island, from Providence to the Pawtucket River, and western Narragansett Bay. Once the most powerful New England group, they were almost entirely wiped out during the tragic Pequot War of 1637, when their population of 5,000 declined radically.

Narváez, Pánfilo de (*c.* 1470–1528), Spanish conquistador. He was the chief lieutenant to Diego de Velázquez in the conquest of Cuba in 1514. In 1520, Velázquez sent him and a force of men to Mexico to arrest Hernán de Cortés. Instead he was defeated and imprisoned by Cortés. Released in 1521, he returned to Spain where Charles V commissioned him to conquer Florida. After a long, hazardous voyage he landed in Florida in 1528. He sent his ships on to Mexico and looked unsuccessfully for gold in the Tallahassee area, then sailed for Mexico in makeshift boats. He was lost at sea.

Narwhal, small, toothed Arctic whale. The male has a twisted "horn"—half as long as its body—protruding horizontally through its upper lip. An overdeveloped tooth, the horn's function is unknown. Length: to 16ft (5m). Species *Monodon monoceros.*

Nashua, city in S New Hampshire, on Merrimack River; one of seats of Hillsborough co; site of Rivier College (1933), Colonial House (1803), Marsh Tavern (1804, stagecoach stop), and New England Aeronautical Institute (1965). Industries: shoes, leather, paper, electronic equipment. Founded 1656 as fur trading post; inc. 1853 as city. Pop. (1980) 67,865.

Nashville, capital city of Tennessee and port of entry, in N central Tennessee, on the Cumberland River; seat of Davidson co. Settled 1779 as Fort Nashborough, it was made capital of Tennessee 1843; taken by Union troops 1862; scene of Battle of Nashville December 1864 in which Union Army overwhelmingly defeated Confederate troops. It is a noted country music and recording center; site of Vanderbilt University (1872), Fisk University (1867), Tennessee State University (1909), capitol (1855) containing tomb of President James Polk, country music hall of fame and museum, "Opryland U.S.A." Industries: railroad shops, automobile glass, clothing, footwear, food products, tires, chemicals, publishing. Inc. 1784 as town, 1806 as city. Pop. (1980) 455,651.

Nassau, port city on NE New Providence Island in the Bahamas, SE of Florida; capital and commercial center of Bahamas, with excellent harbor (sheltered by Hog Island); tourist resort; site of airport, cathedral, 18th-century forts, sea gardens. Founded 1660s by English as Charles Towne, it was renamed 1695; destroyed by French and Spanish 1703; rebuilt 1718 and later fortified; was 18th-century stronghold of Blackbeard and other pirates; free trade port after 1738. Exports: sponge, citrus fruit, tomatoes, sisal hemp. Pop. 100,000.

Nassau, House of, royal European family named for county on east bank of Rhine, founded by Walram I. The elder or German branch ruled Nassau until it was annexed by Prussia in 1866. Since 1890, Nassau has been the ruling house of the Duchy of Luxemburg. The younger (Dutch) branch, founded by Otto I (died 1292?), inherited Orange in 1544. Since William the Silent in 1579, members of this house have ruled the Netherlands almost continuously under the name of the House of Orange.

Nasser, Gamal Abdel (1918–70), Egyptian political figure, first president of the republic of Egypt (1956–70). A revolutionary since his youth, he was expelled from school in 1935 after being wounded while leading an anti-British demonstration. He graduated from the Royal Military Academy in 1938. In 1942 he founded the secret Society of Free Soldiers to combat corruption and foreign domination. He was wounded in action in the 1948 Arab-Israeli War. In 1952 he led the army coup that ousted King Farouk. As head of the Revolutionary Command Council he controlled Egypt, although Gen. Muhammad Naguib was nominal premier.

Narcissus

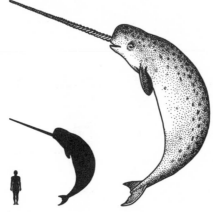

Narwhal

Nashville: The Parthenon

In 1956 he was chosen president in an unopposed election. In 1956 he nationalized the Suez Canal, provoking the brief Anglo-French occupation. Between 1958–61 Syria was merged with Egypt as the United Arab Republic. In 1967 he brought on the third Arab-Israeli War by blocking the Israeli port of Elat. After Egypt's defeat he resigned but reconsidered after massive demonstrations in his support. He promoted land reform and economic and social development through a program he called Arab Socialism. The completion of the Aswan Dam (1970), built with Soviet assistance after the United States withdrew, was a high point in this program. Nasser sought to speak as a leader for all Arab people and pursued a neutralist policy encouraging Third World cooperation.

Nasser, Lake, lake in S Egypt and N Sudan; formed in 1960s by Aswan High Dam, in the process flooding many archeological sites, including Abu Simbel. Length: approx. 300mi (483km).

Nasturtium, annual trailing plant native to Central and South America. Cultivated as a garden ornamental, it has round leaves and spurred, trumpet-shaped flowers of yellow, salmon, or scarlet. Among 50 species is the common nasturtium, or Indian cress, *Tropaeolum majus.* Family Tropaeolaceae.

Natal Province, province in E Republic of South Africa, bordered by Indian Ocean (E), Transvaal, Mozambique, and Swaziland (N), Orange Free State and Lesotho (W); capital is Pietermaritzburg. Visited by Boers on the Great Trek (1836–38), it became a British colony 1843; annexed to Cape Colony 1844; made separate colony 1856; granted internal self-government 1893; joined Union of South Africa 1910. The province is a narrow coastal belt, extending inland, bordered by Drakensberg Mts; highest point is Natal, approx. 11,200ft (3,410m); site of University of Natal, University of Durban, Natal National Park, railway. Industries: sugar, fruit, coal, cereals, textiles, cigarettes, furniture, gold, tin, livestock, rubber, oil refining, tanning, fertilizers, paper. Area: 33,578sq mi (86,967sq km). Pop. 4,236,700.

Natchez, an important tribe of Muskhogean-speaking North American Indians, once the largest and strongest tribe of the southern Mississippi region, although they never numbered more than 2,000 people. They are noted for their religious-political structure, in which the Sun played a major role. Today only a handful of Natchez people survive in Oklahoma.

Nathanael, in the New Testament, one of Christ's disciples. Almost nothing of him is related but his birthplace, Cana, and the genuineness of his calling. Some think he is identical with Bartholomew.

Nation, Carry Amelia Moore (1846–1911), US social reformer, temperance leader, b. Garrard co, Ky. Her first husband, an alcoholic, turned her against liquor for life. Wielding a hatchet, which became her symbol, she began her anti-saloon campaign in Kansas in the 1890s where saloons were illegal. She carried her crusade into several states. She was arrested more than 30 times and was considered too fanatical by other temperance groups, which would not endorse her tactics.

National Aeronautics and Space Administration (NASA), federal agency set up by Congress (1958) to supervise US space activities for peaceful purposes. NASA was responsible for all US space flights and all phases of space exploration—research, building and testing space vehicles, manned and unmanned spacecraft, and international cooperation and exchange.

National Anthem. *See* Star-Spangled Banner.

National Association for the Advancement of Colored People (NAACP), civil rights organization. Its objectives are "to achieve through peaceful and lawful means, equal citizenship rights for all American citizens by eliminating segregation and discrimination in housing, employment, voting, schools, the courts, transportation, and recreation." Early leaders were W.E.B. Du Bois and Booker T. Washington. Whites were influential in the founding, but control of NAACP has been exercised by blacks. It set up the successful Legal Defense and Educational Fund to finance court battles over discriminatory practices, of which *Brown* v. *Board of Education of Topeka* (1954) was a major victory. It also cooperates with other minority protection groups. In the late 1970s, the organization resolved to become more involved in equal rights worldwide. Its publications include *Crisis.* Members, about 500,000. Founded 1909.

National Convention, The, legislative body during the height of the French Revolution (1791–95). The National Assembly ordered the election of members to the Convention by universal suffrage. Within days the Convention made France a republic and condemned King Louis XVI to death. The Convention was dominated by the Mountain, a leftist group, and increasingly by Robespierre's faction. Excesses of the Reign of Terror led to a moderate reaction under the Thermidoreans. The constitution drawn up by the National Convention was implemented by its successor, the Directory.

National Debt, money owed by the government to purchasers of government securities, usually financial institutions and individuals within the country. When government spending exceeds tax revenues, the government must borrow money through deficit financing to make up the difference. While the US national debt has grown significantly over the past 25 years, its size relative to the level of the economy (measured by Gross National Product, GNP) has remained relatively constant. The major burden of the national debt is the interest that must be paid annually in order to maintain it. This interest has also remained a relatively constant percentage of the GNP. Deficit financing allows the use of discretionary policy, which, for the past several years, has always increased the national debt.

National Guard, volunteer citizen militia in the United States. Units of the National Guard are under state jurisdiction in peacetime and in times of national emergency may be activated for federal duty. Units are also activated during disasters and civil unrest. The 7th Regiment of the New York State Militia took the title "National Guards" (1824), and the term came into general use for state militias after the National Guard Association was formed in 1878. Units are located in all the states, and members are trained in the regular armed services. They thereafter attend regular meetings and field exercises.

Nationalism, political and social force based on identification with the state. It has been instrumental in the emergence of the modern independent nation-state. Nationalist sentiment, drawing upon and extolling a common culture, language, and history emphasizes a sense of uniqueness and can be a powerful unifying agent. Conversely, it may exploit a distrust or hatred of other groups to condone aggressive action, as in Nazi Germany and Fascist Italy. Nationalism remains a significant political factor, especially among the underdeveloped "third world" nations.

National Labor Relations Board v. Jones and Laughlin Steel Corp (1937), landmark US Supreme Court case. It was decided during the famous "court-packing" attempts of Pres. Franklin D. Roosevelt to add enough members to the court to get his programs upheld. The court upheld the National Labor Relations Act allowing collective bargaining rights enforceable under the commerce clause and gave virtually limitless jurisdiction to the NLRB. This decision insured success for many New Deal economic programs.

National Socialism or **Nazism,** doctrine of the German National Socialist party under Adolf Hitler. Originating after World War I, national socialism was initially a leftist philosophy. Following the advent of Hitler as party leader (1921), the doctrine emphasized annulment of the Treaty of Versailles, Aryan supremacy, anti-Semitism, anti-Communism, German expansionism, and the cult of the führer. Nazi ideology was implemented during the Hitler regime in Germany (1933–45). *See also* Fascism.

Nativism, anti-Roman Catholic political movement in the United States in the 1840s. Fired by the influx of German and Irish immigrants, Native Americans, as they called themselves, feared the growing influence of the immigrants and the effects that their culture and beliefs might have on US society. The nativists formed organizations, often secretly, to keep immigrants from public office. Some of these groups were the Native American party, the Order of the Star Spangled Banner, the Know Nothing party, and the American Protective Association. A nativist convention in 1845 called for a change in the naturalization laws.

Natural Monopoly, single-firm industry in which competition is not practical; a monopoly whose existence is deemed to be in the public interest, for example, the telephone industry or local utilities. *See also* Monopoly.

Natural Philosophy, a term in common usage during the 17th and 18th centuries, roughly correlative in meaning with the contemporary phrase, natural science. Natural philosophy embraced both the physical and life sciences as well as mathematics. Isaac Newton entitled his great treatise in mathematical physics *Philosophiae Naturalis Principia Mathematica* (Mathematical Principles of Natural Philosophy, 1687).

Natural Selection, tendency for only the best adapted organisms to survive and reproduce in a particular environment. It is commonly referred to as survival of the fittest. *See also* Darwinism; Evolution.

Naucalpan (Naucalpan de Juárez), city in central Mexico, 7mi (11km) NW of Mexico City; site of annual religious fiesta, held in September. Industries: textiles, agriculture. Pop. 373,605.

Nauru, formerly Pleasant Island; island republic in W Pacific Ocean, S of the equator and W of the Gilbert Islands; discovered 1798 by John Fearn, British navigator, who named it Pleasant Island. Annexed by Germany 1888; it came under League of Nations Mandate and was administered by Australia after WWI; occupied by Japanese during WWII; made a trusteeship of United Nations 1947–68, after which it became an independent republic and member of the British Commonwealth of Nations. The native inhabitants are of Polynesian, Micronesian, and Melanesian descent. The economy is based on extensive phosphate mining, controlled by the Nauruans since 1970. It is expected that phosphate deposits will be completely depleted by 1995. Area: approx. 8sq mi (21sq km). Pop. 7,254.

Nautilus, or chambered nautilus, cephalopod found in W Pacific and E Indian oceans at depths to 660ft (201m). Its large, coiled shell is divided into numerous, gas-filled chambers with the body located in the foremost chamber. Its head bears (60–90) retractible, thin, unsuckered tentacles, and it moves by squirting water from a funnel. The eyes have no lens and so function as pin-hole cameras. Shell size 4–8in (10–20cm). There are three surviving species of the formerly dominant suborder Nautiloid. Genus *Nautilus. See also* Cephalopod; Mollusk.

Navajo, Athapascan-speaking tribe, the largest Indian group in the United States. Their reservation lands in Arizona and New Mexico are the largest in the country. In 1981, 1,800,000 acres (728,000 hectares) in Arizona were partitioned equally between the Navajo and Hopi Indians. Some relocation in both tribes was necessary. Famed for their fine weaving and silversmithing, they number over 125,000 persons.

Navarre (Navarra), province and former ancient kingdom in N Spain, on French border; capital is Pamplona. Originally inhabited by Vascones, it was conquered by Romans in 1st century BC; after the fall of Rome in 5th century, Navarre resisted invasions by the Visigoths, Arabs, and Franks for 400 years; it became an independent kingdom 10th century and was divided into three kingdoms 1035; ruled by French dynasties 1234–1512, when S part was conquered by Ferdinand II of Aragon and inc. into Castile 1515; N part passed to Henry IV, King of France, 1589. Industries: lumber, livestock, cereals, wine, grapes, sugar beets. Area: 4,024sq mi (10,422sq km). Pop. 464,867.

Navigation, the science of determining the position of a craft and charting a course for guiding the craft from one point to another. Four main techniques are used: dead reckoning, piloting, celestial navigation, and electronic navigation. Position (the point of the earth's surface, established by latitude and longitude), direction (indicated as angular distance and measured in degrees of arc from true north), speed (rate of travel in nautical miles per hour), and distance must be plotted with special charts and instruments. *See also* Dead Reckoning.

Navigation Acts, corpus of laws imposing protectionist trade restrictions upon foreign commercial shipping. In Britain, the term specifically applies to the series of shipping laws passed in 1651, whereby British sea trade could only be carried on by ships flying the British flag, under the ownership and command of British subjects, and having partly British crews. These acts seriously hampered colonial and foreign trade, since no country could export goods to Britain in any ship that failed to meet the acts' conditions. They contributed to the unrest that led to the American Revolution and were not fully repealed until 1854.

Navy, United States, the naval service of the US armed forces. It consists of over 500,000 personnel under the president, who is commander in chief of the armed forces, and the general supervision of the secretary of the Navy and his advisor, the chief of naval operations (CNO), who is the Navy's highest ranking officer. The CNO is a member of the joint chiefs of staff. The Department of the Navy provides the manpower, material, facilities, and services to support the naval operating forces. The CNO is responsible for the administration of these forces but not their military employment. Currently the Navy operates cruisers, destroyers and patrol ships, aircraft carriers, amphibious warfare ships, conventional and missile submarines, and aircraft. Major commands include the Sixth Fleet in the Mediterranean, the Second Fleet in the N Atlantic, the Third Fleet off the US Pacific coast, and the Seventh Fleet in the W Pacific. The Marines are under the Navy's authority. The Navy was established by Congress in 1798, although naval activities had begun during the Revolutionary War. In 1948 the Navy became a part of the Department of Defense. The Navy has taken an active part in US military operations from the Barbary coast wars in the early 19th century to the Civil and Spanish-American wars later in the 19th century and to the two world wars, the Korean War, and Vietnam conflict in the late 20th. *See also* Defense, Department of; Joint Chiefs of Staff; Marine Corps, United States.

Náxos, island in SE Greece in Aegean Sea; largest of the Cyclades Islands; ancient center of worship of Dionysus; member of Delian League but captured by Athens when it attempted to secede 470 BC; passed to Greece 1829. Industries: white wine, olive oil, fruit, white marble, granite, emery mining. Area: approx. 160sq mi (414sq km). Pop. 14,201.

Nazarenes, group of 19th-century German painters, founded in Vienna in 1809 by Friedrich Overbeck and Franz Pforr, whose primary interest was in painting religious subjects in a primitive style. They were especially influenced by the simplicity of the painting style of the late Middle Ages and early Renaissance. Living in an abandoned monastery near Rome, the group attempted to revive the art of fresco painting of these earlier eras.

Nazareth (Nazerat), town in N Israel, 15mi (24km) SW of Sea of Galilee; capital of Northern District. In biblical times, it was the home of Mary, Joseph, and Jesus Christ; now a pilgrimage center and tourist resort; scene of Christian massacre by Baybar Muslims 1263; it was annexed to the Ottoman Empire 1517; during WWI, it was captured by Australian troops (1918); it came under British rule (1922–48) as part of the League of Nations Palestine mandate; captured by Israeli troops during Arab-Israeli war 1948 and inc. as part of Israel. Town is site of many religious monuments: Church of the Annunciation, containing Our Lady of American pilgrim house (built from donations by US Roman Catholics), Fountain of the Virgin, workshop of St Joseph, and the Table of Christ, traditional site of a meal shared by Christ and his disciples. Industries: food processing, cigarettes, pottery, mineral water bottling, textiles, leather goods. Pop. 36,700.

Nazca (Nasca), Indian civilization located in the southernmost coastal valleys of Peru, flourished 200 BC—AD 600. The Nazca, who developed without outside influence, were a relatively small group of farmers notable for their unique and highly stylized ceramics and textiles.

Nazi Party, German. *See* National Socialism.

N'Djamena. *See* Fort Lamy.

Ndola, city in N central Zambia, S Central Africa, near Zaïre, 170mi (272km) N of Lusaka; site of Northern Technical College (1964); center of copper mining region. Industries: cement, footwear, soap. Pop. 240,000.

Neanderthal Man, extinct race of Middle Paleolithic man, distinct from the ancestors of modern man, known from remains in Europe, N Africa and Asia. First discovered in 1856 in the Neander River Valley of Germany, he was once regarded as ape-like in appearance. Modern studies have shown him to be fairly modern in skeletal anatomy with large bones and powerful muscles, a low forehead, and projecting brow ridge. His brain capacity is comparable to modern man's. Neanderthal skeletons are everywhere found in association with so-called Mousterian stone implements, typical of which are large D-shaped scrapers for dressing skins and triangular spearpoints. Neanderthal man became extinct 35,000–40,000 years ago. *See also* Paleolithic Age

Nearsightedness, or **myopia,** a condition in which visual images come to focus in front of the eye's retina, due to defects in refractive media or to abnormal length of the eyeball. It results in defective vision of distant objects and may be corrected by glasses that are concave on both surfaces.

Nebraska, state in the W central United States, in the Great Plains region.

Land and Economy. Nebraska is a rolling prairie that rises steadily from E to W. Grasses are the principal native vegetation; trees appear mostly along rivers and streams. The Missouri River forms the E and part of the N boundary. The main rivers within the state are the Platte in the central area and the Niobrara in the N. Agricultural production is distributed throughout the state. Manufacturing industries, largely related to agriculture, are situated in the E cities. Petroleum drilling is in the SW area.

People. Early immigration came from E states. In the late 19th century, Germans, Swedes, and Danes arrived to work the farmlands. Most of the present population was born in the United States. About 60% lives in urban areas.

Education. There are nearly 30 institutions of higher education.

History. The region, part of the Louisiana Purchase from France in 1803, was little known until the Lewis and Clark expedition (1804–06) reported its findings. A few military posts were established in the SE. After 1830, the migration of pioneers bound for Oregon and California followed the Platte Valley westward. Nebraska Territory was created in 1854. After the Homestead Act was passed in 1862, thousands of settlers occupied the free lands that it offered. Building of the transcontinental railroads brought prosperity to the farms. Occasional instability of farm prices, as after the boom of WWI, led the state to develop industry to diversify and broaden the base of the economy.

PROFILE

Admitted to Union: March 1, 1867; rank, 37th
US Congressmen: Senate, 2; House of Representatives, 3
Population: 1,570,006 (1980); rank, 35th
Capital: Lincoln, 171,932 (1980)
Chief cities: Omaha, 311,681; Lincoln; Grand Island, 33,180
State legislature (unicameral): 49 members
Area: 77,227sq mi (200,018sq km); rank, 15th
Elevation: Highest, 5,426ft (1,655m), Johnson Township, SW Nebraska; lowest, 840ft (256m), SE Nebraska
Industries (major products): processed meat, grain, dairy products, farm equipment, electrical machinery, railroad equipment
Agriculture (major products): cattle, hogs, wheat, corn, rye, soybeans, sorghum
Minerals (major): petroleum, cement, sand, gravel
State nickname: Cornhusker state
State motto: Equality Before the Law
State bird: Western meadowlark
State flower: goldenrod
State tree: cottonwood

Nebuchadnezzar II or **Nebuchadrezzar** (died 562 BC), Chaldean King of Babylon (605–562 BC). During his reign of 43 years he defeated Necho II of Egypt in 605, captured Jerusalem and appointed Zedekiah king in 598, destroyed that city in 587 BC and for a second time carried Jews in exile to Babylon, conquered Tyre in 573, again overran Egypt in 568, and rebuilt the city of Babylon.

Nebula (plural nebulae), diffuse concentration of gas (chiefly hydrogen) or gas and dust particles in interstellar space. Formerly referred to as galactic nebulae, these objects, from which stars are thought to originate, are assigned to two main classes: bright nebulae (emission nebulae and reflection nebulae) and dark nebulae. Emission nebulae are largely gaseous and shine by the absorption and re-emission of energy from stars located within or near them. Reflection nebulae, containing much more dust, shine by reflecting light from nearby stars. Dark nebulae absorb energy but do not re-emit it as visible light and are only rendered visible when they happen to obscure light from star fields lying beyond them.

Necessary and Proper Clause, found in Article I, Section 8, Paragraph 18 of the Constitution, which deals with the powers of Congress. *See also* Elastic Clause; Implied Powers.

Neckar River, river in SW West Germany; rises in Black Forest; flows N past Stuttgart to Rhine River at Mannheim; connected to Danube by canal; navigable to Stuttgart; supports several hydroelectric plants. Length: 228mi (367km).

Necker, Jacques (1732–1804), financier, finance minister (1776–81) under Louis XVI of France, although a foreigner (Swiss) and a Protestant. He attempted financial reforms but was more attuned to politics than to economics. In his account of the king's finances (1781), he disguised a large deficit to encourage French participation in the American Revolution and revealed the large sums distributed to royal courtesans. Dismissed, but recalled in 1788, his second dismissal was the immediate cause of the storming of the Bastille. He resigned (1790).

Nectarine, smooth-skinned peach grown in the E United States and California. Propagated from a peach seed or bud mutation, the tree shape and leaf characteristics are indistinguishable from those of a peach. The fruit, resembling a large plum, is cling or freestone. Family Rosaceae; species *Prunus persica nectarina. See also* Peach.

Needlefish, primarily marine fish found in tropical and temperate waters and identified by its long jaw filled with fine, needle-sharp teeth and by its long, slender body. It is a ferocious fish capable of tremendous leaps; length to 4ft (121.9cm). Among the 60 species are the Indo-Pacific *Strongylura crocodilus.* Family Belonidae. *See also* Garfish.

Needlegrass. *See* Esparto.

Nefertiti or **Nefretete** (*fl.* 14th century BC), queen of ancient Egypt; wife of Ikhnaton; noted for her influence on her husband's religious ideas and for her exceptional beauty.

Negative Number. *See* Number, Natural.

Negev (Hanegev), desert region in S Israel; covers approx. 50% of Israel's total land area. In NW, Beersheba is the chief city and has fertile land irrigated by National Water Carrier Project; as it extends S, the area becomes more desolate. Region was scene of conflict between Egyptian and Israeli forces after

Navajo hogan

Scott's Bluff, Nebraska: replica of a conestoga wagon

Horatio Nelson

Palestine mandate 1948; Egyptian blockage of Gulf of Aqaba (S Negev) was one of primary reasons for 1967 Arab-Israeli War. Mineral deposits include copper, phosphates, natural gas, gypsum, ceramic clay, feldspar, glass; oil, discovered 1955 and 1963, provides 8% of Israel's fuel needs. Area: 5,140sq mi (13,313sq km).

Negrillo Subrace, subdivision of the Negroid race, comprising the African pygmies, such as the Bambuti. Males average less than 59in (150cm) in height; other physical features are generally Negroid. *See also* Pygmy.

Negrito Subrace, subdivision of the Australoid race, comprising isolated Pacific and Indian Ocean pygmy peoples, such as the Malaysian Semang. Average male height is less than 60in (152cm); other physical features are generally Australoid. *See also* Pygmy.

Negritude, primarily a movement in poetry. It has developed into a philosophy in the works of its followers. Aimé Césaire used the term originally in his *Return to My Native Land* (1939) and defined it as "the simple recognition of the fact of being a Negro and the acceptance of this fact and of its cultural and historical consequences." The concept of Negritude was developed by Césaire, Léopold Senghor, and Léon Damas. *See also* Césaire, Aimé.

Negroid Race, one of the major human racial groupings, sometimes divided into Congoid and Capoid races, and including pygmy (Negrillo) populations. Negroid physical characteristics include heavy skin pigmentation; curly to spiral-tuft hair; thick lips; wide noses; high incidence of RO blood group. Negroids are indigenous to sub-Saharan Africa.

Nehemiah, biblical author and book that is called Esdras II in the Douay Bible. This book recounts Nehemiah's efforts to rebuild the city of Jerusalem, including the reconstruction of the city's walls and sealing of the covenant. Several chapters are an apparently unaltered excerpt from Nehemiah's memoirs.

Nehru, Jawaharlal Pandit (1889–1964), Indian leader, the first prime minister of India (1947–64). The son of a leading Indian nationalist, Motilal Nehru, he was educated in England. He returned to India in 1912 and met Mohandas Gandhi in 1916. He actively joined the Indian independence movement in 1919. In 1929 he was elected president of the Indian National Congress. Between 1930–36 he spent much time in prison for his part in civil disobedience campaigns. He was imprisoned 1942–45 for failure to fully support the British war effort. With the founding of an independent India in 1947, he became the first prime minister and foreign minister of India. He led the new nation through its troubled beginning. He launched five-year plans to bring industrialization and socialization to India. In 1948 he seized the princely state of Hyderabad and went to war with Pakistan over Kashmir. In 1959 he dissolved the Communist government of Kerala state. He advocated neutralism and sought to lead the Afro-Asian bloc. In 1961 he seized Goa from the Portuguese and in 1962 had to contend with Communist Chinese incursions across the northern border.

Neisse River (Nysa Luzycka), river rising in NW Czechoslovakia; flows N to Oder River near Guben, East Germany; part of border between East Germany and Poland since 1945. Length: 140mi (225km).

Nejd (Najd), region in central Saudi Arabia; vast plateau land; taken from Turkey by Wahabi leader Ibn Saud 1899–1912; after conquering Hejaz and Al Hasa,

Nejd became part of Saudi Arabia 1932; site of oasis settlements; inhabited by Bedouins. Area: 447,000sq mi (1,157,730sq km).

Nekton, one of the large groups of the sea's population. It includes the large swimming migrating animals such as adult squid, fishes, and whales. *See also* Benthos; Pelagic Division; Plankton.

Nelson, Horatio Nelson, Viscount (1758–1805), English naval commander. Entering the navy in 1770, he first saw action in the Caribbean (1780). At the outbreak of war with France (1793), he served in the Mediterranean with distinction under Admiral Hood and his successors, losing his right eye and right arm. He rendered effective service at Cape St Vincent (1797) and won a crushing victory over the French at the Battle of the Nile (1798). Promoted to vice admiral, he fought the Battle of Copenhagen (1801) to disrupt the armed neutrality. Recalled to the Mediterranean (1803), he blockaded Toulon for two years until the French fleet finally eluded him. He was killed at the ensuing Battle of Trafalgar, in which the French fleet was destroyed. His long liaison with Emma, Lady Hamilton, was well publicized. *See also* Trafalgar, Battle of.

Nelson, Thomas, Jr. (1738–89), American patriot and a signer of the Declaration of Independence, b. Yorktown, Va. Virginia's delegate to the Continental Congress (1775–77, 1779), he succeeded Thomas Jefferson as governor of that state in 1781.

Nelson River, river in Manitoba, Canada; flows from Lake Winnipeg into the Hudson Bay. The mouth was discovered 1612; route for fur traders; site of first Hudson's Bay Co. trading post (1670). Length: 400mi (644km).

Neman (Nyeman), river in Belorussian SSR, USSR, and Lithuania; rises in Belorussia 30mi (48km) SSW of Minsk, flows W past Stolbtsy, Masty, Grodno, then N into Lithuania, past Alytus, and then W again past Kaunas, Jurbackas, Neman, Sovetsk, to Courland Lagoon, forming a small delta mouth. It receives the Viliya, Nevezys, and Dubysa rivers on the right and the Shchara and Sheshupe on the left. It is navigable for most of its 582mi (937km) and is used as timber route. The Lithuanian resorts of Druskininkai and Bristonas lie on its banks.

Nematode, or **roundworm,** phylum of marine, freshwater, and parasitic worms identified by elongated, cylindrical body pointed at both ends, thick cuticle covering, and longitudinal muscles. Reproduction is sexual. Length: to 1ft (30.5cm). The 10,000 species include *Ascaris* (parasitic in intestine), hookworm, filaria (causes elephantiasis), and *Trichina.*

Nemea, ancient city in S Greece; mythical site of slaying of Nemean lion by Hercules; site of temple of Zeus where and in whose honor the Nemean Games were played; games were est. 573 BC and held in the 2nd and 4th years of each Olympiad; 11 of Pindar's odes celebrated Nemean victories.

Nemertea, ribbon worm, proboscis worm, also called Nemertinea, marine phylum of flatworms similar to Platyhelminthes and identified by protrusile proboscis, anus, and circulatory system. Reproduction is sexual. Length: 1in (2.54cm) to several feet. The 550 species include the bootlace worm *Lineus* and *Eunemertes.*

Nemours, town in N France, 12mi (19km) S of Fontainebleau, on Loing Canal. Made duchy 1404, it was part of House of Savoy 1528–1659; site of 12th-century castle from which Henry III issued edict revoking

privileges of Huguenots (1585); 13th-century church, and bridge (1803). Industries: agriculture, brewing, glassmilling. Pop. 6,605.

Neoclassical Architecture, late 18th and early 19th century architectural style in the United States and Europe. The Napoleonic revival of the idea of the Roman Empire, as exemplified in the Louvre Colonnade (1667–70) by Claude Perrault, and the enthusiasm for archaeological knowledge stimulated by the excavations at Pompeii and Herculaneum, brought an international burst of imitation of classicism in architecture. The influence of monumental Roman temples was particularly dominant in the design of public buildings in the new United States, including Virginia's state capitol (1785) by Thomas Jefferson. James Stuart, co-author of the influential *Antiquities of Athens* (1762), designed the first example of Greek revival in Western Europe, a garden temple at Hagley, England (1758). The trend culminated with the Greek revival buildings of Karl Schinkel, such as the Royal Theater (1818–21) and Old Museum (1822–30) in Berlin. Neoclassicism emphasized a return to the pure forms of Greek and Roman architecture—solidity, severity, and rigid definition of masses. The classical orders were used for structure rather than ornamentation. This geometric clarity opposed the fluid, sculptural principles of Baroque architecture.

Neoclassical Music, music composed from roughly 1920 to 1950. The movement reacted against the emotionalism and subjectivity of Romanticism and sought to return to the ideals and some of the methods of music prior to the Romantic period, using as models the music of Bach, Handel, Mozart, and others. Thus, old forms were revived, such as the toccata, fugue, and concerto grosso, and the older ideal of objectivity with less emotion was stressed in musical composition. Some of the important composers who participated in the movement were Busoni, Prokofiev, Stravinsky, Hindemith, Bartok, Casella, and Piston.

Neodymium, metallic element (symbol Nd) of the Lanthanide group, first isolated in the form of its oxide in 1885. The pure metal was first obtained in 1925. Chief ores are monazite (phosphate) and bastnasite (fluorocarbonate). It has no important use. Properties: at. no. 60; at. wt. 144.24; sp gr 6.8–7.0, melt. pt. 1,875°F (1,024°C); boil. pt. 5,661°F (3,127°C); most common isotope Nd[142] (27.11%). *See also* Lanthanide Elements.

Neo-Impressionism, artistic style developed in the 1880s by French post-Impressionist painters Georges Seurat and Paul Signac and sometimes referred to as divisionism or pointillism. Painting in this precise style was done according to a scientific formula, in which tiny dots of color were used in varying proportions to delineate subjects and to create atmosphere and mood. *See also* Pointillism.

Neolithic Age, or **New Stone Age,** period in man's evolution following the Mesolithic, in which man first lived in settled villages, domesticated and bred animals, cultivated grain crops, and practiced pottery, weaving, and flint-mining. Stone axes were fitted with handles for the first time. *See also* Mesolithic Age.

Neon, gaseous nonmetallic element (symbol Ne) of the rare-gas group, first discovered (1898) by William Ramsay and M. W. Travers. Neon is present in the Earth's atmosphere (0.0018% by volume) and is obtained by the fractionation of liquid air. Its main use is in discharge tubes for advertising signs. The element forms no compounds. Properties: at. no. 10; at. wt. 20.179; density 0.8999 g dm^{-3}; melt. pt. −415.6°F (−248.67°C); boil. pt. −410.89°F (−246.05°C); most common isotope Ne^{20} (90.92%). *See also* Noble Gases.

Neo-Platonism, a school of philosophy that had its greatest importance between about 250 and 550. *Neo* means new, but this school was more than a new version of Platonic thought. It combined Pythagorean, Stoic, Platonic, and Aristotelian ideas with strains from Jewish, Oriental, and Christian religions. In their view of the basic problem of good and evil, Neo-Platonists tended to be mystical and poetic more than philosophical. Formative leaders of the movement were two 3rd century philosophers, Plotinus and Porphyry. One aim of these and other Neo-Platonists in Rome and Greece was to build a philosophy that could compete with the rising influence of Christianity. This effort failed, and the Emperor Justinian closed the Neo-Platonic academies in 529. Yet influences of Neo-Platonism persisted through medieval times.

Neo-Pythagoreans, philosophical movement begun in the 1st century BC and continuing until diluted by the rise of Neo-Platonism in the 3rd century AD. Developing at the start of the Christian era, neo-Pythagoreanism combined Jewish and Hellenistic elements with the more religious and mystical aspects of Pythagorean thought and was an influence on Neo-Platonism. *See also* Neo-Platonism.

Neoteny, the persistence, in the adult animal, of larval characteristics, such as retention of gills, as in some salamanders. An entire order of tunicates, the Larvacea, is permanently larval, never reaching typical adult form. *See also* Mudpuppy; Salamander.

Nepal, an independent kingdom between India (S) and China (N). One frontier cuts through Mt Everest, the world's tallest mountain. The nation consists of three regions: the Terai, S lowland region with arable land; a central mountain area, including the populated Katmandu Valley; and high mountains in the N, extending to the Himalayas. Two-thirds of the nation's income is from agriculture; less than 1% of the population works in industry. Literacy is estimated at 15%. The population is a mixture of Mongoloid and Indian backgrounds, resulting in many divergent languages. In the 18th century numerous small principalities were united under one rule. The expansion of the dominant Gurkhas was checked in 1792 by the Chinese, and in 1816 by a border clash with Britain, which was consolidating its Indian colony. In 1846 the Rana family assumed power, reigning by heredity until a revolution in 1951, and a constitution in 1959, followed by a return to Rana rule. In 1962 the king, Mahendra (reigned 1952–72), dissolved parliament and started a system of "basic democracy," which included an elected village council (panchayat), with zonal and district councils. These councils are responsible to the king, who is aided by an advisory state council and council of ministers. Upon the king's death (1972), his son, Crown Prince Birendra, took control. In 1980, despite persistent violations of human rights by the government, Nepalese voters voted against the return to a multi-party political system.

PROFILE

Official name: Kingdom of Nepal
Area: 54,362sq mi (140,798sq km)
Population: 14,010,000
Chief cities: Katmandu (capital); Bhadgaon
Government: Constitutional
Religion: Hinduism, Buddhism, Islam
Language: Nepali
Monetary unit: Nepali rupee

Nephritis, or glomerulonephritis or Bright's disease, an inflammatory disease of the kidney. Frequently caused by streptococcal infection, it may be chronic or acute. Acute nephritis is treated with bedrest; chronic cases may be helped with artificial kidneys or kidney transplants.

Nephrosis, a syndrome characterized by the presence of edema, large amounts of albumin in the urine, and cholesterol in the blood.

Neptune, eighth planet from the Sun, observed in 1846 by J.C. Galle and H. d'Arrest. Neptune has two known satellites, Triton and Nereid. Mean distance from the Sun, 2,793,000,000mi (4,496,730,000km); mass, approx. 17 times that of Earth; equatorial diameter, 31,200mi (50,232km); rotation period, 15hr, 48min; period of sidereal revolution, 164.8 years. Astronomers' recent observations have indicated the presence of a ring, which will be investigated during *Voyager 2*'s flyby in 1989. *See also* Solar System.

Neptune, in Roman religion originally a god of fresh water. Eventually he became identified with the Greek Poseidon and became a deity of the sea. His female counterpart was Salacia. Neptune's festival took place in summer, when water was scarcest. Thus its purpose was probably the propitiation of the freshwater deity. In art his attributes are the trident and dolphin.

Neptunium, radioactive metallic element (symbol Np) of the actinide group, first made in 1940 by neutron bombardment of uranium. It is found in small amounts in uranium ores. Np^{237} is a by-product obtained in producing plutonium. Properties: at. no. 93; at. wt. 237.0482; sp gr 20.25; melt. pt. 1,184°F (640°C); boil. pt. 7056°F (3905°C); most stable isotope Np^{237} (2.14×10^6 yr). *See also* Transuranium Elements.

Nereis, or **clamworm,** polychaete worm that lives in sand or mud on the seashore. It is usually red or orange with numerous "paddles" on each side of its body. The forepart of its gut can be extended as a proboscis with a pair of jaws. Length: to 3ft (91cm). Family Nereidae. *See also* Annelida.

Nernst, Walther Hermann (1864–1941), German chemist. He became professor at Gottingen and then in Berlin and was awarded the Nobel prize in chemistry in 1920 for his discovery of the third law of thermodynamics. His other important work was concerned with chain reactions in photochemistry. Although he served in World War I, he earned Nazi disfavor because two of his daughters married Jews.

Nero (Claudius Caesar) (37–68), Roman emperor (54–68), b. as Lucius Domitius Ahenobarbus. He was the son of Agrippina II, great-granddaughter of Augustus Caesar, and the stepson of Emperor Claudius I. He murdered his brother Britannicus (55), his mother (59), and his wife Octavia (62). He blamed the Christians for the burning of Rome (64) and began the first official persecution against them. After discovering a plot against him (65), he had many distinguished Romans, including Seneca, Lucan, and Thrasea Paetus, executed. But he was overpowered in a revolt in 68 and committed suicide. He was the last emperor of Julius Caesar's family.

Neruda, Pablo (1904–73), Chilean poet and winner of the Nobel Prize for literature in 1971. Neruda occupied a number of diplomatic posts and was active in politics; he was a Communist-party senator (1945–48) and supported the Marxist regime of Salvador Allende (1970–73). Neruda's poetry transcended politics and dealt with the question of the human condition in general. His best-known work is *Canto General* (1950).

Nerve, any collection of neurons (specifically axons), arranged like the wires of a cable, that travel between nervous system structures and other organs. *Afferent nerves,* or sensory nerves, transmit toward the central nervous system. *Efferent* nerves, or motor nerves, transmit from the central nervous system toward the periphery. Some nerves have both afferent and efferent fibers. For example, 12 cranial nerves (such as the optic nerve and the auditory nerve) originate in the brain and transmit to and away from sensory organs. *See also* Neuron.

Nervous System, one of the major organ systems of the body, with the overall function of relating an individual to his surroundings. It is made up of nervous tissue, that type of tissue that is irritable and conducts impulses, and its basic structural unit is the *neuron,* or nerve cell. In man the nervous system may be divided into three parts: the central nervous system, the peripheral nervous system, and the autonomic nervous system. The *central nervous system* consists of the brain and spinal cord. No function can be performed without some activity of the central nervous system, the major controlling mechanism of the body. The *peripheral nervous system* is a system of nerves and ganglia (nerve aggregations) that connect the peripheral parts of the body to the central nervous system. It has sensory nerves, carrying impulses from sense organs to the central nervous system; motor nerves, carrying motor impulses from the central nervous system to the muscles of the body; and some so-called mixed nerves, containing both sensory and motor nerve fibers. There are 12 cranial nerves originating from the brain, and 31 spinal nerves originating from the spinal cord.

The *autonomic nervous system,* sometimes considered a part of the peripheral nervous system, has an extensive network of nerves away from the brain and spinal cord that control the body's internal environment, regulating such activities as heart rate, peristaltic movements of the digestive tract, urinary bladder contraction, and such emotional reactions as blushing, sweaty palms, and pounding heart. The autonomic nervous system is itself divided into two parts: the *parasympathetic,* or craniosacral, part, which includes some facial-acting nerves and the pelvic nerve, controlling the lower colon and bladder; and the *sympathetic,* or thoracolumbar, part, which can accelerate heart rate, inhibit salivary secretion, stimulate adrenal secretion, among other functions. Functioning through its ganglionic fibers, the two branches of the autonomic nervous system are somewhat antagonistic, yet have independent functions as well. *See also* Brain; Nerve; Neuron; Spinal Cord.

Ness, Loch, freshwater lake in N Scotland, running SW to NE along the geological fault of Glen More; part of Caledonian Canal; legendary home of one or more aquatic monsters. Length: 23mi (37km). Depth: 754ft (230m).

Nest, construction built by an animal to house its eggs, young, or sometimes itself. It is made by some invertebrates, such as social insects, some fish, some amphibians, some reptiles, most birds, and many small mammals. Bird nests vary from the loose structures of owls and many seabirds to the elaborate retorts of weaverbirds. The majority are cup-or dome-shaped and made with twigs, leaves, and mud. Usually a solitary dwelling, some are shared, willingly with ostriches or unwillingly with Old World cuckoos and New World cowbirds.

Nestorius (died *c.*451), patriarch of Constantinople. He was of Persian parents. As patriarch he became involved in a theological dispute on the persons of God. He was charged with believing in two distinct natures: a divine being, God, and a man, Jesus. It is true that Nestorius objected to the title *Theotokos* (Mother of God) for the Virgin Mary, preferring the title Mother of Christ. He distinguished divine and human natures in Christ, but he believed in some kind of moral union of the two natures. The Council of Ephesus (431) condemned the belief in two natures as a heresy, and Nestorius was deposed as patriarch. The Nestorian heresy was named for him, but some historians doubt he held these heretical beliefs. *See also* Nestorianism.

Netanya (Natanya), city in W Israel, 35mi (56km) SSW of Haifa on the Mediterranean Sea coast; site of Jewish Legion Museum; grave of Baron Edmond Rothschild and Wingate Institute for Physical Education are nearby. Industries: diamond processing, tourism, textiles, rubber products, citrus packing. Founded 1928 and named for Nathan Straus, US philanthropist who donated money to further Palestinian education and social services. Pop. 65,400.

Netherlands, independent nation in NW Europe. Low-lying and heavily populated, its economy and history have been shaped by its proximity to the sea.

Land and Economy. A low, flat land averaging 37ft (11m) above sea level, and with much land below sea level, it is bounded N and W by the North Sea, S by Belgium, E by West Germany. Dike systems have been used to reclaim land from the sea to add fertile lands to a densely populated country. Most of the land is used for pasture (43%) and farming (22%). About 80% of the arable land is in farms of less than 50acres (20hectares). Six percent of the work force is engaged in agriculture and fishing. Limited resources place unusual dependence on imports, both for industry and agriculture. The port complex at Rotterdam/Europoort is the world's busiest.

People. The Netherlands has one of the highest population densities in the world. Primarily of German stock (Frisians and Franks), the Dutch also include a Gallo-Celtic mixture. History and social and political attitudes have been largely shaped by their religion. Political parties are divided along ideological lines, and religion influences schools, trade unions, recreational societies, and the media. Freedom of religion is guaranteed: 40.4% is Roman Catholic; 28.3% Protestant Reformed; 9.3% Protestant Calvinist; and about 20% has no religious affiliation. Literacy is about 98%.

Government. The Netherlands is a hereditary constitutional monarchy; the 1954 constitution provided for a council of ministers, an elected parliament, and a prime minister, leader of the majority party or coalition in the parliament.

History. When Julius Caesar invaded the Netherlands, he found it inhabited by German tribes. In the 8th century, as part of Charlemagne's empire, it was passed to the house of Burgundy and the Hapsburgs, and in the 16th century Spain claimed it. Led by William of Orange, the Dutch revolted against the Spanish in 1568. In 1579 the seven N provinces became a republic—the United Netherlands, which became a great sea and colonial power. It came under French domination until Napoleon was defeated in 1813, when it joined with Belgium under a monarchy. Belgium withdrew in 1830, and the Dutch, led by William II, promulgated a liberal constitution in 1848. He was followed by Wilhelmina in 1898. Though neutral in WWI and II, the Netherlands was invaded by the Germans in 1940. The Queen and her daughter, Crown Princess Juliana, established a government-in-exile in London, and returned in 1945 when the Germans had capitulated. Queen Juliana succeeded to the throne in 1948. Some

Nepal

Pablo Neruda

Netherlands

of the Netherlands' many overseas territories are still retained, but have increasing autonomy. Indonesia was given independence in 1949 and Surinam in 1975. In 1980, Queen Juliana abdicated the throne in favor of her daughter Beatrix who became the Netherland's new queen.

PROFILE

Official name: Kingdom of the Netherlands
Area: 15,770sq mi (40,844sq km)
Population: 14,100,000
  Density: 894per sq mi (345per sq km)
Chief cities: Amsterdam (capital); Rotterdam; The Hague
Government: Constitutional monarchy
Religion: Roman Catholic and Protestant
Language: Dutch
Monetary unit: Guilder
Gross national product: $153,000,000
Per capita income: $9,500
Industries: metal, machinery, food processing, chemicals, textiles, oil refining, diamond cutting, pottery, electrical appliances, clothing, cheese
Agriculture: sugar beets, potatoes, cereals, flowers, cattle, fish, hogs, seeds, forests, wheat, barley, rye, oats, flax
Minerals: gas, oil, coal
Trading partners: Federal Republic of Germany, Belgium, France, United States

Netherlands Antilles, autonomous group of five main islands and part of a sixth in West Indies, Caribbean Sea, including Aruba, Bonaire, Curaçao (largest), Saba, St Eustatius, and S half of St Martin. Capital is Willemstad. The Islands have enjoyed full autonomy in internal affairs since 1954. They were discovered 1490s by Christopher Columbus, Alonso de Ojeda, and Amerigo Vespucci; settled by Spanish 1527 at Curaçao; captured by Dutch 1634. Although the Netherlands established (1979) a timetable for complete independence by the end of the 1980s, most of the islands favor continued dependent status because of its economic advantages. Industries: oil refining (Curaçao and Aruba), seasalt, phosphates, tourism. Pop. 246,540.

Nettle, annual and perennial weed found worldwide. It has heart-shaped, toothed leaves, tiny, greenish flowers, and stinging hairs along the stem. Among 500 species is the stinging nettle *Urtica dioica*. Height: 2–4ft (61–121.9cm). Family Urticaceae.

Netzahualcóyotl, city in central Mexico; suburb of Mexico City. Pop. 571,035.

Neuchâtel, capital of Neuchâtel canton in Switzerland, on N shore of Lake Neuchâtel, at mouth of Seyon River. Governed 1648–1707 by counts under Holy Roman Empire, it passed to Prussian rule 1815; site of university (1838), museum, library, Romanesque cloisters, 12th–17th-century castle, observatory. Industries: chocolate, tobacco, watches, printing. Pop. 36,400.

Neumann, (Saint) John Nepomucene (1811–60), Roman Catholic prelate. Born in Bohemia, he studied at the University of Prague before coming to the United States in 1836 where he was ordained a priest. He became a Redemptorist (1840) and head of the Redemptorist community in Pittsburgh (1847). In 1852, Pope Pius IX named him bishop of Philadelphia. He did much work with the poor and with building parochial schools and furthering education. He was beatified in 1963 and canonized June 19, 1977, as the first American male saint.

Neuralgia, pain along a nerve trunk or its branches. It may be the result of a virus infection of the nerve, alcoholic or lead poisoning, physical injury, or vitamin deficiency. It may also be purely psychological. Drugs are used for relief of neuralgic pain.

Neuritis, inflammation or degenerative lesion of the nerves accompanied by pain, paralysis, and impaired reflexes. Causes are many and treatment is directed toward the causative agent.

Neurology, branch of medicine that involves the diagnosis and nonsurgical treatment of diseases of the nervous system.

Neuron, or **nerve cell,** the basic structural unit of the nervous system. It is composed of a cell body and one or more dendrites and one axon. The dendrites and axon are nerve cell processes, extending beyond the cell body. Dendrites carry impulses to the cell body; they are often short and branched. An axon is usually a longer, unbranched process; it carries impulses away from the cell body. *See also* Axon; Dendrite.

Neuroptera, order of carnivorous insects, including lacewings, ant lions, and owl flies, found worldwide. They have a complete life cycle: egg, larva, pupa, and adult. Wing span: 0.7–5.9in (18–150mm). *See also* Ant Lion; Hellgramite; Lacewing.

Neurosis, personality disturbance involving persistent anxiety that is either directly experienced or controlled through the use of psychological defense mechanisms. *See also* Neurotic Personality; Psychoneurotic Disorders.

Neustria, the W section of the Frankish empire (the E section being Austrasia). It was formed when the empire of Clovis I was divided among his four sons (511). In 687, Pepin of Austrasia overcame Neustria. In 912 part of it was ceded to the Scandinavian pirates and became Normandy. Although it was originally the area between the Meuse, the Loire, and the Atlantic Ocean, the name came to mean only Normandy and finally fell into disuse.

Neutrality, policy of noninvolvement in hostilities existing between other states. This status was recognized by international law as early as the 15th century. The rights and obligations of neutral powers have been codified by international treaties and conventions. A nation proclaiming its neutrality must be wholly impartial and refrain from helping or hindering any side. It must furthermore protect its own territory from encroachment by belligerents.

Neutralization, chemical reaction conducted in an aqueous medium between equivalent weights of an acid and a base to produce water and a salt, which is neither acidic nor basic, but has a pH of approximately 7, often accompanied by the generation of heat.

Neutrino, uncharged massless elementary particle with spin ½ that has little reaction with matter and is difficult to detect. There are two sorts: the electron neutrino (symbol e) is closely associated with the electron and is produced when protons and electrons react to form neutrons, as in the Sun. The more common antineutrino occurs when a neutron decays. The muon neutrino (symbol μ), associated with the muon, occurs in high-energy reactions. *See also* Lepton.

Neutron, uncharged elementary particle (symbol n) that occurs in the atomic nuclei of all chemical elements except the lightest isotope of hydrogen. It was first identified by James Chadwick (1932). In isolation it is unstable, decaying with a halflife of 11.7 minutes into a proton, electron, and antineutrino. Its neutrality allows it to penetrate and be absorbed in nuclei and thus to induce nuclear transmutations and fission. It is a baryon with spin ½ and a mass slightly greater than that of the proton.

Neutron Activation Analysis, highly sensitive method of identifying the chemical contents of something by bombarding it with high-energy neutrons that are absorbed by the atoms present in the sample. The resulting radioactive nuclei emit radiation of an energy and decay rate characteristic of the original atoms. The quantity present can also be found with extreme precision.

Neutron Bomb, small hydrogen bomb, commonly called an enhanced radiation weapon, that produces a small blast but a very intense burst of high-speed neutrons. The lack of blast means that buildings are not heavily damaged. The neutrons, however, produce intense radiation sickness in people located within a certain range of the explosion, killing those affected within a week. The bomb is designed for tactical use—for example, to kill an invading force while sparing buildings and nearby civilian populations.

Neutron Star. *See* Pulsar.

Neva, navigable river in Russian SFSR, USSR; issues from the SW corner of Lake Ladoga as Petrokrepost; flows W to the Gulf of Finland at Leningrad. It receives the Mga, Tosna, and Izhora rivers and is connected by the Mariinsk, Tikhvin, and Vyshnevolotsk canal systems with the Volga River, and by the White Sea-Baltic Canal with the White Sea. Length: 40mi (64.4km).

Nevada, state in the W United States, in the Great Basin region.

Land and Economy. At an average altitude of 5,500ft (1,676m), Nevada is a semi-desert region of nearly 100 basins separated by short mountain ranges running N to S. Its climate is dry; moisture-bearing winds are blocked by mountains in California to the W. There are few rivers within the state; the Humboldt, which is the longest, runs 290mi (467km) to disappear in the Humboldt Sink. Pyramid Lake is the only natural lake. Grazing and mining are important to the economy, but tourism is the state's major source of income. Visitors are drawn by the legalized gambling and the lenient divorce laws, which require only brief residence. The city of Las Vegas offers a wide range of entertainment. Resort areas such as Lake Tahoe, which is partly in California, and Lake Mead, formed by dams on the Colorado River on the S border, are year-round recreation centers.

People. Nevada is one of the least densely populated states in the country, but, according to the 1980 census, is the fastest growing, 63.5% between 1970 and 1980. Most of the new residents move to Nevada's cities, and the population is more than 80% urban.

Education. There are six institutions of higher education, including the state-supported University of Nevada.

History. Spaniards visited the area in 1776, but the first explorations were not begun until 1825 by British fur trappers who were followed by US "mountain men." In 1833 a party bound for California crossed the region along the Humboldt River. Their route became the Overland Trail, which took thousands westward after gold was discovered in California in 1848. In that year, the United States acquired Nevada by the treaty that ended the Mexican War. When the Comstock Lode, a rich deposit of silver and gold, was found in W Nevada in 1859, settlers flocked to the land. Nevada Territory was organized in 1861, only three years before it became a state. The mining rush created several boom towns and a number of personal fortunes, but changes in the prices of precious metals and depletion of the ores depressed activity; some boom towns became ghost towns and are now tourist attractions. The WWII quest for useful metals revived the mining industry, especially in copper. Because 88% of the state's land is federally-controlled, by the late 1970s Nevada had become part of the so-called Sagebrush Rebellion, with residents calling for a larger share of control over the state's resources.

PROFILE

Admitted to Union: Oct. 31, 1864; rank, 36th
US Congressmen: Senate, 2; House of Representatives, 1
Population: 799,184 (1980); rank, 43th
Capital: Carson City, 32,022(1980)
Chief cities: Las Vegas, 164,674; Reno, 100,756; North Las Vegas, 42,739
State legislature: Senate, 20; Assembly, 40
Area: 110,540sq mi (286,298sq km); rank, 7th
Elevation: Highest, 13,140ft (4,005m), Boundary Peak; lowest, 470ft (143m), Colorado River
Industries (major products): electronic devices, gaming devices, stone-clay-glass products
Agriculture (major products): cattle, other livestock
Minerals (major): copper, gold, mercury, lithium
State nickname: Sagebrush State, Silver State
State motto: All for Our Country
State bird: mountain bluebird
State flower: sagebrush
State tree: single-leaf piñon

Nevelson, Louise (1900–), US sculptor and painter, b. Russia. Her first sculpture show was in 1940 at the Nierendor Gallery in New York City. In the 1950s she began constructing her famous painted collection of boxes, wooden objects, and castoffs from old houses. Her "environmental sculptures" include "Sky Cathedral" and "Daun's Wedding Feast" (1959). Her later pieces are free-standing, including bins and barrels filled with long flexible poles. She was elected to the American Academy and Institute of Arts and Letters in 1979.

Neville, Richard. *See* Warwick, Richard Neville, Earl of.

New Amsterdam. *See* New York City.

Newark, city in NE New Jersey, on Passaic River and Newark Bay, W of lower Manhattan; seat of Essex co; largest city in New Jersey; connected to New York City by tunnel; site of George Washington's supply base as he retreated across state in 1776; scene of major 1967 race riot; site of Newark College of Engineering (1881), Essex County College (1968). Industries: electrical equipment, paints, chemicals, insurance. Settled 1666 by Puritans; inc. as town 1833, as city 1836. Pop. (1980) 329,248.

New Bedford, city in Massachusetts, 50mi (81km) S of Boston on Buzzard's Bay; seat of Bristol co; Revolutionary War haven for American privateers, burned by British in 1778. City was a whaling capital until the late 1850s, when whaling declined; it was a textile center until 1920s; today it is an important fishing and scalloping port; site of Seamen's Bethel (1832, described in Herman Melville's *Moby Dick*), Bourne Whaling Museum, and a Whaleman Statue by Bela Pratt (1913). Industries: textiles, machinery, tools, copper, brass. Founded 1652; inc. as town 1787, as city 1847. Pop. (1980) 98,478.

New Britain, industrial city in N Connecticut, 9mi (14km) SW of Hartford. Industries: hardware, tools, household appliances, ball bearings. Settled 1687; inc. 1870. Pop. (1980) 73,840.

New Britain Island, largest island of the Bismarck Archipelago and part of Papua New Guinea, in SW Pacific Ocean, approx. 55mi (89km) E of New Guinea Island; chief town is Rabaul. Discovered 1606 by Dutchman Jacques Lemaire, it became German protectorate 1884; after WWI it was mandated to Australia, and reestablished as territory of Australia following Japanese occupation in WWII. Island has a mountainous terrain, with volcanoes exceeding 7,000ft (2,130m); noted for hot springs. Exports: copra, coconuts, cocoa. Industries: mining of gold, copper, iron, coal. Area: approx. 14,160sq mi (36,674sq km). Pop. 175,369.

New Brunswick, province in E Canada; one of the Maritime Provinces, bordered on the W by the state of Maine.

Land and Economy. The Gulf of St Lawrence, an arm of the Atlantic Ocean, is on the E, and the Bay of Fundy, which has the highest tides in the world, is on the S. The land rises gradually inland; the highest parts are in the NW. The St John is the principal river. More than 75% of the province is forest-covered, a valuable resource for the economy. Mineral deposits discovered in the N in the mid-20th century are important. Fisheries along the coasts are a source of income, and forestry is also a major industry.

People. The original settlers were French, and 37% of the population is French speaking. The remainder are principally of English and Scots descent.

Education. Institutions of higher education are the University of New Brunswick, St Louis-Maillet, Le Collège de Bathurst, St Thomas University, and the University of Moncton.

History. The region was discovered by the French explorer Jacques Cartier in 1534. With Nova Scotia, it formed the French colony of Acadia. The colony was ceded to Great Britain by treaty in 1713, but British settlement was slow. More than 12,000 Loyalists from the American colonies fled into the area during the American Revolution, and this influx spurred the creation of the province in 1784. A boundary dispute with the United States was settled in 1842 and in 1867 New Brunswick joined Nova Scotia, Quebec, and Ontario to establish the Dominion of Canada. The economy has continued to rely heavily on primary production. The mining industry experienced dramatic growth during the 1960s, but many of the small coastal villages have become depressed.

PROFILE

Admitted to Confederation: July 1, 1867; one of the four provinces that were joined to form the Dominion of Canada
National Parliament Representatives: Senate, 10; House of Commons, 10
Population: 664,525
Capital: Fredericton
Chief cities: Saint John; Moncton; Fredericton
Provincial legislature: Legislative Assembly: 58 members
Area: 28,354sq mi (73,437sq km); rank, 8th
Elevation: Highest: 2,690ft (820m), Mt Carleton; lowest, sea level
Industries (major products): pulp and paper
Agriculture (major products): potatoes, hay, fruit, dairy products
Minerals (major): copper, zinc, lead, silver
Floral emblem: purple violet

New Caledonia Island, largest island in French Overseas Territory of New Caledonia, in SW Pacific Ocean approx. 750mi (1208km) E of Australia; chief city and capital of territory is Nouméa. Discovered 1774 by Captain Cook, it was site of French Roman Catholic mission est. 1843; used as penal colony 1864–94; became part of official French Overseas Territory 1946. Inhabitants are mainly Melanesians, with some Europeans and Vietnamese; island has irregular climate and geography. Products: copra, coffee, cotton, nickel, iron, manganese, cobalt, chrome. Area: 6,531sq mi (16,915sq km). Pop. 113,680.

Newcastle, Thomas Pelham-Holles, Duke of (1693–1798), English political figure. A Whig, he supported Walpole and became secretary of state (1724–54). He succeeded his brother, Henry Pelham, as prime minister (1754) but resigned (1756). Though prime minister again (1757–62), his secretary of state, William Pitt, directed foreign policy.

Newcastle, formerly King's Town; city in SE Australia, 100mi (161km) NE of Sydney; site of University of Newcastle (1965). Industries: iron, steel, chemicals, textiles, shipbuilding, fertilizers. Founded 1804. Pop. 144,860.

Newcastle Disease, a viral disease of birds, characterized by respiratory difficulty and nervousness. Adult birds may survive. Man can be infected when holding sick birds, usually developing conjunctivitis. No treatment exists, but preventive vaccines are available.

Newcastle-upon-Tyne, county town of Tyne and Wear, NE England; port on Tyne River; linked by tunnel and five bridges to Gateshead; home of University of Newcastle-upon-Tyne. Industries: shipbuilding, heavy engineering. Exports: coal, iron, steel. Pop. 295,700.

Newcomen, Thomas (1663–1729), English inventor of the first economical atmospheric steam engine. In 1705 he built a model of the engine that consisted of a piston moved by atmospheric pressure within a cylinder in which a partial vacuum had been created by condensing steam. He shared the patent with Thomas Savery (1650–1715) who had invented (1698) an earlier but inferior steam engine.

New Criticism, type of literary criticism, primarily of poetry, that emphasizes close analysis of a work as an independent unit. It developed in the 1920s and 1930s in the United States through the influence of various critics and university professors, including John Crowe Ransom, Cleanth Brooks, René Wellek, and Allen Tate. It flourished particularly in the 1940s and 1950s. Although there is diversity among the New Critics, they agree that literary analysis should concentrate on the language and tone of a work rather than on its relation to a period, a tradition, or its author.

New Deal, in US history, the social and economic programs of the administration of Pres. Franklin D. Roosevelt. Elected in 1932 at the depths of the Great Depression, Roosevelt promised a "new deal" to the American people, hence the name that was given to all the domestic reforms of his administration. Although most historians do not credit the New Deal programs with ending the depression—only the defense spending of World War II did that—those programs were extremely important in restoring the confidence of the people during the 1930s and in relieving the worst effects of the Great Depression. Most of the New Deal programs have remained in effect and have been broadened by the policies of succeeding Democratic administrations, including the Fair Deal of Harry S. Truman, the New Frontier of John F. Kennedy, and the Great Society of Lyndon B. Johnson.

Promptly upon inauguration in 1933, Roosevelt embarked upon the most ambitious and revolutionary set of domestic reforms in the nation's history. Assisted by his group of advisors known as the Brain Trust, the President's first action was to declare a "bank holiday" in which the entire US banking system was reformed by the National Banking Act, and the nation in effect was taken off the gold standard. In the first months of the New Deal, the so-called Hundred Days, Roosevelt proposed, and Congress created, such important federal agencies as the Agricultural Adjustment Administration, the National Recovery Administration, the Civilian Conservation Corps, the Public Works Agency, and the Tennessee Valley Authority. In 1934 he established the Securities and Exchange Commission and the Federal Communications Commission. In 1935 were founded the National Youth Administration, the Social Security system, the Works Progress (later, Projects) Administration, and the National Labor Relations Board. A minimum wages and hours law was passed, and the nation's tax system was overhauled.

Despite the cooperation of a Democratic Congress, Roosevelt's New Deal programs were not without opposition. Republicans and conservative Democrats considered them socialistic threats to the free-enterprise system. The unprecedented power they gave to the federal government was a source of concern to states-rights advocates and to old-line liberals who looked with suspicion on all government activity. The most effective opposition, however, came from the Supreme Court. It struck down as unconstitutional several of the central agencies of the New Deal, including the National Recovery Administration and the Agricultural Adjustment Administration. Roosevelt's attempts to "pack" the court by naming additional pro-administration justices met with defeat, but eventually the court came to accept most of the New Deal.

Roosevelt—along with a Democratic Congress—was reelected in 1936, thereby giving him the voters' endorsement to continue the New Deal. His second term, while less revolutionary than the first, nevertheless consolidated and expanded the programs of the first term. By the end of the second term, however, the approaching World War II was engaging more and more attention. The defense spending in preparation for that conflict finally ended the Great Depression, but the social and economic reforms of the New Deal had become permanent parts of American society. *See also* Agricultural Adjustment Act; Civilian Conservation Corps; Federal Communications Commission; National Labor Relations Board; National Recovery Administration; Public Works Administration; Securities and Exchange Commission; Social Security Act; Tennessee Valley Authority; Works Project Administration.

New Delhi, capital of India, in N India, on the Yamuna River in Delhi Union Territory. Planned by English architects Edwin Lutyens and Herbert Baker, it was constructed 1920–30 to replace Calcutta as the capital of British India; where the old city of Delhi (SW) is primarily a commercial center, New Delhi's broad streets are lined with government buildings making it a busy administrative center; site of war memorial arch (1921), marble residence of the president of India, prayer ground where Mahatma Gandhi was assassinated (1948), and Balmiki and Lakshminarayan temples. Pop. 301,800.

Caraquet, New Brunswick

New Delhi, India: WWI memorial at the India Gate

Concord, New Hampshire: state capitol

New Economic Policy (NEP) (1921–28), program of the Soviet government to restore the Russian economy and appease a hostile peasantry after the civil war. It replaced the seizure of grain from peasants with a fixed amount paid as a tax, allowed the surplus to be sold on the open market, loosened controls on trade and light industry, and stabilized the currency. A relatively liberal period, the NEP ended with forcible collectivization in 1928 under the first Five-Year Plan.

New England Confederation, formed (1643) by New England colonies of Plymouth, Connecticut, Massachusetts Bay, and New Haven for mutual safety and welfare. Rhode Island was refused admittance because of religious differences. The confederation was dissolved (1684) with direct English rule over Massachusetts Bay.

Newfoundland, province in E Canada, on the Atlantic Ocean. It consists of the large island of Newfoundland, which was England's first New World colony, and of Labrador, a portion of the mainland to the N that extends inland about 400mi (640km) from the coast. The Strait of Belle Isle separates the parts.

Land and Economy. The surface of the island and of the mainland is generally rolling. The highest elevation on the island is Gros Morne, 2,666ft (813m). The highest in the province is in the far N of Labrador. The entire coastline is broken by deep bays and inlets with many islands. Thick forests cover much of the land, the exploitation of which is a major sector of the economy. Newfoundland's cod fisheries have been famous for nearly 500 years; in the late 20th century international competition and market uncertainties have affected them. Great reserves of mineral deposits, especially of iron in Labrador, remain to be developed. Agriculture is primarily subsistence farming.

People and Education. Almost all the population is in the island of Newfoundland; Labrador is sparsely settled. Most people live in small communities along the coasts. They are descended from the original settlers from the British Isles. Memorial University of Newfoundland at St John's is the only institution of higher education.

History. Norsemen are believed to have touched the coast of Labrador about AD 1000 and to have established a short-lived settlement on the N tip of Newfoundland. The recorded discoveries of the region were by the English navigator John Cabot, who found the island in 1497 and the Labrador coast in 1498. Sir Humphrey Gilbert formally claimed the island for England in 1583. It was a fishing station loosely administered from London, but as the population grew slowly it became a British colony by 1832. Labrador was under the jurisdiction of the governor of Newfoundland, and both remained apart from the Dominion of Canada until they joined the Confederation in 1949 as the province of Newfoundland. Huge offshore oil and natural gas fields were discovered in 1979 and 1980.

PROFILE

Admitted to Confederation: March 31, 1949; rank, 10th
National Parliament Representatives: Senate, 6; House of Commons, 7
Population: 557,725
Capital: St John's
Chief cities: St John's; Corner Brook
Provincial legislature: Legislative Assembly, 43 members
Area: 156,185sq mi (404,520sq km); rank, 7th
Elevation: Highest: 5,500ft (1,678m), Torngat Mts, Labrador; lowest, sea level
Industries (major products): pulp and paper, wood products, processed fish
Fisheries (major products): cod, lobster

Minerals (major): iron ore, lead, zinc, copper, fluorspar
Agriculture (major products): hay, potatoes, turnips, cabbage
Floral emblem: pitcher plant

Newfoundland, rescue and draft dog (working group) bred by Newfoundland fishermen. This dignified dog has a massive head with square, short muzzle; small, triangular ears close to the head; a full-chested, broadbacked body; shortish, strong legs with webbed feet; and broad, long tail. The long, full double coat is short on head, muzzle, and ears. Color is black, bronze, or white and black. Average size: 25–28in (63–71cm) high at shoulder; 110–150lb (50–68kg). *See also* Working Dog.

New France, French colony in North America corresponding roughly to Quebec, Ontario, and the Maritime provinces of Canada. Jacques Cartier claimed the region for France in 1534. The Company of New France was chartered to establish settlements and exploit the fur trade. In 1605 the first permanent white settlement was founded at Port Royal (now Annapolis Royal, Nova Scotia). Quebec was founded in 1608. By 1640 there were fewer than 300 colonists and subsequent wars with the Iroquois almost totally exterminated the population. The Company of New France was disbanded in 1663 and the colony was placed under a royal governor. In 1713 Acadia (Nova Scotia), Newfoundland, and the Hudson Bay area were lost to Britain. In 1763 France lost the complete colony to Britain. The approximately 65,000 colonists became British subjects.

New Granada, an administrative area centered in present-day Bogotá, Colombia. The Kingdom of New Granada was founded in 1538. The *audiencia* (high court) of New Granada was installed in 1549. The captaincy-general of New Granada was created in 1564. The Spanish Crown established the viceroyalty of New Granada in 1717, disbanded it in 1723 and reestablished it in 1739. The term was used to describe present-day Colombia from 1830–61, when it was changed to the United States of Colombia.

New Guinea, island in the SW Pacific Ocean, N of Australia, in the E Malay Archipelago; second largest island in the world. It is administratively divided into two sections. Irian Barat (W), a province of Indonesia, and Papua New Guinea, a self-governing country since 1973. First sighted 1511 by Portuguese explorer Antonio d'Abreu; Dutch claimed the W side 1828, and British the SE side and nearby islands 1885. Australia gained control of the British section 1905, and the Netherlands transferred control of W section to Indonesia 1963. Area: 319,713 sq mi (828,057sq km). Pop. 2,800,000. *See also* Papua New Guinea.

New Hampshire, state in the NE United States, in the New England region, bordered on the N by the province of Quebec, Canada. During presidential election years, New Hampshire receives considerable national attention as the site of the first primary election.

Land and Economy. In the SE, New Hampshire touches the Atlantic Ocean for 13mi (21km). Portsmouth is the only port. To the W and N the land is hilly, with occasional elevations of 3,000ft (915m). In the N are the rugged White Mts, where Mt Washington is the highest peak in the NE United States. The Connecticut River forms the W boundary; the Merrimack is the largest river in the state. There are more than 1,300 lakes, of which Winnipesaukee, Newfound, and Sunapee are the largest. About 85% of the state is forested. The scenic attractions and year-round recreational opportunities of the terrain have made tourism a mainstay of the economy. Industry is concentrated in the cities of

the S and central portions and along the Connecticut and Merrimack rivers. The rigorous climate curtails the growing season for farming.

People. Most of the inhabitants, especially in rural sections and the smaller towns, are descended from the original settlers, but throughout the state there is a strong French-Canadian element that tends to concentrate in the larger cities. Urban areas contain about 60% of the population. The SE is the home of many who commute to jobs in Massachusetts.

Education. There are about 25 institutions of higher education. The state-supported University of New Hampshire has several campuses. Dartmouth College at Hanover is a notable privately endowed institution. The first free public library in the United States was est. at Dublin in 1822.

History. English explorers visited the coast as early as 1603, and the first settlement was made at the mouth of the Piscataqua River in 1623; New Hampshire became an English royal province in 1679. Indian raids harassed the frontier towns until 1759. In one of the first armed moves in the colonies against the British Crown, New Hampshire men captured Fort William and Mary at Portsmouth on Dec. 12, 1774. After joining the Union, the state had a population surge, but the growth rate declined as many left the farms in the westward migration. Expanding industry in the cities drew immigrants in the early 20th century, and the growth rate exceeded that of the nation as a whole, but during the latter part, economic growth stagnated, and population growth was much less than that of the country as a whole.

PROFILE

Admitted to Union: June 21, 1788; 9th of the 13 original states to ratify the US Constitution
US Congressmen: Senate, 2; House of Representatives, 2
Population: 920,610 (1980); rank, 42nd
Capital: Concord, 30,400 (1980)
Chief cities: Manchester, 90,936; Nashua, 67,865; Concord
State legislature: Senate, 24; House of Representatives, 400
Area: 9,304sq mi (24,097sq km); rank, 44th
Elevation: Highest, 6,288ft (1,918m), Mt Washington; lowest, sea level
Industries (major products): shoes, textiles, electrical and electronics equipment, pulp, paper, lumber, wood products
Agriculture (major products): dairy and poultry products, maple syrup, apples
Minerals (major): sand, gravel, stone
State nickname: Granite State
State motto: Live Free or Die
State bird: purple finch
State flower: purple lilac
State tree: paper (white) birch

New Harmony, town in SW Indiana, on Wabash River. Originally settled by Harmony Society under George Rapp, it was sold to Robert Owen (1825), who founded a Utopian communistic colony attracting numerous educators, scientists, and other intellectuals; est. nation's first kindergarten, free public school, free library. It was dissolved in 1828 due to internal dissensions; 25 Rappite buildings remain. Founded 1814. Pop. (1980) 945.

New Haven, in S Connecticut, New Haven co, third largest city in the state, and the site of Yale University; located 70mi (110km) NE of New York City. The presence of Yale, one of the nation's oldest and most famous schools, has made the city a cultural center. Its elm-lined streets feature many old buildings as well as noted examples of modern architecture. Puritans founded New Haven in 1638. A bustling port in the 18th and 19th centuries, the city shared the role of Connecticut capital with Hartford 1701–1875. Noah Webster and Eli Whitney lived in the city.

Points of interest: Peabody Museum of Natural History, Yale University Art Gallery. Industries: firearms and ammunition, rubber products, locks, and tools. Inc. 1784; pop. (1980) 126,109.

New Haven Colony, colony in Connecticut founded in 1637–38 by Puritans under the leadership of Theophilus Eaton and John Davenport on land bartered from Indians. It was run as a strict theocracy with proper religious belief entitling citizenship. It was expanded (1643) to include Milford, Guilford, and Stamford. It joined the New England Confederation (1643) and later merged with the Connecticut Colony (1655) under a charter obtained by John Winthrop.

New Hebrides (Nouvelles Hébrides). *See* Vanuatu.

New Jersey, state in the E United States, on the Atlantic Ocean S of New York City. It is the most densely populated of the 50 states, and one of the most highly industrialized.

Land and Economy. The S 60% of the state is nearly level or gently sloping up to the W. In the N, hill ranges run SW to NE; the highest elevations are on Kittatinny Mt in the extreme NW. The Delaware River forms the W boundary and the Hudson, part of the E. The Hackensack, Passaic, and Raritan are the principal rivers in the state. The economy is greatly influenced by the cities of New York across the Hudson River and Philadelphia across the Delaware. Much of the state's industry is concentrated in the 90mi (145km) between these cities, which constitutes virtually a continuous metropolitan area. Each of the cities is one of the nation's leading ports, with huge docking facilities on the New Jersey side of the rivers. A network of highways and railroads, feeding from the cities, crosses the state. Thousands of New Jersey residents commute to jobs in New York and Philadelphia. Agriculture, centered in great truck farms, is principally in the center and the S. The Atlantic coast is a notable tourist area.

People. New Jersey has a population density of 915 persons per sq mi (353 per sq km). Nearly 90% of the people resides in urban areas. In the 19th century, immigrants from overseas settled in the industrial cities, and their descendants form a large segment of the population. About 10% of the residents are blacks; they account for more than half the population of Newark, the largest city.

Education. There are more than 60 institutions of higher education. Rutgers University, with its main campus at New Brunswick, is the state university; until 1956, it was a private institution. Princeton University, the 4th-oldest college in the United States, founded in 1746, is the leading privately endowed institution.

History. The Italian explorer Giovanni da Verrazano, in the service of France, explored the coast in 1524, but white settlement did not begin until the 1620s, when the Dutch founded the colony of New Netherland (later New York). Some of these pioneers settled in NE New Jersey. In 1664, the English seized New Netherland. The land between the Hudson and the Delaware was separated and renamed New Jersey. The colony supported the Revolution, and almost 100 engagements between American and British troops were fought on its soil. After achieving statehood, New Jersey began the development of its industry and transportation system. In the Civil War and both world wars, the state was a prime supplier of war material. The administration of Woodrow Wilson, governor 1910–13, when he resigned to become president of the United States, initiated many progressive measures of government. During the post-WWII era, this heavily urbanized state has faced the problems of decaying city centers and flight to the suburbs. In 1978 the state legalized casino gambling in Atlantic City in an effort to revitalize its tourism industry.

PROFILE

Admitted to Union: Dec. 18, 1787, 3d of 13 original states to ratify US Constitution
US Congressmen: Senate, 2; House of Representatives, 15
Population: 7,364,158 (1980); rank, 9th
Capital: Trenton, 92,124 (1980)
Chief cities: Newark, 329,248; Jersey City, 223,532; Paterson, 137,970
State Legislature: Senate, 40; General Assembly, 80
Area: 7,836sq mi (20,295sq km); rank, 46th
Elevation: Highest, 1,803ft (550m), High Point; lowest, sea level
Industries (major products): chemical products, apparel, processed foods, electrical machinery, petroleum products
Agriculture (major products): tomatoes, corn, asparagus, apples, cranberries, poultry
Minerals (major): stone, sand, gravel
State nickname: Garden State
State motto: Liberty and Prosperity
State bird: eastern goldfinch
State flower: purple violet
State tree: red oak

New Jersey Plan (1787), plan for national government. It was introduced by William Paterson and offered by the small states at the Constitutional Convention in Philadelphia. An alternative to the Virginia plan, which favored the large states, it called for a single legislative body in which each state was represented equally, the delegates to be chosen by the state legislatures. It included a supremacy clause, which made the national government the authority over the states, which became a part of the Constitution. Elements of the plan were incorporated in the Connecticut Compromise. *See also* Connecticut Compromise.

Newlands, John Alexander Reina (1838–98), English chemist. In 1864 he announced his law of octaves, arranging the elements into eight columns according to increasing atomic weight. The law was ridiculed until Mendeleev announced his periodic law five years later.

Newman, John Henry (1801–90), English theologian. Ordained in the Anglican Church (1824), he associated with Edward Pusey and John Keble, and became a leader of the Oxford Movement. In 1841 he wrote *Tract 90,* showing that the Thirty-Nine Articles of the Church of England were consistent with Roman Catholicism, and began to question his own Anglicanism. He became a Roman Catholic (1845), was ordained and received a doctorate of divinity in Rome (1846), and established a branch of the Oratorians in Birmingham (1847). As rector of the Catholic University of Dublin he delivered the lectures later published as *Idea of a University Defined* (1873). His *Apologia Pro Vita Sua* (1864), written in reply to accusations by Charles Kingsley, justifies his life as an Anglican. Newman was attacked by Cardinal Henry Manning and the Ultramontanes on the doctrine of papal infallibility, but was created cardinal by Leo XIII (1879).

New Mexico, state in the SW United States, bordered on the S by Mexico.

Land and Economy. The state occupies a plateau with a mean elevation of 5,700ft (1,739m). The Sangre de Cristo Mts, a S extension of the Rocky Mts, are in the N central part. Shorter ranges rise in other sections. The Rio Grande, flowing S through the center, is the principal river. Dams on the Rio Grande and other rivers have created artificial lakes for water storage and irrigation. Mineral production is the major sector of the economy. Military installations and nuclear and space research, directed by the US government, are important. The chief centers are Los Alamos, White Sands Proving Ground, and Hollaman and Kirtland Air Force bases. Tourism is a valuable source of income.

People and Education. Besides descendants of immigrants from other states, there are many residents of Spanish, Indian, or mixed ancestry. The blend of races is reflected in the state's culture. About 70% of the population lives in urban areas. There are 13 institutions of higher education.

History. Beginning in 1539, Spanish adventurers seeking gold traversed the region. In 1609 it became a province of the Spanish colony of Mexico; Santa Fe was founded and became the capital the next year. When Mexico won independence in 1821, the area remained a Mexican prov. In that year the Santa Fe Trail, a major trade route from Missouri, was opened. US troops occupied the province on the outbreak of the Mexican War in 1846, and the Territory of New Mexico was organized in 1850. In the Civil War, a Confederate invasion attempt was repulsed; fighting with hostile Indians continued until the 1880s. The New Mexican desert was the site of early research on nuclear weapons. The first atomic bomb was produced at Los Alamos and exploded at Alamogordo on July 16, 1945. Uranium mining began during the 1950s, and both the mining and research industries expanded during the 1970s and early 1980s.

PROFILE

Admitted to Union: Jan. 6, 1912; rank, 47th
US Congressmen: Senate, 2; House of Representatives, 2
Population: 1,299,968 (1980); rank, 37th
Capital: Santa Fe, 48,899 (1980)
Chief cities: Albuquerque, 331,767; Santa Fe; Las Cruces, 45,086
State legislature: Senate, 42; House of Representatives, 70
Area: 121,666sq mi (315,115sq km); rank, 5th
Elevation: Highest, 13,161ft (4,014m), Wheeler Peak; lowest, 2,817ft (859m), Red Bluff Reservoir
Industries (major products): food products, chemicals, ordnance, lumber
Agriculture (major products): sheep, cotton, pecans, sorghum
Minerals (major): uranium, potash, petroleum, natural gas, copper, zinc, lead
State nickname: Land of Enchantment
State motto: Crescit eundo ("It Grows as It Goes")
State bird: roadrunner
State flower: yucca
State tree: piñon (nut pine)

New Netherland, Dutch colonial territory in North America, stretching from the Hudson to the Delaware River. The Dutch claim was based on the explorations of Henry Hudson. Under charter to the Dutch West India Co., settlers founded Ft Nassau (Albany) and New Amsterdam (New York City). The latter was settled by Peter Minuit (1626). The last and most able governor, Peter Stuyvesant, annexed New Sweden (1655). The area was taken over by England in 1664. *See also* Minuit, Peter; New Sweden; Stuyvesant, Peter.

New Orleans, city and port of entry in SE Louisiana, 75mi (121km) SE of Baton Rouge, between Lake Pontchartrain and Mississippi River; seat of Orleans parish and largest city in Louisiana. It remained under French rule until 1762 when it was secretly passed to Spain by Treaty of Fontainebleau; returned to France by Treaty of Ildefonso (1800); incorporated into the Louisiana Purchase (1803); served as capital of Louisiana 1812–49; scene of British defeat (1815) by Andrew Jackson in the War of 1812; fell to Union naval forces led by Adm. David G. Farragut in the Civil War. Additional commercial impetus came with improvement and expansion of harbor facilities (1930s), and installation of Saturn rocket booster plant (1960s). New Orleans is known nationwide as the home of jazz, with its many nightclubs located on Bourbon Street in the French Quarter; site of the annual Mardi Gras, French Market, St Louis Cathedral (1794), Southern Yacht Club (1849), Sugar Bowl, Louisiana Superdome, jazz museum, and many antebellum houses; among its many educational institutions are Tulane University (1834), Loyola University (1849), Dillard University (1869), Louisiana State at New Orleans (1958); transportation center. Imports: coffee, sugar, bananas. Exports: oil, petrochemicals, rice, cotton, lumber, sulfur. Industries: food processing, petroleum, natural gas, oil and sugar refining, shipbuilding and repair, tourism, aluminum, petrochemicals, paper products, furniture. Founded 1718 by the Sieur de Bienville; inc. 1805. Pop. (1980) 557,482.

Newport, city and port in SE Rhode Island, on S Aquidneck Island in Narragansett Bay; seat of Newport co. It was founded 1639 by religious refugees from Massachusetts Bay led by William Coddington and John Clarke; united with Portsmouth 1640; joined Incorporation of Providence Plantations 1644; held by British during the American Revolution. Newport served as joint state capital with Providence until 1900. During 19th century, it developed into a fashionable resort area; its houses remain a popular tourist attraction; site of The Breakers (former summer residence of Cornelius Vanderbilt), Trinity Church (1726), Wanton-Lyman-Hazard House (1675), state house (1739), Touro Synagogue (1763), America's Cup races, National Tennis Hall of Fame, jazz and folk festivals, Salve Regina College (1934), US Naval War College (1885), US Naval Underwater Ordnance Station. Tourism is the chief industry. Inc. 1784. Pop. (1980) 29,259.

Newport Beach, city in S California, 18mi (29km) SE of Long Beach; tourist resort and yachting center. Industries: electronic equipment, boats, plastics. Inc. 1906. Pop. (1980) 63,475.

Newport News, city in SE Virginia, 11mi (18km) NNW of Norfolk, on James River; comprises Port of Hampton Roads, together with Norfolk and Portsmouth; scene of Civil War naval battle between *Monitor* and *Merrimac* (1862); embarkation point during both world wars; site of Mariners' Museum (1930); one of world's largest shipbuilding and repair centers. Exports: coal, oil, tobacco, grain. Industries: food processing, metal products, building materials, textiles, paper, oil refining. Settled 1620 by Irish colonists; inc. 1896. Pop. (1980) 144,903.

New Rochelle, city in SE New York, on Long Island Sound; site of College of New Rochelle (1904), Iona College (1940), preserved home of Thomas Paine. Settled by Huguenots 1688, and named for La Rochelle, France; inc. as village 1858, as city 1899. Pop. (1980) 70,794.

New South Wales, state in SE Australia, bordered by the Tasman Sea (E) which forms 680mi (1,095km) of coastline. The natural-surf beaches, Blue Mts, and

Taos pueblo, New Mexico

Isaac Newton

New York City

snowfields in the Alps are popular tourist attractions. Sydney is the capital city, center of transportation and commerce, and has one of the world's finest harbors. Industries: iron, steel, textiles, agricultural machinery, cement, paper, petrochemicals, electrical equipment. Discovered by Captain Cook 1770; first settled at Botany Bay 1788; became part of the Commonwealth of Australia 1901. Area: 309,433sq mi (801,431sq km). Pop. 4,567,000.

New Spain, an administrative area within the Spanish colonial empire, centered in Mexico City. New Spain, the first permanent viceroyalty on the American mainland, was created in 1535. The viceroyalty covered a vast area: present-day Mexico; Central America; the SW United States; Florida; the West Indies; the Philippines.

New Stone Age. *See* Neolithic Age.

New Sweden (1638–55), colony on the Delaware River, including parts of Delaware, New Jersey, and Pennsylvania. First settled by Peter Minuit for the New Sweden Co. (1638), the area was absorbed into New Netherland by Peter Stuyvesant in 1655.

Newt, tailed amphibian, often called salamander, of Europe, Asia, and North America. European newt is terrestrial except during the breeding season when it is aquatic and the male develops ornamental fins. Fertilization is internal. Family Salamandridae. *See also* Amphibia; Salamander.

New Testament, 27 books of the Christian Bible consisting of the 4 Gospels, Acts of the Apostles, 21 Epistles, and Revelation. They were written in Greek during the early Christian era. They were approved in this order and form by 367. *See also* individual books.

Newton, (Sir) Isaac (1642–1727), English scientist. He became professor of mathematics at Cambridge in 1669, remaining there until 1696 when he was appointed warden of the mint. He was a member of Parliament for Cambridge and was knighted in 1705. Working at home during the 18-month closure (starting in 1664) of Cambridge University during the plague, he made his greatest discoveries: the law of gravitation, the laws of motion, the binomial theorem and the method of fluxions (the basis of calculus), and the combination of the colors of the spectrum to form white light (leading to the invention of the reflecting telescope). He invented infinitesimal calculus, of which the two divisions are differential and integral calculus, and derived the inverse square law.

Newton's major scientific discoveries were published in two works: *Philosophiae Naturalis Principia Mathematica* (1687) and *Opticks* (1704). The latter postulated a combination of the wave and corpuscular theories of light similar to the present view. He was a querulous man frequently in dispute with his contemporaries (notably Robert Hooke, who claimed he had stolen his ideas, and Gottfried Leibniz, who claimed to have invented the calculus). *See also* Calculus; Gravity; Spectrum.

Newton, city in NE Massachusetts, 7mi (11km) W of Boston, on Charles River; site of Newton College of Sacred Heart (1946), Andover Newton Theological Seminary (1825), Mount Alvernia College (1959), Mount Ida Junior College (1889), and homes of Samuel Francis Smith, Horace Mann, Nathaniel Hawthorne; birthplace of Roger Sherman (1721), signer of Declaration of Independence. Industries: paper, thread, yarn. Founded 1631. Pop. (1980) 83,622.

Newton, the unit of force in the metric meter-kilogram-second (mks) system of units. One newton is the force that gives a mass of one kilogram an acceleration of one meter per second per second. One pound is equivalent to 4.45 newtons. *See also* Dyne.

New York, state in the NE United States, on the Atlantic Ocean. New York City is in the extreme S.
Land and Economy. The seacoast is short, but New York harbor is one of the world's finest. The state's interior is mountainous in the E; the Catskills in the SE and the Adirondacks in the NE are the main systems. To the W stretches a gently rolling plateau. The Hudson River in the E empties into New York Bay. Its main tributary is the Mohawk River. Other important rivers are the Delaware and the Genesee. In the W, the state borders on two of the Great Lakes—Ontario and Erie. It is the only state that touches the ocean and the Great Lakes. In the NE, Lake Champlain forms a border with Vermont. There are more than 2,000 other lakes. New York's economy is one of the nation's richest. Its manufacturing and agriculture are varied. The port of New York is among the world's leaders, and the city is a transportation and distribution center, the focus of highways, air and rail lines, and water routes. It is also the nation's financial capital and many corporations have their headquarters in the city and its suburbs. Heavy industry is concentrated in the "upstate" cities.
People. From 1820–1964, when California surpassed it, New York was the most populous state in the Union. About 85% of its inhabitants live in urban areas. Traditionally, the population has been ethnically diverse. In the 19th century, New York—still the nation's largest city—was the port of entry for hundreds of thousands of immigrants from overseas, and many remained in the state to work in the factories or on transportation lines. Their descendants constitute a large segment of the population.
Education. There are more than 250 institutions of higher education. The State University of New York comprises about 25 university and college campuses. Columbia University and New York University in New York City are leading privately endowed institutions. The US Military Academy is at West Point.
History. Henry Hudson, an English navigator in the service of the Netherlands, discovered New York Bay and sailed up the river that bears his name in 1609, laying claim to the surrounding territory. Settlement began up the Hudson Valley, and the colony was named New Netherland. The English seized it in 1664 and renamed it New York. As a royal province, New York became a leader among the American colonies. It played a major part in the Revolution. Almost 100 engagements were fought in the colony, including the Battle of Freeman's Farm, or Second Battle of Saratoga, which was a turning point of the war. The opening of the Erie Canal in 1825, linking the Hudson with Lake Erie and creating a water route to the West through the Great Lakes, was an enormous stimulus to economic growth. New York sent about 500,000 men into the Union army in the Civil War. In later decades, its economic power, great population, and voting strength in national elections exerted tremendous influence in the nation's affairs. During the late 1970s, New York City narrowly avoided defaulting on its loans, and many other cities were affected by an industrial slowdown.

PROFILE

Admitted to Union: July 26, 1788; 11th of the 13 original states to ratify the US Constitution
US Congressmen: Senate, 2; House of Representatives, 39
Population: 17,557,288 (1980); rank, 2d
Capital: Albany, 101,727 (1980)

Chief cities: New York, 7,071,030; Buffalo, 357,870; Rochester, 241,741
State legislature: Senate, 60; Assembly, 150
Area: 49,576sq mi (128,402sq km); rank, 30th
Elevation: Highest, 5,344ft (1,630m), Mt Marcy; lowest, sea level
Industries (major products): apparel, publications, instruments, processed foods, paper and paper products, jewelry, sporting goods
Agriculture (major products): dairy products, apples, grapes, vegetables, poultry
Minerals (major): talc, titanium, garnet, salt, zinc
State nickname: Empire State
State motto: Excelsior (Higher)
State bird: bluebird
State flower: rose
State tree: sugar maple

New York City, largest city in population in the United States, in SE New York State at the mouth of the Hudson River; comprised of five boroughs: Manhattan, the Bronx, Brooklyn, Queens, and Richmond. The greater metropolitan area extends into SW Connecticut, SE New York state, and parts of NE New Jersey and W Long Island. New York is a great world trade center and financial hub.

Originally a trading post under Henry Hudson and Adriaen Block (c.1610), Manhattan Island was bought 1626 from Indians by Peter Minuit of the Dutch West India Co., allegedly for $24 worth of beads and trinkets. New Amsterdam was the chief settlement, at the S end of Manhattan. In 1664 the British took the colony and renamed it New York, for the Duke of York; Dutch regained power for brief period (1673–74). A new charter was est. 1686 as citizens' dissent from British rule grew, culminating in an unsuccessful uprising 1689–91 led by Jacob Leisler; revolutionary sentiment increased with British imposition of the Stamp Act (1765), and solidified under the New York Sons of Liberty, who banished Governor Tryon and a British regiment from the city 1775; the city was unsuccessfully defended by George Washington 1776 and Britain held the city until 1783. New York served as the nation's capital 1789–90; Pres. George Washington was inaugurated at New York's Federal Hall.

The founding of the Bank of New York by Alexander Hamilton, and the opening of the Erie Canal (1825) made New York the principal US commercial and financial center. Following the Civil War, New York experienced a great influx of immigrants. The Greater New York Charter, unifying the five boroughs, was passed May 21, 1897. New York became the home of the United Nations 1945.

Noted areas of New York include Wall Street, Harlem, Fifth Avenue, Greenwich Village. Monuments and notable buildings include Grant's Tomb, Statue of Liberty, Fraunces Tavern (built 1719), St Patrick's Cathedral, the Cathedral of St John the Divine, Empire State Building, the World Trade Center, the United Nations Building, and the Pan Am Building. New York is the site of the Metropolitan Museum of Art, Museum of Modern Art, Museum of Natural History, Radio City Music Hall, Lincoln Center, and Carnegie Hall. The city hosts over 30 colleges and universities. Professional sports teams include New York Yankees and New York Mets (baseball), New York Jets (football), New York Rangers (hockey), New York Knickerbockers (basketball), and it is a boxing center. Area (with water surface): 365sq mi (945sq km). Pop. (1980) 7,071,030.

New York Times v. Sullivan (1964), landmark US Supreme Court decision reversing a libel conviction on the grounds that a state law did not afford enough protection for the freedoms of speech and the press. The court recognized that some falsehood was inevitable under a system of free debate and said only knowing lies regarding public officials could be considered actionable.

New Zealand, independent nation in S Pacific, a member of the Commonwealth of Nations. Populated mainly by descendants of English-speaking immigrants and indigenous Maoris, it has developed a high standard of living in an economy based on sheep-raising and dairy products.

Land and Economy. Located 1,200mi (1,932km) SE of Australia in the SW Pacific, New Zealand is composed of two islands, North Island and South Island, separated by the Cook Strait. With the exception of the flat Canterbury Plain, 3,000,000acres (1,215,000hectares) of rich grain-growing and sheep-raising land, much of South Island is formed by the Southern Alps, with peaks above 10,000ft (3,050m). Along the SW coast are fjords and mountains. The center of North Island is a volcanic plateau, and the base is the fertile plain of three rivers, constituting the major butter-producing area. The longest river in the country is the Waikato, 270mi (435km). Climate is delineated by regional contrasts, without extremes. Agriculture supports a high standard of living although 1971 inflation resulted in wage and price controls. Meat is the largest single export (24%), followed by wool and hides (22%) and butter and cheese (9%). Imports are principally manufactured products and petroleum. After the United Kingdom—formerly New Zealand's leading purchaser of meat and dairy products—joined the European Economic Community (1973), the UK greatly restricted its imports of New Zealand's products, resulting in a serious trade deficit.

People. Of New Zealand's total population, about 250,000 are indigenous Maoris of Polynesian descent; the remainder are mostly British. Dominant religions are Anglican (35%), Presbyterian (22%), and Roman Catholic (16%). The official language is English; Maori is still spoken. The literacy rate is 90%. About half the population lives in the four main cities—Auckland, Wellington, Christchurch, and Dunedin. Education is free and compulsory. The social security system includes education, medical, and pension benefits.

Government. New Zealand has a parliamentary system as an independent member of the British Commonwealth. The leader of the political party winning the majority of seats in the elected unicameral body is prime minister.

History. The discovery of New Zealand in 1642 by the Dutch navigator Abel Janszoon Tasman was followed by Capt. James Cook's exploration for the British (1769–70). Sealing, whaling, and lumbering attracted white settlers, and in 1840, Great Britain annexed New Zealand and signed a treaty with Maori tribes, who nevertheless continued their struggle against colonization. Parliamentary government came in 1890, and full autonomy was granted in 1947 through the Statute of Westminster. The global recession in the 1970s that depressed New Zealand's economy was a major factor in a landslide victory for the National party over the Labour party in 1975 elections. The National Party introduced austerity measures, including wage freezes; rising unemployment, a problem during the late 1970s and early 1980s, seemed to be reversed by 1983. New Zealand's antinuclear policy strained relations with the US and France in 1985 when it protested the presence of US warships in its harbors and the French nuclear tests nearby.

PROFILE

Official name: New Zealand
Area: 103,736sq mi (268,676sq km)
Population: 3,095,000
Density: 30 per sq mi (12 per sq km)
Chief cities: Wellington (capital); Auckland; Christchurch
Government: parliamentary, member of Commonwealth of Nations
Religion: Anglican and Presbyterian
Language: English
Monetary unit: New Zealand dollar
Gross national product: $11,700,000,000
Per capita income: $3,930
Industries: processed foods, meat products, wood products, cement, fertilizers, pulp, paper, steel, aluminum
Agriculture: wheat, sheep, beef cattle, forests, potatoes
Minerals: iron, natural gas
Trading partners: United Kingdom, United States, Australia

Ney, Michel, Duc d'Elchingen, Prince de La Moskova (1769–1815), French marshal, fought in Revolutionary and Napoleonic armies, called by Napoleon "the bravest of the brave" at Friedland (1807) and in the retreat from Russia. Urged Napoleon to abdicate and was sent by the Bourbons to stop Napoleon's return to Paris at the beginning of the Hundred Days (1815); instead he joined Napoleon and distinguished himself for bravery at Waterloo. Condemned for treason, he was executed by firing squad.

Nez Percé, from the French for "pierced nose," referring to their custom of wearing nose ornaments. A major Shahaptian-speaking tribe of North American Indians living in central Idaho, SW Washington, and NE Oregon. Famous for their skill as breeders of fine horses, about 1,750 reside on the Lapwai Reservation in Idaho.

Niagara Falls, city in SE Ontario, Canada, on the Niagara River; noted for view of falls from Queen Victoria Park. Industries: hydroelectric power, chemicals, fertilizers, silverware, sporting goods. Founded 1853; inc. 1904. Pop. 65,271.

Niagara Falls, city in W New York, 17mi (27km) NW of Buffalo, on the Niagara River above and below the falls of the river; site of Niagara Reservation State Park, Niagara Falls power plant (1890), Niagara University (1856), Niagara County Community College (1963); connected with Niagara Falls, Canada, by two bridges over Niagara River. Industries: electrochemicals, electrometallurgy, batteries, paper products, breakfast foods, tourism. Founded as two separate villages (Niagara Falls and Suspension Bridge) that combined and inc. as a city 1892. Pop. (1980) 71,384.

Niagara Falls, great falls of Niagara River on boundary of United States (W New York) and Canada (SE Ontario). Divided by Goat Island into Horseshoe or Canadian Falls and American Falls, the falls were discovered by Father Louis Hennepin in 1678; power from falls was first used in 1882 to light streets of Niagara Falls. Falls drop 158ft (48m) on Canadian side and 167ft (51m) on American side. Face of Canadian Falls is 2,600ft (793m) and American is 1,000ft (305m). Cave of Winds, Whirlpool Rapids, Luna Falls are part of US Niagara Reservation State Park; Canadian government maintains Queen Victoria Park.

Niamey, capital of Niger, Africa, in SW Niger on the Niger River. Located at junction of two main highways, it has port facilities on river; largest city and economic, commercial, and cultural hub of country; became capital 1926. Industries: oil, bricks, food products (especially nuts). Pop. 102,000.

Nibelungenlied, a popular epic taken from Germanic sources and written in Middle High German *c.* 1203 by an unknown author. It resembles the Old Norse *Edda* poems and deals with some of the same characters (Siegfried, Kriemhild, Brünhilde, Gunther, Gudrun, and Hagen), but was written earlier than the *Edda.* The work features the Nibelung treasure, dragons, mermaids, and magic elements, but unlike the *Chanson de Roland* and other national epics, it deals primarily with the personal rivalries and adventures of the characters, not with events of national interest performed by idealized heroes.

Nicaea, one of the chief cities of ancient Bithynia, Asia Minor. The seat of two ecumenical councils (AD 325,-787), it fell to the Seljuk Turks in 1078, then to the Crusaders in 1097. After 1333 the Turks held the city permanently.

Nicaea, Councils of. The First Council of Nicaea (AD 325) met at the order of Constantine I (the Great) of Rome. This first ecumenical council was attended by the major Eastern bishops, four Western bishops, and two papal legates. In conflict with Arianism, the council adopted a creed or test of faith that stated the divinity of Christ the Son and His position of equality within the Trinity. Arius and the two other bishops who refused to accept the creed were exiled to Illyricum. The council deliberated on other church matters and was the model for later church councils including the Second Council of Nicaea (787) convened by Irene, the Byzantine Empress. This was the seventh ecumenical council and the last to be recognized as such by both branches of the Catholic church. Its members ruled against the worship of images (iconoclasm). *See also* Arianism.

Nicaea, Empire of (1206–61), Greek empire founded by Theodore I (Lascaris) after the 4th Crusade overthrow of the Eastern Roman (Byzantine) Empire. Through conquest and alliance, the empire grew more powerful until, in 1261, Constantinople was finally recaptured from the Latins and the Byzantine Empire was restored.

Nicaragua, republic in Central America, bounded by the Caribbean Sea (E), Honduras (N), Costa Rica (S), and Pacific Ocean (W); the capital is Managua. The land area can be viewed as 3 main regions: a triangular area S inland from the Caribbean Sea, consisting of folded faulted structures; a low E coastal plain, Mosquito; and the most inhabited region, a lowland area extending from the Gulf of Fonseca NW to Costa Rican border. Approx. 50% of the land is forested, yielding products of fibers, medicines, balsams, resins, gum, and various woods. Agriculture, the chief economic activity, has been aided by the 1951 National Development Institute and the Nicaraguan Technical Agricultural Service (STAN) 1933, a joint project with US technical assistance. The United States proposed construction of a canal, by the Bryan-Chamorro Treaty 1916, to connect the Pacific Ocean and Caribbean Sea; however due to continuing political disputes, negotiations were terminated 1970. Chief crops are cotton, coffee, corn, beans, rice, sugar cane, cottonseed, cacao, citrus fruits, tobacco, sesame seeds, wheat. Industries include lumbering, refining sugar, cigars, matches, soap, cement, leather, textiles, clothing, soft drinks, beer, shoes. Chief minerals are gold, silver, salt, gypsum, marble. The majority of Nicaraguans are mestizos (85%), mulattoes (10%), and pure Indians (5%); about 90% are Roman Catholic.

Nicaragua's coast, inhabited by Indian tribes called Miskitos, was discovered by Columbus 1502; Fernandes Córdoba founded Granada and León in 1523. In mid-17th century the Mosquito coast in Nicaragua and Honduras became a British protectorate, but in 1786 Great Britain recognized Spanish title to Caribbean coast and in 1838 Nicaragua became independent; Managua was made capital 1855. William Walker, from Tennessee, seized Nicaragua and made himself president 1856; he was driven out of Nicaragua 1857, returned 1860 and was executed; his death helped unite Nicaragua's two political parties. The conservatives won power in 1863, and ruled stably for 30 years. In 1936, Anastasio Somoza Garcia, commander of the National Guard, seized power and ruled until 1956 when he was assassinated. In 1967 his son, Anastasio Somoza Debayle, was elected president. Widespread opposition to the Somoza regime erupted into civil war (1979) between the Sandinista National Liberation Front and other rebel groups and the National Guard. When the Sandinistas took the capital, Somoza fled the country, and a Sandinista junta seized control of the government. As the new government developed ties with Cuba and the USSR, relations with the United States, which during the mid-1980s openly called for support of the Contras (anti-Sandinistas), were increasingly strained. Border skirmishes with Honduras continued.

PROFILE

Official name: Nicaragua
Area: 49,579sq mi (148,000sq km)
Population: 2,587,000
Chief cities: Managua, capital; León; Matagalpa
Religion: Roman Catholic
Language: Spanish
Monetary unit: Cordoba

Nicaragua, lake in SW Nicaragua; largest lake in Central America, receives waters of Lake Managua via Tipitapa River. Area was part of ocean until land rose around it; salt water fish such as sharks have adapted to the change from saline to fresh water. San Juan River drains the lake into the Caribbean Sea. Area: 3,089sq mi (8,001sq km).

Nice, city in SE France, on Mediterranean Sea; capital of Alpes-Maritimes dept. Part of the House of Savoy in 13th and 14th centuries, it was held by France 1792–1814, when it was returned to Savoy until passed to France in 1860. The major French Riviera tourist center, it is scene of the Carnival of Nice held annually in January and February, ending on Shrove Tuesday; noted for villas and boulevards, of which Promenade des Anglais (1822) is the most outstanding; site of 17th-century cathedral, and the Croix de Marbre. Industries: tourism, olive oil, perfumes, electronics, cut flowers. Founded 5th century BC as Greek colony. Pop. 346,620.

Nicene Creed, a statement of Christian faith adopted at the Council of Nicaea in 325. The creed was formulated to uphold orthodox Christian doctrine against the Arian heresy. Followers of Arius held that Jesus was neither wholly God nor wholly man. The Nicene Creed affirms belief in". . .the only-begotten Son of God. . . Being of one substance with the Father." This creed is used by the Roman Catholic and Anglican churches and, with one difference in wording, by the Orthodox Eastern Church.

Nicholas I (800?–867), Roman Catholic pope (858–67) and saint, also known as Nicholas the Great. A stern ruler, he upheld apostolic succession and supported St Ignatius of Constantinople against Photius, who objected to the filioque clause in the Nicene Creed. This controversy led to the split between Eastern and Western Christianity.

Nicholas I (1796–1855), tsar of Russia (1825–55). Ascending the throne in 1825, he was immediately confronted with and crushed the Decembrist revolt that

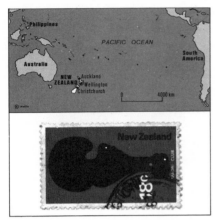

New Zealand

Nicaragua

Niger

sought a constitutional monarchy (1825). He was successful in wars against Persia (1826–28) and Turkey (1828–29), gaining strategic territory for Russia. In 1830–31 he brutally suppressed a Polish revolt, abrogating Polish autonomy. Between 1832–33 Russian law was codified. Modest improvements were made in the position of serfs, but the secret police was expanded, censorship increased, and minorities and liberals suppressed. In 1849 Russia assisted Austria in suppressing the Hungarian revolt. Russian pressure on Turkey led to the Crimean War (1853–56).

Nicholas II (1868–1918), last tsar of Russia (1894–1917). During his reign, Russia occupied Port Arthur (1896) and Manchuria (1900), fought the disastrous Russo-Japanese War (1904–05), and saw the Revolution of 1905 that forced him to approve a legislative assembly *(Duma)*. In World War I he supervised the armed forces, leaving the government to his wife, who was under the influence of Rasputin. Ineffectual and reactionary, after the revolution of March 1917 he abdicated and was sent to Siberia. He and his family were executed in July 1918.

Nicholas of Myra, Saint, the saint whose legends gave rise to the story of Santa Claus. Almost nothing is known about his life, but by tradition he was Bishop of Myra in the first half of the 4th century. He became a popular saint in the Middle Ages and is the patron saint of Greece and Russia. Many legends were told about him. In one, he restored to life three murdered boys; hence he is the patron of children. In another, he secretly gave gold to three poor girls as their dowry. From this came the custom of giving presents on the Eve of St Nicholas—a custom later transferred to Christmas Eve. The saint's name in Dutch, Sant Nikolaas, became Santa Claus.

Nicholson, Ben (1894–1982), English painter. He was a leading member of the abstract art movement in England. Influenced by the cubism of Georges Braque and the neoplasticism of Piet Mondrian, his work consisted mainly of semi-abstract still lifes in the 1920s. In the 1930s he began working on reliefs and in the 1940s on landscapes containing elements of still lifes. His later work took a geometrical form.

Nickel, metallic element of the first transition series, discovered in 1751 by A.F. Cronstedt. Chief ore is pentlandite. The main commercial use is in stainless steels and other special alloys. Nickel is also used in coinage and as a hydrogenation catalyst. The metal is ferromagnetic. Properties: at. no. 28; at. wt. 58.71; sp gr 8.902; melt. pt. 2,647°F (1,453°C); boil. pt. 4,950°F (2,732°C); most common isotope Ni^{58} (68.274%). *See also* Transition Elements.

Nicklaus, Jack (William) (1940–), US golfer, b. Columbus, Ohio. He won the US Amateur title (1959, 1961), turned professional in 1961, and won six Masters Tournaments (1963, 1965, 1966, 1972, 1975, 1986). He also won four Professional Golf Association championships (1963, 1971, 1973, 1980), three US Opens (1962, 1967, 1972), and three British Opens (1966, 1970, 1978). Often acclaimed as the sport's greatest player, he is the leading money winner of all time in professional golf.

Nicobar Islands, island group in Bay of Bengal, India; includes 19 small islands, divided into three groups. Population is mainly Mongoloid stock; held by Japanese during WWII; exports tropical fruit. Area: 707sq mi (1,831sq km). Pop. 14,563.

Nicola, Pisano (*fl.* 1260–78), Italian sculptor. His innovative work helped lay the foundation of the classic

Renaissance style. His works include the pulpit in the Pisa Baptistry, the pulpit in Siena Cathedral (1265–68), and the design for the Arca of St Dominico, Bologna (1267).

Nicosia (Levkosia), capital city of Cyprus, in the N central part of island; capital of Nicosia district. For 300 years descendants of France's Guy Lusignan ruled the island, and Nicosia was their capital. Their reign ended in 1489 when Venetians took the city; ruins of circular walls and fortifications survive from this period. Turks held city 1571–1878, when it passed to British. In 1960 Cyprus became an independent nation and Nicosia continued as capital; site of 13th-century church of St Sophia (now a mosque). Industries: cigarettes, pottery, leather, textiles. Pop. 115,700.

Nicotiana, genus of mainly New World herbs resembling henbane; it is the source of tobacco. There are about 60 species: 45 native to the Americas, 14 to Australia, and 1 to Pacific islands. *N. tabacum,* originally a tropical species, is the source of commercial tobacco, although *N. rustica,* a shrubby plant native to eastern North America, has a higher nicotine content and was used by the Indians. Other species include jasmine tobacco, *N. alata,* which has tubular flowers that open at dusk and emit a jasmine odor. Family Solanaceae. *See also* Tobacco.

Nicotinic Acid, vitamin of the B complex, lack of which causes the disease pellagra. *See* Vitamin.

Niebuhr, Reinhold (1892–1971), US Protestant theologian, b. Detroit. He became a professor of theology at Union Theological Seminary (1928) after having been a pastor in Detroit. An activist and controversialist, he participated in the formation of the National Council of Churches and Americans for Democratic Action and wrote 17 books, including *Moral Man and Immoral Society* (1932). Niebuhr became increasingly more conservative in later life, and critical of the socialism and pacifism he once espoused.

Niello, method of decorating silver or gold objects with incised designs filled with a black alloy. This method was used in Byzantine and Oriental art and became extremely popular in Italy in the 15th century.

Nielsbohrium. *See* Element 105.

Niépce, Joseph (Nicéphore) (1765–1833), French chemist, inventor of the heliography process. Using camera and lens, he obtained unstable negatives in 1816 and permanent images by 1822. He worked with Louis Daguerre from 1829 until his death, after which Daguerre perfected their process, known as daguerreotypy.

Nietzsche, Friedrich (1844–1900), German philosopher. He studied classical philosophy at Bonn and taught at Basel (1869). He met and broke with Richard Wagner (1874). His *Birth of Tragedy* (1872) betrays the influence of Wagner's art. In 1879 he abandoned philology for philosophy, and celebrated his new notion of the "free spirit" in *Thus Spake Zarathustra* (1883–91). His aphoristic method was either misunderstood or ignored, and his later works, *Beyond Good & Evil* (1886), *On the Genealogy of Morals* (1887), *Ecce Homo* (1888) became increasingly shrill.

Niger, republic in W Africa, bounded by Nigeria (S), Benin and Upper Volta (SW), Mali (W), Chad (E), Algeria and Libya (N). The country is land-locked and mostly arid, except along the Niger River in the SW and near the Nigerian border in S where there are strips of savanna land.

The economy is based on agriculture, employing about 90% of the labor force. Chief crops are corn, millet, groundnuts, rice, sorghum, cassava, sugar cane, dates; livestock including camels are raised. Industries are few, and include processed foods, bricks, cement, beverages, shoes, ginned cotton, construction materials, radios, and fishing. In the 1970s a processing plant was opened for production of high grade uranium found in the Air Mts, N central region. In 1974, Niger became a charter member of the West African Economic Community. During the dry season (September–May), approx. 100,000 farmers migrate to the Ivory Coast and Ghana for employment. The people are predominantly black Africans, 55% Hausa, 24% Djerma and Songhai tribes, 3% Tuareg; most live in the S, and are overwhelmingly Islamic.

History and Government. In the 14th century the Hausa people founded several city-states in S Niger; the 16th century brought Songhai empire rule to Niger; and by the 17th century, Djerma people had settled the SW. The Fulani tribe took control of S Niger in the early 19th century. The Conference of Berlin (1884–85) granted Niger territory to French, and it became a separate French colony 1922 with Zinder as capital, replaced by Niamey 1926. In 1946, Niger was granted an autonomous assembly, and in 1960 independence was granted; the leader of the Niger Progressive Party (PPN), Hamani Diori, became the republic's first president. Diori was reelected 1965 and 1970. Niger was the country most seriously affected by the Sahel drought of 1968–74. Diori was unable to control the resulting economic dislocation and in 1974 was deposed in a military coup. During the late 1970s civilians were added to the cabinet. Drought, lasting until 1985, created a serious famine.

PROFILE

Official name: Republic of the Niger
Area: 489,189sq mi (1,267,000sq km)
Population: 4,992,000
Chief cities: Niamey (capital); Maradi; Tahoua
Religion: Islam, Animism, Christianity
Language: French (official)
Monetary unit: Franc CFA

Niger, major river in W Africa; rises in the Fouta Djallon plateau in SW Republic of Guinea; flows NE through Guinea into Mali Republic where it forms an extensive inland delta, then flows in a great curve NE, E, and SE across border into Nigeria, then S into Gulf of Guinea through another vast delta. The river's course was determined by explorations by Mungo Park (1795–97) and Richard and John Lander (1830). The inland delta in Mali Republic has supported an irrigation project that has reclaimed 100,000acres (40,500hectares) since 1930; the delta at the Gulf of Guinea is a source of petroleum and palm oil; the river is also a major source of tigerfish and perch; at various points it has been dammed to create hydroelectric power. It is navigable (but not continuously due to rapids and bars) for over 1,000mi (1,610km) of its 2,600mi (4,186km) course.

Nigeria, independent nation in W Africa. Divided by tribal rivalries, it has experienced considerable unrest since independence. Petroleum is its economic mainstay. Nigeria is the most populous country in Africa.

Land and Economy. The most populous African country, Nigeria sits on the W coast of the continent bounded on the S by the Gulf of Guinea, with Cameroon (W), Chad (NW), Niger (N), and Benin (E) on its borders. Topographic regions, divided according to altitude and climate, are: hot, humid coast of mangrove swamps; a zone 50–100mi (81–161km) wide N of the swamps with tropical rain forest and palm oil plantations; a relatively dry central plateau making up the largest N portion; and the semi-desert in the extreme

N. Its navigable rivers—the Niger, the Benue, and the Cross—provide major transportation routes. Nigeria has two seasons, dry and wet. Annual rainfall varies from 150in (381cm) on the coast to 23in (58cm) in the N. Only 23% of the gross domestic product is derived from agriculture, forestry and fishing. By 1970, Nigeria's offshore and river petroleum deposits had made it one of the 10 largest oil-exporting lands in the world, accounting for 90% of export revenue. Oil profits are being used to develop heavy industry and improve agriculture to make Nigeria self-sufficient in food crops.

People. An ethnically diverse country, Nigeria has about 250 separate tribal groups, each speaking its own language. English is the official tongue. The three largest groups, constituting 60% of the total, are the Ibo of the E; the Muslim Yoruba of the W; and Hausa and Fulani, also Muslim, of the N. Islam is practiced by 44% of the population, animism by 34%, and Christianity by 22%.

Government. According to the constitution of 1979, legislative power is vested in the popularly-elected National Assembly, composed of a 95-member Senate and 449-member House of Representatives. Executive authority is vested in the popularly-elected president, who appoints the cabinet. Each of the 19 states has partial autonomy.

History. Europeans in search of trade brought colonial rule to Nigeria. By 1886, British interests had chartered the Royal Niger Co. The Crown, in an effort to consolidate the slave trade and to promote commercial interests, united the area in 1914 as a colony and protectorate. Africans were slowly added to the government structure, and in 1960, Nigeria was granted full independence as a federation under a parliamentary form of government. In 1963, Nigeria took another step and declared itself a federal republic. Tribal and racial tensions evoked a successful revolt in 1966 by army units under Maj. Gen. J.T.U. Aguiyi-Ironsi. He was killed in a second coup later in the year, and Lt. Col. Yakubu Gowon emerged as head of the Federal Military Government (FMG). Tribal unrest continued, and in 1967 the Ibos in the E announced secession from Nigeria and the formation of the Republic of Biafra. After a savage civil war, Biafra was conquered and reunited with Nigeria (1970). A lack of reprisals after the conflict helped to heal the wounds of war. Gowon ruled until 1975 when he was overthrown in a bloodless military coup. In 1979 the military returned the country to civilian democratic government. Coups in 1983 and 1985 returned the government to military rule. Despite dramatic economic growth in the 1960s and 1970s, Nigeria experienced economic difficulties during the late 1970s and 1980s due to inflation and a worldwide fall in demand for oil.

PROFILE

Official name: Federal Republic of Nigeria
Area: 356,669sq mi (923,773sq km)
Population: 82,503,000
Density: 231per sq mi (89per sq km)
Chief cities: Lagos (capital); Ibadan; Ogbomosho; Kano
Government: military
Religion: Muslim, Christian, Animist
Language: tribal tongues and English
Monetary unit: Naira
Gross national product: $55,310,000,000
Per capita income: $250
Industries: processed food, cotton, textiles, cement, petroleum products, rubber goods, forest products
Agriculture: nuts, palm kernels, cacao, rubber trees, cotton, cattle, fish, tobacco, forests
Minerals: oil, coal, iron, limestone, natural gas, tin
Trading partners: European Economic Community, United Kingdom, United States, Japan

Night Blindness, an early symptom of vitamin A deficiency. The vitamin is necessary for the production of rhodopsin, a retinal substance vital to vision during times of low illumination.

Nighthawk, North American goatsucker with buff to black mottled feathers. It lays its eggs on a gravel-covered roof that hides them. Species *Chordeiles minor. See also* Goatsucker.

Night Heron, thick-billed night-feeding bird with well-developed, ornamental head plumes, especially at breeding time. Length: 2ft (0.6m). Genera: *Nycticorax* and *Gorsachius. See also* Heron.

Nightingale, Florence (1820–1910), British nurse, *b.* Italy. She founded modern nursing and is best known for activities in the Crimean War. In 1854 she took a unit of 38 nurses to care for wounded British soldiers. Called "the Lady with the Lamp," she believed that nursing should continue night and day. In 1860 she founded the Nightingale School and Home for nurses' training at St. Thomas's Hospital, London. She was widely honored and in 1907 became the first woman to be awarded Britain's Order of Merit.

Nightingale, European thrush known for its beautiful nocturnal song. It has a brownish back and pale brown underparts with a reddish tail and rump, similar to the North American hermit thrush. Some tropical American thrushes (genus *Catharus)* are also called nightingales. Length: 6.5in (16cm). Species *Luscinia megarhynchos. See also* Thrush.

Nightmonkey. *See* Douroucouli.

Nightshade, family (Solanaceae) of herbs and shrubs characterized by alternate leaves; 5-petaled, bell-shaped flowers; a fleshy berry or dry capsule fruit; and the presence, in many, of toxic and fatal alkaloids. The 75 genera and 2,000 species include tobacco, petunia, potato, deadly nightshade, and henbane. The common black nightshade, *Solanum nigrum,* is a bushy, spreading plant, 2ft (61cm) tall; its berries are poisonous when green but harmless when ripe.

Nihilism, historically, a 19th-century Russian political philosophy brought to public attention by Ivan Turgenev in the novel *Fathers and Sons* (1861). The nihilists believed that the existing social and economic order must be totally destroyed but had few constructive alternatives. They practiced terrorism and claimed responsibility for the assassination of Tsar Alexander II (1881). Because nihilist doctrines were so vague the movement eventually disintegrated. In the 20th century nihilism has come to signify a philosophical stance that denies an objective basis or intrinsic worth for moral or social values.

Niigata, port city on NW coast of Honshu, Japan, at mouth of Shinano River, opposite Sado Islands; capital of Niigata prefecture; opened to foreign trade 1869. Industries: textiles, fishing, machinery, paper, shipbuilding. Pop. 423,000.

Nijinsky, Vaslav (1890–1950), Russian dancer. Although his career lasted only 12 years (1907–19), he was one of the greatest male ballet dancers. With the Ballet Russe, his most noted roles were in *Pétrouchka, Prince Igor, Les Sylphides,* and *Schéhérazade.* He toured South America, Europe, and the United States. Having become insane, he spent the rest of his life in retirement in England and Switzerland.

Nijmegen, city in E Netherlands, on Waal River, near West German border; site of 16th-century church and town hall; former member of Hanseatic League. Industries: machinery, electronic equipment, shoes, paper. Pop. 148,493.

Nikolayev (Nikolajer), seaport city in Ukrainian SSR, USSR, at confluence of Ingul and Bug rivers; taken by Germans 1941, recaptured by Russia 1944. Industries: shipbuilding, building materials, chemicals, cast iron works. Founded 1784. Pop. 456,000.

Nile (Nahr an-Nil), river in NE Africa; longest river in the world; trunk is at Khartoum at convergence of White Nile and Blue Nile; flows N from E Africa draining basin covering 1,100,000sq mi (2,590,000sq km) or 10% of Africa; enters delta 12mi (19km) N of Cairo, to empty into Mediterranean; site of ancient Egyptian irrigation works dating from 4000 BC; Egypt, Sudan, and other African nations depend almost completely on the Nile as a source of hydroelectric power and irrigation by means of an advanced system of dams, including Aswan High Dam, Gebel Aulia, and Makwar. Length: 4,160mi (6,698km).

Nilgai, or blue buck, large antelope native to the Indian peninsula, mostly in wooded areas. Only males have a throat tuft and small spiked horns. Gray-brown with white markings, its superficial resemblance to Brahman cattle makes it sacred to Hindus. Length: to 82in (2.1m); weight: 440lb (198kg). Family Bovidae; species *Boselaphus tragocamelus.*

Nilotes, large group of Negroid peoples of the upper Nile region of the Sudan and Uganda. They are characteristically tall and slender. Nilotic languages form a closely related group, classified as a branch of the Chari-Nile family. Nilotic peoples include the Luo of Kenya and Uganda, the Masai of Tanzania, and the Dinka and Nuer of the Sudan. There is a great variety of cultures, ranging from the concept of divine kingship among the Shilluk to the political egalitarianism of the Luo and Nuer.

Nimbus, a cloud from which rain is discharged. In meteorological cloud classification it is added to the names of clouds that typically produce rain or snow. Nimbostratus are the true rain clouds, dark and wet-looking with streaks of rain extending to the ground. Cumulonimbus are thunderhead clouds, with bases almost touching the ground and extending upward to 75,000ft (22,875m). These clouds can produce tornadoes.

Nimeiry, Gaafar Muhammad Al (1930–), president of the Sudan (1971–85). Nimeiry took control during a bloodless coup (1969) and was later elected the Sudan's first president. A career army officer, Maj. Gen. Nimeiry stayed in power longer than any other leader since the Sudan's independence in 1956. He was reelected for a six-year term in 1979, but was ousted in a bloodless coup in early 1985. Nimeiry was committed to the reconstruction and development of the Sudan through intensive agricultural programs, but was opposed for his policy of adhering to Islamic law and for his handling of the famine crisis.

Nîmes, city in S France, 64mi (103km) NW of Marseilles; capital of Gard dept. A Roman colony 120 BC, it has been united with French crown since AD 1258; Huguenot stronghold; suffered after Revocation of Edict of Nantes (1685); site of impressive 1st-century Roman Arena (still in use), 2nd-century temple of Diana, 11th-century Cathedral of St Castor, Maison Carée (1st and 2nd centuries), museum of Roman antiquities. Industries: silk, coal, chemicals, metals. Pop. 133,942.

Nimitz, Chester William (1885–1966), US admiral, b. Fredericksburg, Tex. He served with the Atlantic Fleet's submarine division during World War I. When World War II broke out, he replaced Admiral Kimmel as commander in chief of the Pacific fleet, a command he held throughout the war. Nimitz led the landings on Midway (1942), the Solomon Islands (1942–43), the Gilberts (1943), Philippines (1944), and Iwo Jima and Okinawa (1945). After the war, he became chief of naval operations (1945–47).

Nimrod, in Genesis, son of Cush and grandson of Ham. A great hunter and conqueror of the Babylonians, he was the first biblical hero.

Nin, Anaïs (1903–77), US author, b. France. Her novels, all intense psychological studies, include *The House of Incest* (1936), *Winter of Artifice* (1939), and *A Spy in the House of Love* (1954). Extensive portions of her diaries and correspondence were published to critical acclaim in the 1960s and 1970s.

Ninety-Five Theses, document by Martin Luther "On the Power of Indulgences," posted in Wittenberg in 1517. Luther felt that the sale by the Roman Catholic Church of indulgences, which remitted some penalties for sin, interfered with proper penitence. He stated his theses to start a debate on this question. The controversy that followed led to Luther's break with the papacy. *See also* Luther, Martin; Reformation.

Nineveh, ancient capital of Assyria. Existing as early as 1950 BC, its greatest development occurred during the reigns of Sennacherib (705–681 BC) and Assurbanipal. When Nineveh fell to Nabopolassar of Babylonia and his allies (612 BC), the Assyrian empire perished with it.

Ningpo (Ningbo or **Ning-po),** city in E China, 90mi (145km) ESE of Hangchow, on Yung River; site of Portuguese trading center 1533–45; port opened to foreign trade by Treaty of Nanking (1842); under communist control 1949; nearby is birthplace of Chiang Kai-shek. Industries: fishing, textiles, food processing, electrical equipment, furniture, lace. Exports: raw cotton, lumber, tea, fish. Pop. 350,000.

Niobe, in Greek mythology, queen of Thebes, daughter of Tantalus and wife of Amphion. She boasted of how many children she had borne (she had either six or seven of each sex), and said that Leto had only two children. Leto's offspring, Apollo and Artemis, killed all of Niobe's children. Distraught, Niobe fled Thebes. Zeus turned her to stone at Mt Sipylus.

Niobium, or **columbium,** metallic element (symbol Nb) of the second transition series, discovered (1801) by C. Hatchett. Chief ore is columbite-tantalite. The metal is used in alloy steels. Properties: at. no. 41; at. wt. 92.9064; sp gr 8.57; melt. pt. 4,474°F (2,470°C); boil. pt. 8,503°F (4,706°C); most common isotope Nb^{93} (100%). *See also* Transition Elements.

Nippon, or **Nihon,** Japanese name for Japan. It is derived from the Chinese *Jeupenn,* literally "origin of the Sun," from which comes the name "Land of the Rising Sun" for Japan.

Nippur, ancient city of Babylonia. As the seat of the important cult of Enlil, it was the chief religious center of ancient Mesopotamia. It declined gradually after the 7th century BC.

Nirenberg, Marshall W(arren) (1927–), US biochemist, b. New York City. He was awarded part of the 1968 Nobel Prize in physiology or medicine for his part in discoveries about how genes determine cell func-

Nigeria

Richard M. Nixon

Alfred Nobel

tion. Nirenberg found the key to the genetic code, deciphering the particular code triplet for the amino acid phenylalanine.

Nirvana, or **Nibbana,** the indescribable state attained by enlightened beings. Upon death, enlightenment is completed in the state of Parinirvana. In Buddhism, Nirvana is the extinction of craving; in Jainism, it is the place of liberated souls; and in Hinduism, it is the home of liberated souls united with the divine. *See also* Buddhism; Hinduism; Jainism.

Niš (Nish), city in E Yugoslavia, on Nišava River; birthplace of Constantine the Great; site of university (1965). City was taken by Turks 1386; passed to Serbia 1878, and served as capital of Serbia until 1901; taken by Germans 1915 and 1941; by USSR 1944. Industries: tobacco, leather goods, machines. Pop. 128,000.

Nishinomiya, city in SW Honshu, Japan, on Osaka Bay; site of 7th and 8th century temples, Kobe Women's College. Industries: tourism, chemicals, textiles, sake. Pop. 401,000.

Niterói, city in SE Brazil on SE shore of Guanabara Bay opposite Rio de Janeiro; capital of Rio de Janeiro state; site of university (1960). Industries: shipbuilding, tobacco products, chemicals. Founded 1573; made city 1836. Pop. 291,970.

Nitrate, a name applied to any member of two classes of compounds derived from nitric acid. Nitric acid esters are covalent compounds with the structure $R-O-NO_2$ ("R" represents an organic combining group such as ethyl in ethyl nitrate). Nitric acid salts are ionic compounds that contain the nitrate ion and a positive ion, such as $(NH_4)^+$ in ammonium nitrate.

Nitric Acid, colorless fuming corrosive liquid (formula HNO_3) obtained by the oxidation of ammonia in the presence of a platinum catalyst. It is used in the preparation of fertilizers, explosives, and a wide range of chemicals. Properties: sp gr 1.504, melt. pt. $-46.9°F$ ($-41.59°C$).

Nitrites, compounds containing the radical $NO_2\breve{g}$. In the US, sodium nitrite is added to hams, sausages, cold cuts, and other cured meats to prevent botulism and to give the meats a fresh, pink appearance. The practice is regarded as dangerous by some scientists because under certain conditions the nitrite can be transformed into other, carcinogenic compounds. Various nitrites are used in the manufacture of drugs, dyes, explosives, and other chemicals.

Nitrocellulose, or cellulose nitrate, range of compounds prepared by treating cellulose (in the form of linters, cotton waste, cotton wool, or wood pulp) with a mixture of concentrated nitric and sulfuric acids. Nitrocellulose containing 12.5–13.5% nitrogen is used in explosives, such as dynamite and gun cotton, while material containing 10.5–12.2% nitrogen is used in plastics, such as celluloid.

Nitrogen, common gaseous nonmetallic element (symbol N) of group VA of the periodic table, discovered (1772) by Daniel Rutherford. It is the major component of the atmosphere (78% by volume), from which it is extracted by fractionation of liquid air. The main use is in the Haber process for producing ammonia for fertilizers—nitrogen is essential for plant growth. The element is chemically inert. Properties: at. no. 7; at. wt. 14.0067; density 1.2506 g cm^{-3}; melt. pt.

$-345.75°F$ ($-209.86°C$); boil pt. $-320.4°F$ ($-195.8°C$); most common isotope N^{14} (99.63%).

Nitrogen Cycle, circulation of nitrogen through plants and animals in the biosphere. Plants obtain nitrogen compounds for producing essential proteins through assimilation. Nitrogen-fixing bacteria, in the soil or legume root nodules, take free nitrogen from the soil and air to form the nitrogen compounds used by plants to grow. The nitrogen is returned to the soil and air by decay or denitrification, accomplished by denitrifying bacteria.

Nitroglycerin, an oily liquid used in the manufacture of explosives and in medicine to relieve chest pain in chronic heart disease.

Nitrous Oxide, a colorless gas with a pleasant odor, used as an anesthetic or analgesic during surgical or dental procedures. Also known as laughing gas since it initially produces exhilaration, sometimes accompanied by laughter.

Nixon, Richard Milhous (1913–), 37th president of the United States (1969–74), b. Yorba Linda, Calif. He was a graduate of Whittier College (1934) and Duke University Law School (1937). In 1940 he married Thelma Patricia Ryan; they had two daughters. In 1946, Nixon, a young lawyer practicing in Whittier, Calif., was chosen by a group of Republican businessmen to run for the US House of Representatives. He won and became a member of the House Un-American Activities Committee. He achieved national fame there by pursuing the Alger Hiss-Whittaker Chambers spy case. He emphasized his anti-Communism in 1950 when he was elected to the Senate against Helen Gahagan Douglas, whom he accused of being pro-Communist. In 1952, Dwight D. Eisenhower chose him as his vice-presidential running mate.

Nixon's eight years as vice president were unusually active, and in 1960 he was the Republican presidential candidate. He lost the election to John F. Kennedy in a close race. In 1962, Nixon ran unsuccessfully for governor of California; he then moved to New York to practice law. Nixon won the 1968 Republican nomination and the subsequent election.

Nixon was pledged to end the war in Vietnam and began the removal of US forces. He also increased the saturation bombing of North Vietnam and ordered the invasion of Cambodia (1970) and Laos (1971). He eased tensions with the Soviet Union and Communist China, visiting the mainland in 1972. Domestically, there was much unrest; antiwar activists created disturbances, and a severe recession accompanied by inflation caused Nixon to institute (1971) wage-and-price controls.

Nixon and his vice president, Spiro T. Agnew, were reelected in 1972 by a landslide. Almost immediately, however, Nixon was engulfed by revelations of unprecedented corruption in his administration, most of them lumped under the heading of the Watergate affair. There were widespread criticisms of public money spent on Nixon's private houses, and he was found to have greatly underpaid his federal income taxes. At the same time, Agnew was accused of taking bribes while governor of Maryland and while vice president. He was forced to resign, and Nixon appointed Gerald R. Ford to replace him.

In 1974 the Judiciary Committee of the House of Representatives voted a bill of impeachment against Nixon. Before the House could act on impeachment, however, the Supreme Court forced Nixon to release secret tapes that he had made of his private conversations. They revealed that Nixon had lied to the public about his involvement in the Watergate coverup. On Aug. 9, 1974, he resigned from office, the first presi-

dent to do so. A month later his successor, Gerald R. Ford, issued a general pardon to Nixon. A number of his top aides, however, were convicted, fined, and imprisoned.

His writings include *Six Crises* (1962), *RN: The Memoirs of Richard Nixon* (1978), and *The Real War* (1980).

Career: US House of Representatives, 1947–51; US Senate, 1951–53; vice president, 1953–61; president, 1969–74. *See also* Vietnam War; Watergate Affair.

Niznij Tagil (Nizhniy Tagil), city in Russian SFSR, USSR, in the central Urals on the Tagil River, 80mi (129km) NNE of Sverdlovsk; site of teachers' college and museum. Industries: metallurgy, machine tools, agricultural machinery, building materials, chemicals, ceramics, woodworking, mining. Founded 1725; became city 1917. Pop. 403,000.

Nkrumah, Kwame (1909–72), African nationalist and statesman of Ghana. He was educated in Africa and the United States and after returning to Ghana (then the Gold Coast) he formed the Convention People's party in 1949. Building an increasing popular support, he was briefly imprisoned for preaching resistance to the British and led his country to independence in 1957, when he became prime minister. In 1960 he became president and worked steadily to increase his control of Ghanaian government. He alienated his following and was ousted by the military in 1966.

NMR. See Nuclear Magnetic Resonance.

Noah, in the Bible, son of Lamech and 10th in descent from Adam. Chosen by God to survive the Flood, he built the Ark for himself, his family, and pairs of all animals. His sons, Ham, Shem, and Japheth, continued the human race after the flood.

Nobel, Alfred Bernhard (1833–96), Swedish chemist, engineer, and industrialist. He invented dynamite and founded the Nobel Prizes. He received a patent for dynamite in Great Britain in 1866 and in the United States in 1867. In 1876 he patented a more powerful form of blasting gelatin, and in 1888 he produced ballistite, one of the first nitroglycerin smokeless powders. The immense fortune he acquired from the manufacture of explosives and from interests in the Baku oil fields in Russia was bequeathed to establish the prestigious international Nobel Prizes, first awarded in 1901.

Nobelium, radioactive metallic element (symbol No) of the actinide group, made in 1958 by bombarding Cm^{246} with C^{12} nuclei. The element has been made only in trace amounts and has not been identified chemically. Properties: at. no. 102; most stable isotope No^{255} (half-life 3hrs). *See also* Transuranium elements.

Nobel Prizes, awards given each year to individuals or institutions for outstanding contributions in the fields of physics, chemistry, physiology and medicine, literature, peace, and economics. Established in 1901 by the will of Swedish scientist Alfred Bernhard Nobel, the prizes are awarded each December 10. The economics prize was first awarded in 1969. Four committees are designated to select the winning candidates: the Swedish Academy of Science for physics, chemistry, and economics; the Caroline Institute in Stockholm for physiology and medicine; the Swedish Academy in Stockholm for literature; and a committee of five, elected by the Norwegian parliament, for peace. The winner of the peace prize is chosen for outstanding work in promoting peace, international brotherhood,

Nobel Prizes

and disarmament. The peace prize is awarded in Oslo; all others are awarded in Stockholm.

NOBEL PRIZE WINNERS

Physics

Year	Winner
1901	Wilhelm C. Roentgen
1902	Hendrik A. Lorentz
	Pieter Zeeman
1903	Antoine H. Becquerel
	Marie S. Curie
	Pierre Curie
1904	John W. S. Rayleigh
1905	Philipp E. A. Lenard
1906	Joseph J. Thomson
1907	Albert A. Michelson
1908	Gabriel Lippmann
1909	Guglielmo Marconi
	Carl F. Braun
1910	Johannes D. van der Waals
1911	Wilhelm Wien
1912	Nils G. Dalén
1913	Heike Kamerlingh-Onnes
1914	Max von Laue
1915	William H. Bragg
	William Lawrence Bragg
1917	Charles G. Barkla
1918	Max K. E. L. Planck
1919	Johannes Stark
1920	Charles E. Guillaume
1921	Albert Einstein
1922	Niels H. D. Bohr
1923	Robert A. Millikan
1924	Karl M. G. Siegbahn
1925	James Franck
	Gustav Hertz
1926	Jean B. Perrin
1927	Arthur H. Compton
	Charles T. R. Wilson
1928	Owen W. Richardson
1929	Louis Victor de Broglie
1930	Chandrasekhara V. Raman
1932	Werner Heisenberg
1933	Paul A. M. Dirac
	Erwin Schrödinger
1935	James Chadwick
1936	Carl D. Anderson
	Victor F. Hess
1937	Clinton J. Davisson
	George P. Thomson
1938	Enrico Fermi
1939	Ernest O. Lawrence
1943	Otto Stern
1944	Isidor Isaac Rabi
1945	Wolfgang Pauli
1946	Percy Williams Bridgman
1947	Edward V. Appleton
1948	Patrick Blackett
1949	Hideki Yukawa
1950	Cecil F. Powell
1951	John D. Cockcroft
	Ernest T. S. Walton
1952	Felix Bloch
	Edward M. Purcell
1953	Frits Zernike
1954	Max Born
	Walther Bothe
1955	Willis E. Lamb, Jr
	Polykarp Kusch
1956	John Bardeen
	Walter H. Brattain
	William B. Shockley
1957	Tsung-Dao Lee
	Chen Ning Yang
1958	Pavel A. Cherenkov
	Ilya M. Frank
	Igor Y. Tamm
1959	Emilio G. Segrè
	Owen Chamberlain
1960	Donald A. Glaser
1961	Robert Hofstadter
	Rudolf L. Mössbauer
1962	Lev D. Landau
1963	J. Hans D. Jensen
	Maria Goeppert-Mayer
	Eugene P. Wigner
1964	Nikolai G. Basov
	Aleksander M. Prokhorov
	Charles H. Townes
1965	Richard P. Feynman
	Julian S. Schwinger
	Shinichiro Tomonaga
1966	Alfred Kastler
1967	Hans A. Bethe
1968	Luis W. Alvarez
1969	Murray Gell-Mann
1970	Louis Néel
	Hannes Alfvén
1971	Dennis Gabor
1972	John Bardeen
	Leon Cooper
	John R. Schrieffer
1973	Leo Esaki
	Ivar Giaever
	Brian D. Josephson
1974	Antony Hewish
	Martin Ryle
1975	Aage N. Bohr
	Ben Mottelson
	James Rainwater
1976	Burton Richter
	Samuel C.C. Ting
1977	John H. Van Vleck
	Philip W. Anderson
	Sir Nevill F. Mott
1978	Arno A. Penzias
	Robert W. Wilson
	Pyotr Leonidovich Kapitsa
1979	Steven Weinberg
	Sheldon L. Glashow
	Abdus Salam
1980	James W. Cronin
	Val L. Fitch
1981	Nicolaas Bloembergen
	Arthur Schawlow
	Kai M.Siegbahn
1982	Kenneth G. Wilson
1983	Subrahmanyan Chandrasekhar
	William A.Fowler
1984	Carlo Rubbia
	Simon van der Meer
1985	Klaus von Klitzing

Chemistry

Year	Winner
1901	Jacobus van't Hoff
1902	Emil H. Fischer
1903	Svante A. Arrhenius
1904	William Ramsay
1905	Adolf von Baeyer
1906	Henri Moissan
1907	Eduard Buchner
1908	Ernest Rutherford
1909	Wilhelm Ostwald
1910	Otto Wallach
1911	Marie S. Curie
1912	F. A. Victor Grignard
	Paul Sabatier
1913	Alfred Werner
1914	Theodore W. Richards
1915	Richard M. Willstätter
1918	Fritz Haber
1920	Walther H. Nernst
1921	Frederick Soddy
1922	Francis W. Aston
1923	Fritz Pregl
1925	Richard A. Zsigmondy
1926	Theodor Svedberg
1927	Henrich O. Wieland
1928	Adolf O. R. Windaus
1929	Arthur Harden
	Hans von Euler-Chelpin
1930	Hans Fischer
1931	Carl Bosch
	Friedrich Bergius
1932	Irving Langmuir
1934	Harold C. Urey
1935	Irène Joliot-Curie
	Frédéric Joliot
1936	Peter J. W. Debye
1937	Walter N. Haworth
	Paul Karrer
1938	Richard Kuhn
1939	Adolf F. J. Butenandt
	Leopold Ruzicka
1943	Georg von Hevesy
1944	Otto Hahn
1945	Artturi I. Virtanen
1946	John H. Northrop
	Wendell M. Stanley
	James B. Sumner
1947	Robert Robinson
1948	Arne W. K. Tiselius
1949	William F. Giauque
1950	Otto P. H. Diels
	Kurt Alder
1951	Edwin M. McMillan
	Glenn T. Seaborg
1952	Archer J. P. Martin
	Richard L. M. Synge
1953	Hermann Staudinger
1954	Linus C. Pauling
1955	Vincent du Vigneaud
1956	Cyril N. Hinshelwood
	Nikolai N. Semenov
1957	Alexander R. Todd
1958	Frederick Sanger
1959	Jaroslav Heyrovsky
1960	Willard F. Libby
1961	Melvin Calvin
1962	John C. Kendrew
	Max F. Perutz
1963	Giulio Natta
	Karl Ziegler
1964	Dorothy C. Hodgkin
1965	Robert B. Woodward
1966	Robert S. Mulliken
1967	Manfred Eigen
	Ronald G. W. Norrish
	George Porter
1968	Lars Onsager
1969	Odd Hassel
	Derek H. R. Barton
1970	Luis F. Leloir
1971	Gerhard Herzberg
1972	Christian Boehmer Anfinsen
	Stanford Moore
	William Howard Stein
1973	Ernst Otto Fischer
	Geoffrey Wilkinson
1974	Paul J. Flory
1975	John Cornforth
	Vladimir Prelog
1976	William N. Lipscomb, Jr.
1977	Ilya Prigogine
1978	Peter Mitchell
1979	Herbert C. Brown
	Georg Wittig
1980	Paul Berg
	Walter Gilbert
	Frederick Sanger
1981	Roald Hoffmann
	Kenichi Fukui
1982	Aaron Klug
1983	Henry Taube
1984	R. Bruce Merrifield
1985	Herbert A. Hauptman
	Jerome Karle

Physiology and Medicine

Year	Winner
1901	Emil A. von Behring
1902	Ronald Ross
1903	Niels R. Finsen
1904	Ivan P. Pavlov
1905	Robert Koch
1906	Camillo Golgi
	Santiago Ramón y Cajal
1907	Charles L. A. Laveran
1908	Paul Ehrlich
	Élie Metchnikoff
1909	E. Theodor Kocher
1910	Albrecht Kossel
1911	Allvar Gullstrand
1912	Alexis Carrel
1913	Charles R. Richet
1914	Robert Bárány
1919	Jules J. P. V. Bordet
1920	S. August Krogh
1922	Archibald V. Hill
	Otto F. Meyerhof
1923	Frederick G. Banting
	John J. R. Macleod
1924	Willem Einthoven
1926	Johannes A. G. Fibiger
1927	Julius Wagner-Jauregg
1928	Charles J. H. Nicolle
1929	Frederick G. Hopkins
	Christiaan Eijkman
1930	Karl Landsteiner
1931	Otto H. Warburg
1932	Charles S. Sherrington
	Edgar D. Adrian
1933	Thomas H. Morgan
1934	George R. Minot
	William P. Murphy
	George H. Whipple
1935	Hans Spemann
1936	Henry H. Dale
	Otto Loewi
1937	Albert von Szent-Györgyi
1938	Corneille J. F. Heymans
1939	Gerhard Domagk
1943	Edward A. Doisy
	C. P. Henrik Dam
1944	E. Joseph Erlanger
	Herbert S. Gasser
1945	Alexander Fleming
	Howard W. Florey
	Ernst B. Chain
1946	Hermann Joseph Muller
1947	Carl F. Cori
	Gerty T. Cori
	Bernardo A. Houssay
1948	Paul H. Müller
1949	Walter R. Hess
	Antônio de Egas Moniz
1950	Philip S. Hench
	Edward C. Kendall
	Tadeus Reichstein
1951	Max Theiler
1952	Selman A. Waksman

Nobelists George Seferis (left) and Par F. Lagerkvist

Nobelist Cordell Hull

Nobelist Paul Samuelson

1953	Fritz A. Lipmann
	Hans A. Krebs
1954	John F. Enders
	Frederick C. Robbins
	Thomas H. Weller
1955	A. Hugo T. Theorell
1956	André F. Cournand
	Werner Forssmann
	D. W. Richards
1957	Daniel Bovet
1958	George W. Beadle
	Edward L. Tatum
	Joshua Lederberg
1959	Arthur Kornberg
	Severo Ochoa
1960	F. Macfarlane Burnet
	Peter B. Medawar
1961	Georg von Békésy
1962	Francis H. C. Crick
	James D. Watson
	Maurice H. F. Wilkins
1963	Andrew F. Huxley
	John C. Eccles
	Alan L. Hodgkin
1964	Konrad E. Bloch
	Feodor Lynen
1965	François Jacob
	André M. Lwoff
	Jacques L. Monod
1966	Charles B. Huggins
	Francis P. Rous
1967	Ragnar A. Granit
	Haldan K. Hartline
	George Wald
1968	Robert W. Holley
	H. Gobind Khorana
	Marshall W. Nirenberg
1969	Max Delbruck
	Alfred D. Hershey
	Salvador E. Luria
1970	Bernard Katz
	Ulf von Euler
	Julius Axelrod
1971	Earl W. Sutherland
1972	Gerald M. Edelman
	Rodney R. Porter
1973	Karl von Frisch
	Konrad Lorenz
	Nikolaas Tinbergen
1974	Albert Claude
	Christian René de Duve
	George Emil Palade
1975	David Baltimore
	Renatto Dulbecco
	Howard Temin
1976	Baruch S. Blumberg
	Daniel C. Gajdusek
1977	Rosalyn S. Yalow
	Roger C. L. Guillemin
	Andrew V. Schally
1978	Daniel Nathans
	Hamilton O. Smith
	Werner Arber
1979	Allan McLeod Cormack
	Godfrey Newbold Hounsfield
1980	Baruj Benacerraf
	George Snell
	Jean Dausset
1981	Roger Wolcott Sperry
	David Hunter Hubel
	Torsten Nils Wiesel
1982	Sune K. Bergström
	Bengt I. Samuelsson
	John R. Vane
1983	Barbara McClintock
1984	César Milstein

	Georges J. F. Köhler
	Niels K. Jerne
1985	Michael S. Brown
	Joseph L. Goldstein

Literature

Year	Winner
1901	René F. A. Sully-Prudhomme
1902	Theodor Mommsen
1903	Björnstjerne Björnson
1904	Frédéric Mistral
	José Echegaray
1905	Henryk Sienkiewicz
1906	Giosué Carducci
1907	Rudyard Kipling
1908	Rudolf C. Eucken
1909	Selma O. L. Lagerlöf
1910	Paul J. L. Heyse
1911	Maurice Maeterlinck
1912	Gerhart Hauptmann
1913	Rabindranath Tagore
1915	Romain Rolland
1916	Verner von Heidenstam
1917	Karl A. Gjellerup
	Henrik Pontoppidan
1919	Carl F. G. Spitteler
1920	Knut Hamsun
1921	Anatole France
1922	Jacinto Benavente y Martínez
1923	William Butler Yeats
1924	Wladyslaw S. Reymont
1925	George Bernard Shaw
1926	Grazia Deledda
1927	Henri Bergson
1928	Sigrid Undset
1929	Thomas Mann
1930	Sinclair Lewis
1931	Erik A. Karlfeldt
1932	John Galsworthy
1933	Ivan A. Bunin
1934	Luigi Pirandello
1936	Eugene G. O'Neill
1937	Roger M. du Gard
1938	Pearl S. Buck
1939	Frans E. Sillanpaa
1944	Johannes V. Jensen
1945	Gabriela Mistral
1946	Hermann Hesse
1947	André Gide
1948	T. S. Eliot
1949	William Faulkner
1950	Bertrand A. W. Russell
1951	Pär F. Lagerkvist
1952	François Mauriac
1953	Winston Churchill
1954	Ernest Hemingway
1955	Halldór K. Laxness
1956	Juan Ramón Jiménez
1957	Albert Camus
1958	Boris L. Pasternak (declined)
1959	Salvatore Quasimodo
1960	Saint-John Perse
1961	Ivo Andric
1962	John Steinbeck
1963	George Seferis
1964	Jean Paul Sartre (declined)
1965	Mikhail A. Sholokov
1966	Samuel Y. Agnon
	Nelly Sachs
1967	Miguel Angel Asturias
1968	Yasunari Kawabata
1969	Samuel Beckett
1970	Aleksander Solzhenitsyn
1971	Pablo Neruda
1972	Heinrich Böll
1973	Patrick White

1974	Eyvind Johnson
	Harry Martinson
1975	Eugenio Montale
1976	Saul Bellow
1977	Vicente Aleixandre
1978	Isaac Bashevis Singer
1979	Odysseus Elytis
1980	Czeslaw Milosz
1981	Elias Canetti
1982	Gabriel García Márquez
1983	William Golding
1984	Jaraslav Seifert
1985	Claude Simon

Peace

Year	Winner
1901	Jean H. Dunant
	Frédéric Passy
1902	Elie Ducommun
	Charles A. Gobat
1903	William R. Cremer
1904	Institute of International Law
1905	Bertha von Suttner
1906	Theodore Roosevelt
1907	Ernesto T. Moneta
	Louis Renault
1908	Klas P. Arnoldson
	Fredrik Bajer
1909	Auguste M. F. Beernaert
	Paul H. Benjamin Estournelles de Constant
1910	International Peace Bureau
1911	Tobias M. C. Asser
	Alfred H. Fried
1912	Elihu Root
1913	Henri Lafontaine
1917	International Red Cross
1919	Woodrow Wilson
1920	Léon Bourgeois
1921	Hjalmar Branting
	Christian L. Lange
1922	Fridtjof Nansen
1925	J. Austen Chamberlain
	Charles G. Dawes
1926	Aristide Briand
	Gustav Stresemann
1927	Ferdinand E. Buisson
	Ludwig Quidde
1929	Frank B. Kellogg
1930	Nathan Söderblom
1931	Jane Addams
	Nicholas Murray Butler
1933	Norman Angell
1934	Arthur Henderson
1935	Carl von Ossietzky
1936	Carlos Saaredra Lamas
1937	E. A. R. Cecil
1938	Nansen International Office for Refugees
1944	International Red Cross
1945	Cordell Hull
1946	John R. Mott
	Emily Balch
1947	Friends' Service Council; American Friends' Service Committee
1949	John Boyd-Orr
1950	Ralph J. Bunche
1951	Léon Jouhaux
1952	Albert Schweitzer
1953	George C. Marshall
1954	Office of the UN High Commissioner for Refugees
1957	Lester B. Pearson
1958	Father George H. Pire
1959	Philip J. Noel-Baker
1960	Albert J. Luthuli

1961	Dag Hammarskjöld
1962	Linus C. Pauling
1963	International Red Cross; League of Red Cross Societies
1964	Martin Luther King, Jr.
1965	UNICEF (UN Children's Fund)
1968	René Cassin
1969	International Labor Organization
1970	Norman E. Borlaug
1971	Willy Brandt
1973	Henry A. Kissinger
	Le Duc Tho
1974	Sean MacBride
	Eisaku Sato
1975	Andrei D. Sakharov
1976	Mairead Corrigan
	Betty Williams
1977	Amnesty International
1978	Anwar Sadat
	Menachem Begin
1979	Mother Teresa
1980	Adolfo Perez Esquivel
1981	Office of the UN High Commissioner for Refugees
1982	Alva Myrdal
	Alfonso Garciá Robles
1983	Lech Walesa
1984	Bishop Desmond Tutu
1985	International Physicians for the Prevention of Nuclear War

Economics

Year	**Winner**
1969	Ragnar Frisch
	Jan Tinbergen
1970	Paul Anthony Samuelson
1971	Simon Kuznets
1972	Kenneth J. Arrow
	John R. Hicks
1973	Wassily Leontief
1974	Friedrich A. von Hayek
	Gunnar Myrdal
1975	Leonid Kantorovich
	Tjalling C. Koopmans
1976	Milton Friedman
1977	Bertil Ohlin
	James Meade
1978	Herbert A. Simon
1979	Theodore W. Schultz
	Arthur Lewis
1980	Lawrence R. Klein
1981	James Tobin
1982	George Stigler
1983	Gerard Debreu
1984	Richard Stone
1985	Franco Modigliani

Noble Gases, or **Inert Gases,** group of colorless, odorless, nonflammable gases forming group O of the periodic table. They are helium (atomic number 2), neon (10), argon (18), krypton (36), xenon (54), and radon (86). All have complete outer electron shells and were formerly thought not to form compounds. However, fluorides of krypton, xenon, and radon have now been produced. Argon occurs to the extent of 1% in the earth's atmosphere and helium and neon are produced commercially. *See also* Periodic Table.

Noctiluca, genus of plantlike flagellate protozoa usually found floating near the surface of the sea. Phosphorescent dinoflagellate, it has a round body and one large and one small flagellum. Width: to .08in (2mm). Class Mastigophora.

Noddy, sooty-colored tern found along rocky tropical seacoasts. Famous for elaborate nodding displays, fearless males defend the colonies. A single blotched gray egg is incubated by both parents on a rocky shelf or stick-and-seaweed nest. Genus *Anous. See also* Tern.

No Drama, the first significant Japanese dramatic form. It was created in the late 14th century by a father and son, Kannami and Zeami. Into the 19th century it was an entertainment for the aristocracy and the warrior class but it is broadly popular today. Formalized, dignified, and nonrealistic, No uses an all-male cast, which also sings and dances. The warriors, demons, and ghosts who often inhabit No frequently illustrate certain weaknesses. Performances traditionally lasted all day but have been shortened since 1945.

Nogales, city and port of entry in NW Mexico, on the Arizona border; occupied for a short time by Americans from Nogales, Ariz., during a border dispute (1918); site of railroad terminus, national highway. Industries: trade, livestock, minerals. Pop. 52,865.

Noguchi, Hideyo (1876–1928), Japanese bacteriologist known for isolating the causative agent of syphilis in the central nervous system. He improved the technique of the Wasserman reaction and devised the Wasserman skin test. Noguchi invented ways of cultivating microorganisms in the test tube, including the spirochetes that cause syphilis.

Noguchi, Isamu (1904–), US sculptor, b. Los Angeles. Influenced by Giacometti and Alexander Calder, his abstract works are marked by great delicacy and employ all sorts of materials. He constructed many open-air sculptures, including the Garden of Peace for the Paris UNESCO Building. His sculptures were commissioned for the East Building at the National Gallery of Art in Washington, D.C.

Noise, any undesired sound. Common sources of objectionable noise are car and truck exhausts, aircraft jet engines, railroad trains, factory machinery. Experiments carried out to determine the effects of noise on work output tend to show that output is only seriously affected if the work is mental. Nevertheless, noise is often regarded as a form of acoustic pollution and many noise-abatement societies exist. Noise is usually measured on a decibel scale.

Nomadism, way of life, usually accompanying pastoralism, in which a group or tribe has no fixed residence but moves around an area on a seasonal circuit. Many peoples are seminomadic, having settled abodes for part of the year. These societies are common in the Middle East where they live by camel or goat herding and follow the availability of fodder. *See also* Pastoralism.

Nomogram, a graphic representation of the relationships of numbers; a calculating chart with value scales of several mathematical variables. Nomograms are used in industry, engineering, and natural and physical science. Usually, it consists of three graduated parallel lines; known values on any two scales determine a transversal passing through the value on the third, which is the solution.

Nonconformists, term used to describe those whose religious beliefs diverged from established doctrine. More specifically, the nonconformists were Protestant dissenters who refused allegiance to the Church of England, as demanded by the Act of Uniformity (1662). Since 1880, non-Anglicans have had full religious and civil rights in England.

Non-Euclidean Geometry, self-consistent geometry that uses a different set of axioms from those of Euclid's geometry, in particular a set that does not include the parallel postulate. Euclid's fifth postulate is equivalent to the statement that if a point lies outside a line, then only one line can be drawn through that point that does not cut the first line. In the early 19th century Farkas Bolyai and, independently, N.I. Lobachevsky developed systems of geometry in which an infinite number of parallels could exist. This system, called a hyperbolic non-Euclidean geometry, was self-consistent; that is, it had no inherent contradiction in the results obtained from the postulates. Later G.F.B. Riemann introduced a form (elliptical geometry) in which no parallel can exist. Development of these systems cast light on the fundamental nature of geometry. Non-Euclidean geometry is also used in relativity theory.

Nonobjective Art, art that has no familiar forms, such as those of landscapes, inanimate objects, or human figures. Kandinsky was a forerunner in nonobjective painting, which began in 1910. Other early artists in this field were Dove, Doesburg, Malevich, Mondrian, and Delaunay. Nonobjective art has become part of the present international style. By extension, this term also applies to the early geometric style of Muslim art in the Near East and to the decorative art of similar cultures.

Non-Proliferation Treaty (1968), signed by the USSR, the United Kingdom, the United States, and over 80 non-nuclear weapon states. This treaty requires that each participating nation, under the auspices of the IAEA (International Atomic Energy Agency of the United Nations), agree that research and use of nuclear energy for peaceful purposes will not be redirected into military channels. The treaty pledges all signatory nations "to facilitate the fullest possible exchange of equipment, materials and scientific and technological information for . . . peaceful uses."

Non-sporting Dog, dog breeds that do not fit into other classification categories. Although many were once used as hunting and guard dogs, they are now pets. This catchall category varies widely in type. Dogs included are Bichon frise, Boston terrier, bulldog, chowchow, dalmatian, French bulldog, Keeshond, Lhasa Apso, poodle, schipperke, and Tibetan terrier.

Nootka, Wakashan-speaking tribe of North American Indians closely related to the Makah. Famous as whale hunters, their original population of 6,000 persons living along the coast of W Vancouver Island from Cape Cook to Cape Flattery now numbers approximately 2,250.

Nordic Subrace, subdivision of the Caucasoid race, characterized by tall stature, fair skin, blond hair, blue eyes, and long heads. This physical type predominates in Norway and Denmark and occurs throughout N Europe.

Norepinephrine, or **Noradrenaline,** a chemical substance which with adrenaline is secreted by the medulla of the adrenal gland. It is also liberated at the ends of sympathetic nerve fibers where it serves as a mediator in transmitting the nerve impulses to the effector organ. The release of norepinephrine may be inhibitory or excitatory depending on the organ involved and its state at that moment. *See also* Adrenal Gland.

Norfolk, Thomas Howard, 2nd Duke of (1443–1524), English nobleman. Captured at the Battle of Bosworth Field (1485), he was imprisoned in the Tower of London (1485–89). Named lord treasurer (1501), he defeated the Scots at Flodden (1513), and his title of duke was restored (1514).

Norfolk, Thomas Howard, 3rd Duke of (1473–1554), English nobleman, brother-in-law to Henry VII. President of the royal council (1529), he suppressed the Pilgrimage of Grace (1536). Two of his nieces, Anne Boleyn and Catherine Howard, married Henry VIII. Condemned as an accessory to his son Henry, Earl of Surrey's treason (1546), Norfolk was imprisoned (1547–53) but released by Mary I.

Norfolk, city in SE Virginia, on Elizabeth River; comprises port of Hampton Roads, together with Newport News and Portsmouth; nearly destroyed by fire (1776) when attacked by Americans during American Revolution; occupied by Union army during Civil War. City is site of Norfolk State College (1935), Virginia Wesleyan College (1961); naval headquarters. Exports: coal, grain, tobacco, seafood, farm products. Industries: shipbuilding, automobiles, chemicals, textiles, agricultural machinery, peanut oil, food processing. Founded 1682; inc. 1845. Pop. (1980) 266,979.

Norfolk Island, island in SW Pacific Ocean, approx. 900mi (1,449km) E of Australia; territory of Australia. Discovered 1774 by Capt. James Cook, it was made British penal colony 1788–1855; came under New South Wales 1896, then Australia 1913; renowned for its beautiful pine forests. Industries: tourism, farming, livestock. Area: 13sq mi (34sq km). Pop. 1,683.

Norfolk Island Pine, stately evergreen pine widely grown as a pot plant 2–10ft (0.6–3m) high. In its native South Pacific it grows to 200ft (61m). Branches, with bright green needles to .5in. (1.3cm), grow in annual tiers of 4–7. Care and propagation: prefers cool temperatures, filtered sun, well-drained soil (equal parts loam, sand, peatmoss) allowed to dry between soakings, daily misting; propagation by seeds or cuttings of tip growth. Species *Araucaria excelsa. See also* Araucaria.

Norman, city in central Oklahoma, 18mi (29km) S of Oklahoma City; seat of Cleveland co; site of University of Oklahoma (1892). Industries: air conditioners, packaged foods, petroleum. Founded 1889; chartered as city 1902. Pop. (1980) 68,020.

Norman Conquest, period following the invasion of England by William, duke of Normandy, who defeated King Harold at Hastings (1066) and was crowned king of England. Anglo-Saxon lords who had survived Hastings were killed or deprived of their lands in the wake of rebellions (1068–76). William strengthened his position by granting English lands to his Norman barons and establishing Norman feudalism. He brought the church into closer contact with the papacy, but chose his own archbishops. Norman influence encompassed architecture, literature, language, and the art of warfare.

Normandy (Normandie), region and former province in NW France, bounded historically by Picardy (NE), Ile-de-France (E), Maine (S), Brittany (SW), and English Channel (W and N); capital was Rouen; includes departments of Manche, Calvados, Eure, Seine-Maritime, and Orne. A Roman province, it was invaded by Northmen mid-9th century; became part of English kingdom 1066; conquered by France 1450; suffered economically when Edict of Nantes was revoked (1685), causing a mass migration of Huguenots; in 18th century prosperity returned; in 1790, France abolished provinces and new departments were devised; scene of Allied invasion (June 6, 1944) during WWII; Battle of Normandy, ended July 31, 1944 with the German retreat and Allied breakthrough. Forests, flat farmlands,

Noddy

Norfolk Island pine

Linville Gorge, North Carolina

and gently rolling hills characterize land. Industries: fishing, tourism, cattle.

Normans, Scandinavian pirates who, beginning in the 9th century, ravaged the coasts of Europe, going as far as Sicily, Greenland, and perhaps North America. Their longboats ascended the Loire; they plundered Paris, retreating only after payment of gold. In 912, Charles the Simple ceded them part of Neustria (afterwards called Normandy) and gave his daughter in marriage to their leader, Marching Rolf. Renamed Rollo, duke of Normandy, he became a vassal of Charles and adopted Christianity for himself and his followers. Meanwhile, England was enduring waves of attacks by Northmen. In 1066, William, duke of Normandy, conquered England and took its throne as William I.

Norris, Frank (1870–1902), US novelist, b. Chicago. Considered one of the most striking naturalistic writers, Norris first drew attention for *McTeague* (1899). He is also noted for his trilogy about wheat: *The Octopus* (1901), *The Pit* (1903), and *The Wolf* (unfinished).

Norrkoping, port city in SE Sweden, at the head of Bravikin; burned 1719 by Russians during Northern War; site of 17th-century Hedvig's Church. Industries: furniture, paper, processed food. Founded 14th century. Pop. 119,169.

Norsemen, Scandinavian vikings who invaded the coasts of Europe from *c.*780–*c.*1030. Navigators and explorers, they raided and settled in northwest Germany, France, Spain, the Low Countries, Britain, Ireland, and Scotland, in search of land, wealth, trade, and adventure. They left an art style and an iconography, but accounts of the pagan vikings, written by Christians, emphasize their barbarism. *Viking,* a Scandinavian word, means pirate or rover.

North, Frederick North, 8th Baron (1732–92), English political figure. Chancellor of the exchequer (1767–70) and prime minister (1770–82), he followed George III's policies, leading to losses in the American colonies. Resigning (1782), he served as secretary of state (1783) with Charles James Fox.

North Africa, area consisting of Morocco, Algeria, Tunisia, and Libya; bounded on the N by the Mediterranean, S by the Sahara, and E by Egypt, from which it is separated by 1,000mi (1,610km) of desert. Population and economic activity are concentrated along the coastline; has desert-type interior.

North America, continent in the Western hemisphere, and third largest continent of the world. Linked to the continent of South America at Panama's E border and only 55mi (89km) from Asia across the Bering Strait; it is bounded by the Arctic Ocean (N), Pacific Ocean and Bering Sea (W), and the Atlantic Ocean, Gulf of Mexico, and Caribbean Sea (E).
　Land. The Appalachian Mts and Laurentian Highlands of E North America are old, worn down ranges, but the Rocky and other W mountains are young and rugged. The highest peak on the continent is Mt McKinley (20,320ft; 6,198m), in Alaska; the lowest point is Death Valley (282ft; 86m below sea level). In the central region vast plains provide good agricultural land; they give way to desert in the SW United States and N Mexico, and tundra in the far N. Mexico and Central America are generally mountainous but have valleys, plateaus, and coastal plains for farming. Northern Alaska and Canada and most of Greenland extend above the Arctic Circle, while southern Mexico, all of Central America, and most of the West Indies fall below the Tropic of Cancer. Greenland is the world's largest island (840,000sq mi; 2,175,600sq km).

Lakes and Rivers. Since Hudson Bay, the largest body of water in North America, is an inlet of the Atlantic Ocean, Lake Superior ranks as the largest lake of North America (31,820sq mi; 82,414sq km), and with Michigan, Huron, Erie, and Ontario it forms the Great Lakes. The St Lawrence River drains them and provides a navigable outlet to the Atlantic Ocean. The longest river is the combined Mississippi-Missouri system with a length of nearly 4,000mi (6,440km); other important rivers include the Yukon, Mackenzie, Colorado, Columbia, Delaware, Rio Grande.
　Climate and Vegetation. Much of North America experiences hot summers and cold winters, but with extremes only in the Arctic, near the equator, in Death Valley, and in the high mountains; rain forests occur in Central America. Evergreens grow over much of the continent and form a belt across the N below the tundra region. Cypress thrive in the SE, oak and maple in the NE, and giant redwoods in the W; the plains support grasses and shrubs.
　Animal Life. Bears, wolves, and pumas have grown scarce, but foxes remain widespread and lynxes occupy many forests. Coyotes range across the SW, and ocelots live S of the United States. These predators catch deer, rabbits, hares, and mice. Beaver and members of the weasel family are important for their fur. Birds include sparrows, robins, blackbirds, blue jays, wrens, doves, hawks, and owls. Snakes live nearly everywhere, with dangerous ones being rattlers and moccasins.
　People. North America's first settlers probably arrived about 35,000 years ago from Asia by way of Alaska. Their descendants occupied the entire continent when Viking explorers came about AD 1000; Christopher Columbus called them Indians when he rediscovered the New World in 1492. Spaniards moved into the West Indies and other southern lands, while the English and French settled farther N; Swedes, Germans, and the Dutch also made early settlements. Europe's problems later drove numbers of Italians, Irish, and Jews to North America. Blacks came as slaves, while Japanese and Chinese arrived with less coercion to be laborers on the W coast. Descendants of the Spanish now dominate in Mexico, Central America, and some Caribbean islands, while French concentrations exist in Quebec province, Canada, and parts of the West Indies. Blacks outnumber whites in many Caribbean islands. Protestants are numerous N of Mexico, and Roman Catholics dominate in Spanish- and French-speaking areas.
　Economy. The plains region produces grains and livestock, although industry has developed near major rivers and lakes. The S areas are also agricultural; major crops include cotton, tobacco, coffee, and sugar cane. The NE is heavily industrialized, the N and E produce forest products, and the W has mining, truck farming, and some manufacturing. Fishing is important along many of the coasts. The West Indies and other southern regions profit from tourist traffic.
　History. About 500 years after the time of Christ, Mayan Indians of Central America developed a notable civilization, as did the Aztecs of Mexico later. Spanish conquerors in the 16th century destroyed their civilizations. In the same century the French started exploring what is now Canada. The English settled at Jamestown in 1607 and at Plymouth in 1620. English-French conflicts finally brought an English victory in 1763. Some colonies revolted against England's colonial practices in 1775 and declared their independence in 1776. After they won their struggle in 1783, they banded together as the United States, drawing up a constitution in 1787. Other colonies also grew restless; Haiti gained freedom from France in 1804, and Mexico and most of Central America threw off Spanish rule in 1821; Panama became part of Colombia, but British Honduras and most Caribbean islands remained under European

domination. During the 19th century Canada and the United States expanded westward, even though the United States underwent a destructive Civil War in the first half of the 1860s. Canada gained dominion status in 1867 but did not become an independent part of the British Commonwealth for another 64 years. The Spanish-American War of 1898 ended Spain's hold in the New World and led to Cuba's independence in 1902 and to Puerto Rico's becoming associated with the United States. Panama, with US aid, broke from Colombia in 1903 and gave the US permission to build the Panama Canal. Since World War II, many islands of the Caribbean have become independent nations. Extremes of wealth and poverty in Central America have resulted in extreme instability, including leftist revolution in Nicaragua, civil war in El Salvador, and guerrilla movements elsewhere. The United States, the continent's dominant political and economic power, has become more reliant on neighboring Mexico and Canada for relatively cheap energy resources.

PROFILE

Area: 9,400,000sq mi (24,346,000sq km). Largest nation: Canada, 3,851,809sq mi. (9,976,185sq km).
Population 361,601,000
　Density: 38.5per sq mi (15 per sq km). Most populous nation: United States, 226,504,825
Chief cities: New York City; Mexico City; Chicago.
Manufacturing (major products): automobiles, iron and steel, petroleum products, pulp and paper, aircraft, drugs
Agriculture (major products): wheat, corn, oats, cotton, tobacco, cattle, hogs
Minerals (major): iron ore, coal, petroleum, gold, silver, nickle, uranium, copper

North America Nebula (NGC 7,000), bright emission nebula in the constellation Cygnus, situated east of Deneb. Its name derives from its shape, which resembles a map of North America.

Northampton, city in England, on Nene River, 60mi (97km) NW of London; county town of Northamptonshire, site of one of four English round churches. Industries: footwear, leather goods, motor accessories. Pop. 139,900.

North Atlantic Treaty Organization (NATO), Western alliance providing for joint action in an attack against any member. It also promotes joint military aid and economic cooperation during peacetime. The original members were Belgium, Britain, Canada, Denmark, France, Iceland, Italy, Luxembourg, Netherlands, Norway, Portugal, and United States. Greece and Turkey joined in 1952, West Germany in 1955, and Spain in 1982. Its headquarters are in Brussels. The 1949 organizational treaty, known as the North Atlantic Pact, was signed in Washington, D.C. The policy body of the organization is the North Atlantic Council. Its military committee, from which France withdrew in 1966, is divided into three NATO military commands and a regional planning group that aids in the defense of Canada and the United States.

North Bay, town in SE Ontario, Canada, on Lake Nipissing; seat of Nipissing district; site of Nipissing College (1967). Industries: mining equipment, lumber, dairy products, tourism. Pop. 51,639.

North Canadian, river in S United States; rises in plateau of NE New Mexico; flows E through Texas and Oklahoma to the Canadian River, near Eufaula, Okla. Length: 760mi (1,224km).

North Carolina, state in the E United States, on the Atlantic Ocean about midway on the E coastline.

Land and Economy. Along the coast stretches a chain of islands enclosing several large sounds. Beyond the broad coastal plain is the Piedmont plateau, a rolling, fertile region. In the extreme W are the Blue Ridge and Great Smoky Mts, some of which rise to over 6,000ft (1,830m). Mt Mitchell is the highest peak in the United States E of the Mississippi River. There are many small rivers. A mild climate and productive soil made agriculture the base of the economy through the 19th century, but abundant water power and natural resources encouraged the development of manufacturing. Much of the textile industry was attracted to the state from New England by lower labor costs.

People. The population is largely of English origin, with elements of Scots-Irish and Germans. Most of the early settlers came from other colonies. The state has a low percentage of foreign-born whites. Less than 50% of its population lives in urban areas.

Education. There are about 100 institutions of higher education. The University of North Carolina is one of the oldest state universities. Duke University is outstanding among the private institutions.

History, The first English colony in North America was established on Roanoke Island in 1585, but was abandoned the next year. Settlers began moving into the region from Virginia about 1660. A royal charter was granted to eight proprietors in 1663, and North Carolina became a royal province in 1729. It was the first colony to assert its will for independence from Great Britain, and in the Revolution contributed strongly to the Continental cause. The important battles of Kings Mountain and Guilford Courthouse were fought in North Carolina. The new state developed slowly. Before the Civil War, opinion was divided between Union and Confederacy, and North Carolina was the last state to secede, which it did on May 20, 1861, after hostilities had begun. On Dec. 17, 1903, Wilbur and Orville Wright made the first successful flight in a propelled heavier-than-air plane at Kitty Hawk on the coast. The industrial development of the state was spurred by both world wars; it was early known for its network of good roads. With a diversified economy, North Carolina now leads the country in output of textiles, tobacco products, and furniture.

PROFILE

Admitted to Union: Nov. 21, 1789; 12th of the 13 original states to ratify the US Constitution
US Congressmen: Senate, 2; House of Representatives, 11
Population: 5,874,429 (1980); rank, 10th
Capital: Raleigh, 149,771 (1980)
Chief cities: Charlotte, 314,447; Greensboro, 155,-642; Winston-Salem, 131,885
State legislature: Senate, 50; House of Representatives, 120
Area: 52,586sq mi (136,198sq km); rank, 28th
Elevation: Highest, 6,684ft (2,039m), Mt Mitchell; lowest, sea level
Industries (major products): textiles, tobacco products, furniture, bricks
Agriculture (major products): tobacco, sweet potatoes, peanuts, cotton, corn
Minerals (major): mica, lithium, feldspar
State nicknames: Tar Heel State, Old North State
State motto: Esse Quam Videri (To Be Rather Than to Seem)
State bird: cardinal
State flower: dogwood
State tree: pine

North Dakota, state in the N central United States, bordered on the N by the provinces of Saskatchewan and Manitoba, Canada.

Land and Economy. The land rises from the fertile valley of the Red River on the E boundary; the highest point is in the SW. The Missouri River flows E and S through the center of the state. Garrison Reservoir, formed by a dam on the Missouri, is the largest of several artificial lakes that supply irrigation and power facilities. Devils Lake is the largest natural lake. Agriculture remains the principal sector of the economy, but petroleum has grown in importance since its discovery in the 1950s; petroleum products provide a major source of manufacturing income.

People. The first settlers came from other states, from Canada, and from Europe, chiefly Russia, Germany, Sweden, and the Netherlands. The state's population reached its peak in 1930. About 45% of the people lives in urban areas.

Education. There are 12 institutions of higher education.

History. French explorers visited the region as early as 1738, and in 1797 a British trading post was established in the NE. The United States acquired roughly the W half of the area from France in the Louisiana Purchase of 1803, and the remainder from Great Britain in 1818, when the boundary with Canada was fixed. Dakota Territory was created in March 1861; it was divided into North and South Dakota in 1889, and both were admitted to the Union on the same day. The Missouri River was a major route for pioneers and goldseekers; after 1873 the railroads helped to expand farming. The International Peace Garden, a 2,200-acre (891-hectare) area that straddles the border with Manitoba, was dedicated in 1932 as a symbol of friendship between the United States and Canada.

PROFILE

Admitted to Union: Nov. 2, 1889, with South Dakota; rank, 39th or 40th
US Congressmen: Senate, 2; House of Representatives, 1
Population: 652,695 (1980); rank, 46th
Capital: Bismarck, 44,485 (1980)
Chief cities: Fargo, 61,308; Grand Forks, 43,765; Bismarck
State legislature: Senate, 51; House of Representatives, 102
Area: 70,665sq mi (183,022sq km); rank, 17th
Elevation: Highest, 3,506ft (1,069m), White Butte; lowest, 750ft (229m), Red River
Industries (major products): petroleum products, processed foods
Agriculture (major products): wheat, barley, flaxseed, rye, oats, cattle
Minerals (major): petroleum, natural gas, lignite coal, clay
State nicknames: Sioux State, Flickertail State
State motto: Liberty and Union, Now and Forever, One and Inseparable
State bird: meadowlark
State flower: wild prairie rose
State tree: American elm

Northern Cross. *See* Cygnus.

Northern Crown. *See* Corona Borealis.

Northern Ireland. *See* Ireland, Northern.

Northern Mariana Islands, Commonwealth of. *See* Pacific Islands, Trust Territory of the.

Northern War (1700–21), war victoriously fought by Russia in alliance with Poland against Sweden. Charles II of Sweden forced Poland to capitulate in 1706, then moved against Peter the Great in 1708. Relying on inadequate support from Ivan Mazepa, the Swedish forces were destroyed at the Battle of Poltava on July 8, 1709. The Swedish navy was defeated by Russia in 1714. In 1719, Russian expeditions began invading Sweden until the Treaty of Nystadt was signed in 1721. As a result Russia gained the Baltic provinces, its "window into Europe," and suddenly emerged as a major European power.

North Island, island of New Zealand, N of South Island, with which it comprises the principal land areas of New Zealand. The more populous of the two, its chief cities are Wellington (capital of New Zealand), Auckland, Hamilton, and New Plymouth; contains Lake Taupo, several mountain ranges, and fertile coastal areas; many natural bays and harbors. Industries: mining, food production and processing, dairying, timber. Area: 44,297sq mi (114,729sq km). Pop. 2,268,393.

North Little Rock, industrial city in central Arkansas, across Arkansas River from Little Rock. Industries: chemicals, furniture, railroad shops and stockyard, cotton and soybean products. Settled 1856; inc. 1903. Pop. (1980) 64,419.

North Pacific Current, warm, broad, slow, cyclical current in the N Pacific Ocean. It moves in a clockwise motion from the North Equatorial current, turns N by Japan and E in the N Pacific; forms the California current, which flows S to join the North Equatorial current.

North Platte, river in mid-West United States; rises at the confluence of many headstreams in the Park Mts, N Colorado; flows N into central Wyoming, E into Nebraska, where it unites with the South Platte River at North Platte, Nebr., to form the Platte River; used for irrigation and hydroelectricity. Length: 680mi (1,095km).

North Pole, northern end of the earth's axis, 90° latitude, 0° longitude; the Arctic Ocean encompasses the entire area. In 1607, explorer Henry Hudson tried to sail an eastern route across the North Pole; Robert E. Peary, US explorer, was the first person to achieve it (1909).

North Rhine-Westphalia (Nordrhein-Westfalen), state of W West Germany; capital is Düsseldorf; bounded by Belgium and Netherlands (W), Lower Saxony (N and E), Hesse (SE), and Rhineland Palatinate (S); highly industrialized area. State was formed in 1946 by uniting Westphalia (former Prussian prov.), N part of former Prussian Rhine prov., and former state of Lippe. Industries: iron, steel, chemicals, textiles, machinery, oil refining, coal mining. Area: 13,111sq mi (33,957sq km). Pop. 17,129,600.

North Sea, arm of the Atlantic Ocean, approx. 600mi (966km) long and 400mi (644km) wide, extending between European continent (S and E) and Great Britain (W). In the S it is connected to English Channel by Strait of Dover. In 1970 oil was discovered under sea floor; Britain and other countries are now tapping reserves in their territorial waters. Cod and herring fisheries are very important. Area: 222,000sq mi (574,980sq km).

North Star. *See* Polaris.

Northumberland, John Dudley, Duke of (?1502–53), English nobleman. He became lord high admiral (1543) and earl of Warwick (1546). He joined the regency council formed during Edward VI's minority and gained victories against the Scots (1547). Through his scheming with both Catholic and Protestant factions, he deposed the protector, Somerset (1549), and had him executed (1552). Gaining great power he proclaimed his daughter-in-law, Lady Jane Grey, queen, on Edward's death (1553), but Mary I had him executed.

Northumberland, county in N England, bounded by Scotland (N) and North Sea (E); includes Holy Isle and Farne Islands; hilly with Cheviot Hills (N) and Pennines (W); drained by Tyne, Blythe, and Tweed rivers. Chief towns are Newcastle-upon-Tyne (county town), Tynemouth, Berwick-on-Tweed; agricultural region, important for sheep and cattle, with industry centered around lower Tyne. Industries: shipbuilding, coal mining, iron works, chemicals, electrical machinery. Area: 2,018sq mi (5,227sq km). Pop. 794,975.

Northumbria, Kingdom of, Anglo-Saxon kingdom in northern England and Scotland. It was formed by the union of Bernicia and Deira under the Bernician King Aethelfrith (593–616), supreme English kingdom in the 7th century. Christianity was introduced under Edwin (616–32) and the arts flourished. With the invasions of the Danes and the rise of Mercia, Northumbria declined to an earldom after 944.

Northwest Ordinance (1787), US territorial legislation based on a proposal by Thomas Jefferson. Under the provisions of the ordinance, Congress would appoint a governor, a secretary, and three judges to govern the territory, and when the population numbered 5,000 adult, free males, a bicameral legislature would be added. Three to five states could be made from the territory, with 60,000 free inhabitants required for admission. The new states would be equal with the original states and have the same freedoms of worship, jury trial, and public education. It also banned involuntary servitude except as punishment for crimes.

Northwest Passage, sea route around northern Canada and Alaska between the Atlantic and Pacific oceans. Its crossing was first attempted by Martin Frobisher in 1576. An unsuccessful attempt by John Franklin (1845) was followed by McClure's crossing, partially by land, in 1854. Roald Amundsen made the first complete crossing (1903–06), across Lancaster Sound. A Royal Canadian Mounted Police schooner crossed in one season (1944), and in 1969 the *John A. Macdonald* was the first commercial vessel to make the journey. The route has never been commercially feasible and requires the use of icebreaking vessels.

Northwest Territories, a territory in N Canada, covering more than one-third of the country. It consists of the mainland N of 60° latitude W of Hudson Bay and of hundreds of islands in the Arctic Archipelago to the N, of which Baffin and Victoria are the largest. The territory extends beyond 80° N latitude. It is divided into three districts—Mackenzie, on the mainland to the NW; Keewatin, the mainland to the NE; and Franklin, which includes the Arctic islands.

Land and Economy. Much of the vast wilderness area is rolling, or level and poorly drained; there are hundreds of lakes, of which the most important are Great Bear and Great Slave in Mackenzie district, and large areas of swamp. The Mackenzie, flowing into the Arctic Ocean, is the principal river. About 15% of the land is forested; beyond the tree line there is virtually no vegetation of importance. Permafrost—perennially frozen ground—underlies most of the territory. The native peoples hunt fur-bearing animals and also engage in fishing. Valuable mineral deposits are widespread, but transportation problems make their exploitation difficult.

People. Semi-nomadic Indians are scattered about the area, and Eskimos live N of the tree line. Together they form a large segment of the population. White inhabitants are concentrated in and around Yellowknife on Great Slave Lake in S Mackenzie.

Grizzly Creek Falls, North Dakota

Norway

Norwegian elkhound

Education. Schools are few and dispersed and can serve only a small part of the population. There are no institutions of higher education.

History. The Hudson's Bay Co., a fur trading enterprise, received from Charles II of England in 1670 a charter to much of the huge lands W of Hudson Bay. In 1870 the Canadian government bought the lands from the company. The boundaries of the territory and of the interior districts were changed several times before the present limits were defined. During the 1960s an extensive road building program made many mineral deposits—especially lead and zinc—more accessible, and exploration boomed during the 1970s and early 1980s.

PROFILE

Created territory: 1870
National Parliament Representatives: Senate, 0; House of Commons, 1
Population: 42,237
Capital and chief city: Yellowknife
Territorial legislature: Territorial Council, 15 members
Area: 1,304,903sq mi (3,379,699sq km); more than one third of Canada
Elevation: Highest: 9,000ft (2,745m), Franklin and Mackenzie mts; lowest, sea level
Economy: furs; mineral resources: uranium, gold, petroleum, nickel, copper, largely undeveloped
Floral emblem: mountain avens

Northwest Territory, region north of the Ohio River, east of the Mississippi River, and south and west of the Great Lakes. Also known as the Old Northwest, it became the first US territory in 1783 by the Treaty of Paris. It was organized by the Northwest Ordinance (1787). The states of Indiana, Ohio, Illinois, Michigan, Wisconsin, and part of Minnesota were created from this territory.

Norwalk, city in S California, SE of Los Angeles in Los Angeles co; site of Cerritos College (1955). Founded 1850; inc. 1957. Pop. (1980) 85,232.

Norwalk, industrial city in SW Connecticut, on Long Island Sound. Industries: electronics, textiles, apparel. Settled 1650; inc. 1893. Pop. (1980) 77,767.

Norway, an independent kingdom in Europe. Its fjords and islands make it an international tourist attraction. Fishing and agriculture are the economic mainstays.

Land and Economy, Bounded E by Finland, Sweden, and the Soviet Union, Norway's coastline faces (S to N) the Skagerrak, the North Sea, the Atlantic Ocean, and the Barents Sea of the Arctic Ocean. A land of mountainous terrain and high plateaus, about 25% of the country is forested and 3% arable, mainly in the high fertile valleys of the highlands and its many lakes. The Gulf Stream moderates the climate, especially along the coast; in the interior winters are harsh. Average temperature in the spring-summer season is 70°F (20°C). North Sea oil, fishing, forestry, and agriculture comprise the economic base. Norway's merchant fleet is one of the largest in the world. Since 1979 oil has been the leading export, earning about 35% of export revenues. Inflation, although slowed down by the mid-1980s, has been its most difficult economic problem.

People. Norwegians are mainly of Germanic descent, mixed with the Finns and Lapps. About 25,000 Lapps continue to live in the N, following their traditional reindeer culture. About 65% of the people lives in the S and along the coast. Over 95% belongs to the Evangelical Lutheran Church, the state church. Education is free through university level and is compulsory to age 16. Literacy is almost 100%.

Government. Norway is a constitutional monarchy, with the king functioning mainly as a figurehead and symbol of national unity, with some executive privileges. Power is in the hands of the elected parliament (Storting). Suffrage is universal.

History. The oldest inhabitants date back 8,000–10,000 years and were hunters and fishermen; beginning in the early Christian era until the 9th century Norway was divided into many small kingdoms comprised of immigrant Germanic tribes. In 1319, Norway joined briefly with Denmark and then Sweden. In 1536 it was part of the Danish kingdom. After the 1814 Napoleonic Wars it joined with Sweden until Norwegian independence in 1905, when the Norwegian government asked Denmark's Prince Carl to take the throne. A plebiscite approved the monarch and Carl took the name of Haakon VII. His descendants still sit on the Norwegian throne. Neutral in WWI, Norway joined the Allies in WWII and was occupied by Germany. Its firm resistance to the German puppet, Vidkun Quisling, aided the liberation movement. Since then Norway has been closely allied with W Europe, and was a founding member of the North Atlantic Treaty Organization (NATO) in 1949. During the late 1970s, Norway was engaged in a dispute with the USSR over territorial water boundaries in the Barents Sea.

PROFILE

Official name: Kingdom of Norway
Area: 125,181sq mi (324,219sq km)
Population: 4,065,000
  Density: 32per sq mi (12per sq km)
Chief cities: Oslo (capital); Bergen; Trondheim
Government: Constitutional monarchy
Religion: Evangelical Lutheran (state church)
Language: Norwegian
Monetary unit: Krone
Gross national product: $43,520,000,000
Per capita income: $4,735
Industries: paper and pulp, shipbuilding, fish processing, chemicals, metals
Agriculture: forests, fish, oats, rye, potatoes, cattle and dairy products, fruits
Minerals: copper, pyrites, nickel, iron, zinc, lead
Trading partners: Sweden, West Germany, United Kingdom, Denmark, United States

Norwegian, the official language of Norway, spoken by virtually all of the country's 4,000,000 people. The major dialect *bokmål,* spoken mainly in the cities, is very similar to Danish; *nynorsk* ("New Norse"), spoken in the countryside, more closely reflects the language as it was spoken in the Middle Ages.

Norwegian Current, ocean current formed by terminus of North Atlantic current; flows N along Norwegian coast into Barents Sea. The warmth of its waters going through the Norwegian Sea keeps that sea generally ice-free.

Norwegian Elkhound, ancient Nordic hunting dog (hound group) dating from 5000–4000BC and used on elk, lynx, and mountain lion. It has a wedge-shaped head; small, high-set, erect ears; square body; straight, medium-length legs; and high-set, tightly curled tail carried over the back. The dense, smooth, gray coat is short on head, ears, and front legs and longer on neck and under the tail. Average size: 20.5in (52cm) high at shoulder; 55lb (25kg). *See also* Hounds.

Norwich, city in E England; administrative center of Norfolk; ancient manufacturing and market town with cathedral and University of East Anglia. Pop. 121,800.

Norwich Terrier, small hunting dog (terrier group) introduced in England in 1880 and brought to US after

World War I. This rugged dog has a wide head; foxy muzzle; prick or drop ears; short, compact body; short, powerful legs; and medium docked tail. The Norwich's hard and wiry coat is all shades of red, wheaten, or black and tan grizzle. Average size: 10in (25.5cm) high at shoulder; 11–12lb (5–5.5kg). *See also* Terrier.

Notochord, a flexible rod that is the primitive backbone present at some point in development in all chordates (a group that includes amphioxus and some not well-known animals as well as all vertebrates), and which distinguishes chordates from invertebrates. In vertebrates (except cyclostomes) the notochord is replaced by the vertebral column.

Notornis, rare, flightless New Zealand bird related to rail and gallinule and once thought extinct. Turkey-sized, it has heavy curved bill, reddish shield on forehead, and bright blue-green plumage. Species *Notornis hochstetteri.*

Nottingham, Charles Howard, 1st Earl of (1536–1624), English nobleman. Appointed lord high admiral by his cousin Elizabeth I and serving (1585–1619), he commanded the English fleet against the Spanish Armada (1588), led the Cadiz expedition with Essex (1596), and was created earl (1597).

Nottingham, city in N central England, on Trent River; formerly center of ancient Sherwood Forest, traditionally associated with Robin Hood. Industries: textiles, tobacco products, pharmaceuticals, lace, electrical equipment. Pop. 287,800.

Nouakchott (Nonakchott), capital city of Mauritania, W Africa, in SW part of country, approx. 4mi (6km) from the Atlantic Ocean. Originally a small fishing village, it was chosen as the capital of the republic 1957. In 1958 a program was started to build up the city; Nouakchott now has an international airport, is located on a major highway, and is site of modern storage facilities for petroleum, and a desalinization plant (opened 1969, the first in Africa). Industries: trade, handicrafts. Pop. 130,000.

Nouméa, seaport city in SW New Caledonia Island, S Pacific Ocean; capital of the French overseas territory of New Caledonia. A french penal colony 1864–97, it served as an Allied airbase during WWII; seat of South Pacific Commission (1947), est. to insure economic and social stability of the island. Pop. 59,869.

Nova (plural novae), faint star that undergoes unpredictable increases in brightness by several magnitudes, and then slowly fades back to normal, the variations apparently being due to explosions in the outer regions. These phenomena, which are mainly hot young stars of Population I, are relatively common, and some—the recurrent novae—show comparatively frequent brightness variations. *See also* Variable Star; Star.

Nova Lisboa, formerly Huambo; town in Angola, SW Africa; site of major railroad maintenance shops. Founded 1912. Pop. 61,885.

Nova Scotia, province in E Canada, one of the Maritime Provinces, on the Atlantic Ocean.

Land and Economy. Nova Scotia is virtually surrounded by the Atlantic Ocean and its bays; a narrow isthmus links it to the province of New Brunswick on the W. Cape Breton Island, the NE tip of the province, is separated from the mainland by a narrow strait. The land is nearly level or gently rolling. There are many lakes but no rivers of importance. Natural resources of extensive forests and rich fishing grounds have been the traditional base of the economy. Sydney, with its steel mills, and the port city of Halifax are important manufacturing centers. The province has been a leader in Canadian coal production for many years.

People. The French were the first colonizers, but after the mid-18th century came a steady immigration from the British Isles, especially of Scots. The descendants of these immigrants form the bulk of the population, although there remains a sizable proportion of French.

Education. Dalhousie University at Halifax is the largest institution of higher education. Others include Acadia University, St Mary's University, St Francis Xavier University, Mount St Vincent University, and the University of King's College.

History. Nova Scotia's strategic position in the North Atlantic made it a prize in a struggle of empires. The first settlement was by the French at Port Royal in 1605, the first permanent white community in North America N of Florida. Other settlers came to the area, and the French named the land Acadia. In the 17th and 18th centuries until 1758, Nova Scotia was taken and retaken eight times by British and French. With the capture of Louisburg the British consolidated their hold. They deported more than 4,000 Acadians who refused to take a loyalty oath. During and immediately after the American Revolution, the province received thousands of immigrants from New England, many of them British Loyalists who had opposed revolution. Nova Scotia joined New Brunswick, Quebec, and Ontario in 1867 to establish the Dominion of Canada. In both world wars, Halifax was a center of naval operations and a principal port of embarkation for armies and supplies bound for Europe. Beginning in the 1950s, many of the coal mines became unprofitable and have been gradually closing. Economic stimulus has been provided by the construction of new deep-water ports at Halifax and Canso Bay, although many of the coastal fishing villages are depressed.

PROFILE

Admitted to Confederation: July 1, 1867; one of the four provinces that were joined to form the Dominion of Canada
National Parliament Representatives: Senate, 10; House of Commons, 11
Population: 812,127
Capital: Halifax
Chief cities: Halifax; Dartmouth; Sydney
Provincial legislature: Legislative Assembly, 46 members
Area: 21,425sq mi (55,491sq km); rank, 9th
Elevation: Highest, 1,747ft (533m), North Barren; lowest, sea level
Industries (major products): iron and steel, pulp and paper, processed fish
Fisheries: lobster, cod, haddock, herring
Agriculture: dairy products, poultry, cattle, hogs, fruits
Minerals (major): coal, gypsum, salt, clay, sand and gravel, stone
Floral emblem: trailing arbutus

Novaya Zemlya (Novaja Zeml'a), archipelago in the Arctic Ocean off NE coast of Russian SFSR, USSR; consists of two main islands and many smaller islands; N island is ice-covered year around, and the S main island has a sparse population that engages in reindeer herding and trapping. Discovered in 16th century. Area: 35,000sq mi (90,650sq km).

Novel, narrative prose fiction that is longer and more complex than a short story. A novel uses plot and characters imaginatively to create a picture of life in past or present time. The word is derived from the Latin *novus* (meaning "new"), through the Italian *novella* (short tales describing intrigues of everyday life). The novel was established as a literary genre in the 18th century. Daniel Defoe's *Moll Flanders* (1722) is generally considered the earliest example in English.

A novel can be classified as a romance, in which a hero lives through somewhat symbolic adventures (Cervantes's *Don Quixote*); a psychological novel, which develops the inner life of one or more characters (J.D. Salinger's *Catcher in the Rye*); a social novel, which portrays a large segment of society in action (Leo Tolstoy's *War and Peace,* John Steinbeck's *Grapes of Wrath*). *See also* Anti-novel; Gothic Novel; Historical Novel; Psychological Novel; Stream-of-Consciousness Novel.

Novella, type of prose narrative. The term is used to describe medieval and Renaissance tales, such as those by Boccaccio, which influenced the evolution of the novel. In modern times novella sometimes refers to a work of prose fiction that is longer than a short story but shorter than a novel.

November, eleventh month of the year. Its name comes from the Latin for ninth because it was the ninth month in the old ten-month calendar. The birthstone is the topaz.

Novgorod, city in NW Russian SFSR, USSR, on the Volkhov River, 100mi (161km) SSE of Leningrad; capital of Novgorod oblast. One of Russia's oldest cities, it was originally a Varangian trading town; conquered by Rurik *c.* 862, and governed by Kiev until the 12th century, when it became capital of a vast territory and was called Novgorod the Great. Ruled by Prince Alexander Nevski 1238–63, the city fell to Moscow 1478; its downfall was completed by Ivan the Terrible in 1570 and the Swedes in 1616. During WWII it was held by the Germans (1941–44) and greatly damaged. Called the "museum city" due to its many architectural relics, the 12th-century kremlin contains the Cathedral of St Sophia (1045), the monument erected 1862 in commemoration of the 1,000th anniversary of the founding of Russia, historical museum, and the seat of the oblast government; site of several churches, cathedrals, and monasteries, and museum of revolution and old Russian art. Industries: distilling, meat packing, flour milling, clothing, shoes, lumber. Pop. 185,000.

Novi Sad, port city in NE Yugoslavia, on Danube River; capital of Vojvodina autonomous region; site of university (1960); held by Hungary (1941–45). Industries: electrochemical equipment, farm machinery, munitions, textiles. Pop. 141,712.

Novokuzneck (Novokuznetsk), city in Russian SFSR, USSR, at the head of the Tom River, 190mi (306km) SE of Novosibirsk; in 1932, Novokuzneck combined with Kuznetsk to form the city of Stalinsk. Industries: coal mining, iron, steel, aluminum, chemicals. Settled 1617. Pop. 543,000.

Novosibirsk, industrial city in Russian SFSR, USSR, on the Ob River, 1,750mi (2,818km) E of Moscow; capital of Novosibirsk oblast. It grew quickly, surpassing Omsk as Siberia's leading city *c.*1930. During WWII it received complete industrial plants moved from war areas of the W USSR; site of an opera house, numerous higher technical institutes, agricultural, medical, and teachers' colleges, the W Siberian branch of the Academy of Sciences (1959), and a regional museum. Industries: diesel trucks, agricultural and mining machinery, hydraulic presses, heavy machine tools, cold-rolled steel, cotton, shipbuilding, lumber, bicycles, plastics, instruments, radios, leather goods. Founded 1896 after construction of Trans-Siberian Railroad. Pop. 1,324,000.

Noyes, Alfred (1880–1958), English poet. Many of his poems were about the sea. His works include *Drake* (1906–08), *Tales of the Mermaid Tavern* (1912), *A Salute to the Fleet and Other Poems* (1915), and *The Torch Bearers* (1922–30). He is probably best-known for his poem "The Highwayman." Noyes also wrote criticism and fiction.

Nu, U (1907–), Burmese political figure. In 1936 he was expelled from the University of Rangoon by the British for his nationalist activities. Early in World War II he was imprisoned by the British and not released until the Japanese takeover. He served as foreign minister in the Japanese-backed government, but at the same time he was organizing anti-Japanese guerrilla forces. He became Burma's first premier on independence (1948), serving until 1956. He returned briefly to power (1957–58) but was forced to resign by the military under Ne Win. He was reelected in 1960, but Ne Win again deposed him in 1962, this time imprisoning him until 1966. In 1969 he went into exile but he returned (1980) when amnesty for political opponents was granted.

Nuba, collective name for a group of several unrelated peoples inhabiting the Kordofan region of S Sudan. Most Nuba peoples are agriculturalists and many tribes maintain cultivation terraces on the rugged granite hillsides of the region. Animal husbandry is also practiced. The Nuba peoples are in constant conflict with the Sudanese administration, whose authority many of them refuse to accept. Although Islam has made some converts, the predominant religious rituals are still closely linked to agricultural fertility rites, and in the more remote regions the men go naked and the women wear lip and nose ornaments piercing the skin.

Nubia, ancient state of NE Africa, dating from *c.* 20th century BC to *c.* AD 1400. At height of its power it extended from First Cataract of Nile (Aswan, Egypt) to Khartoum in Sudan between Red Sea and Libyan Desert. Remains have been found of ancient temples, palaces, tombs and towns. From 725–670 BC kings from this area ruled all of Egypt.

Nubian Desert, uninhabited region in NE Republic of Sudan; W part of the Sahara Desert, between the Nile River and the Red Sea; consists of a large sandstone plateau, E of the Nile River. Area: approx. 157,000sq mi (406,630sq km).

Nuclear Energy, or **atomic energy,** energy released during a nuclear reaction as a result of the conversion of mass into energy according to Einstein's equation, $E = mc^2$. Nuclear energy is released in two ways: by fission and by fusion. Fission is the process responsible for the atom bomb and for the fission reactors now contributing to energy requirements throughout the world. Fusion provides the energy for the Sun and the stars and for the hydrogen (thermonuclear) bomb. It also offers the prospect of cheap energy once a method has been perfected for controlling fusion reactions.

Both methods of producing nuclear energy depend on the release of the binding energy of the nucleus. When fission occurs the nucleus of a heavy atom disintegrates into two smaller nuclei in which the binding energy per nucleon is higher than in the original nucleus; the difference in total binding energy is carried away by the two or three neutrons released in the fission. In a fusion reaction, two light nuclei combine to form a heavy nucleus, with the release of binding energy. *See also* Binding Energy; Fission, Nuclear; Fusion, Nuclear.

Nuclear Family, family consisting of two adults joined by conjugal link and their immediate offspring (joined by conjugal bond) only. *See also* Family; Kinship.

Nuclear Fuel Breeding. *See* Breeder Reactor; Fission Reactor.

Nuclear Fuel Enrichment, separation of the fissionable isotope uranium-235 from the more abundant uranium-238 isotope. Gaseous uranium hexafluride undergoes diffusion separation utilizing cascades of barriers with microscopically small pores. The difference in mass between the two isotopes is minimal, but sufficient so that the heavier, slower-moving U-238 molecules are concentrated on one side. High-speed centrifugal-force separation methods are also used. *See also* Nuclear Fuels.

Nuclear Fuels, various chemical and physical forms of uranium used in nuclear reactors. Fluid fuels are required in homogeneous reactors. Heterogeneous reactors use many types of fuel—the pure metal, alloys of uranium, as well as its oxide or carbide. Thermal conductivity must be high, and the fuel must be resistant to radiation damage and easy to fabricate. *See also* Fission Reactor.

Nuclear Magnetic Resonance (NMR), absorption of radio waves by certain nuclei in the presence of a strong magnetic field. In this field the nucleus, as a result of its spin, can have slightly different energy values. It can make transitions between these, acquiring the energy by absorbing radiofrequency radiation of the appropriate wavelength.

Nuclear Physics, the scientific discipline involved with the structure of the atomic nucleus. The constituent particles of the nucleus (smaller than the atom by a factor of about 10,000) attract one another so strongly that nuclear energies are about one million times larger than atomic energies. The principal tool for the explication of nuclear structure is the quantum theory. The fission and fusion of nuclear reactions are characterized by energy far exceeding that of chemical reactions, such as the bonding of atoms into molecules. The increasingly prominent role of nuclear physics in other branches of study has resulted in further emphasis on this specialty.

Nuclear Reactor. *See* Fission Reactor.

Nuclear Regulatory Commission (NRC), federal agency created (1974) to assume the licensing and regulatory functions of the former Atomic Energy Commission. The NRC oversees 3 regulatory offices concerned with reactors, materials safety and safeguards, and research. Its purpose is to regulate civilian uses of nuclear materials; its major focus is on nuclear electric power generation. Headquarters are in Bethesda, Md., and there are 5 regional offices.

Nuclear Test-Ban Treaty (1963), treaty signed in Moscow by the USSR, Great Britain, and the United States. It committed these three major powers to halt all nuclear tests in the atmosphere, under water, and in outer space and permitted only underground explosions. It was the first treaty pertaining to a major East-West issue that the United States had made with the USSR in almost 10 years.

Nuclear Weapon, or **atomic weapon,** devastating weapon whose enormous explosive force derives from a nuclear fusion or fission reaction. The first atomic bombs, dropped by the United States on Hiroshima and Nagasaki in August 1945, consisted of two stable subcritical masses of uranium or plutonium. On being brought forcefully together the critical mass is ex-

Nubia, Egypt

Nuclear energy: National Accelerator Laboratory

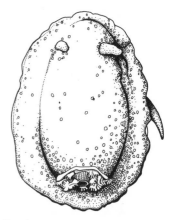

Nudibranch

ceeded, initiating an uncontrolled nuclear fission reaction. Huge amounts of energy and harmful radiation are released: the explosive force can be equivalent to 200,000 tons of TNT. The much more powerful hydrogen bomb (or thermonuclear bomb), first tested in 1952, consists of a fission bomb that on exploding provides a high enough temperature to cause nuclear fusion in a surrounding solid layer, usually lithium deuteride. The explosive power can be that of several million tons (megatons) of TNT. Devastation from such bombs covers a wide area: at 12 mi (19km) from a 15 megaton bomb all flammable material bursts into flame. *See also* Fallout, Atomic; Manhattan Project.

Nuclease, an enzyme found in animal organs. It can split nucleic acids into nucleotides and into nucleosides or their components.

Nucleic Acid, complex organic acid forming the genetic material of living cells. There are two types, deoxyribonucleic acids (DNA) and ribonucleic acids (RNA). The molecule consists of linked units called nucleotides, each containing a 5-carbon (pentose) sugar (ribose for RNA, deoxyribose for DNA), a purine or pyrimidine base (adenine, guanine, cytosine, thymine, or uracil), and phosphoric acid. Nucleotides may be partially hydrolyzed to form nucleosides (eg, adenosine), consisting of ribose or deoxyribose and a purine or pyrimidine base.

Nucleon, collective term for the nuclear constituents, the neutron and proton, the baryon members of a multiplet of two (doublet). As electric charge plays no part in strong interactions, they are considered as manifestations of a single state of matter. *See also* Baryon; Pion.

Nucleoside, sub-unit of nucleic acids consisting of a sugar and a nitrogenous base. *See also* Nucleic Acid.

Nucleosynthesis, the production of all the different kinds of chemical elements that exist in the universe from one or two simple atomic nuclei. This is believed to have occurred by way of large-scale nuclear reactions during cosmogenesis and to be in progress in the Sun and stars now. Starting with hydrogen and helium repeated nuclear fusion reactions can account for most of the elements up to iron. Elements heavier than iron can be explained by repeated neutron capture reactions.

Nucleotide, unit of nucleic acids; may also occur free in the cell acting as a coenzyme. *See also* Nucleic Acid.

Nucleus, Cell, central mass of protoplasm present in all plant or animal cells except bacteria and blue-green algae.

Nudibranch, marine gastropod, usually found on seaweeds. The shell and mantle cavity have been lost and there are fingerlike respiratory organs along the sides of the body. Length: 0.4in (10mm) to several inches. Species include the sea lemon *Archidoris. See also* Slug.

Nuevo Laredo, city in E Mexico, opposite Laredo, Texas, on the Rio Grande River. It was separated from Laredo during Mexican War (1848); site of chief US port of entry, Inter-American Highway, rail terminus, international trade center. Industries: trade (cotton and livestock), tourism. Founded 1755. Pop. 193,145.

Nuevo León, state in NE Mexico; capital is Monterrey. Occupied by US troops during Mexican War, it became a state 1824. It has a mountainous terrain, with lowland plains and numerous rivers; enjoys one of the highest standards of living in Mexico; site of rail and road crossings. Products: maguey, sugar cane, cotton, grains. Industries: steel, iron, chemicals, textiles, beer, beverages, tourism. Settled late 16th century by Spain. Area: 25,136sq mi (65,102sq km). Pop. 2,344,000.

Nukualofa, capital town of independent kingdom of Tonga, in SW Pacific, on N coast of Tongatabu Island; site of royal palace and government buildings. Pop. 15,545.

Numantia, ancient town in Spain, on the Douro River north of the modern Soria, in Old Castile. The Celtiberian tribespeople of Numantia fiercely resisted Roman conquest from 195 BC until 133 BC against overwhelming odds. The Roman general Scipio Aemilianus finally entered the town after an eight-month blockade; he found the town in smoking ruins. The Numantians had set fire to their buildings and committed mass suicide. There are numerous archaeological sites in the area.

Number, Complex, number of the form $a + bi$, where a and b are real numbers and i is the imaginary unit. Every number is a complex number with a real and an imaginary part, either of which may be zero. If b is zero it is a real number (a); if b is not zero it is an imaginary number; if a is zero it is a pure imaginary number (bi).

Number, Irrational, number that cannot be expressed as a ratio of two integers, that is, any real number that is not a rational number. Examples include $\sqrt{2}$ and π (ratio of the circumference to the radius of a circle).

Number, Natural, or **whole number,** any of the numbers 1,2,3,4. . . . as used in counting, that are the simplest numbers, with no fractional, decimal, or imaginary part, and of which there is a limitless (infinite) number. They are all positive numbers, that is, greater than zero. Negative numbers are all less than zero. *See also* Integer.

Number, Prime, positive or negative integer, excluding one and zero, that has no factors other than itself or one. Examples are 2, 3, 5, 7, 11, 13, and 17. The integers 4, 6, 8, . . . are not prime numbers since they can be expressed as 2×2, 2×3, $2 \times 2 \times 2$, . . ., that is, as the product of two or more primes.

Number, Rational, number that can be expressed as a ratio of two integers. Thus ⅛, − 0.75 (− ¾), 3 (3/1), and 572/79 (7.240506 . . .) are rational numbers.

Number, Real, number that is either a rational or an irrational number. Numbers in the decimal system are real numbers. The position of any point on a scale, however long, can be represented by a real number. Real and imaginary numbers taken together are complex numbers.

Numbers, biblical book, fourth book of the Pentateuch. It includes two census lists of the Israelites; a history of events during their 40-year march to the Promised Land; the laws of God through Moses; and the announcement of Joshua as Moses' successor.

Number System, system for writing numerals to represent numbers and the rules for addition, subtraction, multiplication, division, etc, in that system. The decimal system, used almost worldwide today, and the binary system, used in computer science, are place-value systems. The relative positions of the digits in a written number indicate the value in terms of a sum of power multiples (squared, cubed, etc) of the number base. The decimal system has a base 10; the binary system, which uses the digits 0 and 1, has a base 2. Thus the decimal number 3718 is equal to $8 \times 1 + 1 \times 10 + 7$

$\times 100 + 3 \times 1000$ or $8 \times 10^0 + 1 \times 10^1 + 7 \times 10^2 + 3 \times 10^3$.

Numeral, symbol used alone or in a group to denote a number. The Arabic numerals are the 10 digits from zero to nine. The Roman numerals consist of seven letters or marks. The formation of numbers from numerals depends on the system used. *See also* Number System.

Numidia, ancient region of NW Africa (including much of modern Algeria) contained by the Carthaginian empire until the Punic Wars. The Numidian king Masinissa allied with Rome and the country prospered independently from 201 BC until the Jugurthine War. Subjugated by Rome, Numidia survived the Vandal invasion (5th century AD) but waned under the Arabs (8th century).

Numismatics, study or collection of coins, tokens, paper money, medals, and similar objects such as works of art. Besides having monetary value the collection also helps in the study of a culture's history.

Nur-ed-Din or **Nureddin** (1118?–74), ruler of Syria who defeated the armies of the 2nd Crusade before Damascus. After his armies led by his nephew Saladin had conquered Egypt, he was proclaimed Sultan of Syria and Egypt.

Nuremberg (Nürnberg), city in SE West Germany, 93mi (150km) NW of Munich on both sides of Pegnitz River. It became free imperial city in 1219; center of German Renaissance during 15th and 16th centuries; passed to Bavaria 1806; scene of annual congress of Adolf Hitler's National Socialist party; after WWII, site of Allied trials of Nazi war criminals (1945–46); birthplace of Albrecht Dürer, whose oil paintings decorate the walls of the town hall; 13th-century church of St Lorenz contains 60-ft (18-m) white stone tabernacle, sculpted by Adam Kraft (born here 1455); a national museum (1852) is housed in 14th-century Carthusian monastery. Industries: chemicals, textiles, precision instruments. Founded 1050; chartered 1219. Pop. 495,400.

Nuremberg Laws, German laws proclaimed on Sept. 15, 1935, by the National Socialist government of Adolf Hitler. They deprived Jews, including all persons who were one-quarter Jewish, of the rights of citizenship and prohibited marriage of Jews and non-Jews.

Nuremberg Trials (1945–46), war crimes trials of World War II German leaders held at Nuremberg, Germany, under the auspices of an international military tribunal established by Britain, France, the USSR, and the United States. Twenty-four leading National Socialists were tried for crimes against humanity. Twelve were sentenced to death, including Hermann Goering, Joachim von Ribbentrop, and Alfred Rosenberg, and others were imprisoned. Additional trials of Germans, including judges and other civilians, were held by a US military tribunal at Nuremberg.

Nureyev, Rudolf (1938–   ) Russian ballet dancer. He was a soloist with the Kirov Ballet (1958) until he defected from the USSR in 1961. He has danced with the Grand Ballet du Marquis de Cuevas (Paris), Chicago Opera Ballet, American Ballet Theatre, the Dutch National Ballet, the Murray Louis Dance Company, and is a permanent guest artist with England's Royal Ballet. He has often been a partner to Margot Fonteyn, Doreen Wells, and Cynthia Gregory.

Nurse Shark, carpet shark found in shallow tropical and subtropical waters of Atlantic and E Pacific, particularly inshore areas. This sluggish fish is yellow to gray-brown above and lighter below. It is recognized by thick, fleshy whiskers near its mouth. Its young are born alive. Length: 8.5ft (2.6m); weight: 330–370 lb (149–167kg). Family Orectolobidae; species *Ginglymostoma cirratum. See also* Chondrichthyes; Sharks.

Nut, dry, one-seeded fruit with a hard woody or stony wall. It develops from a flower that has petals attached above the ovary (inferior ovary). Nuts are often formed in association with modified leaves (bracts); the cup of an acorn is formed from fused bracts. A nut does not open at maturity. Examples are filbert, beech, chestnut, hickory, and walnut.

Nut, in Egyptian mythology, the goddess of the sky, depicted touching the earth with her fingertips and toes while her star-studded belly forms the vault of the sky. She also appears in the form of a cow supported at each of her legs by a god and at her starry underside by Shu, the Egyptian Atlas. Nut serves also as protector of the dead and can be found painted on the lids of sarcophagi.

Nutation, oscillating movement (period 18.6 years) superimposed on the steady precessional movement of the Earth's axis so that the precessional path of each celestial pole on the celestial sphere follows an irregular rather than a true circle. It results from the varying gravitational attraction of the Sun and Moon on the Earth, due to variations in their distances from Earth and in their relative directions.

Nutcracker, widely distributed, crowlike bird of evergreen forests of the Northern Hemisphere that stores nuts in autumn and eats them during winter. The European thick-billed nutcracker *(Nucifraga caryocatactes)* is a typical species. Length: 12in (30cm).

Nuthatch, bird found mainly in the Northern Hemisphere and occasionally in Africa and Australia. It walks in all directions on tree trunks and limbs where it wedges a nut into a crevice, opening it with its sharp bill. It also feeds on insects, spiders, and seeds, often visiting parks and gardens. Many nest in a tree or rock cavities; some erect mud barriers around the nest. Whitish eggs (5–8) are laid. Length: 3.5–7.5in (9–19cm). Family Sittidae.

Nutmeg, evergreen tree native to tropical Asia, Africa, and America. Cultivated commercially, it has dark brown leaves, pale yellow flowers, and yellow, apricot-like fruits. Among 300 species is *Myristica fragrans,* native to E India. Height: to 60ft (18.3m). First known to Europeans during the 12th century, its seeds yield the spice nutmeg and its seed covering, the spice mace. Family Myristicaceae.

Nutrition, the study of all the processes by which whole plants and animals take in and make use of food substances. It involves identifying the kinds and amounts of nutrients necessary for growth and health. Nutrients are generally divided into proteins, carbohydrates, fats, minerals, and vitamins. Human nutrition and diet is a special discipline and its study is undertaken by doctors, physiologists, biochemists, and agriculturalists.

Nyala. *See* Kudu, Nyala, Sitatunga, and Bushbuck.

Nyasa, Lake (Malawi, Lake), lake in SE Africa, bounded by Malawi (S and W), Tanzania (N and NE), Mozambique (E); 3rd-largest lake in Africa; numerous rivers flow into it from E; however, the Shire River is its only outlet, flowing S into the Zambezi River. Discovered *c.* 1616 by Caspar Boccaro. Area: 11,430sq mi (29,604sq km). Depth (max.): 2,226ft (679m).

Nyasaland, former territory of S Africa, once part of the Bantu Malawi kingdom. It was a British protectorate from 1891 to 1964, when it achieved independence as Malawi. *See also* Malawi.

Nyerere, Julius Kambarage (1921–), president of Tanzania (1964–85). He served as a legislator and chief minister in the Tanganyikan territorial government. An African nationalist leader, he became president of an independent Tanganyika in 1962 and in 1964 oversaw the merger of Tanganyika and Zanzibar as Tanzania. Under a new constitution, he was reelected president in 1980 but retired in 1985. He continued as chairman of the country's sole political party.

Nyköping, port town in SE Sweden, on Baltic Sea; seat of Södermanland co.; site of Nyköpingshus castle (13th century), St Nicholas Church (13th-18th centuries), city hall (17th century). Industries: textiles, sawmills, furniture. Founded 13th century. Pop. 32,205.

Nylon, any of numerous synthetic materials consisting of polyamides formed into fibers, filaments, bristles, or sheets by extrusion through spinnarets and drawing. Nylon is characterized by elasticity and strength and is used chiefly in yarn, cordage, and molded products. Hard and tough or soft and rubbery nylon products can be made by varying the chemical balance.

Nystagmus, involuntary eye movement, resulting from an early loss of central vision, dizziness, barbiturate intoxication, or inner ear or brain disease.

O

Oahu, mountainous island in Hawaii, between Molokai and Kauai islands; 3rd-largest and economically most important of the Hawaiian Islands; Honolulu, the state capital, is on the S coast. It is the site of noted extinct volcanoes: Diamond Head, Punchbowl, and Koko Head; important military installations including Pearl Harbor. Industries: tourism, pineapples, sugar cane, fishing, dairy products. Area: 593sq mi (1,536sq km). Pop. (1970) 629,145.

Oak, hardwood trees and shrubs native to northern temperate regions and high elevations in the tropics. Most have a rounded and broadly spreading shape. The foliage turns red, yellow, or brown in the fall. The fruit, acorns, may take 1–2 years to mature and are relished by squirrels. These trees resist storm damage well and so are long-lived. Often too massive for small yards, they are excellent shade trees where space is available. They are also valuable timber trees. Family Fagaceae; genus *Quercus.*

Oakland, city in W California, opposite Golden Gate Bridge; seat of Alameda co; site of San Francisco-Oakland Bay Bridge (1936); also center of the Bay Area Rapid Transit system (1972); site of Mills College (1852), Holy Name College (1868), and California College of Arts and Crafts (1907); home of baseball's Oakland A's. Industries: chemicals, food processing, shipping port, glass works. Founded 1820; inc. 1852. Pop. (1980) 339,288.

Oakley, Annie (1860–1926), US entertainer, b. as Phoebe Anne Oakley Mozee in Patterson Township, Ohio. She was an expert marksman and long the star of Buffalo Bill's Wild West Show from 1875.

Oak Park, city in NE Illinois; W suburb of Chicago; birthplace of Ernest Hemingway; residence of Frank Lloyd Wright, who designed many buildings here. Settled 1833; inc. 1901. Pop. (1980) 54,887.

Oak Ridge, city in E Tennessee, 17mi (27km) NW of Knoxville, on Clinch River; site of three Atomic Energy Commission installations: Oak Ridge National Laboratory (est. 1943), research and development; Oak Ridge Gaseous Diffusion Plant, uranium production; Oak Ridge Institute of Nuclear Studies (est. 1948), production of U-235; site was closed to public 1942–49 when it was producing uranium for atomic bomb. Inc. 1959. Pop. (1980) 27,662.

Oakville, city in Ontario, Canada, on Lake Ontario between Toronto and Hamilton. Industries: automobiles, electrical equipment, paint. Pop. 68,950.

Oak Wilt, a usually fatal fungus disease of oak trees whose symptoms include wilting and discoloration of leaves. Like its close relative the Dutch elm disease fungus, the oak wilt fungus kills trees by plugging water-conducting tissues in sapwood.

Oat, cereal plant native to W Europe and introduced worldwide. It grows well even in poor soils. The flower is composed of numerous florets that produce one-seeded fruits. Mainly fed to livestock, oats are consumed by humans as breakfast foods. Family Gramineae; genus *Avena.*

Oates, Joyce Carol (1938–), US novelist, short story writer, and poet, b. Lockport, N.Y. Her first book of short stories, *By the North Gate,* appeared in 1963. Oates' works are chronicles of violence and economic and emotional deprivation. In addition to *Them* (1969), the novel for which she won the 1970 National Book Award, her works include the novels *A Garden of Earthly Delights* (1967), *The Assassins* (1975), *Bellefleur* (1980), *Angel of Light* (1981), *A Bloodsmoor Romance* (1982), and *Marya: A Life* (1986).

Oates, Titus (1649–1705), English conspirator. He and some accomplices invented the Popish Plot (1678), described as a Jesuit plan to assassinate Charles II and put James, duke of York, on the throne. Anti-Catholic hatred swept the land, and many Catholics were murdered. Oates was eventually found guilty of perjury (1685) and imprisoned; pardoned by William III (1689).

Oaxaca, city in S Mexico; capital of Oaxaca state. Taken by Spain 1521, it played a significant role in the Mexican revolution; site of gardens, university (1825), monastery of Santo Domingo, Inter-American Highway. Industries: tourism, pottery, silver filigree, sarapes. Founded 1486 as Aztec Huasyacac. Pop. 118,810.

Ob (Ob'), one of the largest rivers in W Siberia, Russian SFSR, USSR; formed by the union of the Biya and Katun rivers SW of Biysk; flows generally NW to the mouth of the Irtysh River, near Khanty-Mansisk, then N; it separates into many arms and flows to Ob Bay, an inlet of the Kara Sea, 75mi (121km) ENE of Salekhard; chief tributaries are the Tom, Chulym, Ket, Vokh, Kazym, Vasyugan, Intysh, Kanda, and N Sasva. Sometimes called the Oki, this major trade route freezes for 6 months; important source of hydroelectric power. Length: 2,287mi (3,682km).

Obadiah, biblical author and fourth of the 12 minor prophets. He condemned the Edomites, tribe of Esau, for their aid in the Babylonian invasion of Judah.

Obeah, or **obi,** system of religious beliefs and witchcraft found among blacks of the Caribbean and SE United States. In some of its magical practices it bears a strong resemblance to voodoo. Like voodoo, obeah is West African in origin. *See also* Voodoo.

Obelia, colonial branching coelenterate found in marine waters. Similar in appearance to delicate plants, the colony is formed of hydralike polyps. The medusa breaks off from the colony and undergoes sexual reproduction to produce new polyps. Order Hydroida.

Oberammergau, town in Bavaria, S West Germany, 42mi (68km) SSW of Munich; famous for its Passion Play, presented by villagers every 10th year since 1634 in fulfillment of a vow for deliverance from the plague (1633). Industries: tourism, lumber, wood carving. Pop. 4,700.

Obesity, condition wherein excessive amounts of fat are stored beneath the skin and within organs. Medically, it is defined as an accumulation of body fat sufficient to impair health. People who are overweight by 30% or more risk diseases of the kidney, arteries, and heart and have a shorter life expectancy than those of normal weight. Obesity is usually caused by consumption of more calories than the body can use. Hormone imbalance, glandular defects, and genetic predisposition are also factors, although less common. Treatment is through reduction of caloric intake.

Oboe, soprano woodwind musical instrument (from the French *hautbois*), ranging 2½ octaves, pitched a fifth above the alto version (English horn). The end-blown conical pipe has a double-reed mouthpiece like the bassoon. The oboe resembles the clarinet. Its mournful A-tone is traditionally sounded to tune symphony and chamber orchestras. The primitive oboe is traced to the Middle East (*c.*1800 BC).

Obote, Milton (1924–), Ugandan political leader, prime minister (1962–66); president (1966–71; 1980–85). He joined the Uganda National Congress (1952–60) and later formed the Uganda People's Congress (1960). He was overthrown by a military coup led by Gen. Idi Amin, who was in turn overthrown (1979). Obote spent nine years in exile in Tanzania, returning to Uganda (1980) after President Godfrey Binaisa was deposed. He was elected president but, accused of fraud and repressive rule marred by violence, was overthrown in 1985.

Obscenity,something, as an act, utterance, picture, or written material, that is judged to offend or corrupt public morals. Application of such judgment is normally directed at the sexual content. Public attitudes toward obscenity have varied over the centuries from place to place, becoming most restrictive in the late 1890s and early 20th century. In 1973, the US Supreme Court, acknowledging the difficulty of formulating a definition of obscenity acceptable to the entire nation, established general standards to guide individual states and municipalities in formulating their own definitions.

Obsidian, a rare gray to black glassy volcanic rock. High in silica, it is the uncrystallized equivalent of rhyolite and granite. Hardness 5.5; sp gr 2.4. Polishes well and makes attractive, semiprecious stone.

Annie Oakley

Ocelot

Sandra Day O'Connor

Obstetrics, branch of medicine that deals with pregnancy, labor, childbirth, and the care of the woman immediately following childbirth. It also treats any disorders and abnormalities of pregnancy.

O'Casey, Sean (1884–1964), Irish playwright. His first play, *The Shadow of a Gunman* (1923), made him famous overnight. *Juno and the Paycock* (1924), a tragedy of the Dublin slums, was followed by *The Plough and the Stars* (1926), a tragedy of the Easter Rebellion of 1916, and *The Silver Tassie* (1928), a realistic play about the horrors of the aftermath of war. His later works, in an expressionistic style, differ considerably from the realism of his early plays. In the 1930s and early 1940s he wrote plays calling for a radical transformation of society, such as *Purple Dust* (1940) and *Red Roses for Me* (1942). Late in his career he returned to Irish themes with such plays as *The Bishop's Bonfire* (1955) and *The Drums of Father Ned* (1958). His most important nondramatic work is a six-volume fictionalized autobiography *Mirror in My House* (1956).

Occam, or **Ockham, William of** (*c.*1285–1350), English theologian and philosopher. Writing against the pope and in favor of the Holy Roman emperor, he was excommunicated and expelled from the Franciscan order on charges of heresy. William was a leader of the nominalist school of philosophy. Contributing to the development of formal logic, he employed the principle of economy, known as "Occam's Razor." *See also* Nominalism; Occam's Razor.

Occam's Razor, principle of economy of explanation named for philosopher William of Occam (*c.*1285–1350), also called Law of Parsimony. It holds that explanatory principles should not be needlessly multiplied; the simplest proof is usually the best.

Ocean, the continuous body of water that surrounds the continents and fills the Earth's great depressions. There are five main oceans, the Atlantic, Pacific, Indian, Arctic, and Antarctic. They cover 71% of the Earth's surface. The ocean floor is not flat but has a varied topography like land, with vast mountain chains, valleys, and plains. Ocean water consists of 3.5% dissolved minerals, hence its salty taste. It is constantly moving in currents and waves.

Oceania, collective name for the islands in central and S Pacific Ocean; includes Micronesia, Melanesia, Polynesia, and Australasia (Australia, New Zealand, and Malay Archipelago). *See also* individual islands.

Oceanography, ocean-going branch of geochemistry, geophysics, meteorology, biology, fluid mechanics, chemistry, and physics. This science studies oceans, past and present, the shorelines, sediments, rocks, muds, plants, animals, temperatures, tides, winds, currents, formation and erosion of abyssal depths and heights, and the effect of neighboring land masses. Since the Earth is largely ocean, the combined efforts of many specialists are necessary to determine a total picture of the effect of oceans on the Earth as a whole.

Ocean Perch. *See* Rosefish.

Oceanside, city in S California, 45mi (72km) N of San Diego; site of San Luis Rey Mission (1798); trading center. Industries: rubber products, flowers and bulbs, electronic equipment. Inc. 1888. Pop. (1980) 76,698.

Ocean Sunfish, huge, flat-bodied, marine bony fish found in open seas of temperate and tropical zones. Dark gray above and white below, it has huge dorsal and ventral fins, but no pelvic bones, pelvic fins, or tail. It swims on its side and drifts at surface. Length: to 11ft

(3.4m); weight: to 2 tons. There are three species including common *Mola mola*. Family Molidae. *See also* Osteichthyes.

Ocelot, or painted leopard, leopard cat, small, spotted New World cat found in scrub, rocky, and forest areas of S United States, Central and South America. A valuable fur animal, its yellowish or rust coat is marked with elongated dark spots. It feeds on small mammals and reptiles. Length: body—27–35in (69–89cm); tail—13–15in (33–38cm); weight: 20–40lb (9.1–18.1kg). Family Felidae; species *Felis pardalis*. *See also* Cat.

Ocher, or **Ochre** (1) an earthy red or yellow iron ore frequently impure and used as a pigment; (2) several ferruginous clays; (3) various pigments, yellow to orange, prepared from natural ochers by washing, grinding, or calcining.

Ochoa, Severo (1905–), US biochemist b. Spain. He shared the 1959 Nobel Prize in physiology or medicine with Arthur Kornberg for work on the synthesis of ribonucleic acid (RNA), the hereditary material of some viruses and deoxyribonucleic acid (DNA), the hereditary material of most cells.

O'Connell, Daniel (1775–1847), Irish political leader, known as the "Liberator." He formed the Catholic Association (1823) and entered the British Parliament (1828) supporting Roman Catholic emancipation, achieved in 1829. Advocating repeal of the union of Ireland with Britain, he formed the Repeal Association (1840). As lord mayor of Dublin (1841), he received support through the *Nation* newspaper. Countermanding a meeting arranged at Clontarf (1843), he was arrested for plotting sedition but subsequently pardoned. He broke with the more militant Young Irelanders (1845) and left Ireland (1847).

O'Connor, Sandra Day (1930–), US Supreme Court justice, b. Duncan, Ariz. Beginning her legal career in private law practice in Arizona, she later became the state's assistant attorney general (1965–68). She won election to two full terms in the Arizona senate and was elected majority leader in 1973. A Republican, she co-chaired the Arizona Committee to Re-Elect the President (Richard M. Nixon) in 1972. She served on the Superior Court in Phoenix (1974–79), until her appointment to the Arizona Court of Appeals. In 1981 she was appointed associate justice of the US Supreme Court, the 102nd justice and the first woman to serve on the high court. She generally took conservative stands.

Ocotillo, or candlewood, desert shrub found in SW United States and Mexico. Its spiny stems have scarlet flowers at tips during the rainy season. Height: 6–25ft (1.8–7.6m). Family Fouquieriaceae, species *Fouquieria splendens*.

Octans, or **The Octant,** faint southern constellation in which the south celestial pole is located. Sigma Octantis, the star closest to the pole, is of the fifth magnitude. Brightest star Nu Octantis.

Octave, in music, the interval between any given tone and another tone that is exactly twice (or half) the frequency of the first tone. In musical notation, such notes are given the same alphabetical designation: for example, a = 440 vibrations per second, a′ = 880 vibrations per second.

October, tenth month of the year. Its name comes from the Latin for eighth because it was the eighth month in the old ten-month calendar. It has 31 days. The birthstone is the opal, beryl, or tourmaline.

Octopus, predaceous cephalopod mollusk with no external shell. Its saclike body has eight powerful suckered tentacles. It moves by jet propulsion and crawling and hides in crevices on the shallow sea bottom. Many of the 150 species are small but the common Pacific octopus (*Octopus vulgaris*) can attain a spread of 32ft (10m). *See also* Cephalopod; Mollusk.

Ode, poetry form used by Greeks. Of moderate length, it usually expressed praise in a lofty, exalted manner. Choral odes had three parts: the first two had identical meter, the third part, a contrasting one. Pindar and Horace wrote odes.

Odense, city and port in S central Denmark, 85mi (137km) WSW of Copenhagen on canal linking it with Odense Fjord; site of Hans Christian Andersen's home (now a museum), 13th-century cathedral of St Knud, 18th-century palace. Industries: metal goods, dairy products, motor vehicles, shipyards. Founded AD 1000. Pop. 102,698.

Oder (Odra), river in Czechoslovakia, East Germany, and Poland; rises in the mountains of NE Czechoslovakia; flows NW through SW Poland, past Wroclaw to junction with Neisse, from here turning N and forming Poland-East Germany border until it departs from the border a few miles from its mouth on the Oderhaft (bay), at Szczecin, NW Poland. River has been an important water route for N Europe since early times, serving a large area with many navigable tributaries, notably the Neisse and Warta rivers; Szczecin, a port on the river, was internationalized between WWI and WWII; lower course was made border between Poland and East Germany by Potsdam Conference 1945. Length: approx. 565mi (910km).

Oder-Neisse Line, boundary between East Germany and Poland formed by the Oder and Neisse rivers. It was est. in 1945 by agreement between Britain, the United States, and the USSR at the Potsdam Conference. By the agreement former German territory was transferred to Poland. The boundary was recognized by the East German government by a treaty with Poland in 1950, but the West German government did not confirm the Oder-Neisse Line until a 1971 treaty. *See also* Potsdam Conference.

Odessa, city in Ukrainian SSR, USSR, 25mi (40km) NE of the mouth of the Dniester River on Odessa Bay; capital of the Odessa oblast. It came under the Turks in 1764, and Russian control in 1791; made a naval base and port 1794; named Odessa in 1795; scene of the mutiny aboard the battleship *Potemkin* 1905; occupied by Axis forces during WWII. A cultural and educational center, it is site of state university (1865), polytechnical, agricultural, medical, and teachers' colleges, maritime academy, conservatory, base of the Soviet Antarctic whaling fleet and fishing fleet. Industries: agricultural machinery, construction equipment, fertilizer, leather goods, foodstuffs, shipbuilding and repairing, oil refining, linoleum. Founded 14th century. Pop. 1,051,000.

Odessa, city in W Texas, 56mi (90km) WSW of Big Spring; seat of Ector co; industrial and shipping center; site of Odessa College (1946). Industries: oil, livestock, chemicals, tile, oil-drilling equipment, limestone, salt, carbon black mining. Settled 1886 by Russian and German colonists; inc. 1927. Pop. (1980) 90,027.

Odin, one of the principal gods in Norse mythology. He was a war god and he appeared in heroic literature as the protector of heroes. Fallen warriors joined him in Valhalla. He carried a spear, rode an eight-legged horse, Sleipnir, and the wolf and raven were sacred to him. Odin was also associated with poets, musicians, and runes.

Odoacer, or **Odovacar** (*c.*435–93), chief of the Germanic Heruli people and conqueror of the West Roman empire. The Heruli were Roman mercenaries until 476 when they declared Odoacer king. He deposed Romulus Augustulus and established his authority over Italy, proving himself a capable ruler. In 488 he was defeated by the Ostrogoth king Theodoric the Great. Odoacer ceded Ravenna and Theodoric invited him to a banquet where he was betrayed and murdered.

Odonata, order of primitive winged insects found worldwide. Those of the suborder Zygoptera (damselfly) have thin bodies with wings held vertically at rest. The long, slender, aquatic nymphs have three leaflike gills on the abdomen. Those of the suborder Anisoptera (dragonfly) have heavy bodies with wings held horizontally at rest. The stout nymphs have gills in the anal end. All prey on insects; none attacks man. Length: 0.75–5in (19–127mm).

Odyssey, ancient Greek epic, generally ascribed to Homer. Written in 24 books, like its predecessor the *Iliad*, the story begins 10 years after the Trojan War. For seven of those years, Odysseus has been detained by the goddess Calypso. His efforts to return home to his loving family are delayed by visits to the land of forgetfulness and to the underworld, as well as encounters with the one-eyed cyclops, sea monsters, and sirens. When Odysseus finally returns to Ithaca, he discovers that his wife Penelope is being urged to remarry by various noblemen who want her fortune. Odysseus kills them all and is reunited with his family. *See also* Iliad.

OECD. *See* Organization for Economic Cooperation and Development.

Oedipus, in Greek mythology and literature, son of Laius, king of Thebes, and Jocasta. Father of Antigone, Electra, Eteocles, and Polynices by his own mother. The 5th-century BC playwright Sophocles tells how Oedipus was saved from death as an infant and raised in Corinth, how he killed his father, solved the riddle of the Sphinx, and became king of Thebes, where he married Queen Jocasta, his own widowed mother.

Oedipus Complex, in psychoanalytic theory, incestuous fantasy in which a child desires the parent of the opposite sex. Sigmund Freud held that children pass through a stage (from about three to six) in which they develop a lively curiosity about sex. The son desires his mother and wants the father dead. The daughter wants sex with the father and hates her mother. ("Electra Complex" may be used to label the girl's feelings.) Freud believed that many adult neuroses originated in conflicts at the Oedipal stage.

Oersted, Hans Christian (1777–1851), Danish physicist and professor at Copenhagen. He took the first steps in elucidating the relationship between electricity and magnetism, thus founding the science of electromagnetism. The oersted unit of magnetic field strength is named after him. He was also the first scientist to isolate pure metallic aluminum.

Oersted, unit of magnetic field strength equal to the magnetic field that would cause a unit magnetic pole to experience a force of one dyne in a vacuum.

Offenbach, Jacques Levy (1819–80), French composer. He composed over 100 operettas, of which *Orpheus in the Underworld* (1858) is the most famous. He turned to serious opera only once with *The Tales of Hoffman* (1880), one of the masterpieces of the French repertory.

Ogaden, arid region in SE Ethiopia, bordering Somalia. Inhabited mainly by ethnic Somali pastoral nomads, it was conquered by Ethiopia in 1891 and was the site of the first battle of the war between Italy and Ethiopia (1935–36). Since 1960, Somali nationalists have called for the union of Ogaden and Somalia. During the late 1970s guerrilla fighting escalated into full-scale war between Ogaden guerrillas, supported by the army of Somalia, and Ethiopian troops. Assisted by Cuban troops and Soviet military equipment, Ethiopia forced Somalian troops to retreat in 1980, and in 1981, Somalia announced its willingness to negotiate with Ethiopia. The dislocation of war combined with severe drought had resulted in famine and massive migration by the people of the Ogaden into Somalia.

Ogbomosho, city in SW Nigeria, approx. 50mi (81km) NNE of Ibadan; it was a Hausa stronghold against Fulani invasions early 19th century; processing and shipping center for region. Products: tobacco, cattle, fruits. Pop. 392,000.

Ogden, city in N Utah, 33mi (53km) N of Salt Lake City; seat of Weber co; site of two Mormon tabernacles, Hill Air Force Base, Weber State College (1889). Industries: dairy products, food processing, electronic equipment, brewing, tourism. Settled 1846 by Mormons and is oldest continuously settled area in state; inc. 1851. Pop. (1980) 64,407.

Oglethorpe, James Edward (1696–1785), English general and colonist. After military service against Turkey, he returned to England and became interested in social reform, particularly the problems of debtors. Taking a group to North America, he settled in Savannah and founded the colony of Georgia for imprisoned English debtors. It was chartered in 1732. Oglethorpe hoped to use the colony as a buffer between South Carolina and the Spanish possessions in Florida, but Georgia did not develop as he had planned.

O'Higgins, Bernardo (1778–1842), Chilean independence leader, became commander of Chile's anti-royalist forces in 1813. O'Higgins issued Chile's declaration of independence in 1818 and was named supreme director by San Martín. In 1823, General Ramón Freire led an army revolt in southern Chile; O'Higgins was forced to resign and leave the country.

Ohio, state in the E central United States. Lake Erie marks most of its N boundary.

Land and economy. The land is a rolling plain with many rivers, including the Muskingum, the Scioto, the Miami, and the Maumee. Water transport on Lake Erie and the Ohio River, which forms the S boundary, is of great importance to the economy. Agriculture is profitable in most sections, and industry is widely distributed in cities and towns. Coal is found in the S and E.

People. Ohio was settled originally by pioneers from New England, Pennsylvania, and Virginia. Immigrants from overseas, principally Germans and Irish, flocked to the state in the early 19th century. For most of the 19th century, the state ranked 3d in the nation in population; its decline in rank reflects the growth of other states rather than a loss in Ohio. About 75% of the inhabitants lives in urban areas.

Education. There are more than 100 institutions of higher education, including twelve state-supported universities.

History. French and English traders operated in the region in the early 18th century. Great Britain acquired it in 1763 at the end of the French and Indian War. It became US soil after the American Revolution, and in 1787 Congress created the Northwest Territory, which included the present states of Ohio, Indiana, and Illinois, and lands to the N. The first settlement in Ohio was at Marietta in 1788. Ohio was separated from the Northwest Territory in 1800 and was accepted as a state three years later. Development of railroads and canals enhanced Ohio's geographical position midway between the Atlantic seaboard and the Mississippi Valley, and the state exerted great influence in national affairs. Seven presidents of the United States after 1868 were born in Ohio. Because of its proximity to iron and coal as well as excellent transportation links, Ohio developed as a major center of heavy manufacturing. By the late 1970s, however, many industries experienced a serious downturn.

PROFILE

Admitted to Union: March 1, 1803; rank, 17th
US Congressmen: Senate, 2; House of Representatives, 23
Population: 10,797,419 (1980); rank, 6th
Capital: Columbus, 564,871 (1980)
Chief cities: Cleveland, 573,822; Columbus; Cincinnati, 385,457
State legislature: Senate, 33; House of Representatives, 99
Area: 41,222sq mi (106,765sq km); rank, 35th
Elevation: Highest, 1,550ft (473m), Campbell Hill; lowest, 433ft (132m), Ohio River
Industries (major products): automobiles, parts and accessories; tires, aircraft, boats, iron and steel, industrial machinery, household appliances, processed foods
Agriculture (major products): cattle, dairy products, hogs, sheep, corn, grapes, soybeans
Minerals (major): bituminous coal, lime, clay, salt, sand and gravel
State nickname: Buckeye State
State motto: With God, All Things Are Possible
State bird: cardinal
State flower: red carnation
State tree: Ohio buckeye

Ohio, navigable river in central United States; rises in Pittsburgh, Pennsylvania at the confluence of the Allegheny and Monongahela rivers; flows W and SW into the Mississippi River in S Illinois. Ohio River basin is populous and heavily industrialized; it has been subject to flood control and anti-pollution measures; used for hydroelectricity and industrial traffic. Discovered 1669 by LaSalle. Length: 981mi (1,579km).

Ohm, Georg Simon (1787–1854), German physicist. He was appointed professor at Munich in honor of his discovery of the law (Ohm's law) relating electrical current intensity, electromotive force, and circuit resistance. His name is also honored in the unit of electrical resistance.

Ohm, unit of electrical resistance equal to the resistance between two points on a conductor when a constant potential difference of one volt between the points produces a current of one ampere.

Ohm's Law, statement that the amount of steady current through a material is proportional to the voltage across the material, propounded by the German physicist Georg Simon Ohm. Ohm's Law is expressed mathematically as $V/I=R$ (V is the unit of volts; I is the amperes; R is the resistance, measured in units called ohms).

Oil. *See* Petroleum.

Oilbird, or guacharo, South American bird equipped with batlike radar that can fly in total darkness. It is maroon-brown with white spots and has stiff bristles around its mouth, a yellowish, hooked bill, and weak legs. Groups feed on palm tree nuts and fruit at night, retreating deep into caves at dawn where they incessantly squeak and squawk. They glue organic matter to form a flattish, pedestal nest high on a ledge for whitish, brown-smudged eggs (2). Odorless oil, obtained from fat of the nestlings, supplied American Indians with oil for lighting and cooking. Length: 13in (33cm); wingspan: 3ft (92cm). Species *Steatornis caripensis.*

Oil-Drop Experiment, experimental method used (1916 onward) by R. A. Millikan to measure the electron's charge by subjecting charged oil drops to a variable electric field.

Oil Painting, painting medium using an oil base for paint pigments. Sometimes a diluting material is used with oil paints, and often a protective varnish is used to cover the paint on the canvas. Jan van Eyck was among the first painters to use an oil base containing resins. Other artists used oils as glazes to make their paintings appear yellow. With the 16th century came the use of canvas as a primary painting surface, and Venetians such as Titian and Tintoretto used oils successfully with little underpainting. In the 17th century Rubens used oils in the Flemish tradition, placing transparent colors over a white priming. Rembrandt used a dark ground and thin paint to make his shadows and heavier paint to make his light portions. Franz Hals and Velazquez also experimented with the use of oils. English painting between 1780 and 1850 has a dark appearance, due to the pigment bitumen. During the 19th century, the traditional use of layers of glazes over a ground was replaced by direct painting. Many 19th-century schools, such as Impressionism and Pointillism, developed different techniques of oil painting, and this experimentation continues today.

Oils, any of numerous plant, animal, mineral, or synthetic substances, usually liquid and greasy to the touch and soluble in organic solvents such as ether but not in water. When combustible, like petroleum, they are used as fuels. Many are used as lubricants and some are important foods. Fats and waxes are similar but solid or semisolid at standard temperatures. Essential oils are odiferous, volatile materials produced by various plant species.

Ojibwa, or **Ojibway,** a variant of the name of the Chippewa tribe. It is more commonly used to refer to this Algonquian-speaking tribe in Canada.

Oka, either of two rivers in central Russian SFSR, USSR. One rises in N part of Kursk oblast; flows N and NE to the Volga River at Gorki; navigable for most of its length. Main tributaries are the Klyazma, Moksha, and Moskva; important for lumber and grain trade. Length: 919mi (1,480km). The other rises in the Sayan Mts, flows N to the Angara River. Length: 530mi (853km).

Okapi, even-toed, hoofed ruminant of African equatorial rain forests. It is purplish colored with striped legs and a tongue so long it reaches to the eyes for cleaning. Males have small, hair-covered horns. Although relatively common, it was unknown to science until 1900. Height: to 8ft (244cm) at shoulder. Family Giraffidae; species *Okapia johnstoni.*

Okayama, city in SW Honshu, Japan, approx. 90mi (145km) W of Osaka; capital of Okayama prefecture; trade center for agricultural region; site of university

Hans Christian Oersted

Great Serpent Mound, Ohio

Oilbird

(1949), 18th-century park and feudal castle. Products: rice, fruits. Industries: agricultural machinery, rubber, textiles. Pop. 513,000.

Okeechobee, lake in S central Florida, N of the Everglades; 3rd-largest freshwater lake in United States. Fed by Kissimmee River and drained by Caloosahatchee River; subject of flood control measures after destructive 1926 hurricane; part of Okeechobee (Cross-Florida) Waterway System. Area: 700sq mi (1,813sq km).

O'Keeffe, Georgia (1887–1986), US painter, b. Sun Prairie, Wis. Her microscopic paintings of flowers brought her popular attention. Her early works were stylized and associated with nonrepresentation ("Abstraction," 1926). Her later works, often involving a series of studies of particular objects, include "Black Iris, Lake George Barns" (1926) and "Stables" (1932).

Okefenokee Swamp, swampland in SE Georgia and NE Florida; drained by the Suwanee and St Mary's rivers; major part of the Okefenokee Wildlife Refuge (est. 1937). Area: 600sq mi (1,554sq km).

Okhotsk, Sea of (Ochotskoje More), NW arm of Pacific Ocean W of Kamčatka Peninsula and Kuril Islands; connected with Sea of Japan by Tatar and La Pérouse straits, and with Pacific Ocean by passages through Kuril Islands; icebound from November to June. Main ports are Magadan and Korsakov in Soviet Union; waters off W Kamčatka Peninsula are source of fish and crabs. Area: 590,000sq mi (1,528,100sq km).

Okinawa, largest member of the Okinawa Islands, Japan, in the Ryuku Islands chain, SSW of mainland Japan, in W Pacific Ocean. A volcanic-coral formation, densely vegetated, it was taken by US forces in WWII after a campaign lasting March–June 1945; it provided the United States with an air base close to mainland Japan; it was returned to Japan 1971. Area: 454sq mi (1,176sq km). Pop. 295,091.

Oklahoma, state in the S central United States in the Great Plains region.

Land and economy. From high plains in the NW, the land slopes to the SE, broken by hills and low mountains. Much of the state is grassland, with some forests in the E. The Arkansas River flows E through the center of the state; the Red River marks most of the S boundary. There are no large natural lakes, but many reservoirs have been created by dams. Oklahoma's grazing land and resources of petroleum and natural gas are widely distributed in the state. Manufacturing is largely involved with processing the products of natural resources.

People. White settlement of the region, which did not come until the 19th century, was principally by immigrants from other states. Oklahoma has one of the largest Indian populations in the United States. There are no reservations as in other states; the Indians mingle with other residents. About 68% of the total population resides in urban areas.

Education. There are about 40 institutions of higher education.

History. Most of the area was acquired by the United States from France in the Louisiana Purchase of 1803. It was successively part of several new larger territories. In 1834, Indian Territory was created as a home for the "Five Civilized Tribes" of Indians—Cherokees, Chickasaws, Creeks, Choctaws, and Seminoles—who had been moved by the federal government from states to the E. Part of the land that had been withdrawn from white settlement was opened in 1889 and was organized in 1890 as the Territory of Oklahoma. This was merged with Indian Territory to

become one state. By the early 20th century oil production had begun, and industry, based on processing oil and natural gas, gradually developed.

PROFILE

Admitted to Union: Nov. 16, 1907; rank, 46th
US Congressmen: Senate, 2; House of Representatives, 6
Population: 3,025,266 (1980); rank, 26th
Capital: Oklahoma City, 403,213 (1980)
Chief cities: Oklahoma City; Tulsa, 360,919; Lawton, 80,054; Norman, 68,020
State legislature: Senate, 48; House of Representatives, 101
Area: 69,919sq mi (181,090sq km); rank, 18th
Elevation: Highest, 4,973ft (1,517m), Black Mesa; lowest, 287ft (88m), Little River
Industries (major products): petroleum products, machinery (construction and oil equipment); processed foods
Agriculture (major products): cattle, wheat, corn, sorghum, peanuts
Minerals (major): petroleum, natural gas, helium, gypsum, coal, zinc
State nickname: Sooner State
State motto: Labor Omnia Vincit (Labor Conquers All Things)
State bird: scissortailed flycatcher
State flower: mistletoe
State tree: redbud

Oklahoma City, largest city and capital of Oklahoma, in central Oklahoma, 88mi (142km) SW of Tulsa on North Canadian River; seat of Oklahoma co. Settled during the land rush, it was opened to homesteaders 1889; made state capital 1910; prospered with discovery of rich oil deposit (1928). It is site of Oklahoma City University (1911), Southwestern College (1946), Oklahoma Christian College (1950), National Cowboy Hall of Fame, Tinker Air Force Base. Industries: oil and oil refining, stockyards, meat packing, grains, cotton processing, steel products, aircraft. Inc. 1890. Pop. (1980) 403,213.

Okra, or gumbo, annual plant native to tropical regions of the Old World. It has yellow flowers with red centers. The sticky, green fruit pods are eaten as a vegetable. Height: 2–6ft (0.6–1.8m). Family Malvaceae; species *Hibiscus esculentus.*

Olaf V (1903–), king of Norway (1957–). He succeeded his father, Haakon VII. Olaf took part in the struggle for liberation during the German occupation in World War II, assuming supreme command of Norwegian forces in 1944.

Olbers, Heinrich Wilhelm Matthäus (1758–1840), German astronomer and physician known for his discovery of the asteroids Pallas (1802) and Vesta (1807), and five comets. He devised a new method of calculating the comets' orbits. Olbers also proposed his famous paradox: if stars are infinite in number and evenly distributed in space, the sky should be solidly bright with no darkness on the Earth. His explanation, that interstellar dust obscures the light, was discarded in the 1970s in favor of the theory that expansion of the universe dims the light from distant objects.

Oldenburg, Claes (1929–), US painter and sculptor. One of the first abstract expressionists, he is noted for his wood, plastic, and plaster sculptures of household items, often grossly oversized. They became a standard pop art form. His works include *Dual Hamburger* (1962), *Giant Light Switches* (1964), and *Lipstick (Ascending) on Caterpillar Track* (1969).

Oldenburg, city in NW West Germany, on Hunte River, 80mi (129km) NW of Bremen; seat of counts of Oldenburg (*c.* 12th century–1667); annexed to Denmark 1667; residence of dukes of Oldenburg 1777–1918; site of two grand-ducal palaces (17th–18th century). Industries: tobacco products, linoleum, knit goods, musical instruments. Inc. 1345. Pop. 134,700.

Old English Sheepdog, drovers' dog (working group) bred in western England early in the 19th century. It has a square head and long, square jaws; medium-sized ears carried flat to the head; short, compact body; medium long, sturdy legs; and docked tail. The shaggy coat is hard-textured and profuse; colors are gray, grizzle, blue—all with or without white. Average size: 21–25in (53.5–63.5cm) high at shoulder; 55–65lb (25–29.5kg). *See* Working Dog.

Oldham, town in NW England, 6mi (10km) NE of Manchester. Industries: cotton spinning, textile machinery, electrical equipment. Pop. 228,400.

Old Norse Literature, literature of the Scandinavian Norsemen from the 9th–12th centuries. It is mainly mythological poetry and sagas. The work was set down in stone and wood, but survived orally and was recorded in eddic and skaldic Icelandic verse.

Old Red Sandstone, a geologic term for freshwater deposits of Devonian age found in Great Britain, especially Scotland. The continental deposits embrace nearly the whole extent of the Devonian and are divided into Lower, Middle, and Upper portions. These strata are noted for their fish fossils among which are jawless fishes (ostracoderms), the first jawed fishes (placoderms), and by the Middle "Old Red," the first true bony fishes (osteichthyes) appear in abundance and variety. Deposits of equivalent age are found in Canada, Greenland, United States, Central Asia, Australia, and Antarctica.

Old Testament, first portion of the Christian Bible or the Hebrew Bible. The number, order, and names of the books vary between Jews and Christians and between Catholics and Protestants. The earliest books of the Old Testament were first collected from older sources around 1000 BC. The Hebrew text, called the Masora, was adopted *c.* AD 100. Christian texts are based on a 3rd-century BC Greek text, the Septuagint. The books include the Pentateuch: Genesis, Exodus, Leviticus, Numbers, Deuteronomy; the prophets, including Joshua, Kings, Isaiah, Jeremiah, Ezekiel; and Hagiographa, including Psalms, Proverbs, Job, Song of Songs, Ruth, Lamentations, Esther, Daniel, Chronicles. *See also* individual books.

Olduvai Gorge, site in northern Tanzania famous for its Pleistocene fossil remains, particularly the sequence of the asteroids Paleolithic cultures revealed there by the Leakey family. The site provides some of the earliest and most controversial evidence for the development of Australopithecines into *Homo erectus. See also* Australopithecus.

Oleander, Eurasian evergreen shrubs with poisonous sap and loose clusters of fragrant red, pink, or white flowers, including *Nerium oleander*—height: to 20ft (6.1m); and sweet-scented oleander *(N. indicum)*—height: to 8ft (2.4m). Family Apocynaceae.

Oleaster, a small, deciduous tree *(Elaeagnus augustifolia)* of the family Elaeagnaceae, native to Eurasia. To 20ft (6m) high, with spines on branches. Narrow leaves are light green with hairy, silver undersides; silver-scaled flowers are small and fragrant. The yel-

Olfaction

low, olive-shaped fruit is edible. Commonly grown as an ornamental hedge.

Olfaction. *See* Smell.

Oligarchy, system of government in which power is concentrated in the hands of a privileged minority, which rules without popular support or any external check on their authority.

Oligocene Epoch. *See* Tertiary Period.

Oligopoly, a situation of imperfect competition, which exists in an industry that contains few firms producing similar products that are usually differentiated by either brand or type. The oligopolistic industry also has significant barriers to entry, either in terms of cost of entry or name recognition. In the automobile industry, for example, the cost of entry by a new firm is almost prohibitive and name recognition is extremely important.

Olive, family (Oleaceae) of trees, shrubs, and vines found in warm regions. Main characteristics are one-seeded fruits and bad smelling wood. The 29 genera and 600 species include ash, lilac, ironwood, and marblewood. The common olive, *Olea europaea,* is native to the Mediterranean and cultivated in other warm regions. Its leathery leaves are lance-shaped; the trunk is gnarled and twisted; 30ft (9m) tall. It may live for 1,000 or more years.

Olive Oil, yellowish liquid oil, containing olein and palmitin, obtained by expressing olives. It is used for cooking, as a salad oil, in soap manufacture, and in medicine. Properties: sp gr 0.910–0.918.

Olives, Mount of, historic ridge in W Jordan, separated from Jerusalem (E) by Kidron stream. The Mt of Olives and its four surrounding hills are associated with the preachings of Christ, his Ascension, David's flight from the city, and Zechariah's prophecy; the Garden of Gethsemane is on its W slope; site of many churches and part of Hebrew University (1925).

Olivier, Laurence, Baron Olivier of Brighton (1907–   ), English actor, producer, and director. He is often referred to as the greatest actor of the 20th century. His first stage appearance was at Stratford-on-Avon in 1922, and he worked with the Old Vic Company from 1937. He entered films after 1930, appearing in *Wuthering Heights* (1939), *Rebecca* (1940), *Othello* (1965), *Three Sisters* (1970), *Boys from Brazil* (1978), and *Clash of the Titans* (1981). He won an Academy Award for *Hamlet* (1948). In 1962 he was appointed director of the National Theatre of England.

Olivine, a group of independent tetrahedral silicates [(Mg,Fe)$_2$Sio$_4$]. The group includes fosterite, tephorite, monticellite, fayalite, and peridote (gem quality). Orthorhombic system crystals, usually granular masses. Green, brown, gray; glassy and brittle. Hardness 6.5–7; sp gr 3.3.

Olmec, one of the earliest known cultural periods of prehistoric New World chronology, covering about 1500–500 BC. The people of the Olmec culture produced some of the most remarkable aesthetic works in Mexican art. Their homeland seems to have been central Mexico, from the Pacific coast of Guerrero to Veracruz, but evidences of their culture have been found as far south as central Guatemala.

Olympia, area in ancient S Greece, near Alpheus River; center of worship of Zeus; scene of the Olympic Games (est. 776 BC), which were held in his honor; the temple of Zeus housed the elaborately adorned statue of Zeus by Phidias, one of the seven Wonders of the World; archeological excavations have unearthed great temples, a stadium, and celebrated statue of Hermes of Praxiteles.

Olympia, capital city and port of entry in SW Washington, on S tip of Puget Sound in Budd Inlet; seat of Thurston co. Settled *c.* 1845 as Smithfield by Edmund Sylvester and Levi Lathrop Smith, it was made first port of entry on Puget Sound by Congress 1851; name changed to Olympia, it was made capital of Washington Territory 1853; development was spurred with coming of railroad 1880s; during WWI and WWII its port was expanded. Olympia is site of capitol (1893), St Martin's College (1895), annual salmon run from Budd Inlet to Capitol Lake. Exports: forest and agricultural products. Industries: food canning, beer, oysters, lumber. Inc. 1859. Pop. (1980) 27,447.

Olympic Games, an athletic competition open to all nations, scheduled every four years, includes a winter and a summer meeting. The modern summer games began in Athens, Greece, in 1896. The winter games began in 1924 at Chamonix, France. The games were canceled during World War I (1916) and World War II (1940, 1944).

Summer events include archery, basketball, boxing, canoeing, cycling, diving, equestrian sports, fencing, field hockey, handball, judo, gymnastics, polo, rowing, soccer, shooting, swimming, track and field (includes decathlon and modern pentathlon), volleyball, water polo, weight lifting, wrestling, and yachting. Winter events include biathlon, bobsledding, ice hockey, luge, skating, and skiing. Additionally, the host country is allowed to name a sport of its choice. Although contestants represent countries, the events are officially won by individuals. A gold medal is awarded for first place, silver for second place, and bronze for the third place. In certain events, the competition is on a team basis. The winning country (unofficially) is the one to accumulate the most medals. Women first competed in 1912.

History. The Olympic Games began in 776 BC in Greece in honor of Olympian Zeus. They were held at Olympia once every four years until they were discontinued by Emperor Theodosius I of Rome at the end of the 4th century AD. Women were not allowed to compete or even watch the games. As a result, they formed their own four-year games (called Heraea) from around the 6th century BC until the 4th century when Greece was conquered by Rome. Although the modern Olympic Games were aimed at emphasizing individual excellence and the spirit of international goodwill, they often have been political in nature. In 1936, Adolf Hitler, who was hosting the games, refused to congratulate Jesse Owens, a black man, after he had won four gold medals. In 1972 the games in Munich were marred by the killing of 11 Israeli athletes by Arab terrorists, and the 1976 Montreal games suffered a boycott by African nations as well as the withdrawal of Taiwan. The 1980 summer games in Moscow were boycotted by the United States and some other western countries to protest the invasion of Afghanistan by the USSR. In turn, the USSR, followed by 13 other Communist countries, boycotted the 1984 summer Olympics held in Los Angeles.

Olympus, Mount, highest mountain peak in Olympus Mts, N Greece. As the highest point in Greece, its summit is covered with clouds, and it was considered in ancient Greek mythology to be the home of the gods, closed to mortal eyes. Height: 9,570ft (2,920m).

Omaha, city and port of entry in E Nebraska, on Missouri River; seat of Douglas co; largest city in Nebraska. Area was ceded to US government 1854; it developed rapidly as a supply depot for westward travelers, and later as an industrial center (1869); capital of Nebraska Territory 1855–67. A leading livestock market and meat processing center, it is site of Creighton University (1878), University of Nebraska at Omaha (1908), College of St Mary (1923), Offutt Air Force Base, Fort Omaha (1868). Industries: packing plants, oil refining, food processing, farm machinery, fertilizers, computer components, telephone and railroad equipment, airplanes, chemicals. Inc. 1857. Pop. (1980) 311,681.

Omaha, a Siouan-speaking tribe of North American Indians that inhabited NW Nebraska, along the Missouri River. They are well known for their participation in a major political action against the US government concerning ownership of Indian lands in the 1880s. Today some surviving 2,000 Omaha people reside in Nebraska and Oklahoma.

Oman (Umān), formerly Muscat and Oman; an independent sultanate on SE Arabian Peninsula, jutting into strategic Strait of Hormuz, bordered by Arabian Sea (SW), Gulf of Oman (NE), extends inland to Rub'al-Khali Desert. The Hajar Mts run parallel to the Gulf of Oman; the highest point is Jebel Sham approx. 9,777ft (2,980m); the interior is a gently sloping, broad plain. The economy is predominantly agricultural and subsistence; chief products are sugar cane, dates, wheat, barley, corn, millet, lime, olives. Industries include petroleum, which is partly limited by claims of the Iraq Petroleum Co., wine, fishing, oil refining. The people are mostly Arab, with minorities of Indians, Baluchis, Iranians,and East Africans. Most of the inhabitants are religious adherents of Ibadism, an Islamic sect.

In 1508 the Portuguese settled the seaport of Muscat and held the area until it was taken by Turkey (1648); in 1741 Oman was recovered by Omans of Yemen, and Ahmad Ibn Said of Yemen founded the present royal line. In the early 19th century Oman was the most powerful of the Arabian states; but in 1856 most of the coasts of Iran, Baluchistan, and Zanzibar were lost, and Oman became politically and economically dependent on Britain. British influence was reaffirmed by a treaty 1939 and renewed 1951 between sultanate and Britain; rebellion against the sultanate 1954–57 was suppressed with British aid. In 1965 the United Nations demanded elimination of Britain's influence in Oman. The ruling sultan was removed 1970 by his son Qabus who promised to use oil revenues for development of Oman. In 1971 Oman joined the Arab League and the United Nations. Qabus has faced guerrilla opposition to his regime and relies heavily on military support from the United Kingdom and United States. Negotiations in 1982 ended hostilities with South Yemen, where guerrillas opposed to Qabus were harbored.

PROFILE

Official name: Sultanate Oman
Area: 82,012sq mi (212,457sq km)
Population: 850,000
Chief cities: Muscat (capital); Matrah
Religion: Islam

Omar Khayyám (c. 1048–1122), Persian poet, mathematician, and astronomer. He received an extensive education, and early in his life wrote a treatise on algebra which so impressed Sultan Jalāl ad-Dīn that he was asked to reform the calendar. He was a master of philosophy and jurisprudence. His fame in the West is due mainly to a collection of verses attributed to him and which were freely translated by Edward Fitzgerald and published in 1859 as *The Rubáiyát of Omar Khayyám.*

Omayyads. *See* Umayyads.

Omdurman (Umm Durman), city in NE central Sudan, on White Nile River, opposite Khartoum; largest city and chief commercial center of Sudan. City served as military headquarters of the Mahdi 1884; captured 1898 by British; site of Mahdi's tomb, Khalifa museum, university (1912). Industries: furniture, tanning, pottery, textiles, livestock, gum arabic. Pop. 305,308.

Omsk, city in Russian SFSR, USSR, on the Irtysh and Om rivers; capital of Omsk oblast; made administrative center of W Siberia 1824; seat of the counter-revolutionary Kolchak government 1918–19; site of medical, agricultural, and teachers' colleges and technical schools. Industries: agricultural machinery, textiles, footwear, flour, lumber, oil, petrochemicals. Founded 1716; chartered 1804. Pop. 1,042,000.

Ona, known as the "foot people," referring to their custom of walking instead of traveling by canoe. A member of the Tshon language family, this tribe of South American Indians was never populous; they were famed for their adaptation to the most rigorous climate in the Americas. About 25 still survive in the Tierra del Fuego region of Chile and Argentina.

Onager, wild ass found in semi-desert areas of Iran and India. It is a dun-colored animal with a triple, light-colored stripe on the back and shoulders. Height 48–51in (121.9–129.5cm) at shoulder. Family Equidae; species *Equus hemionus onager. See also* Ass.

Onchocerciasis, infection with microfilarial worms that dwell in cysts in the skin, in the lymphatics, or in the eye, causing a local dermatitis. It is transmitted by bite of the blackfly.

Onega (Onezskoje), lake in S Karelian ASSR, Russian SFSR, USSR, between Lake Ladoga and the White Sea. The second largest lake in Europe, its outlet is the Svir, flowing from the SW corner to Lake Ladoga; main affluents are the Vodla, Vytegra, and Andoma rivers on the E; site of numerous inlets and islands along N shore, and supports fisheries and timber industries. Petrozavodsk is the only large town on its shores. Area: 3,710sq mi (9,609sq km).

Oneida, the smallest, but most warlike, tribal member of the Six Nations of the Iroquois. Its homeland was around Lake Oneida in New York State. Most of the tribe was removed after the American Revolution to Wisconsin. Today 4,100 live on the Oneida Reservation in New York, and in northern and east-central Wisconsin.

O'Neill, Eugene (Gladstone) (1888–1953), US playwright, b. New York City. He wrote 45 plays, covering a wide range of subjects and dramatic styles. His plays reflect his pessimistic philosophy that man, robbed of his traditional faith by science, has nothing with which to replace it. He won the Nobel Prize for literature in 1936 for his dramas, and four Pulitzer prizes for *Beyond the Horizon* (1919), *Anna Christie* (1922), *Strange Interlude* (1928), and *Long Day's Journey into Night* (1967), produced after his death. His 11-act trilogy *Mourning Becomes Electra* (1931) transfers the Orestean story to New England. At the time of his death he was engaged on a cycle of plays about a long period in American life, including *The Iceman Cometh* (1946) and *A Moon for the Misbegotten* (1947). He is viewed as the United States' most important playwright.

Oman

Eugene O'Neill

J. Robert Oppenheimer

Onion, hardy, bulbous, biennial plant native to central Asia. It has long been cultivated for its large, strong smelling, edible bulb. It has hollow leaves, white or lilac flowers, and prefers dryish, well drained soil and a sunny location. Height: to 18in (46cm). Family Liliaceae; species *Allium cepa.*

Onondaga, one of the members of the Six Nations of the Iroquois, and regarded as "Keepers of the Central Fire." This major group of North American Indians occupied the region around Onondaga co, New York, where some 1,400 still live.

Ontario, province in SE Canada, bordered on the S by four of the Great Lakes—Superior, Huron, Erie, and Ontario. As the most populous province and the site of the federal capital at Ottawa it exerts considerable influence in national affairs.
  Land and economy. The country is rolling or level, of generally even elevation. Forests cover the land in the N toward Hudson Bay, while the center and S offer good farming land. Many rivers supply hydroelectric power for industry. The famous Niagara Falls are on the Niagara River on the SE border. The Great Lakes and the St Lawrence River provide excellent water transport; since the opening of the St Lawrence Seaway, oceangoing vessels can use Ontario's ports. Ontario is Canada's most industrialized province, with transportation equipment, iron and steel, paper, and processed foods the leading products.
  People. Most of the population traces its ancestry to the British Isles. About 10% of the population is French speaking. After WWII, Ontario received about 1,500,-000 immigrants from war-torn countries in Europe. About 90% of the population is in the S part, which covers only about 15% of the total area. About 80% lives in urban areas.
  Education. There are about 20 institutions of higher education. Among the most important are the University of Toronto, the University of Western Ontario, the University of Ottawa, Queen's University, McMaster University, and the University of St Michael's.
  History. French explorers on the Great Lakes and up the rivers roamed through the region early in the 17th century and established a number of fur trading posts. The area became part of New France, the French colonies in North America, but was ceded to Great Britain by treaty at the end of the French and Indian War in 1763. The British ruled the region from Quebec. Its population expanded by the influx of thousands of British Loyalists fleeing the American colonies during and after the Revolution. For 50 years after 1791, Ontario was known as Upper Canada, separate from Quebec, but the two were reunited in 1841, and known as Canada until 1867, when the separate provinces of Ontario and Quebec were created and the Dominion was formed. Ontario's mining industries began to develop during the late 19th century; the 1950s was a decade of intense industrial development.

PROFILE

Entered Confederation: July 1, 1867; one of the four provinces that were joined to form the Dominion of Canada
National Parliament Representatives: Senate, 24; House of Commons, 88
Population: 8,264,465
Capital: Toronto
Chief cities: Toronto; Hamilton; Ottawa (federal capital)
Provincial legislature: Legislative Assembly, 117 members
Area: 412,582sq mi (1,068,587sq km); rank, 2d
Elevation: Highest: 2,183ft (665m), Ogidaki Mt; lowest: sea level at Hudson and James bays

Industries (major products): motor vehicles and parts, aircraft and parts, iron and steel, metal products, copper products, agricultural and industrial machinery, pulp and paper, food products
Agriculture (major products): dairy products, beef cattle, hogs, poultry, oats, barley, winter wheat
Minerals (major): nickel, copper, uranium, gold, platinum, silver, zinc
Floral emblem: white trillium

Ontario, city in SE California, 20mi (32km) W of San Bernardino; site of Chaffey College and Ontario Motor Speedway. Industries: citrus fruits, iron products, mobile homes, clothing. Founded 1882; inc. 1891. Pop. (1980) 63,140.

Ontario, Lake, smallest of the Great Lakes, bounded by New York (S and E) and Ontario prov., Canada (S, W, and N), fed by Lake Erie, the lake is drained to the NE by the St Lawrence River and carries oceangoing vessels via the St Lawrence Seaway; they bypass Niagara Falls by the Welland Canal to reach Lake Erie. Discovered in 1615 by Étienne Brulé. Pollution has decreased its supply of fish. Many resorts are on the lake. Chief Canadian cities are St Catherines, Toronto, Hamilton, Kingston; on the US side are Rochester and Oswego. Area: 7,540sq mi (19,529sq km).

Onychophora, a class of about 90 species of terrestrial invertebrates mainly tropical in distribution, lying between annelid worms and arthropods in evolutionary development. They are free-living and elongated and range in size from .6 to 6in (15–152mm) long, have up to 44 pairs of legs, and soft, velvety skin. The most common genus is *Peripatus.*

Onyx, a striped variety of chalcedony. Black and white onyx used in cameos. White and red called carnelian onyx; white and brown, sardonyx. Most found in India and South America.

Oogenesis, process of preparing ovum, or female reproductive cell, for fertilization. The diploid, primary egg cell develops into a haploid ovum through meiosis, yielding one mature egg and three polar bodies that will degenerate.

Ooze, a fine-grained pelagic deposit containing material of more than 30% organic origin, with the rest comprised of clay derived from colloidal matter. Oozes are divided into two main types according to their chief constituents. Calcareous ooze at depths of 2,000m to 3,900m (6,560–12,792ft) contains the skeletons of animals such as foraminiferans and pteropods. Siliceous ooze at depths of more than 3,900m contains skeletons of radiolarians and diatoms.

Opal, a noncrystalline variety of quartz, found in recent volcanoes, deposits from hot springs, and sediments. Usually colorless or white with rainbow play of color in gem forms, most valuable of quartz gems. Hardness 5.5–6.5; sp gr 2.1.

Op Art, US art movement of the 1960s that rejects all signs of representation and insists on nonobjectivity. It often incorporates kinetic energy into designs of squares, lines, circles, and dots to create optical illusions. Often color is used in a powerful way to give a sense of depth to pictures. Also common are the "invisible paintings," in which shapes emerge as the viewer's eye becomes accustomed to the colors of the canvas.

OPEC. *See* Organization of Petroleum Exporting Countries.

Open Door Policy, arrangement allowing all nations equal commercial access to a particular country. Most often associated with China's early relations with the West, it was first formally espoused in 1899 by US Secretary of State John Hay. After the anti-foreign Boxer Rebellion (1900), the policy was modified, allegedly to protect China's territorial integrity but also, later on, to hinder Japanese encroachment. The policy ended during World War II with the recognition of China as a sovereign state.

Opera, stage drama where most or all of the dialogue is sung and accompanied by an orchestra. The first opera is reckoned to be *Dafne* by Jacopo Peri, introduced in Florence, Italy, in 1597. Important opera composers after Peri were Monteverdi, Lully, Rameau, Gluck, and Mozart through the 18th century. During the 19th century opera reached the heights of popularity with the Italian Romantic school (eg, Verdi, Puccini) and the great music dramas of Richard Wagner. Among the most notable opera companies of the 20th century are the Metropolitan Opera in New York City, the Paris Opera, Covent Garden in London, and La Scala in Milan, Italy.

Operetta, music drama involving songs, dialogue, dancing, and a light, romantic story. Operettas developed largely as attempts by opera composers to reach wider audiences. Among the more significant operetta composers were Johann Strauss, Jr., Gilbert and Sullivan, and Victor Herbert.

Operon, region of a chromosome consisting of structural genes and an operator gene. This was a concept elucidated to explain control of gene activity. The structural genes direct the synthesis of enzymes involved in forming a cell constituent or the utilization of a nutrient. The operator gene responds to a molecule (called a repressor) and can exist open or closed. When the operator gene is open, the genes it controls are functional, producing proteins. When interacting with the repressor, the operator gene is closed.

Ophthalmology, that branch of medicine that deals with the structure, function, and diseases of the eyes. It includes surgical and other treatment of eye disorders and the correction of defective vision. *See also* Optometry.

Opium, drug derived from the juice of unripe seedpods of the opium poppy. Its components and derivatives have been used as narcotics and analgesics as long as history has been recorded. It produces drowsiness and euphoria, reduces pain, and has a noninhibitory effect. Morphine, codeine, and papaverine are common opium compounds. *See also* Heroin.

Opium War (1839–42), war fought by the British with China over issues of restrictions on trade by the Chinese and illegal opium smuggling by the Western traders, mainly British, into China. By the Treaty of Nanking in 1842 the Chinese were saddled with an indemnity for the cost of the war, forced to cede Hong Kong to the British, and required to open five ports for international trade. This marked the beginning of the so-called unequal treaties forced on China by the West.

Oppenheimer, J(ulius) Robert (1904–67), US physicist, b. New York City. He directed atomic energy research at the Los Alamos, N. Mex., project that produced the atom bomb in 1945. After the war, he was chairman of the Atomic Energy Commission's general advisory committee (1946–52) and worked for civilian and international control of atomic energy. Opposing development of the hydrogen bomb (1949), he was dropped from the AEC as a security risk (1953). He was director of the Institute for Advanced Study at Princeton University (1947–66).

Opposition, celestial configuration characterized by a difference of 180° in the longitude of the Sun and a superior planet, as viewed from the Earth. A planet is thus at opposition when it completes a straight line passing through Sun and Earth respectively. It is then usually at its closest to the Earth and is most clearly observable.

Optical Rotation, angle through which a molar solution of a compound rotates the plane of polarization of a beam of light at a given temperature. Optical activity is associated with an asymmetrical assembly of groups about an atom. Many natural products show an ability to rotate polarized light counterclockwise; few rotate clockwise.

Optic Nerve, second cranial nerve, which carries the visual stimuli from the retina of the eye to the visual center in the cortex of the brain. That part of the retina where the optic nerve enters the eye is known as the blind spot. *See also* Blind Spot.

Optics, Crystal. *See* Crystal Optics.

Optometry, science that deals with the examination of eyes and the prescribing of lenses and exercises to correct vision defects. It should not be confused with ophthalmology, the medical and surgical treatment of the eyes.

Opuntia, cactus plants found from Canada to Argentina and characterized by small barbed bristles. Chollas have cylindrical joints and prickly pears have flattened joints. Others have rounded joints. Family Cactaceae; genus *Opuntia*. *See also* Cactus; Cholla; Prickly Pear.

Oracles, intermediaries between gods and men in ancient Greece who answered questions about the will of the gods at their shrines. Consultations were highly ritualized; answers were often ambiguous. The oracle of Zeus at Dodona was the oldest; that at Delphi, the most famous.

Oral Surgery, the dental specialty that deals with the diagnosis and subsequent surgery necessary because of certain diseases, injuries, and defects of the jaws, gums, and teeth. Included are the removal of impacted and infected teeth, the treatment of tumors and lesions of the jaws, and the repair of jaw and facial injuries and of cleft palate and lip.

Oran (Ouahran), leading port city and department capital in NW Algeria, on Gulf of Oran; an important trade center; scene of civil strife in 1950s involving many terrorist attacks, which led to exodus of European population. Industries: wine, wool, iron ore, wheat, tobacco, vegetables. Inhabited since prehistoric times, probably founded by Moorish Andalusians, 10th century. Pop. 1,075,000.

Orange, House of, royal house of the Netherlands. Orange, a principality (from 11th century) in southern France, was inherited by the Nassau house of western Germany. The prince of Orange, William the Silent, became stadtholder (1579) of the Netherlands. Except for brief intervals, the House of Orange has ruled the country ever since, usually with the strong support of the people. King William III of England was a prince of Orange. *See also* Nassau, House of.

Orange, city in S California, 22mi (35km) E of Long Beach; site of Chapman College (1861). Industries: fruit packing and processing, rubber products, industrial furnaces. Inc. 1888. Pop. (1980) 91,788.

Orange (Oranje), principal river of S Africa; rises in Maluti Mts, N Lesotho; runs in an irregular E direction, forming boundary between Orange Free State and Cape prov., and part of that of Republic of South Africa and Namibia before reaching the Atlantic Ocean at Alexander Bay; supports many hydroelectric power plants and irrigation systems. Length: approx. 1,300mi (2,093km).

Orange, evergreen citrus fruit tree. There are two types. The sweet orange is native to Asia and widely grown in California and Florida. Fruit develops without flower pollination and is often seedless. There are many varieties of sweet oranges. The sour orange is widely grown in Spain as an ornamental and for marmalade production. It is grown in the United States for use as a rootstock for less hardy species. Height: to 30ft (9m). Family Rutaceae; genus *Citrus*.

Orange Free State (Oranje-Vrystaat), province in E central Republic of South Africa; bounded E by Natal, N by Transvaal, SE by Lesotho, S and W by Cape prov.; capital is Bloemfontein. Annexed 1900 by Great Britain, it was called Orange River Colony until 1910, when it became a province of Union of South Africa; site of several technical and agricultural schools, University of Orange Free State (1855). Products: grains, fruit, livestock. Industries: gold, gypsum, coal, diamond mining, meat processing, matches, vinegar. Area: 49,866sq mi (129,153sq km). Pop. 1,716,350.

Orangemen, members of the Loyal Orange Institution. It was an Irish political and sectarian society founded in Ulster (1795) and named for Britain's Protestant William III, formerly prince of Orange. The society sought to maintain the Protestant succession, and eventually spread to Great Britain. The Orange society strengthened its position in Ireland and continued as bastion of Protestant Unionist opinion in the late 20th century.

Orangutan, stout-bodied, thick-necked great ape native to forests of Sumatra and Borneo. Orangutans have bulging bellies and a thin, shaggy, reddish-brown coat. In trees, they swing by their arms or walk on branches; on the ground, they walk on all fours. Their favorite food is the durian fruit. Height: 5ft (1.5m); weight: to 220lb (100kg); arm span: over 7ft (2.13m). Species *Pongo pygmaeus*. *See also* Primates.

Oratorio, form of musical composition on religious themes for solo voices, chorus, and orchestra. Usually performed in church or concert hall without acting, scenery, or costumes, the term came originally from 17th-century Italy, where liturgical plays set to music were presented in oratories (chapels). Emilio de Cavalieri and Giacomo Carissimi, the first oratorio composers, used Latin texts; Heinrich Schutz and his followers used their national languages. Some outstanding examples, still popular, include Bach's *Christmas Oratorio* (1734), Handel's *Messiah* (1742), Haydn's *Creation* (1797), Mendelssohn's *Elijah* (1846), Honegger's *King David* (1921), Kodaly's *Psalmus Hungaricus* (1923), and Stravinsky's *Oedipus Rex* (1927).

Oratory, the art of speaking in a manner that inspires listeners to intense emotion or action. It usually includes eloquent quotations and gestures and is used in politics, religion, and the law to gain support for a specific opinion. It conforms to a set of rules formed and revised since 460 BC. Pericles, Aristotle, and Cicero were teachers of the art. In the 20th century the trend has been toward a more informal style than oratory allows.

Orbit, path, usually elliptical, followed by a celestial body moving around another body that acts as a center of gravitational attraction. Planetary orbits are described in terms of numerical quantities (elements), including the semimajor axis and eccentricity of the ellipse, the inclination of the orbital plane to that of the ecliptic, and the longitude of the ascending node and of the perihelion. The period of revolution and the mean orbital velocity can be derived from the values of these quantities. *See also* individual planets.

Orbitals, regions in space around the atomic nucleus in which electrons can move. In the simple "planetary" theory of the atom, the electrons are visualized as moving in circular or elliptical orbits. More advanced quantum mechanics replaces these localized, well defined paths by a probability distribution in space. The atomic orbitals are regions within which there is a high probability of finding the electron. Each orbital can accommodate two electrons and has a shape and energy characterized by the quantum numbers. Orbitals corresponding to *s* sub-shells of the atom are spherical, *p*-orbitals have 2 lobes, and *d* orbitals have 4 lobes. In molecules, the bonding electrons move in the combined electric field of all the nuclei. The atomic orbitals then become molecular orbitals—regions encompassing two nuclei, having a characteristic energy and containing two electrons. These molecular orbitals, which can be thought of as formed by overlap of atomic orbitals, constitute chemical bonds. *See also* Atom; Numbers.

Orchestra, group of musicians who perform together. The development of the modern symphony orchestra began in the 17th century, stimulated by the needs of composers to express themselves in new ways and by the development of new instruments and new ways of playing old instruments. Modern orchestras comprise about 80 to 120 musicians divided into sections playing strings (violin, viola, cello, bass, and harp), woodwinds (flute, piccolo, oboe, clarinet, and bassoon), brass (trumpet, trombone, French horn, and tuba), and percussion instruments (drum, cymbal, piano, etc).

Orchid, any member of the family Orchidaceae. Depending on the authority, there are from 15,000 to 35,000 species found worldwide in all regions, but especially common in the tropics. All are nonwoody perennials and grow in soil or as epiphytes (air plants) on other plants. All have a bilaterally symmetrical flower structure, with three sepals. Color and shape vary greatly, and flowers can be borne singly or in erect or pendant clusters. Flowers range in size from about 0.1in (2mm) to 15in (38cm) in diameter. One of the petals, called the lip, is often markedly different from the others. A club-shaped structure in the middle (columna) results from the fusion of male and female reproductive parts. Most, but not all, species are cross-fertilized by insects or birds. The only economically important orchid product is vanilla, obtained from several species of the genus *Vanilla*.

Orchis, genus of orchids found on rich, wooded slopes of central United States. The upper petals are purple-rose; the large lower petal is white. The blooms are borne in clusters of 2 to 15 flowers; the 2 leaves are smooth and long. Height: to 1ft (30cm). Species include the showy *Orchis spectabilis*. Family Orchidaceae.

Orchitis, flamed and swollen testes, resulting from injury or infection. Symptoms are usually high fever, pain, nausea, and tenderness. Treatment may be antibiotics, bed rest, compresses, or drainage.

Orders of Architecture, types of classical columns, which fall into five orders: the Doric, Ionic, Corinthian, Tuscan, and Composite. Each order consists of a column with its base, shaft, and capital and an entablature above, and each has its own distinctive proportions and details. Of the five orders, the Doric, Ionic, and Corinthian are Greek; the Tuscan and Composite are Roman. *See also* individual orders.

Ordovician Period, the second oldest division of the Paleozoic Era, lasting from 500 to 430 million years ago. All life was still in the seas. Numerous invertebrates flourished, and included trilobites, brachiopods, corals, graptolites, mollusks, and echinoderms. Fragmentary remains of jawless fishes found in coastal deposits mark the first record of the vertebrates. *See also* Geologic Time; Paleozoic Era.

Ore, mineral or combination of minerals from which useful substances, especially metals, can be separated. Ores are divided into metallics (usually oxides and sulfides) and nonmetallics (such as sulfur and fluorite). Industrial rock deposits in beds (for example, gypsum and limestone) are not called ores. Occurrence is in veins, usually sharply angled tabular deposits; in beds or seams parallel to the enclosing rock; or in irregular masses. *See also* Lode.

Oregano, the dried leaves and flowers of any of several perennial herbs of the mint family, native to hilly lands in Mediterranean countries and W Asia. Introduced into the Western Hemisphere for use as a food seasoning. The strong aroma and pungent taste make it popular in Italian and Mexican dishes.

Oregon, state in the NW United States, on the Pacific Ocean N of California.

Land and economy. The fertile Willamette Valley stretches N and S between the Coast Range (W) and the Cascade Range (E). About 65% of the state is a plateau E of the Cascades. The Columbia River on the N boundary is of great economic importance, supplying hydroelectric power to a wide region; its lower section is navigable by ocean vessels. Portland, on the Willamette River near its junction with the Columbia, is a major seaport. Dense forests of Douglas fir and ponderosa pine, especially in the mountains, support the lumber industry. Agriculture is largely centered in the Willamette Valley.

People. Most of the population is descended from the 19th-century settlers who came from other states. About 72% lives in urban areas.

Education. There are about 40 institutions of higher education.

History. Robert Gray, US sea captain, discovered the mouth of the Columbia River in 1792. The Lewis and Clark expedition, marching overland from the Middle West, reached this point in 1805 and a US trading post was est. there in 1811. This was sold to British interests, and the British regarded the region as their territory. The United States claimed it by right of prior discovery and settlement, and in 1846 the boundary with Canada was fixed at its current latitude 49°. US pioneers had been entering the area since the 1830s, and Oregon Territory was organized in 1848. It included the present state of Washington, which was separated in 1853. After Oregon became a state, settlement and development proceeded steadily in spite of occasional Indian uprisings during its first 15 years of statehood. Industrial development took place during the 20th century, but still heavily dependent upon timber, Oregon's economy has remained sensitive to fluctuations in the US building industry.

Orangutan

Orchis

Oriole

PROFILE

Admitted to Union: Feb. 14, 1859; rank, 33rd
US Congressmen: Senate, 2; House of Representatives, 4
Population: 2,632,663 (1980); rank, 30st
Capital: Salem, 89,233 (1980)
Chief cities: Portland, 366,383; Eugene, 105,624; Salem
State legislature: Senate, 30; House of Representatives, 60
Area: 96,981sq mi (251,181sq km); rank, 10th
Elevation: Highest, 11,235ft (3,427m), Mt. Hood; lowest, sea level
Industries (major products): forest products, lumber, furniture, paper, processed foods, transportation equipment
Agriculture (major products): wheat, fruit, nuts, potatoes, oats, cattle, dairy products
Minerals (major): nickel, stone, sand and gravel
State nickname: Beaver State
State motto: The Union
State bird: western meadowlark
State flower: Oregon grape
State tree: Douglas fir

Orel (Or'ol), city in Russian SFSR, USSR, on the Oka River, 200mi (322km) SSW of Moscow; capital of Orel oblast; place of exile for Polish revolutionaries of the 1860s; held by Germans 1941–43; site of triumphal arch (1786), the Turgenev museum, museum of revolution and of natural history, and a teachers' college. Industries: weaving machines, glass, leather goods, construction equipment, clocks, beer, flour, grain, brewing, meat packing. Founded 1564 as S outpost of Moscow territory. Pop. 295,000.

Orem, city in N central Utah, 7mi (11km) NNW of Provo. Industries: steel, electronic equipment, skis, truck farming, fruit growing. Settled 1861; inc. 1919. Pop. (1980) 52,399.

Ore Mountains. See Erzgebirge.

Orenburg, formerly Chkalov; city in Russian SFSR, USSR, on the Ural River, just E of the Sakmara River mouth; capital of Orenburg oblast; scene of heavy fighting after the Revolution of 1917; capital of the Kirgiz Autonomous Republic 1920–24; renamed Chkalov after the Russian polar aviator; renamed Orenburg in 1957; site of medical, agricultural, and teachers' colleges, museums, cathedrals, churches, and a mosque. Industries: locomotive and car repair, flour, hides, meat processing, dairy products, grain, hops, animal feed, aircraft and tractor parts. Founded 1735. Pop. 459,000.

Oreopithecus, ancient primate of the Pliocene and Miocene epochs; a relative of the forerunners of both modern man and the Old World monkeys. In a genus by itself, fossil remains of the now extinct *Oreopithecus* have been found in southern Europe and East Africa from over 7,000,000 years ago. About 4ft (122cm) tall and semi-erect, *Oreopithecus* was apparently a vegetarian.

Oresteia, a trilogy of tragedies by Aeschylus, produced in 458 BC and consisting of *Agamemnon, The Libation Bearers,* and *Eumenides.* The last and greatest work of Aeschylus, it is also the only surviving Greek trilogy. Each play is complete and stands alone; together they explore the themes of crime, revenge, and expiation.

Orestes, in Greek mythology, son of Agamemnon and Clytemnestra. With his sister Electra he killed Clytem-

nestra (his mother) and her lover Aegisthus to avenge the death of Agamemnon, whom Clytemnestra and Aegisthus had murdered. Orestes is a character in a number of Greek plays including Aeschylus' *Oresteia,* Sophocles' *Electra,* and Euripides' *Orestes.*

Organ, largest, most complicated keyboard musical instrument. The player, at a console, regulates the flow of air, mechanically pressurized in the wind-chest, to ranks of pipes, producing diapason tones of solemn timbre, especially suitable for churches. Organs were built in Constantinople in the 7th century; large ones were constructed in England in the 10th century. Keyboards appeared c. 1300; reed pipes imitating other instruments c. 1500. Modern organs date from the Baroque period, when J.S. Bach wrote great compositions for them. Organs acquired crescendos and full orchestral effects in the 19th century. Electrification encouraged the building of elaborate machines in US film theaters (c. 1930) with the sound effects of horses, cannon, and airplanes. Purists such as Albert Schweitzer revived interest in Baroque organ music (c. 1900).

Organic Chemistry, one of the main branches of chemistry. Originally the study of substances produced by living organisms (hence its name), it has been broadened to include the study of all the compounds of carbon with the exclusion of the oxides, metal carbonates, and sulfides. See also Inorganic Chemistry.

Organic Functional Groups, groups of atoms that determine the chemical properties of organic compounds. For example, compounds containing the carboxyl group (-COOH) are fatty acids and behave accordingly. Similarly, compounds containing the hydroxyl group (OH) are alcohols, those containing a carbonyl group (CO) are ketones, and those with a -CHO group are aldehydes.

Organization for Economic Cooperation and Development (OECD), organization of non-Soviet Bloc western, northern, and southern European countries, the United States, Canada, Japan, Australia, and New Zealand; Yugoslavia participates with special status. OECD's purpose is to promote economic and social welfare among member nations, and coordinate their development efforts. The OECD was founded in 1961.

Organization of African Unity (OAU), association of 50 African countries. Its purpose is to promote African unity, coordinate economic growth, defend the sovereignty of independent countries, and eradicate colonialism. Founded in 1963 at Addis Ababa (Ethiopia), the organization holds yearly summit conferences. The Republic of South Africa is the continent's only independent country that does not belong to OAU. During the early 1980s the OAU played an active role in mediating disputes in Chad and Western Sahara, but in a continent plagued by economic problems, ethnic conflicts, and political unrest, the OAU was unable to forge true unity.

Organization of American States (OAS), regional organization that seeks peaceful settlements of disputes and regional cooperation in self-defense. It consists of 27 Latin American and Caribbean countries and the United States and is an outgrowth of the 1948 Pan American Union held in Bogotá, Colombia. Its charter became effective in 1951. In 1962, it voted to exclude Cuba because of its Communist government and supported the US blockade of Cuba to prevent the installation of Soviet missiles. The OAS assisted in restoring diplomatic relations between Panama and the United States in 1964. Economic and diplomatic sanctions imposed on Cuba in 1964 were ended in

1975. Under OAS auspices El Salvador and Honduras signed a peace treaty in 1976, ending long-standing hostilities between the two countries. The headquarters are in Washington, D.C.

Organization of Petroleum Exporting Countries (OPEC), organization formed in 1973 to control the world price of petroleum supplies. This powerful cartel includes the countries of Algeria, Ecuador, Gabon, Indonesia, Iran, Iraq, Kuwait, Libya, Nigeria, Qatar, Saudi Arabia, United Arab Emirates, and Venezuela. The cartel has been successful in increasing world petroleum prices dramatically, but saw prices fall in the early 1980's as world petroleum surpluses developed.

Organometallic Compound, compound in which one or more organic groups of radicals are bonded to an atom of a metal. Metallic carbonates (such as sodium carbonate) and salts of common fatty acids (such as sodium acetate) are usually excluded from this classification. Typical examples are metallic alkyl compounds (such as tetraethyl lead and triethyl aluminum), Grignard reagents (such as ethylmagnesium iodide), and a number of compounds of transition metals.

Organ-pipe Cactus, cactus native to SW North and South America. It has long columns of stems; its night-blooming blossoms open in May, and the fruit is edible. Height: to 33ft (10m). Family Cactaceae; species *Lemairocereus thurberi. See also* Cactus.

Organ Transplant, the surgical implantation of an organ (such as a kidney or heart) from another individual to substitute for a malfunctioning or diseased organ in the patient. Careful pre-operative preparation and matching followed by post-surgical procedures are necessary to ensure that the tissue of the transplanted organ is not rejected by the immune system of the body into which it is placed. See also Immunology.

Original Sin, in Christian theology, the condition of every human being resulting from the fall of Adam and Eve. Due to this first sin, humanity lost the grace of God. The sin of Adam and Eve is endlessly transmitted to all human beings.

Orinoco River, river in Venezuela; rises in Guiana Highlands; flows NW to Colombia, then N forming part of Venezuela-Colombia border, then E to Atlantic Ocean. Length and volume vary with season; navigable by small vessels; source of hydroelectric power. Sighted by Christopher Columbus 1498; navigated by Diego de Ordaz 1530–31. Length: approx. 1,500–1,700mi (2,415–2,737km).

Oriole, Old World songbird that is medium-sized, brightly colored, arboreal, and feeds on insects and builds cup-shaped nest for speckled white eggs (2–4). New World orioles, closely related to blackbirds, are frequently brightly colored and build hanging nests high in trees for speckled white eggs (2–6). Family Oriolidae. See also Baltimore Oriole.

Orion, spectacular equatorial constellation situated south of Taurus and Gemini. Four stars form a conspicuous quadrilateral containing a row of three other stars representing Orion's Belt. The five brightest stars of the first magnitude, include Beta (Rigel), Alpha (Betelgeuse), and Gamma (Bellatrix). This constellation contains the Orion Nebula and several binary stars. See also Betelgeuse; Orion Nebula.

Orion Nebula (M42; NGC 1976), emission nebula in the constellation Orion, located in the Hunter's Sword. It is a mass of gas surrounding a quadrilateral grouping of four hot O-type stars (The Trapezium), from which it absorbs energy and re-emits it as visible light.

Orkneys, islands of United Kingdom in the North Sea, off the NE coast of Scotland, forming an insular administrative area (Orkney region). Pomona (Mainland) is the largest in the group of about 70 islands. Chief industry is dairy products. Area: 376sq mi (974sq km). Pop. 17,675.

Orlando, commercial and residential city in central Florida, 78mi (126km) NE of Tampa, seat of Orange co. Center of citrus region; site of Walt Disney World. Over 30 lakes within city limits. Industries: electronic and missile components, textiles, regional offices of major companies. Settled 1844; inc. 1875. Pop. (1980) 128,394.

Orléans, name of a royal family of France. The title was first created by Philip VI for his son, who died without heirs (1375). The 2d duke of Orléans was the younger son of Charles V (1391). In 1492 the duchy was united to the royal domain when its duke became Louis XII. Louis XIII gave the title to his brother, who also died without issue. In 1661, Louis XIV gave the title to his brother Philip, whose descendants have held it since. The only member of this line to become king was Louis-Philippe (r. 1830–48), although his father, Philippe-Egalité, and his heirs, the counts of Paris, have had their supporters, called Orléanists. Because of their close, but junior, position with the Bourbons, the house of Orléans was a real or threatened source of intrigue and opposition to the crown. Since the French Revolution the House of Orléans has been identified with constitutional monarchy and 19th-century liberalism.

Orléans, Gaston Jean Baptiste, Duc d' (1608–60), French prince, inveterate but unsuccessful intriguer against his brother, Louis XIII, and nephew, Louis XIV. He plotted to assassinate Richelieu; raised troops to support Marie de Medicis against her son, Louis XIII; and twice more rose against Louis and Richelieu. Drawn into the Fronde uprising (1652) and exiled, he was eventually reconciled with Louis XIV.

Orléans, Louis, Duc d' (1372–1407), French prince, younger brother of Charles VI. He became duc d'Orléans (1392). When the king became insane, he and Philip the Bold, duke of Burgundy, were bitter rivals for power. Philip's son John caused Louis's death, beginning a struggle between the two houses, the Armagnacs (Orléanists) and the Burgundians, that dominated French history in the 15th century.

Orléans, Louis-Philippe, Duc d', known as Philippe-Egalité (1747–93), French prince, supporter of democracy in the Revolution. In 1789 he was elected to the Estates-General by the nobility but chose to sit with the third estate. As a member of the National Convention, he supported the leftists (the Mountain), voted the guillotine for Louis XVI, and took for himself the new family name Egalité. His role during the Revolution was difficult and ambiguous, as many suspected him of personal ambition to be king. In 1792 his son, the future King Louis-Philippe, and friends fled France. Suspected of complicity, Philippe-Egalité was arrested and died on the guillotine.

Orléans, city in N central France, on Loire River, 70mi (113km) SW of Paris; capital of Loiret dept. The principal residence of French kings in 10th century, it was besieged by English 1428–29, and relieved by Joan of Arc. Briefly held by Huguenots during the 16th-century Wars of Religion, it was besieged by Roman Catholics in 1563 and held by them until Edict of Nantes in 1598; site of 17th–19th-century cathedral, 16th-century town hall, bronze statue of St Joan; scene of elaborate Feast of Joan of Arc, held each May. Industries: tobacco, textiles, chemicals. Founded c. 52 BC as Aurelianum by Romans. Pop. 109,956.

Ormolu, elaborate mounts applied to furniture and clocks during the reign of Louis XV and Louis XVI in 18th-century France. They were usually made of bronze or copper, which was gilded, and were known for their finely sculpted details of mythological subjects and floral designs.

Ornithischian Dinosaur, dinosaur with a birdlike pelvis. These herbivores appeared later in the fossil record than saurischian types. The earliest forms were bipedal, but later species became quadrupedal. The main divisions are Ornithopoda, Stegosauria, Ceratopsia, and Ankylosauria.

Ornithology, scientific study of birds. Included are classification, structure, function, evolution, distribution, migration, reproduction, ecology, and behavior. In this science, nonprofessionals make substantial contributions in field research and observation. Museums and universities house collections of bird skins, skeletons, and preserved specimens. *See also* Bird; Bird Banding; Bird Migration.

Ornithopoda, ornithischian dinosaurs, including all semi-bipedal herbivorous forms. Early representatives were Camptosaurus and Iguanodon. Later kinds were hadrosaurs or duck-billed dinosaurs. *See also* Trachodon.

Orogeny, in its modern, narrowest usage, the process by which structures within mountainous areas are formed and deformed. Thus, all folding and faulting in upper layers and metamorphism in deeper ones result from orogenic activity. Each mountain region has its own very distinct features, but there are similarities of all processes of change that are common and part of the study of orogeny. *See also* Faulting; Folding.

Orpheus, in Greek mythology, the finest poet and musician, son of Calliope the muse of epic poetry, husband of Eurydice. After his wife died Orpheus descended into Hades to rescue her. He was successful but lost Eurydice when he disobeyed the command not to look back at her. Orpheus was killed by Maenads and rejoined his wife in Hades. Orpheus is usually depicted with the lyre he received as a gift from Apollo.

Orphic Mysteries, mystic rites of Orphism, an ancient Greek religious movement popular in the 6th and 7th centuries BC. The mysteries take their name from Orpheus. Purification and initiation were important rites in the mysteries, which promised deliverance of the soul in the afterlife.

Orpine, any member of the stonecrop (or orpine) family, Crassulaceae, comprising 1,500 species of perennial herbs or low shrubs native to warm, dry parts of the world. Many are grown as pot plants or cultivated in rock gardens. All have thick leaves and red, yellow, or white flower clusters. Stonecrop (Sedum) and houseleek (Sempervivum) are well known representatives.

Orsini, Roman princely family dating from the 10th century. The traditional rivalry between the Guelph (pro-papal) Orsinis and Ghibelline (pro-imperial) Colonna family often kept Rome in a state of civil war until the 16th century. Orsini popes were **Celestine III** (1191–98), **Nicholas III** (1277–80), and **Benedict XIII** (1724–30). The Orsinis were made princes of the Holy Roman Empire in 1629 and of Rome in 1718.

Ortega Saavedra, Daniel (1945–), Nicaraguan revolutionary, president 1985– . The son of a man who had fought under Augusto Sandino, for whom the Sandinista movement (FSLN) is named, he dropped out of law school to join the FSLN (1963). Imprisoned by the Somoza government (1969–74), he then went into exile in Cuba, where he studied guerrilla tactics. Returning secretly, he led with his brothers a moderate faction of the FSLN, which united with 2 other groups (1979) and succeeded in toppling the Somoza government. He was a member of the 5-man junta that controlled Nicaragua for 5 years before being elected president.

Orthodox Eastern Church. See Eastern Orthodox Church.

Orthopedics, branch of medicine that deals with the diagnosis and treatment of diseases, disorders, and injuries to bones, muscles, tendons, ligaments, and associated tissues.

Orthoptera, insect order found worldwide. It includes crickets, mantids, walking sticks, leaf insects, grasshoppers, cockroaches, and others. These insects may be winged or wingless and have chewing mouthparts. They have three life stages: egg, nymph, and adult.

Ortolan, small European bunting often eaten as a delicacy and often trapped when flocks migrate to Africa. An insect and seed eater, it has an olive head and chest, yellow throat, brown-streaked black back, and pinkish underparts. The light-colored, spotted eggs (3–6) are laid in a cup-shaped nest amid plants. Length: 6in (15cm). Species *Emberiza hortulana.*

Orwell, George (1903–50), pseud. of Eric (Arthur) Blair; English journalist, critic, and novelist, b. India. Orwell fought with the Republicans in the Spanish Civil War. His books include the autobiographical *Down and Out in Paris and London* (1933) and *Homage to Catalonia* (1938); the antitotalitarian fable *Animal Farm* (1945); and *Nineteen Eighty-four* (1949), a novel.

Oryx, or **Gemsbok,** four species of large, rapier-horned antelopes found in Africa. Both sexes carry long horns ringed at the base; female's are longer and slimmer. They are cream to brown with black markings on face and legs. Males have a tuft on the throat. Living in herds up to 60, they can kill lions. The Arabian *Oryx leucoryx,* the smallest, is almost extinct. The scimitar-horned *O. tao* of the Sahara, the only species with curved horns, domesticated in ancient Egypt, is also nearing extinction. *O. gazella beisa* lives in E Africa. Gemsbok *O. gazella gazella* of southern Africa survives mainly in Kalahari. Height: to 86in (2.2m); weight: to 462lb (208kg). Family Bovidae.

Osage, river in W Missouri; rises at the confluence of the Marais des Cygnes and Little Osage rivers, flows NE to join the Missouri River near Jefferson City; used for hydroelectricity; its waters, impounded by Bagnell Dam, form the Lake of the Ozarks. Length: 360mi (580km).

Osage Indians, about 5,000 native Americans of Siouan linguistic stock who enjoy considerable prosperity on their oil-rich lands in Oklahoma. The Osage migrated steadily westward from the Atlantic coast and in the early 1800s sold their land in Missouri, moved to a reservation in Kansas, and later bought land in Oklahoma. Farmer-hunters of the Plains type, their society was divided between earth and sky people, or meat-eaters and vegetarians, and was known for its adherence to tradition.

Osage Orange, or bow wood, bodark (from Fr. *bois d'arc*), thorny tree native to the Red River Valley, Okla., and cultivated as an ornamental. Deciduous, it has dark orange bark, oblong leaves, and warty orangelike fruit. Family Moraceae; species *Maclura pomifera.*

Osaka, port city in S Honshu, Japan, at mouth of the Yodo River, head of Osaka Bay; capital of Osaka prefecture and 2nd-largest city and industrial center of Japan. It was capital of Japan 4th century (then called Naniwa); modern city grew around 16th-century castle of Hideyoshi; site of university (1931) and 1970 World's Fair. Industries: textiles, machinery, steel, chemicals, shipping and shipbuilding. Pop. 2,980,487.

Oscillating Theory of the Universe, cosmological theory postulating that the expansion of the universe will eventually slow down as it approaches a critical radius. Because a static universe is unstable it would then contract back to zero size, at which point expansion would recommence to produce an oscillating (expanding-contracting) system. The validity of the theory depends on the density of matter in the universe being less than 3×10^{-29} grams per cc. *See also* Big-Bang Theory of the Universe.

Oscillator, a device for producing alternating electric current. It employs tuned circuits and amplifying components. In radio broadcasting, where oscillators are used to generate high-frequency currents for carrier waves, they are stabilized by coupling the vibrations of a piezoelectric crystal with the electronic circuit.

Oscilloscope, an instrument in which the variations in a fluctuating electrical quantity, such as voltage, appear temporarily as a visible wave form on the fluorescent screen of a cathode ray tube.

Oshawa, city in Ontario, Canada, on Lake Ontario; prosperous farming area. Industries: automotive works, glass, textiles. Founded 1795 as Skaes Corner. Inc. 1924. Pop. 107,023.

Oshogbo, city in SW Nigeria, 50mi (81km) NE of Ibadan on Oshun River. Part of Ijesha, a Yoruban kingdom in 17th century, in 1839 it was scene of a battle in which Ibadan, a Yoruban city state, defeated Ilorin, a Fulani state. Industries: textiles, cigarettes, cotton ginning, trading. Pop. 208,966.

Osiris, in Egyptian mythology and religion, the god of the dead, son of Geb the earth and Nut the sky, husband and brother of Isis and father of Horus. He is generally depicted as a mummified man wearing a feathered crown and bearing the crook and flail of a king. In the myths Osiris was killed by his brother and dismembered; Isis retrieved the corpse and Horus avenged his death.

Oslo, capital of Norway, in SE Norway at the head of Oslo Fjord, an inlet of the Skagerrak. Founded 1050 by King Harold III, city became capital 1299; suffered fire 1624, after which it was rebuilt by Christian IV who named it Christiania (renamed Oslo 1924). Largest city and chief industrial and commercial center of Norway, it contains many historic structures, including 17th-century church, national theater (1899), university (1811); site of 1952 Winter Olympics. Industries: metals, wood products, food processing, textiles, chemicals, shipping, tourism. Pop. 463,022.

Orléans, France

Orpine

Oslo, Norway

Osmium, metallic element (symbol Os) of the third transition series, discovered (1803) by Smithson Tennant. It occurs associated with platinum; chief source is as a by-product from smelting nickel. Like iridium, it is used in producing hard alloys. The tetraoxide (OsO_4) is a powerful oxidizing agent. Properties: at.no. 76; at. wt. 190.2; sp gr 22.57; melt. pt. 5,513°F (3,045°C); boil. pt. 9,081°F (5,027°C); most common isotope Os^{192} (39.952%). *See also* Transition Elements.

Osmosis, diffusion of a solvent through a natural or artificial membrane, which blocks the passage of selected dissolved substances, into a more concentrated solution. Plant roots absorb water by osmosis; walls of living cells selectively allow passage of required substances.

Osmotic Pressure, pressure exerted by a dissolved substance by virtue of the motion of its molecules. In dilute solutions, it varies with the concentration and temperature as if the solute were a gas occupying the same volume. It can be measured by the pressure which must be applied to counterbalance the process of osmosis into the solution.

Osprey, hawk of seacoasts, rivers, and lakes that dives for food, seizing fish with its talons. It has a short, hooked bill, broad, pointed wings, white head, and brownish-black plumage above, whitish below. Brown-blotched, white eggs (2–3) are laid in a large stick nest on or above ground. Length: 20–25in (51–63.5cm). Species *Pandion haliaetus*.

Ossa, Mount, mountain peak in NE Greece. In Greek mythology, the Aloadae, two giants who fought against the gods, piled Mt Ossa on top of Mt Olympus, and Mt Pelion on top of Mt Ossa, in attempt to reach heaven and overthrow the gods. Height: 6,490ft (1,980m).

Ossian, legendary Gaelic warrior and poet of the third century whose name was used by James MacPherson as the original author of his Ossianic poems (1763). Challenged by Dr. Samuel Johnson, MacPherson was forced to compose Gaelic poems purporting to be source material but later discovered to be faked.

Ossification, the process of bone formation. In humans it begins at about the second month of embryonic development, continues through childhood and adolescence, and is completed by about age 25. Some bones, known as intramembranous bones, including the flat bones of the skull roof, develop from connective tissue cells. These cells become osteoblasts, or bone-forming cells, and secrete collagen fibers that combine with minerals and gradually lead to the formation of hard bone matrix. Other bones, known as endochondral bones, such as the long bones, develop from cartilage, with certain cartilage cells changing to osteoblasts. Epiphyseal plates, located typically at the ends of the long bones, are areas of continued bone growth. *See also* Bone.

Ossory, ancient kingdom of Ireland, possibly within Kingdom of Leinster; founded 1st century AD, ruled in 9th century by Cerball. It probably disappeared by the 11th century, but its extent is indicated by the modern diocese of Ossory, centering on Kilkenny.

Osteichthyes, class of fish with bony skeletons, found in almost every water environment. It includes Actinopterygii (spiny-rayed fish) and Sarcopterygii (lungfish and lobefin). Characteristics include a single flap, or opercle, covering gill openings; an air bladder or primitive lung; and fins supported by bony rays. Most members of this class have scales. Fertilization is usually external, and the number of eggs laid at one time ranges from 100 to millions. Osteichthyes first appeared during Devonian period (350–400,000,000 years ago). They were heavily armored and originally were adapted to fresh water. There are more than 20,000 living species. Superclass Pisces.

Osteoarthritis, disease in which the cartilage of the joints is destroyed. It may be caused by aging or by postural or orthopedic abnormalities and may be relieved by physical therapy, analgesics, or cortisone.

Osteomalacia, loss of calcium and phosphorus from the bones in adults. It is caused by deficiency of calcium and vitamin D in the diet. Treatment involves a diet high in protein and calcium, supplemented with vitamin D concentrates.

Osteomyelitis, inflammation of the bone or bone marrow. It is usually caused by infection and accompanied by fever, swelling, and pain. Treatment is with antibiotics or surgery.

Osteopathy, an approach of medicine based on the theory that structural defects interfere with normal body functioning and cause disease and disorders. In the United States osteopaths may be licensed to practice osteopathic medicine, surgery, or other specialty. They use skeletal manipulations and other medical and surgical techniques to try to correct structural defects.

Ostia, ancient Italian city 16mi (26km) from Rome at the mouth of the Tiber; the naval base and important commercial harbor of Rome from the 4th century BC to the 3rd century AD. The town was deserted by the 9th century and became a builder's quarry and treasure trove until systematic excavations were begun in the 19th century.

Ostracism, a procedure peculiar to Athens, instituted by Cleisthenes in 507 BC to prevent the growth of tyrants. If 6,000 citizens voted to do so, any individual aspiring to dictatorship was banished for 10 years.

Ostracod, or seed shrimp, small crustacean common in seas and fresh water. It has a rounded or elliptical carapace, resembling two halves of a clam shell. Although some swim, others scurry along muddy bottoms. Length: 3/16–3/4in(5–19mm). There are a few terrestrial species.

Ostrava, city in N central Czechoslovakia, near junction of Oder and Opava rivers; center of industrialized area and one of country's largest cities. Industries: coal, iron, steel, ship and bridge parts. Pop. 300,945.

Ostrich, largest living bird, found wild in central Africa where groups roam grasslands, feeding on plants and small animals, in company with grazing animals. It has a reddish or bluish, down-covered, small flat head and long neck. Its plump body is covered with soft black feathers and white wing and tail plumes. Flightless, it runs fast. Females scoop a hole in sand for large, shiny yellow eggs (12–16) incubated by the female by day and the male at night. Height: to 8ft (2.4m); weight: over 300lb (135kg). Species *Struthio camelus*.

Ostrogoths, or East Goths, ancient Germanic people. They were subjected to the Huns in the 4th century and settled in Pannonia (modern Hungary). Under King Theodoric (AD 471–526), the Ostrogoths conquered Italy (493) and set up a kingdom based at Ravenna. They were defeated by Byzantium in 552 and expelled from Italy. They were soon absorbed by other peoples.

Ostwald, Wilhelm (1853–1932), Russian-German chemist. He was a professor in Riga but later moved to Leipzig, remaining in Germany for the rest of his life. His interest in the work of Arrhenius on solutions led him to the dilution law that bears his name. His work on catalysis was of considerable industrial importance and was rewarded by the Nobel Prize for chemistry in 1909.

Oswald, Lee Harvey (1939–63), alleged assassin of Pres. John F. Kennedy, b. New Orleans. He went to the USSR in 1959 and renounced his US citizenship, but he returned in 1962 with his Russian-born wife, Marina. In Dallas (1963), he allegedly shot President Kennedy twice, fled and was captured. He was killed by Jack Ruby, a nightclub owner, while being held by Dallas police.

Othello (1604), 5-act tragedy by William Shakespeare, from Giovanni Battista Giraldi's (called Cynthio) *Il Moro de Venezia*. Its earliest recorded performance was at Whitehall Palace, London, in 1604. First performed in the United States in New York (1751), it has been revived countless times. In 1943 a Theatre Guild production ran for 295 performances, a record run for a Shakespeare play on Broadway. It was also the basis for an opera by Giuseppe Verdi (1887). Othello, a noble Moor in the service of Venice, marries Desdemona and sails to Cyprus, followed by Roderigo, who loves Desdemona. Iago, who hates Othello for appointing Cassio as his lieutenant instead of Iago, resolves to kindle Othello's suspicions by suggesting that Desdemona and Cassio are overly familiar. He also has his wife, Emilia, steal a handkerchief Othello gave Desdemona and put it in Cassio's room. When Othello sees Cassio with the handkerchief and is told by Iago that Cassio has confessed to having an affair with Desdemona, Othello resolves to kill the lovers. He gets Roderigo to kill Cassio, but he only wounds him; Iago then kills Roderigo. Othello smothers Desdemona in her bed. Emilia enters the room and Othello confesses and mentions the handkerchief. When Emilia declares she had given the handkerchief to Iago, Othello lunges at him. Iago kills Emilia and flees, is captured and brought back. Othello stabs him, then kills himself and dies upon the body of Desdemona.

Otosclerosis, disease of the bone surrounding the inner ear. The base of the stapes (one of the middle ear bones) is prevented from rocking against the oval window of the inner ear which impairs hearing. It can be treated with surgery.

Ottawa, a group of native North Americans of the Algonkian linguistic family. They originally lived north of the Great Lakes with the Potawatami and Ojibway, but were famous traders and island-dwellers by the arrival of the French. Hunter-farmers of the Eastern Woodlands type, allied with the French and Hurons, they were broken into five groups by the Iroquois and Anglo-Americans and now live in the Great Lakes area, Kansas, and Oklahoma. Pontiac was a famous Ottawa.

Ottawa, capital of Canada, in SE Ontario on the Ottawa River and Rideau Canal; canal divides city into upper and lower towns. Queen Victoria chose it as capital of United Provinces of Canada in 1858, and in 1867 it became capital of Dominion of Canada; site of Ottawa University (1848), Grand Séminaire d'Ottawa (1847), Scholasticat St-Jean (1902), Petit Séminaire d'Ottawa (1925), Bruyère College (1925), St Patrick's College (1932), Carleton University (1942), 1200-acre (486-hectare) Dominion experimental farm, Dominion Observatory, and National Art Gallery (1880). At Chaudière Falls in Ottawa River hydroelectric power is generated for municipal and domestic use. Industries: printing, publishing, logging, pulp, paper, food, beverages. Area was discovered 1613 by Samuel de Champlain; settled 1826 with building of Rideau Canal; inc. as city 1854. Pop. 304,462.

Otter, semi-aquatic carnivore found all over the world except in Australia. Otters have narrow, pointed heads with bristly whiskers, sleek, furred bodies, short legs with webbed feet, and long, tapering tails. The river otters *(Lutra)* of North and South America, Europe, Asia, and Africa are small to medium-sized, freshwater mammals that spend some time on land. The giant otters *(Pteronura brasiliensis)* may be 5ft (1.5m) long with a 2-ft (0.6-m) tail. They eat fish, frogs, reptiles, and birds. Their fur is valuable. Otters are sometimes tamed but may be difficult pets because they are playful and curious animals with great physical strength. Family Mustelidae.

Otter Hound, hunting dog (hound group) used for otter as early as 14th-century England. A boisterous dog with good scenting ability, it has a slightly domed, large but narrow head with long, square muzzle; low-set, long, hanging ears; level-backed body; heavy-boned legs with webbed feet; and a long, sickle-shaped tail. The rough coat, which may be any color, is 3–6in (7.5–15cm) long. Average size: 24–27in (61–68.5cm) high at shoulder; 75–115lb (34–52kg). *See also* Hounds.

Otto I, or **Otto the Great** (912–73), Holy Roman emperor (962–73) and German king (936–73). He succeeded his father, King Henry I, in Germany. After subduing rebellious German nobles, he invaded (951) Italy to aid Queen Adelaide against Berengar II, who had succeeded her husband. Otto defeated Berengar, assumed the title king of the Lombards, and married Adelaide. In 955 he vanquished the Magyars at Lechfeld. He was crowned emperor in 962, reviving the Carolingian imperial title and founding the Holy Roman Empire.

Otto II (955–83), Holy Roman emperor (973–83). He was the son and successor of Otto I. After his accession he subdued a revolt by Henry, duke of Bavaria. In 978 Otto invaded France in retaliation against French efforts to obtain Lorraine. Shortly afterward he led an expedition to Italy to secure lands in S Italy that he claimed through his Byzantine wife. He was defeated by the Byzantines in 982.

Otto III (980–1002), Holy Roman emperor (983–1002). He was the son and successor of Otto II. Until he assumed the government in 996, a regency ruled for him, first under his mother Theophano, then under his grandmother, Adelaide. Shortly after taking over the government, he established his imperial seat at Rome. In 999 he raised his former tutor Gerbert of Aurillac to the papacy as Sylvester II.

Otto IV (1174–1218), Holy Roman emperor (1198–1215). He was elected German anti-king to Philip of Swabia in 1198. After Philip's death (1208), he was recognized as king and crowned emperor by Pope Innocent III. Otto's invasion of Italy led the pope to withdraw his support. In 1214, Otto was defeated at Bouvines by the French, who were allied with Frederick II, who had been elected by dissident nobles. The pope declared Otto deposed in 1215.

Ottoman Empire, former state in Asia Minor, founded by Osman I in the 13th century. By the end of the 15th century, it had destroyed the Byzantine empire and conquered Egypt and Syria. At the height of its power under Suleiman the Magnificent (1520–66), the empire included much of SE Europe, W Asia, and N Africa. In the 17th and 18th centuries, a series of exhausting wars were fought against Poland, Austria, and Russia. The empire continued to decline until its dissolution after World War I, when the nationalist government convened at Ankara (1919) and finally proclaimed the republic of Turkey in 1923.

Ouachita, river in Arkansas and Louisiana; rises in the Ouachita Mts, W Arkansas; flows E and SE into Louisiana to the Red River system near Monroe. Length: 600mi (966km).

Ouagadougou, largest city and capital of Upper Volta, in W Africa; trade and distribution center; served as capital of a Mossi Empire from 11th century until 1896 when French captured it. Industries: handcrafts, food processing, peanuts. Pop. 124,779.

Ouakari, or **Ukari, Uakari,** medium-sized, day-active monkey inhabiting treetops of the upper Amazon basin. The only short-tailed monkey of America, ouakaris have long shaggy coats and naked faces. They feed chiefly on fruit. Genus *Cacajao. See also* Monkey.

Ouananiche, small, landlocked Canadian race of Atlantic salmon found only in the upper Saguenay and its tributaries and rivers flowing into the Gulf of St Lawrence. It is blue-green on its back and has cross-shaped black spots on its upper body. Weight: 3lb (1.4kg). Family Salmonidae; species *Salmo salarouananiche. See also* Salmon.

Oubangui (Ubangi), river in central Africa; originates at the confluence of the Bomu and Uele rivers; flows W and S forming part of boundary between Zaïre and Central African Republic; empties into the Congo River. Upper section is navigable only during wet season. Length: 660mi (1,063km).

Oudh, an ancient city of India in the district of Uttar Pradesh. It is one of the seven holy places of Hinduism and has many monuments and shrines, including the mosque of Rama's birthplace. It was the center of the Mogul Empire.

Outbreeding. *See* Crossbreeding; Cross-pollination.

Outer Hebrides. *See* Hebrides.

Ouzel, heavy-bodied, perching birds found in the mountains of Asia, Europe, and the Western Hemisphere. The ring ouzel has black plumage with a white chest collar and bright bill and facial markings. Family Cinclidae. *See also* Dipper.

Ovary, that part of a multicellular animal or a flowering plant that produces the egg cells, or female reproductive cells, and in vertebrates also produces the female sex hormones. In humans, an ovary—grayish-pink, about 1.5in by 1in (3.8cm by 2.5cm)—occurs on each side of the uterus. From puberty to menopause each month (except during pregnancy) one egg cell matures, ruptures from the ovary at ovulation, and passes into the Fallopian tube where it can be fertilized or will pass through into the uterus to be shed in menstruation. Under pituitary control, the ovary produces two female sex hormones: estrogen and progesterone, which control development and functioning of the female reproductive system.

Ovenbird, perching bird found in varying habitats of South America and named for the oven-shaped nests built by some species. Included are the shaketail, spinetail, leafscraper, and other groups of woodcreeperlike birds. They are generally brownish or reddish-brown. Most feed on insects and some on seeds. Some species nest in cavities and others build globular mud-and-cow-dung or twig-and-leaf nests. A nest may have a side entrance, several chambers, and a tunnel approach. The eggs (2–9) are often white and usually incubated by both parents. Length: 5–9in (12.5–23cm). Family Furnariidae.

Overland Park, city in NE Kansas; residential suburb of Kansas City (S). Inc. 1960. Pop. (1980) 81,784.

Overture, piece of orchestral music that opens an opera, oratorio, or stage play, or occasionally stands on its own, usually lively in character. Famous operatic overtures were composed by Mozart, Rossini (eg, *William Tell*), and Wagner. Noted concert overtures include the *1812 Overture* by Tchaikovsky.

Ovid (43 BC–AD 17), Roman poet, name in full Publius Ovidius Nasso. A popular, prolific poet, for no known reason he was exiled to a Black Sea outpost in AD 8. His works include *Amores,* 49 short love poems, many praising Corinna; *Ars Amatoria (The Art of Love),* a didactic work on how to get and keep a lover; and his masterpiece, the *Metamorphoses,* a collection of skillfully woven together mythological stories. *Tristia (Sorrows)* is an autobiographical work written while in exile.

Oviduct, tube that connects the ovaries and uterus, and through which egg cells are released from the ovary. In mammals it is known as the Fallopian tube. *See also* Fallopian Tube.

Oviedo, city in NW Spain, 230mi (370km) NW of Madrid; capital of Oviedo prov.; important industrial, mining, and agricultural center. City prospered in 9th century as the capital of Asturian kings; its importance declined in 10th century when capital was transferred to León; site of 8th-century Gothic cathedral, University of Oviedo (1604), meteorological observatory, courthouse, hospital, 14th-century cathedral, containing tombs of the Asturian kings. Industries: livestock, firearms, gunpowder, textiles. Founded *c.*760. Area: (prov.) 4,079sq mi (10,565sq km). Pop. (city) 154,117; (prov.) 1,045,635.

Ovimbundu, or **Mbundu,** Negroid people of Angola. Their society is basically agricultural: crops include corn and beans, but hunting and animal husbandry are also practiced, and there is a trade in beeswax. Descent is matrilineal with regard to personal property and patrilineal with regard to land.

Ovulation, mature ovum released from the ovary, enabling fertilization to occur. In human females, one egg is released midway through the menstrual cycle. Occasionally two eggs are released simultaneously. Ovulation is stimulated by hormones from the pituitary gland: follicle-stimulating hormone (FSH) and luteinizing hormone (LH).

Ovum, egg or female gamete produced in the ovary and, after fertilization, capable of developing into a new individual. Oval or spherical, it is immobile and larger than a sperm.

Owen, David (1938–   ), British politician. He received a medical education and began his career as a neurologist. His concern for the poor and homeless led him to join the Labour party (1961) and become a member of Parliament (1966). He held various government posts before being named foreign secretary (1977). In 1981 he and 3 other Labour cabinet ministers formed the Council for Social Democracy, which created the Social Democratic party. Owen became the party's outspoken leader.

Owen, Robert (1771–1858), Welsh social reformer. He was the most famous of the early utopian socialist writers. His most important work was the three-volume *New View of Society* (1813–14). He felt people could be improved by bettering their environment and founded communities based on his concept of "villages of cooperation." In his model community in Scotland (New Lanark Mills) he paid high wages in the spinning mills, provided for better living generally for his employees, and made a profit. The New Harmony Venture he took over in Indiana in 1825 failed in 1829.

Owen Glendower (1359?–?1416), Welsh leader. Calling himself the Prince of Wales, he led a revolt against Henry IV (1399). As an outlaw he continually harassed the English. He captured and won over Edmund Mortimer (1402) and made an alliance with the Percys, thereby posing a serious threat to the English throne. Although defeated after Henry V's succession (1415), he remained a Welsh national hero.

Owens, Jesse (1913–80), US athlete, b. John Cleveland Owens in Alabama. While a student at Ohio State, he broke several world track and field records. At the 1936 Olympics (Berlin, Germany), he deflated Hitler's "Aryan" theory by winning the 100 meter race, the 200 meter race, the broad jump, and the 400 meter race. In the 200 meter race and the broad jump, he set world records.

Owensboro, city in W Kentucky, on Ohio River; seat of Daviess co; site of Kentucky Wesleyan College (1866) and Brescia College (1874). Industries: chemicals, electrical equipment, steel, whiskey, tobacco. Settled 1800 as Yellow Banks; inc. 1817 as Rossborough; chartered as city 1866 and renamed for Col. Abraham Owen. Pop. (1980) 54,450.

Owl, nocturnal bird of prey found worldwide. Known for their forward-directed eyes and screams, hoots, and other sounds, the birds have come to be considered bad omens. Owls have rounded heads, hooked bills, rounded wings, short squarish tails, and long curved talons or claws. Their soft downy feathers are usually brown, black, or gray with white or lighter-colored markings. Using their keen eyesight and hearing, they feed at night on small mammals and birds, frogs, snakes, and sometimes fish. Most owls nest in hollow trees, rock niches, or on the ground. Round white eggs (1–11) are laid. The family Strigidae includes the horned, snowy, screech, and elf owls. Barn owls make up the family Tytonidae. Length: 5–27in (12.5–69cm). Order Strigiformes.

Ox, (1) bovine member of a subdivision of the family Bovidae that includes true cattle and buffalo, water buffalo, and bison. (2) True cattle belonging only to the genus *Bos.* (3) Castrated male of domesticated cattle used as draft animal in various countries. *See also* Bison; Buffalo; Cattle; Water Buffalo.

Oxalic Acid, poisonous colorless crystalline fatty acid whose salts occur in some plants. It is prepared from carbon monoxide and sodium hydroxide and used for metal cleaning, textile cleaning, and in tanning. Properties: sp gr 1.653; melt. pt. 214.70°F (101.5°C).

Oxalis, or wood sorrel, creeping plants found in wooded areas. Common wood sorrel *(Oxalis acetosella)* is a stemless perennial native to temperate North America and Europe. Its flowers are white, veined with purple.

Oxbow, tightly looping stream meander with such an extreme curvature that only a neck of land is left between two parts of the stream, thus it resembles a

Otter

Owl

Oxford, England

U-shaped ox collar. Also called a horseshoe bend. *See also* Meander.

Oxford, city in England, at confluence of Thames (known locally as Isis) and Cherwell rivers; county town of Oxfordshire; seat of Oxford University (dating from 12th century); industrial center with major automobile works. Pop. 116,600.

Oxford, University of, English university, located in Oxford. The institution is a complex of several independent colleges with noted faculties in theology, modern languages, anthropology, humanities, physical sciences, music, and Oriental studies. Noted colleges include University (founded 1249), Balliol (1263), Merton (1264), Oriel (1326), Queen's (1340), New (1379), All Souls (1437), Magdalen (1458), Trinity (1554), and Jesus (1571). Women have been granted degrees from 1920 but it was not until 1959 that they were allowed full university status. Instruction is by lectures and a tutorial system.

Oxford and Asquith, Herbert Henry Asquith, 1st Earl of (1852–1928), English political figure. As a Liberal member of Parliament (1886–1918; 1920–24), he became home secretary (1892–95), chancellor of the exchequer (1905–08), and prime minister (1908–16). The Liberal party prospered in these years, and he is noted for his success, against heavy opposition, in abolishing the veto power of the House of Lords (1911) and promoting the Home Rule Bill. He retired from leadership of his party (1926). In the same year his book *Fifty Years of Parliament* appeared.

Oxford Movement (1833–43), efforts by the Church of England to restore the ideals of the earlier church, caused by a decline in religious interest and the development of liberal theology. Its main influence was in the ritual life of the church. John Newman, a leader, converted to the Roman Catholic Church. *See also* Newman, John Henry.

Oxidation-Reduction, or redox, chemical reaction involving simultaneous oxidation and reduction. In general, oxidation and reduction reactions occur together; thus in the reaction $Fe_2O_3 + 3C\_2Fe + 3CO$, the iron oxide is reduced by the carbon, the carbon is oxidized by the iron oxide. Carbon is the reducing agent; iron oxide the oxidizing agent. The term "oxidation-reduction" is often used in a more restricted sense, to describe reversible reactions of this type. An example is reaction between iron and tin compounds: $2FeCl_2 + SnCl_4 \rightleftharpoons 2FeCl_3 + SnCl_2$. Another is the quinone-hydroquinone electrode reaction: $C_6H_4O_2 + 2H^+ + 2e \rightleftharpoons C_6H_4(OH)_2$. Oxidation-reduction reactions are important in many biochemical systems.

Oxidation State, measure of the extent to which an atom has lost electrons in a compound. It is stated as a number indicating the degree of ionization. Thus in sodium oxide, Na_2O, the sodium (Na^+) has an oxidation number of $+1$; the oxygen (O^{2-}) has an oxidation number of -2. In covalent and coordination compounds the oxidation number is the electric charge that the atoms would have if the compound were ionic. For example, in the ion $[CuCl_4]^{2-}$, regarded as formed from Cu^{2+} with 4 Cl^-, the copper has an oxidation number of $+2$. Oxidation numbers are often used in the names of chemical compounds, as in iron II chloride ($FeCl_2$) and iron III chloride ($FeCl_3$).

Oxide, chemical compound formed between oxygen and another element. Most elements form oxides, which fall into two main classes. Metallic oxides, such as CaO, TiO_2, etc, are mainly ionic compounds that are basic or, in some cases, amphoteric. Nonmetals have

covalently bonded oxides, such as SO_2, CO_2, etc, that form acids in solution. Some, such as CO, are neutral.

Oxidizing Agent, chemical substance that causes oxidation reactions. Thus in the oxidation of carbon: $2C + O_2\_2CO$, oxygen is the oxidizing agent. Other common oxidizing agents include nitric acid, hydrogen peroxide, ozone, potassium dichromate, ferric compounds, and stannic compounds.

Oxnard, city in S California, 22mi (35km) E of Long Beach; originally founded 1868 as Richland, renamed 1875; departure point for tourists to the Santa Barbara Islands and Los Padres National Forest. Industries: electronic components, copper wire, agriculture, mining. Inc. 1903. Pop. (1980) 108,195.

Oxpecker, two species of African birds of the genus *Buphagus.* Both are brown with wide bills and stiff tails and reach 8in (20cm) in length. They cling to cattle and big game animals to remove ticks and maggots. Family Sturnidae.

Oxygen, common nonmetallic gaseous element (symbol O), discovered (1774) by Joseph Priestley and independently (c.1772) by K.W. Scheele. It is the most abundant element in the Earth's crust (49.2% by weight), a constituent of water and many rocks. It is also present in the atmosphere (23.14% by weight), from which it is extracted by fractionation of liquid air. The element is used in steelmaking, in welding, in the manufacture of industrial chemicals, and in breathing and resuscitation apparatus. It is necessary for combustion and for the respiration of plants and animals. Chemically reactive, it forms compounds with nearly all other elements. Properties: at. no. 8; at. wt. 15.9994; density 1.429 g dm^{-3}; melt. pt. $-361.12°F$ ($-218.4°C$); boil. pt. $-297.33°F$ ($-182.962°C$); most common isotope O^{16} (99.759%). *See also* Ozone.

Oxygen Cycle, release of oxygen into the atmosphere and water by plants during photosynthesis. This oxygen is utilized by plants and animals during respiration and in burning. The oxygen then combines with hydrogen to form water and carbon dioxide, again used in photosynthesis.

Oxygen Process, in steel production, a method of producing steel, using pure oxygen instead of air. A special pipe, called a lance, is employed through which a supersonic jet of oxygen is blown to a point above the pig-iron and scrap mixture. This method, superior to the Bessemer and open-hearth processes, is used widely in Japan, North America, and Europe.

Oxytocin, or **Pitocin,** peptide hormone secreted by the posterior pituitary. Its principal effect is on myoepithelial cells of the breast causing contraction of the ducts and ejection of milk. It also stimulates the contraction of the smooth muscle of the uterus, and it may play a part in the initiation of labor. It is used for the induction of labor.

Oyster, edible bivalve mollusk found worldwide in temperate and warm seas. Its porcelainlike shell, usually with unequal-sized valves, varies in shape according to environment. The eastern oyster *(Crassostrea virginica)* occurs along the Atlantic seaboard of the United States. Family Ostreidae. *See also* Bivalve; Pearl.

Oyster Catcher, warm area shorebird with a black and white stocky body and brightly colored, sharp-edged bill used to spear oysters and other seafood. After courtship, sand-colored eggs (2–4) are laid. Length: 21in (53cm). Family Haematopodidae.

Oyster Mushroom, a common arboreal fungus, *Pleurotus ostreatus,* that has a medium-size fleshy oyster- or fan-shaped cap and prominent gills. It usually has no stalk. It is edible. Oyster mushrooms are a favorite nesting ground for beetles.

Ozark Mountains (Ozark Plateau), mountainous upland region in S central United States, extends from SW Missouri across NW Arkansas into Oklahoma. The four main divisions include the Salem Plateau, Springfield Plateau, St Francis Mts, and Boston Mts, which contain the highest peaks exceeding 2,000 ft (610m). An eroded tableland, composed of limestone and dolomite rocks, the Ozarks are a source of lead and zinc. Noted for their scenery, forests, and numerous lakes, they are popular tourist region. Area: approx. 50,000 sq mi (129,500 sq km).

Ozone, unstable bluish gaseous allotrope of oxygen with characteristic odor (formula O_3) that decomposes into molecular oxygen. Ozone in the atmosphere is mainly present in the ozone layer 10–20 mi (16–32 km) above the Earth's surface, where it is responsible for absorbing a large portion of the Sun's dangerous ultraviolet radiation. Studies have shown that certain pollutants, such as aerosol-powered sprays, have upset the ozone-layer balance. Ozone is prepared commercially by irradiation of air and used as an oxidizing agent, in the purification of water, and for bleaching.

P

Paca, William (1740–99), US political figure, b. near Abingdon, Md. A Maryland delegate to the Continental Congress (1774–79), he was a signer of the Declaration of Independence. He later served as Maryland's governor (1782–85) and as a US district judge (1789–99).

Paca, or spotted cavy, big-headed nocturnal rodent of Central and South America hunted for food by man and other animals. A plant-eating burrow-dweller, it has brown to black fur with rows of white spots. Length: to 30in (76cm); weight: over 20lb (9kg). Species *Cuniculus paca.*

Pachuca, city in central Mexico, surrounded by foothills of the Sierra Madre Oriental; capital of Hidalgo state; formerly inhabited by Aztecs; site of meteorological observatory, university (1869), mining and metallurgy school, 16th-century convent. Chief industry is silver mining. Founded 1534 on site of ancient Toltec city. Pop. 84,543.

Pacific, War of the (1879–83), conflict between Peru and Bolivia on one side, Chile on the other. The expropriation of Chilean holdings in the nitrate-rich province of Antofagasta induced Chile to declare war. Chile was victorious: Peru lost the provinces of Tarapacá and Arica; Bolivia became a land-locked nation.

Pacific Islands, Trust Territory of the, US trust territory in the Pacific Ocean, N of the Equator mostly in Micronesia; comprised of more than 2,000 islands, major ones include Caroline, Marshall, and Mariana (except Guam) islands; capital is Saipan. The Mariana Islands approved the Mariana Commonwealth Covenant (February 1976), a move toward a more permanent political relationship with the United States. The islands were seized by Japan 1914; occupied by US forces during WWII; they were approved as a US trusteeship by the United Nations 1947. Exports: fish, copra. Area: 700sq mi (1,813sq km). Pop. 102,250.

Pacific Ocean, the world's largest ocean, lying W of the North and South American continents, and E of Asia, Malaysia, and Australia, and extending N to S from the Arctic Circle to Antarctica. Its many arms include (N to S): Sea of Okhotsk, Sea of Japan, and the Philippine, South China, Coral, Tasman, Ross, Amundsen, Bering, and Bellingshausen seas.

With an area of approx. 69,000,000sq mi (178,700,000sq km), including its arms, the Pacific Ocean occupies about 33% of the surface area of the globe, and contains over 50% of the world's seawater, continually circulated by the two major Pacific Ocean currents, the North and South Equatorial currents. The E and N quarters of the Pacific Ocean floor comprise a great undersea plateau, occasionally pocked by deep troughs, and interrupted by long undersea mountain ranges. A series of long fracture zones runs E to W. The S, W, and central portions are characterized by an extensive volcano series, the Circum-Pacific Ring of Fire, which, with numerous coral formations, accounts for some 20,000 islands which dot this vast region.

The greatest known depth of the Pacific is 36,198ft (11,033m), in the Marianas Trench.

The continental shelves of the Pacific are a major commercial fishing ground, and, with advancements in undersea technology, the Pacific is becoming an increasingly important mineral resource.

The first settlers of the Pacific Islands were Asian migrants; their specific origins and settlement dates are unknown. European recognition of the Pacific as a separate ocean dates from the early 16th century when Vasco Nuñez de Balboa arrived at its E shore in 1513 and Ferdinand Magellan explored beyond the Philippines in 1520. Spain and Portugal dominated in early exploration of the Pacific; they were joined by the English and Dutch in the 17th century and France and Russia in the 18th, as the Pacific became important to European whalers. Although many islands had been charted prior to the 19th century, reliable undersea exploration did not begin until the 19th century led by expeditions of the US and British navies.

Pacifism, philosophy opposing war or violence as a means of settling disputes between nations. Elements can be found in ancient Hebrew and early Christian theology and in later Anabaptist and Quaker beliefs. International pacifist groups were organized during the 19th century, foremost among them the American Peace Society (1828), which later numbered Woodrow Wilson among its members. Eastern religions, the doctrines of Mohandas Gandhi, and the British Fellowship of Reconciliations were based on this philosophy.

Pack Rat, name for over 20 species of nocturnal rodents of North and South America that build large aboveground nests. In carrying nest material they often drop one object to pick up another; from this habit comes the name pack (= trade) rat. Length: 8in (203mm). Family Cricetidae.

Paddlefish, flatbill, or spoonbill sturgeon, primitive bony fish closely related to sturgeon and found in the Mississippi and Yangtze river valleys. Bluish gray to olive brown, it has a long paddlelike nose extension, cartilaginous skeleton, and huge jaws. Length: 6ft (1.8m); weight: 30–50lb (13.5–22.5kg). Family Polyodontidae; species Chinese *Psephurus gladius,* American *Polyodon spathula. See also* Osteichthyes.

Paderewski, Ignace Jan (1860–1941), Polish pianist, composer, statesman. Shortly after his professional debut in 1887 in Vienna he established himself as the most popular concert pianist since Franz Liszt. Famous for his interpretation of another Pole, Frederic Chopin, as well as Schumann, Liszt, and Rubenstein. He was especially popular in the United States. Among his compositions is the well known *Minuet in G.* From 1910 to 1920, he devoted himself to the cause of Polish nationalism and raised funds to assist the victims of World War I on US concert tours. After the war he served as prime minister and foreign minister of Poland in a coalition ministry (1919).

Padua (Padova), industrial city in N Italy, 22mi (35km) W of Venice; capital of Padova prov. First mentioned 302 BC, it was a leading Italian commune 11th–13th centuries; it was ruled by Carrara family 1318–1405, when it passed to Venice; site of University (1222, 2nd-oldest in Italy; Galileo taught here), 13th-century cathedral, oldest European botanical garden (1545), 12th-century Palazzo della Ragione, and several medieval and Renaissance buildings. Industries: agricultural machinery, motorcycles, textiles, distilling, wine. Pop. 242,130.

Paganini, Niccolo (1782–1840), Italian violinist and composer. From 1805 on he made a series of triumphant appearances in the European capitals, mesmerizing audiences with his unequaled technical virtuosity. A charismatic showman, he did nothing to discourage rumors that he was in league with the devil. His style influenced many other Romantic musicians, notably Franz Liszt. He often played his own difficult, virtuosic compositions, which include six violin concertos and 24 caprices.

Paget, (Sir) James (1814–99), English surgeon known as a founder of the science of pathology. He discovered the parasitic worm *Trichina spiralis* that causes trichinosis, described the bone disease osteitis deformans (Paget's disease), and was also among the first to recommend surgical removal of bone-marrow tumors rather than amputation.

Pagoda, Eastern building in the form of a tower, which originated in India and spread with Buddhism to China and Japan. The form of the tower is polygonal. Its height is determined by the number of superimposed stories. Elaborately ornamented roofs often project from each story.

Pago Pago, town on Tutuila Island in SW Pacific Ocean, at shore of an inlet which forms an excellent harbor; site of US naval base; capital of American Samoa since 1899. Pop. 2,491.

Pahlevi Dynasty, the dynasty of modern Iran that came into existence in Persia in 1925, when Riza Khan Pahlevi (1877–1944) overthrew Ahmed Shah and was himself elected Shah, assuming the name Riza Shah Pahlevi. In 1935, he officially changed the name of Persia to Iran, its ancient designation. He was forced by the British and Russians to abdicate in 1941 because of his close relations with Germany. He was succeeded by his son Mohammed Riza Pahlevi (1919–80), whose reign saw Iran's emergence as a military and economic power, but political repressiveness led to his overthrow by Islamic revolutionaries in 1979 and he went into exile. His son Riza Pahlevi (b. 1960) assumed the title of Shah in 1981. *See also* Mohammed Riza Pahlevi; Riza Shah Pahlevi.

Pain, distinct, intense, and highly negative sensation, possibly the least understood of all the senses. Pain may arise from the skin or from the deeper tissues of the body, possibly through the overexcitation of free nerve endings in those tissues. Individual tolerance of pain varies, perhaps because of genetic differences but more likely because of cultural conditioning (for example, members of different ethnic groups have different average pain tolerances).

Paine, Robert Treat (1731–1814), US political figure and jurist, b. Boston, Mass. A Massachusetts delegate to the Continental Congress (1774–78), he signed both the Olive Branch Petition (1775) and the Declaration of Independence (1776). He served as Massachusetts' attorney general (1777–90), helped draft the state's constitution, and was a state supreme court judge (1790–1804).

Paine, Thomas (1737–1809), American political writer and leader, b. England. He was an influential voice of colonial public opinion, and his pamphlet *Common Sense* (1776; published anonymously) became a rallying point for colonial patriots. His series of 16 papers, *The Crisis,* encouraged the patriots during the Revolutionary War. While in England he wrote (1791) *Rights of Man,* defending the French Revolution. For this he was indicted for treason and fled to France. He was jailed by the Jacobins (1793–94) when he advocated exile instead of death for King Louis XVI. Paine returned to the United States (1802), where he died in poverty. His main beliefs included the power of reason where there is freedom to debate, tolerance, equality of rights, and the dignity of man.

Paint, a coating applied to a surface for protective and decorative purposes. Paint—composed of pigment, or color, and a vehicle, a liquid that suspends the pigment—adheres to the intended surface and hardens when dry. Pigments are made of earth, oxides of metals, or synthetic materials. Vehicles may be oils, water mixed with a binding agent, organic compounds, or synthetic resins. Synthetic resins (alkyd or acrylate polymers) may be soluble in water or oil. Water-base paint is water-soluble; oil-based paint is soluble in turpentine or other oil-based solvents.

Painted Desert, badlands in N central Arizona, E of Colorado and Little Colorado rivers; erosion and heat have exposed colorful bands of red and yellow sediment and bentonite clay; includes Petrified Forest National Park (SE). Area: approx. 7,500sq mi (19,425sq km).

Painted Lady Butterfly, or thistle butterfly, insect whose larvae feed on thistles. Like the painted beauty *Vanessa virginiensis,* this butterfly's wing markings are brownish-black and orange-gold with small white spots near the front wing tips. Species *Vanessa cardui.*

Painted Turtle, freshwater turtle of the United States. It has bright orange or red markings around the periphery of its smooth, dark olive shell. Males have long front claws. Length: to 6in (15.2cm). Family Emydidae; species *Chrysemys picta. See also* Turtle.

Painting, the art of producing pictures on flat surfaces, one of the oldest of the arts. Such pictures are usually painted on canvas by using a brush and either oil or watercolor paints. Paintings produced on fresh wet plaster are called frescoes. For articles on the history of painting, *see* Abstract Art; Baroque Art; Cubism; Dadaism; Expressionism; Fauvism; Futurism; Impressionism; Mannerism; Neo-Impressionism; Op Art; Pop Art; Post-Impressionism; Realism; Romanticism; Rococo; Primitivism; Renaissance Art; and Surrealism. *See also* the names of individual painters. For different kinds of art, *see also* Genre Painting; Landscape Painting; Still-Life.

Paisley, Ian (Richard Kyle) (1926–), Northern Ireland political leader; Protestant clergyman. After his ordination (1946), he began preaching anti-Roman Catholic sermons and rallying Protestant support against the "forces of popery." Through the 1960s he led anti-Catholic demonstrations, culminating in the riots of 1969. He became a member of the Ulster Parliament and the British House of Commons (1970) in order to have a platform from which to air his views and continued to incite his followers to violence. In the 1980s he opposed Britain's direct intervention in Northern Ireland.

Paiute, a Shoshonean-speaking tribe of North American Indians divided into two major groups: the Southern Paiute (commonly called "Digger Indians" in the Gold Rush days), who occupied W Utah, N Arizona, SE Nevada, and California; and the so-called Northern Paiute (or "Snake Indians"), also known as the Mono-Paviotso, who inhabited W Nevada, S Oregon, and E California. About 4,000 live in both areas today.

Pakistan, nation in S Asia. The people, a mixture of ethnic groups, are overwhelmingly Muslim. The country was created in 1947 from W India.

Land and economy. The Indus River, flowing S through the heartland of Pakistan, causes fertile, alluvial plains the length of the country. The Hindu Kush Mts lie to the NW and the Himalayas to the NE. A plateau covers most of Baluchistan in the W and the Sind Desert occupies most of the SE. Annual rainfall varies from 5in (13cm) in the Sind to 30–40in (76–102cm) in the NW. The country's economy is based upon agriculture, employing 80% of the work force. Cotton is the most important crop, providing adequate amounts for the country's needs plus substantial surpluses for export. Wheat is the most important food crop. Little has been done in the way of mineral development, and fewer than 1% of the people are employed in industry. The government has been successfully introducing new industries to aid employment.

People. The cosmopolitan make-up of the population can be attributed to its location. Long the favorite invasion route of the Indian subcontinent, many of the invaders remained and settled among the local tribes. Five major languages and several dialects are spoken; however, Urdu and English are the official languages. About 97% of the people are Muslim; most of the rest are Hindu. The people are 75% illiterate, but the government has instituted improved educational programs.

Government. In 1977 the constitution calling for a parliamentary democracy was suspended, and martial law was imposed. Executive power is vested in the president, Gen. Zia ul-Haq since 1978, who appoints a 20-member cabinet.

History. After a period of agitation in the 1930s, Muhammad Ali Jinnah led Pakistan to its independence in 1947. Fashioned from India, the original country was in two sections, East and West Pakistan, separated by 900mi (1,450km). A great migration—accompanied by wide spread bloodshed—followed, which disrupted the country's economy for many years: about 6,000,000 Hindus and Sikhs left Pakistan for India, and at the same time about 7,000,000 Muslims left India for Pakistan. Subsequently, tensions between India and Pakistan erupted into war during 1947–49 and 1965–66. In 1971, East Pakistan, which had demanded more autonomy within Pakistan, revolted and war broke out. With India's help, East Pakistan became independent as Bangladesh. The W sector, under Prime Minister Zulfikar Ali Bhutto, initially had strained relations with Bangladesh, but diplomatic relations were resumed in 1971. In 1977, Bhutto was deposed in a military coup,

Pagoda

Thomas Paine

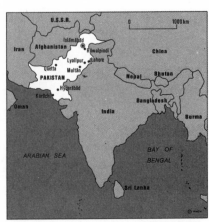

Pakistan

and he was executed in 1979. His daughter, Benazir, leader of the People's Party, returned to Pakistan briefly in 1985 and again in 1986 to lead opposition to Gen. Zia. During the early 1980s dissatisfaction grew with Gen. Zia's increasingly authoritarian rule and by 1985 elections, as promised in his "civilianization" program, were held. After Soviet intervention in neighboring Afghanistan (1979), the United States increased its military assistance to Pakistan.

PROFILE

Official name: Islamic Republic of Pakistan
Area: 310,401sq mi (803,944sq km)
Population: 81,500,000
  Density: 263per sq mi (101per sq km)
Chief cities: Islamabad (capital); Karachi; Lahore
Government: Republic
Religion: Islam
Language: Urdu, English
Monetary unit: Pakistan rupee
Gross national product: $23,000,000,000
Per capita income: $280
Industries (major products): textiles, processed foods, cement, petroleum products
Agriculture (major products): wheat, cotton, rice, sugar cane
Minerals (major): limestone, rock salt
Trading partners (major): United States, West Germany, Japan, United Kingdom

Palate, the roof of the mouth, the bony front part known as the hard palate, the softer fleshy part in the back known as the soft palate. It separates the mouth and nasal cavities.

Palatinate, two regions of West Germany. The Lower, or Rhenish, Palatinate is on the Rhine River. The Upper Palatinate is on the Danube River in Bavaria. The regions were often united historically and were important in the affairs of the Holy Roman Empire from 1356, when the count palatine of the Rhine became an imperial elector. Both regions were part of Bavaria during 1815–1946. In 1946 the Lower Palatinate became the state of Rhineland-Palatinate. The Upper Palatinate remained in Bavaria. *See also* Thirty Years' War.

Palembang, port city in SE Sumatra, on both sides of Musi River; capital of South Sumatra prov. City served as capital of Hindu-Sumatran kingdom of Sri Vijaya (8th century); Dutch settled in city 1617 and est. a trading post and fortress 1659; scene of massacre of Dutch by sultanate 1811; sultanate was abolished 1825; occupied by Japanese during WWII; site of Sriwidjaja State University (1960). Exports: oil, rubber, coffee, coal. Industries: food processing, textiles, oil refining, rubber, fertilizer. Pop. 582,961.

Paleobotany, study of preserved remains of plants. Fossil plants occur as imprints of leaves, as spores and seeds, and as parts of branches and trunks. This division of paleontology has permitted the tracing of various evolutionary relationships among plants. *See also* Paleontology.

Paleocene Epoch. *See* Tertiary Period.

Paleoclimatology, study of ancient climates. The main clues are the remains of plants and animals and the interpretation of various kinds of sediments.

Paleogeography, science that studies ancient geography. It seeks to determine what the physical and biological conditions of the Earth were during its various geological periods. The science also seeks to determine how conditions in one period led to conditions in the next and succeeding periods. Much of the data

needed for good analysis is lacking, and most studies in this area are general.

Paleolithic Age, or Old Stone Age, period in man's evolution in which he used stone tools and weapons and had a hunting and food-gathering economy. Lower Paleolithic man (before about 220,000 BC) used chipped stone artifacts; Middle and Upper Paleolithic cultures also ground and polished stones. *See also* Eolithic Age.

Paleolithic Art, or "cave art," was practiced by early European man in caves, starting in around 30,000 BC. Beasts of chase such as bison and deer were represented naturalistically on the cave walls, probably as a part of some ritual. The first such cave was discovered in 1879 in the Spanish cavern of Altamira.

Paleomagnetism, the study of both direction and intensity of Earth's magnetic field and the changes in it with geologic time. This is important in the investigation of the theory of continental drift. Since the "magnetic memory" of rocks is measurable, this determines their orientation in relation to magnetic north at the time of their solidification. Since neither the location nor intensity of the magnetic poles has changed very much, although the field of Earth has reversed at least once, the gross displacement of large rock formations as measured by their magnetic qualities can be explained by the continental drift theory. *See also* Continental Drift; Magnetic Field, Earth.

Paleontology, geological study of animal and plant fossils. It is important in tracing the evolutionary history of existing and extinct organisms, as well as determining relative ages of geological deposits. The geological periods are: Precambrian, Cambrian, Ordovician, Silurian, Devonian, Carboniferous, Permian, Triassic, Jurassic, Cretaceous, Tertiary, and Quaternary. *See also* Evolution; Fossil; Geologic Time.

Paleozoic Era, one of the major divisions of geologic time lasting from about 570 million to 225 million years ago. Its beginnings mark the earliest occurrence of a good fossil record. All the major animal phyla were present in the early seas of the era; later, some groups took to the land. The Paleozoic is subdivided into the Cambrian, Ordovician, Silurian, Devonian, Carboniferous and Permian periods. *See also* Geologic Time.

Palermo, seaport city in Italy, on Gulf of Palermo, 200mi (322km) SSW of Naples; capital of Sicily and province of Palermo. Founded by Phoenicians *c.* 8th century BC; it passed to Romans 254 BC; prospered under Saracens 9th–11th centuries; it was taken by Normans 1072 and became capital of kingdom of Sicily; seized by Giuseppe Garibaldi 1860; site of 12th–15th-century cathedral, 11th-and 12th-century churches, 12th-century Arab-Norman Palatine Chapel, academy of medical science, letters and arts (1621). Industries: shipbuilding, textiles, food products, chemicals. Pop. 675,501.

Palestine, region on the E shore of the Mediterranean. It has been the Holy Land for Jews, Christians, and Muslims. It was a country of herders and farmers from 4000 BC. Moses led the Jews out of Egypt and into Palestine (*c.* 2000 BC), where they became subjects of the Philistines until 1100 BC, when Saul, David, and Solomon established Hebrew kingdoms. Macedonia ruled 333–142 BC, when Pompey conquered the land for Rome. In succeeding centuries Christianity was dominant until Muslim Arabs seized power in 640. In 1099, Palestine fell to the Crusaders; in 1291 they were routed by the Ottoman Turks. Western influence filtered in through Russian Jews, immigrating after

1882, who embraced the Zionist movement. Arab nationalism was rising, and the British, with a League of Nations mandate over Palestine, attempted unsuccessfully to divide the country between Arabs and Jews. The Arabs feared economic and political results of immigration as WWII and Nazi persecution brought many Jews to Palestine. In 1947, Britain consigned the problem to the United Nations. Ancient Palestine was divided (1948) into the Jewish state of Israel and Arab Jordan. War immediately erupted between Israel and its Arab neighbors and thousands of Palestinian Arabs fled Israel. Arab countries refused to recognize Israel. Since the 1967 Six Day War, Israel has occupied East Jerusalem and the West Bank of the Jordan River. Palestinian refugees have become a powerful political force and, with the patronage of oil-rich Arab states, have demanded the creation of an independent Palestinian nation.

Palestine Liberation Organization (PLO), a council formed (1964) to coordinate the activities of the Arab guerrilla groups and refugee organizations of which it is composed. Since 1968, Yasir Arafat has headed the PLO. In 1974 the PLO was granted full membership in the Arab League, and in 1976 the United Nations recognized the PLO as the legitimate representative of the Palestinian people. The PLO subsequently gained more worldwide support in its demands for an independent Palestinian nation.

Palestrina, Giovanni Pierluigi da (1526–1594), Italian composer of motets, masses, and other religious music. He is often regarded as the greatest composer of the Renaissance period, and his music was long taken as the standard of traditional Roman Catholic liturgical music. *See also* Renaissance Music.

Palladian Architecture, architectural style derived from the buildings and theories of the great Italian architect Andrea Palladio (1508–80), emphasizing symmetrical planning and musically based harmonic proportions. The style became popular in England in the Palladian revival of the early 18th century led by Colen Campbell and Lord Burlington.

Palladio, Andrea (1508–80), Italian Renaissance architect. He studied Roman architecture and published drawings of Roman ruins together with his own designs in *Four Books of Architecture*. In so doing, he revived symmetrical planning and harmonic proportions. His most notable buildings were villas and palazzos, typically with arch and column facades, such as the Villa Rotunda, Vicenza.

Palladium, precious metallic element (symbol Pd) of the second transition series, discovered 1803 by W.H. Wollaston. It is found associated with platinum in nickel ores. Chemically, it is similar to platinum, but more reactive. Properties: at. no. 46; at. wt. 106.4; sp. gr 12.02; melt. pt. 2,826°F (1,552°C); boil. pt. 6,021°F (3,329°C); most common isotope Pd^{106} (27.3%). *See also* Transition Elements.

Pallas, asteroid discovered (1802) by H. W. M. Olbers; the second largest asteroid. Diameter 280mi (450 km); mean distance from Sun 257,000,000mi (414,000,000km); mean sidereal period 4.61 yr.

Pallas' Cat, or manul, rare, small, longhaired cat found from the Caspian Sea to Tibet and north to Siberia, but always in the mountains. It has small rounded ears, circular pupils, short legs, and a compact body. Color is silvery to buff yellow with a pattern of dark spots and stripes. It has a fierce disposition. Length: body—20in (51cm); tail—10in (25cm). Family Felidae; species *Octolobus manul.*

447

Palm, family of trees found in tropical and subtropical regions. Ancient flowering plants that date to the early Triassic (225,000,000 years ago), they have a woody, unbranched, columnar trunk with a crown of large, stiff leaves. The leaves may either be fanlike (palmate) or featherlike (pinnate). Rather than having a true bark covering, palm trunks are covered with fibers. Palm flowers are small, in large clusters, and green, yellow, or red in color. The fruits, which vary according to species, are berries, drupes, or nuts. An economically important family, palms are the source of wax, oil, fiber, sugar, and food; they are also ornamental plants. Family Palmaceae.

Palma, seaport city in Spain, in Balearic Islands, on Bay of Palma; capital of Majorca Island and Baleares prov.; site of Gothic cathedral (1230–1601) containing tomb of King James II of Aragon, 13th-century church of San Francisco containing tomb of Raymond Lully, a Catalan philosopher, Moorish palace, 16th-century town hall. Industries: alcohol, pottery, leather, tourism, jewelry, wine, oil, livestock, flour, sugar, starch, silks. Area: (prov.) 1,936sq mi (5,014sq km). Pop. (city) 234,098; (prov.) 558,287.

Palmerston, Henry John Temple, 3rd Viscount (1784–1865), English political figure. Elected a Tory member of Parliament (1807), he served as secretary of war (1809–28). He left the Tories in support of George Canning (1828). Joining the Whigs, he became foreign secretary (1830) and prime minister (1855), playing a major role in European affairs. Except for a short period in 1858, he remained prime minister until his death. He is noted for effecting the independence of Belgium (1830–31), protecting Portugal and Spain from the threat of absolutism (1834), and annexing Hong Kong (1840–41). He maintained strict neutrality throughout the US Civil War.

Palmetto, fan-leaved palm native from S United States to Central America. The trunk is often covered with dead leaf bases. The 25 species include *Sabal palmetto,* the 90ft (27.4m) cabbage palm of SE United States; *S. bermudiana,* the 40ft (12m) Bermuda palmetto, with a crooked trunk; *S. umbraculifera* native to the West Indies with a massive trunk; and *S. texana,* the 50ft (15m) Texas palmetto, which has a bright red-brown trunk. Family Palmaceae.

Palm Sunday, in the Christian year, the Sunday before Easter and the beginning of Holy Week. Palm Sunday commemorates Christ's triumphal entry into Jerusalem, when the people spread palm branches before him.

Palmyra Palm, fan-leaved palm tree native to India and Malaya. The sap is used to make a fermented drink; the seeds are edible. Height: to 100ft (30.5m); family Palmaceae; species *Borassus flabellifer.*

Palo Alto, suburban city in W California, 17mi (27km) NW of San Jose; site of "El Palo Alto," a 1,000-year-old tree, and Stanford University (1885). Industries: electronic equipment, missile production. Founded 1891; inc. 1894. Pop. (1980) 55,225.

Palolo Worm, polychaete annelid of the South Pacific that lives in holes among coral reefs. A nocturnal swimmer at breeding time, its posterior portion is filled with eggs or sperm. This portion develops an eyespot, separates from the body, and swims to the surface to mate. Family Eunicidae; species *Eunice viridis. See also* Annelida.

Palomino, light horse developed from Spanish horses in the United States and Mexico. A riding horse, it is cream, golden, or light-chestnut, with white, silver, or ivory mane and tail. Height: 56–64in (142.2–162.6cm) at shoulder; weight: 900–1,300lb (405–585kg).

Palynology, originally the study of spores and pollen, now also investigates tiny fragments of animals and plants found in sediment. Neopalynology deals with living microorganisms and parts of plants. Paleopalynology explores fossils of plants and the ancient pollens and spores they produced.

Pamir, mountainous region mostly in Tadzhik SSR, USSR, partly in Sinkiang, Uighur, China, Jammu and Kashmir, India, and along Afghanistan borders; the region forms a geologic structural knot from which the great Tien Shan, Karakorum, Kunlun, and Hindu Kush mountain ranges radiate. The climate is cold during winter and cool during summer; terrain includes grasslands and sparse trees; nomads herd sheep and coal is mined; site of several glaciers and of Terak Pass, used by Marco Polo enroute to China (1271). Highest peaks are Mt Communism, 24,590ft (7,500m) and Lenin Peak, 23,508ft (7,170m).

Pampas (Pampa), plain in S South America, mostly in E Argentina. Divided into two regions: the humid Pampas is very fertile, the heart of the economy of Argentina; the larger dry Pampas includes Buenos Aires, La Pampa, Santa Fe, and Córdoba prov. Area: 294,000sq mi (761,460sq km).

Pampas Grass, species *(Cartaderia selloana)* of tall, reedlike grass of the family Poaccae, native to South America and widely cultivated in warm parts of the world as a lawn ornamental. Female plants bear flower clusters, 3ft (91cm) tall, which are silvery and plumelike.

Pamplona, city in N Spain, 20mi (32km) from French border, on Arga River; capital of Navarra prov.; former capital of French kingdom. Taken 778 from Arabs by Charlemagne, it passed to Ferdinand of Aragón 1512; occupied by French during Peninsular War (1808–13); site of annual fiesta of San Fermín, including celebrated running of bulls; 1397 Gothic cathedral. Industries: sugar milling, brewing, canning, textiles, wine, candies, firearms, furniture, shoes, flour, musical instruments. Area: (prov.) 4,024sq mi (10,422sq km). Pop. (city) 147,168; (prov.) 464,867.

Pan, in Greek mythology, the son of Mercury and a dryad, god of woods and fields, the shepherd and his flock. He is depicted with the horns, legs, and hooves of a goat. A forest dweller, he pursued and loved the dryads and led their dances, while playing the syrinx, the pipes of his invention.

Pan-African Movement, a loosely organized effort for the unification and independence of African nations and black people everywhere. The movement officially began at the Pan-African Congress of 1900 in London, organized by W.E.B. Du Bois and other Western blacks, and was followed by several other meetings in succeeding decades. The Pan-African Federation, created in 1944, was the first strong voice in the call for African rights, leading to considerable activity toward a unified Africa. Although still plagued by differences in structural concepts, the movement materialized in 1963 as the Organization of African Unity, which has enjoyed a limited success. *See also* Organization of African Unity.

Panama, independent Central American nation at the tip of the isthmus connecting North and South America. It is governed by a military junta. The economy is heavily dependent on the Panama Canal Zone.

Land and economy: Panama is divided into 5 areas. The 60-mi (97-km) strip running E–W and including Colón produces most of the country's food, while the Pacific plains have fertile valleys with bananas, pasture land, and grains. Veraguas, a region of rugged, rainy, dense forests, produces coffee. The Caribbean plains, W of Canal Zone, produce cocoa and rubber, and the lowlands E of the Canal Zone have bananas and fishing. Two mountain systems, Sierra de Chiriquí and Cordillera de Veraguas, include volcanic peaks; the highest is Chiriquí, 11,401ft (3,475m). About 30% of the labor force is engaged in agriculture in an economy dominated by trade and international commerce associated with the Panama Canal Zone.

People: Panamanians are largely Roman Catholic, and include descendants of Spanish colonials, immigrant West Indian blacks, and indigenous Indians. The literacy rate is 85%.

Government: In 1978 a national assembly was elected. The assembly, in turn, elected the president to a six year term.

History: Spain's major explorers all had contact with Panama: Rodrigo de Bastidas explored it in 1501; Christopher Columbus sighted it the same year; Vasco de Balboa landed on his way to find the Pacific Ocean; and Francisco Pizarro stopped on his way to Peru in 1531. It remained under Spanish rule until 1821, when it joined the Confederation of Greater Colombia, and in 1903 it declared its independence. Pres. Arnulfo Arias was deposed in a 1968 military coup led by Gen. Omar Torrijos Herrera. After serious anti-US riots in 1974 and 1976, Panama and the United States began renegotiating the treaty. Two new treaties ratified in 1978 came into effect in 1979, gradually handing administration of the zone to Panama. The operation of the canal was completely in the hands of the Panamanians by 1982. Gen. Torrijos resigned the presidency in 1978 but remained the strongman of the government until his death in 1981. Since then, his successors have been unsuccessful in attempts to solidify the government and to solve Panama's economic problems. *See also* Panama Canal; Panama Canal Zone.

PROFILE

Official name: Republic of Panamá
Area: 29,209sq mi (75,651sq km)
Population: 1,837,000
Density: 63per sq mi (24per sq km)
Chief cities: Panamá City (capital); Colón
Government: Provisional junta
Religion: Roman Catholic
Language: Spanish (official)
Monetary unit: Balboa
Gross national product: $1,360,000,000
Per capita income: $1,252
Industries: petroleum products, textiles, wood products, processed foods
Agriculture: bananas, mahogany, pineapple, cocoa, coconut, sugar, shrimp
Minerals: clay, salt, traces of copper
Trading partners: United States, Canada, Mexico, South American countries

Panama Canal, waterway built by the United States (1904–14) to connect the Atlantic and Pacific oceans, opening a shorter route for trade to the Far East. The Isthmus of Panama, owned by Colombia and also the narrowest point of Central America, was chosen as the location. After territorial disputes with Britain were settled in 1850 by the Clayton-Bulwer Treaty, the United States entered into the Hay-Herran Treaty with Colombia (1903), agreeing to pay $10 million and an annual rental of $250,000 in return for a 99-year lease over a 6-mile (9.7km) wide strip of land. When Panama gained independence, the US signed the Hay-Bunau-Varilla Treaty (1903) allowing US control of a canal zone 10 miles (16km) wide for all time with the same fees set in the Colombia treaty. Construction was carried on under US army engineer George W. Goethals. Advances in treating malaria and yellow fever were made while treating victims working on the canal. In 1977, Panama and the United States renegotiated the treaty. Two new treaties, ratified in 1978 and effective beginning in 1979, called for gradual assumption of administrative duties for the canal by Panama (completed in 1982), and by 2000, permanent neutrality of the canal, guaranteed by joint US-Panamanian defense.

Panama City, city in central Panama, capital of Panama since 1903 and Panama prov.; E of Balboa, at the head of the Gulf of Panama; administrative, commercial, and transportation hub; site of University of Panama (1935) and Santa Maria University (1965). Founded (old city) 1519. Pop. 438,000.

Pancreas, an elongated, somewhat triangular-shaped, soft gland lying behind the stomach to the left of the midline. It functions in digestion and as an endocrine organ. As a digestive organ, the pancreas secretes enzymes: trypsin that digests proteins, steapsin that acts on lipids, amylopsin that acts on carbohydrates, and other minor secretions. These pour into the pancreatic duct and then empty into the common bile duct, which opens into the small intestine. The pancreas also contains the islands of Langerhans that secrete the hormone insulin, which plays a major role in the body's metabolism of carbohydrates. *See also* Diabetes Mellitus; Insulin.

Pancreatitis, inflammation of the pancreas caused by alcohol intake or obstruction of the pancreatic ducts. It is characterized by severe pain, fever, and high blood pressure. Treatment involves diet, alcoholic abstinence, and administration of pancreatic extracts.

Panda, or wah, cat-sized mammal of the raccoon family native to Himalayan region. Mostly nocturnal vegetarians, pandas have long, soft red to brown fur, long bushy ringed tails, and dark eyepatches on their white faces. Length: 23in (584mm); weight: 8.5lb (3.9kg). Family Procyonidae; species *Ailurus fulgens. See also* Giant Panda.

Pandora, in Greek mythology, first woman. She was made at Zeus' orders for revenge against Prometheus, who had created man and stolen fire from heaven for man. Pandora was endowed with charm as well as with guile. She was sent to Prometheus' brother Epimetheus, and brought with her a box that she had been forbidden to open. When she opened it all the evils of the human race flew out. Hope remained at the bottom of the box.

Pangaea, the name for the single supercontinent that is hypothesized to have existed 200,000,000 years ago. Using calculations based on computer data, present land masses plus their continental shelves can be fitted together into this one continent. Pangaea was surrounded by Pantalassa, the ancestral Pacific.

Pangolin, or scaly anteater, toothless scale-covered insect-eating mammal of Asia and Africa. When attacked it curls into a ball and raises its sharp scales. Length: 25–70in (64–178cm). They are the only members of the order Pholidota.

Pankhurst, Emmeline Goulden (1858–1928), English political leader, leader of the women's suffrage move-

Panama

Panama Canal

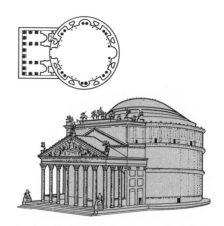

Pantheon: Rome

ment, popularly known as Emily. With her husband, Richard Pankhurst, she worked to secure married women's property rights. When she set up the Women's Social and Political Union (1903), the movement for women's suffrage became militant (including arson, bombing, and hunger strikes), and she was imprisoned. During World War I she supported the cessation of women's suffrage militancy. *See also* Woman Suffrage.

Pannonia, province of ancient Rome SW of the Danube encompassing areas of modern Yugoslavia, Austria, and Hungary. The Romans fought the fierce Pannonians from 119 BC until completing their subjugation in AD 9. The province was split into Upper and Lower Pannonia c. AD 103 and subdivided again by Diocletian. Pannonia fell victim to the barbarian invasions of the 4th century and was abandoned by the Romans c. AD 405.

Pan Pipes (Syrinx), primitive musical wind instrument, probably from Asia. Several tubes of cane, reed, bamboo, or clay are joined like a raft; blown across one end, each pipe produces one note of a scale. Pan pipes are associated with the pastoral Greek god of fertility.

Pansy, common name for a cultivated hybrid violet (*Viola tricolor* var. *hortensis*). It is one of the oldest of European cultivated flowering plants. An annual or short-lived perennial, it grows to about 6 to 12in (15–30cm) tall. The velvety flowers, usually in combinations of blue, yellow, and white, have five petals. Heart-shaped or rounded leaves grow at the base and oval leaves grow from the stem. The wild pansy with mostly purple flowers has been introduced into North America. *See also* Violet.

Pantheism, religious system, contrasted with deism, that identifies God and the universe. All life is infused with divinity, as seen in Hinduism. No distinction is recognized between the Creator and creatures. Mysticism frequently shows a pantheistic language. John Toland first used the term *pantheist* in 1705.

Pantheon, in ancient times, temple for the worship of all the gods in a specific area; by extension, a building honoring illustrious public figures. The Pantheon in Rome was built by Agrippa (27 BC), destroyed, and rebuilt in the 2d century by Hadrian. Well preserved today, its dome, the largest built until modern times, is supported only by the walls of concrete it rests upon. The Panthéon in Paris was designed as a church by J.G. Soufflot and begun in 1764. During the French Revolution it was dedicated to the memory of great Frenchmen. Several times reconsecrated and secularized, it is today a public building.

Panther, or black panther, an all-black (melanistic) leopard or jaguar. In leopards, this form most frequently occurs in the Bengal and Javan varieties. Panthers appear in the same litter as normally colored leopards or jaguars and spots in their black coat can be seen when viewed at a certain angle. Panther tigers have also been reported. *See also* Jaguar; Leopard.

Pantomime, form of theater in which actors use symbolic movement, facial expression, and gesture without dialogue to convey meaning. This is sometimes accompanied by music. Its classical form was a group of dancers enacting a story sung by a chorus. One of the founders of modern pantomime was Jean-Louis Barrault (*Les Enfants du Paradis*); among his students were Marcel Marceau (*The Over Coat* and *The Mask Maker*).

Paotow (Baotou, or **Pao-t'ou),** industrial city, N China, 90mi (145km) W of Huhehot on the Yellow River. Japanese occupied 1937–45. Industries: steel, textiles, automotive, fertilizer. Pop. 800,000.

Papacy, the pope and his authority as the head of the Roman Catholic Church. The doctrine of apostolic succession traces the authority of the pope, the bishop of Rome, from Christ through the apostles, particularly St Peter. The hierarchy developed in the early centuries and underwent many crises and changes throughout history. Basically, it is a system similar to that of the Roman Empire. *See also* Apostolic Succession. *See also* individual popes.

Papago, a Piman-speaking tribe of North American Indians who inhabited the Gila and Santa Cruz river valleys of S Arizona, and N Sonora, Mexico. Less acculturated than their kinsmen the Pima, about 11,000 Papago people live south of Tucson, Ariz. today.

Papal States, central Italian temporal realm of the popes from 754 to 1870, generally including the modern Italian regions of Lazio, Umbria, Marche, and part of Emilia-Romagna. In 756, Pepin the Short, Frankish ruler, granted the exarchate of Ravenna (Donation of Pepin) to Stephen II, establishing the pope's temporal power. Because of rising power of communal governments, the "Babylonian Captivity" (1309–77), and the Great Schism (1377–1417), papal control was weakened in the Middle Ages, never to recover fully. Largely annexed by France between 1797 and 1809, they were restored in 1814, only to be annexed to Italy in 1860 and 1870.

Papandreou, Andreas (1919–), Greek Socialist leader, prime minister 1981– . Educated at the American College and Athens University law school, he earned his PhD at Harvard (1943) and taught in the US for 20 years before giving up his career and his US citizenship to return to Greece and enter politics at the request of his father, then prime minister. Jailed by the ruling military junta (1967), he went abroad on his release and formed the Panhellenic Liberation Movement (PAK), the forerunner of the Panhellenic Socialist Movement (Pasok), which gained strength throughout the 1970s. Its 1981 landslide victory gave Greece its first socialist government in history. As prime minister, he was conciliatory toward socialist and communist regimes.

Papantla, city in E central Mexico, approx. 70mi (113km) NNW of Jalapa; site of nearby ancient pyramid, contains hieroglyphics and small idols. Main industry is tourism. Pop. 94,623.

Papaw, or pawpaw, tree found in central and S United States. It has large, oval leaves, dull purple flowers, and sausage-shaped, yellowish, edible fruits that have a bananalike flavor. Height: to 40ft (12m). Family Annonaceae; species *Asimina triloba.*

Papaya, or tropical pawpaw, palmlike tree widely cultivated in its native American tropics for fleshy, melonlike, edible fruit. Height: to 20ft (6m). Family Caricaceae; species *Carica papaya.*

Papeete, port town and capital of Tahiti and French Polynesia, on NW coast of Tahiti in Society Islands, S Pacific Ocean; trade center of the islands; site of an international airport. Exports: copra, mother of pearl, vanilla. Pop. 24,000.

Paper, flat sheet of compacted cellulose fibers used for packaging, writing or painting upon, as a wall covering, etc. The word "paper" derives from papyrus, the

plant that the Egyptians used at least 5,500 years ago to make sheets of writing material. The papyrus reed was soaked and slit into strips that were laid at right angles and pounded and pressed into a sheet. The modern process of manufacture originated about 2,000 years ago in China and consists of reducing wood fiber, straw, rags, and grasses to a pulp by the action of an alkali, such as caustic soda. The lignin and other noncellulose material is then extracted and the residue is bleached. After washing and the addition of a filler to provide a smooth and flat surface, the pulp is rolled into thin sheets and dried. Newsprint and other cheap papers are mechanical pulps made without chemical treatment and consist of finely divided wood without purification. The better quality papers are made from chemical pulps prepared as described.

Papillon, small dog (toy group) developed from 16th-century dwarf spaniel. A fine-boned dog, it has a small head and thin muzzle and distinctive erect, butterfly-type ears (drop, or Phalene-type, ears also occur). The straight-backed body is set on very slender legs, and the long, well arched tail is carried over the back. The long, silky coat is full on chest, ears, legs, and tail; it is white with patches of any color in a particular pattern. Average size: 8–11in (20–28cm) at shoulder; 5–11lb (2.3–5kg). *See also* Toy Dog.

Pap Smear, a sample of cells, often from the female genital tract, specially stained to detect malignant or premalignant disease. Named for its discoverer, George Papanicolaou.

Papua New Guinea, independent nation of the W Pacific Ocean; consisting of the E half of New Guinea and the neighboring islands of the Bismarck Archipelago, and the northern portion of the Solomon Islands. Most of the terrain is mountainous, and there are many volcanoes, especially in the Bismarck Archipelago. Lowland areas of size are restricted to New Guinea island N and S of the Central Highlands. Situated just S of the Equator, the climate is hot and wet throughout the year, giving rise to the natural vegetation of rain forest. The vast majority of the population practices subsistence agriculture, some with very primitive methods, growing yams and taro. Because of the rugged terrain, many tribes are very isolated. The principal cash crops grown for export are coffee, copra, and cocoa. The forests are exploited for hardwoods, and the country is one of the world's leading producers of gold and copper. Although discovered by the Spanish in the 16th century, little was known about the region until German traders began operating there in the 1870s. Germany claimed New Guinea in 1884; Australia occupied it during WWI, and it became an Australian mandate in 1921. In 1975, Papua New Guinea became independent of Australia, joining the British Commonwealth. Government is by a house of assembly elected by citizens over 18. Since independence, the government has faced unrest from some highland tribes.

PROFILE

Official name: Papua New Guinea
Area: 178,221sq mi (461,691sq km)
Population: 3,078,000.
 Density, 17 per sq mi (7 per sq km).
Chief cities: Port Moresby (capital), 66,244; Lae, 34,-699; Rabaul, 24,778
Religion: Traditional, Christian
Language: English
Trading partners: (major) Australia, United States, Japan, Great Britain

Papyrus, stout perennial plant that Egyptians used to make paperlike writing material. Native to S Europe and N Africa, it grows in shallow water. Height: to 10ft (3m). Family Cyperaceae; species *Cyperus papyrus.*

Parabola, conic formed by cutting a right circular cone with a plane parallel to one of the cone's generators. A parabola is a conic with an eccentricity equal to 1. In rectangular Cartesian coordinates its standard equation is $y^2 = 4ax$, where a is a constant: the curve is symmetrical about the x-axis. A useful property of the parabola is that a line parallel to the x-axis is "reflected" at the curve through the focus, which lies on the x-axis (that is, a line from the focus to a point on the curve makes an angle with the normal at that point equal to the angle between the normal and a line from the point parallel to the x-axis). This property is used in parabolic reflectors in telescopes, searchlights, etc.

Paracelsus, Philippus Aureolus (1493–1541), Swiss physician and alchemist, b. Philippus von Hohenheim. He believed that alchemy should be devoted to the preparation of chemical remedies for disease rather than the discovery of methods for manufacturing gold. In addition to writing on mental disease problems, he was the first to describe zinc.

Parachute Jumping. *See* Sky Diving.

Paradise Lost (1667), epic poem by John Milton in blank verse.

Paradox, apparently contradictory statement intended to contain within it a germ of truth. It is often used in epigrams as in Shaw's "Youth is wasted on the young," meaning youth lacks wisdom and age lacks the energy to profit from its wisdom. *See also* Epigram.

Paraffin, or paraffin wax, white translucent waxy substance consisting of a mixture of solid alkanes (paraffins). It is obtained during petroleum distillation and used to make candles, waxed paper, polishes, and cosmetics. Properties: sp gr 0.88–0.915; melt. pt. 116–149°F (47–65°C).

Paraguay, independent nation in central South America. It is an entirely landlocked country whose capital, Asunción, was established in 1537. Its homogeneous population is Indian and Spanish in an agricultural economy.

Land and economy. Surrounded by Argentina, Brazil, and Bolivia, it reaches the Atlantic Ocean through a river system flowing through Argentina. The 1,584-mi (2,550-km) Paraguay River divides the country into two regions, the temperate E zone of rolling hills, forests, and grasslands, and the W (Chaco) portion of dense forests, unnavigable rivers, and little rainfall. Stockraising and agriculture dominate the economy. With very few minerals and no petroleum, 90% of exports are meat, lumber, cotton, oils, coffee, tobacco. Since 1968 a $33 million hydroelectric plant has provided most of its power needs. Industry, growing rapidly, processes the country's primary products.

People. With 90% of the people of mixed Indian (Guaraní) and Spanish descent, the country is culturally and socially homogeneous. Spanish is the official language; 90% understand Guaraní. Literacy is 30%. Roman Catholicism is the principal religion.

Government. Based on a 1967 constitution, the highly centralized government includes a five-year term for an elected president with broad powers, bicameral congress with elected members. Power rests in the executive branch. Decrees are allowed when congress is not in session. Gen. Alfredo Stroessner has been president since 1954.

History. The Spaniard Alejo García was probably the first European to reach Paraguay. About 1520 he headed an expedition into the Inca Empire, and his reports inspired Sebastian Cabot's explorations (1526–29). Jesuits, who established agricultural colonies and tried to Christianize the Indians, were expelled in 1767. Paraguay gained independence from Spain in 1811 and in 1870 adopted a democratic constitution. Paraguay fought two devastating wars with its neighbors, the War of the Triple Alliance (1864–70) and the Chaco War (1932–35). By the early 1980s it had the fastest growing economy in South America, although a slowdown occurred from 1982.

PROFILE

Official name: Republic of Paraguay
Area: 157,047sq mi (406,752km)
Population: 3,100,000
Density: 20per sq mi (8per sq km)
Chief cities: Asunción (capital); Villarrica
Government: Constitutional democracy
Religion: Roman Catholic
Language: Spanish (official), Guaraní (national)
Monetary unit: Guaraní
Gross national product: $3,100,000,000
Per capita income: $1,038
Industries: meat products, leather, wood products, tannin extract, vegetable oil
Agriculture: corn, wheat, beans, peanuts, tobacco, citrus fruits, beef cattle, timber
Minerals: ore
Trading partners: United States, Argentina, Brazil

Paraguay, river in S central South America; rises in SW Brazil; flows S to form part of the Brazil-Paraguay and Paraguay-Argentina borders; empties into the Paraná River at SW corner of Paraguay; chief tributaries are Pilcomayo and Bermejo rivers; Asunción is the chief port. Length: 1,584mi (2,550km).

Parakeet, name given several different small, brightly colored parrots that are popular pets. Affectionate and clever, they are natural acrobats, climbing toy ladders and playing on swings in their cages. Some hobbyists breed parakeets. The eggs (5) hatch in less than 21 days. The most common pet parakeet is the Australian budgerigar *(Melopsittacus undulatus)* that can often be taught to mimic speech. The males have bluish nostrils, females brownish.

Parallax, apparent change in position of an object, seen against a remote background, when the viewpoint is changed. The parallax of a star (annual parallax) is the angle subtended at the star by the mean radius of the Earth's orbit (one astronomical unit); the smaller the angle, the more distant the star. *See also* Parsec.

Paramecium, freshwater, ciliated protozoan characterized by streamlined "slipper" shape, front and rear ends, oral groove for feeding, food vacuoles for digestion, anal pore for elimination, and two nuclei. Its stiff outer covering is studded with small cilia. Reproduction is by asexual division and sexual conjugation, during which nuclear material is exchanged. Order Holotricha; species include *Paramecium bursaria* and *Paramecium aurelia.*

Paraná, formerly Bajada de Santa Fe; city in E Argentina, 235mi (378km) NW of Buenos Aires; capital of Entre Ríos prov. Capital of the Argentine Confederation 1853–62. Industries: cement, dairy products, furniture; trade in beef and grain, fruit, poultry, fishing, lumber. Founded 1730. Pop. 127,836.

Paraná, river in SE central South America; important passage for inland communications; rises in SE Brazil, flows S into Argentina, forming SE and S border of Paraguay; joins the Uruguay River to form Río de la Plata. Length: 1,827mi (2,941km).

Parasite, any organism that depends entirely upon another organism for its existence. The parasite usually lives in or on its host, nourishes itself at the expense of the host without rapidly destroying it, but often inflicting some degree of injury. Among the parasites that can infect man are single-celled animals such as *Plasmodium* (malaria) and ameba; several types of worms, insects, and arthropods.

Parasitism, relationship involving two different organisms. The parasite benefits, deriving nourishment from the host that is harmed but not usually killed. For example, a fungus (parasite) causes athlete's foot in humans (host).

Parasitology, branch of biology that deals with the study of parasites, organisms that live on other organisms. Some parasitologists concentrate on the study of those parasites responsible for diseases in humans or other animals.

Parasol Mushroom, any of a family of common terrestrial mushrooms (Lepiotaceae) that have shaggy umbrella-shaped caps, especially *Lepiota procera,* which is considered one of the best edible species. Some parasols are toxic and many resemble amanitas.

Parathyroid Gland, any of the four pea-sized bodies, usually embedded in the back part of the thyroid gland, that secrete the hormone parathormone, which controls the amount of calcium and phosphorus in the blood. Abnormalities of this endocrine gland can usually be treated with parathyroid extract and regulation of calcium and phosphorus intake.

Parchment, the processed skins of animals such as sheep, goats, and calves, used as writing material; invented in the 2nd century BC. When made from calf or kid skin, parchment is called vellum. In modern usage, "parchment" and "vellum" refer to high-quality paper made from wood pulp and rags.

Parenchyma, soft tissue made up of nonspecialized, thin-walled cells. It is the chief substance of plant stems, leaves, and fruit pulp and stores nutrients and water. It also helps support plants along with woody cells (sclerenchyma).

Paresis, condition involving deterioration of personality, impaired judgment and disorientation, and paralysis caused by destruction of brain tissue in tertiary syphilis. Antibiotics are used in treatment.

Pareto, Vilfredo (1848–1923), Italian economist and sociologist who emphasized a theoretical approach to economics. Pareto's main area of interest was the distribution of a country's income. He developed criteria for demonstrating the "optimum" (or best) social position and attempted to show empirically that the actual distribution of income in an economy followed an invariant law. His basic conclusion was that policies aimed at redistributing a country's income were ineffective.

Pareto Optimum, named for Vilfredo Pareto, specific situation that exists in a society where society's welfare could not be improved through the exchange of commodities by individuals within the society or by any reallocation of resources within that society. The Pareto optimum implies that a maximum welfare position is being achieved. It implies also that the exchange of goods or services by individuals in the society would result in the decrease in utility to one of the individuals exceeding the increase in utility to the other.

Paris, capital city of France; located on Seine River 100mi (160km) from its mouth on the English Channel. The city proper consists of Paris department, and its suburbs lie in departments of Seine-St-Denis, Val-de-Marne, Hauts-de-Seine, Val-d'Oise, Yvelines, and Essonne. When the Romans took Paris in 52 BC, it was a small village on the river's Ile de la Cité. Under the Romans it grew in importance as an administrative center and bridging point of the Seine; Roman influence is still evident, especially in the catacombs of Montparnasse. The city became the capital of the Merovingian Franks in the 5th century; after raids by the Norse in the 9th century it was reestablished as the French capital by Capetian kings in the 10th century; this spurred growth on the right bank. During the 14th century, Paris rebelled against the crown and declared itself an independent commune, and it suffered from civil disorder during the Hundred Years War. In the reign of Louis XIII (1601–43), Cardinal Richelieu established Paris as the cultural center of Europe. The French Revolution began in Paris when mobs stormed the city prison (Bastille). Under the emperors Paris became a modern city, especially during the reign of Napoleon III (1852–70), when Baron Haussmann was commissioned to plan the boulevards and parks. Although occupied in the Franco-Prussian War (1870–71) and WWII the city was not badly damaged. Site of Cathedral of Notre Dame, Louvre, Les Invalides, Palais de Justice, Palais de Luxembourg, L'Opéra, Panthéon, Bibliothèque Nationale, Tribunal de Commerce, St-Chapelle, Palais de l'Élysée, La Madeleine, St-Germain-des-Prés, Bourse, Sorbonne, Hôtel-Dieu, Eiffel Tower, and Georges Pompidou National Center for Art and Culture. Paris remains the hub of France despite recent attempts at decentralization and retains its importance as a cultural, commercial, and communication center of Europe. Industries: auto, marine, and railroad engineering, other mechanical and electrical engineering, chemicals, textiles, clothing, printing and publishing, luxury goods production. Pop. (city proper) 2,317,227; (metropolitan area) 8,196,746.

Paris, Congress of (1856), peace conference of the Crimean War in which England and France defended Turkey from Russian aggrandizement. It called for demilitarization of the Black Sea, liberty for Turkish Christians, and free navigation of the Danube River.

Paris, Treaty of (1763), diplomatic agreement signed by Britain, France and Spain ending the Seven Years War (1756–63). France ceded most of Canada to Britain in return for Guadeloupe and Martinique, and Spain ceded all its territories east of the Mississippi River to Britain. French settlers were allowed to leave the new British territories with their possessions.

Parity Principle, principle of physics that there is no distinction to be made between the behavior of a system and that of its mirror image. The principle is usually formulated in terms of mathematical transformation between left- and right-handed coordinate systems. It holds for classical physics and for behavior involving strong interactions; parity is then said to be conserved. However, this symmetry does not apply to weak interactions, as in beta decay, in which the spin of the emitted electrons always has a preferred sense. *See also* Spin, Nuclear.

Parkinson's Disease, a chronic, progressive nervous disease occurring mostly in older males. Tremors, muscle weakness, and rigid facial expression are characteristic. Cause is not known, but influenza and hardening of the arteries are frequently associated with the disease. No cure exists, but physical therapy and a new drug, L-dopa, may relieve symptoms.

Paraguay

Paris: Eiffel Tower

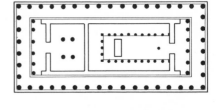

Parthenon

Parlements, highest judicial courts in France before the Revolution. The word is used particularly to mean the Paris parlement. The parlement evolved out of a medieval body with advisory functions, partly because the king wished to rationalize disputes between vassals, and partly because the vassals were eager to restrain royal power. Involved in the revolt of the Fronde (1651–53), the Paris parlement during the 18th century became a symbol of opposition to arbitrary royal rule. Louis XV's chancellor abolished the parlements (1771) to streamline the judicial system, but popular opposition to the move led Louis XVI to reinstate them (1774). They were abolished permanently by the 1790 constitution.

Parliament, British, bicameral legislative assembly at Westminster, England, having supreme political authority in Great Britain and Northern Ireland. In Henry III's reign (1216–72), Parliament emerged as a representative body of knights and burgesses. Gaining influence in the 14th century, it advised the king on domestic and foreign policy, dispatched justice, and passed legislation. Although summoned and dismissed on the king's initiative, its power lay in its right to control taxation, which is why monarchs tended to summon Parliament only when they wanted money. By 1400 a formal division had appeared between the "higher house" or "House of Lords" (evolved from the former *Curia Regis* or Great Council) and the "common house" or "House of Commons." As Parliament's power increased so did its clashes with the crown. The Long Parliament's victory over Charles I (1640) ensured Parliament's political ascendancy. The Hanoverian kings' withdrawal from governing facilitated the establishment of the authority of the prime minister, leaving the crown only a nominal supremacy. The 19th- and 20th-century evolution of universal adult suffrage made Parliament a democratically representative legislature, controlling administration and the nation's policies.

Parliamentary Law, rules governing procedures of deliberative bodies. The English Parliament, particularly the House of Commons, is the basis for most of the accepted rules, which have been adapted for use in other legislatures. A manual of parliamentary law formulated by Thomas Jefferson when he was presiding officer of the US Senate, is generally used by US Congress. Robert's *Rules of Order* (1876), taken from the practices of Parliament and Congress, is a widely accepted authority on parliamentary law, but it is neither prescribed by statute nor by court decision and is not legally binding.

Parma, city in N Italy, 75mi (121km) SE of Milan; capital of Parma prov. Est. by Romans 183 BC, it was an important Roman road junction along the Via Aemilia; rebuilt during the Middle Ages; made a duchy by Pope Paul III; given to Marie Louise of Austria by Napoleon 1815; heavily damaged by Allied bombing WWII; site of cathedral (rebuilt 12th century), Palazzo della Pilotta (begun 1583), abbey of St Paolo (16th century); agricultural economy. Industries: cheese, machinery, pharmaceuticals, fertilizer. Pop. 177,934.

Parma, city in N Ohio, 8mi (13km) S of Cleveland. Industries: automobile parts, tools, dies, industrial research. Founded 1816; inc. as city 1932. Pop. (1980) 92,548.

Parmigianino, or **Parmigiano, Il,** real name **Girolamo Francesco Maria Mazzuola** (1503–40), northern Italian artist. He was a master of the Mannerist style. One of the first Italian painters who was also an important etcher, he is famous for his drawings as well. His works include "Madonna with St Zachary," "Marriage of St Catherine," "Vision of St Jerome," and "Madonna of the Long Neck."

Parnassus (Parnassós), Mount, mountain peak in central Greece. In ancient times, it was considered sacred to Apollo, Dionysus, and the Muses; site of the sacred fountain of Castalia, just above Delphi, at the S foot of the mountain. The Corycian Cave, associated with the Bacchic festivals, lies on a plateau between Delphi and the summit. Height: 8,060ft (2,458m).

Parnell, Charles Stewart (1846–91), Irish nationalist. He entered the British Parliament (1875), vigorously supporting home rule for Ireland and rapidly taking over leadership of the Home Rule Bill. To gain concessions, he embarked upon a policy of parliamentary obstruction. He united all the Irish parties hostile to English rule, including the Fenians in Ireland and the United States. Supporting the Land League (1879), he was imprisoned (1881) for directing tenants to withold rent. Released under the Kilmainham treaty (1882), he found the Liberal government more tolerant than the Conservative. This trend was frustrated by the Phoenix Park assassinations (1882) and the subsequent defeat of William Gladstone's government. Reinstated, Gladstone introduced the Home Rule Bill (1886), marking the zenith of Parnell's power. The bill was defeated, however. Parnell's fall was assured by his suspected implication (1887; shown to be false 1890) in the Phoenix Park murders, and his proven adultery with the wife of one of his supporters (1890). *See also* Home Rule.

Parody, literary composition in which another author's language and style are imitated and exaggerated for comic effect. In ancient Greece, Aristophanes wrote parodies of Aeschylus and Euripides. In England, Henry Fielding's *Joseph Andrews* (1742) was a successful parody of Samuel Richardson's novel *Pamela, or Virtue Rewarded.* 20th-century writers who have made use of parody include Max Beerbohm, James Joyce, and Stephen B. Leacock.

Parotid Gland, largest of the salivary glands, located just in front of and a little below the opening of the ear. Along with the other salivary glands, it forms and secretes saliva. It is the gland that becomes swollen during mumps. *See also* Salivary Glands.

Parr, Catherine (1512–48), queen consort and sixth wife of Henry VIII. She was married four times, marrying her fourth husband, Thomas Seymour, after the king's death (1547). Because of her intercession, the princesses Elizabeth and Mary were reinstated at court. As queen, she tried to alleviate religious persecution.

Parrot, any of numerous tropical and subtropical birds that are popular as pets, including macaws, lories, lorikeets, parakeets, keas, kakas, and others. Brightly colored, they have thick, hooked bills. All nest in tree holes, rock cracks, or on the ground. Pet parrots should be kept in clean, warm, large cages and provided with fresh air, water, and proper food. Some can be taught to mimic speech. Length: 3in–3ft (7.6–92cm). Family Psittacidae.

Parrot Fever. See Psittacosis.

Parrotfish, marine fish of tropical Atlantic and Indo-Pacific identified by heavy, platelike teeth resembling a parrot's beak. A coral-eating fish that goes through many color changes, it builds a mucous cocoon for sleeping. Length: 4.5in–12ft (11.4–366cm). The 80 species include the rainbow *Scarus guacamaia.* Family Scaridae.

Parsec (symbol pc), astronomical unit of length equal to the distance at which the radius of the Earth's orbit subtends an angle of one second. It is thus the distance at which an object would have a parallax of one second, using the Earth-Sun distance as the baseline. One parsec is equal to 3.2616 light-years or 1.917×10^{13} mi. (3.086×10^{13}km).

Parsi, or Parsee, modern descendant of a small number of ancient Persian Zoroastrians who emigrated to Gujerat in India in the 8th century. The modern Parsis follow a mixture of Zoroastrianism and some Indian beliefs and practices. Concentrated today mostly in Bombay, the Parsis are a small but active Indian minority of about 125,000. *See also* Zoroastrianism.

Parsley, smooth branching biennial herb, native to the Mediterranean region and widely cultivated for its tender, curled aromatic leaves used as flavoring and a garnish. It has greenish-yellow flowers and tiny, seedlike fruits. Height: to 3ft (0.9m). Family Umbelliferae; species *Petroselinum crispum.*

Parsnip, biennial plant native to Eurasia and widely cultivated for its edible white taproot. It has tall, ovate leaflets. Family Umbelliferae; species *Pastinaca sativa.*

Parson Bird, or tui, honey eater of New Zealand with greenish-blue plumage and white feathers under the throat. Once valued as a cage bird, it can be taught to whistle or repeat words. Length: 11in (28cm). Species *Prosthemadera novaeseelandiae.*

Parthenogenesis, form of asexual reproduction that produces a new individual by development of an unfertilized ovum. It can occur in animals capable of sexual reproduction. An example of natural parthenogenesis is when a queen honeybee decides whether or not to fertilize her eggs. Artificial parthenogenesis may be induced by electric shock, mechanical stimulation, inorganic salts, organic acids, or temperature change.

Parthenon, temple of the goddess Athena, erected (447–432 BC) by Pericles on the Acropolis in Athens. The architects, Ictinus and Callicrates, and the chief sculptor, Phidias, constructed a peripteral temple of the Doric order. The huge gold and ivory statue of Athena was destroyed in ancient times, and the inner chambers and porticos were ruined in the 17th century, but the surviving outer structure and sculptural pediments testify to the perfection of its design.

Parthia, ancient country in W Asia; originally a province in the Assyrian and Persian empires, the Macedonian empire of Alexander the Great, and the Syrian empire. Led by Arsaces, its first king, it freed itself from the rule of the Seleucidae (c. 2500 BC) and reached the height of its power under Mithridates I (1st century BC). The empire was overthrown c. AD 226 by Ardashir I, the first Sassanid ruler of Persia.

Partial Differential Equation, type of differential equation used when a function depends on two or more independent variables. For example, a wave in three dimensions has an amplitude *(U)* that depends on time and also on the three distance measurements x, y, and z, along mutually perpendicular axes. The differential equation representing the wave is
$$\frac{\partial^2 U}{\partial^2 x} + \frac{\partial^2 U}{\partial^2 y} + \frac{\partial^2 U}{\partial^2 z} = \frac{1}{c^2}\frac{\partial^2 U}{\partial t^2}$$
Here c is the wave's velocity. The symbols
$$\frac{\partial^2 U}{\partial x^2}$$
etc., are called partial derivatives and express the rate of charge of U in the x direction, etc, only. Partial differ-

ential equations are extensively used in physical science. *See also* Differential Equation.

Partial Pressure, pressure that a given component of a gas mixture would have if it alone were present. The pressure of an ideal-gas mixture is the sum of the partial pressures of its components (Dalton's Law of partial pressures).

Partridge, any of several Old World game birds, but in particular, the true partridge *(Perdix perdix),* also known as the European gray partridge and as the Hungarian partridge, a highly valued game bird native to Eurasia and now established in the Americas. A medium-sized bird, it has gray plumage with transversely barred sides and a blackish, sometimes horseshoe-shaped, patch on the belly. It typically takes off fast and is very swift flying. Some partridges (genus *Alectoris*) have reddish breast and legs (chukar or rock partridge); some barring and collar; and some, mainly Asian, are brightly colored.

Partridgeberry, or twinberry, squawberry, evergreen trailing plant native to North America. A popular decorative plant, it prefers shady areas and has white flowers and red berries. Family Rubiaceae; species *Mitchella repens.*

Parzival, late 12th-century romance epic (begun 1197 or 1198) composed in Middle High German by Wolfram von Eschenbach. Based largely on works by Chrétien de Troyes and Hartman von Aue, it deals with the legendary knights of King Arthur and the quest for the Holy Grail. Unique in the period and genre is its emphasis on married love, the lives of children, and inner development of the hero.

Pasadena, city in S California, 8mi (13km) NE of Los Angeles; site of California Institute of Technology (1891), the annual Tournament of Roses Parade (1890), and Rose Bowl football game. Industries: electronic equipment, ceramics, plastics, aircraft components, cosmetics. Founded 1874; inc. 1886. Pop. (1980) 119,374.

Pasadena, city in SE Texas, 10mi (16km) S of Houston, on Houston ship channel; trade and shipping center; site of San Jacinto College (1961); scene of Gen. Santa Anna's capture (1836). Industries: oil refining, synthetic rubber, chemicals, paper, agriculture, cattle. Settled 1892; inc. 1928. Pop. (1980) 112,560.

Pascal, Blaise (1623–62), French mathematician. A prodigy, he had written a book on conics by the age of 16 and later, with Pierre de Fermat, laid the foundations of the theory of probability. He also contributed to calculus and hydrodynamics before retiring from science in 1655 to devote himself to religious and philosophical writing, of which his *Pensées* are the best known example.

Pascal's Law, a concept, formulated by the French mathematician Blaise Pascal in 1647, which states that the pressure applied to an enclosed fluid is transmitted equally in all directions and to all parts of the enclosing vessel, if pressure changes due to the weight of the fluid can be neglected. This law has important applications in hydraulics.

Pashto or **Pushtu,** one of the two major languages of Afghanistan, spoken by about 10,000,000 people there, or about 60% of the population. It is also spoken in NW Pakistan by about 6,000,000 people. Pashto historically is the language of the Pathans, the indigenous inhabitants of this area. It is one of the Iranian languages and thus part of the Indo-European family.

Passenger Pigeon, an extinct species *(Ectopistes migratorius)* of pigeon. Once extremely numerous in the United States, the passenger pigeon was slaughtered for meat and finally the wild birds disappeared; in 1914 the last captive representative died.

Passionflower, also maypops, maracock, climbing tropical plant found in America, Asia, Australia, and Polynesia. Flowers are red, yellow, green, or purple. The outer petals ring a fringed center. Leaves are lobed and some species produce small, egglike, edible fruits. 400 species *(Passiflora);* Family Passifloraceae.

Passion Music, a musical presentation of the New Testament story of Easter according to the gospels of St Matthew, St Mark, St Luke, and St John. This musical form grew out of the "passion plays" presented in the 12th century and developed into large choral works with orchestral accompaniment during the Renaissance and Baroque periods; for example, J. S. Bach's *St Matthew Passion.*

Passion Play, dramatization of Christ's passion, originally performed in medieval Europe. The most important survival is held every 10 years in Oberammergau, Germany, where the first performance of the present text was given in 1634 to fulfill a vow made by the villagers during a plague epidemic. The players are all townspeople.

Passover (Pesach), the Jewish festival of eight days that commemorates the Exodus from Egypt and the redemption of the Israelites. Also called the Feast of the Unleavened Bread. Symbolic dishes are prepared, including bitter herbs (maror) and matzo, or unleavened bread, which remind the Jew of his heritage and the haste with which the Jews fled Egypt. It is also a celebration of thanksgiving for freedom. The Seder, a ceremonial dinner, is a family celebration, in which the Haggadah is read. In Israel, it lasts for 7 days.

Pastel Painting, type of painting used especially for portraits, done with sticks of finely ground pigments usually used on paper. Because they are so soft, pastel colors smudge easily, and a fixative solution is therefore used. Pastels first came into use in the 16th century in northern Europe. They were used for portraits by such painters as Holbein and Clouet and later by the Impressionists, especially Renoir. During the 18th century, pastels were mixed with white to obtain the pale colors in vogue during the Rococo style, and since then the term "pastel" has also meant lightened color.

Pasternak, Boris (1890–1960), Soviet poet, translator, and novelist. The son of a painter and a concert pianist, he was early influenced by the family friends Leo Tolstoy and Aleksandr Scriabin. After studying music and philosophy, he turned to literature. His first book of poetry, *The Twin in the Clouds,* appeared in 1914. Another volume of poetry, *My Sister, Life,* published in 1922, established his reputation. At first he welcomed the Russian Revolution. His autobiographical *Safe Conduct* appeared in 1931 followed by the poems *Second Birth* (1932). By this time his individualistic works were being condemned by party regulars. He published no more original works during the next decade, turning instead to translation. Two books of simpler, more conforming poetry published during World War II were still criticized. After the death of Stalin, Pasternak began work on the novel *Dr. Zhivago.* Its hero, the poet-physician Yuri Zhivago, much like Pasternak, welcomes the Revolution but then finds his search for personal happiness barred by political circumstances. Denied publication in the Soviet Union, it first appeared in Italy in 1957. Pasternak was awarded the Nobel Prize for literature in 1958. Soviet authorities compelled him to retract his acceptance and expelled him from the Soviet Writers Union.

Pasteur, Louis (1822–95), French chemist and founder of microbiology. He made many important contributions to chemistry, bacteriology, and medicine. Among the most significant was his conclusive proof that spontaneous generation (life arising from nonliving matter) does not occur. In his best known work, Pasteur discovered that microorganisms can be destroyed by heat, a technique, now known as pasteurization, used to destroy harmful microorganisms in food. Pasteur also discovered that he could weaken certain disease-causing microorganisms—specifically the microorganisms causing cholera and anthrax in animals and rabies in man—and then use the weakened culture to vaccinate against the disease. He also conducted studies on the diseases of silkworms. He taught at many institutions, including the Sorbonne (1867–89), and directed the Pasteur Institute (1888–95).

Pasteurization, process of controlled heat treatment to kill bacteria, discovered by Louis Pasteur in 1862. Milk is pasteurized by heating to 161° F (72°C) and holding at that temperature for 15 seconds. Alternatively, it may be heated to 143°F (62°C) and held for 30 minutes. Sterilization uses higher temperatures, which would damage some foods.

Pastoral, literary work portraying shepherds or rural life in an idealized manner in order to contrast their innocence with the corruption of the city or royal court. The pastoral in poetry, fiction, and drama has often been used as a vehicle for discussion of politics, religion, and other serious subjects. In classical times Theocritus and Virgil wrote notable pastoral poems, which were known as eclogues. Eclogues were revived during the Renaissance by Edmund Spenser and others. John Milton and Percy Shelley were noted for their pastoral elegies. Certain poets, such as William Wordsworth and Robert Frost, have sometimes been referred to as pastoral poets because of the pastoral or rural nature of their writing.

Pastoralism, mode of subsistence involving the herding of domesticated livestock. Pastoral societies are small scale due to the restrictively large amount of grazing land needed for each animal. In the Americas indigenous pastoralism is confined to the Andes but it is widespread in North Africa and central Asia. *See also* Nomadism.

Patagonia, region in Argentina, E of the Andes Mts, extending to the Strait of Magellan. Magellan was first to visit the area 1520; colonized after wars with Tehuelche Indians 1880. Part of the region lies in S Chile but the name refers to the Argentinian part; the division was disputed between the two countries (1881) and the present boundaries were set 1902; sheep-raising region. Area: 311,000sq mi (805,490sq km).

Patas, large, reddish-gray monkey native to grassy woodlands and scrub forests of central Africa. It is day-active, ground-foraging, omnivorous, and lives in groups often led by a large male. Species *Erythrocebus patas. See also* Monkey.

Patch Test, a test for hypersensitivity to a substance in which patches of linen or paper containing it are placed on the skin and the reaction on removal is observed.

Patella, or kneecap, a large, flattened, roughly triangular bone just in front of the joint where the femur and tibia link. It is surrounded by bursae, sacs of fluid that cushion the joint.

Paterson, William (1745–1806), US jurist, b. Ireland. As a New Jersey delegate to the Constitutional Convention (1787), he proposed the New Jersey Plan, giving more power to the states and less to the federal government. Paterson later served as a US senator (1789–90), resigning to become governor of New Jersey (1790–93). He was an associate justice on the US Supreme Court (1793–1806). Paterson, N.J., is named for him.

Paterson, city in NE New Jersey, at falls of Passaic River 14mi (23km) N of Newark; seat of Passaic co. Founded by Alexander Hamilton and the Society for Establishing Useful Manufacturers, it was formed as a planned community to promote industry. In 1792–94 cotton spinning mills were set up; by 1835 Samuel Colt began the manufacture of the Colt revolver; silk industry started shortly after. A national historic site was est. 1970 around falls in river; site of preserved cobblestone streets, Colt gun factory, mill owners' and workers' houses, spinning mills, waterworks and old bridges. Industries: clothing, chemicals, plastics, paper, food products. Founded 1791; inc. 1851. Pop. (1980) 137,970.

Pathans, or **Pashtuns.** Muslim tribes who constitute the major racial group in SE Afghanistan and NW Pakistan. They speak an eastern Iranian language, Pashto, and are composed of 60 tribes practicing both pastoralism and farming. Disputes among the warlike Pathans commonly result in fierce bloodfeuds.

Pathology, branch of medicine that deals with the nature of disease and the changes it produces in the cells, tissues, and organs of the body. Pathologists usually do not treat patients but examine tissues to study pathologic, or abnormal, changes in the body.

Patna, city in NE India, 290mi (467km) NW of Calcutta on the Ganges River; capital of Bihar state and Patna division; served as the capital of ancient Mauryan empire 325–185 BC and Gupta empire AD 320–545; taken by British 1763; site of Asoka palace (*c.* 270–230 BC), and University of Patna (1917); railroad, commercial, and rice center. Pop. 490,265. *See also* Palaiputra, India.

Paton, Alan Stewart (1903–), South African novelist and reformer. He gave up teaching in 1935 to take charge of a school for delinquent African boys. Strongly opposed to apartheid, he helped found and became president of the Liberal party (1953), a post he held until the party's dissolution by the government in 1968. *Cry the Beloved Country* (1948), his most famous and most popular novel, and *Too Late the Phalarope* (1953), and *Ah, But Your Land Is Beautiful* (1982) deal with racial exploitation. Other works include *The Long View* (1968) and *For You Departed* (1969).

Pátrai, seaport city in central Greece, on Gulf of Pátrai; capital of Akhaía dept. As member of Second Achaean League, city led battle against Macedonians 218 BC; served as Roman military colony (late 1st century BC) under Augustus who developed it into a prosperous seaport; held by Ottoman Turks 1458–1687, 1715–1828, when it passed to Greece; site of university (1966). Exports: currants, tobacco, wine, olive oil. Pop. 112,238.

Patriarchy, term that is employed to describe a social system in which property is inherited through the male

Partridge

Louis Pasteur

Ivan Pavlov

line and in which the family group is ruled by the father or an elderly male. *See also* Matriarchy.

Patricians, privileged upper class or aristocracy of ancient Rome. The term may derive from *pater* ("senate member"). Patricians could hold political and religious office but could not marry plebeians. They wore distinctive clothing. As the lower classes sought and gained political equality, the significance of patrician birth diminished.

Patrick, Saint (*c*.389–461), patron saint of and missionary bishop to Ireland, b. as Succat in Britain. The facts of his career are much interwoven with legend. Abducted by marauders at 16, he was carried to Ireland and sold to an Antrim chief. After six years he escaped to France, where he took holy orders. Returning to Ireland, he was ordained bishop (432). His missionary work was so successful that in his lifetime almost all the Irish were Christianized. He also introduced the Roman alphabet to Ireland. His grave at Downpatrick became a center of pilgrimage.

Patroonships, colonization scheme used in New Netherland after 1629 in which land and manorial privileges were granted a "patroon" for settling a colony of 50 or more people on land purchased from the Indians. The first patroonships were Zwanendal on the Delaware River and Rensselaerwick on the Hudson River, the latter including all of Albany and Rensselaer counties.

Patton, George Smith, Jr. (1885–1945), US military officer, b. San Gabriel, Calif. A graduate of the US Military Academy at West Point (1909), he was with the American Expeditionary Force (AEF) in France during World War I, where he became familiar with tanks. A controversial and highly successful officer, he commanded a tank corps in North Africa and the 7th Army in Sicily in World War II. After the D-Day invasion (1944), he commanded the Third Army in its dash across France and into Germany. His troops broke the German ring around Bastogne. He was known as "Old Blood and Guts."

Pau, city in SW France, 109mi (175km) S of Bordeaux on E bank of Gave de Pau; capital of Pyrenees-Atlantiques dept.; capital of former province of Bèarn (15th century); residence of kings of Navarre 1512; site of 12th-century castle in which Henry IV of France was born (1553); noted winter sports center. Industries: oil refining, wood, shoes, clothing. Founded 11th century. Pop. 85,860.

Paul, in the New Testament, the first Christian theologian and evangelist. He was born Saul in Tarsus of Jewish parents and became a Pharisee and well-educated Roman citizen. Enroute to Damascus to persecute Christians, he received a vision of Jesus. His conversion to Christianity after Christ's death made him a zealous disciple. He proclaimed that Jesus was the Messiah and was sacrificed to atone for the sins of man. His many epistles, recounting his travels and successful labors, were written to the Corinthians, Romans, Philippians, Hebrews, and others, and are a central part of the New Testament.

Paul VI (1897–1978), Roman Catholic Pope (1963–78), b. Giovanni Battista Montini. Educated by Jesuits, he completed the Second Vatican Council begun by John XXIII and carried out the reforms decided at the Council, including revision of the Mass, sacraments, and church government. He traveled extensively, fostering international peace and ecumenism.

Paul I (1754–1801), tsar of Russia (1796–1801). The son and despotic heir of Catherine II, he reestablished the principle of hereditary succession and instituted repressive measures to protect the autocracy from the influence of the French Revolution. Paul's hostility toward his son Alexander led to the murder of the unpopular sovereign by guard officers in March 1801.

Paul I (1901–1964), king of the Hellenes (1947–64). He succeeded George II and ruled during the insurrection of the Greek Communists. He received US aid to help Greece's economic recovery from World War II and was married to the popular Frederika of Brunswick.

Pauli, Wolfgang (1900–58), US physicist, b. Vienna. His work on quantum theory led him to his exclusion principle (the Pauli principle), which relates the quantum theory to properties of atoms. He received a Nobel Prize in 1945 for this work. In 1931 he postulated the existence of the neutrino and lived to see his prediction verified in 1956. *See also* Exclusion Principle; Quantum Theory.

Pauling, Linus Carl (1901–), US biochemist, *b.* Portland, Ore. He studied in Europe and at the California Institute of Technology, where he later became professor. His early work on the application of wave mechanics to molecular structure, detailed in his book *The Nature of the Chemical Bond* (1939), was rewarded by the Nobel Prize in chemistry in 1954. He also worked on the structure of proteins. A keen protagonist of nuclear disarmament, he was awarded the 1962 Nobel Peace Prize. Later, he was an advocate of large doses of vitamin C as a treatment for the common cold.

Paulownia, genus of E Asian deciduous trees grown for their large, heart-shaped leaves and showy clusters of violet flowers. *P. tomentosa* has large clusters of fragrant flowers; height: 40ft (12m). Family Scrophulariaceae.

Pavia, city in N Italy; capital of Pavia province on the Ticino River; political center of 14th-century Italy under Visconti; scene of 1525 Spanish victory over Francis I of France; active in Risorgimento campaigns; liberated in 1859; site of 14th-century Carthusian monastery, church of 12th-century St Michael, 14th-century university; agricultural, industrial, and communications center. Industries: sewing machines, machinery, foundry products. Pop. 87,804.

Pavlov, Ivan P(etrovich) (1849–1936), Russian neurophysiologist. He made pioneer contributions to medicine, physiology, and psychology. His early work centered on the physiology and neurology of digestion, for which he received a Nobel Prize in 1904. However, he is best known for his work in describing the classical (Pavlovian) conditioning of behavior in animals. This work had a permanent effect on Russian psychology and a profound effect on behaviorism in the United States and on subsequent theories of how organisms learn. His major works (in English translation) are *Conditioned Reflexes* (1927); *Lectures on Conditioned Reflexes* (1928); and *Conditioned Reflexes and Psychiatry* (1941). *See also* Behaviorism; Pavlovian Conditioning.

Pavlova, Anna (Matveyevna) (1885–1931), Russian ballerina. She was prima ballerina with the Maryinsky Theatre Company in St Petersburg, Russia, touring Europe and the United States. She left Russia in 1913 to tour with her own troupe, which introduced ballet to Japan, China, India, Egypt, and South Africa. She was known for her extraordinary grace and dramatic ability.

Pavlovian Conditioning or **Classical Conditioning,** in psychology, a basic pattern of how learning takes place, from the work of the Russian psychologist Ivan Pavlov. For example, an event (such as a bell sounding) is repeatedly paired with a stimulus (such as an electric shock) that always elicits a given response (such as leg withdrawal). Continued pairings of the bell and shock will eventually result in a "conditioned response"—the bell itself will elicit leg withdrawal. This pattern has had considerable impact on learning theories and has important applications in changing human behavior, such as that of the mentally ill. *See also* Behavior Modification; Extinction; Reinforcement.

Pawnee, a Caddoan-speaking tribe of North American Indians related to the Arikara, who occupied the Central Platte and Republican river areas in Nebraska. Today 1,200 inhabit a reservation set aside for their use in Oklahoma.

Pawtucket, city in N Rhode Island, 4mi (6km) NE of Providence, on Blackstone River; site of Slater Mill, first US textile mill, also first to use water power to spin cotton thread. Industries: textiles, yarn, hosiery, clothing, brass and iron foundries. Founded 1671; inc. 1885. Pop. (1980) 71,204.

Pax Romana, the 200-year period of peace in the Roman Empire that began in 31 BC with the rule of Augustus, following an era of violence and civil strife. It ended with the decline of the empire that began *c.* AD 180.

Paz, Octavio (1914–), Mexican poet. He is considered the outstanding Spanish American poet. His work has gone through many phases, from Marxism to surrealism to Oriental philosophies, but its dominant characteristics are a search for harmony, notably in erotic experience; an emphasis on objects; and, especially in his later work, a desire to make language more melodious. His writings on the theory of poetry have also been influential. The collection *Parole: Poetic Works* (1960) contains what he regards as his best poems. He added to it in 1968.

PCB. *See* Polychlorinated Biphenyl.

Pea, climbing annual plant *(Pisum sativum)*, probably native to W Asia. It has small, oval leaves and white flowers. The pods contain wrinkled or smooth seeds that are a popular vegetable. There are several varieties. The early dwarf pea (var. *humile*) is a low-growing plant and has small pods. The snow, or sugar, pea (var. *macrocarpum*) has soft, unlined edible pods. It grows to 6ft (1.8m). Family Leguminosae.

Peace Corps, a branch of ACTION (an independent US government agency). The purpose of the Peace Corps is to promote world peace and friendship by sending skilled US volunteers to countries overseas to provide trained manpower and to promote a better understanding between peoples. It was established in 1961 by Pres. John F. Kennedy.

Peace River, river in Canada formed by merger of the Finlay and Parship rivers in N central British Columbia; joins the Slave River near Lake Athabaska; explored 1792–93 by Sir Alexander Mackenzie. Length: 945mi (1,521km).

Peach, small fruit tree native to China or Iran and grown throughout temperate areas. The oblong leaves appear after the pink flowers in spring. The fruit has a thin, downy skin, white or yellow flesh, and is freestone or cling. It is eaten fresh or preserved. Height: 20ft (6.1m). Family Rosacea; species *Prunus persica*.

Peacock, technically the male peafowl, but the term is often used loosely for several species of peafowl (family Phasianidae) that are known for the male's brilliant ornamental tail feathers that he typically raises and spreads fanlike behind him during courtship display. Peacocks are native to Asia and Africa but are also widely kept in zoos. About 40–45in (102–114cm) long, with a train of that length, the typical peacock has a thin neck, small head with fan-shaped crest, blue neck and body, and metallic-green train covered with eyelike spots. They feed on the ground and in the wild lay 3 to 6 light-brown spotted eggs in a hidden ground nest.

Peacock Butterfly, any of several butterflies that have eyespots, resembling those of peacocks, on their wings. In Europe the name is often applied to *Vanessa io* and in E North America, to *Junonia coenia.*

Peale, family of US painters of portraits, miniatures, still lifes, historical scenes, and landscapes, active in the 18th and 19th centuries. The first and most noted member was Charles Willson (1741–1827); his sons included Raphael, Rembrandt, Rubens, Franklin, and Titian. Charles' brother James was also an artist.

Peanut, spreading annual native to Brazil and grown widely in the United States. It has small leaflets and yellowflowers. Valued as a food crop, the subterranean seeds, or peanuts, are eaten in various forms. Height: 20 in (51cm). Family Leguminoseae; species *Arachis hypogaea.*

Pear, fruit native to N Asia and S Europe and grown worldwide in temperate regions. It has a pyramidal shape and clusters of white flowers appear among the glossy, green leaves. The greenish-yellow, brownish, or reddish fruit, picked unripe and allowed to mature in storage, is eaten fresh or preserved. Height: 50–75ft (15.3–22.9m). Family Rosaceae; species *Pyrus communis.*

Pearl, river in Mississippi and Louisiana; rises in E central Mississippi; flows SW and S into the Gulf of Mexico; forms a natural border between Mississippi and Louisiana. Length: 485mi (781km).

Pearl, iridescent concretion produced by certain marine and freshwater bivalve mollusks. Composed almost entirely of nacre, or mother-of-pearl, the calcium carbonate compound forms the inner layer of mollusk shells. A pearl, the only gem of animal origin, results from an abnormal growth of nacre around minute particles of foreign matter, such as sand. The pearl oyster of the Persian Gulf produces the most valuable pearls. *See also* Bivalve; Mother-of-Pearl.

Pearl Harbor, inlet on the S coast of the island of Oahu, Hawaii, 6mi (10km) W of Honolulu, site of US naval base. By treaty of 1887, United States was permitted to use harbor for coaling and repairing station; Congress authorized construction of naval station 1908, drydocks completed 1919. On Dec. 7, 1941, the US Pacific fleet was largely destroyed by the Japanese attack on Pearl Harbor, signaling hostilities between those two countries in the Pacific theater of WWII.

Pearse, Patrick (or **Padraic**) **Henry** (1879–1916), Irish educator, author, and political figure. He headed the revival of interest in Gaelic culture, writing poems, short stories, and plays. Leader of the insurgents in the Easter Uprising against British rule (1916), he was court-martialed and shot.

Pearson, Lester Bowles (1897–1972), prime minister of Canada (1963–68). A combat pilot in World War I and professor of history (1924–28), he joined the department of external affairs (1935–41). He was US ambassador (1945–46), chairman of NATO (1951–52), and UN General Assembly president (1952–53). A Liberal member of Parliament and secretary of state from 1948, he assumed party leadership in 1958. He received the 1957 Nobel Prize for peace for his work in the Middle East. An energetic leader, he ruled as prime minister without a majority and retired in 1968 to become chancellor of Carleton University. He wrote several works on politics.

Peary, Robert Edwin (1856–1920), US arctic explorer. He made the first of several explorations of Greenland in 1886. Accompanied by his wife in 1891, he found evidence that Greenland was an island. In 1898, he announced plans for an expedition to the North Pole, and received financial aid from the Peary Arctic Club of New York. He reached his goal by sled in 1909, along with Matthew Henson, his black assistant, and four Eskimos, but Frederick A. Cook was said to have beaten him by a year. *See also* Cook, Frederick Albert.

Peary Land, region of Greenland; Morris Jesup, its N cape, is most northerly point of land in Arctic Region; explored by Robert Peary in 1892 and 1900. Highest point: 6,300ft (1,922m).

Peat, dark brown, decayed organic material with a high carbon content built up in bogs. It is the first stage in coal development. Sphagnum mosses form most peat in the Northern Hemisphere; cord grass forms salt peat in salt marshes. Dried peat is used as fuel.

Peat Moss, humus obtained from disintegrated sphagnum moss. The most widely obtainable source of humus, it is dug into soil to retain moisture and increase productiveness. It is also added to compost piles for aeration.

Pecan, deciduous tree, native to S central United States, grown primarily as a nut crop. Its oblong nut has a sweet edible kernel. Height: 130ft (40m). Family Juglandaceae; species *Carya illinoensis.*

Peccary, omnivorous piglike mammal native to SW United States and Central and South America. It has thick fur and scent glands on its back. Collared peccaries, or javelinas *(Tayassu tajaçu)*, have dark gray fur with a whitish collar. White-lipped peccaries *(Tayassu pecari)* have brown fur. Weight: 50–66lb (23–30kg). Family Tayassuidae.

Pecking Order, hierarchical system of social organization based on dominance and submission operating on a descending scale. The leader has power over the entire community, the second in command has power over everyone but the leader, and so on. The term derives from the behavior of hens, which express their dominance by pecking their inferiors. *See also* Dominance Relationships.

Pečora, river in N Russian SFSR, USSR, rising in Middle Ural Mts; flows N, W, and N again to Pečora Bay of the Barents Sea, forming a delta mouth at Naryan-Mar; it receives the Ilych, Shchugor, Usa, Kozhva, Izhma, and Tsilma rivers; supports fisheries, farming, and livestock raising along its course, and coal fields in its basin. Both the main river and tributaries are navigable for most of their 1,110mi (1,787km).

Pécs, city in S Hungary; capital of Baranya co; originally the Roman colony of Sopianae; site of Hungary's first university, founded by Louis the Great 1367. Industries: coal mining, wine, leather. Pop. 163,000.

Pectin, water-soluble sugar found in certain ripe fruits or vegetables. It is the removal of this substance that causes fruits and vegetables to soften when cooked. It also yields a gel that is the basis of jellies and jams.

Pedalfer, acid soil, rich in iron and aluminum, formed in humid areas with high temperatures, especially tropical forests. *See also* Pedocal; Podzol; Soil.

Pedocal, soil, rich in lime, that commonly forms in prairie regions with low rainfall, the lack of subsequent leaching, and low temperatures. *See also* Pedalfer; Podzol; Soil.

Pedophilia, sexual deviation either heterosexual or homosexual in nature, in which a child becomes the object of sexual arousal, interest, or gratification. In its overt form it leads to child molesting.

Pedro I (1798–1834), king of Portugal and emperor of Brazil. Pedro became regent of Brazil when his father, João VI, returned to Portugal in 1821. The Portuguese parliament asked Pedro to return to Europe in 1822; instead, Pedro declared Brazil independent and himself emperor. His preoccupation with affairs in Portugal and his inability to mediate political rivalries prompted his abdication in favor of his Brazilian-born son in 1831.

Pedro II (1825–91), emperor of Brazil (1831–89), ruled as regent until 1840 when he was declared old enough to be crowned. Despite internal revolts in the 1830s and 1840s and external threats from Argentina and Paraguay, Pedro II demonstrated greater skill than his father in governing. Slavery was abolished during his tenure (1888). He was forced to resign in 1889; Brazil became a republic.

Peel, (Sir) Robert (1788–1850), English prime minister. Entering Parliament as a Tory (1809), his offices included chief secretary for Ireland (1812–18), home secretary (1823–30), first lord of the treasury, chancellor of the exchequer, and prime minister (1834–35; 1841–45). As home secretary he founded the London police force (1829). In his later offices he lightened the burden of indirect taxation and by alleviating trade impositions enabled Britain to dominate world trade. He reorganized the Bank of England and launched a policy of reform in Ireland (1845). Losing support after repealing the Corn Laws (1846), he resigned. He is credited with the major role in the development of the Conservative party.

Pegasus, in Greek mythology, winged horse. Born out of the blood of Medusa, it carried the thunderbolt of Zeus. It was tamed by Bellerophon and helped him in his battles. According to legend, Pegasus threw Bellerophon when the latter attempted to fly to heaven. The Hippocrene, a sacred spring, was produced by a stamp of Pegasus' hoof.

Pegasus, or the Winged Horse, northern constellation situated southwest of Cygnus. Three of its brightest stars form a giant square with Alpha Andromedae. It contains no stars brighter than the second magnitude.

Peking (Beijing, or **Peiping),** capital of the People's Republic of China, on a vast plain between the Pei and Hun rivers, NE China. City served as China's capital 1421–1911; after est. of Chinese Republic 1911–12, the capital alternated between Peking, Canton, and Han-k'ou; seat of government was transferred to Nanking 1928, and Peking, meaning "northern capital," was known as Peiping. Occupied by Japanese 1937, it was restored to China 1946; under Communist control January 1949, who restored its name and made it the capital of the People's Republic. The city is comprised of two walled sections: Inner or Tartar City, which houses the Forbidden City, and the Outer or Chinese city; political, cultural, educational, financial, and transportation center of China. Pop. 7,570,000.

Pekingese, breed of dog (toy group) considered sacred in China in the past; dating from 8th century and introduced to West in 1860. It has a broad skull; short, wrinkled muzzle; and broad, flat nose. Heart-shaped ears have long drooping feathering; eyes are prominent. The medium-length body is heavy in front; the legs are short and bowed. A high-set tail is carried over the back. The long, thick, straight coat may be any color. Average size: 6–9in (15.2–23cm); 6–14lb (2.7–6.3kg). *See also* Toy Dog.

Peking Man, or *Sinanthropus pekinensis,* extinct Pleistocene man known from remains first discovered in 1927 at Choukoutien, China. A hunter and user of stone tools and fire, *Sinanthropus* was more advanced than related Java Man. *See also* Java Man.

Pelagianism, heretical Christian belief in the 5th century. In opposition to St Augustine's belief that man could only attain salvation through God's grace, the Pelagians saw man as a creature of inherent spiritual grace and strong will and further denied original sin and the need of the Church for salvation. Pelagius (360?–?420) and his followers were rigorously discouraged, but established an argument that thrives even now.

Pelagic Division, the whole mass of ocean water. Its neritic zone extends from the low tide mark on shore out to a 200m (656ft) depth and represents an inshore environment. The oceanic or open-sea zone has an upper lighted part and a lower dark one. The term pelagic is also applied to all life that is not attached to the ocean floor.

Pelargonium, the garden geranium native to South Africa. The circular or lobed leaves of these perennials alternate on the stalk and are often aromatic. Five-petaled flowers are red, pink, purple, or white. Family Geraniaceae; Genus *Pelargonium. See also* Geranium.

Pelayo (died 737), Spanish king of Asturias (718–37). When the Moors conquered Spain from the Christians, beginning in 711, many of the local petty rulers retreated to the Asturian mountains. There they elected one of their members, Pelayo, as leader. His victory over the Moors at Covadonga (probably in 718) is traditionally regarded as the beginning of the long Christian reconquest of Spain.

Pelecypod, or bivalvia, marine mollusks including clams, oysters, mussels, and scallops. Class characteristics are two shells hinged together; laterally compressed foot; reduced head; huge mantle cavity; and complex, sheetlike gills. The two shells are fastened with an elastic horny ligament and closed by two large muscles. The shell's elevated knob near the ligament is the umbo, the oldest part of the shell. As the animal grows, its mantle produces calcareous layers along shell edges. Pelecypods feed by passing water through the body and straining out microscopic particles of food. Class Lamellibranchiata.

Pelée, Mount, volcanic peak in N Martinique, in Windwards, West Indies; it has erupted many times, most notably May 8, 1902, when it engulfed town of St Pierre killing approx. 40,000 people. Highest peak on the island, 4,429ft (1,351m).

Robert Peary

Sir Robert Peel

William Penn

Pelican, stout-bodied inland lake and marsh bird. Each has a pouch under its bill for scooping up fish driven into shallow areas. They are generally white or brown and have long hooked bills, long wings, short thick legs, and webbed feet. They lay white eggs (1–4) in a tree or ground nest. Length: 4–6ft (1.2–1.8m). Family Pelecanidae.

Pelican Flower, or swan flower, perennial creeping vine of West Indies. Its 20-in, (51-cm) maroon and cream mottled tubelike flower has a repulsive odor that attracts flies. Family Aristolochiaceae; species *Aristolochia grandiflora.*

Pellagra, a disease characterized by dermatitis, inflammation of mucous membrane, and gastrointestinal disorders caused by an inadequate intake of niacin, in protein-poor diets. Although common worldwide, it is especially prevalent in the Mediterranean region and Central America. Treatment involves administration of niacin and other B-complex vitamins and a well-balanced diet.

Pelly, river in Canada, in S central Yukon territory, rises in Mackenzie Mts; flows W to join Lewes River to form the Yukon River. Length: 330mi (531km).

Peloponnesian Wars (431–404 BC), conflicts between Athens (Delian League) and Sparta (the Peloponnesians). In the early years Athens maintained her position, but in 430 plague killed over one quarter of her people and in 429 Pericles died. Still, Sparta sued for peace which the demagogue Cleon refused. In 424 Sparta saved Megara from Athens and won other victories. A one year truce then prevailed, till Cleon marched on Thrace. The Peace of Nicias was concluded and was in effect a victory for Athens. The Athenian Alcibiades wrecked the peace with his losing Sicilian campaign (413). In the ensuing years grave internal troubles weakened Athens, which capitulated in April 404. Thucydides called the conflict the worst disturbance in Greek history.

Peloponnesus (Pelopónnisos), peninsula in S Greece, connected to central Greece by the Isthmus of Corinth; site of ancient Sparta, Corinth, Argos, and Megalopolis. The entire peninsula was involved in the Persian Wars 500–449 BC; site of many battles between Sparta and Athens for Grecian hegemony during Peloponnesian Wars (431–04 BC); dominated by Sparta, the peninsula fell to the Romans 146 BC who reduced it to a provincial state. It was awarded to the Villehardouin princes of France (1204) by leaders of the Fourth Crusade; held by Venetians 1687–1715; passed to Greece after its war of independence (1821–29). Industries: textiles, fishing, mining, tourism, fruit, olives, tobacco, wheat. Area: 8,300sq mi (21,500sq km). Pop. 986,912.

Pelvis, bowl-shaped structure that supports the soft internal organs of the lower abdomen. The pelvis is formed by the hip bone on each side, joined at the sacroiliac joint, with the sacrum in the back, and with the pubic bones in front. The pelvis is broader in females than in males.

Pembroke Welsh Corgi, cattle dog (working group) brought to British Isles in 1107 by Flemish weavers; related to Keeshond and Pomeranian types. It has a fox-shaped head; medium-sized, erect ears tapering to a rounded point; long body; short, slightly turned-in legs; and a docked tail. The short, straight coat is slightly longer on neck, chest, and backs of legs; colors include red, sable, fawn, black and tan—all with or without white marks. Average size: 10–12in (25.5–

30.5cm) high at shoulder; to 30lb (13.5kg). *See also* Keeshond; Pomeranian; Working Dog.

Penates, in Roman mythology, gods of the household. Initially gods of the storeroom, their protection eventually extended over the entire household.

Penda (577?–655), king of Mercia. He consolidated the Anglian tribes of midland England. A champion of heathenism, he killed the Northumbrian kings Edwin (633) and Oswald (642). Defeating Cenwealh of Wessex (645), he temporarily ruled England. He was slain by Oswy of Northumbria.

Pendulum, any swinging body supported at a point. A simple pendulum consists of a small heavy mass attached to a string or light rigid rod. Small oscillations of such a pendulum have a frequency of $(L/g)\frac{1}{2}$, where L is the length and g is the acceleration due to gravity. A compound pendulum has a supporting rod whose mass is not negligible, and its motion cannot be described as a simple relation.

Penelope, in Greek mythology, the wife of Odysseus, depicted as a woman of great beauty, fine character, and righteous conduct. As described in Homer's *Odyssey,* she had been married for only a year when her husband left for 10 years of war and 10 of wandering. She remained faithful, putting off her many suitors with the promise that she would choose one when her weaving was done. By day she worked, by night she undid her work.

Penguin, stocky, black and white flightless aquatic bird of Antarctica and nearby coastlines and islands. It has a strong bill, short neck, flipperlike wings, short tail and legs, and webbed feet. It walks upright, bellyflops on the snow and swims well, even in rough seas. Feeding on fish and mollusks, penguins nest and court in colonies, sometimes forming long-lasting pairs. Its many species include the Adélie, the fairy (the smallest), the Galápagos (only species that lives in the tropics), the king, and the emperor (the largest). Fasting males incubate white eggs (1–2) in ground or hole nest. The king penguin holds eggs in an abdominal fold. Height: to 4ft (1.2m); weight: to over 75lb (34kg). Order Sphenisciformes.

Penicillin, antibiotic agent considered the greatest discovery of 20th-century medical science. Developed by Sir Alexander Fleming in 1928, it is derived from molds and can also be produced synthetically. It is effective in combating many bacterial diseases. Allergic reactions range from itching to fatal shock.

Penki (Benxi, or Pen-ch'i), city in NE China, 30mi (48km) E of Liaoyang. Industries: steel, foundry, iron and coal mines. Pop. 750,000.

Penn, John (1741–88), US patriot and a signer of the Declaration of Independence, b. Caroline co, Va. A successful lawyer, he was a North Carolina delegate to the Continental Congress (1775–77, 1778–80).

Penn, William (1644–1718), founder of Pennsylvania, b. England. He joined the Quakers in 1666 and was imprisoned several times for his religious views (1666–70). He wrote *No Cross, No Crown,* explaining the Quaker-Puritan morality (1669), in prison. In 1681, to create a refuge for Quakers, he pressed King Charles II to honor loans made to Penn's father. He received a land grant, which he named Pennsylvania after his father. In organizing a government for the colony, he drew up a Frame of Government, the first constitution with an amendment clause. He also designed the city of Philadelphia. He first came to Pennsylvania in 1682.

In an effort to settle the boundary dispute with Maryland, he left for England (1684), where he drafted the first plan for a union of the American colonies (1696). He was once again in Pennsylvania (1699–1701).

Pennacook, native Americans of the Algonquian linguistic family; originally lived as semi-sedentary hunters, farmers, and sea-fishermen in east-central New England. Although primarily peaceful, the 1,300 Pennacook (reduced from 2,000 by European disease) were so miserably treated by white settlers during King Philip's War (1675) that they fled to Quebec and New York State.

Pennsylvania, state in the E United States, in the Middle Atlantic region.
   Land and Economy. Mountain ranges of medium height run roughly NE to SW across much of the state, interspersed with fertile valleys. In the SE lies a rich agricultural area. The Delaware River, forming the E boundary, enters Delaware Bay, an arm of the Atlantic Ocean. The Susquehanna, flowing N to S in the state's center, and the Allegheny in the W are important rivers. In the extreme NW the state borders Lake Erie. Pennsylvania's productive soil and abundant mineral deposits, especially of coal and iron, contributed to the growth of the manufacturing industries that have kept the economy in a prosperous balance. Manufacturing is centered in 12 metropolitan areas, notably Philadelphia, Pittsburgh, and Allentown-Bethlehem-Easton. Philadelphia, with access to the sea by the Delaware River, is one of the nation's major ports.
   People. The original settlers were mostly from the British Isles. They were followed in the 18th century by Germans, erroneously called "Pennsylvania Dutch," who occupied farming lands in the E and SE. Mines and mills drew immigrants from Italy, Poland, Russia, Czechoslovakia, and Hungary. More than 70% of the population lives in urban areas.
   Education. There are about 150 institutions of higher education. Pennsylvania State University is state-supported. The University of Pennsylvania is the leading private institution.
   History. Swedish and Dutch settlements were made along the Delaware in the mid-17th century, but by 1674 the area was controlled by England. William Penn received a charter from Charles II of England in 1681 for what is now Pennsylvania. Philadelphia became the provincial capital and was the capital of the colonies during the American Revolution. The Declaration of Independence (1776) and the US Constitution (1787) were signed there. The city was the national capital 1790–1800. The Union victory at the Battle of Gettysburg (July 1863), which repulsed a Confederate invasion of the state, was a turning point of the Civil War. In both world wars, Pennsylvania was a major source of military supplies, shipbuilding being especially important. In 1979 a nuclear power plant at Three Mile Island was closed because of a serious malfunction, the country's most serious nuclear accident.

PROFILE

Admitted to Union: Dec. 12, 1787; 2nd of the 13 original states to ratify the US Constitution
US Congressmen: Senate, 2; House of Representatives, 25
Population: 11,886,728 (1980); rank, 4th
Capital: Harrisburg, 53,264 (1980)
Chief cities: Philadelphia, 1,688,210; Pittsburgh, 423,-938; Erie, 119,123
State legislature: Senate, 50; House of Representatives, 203
Area: 45,333sq mi (117,412sq km); rank, 33d
Elevation: Highest, 3,213ft (980m), Mt Davis; lowest, sea level, Delaware River

Industries (major products): steel, metal products, machinery and electrical machinery, chemicals and drugs, processed foods, apparel
Agriculture (major products): dairy products, poultry, grapes, peaches, apples, cherries
Minerals (major): anthracite and bituminous coal, cement, petroleum, zinc, clay
State nickname: Keystone State
State motto: Virtue, Liberty, and Independence
State bird: ruffed grouse
State flower: mountain laurel
State tree: eastern hemlock

Pennsylvanian Period. *See* Carboniferous Period.

Pennyroyal, common name for a number of plants, including the European *Mentha pulegium,* and the American *Hedeoma pulegioides,* sweet herbs of the mint family. They have purple flowers and leaves said to be offensive to mosquitoes.

Penobscot, native Americans of the Algonquian linguistic group. They were prominent members of the Abnaki Confederacy and active allies of the French until 1749. A seasonally nomadic Eastern Woodlands people, the 700 Penobscot lived in the Penobscot Bay and Penobscot River areas of Maine. They received a reservation at Old Town, Maine, after helping the colonists to independence. They are entitled to limited representation in the Maine legislature.

Pensacola, city in extreme NW Florida on Gulf of Mexico, seat of Escambia co, 10mi (16km) NE of Alabama border. Used as base by both Union and Confederacy in Civil War; site of Navy air station. Industries: paper and cork products, chemicals. Settled 1559 by Spain; passed to United States 1821. Pop. (1980) 57,619.

Pentagon, five-sided plane figure. Its interior angles add up to 540°. For a regular pentagon, one whose sides and interior angles are all equal, each interior angle is 108°.

Pentameter, verse line of five metrical feet, introduced into English literature by Chaucer. Iambic pentameter is the most durable form of English poetry. William Shakespeare's *Sonnets,* Edmund Spenser's *The Faerie Queene,* and John Milton's *Paradise Lost* are outstanding examples.

Pentateuch, first five books of the Old Testament: Genesis, Exodus, Leviticus, Numbers, and Deuteronomy. It covers the period from the creation of the universe to the death of Moses.

Pentathlon, an athletic competition. It originated in ancient Greece, where it consisted of five events—foot racing, leaping, wrestling, discus throwing, and javelin throwing—all taking place on the same day. The modern pentathlon, held over a five day period, comprises a cross-country horse-back race, a swimming race, épée fencing, pistol shooting, and a 2.5 mile (4km) cross-country run. The competition has been an Olympic Games event since 1912.

Pentecost, in the Jewish calendar, a festival held seven weeks after the second day of Passover. It commemorates the giving of the law to Moses, but it is also a feast of harvest or Day of the First Fruits. In the Christian calendar Pentecost is a feast held 50 days after Easter to commemorate the descent of the Holy Spirit on the Apostles. After Christ's Ascension, the Holy Spirit gave special strength to his Apostles, as related in Acts 2:1—4. The day is called Pentecost in the Roman Catholic Church and Whitsunday in the Anglican churches.

Pentecostalism, dramatic religious movement of 20th century America, grew from the Fundamentalist and Holiness churches of the 19th century. Involving a number of churches, such as the Assemblies of God, with varying beliefs, Pentecostalism often entails speaking in tongues, faith healing, the baptism of the faithful, and a firm belief in the Second Coming of Christ.

Pentstemon, or beardtongue, genus of North American perennial plants and shrubs with terminal clusters of tubular, white, pink, red, blue, or purple flowers. They have five stamens; one is sterile and bearded. Family Scrophulariaceae; genus *Pentstemon. See also* Figwort.

Penza, city in Russian SFSR, USSR, on the Sura River, 350mi (564km) SE of Moscow; capital of the Penza oblast; site of industrial and teachers' colleges, and agricultural and regional museums. Industries: machine tools, calculators, washing machines, printing presses, agricultural implements, watches, bicycles, medical instruments. Founded 1663 as Moscow fortress; chartered 1682. Pop. 451,000.

Peony, perennial plant native to Eurasia and North America. They have glossy, divided leaves, large white, pink, or red flowers, and are frequently cultivated in gardens. Height: to 3ft (0.9m). Tree peonies grow only in hot, dry areas and have brilliant blossoms of many colors; height: to 6ft (1.8m). Family Ranunculaceae; genus *Paeonia.*

Peoria, port city in central Illinois, on Lake Peoria and Illinois River; seat of Peoria co; transportation and commercial center; site of Bradley University (1896) and marker commemorating Abraham Lincoln's Peoria address condemning slavery (1854). Area first visited by Père Marquette and Louis Jolliet 1673; Fort Creve Coeur was built here 1680 by Robert La Salle. Industries: brewing, distilling, farm machinery, brick, tile, stone. Settled 1819; inc. as town 1835, as city 1845. Pop. (1980) 124,160.

Peperomia, genus of succulent house plant native to tropical America with waxy, ridged or smooth oval or rounded leaves of green, green and white, or copper-black. Care: bright indirect light, soil (equal parts loam, peat moss, sand) kept dry between waterings. Propagation is by stem cuttings. Height: to 10in (25cm).

Pepin II, or **Pepin of Herstal** (died 714), ruler of Austrasia (*c.*679); mayor of palace and ruler of all the Franks (687–714). His defeat of the Neustrians at the Battle of Tertry (687) marked the ascendance of the Carolingians over the Merovingians.

Pepin the Short (714?–768), son of Charles Martel, ruler of Neustria and king of the Franks (751–768), the first Carolingian king. He deposed Childeric III (751), the last Merovingian ruler. He supported the extension of papal control and was anointed by St Boniface in a ceremony of symbolic importance. Again anointed by Pope Stephen II (754), he defeated the Lombards on the pope's behalf. The new papal lands thus acquired were known as the Donation of Pepin. The close relationship between the pope and the Carolingian kings tied papal development to the West rather than to Italy and the East. Pepin was the father of Charlemagne.

Pepper, annual woody plant native to tropical America. The fruit is a many-seeded, pungent berry with size depending on species. Included are bell, red, cayenne, and chili peppers. Family Solanaceae; genus *Capsicum.*

Peppermint, common name for *Mentha piperita,* a perennial herb of the mint family widely cultivated for its essential oil, which is distilled and used as a medicine and for flavoring.

Pepper Tree, or Peruvian mastic tree, evergreen tree native to tropical South America. Grown as an ornamental, it has featherlike leaves, yellow flowers, and reddish berries. Height: to 50ft (15m). Family Anacardiaceae; species *Schinus molle.*

Pepsin, enzyme secreted by glands of the vertebrate stomach as part of the gastric juice. In the presence of hydrochloric acid it catalyzes the splitting of whole proteins into smaller peptide fractions.

Peptide, compound consisting of two or more amino acids linked by bonds between the amino group ($-NH_2$) of one and the carboxyl group (-COOH) of the next. This type of linkage is called a peptide bond, and peptides containing three or more amino acids are called polypeptides. Proteins consist of polypeptide chains, containing up to several hundred amino acids, cross-linked to each other in a variety of ways.

Pepys, Samuel (1633–1703), English diarist and naval administrator. He was secretary of the admiralty (1669–1688) except for a brief imprisonment for alleged complicity in the Popish Plot. His *Diary* (1661–69) frankly describes his private life and English society during the Restoration. It includes a vivid account of the Restoration, the coronation ceremony (1661), the plague (1663), and the Great Fire of London (1666). Pepys' *Diary* was written in cipher (a system of shorthand) and was not deciphered until 1825 by Rev. John Smith.

Pequot, a major tribe of Algonquian-speaking North American Indians formerly inhabiting the New London-Thames River valley region of Connecticut and W Rhode Island. Their unfortunate participation in the Pequot War of 1636–37 reduced their original population of 2,500 to less than 1,200. Today no more than 100 to 175 persons claim any measurable amount of Pequot blood, most of whom live around the Mystic River in Connecticut.

Percentage, quantity or amount reckoned as a part of a whole, expressed in hundredths; the rate or proportion per hundred. A ratio is converted to a percentage by multiplication by 100, thus, ¾ is equivalent to 75 percent (75%).

Perception, process by which the nervous system transforms energy into an impression of the world. The energy may be external (light, sound waves) or internal (stimulation of muscles and tendons). The end-product of the process is sometimes described as experience and sometimes as behavior. Perception is often called information processing. In this view, the central nervous system is analogous to a computer, the energy as input, and perception as the output of the process.

Perch, freshwater fish found in lakes, ponds, and slow-moving streams of the United States east of the Rockies and in Europe. A food fish, it is brass or gold-colored with 6–9 black side bars. Eggs are laid in long sticky ribbons. Genera include the yellow perch *(Perca flavescens)* that grows to 15in (38.1cm); 1lb (0.5kg). The European perch *(Perca fluviatilis)* is found throughout most of Europe except Spain, Italy and N Scandinavia; it grows to 5–6lb (2.3–2.7kg). Family Percidae.

Percheron, draft horse breed developed in La Perche region of NW France from Flemish and Arabian breeds. Introduced in United States about 1840, it was the most popular draft breed, particularly for farm work. Color is black or gray. Height: 65–67in (165–170cm) at shoulder; weight: 1,900–2,100lb (855–945kg).

Perching Bird, largest bird order that includes over 5,000 or more than half the known species. Primarily land birds, many are migratory and found worldwide except in polar areas and a few isolated islands. Their habitats range from desert to tropical jungle to mountainous cliff. Some species are widespread, others are limited to small areas. Mostly songbirds, they evolved about 60,000,000 years ago and are today the most specialized of all birds.

All perching birds have grasping feet with the first toe placed backward; nine or ten flight feathers; and a symmetrical molting pattern. Species vary in size; beak formation—from birds of prey with strong, hooked beaks to nectar feeders with slender beaks and specialized tongues; coloring—drab to bright or multicolored; egg color; and nest formation. Length: 3–40in (7.6–102cm). Order Passeriformes.

Percussion Instruments, instruments producing music by the striking together of solid objects. In drums a stick hits a membrane stretched across a frame. Some percussion instruments have indefinite pitch, for example, snare and bass drums, castanets, and gongs. Others are tuned: timpani, glockenspiels, chimes, and xylophones. Certain instruments normally melodic, such as piano or guitar, may be used for percussion. In jazz, along with drums, they form the rhythm section, providing the basic beat and freeing the band leader to play an instrument.

Percy, (Sir) Henry (1364–1403), English nobleman, known as Hotspur. The son of Henry, 1st earl of Northumberland, he supported Henry IV's accession to the throne, defended the Scottish border, and defeated Scottish invaders at Homildon Hill (1402). He revolted (1403) against the king when he was forbidden to ransom his brother-in-law, Edward Mortimer. He was killed at Shrewsbury before joining the forces of his father and Owen Glendower.

Pere David's Deer, or mi-lu, deer extinct in its native Chinese marshlands but found in zoological parks throughout the world. It has long, three-tined antlers. Height: 45in (1,143mm) at shoulder. Family Cervidae; species *Elaphurus davidianus.*

Peregrine Falcon, or duck hawk, North American gray falcon found along coastal lowlands, nesting high on seacoast cliffs. A fast flyer, it dives at fantastic speeds. Species *Falco peregrinus. See also* Falcon.

Pereira, Nuno Alvares (1360–1431), Portuguese general and statesman. He was the chief supporter of John I in his successful campaign to rid Portugal of Castilian domination. Pereira became a national hero, known as the Great Constable, after defeating the Castilians at Aljubarrota in 1385, a defeat that assured Portuguese independence. After a long career as soldier and statesman, he became a Carmelite monk and retired to a monastery, He was beatified in 1918.

Pereira, city in W central Colombia, S of Manizales; capital of Risaralda dept.; site of technical university (1958); shipping center for livestock. Pop. 211,965.

Perennial, plant with a life cycle of three or more years. It is a common term for flowering herbaceous plants that die before winter and blossom the next season. Perennials are easy to grow and thrive with little attention. Used in all types of gardens and as

Peony

Samuel Pepys

Javier Pérez de Cuéllar

borders, some popular perennials are lily, chrysanthemum, peony, daisy, iris, and delphinium. *See also* Annual; Biennial.

Peres, Shimon (1923–), Israeli political leader, prime minister 1984– . He moved to Palestine from Poland with his family (1934) and joined Haganah, the Jewish resistance organization (1947). After Israeli independence (1948) he worked in the defense ministry, becoming a protégé of Prime Minister Ben Gurion. Elected to the Knesset (parliament) (1959), Peres became deputy defense minister until (1965) he resigned to enter politics, gaining prominence in the Labor party. He was named defense minister (1974) and was briefly acting prime minister (1977). He regained the premiership (1984) in a political agreement to relinquish the post after 25 months to the Likud party leader Yitzhak Shamir.

Pérez de Cuéllar, Javier (1920–), Peruvian diplomat, secretary general of the UN (1982–). Peru's first ambassador to the Soviet Union (1969–71), he headed Peru's UN mission (1971–75) and then became a UN under secretary general. His work as an international negotiator was highly regarded by UN members, and he emerged as a successful compromise candidate in 1981 when there was opposition to the reelection of Kurt Waldheim as secretary general. In 1982, Pérez de Cuéllar tried to implement negotiations in crises caused by Israel's intervention in Lebanon and the Falkland Islands war between Britian and Argentina.

Pérez Esquivel, Aldolfo (1931–), Argentine human rights activist and sculptor. He taught architecture at the National Institute of Fine Arts in Buenos Aires until 1974 and was appointed (1966) secretary-general of Service for Peace and Justice in Latin America, a human rights organization. Long a human rights activist and an advocate of nonviolence, Pérez Esquivel was jailed and tortured (1977–78) by the Argentine government. He was the recipient of the Nobel Prize for peace (1980).

Perfume, aromatic substance that emits a pleasing fragrance. The scents of rose, citrus, lavender, sandalwood, etc, are provided by the essential oils of these plants. These are blended and combined with a fixative of animal origin, such as musk, ambergris, or civet. Fixatives add pungency and prevent the more volatile oils from evaporating too quickly. Liquid perfumes are usually alcoholic solutions containing 10–25% of the perfume concentrate; colognes and toilet waters contain 2–6% of the concentrate.

Pergamum, ancient city of NW Asia Minor in Mysia (Turkey). It became the capital of a Hellenistic kingdom under the Attalid dynasty (3rd century BC). Pergamum's grandeur and influence were enhanced by the Attalids. An agricultural, industrial, and mining center, it was also renowned for its arts, library, and cultural development. Bequeathed to Rome by Attalus III (133 BC), it declined under Roman rule.

Pergolesi, Giovanni (1710–36), Italian composer.

Pericarditis, inflammation of the pericardium, a membranous sac enclosing the heart. It usually develops during rheumatic fever but also may be associated with other diseases. Treatment is directed toward underlying infection and in acute cases, surgical removal.

Pericardium, a double-walled sac that surrounds the heart, separating it from the rest of the chest cavity and protecting it from mechanical injury. Its lower margin is anchored to the diaphragm, its upper part to the base of large blood vessels entering and leaving the heart.

The outer tough fibrous pericardial layer is separated from the inner thin serous layer by pericardial fluid.

Pericles (*c.*495–429 BC), Athenian statesman who introduced many reforms including a daily allowance so that non-wealthy Athenians could serve in government. Although frequently criticized, he was reelected to high office every year from 443 on. Pericles worked to prepare Athens for war with Sparta and at the same time attempted to make Athens the cultural center of the world. He is responsible for constructing the Parthenon (447–432 BC) and other notable buildings. His character, wise policy, and rebuilding of the Acropolis caused later historians to christen his entire period the "Age of Pericles."

Pericles, Prince of Tyre (*c.*1607), 5-act dramatic romance, partly attributed to William Shakespeare. Many scholars believe that Shakespeare had nothing to do with Acts I and II, but he is often considered to be the author of Acts III, IV, and V. The main source of the work was John Gower's *Confesio Amantis* (1385–93), although the legend of Pericles is Greek in origin.

Peridot, a gem variety of transparent green olivine, a silicate mineral. Large crystals found on St John's Island in Red Sea and in Burma; those of United States smaller. *See also* Olivine.

Peridotite term derived from *peridot,* the French word for olivine. It is a heavy igneous rock of coarse texture composed of olivine and pyroxene with small flecks of mica or hornblende. It alters readily into serpentine. Rocks that consist essentially of olivine are called dunites. *See also* Igneous Rocks.

Perigee, point in the orbit about the Earth of the Moon or an artificial satellite, at which the body is nearest to the Earth. *See also* Apogee.

Period. *See* Geologic Time.

Periodic Law, law first stated by D.I. Mendeleev (1834–1907) in 1869 asserting that the properties of the chemical elements are a periodic function of their atomic weights. The groupings of the elements based on this law formed the forerunner of the periodic table. From gaps in these groupings Mendeleev was able to predict the existence and properties of undiscovered elements. However, his table contained anomalies, which were not resolved until H.G.J. Moseley (1887–1915) discovered that periodicity was related to atomic number (rather than atomic weight) and the later discovery of isotopes. *See also* Periodic Table.

Periodic Table, arrangement of the chemical elements in order of their atomic numbers in accordance with the periodic law stated by D.I. Mendeleev and later modified by H.G.J. Moseley. In the modern form of the table, the elements are arranged into 18 vertical columns and seven horizontal periods. The vertical columns are numbered I to VIII, each of which is divided into two subgroups, the A subgroup forming the main group and the B subgroup containing the transition elements: in addition, the noble gases are collected into a ninth group, group O. The elements in each group have the same number of valence electrons and accordingly have similar properties. Elements in the same horizontal period have the same number of electron shells. The elements are arranged in the periods in order of increasing atomic number from left to right.

Peripatetic School (*fl.* late 4th–early 3rd centuries BC), Greek philosophers who followed the doctrines of Aristotle. The name derives from Aristotle's practice of walking (Greek: peripatein) while he taught.

Peripatus, or velvet worm, any of 65 living species of the subphylum Onychophora, intermediate in structure, between annelids and arthropods. It is confined to humid habitats in tropics and subtropics. The sluglike body has many pairs of legs ending in tiny claws. Length: to 6in (15cm).

Peripheral Nervous System (PNS), the portion of the nervous system not in the central nervous system; includes skin neurons and underlying organs. *See also* Nervous System.

Perissodactyla, order of mammals characterized by hoofs with an odd number of toes. The only living members of the order are horses, tapirs, and rhinoceroses. There are 152 extinct genera known from fossils. Perissodactyls bear their body weight on the central toes of their four feet. In horses only one toe is functional.

Peristalsis, a series of involuntary muscular contractions that move food along the digestive tract: from the pharynx along the esophagus to the stomach; from the stomach through the small intestines; and, in what is known as mass peristalsis (occurring about once every 24 hours), through the large intestine, pushing feces to the rectum, where nervous impulses lead to the urge to defecate. Under certain conditions, peristalsis motions are reversed and vomiting occurs.

Peritoneum, strong, colorless membrane that lines the abdominal wall and contains the abdominal organs. The greater omentum, a fold in the peritoneum, forms an apron over the intestines. Inflammation of the peritoneum is known as peritonitis.

Peritonitis, inflammation of the peritoneum, a membrane that lines the abdominal cavity and organs within. It may be general or local and is caused by infection or chemically irritating materials. Its principal symptom is severe abdominal pain with vomiting. Treatment is directed at the underlying cause.

Periwinkle, gastropod mollusk found in clusters along marine shores. Herbivorous, it nestles rather than clings in cracks of rocks. Its coiled shell has a horny plate covering its opening. Length: 0.5–1in. (1.3–2.5cm). Family Littorinidae; species include the common *Littorina littorea.*

Periwinkle, trailing or erect evergreen plants popular as ground covers and for hanging baskets. The common creeping periwinkle (*Vinca minor*) has small blue, white, or pink flowers. Some varieties have white to purple or even variegated colors. Family Apocynaceae.

Perm, formerly Molotov, city in Russian SFSR, USSR, in the central part W of the Ural Mts, on the Kama River; capital of Perm oblast. In the early 18th century the old village settlement was enlarged by Russian merchant princes, made a district town, and later named Perm (1781). Industries: lumber products, leather, agricultural machinery, metallurgy, oil. Pop. 985,000.

Permian Period, the most recent division of the Paleozoic Era lasting from 280 to 225,000,000 years ago. A time of widespread geologic uplift and mostly cool, dry climates with periods of glaciation in the southern continents. Reptiles diversified, especially the mammal-like reptiles. Some groups of amphibians continued to flourish. At the end of the period, many ancient marine invertebrate groups became greatly reduced or died out. The ancestral Alps, earliest Appalachians and Ural Mountains were formed. *See also* Geologic Time; Paleozoic Era.

Pernicious Anemia, severe anemia involving progressive decrease in number of red blood cells, which grow larger in size. It is caused by deficiency of vitamin B_{12}. Treatment is administration of B_{12} by injection.

Perón, Juan Domingo (1895–1974), president of Argentina (1946–55, 1973–74), one of the most important political figures of Latin America. When Ramón Castillo was overthrown in 1943, Perón, a career military officer and leader of a politically active military club, became head of the labor department. Through working-class and union support, Perón was elected president in 1946 and again in 1951. The Peronist program of economic nationalism and social justice gave way to monetary inflation and political violence; Perón was ousted by a military coup in 1955. Perón, in exile, continued to be a powerful force in Argentine politics. He was re-elected in 1973 by a clear majority.

Perón, María Estela ("Isabel") Martínez de (1931–), Argentine political figure. The first woman chief of state in the Americas, she became president of Argentina when her husband, Juan Perón, died in office in 1974. She was overthrown in 1976, in a coup led by the commanders of the armed forces. She was held under house arrest until 1981, when she was released on the condition that she not participate in any political activities, and then went into exile in Spain.

Peroxide, a compound consisting of two oxygen atoms united to each other and yielding a solution of hydrogen peroxide when treated with acid.

Perpendicular Style, style of the last period of English Gothic architecture (*fl.* late 14th–mid-16th century). Named for the strong vertical lines of its window tracery and paneling, its characteristic fan vaulting can be seen in the Chapel of Henry VII, Westminster, and King's College Chapel, Cambridge.

Perpignan, city in S France, 96mi (155km) SE of Toulouse on Têt River; capital of Pyrénées-Orientales dept. Capital of kingdom of Mallorca 13th century, it passed to France in 1659; site of Cathedral of St Jean (1324–1509), and 15th-century castle of kings of Majorca. Industries: tourism, distilleries, chocolate, clothing. Founded 10th century; chartered 1197. Pop. 107,971.

Perry, Matthew Colbraith (1794–1858), US naval officer, b. Newport, R.I. The brother of Oliver Hazard Perry, he established the navy's apprentice system (1837) and organized the first navy engineer corps. In 1833 he supervised the construction of the first naval steamship and was called the father of the steam navy. He also was responsible for opening up Japan to the West (1852–54), negotiating a treaty that secured US trading rights there.

Perry, Oliver Hazard (1785–1819), US naval officer, b. South Kingston, R.I. After serving in the Tripoli campaign (1801–05), Perry began building warships. In the War of 1812 he built and manned a fleet in Lake Erie. In September 1813, near Put-In-Bay, Ohio, he met the British fleet. When his flagship, the *Lawrence,* began to sink, he moved to another ship and forced the British to surrender. This battle gave the United States control over the lake. His message following the battle, "We have met the enemy and they are ours," is often quoted. He died on a diplomatic mission to South America.

Perse, Saint-John (1887–1975), pseud. of Alexis Léger, French poet and diplomat. He served in the foreign service in Peking (1916–21), becoming an expert on East Asia. From 1933–40 he served as secretary general of the French Foreign Service. He was dismissed from his post for opposing appeasement and went into exile in the United States. His elaborately stylized verse epics include *Eloges* (1911), *Anabase* (1922), *Pluies* (1943), *Chronique* (1959), and *Oiseaux* (1962). *Evil* (1942) was inspired by World War II. He was awarded the Nobel Prize for literature in 1960.

Persephone, in Greek mythology, goddess of spring and queen of Hades. She was the daughter of the Earth goddess Demeter and Zeus. As goddess of death she sent the Furies on their errands. In her role as goddess of spring she is depicted as bearing a cornucopia overflowing with flowers, as she was before Hades stole her from earth.

Persepolis, ancient ruined city in Persia, approx. 30mi (48km) NE of Shiraz, SW central Iran; served as capital of the Achaemenid empire 550–330 BC; site of palaces of Darius I and Xerxes; inscriptions of Shutruk-Nakhkhunte, a famous Elamite king (*c.* 1207–1171 BC); citadel containing a treasury looted by Alexander the Great (*c.* 300 BC); nearby Stakhr which served as the capital of the Sassanids *c.* AD 200; nearby archeological excavations have unearthed villages dating from 4000 BC.

Perseus, in Greek mythology, son of Danae and the disguised Zeus, who came to Danae as a shower of gold. Perseus is a major hero in the myths. He severed the snake-haired head of the Gorgon Medusa, turned Atlas to stone, and rescued the princess Andromeda from sacrifice to a sea monster.

Perseus, a constellation close to Cassiopeia and Auriga and typical of the autumn sky. It is roughly K-shaped with the downward arm of the K pointing toward the Pleiades and the upward arm ending in Algol, the "demon star" or "head of Medusa," which is actually an eclipsing binary.

Pershing, John Joseph (1860–1948), US military officer, b. Laclede, Mo. A graduate of the US Military Academy at West Point, he served in Indian campaigns, the Spanish-American War, and helped suppress the Philippine insurrection. In 1916 he led a punitive expedition against Pancho Villa into Mexico. He became a general (1917) and commanded the American Expeditionary Force (AEF) in World War I (1917–19). He insisted on the autonomy of his troops within the Allied Command and led the actions at Château Thierry and Belleau Woods. Returning as a hero in 1919 he became the first to hold the rank of general of the armies. He was army chief of staff (1921–24). His book, *My Experiences in the World War* (1931), won a Pulitzer Prize.

Persia, empire in SW Asia, bounded by the USSR and the Caspian Sea (N), Afghanistan and Pakistan (E), the Persian Gulf and the Gulf of Oman (S), Iraq (W), and Turkey (NW). *See also* Iran.

Persian, the principal language of Iran and one of the two official languages of Afghanistan. It is spoken by about 20 million people in Iran , and by about 5 million more in Afghanistan. An Iranian language and thus part of the Indo-European family, it is one of the world's oldest languages and was a major language of ancient times. Since the 7th century it has been written in the Arabic script.

Persian Cat, longhaired domestic cat breed that first appeared in Europe at the end of the 16th century. It has a wide head with small, well covered ears, wide-set eyes, short nose, full cheeks, and broad muzzle. The compact massive body is set on short, thick legs. The tail is short and full. Its coat is fine-textured and fluffy. Varieties are according to color and include Black, Blue, Red Tabby, Cream, Smoke, and White, all with copper eyes, and Blue-eyed White.

Persian Gulf, shallow extension of the Arabian Sea between Iran and Arabia, connected to the Gulf of Oman by the Strait of Hormuz; among its many islands, Bahrain is the largest. It was an ancient trade route; European conquests started in the 17th century with British capture of the Portuguese city of Hormuz 1622; the Perpetual Maritime Treaty (1853) between Britain and Arabs est. British supremacy of the gulf; this was supported by an international treaty 1907. The discovery of rich oil deposits in the 1930s increased the gulf's importance; after British withdrawal, the United States and USSR sought to gain some control in the 1960s. With Arab-Israeli conflicts, border clashes, and disputes over oil rights, the Persian Gulf has been the scene of much disturbance in the 1970s and early 1980s. Saudi Arabia has led the efforts to unite against the Soviet threat. Area: 90,000sq mi (233,100sq km). Length: 600mi (966km).

Persian Lamb. *See* Karakul.

Persian Literature. Pre-Islamic Persian literature (5th–7th centuries) was written in Avestan and Old Persian. The major work of the period is the *Avesta,* the sacred book of the Zoroastrians. Writings in modern Persian began to appear in the 9th century and for the next 500 years Persian writers produced a rich variety of verse. Among the most famous poets were Omar Khayyam (11th century), Rumi, Sa'di (13th century), and Hafiz (14th century). Persian literature declined in the 15th century, but there was a revival in the 19th–20th centuries with the introduction of modern literary forms and experimentation.

Persian Wars, conflicts during the first half of the 5th century BC, beginning when Athens aided revolting Ionians. In 492 10,000 Athenians encountered a far greater Persian army at Marathon and won. Ten years later Athens and Sparta were defeated at Thermopylae but had a great naval victory at Salamis. In the campaign of 479 the Greeks destroyed the remainder of the Persian fleet and supported further revolts. In 467 Cimon destroyed a Persian army. An agreement favorable to Greece was reached in 449. The wars resulted in increased Greek nationalism and sense of superiority to Orientals.

Persimmon, tropical Asian tree of the genus *Diospyros* with reddish-orange fruit that is sour and astringent until it is dead ripe. Commercially sold persimmons come from the Japanese persimmon *(D. kaki).* The common persimmon *(D. virginiana)* of E United States has delicious fruit but it is too small and pulpy to have commercial value. Family Ebenaceae.

Personality, global term referring to the totality of emotional, attitudinal, and intellectual characteristics of an individual. Psychologists use the term to refer to the more enduring, long-term characteristics of a person rather than short-lived traits or momentary emotional states. Personality traits are assessed in psychology by means of a variety of devices including personality inventories and projective techniques. Among the most influential theories of personality in psychology have been the Freudian approach (psychoanalysis) and theories of behaviorism.

Perspective, in art, way of showing three-dimensional objects and spatial relationships on a two-dimensional plane. The linear perspective system is based on the idea of parallel lines and planes converging in a vanishing point as they recede into the distance. Using this principle, the artist can give a sense of perceptual space and volume on his canvas. Instead of using central perspective, with a single vanishing point, the artist can also use angular, or oblique, perspective, with two vanishing points. Another kind of parallel perspective, with the viewpoint from above, is common in Chinese painting. Linear perspective was not used in painting until the late 15th century in Italy, when the architect Brunelleschi developed mathematical rules for perspective that involved a horizon line, or viewer's eye level, and a vanishing point. Masaccio used these principles in his painting. The use of linear perspective dominated in European painting until the end of the 19th century when Cézanne intentionally flattened his canvases and other artists used color and shading to create depth. In modern art, perspective is often used in a distorted way to change space, such as in the optical illusion paintings of op art.

Perspiration, a clear liquid secreted by the sweat glands as a way of regulating body temperature. Rate of perspiration increases in warm weather, after exercise, and for emotional reasons. *See also* Sweat Gland.

Perth, city in W Australia, on the Swan River; capital city of Western Australia state; site of the University of Western Australia (1911), and St George's and St Mary's cathedrals. The city grew rapidly after the discovery of the Coolgardie goldfields in 1890. Industries: automotives, cement, textiles, munitions, processed food. Founded 1829; inc. 1856. Pop. 787,300.

Pertussis. *See* Whooping Cough.

Peru (Perú), the third-largest South American nation and home of the ancient Inca Empire. Its economy is based on rich mineral deposits. Fifty percent of the population is Indian. The country is ruled by a military junta.

Land and economy. Peru is bounded by Ecuador and Colombia (N), Chile (S), and Brazil and Bolivia (E). It has a 1,400-mi (2,254-km) Pacific coastline (W). Its immense mountain system, Cordillera de los Andes, divides the country into three regions. The coastal is a dry strip of desert that contains 40% of the population and produces 50% of the gross national product. The Sierra is a dry and cold mountain chain that limits transportation and communication. It contains rich mineral deposits and 50% of the country's population. Mt Huascarán, 22,205ft (8,882m), is in the Sierra. The third division, Montaña, is the hot, moist low country of tropical forests and largely unexplored jungles. Since the time of the Incas, Peru has been known for its abundant minerals—lead, copper, zinc, iron, silver, cadmium, tin, gold, coal, marble, limestone, and now oil. With half the population employed in agriculture, cotton, rice, coffee, and sugar are exported. Fishing is also important.

People. Descendants of the Incas make up 40% of Peru's population. Of the rest, 11% are Caucasian and 43% mestizo (mixed). Roman Catholicism is the state religion, practiced by 90% of the people. Spanish is the official language; many Indians speak Quechua and Aymara. Literacy is estimated at 60%. The forest Indians, still living a stone age existence, are said to be the most primitive tribe in the world today.

Government. According to the constitution of 1979, executive power is vested in the president, who is popularly elected to a five-year term. Members of the bicameral national congress are also popularly elected.

Matthew Perry

John J. Pershing

Peru

History. When the Spanish landed in 1531, Peru was the center of the highly developed Inca civilization. Francisco Pizarro, in search of Inca treasure, conquered the country and by 1542 it had become a source of Spanish wealth and power. In 1820–24 José de San Martín and Simon Bolívar led a successful War of Independence and declared Peru independent. Since independence, government has been dominated by dictators and the military. In 1968 a leftist military coup took place, and the new government began restructuring the economy. A new, more conservative military government assumed control in 1976, returning the country to civilian democracy in 1980. The new government, however, faced a high rate of inflation, a large national debt, and growing terrorism and was defeated in 1985 by a government that pledged to combat these problems.

PROFILE

Official name: Republic of Peru
Area: 496,223sq mi (1,285,218sq km)
Population: 18,000,000
  Density: 36per sq mi (14per sq km)
Chief cities: Lima (capital); Cuzco; Callao; Arequipa
Government: Military junta
Religion: Roman Catholic
Language: Spanish
Monetary unit: Sol
Gross national product: $9,500,000,000
Per capita income: $617
Industries: fish meal, processed foods, textiles, chemicals, metal products, automobiles
Agriculture: beef cattle, cotton, sugar cane, rice, coffee, sheep, fish, corn, tobacco
Minerals: copper, iron ore, lead, petroleum
Trading partners (major): United States, Japan

Perugia, city in central Italy; capital of Perugia prov. and Umbria region. One of major Etruscan cities, it passed to Rome 310 BC; became papal possession 1540; center of Umbrian school of painting that peaked 15th century; active in Risorgimento movement; site of 13th-century city walls and Maggiore fountain, Palazzo dei Priori (13th—16th centuries). Industries: chocolate, food, textiles, machines. Pop. 136,933.

Perugino, Il, real name **Pietro di Cristoforo Vannucci** (1446–1523), Italian painter. His works show a good sense of perspective and are executed with an ordered simplicity in the style of the Florentine school. His works include the fresco "St Sebastian" (1478). In 1481 he was commissioned with others, including Botticelli, to execute mural decorations of the Sistine Chapel in Rome.

Peruvian (Humboldt) Current, cold water current in the SE Pacific Ocean; runs N along the SW coast of South America, turning E by Peru.*See also* Humboldt's Current.

Pesach. *See* Passover.

Pescadores (P'enghu Liehtao), group of several small islands of Nationalist China, in the Formosa Strait, between Taiwan and the Chinese mainland. Named by Portuguese in 16th century, the group was ceded to Japan by China 1895; retroceded 1946; part of Nationalist China since 1949. Main islands are P'enghu, Yuweng, Paisha. Products: sweet potatoes, peanuts, coral. Chief industry is fishing. Area: approx. 50sq mi (130sq km).

Pescara, seaport city in central Italy, 95mi (153km) ENE of Rome, on the Adriatic Sea; capital of Pescara prov. As Roman Aternum, it was nearly destroyed by barbarian attacks; heavily damaged WWII; seaside re-

sort and tourist center. Industries: fishing, machinery, textiles, shipbuilding. Made provincial capital 1927. Pop. 135,612.

Peshawar, city in NW Pakistan, 10mi (16km) E of Khyber Pass; capital of North-West Frontier prov. City has been of historical strategic importance, and was repeatedly attacked from 1st century on by Afghan, Persian, and Mongol invaders; held by Sikhs 1823–49, when it was annexed to Britain; site of Buddhist relics, 2nd-century stupa, university (1950). Modern city is famous for handicrafts, carpets, leather goods. Industries: tobacco, textiles, firearms. Pop. 273,000.

Petah Tiqwa, city in central Israel, 7mi (11km) NE of Tel Aviv-Jaffa; commercial center. Industries: asbestos, chemicals, textiles, farm equipment, food processing, rubber products, stone quarries. Founded 1878 as first modern Jewish agricultural colony in Palestine; inc. 1937. Pop. 103,000.

Pétain, Henri Philippe (1856–1951), French general and chief of state in the Vichy government during World War II. He distinguished himself by holding Verdun against the Germans (1916) and was appointed commander-in-chief under Marshal Foch (1917). Between the wars he served on the Higher Council of War (1920–30); commanded in Morocco (1925–26); served as war minister (1934) and ambassador to Spain (1939). He was recalled in 1940 to form the government that signed the armistice with Germany. Old, ill, perhaps senile, Pétain was chief of state and the symbol of French collaboration with Germany. His death sentence (1945) was commuted to life imprisonment by Charles de Gaulle.

Petal, organ that forms the corolla of a flower. Located inside the sepals, flower petals are usually conspicuous and brightly colored. Forms include: corolla tube; ray-formed (petunia); pair-formed—top petal enlarged, side petals smaller, and lower two fused (snapdragon, orchid); and reduced (grasses and some trees).

Peter, Saint, chief of the 12 Apostles of Jesus Christ. Peter and his brother Andrew were fishermen, whom Jesus called to follow him (Mark 1:16). Peter's original name was Simon, and Jesus gave him his new name from the Greek *Petros* (rock): "thou art Peter, and upon this rock I will build my church" (Matthew 16:18). There are many other references to Peter in the Gospels, and he is named first in lists of the Apostles. He failed his lord in one crisis. After Jesus was arrested, the night before his crucifixion, Peter three times denied he knew the master (John 18:15–27). But Peter was the first of the Apostles to see Christ after the Resurrection. The Acts of the Apostles show Peter as a leader of the Christians. It is believed that he founded a church in Rome and was martyred under Emperor Nero, around 64. As the first bishop of Rome, Peter is first in the list of popes.

Peter I, the Great (1672–1725), Russian tsar (1682–1725). Educated by foreigners, Peter ruled jointly with his half-brother Ivan (1682–89) and assumed the throne alone in 1689. After creating a disciplined army and a navy, he declared war on Turkey in 1696. He visited Europe 1696–97 and brought back technical specialists to aid Russia's development. In 1700, Peter allied Russia with Poland against Sweden, which was defeated at the Battle of Poltava in 1709. He married his mistress, the future Catherine I, in 1712, and again visited Europe 1716–17. In 1722 he successfully fought against Persia. An ambitious, tyrannical monarch, he fundamentally altered the character of Russia through westernization. He built a remarkable capital city at St Petersburg (Leningrad), checked the church's author-

ity, reformed the central government, the military, and the civil service, and suddenly transformed Russia into a major European power. *See also* Northern War.

Peter II (1715–30), Russian tsar (1727–30). He succeeded Catherine I and was at first guided by Aleksandr Menshikov and later by his rival Vasili Dolgoruki. He died of smallpox.

Peter III (1728–62), Russian tsar (1762). Named in 1741 to succeed Elizabeth, Peter married the future Catherine II in 1745. On gaining the throne in 1762, he at once returned to Frederick II all conquered Prussian territory. He also issued an important edict releasing the gentry from conscription. He was murdered after a coup organized by guard officers, under his wife's direction, put her in power.

Peter I (1320–67), king of Portugal (1357–67), son and successor of Alfonso IV. As crown prince, he fell in love with his wife's lady in waiting, Inés de Castro. He refused to give her up, and the King connived to have her murdered (1335). In retaliation, Peter raised a revolution against his father, but peace was soon restored and Peter publicly forgave his lover's murderers. Nevertheless, after he became king, he enacted revenge against two of them; he had their hearts cut out. The tragic love affair is one of the favorites of Portuguese literature. Peter was succeeded by his son, Ferdinand I.

Peter IV, king of Portugal. See Pedro I, emperor of Brazil.

Peter, First and Second Epistles, New Testament letters written by Simon Peter who was crucified for his devotion to Christ. Relying heavily on Paul's teachings, he addressed his writings to converts to Christianity from Judaism and encouraged faith in the Second Coming of Christ. Warning against false teachers, he emphasizes the importance of apostolic witness.

Peterborough, city in SE Ontario, Canada, on the Otonabee River and Trent Canal, with one of the world's largest hydraulic lift locks; site of Trent University; center of a rich agricultural area. Exports: lumber, peas, leather, wool, cheese. Inc. 1905. Pop. 59,683.

Peterborough, city in E central England, in Cambridgeshire, on Nene River; site of 7th-century abbey; railroad and industrial center. Industries: machinery, bricks. Pop. 115,000.

Peterloo Massacre (1819), killing by militia of several people in a crowd assembled at St Peter's Fields, Manchester, England, to demand redress of grievances and fair parliamentary representation. Magistrates read the Riot Act to part of the crowd and called in the militia almost immediately to scatter them. The deaths caused great public indignation.

Peter Pan (1904), 5-act fantasy by James M. Barrie, published in 1928. A favorite with children, it concerns Peter Pan, the boy who never grew up. He flies in the nursery window, teaches Wendy and her two brothers to fly, and takes them to exciting adventures in Never-Never Land. They encounter Indians, Captain Hook and his pirate band, and a crocodile with a ticking clock in his stomach.

Peter the Cruel (1334–69), Spanish king of Castile and León (1350–69), son and successor of Alfonso XI. He was constantly at war with his illegitimate brother, Henry of Trastámara (later Henry II). Peter was generally backed by England in the person of Edward the Black Prince; Henry had the backing of Aragón and

French troops under the command of Bertrand du Guesclin. Henry defeated Peter in 1366 and had himself crowned. The next year, however, Peter and Edward defeated Henry. In 1369, Henry won the decisive battle of Monteil and killed Peter in a duel.

Petit Mal, type of epilepsy in which brief episodes of unconsciousness, lasting less than 15 seconds, occur several times a day. It is found mainly in children. *See also* Epilepsy.

Petra, ruined ancient city in SW Jordan. Held by Nabataeans (Arab Tribe) from 4th century BC until it was occupied by Rome AD 106, it was an early seat of Christianity; captured by Muslims 7th century and in 12th century by Crusaders; served as a center for caravan trade routes. Ruins were discovered 1812 by Johann Burckhardt; they include temples, palaces, homes, and theaters carved in varying shades of pink limestone. City is referred to as Sela in Bible and Wadi Musa by Egyptians.

Petrarch, Anglicized form of Francesco Petrarca (1304–74), Italian lyric poet and scholar. One of the most famous and widely imitated poets of the Middle Ages, he is considered, with Giovanni Boccaccio, one of the heralds of the Italian Renaissance. His works, including a collection known as *Rime spare* (scattered lyrics) and *Trionfi* (Triumphs), were read and imitated by Geoffrey Chaucer and other English and European poets through the 19th century. Most of his poems have as their subject "Laura," a woman whom Petrarch idealized in the style of earlier Italian lyric poets, but who was seen in a more realistic and human light.

Petrified Forest National Park, park in E Arizona; an extensive natural exhibit of petrified wood, it also features Indian ruins and petroglyphs, as well as a portion of the Painted Desert. Area: 94,189acres (38,147hectares). Est. 1906.

Petrified Wood, the replacement of wood fibers with opal or chalcedony as a result of hot, silica-bearing waters, forming a fossil. *See also* Chalcedony; Opal.

Petrochemical, chemical substance derived from petroleum or natural gas. The refining of petroleum is undertaken on a very large scale not only for the fuels obtained (gasoline, kerosene, fuel oil, and natural gas) but also for the wide range of chemicals that can be obtained or derived from it. These chemicals include the common alkanes and alkenes, cyclohexone, benzene, toluene, and naphthalene. Ammonia is also regarded as a petrochemical as the hydrogen used in its manufacture is usually derived from petroleum.

Petroleum, a complex mixture of organically derived hydrocarbons, mostly liquids but including gases and solids. It is used as a fuel and raw material in chemical industries. An accepted theory of petroleum formation is that millions of years ago the fats and waxes of dead planktonic plants and animals accumulated on the bottom of seas and large lakes, where they were covered by sand and clay sediments. As pressure increased, the sand and clay were compacted, forcing the organic matter into more porous and permeable rock, such as sandstone or porous carbonates. The organic matter migrated until it became trapped, forcing the petroleum into pools. Oil shale is an organically derived rock, yielding petroleum after a difficult refining stage.

Petroleum Refining, the process in which crude oil is separated into useful products. The primary method of separation is fractional distillation. Crude oil is heated to about 650°F (343°C), and is injected as a vapor into a fractioning column, a tower as high as 150ft (46m) containing 30 to 40 perforated trays. The vapor rises to the top of the column where it condenses and falls back through the trays, mixing with rising vapors. The process of evaporation and condensation continues until an equilibrium is reached, with lighter molecules at the top of the tower grading to heavier molecules at the bottom. The grades are siphoned off individually as a refined product. Less valuable products may be chemically changed. Lighter molecules may be made heavier through alkylation, isomerization, or catalytic reforming. Heavier molecules may be "cracked," or broken down into lighter ones by thermal or catalytic cracking.

Petrology, study of rocks, their origin, chemical composition, and occurrence. Formation of the three classes of rocks—igneous, of volcanic origin; sedimentary, deposited by water; and metamorphic, either of the other two, changed by temperature and pressure—are studied. Experimental petrology simulates in the laboratory those conditions necessary to produce the rocks and minerals found on earth and elsewhere in the solar system. *See also* Geochemistry; Mineralogy.

Petronius, Gauis (died 66), Roman satirist. He was known as Petronius Arbiter because, according to Tacitus, he was the arbiter of elegance at Nero's court. He committed suicide after Nero had him arrested on the charges of a jealous rival. His *Satyricon,* a romance in prose and verse, remains in fragments. It uses both sophisticated Latin and colloquial language to mockingly portray the pretenses of the time. The best known extant episode describes the extravagant dinner party of Tremalchio, a parvenu.

Petunia, genus of herbs native to Argentina and grown as garden ornamentals. The tubular, 5-petaled flowers range in color from white to blue, yellow, pink, red, and purple. Species include *Petunia axillaris,* an erect plant with long white blooms lin (2.5cm) wide; the purple *P. integrifolia* and *P. violacea;* and *P. hybrida,* produced from natural species to provide blooms for cultivation. Family Solanaceae.

Pewee, small olive-brown North American woodland birds that have a *pee-a-wee* whistle. Genus *Contopus.*

Pewter, several alloys that consist mainly of tin and lead. The most common has four parts of tin to one of lead, combined with small amounts of antimony, copper, and bismuth. Pewter is soft, bluish-grey, and similar to tin in appearance. It was formerly used extensively for household objects but declined in popularity in the 19th century. Because of poisonous properties of lead and antimony, pewter has been replaced by other alloys in the making of domestic utensils, but is highly prized by antique collectors.

Peyote, two species of cactus of the genus *Laphophora* (family Cactaceae), native to North America and found in limestone soils of the Chihuahuan desert of Texas and northern Mexico. To 2in (5cm) tall and 3in (8cm) wide with a soft stem, *L. williamsii* has pink or white flowers in summer and a blue-green stem. *L. diffusa* has white or yellow flowers. Peyote contains many alkaloids, the principal one being mescaline, well known as a hallucinogenic. Its use is now prohibited by law in some places.

Phaeton, in Greek mythology, son of Apollo, who drove his father's sun chariot across the sky but lost control of the horses causing the Earth to burn and Olympus to smoke. To save the world, Zeus struck him from the reins with a thunderbolt.

Phagocytosis, process by which cells can engulf extracellular particles to be later digested. For example, white blood cells phagocytose bacteria and kill them.

Phalarope, small, long-necked, web-footed shorebird. The female woos the male, and builds a grass-and-moss nest and incubates the pear-shaped, light-colored, blotched eggs (3–4). Length: 8–10in (20–25cm). Family Phalaropodidae.

pH and pOH, measures of the concentrations of hydrogen ions (pH) and hydroxide ions (pOH) in solution. Since the hydrogen-ion concentration may be small, e.g. 10^{-5} gram molecules per liter, it is more conveniently expressed as the logarithm to the base 10 of its reciprocal, which is called its pH value, e.g. 5.0. A solution with a pH value less than 7 is acid; more than 7 basic; a neutral solution, such as NaCl in water, will have a pH of 7. pOH is a little-used unit defined as $-\log_{10} OH^-$, related to pH through the solubility product of water. The pH can be determined with a glass electrode or, less accurately, by colored indicators. *See also* Indicator.

Pharisees, a sect within Judaism, prominent in Israel in the 1st century AD, before the destruction of the 2nd temple in 70. The name of the sect means "separated," indicating their emphasis on purity and freedom from sin. Stressing oral tradition, they were concerned with the education of the people, and for this reason, are seen as the ancestors of the rabbis of today. They were unjustly condemned in the New Testament as hypocrites, while they strove for imitation of God.

Pharmacology, science that deals with the sources and properties of drugs, their use in treating disease, and their action on living organisms. It includes toxicology, the study of the poisonous effects of drugs.

Pharmacopeia, a standard, authoritative, and usually official reference book containing selected lists of drugs, chemicals and medicinal preparations. Included are exact descriptions; tests for identity, purity, and strength and formulas for their preparation.

Pharos, island off coast of N Egypt, in Mediterranean, connected to mainland by mole (stone structure) built by Alexander the Great *c.* 331 BC. Lighthouse completed by Ptolemy II (280 BC) and considered one of Seven Wonders of World was on Pharos; it was destroyed by an earthquake 1346. Pharos is part of city of Alexandria.

Pharynx, region at the back of the mouth that is the common passageway for food and air. It extends from the nasal cavities (from which it is separated by a flap of tissue called the uvula in the back of the mouth) to the glottis, the opening into the trachea, which is closed off by a "trap door," the epiglottis. The pharynx becomes continuous with the esophagus, which leads to the stomach.

Phase Diagram, diagram showing the conditions under which different equilibrium phases of substances exist. For example, a curve of melting point against pressure of a pure solid divides the graph into two regions. Points in one represent temperatures and pressures at which the substance is solid; points in the other represent the liquid conditions. Systems of two or more components cannot be represented fully by a two-dimensional graph. Graphs of composition against temperature are used to show solubilities, ranges of stability of alloy phases, etc.

Phases, in astronomy, or figures, apparent changes in shape presented by the Moon in a manner corresponding to the amount by which its surface is illuminated by the Sun at various stages during each lunar orbit. The phases range from new, when the Moon lies between Earth and Sun and is totally invisible, to full, when the moon reaches opposition. Similar phases are seen from Earth for the inferior planets Mercury and Venus.

Pheasant, chickenlike game birds sometimes valued as ornamentals. The males are often brilliantly colored, especially on the wings and tail feathers. Females are smaller and brownish. In North America, the widely distributed ring-necked pheasant *(Phasianus colchicus)* has a dark green head, white neck ring, bronze breast, and coppery, black-spotted sides. It frequents fields and farmlands. After courtship rituals, the female lays olive-brown or pale bluish-green eggs (8–15) in a shallow grass nest. Length: 1.5–8ft (0.46–2.4m), including the long tail. Family Phasianidae.

Phenol, any of a family of organic compounds that are known by the attachment of a minimum of one hydroxyl group to a carbon atom forming part of the benzene ring. "Phenol" is the specific name for monohydroxybenzene (C_6H_3OH) and the generic name for compounds containing one or more hydroxyl functions attached to an aromatic ring. Phenols are colorless liquids or white solids at room temperature with higher melting and boiling points than the parent hydrocarbons from which they are derived. Phenol is used by the chemical and pharmaceutical industries for conversion to such products as aspirin, dyes, fungicides, and bactericides, in addition to its application as a starting material for nylon and epoxy resins. See also Carbolic Acid.

Phenolphthalein, a derivative of phenol. It is a chemical compound ($C_{20}H_{14}O_4$), prepared by a reaction between phenol and phthaleic anhydride in the presence of sulfuric acid. It is used as an indicator for alkalinity, in laxatives, and in dyes.

Phenotype, observable characteristics of an individual, often contrasted with genotype, the genetic makeup. *See also* Genotype.

Phenylketonuria (PKU), or phenylpyruvic oligophrenia, condition in which proteins cannot be metabolized normally because the enzyme phenylalinase is absent. Infants with PKU excrete phenylpyruvic acid in the urine. Special diets are used to treat the condition; untreated, it will usually produce severe mental deficiency.

Pheromone, or ectohormone, sociohormone, substance secreted externally by certain animals to elicit specific responses from members of the same species. Common in mammals, insects, and fish, these substances may be a component of body products, such as urine, or secreted by specific glands.

Phidias (Pheidias) (*fl.*470–425 BC), Greek sculptor. His direction of Pericles' program for the beautification of Athens allowed his thinking and work to direct the art of the Periclean age. Although all of his works are now lost, it is probable that he designed the Parthenon sculptures. The sculptures display a style and form that were to become hallmarks of the classic tradition.

Philadelphia, city and port of entry in SE Pennsylvania, bounded by Delaware River (E) and Schuylkill River (W); seat of and coextensive with Philadelphia co. Known as "city of brotherly love," it was founded by William Penn 1681 as a haven of religious and racial freedom; by *c.* 1774 it was the commercial, cultural, and industrial center of the American colonies. Phila-

Petrarch

Petrified Forest National Park, Arizona

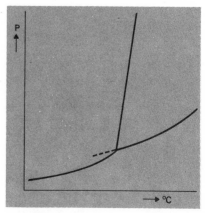

Phase diagram

delphia was paramount in shaping the policies of the colonies; Carpenter's Hall and the State House were sites of the First and Second Continental Congresses (Sept. 5, 1774 and May 10, 1775); at Independence Hall, the Declaration of Independence was signed July 4, 1776; the Constitutional Convention met here and adopted the US Constitution Sept. 17, 1787. Philadelphia served as capital of Pennsylvania 1683–1799, and of the United States 1790–1800; it was scene of first abolitionist movement in North America (1775), with American Anti-Slavery Society est. 1833; during WWI and II, Philadelphia was prominent in production of war materials. Benjamin Franklin est. the University of Pennsylvania (1740), Pennsylvania Hospital (1751), and first daily newspaper (1784); home of Betsy Ross, seamstress of the first American flag. Its landmarks include Liberty Bell, Independence National Historic Park (est. 1956), Christ Church (1727), Edgar Allan Poe's house, Rodin Museum, Academy of Fine Arts (1805), Philadelphia Zoo, Philadelphia Museum of Art, Benjamin Franklin Memorial (1933), Drexel University (1891), Temple University (1884), Philadelphia College of Art (1876), US Mint. Professional sports teams include Phillies (baseball), Eagles (football), '76ers (basketball), and Flyers (ice hockey). Industries: shipbuilding, textiles, chemicals, clothing, electrical equipment, metal products, publishing, printing, oil refining, food products. Laid out 1682; chartered 1701. Pop. (1980) 1,688,210.

Philip, Saint, one of the 12 Apostles of Jesus Christ. The Gospel of John tells that Philip was from "Bethsaida, the city of Andrew and Peter" (John 1:44). Philip's name appears in all the lists of the disciples in the Gospels and Acts of the Apostles. He was present at the feeding of the five thousand (John 6:5–14).

Philip I (1052–1108), king of France. He enlarged his kingdom and fought repeatedly with the kings of England, William I and II, who as dukes of Normandy were technically his vassals. For his illegal marriage to Bertrada de Montfort (both were already married), he was excommunicated by Pope Urban II, but restored on the understanding (openly disregarded) that he have no further converse with her.

Philip II or **Philip Augustus** (1165–1223), king of France. He doubled the area of his domain during a 43-year reign. He conducted many wars against Henry II of England and his sons, Richard and John. In 1202, Philip confiscated the French holdings of John, and at the Battle of Bouvines (1214) defeated the coalition John put together to support his claims, including Holy Roman Emperor Otto IV and the counts of Boulogne and Flanders. A strong ruler, Philip supported the Church and towns, improved the fortifications and streets of Paris, and sent out new administrative officers to call up the army, to collect revenues, and to promulgate his laws.

Philip IV, called **the Fair** (1268–1314), king of France (1285–1314). Described by contemporaries as "the handsomest man in the world, but unable to do anything but stare fixedly at people without saying a word," later recognized as a skilled statesman, the first modern king. He recognized that wealth was the key to a monarch's power over church and rival lords. Claimed the right to tax the clergy for the defense of the realm, using as precedent the levies for the Crusades. Pope Boniface VIII opposed Philip, denouncing him by papal bull and threatening him with excommunication, but Philip refused to back down and convoked the first Estates-General (1302) of nobility, clergy, and commons to hear his justification. Philip secured the election of Pope Clement V and transferred him to Avignon (1309), beginning the "Babylonian captivity"

of the papacy. Philip married Jeanne de Navarre (1284).

Philip VI (1293–1350), king of France, grandson of Philip III, became king (1328) on the death of his cousin, Charles IV, managing to avert successionary wars. He then defeated the rebellious towns of Flanders, restoring their count, whose despotic rule caused further trouble at the outbreak of the Hundred Years' War in 1337. Losing control of Flanders after a severe naval defeat (1340), Philip violated the subsequent treaty, was crushed in Normandy (1346), and made a peace that survived him.

Philip II (382–336 BC), king of Macedon 359–336 BC. A superior statesman, diplomat, and general, he laid the foundations of Macedonia's greatness by uniting the country and promoting urbanization and trade and making an excellent professional army. His military genius enabled him to crush Athens and Thebes at Chaeronea in 338 BC. He was assassinated at the age of 46 and succeeded by his son Alexander the Great.

Philip V (238–179 BC), king of Macedon (221–179), son of Demetrius II, adopted by Antigonus III whom he succeeded. He fought well in Greece against the Aetolian League and Sparta and tried to take Illyria from Rome. His pact with Hannibal precipitated the First Macedonian War (215–205), which he won. By attempting to expand his power in the Aegean he alarmed Pergamum and Rhodes and they convinced Rome to enter the Second Macedonian War (200–197) in which Philip was badly beaten. Thereafter he complied with Rome and strengthened Macedon internally. He was succeeded by his son Perseus. *See also* Macedonian Wars.

Philip II (1527–98), king of Spain (1556–98), son of Holy Roman Emperor Charles V and Isabella of Portugal. His father gave him the duchy of Milan (1548), the kingdom of Naples and Sicily (1554), the Spanish Netherlands (1555), and upon his abdication, Spain (1556) along with its fabulously rich colonies in the New World. Thus, like his father, Philip ruled one of the great empires of history. A hardworking, pious ruler, Philip mostly allied himself with Roman Catholic interests on the continent, plunging Spain into the numerous religious wars of the time. He sent the Spanish Armada to England to topple the Protestant Elizabeth I from the throne. Its defeat marked the turning point in Spanish power. Of more general significance was the great drain on Spanish resources caused by Philip's expensive forays into European wars.

Philip married four times. His second wife was Mary I of England; he proposed marriage after her death to Elizabeth I but was refused. Philip built and held court at the Escorial, a somber but impressive combination palace, monastery, and fortress. He died there and was succeeded by Philip III, his son by his fourth wife. Another son, the legendary Don Carlos (1545–68), died early. John of Austria was his half-brother and Margaret of Parma his half-sister. *See also* Spanish Inquisition.

Philip III (1578–1621), king of Spain, Naples, and Sicily (1598–1621), and king of Portugal (as Philip II, 1598–1621), son of Philip II. Most of the affairs of government were left to his chief minister, the duque de Lerma. His reign was generally peaceful although he did allow Spain to get involved (1620) in the Thirty Years' War. He expelled the Moriscos, an action that accelerated Spain's economic decline. Philip was a great patron of the arts; Cervantes, El Greco, Zurbarán, and Lope de Vega all flourished in his reign. He was succeeded by his son Philip IV. *See also* Thirty Years' War.

Philip IV (1605–65), king of Spain, Naples, and Sicily (1621–65) and king of Portugal (as Philip III, 1621–40), son of Philip III. Spain continued to decline during Philip's reign. The Conde de Olivares was in charge of the government until 1643. The Thirty Years' War ended disastrously for Spain; most of the Netherlands was lost, as was Rousillon. Portugal rebelled and forced out the Spanish (1640). Velazquez was court painter during his reign, and Philip was patron to Rubens and Cano. He was succeeded by his son Charles II. *See also* Thirty Years' War.

Philip V (1683–1746), king of Spain (1700–46), first Bourbon king of Spain. A grandson of Louis XIV of France, his designation as successor of Charles II precipitated the War of the Spanish Succession. That war's conclusion put Philip on the throne of a greatly weakened Spain; Gibraltar was lost to Britain during his reign. Philip was first under the influence of the princesse des Ursins, lady in waiting to his wife. After he remarried in 1714, the princesse's influence was replaced by that of the new queen, Elizabeth Farnese. Thereafter she and Cardinal Alberoni ran the government.

In 1724, Philip briefly abdicated in favor of his son, Louis I, but he resumed the throne after Louis' death. Spain under Philip was involved in the great European wars of the period: the War of the Polish Succession; the War of the Austrian succession; and the War of Jenkins' Ear, with Great Britain. He was succeeded by his son Ferdinand VI. *See also* Spanish Succession, War of the.

Philip (the Good) (1396–1467), duke of Burgundy (1419–67), most prominent of the Valois dukes, and perhaps the most powerful man in Europe during his reign. Maintaining a long alliance with England (in which Henry V was recognized as heir to the French throne), Philip nonetheless managed friendly relations with France, turning his attention to the enlargement and welfare of his own lands. A colorful patron of the arts, Philip loved pageantry and established the chivalrous Order of the Golden Fleece in honor of his marriage (1429) to Isabella of Portugal.

Philippi, ancient city of E Macedon renamed by Philip II (c. 356 BC). It was the site of two battles in which the armies of Cassius and Brutus were defeated by Antony and Octavian (42 BC). It became a colony for veterans and later received the first Christian missionaries.

Philippians, New Testament epistle written by Paul during his first imprisonment in Rome. In this letter to the church he established at Philippi in Macedonia, he stresses his joy in serving Christ, even when threatened with death.

Philippines (Filipinas), island-nation in SE Asia. The people are mostly farmers and predominantly Roman Catholic.

Land and economy. The country, an archipelago, approx. 500mi (805km) off the SE coast of Asia, consists of over 7,000 islands extending roughly 1,100mi (1,771km) N–S and 650mi (1,047km) E–W at its widest point. Two large islands, Luzon in the N and Mindanao in the S, are separated by a number of smaller islands known as the Visayan group. Most of the islands are mountainous, some volcanic, with the densest population concentrated in mountain plains. The climate is tropical and about 40% of the land area is covered with forest; timber is the principal export. The mountains are rich in mineral deposits, metallic and non-metallic, many still undeveloped. The country's economy is based on agriculture, with rice the principal food staple; however, the Philippines is the world's largest producer and principal exporter of coconuts and coconut products. The government has encouraged and furthered the development of industry, and the production of offshore oil began in 1979.

People. Most of the Filipinos' ancestors came to the islands from SE Asia or Indonesia. The Aetas (Balugas), a short, black-complexioned people, are the only remaining aboriginals. Although a large number of languages and dialects is spoken throughout the islands, almost everyone speaks Pilipino, a national language rooted in Tagalog, and English. The vast majority of the people is Roman Catholic.

Government. The Philippines were under martial law from 1972 to 1981. Executive power is vested in the president, popularly elected to a six-year term. An interim national assembly was convened in 1978; 165 of its 200 members are popularly elected. President Marcos ruled as a virtual dictator from 1965 until 1986.

History. Although Muslims arrived in the 15th century, the first mass contact with the outside world was in the 16th century with the arrival of the Spanish. Ferdinand Magellan, who was killed there, discovered the islands in 1521. The first permanent settlement was established on Cebu in 1565, and Manila was settled in 1571. Spanish soldiers methodically conquered the major islands, and the friars, who accompanied them, systematically converted the people to Roman Catholicism. Spain exploited the natural resources until the 19th century when, plagued by European troubles, their grip was relinquished. The opening of the Suez Canal in 1869, improving access to European markets, boosted the economy. In 1898, after the United States defeated Spain at the Battle of Manila Bay, the Philippines were ceded to the United States. Although promised independence, the Philippines were not established as a republic until 1946, the procrastination of the US government and the islands' involvement in WWII causing the delay. In the 1970s a program of rapid economic development was launched. Faced with Communist guerrillas and Muslim separatists, and unable to run legally for president again, Marcos declared martial law in 1972, ruling by decree and becoming increasingly repressive. Although martial law was lifted in 1981, Marcos remained firmly in control until repercussions of the murder (1983) of opposition leader Benigno Aquino, Jr. and charges of election fraud forced him to flee the country in 1986. He was succeeded by Aquino's wife, Corazón.

PROFILE

Official name: Republic of the Philippines
Area: 115,830sq mi (300,000sq km)
Population: 47,720,000
Density: 412per sq mi (159per sq km)
Chief cities: Quezon City (capital); Manila; Cebu
Government: Head of State, President
Religion: Christian
Language: Pilipino, English (official)
Monetary unit: Peso
Gross national product: $28,110,000,000
Per capita income: $210
Industries (major products): petroleum products, tobacco products, plywood, veneers, paper
Agriculture (major products): rice, corn, coconuts, sugar cane, lumber, sweet potatoes
Minerals (major): silver, gold, copper, zinc
Trading Partners (major): Japan, United States

Philippine Sea, arm of the W Pacific Ocean lying E of the Philippine Islands, S of Japan, W of Mariana Islands, and NW of New Guinea and the Caroline Islands. The Philippine Sea lies in the Philippine Trench following the line of the E coast of the archipelago; S arm of the sea was site of US defeat of Japanese fleet June 19–20, 1944. Depth: (max.) 34,578ft (10,546m).

Philistines, a non-Semitic people who probably came to Philistia from Crete in about the 12th century BC.

Philodendron, genus of trailing house plant native to tropical America with shiny, heart-shaped leaves, sometimes split. Large-leaved, climbing tyƥes need support. Care: bright indirect light, well-watered soil (equal parts loam, peat moss, sand). Propagation is by stem cuttings. Height: 4in–6ft (10cm–1.8m). Family Araceae; genus *Philodendron.*

Philology, an older name for linguistics. It is the study of both language and literature. Besides phonetics, grammar, and the structure of language, philology includes textual criticism, etymology, art, archaeology, religion, and any system related to ancient or classical languages. In the 1700s Englishmen discovered that Hindustani resembled Latin and Greek and began the "comparative philology movement" to find the common root.

Philosophes, French term designating a group of 18th-century thinkers with diverse special interests who nevertheless shared a strong commitment to the ideals of the Enlightenment. These ideals included rationalism, toleration, secularization, and the practical improvement of the conditions of life. Voltaire, Hume, and Lessing were eminent philosophes. *See also* Enlightenment.

Philosophical Linguistics. *See* Linguistic Analysis.

Philosophy, term derived from a Greek word meaning "love of wisdom." Those ancient Greeks called philosophers sought wisdom in all fields—the structure of matter, the nature of the good, the reality of God. In modern times scholars specialize—physicists conduct experiments to identify the particles of matter, theologians study about God, philosophers still ponder about questions such as "What is good?" The range of interests still pursued by philosophers can be shown by listing major fields: metaphysics, the study of the first principles of reality; epistemology, the theory of knowledge; logic, the principles of inductive and deductive reasoning; ethics, the study of right and wrong; aesthetics, the study of what is beautiful. Historically, philosophy evolved from the classical, or the Greek and Roman, period characterized by a quest for the meaning of reality as exemplified in the philosophies of Socrates, Plato, Aristotle, and Plotinus. Early Christian thought, or medieval philosophy, explored the relationship between faith and reason under such teachers as St. Augustine and Thomas Aquinas. By the Renaissance period, modern philosophy began to take shape. Philosophers, such as René Descartes, Baruch Spinoza, John Locke, Immanuel Kant, Georg Hegel, John Stuart Mill, and Bertrand Russell, applied science to philosophy. *See also* Aesthetics; Metaphysics; Individual philosophers.

Phlebitis, inflammation of the wall of a vein, usually in the leg. It may be caused by infection, trauma, underlying disease, or by presence of varicose veins in the legs. Symptoms are pain, swelling, redness, and heat of the vein. Phlebitis may be long-lasting and complicated with blood clot. Treatment includes bed rest and anticoagulant therapy.

Phloem, vascular tissue for distributing food materials in plants. It consists mainly of elongated sieve tubes and parenchyma, sometimes with companion cells.

Phlogiston Theory, theory of combustion proposed in the 17th century by Johann Becher (1635–82) and popularized in the 18th century by Georg Stahl (1660–1734). It postulated that combustible materials contained an odorless, colorless, weightless material called phlogiston; combustion involved loss of this phlogiston and it thereby became dephlogisticated in turning to calx (ash). The theory was disproved by A.L. Lavoisier's (1743–94) discovery of the true nature of combustion.

Phlox, a genus of mostly perennial plants native to North America. The flowers are yellow, blue, purple, pink, red, or white. Height: to 5ft (1.5m). Family Polemoniaceae. The phlox family includes plants, shrubs, and small trees native to Eurasia and North America.

Phnom Penh, or **Phnum Penh,** capital city of Cambodia, in S Cambodia at junction of Mekong and Tonle Sab rivers. The city was the capital of the Khmers in 1434; its royal palace was erected 1813. It is now the site of an international airport and is an industrial center for regional products. The city was extensively damaged before Communist capture in 1975. The population was initially swelled by refugees and then drastically reduced as the new regime evacuated its inhabitants. Industries: rice milling, brewing, distilling, textiles, lumber. Founded 1371. Pop. 400,000.

Phoebe, several American tyrant flycatchers, including the black phoebe *(Sayornis nigricans),* found from California to South America. It has a white belly and lives near water, hawking insects in flight and from water surfaces. It lays its eggs (3–6) in a mud-and-foliage platform nest near a cave or bridge. Length: 6 in (15cm).

Phoenicia, ancient region of E Asia, along the E Mediterranean Sea coast; its great city-states included Tyre, Sidon, Tripoli, Byblos. It was founded *c.* 1600 BC; the Phoenicians were traders and colonizers by 1250 BC and by the 12th century BC, controlled the Mediterranean Sea trade; during the 6th century BC, Persia began to absorb Phoenicia, completing the process by Roman times. The Phoenicians originated an alphabet that was later developed by the Greeks; they were famous for their purple "Tyrian" dye and carved ivory.

Phoenix, capital city in SW central Arizona, on Salt River; largest city of Arizona; seat of Maricopa co. Development began with diversion of Salt River for irrigation in the 1880s; it was made territorial capital 1889. Completion of Roosevelt Dam (1911) revitalized farming in the area; it was made state capital 1912. It is site of Phoenix College (1920), Grand Canyon College (1949), Heard, Arizona, and Pueblo Grande museums. Industries: data processing, electronic research and production, tourism, aircraft, fabricated metals, machinery, textiles, clothing, food products. Founded 1870; inc. 1881. Pop. (1980) 764,911.

Phoneme, minimum unit of distinctive sound (phone); a speech sound distinguishing meaning. The phoneme "p" distinguishes "tap" from "tab." A phoneme may include a phonetic variant, such as "th," as long as it is perceived as one sound. As long as there is no contrast in sound it is a single phoneme.

Phonetics, the science of speech sounds and the symbols by which they are shown in writing. It is based on a study of parts of the body and their position when making a particular sound. Speech sounds are classified by manner of articulation and point of articulation, the loudness or stress, and pitch or tone.

Phonology, the study of the nature, production, and reception of speech sounds (phonetics) and the functioning of speech sounds in their linguistic system. The sound patterns that occur in language and the changes that they undergo are studied, and changes in the phonemic system are recorded.

Phosphate, a name for numerous chemical compounds related to phosphoric acid (H_3PO_4). One group is composed of salts with the phosphate ion, the hydrogen phosphate ion, or the dihydrogen phosphate ion, and positively charged ions (eg those of sodium). Another group is composed of esters in which organic combining groups (eg ethyl) replace the hydrogen atoms.

Phosphor, substance that is capable of luminescence (storing energy and later releasing it as light). They are of two main types: the zinc sulfide phosphors, as used on cathode-ray tubes, and the oxygen type, as used on fluorescent light tubes. Zinc sulfide is often mixed with cadmium sulfide and a small quantity of metallic phosphates, silicates, borates, or tungstates.

Phosphorescence, a glow of light produced by some substances after having been illuminated or, in biology, production of light in an organism without noticeable heat. *See also* Bioluminescence.

Phosphoric Acid, group of acids the chief forms of which are orthophosphoric acid (H_3PO_4), metaphosphoric acid (HPO_3), and pyrophosphoric acid ($H_4P_2O_7$). Orthophosphoric acid is a colorless deliquescent substance obtained by the action of sulfuric acid on phosphate rock and used in fertilizers, soaps, and detergents. Metaphosphoric acid is obtained by heating orthophosphoric acid and is used as a dehydrating agent. Pyrophosphoric acid is formed from phosphorus pentoxide and water and is used as a catalyst and in metallurgy.

Phosphorus, common nonmetallic element (symbol P) of group V of the periodic table, discovered (1669) by the alchemist Hennig Brandt. It occurs, as phosphates, in many minerals; apatite is the chief source. The element is used in making phosphoric acid for detergents and fertilizers (phosphorus is an essential element for plant growth). Small amounts are used in rat poison and in matches. Phosphorus has several allotropes including the highly reactive white phosphorus and the more stable form, red phosphorus. Properties: at. no. 15; at. wt. 30.9738; sp gr 1.82 (white), 2.20 (red); melt. pt. 111.38°F (44.1°C) (white); boil. pt. 536 °F (280°C) (white); most common isotope P^{31} (100%).

Photocopying, the process of producing copies of drawings or written material by the use of light, heat, chemicals, or electrostatic charges. The devices used usually employ diffusion transfer or dye line processes. Diffusion transfer involves a master copy made by typing or drawing on translucent paper which is then placed on sensitized negative paper and exposed to light. Negatives are placed in contact with positive transfer and fed into the developer. When peeled apart the image is transferred to the positive paper. Dye line requires a translucent original and uses only one sheet of sensitized paper.

Photoelectric Cell, or photocell, type of electric cell whose operation depends upon the extent to which it is exposed to light. Formerly consisting of an electron tube with a photosensitive cathode, they are now almost exclusively made of light-sensitive semiconductors. They are used as switches (electric eyes), devices to measure light intensity (lightmeters), or as power sources. *See also* Solar Cell.

Philodendron

Phnom Penh, Cambodia

Phoebe

Photoelectric Effect, liberation of electrons from matter by light, ultraviolet radiation, X rays, or gamma rays falling on the surface. The effect can only be explained by the quantum theory. Photons in the incident radiation are absorbed by atoms in the substance and enable electrons to escape by transferring the requisite amount of energy to them.

Photoengraving, a process of preparing illustrations for letterpress printing in which their image is transferred by photography upon metal or plastic. It includes two steps: the preparation of a photographic negative copy of the material to be reproduced, and the making of a positive printing plate. The negatives are made on sensitized films with a copy camera which can produce an image of any size desired. Plates are made of zinc, copper, magnesium, or nylon coated with a photosensitive solution. The light passing through clear sections of the negative affects the coating and makes it insoluble in water. After exposure the plates are washed, leaving an image formed by the insoluble portions. The nonprinting surface is then etched with an acid.

Photographic Memory. See Eidetic Imagery.

Photography, process of obtaining a permanent record of an object, either in black-and-white or in color, on treated paper or film. In black-and-white photography a camera is used to expose a film to an image of the object to be photographed for a controlled time. The film is covered on one side with an emulsion containing silver bromide or chloride. The effect of the exposure is to make the silver compound easily reduced to metallic silver when treated with a developer. The action of the developer is to produce a black deposit of metallic silver particles on those parts of the film that were exposed to light, thus providing a "negative" image. After fixing (in "hypo") and washing, the negative can be printed by placing it over a piece of sensitized paper and exposing it to light so that the silver salts in the paper are affected in the same way as those in the original film. The dark portions of the negative let through the least light and the image on the paper is thus reversed back to a positive. Color photography works on a similar, but more complex, process. *See also* Camera.

Photon, quantum of electromagnetic radiation, which can be considered as streams of photons, the energy of the photons equaling the frequency of the radiation multiplied by the Planck constant. Absorption of photons by atoms and molecules of matter can cause excitation or ionization. A photon may be classified as a stable elementary particle of zero mass, zero charge, and spin 1 traveling at the velocity of light. It is its own antiparticle. Virtual photons are thought to be continuously exchanged between charged particles and thus to be the carrier of the electromagnetic force.

Photosphere, surface of the sun, which radiates the light and heat produced in the solar interior. Having a general temperature of 6,000K, it presents a granular appearance, often disturbed by sunspots, faculae, and associated transient phenomena. *See also* Sun.

Photosynthesis, chemical process occurring in green plants that manufactures food from water and carbon dioxide by using energy absorbed from sunlight. The reactions take place almost instantaneously in the chloroplasts—chlorophyll-containing bodies in the leaf cells. During the first part of the process, light is absorbed by the chlorophyll and splits water into hydrogen and oxygen. The hydrogen attaches to a carrier molecule and the oxygen is set free. The hydrogen and light energy build a supply of cellular chemical energy (adenosine triphosphate, ATP). Then the hydrogen and

ATP convert the carbon dioxide into sugar (including glucose) and starch. Photosynthetic equation: $6CO_2 + 6H_2O + \text{light energy} \rightarrow C_6H_{12}O_6 + 6O_2$.

Phototropism, or **Heliotropism,** plant growth in response to a light stimulus that increases cell growth on the shaded side of plant. Leaves and stems respond positively to light and roots respond negatively or not at all. Examples include indoor plants leaning toward windows; leaves growing at right angles to light; and leaf positioning so overlapping occurs as little as possible.

Phrygia, ancient region in central Asia, generally corresponding to modern central Turkey. It was originally settled by Balkans *c.* 13th century BC; slaves were exported to Greece; art and culture peaked *c.* 600 BC; it was ruled by Lydia 7th century BC, and by Persia 546 BC; N Phrygia passed to Galatia 3rd century BC and the remainder came under Roman rule 133 BC; it was associated in legend with Midas and Gordius.

Phylacteries, two leather boxes containing scriptural passages worn by adult Jewish males in Orthodox and Conservative services. These are ceremonially put on with leather straps for certain ritual prayers. Reform Judaism discarded their use.

Phylloxera, or **Grape Phylloxera,** a small yellowish insect of the order Homoptera that is a pest on grape plants in Europe and western United States. It attaches to the leaves and roots and sucks the plant's fluid, resulting in galls and nodules and leading to eventual rotting of the plant. The complex life cycle includes wingless stages that reproduce parthenogenetically. Females lay eggs that survive the winter. Species *Phylloxera vitifoliae.* Family Phylloxeridae.

Phylum, major group within the animal kingdom or a subdivision in the plant kingdom. It is comprised of a diverse group of organisms with a fundamental characteristic in common. For example, fish and humans are in the phylum Chordata because they both have a notochord.

Physical Chemistry, study of the physical changes associated with chemical reactions and the relationship between physical properties and chemical composition. The main branches are thermodynamics, concerned with the changes of energy in a physical system; chemical kinetics, concerned with rates of reaction; and molecular and atomic structure. Other topics included are electrochemistry, thermochemistry, and some aspects of nuclear physics, radiation physics, and combustion chemistry.

Physical Units, units used in measuring physical quantities. In specifying a unit it is necessary to define an instance of that physical quantity and a way in which it can be compared in making a measurement. For example, the kilogram unit of mass is defined as the mass of a specified block of platinum. Other masses are measured by comparing them, directly or indirectly, with this by weighing. Units are of two types: base units, which like the kilogram have fundamental definitions, and derived units which are defined in terms of these base units. Various systems of units exist, founded on certain base units. They include Imperial units (foot, pound, second), CGS units (centimeter, gram, second), and MKS units (meter, kilogram, second). For all scientific purposes SI units have been adopted (Système International d'Unites), which has seven base units: meter (length), kilogram (mass), second (time), ampere (electric current), kelvin (temperature), candela (luminous intensity), and mole (amount of substance). Derived units are expressed in terms of

these: for example the newton (force) is $1 kg\, m\, s^{-2}$, and the pascal (pressure) is $1 kg\, m^{-1} s^{-2}$.

Physics, study and understanding of natural phenomena in terms of energy and matter. The scientific knowledge thus acquired is put to use by the technologist and engineer. The forms of energy studied include heat, light, mechanical, electrical, sound, and nuclear. The properties of matter itself and the interaction of these different energy forms with matter are also part of physics. It was thought that the properties of matter could be described completely by Newton's laws of motion and gravitation. Although large-scale systems are adequately explained so, classical physics must be replaced by quantum theory (1900) to describe the properties of atoms, etc, and by relativity (1905, 1915) to describe gravitational and very high velocity events.

Physiocrats, school of 18th-century French economists, led by François Quesnay, that attempted to discover basic economic laws and to combat the mercantilists. Their contributions include the *Tableau économique,* which treated the French economy as a system of flows and clearly showed that money spent initially generated successive multiple spending rounds, and the expansion of the idea of wealth to include the "surplus" produced by the land (as opposed to the mercantilists' concept of wealth as silver and gold). *See also* Mercantilism.

Physiology, branch of biology concerned with physical and chemical functions necessary to maintain life. Vast in scope, it includes the study of single cells as well as multicellular organisms. *See also* Biochemistry.

Phytohormone. See Plant Hormone.

Pi (π), symbol used for the ratio of the circumference of any circle to its diameter; its value is irrational, $3.14159 \ldots$; is a reasonable approximation.

Piacenza, city in N Italy, 40mi (64km) SE of Milan; capital of Piacenza prov. It was the terminus of Aemilian Way 187 BC; 12th-century member of Lombard League; given to Farnese family 1545 by Pope Paul III; joined kingdom of Italy 1860; site of 12th–13th century Lombard Romanesque cathedral, uncompleted 16th-century Farnese palace. Industries: chemicals, machinery, food products. Founded 218 BC by Romans. Pop. 109,302.

Piaget, Jean (1896–1980), Swiss psychologist. He was the director (1929–1980) of the Institut Jean-Jacques Rousseau in Geneva. He spent many years developing and writing about a comprehensive theory of the intellectual development of children. His theory describes a number of stages of thinking that children go through as they grow from early infancy to adulthood. Largely ignored in the United States prior to the 1950s, he is now universally recognized as a major figure in contemporary psychology. Major works include *The Origins of Intelligence in Children* (1952) and *Six Psychological Studies* (1968).

Piano, or pianoforte, major keyboard stringed instrument of Western music. The piano ranges 7½ octaves with 88 keys; hammers strike metal strings, one to three for each tone. The grand piano, like the harpsichord, has a horizontal frame, the box-shaped upright piano and smaller spinet have vertical frames. Of three pedals, left (soft) acts to mute, right (damper) lifts pads from strings prolonging vibrations, and center (sustaining) modifies dampening effect in lower register.

The basic tool of composers and conductors, it is a versatile, expressive, and popular solo instrument. It also used for accompaniment and with all types of orchestras and is prominent in jazz band rhythm sections. Evolving from the harpsichord and clavichord, but with improved dynamic possibilities, the earliest pianos were built by Bartolomeo Christofori in Florence (1709). They were in general use by the late 18th century. Mozart and Haydn were the first major piano composers; Beethoven developed orchestral sonority and variety of color; Schumann, Chopin, and Liszt composed and performed great romantic piano music in the 19th century.

Piazzi, Giuseppi (1746–1826), Italian astronomer, known for his discovery of the first known asteroid, Ceres (1801). He also founded the observatory of Palermo and there produced a catalog of 7,646 stars (1814). Piazzi demonstrated that most stars are in motion relative to the sun.

Pica, abnormal craving for unnatural foods, such as chalk or ashes. It occurs both in man and animals, usually those who are suffering from nutritional deficiencies.

Picardy, region and former province in N France, bounded by Strait of Dover, Artois and Flanders (N), Champagne (E), Île-de-France (S), Normandy (SW), and English Channel (W); includes Somme, Oise, and Aisne depts.; capital was Amiens. It was a French province 1477 until French Revolution, when all provinces were replaced by smaller departments; scene of heavy fighting in WWI. Area is predominantly farmlands (wheat, sugar beets, potatoes); major centers are seaports of Boulogne-sur-Mer and Calais. Industries: tourism, fishing, textiles.

Picaresque Novel, novel form relating the adventures of a rogue (Spanish picaro), usually in episodic narrative form. It was partly a reaction against idealistic tales of chivalry and romance and usually covered a cross section of society. The first novel in this genre is the Spanish *Lazarillo de Tormes* (1554).

Picasso, Pablo (Pablo Ruiz y Picasso) (1881–1973), Spanish artist. He was a founder of the abstract movement in 20th-century art. In 1900 Picasso went to Paris and there executed the works of his Blue Period (1900–05), a term that referred to both the color and mood of his work. During this time he painted mostly outcasts of society, emphasizing in subject the isolation depicted in style ("The Old Guitarist," 1903). He moved toward a more vigorous style in 1905. "Les Demoiselles d'Avignon" (1906–07) was his first work, dubbed Cubist by critics who stressed the angular, boxlike structure style. "Ambroise Vollard" (1909–10) was a further development of the style, marked by greater balance, refinement, and subtlety. By 1910 Cubism was a strongly established style with many practitioners, including Georges Braque, who worked closely with Picasso. Together they developed the technique of pasting cut materials onto canvas, which became known as collage ("Still Life," 1911–12). Further development of the collage effect, utilizing only the painted surface, was evidenced in "Three Musicians," a masterpiece of collage Cubism. Picasso's simultaneously developed Neoclassic style ("Mother and Child," 1921–22) merged with the cubist in "Three Dancers" (1925) and was extended in "Guernica" (1937), which depicts the agonies and horrors of war in a powerful manner.

Piccolo, woodwind musical instrument of the flute family, but half its size, and pitched one octave higher. It is played the same way, by blowing across the mouth hole and fingering the keys. It has a bright, penetrating tone and is used in symphony orchestras.

Pickerel, freshwater sport and commercial fish found in E United States. Related to the pike, it has a shovel-shaped bill and elongated body. Length: 12–24in (30.5–61cm). Species include the grass pickerel *Esox americanus* and the chain pickerel, *E. niger.* Family Esocidae.

Pickerel Frog, true frog native to S Canada and E United States in streams, bogs, and meadows. It has distinctive rows of dark, rectangular spots on its back and an orange undersurface on hind legs. Its skin secretion is lethal to other frogs and irritating to humans. Length: to 3.5in (9cm). Family Ranidae; species *Rana palustris. See also* Frog.

Pico Rivera, city in S California, SE of Los Angeles. Industries: chemicals, automobiles, furniture, toys. Formed by union of Pico and Rivera communities; inc. 1958. Pop. (1980) 53,459.

Pictography, system of using pictures to communicate ideas, often used with ideographs. These drawings became very stylized, but it is not considered writing because it represents the object, not the word for the object.

Picts, ancient people of Scotland. First mentioned (AD 297) by Eumenius as invaders of Roman Britain, they had a united kingdom extending between Caithness and Fife by the 7th century and adopted Christianity. In 843, Kenneth I of Dalriada united the Pict lands with his own kingdom and formed Scotland.

Pidgin, a simplified form of a language, usually containing no more than 1,500 words, used for communication between people who do not speak the same language. Most pidgins in use today are based on English, French, Spanish, or Portuguese, with a certain number of native words added. By far the most widely spoken pidgin is the Pidgin English of Papua New Guinea, which is one of the official languages of the country.

Pieplant. *See* Rhubarb.

Pierce, Franklin (1804–69), 14th president of the United States (1853–57), b. Hillsborough, N.H. He graduated from Bowdoin College in 1824, and was admitted to the bar in 1827. In 1834 he married Jane Appleton; they had three sons. The son of a Jacksonian Democrat who was twice governor, Franklin Pierce became a member of the New Hampshire legislature in 1829. After serving in both houses of Congress, he retired (at 36) to a successful practice in Concord, N.H.

Known for his pro-slavery views and for his support of the Compromise of 1850, Pierce was acceptable to the southern Democrats in 1852. He was nominated for the presidency on the 49th ballot and went on to win the election.

As president in the turbulent years before the Civil War, Pierce tried to mediate the differences between North and South. The Gadsden Purchase was made during his administration. His support of the Kansas-Nebraska Act (1854) lost him most northern support, and the Ostend Manifesto (1854) further eroded his popularity; he was not renominated by the Democrats in 1856.

Career: New Hampshire legislature, 1829–33; US House of Representatives, 1833–37; US Senate, 1837–42; president, 1853–57. *See also* Compromise of 1850; Gadsden Purchase; Kansas-Nebraska Act;

Piero della Francesca (Piero de' Franceschi) (*c.* 1429–92), Italian painter. An early group of his frescoes in the Este Palace (1450) have been lost. His early work was influenced by Sienese, Florentine, and Umbrian painting. Two other outstanding early works are the "Flagellation," which demonstrates his spatial organization, and "Baptism of Christ" (*c.* 1450–55). His well-known works include his series of frescoes, the "Legend of the True Cross," in the choir of S. Francesco in Arezzo (completed *c.* 1459) and "Madonna del Parto" for his mother's tomb.

Pierre, capital city of South Dakota, in central South Dakota, on Missouri River opposite Fort Pierre; seat of Hughes co. Originally Aricara Indian capital, it developed as trade area 1822–55, steamboat head for Black Hills gold market 1876–85, and railroad trading and shipping center 1880; made state capital 1889. It is site of capitol (1910), Soldiers and Sailors Memorial Building. Its economy is based on state government and agriculture (grain, cattle). Inc. 1883. Pop. (1980) 11,973.

Piers Plowman (*c.* 1362–92), poem attributed to William Langland. Three different versions survive of this moral allegory on the theme "How may I save my soul?" In a dream the poet meets representatives of medieval humanity, personifications of vices and virtues, and finally Piers Plowman, a Christlike figure.

Pietermaritzburg, city in the Republic of South Africa, 40mi (64km) W of Durban, on the Umsunduzi River; became capital of Natal 1843 when the province was annexed to Great Britain; site of Fort Napier (1843), Natal University (1909), teachers' college, technical institute, Voortrekker Museum (1912), Natal museum (1903), art gallery, botanical gardens. Industries: metal, furniture, shoes, tiles, rubber, bricks. Founded 1838 by Boers. Pop. 158,921.

Pietists, religious group that began as a movement within the Lutheran Church in Germany. Led by Philipp Jacob Spener and August Hermann Francke, the Pietists devoted themselves to the "practice of piety." Pietism, which was strongest during the first half of the 18th century, influenced other Protestant sects, such as the Moravian Brethren and Methodism.

Piezoelectricity, electric charge produced by certain asymmetric crystals when they are subjected to pressure. A crystal of quartz or Rochelle salt will produce positive and negative charges on opposing faces when subjected to pressure; the signs of the charges are reversed when the pressure is changed to tension. This property is used in crystal oscillators and pick-ups for record players.

Pig, any of numerous species and varieties of domestic and wild swine of the family Suidae. The male is generally called a boar; the female, a sow. A castrated boar is usually known as a hog. It is generally a massive, short-legged omnivore with a thick skin bearing short bristles. Wild pigs include the warthog, wild boar, bush pig, and babirusa.

Pigeon, also often called dove, any of a large family (Columbidae) of wild and domestic birds found throughout temperate and tropical parts of the world, but concentrated in southern Asia and the Australian region. Many have long been domesticated, used for food, and some for carrying messages. Generally less than 18in (46cm) long, pigeons have small heads, short necks, plump bodies, and scaly legs and feet. Loosely but thickly plumaged, they may be brown, gray, white, blue, green, yellow, or orange. They usually feed on seeds, fruits, grain, sometimes on insects, and drink in a unique way by sticking their short slender bill into water and sucking water up. Both sexes typically build a flimsy stick nest in a tree or on the ground, on a ledge, or in a hole, and both incubate the white eggs until the young, or squabs, hatch, at which time they are fed pigeon's milk, a cheesy substance secreted by crop of both sexes. Among well-known pigeons are rock pigeon, ground dove, mourning dove, carrier pigeon, and homing pigeon.

Pigeon Hawk, small brownish or grayish falcon. Species *Falco columbarius. See also* Merlin.

Piggyback Plant, widespreading house plant native to North America. It has long-stemmed, hairy leaves. New plants grow in the leaf bases. Care: bright indirect light, moist soil (equal parts loam, peat moss, sand). Propagation is by leaves with plantlets. Height: to 8in (20cm). Family Saxifragaceae; species *Tolmiea menziesii.*

Pigment, colored insoluble substance used to impart color to an object and incorporated for this purpose into paints, printing inks, plastics, cosmetics, floor coverings, etc. They generally function by absorbing light, though some modern luminescent pigments emit colored light. White pigments include titanium and zinc oxides; black pigments are usually based on carbon black. Colored pigments may be either organic or inorganic compounds.

Pigmentation, in anatomy, the coloration of tissues by pigments. In humans, the pigmented areas are skin, hair, and iris of the eye, with the pigments melanin and carotene, combined with the body's hemoglobin, giving the color.

Pigou, Arthur Cecil (1877–1959), English economist, best known for defending the position of classical economists in the face of the Keynesian revolution in the 1930s. According to the classical economists, supply creates its own demand. However, according to Keynes, effective aggregate demand is the immediate determinant of current output (supply). The Pigou effect in economics is concerned with showing that an unregulated economy has a "natural" tendency to gravitate toward full employment. Economists still debate the accuracy of Pigou's position.

Pika, short-haired relative of rabbits that cures hay and stores it underground for winter use. The 12 species live in cold regions of Asia and W North America. Most are gray. Length: under 8in (203mm). Genus *Ochotona.*

Pike, Zebulon Montgomery (1779–1813), US explorer, b. Lamberton, N.J. He explored widely in the newly purchased Louisiana Territory, seeking the source of the Mississippi River (1805–06). He later led expeditions to Colorado and New Mexico (1806–07), where he discovered Pikes Peak. He wrote *Account of the Expeditions to the Sources of the Mississippi and Through the Western Parts of Louisiana* (1810), which proved a valuable source of information.

Pike, freshwater fish found in E North America and parts of Europe and Asia. A popular sport and commercial fish, it has a shovel-shaped bill, elongated body, and mottled coloration. It is a long-living fish (40–50 years). Length: to 54in (137.2cm); weight: to 46lb (20.9kg). Family Esocidae, species northern pike *Esox lucius,* Amur pike *Esox reichteri.*

Pike-Perch, freshwater food and game fish of North America, closely related to the walleye and sauger. A dark olive and brass mottled fish, it has an elongated

Franklin Pierce

Zebulon Pike

Thomas Pinckney

body and large head and mouth. Length: to 3ft (91.4cm); weight: to 25lb (11.3kg). Family Percidae; species *Stizostedion vitreum*.

Pikes Peak, isolated mountain peak in E central Colorado, in the front range of the Rocky Mt system, 10mi (16km) W of Colorado Springs; tourist area, noted for its view. Discovered 1806 by Zebulon Pike, for whom it is named. Height: 14,110ft (4,304m).

Pilate, Pontius, Roman governor of Judea when Jesus Christ was crucified. Pilate was made procurator of Judea, Samaria, and Idumea in AD 26 and earned a reputation for arrogance and cruelty. Pilate passed the death sentence on Jesus but denied responsibility for the death. He may have died in 39. The New Testament Gospels tell of Pilate's role in condemning Jesus (Matthew 27; Mark 15; Luke 23; John 18–19).

Pilchard, marine, schooling, herringlike food fish found along European and Australian coasts. The young are sometimes called sardines. Length: less than 18in (45.7cm). Family Clupeidae, Species *Sardinia pilchardus*.

Pilcomayo, river in S central South America; rises in E Andes Mts in W central Bolivia; flows SE to form Argentina-Paraguay border; empties into the Paraguay River at Port Asunción. Chief tributary is Pilaya River in Bolivia. Length: approx. 700mi (1,127km).

Pilgrimage of Grace (1536), uprising of English Roman Catholics protesting against the enclosure movement and dissolution of the monasteries following the abolition of papal supremacy in England. After a small rising in Lincoln had failed, Robert Aske, the leader, and his followers occupied York and then marched to Doncaster with 35,000 men. The duke of Norfolk, King Henry VIII's emissary, held talks with Aske, and he dispersed his men. Further minor outbreaks were suppressed, and Aske was executed (1537).

Pilgrims, group of colonists who were the first settlers of New England. Most were English separatists who withdrew from the Anglican Church and migrated to Holland. Economic difficulties forced a group of Pilgrims under William Bradford and William Brewster to obtain a land patent from the Virginia Company of London to emigrate to Virginia. The colonists, on the *Mayflower,* landed instead in Massachusetts (1620), establishing the Plymouth Colony. *See also* Mayflower Compact; Plymouth Colony.

Pilgrim's Progress, The (1678), allegory by John Bunyan recounting the perilous and adventurous journey of Christian from the doomed City of Destruction to the Celestial City. Full of allegorical characters and situations, the book also includes a sequel relating the same journey made by Christiana, Christian's wife, and her children. While sustaining its moral, Puritan standpoint, the book is remarkable for its simple style and has greatly influenced English prose.

Pillars of Hercules, in Greek mythology, two promontories in the Mediterranean. They were called Calpe and Abyla in ancient times. They are usually identified as Gibraltar in Europe and Mt Acha (Mt Hacho) in Africa. According to some legends they were joined together until Hercules tore them apart in order to reach Cadiz.

Pilot Fish, marine fish found in warm seas, often around sharks and ships. A blue fish with 5–7 dark side bar markings and a white tail, it feeds on food and

parasites near sharks. Length: to 2ft (61cm). Family Carangidae; species *Naucrates ductor.*

Pilot Whale, or blackfish, small, black, toothed whale distributed in nonpolar seas. They are trained to perform in captivity. Length: to 28ft (8.5m). Genus *Globicephala. See also* Dolphin.

Pilsudski, Józef (1867–1935), Polish general and statesman. He joined the Young Poles; the Russians imprisoned him in Siberia for five years (1887–92). He became a leader of the Polish Socialist party in 1892, was arrested but escaped to England (1902) and formed a secret, private army of 10,000 anti-Russian Poles to fight for independence from Russia. He fought on the side of Austria against the Russians (1914–16); the Germans interned him when he refused to fight further because of their interference. After the war he was hailed as a national hero when he proclaimed the Polish Republic in 1919. With French help he defended Warsaw from the Russians in 1920. From 1926 until his death in 1935 he was dictator of Poland.

Piltdown Man, name given to fossil skull found in Sussex, England (1909–15), believed for years to be the "missing link" between apes and men. In 1953 modern tests conclusively exposed it as a fake.

Pima, a tribe of North American Indians speaking the Uto-Aztekan tongue, and closely related to the Papago. They occupied the Gila and Salt river valleys in S Arizona, where some 8,000 still reside today. They are the descendents of the ancient Hohokam people.

Pimento, a tropical evergreen tree *(Pimento diocia)* of the myrtle family (Myrtaceae), native to the West Indies and Central America. The nearly ripe berries are dried in the sun to furnish the aromatic and pungent spice allspice used in baking. The tree grows to 30ft (9m). *See also* Allspice.

Pimpernel, or shepherd's clock, small, trailing annual plant of the Old World and naturalized in England and North America. The scarlet, white, or blue flowers are born at the leaf axils and close during cloudy weather and at night. Family Primulaceae; species *Anagallis arvensis.*

Pinckney, Charles (1757–1824), US statesman, b. Charleston, S.C. He was a member of the Continental Congress (1784–87) and played a major role at the Constitutional Convention (1785–87) suggesting a number of provisions that became part of the Constitution. He later served as South Carolina's governor (1789–92, 1796–98) and as a Democrat in the US Senate (1798–1801). As minister to Spain (1801–05), at the time of the Louisiana Purchase, he failed in his attempts to acquire Florida for the United States. He served again as governor (1806–08), and in the House of Representatives (1819–21).

Pinckney, Charles Cotesworth (1746–1825) American patriot and political figure, b. Charleston, S.C. The brother of Thomas Pinckney, Charles was a member of the first provincial congress (1775) and served as a Continental officer and aide to Gen. George Washington during the Revolution. As a delegate to the Constitutional Convention (1787), he supported the ratification of the Constitution. He was appointed minister to France in 1796 but was not recognized by the French government. He returned home (1797) after negotiations with France were terminated during the scandalous XYZ Affair. He ran unsuccessfully as the Federalist candidate for vice president in 1800 and for president in 1804 and 1808.

Pinckney, Thomas (1750–1828), US soldier and diplomat, b. Charleston, S.C. A Revolutionary War veteran, he served as South Carolina governor (1787–89) and minister to Great Britain (1792–96). He went as a commissioner to Spain (1794–95); he negotiated Pinckney's Treaty, which marked the southern and western boundary lines between the United States and Spain's New World territories. It also opened up the Mississippi River to US boats. He was the Federalist vice-presidential candidate (1796) and served in the US House of Representatives (1796–1801). During the War of 1812, he was a major general.

Pincushion Cactus, cactus native to W United States, Mexico, and Cuba. It has round or oval globular stems, large brilliantly colored flowers, and bright edible berries. Diameter: 0.5in–2ft (1–61cm). Family Cactaceae; genus *Coryphantha. See also* Cactus.

Pindar (*c.*522–440 BC), Greek lyric poet. Few of his poems exist in complete form—among them the *Triumphal Odes*, written in honor of the Panhellenic games. Noble by birth, he sometimes revealed his aristocratic attitudes in his poems. His style seemed unorganized, as he rushed through his work in order to develop all of his ideas. He used a variety of meters and wrote all forms of choral lyrics, in colorful language. Much respected by his peers, he was later imitated by Horace, Dryden, and Swift.

Pine, evergreen trees mostly native to cooler temperate regions of the Northern Hemisphere; several grow in warm climates. They have scalelike deciduous leaves or evergreen needlelike clusters. The flowers are catkinlike stalks or pine cones. Many are valued for soft wood, oils, and resins. Family Pinaceae; genus *Pinus. See also* Conifers; Evergreen.

Pineal Body, small organ attached to the lower surface of the brain, the function of which is unknown. In humans, the pineal gland degenerates in childhood and is represented only by fibrous tissue in the adult. In some lizards it forms a "third eye" during embryonic stages. Evidence suggests that the pineal may be an endocrine gland.

Pineapple, common name for a tropical herbaceous perennial and its fruit, native to South America and cultivated commercially first in 1850 in the Azores. Grown also in the United States, Cuba, Mexico, Southeast Asia, South Africa, and Australia, the plant has a short, stout stem bearing stiff fleshy leaves and grows to 2–4ft (0.6–1.2m). The fruit is eaten fresh or canned or made into juice. Family Bromeliaceae; species *Ananas comosus.*

Pine Bluff, commercial city in SE central Arkansas, 43mi (69km) SE of Little Rock; seat of Jefferson co, Industries: cotton, textiles, lumber products, chemicals. Founded 1818 as Mount Marie, renamed 1832; inc. 1839. Pop. (1980) 56,576.

Pine Nut, the edible seed obtained from any of several species of low-growing pines called piñon pines (eg *Pinus edulis, P. parryana*) of W North America. It was collected by American Indians as a valuable food resource and is now used in confectionery.

Pine Snake, common, harmless snake found in pine barrens and dry areas of the United States. It is black and white or brown with a faded pattern. Length: to 5.5ft (168cm). Family Colubridae; species *Pituophis melanoleucus. See also* Bull Snake.

Pink, common name for the several genera of the pink family, especially the genus *Dianthus* of over 300 species, found chiefly in the Mediterranean region. Primarily short herbaceous perennials, many are hardy evergreens with showy flowers. The stems are often woody at the base, leaves are simple and usually opposite, and the radially symmetrical flowers are usually bisexual. The Deptford pink, maiden pink, Cheddar pink, and proliferous pink grow wild in Great Britain. A few other species, including clove pink and garden pink, have been naturalized in the United States. The florists' carnation is a modification of the clove pink. Family Caryophyllaceae. *See also* Carnation.

Pinnipedia, meat-eating aquatic mammals formerly classified as carnivores. Comprised of eared seals (Family Otariidae), including fur seals and sea lions; earless, true, or hair seals (Family Phocidae); and the walrus (Family Odobenidae).

Pinochle, card game for two to four players with a 48-card deck made up of two each of nine through ace from each suit. With 3 players, each receives 15 cards, with the remaining 3 turned face down on the table. Players, in turn, then bid for the three cards. The bidding usually starts at 300 points. The cards rank ace, 10, king, queen, jack, and 9. Points are awarded according to runs (a sequence from ace to jack), marriages (king and queen of a suit), four of any rank (except 10s and 9s), and the jack of diamonds and queen of spades (a pinochle). After each player lays the cards he is going to declare as points face up on the table, the bidder "buries" three cards from his hand. Tricks are then collected, and the bidder, through the points he originally declared and those he wins during the course of the game, must at least reach the amount he bid.

Pinocytosis, the taking up of fluid by living cells. Rather than passing through the cell membrane as individual molecules, a droplet becomes bound or absorbed on the membrane which forms a pocket and pinches off to form a vesicle in the cytoplasm.

Piñon, or Mexican stone pine, evergreen tree native to Mexico and SW United States. It has large, edible seeds (pine nuts). Height: to 25ft (7.6m). Family Pinaceae; species *Pinus cembroides.*

Pinter, Harold (1930–), English playwright. He was an actor under the name of David Baron and played repertory. His first play, *The Room* (1957), was followed by such other plays as *The Birthday Party* (1958), *The Caretaker* (1960), *The Homecoming* (1965), *Old Times* (1970), *No Man's Land* (1975), and *Betrayal* (1980). Most of his plays juxtaposed farcical dialogue with an evocation of terror, called by critics the "comedy of menace." He also wrote extensively for radio and television as well as for films.

Pinworm, or seatworm, a tiny worm, which upon infection by ingestion of fecally contaminated material, dwells in the small intestine. Itching in the anal region is a common symptom. Worms can occasionally lodge in the appendix causing symptoms similar to acute appendicitis. Pinworms can be treated with piperazine.

Pion, elementary particle (symbol π) that is a meson. There are three types, forming a nuclear multiplet (triplet). The charged pions, π^+ and π^-, have equal mass, about 280 times the electron mass, and are antiparticles of each other; the neutral π°, of slightly lower mass, is its own antiparticle. All have zero spin. Charged pions decay into muons and muon neutrinos; the π° decays into photons. Virtual pions are thought to be exchanged between nucleons bound together by strong interaction. *See also* Hadron.

Pipefish, marine fish found in the shallow warm and temperate waters of the Atlantic and Pacific. Closely related to the seahorse, it has a pencillike body covered with bony rings. Its mouth is at the end of a long snout. The male incubates the young in a brood pouch. Length: to 23in (58.4cm). Family Syngnathidae; species include *Syngnathus fuscus.*

Pipestone, or **Catlinite,** a pink stone carved by Plains Indians into ceremonial pipes. The name catlinite is from George Catlin (the US artist famous for his paintings of Indians). The stone, found at the Pipestone National Monument in SW Minnesota, is reserved for the Indians who quarry it under special permits.

Pipit, two small North American sparrowlike songbirds that frequent wetlands and meadows, often near large animals, feeding on insects. They have a straight beak, short tail, elongated hind claw, and are protectively colored. Nesting on the ground, the male feeds the female while she incubates the blotched whitish eggs. Family Motacillidae; genus *Anthus.*

Pipsissewa, evergreen shrub native to E North America and N central Eurasia. It has pink or white flowers and jagged leaves. Height: 6–12in (15–30cm). Family Ericaceae; species *Chimpaphila umbellata.*

Piraeus, seaport city in E central Greece, on Saronic Gulf; capital of Piraeus dept. and chief port of Athens. City was besieged by Sulla 86 BC; modern development began after Greece achieved independence (19th century). The ancient Long Walls connected it with Athens; preceded Salamis as Athens' naval and maritime headquarters (480 BC). Industries: shipbuilding, chemicals, textiles. Planned *c.* 490 BC by Themistocles, city was built *c.* 450 BC by Hippodamus of Miletus. Pop. 186,223.

Pirandello, Luigi (1867–1936), Italian author of naturalistic plays, novels, and short stories. His work, expressing his philosophy of disillusionment and uncertainty, was widely translated. He won the Nobel Prize for literature in 1934. His plays include *Six Characters in Search of an Author* (1921), *Henry IV* (1922), and *As You Desire Me* (1930). His novels include *The Late Mattia Pascal* (1923) and *The Young and the Old* (1928).

Piranha, or **Piraya,** vicious, freshwater bony fish found in tropical rivers of South America. It has blunt, powerful jaws, and sharp teeth. It usually travels and attacks in schools. Length: to 2ft (61cm). Family Serrasalmidae; genera *Serrasalmus, Rooseveltiella, Pygocentrus.*

Pirarucu, tropical fish native to rivers of South America. A valuable food fish, it has a greenish, pointed head and reddish broad tail. Length: to 8ft (2.4m); weight: 200lb (90kg). Family Osteoglossidae; species *Arapaima gigas.*

Pisa, city in central Italy, 12mi (19km) NNE of Leghorn, on the Arno River; capital of Pisa prov. A member of Etruscan confederation, it attained Roman citizenship 89 BC; prospered as maritime republic end of 11th century; defeated by Genoa 1284; sold to Florence 1406; scene of council of Pisa (1409) electing Pope Alexander V; birthplace of Galileo; site of famous Leaning Tower, 11th–12th-century cathedral, Palazzo di Medici, university (1343). Industries: textiles, glass, tourism, machine tools. Pop. 103,849.

Pisano, Nicola or **Niccolò** (1220–84), Italian sculptor and architect. He founded a new school combining Gothic and classical architectural elements, and is best known for designing four pulpits, including the marble pulpit for the Pisa baptistery (*c.* 1260). He also designed the great fountain of Perugia and was assisted by his son Giovanni Pisano (*c.* 1245–*c.*1314), also a sculptor.

Pisces, or the Fishes, inconspicuous equatorial constellation situated on the ecliptic between Aquarius and Aries; the 12th and last sign of the zodiac. Lacking any stars brighter than the fourth magnitude, it contains a distant spiral galaxy M74 (NGC 628) only visible telescopically. The astrological sign for the period Feb. 19–Mar. 20.

Pisgah, Mount (Nebo, or Jabal an-Naba), peak in N Jordan, in the Abarim Mountains; traditional site where Moses viewed the Promised Land before his death. Height: 2,644ft (806m).

Pissarro, Camille (1830–1903), French painter. An artist after the Impressionist style, he was variously influenced by Paul Cézanne, Claude Monet, Hilaire Degas, and Georges Seurat, all close friends of his, along with Vincent van Gogh. After the Franco-Prussian war, he was influential in developing the Impressionist movement in France; he was the only member of the Impressionist group to show in all eight of their exhibitions. His works include "Entrance of the Village of Voisino" (1872) and "Avenue de l'Opéra" (1898).

Pistachio, deciduous tree native to the Mediterranean region and E Asia. It is grown commercially for the edible greenish seed of its wrinkled red fruit. Height: to 20ft (6m). Family Anacardiaceae; species *Pistacia vera.*

Pitcairn Island, island and British possession in central S Pacific Ocean, SE of the Tuamotu group. Its residents are descendants of the mutineers from the British ship *Bounty* (1790); when discovered in 1831, the original mutineers were moved to Tahiti, and to Norfolk Island 1856; some descendants later returned to Pitcairn. Exports: oranges, pineapples. Area: under 2sq mi (5sq km). Pop. 74.

Pitch, subjective quality of sound that determines its position in a musical scale; measured in terms of frequency, it also depends on loudness and timbre. Increasing the intensity of a note decreases the pitch of a low note but increases the pitch of a high note.

Pitcher Plant, insect-eating bog plant of North America. The pitcher-shaped leaves, veined with red and green, are lined with bristles. Trapped insects decompose and are absorbed as nutrients by plant cells. The flower is usually red. Height: 8–24in (20–61cm). Species include yellow-flowered *Sarracenia flava.* Family Sarraceniaceae.

Pith, a central strand of parenchymous tissue that occurs in the stems of most vascular plants. It is usually surrounded by vascular tissue and is believed to function chiefly in storage. The term is also used for the soft core at the center of the heartwood of logs, consisting of the dried remains of the pith.

Pithecanthropus, name given to primitive extinct species of man known first from skeletal remains discovered in Java and then from further finds at Choukoutien near Peking. Pithecanthropines lived about half a million years ago, walked erect, made and used crude stone tools, and were possibly capable of speech. Their cranial capacity was about halfway between apes and men; modern man may be descended from them. *See also* Australopithecus; Java Man; Peking Man.

Pitot Tube, a device for determining pressure in a moving fluid. It is a manometer with one open end facing upstream and the other open end out of the stream. The different pressures at the two ends cause the liquid in the tube to shift position within the two arms of the tube.

Pitt, William, 1st Earl of Chatham (1708–78), English political figure, known as the Great Commoner. In Parliament from 1735 he became noted for his brilliant oratory and his opposition to the foreign policies of prime ministers Walpole and Carteret and King George II. Pitt sought to shift Britain's emphasis from support of Hanover and Austria to acquisition of colonies abroad and advancement of commercial interests. As paymaster general of the armed forces (1746–55), he won great esteem by his honesty, unusual in the holders of that office. The crisis of the Seven Years' War (1756–63) made him effective head of the government, first as secretary of state (1756–57). Widespread criticism of his dismissal from that post (1757) brought about his reappointment as head of the government in coalition with the Duke of Newcastle.

His ministry was a brilliant one, preserving and consolidating Britain's old empire and gaining a new one. Pitt subsidized the forces of Frederick the Great, managed military supply problems efficiently, chose commanders shrewdly, expanded the British navy and harassed the French along their coasts and in Africa and the West Indies, placed his main efforts on successful attempts to conquer Canada and India, and mobilized public opinion behind his policies. He resigned in 1761 when George III refused to declare war on Spain, and he opposed the Treaty of Paris (1763) ending the Seven Years' War as inadequate. After the war he spoke out against the prosecution (1763) of John Wilkes and the imposition of the Stamp Act (1765) on the American colonies. The ministry he nominally headed from 1766 to 1768 was a confused and divided one, partly as as result of his physical illnesses (which had plagued him all his life) and periods of mental illness. Created Earl Chatham in 1766, he retired from the House of Commons to the House of Lords in 1768. There he periodically made speeches against repression of the American colonies and in favor of any peace settlement with them short of one granting them independence. He collapsed in Parliament after the last of these speeches and died a month later in the arms of his son William.

Pitt, William, the Younger (1759–1806), British prime minister (1783–1801, 1804–06); son of William Pitt, the Elder. Entering Parliament (1781), he became chancellor of the exchequer (1782) and prime minister (1783). His financial policy, influenced by Adam Smith's theories, aimed at reducing the national debt. He consolidated colonial power in India (1784) and Canada (1791). Forming coalitions against France (1793–1798), he resigned (1801) when George III refused to accept the Catholic Emancipation Bill in the Union with Ireland Act (1800). He returned as prime minister (1804) and formed (1805) a third coalition of powers against Napoleon. Already ill, his death was accelerated by news of defeat at Austerlitz (1805).

Pitta, bright multicolored bird living in the dark jungles of Africa, S Asia, Malaysia, the Philippines, New Guinea, and Australia. Plump birds, they have large heads, short rounded wings, short square tails, and long legs. Some are migratory. Most feed on termites, other insects, and worms and build large, globular nests with side entrances in the fork of a bush or low tree for their glossy white or buff eggs (2–6). The blue-winged pitta *(Pitta brachyura)* has black mask, white throat, green back, red abdomen, and brown under-

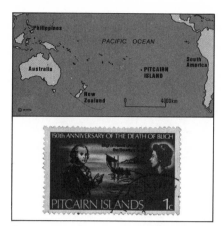

Pitcairn Island

Pitta

Max Planck

sides with blue patches on its rump and wings. Length: 7in (17.5cm). Family Pittidae.

Pittsburgh, industrial city and port of entry in SW Pennsylvania, at confluence of Allegheny and Monongahela rivers; seat of Allegheny co; 2nd-largest city in Pennsylvania. Fort Duquesne was erected on site by French *c.* 1750s; it was captured by British 1758 and renamed Fort Pitt; village developed around the fort by 1760, and grew rapidly as a steel manufacturing center (19th century). Pittsburgh is site of Carnegie Institute (1895), Mellon Institute (1913), Carnegie-Mellon University (1900), University of Pittsburgh (1787), Duquesne University (1878), Chatham College (1869), Three Rivers Stadium (1970); home of Pittsburgh Pirates (baseball) and Steelers (football); birthplace of Stephen Foster. Dr. Jonas Salk developed poliomyelitis vaccine at University of Pittsburgh 1958. Industries: steel, glass, machinery, petroleum products, paper goods, electrical equipment, printing, publishing, railroad shops, coal mining, oil, gas, mine safety equipment. Inc. 1794 as borough, 1816 as city. Pop. (1980) 423,938.

Pituitary Gland, endocrine gland, sometimes considered the master gland. About the size of a small cherry, the pituitary is connected to the lower surface of the brain by a stalk, the infundibulum. It is composed of three parts: an anterior lobe, a connecting pars intermedia, and a posterior lobe, each of which has its own functions. The anterior lobe, the most active part, secretes at least six hormones: thyroid-stimulating hormone (TSH); adrenocorticotropic hormone (ACTH) that stimulates adrenal secretion; follicle stimulating hormone (FSH) that stimulates ovarian function in females and testicular function in males; luteinizing hormone (LH) that stimulates ovulation in females and testosterone secretion in males; luteotropic hormone (LTH) that functions during pregnancy and the postpartum period; and growth hormone, sometimes called somatotropin, that accelerates body growth. The poorly understood intermediate lobe secretes hormones that affect pigmentation. The posterior pituitary secretes vasopressin, which promotes water retention, and oxytocin, which functions in lactation.

Pit Viper, poisonous snake, including the rattlesnake, copperhead, moccasin, lancehead, and bushmaster, found chiefly in the New World, Europe, and Asia. They are characterized by a heat-sensitive pit on each side of the head, used for detecting warm-blooded prey in the dark. The bushmaster is the largest. There are 100 species. Family Crotalidae. *See also* Viper.

Pius XI (1857–1939), Roman Catholic pope (1922–39), b. Achille Ambrogio Ratti. He founded the Catholic Action movement, supervised the program for world relief, supported missionary work, and improved the Vatican library. In 1929 he signed the Lateran Treaty with Mussolini creating the State of the Vatican City. He recognized Franco's government in 1938, after denouncing Hitler in 1937.

Pius XII (1876–1958), Roman Catholic pope (1939–58), b. Eugenio Pacelli. He served as secretary of state to Pope Pius XI. As pope, he took a neutral position during World War II. He renewed the Catholic Action movement to fight Communism and encouraged Marian devotion. He recognized the need for modernization, and the first Vatican City bank was established during his papacy.

Pizarro, Francisco (*c.* 1471–1541), leader of the Spanish conquest of Peru; arrived in the New World in 1502. Of modest origins, Pizarro became a prosperous landholder in Panama City before receiving a commis-

sion from the Crown for the conquest of Peru. At the end of 1530, Pizarro set sail for the western coast of South America, and arrived at a time when the Inca empire already was disintegrating. The Inca ruler Atahualpa was captured in 1532; the stronghold of Cuzco fell in 1534. The conquest was completed by 1535. Civil war among the conquerors resulted in the death of Pizarro's partner and rival, Diego Almagro; Francisco Pizarro, in turn, was assassinated by Almagro's son.

PKU. *See* Phenylketonuria.

Placenta, vascular organ in mammals (except monotremes and marsupials) that connects the fetus to the uterus of the mother and serves as an organ of nutrition, respiration, and excretion for the fetus. In humans, the placenta has three parts: the fetal part, derived from the chorion membrane surrounding the fetus; the maternal part, which is really the decidua basalis layer of the uterine lining; and the intervillous space between these two plates, containing enormous numbers of tiny blood vessel branches and projections through which oxygen and food are carried from the mother to the embryo and wastes are carried from the embryo to the mother to be excreted. The placenta is discharged from the mother's body as the afterbirth, immediately after birth of the baby.

Placental Mammals, mammals whose young develop to an advanced stage attached to a temporary life-support organ—the placenta—inside the mother's uterus. All mammals except the monotremes and marsupials are placentals.

Placer Mining, methods of surface mining employed to obtain valuable minerals (especially gold, platinum, and tin ore) from secondary gravel deposits (placer deposits). Generally, dredging or hydraulic techniques are used. The site is either flooded in order to operate dredging equipment, or, in the case of terraced placer deposits, sluicing with jets of water is customary. *See also* Dredging; Hydraulic Mining.

Placoid Fish, fish, including sharks, rays, and sawfish, with platelike scales that are actually dermal teeth. Placoid scales are the bony part of cartilaginous fish, tip of scale is dentine layered with enamel and lower part is bone anchored to skin. Dermal teeth are modified into large spines in rays and into teeth on snout of the sawfish.

Plagioclase, type of feldspar, itself the most abundant group of minerals on Earth. Plagioclases show an oblique cleavage, as opposed to orthoclase or microclive. These feldspars are composed of varying proportions of sodium- and calcium-aluminum silicate.

Plague, an acute infectious disease of man and rodents caused by the bacillus *Pasteurella pestis.* In man it occurs in three forms: bubonic plague, most common and characterized by buboes; pneumonic plague, in which the lungs are infected; and septicemic plague, in which the bloodstream is invaded. Treatment is administration of vaccines, bed rest, fluids, and sulfa drugs.

Plaice, or European flounder, marine flatfish found along the W European coast. An important food fish, its eye side is brown or gray with orange spots. Length: to 4ft (122cm); weight: 261lb (11.8kg). Family Pleuronectidae; species *Pleuronectes platessa.*

Plainsong, or **Plain Chant,** religious vocal music sung without accompaniment and with voices in unison, particularly that of the Roman Catholic Church. It includes

Gregorian Chant as well as Ambrosian and Roman chants and those of other Mediterranean cultures.

Planaria, marine and freshwater flatworm identified by triangular head with two light-sensitive eyespots; flat, taillike body; and extendable pharynx for sucking in food. Reproduction is hermaphroditic or by asexual splitting, or regeneration. Length: 1in (2.54cm). Phylum Platyhelminthes; class Turbellaria; species include *Dugesia* and *Polycelis.*

Planck, Max Karl Ernst Ludwig (1858–1947), German theoretical physicist, professor at Kiel and later in Berlin, where he studied the characteristics of the radiation emitted by black bodies. In 1900 he came to the conclusion that the frequency distribution of the radiation could only be accounted for if the radiation was emitted in quanta, rather than continuously. An explanation of radiant heat energy distribution given off from a heated surface was proved by Planck's radiation law (1900). Planck's constant (1900) indicates wave and particle behavior on the atomic scale. His equation, relating the energy of a quantum to the frequency, is the basis of the quantum theory. He was awarded the 1918 Nobel Prize for his work. *See also* Black body; Quantum Theory.

Planck's Constant, universal constant (symbol h) of value 6.626×10^{-34} joule second, equal to the energy of a quantum of electromagnetic radiation (photon) divided by the radiation frequency. It appears in formulas describing physical quantities that can only assume certain discrete values. *See also* Quantum Theory.

Plane, flat surface such that the straight line joining any two points on it lies entirely within the surface. Its general equation in three-dimensional Cartesian coordinates takes the form $ax + by + cz + d = 0$ where a,b,c,d are constants.

Planet, a celestial body that revolves in an orbit around the Sun or some other star. The nine planets revolving around the Sun are: Mercury, Venus, Earth, Mars (the terrestrial planets), Jupiter, Saturn, Uranus, Neptune (the giant planets), and Pluto. Between the two groups numerous small bodies, called minor planets or asteroids, are found. *See also* Earth; Jupiter; Mars; Mercury; Saturn; Uranus; Venus.

Planetary Nebula, type of celestial object consisting of a shell or ring of highly ionized gas surrounding a very hot central star. Such objects, which superficially resemble planets when viewed through a telescope of low magnification, appear to be stars departing from the red giant stage, which have thrown off their atmospheres (thus producing the gaseous rings) and are evolving into white dwarfs.

Plane Tree, common name for an attractive tree native to Greece and Asia and later introduced into Europe and America. This large tree with widely spreading branches has five-lobed, palmate leaves and tiny unisexual flowers borne in thick groups containing male or female flowers. With its peeling brownish bark, this shade tree resembles the sycamore. Family Platanaceae; species *Platanus orientalis. See also* Sycamore.

Plane Trigonometry, branch of mathematics that deals with the sides and angles of plane triangles and their measurements and relations. *See also* Trigonometry.

Plankton, drifting mass of plants and animals at the surface of marine and fresh waters. Ranging from tiny algal cells to shrimp, this "meadow of the sea" is an important food source for fish and whales.

Plant, living organism, diverse in size, form, activity, and habitat, generally able to manufacture its own food. Over 500,000 plants have been classified. They vary from the short-lived, single-celled bacteria to the slow-growing oaks and redwoods. Sizes vary from a few millimeters to giant forest trees.

Fundamental differences between plants and animals are mode of nutrition, scheme of growth, cell wall composition, and locomotion. Plants depend on inorganic food materials from soil, water, and air to manufacture their own food. Some non-green plants, such as fungi, are parasites, existing on other organisms.

Botantists have named 11 divisions of plants and include 9 small primitive groups under thallophytes. Thallophytes are fungi, bacteria, algae, and lichens. Bryophytes have a more highly developed reproduction system and include mosses and liverworts. Tracheophytes, or vascular plants, have strong roots, a water-conducting system, and green tissue. They include the club mosses, horsetails, ferns, conifers, and flowering plants.

Plantagenets. *See* Angevins.

Plantain, plant with a rosette of basal leaves and spikes of tiny, greenish flowers that grows in temperate regions. Family Plantaginaceae; genus *Plantago.* Or, tropical banana plant believed native to SE Asia and now cultivated throughout tropics. It has fleshy stems, bright green leaves, and green fruit that is larger and starchier than a banana and eaten cooked. Height: to 33ft (10m). Family Musaceae; species *Musa paradisiaca. See also* Banana.

Plantation System, system of slave-labor agriculture used in the South before the Civil War. Large plantations were usually broken up into separate farms, each with an overseer. The principal plantation crops were cotton, rice, tobacco, and sugar cane. Less than one-third of all white southerners were involved with the plantation system.

Plant Breeding, controlled reproduction of agricultural and horticultural plants by the practical application of genetic theory. Plant breeding has resulted in new varieties characterized by greater productivity, uniformity, adaptability for growth, food value, disease resistance, flower size, and variety of color and form.

Plant Hormone, or phytohormone, organic chemical produced in plant cells and functioning at various sites to affect plant growth, leaf and fruit drop, healing, cambial growth, and possibly flowering. Hormones are transported away from the stem tip. Hormones include abscisin (leaf fall); auxins (growth); cytokinins (leaf and bud growth); gibberellins (growth); florigen (thought to stimulate flowering); and vitamin B_1 (root growth).

Plant Pigment, organic compound present in plant cells and tissues that colors the plant. The most common is green chlorophyll, existing in all higher plants. Carotenoids color plants yellow to tomato red. Located in chloroplasts and chromoplasts, there are more than 60 varieties of these durable pigments. They are a function of photosynthesis and a source of vitamin A. Anthocyanins, responsible for pink, red, blue, and purple, are found in the cell sap. The shorter days and lower temperatures of autumn cause these pigments to combine with other substances and produce the brilliant foliage colors of deciduous trees. *See also* Chlorophyll.

Plant Response, spontaneous or induced reaction of a plant to internal or external stimuli. Spontaneous movements result from internal stimuli, for example, nutation, the circular movement of a plant tip in twining plants. Induced movements, resulting from external stimuli, include tropism and nastic movement that occur as cell turgor changes or growth increases. A tropism is a plant response to stimuli direction and includes geotropism, phototropism, and stereotropism. Nastic movements are responses independent of stimuli direction and include flowers opening or closing and leaves rapidly folding or dropping. Growth responses include photoperiodism, flowering in relation to light intensity, increased growth with higher temperatures, and growth resulting from hormone stimuli.

Plasma, highly ionized state of matter in which substances consist almost entirely of electrons and atomic nuclei. This state, often described as the fourth state of matter, occurs at enormous temperatures, as in the interior of stars and in fusion reactors. *See also* Fusion, Nuclear; Fusion Reactor.

Plasma, Blood, the fluid portion of the blood. It contains an immense number of ions, inorganic and organic molecules such as immunoglobulins, and hormones and their carriers. It will clot upon standing. *See also* Blood.

Plasma Expanders, substances used to temporarily expand the volume of plasma in the body in order to restore blood flow in disorders such as thrombosis or critical blood loss. The substance most often used is a glucose compound called dextran.

Plasmodium, genus of parasitic protozoa that causes malaria. It infects the red blood cells of mammals, birds, and reptiles throughout the world, being transmitted by the bite of a female *Anopheles* mosquito. Four species cause human malaria, passing from mosquito to man as sporozoites in the mosquito's saliva. Once in the red blood cells, they divide, forming up to 24 daughter parasites, then destroy the red blood cells. Entering the plasma, they infect new cells. *See also* Malaria.

Plaster, mixture of slaked lime (calcium hydroxide), sand, and water, often with hair or fibers added as a binder, that is applied wet to interior walls and ceilings to form a smooth hard surface for papering or painting when dry.

Plaster of Paris, or gypsum cement, powdered form of calcium sulphate hemihydrate obtained by heating gypsum to 262.4°F (128°C). After the addition of water it sets and hardens and is used as a plaster for a wide range of purposes.

Plastics, synthetic materials composed of organic molecules in predetermined complex combinations. The weight and structure of the molecule determine the physical and chemical properties of a given compound. Plastics are synthesized from such common materials as cellulose from cotton or wood pulp; organic acid from coal tar; casein from skim milk; as well as from petroleum, corn, potatoes, peanuts, and soybeans. The plastics industry began in the 1860s with the development of celluloid by John Wesley Hyatt. Since then many types of plastics have been invented, based on Hermann Staudinger's work on polymerization.

Plastic Surgery, branch of medicine that involves the use of surgical techniques to correct disabling or disfiguring conditions that may be congenital or the result of injury. It usually involves superficial parts of the body.

Plata, Río de la, river in SE South America, formed by the confluence of the Paraná and Uruguay rivers; serves as the major channel into the interior of SE South America; chief ports are Buenos Aires and Montevideo. Discovered 1516 by Juan Diaz de Solis, it was explored 1520 by Ferdinand Magellan, and 1526–30 by Sebastian Cabot. Length: approx. 170mi (274km).

Plataea, ancient city in E central Greece, on Mt Cithaeron; it allied with Athens at Marathon 490 BC; scene of Persian defeat by Greek forces under Pausanias 479 BC, which assured Grecian independence; twice beseiged (429–427, 373 BC) by Thebes and destroyed; rebuilt by Alexander the Great.

Platelet, a light-gray, round or egg-shaped structure found in all mammalian blood. Chemical compounds in platelets, known as factors and cofactors, are essential to the coagulation of the blood. The normal platelet count is 250,000 to 400,000 per cubic millimeter of blood.

Plate Tectonics, a theory proposed in 1960 by H.H. Hess to explain the mechanism of continental drift. Using the evidence of the mid-ocean ridges and deep trenches, he suggested that magma rises by convection from the deep Earth and spreads along the ocean floor and cools. At the same time a heavier layer under the continental crust, the lithosphere, is also being spread apart by the rising magma. The plates of lithosphere push against each other at a rate of more than 2.4in (6cm) per year and one plate is forced to bend down into the deep mantle, or asthenosphere, where it becomes liquid magma again. When one edge of the top crust pushes against another, it wrinkles, forming new mountains like the Andes.

Platform Tennis, a sport played by two sets of partners on a court raised off the ground and enclosed by wire-fence screens. A large-faced, short-handled paddle made of perforated plywood is used along with a sponge rubber ball. The overall dimensions of the court are the same as for a badminton court, and the playing rules are similar to lawn tennis except that only one serve is allowed and the ball may be played off the wire screens. The game originated in Scarsdale, N.Y., in 1928.

Plath, Sylvia (1932–63), US poet, b. Boston. Her intensely personal verse includes *The Colossus and Other Poems* (1960) and *Ariel* (1968). She committed suicide, and the latter volume contains poems written near the end of her life. She also wrote a novel, *The Bell Jar* (1963; under the name Victoria Lucas). She was married to the poet Ted Hughes. Her journals, published in 1982, were awarded a Pulitzer Prize (1982).

Plating, the electrical, chemical, or mechanical process of applying a metal covering to the surface of an object. When gilding is practiced, base metals are dipped into a chemical salt solution to deposit mercury, then rubbed with gold and mercury amalgam. The mercury is then removed by firing. Mechanical plating involves rolling on gold or silver plate. In electroplating, the layer of metal is deposited by electrolysis.

Platinum, precious metallic element (symbol Pt) of the third transition series, discovered (1735) by Antonio de Ulloa. Chief source is from certain ores of nickel. It is used in jewelry and in resistance wire, thermocouples, electrodes, and other laboratory apparatus. It is chemically unreactive; it does not react with oxygen at normal temperatures nor with common acids. Properties: at. no. 78; at. wt. 195.09; sp gr 21.45; melt. pt. 3,217 °F (1,754°C); boil. pt. 6,882°F (3,808°C); most common isotope Pt^{195} (33.8%). *See also* Transition Elements.

Plato (427–347 BC) Greek philosopher. Spending eight years as Socrates' disciple, he founded his Academy of philosophy near Athens, in 387, and taught there until his death. His works are well-preserved, including more than 25 dialogues and some letters. Believing the human mind can attain absolute truth, Plato's is a spiritualistic view of life. His works include *The Republic, Theaetetus, Timaeus, Phaedo,* and *Gorgias.*

Platte, unnavigable river in central Nebraska; rises at the confluence of the North and South Platte rivers; flows E into the Missouri River just S of Omaha; used for irrigation and hydroelectricity. Length: approx 310mi (500km).

Platyhelminthes, or flatworms, most primitive phylum of worms, characterized by bilateral symmetry, they have one gut opening, no coelom or blood system, an excretory system of flame cells, and three cell layers. Flatworms have a definite head, central nervous system, and dorsal and ventral surfaces. Reproduction is sexual and asexual. The 15,000 species include flukes, tapeworms, and planaria.

Platypus, an egg-laying mammal, up to 2 feet (0.6 meters) in length, with sleek greyish-brown fur, native to Australia and Tasmania. It and the echidna (spiny anteater) are the only egg-laying mammals. Together they are called the monotremes. The platypus is also called duck-billed platypus because of its broad, duck-like beak. It lives in burrows on stream banks and feeds on worms, grubs, insects, and small stream animals such as crayfish. One to three eggs are laid at a time and hatch after about 10 days of incubation. Species *Ornithorhynchus anatinus.*

Plautus, comic dramatist of ancient Rome who probably flourished in the late 3rd and early 2nd centuries BC. According to Jerome, Plautus was born at Sarsina in Umbria and died in 200 BC. Cicero dates his death in 184 BC. Perhaps involved in the theater from an early age, he may have been an actor. Aulus Gellius' record of Plautus' life is historically questionable. Manuscripts containing 21 of his plays have survived, including his *Pseudolus, Truculentus,* and *Amphitruo.*

Plebeians, or **Plebs,** term for the main body of Roman citizens other than the patricians, or privileged class. They were originally forbidden to hold political or religious office and prohibited from marriage with patricians. By 287 BC they had obtained political equality after a long, fierce struggle.

Plebiscite, from the Latin *plebis citum* (decree of the common people), election in which a decision on an issue is made by a simple "yes" or "no" vote.

Pléiade, group of seven 16th-century French poets (Ronsard, du Bellay, Baif, Belleau, Jodelle, Tyard, and Dorat). Under the leadership of Pierre de Ronsard, they championed the dignity of the French language against the academic tradition of Latin and Greek and advocated linguistic and stylistic reforms. Strict rules were evolved for literary composition, and the alexandrine verse form was revived.

Pleiades (M45), spectacular open star cluster in the constellation Taurus, easily visible with the naked eye. The cluster is enveloped in nebulosity, which causes some distortion of the stellar images as viewed from

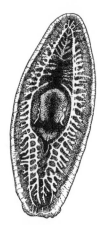

Platyhelminthes

Plovdiv, Bulgaria

Plover

Earth. Brightest star Eta Tauri (Alcyone); distance 500 light-years.

Pleistocene Epoch, geological time period beginning about 2,000,000 years ago, during which man and most forms of familiar mammalian life evolved. Episodes of climatic cooling in this epoch led to widespread glaciation in the Northern Hemisphere—the Ice Ages. The present Holocene epoch succeeded the Pleistocene around 10,000 BC.

Plesiosaur, extinct marine reptile of Jurassic to Cretaceous times. It had a stout body propelled by powerful paddlelike limbs. Some were long-necked with small heads; others short-necked with large heads. Length: 15–40ft (4.5–12m).

Plessy v. Ferguson (1896), US Supreme Court decision following the Civil Rights Cases of 1883. Plessy held that a state law requiring separation of races on public transportation facilities did not violate the Fourteenth Amendment. The court adhered to a doctrine of "separate but equal" facilities and reasoned that the 14th Amendment was not intended to abolish all distinctions based on race. Thus, state-enforced segregation was acceptable until Plessy was overruled in *Brown* v. *Board of Education of Topeka* in 1954. *See also* Brown v. Board of Education of Topeka (1954); Civil Rights Cases (1883).

Pleurisy, painful inflammation of the pleura, a membrane lining of the chest cavity, caused by infection in the lung. Treatment is directed toward the cause; pain is controlled with analgesics.

Plexiglass. *See* Lucite.

Pliny the Elder (*c.* 23–79), Roman naturalist, full name Gaius Plinius Secundus. His *Natural History* is an encyclopedic work dealing with the nature of the universe, anthropology, geography, mineralogy, botany and zoology, medicine, and a history of the fine arts. He died while investigating the eruption of Vesuvius.

Pliny the Younger (61/62–113), Roman writer and political figure, full name Gaius Plinius Caecilius Secundus, the adopted son of Pliny the Elder. He held many important posts in Rome, including consul (100). He died in Pontuo-Bithynia where he was serving as proconsul. His letters, written for publication, are a valuable source for information on contemporary Roman life.

Pliocene Epoch. *See* Tertiary Period.

Pliohippus, pony-sized fossil horse that lived during Pliocene Epoch (12,000,000 years ago). The first one-toed horse, it is the immediate forerunner of *Equus,* modern horse. Side toes were reduced to splints, and teeth were high-crowned for grazing.

Ploiesti (Ptoiesh), city in SE central Romania, 35mi (56km) N of Bucharest; capital of Prahova co; prospered as largest oil-producing center in SE Europe in 19th century. As a result of a cooperation pact Romania signed with Axis powers (1940) supplying Germany with Romanian oil, the city was heavily bombed by Allied powers. Industries: oil refining, petrochemicals. Founded 1596. Pop. 178,256.

Plovdiv, city in central Bulgaria, on the Maritsa River, on main route between Europe and Asia Minor; capital of Plovdiv prov. Seized by the Turks in 1364, it remained under Turkish rule for 500 years; center of leading tobacco; railroad junction. Industries: rice, fruit, wine, tobacco, lead, zinc. Pop. 309,242.

Plover, 38 species of wading shorebirds, many of which migrate long distances over open seas from arctic breeding areas to Southern Hemisphere wintering areas. They have large heads, plump bodies with concealing coloration, and short legs. Speckled, pear-shaped eggs (4) are laid in a depression. Length: 11in (28cm). Family Charadriidae. *See also* Golden Plover.

Plow, agricultural machine used to cut, lift, turn, and partially pulverize soil in preparation for planting. Almost as old as agriculture itself, the plow is one of the most important inventions in farming. Originally single-shared implements drawn by humans, oxen, or horses, modern multiple-shared plows, pulled by tractors, turn over 10-ft (3-m) swaths. *See also* Farm Machinery.

Plum, small fruit tree mostly native to Asia and naturalized in Europe and North America. The Japanese plum *(Prunus salicina)* is native to China; 12 species are native to North America. They have alternate simple leaves, white flowers, and edible, smooth-skinned, oval fruit of purple, red, blue, or green. In the United States plums dried to make prunes are grown mostly on the West Coast. Height: to 30ft (9.1m). Family Rosaceae.

Pluralism, socio-political theory advocating the participation of all groups in a society in the decision-making process. A pluralist society is one made up of a number of different interests whose views, theoretically, are ultimately synthesized into one policy. Pluralism is considered a hallmark of a democratic society.

Plutarch (*c.*46–120 AD), Greek author, born in Chaeronea. Known as a biographer and Academic philosopher, Plutarch was the last important writer of ancient Greece. Of his many works, approximately one-third survive today. The best known are Plutarch's *Lives,* biographies of soldiers and statesmen. The work presents the lives in pairs, first a Greek, then a Roman, and concludes with a comparison. Plutarch's style is pleasant, though his thoughts are not profound.

Pluto, Latin name for the Greek god Hades, sovereign of the lower world and lord of the shades of the dead. He was brother of Zeus and husband of Persephone, and of hard and inexorable character who dwelt beneath the secret places of the Earth in a gloomy palace in barren fields. Pluto was considered also to be the giver of wealth in that he possessed all that sprang from the Earth.

Pluto, ninth planet from the Sun, discovered in 1930 by C.W. Tombaugh. Mean distance from the Sun, 3,658,000,000mi (5,900,000,000km); estimated mass, 0.10 times that of Earth; estimated diameter, approx. 3,725mi (5,998km); rotation period, 6.3 days; period of sidereal revolution, 247.7 years; estimated surface temperature, about $-382°F$ ($-230°C$). *See also* Solar System.

Plutonium, radioactive metallic element (symbol Pu) of the actinide group, first made in 1940 by Seaborg, McMillan, Kennedy, and Wahl by deuteron bombardment of uranium. It is found in small amounts in uranium ores. Pu^{239} (half-life 24,360yrs) is made in large quantities in breeder reactors. It is a fissionable material used in nuclear reactors and nuclear weapons. The element is a strong alpha emitter and is absorbed in bone, making it a dangerous radiological hazard. Properties: at. no. 94; sp gr 9.84; melt. pt. 1,186°F (641°C); boil. pt. (6,021°F) (3,329°C); most stable isotope Pu^{244} (half-life 8×10^7 yr). *See also* Transuranium Elements.

Plymouth, major port in SW England, in Devon, one of the Three Towns with Plymouth (E), Stonehouse (cen-

tral), and Devonport (W). On the peninsula between Plym and Tamar estuaries, it is England's 2nd-most important naval base. The *Mayflower* set sail for America from here in 1620. Pop. 257,900.

Plymouth, town in SE Massachusetts, on Plymouth Bay, 18mi (29km) SE of Brockton; seat of Plymouth co. In 1620 Pilgrims established the first permanent white settlement in New England here; Mayflower Compact was drawn up to govern colony; site of Plymouth Rock, replica of the original *Mayflower,* 80-ft (24-m) granite monument to National Forefathers (1889), several 17th-century houses, and Cole's Hill and Burial Hill, containing graves of many of the first settlers. Industries: tourism, cranberry packing, fisheries, rope, twine. Pop. (1980) 35,913.

Plymouth Colony, settlement on the coast of Massachusetts (1620). About 100 Pilgrims and other colonists from the *Mayflower* landed near Cape Cod after poor weather diverted the ship from Virginia. Government by majority rule was established by the Mayflower Compact since no royal charter existed: this form lasted until 1636, when a government and series of laws were established by the Great Fundamentals. The hardships of the first winter killed nearly half the settlers, but, under the leadership of Gov. William Bradford and the aid of friendly Indians, the colony grew slowly. Prior to 1623 all property was held in common, but a system of private property proved more acceptable. The colony received a new land patent called the Plymouth Patent (1630) from the Council for New England. It was merged with the Massachusetts Bay Colony and Maine (1691) under royal rule. *See also* Mayflower Compact; Pilgrims; Plymouth Patent.

Plywood, a panel made of three or more layers of wood glued together with the grain of plies at right angles to each other. Thin panels are made only of veneer. Thicker panels are comprised of sawed lumber at the center surrounded by veneer. Interior plywood is used in dry locations; exterior plywood employs water-resistant glues.

Plzeň (Pilsen), city in W Czechoslovakia, 52mi (84km) WSW of Prague; famous for its Pilsner beer. Industries: heavy machinery, automobiles, locomotives, armaments, brewing. Founded 1290 by King Wenceslaus II. Pop. 156,461.

Pneumoconiosis, an occupational disease affecting the lungs, caused by inhalation of irritants such as carbon particles inhaled by coal workers.

Pneumonia, an inflammation of the tissue of the lungs as a result of infection, caused by a number of organisms. Mycoplasmal pneumonia is more severe and attacks adults. Symptoms are high fever, chest pain, coughing, and bloody sputum. Treatment is with antibiotics.

PNS. *See* Peripheral Nervous System.

Po, longest river in Italy; rises in Cottian Alps of NW Italy, flows generally E through the Piedmonte; empties into the Adriatic through several mouths. Po valley is important industrial and agricultural region; the river is a major source of irrigation; navigable for 345mi (555km) to Pavia. Length: 405mi (652km).

Pocahontas (1595–1617), daughter of Indian chief Powhatan and wife of Jamestown settler John Rolfe. Famous for saving life of Jamestown leader John Smith, she converted to Christianity before her marriage to Rolfe. She bore one son in England, Thomas Rolfe. *See also* Powhatan; Rolfe, John; Smith, John.

Pochard, diving duck that lives in fresh water. Males typically pursue females with mock brutality. Included are the red-crested pochard *(Netta rufina)* of Europe and the prized sporting North American canvasback. *See also* Canvasback Duck; Duck.

Pocket Gopher, any of about 30 species of thickset rodents found in North and Central America. Short-tailed, they have external fur-lined cheek pouches. They make extensive burrows, eating underground portions of plants. Length: 5–18in (13–45cm). Family Geomyidae. *See also* Gopher.

Pocono Mountains, range of the Appalachian system in NE Pennsylvania reaching to Delaware River on New York and New Jersey lines. A year-round vacation area. Height: approx. 2,000 ft (610m).

Podzol, light-colored, infertile soil, poor in lime and iron, found in cool, humid regions, such as coniferous forests. The name comes from the Russian world for "ash soil." *See also* Pedalfer; Pedocal; Soil.

Poe, Edgar Allan (1809–49), US poet and short-story writer, b. Boston. Orphaned in 1811, he was raised in Richmond, Va., by a wealthy merchant, John Allan. He briefly attended the University of Virginia (1826), enlisted in the army, was appointed to West Point, and then, after a final breach with Allan, went to New York City, where a volume of poetry, his third, was published (1831). To support himself he began to write short stories and held several editorial jobs. During 1835–37 he edited the *Southern Literary Messenger* in Richmond, but he began drinking and lost the job. Subsequently, he was editor of *Burton's Gentleman's Magazine* (1839–40) and *Graham's Magazine* (1841–42) in Philadelphia and of the *Evening Mirror* and *Broadway Journal* (1845–46) in New York. He gained repute for his literary criticism, as well as for his numerous short stories. His stories include "The Fall of the House of Usher" (1839), "The Murders in the Rue Morgue" (1841), "The Gold Bug" (1843), "The Tell-Tale Heart" (1843), "The Pit and the Pendulum" (1843), and "The Purloined Letter" (1844), tales of mystery and horror. Although plagued by alcoholism before his death, he produced his finest verse, including "The Raven" (1845), "To Helen" (1848), and "Annabel Lee" (1849). He is regarded as the creator of the modern detective story and greatly influenced other writers.

Poetry, art form using words for sound and rhythm as well as for speech communication so as to express a poet's feelings or imagination. Good poetry is characterized by succinct, allusive, often figurative language and by pleasing rhythm, often enhanced by metrical patterns and rhyme. The earliest of the literary arts, poetry probably evolved from emotional expressions connected with song and dance. Poetry can be classified by its style—lyric, narrative, dramatic, etc—by its form—sonnet, epic, ballad, ode, free verse, etc—by historic period—Greek, Latin, medieval, Renaissance, Romantic, Victorian, etc. *See also* Versification.

Poikilothermal Animal, cold-blooded organism, incapable of regulating its body temperature independently of environmental temperature.

Poincaré, Raymond (1860–1934), French statesman; prime minister in 1912, 1922–24, and 1926–29; and president of the republic from 1913–1920. He struggled, through skillful diplomatic peace-making and strengthening of alliances, to prevent World War I, and proved a selfless and determined leader in the ensuing conflict. After the war he helped settle the problem of German reparation and managed to stabilize France politically and financially.

Poinciana, evergreen trees native to E Africa and Madagascar. They have feathery, oblong leaves and red, orange, or yellow flowers. *Poinciana regia* has orchidlike yellow-striped, scarlet flowers. Height: to 40ft (12m). Family Leguminoseae.

Poinsettia, showy houseplant native to Mexico with tapering leaves and tiny yellow flowers centered in leaflike red, white, or pink bracts. It is a favorite Christmas plant. Care: bright light, soil (equal parts loam, peat moss, sand) kept dry between waterings. Propagation is by tip cuttings. Height: 2ft (61cm). Family Euphorbiaceae; species *Euphorbia pulcherrima.*

Pointer, type of sporting dog used to find birds, point accurately, and hold until the hunter flushes and shoots. It then retrieves on command. The ideal pointer stands on game with high head and tail and is steady on shot and when birds take flight. Pointing breeds include the pointer, setter, Brittany spaniel, Weimaraner, Vizsla, and wirehaired pointing griffon.

Pointer, gun dog (sporting group) developed about 1650 in England, Spain, and Portugal, and the first breed to stand game. The pointer's wide head has a substantial muzzle. Hanging ears are set at eye level. A solid, strong body is set on muscular, powerful legs, and the tail tapers to a fine point and is carried straight. Colored liver, lemon, black, or orange combined with white, the coat is short, dense, and smooth. Average size: 25–28in (63.5–71cm) high at shoulder; 55–75lb (25–34kg). *See also* Sporting Dog.

Pointillism, a branch of Impressionist painting, also called Pointillisme, Divisionism, or Neo-impressionism. Color is applied in carefully spaced detached specks which merge in the beholder's eye and produce intermediary tints more luminous than those obtainable from premixed pigments. Forms are discernible only from a distance. Its inventor and chief exponent was French painter Georges Seurat (1859–91); his masterpiece was "Sunday Afternoon on the Grande-Jatte." Paul Signac (1863–1935), another leading Pointillist, originated its color system.

Poisoning, the adverse effects of substances, either natural or synthetic, introduced into the body or produced as side-products of the organism itself. Pharmaceuticals can have poisonous side-effects. Industrial and pesticidal products include highly toxic chemicals. Environmental poison hazards exist in air, water, and food. Bacterial, plant, and animal toxins comprise some of the most lethal substances known. Levels of sensitivity and treatments vary, depending on whether acute or chronic poisoning is involved.

Poison Ivy, Poison Oak, and **Poison Sumac,** several plants that cause a severe, itchy rash on contact; all members of the sumac family. Poison ivy *(Rhus radicans)* is a North American creeping shrub, identified by its toothed leaves of three leaflets. It has greenish flowers and white berries. Poison oak *(Rhus diversiloba),* a climbing shrub of NW North America also has toothed, three-part leaves and whitish fruit. Poison sumac *(Rhus vermix)* is a shrub native to E North America. It has long, featherlike leaves and whitish fruit and grows to 20ft (6m).

Poitiers, city in W central France, 100mi (161km) ESE of Nantes; capital of Vienne dept. The old Gallic settlement of Limonum, it was captured by Romans and made part of Aquitania 56 BC; scene of Charles Martel's defeat of invading Saracens 732; site of University (founded 1432 by Charles VII), Roman amphitheaters and baths. Industries: farming, trading, wheat, wine, livestock. Pop. 85,466.

Poitou, region and former province in W France; now contains depts. of Vienne, Deux-Sèvres, and Vendée; bounded by Brittany (NW), Anjou and Samurois (N), Touraine (NE), Marche (E), Limousin (SE), Angoumois and Aunis (S), Atlantic Ocean (W); capital was Poitiers. Part of duchy of Aquitania, it was taken by England and held 1152–1204, 1356–69; made part of French crown lands 1416; it was a French province until 1790, when France was broken up into present departments. A level area between two uplands, chief industries are cattle, wheat, and dairying.

Poker, one of the most popular card games, played with a standard deck. There are many variations of the game, using two or more players. The variations mostly played are five- and seven-card stud and draw. In the five-card game, each player receives one card face down and the others, one at a time, face up. After each card is dealt, bets are made. In seven-card, the first, second, and seventh are dealt face down and the others face up. Draw consists of each player getting five concealed cards, three of which may be exchanged for new cards after the initial bets have been made. In all forms of poker, except when wild cards are employed, the order of ranking is as follows: straight or royal flush (a five-card sequence in one suit—ace, king, queen, jack, ten), four of a kind, full house (three of a kind plus a pair), flush (five of one suit), straight (a five-card sequence regardless of suit), three of a kind, two pairs, one pair, highest card.

Pokeweed, any of about 150 species of plants of the family Phytolaccaceae, most of which are native to tropical America. Included are herbs, shrubs, trees, and vines, all with toothed, alternate leaves, stalked clusters of petalless flowers, and either dry or fleshy fruit. The most common species, *Phytolacca americana,* is a weed with white flowers, reddish berries and red-veined leaves. Its poisonous root resembles a horseradish. It is found in wet or sandy parts of E North America. The berries are used to color wine, candy, and cloth.

Poland (Polska), independent communist nation in N central Europe. The state has moderated its position to cope with workers' grievances concerning wages, housing, and food supplies.

Land and economy. Located in NE Europe, Poland is bounded N by the Baltic Sea, S by Carpathian Mts and Czechoslovakia, W by East Germany, and E by the USSR. With the exception of the S ranges, it is mainly lowlands with a continental climate. About 30% of the labor force is engaged in agriculture, and Poland is a leader in growing rye, oats, potatoes, and sugar beets. Its generally poor soil, inefficient farming methods, and a poor distribution system make food imports necessary. Private farmers cultivate nearly 80% of the land; state farms make up the remainder. Since WWII the industrial base has been expanded and now employs 60% of the work force. Poland is a major coal producer and has begun to develop artificial fertilizers and petrochemicals.

People. Since WWII, 96% of the population has been ethnically Polish. Before the war, the 35,000,000 people occupied 150,000sq mi (388,500sq km) and included Ukrainians, Germans, Jews, and Belorussians. About half the pre-war area was annexed to the USSR, and the minorities either fled or were killed. The Jews were exterminated during the 1943–44 Nazi occupation. More than 90% of the Poles are Roman Catholic, and the church plays an important role in political affairs. Education is free and compulsory. Literacy is about 98%.

Government. A 1952 constitution set up an elected parliament which, in turn, elects a Council of State and Council of Ministers. The Polish communist party decrees policy.

History. The shaping of the modern Polish state began in the 9th and 10th centuries as the Piast dynasty gained power and introduced Christianity. United to Lithuania by marriage in 1386 and formally in 1569, Poland was one of Europe's most powerful medieval states. After a golden age in the 16th century, Poland was weakened by independent nobles, attacks by the Turks, and encroachment by its neighbors. Poland disappeared through three partitions (1772,1793,1795) that divided its lands among Prussia, Russia, and Austria. During WWI, it was invaded by German armies, declared its independence in 1918, and was recognized by the 1919 Treaty of Versailles. Its coalition governments were patterned on the French, with ultra-conservative, nationalistic, and army regimes dominant. In a brief 1939 coalition of Germany and Russia, Poland was invaded and divided and remained under foreign domination until the end of WWII. The United States recognized the Polish government-in-exile; however, the Soviets backed a left-wing rival group. The communists won a 1947 election, conducted without supervision and criticized by noncommunist powers. Industry was nationalized, estates abolished, schools secularized, and some churchmen jailed. In 1956, Poland moved to a more moderate brand of communism. Many collective farms were abolished, more emphasis was placed on housing and consumer goods. Better relations with the West were symbolized by the ratification (1972) of a treaty with West Germany establishing diplomatic relations and recognizing the Oder-Neisse Line as Poland's W frontier. Economic problems and food shortages resulted in rioting in 1970 and 1976. In 1980 a prolonged workers' strike culminated in the creation of Solidarity, the first independent labor movement in the Soviet bloc, led by Lech Walesa. Strikes continued, however, and the government announced a program of economic reforms. Despite the threat of Soviet intervention, strikes and protests intensified in 1981 due to food shortages, leading to the imposition of martial law and mass arrests of labor leaders late in the year. Although martial law was lifted in 1983, unrest and the demonstrations of the banned Solidarity union continued. Pope John Paul's 1983 visit to his native country signalled somewhat better church-state relations.

PROFILE

Official name: Polish People's Republic
Area: 120,724sq mi (311,380sq km)
Population: 35,641,000
Density: 295per sq mi (114per sq km)
Chief cities: Warsaw (capital); Lód; Kraców
Government: Communist
Religion: Roman Catholic
Language: Polish
Monetary unit: Zloty
Gross national product: $103,000,000,000
Industries: petroleum products, transport equipment, chemicals, machinery, motor vehicles, aircraft, aluminum
Agriculture: rye, oats, potatoes, sugar beets, wheat, tobacco, cattle, hogs, sheep, barley, flax
Minerals: coal, zinc, sulphur, salt, oil, natural gas
Trading partners: USSR, E Europe

Poland, Partitions of, divisions of Poland (1772, 1793, 1795) that led to the elimination of the state in the 18th century. The first partition (1772) was proposed by Russia and agreed to by Austria and Prussia. Polish

Edgar Allan Poe

Poland

James K. Polk

territory was reduced by one-fourth. Poland lost all of its part of Prussia except Danzig and Toruń(to Prussia); Red Russia, Galicia, and western Poldolia and part of Krakó W (to Austria); and White Russia and everything east of the Dvina and Dnepr rivers (to Russia). Consent from the Sejm in 1773 was obtained by bribery. The second partition in 1793 reduced Poland's size by another two-thirds. Danzig and Toruń as well as Great Poland went to Prussia; Russia took most of Lithuania and Western Ukraine. What remained became a Russian puppet state. The third partition in 1795 eliminated Poland as Austria, Prussia, and Russia shared the spoils.

Polar Bear, large white bear that lives on Arctic coasts and ice floes. They spend most of their time at sea on drifting ice floes, often swimming for many miles. On land, they can briefly outrun a reindeer. Only pregnant females seem to hibernate during winter. Polar bears prey chiefly on seals and fish. Their chief enemies are Eskimo hunters. Length: 7.5ft (2.3m); weight: to 900lb (405kg). Species *Thalarctos maritimus. See also* Bear.

Polar Exploration, efforts to discover and learn about the Arctic and Antarctic regions of the Earth. Early exploration was stimulated by search for the Northwest Passage. The North Pole was reached (1909) by Admiral Robert Peary. Airplanes and submarines have allowed systematic exploration of the Arctic ice cap. Whalers and sealers touched upon Antarctica, but permanent bases were established only after World War II. Internationalization of the continent was set forth in a treaty in 1959.

Polaris, or Alpha Ursae Minoris, brightest star in the constellation Ursa Minor, and also the star that is currently marking the Earth's north celestial pole. Located at the end of the Little Dipper's handle, Polaris is a triple star system; the main component, a classical Cepheid variable, is associated with a faint companion, and is itself a spectroscopic binary. Characteristics: apparent mag. +2.0; absolute mag. −4.5 (main component); spectral type F8 (main component); distance 650 light-years. *See also* Ursa Minor.

Polarization of Light, suppression of certain directions of vibration of the electric and magnetic fields of a light wave so that the wave form is no longer symmetrical about the direction of propagation. In plane-polarized light the electric vibrations are confined to one direction only, the magnetic vibrations occurring at right angles. Plane-polarized light can be produced by reflection, as from a sheet of glass or a water surface, or by passing light through certain crystals, such as quartz, tourmaline, or calcite.

Polar Solution, solution in which the solvent molecules have substantial dipole moments, such as water. Hydrogen bonding and solvent-solute complexes form, encouraging the association of solvent and solute molecules in preferred orientations in solution. *See also* Aqueous Solution.

Polar Wander, Apparent, the change in position of the Earth's rotational and magnetic poles. Magnetized magma shows that the magnetic poles have reversed numerous times in recent geologic ages and tropical fossils found in Antarctica indicate the movement of the rotational poles. But whether this movement reflects polar wandering or continental drift remains a question.

Polar Wander, Magnetic, the fluctuation of the latitude and longitude of the magnetic poles in a regular pattern (diurnal change) or erratically during magnetic storms and disturbance. The latter changes are temporary. *See also* Magnetic Poles; Magnetic Storm.

Pole, de la, English noble family descended from **Sir William de la Pole** (died 1366), a rich Hull merchant and baron of the exchequer (1339). His son **Michael** (1330–89), created 1st earl of Suffolk (1385), was chancellor to Richard II but died in exile. Michael's grandson **William** (1396–1450), created duke of Suffolk (1447), was also exiled, after faithfully serving Henry VI. William's son **John** (1442–91) married Elizabeth, sister to Edward IV, and their sons **John** (1464–87), **Edmund** (1472–1513), and **Richard** (died 1525) unsuccessfully claimed the English throne. The line ended with Richard's death at the Battle of Pavia.

Pole, Reginald (1500–58), English Roman Catholic churchman. He opposed King Henry VIII's plan to divorce Catherine of Aragon and wrote a treatise condemning Henry's policy of rejecting the authority of the pope. Pope Paul III made Pole a cardinal. During the reign of Queen Mary, a Catholic, Pole was made archbishop of Canterbury to succeed Thomas Cranmer.

Polecat, small, carnivorous, nocturnal mammal native to wooded areas of Eurasia and N Africa. It has a slender body, long bushy tail, anal scent glands, and brown to black fur commercially known as fitch. Polecats eat small animals, birds, and eggs. American skunks are sometimes called polecats. Length: 18in (45.7cm). Family Mustelidae; species *Mustela putorius. See also* Ferret; Weasel.

Polio, or infantile paralysis, viral disease of the central nervous system. It frequently attacks young children, although adults are also afflicted. Symptoms vary from mild fever, headache, and nausea to paralysis. Treatment is symptomatic: use of moist heat with physical therapy is effective in stimulating muscles; antibiotics and sulfa help to control secondary infections; a mechanical apparatus called an "iron lung" is used when nerve cells in respiratory centers are destroyed. Vaccines are now available to provide protection against the polio virus.

Polish, the national language of Poland, spoken by virtually all of the country's 35,000,000 people. It is one of the Slavic languages and thus part of the Indo-European family. Polish is written in the Roman (Latin) alphabet, but with a large number of diacritical marks to represent the various Slavic vowels and consonants.

Polish Corridor, established in 1919 by the Treaty of Versailles, a narrow belt of land along the Vistula River to allow Poland access to the Baltic Sea. The city of Danzig was to be a free city, linked to Poland. This settlement was the source of much dispute with Germany.

Political Party, group organized for the purpose of electing candidates to office and promoting a particular set of political principles. The British two-party system was used as a model for the United States, despite the admonition against parties, or "factions," in the *Federalist Papers* (1789). A two- or multi-party system, in which the party or parties in power represent a majority of plurality of voters, is a feature of democratic societies.

Political Science, study of governments. The study includes analysis of governments at the state and local as well as the national and international levels. In addition to the structure and functions of governments, political science also looks at the relationship of citizens with a government.

Polk, James Knox (1795–1849), 11th president of the United States (1845–49), b. Mecklenburg co, N.C. As

a child he moved to Tennessee with his family. He graduated (1818) from the University of North Carolina and began (1820) to practice law in Columbia, Tenn. In 1824 he married Sarah Childress.

Polk was an ardent Jacksonian Democrat. He entered the US House of Representatives in 1825 and was House leader while Andrew Jackson was president and speaker under President Van Buren. He was governor of Tennessee for one term, and in 1844 he was the compromise candidate of the Democrats for president. He defeated the Whig candidate, Henry Clay, in a close election. Polk's one-term presidency was remarkably productive. He reduced the tariff, restored the Independent Treasury System, settled the Oregon boundary dispute with Great Britain, and admitted Texas and California as states. Relations with Mexico over Texas resulted in the Mexican War. Although the war was unpopular in the North, it was conducted with dispatch and efficiency; its successful completion secured the entire Southwest for the United States. Polk's poor health prevented his running for a second term.

Career: Tennessee legislature, 1823–25; US House of Representatives, 1825–39; governor of Tennessee, 1839–41; president, 1845–49. *See also* Mexican War.

Pollack, or **Pollock,** also coalfish, marine food fish of the cod group found in large schools on both sides of the North Atlantic. Colored green with yellow or gray, it has a jutting lower jaw. Length: to 3.5ft (106.7cm); weight: 35lb (15.9kg). Family Gadidae; species include *Pollachius pollachius* and *Pollachius virens*.

Pollaiuolo, Antonio del (c.1429–1498), Italian painter, sculptor, engraver, and goldsmith. His work is similiar in style to that of his brother Piero, making it difficult to distinguish between the two. One of the best known artists in Florence, he was influential in promoting vitality and motion in Florentine art. His works include three compositions on the "Labors of Hercules" (c.1460) and "Martyrdom of St Sebastian" (1475).

Pollen, yellow, powderlike male sex cells of a plant. Pollen grains are produced in the anther chambers on the stamen and have thick walls with a pattern of spines, plates, or ridges, according to species. These markings are the basis of pollen analysis (palynology) used to identify fossil plants and sediments.

Pollination, transfer of pollen from the stamen to the stigma on a flower. Self-pollination occurs on one flower and cross-pollination between two flowers. Cross-pollination is more common and results in diverse genetic combinations and greater plant vigor. Pollination occurs mainly by wind (anemophily) and insects (entomophily). Wind-pollinated flowers are usually small and clustered with a large quantity of small, light, dry pollen grains. Insect-pollinated flowers are brightly colored, strongly scented, contain nectar, and produce heavy, sticky pollen. These flowers are incapable of self-pollination.

Pollock, Jackson (Paul Jackson) (1912–56), US painter, b. Cody, Wyo. His work was influential in making the United States a force in international art. One of the most important members of the Abstract Expressionist movement, he is one of the most important 20th-century artists. His early works include "Male and Female" (1942). He introduced his "dripping" technique in the 1940s and '50s in a number of masterpieces: "Cathedral" (1947), "Number I" (1948), and "Lavender Mist" (1950). His later works returned to earlier circular forms.

Pollution. *See* Air Pollution; Noise; Waste Disposal, Nuclear; Water Pollution.

Pollux, in Greek mythology, son of Zeus and Leda, brother of Helen and twin brother of Castor, whose father was Tyndareus, king of Sparta. The twins were inseparable adventurers. They fought the boar on the Calydonian hunt and rescued Helen from her kidnapper, Theseus. When Castor was slain in a battle over possession of a herd of oxen, the inconsolable Pollux offered his life instead. Zeus rewarded him by permitting each of the twins alternate days on Earth and in the underworld.

Pollux, or **Beta Geminorum,** the brightest star in the constellation Gemini; a red giant. Characteristics: apparent mag. 1.15; absolute mag. 0.7; spectral type KO; distance 35 light-years.

Polo, Marco (*c.*1254–1324), first European traveler to cross the length of Asia. As a boy he went with his father, Nicolo, and uncle, Maffeo, on a trading mission (1275) that took them to Kublai Khan, Mongol ruler of China. Returning to Venice from the Chinese coast in 1295, Polo became involved in a war with Genoa and was taken prisoner, during which time he narrated an account of his travels. He was released in 1299 after less than a year in prison. He died in Venice.

Polo, game played on horseback by two teams of four persons each on an outdoor field. The game is also played indoors by two teams of three persons each. A match consists of six or eight periods (chukkers) that are 7.5 minutes long with a 3-minute time-out between periods to change horses. The outdoor field is 200 by 300 yards (182 by 273m) with 2 goal posts 8 feet (2.4m) wide and about 10 feet (3m) high. Players wear a protective helmet and use a flexible-stemmed mallet 48 to 52 inches (122–132cm) in length. The ball used is made of rubber and inflated, weighing 6–6.5 ounces (170–184 grams). No substitutions are allowed except for injury, and penalties (carrying the ball, dangerous riding, or illegal use of the mallet), which result in automatic goals, free hits, and disqualification, are meted out by an umpire, also on horseback. Play begins by the umpire throwing the ball in a marked-off center court between the two lines of opposing players (this same procedure occurs after every goal). Players are ranked by handicap (descending from 10), based upon the goals they are expected to score in a game.

History. Polo is considered a rich man's sport. The game is believed to have originated in Persia. It then spread to Turkey, India, Tibet, China, and Japan. It was revived in India in the 19th century, where it became popular with British army officers. After being introduced in England in 1869, it was imported to the United States by James Gordon Bennett, a US newspaper publisher. Polo is now played in colleges, as well as on an international basis. Matches for US teams are sanctioned by the US Polo Association.

Polonium, rare radioactive metallic element (symbol Po) of group VIA of the periodic table, discovered in 1898 by Mme. Curie. It is found in trace amounts in uranium ores and may also be synthesized. Properties: at. no. 84; sp gr 9.40; melt. pt. 489°F (254°C); boil. pt. 1,764°F (962°C); most stable isotope Po^{209} (half-life 103yrs).

Poltava, city in Ukrainian SSR, USSR, on the Vorskla River, 180mi (290km) ESE of Kiev; capital of Poltava oblast. It was ceded by Lithuania to the Tartars in 1430; it was a 17th-century Cossack stronghold. On July 8, 1709, the Russians, under Peter the Great, defeated the Swedes, under Charles XII, marking Russia's emergence as a major European power; it was occupied by Germans 1941–43; site of teachers' and agricultural colleges, regional historical museum, Shevchenko monument. Industries: sugar, wheat, bacon packing, flour milling, sunflower oil extraction, bakery products, machinery works, leather goods, canned foods, textiles, railroad shops. Pop. 278,000.

Polybius (*c.*200–*c.*120 BC), Greek historian and politician, b. Megalopolis. A leader in the Achaean League, he was deported to Rome (167) where he obtained the patronage of Paullus and Scipio. He served as Roman ambassador to Spain, Achaea, and Africa and wrote his universal history (40 vols. of which only the first five are wholly extant) describing the rise of Rome in the Mediterranean world from 220 to 146 BC. A work of detailed scholarship, it includes didactic essays on the lessons of history.

Polychlorinated Biphenyl (PCB), several stable mixtures—liquid, resinous, or crystalline—of organic compounds made via the reaction of chlorine with biphenyl. These are used as lubricants, heat-transfer fluids, and fluids in transformers. They are also used to impregnate condensers and capacitators and to give flexibility to protective coatings for wood, concrete, and metal. PCBs are toxic, and their resistance to decomposition in streams and soils poses a threat to wildlife.

Polycythemia, any condition characterized by an abnormal increase of red blood cells, resulting in a danger of clot formation in the circulatory system. Symptoms are headache, dizziness, an enlarged spleen, and reddening of the face.

Polygamy, conjugal union where more than one spouse is permitted. It is used only to describe those situations where these unions are legal and more often denotes polygyny (several wives) than polyandry (several husbands).

Polygon, plane geometric figure having three or more sides intersecting at three or more points (vertices). They are named according to the number of sides or vertices: triangle (three-sided), quadrilateral (four-sided), hexagon (six-sided). A regular polygon is equilateral and equiangular.

Polymer, substance formed by the union of from two to several thousand simple molecules (monomers) to form a large molecular structure. Polymers are formed in three ways: addition, as in the formation of polyethylene from ethylene (C_2H_4); condensation (the elimination of a water molecule between monomer units) as in the formation of phenol-formaldehyde resins; or by copolymerization (the union of two or more different monomers), as in copolymers of polyvinyl acetate. Some polymers, such as cellulose, occur in nature, others form the basis of the plastics and synthetic resin industry.

Polymerization, chemical combination of several molecules to form straight-chain and/or cross-linked giant molecules called polymers. Reaction can proceed either by simple addition, such as the polymerization of styrene, or by the elimination of a small molecule such as H_2O, as in terylene manufacture from phthalic acid and ethylene glycol. Nature synthesizes natural polymers, such as proteins and nucleic acids, by the latter mechanism.

Polymorphism, any variation among members of a biological species. Such difference in structure or function may be genetically determined or due to differing environments. The most common variations involve color and body proportions, blood groups and other chemical factors, and behavior. Polymorphism is common in many plant and animal species and is frequently found to be of adaptive advantage.

Polynesia, E subdivision of Oceania and general term for islands in the central Pacific Ocean; Micronesia and Melanesia lie to W; includes Hawaiian Islands, Phoenix Islands, Tokelau Islands, Samoa group, Cook Islands, French Polynesia as well as many other groups; islands are chiefly of coral or volcanic formation; inhabitants share a similar cultural and linguistic background.

Polynesians, group of people found in the Pacific Ocean area bounded by Hawaii, New Zealand, and Easter Island. They are typically of medium height, stocky build, and light-to-medium skin tone. They are predominantly Caucasoid, similar to the Melanesians and Micronesians, and probably entered the Pacific area through Southeast Asia, although they could have come from South America. They speak languages of Malayo-Polynesian origin.

Polynomial, a sum of terms that are powers of a variable: for example $5^4 - 3^3 + 2^2 + \; + 5$ is a polynomial of the fourth degree. In general a polynomial has the form $a_0{}^n + a_1{}^{n-1} + a_2{}^{n-2} + \ldots\ldots\ldots a_{n_2}{}^2 + an_1 + a_n$, although certain powers of and the constant term a_n may be missing. The values a_n, a_{n-1}, etc, are the coefficients of the polynomial.

Polypeptide, chain of three or more amino acids linked by peptide bonds. *See* Peptide.

Polyphemus Moth, large American moth whose yellowish-brown wings are banded with pink and have transparent eyespots centered on each wing. Family Saturniidae; species *Antheraea polyphemus.*

Polyphony, music characterized by the interweaving of two or more relatively independent melodic lines (ie, counterpoint). It is often contrasted with homophony and monody. The great age of polyphonic music was the 16th century, culminating in the music of J. S. Bach and Handel.

Polytheism, belief in or worship of many gods. Such gods usually have specific attributes or functions. For example, Neptune is the Roman god of the sea, represented with trident. *See also* Ancestor Worship; Animism; Monotheism.

Pomace Fly. *See* Fruit Fly.

Pombal, Sebasti'ão, José de Carvalho e Melo, marquês de (1699–1782), Portuguese statesman. He was chief minister to King Joseph after 1756 and was virtual ruler of the country. He greatly increased royal power at the expense of the old nobility, the Inquisition, and the Jesuits, whom he expelled in 1759. His economic policies, both at home and in the colonies (particularly in Brazil), enriched the country. He ruled autocratically and strong opposition to him arose. He was ousted when Maria I became queen.

Pome, fleshy fruit formed from the flower receptacle or base. Because it is not developed from the carpel, it is a false fruit. Familiar examples are the apple, pear, and quince. *See also* Flower; Fruit.

Pomegranate, deciduous, spiny shrub or small tree native to W Asia and North Africa. It has shiny, oval leaves and showy, orange-red flowers. The round fruit has a red, leathery rind and numerous seeds coated with edible pulp. Family Punicaceae; species *Punica granatum.*

Pomerania (Pomorze), region in N central Europe, running along Baltic Sea from W of Stralsund, East Germany, to Vistula River in Poland, including Rügen Island; passed to Prussia 1815; after WWI it was German state. The USSR occupied Pomerania March–April 1945, when the Potsdam Conference assigned area E of Oder River to Poland.

Pomeranian, small spitz-type dog (toy group) descended from the sled dogs of Iceland and Lapland. Its wedge-shaped head; small, erect ears; and bright eyes give it a foxlike expression. The short body is set on straight, medium-length legs; the tail turns over the back. Its double coat has a short and thick undercoat and a long, coarse outer coat that stands straight out. Coat may be any color, with sable or black shadings; or sable, black, and tan. Average size: 6in (15.5cm) high at shoulder; 3–7lb (1.5–3kg). *See also* Toy Dog.

Pomona, city in S California, 25mi (40km) E of Los Angeles; site of California State Polytechnic University (1956) and Los Angeles County Fair. Industries: canning, shipping, missile components, paper products. Inc. 1888. Pop. (1980) 92,742.

Pompadour (Pomorze), Jeanne Antoinette Poisson Le Normant d'Etioles, Marquise de (1721–64), influential mistress and confidante of Louis XV. Well-educated as a rich man's prospective wife, she rose to prominence in Parisian society, attracting, and becoming the mistress of, the king. A great patron of the arts, she included among her friends the encyclopedist Voltaire. She urged the rearrangement of alliances, which caused the crushing French defeat of the Seven Years' War.

Pompano, marine and sport fish found worldwide in tropical and temperate waters. It is a blunt-headed and deep-bodied fish. Length: 18in (46cm); weight: 2lb (9kg). Species include the common or Florida *Trachinotus carolinus* and the round pompano *T. falcatus.* Family Carangidae.

Pompeii, ancient city in S Italy, at foot of Mt Vesuvius, 14mi (23km) SE of Naples. A Roman settlement 80 BC, it was destroyed AD 79 by eruption of Mt Vesuvius; ruins were first discovered 1748; excavations began 1763; remains include the forum, temples, baths, theaters, and many homes. Settled by Oscans 5th or 6th century BC.

Pompey, Gnaeus, called Pompeius Magnus (106–48 BC), Roman general. He fought for Sulla and campaigned in Sicily, Africa, and Spain, and with Crassus ended the Servile War. He was named consul illegally and, enjoying vast power, crushed the pirates and fought brilliantly against Mithradates VI, establishing Roman organization of the East. In Rome he formed the first triumvirate with Crassus and Caesar, his fierce rival and father-in-law. As consul he ruled Spain and sided with the senate against Caesar. He met Caesar with a great army in civil war in Greece where he was utterly defeated at Pharsala (48). Fleeing to Egypt he was stabbed by a soldier of his army. *See also* Spartacus.

Pompidou, Georges (1911–74), French prime minister (1962–68) and president of the Republic from 1969 to his death. A teacher until 1944, Pompidou served with de Gaulle's postwar government, becoming a close aide. After some years as a banker, he helped formulate the constitution of the Fifth Republic, arranged a cease-fire in Algeria, and was appointed prime minister in 1962. He helped settle the student worker riots of 1968 and was elected president when de Gaulle resigned. He concentrated on the economy and foreign relations.

Polynesia

Pompeii, Italy: Temple of Apollo

Alexander Pope

Ponce, seaport city in S Puerto Rico, 140mi (225km) SW of San Juan; Puerto Rico's chief Caribbean port; site of Catholic University of Puerto Rico (1948), 18th-century fort, cathedral; trade and distribution center. Exports: sugar. Industries: cement, oil refining, paper products, rum distilling, tourism. Founded 1692, one of the oldest cities in the Americas. Pop. 207,500.

Ponce de León, Juan (1460?–1521), Spanish explorer. He served in the Moorish wars and was with Columbus on second voyage (1493). He was governor of Puerto Rico (1510–12) and founder of San Juan. Searching for the legendary Fountain of Youth, he explored the coasts of Florida (1513).

Pond Skater. *See* Water Strider.

Pondweed, any of some 60 species of a large family of aquatic perennial seed plants; found mostly in temperate zone regions in freshwater lakes and ponds, but also in brackish and salt water. Pondweeds survive the winter by using food stored in underground stems and tubers. They usually have emergent spikelike flowers and submerged or floating leaves arranged alternately along stem. Common species are leafy pondweed (*Potamogedon foliosus),* found in North America, with thin leaves; and crisp pondweed (*P. crispus),* introduced into North America from Europe, with crinkled broader leaves. Many ducks feed almost exclusively on pondweed. Family Potamogedonaceae.

Pontchartrain, Lake, large shallow lake in SE Louisiana, just N of New Orleans; Lake Borgne connects it with the Mississippi River, also connected to Gulf of Mexico; spanned N–S by 10-mi (16-km) bridge; site of Fontainebleau State Park and other resort areas. Area: 630sq mi (1,632sq km). Depth: 10–16ft (3–5m).

Pontiac (died 1769), American Indian chieftain, leader of the Chippewa, Potawatomi, and Ottawa tribes. He helped the French against the British in the French and Indian War (1754–63) and toward the end of it organized the "Conspiracy of Pontiac," an alliance with the French to drive the British and American colonists from west of the Allegheny Mountains. Peace with the British was made in 1766.

Pontiac, city in SE Michigan, on Clinton River, 25mi (40km) NW of Detroit; seat of Oakland co; site of St Mary's Seminary College. Industries: trucks, taxicabs, oil seals, varnishes. Founded 1818; inc. as village 1837, as city 1861. Pop. (1980) 76,715.

Pontus, an ancient country in NE Asia Minor. It gained its independence from Persia (4th century BC) and reached the height of its power under Mithradates the Great who conquered Asia Minor, gained control of the Crimea, and threatened Rome. After his defeat by Pompey (65 BC), the size and power of the country diminished. In 47 BC Pontus was made a Roman province.

Pony, small horse. Usually gentle with children, it is used as a child's mount and for show and work in harness and heavy harness. Types include Shetland, Welsh, Welsh Cob, Highland, Dale and Fell, Dartmoor, Exmoor, New Forest, and Hackney. Height: under 58in (147cm) at shoulder; weight: 500–900lb (227–408kg). An American breed, Pony of the Americas, is a western type; height: 46–54in (117–137cm) at shoulder. *See also* Hackney; Shetland Pony; Welsh Pony.

Pony Express, a relay mail service between St Joseph, Mo., and Sacramento, Calif. (1860–61). Established by the freight-carrying company of Russell, Majors, and Waddell, it involved using riders who changed

their horses about every 10 miles (16km). It took the pony express about eight days to carry the 20-lb (9kg) mail bags the 2,000 miles (3,220km) between the two cities, a saving of about two weeks over the stagecoach. The express was soon replaced by the telegraph.

Poodle, water retriever breed of dog believed to have originated in Germany in the 15th–16th centuries, but now considered the national dog of France. This elegant, popular dog has a rounded skull and long, straight body; small feet; and high-set, docked tail carried up. The profuse, harsh-textured coat is a solid color—blue, gray, silver, brown, apricot, or cream. The coat is clipped (originally to facilitate swimming) in either puppy, English saddle, or Continental styles. Sizes —three varieties: standard, over 15in (38cm) high at shoulder, and miniature, over 10 and to 15in (25.5– 38cm), both in nonsporting group; toy, 10in or less (25.5cm) in toy group.

Poole, port city in S England, in Dorset, 5mi (8km) W of Bournemouth. On Poole Harbour; resort and naval supply base. Industries: shipbuilding, pottery. Pop. 106,697.

Poona (Pune), city in W India, 80mi (129km) ESE of Bombay; capital of Poona district and division. City served as capital of Maratha confederacy (18th century) until 1817, when it came under British control; used as British military station; site of temple of Parvati, headquarters of southern command and National Defense Academy, Poona University (1948). Industries: metal works, pharmaceuticals, textiles, paper, ammunition. Pop. 1,135,034.

Poor Laws, English legislation designed to alleviate poverty and prevent begging and vagrancy and requiring individual parishes to provide for the local poor. It distinguished between the genuinely poor, such as the old and sick, and the able-bodied, for whom workhouses were provided. The first poor laws were passed in 1601.

Poorwill, W North American goatsucker with unusual hibernating habits. It lowers its body temperature, lapses into a state of torpor, and hibernates in a rock niche. Species *Phalaenoptilus nuttalli. See also* Goatsucker.

Pop Art, an art form that emerged in the mid-1950s, inspired by the mass media, consumer sphere, industrial products, science fiction, and movies. Some pop artists saw the world critically; others simply reproduced or enlarged it. English pop art was formulated by the Independence Group. Jasper Johns and Robert Rauschenberg continued the trend in New York, using abstract techniques to depict everyday objects. Roy Lichtenstein and Andy Warhol used commercial techniques.

Pope, Alexander (1688–1744), English poet, b. London. Small, deformed, and self-taught, he achieved mastery over classical poetic forms, showing early metrical skills in *Pastorals* (1709). He also wrote lyric and elegiac poetry and published fine translations of Homer (1720 and 1726) and *Imitations of Horace* (1733). His great talent was for satire, notably in *The Dunciad* and *An Epistle to Dr. Arbuthnot.*

Pope, head of the Roman Catholic Church. Originally the title was used for all bishops and priests, but in the 11th century St Gregory VII decreed that in the Roman Catholic Church, "pope" would refer only to the bishop of Rome. Sucession is accomplished by the Conclave, a meeting of the college of cardinals that is sequest-

ered in the Vatican 15 to 18 days after a pope's death. Each day the cardinals cast ballots for one of their number in the Sistine Chapel. If the required two-thirds plus one vote has not been attained, the ballots are mixed with wet straw and burned. The resulting black smoke demonstrates to the crowd waiting outside that the new pope has not yet been chosen. When a pope is elected, the ballots are burned with dry straw and the smoke is white. If the election is accepted by the cardinal chosen, he is declared pope and resides in the Vatican, Rome. He is recognized by his followers as the successor of St Peter, head of Christ's apostles. *See also* Papacy.

Poplar, deciduous, softwood trees native to cool to temperate regions of the Northern Hemisphere. The oval leaves grow on stalks and flowers are borne in catkins. Some species are called cottonwoods because of the cottonlike fluff on their seeds. Height: to 90ft (27m). Family Salicaceae; genus *Populus.*

Poppy, common name for plants of the poppy family, especially of the genus *Papaver* of about 100 species of annual and perennial erect herbs, most native to central and S Europe, but also found in the Orient, Great Britain, and Iceland. The plants contain a milky juice, are long-stalked, and have showy blooms. The opium poppy of Greece and the Orient is grown for medical and illicit purposes. Family Papaveraceae.

Population, in sociology, either the total number of persons living in a specified area—neighborhood, town, county, state, country—or the group of people sharing certain traits, as in "the female population" or the "adolescent population." Also used as a synonym for the adjective "demographic," as in "population studies," or "population statistics." *See also* Demography.

Populism, socio-political movement arising out of the agrarian economies of the southern and western United States and rooted in a basic distrust of the Eastern industrial establishment. First espoused in the 1870s, the movement coalesced around the Populist party, formed in 1891, which advocated free coinage of silver, abolition of national banks, tariff reform, and a graduated income tax, among other measures. These measures were later adopted into law by Democratic administrations and the Populist party disbanded.

Porcelain, white, vitreous, nonporous, translucent ceramic that gives a clear note when struck. The term is derived from the Italian *porcellus,* meaning little pig and was used by the Portuguese to describe Chinese ceramics that curved and glistened like the upper surface of a pig's back. Porcelain was first developed by the Chinese (7th or 8th century) and made of kaolin (well-decayed feldspar) and petuntse (powdered feldspar or partially decomposed granite). This true, or hard paste, ceramic ware is fired at 1400°C. Meissen ware (early 18th century) was the first successful European attempt to imitate this hard paste porcelain, referred to as "china." Other kinds are English soft paste, composed of clay and powdered glass or frit, fired at a comparatively low temperature, lead glazed, and refired; and English bone china, a soft paste, modified with the addition of calcined bone. *See also* Ceramics; Pottery.

Porcupine, river in Alaska and Canada; rises in the mountains of N Yukon Territory, Canada; flows NE and turns W to Yukon River at Fort Yukon, Alaska. Discovered 1842 by John Bell. Length: 448mi (721km).

Porcupine, short-legged, mostly nocturnal plant-eating rodent with long quills on its back for defense. Old

World porcupines (family Hystricidae) are heavy, have brown to black fur with white-banded quills, and live on the ground. New World porcupines (family Erethizontidae) are smaller with yellow to white quills and can climb trees. A South American porcupine, *Coendou prehensilis,* can hang by its tail. Weight: to 60lb (27kg).

Porcupine Fish, or **Balloon Fish,** tropical marine puffer fish found worldwide. A whitish and brown fish with sharp erectile spines, it can gulp air and swell to a sphere. Length: to 3ft (91.4cm). Among the 15 species is *Diodon hystrix.* Family Diodontidae.

Porgy, commercial and sport marine fish found in tropical and temperate waters. It is a deep-bodied, blunt-headed fish with powerful teeth. Length: to 2ft (61cm). Among the 100 species are the northern *Stenotomus chrysops* and Holbrook's *Diplodus holbrooki.* Family Sparidae.

Porgy and Bess (1935), 3-act opera by George Gershwin, English libretto by Ira Gershwin and Du Bose Heyward, from Dorothy and Du Bose Heyward's play *Porgy.* Its premiere was held in Boston, with an all-black cast. The plot concerns a tragedy in a Carolina coastal town. Crown (bass) kills Robbins (baritone) and escapes. Sportin' Life (tenor) tries to get Crown's lady friend Bess (soprano) to go with him to New York, but she goes to live with the crippled Porgy (baritone). Porgy kills Crown and goes to jail; Sportin' Life lures Bess to New York. When Porgy is released he goes to find Bess.

Porifera, or pore-bearers, also called parazoa, animal phylum containing sponges. They are many celled, nonmobile animals representing an evolutionary dead end. *See also* Sponge.

Porphyria, an often genetic disease of man and some animals, characterized by abnormalities of porphyrin metabolism and subsequent excretion of porphyrins in the urine as well as extreme sensitivity to light. There is no specific treatment, but therapy can alleviate the symptoms.

Porphyry, textural term applied to rocks that contain large crystals (phenocrysts) in a fine-textured igneous matrix. They are found in both intrusive and extrusive rocks. Different varieties are named after the phenocrysts.

Porpoise, small, toothed whale with blunt beakless snout, inhabiting most oceans. The best known porpoise is the common, or harbor, porpoise of Northern Hemisphere. Its body is black above and white below. Length: 5ft (1.5m). Family Phocaenidae; species *Phocaena phocaena. See also* Whale.

Port Arthur, city in SE Texas, 17mi (27km) SE of Beaumont, on Sabine Lake; connected to Gulf of Mexico by canal system; port of entry; industrial, shipping, and recreational center. Exports: oil, petrochemicals, lumber, grain. Industries: oil, livestock, rice, foundries, rubber. Founded 1895; inc. 1898. Pop. (1980) 61,195.

Port-au-Prince, capital city of Haiti, on SE shore of Gulf of Gonâve; served as capital of Saint-Domingue 1770; site of University of Haiti (1944), technical institute (1962). Exports: coffee, sugar, sisal, bananas, rum. Industries: sugar, rum, cottonseed oil, textiles, flour. Founded 1749 by French as L'Hôpital. Pop. 550,000.

Port Elizabeth, port city in S Republic of South Africa, on Algoa Bay and Indian Ocean; developed after completion of railroad line to Kimberly 1873; site of Fort Frederich (1799), art gallery, museum, Snake Park, University of Port Elizabeth (1964). Industries: automobiles, tires, chemicals, glass, soap, candy, shoes, woodworking, fishing, electrical engineering, timber processing, tanning. Founded 1799 by British settlers. Pop. 406,000.

Porter, Cole (1893–1964), US composer and lyricist of musical comedies, b. Peru, Ind. His plays include *The Gay Divorcee* (1932), with the song "Night and Day"; *Anything Goes* (1934), with the song "You're the Top"; *Jubilee* (1935) with "Begin the Beguine"; and *Rosalie* (1937) with "In the Still of the Night." After a fall in 1937, he continued to compose even though he was confined to a wheelchair. *Kiss Me Kate* (1948) and *Silk Stockings* (1955) were two of his later works.

Porter, William Sydney. *See* Henry, O.

Port Harcourt, city in S Nigeria, on Bonny arm of Niger River delta system approx. 275mi (443km) ESE of Lagos; shipping center and terminus of railroad from interior. Exports: coal, tin, palm products, peanuts, cacao, cigarettes. Est. 1912. Pop. 220,000.

Portland, city and port of entry in SW Maine, on Casco Bay; seat of Cumberland co; largest city in Maine. Settled 1632 by George Cleeve and Richard Tucker, city grew, as Falmouth, into commercial area under Massachusetts Bay Colony (17th century); served as state capital 1820–32; birthplace of Henry Wadsworth Longfellow, and home of Robert E. Peary. It is site of lighthouse (1791), University of Maine at Portland-Gorham, Westbrook College (1831). Industries: shipyards, canneries, fishing, chemicals, lumber, paper, textiles, tourism. Inc. 1786 as town and renamed; inc. 1832 as city. Pop. (1980) 61,572.

Portland, city and port of entry in NW Oregon, on Willamette River; seat of Multnomah co; largest city in Oregon. Settled 1845, it was named for Portland, Maine; it developed as major port for lumber and grain (1850), and as supply station for California gold miners (1860s and '70s), and Alaskan Gold Rush (1897–1900). Portland is the site of Lewis and Clark College (1867), University of Portland (1901), Reed College (1904), Concordia College (1905). Industries: shipyards, lumber, wood products, textiles, metals, machinery. Inc. 1851. Pop. (1980) 366,383.

Port Louis, capital and seaport city in NW Mauritius in Indian Ocean. Founded in 1736 by Bertrand François Mahé de la Bourdonnais, governor of French colony on the island, to be used as a base of operations against British in India; seized by Great Britain in 1810. It is the site of Citadel (1838) and the Mauritius Institute (1880). Industries: sugar processing, storing and shipping, cigarettes, rum, food products. Pop. 136,000.

Port Moresby, capital city of Papua New Guinea, on Coral Sea, on SE shore of New Guinea island; excellent sheltered harbor; site of Allied base in WWII. Exports: minerals, rubber, and coffee. Discovered 1873; settled 1888; became capital 1946. Pop. 76,507.

Porto (Oporto), port city in NW Portugal, on the Douro River 2mi (3km) from its mouth on the Atlantic Ocean; capital of Porto district and 2nd-largest city in Portugal. An ancient Roman settlement, it was founded *c.* 138 BC; the port was occupied by the Visigoths 540–716 and the Moors 716–997, from whom Alfonso I of Portugal captured it. Porto grew as wine center in 17th century; scene of the unsuccessful "tipplers revolt" against the wine monopoly 1757. City revolted against French rule 1808 during the Peninsular War, and withstood the siege of Don Miguel 1832–33 during the Miguelist Wars; 12th- and 14th-century structures survive, with 18th-century baroque tower, Torre dos Clérigos; site of university (1911). Harbor of Porto is Leixoes. Industries: port wine, olives, fruits, cork, chemicals, textiles, canning, fishing. Pop. 300,925.

Pôrto Alegre, city in SE Brazil, on Guaíba River; capital of Rio Grande do Sul state. Chief river port in S Brazil, it is a large commercial center. Industries: meat packing, agriculture, brewing. Founded 1742 by colonists from the Azores, later settled by German and Italian immigrants. Pop. 869,795.

Port of Spain, capital city of Trinidad and Tobago, on Gulf of Paria; former capital of West Indies Federation (1958–62); industrial and commercial center, major Caribbean shipping hub; site of botanical gardens. Tourism is main industry. Pop. 67,867.

Porto-Novo, capital city and port in Benin (Dahomey), W. Africa; settled in 16th century by Portuguese traders; used as a shipping point for African slaves to America; administrative, trade, and shipping center. Founded 16th century. Pop. 120,000.

Port Said (Būr Said), city in NE Egypt, at entrance to Suez Canal, on a narrow peninsula between Lake Manzala and Mediterranean Sea. In 1956 French and British paratroops landed here during Suez Campaign and occupied city for seven weeks; in Arab-Israeli Wars the Israelis attacked the city; harbor was closed to shipping 1967–1974. Industries: fishing, salt, canal workshops. Founded 1859 by builders of Suez Canal. Pop. 310,000.

Portsmouth, port city in S England, in Hampshire, on Spithead Channel; Britain's chief naval base since the reign of Henry VII. It comprises Landport, Portsea, Cosham, and the resort of Southsea. Nelson's flagship, *H.M.S. Victory,* stands here in dry dock; birthplace of Charles Dickens. Pop. 200,900.

Portsmouth, city in SE Virginia, on Elizabeth River opposite Norfolk; comprises port of Hampton Roads, together with Norfolk and Newport News; site of large naval facilities including Norfolk Navy Yard (est. 1801) where the *Merrimack* was converted to the ironclad *Virginia* (1861–62), Portsmouth Naval Hospital (est. 1830), and Frederick College (1958); transportation, shipping, and commercial center. Industries: shipyards, chemicals, fertilizer, railroad equipment and shops, tools, plastics. Founded 1752; chartered as city 1858. Pop. (1980) 104,577.

Portsmouth Peace Conference (1905), peace negotiations to settle the Russo-Japanese War. The meeting brought Russia and Japan together with Pres. Theodore Roosevelt acting as mediator in Portsmouth, N.H. It established Japan as the dominant Far Eastern power. Japan gained territory in Manchuria, and influence in Korea, plus the South Manchurian Railway, but won no indemnity to repair its impoverished treasury. For his efforts at Portsmouth, Roosevelt received the 1906 Nobel Peace Prize.

Port Sudan (Bur Sudan), city in NE Sudan, on Red Sea; chief port of entry of Sudan; rich cotton growing region. Exports: peanuts, hides, gum, cotton, oilseed. Founded during construction of railroad in 1905, linking Nile River with Red Sea. Pop. 123,000.

Portugal, independent nation in SW Europe, on the Iberian Peninsula. Internal politics were unstable during the mid–1970s and early 1980s as Portugal shifted away from right-wing government and tried to deal with the dislocations caused by the loss of its overseas territories.

Land and economy. A mountainous agricultural country located on one-sixth of the Iberian Peninsula, it is bordered by Spain N and E and the Atlantic Ocean S and W and includes the Azores and Madeira islands. The Tagus River divides the country into two topographical regions. The N part of the mainland is covered with mountains, has a heavy rainfall and a moderate climate. To the S are rolling plains with less rainfall and a warmer climate. Long sandy beaches mark its 500-mi (805-km) coastline. Forests cover 19% of the land. About 40% of the land is arable; wheat is the most valuable crop, followed by olives. Port wine is a principal export, and Portugal leads the world in cork production. A large part of the economy comes from tourism and money earned by Portuguese workers abroad. Portuguese overseas possessions now consist only of Macao and enclave at the mouth of the Canton River in China.

People. Although the Romans put their stamp on Portugal with their language, institutions, and culture, ethnically the country reflects invasion by the Goths, Arabs, and Berbers, then settlers from N Europe, Jews who came in the Middle Ages, and slaves from Africa. Before WWII, a poor economy led unskilled workers to emigrate to the United States and Africa. The population is relatively homogeneous with no significant minorities. The principal religion is Roman Catholicism. Literacy is estimated at 65%.

Government. According to the constitution of 1976, the president is popularly elected and appoints the prime minister, who represents the majority party or coalition in the 250-member national assembly. The Council of Revolution, composed of military officers, that advised the government, was disbanded in 1982.

History. An independent state since the 12th century, Portugal's modern history began in 1140. Before that time it had been ruled by Romans, Visigoths, and Moors. Galician, Leonese, and Castilian kings revolted and established the nation of Portugal in 997. Between 1130–39, Alfonso Henriques, son of the Count of Portugal, defeated the small kingdoms, then the Moors, and became Portugal's first king in 1150. Portuguese exploration started about 1336 when navigators reached the Canary Islands. Prince Henry the Navigator encouraged overseas expansion, which led to the 15th–16th century voyages of Vasco da Gama, Bartolomeu Dias, and Pedro Cabal, who claimed vast territories and brought wealth to the Portuguese kingdom. Conflict with neighboring Spain was a constant problem, and Spain ruled Portugal 1580–1640. Independence was reestablished under the Braganzas, who ruled, with interruptions, until 1910, when Manuel II abdicated, and a republic was established. Political instability characterized the next two decades. António de Olivera Salazar took an increasingly prominent role in the government from 1928 and in 1932 gained control as premier. He maintained domestic stability but also repressed all opposition. He retired in 1968, and in 1974 a military junta seized the government, instituting a socialist program. In the next two years Portugal's vast overseas empire disintegrated as colonies gained independence (including Angola and Mozambique). In April 1976 elections brought moderate, democratic leaders to power. Since then there has been a succession of moderate and conservative governments, although the military still retains some control of the government.

PROFILE

Official name: Republic of Portugal
Area: (continental Portugal) 35,553sq mi (92,082sq km); Azores, 905sq mi (2,344sq km); Madeira, 308sq mi. (798sq km)

Cole Porter

Portugal

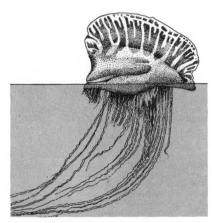

Portuguese man-of-war

Population: (continental Portugal) 9,870,000; Azores, 336,100; Madeira, 268,700
  Density: (continental Portugal) 278 per sq mi (107 per sq km)
Chief cities: Lisbon (capital); Oporto
Government: Parliamentary democracy
Religion: Roman Catholic
Language: Portuguese
Monetary unit: Escudo
Gross national product: $12,200,000,000
Per capita income: $1,308
Industries: canned fish and seafood, olive oil, wine, textiles, ships, forests, sisal cordage, forest products, paper, glassware, petrochemicals
Agriculture: wheat, olives, citrus fruits, fish, forests, almonds
Minerals: wolfram, pyrites
Trading partners: European Economic Community, United States

Portuguese, the national language of both Portugal and Brazil, spoken by about 10,000,000 people in the former and 100,000,000 in the latter. A Romance language, it is closely related to Spanish, but its pronunciation is softer and contains more nasal sounds.

Portuguese Guinea. *See* Guinea-Bissau, Republic of.

Portuguese Man of War, colonial coelenterate found in marine subtropical and tropical waters, recognized by its bright blue gas float and long, trailing tentacles with poisonous stingers. The tentacles are actually a cluster of several kinds of modified medusae and polyps. Length: 60ft (18.3m). Class Hydrozoa, phylum Cnidaria, species *Physalia*.

Portulaca, common name for the purslane family of annual or perennial flowering plants and small shrubs in the United States. They have cylindrical leaves. There are over 500 species. Also, low-growing annual plant *(Portulaca grandiflora)* with red, yellow, or white flowers that open only in sunshine.

Poseidon, in Greek mythology, the god of all waters, Earth-shaker, brother of Zeus. Poseidon controlled the monsters of the deep and sired by gods and mortals the Laestrygonians, Orion, Polyphemus, and Procrustes. Zeus called upon him to bring the Flood when he was displeased with men. He is the Roman Neptune.

Positive Integer. *See* Number, Natural.

Positron, positively charged antiparticle of the electron (symbol e$^+$) postulated as the first antiparticle by P. Dirac (1928) and observed (1933) in cosmic rays. It is also emitted from certain radioactive nuclei. It can only exist a brief period before annihilating with an electron. When gamma rays interact with matter, electron-positron pairs can be produced. *See also* Annihilation; Lepton.

Post-impressionism, term invented by English critic Roger Fry to denote the movement associated with Paul Gauguin, Vincent van Gogh, and Paul Cézanne. It is generally used for art trends from the mid-1880s to the early 1900s. It stressed subjective and emotional content and was later referred to as Expressionism.

Post-partum Depression, series of depressive symptoms that occasionally appear in mothers shortly after the birth of a child. Some authorities stress psychological causes, others emphasize endocrine and other chemical changes engendered by the termination of pregnancy.

Postulate, statement or proposition that is to be assumed to be true without proof and that forms a framework for the derivation of theorems. The term as now used is synonymous with "axiom." Euclid drew a distinction between postulates, which dealt with geometric properties, and axioms, which were more general statements about equality and inequality.

Potassium, common metallic element (symbol K) of the alkali-metal group, first isolated in 1807 by Sir Humphry Davy. Chief ores are sylvite (chloride), carnallite, and polyhalite. The metal is used as a heat-transfer medium but has few other commercial uses. Chemically it resembles sodium, being rather more reactive. The natural element contains a radioisotope K^{40} (half-life 1.4×10^9yrs), which is used in radioactive dating of rocks. Properties: at. no. 19; at. wt. 39.102; sp gr 0.86; melt. pt. 153.77°F (67.70°C); boil pt. 1,425°F (774°C); most common isotope K^{39} (93.1%). *See also* Alkali Element; Dating, Radioactive.

Potassium-Argon Dating, a method of assessing geological age up to about ten million years. *See also* Dating, Radioactive.

Potassium Carbonate, a commercially produced white solid (K_2CO_3), usually produced by electrolysis of potassium chloride, followed by treatment of the resulting potassium hydroxide with carbon dioxide. It is used in the manufacture of glass and textile dyes and in cleaning and electroplating metals.

Potassium Chloride, a potassium salt (KCl) extracted from lake brines as well as from minerals (sylvite, kainite, carnallite). Colorless or white, with a specific gravity of 1.9, it is used as a fertilizer and as a raw material in the production of potassium hydroxide and potassium carbonate.

Potassium Hydroxide, a commercially produced white solid (KOH) prepared by electrolysis of potassium chloride. It is an alkaline substance used for making soaps and detergents.

Potassium Nitrate (KNO_3), (1) a naturally occurring (nitre) mineral which is a source of nitrogen. It appears as a white crust on rocks, in caves, and in some soils in hot, dry areas. (2) A synthetically produced transparent solid salt prepared by the reaction of sodium nitrate and potassium chloride or by the reaction of nitric acid and potassium hydroxide. Potassium nitrate is used as a fertilizer, in the manufacture of explosives, and as a food preservative.

Potassium Permanganate, purple soluble crystalline salt (formula $KMnO_4$) obtained from pyrolusite (manganese dioxide) and potassium hydroxide. It is used as an oxidizing agent, disinfectant, dye, and in the preparation of other chemicals. Properties: sp gr 2.70; decomposes at 464°F (240°C).

Potato, also white potato, Irish potato; herb native to Central and South America and introduced to Europe by the Spaniards in the 16th century. Best grown in a moist, cool climate, it has oval leaves and violet, pink, or white flowers, which produce a greenish berry fruit. The potato itself is a tuber (underground modified stem). The leaves and green potatoes contain the alkaloid solanine and are poisonous if eaten raw. Family Solanaceae; species *Solanum tuberosa*.

Potato Beetle. *See* Colorado Potato Beetle.

Potawatomi, American Indians of the Algonquian linguistic family. Originally united with the Ottawa and the Ojibwa, these semi-sedentary hunter-farmers were driven by the Sioux southeast from Wisconsin, migrating as far as Indiana before the whites drove them west. They were eventually settled on reservations in Oklahoma, Kansas, Michigan, and Wisconsin, where they now number about 1,300.

Potemkin, Grigori Aleksandrovich (1739–91), Russian statesman. Involved in the coup that brought Catherine II to power (1762), he became her lover and favorite in 1771 and remained until his death the most powerful man in Russia. Governor general of "New Russia" (Ukraine), he engineered the colonization of the Ukrainian steppes and the conquest of the Crimea. He became a field marshal in 1784 and was commander in chief during the second Turkish War (1787–91).

Potential Energy, in mechanics, energy that can be transformed into kinetic energy. For example, a swing at the top of its motion has a potential energy equal to its kinetic energy at the bottom of its path. A body of mass m and height h in the Earth's gravitational field g has a potential energy of mgh. *See also* Kinetic Energy.

Potentiometer, a special type of rheostat that measures an unknown voltage or potential difference by balancing it by a known potential difference. The simplest form is a resistor with two fixed terminals and a third terminal connected to a variable contact arm. Potentiometers are used as volume controls in audio equipment.

Pothole, in geology, term used for many formations with pot shapes but most commonly denoting a circular, bowl-shaped hollow formed in a rocky stream bed by the grinding action of sand and stones whirled around by eddies or the force of the stream. They are usually found in rapids or at the foot of a waterfall.

Pothos, or devil's ivy, trailing house plant native to the South Pacific islands. It has waxy, heart-shaped leaves marked with yellow or white. Care: bright indirect light, soil (1 part loam, 2 parts peat moss, 1 part sand) kept dry between waterings. Propagation is by stem cuttings. Family Araceae; species *Scindapsus aureus*.

Potomac, river in SE United States; rises in West Virginia at the confluence of the North Branch and South Branch rivers, flows E and SE to Chesapeake Bay, forming natural boundaries of Maryland-West Virginia, Virginia-Maryland, and Virginia-District of Columbia; navigable for large ships to Washington, D.C.; site of many historic landmarks including Mount Vernon. Length: 285mi (459km).

Potsdam, city in central East Germany, on an island in the Havel River, 17mi (27km) SW of West Berlin; capital of Potsdam district. Residence of Frederick William of Brandenburg (1660), who opened city to French refugees by Edict of Potsdam (1685); scene of Peace of Potsdam (1805), which strengthened alliance between Russia and Prussia against France, and Potsdam Conference (July 17–Aug. 2, 1945) which determined administration of Germany after WWII; site of New Palace (1763–69), Town Palace (1745), park Sans Souci (1745–47), Garrison Church (1731–35); center of East German movie industry. Industries: food processing, textiles, pharmaceuticals, electrical equipment. Founded *c.* 10th century. Pop. 119,482.

Potsdam Conference (1945), meeting to settle European problems following World War II. The principal participants included Pres. Harry S. Truman of the United States, Prime Minister Winston Churchill of Britain, and later Prime Minister Clement P. Attlee, and Premier Joseph Stalin of the USSR. Held in Potsdam,

Germany, the conference established the Council of Foreign Ministers to prepare draft treaties and to make proposals for settling territorial issues. The occupation of Germany was planned. An "unconditional surrender" ultimatum was issued to Japan.

Potsherd, pottery fragment, one of the archeologist's chief aids in dating sites and tracing cultural contacts after the invention of pottery in Neolithic times. Potsherds are useful because they are often found in large numbers and because potters' conservatism supplies the basis for typological dating.

Pottery, in its widest sense includes all objects shaped of clay and hardened by fire or dried in the sun. The term is from the French *poterie,* related to the Latin *potare* (to drink). Pottery is dependent on two properties of clay, its plasticity and its durability after firing. It can be divided into three categories according to the degree of hardness and special constitution: earthenware, the ordinary pottery dating back to primitive times, baked at 700°C (1292°F) or lower; stoneware, fired at up to 1,150°C (2102°F), more vitrified or close-grained and nonporous, and produced more commonly in the Far East than in Europe until modern times; and porcelain, fired at 1,400°C (2552°F), a Chinese invention, and the most refined ceramic material, known as hard paste because of its homogeneous composition.

Clay is dug from the Earth's surface and prepared by beating and kneading with the hands, feet, or mallets. A potter's wheel, dating back to ancient times, rotated by feet and later by power, leaves the potter free use of his hands for manipulating the clay. After the object is formed and dried, it is fired in a kiln; glaze is applied, and it is refired. A glaze is a thin layer of glass applied to prevent seepage of liquids and impart a pleasing finish. Different glazes include alkaline, lead, feldspathic, and salt. *See also* Ceramics.

Potto, slow-moving squirrel-sized primitive African primate with big eyes and pointed face. The common potto has short tail, and golden, or Calabar, potto is nearly tailless. Species: common *Perodicticus potto,* golden *Arctocebus calabarensis.*

Poulenc, Francis (1899–1963), French composer. Many of his works are characterized by a light, witty style with simple melodies. Later works are more serious, many with a religious theme, eg, the opera *Les Dialogues des Carmélites* (1957). He is regarded as the most significant 20th-century French composer of songs.

Poultry, domesticated birds raised as a source of meat and eggs. In the United States, important poultry species include chickens and turkeys. In other parts of the world, guinea fowl, pheasant, pigeons, quail, and others are raised for food.

Pound, Ezra (Loomis) (1885–1972), US poet and critic, b. Hailey, Idaho. He published *A Lume Spento,* his first volume of poetry, in Venice in 1908; and then settled in London. In England from 1908 to 1920 he wrote *Exultations* (1909) and *Personae* (1909), which made him noted as a poet, and *The Spirit of Romance* (1910), a collection of critical articles. Emphasizing direct and precise language in poetry, he became a leader of the Imagist and Vorticist movements in the years around World War I and the dominant influence in Anglo-American poetry. Distressed by World War I, he began to emphasize the interconnections of the arts and society, beginning his complex epic *The Cantos* in 1915.

He developed an admiration for Fascist dictator Benito Mussolini and during World War II broadcast against the US war effort. Arrested in 1945, he was taken to the United States, found unfit to stand trial by reason of insanity, and confined to a hospital in Washington, D.C. In 1958 the charges against him were dropped, and he returned to Italy. *See also* Cantos, The.

Pound, the unit of force in the English foot-slug-second system of units. One pound is the force that would give a mass of one slug an acceleration of one foot per second per second.

Poussin, Nicolas (1594–1665), French painter of religious and mythological scenes and classical landscapes. His mature works evoked the spirit of the French classic ideal as no other paintings of that period did. His early works include "Victory of Joshua over the Amorites" (1625–26), executed in a Mannerist style, and "The Martyrdom of St Erasmus" (1628–29), in a Baroque style. His mature works include "The Eucharist" (1647) and "The Ashes of Phocion" (1648). After 1653 he enjoyed international prestige.

Powder Metallurgy, the manufacture of metal powders and their use in producing metal parts. Powder particles are compressed to the desired shape and then sintered. Use of powders is more economical than molten metal in making such items as small gears. Melting may also prove impractical when a metal has a very high melting temperature or when an alloy of unfusable materials is involved. Powder metallurgy is also used for porous end products.

Powell, Anthony (Dymoke) (1905–), British novelist specializing in social comedies; he was also a scriptwriter and journalist. His work includes *A Dance to The Music of Time,* a series of novels which portray the snobbish, insular world of the English upper classes after WWI, beginning with *A Question of Upbringing* (1951) and including *At Lady Molly's* (1957), *Temporary Kings* (1973), and *Hearing Secret Harmonies* (1975).

Powell, Lewis Franklin, Jr., (1907–), US jurist and lawyer, b. Suffolk, Va. He is noted for his role on the Richmond, Va., Board of Education (1952–61) where he helped to achieve peaceful integration. He also served as president of the American Bar Association (1964–65) and president of the ABA Foundation (1969–71). He was nominated an associate justice of the US Supreme Court by Pres. Richard M. Nixon and confirmed in 1971.

Power, rate of doing work. An engine that can lift 550lbs (247.5kg) through a height of one foot in one second is rated at one horsepower. The unit of electrical power is the watt; 746 watts equal one horsepower. Power multiplied by the time of operation gives the total energy consumed.

Power (of a number), the result of multiplying a number or variable by itself a specified number of times. Thus a^2 ($= a \times a$) is the second power of a; a^3 is the third power; a^4 the fourth, etc. The superscript, 2, 3, 4, etc, is the exponent.

Power Plant, any installation that generates electricity. Such installations are typically hydroelectric, thermal or fossil fuel, or nuclear power plants. In each case potential or unusable energy is converted into easily used electricity. Power plants consist of reservoirs in which fuel is stored, an energy release mechanism (dam, boiler, reactor), turbines, generators, transformers, and a transmission or electrical distribution system. *See also* Hydroelectric Power Plant.

Powhatan, or **Wahunsonacock** (1550–1618), chief of Indian tribes in vicinity of Jamestown settlement. Powhatan was not friendly to the colonists until the marriage of his daughter Pocahontas to John Rolfe.

Powhatan, a major Algonkian-speaking confederacy of North American Indians formerly occupying the region from the Potomac River south to Albemarle Sound, in Virginia. They were famous in early American history for their role in the development of the eastern Atlantic area, and the position of two major personages—Powhatan and his daughter Pocahontas. From 9,000 individuals in 30 tribal groups, they have declined in numbers to about 2,000 today.

Poznán, city in W Poland, on the Warta River, approx. 170mi (274km) W of Warsaw. One of the oldest cities of Poland, it became first Polish episcopal see (10th century), was a member of the Hanseatic League, and the central power of the Polish state, growing in prosperity until it passed to Prussia 1793; part of Grand Duchy of Warsaw 1807; passed back to Prussia 1815; ceded to Poland 1919; site of a Gothic cathedral, annual international spring fair, university (1919). Industries: metal, chemicals, textiles, food processing, marketing. Pop. 469,000.

PPLO, or pleuropneumonia-like organism, smallest organisms capable of growth and reproduction outside of living host cells. At about 0.25μm (1μm = 1/25,400 of an inch) in diameter, they are smaller than bacteria, but larger than viruses. This group is now classified under the genus *Mycoplasma;* the original name derived from the first such organism isolated which caused pleuropneumonia. Although widespread in humans, only one known disease is caused by mycoplasma—primary atypical pneumonia.

Prado, Madrid, the Spanish National Museum of Fine Art. Founded in 1818, it is an example of Spanish Neoclassical architecture. The major part of its collection derives from the royal collection of the Hapsburg and Bourbon kings of Spain. Almost all the important works of Velázquez and a full representation of El Greco and Goya are contained there. Bosch, Titian, Tintoretto, Veronese, Rubens, van Dyke, and Brueghel are also well represented.

Praesepe, a galactic or open cluster of several hundred stars in the constellation Cancer. It is visible to the unaided eye as a small bright hazy patch. First distinguished as a group of stars by Galileo. The name Praesepe means "cradle" and has been used since early Greek times. An alternative name, Beehive, is of more recent origin.

Praetorian Guards, bodyguard of the Roman emperors from Augustus to Constantine I. They were first selected by Augustus in 27 BC from the *cohort praetoria* that had guarded generals of the republic. Numbering from 9,000 to 16,000 men, they attended the emperor's family and enjoyed special privileges.

Pragmatic Sanction, solemn ordinance or decree by a head of state relating to matters of prime importance and having the force of law. Charles VI, Holy Roman emperor, decreed in 1713 that if he died without male heirs, his eldest daughter would inherit the Hapsburg dominions. This pragmatic sanction was initially agreed to by the major powers, but Prussia disputed it in 1740 when Charles died. The ensuing War of the Austrian Succession decided the issue in favor of Maria Theresa, Charles' daughter.

Pragmatism, development of British Empiricism, associated with the US philosophers C.S. Peirce and William James. Stemming from the Greek *pragma,* things done, pragmatism is both a doctrine of meaning and a definition of truth. The meaning of a symbol is understood in terms of the rational conduct inspired, and a proposition is true when its consequences prove useful and practical. What works best is true. *See also* James, William; Peirce, Charles S.

Prague (Praha), capital of Czechoslovakia, on Vitava River, 160mi (256km) NW of Vienna, Austria. Its location on a strategic trade route and establishment of Charles University (1348) caused rapid growth. It became the capital in 1918 when Czechoslovakia was created. In 1945 the people drove out the Germans who had occupied it since 1939; Russians then took possession; site of Stavovske Theater (where Mozart's "Don Giovanni" was first performed), Old Synagogue (13th century), and 17th-century palace, Waldstein, all in Old Town part of Prague. Industries: automobiles, printing, publishing, airplanes. Founded AD 722. Pop. 1,169,567.

Praia, seaport town on S shore of São Tiago Island, Cape Verde. It has served as the capital of the archipelago and seat of the governor general and his palace since 1770; site of meteorological observatory; cable station, important link between South America, Europe, and W Africa. Exports: castor oil, sugar cane, oranges, coffee. Industries: straw hats, fish processing, distilling. Pop. 45,079.

Prairie Chicken, chicken-sized, pale brown grouse of W United States. It has brown and black, stiffly pointed neck feathers that stand up when the male inflates orange neck air sacs during courtship displays. Groups of males shuffle about with necks erect and bills pointed down until mating. The female incubates the eggs (12) in a small scraped area and cares for the young. Species *Tympanuchus cupido. See also* Grouse; Heath Hen.

Prairie Dog, squirrellike rodent of North America named for its barking cry. Short-tailed plant and insect eaters, they have grizzled brown to buff fur. Active by day, they live in communal burrows that are connected to form colonies. Length: 12in (30cm). Genus *Cynomys. See also* Ground Squirrel.

Prairie Falcon, common falcon generally found in dry inland areas. Species *Falco mexicanus. See also* Falcon.

Praseodymium, metallic element (symbol Pr) of the Lanthanide group, first identified spectroscopically (1879) by Lecoq de Boisbaudran. Chief ores are monazite (phosphate) and bastnasite (fluorocarbonate). Praseodymium is used in carbon-arc lamps. Its salts are used in colored glasses. Properties: at. no. 59; at. wt. 140.9077; sp gr 6.773(), 6.64 (); melt. pt. 1,708°F (931°C); boil. pt. 5,814°F (3,212°C); most common isotope Pr^{141}(100%). *See also* Lanthanide Elements.

Pratincole, any of about seven species of Old World birds, related to shorebirds. All are brown with white rumps, to about 8in (20cm) long, with forked tails and long, pointed wings. They feed on insects near rivers and nest colonially on the ground. The black-winged pratincole *(Glareola pratincola),* native to the Middle East, is sometimes called the locust bird in its winter home in Africa. Family Glareolidae.

Praxiteles (*fl.* 370–330 BC), Greek sculptor. His graceful style encompassed the 4th-century Greek ideal. One of the most widely imitated of Greek sculptors, he is the author of "Hermes Holding the Infant Dionysos," a work found in Olympia in 1877 and now in the mu-

Potto

Ezra Pound

Maurice Prendergast: Central Park (detail)

seum there. It may possibly be the original work, but it is more likely a good Roman copy. His most famous work is "Aphrodite (Venus) of Cnidus," a sensuous work that created a new ideal model. The best of several extant copies is at the Vatican museum.

Praying Mantis. See Mantis.

Precambrian Era, the oldest and longest major division of Earth history, lasting from the beginning of the Earth over 4,000,000,000 years ago to the beginnings of a good fossil record 570,000,000 years ago. Precambrian fossils are extremely rare because the earliest life forms are presumed not to have had hard parts suitable for preservation. Also, Precambrian rocks have been greatly changed and deformed. Nonetheless, primitive bacteria and blue-green algae have been identified from deposits 3,300,000,000 years old and later Precambrian localities have yielded some questionable finds of more advanced organisms such as jellyfish, worms, and arthropods.

Precession, slow revolution of the Earth's axis of rotation about the poles of the ecliptic. It is caused by lunar and solar perturbations acting on the Earth's equatorial bulge and causes a westward motion of the stars that takes 25,800 years to complete.

Precipitate, formation of an insoluble solid in solution either by direct reaction or by varying the solution composition to diminish the solubility of the dissolved compound. This technique is used for the separation and identification of compounds in chemical processes.

Precipitation, all forms of water particles, whether liquid or solid, that fall from the atmosphere to the ground. Distinguished from cloud, fog, dew, and frost, in that it must fall and reach the ground, precipitation includes rain, drizzle, snow, snow and ice pellets and crystals, and hail. Measured by rain and snow gauges, the amount of precipitation is expressed in inches (or mm) of liquid water depth. Precipitation occurs with the condensation of water vapor in clouds into water droplets that coalesce into drops as large as 0.25in. (6mm) in diameter or form from melting ice crystals in the clouds. Drizzle consists of fine droplets, and snow of masses of six-sided ice crystals or prisms. Sleet is produced by freezing of raindrops into small ice pellets, and hail by the freezing of concentric layers of ice in cumulonimbus clouds, with lumps measuring from 0.2 up to 2in. (0.5 to 5cm) in diameter. Ice storms result when rain falls on frozen ground or other objects like trees and wires, freezing into a heavy glaze. Fog is like a cloud in that water vapor condenses, in this case at or near the ground. Dew is water condensed on grass and other objects near the ground when temperatures fall below the dewpoint, and frost forms when the dewpoint is below freezing.

Precipitator. See Electrostatic Cleaner.

Pre-Columbian Art and Architecture, the art and architecture of Mexico, Central America, and the Andean region of South America before the arrival of Europeans.

Predestination, theological concept whereby certain souls are guaranteed salvation before birth by the grace of an omniscient God. A basic belief (in some form) of Muslims, Roman Catholics, and Jews, predestination took on renewed significance with the Calvinists, who believed that God from eternity had blessed certain souls and damned others, the difference to be seen in the individual's works.

Prefabrication, the assembly of buildings or their components at locations other than their final position. Prefabrication methods are used for kitchen cabinets and appliances, wall and floor panels, roof trusses, window-wall elements, and total buildings. Custom fabrication is used when the design calls for several identical components in a single structure, such as might be used in hospitals, apartment buildings, and schools. General prefabrication is designed for a wide range of building types, such as residential roof trusses, warehouse frames, and bowling alleys.

Pregnancy, the period of time from conception until birth. In the human it is generally divided into three 3-month periods called trimesters. In the first trimester the fetus grows from a small ball of cells to about 3in (7.6cm) in length, during which time all the vital organs, such as the heart, lungs, skeleton, and brain develop. In the second trimester the fetus grows to about 14in (36cm), and movements are first felt about midway. In the third trimester the fetus gains full body weight.

Pregnancy Tests, methods of determining whether or not a developing embryo or fetus is present in the uterus. Pregnancy is suggested or confirmed by the following: elevation of basal body temperature (taken on first waking in the morning) continuing after the first missed period; absence of the "fern" pattern on microscopic examination of cervical mucus; failure to induce menstruation by administering progesterone or neostigmine; finding of high levels of the hormone human chorionic gonadotropin (HCG) in the urine. Tests for HCG are now so refined that an accurate diagnosis of pregnancy can be made by this method on the first day after the missed period.

Prejudice, a preconceived feeling or attitude, most often unfriendly. A prejudiced person resists change in his view of ideas or people he does not like, and he may use discrimination or violence against them. Prejudice may grow out of individual conflicts or be taught by society. See also Apartheid; Discrimination.

Premature Birth, birth of a human less than 36 weeks after conception. 85% of liveborn premature babies survive, those of higher weight having the greater potential for life. Multiple births are frequently premature; poor maternal health and nutrition are also major factors.

Prendergast, Maurice Brazil (1861–1924), US painter, b. Roxbury, Mass. One of the most advanced artists of his time, he exhibited with The Eight in their famous show of 1908. His works include "Seashore" (1910), "Promenade" (1914–15), and the watercolors "The Balloon" and "Cape Ann."

Pre-Raphaelite Brotherhood, formulated in 1848 by Dante Gabriel Rossetti, John Everett Millais, and William Holman Hunt, three young English painters. Reacting against the inflated forms and sentiments that they found in the followers of Raphael, they preferred the sincerity they saw in the Florentine and Sienese who predated him. They tried to bring a new moral and literary seriousness to painting and to study nature directly.

Presbyterianism, a Protestant faith emphasizing a form of church government with a ranking of elders and ministers. John Calvin did not found but laid the foundation of the Presbyterian faith. John Knox established the church in Scotland where it remains dominant. Today it is one of the largest Protestant groups in the world.

Prescriptive Linguistics, investigation of the problems of language, as it is influenced by reasoning and behavior consistency. Prescriptivism holds that moral principles have more to do with reasoning and with consistency of behavior than with emotion and persuasion.

Presidential Government, system of government in which the center of authority resides in the president, who is the chief executive officer. The US Constitution bestows on the president both defined and implied powers which give him a vast amount of influence over both foreign and domestic policy. In most presidential governments, the chief executive is popularly elected to a specific term of office.

Presidential Powers, authority vested in a president as chief executive to carry out the laws of the land. In the United States, these include the powers of commander-in-chief of the armed forces; the appointment of executive agency heads, of ambassadors, and of Supreme Court justices; veto power over legislation; and the power to make treaties with senatorial consent. The influence of office further invests the president with the political power to ensure favorable action on his legislative program. A system of checks and balances allows the legislative and judicial branches to curb presidential excesses. See also Presidential Government; President of the United States.

Presidential Range, mountain chain of the White Mt system in N New Hampshire; culminates at Mt Washington, 6,288ft (1,918m).

Presidential Succession, procedure for filling a presidential vacancy occurring before the end of the prescribed term. The procedure was first outlined in the US Constitution and later amplified in the Presidential Succession Act of 1947. The vice president is first in line to succeed under the Constitution, followed by the speaker of the House of Representatives, the president pro tempore of the Senate, and the secretary of state according to the 1947 act. Amendment XXV to the Constitution, adopted Feb. 10, 1967, covers such emergencies as an incapacitating illness of the president. Under the amendment, the vice president's office is protected from vacancy and the method by which he takes the president's place, should the president be unable to discharge his duties, is specified.

President of the United States, US chief executive officer, as defined in Article II of the Constitution; elected by eligible voters through the Electoral College for a term of four years. No president may serve more than two terms under the provisions of Amendment XXII. The president must be a natural-born citizen and at least 35 years of age.

The Constitution specifies that presidential powers include those of commander-in-chief of the armed forces; the appointment of Supreme Court justices, ambassadors, and other officials; and the authority to grant pardons, make treaties with foreign countries with the advice and consent of two-thirds of the Senate; and veto legislation. The president is required to report to the Congress from time to time on the state of the union; to preserve, protect, and defend the Constitution; and to "faithfully execute" the laws. Presidential power is limited by the system of checks and balances.

Following is a chronological list of the US presidents and their terms of office. See also Presidential Powers.

Presidents of the United States
George Washington (1789–97)
John Adams (1797–1801)
Thomas Jefferson (1801–09)

James Madison (1809–17)
James Monroe (1817–25)
John Quincy Adams (1825–29)
Andrew Jackson (1829–37)
Martin Van Buren (1837–41)
William Henry Harrison (1841)
John Tyler (1841–45)
James Knox Polk (1845–49)
Zachary Taylor (1849–50)
Millard Fillmore (1850–53)
Franklin Pierce (1853–57)
James Buchanan (1857–61)
Abraham Lincoln (1861–65)
Andrew Johnson (1865–69)
Ulysses Simpson Grant (1869–77)
Rutherford Birchard Hayes (1877–81)
James Abram Garfield (1881)
Chester Alan Arthur (1881–85)
Grover Cleveland (1885–89, 1893–97)
Benjamin Harrison (1889–93)
William McKinley (1897–1901)
Theodore Roosevelt (1901–09)
William Howard Taft (1909–13)
(Thomas) Woodrow Wilson (1913–21)
Warren Gamaliel Harding (1921–23)
(John) Calvin Coolidge (1923–29)
Herbert Clark Hoover (1929–33)
Franklin Delano Roosevelt (1933–45)
Harry S Truman (1945–53)
Dwight David Eisenhower (1953–61)
John Fitzgerald Kennedy (1961–63)
Lyndon Baines Johnson (1963–69)
Richard Milhous Nixon (1969–74)
Gerald Rudolph Ford (1974–77)
James Earl Carter, Jr. (1977–81)
Ronald Wilson Reagan (1981–)

President Pro Tempore of the Senate, US Senator elected by his colleagues to preside over the Senate in the absence of the vice president or when the vice president has assumed the presidency.

Pressure Gauge, an instrument used to measure fluid pressure. Liquid-column gauges, such as manometers or pitot tubes, use shifts of liquid positions in U-shaped tubes to measure pressure. Mechanical gauges, such as Bourdon tubes or Bellows-element gauges, utilize elasticity of metals to measure pressure.

Pressurized-Water Reactor. *See* Fission Reactor.

Prester John, also John the Elder, legendary Christian king in either Asia or Africa. Supposedly descended from one of the Magi, he became the subject of much speculation during the European crusades—he was reported to have severely defeated the Persians. Several explorers joined the search for this possible ruler of either Mongolia or Ethiopia.

Preston, city in NW England, on the River Ribble; administrative center for Lancashire; market town and port. Industries: engineering, textiles, paper, chemicals. Pop. 97,365.

Prestressed Concrete, a type of strong concrete used in bridges and large, roofed structures. While it is settling, tightly drawn steel wires are extended through it, which, after bonding, are cut, releasing tension and compressing the concrete.

Pretoria, city in Republic of South Africa, on the Limpopo River 34mi (54km) N of Johannesburg; administrative capital of Republic of South Africa (since 1910) and capital of the Transvaal (since 1860). It was the scene of the imprisonment of Winston Churchill (1899) during the Boer War and of the signing of the Peace of Vereeniging (1902) ending the war; site of the National Cultural History Museum, National Zoological Gardens, several cathedrals, and universities of Pretoria (1930) and South Africa (1873). Founded 1855 by Marthinus Pretorius. Industries: iron, steel, diamonds, food processing. Pop. 595,000.

Preventive Medicine, branch of medicine concentrating on attempts to prevent disease through the use of immunization, public health measures, and other means.

Priam, in Greek mythology, the king of Troy at the time of the war with Greece. He had been installed as king in his youth by Hercules, but by the time of the ten-years' war had become a very old man. He lived to see his sons Hector and Paris and his daughter Polyxena killed by the enemy.

Pribilof Islands, group of four volcanic islands in SE Bering Sea, Alaska, 230mi (368km) N of Aleutian Islands. Discovered 1786 by Russian navigator, Gerasim Pribilof, it was purchased by the United States from Russia as part of Alaska purchase 1867. St Paul and St George, the larger islands, are breeding places for blue and white foxes and Alaska fur seals. Since 1911, when extinction of seals was threatened, the United States has administered a strict code of standards for commercial hunting of these animals. Pop. 642.

Price Theory, in economics, deals with the way prices are determined, including both the demand and the supply components. Price theory involves the study of the individual units within the economy, both the way the individual consumer seeks to maximize his utility position and the theory of the individual firm or business enterprise and its decisions in its attempts to maximize profits.

Prickly Pear, cactus, characterized by flat or cylindrical joints, native to North and South America. The jointed pads have tufts of bristles and the edible fruit is red and pulpy. Its showy yellow blossoms and interesting shape make it a popular house plant. Family Cactaceae; genus *Opuntia. See also* Cactus; Opuntia.

Pride's Purge (1648), expulsion of 140 moderate members of the English House of Commons. It was carried out by Col. Thomas Pride's regiment, on the orders of the republican army council, in preparation for the trial of King Charles I.

Priestley, J(ohn) B(oynton) (1894–1984), English author and playwright. His best known novel, *The Good Companions* (1929), is about a wandering music-hall troupe. He also wrote the nostalgic *Lost Empires* (1965) about the music-hall world, as well as several other novels. His nonfiction work includes *Literature and Western Man* (1960). His writing for the theater began with *Dangerous Corner* (1932), a satire on middle-class life, and includes *An Inspector Calls* (1945), another satire; *Time and the Conways* (1937), a science-fiction play; *Johnson Over Jordan* (1939), a modern morality play; and *The Glass Cage* (1957). He was awarded Britain's Order of Merit in 1977.

Priestley, Joseph (1733–1804), English chemist. A Unitarian minister, his involvement in science grew from his interest in the gases produced by fermentation in a local brewery. He studied the properties of carbon dioxide (then called "fixed air") and invented carbonated drinks. Although an advocate of the phlogiston theory, he discovered oxygen (which he called "dephlogisticated air") and a number of other gases, including ammonia and the oxides of nitrogen. Because of his support for the French Revolution his house was burned by an angry mob and he emigrated to the US, where he renewed a friendship with Benjamin Franklin. *See also* Phlogiston Theory.

Primates, order of mammals including monkeys, apes, and humans. Primates, native to most tropical and subtropical regions, are primarily herbivorous, day-active, tree-dwelling animals. Their hands and feet, usually with flat nails instead of claws, are adapted for grasping. Most species have opposable thumbs, and all but man have opposable big toes. They have a poor sense of smell, good hearing, and acute stereoscopic color vision. The outstanding feature of primates, especially man, is the large, complex brain and high intelligence. Primate characteristics are least pronounced in the relatively primitive *prosimians* (including tree shrews, lemurs, bush babies, lorises, and tarsiers) and are most pronounced in the more numerous and advanced *anthropoids* (monkeys, apes, and humans).

Prime Meridian, meridian adopted as the zero of longitude on a planet, the prime meridian on Earth passing through Greenwich, England.

Primer, Paint, a coat of paint, varnish, or sealer applied to a surface on which a second coating will be applied to ensure complete protection and covering to the surface. Primers are particularly important when the surface to be covered is porous, as cinder block; when the surface is a darker color than the finishing coat; or when the surface is extremely smooth and hard, as in some metals.

Primitivism, in art, a style sometimes practiced by highly skilled but untrained, nonacademic artists. The style features everyday subjects, great elaboration of detail, flat colors, unrealistic perspective, and often landscape. Leading primitivistic painters include Henri Rousseau in France and the Americans Grandma Moses, Morris Hirschfield, Israel Litwak, and Joseph Pickett.

Primo de Rivera, Miguel (1870–1930), Spanish general and political leader. After a distinguished military career, he staged a coup in 1923 with the full support of King Alfonso XIII. He dissolved the Cortes, rescinded the constitution, and ruled over a military dictatorship. In 1925 he instituted a civilian regime but continued as sole dictator. He ended the war in Morocco but faced varied opposition at home, especially from the Catalans. He was forced from office in 1930 and died in exile.

Primogeniture, under feudalism, the law or practice that entitled the eldest son to inherit his father's estate, necessary if fiefs were to remain intact. In most parts of France and Germany, partition of properties held in fief, known as *parage,* was more common, but in England, primogeniture became the prevailing custom by the 12th century. Although under the feudal system direct inheritance of real property was inconsistent with the concept of fiefs and vassalage, the vassal's son did have the right to apply to his father's lord for the privilege of assuming his father's lands and obligations under a new contract of vassalage. *See also* Feudalism.

Primordial Fireball, in cosmology, hypothetical object of enormous density and temperature that, according to the big-bang theory, existed prior to the explosion with which the universe originally came into existence. The entire mass and energy of the universe was originally contained in this object, which consisted of interacting atomic nuclei, became unstable and exploded at the zero point of cosmic time (2×10^{10} years ago). Energy radiation, chiefly in the form of photons, then dominated the expanding universe, the temperature decreasing until gravitation commenced to bind particles together and form matter. *See also* Big-Bang Theory of Universe.

Primrose, herbaceous perennial plant that grows in the cooler climates of Europe, Asia, Ethiopia, Java, and the United States. It has a tuft of leaves rising from the rootstock and clustered flowers of pale yellow to deep crimson. There are about 500 species. Family Primulaceae; genus *Primula.*

Prince Edward Island, province of E Canada, in the S part of the Gulf of St Lawrence, an arm of the Atlantic Ocean.

Land and economy. High cliffs rise along the coast, but the land is low and rolling. Fertile soils and a temperate climate are favorable to agriculture, which has long been the province's chief source of income. Fishing and tourism are also important. Manufacturing is limited to a few small plants.

People and education. Because of its small size, Prince Edward Island is the most densely populated province in Canada. English, Irish, and French stocks are predominant. The University of Prince Edward Island is at Charlottetown.

History. The island was discovered by Jacques Cartier in 1534. Known as Île St Jean (St John's Island), it was a French fishing station until it was captured by the British in 1745. Retaken by the French, it finally passed to the British by treaty in 1763. The name was changed to Prince Edward Island in 1798. As the forest was cleared, agriculture broadened the economic base, which had been founded on fishing. Hoping to alleviate its economic difficulties, Prince Edward Island joined the Dominion of Canada in 1873. The province was granted extensive economic aid during the 1940s, and in 1969 a comprehensive economic development plan was launched.

PROFILE

Admitted to Confederation: July 1, 1873; rank, 7th
National Parliament Representatives: Senate, 4; House of Commons, 4
Population: 116,251
Capital: Charlottetown
Chief Cities: Charlottetown; Summerside
Provincial Legislature: Legislative Assembly, 32
Area: 2,184sq mi (5,657sq km); rank, 10th
Elevation: Highest, 450ft (137m); lowest, sea level
Industries (major products): prefabricated homes, boats
Agriculture (major products): potatoes, dairy products, oats, barley
Fisheries: lobster, oysters, codfish, herring, haddock
Floral Emblem: lady's slipper

Princeton, borough in W central New Jersey, on Millstone River; scene of British defeat by US forces (1777) during American Revolution, Continental Congress (1783), and headquarters of Lord Cornwallis in home of Richard Stockton. Educational facilities include Princeton University (1746) and St Joseph's College (1938). Founded 1696 by Quakers; inc. 1813. Pop. (1980) 12,035.

Printed Circuit, electrical device. The wiring and some components consist of a thin coat of electrically conductive material on an insulating base in a pattern. Printed circuits replaced conventional wiring in radios, television sets, and computers for a time after World War II. But in the 1970s smaller and more compact circuits replaced the printed circuits, rendering them obsolete.

Malpeque, Prince Edward Island

Progressive Party: candidate Theodore Roosevelt

Sergei Prokofiev

Printmaking, process in graphics of making impressions from wood blocks, plates, stones, or silk. There are four main groups of graphic techniques. The first is the relief method, in which the parts of the wood block or metal plate that are to be printed are left in relief, and the remainder is cut away. Ink is rolled over and adheres to the raised portions. A print may be made by hand; a press is unnecessary. Some examples are woodcuts, wood engravings, linocuts, and metal cuts. The second is the intaglio method. Here the surface does not print; ink is held in the engraved furrows. Damp paper is pressed by a copper plate press into these cuts and picks up the ink from them. Examples are line engravings, drypoints, etchings, and aquatints. The third method is the surface or planographic method (lithography), in which greased areas on a slab of limestone or a metal plate reject printing ink. In the fourth method, the stencil, color is brushed through a hole in a protecting sheet onto the surface below. Examples are silkscreens and serigraphs.

Pripyat (Pripet or **Pinsk) Marshes,** marshlands in S Belorussian SSR and NW Ukrainian SSR, USSR; extending along Pripyat River 300mi (483km) E and W and 140mi (225km) N and S; largest tract of swamp in Europe, formerly in E Poland. Heavily wooded, largely uninhabited, nearly impassable area forms a natural defense barrier; site of battlefield during WWI, bypassed during WWII. Drainage of area was begun 1870 to reclaim land for cultivation and pasturage.

Prism, piece of transparent glass, plastic, quartz, etc, usually with a rectangular base and triangular ends, in which a light beam is refracted and is also split into its component colors by dispersion. Prisms are thus used to produce spectra in spectrometers. A light ray inside a prism can undergo total internal reflection from one of the sides so that a prism can also be used for inverting an image, as in binoculars, or changing the direction of a beam, as in a periscope.

Prism (in geometry), solid figure having two identical ends that are polygons in parallel planes, the other faces being parallelograms equal in number to the number of sides of one of the bases.

Privet, deciduous shrub native to Europe and N Africa. It is frequently planted in England and the United States as a hedge. It has smooth, lance-shaped leaves and loose clusters of tiny, white flowers that appear in June and July. It bears small black berries. Species include the common, or European, privet *(Ligustrum vulgare)* and the hardier California privet *(L. ovalifolium)* popular in the United States. Height: to 15ft (4.6m). Family Oleaceae.

Probability, number representing the likelihood of a given occurrence. The probability of a specified event is the number of ways that event may occur divided by the total possible number of outcomes. For instance, in one throw of a six-sided die there are six possible outcomes, and three of these results in an even number: the probability of throwing an even number is thus $3/6 = ½$. This assumes that each possibility is equally "likely." A less circular idea of probability utilizes the concept of a limit. If the die were thrown a large number of times the number of even numbers resulting divided by the total number of throws would tend to the value ½. Probability theory is concerned with the analysis of random events of this type.

Proboscis Monkey, large monkey of Borneo with protruding nose that is upturned in young monkeys and long and pendulous in older males. They are gregarious, day-active leaf and fruit eaters and swim and dive freely. Species *Nasalis larvatus. See also* Monkey.

Proclamation of Amnesty and Reconstruction (May 1865), declaration by President Andrew Johnson providing for restoration of the Confederate states to the Union. Under the plan, pardons were granted to Southerners who took an oath to support the United States. Elected government was restored in former Confederate states after state constitutional conventions repealed ordinances of secession and abolished slavery. Johnson's plan was negated by congressional action. *See also* Reconstruction.

Proclamation of 1763, British document designed to establish government in territories acquired in the French and Indian wars. Written by Lord Shelburne, head of the Board of Trade, and modified by his successor, the Earl of Hillsborough, it attempted to formulate a policy that would not antagonize the Indians. The provisions forbade American settlement west of the line formed by the Appalachians and ordered all settlers to vacate the area, which was to be reserved for the Indians. Three new provinces were established —Quebec, East Florida, and West Florida. Quebec was to be governed by British law.

Procrustes, in Greek mythology, a brigand in Attica. He tortured travelers that he captured by placing them on a bed and stretching them to fit it if they were too short, or cutting off their limbs if they were too long. Theseus had him killed by his own methods. He is also known as Damastes.

Proctology, branch of medicine dealing with the diagnosis and treatment of diseases of the rectum and lower intestine.

Procyon, or **Alpha Canis Minoris,** the brightest star in the constellation Canis Minor. Procyon A has a faint companion, Procyon B (white dwarf). Characteristics: apparent mag. 0.34 (A), 10.8 (B); absolute mag. 2.8 (A), 13.1 (B); spectral type F5 (A), wF (B); distance 11.4 light-years.

Producer Gas, a mixture of gases, flammable (eg carbon monoxide and hydrogen) and nonflammable (eg nitrogen and carbon dioxide) made by partial combustion of carbonaceous substances (such as coal) in air and steam. It has a lower heating value than other fuels, but can be manufactured with simple equipment. Producer gas is used as a fuel in large industrial furnaces.

Progesterone, steroid hormone secreted mainly by the corpus luteum of the mammalian ovary. Its principal function is to prepare and maintain the uterus for pregnancy. *See also* Hormones; Steroid.

Program, Computer, detailed, explicit set of directions for accomplishing some computation or manipulation of data by a computer. The program must be stated in a language suitable for use by the computer input compiler, assembler, or translation input device, or directly in machine language. Computer programming is an activity by human beings that begins with an understanding of the problem, follows with coding the request for solution of the problem in appropriate computer language, entering, and running tests until satisfactory results are achieved from the computer.

Program Music, music without words, intended to describe and represent events, people, or a story. Significant examples of program music are Beethoven's "Pastoral" *Symphony No. 6* (about an outing in the country) and Berlioz's *Symphonie Fantastique.* Program music reached great popularity in the late 19th century in such works as Moussorgsky's *Pictures at an Exhibition* and the tone poems of Richard Strauss.

Progression. *See* Arithmetic Progression.

Progressive Education, movement in 20th-century US education, commonly associated with the philosophy of John Dewey. Educators such as William Heard Kilpatrick applied Dewey's ideas, with additions and distortions, to schooling. Efforts to democratize the classroom, to consider children's needs, and to have them "learn by doing," led in some cases to what critics termed laxness.

Progressive Party, third party movement that split off from the Republicans in 1912, also called the Bull Moose Party. Under the leadership of Theodore Roosevelt, who praised the strength and vigor of the bull moose, the party advocated direct government and promoted advanced social and industrial legislation. Progressives also favored the establishment of a federal labor department in the cabinet and liberal extension of credit to farmers. Support for Progressive party presidential candidate Roosevelt seriously split the Republican vote in 1912, insuring the election of Democratic candidate Woodrow Wilson. However, by 1914, the Progressives were suffering setbacks, and in 1916, the party joined with the Republicans to endorse the nomination of Charles Evans Hughes.

Prohibition, era in which the manufacture and sale of alcoholic beverages was illegal. It was enacted through the 18th Amendment to the Constitution (1919) and was later repealed by the 21st Amendment (1933). Although the regulation of liquor had previously been under the jurisdiction of the states, the amendment made national previous state and local legislation and engendered widespread conflict between rural and urban groups. The refusal of most citizens to obey the Volstead Act, which enforced the 18th Amendment, led to the condoning of lawlessness, invasion of personal rights by federal agents, corruption of government officials and local police, paralysis of the courts, and the growth of organized crime financed by immense bootlegging profits.

Projective Geometry, a branch of geometry dealing with the properties of geometric configurations that are unaltered by projective transformation and in which the notion of length does not appear.

Prokofiev, Sergei (1891–1953), Soviet composer and pianist. He used a post-Romantic style featuring melody, biting dissonances, and orchestral brilliance. His most popular works are the ballets *Romeo and Juliet* (1940) and *Cinderella* (1944); the "Classical" *Symphony No. 1* (1917); *Peter and the Wolf* (1936), an orchestral suite for children; and the suite from the opera *The Love for Three Oranges* (1925). He also composed a great deal of piano music, nine piano sonatas, seven symphonies, five piano concertos, chamber music, film music, and an opera, *War and Peace* (1952), based on Tolstoy's novel.

Prolactin, also known as luteotropic hormone, synthesized in the anterior pituitary gland and stimulates milk production by the mammary gland.

Proletariat, term used to describe the working class. It was popularized by Karl Marx in his *Communist Manifesto* (1848). According to Marx, the exploited laboring class must seize power from the capitalists as the first step toward establishing a classless society.

Proline, white crystalline amino acid found in proteins. *See also* Amino Acid.

Promethea Moth, large moth of the giant silkworm family. Males are dark brown or black; females are much lighter. The caterpillar has a yellow head and blue body with rows of mostly black tubercles. Length: 2-3in (5-7.5cm). Family Saturniidae; species *Callosamia promethea.*

Prometheus, in Greek mythology, the fire-giver. His brother Epimetheus (afterthought) created the animals that turn their faces to Earth. Prometheus (forethought) created man who gazes at the stars, provided him with reason, and brought fire down from the Sun for his comfort. For his devotion to humanity Zeus had him chained to a rock in the Caucasus where an eagle consumed his liver for eternity.

Promethium, radioactive metallic element (symbol P) of the Lanthanide group, made (1941) by particle bombardment of neodymium and praseodymium. The element does not occur in the Earth's crust. Properties: at. no. 61; melt. pt. (approx) 1,976°F (1,080°C); boil. pt. (approx) 4,460°F (2,460°C); most stable isotope Pm^{145} (half-life 17.7yr). *See also* Lanthanide Elements.

Prominence, Solar, gaseous jet or cloud of hydrogen or helium that erupts from the Sun's surface and can extend a quarter of a million miles above it. Prominences present beautiful filamentous archlike or ribbonlike structures best seen at the Sun's limb during a total solar eclipse.

Pronghorn Antelope, North American ruminant native to desert and grasslands of SW Canada, W United States, and N Mexico. Both sexes have horns, shedding the outer sheath annually. Not a true antelope, its upper parts are reddish-brown to tan with black markings on face and neck. Erectile white rump hairs form a conspicuous white patch. It runs 40mi (64km) per hour. It is the only survivor of New World family Antilocapridae. Length: to 4.5ft (1.5m). Species *Antilocapra americana.*

Pronoun, the part of speech used to replace a noun. The noun replaced becomes the antecedent. Classifications: personal, relative, intensive, reflexive, interrogative, indefinite, and demonstrative.

Propaganda, use of words or familiar symbols to communicate ideas and information to a great number of people quickly and efficiently.

Propane, colorless flammable gas (formula C_3H_8), the third member of the alkane series of hydrocarbons. It occurs in natural gas, from which it is obtained; it is also obtained during petroleum refining. It is used (as bottled gas) as a fuel, as a solvent, and in the preparation of many chemicals. Properties: melt. pt. −310°F (−189.9°C); boil. pt. −44.5°F (−42.5°C).

Propellant, Rocket, material that undergoes chemical, nuclear, or thermoelectric reactions to propel a rocket.

Proper Motion, very small continuous change of a star's position on the celestial sphere, thus indicating the star's movement relative to the Sun. The largest annual proper motion is about 10 seconds of arc (Barnard's star) but for most stars it is negligible.

Prophet Zachariah, The. *See* Well Of Moses.

Proportion, mathematical relation of equality between two ratios, having the form $a/b = c/d$. A continued proportion is a group of three or more quantities, each bearing the same ratio to its successor, as in 1:3:9:27:81.

Proportional Representation, legislative representation based on percentage of either the electoral vote or the population. For example, in Europe political parties are awarded seats according to their percentage of the vote, an arrangement conducive to multi-party systems. In the US House of Representatives, each state is represented according to its percentage of the total population, an arrangement favorable to the larger states.

Proserpina, Latin equivalent to Persephone. She was also identified by some with Libitina, who became the goddess of funerals. Whenever anyone died, a piece of money had to be brought to her temple.

Prosody, systematic study of the principles of verse structure, especially meter. *See also* Meter; Versification.

Prostaglandins, hormonelike substances normally present in low levels in blood and various tissues. Biological effects include stimulation of muscle contraction, control of dilation and constriction of blood vessels, and a role in reproduction as well as joint inflammation in rheumatoid arthritis.

Prostate Gland, a gland in the male reproductive tract surrounding the urethra. It secretes specific chemicals that mix with sperm cells and secretions of other accessory glands to make up the sperm-containing fluid, semen, that is released at ejaculation.

Prostatitis, inflammation of the prostate gland caused by bacteria or their toxins. Chronic prostatitis sometimes occurs in men over 50, following an acute inflammation.

Prosthesis, manufactured substitute for a missing organ or part, originally an arm or leg. Until the 17th century artificial limbs were either wooden or solid metal, but innovations in metallurgy and engineering design have enabled lighter, jointed limbs to be made. Methods of attachment, too, have greatly improved. More recent prosthetic devices include artificial heart valves made of silicones that have now given excellent service for many years.

Prosthodontics, the dental specialty that deals with the replacement of missing teeth and surrounding tissue with artificial substitutes. The proper fitting of such devices requires a precise knowledge of occlusion and jaw movements and the skills necessary for preparation, impression making, placement, and follow-up care.

Protactinium, rare radioactive metallic element (symbol Pa) of the actinide group, first isolated 1917 by three independent groups. Chief source is pitchblende. Properties: at. no. 91; at. wt. 231.0359; sp gr 15.37; melt. pt. 2,012°F (1,100°C); boil. pt. 7,232°F (4,033°C); most stable isotope Pa^{231} (half-life 3.25×10^4 yrs. *See also* Actinide Elements.

Protectionism, policy of restricting foreign imports through a system of high tariffs and quotas, thus stimulating the domestic economy and "protecting" domestic manufacturers from foreign competition. Protectionist ideology was the basis of United States economic policy since its formulation by Alexander Hamilton in the late 18th century, but was disputed by the South in the decades preceding the Civil War.

Protective Coloration, natural camouflage or warning colors that organisms have to blend in with their surrounding environment or to warn off predators. Tigers and some moths have permanent protective coloring. Chameleons and some flatfish can change color to match the background. Warning colors of an animal usually mean it is poisonous or distasteful to most predators. Predators learn to recognize and avoid these distinctive warning colorations. *See also* Mimicry.

Protectorate, period of English government (1653–59). The Protectorate was established when Oliver Cromwell dissolved the Rump Parliament and instituted the nominated Parliament. When it proved ineffective the army presented and Cromwell accepted a constitutional document, the Instrument of Government. Cromwell became lord protector of the commonwealth of England, Scotland, Ireland, ruling with one house of Parliament and a council. The Protectorate was actually a military dictatorship. Following Cromwell's death the Rump Parliament was recalled and Charles II was returned to the throne (1660).

Protein, organic compound containing many amino acids linked together. Living cells use about 20 amino acids, but as proteins have thousands of amino acids in each molecule the number of possible proteins is very large. The order of amino acids in proteins is controlled by the genes in the cell's DNA. The most important proteins are the enzymes, which determine all the chemical reactions in the cell. Other proteins are used in structures such as the cell walls and internal membranes. Basic proteins are associated with DNA in the cell nucleus. Tough, flexible proteins include cartilage and keratin, which is used in hair, nails, and horn. *See also* Amino Acid; Enzymes; Peptide.

Protestant Episcopal Church, US branch of the Anglican Communion, formally organized in Philadelphia in 1789. It is self-governing, with the laity having a large role in administration duties. A presiding Bishop is elected by the General Convention. The Apostles' Creed and the Nicene Creed are accepted. Membership is approximately 3,200,000. *See also* Apostles' Creed, The; Nicene Creed, The.

Protestant Ethic, social theory devised by Max Weber (1864–1920) that explains the origins and development of capitalism in terms of the Calvinist doctrine of predestination. Calvinists in the 17th century interpreted worldly success as a sign of spiritual salvation. Therefore they worked hard and lived frugally in order to accumulate the symbols of salvation and convince themselves and others of their membership in the elect. This syndrome created a pattern of behavior that fostered the growth of capitalism and individual achievement.

Protestantism, system of Christian faith and practices first developed in the 16th century. It differs from Roman Catholicism mainly in the question of papal authority. The Protestant church is understood as a fellowship of believers, with Scripture as the source of faith. It began as a number of independent reform attempts, therefore there are many different churches within the Protestant tradition: Lutheran; Calvinist; Anglican or Episcopal; and "free church" are the four main forms of Protestantism. They are usually understood as complementary rather than in opposition in their search for Christian truths. A large body of conservatives, known as fundamentalists, developed in reaction to 18th-century liberalism.

Generally, preaching is stressed as primary before sacramental practices. The Word is the focal point of faith and of Christian living. Asceticism is largely rejected, while personal morality is stressed. Justification is through faith alone. In 1948, the World Council of Churches, open to all denominations, was formed in the effort to unite in an ecumenical movement. *See also* individual Protestant churches.

Proteus, in Greek mythology, a sea god, son of Poseidon and Amphitrite. He is depicted as a little old man of the sea. Proteus possessed the gift of prophecy and the ability to alter his form at will. In an instant he could become fire, flood, or a wild beast.

Prothrombin, precursor of the blood enzyme thrombin; converted into thrombin by thromboplastin. *See also* Blood Clotting.

Protista, large group of unicellular and simple multicellular organisms including protozoa, algae, bacteria, and fungi. Used to overcome the difficulty of distinguishing simple plants from simple animals, the term also may include organisms with many nuclei within one cell wall (coenocytes).

Protoceratops, horned ornithischian dinosaur of Cretaceous times from Central Asia. It had a frill of bone on the back of its skull but, unlike later forms, its nose was hornless. Fossilized nests of eggs of this reptile have been found. Length: 6ft (1.8m). *See also* Triceratops.

Proton, stable elementary particle (symbol p) with a positive charge that is equal in magnitude to that of the electron. It forms the nucleus of the lightest isotope of hydrogen and with the neutron is a constituent of the nuclei of all other elements. It also occurs in primary cosmic rays. It is a baryon with spin ½ and a mass 1836.12 times that of the electron. Beams of high-velocity protons, produced by particle accelerators, are used to study nuclear reactions. *See also* Atomic Number.

Protonation, the addition of a proton (an elementary particle identical with the nucleus of the hydrogen atom). *See also* Proton.

Protoplasm, semifluid, essential living matter within all plant and animal cells. *See also* Cell.

Protozoa, phylum of one-celled animals found throughout the world in marine or fresh water and as parasites. First seen in 1674 by van Leeuwenhoek, these microscopic animals have the ability to move (by cilia or psoudopodia) and have nucleus, cytoplasm, and cell wall; some contain chlorophyll. They are transparent, green, iridescent, blue, rose, or yellow. Reproduction is by fission or encystment. Length: 2/25000in (2/1000mm) to 0.2in (5mm). The 30,000–80,000 species are divided into four classes—Flagellata, Rhizopoda, Ciliophora, and Sporozoa.

Proust, Marcel, (1871–1922), French novelist. The son of a doctor, he studied law at the Sorbonne, and deliberately infiltrated the Parisian social élite. Proust was interested in philosophy and translated some works of John Ruskin. He suffered from asthma and nervous disorders and in 1908 withdrew into his cork-lined bedroom. Here he wrote the seven-part novel cycle *A la recherche du temps perdu (Remembrance of Things Past),* published between 1913–1927. The first volume, *Swann's Way,* was published at his own expense, since his eccentricities and his reputation for dilettantism prevented him from finding a publisher. The second volume (*Within a Budding Grove,* 1918), however, won the Prix Goncourt. With his health failing, Proust raced to complete his work; the last three books were published posthumously.

Provençal, Romance language spoken in SE France, in the historic region of Provence. With most of its

Pronghorn antelope

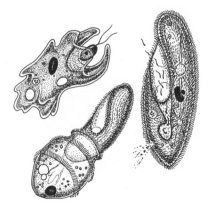

Protozoa

Psychological Novel: James Joyce

speakers fluent in French, it has no official status in the country and is gradually dying out.

Provence, region and former province in SE France; it included present depts. of Var, Vaucluse, and Bouches du Rhône, and parts of Alpes-de-Haute-Provence and Alpes-Maritimes; capital was Aix-en-Provence. Coastal area was settled 600 BC by Greeks; Romans set up colonies 2nd century BC; passed to Louis XI of France 1481; it was a province of France until the French Revolution, when France was divided into departments. Region includes French Riviera, famous vacation spot; valley of Rhône produces many crops; cattle are raised in Camargue; scenery, historic remains, and old towns attract many tourists.

Proverbs (of Solomon), biblical book of the Old Testament, probably the oldest existing example of Hebrew Wisdom literature. Poetic, as is the Song of Solomon, Proverbs deals with practical piety. It makes no mention of Israel's history; instead, God's revelation is seen more in patterns of nature than historical events.

Providence, capital city and port of entry in NE Rhode Island, on Providence Bay; largest city of Rhode Island; seat of Providence co. Founded 1636 by Roger Williams, the city developed as refuge for religious dissenters from Massachusetts; joined Providence Plantations 1644; prospered as trading port with West Indies and as textile center 18th century. In 1772, the city's men captured and burned Britain's ship *Gaspee*; on May 4, 1776, city was scene of signing of Rhode Island Independence Act; made capital of Rhode Island 1900. Landmarks include Stephen Hopkins House (1755), John Brown House (1786), First Baptist meetinghouse (1775); site of Brown University (1764), Bryant College (1863), Rhode Island School of Design (1877), Rhode Island College (1854), Pembroke College (1891), Providence College (1917). Industries: jewelry, electrical equipment, silverware, machine tools, rubber goods. Inc. 1832. Pop. (1980) 156,804.

Provo, city in N central Utah, 38mi (61km) SSE of Salt Lake City, on Provo River; seat of Utah co; site of Brigham Young University (1875); distribution, manufacturing, processing center. Industries: steel, farming, fruit, electronic equipment, mining, tourism. Founded 1849 by Mormons; inc. 1851. Pop. (1980) 73,907.

Prud'hon, Pierre-Paul (1758–1823), French painter. His work served to link the 18th-century Neoclassic style with 19th-century Romanticism. In 1794 he executed a fine series of portraits, which includes "Madame Anthony and Her Children." His best works were produced after 1799 and include "Justice and Divine Vengeance Pursuing Crime."

Prune, variety of plum that can be dried without fermentation at the pit. It is grown in Europe, especially Yugoslavia, and Australia, Chile, South Africa, and United States. The flesh of the fruit easily separates from the pit. Family Rosaceae; species *Prunus domestica. See also* Plum.

Pruning, the removal of branches, stems, or buds from a tree or shrub. Pruning is usually done to improve the appearance of ornamental trees and shrubs and the productivity of fruit trees and berry bushes. Fruit trees are usually pruned in the winter or early spring, as are hydrangeas, rose of sharon, and other flowering shrubs that bloom on new wood. Lilac, forsythia, and other spring-blooming shrubs—all of which bloom on old wood—are usually pruned after they have bloomed in order to avoid removing flower buds.

Prussia, former German state, occupying most of N and central Germany; capital was Berlin. Conquered by Teutonic Knights 13th century, it was a secular hereditary duchy under Hohenzollern dynasty of Brandenburg (1525); independent of Poland (1660). Region became strong German military state, especially under Frederick the Great (1740–86); it was expanded to include Rhineland territories (1720), Silesia (1742–63), Poland (1772–95), Saxony (1815), Lauenburg and Schleswig (1865). Region was under Chancellor Otto von Bismarck through three wars, with Denmark (1864), Austria (1866), and France (1870–71). William I of Prussia was proclaimed emperor of Germany 1871, giving Prussia great power in the new German Empire. Prussia became a republic 1918 and joined the Weimar Republic (Germany) as one of its states. Formally abolished by the Allied Control Council, March 1, 1947, Prussian territories were divided between Soviet Union and Poland.

Przewalski's horse, or **Mongolian Wild Horse,** only surviving species of original wild horse. Once common on Eurasian plains, it is now found only in Mongolia and Sinkiang. It is a small and stocky horse with an erect black mane and no forelock. Its red-brown coat is marked with a darker line on the back and shoulders and leg stripes. Height: 47.2–57.5in (120–146cm) at shoulder; weight: 441–661lb (200–300 kg). Family Equidae; species *Equus caballus przewalski.*

Psalms or **Psalter,** book of the Old Testament, consists of 150 poetic pieces in the form of poems, songs, hymns, or laments; divided into five books; most are dated between *c.* 537BC and *c.* 100BC, and vary in tone and subject.

Psaltery, medieval stringed musical instrument similar to the dulcimer or zither. Several strings on a frame with a shallow sounding board are plucked with fingers or with a plectrum. Originally used in Hebrew services, it was used to accompany the singer of Psalms. It was depicted in classic art as a variant of the kithara or lyre.

Psilophytales, an order of simple dichotomously branched plants of the Paleozoic Era. They were native to Europe and Canada. This order includes the oldest known land plants with vascular structure.

Psi Particles, two elementary particles (mesons), discovered 1974, each with an anomalously long lifetime. *See also* Quark.

Psittacosis, or parrot fever, usually a disease affecting the respiratory system of birds. Probably caused by bacteria, it is transmissible to man through handling of infected birds, bites from them, or dust surrounding them. In birds, there is diarrhea and breathing difficulty; in man, headache and vomiting. Treatment is administration of antibiotics.

Pskov, city in NW Russian SFSR, USSR, on the Velikaya River near the SE shore of Lake Pskov, 155mi (250km) SW of Leningrad; capital of Pskov oblast. Historically important, Pskov dates from the 8th century; originally an outpost of Novgorod, Pskov gained independence in the 13th century and was annexed to Moscow 1510; it was a medieval commercial center; in WWII, it was occupied by the Germans 1941–44 and suffered extensive damage; site of teachers' college, 12th–16th-century Kremlin, 17th-century cathedral containing the tombs of the Pskov princes, many churches, monasteries, and art museums. Industries: flax processing, agricultural machinery, railroad shops, linen, rope, tanning, distilling, flour milling, footwear. Pop. 171,000.

Psoriasis, chronic disorder of the skin in which there are patches, plaques, or papules. The red or brown lesions are slightly elevated and usually covered with white scales. They frequently appear on chest, knees, elbows, and scalp. Cause is unknown and there is no specific treatment, though sunlight helps.

Psyche, in Greek mythology, a beautiful mortal loved by Eros (Cupid). Psyche is the Greek word for butterfly and for soul. Apuleius, a writer of the 2nd century AD, tells how the Pythian oracle warned her she would love no mortal, how she wed Cupid, lost him, and how they were reunited. The allegory suggests the freeing of the soul after purification through suffering.

Psychiatry, branch of medicine specializing in analyzing, diagnosing, and treating behavior disorders and mental illnesses. A psychiatrist must first earn an M.D. degree and then take special training in psychology. Methods of treatment range from talking out problems in psychotherapy to more specifically medical measures such as drug therapy. *See also* Abnormal Psychology; Psychoanalysis.

Psychoanalysis, method for treating behavior disorders and a theory that attempts to explain both normal and abnormal behavior. Sigmund Freud pioneered in treating psychoneurotic patients by such methods as encouraging free association and interpreting dreams. Traditional psychoanalysis requires a patient to spend three or more sessions a week with the analyst for a period of years. Freud also proposed theories of personality development, which, despite challenges, remain major influences on psychology, psychiatry, and other fields such as literature. *See also* Freud, Sigmund; Psychiatry.

Psychobiology, field, closely related to physiological psychology, that studies anatomical and biochemical structures and processes as they affect behavior.

Psycholinguistics, study of language, its patterns, its forms, and the way it is acquired and used. The development of language is studied by observing young children as they learn to speak. It is not known if certain linguistic potentials are innate or learned, and it has not been determined whether other species can learn abstract communication. David Premack's experiments with "Sarah" have shown that this chimpanzee is capable of understanding the concept of words.

Psychological Novel, type of novel whose main emphasis is on characterization and motivation rather than on plot or setting. In a psychological novel internal action explains and develops external action. The term was first applied to certain 19th-century novels, such as those by George Eliot. Its chief use, however, is to describe 20th-century novels influenced by Freudianism. James Joyce's *Ulysses* (1922) is an outstanding example.

Psychology, biosocial science that studies the behavior of humans and other animals. Psychology draws on the biological sciences to study, for example, the structure and functions of the brain, to find out how the eye, ear, and other sense organs work, and to assess the effects of drugs. Psychology is also a social science because it focuses on how humans interact, react, and adjust to other individuals and groups. The stress is on human behavior, but experiments with other animals provide useful information. *See also* individual fields in psychology.

Psychopharmacology, study of how drugs affect behavior. Drugs are classified according to their chemical structure and effect, for example: sedative hypnotics like barbiturates and alcohol, stimulants like amphetamines, opiate narcotics like heroin, and psychedelics and hallucinogens like LSD. Psychologists are particularly concerned with the effect of drugs on behavior, tolerance levels, physical dependence, and drug treatment of mental illness.

Psychophysics, measurement of stimuli and the sensations they produce. Beginning with the 19th-century experimentalists Ernst Weber and Gustav Fechner, specialists in this field have studied the relation between intensity of stimulus (sound, for example) and intensity of sensation (hearing, in this case).

Psychosomatic Disorders, physical by products of psychological disturbances. Continued stress, whether caused by internal or external conditions, will often lead to a physical disturbance, eg, changes in respiration, circulation, digestion, sweat-gland activity, and other hormone regulated activities. Any of these body mechanisms may become the target of a psychosomatic disturbance. For example, continued erosion of the gastric mucosa resulting from stress will lead to gastric ulcers; continued blood-pressure elevation will produce hypertension and greatly increase the risk of heart disease or stroke. A psychosomatic basis has been discovered in some varieties of asthma and dermatitis.

Psychosurgery, any surgical procedure practiced on the central nervous system that is intended to alter behavior; performed upon animals for experimental purposes or upon humans to treat mental illness.

Psychotherapy, techniques (verbal, social, interpersonal, and expressive) used to modify behavior or psychological disturbance. Psychoanalysis (Freudian psychotherapy) emphasizes discovery of the unconscious determinants of behavior and personal-historical antecedents of personality. Humanistic psychotherapists reject the more mechanistic aspects of Freudian therapy in favor of a more optimistic, interpersonal, and integrated approach. Behavior therapy seeks to modify behavior through the application of principles of learning. Other varieties include group therapy; psychodrama; play, music and art therapy; and encounter therapy. *See also* Psychoanalysis.

Psychotic Disorders, severe mental disturbances in which there is a profound loss of ability or a basic incapacity adequately to test reality. Psychotic disorders may be of organic or psychogenic origin and are expressed through a wide variety of syndromes, including schizophrenic and paranoid reactions. Delusions and hallucinations are often, though not necessarily, present. Other symptoms often observed are confusion in orientation to time, place, or person; poor judgment; communication disturbance; and social withdrawal. *See also* Brain Disorders; Paranoid Personality; Schizophrenia.

Ptah, in Egyptian mythology, the god of craftsmen and creator of the universe, depicted as a standing, mummified man. He was thought to have created the world. The center of his worship was at Memphis.

Ptarmigan, northern or alpine grouse. Pairs are seasonally monogamous and the male engages in courtship displays and takes a vigorous role in defending the nest and rearing young. The N Eurasian rock ptarmigan *(Lagopus mutus)* has three protective color phases: white in winter, brown in spring and summer, gray in autumn; length: 14in (35cm). The white-tailed ptarmigan *(Lagopus leucurus)* is found in N New World; length: 12in (30cm). *See also* Grouse.

Pteranodon, short-tailed, toothless Cretaceous pterosaur of United States and Europe. A long, bony crest at back of skull balanced its three-foot (0.9m) beak. Its wing span 25ft (7.6m) allowed for gliding rather than active flight as it soared over ancient seas in search of fish.

Pteridophyte, obsolete name for any of a group of spore-bearing plants. At one time, pteridophytes included club moss, horsetails, and ferns, and several fossil groups. These plants have similar life cycles but in other respects are quite distinct.

Pterosaur, extinct reptile characterized by flying membranes, supported by single, elongated finger on each side. Worldwide in distribution during Jurassic and Cretaceous times, early forms had teeth and tails; later forms were tailless and had toothless beaks. They ranged from sparrow to goose-sized with a wing span to 50ft (15m).

Ptolemaic System, an arrangement of celestial bodies and their motions, formulated by Ptolemy about AD 140, in which the Earth was considered the center of the universe. The stars were thought to be fixed to a sphere, with another sphere, the prime mover, outside. The prime mover provided the force operating the whole system as well as the daily rotation of the heavens. Gradually the Ptolemaic system was superseded by the heliocentric system, from the 16th century onward.

Ptolemy, the name of a 14-member Greek dynasty that ruled Egypt for 300 years (323–30 BC). **Ptolemy I,** one of Alexander the Great's best generals, obtained Egypt upon the latter's death in 323 BC. After struggling for years to maintain his position, he assumed the title of king (305) and built Alexandria into a cultural and commercial center. His son **Ptolemy II** succeeded him and during his reign (285–246) Egypt attained its greatest height. Under **Ptolemy III** (246–221), Egyptian fleets gained control of the eastern Mediterranean. **Ptolemy IV** (221–205) began his reign by murdering his mother and brother to preserve his throne. Weakened by the king's continued decadence, the administration disintegrated, and soon after Ptolemy's death (205) the kings of Syria and Macedonia seized all of Egypt's provinces. The ministers of the infant king **Ptolemy V** appealed to Rome for help and from about 200 BC on the power of the dynasty was superseded by the influence of Rome. The rest of the Ptolemy line ruled ineffectually down to the time of Cleopatra (30 BC), after which Egypt became a Roman province.

Ptolemy, anglicized form of Claudius Ptolemaeus (fl. 2nd century AD), Greek scientist, whose influence on scientific thought, especially astronomy, extended well into the 17th century, b. in Ptolemais Hermii, Egypt. Active in Alexandria, he wrote several books on geography, geometry, and optics, but his most famous work is the *Almagest,* a treatise on the motions of the heavenly bodies according to the Ptolemaic system.

Ptomaine Poisoning. *See* Food Poisoning.

Puberty, the period of development climaxed by maturation of sexual organs in both sexes such that reproduction is possible. Secondary sexual characteristics start to become evident. It occurs in males at about 14 years, and 12 in females.

Puberty Rites, rites that are symbolic representations of an adolescent reaching maturity. With boys they occur between the ages of nine and twenty whereas with girls they usually accompany the first menstruation. The rites initiate young people into the society of adults and often involve, in the case of boys, an ordeal (such as scarification among the Nuer) and, with girls, purification. *See also* Rites of Passage.

Public Health, branch of medicine that attempts to protect and improve the health of people in a community. It is involved with disease control, such as mass vaccination programs, and with establishing and maintaining health standards for housing, food, water, waste disposal, and air quality.

Puccini, Giacomo (1858–1924), Italian composer of operas, some of which are among the most popular ever composed. His operas include *Manon Lescaut* (1893), *La Bohème* (1896), *Tosca* (1900), *Madame Butterfly* (1904), *The Girl of the Golden West* (1910), and *Turandot* (left incomplete at his death and first performed posthumously, 1926).

Pudu, genus of South American deer that is almost tailless and has short, spikelike antlers. Rivaling musk deer and muntjacs in its small size, it measures only 15in (38cm) at the shoulder. Adults are a rich brown to gray. Family Cervidae. *See also* Deer.

Puebla (Puebla de Zaragoza), city in E central Mexico, 75mi (121km) SE of Mexico City; capital of Puebla prov. The area was occupied by US forces (1847) during Mexican War; scene of French defeat by Mexicans (1862), later occupied by French (1863). Puebla is the site of many old buildings including a cathedral (1552–1649), theater (1790), university (1537). Industries: pottery, glass, soap, leather products, textiles. Founded *c.*1535 as Puebla de los Angeles; renamed *c.*1870 for Gen. Ignacio Zaragoza. Pop. 516,000.

Pueblo, industrial and commercial city in SE central Colorado, 40mi (64km) SSE of Colorado Springs. Industries: steel, iron, aluminum, concrete products, auto parts, beer, lumber. Founded by gold miners 1858; inc. 1873. Pop. (1980) 101,686.

Pueblo, a generic name for the several North American Indian tribes inhabiting the mesa and Rio Grande region of Arizona and New Mexico. These include four language families: the Queres, Tewa (or Tanoan), Shoshonean, and Zuni. Their mud-and-stone architecture is famous throughout the Southwest, and the seven-story structure at Zuni gave rise to the legendary "Seven Cities of Cibola" eagerly sought by the Spaniards.

Puerperal Fever, an infection occurring in women after childbirth. It is caused by streptococci entering the body through lack of aseptic techniques. With modern hospital methods, the fever has become a rarity.

Puerto Rico, an autonomous commonwealth in union with the United States; it comprises the smallest and easternmost island of Greater Antilles; includes Vieques, Mona, Culebra. Puerto Rico is located in the N part of the tropical zone and dominates the principal entrance from the Atlantic Ocean to the Caribbean Sea. The land is mountainous, highest peak at Cerro de Punta 4,389ft (1,339m), surrounded by broken coastal plain. Only 1/3 of Puerto Rico's land area is arable; the economy is supported mostly by the production of sugar and sugar products; tobacco, coffee, pineapples, cabbages, corn, tomatoes are also grown. Industries include pharmaceuticals, electronics assembly, appliances, cement, canning, cigars, dairying, molasses, and refrigerators. Tourism is also important. The 20th century has seen a great increase in the middle class as opposed to the distinct minority of wealthy upper class and majority of poor class of the past. Nevertheless, unemployment remains high, and many Puerto Ricans leave the island for the mainland, many settling in the urban slums of the large cities. Most of the people are Roman Catholic and engage in Spanish customs, modified by US influences. Puerto Rico has public school systems and universities for higher education.

The government is modeled after the United States; the head of executive branch is a governor, elected for a 4-year term. The United States handles all foreign affairs. The island was discovered by Christopher Columbus in 1493; colonization began with Ponce de León, who was made governor 1510. In 1515 sugar cane was introduced; and by 1518 the first black slaves were brought to Puerto Rico. The Spanish concentrated on the exploitation of gold, by 1570 approx. four million dollars' worth of gold was mined but the resources were exhausted. In 1804 island ports were opened for foreign trade; economic development brought with it the desire for autonomy of native Puerto Ricans. In 1873 slavery and forced labor were abolished; 1898 Spain ceded Puerto Rico to the United States, following the Spanish-American War. Since 1898 the United States has aided development of Puerto Rico, in education, economy, transportation, and communication. In 1917 the Jones Act secured local elections of legislature and US citizenship for all Puerto Ricans. In 1932 the name Porto Rico was officially changed to Puerto Rico. During the 1970s a militant Puerto Rican nationalist group committed some terrorist acts. In 1976, Romero Barcelo was elected governor on a platform of statehood for the island but was voted out of office in 1984. He was succeeded by Rafael Hernández Colón, a former governor and proponent of commonwealth status. The United Nations has called for the United States to withdraw from the island.

PROFILE

Official Name: Commonwealth of Puerto Rico
Area: 3,435sq mi (8,897sq km)
Population: 3,410,000
Chief Cities: San Juan 522,700; Ponce 207,500; Mayaguez 106,500
Religion: Roman Catholic
Language: Spanish, English
Monetary Unit: US dollar

Puff Adder, widely distributed African and Arabian viper that hunts large rodents in open country. Its skin pattern varies, but it usually has yellow, crescentic markings on brown. Its bite is often fatal to man. Up to 70 live young are born at one time. Length: to 4ft (1.2m). Family Viperidae; species *Bitis arietans. See also* Hognose Snake; Viper.

Puffball, any of a large family of mushrooms (Lycoperdaceae) whose spore masses become powdery at maturity and are expelled in "puffs" when the case is pressed. True puffballs are stemless and mostly edible; false ones have stems and are inedible.

Puffbird, tropical New World dull-colored bird with a large head and loose, puffy plumage. It appears unwary, stupid, seldom fleeing and always perching in the same place, where it catches insects on the wing. It nests in an earth bank. Family Bucconidae.

Puffer, or **Blowfish,** also swellfish, marine fish found in warm and temperate seas. When taken from the water it swallows air and inflates its body. Colors are dusky brown and green with band markings. Smaller, sharp-nosed varieties are often kept in home aquariums. Length: to 36in (91.4cm). Family Tetraodontidae;

Pterosaur

Puerto Rico

Joseph Pulitzer

among the 100 species are the northern *Sphaeroides maculatus.*

Puffin, awkward looking, migratory seabird found in N Northern Hemisphere. The Atlantic puffin *(Fratercula arctica)* has a short neck, long reddish bill, and reddish legs and feet; length: 10in (25cm). A single white, sometimes spotted, egg is laid in a crude nest on an oceanic cliff.

Pug, small dog (toy group) first popular in Holland; probably originated in China and brought West by Dutch East India Company traders. It has a large, round head; blunt, square muzzle; deep face wrinkles; and a well-defined black face mask. Small, thin ears are folded forward or fold over and back. A wide-chested, short body is set on strong, straight, medium-length legs. The tail is tightly curled over the hip. Colored silver, apricot, or fawn with black, the coat is short and soft. Average size: 11in (28cm) high at shoulder; 14–18lb (6.5–8kg). *See also* Toy Dog.

Pugachev, Emelyan Ivanovich (*c.*1742–75), Cossack leader. He led a massive popular revolt against Catherine II that spread along the Ural River and across the Volga basin. In 1773 he proclaimed himself Peter III, promising freedom from serfdom, taxes, and military service, and the elimination of landlords and officials. He was defeated in late 1774, brought to Moscow for trial, and executed.

Puget Sound, arm of the Pacific Ocean in NW Washington, connected with the ocean by Juan de Fuca Strait through Admiralty Inlet; Bremerton, on W shore opposite Seattle, is site of a large navy yard. Explored and named 1792 by Capt. George Vancouver. Area: approx. 561sq mi (1,453sq km).

Pulaski, Casimir (1748?–79), Polish nobleman, patriot, and soldier. He participated in the founding of the Confederation of Bar (1768), and in the subsequent unsuccessful revolt against Russian control of Poland. He fled first to Turkey and then to France, where Benjamin Franklin persuaded him to join the American colonists' revolt (1777). He was appointed brigadier general by the Continental Congress. He was mortally wounded at the siege of Savannah, Georgia (1779).

Puli, Hungarian shepherd dog (working group). Breed is at least 1,000 years old. A vigorous dog, it has a medium-sized, slightly domed head with medium-long muzzle and large nose; V-shaped hanging ears; medium-length, straight-backed body; strong legs; and tail curved over the back. The unusual long, double coat mats into feltlike cords; color must be solid to be acceptable to kennel clubs. Average size: 17–19in (43–48cm) high at shoulder; 25–35lb (11.5–16kg). The puli is considered a good guard and watch dog. *See also* Working Dog.

Pulitzer, Joseph (1847–1911), US journalist, b. Hungary. He emigrated in 1864 and served in the Union Army. He pioneered sensational journalism and founded the Pulitzer prizes. He bought (1878) the St Louis *Post,* merging it with the *Dispatch.* In 1883 he bought the *New York World* and made it the nation's biggest daily by crusading powerfully for oppressed workers and against alleged big business and government corruption, using the "yellow-press" techniques that William Randolph Hearst copied successfully. Part of Pulitzer's $2 million bequest to found Columbia University's School of Journalism finances the annual Pulitzer prizes.

Pulitzer Prizes, annual awards presented for outstanding achievement in journalism, letters, and music.

The prizes are paid for by the income of a trust fund of the estate of Joseph Pulitzer (1847–1911) to the trustees of Columbia University. There are eight awards in journalism including best cartoon, best news photograph, and outstanding editorial writing. There are prizes for fiction, drama, history, biography, poetry, and musical composition. Four scholarships are also awarded. Journalism awards are $1,000 each and the letters and music awards are $500 respectively.

Pulleys and Hoists, commonly known as block and tackle, used to gain a mechanical advantage in lifting or moving heavy loads. The system consists of a combination of a flexible material, such as rope or chain, and a wheel (pulley), which changes the direction of motion and the applied force. The mechanical advantage in an ideal system, discounting friction, is determined by counting the number of lines leading to the movable pulley.

Pullman, George Mortimer (1831–97), US industrialist and inventor of railroad sleeping car, b. Brocton, N.Y. He was president of Pullman Palace Car Co. and started a paternalistic model town for employees.

Pulmonary Embolism, chronic and sometimes fatal obstruction of a pulmonary blood vessel by a massive traveling clot. It generally leads to symptoms of shock, acute high blood pressure in the pulmonary arteries, and eventual failure of the right ventricle of the heart. *See also* Embolism.

Pulsar, rapidly rotating star of extreme density that, although only between about 1.4–3 times as massive as the Sun, has been compressed by gravitational collapse to only a few miles across. Pulsars emit regularly spaced radio pulses and in some cases X-ray and visible pulses; they were first detected in 1967. The magnetic field and force of gravity are also extreme by terrestrial standards. Pulsars are now identified with neutron stars, postulated in the 1930s as dying stars that would be too massive to become stable white dwarfs and that would collapse further with tremendous release of energy. In the ensuing supernova explosion much of the star's mass is blown off to leave a tiny compressed body composed of tightly packed neutrons formed from proton-electron interactions. *See also* Black Hole; Crab Nebula.

Pulsating Star, variable star whose luminosity is intrinsically altered as a result of periodic expansions and contractions arising from changes in the star's atmosphere. Most pulsating stars are relatively short-period variables, including the classical Cepheids and the RR Lyrae variables. *See also* Variable Star.

Pulse, a regularly recurrent wave of distention in arteries that results from the flow of blood injected into the arterial system at each contraction of the heart's ventricles. The pulse is usually taken at the wrist, over the radial artery. It may be observed at any point where an artery appears near the surface of the body. Women usually have a higher (78–82 per minute) pulse rate than men (70–72). Abnormalities in pulse rate may indicate disorders of the circulatory system and the heart.

Puma, or mountain lion, cougar, panther, catamount, large New World cat found in mountains, forests, swamps, and jungles of W United States, S Florida, and Central and South America. It has a small round head, erect ears, and heavy tail. It is tawny with dark brown on ears, nose, and tail; underparts are white. The gestation period is 88–97days and 1–6 young are born. Length: body—42–54in (107–137cm); tail—30–

36in (76–91cm); weight: 80–200lb (36–91kg). Family Felidae; species *Felis concolor* or *Felis cougar.*

Pumice, rhyolitic lava blown to a low density rock froth by the sudden discharge of gases during a volcanic action. When ground and pressed into cakes it is used as a light abrasive.

Pump, a mechanical device for raising, compressing, propelling, or transferring fluids. The volute centrifugal pump, with rotating blades that are immersed in the liquid to increase its pressure through centrifugal force, is most common for general use.

Pumpkin, or squash, trailing annual vine from warm regions of Old World and United States. The orange, hard-rind garden pumpkin used for pies and Jack-o-lanterns is usually a *Cucurbita pepo* variety. Summer squash *(C. pepo melopepo),* picked when immature, have soft white or yellow flesh. Winter squash *(C. bita maxima* and *moschata),* harvested when ripe, have solid yellow flesh. Family Cucurbitaceae. *See also* Gourd.

Pumpkinseed, or common sunfish, freshwater fish found in E North America. A colorful, iridescent fish, it is identified by a bright red spot on the rear of the gill cover. The male builds a nest in sand and guards the eggs and young. Length: to 9in (22.9cm). Family Centrarchidae; species *Lepomis gibbosus.*

Pun, play on words, usually humorous, exploiting the fact that words sounding alike may mean different things. Although they are often considered a low form of humor, Shakespeare makes frequent and effective use of puns. Hamlet puns on "fret," exclaiming "Call me what instrument you will, though you can fret me, you cannot play upon me," where "fret" may mean to "vex," or the ridges on the neck of a guitar.

Punic Wars, three wars (264–261, 218–201, 149–146 BC) during which Rome, dominant in Italy, wrested from Carthage control of NW Africa and the W Mediterranean. At first Rome negotiated with Carthage, the undisputed commercial power of the area, to protect Italian coastal communities from Punic (Carthaginian) attack. Then two rival Sicilian factions called upon the two powers to settle a dispute and, as the Straits of Messana (Messina) separating Italy from Sicily were of great value to both, their armies met in Sicily. The Carthaginians occupied Messana (264 BC), and the Romans soon drove them from their garrison, precipitating the First Punic War.

After inital successes at Segesta and Agrigentum, the Romans sought to expel Punic forces from Sicily entirely. They built a fleet and won naval victories at Mylae (260) and Cape Ecnomus (256), after which they sent an expeditionary force into Africa under Regulus. It was routed by the Spartan mercenary general Xanthippus (255). The Romans captured Panormus (Palermo) in 254 and Lucius Metellus held it against Punic assault, but they could not take Lilybaeum, the Punic stronghold defended with guerrilla strategy by Hamilcar Barca. The Roman fleet was wrecked and had to be rebuilt. Under Catulus it won the final naval battle of the war near the Aegates islands. Carthage was forced to pay a huge indemnity and evacuate Sicily, then Corsica and Sardinia.

Carthage achieved control of Spain (237–219) through campaigns led by Hamilcar and his sons Hannibal and Hasdrubal. When Hannibal took Rome's ally Saguntum in 219, Rome declared the Second Punic War (218–201). Hannibal marched over the Alps into Italy with select troops and an elephant corps. The Roman armies in Spain led by the brothers Gnaeus and Publius Scipio cut off his supply lines and won

Roman dominance at sea. Hannibal destroyed Roman armies at Trebia (218), Trasimene (217), and Cannae (216) but, lacking reinforcements and faced with united Italian opposition, could not take Rome. Hasdrubal was defeated in Spain (215) and in Italy (207). Fabian Cunctator exhausted Hannibal's army with his policy of avoiding pitched battle. Scipio Africanus Major pushed the Punic army from Spain and attacked Africa. Hannibal was recalled to defend Carthage and was defeated at Zama (202) by Scipio and the Numidian king Masinissa.

Carthage became a dependent of Rome. Roman senator Cato the Elder insisted upon the total destruction of Carthage. Rome declared the Third Punic War (149–146), using the Punic resistance to Numidian aggression as an excuse. As described by Polybius, Carthage died without surrender, building by building razed at the command of Scipio Africanus Minor. Her survivors became slaves and her lands the Roman province of Africa. *See also* Carthage.

Punjab, state in N India; Chandigarh is the capital. Formed 1956 with the partitioning of the former Punjab prov. of British India between Pakistan and India, it is largely an irrigated agricultural area. Products: wheat, cotton, millet, barley, cotton, sugar. Industries: animal husbandry, textiles, cloth weaving, woolens, cement, machine tools, steel, farming equipment. Area: 19,495sq mi (50,492sq km). Pop. 15,230,000.

Punjabi, the major spoken language of Pakistan and also one of the constitutional languages of India. It is spoken by about 50,000,000 of Pakistan's 70,000,000 people, and by about 15,000,000 more in NW India. Punjabi is one of the Indic languages and thus part of the Indo-European family.

Pupa, quiescent, nonfeeding developmental stage of insects that undergo complete metamorphosis, such as the fly, butterfly, and beetle. It occurs between the larval and adult stage. *See also* Chrysalis; Cocoon.

Puppet Theater, theater for puppet shows. They existed as far back as the 5th century BC in Greece, China, and Java, and reached peak popularity in 18th-century Europe. They also flourished in the Puritan period in England when other forms of theater were prohibited. They are often used for religious allegory or satire as well as entertainment. A 20th-century example is *Kukla, Fran, and Ollie.*

Purcell, Henry (1659–95), English composer and organist. Purcell's incidental music for the plays *The Fairy Queen* and *King Arthur* and his opera *Dido and Aeneas* (1689) made him the greatest English composer of the Baroque period. He also composed anthems, instrumental music, and secular songs. *See also* Baroque Music.

Purim, an ancient Jewish celebration of thanksgiving, which usually takes place in March, commemorating the deliverance of the Jews of Persia from Haman's plot to destroy them. The story appears in the Book of Esther in the Old Testament, which is read on this day in a synagogue service. Charity is stressed on this occasion.

Puritanism, religious reform movement that developed within the Church of England during the late 16th century. The movement found its origin in the writings and thinking of early reformers, such as Thomas Cranmer, and was influenced by contemporary reformers, such as John Calvin. Through church reform, Puritans sought to purify the church of any remaining Roman Catholic influence. Faithful to the Bible, Puritanism provided the format for worship services, which included preaching, prayers, and psalms. Making their pattern of religious reform the life style of the society, Puritans influenced all aspects of life. They were responsible for the founding of the North American colonies. *See also* Calvin, John; Cranmer, Thomas.

Purple Martin, gregarious swallow of North America and the West Indies. Males are glossy blue-black; females are duller. They lay their eggs (4–6) in tree cavities. Length: 8in (20cm). Family Hirundinidae; species *Progne subis. See also* Swallow.

Purpura, or wide-mouthed dye shell, gastropod mollusk found in all seas. Having a dull gray-green or brown shell with pink inside, the animal's body secretes a deep purple fluid used for dye. Length: 3in (76.2mm). Family Thaisidae; species *Purpura lapillus.*

Purpura, hemorrhage in the skin usually associated with bleeding in tissues and body cavities, as a result of failure of homeostasis. *See also* Homeostasis.

Pus, yellowish-white fluid matter produced by inflammation of body tissue due to microorganisms. It consists of a mass of degenerating leukocytes and tissue debris in a fluid called liquor puris.

Pusan, seaport city in SE South Korea, 200mi (322km) SSE of Seoul; capital of Kyŏngsang prov.; under Japanese domination 1910–45; during Korean War, it was the only port through which the UN army could be supplied; in September 1950, UN troops broke out from this area. Industries: shipbuilding, textiles, metallurgy. Pop. 2,454,051.

Pushkin, Aleksandr (1799–1837), Russian Romantic poet and novelist. His first major work, *Ruslan and Lyudmila,* was published in 1820. In exile for his political views he wrote *The Prisoner of the Caucasus* (1822) and the historical drama *Boris Godunov* (1831). Later, under the protection of Tsar Nicholas I, he completed his masterpiece *Eugene Onegin* (1833) and "The Bronze Horseman" (1833), "The Queen of Spades" (1834), and *The Captain's Daughter* (1836). He was mortally wounded in a duel.

Pussy Willow, deciduous shrub or small tree native to E North America. It has long, oval leaves with bluish-green undersides. The large, silvery, fuzzy female catkins appear before the leaves in late winter or early spring. Height: to 20ft (6m). Family Salicaceae; species *Salix discolor.*

Putrefaction, decomposition of organic matter, especially proteins, by fungi, bacteria, and oxidation. It results in foul-smelling products. Putrefaction of meat yields hydrogen sulfide, ammonia, and mercaptans.

Putumayo (Icá), river in NW South America; rises in SW part of Colombia, on slope of Andes; flows SE forming a large part of Colombia–Peru border; flows into Brazil, where it is known as the Icá, then into Amazon River. Length: 1,000mi (1610km).

Puyallop, tribe of about 170 native Americans of coastal Washington. Speaking a Salishan tongue of the Algonquian-Wakashan family, the Puyallop were living near present-day Tacoma when the whites came. Giving up their lands in the Treaty of Medicine Creek in 1854, they were assigned a reservation on Puget Sound.

Pygmalion, in Greek mythology, a misogynistic sculptor who carved an ivory woman of surpassing beauty. He fell in love with it and offered to build a golden altar to Aphrodite if the statue were brought to life. The name of their son, Paphos, was given to a city sacred to the love goddess.

Pygmy, anthropological term denoting groups whose males average less than 59in (150cm) in height. African Pygmies, or Negrillos, inhabit three areas of central Africa and Zaire; Asian Pygmies, or Negritos, are found in the Philippines, Malaysia, and elsewhere. Pygmies are generally hunters and gatherers with few crafts. Most Pygmy populations are declining rapidly and they seem likely to become extinct fairly soon.

P'Yŏngyang, industrial city in W North Korea, on the Taedong River; capital of North Korea with provincial status. An ancient city, it served as the capital under the Choson (300–200 BC), Koguryo (c. 77 BC–AD 668), and Koryo (10th–12th centuries) kingdoms; made capital of North Korea 1948; during Korean War (1950–53), P'Yŏngyang was taken by UN forces but later fell to communists (1950); site of ancient city walls and tombs, university (1946). Industries: cement, iron and steel, chemicals, rubber, textiles, railroad workshops. Founded c. 1122 BC. Pop. 1,500,000.

Pyorrhea or **Periodontitis,** inflammatory condition of the gums and associated tissues that surround and support the teeth. It is thought to be caused by local irritants and bacterial plaques. If untreated it destroys the gums and leads to loss of teeth.

Pyracantha, or firethorn, thorny evergreen shrub native from SE Europe to China and easily grown in subtropical and temperate regions. It has toothed, leathery leaves, white flowers, and red, orange, or yellow berries. Varieties of *Pyracantha coccinea* are popular in the United States. Family Rosaceae.

Pyramid, in architecture, huge monument with a square or rectangular base and, usually, triangular sides rising to an apex. In the 4th through 6th dynasties in Egypt pyramids reached their greatest size and significance. The three 4th-dynasty pyramids at Giza are the best known. That built by Khufu is the largest: 756ft (231m) on a side and 481ft (147m) tall. In the New World, the largest pyramid is at Teotihuacán, northeast of Mexico City. The Temple of the Sun, a truncated, terraced structure, was about 1,450ft (442m) wide at the base and 216ft (66m) high.

Pyramid, in geometry, solid figure having a polygon as one of its faces (base), the other faces being triangles with a common vertex. Its volume is one-third of the base area times the vertical height.

Pyrenees, mountain range in S France and N Spain; extends in almost straight E-W line from Mediterranean (Cape Creuse) to Bay of Biscay (Cape Higuer) for 258mi (415km). There are few passes through this very compact, high range. Hannibal crossed Pyrenees 218 BC; Charles Martel forced Muslim invaders to retreat beyond Pyrenees at Battle of Tours, AD 732. Range contains deposits of marble, gypsum, oil. Cattle grazing is important industry. Rainfall increases toward W part of range where farming is carried on. Highest peak is Pico de Aneto, 11,168ft (3,406m).

Pyrenees, Peace of the (1659), treaty ending conflict between France and Spain. France received extensive territory in Flanders and the Franco-Spanish border was established at the Pyrenees. A marriage was arranged between Louis XIV and Marie Therese, daughter of Philip IV of Spain. If Marie Therese renounced her claim to the Spanish throne, she was to receive a payment. When the payment was not made the War of Devolution resulted.

Pyrethrum, popular name for the painted daisy (*Chrysanthemum coccineum*) and for several other species of *Chrysanthemum* and *Matricaria.* It is also the name for the insecticide made from the dried flower heads of the Dalmatian chrysanthemum (*C. cinerariaefolium*).

Pyridine, a compound (C_5H_5N) of the heterocyclic series characterized by a six-membered ring structure composed of five carbon atoms and one nitrogen atom. It occurs in bone oil and coal tar and is synthetically produced from acetaldehyde and ammonia. Pyridine is used as a solvent and converted to sulfapyridine (a drug used to combat bacterial and viral infection), pyribenzamine and pyrilamine (antihistamines), piperidine (a product used in processing rubber), and various water repellants, bactericides, and herbicides.

Pyridoxine, vitamin of the B complex involved in the metabolism of amino acids. *See also* Vitamin.

Pyrimidine, a colorless liquid ($C_4H_4N_2$) of the heterocyclic series characterized by a ring structure composed of four carbon atoms and two nitrogen atoms. It may be prepared from uracil, a dihydroxy pyrimidine compound, by chemical reactions that remove two oxygen atoms. Cytosine, uracil, thiamine, sulfadiazine, sulfamerazine, and sulfamethazine are well-known pyrimidine compounds.

Pyrite, the most common and widespread sulfide mineral (FeC_2), occurring in all types of rocks and veins. Often called "fool's gold" because of its deceptive color, it is used chiefly to produce sulfuric acid. Crystallizes as cubes, pyritohedra, and octahedra, often twinned; also as granules and globular masses. Opaque, metallic, and brittle; hardness 6.5; sp gr 5.01.

Pyrolysis, chemical decomposition of a complex substance into simpler ones by the action of heat alone. Garbage and coal may be pyrolyzed to produce valuable fuels and chemicals.

Pyrometallurgy, chemical metallurgy dependent upon roasting or smelting. Roasting involves heating ore in air without fusion. It transforms sulfide ores into oxides. Smelting involves blast furnaces to reduce iron, tin, copper, and lead ores.

Pyrometer, a thermometer for use at extremely high temperatures, above the melting points of ordinary thermometers. The optical pyrometer consists essentially of a small telescope, a rheostat, and a filament. When the telescope is aimed at a furnace or other hot object, the filament appears dark against the background. As electric current is increased slowly using the rheostat, the filament grows brighter until it matches the intensity of the furnace.

Pyroxene, any of a group of numerous single-chain silicates. They include many important rock-forming minerals. Diagnostic features are prismatic crystal form with interfacial angles of 87° and 93° and good cleavage parallel to these faces. Enstatite, augite, jadeite, and wollastonite are well-known pyroxenes.

Pyrrhus (319–272 BC), king of Epirus (295–272). He greatly expanded his kingdom into Illyria, Macedon, and Thessaly and aiding Tarentum he defeated the Romans at Heraclea (280) and Asculum (279) but sustained grievous losses (hence "Pyrrhic victory"). After building a magnificent Hellenized capital at Ambracia, he was killed by a street mob in Argos.

Aleksandr Pushkin (left)

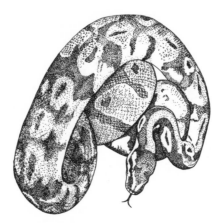

Python

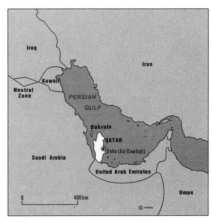

Qatar

Pythagorean Theorem, geometric theorem stating that in a right-angled triangle the square of the hypotenuse is equal to the sum of the squares of the other two sides. The theorem is named after Pythagoras of Samos (c. 580–c. 500 BC).

Python, any of about 20 species of constricting snakes found in tropical regions of Asia, Africa, and Australia. They are distinguished from boas by certain features of skull, geographic distribution, and hatching young from eggs. True pythons (Python) of Africa and Asia include several giant species, such as the reticulated python, to 25ft (7.6m). Most are terrestrial, but some are arboreal, and one is a burrower. Family Boidae. See also Boa.

Q

Qaddafi, Muammar al- (1938–), Libyan political leader. An army officer, he led a coup against the monarchy of Idris I (1969), naming himself Libya's commander-in-chief and chairman of the Revolutionary Command Council, which was dissolved in 1979 and replaced with the 21-member General People's Committee. A militant Arab nationalist, he helped support the Palestinian guerrillas and sought to unite Libya with other Arab countries. He clashed often with Egypt and was accused of meddling in other African countries' internal affairs. A rash of Qaddafi-backed terrorist attacks, often targeted at Americans abroad, precipitated US bombings of Libyan terrorist centers of activity in 1986.

Qatar, State of, nation in Asia occupying a peninsula extending N into the Persian Gulf from the Saudi Arabian mainland. The peninsula, running almost due N–S, is about 125mi (201km) long and 55mi (89km) wide. From the coast the terrain rises sharply to a low, barren plateau. The climate is hot with high humidity along the coast. Rainfall is meager and vegetation scarce. The economy is based almost entirely on petroleum production; the income is used to aid the general welfare. In 1975 the government completed the nationalization of the major independent oil companies. A new three-year industrial plan was introduced to diversify the economy and reduce dependency upon the oil industry. The majority of the people are Arabs, living in villages along the coast. About 50% are indigenous Qataris, with a large minority of Palestinian refugees. Most of the people are Muslims.

Although the country is a monarchy ruled by an emir, the Basic Law of 1970 (similar to a bill of rights) provides for a Council of Ministers and an Advisory Council, all elected for a term of three years. With the move toward constitutional monarchy, an independent judiciary system was installed. A general maritime treaty in 1868 allowed Great Britain to gain predominance in the area. The treaty of 1916 gave Britain control over Qatar's defense and foreign affairs. Oil discoveries in the 1940s stimulated the economy. Qatar became an independent state in 1971, joining the United Nations and the Arab League the same year.

PROFILE

Official name: State of Qatar
Area: 4,400sq mi (11,400sq km)
Population: 250,000
  Density: 57per sq mi (22per sq km)
Chief cities: Doha, capital; Dukhan

Government: Monarchy
Religion: Muslim (official)
Language: Arabic (official)
Monetary unit: Qatar riyal
Gross national product: $4,500,000,000
Per capita income: $18,000
Minerals (major): petroleum, natural gas
Trading partners (major): Great Britain, Japan

Qattara Depression, desert basin in NW Egypt, in Libyan Desert. Impassable by armies and vehicles, it was S end of British defense at Al-Alamein 1942; stopped Rommel's invasion. Contains lowest point in Africa, 436ft (133m) below sea level. Area: approx. 7,000sq mi (18,130sq km).

Q Fever, mild systemic disease, resembling typhus, caused by the microorganism Rickettsia burneti. Commonly accompanied by atypical pneumonia, it is widespread in ruminants and can be transmitted to man in raw milk or by contact.

Qom, city in W central Iran, 75mi (121km) SSW of Tehran; site of many mosques; burial place of Fatima (816), sister of Imam Riza; since 17th century noted pilgrimage place of Shiite Muslims. Industries: textiles, pottery, glass, shoes. Pop. 170,000.

Quadrant (graph), one of the four sections into which a plane is divided by rectangular axes. The four quadrants are called the first, second, third, and fourth, traveling counterclockwise from the first, which contains all points having positive x and y coordinates.

Quadratic Equation, mathematical equation in which the highest exponent of the variable is 2; an equation of the second degree. Quadratic equations have the form $ax^2 + bx + c = 0$, where a, b, and c are constants. In general a quadratic equation has two solutions (roots) given by the formula.
$$x = \frac{-b \pm \sqrt{b^2 - 4ac}}{2a}.$$

Quadratic Function, mathematical function the value of which depends on the square of the independent variable, x, and is thus given by a quadratic polynomial, as in $f(x) = 4x^2 + 17$ or $f(x) = x^2 + 3x + 2$.

Quaestor, Roman financial magistrate. During the republic the two quaestors were responsible for the treasury. When plebeians were admitted to the office their number rose to four (421 BC) and under Caesar to 40, many being stationed outside Rome and holding military power. The office declined during the empire.

Quagga, extinct zebra once common in South Africa. Exterminated by the Boers by 1870s, its brown coat was marked with black and cream stripes on head and neck; underparts were white. Family Equidae; species Equus quagga quagga. See also Zebra.

Quail, any of a group of Old World chickenlike game birds. The European quail (Coturnix coturnix), a small, short-tailed bird with white throat and mottled brownish plumage, is found throughout Eurasia and Africa. The Australian quail (Synoicus ypsilophrus) is a stocky, sedentary, brownish bird. Mainly ground birds, they scrape for fruits and seeds and nest on the ground. New World quails (subfamily Odontophorinae), found from temperate North America to S Brazil, are frequently called bobwhite.

Quakers, members of the Society of Friends. They regard George Fox as their founder. Puritan in spirit, they suffered persecutions in England and encountered difficulties in the American colonies. Through vol-

untary suffering, they bear witness to God. The purpose of life is to worship God, and fellowship of spirit is the group form of worship. They approach God directly, with no need to distinguish a clergy. See also Friends, The Religious Society of.

Qualities, Primary and Secondary, distinction between primary and secondary qualities, first asserted by Galileo and affirmed by John Locke. Objects exhibit inherent (primary) characteristics—extension, motion, rest, and number or so-called "mathematical" qualities; sensible (secondary) characteristics are only apparent and may vary—for example, color or texture.

Quantum Numbers, any of a set of numbers corresponding to the discrete values of a quantized physical property. Quantum numbers are either integers (1, 2, 3, etc) or half integers (1/2, 3/2, 5/2, etc). For example, an electron in a hydrogen atom can have energies n^2E_0, where n, the principal quantum number, can take values of 1, 2, 3, etc, and E_0 is the lowest energy level ($n = 1$). Similarly the charge of a particle can be thought of as quantized in units of electron charge, so a proton has a charge of $+1$. An elementary particle is defined uniquely by its mass and quantum numbers.

Quantum Theory, theory proposed by Max Planck (1900), based on the fact that certain physical properties can only assume discrete values; that is, they are quantized. For example, an oscillator cannot gain or lose energy continuously but only in discrete amounts, termed quanta (sing. quantum). A quantum has energy $h\nu$, where h is Planck's constant and ν is the frequency. The quantum of electromagnetic radiation is the photon. Planck used quantum theory to explain black-body radiation, Einstein used it to explain the photoelectric effect (1905), and Bohr applied it to atomic spectra (1913). The older quantum theory has developed into quantum mechanics—a mathematical formalism applied to the behavior of atoms, molecules, and elementary particles. Quantum electrodynamics is an extension of these satisfying relativistic effects, especially those concerning charged particles.

Qu'Appelle River, river in S Saskatchewan, Canada, rises NW of Moose Jaw, flows E through Buffalo Pound Lake and Fishing Lakes across Manitoba border into Assiniboine River; excellent source of whitefish. Length: 270mi (435km).

Quark, particle postulated as a constituent of the hadron group of elementary particles. Baryons consist of three quarks, antibaryons of three antiquarks, and mesons of a quark and an antiquark, all tightly bound together. Originally three kinds of quarks, with fractional charges ($+2/3$ or $-1/3$ that of the electron) and slightly different masses, were suggested. The discovery in 1974 of the long-lived psi (or J) particles and their decay products, the chi particles, indicates four or possibly twelve quarks. Evidence has also been found for free, unbound quarks with a unit of charge 1/9 or 4/9 the signal of some other particle. See also Subparticles, Elementary.

Quarrying, methods employed in obtaining dimension (cut) stone or other types of nonmetallic rock from shallow, open-pit mines. Dimension stone for building (sandstone, granite, marble) is obtained by separating large blocks from the parent mass by hand, explosives, or machine. Crushed stone for road building is obtained by drilling and blasting. It is then crushed, screened, and sized.

Quarter Horse, or cow pony, light horse breed developed in 18th-century North America to race on quarter-mile track. Now used for racing and working cattle, it is a sturdy horse capable of short bursts of speed. It has a short head; short, muscular back and loin; and short legs. Colors are chestnut, sorrel, bay, or dun. Height: to 60in (152cm) at shoulder; weight: 1,000–1,200lb (450–540kg).

Quartz, silicate mineral, silicon dioxide (SiO_2). Most surface rocks contain quartz. It occurs in two basic forms: (1) well-formed, transparent, hexagonal system, short to long prismatic crystals variously hued (gem varieties include smoky quartz, amethyst, and citrine), and (2) cryptocrystalline varieties of microscopically small crystals divided into two types—chalcedony (agate, onyx, sardonyx, carnelian, and chrysoprase are gem varieties) and the more opaque chert (of which aventurine and jasper are the best-known gem stones).

Quartzite, metamorphic rock, usually produced from sandstone, in which the quartz grains have recrystallized. Fracturing through these grains rather than between them, quartzite is a hard and massive rock. Its color is usually white, light gray, yellow, or buff, but it can be colored green, blue, purple, or black by various minerals. *See also* Metamorphic Rocks.

Quasar or **Quasi-stellar Object,** astronomical object, first observed in the 1960s, that appears to be a massive, highly compressed, extremely powerful source of radio and light waves, characterized by very large red shifts. If the red shift is due to the Doppler effect, quasars must be very remote, thus occurring early in the universe's history, and be receding at velocities close to that of light. Alternatively gravitational red shifts might be involved. The cause of the prodigious energy output is unknown but could result from gravitational collapse, as of a galaxy, or from a gigantic thermonuclear explosion in an unstable object.

Quasimodo, Salvatore (1901–68), Italian poet and translator. His early poetry, such as *Acque e terra* (1930), is hermetic in style. He was imprisoned for antifascist activities during World War II, and his poetry increased in sensitivity, as in *The Promised Land* (1957) and *Debit and Credit* (trans. 1972). Awarded the Nobel Prize (1959).

Quasi-stellar Object. *See* Quasar.

Quaternary Period, the most recent period of the Cenozoic Era, beginning about 2 million years ago and extending through the present. It marks the beginnings of man. It is divided into the Pleistocene or Glacial Epoch, characterized by a periodic succession of four great ice ages, and the Holocene or Recent Epoch, starting some 10,000 years ago.

Quatrain, four-line stanza with a particular rhyme scheme. Quatrains frequently follow the pattern of four iambic pentameters rhyming *abab;* ie, the first and third lines rhyme and the second and fourth lines rhyme. An example is this first quatrain from Thomas Gray's "Elegy Written in a Country Churchyard":

The curfew tolls the knell of parting day,
The lowing herd winds slowly o'er the lea,
The ploughman homeward plods his weary way,
And leaves the world to darkness and to me.

Quatre Bras, village in central Belgium, 20mi (32km) SSE of Brussels; scene of battle June 16, 1815, in which British under the Duke of Wellington defeated French under Marshal Michel Ney.

Quebec, province in E Canada, largest in area and 2nd in population among the 10 provinces.

Land and economy. A broken wilderness covers most of the N, reaching along the E shore of Hudson Bay to Hudson Strait. This land is rich in minerals. The St Lawrence River in the extreme S, flowing from the Great Lakes to the Atlantic Ocean, has been vital in Quebec's history and economy. In its valley and to the S lie the agricultural lands. The Appalachian Mts of E North America extend into the far SE. Quebec's wealth in natural resources, especially timber and minerals, has sustained its economy at a high level. Manufacturing is centered in the cities along the St Lawrence and in the S. Montreal is a major port and financial center. Tourism makes an important year-round contribution to the province's income.

People. Quebec was the seat of the French colonial empire in North America in the 18th century, and the French heritage remains dominant. More than 80% of the population is of French descent, and is French-speaking. The remainder of the population is chiefly of English ancestry.

Education. There are seven major institutions of higher education: Laval University, the University of Montreal, the University of Sherbrooke, McGill University, Sir George Williams University, Bishop's University, and Concordia University.

History. The Frenchman Jacques Cartier found the E coast in 1534 and later sailed up the St Lawrence. The first permanent settlement in the area was Quebec city, founded on the St Lawrence by Samuel de Champlain in 1608. Montreal was est. in 1642. From the expanding colony, the French pushed trading and military posts to the W. Quebec city fell to the British in 1759 during the Seven Years' War, Montreal surrendered in 1760, and in 1763 the entire area was ceded by treaty to Great Britain, and became a British colony. In 1791, Canada was divided into Lower and Upper Canada, Quebec being known as Lower Canada, but in 1841 the parts were united as the province of Canada. With the establishment of the Dominion of Canada in 1867, Quebec became a province under that name. In the mid-20th century French-speaking elements intensified their demands for recognition of their cultural heritage. In 1976 the militant separatist party, Parti Québécois, under the leadership of René Lévesque was elected, and the following year French was made the official language of the province, although the Canadian Supreme court struck down the law in 1979. In 1980, Quebec voters rejected a referendum on separate status for the province thus preserving national unity, but Lévesque was opposed to Canada's new constitution (1982). Lévesque resigned in 1985 and was succeeded briefly by Pierre Marc Johnson before a Liberal party landslide put Robert Bourassa in office.

PROFILE

Admitted to Confederation: July 1, 1867; one of the four provinces that were joined to form the Dominion of Canada.
National Parliament Representatives: Senate, 24; House of Commons, 74
Population: 6,141,491
Capital: Quebec
Chief cities: Montreal; Laval; Quebec
Provincial legislature: Provincial Assembly, 110
Area: 594,860sq mi (1,540,687sq km); rank, 1st
Elevation: Highest, 4,160ft (1,269m), Mt Jacques Cartier; lowest, sea level
Industries (major products): pulp and paper, aluminum, petroleum products, electrical equipment, railroad equipment, textiles, clothing, shoes, food products
Agriculture (major products): dairy products, hay, oats, potatoes, cattle, maple sugar and sugar, sugar beets
Minerals (major): iron, copper, asbestos
Floral emblem: madonna lily

Quebec, port city in S Quebec province, Canada, 150mi (242km) NE of Montreal at the confluence of the St Lawrence and St Charles rivers; capital of Quebec prov. and Canada's oldest city. French is the official language as a majority of the population is of French heritage; 98% is Roman Catholic. The city is divided into two sections: Lower Town, built on the waterfront, and Upper Town on Cape Diamond. The site of Quebec, an Indian town of Stadacona, was visited by Jacques Cartier in 1535 and 1541. Samuel de Champlain est. a French trading post 1608 and became its first governor; it was captured by British forces 1629 and held until 1632, when it was returned to France. Quebec served as capital of New France 1663–1763 and rapidly grew as the center of French fur trade. The famous battle on the Plains of Abraham (1759) resulted in a British victory against the French, forcing Quebec to surrender and ultimately to become a British colony (1763). During the American Revolution, Quebec withstood an American siege led by Benedict Arnold and Richard Montgomery (1775). It served as capital of Lower Canada and seat of governor general 1791–1841, when Upper and Lower Canada united; it was twice capital of the United Provinces of Canada (1851–55, 1859–67); scene of Quebec Conference (1943 and 1944). Quebec is the site of Hôtel-Dieu du Précieux-Sang (1639) one of the oldest hospitals in North America, Kent House (1636), Ursuline Convent (1639), Basilica of Notre Dame (1647), Quebec Seminary (1663), Château Frontenac, Laval University (1852), University of Quebec (1969), General Hospital (1692), Citadel (1823), Chapel of Notre Dame des Victoires (1688). Exports: petroleum products, grain, paper and pulp, asbestos. Industries: shipbuilding, tourism, bricks, pulp and paper, leather, textiles, clothing, machinery, canned food, beverages, tobacco, cigars, cigarettes, chemicals. Pop. 177,082.

Quebec Act (1774), act by British Parliament setting up civil government for Canada. A council appointed by the crown was the legislative authority, subject to royal veto. Parliament retained all powers of taxation except for local taxes. Religious tolerance and civil rights were granted to Roman Catholics. Quebec's boundary was extended south to the Ohio River, thus cutting off western claims of Massachusetts, Virginia, and Connecticut. The latter two provisions greatly disturbed the colonists.

Quechua, the most widely spoken of all the American Indian languages, with about 5,000,000 speakers in Peru, 1,500,000 in Bolivia, and 500,000 in Ecuador. Originally the language of the great Inca Empire, it is related to Aymara, the two forming the Quechumaran family.

Queen Anne Style, originally applied to architecture and furniture produced in England between 1702 and 1714 but often extended to include red brick houses and their decoration built *c.*1660–1720. It is also applied to graceful yet solidly built furniture with modern upholstery.

Queen Anne's War (1702–13), North American extension of the War of Spanish Succession. It involved Indian raids in the southern colonies and French and Indian raids in New England. Deerfield, Mass., was destroyed (1704). Expeditions against French Canada were partially successful, with the English capturing Port Royal and Acadia. The war ended with the Treaty of Utrecht (1713), in which France ceded Acadia, Newfoundland, and Hudson Bay to England.

Queen Charlotte Islands, archipelago off W British Columbia, Canada; separated from mainland by Hecate Strait. Chief islands are Graham, Moresby, Louise, and Lyell; inhabitants are mostly Haida Indians. Industries: mining, timber, fishing. Area: 3,705sq mi (9,596sq km). Pop. 2,222.

Queen Elizabeth Islands, formerly Parry Islands; northernmost part of Arctic Archipelago, in Northwest Territories, Canada; includes Ellesmere Island (largest), the Sverdrup and Parry groups, along with many smaller islands. Islands extend to within 500mi (805km) of North Pole; oil drilling is underway. Area: 160,000sq mi (414,400sq km).

Queens, largest borough of New York City, New York, on W end of Long Island; coextensive with Queens co; connected with mainland by Hell Gate Bridge (between Bronx and Astoria) and Triboro Bridge, and with Manhattan by Queensboro and Triboro bridges; also connected by railroad tunnels beneath East River. Mainly residential area, it manufactures consumer products for the area; site of New York World's Fairs 1939–40 and 1964–65 in Flushing Meadows Park; LaGuardia and Kennedy International airports; Queens College (1937) in Flushing, and St John's University (1870) in Jamaica. Industries: baking products, clothing, hosiery, pianos, paint, silk. First settled by Dutch 1635; chartered as borough 1898. Area: 108sq mi (280sq km). Pop. (1980) 1,891,325.

Queensberry, John Sholto Douglas, 8th Marquess of (1844–1900), British sportsman credited with drafting (1865) the rules that govern modern boxing. The rules, standardized in 1889, called for 3-minute rounds with a 1-minute rest period in between and the use of gloves. John Graham Chambers, who helped draft the rules, is sometimes credited as their sole originator.

Queensland, state in NE Australia, bounded by the Coral Sea and Pacific Ocean (NE and E) and the Gulf of Carpentaria and Torres Strait (NW); Brisbane is the capital city. An agricultural state, chief crop is sugar cane; largest cattle-producing state. Major industries: dairying, food processing, mining of copper, coal, lead, zinc. First visited by Capt. James Cook 1770, settled 1824–43 as a penal colony; became Commonwealth state 1901. Area: 667,000sq mi (1,727,530sq km). Pop. 1,799,200.

Quemoy (Chinmen, or **Chin-men),** island group off SE China, on Formosa Strait, 150mi (242km) W of Taiwan; comprised of Quemoy and Little Quemoy islands and 12 islets. Quemoy Island has been garrisoned by Taiwan since Communist takeover 1949; fishing and agricultural area. Crops: sweet potatoes, peanuts, barley, wheat, vegetables, rice. Pop. 61,305.

Quercy, region and former co of SW France, now occupied by Lot and Tarn-et-Garonne depts. Of Gallo-Roman origin, it was held by English 1360–1440; made part of French crownlands 1472 when it was included in Guienne prov. Region is composed of arid limestone plateaus and fertile river valleys. Industries: sheep, Rocamadour cheese.

Querétaro, state in central Mexico; capital is Querétaro; N terrain is mountainous, plains and valleys are in S. Spanish conquered area 1531 from Chichimec Indians; it was made separate Mexican state 1824. Industries: sugar cane, cotton, tobacco, livestock; mining of opals, silver, iron, copper. Area: 4,544sq mi (11,769sq km). Pop. 618,000.

Querétaro, city in central Mexico, 160mi (258km) NW of Mexico City. Formerly an Aztec city, it was taken 1531 by Spanish; scene of 1867 execution of Emperor Maximilian; revolution against Spain was planned here 1810; site of several colonial landmarks, university,

Salvatore Quasimodo

Quebec City

Manuel Luis Quezon

16th-century cathedral. Industries: cotton, agricultural equipment, tourism, opal mining. Pop. 150,226.

Quesnay, François (1694–1774), leader of the 18th-century French Physiocrats, who invented an economic table for France, which demonstrated the circular flow of economic activity throughout the society. *See also* Physiocrats.

Quetzal, inactive, tree-perching Central American forest bird. The male is bright green above and crimson below with 3-ft (91-cm) tail feathers, once used as authority symbols by the Maya. The duller-colored female nests in a tree hole, laying light blue eggs (2) that are incubated by both parents. Species *Pharomachrus mocinno.*

Quetzalcoatl, in ancient Mexican mythology, the ruler god of the Toltec empire. The Aztecs worshiped him as the bringer of maize and of civilization. He was depicted as a plumed serpent. Montezuma, the Aztec ruler, believed that Hernán Cortés was the god returning to fulfill a prophecy, easing the way for the Spanish conquest.

Quezon, Manuel Luis (1878–1944), Filipino political figure. He was an early leader in the fight for Philippine independence. In 1909 he went to Washington, D.C., as a resident commissioner for the Philippines to the US Congress. When the United States refused to specify a time for Philippine independence in the Jones Act (1916), Quezon resigned and returned to the Philippines, where he led the Nationalist party. In 1935 he was elected first president of the Commonwealth of the Philippines. His term saw improvements and reforms in housing, the military, and government organization. After the Japanese occupation in 1942, he served the Pacific War Council in the United States.

Quezon City, capital city of the Republic of the Philippines, on Luzon island, adjacent to Manila (SW). The 2nd-largest city of the Philippines, it is mainly a residential section, with textile mills and the University of Philippines; made capital 1948. Pop. 994,679.

Quiché, Mayan Indian group located in the highlands of W Guatemala. Archeological remains show large pre-conquest population centers and an advanced civilization; the *Popul Vuh,* an account of the Quiché myth of creation, is another important source of knowledge about the Quiché.

Quicksand, smooth grains of sand which do not adhere to each other, and are saturated with upward flowing water. It is a soft, shifting mass, yielding easily to pressure. Objects resting on its surface are usually sucked down and engulfed. Where the density of the suspension is exceeded by the object (as in the case of a human body), the object cannot sink below the surface, although struggling may lead to loss of balance and drowning.

Quietism, heretical doctrine of religious spirituality and mysticism, identified with Miguel de Molinos, a 17th-century Spanish priest. The meaning of Quietism is that perfection consists of complete passivity of the soul and the suppression of individual effort, so that divine love and action may reign freely; therefore, the soul, which has undergone mystical death, can will only what God wills. Although his teachings were begun within the Roman Catholic Church, Molinos' teachings were condemned and he was sentenced to prison by Pope Innocent XI in 1687.

Quilmes, city in E Argentina, 9mi (14km) SE of Buenos Aires; site of British landing 1806, capturing Buenos Aires for a short time. Industries: brewing, tourism, textiles, rope, tiles. Founded 1665. Pop. 355,265.

Quince, shrub or small tree native to Asia. It is popular for its greenish-yellow, hard fruit used in preserves. Height: 20ft (6.1m). Family Rosaceae; species *Cydonia oblonga.*

Quincy, city in Massachusetts, on Boston Bay; S suburb of Boston; birthplace of presidents John Adams and John Quincy Adams, whose homes are National Historic sites, and of John Hancock; site of Quincy Junior College (1958), Eastern Nazarene College (1900), First Parish Church (1828). Industries: shipbuilding, packaging machinery, soaps, television tubes. Founded 1625 as trading post; separated from Braintree 1792; inc. as city 1888. Pop. (1980) 84,743.

Quinine, drug derived from cinchona bark, used principally to treat malaria, if modern drugs are unavailable, and provide relief from chronic leg cramps. It is toxic if taken in large doses.

Quintana Roo, state in SE Mexico, on Caribbean Sea; occupies most of the Yucatán Peninsula; flat plain area with dense forests; climate is hot and humid; inhabited mostly by Indians. Products: lumber, chicle, sponge, coconuts, turtle fishing. Area: 16,228sq mi (42,031sq km). Pop. 91,044.

Quirinus, in Roman mythology, a major deity, husband of Hora. His festival was held Feb. 17.

Quisling, Vidkun (1887–1945), Norwegian fascist. He was minister of defense (1931–32) and then left the Agrarian party to found the fascist National Union party. In 1940 he collaborated with Germany in the invasion of Norway; he was made premier in 1942. The Norwegians opposed his attempt to nazify church and school, but he stayed in power until Norway's liberation when he was arrested, convicted of high treason, and shot.

Quito, capital city of Ecuador, in N central part of country, 114mi (184km) from Pacific coast almost on Equator. Site was originally settled by Quito Indians and captured by Incas (1487); taken by Spain in 1534; liberated 1822 by Antonio José de Sucre. Located at foot of Pichincha volcano it has suffered many earthquakes. A cultural and political center with little industry, it is the site of Central University of Ecuador (1787), the oldest art school in Latin America, Catholic University (1946), and an observatory. Industries: textiles, handcrafts. Pop. 599,828.

Quoits, a game played by two or more persons, similar to horseshoe pitching. The metal, circular quoits, with one rounded and one flat surface, are thrown at a peg in the ground 1 inch (2.54cm) high. The pitching distance for men is 30 feet (9.1m) and the distance for women is 20 feet (6.1m). Points are scored similar to horseshoe pitching, except that only 21 points are needed to win. *See also* Horseshoe Pitching.

R

Rabat, capital city of Morocco, in N Morocco, on Atlantic coast, approx. 55mi (89km) NE of Casablanca. Settlement dates from Phoenician times, but fortified city was founded in 12th century; French protectorate est. 1912: became independent 1956; site of 180-ft (55-m) Hassane Tower (12th century), and University of

Rabat. Industries: hand-woven rugs, textiles, food processing. Pop. 724,100.

Rabbi, (Hebrew "my master"), since the Middle Ages, the individual responsible for religious education, guidance, and services in the synagogue. His position is based on his learning, but entails no special privileges. His duties include interpreting Jewish law and guiding the spiritual lives of people.

Rabbit, long-eared, herbivorous, prolific mammal of the family Leporidae, including the European common rabbit and the American cottontail. Although usage varies, most so-called rabbits typically are smaller than hares (Lepus), have shorter ears, run without leaping, and their young are born furless, blind, and helpless. The common rabbit *(Oryctolagus cuniculus)* of S Europe and Africa has been introduced in many other regions—notably Australia. It has thick, soft, grayish-brown fur. The wide variety of domesticated rabbits are of this species. Length: 14–18in (35–45cm); weight 3–5lb (1.4–2.3kg). *See also* Cottontail; Hare.

Rabelais, François (*c.*1494–*c.*1553), French humanist and satirist. He left convent life to study medicine and was appointed hospital physician at Lyons in 1532. He traveled widely in Italy. His life work (*Pantagruel* 1532; *Gargantua* 1534; *Tiers Livre* 1546; *Quart Livre* 1548, 1552) is a series of vivid, hedonistic, satirical digressions. Condemned by theologians and the Sorbonne, his works were widely popular and gained him the protection of important patrons. *See also* Gargantua, *La vie tres horrifique du grand.*

Rabi, Isidor Isaac (1898–   ), US physicist, b. Austria, who was awarded a 1944 Nobel Prize for his invention of a magnetic resonance method of observing atomic spectra. This invention, in addition to shedding light on atomic and molecular structures, helped determine the nucleus shape of an atom. He also worked on the development of microwave radar.

Rabies, or hydrophobia, acute contagious viral infection of the central nervous system. It occurs in all warmblooded animals, especially canines, mustelids, and bats, and is transmissible to man through the bite of an affected animal.

Rabin, Itzhak (1922–   ), Israeli statesman. After a distinguished military career, he served as ambassador to the US (1968–73) and minister of labor (1974). Following Golda Meir's resignation, he became (1974) Israel's first native-born premier until 1977 when he was replaced by Menachem Begin. His controversial book, *The Rabin Memoirs* (1979), was censored in Israel.

Raccoon, stout-bodied, omnivorous, mostly nocturnal mammal of North and Central American wooded areas near water. They have a black masklike marking across their eyes and a long, black-banded tail. They have agile and sensitive front paws and typically dip food and other objects in water. Their footprints look human. The seven species include the North American *Procyon lotor.* Length: 16–24in (40–61cm); weight: 10–30lb (4.5–13.6kg). Family Procyonidae.

Race, biological classification of the human species according to hereditary (genetic) differences. The term "geographical race" denotes large groupings of man that contain many "local races," varying in numerical strength from a few hundred to many million. Different racial characteristics arise through genetic mutation, selective breeding, and adaptation to a particular environment. Many aspects of anthropological taxonomy are still confused and debatable. *See also* Australoid

Race; Caucasoid Race; Mongoloid Race; Negroid Race.

Racematization, transformation of an optically active substance into a mixture of equal quantities of two mirror-image crystals (enantiomorphs), usually by heat or the action of acids or bases. Individually each enantiomorph rotates the plane of polarized light through a characteristic angle, but an equal quantity of each will cancel each other's rotatory effect.

Racer, any of several species of slender snakes ranging from S Canada to Guatemala. They are broad-headed, large-eyed, and varied in color. The E United States species is black. Length: to 5ft (1.5m). Family Colubridae; species include *Coluber constrictor constrictor*

Racerunner, active, slim, long-tailed lizard distributed throughout the Americas. There are 12 species in the United States, chiefly in the southwest. They are generally dark-colored with light, longitudinal stripes. Some forms develop from unfertilized eggs. Length: to 16in (41cm). Family Teiidae; genus *Cnemidophorus.*

Rachel, in the Bible, daughter of Laban, Jacob's second wife, and the mother of Joseph and Benjamin. Having labored seven years for Rachel's hand, Jacob was tricked by her father into marrying Leah, her older sister. He worked seven more years to marry Rachel.

Rachmaninoff, Sergei (1873–1943), Russian composer and pianist. He composed in a basically conservative, post-Romantic style modeled after Tchaikovsky and was one of the foremost pianists of the 20th century. His *Piano Concerto No. 2* (1901), *Rhapsody on a Theme of Paganini* (1934), and second symphony are among his most popular works. He also composed songs, preludes and etudes for piano, four piano concertos, and other works.

Racial Discrimination, denial of rights, privileges, and opportunities to an individual or group because of race. In the United States, such action has been outlawed in the public sector by a series of constitutional amendments (eg the 15th Amendment), judicial decisions (eg *Brown* v. *Board of Education of Topeka,* 1954), and legislative acts beginning with the Civil Rights Act of 1866 and culminating in the Civil Rights Acts of 1964 and 1968. The constitutions of other governments, including that of the Soviet Union, also contain prohibitions against racial discrimination. *See also* Civil Rights and Liberties; Racism.

Racine, Jean Baptiste (1639–99), French classical dramatist who perfected disciplined 17th-century tragedy. A theatrical rival of Corneille and Molière, he was encouraged by Louis XIV. Racine wrote *Andromaque* (1667), *Iphigénie* (1674), *Phèdre* (1677), *Esther* (1689), and *Athalie* (1691), the last two in retirement.

Racine, city and port of entry in SE Wisconsin, 25mi (40km) S of Milwaukee, on Lake Michigan and mouth of Root River; seat of Racine co. Industrial growth was spurred by establishment of threshing machine plant (1842), harbor improvements (*c.* 1844), and the introduction of railroad to the area (1855). Industries: farm machinery, floor wax, electrical equipment, printing, clothing, automobile parts. Settled 1834; inc. 1848. Pop (1980) 85,725.

Racism, doctrine advocating the superiority of one race over any and all others. Racism has, from time to time, been the avowed policy of governments and, as such, the root cause of slavery and discriminatory legislation, such as in the United States before the Civil War, in Nazi Germany during the 1930s, and in several African nations. It has been perpetrated by both white and black administrations. *See also* Civil Rights and Liberties; Racial Discrimination.

Rackets, game played by two or four persons on a court. The court is 60 by 30 feet (18.3 by 9.2m) and is surrounded by three walls 30 feet (9.2m) high and a back wall 15 feet (4.6m) high. Each player uses a gut-strung racket 30 inches (76.2cm) long that has a circular head 7–8 inches (17.8–20.3cm) in diameter and that weighs 8–10 ounces (226–283 grams). The ball with a diameter of 1 inch (2.5cm) is tightly wound cloth and twine and covered by leather. A service line is painted on the front wall at a height of 9 feet, 7.5 inches (2.9m) and a fixed wooden board *(telltale),* also on the front wall, extends 27 inches (68.6cm) up from the floor. These are the markers that determine when a ball is in play. The serve must be put in play above the service line and must then land behind a short line, marked 24 feet (7.3m) from the back wall. Games are played to 15 points. Rackets originated in debtors' prison in England in the 18th century. The game soon spread to the wealthier classes. It was introduced to the United States, where it is governed by the Racquet and Tennis Club (1890), from Canada.

Radar, a contraction of RA(dio) D(etecting) A(nd) R(anging), a method of detecting the position, velocity, and other characteristics of a distant object by analyzing the high frequency radio waves reflected from its surface. The technique was developed simultaneously (*c.* 1935–40) in several countries. Current fields in which radar is used include navigation, meteorology, astronomy, defense systems, and geographical studies.

Radhakrishnan, (Sir) Sarvepalli (1888–1975), Indian political figure and author. As writer and teacher, he attempted to spread Indian thought in the West and teach Indians the worth of the individual and the value of a casteless society. His works include *East and West in Religion* (1933) and *Religion in a Changing World* (1967). He was Indian delegate to UNESCO (1946–52) and ambassador to the Soviet Union (1949–52). He became president of India in 1962 and served until 1967.

Radian, unit of plane angle given as the angle subtended at the center of a circle by an arc of length equal to that of the radius of the circle. Thus 2π radians is equal to 360°; one radian is equal to 57.296°.

Radiation, a process of energy transfer by electromagnetic waves propagating through space and other media, as distinguished from conduction and convention. Principal components of solar radiation include waves in radio frequencies, microwaves, long-wave (infrared) radiation, visible light or radiation, and short-wave (ultraviolet) radiation, as well as X and gamma rays of even shorter wavelengths. *See also* Heat Transfer; Solar Constant.

Radiation, Heat, the energy given off by a body in the form of electromagnetic waves. Heat energy is simply a measure of the vibrations of atoms and electrons within a body. But vibrating electrons also give off electromagnetic waves continuously; thus all objects, even ice, radiate heat.

Radiation, Nuclear, particles or electromagnetic radiation emitted spontaneously and at high energies from atomic nuclei. It can result from radioactive decay to yield alpha particles (helium nuclei), beta particles (electrons), gamma rays, and, more rarely, positrons (antielectrons). It can also result from spontaneous fission of the nucleus, with ejection of neutrons or gamma rays. Spontaneous fission occurs in some heavy atoms without the supply of energy.

Radiation Biology, study of the effects of ionizing radiations (X rays and radioactive radiation) on living organisms. All forms of life are destroyed by large doses of radiation, the main effect being on cell division and therefore it is the parts of the body that replace themselves most frequently that are the most susceptible. It is for this reason that cancer cells can be destroyed by radiation. Whether or not radiation causes cancer or destroys neoplastic tumors depends on careful control of the dosage.

Radiation Sickness, illness resulting from exposing the body to ionizing radiation (X rays or gamma rays). Diarrhea, vomiting, fever, and hemorrhage are symptoms. Sickness may occur immediately or be delayed. Severity depends upon the degree of radiation. Treatment is effective in mild cases.

Radiation Therapy, the use of X-ray and gamma-ray radiation to treat disease; often used alone or in combination with surgery to eradicate malignant tumors.

Radical, root of a number or quantity, such as its square root or cube root. The radical sign ($\sqrt{}$) is qualified, except for a square root, by a superscript number that indicates a particular radical, as with $\sqrt[3]{}$ (cube root).

Radical, single atom or group of atoms in which all the atomic valences are not satisfied by chemical bonding. Thus, removal of a hydrogen atom from methane, CH_4, gives the methyl radical CH_3. The term is usually taken to mean a free radical, that is, one existing free for a short time in a reaction. Free radicals are highly reactive: they can be produced by ultraviolet light, pyrolysis, electron impact, and other means, and play an important part in the mechanisms of many chemical reactions.

Radio, the use of electromagnetic waves in the radio frequency range to transmit or receive electric signals through the intervening space without wires. Guglielmo Marconi first realized the potential of these waves as a wireless communications system, and in 1901 transmitted the letter *S* across the Atlantic Ocean. The development in 1904 of the vacuum electron tube by Sir John A. Fleming made possible the transmission of speech and music. Lee de Forest in 1906 invented a three-element tube that could both detect and amplify radio waves. The invention by Edwin H. Armstrong of the circuit for the regenerative receiver made possible long-range radio reception.

Radioactive Isotope. *See* Isotope.

Radioactive Waste Disposal, the process involved in rendering still-radioactive "hot" nuclear material safe. In the case of nuclear fuel when the reaction producing energy becomes too loaded with impurities to be efficient, the "spent" fuel is still radioactive. Cooling and reprocessing are necessary to remove still-useful material. Long-lived isotopes are buried in deep mines until they are no longer radioactive. These wastes can also be fused into nondegradable ceramic containers and then dumped into deep ocean trenches. Some such isotopes may remain radioactive for thousands of years. In the United States, the dangers of transportation and disposing of radioactive waste and the long-term potential dangers of waste disposal sites have prompted many states to enact regulatory legislation.

Radioactivity, spontaneous disintegration of the nuclei of radioactive isotopes (radioisotopes) with, in most cases, the emission of alpha particles (helium nuclei) or beta particles (electrons) often accompanied by gamma rays. These two processes of radioactive decay, alpha decay and beta decay, cause the radioisotope to be transformed into a chemically different atom. Alpha decay results in the nucleus losing two protons and two neutrons; beta decay occurs when a neutron changes into a proton, an electron (beta particle) being emitted in the process. Thus the atomic number changes in both cases and an isotope of another element is produced, which might also be radioactive. The stability of different isotopes varies widely. It is impossible to predict when a nucleus will disintegrate but in a large collection of atoms there is a characteristic time (half-life) after which one-half of them can be expected to have decayed. This time varies from about ten billion years to ten billionths of a second. The activity of any radioactive sample decreases exponentially with time, never completely disappearing. *See also* Dating, Radioactive; Isotope.

Radiocarbon Dating, or carbon-14 dating, method of determining age of dead organic matter (such as wood, cotton). Living matter assimilates a certain amount of radioactive carbon-14, which comes from the CO_2 in the air. This balances its amount disintegrating in the tissues. After death only the decay process remains and measurement of the amount of carbon-14 gives an indication of age.

Radio Galaxy, galaxy emitting strong electromagnetic radiation of radio-frequency wavelengths. These emissions seem to be produced by the high-speed motion of subatomic particles in strong magnetic fields. They probably result from explosions occurring in the nuclei of the galaxies concerned. Some radio galaxies correspond to visual sources, such as Cygnus A, which is a distant double galaxy. Radio galaxies are frequently double and many are of immense dimensions. One, 3C236, appears to be the largest galaxy known, being 18,000,000 light years across. *See also* Radio Source.

Radiography, production on photographic material of the interior of opaque bodies by irradiating with X rays. Industrial X ray photographs can show assembly faults, metal defects, etc. In medicine and dentistry they are invaluable for diagnosing bone damage, tooth decay, and internal disease. The images normally only show bones, some tissue structure, and air spaces. Using very sensitive modern techniques, cross-sectional areas of the body can now be obtained showing organs, blood vessels, and diseased parts. *See also* CAT Scanner.

Radioisotope Tracer, radioactive isotope of an element used to trace the course of that element through a biological system. As the stable isotope and radioisotope behave identically from a chemical point of view, the radioisotope will follow exactly the same path as the stable isotope, but its presence in the cells and tissues of the organism can be monitored by the radiation it emits. Compounds labeled with radioisotopes are used in research and diagnosis.

Radiolaria, order of marine, planktonic, ameboid protozoans characterized by a spherical body and silica skeleton. The skeletons, which are the main components of ocean bottom ooze and flint, are patterned according to species. Shapes include long spines, latticed spheres, polyps, and basket-, bell-, and helmet-like shapes; 5,000 species including *Actipylina, Peripylaria, Hexacontium.* Class Rhizopoda.

Sergei Rachmaninoff

Jean Baptiste Racine

Chandrasekhara Raman

Radiology, branch of medicine dealing with the use of X rays and other forms of radiation to diagnose and treat disease.

Radio Source, discrete astronomical source of radio waves, detected by radio telescope. Radio sources include the Sun, supernova remnants and pulsars, quasars, and certain nebulae and galaxies, many of which have been identified optically. The strongest sources are the Andromeda Galaxy, Perseus, Taurus A, Puppis A, Virgo A, Centaurus A, Cygnus A, and Cassiopeia A.

Radish, annual garden vegetable developed from a wild plant native to cooler regions of Asia. Its leaves are long, deeply lobed, and prickly. The fleshy root, red, white, or black, is eaten raw. Red radishes are small and globular; white radishes are long and cylindrical. They mature in 24–45 days; winter crops take 60 days. Family Cruciferae; species *Raphanus sativus*.

Radium, radioactive metallic element (symbol Ra) of the alkaline-Earth group, first isolated as radium salts (1898) by Pierre and Marie Curie. The metal was isolated by Mme. Curie in 1911. It is present in uranium minerals. The metal is used in research, luminous paints, and medical radiotherapy. It has 13 isotopes that emit alpha, beta, and gamma radiation: radon is a decay product. Properties: at. no. 88; at. wt. 226.0254; sp gr 5 (approx.); melt. pt. 1,292°F (700°C); boil. pt. 2,084°F (1,140°C); most stable isotope Ra^{226} (half-life 1,600 yr). *See also* Alkaline-Earth Elements.

Radius, distance, or line segment, from the center to any point on the circumference of a circle or the surface of a sphere.

Radon, radioactive nonmetallic gaseous element (symbol Rn) of the noble-gas group, first discovered in 1900. Rn^{222} (half-life 3.8 days) is a decay product of radium. Thorium decays to Rn^{220} (half-life 54.5s) and actinium gives Rn^{219} (half-life 3.92s). The isotopes, which are alpha emitters, are present in the Earth's atmosphere in trace amounts. Chemically, the element is known to form fluorides. Properties: at. no. 86; density 9.73 g dm^{-3}; melt. pt. −95.8°F (−71°C); boil. pt. −79.24°F (−61.8°C); most stable isotope Rn^{222} (half-life 3.823 days). *See also* Noble Gases.

Ragnarok, in Scandinavian mythology, the end of the world of gods and men. Chaos and tempests will prevail before Ragnarok. Afterward the Earth will rise again.

Ragweed, wind-pollinated plant that is the chief cause of hay fever in late summer and early fall. The common ragweed *(Ambrosia artemisiifolia)* is widespread in N United States and produces large amounts of pollen from branching greenish, tassellike flowers; height: 1–8ft (0.3–2.4m). The giant ragweed *(A. trifida)* is most common on E and SE United States coasts; height: 1.5–20ft (0.45–6m). Family Compositae.

Ragwort, ragged-leaved plants, including golden ragwort or golden groundsel *(Senecio aureus),* a biennial or perennial that bears flat-topped clusters of yellow flower heads; height: to 4ft (1.2m). Family Compositae. *See also* Groundsel.

Rahu, in Hindu mythology and religion, the mischievous four-armed deity who causes eclipses and the fall of meteors, and who presages trouble and sickness. Rahu is especially worshiped by the Dosadhs and Dhangars of India who show their devotion by walking on a path of hot coals.

Rail, slender, long-legged, drab-colored marsh bird that is well camouflaged in its dense swampland home. They are shy, generally nocturnal, and often emit melodious calls. They lay marked white or buff-colored eggs (8–15) in a reed-and-grass ground nest. Length: 4–18in (10–46cm). Family Rallidae.

Rainbow, a bright band in a circular arc with colors of the spectrum arranged from red inside to blue outside, usually formed opposite to the sun or other light source in sheets of water droplets from which the light is refracted and reflected.

Rainier, Mount (Mount Tacoma), peak in W central Washington, in Mt Rainier National Park (est. 1899); greatest single peak glacier system in the United States radiates from the summit of this ancient volcano. Highest point in the Cascade Range, 14,410ft (4,395m). Discovered and named 1792 by Capt. Vancouver; first scaled 1870.

Rain Tree, or saman, tree native to tropical regions in the West Indies and Central America. It is grown in other tropical areas as a shade tree. The leaflets fold up at night or if rain is imminent. Height: to 80ft (24m). Family Leguminosae; genus *Samanea*.

Raisin, dried, sweet grapes, usually seedless, for eating. *See also* Grape.

Rákóczy, name of a noble Hungarian family, princes of Transylvania. During the 16th and 17th centuries these noble Magyars were closely linked with the fortunes of Hungary. **Sigismund** (1544–1608) supported István Bocskay against the Jesuits. **George I** (1591–1648), prince of Transylvania (1631–48), a staunch Protestant, allied himself with Sweden and France to invade Austria in 1644 to protect Protestant rights. **George II** (1621–60) allied with the Swedes and invaded Poland to secure the throne but was forced to retreat. The Turks deposed him. **Francis II** (1676–1735), a Protestant, headed revolt against Austria in Hungary and held power over Hungary and Transylvania before he was defeated by the Austrians (1708) and driven into exile.

Raleigh, (Sir) Walter (1552?–1618), English soldier, political figure, and author. Finding favor at court with Queen Elizabeth I, he was knighted (1585). His captains explored the coast from Florida to North Carolina (1584), and he sent settlers (1585) to Roanoke Island, N.C., but no permanent settlement was made. In 1587 he obtained a patent to take possession of unknown lands in North America, to be named "Virginia." He is credited with the introduction to England from North America of the potato plant and tobacco. Supplanted as the Queen's favorite by the Earl of Essex, he was expelled from court (1592). After the accession of James I he was found guilty of conspiracy and imprisoned (1603–16). While in prison he wrote his *History of the World* (1614). In 1617 he led an unsuccessful expedition to the Orinoco River in search of gold, was arrested on his return, and was executed under terms of his original sentence.

Raleigh, capital city of North Carolina, in E central part of state, 50mi (81km) S of Virginia border; seat of Wake co; occupied during Civil War by Gen. William Sherman and Union forces (April 1865); birthplace of Pres. Andrew Johnson (1808); site of St Mary's Junior College (1842), Pearce College (1857), Shaw University (1865), St Augustine's College (1867), North Carolina State University at Raleigh (1887), Meredith College (1891); market center for cotton and tobacco trade. Industries: food processing, textiles, electrical

equipment. Founded as state capital 1788; inc. 1792. Pop. (1980) 149,771.

Ram, The. *See* Aries.

Rama, figure in Hindu mythology, specifically the great epic tale the *Ramayana*. He is the perfect Hindu, devoted and chivalrous husband, obedient to sacred law, courageous, patient, and possessed of a great sense of duty. He was considered in the folk legends to be an incarnation of the god Vishnu and his name became synonymous with God.

Ramadan, the 9th month of the Muslim year, set aside for fasting. One of the Five Pillars of Islam, the basic duties of Muslims, is to fast during Ramadan. The month begins with the sighting of the new moon. For 29 days thereafter the faithful do not eat or drink between sunrise and sunset. Since this is a month in a lunar calendar, it comes at a different time each year in the Western calendar. *See also* Islam.

Raman, (Sir) Chandrasekhara Venkata (1888–1970), Indian physicist who greatly influenced and contributed to the growth of science, and to research facilities in his country. He was awarded a 1930 Nobel Prize for his discovery of the Raman Effect. He indicated that in conjunction with the diffusion of light through a transparent material, there are some changes in the wavelength of the light.

Ramat Gan, city in W Israel, 2mi (3km) E of Tel Aviv-Jaffa; site of Bar Ilan University (1953), and Israel's largest sports stadium. Industries: diamond processing, tourism, food processing. Founded 1921. Pop. 121,000.

Ramayana, along with the *Mahabharata,* one of India's two great epic poems. Consisting of seven books and 24,000 couplets in Sanskrit, it was probably written sometime between 500 and 300 BC. Valmiki was the author. It relates the adventures of Rama, his wife Sita, his brother Lakshmana, and others amid royal intrigues and battles.

Rambouillet, Catherine de Vivonne de Savelli (1558–1665), French social figure. She held a famed literary salon in her home, Hôtel de Rambouillet. Notable figures who frequented her salon included Pierre Corneille, Cardinal Richelieu, and Jean Louis Guez de Balzac. Her salon had a profound influence on 17th-century literature.

Rameau, Jean Philippe (1683–1764), French composer and music theorist. His *Treatise on Harmony* (1722) was an important contribution to musicology. He composed harpsichord suites and many operas such as *Les Indes Gallantes* (1735) and *Castor et Pollux* (1737).

Ramesses or **Rameses,** the name of 12 kings of the XIXth and XXth dynasties of ancient Egypt. **Ramesses I** (*r.* 1315–1314 BC) succeeded Horemheb but died soon after. **Ramesses II** (grandson of Ramesses I) (*r.* 1292–1225), conducted war against the Hittites in Palestine and Syria, built many luxurious temples, including the temple at Abu Simbel, and is believed to be the Pharaoh of the Hebrew oppression. **Ramesses III** (*r.c.*1198–1166), second king of the XXth dynasty and husband of Tiy, defended Egypt from the attacks of Libya and Syria, but the great wealth of the nobility and the vast accumulation of slaves led to the dynasty's decline, with the priesthood becoming its center of power. The dynasty ended with **Ramesses XII** (*r.* 1118–1090 BC).

Ramsay, (Sir) William (1852–1916), British chemist. Working with Lord Rayleigh he discovered argon in air and later discovered helium, neon, and krypton spectroscopically. For this work he was awarded a Nobel Prize in 1904 and was knighted in 1902. He was also interested in radioactivity and showed that helium is produced by radioactive decay.

Rand, Ayn (1905–82), US author, b. St Petersburg (now Leningrad), Russia. She emigrated to the US in 1926 and was naturalized in 1931. Her first novel, *We the Living,* appeared in 1936. Other works include *Anthem* (1938), *The Fountainhead* (1943), and *Atlas Shrugged* (1957). The last two are massive narratives that serve as vehicles for her philosophy of objectivism. Objectivism espouses the self-fulfillment of the individual in a capitalist society. Rand scorns weakness and altruism and regards selfishness as a virtue. The heroes of her novels, such as the architect in *The Fountainhead,* are independent, strong-willed people.

Randolph, A(sa) Philip (1889–1979), US labor leader and civil rights activist, b. Crescent City, Fla. Randolph was editor of the radical black journal *The Messenger* until 1925, when he founded the Brotherhood of Sleeping Car Porters. He organized the 1941 March on Washington that prompted President Roosevelt to issue a fair employment practices executive order, and helped organize the 1963 March on Washington. He resigned as president of the Brotherhood in 1968 to devote his time to the A. Philip Randolph Institute, a civil rights organization established in 1964.

Randolph, Edmund (1753–1813), US lawyer and statesman, b. near Williamsburg, Va. Randolph was an active participant in the American Revolution and served his state in a number of high political offices. As a delegate to the Federal Convention of 1787, Randolph proposed the Virginia Plan, foreshadowing the stronger federal government subsequently adopted. He was appointed attorney general by George Washington and fulfilled Jefferson's term as secretary of state (1794–95). Randolph later served as senior counsel for Aaron Burr in the famous treason trial of 1807.

Rangoon, capital and largest city of Burma, on Rangoon River, approx. 21mi (34km) N of Andaman Sea; one of SE Asia's largest seaports. Rangoon was won by Burma 1755; occupied by Britain 1824–26 and taken in Second Anglo-Burmese Wars 1852; occupied by Japan during WWII; site of airport, railhead, university (1920), technical university (1963), extensive parks and gardens; city proper is dominated by the massive 368-ft (112-m) Buddhist shrine, Shwe Dagon Pagoda (588BC). Industries: rice, lead, zinc ore, timber, oil refining, cotton, tobacco. Pop. 2,300,000.

Rankine, William John Macquorn (1820–72), Scottish engineer and physicist. He became professor of engineering at Glasgow, using his training in physics to acquaint engineers with the fundamentals of thermodynamics. His *Manual of the Steam Engine* (1859) introduced a practical notation system into engineering thermodynamics, and he devised the absolute temperature scale based on the degree Fahrenheit, which is known as the Rankine scale. He also determined the Rankine cycle, which functions as a model for steam-power installation performance.

Rann of Kutch. *See* Kutch, Rann of.

Raoult's Law, a statement that the changes in certain properties of a liquid that occur when a substance is dissolved in it are proportional to the number of molecules of solute present for a given quantity of solvent molecules. Discovered by François-Marie Raoult in 1886, it has been fundamental to many theories of solution.

Rape of Lucrece, The (1594), narrative poem by William Shakespeare, written in rhyme royal. It is based on Ovid's tale of Lucrece, wife of Collatinus. Revered as the most chaste woman in Rome, she is raped by Sextus Tarquinius, the king's son.

Raphael, biblical archangel who, with Michael, Gabriel, and Uriel, serves as a messenger of God, healing and relieving the suffering and sick.

Raphael (Raffaello Sanzio) (1483–1520), Italian painter. The major artist of the High Renaissance, he was influential in establishing the standards of that style. Raphael merged the poetic and the dramatic, the rich and the solid to achieve a personal and unique power evidenced even in his early work "Madonna del Granduca" (*c.*1505). While Michelangelo worked on the Sistine Chapel, Raphael executed a series of frescoes on the walls and ceiling of the Stanza della Segnatura in the Vatican Palace, a commission he received from Julius II. His frescoes depicted the four areas of learning, and "School of Athens" (1510–11) is considered his masterpiece. The epitome of the classical spirit of the High Renaissance, it is not unlike Michelangelo's "Last Supper" in spirit and scope. His subsequent works did not approach the magnitude of "School of Athens." "Galatea" (1513), a fresco, is sensuous in comparison to the earlier, more somber, and idealistic work, although both are in the classical tradition. Raphael was an extremely talented portrait painter, merging 15th-century realism with the human ideal of the High Renaissance. "Pope Leo X" (*c.*1518) is typical of his powerful style.

Rapid Eye Movement. *See* REM.

Rappahannock, river in Virginia; rises in the Blue Ridge Mts, N Virginia; flows SE to Chesapeake Bay, just S of Potomac River mouth; scene of many Civil War battles. Length: 212mi (341km).

Rare Earths. *See* Lanthanide Elements.

Ras al Khaymah, sheikdom in E Arabia and a member state of the United Arab Emirates on the Persian Gulf; part of Sharjah sheikdom until 1921; joined United Arab Emirates 1972; oil producing area. Area: 650sq mi (1,684sq km). Pop. 31,480.

Rasbora, freshwater fish found in SE Asia. A minnow popular with home aquarists, it has distinctive black markings according to species. Length: to 2in (5.1cm). Species include the Harlequin *Rasbora heteromorpha,* pygmy rasbora *R. maculate.* Family Cyprinidae.

Rash, pimples, hives, or wheals on the skin. It may accompany fever, measles, chicken pox, small pox, and scarlet fever. It also occurs as a reaction to some drugs and other substances to which the body is sensitive. Most rashes do not leave scars after drying.

Raspberry, bramble fruit grown in polar and temperate regions of North America, Europe, and Asia. The black, purple, or red fruit is eaten fresh or preserved. Canes, rising from perennial roots, bear fruit the second year. Family Rosaceae; genus *Rubus.*

Rasputin, Grigori Efimovich (1871?–1916), Russian peasant mystic who exercised great influence at the court of Nicholas II. Arriving in St Petersburg in 1904, he impressed the royal family with his ability to cure the tsarevich Alexis' hemophilia. In 1911 he created a major scandal through his frivolous appointments. During World War I he virtually ruled Russia. He was assassinated in 1916 by a group of conservative noblemen.

Rat, any of over 500 groups of small rodents found worldwide in almost all habitats. Most are herbivores and inoffensive. But the best known are the black rat *(Rattus rattus)* and brown rat *(Rattus Norvegicus),* both of the family Muridae. They are prolific, aggressive, and eat practically anything and carry many deadly diseases and destroy or contaminate property and food. Both are of Asiatic origin, but now live everywhere man does. Black rats are dark gray, under 8in (20cm) long, weigh under 12oz (350g), and have long tails and big ears. Brown rats are slightly heavier and longer with shorter tails and smaller ears. Most lab rats are albino strains of brown rats.

Ratel, or honey badger, solitary, aggressive, burrowing mammal of the weasel family, native to Africa and S Asia. It has a heavy body with light back and dark underparts. Omnivorous, it also is fond of honey and sometimes forms an association with a honey guide bird to locate wild bees' nests and share the spoils. Length: to 30in (76cm). Family Mustelidae; species *Mellivora capensis.*

Ratfish. *See* Chimaera.

Ratio, quotient of two numbers or of two quantities of the same kind, such as two prices, both in dollars, or of two lengths, both in meters, that indicates their relative magnitude. Ratios, as of the numbers 3 and 4, can be written as a fraction (3/4) or with a colon (3:4).

Rat Islands, group of islands in the W Aleutians, off SW Alaska; comprised of Kiska, Amchitka, Semisopochnoi, Rat, and smaller islets; scene of WWII conflicts.

Ratite Birds, large, usually flightless birds with flat breastbones rather than the keellike prominences found in most flying birds. Ratites include the ostrich, rhea, cassowary, emu, kiwi, the unusual flying tinamou, and extinct forms such as the moa and elephant bird. *See also* individual birds.

Rat Snake, any of some 50 species of terrestrial and arboreal snakes, distributed widely in North America and Europe. Common in North America are the black and yellow rat snakes, fox snakes, and corn snakes. The four-lined and Aesculapian snakes are European. Length: to 5ft (1.5m). Family Colubridae; genus *Elaphe.*

Rattan, climbing palm native to the East Indies and Africa. Its stems grow to 500ft (152m) by climbing over other trees and plants. They are used for making ropes, furniture, and mats. Family Palmaceae; species *Calamus.*

Rattlesnake, any of about 30 species of New World pit vipers characterized by a tail rattle of bony, loosely connected segments, found from Canada to South America, mostly in arid regions. A few are banded but most are blotched with dark diamonds, hexagons, or spots on lighter background. They feed mostly on rodents and bear their young live. The genus *Sistrurus* includes the massasauga and pygmy rattler. *Crotalus* includes all others. Common North American species are timber *(Crotalus horridus),* prairie *(C. viridis),* eastern diamondback *(C. adamanteus),* and western diamondback *(C. atrox)* rattlesnakes. The South American cascabel *(C. durissus)* has the most potent venom. Length: 1–8ft (30cm–2.5m). Family Viperidae. *See also* Pit Viper; Snake.

Rauschenberg, Robert (1925–), US painter and graphic artist, b. Port Arthur, Texas. He gained recognition in 1953 with his collages and assemblages. These works combined techniques, including dripped paint and collage ("Rebus," 1955). From 1955 he composed works that juxtaposed common objects such as stuffed birds, buckets, and hats with abstract expressionist painting ("Monogram," 1961). Rauschenberg's work is considered a link between abstract expressionism and pop art. He was elected a member of the American Academy and Institute of Arts and Letters in 1978.

Rauwolfia, drug derived from a shrub native to India. Its compounds are used to treat hypertension, anxiety, and psychoses. *See also* Reserpine.

Ravel, Maurice (1875–1937), French composer and pianist. Influenced by Franz Liszt and Claude Debussy, Ravel developed a style featuring exotic harmonies and orchestral brilliance. His piano piece *Jeux d'Eau* (1901) influenced Debussy and the Impressionist movement in music. He composed relatively few works, a number of which are very popular, eg, *Rhapsodie Espagnole* (1907), *La Valse* (1920), and *Bolero* (1928). His other important works include the ballet *Daphnis et Chloé* (1912), two piano concertos, sonatas, songs, and piano music.

Raven, large crow found in deserts, forests, and mountainous areas of the Northern Hemisphere. They have long conical bills, shaggy throat feathers, wedge-shaped tails, and black plumage with a purple sheen. They eat any plant or animal matter and build twig, stick, and bark cliff or tree nests for their greenish eggs (5–7). The common raven *(Corvus corax)* lives in central North America; the white-necked raven *(Corvus cryptoleucus)* lives in the SW United States and Mexico. Length: to 27in (68cm). Family Corvidae.

Ravenna, city in N Italy, 45mi (72km) ESE of Bologna; capital of Ravenna prov. A Roman naval base 1st century BC, it was capital of W Roman Empire AD 5th century; became capital of Byzantine Empire in Italy 6th century; independent republic 13th century; under papal dominion 16th–19th centuries; passed to Italy 1860; site of outstanding Roman and Byzantine architectural remains, including 5th–8th-century churches. Industries: petroleum, furniture, cement, fertilizer, sugar. Pop. 138,352.

Rawalpindi, city in NE Pakistan, approx. 160mi (258km) NNW of Lahore; industrial center. Great Britain signed treaty here Aug. 8, 1919, recognizing independence of Afghanistan. Industries: iron foundries, oil refining, machine shops. Pop. 615,000.

Ray, Man (1890–1976), US photographer and painter, b. Philadelphia. In 1917 he founded the New York Dada movement with Marcel Duchamp and Picabia. His early works utilized an airbrush technique. In the 1920s he began making his "Rayographs," in which he placed objects on light-sensitive photograph paper and exposed and developed them (Manikin).

Ray, flat-bodied, bottom-dwelling elasmobranch found throughout tropical and subtropical marine waters. Its color ranges from mottled black or brown to purple and white. Gills are located underneath enlarged winglike pectoral fins; many rays also have a tail spine. Young are born alive. There are several families including butterfly, eagle, manta, cownosed, electric, and sting rays. Order Raiiformes (also called Batoidei). *See also*

Raphael: Madonna of the Chair

Maurice Ravel

Sam Rayburn

Devilfish; Guitar Fish; Sawfish; Sting Ray; Torpedo Ray.

Rayburn, Samuel Taliaferro (1882–1961), US political leader, b. Roane co, Tenn. Beginning his political career in the Texas state legislature (1907–12), he was elected to the US House of Representatives (1913) and served until his death. He helped Pres. Franklin D. Roosevelt get his New Deal laws passed in the House (1931–37), and held that position, except for 4 years, as long as he was in the House, twice as long as any predecessor. He was noted for his knowledge of House rules and his parliamentary skill.

Rayleigh, John William Strutt (Lord) (1842–1919), English physicist, professor at Cambridge and later at the Royal Institution of London. His work was chiefly concerned with various forms of wave motion: the scattering of light, black-body radiation, sound waves, and water and earthquake waves. For his discovery of the inert atmospheric gas argon (with William Ramsay), he was awarded a 1904 Nobel Prize.

Raynaud's Disease, disorder in which spasms of the arteries to the fingers cause fingertips to become pale and then blue when exposed to cold. It occurs mainly in women.

Rayon, a fine, smooth, man-made textile fiber produced from solutions of modified cellulose of softwood pulp or cotton linters. Cellulose is extruded through spinnerets and solidified in chemicals or in warm air. Viscose rayon, the most common, is spun-dried and has strength approaching that of nylon. The more costly cuprammonium rayon, known as Bemberg, resembles silk.

Razor-billed Auk, or razorbill, chunky seabird of cold Northern Hemisphere coastlines that resembles a small penguin. It is black and white with a white-ringed narrow bill and dives for food. Nesting in large colonies, it lays a single conical egg on bare oceanic cliffs. Length: 17in (43cm). Species *Alca torda*.

Re, or **Ra,** in Egyptian religion, the Sun god and lord of the dead, whose center of worship was at Heliopolis. In some traditions he is identified with Osiris or sometimes as the creator of men. In the myths, Re sailed his sun boat across the sky by day and through the underworld by night. He is depicted as a falcon-headed man with a solar disc on his head.

Reactant. See Chemical Reaction.

Reaction, Chemical. See Chemical Reaction.

Reaction Propulsion, propulsion utilizing Newton's Third Law of Motion: For every action there is an equal and opposite reaction. Both rocket and jet engines build up internal pressure from gases or plasmas that are allowed to escape in one direction, creating an unbalanced force in the other direction.

Reactor, Fission. See Fission Reactor.

Reactor, Fusion. See Fusion Reactor.

Reading, county town of Berkshire, S central England, at confluence of Thames and Kennet rivers; railroad and industrial center; seat of University of Reading. Industries: engineering, brewing. Pop. 132,900.

Reading, city in SE Pennsylvania, on Schuylkill River; seat of Berks co; military base during French and Indian War; cannons were made here during Revolution

and Civil War; site of Albright College (1856), Albernia College (1958), and the Pagoda, a Japanese-style observatory on Mt Penn; a rich agricultural region in Pennsylvania Dutch country. Industries: textiles, clothing, leather goods, iron and steel products, batteries. Founded 1748 by Thomas Penn; inc. as borough 1783, as city 1847. Pop. (1980) 78,686.

Reagan, Ronald Wilson (1911–), 40th president of the United States (1981–), b. Tampico, Ill. In 1940 he married actress Jane Wyman, and they had one child and adopted another before their divorce (1948). In 1952 he married Nancy Davis, with whom he had two children. Reagan graduated from Eureka (Illinois) College in 1932 and began working as a radio sportscaster and newspaper sportswriter in Des Moines, Iowa. On assignment near Los Angeles in 1937, he took a successful screen test and in the same year appeared in the first of over 50 films he made during the following three decades. After serving in the US Army (1942–45), he returned to Hollywood where he was active in liberal causes, at the same time developing strong anti-Communist sentiments. In 1947 he was elected president of the Screen Actors Guild, serving five successive terms, until 1952. Working (1954–62) for the General Electric Company, he appeared on the television program *General Electric Theater* while serving again (1959–60) as president of the Screen Actors Guild. In 1962 he joined the Republican party and became a crusader for conservative causes and candidates. Despite his lack of political experience, he won a landslide victory over California's incumbent governor, Edmund G. Brown, in 1966. Reagan was reelected in 1970, serving until 1974. He ran unsuccessfully for the Republican presidential nomination in 1968 and 1976. In 1980, on a ticket with George Bush, he defeated incumbent President Jimmy Carter. Reagan's campaign platform called for a balanced budget, with reduced federal spending and taxes, and a strengthening of military defense. During 1981–83, a time of recession, his economics ("Reaganomics") drew much criticism. In March 1981, he was wounded in an assassination attempt. Reelected in 1984, Reagan took a hard line against terrorism and ordered the US bombing of Libya in 1986. Career: governor of California (1966–74); president (1981–).

Reagent, substance that takes part in a chemical reaction. The term is often understood to mean a common laboratory reagent, that is, a substance used in routine qualitative or quantitative analytical tests.

Realism, doctrine that universal concepts and tangibles exist outside the mind, that is, independently of human perception—the opposite of idealism. The term is also applied to the literary school, of whom Gustave Flaubert, to depict life as it is, without idealizing or romanticizing any of its aspects. Flaubert's realism was extended by the naturalist school, of whom Theodore Dreiser and Emile Zola were chief exponents, to espouse a totally objective inquiry into the social order. Realism was also a 19th-century movement in painting and architecture. Reacting against the subjectivity of Romanticism, realistic artists insisted on portraying everyday matters of ordinary people, including their baser aspects. Gustave Courbet was the first major realist painter.

Rebekah, in the Bible, daughter of Bethuel, sister of Laban, wife of Isaac, and mother of twins Esau and Jacob. Jacob was her favorite and she helped him win, through deception, Isaac's blessing from the elder Esau.

Rebellion of 1837, uprising in opposition to the power of the Family Compacts and the Church of England in

Canada, and French-Canadian desire for cultural autonomy, touched off two years of armed rebellion led by William Lyon Mackenzie and Louis Papineau. The rebellion was poorly organized and militarily unsuccessful but the revolt led to the Durham Report (1839) and Act of Union (1841). *See also* Durham Report; Family Compacts.

Recall. See Memory.

Receptor, any of several kinds of neurons specialized to transform physical energy into the electrochemical impulses of the nervous system. For example, the rods and cones of the retina are receptors that transform light energy into impulses sent to the brain.

Recession, phase of the business cycle associated with a declining economy. It is associated with increasing unemployment, contracting business activity, and decreasing consumer purchasing power. A recession may have a number of causes and is generally associated with pessimistic business attitudes. Government expansionary policy, such as government spending or tax cuts, may be used to stimulate the economy during a recession. If the recession is not checked, the economy may head into a depression. *See also* Business Cycles.

Recessive Gene, any pair of hereditary genes that remains latent. *See also* Dominance; Heredity.

Recife (Pernambuco), city in NE Brazil; capital of Pernambuco state. Located partly on an island and connected to mainland by numerous bridges, it is an excellent port and shipping center. Founded 1548 by Portuguese fishermen. Pop. 1,249,821.

Reciprocal, number or quantity equal to one divided by a specified number or quantity: the reciprocal of 2 is ½; the reciprocal of ½ is 2. The product of a number and its reciprocal is one: $2 \times \frac{1}{2} = 1$.

Recombinant DNA Research, also called gene splicing, a branch of genetic engineering involving the transference of a segment of DNA (deoxyribonucleic acid, of which the genetic code is made up) from a source organism (which may be a human) into a host mechanism (typically a microbe). The transferred segment is spliced into the overall DNA structure of the host, thus becoming part of its DNA structure and altering its genetic information. When the host undergoes asexual cell division, each product cell carries a replica of the new DNA. In this way numerous clones of the new cell can be made. Gene splicing can be used to design cells to produce medicines, to digest spilled oil or waste products, or for other purposes. *See also* Deoxyribonucleic Acid (DNA).

Reconstruction (1865–77), period in US history after the Civil War. Conflict arose almost immediately between the conflicting policies of President Andrew Johnson and Congress concerning plans and authority for reestablishing the 11 Confederate states within the Union. By overriding presidential vetoes and by limiting the president's powers, Congress, led by Radical Republicans, prevailed. When Johnson attempted to challenge congressional authority, he was impeached (1868), but not convicted. Under the congressional plan, the South was divided into five military districts. The rights of newly-freed blacks were protected by civil rights acts and constitutional amendments. By 1870, all the Southern states had been readmitted to the Union. State governments were, however, controlled by Radical Republicans and their black and Scalawag allies. With the aid of the Ku Klux Klan, white Southerners, many of whom were reenfranchised by the General Amnesty Act (1872), recaptured the state governments. Reconstruction ended in 1877 when the last Federal troops were withdrawn from the South. *See also* Civil Rights Act of 1866 and 1870; Freedmen's Bureau; Ku Klux Klan.

Recorder, simple woodwind musical instrument dating from 15th- to 18th-century Europe. Easy to play, it has a whistle-shaped mouthpiece and an end-blown straight tube with eight finger holes. It is made in four sizes: bass, tenor, treble (alto), and descant (soprano), each ranging two octaves. Revived by Arnold Dolmetsch in England (1926), it is popular with amateur musicians.

Rectangle, four-sided geometric figure (quadrilateral) the interior angles of which are right angles and each pair of opposite sides is of equal length and is parallel. It is a special case of a parallelogram.

Rectangular Coordinate System, Cartesian coordinate system in which the axes are at right angles to each other. *See also* Cartesian Coordinate System.

Rectifier, device for converting an alternating current into a direct current. It consists of an electron tube or semiconductor that presents a high resistance to a current flowing in one direction and a low resistance to current flowing in the opposite direction. *See also* Semiconductor.

Red (Yuan), formerly Koi: a chief river of Vietnam; rises in S China, flows SE across northern Vietnam, passing Hanoi, to Gulf of Tonkin. Important transportation link between China and Vietnam; forms wide fertile delta E of Hanoi (rice-growing region); receives Clear and Black rivers NW of Hanoi. Length: approx. 500mi (805km).

Red Admiral Butterfly, anglewing butterfly common in North America and Europe. Its dark front wings are crossed by a broad, bright orange band. The caterpillars feed on elms, nettles, and other plants. Species *Vanessa atalanta.*

Red Algae, a group of typically reddish mostly marine algae (division Rhodophyta) especially numerous in tropical and subtropical seas. Some, including dulse and Irish moss, are common on Northern coasts. The reddish color is caused by a red pigment that conceals the green chlorophyll. Some red algae are single-celled, but most are many-celled plants growing in tentaclelike strands forming shrublike masses.

Red-Bellied Snake, species of small, secretive snake of open woods and bogs of E and central United States. It is usually brown or gray with four narrow dark stripes, a plain red belly, and three pale spots on neck. Length: to 10in (25cm). Family Colubridae; species *Storeria occipitomaculata.*

Red Blood Cell. *See* Erythrocyte.

Red Clay, a component of the benthic division of the ocean, occurring with oozes or alone below depths of 16,400ft (5,000m), and consisting of ultrafine organic particles, wind-blown volcanic ash, and meteoric material. Its red-brown color is due to the ferric iron and manganese compounds in it.

Red Cross, founded 1863, international organization that seeks to lessen human suffering, particularly through disaster relief, neutral aid to war victims, and services to members of the armed forces. The Red Cross was created as a result of the urging of Jean Henri Dunant, a Swiss citizen, who had been shocked by the suffering of the wounded after the battle of Solferino in 1859. Composed of over 100 independent national societies with central headquarters in Switzerland and staffed largely by volunteers, the Red Cross' name comes from its symbol, a red cross on a white field, which reverses the colors of the Swiss flag.

Red Hake. *See* Ling.

Redheaded Woodpecker, black and white woodpecker with a crimson head found in North America. An insect eater, it hunts like a flycatcher. Species *Melanerpes erythrocephalus. See also* Woodpecker.

Redondo Beach, suburban city in S California, 17mi (27km) SE of Los Angeles; supports tourism and light manufacturing. Inc. 1892. Pop. (1980) 57,102.

Redpoll, seed-eating finch found in colder parts of the Northern Hemisphere. They have pointed conical bills, short forked tails, and brownish plumage with a red patch on the crown. Length: 5in (12.5cm). Genus *Acanthis.*

Red River, river in S United States; rises in highlands of E New Mexico; flows E across Texas panhandle, forms natural boundary between Texas and Oklahoma, turns S in SW Arkansas to Louisiana and empties into the Atchafalaya River (to Gulf of Mexico) and Old River (to the Mississippi River); used for irrigation, hydroelectricity, and industrial traffic. Length: 1,222mi(1,967km).

Red River of the North, river in United States and Canada; rises in North Dakota at the confluence of the Bois de Sioux and Otter Tail rivers; flows N between Minnesota and North Dakota, empties into Lake Winnipeg, Manitoba, Canada; used for irrigation. Length: approx. 310mi (500km).

Red Sea, narrow arm of the Indian Ocean, between NE Africa and the Arabian Peninsula; connected with the Mediterranean Sea by the Gulf of Suez and Suez Canal. Known in biblical times as the passageway for the Israelite exodus from Egypt, it was an ancient trade route whose importance declined with the discovery of an all-water route around Africa (1498). Its importance greatly increased (1869) with building of Suez Canal, but with the closing of Suez Canal (1967–75) during Arab-Israeli conflicts, building of vessels too large for the canal, and initiation of pipelines, the Red Sea's importance as a trade route diminished. Area: 170,000sq mi (440,300sq km).

Red Shift, shift in the spectral lines of a star, galaxy, or other celestial object toward the red end of the visible spectrum, relative to their positions in an equivalent spectrum produced on Earth. Although sometimes a gravitational effect, it is usually due to the Doppler effect and results from a recessional velocity of the object (a star approaching the Sun has a blue shift). The red shift of galaxies is evidence for the expansion of the universe. *See also* Quasar.

Red Snapper, tropical marine food fish found from West Indies to Florida. Bright scarlet, it has sharp teeth and a flattened snout. Length: 2–3ft (61–91cm). Family Lutjanidae; species *Lutjanus campechanus.*

Red Spider, or spider mite, red vegetarian mite found worldwide. A serious plant pest, it spins webs, revealing its presence. Length: 0.01–0.03in (0.03–0.8mm). Family Tetranychidae. *See also* Mite.

Redstart, two unrelated warblers. The American flycatching redstart (*Setophaga ruticila*) is a wood warbler. The male is black and orange above and white underneath; length: 5 in (12.5cm). The European redstart (*Phoenicurus phoenicurus*) is slightly larger and the male is grayish with a rust-red breast and tail. *See also* Warbler.

Red Tide, marine phenomenon occurring in subtropical water in which sea water turns red and fish are killed. It is caused by an overabundance of plantlike flagellate protozoans called dinoflagellates. Their pigment causes the water to appear reddish and they produce a toxin that kills fish. One species is *Gonyaulax catanella.*

Reduction Reaction, chemical process in which a specified substance loses oxygen. The term has been extended to include reaction with hydrogen and, more generally, to any reaction involving gain of electrons or other decrease in oxidation number. For instance, the change from a ferric to a ferrous compound is reduction of the ferric compound. *See also* Oxidation-Reduction.

Redwood City, city in W California, 18mi (29km) SE of San Francisco; seat of San Mateo co; noted since 1900 for its chrysanthemum industry. Industries: food-processing, electronic equipment, chemicals, cement, plastics. Inc. 1868. Pop. (1980) 54,965.

Reed, Stanley Forman (1884–1980), US jurist and lawyer, b. Mason co, Ky. A Kentucky state legislator (1912–16), he was appointed by Pres. Herbert Hoover and served as general counsel for both the Federal Farm Board (1929–32) and the Reconstruction Finance Corporation (1932–35). He was then made US solicitor general (1935–38). He was associate justice of the US Supreme Court (1938–57), appointed by Pres. Franklin D. Roosevelt.

Reed, Walter (1851–1902), US military surgeon, b. Belroi, Va. He headed the commission of physicians sent to Cuba that established that yellow fever was transmitted by the *Aedes aegypti* mosquito. Later he proved that the disease was caused by a virus carried by the mosquito.

Reed, aquatic grass native to wetlands throughout the world. The common reed *(Phragmites communis)* has broad leaves, feathery flower cluster, and stiff smooth stems. Dry reed stems are used for thatching, construction, and musical pipes. Height: to 10ft (3m). Family Gramineae. *See also* Grass.

Reedbuck, light, graceful antelope native to Africa, south of the Sahara, usually near water. Brown to gray, its bushy tail is erect when disturbed. Male has short horns, curved forward at tips. Length: to 4.5ft (1.4m). Family Bovidae; genus *Redunca.*

Reed Instruments, instruments producing tones when air current vibrates a fiber or metal tongue. The accordion, where wind flows in both directions, uses a free reed. In a clarinet or reed organ pipe, where air passes in one direction, a beating reed vibrates against a hole at the end of the tube. The oboe has a double-reed mouthpiece, the two tongues vibrating against each other when blown.

Reef. *See* Coral Reef.

Refining, Ore, the process employed in removing impurities or changing the composition of various ores to obtain the desired metal in reasonably pure form. Employed are pyrometallurgy, or smelting and distillation methods; electrometallurgy, for example, electrolytic refining in which the pure metal forms on one electrode; and hydrometallurgy, or extraction from aqueous solution. *See also* Ore.

Reflection, change in direction of part of a wave motion when a wave, such as a light wave, encounters a surface separating two different media, such as air and metal, and is thrown back into the original medium. The remaining part passes into the second medium. The incident wave, reflected wave, and the line perpendicular to the surface at the point of incidence (the normal) all lie in the same plane. The incident and reflected waves make equal angles with the normal.

Reflector. *See* Telescope, Optical.

Reflex, simple type of unlearned and involuntary behavior, for example, the patellar or "knee-jerk" reflex that occurs when the bent knee is struck by an object. At least two neurons (receptor and effector) must be involved in the reflex arc, although one or more intervening neurons (interneurons) are often present. Additional nerve impulses travel from the arc to the brain via the central nervous system; they inform the individual that the involuntary reflex is occurring.

Reformation, major change within Western Christianity that developed between the 14th and 17th centuries. A large segment of Christianity separated from the Roman Catholic Church. Several intellectuals guided the change. The papacy became the focus of the critics' attack. Apostolic succession, as interpreted by Rome, was seriously questioned and threatened by the reformers. Martin Luther's dispute over the sale of indulgences is claimed as the clear beginning of the reform movement. The worldliness of the papacy was criticized. Ulrich Zwingli's reforms were more radical than those of Luther. John Calvin developed the doctrine of predestination and the concept of the elect. Individual churches eventually developed around the teachings of the reformers. Scripture was the basis of these changes as well as the doctrine of the priesthood of believers and concepts of faith and grace. *See also* Calvin, John; Luther, Martin; Zwingli, Ulrich.

Reformation, Catholic, internal 16th-century reform movement of the Roman Catholic Church. In part a response to the Protestant Reformation, this reform involved a strengthening and purification of church organization and tradition, as well as an ambitious reclamation of certain former Catholic territories. Greatly aided by the Jesuits, this renewed vigor spread throughout Europe and America.

Reform Bills, a series of 19th-century British electoral measures making parliamentary democracy more representative. Prime Minister Grey's 1832 bill, hotly contested by the House of Lords, abolished obsolete constituencies, redistributed seats in favor of the new industrial population centers, and extended the franchise to the industrial middle class. Benjamin Disraeli's 1867 bill, by lowering property qualifications, enfranchised the urban working class, which almost doubled the electorate. William Gladstone's 1884 bill added 2,000,000 new voters to the list by enfranchising most agricultural workers and miners. The franchise was not extended to women until the 20th century.

Reform Judaism, one of the three divisions that has developed within modern Judaism. It is also called Progressive or Liberal Judaism. It originated in 19th-century Germany. Israel Jacobson, one of the founders, made changes in rituals and used the vernacular for some prayers. Its main tenet stresses the progressive nature of revelation. Customs that had no contempo-

Redpoll

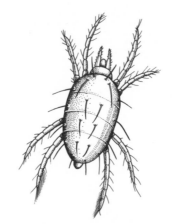

Red spider

Reims, France

rary meaning were changed or discarded. In 1929 the World Union for Progressive Judaism was founded, uniting world reform congregations.

Refraction, change in direction of a wave, such as a light wave, when it crosses the boundary between one medium and another transparent medium, such as air and glass, and undergoes a change in velocity. The incident wave, refracted wave, and the line perpendicular to the surface at the point of incidence (the normal) all lie in the same plane. The incident and refracted waves make an angle of incidence, i, and an angle of refraction, r, respectively, with the normal. The new direction of motion is such that the ratio of the sines of these angles, $\sin i / \sin r$, always has the same value for two particular media. This constant value is the index of refraction for the two media.

Refractor. See Telescope, Optical.

Refractory, any nonmetallic material having high compressive strength at furnace temperatures with low thermal conductivity and a low coefficient of expansion (such as insulating bricks). Most important of the refractory materials are magnesite and dolomite used in open-hearth steel furnaces and portland cement kilns. High-melting oxides, carbides, nitrides, and sulfides are refractories used in nuclear power plants.

Refrigeration, process by which the temperature in a given area is lowered. The use of ice or dry ice (solid carbon dioxide), which absorb heat while melting, is still common. Refrigerants include Freon, methyl chloride, or ammonia.

Regal moth, large American moth with a wingspread up to 6in (15cm). Its olive-gray front wings are marked with reddish veins and yellow spots; its orange-red hind wings have yellow markings. The caterpillars are known as hickory horned devils because of prominent hornlike appendages. Length: 4–5in (10–12.5cm). Species *Citheronia regalise.*

Regency Period (1811–20), the period of British history when because of King George III's mental incapacity his powers were transferred to his son George, Prince of Wales, as prince regent. Various limitations on the regent's powers were removed in 1812.

Regensburg, city in SE West Germany, at confluence of Danube and Regen rivers, 65mi (105km) NE of Munich. City flourished as trade center with Near East and India during the 13th century; seat of imperial diet 1663–1806; annexed to Bavaria 1810; became free port 1853. Notable buildings include Gothic cathedral (13th–16th century), remains of Porta Praetoria (179), Schottenkirche St Jakob (12th century), St Emmeram (7th century). Industries: machines, precision instruments, printing, pottery, wood products, chemicals. Pop. 131,000.

Reggio Calabria (Reggio di Calabria), seaport city in S Italy, 7mi (11km) SE of Messina; capital of Reggio di Calabria prov. and former capital of Calabria region. Founded by Greek colonists 8th century BC, it was allied with Rome 270 BC; conquered by Normans 1060; site of Roman and Greek remains, museum housing fine archaeological collection. Exports: fruit, silk, wine, olive oil, figs. Industries: tourism, perfumes, fisheries, pharmaceuticals, fruit canning. Pop. 178,094.

Regina, capital and largest city in Saskatchewan, Canada, 355mi (572km) W of Winnipeg. Canadian Pacific Transcontinental Railway and the Transcontinental Highway pass through Regina, making it a very impor-

tant trade and cooperative business center for the provinces. Originally called Pile O' Bones, for buffalo bones found there. Founded 1882. Pop. 149,593.

Regulus, or Alpha Leonis, bluish main-sequence star in the constellation Leo. Characteristics: apparent mag. 1.33, absolute mag. 1.0, spectral type B7; distance 85 light-years.

Rehnquist, William Hubbs (1924–   ), US jurist and lawyer, b. Milwaukee. A law clerk to Supreme Court Justice Jackson (1952–53), he practiced law 1953–69. A political conservative, he was chosen by President Nixon to direct the Office of Legal Counsel of the Department of Justice (1968–71). In 1971, Nixon appointed him an associate justice of the US Supreme Court. He took his seat in 1972 and quickly won a reputation for well-written opinions. In 1986 he succeeded Warren Burger as chief justice.

Reichstag Fire (1933), conflagration that destroyed part of the German Reichstag (lower house of parliament) building. Hitler used the subsequent trial of a Dutchman who set the fire to indict Communist party leaders and discredit the party.

Reign of Terror (1793–94), stage of the French Revolution. It involved a military dictatorship, directed by a Committee of Public Safety in which Maximilien Robespierre wielded the greatest power. It was established to preserve the Revolution in a period of emergency. The committee sought to reorganize the military, crush counterrevolution, and stabilize the economy. The committee's tactics were harsh. There were many executions for treason and economic problems worsened. In 1794 the National Convention overthrew Robespierre, and the Reign of Terror ended.

Reims (Rheims), city in NE France, on Vesle River, 83mi (134km) ENE of Paris; port on Aisne-Marne Canal; important town of Roman Gaul. Clovis I was baptized and crowned king of all Franks in cathedral by St Remi, bishop of Rheims (AD 496). Present cathedral is monument of French Gothic architecture; scene of crowning of Charles VII with Joan of Arc at his side (1429). In WWI much of cathedral was destroyed, including outstanding stained glass window. Its restoration 1927–38 was aided by funds from Rockefeller Foundation. City was scene of signing of German unconditional surrender May 7, 1945. Pope Paul III founded university here 1547; birthplace of Jean Baptiste Colbert, French statesman (1619), and St John Baptist de la Salle, founder of the Christian Brothers (1651). Industries: grapes, woolens, glass, baked goods. Pop. 183,610.

Reincarnation, transmigration, rebirth, or metempsychosis, the passage of the soul through successive bodies. This view of life as being cyclical has appeared in primitive speculations about the fate of the soul after death. In the 6th century BC it was taught as religious-philosophical doctrine in both Greece and India. This belief appears in Hinduism, Buddhism, Jainism, and Sikhism.

Reindeer. See Caribou.

Reindeer Moss, a gray tufted, much-branched lichen *(Cladonia rangiferina)* that grows erect on the soil. Large patches of reindeer moss are an important food for caribou and reindeer and are sometimes eaten by people. See also Lichen.

Reinforced Concrete, a type of strong concrete used widely in bridge construction. It is hardened onto embedded steel (in the form of rods, bars, or mesh), which

adds tensile strength. Reinforced concrete can sustain heavy stresses over considerable spans.

Relapsing Fever, infectious disease caused by spirochetes and transmitted by tick and lice bites. It is characterized by fever, headache, muscle pain, and vomiting. An attack ends after nine days and then recurs after a few days. Treatment is antibiotics, bed rest, and fluid diet.

Relative Molecular Mass. See Molecular Weight.

Relativity Tests, observable phenomena that are outside the scope of Newtonian mechanics but can be explained by, and used to test, relativity theory. They include the small discrepancy between the actual orbit of Mercury and that predicted by Newton's theory; the apparent displacements of the positions of stars through the bending of their light rays; the effect of a gravitational field on the wavelength of light emitted by atoms. This proved difficult to detect with certainty, but was verified in 1960 by comparing the atoms at the top and bottom of a water tower, the wavelength difference being measured by means of the Mössbauer effect.

Relativity Theory, theory, proposed by Albert Einstein, based on the postulate that the motion of one body can be defined only with respect to that of a second body and that no absolute meaning can be given to the statement that a body is at rest. This led to the concept of a four-dimensional space-time continuum in which the three space dimensions and time are treated on an equal footing. The special theory, put forward in 1905, is limited to the description of events as they appear to observers in a state of uniform relative motion. The need for it arose from the negative result of the Michelson-Morley experiment (1887), which showed that there was no difference between the velocity of light as measured in the direction of the Earth's motion and its velocity at right angles to this direction. The more important consequences of the theory are: (1) that the velocity of light is absolute, that is, not relative to the velocity of the observer; (2) that the mass of a body increases with its velocity; (3) that mass (m) and energy (E) are equivalent, that is, $E = mc^2$, where c is the velocity of light (this shows that when mass is converted to energy, a small mass gives rise to large energy); (4) the Lorentz-Fitzgerald contraction, that is, bodies contract as their velocity increases; and (5) time dilation. The general theory of relativity, completed in 1915, is applicable to observers not in uniform relative motion and leads to the concept of gravitation. The presence of matter in space causes space to "curve," forming gravitational fields, thus gravitation becomes a property of space itself. Later modifications of the geometry of relativity have attempted to combine a representation of the gravitational and electromagnetic fields to form a unified field theory.

Religion, particular system of beliefs and resulting practices stimulated by some awareness of a supreme being or power. Throughout the historical development of all cultures, some religious system is present. Many stress the individual nature of religion as a personal experience, while others emphasize its social dimension. It necessarily develops according to man's self-understanding in relation to the infinite. It should be seen as a dynamic, rather than a static, process. Institutional organization shapes religious life into specific forms. Distinctions are made between authoritarian and humanitarian forms and denominations are viewed as different paths to the Divine. The paradoxical nature of religion is evident; some deny the necessity of faith and its universality, while it is also seen as basic to man's nature. Feeling is generally seen as essential to religion as well as knowledge and response in actions. The religious needs of man are generally formalized and given direction through denominations. Individual religious bodies are innumerable, and united only in their search for truth. One main division is between Christian and non-Christian religions. Christianity, Judaism, and Islam are generally regarded as the most influential religions in the world today. The ecumenical movement is developing within varied religions. It recognizes the common ground of religious drives and experiences, and strives to unify men as religious beings. Agnosticism and theism are frequently studied as religions. *See also* individual religions.

Religion, Primitive, religions of poor small-scale societies without literary cultures. Christianity and other "advanced" religions are difficult to distinguish from "primitive" religions. Few other generalizations can be made, since primitive religions are numerous and show tremendous variety. They tend to take the place of science and philosophy in explaining life and the natural world; through ritual and other practices attempts are made to affect this world. Similarly, primitive religions often back up their culture's morality. Phenomena such as shamanism and totemism are aspects of such religions rather than types of primitive religion. *See also* Animism; Monotheism; Polytheism; Shaman; Taboo; Totem.

Religion, Wars of (1562–98), series of religious conflicts in France. At stake was freedom of worship for French Protestants. There was also a struggle among the French nobility for power and influence with the French king. The conflicts, also known as the Huguenot Wars, were ended following the Edict of Nantes giving freedom of worship to the Protestants and the Treaty of Vervins (1598). In 1685 Louis XIV revoked the edict.

REM, or rapid eye movement sleep; occupies about 20% of a usual night's sleep, and is a recurring 20-minute period every 90 minutes. Dreaming is believed to occur during REM sleep.

Rembrandt (Harmenszoon van Rijn) (1606–69), Dutch painter and graphic artist. His early career, the Leyden period (1625–31), during which he executed small, realistic works, was influenced by the work of Caravaggio. Typical of this period is "Tobit and Anna with the Kid" (1626). By 1636 he was in the midst of his High Baroque style ("The Blinding of Samson," 1636). He had also become a popular and wealthy painter of portraits. After 1650 his style shows a new emotional depth and subtle lyricism. "Jacob Blessing the Sons of Joseph" (1656) is typical of this period. In his later works Rembrandt often alludes in mood or composition to works of the Northern Renaissance, as in "The Polish Rider" (*c.*1656), which likens to Albrecht Dürer's "Knight, Death and Devil." "The Return of the Prodigal Son" (1665) is one of Rembrandt's most subtle and expressively emotional religious works. It is evidence of his lifelong sympathy with the downtrodden and the poor. Rembrandt is an important graphic artist whose talent rivals that of Dürer. He was a master of the etching and its wide tonal range not available through techniques in woodcutting or engraving. "Christ Preaching" is a typical print.

Remington, Frederic (1861–1909), US painter and sculptor, b. Canton, N.Y. For health reasons he moved to the West and began painting scenes of western life. His romantic depictions of cowboys and Indians became immensely popular. His works include "The Scout, Friends or Enemies" (1908) and the bronze "Bronco Buster." His style is detailed and realistic. The Remington Art Memorial, Ogdensburg, N.Y., houses a notable collection.

Remora, or sharksucker, marine fish found worldwide in tropical and temperate seas. Gray, reddish, or brown, it has a ridged sucking disc on top of its head that it uses to cling to sharks, turtles, rays, whales, and boats. Length: 7–36in (18–91cm). The eight species include *Echeneis naucrates* and the whalesucker *Remilegia australis.* Family Echeneidae.

Renaissance Architecture, architectural style that began in Italy in the 15th century and spread throughout Europe until the advent of Mannerism and the Baroque in the 16th and 17th centuries. Revolting against Gothic architecture, this rebirth of Roman motifs was readily adapted in Italy, where Roman ruins were prevalent and Gothic styles least firmly entrenched. Brunelleschi and Alberti studied actual Roman ruins; Michelozzi, Bramante, and others used the classical orders of architecture and structural elements. In France the style was first employed by Lescot, commissioned by Francis I to work on the Louvre (1546). In England and other European countries classical forms were integrated with medieval motifs.

Renaissance Art, usually refers to Italian art from 1400–1600 and its spread to the rest of Europe by the early 16th century. The artistic movement is characterized by a revival of interest in classical antiquity, with its ethical and aesthetic values, a new humanistic outlook, and a new interest in naturalism and science. The scientific studies in anatomy, optics, and perspective led to a new realism in painting and sculpture. The new criteria of beauty included harmony, defined as a resolution of complex and conflicting elements, and proportion. Italian Renaissance is grouped into several schools. The Florentines include Giotto, the first artist to apply the new humanism and the rediscovery of the human body to painting; Masaccio, interested in perspective; Uccello; Mantegna; Botticelli, with his classical subject matter; Verrocchio; Leonardo da Vinci; and Michelangelo. The main architects were Ghiberti and Brunelleschi. The Venetian school, including Bellini, Titian, and Tintoretto, stressed light and color and introduced landscape backgrounds.

Renaissance Music, music composed in Europe from roughly 1400 to 1600. This music was mainly vocal polyphony, ie, works sung by an unaccompanied chorus divided into four to six separate parts. Composers produced many masses and motets in this style, often for religious occasions. Nonreligious music at this time was mainly in the form of songs—Italian and English madrigals. French chansons, German lieder—and some instrumental music composed for organ, clavier, lute, or for small ensembles of musicians. Masters who composed during this period include Ockeghem, Palestrina, Lasso, Byrd, and Gabrieli. *See also* Madrigal; Motet; Polyphony.

Renal Tubular Acidosis (RTA), an inherited kidney disorder in which there is failure to acidify the urine. There are two types—proximal and distal. The distal type usually occurs in women and is caused by the inability of the distal tubules of the kidney to maintain an acid urine. The distal-type condition can be accompanied by kidney failure, deposits of calcium phosphate in the kidney tubules, and retardation. The proximal type, which usually occurs in males, is characterized by excess bicarbonate, a base, in the urine.

Renin, polypeptide hormone produced by the kidney in response to lowered blood pressure. It activates angiotensin, a powerful vasoconstrictor, which then increases blood pressure.

Rennes, city in NW France, at junction of Ille and Vilaine rivers, 193mi (311km) WSW of Paris. During Middle Ages it served as capital of Brittany; partially destroyed by fire 1720; site of Palais de Justice (1618–54), and cathedral of St Pierre (1787–1844). Industries: leather, printing, linen, cotton yarns. Founded as old Gallic town. Pop. 205,733.

Reno, city in W Nevada, on Truckee River; seat of Washoe co. Founded 1858, it was known as Lake's Crossing; it was renamed Reno after Civil War Gen. Jesse Lee Reno; it grew with coming of Central Pacific Railroad (1868). It is known nationwide for its free port privileges, legalized gambling, and quick divorces; site of University of Nevada (1874), Mackay School of Mines (1907), and annual rodeo, state fair, and national air race. Industries: tourism, mining, agriculture, meat packing, flour milling, beverages, sheet metals. Inc. 1903. Pop. (1980) 100,756.

Renoir, Jean (1894–1979), French filmmaker and actor, son of the painter Auguste Renoir. Internationally famed for lyric response to nature and humanity and for subtlety of style, Renoir's foremost films include *Nana* (1926), *Madame Bovary* (1934), *La Grand Illusion* (1937), *La Règle du Jeu* (1939), *French Cancan* (1955), and *C'est la Revolution* (1967). In 1975, he was awarded a special Oscar for his lifetime achievements.

Renoir, Pierre Auguste (1841–1919), French painter and sculptor. His "Lise" was accepted by the 1865 Salon, Paris, although "Diana," after the style of Edouard Manet, was rejected in 1867. "Odalisque" (1870) showed influences of Delacroix. He exhibited in the first Impressionist show (1874) and also in that group's second and seventh exhibitions. One of the finest works of 1874 was "La Loge." At this point he was developing a personal style that culminated in "Le Moulin de la Galette" (1876), a work both sensuous and ethereal. "Les Parapluies" (1882–83) was an attempt to discipline the Impressionist style. In the 1890s he moved to a warmer style, primarily painting women and domestic scenes. His female nudes were soft and of epic proportions. Works of this period include "Young Girls at the Piano" (1892). After 1912 arthritis forced him to paint with a brush strapped to his arm.

Representative, member of US House of Representatives. Chosen for a two-year term, a representative must be a US citizen for at least seven years, 25 or older, and, with some exceptions, must reside in the district represented. Responsible to his constituency, a representative must answer also to his party.

Representative Government, system where representatives are authorized to act on behalf of the citizenry.

Repression, defense mechanism in which an idea or an impulse is excluded or banished from consciousness. Though repression is a form of motivated forgetting, the process is automatic and unconscious. Freud viewed repression as the most fundamental defense mechanism.

Reproductive System, the organs of a plant or animal necessary to the reproductive processes. *See also* Urogenital System.

Reptile, vertebrates, including turtles, crocodilians, lizards, snakes, and tuatara, distributed worldwide. Majority are found in warm areas. The first true land vertebrates, they lay shelled, fluid-filled, yolky eggs on land. Some species carry eggs in the body and bear live young. Body temperatures are dependent on external environment. The skin is dry and covered with scales or embedded with bony plates. The first reptiles appeared during the Carboniferous Period and 23 orders flourished during the Mesozoic Era. There are now four living orders of about 6,000 species. *See also* Vertebrate.

Republic, state where sovereignty is vested in the people (either actually or theoretically) rather than in a king or prince. A republic may be a pure democracy, representative democracy, aristocracy, or dictatorship. Modern usage, however, limits republic to a sovereign state ruled by representatives of a broad electorate, thus a form of democratic representative government.

Republicanism, doctrine that the government should represent and serve the common interests of all members and not the special interests of an elite. Originating in the time of the Roman Empire, the concept declined during the Dark Ages but was then revived in the Italian city-states under men such as Marsilius of Padua(*c.* 1270–1342), who espoused popular sovereignty. The provinces in the Netherlands set up a republic after gaining their independence from Spain, as did Switzerland after gaining independence from Austria. France formed a republic in 1792. The United States established an effective republic and this became a popular form of government. Many countries with differing political systems call themselves republics; the USSR is a totalitarian republic, while Great Britain has a democratic republic.

Republican Party, US political party, also known as the G.O.P., or Grand Old Party. It was organized in 1854 as an amalgamation of Whigs and Free Soilers with businessmen, workers, and professional people who formerly had called themselves Independent Democrats, Know-Nothings, Barnburners, and Abolitionists. John C. Fremont was the party's first presidential candidate in 1856. Its first successful candidate was Abraham Lincoln, elected in 1860. The party was particularly strong in the period from the Civil War to 1932. After 1932, Dwight Eisenhower (1952, 1956) and Richard Nixon (1968, 1972) each won election victories but both had to work with largely Democratic Congresses. When Ronald Reagan was elected president in 1981, the Republican representation in Congress increased substantially.

Republican River, river in Nebraska and Kansas; rises at the confluence of the North Fork Republican and Arikanee rivers, SW Nebraska; flows NE and E through S Nebraska, SE into Kansas to join Smoky Hill River at Junction City and form the Kansas River; subjects of flood control projects; used for irrigation. Length: 422mi (679km).

Reserpine, derivative of rauwolfia used to treat hypertension by acting as a sedative or reducing cardiac output. Its side effects include serious depression. Also known under the trademark Serpasil.

Reservoir, a storage place for water to be used by man. Water may be impounded during periods of higher flows to prevent floods, then released during times of lower flows. Beginning early in man's history in southern Asia and northern Africa, the use of reservoirs spread to Europe and then worldwide. They are usually formed by dams, but sometimes pipelines are used to carry water from rivers to depressions. Sedimentation causes most reservoirs to become useless after several decades; few last more than 100 years.

Jean Renoir (right)

Paul Revere

Joshua Reynolds

Reservoirs serve a number of functions: water supply, irrigation, power generation, flood control, and recreation. The world's largest reservoirs include Lake Victoria in Uganda, artificially raised by the Owen Falls Dam; Aswan on the Nile in Egypt; Bratsk on the Angara in the Soviet Union; the Kariba on the Zambezi in Zambia-Rhodesia; and the Akosombo-Main on the Volta in Ghana.

Resin, or rosin, viscous substance secreted by various plants or trees. It is impermeable to water and when present in large amounts (pine), it makes the wood resistant to rot and weather. Oleoresin secreted by conifers is distilled to produce turpentine, and rosin, a yellow-to-black material, remains after oil of turpentine has been distilled.

Resistor, electrical or electronic circuit component that has a specified resistance. For electronic circuits resistors usually consist of finely ground carbon particles mixed with a ceramic, enclosed in an insulated tube. The value of the resistance is denoted by a set of colored rings on the outside of the tube. Resistances for high currents consist of a coil of insulated wire.

Resonance, Wave, phenomenon in which a mechanical or acoustic system, set into forced vibrations by the application of an external vibration, responds with maximum amplitude. It occurs when the frequency of the applied force becomes equal to the natural vibrational frequency of the system. The large vibrations can cause damage to the system.

Resonances, Particle, extremely short-lived elementary particles that are produced in high-energy nuclear reactions occurring in particle accelerators and decay in a time (10^{-23} second) characteristic of hadrons. Over 150 have been detected, all since the 1960s. A resonance can be considered as a marked increase in the probability of interaction between two energetic colliding particles, occurring when the combined energy of the particles attains a particular energy, the resonance energy.

Resource Allocation. *See* Allocation.

Respiration, transfer of gases, usually oxygen and carbon dioxide, between living things and their environment. In simple, single-celled organisms this exchange occurs directly through the cell wall. In higher animal forms, lungs or gills have evolved to transport the gases in and out of the body. Plants use openings (stomata) in their leaves.

Respiration, Cellular, processes used by a cell to release energy for metabolism. This involves the oxidation, or breakdown, of fuel compounds within the cell and the release of simpler compounds, such as carbon dioxide.

Respiratory System, that system of the body concerned with external respiration, the process whereby air travels from outside to the lungs. The respiratory tract begins with the nose and mouth, through which air enters the body. The air then passes through the pharynx; into the larynx, or voice box; and into the trachea. The trachea at its lower end branches into two bronchi, each of which leads to a lung, where the exchange of gases between air and blood takes place. Exhaled air leaves through the same pathway.

Rest Mass, mass of an elementary particle, etc, when it is at rest. By the theory of relativity, motion will increase a body's mass although this is only noticeable at velocities approaching that of light. Such velocities are reached in particle accelerators.

Retention, Memory. *See* Memory.

Reticuloendothelial System, body system made up of reticular tissue, a specialized type of connective tissue that lines and supports the spleen, lymph nodes, and some other organs. Reticular tissue also contains cells that have macrophage action, destroying worn-out red blood cells in the spleen or invading organisms in the lymph nodes.

Retina, inner layer of the wall of the eye, composed mainly of different kinds of neurons (nerve cells), some of which are the actual visual receptors of the eye. These receptor cells are stimulated by light. Some, known as cones, respond primarily to the spectrum of visible colors; others, known as rods, respond mainly to shades of gray and to movement. The rods and cones connect with sensory neurons that in turn connect with the optic nerve that carries the visual stimuli to the brain.

Retinal Detachment, separation of the layers of the retina, after which the outermost layer, the pigment epithelium, remains attached to the choroid. Occurring in older people, it results in blurred vision. The retina is restored to its position by draining fluid and applying heat or cold to the eye's wall.

Retrievers, sporting dog breeds originally used only as water dogs to kill or cripple downed game and return it to the hunter. Today, they are also used to locate game. They have water-repelling coats, good swimming and scenting abilities, and tender mouths. Retrievers were developed in early 19th-century England. Breeds include curly-coated and wavy or flat-coated retrievers, Labrador and golden retrievers, Irish water spaniel, American water spaniel, and poodle.

Reuben, in Genesis, oldest son of Jacob and Leah. He saved his brother Joseph's life, offered his sons to Jacob as pledges for the safe return of his brother Benjamin, and had intercourse with his father's concubine.

Réunion, island constituting an overseas territory of France, in the Indian Ocean 425mi (684km) E of Malagasy Republic; member of the Mascarene group; Saint-Denis is the capital. First visited by Portuguese 16th century, it was claimed (1638) for France, which later colonized it; occupied by British 1810–15; made an overseas territory 1946. Exports: rum, sugar. Industries: agriculture, sugar mills, rum and alcohol distilling, canning. Area: 970sq mi (2,512sq km). Pop. 476,700.

Revelation, last book of the New Testament, written by the apostle John. Often called the Apocalypse, this book shows great imagery in its treatment of God's relation to all and concentrates on depicting the end of all creation.

Revere, Paul (1735–1818), American patriot, skilled craftsman, silversmith, engraver, and printer, b. Boston. He is best known for his ride (April 18, 1775) warning Massachusetts colonists that British troops were marching toward Lexington and Concord to seize militia supplies. He was an express rider for the Boston Committee of Safety, a leader of the Boston Tea Party (1773), and a lieutenant colonel during the Revolutionary War. He was immortalized in a Longfellow poem.

Revolution, orbital motion of a planet or satellite around its primary. A single revolution is the planet's or satellite's "year" and its length is determined according to any of several different methods. *See also* Geologic Time.

Revolution, the overthrow of the established government by its citizens, a large-scale, successful revolt. A revolution is not always violent (for example, the English Revolution of 1688) nor is it simply the overthrow of one government by another, as in a coup d'état, since the mass of citizenry is not involved. The American, French, and Russian revolutions are classic examples of revolution, but the term is also extended to mean vast changes in ways of doing things and of thinking about them (for example, the Industrial Revolution, the Scientific Revolution).

Revolutionary War, American. *See* American Revolution.

Rex Cat, domestic cat, coat type recently developed. Each hair is waved and guard hairs are short, giving the coat a marcelled effect. These curly-coated cats are often called "poodle" cats. The type can be transferred to any breed, color, or type of cat. It is a mutation.

Reye's Syndrome, an acute disease that can occur in children after viral infections such as chicken pox, influenza, and gastrointestinal diseases. Asprin, thought to be a contributing factor in the occurrence of Reye's Syndrome, should not be given to children with such infections. Clinical symptoms are fever and vomiting followed by loss of consciousness, convulsions, and coma. Pathological characteristics are swelling of the brain and infiltration of the liver and kidney by fatty deposits. It is named after the Australian pathologist R.D.K. Reye.

Reykjavík, seaport and capital city of Iceland, on SW coast of the island; major port between Europe and North America; Episcopal see 1796; made seat of Danish administration 1801; became capital of Iceland 1918; served as British and US air base during WWII; site of University of Reykjavík (1911), House of the Althing, National Museum, National Library, a statue of Leif Ericson given by United States on the 1000th anniversary of the Althing (parliament); commercial and fishing center. Industries: food processing, textiles, metallurgy, fishing, printing, shipyards. Founded c. 870. Pop. 84,856.

Reymont, Ladislaus (c.1867–1925), Polish novelist. His concern with social themes is evident in his first novel, *The Promised Land* (1899), and the four-volume novel of peasant life, *Chlopi* (1902–09), a comprehensive panorama of rural life. In 1924 he was awarded the Nobel Prize for literature.

Reynolds, (Sir) Joshua (1723–92), English portrait painter and writer. The first president of the Royal Academy of Arts, he was an important artist in linking English painting with that of Europe. His fashionable portraits include the famous "Nelly O'Brien." His classic manner of the late 1760s evolved into a more relaxed, naturalistic style in the 1780s ("Mrs. Thomas Meyrick," c.1782).

Rhaetian Alps (Ratioche Alpen), range of mountains along Italian-Swiss border and Austrian-Swiss border, but primarily in Grisons canton, Switzerland; division of Central Alps. They extend from Splügen Pass (WSW) between Lepontine and Rhaetian alps to Otztal Alps (ENE) and Lechtal Alps (NE). Highest peak is Piz Bernina, 13,304ft (4,058m).

Rhaeto-Romanic, term used to refer to three Romance dialects spoken in SE Switzerland and NE Italy. One of them, Romansch, spoken in the Swiss canton of Graubünden by about 50,000 people, is one of the official languages of the country. The other two are

Friulian, with about 500,000 speakers in Friulia, and Ladin, with about 10,000 speakers in Alto Adige.

Rh Disease, anemic disease of fetuses and of newborn infants due to Rh-factor incompatibility between mother and developing embryo. It is marked by destruction of mature red blood cells, presence of many immature red cells, and jaundice. It develops after the first pregnancy; severity varies and increases with each successive pregnancy. Exchange transfusions in which compatible blood is substituted in the newborn now save most afflicted infants. There is also a vaccine that prevents formation of Rh antibodies in the Rh negative mother. *See also* Rh Factor.

Rhea, large, brownish, flightless, fast-running South American bird resembling a small ostrich. It feeds mostly on plant matter. Males engage in noisy courtship displays, after which several females lay a total of 12–30 eggs in a single concealed ground-scraped nest prepared by the male. Height: to 5ft (1.5m). Species *Rhea americana.*

Rhea, satellite of Saturn.

Rhee, Syngman (1875–1965), president of the Republic of Korea (South Korea) (1948–60). Imprisoned (1898–1904) for his work to free Korea from Japanese rule, he spent more than 30 years in exile (1912–45). Elected South Korea's first president (1948), he was a dictatorial leader purging all opposition and outlawing the Progressive party. Bloody rioting after his reelection in 1960 caused his resignation and retirement to Hawaii. *See also* Korean War.

Rhenium, metallic element (symbol Re) of the third transition series, discovered in 1925. It is found in molybdenite (MoS_2), from which it is obtained as a by-product. It is used in thermocouples and in certain alloys and is also a useful catalyst. Properties: at. no. 75; at. wt. 186.2; sp gr 21.02; melt. pt. 5,756°F (3,180°C); boil. pt. 10,160°F (est.) (5,627°C); most common isotope Re^{103}(100%). *See also* Transition Elements.

Rhesus, medium-sized, yellow-brown macaque monkey of India. Short tailed, it has a large head with bare face, big ears, and closely spaced, deep-set eyes. Omnivorous, day-active, and gregarious, they occupy a wide range of habitats—from densely forested to treeless and from tropical lowlands to temperate uplands. Used in scientific work, the rhesus gave the first two letters of its name to the Rh blood factor. Height: 2ft (61cm). Species *Macaca rhesus. See also* Monkey.

Rhetoric, the art of presenting facts and ideas in clear, convincing, and attractive language. It is designed to instruct, to move, or to delight and requires an understanding of the effect of words and their arrangements as well as an imaginative approach. At one time the Sophists used rhetoric "to make great matters small and small things great," and it became associated with oratorical emptiness, but the basic rhetorical principles are still valid.

Rheumatic Fever, inflammatory disease caused by streptococcal infection and characterized by fever and swelling and pain in the joints. It is associated with inflammation of the heart and often results in rheumatic heart disease. Most frequent in children of ages 5–15, it also affects adults. Treatment is by antibiotics and cortisone. Prevention entails immediate treatment of streptococcal infections.

Rheumatism, general term for disorders characterized by stiffness and pain in the joints or muscles, such as bursitis and rheumatoid arthritis.

Rh Factor, any of a group of antigens (substances that stimulate antibody production) found on the surface of red blood cells, so called because first discovered in the rhesus monkey. Rh-negative blood lacks Rh factor, and Rh-positive blood contains it; it is present in about 85% of the population. Rh incompatibility (Rh-negative mother and Rh-positive fetus) is a major cause of a serious condition in infants, hemolytic disease of the newborn (anemia). It occurs in the Rh-positive fetus of an Rh-negative mother who has previously borne an Rh-positive child and has thus developed antibodies (has become sensitized) against Rh factor at the time of delivery.

Rhine (Rhein, Rhin, or Rijn), river in W Europe, rises in SE Switzerland in the Swiss Alps and forms a natural boundary between Switzerland, Austria, and Liechtenstein on the W; flows NW, and forms the boundary between Switzerland and Germany. Along its route it connects with numerous other rivers; after joining with the Sieg, Wupper, Ruhr, and Lippe rivers, it flows to the Netherlands and the North Sea. The Rhine has played a prominent part in German history and trade. Length: 820mi (1,320km).

Rhineland, region in W West Germany, along W bank of Rhine River; includes Rhineland Palatinate, Rhenish Hesse, SW Hesse, and W Baden. The Treaty of Versailles (1919) provided for Allied occupation and demilitarization of the area; the last occupational troops were removed in 1930, five years early, but by 1936 Hitler had formed the Siegfried Line, a German defense system, which caused League of Nations' censorship of Germany. This defense was infiltrated by Allies during WWII. Area: 9,000sq mi (23,310sq km).

Rhinoceros, massive, horned and hoofed, herbivorous mammal native to Africa and Asia. Depending on the species, they have either one or two horns on the snout. They have thick skins and poor eyesight. Mostly solitary grazers or browsers, they rest during the heat of the day and like to wallow in muddy pools. When alarmed they may charge. Now rare except in protected areas, rhinos were hunted heavily for their horns. Weight: 1–3.5ton. Family Rhinocerotidae.

Rhinoceros Beetle, mostly tropical and subtropical plant-eating scarab beetle named for rhinoceroslike horns on males of some species. Length: to 7.5in (19cm). Subfamily Dyanstinae.

Rhizopoda, class of protozoa found in fresh and salt water, damp soil, and animal digestive tracts. They move and capture food by pseudopodia—extensions of protoplasm. They include amoebas, foraminifera, radiolaria, and heliozoa.

Rhode Island, state in the NE United States, on the Atlantic Ocean in the New England region. It is the smallest and second most densely populated of the states.

Land and Economy. The land is level or gently rolling. Narragansett Bay, which contains many islands, cuts deeply into the E section. There are no rivers of importance, but nearly 300 lakes and ponds. Manufacturing, centered in the larger cities, is the economy's mainstay. Fish and shellfish are harvested in coastal waters. Tourism is a valuable source of income.

People. About 87% of the population lives in urban areas, most in the Providence metropolitan area.The first settlers were mostly English, but immigrants from many European countries arrived in the 19th century to work in the factories. There is a significant Portuguese community.

Education. There are 13 institutions of higher education. The University of Rhode Island is state-supported.

History. The first white settlers came in 1636, led by Roger Williams, who had been banished from Massachusetts for his liberal religious and political views. The town he founded at Providence joined later settlements in 1644 to form the colony of Providence Plantations, but in 1663 the charter was revoked by Charles II of England and the area, including some islands that had been governed separately, became the Colony of Rhode Island and Providence Plantations. This remains the official name of the state. Wars with the Indians shook the colony in the late 17th century. Rhode Island was one of the first colonies to show a spirit of revolt against the British Crown. A British revenue cutter was burned by colonists in 1772, and on May 4, 1776, two months before the national Declaration of Independence, the General Assembly declared Rhode Island free of Great Britain. A French fleet aiding the Americans was based at Newport during the Revolution. In the 19th century, the state became a center of the textile industry, but by 1940 most of these enterprises had moved to southern states. Providence has continued to be troubled by a decline in industry and a deteriorating urban core.

PROFILE

Admitted to the Union: May 29, 1790; 13th of the 13 original states to ratify the US Constitution
US Congressmen: Senate, 2; House of Representatives, 2
Population: 947,154 (1980); rank, 40th
Capital: Providence, 156,804 (1980)
Chief cities: Providence; Warwick, 87,123; Pawtucket, 71,204
State legislature: Senate, 50; House of Representatives, 100
Area: 1,214sq mi (3,144sq km); rank, 50th
Elevation: Highest, 812ft (247m), Jerimoth Hill; lowest, sea level
Industries (major products): jewelry, silverware, metal products, machinery, rubber, plastics, apparel
Agriculture (major products): poultry, dairy products
Minerals (major): stone, sand, gravel
State nickname: Little Rhody, Ocean State
State motto: Hope
State bird: Rhode Island red (chicken)
State flower: violet
State tree: red maple

Rhode Island (formerly Aquidneck Island), island in S Rhode Island, largest island of Narragansett Bay; Newport, Portsmouth, and Middletown located on it. First settled at Portsmouth 1638 as Aquidneck; name changed 1644. Length: 15mi (24km); width: 5mi (8km).

Rhode Island Red, chicken breed raised for its brown-shelled eggs. They have yellow skin and a single comb. Weight: 8.5lb (3.9kg) cock; 6.5lb (3kg) hen.

Rhodes, Cecil John (1853–1902), English capitalist, imperialist, and statesman of Africa. He went to Africa for his health in 1870, where he started a diamond mine. He greatly increased his mining operations and became a firm believer in British colonial expansion. He formed the British South Africa Company in 1889 and with it controlled the large areas of SE Africa later called Rhodesia. Legislator and prime minister (1890–96) of the Cape Colony, he helped exclude black Africans from the democratic process, but his attempt to gain control of Boer Transvaal through the Jameson Raid of 1895 destroyed his political ambitions. He subsequently concentrated on the development of railroads and Rhodesia. He willed his vast fortune to various public works, including noted scholarships for education.

Rhodes (Rodhos), island in SE Aegean Sea, Greece, in the Dodecanese islands; mountainous interior, fertile coastal areas, fine climate. Colonized by Dorians *c.* 1000 BC; conquered at different times by Persia, Sparta, Athens, Caria, Alexander the Great; part of Byzantine Empire (1204); taken by Turks 1522; ceded to Italy 1923; annexed to Greece 1947. Chief city and capital of Dodecanese dept. is Rhodes. Industries: shipbuilding, sponge diving, fishing, tourism. Area: 540sq mi (1,399sq km). Pop. 68,873.

Rhodesia, located in S Africa, was officially the British Colony of Southern Rhodesia until 1980, when the territory became the independent country of Zimbabwe. In 1890 white settlers from the Republic of South Africa arrived there, and in 1923 it became a self-governing British colony. When the British demanded participation of the black majority in the government, Rhodesia made (1965) a unilateral declaration of independence unrecognized by other countries. Following a period of fighting between Rhodesian forces and black nationalist guerrillas, the British helped negotiate the creation of independent Zimbabwe, with a black majority government. *See also* Zimbabwe.

Rhodesian Ridgeback, South African hunting dog (hound group) bred by Boers and introduced to Rhodesia in 1877; also called African lion hound. It has a long, flat, broad head with a long, deep muzzle; high-set, medium-sized ears close to the head; a powerful body with slightly arched loin; long, heavy legs; and a long, tapered tail. The short, dense, light- to red-wheaten coat has a characteristic ridge of hair on the back. Average size: 25–27in (63.5–68.5cm) high at shoulder; 65–75lb (29.5–34kg). *See also* Hounds.

Rhodium, metallic element (symbol Rh) of the second transition series, discovered (1803) by W. H. Wollaston. It occurs associated with platinum; chief source is as a by-product of nickel smelting. It is used in hard platinum alloys. Properties: at. no. 45; at. wt. 102.9055; sp gr 12.41; melt. pt. 3,571°F (1,966°C); boil. pt. 6,709 °F (3,709°C); most common isotope Rh^{103} (100%). *See also* Transition Elements.

Rhododendron, a large genus of shrubs and small trees that prefer the acid soil of cool temperate regions in North America, Europe, and Asia. Primarily evergreen, they have leathery leaves and bell-shaped white, pink, or purple flowers. Many species are used in landscaping. Family Ericaceae. *See also* Azalea; Heath.

Rhodopsin, or visual purple, visual pigment present in the rod cells of the retina of the eye. It absorbs light, producing a nerve impulse that is perceived as vision.

Rhône River, river that rises in Rhône Glacier in Bernese Oberland of Switzerland, flows W through narrow valley to Lake Geneva; from SW end of lake it crosses French border through opening in Jura Mts; continues S through Lyons, Avignon, and Tarascon to Arles, where it branches into Grand Rhône and Petit Rhône. They join the Mediterranean at Marseilles. It is linked with other rivers by extensive canal system; navigable for about 300mi (483km) of its 505mi (813km).

Rhubarb, or pieplant, perennial herbaceous plants native to Asia and cultivated worldwide in cool climates for its large, edible leaf stalks. It has large poisonous leaves and small white or red flowers. The stalks are used in pies, compotes, and preserves; the roots in medicine. *Rheum rhaponticum* is the common cul-

Rhine River

Providence, Rhode Island

Rhode Island red

tivated plant found in gardens. Height: to 8ft (2.5m). Family Polygonaceae.

Rhyme, identity or similarity of final sounds in two or more words, such as *keep/deep; baking/shaking*. Rhyme is used in poetry to reinforce meter and to organize related lines into a stanza. End rhymes, the most common, establish verse lines. Internal or Leonine rhymes emphasize rhythmic structures. Rhymes are also classified as male (one-syllable); female (two-syllable); triple (three-syllable); quadruple (four-syllable).

Rhythm, in music, one of the prime elements, referring to how long musical notes last (duration), how fast one note follows another (tempo), and the pattern of sounds formed by changes in duration and tempo. Rhythm in Western cultures is normally metrical, that is notes follow one another in a regular pattern at some specified rate. In Oriental and primitive music rhythms may be more free; there is more improvisation and rhythm is not related to some fundamental pattern.

Rhythm, in poetry, tempo or flow of speech sounds and silences that is essential to poetry. A poem may have rhymed or unrhymed lines; it may be composed according to strict metrical form or in free verse, but it must offer sounds and silences that fill equal or balancing time periods, recurring with pleasing regularity. In true rhythm, rhythm is organic; that is, the tempo of the lines follows the rhythm of the feeling intended to be conveyed. *See also* Meter.

Rhythm Method, a technique for preventing pregnancy by abstaining from sexual intercourse at the time during the monthly menstrual cycle that ovulation is presumed to take place.

Rib, curved bones arranged in pairs that form part of the front and side support of the chest. In man there are 12 pairs. The first seven pairs, known as true ribs, are joined by costal cartilage to the sternum; the next three, called false ribs, to the costal cartilage of the seventh pair; the last two, called floating ribs, are not attached to the sternum. The head of each rib joins with a thoracic vertebra in the back. The shafts (main curved part of the bone) of adjacent ribs are joined by intercostal muscles that act to change chest capacity during breathing.

Ribbon Fish, also Seyth or deal fish, marine fish found in cold deep waters. It is identified by its long, thin body and plumelike dorsal fin extending along the entire length of the body. Length: 8ft (243.8cm). Species include *Trachipterus arcticus* and the Pacific northwest king of the salmon fish *Trachipterus attivelus*. Family Trachipteridae.

Ribbon Snake. *See* Garter Snake.

Ribbonworm. *See* Nemertea.

Riboflavin, vitamin of the B complex, lack of which impairs growth and causes skin disorders. *See* Vitamin.

Ribonucleic Acid (RNA), nucleic acid that controls the synthesis of proteins in the cell and in some viruses is the genetic material. The molecule consists of a single strand of nucleotides, each containing the sugar ribose, phosphoric acid, and one of four bases: adenine, guanine, cytosine, or thymine. Messenger RNA carries the information for protein synthesis from DNA in the nucleus to the ribosomes in the cytoplasm. Each amino acid to be formed is specified by a sequence of three bases in messenger RNA. Transfer RNA brings the amino acids to their correct position on the messenger RNA.

Ribosome, a ribonucleoprotein particle in cells, the site of protein synthesis in the cells.

Ricardo, David (1772–1823), English economist. His book *Principles of Economics and Taxation* (1817) made an important contribution to the field of international trade. According to Ricardo, two principles, absolute and comparative advantage, mean that the best policy a nation can pursue is free international trade. According to Ricardo's theory, a nation should erect no trade barriers (eg, tariffs or quotas). Basically, Ricardo posits that people should spend their working time doing the things they do best. In fact, Ricardo would say that if a nation is not "best" at anything, it should devote its energies to the tasks at which it is "least bad." If this is done, total world production will be maximized.

Rice, annual cereal grass cultivated since 3000 BC on tropical and temperate submerged lowlands throughout the world. It has long, flattened leaves and flowers that produce the starchy, seedlike grains, usually milled to remove the husk and bran. When only the husk is removed, it is called brown rice and is more nourishing. Rice is used in brewing, distilling, and for flour; bran as animal food; hulls as fuel and fertilizer; and straw as feed, mats, and brooms. Height: to 4ft (1.2m). Family Gramineae; species *Oryza sativa. See also* Grass.

Richard I (1157–99), king of England, son of Henry II and Eleanor of Aquitaine, known as Richard Coeur de Lion, Richard the Lion-hearted. Richard fought against his father (1173–74; 1188–89) and succeeded Henry in 1189. Although popular, Richard spent little time in England, the country being governed by regents, including his brother, John. Richard joined the Third Crusade (1189) and took Cyprus and Acre (1191) but failed to gain Jerusalem. On his return, he was captured (1192) and held for ransom in Austria. The ransom raised, he returned to England (1194), was again crowned, but spent the rest of his life in France.

Richard II (1367–1400), king of England (1377–99), son of Edward the Black Prince. He married Anne of Bohemia (1382) and Isabella of France (1396). He succeeded his grandfather Edward III. His uncle, John of Gaunt, controlled the government, but Richard met and put down the Peasants Revolt (1381), and Gaunt soon retired to Europe. In 1386 the duke of Gloucester led other lords to confront the king and called for the dismissal of his closest counselors. The king opposed them but his army was defeated at Radcot Bridge (1387) and in 1388 Gloucester, and four other lords, forced the dismissal or execution of Richard's advisers and assumed control of the government. Richard regained authority (1389) and banished or executed the opposition lords. On John of Gaunt's death (1399), Richard confiscated his Lancastrian estates and Gaunt's heir, Henry, duke of Hereford, raised an army against him. Richard was imprisoned and Hereford was crowned as Henry IV in 1399. Richard either starved himself to death or was murdered in 1400.

Richard III (1452–85), king of England (1483–85), brother of Edward IV. He was made duke of Gloucester (1461) at Edward's coronation. Suspected of complicity in the murders of Henry VI and his own brother; he assumed protectorship of the young Edward V on Edward IV's death (1483). He put Edward and his brother, the duke of York, in the Tower of London and crowned himself king. His old supporter, the duke of Buckingham, led a revolt in favor of Henry Tudor, but

was executed. Henry landed in Wales (1485) and killed Richard, the last Yorkist king, at Bosworth. His death ended the Wars of the Roses.

Richard, Earl of Cornwall (1209–72), brother of Henry III of England. He recovered Gascony (1225–26) and returned to force Henry to grant him lands and the title earl of Cornwall (1231) and sided with the barons against the crown. He then married Isabella, daughter of the earl of Pembroke (1231) and sided with the barons against the crown. After leading a crusade (1240–41), he married the queen's sister (1243) and supported Henry in the Barons' War (1263–67). Captured at Lewes (1264), he was freed after the battle of Evesham (1265). He had himself crowned Holy Roman emperor (1257) but he was only a titular ruler.

Richard II (c.1595), 5-act historical play by William Shakespeare. His historical source was Raphael Holinshed's *Chronicles* (1587). The structure of the play is like Marlowe's *Edward II* (c.1593). Richard II, weak and self-indulgent, yields his throne to his powerful cousin Henry Bolingbroke, who becomes Henry IV. Richard is imprisoned, then murdered.

Richard III (c.1594), 5-act history play by William Shakespeare. For his hunchbacked royal criminal, Shakespeare draws on many sources—morality plays, the tragedies of Seneca and Niccolò Machiavelli's *The Prince,* and Thomas More's *History of Richard III.* Misshapen Richard, duke of Gloucester, murders his brother, the duke of Clarence. When his other brother, King Edward IV, dies, Richard has Edward's two young sons imprisoned and killed and takes the crown for himself. He is defeated in battle at Bosworth field and killed by the future King Henry VII.

Richardson, Samuel (1689–1761), English novelist and printer. His novels include *Pamela* (4 vols., 1740–41), *Clarissa Harlowe* (1747–48), and *Sir Charles Grandison* (1753–54). He contributed to the development of the psychological novel. *See also* Pamela.

Richardson, city in NE Texas; N suburb of Dallas; mainly residential area with few light industries. Founded 1873; inc. 1925. Pop. (1980) 72,496.

Richelieu, Armand Jean du Plessis, Cardinal Duc de (1585–1642), French statesman. Bishop of Luçon at 21 (1606), he was sent to the States-General (the legislative assembly) in 1614. He became a cardinal (1622) and was advisor to the exiled Marie de' Medici, Louis XIII's mother. He helped make peace between the two, becoming prime minister 1624–42. He established an ever-increasing royal power that lasted until the French Revolution. In foreign affairs, Richelieu turned the Swedes and Protestant Germans against the Hapsburgs, and in a series of French victories advanced the French cause in the Thirty Years' War. Author and wealthy literary patron, he established the Académie Française (1635). He is buried in the chapel of the Sorbonne, which he built.

Richmond, city in W California, 9mi (14km) NNW of Oakland. Industries: oil refineries, chemicals, electronic equipment, port. Founded 1823 as part of a Spanish ranch; inc. 1905. Pop. (1980) 74,676.

Richmond, capital city and port of entry in E central Virginia, on James River; seat of Henrico co. Built on site of Fort Charles (1645), city developed as trading center; it was made capital of Commonwealth of Virginia 1779, of state 1785; scene of 2nd and 3rd Virginia Conventions (1775). It was made capital of Confederacy July 1861, and fell to Union forces in 1865. It is site of Hollywood Cemetery (1847) containing tombs of James Monroe, John Tyler, Jefferson Davis; St John's

Church (1741), state capitol (1785), Richmond National Battlefield Park, Robert E. Lee's house (1844), Commonwealth University (1804), University of Richmond (1832), Virginia Union University (1865). Industries: metal items, tobacco and tobacco processing, textiles, clothing, chemicals, foodstuffs, paper and paper products, machinery, printing, publishing. Settled 1637; inc. 1782 as town, 1842 as city. Pop. (1980) 219,214.

Richter, C(harles) F(rancis) (1900–85), US geophysicist and seismologist, b. Butler Co, Ohio. With Beno Gutenberg he developed a scale to measure earthquake intensity at any distance from the recording station. That scale now bears his name.

Richthofen, Manfred, Baron von (1892–1918), German World War I flying ace. As an aviator in World War I, he shot down 80 enemy aircraft. His combat group was called "Richthofen's Circus," and he was known as the "Red Baron." He was killed in action.

Rickets, nutritional disorder characterized by deformities of the skeleton. It is caused by lack of calcium and phosphorus in the blood due to insufficient vitamin D in the diet or inadequate exposure to sunlight.

Rickettsial Disease, a number of illnesses of vertebrate animals, caused by various rickettsiae, a group of microorganisms, usually carried by fleas, lice, and ticks. Typhus, Rocky Mountain spotted fever, and Q Fever can be transmitted to man. Dogs are afflicted with canine rickettsiosis, in which they have fever and nervous system disorders. It is often fatal.

Ride, Sally (Kristen) (1951–), US astronaut, b. Encino, Calif. Educated at Swarthmore College and Stanford University (1973), she earned a PhD in astrophysics (1978) from Stanford and joined NASA, where she qualified as a jet pilot while undergoing astronaut training. She was capsule communicator for 2 space shuttle flights (1981, 1982) before becoming the first American woman to fly in space (1983) when she was mission specialist aboard the space shuttle *Challenger.*

Riel, Louis (1844–85), Canadian political leader. In 1869 he led the Métis (people of mixed French and Indian descent) against the transfer of the western territories from the Hudson Bay Company to Canada, and established and headed a provisional government in the West. In 1870 Manitoba became a province, and in 1873 Riel was elected to the House of Commons. He never took his seat, and in 1875 he was exiled for five years. He settled in Montana and became a US citizen in 1883. He returned to Canada in 1884 and in 1885 led a Métis uprising. The rebellion was suppressed, and Riel was tried and hanged for treason.

Rif (Er Rif), range of Atlas Mts, in NE Morocco, NW Africa; extends from Ceuta to Melilla along Mediterranean coast. It was inhabited by independent Berber tribes until 1925–26, when they were conquered by French and Spanish forces. Highest point is Tidighin, 8,056ft (2,457m).

Rift Valley (Great Rift Valley), geological depression extending from Jordan in SW Asia to Mozambique in SE Africa. Volcanic eruptions caused chain of geological faults, resulting in the Dead Sea, Gulf of Aqaba, Red Sea, lakes in S Ethiopia, and lakes Albert, Edward, Kivu, Tanganyika, and Nyasa.

Riga, capital city of the Latvian republic, NW USSR, at the S extremity of the Gulf of Riga, on the Western Dvina River 9mi (14km) above its mouth. City joined the Hanseatic League in 1282; it was burned 1558 during the Livonian War; it came under Polish domination in 1581; in 1621, Gustavus Adolphus of Sweden took Riga and instituted self-government; it was ceded to Peter the Great of Russia 1710; the port was closed 1915 and evacuated by the Russians; in 1917 it came under Germans. Latvia's independence was declared at Riga in November 1918; from 1920–40, Riga was capital of Vidzeme in independent Latvia; in WWII, it was taken by the Germans (1941) and retaken by the USSR (1944); site of the Latvian State University (1919), agricultural and art academies, teachers' college, conservatory, 16th-century castle, Renaissance parliament building, national opera house. Industries: electric machinery, telephone and radio equipment, superphosphates, glass, wood products, paper, textiles, rubber and leather goods. Exports: timber, paper, linseed oil, dairy products. Founded 1201 by Bishop of Livonia. Pop. 827,000.

Rigel, or Beta Orionis, the brightest star in the constellation Orion; a bluish-white supergiant. Characteristics: apparent mag. +0.08; absolute mag. −7.0; spectral type B8; distance 600 light-years.

Rights of Man and of the Citizen, Declaration of the, proclamation of human liberties of the French Revolution (1789). It was adopted by the newly formed National Assembly to express the new spirit of liberty and equality in France. It was inspired by the US Declaration of Independence. Longer than its US counterpart, it further established the duty of each man to further personally his own political views. Drafted by Abbé Sieyès, it guaranteed rights of "liberty, property, security, and resistance to oppression," as well as freedom of speech and press.

Right Whale, small-to-large whalebone whale with a huge head and stocky body. Slow and unsinkable when killed, right whales were the mainstay of the whaling industry and, thus, are near extinction. Length: 45–60ft (14–18m). Family Balaenidae. *See also* Whale.

Rig Veda, one of the four sacred books of the Hindu religion, consisting of a collection of 1,017 prayers and hymns contained in 10 chapters. The hymns are generally directed to the gods of the forces of nature such as Indra, Agni, and Varuna.

Rijeka (Fiume), city in NW Yugoslavia, on Adriatic Sea and Gulf of Ouarnero; largest seaport in Yugoslavia; site of Roman triumphal arch, naval base. Settled by Romans, it was held at various times by Franks, Croatian dukes, Austria-Hungary. Long disputed between Italy and Yugoslavia, it was annexed to Italy 1924, then to Yugoslavia 1947. Industries: shipbuilding, oil refining, engineering. Exports: ores, timber, cotton, tobacco, grain. Pop. 132,933.

Riley, James Whitcomb (1849–1916), US poet and journalist, b. Greenfield, Ind. After working at odd jobs, he became a newspaperman. During 1877–85, he was affiliated with the Indianapolis *Journal.* Many of his poems, which were sentimental and often in Indiana (Hoosier) dialect, first appeared there under the name "Benj. F. Johnson, of Boone." His verse was collected in *The Old Swimmin' Hole* and *'Leven More Poems* (1883) and other books. One of his best-known poems is "Little Orphant Annie" (1905).

Rilke, Rainer Maria (1875–1926), Austrian lyrical poet and translator. His first cycle of poems, *The Book of the Hours* (1905), was inspired by his visits to Russia. *New Poems* (1907–08) showed the influence of the French sculptor Auguste Rodin, whose secretary Rilke had been (1905–06). *Sonnets to Orpheus* (1923) demonstrated the poet's new affirmation of life. He also translated the works of several French authors.

Rimbaud, Arthur (1854–91), French poet. After an unhappy childhood, he lived with the poet Verlaine. They separated (1873) when Verlaine shot him. His prose-poem *A Season in Hell* (1873) appeared soon after, recording his disillusionment with life and art. He traveled in Europe and Africa, working as a gunrunner and merchant, and returned to France in 1891. Verlaine published a collection of Rimbaud's early poetry, *Les Illuminations,* in 1886.

Rimini, city in N Italy, 27mi (43km) ESE of Forlí, on the Adriatic. Founded by Umbrians, it was taken by Rome 286 BC; independent commune 12th century; passed to papal states 1509; site of Roman ruins including triumphal arch and bridge, the Malatesta temple (renovated 15th century). Industries: tourism, food products, wineries, textiles, pharmaceuticals, shipyards. Pop. 126,025.

Rimski-Korsakov, Nikolai (1844–1908), Russian composer and influential musical figure of the late 19th century. He was the leader of the "Russian Five," who were dedicated to promoting Russian nationalism in music. A master of orchestral color, he also taught and influenced Igor Stravinsky. He composed many operas including *The Snow Maiden* (1881) and *Le Coq d'Or* (1907). His most popular works are the orchestral pieces *Scheherazade* (1888), *Capriccio Espagnol* (1886), and the "Flight of the Bumblebee" from the opera *Tsar Saltan* (1900).

Ringed Snake. *See* Grass Snake.

Ring of the Nibelung, The (1848–74), cycle of four operas by Richard Wagner. Called a tetralogy by the composer—the first drama being a prelude to the other three—the entire cycle took more than 26 years to compose. The Ring was first performed as a whole in Bayreuth (1876), in Wagner's own theater. Based on ancient Scandinavian, Germanic, and Icelandic sagas, the four operas include *Das Rheingold* (first performance 1869), *Die Walküre* (1870), *Siegfried* (1876), and *Die Götterdammerung* (1876). Throughout, each principal character is identified by a *leitmotiv,* an individual theme.

Ringworm, an infection of the skin, hair, or nails caused by fungi and named for its growth pattern. It is a red eruption on the skin that spreads at the edges as it heals in the center, forming a ring of inflammation. If on the scalp, it is accompanied by burning, itching, and loss of hair.

Rio de Janeiro, city in SE Brazil, on Guanabara Bay; capital of Guanabara state. Former capital of the country, it was settled by the Portuguese, later colonized by French, who were driven out by Mem de Sá, governor of Portuguese colony of Brazil; by 18th century it had grown as the export center of all gold mined in the hinterlands. The 2nd-largest city in the country, it is the cultural hub of Brazil; contains a major port and scenic harbor; import-export and tourist center. Festive Mardi Gras is celebrated on Shrove Tuesday, the day before Lent begins. Founded 1504. Pop. 4,251,918.

Rio Grande, river in S United States and N Mexico; rises in the San Juan Mts of SW Colorado; flows generally S through New Mexico, forming the border between New Mexico, Texas, and Mexico, continues to run between the border cities of Texas and Mexico, and empties into the Gulf of Mexico just E of Brownsville, Tex. Used for irrigation, hydroelectricity; subject of flood control projects; made international boundary in 1848 by the Treaty of Guadalupe Hidalgo. Length: approx. 1,885mi (3,035km).

Rio Muni, mainland province in Equatorial Guinea, bordered N by Cameroon, E and S by Gabon, and W by Atlantic Ocean; has mostly mountainous interior with fertile coastal lowland. Industries: lumbering, subsistence farming. Area: 10,040sq mi (26,004sq km). Pop. 290,000.

Rio Negro, river in South America; rises in E Colombia; flows E to Venezuela, S along Colombia-Venezuela boundary, into Brazil and the Amazon River. Length: approx. 1,400mi (2,254km).

Risorgimento, 19th-century Italian national unification movement culminating in the 1861 establishment of the kingdom of Italy. After Napoleon's defeat (1815), the Austrians regained control of Italy and initially were opposed by the Carbonari and Giuseppe Mazzini's Young Italy group. With the failed liberal and republican revolutions of 1848, the Piedmontese house of Savoy led the unification, ousting Austria (1859) and uniting most of Italy by 1861. The Risorgimento was completed with annexation of Venetia (1866) and papal Rome (1870).

Risso's Dolphin. *See* Grampus.

Rites of Passage, rites carried out at times of life crises. Such rites accompany an individual's passage from one social status to another and can be divided into three types or stages: rites of separation, marginal rites, and rites of aggregation. Rites of passage (such as marriage, initiation, or funerals) are characterized by ceremonials. *See also* Birth Rites.

Rittenhouse, David (1732–96), American astronomer, b. near Germantown, Pa. He constructed the first apparatus in the colonies for displaying planetary motions. He also built an observatory and transit telescope in the colonies. In 1785 he invented the collimating telescope. He was president of the Council of Safety (1777), Pennsylvania's first treasurer (1777–89), and first director of US Mint (1792–95). He was elected to the Royal Society (1795).

River, natural stream of water of considerable volume and velocity, and larger than a brook or creek. By erosion of the underlying earth and/or rock, the water's flow becomes permanent or seasonal.

Rivera, Diego (1886–1957), Mexican painter. Influenced by Cubism in his early work, he painted many oils, watercolors, and portraits. He is primarily known as a muralist. Characteristic of his style are carefully drawn, simplified, flat geometric forms in expressive colors. His murals at the Ministry of Education's Court of Labor in Mexico City reach three stories high and deal with Mexico's activities in industry, agriculture, and the arts. Often, he used symbolism and allegory in his murals to show Mexico's triumph over repression and his hope for a Marxist future.

Rivers, Larry (1923–), US painter, b. New York City. His early works included naturalistic paintings of figures. After a period of abstract expressionism in the 1950s, he returned to a realistic portrayal of the human figure in a style that was a forerunner of pop art. He received a 1980 American Book Award for *Drawings and Digressions.*

Riverside, city in S California, 10mi (16km) SSW of San Bernardino; seat of Riverside co; noted for its or-

James Whitcomb Riley

Rainer Maria Rilke

Nikolai Rimski-Korsakov

ange industry since 1873; site of University of California at Riverside (1907). Founded 1870; inc. 1883. Pop. (1980) 170,876.

Riviera, region in SE France and NW Italy, on Mediterranean Sea, extending 230mi (370km) from La Spezia, Italy and Hyères, France. Scenery and mild climate make it leading resort area of W Europe. Crops: olives, grapes, citrus fruits. Leading cities include Nice, Cannes, Menton, Antibes, and Monte Carlo, Monaco.

Riyadh (Ar-Riyad), city in E central Saudi Arabia, approx. 240mi (386km) inland from Persian Gulf; capital of Saudi Arabia; center of desert trade and travel; focal point of Wahabi movement; site of Riyadh University (1957), royal palace, several mosques. Chief industry is oil production. Pop. 450,000.

Riza Shah Pahlevi (1877–1944), shah of Iran (1925–41). He led a coup d'état in 1921, served as prime minister (1923–25), and after Ahmed Shah was deposed in 1926, became shah. He reduced the power of the tribal chieftains, reorganized government administration, improved finances, and encouraged industrialization. In 1941 he abdicated in favor of his son Mohammed Riza Pahlevi. *See also* Mohammed Riza Pahlevi, Pahlevi Dynasty.

RNA. *See* Ribonucleic Acid.

Roanoke, formerly Big Lick; city in Virginia, 148mi (238km) SW of Richmond, on Roanoke River; area developed around Shenandoah Railroad (June 18, 1882); site of National Business College (1886), Virginia Southern College (1933), Virginia Western Community College (1966); industrial and railroad center. Industries: railroad cars, electrical equipment, rayon fabric, clothing, foundry products, tourism. Founded 1740; inc. 1884. Pop. (1980) 100,427.

Roanoke Island Colony, two settlement attempts made by Sir Walter Raleigh on an island off North Carolina. First settlers returned to England (1585–86), the second colony was found deserted (1591); those lost included Virginia Dare, first English child born in America. *See also* Raleigh, (Sir) Walter.

Roanoke River, river in S Virginia, formed by confluence of rivers in W Va., and flows SE across Blue Ridge Mts to Albemarle Sound in NE North Carolina. Flood control and hydroelectric projects are used on the river. Length: 410mi (660km).

Robber Fly, gray to black fly to 1 in (25mm) or more in length, found worldwide. It is predaceous on other insects, often attacking those as large or larger than itself. Family Asilidae. *See also* Diptera.

Robbia, Luca della (1400?–82), Italian Florentine sculptor. He worked in bronze and marble, but his fame resulted chiefly from his numerous, glazed, terra-cotta half-length Madonnas, represented against a blue background. He was commissioned to execute many religious sculptures, such as his "Singing Gallery" in the Cathedral of Florence.

Robert I (865?–923), king of the Franks. The brother of Eudes, he ruled the western Franks, at first accepting the succession of Carolingian Charles III the Simple when Eudes died (898). After fighting the Normans for several years in northern France, Robert gained considerable support and in 922 drove Charles from the throne. Charles gathered an army and killed Robert in battle the following year. Robert's grandson, Hugh Capet, founded the Capetian dynasty.

Robert II (?970–1031), king of France (996–1031). He succeeded his father, Hugh Capet, in 996. He repudiated his wife in 989 and became interested in a relative, Bertha, wife of Eudes I, Count of Blois. They were married after Eudes's death, and Robert was excommunicated (998). Separated (1001), he remarried, fathering four sons. He conquered Burgundy (1015) adding it to the French crown.

Robert I, or **Robert the Bruce** (1274–1329), king of Scotland (1306–29). He swore fealty to Edward I of England (1296) but joined the Scottish revolt against him in 1297. He murdered the Scottish nationalist leader, John Comyn (1306), and was crowned king of Scotland, but, defeated at Methven (1306) by the English, he fled to Ireland. Returning (1307), he defeated the English at Loudon Hill and Bannockburn (1314). After a short truce (1323–27), England recognized Scotland's independence in the Treaty of Northampton (1328).

Robert I Guiscard (c. 1015–85), also called Robert de Hauteville, Norman conqueror of southern Italy. He led invasions against Arabs and Byzantines in the Mediterranean islands and southern Italy and established his dominion in Calabria. By allying himself to Pope Nicholas II and extending Norman power into Sicily, he laid foundations for the future kingdom of Sicily and French claims there.

Robert II (1054?–1134), also Robert Curthose, duke of Normandy. He was the eldest son of William the Conqueror. He was deprived of the English throne by his brother, King William II; he became duke of Normandy (1087–1134). After a short war with William (1089–94), Robert went on a crusade (1096–99). In his absence William died, and his brother Henry became King Henry I of England. After initial peace, Henry invaded Normandy (1106) and took Robert prisoner for life.

Robespierre, Maximilien François Marie Isidore de (1758–94), one of the leaders of the French Revolution. He was elected to the newly formed National Assembly in 1789. There he helped form the new constitution, allied himself with the Jacobins, and gained the support of the Parisian people, who named him an incorruptible patriot. He became involved with the Paris commune, urged the execution of King Louis XVI, and was elected to the Committee of Public Safety in 1793. Here he supported the Reign of Terror, in which thousands were executed, and tried to establish a worship of Reason. Partly in revenge for his past executions, he was himself guillotined in the Thermidorean Reaction of July 1794.

Robin, thrush found throughout most of North America. It has a reddish breast, black and white striped throat, and blackish head; length: 10in (25cm). Species *Turdus migratorius*. The European robin (*Erithacus rubecula*) is a warbler and has a yellowish-red breast; length: 6in (15cm). The American robin builds a cup-shaped nest; the European robin nests in tree holes and other cavities. Family Turdidae.

Robin Hood, legendary English folk hero generally portrayed as a benevolent outlaw of Sherwood Forest whose traditional adversary was the Sheriff of Nottingham. Many attempts have been made to establish his authenticity, the most popular placing him in Richard I's reign (1189–99). Another attempt sets him in the 13th century as an ex-follower of Simon de Montfort. His exploits have been chronicled in books and films.

Robinson, Edwin Arlington (1869–1935), US poet. b. Head Tide, Me. When a child his family moved to Gar-

diner, Me., which became the Tilbury Town of his poetry. His first volume of poetry, *The Children of the Night,* was published in 1897. In 1904 Pres. Theodore Roosevelt appointed him to a clerkship in the N.Y. Custom House. Upon publication of *The Town down the River* (1910), Robinson left this job and gained financial security with *The Man against the Sky* (1916) and *The Three Taverns* (1920). In simple, realistic, but intellectual verse, Robinson analyzed people and the motivations that moved them to succeed or fail. He was awarded the Pulitzer Prize in 1921, 1924, and 1927.

Robinson, Jack Roosevelt (Jackie) (1919–72), US baseball player, b. Cairo, Ga. Signed by the Brooklyn Dodgers in 1947 after a year in the International League, he was the first black to play in the major leagues. He had a batting average of .311 during his career (1947–56). In 1962 he became the first black elected to the Baseball Hall of Fame.

Robinson Crusoe (1719), novel by Daniel Defoe. It purports to tell the true story of a man shipwrecked on a desert island. With industry and ingenuity this man salvages materials from the ship, builds homes, sows crops, makes clothes, and domesticates animals. He also rescues and befriends Friday, a savage, before they are themselves rescued.

Robot, an instrumented mechanism used in science or industry to take the place of a human being. It may resemble a human and perform in a human way the tasks set it. But frequently it does not and the line separating a robot from other automated machinery is not always distinct. Sophisticated, individualized machines are most likely to be classed "robots." The word was first used in *R.U.R.,* a play (1921) by Karel Capek.

Rob Roy (1671–1734), Scots freebooter, whose reputation is enhanced in Sir Walter Scott's novel *Rob Roy* (1818). A Macgregor, he assumed the name of Campbell and held territory between the Montrose and Argyll estates. He took advantage of their rivalry and the Jacobite Rebellion (1715) to further his cattle-stealing and brigandage. Sentenced to transportation (1727), he was finally pardoned.

Rochambeau, Jean Baptiste Donatien de Vimeur, Comte de (1725–1807), French military commander. He served in the French cavalry in his youth and was promoted to brigadier of infantry (1761) after the Minorca expedition. After several conflicts he led a French force in the American Revolution, aiding the Marquis de Lafayette and George Washington in the defeat of Lord Cornwallis at Yorktown. He was made governor of Picardy as a reward. He also fought during the French Revolution, but resigned in 1792.

Rochester, city in SE Minnesota, 70mi (113km) SSE of St Paul; seat of Olmsted co, site of Mayo Clinic, founded by Dr. W. W. Mayo and his sons Drs. William J. and Charles H. Mayo in 1889; and Rochester Junior College (1915). Industries: hospital supplies, data processing machines, dairy products. Settled 1854; inc. 1858. Pop. (1980) 57,855.

Rochester, city and port of entry in W New York, 70mi (113km) ENE of Buffalo on Lake Ontario and Genesee River; seat of Monroe co. First permanent settlement was made 1812; industrial growth was spurred by Erie Canal through Rochester; a center of abolitionist movement during Civil War; specialized industries developed between 1850–1900, including Eastman Kodak (est. 1888). Landmarks are St Luke's Episcopal Church (1824), Rochester Institute of Technology (1829), University of Rochester (1850). Industries:

cameras, photographic films and supplies, office equipment, food processing, clothing. Inc. 1817 as village, 1834 as city. Pop. (1980) 241,741.

Rock, solid material that comprises the Earth's crust. Although solid, it is not necessarily hard, as clay or volcanic ash are also considered to be rock. It can be composed of a single mineral or can be a compound of several. Rocks are classified by origin into three major groups: (1) Igneous rocks are those formed by the cooling and solidification of molten material from the earth's interior. Volcanic lava and granite are igneous rocks. (2) Sedimentary rocks are formed from older rock that has been transported from its original position by water, glacier, or the atmosphere, and consolidated again into rock. Limestone and sandstone are sedimentary rocks. (3) Metamorphic rocks originate from igneous or sedimentary rocks, but have been changed in texture or mineral content or both by extreme pressure and heat deep within the earth. Marble, derived from limestone, is a metamorphic rock.

Rockefeller, John Davison (1839–1937), US industrialist and philanthropist, b. Richford, N.Y. In 1863, following the drilling of the first US oil well, Rockefeller, with Samuel Andrews and Maurice B. Clark, started an oil refining business. Two years later his brother, William, established a second refinery, and the two firms were consolidated into a joint stock company (1870), Standard Oil of Ohio. With mergers, rebates, and other devices the Standard Oil trust was organized (1882). It soon controlled over 90% of the oil business. In 1892 the Ohio Supreme Court declared the trust in violation of the Sherman Antitrust Act and it was dissolved. It was replaced by a holding company, Standard Oil of New Jersey, and in 1911 the US Supreme Court declared this illegal. When he retired he devoted his attention to charitable corporations, to which his donations amounted to about $500,000,000. His philanthropic work includes the endowment of the University of Chicago (1892), the Rockefeller Institute for Medical Research (1901), and the Rockefeller Foundation (1913). His grandsons included Nelson Rockefeller.

Rockefeller, Nelson Aldrich (1908–79), US vice president (1974–77) and New York governor, b. Bar Harbor, Me. A member of the wealthy Rockefeller family, he held a number of appointive government posts before being elected governor in 1958 as a Republican. He was re-elected three times (1962, 1966, 1970) before resigning in 1973. In 1974, President Gerald Ford picked him to fill the vacant office of vice president. He was an unsuccessful contender for the Republican presidential nomination in 1960, 1964, and 1968. In 1975 he announced that he would not run for election as vice president in 1976.

Rocket, missile or craft powered by a rocket engine. First mentioned in accounts of 13th-century battles involving Chinese, Mongols, and Arabs. Major applications are military (projectiles and ballistic missiles) and scientific (spacecraft and satellite launchers). Developers of modern rockets include Konstantin Tsiolkovsky (USSR), Hermann Oberth (Germany), and Robert Goddard (United States).

Rocket Engine, reaction engine carrying its own supply of both fuel and oxidizer, as distinguished from the jet engine, which obtains oxidizer from the surrounding atmosphere. Chemical rocket engines are powered by solid or liquid propellants that are burned in a combustion chamber and expelled at supersonic velocities from the exhaust nozzle. Nuclear engines heat fuel by radiation from reactor cores. Ion engines use thermoelectric power to expel ions rather than gases.

Rockford, city in N Illinois, on Rock River near Wisconsin line; seat of Winnebago co; 2nd-largest city in state; site of Rockford College (1847), Rock Valley College (1964), and noteworthy clock museum. Industries: machine tools, air conditioning and heating equipment, textiles, hardware. Founded 1834 on Black Hawk War battlefield; inc. 1839. Pop. (1980) 139,712.

Rock Music, form of US popular music, which developed in the 1960s out of the "rock 'n' roll" of the 1950s. It features a steady "beat," intense vocals about love, accompaniment by guitars, and a small group of musicians rather than a whole band. It achieved great popularity, especially with young people, when the English singing group The Beatles began to be heard in 1963.

Rock River, river in S Wisconsin and N Illinois, rises in SE Wisconsin, flows S and SW across NW Illinois to Mississippi River near Rock Island. Statue of Black Hawk by Lorado Taft stands on bluff above river near Oregon, Ill. Length: 285mi (459km).

Rockweed, or **wrack**, coarse brown seaweeds (especially *Fucus* or *Ascophyllum*) growing on rocks, attached by rootlike holdfasts. *See also* Brown Algae.

Rockwell, Norman (1894–1978), US illustrator, b. New York, N.Y. An immensely popular painter of rural and small-town life in America, he was best known for the more than 300 homespun covers he created for *The Saturday Evening Post* (1916–63), among which were the "Four Freedoms" series used as posters by the Office of War Information during World War II. In 1977 he was presented the Presidential Medal of Freedom by Pres. Gerald Ford.

Rockwell Hardness Test, a method of measuring the hardness of a metal or alloy using an apparatus with a diamond-pointed cone. The cone is pressed into the metal to a standard depth. Resistance to penetration is automatically indicated by a calibrated dial.

Rocky Mountains, major mountain system in W North America, extends from Mexico to the Bering Strait, N of Arctic Circle. They form the Continental Divide, which separates rivers draining to the Atlantic and Arctic oceans from those draining to the Pacific Ocean; geologically formed as a series of pulses over millions of years. Highest point is Mt Elbert in Colorado, 14,431ft (4,401m). Length: approx. 3,000mi (4,830km).

Rocky Mountain Sheep. *See* Bighorn Sheep.

Rocky Mountain Spotted Fever, an infectious disease caused by a rickettsia and transmitted by a wood tick that lives on cattle, sheep, and rodents in addition to man. Symptoms are similar to typhus with rose-colored spots on the body.

Rococo, originally a demeaning expression for 18th-century decorative art but now used objectively by art historians. The style is colorful, fragile, pastoral, with trivial subject matter. It developed in four phases: late Louis XIV; Regency; early-middle Louis XV, the style Pompadour; and late Louis XV. Antoine Lepautre's chapel at Versailles and the paintings of Jean Watteau and François Boucher are examples.

Rodchenko, Aleksandr (1891–1956), Russian painter, sculptor, and designer. Influenced by K. S. Malevich, he turned from the futurist style of his early works to a completely abstract style, in which he used a ruler and compass to create geometric forms. In his later work, he used metals and wood in abstract three-dimensional compositions, such as mobiles, and he became a leading artist in the constructivist movement.

Rodent, any member of the vast mammalian order Rodentia, characterized by a pair of gnawing incisor teeth in both the upper and lower jaws. Numbering close to 2,000 species, rodents live all over the world. They may live in underground burrows (rabbits), on the ground (mice), in trees (squirrels), or in water (beavers). Most rodents are small and lightweight, but one species, the South American capybara, weighs up to 110lb (50kg).

The distinctive incisor teeth continue to grow as long as the animal lives. Because the soft inner layer is ground down faster than the hard outer layer, rodent incisors are chisel-shaped and sharpened by use. Most rodents are herbivorous, but some are omnivorous. Some, like chinchillas, are valuable for their fur. Some, like guinea pigs, are important scientific tools. Some rats and mice are pests that carry disease and destroy property. Because there are so many of them, rodents are a major factor in the ecology of the world.

Rodeo, a sport that features calf roping, steer wrestling, bronco riding, and Brahma bull riding. Other events may include bulldogging, bareback riding, quarterhorse cutting, team roping, barrel racing, and greased-pig chasing. Most popular is saddle-bronco riding. In this event a rider carries a rope rein in his hand and uses it to get the animal to buck. Minimum time aboard the horse to qualify for prize money is eight seconds. The rodeo developed in the cattle-raising industry in the W United States in the early 1880s. The Rodeo Cowboys Association controls events for men, and the women's aspect of the sport is governed by the Girls' Rodeo Association.

Rodin, Auguste (1840–1917), French sculptor and painter. In his early decorative style, he painted landscapes, made reliefs of mythological figures, and sculpted busts and small figurines. He visited Rome, where he was influenced by Michelangelo's work. His first major work, "The Age of Bronze" (1876) was so realistic that he was accused of having cast it from a living figure. Many of Rodin's most famous sculptures, such as "The Thinker" (1880) and "The Kiss" (1886), are taken from his huge "Gates of Hell" design, a maze of twisted, tortured figures. Characteristic of his Romantic style was his interest in movement and his use of modeling to express the intensity of the subject's personality.

Roe Deer, small agile Eurasian deer frequently found among dense human populations. It has short, erect antlers. The gestation period is almost one year, with the fertilized egg dormant for over four months. Height: to 31in (79cm) at shoulder. Family Cervidae; species *Capreolus capreolus. See also* Deer.

Roentgen or **Röntgen, Wilhelm Konrad** (1845–1923), German physicist. In 1895, while at Würzburg, he discovered X rays, which led to modern physics and medical diagnostic practices. He was awarded the first Nobel Prize for physics (in 1901), and X radiation is also known as Röntgen radiation. His work was also concerned with specific heats of gases, fluid capillary action, and elasticity.

Roentgen, unit (symbol R) used to measure the X rays or gamma rays to which a body is exposed (exposure dose). One roentgen causes sufficient ionization to produce a total electric charge of 2.58×10^{-4} coulomb on all the positive (or negative) ions in one kilogram of air, all the electrons released being stopped. Named for Wilhelm K. Roentgen, discoverer of X rays.

Roger II (1095–1154), son of Roger I Guiscard and count (1101–30) and king (1130–54) of Sicily. Acknowledged as duke of Calabria (1122) and Apulia (1127), he thus united Norman holdings in Italy and Sicily. In 1130 anti-Pope Anacletus II crowned him king of Sicily; and after 1139, with recognition from Pope Innocent II, he aquired the lands that for seven centuries would constitute the kingdoms of Sicily and Naples (the two Sicilies).

Rogue River, river in SW Oregon; rises in Cascade Range, N of Crater Lake; flows S and W across Coast Range to Pacific Ocean at Gold Beach. Length: 200mi (322km).

Role, in social science, the way a person usually behaves in a given situation. One individual may take several roles. Feminists point out that a woman may be expected to be housekeeper, cook, mother, counselor, and sex object. Acquiring some roles is central to the process of socialization. From families, friends, teachers, and other sources most people learn roles that are considered appropriate for the society they live in. *See also* Internalization; Role Conflict; Role Model; Socialization; Status.

Role Model, in social science, a person whom others copy when they are acquiring their attitudes and ways of behaving. A girl may take her mother as a model, or she may learn a role by observing and emulating a singer or a writer or a business executive. *See also* Role.

Rolfe, John (1585–1622), English colonist. He was the first colonist to cultivate tobacco in the Jamestown Colony. He married Pocahontas (1614), and went to England where she died. He returned to Virginia as member of the colony council (1617). *See also* Jamestown Colony; Pocahontas.

Rolland, Romain (1866–1944), French novelist, biographer, and dramatist. Although chiefly remembered for his novel *Jean Christophe* (10 vols., 1904–12), he wrote many biographies including *Beethoven* (1903), *Tolstoy* (1911), and *Mahatma Gandhi* (1926). He was awarded the Nobel Prize in literature for 1915.

Roller Skating, recreation and sport. It consists of gliding on a smooth surface on skates with wheels that are cushioned by ball bearings. The sport first gained popularity in the early 20th century and, aside from a recreational use, has several competitive forms. Much like its counterpart, ice skating, there are events in figure and dance skating, speed skating, and roller derby (a team sport) and roller hockey. Except for speed skating, which uses oval outdoor tracks, most skating is an indoor activity. The sport is popular in many countries, and in the United States enjoyed a resurgence of interest in late 1970s and early 1980s.

Rolling, Metal, the most widely used method of shaping metal, hot or cold. It consists of passing the material between revolving rolls. Hot rolling is most common and involves reducing the heated metal to thinner and thinner cross-section (as from ingot to sheet). Cold rolling is used on relatively soft metals to develop new mechanical properties.

Roman Art, the art of ancient Rome. Prior to 400 BC Roman art was largely Etruscan art in the form of tomb decorations. After that Roman art became a welding of Etruscan with Greek influences. Roman painting was largely decorative, consisting of large murals embellishing buildings. In sculpture, the Romans excelled in

John D. Rockefeller

Auguste Rodin: sculpture

Romania

portrait busts. In architecture the Romans made many notable contributions, most conspicuously the invention of the dome, first exemplified in AD 124 in the erection of the Pantheon in Rome—perhaps the parent of all later domes.

Roman Catholic Church, Christian denomination claiming the pope in Rome as the visible head and authority in church affairs. Christ is the invisible head of the church, with the members composing its body. It is founded in tradition, claiming to be one, holy, catholic, and apostolic. The apostle Peter is considered the first pope. The pope, imperfect himself, cannot lead the church into doctrinal error. This is the doctrine of papal infallibility. The pope governs the church through the Roman Curia. It is a hierarchical system of government; the clergy, consisting of bishops, priests, and deacons, are clearly distinguished from other Catholics, the laity. There are seven sacraments that convey grace. There are devotions to the saints, such as novenas. The Mass is the central act of worship in the church, and the focus of its liturgical life. Weekly attendance is required of all members. Religious education is of primary importance. Missionary activity has continued throughout the world. *See also* Papacy; Pope.

Romance Languages, the languages that evolved out of Latin, the language of the Roman Empire. The major Romance languages are Italian, French, Spanish, Portuguese, and Romanian. Others include Catalan, Provençal, and Rhaeto-Romanic. The Romance languages are related to the Germanic, Slavic, Iranian, Indic, and other languages, all of them belonging to the Indo-European family.

Roman de la Rose, an Old French romance of the 13th-century written by Guillaume de Lorris and Jean de Meun. Guillaume began the poem *c.*1230 as an allegory of the progress of a courtly lover. The main narrative, in which the hero dreams of a beautiful garden where he falls in love with a rosebud he sees reflected in a pool, breaks off after 4,000 lines. When Jean continued it *c.* 1275, more than a generation later, he mocked the values of the first half and instead saw love as a means of continuing the species.

Romanesque Architecture, architectural style found throughout Western Europe *c.* 1000 and consisting of a variety of closely related regional styles. Northern Romanesque churches are characterized by the round arch; staggered apse at the east end; radiating chapels along the sides; square bays in the nave, transept, and chancel; vaulted ceilings; and buttressed walls. Regional differences vary the western facade of these churches. Two towers plus a tower over the crossing are found in England and Normandy, a screen facade with no tower is characteristic of southern France, and many towers on both east and west facades can be seen in Germany.

Romania, independent nation in SE Europe. A socialist republic and member of the Warsaw Pact, it has developed economic and political policies increasingly independent of the USSR.

Land and economy. A Balkan state in SE Europe, its S border is the lower course of the Danube River. It extends on either side of the Carpathian and Transylvanian alps which, together with the Balkan Mts, serve as natural barriers. It is bounded by the Black Sea (E), USSR (N and E), Bulgaria (S), Yugoslavia (SW), and Hungary (NW). There are three principal seasons: a severe winter, a brief spring, and a hot summer. Patterned on the centralized and nationalized communist system, Romania, with abundant natural resources, has developed an industrialized economy that ac-

counts for more than 65% of the national income. About 30% of the labor force is in agriculture, and farms and forests contribute 29% of the GNP. State farms and cooperatives maintain 96.4% of the arable land.

People. A Roman colony in the first and second centuries, Romanians trace their lineage back to French, Spanish, and Italian ancestry and consider themselves of Latin origin in contrast to their Magyar and Slavic neighbors. Both the Romanian language and culture contain some Slavic and German elements. Principal minorities are Hungarians, Germans, and Jews. The 28% minority population before WWII was decreased by USSR annexation of several provinces and by postwar expulsion of Germans. Religious choice follows ethnic lines; 80% belongs to the Romanian Orthodox Church. Literacy is over 90%.

Government. Governed by a centralized executive appointed by the legislative branch, power lies in the leadership of the Romanian Communist party.

History. From 400 BC, when it was colonized by the Dacians, Romania had a turbulent history. The principalities of Walachia and Moldavia emerged in the Middle Ages, and the Ottoman Empire exerted considerable influence from the 15th century. From 1829–56 the principalities were under Russian protection; independence was assumed gradually. Carol I became king in 1866, and Romania proclaimed itself independent in 1881. Fighting with the Allies in WWI, Romania gained new territory after the war and became an ally of France and a member of the Little and Balkan ententes. In the 1930s the anti-Semitic, anti-Soviet Fascist Iron Guard brought Romania into WWII on the Axis side. Romania's surrender in 1944 was followed by Russian occupation in 1945 and the establishment of a Communist regime. The king abdicated in 1947 when a Romanian People's Republic was declared. Gheorghe Gheorgiu-Dej, the long-time head of the Communist party, died in 1965. He was succeeded by Nicolae Ceausescu, who broadened Romania's contacts—especially economic ties—with the West, cautiously liberalized the government, and became increasingly independent in foreign affairs.

PROFILE

Official name: Socialist Republic of Romania
Area: 91,700sq mi (237,503sq km)
Population: 22,053,000
   Density: 240per sq mi (93per sq km)
Chief cities: Bucharest (capital); Cluj
Government: Socialist Republic
Religion: Romanian Orthodox (major)
Language: Romanian
Monetary unit: Leu
Gross national product: $31,000,000,000
Per capita income: $1,450
Industries: iron and steel, machinery, oil products, chemicals, building materials, footwear, food processing, textiles
Agriculture: forests, corn, wheat, maize, rye, sugar beets, grapes, fruits, sheep, hogs, cattle
Minerals: oil, natural gas, coal, salt, bauxite, manganese, lead, zinc, gold, silver
Trading partners: USSR, W Europe, Czechoslovakia

Romanian, the official language of Romania, spoken by about 18,000,000 people, or about 90% of the country's population. It is a Romance language, having descended from the Latin that was introduced into the area when it was conquered by the Romans AD. Originally written in Cyrillic characters, Romanian has used the Latin (Roman) alphabet since 1860.

Roman Law, legal system developed by the ancient Romans. The law of twelve tables (450 BC) applied only

to Rome proper. In the 3rd century BC *jus gentium* was added. This was the law applied in dealing with a foreigner, which embodied the highly developed commercial law of the Greek city-states. After the establishment of the Roman Empire, law was enacted by imperial edicts, senate legislation, and judicial officers, growing in complexity and confusion until the codification of Justinian (*c.* 529–34) made Roman law the source of legal knowledge for centuries. It became the basis of Germanic law, and during the Renaissance it spread throughout the world as modern civil law, influencing development of English common law. *Jus gentium* became the basis for commercial law. *See also* Civil Law; Commercial Law; Law; Twelve Tables.

Roman Mythology. The Romans did not develop a true hierarchical pantheon of gods even as they acquired the deities of their conquered enemies, but rather paid homage to a catalog of powers. With formal rites and sacrifice, they paid or withheld payment to each of their heavenly protectors as occasion demanded. The legends of the Greeks, which strongly influenced Roman mythology as early as the 8th century BC, involved gods of more capricious nature.

Roman Numeral, any of the letters, or their variants, used originally in the counting system of the Romans. Numbers are formed, by simple rules, from combinations of the letters I (one), V (five), X (ten), L (50), C (100), D (500), and M (1000). Zero was an unknown notion, as were multiplication and division. *See also* Numeral.

Romanov, House of, the Russian imperial family from 1613 until the March 1917 revolution. The first tsar, **Michael** (1596–1645), was elected by a general assembly at the end of the Time of Troubles. Male primogeniture operated until **Peter the Great** (1672–1725) established the principle of a choice of successor by the ruling monarch (1722). **Paul I** (1754–1801), however, restored the earlier system (1797). **Nicholas II** (1868–1918), the last tsar, abdicated (1917) and was executed after the Bolshevik seizure of power.

Romans, New Testament epistle written by apostle Paul in Corinth *c.*56. He had never been to Rome when he wrote his letter to discuss difficulties existing between Jewish and Gentile members of the Roman church. It shows his pastoral concern for the young churches and states that Christ offers a new life for man.

Romansch. *See* Rhaeto-Romanic.

Romanticism in Architecture, architectural movement of the late 18th and 19th centuries of many different tendencies, united by a common reaction against the supposed artificiality and irrationality of the Baroque. It includes the archeologically inspired Neoclassicism of the late 18th century, as well as the Gothic revival, the revival of medieval forms, and the picturesque cultivation of rustic motifs.

Romanticism in Art, the chief movement in painting and sculpture in the 19th century. As in literature and music, Romanticism stressed the importance of the senses, the emotions, and nature over rationalism and classical forms. Thus, emotional and spiritual themes were emphasized, while subject matter was often drawn from simpler, even everyday ways of living, rather than from religious history or myth. These romantic trends are perhaps best exemplified by landscape painting of the period. Romantic elements are present in the arts of all periods, but reached their height in the 19th century in the works of such artists as Turner, Constable, Whistler, Gericault, Delacroix, Corot, and Friedrich.

Romanticism in Music, music composed from roughly 1820 to 1920. Romanticism in music refers to preferences for subjectivity, fantasy, emotionality, and theatricality over the formal or intellectual aspects of music, sometimes at the expense of sound musical structure. Early Romanticism (*c.* 1820–50) began with the late works of Beethoven and Schubert, followed by Weber, Berlioz, Mendelssohn, Schumann, Chopin, and Rossini. Here the forms of the Classical Period were predominant, but with greater emotional intensity. Middle Romanticism (*c.* 1850–90) is represented by Liszt, Franck, Wagner, Bruckner, Smetana, Verdi, Brahms, Tchaikovsky, Dvorak, and Mussorgsky. Here the symphonic poem emerged as a distinct form and nationalistic trends were very evident as serious composers adopted styles of music from their native folk music. Late Romanticism (*c.* 1890–1920) is represented by Elgar, Mahler, Rachmaninoff, R. Strauss, Nielsen, Sibelius, Reger, Holst, and Vaughan-Williams. They enlarged the symphony orchestra and wrote Romantic music more complex than their predecessors'. Romanticism has continued into contemporary music in the works of such composers as Barber and Shostakovitch. *See also* the above composers; Classical Music.

Romany, the language of the gypsies. It is an Indic language, related to Sanskrit and Hindi, and is known to have originated in India. The gypsies are thought to have begun their migration westward about AD 1000.

Rome (Roma), capital city of Italy, in central Italy, on both sides of the Tiber River; capital of Latium region and Roma prov. Hill settlements combined to form one city 8th century BC; it was traditionally founded by Romulus 735 BC, and was an Etruscan city-kingdom to 6th century BC. The Roman Republic was founded *c.* 500 BC; by the 3rd century BC, Rome ruled most of Italy and began overseas expansion. Julius Caesar ruled 46–44 BC; Roman Empire was founded 30 BC with defeat of Marc Antony by Octavian, who reigned as the emperor Augustus 27 BC–AD 14. Rome was capital of Roman Empire until 330 AD, when Constantinople was named capital, Rome was the medieval spiritual center of Western World; capital of Papal States, which were annexed to France by Napoleon 1809; inc. into Kingdom of Italy 1870; liberated by Allied troops June 4, 1944. It is site of Vatican City, the autonomous papal see housing fine museums and libraries. Roman remains include the Colosseum, catacombs, Forum; five basilicas, including St Peter's and St John Lateran; notable churches, many palaces, including the Farnese (16th century), and villas; site of University of Rome (1303); scene of 1960 Summer Olympics. Industries: tourism, motion pictures, fashion, metallurgy. Pop. 2,600,000.

Rome, Ancient. The earliest Roman settlement was built in the 8th century BC according to legend by Romulus and Remus in 753, on the Palatine, the central hill of the seven hills of Rome on the east bank of the Tiber. The Tiber separated the Etruscans from the Latins (of the plain of Latium) and the Sabines and Samnites to the north. The Etruscans affected Rome's culture through the influence of the two Etruscan kings of Rome, Tarquinius Priscus and Tarquinius Superbus. By 500 BC the Romans had rid themselves of Etruscan rule and developed a stable republic that was to endure for four centuries. It was at first governed by patricians, the upper class elite, with two consuls elected by and representing the plebeians, or main body of the population. The plebeians fought a long, bitter struggle for political equality, which they gained by the 3rd century BC. They elected powerful tribunes who came to hold the right of veto over the resolutions of the senate, which enacted legislation and determined policy. The first major code of law, known as the Twelve Tables, was set down in writing by plebeian demand c.450 BC and became the basis of later legislation. The plebeians convened in three comitia, assemblies that gained power from the patricians. Magistrates designated quaestors, aediles, praetors, and censors took up the increasingly complicated business of running the burgeoning state.

The Romans developed their superb military organization as they extended their influence over Italy beginning in the 4th century BC. The Gauls invaded from the north and sacked Rome in 390. The city, rebuilt, recovered gradually and forged its supremacy over its neighbors in Latium and Etruria, dissolving the Latin League. They defeated the warlike Samnites in the drawn-out Samnite Wars, absorbed the Sabines, and made alliances with other peoples. Pushing south, they occupied Greek colonial territories and waged a mutually costly war with Pyrrhus, king of Epirus, who later withdrew to Greece.

Rome thereby retained control of central and S Italy and looked to the Mediterranean for further expansion, coming into fierce conflict with Carthage, the greatest naval and commercial power of the area. Their armies met in Sicily in dispute over the strategically valuable Straits of Messina, beginning the long Punic Wars (264–146 BC). The greater manpower, wealth, perseverance, and discipline of the Roman armies, the loyalty of the Italian peoples to Rome, and the failure of the Carthaginian supply line were all factors in the crushing defeat of Carthage. At the insistence of the influential senator Cato the Elder, Carthage was razed. Rome was the dominant power in Spain, the Mediterranean islands, and N Africa.

The Romans then focused their expansion on the East. They defeated Philip V and Perseus in the Macedonian Wars (215–168 BC), took much of Syria from Antiochus III and Magnesia (189 BC), and dissolved the Achaean League. After subjugating Bithynia, Galatia, Pergamum, and Rhodes, they established their supremacy over Egypt (168 BC). This rapid and gross expansion had dire consequences for Rome. The senate grew corrupt administering the vast wealth of the new provinces and dependent peoples to its own advantage, suppressing the introduction of social reforms supported by Tiberius and Gaius Gracchus. Slave revolts (134–132 and 104–101 BC) were brutally put down. Marius, the leader of the *populares,* defeated Jugurtha (106), the Cimbri, and the Teutones (102), and took the Roman army for the first time into Transalpine Gaul. He and his followers were slaughtered by Sulla who gained support of the optimates and equites. The Social War, led by the Marsi, forced the Romans to grant citizenship to all Italian allies south of the Po (87). The Third Servile War (73–71), led by the gladiator Spartacus, was ruthlessly ended by Crassus and Pompey. Sulla marched in civil war against Rome and established himself as dictator. He introduced constitutional reforms to revive the dying republic and then retired. His former legates, the ambitious general Pompey and the wealthy Crassus, elected consuls, reversed his reforms. Pompey vanquished the Mediterranean pirates, ended the Mithradatic Wars (63), and added Pontus, Syria, and Phoenicia to the empire.

Crassus and Pompey formed an uneasy coalition called the First Triumvirate (60) with the illustrious patrician and popular leader Julius Caesar. While Caesar campaigned brilliantly in the Gallic Wars (58–51), Crassus died (53) and Pompey's hatred of Caesar came to a head. He took up the senate's opposition to Caesar and Caesar, crossing the Rubicon, entered into civil war with Pompey's army, defeating him at Pharsala (48). Caesar was acknowledged dictator of Rome and set about to secure and consolidate the empire and promote liberal legislation at home. His administration ended abruptly with his assassination (44). At the time of Caesar's death Rome was experiencing a period of advanced cultural achievement in arts and letters as exemplified by the works of Cicero. Further civil war followed as Caesar's heir Octavian formed a Second Triumvirate (43) with Antony and Lepidus and defeated the forces of the conspirators Brutus and Cassius at Philippi (42). At Actium (31) Octavian destroyed the armies of Antony and Cleopatra, annexed Egypt, and restored a long-lasting peace (Pax Romana) to Rome as Augustus, imperator.

Romeo and Juliet (*c.*1596), 5-act tragedy by William Shakespeare, from a poem by Arthur Brooke (1562). It has been the most often and successfully produced of all Shakespeare's plays and has been filmed more often than any other Shakespeare play, from a silent version in 1916 to a 1968 production. In Verona, Italy, the Montague and Capulet families bear an "ancient grudge." Juliet, a Capulet, and Romeo, a Montague, fall in love and are secretly married in defiance of their parents' opposition. When the two lovers die the families make a belated peace.

Rommel, Erwin (1891–1944), German military commander. He rose in the German army during Adolf Hitler's regime and led troops in Austria, Czechoslovakia, Poland, and France in early World War II. In 1942 as commander of the Afrika Korps, a tank corps, he drove the British back almost to Alexandria, Egypt. Known as "the desert fox," he was defeated by the British in November 1942 at El Alamein. In 1944, disenchanted with Hitler's military leadership, he joined an unsuccessful plot to kill him. He was arrested and forced to take poison.

Romulo, Carlos Pena (1901–85), Filipino military and political figure. In 1941 he won the Pulitzer Prize in journalism for his reports on the Pacific military situation before World War II. After the Japanese attack on the Philippines in late 1941, he became an aide-de-camp to Gen. Douglas MacArthur. His "Voice of Freedom" radio broadcasts were famous. He joined the Philippine government in exile in the United States as secretary of information. Returning to the Philippines in 1945, he served variously as president of the United Nations General Assembly (1949–50), ambassador to the United States (1952), president of the University of the Philippines (1962–65), secretary of education and foreign minister.

Romulus and Remus, legendary founders of Rome. According to a myth of the late 4th century BC, Rhea Silvia, daughter of Numitor, the king of Alba Longa, bore twins by the god Mars. Amulius, Numitor's brother, deposed him and threw the twins into the Tiber. They were rescued and suckled by a wolf and reared by a shepherd. They grew strong and killed Amulius, restoring Numitor to his throne. In 753 BC they founded the settlement on the Palatine hill that became Rome. Romulus walled it and Remus was slain for leaping the wall after a quarrel. Romulus led the rape of the Sabines to obtain wives for his settlement of fugitives. After a long reign he disappeared in a thunderstorm and came to be revered as the god Quirinus.

Rondeau, French medieval verse form, popularized by Guillaume de Machaut in the 14th century. It consisted of four stanzas, the second and third usually containing a refrain echoed from the first line of the first stanza. Rondeaux were sung to music composed for several voices.

Ronsard, Pierre de (1524–85), French poet. In 1549 he formed the Pléiade, a literary group that aimed to reform French verse on classical principles. His *Odes* (1550) and *Amours* (1552) brought him fame and royal patronage, and he wrote several patriotic political poems. After 1574 he retired from public life, but his late *Sonnets pour Hélène* (1578) contained some of his finest work. *See also* Pléiade.

Rook, Old World crowlike bird that nests in colonies near the tops of trees. Family Corvidae; species *Corvus frugilegus.*

Roosevelt, Anna Eleanor (1884–1962), US reformer and humanitarian, b. New York City. She was the niece of Theodore Roosevelt and a distant cousin of Franklin Delano Roosevelt, whom she married (1905). She worked for social causes both before and after her marriage. She raised a large family and helped her polio-stricken husband regain his vigor. After she became first lady (1933) she was active in the National Association for the Advancement of Colored People and other social reform organizations, wrote a newspaper column, was a lecturer, and was assistant director of the Office of Civilian Defense (1941–42). She visited battlefronts in World War II and after the war, became the US ambassador to the United Nations (1945, 1949–52, 1961–62). Her books include *This is My Story* (1937) and *This I Remember* (1949).

Roosevelt, Franklin Delano (1882–1945), 32nd president of the United States (1933–45), b. Hyde Park, N.Y. He graduated from Harvard University (1904), attended the Columbia University Law School, and was admitted to the New York bar. In 1905 he married a distant cousin, Eleanor Roosevelt; they had six children.

A distant relative of Theodore Roosevelt, Franklin Roosevelt became a Democrat early in life. He gained notice as an insurgent member of the New York legislature and was chosen by Woodrow Wilson as assistant secretary of the navy. In 1920 he was the unsuccessful Democratic vice-presidential nominee.

In August 1921, Roosevelt was stricken with poliomyelitis, which left him unable to walk. With his wife's encouragement, however, he soon resumed an active political life and was elected (1928) governor of New York. In 1932 he was the Democratic candidate for president and won by a wide margin.

Roosevelt took office at the depths of the Great Depression. He immediately instituted a program, known as the New Deal, that included a wide variety of measures aimed at bringing about an economic recovery. Collectively, the New Deal programs had the effect of revolutionizing US economic, political, and social life. Vigorously denounced by Republicans and conservatives in general, Roosevelt nevertheless was reelected by a landslide in 1936. Roosevelt's second term saw some lessening of public support. His attempt to "pack" the Supreme Court by adding new members was defeated. Although the Republicans had shown some resurgence of strength, Roosevelt decided to run for an unprecedented third term in 1940. He was easily reelected.

Roosevelt's remaining years in office were almost totally concerned with US involvement in World War II. Even before the United States entered the war, Roosevelt had forged strong alliances with the Allies, particularly through the lend-lease program. Once the United States was at war, Roosevelt commanded the most massive war effort in history. He attended a number of conferences where the strategy of the war was determined and where the postwar world was planned. In 1944, Roosevelt ran for a fourth term although clearly in poor health. He won the election but died shortly

Eleanor Roosevelt

Franklin D. Roosevelt

Theodore Roosevelt

after inauguration. He was succeeded by Harry S. Truman.

Career: New York legislature, 1910–13; assistant secretary of the navy, 1913–20; governor of New York, 1929–33; president, 1933–45. *See also* New Deal; World War II.

Roosevelt, Theodore (1858–1919), 26th president of the United States (1901–09), b. New York City. He graduated from Harvard University in 1880. He married Alice Lee (1880) and Edith Carow (1886) and had six children. After deciding against becoming a lawyer, Roosevelt settled into the vocations of author, rancher, and politician. He wrote books and journalism, bought a ranch in Dakota, and was elected as a Republican to the New York legislature.

He quickly won a reputation as a reformer and was appointed to the US Civil Service Commission by Benjamin Harrison; he was reappointed by Grover Cleveland. In 1895 a reform mayor named him president of the New York City police board. In 1897, President McKinley made him assistant secretary of the navy. During the Spanish-American War, Roosevelt organized and fought with the Rough Riders regiment and returned from Cuba a great war hero.

He was chosen in 1898 to run for governor of New York largely because he was a hero. Once elected, however, he alienated Republican regulars by his independence. Partly to remove him from the governor's chair, the Republicans named him (1900) vice-presidential candidate to run with President McKinley in his successful bid for a second term.

When McKinley was assassinated on Sept. 14, 1901, Roosevelt became president. Conservative Republican fears of "that damned cowboy" (as they called him) were soon realized. He forced coal mine owners to negotiate with striking miners; he energetically enforced the Sherman Antitrust Act; and he pushed through land reclamation and conservation laws. In 1904 he ran for and won a full term. Roosevelt's foreign policy was one of increasing US influence, particularly in Latin America. The Panama Canal was begun, and the Monroe Doctrine was strengthened. In 1906 he won the Nobel Peace Prize for helping to end the Russo-Japanese War.

Roosevelt virtually hand-picked his successor, William Howard Taft. By 1912, however, he had become disenchanted with the conservative drift of the Republicans. After failing to win the nomination away from Taft, he organized his own Progressive, or Bull Moose, party. He polled more votes in the election than Taft but Democrat Woodrow Wilson won.

Career: New York legislature, 1882–84; US Civil Service Commission, 1889–95; president, New York City police board, 1895–97; assistant secretary of the navy, 1897–98; governor of New York, 1899–1901; vice president, 1901; president, 1901–09.

Root, Elihu (1845–1937), US lawyer and statesman, b. Clinton, N.Y. The leader of the American bar, Root became secretary of war immediately following the end of the war with Spain; he supervised the affairs of Cuba and of the newly acquired territories of the Philippines and Puerto Rico. Root was appointed secretary of state in 1905; he was awarded the Nobel Peace Prize in 1912 for his contribution to peace in the Western hemisphere. Root also served in the US Senate (1909–15) and as president of Andrew Carnegie's philanthropic trusts.

Root, underground portion of a vascular plant that serves as an anchor and absorbs water and nutrients. The primary root develops from the lower end of the plant embryo. Some plants have taproots with smaller lateral branches (dandelion). Others develop fibrous roots with lateral branches equalling the main root in

growth (grasses). Adventitious roots are produced from the above-ground portion of the stem (mangrove) and provide additional support and absorption of water and minerals. Some plants have large taproots that store nutrients (beet, parsnip, carrot).

Rorqual, five species of whalebone whales distributed worldwide. Gregarious, they travel in groups of several hundred. Genus *Balaenoptera*. *See also* Finback Whale; Whale.

Rosario, city in E central Argentina, on the Paraná River, 90 mi (145km) S of Santa Fe; export and import hub. Exports: grain, hay, meat, hides, cattle, wool, sugar. Industries: grain, flour mills, tanneries, distilleries. Founded 1725. Pop. 810,840.

Rosas, Juan Manuel de (1793–1877), Argentine caudillo and governor of Buenos Aires province (1829–32, 1835–52), one of the most important political figures of post-independence Latin America. A rancher, Rosas organized the local militia; by 1835, his rivals in exile or dead, he had become a virtual dictator. Rosas controlled access to markets by controlling Buenos Aires; he survived blockades imposed by the French and the English. It was not until 1851, when Justo José de Urquiza rose in revolt, that the era of Rosas was ended. Rosas went into exile in England.

Rose, wild or cultivated flowering shrubs. The majority are native to Asia, several to America, and a few to Europe and NW Africa. Growing mostly in temperate regions of the Northern Hemisphere, some species are found at high elevations in the tropics and even above the Arctic Circle.

Roses are divided into groups according to type or use: hybrid tea, floribunda, grandiflora, climbing, polyantha, hybrid perpetual, tea, old, and special purpose. The stems are thorny and erect, climbing, or trailing. The leaves have leaflets in pairs with the odd one at the tip. Flowers appear singly or in loose clusters and colors range from white to yellow, pink, crimson, and maroon. About nine species have been involved in the breeding of today's many garden roses. Prized for their fragrant blossoms, roses are also used in medicines, cosmetics, and, a regional favorite, rosehip jelly. Rose hips are considered an excellent source of vitamin C. There are about 200 species. Family Rosaceae; genus *Rosa*.

Rose Beetle, or rose chafer, small, long-legged, tan scarab beetle ranging from New England to Virginia and west to Texas. It feeds on fruit and foliage of grapes, peaches, roses, and other fruit. Species *Macrodactylus subspinosus.*

Rosefish, or ocean perch, marine food fish found in the North Atlantic and usually fished by trawlers at 300–700ft (91–213m). It is bright red or rose. Family Scorpaenidae; species *Sebastes marinus.*

Rosemary, common name for *Rosmarinis officinalis,* a perennial evergreen undershrub of the mint family with aromatic lance-shaped leaves used in seasoning and yielding an oil used in medicine. Its flowers are pale blue.

Rosenberg Case (1951–53), US espionage case. A New York couple, Julius and Ethel Rosenberg, were found guilty of passing atomic bomb secrets to Soviet agents. The couple were executed (June 19, 1953) for the crime. Their trial gained international attention because many felt the couple were the victims of Cold War hysteria. The couple's two sons campaigned to vindicate their parents.

Rose of Sharon, hardy shrub, *Hibiscus syriacus,* native to China. It can be grown farther north than many hibiscus plants. The flowers are red, purple, rose, or white. Height: to 15ft (4.6m). Family Malvaceae. *See also* Hibiscus.

Roseola Infantum, an infectious disease of young children, probably caused by a virus. It is characterized by high fever, followed by a mild rash on the trunk and neck.

Roses, Wars of the (1455–85), English civil wars fought for the possession of the crown and taking their name from the badges of the House of Lancaster (red rose) and the House of York (white rose). By 1455 the incompetence of the Lancastrian Henry VI had led to widespread civil disorder. Henry's interests were promoted by his wife, Margaret of Anjou, who was determined to protect the right of their son Edward (b. 1453). Richard, duke of York, and a small group of lords attempted to gain control of the government but were strongly resisted. York was killed in 1460, but his son Edward IV claimed the throne and defeated Henry VI at Towton in 1461. In 1470, Edward's closest ally, the earl of Warwick, deserted him for the Lancastrians. Briefly deposed, Edward regained his throne and defeated his enemies in 1471. Henry VI and his son were killed. After Edward IV died in 1483, his brother usurped the throne as Richard III and Edward's sons were murdered. Their deaths allowed Henry Tudor to rally the Lancastrian faction and Richard was overcome at Bosworth in 1485 by Henry who as Henry VII, married Edward IV's daughter Elizabeth in 1486, thus uniting the two warring factions. The wars illustrated the weakness of the English kings because of their dependence on the armed retinues of the nobility and marked the transition from feudalism to a stronger monarchy. *See also* Henry VI; Henry VII; Richard III.

Rosetta Stone, a slab of black basalt that was the key to deciphering Egyptian hieroglyphics. It was erected in 195 BC to honor Ptolemy Epiphanes. The stone was discovered in Rosetta, Egypt, in 1799 by an officer in Napoleon's army. It bears an inscription in three languages: Greek, hieroglyphics, and demotic or common characters. Using the Greek inscription as a basis, English physicist Thomas Young in 1818 and Jean François Champollion in 1822 were able to decipher the hieroglyphic inscription. The stone is now in the British Museum.

Rosewood, any of several kinds of ornamental wood derived from various kinds of New World and Old World tropical trees. The most important are Honduras rosewood, *Dalbergia stevensoni,* and Brailian rosewood. *D. nigra.* It varies from deep, ruddy brown to purplish and has a black grain, hard to polish because of high resin content. Once much in demand by cabinetmakers, it is now scarce.

Rosh Hashanah, meaning New Year, begins the Jewish year with the Ten Days of Penitence. The festival ends with the Day of Atonement, the 10th day. It does not commemorate a particular event but is a day of reflection and prayer. Man must realize his sins and unite in God. It is celebrated as a day of judgment for man and Israel as a nation.

Rosin, or colophony, yellowish amorphous resin obtained as a residue from the distillation of turpentine. Chief constituent is abietic acid; used in varnishes, soldering fluxes, linoleum, and printing inks. Properties: sp gr 1.08; melt. pt. 212–308°F (100–153°C).

Ross, Betsy (1752–1836), US seamstress, said to have made the first American flag with stars and stripes, b. Philadelphia as Elizabeth Griscom. According to the account of her grandson William Canby, Gen. George Washington and a committee came to her with a rough drawing of a flag and commissioned her to make it, which she did. Congress then adopted the stars and stripes design as the official flag of the United States. The story is disputed, but Betsy Ross remains a folk hero.

Ross, (Sir) James Clark (1800–62), British naval officer and explorer; participated in six Arctic expeditions in search of a northwest passage linking the Atlantic and Pacific Oceans (1818–33). During the last Arctic expedition, Ross discovered the magnetic north pole (June 1831). Ross later commanded an Antarctic expedition (1839–43), which earned him a knighthood and awards from the Geographical Societies of London and Paris.

Ross Dependency, area of Antarctica, includes Ross Island, coasts along Ross Sea, and nearby islands. Under jurisdiction of New Zealand by act of British Parliament. Area: 175,000sq mi (453,250sq km).

Rossetti, Dante Gabriel (1828–82), English poet and painter. He was a founding member, with John Everett Millais and Holman Hunt, of the Pre-Raphaelite Brotherhood. Although his poem *The Blessed Damozel* was first published when he was 19, recognition as a poet came long after his paintings had won acclaim. Apart from a volume of translations (1861), no collection of poems appeared until 1870, when one he had buried in his wife's grave in 1862 was dug up and published with others. This sonnet sequence was *The House of Life*. A further volume, which completed the sequence, appeared in 1881. *See also* Pre-Raphaelite Brotherhood.

Rossini, Gioacchino (1792–1868), Italian operatic composer. He produced 38 operas before the age of 37, after which he never composed another. His operas include *The Italian Girl in Algiers* (1813), *The Thieving Magpie* (1817), *The Journey to Reims* (1823), *Semiramide* (1823), and his masterpiece, the still popular comic opera *The Barber of Seville* (1816); other works include the overture to the opera *William Tell* (1829).

Ross Sea, extension of S Pacific Ocean, in Antarctica, between Edward VII Peninsula and Victoria Land. Discovered 1841 by Capt. James C. Ross.

Rostand, Edmond (1868–1918), French dramatist. His early verse dramas include *Les Romanesques* (1894), *La Princesse Lointaine* (1895), and *La Samaritaine* (1897). His best-known work is *Cyrano de Bergerac* (1897), a tragicomedy about unrequited love. *L'Aiglon* (1900) about Napoleon II, and *Chantecler* (1910), a barnyard fable, are also well known.

Rostock, seaport city in N East Germany, on Warnov River, near Baltic Sea, 41mi (66km) WSW of Stralsund; capital of Rostock district; powerful Baltic member of the Hanseatic League (14th century); seat of university (1419); birthplace of Gebhard von Blücher, Prussian general; site of Church of St Mary (13th century), town hall (15th century), tower (16th century). Industries: shipyards, petroleum storage, farm machinery, fishing, watches, chemicals, food processing, diesel engines, furniture. Founded 1189; chartered 1218. Pop. 213,475.

Rotation, turning of a celestial body about its axis. In the solar system the Sun and all the planets, except for Uranus and Venus, rotate from west to east (that is, in a counterclockwise direction).

Roth, Phillip (1933–), US author, b. Newark. A novelist and short story writer, he often draws on his Jewish background to produce amusing works. He won the National Book Award (1960) for *Goodbye, Columbus* (1959), a work comprised of a novella and five short stories. His novels include *Letting Go* (1962), *Portnoy's Complaint* (1969), *The Great American Novel (1973), The Ghost Writer (1979), and Zuckerman Unbound* (1981).

Rothko, Mark (1903–70), US painter, b. Latvia. His early style was realistic. He was briefly influenced by Surrealism and then became increasingly abstract in style. His abstract expressionistic paintings are characterized by two or three vertically arranged rectangular shapes with somewhat blurred outlines painted parallel to each other on a colored background. Depending on the relationship between the colors of the rectangles and their background, the shapes seem either to advance or recede. Most of Rothko's canvases are quite large.

Rothschild, Nathan Mayer (1777–1836), member of the German banking family who established the British house. Designated his father's representative in commercially active Manchester, in 1798, Nathan transferred his operation to London in 1805, where he was instrumental in financing British obligations incurred during the Napoleonic Wars. His success guaranteed close cooperation with the government after peace was concluded and generated an even greater expansion of the family's financial interests.

Rothschild Family, commercial and banking dynasty founded in 19th century Germany by **Meyer Amschel Rothschild** (1743–1812). The five sons of Meyer Amschel established branches in the financial centers of London, Frankfurt, Paris, and Naples. Profits earned during the Napoleonic Wars were invested throughout Europe. Control over the vast empire passed to capable male heirs and came to include branches influential in the sciences and politics as well as finance.

Rotifer, microscopic metazoan found in fresh water. Although they resemble ciliate protozoans, they are many-celled with a general body structure similar to simple worms. Elongated to round, they are identified by a crown of cilia around the mouth. Reproduction is sexual. Class Rotifera; species include *Philodina* and *Conochilus*.

Rotterdam, major seaport and industrial city in W Netherlands, on New Meuse River, 15mi (24km) from North Sea; site of 15th-century church, 18th-century stock exchange. Heart of city was demolished by German bombing, May 14, 1940. Exports: coal, dairy and vegetable products. Industries: chemicals, textiles, paper, ship, rail, and automobile manufacturing, brewing, oil refining, machinery. Chartered 1328. Pop. 614,-767.

Rottweiler, German cattle dog (working group) descended from dogs brought over the Alps by Romans, 1,900 years ago. It has a medium-length head that is broad between the ears; strong, muscular jaws; hanging ears set high; a short-backed, strong body; muscular, medium-length legs; and high-set short or docked tail. The short, coarse, flat coat is black with brown markings. Average size: 23–27in (58–68.5cm) high at shoulder, 75–90lb (34–41kg). *See also* Working Dog.

Rouault, Georges (1871–1958), French painter and printmaker. His early training was in stained glass. He also painted naturalistic landscapes and pictures with religious and mythological themes. Influenced by Fauvism, his style became less realistic. He used dark reds and blues to paint corrupt judges and prostitutes. He then turned to printmaking for a decade and then back again to painting. This time, his style evolved to the point where he used heavy black lines to delineate his expressionistic clowns and prostitutes who were painted in thick, primary colors.

Rouen, seaport in France, on Seine River, 70mi (113km) NW of Paris; capital of Seine-Maritime dept. An archepiscopal see since 5th century, by 10th century it was capital of Normandy and one of Europe's leading cities; scene of Joan of Arc's trial and burning (1431); site of Cathedral of Notre Dame (12th–15th centuries) with its Tour de Beurre (butter tower), 14th-century Gothic church of St Ouen, and 14th-century Tour de la Gros Horloge (clock tower). Industries: textiles, flour, foundries, perfumes, leather goods. Pop. 118,332.

Roulette, gambling game, popular in casinos. The game consists of a ball, and a wheel with its outer area marked off into 38 squares. The numbers on these squares alternately range in red and black from 1 to 36, with a 0 and double 0 marked in green. Near the wheel is a table with an arrangement of squares corresponding to the wheel. There are many types of bets that may be made, with the odds varying according to the number and/or color selected. After the bets are made, the wheel is spun and the ball tossed into it; its final resting place indicates the winning bets.

Roundworm. *See* Nematode.

Rousseau, Henri (1844–1910), French primitive painter. He received no formal training and taught himself to paint by copying works from the Louvre. His style is characterized by a strong sense of pattern and color combined with the use of imaginative, exotic jungle themes showing tropical plants and beasts. Pablo Picasso viewed Rousseau's directness of expression as an important contribution to 20th-century art.

Rousseau, Jean Jacques (1712–78), French philosopher and author. One of the most original prophets of modernity, he went to Paris in 1741 and was associated with Denis Diderot and the Encyclopedists. Although often living in the provinces or in Switzerland, Rousseau remained in contact with Parisian intellectuals thereafter. In his celebrated *Discourses on the Sciences and Arts* (1750) and in *On Equality* (1754) he argued that man's natural goodness is perverted by artificial and inequitable societies. *The New Héloise* (1761) celebrated love in a new romantic style. In *The Social Contract* (1762) he envisioned a liberated society that would conform with a kind of humanistic, individualized education, also outlined in *Émile* (1762). His *Confessions* (1781–88) convey the impression of a passionate and often persecuted human spirit. *See also* Social Contract.

Rove Beetle, small, slender, generally beneficial beetle found chiefly near decaying plant and animal matter. They have short wing covers. Family Staphylinidae.

Rowing, a sport that includes events for eights, fours, and pairs. A coxswain steers the shell for eights by means of tiller ropes attached to a rudder; he also directs the crew. Each crew member uses both hands on one oar. The oars are alternately attached to riggings on opposite sides of the shell. The shell for eights is between 55 and 60 feet (16.8–18.3m) long and 2 feet wide (0.6m). Rowing has been included in the Olympic Games since 1900. The sport has been popular in England since 1829, when the first Oxford and Cambridge crew races were held. In the United States, the first intercollegiate event matched Harvard and Yale in 1852.

Royal Canadian Mounted Police, federal police of Canada. Organized in 1873 as the Northwest Mounted Police to protect western settlements, railroads, and liquor revenues. The Mounties opened their first post at Emerson (1874). Active in the Riel rebellion (1884–85), Yukon gold rush, and both world wars, they enforce all federal laws in Canada and provide police manpower to most provinces.

Royal Fern, or flowering fern, common, widely distributed bush fern of wetlands. It has large leaves rising from a heavy rootstock that forms a mat. The cylindrical pinnae on frond ends are densely covered with sporangia and look like flowers. Height: to 6ft (1.8m). Family Osmundaceae; species *Osmunda regalis. See also* Fern.

Royal Oak, city in SE Michigan; residential suburb 13mi (21km) NW of Detroit. Industries: tools, paints, mattresses. Settled 1820; inc. as village 1891, as city 1921. Pop. (1980) 70,893.

Royal Palm, ornamental palm native to the Caribbean islands and Central America. It has a tall, light-colored trunk and feather-shaped leaves. Species include *Roystonea elata*, the Florida royal palm, to 70ft (21m); *R. oleracea,* the cabbage palm or palmiste, to 120ft (37m); and *R. regia,* the Cuban royal palm, to 70ft (21m). Family Palmaceae.

Royal Waterlily, aquatic plant with floating leaves and fragrant white flowers that turn pink and then red on the second day. Leaf diameter: to 6ft (1.8m). Family Nymphaeaceae; species *Victoria regia*.

RR Lyrae Variable, or cluster variable, intrinsic regular short-period variable star of the Cepheid type, usually completing one cycle of luminosity fluctuations in less than one day. Stars of this type are of Population II, that is, they are old stars commonly found in globular clusters, and appear to be of uniform intrinsic brightness. Like the classic Cepheids, they have been effectively used in distance measurement.

Rubáiyát of Omar Khayyám, collection of quatrains written by an 11th-century Persian poet and scholar and translated into English by Edward Fitzgerald in 1859. The verses exalt the sensual, pleasure-seeking life. The epicurean philosophy of the poems made them extremely popular in the Victorian age.

Rub al-Khali (Ar-Rab' al Khalil), vast desert of S Arabian Peninsula, in SW Saudi Arabia and N Oman; translation of Arabic name is "empty quarter." Length: 750mi (1,208km). Width: 400mi (644km). Area: 250,000sq mi (647,500sq km).

Rubber, elastic solid obtained from the latex of the rubber tree *(Hevea brasiliensis).* Natural rubber consists of a polymer of cis-isoprene and is widely used for tires and other applications, especially after vulcanization. Synthetic rubbers are polymers tailored to excel in specific properties for specific purposes; none has the overall advantages of natural rubber. They include styrene-butadiene rubber (SBR), neoprene, nitrile rubber, and the newer stereo-regular rubbers based on synthetic cis-polyisoprene.

Rubber Plant, evergreen fig native to India and Malaysia. Tree-sized in the tropics, it is grown as a pot plant in temperate regions. Once cultivated for its white

Gioacchino Rossini

Jean Jacques Rousseau

Arthur Rubinstein

latex to make India rubber, it has large, glossy, leathery leaves and a stout, buttressed trunk. Size: to 100ft (30.5m). It begins as an epiphyte (air plant) and later anchors to the ground; fruits are egg-shaped. Height: to 100ft (30.5m) Family Moraceae; species *Ficus elastica.*

Rubber Tree, any of several South American trees whose exudations can be made into rubber; especially *Hevea brasiliensis* (family Euphorbiaceae), a tall softwood tree native to Brazil. The milky exudate, called latex, is obtained from the inner bark by tapping, and then coagulated chemically or by smoking over fires.

Rubella. *See* German Measles.

Rubeola. *See* Measles.

Rubens, Peter Paul (1577–1640), Flemish painter and engraver. During a stay in Italy (1600–08), he painted religious works, in which he paid much attention to careful drawing and decorative detail. He was greatly influenced in his style by the works of Italian High Renaissance masters. Monumental muscular figures in action are characteristic of his heroic, Mannerist style. When he returned to Antwerp (1608), he established a workshop that became highly successful, producing huge portraits and allegorical series for the wealthy and nobility of western Europe. Rubens' best-known works are his many decorative series for churches and palaces, dating from 1620 to 1630. He crowded his Baroque canvases with dynamic bodies and used light and color to give a dramatic sense of action. His 21 paintings of ''The Life of Marie de Médicis'' (Louvre) are from this period. His later landscapes show a softening of colors.

Rubidium, metallic element (symbol Rb) of the alkali-metal group, discovered (1861) by R.W. Bunsen and G. R. Kirchhoff. Lepidolite contains small amounts of rubidium salts and is the chief source. The element has few commercial uses: small amounts are used in photoelectric cells. Chemically it resembles sodium, but is more reactive. Natural rubidium contains 27.85% of the radioisotope Rb^{87} (half-life 6×10^{10}yr). Properties: at. no. 37; at. wt. 85.468, sp gr 1.532; melt. pt. 102 °F (38.89°C); boil. pt. 1270°F (688°C); most common isotope Rb^{85} (72.15%). *See also* Alkali Elements.

Rubinstein, Arthur (1886–1982), US pianist, b. Poland. He studied in Germany, made his debut there at the age of 12, and first performed in the United States in 1906. He moved permanently to the United States in 1937. He enjoyed the longest active concert career of any musician—more than three-quarters of a century—touring the world many times. He was especially known for his interpretations of Spanish composers, and of Chopin and other Romantic composers. He wrote his memoirs in two volumes, *My Young Years* (1974) and *My Many Years* (1980).

Ruby, a transparent red gemstone variety of corundum with high refraction, found mainly in Burma. Brilliant when cut and polished, the ruby lacks fire. Turns green when heated, but regains color. Deep red rubies are valued more highly than diamonds. *See also* Corundum.

Ruddy Duck, North American stiff-tailed duck with a black and white head and, in the male, brownish-red upper plumage. It typically holds its tail at a jaunty angle while swimming. Length: 15in (8cm). Species *Oxyura jamaicensis. See also* Duck.

Rudolf I (1218–91), German king (1273–91). The first Hapsburg monarch, his election as king ended the pe-

riod (1250–73) during which there was no accepted German king or Holy Roman emperor. Rudolf laid the foundations of the Hapsburg dominions by obtaining in 1278 Austria, Styria, and Carniola from Bohemia. Although he was conciliatory toward the papacy, he was never crowned Holy Roman emperor by the pope.

Rudolf II (1552–1612), Holy Roman emperor (1576–1612), king of Bohemia (1575–1611), and of Hungary (1572–1608). He was the son and successor of Holy Roman Emperor Maximilian II. Opposed to the Protestant Reformation, his attempt to force Catholicism on Hungary led to a revolt (1604) that his brother Matthias ended. Matthias soon forced Rudolf to cede rule of Hungary, Austria, Moravia (1608), and Bohemia (1611) to him.

Rudolf, Lake, lake in NW Kenya, in Great Rift Valley; N part is between Ethiopia and SE Sudan; serves as focus for interior drainage; has no outlet; is becoming increasingly saline. Area: approx. 2,500sq mi (6,475sq km).

Rue, evergreen plants or shrubs native to warm regions of S Europe and SW Asia. They have aromatic leaves used in medicine or as flavoring. Family Rutaceae; genus *Ruta.*

Rugby, game, also called rugby football, played with a ball by 2 teams of 15 persons each on a field. The field cannot exceed 110 yards (100m) in length or 75 yards (68m) in width. At each end of the 110-yard field is a 25-yard (22.9m) deep in-goal area and a goal post (about the size used in football). The ball is similar to the one used in football, except that it is rounder and larger. A game is divided into two 40-minute periods and may end in a tie. No substitutions are allowed. In the case of a serious injury, the team must play short-handed.

In 15-man rugby (eight forwards, seven backs), the scoring consists of grounding the ball over the opponent's goal line (a try, worth four points), a conversion (kicking the ball between the goal posts) after the try, worth two points; and a penalty goal, dropped goal, and goal from a fair catch, worth three points each. The ball may be kicked, carried, or passed (sideward and to the rear). Tackling is allowed, but not blocking. Professional rugby uses 13-man teams and two substitutes. A try is worth three points, a conversion after the try two points, penalty goals two points, and a dropped goal one point.

History. The sport originated in England in 1823 on the playing fields of Rugby School. Amateur play was organized in 1871 when the English Rugby Union was formed to standardize the game. Professional play was begun in 1895 and now includes unions (leagues) in England, Wales, Scotland, and Ireland. The sport is also popular in France, New Zealand, Australia, and South Africa. In the United States, the game is played by clubs and colleges.

Rugs and Carpets, Oriental, floor coverings of felt, tapestry, a shuttle-woven material, or most frequently a pile fabric, produced by hand and originating in the Indo-European area centering around Persia (Iran). Carpets are named for the town or tribe from which they originate. One of the principal centers for rug weaving is Persia, known for the great court carpets of the 16th century. Some Persian centers are Kerman, Shiraz, Hamadan, Kashan, and Tabriz. Turkey and Asia Minor are also rug-weaving centers, known for carpets of broad spacious designs, rich in harmonious colors, with simpler patterns than the Persians. The Caucasus, another center, is known for simple designs with a coarse weave, eg., Shirvan, Kazak, and the dragon carpets of Kuba. Turcoman carpets are made by

nomadic tribes and have dark red coloring and geometric octagon designs in rows and columns. Oriental rugs are also made in Afghanistan, India, Chinese Turkestan, and Tibet.

Ruhr, river in West Germany; rises in hills of N central West Germany and flows NW and W to join Rhine River at Duisburg; the Ruhr valley, an industrial mining district, contains large coal deposits. Area along river was occupied by French and Belgian troops 1923–25 because of Germany's default on reparations; strategically important in WWII. Length: 146mi (234km).

Rumelia, name used by the Turks for possessions in the Balkans, including parts of Salonika, Kosovo, Janina, Scutari, and Bosnia-Herzegovina, the ancient provinces of Thrace and Macedonia. During the darkest period of its history (1396–1878), the province was ruled from Sophia under a feudal system of agricultural taxation. Boys between 10 and 12 years of age were abducted as ''janissaries'' for the Turkish Army. After the first Russo-Turkish War in 1877, the Congress of Berlin proclaimed Eastern Rumelia an autonomous province of the Turkish Empire. Eastern Rumelia revolted against Turkey in 1885 and was reunited with Bulgaria despite Russian protests.

Rumford, Benjamin Thomson, Count (1753–1814), American-British scientist and administrator, b. Woburn, Mass. A loyalist, he moved to England during the American Revolution. He later went into service of the elector of Bavaria as an administrator, for which in 1791 he was made a count of the Holy Roman Empire. In science, he devised a photometer and a calorimeter; improved home cooking and heating apparatuses; and helped to demolish the phlogiston theory by showing that heat is a form of motion. He measured the equivalence of mechanical energy and heat. In 1799 he returned to England and founded the Royal Institution.

Ruminant, cud-chewing, even-toed, hooved mammals, including camels, chevrotain, deer, giraffes, antelope, cattle, sheep, and goats. All have four-chambered stomachs except camel and chevrotain.

Rummy, two-to-six-player card game with a standard deck. In the three-or-four hand game, several cards are dealt to each player, and one card is turned up on the table. Players, in order, then either select the most recent discarded card or select a new card from the deck. The first person to meld—set his cards on the table—wins. A player may meld 7 cards of the same suit in sequence, three or four cards in a sequence, or three or four of the same rank. The cards usually rank from king down to ace. One of the popular variations is knock rummy, where a player, except for sequences of three or four cards of the same rank, must total fewer points in his hand than any other player in the game. Aces count one point, picture cards are 10, and all others their face value. *See also* Gin Rummy.

Runcie, Robert Alexander Kennedy (1921–), archbishop of Canterbury who succeeded Donald Coggan in 1980. He was ordained in 1951 and was co-chairman of the Anglican-Orthodox Joint Doctrinal Commission for six years. He was appointed bishop of St. Albans in 1970. A man with a warm, outgoing personality, he showed interest in improving the accessibility of the Anglican communion and in making the Anglican image and position more clearly defined. He signed a pledge to move toward unity with the Roman Catholic church during Pope John Paul II's historic trip to Britain in 1982.

Runnymede, meadow in S England, on S bank of Thames River at Egham, Surrey, W of London. It was either here or on a nearby island in the Thames that King John granted the Magna Carta in 1215. The meadow was given to the British nation in 1929. Today it also has a memorial to President John F. Kennedy.

Rupert (1352–1410), German king. Elector palatine (1398), he succeeded Emperor Wenceslaus as king of Germany (1400). Rupert was defeated in Italy while attempting to recover Milan and receive the imperial crown (1401–02). His title was recognized by Pope Boniface IX (1403). Rupert supported the Roman popes during the Great Schism, but was constantly at war within his domain.

Rurik (died 879), semi-legendary leader of the Varangians who ruled as prince of Novgorod after 862, from which the beginning of the Russian state is dated. His successor Oleg founded the Kievan state.

Rush, Benjamin (1745?–1813), US physician, reformer, and signer of the Declaration of Independence, b. Byberry, Pa. He practiced medicine in Philadelphia and was professor of chemistry at the College of Philadelphia (1769–89). In 1789 he became professor of medicine in the University of Pennsylvania, a post he held until his death. As a member of the Continental Congress (1776–77), he signed the Declaration of Independence. An avid reformer, Rush established the first US free medical dispensary (1786), worked for the abolition of slavery and capital punishment, and advocated a modern prison system and education for women. He was the author of *Medical Inquiries and Observations upon the Diseases of the Mind* (1812), the first American treatise on mental illness. He was treasurer of the US Mint (1797–1813).

Rush, tufted, perennial bog plant found in temperate regions. It has long, narrow leaves and small flowers crowded into dense clusters. Among 350 species is *Juncus conglomeratus* of Europe and N Africa. It has dense, brown flowers and ridged stems; height: 1–5ft (30–152cm). *Juncus effusus*, or soft rush, has smooth stems. Family Juncaceae.

Ruskin, John (1819–1900), English art and social critic. His strict religious upbringing combined with appreciation of European painting and architecture imbued his art criticism with ethical and social concerns. He revolutionized art criticism with *Modern Painters* (5 vols., 1843–60), which, most significantly, defended the paintings of J.M.W. Turner. *The Seven Lamps of Architecture* (1849) and *The Stones of Venice* (3 vols., 1851–53) are important studies of architecture. *Sesame and Lilies* (1865) discussed the role of women in society, and *Unto This Last* (4 essays, 1860–62) attacked laissez-faire economics and Victorian business ethics.

Russell, English noble family. The Russells first became prominent among the nobility in the 16th century. **John Russell** (1486?–1555), lord keeper of the privy seal to Henry VIII and Edward VI, was made 1st earl of Bedford in 1550. His successors were influential in government, and in 1694 the fourth earl was created first duke of Bedford. The family seat is at Woburn, Bedfordshire. The two most notable members of the family, both outside the main line of succession, were **Lord John Russell** (1792–1878), later 1st earl Russell, who played an important part in 19th-century parliamentary reform, and the philosopher **Lord Bertrand Russell** (1872–1970). *See also* Russell, Bertrand; Russell, John.

Russell, Bertrand Arthur William (1872–1970), British philosopher and mathematician. He wrote numerous books on various topics including mathematical logic, the theory of knowledge, and social issues. His philosophy was of logical contructionism, which he first applied to mathematics. He demonstrated that mathematics could be explained by the rules of formal logic. Later he applied this technique to other concepts. His most famous work, *Principia Mathematica* (3 vols., 1910–13), was written in collaboration with his teacher, Alfred North Whitehead. A pacifist except during World War II, Russell organized demonstrations against nuclear weapons and the Vietnam War. He was imprisoned twice for his activities on behalf of peace and nuclear disarmament. He won the Nobel Prize in literature (1950). *See also* Principia Mathematica.

Russell, John Russell, 1st Earl (1792–1878), English statesman. He was the son of the 6th duke of Bedford and made an important contribution to the development of British politics in the 19th century. A Whig, he was associated with the major reform issues of the day, such as Roman Catholic emancipation (1829), parliamentary and municipal reform (1832), and the repeal of the Corn Laws (1846). He led the Whigs in opposition to Sir Robert Peel and was prime minister during 1846–52 and 1865–66. He became an earl in 1861.

Russia. *See* Union of Soviet Socialist Republics.

Russian, the official language of the Soviet Union, the mother tongue of about 150,000,000 people there, or about 60% of the population, and spoken as a second language by about 40,000,000 more. It is the most important of the Slavic languages, which form a subdivision of the Indo-European family. Russian is written in the Cyrillic alphabet, a combination of Latin, Greek, and other characters that was developed in the ninth century.

Russian Architecture, architectural style that began as a regional variety of Byzantine architecture in the 10th century with the Christianization of Russia. Important centers of architectural activity developed at Kiev, Novgorod, and Pskov. Early churches were built of wood, but beginning with the construction of the Cathedral of Sancta Sophia, Kiev (1018–37), stone was used. Early churches also used the characteristic Byzantine design of the inscribed cross and five domes, but in later structures domes, apses, and aisles proliferated. The distinctive onion-shaped dome was introduced in the 12th century at the Cathedral of Sancta Sophia, Novgorod. Although the Byzantine influence remained strong, during the 15th century Russia was subject to a series of western European trends. During the reign of Ivan the Great (1462–1505), Italian architects built the Kremlin in a Renaissance style. Peter the Great and, later, Catherine brought Rococo and Neoclassical principles to the building of St Petersburg. In the 19th century a revival of medieval Russian architecture occurred.

Russian Blue Cat, or American Blue, short-haired domestic cat breed. Of unknown origin, this quiet, fine-boned cat has a longish face, almond-shaped, emerald green eyes, and large, pointed ears. The coat is medium to dark blue with silver.

Russian Revolution (1917), the overthrow of the Russian monarchy and Bolshevik seizure of power. Misconduct of the war, loss of confidence in the regime, and riots in the capital forced Nicholas II to abdicate in March (February Old Style) 1917. A Provisional Government was formed by liberals in the Duma (legislative assembly), but had to contend with the growing influence of the soviets (workers' and soldiers' councils). The new government was characterized by vacillation, postponing crucial issues until the constituent assembly met. The decision to continue the war and failure to introduce land reform caused popular support to shift to the Supreme Soviet. In July the Bolsheviks tried to seize control, but lacked the support of the Soviet. V.I. Lenin, who had arrived in April, had to flee to Finland. In September the socialist Prime Minister Kerensky summoned troops under General Kornilov to Petrograd to suppress opposition, but changed his mind and called for its defense. After the "Kornilov Affair" the Bolsheviks gained a majority in urban soviets, and in October Lenin returned in disguise. On November 7 (October 25) Bolshevik troops stormed the Winter Palace and captured the government. In January 1918 they disbanded the constituent assembly, and in July executed the royal family.

Russian Soviet Federated Socialist Republic (Rossijskaja Sovetskaja Federativnaja), largest constituent republic of the USSR, commonly abbreviated RSFSR, bordered by seas of the Arctic Ocean (N); seas of the Pacific (E); China, Mongolia, and Kazakh (S); Azerbaijan and Georgia (SW); and Ukraine, Belorussia, Baltic republics, and Finland (W). The main cities are Moscow (capital), Leningrad, Gorky, Novosibirsk, Kuibyshev, Sverdlovsk. Republic contains the E European lowland, the Urals, W Siberian Plain, Central Siberian Plateau drained by the Volga, Ob, Jenisej, Lena, and Amur rivers. It was a major portion of the tsarist empire and the first part to come under Soviet control (1917); joined Ukrainian and Belorussian republics and Transcaucasian federated republic to form the USSR 1922. Industries: machinery, chemicals, textiles, leather goods, fish, lumber products, wheat, flax, sugar beet, livestock, coal, iron ore, copper, nickel, lead, manganese, zinc, platinum, oil. Area: 6,592,812sq mi (17,075,383sq km). Pop. 136,546,000.

Russo-Japanese War (1904–05), military conflict between Russia and Japan. Rivalry over Manchuria and Korea caused Japan to break off relations with Russia in February 1904. Declarations of war followed a few days later. In May, Japan crossed the Yalu River from Korea into Manchuria, while its naval forces seized Dairen and besieged Port Arthur, which fell in January 1905. In March 1905 the Japanese captured Mukden, and on May 27 the Japanese annihilated Russia's Baltic fleet, its last hope, at Tsushima. Following US Pres. Theodore Roosevelt's initiative, both parties signed the Treaty of Portsmouth (N.H.) on Sept. 15, 1905. Having proved itself equal to Western forces, Japan required Russia to recognize Japan's "paramount interest" in Korea, recognize Chinese sovereignty in Manchuria, and cede the Kwantung Peninsula and the South Manchurian Railway as far north as Changchow to Japan. Although Japan received no indemnity, it was also given the southern half of Sakhalin by the Russians under the treaty. The Russian defeat was a primary cause of the Russian Revolution of 1905 and established Japan as a world power.

Rust, in botany, any of many fungal plant diseases characterized by "rusty" reddish-brown or orange blisters and streaks on affected leaves and stems. Rusts stunt plant growth and often kill infected plants. Rust fungi, also called rusts, are particularly serious pests of wheat.

Rutabaga, or **Swede turnip,** garden vegetable best grown in cool weather. It has large lobed leaves and yellow flowers. The globular, edible root is purplish with yellow flesh. Family Cruciferae; species *Brassica napobrassica*.

Ruth, biblical book that recounts the story of Ruth, a Moabite woman and mother of Obed, father of Jesse who sired David. A hagiographical book, its main purpose is to give an account of David's ancestors, following Ruth through her marriage to Naomi's son, Mahlon; his death; her decision to stay with Naomi; her marriage to Naomi's husband, Boaz; and Obed's birth.

Ruth, Babe (1895–1948), US baseball player, b. George Herman Ruth in Baltimore. The all-time home run hitter (714) until surpassed by Hank Aaron in 1974, he played for three teams: Boston Red Sox (1914–19), New York Yankees (1920–34), and Boston Braves (1935). He began his career as a pitcher and established a World Series record of 29 2/3 consecutive scoreless innings that lasted until 1961. In 1936, he was elected to the Baseball Hall of Fame.

Ruthenia, now constitutes Transcarpathian oblast, Ukrainian SSR, USSR; capital is Uzhgorod; formerly an autonomous region, the name is Latin word for Russia. During Middle Ages it referred to the Ukraine. After 1918 the term applied only to the easternmost province of Czechoslovakia. Present day Transcarpathian oblast is made up of land ceded to USSR by Czechoslovakia in 1945. Economy is largely agricultural; much of area is heavily forested. Industries: mining, lumbering, furniture, cartons, wood chemicals. Area: 4,981sq mi (12,901sq km). Pop. 1,057,000.

Ruthenium, metallic element (symbol Ru) of the second transition series, first isolated in 1844. It is found associated with platinum. Ruthenium is alloyed with other platinum metals for electrical contacts and is also used as a catalyst. Properties: at. no. 44; at. wt.101.07; sp gr 12.41; melt. pt. 4190°F (2310°C); boil. pt. 7,052°F (3,900°C); most common isotope Ru^{102} (31.61%). *See also* Transition Elements.

Rutherford, Ernest, 1st Baron (1871–1937), English physicist, b. New Zealand. Leaving New Zealand in 1895, he went to Cambridge to work with J.J. Thomson. After a period at McGill University he returned to Manchester and then to Cambridge, where he succeeded Thomson at the Cavendish Laboratory. His work was the study of radioactivity and atomic structure. He discovered alpha, beta, and gamma radiation, correctly identifying each. He was the first to show that the atom had a nucleus and he carried out the first nuclear reactions. He also identified and named the proton. In 1908 he was awarded a Nobel Prize and in 1931 was created a baron. Although his work led to release of atomic energy, he never believed that the nucleus would provide a source of usable energy.

Rutherfordium. *See* Element 104.

Rutile, an oxide mineral, titanium dioxide (TiO_2). Found in igneous and metamorphic rocks and quartz veins. Tetragonal system long prismatic and needle-like crystals; also granular masses. Black to red-brown; metallic luster; brittle. Hardness 6–6.5; sp gr 4.2. Used as a gemstone.

Rutledge, John (1739–1800), US political figure and chief justice of the US Supreme Court (1795), b. Charleston, S.C. He was a delegate to the Stamp Act Congress (1765) and two Continental Congresses (1774–76, 1782–83). He was a member of the committee to draft a state constitution (1776) and both president (1776–78) and governor (1779–82) of South Carolina. He played a key role at the federal Constitutional Convention (1787). He was an associate justice on the US Supreme Court (1778–91) and resigned to become chief justice of the South Carolina supreme court (1791–95). He was nominated to be chief justice (1795) but the Senate refused to confirm the appoint-

Babe Ruth

Rwanda

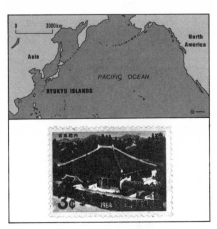

Ryukyu Islands

ment because of his adamant criticism of Jay's Treaty.

Rutledge, Wiley Blount, Jr. (1894–1949), US jurist and lawyer, b. Cloverport, Ky. A law professor at Washington University (1926–31) and dean of its law school (1931–35), he was also dean of the University of Iowa law school (1935–39). A US Appeals Court judge (1939–43) and a staunch liberal, he was appointed, by Franklin Delano Roosevelt, associate justice of the US Supreme Court, serving 1943–49. He was noted for his dissents favoring civil liberties, and cast the deciding votes in important cases such as *West Virginia State Board of Education* v. *Barnette* (1942).

Ruwenzori, mountains in central Africa, on the Uganda-Zaire border between lakes Albert and Edward; discovered 1889 by Henry Stanley. Range includes snowcapped peaks; highest is Mt Margherita, 16,763ft (5,113m). Length of range: 75mi (121km); width: 40mi (64km).

Ruysdael. *See* Ruisdael.

Rwanda, republic in E central Africa, bordered by Uganda (N), Tanzania (E), Burundi (S), and Zaïre (W). It is one of the most densely populated countries in Africa. The land is mountainous, rugged, with plateaus and deep valleys. The volcanic Virunga Mts (NW) separate the Congo Basin from the Nile Basin; a savanna zone (E) ranges from arid flat lands to low scrublands and bamboo forests; Lake Kivu, country's largest lake, comprises part of the Rwanda-Zaïre border. The great abundance of cattle overgrazing grasses growing on the thin soil has sped up the erosion process, limiting present and future cultivation for the land. Most of the farming is done on a subsistence level. The major crops include: (subsistence) bananas, beans, peas, sweet potatoes; (cash) coffee, tea, pyrethrum, rice, cotton. Rwanda has put approx. 30,000 families on paysannats (farming communities), to expand the tea crop and ease the economic importance of coffee. With no railroad, and inadequate roads, the social and economic development has been hampered greatly. Industries include textiles, chemicals, tourism, and food processing.

There are 3 major ethnic groups in Rwanda. The Tutsi or Watutsi make up approx. 4% of the population; they are characteristically tall, and have played the role of dominant caste in Rwanda history. The Hutu or Bahutu account for 85% of the population and are mostly farmers, formerly employed by Tutsi landowners. The pygmoid Twa or Batwa are hunters and potters, and make up approx. 1% of total population.

History. The area of Rwanda was first inhabited by the Twa, later the Hutu; the Tutsi were last to come to Rwanda. In the late 19th century Rwanda became part of German East Africa; after WWI administered by Belgium as League of Nations mandate of Rwanda-Urundi, and later a United Nations trust territory. The Belgians governed Rwanda through the Tutsi established supremacy. After two Hutu rebellions, 1928 and 1959, Belgium supported the Hutu provisional government (1960), and in 1962, Rwanda became independent with a presidential democracy. In 1972 strife between Rwanda's ethnic groups resulted in a military coup. In 1978 a new constitution was promulgated, and elections were held for a return to democratic government, but the head of the military junta remained in office as president. In 1982, Rwanda's first elected Parliament was established. Rwanda is a member of the United Nations and the Organization of African Unity.

PROFILE

Official name: Republic of Rwanda
Area: 10,169sq mi (26,338sq km)
Population: 5,100,000
Chief cities: Kigali (capital); Butare; Nyanza
Religion: Christianity; tribal
Language: Kinyarwanda, French (both official)
Monetary unit: Rwanda franc

Ryazan (R'azan), city in Ryazan oblast, W central USSR, 120mi (193km) SE of Moscow on Oka River; annexed by Moscow 1521 and held until it became a city 1778; site of Archangel Cathedral (begun late 15th century), Assumption Cathedral (1693–99), and a kremlin wall (1208). Industries: agricultural machinery, radios, machine tools, oil refining. Pop. 452,000.

Rybinsk, formerly Shcherbakov; city in Russian SFSR, USSR, on the Volga River at its efflux from the Rybinsk Reservoir. First mentioned in 1504, it was chartered 1777. It became an important trading and transshipment center after 1703 founding of St Petersburg and construction of Volga-Neva canal systems; site of mid-19th-century cathedral and regional museum. Industries: shipyards, agriculture, matches, machinery, linen, aircraft motors, fish canneries, flour, lumber. Pop. 239,000.

Rye, hardy cereal grass originating in SW Asia and naturalized worldwide. It grows where many other cereals cannot. It has flower spikelets that develop one-seeded grains. It is used for bread flour, animal feed and pasture, and in alcoholic beverages. Height: to 6ft (1.8m). Family Gramineae; species *Secale cereale.*

Ryukyu Islands (Nansei-shoto), Japanese archipelago in W Pacific Ocean, extends approx. 600mi (966km) between Kyushu and Formosa; separates the East China Sea (W) from the Pacific Ocean (E). Island groups include Amami, Okinawa, and Sakishima. Volcanic and coral formations, they have been inhabited since early times; invaded by China 7th century, and by Satsuma of Japan in 17th century; tribute of both countries until relinquished by China to Japan in 1879. After WWII they were administered by the United States; restored to Japan 1971. Agriculture and fishing are chief occupations. Area: approx. 850sq. mi (2,202sq km). Pop. 1,235,000.

S

Saadiah, Ben Joseph (892–942), a prolific writer and Jewish scholar, b. Egypt. He became well known for his involvement in the controversy with Aaron ben Neir in Babylonia over the Jewish calendar. At this time, he produced many works against heretical thought. He also translated the Old Testament into Arabic. The academy of Sura (Baghdad) was under his leadership (928–35).

Saarbrücken, city in W West Germany, on Saar River, 39mi (62km) SE of Trier; capital of Saarland; seat of counts of Nassau-Saarbrücken 1381–1793; annexed to France 1793–1815, to Prussia 1815; capital of Saar Territory 1919–35, 1945–57; returned to Germany 1935; scene of heavy fighting during WWII; seat of university (1948). Notable buildings include Gothic

Castle Church (15th century), city hall (1750), the Ludwigskirche, a baroque church, (1762–75). Industries: coal mining, iron, steel, precision instruments, machinery, printing, beer, cement, sugar. Founded 999; chartered 1321. Pop. 204,300.

Saarland, formerly Saar or Saar Territory; state in SW West Germany; capital is Saarbrücken. Annexed to France 1797; divided between Bavaria and Prussia by Treaty of Paris (1815); made autonomous territory by Treaty of Versailles (1919); restored to Germany by plebiscite 1935; after WWII autonomous under French economic protection; became a German state 1957. Industries: coal and coke mining, iron, steel, glass, chemicals, textiles. Area: 991sq mi (2,567sq km). Pop. 1,096,300.

Sabbath, the seventh day (Saturday), observed as a day of rest by Jews. It is observed to mark God's day of rest after the creation. The Sabbath has become the principal day of worship and work is not permissible. In Christian churches this day of worship and rest was changed to the first day (Sunday) in observance of the Resurrection.

Saber Tooth, extinct cat having long upper canines, for stabbing and slicing thick-skinned prey, often Mastodons. They were worldwide in distribution from Oligocene to Pleistocene epochs. *Smilodon,* last of the North American saber tooths, had 9-inch (23-cm) sabers. Height: 40in (102cm). *See also* Felidae.

Sabin, Albert Bruce (1906–   ), US virologist, b. Bialystock, Russia. Sabin developed a live virus oral vaccine against poliomyelitis, in contrast to Jonas Salk's inactivated virus vaccine, and began testing Sabin vaccine in 1957. In 1980, he worked to make vaccine available in order to eradicate polio in Brazil.

Sabine River, river in Texas and Louisiana; rises at confluence of many headstreams, NE Texas; flows SE to form Texas-Louisiana border, empties through Sabine Lake and Sabine Pass into the Gulf of Mexico. Length: approx. 360mi (577km).

Sabines, or **Sabini,** people of ancient central Italy inhabiting the Sabine Hills NE of Rome. They were intensely religious and politically diffuse. The legend of Romulus' rape of the Sabine women may have been recounted to explain the Sabine part of the early Roman population. After sporadic fighting they were gradually Romanized while the Romans adopted a number of their customs, including burial rituals.

Sable, marten native of forested areas of N Europe and Siberia. It has been hunted almost to extinction for its thick, soft, durable fur that is dark brown to black, sometimes flecked with white. Now protected in N USSR, they have long bushy tails. Length: 1–2ft (30–60cm). Family Mustelidae; species *Mustela zibellina.*

Sable Antelope, large, heavy antelope native to Africa, south of the Sahara. Both sexes have long, stout horns, curving backward, that are used for defense. Color is brown to black or roan gray. Height: to 6.5ft (165cm) at shoulder; weight: to 616lb (280kg). Family Bovidae; genus *Hippotragus.*

Sacagawea (1787?–?1812), American Indian interpreter for the Lewis and Clark Expedition (1804–06), b. Idaho. She was born a Shoshone but was captured and sold as a slave to French trapper Toussaint Charbonneau, who later married her. They joined Lewis and Clark, and she became their guide taking them to the Pacific Ocean, befriending the Indians they met on the way. Monuments to her are found in Oregon, Montana, Idaho, and North Dakota.

Saccharide, organic compound based on sugar molecules. Monosaccharides include glucose and fructose, found in fruit and honey. Two sugar molecules join together to make a disaccharide, such as cane sugar. Polysaccharides have more than two sugar molecules. *See also* Carbohydrate.

Saccharin. *See* Sweetener, Artificial.

Sacco and Vanzetti Case, controversial robbery-murder trial taken up as a cause by intellectuals, radicals and liberals in the 1920s. At the height of the Red Scare (April 1920), two men robbed and killed a paymaster and his guard in South Braintree, Mass. Italian immigrant anarchists Nicola Sacco and Bartolomeo Vanzetti were convicted and executed for the crime. Their supporters claimed the verdict was a reflection of anti-Italian, anti-radical bigotry. There is continued belief in Vanzetti's innocence, although a 1961 ballistics test suggested the fatal bullet came from Sacco's gun.

Sachs, Nelly (1891–1970), German-Jewish poet. Having escaped from Nazi Germany, her early stories and later poetic works, including *In the Houses of Death* (1946) and *Later Poems* (1965), bore witness to the sufferings of her people. Her later works included *O the Chimneys: Selected Poems* (1967) and *Seeker and Other Poems* (1970). She shared the Nobel Prize for literature in 1966 with S.Y. Agnon.

Sackville-West, Victoria Mary (1892–1962), English poet and novelist. Wife of Harold Nicolson and with him a member of the Bloomsbury Group. Her best-known novels are *The Edwardians* (1930) and *All Passion Spent* (1931). Her interest in her ancestors and in her family home at Knole dominated her work. *See also* Bloomsbury Group.

Sacral Bone. *See* Sacrum.

Sacramento, capital city and port in central California, 72mi (116km) NE of San Francisco; seat of Sacramento co. Originally a Mexican land grant to John A. Sutter, the city grew around site of fort built 1840, and was called New Helvetia; it experienced a population and prosperity boom after discovery of gold near Sutter's mill (1848); made state capital 1854, W terminus of Pony Express 1860, and W terminus of first transcontinental railroad 1863. It is site of Sacramento City College (1916), California State at Sacramento (1947), American River College (1955), Sutter's Fort; nearby are Mather and McClellan Air Force bases. Industries: food processing, jet fuels, soap, machinery, bricks. Settled 1839; inc. 1850 as town, 1863 as city. Pop. (1980) 275,741.

Sacramento Mountains, range in S New Mexico and W Texas between Pecos and Rio Grande rivers; site of Lincoln National Forest and Mescalero Indian Reservation. Highest peak, Sierra Blanca, 12,003ft (3,661m).

Sacramento River, longest river in California; rises NW near Mt Shasta; flows SW to Suisan Bay, arm of San Francisco Bay, where it joins San Joaquin River at a large delta. Waters have been inc. into Central Valley Project for irrigation of the San Joaquin Valley; navigable by small steamers for approx. 260mi (419km) of its 320mi (515km).

Sacrifice, offering or destruction of precious objects, food and drink, flowers and incense, animals and humans for religious purposes. Sacrifices are important in many religions. They are made in the hope of winning divine favor, atoning for guilt, or for some other mystical purpose.

Sacroiliac Suture, immovable joint, or seam, that joins the sacrum and the ilium part of the hip bone to form the pelvis. *See also* Pelvis; Sacrum.

Sacrum, or sacral bone, region of the vertebral column, formed by the fusion of five vertebrae. The sacrum and the two hipbones form the pelvic girdle for the attachment of the legs to the body.

Sadat, Anwar al- (1918–81), Egyptian political leader. He succeeded Gamal Abdel Nasser as president of Egypt (1970). In 1973 he led Egypt into war against Israel, demanding the return of Egyptian land occupied by Israel after the Arab-Israeli war of 1967. Sadat later demonstrated his willingness to consider a negotiated peace settlement by his support of the 1974 troop disengagement accord. In 1977, he made a historic peace mission visit to Israel and, in 1978, worked out peace terms with Israeli premier Menachem Begin at Camp David, Maryland. Sadat and Begin shared the 1978 Nobel Peace Prize for efforts to end the 30-year Arab-Israeli conflict. In 1981, Sadat was assassinated, apparently by Egyptian Muslim fundamentalists opposed to his policies towards Israel.

Sadducees, a sect of Judaism, developed around 200 BC. The members were wealthy priests and aristocrats. They stressed a literal interpretation of written law, and rejected oral law. They were often in opposition to the Pharisees. Sadducees were based on the temple cult with the priest as central. They rejected the soul's immortality and the existence of angels. The sect disappeared with the destruction of the Temple, AD 70.

Sade, Marquis de (1740–1814), popular name of Donatien Alphonse François, Comte de Sade; French novelist. He spent over 30 years in prison for sexual offenses and produced several works dealing with sexual pathology, including *Justine* (1791) and *Aline et Valcour* (1795). He was eventually committed to the insane asylum at Charenton. The brilliance of his work has only recently been acknowledged. *See also* Sadism.

Sadism, taking pleasure in hurting or abusing others physically or psychologically. Sadism is frequently connected with deviant sexual behavior in which beating or abuse of the other is a necessary part of sexual arousal or gratification. The sadist often takes pleasure in dominating others or in watching them suffer. As a characteristic it may be linked with *masochism* and a person may alternate between these two forms of aggression. The term is derived from the Marquis de Sade, whose writing included examples of cruelty and sexual abuse.

Safad (Zefat), town in N Israel, 7mi (11km) NNW of the Sea of Galilee; fortified by invading Crusaders (11th century) who devastated Jewish community; by 16th century the Jewish population was reinstated, and Safad grew to be a center of Jewish learning and mysticism, and one of Palestine's four holy cities; scene of conflict between the Arabs and the Israelis during 1948 war of independence; popular health and tourist resort. Pop. 13,100.

Safflower, annual plant with large, orange flower heads that yield a dyestuff. The seeds yield an oil low in saturated fats that is used in cooking, paints, and cosmetics. Family Compositae; species *Carthamus tinctorius.*

Saffron, bulbous perennial crocus native to Asia Minor and cultivated in Europe. It has purple or white flower blooms in autumn. Family Iridaceae; species *Crocus sativus.* Or, the golden, dried stigmas of this plant used as flavoring or dye. Or, the color this dye produces.

Saga, prose tale usually written in Old Norse or Gaelic between the 7th and 14th centuries. Old Norse sagas were generally written in Iceland by anonymous Norwegian expatriates during the 12th and 13th centuries and fall into several types. The "fornaldar sagas," the oldest form, deal with heroic, often mythological figures from Scandinavian and Germanic traditions. The best known of these is *Ragnar Lothbok.* "Family sagas" trace the genealogy of Icelandic families, and "Kings' sagas" (after *c.*1220) are histories similar to Latin chronicles, eg, Snorri Sturluson's *Heimskringla.* Some 13th-century sagas are translations of French romances.

Irish sagas, written in Gaelic, derive from an oral tradition going back to the 6th century or earlier. The oldest extant manuscript is the *Wurzburg Codex* (*c.* 700). They are perhaps the most pagan of any form of Medieval literature and are characterized by a hero of both human and divine descent, the intervention of supernatural and magic forces in men's affairs, taboos, and personal quarrels between brothers or near kinsmen. These sagas provided many of the story lines for Arthurian romances in other languages, although the characters and social milieu are different. *See also* Arthurian Romance; Fenian Cycle.

Sagan, Françoise (1935–), pseud. of Françoise Quoirez, French novelist and playwright. Her works portray the tragic disillusionment of the young and innocent, as in *Bonjour Tristesse* (1954). This theme was developed in *A Certain Smile* (1956) and *Those Without Shadows* (1957). Later works included *Chamade* (1970), *The Heart Keeper* (1974), *Lost Profile* (1976), and *Silken Eyes* (1977).

Sage, common name for a number of plants of the mint family, principally *Salvia officinalis,* an aromatic perennial herb used for seasoning. Scarlet sage, common name for *Salvia splendens,* is grown for its showy flowers. Blue sage *(S. pitchere)* is a perennial native to the prairies of central United States.

Sagebrush, aromatic shrubs common in arid areas of W North America. The big sagebrush, *Artemisia tridentata,* has small, silvery-green leaves and bears clusters of tiny white flower heads; height: to 12ft (3.6m). Family Compositae.

Sage Grouse, or sage hen, largest North American grouse. The male fans its long slender tail as background for its inflated orange neck air sacs while it bows, dances, and utters groaning sounds during courtship displays. The female builds the nest, incubates the eggs (7) and cares for the young. Length: to 30in (76cm). Species *Centrocercus urophasianus. See also* Grouse.

Saginaw, city in E Michigan, on Saginaw River, 80mi (129km) NW of Detroit; seat of Saginaw co. Industries: automobile parts, graphite, paper products, mobile homes. Settled 1816 as fur trading post; inc. as city 1857. Pop. (1980) 77,508.

Sagittarius, or the Archer, southern constellation situated on the ecliptic between Scorpius and Capricornus; the ninth sign of the zodiac. Rich in stellar clusters, this constellation also contains much interstellar matter obscuring the central region of the Milky Way Galaxy and is only penetrable with radio telescopes. Two interesting features of Sagittarius are the Lagoon and Trifid nebulae. Brightest star Epsilon Sagittarii (Kaus Australis). The astrological sign for the period Nov. 22–Dec. 21.

Sago Palm, or fern palm, a feather-leaved palm tree native to swampy areas of Malaya and Polynesia. Its thick trunk contains a starch used in foodstuffs. The sago palm flowers once after 15 years of age and then dies when the fruit ripens. Height 4–30ft (1.2–9.1m). Species include *Metroxylon sagus* and *M. rumphii.* Family Palmaceae. Some cycads are called sago palms, but they are not true palms.

Saguaro, large cactus native to Arizona, California, and Mexico. It has 5–6 branches. White, night-blooming flowers appear when the plant is 50–75 years old. Its edible fruit is red. Height: to 40ft (12m). Family Cactaceae; species *Carnegiea gigantea. See also* Cactus.

Sahara, desert in N Africa; extends from Atlantic Ocean to the Red Sea and from the Atlas Mts to the S Sudan region. It is the world's largest desert with an area of more than 3,500,000sq mi (9,065,000sq km). Terrain varies from rocky plateaus and gravel-covered plains (N) to low plateaus and broad plains (S); contains many oases. Region is rich in minerals, especially oil, natural gas, and iron ore.

Sahel, semi-arid region of Africa, bordered by Sahara (N), Senegal (W), savannas (S), and Ethiopia (E); extends through Mauritania, Mali, Upper Volta, Niger, N Nigeria, and Sudan. Normally a land of very little rainfall, a serious drought from late 1960s to mid-70s caused starvation of many.

Saiga, Eurasian antelope, found only in S Russia and central Asia. Sheeplike with "swollen" nose, ending in a piglike snout, it is brown in summer, white in winter. Males carry short, ridged, slightly curved horns. Length: to 5.5ft (1.7m); height: to 32in (81cm). Family Bovidae; species *Saiga.*

Sailboat, boat propelled by sails utilizing the power of the wind. Most important of all vessels until the late 19th century, when they were replaced by steam-driven craft, sailboats are now used for recreational purposes. Most are small and designed for coastal and inland waters. Timber hulls are decreasing in number, being supplanted by fiberglass, metal, and ferro-cement constructions. Catboats, sloops, and cutters are single-masted vessels; yawls and ketches are two-masted.

Sailfish, marine billfish found worldwide in tropical seas. A popular sport fish, it is identified by a large, saillike dorsal fin and sword-shaped upper jaw. Length: to 11ft (3.4m); weight: 221lb (99kg). Species include *Istiophorus platypterus* and the smaller Atlantic *I. Americanus.* Family Istiophoridae.

Sailing. *See* Yachting.

Saint, an individual who has manifested exceptional love of God and holiness in life. In some Christian writings all believers are called saints, but the title is usually reserved for men and women of the most outstanding merit, such as St Peter and other Apostles, St Augustine and other theologians, St Agnes and other martyrs. The Roman Catholic Church has a process by which additional saints can be named—Joan of Arc was canonized in 1920. Many shrines have been built to honor saints, and Catholics pray to saints to intercede with God for them. *See also* Beatification.

Anwar al-Sadat

St. Helena Island

St. Kitts-Nevis-Anguilla

Saint Bartholomew's Day Massacre, the slaying of French Protestants, called Huguenots, which began in Paris on Saint Bartholomew's Day, Aug. 24, 1572. Catherine de Médicis, mother of Charles IX, plotted to assassinate Admiral Gaspard de Coligny, a Huguenot who advocated war with Spain. When the assassination attempt failed and her involvement was about to be discovered, Catherine convinced Charles to order the death of Huguenot leaders, many of whom were in Paris for the wedding of Henry of Navarre (later Henry IV). The ensuing bloodbath—3,000 deaths in Paris alone—was justified by Charles' claim of a Huguenot plot against the crown. The massacre horrified Protestant countries and solidified Protestant opposition to the crown within France.

Saint Bernard, Swiss mountain and rescue dog (working group). A dog of excellent scenting abilities, it has a massive head with forehead wrinkles; short, deep muzzle; hanging lips; high-set, triangular, drop ears; broad, straight body; long, muscular legs; and long, heavy tail. The white and red dense coat may be short-haired (smooth with bushy tail) or long-haired (medium-long, slightly wavy). Average size: 25–29in (63–74cm) at shoulder; 140–170lb (63–76kg). First brought to Hospice of Great St Bernard Pass in 1660–70, this dog has worked with monks to find people lost in the snow. *See also* Working Dog.

Saint Bernard Passes, two alpine passes in Switzerland; link Valais, Switzerland with Valle d'Aosta, Italy; referred to as Great St Bernard and Little St Bernard passes. The passes were used as invasion routes by Gauls, Romans, Charlemagne, Emperor Henry IV, Frederick Barbarossa, and Napoleon I; site of two hospices, ruined temple of Jupiter, scientific institute, hotel, library, church, Great St Bernard Tunnel (opened 1964). Height: 8,098ft (2,470m).

Saint Catharines, city in S Ontario, Canada; seat of Lincoln co, on Welland Canal. Industries: shipbuilding and repair, automotive parts, food processing, fruit trade center. Inc. 1876. Pop. 123,351.

Saint Clair Shores, city in SE Michigan, on Lake St Clair, 13mi (21km) NE of Detroit; pleasure boating center. Inc. as village 1925, as city 1950. Pop. (1980) 76,210.

Saint Croix Island (Santa Cruz), largest of US Virgin Islands, in the West Indies; Christiansted, on NE coast, is chief town; agricultural and tourist center. Discovered 1493 by Christopher Columbus, it was taken at various times by Dutch, English, Spanish, and French; purchased by Denmark 18th century; sold to United States 1917. Industries: rum, sugar, livestock. Area: 84sq mi (218sq km). Pop. 51,570.

Saint Croix River, river on boundary of SE Maine and SW New Brunswick, Canada; rises in Chiputneticoo Lakes; flows SE to Passamaquoddy Bay; used for power and transporting logs downstream. St Croix Island in the river is site of a national monument commemorating the French settlement est. 1604 by Samuel de Champlain and colonist Pierre du Gua, Sieur de Monts. Length: 129mi (208km).

Saint-Denis, city in N France, 7mi (11km) NNE of Paris. City grew up around abbey (AD 626) built on site of St Denis' tomb (patron saint of France). It was rebuilt in 18th century. Much-copied basilica of St Denis (1136–47) is outstanding example of a Gothic cathedral; contains tombs of Louis XVI, Marie Antoinette, and other French rulers. Industries: metals, chemicals, glass, paper, soap. Pop. 96,759.

Saint Elmo's Fire, an electrical discharge illuminating the tops of tall objects, also called a corposant. It usually occurs during a storm when the atmosphere becomes charged strongly enough to create a discharge between the air and an object. Early sailors named this phenomenon after their patron saint.

Saint-Etienne, city in E central France, 32mi (51km) SW of Lyons on Furens River; capital of Loire dept. Textile and silk industries were est. here 11th century; in 16th century firearms were produced; in 1815 city had its first steel plant and in 1827 terminus of first French railroad was built here; site of arms museum, 17th-century Church of St Louis and Notre Dame. Industries: textiles, small arms, ammunition, alloy steels. Pop. 221,775.

Saint Francis River, river in SE Missouri and E Arkansas; rises in hills of SE Mo.; flows S to Mississippi River near Helena, Ark.; forms part of Missouri-Arkansas boundary. Wappapello Dam (1941) near Poplar Bluff, Mo. forms reservoir and recreation area. Navigable for 125mi (201km) of its 470mi (757km).

Saint-Gaudens, Augustus (1848–1907), US sculptor, b. Ireland. An influential neoclassical sculptor, he received numerous commissions for decorative and monumental sculptures, including Lincoln (Lincoln Park, Chicago) and General Sherman (New York City).

Saint George's (St George), port town on SW coast of Grenada, in the West Indies; capital of Grenada; beautiful harbor; site of St George's church, Fort George; was capital of former British colony of Windward Islands. Industries: rum and sugar processing. Exports: cacao, nutmeg, mace. Founded 1650 as French settlement. Pop. 6,657.

Saint-Germain, Treaty of (1919), World War I peace agreement between the Allies and the Republic of Austria. Signed in Saint-Germain-en-Laye, France, it was concerned with the status of Austria. It established boundaries for the new republic, which was reduced by the loss of a great deal of territory, and declared the Austro-Hungarian monarchy dissolved. It further stated that Austria refrain from entering into political or economic union with Germany, without agreement by the League of Nations, the covenant of which was included in the treaty.

Saint Helena, island in S Atlantic Ocean, 1,200mi (1,932km) W of Africa; capital is Jamestown. Discovered 1502 by Portuguese navigator João da Nova Castella, it was annexed by Dutch 1633; annexed by British East India Co. 1659 and made a British crown colony 1834; place of exile of Napoleon I in 1815; his home is maintained as a memorial. St Helena, Ascension Island, and Tristan da Cunha comprise the British dependency of St Helena. Industries: hemp, vegetables, sweet potatoes, livestock. Area: 47sq mi (122sq km). Pop. 5,147.

Saint John, Henry, Viscount Bolingbroke (1678–1751), English political figure and philosopher. He was an influential Tory during Queen Anne's reign, rising to prominence under the patronage of Robert Harley and Abigail Masham. He became Viscount Bolingbroke (1712) but sacrificed his career in an attempt to prevent the Hanoverian succession to the British throne. His secret negotiations with the Stuart pretender were discovered, and he fled the country (1714). He was pardoned for his contacts with the Stuarts in 1723. In his latter years he enjoyed a reputation as a political theorist. His *The Idea of the Patriot King* (1749), advocating benevolent despotism, influenced George III.

Saint John, port city in S New Brunswick, Canada, on N shore of Bay of Fundy, at mouth of St John River; seat of St John co; first Canadian city to be inc. (1785). Industries: shipping, shipbuilding and repair. Pop. 85,956.

Saint John River, river in NE United States and SE Canada; rises in NW Maine; flows NE into Canada, then SE to St John, New Brunswick, emptying into the Bay of Fundy; Reversing Falls, located at the river's mouth, are caused by the strong tides of the Bay of Fundy; used for lumber transportation and hydroelectricity. Discovered 1604. Length: 418mi (673km).

Saint John's, capital city and principal port of Newfoundland, Canada, on SE coast; site of Queens College, and Memorial University of Newfoundland. Industries: fishing and fish processing, shipping and shipbuilding, textiles, iron works. Colonized 1583 by British. Pop. 86,576.

Saint Johns River, river in E Florida; rises in E central Florida 28mi (45km) W of Melbourne; flows N to Jacksonville, turns E and enters Atlantic Ocean 28mi (45km) downstream. Lower section is part of Intracoastal Waterway; navigable for 170mi (274km) of its 285mi (459km).

Saint Joseph, city in NW Missouri, on Missouri River, 46mi (74km) NNW of Kansas City; seat of Buchanan co; served as E terminus of Pony Express (1860); site of Missouri Western College (1915), Pony Express Stables (now a museum), and house where Jesse James was killed; railroad center; livestock and grain market. Industries: electrical products, meat packing, flour milling, wire rope. Founded 1826; inc. 1851. Pop. (1980) 76,691.

Saint Joseph River, river in Michigan and Indiana; rises in S Michigan; flows S and W into Indiana, and turns NW to empty into Lake Michigan at St Joseph, Michigan. Length: 210mi (338km).

Saint Kitts-Nevis (Saint Christopher-Nevis), independent state of Leeward Islands, British West Indies; includes islands of St Kitts, Nevis, and Sombrero; Basseterre is capital, on St Kitts; chief town of Nevis is Charlestown; agricultural processing and tourism are important on both Nevis and St Kitts; islands are volcanic, mountainous, and scenic. Discovered 1493 by Christopher Columbus, the islands were settled 1623 by British (under Thomas Warner) at St Kitts, 1628 at Nevis, to be followed shortly after by French settlers. Anglo-French disputes over possession were settled in British favor 1783 by terms of the Treaty of Paris; the islands were part of colony of Leewards 1871–1956; belonged to the West Indies Federation 1958–62; became self-governing (associated with Great Britain) 1967 with Anguilla, which seceded from state 1971. Full independence for St.Kitts-Nevis was scheduled for the early 1980s. Nevis is site of thermal baths and birthplace of Alexander Hamilton. Tourism dominates the economy. Exports: cotton, yams, molasses, sugar, coconuts. Area: 118sq mi (306sq km). Pop. 40,434.

Saint Laurent, Louis Stephen (1882–1973), Canadian prime minister (1948–57). A bilingual lawyer, he was minister of justice and attorney general (1941–46). As prime minister he effected court reform and was a moving force in the formation of the North Atlantic Treaty Organization. He led the Liberal party after 1948, succeeding Mackenzie King.

Saint Lawrence, Gulf of, broad, deep, gulf in Atlantic Ocean between Newfoundland and the E coast of mainland Canada (coastal Quebec, NE coastal New

Brunswick, and Nova Scotia); joins NE Atlantic Ocean through Cabot Strait (SE) and Strait of Belle Isle (NE); door of the St Lawrence Seaway; contains many islands.

Saint Lawrence River, a principal river of North America, in SE Ontario and S Quebec provinces, Canada; flows from NE end of Lake Ontario, about 760mi (1,224km) to the Gulf of St Lawrence on SE Canadian shore. Length from W end of Lake Superior to the river mouth is over 2,000mi (3,220km), and has been entirely navigable since the completion of the St Lawrence Seaway (1959). River forms boundary between New York and Ontario for approx. 120mi (193km) (this section includes the Thousand Islands); supports extensive lumbering and many hydroelectric power stations.

Saint Lawrence Seaway, deep international waterway in Canada and United States, on the St Lawrence River between Montreal and Lake Ontario, Quebec and New York; connects Great Lakes with Atlantic Ocean. Authorized by Canada 1951, and by the United States 1954, it was planned to break the congestion caused by an outdated canal system along the rapids section of the St Lawrence River. Constructed 1955–59, the seaway has seven locks, and a large hydroelectric power project was built in the international rapids section between Ogdensburg, N.Y. and Cornwall, Ontario. The busiest period for this waterway system, which can now accommodate deep draft vessels, is May-October. The navigation and hydroelectric power project has spurred industrial and agricultural development. Length: 2,342mi (3,771km).

Saint-Louis, port city in Senegal, W Africa, on an island in the Senegal River; oldest French settlement in Africa; site of railroad junction, research institute, airport. Industries: meat processing, hides, exporting. Founded 1658 as trade base. Pop. 81,204.

Saint Louis, port city in E Missouri, on Mississippi River; largest city in Missouri. City site was chosen by Pierre LaClède, who est. post here 1764. By terms of secret treaty of Fontainbleau (1762) city was transferred to Spain (1770–1800) and made seat of Upper Louisiana government; it was returned briefly to France 1800; ceded to the United States in Louisiana Purchase 1803; became seat of government for District of Louisiana and capital of Territory of Missouri 1812–21; served as Union supply and hospital center during the Civil War. It was site of Louisiana Purchase Exposition (1904), first international aviation meet (1910), sponsorship of Charles A. Lindbergh's *Spirit of St Louis* transatlantic flight (1927). Landmarks include Jefferson National Expansion Memorial, a national historic site (est. 1935), Missouri Botanical Gardens (1858), Wainwright Building (1891), Busch Memorial Stadium (1966); professional sports teams include baseball's and football's Cardinals and ice hockey's Blues; site of Washington University (1853), St Louis University (1818), University of Missouri at St Louis (1960). Industries: automobiles, brewing, chemicals, aircraft, space capsules, food processing, iron, lead, zinc, copper, aluminum, magnesium. Inc. 1809 as town, 1822 as city. Pop. (1980) 453,085.

Saint Lucia, island nation in Windward Islands, British West Indies, between Atlantic Ocean (E) and Caribbean Sea (W); Castries is capital. A volcanic, mountainous, forested island it was first inhabited by Carib Indians; discovered 1502 by Christopher Columbus; first colonized 17th century by British; later settled by French; island was point of Anglo-French contention until British gained control 1803; member of Federation of West Indies 1958; part of British Windwards colony until 1959; Caribbean Common Market member; in 1967 it became one of six associate states of West Indies, with internal self-government and, in 1979, gained full independence. Bananas are main export. Area: 238sq mi (616sq km). Pop. 120,000.

Saint Martin (Sint Maarten), island of NW Leeward Islands in West Indies, between Atlantic Ocean (NE) and Caribbean (SW). It has been politically divided since 1648: N is a dependency of French dept. of Guadeloupe; S (Sint Maarten) is administered by Netherlands Antilles. Principal towns are Marigot (N) and Philipsburg (S). Products: cotton, sugar cane, fruit, cattle, salt. Pop. (combined sections) 14,230.

Saint Michel, residential city in Canada; N suburb of Montreal. Pop. 71,446.

Saint Moritz (Sankt Moritz), village in E Switzerland, on the Imr River, 28mi (45km) SSE of Chur; scene of Olympic games 1928 and 1948; famous tourist resort, noted for curative mineral springs; site of Romanesque church, Engadine historical museum, Leganti museum. Chief industry is tourism. Pop. 5,699.

Saint Paul, capital city and port of entry in E Minnesota, on Mississippi River just E of Minneapolis, its twin city; seat of Ramsey co. Included in Louisiana Purchase (1803), fur-trading post est. 1838; it was named after Father Galtier's St Paul's Church 1841; made territorial capital 1849, state capital 1858. It is site of Hamline University (1854), College of St Thomas (1855), Bethel College (1871), Concordia College (1893), College of St Catherine (1906), capitol (1904), Cathedral of St Paul (1906–15), Indian Mounds Park. Industries: steel, iron, automobiles, machinery, chemicals, paper, tapes, computers, food products. Inc. 1854. Pop. (1980) 270,230.

Saint Petersburg, residential city in W central Florida peninsula, on Tampa Bay; known as Sunshine City. Yachting and fishing resort; site of Sunshine Skyway Bridge, 15mi (24km) long. Industries: concrete, aluminum products. Settled 1888; inc. 1892. Pop. (1980) 236,893.

Saint Pierre and Miquelon, group of nine small islands, 10mi (16km) SW of Newfoundland in Gulf of St Lawrence. Capital is St Pierre on St Pierre Island; French territory. Area: 93sq mi (241sq km). Pop. 5,232.

Saint Quentin, city in N France, on Somme River, 25mi (40km) NW of Laon. Originally a Roman town, during Middle Ages it was site of pilgrimage to tomb of St Quentin, believed to have been persecuted here 284–305 by Emperor Diocletian; became part of French crownlands 1191; scene of many battles due to its strategic location; site of Musée Lécuyer with a collection of pastels by Maurice Quentin de la Tour (born here), 15th-century town hall, and the large Gothic church, Collegiale Saint-Quentin (13th–15th centuries). Industries: textiles, furniture, rubber, food products. Pop. 69,153.

Saint-Simon, Claude Henri de Rouvroy, Comte de (1760–1825), French political reformer, one of the founders of socialism. As a young man he fought in the American Revolution and supported the French Revolution. In *Memoire sur la science de l'homme* (1813) and other writings (*L'industrie,* for example, written in collaboration with Auguste Comte), Saint-Simon proposed a productive industrialized state directed by scientist-businessmen. Although his writings were largely ignored during his lifetime, they influenced both later socialists and Marxists and advocates of the modern capitalist state.

Saint Sophia Church. *See* Hagia Sophia.

Saint Thomas Island, second-largest island of US Virgin Islands, West Indies. Of volcanic origin, the island has a hilly terrain and many coastal inlets including St Thomas Harbor. Charlotte Amalie, capital of US Virgin Islands, is on S shore. Discovered and named by Christopher Columbus 1493, island was first settled by Dutch. Industries: rum, tourism. Area: 28sq mi (72sq km). Pop. 47,260.

Saint-Tropez, town of French Riviera, in SE France, on bay of St Tropez. From 15th–17th centuries it was an independent republic; beach resort and fishing village. Pop. 5,689.

Saint Vincent, Cape, SW extremity of Portugal and continental Europe, 60mi (97km) W of Faro; scene of 1797 battle in which British, under command of Commodore Horatio Nelson, defeated Spanish naval forces; contains 15th-century ruins of Prince Henry the Navigator's town.

Saint Vincent and the Grenadines, independent island nation in the Windward Islands of the Caribbean Sea, composed of the larger volcanic island of Saint Vincent and five smaller islands, part of the Grenadine island group. Saint Vincent was reputedly discovered by Christopher Columbus in 1498, but the indigenous Carib Indians were left to inhabit the island until 1797, when the British solidified their control and deported most of the Caribs. Self-government was granted in 1969, followed by full independence within the Commonwealth of Nations in 1979. Since then a Grenadine separatist movement has been active. The majority of the population is descended from black African slaves and belongs to the Anglican church. Agriculture dominates the economy, with bananas and arrowroot the leading exports. Capital: Kingstown. Area: 150sq mi (380sq km). Pop. 118,000.

St. Vitus Dance. *See* Chorea.

Saipan, island in Mariana Islands, W Pacific Ocean; member of US Trust Territory of the Pacific Islands. A Spanish possession 1565–1899, it came under Germany 1899; mandated to Japan 1919 and used as a naval and air base in WWII; taken by the United States 1944. Products: tropical fruits, sugar cane, coffee; mineral deposits have been found. Chief city is Chalan Kanoa; chief port is Tanapag Harbor; Trust Territory government seat is Capital Hill. Area: 70sq mi (181sq km). Pop. 14,000.

Saithe. *See* Pollack.

Sakai, industrial city in S Honshu, Japan, on Osaka Bay approx. 6mi (10km) S of Osaka, in Osaka industrial belt. An important port 15th–17th century, since the harbor silted up its port business has declined; site of Emperor Nitoku's tomb. Industries: machinery, automobiles, chemicals, dyes, fertilizer, iron, steel, textiles. Pop. 751,000.

Sakhalin Island, island off the E coast of Siberian Russian SFSR, USSR, between Tatar Strait and Sea of Japan and Sea of Okhotsk, extending from Cape Yelizaveta to Cape Crillon, separated from Hokkaido, Japan by La Pérouse Strait, containing two parallel mountain ranges. Main urban centers are Aleksandrovsk, Okha, Uglegorsk, Kholmsk, Korsakov, Dolinsk, Yuzhno-Sakhalinsk. Chinese in ancient times, it was first visited by Japanese *c.* 1630; explored by Japanese in late 18th century; disputed between Japan and Russia 1853–75; settled by Russians 1853; came under Russian control 1875 when ceded by Japan in exchange for Kuril Island; occupied by Japanese 1905; returned to USSR 1946 after Allied defeat of Japan. Industries: grains, vegetables, coal, paper, pulp, fish canning, oil. Area: 8,597sq mi (4,066sq km). Pop. 600,000.

Sakharov, Andrei Dimitrievich (1921–), Soviet physicist and social critic. His work in nuclear fusion was instrumental in the development of the Soviet hydrogen bomb. He received international recognition as a scientist and was a member of the American Academy of Arts and Sciences. An outspoken defender of civil liberties, he created the Human Rights Committee in 1970 and received the Eleanor Roosevelt Peace Award (1973) and the Cino del Duca Prize (1974). He believed in the possible unification of East and West through democratic socialism and received the Nobel Peace prize in 1975. Sakharov was arrested, stripped of all honors, and exiled to Gorky in 1980.

Saki. *See* Munro, Hector Hugh.

Saki, dark, slender monkey of tropical South American forests. They have long bushy tails and are day-active, tree-dwelling omnivores. Weight: 1.5–3.7lb (0.7–1.7kg). Genera *Pithecia* and *Chiropotes. See also* Monkey.

Sakti, in Hinduism, the female consort of male deities. Its origin is the story of the inactive god Shiva's ineffectiveness without his wife Sakti's pure activity.

Saladin (*c.* 1137–1193), sultan of Egypt and Syria. As a lieutenant of Nur-ad-din, he suppressed the Fatimite dynasty of Egypt, became vizier, and then proclaimed himself sultan in 1174. After conquering most of Syria, he launched a campaign to drive the Christians from Palestine. His capture of Jerusalem in 1187 brought on the arrival of an army of the third Crusade led by Richard I of England and Philip II of France. After three years of fighting, the Muslims retained most of the territory but conceded to the Christians the right to enter Jerusalem.

Salamanca, city in central Mexico, 17mi (27km) S of Guanajuato, on the Lerma River; rail junction. Products: corn, wheat, sugar cane, alfalfa, cotton. Industries: chemicals, oil refining, cotton goods, flour milling, handicrafts. Pop. 103,740.

Salamanca, city in W Spain, on Tormes River; capital of Salamanca prov.; conquered by Hannibal 220 BC; city was partially destroyed by French during Peninsular War 1808–13; served as capital for the insurgents during Spanish civil war 1937–38. It is the site of a 15th-century university founded by Alfonso IX, containing several precious manuscripts, 12th-century Gothic cathedral, 17th-century Plaza Mayor, Roman bridge. Industries: food processing, chemicals. Area: (prov.) 829sq mi (2147sq km). Pop. (city) 125,220; (prov.) 371,607.

Salamander, amphibian found worldwide, except in Australia and polar regions. The 280 species are characterized by slimy, elongated bodies, long tails, and short legs. Most lay eggs, but some give birth to live young. Fertilization is usually internal. The male deposits spermatophore into the female's cloaca. She lays eggs on moist land or in water. Those laid in water hatch into aquatic larvae with gills. Order Caudata (Urodela). *See also* Amphibia.

Salamis, island in E Greece, in Saronic Gulf; scene of Persian War naval battle during which Greek forces,

St. Vincent, British West Indies

Andrei Sakharov

Jonas Salk

under Themistocles, defeated Persian fleet 480 BC; site of naval base. Industries: wheat, olive oil, wine, fisheries. Area: 37sq mi (96sq km). Pop. 20,000.

Salazar, António de Oliveira (1889–1970), Portuguese dictator. He was a professor of political theory with right-wing, pro-Roman Catholic Church leanings. He was briefly finance minister in the right-wing government that came into power in 1926. He was called back to office in 1928 and succeeded in stabilizing Portugal's financial situation. He became premier in 1932 and thereafter ruled as virtual dictator. He supported the Nationalists in the Spanish Civil War, and although sympathetic to the Axis powers in World War II, managed to keep Portugal neutral. He presided over Portugal's economic revival after the war but fought a futile battle to save the Portuguese colonies in Africa. He suffered a stroke in 1968 and died two years later.

Salem, city in NE Massachusetts, on Massachusetts Bay, 14mi (22km) NE of Boston; seat of Essex co; scene of witchcraft trials (1692) during which 20 people were put to death; site of Massachusetts State College at Salem (1854), House of Seven Gables (1668), Nathaniel Hawthorne's birthplace (c. 1750), Peabody Museum, Witch House (1642), home of Jonathan Corwin, a judge at witchcraft trials. Industries: leather, precision machines. Founded 1626 as Naumkeag; name changed in 1630; inc. as city 1836. Pop. (1980) 38,220.

Salem, capital city of Oregon, 44mi (71km) S of Portland on Willamette River; seat of Marion co; site of Willamette University (1842), and Salem Technical Vocational Community College (1954). Industries: meatpacking, lumber, canneries, paper, linen, woolens. Founded 1840 by Methodist Episcopal missionaries as a mission station and manual training school for Indians; made territorial capital 1851 and chartered 1857; continued as capital when Oregon joined Union in 1859. Pop. (1980) 89,233.

Salerno, seaport city in S Italy, 29mi (47km) SE of Naples, on the Gulf of Salerno; capital of Salerno prov. Founded by Romans 197 BC, it was conquered by the Normans 1076; sacked by the Swabian Hohenstaufens 1194; became part of Italy 1860; scene of heavy fighting September 1943. First European medical school was founded here 9th century, closed 1817; site of cathedral of San Matteo (founded 845), said to contain tomb of St Matthew and Pope Gregory VII. Industries: textiles, machinery, cement, macaroni, flour, lumber. Pop. 161,598.

Salic Law, rule of succession denying the right of women to inherit royal titles or offices and eliminating royal succession through the female line. In the later Middle Ages the practice was called the Salic Law because it was mistakenly supposed to have been outlined in the *Lex Salica* (c. 510), the law of the Salian Franks under Clovis I. Actually, the rule was first applied after the death of Louis X in France (1316), when Philip V took the throne in preference to Louis' daughter Joanna.

Salinas, city in W California, 47mi (76km) SSE of San Jose; seat of Monterey co; birthplace of John Steinbeck. Industries: shipping and processing center; fruits, dairy goods, jams, jellies. Founded 1856; inc. 1874. Pop. (1980) 80,479.

Salinas River, river in W California; rises in Santa Lucia Mts; flows NW past King City and Salinas to Monterey Bay; its irrigated valley is one of the chief US lettuce-producing regions. Length: 150mi (241km).

Salinger, J(erome) D(avid) (1919–   ), US author, b. New York City. He began publishing stories in magazines. His first book, a novel, was *Catcher in the Rye* (1951). Subsequent works include *Nine Stories* (1953), *Franny and Zooey* (1961), two novellas, and *Raise High the Roof Beam, Carpenters* and *Seymour: An Introduction* (1963), two stories.

Salisbury, Robert Arthur Talbot Gascoyne-Cecil, 3rd Marquess of (1830–1903), English statesman and diplomat. A conservative, he placed great faith in the efficacy of aristocratic and paternalist government. He distrusted reform of Parliament throughout his political career (1853–1902). He was prime minister three times (1885–86, 1886–92, and 1895–1902) and also foreign secretary. His eminence in foreign affairs was established by his leadership of the Congress of Berlin (1878). After the Boer War he retired (1902) and was succeeded by Arthur Balfour, his nephew.

Salisbury, Robert Cecil, 1st Earl of (1563–1612), English statesman. The son of Elizabeth I's secretary of state, Lord Burghley, he succeeded his father in office (1596) and continued as chief minister until his death, assuming the office of treasurer as well in 1608. His financial acumen secured James I an independence that influenced his dealings with Parliament. He was made an earl in 1605.

Salisbury (New Sarum), county town of Wiltshire, S England; a market town, 10mi (16km) S of Stonehenge. Its great 13th-century Early English cathedral has the highest spire in England, 404ft (123m) and was added to original cathedral about 1330. Its library contains one of the four original copies of the Magna Carta. Some of the building materials for this edifice were brought from the razed cathedral at Old Sarum. Town was founded 1220 as site of cathedral. Pop. 103,200.

Salisbury, former name of capital of Zimbabwe, named after British Prime Minister R.A. Salisbury. *See also* Harare.

Salish, a tribe of North American Indians formerly occupying an area in W Montana; they later moved to the Flathead Lake region. They gave their name to one of the major language families of the American Indians. Today approximately 3,000 Salish-speaking Indians occupy several reservations in Washington, Oregon, and Idaho.

Salivary Glands, three pairs of glands located on either side of the mouth that form and secrete saliva. The parotid gland, just below and in front of the ear, is the largest of the salivary glands and the one that becomes enlarged in mumps; the submaxillary is found near the lower jaw angle; and the sublingual under the side of the tongue.

Salk, Jonas Edward (1914–   ), US medical researcher, b. New York City. He developed the first vaccine against poliomyelitis in 1952, using inactivated polio virus as an immunizing agent. Mass tests of the vaccine began in 1954, and mass immunization programs followed.

Salmon, marine and freshwater fish of the N Hemisphere. A popular sport and commercial fish, it is silvery and spotted until spawning season when it turns black or red. The Pacific salmon (*Oncorhynchus*) hatches, spawns, and dies in freshwater, but spends its adult life in the ocean. Pacific species include the pink, sockeye, chinook, dog, silver, and masu varieties. The Atlantic salmon (*Salmo salar*) is actually an ocean-run trout. A marine fish, it spawns in rivers on both sides of the Atlantic and then returns to the sea. It does not die

after spawning like the Pacific salmon. Weight: to 80lb (36kg). Family Salmonidae.

Salmonellosis, group of diseases caused by bacteria of the *Salmonella* genus. Some species, attacking animals, cause abortion, others cause blood poisoning and intestinal inflammation to man as well. Other species are a cause of human food poisoning.

Salome, two women in the Bible. The first was the daughter of Herod Philip and Herodias. Although not mentioned by name, she is supposed to be the woman who danced for the head of the executed John the Baptist (Mark 6:16–28). The second was a witness to the Crucifixion and brought offerings to Christ's tomb (Matt. 27:56).

Salonika (Thessaloníki), seaport city in NE Greece, on Gulf of Salonika; 2nd-largest city in Greece and capital of Thessaloniki dept. City served as capital of Macedon 146 BC; site where Paul delivered his two epistles to the Thessalonians; scene of massacre of insurrectionists AD 390 by Theodosius. City was under Ottoman Turks 1430–1912, when it was taken by Greece during Balkan Wars; scene of mass liquidation of Jewish population by Germans during WWII; site of White Tower (15th century), triumphal arch of Constantine, and several Byzantine churches. Exports: grain, livestock, tobacco, manganese, chrome, livestock. Industries: textiles, wine, beer, soap, machinery, flour, cement, explosives. Founded c. 315 BC by Cassander, King of Macedon. Pop. 339,496.

Salt, chemical compound formed, along with water, when an acid and a base react together. Salts are typically high melting crystalline compounds that tend to be soluble in water. They are formed of ions held together by electrostatic forces and in solution they conduct electricity. Sodium chloride—common table salt—is a typical example. *See also* Halite; Sodium Chloride.

SALT Agreements, arms control agreements worked out at Strategic Arms Limitations Talks and signed May 26, 1972, by US Pres. Richard Nixon and Soviet General Secretary Leonid Brezhnev. The SALT agreements limited anti-ballistic missile systems and offensive missile launchers. Talks continued concerning offensive strategic weapons.

Salt Dome, body of salt that has intruded into a sedimentary rock overlay. The flow of the relatively plastic salt into a dome may be the result of a difference in density between the salt and the overlying rock. This process is not completely understood, however.

Saltillo, city in NE Mexico, on plateau of Sierra Madre Oriental; taken by US forces during Mexican War; site of rail junction, resort, university, cathedral; mining center, for silver, gold, copper, lead, zinc, iron. Industries: textiles, flour, shoes, clothing, kitchen utensils, handicrafts. Founded late 16th century. Pop. 233,600.

Salt Lake City, capital city in N central Utah, 13mi (21km) E of Great Salt Lake on Jordan River; largest city of Utah; seat of Salt Lake co. Founded 1847 by the Mormon Community under Brigham Young, city developed as trading and supply point for westward travelers to California; it was made capital of Provisional State of Deseret 1849, Territory of Utah 1850, state of Utah 1896. Landmarks include Mormon Temple (1853–93), Brigham Young's House (1877) and Museum (1897), Fort Douglas (1862); site of University of Utah (1850), Westminster College (1875), Stevens Henager College (1907); world headquarters of Mormon Church. Industries: food processing, missiles, rocket engines, tourism, oil refining, printing, publishing; zinc, gold, silver, lead, and copper mining. Inc. 1851. Pop. (1980) 163,033.

Saluda River, river that rises in Blue Ridge of NW South Carolina, flows SE through Lake Murray; near Columbia it joins the Broad River to form the Congaree River. The Saluda Dam (1930) furnishes hydroelectric power to area. Length: 200mi (322km).

Saluki, royal coursing dog of Egypt (hound group) and perhaps the oldest domesticated breed dog. Known 7000–6000 BC; brought to England in 1840; also called Persian greyhound. A graceful dog of strong constitution and remarkable vision, it has a long, narrow head; long, hanging ears; deep but narrow-chested body with broad back and slightly arched loin; long legs and tail. The smooth, silky coat is feathered on legs, ears, and tail (no feathering in smooth variety). Colors include white, golden, red, black, and tan. Average size: 23–28in (58–71cm) high at shoulder; 45–60lb (20–27kg). *See also* Hounds.

Salvador (Bahia), seaport city in E central Brazil, 750mi (1,207km) N of Rio de Janeiro; capital of Bahia state. Settled by the Portuguese as Bahia, it was the first formally established colony in Brazil; slave market in 17th and 18th centuries; capital of Brazil until 1763. Industries: exporting, food and tobacco processing, textiles. Founded 1549 by order of King John III of Portugal. Pop. 1,007,195.

Salvation Army, Christian organization formed after a military pattern, with a general as head. Founded in 1865 by William Booth, a Methodist minister and his wife, it concentrates on evangelistic and social work. The Salvation Army in the United States began in 1880. With the Bible as the guide for life, constant conversion programs are enacted. Members must give complete obedience, denying one's self. International headquarters are in London.

Salween (Nujiang), river in SE Asia; rises in Tibetan Plateau, E Tibet; flows SE through Yunnan prov. cutting deep gorges through the rough terrain almost parallel to Mekong, Yangtze, and Irrawaddy rivers; continues into Shan and Karen states of Burma to empty into the Gulf of Martaban, near Moulmein. Along its course, it forms many rapids and is only navigable for 75mi (121km) upstream, limiting its commercial importance as an E-W transportation route. Length: approx. 1,750mi (2,818km).

Salzburg, city in Austria, on the Salzach River 71mi (114km) ESE of Munich, West Germany; site of two archepiscopal palaces, a 17th-century cathedral, and several notable churches and houses; ruled by prince-archbishops for over 1,000 years; birthplace of Mozart; music center. Founded late 7th century. Pop. 128,845.

Samarium, metallic element (symbol Sm) of the Lanthanide group, first identified spectroscopically in 1879 by Lecoq de Boisbaudran. Chief ores are monazite (phosphate) and bastänite (fluorocarbonate). The element is used in pyrophoric alloys and carbon-arc lamps; some samarium alloys are used in making powerful permanent magnets. Properties: at. no. 62; at. wt. 150.35; sp gr 7.5 (α), 7.4 (β); melt. pt. 1962°F (1072°C); boil. pt. 3200°F (1778°C); most common isotope Sm^{152} (26.72%). *See also* Lanthanide Elements.

Samarkand, formerly Maracanda; city in Uzbek SSR, USSR, on W spur of Alai Mts, 180mi (290km) SW of Tashkent, near Zerayshan River; capital of Samarkand oblast. One of the oldest cities in the USSR, it was destroyed by Alexander the Great 329 BC; important 7th-century point on the "Silk Route" from China to Europe, it was again destroyed 1221 by Genghis Khan; it was made capital of Tamerlane's empire 1370; almost uninhabited by 1700, the Russians took it 1868 and it was inc. in the Uzbek SSR 1924; site of Tamerlane's mausoleum (1404), 14th–15th-century mosque and mausoleum of Shakh Zinda, Uzbek State University, institute of tropical medicine, regional museum, agricultural, medical, and teachers' colleges. Industries: cotton, silk, clothing, shoes, wine, tea, food canning, motor vehicle parts, leather. Pop. 312,000.

Samnium, ancient state in S Italy; confederation of Caraceni, Pentri, Caudini and Hirpini; Samnites were enemies of Rome, with whom they fought the three Samnite Wars; they were conquered by Rome *c.* 290 BC. The Samnites were probably of Sabine origin and spoke Oscan.

Samoa. *See* American Samoa; Western Samoa.

Sámos, island in SE Greece; member of the Sporades Islands in Aegean Sea; forms department of Greece with Ikaria and other islands. Developed into maritime power and cultural center under Polycrates 6th century BC, it was a member of Delian League, allied with Athens during Peloponnesian War; held by Ottoman Turks 1475–1912, when it was annexed to Greece; occupied by Axis powers during WWII; home of Aesop, Anacreon, and Rhuecus; birthplace of Pythagoras and Conon; site of Temple of Hera. Industries: shipbuilding, tobacco, silk, wine, fruits, currants, grapes. Area: 184sq mi (477sq km). Pop. 41,709.

Samothrace, island in NE Greece, in NE Aegean Sea; An independent community under Roman protection 2nd century BC, it was occupied by Ottoman Turks 1456–1912, when annexed to Greece. Excavations have unearthed the famous Winged Victory of Samothrace (*c.* 200 BC), ruins of the Sanctuary of the Great Gods, a stoa, and much pottery. Industries: grains, olive oil, honey, sponges. Area: 69sq mi (179sq km). Pop. 3,012.

Samoyed, ancient sled and guard dog (working group) bred in northern Asia. A dog with a smiling expression, it has a broad, wedge-shaped head; thick, erect, triangular ears; dark, almond-shaped eyes; deep-chested, medium-length body with slightly arched loin; moderately long, sturdy legs with large feet; and long tail curved over the back or side. The white, biscuit, or cream double coat stands straight out. Average size: 19–23.5in (48–60cm) high at shoulder; 35–65lb (16–29kg). *See also* Working Dog.

Samoyeds, Uralic-speaking people, who inhabit N Soviet Union and consist of a number of groups including the Nentsy, Yenisy, Tavgis, and Selkups. They practice fishing, hunting, pastoralism (reindeer and horses) and trapping, but their traditionally nomadic lifestyle has been modified by the implementation of Soviet collective farming.

Samson, biblical Israelite judge and hero. His Philistine wife was given to another man by his father and Samson, in reprisal, ruined Philistine crops. After he killed 1,000 Philistines with the jawbone of an ass, his mistress Delilah discovered his great strength came from his long hair. She had his hair cut and gave him to the Philistines. Though weak and blind, he destroyed a building, killing himself and his captors.

Samsun, city and port in Turkey, on Black Sea, 200mi (322km) NW of Ankara; capital of Samsun prov. Captured by Romans 1st century BC, it became part of Byzantine Empire during Middle Ages. In 14th century it fell to Ottoman Turks. In 1919, Kemal Atatürk landed at Samsun to organize a nationalist movement against Greece; an equestrian statue commemorates his landing. City now serves as Turkey's most important Black Sea port. Industries: cigarettes, textiles. Founded 562 BC by Greek colonists. Pop. 169,060.

Samuel I and II, two books of the Old Testament describing the transition of Israel from a collection of tribes under separate chiefs to a single nation under a king through the stories of the prophet Samuel and of Saul and David, Israel's first two kings. The song of Hannah, Samuel's prayer, and God's prophecy to David are the most important passages.

Samuelson, Paul Anthony (1915–), US economist, b. Gary, Ind. He was noted for his work in macroeconomics and mathematical economics. His best-known work is *Economics: An Introductory Analysis,* a widely used text . Other works include *Foundations of Economic Analysis* (1947). In 1970 he received the Nobel Prize for economics.

Samurai, warrior class of feudal Japan. Beginning its rise to importance in the 12th century, the samurai (or *bushi*) class was firmly fixed at the top of the social order of the Tokugawa era (1603–1867). Samurai alone were privileged to bear arms, usually wearing two swords, and received a pension from their daimyo (feudal lords), to whom they pledged allegiance. Samurai intermarried in their own caste, and their children were samurai from birth, although only the heir received a pension. Samurai followed Bushido, a special code of conduct. Many modern military men had samurai origins, and events such as the Satsuma Rebellion (1877) had their roots in samurai feudalism.

Sana (San'a), capital city of Yemen Arab Republic, 40mi (64km) from Hodeida; largest city in S Arabia; agricultural and trade center; Islamic cultural center, site of Muslim University, the Great Mosque (built on site of 6th-century church). Walled city was settled in pre-Islamic times; first became Yemen's capital 4th century; ruled by Ethiopians during Middle Ages; occupied by Ottoman Turks in 17th century, after which it became seat of Rassite dynasty until second Turkish occupation 1872–1918. Modern kingdom of Yemen began 1904 with revolt against Ottoman Turks; independence was achieved in 1918; became capital of Yemen Arab Republic 1962. Industries: leather, jewelry work, vineyards, coffee, raisins. Pop. 150,000.

San Andreas Fault, a right-lateral, strike-slip fault that forms the boundary between the North American plate and the North Pacific plate and separates SW California from the rest of North America. Over the past 60,000,000 years the total movement along the fault has amounted to more than 345mi (555km). The fault is a center for earthquakes; the great San Francisco quake of 1906 occurred along it.

San Angelo, city in W Texas, 180mi (290km) NW of Austin, at confluence of North and Middle Concho rivers; seat of Tom Green co; site of San Angelo State College (1928), Goodfellow Air Force Base, livestock and trading center. Industries: wool, mohair, dairy products, oil, gas, farming, food processing. Settled 1867; inc. 1888. Pop. (1980) 73,240.

San Antonio, city in S central Texas, 74mi (118km) SW of Austin on San Antonio River; seat of Bexar co. Founded 1793 with inc. of Villa de Bejar, San Fernando de Bejar, and mission San Antonio de Valero (later the Alamo); scene of Mexico-Texas struggles at the Alamo (1836). A military center, it is site of Lackland, Randolph, Brooks, and Kelly Air Force bases, Fort Sam Houston, Alamo (1718), Spanish governor's palace (1749), HemisFair Plaza (1968), Trinity University (1869), St Mary's University (1852), Incarnate Word College (1881). Industries: food products, aircraft, building materials, chemicals, wood products, livestock, tourism. Inc. 1837. Pop. (1980) 785,410.

San Bernardino, city in S California, 55mi (89km) E of Los Angeles; seat of San Bernardino co. A Spanish settlement, it was explored in 1772 and named in 1810; Mormons emigrated from 1850. Industries: missiles, steel and iron products, cement, foodstuffs. Founded 1851; inc. 1854. Pop. (1980) 118,057.

San Bernardino Mountains, range in S California; extends about 60mi (97km) NW-SE between San Gabriel and San Jacinto Mts. Highest peak is San Gorgonio, 11,502ft (3,508m).

San Cristóbal, city in W Venezuela, at SW end of Cordillera Mérida in Andean uplands; capital of Tachira state; trade center. Industries: coffee, cacao, cotton, sugar, grains, cattle, cement, iron, coal, asphalt mining. Founded 1561. Pop. 151,717.

Sancti-Spiritus, city in W central Cuba, 45mi (72km) SE of Santa Clara on Yayabo River; taken by Fidel Castro 1958; site of 16th-century bridge over Yayabo River, 16th-century church, theater (1839). Industries: processing center for sugar, tobacco, cattle. Founded 1516. Pop. 146,450.

Sand, George (1804–76), pseud. of Amandine Aurore Lucie Dupin, French novelist. After an unhappy marriage to Baron Dudevant, she returned to Paris from her native Nohant. She became famous for her affairs with Alfred de Musset and Frédéric Chopin. Her novels from this period, including *Lélia* (1833) and *Mauprat* (1837), examine women's right to independence. *Le Meunier d'Angibault* (1845) reflects her socialist and republican interests, while her last novels, such as *Francis the Waif* (1847–48), are pastoral studies.

Sandalwood, tree whose fragrant, reddish wood is used for carved boxes and screens or burned as incense. Many are semiparasitic on roots of other plants. The evergreen *Santalum album* is native to S Asia. Its oval leaves are hairy, and the flowers turn from straw-color to blood red. Height: to 40ft (12m). Family Santalaceae.

Sandburg, Carl (1878–1967), US poet, biographer, and folklorist, b. Galesburg, Ill. The son of Swedish immigrants, he left school at 13 to become a laborer. After serving in the Spanish-American War, he put himself through college, graduating in 1902. He went to work as a newspaper reporter in Milwaukee. In 1908 he married Lillian Steichen, sister of photographer Edward Steichen. He moved to Chicago in 1913 and began contributing to Harriet Monroe's *Poetry* magazine. His first volume of poetry, *Chicago Poems,* appeared in 1915. It contains his most famous poem, "Chicago." Other volumes of poetry include *Cornhuskers* (1918), *Smoke and Steel* (1920), *Good Morning, America* (1928), *The People, Yes* (1936), *Honey and Salt* (1963). He won the Pulitzer Prize for poetry in 1951 for his *Complete Poems* (1950). His poetry, inspired by Walt Whitman, vigorously draws on American history and idiom. He won the 1940 Pulitzer Prize for history for his six volume biography of Abraham Lincoln (1926–39). A novel, *Remembrance Rock* appeared in 1948. *The American Songbag* (1927) and *New American Songbag* (1950) are collections of folk

Samoyed

Carl Sandburg

Margaret Sanger

ballads and songs. *Rootabaga Stories* (1922) was the first of several collections of children's stories.

Sand Crab. *See* Ghost Crab.

Sand Dollar, marine echinoderm with round, flattened body covered with short spines; a fused skeleton; and five radiating double rows of respiratory tube feet on both sides. Class Echinoidea; species *Echinarachnius parma.*

Sand Fish. *See* Skink.

Sand Grouse, terrestrial bird of central and S Eurasia and Africa that lives in large flocks in open arid areas, feeding on seeds and vegetable shoots, and sometimes resting in shallow sand depressions. They look like grouse but are related to pigeons and, like pigeons, drink with their bills held in the water at water holes at dusk and dawn. They lay elongated, smudged eggs (2–3) in a grass-lined sand depression. The female incubates the eggs during the day, the male at night. Length: 9–16in (23–41cm). Family Pteroclidae.

San Diego, city in S California; seat of San Diego co; important medical center and port of entry for S California, Arizona, New Mexico, lower California; site of four universities and two colleges, large naval and marine bases, zoological park. Industries: aerospace, electronics, shipbuilding. Mission San Diego de Alcalá was founded 1769 by Júnipero Serra; inc. 1850. Pop. (1980) 875,504.

Sand Painting, practiced by the Indians of the Southwest and regarded as the vital core of a powerful magic performance designed to heal. The sand picture is believed to absorb the illness from the sick man sitting in its center.

Sandpiper, shorebird that breeds in cold regions and migrates long distances to winter in warm areas, settling in grass or low bushes near water. They feed on invertebrates, nest in colonies, and lay pointed eggs (4) in a grass-lined ground hole nest. Length: 6–12in (15–30cm). Family Scolopacidae.

Sandstone, sedimentary rock composed of sand grains cemented in such materials as silica, iron oxide, or carbonate of lime. Its hardness depends on the character of the cementing material. Its color may be gray, red, buff, brown, or green. *See also* Sedimentary Rocks.

Sandstorm, a strong wind carrying with it dense clouds of desert sand more coarse-grained than the particles in dust storms. *See also* Dust Storm.

Sanford, Edward Terry (1865–1930), US jurist and lawyer, b. Knoxville, Tenn. He was an assistant attorney-general (1907–08) and US District Court judge (1909–23). He became an associate justice of the US Supreme Court (1923–30), appointed by Pres. Warren G. Harding. He wrote the opinion in the *Gitlow* v. *New York* (1925) freedom of expression case.

San Francisco, city and port of entry in W California, on S tip of a peninsula bounded by Pacific Ocean (W) and San Francisco Bay (E), connected by Golden Gate Strait (N); seat of and coextensive with San Francisco co. Founded 1776 as Yerba Buena by Spanish who est. a presidio and mission, it continued under Spanish control until July 9, 1846, when it was taken for the United States by Com. John D. Sloat. Growth was spurred by California gold rush (1848), development of its harbor for foreign trade and fishing (1860s), pony express (1860), and coming of transcontinental rail-

road (1869). Devastated by San Andreas earthquake and fire (April 1906), it was quickly rebuilt and prospered from opening of Panama Canal (1914). During WWII, city served as embarkation point for Pacific campaigns; scene of drafting of UN Charter (1945), and signing of Japanese Peace Treaty (1951). Landmarks include Chinatown, Fisherman's Wharf, Coit Memorial Tower, Nob Hill, Telegraph Hill, Russian Hill, Treasure Island, Golden Gate Bridge (1937), cable cars, Market Street, Latin Quarter, Presidio of San Francisco (1776), Mission Dolores (1782), Golden Gate Park; site of University of San Francisco (1855), University of California Medical Center (1864), Heald Engineering College (1863), San Francisco State College (1899), City College of San Francisco (1935); many military installations. Industries: tourism, shipbuilding, food processing, oil refining, chemicals, aircraft, fishing, publishing. Inc. 1850. Pop. (1980) 678,974.

San Francisco Bay, inlet of Pacific Ocean on W central coast of California, entered through the Golden Gate, a strait between two peninsulas. San Francisco is on S peninsula and is connected to N peninsula by Golden Gate Bridge (1933–37). Bay was discovered 1579 by Francis Drake. Length: 60mi (97km). Width: 3–12mi (4.8–19km).

San Francisco Conference on International Organization (1945), meeting that drafted the charter forming the United Nations. Delegates representing 50 nations met in San Francisco, beginning on April 25. With World War II ending, the Allies wanted to safeguard peace in the future. The UN charter, which provided the structure of the organization, was signed on June 26.

Sanger, Margaret Higgins (1883–1966), US social reformer, b. Corning, N.Y. As a public health nurse, she became convinced of the necessity of birth control, especially for the poor. Her crusade for birth control, which began in 1912, was unpopular at first, and she was jailed for sending birth control information through the mail. She established the first birth control clinic in the United States (1916) in Brooklyn, N.Y., and founded the American Birth Control League (1921), which grew into the Planned Parenthood Federation of America (1942). She was the first president of International Planned Parenthood (1953).

Sangre de Cristo Mountains, part of the Rocky Mts, stretching from central Colorado to N central New Mexico; culminates at Blanca Peak, 14,317ft (4,367m). Length: 220mi (354km).

Sanhedrin, the council or court of Judaism, prominent during the period of the Second Temple, before its destruction in 70 AD. There is little information on its development and function. It served as a legislative body on both religious and political issues. It was in essence a rabbinical court, whose authority was accepted by the Jews. It disappeared in the 5th century.

Sanitary Engineering, a branch of civil engineering dealing with problems of water supply and treatment, waste disposal and reclamation of useful waste, pollution control, food and housing sanitation, insect and vermin control, and industrial hygiene.

San Jacinto, Battle of (April 1836), engagement on the San Jacinto River, Tex. Led by Sam Houston, the Texans defeated 1,200 Mexicans and captured General Santa Anna.

San José, capital city of Costa Rica, in central Costa Rica, 70mi (113km) E of Puntarenas on the Inter-American Highway; largest city and nation's economic, political, and commercial center; capital of San José

prov. Founded *c.* 1736 as Villa Nueva, after Costa Rica declared independence 1821, it developed as the center of liberal faction and was the rival of Cartago; San José succeeded Cartago as capital of Costa Rica 1823. The city soon became the center of a lucrative coffee trade; site of two conferences for the Organization of American States (OAS) 1960. Notable buildings include the National Palace (1855), Municipal Palace (1937), National Museum, National Library, National Theater, cathedral, and the University of Costa Rica (1844). Products: coffee, sugar cane, cacao, vegetables, fruit, tobacco. Industries: livestock, food processing, wine, beer, chocolate, leather goods, textiles, furniture. Pop. 228,302.

San Jose, city in W California, 40mi (64km) SE of San Francisco; seat of Santa Clara co; California's capital 1849–52; site of Rosicrucian Park, Kelley Park, Alum Rock Park, and California State University at San Jose. Industries: fruit orchards, wineries, food-processing, atomic-power equipment. Founded 1777; inc. 1850. Pop. (1980) 636,550.

San Jose Scale, conelike scale insect introduced to California about 1880 from the Orient. Now spread across the United States, they suck juices from trees and shrubs, often destroying the plants. Length: 0.1in (2.5mm). Family Diaspididae; species *Quadraspidiotus perniciosus. See also* Scale Insect.

San Juan, capital and largest city of Puerto Rico, on NE coast; made up of Old San Juan, built on an island and connected to the mainland by bridges. Major seaport, governmental and commercial center of Puerto Rico; under US administration since 1898. It prospered as a West Indian Port during 18th and 19th centuries; site of El Morro castle (1539), San Cristobal castle (1631), governors' official residence (1529), San Jose Church (c.1523), Casa Blanca (1523), Cathedral of San Juan Bautista, containing tomb of Ponce de Leon, University of Puerto Rico, school of tropical medicine, and several other institutions of higher learning; US air base. Exports: (mainly to United States) sugar, tobacco, fruit. Industries: tourism, cigars, clothing, publishing, sugar refining, rum distilling, jewelry, furniture, pharmaceuticals, plastics. Discovered 1508 by Ponce de Leon who settled 1509 at nearby Caparra; the settlement moved to present site of San Juan 1521. Pop. (1980) 522,700.

San Juan Hill, Battle of (July 1898), decisive battle in the Spanish American War. It was a US victory of the 1st US Volunteer Cavalry organized by Col. "Teddy" Roosevelt. His Rough Riders lacked military form, but their enthusiastic charge won the battle and the strategic hill overlooking Santiago and controlling the Spanish harbor below.

San Juan Islands, archipelago of 172 islands off NW Washington, E of Vancouver Island between Haro and Rosario Straits; comprises the co of San Juan. Discovered 1790 by Spanish explorers, it was subject of US-British boundary dispute decided in 1872. San Juan, Orcas, and Lopez islands are largest. A national park has been est. on San Juan Island (1966), dedicated to peaceful relationship between the United States, Canada, and Britain. Pop. 3,856.

San Leandro, city in W California, 15mi (24km) SE of Oakland. Industries: paper products, foodstuffs, transportation equipment, flowers. Founded by José Joaquin Estudillo 1837; inc. 1872. Pop. (1980) 63,952.

Sanlúcar de Barrameda, seaport in SW Spain, at the mouth of the Guadalquivir River 18mi (29km) NW of Cadiz; departure point for voyages of Christopher Columbus (1498) and Ferdinand Magellan (1519). It is the site of palace of duke of Montpensier, medieval castle, St George Hospital, 14th-century church. Industries: flour, wine, salt, fisheries. Pop. 41,072.

San Luis Potosi, state in central Mexico, primarily on Mexico's northern plateau; capital is San Luis Potosi. It is the chief mining state of Mexico; some mines have yielded silver, gold, copper, zinc, and bismuth since 18th century. Arid conditions result in little farming. Pánuco River Valley produces coffee, tobacco, sugar, and fiber plants. Area: 24,266sq mi (62,849sq km). Pop. 1,527,000.

San Marino, republic of Europe, in Apennines, 11mi (18km) SSW of Rimini, Italy; capital is San Marino. One of the world's smallest independent states, it is totally surrounded by Italy, and claims to be the oldest existing European state; receives a subsidy from Italy in return for concessions such as not raising tobacco and not having a radio station. Government includes 60-member grand council elected for 5 years; every 6 months they elect 2 regents who, along with a 10-member council of state, are the executive branch. Women were given suffrage in 1960, and the right to hold public office in 1973; site of 19th-century Basilica Santo Marino, 10th-century church. Industries: tourism, postage stamps (mainly for collectors), light manufacturing, agriculture. Republic founded 4th century by St Marinus.

PROFILE

Official name: Republic of San Marino
Area: 24sq mi (62sq km)
Population: 21,000
Density: 875 per sq mi (338 per sq km)
Chief cities: San Marino, capital; Serravalle
Government: Parliamentary democracy
Religion: Roman Catholic
Language: Italian
Unit of currency: Lira
Industries (major products): wine, ceramics, building stone, postage stamps.
Agriculture (major products): grapes, grain, corn.

San Martín, José de (1778–1850), South American independence leader, served as an officer in the Spanish army prior to joining the rebel forces in Argentina in 1812. His reputation as a brilliant military strategist was well-established by 1817, the year he took his army across the Andes into Chile. He combined forces with Bernardo O'Higgins to defeat the royalists. San Martín sailed for Peru in 1820 and entered Lima in victory in 1821. He assumed power in Peru, but in 1822 voluntarily withdrew in favor of Bolívar and left for Europe.

San Mateo, city in NW California, on the SW shore of San Francisco Bay; a Mexican possession 1822–1846. Introduction of railroad (1863) and influx of San Francisco earthquake victims (1906) led to population boom and prosperity. Founded 1863, inc. 1894. Pop. (1980) 77,561.

San Salvador, capital and largest city of El Salvador, in central part of country; trade and communications center. City has suffered from many earthquakes; served as capital of a federation of Central American states 1831–39. Industries: soap, sugar, beer, textiles, cigars. Founded 1524 by Jorge de Alvarado. Pop. 368,313.

San Sebastián, seaport city in N Spain, on Bay of Biscay 48mi (77km) E of Bilbao; capital of Guipuzcoa prov. Noted for its beautiful scenery and beaches, it is a popular resort area and former royal residence. Industries: metalworking, chemicals, fisheries, cement, tobacco, brewing. First mentioned 1014; inc. late 12th century. Area: (prov.) 771sq mi (1,997sq km). Pop. (city) 165,829; (prov.) 631,003.

Sansevieria, or snake plant, genus of house plant native to tropical Africa with erect, sword-shaped leaves that are green with various markings. Shorter types grow in spreading rosettes. Care: any light, soil (equal parts loam, peat moss, sand) kept dry between waterings. Propagation by suckers of leaf cuttings. Height: 18–30in (46–76cm). Family Agavaceae.

Sanskrit, the ancient classical language of India, the sacred language of the Hindu religion, and the forerunner of the modern Indic languages. Like Latin and Greek, it is an Indo-European language, and was brought to India from the north about 1500 BC. Only a handful of people are able to speak it today but it has nevertheless been designated one of the constitutional languages of India.

Sanskrit Literature. The Sanskrit language was brought to India by the Aryans, immigrants who entered from the northwest in the second millennium BC. After 1000 BC the language spread throughout India. The two main periods in Sanskrit literature are the Vedic (*c.*1500–*c.*200BC) and the overlapping Classical (*c.*500 BC–*c.*AD1000). The Vedic period produced the Vedas, the earliest works in Sanskrit literature and among the most important. They are sacred hymns praising the Aryan gods and containing the liturgy for ritual sacrifices. The foremost collection of Vedas is the *Rigveda.* Later Vedic literature included the *Brahmanas,* which explain the significance of the sacrifices, and the *Upanisads* (Upanishads), which discuss the essence of the universe. The early Classical period contributed India's two great national epics, the *Mahabharata* and the *Ramayana.* They are significant both as literature and Hindu sacred works. Later Classical epics called the *Puranas* have become the main source of modern Hindu mythology. *See also* Brahmanas; Mahabharata.

Santa Ana, city in W El Salvador; capital of Santa Ana dept.; 2nd-largest city of country. Industries: coffee, sugar refining. Pop. 174,546.

Santa Ana, city in S California, 20mi (32km) E of Long Beach; seat of Orange co; hub of the Anaheim-Santa Ana-Garden Grove metropolitan area, containing governmental, industrial, medical, and commercial establishments. Industries: electrical equipment, aircraft and nuclear parts, sporting goods, perfume, soft drinks. Founded 1869; inc. 1886. Pop. (1980) 203,713.

Santa Anna, Antonio López de (1794–1876), an enigmatic figure who weaved in and out of the political life of Mexico from 1822 to 1855. Santa Anna seemed at times to be a federalist, at other times a centralist; he identified himself with both liberal and conservative ideologies. He was unable to crush the movement for the independence of Texas and was defeated by General Winfield Scott in the war with the United States (1846–48). He led revolts against the governments of Iturbide, Guerrero, and Bustamante. Santa Anna was president of Mexico on several occasions, each time removed from office but recalled to head it again.

Santa Barbara, city in S California, 80mi (128km) NW of Los Angeles; seat of Santa Barbara co; site of Spanish Mission (1786), and Santa Ynez Mts, encompassing the Los Padres National Forest. Industries: oil, aerospace research, orchids. Founded 1782; inc. 1850. Pop. (1980) 74,542.

Santa Catalina Island, resort island, off the coast of S California, member of the Santa Barbara group; picturesque, resort island with many coves and beaches. Discovered 1543 by Juan Rodriguez Cabrillo. Area: 70sq mi (181sq km).

Santa Clara, city in W California, 5mi (8km) NW of San Jose; location of University of Santa Clara (1851). Franciscans' Santa Clara de Asís Mission (1777) was the original settlement. Industries: fiberglass, chemicals, paper products, truck farming. Inc. 1852. Pop. (1980) 87,746.

Santa Cruz de Tenerife, port city in Spain, on NW coast of Tenerife Island, in the Canary Islands; capital of Tenerife prov. One of two provinces comprising the Canary Islands, it has an excellent harbor; site of San Cristobal castle, Concepcion parochial church, and many institutions of higher learning. Exports: onions, wine, vegetables, tobacco, sugar cane, bananas. Industries: tourism, wine, pottery, oil refining. Area: (prov.) 1,239sq mi (3,209sq km). Pop. (city) 151,361; (prov.) 590,514.

Santa Fe, formerly Santa Fe de Vera Cruz; city in N Argentina, 12mi (19km) WNW of Paraná; capital of Sante Fe prov. Settled by Juan de Garay, it was the center of Jesuit missions and fortification against indians; constitutional seat 1853. Industries: ships, grain, cotton, lumber. Founded 1573. Pop. 244,579.

Santa Fe, city in N New Mexico, 55mi (89km) NE of Albuquerque; capital of New Mexico and seat of Santa Fe co. As the seat of region's government since its founding *c.* 1609 by Spanish, it is the oldest capital in the United States; became W terminus of Sante Fe Trail (1821); made capital of territory 1851, and of state 1912. It is site of San Miguel Mission Church (1636), Cathedral of St Francis (1869), Palace of the Governors (1610, now a museum), Cristo Rey Church, College of Santa Fe (1947); seat of archbishopric since 1875. Industries: tourism, Indian and Mexican handicrafts. Pop. (1980) 48,899.

Santa Fe Trail, famed wagon trail from Independence, Mo., to Santa Fe, N.M. It was a main trail for western settlement and an important commercial route from about 1820 to 1850, until outdated by the railroad.

Santa Gertrudis. *See* Zebu.

Santa Marta, city on the N coast of Colombia; capital of Magdalena dept.; Colombia's oldest city. Built on cliffs, it overlooks a deep bay in the Caribbean and is at the base of Sierra Nevada de Santa Maria; tourist resort and banana shipping center; connected with Bogotá by rail since 1961. Founded 1525. Pop. 102,484.

Santa Monica, city in S California, 15mi (24km) W of Los Angeles; site of the J. Paul Getty Museum and several state parks. Industries: missiles, aircraft, tourism, chemicals. Inc. 1885. Pop. (1980) 88,314.

Santander, port city in N Spain, on the Bay of Biscay; capital of Santander prov. Linked with Castile during the Middle Ages, it is site of Gothic cathedral with Moorish facade, containing ancient crypts; nearby are caves of Altamira, with prehistoric wall paintings. Industries: shipping, tourism, grain, fishing, livestock. Area: (prov.) 2,042sq mi (5,289sq km). Pop. (city) 149,704; (prov.) 467,138.

Santa Rosa, city in W California, 50mi (80km) NNW of San Francisco; seat of Sonoma co; site of the Church of One Tree (1874) built from one redwood, and the Jack London "Wolf House." Inc. 1868. Pop. (1980) 83,205.

Santiago, capital of Chile, in central Chile on the Mapocho River; capital of Santiago prov. Founded 1541 by Pedro de Valdivia, it was destroyed by earthquake 1647; President Salvatore Allende died here 1973 during a coup d'état; economic and cultural center of Chile; site of the University of Chile (1843), military academy, presidential palace. Industries: textiles, footwear, foodstuffs, iron and steel foundries. Pop. 2,661,920.

Santiago de Compostela, city in N central Spain, 32mi (51km) S of La Coruna; major pilgrimage site in Europe. Founded in the 9th century by Alfonso II, who built a chapel on site of St James tomb, the city became the major pilgrimage center in Europe; it was destroyed 997 by the Moors. It is the site of annual festival of St James, cathedral of St James (built 11th–13th centuries on site of original chapel), state university Colegio Fonseca (1525), pontifical university. Industries: tourism, religious articles, livestock, handicrafts, wood carvings, drugs, furniture, tires, leather goods. Pop. 70,893.

Santiago de Cuba, seaport in E Cuba, on cliff overlooking bay at the E end of Sierra Maestra; 2nd-largest city in Cuba and capital of Oriente prov. City was capital of Cuba 1522–1589; Fidel Castro's campaign against Fulgencio Batista began by attacking military garrison here July 26, 1953; site of historical French and Spanish buildings. Exports: agricultural produce, exotic woods. Founded 1514. Pop. 277,600.

Santiago de los Caballeros, city in N central Dominican Republic, on Rio Yaque del Norte; nation's 2nd-largest city. Industries: tobacco products, honey, beeswax. Founded 1500. Pop. 155,000.

Santo Domingo, name of the Dominican Republic before it became an independent state in 1844. *See* Dominican Republic.

Santo Domingo, capital city and seaport of Dominican Republic, on S coast of Island of Hispaniola, 150mi (241km) E of Port-au-Prince, Haiti. Founded by Bartholomé Columbus in 1496, it is the oldest continuously-settled European-founded community in Western Hemisphere. By 1550 most of the native Indian population had died of disease and warfare; city was almost destroyed by 1930 hurricane. Christopher Columbus' remains are reportedly buried here in the Cathedral of Santa Maria (1514). Industries: sugar, textiles, woodworking. Exports: tobacco, coffee, cacao. Pop. 980,000.

Santos, city in SE Brazil, 45mi (72km) SE of São Paulo on São Vincentes Island; contains largest harbor in Latin America; port is world's largest exporter of coffee and major distributor of other Brazilian products. Founded by Portuguese 1540. Pop. 341,317.

Saône River, river in E France, in Vosges Mts; flows SW past Gray, Chalon-sur-Saône, and Mâcon to join Rhône River at Lyons; connected by canals to Moselle, Marne, Yonne, and Loir rivers. Length: 298mi (480km).

São Paulo, city in SE Brazil, on Tietê River; capital of São Paulo state: was 17th-century base for expeditions into interior seeking slaves and mineral riches. Here Dom Pedro of Portuguese royal house declared Brazil's independence from Portugal in 1822; he later became Emperor Pedro I of Brazil. São Paulo was finance and trading center of coffee industry in the 19th

San Marino

São Tomé and Príncipe

John Singer Sargent

century. Largest city in Brazil and South America, it is the commercial, industrial, and financial hub of Brazil. Industries: car manufacture, metallurgy, chemicals, marketing agricultural products. Founded by Jesuits 1554; inc. 1711. Pop. 5,186,752.

São Tomé and Príncipe, independent W African republic in the Gulf of Guinea, off the W coast of Africa, consisting of the islands of São Tomé, approx. 150mi (241km) NW of Cape Lopez, Gabon; Príncipe, about 90mi (145km) NE of São Tomé; and several additional islets. The capital of São Tomé is on island of the same name.

Located on the equator, climate is humid with high temperatures and heavy rainfall from September to May of 40–100in (102–254cm). São Tomé island is 30mi (48km) long and 20mi (32km) wide; the highest point is Pico de São Tomé at 6,640ft (2,025m). Príncipe is 10mi (16km) long and 5mi (8km) wide with less rugged surface.

The islands' official language is Portuguese. People are descendants of original Portuguese and Africans with many Portuguese laborers who work on the islands' plantations. Religion is mainly Roman Catholic. Cacao is the chief export. Also grown and exported are coffee, bananas, coconuts, and copra and palm oil from coconuts.

Discovered by Portuguese navigators Pedro Escobar and João de Santarém 1470–71, the islands were officially claimed by Portugal in 1522 (claimed briefly by the Dutch in mid-17th century). Uninhabited at time of discovery, Portuguese came and brought Africans in as slaves. The islands began preparing for independence in 1974 and became independent in July 1975, with Manuel Pinto da Costa as the first president. Since independence he has faced several unsuccessful attempts to take over his government.

PROFILE

Official name: Democratic Republic of São Tomé and Príncipe
Area: 372sq mi (964sq km)
Population: 83,000
Chief city: São Tomé (capital)
Religion: Roman Catholic
Language: Portuguese (official)

Sapphire, a transparent to translucent gemstone variety of corundum, varying in color, the most valuable being deep blue. Most sapphires change color with direction of view. Star-sapphires reflect light in a six-pointed star. Brilliant when cut and polished, but lacking fire. *See also* Corundum.

Sappho, (late 7th–early 6th century BC) , Greek poetess from Lesbos. Regarded by other poets as the Tenth Muse, she was a noblewoman who ran a girls' school devoted to the study of music and poetry. Her theme was love, and she used nature to express her emotions. Amorous and passionate in style, she wrote love poems, of which large fragments remain, to her students. The Sapphic meter was named for her.

Sapporo, city in W Hokkaido, Japan; capital of Hokkaido prefecture. A growing industrial-commercial city, it has become the business center of Japan's N main island; situated at E foot of a mountain range, the city hosted the 1972 Winter Olympics; site of Hokkaido University. Industries: lumber, food processing, printing, publishing, tourism. Pop. 1,241,000.

Saprophyte, plant that obtains its food from dead or decaying plant and animal tissues. They usually have no chlorophyll and grow in humus. Saprophytes include bacteria, fungi (puffballs, mushrooms, and molds), and flowering plants (Indian pipe).

Sapsucker, North American woodpecker that drills rows of holes in trees to drink the sap. It also eats insects attracted by the flowing sap. They are blackish above with white mottling and yellowish below with a black chest patch. Males have crimson heads and throats. Genus *Sphyrapicus. See also* Woodpecker.

Saracens, a term first applied only to the people of NW Arabia and then extended to cover all Arabs and all Muslims. A Saracen invasion of France in the 8th century met defeat, but they were more successful in S Italy and in Sicily which they held from the 9th to the 11th century.

Saragossa, city in NE Spain, on the Ebro River; capital of Zaragoza prov.; traditional capital of Aragon. Originally an Iberian settlement, it was taken by Romans 1st century BC; fell to Visigoths 5th century; captured by Moors 713; taken 1118 by Alfonso I of Aragon. A major industrial and commercial center, it is site of 15th-century arched bridge, cathedral of La Seo (1119), University of Saragossa (1474). Industries: agricultural machinery, chemicals, glass, textiles. Area: (prov.) 6,639sq mi (17,195sq km). Pop. (city) 479,845; (prov.) 760,186.

Sarah, in the Bible, wife and half sister of Abraham and mother of Isaac. Childless, she gave Abraham her maid Hagar, who bore Ishmael. In her old age, Sarah bore Isaac.

Sarajevo, city in SW central Yugoslavia, on Bosna River; capital of Bosnia and Herzegovina; site of university (1946), 15th-century mosque. Founded as Vrh-Bosna citadel, city fell to Turks 1429; passed to Austria-Hungary 1878; inc. into Yugoslavia 1918. City was scene of assassination of Archduke Francis Ferdinand and his wife, June 28, 1914, precipitating WWI. Industries: textiles, steel, tobacco, sugar, beer, carpets, handicrafts, electrical equipment. Founded 1263. Pop. 244,045.

Sarasota, city in W central Florida, on Gulf of Mexico, 51mi (82km) S of Tampa. Winter home of Ringling Brothers Circus; site of Ringling Museum of Art. Settled 1886; inc. 1914. Pop. (1980) 48,868.

Saratoga, Battle of, Revolutionary War battle in which British Gen. John Burgoyne's forces were defeated at Saratoga, N.Y. (Oct. 17, 1777). It was a turning point in the war, influencing France to recognize the colonies. Burgoyne's expedition, marching from Canada to Albany, suffered heavy losses. Overwhelmed, he surrendered his entire army to Gen. Horatio Gates.

Saratov, city in Russian SFSR, USSR, on the Volga River; capital of Saratov oblast. Founded 1590 it moved to the present site in 1674; chartered 1780; developed into a major 19th-century grain trade center; it was successfully defended by Soviet troops in the civil war (1918–19); in 1943 it came under jurisdiction of Russian SFSR government; site of university (1919), institutes for road construction and agricultural mechanization, conservatory, agricultural, medical, and teachers' colleges, archeological and ethnographic museums. Industries: natural gas, chemicals, cotton textiles, leather goods, soap, flour, oilseeds, oil, lumber, shipbuilding, precision instruments. Pop. 866,000.

Sarcodina, term meaning "living jelly," it is a class of protozoa that includes the amoeba. The original name for this class, it is used alternatively with "Rhizopoda." *See also* Rhizopoda.

Sarcoma, cancerous growth or tumor made up of tissues from muscles and bones or cells embedded in connective tissue. It is usually highly malignant.

Sardegna. See Sardinia.

Sardine, small marine food fish found worldwide. It has a laterally compressed body, large toothless mouth, and oily flesh. Length: to 1ft (30cm). Species include the California *Sardinops Caerulea,* South American *Sardinops sagax,* and the European sardine, or pilchard, *Sardinia pilchardus.* Family Clupeidae.

Sardinia (Sardegna), island in Mediterranean Sea; forms autonomous region of W Italy, with islands of Asinara, Caprera, San Pietro, and La Maddalena; capital city is Cagliari. Major portion of the island is mountainous; Campidano Plain in SW is major agricultural area. Prehistoric civilization existed; island was settled by Phoenicians c. 800 BC, Carthaginians c. 500 BC; taken by Rome 238 BC; under Vandals AD 5th century; made a Byzantine province 6th–8th centuries; attacked by Saracens 8th-11th centuries; disputed 11th-14th centuries by Pisa and Genoa; given to Aragonese by Pope Boniface VIII 13th century; passed to Spain 15th century, Austria 1713, Savoy 1720 and was included in kingdom of Sardinia. Products: wheat, barley, grapes, olives, livestock. Industries: fishing, processed foods, wine, refined petroleum, paper, cement, textiles. Area: 9,301sq mi (24,090sq km). Highest point is Mt Gennargentu, 6,017ft (1,835m). Pop. 1,571,499.

Sardinia, Kingdom of, the possessions of the House of Savoy from 1720, when they were ceded Sardinia to compensate for the loss of Sicily. It comprised Sardinia, Savoy, Nice, Aosta, Montferrat, Piedmont, and Genoa. Fighting with the Allies against France during the French Revolution, it lost most of its mainland possessions to France from 1798 to 1814 (Napoleon's defeat). Lombardy became part of the kingdom in 1859; most of the Papal States in 1860; the Two Sicilies in 1861—so that from the Risorgimento the kingdom of Sardinia included almost all of modern Italy, and Victor Emmanuel II of Sardinia became king of Italy.

Sardis, ancient city in Asia Minor, 50mi (80km) E of Smyrna in the Hermus valley; served as capital of ancient Lydia c. 650–519 BC; site of first minting of coins (6th century BC); passed to Rome AD 133; one of Seven Churches of Asia Minor; ruined 14th century by Tamerlane. Archeological excavations uncovered the city 1958,; further excavations (1962) revealed temple of Artemis (4th century BC).

Sargasso Sea, the eddy within the North Atlantic gyre, named for the large quantities of floating seaweed *Sargassum* which covers it. Though filled with the seaweed, in reality it is like a great oceanic dessert, with the lowest amount of life of any sea water. *See also* Gyre.

Sargassum Fish, marine bony fish found in tropical seas worldwide. A voracious predator, its balloon-shaped body is covered with loose skin camouflaging it as floating seaweed; it also has a "fishing pole" lure on its head. Length: 6in (15.2cm). Family Antennariidae; species *Histrio histrio.*

Sargent, John Singer (1856–1925), US painter, b. Italy. The son of wealthy expatriate parents, he lived and studied abroad. He is best known for his numerous portrait commissions, especially those of society ladies. His infamous portrait of Madame Gautreau (Mme. X) was rejected by his client and also by the French art public because he lowered the neckline of her dress and also exposed her vanity. His later works included Impressionistic watercolors.

Sargon (*fl. c.*2600 BC), founder of first Semitic dynasty of Akkad in ancient Mesopotamia. His empire lasted over 100 years and stretched from the Persian Gulf to the Mediterranean Sea.

Sargon II (died 705 BC), powerful King of Assyria (721–705), succeeding Shalmaneser V. He conquered Samaria (721), subjugated Babylonia and the other major unconquered states of Syria, and broke the power of Urartu (Armenia).

Sark, island in the English Channel; one of the Channel Islands, E of Guernsey; comprises Great Sark and Little Sark, linked by the Coupée isthmus. Its economy is based on agriculture and tourism. Area: 2sq mi (5sq km). Pop. 590.

Sarmatians, ancient nomadic and pastoral people who in the 5th century BC lived in the area between the Caspian Sea, the Don River, and the Sea of Azov. By the 3d century BC, their territory extended from the Baltic to the Black Sea, from the Vistula River to the Volga. They were overpowered by the Goths from the west and the Huns from Asia in the 4th century AD.

Sarney, José (1930–), Brazilian political leader, president (1985–). He began his political career as assistant to a state governor (1950). In 1956 he entered Congress, being reelected twice (1958, 1962). He was later governor of Maranhão (1965–70) then state senator for Maranhão (1970), representing what became the Social Democratic party (PDS) (1979). After heading the PDS (1981–84), he left to lead a faction that joined with an opposing group to form the Liberal party, which nominated him for vice-president (1984). Sarney became president when President-elect Tancredo Neves died before assuming the office.

Sarnia, city in SW Ontario; pipeline terminus for oil from Texas and Alberta. Industries: oil refineries, chemical products, lumber. Founded 1807 by French, 1833 by English. Pop. 56,727.

Sarsaparilla, wild perennial plant native to North America. It has greenish flowers. Family Araliaceae; species *Aralia nudicaulis.* Or, several species of *Smilax* (family Liliaceae) cultivated for their roots formerly thought to have medicinal value.

Sarto, Andrea del (1486–1531), Florentine artist known as "the faultless painter" after decorating the Cloisters of the Annunziata in Florence. His work, in which figure and background are closely related, is represented in New York City's Metropolitan Museum by "Holy Family."

Sartre, Jean-Paul (1905–80), French novelist, playwright, and philosopher. He participated in the French Resistance in World War II. The foremost exponent of Existentialism, he was also involved in Marxist politics. For many years he lived with author Simone de Beauvoir. His important works include *Nausea* (1938), *Being and Nothingness* (1943), *The Roads to Freedom* (1949), *Critique of Dialectical Reason* (1964), and *Black Orpheus* (1971). In 1964 he refused the Nobel Prize for literature. *See also* Existentialism.

Saskatchewan, province in W central Canada, in the plains region, bordered on the S by the states of Montana and North Dakota.

Land and Economy. The country is gently rolling; the highest elevations are in the SW. The S half is chiefly agricultural land; the N is forested wilderness. Rivers, of which the most important are the North and the South Saskatchewan, cut deep valleys; there are hundreds of lakes. The province has long been a major wheat producer. Oil drilling, tapping of natural gas resources, and uranium mining have developed largely since WWII.

People. Settlement did not begin until the late 19th century, when immigrants came from E Canada, the United States, and Europe. People of English descent form the largest sector of the population, with elements of Germans, Ukrainians, Scandinavians, and French.

Education. The University of Saskatchewan at Saskatoon and the University of Regina are the only institutions of higher education.

History. Henry Kelsey, an agent of the Hudson's Bay Co., fur traders, visited the region in 1690. The first trading post, Fort Lacorne, was built in 1753; the first permanent settlement was Cumberland House, built by the Hudson's Bay Co. in 1774. Slow immigration created farming communities through the 19th century, but the population influx did not begin until after the completion of the transcontinental Canadian Pacific Railroad in 1885. Saskatchewan joined the Confederation on the same day as Alberta in 1905. Under Saskatchewan's Socialist government (1944–64), many innovative social welfare programs were introduced that were subsequently adopted by Canada's national government.

PROFILE

Admitted to Confederation: Sept. 1, 1905; rank, 9th
National Parliament Representatives: Senate, 6; House of Commons, 13
Population: 907,650; rank, 6th
Capital: Regina
Chief cities: Regina; Saskatoon; Moose Jaw
Provincial Legislature: Legislative Assembly, 60
Area: 251,700sq mi (651,903sq km); rank, 5th
Elevation: Highest, 4,546ft (1,386m), Cypress Hills; lowest, 699ft (213m), Lake Athabaska
Industries (major products): petroleum products, processed foods
Agriculture (major products): wheat, barley, oats, rye, beef cattle, hogs, flax
Minerals (major): petroleum, natural gas, uranium, potash
Floral emblem: wood lily

Saskatchewan, river in S central Canada; has two tributaries—North and South Saskatchewan rivers. Both rise in E region of the Rocky Mts, continuing E and emptying into Lake Winnipeg, 25mi (40km) E of Prince Albert, Saskatchewan. Discovered 18th century by Sieur de La Vérendrye, it was a well-traveled route for fur trapping companies. Agriculture is prominent around the river's mouth, where irrigation began in 1901. Length: approx. 340mi (547km).

Saskatoon, city in S central Saskatchewan, Canada, on South Saskatchewan River; est. as capital of a temperance society under the direction of the Temperance Colonization Society of Ontario; site of the University of Saskatchewan; commercial and distributing center for surrounding grain farms. Industries: flour, cereal mills, meat packing, dairy products. Founded 1883; inc. 1906. Pop. 133,750.

Sassafras, small E North American tree with furrowed bark, green twigs, yellow flowers, and blue berries. Its leaves have three shapes (3-lobed, 2-lobed, or smooth egg-shape) often on the same branch. An aromatic tea is made from the outer bark of its roots and oil from the roots is used to flavor root beer. Family Lauraceae; species *Sassafras albidum.*

Sassanids, or **Sassanians,** last native dynasty of Persian kings, founded by Ardashir I *c.* AD 226. There were approximately 25 Sassanid rulers, the most important after Ardashir being Shapur II (309–79); Khosrau I (531–79), who invaded Syria; and Khosrau II (590–628), whose conquest of Egypt marks the height of the dynasty's power. The line ended when Persia fell to the Arabs *c.*641.

Satan, a name for the devil. Originally, Satan simply meant an opponent, and not a particular being. Around the 6th century BC, he appears in the Old Testament as an individual angel, subordinate to God. Gradually, Satan became the source of all evil, responsible for leading man into sin, and thus the tempter opposed to God.

Satellite, a body that orbits around a much more massive body. The Moon, for example, is a satellite of Earth. The two objects actually both orbit around the center of mass between them. However, because this point is deep inside the Earth, not far from the Earth's center, the effect is as though the Moon orbited around a stationary Earth. The Earth and the other planets orbit around the Sun. The physical laws that govern these motions also govern the motions of artificial satellites.

Satellite, Artificial, man-made object orbiting a planet. The first Earth satellite was Sputnik 1, launched Oct. 4, 1957, by the Soviet Union. The main uses of satellites are military reconnaissance, weather studies, communications, and scientific studies. Artificial satellites are distinguished from space probes, which do not orbit planets. *See also* Satellite, Communications; Satellite, Geodetic; Satellite, Weather; Sputnik.

Satellite, Communications, satellite used to beam or reflect electromagnetic signals. Passive satellites such as the aluminized 100-ft (30.5m) high "balloon" (Echo series) serve as reflectors. Active satellites such as Intelsat can handle thousands of telephone circuits or 12 television channels. Synchronous satellites such as Syncom provide 24-hour coverage to large areas. *See also* Synchronous Orbit, Satellite.

Satellite, Geodetic, satellite whose orbit is studied from widely separated places to provide more accurate maps of oceans and continents. The Geodetic Earth Orbiting Satellite program of 1971 (GEOS) reduced intercontinental distance errors to 10 meters. Laser measurements of vertical Earth movements to forecast incipient earthquakes are also possible.

Satellite, Natural, any of several minor bodies orbiting some of the planets of the solar system. Six planets are known to have satellites, ranging in numbers from one for Earth to possibly more than 20 for Saturn. Some satellites appear to be asteroids captured after the solar system was already formed. Others, such as the Moon, may have formed with the planets or coalesced from particles orbiting them.

Satellite, Weather, a satellite studying weather patterns on Earth by photographic, infrared, or other means. Photographic histories of hurricane development and discovery of large-scale coherence in cloud and other weather patterns have had great impact on weather forecasts.

Satinwood Tree, tree native to E India with smooth, hard wood that is valued for furniture and veneer. Height: to 50ft (15m). Family Rutaceae; species *Chloroxylon swietenia.*

Satire, Roman, invented by the poet Gaius Lucilius in the 2nd century BC. Only fragments of his works remain. Satire became agreeably persuasive in Horace's *Satires* and the instructional quality was emphasized even more in the works of Persius. Juvenal was the first great tragic satirist and the satirical romance appeared with the works of Petronius and Apuleius. *See also* Horace; Juvenal; Lucilius, Gaius.

Sato, Eisaku (1901–75), Japanese political figure. In 1947 he became vice-minister of transportation after work with the railway ministry and was finance minister (1958–60). A Liberal-Democratic member of the Diet, he was prime minister (1964–72). His chief foreign policy successes were normalization of relations with South Korea and the signing of a treaty returning Okinawa and the Bonin Islands to Japanese jurisdiction (1969). In 1974 he was awarded the Nobel Prize for peace.

Saturation, condition of a solution when the maximum amount of the dissolved substance, the solute, has been taken into solution at a given temperature. Conditions of supersaturation—excess solute over the limiting condition of the saturated state—can exist for a few seconds, but are unstable.

Saturn, sixth planet from the sun and second largest in the solar system, encircled by at least 17 and possibly as many as 23 satellites and a complicated ring system consisting of thousands of ringlets composed of icy or ice covered particles. Mean distance from the Sun, 886,000,000mi (1,427,000,000km); mass and volume, 95.2 and 744 times that of Earth, respectively; equatorial diameter, 75,000mi (120,911km); rotation period, 10hr 14min; period of sidereal revolution, 29.46 years; composition, principally hydrogen, methane, ammonia, and helium. *See also* Solar System.

Saturn, in Roman religion, the god of sowing or seed. Saturn's cult partner was the goddess Lua. He is also associated with Ops. His great festival, the Saturnalia, became the most popular of Roman festivals and its influence is still felt throughout the Western world in the celebrations of Christmas and New Year's.

Satyr Butterfly, brown and gray butterfly often having eyespots on wings. Veins of the front wings are typically swollen at wing base. Family Agapetidae; genus *Neonymphia.*

Satyriasis, insatiable sexual appetite in a male. Compulsive sexual activity in which sexual thoughts and behavior completely dominate all else. As in the case of nymphomania, it is the insatiable nature of the need for sexual gratification that defines the syndrome.

Satyrs, in Greek mythology, gods of the woods, fields, and mountains of sensual and lascivious character. They are depicted as goat-bearded and goat-legged, but with the head (though horned) and trunk of a man. In later art their countenance became milder, less animal. They became men with small horns and pointed ears.

Saud (1902–69), king of Saudi Arabia (1953–64). His name in full was Ibn Abd al-Aziz Al Faisal Al Saud. The son and successor of Ibn Saud, he became crown prince (1933). His fiscal mismanagement and personal extravagance caused a severe financial crisis in 1958. Soon after, his brother Faisal took over all administrative powers, formally replacing Saud as king in 1964.

Saudi Arabia, Kingdom of, nation of Arabian Peninsula. The people are Arabic and overwhelmingly Muslim. The country is the birthplace of Islam and site of the holy city of Mecca. The leading oil producer of the

Jean-Paul Sartre

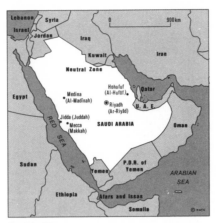

Saudi Arabia

Mecca, Saudi Arabia

Middle East and the foremost Arab leader, Saudi Arabia played a vital role in world economics and politics in the 1970s and early 1980s.

Land and Economy. There are two major geologic regions. The Arabian Shield, in the W, is composed of ancient crystalline rock piled up into mountain chains (7,000–9,000ft; 2,135–2,745m) paralleling the Red Sea. The E region, of sedimentary rock, slopes gently toward the Persian Gulf. The hot, humid Tihamah plain lies between the mountains and coast. The interior is less humid and hot than the coasts. Most of Saudi Arabia is arid; the largest deserts, connected by the Dahna sand belt, are the Rub al-Khali in the S (230,000sq mi; 595,700sq km) and the Great Nafud in the N (26,000sq mi; 67,340sq km). The economy is dominated by oil, exploited from 1938, which furnishes over 90% of revenue. The government has bought control of the Arabian American Oil Company (Aramco), the primary producer. Enormous natural gas deposits occur in conjunction with the oil. Some salt and gypsum are extracted, and clay and limestone are used in cement manufacture. Saudi Arabia falls short of self-sufficiency in food. Dhahran, Jidda, Riyadh, and Medina have international airports. Jidda and Damman are the major ports. Profits from oil and natural gas are being invested in industrial development.

People. The vast majority of the Saudis are descended from indigenous tribes; different Arabic dialects are spoken. About 90% of the people are Sunnite Muslims of the Wahhabi sect; some Shiite Muslims live in the E. Over 50% of the population is nomadic or semi-nomadic; about 25% city-dwellers; the remainder primarily farmers. The family and tribe are the main social units. The population is about 90% illiterate, but extensive education programs have been inaugurated, including expanded opportunities for women.

Government. The constitution is based on Islam's Wahhabi reform movement. The king's power is by the law of Islam and by the Council of Ministers. The principal decisions of the Council are issued as royal decrees. Elections are held only at the municipal level; there are no political parties. Local government is largely in the hands of appointed officials, many of whom are members of the royal family. Religious judges preside over the courts, but local administrative officials have certain judicial functions.

History. The area's early history is covered under Arabia. The power of the Saud family, originally rulers of an oasis, grew from 1774 as the Wahhabi movement, which it led, spread in the Nejd. Mecca was occupied (1803), but the Turks then conquered the Nejd (1818). The house of Saud revived, and Ibn Saud recaptured (1902) the ancestral capital of Riyadh. In 1932 he named his kingdom Saudi Arabia. Neutral in World War II, Saudi Arabia was a founding member of the United Nations (1945) and the Arab League. Ibn Saud was succeeded (1953) by his son Saud, deposed in 1964 in favor of his half-brother Faisal. Faisal, assassinated in 1975, was succeeded by his brother Khalid, who died in 1982, and was succeeded by Crown Prince Fahd. Saudi Arabia's power has increased as its petroleum has become more valuable, and although it remains opposed to Israel, Saudi Arabia, closely allied with the United States, is the leading moderate voice among the Arab countries. An important member of the Organization of Petroleum Exporting Countries (OPEC), Saudi Arabia has been opposed to rapid increases in the price of oil and was slow to curtail production to reduce the oil glut during the 1980s. By 1985, dissatisfied with the actions of other OPEC countries, Saudi Arabia became more competitive in the world oil market. *See also* Arabia; Arab League.

PROFILE

Official name: Kingdom of Saudi Arabia
Area: 830,000sq mi (2,149,700sq km)

Population: 7,100,000
Density. 8.5per sq mi (3per sq km)
Chief cities: Riyadh (capital); Jidda; Mecca
Government: Head of state, King Khalid (acceded 1975)
Religion: Islam (official)
Language: Arabic (official)
Monetary unit: Riyal
Gross national product: $62,640,000,000
Per capita income: $11,500
Manufacturing (major products): petroleum products, cement, fertilizers, iron, and steel
Agriculture (major products): dates, vegetables, wheat
Minerals (major): petroleum
Trading partners (major): United States, West Germany, Japan

Sauk, or **Sac,** an Algonquian-speaking tribe of North American Indians originally occupying the Saginaw Bay region of Michigan. Closely related to the Mesquakie, Potawatomi, and Kickapoo peoples, they are famous for their role in the Black Hawk War of 1832. Approximately 1,200 live on lands in Kansas, Iowa, and Oklahoma today.

Saul, in the Bible, first king of Israel and son of Benjaminite Kish. Anointed by the prophet Samuel to be Israelite leader, he became king after his victory over the Ammonites. His jealousy led to conflicts with Samuel, David, and his son Jonathan. After hearing his defeat and death prophesied, he committed suicide rather than be captured by the Philistines.

Sault Sainte Marie, city in S Ontario, Canada, across St Mary's River from Sault Ste Marie, Michigan; seat of Algoma district. During 17th century it was populated by missionaries, fur traders, and explorers; North-West Fur Co. est. a trading post here in 18th century. City is chief port, close to lakes Huron, Superior, and Michigan. Industries: paper, lumber, steel, iron, farming, chemicals. Founded 1668; inc. 1912. Pop. 81,048.

Sault Sainte Marie Canals (Soo Canals), artificial waterway system on the US-Canadian border, between lakes Huron and Superior at the twin cities of Sault Sainte Marie, N Michigan, and Sault Sainte Marie, S central Ontario. A canal system was needed to bypass the rapids of the St Marys River and connect the vital water routes of the Great Lakes; the Canadian canal was completed in 1799 but was later destroyed by US attacks during the War of 1812; it was rebuilt in 1895. A parallel route on the US side was built 1853–55; this was replaced and enlarged 1881–1919. The US canal is 1.6mi (3km) long with two channels and four locks. Two of the locks, 1,350ft (412m) long and 80ft (24m) wide, are among the largest in the world. The Canadian canal is 1.4mi (2km) long and has one lock. This system, although ice-bound in winter, is one of the world's busiest waterways.

Saurischian, "lizard-hipped" dinosaur, carnivorous as well as herbivorous. Theropoda were meat-eaters, and Sauropoda were plant-eaters. The pelvis was characteristically three-pronged, resembling lizard's.

Sauropoda, saurischian dinosaur that was a swamp-dwelling, semiaquatic giant flourishing worldwide during the Jurassic period until Cretaceous times (65–136,000,000 years ago). Included were all large, peg-toothed herbivorous types such as Brontosaurus and Diplodocus.

Sava, longest river in Yugoslavia; rises in Julian Alps in NW Slovenia, flows ESE across N Yugoslavia into

Danube River at Belgrade; navigable to Sisak. Length: approx. 584mi (940km).

Savannah, city and port of entry in E Georgia, on Savannah River; seat of Chatham co; oldest city in Georgia. Chosen as the seat of colonial government and capital of Georgia Colony 1754, it was captured by British 1778 during American Revolution and held until end of the war; served as state capital 1754–86; grew quickly as cotton center. A Confederate supply depot during Civil War, it was taken by Gen. William Sherman Dec. 21, 1864. Its colonial homes include Pirate's (1754), Herb (1734), Pink (1789), and Wormsloe (1733) houses; birthplace of Juliette Gordon Low; site of Armstrong State College (1935), Savannah State College (1890). Industries: paper, petroleum products, paint, wallboard, refined sugar, food processing, shipbuilding and repair, wood products. Founded 1733 by Gen. James Oglethorpe; inc. 1789. Pop. (1980) 141,634.

Savannah River, river in E Georgia and NW South Carolina; formed by confluence of Tugaloo and Seneca rivers in South Carolina; flows SE forming major part of boundary between Georgia and South Carolina; empties into Atlantic Ocean at Savannah; site of Hartwell and Clark Hill Dams, part of Savannah River Basin development plan. Length: 314mi (505km).

Savonarola, Girolamo (1452–98), Italian religious reformer. He abandoned medicine to become a monk, when convinced of the sinfulness of the world. Sent to Florence (1482) he was first enchanted and then horrified by Florentine culture. When he returned to Florence (1490) it was as a famous pulpit orator. As prior of St Marks, he was led by visions in a crusade against corruption, and after the collapse of Medici rule (1494) Savonarola became virtual dictator of the city. Consequent to the civil disturbances that ensued, he was executed. Florence, apparently, could only be persuaded to rid itself momentarily of "vanities," against which Savonarola had preached.

Savory, common name for hardy aromatic herbs of the mint family with leaves used, green or dried, for flavoring. Summer savory (*Satureia hortensis*) is an annual. Winter Savory (*S. montana*) is a perennial.

Savoy, royal European dynasty and ruling house of Italy from 1861–1946. Descended from Humbert the Whitehanded (died *c.* 1048), the first count of Savoy, they were dukes from 1416, kings of Sicily from 1720, and kings of Italy from the Risorgimento (1861) through World War II (until 1946). It was under the house of Savoy that Italian unification was achieved (1860–70) and Benito Mussolini's Fascists ruled Italy (1922–43).

Savoy, historic region between Italy and France. Historically important for its control of western Alpine passes, it was part of the first Burgundian kingdom, the kingdom of Arles, and, in the 11th century, the Holy Roman Empire (as a county). In 1416 it became a duchy and then greatly expanded into France, Switzerland, and Italy. Savoy became part of France permanently in 1860, while its rulers became kings of Italy.

Sawfish, flat-bodied elasmobranch found in tropical marine and brackish waters. Actually a ray, its dark gray or black-brown body has a long saw-toothed sword attached to its nose. It uses it to dig up the ocean bottom and to club prey. Length: to 16ft (5m). Family Prisidae; species W Atlantic common *Pristis pectinotus; See also* Ray.

Sawfly, primitive, plant-feeding wasp that lacks a thread waist. Its larvae are caterpillarlike, with 8 abdominal legs. The females have a two-bladed, sawlike ovipositor for laying eggs in plant tissue. Found worldwide, they rarely exceed 0.8in (20mm) in length. Family Tenthredinidae. *See also* Hymenoptera.

Saxe-Weimar, former duchy in central Germany; became separate entity 1547 when Ernestine lands were divided into duchies of Weimar, Gotha, Coburg, Eisenach, and Altenburg. In 1741 it became Saxe-Weimar-Eisenach duchy and developed into a European cultural center under Duke Charles Augustus, patron of Johann Wolfgang Von Goethe. In 1920 the duchy was inc. into German state of Thuringia.

Saxifrage, perennial plants native to temperate and mountainous regions of Europe and North America. Leaves are massed at the base and the small flowers are white, pink, purple, or yellow. Height: to 2ft (61cm). Family Saxifragaceae; genus *Saxifraga.*

Saxons, ancient Germanic people. Originating in N Europe, they extended south and west, eventually colonizing Britain (*c.*450). There they amalgamated with the Angles to form the Anglo-Saxon civilization. The continental Saxons warred with the Franks and were finally subjugated by Charlemagne in the early 9th century. Their lands became part of what is now modern Germany.

Saxony, former German state; since WWII it has been part of East Germany. Est. late 9th century by the Duchy of Saxony, it was one of five primary duchies of medieval Germany and included almost all land between Elbe and Saale rivers (E), Rhine (W), and Franconia and Thuringia (E). By 1435 its area had shifted from NW to E central Germany; in 1815 over half of Saxony was ceded to Prussia and, with several Prussian districts, it became the province of Saxony, which included Wittenburg and Thuringia, plus territories between Elbe River and Harz Mts. In 1945 state of Anhalt was added to form Saxony Anhalt state; in 1952 East Germany reorganized its land into smaller administrative units and eliminated Saxony-Anhalt. Industries: agriculture, mining, chemicals, textiles.

Saxophone, wind musical instrument with single-reed, curved conical pipe of metal and holes with keys. Invented by Adolphe Sax in Paris (1840), it is made in seven sizes, soprano to bass, pitched alternately Eb and Bb, with alto and tenor most common. It was used symphonically by Bizet, Debussy, Ravel, Richard Strauss, and Prokofiev. Associated with dance halls after World War I, the hybrid saxophone with its rich, voicelike timbre was accepted in the late 1920s by jazz musicians.

Sayers, Dorothy (1863–1957), English novelist and playwright. Her first novels were detective stories featuring Lord Peter Wimsey, including *Whose Body?* (1923) and *Strong Poison* (1930). Her plays are religious dramas, such as *The Zeal of Thy House* (1937) and a sequence of radio plays *The Man Born to be King* (1941). She also wrote critical essays on medieval literature.

Scab, in botany, any of various plant diseases whose symptoms include scabby scaly spots on fruit and twigs or velvety spots on leaves. Scabby fruit is often stunted or deformed. Scab diseases are serious pests of apples, pears, pecans, peaches, cucumbers, and potatoes.

Scabies, inflammation of the skin brought about by a female mite, *Sarcoptes scabei,* burrowing in the skin to lay eggs. It can be seen as a dark wavy line on the skin.

Scafell Pike, mountain in NW England, in Cumbria; highest peak in England, 3,210ft (979m). Neighboring Scafell (Sca Fell) is the second-highest, 3,162ft (964m).

Scalar, quantity that has only a magnitude, as contrasted with a vector. Mass, energy, and speed are scalars, while weight, force, and velocity are vectors. *See also* Vector.

Scale, flat plates that form the outer covering of most fishes and many reptiles and which cover a few mammals (scaly anteater) and occur on certain body parts of other animals. Scales often overlap one another like shingles and protect softer inner body parts. In bony fishes, the scales are bony disks developed from under the skin; in sharks they are enamel and bone; in reptiles they are usually hardened and horny folded skin. The term is also used for the small flaky leaves that cover plant buds.

Scale Insect, small insect destructive to plants found worldwide. All are covered by a waxy or scalelike covering secreted by the insect. They feed by sucking

plant juices. Length: to 1in (25mm). Family Coccidae. *See also* Cochineal, Lac Insect, San Jose Scale.

Scallop, edible bivalve mollusk. Generally the bottom valve is convex with the upper valve almost flat. The shell's surface is ribbed and scalloped. Most possess well-developed eyes that fringe the fleshy mantle. Width: 1–8in (2.5–20cm). Family Pectinidae. *See also* Bivalve, Mollusk.

Scaly Anteater. *See* Pangolin.

Scanderbeg, or **Skanderbeg** (1403–68), national hero of Albania. His real name was George Castriota; his Turkish name was Iskender Bey. A Serb, he was abducted by Turks at age seven, and became a favorite army commander of Sultan Murad II. In 1443 he renounced Islam, married the daughter of an Albanian chieftan, and drove the Turks out of Albania. For 20 years he maintained the area's independence against every force. His empire collapsed immediately after his death, however, and the Turks took control.

Scandinavia, region of N Europe, consisting of kingdoms of Sweden, Norway, and Denmark; culturally and historically Finland and Iceland are often considered part of this area. It is bordered by the Gulf of Bothnia, the Baltic Sea, the Kattegat and Skagerrak straits, North Sea, and Atlantic and Arctic oceans. Mountainous in W with swift-flowing streams, its coastline has many fjords; land in E and S is gently sloped and has many lakes. Approx. 25% of peninsula lies in Arctic Circle where tundra predominates. S Sweden contains best farmlands; there is much forested land and mineral wealth, and coastal waters supply abundant fish. Largest cities are: Stockholm and Göteborg, Sweden; Oslo, Norway; and Helsinki, Finland. Area of peninsula: 300,000sq mi (777,000sq km).

Scandium, metallic element (symbol Sc) of group IIIB of the periodic table predicted (as ekaboron) by Mendeleev and discovered in 1879 by Lars Nilson. It is found in thortveitite and, in small amounts, in many other minerals. It is a soft metal with few commercial uses. Chemically it resembles the lanthanides. Properties: at. no. 21; at. wt. 44.9559; sp gr 2.99 (25°C); melt. pt. 2802°F (1539°C); boil. pt. 5130°F (2832°C); most common isotope Sc^{45} (100%).

Scansion, analysis of the meter of a poem by breaking down each line into metrical feet. Each foot consists of a group of two or three syllables, one of which is stressed, or long. Metrical feet are scanned as: iambs (one short, one long ∪–); trochees (one long, one short –∪); anapests (two shorts, one long ∪∪–); dactyls (one long, two shorts –∪∪); spondees (two longs ––); pyrrhics (two shorts ∪∪). *See also* Meter; Rhythm.

Scapa Flow, landlocked anchorage in Scotland, S of Pomona (Mainland) in the Orkney Islands. The main entrance is from Pentland Firth(S). In both world wars the British fleet was stationed at Scapa Flow; here the German fleet was scuttled 1918, and the battleship *Royal Oak* sunk 1939. Length: 15mi (24km). Width: 8mi (13km).

Scapegoat, in ancient Israel, a goat used in the ritual on the Day of Atonement. The high priest touched the goat and confessed the sins of the community. The animal was then driven from the village, symbolically bearing the sins of the people. Later, as the ritual developed, the scapegoat was pushed to his death from a cliff. The term has come to mean one blamed unfairly for others' misfortunes.

Scapula, or shoulder blade, a large, roughly triangular, flat bone, that serves to hold the upper arm bone, or humerus, in place. It allows for the attachment of muscles that function in arm movement. The scapula joins with the clavicle at a point called the acromion process and with the humerus at the glenoid cavity.

Scarab Beetle, robust, broad beetle distributed worldwide. Most scarab beetles, including the June bug, Japanese beetle, and rhinoceros beetle, are leaf chafers. A smaller group, including the dung beetle or tumblebug, are scavengers. Family Scarabaeidae.

Scarlatti, Alessandro (1660–1725), Italian composer known primarily for his vocal music, which appeared in his 115 operas, 200 masses, and over 700 cantatas and oratorios.

Scarlatti, Domenico (1683–1757), Italian composer, son of Alessandro Scarlatti. A harpsichord virtuoso, he settled in Spain and is primarily known for his 545 short pieces for the harpsichord. These pieces advanced keyboard technique and place Scarlatti as the greatest Italian composer of keyboard music of the Baroque period. *See also* Baroque Music.

Scarlet Fever, or scarlatina, acute contagious disease, usually of children, caused by streptococcal bacteria. It is characterized by body rash, fever, and throat infection. It may be transmitted from person to person by direct contact or through use of the same utensils.

Scattering, Light, deflection of light waves from the main direction of a beam by fine particles of solid, liquid, or gaseous matter. The effects observed depend on the size of the particles, smaller particles causing diffraction while larger particles produce diffraction and reflection. *See also* Diffraction, Reflection.

Schechter Poultry Corporation v. United States (1935), US Supreme Court decision invalidating Pres. Franklin Roosevelt's National Recovery Administration (NRA). The court declared that the NRA codes could not be applied to a firm not engaged in interstate commerce. This limited view of the commerce clause was short lived, and *NLRB* v. *Jones and Laughlin* subsequently insured success for Roosevelt's New Deal programs. *See also* National Labor Relations Board v. Jones and Laughlin Steel Company (1937); National Recovery Administration.

Scheel, Walter (1919–), West German political figure. As head of the Free Democratic party (1968–74), he formed a coalition government (1969) with the Social Democrats and served as foreign minister in the cabinet of Willy Brandt. When Brandt resigned in 1974, Scheel was briefly chancellor. He then became president of West Germany (1974–79).

Scheele, Karl Wilhelm (1742–86), Swedish chemist. An apothecary, his interest in chemistry led to an investigation of combustion and the discovery of oxygen. Publication of this discovery was delayed and the credit went to Joseph Priestley. He made other important discoveries, including chlorine, glycerine, and a number of organic acids.

Scheelite, a molybdate mineral, calcium tungstate-molybdate [Ca (WO$_4$,MoO$_4$)]. An important ore of tungsten. In metamorphic deposits and in pegmatites. Tetragonal system bipyramidal crystals; also massive and granular aggregates. In various tints with adamantine luster; brittle. Hardness 4.5–6; sp gr 5. Fluoresces under ultraviolet light.

Schefflera, or umbrella tree, genus of slow-growing ornamental tree native to the South Pacific islands. It has shiny, round leaves of up to 16 oval leaflets on branches rising from a single stem. Care: bright light, soil (equal parts loam, peat moss, sand) kept dry between waterings. Propagation is by seeds. Height: to 6 ft (1.8m).

Schelde (Sheldt or **Escaut),** river rises in N France, flows N and NE through W Belgium to Antwerp, then NW into North Sea through 2 estuaries (East and West Schelde) in the Netherlands. It is a master stream for a dense network of canals in N France and Belgium; navigable for most of its 270mi (435km).

Schenck v. United States (1919), landmark US Supreme Court case in which Justice Holmes emerged as the court's spokesman in free speech matters. He stated the "clear and present danger" test defining the limits of 1st Amendment protection. The court ruled that no speech was protected if illegal action was the likely result of such speech. The test adopted has been the subject of continuous debate and the subsequent cases of *Gitlow* v. *New York* and *Whitney* v. *California* refined it.

Schenectady, industrial city in E New York, 13mi (20km) NW of Albany on Mohawk River; seat of Schenectady co. In 1661, Arent Van Curler bought the land from Mohawk Indians; it was scene of Indian raid 1690; industrial growth was spurred by completion of Erie Canal (1825) and railroads (1830s); locomotive works (1848) and General Electric plant (1892) still remain as major Schenectady employers; site of Union College and University (1795). Industries: electrical materials, locomotives, chemicals, aerospace, plastics. Inc. 1798. Pop. (1980) 67,972.

Schick Test, a test of immunity to diphtheria, devised by the Hungarian-born US pediatrician Béla Schick, in which lack of immunity is demonstrated by the appearance of an area of inflammation at the site of injection of a minute amount of diphtheria toxin.

Schiller, Johann Christoph Friedrich von (1759–1805), influential German dramatist, historian, and democratic philosopher. He wrote blank verse *Sturm und Drang* plays: *Don Carlos* (1787), a trilogy on Wallenstein (1799), *Mary Stuart* (1800), *Maid of Orleans* (1810), and *William Tell* (1804). Beethoven's *9th Symphony* uses his "Hymn to Joy."

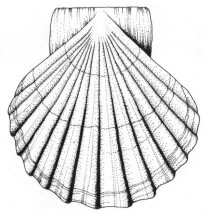

Scallop

Johann Schiller

Franz Schubert

Schipperke, Flemish watchdog (nonsporting group) bred several hundred years ago; name means Little Captain, from use on canal boats. Its foxlike face bears a questioning expression. Small, triangular ears are erect. The short, thickset body is set on medium-length legs. Tail is docked. Its abundant harsh coat is short on the ears, legs, and body and longer on the ruffed neck and the back of the hind legs; color is solid black. Average size: 13in (33cm) high at shoulder; 14–18lb (6.3–8kg). *See also* Non-sporting Dog.

Schism, in religion, a division within a church or a break away from a church. In the history of the Christian Church the name is particularly applied to the Great Eastern Schism, the separation of the Roman and Eastern Churches that began in the 9th century, and the Great Western Schism, the period when there were two or three rival popes (1378–1417).

Schist, large group of metamorphic rocks characterized by a preponderance of platy minerals that cause the rocks to split leaving a wavy, uneven surface. They are named for their predominant mineral, eg mica schist. Most probably metamorphose from mud or clay, with slates, shales, and phylites the intermediate products. *See also* Metamorphic Rocks.

Schistosomiasis, or **Snail Fever,** a visceral venous infestation of the human body by certain blood flukes occurring mainly in the tropics. Next to malaria, it is man's most serious parasitic infection. Symptoms are inflammation, cough, fever, skin eruption, and swelling of the liver. It is contracted by working or swimming in water contaminated with miniature stages of the parasite released by snails. Chemotherapy is used to kill adult flukes.

Schizophrenia, functional psychotic disorder marked primarily by disturbances of cognitive functioning, particularly thinking. Bleuler, who introduced term in 1911 viewed it as a "splitting of the personality" (from reality), a tendency of thinking to become wish-fulfilling, idiosyncratic, and dominated by fantasy. Currently term is used to describe a diverse assortment of clinical entities. Subtypes include: simple, hebephrenic, catatonic, paranoid, undifferentiated, schizo-affective, and childhood. *See also* Bleuler, Paul Eugen; Psychotic Disorders.

Schleswig-Holstein, state in N West Germany; capital is Kiel. Formerly consisting of duchies of Denmark, by 1815 Holstein became German state; Denmark declared union with Schleswig causing revolt with German Confederation; by 1850 peace was declared. By terms of the Treaty of Gastein (1865) Schleswig was awarded to Prussia, Holstein to Austria, and Lauenburg (lost by Denmark to Prussia and Austria 1864) also to Prussia; settlement led to Austro-Prussian War (1866) and all three areas were annexed to Prussia; N Schleswig went to Denmark 1920; it was constituted as a state 1946. Industries: farming, cattle, shipping, fishing, tourism, textiles, shipbuilding, food processing, oil, clothing, machinery. Pop. 2,582,400.

Schliemann, Heinrich (1822–90), German archeologist and excavator of Troy, Mycenae, and Tiryns. In 1871 he began excavations at his own expense at Hissarlik, Turkey, which he believed to be the site of the Homeric city of Troy. He uncovered four superimposed towns. From 1874 to 1876 he excavated in Greece, and in 1875 in Mycenae. His findings in the various excavations were published respectively as *Trojanische Altertümer* (*Antiquities of Troy,* 1874), *Troja und seine Ruinen* (*Troy and Its Remains,* 1875), and *Mykenä* (*Mycenae,* 1878). *See also* Troy.

Schmidt, Helmut (1918–), West German statesman. A member of the SPD (Social Democratic party), he replaced Willy Brandt as chancellor in 1974, receiving the unanimous support of SPD and Free Democratic party Bundestag members. He worked toward bettering economic conditions and easing East-West tensions worldwide. He stabilized West Germany's position in international affairs before leaving office in 1982, when he was succeeded by Helmut Kohl.

Schmidt-Rottluff, Karl (1884–1976), German painter. His early woodcuts were Impressionistic in style and then became more abstract, with contrasts of black and white. A member of Die Brücke, he used decorative color in his paintings.

Schnauzer. *See* Giant Schnauzer; Miniature Schnauzer; Standard Schnauzer.

Scholasticism, attempt to analyze the articles of faith through intellectual processes, with a view to deeper understanding of Christian doctrine. Arising in medieval schools, based on teachings of Augustine and Boethius, Scholastic thought was advanced by Johannes Scotus Erigena in the 9th century and by Anselm in the 11th century. After the important work of Duns Scotus and Aquinas, scholasticism declined rapidly in the face of Ockham's nominalism, which denied the possibility of objective knowledge.

Schönberg, Arnold (1874–1951), Austrian composer, a seminal figure in 20th-century music. His early works were characterized by a post-Romantic style akin to Richard Wagner, eg, *Verklärte Nacht* (1899). In 1914 he broke from the traditional musical stream and devised his own compositional system called 12-tone music. Though never popular, the 12-tone system has exerted an enormous influence on composing techniques used by many other composers, especially by Schönberg's students such as Alban Berg, Anton von Webern, and Ernst Křenek. Schönberg's works include a violin concerto (1936), five string quartets, and chamber, vocal, and piano music.

Schooner, usually a two-masted commercial vessel with bowsprit and fore-and-aft sails rather than square sails.

Schopenhauer, Arthur (1788–1860), German philosopher. He was overshadowed by G.W.F. Hegel until 1852, when Schopenhauer's system was popularized. His main work, *The World as Will and Idea* (1818), establishes will as the moving force behind the world. A primordial drive to endure, it creates the possibility of its own negation as Nirvana. *On Basis of Morality* (1841) cites compassion as the foundation of ethics. Schopenhauer's fame was established by his caustic and witty essays, *Parerga and Paralipomena* (1851).

Schouten, Willem Cornelis (?1567–1625), Dutch navigator. During one of his voyages (1615–16) he found a new trade route to the East. Sailing around the tip of South America, he named Cape Horn after his birthplace, Hoorn. He then sailed on to visit islands in the SW Pacific. Charged with violation of a Dutch East India Company monopoly, he was arrested and his ship seized in Java.

Schrödinger, Erwin (1887–1961), Austrian theoretical physicist who discovered the basic quantum mechanics equation. He was awarded the 1933 Nobel Prize for the development of his wave equation, which is capable of describing electron and small particle behavior. In 1938, he left Austria and became a professor in Dublin.

Schubert, Franz (1797–1828), Austrian Romantic composer. A melodic genius, he lived in poverty and was largely unappreciated in his own time. Now his talent, especially as a composer of songs, is recognized. His over 600 songs include those in the cycle *Die Schöne Müllerin* (1823), those in the cycle *Die Winterreise* (1827), "The Erl King" (1815), and "Ave Maria" (1825). Among his other popular works are the "Unfinished" *Symphony No. 8* and the C Major *Symphony No. 9,* piano sonatas, chamber music, masses, and incidental music. *See also* Romanticism in Music.

Schuman, Robert (1886–1963), French political figure. He was noted for his efforts to achieve European economic and political unity. While foreign minister (1950), he successfully proposed the creation of a single authority to control the production of coal and steel in Europe. This agreement was the first of several leading to the formation of the European Economic Community (Common Market) in 1958, which he served, first as president of the assembly, then as assembly member, until his death.

Schumann, Robert (1810–56), German Romantic composer. He married the outstanding pianist Clara Wieck and was a friend to Johannes Brahms, but he spent his last years in madness. He composed many sets of piano pieces, eg, *Kinderscenen, Carnival,* and *Waldscenen.* His best known works include concertos for cello and for piano, four symphonies, chamber music, and about 150 songs. Schumann was also one of the most important music critics of his day.

Schuylkill River, river in SE Pennsylvania, rises in E central Pa., flows SE to Delaware River at Philadelphia. Length: 130mi (209km).

Schwann, Theodor (1810–82), German biologist. With Matthias Jakob Schleiden he established the cell theory. Schwann extended the theory from plants to animals, stating that all living organisms are composed of cells, and that these cells have a life of their own that is subject to the life of the organism as a whole.

Schweitzer, Albert (1875–1965), humanitarian, musician, mission physician, philosopher, and Christian theologian, is perhaps best known for his medical work in Gabon (Africa), where he founded the Lambaréné Hospital in 1913. Although he stayed in Gabon most of his life, he was famous for his work as an organist, as an expert on J.S. Bach, for his theories of Christian history, and for his ethic of "reverence for life." His works included *Kant's Philosophy of Religion* (1899) and *On the Edge of the Primeval Forest* (1922). He received the Nobel Peace prize in 1952.

Schwitters, Kurt (1887–1948), German artist. His early work showed the influence of Vasili Kandinsky and the Dada movement. He is best known for his technique of combining ticket stubs, newspaper pieces, and other scraps into collages. He used the term *"merz"* to label his style and made huge works from trash and scraps, which he called Merz-bau constructions.

Schwyz, canton in central Switzerland; borders on Lake of Zurich (N) and Lake of Lucerne (SW); capital is Schwyz. One of original Four Forest cantons, it is forested and mountainous. Industries: livestock, fruit, cotton and silk textiles, wood products, tourism. Area: 351sq mi (909sq Km). Pop. 92,400.

Sciatica, neuralgia or neuritis associated with excruciating pain. It is caused by irritation or swelling of the sciatic nerve, which passes from the lower spinal column down the back of thighs and legs. It can be treated with bedrest, sedation, or corrective exercise.

Science Fiction, form of fiction in which the improbable becomes probable, where scientific discovery allows man to supersede preconceived limits, often by the use of mechanical devices still not invented. The first successful science-fiction writer was France's Jules Verne, the first successful English writer was H.G. Wells; and the first American, Edgar Allan Poe. Little science fiction was printed in the 1800s, but the pulp magazines pushed it into prominence in the 1900s. The first magazine to contain only science fiction was *Amazing Stories* (1926), but science fiction did not really come into its own until the mid-1900s. Early pulp stories were criticized as "space operas" where life was cheap and violence and cruelty common. Modern science fiction has taken on a new sophistication, often bringing to the reader a thoughtful message packaged in a plausible well-written story. Among the better-known writers are Isaac Asimov, Ray Bradbury, Arthur C. Clarke, and John Wyndham.

Scientific Method, general logic and procedures common to all the physical and social sciences, which may be outlined as a series of steps: (1) stating a problem or question; (2) forming a hypothesis (possible solution to the problem) based on a theory or rationale; (3) experimentation (gathering empirical data bearing on the hypothesis); (4) interpretation of the data and drawing conclusions; and (5) revising the theory or deriving further hypotheses for testing. Putting the hypothesis in a form that can be empirically tested is one of the chief challenges to the scientist. In addition, all of the sciences try to express their theories and conclusions in some quantitative form and to use standardized testing procedures that other scientists could repeat.

Scilly, Isles of, group of more than 140 islands off SW England; part of Cornwall, 28mi (45km) SW of Land's End. Largest island is St Mary's. The mild climate makes the islands a resort and a center for early spring flowers and vegetables. Pop. 2,020.

Scintillation Counter, instrument containing a crystal that emits scintillations of light when bombarded by radiation. Each light flash, corresponding to a single particle, is converted into an electric pulse by a photomultiplier. The number of pulses, counted electronically, indicates the activity of the source.

Scipio, distinguished Roman family. Lucius Cornelius, consul (259 BC) and censor, won naval victories against Algeria and Corsica. His son Gnaeus Cornelius Scipio Calvus (died 211) attacked Hannibal's supply line in Spain (218) and with his brother Publius defeated Hasdrubal and took Saguntum (212). Publius' son was Scipio Africanus Major whose eldest son adopted the son of Aemilius Paullus, who came to be known as Scipio Africanus Minor. Publius Scipio Nasica Serapio (died *c.*132 BC) fled Rome after leading the senate riot in which Tiberius Gracchus was killed. His descendant Quintus Caecilius Metellus Pius Scipio (died 46 BC) led troops for Pompey at Pharsala and, fleeing to Africa, was defeated by Caesar.

Scipio, Publius Cornelius (died 211), Roman general, younger brother of Gnaeus and father of Scipio Africanus Major. As consul (218) his attempt to halt Hannibal failed because he was forced to put down a revolt of Gauls in N Italy first. He lost two-thirds of his army fighting Hannibal at Trebia (218). He and his brother were killed in Spain after defeating Hasdrubal (216) near Ibera.

Scipio Africanus Major (Publius Cornelius Scipio) (*c.* 234–183 BC), greatest military genius of the Scipio family and conqueror of Hannibal. Son of Publius Cornelius Scipio, he fought at Cannae and became proconsul of Spain after his father. Supremely self-confident, he pursued an aggressive policy, took Cartagena (209), defeated Hasdrubal, and established Roman rule in Spain. Defying the senate he captured Tunis with a volunteer army and defeated Hannibal's Carthaginians at Zama (202) through brilliant deployment of cavalry. As censor and chief senator (199) he made strong enemies including Cato the Elder. Brought to trial for corruption (on presumably false charges), his influence waned and he retired in anger to Liternum where he died. *See also* Punic Wars.

Scipio Africanus Minor (Publius Cornelius Scipio Aemilianus Africanus Numantius) (*c.*185–129 BC), Roman general and scholar, second son of Lucius Aemilius Paullus, adopted son of Publius Scipio (eldest son of Scipio Africanus Major). An orator and patron of letters, he improved the army and destroyed Carthage (147) during the Third Punic War. In 134 he devastated Numantia in Spain. He sought to reverse the reforms of Tiberius Gracchus but died suddenly (possibly murdered) during the ensuing crisis. He is celebrated in Cicero's works.

Sclerosis, degenerative hardening of tissue, especially in the arteries and central nervous system, in which normal tissue is replaced by connective tissue, as in a scar.

Scone, village in central Scotland; Old Scone was the Pictish and Scottish capital where kings of Scotland were crowned 1157–1488. The Coronation stone, or Stone of Scone, was removed to Westminster Abbey by Edward I of England 1296, where it has remained, in spite of an attempt (1950) by Scottish nationalists to return it to Scone.

Scopus, Mount, peak in Israel that has always been important to the defense of Jerusalem. From 1948 to 1967 it was held by the Israelis but was completely surrounded by Arab territory.

Scorpion, variously colored arthropod found in warmer regions worldwide. It has two body parts, two eyes, one pair of pincers, and long slender tail ending in a curved, poisonous stinger. It feeds at night on insects and spiders. It stings in self-defense; some are dangerous. Length: 1.5–7in (4–18cm). Class Arachnida; order Scorpionida.

Scorpion-fish, or rockfish, family of marine fish found in temperate waters at or near rocky bottoms and identified by venomous fin spines capable of inflicting painful and sometimes fatal injury. Young are born alive. Length: 12in (30.5cm). Family Scorpaenidae; species include *Scorpaena scrofa,* lionfish *Pterois volitans,* and ocean perch *Sebastes marinus.*

Scorpion Fly, brown to gray insect limited to the Northern Hemisphere. Its chewing mouthparts are at the end of a long, beaklike structure. The males of some species have abdomens resembling a scorpion's. They are harmless and feed on insects. Length: 0.5–1.6in (13–41mm). Order Mecoptera.

Scorpius, or the Scorpion, southern constellation situated on the ecliptic between Libra and Sagittarius; the eighth sign of the zodiac. Usually referred to as Scorpio only for astrological purposes, this constellation contains several open and globular clusters. The Milky Way also passes through it. Brightest star Alpha Scorpii (Antares). The astrological sign for the period Oct. 24–Nov. 21.

Scotland, N part of Great Britain, bounded N and W by the Atlantic Ocean, E by the North Sea, and S by England.

Land and Economy. Scotland has an indented coastline with many lochs and offshore islands; the main island groups are the Inner and Outer Hebrides (W) and the Orkneys and Shetlands (N). High land in the N and W rises from high moorland to Cairngorm Mts and Ben Nevis, 4,406ft (1,344m). The country is drained by fast-flowing rivers providing hydroelectric power and has many lakes (lochs), particularly along Great Glen (Glen More), a fault running SW-NE from Loch Linnhe to the Moray Firth. Low land occurs in central Scotland; it is hilly in S. The principal rivers are the Clyde, Forth, Tay, Tweed, Dee, and Spey. Forestry and lumbering take place in the Highlands, with rough grazing in moorland regions, and stock farming in the hills. The main agricultural crops are cereal and potatoes in river valleys, fruit growing in the E. Scotland's industries are concentrated in the Clyde and Forth river basins and lowlands, and include mining, engineering, shipbuilding, fishing, textiles, chemicals, brewing, and distilling.

People. The population is largely a mixture of Celt, Anglo-Saxon, and Norman, with some Norse influence in the islands and NW. The main religious group is the Church of Scotland (Presbyterian). Less than 2% of the population speaks Gaelic, but national identity is strong.

Government. Scotland is part of the United Kingdom, sending more than 70 members to the British Parliament, including members of the Scottish Nationalist Party. Traditional regions were abolished in 1974, and new administrative regions were established for local government.

History. Most of Scotland was united under one king, Kenneth I, in the 9th century. The country first came under English control in 1174 as a result of a treaty obtained by Henry II. In 1292 John de Baliol was crowned king after a struggle among several claimants, and acknowledged Edward I of England as overlord. Edward II of England was defeated at Bannockburn 1314, but over the next century Scotland was torn by civil strife. In 1513 the Scots were badly defeated at Flodden Field. The country was finally united with England in 1603 when James VI succeeded to the English throne as James I. During the 18th century the Jacobite rebellion was fought by Scots seeking to restore the Stuarts to the British throne. During the 1970s, Scottish nationalistic feeling grew, and the British Parliament promised limited home rule, or devolution. In 1979, however, Scottish voters rejected devolution in a referendum.

PROFILE

Official name: Scotland
Area: 30,405sq mi (78,749sq km)
Population: 5,167,600
Density: 171per sq mi (66per sq km)
Chief cities: Glasgow; Edinburgh (capital); Dundee

Scott, Robert Falcon (1868–1912), English antarctic explorer and naval commander. He entered the navy in 1880, and in 1899 was made commander of an expedition into the antarctic. He led another expedition with the intention of reaching the south pole in 1910. Traveling by sled, he and four others came to the pole in January 1912, only to find that Amundsen had been there first. Plagued by fierce weather, sickness, and shortness of supplies, Scott and his men died by March. They were found later that year by a search party.

Scott, (Sir) Walter (1771–1832), Scottish novelist and poet, b. Edinburgh. Scott left Edinburgh University to become a lawyer (1792), but his interest in Border history gave rise to a collection of ballads, *Minstrelsy of the Scottish Border* (3 vols., 1802–03) and *The Lay of the Last Minstrel* (1805). His works appeared continually from 1808 *(Marmion)* until his death, which was hastened by Scott's efforts to pay off debts following the ruin in 1826 of his partner in a printing business. His other works included *Lady of the Lake* (1810), *The Heart of Midlothian* (1818), *Ivanhoe* (1819), *Kenilworth* (1821), *Quentin Durward* (1823), and *The Talisman* (1825).

Scott, Winfield (1786–1866), US military officer, b. Petersburg, Va. He served in the War of 1812, and from 1846–48 in the Mexican War where he led the triumphant march from Vera Cruz to Mexico City which he governed (1847–48). In 1852 he was the Whig candidate for the presidency but lost to Franklin Pierce. Called "Old Fuss and Feathers," he was regarded as the outstanding military figure between George Washington and Robert E. Lee.

Scottish Deerhound, graceful hunting dog (hound group) dating from at least the 16th century and known as royal dog of Scotland. A keen scenter, it has a long, flat head and pointed muzzle; small, high-set ears, folded back; long neck; deep chest; and well-arched loin; long, broad-boned legs; and long, tapering tail. The 3–4in (8–10cm) long, harsh, and wiry coat is usually dark blue-gray. Average size: 28–32in (71–81cm) high at shoulder; 75–110lb (34–50kg). *See also* Hounds.

Scottish Terrier, ancient Highland breed (terrier group) dating from the 16th century and brought to US in 1883. The Scottie's head is long and slightly domed, with whiskers and dark, piercing eyes set under bushy eyebrows. The short, deep-chested body is set on short, heavy legs. The curved tail is 7in (18cm) long. Coat is short (2in–5cm), hard, and wiry; colors may be steel or iron gray, brindle, grizzle, black, sandy, or wheaten. Average size: 10in (25.5cm) high at shoulder; 19–22lb (8.5–10kg). *See also* Terrier.

Scottsdale, residential city in SW central Arizona, 10mi (16km) E of Phoenix; old western shopping town. Industries: women's clothing, ceramics. Inc. 1951. Pop. (1980) 88,364.

Scranton, city in NE Pennsylvania, on Lackawanna River, 120mi (193km) N of Philadelphia; seat of Lackawanna co. Known as world's major anthracite coal capital until the end of WWII, it is now a city of diversified manufacturing; site of University of Scranton (1888), Lackawanna Junior College (1894), and Marywood College (1915). Industries: textiles, clothing, paints and varnishes, printing supplies. Founded 1788; inc. as borough 1853, as city 1866. Pop. (1980) 88,117.

Screech Owl, common North American owl that is usually brown or gray and has earlike tufts of feathers on its head. Despite its name, it utters a pleasant whistling sound. It is related to the smaller scops owl *(Otus scops)* of Europe, Asia, and Africa. Length: 10in (25cm). Family Strigidae; species *Otus asio. See also* Owl.

Screw Pine, woody Old World plant native to tropical Asia, Africa, and Indian Ocean and Pacific islands. Not a true pine, its long, narrow, spiny leaves rise from a rosette in a spiral, like threads of a screw. Stilt roots steady the plant in high winds. It bears conelike fruits. Height: to 40ft (12m). Family Pandanaceae. Species include *Pandanus odoratissimus.*

Robert F. Scott

Sir Walter Scott

Sea otter

Screwworm, bluegreen fly 0.56 to 0.72in (14–18mm) long. A parasite of warm-blooded animals, the larva enters through wounds in the skin. It is a serious pest of domestic animals in North and South America. Family Calliphoridae, species *Callitroga hominivorax. See also* Diptera.

Scriabin, Alexander (1872–1915), Russian composer and pianist. He composed highly original piano music according to his own principles of harmony, foreshadowing many of the musical developments of the 20th century. His most significant works include nine piano sonatas, five symphonic poems, and numerous short piano pieces.

Scriptures, the books of the Old and New Testaments, often including the Apocrypha; also a text or passage from one of these books of the Bible. The term, as used in the New Testament, refers primarily to sacred Hebraic writings, as in Mark 12:10. *Scripture,* in the singular form, usually refers to the collection of writings thought of as a single book; the plural *Scriptures* refers to the many writings. The term *Scriptures* can also be applied to other sacred writings such as the Koran of the Muslims. *See also* Apocrypha; New Testament, Old Testament.

Scrofula, general name used variously through time in medicine, especially to describe tuberculosis of the bones and lymphatic glands.

Scuba Diving, a water sport. It consists of diving with the use of Self-Contained Underwater Breathing Apparatus, known as the aqualung. Other equipment includes a wet suit and rubber fins for the diver's feet. The sport has attracted many enthusiasts since the design of the modern aqualung by Jacques Yves Cousteau and Emil Gagnan.

Sculpin, bottom-dwelling marine fish found in temperate and cold waters of the North Atlantic. A grayish fish mottled with yellow, it has a large bony head covered with prickles. Its eyes are set high on its head and the pectoral fins are large and fanlike. Length: to 3ft (91.5cm). Family Cottidae. The 300 species include the shorthorn *Myoxocephalus scorpius.*

Sculpture, the art of creating forms and objects in three dimensions or in relief. Works of sculpture may be carved (in marble, stone, wood, ivory, etc) or built up from some flexible or plastic material (plaster, metals, bronze, etc) and range in size from tiny to monumental. The history of sculpture basically parallels that of painting. *See also* Painting and related articles on the history of painting.

Scup, or northern porgy, Atlantic marine food and sport fish found in tropical and temperate waters. It is a deep-bodied silver blue fish. Length: to 18in (45.7cm); weight: to 41lb (1.8kg). Family Sparidae; species *Stenotomus chrysops.*

Scurvy, disease caused by a prolonged deficiency of vitamin C. It is characterized by weakness, inflamed gums, loose teeth, and swollen joints and also absorption by tissues of blood from ruptured vessels, which causes anemia.

Scylla and Charybdis, in classical mythology, two monsters of the Sicilian seas. Scylla, a beautiful nymph, daughter of Poseidon, had been changed by the enchantress Circe into a long-necked, six-headed beast who lived in a dark cave in the sea and subsisted on passing dolphins and sailors. Charybdis, another daughter of Poseidon, was a creature out of Homer, who was changed into a violent whirlpool by the thun-

derbolt of Zeus. She swallowed the waves of the sea and three times each day vomited them forth.

Scythians, an ancient people who ruled an empire in southern Russia from the 7th century BC until defeated by the Sarmatians in the 4th century BC. Of Iranian stock, the Scythians were a nomadic and warlike tribe with a well advanced civilization. They were ferocious warriors, skilled craftsmen, active hunters and fishermen, and good agriculturists.

Sea Anemone, polyp-type coelenterate found in marine tidal pools and along rocky shores. Cylindrical with many tentacles around its mouth and color varying according to species. There is no medusa phase; reproduction is asexual and sexual. Height: 8in (203.2mm). Class Anthozoa; species include *Metridium.*

Sea Bass, marine food fish found in tropical and some temperate waters. It includes white, yellow, and striped bass in the genus *Roccus;* groupers; butterfish; and the black bass *Centropristis striatus.* Many of these species are self-fertilizing. Family Serranidae. *See also* Bass; Grouper; Jewfish.

Seaborg, Glen Theodore (1912–   ), US physicist, b. Ishpeming, Mich. He became chancellor of the University of California at Berkeley in 1958 and chairman of the US Atomic Energy Commission in 1961. His scientific work was concerned with the transuranic elements and the discovery of the actinide series, for which he was awarded a Nobel prize (jointly with Edwin McMillan) in 1951. In 1942 he was responsible for isolating uranium-233.

Sea Bream, any of numerous marine, spiny-finned (percoid) fishes, usually of the families Sparidae or Bramidae.

Sea Cow. See Dugong.

Sea Cucumber, marine echinoderm found in rocky areas. A cylindrical animal with a soft, fleshy body, it has branched tentacles around the mouth. Edible species are smoked and dried; the end product is trepang. Species include the cotton-spinner *Holothuria* and the burrowing *Leptopentacta.* Class Holothuroidea.

Sea Dragon, or leafy sea dragon, marine fish found off the coast of Australia. A pipefish, closely related to the seahorse, its reddish-brown body is covered with leafy and spine-like projections, making it resemble floating seaweed. Family Syngnathidae; species *Phycidurus eques* and *Phyllopteryx foliatus.*

Sea Fan, or gorgonian, colonial coelenterate found in coral reefs in tropical marine waters. Colonies are branching but flat; eight-tentacled polyps live in tiny pits along horny branches. Class Anthozoa; subclass Alcyonaria; species *Eunicella verrucosa.*

Sea-floor Spreading, the systematic increase in the Earth's crust occurring along the mid-ocean ridges. Here basaltic magma rises, cools, and is pushed along by new magma eruptions. As the magma cools, it becomes magnetized in the direction of the Earth's current magnetic field. These magnetized strips form identical patterns on either side of the ridges, evidence that new crust is being produced. The spreading has been plotted at rates of 1 to 10 cm (0.4–4in) per year.

Sea Hare, marine gastropod found on shore or in shallow offshore waters. It has no shell and in some cases has lost the mantle cavity. Gills are visible externally.

It secretes a purple mucus for defense. Class Gastropoda; order Anaspidea; genus *Tethys.*

Sea Islands, chain of more than 100 islands off Atlantic coast of South Carolina, Georgia, and Florida. Notable islands include Port Royal, containing chief city of Beaufort, Paris Island, site of a US Marine Corp. training center, and St Simons, Sea, Jekyll, and Hilton Head islands, all popular resorts.

Seal, large fish-eating aquatic mammal of coastal regions in all oceans, especially colder waters. They have a streamlined body and flippers for limbs. A thick layer of blubber—nearly half the seal's weight—provides insulation, buoyancy, and reserve energy for long periods without food. They return to land to breed; some form breeding colonies of over one million individuals. Skillfull swimmers, they are awkward on land. Fur seals are hunted for their pelts; hair seals, for leather, blubber oil, and meat. Seals range in size from the ringed seal: length 55in (140cm); weight: 200lb (90kg), to the elephant seal: length: 22ft (7m); weight: to 4 tons. Eared seals Family Otariidae. Earless seals Family Phocidae. *See also* Pinnipedia; Sea Lion.

Sea Lily, crinoid echinoderm found in deep marine waters. Seldom seen, it has many branched arms with ciliated grooves for food collecting radiating from a tiny body disk. Spineless, it attaches itself to the ocean bottom with a stalk. Class Crinoidea.

Sea Lion, eared seal with coarse pelt of little commercial value, found in Southern Hemisphere and N Pacific coastal waters. Largest is the N Pacific Steller's sea lion. Length: over 11ft (3m); weight: over 1ton. Species *Eumetopias Jubata.* The smallest is the gregarious, playful Californian or Japanese sea lion that is the familiar trained seal of circuses and animal shows. Length: 8ft (2.4m); weight: 615lb (277kg). Species *Zalophus californianus. See also* Pinnipedia; Seal.

Sealyham Terrier, dog (terrier group) named for Sealyham Estates, Wales, where the breed was developed 1850–91 to hunt out fox, badger, and otter. The Sealyham's long head is emphasized by whiskers; rounded ears are folded; oval eyes are dark and deep set. The forepart of the body is well let down between the short, strong forelegs. The docked tail is carried up. A hard, wiry top coat is all white. Average size: 10.5in (27cm) high at shoulder; 23–24lb (10–11kg). *See also* Terrier.

Sea Mouse, large marine annelid worm with iridescent matted bristles on sides and top of body. Length: to 4in (10cm). The common sea mouse *Aphrodite aculeata* lives in sandy mud on both sides of North Atlantic. Family Aphroditidae. *See also* Annelida.

Sea Otter, marine otter of the weasel family, originally native to the Pacific coast of N America. Now protected, it was almost exterminated for its valuable dark brown fur. Its hind feet are flattened into flippers and it likes to swim and float on its back within a mile of shore. It eats fish and invertebrates and often uses stones to open hard shells. Length: 40–50in (1–1.2m); weight: 20lb (9kg). Family Mustelidae; species *Enhydra lutris.*

Sea Perch, or surf perch, marine fish found in temperate Pacific waters. Often quite colorful, its young are born alive. Length: 18in (45.7cm). Family Embiotocidae; Species include the rubberlip *Rhacochilus toxotes,* the striped *Embiotoca lateralis,* and a commercial species, white *Phanerodon furcatus.*

Sea Raven, marine fish found in temperate waters. A sculpin identified by its large head with prickles and its ability to gulp air to inflate itself, it varies in color from red and purple to yellow and brown. Length: to 25in (63.5cm); 5lb (2.3kg). Family Cottidae; species *Homotripterus americanus.*

Sea Robin, marine fish found worldwide in tropical and temperate waters. Edible but not popular, it has a bony head, can produce sound, and "walk" on sea bottom with its large pectoral fins. It is red, gray, yellow, or green with dark blotches. Length: to 3ft (91.5cm). Family Triglidae; Among the 85 species are the northern *Prionotus carolinus* and the striped *Prionotus evolons.*

Sea Snake, any of about 50 species of colorful, poisonous marine snakes found in coastal waters of Indian, Pacific, and Atlantic oceans. The posterior half of its body is flattened and ends in a paddlelike tip. It has valved nostrils on top of its head. Most bear live young; a few lay eggs on shore. Length: to 4ft (1.2m). Family Hydrophidae.

Seasons, four astronomical and climatic periods of the year based on differential solar heating of the Earth as it makes its annual revolution of the Sun. Due to the parallelism of the Earth's axis of rotation, pointed near the Pole Star throughout the year, the Northern Hemisphere receives more solar radiation when its pole is aimed toward the Sun in summer and less in winter when it is aimed away, while the opposite holds for the Southern Hemisphere. The seasons are conventionally initiated at the vernal (spring) and autumnal (fall) equinoxes and the winter and summer solstices. *See also* Equinox; Solstice.

Sea Squirt. *See* Tunicate.

SEATO. *See* Southeast Asia Treaty Organization.

Seattle, city and port of entry in W Washington, between Lake Washington and Puget Sound; seat of King co. Settled during California building boom (1851), it profited as busy port to Orient (1893); it was gateway to Alaska Gold Rush (1897); scene of Alaska-Yukon-Pacific Exposition (1909–10); scene of first labor strike (1919) in US history led by Industrial Workers of the World; site of University of Washington (1861), Seattle University (1900), Seattle Pacific College (1893), 1962 World's Fair—Century 21 Exposition. Industries: aerospace, shipbuilding, precision instruments, building materials, chemicals, lumber, food processing, agriculture, fishing, clothing. Inc. 1869. Pop. (1980) 493,846.

Sea Urchin, spiny echinoderm found in marine tidal pools along rocky shores. Round with long, radiating often poisonous, moveable spines, it has a mouth on its bottom and anus at the top. Its skeletal plates fuse to form a perforated shell. Class Echinoidea; species include (edible sea urchin) *Echinus* and (purple heart urchin) *Spatangus.*

Sea Walnut, comb jelly or ctenophore, large swarms live in marine waters. A luminescent animal, it is globular, jellylike, and has eight rows of ciliated plates. Diameter: 0.25in–1ft (0.6–30.5cm). Phylum *Ctenophora.*

Seaweed, any of various marine plants, or algae, especially large kinds such as kelp, gulfweed, dulse, rockweed, and sea lettuce. *See also* Algae.

Sebaceous Gland, a skin gland, often occurring along the walls of hair follicles. It secretes sebum, a waxy substance containing fats, proteins, salts, and water, which keeps the hair and skin surface flexible and prevents excessive loss of water from the surface of the body.

Sebastian (1554–78), king of Portugal (1557–78), grandson and successor of John III. His grandmother, Catherine of Austria, and his uncle, Cardinal Henry, acted as regents until he came of age in 1568. Highly religious, he became obsessed with leading a crusade against the Muslims in Morocco. He spent vast sums on the project and led a large expedition there in 1578. He was defeated (and the Portuguese army destroyed) at the battle of Alcazarquivir. Sebastian himself was killed in the battle, but reports of his survival led to the cult known as Sebastianism and to the appearance of several impostors. He was succeeded by Cardinal Henry.

Seborrhea, disease of the sebaceous glands, characterized by an increased and altered secretion of fatty matter that results in oily or scaly skin. It may cause baldness and dandruff.

Secession, formal separation from an organized body. The best-known secession in history occurred in 1860–61 when 11 states (South Carolina, Mississippi, Florida, Alabama, Georgia, Louisiana, Texas, Virginia, Arkansas, Tennessee, and North Carolina) seceded from the United States and formed the Confederate States of America.

Second, fundamental unit of time (symbol s) defined as the time of 9,192,631,770 periods of the electromagnetic radiation corresponding to a transition in the cesium-133 atom. *See also* Physical Units.

Second Empire (1852–70), French government under Napoleon III. On Dec. 2, 1851, Louis Napoleon Bonaparte, then president of the Second Republic, staged a coup d'état. Shortly afterward he acquired dictatorial power. The Second Empire was formally established by plebiscite in November 1852. The Senate was no longer elected; the lower house met only briefly and did not choose its president or publish its debates. The press was strictly controlled, and officials took an oath of allegiance to the emperor, who had assumed the title Napoleon III. Under the empire industrial development spread; railways tripled in mileage; overseas trade quadrupled in value (1851–69); and credit and banking grew with formation of the Crédit Mobilier and the Société Générale. Napoleon III bettered relations with Britain, allying with it in the Crimean War (1854–56) and signing a commercial treaty (1860) that moved France toward greater freedom of trade. The rise of Prussia, with its defeat of Austria (1866) and drive toward unification of Germany, caught France unprepared. Popular anti-Prussian sentiment swept the emperor into the disastrous Franco-Prussian War (1870–71). After the French defeat at Sedan (October 1870), a republic was proclaimed, and the emperor fled to England, where he died (1873). *See also* Franco-Prussian War; Napoleon III.

Second Republic (1848–52), government of France. Popular insurrection against the reign of King Louis Philippe brought about his abdication and the establishment of a republic in early 1848. In June, Parisian workers rose against the conservative tendencies of the provisional government. The constitution of 1848 provided for election by universal suffrage of a president and assembly but failed to foresee potential conflicts between them. Louis Napoleon, president of the republic, replaced it with the Second Empire in 1852. *See also* Second Empire.

Secretary Bird, bird of prey found in Africa south of the Sahara. It is pale gray with black markings, has quill-like feathers behind its ears, large wings, and long legs and tail. It feeds on reptiles, birds, and mammals and lays reddish-white eggs (2–3) in a tree nest. Height: 4ft (1.2m). Species *Sagittarius serpentarius.*

Securities and Exchange Commission (SEC), US federal agency. Its general objective is to provide the fullest possible disclosure to the investing public and to protect the interest of the public and investors against malpractice in the securities and financial markets. This includes stock exchange, investment and holding companies. The 5-man commission, appointed by the president, advises district courts on reorganization proceedings for debtor corporations. The commission is vested with quasi-judicial functions and its decisions may be appealed in the courts. It was established in 1934 by the Securities Exchange Act.

Sedan, town in NE France, on Meuse River, 11mi (18km) ESE of Mézières; became part of French crownlands in 1642; Protestant stronghold in 16th and 17th centuries; in 1870 French were defeated here, and Napoleon III surrendered to Prussian forces; site of heavy fighting WWI; in WWII it was Germany's initial capture in French invasion. Pop. 25,430.

Sedative, any drug used to reduce excitement, induce sleep, or control convulsions. Sedatives are classified as barbiturates and non-barbiturates, the latter including bromides and chloral compounds. An overdose can produce serious side effects or death.

Seder, meaning "order" in Hebrew, is a religious observance held on the first night of Passover in Jewish homes in Israel, and the first two nights outside Israel. The Haggadah is recited. The ancient temple service is commemorated and is based on the Mishnah.

Sedge, grasslike perennial plants widely distributed in temperate, cold, and tropical mountain regions, usually on wet ground or in water. Cultivated only as border plants, they have flat leaves and spikes of flowers. Family Cyperaceae; genus *Carex.*

Sediment, in geology a general term used to describe (1) any material in suspension in air or water; (2) the total load transported by a stream, including materials moved along its bed and those that are in solution as well as sediment in suspension; and (3) any unconsolidated sand and gravel deposit in river valleys and along coastlines.

Sedimentary Rocks, mineral or organic particles that have been moved by the action of water, wind, or glacial ice (or have been chemically precipitated from solution) to a new location. Following a process of compaction and cementation the particles form strata of sedimentary rock. Those formed by particles of volcanic rock are said to have pyroclastic characteristics; derived from other rocks, they are described as clastic.

Sedimentation, any process or processes that deposit rock-formation materials. The materials deposited are continental in origin and the debris of landforms worn down and carried off by wind, water, or ice. Whenever the flow of the transporting medium is interrupted or diverted, the carried material is deposited either on land; in desert, lake, or river bed; or on coasts; or as marine sediments. *See also* Deposition; Erosion; Transportation.

Sedum, genus of succulent perennials that grow in dry areas throughout the world. Clusters of tiny flowers are yellow, pink, or blue. Among the hundreds of species are *Sedum acre,* the yellow stonecrop, with small triangular leaves and yellow, star-shaped flowers; *S. rosea,* or roseroot, to 6–12in (15.2–30.5cm), with greenish yellow flowers; and *S. spectabile,* to 12–18in (30.5–45.7cm), with rose pink blooms. Family Crassulaceae.

Seebeck Effect. If wires of two different metals are joined at their ends to form a circuit, a current will flow around the circuit if the ends are maintained at different temperatures. Named after T. J. Seebeck (1770–1831).

Seed, part of a flowering plant that contains the embryo with its coating and stored food. The seed is formed in the ovary by fertilization of the female gamete by two sperm nuclei. The seed coating may be thin (peanut, garden bean) or hard (Brazil nut). The embryo consists of an axis, two cotyledons, growing shoot, and root. In some seeds, an endosperm develops from nutrients supplied by the parent plant rather than the embryo (corn and cereals). In others, food is stored in the embryo itself (bean).

Seed Fern, extinct group of ferns, thought to be ancestral to gymnosperms. Its fossil history extends from the late Devonian period to the Triassic period. Many had stout trunks bearing crowns of large, feathery leaves; height: to 50ft (15m). Order Cycadofilicales. *See also* Fern; Gymnosperm.

Seferis, George (1900–71), pseud. of Giorgos Seferiades, outstanding Greek writer and diplomat, b. Turkey. Educated in Paris, he had a distinguished diplomatic career and was Greek ambassador to the United Nations (1956–57) and to Great Britain (1957–62). His writing, especially his lyric poetry, earned him a Nobel Prize for literature in 1963.

Segmented Worms. *See* Annelida.

Segou, city and port in S Mali, W Africa, on Niger River; part of Bambara kingdom until 1861 when it was captured by a militant Muslim reformer, Al-haji Umar; in 1890 it was occupied by French. Industries: cotton, textiles. Pop. 300,627.

Segovia, Andrés (1893–), Spanish guitarist. He successfully established the guitar as a concert instrument and created many new guitar techniques. Many 20th-century composers created works specifically for him.

Segovia, city in Spain, 40mi (64km) NW of Madrid between Eresma and Clamores rivers; capital of Segovia prov. A Roman settlement in 1st century, it was a major textile center in the Middle Ages; taken by Moors in 8th century; captured 1079 by Alfonso VI. It is the site of 2nd-century Roman aqueduct, 16th-century cathedral. Industries: chemicals, rubber, cement, flour, fertilizers. Est. 700 BC. Area: (prov.) 2,683sq mi (6,949sq km). Pop. (city) 41,880; (prov.) 162,770.

Seifert, Jaroslav (1901–), Czech poet. His work always reflected his interest in politics, especially those of his native country. His work was, however, little known outside Czechoslovakia until 1984, when he became the first Czech to be awarded the Nobel Prize in literature. *The Plague Monument* (1980) and *The Casting of Bells* (1983) have been translated into English.

Seine River, river in N central France; rises in Plateau of Langres, flows NW through Paris and empties into English Channel near Le Havre. It is connected to Loire, Rhône, Meuse, Scheldt, Saône, and Somme rivers by canals. The first settlement at Paris was Île de la Cité, an island in the Seine. Other cities on the river are Le Havre, Rouen, and Troyes. The most important river of N France, it is navigable for ocean-going vessels as far as Rouen, and for barges to Nogent-sur-

Secretary bird

Andrés Segovia

Seine River, Paris

Seine; has been important commercially since Roman times. Navigable for 350mi (564km) of its 482mi (776km).

Seismic Array, the continuous and composite picture accumulated from all the continuous-recording seismographs that are a part of the World Wide Standard Seismograph Network (WWSSN) and the generation of equipment such as Large Aperture Seismic Array (LASA). *See also* Earthquake; Seismology.

Seismic Profile, continuous record of sound waves as bounced off sea-bottom sediments. The sounds become seismic waves and as such are used to determine the thickness and structure of bottom sediments. *See also* Echo Sounder.

Seismic Survey, a method of petroleum exploration involving an underground explosion which sends shock waves through the ground at speeds relative to the transmitting ability of the rock. Calculation of the speed of transmission, taken from readings in many places around the explosion, yeilds a profile of the land's folds and faults, which indicates possible locations of petroleum reservoirs.

Seismic Waves, waves produced by earthquakes. These shock waves go through Earth and emerge on the surface and are recorded. Primary (P) and secondary (S) waves are transmitted by the solid Earth. P waves vibrate in the direction of propagation; S waves vibrate at right angles to the direction of propagation. Only P waves are transmitted through fluid zones. Thus, information about the state of Earth can be gathered by the study of the effect and transmission of the P and S waves. The waves are also affected by differing layers. *See also* Earthquake; Seismology.

Seismograph, or **Seismometer,** a device for measuring and recording Earth's crustal movement. The seismographs may be of the pendulum or strain type. The pendulum type is used most frequently to record earthquakes and is an electromagnetic device. A coil on a pendulum is wired to a galvanometer. Motion activates the pendulum in a magnetic field, the coil moves and deflects a beam of light, which is reflected onto a photosensitive paper and recorded. *See also* Seismic Waves.

Seismology, the study and measurement of the propagation of strain waves. The field began developing in the 1880s and has since been applied to the detection of earthquakes and underground explosions (nuclear and other). The detection involves the separation of events from the ever-present background of seismic noise. Pinpointing sites of events is now very accurate since the development of precise instrumentation and the establishment of the World Wide Standard Seismograph Network (WWSSN). *See also* Earthquake; Seismic Waves.

Selaginella, or spike moss, genus of small-leaved, mosslike plants found worldwide, mostly in the tropics. Two kinds of spores are borne in cones at branch tips. Some grow on trees, others on the ground. The North American rock spike moss *(Selaginella rupestris)* is grayish-green and grows in dense mats on rocks or sand; height: 3in (7.6cm). There are over 700 species. Family Selaginellaceae. *See also* Club Moss.

Selection, in genetics, the probability that one genetic factor or allele will be passed on in favor of another. *See also* Natural Selection.

Selenium, metalloid element (symbol Se) of group VIA of the periodic table, discovered (1817) by J.J. Ber-

zelius. Chief source is as a by-product in the electrolytic refining of copper. The element is photoactive and is extensively used in photocells, solar cells, and xerography. Properties: at. no. 34; at. wt. 78.96; sp gr 4.79 (gray); melt. pt. 423°F (217°C); boil. pt. 1233°F (684°C); most common isotope Se^{80}(49.82%).

Selenology, study of the Moon's physical and chemical composition and formative processes. Current research reveals that the moon greatly resembles the Earth in physico-chemical makeup. Its surface is composed mainly of volcanic basalts but evidence of considerable chemical differentiation has been found, suggesting that the Moon was formed at a very high temperature along with the other planets of the solar system.

Seleucids, a Hellenistic dynasty (312–64 BC) founded in Syria by Seleucus I. The most notable rulers of this dynasty were Seleucus I, Antiochus I, and Antiochus III, who founded new cities and brought prosperity to the Near East through their gifted administrations.

Selim I (1467–1520), Ottoman sultan (1512–20) under whom the empire reached its greatest power. A bloody despot, but able administrator, he conquered parts of Persia, all of Syria and Palestine, and Egypt (1514–17). As caliph, he was acknowledged by the holy cities of Arabia as spiritual as well as temporal leader.

Selim III (1761–1808), Ottoman sultan (1789–1807). After ending a war against Russia and Austria in *c.* 1791, he began a program to westernize the state's finances and armed forces. In 1801 Egypt was recovered after being occupied by the French under Napoleon. In 1808 he was strangled during a revolt of the janizaries and conservatives who opposed his reforms.

Seljuk Turks, nomadic tribe which traveled to the Middle East and converted to Islam after the breakup of the Mongolian Empire. In the early 11th century they began long and destructive attacks on the Byzantine Empire.

Selkirk, Thomas Douglas, 5th Earl of (1771–1820), Canadian settler leader and financier, b. Scotland. He established settlements in Prince Edward Island and Ontario in 1803. In 1811 he bought a controlling interest in the Hudson's Bay Co. and founded the Red River settlement in Manitoba. Sued by the North West Co. in 1818, he returned to Britain in ill health, leaving a struggling community on the Red River. A friend of Sir Walter Scott, he also wrote widely on the politics and mores of western Canada.

Selkirk, mountain range in SE British Columbia, Canada. An extension of the Rocky Mts, it is traversed by Canadian Pacific Railway; site of portions of Glacier National Park and Mt Revelstok National Park. Highest peak is Mt Sir Sanford, 11,591ft (3,535m). Length: 200mi (322km).

Semantics, study of words, their meanings and uses, and how accurately they reflect reality. Words stand for concepts, and concepts themselves are based on human perceptions of reality that are not necessarily accurate. Thus semantic confusion is possible; people may use the same word to refer to different realities.

Semaphore, device or technique that communicates messages visually. The railroad semaphore consists of a vertical post on which is mounted a single projecting arm. This arm can take three positions, indicating "all clear," "caution," or "stop." The marine semaphore is equipped with two pivoted arms. Letters and numerals are indicated by different placing of these arms.

Semarang, seaport city in N Java, Indonesia, on Java Sea; capital of Central Java prov. and Semarang residency; occupied by Dutch 1748 and Japanese during WWII; site of Diponegoro University (1957). Exports: kapok, rubber, coffee, sugar, tobacco. Industries: fishing, shipbuilding, textiles. Pop. 646,500.

Semen, thick, milky-white fluid ejaculated by the male at orgasm; contains sperms, and the secretions of various accessory sexual glands. Volume is about .085 to .118 ozs. (2.5 to 3.5 ml) and contains about 200 to 300 million sperms per ejaculate.

Semenov, Nikolai Nikolaevich (1896–), Russian chemist. After studying at Leningrad he moved to Moscow State University. In 1956 he shared a Nobel prize with C.N. Hinshelwood for his work on branched chain reactions in combustion processes.

Semiconductor, substance with electrical conductivity intermediate between that of a conductor and an insulator, whose resistance decreases as its temperature increases. It consists of elements or compounds, such as germanium, silicon, and lead telluride, made up of covalent crystals. At normal temperatures some of the electrons in the atoms have sufficient energy to break free of the covalent bonds and will drift against an imposed field giving rise to n-type conductivity. The vacancies, or holes, left by these electrons behave as if they were positive charges that are free to move about the crystal, giving rise to p-type conductivity. In practical semiconductors impurities are added in controlled amounts during manufacture, the number of valency electrons of the impurity atoms determining whether the majority of the current carriers will be p-type holes or n-type electrons. A semiconductor junction is formed when there is an abrupt change along the length of the crystal from one type of impurity to the other. Such a p-n junction acts as a very efficient rectifier and is the basis of the semiconductor diode. *See also* Transistor.

Seminole, North American Indian tribe that dates only from about 1725, when the original members separated from the main Creek Indian group under the pressure of wars with whites, and fled into Georgia and Florida, eventually arriving at the Everglades. About 5,000 inhabit Florida and Oklahoma today.

Semipalatinsk, city in Kazakh SSR, USSR, on Irtysh River; capital of Semipalatinsk oblast; site of a teachers' college. Industries: agriculture, livestock, gold mining, lumbering, food processing, meat packing, textiles. Founded 1718 as a Russian frontier post and transferred to present site 1778. Pop. 282,000.

Semipermeable Membrane, membrane that permits the passage of solvent, such as water, but is impermeable to larger dissolved molecules, such as salt and sugar molecules. The property of permeability depends on the molecular diameter of the dissolved substance and the nature of the membrane. Common membranes include thin palladium foil, pig's bladder, cellophane, copper cyanoferrate, and the cell wall, which allows passage of certain molecules and ions into and out of the cell. *See also* Osmosis.

Semiramis, Greek form of Sammu-ramat, legendary queen of ancient Assyria. Historically she was the wife of Shamshi-Adad V and was queen regent for her son (811–808 BC), but myths have attached to her name that overshadow her historical person. In Assyrian mythology she was daughter of a goddess who abandoned her. Doves nourished her until a kindly shepherd saved her. She eventually became queen by killing her royal husband, and in the myths she is acclaimed as the builder of Babylon.

Semitic Languages, family of languages of peoples native to Asia Minor and N Africa. They have a non-Roman alphabet in which characteristically only the consonants are written, with vowels indicated by marks above or below them, such as Hebrew, Arabic, and Aramaic. Egyptian and Abyssinian languages are often distinguished as belonging to the subgroup of Hamitic languages. The words Semitic and Hamitic are derived from the names of Noah's sons, Shem and Ham (Gen. 10).

Senate, Roman, governing body of the Roman republic, first convened during the monarchy as the king's council. By the 2nd century BC it controlled military, religious, financial, domestic, and foreign policy. The senators, chosen for life by the censors, increased to 600 under Sulla, 900 under Caesar, and fell to 600 under Augustus. Patricians had privileges of precedence over plebeian members; all enjoyed freedom of speech during the republic. The Senate met in Rome to debate legislation; resolutions could be vetoed by the tribunes. After Sulla's defeat of Marius (182 BC), the Senate was controlled by generals until Caesar, leading the populares, destroyed Pompey (48 BC). During the empire the Senate's power was reduced to judicial functions and freedom of debate was lost.

Senate of the United States, upper house of the legislature. It is composed of two senators from each state who are popularly elected and serve six-year terms. Senators are elected in even-numbered years, with about one third of the Senate elected at a time. There are 17 standing committees in the Senate and committee chairmen retain their positions for as long as their party has a majority of the votes. Senate approval by a simple majority is necessary for some presidential appointments and a two-thirds majority for treaties. The vice president serves as the presiding officer and, in his absence, the majority party chooses a "pro-tem" leader. The Senate acts as a court during impeachment proceedings, which are brought by the House. The Senate allows unlimited debate, and the filibuster technique is often employed.

Sendai, city in NE Honshu, Japan, near shore of Sendai Bay; capital of Miyagi prefecture; seat of the powerful daimyo of Date Masamune 17th–19th centuries. It is chief industrial and commercial center of N Honshu; site of Tokohu Imperial University (1907) and Industrial Art Research Institute (1928). Industries: textiles, yarn, silk, wood products, brewing. Pop. 615,000.

Seneca (the Elder), Lucius Annaeus (*c.*60 BC–*c.*AD 37), Roman rhetorician and writer. He lived most of his life in his native Spain. His *Controversies* contains model arguments for legal cases while *Persuasions* contains model orations. He also wrote a book on declamations and a history of Rome.

Seneca (the Younger), Lucius Annaeus (4 BC?–AD 65), Roman philosopher, dramatist, and political figure, the son of Seneca the Elder. Tutor for the young Nero, he was highly influential in the first years of the emperor's reign. A Stoic, he wrote many philosophical essays including *De elementia* on the duty of a ruler to be merciful. His *Dialogue* contained essays on anger, impassivity, divine providence, and other topics. *Quaestiones Naturales* viewed nature from a philosophical perspective. He wrote nine tragedies based on Greek models, the best known of which is *Phaedra.* The tragedies were written to be recited, not performed. Seneca resigned his offices out of alarm and disgust with Nero's excesses. He was compelled by Nero to commit suicide.

Seneca, the most populous division of the League of the Iroquois; a tribe of North American Indians inhabiting N New York; a few live in Canada. Today, about 850 so-called "Seneca" live in Oklahoma, where they moved in 1832; the main eastern group totals about 7,000 in New York, Ontario, and Pennsylvania.

Seneca Lake, lake in W New York, one of the Finger Lakes, joined by Seneca River to Cayuga Lake; part of New York State Barge System. Area: 67sq mi (174sq km).

Senegal, independent republic in W Africa, formerly a French protectorate. Peanuts are the principal crop.

Land and Economy. Located on the bulge of West Africa, it is bordered by the Atlantic Ocean (W), Mauritania (N), Mali (E), Guinea and Guinea-Bissau (S). Mostly a low altitude country of rolling plains, it includes a SE plateau at the foothills of the Fouta-Djallon Mts. Tropical rain forests cover the SW. Four major rivers, all navigable for large vessels, cross the country —the Senegal, Saloumn, Gambia, and Casamance. The seasons include two hot and two dry periods. Peanuts provide Senegal's main crop, accounting for about half of export earnings. Attempts to diversify agriculture have added cotton as a cash crop. Commercial fishing is expanding. A high degree of industrialization allows Senegal to process raw materials for export—peanut oil, canned fish, and phosphates, the major mineral resource.

People. Among the chief ethnic groups 35% of the population is Wolof, 17.5% Fulani, 16.5% Serere, 9% Toucouleur, and 9% Diola. Although French is the official language, each separate ethnic group speaks its own language. About 80% of the country is Muslim; of the remaining most are animist, with a small percentage of Catholics. The literacy rate is about 10%.

Government. A constitution provides for an executive-presidential system with an elected unicameral legislature. The president is elected by universal adult suffrage, and a prime minister is appointed by the president.

History. Fossils show that Senegal was probably inhabited in prehistoric times. During the 13th and 14th centuries it came under the influence of the Mandingo Empire, and the Djoloff Empire of Senegal was formed. French control over the region started in the 17th century. Senegal became a French protectorate in 1920. By 1956 the franchise had been broadened, and Senegal became a member of the French Community with internal autonomy. An attempt at federation with French Sudan, as the Mali Federation (1959–60) was not successful, and in 1960 Senegal seceded and declared itself a republic. From independence the country was led by Léopold Senghor until 1981, when he stepped down. In 1980 and again in 1981, Senegal sent troops to neighboring Gambia to assist in putting down attempted coups. In 1981 the two countries announced the creation of Senegambia, a confederation of the two nations, which was formalized in 1982. In 1983, the Pan-African News Agency (PANA) was established and headquartered in Dakar. Senegal continued to work for peace in the area through the 1980s. *See also* Senegambia.

PROFILE

Official name: Republic of Senegal
Area: 76,124sq mi (197,161sq km)
Population: 5,518,000
Density: 73per sq mi (28per sq km)
Chief city: Dakar (capital)
Government: Republic (elected president and appointed prime minister)
Religion: Islam
Language: French (official)
Monetary unit: CFA franc
Gross national product: $2,370,000,000
Per capita income: $252
Industries: canning, chemicals, cement, food processing, textiles
Agriculture: peanuts, rice, millet, sorghum
Minerals: phosphates
Trading partners: United States, France

Senegal River, river in Senegal, W Africa; formed by the confluence of the Bafing and Bakarg rivers; rises near the Sierra Leone border; flows N then NW to form Mauritanian-Senegal border; empties into the Atlantic Ocean at St Louis; chief tributary is Falémé River; serves as source of irrigation for rice growing region. Length: approx. 1,015mi (1,634km).

Senegambia, confederation formed (1981) and made official (1982) between Senegal and Gambia, the tiny country enclosed on three sides by Senegal. In 1980 and 1981, Senegal sent troops to Gambia to support the government during attempted coups. Although the two countries were formally united, they each maintained separate sovereignty, and the confederation's first stated goal was the integration of security and military forces. *See also* Gambia; Senegal.

Senghor, Léopold Sédar (1906–), African intellectual and president of Senegal. He studied in France and fought against Germany in World War II. A skillful writer and champion of black African culture, he became involved in the government of Senegal and was elected president of the new republic in 1960. He worked toward greater African unity and the development of W Africa. He resigned as president at the end of 1980.

Senility, a serious decline in mental and physical abilities in old age. Some old people develop mental disorders marked by such symptoms as lack of attention, forgetfulness, or delusions. Many elderly people do continue to live productive and creative lives, however.

Senna, plants, shrubs, and trees native to warm and tropical regions; some species grow in temperate areas worldwide. They have oblong, featherlike leaves and yellow flowers. Family Leguminosae; genus *Cassia.*

Sennacherib, King of Assyria (704–681 BC), son and successor of Sargon II. His main military campaigns were directed against the Babylonian and Elamite alliance, ending with the capture in 703 then destruction of Babylon in 689 and the defeat of Elam in 691. He led another major campaign against Phoenicia, Palestine, and Philistia in 701. The rest of his reign was spent restoring Nineveh.

Sensitive Fern, a single species of North American fern, found in damp places, and noted for fragility of its leaves, which wilt when picked and are susceptible to early frosts. Long, coarse, triangular sterile fronds; fertile fronds small and beadlike enclosing sori, to 2ft (61cm) high. Family Polypodiaceae; species *Onoclea sensibilis. See also* Fern.

Sentence, a complete thought expressed in words. It begins with a capital letter and ends with a period (declarative), a question mark (interrogative), or exclamation point (imperative or exclamatory). Classifications: simple, compound, complex. Parts: subject and predicate for each clause.

Seoul (Soul), capital city of South Korea, in NW South Korea, 40mi (64km) E of its port of Inch'ŏn; capital of Kyonggi prov. As Hansung, it served as the capital of the Yi dynasty (1394–1910); occupied by Japan 1910–45; headquarters of US forces and US military government 1945; made capital of South Korea 1948; occupied by Communist forces 1950–51; sustained heavy damages during Korean War (1950–53); site of Seoul National University (1945); political, economic, cultural center. Industries: textiles, metallurgy, food processing, chemicals, farm equipment. Pop. 6,889,470.

Separation of Powers, a fundamental principle of the US federal and state governments. Fearing the power of a despot, the framers of the Constitution saw the need for separating the powers of government among the legislature, which makes laws; the president, who executes the laws; and the courts, which interpret the laws. The principle was early enunciated in the writings of Locke and Montesquieu.

Sephardim, the classification of all Jews and their descendants who settled in Spain and Portugal before 1492, when Spanish Jewry was expelled and dispersed. Their language is Ladino or Judeo-Spanish. They now comprise about 17% of the world Jewish population. Today, this category generally includes all Oriental Jews as well.

Sepoy Mutiny. *See* Indian Mutiny.

Septal Region, region of the brain centered about the septum lucidum, a band of tissues that separate the lateral ventricles. *See also* Brain.

September, ninth month of the year. Its name comes from the Latin for seventh because it was the seventh month in the old ten-month calendar. It has 30 days. The birthstone is the sapphire.

Septicemia, generalized bacterial infection in which bacteria, usually staphylococcus, streptococcus, or pneumococcus, multiply in the bloodstream. They may enter from a wound or from an infection within the body.

Septic Tank, a unit for sewage disposal, usually in residences not connected to sewer lines. The compartmented tank is buried in the ground and arranged so that settled sludge contacts waste water flowing through the tank and beyond into a drain field. Bacteria in the sludge decompose solids.

Septimius Severus, Lucius. *See* Severus, Lucius Septimius.

Septuagint (3rd/2nd century BC), Greek translation of the Hebrew Old Testament, written for the Greek-speaking Jewish community in Egypt. It is the oldest Greek translation of the Bible. The Septuagint contains the entire Jewish Canon plus the Apocrypha. It is divided into four sections: the law, history, poetry, and prophets. The books of the Apocrypha do not form a separate section, but are inserted throughout where suitable. It is still used by the Greek Orthodox Church. *See also* Apocrypha; Old Testament.

Sequoia, two species of mammoth evergreen trees found only in California and S Oregon. They are the giant sequoia or big tree *(Sequoia giganteum)* and the redwood *(Sequoia sempervirens).* The size and scarcity of these trees have made them a natural wonder of the United States. Height: over 300ft (91.5m). Family Pinaceae.

Sequoya (1770?–1843), scholar of the Cherokee tribe of American Indians. He invented an alphabet for the

Senegal

Seriema

Saint Elizabeth Seton

Cherokee language so that his people could learn to read and write. He completed his system in 1821 after 12 years' work. With his alphabet he was able to write the history of his people. In 1828 he went to Washington to represent his people to the US government. The sequoia trees are named for him.

Seraphim, heavenly beings described in the Old Testament as having human form but six wings (Isaiah 6:2–6). Though this is the only mention of them in the Bible, the Seraphim became high ranking angels in Jewish and Christian theology.

Serbia (Srbija), largest constituent republic of Yugoslavia, in E Yugoslavia; capital is Belgrade. Mostly mountainous terrain, the fertile NE is drained by the Danube River. Settled by Serbs, it emerged as a state in the 10th century; ruled as a dynasty by Stephen Nemanja (r.1168–96); became chief Slav kingdom under Stephen Dushan (1331–55); taken by Turks 1389 and made part of Ottoman Empire 1459. Serbia rebelled against Turkish rule and was guaranteed autonomy 1829; gained independence 1878, defeated by Bulgaria 1885; gained power and prestige after accession of Peter I (1903). It was drawn into anti-Austrian policy and the First Balkan War (1912); received part of Macedonia after Second Balkan War (1913). Austria declared war on Serbia in 1914, beginning WWI. Defeated by the Central Powers, formed the united kingdom of Serbs, Croats, and Slovenes 1918 (Yugoslavia); region was divided 1929 and made a constituent republic 1946. Industries: agriculture, vineyards, mining. Area: 34,115sq mi (88,358sq km). Pop. 8,447,000.

Serbo-Croatian, the principal language of Yugoslavia, spoken by about three-fourths of the country's population, or about 15,000,000 people. It is spoken by two major ethnic groups—the Serbs, who write it in the Cyrillic alphabet, and the Croats, who use the Roman (Latin) alphabet. Serbo-Croatian is a Slavic language.

Serbs, Croats and Slovenes, Kingdom of, a kingdom formed in 1918 following the Allied victory in World War I, which for the first time united all the South Slavs except Bulgaria in a single government, and which became Yugoslavia in 1929.

Serf, during the Middle Ages in Europe, a peasant bound to his lord's land, part of which he held and developed to provide for his own needs. In the 11th century a peasant voluntarily entered himself and his descendants into serfdom by a symbolic act, similar to fealty and homage for a vassal, consisting of the payment of "head money" and a gesture, such as hanging a bellrope around his neck. By the 13th century, the only serfs were those descended from serfs. Called *villeins* in England, serfs held a social position inferior to that of freemen and superior to that of slaves. *See also* Manorial System.

Seriema, or cariama, large, cranelike, South American bird with erectile crests above short broad bill. Brownish-crested seriema *(Cariama cristata)* lives in grasslands; grayish Burmeister's seriema *(Chunga burmeisteri)* in woodlands. Both feed on small animals, including reptiles, and lay white or buff-colored eggs(2).

Series, mathematical expression obtained by adding the terms of a sequence. Thus, the series $1 + 4 + 9 + 16 + \ldots$ is formed from the sequence 1, 4, 9, 16, …. Like sequences, series may be finite or infinite and infinite series may converge or diverge. A series formed from increasing powers of a variable is a power series; convergent power series are used for repre-

senting many functions. *See also* Arithmetic, Geometric, and Harmonic Progressions; Exponential Function; Trigonometric Function.

Serigraphy, or silk-screen printing. A technique in which multiple images are produced by means of a stencil, or mask, glued or painted onto a fine-meshed fabric screen. When certain areas or patterns have been blocked out, paint or ink is applied to the screen and forced onto the surface of the paper by means of a roller or squeegee. Although devised as a commercial reproductive process, it has been used since the 1930s as a fine-arts medium.

Serine, white crystalline amino acid found in proteins. *See* Amino Acid.

Sermon on the Mount, in the New Testament, a dissertation spoken by Jesus to his disciples and others in the hills of Galilee. Delivered early in his ministry, it is recorded in the Gospel of Matthew. Beginning with the Beatitudes, it continues with a discussion of social responsibility, specifically contrasting Jesus' teaching with Jewish legalistic traditions, and a discourse on individual religious observances.

Serpens, or the Serpent, extensive equatorial constellation situated east of Virgo and divided into two parts, Serpens Canda in the east and Serpens Caput in the west, by Ophiuchus, the Serpent-bearer. Serpens Caput contains the bright globular cluster M 5 (NGC 5904), while Serpens Canda includes M 16 (NGC 6611), an open cluster shining through surrounding nebulosity. Brightest star Alpha Serpentis (Unukalhai).

Serpentine, a group of sheet silicate minerals, with a pattern of green mottling like a snake's; hydrous magnesium silicate. Greasy, of varied hues; hardness 2–5; sp gr 2.4. Commonly used in decorative carving, fibrous varieties are used in asbestos cloth.

Serum, the fluid that remains if whole blood is allowed to clot, and the clot removed; essentially the same composition as plasma, with fibrinogen and clotting factors gone. *See also* Plasma.

Serval, or Bush Cat, orange and black spotted doglike cat found in grassy areas of sub-Saharan Africa. It has a narrow head and long legs, neck, and ears. The gestation period is 74 days and 1–3 young are born. Length: body—30–39.4in (70–100cm); tail—13.8–15.7in (35–40cm); weight: 15–25lb (6.8–11.3kg). Family Felidae; species *Felis serval.*

Servetus, Michael (1511–53), Spanish physician and theologian. While studying in France and Germany, he became interested in ideas of the Protestant reformers, but his theological writings were denounced by reformers as well as Rome. He lived under another name in France, practicing medicine. In medical history he is known for discovering that blood is aerated in the lungs before passing into the heart. Forced to flee from France because of his religious beliefs, Servetus was arrested as a heretic and burned by Calvinists in Geneva.

Servius Tullius (578–535 BC), sixth king of Rome who, although of Roman or Latin birth, ruled during a period of Etruscan supremacy. He built a temple to the Latin Diana and, according to tradition rejected by modern scholars, built the walls of Rome. He is credited with the Servian Reforms.

Servomechanism, automatic device in which one mechanism is controlled by another mechanism, which has an independent power supply. The device usually

forms part of a control system: power steering in a car relies on a servomechanism to provide independent power to turn the wheels in accordance with instructions imparted by the driver through the steering wheel. Some servomechanisms, such as the automatic pilot of an aircraft, incorporate a feedback mechanism that makes the aircraft independent of human control.

Sesostris, the name of three kings of the XII dynasty of ancient Egypt. Sesostris I, coregent with his father Amenemhet I, became sole ruler c.1970 BC. During his reign Nubia was conquered. Sesostris II was also a coregent before succeeding (1906 BC) his father Amenemhet II. Under Sesostris III (reigned c.1887–1849), Egypt became very powerful, its southern boundary extending above the 2nd cataract of the Nile.

Sessions, Roger (1896–1985), US composer, b. Brooklyn, N.Y. He has employed a complex, atonal style in numerous works including his *Violin Concerto* (1935), eight symphonies, and choral, chamber, piano, and organ music. His symphonic piece, *When the Lilacs Last in the Dooryard Bloom'd,* had its first US performance in 1976.

Seth, in the Bible, third son of Adam and Eve, thought by Eve to be recompense from God for the slain Abel. Seth is an ancestor of Christ, according to the New Testament.

Seton, (Saint) Elizabeth Ann (1774–1821), US teacher and organizer of charity, b. New York City. Elizabeth Ann Bayley was the daughter of a physician and professor of anatomy. She married William Seton in 1797 and had five children. Her husband died in 1803; she joined the Roman Catholic Church in 1805 and soon became a leader in church works. She founded a school for girls in Maryland, prepared the way for the US parochial school system, and organized the American Sisters of Charity. Her sainthood was proclaimed in 1975. She was the first US citizen to be canonized.

Sets, distinct collections of definite objects of perception or thought that can be conceived and considered as a whole. The objects are called the elements or members of the set. The number of members can be finite or infinite or be zero (empty set) or the maximum possible (universal set). Various relations can exist between two sets, A and B: A equals B (written $A = B$) if both sets contain exactly the same members; A is included in or is a subset of B ($A{\subset}B$) if all members of A are members of B; disjoint sets have no members in common; overlapping sets have one or more common members. Operations on sets produce new sets: the union of A and B ($A{\cup}B$) contains members of both A and B with no duplicate members; the intersection of A and B ($A{\cap}B$) contains only those members common to both sets; the complement of A contains all members that do not belong to A.

Setter, sporting dog used to locate game and stand on point until the hunter arrives. After the shot, it retrieves on command. Setters have a long, more classically shaped head than spaniels, good scenting powers, endurance, and personality. Developed in 16th-century England, types of setters are English, Irish, and Gordon.

Set Theory, theory that attempts to give mathematics a rigidly logical basis, developed by Georg Cantor in the late 19th century and only later recognized as an important branch of mathematics. It is concerned with the properties of sets, relations between sets, and operations that can be made on sets. Set theory is based on George Boole's work on mathematical logic but manipulates sets of abstract or real objects, finite or infinite in number, rather than logical propositions.

Settlement, Act of (1701), statute designed to regulate and define the rights of the English monarchy. It provided that, if William III and the future Queen Anne died without heirs, the crown would pass to James I's granddaughter, Sophia of Hanover, or her heirs, if they were Protestants. The act ensured the Protestant Hanoverian succession to the throne and restricted the rights of the crown to appoint foreigners.

Seurat, Georges (1859–91), French painter. A post-Impressionist artist, he was interested in the use of color and atmosphere by the Impressionists and brought order and a sense of brilliantly shimmering light to his pictures by using organized color. He developed a style known as Pointillism, in which he painted forms by using colored dots of a uniform size, as in his masterpiece "A Sunday Afternoon on the Island of La Grande Jatte" (1884–86). He also painted many port scenes at Honfleur. Seurat's style influenced that of other artists, especially Paul Signac and Camille Pissarro.

Sevan Lake, lake in N Armenian SSR, USSR; largest lake in Caucasus; fed by 30 streams, drained by Razdau River; ice-free in winter; surrounded by high mountains. It is excellent source of fish; part of an extensive hydroelectric system. Area: 540sq mi (1,400sq km).

Sevastopol, formerly Sebastopol; city in Russian SFSR, USSR, on the Black Sea, 190mi (306km) SE of Odessa; site of a late 6th-century Greek colony; in 100 BC it was absorbed into kingdom of Cimmerian Bosporus; site of a 13th-century Tartar settlement; came under Russian control in 1783; site of a naval base since 1784; a commercial port since 1808. It has been the main base of the Russian Black Sea fleet since early 19th century; fell to the Allies in the Crimean War (1855); it fell to the Germans in WWII (1942); recaptured 1944 by Soviet troops; site of institute of physiotherapy, biological marine research station, regional museum, and the Peter-Paul cathedral, a copy of the temple of Theseus at Athens. Industries: shipbuilding, fish processing, tanning, flour milling. Pop. 291,000.

Seveners. *See* Isma'ilis.

Seventeen-year Locust. *See* Cicada.

Seventh-Day Adventists, Christian denomination whose members expect Christ to return to Earth in person. They also hold the Sabbath on Saturday, the seventh day, and accept the Bible literally as their guide for living. This church was formally organized in 1863. With a worldwide membership of 1,600,000, this is the largest Adventist denomination. *See also* Adventists.

Seven Weeks War. *See* Austro-Prussian War.

Seven Years' War (1756–63), a worldwide conflict growing from the competition between France and England for an overseas empire and between the house of Austria and the kingdom of Prussia for power in Germany. Austria, humiliated by the loss of Silesia to Prussia under the terms of the Treaty of Aix-la-Chapelle (1748), worked toward Russian and French alliances under Prince Kaunitz. He brought about the Diplomatic Revolution, as this reversal of traditional alliances came to be known. He persuaded Louis XV to sign a defensive alliance with Austria (May 1756), and in the following month war broke out between France and England. Frederick II of Prussia, taking the initiative while his enemies were unprepared, invaded Saxony whose wealth he used to finance later campaigns. By January 1757, war was declared on Prussia by most of the German states in the name of the Holy Roman Empire. Austria and Russia signed an agreement to partition Prussia and were joined in alliances with France and Sweden. Frederick responded by invading Bohemia and besieging Prague. When defeated at Kolin (June 1757), he was forced to leave Bohemia. The Anglo-Prussian cause was further harmed by the French victory over the British at Hastenbeck (July 1757) and Russian victories in East Prussia. Frederick, surrounded, responded with military genius. He surprised the French and was victorious at Rossback (November 1757) and defeated the Russians at Zorndorf (August 1758). The English and Hanoverians also began to have more success when William Pitt was put in charge of foreign affairs and pursued the war vigorously on the continent and in the colonies. The tide turned against the Anglo-Prussians when the Russians and Austrians joined forces to defeat them at Kunersdorf (August 1759), and Daun took a Prussian army of 13,000 captive at Maxen (November 1759). The Russians burned Berlin (1760), and in spite of successes at Liegnitz and Jorgan, Prussian losses continued. Frederick lost his English subsidy with the fall of Pitt in 1761. He maintained a defensive position that year, husbanding resources, but was unable to save Schweidnitz from the Austrians or Kolberg from the Russians. He was saved from a critical position by the succession of his admirer Peter III in Russia (January 1762), who immediately made peace and restored all conquests. Sweden made peace the same year. Fighting alone, the Austrians were defeated at Burkersdorf (July 1762). During this same period, the Anglo-French conflict, called the French and Indian Wars in North America, was being decided in favor of the British. The French lost Louisburg in 1758, Quebec in 1759, and Montreal in 1760. In India, the competition between the English and French was decided by British victories at Plassey (1757) and at Pondicherry (1761). Initial French sea superiority was reversed by English naval commander Edward Hawke's victory in Quiberon Bay (1759). Spain's entry into the war in 1761 did little to help France. After long negotiations, the war-weary nations made peace. England, France, and Spain signed the Treaty of Paris (1763), out of which Great Britain emerged as the strongest colonial empire. Austria, Saxony, and Prussia concluded the Treaty of Hubertusburg (1763), restoring the prewar status quo. *See also* French and Indian Wars.

Severnaya Zemlya (Severnaja Zeml'a), archipelago in the Arctic Ocean, Russian SFSR, USSR, N of Taimyr Peninsula, separating Kara and Laptev seas. Main islands are Komsomolets, Pioner, Oktyabrskaya Revolyutsiya, Bolshevik. They were discovered 1913 by Boris Vilkitski. Area: 14,286sq mi (37,001sq km).

Severn River, river in NW Ontario, Canada; rises in Finger Lake area; flows NE through Severn Lake into Hudson Bay; site of Hudson Bay trading post; Fort Severn, at river's mouth, has been in operation since it was rebuilt 1759. Length: 610mi (982 km).

Severn River, one of Britain's chief rivers; rises on Mt Plynlimon, W Wales, flows NE to Shrewsbury, curves SE and then SW to empty into the Bristol Channel. Tributaries include the Vyrnwy, Teme, Stour, Wye, and Upper and Lower Avon rivers; crossed by the Severn Road Bridge. Length: 180mi (290km).

Severus, Lucius Septimius (AD 146–211), Roman emperor (AD 193–211), b. Africa. He was governor of Upper Pannonia. His cohorts murdered Didius Julianus, avenging the death of Pertinax. He defeated and killed Pescennius Niger (194), took Byzantium (196), repulsed Clodius Albinus (197), reoccupied Mesopotamia (198), and invaded Scotland (209). To achieve his military aims, he doubled taxation. He reconstructed the Praetorian Guard with frontier legionnaires. He erected the triple Arch of Septimius Severus and was Papinian's patron. He died in Britain, and Geta and Caracalla succeeded him.

Seville (Sevilla), inland port city in SW Spain, on Guadalquivir River, 337mi (543km) SW of Madrid; capital of Sevilla prov. Occupied by Romans 2nd–5th centuries, it was taken by Moors 712; in 1248 Ferdinand III, king of Castile and Leon, conquered Seville; the city prospered in 16th–17th centuries due to trade monopoly between Spanish empire and the New World; prosperity declined in 18th century when powerful mercantile association was transferred to Cadiz (1720), and freedom to trade with America was given to other Spanish ports. It is the site of 15th-century cathedral containing tomb and library of Christopher Columbus and paintings by Goya and El Greco; Giralda tower 1189, crowned by Renaissance bell tower added in 16th century; 14th-century Alcazar Palace. Industries: agricultural machinery, shipbuilding, chemicals, textiles, shipping. Area: (prov.) 5,402sq mi (13,991sq km). Pop. (city) 560,000; (prov.) 1,434,900.

Sewage. *See* Sanitary Engineering; Solid-Waste Disposal.

Sewall, Samuel (1652–1730), merchant and magistrate in colonial Massachusetts, b. England. He was the only judge to admit he was in error in sentencing 19 to death for practicing witchcraft in Salem (1692). Considered one of the most distinguished colonial magistrates, Sewall is best-remembered for his diary covering the years 1674–77 and 1685–1729.

Seward, William H. (1801–72), US statesman, b. Florida, N.Y. He was an influential senator in 1860 but lost the Republican nomination for president to Abraham Lincoln. During the Civil War, he served as Lincoln's secretary of state. After the war, he served Andrew Johnson in the same capacity and in 1867 purchased Alaska, called at the time "Seward's Folly."

Sewellel, or mountain beaver, small, short-legged rodent native to humid areas of W North America. Not a beaver, it has gray to brown fur and is a burrowing plant-eater. Length: lft (.305m). Family Aplodontia.

Sex Determination. The sex of an organism is determined through the combination of chromosomes. There are two types of sex chromosomes, the X type and the Y type. All female eggs have one X chromosome. The sperm may either have the X or the Y. If the sperm that fertilizes the egg has an X chromosome, the resulting zygote will be XX, or female. If the egg is fertilized with a Y carrying sperm, the zygote will be XY, or male.

Sex Discrimination, unequal treatment because of sex. This usually involves denial of economic and social opportunities. Efforts to eliminate such discrimination include women's liberation movements, women's political coalitions, consciousness raising groups, and the establishment of various governmental committees on the status of women. The Equal Rights Amendment would prohibit discrimination based on sex. *See also* Woman Suffrage; Women's Liberation.

Sex Drive, need of an organism for sexual gratification. In lower animals sex drive is primarily controlled by hormones, while in more complex organisms such as humans psychological factors play a more dominant role. *See also* Drive.

Sex Hormones, hormones produced mainly in the reproductive organs and controlling reproduction and the development of secondary sex characteristics. *See also* Androgens; Estrogens.

Sex Organs. *See* Gonads.

Sextant, a navigational instrument to establish latitude by determining the angle between the horizon and the Sun or a star. It consists of an arc, marked in degrees, a movable arm with a mirror pivoted at the center, and a telescope mounted to the framework. The telescope is focused on the horizon and the arm moved until the mirror image of Sun or star is reflected in line with the telescope, so that it coincides with the horizon. The angle, which can be read on the arc, and the exact time of day (as registered by a chronometer) allow the latitude to be established by means of printed tables.

Sexual Reproduction, fusion of the nuclei of two cells.

Seychelle Islands, independent republic in the Indian Ocean, 1,000mi (1,610km) off E coast of Africa. The group consists of approx. 85 islands; the largest is Mahe, location of the capital city Victoria. The population is mainly of African, European, Indian, and Chinese descent; and overwhelmingly Roman Catholic. Industry is centered around the exportation of tea, coconuts, and cinnamon, and is heavily dependent on tourism. The Seychelles were discovered by Vasco da Gama 1502; and claimed by France 1756. The British took possession 1794, and ruled until 1976, when the Seychelles became an independent republic, joining the United Nations and Commonwealth of Nations. Following a coup in 1977, the new Marxist government promulgated a new constitution, establishing the Seychelles as a one-party socialist state. Coup attempts by European and South African mercenaries in 1981 and the military in 1982 were unsuccessful.

PROFILE

Official name: Seychelles
Area: 107sq mi (172sq km)
Population: 62,686
Density: 586per sq mi (226per sq km)
Chief city: Victoria (capital)
Government: Republic
Language: English and French (both official); Creole

Seymour, Jane (1509–37), queen of England, the daughter of Sir John Seymour and sister of Thomas Seymour. She was the third wife of Henry VIII, whom she married in 1536. She died in 1537 after the birth of her son, the future Edward VI.

Seymour, Thomas, Baron Seymour of Sudeley, (1508–49), English lord high admiral. He was the brother of Jane Seymour and Edward Seymour, Lord Protector Somerset, and the husband of Henry VIII's widow, Catherine Parr. His ambition to supplant his brother as guardian of Edward VI and his attempt to marry Princess Elizabeth led to his trial and execution for treason in 1549.

Sforza, Italian family that ruled Milan from 1450 to 1535. **Muzio Attendolo** (1369–1424), a *condottiere* (mercenary military leader), founded the family and took the name "Sforza." Thereafter the family's control of Milan was based upon military power. Their first duke of Milan was **Francesco** (1401–66), whose son **Galeazzo Maria** (1444–76) succeeded him and married Louis XI of France's sister-in-law. **Ludovico**

William H. Seward

Sewellel

Shantung Province, China

Sforza (1451–1508) was driven from the duchy by Louis XII of France in 1499. His son **Francesco Maria** (1492–1535) was restored by Emperor Charles V as duke in 1522; but with Francesco Maria's death the duchy passed to Charles and the Hapsburgs.

Sforza, (Count) Carlo (1873–1952), Italian anti-fascist statesman and foreign minister, from a collateral branch of the Renaissance Sforzas. In protest against Benito Mussolini he was in voluntary exile from 1927–1943. After Mussolini's fall, he returned to Italy, a prominent anti-Fascist and anti-monarchist, to serve the government. He was minister of foreign affairs from 1947 to 1951.

Shad, saltwater food fish of the herring family that swims upriver to spawn. They are prized for their roe. Deep-bodied, they have a notch in the upper jaw for the tip of the lower. The American shad (*Alosa sapidissima*), formerly only on the Atlantic coast, was introduced on the Pacific coast; the allice and twaite shad are European. Length: to 30in (76cm). Family Clupeidae.

Shaftesbury, Anthony Ashley Cooper, 1st Earl of (1621–83), English political figure. One of the proprietors of the colony of Carolina, he is chiefly remembered for his opposition to the crown and his friendship with philosopher John Locke. Shaftesbury achieved prominence during the Civil War and Commonwealth as a general and a member of the Council of State. He supported the Restoration (1660), becoming chancellor of the exchequer (1661), and lord chancellor (1672). A leader of the Whigs, he always remained a champion of Parliament, a role that brought him into conflict with the king. He was instrumental in the passage of the Habeas Corpus Act (1679) and supported the duke of Monmouth's claim to the throne.

Shakers, religious organization, also known as the United Society of Believers in Christ's Second Appearing, or The Millennial Church. In a state of spiritual excitement, their bodies shake. It developed in England from 1747. Numerous US communities were founded from 1776, but by the 1980s few Shakers were in existence, and they disagreed among themselves about the ultimate disposition of their valuable property. With a communistic form, the Shakers stress separation from the world. Shakers stress separation of the sexes and complete celibacy.

Shakespeare, William (1564–1616), English playwright and poet. Considered by many to be the greatest playwright of all time, he is the most frequently quoted individual writer in the world. His plays have been presented continuously since their writing. He arrived in London sometime around 1590, when his first plays, the three parts of Henry VI, were written. In 1594 he joined the Lord Chamberlain's (later, King's) Men as an actor and playwright. In 1599 he became a partner in the Globe Theatre; in 1608 of the Blackfriars Theatre. He retired to his birthplace, Stratford-on-Avon, in 1613. His poetry includes the heroic poems *Venus and Adonis* (1593) and *The Rape of Lucrece* (1594), the love poem *The Phoenix and the Turtle* (1601), and the 154 *Sonnets,* first published 1609.

Following is a list of Shakespeare's plays, with the dates of first performances.

Henry VI (Part II)	1590
Henry VI (Part III)	1590
Henry VI (Part I)	1590
Titus Andronicus	1593
Richard III	c. 1594
The Comedy of Errors	1594
The Taming of the Shrew	c. 1594
Love's Labour's Lost	1594
The Two Gentlemen of Verona	1594–95
Richard II	c. 1595
A Midsummer Night's Dream	c. 1595
Romeo and Juliet	c. 1596
King John	1596
The Merchant of Venice	1596
Henry IV (Part I)	1597
Henry IV (Part II)	1597
The Merry Wives of Windsor	c. 1597
Much Ado About Nothing	c. 1598
Henry V	1598
Julius Caesar	1599
As You Like It	1599
Twelfth Night	1599
Hamlet	1600
Troilus and Cressida	1601
All's Well That Ends Well	1602
Measure for Measure	1604
Othello	1604
King Lear	1605
Macbeth	1605
Antony and Cleopatra	1606
Coriolanus	1607
Timon of Athens	1607
Pericles	c. 1607
Cymbeline	1609
The Winter's Tale	1610
The Tempest	1611
Henry VIII	1612
Two Noble Kinsmen	c. 1613

See also individual plays.

Shale, is a sedimentary rock made from mud or clay. Shales are quite common, comprising over half the world's sedimentary rock, and may contain different materials such as fossils, alumina, carbonaceous matter, and oil. *See also* Sedimentary Rocks.

Shaman, or medicine man, person with magical powers and ability to communicate with the dead and spirits through trances and rituals. By controlling spirits, Shamans ward off evil, heal, and tell the future. *See also* Animism; Sorcery.

Shamir, Yitzhak (1915–), Israeli political leader. He immigrated to Palestine from his native Poland (1935) and received a law degree from the Hebrew University. He worked to overthrow British rule in Palestine and establish a Jewish homeland there, despite arrests and deportation by the British. He returned from exile in 1948 but did not enter political life until 1973, when he was elected to the Knesset (parliament). He became speaker of the Knesset (1977–80), foreign minister (1980–83), and prime minister (1983–84). After narrowly losing an election (1984), he agreed to share the prime ministership with Shimon Peres, taking the first half of the term as deputy premier and foreign minister.

Shamrock, plant with three-part leaves, usually *Trifolium repens* or *T. dubium,* grown for forage. Other plants also called shamrock include *Oxalis acetosella* and *Medicago lupulina.*

Shang Dynasty (1766–1122 BC), Chinese dynasty, the earliest dynasty for which accurate records exist. The Shangs, who ruled in the Yellow River Valley, willed to China its complex and sophisticated written language, techniques of flood control and irrigation, and a high level of artistry in bronze works. It eventually grew weak and was overthrown by the Chou Dynasty.

Shanghai (Shang-hai), seaport city in E China, on Hwangpu River, 13mi (21km) from Yangtze delta; largest city in China, most populous in mainland Asia, and a leading world port. City was made a treaty port 1843 and opened to foreign trade; this spurred tremendous economic growth and created concessions held by United States, Great Britain, France, and Japan. By the end of WWII, the entire city was under Chinese control; fell to Communists 1949; industrial, commercial, educational, transportation center. Industries: textiles, steel, chemicals, publishing, food processing, rubber products, farm machinery, shipbuilding, pharmaceuticals. Pop. 10,820,000.

Shannon River, river in Republic of Ireland; rises on Cuilcagh Mt in Cavan and flows S through Loughs Allen, Ree, and Derg to Limerick, then W into Atlantic between Loop Head to N and Kerry Head to S. Length: 230mi (370km).

Shansi (Shanxi), province in NE China; bounded by Yellow River (W and S), Great Wall (N), North China Plain (E); capital is Taiyuan. Ruled 1911–49 by Yen Hsishan, it was occupied by Japanese (1937–45) during Sino-Japanese War; site of Buddhist caves dating from Northern Wei dynasty (386–535). Industries: coal and iron mining, salt, fertilizer, chemicals, machinery, cement, locomotives, lumber, livestock, cotton, grapes, tobacco, grains. Area: approx. 60,656sq mi (157,099sq km). Pop. 18,010,000.

Shantung (Shandong), province in NE China; bounded by Hopeh and Honan provs. (W), Honan and Kiangsu provs. (S); the E is a peninsula between the Potlai Gulf (N) and Yellow Sea (E and S); capital is Chi-nan. Strategically located near Manchuria, it was held by Germany 1898–1914, Japan 1919–22, Great Britain 1898–1930; during the Sino-Japanese War, Japan occupied the entire province (1937–45); it was under Communist control 1948; traditional birthplace of Confucius and Mencius; site of China's most sacred Buddhist and Taoist mountain peak, Tai Shan. Industries: agriculture, forest products, fishing, salt. Area: 59,189sq mi (153,299sq km). Pop. 55,520,000.

Shaping, in psychology, a procedure used to teach an organism a behavior it would not normally perform; a form of operant conditioning. Approximations to the desired behavior are gradually encouraged by rewards until the organism performs the final behavior; eg, a dog is taught to roll over by first rewarding it when it lies down, then when it also gets up, and finally rewarding only the entire sequence of behaviors when it occurs on command. *See also* Operant Conditioning.

Sharecroppers, type of US tenant farmers. In return for their labor and one-half of their crop they are provided with land, seed, stock, tools, and living facilities. After the Civil War, many former slaves became sharecroppers in the South.

Sharett, Moshe (1894–1965), Israeli political leader, b. Russia. Born Moshe Shertok, he emigrated to Palestine (1906) and he was a member of the Jewish Agency (1933), which represented the Palestinian Jews under the British mandate. He became the agency's political secretary and argued for a Jewish national home before the British government and the United Nations. With the creation of Israel, he became foreign minister (1948–53). He was prime minister of Israel (1954–55).

Sharks, torpedo-shaped elasmobranch found in subpolar to tropical marine waters. They have well-developed jaws; cartilaginous skeleton; bony teeth; skin denticles; 5–7 gill slits on each side of the head; and a characteristic lobe-shaped tail with longer top lobe. Pit organs are used to detect hydrostatic pressure, sound, chemical composition of water, and possibly the presence of blood. Sharks are carnivorous; at least 10 species are known to attack man. Fertilization is internal, and young are born alive. A few species lay leathery eggs. Sharks first appeared about 240–350,-000,000 years ago. There are about 250 living species. Order Selachii. *See also* Chondrichthyes; Dogfish; Hammerhead Shark; Nurse Shark; Tiger Shark; Whale Shark; White Shark.

Sharm al-Sheikh (Sharm ash Shaykh), promontory at S end of Sinai Peninsula, overlooking Strait of Tiran. Captured by Israel from Egypt during 1967 Arab-Israeli War, it has since been surrendered by Israel as result of 1973 war and United Nations negotiations in 1974.

Sharon, Plain of (Plain of Saron), fertile coastal plain in W Israel, extending from Caesarea to Tel-Aviv Jaffa. Area: 500sq mi (1,295sq km).

Sharp-shinned Hawk, small North American hawk, perhaps the smallest, with short rounded wings and a long tail. Species *Accipiter velox. See also* Hawk.

Shatt-al-Arab, channel in SE Iraq, formed by confluence of Tigris and Euphrates rivers; flows SE to Persian Gulf through wide delta containing extensive date palm groves. Navigable for ocean-going vessels as far as Basra, it forms part of Iran-Iraq border. Length: 120mi (193km).

Shaw, George Bernard(1856–1950), British dramatist, novelist, essayist, and critic, b. Ireland. He moved from Dublin to London in 1876, joined the Fabian Society, and became a notable public speaker and writer of political and economic tracts. By the 1880s he was highly respected for the excellence of his art, music, and drama criticism, written for London newspapers. He began writing plays in the early 1890s, achieving finally a large lifetime output that established him as the leading British playwright of his time. Many of his plays were provided with extended and pertinent prefaces. Among the most notable are *Arms and the Man* (1894); *Candida* (1897); *The Man of Destiny* (1897); *The Devil's Disciple* (1897); *Captain Brassbound's Conversion* (1900); *Caesar and Cleopatra* (1901); *Mrs. Warren's Profession* (1902); *Man and Superman* (1903); *Major Barbara* (1905); *The Doctor's Dilemma* (1906); *Misalliance* (1910); *Androcles and the Lion* (1912); *Pygmalion* (1913); *Heartbreak House* (1919); *Back to Methuselah* (1921); *Saint Joan* (1923); *The Apple Cart* (1929); *Too True to Be Good* (1932); and *In Good King Charles's Golden Days* (1939). Other important writings by Shaw are the novel *Cashel Byron's Profession* (1886); the essays *The Quintessence of Ibsenism* (1891) and *The Perfect Wagnerite* (1898); the political tracts *Fabian Essays on Socialism* (1889) and *The Intelligent Woman's Guide to Capitalism and Socialism* (1928); and the collections of his music and drama criticism. He received the Nobel Prize for literature in 1925.

Shawnee, a major Algonquian-speaking tribe of North American Indians who have moved around the United States more than any other tribe. Their early home is recorded as along the Cumberland River in Tennessee, but today most of the 3,000 live in Oklahoma. This includes many Delaware, who are closely related to them. Two famous Shawnee people were Tecumseh and his brother Tenskwatawa, the Shawnee prophet.

Shear, or shear stress, a force tending to cause deformation of a material by slipping along a plane parallel to the imposed stress. In nature, the resulting shear is related to the downslope of Earth materials as well as to earthquakes.

Sheathbill, strong-flying, shore-loving white bird of Antarctica. Pigeon-sized, with short, horny, sheathed bill; spurred, long, wings; and short legs, they feed on seaweed and small crustaceans. Dark-blotched white eggs (2–3) are laid in a rock-or-burrow-sheltered nest. Genus: *Chionis.*

Sheep, common name for eight ruminants of genera *Ovis, Pseudois,* and *Ammotragus,* closely related to goats. Wild species occur in mountains of Europe, Asia, Africa, and North America. One to three young are born after 5–6 months pregnancy. Males are called rams; females, ewes; young, lambs. Sheep were domesticated 7000 years ago in SW Asia. All domestic sheep are *Ovis aries;* no wild specimen survives. Common breeds of domestic sheep are of three types: fine wool, mutton, and fur (karakul). The long fur of wild types has disappeared from domestic breeds that retain only the woolly undercoat. The blue sheep, or bharal *(Pseudois nayaur),* of W China is the only wild sheep that does not interbreed with domestic sheep. The N African aoudad *(Ammotragus lervia)* is the only wild sheep indigenous to that continent. The genus *Ovis* contains six wild species: bighorn and Dall sheep are North American; argali, Asiatic mouflon, laristan, and European mouflon are Old World species. Family Bovidae. *See also* Wool.

Sheep Liver Fluke, parasitic flatworm that collects in liver bile passages of cattle and sheep. It develops in a host snail—the tailed cercaria escapes, encysts on grass, and is eaten by livestock. Length: 0.75in (19mm). Phylum Platyhelminthes; class Trematoda; species *Fasciola hepatica.*

Sheepshead, or sea bream, marine food and game fish found in tropical and temperate waters. Deep-bodied, it is greenish yellow with seven dark bars on each side. Length: 2.5ft (76.2cm); weight: 30lb (13.6kg). Family Sparidae; species *Archosargus probatocephalus.*

Sheep Tick, or sheep mite, sheep ked, reddish brown, wingless fly, that is a worldwide external parasite of sheep and goats. It is flat and leathery. Length: 0.25in. (6mm). Family Hippoboscidae; species *Melophagus ovinus.*

Sheffield, industrial city in N England, in South Yorkshire, at confluence of Don and Sheaf rivers. A leading industrial city famous for its special steels and their products, it has been noted since 14th century for manufacture of cutlery; first Bessemer steel plant was built here 1859; seat of University of Sheffield. Pop. 559,800.

Shell, Atomic, any of the groupings of orbital electrons around the nucleus of an atom, named K, L, M, etc, outward, each containing a limited number of electrons of a particular energy. *See also* Atom.

Shellac, a purified resin made from the secretions of the lac insect, *Laccifer lacca.* Shellac is fluid when heated and rigid at room temperature and is used in the production of adhesives, hair sprays, varnishes, and sealers.

Shelley, Mary Wollstonecraft (1797–1851), English novelist, daughter of William Godwin and Mary Wollstonecraft. She went abroad with Percy Bysshe Shelley in 1814, marrying him in 1816. Her works include *Frankenstein* (1818), *The Last Man* (1826), and *Lodore* (1835). *See also* Frankenstein.

Shelley, Percy Bysshe (1792–1822), English author. One of the greatest Romantic lyric poets, he visited Italy and Switzerland and associated with Byron, Keats, and William Godwin, whose daughter he married. His poetry included "Queen Mab" (1813), "Ozymandias" (1818), "Ode to the West Wind" (1819), *Prometheus Unbound* (1820), "Ode to a Skylark" (1820), and "Adonais" (1821). His prose includes *A Philosophical View of Reform* (1819) and *A Defence of Poetry* (1821). He died while sailing off the Italian coast.

Shellfish, common name for shelled mollusks and crustaceans used as food by man. Shelled mollusks include clams, oysters, and scallops; crustaceans include shrimp, lobsters, crabs, and crayfish.

Shells and Shell Collecting, shells, the limy protective cases secreted by various mollusks, have been important to man as tools, decorations, jewelry, and money (cowrie shells in Africa and Pacific islands and wampum of North American Indians). They also have had great economic value—*Murex* was used to make Royal Tyrian purple dye, the basis of Mediterranean trade 3000 years ago, and pearls produced by oysters are sold as precious jewels. Most collectible shells are produced by gastropods. The ideal shell is found alive and then properly cleaned. A famous shell collection is owned by Japan's Emperor Hirohito. The most expensive shell is Glory-of-the-Seas found in the SW Pacific; one of the rarest is Glory-of-India.

Shem, in Genesis, eldest son of Noah. He received the first blessing of Noah after the Flood. He settled land between that of his brothers Ham and Japheth.

Shenandoah Valley, valley in N Virginia, between the Blue Ridge and Allegheny Mts, part of Great Appalachian Valley; scene of much activity during the Civil War; site of Shenandoah National Park and source of Shenandoah River. Explored early 18th century; settled *c.* 1730. Length: 150mi (242km).

Shensi (Shaxi), province in E central China, W of the T'ung-kuan Pass; capital is Sian. The province is divided into four geographical regions: (1) N is a plateau, used for agriculture, with rich coal deposits and some oil production; (2) S is Wei-ho valley, a very fertile and populated region, called "cradle of Chinese civilization;" (3) further S are the Chinling Mts, running E-W for 930mi (1,497km); (4) S of the mountains is Han River valley with mild climate. Province was scene of Muslim rebellion 1860s; seat of Chinese communists 1935–49. Area: 76,000sq mi (196,840sq km). Pop. 21,-000,000.

Shepard, Alan Bartlett, Jr. (1923–), US astronaut, b. East Derry, N.H. A naval officer, he was the first American to be launched into space (1961), going 115 miles (185km) above the Earth. He participated in the Apollo 14 flight to the moon in 1971 and was the fifth man to walk on the moon. In 1978 he was awarded the Space Medal of Honor.

Sheraton, Thomas (1751–1806), English furniture designer. His furniture style, which is known for its slim legs and simple outlines, had much influence on furniture design. His chair designs show the influence of curving ancient Greek chairs.

Sherbrooke, city in S Quebec, Canada, 93mi (150km) E of Montreal, at the confluence of Magog and St Francis rivers; seat of Sherbrooke co; site of Université de Sherbrooke, and St Peter's cathedral (1844). Industries: textiles, clothing, soft drinks, rubber products, machinery. Inc. 1852. Pop. 76,804.

Sheridan, Philip Henry (1831–88), Union Civil War general, later commanding general of the US Army, b. Albany, N.Y. Known as a fiery leader, he commanded an Army of the Potomac cavalry corps, winning two important victories in the Shenandoah Valley. He forced Confederate Gen. Robert E. Lee's surrender by cutting off his retreat at Appomattox, Va. (1865).

Sheridan, Richard Brinsley (1751–1816), English dramatist b. Dublin. A politician, actor, and partner (1776) in the Drury Lane Theatre, Sheridan excelled in comedies of manners, such as *The Rivals* (1775), *The School for Scandal* (1777), *The Critic* (1779). Sheridan abandoned the theater in 1780 and won fame for oratory as a Whig member of Parliament.

Sherlock Holmes, fictional private detective, a character in works by Arthur Conan Doyle. He first appears in *A Study in Scarlet* (1887). Holmes has many eccentricities and mannerisms, the chief of which are his dressing gown, hypodermic syringe, violin playing, and amazing deductive powers. Dr. Watson acts as his ponderous foil, and Professor Moriarty as a worthy villain-antagonist.

Sherman, William Tecumseh (1820–91), US military officer, b. Lancaster, Ohio. A graduate (1840) of the US Military Academy at West Point, he became brigadier general of volunteers during the Civil War (1861). He took part in the battles of Bull Run, Shiloh, Corinth, and the capture of Vicksburg. His most noted exploit was his march eastward through Georgia, including the "march to the sea" from Atlanta to Savannah (1864). By the end of the war he was General Grant's most dependable general, and Sherman took over from Grant as general and commander of the army in 1869. He retired in 1884. His often-quoted remark "War is hell" was made in 1880.

Sherrington, (Sir) Charles S(cott) (1861–1952), English physiologist. He was a pioneer in the study of how the nervous system works. His book *The Integrative Action of the Nervous System* (1906) helped establish physiological psychology. For his work he received a Nobel Prize in 1932.

Sherwood, Robert Emmet (1896–1955), US writer, b. New Rochelle, N.Y. He wrote comedies and socially significant dramas such as *Waterloo Bridge* (1930), *Reunion in Vienna* (1931), *The Petrified Forest* (1934), the Pulitzer Prize winner *Idiot's Delight* (1936), and *Abe Lincoln in Illinois* (1938). He was a political propagandist in World War II and worked as a speech writer for President Franklin D. Roosevelt. The memoir *Roosevelt and Hopkins* was published in 1948.

Shetland Islands, group of about 100 islands and islets NE of the Orkneys, about 130mi (209km) off N Scotland; administratively the county of Zetland. Main islands are Mainland, Yell, Unst; Lerwick is the chief town. Severe gales hamper agriculture, but Shetland ponies, cattle, and sheep are raised. Patterned "Fair Isle" knitwear is a traditional product.

Shetland Pony, one of the smallest and oldest light horse breeds. Dating from the 6th century in the Shetland Islands of Scotland, it was introduced in the United States in the middle 1800s. A small, hardy horse, it was used for draft or road work and makes an ideal children's mount. It can be any horse color, broken or solid. Height: under 46in (116.8cm) at shoulder; weight: 350lb (158kg).

Shetland Sheepdog, miniature collie (working group) used as guard and farm dog; also called Sheltie. Probably bred from small collies, it has a long, blunted,

George Bernard Shaw

Philip Sheridan

William Sherman

wedge-shaped head; high-set, small ears held ¾ erect; a moderately long body; medium-length legs; and a long tail. The long, straight double coat is black, blue merle, or sable with white or tan marks; it is short and smooth on face, feet, and ears. Average size: 13–16in (33–41cm) high at shoulder; 15lb (7kg). *See also* Working Dog.

Shi'a, Muslim sect, including about 10% of the followers of Islam. Shiites differ with the majority sect, the Sunnis, about sources of authority in their faith. Sunnis find the source in the Sunna, the customary practice of Mohammed and his close followers. Shiites started as a political party. They find authority in the inspired leadership of a succession of imams starting with Ali, Mohammed's son-in-law. There are two main Shi'a subsects, the Imamis and the Isma'ilis. The largest Shi'a communities are found in Iran, Iraq, Arabia, and India. *See also* Islam.

Shield, a large, low-relief, exposed mass of Precambrian rock, commonly having a very gently convex surface and surrounded by belts of younger rock. Within shields are the Earth's most ancient rocks, more than 2 billion years old, now changed by metamorphism but originally composed of basaltic lava. Shields form the nucleus of continents. Such a region occupies two-thirds of Canada and is known as the Canadian Shield.

Shield Constellation. See Scutum Constellation.

Shih-Huang-ti (246–209 BC), the first emperor of the Ch'in Dynasty in China (221–207 BC). He centralized rule in ancient China by conquering six feudal states and replacing the feudal system of the Chou Dynasty while king of the northwestern state of Ch'in (246–221 BC). He drove back the Hsiung-Nu and began the Great Wall to keep out nomad tribes. To ensure unity in the new empire he imposed the Ch'in code of law, standardized weights and measures, and created an intelligible written language by standardizing Chinese script. To suppress diversity in customs and thought, he ordered the burning of all but practical books in 212. Defying the decree, 460 scholars were killed. The Shih's son was murdered in retribution for his tyranny, and the Han Dynasty was established in 202.

Shihkiachwang (Shijiazhuang, Shihchiachuang), city in China, 160mi (258km) SW of Peking; capital of Hopeh prov. Industries: textiles, fertilizer, pharmaceuticals, iron, steel, machinery, food processing, paper. Pop. 1,500,000.

Shih Tzu Dog, (toy group) bred in imperial court of China as pet of nobility; first brought West about 1930. Name means "lion." It has a broad, round head; square, short muzzle with long moustaches; dark, large eyes; long, drooping ears; long, broad-chested body; short muscular legs; and tail carried curved up over the back. The long, luxurious coat is slightly wavy and may be any color. Average size: 9–10.5in (23–25.4cm) high at shoulder; 12–15lb (5.4–7kg). *See also* Toy Dog.

Shiites. See Shi'a.

Shikoku, smallest of the four main islands of Japan, S of Honshu and E of Kyushu; mostly settled along coast; interior is mountainous and heavily forested. Industries: rice, tea, salt, lumber, fishing, tobacco, copper mining. Area: 7,245sq mi (18,765sq km). Pop. 3,904,014.

Shiloh, ruins of Biblical city in Jordan, on Mt Ephraim, 15mi (24km) W of Jordan River. Ark of the Covenant was kept here until captured by Philistines, and a tabernacle established; modern town called Khirbet Seilun.

Shimonoseki, seaport in SW Honshu, Japan, across Shimonoseki Strait, W door to Inland Sea. A major industrial center and port, it is connected with Kitakyushu (Kyushu Island) by tunnels under the narrow strait; seat of daimyos 10th–19th centuries; scene of attack by European and US ships Sept. 5–8, 1864; treaty ending Sino-Japanese War was signed here 1895; bombed by United States during WWII. Industries: shipbuilding and repair, metal works, machinery, fish canning, textiles, tobacco. Pop. 267,000.

Shin Bone. *See* Tibia.

Shiner, small freshwater minnow often used for bait. Among the 100 species are the spottail *Notropis hudsonius,* the golden *Notemigonus crysoleucas,* and the sailfin *Notropis hypselopterus.* Family Cyprinidae.

Shingles, or herpes zoster, an acute viral infection of the skin and nerves. Groups of small blisters appear along segments of nerves, usually on the back, sometimes preceded by pain in the affected place.

Shinto, the "Way of the Gods," native religion of Japan. It originated as a cult of nature-worship. Confucian and Buddhist influences shaped Shintoism from the 5th century until the 17th-century revival and codification of state Shinto. Shinto is polytheistic and concerned with ceremonial purity, believing that the emperor and the Japanese people are descended from the Gods. Today Shintos number over 60,000,000.

Shipworm, or teredo, pileworm, wood-boring, elongated clam that burrows with the edge of its tiny shell into ships and wood pilings. The viscera are contained in a wormlike siphon; a limy tube is secreted in burrowed tunnels. Length: 0.25in (6.4mm). Family Teredinidae; species include *Teredo navalis.*

Shiraz, city in SW central Iran, approx. 200mi (322km) SE of Isfahan; capital of Fars prov. Active trade center from 10th century, city served as capital of Persia 1750–59; site of tombs of Hafiz and Sadi, Persian poets; pilgrimage center for Shiite Muslims; seat of Pahlavi University (1945). Nearby are the ruins of Persepolis; industrial and commercial center. Industries: textiles, cement, sugar, fertilizer, wine, carpets, metalworks, petrochemicals, handicrafts. Pop. 373,000.

Shire, earliest draft horse breed. It was developed in England during the 1700s and is a descendant of the Middle Ages' Great Horse. Also called Great Horse, War Horse, and Cart Horse, this heavy-boned horse has a sluggish temperament. Colors are bay, brown, or black with white markings. Height: 64–70in (163–178cm) at shoulder; weight; over 2,000lb (900kg).

Shiva, one of the three great Hindu gods, along with Brahma and Vishnu. A complex god, he represents both reproduction and destruction, although the combining of contradictory qualities is not uncommon in Hinduism. His name means "Auspicious One" in Sanskrit. In paintings and statues he often has three eyes (the third eye provides inward vision and outward destruction), coiled hair, and a serpent and a garland of skulls around his blue neck. In modern Hinduism, Shiva's cult is one of the most popular.

Shizuoka, city in E Honshu, Japan, approx. 55mi (89km) SW of Tokyo; capital of Shizuoka prefecture; seat of Tokugawa shogunate, founded 1607 by Ieyasu; agricultural trade center for prefecture. Products: textiles, tea, oranges, metals, wood products. Pop. 447,000.

Shock, acute progressive circulatory failure, the result of the heart's inability to pump enough blood through the major organs. It may be caused by injury, burns, hemorrhage or major surgery, or poisoning. It is characterized by weakness, shallow breathing, rapid heartbeat, and low blood pressure. Treatment involves keeping the patient warm and giving oxygen and sedation.

Shock Wave, in fluids, a region across which sharp discontinuities in pressure and density occur. Shock waves are brought about by supersonic velocities of a solid or fluid; since the surrounding fluid can propagate disturbances only at the local speed of sound, the moving body "piles up" the disturbances it is causing into a V-shaped "wake" attached to the body. The "sonic boom" of supersonic aircraft is simply the passage of this shock wave past the eardrum.

Shoebill, tall, strange-looking, storklike wading bird found in papyrus marshes of tropical E Africa. Also known as whale-headed stork, it has a swollen, shoe-shaped bill with a sharp hook; short neck, darkish plumage, and long black legs. It feeds at night on small animals, including lungfish, frogs, and turtles, and lays a single chalky white egg in a reed nest in tall vegetation. Height: to 54in (137cm). Species *Balaeniceps rex.*

Shofar, ancient musical instrument, it is sounded in synagogues on Rosh Hashanah and Yom Kippur. Made from the curved horn of a ram, it produces tones one fifth apart. Joshua's trumpet at Jericho was a shofar.

Shōgun ("Barbarian-quelling generalissimo"), military ruler of Japan (1192–1867), conferred upon Yoritomo in 1192, acknowledging him as the supreme military commander in Japan. The Minamoto (1192–1333), Ashikaga (1338–1568), and Tokugawa shogunates (1603–1867) provided the de facto rulers of feudal Japan. Although their authority was in theory purely military, the bakufu ("tent government") exercised control over all aspects of life. Originally based on a system of estates and a code, Japan's particular feudal system evolved, reaching its height during the Tokugawa period, when the combination of the influences of the daimyo (feudal lords) and Confucian ethics provided a stable central government ruling "in the name of the emperor." This period was one of the most active, creative, and prosperous in Japanese history because of its strong and stable government and economy. It ended with the Meiji Restoration. *See also* Ashikaga.

Sholokhov, Mikhail (1905–84), Soviet novelist. His novels are frequently set in his native Don region and include the epic *The Silent Don* (1928–40); trans. as *And Quiet Flows the Don* and *The Don Flows Home to the Sea,* and the propagandistic *Virgin Soil Upturned* (1932–60). Several of his short stories are collected in *Tales of the Don* (1926). He was awarded the Nobel Prize for literature (1965).

Shooting Star. See Meteor.

Shorebird, birds that live close to water. Most nest in the Arctic and are migratory, making transoceanic trips to winter in warmer areas. They are strong and swift in flight, feeding on fish, shellfish, small worms, and insects, often using a long, specially adapted bill for capturing food. Included are the web-footed gull, tern, skua, jaegar, and skimmer. Others not having webbed feet include the plover, lapwing, sandpiper, snipe, woodcock, curlew, oyster catcher, stilt, sheathbill, auk, puffin, and guillemot. Order Charadriiformes. *See also* Separate entries.

Shorthorn

Shorthorn, most widespread beef cattle breed. It is red, red and white, or roan. Developed in Durham, England, there are two types: strictly beef and dual-purpose, used also for milk. Some varieties are hornless or polled. *See also* Beef Cattle; Cattle.

Short Parliament (1640), English parliament ending 11 years of personal rule by Charles I. Its calling was occasioned by his need for money after defeat (1639) in the first of the Scottish Bishops' Wars. It was dissolved after three weeks when its members made redress of political grievances the condition for financial subsidy of the king.

Short Story, brief prose fictional narrative, established as a modern art form by the 19th-century US master Edgar Allan Poe. A short story deals with few characters; aims for unity of effect; often concentrates on mood rather than plot. Two 14th-century works, Geoffrey Chaucer's *Canterbury Tales* and Giovanni Boccaccio's *Decameron* greatly influenced its development. Famous short story writers include Guy de Maupassant, Anton Chekov, Nathaniel Hawthorne, Washington Irving, Bret Harte, and Ernest Hemingway.

Short Wave, electromagnetic wave that has a wavelength of less than 80 meters. When a short wave hits certain layers of the ionosphere it is bounced back toward Earth, where it can be picked up and bounced out again. Through repetition of this process a short wave can be transmitted long distances.

Shoshoni, a major Indian tribe, divided into two important subgroups, who have given their name to one of the most prominent American Indian language families; also known as Snake Indians. The total population today is perhaps 50,000 persons, living in Idaho, Wyoming, Nevada, and Utah.

Shostakovich, Dmitri (1906–1975), Soviet composer, b. St. Petersburg, Russia. He composed prolifically in every form and was perhaps the most important modern Russian-born composer after Stravinsky. His style is basically post-Romantic with emphasis on melody. His works include 15 symphonies, 13 string quartets, ballets, concertos, piano music, film music, and vocal works. His opera *Lady Macbeth of Mzensk* (1934) was condemned by the Soviet government but was later revised and accepted as *Katerina Ismailova* (1963). Shostakovitch was the Soviet Union's most honored composer, receiving a number of Lenin and Stalin prizes and the designation Hero of Socialist Labor.

Shoulder Blade. *See* Scapula.

Shoveler, widely distributed river duck that dabbles, or feeds from the water surface. The male engages in a complex courtship to attract a female. Species *Anas clypeata. See also* Duck.

Shreveport, city in NW Louisiana, on Red River; seat of Caddo parish. Founded 1835, it was made capital of Confederacy of Louisiana 1863; developed after the discovery of oil at Caddo Lake 1906. It is site of ruins of Confederate Fort Humbug, annual Louisiana State Fair, Centenary College (1825). Industries: cotton, oil, natural gas, clothing, food products, lumber, chemicals, printing, machinery. Inc. 1839 as town, 1871 as city. Pop. (1980) 205,815.

Shrew, tiny, mouselike insectivore. It is an active, voracious carnivore that eats more than three times its own weight daily. Some have poisonous saliva. The smallest of all mammals, some weigh only 1/15oz (2g). Family Soricidae. See also Insectivore.

Shrewsbury, county town of Salop, W England, on Severn River; market town and rail and road junction; occupies strategic position on border with Wales; site of 11th-century castle, many half-timbered houses of 15th–17th centuries, a famous public school (1552). Industries: engineering, brewing, tanning. Pop. 83,900.

Shrike, or butcherbird, small bird of prey found worldwide, except in South America and Australia. It dives at prey—insects, small birds, mice—hitting it with its strong hooked bill and then impaling it on a sharp fence post, twig, or thorn. Food is sometimes left impaled for later use. Most, including the North American northern shrike *(Lanius excubitor)* and loggerhead shrike *(Lanius ludovicianus),* are brown or gray above with darker markings on the head, wings, and tail. They lay spotted whitish eggs (3–6) in a bulky cup-shaped twig nest. Family Laniidae.

Shrimp, mostly marine, swimming decapod crustacean including true, sand, and pistol shrimps. Its compressed body has long antennae, stalked eyes, a beaklike prolongation, segmented abdomen with five pairs of swimming legs, and a terminal spine. Large edible shrimp are often called prawns. True prawns include European and American genera *Palaemon* and *Penais.* Length: 2–3in (5–7.6cm); some freshwater shrimp reach 2ft (61cm). *See also* Crustacean; Decapod.

Shrub, low, woody perennial plant of limited height. Instead of having a main stem, it branches at or slightly above ground level into several equally strong stems. Environment is often a determining factor: species that are shrubs in one climate may be trees in another.

Shuara. *See* Jívaro.

Shute, Nevil (1899–1960), English novelist. His real name was Nevil Shute Norway. He wrote a number of novels whose exciting, fast-moving plots made them immensely popular. Among his books are *An Old Captivity* (1940), *No Highway* (1948), *A Town Like Alice* (1950), *The Far Country* (1952), and *On the Beach* (1957).

Siam, Gulf of, shallow inlet of South China Sea, in Thailand; separates Malay Peninsula from E Thailand, Cambodia, and S Vietnam. Chao Phraya and Tha Chin rivers enter at NW point; Bangkok is the gulf's chief port. Length: 500mi (805km). Width: 350mi (564km).

Siamese Cat, exotic short-haired domestic cat breed of disputed origin. An affectionate pet with a distinctive cry, it has a wedge-shaped head, blue almond-shaped eyes, large ears, long slim body, and long tapered tail. A small- to medium-sized cat, its albino to fawn-colored coat has darker colored points on ears, mask, feet, and tail. Recognized varieties in the United States are seal point, chocolate, blue, and lilac.

Siamese Twins, conjoined, identical twins sometimes sharing organs. Usually fusion is along the trunk or at the head. When both are normal, except for fusion, surgical separation is sometimes possible. If one twin is underdeveloped and therefore parasitic, it is usually separated surgically so the other might live.

Sian (Xi'an, or Hsi-an), city in N China, in Wei River Valley; capital of Shensi prov.; early center of Buddhism, Islam, Judaism, and Nestorian Christianity (7th–10th centuries); scene of the "Sian Incident" where Chiang Kai-shek was kidnapped and held until he agreed to form a united front with Communists against Japan (1936); site of Nestorian monument (781), pagodas dating from T'ang dynasty, and city wall constructed during Ming dynasty (1368–1644); seat of Northwestern University (1937), and Northwestern Institute of Technology (1960). Industries: agriculture, textiles, food processing, chemicals, cement, motor vehicles, iron, steel. Pop. 1,600,000.

Siangtan (Xiangtan or Hsiang-t'an), city in SE China, 20mi (32km) SW of Changsha, on Siang River; nearby is Shaoshan, birthplace of Mao-Tse-tung. Industries: food processing, machine tools, textiles, manganese ore, engineering, cement, trucks. Pop. 300,000.

Sibelius, Jean (1865–1957), Finnish composer. He promoted Finnish nationalism in such works as the popular orchestral piece *Finlandia* (1899). Among his best works are *The Swan of Tuonela* (1893), a violin concerto (1903), the *Valse Triste* (1903), and seven symphonies.

Siberia (Sibir'), vast region in NE Asia, in the USSR, comprising most of the Asiatic part of Russian SFSR, extending from the Ural Mts. to the Pacific Ocean, and from the Arctic Ocean to Kazakhstan and the S border with China and Mongolia. The Tartar Khanate of Siberia was conquered by Russian Cossacks 1581–98; in 1644 Russians reached the Amur River region, but abandoned it to Chinese; it was ceded to Russia 1860; anti-Bolshevik activities led by Admiral Kolchak promoted invasion by Bolsheviks, who made it part of Russian SFSR (1919) and re-established Bolshevik rule; site of large-scale colonization since WWII. Main cities are Novosibirsk, Omsk, Krasnoyarsk, Novokuznetsk, Irkutsk, Barnaul, Kemerovo, Tomsk, Ulan-Ude, Chita. Industries: coal, iron ore, manganese, gold, copper, lead, zinc, tungsten, oil, grains, lumbering, fishing. Area: 5,330,896sq mi (13,807,021sq km). Pop. 35,605,000.

Siberian Husky, endurance sled dog (working group) bred by Chukchi people of northeastern Asia; brought to Alaska in 1910. A gentle, friendly dog, it has a medium-sized, slightly rounded head with medium-length tapered muzzle; high-set, erect, triangular ears; almond-shaped blue, brown, or one of each color, eyes; strong-chested body with lean loin; moderately long legs; and fox brush tail carried in sickle curve. The medium-length double coat is straight and smooth; color ranges from black to white with characteristic head markings. Average size: 21–23.5in (53–60cm)

high at shoulder; 40–60lb (18–27kg). See also Working Dog.

Sibyl, prophetess in Greek legend and scripture. A famous collection of Sibylline prophecies, the Sibylline Books, were bought by Tarquinius Superbus, the last of the seven kings of Rome, from the Cumaean Sibyl. The books were kept in the temple of Jupiter on the Capitoline Hill.

Sichuan. *See* Szechwan.

Sicilia. *See* Sicily.

Sicilian Vespers (1282), massacre of the French, which began the Sicilian revolt against the Angevin King Charles I of Naples-Sicily. The massacre of 2,000 French began at vespers on Easter Monday at Palermo in response to oppressive French policies and with Peter III of Aragon's support. In the ensuing war the French Angevins fought with the papacy and the Italian Guelphs; the Italian Ghibellines supported the Aragonese.

Sicily, island of Italy in the Mediterranean Sea at the toe of the Italian boot. With nearby islands it forms an autonomous region of Italy. The largest island in the Mediterranean Sea, it has an area of 9,927sq mi (25,711sq km). Once part of the mainland, it is separated from Italy by the narrow Straits of Messina. Mostly mountainous, it has three active volcanoes, Vulcano, 1,637ft (499m), Stromboli, 3,038ft (911m), and Mt Etna, 10,705ft (3,265m). Fertile valleys cover the central plateau. The E coast is famous for its beauty and tourism; the shore is a flat, sandy plain, the least productive portion of the island. Fishing and small farms provide the major occupations in an essentially poor economy. The island's chief cities are Palermo (pop. 661,477), Catania (pop. 413,670), and Messina (pop. 273,526). Sicily was occupied by three peoples —Siculi, Sicani, and Elmyi—when the Greeks came before 413 BC. The modern population of Sicily is 4,867,650, one-third of which lives in the towns on the coast and the fertile slopes of Mt Etna. Most are Roman Catholics. Economic decline increased emigration, and between 1906–10 22% of all Italian emigrants came from Sicily, mostly to the United States.

History. Strategically situated between Europe and Africa, Sicily has frequently been a battlefield. Early settlers came from S Italy and were conquered by Greeks, who were defeated in 415 BC. Invasions by Phoenicia, Carthage, and Rome followed. In AD 535 Sicily became part of the Byzantine Empire. The Normans ruled the islands in the 2nd century until an uprising in 1282. Spain, Savoy, and Austria successively held power until the island passed to the Bourbon kings of Naples in 1738. In 1860, Guiseppe Garibaldi freed Sicily and it joined the newly united Italy (1861).

Sickle Cell Anemia, inheritance of an abnormal hemoglobin, occurring mainly in blacks. The hemoglobin is sensitive to a deficiency of oxygen, and red cells become rigid and sickle-shaped. When oxygen is supplied, the phenomenon is reversed. If anemia becomes chronic, there are bone and kidney changes.

Side-necked Turtle, freshwater turtle characterized by the ability to bend the neck sideways under the shell to hide its head. They are found only on southern continents. There are two families: hidden-necked turtles (Pelomedusidae) of Africa and South American and snake-necked turtles (Chelidae) of Australia and South America. Length: 6–32in (15–81cm). *See also* Matamata; Turtle.

Sidereal Period, time taken for a planet or satellite to complete one orbit around its primary with respect to the fixed stars. Earth's sidereal period is 365.25 days. The sidereal period of rotation of a planet is the interval between successive meridian transits of a given star or celestial point as seen from the planet.

Siderite, carbonate mineral, iron carbonate ($FeCO_3$), found in sedimentary iron ores and as vein deposits with other ores. Hexagonal system rhombohedral crystals or massive or granular. Pearly brown or white; hardness 3.5–4; sp gr 3.8.

Sidewinder, or horned rattlesnake, nocturnal rattlesnake found in deserts of SW United States and Mexico. It has hornlike scales over the eyes and is usually tan with a light pattern. It loops obliquely across the sand, leaving a J-shaped trail. Length: to 30in (76cm). Family Viperidae; species *Crotalus cerastes. See also* Rattlesnake.

Sidon (Sayda), town in SW Lebanon, 22mi (35km) N of Tyre; site of oil pipeline terminus; most ancient city of Phoenicia, was an important port and trade center; glass-blowing invented here; destroyed in war several

Dmitri Shostakovich

Siamese cat

Sierra Leone

times. Industries: oil refineries, textiles, furniture; founded c. 2 BC. Pop. 40,000.

Siegfried Line, a system of fortifications built along Germany's western frontier before World War II. In 1944 it provided a brief respite for the retreating German army, preventing a US breakthrough until the spring of 1945.

Siemens-Martin Process. See Open-Hearth Process.

Siena, city in central Italy, 33mi (53km) S of Florence; capital of Siena prov. A self-governing commune in 12th century, it was conquered by Charles of Anjou 1270; developed into important art center 13th-14th centuries; ravaged by Black Death 1348; known for its artistic treasures; site of 13th-century Palazzo Pubblico, 11th-14th-century cathedral, 14th-century chapel. Industries: tourism, wine, fertilizer, chemicals. Pop. 64,745.

Sienkiewicz, Henryk (1846–1916), Polish novelist and short-story writer. His war novels include the trilogy *Ogniem i Mieczem* (With Fire and Sword, 1884), *Potop* (The Deluge, 1886), and *Pan Michael* (1888), set in 17th-century Poland. He gained international recognition with *Quo Vadis?* (1896), a story of Nero's Rome. He was awarded the Nobel Prize for literature in 1905.

Sierra Leone, independent nation of West Africa, within the Commonwealth of Nations; bordered by Guinea (N and E), Liberia (S), Atlantic Ocean (W). Mountains in the NE, highest Loma Mansa 6,390ft (1,948m), slope down through a plateau region of savannah to the coastal plains of the SW. Along the coast mangrove swamps and lagoons are the main features. Numerous small rivers flow NE to SW into the Atlantic. The climate is hot throughout the year, and there is a marked seasonal difference in rainfall, with most falling in the summer months. Subsistence farmers produce maize and rice, while cocoa, coffee, palm kernels, and ginger are produced for export. The greatest source of foreign currency comes from the export of diamonds, iron, bauxite, and rutile. Industry refines products such as palm oil, rice, and lumber. The main tribes are the Mende, Temne, Limba, Kuranko, and Susu. Government is by an elected house of representatives, some of its members being hereditary chiefs. First discovered in the 15th century by Portuguese; became a British colony in 1787 when land was sold by local chiefs to the English who later made it a settlement for Africans rescued from slave ships. Independence was granted in 1961. In 1967 the army assumed control of the government, but returned it to civilian rule the following year. In an effort to stem political instability a new constitution was promulgated in 1978, making Sierra Leone a one-party state. The government has faced continuing civil unrest, however and in 1985, Siaka Stevens, president-for-life since 1961, voluntarily stepped down to make way for newly-elected president Joseph Momoh.

PROFILE

Official name: Republic of Sierra Leone
Area: 27,693 sq mi (71,740sq km)
Population: 3,500,000
  Density: 126 per sq mi (49 per sq km)
Chief Cities: Freetown (capital), Bo, Kenema, Makeni
Government: Republic
Religion: animist, Muslim, Christian
Language: English (official), Krio
Gross national product: $490,000,000
Trading partners (major): Great Britain, United States, Japan, Netherlands

Sierra Madre, mountain range in SE Mexico; extends S into Guatemala; made up of Sierra Madre Occidental, Oriental, and del Sur. The Occidental stretches from N Mexican border to Rio de las Balsas valley; a transportation barrier, it is crossed by a single highway between Mazatlán and Durango. The Oriental extends from Coahuila state to the Isthmus of Tehuantepec. The del Sur extends parallel to the Pacific Ocean, from Guatemala to Rio de las Balsas valley; terrain ranges from hot tropical valleys to permanently snow-covered peaks. Industries: lumber, agriculture, hydroelectric power, silver, copper. Height: 6,000–12,000ft (1,830–3,660m).

Sierra Morena, mountain range in SW Spain, between Guadiana and Guadalquivir rivers, along S border of the Meseta (central plateau), from Portuguese border to the Sierra de Alcaraz. Despenaperros Pass is the main route through the mountains linking Andalusia and Castile. Length: 375mi (604km). Highest peak is Banuelo, approx. 4,339ft (1,323m).

Sierra Nevada, chief mountain range in S Spain; extends E to W in Granada and Almeria prov.; source of iron, lead, copper, zinc, mercury; S slopes are highly agriculturally developed. Contains highest peak in continental Spain, Mt Mulhacen, 11,408ft (3,479m). Length: 60mi (97km).

Sierra Nevada Mountains, mountain system in E California, runs parallel to Coast Ranges; site of Donner Pass, made famous during California Gold Rush of mid-19th century; source of many rivers which are used to irrigate and supply hydroelectricity to surrounding area; famous for their magnificent scenery and popular resort region; contains Yosemite, Sequoia, and Kings Canyon National Parks; culminates at Mt Whitney, 14,494ft (4,421m). Length: 400mi (644km).

Sigismund (1368–1437), Holy Roman emperor (1411–37) and king of Germany (1410–37), Hungary (1387–1437), and Bohemia (1419–37). Crowned king of Hungary in 1387, he was plagued from the outset with much foreign, domestic, and dynastic opposition, suffering a tremendous defeat by the Turks at Nikopol in 1396. Because, as emperor, he was implicated in the execution of John Huss (1415), the Czechs rose against him when he inherited Bohemia in 1419, resulting in 17 years of fighting. He was also active in attempting to end schisms in the Roman Catholic Church.

Sigismund I (1467–1548), king of Poland (1506–48), grand duke of Lithuania (1505–48). During his reign, Polish domains were expanded, he fought successful wars against Russia, and concluded a war with the Teutonic Order in 1525. He also aided the Hungarians against the Turks at the Battle of Mohács in 1526 and at the seige of Vienna in 1529. Lutheranism was introduced in Poland at this time and the diet passed laws initiating serfdom in Poland (1511).

Sigismund II Augustus (1520–72), last of the Jagellon kings of Poland (1548–72), son of Sigismund I, united Lithuania and Ukraine with Poland. Struggles with the nobility and the spread of Protestantism characterized his reign. Married to an Italian princess, he held a brilliant court at Cracow where Renaissance art and poetry flourished.

Sigismund III, or **Sigismund Vasa** (1566–1632), son of John III of Sweden, elected king of Poland (1587), king of Sweden (1592–1604). An unstatesmanlike ruler, he fought numerous wars with Sweden to win its throne and intervened in Russia during the Time of Troubles. For his attempts to convert Russia to Catholicism, all Poles were expelled from Moscow. He joined the Holy Roman emperor at the outbreak of the Thirty Years' War.

Sigma Particle. See Hyperon.

Sigurd, also called Siegfried. A hero of ancient Germanic literature, he was known for his strength and courage. He appears in many stories, most notably, the story of Brunhild.

Sihanouk, Norodom (1922–   ), Cambodian political figure; king (1941–55); prime minister (1955–60); head of state (1960–70, 1975–76). Exiled in 1970, when his government was overthrown, he returned as titular head of state in 1975. He resigned in 1976 and was kept under house arrest until 1979 when he appeared before the United Nations to plead for Vietnam's withdrawal from Cambodia. He returned to China to live. In 1982, he became president of a coalition government with the Khmer Rouge and National Liberation Front to oppose the Vietnamese-backed government in Cambodia.

Sikhism, Indian religion that came into being in the 16th and 17th centuries. Combining Hindu and Muslim teachings, Sikh scripture, the *Adi Granth,* stressed the need for a guru's guidance in seeking the One Lord. Sikh means "disciple." Begun by Nanak as a passive way of life, Sikhism later became an activist faith. Today there are some 6,000,000 Sikhs, mainly in the Punjab.

Sikh Wars (1845–46, 1848–49), military conflicts between the Sikhs and the British in India. Overrun by the Moguls, the Sikhs fled to the mountains but returned to form a powerful state at Lahore with Ranjit Singh (1780–1839) as maharaja. By 1824 they controlled most of northern India. The British took Lahore in the first Sikh War, and the Sikhs were completely defeated in the second one.

Sikkim, a tiny, associate state of India in the high Himalayas. Its climate ranges from subtropical to arctic. Known for its Buddhist monasteries, Sikkim's economy is largely undeveloped.
  Land and economy. Located in the main chain of the Himalayas, it has perpetual snow above 17,000ft (5,185m). Between 12,000–15,000ft (3,660–4,575m) there are plateaus and summer grazing for cattle. Forests are found from 9,000–12,000ft (2,745–3,660m) and crops such as maize and millet are grown from 4,000–6,000ft (1,220–1,830m). Rice is grown on the lower level. The highest peak is Kanchenjunga, 28,208ft (8,603m). The only urban center is its capital, Gangtok, and the main river is the Tista. Woolen cloth and cotton are produced by home industry, and there is some primitive copper mining. Monsoons from the Bay of Bengal bring an average annual rainfall of 137in (348cm) in the capital. The area is 2,818sq mi (7,299sq km); the population is 250,000.
  People. Sikkim's people are mainly Nepalese with Bhotias, herders in the high altitudes, and Lepchas, pastoral people who were the earliest inhabitants. Buddhism is the state religion. Most of the Nepalese are Hindu. Tibeto-Burmese dialects are the main tongues.
  Government. Under a constitution passed by India's parliament, Sikkim is governed by a chief minister appointed by India and a five-member council of ministries.
  History. Sikkim's ruling family claimed it was descended from E Tibetan princes who came to Lhasa in 1641, defeated the Lepchas, and established Buddhist Lamaism as the state religion. British influence started in 1816 when they ousted invading Nepalese Gurkhas,

and Sikkim became a British protectorate. When India won independence in 1947, British control over Sikkim declined. In 1950, independent Sikkim became an Indian protectorate. In 1975, Sikkim became a state of India. The office of Chogyal, the traditional ruler, was then abolished.

Silas, in the New Testament, the man who replaced Barnabas as St Paul's companion in his missionary labors. After considerable travel, he was left with Timothy at Beroea, only to rejoin Paul at Corinth. It is held that he was both Jewish by birth and, like St Paul, a Roman citizen.

Silenus, in Greek mythology, a companion of Dionysus. He was a perpetually drunk, fat old man who followed the god while swaying awkwardly on the back of a donkey. Nevertheless, he was more than tolerated for he knew the past and could fortell the future and had given Dionysus much of his wisdom. King Midas' golden touch was a reward for his considerate care of Silenus after one of the deity's drunken bouts.

Silesia, former province of Czechoslovakia, formed in 1919 from a portion of Austria-Hungary and Upper Silesia. It is also a former Prussian province and is now mostly Polish. In 1927, it was united with Moravia, and by the terms of the Munich Pact of 1938 it was ceded to Germany. At the end of WWII, it returned to Czechoslovakia and in 1960 was made part of the region of Severomoravsky (North Moravia).

Silica, silicon dioxide, a compound of silicon and oxygen (SiO_2). Silica is the main constituent of 95% of the Earth's crust. It has three main crystalline varieties: quartz, tridymite, and cristabolite. Silica sand (in the form of portland cement) is used in buildings and roads. It is also used for grinding and polishing glass and stone and in the manufacture of glass, ceramics, and silicone. It is a refractory material and is frequently of gemstone quality.

Silicon, common nonmetallic element (symbol Si) of group IVA of the periodic table, discovered by J.J. Berzelius (1824). It is the second most abundant element in the Earth's crust (25.7% by weight), a common constituent of rocks and minerals. The element is extensively used in transistors and similar devices. Two allotropes exist: a brown amorphous form and a gray crystalline variety. Properties: at. no. 14; at. wt. 28.086; sp gr 2.33 at 25°C; melt. pt. 2570°F (1410°C); boil. pt. 4271°F (2355°C); most common isotope Si^{28} (92.21%); *See also* Silicone.

Silicone, any of a group of polymers lacking carbon. Atoms of silicon and hydrogen alternate in a polysiloxane chain. Silicone is manufactured as a liquid, a resin, or an elastomer and resists decomposition by heat, water, or oxidizing agents. It is used as a liquid to waterproof textiles and paper; as a resin in protective coatings and for laminating glass cloth; and as a elastomer in electrical insulation.

Silicosis, chronic occupational lung disease, caused by prolonged inhalation of silica dust. It affects people employed in such occupations as mining, metal grinding. No treatment exists, but prevention is possible by reducing the amount of dust inhaled.

Silk Screen Printing. *See* Serigraphy.

Silkworm, moth caterpillar that feeds chiefly on mulberry leaves. The common domesticated *Bombyx mori* is raised commercially for its silk cocoon. The creamy white caterpillar spins its cocoon from a silk fiber secreted by glands in its body. Length: 3in (7.6cm). Family Bombycidae.

Silky Terrier, small Australian dog (toy group) also called Sidney Silky; bred from Australian and Yorkshire terriers. It has a wedge-shaped head; small, V-shaped, prick ears; long, low-set body; straight, fine-boned legs; and docked tail carried up. The flat, silky, fine coat is 5–6in (12.5–15cm) long and parted from head to tail; there is a topknot on the head. Colors are blue and tan. Average size: 9–10in (23–25.4cm) high at shoulder; 8–10lb (3.6–4.5kg). *See also* Toy Dog.

Sill, sheet-like intrusion of igneous rock that parallels the bedding or other structure of the surrounding rock. Sill rock is normally medium-grained and basic sills (dolerite) are the most common. *See also* Dike.

Sillanpää, Frans Eemil (1888–1964), Finnish author. His novels include *Life and Sun* (1916), *Meek Heritage* (1919), and *The Maid Silja* (1931). He was awarded the Nobel Prize for literature in 1939.

Sillitoe, Alan (1928–), English novelist and short-story writer. His angry, blunt accounts of the frustrations of working class life include *Saturday Night and Sunday Morning* (1958), *The Flame of Life* (1974), *The Widower's Son* (1977), *The Storyteller* (1980), and *Her Victory* (1982), and the short stories *The Loneliness of the Long Distance Runner* (1959) and *The Second Chance* (1981).

Sills, Beverly (1929–), US coloratura soprano, b. Brooklyn, N.Y. She made her debut in 1946, sang with the San Francisco Opera (1953–55), and sang with the New York City Opera (1955–80). In 1975 she made her long awaited Metropolitan Opera debut. When she retired in 1980, she became managing director of the New York City Opera.

Silurian Period, the third oldest division of the Paleozoic Era, lasting from 430 to 395,000,000 years ago. Marine invertebrates continue much as in Ordovician times. Fragmentary remains of jawless fishes increase in coastal deposits. The earliest land plants (psilopsids) and first land animals (archaic scorpions) developed. Mountains formed in NW Europe. *See also* Geologic time; Paleozoic Era.

Silver, metallic element (symbol Ag) of the second transition series, known from the earliest times. It occurs native and in argentite (sulfide) and horn silver (chloride). It is also obtained as a by-product in the electrolytic refining of copper. It is the most efficient conductor of heat and electricity known and is used in electrical contacts and printed circuits. Other uses include jewelry and other decorative items, mirrors, and silver salts for photography. The metal does not oxidize in air but quickly tarnishes when exposed to sulfur compounds. Properties: at. no. 47; at. wt. 107.868; sp gr 10.5; melt. pt. 1763°F (961.93°C); boil. pt. 3850°F (2121°C); most common isotope Ag^{107} (51.82%). *See also* Transition Elements.

Silverfish, or bristle tail, gray, primitive, wingless insect found worldwide. It lives in cool damp areas, feeding on starches in books, clothes, and wallpaper. Length: 0.5in (13mm). Family Lepismatidae; species *Lepisma saccharina.*

Silver Spring, community in central Maryland, about 7mi (11km) N of Washington, D.C.; site of Xaverian College (1931); scene of drive toward Washington (July 1864) by Gen. Jubal Early's Confederate raiders, which posed grave threat to the Union government. Chief industry is scientific research. Pop. (1980) 72,893.

Silverside, or spearing, smelt, small marine fish found in temperate and tropical seas. Not a true smelt, it is identified by broad silvery side bands. Length: 3–20in (7.6–50.8cm). Family Atherinidae. *See also* Grunion.

Silviculture, the study of the relationship of a forest to its environment as well as the effects of such practices as planting, pruning, and harvesting on the forest.

Simeon I (*r.* 893–927), Bulgarian tsar, younger son of Boris I, brilliant administrator and military leader. Waged many battles against Byzantium; advanced to the gates of Constantinople four times 919–24, but was unable to take it for want of a fleet; defeated Magyars; conquered Serbs in 926. Proclaimed himself tsar of Bulgaria and Serbia in 925, and was the strongest ruler in eastern Europe. At his capital at Preslav, advances in education were made.

Simferopol, city in Russian SFSR, USSR, 37mi (60km) NE of Sevastopol. It was the site of the ancient Greek settlement of Neapolis and a Scythian capital. This site was occupied after the 16th century by Tartar town of Ak-Mechet; it was seized and destroyed by Russians 1736; refounded and fortified under present name after Russian conquest 1783; occupied by Germans 1941–44; site of agricultural, medical, and teachers' colleges. Industries: fruit, tobacco, canning of fruits and vegetables, flour milling, tanning. Pop. 301,000.

Simile, figure of speech comparing two things. It differs from ordinary comparisons by comparing things usually considered dissimilar although sharing, in most cases, one common characteristic: "fleece as white as snow" is a simile. A simile is most often recognized by its use of "like" or "as." *See also* Metaphor.

Simon, Claude (-Eugene-Henri) (1913–), French novelist. His works, written in the unorthodox "new novel" genre, emphasized narrative style rather than plot or character development. His first novel, *Le Tricheur* (The Trickster), was written during WWII. *Histoire* (1967; *History,* 1968) won the Prix de Medicis. He was awarded the 1985 Nobel Prize in literature.

Simple Multiple Proportions, Law of, a law announced in 1804 by the English chemist John Dalton. It states that when two elements combine to form more than one compound, a fixed weight of one element always combines with weights of the other that can be reduced to ratios of small whole numbers. It was a powerful argument for Dalton's atomic theory.

Simultaneous Equations, set of two or more mathematical equations involving two or more unknowns, for which common solutions are required. For example, in the simultaneous equations $x + 2y = 7$ and $5x + y = 4$, the problem is to find values of x and y that satisfy both equations: this can be done by substituting the value of x from one into the other to give a single equation in y. Simultaneous equations can be solved only if the number of equations equals the number of unknowns.

Sinai (Sinā') Peninsula, Egyptian desert region constituting a governorate of Egypt, bounded by Gulf of Suez and Suez Canal (W), Gulf of Aqaba and the Negev Desert of Israel (E), Mediterranean Sea (N), Red Sea (S). The petroleum center of Al-'Arish is the principal urban center. A barren plateau region inhabited chiefly by nomads, it is site of Gebel Musas, S mountain group where in tradition Moses received the ten commandments; nearby is St Catherine Monastery (*c.* 250) where the Codex Sinaiticus, early New Testament manuscript, was discovered 1844. The Sinai Peninsula has been the scene of Arab-Israeli conflicts since Oct. 29, 1956, when it was briefly occupied by Israeli forces; during the Six-Day War of 1967, Israel forced Egyptian evacuation of the Sinai June 5, and seized strategically located posts on Gulf of Aqaba; the Suez Canal was closed during the conflict. Egypt successfully recaptured the territory 1973; by January 1974, an agreement was signed calling for Israeli withdrawal from the Sinai, and UN forces were positioned between Egyptian and Israeli troops. This led to the lifting of the oil embargo and reopening of the Suez Canal. On Sept. 4, 1975, delegates from Egypt, Israel, and United States met in Geneva, Switzerland to sign another agreement which included an Israeli withdrawal from Sinai Peninsula, Mitla and Gidi passes, an increased Sinai UN buffer zone, and a 200-man US "early-warning" system in the area; Suez Canal reopened June 5, 1975. In 1979, Israel and Egypt signed a peace treaty calling for the phased withdrawal of Israeli troops between 1979 and 1982, after which an international peacekeeping force patrolled the region. Industries: oil, manganese, limestone. Area: 23,442sq mi (60,715sq km). Pop. 140,000.

Sindhi, language of Pakistan and India, spoken by about 7,000,000 people in the province of Sind, S Pakistan, and by about 1,500,000 more across the border in India. It is an Indic language, related to Sanskrit and Hindi.

Sine, ratio of the length of the side opposite to an acute angle to the length of the hypotenuse in a right-angled triangle. The sine of angle A is usually abbreviated to "sin A." *See also* Trigonometric Functions.

Sinews. *See* Tendons.

Singapore, island republic in SE Asia, at S end of Malay peninsula, between the Indian Ocean and South China Sea. Its parliamentary government is led by the prime minister, with the president serving as head of state. Once covered by a tropical rain forest, more than 60% of the land has been cleared to accommodate the rapidly urbanizing economy. Less than 25% of the land is used for agriculture; vegetables, tobacco, fruits, rubber, and coconuts are the chief products. Singapore is one of the world's greatest commercial centers and busiest harbors; 70% of its trade is transshipment traffic. Principal industries include shipping, shipbuilding, tourism, food processing, steel products. More than 75% of its 2,122,456 inhabitants lives in the capital city of Singapore. Of the total population, 76% is Chinese; the island has one of the highest standards of living in Asia, a high literacy rate, and excellent health facilities. It is the site of University of Singapore (1963) and Nanyang University (1953).

The government, under the constitution of 1966, is a parliamentary democracy. Effective power rests with the prime minister, who heads the majority party or coalition in the 69-seat parliament. Singapore was ceded (1819) to British East India Co. by the Sultan of Johore, through the efforts of T. Stanford Raffles, who founded the city of Singapore the same year. It grew, with influx of Chinese and Malay merchants, into a major exporter of rubber and tin; became one of the Straits Settlements (1867–1946). During WWII, Singapore was occupied by the Japanese. At the end of the war, returned to British control, the Straits Settlements were abolished, and Singapore joined Christmas Island and Cocos-Keeling islands as a crown colony of Britain (1946); it was made a self-governing state 1959. In 1962, it merged with Malaya, Sarawak, and Sabath to form the Federation of Malaya but due to internal and racial strife it involuntarily agreed to separate 1965 and became an independent republic.

Beverly Sills

Singapore

Sitting Bull

Since then Singapore has pursued a moderate nonaligned foreign policy.

PROFILE

Official name: Republic of Singapore
Area: 225sq mi (583sq km)
Population: 2,362,700
Density: 10,222per sq mi (3,947per sq km)
Chief city: Singapore (capital)
Religion: Islam, Christianity, Buddhism, Hinduism
Language: Malay (national), Chinese, Tamil, English (all official)
Monetary unit: Singapore dollar

Singer, Isaac Bashevis (1904–), US novelist and short story writer, b. Poland. In 1935 he emigrated to New York City. Although all his works are written in Yiddish, they have been translated into English. They include *The Family Moskat* (1950), *The Estate* (1969), *A Crown of Feathers and Other Stories* (1973), for which he won a 1974 National Book Award, *Shosha* (1978), *Old Love* (1979), and *Lost in America* (1981). He was awarded the Nobel Prize for literature in 1978. Many of his stories appeared in *Collected Stories of Isaac Bashevis Singer* (1982) and *The Image and Other Stories* (1985).

Single Tax, form of taxation where the only form of government revenue is a tax on land. Based on the idea that the profit derived from natural resources and the increased value of land should benefit all of society, the theory was popularized by Henry George in his book *Progress and Poverty* (1879). George believed that such a tax would prove sufficient to meet all government costs and eradicate poverty.

Sinhalese, people constituting the largest ethnic group of Sri Lanka (Ceylon). Speaking Sinhala, an Indo-Aryan language, and practicing Theravāda Buddhism, the mainly agriculturalist Sinhalese are divided into two groups: the lowland dwellers, influenced by commercial and social change, and the more traditionalist highlanders around Kandy.

Sinn Fein, Irish nationalist movement founded 1899 by Arthur Griffith. Its aim to achieve Irish independence was partially realized with the establishment of the Irish Free State (1921). In 1938, it joined with the Irish Republican Army.

Sino-Japanese War (1894–95), military conflict between China and Japan. Disagreement over Korea and clashes in 1892 and 1894 foreshadowed the Japanese declaration of war against China on Aug. 1, 1894, following a conflict between Japanese and Chinese armies during a Korean revolt. The Japanese seized control over the Korean government. Japan's modernized military had the advantage, and after crippling the Chinese fleet at the mouth of the Yalu River (Sept. 17, 1894), Japanese forces went on to capture Port Arthur and Weiheiwei and the remainder of the Chinese fleet. The war ended with the signing of the Treaty of Shimonoseki (April 17, 1895), by which China ceded territory to Japan and agreed to pay an indemnity.

Sino-Tibetan Languages, large family of languages which includes Chinese; the Tibeto-Burman languages; the Tai languages; and Miao (Meo) and Yao, spoken in S China and Southeast Asia. That these four groups of languages are actually related to each other is still questioned by many linguists.

Sinus, a normal cavity, or opening, in a bone or other organ. The most familiar sinuses are the paranasal sinuses, located in the facial region and lined with epithelium, that normally drain into the nasal cavity.

Sinusitis, acute or chronic disease of the paranasal tissues. Acute sinusitis involving pain and nasal obstruction occurs as an aftermath to a cold, a secondary bacterial infection, improper breathing while swimming, or sudden changes in barometric pressure. Chronic sinusitis causes tendency to colds, obstructed breathing, and loss of the sense of smell.

Siouan, family of American Indian languages. It includes Sioux (Dakota), spoken mainly in South Dakota; Crow, of Montana; Winnebago, of Wisconsin; Omaha, of Nebraska; and Osage, now spoken mainly in Oklahoma.

Sioux. *See* Dakota Indians.

Sioux City, city in NW Iowa, on Missouri River at confluence of Big Sioux and Floyd rivers; seat of Woodbury co; site of Morningside College (1889), Briar Cliff College (1930), and nearby monument in state park commemorating death (1804) of Sgt. Charles Floyd of Lewis and Clark expedition. Industries: fabricated metals, lumber, tools, grain, meat packing. Inc. 1857. Pop. (1980) 82,003.

Sioux Falls, city in SE South Dakota, 180mi (290km) SE of Pierre, on Big Sioux River; seat of Minnehaha co; largest city in state; site of Augustana College (1860), Sioux Falls College (1860); trading and distribution center. Industries: meat packing, food processing, farm machinery, fertilizer, textiles, granite quarrying, baked goods. Original settlement (1857) abandoned after Sioux Indian attacks; resettled 1865 as military post; inc. 1877 as village, 1883 as city. Pop. (1980) 81,343.

Siqueiros, David Alfaro (1898–74), Mexican painter. He viewed art as a vehicle for social and political expression. Active as a socialist, he did much easel painting but is best known for his murals of revolutionary themes. *The New Democracy*, painted for the Palace of Fine Arts in Mexico City, and *Death to the Invader*, painted in Chile, are examples. He experimented with synthetic lacquer paints and spray painting techniques. His works are realistic and often show struggle and violence.

Siren, aquatic, tailed amphibian of North America. The adult is neotenic, that is, it reaches sexual maturity while retaining the larval physical form. These eel-like animals have external gills, tiny forelegs, and minute eyes. They have no hind legs. Length: to 36in (91cm). Family Sirenidae. *See also* Amphibia; Salamander.

Sirenia, order of plant-eating aquatic mammals with paddlelike flippers for forelimbs, no hind limbs, and a horizontally flattened tail fin. The four species include the dugong (family Dugongidae) and three manatees (family Trichechidae). Length: 8–13ft (2–4m); weight: to 790lb (356kg).

Sirens, in Greek mythology, sea nymphs that were birds with women's heads. They lived on an island surrounded by rocks onto which they enticed sailors by their songs, devouring their shipwrecked prey. Jason escaped them because the songs of Orpheus were more beautiful, and Odysseus survived by stopping his men's ears with wax and having himself tied to the mast.

Sirius, or **Alpha Canis Majoris,** white main-sequence star in the constellation Canis Major, the brightest star visible from Earth. Also called the Dog Star, Sirius is actually a binary star, situated 8.7 light-years from the Sun. It has an 8th-magnitude white dwarf, Sirius B, as its companion. Characteristics: apparent mag. −1.47

(Sirius A), 8.5 (Sirius B); absolute mag. 0.7 (A), 11.4 (B); spectral type A1 (A), DA (B).

Sisal, or **Sisal Hemp,** fiber plant native to the West Indies and cultivated in Mexico, Java, E Africa, and the Bahamas. Fibers from the leaves are used for rope, insulation, and binder twine; fiber length: 3–5ft (1–1.5m). Family Agavaceae; species *Agave sisalana*. *See also* Agave.

Sisley, Alfred (1839–99), English painter. He spent most of his life in France, often painting outdoors with Claude Monet. He used an Impressionistic style to show the effects of sunlight on color at various times of the day. His outlines were carefully drawn, and unlike Monet, he did not dissolve his colors or forms. He concentrated on landscapes, especially of the countryside around Paris.

Sitar, stringed musical instrument of northern India. A smaller, simplified variant of the traditional vina, it has 3 to 7 strings stretched over a metal plate between a drum and a gourd resonator and played tremulously with a plectrum. Ravi Shankar popularized the sitar on world tours (c.1960).

Sitatunga. *See* Kudu, Nyala, Sitatunga, and Bushbuck.

Sitting Bull (c.1831–90), Indian leader, b. Grand River, S.D. He became chief of the northern hunting Sioux (1866) and participated in the peace with the United States that granted the Indians a reservation above the North Platte River (1868). When the terms of the peace were violated, 2,500–4,000 Sioux, Arapahoe, and Cheyenne gathered around him and defied the army. In 1876 this force wiped out the 7th Cavalry detachment led by Col. George Custer at Little Big Horn. He led his men to Canada (1877) and finally surrendered to the Army (1881). He was killed during Indian unrest on the Standing Rock Reservation.

Sitwell, (Dame) Edith (1887–1964), English poet, sister of Osbert Sitwell. Her anthology *Wheels* (1916) encouraged experimentalism in British verse. Her own verse is witty and inventive. Her purpose was to shock the middle-class public, though her wartime poetry has great compassion. She was a generous patron of younger writers, artists, and musicians.

Sitwell, (Sir) Osbert (1892–1969), English poet and novelist. Brother of the poets Edith and Sacheverell Sitwell, he shared their aristocratic tastes in life and literature. His verse, novels, and criticism are all marked by wit and a graceful style.

Six-Day War. *See* Arab-Israeli War.

Six Nations, the League of the Iroquois, after it was joined by the Tuscarora in 1722. The original members were the Cayuga, Oneida, Onondaga, Mohawk, and Seneca.

Sixtus IV, Roman Catholic pope (1471–84), b. Francesco della Rovere (1414). He became a famed preacher and theologian. He was a nepotist and drained the papacy of funds. He erected the Sistine Chapel, and opened the Vatican Library to scholars.

61 Cygni, star situated near the sun in the constellation Cygnus. It is historically important in astronomy since it was the first star to have its distance accurately calculated by parallax measurement (by F. W. Bessel in 1838). It is a binary star, both components of which are orange. 61 Cygni A has a planetary companion. Characteristics: apparent mag. +5.2 (A), +6.0 (B);

absolute mag. +7.5 (A), +8.4 (B); spectral type K5 (A), K7 (B); distance 11.2 light-years.

Sjaelland, largest of islands that form Denmark, bounded N and NW by Kattegat, on W by the Great Belt, S by the channel separating it from smaller islands, and E by the Baltic Sea and Øresund. Area: 2,709sq mi (7,016sq km). Pop. 1,855,500.

Skagerrak, strait between Norway and Denmark, connecting North Sea and Baltic Sea by way of Kattegat. Shallow on Danish coast, it deepens as it approaches Norway. Length: 150mi (242km). Width: 85mi (137km).

Skanderbeg. See Scanderbeg.

Skate, flat-bodied, bottom-dwelling cartilaginous fish found in most shallow temperate and tropical waters. Brown, white, or gray with spots, it has enlarged pectoral fins attached at the sides of the head, and a short, slender tail, which sometimes has electric organs. Length: 20–96in (50.8–243.8cm). Family Rajidae; species, about 100 including large Pacific *Raja binoculata* and smaller *Raja erinacea. See also* Chondrichthyes.

Skeletal System, or **Skeleton,** the bony connective tissue that makes up the general framework of the body. It supports and protects the soft inner organs; serves as a place of attachment for muscles, ligaments, and other structures; provides storage for some minerals; and produces some blood cells. In man the skeleton is divided into two parts: the axial skeleton, or main axis of the body, includes the cranium, or skull; the spinal, or vertebral, column; the sternum, or breastbone; and the ribs. The appendicular skeleton, serving for the attachment of appendages, includes the shoulder girdle and arm bones and the pelvic, or hip, girdle and leg bones. The human skeleton has 206 named bones, with most of them specialized for one or two particular functions. Some of these bones are: the cranium, protecting the brain; the sternum and ribs, protecting the heart and lungs and serving for muscle attachment; and the long arm and leg bones, serving as a framework for muscle attachment and for blood cell formation.

Skiing, winter sport and recreational activity. It is the national sport of Norway, where skiing began as a competitive sport in the late 19th century. Competition includes four events: jumping, downhill, slalom, and cross-country. In jumping, each participant leaps twice from a specially designed jump slope and scores points on distance and form. Downhill is a straight descent on a sharply twisting course marked off by flags. Most grueling is cross-country, which is over a course from 10 to 50km (6–31mi). Except for jumping, women compete in all events. The first ski club formed in the United States was in 1872. The sport is governed by the Fédération Internationale de Ski, founded in 1924, the same year the first Winter Olympic Games were held at Chamonix, France. As a recreational sport, it has been popular since the 1930s, but it enjoyed a surge in participation in the 1970s.

Skimmer, nocturnal shorebird that frequents warm seas, rivers, and lakes using its knifelike bill to plow the water for food. After courtship, oval, stone-colored blotched eggs (3–5) are laid in deep scrape. Family Rynchopidae.

Skin, continuous, tough, elastic and sensitive covering of the body serving many functions. The skin protects the body from mechanical injury, water loss, and ultraviolet rays. It provides the sensations of touch, warmth, cold, and pain, each perceived at discrete points on the skin surface. It helps regulate body temperature through sweat secretion and reduces moisture loss and keeps itself smooth and pliable with an oily secretion from sebaceous glands.

Structurally the skin consists of two main layers: the outer layer, or epidermis, and the inner layer, called the dermis, corium, or cutis. The epidermis is itself composed of several layers: the stratum corneum, a horny layer made up of closely packed dead cells constantly shed as microscopic scales; the stratum lucidum, a layer of flattened cells best seen on palms and soles; the stratum granulosum, layers of elongated cells; lower layers of stratum germinativum and stratum mucosum, living cell layers which contain pigment and nerve fibrils and which divide to replace outer shed layers. The dermis, or corium, contains dense networks of connective tissue, blood vessels, nerves, glands, and hair follicles.

Skink, any of about 600 species of secretive, agile lizards, mostly small with shiny scales found worldwide, but most numerous in Australia, Asia and Africa. Most are terrestrial; the burrowing species have reduced limbs or are legless. Length: 8–24in (20–61cm). Family Scincidae. *See also* Lizard.

Skinner, B(urrhus) F(redric) (1904–), US psychologist, b. Susquehanna, Pa. He was a pivotal figure in psychological behaviorism. Skinner has made substantial contributions to psychology using rigorous, objective methods. Much of his work has centered on the process of operant conditioning, ie, how behavior is controlled by its consequences or reinforcements. His work led to the development of behavior modification for the treatment of the mentally disturbed and the development of teaching machines in the classroom. Skinner has also expressed concern about the future of mankind in such works as *Walden Two* (1948) and *Beyond Freedom and Dignity* (1971). Other works include *Particulars of My Life* (1976) and *Notebooks* (1981). *See also* Behaviorism; Behavior Modification; Operant Conditioning.

Skinner Box, device used in psychological studies of operant conditioning, named for B. F. Skinner, its inventor. An animal placed in the box learns to press a lever in order to get food or water (reinforcement). The device allows precise control of learning conditions and measurement of changes occurring in behavior during the learning process. *See also* Behaviorism; Operant Conditioning.

Skin Senses, or cutaneous senses, touch, pain, and temperature (hot and cold). In addition to free nerve endings, other types of receptors seem to be involved although their precise function is unclear. Some receptors are located near hair follicles and "fire" when the hair is moved; others operate in more complex ways.

Skipper, day-active insects characterized by darting or skipping flight. They have stouter bodies than butterflies but more slender than moths. There is usually a hooklike extension at the end of each knobbed antenna. Order Lepidoptera; superfamily Hesperioidea. *See also* Lepidoptera.

Skokie, city in NE Illinois, 15mi (24km) N of Chicago; site of Hebrew Theological College (1922). Industries: pharmaceuticals, communications equipment. Founded as Niles Center; inc. 1888, name changed 1940. Pop. (1980) 60,278.

Skopje (Usküp), city in S Yugoslavia, on Vardar River; capital of Macedonia; industrial, transportation, and trade center; site of Macedonian University (1949), Stephen Dušan bridge, mosques of Mustafa Pasha and Sultan Murad (15th century). Medieval Serbian capital (est. 1282), city fell to Turks 1392; inc. into Yugoslavia 1918; severely damaged by 1963 earthquake. Industries: iron, steel, textiles, chemicals, glass, handicrafts. Pop. 313,000.

Skua, dark-colored, swift-flying, sharp-billed shorebird that pirates food from other birds in flight. Skuas nest in colonies, laying spotted, earth-colored eggs (2) on isolated polar islands. Length: 24in (61cm). Family Stercorariidae; species *Stercorarius skua.*

Skull, part of the body at the anterior end of the vertebral column. It consists of the cranium, or brain case, which is made up of eight bones; and the facial bones, 14 irregularly shaped bones that support and protect the eyes, nose, and mouth. *See also* Cranium.

Skunk, nocturnal omnivorous mammal native to North, Central, and South America with powerful scent glands used in defense. The size of large house cats, skunks have small heads and slender, thickly-furred bodies with short legs and big bushy tails. They have bold black and white markings. Best known is the striped skunk *(Mephitis mephitis)*—length: 15in (38cm); weight: 10lb (4.5kg). Family Mustelidae.

Skunk Cabbage, evil-smelling perennial plant of E North American and Asian woods and swamps. It has a mottled hood of green or purple enveloping a small, tight, knob-shaped flower cluster and cabbagelike leaves. Height: 1–3ft (30–91cm). Family Araceae; species *Symplocarpus foetidus. See also* Arum.

Skye, island off the NW coast of Scotland; largest island in the Inner Hebrides; chief town is Portree. Industries: livestock, tourism. The Cuillin Hills (S) reach 3,309ft (1,009m). Area: 670sq mi (1,735sq km).

Skye Terrier, 400-year-old game breed (terrier group) from Skye Island region, Scotland. Most widely known of the terriers until the end of the 19th century. Once pet of the nobility, the Skye has a long, powerful head with prick or drop ears and brown eyes. The body is long and low, with short legs and long tail. The straight, flat coat is 5.5in (14cm) long and worn parted from head to tail; one overall color of blue black, gray, silver, fawn, or cream is acceptable to kennel clubs. Average size: 10in (25.4cm) high at shoulder; 25lb (11kg). *See also* Terrier.

Skylab, US program of manned orbiting space laboratories. In the mid-1970s three 3-man Skylab crews spent 655 man-days in space. Expanded activities in conjunction with Space Shuttle were planned for the 1980s. However, in 1979, a Skylab fell to Earth on Australia and the Indian Ocean while unmanned. *See also* Space Shuttle; Space Station.

Skylark, Eurasian bird known for the male's flutelike song and elaborate courtship rite. It is black streaked with dull brown and has white tail feathers. It is an insect and berry eater. Its eggs (3–5) are hatched in a cup-shaped ground nest. Length: 7in (18cm). Species *Alauda arvensis. See also* Lark.

Skyros (Skiros), island in Greece, largest of N Sporades group, in Aegean Sea; connected in legend to Theseus, hero of Athens; Rupert Brooke, English poet, is buried here. Industries: wheat, figs, citrus fruits, olive oil, cheese, marble, chromite, iron. Area: 81sq mi (210sq km). Pop. 3,000.

Skyscraper, a very tall building, constructed on a steel skeleton, generally for commercial use. The invention of practical electric elevators and the need for space in central cities spurred construction of taller buildings in the late 19th century. The first were all masonry construction. Next came cage construction—the building's metal framework supported the floors; the masonry walls supported themselves. True skyscraper construction, in which the metal skeleton supported both floors and walls, was introduced in the Home Insurance Building in Chicago (1883). Later skyscrapers have riveted metal skeletons, and the walls merely enclose the internal space. The first design to show concern for environmental impact was that of Rockefeller Center in New York City (1929–40). The tallest skyscraper now in use is Chicago's Sears Tower (110 stories, 1,454ft (443.5m) plus a TV antenna).

Slash-and-Burn Agriculture, a primitive agricultural technique that involves the felling and girdling of trees, which are then burned to make land arable. This is a temporary measure, as the land is rarely usable for a second season, and the farmer moves on to new woodland to follow the same procedure.

Slate, a fine-grained homogeneous metamorphic rock, which splits into smooth, thin layers. Formed by the metamorphosis of shale, its regular fissility makes it valuable as a roofing material. The characteristic color is gray-blue. *See also* Metamorphic Rocks.

Slater, Samuel (1768–1835), US textile manufacturer, b. England. Britain, to protect its cotton industry, forbade textile workers to emigrate. Slater traveled secretly to the United States. From memory he recreated complex English textile machinery in a mill in Pawtucket, R.I. (1790). This was the first textile factory in the United States. In 1815 he started wool fabric production.

Slave Coast, name given to a portion of Africa's Guinean coast that supplied vast numbers of slaves from *c.* 1500–1800.

Slavery, condition in which persons are held as property by other persons, and the slave is obliged to perform labor or services for the master. Practiced since prehistoric times, the institution probably began with enforced servitude of prisoners of war and then was extended to include countrymen who broke the law. Very common among the classical Greeks and Romans, slavery became fairly rare in the Middle Ages, though more because of economic considerations than any general acceptance that it was immoral. Beginning in the late 15th century, in the New World, slavery provided a supply of much-needed labor. Though native Indians were the first slaves there, trade in African slaves became highly profitable and was carried on with almost unimaginable brutality.

The antislavery movement, which was stimulated by the spread of Enlightenment humanitarian ideals in the 18th century, led to Britain's abolition of slavery in its territories in 1833 and eventually to growing feeling against the institution in the United States. Resistance to abolition, among other things, led to the US Civil War and eventual emancipation. Other countries followed suit, but a 1966 UN report stated that slavery still existed in parts of Asia and Africa.

Slavic Languages, group of languages spoken in the Soviet Union and E Europe and constituting a major subdivision of the Indo-European family. The Slavic languages spoken today are Russian, Ukrainian, Belorussian, Polish, Czech, Slovak, Bulgarian, Serbo-Croatian, Slovenian, Macedonian, and Sorbian (Lusatian), the last-mentioned spoken in East Germany. Some Slavic languages are written in the Cyrillic alphabet, others in the Roman, depending mainly on whether its speakers are Eastern Orthodox or Roman Catholic.

Skeletal system

Skunk

Bedřich Smetana

Slavonia, historic area in N Yugoslavia, between Sava River (S) and Drava and Danube rivers (N and E); now part of constituent republic of Croatia; Croatia and Slavonia were united with Hungary 1102; taken by Turkey 16th century; returned to Hungary 1699; part of Yugoslavia since 1918.

Sleep and Dreams, relatively new psychological discipline that studies the interrelated phenomena of sleep and dreams. Nobody knows exactly why organisms sleep but one theory suggests that this rest period allows the organism to live longer. Sleep varies from light to deep, with each stage corresponding to specific brain wave patterns. It is also related to the activity of the brain's reticular activating system (RAS). The function of dreaming is also obscure, and some researchers feel that it is merely random brain activity during sleep. Earlier theorists, notably Sigmund Freud, believed that dreams reflected conscious thought, and the concept is a central one in psychoanalysis. Dreaming is often accompanied by rapid eye movements (REM), which can be measured electrically. Some researchers report that depriving an individual of REM sleep produces irritability and even hallucinations. All sleep stages are accompanied by considerable neural activity, suggesting that sleep is not passive. *See also* Sleep Deprivation.

Sleeping Sickness, infection with a flagellate protozoan transmitted by the tsetse fly. It is characterized by fever, inflamed lymph nodes, and involvement of brain and spinal cord, leading to profound lethargy. Treatment with drugs is helpful in early stages, but useless later. *See also* Trypanosomiasis.

Slider, freshwater turtle common to the New World. Its oval, wrinkled shell is olive with black or brown markings. Males have elongated front claws used in courtship. Pond sliders have red or yellow blotches on sides of head. Length: to 12in (30.5cm). Family Emydidae; genus *Chrysemys. See also* Turtle.

Slide Rule, mechanical calculating device consisting of two rules engraved with logarithmic scales of numbers, one of which slides along the other. Multiplication and division of numbers, and often of their squares, squares roots, and other functions, is thus reduced to mechanical addition and subtraction.

Slime Mold, any of a small group of strange, basically single-celled organisms that are intermediate between the plant and animal kingdoms. During their complex life cycle they pass through several stages, including a flagellated swimming stage; an amebalike stage; and a stage consisting of a slimy mass of protoplasm with many nuclei.

Slipped Disk, or herniated disk, an intervertebral disk in which the center has slipped out from between abutting vertebrae, causing pressure against the spinal cord. Subsequent pain may be in the arms or in the lower back and legs, depending on which disks are displaced. Treatment involves bedrest, analgesic medication, traction, support, physical therapy, and, occasionally, surgical removal of protruded portion.

Sloan, John (1871–1951), US painter, b. Lock Haven, Pa. He worked as a newspaper illustrator in Philadelphia and New York City. He became a member of The Eight (Ashcan school) and painted realistic city scenes of working-class people engaged in their daily activities. Neutral colors prevail in his works.

Sloop, term used to designate a small single-masted sailing vessel with fore and aft sails, and, in the 18th century, a sail-powered warship with 10 to 32 cannon.

The term is also used for a small warship, similar to the destroyer, but much slower and often better armed, providing escort for merchant ships.

Sloth, slow-moving herbivorous tropical American mammal. It has long limbs tipped with two or three long claws and spends most of its life in trees. Length: 2ft (61cm); weight: 12lb (5.4kg). Family *Bradypodidae. See also* Edentate.

Sloth Bear, omnivorous, medium-sized bear of Indian and Sri Lankan forests. It has a shaggy black coat with a yellow or white v-shaped marking on its chest. Species *Melursus ursinus.*

Slovak, the second of the two major languages of Czechoslovakia, spoken by about 5,000,000 people in the E third of the country, which is known as Slovakia. It is closely related to Czech and is thought by some to be a dialect of that language.

Slovakia (Slovensko), region of E Czechoslovakia, bounded by Poland (N), USSR (E), Hungary (S), and Austria and Moravia (W). Capital is Bratislava; most of region is crossed by Carpathian Mts. Until 1918 it was primarily under control of Hungary; became part of new country of Czechoslovakia 1918, but retained broad powers of autonomy; occupied by Germany in WWII; occupied by Soviet Union 1968. Mountainous parts of country are rich in minerals; sheep grazing and farming in the valleys are important. Area: 18,923sq mi (49,010sq km).

Slovenia, constituent republic of Yugoslavia, in NW part of country, primarily in Karst plateau and Julian Alps; bounded by Austria (N), Hungary (NE), Croatia (S), Trieste (SW), and Italy (W); capital is Ljubljana. It was part of kingdom of Austria 1335–1918, when it was included in kingdom of Serbs, Croats, and Slovenes (known as Yugoslavia since 1929). In 1945 it was made a constituent republic of Yugoslavia and added part of Venezia Giulia (formerly part of Italy); most industrialized of all Yugoslav republics. Chief rivers are Sava and Drava. Industries: farming, livestock, iron, steel, textiles, aluminum. Area: 7,819sq mi (20,251sq km). Pop. 1,727,000.

Slug, land gastropod mollusk identified by evolutionary loss of shell and untwisted viscera. It secretes a protective slime also used for locomotion. Length: to 7.9in (201mm). Class Gastropoda; subclass Pulmonata; species include garden *Arion hortensis* and great gray *Limax maximus.*

Small Intestine, that part of the digestive system that extends—some 23ft (7m) coiled and looped—from the stomach to the large intestine, or colon. Food passes from the stomach through the pyloric sphincter to the duodenum, the first part of the small intestine, then to the jejunum, the second part, and then to the ileum, the third part of the small intestine, from which it passes through the colic valve to the colon. The small intestine secretes intestinal juices that combine with bile from the liver and gall bladder and with pancreatic juice to complete the digestion of foodstuffs. The final products are then absorbed through the thin membranes of fingerlike projections (villi) on the intestinal walls into tiny blood and lymph vessels that carry the nutrients to cells throughout the body.

Smallpox, or variola, highly contagious, often fatal viral disease. Its symptoms are high fever and rash on face and extremities, which becomes papular, then pustular. Pustules become crusted, leaving scars. Death is caused when lungs, heart, and brain are in-

fected. Through a vigorous program of vaccination, smallpox has been virtually eradicated.

Smell, or olfaction, a chemical sense, in which the stimulus is a chemical diffused in air. Smell is mediated by olfactory receptors located in a membrane at the top of the nose. When operating properly, olfaction can detect a few molecules per million parts of air. The olfactory cortex is more highly developed in some other species (for example, dogs and cats), than in humans.

Smelt, inshore marine food fish found in temperate and cold waters of N Pacific. It is olive green and silver. Length: to 14in (35.6cm). Family Osmeridae; genus *Osmerus.*

Smetana, Bedrich (1824–84), Czech romantic composer who promoted Czech nationalistic style in operas and orchestral music. His masterpiece is the folk opera *The Bartered Bride* (1866). Also popular is his symphonic poem *The Moldau* (1879).

Smith, Adam (1723–90), Scottish economist. He was appointed professor of moral philosophy at Glasgow University (1752). He wrote the economic treatise *An Enquiry into the Nature and Causes of the Wealth of Nations* (1776), after meeting French Physiocrats. He argued that a laissez-faire economy and free trade would stimulate production and thus act in the interests of the public but also recognized the necessity for legal and moral restrictions.

Smith, Bessie (1898–1937), US blues singer, b. Chattanooga, Tenn. The most famous of all blues singers, she started recording in 1923, toured with bands as a soloist, and became a highly paid and successful artist. Her many mournful, moving recordings of blues became a part of jazz history. She died from injuries received in an auto accident.

Smith, David (1906–65), US sculptor, b. Decatur, Ind. He is perhaps the most important US sculptor of the 20th century. It was only in 1930–33, however, that he became interested in welded metal sculpture, and he continued to work with metal for the rest of his career. Some of his work has been called "drawing in space" because it seems two-dimensional and linear instead of solid and bulky. Until the 1960s his sculpture was rarely completely abstract, and there were usually suggestions of human figures in it. Later his work became geometric and smooth, as in the "Zig" and "Cubi" series of wholly abstract pieces.

Smith, Ian Douglas (1919–), Rhodesian prime minister (1964–79). He fought in World War II and then entered Rhodesian politics. He became prime minister in 1964 and declared Rhodesia's independence from Great Britain in 1965. Although he suppressed all dissent to white administration of his overwhelmingly black country, during the mid-1970s Smith made some efforts to negotiate with black leaders. In 1976 he agreed to eventual black majority rule in Rhodesia and stepped down in 1979 when Rhodesia became the independent Zimbabwe.

Smith, John (1580–1631), English soldier and colonial leader. He served with the Huguenots in France and against the Turks in eastern Europe. He took a leading part in establishing the Jamestown settlement (1607) and was instrumental in obtaining corn from the Indians, thus saving the colony from destruction during three years of hardship. According to his story, he was rescued from death at the hands of Powhatan by the chief's daughter Pocahontas. He explored the New

England coast and gave the region its name. *See also* Jamestown Settlement; Pocahontas.

Smith, Joseph (1805–44), founder of the Church of Jesus Christ of Latter-day Saints, also known as the Mormons, b. Sharon, Vt. From 1820–27 he experienced visions in which the angel Moroni told Smith to establish a church. In 1827, he discovered a set of gold plates whose hieroglyphic inscriptions were later published as The Book of Mormon, and in 1830 he formally founded the Mormon church at Fayette, N.Y. Later he and his followers moved west, finally settling in Nauvoo, Ill. A controversial figure, he was pressured by outside groups, especially concerning Mormon polygamy. In 1844 he was arrested for destroying the presses of a critical local newspaper. He was murdered by a mob and was succeeded by Brigham Young as the Mormons' leader. *See also* Mormon, The Book of; Mormons.

Smith, William (1769–1839), English geologist. A founder of stratigraphic geology, he studied the geological strata of England and Wales and published his findings in a *Geological Atlas of England and Wales* (1815–22). *See also* Stratigraphy.

Smithson, James (1765–1829), English scientist. A chemist and mineralogist, he traveled widely in Europe, the mineral zinc carbonate (Smithsonite) being named after him. He died without issue and left his fortune to a nephew on the condition that if he died without issue the money should be used to found an establishment for the increase and diffusion of knowledge in Washington, D.C., to be known as the Smithsonian Institution. As the illegitimate son of the duke of Northumberland his bequest may have been an attempt to perpetuate his own name.

Smithsonian Institution, US independent trust establishment. It was created in 1846 to carry out the will of James Smithson of England who bequeathed (1829) his entire estate to the United States "to found at Washington, under the name of the Smithsonian Institution, an establishment for the increase and diffusion of knowledge among men." The institution is administered by a Board of Regents, composed of the chief justice of the Supreme Court, the vice-president, three members of the Senate, three members of the House of Representatives, and nine citizens appointed by joint resolution of Congress. The institution performs fundamental research, publishes the results of studies, explorations, and investigations, and preserves for study and reference over 65,000,000 items of scientific, cultural, and historic interest. Under it are a number of museums, galleries, parks, cultural centers, and information exchange services.

Smog, a dense atmospheric mixture of fog and smoke or chemical fumes, particularly noted in urban or industrial settings with many sources of air pollution and densest during temperature inversions. *See also* Air Pollution; Inversion.

Smoke Detector, a device that gives a loud alarm when smoke particles enter it. Smoke detectors may be powered by batteries or by house current. One type of detector contains a photoelectric cell. Smoke entering the detector cuts down on the amount of light entering the cell, thereby reducing the amount of current flowing through the cell. The drop in current sets off the alarm. In another type of detector, a steady current is sustained by ions produced by a tiny radioactive source. Smoke particles become attached to the ions, reducing the current and setting off the alarm.

Smolensk, city in Russian SFSR, USSR, on Dnieper River, 220mi (354km) WSW of Moscow; capital of Smolensk oblast. It was first mentioned 882; early important commercial center; 12th–14th-century capital of Smolensk principality; sacked by Tartars *c.* 1240; taken by Lithuania 1408; ceded to Russia 1686; burned when French invaded Russia 1812; occupied by Germany 1941–43; site of medical and teachers' colleges, cathedral, regional museum, monument to 1812 battle. Industries: linen, textile machines, electrical goods, clothing, flour milling, distilling, brewing, lumber, bricks, glass, Pop. 271,000.

Smollett, Tobias George (1721–71), Scottish novelist and surgeon. His novels include *Roderick Random* (1748), *The Adventures of Peregrine Pickle* (1751), and *Humphrey Clinker* (1770). Smollett also translated Voltaire and edited several periodicals.

Smut, any of a group of plant diseases caused by parasitic fungi, also called smuts, that attack many flowering plants including corn, wheat, and other cereal grasses. The diseases are named after the sooty black masses of reproductive spores produced by the fungi.

Smuts, Jan Christiaan (1870–1950), South African political leader. A lawyer, he was alarmed by the Jameson Raid of 1895 and entered Boer politics. He was a guerrilla leader during the Boer War (1899–1902) but afterwards worked for the establishment of a unified republic, repressing Boer rebellion during World War I. He helped form the Union of South Africa in 1910, served in various ministries under Louis Botha, and predicted the disastrous failure of the Treaty of Versailles following World War I. A supporter of the League of Nations, he was prime minister from 1919–24 and 1939–48 and helped form the United Nations following World War II. His government was replaced by the anti-British and white supremacist nationalists of D. F. Malan.

Snail, gastropod mollusk found in fresh and marine waters and on land. It has coiled protective shell encasing an asymmetric visceral mass; large, fleshy foot and head with tentacles; one or more gills; and radula. Often brightly colored, snails are born with a shell. Many snails are intermediate hosts for parasites such as sheep liver fluke. Height: to 2in (51mm). Class Gastropoda; species include common garden *Helix aspersa,* Roman or edible *Helix pomatia,* pond *Limnea stagnalis.*

Snail Darter, a rare and endangered species of fish native to the Little Tennessee River in Tennessee. It is a bottom-dweller with a maximum length of about 3 inches (7.5 cm). Some scientists fear that the Tellico Dam on the river may threaten the snail darter's existence. However, since the completion of the dam in 1980, the snail darter has been found in a different stream. Species *Percina tanasi.*

Snail Fever. *See* Schistosomiasis.

Snake, any of some 2,700 species of legless, elongated reptiles forming the suborder Serpentes of the order Squamata (which also includes the lizards). There are 10 families. Some are small burrowers, others are large, constricting types. They range in size from 4in (102mm) to over 30ft (9m). There are terrestrial, arboreal, semiaquatic, and aquatic species; one group is entirely marine. Many are poisonous. They have external ear openings, eardrums, or middle ears; sound vibrations are picked up via the ground. Their eyelids are immovable and fused into a transparent protective window. Internal organs are elongated with the left lung reduced or absent. The long, forked, protractile tongue is used to detect odors. Their bodies are scale-covered. Males have paired copulatory organs called hemipenes. Upper and lower jaws are moveable and each half of either jaw can be moved independently of the other, allowing snakes to swallow outsized prey. *See also* Reptile.

Snakebird, or anhinga, bird found in freshwater and nearby brush of warm temperate areas. Dark with metallic plumage, it has a straight bill, small head on a long neck, a slender body, long tail, and webbed feet. It swims well and feeds mostly on fish. It lays pale blue eggs (3–5) in a shallow, leaf-lined, cup-shaped stick nest in a bush or tree overhanging water. Length: 35in (90cm). Family Anhingidae.

Snakebite, injection of a poisonous substance (venom) secreted by a snake into the bloodstream, causing damage to blood cells or nervous tissue and often fatal if not treated immediately. Among the venomous snakes are cobras, copperheads, bushmasters, coral snakes, rattlesnakes, mambas, vipers, and water moccasins.

Snakehead, freshwater food fish found in Africa and Asia. An air breather, it wriggles over ground from pond to pond. It has a cylindrical body and flattened head. Length: 6in–3ft (15.2–91.4cm). Family Channidae; species *Channa asiatica.*

Snake River, river in NW United States; rises in Yellowstone National Park, NW Wyoming; flows SW and N across Idaho; turns N, then W across SE Washington and empties into the Columbia River, near Pasco; site of Hell's Canyon gorge reaching a 7,900-ft (2,410-m) depth; major source of hydroelectricity, and irrigation. Discovered *c.* 1803 by Lewis and Clark. Length: 1,038mi (1,671km).

Snapdragon, any of a genus *(Antirrhinum)* of perennial plants with saclike, two-lipped, purple, red, yellow, or white flowers. The common snapdragon *(A. majus)* is a popular garden plant; height: 0.5–3ft (15–91cm). Family Scrophulariaceae.

Snapper, marine food fish found in tropical waters of the Indo-Pacific and Atlantic. It is usually red or yellow. Length: to 3ft (91cm); weight: 110lb (50kg). The 250 species include red *Lutjanus campechanus,* yellowtail *Ocyurus chrysurus,* and Atlantic gray *L. griseus.* Family Lutjanidae.

Snapping Turtle, large aquatic turtle found in North and South America. It has a large head, broad neck, powerful limbs, and a long saw-toothed tail too bulky to be retracted into its shell. Length: 15in (38cm). Genus *Chelydra.* The much larger related alligator snapper *(Macrochelys temmincki)* of SE United States has a wormlike appendage on its tongue to lure fish. Family Chelydridae. *See also* Turtle.

Snipe, migratory, long-billed shorebird, found in swamp grasslands over most of the world. Often valued as game birds, they are mottled black, brown, and buff. Length: 12in (30cm). Family Scolopacidae; Genus *Capella.*

Snook, or robalo, marine and freshwater fish found in tropical waters. Large snooks—Atlantic *Centropomus undecimalis.* Length: 56in (142cm); weight: 50lb (22.7kg); freshwater Nile perch *Lates niloticus* (weight: to 200lb, 90kg)—are commercial and sport fish. Small snooks are popular aquarium fish. Family Centropomidae. *See also* Glass Fish.

Snorri Sturluson (1178–1241), Icelandic historian. His *Prose Edda* is a collection of Norse mythology and a discussion of the art of poetry. *Heimskringla,* sagas of the Norwegian king to 1177, mingles history and legend and is an important source for Norwegian history. A lawyer from an aristocratic family, he was politically active, supporting Haakon IV in annexing Iceland to Norway. His son-in-law killed him during political intrigues.

Snow, C(harles) P(ercy) (1905–80). English novelist and physicist. He was knighted in 1957 for government work and created baron in 1964. From 1935 he has written a sequence of novels, which included *Strangers and Brothers* (1940), *The Masters* (1951), *The Affair* (1960), *Corridors of Power* (1964), *Last Things* (1970), and *In Their Wisdom* (1974). His nonfiction included *The Two Cultures and the Scientific Revolution* (1959), *Science and Government* (1961), *Public Affairs* (1971), *A Coat of Varnish (1979),* and *The Physicists* (posthumously, 1981).

Snow, aggregates of frozen water that fall from clouds to Earth's surface, as opposed to frost. *See also* Ice or Snow Crystals.

Snowball, showy shrub widely cultivated in gardens. The snowball or guelder-rose *(Viburnum opulus roseum)* has round-topped, sterile, white or pinkish flower clusters. The Chinese snowball *(Viburnum macrocephalum sterile)* has large balls of white flowers. Family Caprifoliaceae. *See also* Viburnum.

Snow Bunting, small, mostly white, seed-eating finch found in circumpolar areas. It builds a cup-shaped nest for its finely spotted eggs (2–6). Species *Plectrophenax nivalis.*

Snowdon, Antony Armstrong-Jones, Earl of (1930–), British designer and photographer who married, in 1960, Princess Margaret, the sister of Queen Elizabeth II. They were divorced in 1976.

Snowdon, mountain in NW Wales, in Gwynedd. One of its five peaks is the highest in England and Wales, 3,560ft (1,086m). A rack-and-pinion railway climbs it from Llanberis. Much of the area is included in Snowdonia National Park (est. 1951).

Snowdrop, low-growing perennial plant of the Mediterranean region, widely cultivated in gardens worldwide. The green and white, fragrant nodding flowers appear early in spring. The common snowdrop *(Galanthus nivalis)* has long narrow leaves; height: 12in (30cm). Family Amaryllidaceae.

Snow Leopard, or ounce, large spotted cat found in central Asian mountains, usually above 8,000ft (2,440m). Not a true leopard, its soft, long fur is whitish to yellow-gray with black spots. The gestation period is 93–103 days and 2–5 young are born. Length: body —47.2–59.1in (120–150cm); tail—35in (89cm); weight: 75–100lb (34–45kg). Family Felidae; species *Uncia uncia. See also* Cat.

Snowmobile, gasoline-powered racing sled with rubber-cleated tracks and ski runners. In rural areas it is used extensively for transportation in the winter and as a recreational vehicle. As a competitive winter sport, it has been popular since the 1960s and includes a variety of events, classified according to engine displacement (250 cc, 340 cc, 440 cc, and 650 cc). A crude form of the snowmobile was invented in 1928 by Carl Eliason, a Wisconsin woodsman, who attached a 2.5 horsepower outboard motor to a toboggan that had

Soccer

Socrates

Sofia, Bulgaria: Alexander II memorial

two wooden skis in front. In 1932 he perfected his invention and recorded speeds over 40 miles (64.4km) per hour.

Snow-on-the-Mountain, annual plant native to W United States. Popular in gardens, it is bushy and has white margins on its upper leaves and small flowers in cuplike clusters. Height: to 2ft (61cm). Family Euphorbiaceae; species *Euphorbia marginata.*

Snowshoe Rabbit, or varying hare, medium-sized hare of N North America with large furry hind feet that act as snowshoes. It is brownish in summer, white in winter. It feeds chiefly on twigs, foliage, and bark. Species *Lepus americanus. See also* Hare.

Snowy Owl, white owl that blends with the snowy barren Arctic tundra where it lives. It feeds mainly on lemmings and hares, hunting in daylight during the Arctic summer. Length: to 2ft (61cm). Species *Nyctaea scandiaca. See also* Owl.

Soap, substance used to remove dirt and grease, made by the action of alkali on fats. Common soaps are sodium or potassium salts of stearic, oleic, or adipic acids. The molecule has a long chain, one end of which attaches to grease, while the other end dissolves in the water, pulling the grease away into solution. Toilet soaps usually contain colorant and perfume. *See also* Detergent.

Soccer, game, also known as association football, played by 2 teams of 11 persons each on a field between 110 and 130 yards (100–118m) long and from 70 to 80 yards (64–73m) wide. Centered at each end of the field is a goal, 8 yards (7.3m) wide by 8 feet (2.4m) high, backed with netting. The round ball is about 28 inches (71cm) in circumference, covered with leather, and inflated. Each team consists of a goalkeeper, two fullbacks, three halfbacks, and five forwards. The object is to advance the ball toward the opponent's goal and between the goal posts by kicking, dribbling, heading, or using any other part of the body other than the arms and hands; the goalkeeper is the only one allowed to use hands. Each goal counts one point. A match consists of two 45-minute periods and may end in a tie. Substitutions are not allowed. The game is controlled by a referee, who is assisted by a linesman, and infractions result in various types of free kicks.

History. Soccer is considered the most popular sport in the world, originating in England in 1863. The sport is governed by the Fédération Internationale de Football Associations, which includes 130 member nations, and sponsors the famed World Cup competition for the Jules Rimet trophy every four years. The game is played on an amateur level throughout the world and professionally in Europe, the United States, and South America. In the United States, where the sport is secondary to US football, interest has increased since the formation of the professional North American Soccer League in 1968. The sport was first included as an event in the Olympic Games in 1900.

Socialism, economic system in which the major portion of large-scale productive resources, man-made and natural, are owned by the state or by agencies of the state. While there are various forms of socialism, most socialists agree that public ownership is a necessary component. Socialist thought is based on the assumption that capitalism is an inefficient way to produce goods and services, and that far greater production is possible under socialism. This production will be divided among the population in a more equitable manner than that characteristic of capitalistic societies, al-

though most socialist writers do not insist on complete equality.

Socialist Realism, artistic style. Generally recognized as the "official" style of the USSR., it usually takes an idealized, heroic form and is intended to advance the doctrines of the state. It is diametrically opposed to Aestheticism.

Social Security Act (1935), US legislation to provide for government-protected social insurance. This act, part of the New Deal of Pres. Franklin D. Roosevelt, required a set amount to be withheld from workers' pay to subsidize old-age and survivors benefits, disability, unemployment insurance, and social welfare. There were grants provided to the states to cover some costs of this system, and a Social Security Board was created to administer it. Historically, benefits and deductions have been raised as prices have increased. By the early 1980s, despite substantial increases in revenues, concern escalated over the ability of the system to survive. President Reagan attempted to tighten the Social Security budget without affecting the truly needy.

Social War, or **Marsic War,** war waged against Rome by her rebellious Italian allies *(socii).* It began in 91 BC and continued to 87 with the hardest battles fought in 90–89. The Marsian people led the fight to gain Roman citizenship, which had been proposed by Drusus and withheld by the senate. The war was a stalemate and ended only when Rome granted citizenship to Italians S of the Po.

Society Islands, island group in S Pacific Ocean; part of W French Polynesia; comprised of the Windward Islands which include Tahiti, Mooréa, Mehetia, and islets, and the Leeward Islands, including Raiatea, Bora-Bora, Huahine, Maupiti, and several others. Islands contain volcanic mountains and coral formations; they were first sighted 1607 by Portuguese navigator Pedro Fernandes de Queirós; claimed for Great Britain 1767 by Samuel Wallis; claimed for France 1768 by Louis de Bougainville; made a French protectorate in 1843. Islands support tropical fruit industry. Exports: rum, sugar, mother-of-pearl, vanilla. Capital is Papeete, on Tahiti. Area: 621sq mi (1,608sq km). Pop. 100,270.

Society of Friends. *See* Quakers.

Sociology, science that examines society by describing and evaluating its institutions and processes. It attempts to discover the factors and causes that form these institutions and the effects the institutions have on the lives and personalities of those who are required to live under them.

Socrates (469–399 BC), Greek philosopher. Written about by Plato, he spent most of his life in Athens, engaging those he met in profound philosophic discussions. Believing that the highest meaning of life is attained through self-knowledge, he tried to convince his fellow men of the value of self analysis. He was loyal to this "mission," having a "demon" inside that would not let him stray from his pursuit. Found guilty of impiety and corruption of the young, he was condemned to death and poisoned himself. He wrote nothing although his verbal teachings influenced many.

Sodalite, a silicate mineral, sodium aluminum silicate with chlorine, found in alkaline igneous rocks. Cubic system small, dodecahedron crystals; also in masses. Glassy colorless, white, blue, pink; hardness 5.5–6; sp gr 2.2. Sometimes used as gem.

Soddy, Frederick (1877–1956), English chemist who received a Nobel Prize in 1921 for his studies of radioactive substances and his contributions to the isotope theory. With Ernest Rutherford he predicted the formation of helium during radioactive decay, and later, with William Ramsay, detected it spectroscopically. He coined the term isotopes to describe elements that exist in more than one form, have different atomic weights, but are indistinguishable chemically. In 1920 he revealed the value of isotopes in computing geological age.

Sodium, common metallic element (symbol Na) of the alkali-metal group, first isolated in 1807 by Sir Humphry Davy. It occurs in the sea and in many minerals. Chief source is sodium chloride, from which it is extracted by electrolysis. The metal is used as a heat-transfer medium and in making some organic compounds. Its compounds are extensively used commercially. Chemically, sodium is a very reactive electropositive element. Properties: at. no 11; at. wt. 22.9898; sp. gr. 0.971; melt. pt. 208.05°F (97.81°C); boil. pt. 1638°F (892°C); most common isotope Na^{23} (100%). *See also* Alkali Elements.

Sodium Chloride. *See* Halite; Salt.

Sodium Hydroxide, or caustic soda, white deliquescent crystalline substance (formula NaOH) obtained by the electrolysis of brine or by treating soda ash with a solution of lime in water. It is used in chemical synthesis and as an alkali in the manufacture of rayon, paper, detergents, soap, and aluminum.

Sofia (Sofija), capital city of Bulgaria and of Sofia prov.; in W central Bulgaria, approx. 35mi (56km) from Yugoslav border. Once residence of Constantine the Great, Sofia was ruled by Byzantine Empire 1018–1185, by the second Bulgarian empire (1186–1382), and by the Ottoman Empire (1382–1877). Sofia was taken by Russia 1877 and chosen for capital of Bulgaria in 1879. City contains opera house, museums, 19th-century Church of St George, a university (1888), and several technical schools; it is Bulgaria's most important commercial center. Industries: machinery, textiles, rubber, leather goods, food processing plants. Founded 2nd century. Pop. 965,728.

Softball, a game similar to baseball. It is played by two teams of nine persons each on a field with no set dimensions other than the infield, which measures 60 feet (18.3m) square. The ball is about 12 inches (30.5cm) in diameter, and the rules are close to those of baseball except for the pitching distance (43 feet; 13.1m), the amount of innings (seven), and the pitching delivery (underhand). Softball was originally invented as an indoor game in Chicago in 1887 by Lewis Rober, a Minneapolis fireman, and was known under several different names ("indoor baseball," "kitten ball," "mush ball," "playground ball," "ladies baseball") until 1926. The game began to increase in popularity when it was first moved outdoors in 1930. The first national tournament was held at the Chicago's World's Fair in 1933. The sport is governed by the Amateur Softball Association, founded in 1934.

Soft-coated Wheaten Terrier, sporting dog (terrier group) known for over 200 years in Ireland; brought to US in 1946. Used to hunt small game and guard stock, the soft-coated wheaten has a medium-long head, dark hazel eyes under a strong brow, compact body, moderately long legs, and a docked tail carried up. Its distinctive soft, wavy coat is clear wheaten-colored. Average size: 18–19in (46–48cm) high at shoulder; 35–45lb (16–20.5kg). *See also* Terrier.

Softener, Water, substance added to water to reduce its hardness, that is, its inability to form a lather with soap as a result of the presence of dissolved calcium, magnesium, and iron compounds. Some hardness, mostly due to bicarbonates of these metals, can be removed by boiling; the remaining "permanent" hardness is mostly due to sulfates of the metals and is reduced by adding such compounds as sodium carbonate, trisodium phosphate, or geolites (hydrated silicates of calcium and aluminum) to remove or sequester the metallic ions.

Soft-shelled Turtle, freshwater turtle widely distributed in Old and New Worlds. It has a soft, leathery shell, beak with fleshy lips, and a snorkel-like proboscis. Length: to 30in (76cm). The most common of seven genera is *Trionyx.* Family Trionychidae. *See also* Turtle.

Soil, surface layer of Earth capable of supporting plant life. An aggregation of mineral and organic particles, it consists of undissolved nonliving substances produced by the weathering and breakdown of surface rocks, organic matter, water, and gases, required by plants and subterranean organisms. Soil acts as a reservoir for plant nutrients, absorbing and oxidizing waste products of plant root growth. The chemical composition and physical structure of soil are determined by its original geological material, vegetative cover, and topography.

Soil Conservation and Reclamation, preserving and reconstituting arable soils through programs to prevent soil erosion and nutrient depletion and to improve crop yields. Proper soil management includes crop rotation, green manuring, fertilization, irrigation, drainage, and cultivation techniques, such as strip cropping. Semiarid soils are being reclaimed by laying asphalt moisture barriers below the soil surface to improve water retention and reduce the amount of water needed for irrigation. *See also* Crop Rotation; Irrigation.

Soil Profile, vertical view of horizontal layers, or horizons, of soil from the surface down to the unaltered parent material. This profile is used in classifying soils, with the ideal being one in which soluble substances from the top horizon have leached into the second horizon and the third horizon is the parent material of the surface soil. Bedrock underlies all three.

Soil Testing, process of analyzing the chemical and mineral composition and porosity of soil to determine its ability to support plant life. The principal nutrients needed by plants are nitrogen, potassium, and phosphorus. Soil alkalinity or acidity (pH) can, in some cases, be adjusted chemically or organically to meet a particular crop's needs.

Sol, in Roman mythology, two Sun gods. One was Sol Indiges. The other was Sol Invictus. Emperor Elagabalus tried to make the worship of Sol Invictus the major religion in Rome.

Solar Cell, device to convert sunlight directly to electric power. A solar cell normally consists of a *p*-type silicon crystal coated with an *n*-type silicon crystal. Solar radiation creates a potential difference between the two crystals and current flows between the electrodes connecting them. All wavelengths shorter than one micron can create electrical energy; the cells are about 10% efficient. Several thousand cells may be deployed in panels to provide power of a few hundred watts.

Solar Constant, the steady rate at which heat from the Sun is received from just outside the Earth's atmosphere, measuring approximately two gram-calories per square centimeter (perpendicular to the Sun's rays) per minute.

Solar Energy, thermal and electromagnetic energy from the Sun. Approximately 35% of the energy reaching the Earth is absorbed; most of this energy is spent evaporating moisture into clouds; some is converted into organic chemical energy by photosynthesis of plants. Man is seeking ways to utilize solar energy in the form of liquid heat storage and generation of electricity through solar photovoltaic cells. The effective use of solar energy is hampered by the diurnal cycle, seasonal and climatic variations, and presently cheaper energy forms. During the 1970s and 1980s, government funding and tax benefits promoted solar energy research and use. The Department of Energy was formed in 1979 for research and regulation. Sun Day (May 3, 1978) promoted solar energy worldwide.

Solar System, the celestial group consisting of the Sun and the assemblage of bodies, gas, and dust particles that revolve around it in closed orbits under the influence of its gravitational attraction. The known constituents include the major planets: Mercury, Venus, Earth, Mars, Jupiter, Saturn, Uranus, Neptune, and Pluto, the planetary satellites or moons, thousands of minor planets, or asteroids (mostly between Mars and Jupiter), many comets, meteorites, dust, and gas.

Solar Time, system of time reckoning based upon the interval between successive transits of the Sun across the observer's meridian (the solar day). Because of variations in the Earth's orbital velocity and changes in the Sun's apparent position as viewed from the orbiting Earth, solar days vary greatly in length throughout the year. An average or mean solar day has therefore been adopted, giving rise to mean solar time. As measured on the 0° meridian at the Greenwich Observatory, mean solar time takes the form of Greenwich Time or Universal Time.

Solar Wind, particles accelerated by high temperatures of the solar corona to velocities great enough to allow them to escape from the Sun's gravity. The solar wind deflects the tail of the Earth's magnetosphere and the tails of comets away from the Sun. When the solar wind meets the magnetic field of the Earth, a shock wave results.

Solder, alloy of low melting point used to join together metals with higher melting points. Soft solders consist of alloys of tin and lead in varying porportions; brazing solders are alloys of copper and zinc.

Sole, marine flatfish found in the Atlantic from NW Africa to Norway. This food fish is green-gray or black-brown with dark spots. Length: 23.6in (60cm). Species include common *Solea solea* and hogchocker *Trinectes maculatus.* Family Soleidae.

Solenodon, endangered species of nocturnal insectivores that resemble large shrews; one species occurs in Cuba, the other in Hispaniola. They have long, scaly tails. At least one species has poisonous saliva. Length: 1ft (30cm). Genus *Solenodon. See also* Insectivore.

Solid, state of matter in which a substance has a relatively fixed shape and size. The forces between atoms or molecules are strong enough to hold them in definite locations (about which they can vibrate) and to resist change in volume of the material or application of shear stress. *See also* Crystal; Liquid; Gas.

Solid State, state of matter in which the constituent atoms and molecules vibrate about fixed positions. Solid-state electronic devices are based on semiconductors, the term being used to distinguish these devices from electron tubes in which electrons pass through a vacuum or low-pressure gas. *See also* Semiconductor.

Solid-State Chemistry, study of the chemical properties of solid chemical compounds. Solid-state chemistry includes investigations into the structure of crystalline compounds and into the mechanism involved in decompositions, oxidations, and other reactions of solids.

Solid-State Physics, the physics of solid materials. From the study of the structure, binding forces, electrical, magnetic, and thermal properties of solids have come the development of the transistor, semiconductor, maser, laser, solar cell, and the printed circuits used in computers, all technological developments of revolutionary significance. Solid-state physics is a relatively recent branch of physics, involving far more complicated quantum mechanical calculations than the preceding studies of gases and liquids. Among the most eminent solid-state physicists are William Shockley, John Bardeen, and Walter Brattain, developers of the transistor; and Charles Townes, inventor of the maser. All won the Nobel Prize for their inventions.

Solid-Waste Disposal, systems for managing refuse in a healthful and economic way. In urban areas, bulk containers are lifted mechanically into compactor-equipped trucks that transport refuse to a disposal site. Combustible wastes may be burned in an incinerator. Garbage ground into small particles may be discharged into the sewer system. Ocean disposal of refuse is now prohibited in many areas; sanitary land disposal sites create areas that can be used later as parks or golf courses.

Solingen, city in W West Germany, on Wupper River, 14mi (23km) ESE of Düsseldorf; annexed as part of Prussia 1815; heavily bombed during WWII; world-famous for cutlery made from Solingen steel. Industries: knives, scissors, surgical instruments, razors, chemicals, machine tools, steel castings. Chartered 1374. Pop. 170,400.

Solomon (died *c.* 922 BC), third king of Israel (*c.* 961–922 BC), son of David and Bathsheba. He succeeded David and consolidated the empire. At first he ruled peacefully, made alliances with Egypt and Phoenicia, and showed wisdom. Later he became despotic, heavily taxed the tribes, and brought on the revolt of Jeroboam I. Solomon is regarded as the author of Proverbs, the Song of Solomon, and Wisdom of Solomon.

Solomon Islands, independent nation in W Pacific, E of Papua New Guinea, extends for 900mi (1,450km), composed of seven large volcanic islands and many small islets; northernmost islands of the Solomon Archipelago are part of Papua New Guinea. The Solomons were discovered (1568) by the Spaniard Álvaro de Mendaña. By 1900 the Solomons had become a British protectorate. In 1942, Japan invaded the Solomons, and they were recaptured the following year by US forces only after fierce fighting on Guadalcanal. In 1976 the islands were granted internal self-government, becoming fully independent within the Commonwealth of Nations in 1978. Since then the principal political issue has been decentralization of government to the country's four far-flung districts. The people are overwelmingly Melanesian, with about 90% of the labor force engaged in subsistence agriculture. Formerly, copra was virtually the only export, but because of a successful government diversification program launched during the 1960s, timber and palm oil are now also leading sources of income. Area: 10,938sq mi (28,446sq km). Pop. 221,000. Capital: Honiara.

Solomon's Seal, or David's harp, perennial plant native to cool temperate regions of Europe and Asia. It has broad, waxy leaves, white or greenish flowers, and blue or black berries. Height: to 3ft (0.9m). Family Liliaceae; species *Polygonatum multiflorum.*

Solon (*c.* 640–559 BC), Athenian poet and statesman who first gained fame with a poem in 612 BC. In 594 he was made archon and is known for his numerous reforms in law and citizen's rights, including abolishing debt laws, instituting habeas corpus, and freeing some of the slaves.

Solothurn, capital city of Solothurn canton in NNW Switzerland, on the Aare River, 19mi (31km) N of Bern. A former free town of the Holy Roman Empire (1218), it joined the Swiss Confederation 1481; served as the residence of the French ambassadors to the Swiss diet until 1797; site of municipal museum, 18th-century Italian baroque church, 15th-century town hall, 17th-century arsenal, 13th-century clock tower. Products: cattle, cereals. Industries: gas and electrical apparatus, radios, watches, printing, metal goods. Pop. 16,200.

Solstice, either of the two days of the year when the Sun is at its greatest angular distance from the celestial equator, leading to the longest day and shortest night (summer solstice) in one hemisphere of the Earth and the shortest day and longest night (winter solstice) in the other hemisphere. In the northern hemisphere the summer solstice occurs on about June 21 and the winter solstice on about Dec. 22.

Solute, gaseous, liquid, or solid substance that is dissolved and dispersed homogeneously in a solvent to form a solution. Solids, such as calcium bicarbonate, sugars, and starch, dissolve in water. Liquids can dissolve in liquids; for example, ethanol and water are miscible in all quantities at room temperature and gases, such as hydrogen chloride (HCl), are soluble in liquid water.

Solution, mixture, homogeneous on a molecular scale, of two or more chemically distinct compounds inseparable by filters. Most common are liquids and solids in liquids, but gases may be dissolved in liquids; and gases, liquids, and solids may also be dissolved in solids. The amount of a substance dissolved in a solvent is called the concentration of a solution and may be expressed in grams per liter, gram equivalents per liter, or as a molar fraction. The ability of one substance to dissolve another depends on the compounds, the temperature, and to a small extent the pressure. An "ideal solution" is one that obeys Raoult's Law: at constant temperature the partial pressure of a component in a liquid mixture is proportional to its mole fraction in the mixture. Heat can be evolved (an exothermic solution) or absorbed (endothermic) when a solution is formed. *See also* Molarity.

Solvent, substance, especially in liquid form, that dissolves and disperses other substances (solutes) to form a solution. This inert medium may be non-polar, exemplified by hydrocarbons or benzene, as utilized in paints, varnishes, and oils, or polar, such as water or alcohol, which are solvents widely found in nature.

Solzhenitsyn, Aleksandr (1918–), Soviet author. Arrested for criticism of Stalin while in the Red Army, he was sentenced to a forced labor camp (1945–53), where he contracted cancer, from which he recovered.

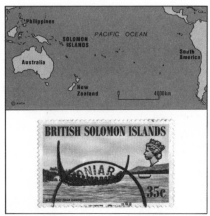

Solomon Islands

Aleksandr Solzhenitsyn

Somalia

Subsequently exiled in Kazakhstan, he was officially rehabilitated in 1957. Now a major spokesman for Soviet dissident intellectuals, his writings include the novels *One Day in the Life of Ivan Denisovich* (1962), *The First Circle* (1964), *Cancer Ward* (1966), *August 1914* (1972), the nonfiction *The Gulag Archipelago* (1974), and his memoirs *The Oak and the Calf* (1980). He encountered growing opposition from the Soviet regime, was deported to the West (1974), and settled in the United States, eventually forming a publishing company. He was awarded the Nobel Prize for literature (1970).

Somalia (Somaliya), independent republic in NE Africa, occupies majority of the strategically important Horn of Africa; bounded by Gulf of Aden (N), Indian Ocean (S and E), and Kenya, Ethiopia, and Afars and Issas (W). Most of the W boundaries, particularly the Ethiopian frontier, are in constant dispute. Somalia's 1,500mi (2,415km) coastline contains no natural harbors and its two rivers, the Shebelle and Juba, are both unnavigable and are used as a source of irrigation. The N section is mountainous with high plateaus; land between the two rivers is low farm country. The climate is tropical and suffers insufficient rainfall, causing disastrous droughts.

The economy is based primarily on livestock and subsistence farming. Chief products are bananas, millet, sesame, sugar, maize, cotton. Main industries include: tuna processing, soap, leather, textiles, and incense; the sea yields fish and resources of salt, limestone, and clay. Somalia is one of the world's poorest countries, heavily dependent upon foreign aid from the United States and W European countries. Somalis, the principal ethnic group, are a Cushitic people of Middle East origin; most are nomadic or seminomadic Muslims following the Sunni sect of the Shafii. Only 10% is literate; there is no national written language and as a result Somali poetry and classical literature are in danger of being lost.

History. The Somalis are believed to have arrived in the NW regions *c.* AD 750; by the 10th century Arab influence predominated the coastal areas. The disputes between Ethiopia and Somalia continued through the 13th–16th centuries. In 1884–86 Britain established a protectorate in N Somalia, while the Italians controlled the S territory. In 1960 the two territories joined to form the independent Somali Democratic Republic. In 1969 the military took control of the government, declaring the country a one-party socialist state (1970). In 1977 the country launched an offensive into the Ethiopian Ogaden region, in support of ethnic Somali guerrillas. The following year Somali national troops were forced to withdraw, but fighting continues in the region and relations with Ethiopia remain tense. By the early 1980s dislocation from war and drought resulted in famine in the Ogaden, and about 800,000 refugees had migrated into Somalia, severely taxing the country's scanty resources, despite assistance from international relief agencies. The refugee situation stabilized and crop yields increased by 1985, although the problem of their future remained.

PROFILE

Official name: Somali Democratic Republic
Area: 246,200sq mi (637,658sq km)
Population: 3,900,000
Chief cities: Mogadisho (capital); Hargeisa; Kismayu
Religion: Islam
Language: Somali, English, Italian, Arabic
Monetary unit: Somali shilling

Somaliland, French. See Djibouti.

Somerset, Edward Seymour, Duke of (?1506–52), protector of England, brother of Jane Seymour. Win-

ning Henry VIII's favor, he commanded successfully in Scotland (1544) and at Boulogne (1545). Appointed protector of Edward VI, a minor, on Henry's death (1547), he obtained almost royal powers. His religious reforms, leading to the Act of Uniformity (1549), established Protestantism in England. Deposed from the protectorate (1549), he was subsequently beheaded.

Somerville, city in E Massachusetts, on the Mystic River; site of Old Powder Mill (1703) and Prospect Hill, where Gen. Rufus Putnam raised first flag of United Colonies (1776). Industries: vehicle bodies, meat packing, clothing. Founded 1630; separated from Charlestown 1842; inc. as city 1872. Pop. (1980) 77,372.

Somme, river that rises in N France, above San Quentin; flows WNW for 150mi (242km) through Amiens and Abbeville to English Channel; scene of heavy fighting July 1–Nov. 18, 1916, between British and Germans; occupied by Germans May–June 1940 and recovered by Allies 1944 in WWII. Length: 152mi (245km).

Somnambulism. See Sleepwalking.

Somoza García, Anastasio (1896–1956), central figure in Nicaraguan politics from 1936, when he ousted President Sacasa, until his death. Somoza created both a dictatorial government and a political dynasty; he was succeeded in office by his two sons, Luis and Anastasio.

Sonar, underwater detection and navigation system. The letters stand for SOund, NAvigation, and Radar. The system emits high frequency sound that is reflected by underwater objects.

Sonata, a composition for one or more instruments (usually including a keyboard instrument) in three movements of fast-slow-fast tempo. A scherzo or minuet is often included before the final movement. Classically, the first movement is in "sonata-allegro form," which involves an exposition of contrasting themes, their development, and a recapitulation. This structure may appear in the later sonata movements as well, and appears in string quartets, symphonies, and concertos. The second movement of a sonata is typically a two- or three-part adagio, and the final movement is presto in rondo form. The term was first used in the 16th century to distinguish an instrumental from a vocal work. Sonatas increased in importance because of increasing emphasis on instrumental music during the baroque era. In the late 17th century the trio sonata emerged as the primary baroque chamber music form. This form was adopted by J.S. Bach and Handel. The outstanding baroque keyboard composer, Domenico Scarlatti, presaged the classical sonata in his explorations of thematic contrast. By the late 18th century, sonatas for groups of instruments became known as string quartets and symphonies, and sonata acquired its modern meaning. The experiments of K.P.E. Bach were particularly influential in this period, culminating in the perfection of the classical form by Haydn, Mozart, and above all Beethoven. In the romantic period the most original development was a striving for thematic unification, most fully realized in Liszt's Sonata in B Minor for piano (1854). Composers of the twentieth century, Paul Hindemith, Stravinsky, Prokofiev, Shostakovich, and Bartok, have introduced dissonant counterpoint and continuing key changes to the sonata.

Song of Solomon, or **Song of Songs,** book of the Old Testament comprised of a series of love poems spoken alternately by a man and a woman. They were perhaps originally written for wedding feasts and edited to their present form in the 3rd century BC.

Sonic Boom, the thunderlike sound produced when the high-pressure shock waves formed at the nose, wing leading edges, and tail of a supersonic aircraft spread out behind the aircraft and strike the ground. *See also* Supersonic Flight.

Sonnet, lyric poem of 14 lines, generally in iambic pentameter, following a definite rhyme scheme. There are two basic rhyme schemes. The Italian or Petrarchan sonnet follows the scheme abbaabba cdecde. The English or Elizabethan sonnet rhymes abab cdcd efef gg. The sonnet was given its greatest expression in the work of Petrarch, Spenser, Shakespeare, and Milton, among others.

Sons of Liberty, American colonial group. This secret organization began, principally in Connecticut and New York, to protest the Stamp Act (1765); it was dedicated to work for freedom and liberty in the 13 British colonies.

Soochow (Suzhou, or Su-chow), city in E central China, 55mi (89km) W of Shanghai on Grand Canal; capital of Wu kingdom 5th century BC; famous silk industry developed under Sung dynasty (12th century). It was declared a treaty port 1896; fell to Communist control 1949; noted since 100 BC for its many gardens, temples, and canals. Industries: silk, cotton, embroidery, food processing, chemicals. Pop. 1,300,000.

Soong Family, term used to refer to the talented children of the US-trained missionary, businessman, and industrialist Charles Jones Soong (1866–1918). The children came to be regarded as the first family of modern China. One son, **T. V. Soong** (1894–1971), occupied many high government positions, including minister of foreign affairs (1942–45) and president of the Executive Yuan (1945–47). Three daughters all married famous Chinese leaders. **Ai-ling** (1890–1973) became Mrs. H. H. Kung; **Ch'ing-ling** (1892–1981) became Mme. Sun Yat-sen and later held positions under the Communists; and **Mei-ling** (1898–) married Chiang Kai-shek.

Sophists, Greek teachers of the 5th to 4th centuries BC. To train young men of political careers, the Sophists provided what higher education was available in their day. They taught all the known subjects, but emphasized rhetoric as a means of convincing listeners. The Sophists were accused of using rhetoric as a device to win points rather than as a way to expound truth. They tended to teach their students what the students wanted to learn, which was often the way to get ahead rather than the way to truth. A leading Sophist, Protagoras, is a figure in one of Plato's dialogues.

Sophocles (496–406 BC), Greek playwright, born at Colonus. Of 120 plays, only 7 tragedies and part of a satyr play remain. These include *Ajax, Antigone* (441), *Electra, Oedipus Rex* (*c.*428), and *Oedipus at Colonus* (produced 401). His works introduced a third speaking actor, added stage scenery, and increased the chorus from 12 to 15 members. A popular, prominent figure in his day, he was often elected to public offices he had not sought. With Aeschylus and Euripides, he was considered one of the three great tragedians of ancient Greece. *See also* Ajax; Antigone.

Sora, Sora Rail, or Carolina Crake, grayish-brown bird, best known of North American rails. Height: 8in (20cm). Species: *Porzana carolina*. *See also* Rail.

Sorbonne, The. *See* Paris, University of.

Sorbs. *See* Wends.

Sorcery, magical manipulation of the natural world for specific ends. Sorcerers often seek the assistance of spirits or try to exercise supernatural powers in carrying out practices designed to cause or cure disease, reveal the future, etc. Anthropologists sometimes distinguish sorcery from witchcraft—witches need inherent spiritual powers whereas sorcerers do not. In many societies, including numerous Amerindian ones, sorcerers enjoy high social status. *See also* Shaman; Witch Doctor.

Sorghum, tropical cereal grass native to Africa and cultivated worldwide. Types raised for grain are varieties of *Sorghum vulgare* that has leaves coated with white waxy blooms and panicles that bear up to 3,000 kernels. It is used for meal, oil, starch, dextrose, and alcoholic beverages. Height: 2–8ft (0.6–2.4m). Family Gramineae.

Sorrel, or dock, herbaceous perennial weeds native to temperate regions. They have large basal or stem leaves and small green or brown flowers. Height: to 9ft (2.7m). Family Polygonaceae; genus *Rumex.*

Sorrel Tree, or sourwood, deciduous tree native to E and SE United States. Cultivated varieties are smaller than wild types. It has oval, sour leaves that are red in autumn and small white flowers. Height: 20–80ft (6–24m). Family Ericaceae; species *Oxydendrum arboreum.*

Sound, physiological sensation perceived by the ear, caused by an oscillating source, and transmitted through a material medium as a sound (acoustic) wave. The human ear can perceive sounds that have frequencies between 20 hertz and 20,000 hertz; the study of oscillations within this range constitutes the branch of physics known as *acoustics*—infrasonics is concerned with oscillations of lower frequencies and ultrasonics with sounds of higher frequencies.

The velocity *(c)* at which a sound wave travels through a medium depends on the elasticity of the medium *(K)* and its density ρ: $c = \sqrt{K/\rho}$. If the medium is a gas, the sound wave is longitudinal and the velocity of propagation depends on the gas temperature $c_e = c_0\sqrt{1+\alpha\theta}$, where c_0 and c_e are the velocities at 0°C and θ°C and α is the coefficient of expansion of the gas. The velocity of sound in dry air at STP is 331.4 meters per second (740.5mph) and depends on the height above sea level.

Every pure sound is characterized by its intensity, pitch, and timbre. The intensity is the rate of flow of sound energy through unit area perpendicular to the direction of flow. *See also* Noise; Pitch; Sound Sensation.

Sounding, any of several techniques used in determining the depth of water. The simplest means of sounding is by dropping a weighted line to the bottom. Acoustical means, using a sonic depth finder, are often used. This underwater device measures the time it takes a sound produced just below the surface to be reflected from the bottom. A transducer converts an electrical pulse into an acoustical pressure wave and, receiving its echo, converts it back to electric energy.

Sound Recording and Reproduction, the storing of sound waves in converted form and their subsequent recovery. Commonly, the sound is first converted into a physical analog, such as vibrations in a microphone diaphragm, which in turn produces electric signals. A tape recorder stores signals by an arrangement of magnetized iron particles on a tape. The sound is recovered when the tape regenerates the voltage pattern, which is then reconverted to sound waves in a loudspeaker. Phonographs store sound as modulations in the spiral groove on a disk. It is reproduced when the groove causes vibrations in a stylus, which are converted to electric signals and back to sound. Optical recording, as in sound tracks, stores sound by exposing the side of a filmstrip to light beams with intensities analogous to the acoustic signals.

Sound Sensation, physiological sensation perceived by the ear when stimulated by a sound wave within the frequency range 20–20,000 hertz. The sensitivity of the ear depends primarily on the intensity of the sound but also to a lesser extent on its frequency. The intensity of a pure tone that is just audible is known as the threshold of audibility. This varies with frequency but is a minimum at about 3,500 hertz when the threshold pressure (RMS) is about 0.0008 pascal. At a frequency of 1,000 hertz the maximum intensity that the ear can perceive is 10^{14} times greater than the threshold. Beyond this intensity the sensation becomes one of pain.

Sousa, John Philip (1854–1932), US composer and bandmaster, b. Washington, D.C. In 1911 he toured the world with his own band. He composed over 100 marches, including *Semper Fidelis* (1888) and *The Stars and Stripes Forever* (1897).

Sousaphone, largest brass wind musical instrument of the tuba family. It was introduced by John P. Sousa to fortify the bass section of the military band. Its range is 2 octaves below the cornet. The tube coils around the player, with the removable flaring bell directed forward, not upward, as with orchestral tubas.

South Africa (Suid-Afrika), independent nation in extreme southern Africa. The government follows an official policy of apartheid (separation of races), and the black majority is not allowed to participate in the government. South Africa has the most highly industrialized economy in Africa and is a major world producer of gold and diamonds.

Land and economy. Situated at the S tip of Africa, it is bordered by Namibia (South West Africa), Botswana, and Zimbabwe (N), and by Mozambique and Swaziland (E). It surrounds the independent Kingdom of Lesotho and the enclave of Walvis Bay, located on the coast of Namibia. With no important rivers or lakes, water control is essential in this country of narrow coastal regions and interior plateaus. The climate is moderate with an average temperature of about 60°F (15°C). Until diamonds were discovered in 1867 and gold in 1886, South Africa had been a country of subsistence farmers. Cut off from essential European supplies during WWI and II, it developed its own industries, which now account for 22% of the gross national product, and include transportation equipment, steel, chemicals, and petroleum refining. Mining accounts for almost 20% of GNP. The government's goal is to make South Africa self-sufficient. Minerals are abundant and crop production is high.

People. South Africa's multi-racial society is composed of four groups: whites, descended from Dutch, English, French, and German settlers (17%); Africans, divided into 10 ethnic groups (70%); colored, descended from Cape of Good Hope indigenous people and early European settlers (10%); and Asians, descended from East Indian workers (3%). More than 2,000,000 whites are members of the Dutch Reformed Church. About 50% of the Africans are animist. Literacy is estimated at 100% for whites, 50% for Africans, 75% for coloreds, and 85% for Asians.

Government. A 1961 constitution provides for two houses of Parliament, whose electoral college names the chief of state. A prime minister is leader of the majority party. Only whites, 18 years and over, are allowed to vote.

History. First sighted by the Portuguese in 1486, white settlers came in the 17th century when the Dutch East Indies Co. established a trading station. Dutch, German, and Huguenot refugees from France followed, forming the basis for the modern Afrikaners. British settlement started in 1836, and Afrikan farmers (Boers), eager to escape British political pressure, moved N, defeated the Zulus, and formed the Republic of Transvaal (1852) and the Orange Free State (1854). The discovery of gold brought hordes of European immigrants, which in turn led the Boers into an 1899 unsuccessful war against the British (Boer War). In 1910, the two former republics and British colonies of Cape and Natal formed the Union of South Africa. In 1948 apartheid, the doctrine of the separate development of the races, became official policy. The government has approved the eventual formation of ten separate black homelands (bantustans) for the black majority, on only 13% of the land area. All blacks are assigned to one of the bantustans as their official home, and in order to work elsewhere in South Africa they must obtain work permits. Because of this system, many men are separated from their families, which must remain in the bantustans. A 1961 referendum approved withdrawal from the British Commonwealth and the establishment of a republic. The increase in black independent nations in Africa from the 1950s led to pressure upon South Africa to change its racial policies, including international censure. Four of the bantustans —Transkei (1976), Bopthuthatswana (1977), Venda (1979), and Ciskei (1981)—have been given independence by South Africa, although their sovereignty is not recognized by any other country. During 1976 rioting and civil unrest erupted, especially in Soweto, a black township outside Johannesburg, and the government passed increasingly repressive measures. Black majority rule in Zimbabwe (formerly Rhodesia) put increasing pressure on the South African government to moderate its policies. Although some apartheid laws were amended, violence increased in 1985, and world attention focused on South Africa's apartheid policies. By early 1986, pass laws, which restricted the movement of blacks from one area to another, were repealed. The United Nations continued to pressure South Africa to relinquish its disputed control of Namibia, where South African troops waged war against SWAPO, a black nationalist guerrilla group. Nonaggression agreements, signed with Mozambique and Angola in 1984, were broken by South Africa. Cuban troops in Angola refused to leave until South Africa abolished apartheid and recognized Namibia as independent. *See also* Boer War.

PROFILE

Official name: Republic of South Africa
Area: 471,444sq mi (1,222,011sq km)
Population: 28,475,000
Density: 60 per sq mi (23 per sq km)
Chief cities: Pretoria (administrative capital); Capetown (legislative capital); Johannesburg; Durban
Government: Parliamentary democracy
Religion: Dutch Reform (major), 50% of Africans are animist
Language: English and Afrikaans (both official)
Monetary unit: Rand
Gross national product: $48,980,000,000
Per capita income: $1,077
Industries: steel, electric motors, textiles, tires, furniture, plastics, automobile assembly, machine tools, fertilizers, chemicals, petroleum products
Agriculture: corn, sheep, wheat, tobacco, sugar, fruits, peanuts, cattle
Minerals: gold, gem diamonds, antimony, platinum, chrome, copper, uranium, vanadium, vermiculite, manganese, asbestos, coal, iron, lead, zinc
Trading partners: United Kingdom, United States, West Germany, Japan

South African Hake. *See* Stockfish.

South African War (1899–1902). *See* Boer War.

South America, fourth largest continent of the world, entirely in the Western Hemisphere, mostly below the equator. Roughly triangular in shape, it consists of two giant nations, Brazil and Argentina, and eleven smaller ones.

Land. South America's W edge towers above the rest of the continent, which slopes toward the Atlantic Ocean except for the Guiana Highlands (N) and the Brazilian Highlands (central E). The Andes contain the highest peaks of the Americas, with the leader Aconcagua at 22,835ft (6,965m). The driest place in the world is a coastal strip W of the Andes, the Atacama Desert. Major islands are the Falkland, a British crown colony near the continent's S tip, and the Galápagos, a territory of Ecuador 650mi (1,046km) offshore in the Pacific.

Lakes and rivers. Lake Maracaibo in Venezuela is an extension of the Gulf of Venezuela; if classified as a lake, its 5,217sq mi (13,512sq km) make it the largest of South America. Otherwise the largest is Lake Titicaca, on the border between Peru and Bolivia, covering 3,200sq mi (8,288sq km). Lengthy rivers combine to form three major systems that reach the Atlantic. The Amazon ranks, after the Nile, as the second longest river in the world (4,000mi; 6,440km) and largest in the world by volume; flowing S is the Paraguay-Paraná system and NE is the Orinoco.

Climate and vegetation. Except in the mountains and the S, the climate remains generally warm and humid. Much of the N supports tropical rain forest, while lowlands in the extreme N and the central region have a cover of tropical grass. The pampas, S of the Tropic of Capricorn, produce temperate grasslands, but vegetation is scarce far SE of the mountains. Pine and other temperate forests grow along the W coast in the S.

Animal life. Mammals include howler and other monkeys, ocelots, pumas, deer, tapirs, peccaries, and coatis. Particular to the Andes are small members of the camel family: llamas, alpacas, and vicuñas, of which only the vicuñas are not domesticated. Colorful birds include large macaws and toucans and tiny hummingbirds. Condors are in the mountains. Dangerous snakes include bushmasters, anacondas, and boa constrictors; piranha fish are in some of the rivers.

People. Some pure-blood Incas (Quechuas) still remain in the Andes, as do some Mapucho (Araucanians) of Chile. But most Indian groups have become mestizos by mixing with the Portuguese in Brazil and the Spaniards in the rest of the continent. Brazil has many blacks, as do the small countries of the N coast. Although many Germans have migrated to Argentina and some, along with Italians, to Chile, people of Spanish and Portuguese descent remain the two main groups and theirs are the dominant languages. Roman Catholicism is the major religion.

Economy. Agriculture occupies most Indians and many of the mestizos, but the land belongs mainly to people of European descent. Valuable ores come from the mountains and the Atacama Desert, with copper, tin, silver, and gemstones being of importance. Venezuela's Maracaibo region yields petroleum. Most countries remain underdeveloped industrially.

History. About 1100, the Incas became the dominant tribe and for 400 years expanded an empire through the central Andes. After Pedro Alvares Cabral discovered Brazil in 1500, the Portuguese gained control there, but the real conquest of South America came with Francisco Pizarro's conquest of the Incas in 1432–33. For nearly 300 years the intruders held the continent. Brazil gained independence peacefully after

Sorrel tree

John Philip Sousa

Mount Rushmore National Memorial, South Dakota

the Portuguese royal family lived there for a time to escape Napoleon in Europe, and determined generals such as José de San Martín, Simón Bolívar, Antonio José de Sucre, and Bernardo O'Higgins freed much of S, W, and NSouth America in the 1820s. Political assassinations, overthrows, and territorial conflicts kept nations from cooperating with one another. As a result, South American republics failed to become world powers until nearly the second half of the 20th century, after the formation of the United Nations in 1945 and the OAS (Organization of American States) in 1948 gave them a say in international affairs. Chile elected a Marxist government in 1970, the first such duly elected regime in the New World, but a right-wing military junta seized control of the government in 1973. Brazil and, to a lesser extent, Argentina have developed well-established industrial sectors, and Venezuela has become a major oil exporter, but the other countries have developing economies, and during the early 1980s many had inflation rates exceeding 100% per year. Throughout South America, extremes of wealth and poverty exist side by side, leading to unrest and instability and frequently resulting in dictatorships, repressive regimes, and military takeovers, including Argentina (1976) and Bolivia (1980). International attention focused on Argentina in 1982 when it unsuccessfully tried to take the Falkland Islands from Britain. *See also* Falklands War.

PROFILE

Area: 6,880,000sq mi (17,819,200sq km)
Largest nations: Brazil, 3,284,426sq mi (8,506,663 sq km); Argentina, 1,072,156sq mi (2,776,884sq km)
Population: 239,077,000
Density: 35per sq mi (13 per sq km)
Most populous nations: Brazil, 122,879,000; Argentina, 26,740,000; Colombia, 26,122,000
Chief cities: São Paulo, Brazil; Rio de Janeiro, Brazil; Buenos Aires, Argentina
Manufacturing (major products): petroleum products, chemicals, foodstuffs, drugs, textiles, iron and steel, paper
Agriculture (major products): wheat, coffee, corn, grapes, sugar cane, cacao, livestock, bananas, cotton
Minerals (major): petroleum, copper, tin, silver, iron ore, gold, zinc, gemstones

Southampton, port in S England, at head of Southampton Water on Test and Itchen estuaries; Britain's chief passenger port and a major commercial port; seat of University of Southampton (1952). The Pilgrim Fathers embarked from here at start of their voyage (1620). Industries: shipbuilding, engines, oil refining, food products. Pop. 215,400.

South Australia, state in S central Australia, including Kangaroo and several smaller islands; the terrain includes deserts, mountains, salt lakes, swampland; 66% of the population lives in the capital city, Adelaide; location of Whyalla, home of Australia's largest shipyards, and the Murray River valley, whose grapes produce the finest Australian wine. Industries: mining, metal processing, textiles, food processing. Coastline reputedly visited by the Dutch in 1627; first British settlement 1836; became a state of the Commonwealth 1901. Area: 380,070sq mi (984,381sq km). Pop. 1,164,700.

South Bend, city in N Indiana, 135mi (217km) N of Indianapolis, on St Joseph River; seat of St Joseph co; scene of 1679 camp of French explorer Sieur de La-Salle; American Fur Co. post 1820; site of St Joseph County courthouse (1855), now a museum; branch of University of Indiana, Notre Dame University (1842). Industries: automotive parts, paints, plastics, farm ma-

chinery. Named South Bend in 1830 for bend of St Joseph River; inc. 1835, chartered (city) 1865. Pop. (1980) 109,727.

South Carolina, state in the SE United States, on the Atlantic Ocean. It was the first state to secede from the Union before the Civil War.

Land and economy. From the seacoast the land rolls gradually up to the Blue Ridge Mt range in the extreme NW. Many rivers flow SE to the Atlantic, including the Pee Dee, the Santee, and the Edisto. The Savannah River forms the SW boundary. The principal lakes are man-made, providing hydroelectric power and flood control. Fertile soils and a mild climate made South Carolina a productive agricultural region from its earliest days. Forests yield an abundant supply of timber. Manufacturing did not become important until the 20th century; it was widely diversified after WWII. The ocean beaches, fine public gardens, and the old-world charm of Charleston attract a lucrative tourist business.

People. The original English settlers were followed by the French Huguenots, Germans, and Swiss. Blacks were brought in to work the plantations, and for many years they were a majority of the population. There are no significant groups of foreign-born residents. About 47% of the people live in urban areas.

Education. There are nearly 50 institutions of higher education.

History. Spaniards and French had short-lived settlements on the coast in the 16th century, but permanent occupation did not begin until the English came a century later. Charles II of Great Britain granted the land to eight proprietors in 1663, and the first settlers arrived in 1670. Charleston (then known as Charles Town) was founded in 1680. Pioneers pushed inland, and in 1729 South Carolina became a royal colony. A plantation society arose; rice, indigo, and cotton were major crops. In the Revolution, the battles of Camden, Kings Mountain, Cowpens, and Eutaw Springs were fought in the area. After joining the Union, South Carolina was a strong defender of states' rights and in 1832 took the extreme step of passing the Order of Nullification, declaring federal tariffs to be null and void in the state. A compromise tariff law settled the dispute, but over the slavery question the state stood firm and was a leader in forming the Confederacy. The first shots of the Civil War were fired on Fort Sumter in Charleston harbor on April 12, 1861. In 1865, a Union army devastated the state and burned Columbia, the capital. Recovery from the catastrophe was long and difficult. Development of the textile industry, beginning during the 1880s, aided by the movement of many mills from Northern states, helped to stabilize the economy. During the 20th century industry became more diversified and now dominates the economy.

PROFILE

Admitted to Union: May 23, 1788; 8th of the 13 original states to ratify the US Constitution
US Congressmen: Senate, 2; House of Representatives, 6
Population: 3,119,208 (1980); rank, 24th
Capital: Columbia, 99,296 (1980)
Chief cities: Columbia; Charleston, 69,510; Greenville, 58,242; Spartanburg, 43,968
State legislature: Senate, 46; House of Representatives, 124
Area: 31,055sq mi (80,432sq km); rank, 40th
Elevation: Highest, 3,560ft (1,086m), Sassafras Mt; lowest, sea level
Industries (major products): textiles, lumber, pulp and paper, chemicals, apparel, machinery
Agriculture (major products): tobacco, cotton, peaches, peanuts, poultry

Minerals(major): clay, cement, limestone, vermiculite
State nickname: Palmetto State
State mottoes: Dum Spiro, Spero (While I breathe, I hope) and Animis opibusque parati (Prepared in soul and resources)
State bird: Carolina wren
State flower: Carolina jessamine
State tree: palmetto

South China Sea, W branch of Pacific Ocean; surrounded by SE China, Indochina, Malay Peninsula, Borneo, Philippines, Taiwan; Formosa Strait connects it to East China Sea: Its chief arms are the Gulf of Tonkin and Gulf of Siam; the Si, Red, Mekong, and Chao Phraya rivers flow into it. Area: approx. 1,000,000sq mi (2,590,000sq km). Depth (max.): 18,000ft (5,490m).

South Dakota, state in the N central United States, in the Plains region.

Land and economy. The land rises gradually from E to W. In the SW are the Badlands, an area of broken terrain, and the Black Hills, a rugged forested region, where the rocky front of Mt Rushmore presents gigantic sculptured portraits of presidents Washington, Jefferson, Lincoln, and Theodore Roosevelt. The Missouri River, flowing from N to S, cuts the state down the middle. Four huge dams have created lakes that supply irrigation and hydroelectric power and control flooding. Fertile farmlands lie generally E of the river; to the W are grasslands for grazing. Rich mineral deposits are found in the Black Hills. Manufacturing is concentrated in the population centers of the E.

People. Settlement did not begin until the 19th century when pioneers from Minnesota, Wisconsin, Illinois, and Iowa occupied the farming country. Some came from Canada and numbers from Sweden, Norway, Germany, the Netherlands, and Russia. After WWI, the influx slowed. A small number of Indians live on reservations. About 45% of the population lives in urban areas.

Education. There are 16 institutions of higher education.

History. French trappers in the 1740s claimed the land for France, from which the United States acquired it in the Louisiana Purchase of 1803. The Lewis and Clark Expedition explored it 1804–05. Fur traders and army garrisons were the only inhabitants until the late 1850s when settlements were made at Sioux Falls, Yankton, and Vermillion. Dakota Territory, which included the present states of North and South Dakota, was formed 1861. Discovery of gold in the Black Hills in 1874 caused a population growth that led to statehood. The last armed conflict between the US Army and the Indians took place at Wounded Knee on Dec. 29, 1890. The state suffered a serious drought during the Depression of the 1930s. During the 1960s new defense installations boosted the economy. In 1973, Wounded Knee was once again the scene of confrontation between Indians and the government, when 200 armed Sioux took over the site.

PROFILE

Admitted to Union: Nov. 2, 1889, the same day as North Dakota; rank, 39th or 40th
US Congressmen: Senate, 2; House of Representatives, 2
Population: 690,178 (1980); rank 45th
Capital: Pierre, 11,973 (1980)
Chief cities: Sioux Falls, 81,343; Rapid City, 46,492; Aberdeen, 25,956
State legislature: Senate, 35; House of Representatives, 70
Area: 77,047sq mi (199,552sq km); rank, 16th

Elevation: Highest, 7,242ft (2,209m), Harney Peak; lowest, 962ft (293m), Big Stone Lake
Industries (major products): processed foods, lumber, wood products, farm equipment
Agriculture (major products): sheep, cattle, hogs, rye, wheat
Minerals (major): gold, beryllium, silver, petroleum, uranium
State nicknames: Coyote State, Sunshine State
State motto: Under God, the People Rule
State bird: ring-necked pheasant
State flower: American pasque
State tree: Black Hills spruce

Southeast Asia, region of Asia, bounded by India (W), China (N), and the Pacific Ocean (E); includes Burma, Thailand, Malaysia, Cambodia, Laos, Vietnam, Philippines, Singapore, and Indonesia. Area: approx. 1,740,000sq mi (4,506,600sq km). *See also* individual countries.

Southern Ape. *See* Australopithecus.

Southern Cross. *See* Crux.

Southern Crown Constellation. *See* Corona Australis.

Southey, Robert (1774–1843), English poet and biographer. He was related to Samuel Taylor Coleridge by marriage. His long epic poems are *Thalaba the Destroyer* (1801), *Madoc* (1805), *The Curse of Kehama* (1810), and *Roderick the Last of the Goths* (1821). He also wrote numerous biographies, including *The Life of Nelson* (1813), and *History of the Peninsular War* (1823–32). He was made poet laureate in 1813.

Southfield, city in SE Michigan, 15mi (24km) NW of Detroit; site of Duns Scotus College (1930) and Lawrence Institute of Technology (1932). Industries: precision tools, sporting goods. Inc. 1958. Pop. (1980) 75,568.

South Gate, city in S California, 7mi (11km) SSE of Los Angeles. Industries: automobiles, chemicals, furniture, glass. Inc. 1923. Pop. (1980) 66,784.

South Island, largest island of New Zealand, SW of North Island, and NE of Stewart Island. Southern Alps mountain range extends length of island, creating many rivers, lakes, and fjords. Principal cities are Christchurch, Dunedin, and Invercargill. Industries: dairying, herding, grain, tourism. Highest peak is Mt Cook, 12,349ft (3,766m). Area: 58,093sq mi (150,461sq km). Pop. 860,990.

South Platte River, river in Colorado and Nebraska; rises at the confluence of many streams in the Rocky Mts, central Colo.; flows SE then NE across Nebraska to join the North Platte River; in SW central Neb. to form the Platte River; used for irrigation and hydroelectricity. Length: 450mi (725km).

South Saskatchewan, river in SW Canada; rises in the Rocky Mts; with its tributary, Bow River, it is the longest branch of the Nelson River, 1,205mi (1,940km).

South Sea Bubble, speculation in the shares of the English South Sea Company, ending in financial disaster (1720). This company, founded by Robert Harley (1711), was formed on the assumption of an eventual British trading monopoly in the Pacific Ocean and South America. Although this monopoly failed to materialize, the government, to fund the national debt, encouraged public confidence in the company, persuading investors to exchange state annuities for its stock. Many were ruined, the whole system of chartered companies was discredited, and the House of Commons' inquiry into the scandal revealed corruption and resulted in the chancellor of the exchequer's expulsion.

South West Africa. *See* Namibia.

Soutine, Chaim (1894–1943), French painter. He began to make a reputation with his distorted, nightmarish painting in the 1920s. Most sensational of his pictures are those of blood-spattered meat.

Soviet ("council"), basic political unit in the USSR according to the 1936 constitution. First established after the 1905 revolution, and revived in 1917 as soviets of workers' and soldiers' deputies, they soon came under Bolshevik influence. The Petrograd soviet was instrumental in the overthrow of the Provisional Government in November 1917.

Soviet Union. *See* Union of Soviet Socialist Republics.

Soybean, hairy, annual plant native to China and Japan. It has oval, three-part leaves and small white or purplish flowers. Grown for food, forage, green manure, and oil, its seed is an important protein source. Height: to 6ft (1.8m). Family Leguminosae; species *Glycine soja.*

Soyuz Flights, Soviet manned orbital missions in Soyuz spacecraft, which are used as small, experimental space stations as well as ferry craft to carry crew and supplies between Earth and the larger Salyut-type of space station. The first manned Soyuz mission, in April 1967, ended in tragedy when the reentry portion of the craft crashed on landing, killing the pilot. The first successful linkup of two Soyuz craft took place in 1969. The program has experienced both successes and notable failures and disasters. In 1981 Soviet officials announced the end of the Soyuz series. However, experiments continued with the slightly larger Soyuz-T series.

Spaak, Paul-Henri (1899–1972), Belgian and international statesman. An advocate of European unity, he was premier of Belgium (1938–39; 1946; 1947–49), and foreign minister (1936–38; 1939–45; 1947–49; 1954–57; 1961–66). First president of the UN General Assembly (1946); secretary general of NATO (1957–61).

Space Flight, flight of manned or unmanned vehicles beyond Earth's atmosphere. Dreamed of by ancient Greeks and by Renaissance scientists such as Galileo, Kepler, and Huyghens, it became a reality on Oct. 4, 1957, with the launching of Sputnik 1. Major milestones: first space probe (Explorer 1, discoverer of Van Allen radiation belts, launched Jan. 31, 1958); first lunar probe (Luna 2, Sept. 12, 1959); first manned flight (Yuri Gagarin, April 12, 1961); first close-up pictures of Mars (Mariner 4, 1965); first manned lunar landing (Neil Armstrong, July 20, 1969); first pictures from surface of another planet (Venera 9, Oct. 22, 1975); first study of another planet's atmosphere and weather conditions on a global scale (Pioneer Venus I, launched May 20, 1978); longest space flight, 185 days (Valery Ryumin and Leonid Popov, *Salyut 6* space station, April 10–Oct. 11, 1980), US space shuttle program, 24 missions (Nov. 1982–Jan. 1986), when *Challenger's* explosion temporarily suspended the program.

Space Probe, craft or mission designed to explore regions above one Earth radius (about 4,000mi, or 6,400km) altitude. The first US space probe was Explorer I, launched Jan. 31, 1958; it discovered the inner Van Allen radiation belt. The first lunar probe was Luna 2, launched Sept. 12, 1959. The first planetary probe was Mariner 2, launched Aug. 27, 1962, which flew by Venus. Pioneers 10 and 11 photographed Venus (Oct. 22, 1975); the Viking lander tested the Martian surface for life (July 20, 1976). New rings and moons were discovered on Saturn (Pioneer 11, Sept. 1, 1979) and Jupiter was found to have a ring and an additional moon (Voyager 2, July 1979).

Space Shuttle, reusable rocket and aerodynamic vehicle carrying men and supplies between Earth and a space station. It consists of a delta-winged, reusable orbiter (110ft, 34m long; 79ft, 24m wing-span) with a 7-person capacity. Total weight is 4,500,000lb (2,000,000kg); payload is 65,000lbs (29,500kg). Uses include launching new satellites and planetary probes, scientific observation, and technological applications. The orbiter is launched by a system of 3 rockets—2 solid-propellant, recoverable boosters, and a large, disposable liquid H and O_2 rocket. The orbiter uses small rockets to leave orbit and then descends and lands without power at long-runway facilities. NASA began development of the space shuttle in 1972; the 1st air test was in 1977 and the 1st orbital flight in 1981. The US space shuttle program had completed 24 flights by 1986, when the shuttle *Challenger,* 74 seconds into its 10th flight on January 28, 1986, exploded due to a faulty fuel booster rocket and icy weather conditions, killing all 7 astronauts, including Christa McAuliffe, the first schoolteacher in space. The US space shuttle program was temporarily suspended.

Space Station, orbiting laboratory in space where men can carry out construction and maintenance of spacecraft and scientific and medical experiments. Early stations included the Russian Soyuz (1971) and the US Skylab (1975). The space station concept was first described by Konstantin Tsiolkovsky in 1895. A basic structure envisioned for the 1990s accommodates 6–12 people, is serviced by a space shuttle, and remains in orbit for up to 10 years. *See also* Skylab; Space Shuttle.

Space-Time, treatment, in relativity theory, of the three space dimensions and the dimension of time as forming a four-dimensional space. Hermann Minkowski devised (1907) a presentation of relativity theory by extending three-dimensional geometry to four dimensions. A line drawn in this space represents the whole history of a particle as its path both in space and time (its world line). *See also* Relativity Theory.

Spadefoot Toad, tailless amphibian with a horny space on the inside of each hind foot. They are squat and smooth-skinned. Genus *Scaphiopus* is found from Canada to Mexico and genus *Pelobates* is found in S Europe and N Africa. Family Pelobatidae.

Spain, independent nation in SW Europe, on the Iberian peninsula. After decades of dictatorical rule by Francisco Franco, Spain entered a new era when King Juan Carlos I took the throne in 1975, and subsequently instituted parliamentary democracy.

Land and economy. Occupying the major portion of the Iberian peninsula in SW Europe, it is bordered N by France and the Atlantic Ocean; E and S by the Mediterranean, W by Portugal and the Atlantic. Spain also includes the Balearic and Canary islands. The Pyrenees Mts, in which the tiny republic of Andorra is located, form a natural barrier between France and Spain. Except for the Andalusian lowlands, the land mass rises from a narrow coastal plain. The center of the country, a high plateau, is divided by ranges and rivers. Wheat growing and sheep raising are the chief products of this arid plateau, which has only a few fertile valleys. Agriculture employs about 20% of the labor force; output suffers from lack of irrigation and mechanization, poor soil, and erosion. Spain is one of Europe's leading producers of automobiles, and tourism is also important to the economy. The country suffers from a perennial balance of payments deficit.

People. The people are descendants of the succeeding waves of N African and European peoples who invaded and colonized Spain. The most recognizable minority are the Basques, whose unique language is not related to any other tongue, but the other regions —Galicia, Catalonia, Valencia, and Aragon—each speak their own dialect of Spanish and also have strong regional identities. Under Francisco Franco, Roman Catholicism was reinstated as the official religion, although a 1966 organic law guarantees freedom of worship. Over 99% of the population is Roman Catholic. Literacy is 97%. Primary education is compulsory and free.

Government. According to the constitution of 1978, Spain is a constitutional monarchy, with the king serving as head of state. Executive authority is vested in the prime minister, who leads the majority party or coalition in the popularly-elected Cortes, the bicarneral legislature.

History. Its strategic geographical position made Spain a center of invasion and resistance for centuries before it became unified. Phoenicians, Greeks, Carthaginians, and Moors came from the sea and Celts came from the continent. A major influence was the Roman invasion in the 2nd century BC; their language, religion, and law prevailed until the Moors invaded from North Africa in 711 and remained for 700 years. The nation was unified by Isabella and Ferdinand in 1492, the year in which Christopher Columbus discovered the New World. Spain became a major power in the 16th century until its Armada was defeated by England in 1588. Spain's decline in the subsequent centuries invited intervention by other powers, notably France; during the French revolutionary wars Spain was a major battleground. The country also lost its colonies in the Americas, its hold over the Low Countries, and much of its influence in Italy. Efforts to establish a more liberal government were rejected by Ferdinand VII, who returned from exile in 1814. Quarrels over succession to the throne provoked the Carlist Wars in the 19th century. In the Spanish-American War (1898), Spain lost the last of its empire in the Americas and the Pacific. Domestic problems led to the dictatorship in 1923 of Primo de Rivera, who was forced out in 1930. A republic was est. in 1931 and lasted until 1936. Uncompromised disputes between the liberals, the church, landowners, and the working class brought unchecked violence and the 1936–39 Civil War. Following the nationalist victory, Gen. Francisco Franco ruled the devastated nation. His military dictatorship lasted until his death in 1975 when he was succeeded by Prince Juan Carlos, who became king. In 1976 gradual political liberalization began, and with free general elections in 1977, parliamentary democracy was begun and formalized by the new constitution of 1978. In 1979 the Cortes approved provisional limited autonomy for Spain's regions, and in 1980 regional parliaments were elected in Catalonia and the Basque region. The Basque separatist party, however, continued its terrorist activities. Spain's new government began forging closer ties with the West, joining NATO in 1982 and the European Economic Community (EEC) in 1986. The democratic government successfully weathered an attempted military coup in 1981. Prince Felipe was sworn in as heir apparent to the throne in 1986. *See also* Carlists; Civil War, Spanish.

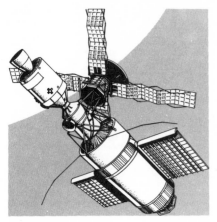

Space station

Spain

Sparrow hawk

PROFILE

Official name: Kingdom of Spain
Area: 194,897sq mi (504,783sq km)
Population: 37,538,262
Density: 193per sq mi (74per sq km)
Chief cities: Madrid (capital); Barcelona; Valencia
Government: Constitutional monarchy
Religion: Roman Catholic (official)
Language: Spanish (official), Catalan, and Basque
Monetary unit: Peseta
Gross national product: $162,330,000,000
Per capita income: $1,850
Industries: machinery, textiles, wine, shoes, paper, automobiles, cork, cement, iron and steel, chemicals, ships, processed foods
Agriculture: wheat, rye, barley, oats, fish, olives, grapes, citrus fruits, onions, almonds, esparto, flax, hemp, tobacco, cotton, rice, sheep
Minerals: lead, iron, copper, zinc, coal, cobalt, mercury, silver, sulfur, phosphates, uranium
Trading partners (major): United States, European Economic Community, Saudi Arabia

Spaniel, sporting dog used to locate and flush game, drop for the hunter's shot, and sometimes retrieve on command. Mentioned as early as 1368, it was called setting spaniel before the gun. Its job then was to locate game and sit while the hunter threw a net over it. Land spaniels include the cocker and toy. Water spaniels are usually retrievers.

Spanish, major world language, spoken in Spain, most of South America (but not in Brazil or Guyana), all of Central America, Mexico, Cuba, the Dominican Republic, Puerto Rico, and a number of other countries. Its total number of speakers is more than 200,000,000. Spanish is a Romance language but its vocabulary contains a number of words of Arabic origin, the result of Spain's being under Moorish domination for many centuries.

Spanish-American War (1898), conflict between Spain and the United States, waged in the Philippines and Cuba. The destruction of the battleship *Maine* in Havana harbor (February 1898) was the immediate cause of US entry; long-range causes included the desire to protect US investments in Cuba and the prevailing climate of jingoism. Beginning in April, the war between Spain and the United States essentially involved two naval engagements and one encounter on land. Adm. George Dewey annihilated the Spanish fleet in Manila Bay (May); Col. Teddy Roosevelt's Rough Riders helped achieve the capture of the heights above the port of Santiago de Cuba and placed the Spanish fleet under bombardment, precipitating the decisive naval battle of Santiago, which ended the war. The terms of the Treaty of Paris (ratified 1899) made Cuba independent; Puerto Rico, Guam, and the Philippines were ceded to the United States, which paid $20,000,000 to Spain.

Spanish Bayonet, erect-stemmed plant native to S United States, Mexico, and West Indies. It has long, pointed leaves and large white or purple flowers. Height: 10–25ft (3–7.6m). Family Agavaceae; species *Yucca aloifolia*.

Spanish Inquisition, tribunal founded in 1478 by Ferdinand II and Isabella I to discover and punish heretics in Spain. It was firmly under royal control, as opposed to the medieval Inquisition, which, regardless of the country in which it operated, was always under the control of the Roman Catholic Church. The original purpose of the Spanish Inquisition was to punish those converted Jews and Muslims who were insincere in their Christian beliefs. Under the direction of Tomás de Torquemada, however, it soon expanded its jurisdiction to include questioning the beliefs of all Christians (both St Theresa of Ávila and St Ignatius of Loyola were brought before the Inquisition). Its excesses are legendary; the auto-da-fé, the ceremony preceding the execution of a heretic, became symbolic of these excesses. The property of condemned heretics was confiscated, creating suspicion of the motives of the inquisitors. At its height, the Spanish Inquisition was established in all of the Spanish colonies, although it never achieved the power there that it did in Spain itself. It was finally abolished in 1834. *See also* Inquisition; Torquemada, Tomás de.

Spanish Literature. Prior to the 15th century Catalan and Galician flourished as literary languages along with Castilian. One of the major early works is the epic poem *Cantar de Mío Cid* (c. 1200). French and Italian influence predominated until the 16th century when a truly Spanish literature emerged. The late 16th century and the 17th century are known as the Golden Age with the work of Miguel de Cervantes, Luis de Góngora, Lope de Vega, and Calderón dominating the era. The 18th century witnessed a decline in Spanish writings. *Costumbrismo,* sketches of Spanish life and customs, flourished in the 19th century, and was incorporated into the realistic novels of Benito Pérez Galdós, Armando Palacio Valdés, and others. In the early 20th century the writers of the Generation of '98 reexamined Spanish traditions and revitalized Spanish culture. Major figures of this group included Pío Baroja y Nessi, Miguel de Unamuno, and Azorín (Jose Martínez Ruiz). Probably the most important Spanish writer of the 20th century was Federico García Lorca. Poet Vincente Aleixandre was awarded the Nobel Prize for literature in 1977.

Spanish Main, term used to refer to the West Indies and the Caribbean coast of Panama, Colombia, and Venezuela during this area's exploration and development.

Spanish Missions, group of 21 Franciscan missions, extending along the California coast; established to convert Indians to Christianity; first built in San Diego (1769) and finished in Sonoma (1823).

Spanish Moss, common name for an epiphytic herbaceous plant, not a true moss. Grown in tropical and subtropical American forests, especially on the live oak of SE United States, the loose gray clumps hang from tree branches. It is used as imitation horsehair stuffing and for insulation. Family Bromeliaceae; species *Tillandsia usneoides*.

Spanish Sahara, former name of Western Sahara. *See* Western Sahara.

Spanish Succession, War of the (1701–14), dynastic struggle for the throne of Spain. When it became apparent that Charles II of Spain would die childless, three pretenders—all with dynastic ties to the Spanish royal family—arose: Louis XIV of France; the elector of Bavaria, Joseph Ferdinand; and Holy Roman Emperor Leopold I. England and Holland, fearing both French and Austrian influence in Spain, supported Joseph Ferdinand. In 1698, after lengthy negotiations and a complicated agreement, all sides agreed that Joseph Ferdinand should succeed. His sudden death the following year, however, caused the agreement to disintegrate.

While new negotiations were going on, the dying Charles II named Philip of Anjou, grandson of Louis XIV, as his heir. When he took the throne as Philip V in 1701, most of Europe was plunged into war. Supporting France were Spain, Portugal, Bavaria, and Savoy.

The Allies consisted of the imperial forces, England, Holland, and most of the German states. The duke of Marlborough, Prince Eugene of Savoy, commander of the imperial forces, and Louis of Baden were the chief commanders of the Allied forces; the dukes of Vendôme and Villars and the count of Tallard were the French commanders. The war dragged on for a decade and, despite impressive Allied victories at Blenheim, Malplaquet, Ramillies, and in Bavaria, no decisive defeat of the French forces resulted. In 1713, France, Britain, and Holland signed the Treaty of Utrecht, but the Holy Roman emperor continued the war for another year. Finally, in 1714 the war was brought to a close with the Peace of Utrecht. Philip V remained on a badly weakened Spanish throne. *See also* Utrecht, Peace of.

Spanish Town, town in SE central Jamaica, West Indies; large agricultural processing and manufacturing center, on Cobre River. The former capital of Jamaica (1535–1872) it is site of old colonial buildings around central square: St Catherine cathedral (1655), Rodney Memorial, House of Assembly. Industries: sugar milling, rum distilling, food processing. Founded c. 1523. Pop. 14,706.

Spark, Muriel (Sarah) (1918–), Scottish novelist. She wrote short stories, plays, verse, and criticism. Her novels include *Memento Mori* (1959), *The Prime of Miss Jean Brodie* (1961), later made into a play and a film, *The Abbess of Crewe* (1974), *The Takeover* (1976), *Territorial Rights* (1979), *Loitering with Intent* (1981), and *The Only Problem* (1984). Her short stories are collected in *The Stories of Muriel Spark* (1985).

Spark Plug, Engine, in an internal combustion engine, a device carrying two electrodes separated by an air gap, across which electric current from the ignition discharges, forming a spark. This ignites the fuel.

Sparrow, two groups of widely distributed seed-eating birds that frequent grasslands and open wooded areas. They have stout, cone-shaped bills; brownish plumage, often streaked with gray; lighter underparts; and medium-sized tails. Old World sparrows, including the house sparrow and tree sparrow, are weaverbirds and nest in rock crevices or holes in trees or buildings, laying speckled white eggs (4–9); Family Ploceidae. New World sparrows, including the song sparrow and field sparrow, are finches and build cup-shaped nests in trees or bushes for white or pale blue eggs (2–3); family Fringillidae. Length: about 6in (15.5cm).

Sparrow Hawk, bird of prey. The American sparrow hawk *(Falco sparverius)*, often called the American kestrel, is reddish-brown and eats small animals; length: to 12in (30cm). The slightly larger European sparrow hawk *(Accipter nisus)* feeds on birds.

Sparta (Spárti), town in SE Peloponnesus, S Greece, on Eurotas River; capital of Laconia department. Just S are ruins of ancient Sparta, a Greek city-state founded by the Dorians c. 900 BC in the province of Laconia. The ancient city-state of three classes: the Spartiates (ruling class), perioeci (free inhabitants with no political power), and helots (slaves). After its conquest of Messenia (c. 743–724 BC), Sparta flourished as an economic and cultural center. Faced with a massive helot revolt in 7th century BC, Sparta changed into an armed camp with a primitive socio-militaristic government ruled by two kings and later by the gerouisa and ephors; in c. 500 BC the Peloponnesian League was formed with Sparta as the most powerful member. After the Persian Wars (500–449 BC), Athens began to rival Sparta, leading to the Peloponnesian War (431–

404 BC), which ended in total defeat of Athens. Sparta dominated the Peloponnesus until 371 BC, when it was defeated by Thebes at Leucta, and Messenia was freed. A revival of prosperity occurred under the Romans; Sparta was destroyed by Goths in 395 AD. The modern town was built in 1834. Industries: citrus fruits, olive oil. Pop. 11,981.

Spartacus (died 71 BC), Thracian gladiator in Rome who led a slave revolt known as the Third Servile War or Gladiators' War. He won victories at Capua (73) and in S Italy, defeating five Roman armies and entering Cisalpine Gaul. His soldiers devastated the land and moved south toward Sicily where they were eventually defeated by Crassus, who, with Pompey's aid, crucified some 6,000 of the rebels. Spartacus died in battle, his army holding 3,000 Roman prisoners unharmed.

Sparticists, German political party of the radical left that broke away from the Social Democrats during World War I. Led by Karl Liebknecht and Rosa Luxemburg, the Sparticists refused to sustain the war effort and rejected participation in the post-Versailles republican government. The Sparticists fomented a number of uprisings, including one in Berlin in 1919 that resulted in thousands of casualties. Volunteer armies of ex-servicemen were employed to suppress the movement.

Spathiphyllum, flowering plant native to Colombia, with shiny, lance-shaped leaves pointed at the tips. It has blooms resembling calla lilies. A popular house plant, it is a rapid grower. Family Araceae; species *Spathiphyllum clevelandii.*

Speaker of the House, presiding officer in the US House of Representatives. He is elected from the majority party by the House. His powers include the recognition of members for debate, the appointment of select and conference committees, the referral of bills to committees, and the signing of documents on behalf of the House. The speaker follows the vice president in presidential succession.

Spearfish, marine billfish popular as a sport fish. Silvery-blue with long bill, its smaller dorsal fin distinguishes it from sailfish. Length: 6ft (183cm); weight: 60lb (27kg). Species include Pacific shortbill *Tetrapturus angustirostris* and W Atlantic *T. pfleugeri.* Family Istiophoridae.

Spearmint, common name of *Mentha spicata,* or *M. viridis,* a hardy perennial herb of the mint family with leaves used for flavoring, especially in vinegar, jelly, and beverages. Oil distilled from spearmint is used as a medicine. Its flowers are pale blue and grow in spikes.

Species, group of physically and genetically similar individuals that interbreed under natural conditions. Over 300,000 plant species and more than 1,000,000 animal species have been identified and 15–20,000 new ones are identified every year. Over half the living species are insects and one-third of these are beetles.

Specific Gravity, the ratio of the density of a substance to the density of water. Thus, the specific gravity of gold is 13.2; that is, it is about 13 times heavier than an equal volume of water.

Specific Heat, the heat energy necessary to raise the temperature of a given amount of some substance by one degree. Bodies with high specific heat, such as water, require much more heat energy to raise their temperature than bodies of low specific heat. Thus oceans exert a moderating influence on the Earth's climate by absorbing excess heat from the land during the day and returning it at night.

Spectacled Bear, small black bear that lives in the Andes. It has white, spectaclelike rings around its eyes and is the only bear in the Southern Hemisphere. Species *Tremarctos ornatus.*

Spectator (1711–12; 1714), English periodical edited and largely written by Richard Steele and Joseph Addison, a successor to the *Tatler.*

Spectrograph, instrument for producing and recording a spectrum. Light from an incandescent source is formed into a parallel beam in the instrument, falls onto a prism or diffraction grating, and is split into its component wavelengths by dispersion. This emission spectrum is then focused onto a photographic plate. To record an absorption spectrum, light from a source emitting a continuous spectrum is passed through the absorbing medium before entering the instrument. X-ray, ultraviolet, and infrared spectra can also be investigated with suitable dispersing and recording media.

Spectrum, distribution of the wavelength or frequency components of a wave, as in a visible spectrum which displays rainbow colors ranging from red to violet. It is characteristic of the source of the radiation and is produced by dispersion in a prism or diffraction grating. An emission spectrum, consisting of bright regions on a dark background, is produced when a source is strongly heated or is bombarded by electrons, etc. The positions and brightness of the regions indicate the frequencies present and their intensities. An absorption spectrum, consisting of dark regions on a bright background, is produced when a continuous range of frequencies passes through a medium that absorbs certain frequencies. In a line spectrum, as produced by gas atoms, the light or dark regions are narrow lines. Molecules produce band spectra with wider light or dark bands.

Speech, verbal or vocal expression of ideas and feelings, specifically intended to convey meaning. Speech is learned by listening and imitating, by assimilating systematic language patterns. The infant's babbling is the first step toward learning to speak; his progress thereafter depends on the maturing of his speech organs, his ability to hear, his sex, intelligence, and his environment (stimulation, attentive parents, absence of bilingualism, reinforcement of vocalization).

Speed, rate of motion. *See* Velocity.

Speedwell. *See* Veronica.

Speer, Albert (1905–81), German architect and Nazi official, a close associate of Adolf Hitler. Speer drew up the plans for Germany's super-highways and for the stadium at Nuremberg. By 1943 his authority over the entire war economy was second only to that of Hermann Goering. Speer was tried in 1946 by the international war crimes tribunal and sentenced to 20 years in Spandau prison. His memoirs, *Inside the Third Reich* (1970), became a best-seller; *Spandau* (1976) is his prison diary. *Infiltration,* a history, was published in 1981.

Speke, John Hanning (1827–1864), British soldier and explorer of Africa. He served in India and after several African expeditions with Sir Richard Burton discovered Lake Victoria, which he proved to be a source of the Nile.

Speleology, the scientific study of caves and cave systems. Exploration and description of the various features of caves are the main object. Included, too, are the hydrological and geological studies concerned with the rate of formation of stalagmites and stalactites and the influence of groundwater conditions on cave formation. A special aspect is the study of the unusual animals that are found in caves.

Spemann, Hans (1869–1941), German zoologist and comparative anatomist. He was awarded the 1935 Nobel Prize in physiology or medicine for his discovery of the organizer effect in embryonic development.

Spender, Stephen (Harold) (1909–), English poet. A prominent poet of the 1930s, his autobiography *World Within World* (1951) is an important account of that period. He served in the Spanish Civil War and was briefly a member of the Communist party. His poetry is often purely subjective and lyrical.

Spengler, Oswald (1880–1936), German philosopher and historian. He expounded a cyclic theory of civilization that quickly established his reputation as a scholar. His *Decline of the West; Outlines of a Morphology of World History* (2 vols., 1918–22) proposed that Western culture was in a period of decline, having passed its creative zenith. Spengler felt that the state needed to have absolute power to reverse this process. After Hitler came into power (1933), however, he went into isolation, since he did not agree with the Nazi belief in Aryan supremacy.

Spenser, Edmund (1552?–99), English poet, b. London. Major works include *The Faerie Queene* (1589, 1596); *The Shepheardes Calender* (1579); elegies, such as *Astrophel* (1586, on Sir Philip Sidney); *Colin Clouts Come Home Againe* (1595), and *Epithalamion* (1595, celebrating his marriage). In 1580 he settled as a colonist in Ireland. He died in distress in London after an Irish uprising had destroyed his home, Kilcolman Castle, and a third part of *The Faerie Queene. See also* Spenserian Stanza.

Spenserian Stanza, poetic form, consisting of nine lines: eight five-foot iambic lines followed by one six-foot iambic line, or alexandrine. It was named after the 16th-century English poet Edmund Spenser, who first used this form in his *The Faerie Queene.* It has been called the stateliest of English measures. It was used in Lord Byron's *Childe Harold's Pilgrimage,* Percy Bysshe Shelley's *Adonais,* and John Keats' *The Eve of St Agnes.*

Spermatozoon, or sperm, male gamete, its function is to fertilize the female ovum. Small and mobile, it consists of a head containing nucleus and chromosomes; midpiece containing mitochondria (energy sources); and flagellum for mobility.

Spermicides. *See* Contraceptives.

Sperm Whale, largest of the toothed whales. Distinguished by its huge, squarish head with an undershot jaw, it feeds chiefly on squid and cuttlefish, which it hunts in all oceans. Species *Physeter catodon. See also* Whale.

Sphere, solid geometric figure formed by the locus in space of points equidistant from a given point (the center); surface generated by rotation of a circle about a diameter. The distance from the center to the surface is the radius *(r).* The volume is $4/3\pi r^3$ and the surface area is $4\pi r^2$.

Spherical Triangle, triangle formed by the intersection, on the surface of a sphere, of arcs of three great circles. The sides of spherical triangles are measured in terms of the angles that these arcs subtend at the sphere's center. Spherical trigonometry, the branch of geometry concerned with the properties of such triangles, is used in navigation.

Spherical Trigonometry, branch of mathematics that deals with the sides, angles, and areas of spherical triangles, that is, portions of the surface of a sphere bounded by three arcs or great circles. *See also* Trigonometry.

Sphygmomanometer, a device for measuring arterial blood pressure.

Spica, or **Alpha Virginis,** bluish-white star in the constellation Virgo. It is a spectroscopic binary; the main star has a fainter companion of the 3rd magnitude. Characteristics: apparent mag. .98; absolute mag. −3.2; spectral type B1; distance 220 light-years.

Spice Islands, group of small islands within the Moluccas islands in Indonesia. Sparsely populated, they were the center of early spice harvesting. *See also* Moluccas.

Spider, land arthropod found worldwide. They have an unsegmented abdomen, attached to the cephalothorax by a slender stalk; eight eyes; and pairs of spinnerets on the abdomen to spin silk for egg cases and webs. Though their prey is killed by a poison injected by chelicerate jaws, only a few are poisonous to humans. Length: 0.1–3.5in (2.5–89mm). Order Araneae; class Arachnida. *See also* Arachnida.

Spider Crab, marine crab of the Atlantic and Pacific. It has a spiny, sac-shaped carapace that is pointed in front and long, thin legs. Japanese spider crab *(Macrocheira kaempferi)* is 10ft (3m) across. There are 600 species. Family Majidae. *See also* Crab; Crustacean.

Spider Mite. *See* Red Spider.

Spider Monkey, medium-sized monkey found from S Mexico to SE Brazil. They have long, spidery legs, a fully prehensile tail, and are agile tree dwellers, using the tail as a fifth hand. They are day-active and eat fruits and nuts. Genera *Ateles* and *Brachyteles. See also* Monkey.

Spider Plant, house plant native to S Africa with green or green and white arching grasslike leaves. Plantlets and tiny flowers grow on long stems from the plant base. Care: bright indirect light, moist soil (equal parts loam, peat moss, sand). Propagation is by plantlets or root division. Height: to 18in (46cm). Species *Chlorophytum comosum.*

Spiderwort, any of a genus *(Tradescantia)* of New World perennial plants having long, keeled, grasslike leaves and blue, rosy-purple, or white flowers in flat-topped clusters. Family Commelinaceae.

Spin, Nuclear, intrinsic angular momentum of an atomic nucleus, which can be thought of as resulting from rotation about an axis. It is a quantized quantity, assuming certain discrete values. The spin quantum number, from which these are derived, can either be zero, a half integer (for protons and electrons), or an integer (for mesons).

Spina Bifida, a congenital cleft of the vertebral column. It is a result of abnormal development of the neural tube and its linings during early embryonic life.

Speleology: Mammoth Cave, Ky.

Spitsbergen

Spoonbill

Spinach, herbaceous annual plant widely cultivated in areas with cool summers. Its dark green leaves contain great food value. Family Chenopodiaceae; species *Spinacia oleracea.*

Spinal Cord, tubular central nerve cord, lying within the vertebral column, or spine. It, along with the brain, makes up the central nervous system, the communication center of the body. It gives off 31 pairs of spinal nerves, each of which has sensory and motor fibers. The spinal cord functions to receive sensory input, interpret the messages, and send messages to the periphery and to the brain. The spinal cord itself, as seen in cross section, is made up of H-shaped gray matter, containing sensory and motor nerve centers, and surrounding white matter, made up of fatty connective sheath around motor nerves, or axons. *See also* Nervous System.

Spinal Fluid. See Cerebrospinal Fluid.

Spine, the vertebral column, or spinal column; in humans a somewhat S-shaped, flexible column made up of 33 separate bones, known as vertebrae, that forms the backbone and surrounds and protects the spinal cord. The human spinal, or vertebral, column is divided into five sections: the cervical region, or neck section, composed of 7 vertebrae; the thoracic region, or chest, composed of 12 vertebrae; the lumbar region, or small of the back, composed of five vertebrae; the sacral region, or sacrum, composed of five vertebrae; and the coccygeal region, or coccyx, composed of 4 vertebrae. Disk-shaped cartilaginous pads located between vertebrae cushion and absorb shock during movement and reduce wear. *See also* Vertebra.

Spinel, oxide mineral, magnesium aluminum oxide ($MgAl_2O_4$) found in igneous and metamorphic rocks. Cubic system frequently twinned octahedral crystals. Glassy black, red, blue, brown, or white; hardness 7.5–8; sp gr 3.8. Red spinel from Sri Lanka is a valuable gemstone.

Spinet, keyboard stringed musical instrument. Originally (15th–18th centuries) it was a small, oblong harpsichord with a single keyboard, ranging 3 octaves. In the 19th and 20th centuries, it became a small upright piano, ranging about 7 octaves, with thinner sound than a grand piano, and used as a parlor instrument.

Spinone Italiano, pointer and gun dog bred in Piedmont region of Italy several centuries ago. This rugged dog has a big, long hound head; large, dropped ears; bushy eyebrows; a pointer's body; and docked tail. The short, hard, rough, weather-resistant coat is solid white or white with yellow or white with light brown patches. Average size: 26in (66cm) high at shoulder; 56lb (25.5kg).

Spinoza, Baruch (1632–77), Dutch philosopher. After his expulsion from the synagogue for "atheism," he worked in seclusion as a lens grinder. Although he was austere and reclusive, his reputation as a philosopher-scientist grew. He refused generous gifts and employment and worked alone on his *Ethica* (Ethics) (1660–66). *The Theological-Political Treatise* (1670) contained the first modern historical interpretation of the Bible. Spinoza declined the chair of philosophy at Heidelberg in order to preserve his independence. Moral autonomy *(Ethics)* and toleration *(Political Treatise),* were among his central ideas.

Spiracle, external opening for respiration in various animals. In insects and spiders, it is the opening to a trachea (air tube); in sharks, rays, and some bony fish, water passes through a pair of spiracles during gill respiration; in whales the nasal opening is called a spiracle.

Spiraea, genus of flowering shrubs native to the Northern Hemisphere. They have small lobed leaves and clusters of small white or pink flowers. Many of the 75 species are grown as ornamentals. Height: 5ft (1.5m). Family Rosaceae.

Spiral Galaxy, type of regular galaxy in which a condensed nucleus of stars is surrounded by streams of younger stars, gas, and dust spiraling out from opposite sides of it. In normal spirals the nucleus is more or less spherical. Such galaxies are graded in three groups, Sa to Sc, according to increasing openness of their spiral arms. *See also* Andromeda Galaxy; Barred Spiral Galaxy; Elliptical Galaxy; Galaxy.

Spirituals, religious folk music, especially that associated with US black culture. The words of spirituals are often based on Biblical stories while the music is often in 4-part harmony with stylistic features peculiar to the spiritual (eg, 5-note melodies). Spirituals are an authentic form of US folk music that have influenced the development of other musical forms such as the blues.

Spirochete, general name applied to group of bacteria that are spiral-rod shaped and capable of flexing and wriggling their bodies as they move about. *See also* Bacteria.

Spitsbergen (Svalbard), island group in the Arctic Ocean, approx. 400mi (644km) N of Norway; Spitsbergen is the chief island. Large coal deposits on Spitsbergen were discovered in the late 19th century, and coal production is now a major industry; copper, asbestos, iron, and other minerals are also mined. The group was discovered in the 12th century by the Vikings, and again in 1596 by Willem Barents. The islands are now occupied by Norway and the USSR. Area: 24,000sq mi (63,158sq km). Pop. 3,431.

Spitteler, Carl Friedrich Georg (1845–1924), pseud. Carl Felix Tandem, Swiss poet. His epics, *Prometheus and Epimetheus* (1881) and *Der Olympische Frühling* (1900), resemble Friedrich Nietzsche's *Zarathustra,* but it is controversial as to who influenced whom. He wrote essays on Nietzsche and a novel *Imago* (1906). He was awarded the Nobel Prize in literature in 1919.

Spittle Bug, or frog hopper, leaping insect found worldwide. Adults are brown to gray. Green to brown nymphs produce frothy masses on plants. Length: 0.5in (13mm). Family Cercopidae. *See also* Homoptera.

Spleen, an important, but nonessential, organ of the circulatory system. It lies in the abdominal cavity to the left of the stomach. The spleen functions to store blood, in an emergency supplying additional blood cells and oxygen. It also destroys, through the action of its macrophages, worn out or damaged red blood cells and produces lymphocytes, a type of white blood cell.

Spleenwort, widely distributed fern with simple or compound fronds. They have crescent-shaped sori and sporangia. The North American ebony spleenwort *(Asplenium playneuron)* has long, stiff, ladderlike, fertile leaves with shorter, less erect sterile leaves; height: to 18in (46cm). Family Aspleniaceae.

Split (Spljet), seaport city in W Yugoslavia, on Dalmatian coast, in Croatia; resort and commercial center; site of palace of Roman emperor Diocletian (295–305),

amphitheater, museum, oceanographic institute, teachers' college. City held by Venice 1420–1797; passed to Austria 1797; inc. into Yugoslavia 1918. Industries: shipbuilding, textiles, chemicals, tourism. Pop. 153,000.

Spokane, city and port of entry in E Washington, on falls of Spokane River; seat of Spokane co. Originally inhabited by Spokane Indians, a trading post was est. 1810; settlement began *c.* 1871; industry was spurred by arrival of Northern Pacific Railroad (1881). Spokane is the site of Gonzaga University (1887), Whitworth College (1890), Fort Wright College (1907). Industries: lumbering, food processing, metal refining, mining, cement. Inc. 1881 as village, 1891 as city. Pop. (1980) 171,300.

Spondee, metrical foot consisting of two stressed syllables, or two longs. The meter is called spondaic. Spondaic meter is found in Greek poetry in the slow, solemn hymns sung at a "spondee" or drink-offering. In English-language verse spondaic meter is found in this line from John Milton's *Paradise Lost.*

Rocks, caves, lakes, fens, bogs, dens,
and shades of death.
See also Meter.

Sponge, mainly marine animal composed of an outer layer of cells; a middle layer of nonliving, jellylike substance; and an inner layer of collar cells. The body is supported by a skeleton of lime, silica, or spongin. There is no nervous system or cellular coordination. Sponges reproduce sexually and by asexual budding. Length: from 0.04in (1mm)–several feet (1–2 meters). Phylum Porifera; 4,200 species including purse sponge *Grantia* and simple sponge *Leucosolenia.*

Spontaneous Combustion, outbreak of fire without external application of heat. When combustible material, such as hay or coal, is slowly oxidized by bacteria or air, the temperature rises to the ignition point, whereupon it catches fire.

Spontaneous Fission. See Radiation, Nuclear.

Spontaneous Generation, or abiogenesis, belief, now discredited, that living organisms arise from nonliving matter. It supposedly explained the presence of maggots on decaying meat.

Spoonbill, widely distributed wading bird with long bill that is flat and rounded at the tip. With large wings, long legs, short tails, and white or pinkish plumage, they feed on small plant and animal matter and lay light-colored spotted eggs (3–5) in a stick nest. Length: 3ft (91.5cm). Family Threskiornithidae.

Spore, small reproductive body that detaches from the parent plant to produce new plants. Mostly microscopic, spores are one- or several-celled and produced in large numbers. Some reproduce rapidly, others rest, surviving unfavorable environmental conditions. Although they occur in all plant groups, spores are particularly characteristic of fungi and ferns.

Sporozoa, class of parasitic protozoa characterized by reproduction by sporulation (asexual multiple fission) and absence of special locomotive apparatus for much of their lives. The best example is the plasmodium that causes malaria.

Sporting Dog, dog breeds that hunt by air-scenting. Also called gun or bird dogs, they locate game, flush it, wait for the hunter's shot, and retrieve on command. Breeds in this category are pointer, retriever, setter, spaniel, vizla, Weimaraner, and wirehaired pointing griffon. *See also* Hounds.

Sports, as a term, includes activities in which skill and physical prowess may be demonstrated. Generally, the term is restricted to a contest incorporating a specified set of rules. The types of activities vary greatly, and are classified either by individual or team sports. While individual sports would include those where one person could achieve success without another person's aid, team sports involve those which are designed to succeed due to a coordinated effort of more than one individual. In amateur sports, the major competition is the Olympic Games, held every four years (winter and summer) at a different site. *See also* specific sports and biographies of sports personalities.

Spring, a natural opening for discharge of water from an underground source. Springs are an important part of the water cycle. They may emerge at points on dry land or in beds of streams or ponds. The composition of spring water varies with the surrounding soil or rocks.

Springbok, or springbuck, small antelope native to S Africa, it is the national emblem of the Republic of South Africa. Reddish-brown on back grades into dark horizontal band just above white underside. Both sexes carry short, black, slightly curved horns. When alarmed, it raises white fold of hair along back. It once migrated in herds numbering over 1,000,000, but now is rare. Length: to 4.5ft (1.4m); weight: to 79lb (36kg). Family Bovidae; species *Antidorcas marsupialis.*

Springfield, capital city of Illinois, in central Illinois on Sangamon River; seat of Sangamon co. It is noted as the home and area where Abraham Lincoln practiced law 1837–61; made state capital 1839; industrial development started *c.* 1870; site of Lincoln's home, now a national historic site (est. 1971), Lincoln's tomb containing his wife and three of four sons, Lincoln Land Community College (1967), Illinois State Fair. Industries: farm machinery, flour, feed, electronic equipment, tourism. Settled 1818; inc. 1832 as town, 1840 as city. Pop. (1980) 99,637.

Springfield, city in S Massachusetts, on E bank of Connecticut River, 80mi (129km) W of Boston; seat of Hampden co. Burned during King Philip's War (1675), it was scene of Shay's Rebellion (1786–87); station on Underground Railroad; site of Springfield College (1885), American International College (1885), Western New England College (1919), and US Armory (1794–1966); Springfield and Garand rifles were developed here), now an arms museum. Industries: hosiery, matches, firearms, paper, printing. Settled 1636 as Agawam; name changed in 1640; inc. 1641, as city 1852. Pop. (1980) 152,319.

Springfield, city in SW Missouri, approx. 150mi (242km) SSE of Kansas City in resort area of Ozarks; seat of Greene co; site of Drury College (1873), Southwest Missouri State College (1905), Central Bible College (1922), Evangel College (1955); nearby is Mark Twain National Forest. Industries: agriculture, flour, food processing, clothing, furniture, typewriters. Settled 1829; inc. 1855. Pop. (1980) 133,116.

Springfield, city in W central Ohio, on the Mad River 23mi (37km) NE of Dayton; seat of Clark co; scene of 1807 regional peace negotiations between Indian chiefs, including Tecumseh; tablet marks spot of tavern in which meeting was held; site of Wittenberg University (1842). Industries: farm machinery, electric motors, incubators, diesel engines. Founded 1799 by Kentuckians; made seat 1818; inc. as town 1827, as city 1850. Pop. (1980) 72,563.

Spring Peeper, tree frog native to E and S United States and S Canada. It is brown with a dark, cross-shaped mark on its back. Found on low tree branches or on the ground, its high peeping mating call is a sign of spring in the north. Length: 1.5in (4cm). Family Hylidae; species *Hyla crucifer. See also* Tree Frog.

Springtail, tiny, wingless insect found worldwide. it varies in color and can jump 3–4in (76–102mm), using a leverlike, forked tail under the abdomen that is forced down and backward. Length: 0.19–0.23in (5–6mm). Order Collembola.

Spruce, evergreen trees, often confused with firs, native to mountainous or cooler temperate regions of the Northern Hemisphere. Pyramid-shaped and dense, they have four-sided needles that fall off easily and pendulous cones. The timber is used in cabinets and some species yield turpentine. Height: to 200 ft (61m); family Pinaceae; genus *Picea.*

Spurge, widely distributed herbs, shrubs, and trees. Some are succulent and others are cactuslike. They

exude a milky juice when cut and have small flowers surrounded by large, colorful, flowerlike bracts, as in the poinsettia. Family Euphorbiaceae; genus *Euphorbia.*

Sputnik, the first artificial satellite, launched Oct. 4, 1957, by the Soviet Union. Weighing 184lb (83kg) and equipped with a radio transmitter, it circled the Earth for several months. The launch date of Sputnik is generally agreed to mark the beginning of the Space Age. *See also* Satellite, Artificial.

Squanto (died 1622), American Indian of the Pawtuxet tribe of Massachusetts. He lived in England (1605–14), was sold as a slave in Spain, but was returned to Massachusetts in 1619. He acted as an interpreter for the Pilgrims of Plymouth Colony, helping them make a treaty with Massasoit and teaching them to plant corn and where to fish.

Square, number or quantity resulting when a specified number or quantity is multiplied by itself: the square of 3 is 9; the square of x is x^2. The squares of both positive and negative numbers are positive: $-3^2 = 9$.

Square, quadrilateral having all its sides equal and all its angles right angles. Its area is the product of adjacent sides.

Square Root (symbol $\sqrt{\ }$), number or quantity that must be multiplied by itself to give a specified number or quantity. As a number it is usually irrational. The square root of 4 is 2, ie, $\sqrt{4} = 2$; $\sqrt{2} = 1.414213$. . . . .A negative number has imaginary square roots.

Squash. *See* Pumpkin.

Squash Bug, brown to gray bug found only in the Western Hemisphere. It sucks juices from leaves of pumpkin, squash, and related plants. There is one generation per year. Length: 0.5in (13mm). Family Coreidae; species *Anasa tristis.*

Squash Rackets, game played by two or four persons on a four-walled court. The court is 18.5 feet (5.6m) wide by 32 feet (9.8m) long, and 16 feet (4.9m) high at the front wall. The back wall is usually 9 feet (2.7m) high. Players use a gut-strung racket (27 inches, 68.6cm, long) that is round-headed, and a black, hard-rubber ball that is 1.75 inches (4.4cm) in diameter. The game begins from a designated area behind the floor service line which is 22 feet (6.7m) away from, and parallel to, the front wall. After striking the ball above the *telltale* (a 17-inch, 43.2-cm, horizontal strip) on the front wall, the ball must land in the opposite service court. Volleying (with caroms off the side walls permitted) continues until a point is scored when one of the players fails to return the ball before it strikes the floor twice. A game is 15 points, unless the score is 13-all, in which case the game is played to 15, 16, or 18 points. The game originated in England in the 19th century.

Squid, marine cephalopod mollusk that has a cylindrical body, eight short, suckered tentacles, and two long armlike tentacles surrounding the mouth. They can attain swimming speeds of 30mph (48km/h). Most squid have a horny, internal support called a pen. The giant squid *Architeuthis* of North Atlantic is the largest. There are about 350 species. Length: 2in–60ft (5cm–18m). Order Decapoda; family Teuthoidea. *See also* Cephalopod; Mollusk.

Squint. *See* Strabismus.

Squirrel, large family (Sciuridae) of rodents living almost worldwide. The busy, noisy diurnal tree squirrels of Eurasia and North and South America are the best known. The smallest is the African pygmy; the largest is the Indian giant. They eat nuts, seeds, fruit, insects, and, occasionally, eggs and young birds. Most have glossy fur and bushy tails. Weight: to 6lb (3kg).

Squirrelfish, coral reef fish found worldwide in tropical seas. Bright red, often with white streaks or spots, it has large eyes and sharp spines on gill covers and fins. Length: 1–2ft (30.5–61cm). The 70 species include Atlantic longspine *Holocentrus rufus.* Family Holocentridae.

Squirrel Monkey, small monkey with a long, non-prehensile tail, found from Costa Rica to Paraguay. They are day-active tree dwellers, feed on fruits and flowers, and travel in troops of up to 100. They make lively pets, but do best with one or two other squirrel monkeys as companions. Genus *Saimiri. See also* Monkey.

Sri Lanka, Republic of, formerly Ceylon; independent island-state in the Indian Ocean, 20mi (32km) off the

SE coast of India. The people are of Indian origin (Sinhalese and Tamil), and the majority is Buddhist.

Land and economy. Sri Lanka, a continuation of the Indian continental shelf, is separated from the mainland by Palk Strait. A mountainous massif dominates the S central island, trailing off to coastal plains to the N, W, and E. The climate is tropical, and 70% of the island is covered by forest and natural grassland. The annual rainfall varies about the island from 40–200in (102—508cm). The economy, primarily agricultural, relies heavily on the export of tea, rubber, and coconuts. Graphite of extremely high quality is the principal mineral export. Industry, once of minor importance, is growing significantly because of government direction of foreign aid funds. The population has more than doubled since 1950, causing serious food and economic problems.

People. The majority of the people is of Indian descent, Sinhalese and Tamil. The Buddhist Sinhalese account for about 66% of the population, and the Hindu Tamils, about 18%. The Tamils divide into two groups: the Ceylonese Tamils, who invaded many centuries ago, and the Indian Tamils, imported for labor by the British in the late 19th century. Education is universal and the majority of the people are literate.

Government. An independent republic, Sri Lanka is a member of the Commonwealth of Nations. According to the constitution of 1978, executive power is vested in the popularly-elected president, who holds broad powers. The cabinet is responsible to the unicameral parliament. Local government is invested in provinces and districts. The judicial system consists of a supreme court and many lesser courts. There are four major political parties, often necessitating coalition governments.

History. Sri Lanka has had a recorded history for over 2,000 years. Influenced by its proximity to India, and its position along the E-W trade route, the island fell under European control in the early 16th century. The island was settled in the 5th century BC by the Sinhalese from India and was controlled by their Buddhist kings until the arrival of the Portuguese in 1505. By 1619 the Portuguese governed the entire island only to be driven out by the Dutch, with the help of Sinhalese kings, in 1648. The English gained control in 1796 and continued their dominance until a series of disturbances beginning in 1915 convinced them to grant independence to the people in 1948. The major figure in the early years of independence was S.W.R. Bandaranaike, who was assassinated in 1959. His widow, Sirimavo Bandaranaike, governed 1959–65 and 1972–77. In 1978 a new constitution abolished the parliamentary government in favor of a presidential system, in an effort to stabilize the country. Civil disorders by Hindu Tamils demanding greater recognition by the government and a separate Tamil state continued, however, as well as clashes among religious and political factions. Attempts by the government to negotiate with the Tamils and grants of greater Tamil autonomy during 1985 failed. Violence and bloodshed continued.

PROFILE

Official name: Republic of Sri Lanka
Area: 25,332sq mi (65,610sq km)
Population: 14,500,000
   Density: 572per sq mi (221per sq km)
Chief cities: Colombo (capital); Jaffna; Kandy; Galle
Government: Republic
Religion: Buddhism
Language: Sinhala (official), English
Monetary unit: Ceylonese rupee
Gross national product: $2,300,000,000
Per capita income: under $200
Industries (major products): milled rice, cement, pharmaceuticals, petroleum products
Agriculture (major products): rice, tea, coconuts, rubber
Minerals (major): graphite, salt
Trading partners (major): United Kingdom, Japan

Srinagar, city in N India, on Jhelum River; capital of Srinagar district and summer capital of Jammu and Kashmir state; site of University of Jammu and Kashmir (1948); summer resort; site of 7th-century Sankaracharya temple, 16th-century fort, many Buddhist remains. Industries: carpets, silk, silver, leather, plywood, cement, tourism. Founded 6th century. Pop. 327,076.

SS (Ger. *Schutzstaffel,* "defense corps"), also known as the Blackshirts, the Nazi party's most elite terror organization. Headed by Heinrich Himmler, it included the Gestapo or secret police, the officers and guards of the concentration camps, and Adolf Hitler's personal bodyguard. After Hitler's rise to power, it became a source of cruelty and terror throughout Europe, responsible for the enforcement and implementation of Hitler's racist ideology. The symbol of the branch of this organization assigned to administer the concentration camps was the skull and crossbones, and it was called the Death's Head Battalion (Ger. *Totenkopfver-*

Sri Lanka

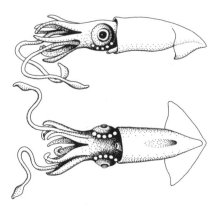

Squid

Henry Stanley

bande). After the war, many of its leaders were captured, tried, and convicted of crimes against humanity.

Staël, Germaine, Madame de (1766–1817), French author. Her full name was Anne Louise Germaine Necker, Baronne de Staël-Holstein. The daughter of Jacques Necker, she married the Swedish ambassador to Paris and established a salon that became an intellectual and political center. She did not hesitate to criticize France and Napoleon and was exiled several times. Her novels *Delphine* (1803) and *Corinne* (1807) are considered the first modern feminist psychological novels. She introduced German Romanticism to France in *De l'Allemagne* (1810). *De l'Allemagne* is an account of Germany which introduced the German philosophy and literature of the romantic era to France. Napoleon had it seized and destroyed for being "un-French" and "subversive."

Staffordshire Bull Terrier, fighting dog (terrier group) bred in England in the 19th century. Now an all-purpose dog, the Staffordshire bull has a short, broad head; small drop or half-prick ears; dark eyes; wide-chested body; wide-set well-boned legs; and medium-length, tapered tail. Its smooth, short coat is red, fawn, black, blue, or any of these with white. Average size: 14–16in (35.5–40.5cm) high at shoulder; 28–38lb (12.5–17kg). *See also* Terrier.

Stag Beetle, or pinching bug, large, usually brown or black beetle named for long, antlerlike mandibles present in many species, particularly among males. Family Lucanidae.

Staggers, disease of horses, cattle, and sheep, causing uncoordination, convulsions, and paralysis. Its cause is unknown.

Stained Glass, artistic medium. It was used primarily in conjunction with church architecture and was brought to its full flower during the Gothic era, particularly in France. Of Byzantine origin, stained glass is produced in its purest form by impregnating the components of glass with colored dyes and arranging shapes cut from the resultant sheets to form decorative patterns or representational images. These shapes are joined and supported by flexible strips of lead that take the form of dark, emphatic contours as natural light filters through the glass and silhouettes the leading. Details are painted onto the glass surfaces in liquid enamel and fused to the surfaces by heat.

Aside from fragmentary examples, the earliest surviving stained glass is to be found in Augsburg Cathedral, Bavaria, although its precise age is debatable, with speculation ranging from 1050 to 1150 as the date of its installation. At about the latter date, stained-glass windows were created for the French Abbey of Saint-Denis, Paris, and shortly thereafter the great west window of Chartres Cathedral was installed. The Ille de France soon became the art's great center, its influence spreading throughout the northwest of Europe. In modern times, concrete has supplanted the more graceful lead as a support for the glass.

Stalactite, icicle-like formation of calcite, made by the precipitation of calcium carbonate out of ground water that has seeped into limestone caves. Stalagmites are similar formations built up from the floor of the cave.

Stalin, Joseph Vissarionovich (1879–1953), Soviet political leader and dictator, b. Georgia. Born Iosif Vissarionovich Dzhugashvili, he was educated at the Tiflis theological seminary, and expelled in 1898 as a revolutionary. He became a Bolshevik in 1903 and joined the Central Committee in 1913, taking part in terrorist activities. Following the Bolshevik revolution,

in October 1917, he served under V.I. Lenin as commissar for nationalities (1921–23), becoming general secretary of the Central Committee in 1922. Following Lenin's death in 1924, Stalin was able to maneuver for supreme power and suppress Lenin's criticism of him. Leon Trotsky was his strongest rival, but Stalin managed to eliminate him and by 1927 he was a virtual dictator. He introduced forced collectivization in 1929. Stalin began a ruthless purge that eliminated possible rivals and resulted in a reign of terror in which millions perished (1936–39). He became premier in 1941, and generalissimo during the war, which he personally supervised. As one of the three Allied leaders, he participated in the Tehran (1943) and Yalta Conferences (1945) in which the political future of the postwar world was determined. After the war, he established a system of Communist "satellite" states in Eastern Europe that were nominally independent but carefully controlled by the Soviet Union. The defection of Titoist Yugoslavia (1948) led Stalin to institute even tighter supervision over Eastern Europe. His last years were dominated by personal eccentricities and paranoia, leading to mass executions of suspected Soviet subversives. After his death, Nikita Khrushchev denounced his tyrannical rule at the 1956 party congress.

Stalingrad. *See* Volgograd.

Stalingrad, Battle of (1942–43), a decisive conflict in World War II, centering on the Soviet city of Stalingrad.

Stamford, city in SW Connecticut, on Long Island Sound and New York border. Industries: electronics, computers, plastics, shipyards. Settled as part of New York 1641; annexed to Connecticut 1662; city inc. within town of Stamford 1893; city and town consolidated 1949. Pop. (1980) 102, 453.

Stamp Act, first direct tax (1765) levied on the colonies by the British Parliament. It was intended to raise revenue to help pay for troops defending the colonies. The act required a tax, in the form of a stamp, affixed to all legal papers, newspaper copies, and other documents. Colonists in secret organizations such as the Sons of Liberty resisted the tax, attacking the stamp distributors and burning stamped paper. The act was repealed in 1766.

Stamp Act Congress, meeting in opposition to the Stamp Act. Convened in New York City, it was composed of representatives of nine colonies (1765). It resolved that only the colonies could tax themselves and demanded repeal of the Stamp Act. The Declaration of Rights and Grievances was issued as a statement of the colonial position.

Stamping, method of forming metal. A flat blank of metal is stretched over a die and struck with a movable punch until the desired shape is attained. Dies also perforate, bend, and shear when necessary. Stampings are limited to metal ¾in (19mm) or less thick.

Standardbred, light horse breed that includes trotters and pacers. An American breed (once the American Trotter), it was developed about 1849 from several breeds for road driving and racing. More rugged than the thoroughbred, it is smaller, has shorter legs, and is longer bodied. Its speed is attained by extending its legs into rapidly repeated long strides. Colors are bay, brown, chestnut, and black. Height: 60–64in (152–163cm) at shoulder; weight: 900–1300lb (405–591kg).

Standard Deviation, in statistics, a measure of dispersion or deviation of scores from the average or mean of the scores. A small standard deviation indicates that scores cluster around the mean, while a large one

indicates that scores are widely dispersed about the mean. The formula for calculating the standard deviation is $\sqrt{\Sigma x^2 \div N}$ where Σ means "the sum of," each x is the deviation of each score from the mean of all scores, and N is the number of scores. *See also* Statistics.

Standard of Living, referring to a country, is measured by the per capita income of the population. It is used to compare the degree of economic development in the various countries. Many economists define an underdeveloped nation as one whose per capita income is less than some percent (25% is sometimes used) of the more developed countries. *See also* Less Developed Countries.

Standard Schnauzer, guard and yard dog (working group) bred in Germany around 15th–16th centuries; oldest of Schnauzer types. It has an elongated, rectangular head with arched eyebrows, moustache, and whiskers. High-set ears are cropped or V-shaped; the compact body has a stiff, straight back. Legs are medium-length and appear heavy because of coat; the high-set tail is docked. The 1.5in (4cm) long coat is hard and wiry; colors are pepper and salt or pure black. Average size: 17–20in (43–51cm) at shoulders; 27–37lb (12–17kg). *See also* Working Dog.

Standard Temperature and Pressure (STP), or normal temperature and pressure (NTP), standard conditions for comparing the volumes of gases, etc. It is a pressure of 760mm of mercury (1.013/25 × 10⁵ pascals) and a temperature of 0°C.

Stanford, Leland (1824–93), US railroad builder and politician, b. Watervliet, N.Y. During the Civil War he was Republican governor of California (1861) and kept it in the Union. He was a founder of the Central Pacific Railroad and president of the Southern Pacific lines. While in the US Senate (1885–93) he secured financial aid for the railroads from state and municipal governments. He founded Stanford University in 1885 and named it for his son Leland.

Stanislas I Leszczyński (1677–1766), Polish nobleman, king of Poland (1704–09, 1733–35). He became king with the support of Charles XII of Sweden, replacing Augustus II, but was forced to relinquish the throne to Augustus after the Swedish defeat at the battle of Poltava (1709). With French help (the result of his daughter's marriage to Louis XV) he regained the throne, but was deposed by Augustus III, who was aided by Russia.

Stanley, (Sir) Henry Morton (1841–1904), British-US explorer of Africa, b. John Rowlands in Wales. After a miserable childhood, he ran away to the United States, taking the name of a merchant who befriended him. He served in the Confederate army and US Navy. As a journalist, he accompanied an expedition to Abyssinia. Later he was sent by the New York *Herald* to central Africa to find David Livingstone, a missing missionary and explorer, which he did in 1871. A courageous and tenacious explorer, Stanley made several other expeditions into Africa, making vital geographic discoveries and establishing the Congo Free State for Belgium. He authored many successful accounts and served in the British parliament (1895–1900).

Stanley, Thomas, 1st Earl of Derby. *See* Derby, Thomas Stanley, 1st Earl of.

Stanton, Elizabeth Cady (1815–1902), US women's rights leader and social reformer, b. Johnstown, N.Y. In 1840, when women were excluded from the world antislavery convention, she joined with Lucretia Mott to fight for equality. In 1848 they organized the first women's rights convention at Seneca Falls, N.Y. In 1851 she joined Susan B. Anthony, and the two worked closely in the struggle for women's rights for 50 years. She edited the feminist journal, *The Revolution* (1868–70). In 1869 she was elected president of the National Women's Suffrage Association, a position she held from 1869–90. She collaborated in the writing of the *History of Women Suffrage* (1881–86). *See also* National Woman Suffrage Association; Seneca Falls Convention.

Stanza, group of verse lines into which a poem is divided. Stanzas are characterized by the number of lines. For example, couplet has two lines; tercet and terza rima, three; quatrain, four; ottava rima, eight. Stanzas can also be characterized by rhyme scheme or meter. Another word for stanza is *stave,* which is closely associated with song.

Staphylococcus, genus of bacteria characterized by gram-positive spherical cells that grow in grapelike clusters. They are facultative anaerobes present normally on the skin and on nasal and other mucous membranes. Some are pathogenic, the basic lesion being an abcess such as in wound infections. They are resistant to most antibiotics and are thus hard to control. *See also* Bacteria.

Star, hot gaseous self-luminous object, such as the Sun, that emits energy principally in the form of heat and light, produced through thermonuclear reactions occurring in its interior. Stars are thought to be formed out of nebular concentrations of interstellar matter, and thereafter follow certain evolutionary patterns governed by their physical characteristics. Their diameters vary considerably, from several hundred million miles for low-density red supergiants to Earthlike dimensions for enormously dense white dwarfs. Stellar temperatures also show wide variations, from about 1,500° K to 80,000° K and stars are grouped into well-defined spectral types and luminosity classes. *See also* Cepheid Variable.

Starch, form of polysaccharide in which carbohydrate is stored in many plants and that is an important source of carbohydrate in the diet of animals. It consists of linked glucose units and exists in two forms: amylose, in which the glucose chains are unbranched, and amylopectin, in which they are branched. It is made commercially from corn, potatoes, etc, and used in the manufacture of adhesives, sizing, and foods.

Star Chamber, meeting place of the king's council in Westminster Palace, London. Under the Tudors, the name referred mainly to councilors and legal experts gathered there as a judicial tribunal. Proceeding without a jury, arbitrary in sentencing, and permitting torture, the Star Chamber court became notorious and was abolished (1641).

Starfish, marine echinoderm with central disk body and radiating arms (8 to 25). The mouth is on the disk underside, and the stomach can be extruded to take in clams and other echinoderms. Calcareous spines are embedded in the skin. They move by varying water pressure in the water vascular system and tube feet. Class Asteroides; 1,000 species include common *Asterias* and 13-armed *Solaster.*

Stark, Johannes (1874–1957), German physicist. He received a 1919 Nobel Prize for describing the Stark effect (the splitting of the spectral lines of dispersed light when a light source is subjected to a strong electromagnetic field). *See also* Doppler Effect.

Starling, widely distributed aggressive bird that generally roosts in large groups, often in cities. They create a nuisance with their droppings and almost constant chattering, clicking, whistling, and other noises. They have stout bodies, pointed, sometimes notched, wings, and short tails. Most are dark, some are brightly colored. They feed on insects and fruit and build nests in tree cavities or on cliffs for bluish-green or whitish eggs (2–9). Length: 7–13in (18–33cm). Family Sturnidae.

Star of Bethlehem, bulbous house plant native to S Africa. Fragrant, star-shaped, white flowers grow on a central spike rising from slender, arching leaves. Care: direct sunlight, slightly dry soil (equal parts loam, peat moss, sand). Propagation is by offsets or seeds. Height: to 18in (46cm). Family Liliaceae; genus *Ornithogalum.*

Star of David, Magen David, or **Shield of David,** has evolved into a symbol of Judaism. It is a 6-pointed star formed by two equilateral triangles. Its origin is unknown. It was used at one time as an emblem by pagans, Christians, and Muslims alike. The Nazis used it to brand Jews. It is often traced to King David and Jewish warriors used it on their shields.

Star-Spangled Banner, The, US national anthem. The words were written by a young lawyer, Francis Scott Key, while he was detained by the British and forced to witness the bombardment of Fort McHenry in 1814. He was inspired by the sight of the US flag still waving above the fort at dawn. The lyrics were published that same year in a Baltimore newspaper. The tune was taken from "To Anacreon in Heaven," a popular English song. Although long sung by the US Army and Navy, "The Star-Spangled Banner" did not officially become the national anthem until so designated by President Woodrow Wilson in an executive order in 1916.

Following is the text of the first verse of the anthem:

Oh, say can you see by the dawn's early light
What so proudly we hailed at the twilight's last gleaming?
Whose broad stripes and bright stars thru the perilous fight
O'er the ramparts we watched were so gallantly streaming?
And the rockets' red glare, the bombs bursting in air.
Gave proof through the night that our flag was still there.
Oh say, does that star-spangled banner yet wave
O'er the land of the free and the home of the brave?

State, Department of, cabinet-level department within the executive branch. It is charged with developing and maintaining the foreign policy of the United States. Originally, the Continental Congress conducted foreign affairs. It had its origins in 1775 in a committee chaired by Benjamin Franklin. In 1777, a Committee for Foreign Affairs was established, but its real power was limited. The Department of Foreign Affairs (1781) was followed in 1789 by the Department of State, with Thomas Jefferson as its first secretary. The department's responsibilities have expanded, but it is no longer responsible for domestic affairs such as census, issuing patents, and handling territorial affairs. It is primarily concerned with the execution of the US foreign policy to promote long-range US security and well-being through continuous consultations with other nations. It also negotiates treaties and agreements with foreign nations and speaks for the United States in the United Nations and other international organizations and conferences.

Staten Island, island in SE New York, in New York Bay, 5mi (8km) SW of Manhattan; separated from Long Island (E) by the Narrows and from New Jersey (W) by narrow Arthur Kill; coextensive with Richmond borough of New York City; connected with Brooklyn by Verrazano-Narrows bridge (1964) and with New York City and Brooklyn by ferries; site of Wagner College (1928), Notre Dame College of Staten Island (1931), US marine and army hospital; Billopp House (1688), Church of St Andrew (1708). Industries: shipbuilding, printing, publishing, oil refining, soap. Settled 1661; inc. with New York City 1898. Area: 64sq mi (166sq km). Pop. (1980) 352,121.

States General. *See* Estates General.

State Sovereignty, doctrine of states' authority. Under Article X of the US Constitution, the states possess those powers not delegated to the federal government and not expressly prohibited to the states.

States' Rights, doctrine that the states have authority in matters not specifically delegated to the federal government. The controversy between federal and state jurisdiction reached a peak with John C. Calhoun's constitutional interpretation that a state could refuse to obey a federal law it deemed unconstitutional. This led to the Nullification Crisis (1832) and ultimately contributed to secession and the Civil War. More recently, it was an issue during the civil rights movement of 1950s and 1960s and in the George C. Wallace presidential campaign of 1968. *See also* Calhoun, John C.

Statistical Mechanics, the study of large-scale properties of matter based on the underlying laws of quantum mechanics in conjunction with the statistical laws of large numbers. Quantum mechanics determines the possible energy states of a substance or system; the large number of molecules in such a system then allows one to use statistics to predict the probability of finding the system in any one of these states. The entropy of the system is related to the number of possible states; a system left to itself will tend to approach the most probable distribution of energy states. *See also* Thermodynamics.

Statistics, the science that deals with methods for analyzing empirical data, or characteristics of the data itself. Statistics can be descriptive (simply summarizing the data) or inferential (leading to conclusions or inferences about larger populations of which the data are one sample). Inferential statistics are used by all the sciences to lend a greater degree of confidence to one's results, since statistics often allow one to calculate the probability that one's conclusions are in error. *See also* Average; Correlation; Factor Analysis; Frequency Distribution; Standard Deviation; Validity.

Statue of Liberty, statue in SE New York, in New York Harbor on Liberty Island, SW of Manhattan Island. A gift from the people of France to the United States in commemoration of the centennial of US independence. Frédéric Auguste Bartholdi conceived the idea and designed it; framework was designed by Gustave Eiffel (creator of Eiffel Tower). Funds were raised by subscription from French people, and the statue was completed in Paris, disassembled, and shipped to the United States. The figure of a woman, it is 151ft (46m) high to top of torch in her uplifted right hand; regally draped, she wears a crown of seven spokes and carries a lawbook inscribed "July 4, 1776." Dedicated by Pres. Grover Cleveland Oct. 28, 1886; national monument since 1924. It was refurbished for centennial celebrations in 1986.

Stavanger, port city in SW Norway, on S bank of mouth of Stavanger Fjord, inlet of the North Sea, capital of Rogaland co. Founded before 10th century, it became bishopric 1125; site of 12th-century church. Industries: shipbuilding, fishing and fish processing. Pop. 86,643.

Stavisky Affair, French financial scandal that led to government crises in 1934. Financier Serge Alexandre Stavisky was found dead shortly after bonds of his credit organization were found to be worthless. Right-wing extremists claimed that the left-wing coalition government was involved in the scandal and hushing up a murder. Riots led to 15 deaths, resignation by two prime ministers, and the establishment of a centrist government under Gaston Doumergue.

Steady-State Theory of Universe, cosmological theory postulating that the universe, though expanding, has the same large-scale structure at all times: it is thus infinitely large, with no beginning and no end. The galaxies are receding, as indicated by their red shift, but matter is being created extremely slowly in the resulting spaces, to form eventually into new galaxies: the average density of galaxies thus remains constant. The theory is incompatible with the existing laws of physics and recent developments in astronomy tend to favor the big-bang theory.

Steam Engine, first machine successfully used in the generation of mechanical power from thermal energy. Pistons driven by high pressure steam move crankshafts providing rotational motion to ships' propulsions, railroad locomotives, and electric generators. The first practical engine was developed by James Watt in 1763, and the origins of the Industrial Revolution can be traced to that time.

Stearate, salt or ester of stearic acid ($C_{17}H_{35}COOH$), the most common fatty acid occurring in natural animal and vegetable fats. Stearates, especially the sodium and potassium salts, are used in soaps, lubricants, cosmetics, food additives, and pharmaceuticals.

Steel, David Martin Scott (1938–), British politician. A Liberal member of Parliament from 1965, he was elected leader of the Liberal Party in 1976. In 1975 he announced the formation of the "Lib-Lab Pact" between his party and the Labour government. He was instrumental in the formation of the Liberal/Social Democratic Alliance in 1981.

Steel, a commercial iron, containing carbon as an essential alloy. Its malleability distinguishes it from cast iron and its freedom of slag from wrought iron. It is the most widely used of all metals. First made in ancient times, it was not until the development of the Bessemer and open-hearth processes in the 19th century, that steel became available for large-scale uses. Carbon steel, used for automobile bodies, machinery, appliances, and ships has only carbon added to iron. Low-alloy steels, with less than 5% of nickel, chromium, and molybdenum or other metals added, are exceptionally strong and are used for structured members of buildings, bridges, and machine parts. High-alloy steels, such as stainless steel, with more than 5% of other metals, are used in tableware and cooking utensils, where lustrous appearance and resistance to rust are required.

Steele, (Sir) Richard (1672–1729), British essayist and dramatist, b. Dublin. His early works include a moral treatise *The Christian Hero* (1701) and a comedy *The Lying Lover* (1704). He edited and wrote for the periodicals the *Tatler* (1709–11) and the *Spectator* (1711–12) with Joseph Addison.

Steenbok, Steinbok, or **Grysbok,** three species of small, slender-legged antelopes native to hills of E and

Statue of Liberty

Gertrude Stein

John Steinbeck

S Africa. Colored shades of reddish brown and stippled with white, they are usually solitary. Males carry short, spiked horns. Length: to 34in (85cm); weight: to 30lb (14kg). Family Bovidae; genus *Raphicerus. See also* Antelope.

Stegosaurus, plated ornithischian dinosaur of Jurassic times of W United States. It was four-footed with a tiny skull and long tail. Its hallmark was á double row of bony, triangular plates running along its neck, back, and tail that carried long spikes. Length: 20ft (6m); weight: 8ton (7,200kg).

Steichen, Edward (1897–1973), US photographer, considered one of the greatest masters of the medium, b. Luxembourg. He helped Alfred Stieglitz open two photographic galleries in New York. First a portraitist and fashion photographer, he pioneered aerial photography during World War I and commanded naval combat photography during World War II. As director of the photography department of the Museum of Modern Art in New York (1947–62), he organized the famous "Family of Man" exhibition (1955). Many of his expressive images are included in *A Life in Photography* (1963).

Stein, Gertrude (1874–1946), US author and critic, b. Allegheny, Pa. She abandoned the study of medicine to devote her life to literature. She joined her brother in Paris (1903) and established a famous salon where she entertained and became a counselor and confidante of many of the great artists and writers of the time: Cézanne, Picasso, Hemingway, Fitzgerald, and many more.
Her first important book was *Three Lives* (1909). Other important works include *Tender Buttons* (1914), a volume of poems, and *The Making of Americans* (1925), a narrative. Her memoirs, *The Autobiography of Alice B. Toklas* (1933), actually a book by Stein about Stein but presented as the work of her secretary and constant personal companion, attained wide popularity. *See also* Lost Generation.

Steinbeck, John (1902–68), US novelist, b. Salinas, Calif. He gained critical notice in 1935 with the publication of his fourth novel, *Tortilla Flat.* His works are characterized by realistic dialogue and concern for the downtrodden. Among his novels are *Of Mice and Men* (1937), *The Grapes of Wrath* (1939, Pulitzer Prize 1940), *Cannery Row* (1945), *East of Eden* (1952), and *The Winter of Our Discontent* (1961). He was awarded the Nobel Prize for literature in 1962.

Stem, main, upward-growing part of a plant that bears leaves, buds, and flowers. The internal structure is composed of vascular tissue arranged in a ring (dicot) or scattered (monocot). Stems usually are erect, but may be climbing (vine) or prostrate (stolon); they can also be succulent (cactus) or modified into underground structures (rhizomes, tubers, corms, bulbs). Stems vary in size from the threadlike stalks of aquatic plants to tree trunks.

Stendhal (1783–1842), pseud. of Marie Henri Beyle, French novelist. After an unhappy childhood, Stendhal sought pleasure in Paris, joined Napoleon's army, and traveled widely in Italy. His literary output ranged from autobiographical studies to a treatise on love, from books on aesthetics through Romanticism into the realism of his two greatest novels, *The Red and the Black* (1831) and *Charterhouse of Parma* (1839). *See also* Charterhouse of Parma.

Stentor, freshwater, ciliate protozoan characterized by cone-shaped body with nucleus resembling long string of beads, clumps of cilia around the mouth, and a stalklike holdfast. Length: to 0.10in (2.5mm). Order Spirotricha; species include *Stentor polymorphus.*

Stephen I, Saint (975?–1038), king of Hungary (997–1038), greatest of Árpád line. Son of Geza, he converted to Christianity during his youth. Stephen married Gisela, sister of Emperor Henry II. He became duke of Hungary in 997. Pope Sylvester II sent a crown for his coronation in 1001 and gave him the title "Apostolic Majesty," which was held by Hungarian sovereigns until the overthrow of the monarchy in 1918. In 1027, Stephen conquered Slovakia. Stephen's rule was a period of great prestige for Hungary, one of consolidation, prosperity, and the suppression of paganism. With the aid of the clergy, he overcame the powerful tribal chieftains and appropriated their lands; established a centralized government; and brought Hungary into the European community.

Stephen (1097?–1154), king of England. Despite acknowledging Matilda as heir (1126), Stephen took the English crown on Henry I's death (1135). Harassed by the Scots and Matilda's supporters, Stephen provoked a revolt (1139) and was temporarily deposed (1141). Although he reestablished himself as king, Stephen could not thereafter control his barons. By the Treaty of Wallingford (1153), he conceded the succession to Matilda's son, Henry. *See also* Matilda.

Stephen Báthory (1533–86), prince of Transylvania (1571–76), elected king of Poland by the nobility in 1575. Renowned as a soldier, he put down a revolt in Danzig (1577) and defeated Russia's Ivan the Terrible in a war (1579–82). In order to defend his northeastern frontiers against Moscow and gain access to the sea at Danzig, he brought the Cossacks into his military system, giving them privileges to secure their help in the war with Russia. He also reformed the judicial system.

Stephens, Alexander Hamilton (1812–83), Confederate vice president (1861–65), b. Wilkes co, Ga. A brilliant man and leader, Stephens often opposed Confederate Pres. Jefferson Davis, particularly about the military draft. He worked for peace and was at the Hampton Roads Peace Conference (February 1865). After the war, he wrote *Constitutional View of the War Between the States,* a closely reasoned defense of the right of states to secede.

Steppe, the extensive, semiarid plains of northern Asia. The word is a Tartar term that has been adopted by geographers. The plains are covered with long rough grass and are only partially wooded. The soil consists of alluvial deposits. Prairies in the United States are similar but not so dry.

Stereophonic Sound, a method of reproducing sound so that it gives the illusion of both location and direction. As this depends on a difference in the time of hearing between the two ears, two separate channels are required. In stereophonic phonograph records, the groove is modulated in two planes—the lateral and the vertical (groove depth). Depth variations correspond to the difference between the left and right channels of the stereorecording and lateral modulations correspond to their sum. Two transducers in the pick-up cartridge feed two separate amplifiers and two widely spaced loudspeakers.

Stereoscope, optical binocular device that produces an apparently three-dimensional image by presenting two slightly different plane images, usually photographs, to each eye.

Stereotyping, tendency to ascribe to an individual characteristics that are attributed to the group or class of which the individual is a member. The stereotyped judgment, however, may or may not apply to the individual, and thus stereotyping is an elementary form of prejudice. The most typical stereotypes involve judging people on the basis of characteristics attributed to their sex, race, ethnic group, nationality, age, or religion. *See also* Prejudice.

Sterilization, killing of all microorganisms, spores, viruses, or other life forms. Sterile conditions may be created by chemical means, such as DDT, organophosphates affecting toxicological penetration, or chlorine in drinking water; by heat as in the use of steam in some foods and hospital supplies; by cold; or by ionizing radiation which eradicates insects (eg, screwworm fly) by sexual sterilization.

Sterling Heights, city in SE Michigan, 19mi (39km) N of Detroit. Industries: missile parts, automotive body stampings, chassis assemblies. Inc. 1968. Pop. (1980) 108,999.

Stern, Otto (1888–1969), US physicist, b. Germany. He won the Nobel Prize in physics (1943) for developing the molecular beam as a tool for studying the characteristics of molecules and for his measurement of magnetic moment of the proton.

Sterne, Laurence (1713–68), English novelist. A clergyman, he began as a political and ecclesiastical satirist, but his later works became more sentimental as he catered to public taste and wrote in a sentimental vein. His writings include a novel *The Life and Opinions of Tristram Shandy* (9 vols., 1760–67), *Sermons of Mr. Yorick* (1760), and *A Sentimental Journey through France and Italy* (1768).

Sternum, or breast bone, the flat, narrow bone in front of the chest between the breasts. It is generally divided into three regions: the manubrium, or upper part; the body; and the xiphoid process, or lower and more flexible cartilaginous part. The top of the manubrium is attached by ligaments to the collarbone on each side, and the body is joined to the ribs by seven pairs of costal cartilages.

Steroid, one of a class of organic compounds characterized by a basic molecular structure of 17 carbon atoms arranged in four rings and bonded to 28 hydrogen atoms. Steroids are widely distributed in animals and plants; the most abundant are the sterols (steroid alcohols), such as cholesterol. Another important group is the steroid hormones, including the corticosteroids, secreted by the adrenal cortex, and the sex hormones. The sex hormones are the estrogens (such as estrone) and progesterone produced by the ovary, and androgens (such as testosterone and androsterone) secreted by the testis. Synthetic steroids are widely used in medicine.

Stettin. *See* Szczecin.

Steuben, Frederick William, Baron von (1730–94), German and American soldier. Receiving his rigorous military training in Prussia, where he was aide-de-camp to Frederick the Great (1762), he transported these ideas to America, successfully training George Washington's troops before Valley Forge. His treatise on regulations was an official US Army manual until 1812.

Stevens, John Paul (1920–), associate justice of the US Supreme Court, b. Chicago, Ill. He began his career by clerking for Supreme Court Justice Wiley B. Rutledge in 1948, before beginning specialization in antitrust law. President Nixon appointed him judge of the 7th Circuit Court of Appeals in 1970. In 1975, he was nominated to the Supreme Court by President Ford. The 101st justice to serve the court, he filled the vacancy left by the retirement of William O. Douglas.

Stevens, Wallace (1879–1955), US poet, b. Reading, Pa. A lawyer, he was for many years an executive of a Hartford, Conn., insurance company. His first book of poems, *Harmonium,* appeared in 1923. His work is rich in metaphors, and in it he contemplates nature and society. His early poems are often set in the tropics and reflect the lushness of their location. Among his works are *Ideas of Order* (1935), *Owl's Clover* (1936), *The Man with the Blue Guitar and Other Poems* (1937), *Parts of a World* (1942), *Notes Toward a Supreme Fiction* (1942), *Transport to Summer* (1947), and *Collected Poems* (1954; Pulitzer Prize 1955).

Stevenson, Adlai Ewing (1835–1914), US vice president, b. Christian co, Ky. He was a Democratic Congressman from Illinois (1875–77, 1879–81) and as assistant postmaster general during the first Cleveland administration. Stevenson headed the Illinois delegation to the 1892 convention and helped re-nominate Cleveland; he was rewarded with the vice presidency (1893–97). Stevenson was William Jennings Bryan's running mate in 1900 and a candidate for governor of Illinois in 1908; he won neither contest.

Stevenson, Adlai Ewing (1900–65), US political leader, b. Los Angeles. He practiced law in Chicago before he went into government service during the early New Deal. He was an advisor at the San Francisco conference (1945) that set up the United Nations. After serving as advisor to the US delegation to the United Nations (1946–47), he was elected governor of Illinois (1949). He was the unsuccessful Democratic candidate for president against Dwight D. Eisenhower in 1952 and 1956. In 1961, he was appointed US ambassador to the United Nations. His writings include *A Call to Greatness* (1954) and *Looking Outward: Years of Crisis at the U.N.* (1963).

Stevenson, Robert Louis (1850–94), Scottish novelist, essayist, and poet. He traveled in Europe and the United States, finally settling in Samoa. His essays, many of them about travel, suffer from an artificiality of style, but his novels, including *Treasure Island* (1883), *Dr. Jekyll and Mr. Hyde* (1886), *Kidnapped* (1886), *The Black Arrow* (1888), and *The Master of Ballantrae* (1889), display a keen sense of adventure and are widely read, particularly by children. *A Child's Garden of Verses,* sentimental poems for children, appeared in 1885.

Stewart. *See* Stuart.

Stewart, Potter (1915–85), US jurist and lawyer, b. Jackson, Mich. An Ohio attorney, he served as a Cincinnati city councilman (1949–53) and vice-mayor of Cincinnati (1952–53). He was appointed a US Appeals Court judge (1954–58) and in 1958, Pres. Dwight D. Eisenhower appointed him an associate justice of the US Supreme Court. He was confirmed in 1959 and served until his retirement in 1981. Considered a political conservative, he maintained a centrist position on the court and was a champion of freedom of the press. He was the only dissenter in *Engel* v. *Vitale* (1962), the school prayer decision.

Stibnite, a sulfide mineral, antimony trisulfide (Sb_2S_3) found in low-temperature veins and rock impregnations. Orthorhombic system aggregates of prismatic crystals or granular masses. Opaque, sometimes iridescent; gray; hardness 2; sp gr 4.6. Important ore of antimony.

Stickleback, small fish found in fresh, brackish, and salt water. Usually brown and green, it is identified by the number of bony plates and spines along its sides and back. It is a popular scientific subject because of its elaborate mating and courtship ritual. The male builds a nest in water plants and, through an elaborate ritual, drives the female into it. He then watches the eggs and cares for the young. Length: 2.5–6.5in (6.4–16.5cm). The 12 or so species include the three-spine *Gasterosteus aculeatus* and the polar nine-spine *Pungitius pungitius.* Family Gasterosteidae.

Stieglitz, Alfred (1864–1946), US photographer, editor, and promoter of modern art, b. Hoboken. He is responsible for establishing photography as a fine art through exhibitions at his New York galleries and through magazines. In 1902 he founded the Photo-Secession Group. His photographs include classic portraits of his wife, Georgia O'Keeffe, studies of Manhattan, and the cloud images known as "equivalents."

Stilbite, a hydrous silicate mineral, hydrous calcium, sodium, aluminum silicate; one of the zeolite group. Monoclinic system radiating tabular crystals and aggregates. White, yellow, red or brown; hardness 3.5–4; sp gr 2.1.

Still Life, the art of painting pictures of everyday objects, flowers, furniture, etc, as viewed close up. It arose as an independent art in around the 16th century in the works of Caravaggio, for example. The art flourished with Flemish artists of the 17th century. Chardin was the first notable French still-life painter, and still lifes were also an important stage in the development of a number of 20th-century artists and nonrepresentational art, as in the works of Cézanne, Van Gogh, and Picasso.

Stilt, wading, long-legged marsh bird. It has an elaborate nest defense that includes playing dead and in-flight distraction displays. Pear-shaped, marked olive eggs (4) are laid. Included are whitish pied or black-winged stilt *(Himantopus himantopus)* and the rarer Australasian banded stilt *(Cladorhynchus leucocephaus).* Length: 14–18in (36–46cm). Family Recurvirostridae.

Stimulant, drug that excites the central nervous system, which results in a mental state associated with heightened alertness and elevation of mood. There are two types: one type affects alertness and has only secondary actions on emotions; the other (called antidepressants) affects the emotions. Stimulants, such as amphetamines, are among the most commonly prescribed drugs; methylxanthines, the ingredients in coffee, tea, and colas that provide stimulation, are the most widely consumed of all drugs.

Stimulus, in psychology, the energy that excites receptors of the nervous system. The term is sometimes applied to the objects that produce or transmit the energy, for example, the light is a *stimulus;* the book or chair that reflects the light is a *stimulus object.*

Sting Ray, bottom-dwelling elasmobranch found in shallow marine waters. Its flattened, disklike body has winglike fins extending around the head and a long slender tail. Its poison tail spine can inflict serious injury. Width: 1–7ft (30.5cm–2.1m); weight: 1.5–750lb (.7–338kg). There are five genera including the southern *Dasyatis americana.* Family Dasyatidae. *See also* Chondrichthyes; Ray.

Stink Bug, shield-shaped, brown bug with a disagreeable odor found worldwide. Barrel-shaped eggs are laid in clusters on leaves. Subfamilies Acanthosomatinae and Asopinae suck insect juices, while Pentatominae suck plant juices. Length: 1/3in (8mm). Family Pentatomidae. *See also* Harlequin Bug.

Stinkhorns, any of several mushrooms (order Phallales) that are egg-shaped when young. At maturity the stalks grow rapidly and rupture the egg, releasing the spore mass in a sticky, smelly slime. The spores are spread by insects that are attracted by the smell and carry the spores away on their bodies.

Stoat. *See* Ermine.

Stock, certificate of ownership in a corporation. A corporation may issue shares of stock upon its formation. It may also issue additional shares when it needs more capital. The ownership of stock implies sharing in the control of the corporation's operations, and the major stockholder may have prime influence upon the operation of the corporation. Stock is divided into two general classes: common stock and preferred stock.

Stockfish, or South African hake, elongated commercial food fish found in cold and temperate marine waters of the S Atlantic. Length: to 4ft (1.2m). Family Merluccidae (or Gadidae); species *Merluccius capensis.*

Stockholm, seaport and capital city of Sweden, on Lake Mälaren at the Baltic Sea; strategic location has made Stockholm most important city in Sweden's history. Stockholm's early history was dominated by the German Hanseatic League; in 1520, Christian II of Denmark and Norway proclaimed himself king of Sweden; rule passed to Gustavus I 1523–60, who made Stockholm the center of his kingdom. It became the capital of Sweden 1643; it is now a modern city with wide streets, and several fine buildings and parks; site of Sweden's stock exchange, 13th-century Church of St Nicholas, Stockholm University (1877), technical institute (1827), national museum, royal palace (1754), Nobel Institute, Court Theatre, Riddarholm Church, which contains the tombs of Sweden's monarchs; scene of annual presentation of the Nobel prizes, the first UN Conference of the Human Environment 1972. Industries: textiles, clothing, publishing, food processing, engineering works, rubber, shipbuilding, beer, motor vehicles, porcelain, communications equipment, liquor. Founded *c.* 1250 by Birger Jarl. Pop. 665,202.

Stockton, city in central California, 53mi (85km) E of Oakland; seat of San Joaquin co; supply center during the gold-rush era. Industries: canning, farm machinery, boats. Inc. 1850. Pop. (1980) 149,779.

Stoichiometry, quantitative proportions in which compounds combine or react together. The term also describes the measurement of these proportions and their use in finding formulas, molecular weights, etc.

Stoicism, dominant philosophy of the Hellenistic-Roman period, founded by Zeno of Citium (*c.*333–262 BC). Chrysippus systematized Zeno's fundamental principles. Stoicism was reworked but remained basically unchanged until it faded after the end of the 3rd century BC. The highest Stoic virtue is to live in harmony with the cosmos. To do this people must live austere and noble lives, above concern for trivial things, and be able to control emotions. The wise man, or sage, puts his own integrity and duty ahead of lesser interests and feelings.

Stoke-on-Trent, industrial city in W central England, on Trent River; covers most of Potteries district; center of pottery industry; comprises the "Five Towns" of Arnold Bennett's novels. Industries: ceramics, bricks, tiles, coal, chemicals, tires. Pop. 255,800.

STOL (Short Takeoff and Landing) Aircraft, aircraft with the ability to operate out of extremely small airfields. Present STOL aircraft are capable of taking off and climbing over a 50-foot (15-m) obstacle in less than 500 feet (152.5m). Wings of great lifting ability and powerful engines allow for unusual performance without sacrificing load-carrying capability. *See also* VTOL Aircraft.

Stomach, a J-shaped organ, lying to the left and slightly below the diaphragm in man; one of the organs of the digestive system. It is connected at its upper end, or fundus, to the esophagus at the cardiac orifice; at its lower end, or pyloric section, to the small intestine at the pylorus. The stomach itself is lined by three layers of muscle (longitudinal, circular, and oblique) and a mucous layer, the gastric mucosa, that lies in folds (rugae) and contains gastric glands. These glands secrete hydrochloric acid that destroys any food bacteria, dissolves salt in the food, and makes possible the action of pepsin, the active stomach enzyme that digests proteins alone. Gastric gland secretion is controlled by sensory stimuli—the sight, smell, and taste of food—and by hormonal stimuli, chiefly the hormone gastrin. As the food is digested, it is churned by muscular action into a thick liquid state, called chyme, at which point it passes through the pylorus to the small intestine. *See also* Digestive System.

Stone, Harlan Fiske (1872–1946), chief justice of the US Supreme Court (1941–46), b. Chesterfield, N.H. He served as dean of Columbia Law School (1910–23), resigning to resume private practice. As US attorney general under Pres. Calvin Coolidge (1924–25), he reorganized the Federal Bureau of Investigation. He was an associate justice of the Supreme Court from 1925 and was appointed Chief Justice by Pres. Franklin D. Roosevelt (1941). Together with Louis Brandeis, Benjamin Cardozo, and Oliver Wendell Holmes, he was a liberal dissenter on social issues, and generally supported New Deal legislation. He supported the protection of individual civil liberties from restrictive state legislation, as in *West Virginia State Board of Education* v. *Barnette* and *Smith* v. *Allwright* (1944), which invalidated all-white political party membership.

Stone, Lucy (1818–93), US feminist, b. near West Brookfield, Mass. A graduate of Oberlin College (1847), she lectured for women's rights and against slavery. With others, she organized the first US women's rights convention (1850). Although she married in 1855, she retained her own name and was known as Mrs. Stone. She organized several organizations for woman suffrage and founded (1870) the *Woman's Journal.*

Stone, (John) Richard (Nicholas) (1913–), British economist. He received the Nobel Prize in economics (1984) for creating "an accounting system for nations that has been indispensable in monitoring their financial position, in tracking trends in national development, and in comparing one nation's economic workings with another's." The system is used by most industrialized countries and is important to international banking and economic organizations such as the International Monetary Fund.

Stone Age, period in man's evolution lasting over 2,-500,000 years, in which he used stone tools and weapons. In this time he progressed from making crude

Adlai E. Stevenson

Lucy Stone

Harriet Beecher Stowe

flaked pebble tools to finely worked arrowheads and polished and hafted axes. *See also* Eolithic Age; Mesolithic Age; Neolithic Age; Paleolithic Age.

Stonecrop, any member of the genus *Sedum* of the family Crassulaceae, especially creeping sedum *(S. acre),* an evergreen mossy plant of European origin with pungent fleshy leaves and yellow flowers widely used as a ground cover.

Stonefish, or stingfish, deadly marine fish found in tropical Indo-Pacific. Ugly with warty, slime-coated body, its neurotoxic poison is injected by 13 spines. The poison is painful and fatal unless immediately treated with an antidote. Length: 13in (33cm). Family Synancejidae; species *Synanceja verrucosa.*

Stonefly, or salmon fly, soft-bodied insect with long, narrow front wings and chewing mouthparts, found worldwide. The aquatic nymphs have branched gills. Often used as fish bait, adults are brown to black. Length: 0.2–4in(5–102mm). Order Plecoptera.

Stone Fruit. *See* Drupe.

Stonehenge, major prehistoric monument in S England; a group of standing stones on Salisbury Plain, Wiltshire, 3mi (4.8km) W of Amesbury. Erected in the 2nd millennium BC, its four series of stones are circled by a ditch 300ft (91.5m) in diameter. The outermost circle of sandstones, 13.5ft (4.1m) high, are connected by lintels. The next circle is bluestone Menhirs (single standing stones); third ring is horseshoe-shaped. The inner ring is ovoid with an Altar Stone within its confines. NE of circle is a huge upright Heelstone. At one time attributed to the Druids, it is now believed they arrived in Britain much later than the erection of this work, but it is generally agreed that stones served some religious purpose. Latest theory by Gerald Hawkins (1963), a British astronomer, proposes that they were used as an astronomical instrument. Others claim that the Bronze Age culture during which Stonehenge was created was not sophisticated enough to support Hawkins' calculations. This site is one of 40 or 50 such prehistoric "henge" monuments in British Isles.

Stony Meteorite, or aerolite, an abundant meteorite type, consisting mostly of silicate minerals, and divided into two groups called chondrites and achondrites. Chondrites are the most common and contain embedded, small spherical bodies called chondrules. Chondrites, mostly with anhydrous silicates, resemble terrestrial volcanic pulp. Those with claylike silicates and carbonaceous material are called carbonaceous chondrites. Achondrites are much rarer, may be secondarily derived from chondrites, and resemble terrestrial igneous rocks low in silica (such as basalt).

Stoph, Willi (1914–), East German politician. He became premier of the German Democratic Republic (1964–73). He met with West Germany's Willy Brandt in 1970 in an effort to normalize relations between the two countries, and in 1972 a basic treaty was signed in which each state recognized the other's post-war boundaries. He was made chairman of the State Council (1974–76) and premier again (1976–).

Stork, long-legged wading bird living along rivers, lakes, and marshes in temperate and tropical regions. Usually black, white, and gray, they have straight bills, long necks, robust bodies, long broad wings, and partially webbed toes. Diurnal, they feed on small animals and sometimes on carrion. They lay white eggs (3–5) in a platform nest in a tree or on a ledge or rooftop. Length: 3–6ft (0.9–1.8m). Family Ciconiidae.

Storm Petrel, small seabird ranging over the oceans. A strong flyer, even in rough weather, it feeds on plankton. Sooty-colored with a white rump, it has a small hooked bill, narrow sharp wings, long thin legs, and webbed feet. Breeding on oceanic islands and rocky coastlines, it burrows a nest for a single white egg. Length: 12–15in (30–38cm). Family Hydrobatidae.

Story, Joseph (1779–1845), US Supreme Court justice (1811–45) and legal scholar, b. Marblehead, Mass. He served as speaker of the Massachusetts legislature (1810–11) and as a US Congressman (1808–09). He was only 32 when selected to sit on the Supreme Court. His best known opinions were in *Martin* v. *Hunter's Lessee* (1816), his dissent in *Charles River Bridge* v. *Warren Bridge* (1837), and in the *Amistad* case (1841). As Harvard's first Dane Law Professor (1829–45), he introduced a number of legal textbooks and wrote his classic *Commentaries on the Constitution* (1833).

Stowe, Harriet Beecher (1811–96), US author, b. Litchfield, Conn. The daughter of Lyman Beecher, a renowned clergyman, she moved with her family to Cincinnati in 1832. There she taught school and began writing stories of New England. In 1836 she married Calvin E. Stowe. An advocate of the abolition of slavery, she began to write her famous novel about slavery, *Uncle Tom's Cabin,* in 1848. It was serialized in 1851–52 and published in book form in 1852 and brought her to fame. She later wrote a second novel about slavery, *Dred* (1856). Other works, none as popular as her first book, include several novels about New England life, *The Minister's Wooing* (1859) and *Oldtown Folks* (1869). *See also* Uncle Tom's Cabin.

STP. *See* Standard Temperature and Pressure.

Strabismus, or squint, abnormal condition in which weak or paralyzed eye muscles prevent binocular vision. The eye may be directed inward or outward with a consistent squint if the deviation remains constant. Strabismus may be corrected with glasses or surgery.

Strachey, (Giles) Lytton (1880–1932), English author. His works include the biographies *Eminent Victorians* (1918), *Queen Victoria* (1921), and *Elizabeth and Essex* (1928), and a critical survey *Landmarks in French Literature* (1912).

Strafford, Thomas Wentworth, 1st Earl of (1593–1641), English nobleman, leading advisor of Charles I. Although a loyal monarchist, he opposed Charles's arbitrary conduct of the war against Spain (1626) but was later appointed lord president of the north (1628) and privy councillor (1629). As lord deputy of Ireland (1632–38), he sought to strengthen royal authority and Protestantism and to stimulate agriculture and trade. He was made an earl in 1640. Strafford's advocacy of sovereign power led to conflict with Parliament and his impeachment (1640). He was convicted and executed, Charles reluctantly acquiescing in the hope of appeasing Parliament.

Strain, the change in dimensions of a body subjected to stress. *Longitudinal* strain is the ratio of the change in length of a bar to its original length while being stretched or compressed. *Shearing* strain describes the change in shape of a body whose opposite faces are pushed in different directions. Hooke's law for elastic bodies states that strain is proportional to stress. *See also* Hooke's Law; Stress.

Strange Particles, elementary particles, all hadrons including the hyperons and kaons, that have an anomalously long lifetime (10^{-10} to 10^{-7} second) compared to that characteristic of most other hadrons (10^{-23} second). The delay is attributed to a property, strangeness, described by a quantum number that is a positive or negative integer for strange particles and zero for other hadrons and must be conserved in particle interactions. *See also* Conservation Law, Nuclear; Hadron.

Strangford, Lord. *See* Smythe, Percy Ellen Frederick William.

Strasbourg, city in NE France, on Ill River, 2mi (3km) W of confluence with Rhine River; capital of Bas-Rhin dept. Known in Roman times as Argentoratum, it was destroyed by Huns in 5th century; became part of Holy Roman Empire in 923; made a free imperial city 1262; seized by France 1681; site of University of Strasbourg (1621) and 11th-century Cathedral of Notre Dame containing astronomical clock installed 1574. Industries: boatbuilding, oil refining, processed foods. Pop. 257,303.

Stratford, town in SW Connecticut, on Long Island Sound at mouth of Housatonic River; site of Housatonic Community College (1966), American Shakespeare Festival Theater (1955), David Judson House (1723). Industries: aircraft engines, helicopters, asbestos products. Founded and inc. 1639. Pop. (1980) 50, 541.

Stratford-upon-Avon, market town in central England, on Avon River; birthplace of William Shakespeare; site of Shakespeare's grave, several places linked with him, and the Memorial Theatre—home of the Royal Shakespeare Company. Pop. 99,400.

Stratification, in geology, the layering in rocks. It occurs in sedimentary rocks and in those igneous rocks formed from lava flows and volcanic fragmental deposits. Layers range in depth and vary in shape. Strata may occur as thin sheets covering many miles or as thick bodies extending only a few feet. Separations between individual layers are called stratification planes. They parallel the strata they bound, being horizontal near flat layers and exhibiting inclination on a sloping surface. In sedimentary rocks, stratification may result from changes during deposition or from pauses in deposition. The sequence may then appear as alternations of coarse and fine particles, a series of color changes, or as similar layers, separated by distinct planes. Folding and faulting are recorded by tilted or broken strata, allowing interpretation of geologic events and the location of mineral deposits, oil fields, and groundwater. *See also* Stratigraphy.

Stratigraphy, branch of geology dealing with stratified or layered rocks. Sediments are layered in the order of deposition by water and hardened. These may then have undergone metamorphism, folding, faulting, or igneous intrusion. Some igneous rocks are also stratified, particularly those associated with volcanic systems that continue to produce material. *See also* Historical Geology; Paleontology; Superposition, Principle of.

Stratosphere, the cloudless shell of gases just above the troposphere in the atmosphere. *See* Atmosphere.

Stratum (pl. strata), distinct layer of sedimentary or igneous rock consisting of material that has been spread out on the Earth's surface. It can be of any thickness but is visibly separated from layers above and below by a change in the kind of material deposited. Sedimentary beds consisting of material transported by ancient rivers and deposited in layers make up a stratum.

Stratus Cloud. *See* Cloud.

Strauss, Johann (the Younger) (1825–99), Austrian composer and conductor known as the "waltz king." He became extremely popular for his more than 400 waltzes, eg, *The Blue Danube, Tales from the Vienna Woods, Wine, Women and Song.* He also composed two popular operettas, *Die Fledermaus* (1874) and *The Gypsy Baron* (1885).

Strauss, Richard (1864–1949), German composer and conductor. Influenced by Richard Wagner, his music is characterized by Romantic themes and rich orchestral colors. His best known works are a number of symphonic poems, eg, *Don Juan* (1888), *Till Eulenspiegel* (1895), *Also Sprach Zarathustra* (1896), and *Ein Heldenleben* (1898). His operas include *Salome* (1905), *Elektra* (1908), and *Der Rosenkavalier* (1911). He also composed chamber works and songs.

Stravinsky, Igor (1882–1971), Russian composer, b. Oranienbaum (now Lomonosov). After studying with Rimsky-Korsakov, he emigrated to Western Europe in 1910 and to the United States in 1939. His early ballets *The Firebird* (1910) and *Petrouchka* (1911) earned him popularity and a reputation as a ballet master. His orchestral masterpiece *Le Sacre du Printemps* (*The Rite of Spring,* 1913) revolutionized orchestral composition and established him as a major composer.

Later works included ballets modeled after Tchaikovsky (eg, *The Fairy's Kiss,* 1928), Neoclassical instrumental and orchestral works (eg, the *Violin Concerto,* 1931) and experiments in serialism and 12-tone music (eg, the ballet *Agon,* 1957). *See also* Neoclassical Music.

Strawberry, fruit-bearing plant native to northern temperate areas and higher altitudes of tropical South America. Having trifoliate leaves and clusters of white or reddish flowers, the plants send out runners that root and produce new plants. There are two types: June bearers that produce one crop in early summer and everbearers that produce a crop in early summer and another in the fall. Plants that are well cared for can produce good fruit for 5–6 years. The sweet, juicy red fruits are eaten fresh or preserved. Family Rosaceae; genus *Fragaria.*

Stream-of-Consciousness Novel, type of 20th-century psychological novel that presents the flow of thoughts and images through the minds of its main characters. The stream-of-consciousness novel contains a mass of seemingly disconnected detail that has an underlying pattern. Events that appear trivial are often actually more important than major happenings. James Joyce, William Faulkner, and Virginia Woolf used the stream-of-consciousness technique in their novels.

Streptococcus, genus of bacteria characterized by gram-positive spherical cells that grow in chains and are generally facultative anaerobes. They occur normally in the mouth, respiratory tract, and intestine of man; some are pathogenic, causing scarlet fever and strep throat; treated with penicillin. *See also* Bacteria.

Streptomycin, antibiotic drug used to treat certain bacterial diseases resistant to penicillin. Its side effects include sensitization and a rash. Its discovery in 1944 by Selman A. Waksman quickly led to the development of other antibiotics.

Stresemann, Gustav (1878–1929), German chancellor (1923) and foreign minister (1923–29), the outstanding statesman of the Weimar Republic. He concluded the Treaty of Locarno in 1925, in one of his many efforts to make a workable settlement with the Allies, for which he shared the Nobel Prize for peace in 1926.

Stress, a tensor quantity describing the internal pressure of a body being stretched, twisted, or squeezed. If any part of the body with cross-sectional area A is subjected to a tensile or compressive force F having components F_n perpendicular to A and F_t tangential to A, then the *normal* stress is F_n/A and the *tangential* (or *shearing*) stress is F_t/A. In a fluid, no shearing stress is possible because the fluid slips sideways—thus all stresses are normal stresses and are denoted by the term "pressure." *See also* Strain.

Stress, a physical and emotional state experienced by the organism when an excessive number of demands are placed upon it. In the human organism its sources may be infections, excessive work load, unfavorable living conditions, emotional strain, and excessive worry. Normally the organism is equipped to cope with a reasonable amount of stress; however, when an accumulation and a prolonged exposure to the above factors are experienced its coping mechanisms undergo physical and/or emotional breakdown. *See also* Psychosomatic Disorders.

Strindberg, Johan August (1849–1912), influential Swedish dramatist. A master of language, he wrote over 50 plays in many styles. He is best known abroad for *The Father* (1887) and *Julia* (1888). In his novels and short stories he fictionalized his unhappy life and marriages.

Stringed Musical Instruments, instruments producing sound by the vibration of strings, usually gut or steel, and tuned by tension. In violins, strings are stroked with a resin-dressed horsehair bow, and sometimes finger-plucked (pizzicato). The strings of harps, lutes, and guitars are strummed or plucked with fingers or a plectrum. In keyboard instruments like the piano, strings are struck with hammers; in the harpsichord, strings are plucked by quills. In both cases keys control the mechanical action.

Strip Cropping, practice of planting strips of deep-rooted crops alternately with strips of short-rooted crops to prevent soil erosion. This method is often used on sloping land. *See also* Soil Conservation.

Strip Mining, or stripping, method of open-pit mining used for coal. Electric excavator shovels with bucket capacities of 40–100cu yd (30–76cu m) uncover coal beds by removing the overburden in parallel paths and dumping the waste to the side. Smaller shovels follow, removing the coal and making room for more waste. *See also* Open-Pit Mining.

Stroboscope, any of various optic devices capable of making moving, rotating, or vibrating objects appear slowed down or stationary. This effect is achieved by interrupting the observer's continuous view of the moving object.

Stroke, or apoplexy, or cerebrovascular accident, interruption of the flow of blood to the brain. It is caused by blockage or rupture of an artery and results in temporary or permanent paralysis, difficulty in articulating, or loss of muscular coordination. It may occur without symptoms or after a period of headaches and irritability. Treatment includes surgery, drugs to reduce clotting, and physical therapy.

Structural Analysis, the study of rock deformation, faulting, folding, and crumpling of rock strata and the effects of these processes. Structural models simulating Earth materials are used. Structural patterns produced by applied stresses are recorded on models.

Structural Isomer. *See* Isomers.

Strychnine, lethal poison formerly believed to have therapeutic value. Symptoms of strychnine poisoning include stiffness and twitching.

Stuart or **Stewart,** Scottish family of Breton origin, the senior branch of which inherited the Scottish crown in 1371 (Robert II) and the English crown in 1603 (James I). The family gained a name for persistent bad luck over several centuries. Seven Stuarts ascended the Scottish throne as minors through sudden deaths. The direct male line died out with James V (1542). His daughter, Mary, Queen of Scots, was succeeded by James VI of Scotland (James I of England). After the execution of James' son Charles I in 1649, Stuarts were excluded from the throne until the restoration of Charles II (1660). They lost the throne with the deposition of James II in 1688. The last male Stuarts of the royal English line were grandsons of James II: Charles (Bonnie Prince Charlie) and Henry, a cardinal. *See also* Charles I and II of England; James I and II of England; James I–VI of Scotland; Mary, Queen of Scots; Robert I of Scotland; Stuart, Charles Edward; Stuart, James Francis Edward.

Stuart, Charles Edward (1720–88), English prince and claimant to the throne, also called "Bonnie Prince Charlie" and the "Young Pretender," b. Italy. A grandson of the deposed James II, he invaded Scotland (1745) to begin the Forty-five, a Jacobite revolt. He was initially victorious at Prestonpans, but the duke of Cumberland annihilated his army at Culloden (1746) and he went into permanent exile in Europe.

Stuart, Gilbert (Charles) (1755–1828), US painter, b. Kingston, R.I. He painted portraits in Europe and eventually settled in Boston. His best known works are his three clearly and precisely rendered portraits of George Washington, for which the subject posed, and his many replicas of these.

Stuart, James Ewell Brown (1833–64), Confederate Civil War general, b. Patrick co, Va. Known as "Jeb" Stuart, he was commander of Robert E. Lee's cavalry at the age of 30. A brilliant leader, he gained fame with his ride around Gen. George McClellan's Army of the Potomac in June 1862. Later exploits included a dash against Gen. John Pope's headquarters and a raid on Manassas Junction, Va., both in August 1862. He was mortally wounded at Yellow Tavern, Va.

Stuart, or **Stewart, James Francis Edward** (1688–1766), also called "The Old Pretender," claimant to the British throne, only son of James II. Brought up in France, he was proclaimed king of England (1701) and tried to take advantage of the 1715 Scottish Jacobite rising, establishing his court at Scone. Forced to flee, he subsequently lived in exile, intriguing in France and Italy.

Stubbs, George (1724–1806), English painter. He began as a portrait painter but gained considerable fame as a painter of animals, especially horses. His book *The Anatomy of the Horse* (1766) is well known.

Stupa, a Buddhist burial mound, found mainly in India, with a domed circular center surrounded by a processional path and a square stone railing.

Sture Family, Swedish noble family that played a key role in Sweden's fight for independence during the 15th and 16th centuries. Sten Sture the elder (*c.*1440–1503) was regent in 1470, had to resign in 1497, was regent again in 1501. Svante Sture succeeded him, followed by Sten Sture the younger, who asserted the state's superiority over the church. His refusal to accept Christian II of Denmark as king of Sweden resulted in the Stockholm Bloodbath.

Sturgeon, largest primitive, bony freshwater fish in North America, found in temperate fresh and marine waters of Northern Hemisphere. The source of caviar, this fish has five series of sharp-pointed scales along its sides, fleshy whiskers, and a tapering snoutlike head. Family Acepenseridae; species giant beluga *Huso huso* of E Europe—length: to 14ft (4.3m); weight: 2,200lb (990kg); Atlantic Sturgeon *Acipenser sturio*—length: 11ft (3.3m); weight: 600lb (272kg). *See also* Ganoid Fish, Osteichthyes.

Stuttgart, city in SW West Germany, on Neckar River, 38mi (61km) ESE of Karlsruhe; capital of Baden-Württemberg state; seat of Württemberg royalty 1320–1806; severely damaged during WWII; site of the Solitude Palace (1763–67), New Palace (1746–1807), Rosenstein Palace (1824–29), technical university (1956), agricultural college, academy of fine arts, and a conservatory. Industries: publishing, textiles, chemicals, paper, wine, iron, steel, machinery, footwear, beer, electrical equipment, motor vehicles, musical instruments, tourism. Founded *c.* 950; chartered 1254. Pop. 594,100.

Stuyvesant, Peter (*c.*1610–72), Dutch colonial governor. He became governor of the Caribbean Islands of Curacao, Bonaire, and Aruba (1643) and in 1647 he was named director general of New Netherlands as well. As governor, he ruled in a dictatorial manner, denying freedom to worship and causing discontent among the colonists. He was successful in curbing the sale of liquor to Indians, raising taxes, and improving defense, but the colony did not prosper. In 1650 he negotiated the Treaty of Hartford, which set the boundary between New York and Connecticut, and he ended Swedish influence in Delaware (1655). He ruled until the colony was taken over by the British (1664) and renamed New York.

Sty, infection of an eyelid gland, caused by a staphylococcus organism. It may occur externally, in the margin of the lid, or internally, under the lining of the lid. A small boil or pimple with a central yellow spot erupts, then breaks and discharges its contents.

Styria, province in central and SE Austria; Graz is capital. Made a duchy 1180; came under Hapsburg domination 1282; S portion passed to Yugoslavia by Treaty of Saint-Germain (1919). Industries: mining, livestock, metals, resorts. Area: 6,324sq mi (16,379sq km). Pop. 1,192,100.

Styron, William (1925–), US novelist, b. Newport News, Va. He achieved considerable success with his first novel, *Lie Down in Darkness* (1951), a story of psychological problems and tangled family relationships. Other novels include *The Long March* (1956); *Set This House on Fire* (1960); *The Confessions of Nat Turner* (1967), which received a Pulitzer Prize in fiction (1968); *Sophie's Choice* (1979), which received an American Book Award (1980); and *This Quiet Dust* (1982).

Styx, in Greek mythology, the river between the land of the living and Hades, the land of the dead. Styx, the nymph who personified the river, was the mother of Nike and the daughter of Jethys and Oceanus. The

Strawberry

Jeb Stuart

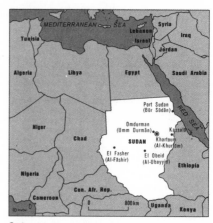

Sudan

river was considered sacred and oaths taken in her name could not be broken, even by the gods. A poisonous river named the Styx actually flowed through ancient Arcadia.

Subconscious, any of the mental processes that occur just below the level of awareness. Psychoanalysts define it as a zone between the conscious and the unconscious and believe that many important psychological activities occur here. Much of the psychoanalytical method involves bringing into awareness subconscious processes.

Sublimation, in physics, a change from the solid phase directly to the gaseous phase, as seen in dry ice (CO_2). Most substances can sublimate at a certain range of pressure but usually not at atmospheric pressures.

Submarine, seagoing warship capable of traveling both on and under the water, armed principally with torpedoes. *See also* Torpedo.

Submarine Canyon, a deep (1km or 0.62mi), steep-sided, V-shaped valley that cuts through the continental shelf. Though some line up with large land rivers, others do not. Therefore, it seems likely that they are formed when sediment deposited on the shelf becomes unstable and gravity causes it to slump, forming a turbid muddy bottom current that races downslope onto the deep-sea floor, scouring out the great canyons.

Submersible, Research, small vessel designed for brief periods of undersea exploration. This type of workboat is meant to remain submerged for a few hours or days and life support, power, and navigation systems are limited. Submersibles have been used to collect water and plankton samples, photograph ocean topography, investigate acoustic and electromagnetic properties at various depths.

Subparticles, Elementary, postulated constituents of the hadron group of elementary particles. Experimental evidence indicates that protons are made up of tiny pointlike bodies, termed partons. There is also evidence that the parton is the theoretical quark. Although the four leptons appear to be pointlike particles, the large number of hadrons could be explained by various combinations of three or possibly four or twelve quarks.

Subsistence Economy, condition in which economic activity is concentrated within each household; items are produced for consumption by the productive unit, not for sale in a market. In such primitive economies, money and trade are not yet in evidence, and the level of living is usually very low.

Substitution, chemical reaction in which one atom or group of atoms replaces (usually in the same structural position) another group in a molecule or ion. Chemists differentiate electron-rich incoming groups, such as the hydroxyl and halogen ions, from electron-deficient groups, such as the hydroxonium ion (H_3O^+) and the nitro group (NO_2^+), and unstable unpolarized species called radicals.

Subtraction, arithmetical operation signified by $-$, interpreted as the inverse process of addition. The difference of two numbers, $a - b$, is the number that has to be added to b to give a. a is called the minuend and b the subtrahend. *See also* Arithmetical Operations.

Succession, orderly change in plant and animal life in a biotic community over a long time period. It is the result of modifications in the community environment.

The process ends in establishment of a stable ecosystem (climax community).

Succulent Plant, plant that stores water in its tissues to resist periods of drought. Usually perennial and evergreen, most of the succulent plant body is made up of water storage cells giving it a fleshy appearance. A well-developed cuticle and low rate of daytime transpiration also conserve water. Succulent plants include cactus, milkweed, lily, and stonecrop sedum.

Süchow (Xuzhou or Hsu-chou), city in E central China, 180mi (290km) NW of Nanking; railroad center. Industries: food processing, textiles, flour, machine tools, steel, iron, coal. Pop. 1,500,000.

Sucker, freshwater fish found mainly from N Canada to Gulf of Mexico. A bottom grubber similar to minnows, it has a protrusible sucking mouth. Among the 100 species is the quillback *Carpiodes cyprinus;* length: 26in (66cm); weight: 12lb (5.4kg). Family Catostomidae.

Suckling, (Sir) John (1609–42), English Cavalier poet, author of witty, mocking lyrics. Once described as "the greatest gallant of his time, and the greatest gamester . . . so that no shopkeeper would trust him for 6d." After plotting against Parliament, Suckling fled to Paris, where he reputedly committed suicide. *See also* Cavalier Poets.

Sucre, Antonio José de (1795–1830), South American independence leader, Bolívar's chief of staff, and a key figure in the liberation of Ecuador, Peru, and Bolivia. Sucre commanded the rebel forces during the decisive battle of the independence struggles, Ayacucho (1824). An assembly chose him as the first constitutional president of Bolivia in 1826. He proved a good administrator, but political rivalries forced him to resign in 1829. He reassumed a battlefield command, defeating the Peruvian force that invaded Ecuador in 1829.

Sucre, formerly La Plata, and Chuquisaca; city in S central Bolivia; constitutional capital of Bolivia and capital of Chuquisaca dept. Renamed 1839 for revolutionary leader and first president of Bolivia, Antonio José de Sucre; site of archbishopric, supreme court, University of San Francisco Xavier (1624), oil refinery. Industries: mining. Founded 1538. Pop. 57,090.

Sucrose, disaccharide sugar (formula $C_{12}H_{22}O_{11}$), consisting of linked glucose and fructose units, that occurs in many plants; its principal commercial sources are sugarcane and sugar beet, but it is also obtained from maple trees, date palms, and sorghum. It is widely used for food sweetening and in the manufacture of preserves.

Suctorida, protozoa having cilia before developing into adults without cilia and with long hollow protoplasmic extensions used to suck in prey. Order Holotricha; class Suctoria; species include *Tokophrya.*

Sudan (As-Sudan), independent nation in N Africa. There are two primary cultural divisions among the people. Agriculture is the most important occupation, with cotton and cottonseed the main crops.

Land and economy. The largest country in Africa, Sudan is bounded on the N by Egypt, W by Libya, Chad, and the Central African Republic, S by Zaïre, Uganda, and Kenya, and E by Ethiopia and the Red Sea. Sudan's diverse geography ranges S to N, through tropical forests, swamplands, tropical grasslands, and arid hills between the Red Sea and the enormous Libyan and Sahara deserts. Flowing through the country for 2,340mi (3,767km) is the White Nile,

main artery of the Nile River. In the N, cultivation is dependent on Nile irrigation. The S has enough rainfall for crops or grazing. Cotton and cottonseed are the principal cash crops, accounting for 60% of export earnings. Gum arabic, the 2nd-most important export item, is sold almost exclusively to the United States. Minerals have been found only in small quantities.

People. The integration of Sudan's divided cultural groups is a major problem. In the N two-thirds of the country are Arab-speaking Muslims, including camel-raising nomads and tribes displaced by the Aswan High Dam, who constitute over 70% of the population. In the S are subsistence rural African tribal peoples, mainly animist in religious beliefs, who make up 30% of the population. The literacy rate is 10%–15%.

Government. Officially governed by an elected president and a People's Assembly, the Sudan is actually ruled through the military.

History. Until unified by Egypt in 1820, Sudan was a conglomeration of independent states. Egyptian exploitation brought a revolt in 1881, conquest by Anglo-Egyptian forces in 1896, and rule as a joint Anglo-Egyptian condominium until 1956, when Sudan was granted independence. Economic and political problems, regional strife, and a series of military coups and civil governments wracked the parliamentary system. Maj. Gen. Jaafar Muhammed Numeiry, who seized power in a military coup in 1969, was elected president in 1971. He declared a socialist state and gave autonomy to the S, and subsequently to the N. Sudan maintained close ties with Egypt, in 1979 approving an agreement for social, economic, and cultural integration between the two countries and in 1982 approving plans to coordinate political and economic policies. Numeiry was overthrown in 1985 amid accusations of corruption and mismanagement. Gen. Abdel Rahman Siwar el-Dahab suspended the constitution and declared martial law.

PROFILE

Official name: Democratic Republic of Sudan
Area: 967,497sq mi (2,505,817sq km)
Population: 17,400,000
 Density: 18per sq mi (7per sq km)
Chief cities: Khartoum (capital); Omdurman
Government: Republic, with military rule
Religion: Islam, Christianity, animist
Language: Arabic (official)
Monetary unit: Pound
Gross national product: $5,600,000,000
Per capita income: $320
Industries: textiles, food processing, vegetable oil, shoes, pharmaceuticals, cement
Agriculture: gum arabic, cotton, peanuts, rice, coffee, sugar cane, tobacco, wheat, dates, cattle, mahogany, forests, camels, sheep
Minerals: chrome, oil, natural gas
Trading partners: United States, Egypt, People's Republic of China, Soviet Union

Sudbury, city in central Ontario, Canada, 38mi (61km) N of Georgian Bay; site of Laurentian University (1960). Canadian Pacific Railroad excavations in 1883 revealed veins of nickel and copper; one of world's richest nickel-producing regions. Industries: nickel, copper, platinum, and palladium mining; lumbering, smelting. Inc. 1892. Pop. 97,604.

Sudden Infant Death Syndrome, or crib death, sudden mysterious, fatal affliction of infants who are unexpectedly found dead in their cribs. It can occur up to about one year after birth. The peak period seems to be around two months of age. Respiratory causes are suspected, with the possible involvement of a virus. Another theory proposed is an abnormal disruption of breathing at critical points in the sleep cycle. Other abnormalities involved include high levels of the thyroid hormone, triiodothyronine, which plays a key role in development of the central nervous system, excess brown fat around the adrenal glands, and abnormalities of the pulmonary arteries and brainstem.

Sudetenland, name given to a strip of territory along the Sudeten mountains, located in Czechoslovakia but inhabited by Germans. From 1526, under Hapsburg rule, Germanic influences permeated throughout Bohemia and Moravia, remaining dominant until a Czech nationalist movement began in the 19th century. The new independent country of Czechoslovakia was created after World War I, but the German speaking parts were ceded to Hitler in the Munich pact of 1938. After World War II, Czechoslovakia reclaimed Sudetenland and expelled the majority of Germans.

Suetonius (Gaius Suetonius Tranquillus) (c. 69–c.140 AD), Roman author. A lawyer and secretary to Emperor Hadrian, Suetonius is best remembered as a biographer. Two collections of his work survive: *De viris illustribus* (*On Famous Men*), biographies of literary figures, and *De vita Caesarum* (*The Lives of the Caesars*), biographies of rulers from Julius Caesar through Domitian. His writing was lively and informative and had a significant effect on later historiography.

Suez (As-Suways), city in NE Egypt, at N end of Gulf of Suez and S terminus of Suez Canal. A naval and trading station in 16th century, it developed into leading port in 1869 after completion of Suez Canal. City was occupied by Israelis in 1973 war and suffered damage during fighting; departure point for pilgrims to Mecca. Industries: oil storage and refining, paper, fertilizer. Pop. 275,000.

Suez, Gulf of (Suways, Khaty as-), NW extension of Red Sea; W of Sinai peninsula; connected on N to the Mediterranean Sea by way of the Suez Canal.

Suez Canal, waterway connecting the Mediterranean with the Red Sea. It was planned and built (1859–69) by the Suez Canal Company under the leadership of Ferdinand de Lesseps. This sea-level, 105mi (169km) canal has been enlarged to 46ft (14m) deep and 196ft (60m) bottom width. Its total cost was about $136,-000,000. After the introduction of steam vessels, its use increased and stockholders in the company realized huge gains. Disraeli purchased (1875) the Egyptian-held stock to make the British government the largest stockholder (though never owning the majority). In 1955 over 120,000,000 tons passed through the canal, much of it petroleum. The Suez Canal Company's 99-year concession was to revert to Egypt in 1968, but the Egyptian government nationalized it in 1956. Israel, Britain, and France attacked Egypt. The canal was closed from Oct. 1956 to April 1957, while repairs were being made, after a United Nation's Task Force entered and stopped the conflict. Egypt gained complete control and closed it during the Arab-Israeli War of 1967 and did not open it again until 1975.

Suffolk, nonmetropolitan county in E England, bounded by the North Sea (E), Stour River (S), and Little Ouse and Waveney rivers (N). County town is Ipswich. The land is mainly level, rising to the chalk hills of the East Anglian Heights in the SW. The area is principally agricultural, producing grain and sugar beets and raising livestock; formerly part of the Anglo-Saxon kingdom of East Anglia.

Suffrage, the constitutional right to vote. The United States Constitution, in several amendments, establishes suffrage. It guarantees that no citizen shall be denied the vote on account of race, color, previous condition of servitude (14th and 15th Amendments), or sex (19th Amendment). In national elections, no citizen shall be subjected to restrictive poll taxes (24th Amendment). The universal voting age is 18 (26th Amendment) and Washington, D.C., residents may vote in presidential elections (23rd Amendment). *See also* Woman Suffrage.

Sufism, communities of Muslim mystics, so named because their ascetic predecessors wore wool (suf). Sufis seek the union with God that is attained through ecstasy. After achieving the cessation of conscious thought, the Sufi attains consciousness of continuous survival in unity with God. Although there have been pantheistic tendencies in Sufism, Sufis are generally faithful to traditional Islamic monotheism. There are numerous orders and suborders within Sufism, including the Dervish. *See also* Dervish.

Sugar, a water-soluble, sweet carbohydrate found in both plants and animals. Sucrose, saccharose, maltose, fructose, and dextrose are among the naturally occurring sugars.

Sugar Act, or **Revenue Act** (1764), British legislation imposed on the American colonies to gain revenue and halt smuggling of foreign sugar into the colonies. Act reduced duty on foreign molasses, increased duties on refined sugar from England, and imposed duty on Madeira wine. It is considered a minor cause of the Revolution.

Sugar Beet, variety of beet grown commercially for its high sugar content. It has a thick white root. Species *Beta vulgaris crassa. See also* Beet.

Sugarcane, perennial grass cultivated in tropical and subtropical regions throughout the world. It has clumps of solid stalks with lancelike leaves and regularly spaced joints; each joint bears a single bud. Color varies. The tassel bears hundreds of flowered spikelets. After harvesting, stems are processed in factories, becoming the main source of sugar. Most cultivated canes are *Saccharum officinarum.* Height: to 26ft (8m). Family Gramineae.

Suharto (1921–), Indonesian military and political figure, president (1967–). A lieutenant colonel in a guerrilla army that fought for independence from the Dutch (1945–49), Suharto seized power from President Sukarno in 1966. He was formally elected president in 1968 by the Consultative Congress and was reelected in 1973, 1978, and 1983.

Suicide, act of terminating one's life voluntarily and intentionally. According to the French sociologist Emile Durkheim, there are three types of voluntary death: (1) *altruistic suicide,* which results from an excessive degree of group interaction; (2) *egoistic suicide,* which occurs because the individual is detached and uninvolved; and (3) *anomic suicide,* which occurs because the individual has inadequate self-discipline. About 90% of suicide attempts are by females. Males, however, are three times more successful in completing the act. Suicide rates per 100,000 population vary from less than 2 in Mexico to about 12 in the United States and Great Britain, 15 in France, 20 in Sweden, 24 in Australia, and 40 in Hungary.

Sui Dynasty (581–618), Chinese dynasty whose two rulers reestablished strong central rule in China following more than 250 years of division and contention. The Grand Canal was completed, military campaigns undertaken, huge palaces constructed, and Chinese prestige restored, all at great human cost leading to revolts and overthrow.

Suite, set of four or more pieces for orchestra or solo instrument, with movements often consisting of dance rhythms. The suite originated in the Baroque Period of music. Orchestral suites are often derived from operas or ballets (eg, Prokofiev's suite from the opera *The Love for Three Oranges* or Copland's suite from the ballet *Appalachian Spring*).

Sukarno (1901–70), Indonesian political figure, president (1949–67). After a four-year struggle with the Dutch, he achieved his goal of seeing Indonesia independent in 1949 and became its president. As president he rejected the country's parliamentary system for more authoritarian rule. In 1966 anti-Communist Indonesian military leaders forced a reduction of his powers, and he was deposed in 1967.

Sukkoth or **Sukkot,** the Jewish festival of tabernacles, which lasts for 7 days. It commemorates the wandering of the Jews in the desert and their salvation through God. A *sukkah,* or simple shelter, is raised in the synagogue and formerly in all Jewish homes, to remind Jews of the temporal nature of possessions. It had been an agricultural event.

Sulawesi (Celebes), island in Indonesia, in the Malay archipelago, separated from Borneo (W) by Makasar Strait; chief city and port is Makasar; with adjacent islands comprises four provinces of Indonesia. Taken from Muslim Malays by Dutch (16th century) for spice trade, it was ruled by Dutch until WWII when occupied by the Japanese; retaken by Dutch at the end of the war; joined Republic of Indonesia 1949: scene of an unsuccessful attempt to form independent government 1957, 1965. Products: rice, yams, maize, cassava, beans, coconuts, coffee, copra, spices, kapok. Industries: handcrafts, asphalt, paper, pearl farming. Area: 72,986sq mi (189,034sq km). Pop. 8,925,000.

Suleiman I or **Suleiman the Magnificent** (1494–1566), Ottoman sultan (1520–66), son and successor of Selim I. He extended his father's conquests in the Balkans and the Mediterranean, captured Belgrade (1521), expelled the Knights Hospitalers from Rhodes (1522), and defeated the Hungarians under Louis II at Mohacs (1526). After the death of John I of Hungary he annexed most of the country. He made an alliance with Francis I of France against the Hapsburgs (1536) and

his admiral, Barbarossa, ravaged the coasts of Spain, Italy, and Greece with his Turkish fleet. Suleiman seized Arabian coastal lands but failed to take Tunis and Malta. He died during the siege of Szigetvar (Hungary), and his stepson Selim II succeeded him.

Sulfa Drug, or sulfonamide, first drugs prescribed to treat bacterial infections. Mostly superseded by modern antibiotics, they are used to treat infections resistant to penicillin or patients allergic to penicillin. Sometimes prescribed as a preventative, they have numerous possible side effects.

Sulfation, preparative method for sulfuric acid esters and salts. Lead sulfate on the plates of lead-acid storage batteries, calcium sulfate on stone are examples of unwanted sulfations. Esters with sulfuric acid and alcohols are used industrially to produce the surfactant, sodium lauryl sulfate.

Sulfonation, preparative method for molecules containing the sulfuric acid group (–SO_2) achieved by reacting aromatic hydrocarbons with sulfuric acid or halogen compounds with inorganic sulfates. Sulfonated anthraquinones (wool dyestuffs) and sulfonamides (antibacterial drugs) are prepared by sulfonation.

Sulfur, common nonmetallic element (symbol S), known from ancient times (brimstone). It occurs in iron pyrites (FeS), galena (PbS), cinnabar (HgS), and other minerals; chief source is from native deposits and as a by-product from gas and oil wells. The element is used as a fungicide, a component of gunpowder, and a reagent for vulcanizing rubber. The main use is in the production of sulfuric acid. Sulfur has several allotropic forms, including two crystalline forms (rhombic and monoclinic). Plastic sulfur is a fine powder formed by sublimation. Liquid sulfur also has a variety of allotropic forms depending on the temperature. Chemically sulfur is a reactive element. Properties: at. no. 16; at. wt. 32.064; sp gr 2.07 (rhombic), 1.957 (monoclinic); melt. pt. 235°F (112.9°C); boil. pt. 832°F (444.4°C); most common isotope S^{32} (95.0%).

Sulfur Butterfly, medium-sized, orange or yellow butterfly with wings bordered or otherwise marked with black. The common yellow butterfly of E United States is the cloudless *Callidryas eubule.* White members of this family are called whites. Family Pieridae.

Sulfur Dioxide, colorless gas with choking odor (formula SO_2) obtained by roasting pyrites (FeS_2) or by burning sulfur. It is used in the manufacture of sulfuric acid and other chemicals, in the solvent extraction of lubricating oils, as a bleach, and as a food and drink preservative. Properties: sp gr (liq. 0°C) 1.434; melt. pt. −105°F (−76.2°C); boil. pt. 140°F (60°C).

Sulfuric Acid, corrosive oily liquid manufactured from sulfur dioxide by the contact process and the chamber process. It is used in the manufacture of fertilizers and chemicals, in petroleum refining, and in many other industries. Properties (pure): sp gr 1.84; melt. pt. 50.7°F (10.4°C).

Sulla, Lucius Cornelius (138–78 BC), Roman general and senate leader. He brought the Jugurthine War with Numidia to an end through diplomacy and opposed Marius to gain control of the Roman forces fighting Mithridates VI. In an unprecedented move he attacked Rome and gained command of the army. He defeated Mithridates, sacked Athens (86), and slaughtered Marius' followers. Proclaimed dictator (82), he instituted political reforms and restored constitutional government before his death. His reforms were soon reversed.

Sullivan, (Sir) Arthur (1842–1900), English composer. He is best known for composing the music for operettas with W.S. Gilbert. Their works included *H.M.S. Pinafore, The Mikado,* and *The Pirates of Penzance.* Sullivan also composed serious operas, songs, and popular hymns such as "Onward, Christian Soldiers."

Sully, Maximilien de Béthune, Duc de (1560–1641), French minister under Henry IV. A Huguenot, he barely escaped the massacre of Protestants on St Bartholomew's Day (1572) and served Henry of Navarre in his struggle for the throne. Once crowned Henry IV, the king entrusted major responsibilities (1597–1610) to Sully. As superintendent of finances he initiated major reforms, encouraged agriculture and trade, and initiated a levy upon officeholders, who, in return, were given their titles to keep or transfer at will.

Sully Prudhomme, René-François-Armand (1839–1907), French poet. A Parnassian poet, his verse includes *Stances et poèmes* (1865), *Les épreuves* (1866), *La Justice* (1878), and *Le Bonheur* (1888). Ini-

Sulawesi

Sumatra

Sunbird

tially a lyric poet, his work became increasingly formal and impersonal. He was elected to the Académie Française in 1881 and was the first to be awarded the Nobel Prize for literature in 1901.

Sulu Archipelago, volcanic island group in extreme S Philippines, separating Sulu Sea (NW) from Celebes Sea (SE); comprises Sulu prov. The archipelago extends SW from Basilan Island to within 40mi (64km) of the E tip of Borneo, and includes over 400 islands and coral formations, chief of which are Jolo, Tawitawi, Pangutaran, and the Tapul group. Chief occupations are fishing, pearl diving, and cattle. Capital is Jolo. Area: 1,086sq mi (2,813sq km). Pop. 427,386.

Sulu Sea, branch of the W Pacific Ocean amid the SW Philippine Islands; the surrounding islands are Borneo (SW), Palawan (NW), Panay and Negros (NE), and the Sulu Archipelago (SE). The sea itself contains only a few small island clusters, and is used as a fishing ground.

Sumac, shrubs and trees widely distributed in temperate regions. They have long featherlike leaves and red, hairy fruit clusters. Some are grown as ornamentals; some species are poisonous to touch. Height: to 30ft (9m). Family Anacardiaceae; genera *Rhus* and *Toxicodendron. See also* Poison Ivy.

Sumatra (Sumatera), island in W Indonesia, 2nd-largest of the Greater Sunda group after Borneo; chief cities are Palembang, Medan, Padang. The terrain of the W coast is rugged and mountainous, containing the Barisan Mts, rising to Mt Kerintji, 12,500ft (3,813m); E and SE are lowland jungles with many rivers. By the 7th century, India had est. two states in Sumatra, Melayu and Srivijaya, which flourished as centers of trade and Buddhist learning. Island was reached by Portuguese 16th century and Dutch 17th century; Dutch East India Co. had fortresses and trading posts erected 18th century on both coasts. Island was occupied by Japanese 1942–45; made part of Republic of Indonesia 1950. Exports: rubber, tobacco, palm oil, tea, coffee, sisal. Industries: agriculture, mining, oil. Area: 183,000sq mi (473,970sq km). Pop. 20,800,000.

Sumer, S region of ancient Mesopotamia, later the S part of Babylonia, now S central Iraq. An agricultural civilization flourished here during the 3rd and 4th millennia BC. The Sumerians built canals, established an irrigation system, and were skilled in the use of metals (silver, gold, copper) to make pottery, jewelry, and weapons. They invented the cuneiform system of writing. Various kings founded dynasties at Kish, Erech, and Ur. Sargon of Agade brought the region under the Semites (*c.* 2600 BC), who blended their culture with the Sumerians. The final Sumerian civilization at Ur fell to Elam, and when Semitic Babylonia under Hammurabi (*c.*2000 BC) controlled the land, the Sumerian nation vanished. *See also* Babylon; Babylonia.

Sumner, Charles (1811–74), US senator from Massachusetts (1851–74), b. Boston. An abolitionist, he was assaulted in the Senate in 1856 after denouncing Sen. Andrew Butler of South Carolina in an antislavery speech. Although incapacitated for three years, he retained his Senate seat. He fought for the Radical Republican plan for Reconstruction and was active in the attempt to remove Pres. Andrew Johnson from office (1868). From 1861–71, he was chairman of the Senate foreign relations committee.

Sumo Wrestling, a sport, popular in Japan. It pits wrestlers who usually weigh more than 350 pounds (158kg) in a match that is quasi-religious in nature and is fought with much ritual. *See also* Wrestling.

Sumter, Fort, fort in SE Carolina, on S shore of mouth of Charleston harbor, just S of Charleston; Confederate attack on fort (April 12, 1861) marked the beginning of the Civil War. It was est. 1948 as national monument.

Sun, Earth's nearest star and the central body in the solar system, radiating light, heat, and other energy by means of nuclear fusion reactions in its highly compressed high-temperature interior. The less dense cooler (about 6,000°C) gaseous surface (photosphere), which is violently active, is surrounded by the chromossphere and corona of much higher temperature. Magnetic fields in these regions give rise to sunspots, prominences, etc. The Sun is a main-sequence yellow-dwarf star situated in a spiral arm of the Galaxy, about 30,000 light-years from the Galactic center. Characteristics: mass 1.99×10^{30} kg; equatorial diameter 865,000mi (1,392,000km); specific gravity 1.41; mean rotation period 25.38 days; apparent mag. -26.86; absolute mag. $+4.7$; spectral type G2. *See also* Eclipse; Solar Energy

Sun Bear, omnivorous, honey-loving, tree-climbing bear found in SE Asia. It has a short-haired black coat with a crescent-shaped yellow mark on its chest and a gray or orange muzzle. It is smallest of all bears. Weight: 100lb (45kg). Family Ursidae, species *Helarctos malayanus.*

Sunbird, tropical nectar-feeding songbird of the Old World, often considered a counterpart of the New World hummingbird. Males are usually brightly colored. After the male's courtship display, the female builds a purselike nest with a spoutlike porch for a single streaked white egg. Length: 3.5–8in (9–20cm). Family Nectariniidae.

Sunburn, an effect on the skin from ultraviolet radiation from the Sun. Redness, swelling, and pain are associated with destruction and coagulation of some of the substances in the cells of the skin, along with enlargement of small vessels beneath the epidermis. In severe cases, blisters and ulcers may form, accompanied by fever. There is a latent period of several hours between exposure and onset of symptoms. Excessive exposure is harmful, hastening the aging process and contributing to the development of keratoses and skin cancer.

Sunderland, industrial city and seaport in NE England, at mouth of Wear River; shipbuilding center. At nearby Monkwearmouth, incorporated in St Peter's Church, are remains of the great Benedictine abbey (founded 674) where the Venerable Bede studied. Industries: precision engineering, glass, chemicals, coal, pottery. Exports: iron, steel. Pop. 298,000.

Sundew, insectivorous plants native to temperate swamps and bogs. They have hairy, basal leaves that glisten with a dewlike substance to attract, trap, and digest insects. When the hairy projections are touched, the leaves close to trap the insect. These plants are often grown indoors as curiosities. Family Droseraceae; genera *Dionaea* and *Drosera.*

Sun Dog, or parhelion, also called mock Sun, for two bright and colored spots appearing 22° to each side of the Sun, caused by refraction of the light from ice crystals.

Sunfish, North American freshwater fish. A popular sport fish, similar in appearance to perch, it has a continuous dorsal fin containing spiny and soft rays. The male guards nest and young. The 300 species range in size from the blue spotted *Enneacanthus gloriosus,* length: 3.5in (8.9cm) to large-

mouth bass, *Micropterus salmoides* length 32in (81.3cm); weight: 22lb (10kg). Family Centrarchidae. *See also* Bluegill; Pumpkinseed.

Sunflower, coarse annual and perennial plant of North America. The flower heads turn to face the Sun and resemble huge daisies with yellow ray flowers and a center disk of yellow, brown, or purple. The common sunflower (*Helianthus annus*) has 1ft (30.5cm) leaves and flower heads over 1ft (30.5cm) across; height: to 15ft (4.6m). Sunflower seeds are a source of an edible oil and are used as feed for poultry and wild birds.

Sungari (Sung-hua), river in NE China; rises in Ch'ang-pai Shan Mts, near North Korean border; flows generally N to Amur River at USSR border; navigable for most of its 1,150mi (1,852km); it is a main trade route in an agricultural area.

Sung Dynasty (960–1279), Chinese dynasty. Divided into the North and South Sung by the Jurchen conquest and establishment of the Chin dynasty in the North, it was a period of refinement and cultural flowering in China. Many of the finest literary, artistic, and cultural treasures of Chinese civilization date from this period including literary essays, prose poems, landscape paintings, and highly valuable ceramics. Southern ports were opened for commerce and relations with South Asia.

Sunnis, or **Sunnites,** the main body of Muslims, including about 90% of the followers of Islam. This sect finds authority in the entire Sunna, the body of orthodox tradition including teachings outside the Koran. On this point the Sunnis differ from the Shi'a sect, which believes in the inspired leadership of a succession of imams. The Shi'a hold that this succession started with Ali, Mohammed's son-in-law. The Sunnis acknowledge three caliphs before Ali as legitimate rulers. Both Sunnis and Shi'ites believe in the basic Islamic faith: one God, Allah, Mohammed as the Prophet of God, and the Koran as the revealed word of God. *See also* Caliph; Islam; Shi'a.

Sunnyvale, city in W California, 8mi (13km) WNW of San Jose; site of Moffet Field Naval Air Station. Industries: electrical equipment, foodstuffs, paper products, chemicals. Founded 1849; inc. 1912. Pop. (1980) 106,618.

Sunspot, short-lived dark areas, often several thousand miles across, that appear periodically on the Sun's photosphere and participate in its rotation. They have a dark center (the umbra) surrounded by a brighter border (the penumbra). Possessing strong magnetic fields that are caused by localized magnetohydrodynamic disturbances below the surface, they appear dark because they are about 2000°K cooler than the surrounding regions. Sunspots usually appear in groups, and usually follow an 11-year cycle between minima and maxima.

Sunstroke, serious disorder caused by exposure to direct sunlight. It is characterized by extreme elevation of body temperature to 106°–110°F (41°–43°C). The fever exerts a harmful effect on the central nervous system. The usual cause is failure of sweating to remove body heat. Cooling of the body is urgent in sunstroke followed by expert medical care.

Sun Yat-sen (1866–1925), first president of the Chinese Republic (1911–12) and revolutionary leader of modern China. Sun became convinced after China's defeat by Japan in 1895 that the Manchu dynasty must be overthrown. In exile 1895–1911, he worked through secret societies and with support from overseas Chinese to bring about his aim. His inspiration eventually brought about the revolution of 1911. He joined in founding the Kuomintang (1912) and became its leader and ideologue.

Superior, Lake, lake in the United States and Canada; world's largest freshwater lake; bounded by NE Minnesota (W), Ontario, Canada (N and E), and NW Michigan and NW Wisconsin (S); it is connected to Lake Huron and St Lawrence Seaway by Sault Ste Marie Canals. A commercial and recreational fishing source, it is also used for transport of grains and iron ore. It is the highest of the Great Lakes and least polluted. Discovered 1616 by Étienne Brulé, it was settled 1649 at Ashland. Length: 350mi (564km). Width: 160mi (258km). Area: 31,820sq mi (82,414sq km).

Supermultiplet. *See* Multiplet.

Supernova (plural supernovae), star that undergoes a cataclysmic outburst of energy and matter as the result of internal imbalances caused by the exhaustion of its fuel. These imbalances, which may occur in stars beyond a certain critical mass, take the form of accelerated nuclear reactions in the core, enormously increased internal temperatures (up to 5,000,000,000 °K), and gravitational collapse. The catastrophic explosion that follows, in which the star blows itself apart, ejecting matter at relativistic speeds, temporarily increases its absolute magnitude to a figure in excess of −14, the brightness of a galaxy. These spectacular but also very rare phenomena usually leave behind a filamentary remnant, such as the Crab Nebula, and the original core may survive as a neutron star or pulsar, or even a black hole.

Superposition, Principle of, geologic principle that the oldest layer in a group of sedimentary strata is the one on the bottom. In the absence of upheavals and folding, or igneous intrusion, the oldest layer of rock and its fossils is the lowest. *See also* Historical Geology.

Supersonic Flight, flight beyond Mach 1, the speed at which sound travels under varying conditions of temperature and pressure. Thus at sea level 760mph (1,223kph) is the critical speed. At high altitude the speed might be 660mph (1,062kph). At these speeds the pressure wave that normally moves away from the airplane is compressed, creating a cone-shaped shock wave. Early attempts to fly through this barrier were unsuccessful. Swept-wing, slender-bodied airplanes fly at supersonic speeds by retarding the formation of the wave.

Supersonic Velocity, velocity in excess of the local velocity of sound. Its magnitude is usually expressed as a Mach Number (named after Ernst Mach, 1838–1916), which is the ratio of the velocity of a body of fluid to the local velocity of sound. Thus a body traveling at twice the speed of sound has a Mach Number 2. A velocity in excess of Mach 5 is said to be hypersonic.

Supplementary Angles, two angles whose sum is 180°. Each is the supplement of the other.

Supply and Demand, Law of. The law of supply indicates that other things being equal, as the price of a good increases, suppliers will be willing to produce more and as the price of a good decreases, producers will be willing to produce less. Thus, price and quantity supplied are directly related. The law of demand states the reverse; that is, as prices increase, consumers will demand less, and as prices decrease, consumers will demand more. Thus, price and quantity demanded are inversely related. Through the interaction of supply and demand, an equilibrium position is reached. *See also* Equilibrium.

Suprematism, abstract art movement. Derived from Cubism and launched in Russia in 1913 by the painter Casimir Malevich.

Supreme Court of Canada, one of two Canadian federal courts. It is generally a court of last resort for both civil and criminal cases. Appeals are brought from superior courts of the provinces where the amount in question exceeds $10,000. Any lesser amount may be granted by the high provincial court, but if refused, the Supreme Court may itself institute appeal. Certain appeals are brought from the Exchequer Court, its companion federal court. In civil cases only, the Supreme Court or superior courts may appeal to the Judicial Committee of the British Privy Council in London. There are nine justices, including a chief justice.

Supreme Court of the United States, US court of last resort. It derives its power from the doctrine of "judicial review" and from its ability to pass on the constitutionality of state and federal legislation and of executive acts. It exercises both original jurisdiction ("in all cases affecting ambassadors, other public ministers, consuls, and those in which a State shall be a party"), and appellate jurisdiction ("both as to law and fact, with such exceptions and under such regulations as Congress shall make," Sect. 2, Art. III, US Constitution). It hears appeals from the courts of appeals, the district courts, and the highest state courts where a federal question is involved. Created by the Judiciary Act of 1789, the Supreme Court consists of justices who are appointed by the president with the advice and consent of the Senate. The number of justices has varied, but since 1869 has remained at nine, including a chief justice. Justices are removeable only by impeachment. The chief justice presides over all sessions and five judges constitute a quorum to hear a case. There must be a majority vote before a decision is made. If a tie exists, the previous decision is upheld.

History. The Supreme Court has heard several hundred cases since it was established, some of which had controversial effects on the country's political and social structure. While some of these decisions were conservative changes, many were quite radical and often openly criticized by the government. Chief Justice John Marshall successfully (*Marbury v. Madison,* 1803) claimed the power to declare acts of Congress unconstitutional. After World War I the Supreme Court's conservative views met opposition by the liberalism of the New Deal Era. After some of Pres. Franklin Roosevelt's most important economic recovery programs were invalidated by the court, he sought to reform the court by filling vacancies with more liberal justices. In 1954 the court issued its landmark desegregation decision, *Brown* v. *Board of Education of Topeka.* This new liberalism continued through Pres. Lyndon Johnson's administration and was most evident in Chief Justice Earl Warren's focusing of the court's attention to civil rights and the enforcement of the Bill of Rights. First Amendment rights of speech, press, assembly, and religious freedom were vigorously enforced. Newspapers were reassured against libel (*New York Times* v. *Sullivan,* 1964), peaceful demonstrators were protected from arrest (*Edwards* v. *South Carolina,* 1963), and civil rights organizations were safeguarded from official harassment (*NAACP* v. *Alabama,* 1958). The provisions of the fair trial rights of federal criminals were extended to the states. The liberalism of all these decisions was openly attacked, and with the election of President Nixon, a change began in the ideological structure of the court with the appointment of the more conservative Warren Burger as chief justice. Several other vacancies were filled with justices who had criticized previous decisions. In 1981, Sandra Day O'Connor became the first woman appointed an associate justice.

Following is a list of the chief justices of the Supreme Court.

CHIEF JUSTICES OF US SUPREME COURT

	Term
John Jay	1789–95
John Rutledge*	1795
Oliver Ellsworth	1796–1800
John Marshall	1801–35
Roger Brooke Taney	1836–64
Salmon Portland Chase	1864–73
Morrison Remick Waite	1874–88
Melville Weston Fuller	1888–1910
Edward Douglass White	1910–21
William Howard Taft	1921–30
Charles Evans Hughes	1930–41
Harlan Fiske Stone	1941–46
Fred Moore Vinson	1946–53
Earl Warren	1953–69
Warren Earl Burger	1969–

*appointment not confirmed by Senate

Surabaja, seaport city in NE Java, Indonesia, across Surabaja Strait from Madura Island; 2nd-largest city in Indonesia and capital of East Java prov.; occupied by Dutch, and a principal Dutch naval base until WWII, when occupied by Japanese; site of Airlangga University (1954) and naval college; trade center. Exports: rice, sugar cane, spices, tobacco, maize, tapioca, coffee, cocoa, rubber, copra. Pop. 1,556,255.

Surat, city in W India, 150mi (242km) N of Bombay on Tapti River. With the est. of British and Dutch trading posts in the early 17th century, Surat developed into one of India's most populated and busiest port cities; in 1664 it was devastated by a Mahrattas invasion and steadily declined in importance; site of several colleges. Industries: textiles, cotton gins, engineering, rice, paper, soap, gold and silverware, carpets. Pop. 471,815.

Surface Tension, the molecular forces associated with the boundary layer of a liquid. Cohesive forces in the liquid tend to resist disruption, so that a pin placed carefully on the surface will "float" even though its density is many times that of the liquid.

Surgery, branch of medicine that uses specialized instrumental techniques and manipulations to treat diseases and injuries.

Suriname (formerly Surinam), independent nation in NE South America, on the Atlantic Ocean, bordered by Brazil (S), French Guiana (E), and Guyana (W). Suriname is made up of the Guiana Highlands plateau, a flat coastal plain, and a forest inland region which covers 80% of the total land area; its many rivers serve as a source of hydroelectric power. The chief agricultural products are rice, bananas, sugarcane, coffee, coconuts, lumber, and citrus fruits. The economy depends greatly on the export of bauxite, of which it is one of the world's largest producers. The main industries include shrimp freezing, processed foods, paint, plywood, and fruit juices. The people are mostly Indonesian, Creoles, Asian, and Indians; they enjoy complete religious freedom, with denominations of Hindus, Roman Catholics, Muslims, Protestants, and Confucians; education is free. The region was discovered 1499 by Spanish explorer Alfonso de Ojeda. The Dutch founded the first colony in 1616. In 1815 the Congress of Vienna gave the Guyana region to Britain and reaffirmed Dutch control of Suriname. Suriname became officially autonomous 1954, and in 1975, Suriname gained full independence from the Netherlands. The new government, dominated by Creoles, attempted to halt the flight of skilled Surinamese, many of them Hindus, most of whom emigrated to the Netherlands. Suriname became a member of the United Nations in 1975, soon after independence was gained. In 1980 the military seized control of the government. Martial law and complete control by the military were in effect from 1982.

PROFILE

Official name: Republic of Suriname
Area: 63,037sq mi (163,266sq km)
Population: 352,041
Chief city: Paramaribo
Government: Republic
Religion: Hindu (majority)
Language: Dutch (official)

Surinam Toad, South American aquatic tailless amphibian characterized by the absence of a tongue. It is brown with a flat, square body. The female carries fertilized eggs embedded in the skin on her back; larvae remain until metamorphosed. Length: to 8in (20cm). Family Pipidae; species *Pipa pipa. See also* Frog.

Surmullet. *See* Goatfish.

Surrealism, influential movement in art and literature, evolved in the mid-1920s from Dadaism. Influenced by psychoanalysis, it represented a reaction against rationalism and advocated creative use of the powers of the unconscious mind. Led by André Breton, who wrote several surrealist manifestos, surrealist writers include Louis Aragon, Paul Eluard, and Benjamin Péret, while painters include Jean Arp, Max Ernst, René Magritte, Yves Tanguy, Salvador Dali, Joan Miró, and Paul Klee. Surrealism in painting took two basic forms, one made up of fanciful, often abstract elements, and the other devoted to the meticulous depiction of dreamlike subject matter.

Surrey, Earl of. *See* Howard (Henry).

Surrey, nonmetropolitan county of SE England, one of the Home Counties bordering Greater London. County town is Guildford. Important towns are Redhill, Riegate, Epsom and Ewell, Weybridge, and Woking. The region is traversed by the North Downs, across which flow the Wey and Mole rivers. Mainly residential, the county has industries in the N and some dairy farming and market gardening. Pop. 1,000,700.

Surveying, the accurate measurement of the Earth's surface. Used in establishing land boundaries, the topography of landforms, and major construction and civil engineering work such as dams, bridges, and highways. Measurements are linear or angular, applying principles of geometry and trigonometry. For smaller areas, the land is treated as a horizontal plane. Large areas involve considerations of the Earth's curving shape and are referred to as geodetic surveys. Various surveys, such as topographic, engineering, land, construction, cartographic, and mining require specialized methods and instruments.

Surya, in Hindu mythology, the personification of the Sun, possessed of 12 names and incarnations, among them Indra, Varuna, and Mitra. As Surya he is depicted as a three-eyed, four-armed man of burnished copper, sometimes seated on a lotus or in a chariot drawn by many horses. He is prayed to as a healer and bringer of luck. His festival, the Suryapuja, occurs in the spring. *See also* Indra.

Joan Sutherland

Swaziland

Sweden

Susa, ruined city in ancient country of Elam, 15mi (24km) SW of modern Dizful, W Iran; served as the winter residence of the Achaemenian kings 7th century–331 BC; scene of the biblical story of Esther and King Ahasuerus. Archeological excavations here unearthed the code of Hammurabi and the stele of Naram-sin.

Suspension, liquid medium in which small solid particles are uniformly disposed. If the particles do not settle out on standing but are unable to pass through a semipermeable membrane the suspension is called a colloid. The particle size in such colloidal suspensions is likely to be in the range 10^{-4} to 10^{-6} millimeters.

Suspension Bridge, a bridge that has its roadway suspended from two or more cables that generally pass over towers and anchor at the ends.

Susquehanna River, river in NE United States, rises in Otsego Lake, central New York; flows S through Pennsylvania to NE corner of Maryland and empties into Chesapeake Bay near Havre de Grace; site of several hydroelectric plants and subject of extensive flood control systems. Length: 444mi (715km).

Sussex, former county of S England, now divided into the nonmetropolitan counties of East Sussex and West Sussex. The area is crossed by the South Downs; its main rivers are the Rother, Duse, and Arun; an agricultural region, with many coastal resorts.

Sussex Spaniel, hunting dog (sporting group) used for upland shooting. Massive and muscular, this determined hunter has a heavy looking head, square muzzle, and hanging lips; thick, large ears are low-set and hanging. The body is round-chested, long, and low; legs are short with large, round feet. Tail is docked and set low. The abundant coat is flat or slightly wavy, with feathering on the legs; the characteristic color is rich golden liver. Average size: about 15in (38cm) high at shoulder; 35–45lb (16–20kg). *See also* Sporting Dog.

Sutherland, Joan (1926–), Australian soprano. She studied at the Sydney Conservatory and made her debut in 1950. She spent a number of years with the Covent Garden Opera in England, establishing a great reputation, before making a spectacular debut at the Metropolitan Opera in 1961 as Lucia in Donizetti's *Lucia Di Lammermoor.* She is highly regarded for both coloratura and dramatic roles.

Sutlej (Langchuhe), tributary of Indus River and longest of the five rivers of the Punjab; rises in SW Tibet, China; flows W through Himalayas and the Punjab plain, joins the Beas River, continues into Pakistan to join Chenab River, forming the Panjnad, which flows to the Indus. Length: approx. 900mi (1,450km).

Sutra, sacred Buddhist text claiming to have been spoken by Buddha himself and recorded by his disciple, Ananda, immediately after Buddha's death in approximately 483 BC. Many Sutras, however, were composed centuries later by unknown authors, and there is disagreement among Buddhists as to their value. *See also* Buddha; Buddhism.

Sutter, Johann Augustus (1803–80), US pioneer, b. Germany. He settled in Sacramento, Calif., in 1839. He acquired a large tract of land and became a prosperous rancher. After gold was found at his mill (1848), he was ruined when miners swarmed over his land.

Suttner, Bertha Felice Sophie, Baroness von (1843–1914), Austrian novelist and free-thinking pacifist. Her best novels include *Lay Down Your Arms* (1889) and *Das Maschinenzeitalter* (1899). Active in the peace movement, she founded the Austrian Society of Friends of Peace (1891) and edited the pacifist journal *Lay Down Your Arms!* (1892–99). She influenced Alfred Nobel to include among his awards the peace prize, which she received in 1905.

Suwannee River, river in SE Georgia and N Florida; rises in Okefenokee Swamp, SE Ga., flows SW across Fla. into Gulf of Mexico at Suwannee Sound. Length: 240mi (386km).

Sverdlovsk, city in Russian SFSR, USSR, in E foothills of the central Urals, on dammed Iset River; capital of Sverdlovsk oblast. Founded as a fortress 1722, it was named Yekaterinburg for Russian empress Catherine I; site of 1918 execution of Tsar Nicholas II and his family; renamed 1924 for Bolshevik revolutionary Yakov Sverdlov; city was placed under direct jurisdiction of Russian SFSR 1943; site of Urals state university (1920), medical, law, mining, forestry, art and teachers' colleges, polytechnic school, conservatory, and branch of USSR Academy of Science. Industries: metallurgical and mining equipment, steel, aircraft, ballbearings, railroad cars, radio, television, building materials. Pop. 1,204,000.

Sverdrup Islands. *See* Queen Elizabeth Islands.

Swabia, a duchy in medieval Germany that took its name from the Suevi tribes, its former inhabitants. Burkhard, count of Raetia, was recognized as the first duke in 919. The duchy was joined to the imperial crown when Emperor Henry IV gave it in 1079 to the house of Hohenstauffen, under whose rule its cities began to achieve great wealth. In 1331, to defend themselves against aggression by the crown, the cities formed an association called the Swabian League, which lasted intermittently until 1534.

Swahili, or Kingwana, a Bantu language of the Niger-Kordofanian family of African languages. The most important, having about 8,000,000 native speakers, it is a lingua-franca in most of E Africa to E portion of Congo Basin. Imposed by foreign rulers as the official tongue, it has a large native literature using a form of the Arabic alphabet.

Swallow, swift-flying bird with long wings and forked tail found worldwide. In some areas, their regular migratory habits make them a symbol of spring. Insect eaters, they lay 3–5 plain whitish eggs. The barn swallow *(Hirundo rustica)* builds its mud nest in a tree hole, house, or barn; the cliff swallow *(Petrochelidon pyrrhonota)* builds on a cliff. Length: 4.8–6in (12.2–15.2cm); family Hirundinidae.

Swallowtail Butterfly, butterfly found worldwide, that typically has taillike extensions on the hind wings. Most swallowtails are large and black with bright markings—usually yellow, but often blue, green, or red. The yellow and black giant *Papilio cresphontes* has a wingspread up to 5.5in (14cm). When a swallowtail caterpillar is disturbed, it emits an unpleasant odor from a protrusible organ behind its head. Family Papilionidae.

Swammerdam, Jan (1637–80), Dutch naturalist. His works, including *General History of Insects,* aided the development of the modern study of entomology. He discovered red corpuscles and identified the lymphatic valves in the human body.

Swan, graceful, white waterfowl that nests in N Northern Hemisphere and migrates south for winter. Three species live in the Southern Hemisphere. They have broad, flat bills, long necks, plump bodies, long legs, webbed feet, and dense plumage over down. They dip their heads under water to feed on plant matter. Swans form life-long pair bonds, build large grass-and-leaf nests in marshes, and lay white eggs (4–6). The young are called cygnets. Length: 3.5–6ft (1.1–1.8m). Family Anatidae; genus *Cygnus.*

Swan, The (constellation). *See* Cygnus.

Swansea (Abertawe), port in South Wales, on Swansea Bay, an inlet of Bristol Channel; administrative center of West Glamorgan; site of university (1920). Industries: metal smelting, tinplate, chemicals, oil refining. Pop. 190,500.

Swatow (Shantou, or Shan-t'ou), city in SE China, 170mi (274km) NW of Hong Kong, on Han Shui River delta, on South China Sea. A small fishing village, its economic growth was spurred when it was declared a treaty port (1869) and opened to foreign traffic; occupied by Japan during WWII. Exports: tea, sugar, oranges, tobacco. Industries: fishing, shipbuilding, machine shops. Pop. 400,000.

Swazi, Negroid people of S Africa, who are mainly agricultural pastoralists. In their traditionally polygamous society power is shared between a hereditary male ruler and his mother (or a recognized substitute). Approximately half the Swazi continue to practice ancestor worship, witchcraft, and sorcery.

Swaziland, kingdom in S Africa, bordering the Republic of South Africa and Mozambique. The region can be looked at as 3 topographical zones: high forestland, middle savanna grassland with some farm lands, and low arable land. The economy has flourished since 1950, due to development and diversification in agriculture. The per capita gross national product of $650 a year does not indicate the income level of indigenous Swazis, because wealth is concentrated in the hands of the white minority. Cattle and dairying are important; industries include food processing, sugar, corn, citrus fruits, cotton, forest products; iron, asbestos, and coal are chief minerals. The construction of a railroad line from Ngwenga to Mozambique and another to the Republic of South Africa have aided economic growth substantially. Most Swazi still practice subsistence farming, but a growing number are working in either skilled or unskilled industrial labor, many in the Republic of South Africa.

Africans comprise approx. 97% of the population, with minorities of Eurafricans and native whites. The majority practices Christianity, the rest adhere to animism. The official language is English, but the Swazi language is SiSwati. There is a university and schools set up by Christian missions; literacy rate is 25%.

History. During the mid-19th century, the traditional Swazi ruler asked for protection from the British against the Zulu. By 1903 the Swazi had ceded much land to Boer and British settlers, and Swaziland formally became a British protectorate. In 1949 the British denied South Africa's desire to control Swaziland; given self government 1963; independence 1968 and a parliamentary government established. In 1973, King Sobhuza II (1899–1982) suspended the constitution and assumed power to rule by decree. Sobhuza died in 1982, having reigned since 1921. Area: 6,704sq mi (17,363sq km); Pop. 550,000.

Sweat Gland, one of many small tubular, subcutaneous glands that open on the skin surface through pores and release perspiration, water, and some salt to regulate body temperature.

Sweden (Sverige), independent nation in N Europe, in Scandinavia. One of the most prosperous countries in

557

the world, its government social welfare programs account for much of the national budget and provide one of the world's highest standards of living.

Land and economy. Located in N Europe on the E half of the Scandinavian peninsula, its neighbors are Norway (W) and Finland (NE). Denmark lies across the Kattegat. The border with Norway is mountainous, sloping gently to the S. Half of the country is forested, lakes cover 9%, and 7% of the total is arable. Along the coast are sandy beaches (S), rocky cliffs (N and W), and the fertile central and S plains (Skane) with farmland covering 40%. Two Baltic Sea islands belong to Sweden: Gotland, a fertile 1,160sq mi (3,004sq km) area, and the smaller Oland. The Gulf Stream moderates the climate, although N winters last 6 months or longer. Sweden is heavily industrialized, oriented toward the production of exports; manufacturing employs 24% of the labor force, producing iron and steel, pulp and paper, and large ships. Sweden is virtually self-sufficient in foodstuffs, although only about 6% of the labor force is engaged in agriculture, forestry, and fishing. Although the government controls transportation, water power, communication, and iron ore mining, 90% of the total output is from private enterprise.

People. The most heavily populated Scandinavian country. The basic population is a homogeneous mixture with about 35,000 Finns and 10,000 Lapps in the N. Ninety-five percent of the people belong to the Lutheran state church. Education is compulsory and literacy almost 100%.

Government. The Swedish constitution, promulgated in 1809, is one of the oldest still in effect in Europe. The king, as chief of state, serves primarily as a symbol of national unity. Executive power is vested in the prime minister, who represents the majority party or coalition in the popularly-elected Riksdag (parliament).

History. During the Viking era (AD 800), Christianity began to emerge in Sweden, and by 1003 the first Christian king was baptized. During the next 700 years Sweden expanded its influence E to the Black and Caspian seas, trading slaves and furs for gold and silver. Expansion lasted until the 18th century when Russia acquired Sweden's Baltic empire, including Finland. Sweden was joined with Norway 1814–1905 when Norway dissolved the union. Parliamentary government came to Sweden in 1917, universal suffrage in 1921. During WWI and WWII Sweden remained neutral. Since the neutrality has been based on the concept of strong self-defense, relations with the Soviet Union were strained in 1981 when a Soviet nuclear submarine ran aground on Sweden's coast near naval installations. Throughout virtually the entire period of 1932–76 the Socialist party governed Sweden, but they were voted out of office, partly out of widespread dissatisfaction with high taxes. They were voted in again in 1982, on election promises to stimulate the economy and lower the unemployment rate. King Carl Gustav succeeded to the throne in 1973. The world was shocked by the 1986 assassination of Olof Palme, premier (1969–76; 1982–86).

PROFILE

Official name: Kingdom of Sweden
Area: 173,649sq mi (449,751sq km)
Population: 8,303,010
Density: 48per sq mi (18per sq km)
Chief cities: Stockholm (capital); Göteborg; Malmo
Government: Parliamentary monarchy (limited)
Religion: Lutheran (state church)
Language: Swedish
Monetary unit: Krona
Gross national product: $98,580,000,000
Per capita income: $6,155
Industries: pulp and paper mills, shipbuilding, machinery, automobiles, aircraft, toolmaking, iron and steel
Agriculture: cattle, pigs, forests, oats, sugar beets, potatoes, wheat
Minerals: iron ore, zinc
Trading partners: United Kingdom, West Germany, Norway, Denmark

Swedenborg, Emanuel (1688–1772), Swedish philosopher and mystic. Early scientific preoccupations and official duties as inspector of mines were followed by psychical conversion. He professed to have special gifts and divine illumination (1747). In his *Divine Love and Wisdom* he characterized divinity as infinite love. His followers, organized as a sect, were known as Swedenborgians.

Swede Turnip. *See* Rutabaga.

Swedish, the national language of Sweden, spoken by virtually all of the country's 8,000,000 people. Closely related to Norwegian and Danish, it is one of the Germanic languages, and thus part of the Indo-European family.

Swedish Ivy, trailing house plant native to Africa and Australia. It has waxy, scalloped-edged, rounded leaves of green or green edged with white, and fleshy stems. Some species are purplish. Care: bright indirect light, soil (equal parts loam, peat moss, sand) kept barely moist. Propagation is by stem-tip cuttings. Genus *Plectranthus*.

Sweet Alyssum, annual plant native to Europe and used in borders and rock gardens. It has lobed leaves and white or purple flower clusters. Height: 3–6in (7.6–15.2cm). Family Cruciferae; species *Lobularia maritima*.

Sweet Flag, or **Calamus,** perennial marsh plant native to the Old World now found in E North America. It has sword-shaped leaves, small green flowers, and a sweet-scented root that yields calamus oil used in liqueurs and perfumes. Height: 1–4ft (30–122cm). Family Araceae; species *Acorus calamus*.

Sweet Gale, or bog myrtle, Scotch gale, fragrant marsh plant found throughout northern temperate wetlands. It has yellowish flowers and bitter leaves used in making medicine. Height: to 6ft (1.8m). Family Myricaceae; species *Myrica gale*. *See also* Bayberry.

Sweet Gum, deciduous tree native to E North America. In autumn, its maplelike leaves turn brilliant yellow, orange, or red. It has spiny brown seedpods often used for indoor decorations. Height: over 120ft (36.6m). Family Hamamelidaceae; species *Liquidambar styraciflua*.

Sweet Pea, tendril-climbing, annual plant native to Italy. It has fragrant, butterfly-shaped flowers of white, pink, rose, lavender, purple, red, or orange. Height: to 6ft (1.8m). Family Leguminosae; species *Lathyrus odoratus*.

Sweet Potato, trailing plant native to South America and cultivated as a vegetable in S United States. Its funnel-shaped flowers are purple. Harvested after the first fall frost, the orange or yellow fleshy, tuberlike root is edible. Family Convolvulaceae; species *Ipomoea batatas*.

Sweet William, common name for a flowering plant of Europe and North America. A smooth plant that reaches about 1ft (30cm) in height, its flowers are pink or white with petals about 0.25in (0.6cm) long. Introduced as a garden plant, sweet william is now a wildflower along roadsides and in waste areas. Family Caryophyllaceae; species *Dianthus barbatus*.

Sweyn I Forkbeard (c. 960–1014), king of Denmark (986–1014), son of Harald Bluetooth. His early attacks on England forced King Ethelred to pay tribute, but after his invasion in 1013 Ethelred fled to Normandy, and Sweyn became king. Sweyn died before the coronation, and his son Canute the Great eventually succeeded him.

Swift, Jonathan (1667–1745), Irish satirist and novelist. He became secretary to Sir William Temple (1689) and was ordained (1694), seeking benefits for Irish clergy. He wrote religious pamphlets and Tory propaganda (*The Examiner* 1710–11). His early works include *A Tale of a Tub* (1704), on religious and scholarly corruption and *The Battle of the Books* (1704), satirizing the controversy over ancient and modern learning. His *Gulliver's Travels* (1726) satirized courts and politicians. Swift had frequent contact with London literary circles until the late 1720s. He wrote numerous works criticizing Britain's treatment of Ireland, including *A Modest Proposal* (1729), which suggested that children be fattened and eaten. His later works were increasingly bitter.

Swift, any of a family (Apodidae) of fast-flying widely distributed birds. From 3.5 to 9 in (9–23cm) long, they generally have a short, sharply hooked bill, wide mouth, long narrow wings, short weak legs, and darkish plumage. They typically feed on insects that they can catch in flight, and build a nest of plant matter held together with saliva, in a chimney or under a ledge, for their one to six white eggs. Among well known species are the chimney swift; palm swift; common swift. *See also* Chimney Swift.

Swimming, recreational activity and competitive sport. Formal competition was first introduced in 1603 in Japan by an imperial edict which ordered interschool competition as an integral part of the curriculum. In 1837 in England, the National Swimming Association was formed, and in 1846 in Sydney, Australia, the first international swimming championships were held. Swimming was first included on a limited basis in the modern Olympic Games in Athens in 1896, and by 1908 the Fédération Internationale de Natation Amateur (FINA), the world governing body, was formed. Recognized distances for men and women include the 100, 200, 400, 800, and 1,500 meters freestyle, the 100 and 200 meters breaststroke, the 100 and 200 meters butterfly, the 100 and 200 meters backstroke, the 4 by 100 meters relay, the 4 by 200 meters relay (for men), the 200 and 400 meters individual medley, and the 4 by 100 meters relay medley.

Swinburne, Algernon Charles (1837–1909), English poet and critic. He became known with *Atalanta and Calydon* (1865), a verse drama, but the pagan and sensual tone of *Poems and Ballads* (1866) brought him widespread notoriety. Rich imagery and stylistic complexity characterize poems such as *The Garden of Proserpine* (1865), *The Triumph of Time* (1865), and *Tristram of Lyonesse* (1882). He was a friend of Rossetti and William Morris but spent the latter part of his life in seclusion.

Swiss Chard, annual plant, related to the beet, grown for its spinachlike green or red leaves. The white or red leaf ribs and stems are often cooked separately. Family Chenopodiaceae; species *Beta vulgaris cicla*.

Switzerland (Schweiz, Suisse, Svizzera), independent landlocked nation of W Europe. Noted for its scenery and manufacture of precision instruments, it has historically been a neutral nation.

Land and economy. The most mountainous country in Europe, it is located between West Germany (N), Italy (S), Austria and Lichtenstein (E), and France (W). It is the main watershed for Europe—the Rhine flows into the North Sea, the Inn leads into the Danube, the Rhone runs to the Mediterranean, and the Ticino is a tributary of the Po. Through the S part of the country is the Alpine range, covering 60% of the land. The Jura Mts, SW to NW, cover another 10%. The remaining 30% is lowlands. About 27% of Switzerland is cultivated, 25% is used for grazing, 24% is covered with forests, and the rest is mountains and glaciers. Dufour Peak, 15,217ft (4,638m) above sea level, is the highest point. The country has a temperate climate, varying greatly with altitude. Its highly skilled labor force is the backbone of a developed manufacturing economy that imports raw materials and exports finished products, especially watches and precision instruments. Tourism, international banking, and insurance comprise important segments of the economy.

People. With so many ethnic groups, the Swiss constitution allows for three official languages—French, Italian, and German—and four national languages, the three official ones plus Romansch, related to Latin and spoken in one canton (state). During the late 1970s there were about 650,000 guest workers in Switzerland. With complete freedom of religion, 47.8% is Protestant, 49.4% Roman Catholic. Primary education is free and compulsory. Literacy is almost 100%.

Government. A federal state of 23 cantons, legislative power rests in the elected Federal Assembly (parliament). The constitution provides for initiative and referendum as the final authorities.

History. In 58 BC, Julius Caesar conquered a Celtic people, the Helvetians, living in what is now Switzerland, and made them part of the Roman Empire. As the empire declined, Teutonic tribes from the N and W invaded and settled. Charlemagne and German emperors ruled from 800 until 1291, the date of Swiss independence when the three forest cantons united. They defeated the Austrians (1315) and established a confederation to preserve independence. In 1848 the 22 cantons were joined under a constitution with federal responsibility for trade and defense. Many controls were retained by each canton. Permanent neutrality was internationally accepted, and the Swiss did not participate in WWI or WWII. The offices of many international organizations are located in Switzerland. Although Switzerland experienced tremendous economic growth following WWII, the country had entered a decline by the late 1970s and early 1980s.

PROFILE:

Official name: Swiss Confederation
Area: 15,491sq mi (40,122sq km)
Population: 6,314,200
Density: 408per sq mi (157per sq km)
Chief cities: Bern (capital); Geneva; Basel; Zurich
Government: Federal republic
Religion: Protestant and Roman Catholic
Language: German, French, Italian (all official)
Monetary unit: Swiss franc
Gross National Product: $38,800,000,000
Per capita income: $6,346
Industries: watches, precision instruments, chemicals, cheese, chocolates, generators, turbines, hydroelectric power
Agriculture: cattle, hogs, goats, sheep, hay, livestock feeds, forests
Minerals: salt, limestone, sandstone
Trading partners: European Economic Community

Swordfish, or broadbill, marine fish found worldwide in temperate and tropical seas. A popular food fish, it is silvery-black, dark purple, or blue. Its flattened sword

Switzerland

Sycamore

Sydney, Australia

is one-third of its length and used to strike at prey. Length: to 15ft (457.5cm); weight: 1,182lb (532kg). Family Xiphiidae; species *Xiphias gladius.*

Swordtail, freshwater tropical fish found from S Mexico to Guatemala. This popular aquarium fish is identified by a long extension of its caudal fin. Young are born alive. Many varieties include red-eyed, red wagtail, and berlin swordtails. Length: to 5in (12.7cm). Family Poecilidae; species *Xiphophorus helleri.*

Sycamore, or buttonwood, common names for a species of shade tree related to the plane tree, native to the United States and grown best in the basin of the lower Ohio and Mississippi rivers. The related Arizona and California sycamores are smaller than the eastern species. Introduced into England in the 17th century, the sycamore is also found in W and central Europe. Family Platanaceae; species *Platanus occidentalis. See also* Plane Tree.

Sydney, capital city of New South Wales state, Australia, on Port Jackson, an inlet on the Pacific Ocean. The largest city and center of finance, commerce, industry, culture, transportation, and communication in Australia; noted for 19th-century buildings, and obelisk (1819); seat of Roman Catholic and Anglican archbishops, site of three universities, the National Art Gallery, and an important naval base; world's leading wool-selling market. Industries: automotive parts, textiles, food processing, building materials, chemicals. Founded 1788 as the first British penal colony in Australia. Pop. 2,922,760.

Syllogism, from the Greek *syllogismos* or "a reckoning all together." A construction of argument consisting of at least three propositions: two or more premises and a conclusion. The premises are related in such a way that the conclusion must be valid.

Sylvester II, Roman Catholic pope (999–1003), b. Gerbert. The first French pope, he stressed learning and encouraged missionary work. He aided in the Christianization of Poland and Hungary and rid the church of simony and the clergy of concubinage.

Symbiosis, relationship between two kinds of organisms that is mutually advantageous. An ectosymbiont is an organism living on its host; an endosymbiont lives within its host. *See also* Mutualism; Parasitism.

Symbolic Logic, also known as modern or mathematical logic. Latest stage in the development of logic, using symbols to represent the forms of sentences expressing propositions. Arising in the 19th century, it is an extension of previous forms of logic. *See also* Logic.

Symbolism, loosely defined art movement in French painting and sculpture. It arose around 1885 as a reaction against the prevailing pragmatism of Gustave Courbet and the Impressionists and strove to give visual expression to spiritual concerns through color and form.

Symbolists, name given to a group of French poets active in the latter part of the 19th century of whom the most famous were Mallarmé, Verlaine, Corbière, Rimbaud, and Laforgue. Influenced by Baudelaire, they had no common technique but shared a desire to transcend reality as portrayed in the realistic novel and to create poetic impressions through suggestion rather than statement.

Symmetry, anatomical description of body form or geometrical pattern of a plant or animal. It is used to help classify living things (taxonomy) and to clarify relationships. There are three types of symmetry: spherical, radial, and bilateral. Spherical, like a ball, as found in simple organisms; radial, like a coin, as in a starfish; and bilateral, two similar halves, as in man.

Symmetry Law, Nuclear, hypothesis that at subatomic levels time reversal would not affect events: there is virtually no distinction between past and future.

Sympathetic Nervous System. *See* Autonomic Nervous System.

Symphony, a work for symphony orchestra, usually having four parts or movements and taking the form of a sonata. The symphony was developed by the Classical composers Haydn and Mozart and reached a pinnacle in the Classical period with the nine symphonies of Beethoven. Significant later composers of symphonies were Schubert, Brahms, and Mahler and, in the 20th century, Vaughan Williams, Sibelius, and Shostakovitch.

Synagogue (Gr. "assembly"), a building constructed for Jewish worship, education, and cultural development. Synagogues serve as communal centers, led by a rabbi. They house the ark and are built facing Jerusalem. They may have developed during the Babylonian exile after 586 BC, and were brought to Israel with the return.

Synapse, space between the axon of one neuron and the receptive area of the next neuron. In a chain of neurons this gap is bridged by a special "transmitter substance," such as acetylcholine, which is produced by structures in the axon endings. *See also* Neuron.

Synchrocyclotron, modification of the cyclotron in which the frequency of the electric field is slowly changed as the particles spiral round the device. This counteracts the increase in particle mass at relativistic velocities and prevents the particles getting out of phase with the field, the radius of the path being proportional to velocity and mass. Energies can reach 700 MeV. *See also* Cyclotron.

Synchronous Orbit, Satellite, circular or near-circular orbit at such a height (22,300mi or 35,900km) that the satellite remains above a single point on the surface. It is used to reflect or actively broadcast television communications to large areas. Spaced correctly, only three synchronous satellites could cover the entire Earth with direct radio or television communications. The first synchronous satellite was Syncom 2 (July 26, 1963).

Synchrotron, field accelerator in which a beam of electrons or protons is focused and guided around a fixed circular path by changing magnetic fields. Millions of revolutions are made. A high-frequency electric field at one point in the path accelerates the particles. Proton energies can reach hundreds of GeV, electron energies tens of GeV.

Syncline, a downward fold in rocks. The bending of rocks is referred to by geologists as folding. When rock layers fold down into a troughlike form, it is called a syncline. An upward arch-shaped fold is called an anticline. The sides of the fold are called limbs, and the median line between the limbs along or through the crest is known as the axis of the fold. *See also* Geosyncline.

Syndicalism, theory of revolutionary action associated with French radical Georges Sorel. The syndicalists argued that bourgeois society can only be cured by coordinated violence known as the "myth of the general strike." Trade unions, or "syndicates," are the centers of revolution.

Synge, John Millington (1871–1909), Irish dramatist who joined W.B. Yeats and Lady Gregory in the Abbey Theatre. Synge, more dramatist than poet, portrayed peasants critically but with sympathy, in early one-acts *The Shadow of the Glen* (1903) and *Riders to the Sea* (1904) as well as in major dramas *The Well of the Saints* (1905) and *The Playboy of the Western World* (1907). He died leaving *Deirdre of the Sorrows* unfinished.

Syntax, the phase of grammar dealing with the construction of sentences, clauses, or phrases. The study of syntax examines the effectiveness of the arrangement of words. It also examines how the meaning of a word changes if the words are rearranged. English is said to be a syntactical language.

Syphilis, systemic disease caused by the spirochete *Treponema pallidum.* It is usually transmitted through sexual contact, but sometimes occurs congenitally. The first symptom is a small, hard swelling at the site of inoculation. In the second stage, there are skin lesions or rash. Tertiary symptoms may be incapacitating or fatal, affecting almost any part of the body. Other forms are endemic and non-venereal and include such diseases as yaws and pinta. Laboratory tests can detect syphilis in its earliest stage, when treatment with penicillin can achieve a complete cure.

Syracuse (Siracusa), seaport city in Sicily, Italy, on Ionian Sea; capital of Syracuse province. Founded by Greek colonists 734 BC, it prospered and est. own colonies, triumphing over Carthaginians 480 BC; became a center of Greek culture; defeated Athens 5th century BC; taken by Romans 212 BC; conquered by Byzantines and made capital of Sicily AD 535; site of 7th-century cathedral built on Greek temple remains, archeological museum, 13th-century castle. Industries: food processing, wine, tourism. Pop. 121,134.

Syracuse, city in central New York, at S end of Onondaga Lake; seat of Onondaga co. Salt springs were discovered here 1654 by Father Simon LeMoyne, French missionary; site of Syracuse University (1870), New York State Upstate Medical Center (1834), Maria Regina College (1934), Le Moyne College (1946), Onondaga Community College (1962), Everson Museum of Art (designed by I.M. Pei), and Lowe Art Center at Syracuse University. Industries: roller bearings, electrical equipment, candles, soda ash, caskets, air-conditioning equipment. Settled 1788; inc. as village 1824, as city, including settlements of Salina and Lodi, 1847. Pop. (1980) 170,105.

Syr Darya (Syrdarja or Syr Dar'ya), shallow river flowing through the USSR, formed by the junction of the Naryn and Kara Darya rivers in the Fergana Valley of Uzbek SSR, flowing W past Leninabad in Tadzhik SSR, and N reentering Uzbek SSR at Begovat, into Kazakh SSR below Chinaz, past Chardara, forming the E and N limits of the Kyzyl-Kum desert between Kzyl-Orda and Kazalinsk, to the Aral Sea. It receives the Angren, Chirchik, and Arys rivers. Important for irrigation, it is unnavigable for all of its 1,370mi (2,206km).

Syria (As-Suriyah), independent nation in the Middle East. It is dominated politically by the Socialist Baath administration.

Land and economy. Situated in the Middle East surrounded by Turkey (N), the Mediterranean, Lebanon, and Israel (W), Jordan (S), and Iraq (E), Syria's dominant geographical features are the Anti-Lebanon and Alawite Mts along the coast from Israel to Turkey, the Euphrates River Valley crossing the country from N to SW, the S Jabal al-Druze mountains, and the desert plateau in the SE. Features of the coastline range from cliffs N of Latakia (seaport), to rugged areas between Tripoli and Beirut, to sandy shores near Tyre. The climate is mainly dry. Annual rainfall varies from 50in (127cm) in the mountains to 0.5in (1.3cm) in the desert. Syria began exporting petroleum in 1968, and although output is low compared to major Middle Eastern producers, oil has come to dominate Syria's economy, providing over 70% of export revenues. Agriculture employs about 32% of the labor force, and raw cotton and cotton textiles are the second-most important export.

People. Mostly of Arab stock, there are also minorities of Kurds, living in the N along the Turkish border, and Armenians, mostly urban dwellers. Probably the only indigenous people are the Alawis, a Muslim sect in the province of Latakia. Literacy is rated at 40%.

Government. A 1973 constitution provides for a 195-member People's Council, with executive power vested in the president.

History. Located where three continents merge, Syria has been a strategic possession since about 2500 BC. Dominated by a series of rulers, it fell into Muslim hands in AD 636, was destroyed by the Mongols in 1400, and was under Turkish rule for 400 years after 1517. It was a French League of Nations mandate after WWI and declared itself a republic in 1941. Full independence came in 1944. For a short time (1958–61), Syria joined Egypt in the United Arab Republic. In 1963 the Socialist Baath party seized power. In 1970, Hafez al-Assad seized power in a coup and was elected president in 1978 and reelected in 1985. Syria has been a strong opponent of Israel and has participated in the Arab-Israeli wars. In 1976, Syrian troops intervened in the Lebanese civil war. The remaining troops have engaged in sporadic fighting with Israeli-backed Christian militia. Tensions increased in 1981 when Syria positioned missiles toward Israel in Lebanon and in 1982 when those missile sites were fired upon by the Israelis. Tensions eased when the missiles were removed in 1986. Domestically, Assad has faced opposition to his regime from conservative Muslim extremists, resulting in repression of dissidence and heavy fighting (1982) against the Muslim Brotherhood in Hamah, although partial amnesty was granted to the Brotherhood in 1985. Syria was thought to support increased terrorism in 1986.

PROFILE

Official name: Syrian Arab Republic
Area: 71,498sq mi (185,180sq km)
Population: 8,347,000
Density: 117per sq mi (45per sq km)
Chief cities: Damascus (capital); Aleppo
Government: Socialist republic
Religion: Islam, Christian
Language: Arabic
Monetary unit: Syrian pound
Gross national product: $8,920,000,000
Per capita income: $345
Industries: textiles, flour milling, oil refining, cement, tobacco products, glassware, brassware, soap
Agriculture: cotton, barley, wheat, fruits, vegetables, sugar beets, sheep
Minerals: oil
Trading partners: USSR, People's Republic of China, Lebanon, France, Italy, Japan, United Kingdom

Syrian Desert (Badiyat ash-Sham), arid wasteland in SW Asia, along the E Mediterranean coast; extends N from Arabian Desert in Saudi Arabia, includes W Iraq, E Jordan, and SE Syria. The desert is crossed by oil pipelines and highway from Damascus to Baghdad; site of several oases including Palmyra; Arabian horses are raised on the outskirts of the desert; inhabited by numerous nomadic tribes.

Syrian War, campaigns of 192–189 BC waged between Antiochus III, Seleucid king, and Rome. In an effort to expand his kingdom Antiochus conquered Ptolemaic Syria and Palestine (202–198). Fighting in Thrace he alarmed Rome. He lost three major battles to the Romans (at Thermopylae, Magnesia, and Sipylum), ending Seleucid power in the Mediterranean with the peace of Apamea (188).

Syringa, genus of flowering deciduous shrubs and trees native to Europe and NE Asia.

Syrinx, vocal apparatus of birds located at base of the windpipe. It is well-developed in songbirds with cartilage, membranes, and muscle groups working in pairs, providing a separate voice on each side.

Szczecin (Stettin), city in NW Poland, on Oder River near its mouth on the Stettiner Haff (bay); capital of Szczecin prov.; a major port and industrial city. Largest city of Pomerania in the 12th century, and a member of the Hanseatic League from 1360, it passed to Sweden 1648 by Peace of Westphalia, then to Prussia at close of Northern War (1720); was returned to Poland by Potsdam Conference 1945. City became an important modern port with the construction of a canal to Berlin (1914); site of technical university (1945) and agricultural college (1954). Industries: shipbuilding, iron works, chemicals, food processing, fishing. Pop. 337,200.

Szechwan (Sichuan), province in SW China; bounded by provs. of Tsinghai, Kansu, and Shensi (N), Hupeh and Hunan (E), Kweichow and Yunnan (S), Tibet (W); completely surrounded by mountains. Capital is Chengtu. Province served as temporary capital of Nationalist China during 2nd Sino-Japanese War (1937–45); seat of Szechwan University. Called the "rice bowl" of China, it is a leading rice producer. Crops: rice, sugar cane, potatoes, fruit, wheat, corn, sugar beets. Industries: forestry, textiles, livestock, salt, oil, natural gas; coal, iron, copper, lead, zinc, asbestos, mercury mining. Area: 220,000sq mi (569,800sq km). Pop. 67,960,000.

Szent-Györgyi von Nagyrapolt, Albert (1893–), US biochemist, b. Hungary. He was awarded the 1937 Nobel Prize in physiology or medicine for his work on biological combustion processes and the isolation of vitamin C. He also studied the biochemistry of muscle, discovering the muscle protein actin that is responsible for muscular contraction when combined with the muscle protein myosin.

T

Tabasco, state of SE Mexico, on the Gulf of Mexico; bounded by Guatemala (SE). First explored by Spanish 1518, it was taken by Francisco de Montejo 1530; it is predominantly a tropical forest plain, with numerous swamps, lagoons, and rivers; the Grijalva and Usumacinta rivers are the main travel routes. Products: hardwood, bananas, cacao, pineapples, rubber, chicle, fruits, oil. Area: 9,783sq mi (25,338sq km). Pop. 1,054,000.

Tabernacle, the place of worship used by the Jews during their wanderings in Sinai. It is also called Mishkan, or the dwelling of God. It was a tent constructed under instructions from God, rectangular in shape and covered with skins. In it the Ark of the Covenant was contained and hidden by a veil.

Tabes Dorsalis, or locomotor ataxia, a form of neurosyphilis in which the dorsal columns of the spinal cord degenerate, causing intense pain and lack of muscular coordination.

Table Tennis, table game, also known as Ping Pong (trademark), played by two or four persons. The table is 9 feet (2.7m) long and 5 feet (1.5m) wide and 30 inches (76.2cm) from the floor. The surface is divided by a transverse net 6 inches (15.2cm) high, and halved longitudinally by a light stripe. A hollow, seamless, celluloid ball, about 1.5 inches (3.8cm) in diameter, is hit with wooden paddles that measure, with the handle, 9.5 inches (24.1cm) long. The surface of the paddle is covered with either sandpaper or rubber. On the serve, the ball must bounce once before clearing the net on the near surface and then bounce once on the far surface before it is returned. After the serve, the ball may not take more than one bounce on either surface. If the ball goes foul or fails to be returned properly, a point is scored. Each player in turn has five consecutive serves until 21 is reached (games tied at 20–20 continue until a two-point margin is achieved). In doubles, the server must deliver the ball into the diagonally opposite box. Table tennis, first popular in England, is believed to have originated in the 19th century.

Taboo, or tabu, prohibition of a form of behavior, object, word, etc. In many cultures a thing may be regarded as taboo because it is either unclean or sacred—there is often a taboo on a totem. Breaking a taboo is believed to bring supernatural retribution and often brings social ostracism or other punishment. The term is of Tongan origin. *See also* Totem.

Tabor (Tavor), Mount, mountain in N Israel, 5mi (8km) E of Nazareth; Biblical scene of Christ's transfiguration. Height: 1,929ft (588m).

Tabriz, city in NW Iran, 38mi (61km) E of Lake Urmia; capital of East Azerbaijan prov. An ancient city, it served as the capital of Armenia under King Tiridates III (AD 3rd century). Ghazan Khan developed it as the chief administrative center for his vast Asian empire (1295); occupied by Ottomans 1514, 1585–1603, 1724–30; held by Russians 1827–28; scene of revolution 1946, led by Tudeh regime and supported by Soviet Union; few historical buildings remain due to devastating earthquakes (858, 1041, 1721); a long-time trade center due to its proximity to Turkey and Soviet Union; site of university (1946). Industries: carpets, textiles, leather, paint, shoes, soap. Pop. 403,413.

Tachinid Fly, white to black fly, 0.25 to 0.5in (6.25–12.7mm) long, found worldwide. It is an important parasite of harmful insects, and several species have been imported into the United States to control insect pests. Family Tachinidae. *See also* Diptera.

Tachyon, hypothetical particle that travels faster than the speed of light. It might be detectable by the Cerenkov radiation it emits. To satisfy the special theory of relativity it would have to have either real rest mass and imaginary energy and momentum, or imaginary rest mass and real energy and momentum.

Tacitus, Cornelius (*c.*55–*c.*117), Roman historian. Often considered the greatest of the Roman historians, he was both an accurate observer of contemporary life and a uniquely effective stylist. His best known works are the *Agricola,* a eulogy on his father-in-law; the *Germania,* a description of the various German tribes; and the *Histories* and the *Annals,* which narrate imperial history from the death of Augustus (AD 14) through AD 96.

Tacoma, seaport and city in W Washington, on Commencement Bay and Puget Sound, 26mi (42km) S of Seattle; seat of Pierce co. The city is beautifully situated between water and the Olympic Mts (NW), and Mt Rainier (E) from which the city's Indian name is derived; the area's growth was spurred by the coming of the North Pacific Railway (1887); site of Tacoma Smelter, Point Defiance Park, Fort Nisqually (1833), Washington State Historical Museum, University of Puget Sound (1888), Pacific Lutheran University, Tacoma Community College; industrial and commercial center. Exports: wheat, flour, lumber. Industries: food and forest products, railroad shops, chemicals, explosives, paints, shipbuilding, copper smelting and refining, aluminum reduction. Settled 1852; inc. 1884. Pop. (1980) 158,501.

Taconite, a kind of chert that contains iron, resulting from replacement processes. It is used as an iron ore in some countries. *See* Chert.

Tactics, the maneuver of troops in combat. In the offense, military units are employed in frontal or flanking assaults against specific objectives, and are supported by automatic weapons, tanks, artillery, and aircraft. Forces with defensive missions usually fight from prepared or dug-in positions with mines, obstacles, artillery barrages, and direct fire positioned along the expected approach route of the enemy. Tactical deployments must consider all forces at the disposal of the commander as well as the terrain, weather, and the forces and dispositions of the enemy.

Tadpole, aquatic, fishlike frog or toad larva with finned tail and gills. It lacks lungs and legs. Unlike adults, most tadpoles are vegetarians, feeding on algae and other aquatic plants. During metamorphosis, limbs are grown, the tail is absorbed, and internal lungs take the place of gills. *See also* Frog; Toad.

Tadzhik Soviet Socialist Republic (Tadzikskaja Sovetskaja Socialisticeskaja Respublik, or Tadzhikistan), constituent republic of the USSR, bounded N and W by the Uzbek and Kirghiz republics, S by Afghanistan, and E by China, including the Garno-Badachsanskaja autonomous oblast; contains the Pamir and Trans Abil mountain systems. Main cities are Dusanbe, Leninabad, Ura-T'ube. It was acquired as part of Russian Turkistan 1895; became part of Russian SFSR 1924 and a constituent republic 1929. Crops: cotton, rice, lucerne, fruits, grains, sesame, vegetables, nuts, sugar cane. Minerals: lead, zinc, silver, uranium, arsenic, antimony, bismuth, molybdenum, tungsten, feldspar, coal, petroleum, salt, gold. Exports: cotton, silk, dried fruit, lead-zinc ores. Area: 55,000sq mi (142,000sq km). Pop. 3,691,000.

Taegu, city in S central South Korea, 56mi (90km) NW of Pusan; capital of North Kyŏngsang since 1895 and 3rd-largest city in South Korea; successfully defended by UN troops against Communist invasions during Korean War (1950–53); textile and agricultural center. Pop. 1,311,078.

Taenia. *See* Tenia.

William Howard Taft

Tahiti

Taj Mahal

Taft, William Howard (1857–1930), 27th president of the United States (1909–13) and 10th chief justice of the Supreme Court (1921–30), b. Cincinnati, Ohio. He graduated from Yale University (1878) and Cincinnati Law School (1880). In 1886 he married Helen Herron; they had three children.

A practicing lawyer in Cincinnati, Taft was active in Republican politics from an early age. He served as a state judge and in 1890 Pres. Benjamin Harrison named him solicitor general and later made him a federal judge. He was the first US governor of the Philippines and did much to improve US-Philippine relations.

In 1904, Pres. Theodore Roosevelt named Taft secretary of war. He became one of Roosevelt's closest advisors, and he was Roosevelt's handpicked candidate to succeed him. The Republicans nominated Taft in 1908, and he defeated the Democratic candidate, William Jennings Bryan. In some respects Taft continued Roosevelt's Progressive Republican policies. The antitrust laws continued to be enforced, and, in foreign affairs, Taft continued the activist, adventurous policies of his predecessor. His administration became increasingly more conservative, however, and Taft's relationship with Roosevelt deteriorated. By 1912, Roosevelt was in active opposition and tried to win the Republican nomination away from Taft. After Taft won, Roosevelt ran on his own Progressive, or Bull Moose, ticket. He polled more votes than Taft but the election went to Democrat Woodrow Wilson.

Taft taught law after leaving the White House, and in 1921 President Harding named him chief justice of the United States. While chief justice, he greatly streamlined the operations of the federal judiciary.

Career: US solicitor general, 1890–92; federal circuit judge, 1892–1900; governor of the Philippines, 1900–04; secretary of war, 1904–09; president, 1909–13; chief justice, 1921–30.

Tagalog, the national language of the Philippines. In 1962 it was made the country's official language and given the new name of Pilipino. It is the mother tongue of about 10,000,000 people, living mainly in southern Luzon, but it is estimated that about 20,000,000 more at least understand the language. Tagalog belongs to the Austronesian family of languages.

Tagore, Rabindranath (1861–1941), Indian poet, philosopher, and social theorist. He received the Nobel Prize for literature in 1913. Written in Bengali, his works reflect his myriad interests. He is most famous in the West for his book of religious verse called *Gitanjali* (1912), but in his own country his poems on love and nature are also popular. He founded an experimental village and a school which eliminated the usual restrictions. He was a dramatist, novelist, painter, and musician as well.

Tagus (Tajo or **Tejo),** river in Spain and Portugal; rises in E central Spain; flows to the Atlantic Ocean at Lisbon. The longest river on the Iberian Peninsula, it forms part of Spanish-Portuguese border; above Lisbon the river widens to form a lagoon approx. 7mi (11km) wide; navigable for approx. 100mi (161km). Length: 626mi (1,008km).

Tahiti, island in S Pacific Ocean, in Windward Island group of the Society Islands, French Polynesia. Largest of the French Polynesian islands, Tahiti has long been regarded as an idyllic island paradise. It was discovered by English navigator Samuel Wallis and explored by Capt. James Cook on several visits 1769–77; missionaries were est. in late 18th century; colonized by France 1880; the French painter Paul Gauguin did many of his works here. Tahiti is mountainous and fertile, producing tropical fruits, copra, sugar cane, and vanilla; pearl fishing is an important industry. Majority

of inhabitants are Polynesians, and most settlements are situated along the coast. Capital is Papeete. Area: 402sq mi (1,041sq km). Pop. 79,494.

Tahoe, Lake, lake on the N central California-W Nevada border, in the Eldorado National Forest and N Sierra Nevada Mts; drained by the Truckee River. A noted resort and tourist area, it has been cited as one of the most beautiful lakes in the world. Discovered 1844 by John C. Frémont. Area: 193sq mi (500sq km). Max. depth: 1,645ft (504m).

Tahr, gregarious, goatlike ruminant found in the Himalayas, S India, and SE Arabia. Unlike goats, the male is beardless with short horns. Long fur varies from light to dark brown. Length: to 3.5ft (1.1m); weight: to 200lb (90kg). Family Bovidae; genus *Hemitragus. See also* Ruminant.

Tai, people of Chinese origins, who inhabit the mainland of Southeast Asia, and who consist of several Tai-speaking groups: the Siamese, Lao, Shan, Lü, Yunnan Tai, and tribal Tai. An agricultural people whose major crop is rice, they practice Theraváda Buddhism, although some animism remains.

Tai Chi, a Neo-Confucian concept, dating from before the 11th century in China, of the Supreme Ultimate, the primary principle and source of all things, the purpose and cause of the evolution of the universe. The philosophic system in which this is regarded as the First Principle was developed in the work of Chou Tun-i (1017–73) and Chu Hsi (1130–1200). The name *Tai Chi* is applied to a system of stylized exercises of Oriental character.

T'ai-chung, or **Taichung,** city in W central Taiwan; site of Chinese National Palace Museum and Chinese National Central Museum. Industries: agriculture, textiles, food processing, chemicals. Pop. 575,000.

Taiga, a Russian word for the vast, cold, swampy, coniferous-forest region of Siberia; the part that lies between the tundra and the steppe. The term is applied to similar areas in Europe and America.

Tai Languages, group of languages spoken in Southeast Asia. It includes Thai, of Thailand, Lao, of Laos, Shan, of Burma, plus a number of languages in S China such as Chuang, Puyi (Chungchia), and Tung. Some scholars place the Tai languages in the Sino-Tibetan family, which includes Chinese, but this is disputed by other scholars.

Tailorbird, tropical Asian and African warbler that stitches leaves together, forming a pocket for its nest. Brown spotted eggs (2–6) are laid. Insect-eaters, most species are dull-colored. Length: 5in (12.5cm). Genus *Orthotomus.*

Taimyr Peninsula (Taymyr, Taimir, or Tajmyr), large peninsula in central USSR, on the Kara and Laptev seas, between the Jenisej and Chatanga river mouths, crossed in the central part by the Taimyr River; site of Cape Cel'uskin, Asia's northernmost point, containing the Byrranga Mts and Lake Taimyr. Length: 700mi (1,127km).

Tainan (T'ainan), city in W central Taiwan, on the Taiwan Strait. Oldest city in Taiwan; held by Dutch 1624–62; served as capital of Taiwan prov. under Koxinga until the 1885 transfer of government to Taipei; site of university (1956), temples, shrine of Koxinga. Industries: textiles, aluminum, rubber, plastics, iron and steel products, food processing. Settled 1590. Pop. 550,000.

Taipei (T'aipei), capital city of Nationalist China, at N end of Taiwan, major trade center for tea in 19th century; in 1885 it replaced T'ainan as the capital of Taiwan prov.; prospered under Japanese rule 1895–1945; became seat of Chinese Nationalist government 1949; site of National Taiwan University (1928). Industries: wood, paper products, chemicals, fertilizers, food products, machinery, electrical equipment, brewing, printing, railroad shops. Founded 1708. Pop. 2,100,000.

Taiping Rebellion (1850–64), an anti-Manchu revolt led by a Hakka fanatic, Hung Hsiu-ch'üan, who imagined himself to be the son of God and younger brother of Jesus Christ. The fighting laid waste 12 provinces of China and resulted in more than 20,000,000 casualties. The Manchus never recovered their control or ability to govern China with the former authority. Chinese scholar-statesmen, including Tseng Kuo-fan and Tso Tsungt'ang, aided the Manchus in suppressing the rebels.

Taiwan (Formosa), island province of China, 100mi (161km) off SE China mainland in the Pacific Ocean; seat of the Chinese Nationalist government; province includes main island of Taiwan, several islets, and Pescadores island group; capital is Taipei. The terrain is mostly mountainous; climate is semitropical and subject to typhoons. Immigration from mainland China began 7th century; Portuguese visited the island 1509 and named it Formosa (beautiful). It was occupied by Dutch 1624 and seized by Ming dynasty 1662; taken by Manchus 1683; made a province of China 1886. It was ceded to Japan 1895 after first Sino-Japanese War; returned to China 1945 and made seat of government 1949. Area: 13,807sq mi (35,760sq km). Pop. 17,000,000. *See also* China, Republic of.

Taiyüan (Taiyuan or **T'ai-yüan),** city in NE China, 265mi (427km) SW of Peking, on Fen River; capital of Shansi prov. under Communist control after long battle in which thousands starved (1948–49); one of richest coal and iron areas in the world; seat of Shansi University. Industries: mining, smelting, iron and steel foundries, chemicals, plastics, food processing. Pop. 1,350,000.

Ta'izz, city in S Yemen, 32mi (52km) E of Mocha; served as administrative capital of Yemen (1948–62); marketing center. Pop. 100,000.

Taj Mahal, a Muslim mausoleum, built 1630–48 in Agra, India, by the Mogul emperor Shah Jahan after the death of his favorite wife.

Talc, a sheet silicate mineral, hydrous magnesium silicate [$Mg_3Si_4O_{10}(OH)_2$]. Monoclinic system; rare tabular crystals and as masses. White, green, blue, brown. Hardness 1; sp gr 2.6. Used as base for talcum powder and in ceramics.

Tale of Genji, The, Japanese novel combining fiction and history, relating the amorous adventures of Prince Genji in Japan's feudal court and perceptively depicts court life. It was written *c.* 1010 by Lady Murasaki Shikibu (*c.* 970–early or mid-11th century). The first significant novel written anywhere, it is rated the greatest work of the Heian period (794–1192) and possibly in all Japanese literature. The long, winding narrative is over 1,000 pages in the English translation, expertly done by Arthur Waley (6 vols., 1925–33; 1 vol., 1935).

Tallahassee, capital city of Florida, in NW Florida, 160mi (258km) W of Jacksonville; seat of Leon co. It was inhabited by Seminole Indians, settlers from other southern states, and Spanish missionaries when Tallahassee was made capital of Florida Territory (1824); made state capital 1845; scene of adoption of secessionist ordinance (1861); 20th-century cultural and administrative center. It is site of Goodwood (1843) and Grove (1830) antebellum houses, Florida State University (1857). Industries: lumber and lumber products, food processing, tourism, truck farming. Inc. 1825. Pop. (1980) 81,548.

Tallahatchie River, river in Mississippi, rises in NE Miss., flows generally S to the Yalobusha River, near Greenwood, forming the Yazoo River; its waters, impounded by Sardis Dam, form Sardis Lake. Length: 301mi (485km).

Tallapoosa River, river in NW Georgia and E Alabama; rises in NW Ga.; flows SW across Ala. border, then S and W to join Coosa River near Montgomery, Ala., forming Alabama River. Length: 268mi (431km).

Talleyrand-Périgord, Charles Maurice de (1754–1838), French political figure and diplomat. Although a member of the Second Estate (the church), he successfully proposed confiscation of church property. In London (1791–93) he tried to keep Britain from joining Austria, Russia, and Prussia in war against the French revolutionary government. Failing, he returned to France after the fall of Maximilien Robespierre (1794) and was grudgingly admitted to the Directory. He supported Napoleon and was foreign minister (1797–1807), but the two fell out over Napoleon's grandiose European ambitions, and Talleyrand was prominent in the restoration of the Bourbons (1814). At the Congress of Vienna (1814–15) he showed superb diplomatic skill, exploiting tensions among the victors to the benefit of France. His unerring political sense led him to support Louis Philippe, whom he served as minister to Britain (1830–34).

Tallinn (Talin), city and capital of Estonian SSR, USSR, on the Gulf of Finland opposite Helsinki, 200mi (322km) W of Leningrad. It was founded 1219 by Danes on the site of an Estonian settlement; joined Hanseatic League 1285; sold to Teutonic Knights 1346; passed to Sweden 1561; occupied by Russia 1710; ceded to Russia by Sweden 1721; developed commercially in the 19th century; occupied and damaged by Germans 1941–44; site of polytechnical and teachers' colleges, conservatory, schools of drama and applied arts, Danish Toompea castle, 13th-century episcopal church, 16th-century watch tower, 13th-century Gothic church of St Olai, Hanseatic "Black Heads" house. Industries: shipbuilding, cotton, textiles, plastics, glass, pulp and paper, plywood, furniture, flour, tobacco products. Exports: textiles, paper, timber. Pop. 422,000.

Tallow Tree, evergreen tree, native to SE China, grown for shade and ornament in the United States. It has heart-shaped leaves that turn yellow to red in autumn. The capsule-contained seeds yield a tallowlike material used in soap and candle making. Height: to 40ft (12m). Family Euphorbiaceae; species *Sapium sebiferum.*

Talmud, 63 books of writings of ancient rabbis, which were developed in the 5th century AD. They are concerned with the whole of Jewish life and use parables and legends. Mishnah, the oral tradition, was recorded and forms part of the Talmud. The interpretation of Mishnah, called Gemara, is included as well. The Talmud includes codes of law as well as legendary accounts of the Jewish people. The study of the Talmud is central to Jewish faith. *See also* Mishna.

Talon, Jean Baptiste (1625–94), French colonial leader in Canada, first intendant of New France (1665–68, 1670–72). Sent to Canada by Jean Colbert, Talon created the seignorial land system, encouraged immigration, established industry, and held the first census in Canada. A tireless, efficient administrator, he developed the political and economic structure of French Canada.

Talus, the heap of rock waste lying at the bottom of a cliff. It is made up of particles, ranging in size from sand grains to boulders, that have been loosened from the cliff rock by mechanical weathering. The accumulated material is called sliderock and as it continues to move within the talus; the movement is known as talus creep.

Tamarisk, family *(Tamaricacae)* of shrubs and small trees found in temperate to subtropical regions. Deciduous, they have slender branches covered with scalelike leaves and feathery clusters of small, white or pink flowers. Foliage is blue-gray. Height: to 30ft (9.1m).

Tamaulipas, state in NE Mexico. First explored by Spanish 1519, its colonization began 1747; became independent 1824. Region is mountainous with plains and coastal strip; climate is predominantly hot and humid; site of several 18th-century Franciscan missions. Products: petroleum, cotton, sugar cane, corn, citrus fruits, livestock. Industries: chemicals, soap, petroleum by-products, vegetable oil, flour, hides, tourism. Area: 30,734sq mi (79,601sq km). Pop. 1,901,000.

Tamerlane, or **Timur** (1336–1405), Oriental conqueror. Descended from Genghis Khan, he controlled a vast empire that extended from the Black Sea to the Indus River and from the Persian Gulf to the Syr Darya River. He made Samarkand, which he took in 1361, his center and personal domain. By defeating the Golden Horde under Toktamysh, Tamerlane inadvertently helped to consolidate Russia. His atrocities have become legendary, and he is the subject of Christopher Marlowe's play *Tamburlaine.*

Tamil, language spoken in S India, chiefly in the state of Tamil Nadu on the E coast, by about 40,000,000 people. There are also about 4,000,000 speakers in NE Sri Lanka, about 1,000,000 in Malaysia, and smaller colonies in Singapore, Fiji, Mauritius, and Guyana. Tamil belongs to the Dravidian family of languages.

Taming of the Shrew, The (*c.*1594), 5-act comedy by William Shakespeare. Some sources believe it was based on an anonymous play *The Taming of A Shrew* (1594), although the latter may be simply a pirated version of Shakespeare's work. The main plot concerns the successful efforts of Petrucchio to subdue his fractious wife Katharina. A subplot deals with the courtship of Katharina's sister Bianca by Lucentio. The play has been produced worldwide and provided the basis for the Broadway musical *Kiss Me Kate* (1948). It was filmed in 1908, 1929, and 1967, and *Kiss Me Kate* was made into a film in 1953.

Tampa, port city, W Florida, seat of Hillsborough co, 81mi (130km) SW of Orlando. Developed as major cigar-making center; fishing resort; processing center for citrus and vegetables. Industries: beer, fertilizers, chemicals. Settled as Fort Brooke, 1824; inc. 1855. Pop. (1980) 271,523.

Tampere, city in SW Finland, on Lake Näsijärvi; Finland's 2nd-largest city. In 1918, White Guards of Finland defeated Finnish Bolsheviks (Red Guards) here; site of technological institute (1965), university (1966), and an open-air theater; textile center of N Europe. Industries: footwear, paper, textiles, machinery. Chartered 1775. Pop. 165,908.

Tampico, seaport city in E Mexico, approx. 6mi (10km) from the Gulf of Mexico, on the Panuco River; former site of the Huastec kingdom, which later evolved into the Aztec Empire; settled by Spanish 1532. Oil was discovered *c.* 1900 by US and British geologists; site of episcopal see, state university. Exports: livestock, hides, oil, agricultural products, copper ore. Industries: machinery, lumber, fishing, tourism. Pop. 240,500.

Tanager, small, brightly colored American forest bird that has a downward-curved, cone-shaped bill and short rounded wings. They feed on insects and fruit and build cup- or dome-shaped nests for their eggs (1–5). The male scarlet tanager *(Piranga olivacea)* of E North America has black on its wings and tail; the female is greenish above and yellowish below. Family Thraupidae.

Tananarive (Madag), capital city of Malagasy Republic, on Madagascar Island; became royal residence 1797 for Merina rulers; it was taken by French 1895 and became part of French protectorate; site of University of Madagascar, Collège Rural d'Ambatobe, astronomical observatory. Industries: rice, food processing, textiles, tobacco, leather goods. Pop. 500,000.

Tancred (died 1194), last Norman king (1190–94) of Sicily. Illegitimate son of Duke Roger of Apulia and grandson of King Roger II of Sicily, he had to fight Emperor Henry VI of Germany (married to Roger of Apulia's sister) for the throne. Although Tancred successfully defended his claim, upon his death Henry deposed Tancred's infant heir, William III, and took Naples.

Tancred (1078?–1112), Norman prince. He was one of the leaders of the First Crusade to the Holy Land, participated in the siege of Nicaea and in the battle of Dorylaeum (1097), and helped capture Jerusalem (1099). When Godfrey of Bouillon became king of Jerusalem, he was made prince of Galilee. He drove the Saracens from Syria.

Taney, Roger Brooke (1777–1864), chief justice of the US Supreme Court (1836–64), b. Calvert City, Md. As attorney general (1831), he aided President Jackson in a struggle with the Bank of the United States, advising him in a veto over the recharter of the bank. As secretary of the treasury (1833), he withdrew US funds from the bank, causing a Senate outrage and its refusal to confirm his appointment. He was appointed associate justice (1835) but was never confirmed by the Senate. The next year a Senate Democratic majority confirmed his appointment by President Jackson as chief justice, succeeding John Marshall. A "states' rightist," he nonetheless extended the scope and power of the Supreme Court. He was associated with *Dred Scott* v. *Sanford* (1857), which refused blacks the right of citizenship and gave Congress power to control slavery in the territories. The decision heightened tensions between North and South.

Tanganyika, Lake, navigable lake in E central Africa, between W Tanzania and E Zaire. Area: 12,700sq mi (32,893sq km); depth: 4,710ft (1,437m).

T'ang Chinese, or **T'ang Jen,** people inhabiting the S Chinese provinces of Kwangtung and Kwangsi. Ethnically indistinguishable from the Han Chinese, but speaking a number of different dialects, the T'ang represent refugees from the 12th- and 13th-century Tatar and Mongol invasions in the north.

T'ang Dynasty (618–907), Chinese dynasty that ruled during imperial China's most vigorous and creative age. The capital Ch'ang-an (modern Sian) was a cosmopolitan center of world trade and relations, and Chinese political and cultural institutions were at their height. This was the golden age of Chinese poetry, the period when China had its greatest impact on Korea and Japan, and the age when the civil service examination system came into full vigor. The dynasty was interrupted briefly by the revolt of the tribal military leader An Lu-shan, but recovered and gave renewed thrust to Chinese tradition and institutions.

Tangent, ratio of the length of the side opposite an acute angle to the length of the side adjacent to the angle in a right-angled triangle. The tangent of angle A is usually abbreviated to "tan A." *See also* Trigonometric Functions.

Tangerine, or mandarin orange, small, edible citrus fruit native to China. It has a thin skin and easily separated segments. Family Rutaceae; species *Citrus reticulata.*

Tangier (Tanger), seaport in N Morocco, on the Strait of Gibraltar. An ancient Roman port, it was later occupied by Moors; taken by Portuguese 1471; received by England 1662 as part of dowry in marriage of Catherine of Braganza to Charles II; abandoned to Moors 1684. City was est. as an International Zone 1924–56, providing a neutralized seaport which developed into a base for European smuggling; became part of independent Morocco 1956; site of casbah and the old Moorish walled city. Industries: rugs, pottery, shipping, tourism. Pop. 243,600.

T'ang-shan, or **Tangshan,** city in NE China, 100mi (161km) SE of Peking. Much of city was destroyed in an earthquake July 1976. Industries: coal mining, iron, steel, chemicals, petroleum products, textiles. Pop. 1,200,000.

Tank, tracked armored vehicle mounting a single primary weapon, usually a gun, and one or more machine guns. Modern tanks all have an enclosed fully-revolving turret and are heavily armored; main battle tanks presently weigh from 35 to 50 tons and have a crew of 4. Developed in great secrecy by the British during World War I, they were first employed at the Battle of the Somme in 1916. It was not until the Germans concentrated their tanks into armored divisions during early World War II that the tank came into its own as a major weapon system.

Tanker, a ship that carries bulk liquids, usually petroleum products, as cargo. The crude oil or gasoline is piped into the cargo spaces and transported. No containers are used and the largest tankers (super tankers), more than 1,000 ft (305m) long, can carry 300, 000 tons. Propelling machinery is located in the stern with the poop above it; a forecastle and a house are amidships.

Tannaim, scholars and teachers of the Jewish Oral Law who flourished from AD 10 to 220. Hillel, a *tanna* (scholar), began to spread the Midrash (a homiletical interpretation of the Jewish scriptures) of the Talmud, and Judah I (the last *tanna*) organized and preserved it. Other important teachers were Johanan ben Zaccai, who established the academy at Jamnia, and Akiba ben Joseph, who systematically compiled the Oral Laws and sided with Bar Kokba against Rome.

Tanning, process of converting skins and hides into leather. Traditionally, tanning liquids are based on tannin and the process takes one month or more. It is still

Charles Maurice de Talleyrand-Périgord

Roger Brooke Taney

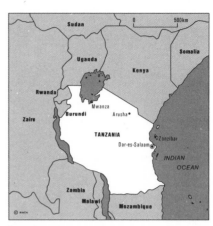

Tanzania

used for heavy leathers. Light leathers are now tanned in a few hours using chromium salts. *See also* Leather.

Tansy, any of several mostly perennial plants characterized by fernlike aromatic leaves and clusters of yellow, buttonlike flower heads. The poisonous *Tanacetum vulgare,* native to Eurasia, is a common weed in North America; height: to 3ft (91cm). Family Compositae.

Tanta, city in N Egypt, 51mi (82km) N of Cairo on Nile River delta; capital of Gharbiyah governorate; site of three annual festivals for Muslim leader, Ahmad al-Badawi, whose grave is in Tanta. Industries: cotton ginning, shipping. Pop. 240,500.

Tantalum, metallic element (symbol Ta) of the third transition series, first isolated in 1903. Chief ore is columbite-tantalite. It is used in steels and other special alloys. Properties: at. no. 73; at. wt. 180.948; sp gr 16.654; melt. pt. 5,425°F (2,996°C); boil. pt. 9,795°F (5,425°C); most common isotope Ta^{181} (99.988%). *See also* Transition Elements.

Tanzania, independent nation in E Africa, uniting the formerly separate nations of Tanganyika and Zanzibar. It contains the earliest fossil evidence of mankind. It came under Arab, British, and German domination before independence in 1961.
Land and economy. Tanzania includes Tanganyika and the islands of Zanzibar and Pemba; the mainland is in E Africa, bordering the Indian Ocean. Its neighbors are Kenya and Uganda (N), Rwanda, Burundi, and Zaire (W), Zambia, Malawi, and Mozambique (S). The land is divided into four main regions: the hot coastal plains, the hot, dry central plateau, the moist lake sections, and the temperate highlands. Mt Kilimanjaro, 19,340ft (5,899m) above sea level, is the highest point in Africa. Development has been hampered by a lack of water and the tsetse fly. About 90% of the labor force is engaged in agriculture, forestry, and fishing. Principal subsistence crops are cassava and maize; cotton, coffee, and sisal represent 40% of all exports; diamonds are the 4th-largest export. From 1972–74 and in the mid-1980s Tanzania suffered from a prolonged drought.
People. In a population 90% rural, density differs widely, from 3per sq mi (1.2per sq km) in arid regions to 347per sq mi (134per sq km) on Zanzibar. Africans are divided into some 130 ethnic groups, each with its own language. The majority is of Bantu origin. On Zanzibar, Shirazis trace their ancestry back to Persian settlers. Literacy is 15%–20%. Non-Africans constitute 1% of the population.
Government. A single party state, Tanzania operates under an elected president with broad powers and unicameral National Assembly.If the president is from the mainland, the vice-president must be from Zanzibar, and vice versa. Zanzibar has its own separate government for internal affairs.
History. Before migrating Bantus replaced the indigenous Bushmen and Hottentots, fossils suggest that E Africa may have been the cradle of mankind. Arabs established trading centers in the 8th century and, with the exception of a Portuguese period in 1506, they remained in control until the British took power in the mid-19th century. Britain was followed by German colonials who brought roads, repression of the natives, and consequent rebellion. German rule ended after WWI. It became a UN trust territory under Britain after WWII. In 1954, Julius K. Nyerere organized the Tanganyika African National Union. Full independence as a republic under the Commonwealth came in 1961; Nyerere was elected president in 1964 and served until his retirement in 1985 when he was succeeded by Ali Hassan Mwinyi, head of Zanzibar. On April 26, 1964,

Zanzibar and Tanganyika united as Tanzania. In 1979, Tanzanian troops invaded neighboring Uganda, to depose its dictator, Idi Amin. The drought in Africa during the early 1980s created severe food shortages by 1985.

PROFILE

Official name: United Republic of Tanzania
Area: 364,882sq mi (945,087sq km)
Population: 17,982,000
 Density: 49per sq mi (19per sq km)
Chief cities: Dar es Salaam (capital); Arusha
Government: Single party state with elected president and National Assembly
Religion: Islam (30%), Christian (30%), animism
Language: Swahili and English (both official)
Monetary unit: Tanzanian shilling
Gross national product: $4,700,000,000
Per capita income: $127
Industries: food processing, clothing, textiles, cement, petroleum products, sugar refining, tanning, aluminum
Agriculture: cloves, sisal, cotton, coffee, tea, tobacco, cattle
Minerals: diamonds, gold, salt, tin, mica
Trading partners: United Kingdom, European Economic Community, China, Japan, India

T'ao Ch'ien (*c.* 365–427), Chinese poet. He is considered China's greatest poet during the period of political division from AD 221–589. He left a minor official post as a protest against corruption and barely eked out a farming existence with his family. His verse, which has a predominantly Taoist outlook, is frequently about nature and wine. His simple style differed from the ornateness of his contemporaries, so he did not earn full recognition until the 8th century.

Taoism, Chinese philosophy and religion considered next to Confucianism in importance. Taoist philosophy is traced to a 6th-century BC classic of Lao-tzu, the *Tao tê Ching.* The recurrent theme is the Tao, or path. To follow the Tao is to follow the path of the cosmos leading to self-realization. Taoist ethics emphasize patience, simplicity, and nature's harmony. As a religion, Taoism dates from the time of Chang Tao-ling, who organized a group of followers in AD 143. It was a state religion in China for a time, but in modern times membership has dwindled.

Taos, northernmost of the Río Grande Pueblo Indians, inhabiting a village erected on both sides of the Taos River in Taos co, N.M., around AD 1700. Although they speak a Tanoan language, their location gave them extensive contact with the Plains Indians and greatly influenced their culture. Today about 3,400 people inhabit the village.

Tapestry, fabric woven by hand of plain weave without shuttle or drawboy, the design being threaded into the warp with a bobbin or by hand. The term now includes many heavy materials that are not true tapestries, as well as imitation tapestries woven on Jaquard looms. Tapestry design is an ancient art; a few survive today from 1500 BC Egypt. Brussels was the leading tapestry center from the 14th to 17th centuries, when Paris took the lead. Tapestry design has generally followed parallel movements and styles in art. Important tapestry collections in the United States are found in the Metropolitan Museum in New York and in the Museum of Fine Arts, Boston.

Tapeworm, parasitic flatworm found in alimentary tract of vertebrate hosts. It has a tiny head, or scolex, with hooks and suckers and a long body of segments, or proglottids, each having its own reproductive sys-

tem. Intermediate hosts include cattle, fish, and pigs. Infection occurs when improperly cooked, infected meat is eaten. Length: to 90ft (27m). Phylum Platyhelminthes; class Cestoda; species include dog *Dipylidium caninum,* pork *Taenia solium,* beef *Taenia saginata.*

Tapir, nocturnal, plant-eating, hoofed mammal native to forests of tropical America, Sumatra, and Malaya. They have big heads, long, flexible snouts, heavy bodies, short legs, and tiny tails. Adult Malayan tapirs have a striking half-white, half-black coat; New World species are dark brown. Length: 7ft (2.1m); weight: 400lb (180kg). Family Tapiridae.

Taranto, city in S Italy, 50mi (81km) SSE of Bari, on Gulf of Taranto. Founded 8th century BC, it was a leading city of Magna Graecia; part of Rome 272 BC; destroyed by Arabs AD 972; Italian fleet was damaged here during harbor bombing WWII; site of national museum, 11th-century cathedral. Industries: agriculture, fishing, steel, chemicals, shipyards. Pop. 244,249.

Tarantula, large, hairy spider of the Western Hemisphere with a mildly poisonous bite. Its legs grow longer than the body. Body length: to 3.5in (90mm). Family Theraphosidae. *See also* Spider.

Tarascans, Indian group located in Michoacán, Mexico. The Tarascans, who developed a powerful state by 1440, remained neutral during the Spanish conquest of the rival Aztec empire. The Tarascans and the Spanish maintained relatively good relations throughout the colonial period. Lázaro Cárdenas, a former governor of Michoacán, revitalized Tarascan culture during his presidency (1934–40).

Tarawa, atoll in W Pacific Ocean; capital of Gilbert and Ellice Islands, located in N part of the group; trade center for the islands; site of hospital; scene of fierce four-day battle, November 1943, during which the United States freed islands from Japanese occupation. Exports: copra, phosphate rock. Pop. 12,642.

Tariff, tax placed on imports either as a percentage of the value of the item (ad valorem tariff) or per unit (specific duty). Tariffs may be used to discourage the importing of certain types of goods or to adjust for price differentials in order to allow the importing country's products to be competitive. Tariffs are placed on such goods as automobiles in order to prevent foreign competition from gaining an excessive share of the national market. Tariffs may be levied on a specific good, regardless of the country it came from, or may be specifically aimed at discriminating among goods on the basis of country or origin.

Tarkington, (Newton) Booth (1869–1946), US novelist, b. Indianapolis. He is best known for his depiction of middle-class life in small Midwestern cities. Originally planning to be an illustrator, he turned to writing and produced his first book, *The Gentleman from Indiana,* in 1899. He served a term in the Indiana legislature and won Pulitzer Prizes for *The Magnificent Ambersons* (1918) and *Alice Adams* (1921). Also noted for his novels about childhood, he produced the popular *Penrod* (1914) and *Seventeen* (1916).

Taro, large tropical plant native to the Pacific Islands and Southeast Asia and cultivated in other parts of the world for its edible tuberous root. In Hawaii it is eaten as poi. Family Araceae; species *Colocasia esculenta.* *See also* Arum.

Tarpon, tropical marine game fish. Blue and bright silver, it has a long, deeply forked tail. Its eggs hatch into a bandlike, transparent larval form, and then metamorphose into the juvenile form. Length: to 8ft (244cm); weight: 340lb (154kg). Main species are the small Pacific *Megalops cyprinoides* and the large Atlantic *M. atlanticus.* Family Elopidae.

Tarquinius Priscus (616–578 BC), traditionally the fifth king of Rome. His history is vague. Of Etruscan origin, he is thought to have established the Etruscan culture in Rome. He is attributed with building the Capitoline Triad temple and draining the marshes for the Forum. He is thought to have been murdered as part of an attempt to return the crown to a solely religious function. *See also* Etruscans.

Tarquinius Superbus (Lat. "Tarquin the Proud") (*r.*534–510 BC), traditionally the last king of Rome, of Etruscan birth. Largely a legendary figure, he is said to have captured several Latin towns. He was expelled by the senate (509) and the efforts of Lars Porsena and of his own sons to restore him to the throne failed. He fled through Italy, dying at Cumae.

Tarragon, perennial plant with 2in (5cm), licorice-flavored leaves used fresh or dried in salads, pickles, etc. Family Compositae; species *Artemisia dracunculus.*

Tarragona, city in Spain, 54mi (87km) SW of Barcelona near the estuary of Francoli River; capital of Tarragona prov. Captured 218 BC from Iberians by Rome's Publius Scipio, it fell to Visigoths AD 469; held by Muslims 714–1085; suffered attacks by French 1640–1811. It is the site of 12th–13th-century cathedral, Roman remains, archeological museum. Exports: wine, olives, almonds. Industries: food processing, distilling, tobacco products. Area: (prov.) 2,426sq mi (6,283sq km). Pop. (city) 78,238; (prov.) 431,961.

Tarsier, nocturnal tree-dwelling primate of Indonesia resembling a squat, big-eyed rat with long tail and monkeylike hands and feet. Tarsiers have silky grayish-brown coat and can turn their heads 180 degrees. Feeding chiefly on insects, tarsiers represent a stage of evolution intermediate between lemurs and monkeys. Genus *Tarsier. See also* Primates.

Tarsus, city in S Turkey, 23mi (37km) W of Adana on Tarsus River near the Mediterranean Sea. Conquered by Romans 67 BC, it became a leading industrial and cultural center; it was destroyed by Arabs AD 660 and rebuilt by them 780; Ottoman Turks took it in 1515; birthplace of St Paul; agricultural trading center for citrus fruit and cotton grown in area. Copper, chromium, zinc, and coal are mined nearby. Settled by Hittites 14th century BC. Pop. 74,510.

Tartars. *See* Tatars.

Tartrates, salt or ester of tartaric acid. Tartrates, such as potassium bitartrate (cream of tartar) and sodium bitartrate, are used in baking powder in the food industry, as a sequestrant, and in tanning. Antimony potassium tartrate (tartar emetic) is used as an emetic and a mordant.

Tasaday, small group of isolated aboriginal people of the rain forests of S Mindanao in the Philippines, first discovered in 1971. They are food-gathering cave dwellers with a Stone-Age culture, although since their discovery they have adopted hunting and trapping techniques.

Tashkent (Ta'škent), capital city of the Uzbek SSR, USSR; also capital of Tashkent oblast, in the Tashkent oasis, watered by the Chirchik River, 1,800mi (2,898km) SE of Moscow. It was founded *c.* 7th century; ruled by Arabs until the 11th century; came under Timurid Empire in the 13th century; came under Mongol rule 1361; captured by Russians 1865 and a new city was built around the old one; site of 1966 India-Pakistan conference on Kashmir dispute; severely damaged by 1966 earthquake; site of Central Asian state university and industrial college, medical, agricultural, law, and teachers' colleges, textile and railroad trade schools, Uzbek Academy of Sciences, state library, historical museum, Uzbek academic theater. Industries: cotton, textiles, flour, wine, canned goods, meat, tobacco, radios, porcelain, abrasives, paper, furniture, pottery, chemicals. Pop. 1,733,000.

Tasmania, formerly Van Diemen's Land; island state 150mi (242km) off SE coast of Australia, separated from the mainland by the Bass Strait. Industries: electrochemicals, metal processing, paper, textiles. Discovered by Abel Tasman, Dutch navigator, in 1642; settled 1803 as a penal colony; became an Australian state 1901. Area: 26,383sq mi (68,332sq km). Pop. 410,222.

Tasman Sea, section of the Pacific Ocean between Australia and New Zealand; named for the Dutch explorer Abel Tasman. Sydney, Australia, is the largest port on the sea. Width: approx. 1,200mi (1,932km).

Tasso, Torquato (1544–95), Italian late-Renaissance poet, Bernardo Tasso's son. He had an unhappy childhood, but after writing the epic *Rinaldo* (1562) he joined the Este court at Ferrara. His most famous works are the drama *Aminta* (1573) and the epic *Gerusalemme liberata* (1575). After 1577 he became psychologically disturbed and was confined intermittently in a hospital (1579–86), where he continued writing.

Taste, or gustation, a chemical sense, in which the stimulus is a chemical molecule dissolved in saliva in the mouth; the receptors are specialized cells located in the raised taste buds of the tongue. Taste often represents an interaction between gustation and the sense of smell; for example, food does not taste as palatable when one has a head cold.

TAT. *See* Thematic Apperception Test.

Tatars, or **Tartars,** Turkic-speaking people spread across central Asia. The name "Tatar" has been used loosely for many central Asian nomads, beginning with those of Kipchak in the 1st century AD. By the 15th century the Tatars were generally Muslims, a farming and herding people skilled in leather work, cloth, and ceramic and metal crafts. Their leaders intermarried with Russian aristocracy after 1600. In the 18th century they flourished as middlemen between Russians and central Asian tribesmen. Their feudal social system lasted until the Russian Revolution (1917). The modern Tatar republic is well forested and rich in oil and natural gas in the Soviet Union. The capital, Kazan, is a center of trade and industry, particularly petroleum refining.

Tattooing, coloring or marking the skin for cosmetic or religious purposes. Pigment is inserted under the skin's surface with needles, or scars are made. An ancient and widespread practice, it was most widely cultivated in Polynesia, especially among the Maori.

Tatum, Edward Lawrie (1909–75), US geneticist and biochemist b. Boulder, Colo. He shared the 1958 Nobel Prize in physiology or medicine with George W. Beadle and Joshua Lederberg for his part in the "discovery that genes act by regulating specific chemical processes," a basic principle explaining how genes determine the characteristics of an organism.

Tau Ceti, main-sequence yellow star situated not far from the Sun and located in the constellation Cetus. Characteristics: apparent mag. +3.5; absolute mag. +5.7; spectral type G8; distance 11.9 light-years.

Taupo Lake, largest lake in New Zealand, in mountainous central North Island; drained by Waikato River. Area: 234sq mi (606sq km). Depth: 552ft (168m).

Taurus, or the Bull, northern constellation situated on the ecliptic between Aries and Gemini, and lying northwest of Orion; the second sign of the zodiac. It contains the Pleiades and Hyades and the Crab Nebula. Brightest star: Alpha Tauri (Aldebaran). The astrological sign for the period Apr. 20-May 20.

Taurus Mountains (Toros Dağlaı), chain of mountains in S central Turkey, extends 350mi (564km) roughly parallel to Mediterranean coast of S Asia Minor; its NE extension is called Anti-Taurus. Mountains have important deposits of chromium. Highest peak is Ala Dağ, 12,251ft (3,737m).

Taxation, method by which central governments and their subdivisions collect revenue in order to defray the cost of providing services to the population. The different forms of taxation include income taxes, sales taxes, tariffs, property taxes, excise taxes, value-added taxes, and payroll taxes. Most US states have sales taxes, income taxes, and property taxes. Federal government revenues come primarily from individual and corporate income taxes.

Taxco de Alarcén, city in S Mexico; major stopping place between Mexico City and Acapulco during Spanish colonial trade with Philippines; mining center during 18th century; site of colonial church (1717), cobbled streets, fine Spanish architecture. Industries: tourism, gold, silver, silverware. Pop. 64,368.

Taxonomy, biological classification of plants and animals into groups that reflect natural relationships. Carolus Linnaeus, Swedish botanist, developed the system during the 1750s.

Taylor, Edward (1642?–1729), colonial American poet, b. England. Considered the finest 17th-century colonial poet, in the tradition of the English metaphysical poets, he came to Boston in 1668. Because he requested that none of his works be published, they did not appear until 1939 (*Poetical Works,* Thomas H. Johnson, ed.) after being discovered in the Yale University library, where they had been placed by his grandson.

Taylor, Zachary (1784–1850), 12th president of the United States (1849–50), b. Orange co, Va., raised in Kentucky. In 1810 he married Margaret Smith; they had six children. Although his father was a wealthy planter, Zachary Taylor had little formal education. He received a military commission in 1808 and became a career army officer. He fought in the War of 1812, the Black Hawk War, and in the Seminole wars in Florida. In the last, he acquired the nickname "Old Rough and Ready."

In 1845 he was sent to the Texas border to command US troops there. He made a foray into territory in dispute with Mexico, thereby setting off the Mexican War. He took Matamoros, occupied Monterrey, and won the crucial battle of Buena Vista. The end of the war found Taylor a popular hero, and he was nominated for the presidency by the Whigs. He was elected but without a majority of popular votes. As president he advocated the quick admission of California and New Mexico as states and was a moderate on the extension of slavery issue. On July 9, 1850, he died of cholera morbus (acute indigestion) and was succeeded by Vice President Millard Fillmore.

Career: US Army, 1808–49; president, 1849–50. *See also* Mexican War.

Taylor, city in SE Michigan, 20mi (32km) SW of Detroit; named for President Zachary Taylor. Industries: machinery, wood products, sand, gravel, concrete, pipe, glass. Founded as town 1847; inc. as city 1968. Pop. (1980) 77,568.

Tay-Sachs Disease, a rare hereditary disorder (found chiefly in Jewish children) of fat metabolism. It is characterized by an accumulation of gangliosides in the central nervous system, resulting in severe mental deficiency, blindness, and death at about three years of age.

Tbilisi (Tiflis), capital of Georgian SSR, USSR, on the upper Kura River. It was founded *c.* 455 as the capital of the ancient Georgian kingdom; long an important trade center, it was ruled at different times by Persians, Byzantines, Arabs, Mongols, Tatars, and Turks; came under Russian rule 1801; center of 1905 rebellion against Russian government; seat of new administration 1917; made capital of the Transcaucasian Federation 1921; made capital of Georgian SSR 1936; site of Georgian Academy of Sciences (1941), state university (1918), polytechnic, teaching, medical, and art schools, opera, Rustaveli Theater, and botanic gardens. Industries: railroad shops, lathes, oil drills, machinery, electrical goods, ceramics, footwear, clothing, silk and woolen goods, furniture, musical instruments, tobacco, food and wine processing, plastics, chocolate, hydroelectricity. Pop. 1,030,000.

Tchaikovsky, Pëtr Ilyich (1840–93), Russian Romantic composer whose melodic, emotional works are very popular. His best known works are the three ballets *Swan Lake* (1876), *The Sleeping Beauty* (1890), and *The Nutcracker* (1892); the *Piano Concerto No. 1* (1875); a *Violin Concerto* (1878); the *1812 Overture* (1882); and the orchestral pieces *Romeo and Juliet* (1870) and *Marche Slav* (1876). He wrote six symphonies, of which the Sixth or *Pathétique* (1893) is very popular. His works also included chamber music, songs, and operas.

Tea, family of trees and shrubs with leathery undivided leaves and five-petalled blossoms. Among 500 species is *Camellia thea (Thea sinensis),* the commercial source of tea. Cultivated in moist tropical regions, tea plants, which can reach 30ft (9.1m) height, are kept low by frequent picking of the young shoots for tea leaves; flowers are white. The leaves are dried immediately to produce green tea and are fermented before drying for black tea. Family Theaceae.

Tea Act (1773), legislation by the British Parliament removing export duties on tea. To give relief to financially failing East India Co., the act withdrew duty on tea exported to the colonies and enabled the East India Co. to sell tea directly to the colonies without first going to Britain. Colonial merchants were undersold, and the act led directly to the Boston Tea Party. *See also* Boston Tea Party.

Teaching Machine, device that presents a planned, step-by-step program of instruction. For example, one such machine displays information or a question on a screen. The learner responds by punching a key on a keyboard. The machine at once shows if the response is correct. If the response is right, the student moves on to the next step; if it is wrong, he or she corrects the mistake and then moves ahead. The learner is continu-

Torquato Tasso

Zachary Taylor

Pëtr Tchaikovsky

ally told whether he or she is on the right track. The machine may be simple, displaying a printed program through an opening in a box, or it may use a computer to present material and evaluate answers.

Teak, hardwood tree, native to India, Burma, and the East Indies, valued for its yellowish-brown wood used in furniture and shipbuilding. Height: to 150ft (45.7m). Family Verbenacea; species *Tectona grandis.*

Teal, small, widely distributed river duck that often has bright plumage. The blue-winged teal *(Anas discors)* of North America is a fast, strong flier. They dabble, or feed from the water surface. *See also* Duck.

Teapot Dome Scandal (1921–24), one of the Harding administration disgraces, it involved fraudulent leases of the naval oil reserves at Teapot Dome and Elk Hills in South Dakota by Secretary of the Interior Albert B. Fall to oilmen Harry Sinclair and Edward Doheny. Fall collected some $409,000 from the two leases. Investigations and litigation, continuing through the decade, ended with Fall's being found guilty of accepting a bribe from Doheny and Doheny and Sinclair's acquittal.

Tears, fluid that moistens the surface of the cornea of the eye, secreted by the lacrimal glands. It is antibacterial in nature, and also improves the optical properties of the eye by forming a thin, smooth film on the cornea and compensating for slight surface imperfections.

Technetium, radioactive metallic element (symbol Tc) of the second transition series, made in 1937 by C. Perrier and E. G. Segrè by bombarding molybdenum with deuterons. It was the first element to be synthesized. No technetium has been found in the Earth's crust, although it is present in some stars. Properties: at. no. 43; at. wt. 98.9062 sp gr 11.5; melt. pt. 3,992°F (2,200°C); most stable isotope Tc^{97} (half-life 2.6 × 10^{6}yrs). *See also* Transition Elements.

Tectonics, study of the Earth's crustal arrangement on large, stable plates that move and the effect of this movement on the rim of continents, ocean basins, and the mountain regions that result from crustal movement compression. Any crustal movement and the results of it are considered within the area of tectonics. *See also* Continental Drift; Deformation; Orogeny.

Tecumseh (?1768–1813), Shawnee Indian chief, b. near Springfield, Ohio. With his brother, The Prophet, Tecumseh worked to unite the Western Indians against white expansion. After his brother's defeat and death at Tippecanoe in 1811, Tecumseh joined the British in the War of 1812. He was killed in action in 1813.

Teething, the growing in place of milk teeth and the replacement of the first dentition by the second in children and young adults. Twenty deciduous teeth usually appear by the first to second year. Between the ages of 5 and 12 these teeth then drop out and are replaced by permanent teeth. In addition, 12 new molars (3 on each side of the upper and lower jaw) grow in place to yield a complement of 32 adult teeth. *See also* Tooth.

Teflon, a trademarked name for polytetrafluoroethylene, a strong, waxy nonflammable resin. It is a polymer composed of large molecules formed by chemical combinations of small ones into chains. Characterized by a slippery surface and resistance to chemicals, it is used in gaskets, bearings, pipe linings, and as a protective coating on cooking utensils and other articles. *See also* Fluorocarbon Plastics.

Tefnut, in Egyptian mythology, a minor deity, who personifies the dew and rain. She was depicted as a woman with the head of a lioness.

Tegucigalpa, capital city of Honduras, located in the S central part of the country and composed of townships of Tegucigalpa and Comayagüela; site of university (1895), teacher training college (1956). Industries: sugar, textiles, cigarettes. Founded *c.* 1579 as silver mining center. Pop. 270,645.

Tehran, city in N Iran, 65mi (105km) S of Caspian Sea; capital of Iran and Tehran prov. City served as capital of Persia 1788; renovation and modernization of the city began in 1797 under Fath Ali Shah and continued through reign of Reza Shah Pahlevi (1941); scene of Tehran Conference (Nov. 26–Dec. 2, 1943) between President Franklin D. Roosevelt, Prime Minister Winston Churchill, and Premier Joseph Stalin. City contains University of Tehran (1934); National University (1960); the Gulistan (Rose Garden) Palace (1786) with its marble throne and jeweled peacock throne; the Shah Mosque, a revolutionary center prior to est. of constitutional government in 1906; Museum of Iranian Ethnology and Museum of Iranian Art, both housing outstanding collections of cultural artifacts; and Masjid Sipah-Silar Mosque with its theological college; industrial, commercial, and administrative center. Industries: automobiles, cement, sugar, textiles, firearms. Pop. 3,150,000.

Tehran Conference (1943), meeting of Allied leaders Winston Churchill, Joseph Stalin, and Franklin D. Roosevelt in Tehran, Iran, to discuss military and political policies in World War II. The leaders agreed to open a western front in occupied France. The USSR was assured control of eastern Poland, while agreeing to enter the war against Japan. Discussions were held on the future of Finland and Manchuria, and the postwar independence of Iran was guaranteed.

Teilhard de Chardin, Pierre (1881–1955), French Roman Catholic priest and scientist. He joined the Society of Jesus (Jesuits) in 1899, was ordained a priest in 1911, and then began studying paleontology. He worked in China at various times from 1923 to 1946 and shared in the discovery of Peking Man. Teilhard is best known for his efforts to produce a synthesis of scientific views of evolution and Christian faith. His book *The Phenomenon of Man* (finished in 1947 but published after his death), drew world-wide attention from Christians and non-Christians.

Tektite, generally dark, glassy objects, ranging in diameter from 20 microns to 2mm (microtektites) and larger (to 10cm) believed to be of either lunar origin or formed from splashes of liquefied rock during meteorite impact on Earth. They occur in limited areas, called strewn-fields, on continents and ocean floors. Specimens from Czechoslovakia are called moldavites.

Tel Aviv-Jaffa (Tel Aviv-Yafo), largest city and commercial center in Israel, 34mi (55km) NW of Jerusalem on the Mediterranean Sea. Founded 1909 as a Jewish suburb by the Jewish population of Arab Jaffa, by 1921, Britain had established it as a separate all-Jewish community. During the period of Britain's Palestine mandate (1923–48) and Adolf Hitler's regime in Germany (1933–45), Tel Aviv's immigrant Jewish population grew rapidly, and it became the cultural, administrative, and commercial center of the Jews in Palestine. Not until the close of the 1948–49 Arab-Israeli War was Tel Aviv able to expand physically inland. It served as the seat of the transitional government and legislature (1948–49), when Israel's capital was moved to Jerusalem; incorporated with Jaffa (1950); site of Tel Aviv University (1953), Afro-Asian Institute for Labor Studies and Cooperation, the quadrennial Maccabiah Athletic Games, Temple of Culture (1957), Haaretz Museum, Tel Aviv Museum, Israel Philharmonic Orchestra, Habima Theater (1945), the national theater of Israel; the ministry of defense, headquarters for labor federation, botanical and zoological gardens, and the memorial and library preserved in the home of H.N. Bialik, the national poet. On N end are Tel Quasile excavations, where ruins of Philistine, Hebrew, Persian, Greek, and Roman civilizations have been found. Industries: construction, pharmaceuticals, electrical appliances, publishing, banking, insurance, tourism, textiles, clothing, food processing, chemicals, furniture, soap, cement, paper, plastics, leather, glass, precision instruments. Pop. 353,800.

Telecommunication(s), the science and technology of communicating signals, images, sounds, or writing by wire, cable, radio, or other electromagnetic equipment. Transmission may be digital, in which case the signals are transformed in a coder before being sent, or analogue, in which case the message is sent directly.

Telegraph, any communications system that transmits and receives visible or audible signals over a distance. Although most devices are electrically operated and connected by wires or cables, telegraph messages can be sent by radio waves, microwaves, and communication satellites. Pioneering work was performed by many, but credit for the device and code is generally given to Samuel F. B. Morse, who, in 1844, during a demonstration to Congress transmitted the message, "What hath God wrought!" In 1866 the first permanently successful telegraphic cable was laid across the Atlantic Ocean, and in 1874 Thomas A. Edison invented the method to transmit several messages simultaneously over the same wire.

Teleki, Count Pál (1879–1941), Hungarian statesman and geographer, a member of the counterrevolutionary government that ruled after Béla Kun was deposed in 1920. Count Teleki served as premier 1920, 1926, and 1939–40. When Germany attacked Poland, Hungary refused to allow German troops to cross its territory. When the German-infiltrated army command made a deal to permit German troops to cross Hungary to attack Yugoslavia, Teleki committed suicide as an act of protest.

Telemann, Georg Philipp (1681–1767), German composer of numerous Baroque concertos, suites, and sonatas, as well as religious music.

Telemetry, Spacecraft, system of transmitting data to the ground via electromagnetic waves, normally in digital (on-off) form. Solar cells or chemical batteries provide power for operating high-gain directional antennae on the spacecraft. These beam high-frequency (but low-power) radio waves to large receiving stations on the ground. Data may be transmitted at rates up to 100,000 bits/sec, or stored on tape for later transmission. Voice telemetry was utilized by the Gemini and Apollo astronauts.

Teleostei, superorder of fish, most progressive of bony fish in class Osteichthyes, which contains 30 orders and 20,000 species—the majority of existing fish. Modern teleost families were established during the late Cretaceous Period (65,000,000 years ago). *See also* Osteichthyes.

Telephone, an instrument that communicates speech sounds via wires in an electrical circuit. In 1876 Alexander Graham Bell invented the prototype, which employed a diaphragm of soft iron that vibrated to sound waves. These vibrations caused disturbances in the magnetic field of a nearby bar magnet, causing an electric current of fluctuating intensity in the thin copper wire wrapped around the magnet. This current could be transmitted along wires to a distant identical device which repeated the process in reverse, finally reproducing the audible sound. Later improvements separated the transmitter from the receiver, and replaced the bar magnet with batteries.

Telescope, Optical, instrument used for producing a magnified image of a distant object, first used in astronomy by Galileo (1609). Two types are employed: the refractor, in which the image is produced by two or more lens systems, and the reflector, in which light is gathered and focused by a concave, usually parabolic, mirror. The image can be recorded photographically or analyzed for its spectrum, etc. Large lenses are difficult to grind accurately and mount and are subject to aberration. These problems are much less severe for mirrors so that large-aperture reflectors are used in many astronomical observatories. *See also* Aberration.

Telescope, Radio, complex electronic system for detecting, amplifying, and analyzing radio waves from space. One basic design is the large steerable wire-mesh dish, parabolic in shape and based on the precision wartime radar dishes, that reflects radio waves from a small area of the sky onto an antenna. The resulting electrical signal is greatly amplified before analysis. A more sensitive design is the radio interferometer employing arrays of antennas, such as the Y-shaped arrangement of 27 antennas in the Very Large Array in New Mexico. VLAs can map large radio structures such as the radio galaxies, which may be 100,000 light years across. *See also* Astronomy; Radio; Interferometer.

Telescope, X-Ray, specially designed telescope in which radiation from an astronomical X-ray source can be focused from a double reflecting mirror system, consisting of a paraboloid and a hyperboloid surface, the reflections (specular) occurring at near grazing incidence.

Teletype, the transmission and reception of messages via an electromechanical typewriter and telegraph or telephone wires. In effect, the system employs a receiving typewriter whose keys are operated from the transmitting station. In the United States both simplex and multiplex systems use the Baudot code, which uses various combinations of five equal length pulses to indicate numerals, letters, and punctuation.

Television, the transmission of scenes, moving or stationary, commonly with accompanying sound, via electromagnetic waves, and the reconversion of those waves into the original scene. Five components are fundamental to television systems: a camera device to record the scene; a transducer to change the light impulses of the scene into corresponding electrical signals; a transmitter; a receiver; and a second transducer to convert the electrical signals back into light impulses, thus reproducing the original scene. An early prototype was patented by Paul Nipkow in Germany in 1884. The development of the electron tube and electronic scanning methods made the marketing of television systems practical in 1945.

Tell el-Amarna, area of ruins and rock tombs on E bank of Nile River, Egypt, 8mi (13km) SE of Mallawi. In 1887, about 400 tablets inscribed in Akkadian cuneiform were found here; they have given much information on ancient Egypt and Middle East. Written by Amenhotep III and Ikhnaton 1411–1354 BC, they are now in British, Berlin, and Cairo museums.

Teller, Edward (1908–), US physicist, b. Hungary. He left Europe because of the Nazis, finally settling in the United States in 1935. He worked on the atom bomb at Los Alamos during World War II. After the war he pioneered the development of the hydrogen bomb and taught at numerous universities. In the late 1970s, he advocated the development of nuclear energy and the release of satellite photos to the world.

Tellurium, metalloid element (symbol Te) of group VIA of the periodic table, discovered 1782. It is found native and in calaverite (AuTe); chief source is as a by-product of the electrolytic refining of copper. It is used in some alloys and semiconductor devices. Properties: at. no. 52; at. wt. 127.60; sp. gr. 6.24; melt. pt. 841°F (449.5°C); boil. pt. 1814°F (989.8°C); most common isotope Te^{130} (34.48%).

Temin, Howard M(artin) (1934–), US oncologist, b. Philadelphia. He was awarded part of the 1975 Nobel Prize in physiology or medicine for his studies of the "interaction between tumor viruses and the genetic material of the cell." Temin (independently of colaureate David Baltimore) discovered reverse transcriptase, the enzyme necessary for viral genetic information to be incorporated into an animal cell.

Tempe, city in SW central Arizona, on Salt River, 9mi (14km) E of Phoenix; site of Arizona State University. Industries: electronic equipment, steel, clothing, agriculture. Founded 1872; inc. 1894. Pop. (1980) 106,743.

Temperament, emotional reactions including characteristic energy level, intensity of reaction moods, mood changes, and threshold of responsiveness. It is presumed that temperament is constitutionally determined, but it is also deeply influenced by life experience. *See also* Personality.

Temperance Movement, campaign in the United States to wipe out the consumption of alcoholic beverages. Beginning in the late 18th century, the temperance crusade reached its peak with the ratification of the 18th Amendment (1919), which brought in the Prohibition Era. The amendment was later repealed (1933) after enforcement proved impossible. Prominent in the movement were Benjamin Rush, Lyman Beecher, Carry Nation, and Frances Willard.

Tempera Painting, artistic medium. It takes its name from the practice of "tempering" powdered pigments with egg yolk diluted in water. Until the late 15th century when it was largely replaced by oil painting, tempera, applied to wooden panels, was the commonest technique used in Western art. Its chief disadvantage is that it turns several shades lighter as it dries, but, unlike oil, it dries at once.

Temperature, a parameter describing the number of energy states available to a substance or system. Observations indicate that two bodies placed in thermal contact exchange heat energy initially but eventually arrive at thermal equilibrium; neither body gains or loses heat. At this point, both bodies are said to have the same temperature; that is, the most probable distribution of energy states of the atoms and molecules composing the bodies has been attained. At high temperatures, the number of energy states available to the atoms and molecules of a system is very large; at lower temperatures, fewer states are available (molecules become locked into position and liquids change to solids). At a sufficiently low temperature, all parts of the system are at their lowest energy levels; this temperature is described as absolute zero. *See also* Absolute Zero.

Temperature, Body, in homeothermic animals such as birds and mammals, the body temperature is maintained within narrow limits regardless of the ambient temperature. This is accomplished by muscular activity and normal basal metabolism. In man, the traditional normal temperature is 37°C (98.6°F), which will vary with degree of activity, reaching 40°C (104°F) during exercise, and lower than 37°C during sleep.

Temperature Scales, scales for measuring temperature. The Fahrenheit scale was devised by the German physicist Gabriel Fahrenheit (1686–1736) using two reference points: the freezing point of water (taken to be 32 degrees) and the temperature of the human body (taken to be 96 degrees, although later found to be 98.6 degrees). The Celsius (formerly Centigrade) scale was introduced by A. Celsius, an 18th-century Swedish astronomer. On this scale water freezes at 0 °C and boils at 100°C. With the development of thermodynamics by Lord Kelvin and the later discovery that temperature has a lower bound of −273°C (−459°F), the Absolute (or Kelvin) scale was introduced, having a zero point coincident with absolute zero. The degree Kelvin (or kelvin) represents the same temperature difference as the degree Celsius; but both are 1.8 times as large as the degree Fahrenheit. To transform from Fahrenheit (F) to Celsius (C), use the formula $C = 5/9\ (F - 32)$.

Temperature Sense, one of the skin senses, which may or may not be distinct from the sense of touch. Although specialized thermoreceptors have been predicted by various theorists, none has yet been found. Temperature detection seems to be related to other more subtle sensory impressions, such as the feeling of wetness.

Tempering. *See* Heat Treatment.

Tempest, The (1611), comedy by William Shakespeare. The play recounts how Prospero, the unseated duke of Milan, regains his throne after a tempest shipwrecks his usurpers on the enchanted isle where he lives with his daughter Miranda, the slave Caliban, and the spirit Ariel. Everyone then returns to Naples for the wedding of Miranda to Ferdinand, the king's son. Shakespeare's last complete work, this romance was revived in New York City in 1916 and 1945.

Temple, city in central Texas, 35mi (56km) S of Waco; site of Texas Soil Conservation Service, Blackland Experiment Station, and Texas branch of Farmers Home Administration; hospital center. Industries: furniture, plastics, footwear, railroad shops, cotton, grain, clothing, cottonseed products. Founded 1881; inc. 1882. Pop. (1980) 42,483.

Temporal Lobes, prominent lobes of the cerebral cortex that, in humans, lie directly below the temples. The temporal lobes are directly involved in the interpretation and generation of language, and injury to them sometimes produces speech disorders. *See also* Brain.

Tenant Farming, system of farming in which a renter works the land and pays the land owner rent in cash or a share of the crop.

Ten Commandments, or **Decalogue,** the code of ethical conduct held in Judeo-Christian tradition to have been revealed by God to Moses. Representing the moral basis of God's Covenant with Israel, they appear in both Exodus 20 and Deuteronomy 5, but with different phrasing. The first "tablet" (commandments 1–4) exhorts obligation and service to the one God. The second "tablet" (5–10) requires respect for basic human rights and individual social responsibility. Protestant, Catholic, and Jewish traditions each have slightly different versions of the laws.

Tendon, strong, elastic band of connective tissue that connects muscle to bone.

Tendonitis, inflammatory condition of any of the white bands of dense connective tissue that unite muscles with other parts of the body and chiefly transmit muscle force to bones and joints. Physical trauma and hereditary and acquired connective tissue diseases, especially rheumatoid arthritis, can be causes.

Tenerife Island, island of Spain, in Atlantic Ocean 40mi (64km) WNW of Grand Canary Island; largest of the Canary Islands. Originally inhabited by Guanches, it was conquered 15th century by Spain. The island is mountainous and covered with lava layers; site of Pico de Teide, highest peak on the island, approx. 12,200ft (3,721m). Industries: tourism, goats, sheep, food processing, linen. Crops: bananas, sugar cane, almonds, tobacco, cereals. Pop. 500, 381.

Teng Hsiao-p'ing (Deng Xiaoping) (1904–), Chinese Communist political leader. He rose in the early 1960s to be secretary general of the Chinese Communist party but was purged during the late 1960s Cultural Revolution. He reappeared on the Chinese political scene from 1973 to 1976 but was purged again following the death of his supporter, Chou En-lai, in early 1976. After Mao Tse-tung's death later in 1976, Teng emerged again as a principal leader and was reinstalled as a deputy premier to lead the Chinese Communist Party. He became chairman of the Central Military Commission in 1981.

Tenia, or **Taenia,** genus of tapeworms including the common beef *(T. saginata)* and pork *(T. solium)* tapeworm that can infest the human intestine as adults. Such an infestation is very debilitating and comes as a result of eating raw or rare beef or pork containing tapeworm larvae. *See also* Tapeworm.

Ten Lost Tribes, the ten tribes composed of descendants from Jacob's sons. Two other tribes formed the southern kingdom of Judah, while the ten tribes formed the northern kingdom, known as Israel. In 722 BC, the Assyrians overcame Israel and the ten tribes wandered into different lands and disappeared. From the Middle Ages onward various explanations developed. Some see them as the Anglo-Saxons, the early Irish settlers, or the American Indians, but they were more likely assimilated into other peoples.

Tennent, Gilbert (1703–64), American religious leader, b. Ireland. A Presbyterian minister and evangelist, he toured the colonies with English revivalist George Whitefield (1739–40) and became prominent in the Great Awakening. When the Presbyterian Church split (1741), he became a leader of the evangelistic New Side. In 1758, he helped reunite the New and Old sides.

Tennessee, state in the SE central United States, between the Appalachian Mts and the Mississippi River.

Land and economy. The Great Smoky Mts of the Appalachian chain, with elevations of more than 6,000ft (1,830m) rise along the E boundary. W of them is the Great Valley of E Tennessee and the Cumberland Plateau. Beyond, the land slopes to the Missis-

Teng Hsiao-p'ing

Tennessee Valley Authority: Hiwassee Dam

Tent caterpillar

sippi River on the W border. The principal river is the Tennessee, which rises in the E, flows S into Alabama, and turns N to flow across the W part of the state. Mountain valleys in the E and the lower lands in the center and W are agricultural regions. Plentiful electric power from the network of the Tennessee Valley Authority, an efficient transportation system, and the state's proximity to major markets have created a diversified manufacturing industry, centered in the E cities and towns, that is unmatched by any Southern state. Industrial research facilities, especially the federal government's nuclear installations at Oak Ridge, which produced material for the first atom bomb and now carry on nuclear studies, are important to the economy.

People. The first settlers were pioneers who crossed the mountains from states on the Atlantic seaboard; their descendants form a major part of the population. Almost 60% live in urban areas.

Education. There are more than 60 institutions of higher education.

History. The region was visited by Spaniards in the 16th century and by English and French a century later. Some forts were built and abandoned; the first permanent settlement was made in the Watauga River Valley in the NE in 1769. Sparsely settled and far removed from theaters of action in the Revolution, the area was little affected by the war. Nashville was founded 1779. North Carolina relinquished its claim to the land in 1784, and dwellers in E Tennessee organized what they called the State of Franklin, which was never recognized by the United States. In 1790, Congress created the Southwest Territory, from which six years later the state of Tennessee was established. As the Civil War approached, Union sentiment was strong in Tennessee, but the state seceded in 1861. Tennesseans served on both sides. More than 400 engagements, including several major battles, were fought in the state. Industrial development began late in the 19th century and was greatly stimulated by WWII. In 1968 civil rights leader Dr. Martin Luther King was assassinated in Memphis.

PROFILE

Admitted to Union: June 1, 1796; rank, 16th
US Congressmen: Senate, 2; House of Representatives, 8
Population: 4,590,750 (1980); rank, 17th
Capital: Nashville, 455,651 (1980)
Chief cities: Memphis, 646,356; Nashville; Knoxville, 183,139; Chattanooga, 169,565
State Legislature: Senate, 33; House of Representatives, 99
Area: 42,244sq mi (109,412sq km); rank, 34th
Elevation: Highest, 6,643ft (2,026m), Clingman's Dome; lowest, 182ft (56m), Mississippi River
Industries: (major products) chemicals, textiles, apparel, electrical machinery, processed foods, forest products
Agriculture: (major products) cattle, dairy products, hogs, tobacco, cotton, soybeans, corn
Minerals: (major): zinc, limestone, marble, sandstone, bituminous coal
State nickname: Volunteer State
State motto: Agriculture and Commerce
State bird: mockingbird
State flower: iris
State tree: tulip poplar

Tennessee River, river in Tennessee, N Alabama, and W Kentucky; formed by confluence of Holston and French Broad rivers near Knoxville, Tenn.; flows SW into N Alabama, N across W Tennessee and W Kentucky into Ohio River at Paducah, Ky. Tennessee Valley Authority (1933) has developed the river's water power and transportation facilities along with flood control. Length: 652mi (1,050km). *See also* Tennessee Valley Authority.

Tennessee Valley Authority (TVA), New Deal agency established as part of a long-range regional planning project (1933). An independent public corporation, it was authorized to build dams and power plants to control the Tennessee River and improve the surrounding area. Sen. George Norris of Nebraska proposed the plan that the river be dammed to prevent flooding, produce electricity, and rebuild the eroded farmland. The success of TVA contributed greatly to the Tennessee River Valley's wealth.

Tennessee Walking, or **Plantation Walking, Horse,** light horse breed developed during the 19th century in Tennessee from several breeds for plantation owners to ride. A comfortable saddle horse with stamina, its three gaits are flat-foot walk, running walk, and canter. It has a plain head and massive body; colors include sorrel, chestnut, black, and golden with white marks on feet and legs. Height: 62in (157.5cm) at shoulder; weight: 1,000–1,200lb (450–540kg).

Tennis, game, played by two or four persons with rackets and a ball. It is played outdoors on a surface of grass, clay, or asphalt and indoors on wood, artificial grass, linoleum, tarmacadam, or carpeting. For singles, the court measures 78 feet by 27 feet (23.8 by 8.2m) and in doubles, 78 feet by 36 feet (11m). The court is divided by a net 3 feet high (.9m). Each half of the court is divided into a service court 21 × 13.5 feet (6.4 × 4.1m) and a backcourt 27 × 18 feet (5.5m). A 4.5 foot (1.4m) alley flanks either side of the court perpendicular to the net; it is used only in doubles play. The ball used is unstitched, felt-covered, inflated rubber about 2.5 inches (6.3cm) in diameter; the oval-headed rackets are usually 27 inches (69cm) long with a strung hitting surface of resilient fiber.

A player serves for an entire game, and is allowed two service tries every time the ball is put into play. The ball is diagonally served from behind the baseline and must bounce into the opposite serving court beyond the net. If the ball fails to enter the opponent's service court on two consecutive services (double fault), a point is awarded the non-server. Also, a foot fault (stepping on or over the baseline on the serve) results in a forfeiture of a point. The players change sides after the first game and then after every two games.

After the serve, the ball may be returned into any area of the opponent's court. Points, which may be won by either the server or the receiver, are scored in a 15, 30, 40, and game procession. In lieu of zero, the term "love" is used. If the game goes to 40–40 (deuce), the first player to win two consecutive points wins. Generally, a game is four points, providing that the margin of victory is at least two points, and every six-game victory constitutes a set. In championship play a match is won by taking two of three sets (women) or three of five sets (men). The game is officiated by an umpire, and sometimes a referee, foot-fault judges, and linesmen.

History. Tennis was invented in Wales in 1873 by Walter C. Wingfield, and has steadily risen to become one of the most popular of international sporting events. The most prestigious tournaments include Wimbledon (Great Britain), Forest Hills (United States), and the singles championships of France and Australia. These four tournaments, for men and women, are now open to professionals and amateurs; if a player captures all four titles in one year, he has won the grand slam. For nations, the most coveted prize is the Davis Cup, originated in 1900.

Tennyson, Alfred, 1st Baron (1809–1892), English poet, poet laureate (1850–1892). His poetry covers the spectrum of lyric, elegiac, dramatic, and epic, taking subject matter from Arthurian legends, classic mythology, and the contemporary crisis in belief. Among his most famous poems are "The Lady of Shalott" (1832), "The Lotus Eaters" (1832), "Locksley Hall" (1842), "Tears, Idle Tears" (1847), "In Memoriam" (1850), "Maud" (1855), and "Crossing the Bar" (1889). Other works include the cycle *Idylls of the King* (1859–85) and the verse drama *Becket* (1884).

Tenochtitlán, Aztec capital, founded *c.*1325 on islands in the midst of Lake Texcoco. The initial Aztec settlement grew into a big population and ceremonial center. Gardens within the lake provided produce; aqueducts brought fresh water from Chapultepec. The city was besieged by Cortés in 1521; Mexico City was erected on its ruins.

Tenrec, burrowing, insect-eating mammal of Madagascar and the Comoro Islands. The common *Tenrec ecaudatus* is a nocturnal, highly prolific animal with a spiny coat like a hedgehog. It is about the size of a cat. Family Tenrecidae. *See also* Insectivore.

Tent Caterpillar, medium-sized, hairy, dark-brown moth caterpillar that, in early spring, spins a large communal nest of silk, usually in a tree crotch. Tent caterpillars defoliate many shrubs and trees and are serious pests in North America and Eurasia. The eastern *Malacosoma americanum* of North America has a white stripe down its back with blue and white spots on its sides.

Tenure, in feudalism, a piece of land, part of a greater estate, granted for a prolonged period by one person to another (the tenant), in exchange for rent, labor, or both. The practice was common in the Frankish empire in France in about the 8th century and was a precursor to the elaborate ownership and land-use systems of feudalism. Unlike some feudal fiefs, the tenure was more directly under the control of the tenant, and was almost always held for life and was hereditary. *See also* Feudalism.

Tenure of Office Act (1867), US law, passed over the veto of Pres. Andrew Johnson, which prohibited the president from removing any federal officeholder approved by the Senate without the Senate's consent to the removal. Impeachment proceedings were initiated against Johnson (1868) for dismissing Secretary of War Edwin Stanton.

Teosinte, cornlike annual grass native to Mexico and Central America and cultivated in SW United States. It grows in large clumps, branching at the base. Like corn, it has tassels but small ears. Family Gramineae; species *Euchlaena mexicana* or *Zea mexicana*. *See also* Corn.

Teotihuacán, ancient city located NW of Mexico City, arose *c.*100 BC and flourished until 900 AD. Built by an Olmec-based culture, the city, at its peak, covered 8sq mi (21sq km) and supported a population of 50,000. The city was laid out in a grid pattern centered on a thoroughfare named the Street of the Dead—the Pyramid of the Sun and Temple of Quetzalcoatl dominated the E limit; the Pyramid of the Moon the N quadrant.

Tepe Gawra, one of the most important archeological sites in northern Iraq. Excavations have uncovered 26 levels of ancient cities, dating from the 5th to the 2nd millennium BC, and including the civilizations of the Tell Halaf (*c.*5000 BC), Al' Ubaid (*c.*4100–3500 BC), and Jemdet Nasr (3500–3000 BC).

Terbium, metallic element (symbol Tb) of the lanthanide group, first isolated in 1843 by C. G. Mosander. Chief ore is monazite (phosphate). The element is used in semiconductors. Properties: at. no 65; at. wt. 158.9254; sp gr 8.234; melt. pt. 2,480°F (1,360°C); boil. pt. 5,474°F (3,041°C); most common isotope Tb^{159} (100%). *See also* Lanthanide Elements.

Terence, or **Publius Terentius Afer** (*c.* 185–159 BC), after Plautus, the greatest Roman author of comedy. Born in Carthage, he was a slave in Rome, educated and freed by his master, the senator Terentius Lucanus. Befriended by certain noble Romans, he produced 6 plays between 166 and 160 BC. His principal works include *Andria, Phormio,* and *Hecyra.* He was interested primarily in character, and his moralizing mood made him an influential force in the Middle Ages.

Teresa, Mother (1910–), Roman Catholic missionary, b. Agnes Gonxha Bojaxhiu, in Skopje, Yugoslavia. She began her missionary work as a teacher in Calcutta, India, with the Sisters of Loretto of Ireland. She took her first vows as a nun in 1928 and was granted permission by the Vatican to leave her convent in 1948 to tend the homeless, starving, and sick in Calcutta's slums. Her Order of the Missionaries of Charity was established in 1950 and in 1965 officially became a pontifical congregation. The order's work expanded to Australia, Britain, Sri Lanka, Jordan, Tanzania, Venezuela, and elsewhere. She won the first Pope John XXIII Peace Prize in 1971 and the Nobel Peace Prize in 1979. In 1980 she visited the United States and in 1982 she went to Lebanon to aid in the evacuation of handicapped children.

Terman, Lewis M(adison) (1877–1956), US psychologist, b. Johnson co, Ind. He devised the first widely used intelligence test in the United States (an adaptation of tests devised by Alfred Binet). He also performed classic studies of highly intelligent individuals that dispelled many misconceptions about the gifted, such as the notion that more intelligent people are not well adjusted. Major publications include *The Measurement of Intelligence* (1916); *Genetic Studies of Genius* (coauthor, 1925); and *The Gifted Child Grows Up* (coauthor, 1947).

Terminator, boundary between the sunlit and dark sides of a planet or satellite. In the case of a body lacking atmosphere, such as the Moon, the terminator is distinct, although often broken up because of reflections from craters or mountains. Bodies with atmospheres have less well defined terminators owing to the atmospheric scattering that causes twilight.

Termite, or white ant, social insect found worldwide in nests ranging from subterranean to aboveground towers. They have a caste system with a king and queen guarded and tended by soldiers, workers, and nymphs. Usually white and wingless, when the nest becomes crowded, they darken, develop wings, and swarm. They can be distinguished from ants by the lack of a narrow waist. Length: 0.08–0.9in (2–22.9mm); queens: to 4in (102mm).

Tern, or sea swallow, graceful seabird found over most waters of the world, diving for fish and crustaceans. They are white and gray with a blackish head, and have pointed bills, long pointed wings, forked tails, and webbed feet. After long migrations and courtship rituals, they lay eggs (2–3) in a scraped depression in sand. Length: 8–22in (20–56cm). Family Laridae.

Terni, city in central Italy, 49mi (79km) NE of Rome; capital of Terni prov.; nearby waterfalls (including Cascata delle Marmore) furnish hydroelectric power; Roman ruins are nearby; site of medieval churches. Industries: metallurgy, firearms, textiles. Pop. 114,534.

Terpander (7th century BC), Greek musician and poet, sometimes called the father of Greek classical music. He developed the *nomos,* a hymn to the gods set to flute and lyre music. He also established the first music school in Sparta and is said to have added 3 strings to the lyre. Little of his work remains.

Terpenes, group of unsaturated isomers having the formula $C_{10}H_{16}$. They occur in most essential oils and are colorless liquids. Pinere, the chief ingredient of turpentine, and limonene, found in the essential oils of citrus fruits, are examples.

Terracing, practice of building terraces into sloping land to prevent soil erosion. Crops are planted on the flat portion of each terrace. In countries where arable land is at a premium, such as Japan, Peru, and Ethiopia, terracing is extensively practiced. It is often avoided in other areas because it involves great labor.

Terra Cotta, fired clay, generally a form made from coarse, porous unglazed clay that assumes a reddish-brown color. Terra cotta figures 5,000 years old have been excavated in Greece.

Terrapin, any of various edible North American turtles of the family Emydidae living in fresh or brackish water. The term refers especially to the salt marsh diamondback terrapin *(Malaclemus terrapin)* of the US Atlantic coast.

Terrarium, container enclosing a garden of small plants; or, any small contained garden. Once established, a terrarium maintains itself for years, recycling moisture supplied by transpiration. A terrarium can be any clear glass or plastic container. The bottom is layered with drainage gravel, charcoal, and soil. Suitable woodland plants are mosses, rattlesnake plantain, conifer seedlings, and ferns. These should be dug in early autumn. House plants used should be small and tolerate humid conditions, such as begonias, small orchids, ferns, and inch plant.

Terre Haute, city in W Indiana, on Wabash River, 67mi (108km) WSW of Indianapolis; seat of Vigo co; site of Indiana State University (1865), Rose Polytechnic Institute, St Mary's-of-the-Woods College (1840); birthplace of Eugene Debs and Theodore Dreiser. Industries: food processing, phonograph records, aluminum and steel products. Founded 1811; inc. as town 1832, as city 1853. Pop. (1980) 61,125.

Terrier, dog breeds that dig the earth to rout game. Referred to as early as 1359 and as black and tan dog in the 1500s, they have been used to hunt badgers, foxes, weasels, and rats. On a hunt, they are carried along while hounds trail the quarry. When it is located, terriers are set down to dig it out of its burrow. The separate breeds emerged in 19th-century England. The 22 terriers recognized by the American Kennel Club include Sealyham, Australian, fox, Manchester, Scottish, and Bedlington. Larger types such as the Kerry blue, Airedale, and Irish are used as guard, police, and war dogs.

Terrigenous Deposits, one of the two main groups of marine deposits. They are found near shore and consist of material eroded from the land surface like sand, silt, mud, and intergrading types.

Territory, area for mating, nesting, roosting, or feeding, occupied by one or more organisms and defended against others of the same species. It is a spacing mechanism to prevent overcrowding and exhaustion of food supplies. Most vertebrates, some arthropods, such as dragonflies, and even some plants (those secreting repulsive chemicals) are territorial. Marking and defense of territory can involve song and other vocalizations, chemical scents, color displays, and physical aggression.

Terry, (Dame) Ellen Alicia (1848–1928), English actress. Her first stage appearance was at age nine in *A Winter's Tale.* She toured extensively with her sister Kate. In 1907 she toured the United States as a Shakespearean lecturer. In 1908 she published her autobiography and her correspondence with Bernard Shaw. She was made a dame of the British Empire in 1925.

Tertiary Period, the lower division of the Cenozoic Era, lasting from 65,000,000 to about 3,000,000 years ago. It is divided into four epochs, starting with the Eocene, the earliest part of which is sometimes called the Paleocene, followed by the Oligocene, Miocene, and Pliocene. Early Tertiary times were marked by great mountain-building activity (Rockies, Andes, Alps, and Himalayas) and continental relationships were beginning to resemble those of today. Both marsupial and placental mammals diversified greatly. Archaic forms of carnivores and plant-eaters flourished, along with primitive primates, bats, rodents, and early whales. Later there was a transition to the more modern kinds of mammals. There was also a gradual change from worldwide warm climates to today's climatic zoning. *See also* Cenozoic Era; Geologic Time.

Tertullian (Quintus Septimius Tertullianus) (*c.*160–*c.*230), one of the Latin Fathers of the Church, b. Carthage. The son of a Roman centurion, he was converted to Christianity *c.*195 and used his training in law and rhetoric to develop a systematic and practical approach to theology and Christian apologetics. His works include *Apologeticus, De Spectaculis,* and *De Anima.* Partly responsible for making Latin the official language of Christian theological writing, he is also remembered for enumerating the Seven Deadly Sins.

Terza Rima, in Italian poetry, a chain rhyme incorporating stanzas of three lines each (tercets). The second line of each tercet rhymes with the first and third lines of the next. The chain ends with either a couplet or an extra line added to the last tercet. This rhyme scheme first appeared in Dante's *Divine Comedy* (*c.* 1321) and was probably invented by him for that work. It later became popular with both Italian and English poets. *See also* Dante Alighieri; Divine Comedy.

Test Act (1673), English legislation intended to exclude Protestant dissenters and Roman Catholics from public offices. It required all candidates for such offices to profess the established religion of the Church of England. It was made less harsh by the Act of Toleration (1689).

Testis (pl. testes), the male sex gland, a pair located in a pouch, the scrotum, external to the body. The testes are made up of a series of seminiferous tubules in which male sex cells (sperm) are formed and mature, after which they drain into ducts, the epididymis, from which they will be discharged.

Testosterone, steroid hormone produced mainly by the mammalian testis. It is responsible for the growth and development of male sex organs and male secondary sexual characteristics. *See also* Hormones; Steroid.

Tetanus, infectious disease of the central nervous system caused by the toxin secreted by the bacterium *Clostridium tetani,* introduced into the body through a skin puncture and not subsequently exposed to oxygen. The symptoms are extreme stiffness, convulsions, and painful generalized muscle spasms. Muscle spasms of the jaw are particularly characteristic and result in difficulty in opening the mouth, which has earned the disease the name "lockjaw." Tetanus has a high mortality but is preventable by immunization with tetanus antitoxin.

Tethys, Sea of, the hypothetical sea which separated the Eurasian part from the African part of the supercontinent Pangaea 200,000,000 years ago. It was ancestral to the Mediterranean. The sea is named for the Greek god Oceanus' wife who was the mother of the seas.

Tet Offensive (1968), in the Vietnam War, a devastating military attack by North Vietnamese and Viet Cong troops on more than 100 cities and towns in South Vietnam. It discredited US military reports that said that victory over North Vietnam was near.

Teton Range, mountain chain in NW Wyoming and SE Idaho, S of Yellowstone National Park; part of Rocky Mt system; forms part of Grand Teton National Park and Targhee National Forest. Highest peak is Grand Teton, 13,747ft (4,193m).

Tetrahedrite, a sulfide mineral; copper, iron, antimony, and arsenic sulfide, found in medium-to-low temperature ore veins. Cubic system well-formed tetrahedral crystals and also massive. Metallic gray to black; hardness 3–4.5; sp gr 4.9. Important ore of copper.

Tetrameter, verse line of four metrical feet. Each tetrameter line is usually broken by a caesura or pause, as is every longer line. The caesura is not counted in the timing. Tetrameter lines can have a monotonous effect. *See also* Meter.

Teutonic Knights, Order of the Knights of the Hospital of St Mary of the Teutons in Jerusalem. A religious, military order restricted to Germans, and knighthood, to nobles, patterned after the Knights Templar, formed by German crusaders in 1190. Beginning in the early 13th century, they took as their mission the Christianization and Germanization of the eastern frontier. During that century, they conquered the heathen Slavs of Prussia. By 1329 they held the entire Baltic region as a papal fief, but their power declined after defeat at the Battle of Tannenberg by Poles and Lithuanians in 1410. The order has kept its identity and today has headquarters in Vienna, where the Knights devote themselves to charitable and nursing work.

Teutons, ancient Germanic tribe who migrated in company with the neighboring Cimbri from Jutland to S France. They were destroyed by Roman general Marius in 102 BC at the battle of Aquae Sextiae. Some few may have survived at Miltenberg. Their name came to mean German after they themselves had disappeared.

Texarkana, city in SW Arkansas, twin city with Texarkana, Tex., 137mi (221km) SW of Little Rock; seat of Miller co. Industries: lumber, railroad products, oil wells. Settled 1873. Pop. (1980) 21,459.

Texarkana, city in NE Texas, 185mi (298km) NE of Dallas; twin city with Texarkana, Arkansas. Industries: lumber, railroad cars, dairy products, creosote, sand, gravel, tires, mobile homes. Inc. 1874. Pop. (1980) 31,271.

Texas: Alamo, San Antonio

Thailand: Bangkok

Thailand: ceremonial dancers

Texas, state in the SW central United States, on the Gulf of Mexico, separated from the republic of Mexico by the Rio Grande. It was an independent republic before joining the Union.

Land and economy. Covering about 12% of the land mass of the 48 coterminous states, Texas exhibits a varied topography. A broad coastal plain lies along the Gulf of Mexico. W and N the land rises to plains and plateaus. Highest elevations are in the far W mountains. Besides the Rio Grande, the principal rivers are the Brazos, the Colorado, the Guadalupe, and the Nueces. There are few natural lakes; throughout the state dams create reservoirs for irrigation and flood control. Irrigation aids the growth of ranching and farming on the plains in the W and N. Manufacturing is largely centered in the populous E and S. Major petroleum deposits and refineries are on or near the Gulf coast, although wells are operated also in the NW. Seaborne transport is a major asset. Houston, linked to the Gulf by a ship canal, is a leading port; others are Beaumont, Port Arthur, Galveston, and Corpus Christi. Networks of railroads and highways cover the state's vast interior. NASA's Johnson Space Center, located outside of Houston, directs US manned space flights.

People. Texas is the third most populous state (after California and New York), and one of the fastest growing. Most Texans were born in the state, descendants of settlers from other states. There is a strong element of Mexican culture, and 20% of the population is Spanish speaking. Urbanization, due to the growth of industry, has been rapid; about 80% of the population lives in urban areas.

Education. There are nearly 140 institutions of higher education. The University of Texas system is a state-supported group of academic and professional schools throughout the state.

History. Over Texas have flown the flags of six nations—Spain, France, Mexico, the Republic of Texas, the Confederate States of America, and the United States of America. Spaniards explored the region after 1519 and claimed it. The Sieur de la Salle, descending the Mississippi River in 1682, asserted a French claim by building a fort on Matagorda Bay. The French went no farther, but the Spaniards made a few settlements, and the area became part of Mexico, then a Spanish colony. Mexico won independence in 1821, and in that year Americans began settling Texas in large numbers. They revolted against Mexican rule, and in 1836, after defeating a Mexican army, they established the Republic of Texas, which was recognized by the United States in 1837. It lasted eight years before being admitted to the Union. Texas seceded in 1861 and was an active member of the Confederacy. The first major oil discovery was at Spindletop in 1901, ushering in modern growth of the economy. In recent years high technology industries, such as aerospace and electronics, have become important. In 1963, Pres. John F. Kennedy was assassinated while visiting Dallas.

PROFILE

Admitted to Union: Dec. 29, 1845; rank, 28th
US Congressmen: Senate, 2; House of Representatives, 24
Population: 14,228,383 (1980); rank, 3rd
Capital: Austin, 345,496 (1980)
Chief cities: Houston, 1,594,086; Dallas, 904,078; San Antonio, 785,410
State Legislature: Senate, 31; House of Representatives, 150
Area: 267,338sq mi (692,405sq km); rank, 2nd
Elevation: Highest, 8,751ft (2,672m), Guadalupe Peak; lowest, sea level
Industries (major products): chemicals, refined petroleum, aircraft, aerospace equipment, automobiles, ships and boats, machinery, processed foods

Agriculture (major products): cattle, sheep, poultry, rice, sorghum, fruits, vegetables, nuts, peanuts
Minerals (major): petroleum, natural gas, sulfur, helium, cement, clay
State nickname: Lone Star State
State motto: Friendship
State bird: mockingbird
State flower: bluebonnet
State tree: pecan

Texas City, city in SE Texas, 35mi (56km) SE of Houston, on Galveston Bay; severely damaged by ship explosion and subsequent fires 1947, city was later rebuilt. Industries: chemicals, oil, tin. Exports: phosphate, petroleum, sulfur, chemicals, metal, cotton. Inc. 1912. Pop. (1980) 41,403.

Texas Rangers, mounted law officers organized in 1835 during the Texas Revolution against Mexico. They became a division of the Texas Department of Public Safety in 1935. Stephen Austin, founder of the first Texas colony, hired rangers in 1823, before they were formally organized, to defend the colony from Indian attack. The first Rangers were left to protect small Anglo-American settlements from the Comanche and Apache Indians while the main Texas army was fighting the Mexican army in the south. In the Mexican War (1846–48) they were effective as guerrilla fighters and scouts. Temporarily disbanding in the Reconstruction period, they were organized into two battalions in 1874, one to control the frontier range wars, and one to stop banditry and cattle theft along the Rio Grande. This was their period of greatest renown. The fast growth of the cattle business brought about rustling, feuding, shootings, and such lawlessness that the Texas Rangers were in great demand. Their responsibilities decreased and they lost their flamboyancy after the turn of the century.

Texas v. White (1869), US Supreme Court decision affirming Abraham Lincoln's position that the Union was indissoluble and upholding Congress' authority to reconstruct the states. It ruled that, despite secession, Texas had remained a state and that Congress, not the executive, would recognize state governments.

Textiles, fabrics produced from natural or synthetic fibers by weaving, knitting, felting, braiding, or netting. They are classified either by the nature of the fiber or of the weave. Fibers include wool, cotton, linen, silk, and synthetics, such as rayon, nylon, and the polyesters. Colored designs are applied to textiles by a variety of methods, ranging from ancient block printing to modern screen printing.

Thackeray, William Makepeace (1811–63), English novelist, comic illustrator, and journalist. A prolific writer in several genres, including satiric, historic, and fairy-tale, his works include *Barry Lyndon* (1842), *Vanity Fair* (1848), *Pendennis* (1850), *Henry Esmond* (1852), and *The Virginians* (1859).

Thai, the national language of Thailand, spoken there by about 35,000,000 people, or 85% of the country's population. Closely related to Lao, spoken across the border in Laos, it belongs to the Tai family of languages.

Thailand (Prathet Thai), independent nation in SE Asia. Formerly known as Siam, it is now a constitutional monarchy. Thailand is one of the world's leading producers of rice.

Land and economy. The Kingdom of Thailand is located in the center of SE Asia, bordered by Burma (W and N), Laos (N and E), Cambodia (SE), and Malaysia (S). Its coastline is on the Gulf of Thailand.

Thailand is made up of four divisions: central, a fertile region with water from the Chao Phraya River and irrigation canals; NE, a large plateau of poor soil, frequent droughts or floods; N, forested mountains and fertile valleys; and S, a long, narrow rain forest from central Thailand to Malaysia. Monsoons dominate the tropical climate. The economy is largely agricultural, with rice and rubber providing about half of export revenues. Thailand is the world's fifth-leading producer of tin, and large deposits of natural gas are located off-shore. Tourism is a growing factor in the economy.

People. Composed mainly of Thai stock, the population includes 2,000,000 urban Chinese and about 800,000 Malay-speaking Muslims with minorities of hill tribes and Vietnamese. A rural society population is centered in the fertile valleys. The official language is Thai; English is the second language. Education is compulsory between ages 7 and 14, and literacy is estimated at 70%. Theravada Buddhism is the religion of 90% of the people. Religious freedom is permitted.

Government. According to the constitution of 1978 the king is the head of state. The prime minister heads the bicameral national assembly. In fact, the military has controlled the government since 1976.

History. Historical records indicate that Thais originally ruled a kingdom in what is Yunnan, China, and migrated to Thailand about 1,000 years ago, encouraged by the Mongol invasion of S China. Contact with the West came with the Portuguese in the 16th century. Burmese conquerors in the 18th century were driven out by Rama I, founder of the present Thai ruling family. European colonialism grew stronger, and succeeding rulers modernized Thailand in an attempt to survive as a state. Thailand was occupied by Japan from 1941 until the Allied victory in WWII. The army seized control of the government in 1947, ruling until popular opposition led to the election of a civilian government in 1973. Since another military coup in 1976, the army has continued to control the government. During the 1960s, Thailand was allied with the United States, but following the collapse of US influence in South Vietnam in 1975, Thailand began forging closer ties with its neighbors. Relations with Vietnam deteriorated, however, after Vietnam invaded Cambodia in 1978. Border fighting between Vietnam and Thailand erupted in 1980 over the issue of Cambodian refugee camps in Thailand and continued in the early 1980s when Vietnam accused Thailand of harboring and aiding the Cambodian Khmer Rouge.

PROFILE

Official name: Kingdom of Thailand
Area: 198,414sq mi (514,000sq km)
Population: 46,455,000
 Density: 234per sq mi (90per sq km)
Chief cities: Bangkok (capital); Thon Buri
Government: Constitutional monarchy
Religion: Buddhist
Language: Thai
Monetary unit: Baht
Gross national product: $27,000,000,000
Per capita income: $232
Industries: textiles, cement, sugar refining and food processing, petroleum refining
Agriculture: rice, rubber, corn, coconuts, tobacco, pepper, peanuts, beans, cotton, jute
Minerals: tin, iron, manganese, tungsten, antimony
Trading partners: Japan, United States, Netherlands, Saudi Arabia

Thailand, Gulf of. *See* Siam, Gulf of.

Thalamus, forebrain area immediately above the hypothalamus. Sometimes called the sensory-motor receiving area, it obtains impulses from sensory neu-

Thalassemia

rons and sends them to other structures in the brain, particularly areas of the cerebral cortex.

Thalassemia, or Cooley's anemia, a genetic condition characterized by a deficiency of hemoglobin in the blood. It is prevalent in Italy, Greece, the Middle East, India, Thailand, and China.

Thales (c.634–546 BC), the first Greek scientist and philosopher of whom we have any knowledge. His parents were Greek and he lived in Miletus in Asia Minor. He made discoveries in geometry, such as that the angles at the base of an isosceles triangle are equal. He predicted the eclipse of the Sun that took place in 585 BC. He founded the Ionian school of natural philosophy, which held that a single elementary matter, water, is the basis of all the transformations of nature.

Thallium, metallic element (symbol Tl) of group IIIA of the periodic table, discovered spectroscopically (1861) by Sir William Crookes and isolated by him (1862). It occurs in some rare minerals; chief source is as a by-product from iron pyrites. Thallium is an extremely toxic compound. It is used in infrared detectors and certain specialized glasses. Properties: at. no. 81; at. wt. 204.37; sp gr 11.85; melt. pt. 578°F (303.5°C); boil. pt. 2,655°F (1,457°C); most common isotope Tl^{205} (70.5%).

Thallophyte, subkingdom of nonvascular plants containing more primitive forms of plant life. They have no distinctive roots, stems, or leaves and range in size from one-celled plants to 200-ft (61m) seaweeds. Asexual reproduction is by spores and sexual reproduction is by gamete fusion. Chlorophyll-containing thallopyhtes are algae, euglenoids, dinoflagellates, and lichens; thallophytes lacking chlorophyll are bacteria, fungi, and slime molds.

Thames, England's chief river. Its four headstreams—Thames, Churn, Coln, and Leach—rise in the Cotswolds, Gloucestershire. It winds E across S England, through London to the North Sea at the Nore. Navigable by barges as far as Lechlade, it is tidal to Teddington. It is crossed by 27 bridges including a new London Bridge. Above London it is mainly a pleasure river with beautiful scenery. Since 1857 the Thames Conservancy has successfully engaged in pollution control.

Thant, U (1909–74), Burmese diplomat, secretary general of the UN (1961–71). From 1947 he represented Burma at the UN. With the death of Dag Hammarskjöld in 1961, he became acting secretary general. He was elected secretary general in 1962 and reelected in 1966. He was involved in settling crises over Soviet missiles in Cuba (1962), civil war in the Congo (Zaïre) (1963) and in Cyprus (1964), and the India-Pakistan War (1965). He was less successful in dealing with the Vietnam War, the Middle East, and the India-Pakistan War of 1971.

Tharp, Twyia (1941–), US choreographer, b. Portland, Ind. She studied with Merce Cunningham for several years before joining the Paul Taylor Dance Company. In 1965 she formed her own company and began her career as an exceptionally original choreographer noted for her blending of classical movement, modern, jazz, pop, and comedy. Her dances include *Eight Jelly Rolls* (1971), *The Bix Pieces* (1971), *As Time Goes By* (1973), and *Push Comes to Shove* (1976).

Thatcher, Margaret Hilda (Roberts) (1925–), British prime minister. The daughter of a grocer, she went to Oxford University and became a research chemist. She was elected to Parliament in 1959 and served in the Conservative government from 1964 to 1970, before becoming secretary of state for education and science (1970–74). She was elected leader of the Conservative Party in 1974, and in 1979 she led the Conservative Party to an election victory. As Britain's first woman prime minister, she used her secure majority in the House of Commons to redirect economic policy along stringent conservative lines in an effort to solve the nation's economic and social woes. These problems and the continuing conflict in Northern Ireland in 1981 eroded her popularity. In 1982 she firmly supported Britain's decision to fight Argentina in order to retain the Falkland Islands and was reelected in 1983. She backed US Pres. Ronald Reagan's decision to bomb Libya (1986) to combat terrorism.

Theater, the art of mimetic representation, has developed among nearly all civilizations throughout known history. Early presentations usually involved honoring gods or mimicking nature. At other times important historical events were reenacted, or ribald and irreverent actions were displayed. Thus, motivations are diverse but are united by a common pleasure; the temporary removal of self-consciousness as feelings merge in a vital, communal flow. Mimetic features can be seen in African tribal dances and in American Indian

dance dramas. In Asian theater a combination of poetry, music, and dance called *sangita* prevails. Abstract, symbolic, and fixed in form, it includes the 4th- and 5th-century Sanskrit plays in India, the popular Chinese opera, and the No and Kabuki theater in Japan. Drama, a form of literature written for stage presentation, had its greatest development in Western theater, and after the 19th century grew in the East as well, existing alongside the classical forms. Generally narrative in form, with an interplay of forces resulting in a conflict which is then resolved, Western drama has its roots in ancient Greece, particularly in the works of Aeschylus, Sophocles, and Euripides, who wrote tragedies, and Aristophanes and Menander, who wrote comedies. The Romans preferred spectacles to drama, and the Christians suppressed it; nevertheless theatrical continuity was created from the ancient to the medieval era by traveling mime troops. Medieval drama began in the church, where sung Latin scripture evolved into mystery, miracle, and morality plays. A rediscovery of classical drama in the Renaissance inspired a great flowering of the art, most brilliantly displayed in the works of Shakespeare. The late 17th century produced the French neoclassical plays of Racine and Molière and English Restoration comedies of manners. A romantic reaction to neoclassicism was expressed in Germany, the *sturm und drang* movement, later occurring in France and England. Realism emerged in the 19th century, powerfully expressed by Russian dramatists and Norway's Henrik Ibsen. Symbolism, foreshadowed by Ibsen and expressed in August Strindberg's dream plays, was a reaction to realism, as were Oscar Wilde's comedies of manners. George Bernard Shaw's uniquely witty and intelligent plays of ideas stand apart from any trend. Naturalism, expressed by Sean O'Casey and Eugene O'Neill, is a strong 20th-century influence, as is expressionism, portraying dehumanization by technology. Federico García Lorca's verse dramas, Bertolt Brecht's epic theater, and Luigi Pirandello's plays pitting illusion against reality are major 20th-century works. Giraudoux elegantly presents an imaginative, rational voice in the French neoclassical tradition. A widespread sense of the meaninglessness of life followed World War II, bringing to the fore the theater of the absurd of Samuel Beckett, Eugene Ionesco, and Jean Genêt. Pessimism has also been expressed in the existential works of Jean Paul Sartre and Albert Camus, in Harold Pinter's "comedies of menace," and in the more realistic works of Arthur Miller and Tennessee Williams. The theater of cruelty vies to see who can be the most shockingly outrageous. Boundaries between audience and players are being crossed by experimental groups worldwide.

Theater of the Absurd, a theater form that abandons traditional devices of drama, including plot, meaningful dialogue, and normal characterization, to display the bewilderment and alienation of man. The roots of this theater form are Surrealism, Dadaism, and Existentialism. Playwrights include Eugene Ionesco (*The Bald Soprano,* 1950) and Samuel Beckett (*Waiting for Godot,* 1952).

Thebes (Thivai), ancient city in central Egypt (now occupied by Karnak and Luxor) on the Nile; most important from 2143 BC until its decline in 10th century BC; site of noted tomb of Tutankhamen.

Thebes, city in ancient Greece; center of Mycenaean power, destroyed c. 1100 BC. Rebuilt, it gained dominance of the Boeotian League 5th century BC; hostility to Athens over the Platae district led to alliance with Persia and later with Sparta in the Peloponnesian Wars. Thebes was victorious (371 BC) in its later clash with Sparta, but was almost destroyed in an uprising against Alexander the Great (336 BC) and fell to the Romans in 197. It was the seat of the legendary king Oedipus and the scene of tragedies by Sophocles and Aeschylus. The modern market town of Thebes is built on the site of the Theban acropolis. Pop. 15,899.

Theism, philosophical and theological systems, developed in opposition to atheism. The creed developed proposes the existence of one supreme being. As the creator of all, he is perfect and merits man's worship. Man is allowed freedom of choice, and revelation is possible.

Thematic Apperception Test (TAT), in psychology, a projective technique used to assess personality characteristics developed in 1938 by Henry A. Murray. The subject is presented with a series of cards with pictures on them, and he or she must make up a story about the characters in each picture. The method assumes that subjects will reveal their unconscious feeling and desires in their stories.

Themistocles (c.528–462 BC), Athenian statesman. Elected archon in 493, he ostracized many, built up the navy in time to save Athens from Persia, and devised

the battle plan for Salamis. Ousted in 471 for association with the Persians, he fled to Asia and governed a territory.

Theocracy, government ruled by religious leaders, who believe they possess divine authority. Theocracies were frequent in primitive societies and existed in ancient Egypt and the Orient. The New England Puritan colony (1620–60) was predominately theocratic.

Theodore Roosevelt National Memorial Park, park in W central North Dakota, in 3 units in the heart of the Badlands, includes bird and animal sanctuaries, museum, camping and picnicking grounds, petrified forest; in memory of President Theodore Roosevelt who owned several ranches in the area. Area: 70,374 acres (28,501hectares). Est. 1947.

Theodoric the Great (454?–526), Ostrogoth king who became king of Italy. Zeno, emperor of the Eastern Roman Empire, encouraged Theodoric to expel Odoacer, the German ruler of Italy. Theodoric defeated Odoacer and established (493) a peaceful reign based on Roman law and administration. Himself an Arian, he tolerated his subjects' Catholicism until an agreement between the churches of Rome and Constantinople (519) raised fears of new persecutions of Arians. *See also* Arianism.

Theodosius I, the Great (346?–395), Roman emperor (379–95). In 380–82 Theodosius reached a peaceful solution to the problem of the Gothic invasions. The Goths were allowed to settle on the Roman frontier but were made federate allies (*foederati*) of the Roman Empire. In this way Theodosius maintained imperial authority throughout the empire. He is best known, however, for his firm adherence to Christian orthodoxy, which later earned him the title of "the Great."

Theodosius II (401–50), Eastern Roman emperor (408–50). A weak ruler, he was dominated throughout his reign by others, among them his elder sister Pulcheria and his wife Eudocia. During his reign, the fortifications of Constantinople were strengthened, making the city virtually invulnerable to foreign attack. In 438 he published the Theodosian Code, an important legal reference work.

Theology, systematic, scientific investigation of the precepts of a given religion. It is intricately related to philosophical and historical studies. It strives to achieve an understanding of various beliefs. Necessarily, it is concerned with concepts of a divine being, man, and moral law or ethics. It has many branches, such as dogmatic, historical, and systematic theology.

Theorem, statement or proposition that is to be proved by logical reasoning from given facts and justifiable assumptions. In geometry a proposition is considered as a problem (a construction to be effected) or a theorem (a statement to be proved). Outside geometry two of the more famous theorems are the "binomial theorem" and the "fundamental theorem of algebra."

Theosophy, religious movement founded in the 19th century by H.P. Blavatsky. Using the Upanishads and Sutras as sources, it claims a natural awareness of the Divine. A personal God is denied, and Christ is seen as wholly human. The belief of the transmigration of souls is a central tenet.

Theresa of Avila, Saint (1515–82), Spanish reformer and author of books on the spiritual life. After 19 years as a Carmelite nun, she had a mystical experience of the nearness of God and Christ. Thereafter, she began to found monasteries following an old and more austere Carmelite rule. Her works include *The Way of Perfection,* written to instruct her nuns, and *The Interior Castle,* a book on spiritual experience. Theresa was one of the first two women to be named Doctors of the Church.

Thermocline, middle layers of ocean water between surface and deep waters, which are defined by differing densities and temperatures. It is up to 1,000m (3,280ft) thick with a lowest temperature only a few degrees above freezing. The thermocline is important as a stable boundary that tends to prevent interchange between layers.

Thermodynamics, the study of the heat content and interactions of systems. Historically, the laws of thermodynamics were developed from observation of large-scale properties of systems, with no understanding of the underlying atomic structure. It is now possible to calculate those laws from statistical and quantum mechanical principles. Thus the historical subject of thermodynamics is now subsumed in the disciplines of statistical mechanics or quantum thermodynamics. The three laws of thermodynamics follow: the First

Theater: The Glass Menagerie by Tennessee Williams

Thebes, Egypt

Third World: rice harvest

Law, basically a restatement of the conservation of energy, states that for any substance a quantity called the internal energy can be defined such that the change in the internal energy is the sum of the work done on the system and the heat absorbed by it. The Second Law states that for any substance a quantity called entropy can be defined such that (a) if the system is left alone, its entropy tends to increase, and (b) if the system absorbs heat, its entropy changes by the ratio of the heat absorbed to the temperature. The Third Law states that as the temperature approaches absolute zero, the entropy approaches a constant value independent of all other parameters. *See also* Statistical Mechanics.

Thermoelectric Propulsion, any of several rocket propulsion systems combining heat and electrical means to accelerate particles to high velocities. The arc jet engine uses an electric arc to heat liquid hydrogen to 50,000°C; the resulting plasma (separate electrons and protons) is accelerated through a conventional nozzle, or, in the plasma engine, through a magnetic field for greater force. Ion rockets accelerate heavy charged particles such as cesium ions. All thermoelectric rockets produce low but long-lasting thrust —superior for interplanetary space trips.

Thermometer, an instrument for measuring temperature by using those physical liquid, gas, or electrical changes in substances that are dependent on their degree of hotness or coldness. For example, air temperature may be measured by the expansion and contraction of mercury in a glass tube against units of a temperature scale. Common temperature scales are Celsius, Fahrenheit, and Kelvin. *See also* Temperature.

Thermonuclear Bomb. See Nuclear Weapon.

Thermonuclear Reaction. See Fusion, Nuclear.

Thermoplastic, type of polymer that becomes plastic on being heated and can be repeatedly melted or softened by heat without change of properties. Typical examples are polyethylene, polystyrene, and polyvinyl chloride. *See also* Plastics; Thermosetting Polymer.

Thermopylae (Thermopilai), mountain pass in E central Greece, between Mt Oeta and S Malian Gulf. Strategically located as N entrance to Greece, it was scene of many ancient battles. During Persian Wars, Spartans, under Leonidas, were defeated by Xerxes and Persians (480 BC); also site of Roman victory over Antiochus III of Syria (191 BC), and of German stalemate of Anzacs (1941).

Thermosetting Polymer, type of polymer that loses its plasticity once it has been softened by heat and pressure. Typical examples are the polymers that form a three-dimensional network of cross linkages, such as the phenolic resins, polyesters, epoxy resins, and silicones.

Thermostat, device for maintaining a constant temperature, usually by cutting off the heat supply when a predetermined temperature is reached. Most thermostats contain a bimetallic strip that breaks an electrical contact by buckling at a certain temperature.

Theropoda, saurischian dinosaur that was a biped, sharp-toothed carnivore. During Triassic times (190,-000,000 years ago), they were a light, running reptile, eg, Coelophysis. Later, they were several large types, such as the Jurassic Allosaurus and the giant Tyrannosaurus during Cretaceous times. *See also* Saurischian.

Theseus, in Greek mythology, a hero of many adventures. Son of Aethra, a princess of Troezen, by two fathers, Aegeus, king of Athens, and the sea god Poseidon. Theseus killed many villains in his youth, among them Procrustes, who forced his victims to lie on a bed that he used as a measure. Procrustes cut off what overlapped or stretched the victim to fit. Theseus slew the Minotaur in the Cretan labyrinth and eventually became king of Attica.

Thespis (6th century BC), Greek writer, credited with the invention of drama. He was the first to add an actor to performances, which had been dominated by the chorus alone. He is also said to have introduced the use of masks. No work remains.

Thessalonians, First and Second Epistles to, two of Paul's earliest letters, written to the church at Thessalonica. He encourages it and adjacent churches in confirmation of their faith and gives courage through Christ's Second Coming, rectifying their mistaken belief that the day of judgment is at hand.

Thessaloniki. See Salonika.

Thessaly (Thessalia), administrative district in N central Greece, almost completely surrounded by mountains. Ancient Thessaly headed the Amphictyonic League (6th century BC); it was subjugated by Philip II of Macedon (344 BC); later under Roman rule, passed to Ottoman Empire 1355; annexed to Greece 1881; site of WWII battle between Germans and troops of Britain and Greece. Crops: grain, cotton, sugar beets. Area: 5,382sq mi (13,939sq km). Pop. 659,913.

Thetis, a daughter of the sea god Nereus, in Greek mythology. She was the mother of the hero Achilles who attempted to make her son immortal to save him from the destiny she perceived for him. At his birth she dipped him in the River Styx, holding him by the heel. Achilles became all but invulnerable. Unfortunately, the Trojan Paris shot him in the heel with a poisoned arrow and he died.

Thiamine, vitamin of the B complex required for carbohydrate metabolism; its deficiency causes the disease beri-beri. See Vitamin, Vitamin B₁.

Thiers, Adolphe (1797–1877), French statesman and historian. He was a founder of the journal *National,* which attacked King Charles X and helped to precipitate the July Revolution of 1830. Under King Louis Philippe, Thiers held cabinet offices (1832–36) until his aggressive foreign policy led to his dismissal. After the Revolution of 1848, he was elected to the constituent assembly. Although supporting Louis Napoleon for president, Thiers opposed his coup d'etat in 1851 and was exiled. Again elected to the legislature in 1863, he attacked Napoleon III's imperial policies and promoted reforms. After the Franco-Prussian War he was chosen chief executive of the provisional government. He harshly suppressed the 1871 Commune of Paris and became president of the republic until 1873, when he was forced to resign.

Thieu, Nguyen Van (1923–), president of the Republic of Vietnam (1967–75). He participated in the overthrow of President Diem in 1963 and ruled with others until his election as president. In 1968 he declared martial law and suspended most freedoms. He was reelected in 1971 amid dispute. Thieu resigned shortly before the fall of Saigon to the Vietcong and went into exile.

Thighbone. See Femur.

Thinking, mental (ideational or cognitive) activity of the brain, the integration of an external stimulus with the person's response to it. Thinking requires some detachment from the outer world in order to understand, predict, and master that world. Objective thinking reaches its highest level in scientific thinking (investigation). The thinking of the mentally ill is impaired, and the thought processes of autistic children, schizophrenics, and neurotic psychotic people are unique. *See also* Austistic Thinking; Repression; Schizophrenia.

Third Party Politics, political action by a group challenging the major parties in a two-party system. Third parties usually represent voters who are dissatisfied with the existing parties or who feel their views are not expressed by them.

Third Reich, the period in German history from 1933–45 when Germany was under the totalitarian dictatorship of Adolf Hitler. The term was used to indicate a closeness with other great periods of German history —the First Reich of the Holy Roman Empire and the Second Reich (1871–1918) founded by Otto von Bismarck.

Third Republic, French government during 1870–1940. It began with the collapse of the Second Empire in the Franco-Prussian War (1870–71), with the bloody uprising of the Paris Commune following soon after (1871). Adolphe Thiers provided the leadership that created republican institutions. Until 1914 the government was marked by bourgeois liberalism and a surge of imperial growth. After 1918 it was beset by economic problems. It collapsed (1940) as it was born, in defeat by Germany. *See also* Franco-Prussian War.

Third World, name given to less developed nations of Asia, Africa, and Latin America. These nations are outside the larger power blocs and are usually agrarian and lacking advanced technology. They often have unstable governments and a variety of social problems.

Thirteen Colonies, name given to the 13 territories that, along with Canada, made up British North America prior to the American Revolution. After the Revolution, the colonies became the first states in the United States. They are New Hampshire, Massachusetts, Connecticut, Rhode Island, New York, New Jersey, Pennsylvania, Delaware, Maryland, Virginia, North Carolina, South Carolina, and Georgia.

Thirty Years War (1618–48), European war. It involved German Protestant princes with France, Sweden, England, and Denmark against the Hapsburgs and Catholic princes of the Holy Roman Empire. Bohemian Protestant princes revolted (1618) against Catholic King Ferdinand (later Emperor Ferdinand II) and the revolt spread throughout Europe. The war left German lands devastated, German population tremendously decreased, the German economy in ruins, the Holy Roman Empire divided, and the Hapsburgs with decreased power. After the war, European religious conflicts decreased; the Peace of Westphalia led to increased religious toleration. *See also* Holy Roman Empire.

Thistle, plant with thorny leaves and purple, pink, yellow, or white flower heads with prickly bracts. Most thistles belong to the genera *Cirsium, Onopordum,* and *Carduus.* Many, such as the Canada thistle (*Cirsium arvense*) are fast-spreading, troublesome weeds in the United States. Family Compositae.

Thomas, Saint, one of the 12 Apostles of Jesus Christ. In the *Gospel of John* he is called Twin (Greek *Didymus*). He has been called "Doubting Thomas" because, after the Resurrection, he at first did not believe he saw the risen Lord (John 20: 24–28). The *Gospel of Thomas* and three other apocryphal works bearing his name were written well after his time.

Thomas, Dylan (1914–53), Welsh poet. His verse is powerfully rhetorical, occasionally willfully obscure, but at its best, as in the poems in *Deaths and Entrances* (1946), both original and simple. His radio play *Under Milk Wood* (1954) makes skillful use of speech rhythms. His obsessive drinking contributed to his early death while on a lecture tour in the United States.

Thomas, Norman Mattoon (1884–1968), US socialist leader, b. Marion, Ohio. A pacifist, he joined the Socialist Party in 1918. In 1926 he became party leader and was its unsuccessful candidate for US president six times (1928–1948). A strong anti-Communist, he campaigned for social welfare measures, civil rights, free speech, and world peace.

Thomas à Kempis (*c.*1380–1471), German theologian. He was born in Germany (family name Hemerken) and entered a monastery in the Netherlands in 1399. There he became a priest and spent most of his life in scholarly work. He was influenced by the "modern devotion," a movement to return to the simple and sincere ways of the early Christians. He is generally believed to be the author of the *Imitation of Christ,* one of the most widely read devotional books, which gives counsel on how to put away worldly interests and follow Christ.

Thomism, the philosophy of St Thomas Aquinas, one of the major systems in Scholasticism. Aquinas blended Aristotle's philosophy with Christian theology. Using Aristotle's views of matter and form, Aquinas conceived a hierarchy in which spirit is higher than matter, soul higher than body, and theology above philosophy. He taught that reason, while essential, can reach only so high. There is a point at which faith becomes the final authority.

Thompson, David (1770–1857), Canadian fur trader and explorer, b. England. He joined the Hudson's Bay Co. (1784), wintered at Calgary (1787), and studied surveying (1789–90). He journeyed to Lake Athabasca (1796), took a 4,000-mile (6,400-km) trip to the Mississippi headwaters (1797–98), and established Kootenae House (1807), the first trading post on the Columbia River. He explored the Columbia to Fort Astoria (1811) and charted the US-Canada boundary (1816–26).

Thompson, river in S British Columbia, Canada; formed by convergence of North Thompson and South Thompson rivers at Kamloops: discovered 1808 by Simon Fraser. Length: 304mi (489km).

Thomson, (Sir) Joseph John (1856–1940), English physicist. His work on the conductivity of gases led him to the discovery of the electron in 1897 and the foundation of the famous atomic research unit at the Cavendish Laboratories in England. He was awarded a Nobel Prize in 1906 for his investigations of electrical conductivity of gases.

Thomson, Virgil (1896–), US music critic and composer, b. Kansas City, Mo. He was chief music critic for the New York *Herald Tribune* (1940–57). Many of his works have been based on American folk music. He is best known for the operas *Four Saints in Three Acts* (1928) and *The Mother of Us All* (1947), both with librettos by Gertrude Stein.

Thomson Effect. A potential difference is developed between two points on a metal conductor if the two points are maintained at different temperatures. Named after Sir William Thomson (Lord Kelvin) (1824–1907).

Thon Buri, city in central Thailand, opposite Bangkok on Chao Phraya River; served as capital of Siam (1767–82). Industries: rice processing, sawmills. Pop. 627,989.

Thor, deity common to all the early Germanic peoples, a great warrior represented as a red-bearded, middle-aged man of enormous strength. Thor was an implacable foe of the harmful race of giants, but benevolent toward mankind. He was generally secondary to the god Odin, who in some traditions was his father. In Iceland he was the supreme deity.

Thorazine. *See* Chlorpromazine.

Thoreau, Henry David (1817–62), US author, b. Concord, Mass. After graduating from Harvard University (1837), he taught school for several years in Concord. There he became friends with Ralph Waldo Emerson and other Transcendentalists. During 1841–43 he lived with Emerson as a handyman and assistant. During this period some of his early prose and poetry appeared in the Transcendentalist journal, *The Dial.*

An ardent individualist, in July 1845, he began to live at Walden Pond, near Concord, in a cabin that he built. He kept a daily journal, recording, among other things, the plant and animal life that he observed and worked on his first book *A Week on the Concord and Merrimack Rivers* (1849). In 1846 he spent one night in jail for refusing to pay a federal poll tax in protest against the Mexican War, which he regarded as a war for the extension of slavery; his famous essay on "Civil Disobedience" (1849) stemming from this incident emphasized his belief that man should live according to his conscience. Thoreau left Walden in September 1847. Subsequently, he worked in his father's pencil factory and at odd jobs. His masterwork, *Walden,* or meditative narrative, appeared in 1854. During the 1850s, he was active in the antislavery movement, helping escaped slaves on their way to Canada, lecturing against slavery, and praising John Brown. He died of tuberculosis. Records of his walking excursions were published in *The Maine Woods* (1864), *Cape Cod* (1865), and *A Yankee in Canada* (1866). His *Poems of Nature* was published in 1895. *See also* Brown, John; Civil Disobedience; Transcendentalism; Walden.

Thorium, radioactive metallic element (symbol Th) of the actinide group, first discovered in 1828 by J. J. Berzelius. The chief ore is monazite (phosphate). The metal is used in photoelectric and thermionic emitters. Chemically reactive, it burns in air and reacts slowly in water. Properties: at. no. 90; at. wt. 232.038; sp gr 11.7; melt. pt. 3,182°F (1,750°C); boil. pt. 6,872°F (3,800°C); most stable isotope Th^{232} (1.41×10^{10}yrs). *See also* Actinide Elements.

Thorn Apple, (1) the fruit of the hawthorn. (2) Any plant of the genus *Datura,* especially Jimson weed *(D. stramomium),* a very poisonous, tall, coarse, annual weed of tropical Asiatic origin, now naturalized all over the world. It has foul-smelling leaves and large white or violet trumpet-shaped flowers that are succeeded by round prickly fruit. *See also* Hawthorn.

Thorndike, Edward Lee (1874–1949), US psychologist and educator, b. Williamsburg, Mass. He devised the first systematic theory of learning, stressing the importance of the "law of effect" (the principle of reinforcement). He was one of the earliest psychological researchers to do laboratory studies with animals, and he also pioneered in applying psychological knowledge to problems in education and human abilities. Major works include *The Fundamentals of Learning* (1932).

Thorpe, James Francis ("Jim") (1888–1953), US athlete, b. Bright Path near Prague, Okla. A Sac Indian, he won both the pentathlon and decathlon in the 1912 Olympics. A year later, however, he was forced to give up his medals when it was discovered he had played semi-pro baseball. He played professional football with several teams (1915–26) and baseball in the National League with three different teams (1913–19). He was elected to the Football Hall of Fame in 1963. In 1973 the Amateur Athletic Union voted to restore his Olympic records and medals.

Thoth, in Egyptian mythology, the scribe of the gods. In various myths he appears as the record keeper of the dead, patron of the arts and learning, inventor of writing, and as creator of the universe. Thoth is depicted as a man with the head of an ibis or of an ape, bearing pen and ink or the lunar disk and crescent.

Thousand Islands, group of more than 1,800 islands in the St Lawrence River extending about 50mi (81km) along the US-Canada border; about equally divided between both countries; site of two New York state parks and Canada's St Lawrence Islands National Park. The Thousand Island Bridge (1938) connects Collins Landing, New York, with Ivy Lea, Ontario.

Thousand Oaks, city in S California, 30mi (48km) WNW of Los Angeles; original name was Conejo Valley. Industries: aircraft parts, citrus fruits, plastics. Inc. 1964. Pop. (1980) 77,797.

Thrasher, New World songbird related to the mockingbird. The brown thrasher *(Toxostoma rufum)* of E North America is brownish above and pale below with white stripes on its wings. It frequents forest edges and grasslands, feeding on insects and fruit. It builds its nest in thick vines and lays pale blue-green eggs (4–5) marked with reddish spots. Length: 11in (28cm). Several genera are confined to the West Indies, including the trembler *(Cinclocerthia ruficauda).* Length: 9in (23cm).

Thread Worm. *See* Horsehair Worm.

Three Mile Island, an island on the Susquehanna River near Harrisburg, Pa. It is the site of a nuclear power-generating plant where a near-disastrous accident took place in March 1979. The accident began with the failure of the feedwater system that picks up heat from another system that has circulated through the reactor core, producing steam to power the turbines. A series of mechanical failures and human errors followed. Radioactive water and gases were released into the environment. Although the ultimate disaster (meltdown of the reactor core) did not take place, the accident demonstrated problems with reactor design, maintenance procedures, and operator training.

Threonine, colorless soluble crystalline essential amino acid found in proteins. *See* Amino Acid.

Thresher, agricultural machine used to separate grain from chaff and straw. The first threshers were the feet of humans and animals or flails. Today, the threshing operation is incorporated into the combine.

Threshold, in psychology, theoretical point along a physical scale of energy that corresponds to the detection of the stimulus (detection threshold) or the discrimination between stimuli (difference threshold). Thresholds are sometimes called *limens.*

Thrip, slender, sucking insects found worldwide. Varied in color, most are plant feeders and some carry plant diseases. Often found in large numbers, they may be irritating to human skin. Length: 0.02–0.5in (0.5–13mm). Order Thysanoptera.

Throat. *See* Pharynx.

Thrombin, blood enzyme that converts fibrinogen to fibrin during clot formation. *See also* Blood Clotting.

Thrombophlebitis, inflammation of a vein, coupled with formation of a blood clot that adheres to the wall of the vessel. Treatment is with anticoagulants and application of heat.

Thrombosis, formation or presence of a blood clot in the heart or any blood vessel. Factors involved are injury to the lining of heart or vessels, alterations in normal blood flow, and changes in the coagulability of the blood.

Thrush, family (Turdidae) of small-to-medium-sized perching songbirds, often seen on the ground; found worldwide. Typical thrushes may be brightly colored or black, but most have yellow or orange bills and eye rings. They feed mainly on insects or fruit and build open nests. Included in the family are the robin, hermit thrush, wood thrush, and nightingale.

Thrust, Rocket, the force developed by a rocket engine. It depends on the velocity *(v)* of the exhaust gases, the difference in pressure between the combustion chamber and exit nozzle gases ($P_c - P_e$), the area of the exhaust nozzle (A_e), and the mass of gas expelled per unit time ($\dot{M}$):$F = \dot{M}v + (P_c - P_e)A_e$. Thus the higher the velocity of the exhaust gases, or the greater their molecular weight, the larger the thrust.

Thucydides (*c.*470–*c.*400 BC), noted ancient historian. After commanding an unsuccessful expedition (424) to Amphipolis in the Peloponnesian War, he went into exile (423–403), during which he wrote his *History of the Peloponnesian War.*

Thugs, members of a secret society in India who would kill in honor of Kali, Hindu goddess of destruction. They strangled their victims. Beginning in 1829 the British stamped out the Thugs through arrests and executions, and by 1848 the menace had ended.

Thule, settlement in NW Greenland, on S shore of Wolstenholme Fjord of Baffin Bay. A large Eskimo population migrated here from Canada 1862–66; its name has been given to an anthropological term describing a pre-European Eskimo culture, also found in other Arctic areas; site of Thule Air Force Base (1952), used for furthering explorations of N Greenland icecap. Founded 1910 by Knud Rasmussen as a Danish trading post. Pop. 749.

Thulium, metallic element (symbol Tm) of the lanthanide group, first discovered in 1879 by P. T. Cleve. Chief ore is monazite (phosphate). The element has few commercial uses. Properties: at. no. 69; at. wt. 168.9342; sp. gr. 9.31 (25°C); melt. pt. 2,813°F (1,545 °C); boil. pt. 3,141°F (1,727°C); most stable isotope Tm^{169} (100%). *See also* Lanthanide Elements.

Thunder Bay, city in SW Ontario, Canada, on Thunder Bay, an inlet of Lake Superior; capital of Thunder Bay

Norman Thomas

Sir J.J. Thomson

James Thorpe

district; major Canadian port; important transportation center in rich mining region; site of Lakehead University (1965) and Confederation College (1967). Industries: shipyards, oil refineries, grain elevators, paper and pulp mills. Est. 1970 by the merging of Port Arthur and Fort William. Pop. 111,476.

Thunderstorm, or electrical storm, a storm produced by a cumulonimbus cloud, accompanied by lightning, thunder, strong winds, heavy rain, and sometimes hail. Forming with strong updrafts, the thunderhead often builds up to heights of 8 to 10mi (13 to 16km), creating centers of opposite electrical charges within it and with the ground, which are discharged with lightning strokes that produce thunder. As the storm dissipates, columns of precipitation occur with strong downdrafts. *See also* Cloud; Lightning.

Thurber, James (1894–1961), US author, b. Columbus, Ohio. He began his career as a reporter. In 1926 he became regular contributor of essays, short stories, and cartoons to the *New Yorker* magazine. A humorist, his work is ironic and satiric. Collections of his essays and stories include *My Life and Hard Times* (1933), *The Middle Aged Man on the Flying Trapeze* (1935), *My World and Welcome to It* (1942)—which contained the fantasy, "The Secret Life of Walter Mitty"—and *The Thurber Carnival* (1945).

Thurgau, canton in NE Switzerland, bordered (N) by Lake Constance; capital is Frauenfeld. Ruled 1264 by Hapsburgs, it was taken 1460 by Swiss cantons; in 1798 it was invaded by France; joined Swiss Confederation 1803. Products: cereals, fruit, cattle. Chief industry is wine. Area: 388sq mi (1,005 sq km). Pop. 184,500.

Thurmond, (James) Strom (1902–   ), US senator, b. Edgefield, S.C. He was a state senator (1933–38) and then served as governor of South Carolina (1947–51). In 1948, he was a candidate for president on the States' Rights ticket. A conservative Southerner, he entered the Senate as a Democrat in 1954, but switched to the Republican part in 1964. He became President Pro Tempore of the Senate in 1981.

Thurstone, Louis Leon (1887–1955), US psychologist, b. Chicago. He was a pioneer in the development of ability tests and statistical methods of analyzing them. Among his publications are *Primary Mental Abilities* (1938) and *Multiple Factor Analysis* (1947).

Thus Spake Zarathustra (1883–85), poetic work of philosophy in aphoristic style by Friedrich Nietzsche.

Thutmose, the royal name of four kings of the XVIIIth dynasty of Egypt (c.1525–1398 BC). The most significant achievement of **Thutmose I** was the subjugation of the Nile Valley up to the 3rd cataract. **Thutmose II** married his half-sister Hatshepsut, who in effect ruled Egypt for 22 years. **Thutmose III** reigned for 54 years either alone or with Thutmose II and Hatshepsut, and built his empire to include all of Syria except Phoenicia, extending it from the 3rd cataract to the Euphrates. **Thutmose IV** was the last king of the dynasty, ruling c.1406–1398 BC.

Thyme, common name for *Thymus,* aromatic herbs of the mint family used as ornamental plants and for seasoning. Common thyme and mother-of-thyme, or creeping thyme, have purplish flowers.

Thymus Gland, one of the endocrine, or ductless, glands, located in the upper chest. Sometimes called the gland of childhood, it is large in infancy and atrophies after puberty. Its function was long unknown but

it is now thought to be primarily a lymphoid organ, secreting a hormone that acts on lymph tissue and producing antibodies that function in the body's immune mechanism. Disorder of the thymus is often associated with auto-immune diseases.

Thyroid Gland, H-shaped endocrine gland lying in the neck region, along the sides of and over the trachea. It secretes the hormone thyroxin, which is essential for the growth and development of the body, regulation of metabolism, and the utilization of some foodstuffs. A lack of thyroxin can produce cretinism in children, myxedema in adolescents and adults. Overactivity of the gland, frequently caused by a goiter, produces weight loss, bulging eyeballs, irritability. *See also* Cretinism; Goiter; Myxedema.

Thyrotropic Hormone, or thyrotropin, glycoprotein produced by the anterior pituitary that stimulates growth and function of the thyroid.

Thyroxin, or thyroid hormone, iodine-containing compound secreted by the thyroid. It regulates the rate of oxygen consumption by stimulation of basic metabolism; required for normal growth and development.

Tiber (Tevere), second-longest river in Italy; rises in Etruscan Apennines; flows S then SW, empties into Tyrrhenian Sea near Ostia; joined to the Arno River by the Chiana Canal; flood-prone; upper Tiber is used to generate electricity. Length: 251mi (404km).

Tiberias (Teverya), lake port town in N Israel, 30mi (48km) E of Haifa on the Sea of Galilee. After the destruction of Jerusalem 2nd century, Tiberius became center of Jewish learning and capital of Jewish Palestine; site of many ancient synagogues and tomb of Maimonides; trade center for rich agricultural community. Industries: tourism, machines. Founded AD 26 by Herod Antipas; named for Roman emperor Tiberius. Pop. 23,900.

Tiberius (42 BC–AD 37), Roman emperor (AD 14–37). He governed Transalpine Gaul and fought well in Germany and Illyricum. He was adopted by Augustus, whose heirs had died, and became emperor at Augustus' death. He pursued Augustan foreign policy and practiced strict economy, leaving Rome great wealth. Harassed by political and family jealousies, he retired from Rome (26), fearing plots upon his life. Unbalanced and unpopular, he commanded numerous executions of suspected conspirators in his last years.

Tibet (Xizang), Land of the Lamas, a high plateau in central Asia annexed by China in 1951. In 1965 it was declared the Tibetan Autonomous Region of China. The capital is Lhasa, and there are 1,740,000 inhabitants.

Land and economy. Its 471,700sq mi (1,221,703sq km), with 1,400,000 population, contains the world's highest mountains, the Himalayas, at the S border. This range, part of four great Tibetan mountain systems formed during the glacier period, is still growing. Lakes in one district are said to be remains of an early sea. The average altitude of the country is over 15,000ft (4,575m) and one city, Jiachan, is 15,870ft (4,840m) above sea level. Asia's largest rivers—Yangtze, Mekong, Yellow, Salween, Irrawaddy, Indus, and Brahmaputra—rise in Tibet. Annual rainfall varies from 200in (508cm) on the S side of the Himalayas to 8in (20cm) in the rest of the country. Over 12,000ft (3,660m) the climate is severe, with gale winds and temperatures dropping from 100°F (38°C) at noon to below zero at night; below 12,000ft (3,660m) the climate is pleasant. Trees in the S valleys include spruce, fir, cypress, oak, and walnut. Crops are barley, buck-

wheat, and medicinal herbs. Sheep, which provide the nomadic N Tibetans with both food and clothing, are raised along with yaks, goats, and horses. Under Chinese administration, irrigation projects and roads have been built and light industry developed.

People. With cultural ties to adjacent Chinese provinces and Burma, Tibetans belong to the Mongolian race and are divided into three groups: Bodpo, Khampa, and Amdo. They have few racial differences, share the same language (based on Sanskrit) and the same religion, Lamaism, an offshoot of Buddhism. Before the Communists' rule, highly endowed monasteries were the learning centers; no public schools existed.

Government. As an autonomous region of China, Tibet is under the control of the Chinese central government and sends representatives to the National Peoples' Congress. Within the region, administration is by Revolutional Council, whose leader also heads the Tibetan Communist Party.

History. Religion and history are tied together in Tibet. From Buddhism in the 11th century, Tibet moved to Lamaism in the 15th century, when a successful reformation movement (Yellow Hats) installed the first Dalai Lama as secular and religious chief. Tibet was independent 1913–50. After a Communist invasion in 1950 a pact was signed with the Dalai Lama; however, Tibetans continued to fight Chinese domination. Following an uprising in 1959, that was harshly crushed by Chinese forces, the Dalai Lama fled to India. During the late 1970s some liberalization was allowed: some temples were allowed to open, and the Panchen Lama (another traditional leader) was elected to the National People's Congress.

Tibetan Terrier, 2,000-year-old breed of dog (nonsporting group) bred in lamaseries of the Lost Valley of Tibet; first brought to West in 1920s. Considered holy and a bringer of luck in Tibet. Not actually a terrier, it has a medium-long head with long furnishings; hanging, V-shaped ears; large, dark eyes; compact body; medium-length legs; and curled tail carried over the back. The double coat is straight or waved, long, fine, and can be any color or colors. Average size: 14–16in (35.5–41cm) high at shoulder; 22–23lb (10–10.3kg). *See also* Nonsporting Dog.

Tibeto-Burman Languages, group of languages spoken in a number of countries of S Asia. It includes Burmese and Tibetan, plus Yi, Lisu, and Lahu, of China; Karen, of Burma; Kachin (or Chingpaw), of Burma and China; Bodo, Garo, Meithei, and Lushei, of E India; and Newari and Murmi, of Nepal. The Tibeto-Burman languages are thought to be part of the Sino-Tibetan family, which includes Chinese.

Tibia, larger of the two lower leg bones. It articulates with the femur, or upper leg bone, at the knee and extends to the ankle, where its lower end forms the projecting ankle bone on the inside of the leg. *See also* Fibula.

Tic Douloureux, or trigeminal neuralgia, a condition of brief, but extremely severe shooting pains along one or more branches of the trigeminal nerve affecting the face. Its cause is unknown and nerve tissue appears unaffected. Surgery and decompression of the nerve roots offer permanent cures.

Ticino River, river in Switzerland and Italy; rises on the slopes of Saint Gotthard Mt; flows SE then S through Ticino canton, joining the Po River in N Italy; scene of Hannibal's victory 218 BC over Scipio in Second Punic War; source of hydroelectricity. Length: 154mi (248km).

Tick, wingless, bloodsucking arthropod found worldwide. It varies in color and is an external parasite on birds, animals, and humans. Several species carry diseases, including relapsing, spotted, and African tick fevers. Their feeding can also cause paralysis. Length: to 1.2in (3cm). Class Arachnida; order Acarina.

Ticonderoga, Fort, formerly Fort Carillon; historic military post in NE New York, strategically located near Lake Champlain. Once on a main water route between Canada and New York City, it was scene of attack by Gen. James Abercromby during French and Indian War (July 1758). Taken by Ethan Allen (May 1775), it became an American base for Canadian invasion; it was occupied by British (July 1777) until Burgoyne's surrender; bought 1820 by New York entrepreneur and restored as museum.

Tidal Flat, an extensive, nearly flat, barren land area that is alternately covered and uncovered by the action of the tide. It consists of mud and sand. A tidal marsh has a covering of salt-tolerant plants and grasses.

Tidal Wave. *See* Tsunami.

Tide, the periodic rise and fall of the surface level of the oceans caused by the gravitational attraction of the Moon and Sun and the opposite force of centrifugal motion. Tides follow the Moon's cycle of 28 days so they arrive at a given spot 50 minutes later each day. When the Sun and Moon are aligned, the greatest tidal range occurs, called spring tides. When they are in quadrature, tidal ranges are lowest and are called neap tides.

Tien Shan, mountain system in central Asia, ranging from Pamir Mts, USSR, through NW China to the border of Mongolia. Highest peak is 24,406ft (7,444m). Length: approx. 1,500mi (2,415km).

Tientsin (Tianjin, or **T'ien-ching),** port city in NE China, 80mi (129km) SE of Peking, at the confluence of Hai River and Grand Canal; 3rd-largest city in China; capital of Hopei prov. Economic and political growth was spurred when it was declared a treaty port 1860, open to foreign traffic, and including agreement with France and Britain to open parts to foreign colonization and military posts; all foreign concessions were abolished by 1946. Suffered severe earthquake damage, July, 1976. Seat of Hopeh University (1960), Nankai University, Tientsin University. Industries: textiles, chemicals, iron, steel, machine shops, flour, food processing, paper, automobiles, tobacco products, fertilizer. Pop. 3,800,000.

Tiepolo, Giovanni Battista (1696–1770), Italian painter. He was a leading artist of the Venetian Rococo. One of his early works is "The Sacrifice of Abraham" (*c.*1715–16) in the Church of Ospedaletto, Venice. He executed ceiling decorations (1720–25) for the vault of the side chapel in the Church of Scalzi, Venice. From 1741 to 1750 he executed his mature works in a classic style. They include "The Miracle of the Holy House of Loreto" (1743–44) and the Cleopatra frescoes (1745–50), a notable group of works in the Labia Palace, Venice. One of his last commissions was the decoration of the Villa Valmarana and "The Apotheosis of the Pisani Family" (1761–62) in the Villa Pisani.

Tierra del Fuego, archipelago of S Argentina and S Chile, forming the southernmost tip of South America; separated from the mainland by the Strait of Magellan; named by Ferdinand Magellan (1520) from Spanish meaning "Land of Fire." Francis Drake discovered Cape Horn (1578), the southernmost point in the archipelago and Western Hemisphere. Industries: sheep, oil, fishing, timber. Area: 28,434sq mi (73,644sq km). Pop. 27,476.

Tiger, powerful large cat found throughout Asia, mainly in forest areas. Its dark-striped coat is yellow-orange with the chin and underparts white. A nonclimbing cat that relies on keen hearing, it feeds on birds, deer, cattle, and reptiles. The gestation period is three months and 1–6 young are born. The largest tiger is the Siberian variety. Length: 13ft (4m); weight: 650lb (292.5kg). The Bengal variety of India may achieve the same weight but is no more than 10ft (3m) long. Other varieties are Indochinese, Sumatran, Javan, Caspian, and south Chinese. Family Felidae; species *Panthera tigris. See also* Cat.

Tiger Beetle, active, usually strikingly colored, medium-sized beetle. Adults and larvae prey on other insects. Family Cicindelidae.

Tiger Moth, stout-bodied, medium-sized moth with bright orange and black wings. Most tiger moth caterpillars, including woolly bears, are covered with long hairs. Family Arctiidae. *See also* Woolly Bear.

Tiger Shark, a large shark found worldwide in inshore and offshore tropical waters. It will enter bays and river mouths. This gray shark is recognized by vertical bars along its sides and its long, lopsided tail. A noted scavenger, its young are born alive. Length: to 18ft (5.5m). Family Carcharhinidae; species *Galeocerdo cuvieri.* See also Chondrichthyes; Sharks.

Tigris, river in SW Asia; rises in the Taurus Mts of E Turkey; flows SSE through Iraq until it joins the Euphrates River at Gurna, SE Iraq, to form the Shatt-al-Arab. Subject to sudden flooding, it is the site of complex flood-control projects, and the source of large irrigation systems since ancient times. Length: 1,180mi (1,990km).

Tigris-Euphrates Region. *See* Babylonia; Mesopotamia; Sumer.

Tijuana, city in NW Mexico, S of US border, on the Pacific Coast; developed around the Rancho de Tia Juana, one of six cattle ranches that merged into a village 1840. Tijuana gained popularity during US prohibition, because of availability of alcoholic beverages; est. as a free port 1933; site of race track, bullfights, casinos. Industries: tourism, food processing, electronics, textiles. Pop. 335,100.

Tilburg, city in S Netherlands, near Belgian border, approx. 15mi (24km) NE of Eindhoven; 19th-century textile manufacturing and research center of Netherlands. Pop. 151,513.

Tilden, Samuel Jones (1814–86), US political leader, b. New Lebanon, N.Y. A lawyer and reform Democrat, he helped oust the Tweed Ring. From 1875–76, he was governor of New York. In 1876, as the Democratic party candidate for president, he won a majority of popular votes but lost the election when contested electoral votes were awarded to Republican Rutherford B. Hayes by a partisan electoral commission.

Tile, thin flat slabs or blocks used structurally or decoratively in building. Traditionally, tiles have been made of glazed or unglazed firing clay, but modern tiles are also made of plastic, synthetic rubber, glass, asphalt, and asbestos cement. Tiles are used in many ways, among them: floors, ceilings, roofs, sound insulation, water-shedding surfaces, partitions, walls, stove linings, and ornaments.

Tilefish, or blanquillos, tropical marine fish of some commercial value. Elongated, it is olive green or blue with yellow and rose markings. Length: 2ft (61cm). The 15 species include the Atlantic sand tilefish *Malacanthus plumieri.* Family Branchiostegidae.

Till, nonsorted, nonstratified sediment or drift that is deposited directly from the ice of glaciers. It is a heterogeneous mixture of clay, sand, gravel, and boulders. Tillite is till that has been converted into solid rock.

Tillich, Paul Johannes Oskar (1886–1965), German-American theologian and philosopher. He was born in Germany, was ordained in the Lutheran Church, and served as a chaplain in World War I. Because he opposed the Nazis, he left Germany for the United States in 1933 and taught at Union Theological Seminary and several universities. He wrote more than 30 books, including *The Courage To Be* (1952), *Dynamics of Faith* (1957), and *Systematic Theology* (three volumes, 1951–63). In his own words he was a thinker "on the boundary" between theology and philosophy, the church and the rest of the world, faith and skepticism. By his "method of correlation" he tried to relate Christian faith to the problems of human living.

Timber, growing trees or their wood, which is used for building construction or carpentry. *See* Lumber; Wood.

Timbuktu (Tombouctou), town in Mali, W Africa; became famous throughout Europe as slave and gold market; destroyed by Moroccan army 1591; seized by France 1893. Chief industry is salt trade. Settled 1000. Pop. 19,500.

Time and Motion Studies, efficiency analyses of labor performances involved in the execution of a given industrial activity. Innovated by Frederick W. Taylor (1856–1915) and Frank B. Gilbreth (1868–1924), the studies involve timing each discrete and overall step for a worker performing a standard task under standard working conditions. The analyses focus on eliminating waste motion and unsafe methods to provide an increase in productivity without creating fatigue. The elemental time standards are used in production scheduling estimates.

Time Zone, any of 24 longitudinal divisions of the Earth established for the purpose of determining local mean solar time. Within each zone the overall local time is standardized and differs from time in a neighboring zone by one hour. Time zones east of the Greenwich (0°) meridian will be so many hours ahead of Greenwich Time, while zones west of it will be so many hours behind. By convention, though zones are meant to be equal, they are usually made to coincide with country or state frontiers for convenience.

Timgad, ruined city in NE Algeria; called the Pompeii of N Africa because of extensive remains that include a forum, theater, capitol, library, triumphal arch, and several baths with mosaic floors. Founded AD 100 by Trajan, as Thamugadi or Thamugadis, city declined in 5th century and was destroyed by native tribes in 7th century. Excavated 1881.

Timisoara (Temesvar), city in W Romania, on the Beja Canal. An ancient Roman settlement, it was ruled by Magyars 896; annexed to Hungary 1010; taken by Turks 1552–1716, liberated by Eugene of Savoy; and passed to Romania 1920; site of 14th–15th-century Hunyadi castle (now a museum), 18th-century town hall, Roman Catholic and Eastern Orthodox cathedrals, university (1945). Industries: engineering works, food processing, tobacco, chemicals, textiles, machinery. Pop. 213,054.

Timor, island in Indonesia, largest member of Lesser Sunda Islands of the Malay archipelago; divided into the Nusa Tenggara Timur prov. of Indonesia (S) and Portuguese Timor territory (N). Portuguese Timor annexed by Indonesia in 1976. Settled by Portuguese *c.* 1520 as trading area; modern boundaries were set by treaties 1859, 1893, 1904; occupied by Japanese WWII. Dutch Timor passed to Indonesia 1949; Portuguese Timor was made a separate colony 1926 and part of Portuguese overseas territory 1951. Industries: fishing, agriculture (tobacco, coffee, sugar, tea). Area: 13,070sq mi (33,851sq km). Pop. 1,450,000.

Timor Sea, branch of the Indian Ocean between Timor Island, S Malay Archipelago, and NW coast of Australia; connects in NE with Arafura Sea. Width: 300mi (483km).

Timothy, First and Second Epistles to, two letters in the New Testament written in the name of Paul, encouraging faith in Christ and demanding Orthodox belief.

Timpani, or kettledrums, principal percussion instruments in the symphony orchestra. Usually paired, they are hemispherical vessels with single skins, tuned by screws and hit with padded mallets. Military kettledrums were played on horseback by Asian nomads and brought to Europe by the Crusaders *c.*1100. Modern timpani were introduced into orchestras in the 17th century; pedal action for quick retuning was invented in the 19th century. In 17th- and 18th-century scores two timpani were used—one tuned to the tonic pitches and the other to the dominant pitches (1st and 5th notes of the scale). In modern orchestras 3 or more timpani are used with a variety of tuning.

Timur. *See* Tamerlane.

Tin, metallic element (symbol Sn) of group IVA of the periodic table, known from ancient times. Chief ore is cassiterite (oxide). It is used as a protective coating for steel in tin plate, and in solder, pewter, type metal, and similar alloys. Two allotropes exist: the common metallic form (white tin) changes slowly below 13.2°C to a brittle nonmetallic form (gray tin). Properties: at. no. 50; at. wt. 118.69; sp gr 5.75 (gray), 7.31 (white); melt. pt. 449.60°F (231.89°C); boil. pt. 4,118°F (2,270°C); most common isotope Sn^{118} (24.03%).

Tinamou, grassland and jungle bird found from Mexico to S South America with a heavy body and camouflaging brown or gray coloration. It has a slender, deeply cleft bill; small weak wings; and a short tail. Glossy pale blue to violet eggs (4–9) are incubated by the male in a leaf-mat nest. Length: 9–15in (23–38cm). Family Tinamidae.

Tinbergen, Nikolaas (1906–), Dutch ethologist, who shared with K. Lorenz and K. von Frisch the 1973 Nobel Prize in physiology or medicine for his pioneering work in ethology. Tinbergen, cited for his ability to design ingenious experiments, studied how certain stimuli evoke specific responses. *See also* Ethology.

Tinguely, Jean (1925–), Swiss sculptor. His work incorporated motion through small motors. He experimented with motorization and produced progressively more complicated machines, some of which were self-destructive.

Tin Processing, the extraction of the metal from its principal ore cassiterite (SnO_2).

Tiger

Tiger shark

Tintoretto

Tintoretto, Il, real name **Jacopo Robusti** (1518–94), Italian painter. A major exponent of the Venetian school, he was a leading painter for patrons and Venetian churches. His style had an amazing versatility, and he worked carefully, often utilizing small wax models and candles to study lighting. One of his earliest works is "Apollo and Marsyas" (1545) in the Mannerist style. Other early works include the important "Last Supper" (1547), "Washing of the Feet" (1547), and "St Marcellinus" (1549). His masterpiece, which brought him recognition, is "St Mark Freeing a Slave" (1548), a work marked by vibrant color and vigorous modeling. His important portraits include "Portrait of a Young Man," "Nicola Pruili," "Miracle of St Mark," and the "Marriage at Cana." His later works include "Alvise Cornaro" and "Philosophers." In its final development Tintoretto's style anticipated the Baroque.

Tippecanoe, Battle of (1811), battle on the Tippecanoe River in Illinois in which US forces, under William Henry Harrison, governor of the Indiana Territory, were attacked by the Shawnee under The Prophet, who opposed Harrison's land-grabbing actions. The battle was inconclusive, but it made a hero of Harrison.

Tiranë (Tirana), city and capital of Albania; approx. 20mi (32km) inland from the Adriatic Sea, in E central Albania; capital of Tirane prov.; modern manufacturing and trade center (textiles, soap, food processing); location of music and art schools, agricultural and teachers' colleges, national library and university, Etehem Bey mosque, and Scanderbeg Square (government buildings) at the city's center. Founded early 17th century by Turks. Pop. 175,000.

Tirpitz, Alfred von (1849–1930), German statesman and admiral. He became secretary of state in 1897 and lord high admiral in 1911. Under him the German navy grew to enormous strength by 1914. His policy of unrestricted submarine warfare against Great Britain led to the sinking of the *Lusitania* (1915).

Tiryns, a prehistoric city in E Peloponnesus, S Greece, just N of Nauplia near Gulf of Argos; port of trade with Crete; flourished as cultural center 1600–1100 BC; fell to ruin c. 468 BC with the invasion of Argives. Archeological excavations by Heinrich Schliemann (1884–85) and Wilhelm Dörpfeld uncovered architectural remains of the pre-Homeric period (7th century BC). It is represented as a great state and birthplace of Hercules in *The Illiad.*

Tisza, (Count) Ist ván (1861–1918), Hungarian statesman. He followed his father Kálmán as prime minister of Hungary (1903–05, 1913–17). In that post, he exercised far-reaching authority both in Hungary and in the councils of the dual monarchy in Austria, attempting to prevent war with Serbia in 1914 to avoid larger complications. He was assassinated in 1918.

Tisza (Tisa), river in E Europe, the major tributary of the Danube River; rises at the confluence of the White Tisza and Black Tisza rivers in Carpathian Mts, W Ukrainian republic, USSR; flows W then SW through Hungary; enters NE Yugoslavia to join the Danube above Belgrade; navigable for 450mi (725km) of its 600mi (966km).

Titan, largest of Saturn's satellites. It is comparable in size with Mercury and is believed to support a thin atmosphere, chiefly of methane. Diameter 2980mi (4800km); mean distance from planet 757,640mi (1,220,000km); mean sidereal period 15.95 days.

Titanic, British luxury passenger ship, considered unsinkable, that sank (April 14–15, 1912) on its maiden voyage. The disaster occurred after the liner collided with an iceberg in the North Atlantic. Out of the 2,224 people on board, many of them US and British notables, 1,513 were drowned. The disaster led to the first International Convention for Safety of Life at Sea (1913).

Titanium, common metallic element (symbol Ti) of the first transition series, discovered in 1791 by William Gregor. It is found in many minerals; chief sources are ilmenite (iron titanate) and rutile (oxide). The element is used in steels and other alloys, especially in aircraft and other applications where strength must be combined with lightness. The dioxide (TiO_2) is a white paint pigment. Properties: at. no. 22; at. wt. 47.9; sp gr 4.54; melt. pt. 3,047°F (1,675°C); boil. pt. 6,548°F (3,620°C); most common isotope Ti^{48} (73.94%). *See also* Transition Elements.

Titchener, Edward B(radford) (1867–1927), English psychologist. With the German psychologist Wilhelm Wundt, he was a leader of the *structuralism* school of psychology in the late 19th century. He tried to determine the contents (structures) of the mind by means of systematic introspection. Though his theories were replaced by functionalism and behaviorism, he had encouraged US psychology to be more scientific and systematic. His major publication is *Experimental Psychology* (1901–05).

Titian, real name **Tiziano Veceli** (c.1477–1576), Venetian painter. Early works that show his vigorous and original style include "St Peter with Donor" (c.1508) and the three frescoes of the "Miracles of St Anthony" (1511) in the Scuola del Santo, Padua. His livelier color erupts in the portraits "Ariosto" (1512) and "Gypsy Madonna" (c.1510) and in the St Mark Altarpiece. Two of his most famous works of grandeur are the "Three Ages of Man" (1515) and "Sacred and Profane Love" (1512–15). Titian began a series of mythological pieces for the Duke of Ferrara in 1516, which include "Worship of Venus" (1518–19), "Bacchanal" (1519–22), and "Bacchus and Ariadne" (1523). After 1530 his canvases are marked by bright, shining color, as in the famous "Venus of Urbino" (1538–39). His works of the 1550s are marked by reduced color—"Martyrdom of St Lawrence" (c.1567) and "Rape of Europa" (c. 1560). After 1560 his colors are once again brighter and his works livelier, as in "The Adoration of the Magi" and the "Annunciation" (c.1565). His final works incorporate a new warmth and pathos ("Pieta," 1576).

Titicaca, lake on Peru-Bolivia border, drains S through Desaguadero River into Lake Poopó; highest large navigable lake in the world. Altitude: 12,500ft (3,813m). Length: 110mi (177km). Depth: 900ft (270m).

Titmouse, small, stubby-bodied and large-headed bird of open woodlands and wooded parks of the Northern Hemisphere and Africa. Active, they move abruptly but agilely, and often hang in awkward positions, feeding on insects. Most true titmice nest in self-drilled holes or abandoned woodpecker holes. Family Paridae; genus *Parus*. The long-tailed titmice and bush tits of Eurasia and W North America are larger and build closed, often hanging, nests. Subfamily Aegithalinae. The penduline tits of Eurasia and Africa build some of the most complicated nests in the bird world. Subfamily Remizinae. Most titmice lay large clutches of freckled white eggs.

Tito, original name Josip Broz (1892–1980), effective head of the Yugoslav state from 1943, premier from 1945, and president (1953–80). As a Croatian soldier in the Austro-Hungarian army in World War I, he was captured by the czar's troops (1915) but released by the Communists after the Revolution (1917). Returning home he helped organize the Yugoslav Communist party, and as one of its key members served jail terms after it was outlawed (1929–34)). In World War II he led the partisan resistance forces in Croatia (Draža Mihajlović led the Chetnik guerrillas in Serbia), becoming so powerful that he was able to set up a Communist government in 1945 that achieved international recognition. Russian efforts to control Yugoslavia soon led to a split between Tito and Stalin, who expelled the nation from the Communist bloc in 1948. Tito then became the first independent Communist leader and an important figure to many Third World powers. His rule was marked by strict controls and intolerance of opposition, but in later years he limited the powers of the secret police and encouraged some economic and political freedom.

Titration, method used in analytical chemistry to determine the concentration of a solution by volumetric means. A solution of known concentration is added in measured amounts from a buret to the liquid of unknown concentration until the reaction is complete (as shown by an indicator). The volume removed from the buret enables the unknown concentration to be calculated.

Titus (40?–81), Roman emperor (79–81), elder son of Vespasian. He campaigned in Britain and Germany and captured and destroyed Jerusalem in the Jewish war (AD 70). He was briefly (AD 79) coruler with Vespasian, then sole emperor. As emperor he stopped prosecutions for treason, built lavish baths, and gained great popularity. He died childless and his brother, Emperor Domitian, erected the Arch of Titus. His death remains mysterious.

Titus Andronicus (1593), early work attributed to Shakespeare, but possibly a collaboration. The play tells the bloody tale of Titus Andronicus' revenge on Tamora, queen of the Goths, for her brutal murders and maimings of his children.

Titus Quinctius. *See* Cincinnatus, Lucius.

Tlalnepantla, city in Mexico, 9mi (14km) N of Mexico City; originally inhabited by Otomi Indians; conquered by Aztecs; site of 1583 colonial church, Santa Cecilia pyramids, noted Aztec monuments. Industries: tin, mercury, cement. Pop. 373,657.

Tlalpán, city in central Mexico, S of Mexico City; residence of early Spanish viceroys; site of Cuicuilco pyramid, thought to be oldest man-made structure on continent, approx. 10,000 years old; church (1532). Industries: textiles, paper. Pop. 115,528.

Tlaquepaque, city in W central Mexico; site of railroad junction. Products: sugarcane, tobacco, corn, peanuts, wheat, vegetables. Chief industry is tourism. Pop. 108,119.

Tlaxcala, city in central Mexico, between Mexico City and Veracruz; capital of Tlaxcala State; ancient capital of Tlaxcalan kingdom, conquered 1519 by Hernán Cortes; site of oldest Christian church in the Americas (1521), Ocolan sanctuary and shrine. Products: wheat, corn, beans, livestock. Industries: shoes, rayon, cotton. Pop. 21,424.

Tlaxcaltec, Nahua-speaking Indian group, became allies of the Spaniards during the conquest of the Aztec empire and provided aid for other campaigns in Mexico.

TNT (Trinitrotoluene), a nitrogen compound ($C_7H_5N_3O_6$) used as an explosive. It is a pale yellow crystalline powder, easily soluble in benzene, toluene, and acetone and has a specific gravity of 1.65. TNT melts at 178°F (82°C), but does not explode below 464 °F (240°C), allowing it to be melted in steam-heated vessels and poured into casings. It is then insensitive to shock and requires a detonator to explode. It is used extensively in munitions and nonmilitary demolition.

Toad, tailless amphibian found worldwide except in Antarctica. It is short and fat with a hopping gait and has no teeth in its upper jaw. Parotid glands behind eyes secrete an irritating substance. Toads are differentiated from frogs by being toothless and having a rougher, bumpier skin and a rounder body with shorter legs. Length: 1–7in (2.5–18cm). Well-known toads are Fowler's toad, American toad, and green toad. Family Bufonidae. *See also* Amphibia; Frog.

Toadfish, marine bottom-dwelling fish found in temperate and tropical seas. Capable of living out of water for a short time, it has a large mouth and head and a tapered body. Colors are green, yellow, or brown with dark blotches. Dorsal fin spines are venomous. Length: to 15in (38cm). Among 40 species is the oyster toadfish *Opsanus tau.* Family Batrachoididae.

Tobacco, herb native to the Americas but cultivated throughout the world. It has large leaves with no stalk, and white, pink, or red star-shaped flowers. Height: 2–9ft (0.6–2.7m). *Nicotiana tabacum* is the principal cultivated species. American Indians smoked the leaves of tobacco and used them medicinally well before the arrival of Europeans in the New World. These plants were more potent than modern blends and often produced unconsciousness in the smoker. Seeds were brought to Europe in 1556–57 by Jean Andre Thevet. Settlers in Virginia obtained seeds from the Spanish colonies (1612) and soon tobacco was the major crop of the Virginia colony and America's first export. Leaves are prepared for smoking by curing (drying) and then aging. Family Solanaceae (nightshade family).

Tobago. *See* Trinidad and Tobago.

Tobit, book in the Roman Catholic and Eastern Orthodox Christian Old Testament, regarded by Protestants and Jews as part of the Apocrypha. A travel narrative of Tobit's son, Tobias, the story involves Tobias' recovery of his family's wealth and Tobit's recovery of his sight through the efforts of the disguised angel, Raphael. *See also* Apocrypha; Old Testament.

Tobogganing, sport in which participants coast down snowy hillsides on a flat-bottomed vehicle made of hard wood. The toboggan is usually 8 feet (2.4m) long and 3 feet (0.9m) wide, and curled at the front end. It is controlled by shifting weight and by trailing one's feet. *See also* Bobsledding.

Tobruk (Tubruq), port town in NE Libya, on the Mediterranean Sea; disputed during WWII, it was taken alternately by British and Germans (1940–42); located on coastal road. Chief industry is trade. Pop. 28, 000.

Togo, independent nation of West Africa; bordered by Ghana (W), Upper Volta (N), Benin (E), and Gulf of Guinea (S). The Togo Hills running centrally from the NE to the SW, highest point Pic Baumann 3,234ft (986m), divide the country into two regions. To the SE rivers flow directly into the Gulf of Guinea, whereas to the NW they drain N and W into the Volta River system. Temperatures are high throughout the year, and rainfall has a pronounced seasonal variation with by far the most falling during the summer; precipitation also declines inland and vegetation changes from coastal mangrove swamps to savannah and then to more arid grasslands. Subsistence farmers grow maize, millet, and cassava; cash crops are cocoa, coffee, palm nuts, and peanuts; livestock is most important in the N. Phosphate is the principal mineral, and marble and limestone are quarried. Industry is of small scale and devoted to processing agricultural products. The population is made up of about 30 ethnic groups, many of which are not indigenous to Togo. A former UN Trust Territory administered by France; became a republic within French Union in 1956; becoming fully independent in 1960. In 1967 the military assumed control of the government. Elections for a civilian government were held in 1979, although Gnassingbe Eyadéma, who had led the coup, became president. During the late 1970s the country's economy was seriously affected by a drought, and in the 1980s by a decrease in the export of phosphates.

PROFILE

Official name: Togolese Republic
Area: 21,617sq mi (56,000sq km)
Population: 2,472,000
Density: 114per sq mi (44per sq km)
Chief cities: Lomé (capital); Sokodé; Palimé
Government: Republic
Religion: Animist, Christian, Muslim
Language: French (official), tribal
Gross national product: (1970) $270,000,000
Trading partners: (major): United Kingdom, Japan

Tojo, Hideki (1885–1948), Japanese general and political figure. As prime minister (1941–44) during World War II, he approved the Pearl Harbor attack and was responsible for all aspects of the war effort. He resigned in July 1944 when Japan lost Saipan. He was tried for war crimes by the Allies after the defeat of Japan, was found guilty and was hanged.

Tokugawa, Japanese family holding the title of shogun and maintaining effective control of Japan (1603–1867). Under their shogunate, centralized feudalism was based on an intricate system of allegiances of "autonomous" daimyo (feudal lords) to the Tokugawa family, who owned much of the country's wealth and a quarter of the farmland in strategic locations. The period of their rule is notable for its intense isolationism, improvements in farming, increase in domestic trade, and advances in overall literacy. The regime weakened in the 19th century and fell because of internal and external pressures in 1867, resulting in the Meiji Restoration. *See also* Meiji Restoration. *See also* Edo period.

Tokyo (Tokio), largest city in Japan, at the head of Tokyo Bay, E Honshu; capital of Tokyo prefecture; administrative, cultural, commercial, and industrial center of Japan. Founded in the 12th century as Yedo (or Edo), the village became increasingly important after it was fortified 1457; it became capital of the powerful Tokugawa shogunate under Ieyaso (1603). The city grew rapidly in the 18th and 19th centuries, and as the Japanese Reformation reestablished imperial power, it was made capital of Japan 1868 (replacing Kyoto) and renamed Tokyo ("eastern capital"). Most of Tokyo was destroyed by earthquake and fire 1923; however, the city was reconstructed as a modern metropolis; it was further modernized after extensive US bombings destroyed most of Tokyo 1944–45; the Imperial Palace and surrounding gardens, however, as well as many temples and shrines, remained intact. Tokyo is now the center of a massive industrial-commercial belt extending along the W shore of Tokyo Bay, and including Kawasaki and Yokohama, the latter serving as seaport for Tokyo and vicinity. Modern Tokyo contains over 150 colleges, universities, and specialized schools, including the University of Tokyo (1877), Kieo-Gijuku University (1867), Rikkyo University (1883), Waseda University (1882), Tokyo Women's Medical College (1900); art museums include the Imperial Museum and the Museum of Arms; Asakusa entertainment district is the center of Tokyo's night life, and Ginza Street is a famous shopping area. The city is governed by a popularly elected governor and assembly, with separate assemblies administering local matters of the city's 23 wards. Industries: metals, machinery, electronic and transit equipment, chemicals, textiles, shipbuilding, automobiles, consumer products, tourism. Pop. 8,500,000.

Tokyo Bay, arm of the W Pacific Ocean, on SE coast of Honshu, Japan; forms a large harbor for Tokyo, Yokohama, and Yokosuka; with Osaka Bay, it is one of the two principal port areas of Japan. Length: approx. 30mi (48km). Width: approx. 10–20 mi (16–32km).

Tolbert, William Richard, Jr. (1913–80), Liberian political leader. He served in the treasury and legislature before he became vice president (1951–71) and then president from 1971 until his assassination in a coup d'état in 1980. He was also leader of the Baptist World Alliance for Africa (1965–70) and chairman of the Organization of African Unity (1979–80).

Toledo, city in Spain, on Tagus River, 40mi (64km) SSW of Madrid; capital of Toledo prov. One of Spain's most historically and architecturally important cities, it was captured by Romans 192 BC; a Visigoth king made Toledo his capital 6th century AD; taken 712 by Arabs, in 1085 it was reconquered by Alfonso VI. It is the site of a cathedral (begun 1226), Santo Cristo de la Cruz (Gothic chapel), Tránsito (14th-century synagogue), 13th-century school of scholars and translators, 7th-century wall, Aleaga (a Moorish citadel), former home of El Greco, now a museum containing his paintings. Industries: silk products, metal work, surgical equipment, shell castings. Area: (prov.) 5,934sq mi (15,370sq km). Pop. (city) 44,382; (prov.) 468,925.

Toledo, port city in NW Ohio, on Maumee River as it enters Lake Erie; seat of Lucas co; formed 1833 by union of two villages, Port Lawrence and Vistula. Port Lawrence was est. 1817 next to Fort Industry, built by Gen. Anthony Wayne 1794 after Battle of Fallen Timbers. In 1835, Toledo was awarded to Ohio by Congress after a boundary dispute with Michigan, in the so-called Toledo War (bloodless); site of University of Toledo (1872) and Mary Manse College (1873). Industries: glass, machine tools, oil refining, plastics, cosmetics, tools, dies. Inc. 1837 as Toledo, named for Spanish city. Pop. (1980) 354,635.

Toleration, Act of (1689), English legislation permitting freedom of religious practice to Protestant dissenters, subject to their taking oaths of allegiance to William and Mary. It modified the Test Act, but it did not remove Protestants' political and social disabilities, nor did it extend to Roman Catholics. *See also* Test Act.

Tolkien, J(ohn) R(onald) R(euel) (1892–1973), English philology scholar who achieved fame with his imaginative epic trilogy, *The Lord of The Rings* (3 vols., 1954–55). Both his prose style and fantastic world are reminiscent of Norse sagas and Anglo-Saxon poetry, which he taught at Oxford University. The trilogy is introduced by *The Hobbit* (1937).

Tolman, Edward C(hace) (1886–1959), US psychologist, b. West Newton, Mass. He was a leading learning theorist. He devised a theory called "purposive behaviorism" involving trial-and error, goal-directed behavior, and cognitive processes in *Purposive Behavior in Animals and Men* (1932).

Tolpuddle Martyrs, name given to six British farm laborers sentenced (1834) to seven years' transportation to Australia for trade union activities in Tolpuddle. The tremendous popular reaction in their favor defeated the government's intention of creating an example to prevent further working-class discontent. Their sentences were remitted in 1836.

Tolstoy, (Count) Leo (1828–1910), Russian novelist and philosopher. While serving in the army, he began the autobiographical trilogy *Childhood, Boyhood, and Youth* (1852–57). After taking part in the defense of Sevastopol (1855), he lived on his estate, Yasnaya Polyana, and in St Petersburg, marrying in 1862. After writing *War and Peace* (1865–69) and *Anna Karenina* (1875–77), he underwent a spiritual crisis, as recorded in *Confession* (1879). Later works, including *The Death of Ivan Ilyich* (1886), *The Kreutzer Sonata* (1889), and *Resurrection* (1899–1900), advocate nonviolence and a simple life and reflect his rejection of Orthodox Christianity. Estranged from his wife, he died after fleeing from his home. *See also* Anna Karenina; War and Peace.

Toltec, the Aztec name from their city of Tollán. A major prehistoric culture in Hidalgo, Mexico, dating from about AD 900–1200. A wide-ranging people, their influence extended from the later capital at Tula to Chichén Itzá in Yucatán, and ultimately as far south as Guatemala.

Toluca, city in central Mexico, at the foot of Nevado de Toluca, 35mi (56km) SW of Mexico City; site of airfield, state museum, El Calvario shrine. Industries: tile, handcrafts, silver, gold, copper, textiles, cigars, brushes, livestock. Pop. 141,726.

Tomato, herb native to the Americas. Not used as food until the 18th century, it was believed poisonous and was grown as an ornamental. The plant was cultivated in Europe as early as 1544 and introduced to the American colonies in 1710. Leaves are deeply toothed or lobed and yellow flowers produce the familiar green fruit which turns reddish-orange as it ripens. Species: *Lycopersicum esculentum.* The small cherry tomato is a variety *(cerasiforme). L. pimpenellifolium,* the currant tomato, is native to Peru and Ecuador and produces a very small fruit. Family Solanaceae.

Tombaugh, Clyde William (1906–), US astronomer, b. Streator, Ill. Working at the Lowell Observatory, Flagstaff, Arizona, he made the discovery of Pluto, the outermost planet of the solar system, in 1930.

Tombstone, city in SE Arizona, about 69mi (110km) SE of Tucson. Primarily a residential town, its legendary past makes it a popular tourist attraction; features Boot Hill, the OK Corral (scene of the Earp and Clanton gunfight) and annual 3-day Helldorado. Inc. 1881. Pop. 1,241.

Tom Sawyer, The Adventures of (1876), autobiographical novel by Mark Twain about the adventures of a young boy (Tom) in and out of his hometown of St Petersburg, Mo., where he lives with his Aunt Polly, friend Huckleberry Finn, and sweetheart Becky Thatcher. Tom and Huck witness a murder in a cemetery and later run away. Thought to be dead, they return to their own funeral and are taken for corpses.

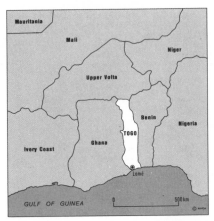

Togo

Leo Tolstoy

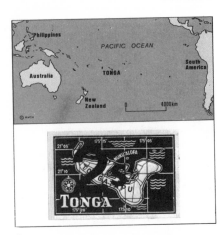

Tonga

Tom reveals the identity of the murderer (Injun Joe), and later Tom and Becky get lost in a cave where Injun Joe is hiding. After their escape Huck and Becky return to find the treasure that Injun Joe buried. One of Twain's best loved and finest novels, it is a combination of well-told adventure and social comment. *See also* Huckleberry Finn, The Adventures of.

Tomsk, city in Russian SFSR, USSR, on the Tom River, 125mi (201km) NE of Novosibirsk; capital of Tomsk oblast. It was founded 1604 by Boris Godunov; became an important trading post; leading 19th-century Siberian city; bypassed by the Trans-Siberian Railroad, it lost leadership after 1900; site of university (1888), polytechnic institute (1900), medical and teachers' colleges, electro-technical and rail transportation schools, library, and botanic gardens. Industries: electric motors, ball bearings, rubber goods, pencils, matches, light bulbs, flour, tobacco, alcohol, meat, vegetable oil. Pop. 432,000.

Tom Thumb (1838–83), US midget, made famous by P.T. Barnum, b. Charles S. Stratton in Bridgeport, Conn. Brought to New York in 1842, he was billed as Gen. Tom Thumb. He later married Lavinia Warren, a dwarf under Barnum's employ. They toured Europe and also met President Lincoln.

Tone, Theobald Wolfe (1768–98), Irish revolutionary leader. Tone, wanting the Irish to ignore religious differences and combine for political independence, founded the United Irishmen (1791) and promoted the Catholic Relief Act (1793). After visiting America (1795), Tone masterminded the abortive French invasion of Ireland (1796). Captured in 1798, he committed suicide.

Tone Languages, languages that use the pitch of the voice as a major device in giving meaning or indicating grammatical relationships. For example, in Efik language of Nigeria, "akpa" spoken with a rising tone means "first," with a descending tone means "he dies"; in Dinka in Sudan "pany" in a high tone means "wall," in a low tone "walls." Many Oriental and African tongues are tonal.

Tonga, independent republic in SW Pacific Ocean; officially, Kingdom of Tonga; an archipelago comprised of approx. 170 islands, which are divided into three groups: Tongatapu, Vavau, and Haapai, traditionally known as Friendly Islands; only 36 are important. N islands are of volcanic origin, S islands are mostly coral formations. The archipelago was discovered 1616 by Dutch; English missions were est. in 1797, and British power gradually increased until the islands became a British protectorate (1900) under King George Tupou II, insuring British control over foreign affairs and trade while the islands remained self-governing; the group became completely independent in 1970. The government is composed of a legislative assembly, a prime minister with a cabinet and a privy council, as well as a king. Native inhabitants are Polynesian; subsistence farming and fishing are chief occupations. At age 16, male Tongans have a legal right to 8acres (3.2hectares) of land, to be used for farming, but overcrowding on some of the islands has made it impossible for all Tongans to take advantage of this right. Tourism is important, and some Tonganese find employment in New Zealand as guest workers. Two devastating storms (1982) destroyed the coconut plantations. Chief exports: copra, bananas. Area, 270sq mi (699sq km); Pop. 96,000.

Tongue, muscular organ that helps move food in the mouth, helps move it to the back for swallowing, and functions in speech. The tongue contains the taste buds, groups of cells that distinguish the four basic tastes: bitter, tasted on the sides and back of the tongue and the palate; sweet and salty, tasted on the tip and front of the tongue; and sour, tasted mainly on the sides of the tongue.

Tonkin Gulf, Resolution of (1964), US Congressional resolution authorizing the president to take military action to defend US forces and US allies in South Vietnam. It was passed at the urging of President Lyndon B. Johnson after US destroyers in the Gulf of Tonkin allegedly were attacked by North Vietnamese torpedo boats. The resolution was later used by Presidents Johnson and Nixon to justify escalation of US military activities in Southeast Asia. It was repealed in 1970.

Tonsil, mass of lymphatic tissue located at the back of the throat, on either side of the opening of the nasopharynx. It has a pitted surface that frequently becomes infected (tonsillitis). Chronic cases are often treated by surgical removal of the tonsils (tonsillectomy), often along with the adenoids.

Tonsillectomy, surgical removal of the palatine tonsils, which are masses of lymphoid tissue lying in the area around the soft palate and the base of the tongue and between the arches of the passages leading to the pharynx.

Tonsillitis, acute or chronic inflammation of the tonsils, often caused by streptococcus infection. Tissues surrounding the tonsils frequently form pus during acute attacks, causing white specks or coating with white exudate.

Tooth, hard, bonelike, structure located on the jaws or other bones of the oral cavity in vertebrates. Teeth are used mainly for seizing and tearing food and for defense. All true teeth are typically made of three layers. Mammalian teeth have (1) an outer layer of enamel, a hard dense substance over the crown of the tooth, (2) a middle layer of dentine, similar in composition to bone and nourished by (3) the innermost pulp, which contains cells, blood vessels, and a nerve. The root of the tooth below the gum line is covered with cementum, which is not quite as hard as dentine. Many vertebrates other than mammals have rootless teeth; a substance called vitodentine, not quite as hard as enamel, covers the dentine layer. Mammals typically have incisors, canines, premolars, and molars; most other vertebrates have teeth that generally resemble each other.

Toothache, any pain associated with malfunctioning of the teeth and their surrounding tissues. The major cause is tooth decay, or caries, but disease of the gums, nerve irritations, or infections can also be involved. Treatment varies but cleaning and filling of cavities is a standard procedure.

Tooth Shell, or tusk shell, any of several hundred marine species of mollusk having a tubular, toothlike shell that is open at both ends. It burrows into sand with a three-lobed conical foot at the wider end. It has small filaments to gather tiny organisms for food. Sexes are separate and fertilization is external. Length: 0.5–5in (13–127mm). Class Scaphopoda. *See also* Mollusk.

Topaz, an orthosilicate mineral, aluminum fluosilicate ($Al_2SiO_4(F,OH)_2$). Found in pegmatites. Orthorhombic system columnar prisms and granular masses. Transparent; glassy; colorless, white, blue, or yellow; hardness 8; sp gr 3.5. Some large crystals are of gem quality. Some gem varieties of quartz are sometimes misnamed "topaz."

Topeka, capital city of Kansas, in NE Kansas, 55mi (89km) W of Kansas City; seat of Shawnee co. Situated on the Kansas River, Topeka is set in the midst of fertile farm region. The city was founded by antislavery settlers in 1854 and became the state capital in 1861. It is celebrated in song as the center of the Atchison, Topeka, and Santa Fe Railroad; site of Menninger Clinic, renowned for its psychiatric research and treatment programs, the state capitol, the Episcopal cathedral, Forbes Air Force Base, Washburn University of Topeka (1865). Industries: marketing, shipping, and processing of cattle, wheat, and other farm products. Inc. 1857. Pop. (1980) 115,266.

Topographic Mapping, representation of the surface of the Earth in relief, using contour lines drawn through points of equal elevation. Intervals are arbitrary. Most topographic maps are made from aerial photographs. Special plotting instruments allow the cartographer to follow a "floating" dot along an elevation, producing contour lines in sequence.

Topography, study of surfaces and their mapping, using fixed points as bases for the calculation. The result of topographic mapping is a relief map or a plan for construction. The terrain of a region is explored using surveyors' instruments or aerial photogrammetry (plotting elevations from photographs). *See also* Surveying.

Topology, basic branch of mathematics concerned with those properties of geometric figures that remain unchanged after a continuous deforming transformation, as by squeezing, stretching, or twisting (but not tearing or breaking). The number of boundaries of a surface is such a property. All plane closed curves are topologically equivalent to a circle; a cube, cylinder, and cone are topologically equivalent to a sphere. These figures can be considered sets of points, each point of one set being transformable into one point in another set. They are also treated as a regular combination of simpler figures.

Torah, meaning "to teach" in Hebrew, is strictly the first five books of the Old Testament, which are Genesis, Exodus, Leviticus, Numbers, and Deuteronomy. These books are also called the Pentateuch. Moses is generally claimed as the author, having received inspiration from God on Mt Sinai. It is kept in the ark in synagogues and read during Sabbath services. Torah may also indicate the entire Jewish Bible and all laws and customs of Judaism.

Tornado, also called cyclone or twister, a funnel-shaped, violently rotating storm column hanging from a cumulonimbus cloud from which it forms, with a center often several hundred yards in diameter in which devastating winds range from 100 to 300mi (160 to 483km) per hour. Tornadoes occur in deep low pressure areas, associated with fronts or other instabilities, on any continent and in the United States most frequently between the Rockies and Appalachians.

Torne (Torneträsk), river in extreme N Sweden; rises from Torneträsk Lake near the Norwegian border; flows SSE to Pajala, from which point it forms the border of Sweden and Finland before emptying into the Gulf of Bothnia. Length: 354mi (570km).

Toronto, commercial port city in SE Ontario, Canada, 360mi (580km) W of Montreal on Toronto Bay at NW end of Lake Ontario; capital of Ontario prov.; seat of York co; 2nd-largest city in Canada. First visited 1615 by French explorer Étienne Brulé, it was the site of a French fur-trading post, Fort Rouillé, which was burned 1759 to prevent British capture. In 1787, British Loyalists purchased the land from the Indians, and York was founded 1793; by 1797, it replaced Niagara-on-the-Lake as capital of Upper Canada. During the War of 1812 it was besieged twice by US troops, which was used as an excuse for British invasion of Washington 1814; site of separatist uprising 1837; served as capital of Canada 1849–51, 1855–59; made provincial capital 1867; the Municipality of Metropolitan Toronto was est. 1953. Toronto is the site of Exhibition Park hosting the annual Canadian National Exposition (since 1912), Art Gallery of Ontario, Royal Conservatory of Music, Royal Ontario Museum, Casa Loma castle (1911), Ontario Science Center (1919); among its many educational facilities are University of Toronto (1827), Victoria College (1836), Knox College (1844), University of Trinity College (1852); seat of Anglican and Roman Catholic archbishops, and home of hockey's Toronto Maple Leafs and football's Toronto Argonauts. Exports: grain, livestock, meat. Industries: electrical equipment, brewing, printing, publishing, iron and steel products, sugar refining, distilling, flour, meat packing, farm machinery. Inc. 1834. Pop. 633,318.

Torpedo, self-propelled underwater missile used by submarines, small surface warships, and aircraft to destroy enemy vessels. Modern torpedoes may be launched by rocket boosters and often have internal electronic equipment for guiding the missile to the target.

Torpedo Boat, small, inexpensive, fast coastal naval craft armed with torpedoes and, recently, with antiship guided missiles. Torpedo boats are generally used to defend or attack coastal shipping and installations, and to conduct hit-and-run attacks against larger warships.

Torpedo Ray, or electric ray, flat-bodied elasmobranch found in all tropical and temperate marine waters from shallow depths to 3000ft (915m). Usually shades of brown above and whitish below, it has winglike fins at the sides of the head and a well-developed tail and tail fin. Electric glands next to the head can produce up to 200 volts. Length: 5ft (1.5m); weight: 160–200lb (72–90kg). There are 11 genera with 36 species including the Atlantic *Torpedo nobiliana*. Family Torpedinidae. *See also* Chondrichthyes: Ray.

Torquay, noted seaside resort and yachting center in SW England; now part of district of Torbay. Pop. 108,888.

Torque, the vector quantity describing the rotational force about an axis. A force F applied at a distance r from an axis of rotation produces a torque $T + r \times F$.

Torquemada, Tomás de (1420–98), Spanish churchman and grand inquisitor. He was a Dominican priest and was confessor to Ferdinand II and Isabella I. In 1483 they named him head of the Spanish Inquisition. He became noted for the severity of his judgments and the harshness of his punishments; he is generally held responsible for most of the excesses of the early Spanish Inquisition. He was chiefly responsible for the expulsion of the Jews from Spain in 1492. Toward the end of his career, his power was somewhat restricted by the pope, but he remained grand inquisitor until his death. *See also* Spanish Inquisition.

Torrance, city in S California, 15mi (24km) SSW of Los Angeles. Industries: aircraft, electronic equipment, oil, chemical, aluminum products. Founded 1912; inc. 1921. Pop. (1980) 131,497.

Torreón, city in NE Mexico, on the Nazas River. Industries: mining, cotton, flour, steel, iron, textiles. Pop. 257,000.

Torrey, John (1796–1873), US botanist and chemist, b. New York City. He conducted major studies of North American plant life and amassed one of the most valuable botanical libraries and herbariums of his time. His works include *Flora of the Northern and Middle Sections of the United States* (1824) and *Flora of the State of New York* (1843), which he wrote after being appointed state botanist (1836).

Torricelli, Evangelista (1608–47), Italian physicist, who served as assistant and secretary to Galileo during the latter's last three months of life. He is credited with the first man-made vacuum (the Torricellian vacuum), and he invented the first barometer. He also constructed a primitive microscope and made some improvements on the telescope. His work in geometry eventually contributed to the development of integral calculus.

Torrid Zone, a belt of the Earth between the tropics over which the Sun is vertical at some period of the year.

Torsion, in mechanics, the strain in a material subjected to a simple twist. In a rod or shaft, such as an automobile drive shaft, the torsion angle of twist is inversely proportional to the fourth power of the rod diameter and the shear modulus of the material.

Tort, a form of law that settles the rights of monetary damages for injuries in both civil and private cases. Usually, parties involved are private persons or business corporations. Injuries caused from actions such as bursting dams, spoiled food, dangerous structures, or swindling usually constitute a tort case.

Tortoise, any turtle that is terrestrial in habit. The main genera are *Testudo* and *Geochelone* with many species in Europe, Africa, Asia, and South America, and *Gopherus* with three species in North America. There are also species of pond turtle (Emydidae) that have become mainly terrestrial (eg, the North American box turtle *Terrapene carolina*).

Tortoiseshell Butterfly, widespread group of medium-sized anglewing butterflies with wings having tortoiseshell-like markings of black, brown, and white. Genus *Nymphalis.*

Tortoiseshell Cat, also Spanish cat, chintz and white, old variety of domestic cat characterized by patched long- or short-haired coat of black, and light and dark red. The addition of cream is calico. This color is sex-linked and most cats of this breed are female; the males are sterile.

Tortuga (Île de la Tortue), island in the West Indies, off N coast of Haiti. In 17th century, it was used by pirates and buccaneers as a base for attacks on European fleets; administered by Haitian government. Area: approx. 70sq mi (181sq km). Pop. 10,000.

Tory Party, British political party, *c.*1680–1815, chiefly representing the interests and opinions of the country gentry and Anglican clergy. Originally applied derisively to James II's supporters, "Tory" became a general term for those opposed to religious toleration, parliamentary reform, and foreign wars. After 1815 new political alignments caused the term "Conservative" generally to replace "Tory."

Toscanini, Arturo (1867–1957), Italian conductor. He was music director of opera houses in Milan (La Scala) and Bayreuth and of the Salzburg Festivals. During his tenure at La Scala he raised that opera house to one of the world's finest. He conducted the Metropolitan Opera (1907–21), the New York Philharmonic Orchestra (1928–33), and the NBC Symphony (1937–54), which was created specifically for him. Famed for his temperamental and dictatorial ways, he strove throughout his career to bring perfection to operatic and symphonic performances.

Totem, plant, animal, or thing with a special relationship to a clan, tribe, or people. Totems are found in many cultures. A group identifies with its totem, which plays a large part in ritual and ceremony. The group often believes the totem to be its ancestor. *See also* Taboo.

Totem Pole, thick carved painted pole erected by the Indians of the Pacific Northwest. A totem pole portrays real and mythical animals and objects, which reveal the lineage of the household that erected it.

Toucan, colorful, gregarious forest bird found from Mexico to Argentina and known for its enormous, swollen, and colorful bill. They have red, yellow, blue, black, or orange plumage, often in vivid patterns, and feed on fruit and berries. They nest in tree holes, laying glossy white eggs (1–4) that are incubated by both parents. Length: 1–2ft (30.5–61cm). Family Ramphastidae.

Toucan Constellation. *See* Tucana.

Touch, the principal skin sense, occurs when the skin is mechanically deformed (moved). In addition to free nerve endings, the skin also has special basket cell receptors, which are particularly prevalent around bases of hairs. Touch probably interacts with the kinesthetic sense to produce sensations about body position; the sense of touch may persist even when a limb has been amputated.

Toulon, seaport city in SE France, on Mediterranean Sea, 30mi (48km) ESE of Marseilles. A Roman naval station in 3rd century, it passed to France 1481; scene of Napoleon's victory over English, Spanish, and French royalists 1793; French fleet was scuttled here after German occupation 1942, site of French naval base, church of Ste Marie Majeure (17th–18th centuries). Industries: tourism, shipbuilding, cork, furniture, chemicals. Pop. 185,050.

Toulouse, city in S France, on Garonne River, 133mi (214km) ESE of Bordeaux; capital of Haute-Garonne dept.; canals connect city to Mediterranean Sea and Atlantic Ocean. Capital of Visigoths 5th century, it was captured by Clovis 508; became part of French crown lands 1271; scene of Protestant massacre 1562; site of University of Toulouse (1230), Romanesque Basilica (11th–12th centuries), 16th-century Assezat mansion; center of French aeronautic industry. Industries: paper, knit goods, fertilizer, ammunition. Founded *c.* 4th century BC. Pop. 383,176.

Toulouse-Lautrec, Henri de (1864–1901), French painter, graphic artist, and designer of posters. A childhood accident in which he broke both legs left him permanently deformed. He led a night life, frequenting Paris music halls, and spent his later days in an asylum, where he died of alcoholism. Nonetheless, his vision of the decadent life gave strength to his work; his depictions of bars and circuses reflect both the superficial gaiety and the underlying pathos. His fine work, influenced by both Degas and Gauguin, retains a biting and satiric quality, which is evident in his famous "Moulin Rouge," where he includes himself in the picture, a tiny and certainly unromanticized figure. He was immensely productive, executing numerous paintings and lithographs, which received little attention at the time.

Touraco, or **Turaco,** inquisitive, agile, cuckoolike bird of SE Africa known for its special feather pigments. Forest-dwelling turacos, with red wings due to the copper-containing turacin pigment, are typified by the white-crested touraco *(Tauraco leucolophus)* that is green with red wings and white cheeks and crest; length: 14in (35cm). Bushland-dwelling touracos are typified by the gray plantain-eater *(Crinifer zonurus)* which is brown and white with a greenish-yellow bill. They build fragile, twig-and-stick nests for whitish or green-tinted eggs (2). Family Musophagidae.

Touraine, historical region of NW central France, bounded anciently by Le Maine (N), Orléanais (NE), Berry (SE), Marche (S), Poitou (SW), Saumurois (W), Anjou (NW); capital was Tours. Region now includes most of Indre-et-Loire and parts of Loir-et-Cher and Indre depts. Known for 15th- and 16th-century chateaux, it was made part of French crownlands 1204; called "Garden of France" for its fertile valleys, vineyards, and orchards; birthplace of Descartes, Rabelais, and Balzac.

Touré, Ahmed Sékou (1922–84), African nationalist and president of Guinea (1958–84). He entered politics as a champion of the labor movement. He helped form black African labor unions and was often chosen as Guinea's territorial representative in the 1950s. He became president of independent Guinea in 1958 and, often in conflict with his African neighbors, severely repressed opposition. He survived an assassination attempt in 1980 and died in office in 1984.

Tourmaline, a silicate mineral, sodium aluminum borosilicate, found in igneous and metamorphic rocks. Hexagonal system; glassy; opaque to transparent; black, red, green, brown, and blue. Hardness 7; sp gr 3.1. Some crystals prized as gems.

Tours, city in NW central France, on Loire River, 129mi (208km) SW of Paris; capital of Indre-et-Loire dept.; scene of battle in which Charles Martel defeated Saracens (AD 732); seat of French government during siege of Paris (1870); birthplace of Honoré de Balzac (1799); site of 18th-century bridge over Loire, 13th–16th-century Cathedral of St Gatien, 17th–18th-century Archbishop's Palace. Industries: tourism, food processing, metals, pharmaceuticals. Pop. 145,441.

Toussaint L'Ouverture, François Dominique (*c.* 1744–1803), Haitian independence leader. The educated son of slave parents, Toussaint became an officer in the French colonial army. He joined the Spanish army when the Spaniards occupied the island in 1793, but withdrew his support in 1794 and emerged as master of the northern part of the colony. By 1800 Toussaint had defeated his rival André Rigaud and controlled all of Hispaniola. In 1802, Napoleon sent troops commanded by Charles Leclerc to re-establish French authority; this they failed to do, but Toussaint was betrayed, captured, and taken to France, where he died in prison.

Tower of London, fortress on the north bank of the Thames River in London.

Towhee, drab-colored North American sparrow. The chewink *(Pipilo erythrophthalmus)* male has black, white, and rust plumage. The green-tailed towhee *(Chlorura chlorura)* of the W United States has a green tail and reddish crown. Family Fringillidae.

Arturo Toscanini

Henri de Toulouse-Lautrec: painting

Spencer Tracy in Old Man and the Sea

Townes, Charles Hard (1915–), US physicist, b. Greenwill, S.C.. He invented the maser, for which he shared a Nobel Prize in 1964 with Alexander Prokhorov and Nikolai Basov. The Michelson-Morley experiment was accurately confirmed with the aid of masers. *See also* Maser.

Townshend Acts (1767), a series of taxes levied on the American colonies by the British Parliament. Proposed by Chancellor of the Exchequer Charles Townshend, they were designed to provide revenue to defray the cost of colonial government. They taxed such imports as glass, paper, lead, tea, and paint. The acts were opposed by the colonists—"Taxation without representation is tyranny" was the popular phrase. The adverse colonial reaction caused repeal of all duties except that on tea (1770).

Toxemia, poisoned condition of the blood due to circulation in it of bacterial, chemical, or hormonal toxins. Toxemia is often the name applied to a condition occurring in late pregnancy marked by high blood pressure, kidney failure, and convulsions.

Toxin, a poisonous substance, usually referring to a product of certain plants, animals, or bacteria, such as the organisms that cause diphtheria and tetanus. The controlled use of bacterial toxins as immunologic agents has been effective in providing protection against those and other diseases. Antibodies produced against diluted toxins are effective immediately against later invasion of bacteria.

Toxoid, a bacterial toxin that has lost its virulence but can still stimulate the production of antibodies against a disease. *See also* Toxin.

Toxoplasmosis, infection occurring in all warm-blooded animals, including man, of microorganisms of the genus *Toxoplasma.* Symptoms resemble the common cold in adult humans, but can be very damaging to the central nervous system or the eyes of infants.

Toy Dog, dog breeds of small size. Toy dogs range from the tiny Chihuahua and Maltese to the large Pekingese and pug. Most toy breeds are dwarfed from larger types, although the Maltese is not. Often pets of nobility, objects of barter, and royal gifts, they were popular since ancient Greece. Also called pillow, sleeve, lap, comforter, and under the table dogs, they remain popular pets. Weight: 1–18lb (0.5–8kg).

Toynbee, Arnold Joseph (1889–1975), English historian. Educated at Winchester and Balliol College, Oxford, he taught at Oxford and the University of London. He worked for the government during both world wars and was a member of the British delegation to the Paris Peace Conference (1919). His masterpiece, *A Study of History* (12 vols., 1934–61), emphasized the need to examine whole civilizations rather than individual nations.

Trachea, tube that extends from the larynx to about the middle of the breastbone. It is lined with cilia that prevent dirt and other substances from entering the lungs. At its lower end, the trachea splits into two branches, the bronchi, one of which then passes into each lung.

Tracheophyte. *See* Vascular Plant.

Tracheotomy, procedure in which an incision is made through the skin into the trachea (windpipe) to enable breathing or give oxygen.

Trachodon, or anatosaurus, large, amphibious, ornithopod dinosaur abundant during late Cretaceous times in North America. The front ends of its upper and lower jaws were toothless and flattened like a duck bill. Farther back in the jaws were hundreds of shearing teeth for chopping vegetation. When swimming, it used its webbed feet and powerful, flattened tail. Unlike many other duck-billed dinosaurs, it had no head crest. Length: 35ft (10.6m). *See also* Ornithopoda.

Trachoma, chronic, contagious rickettsial conjunctivitis characterized by inflammatory granulations on the conjunctival surfaces. In early stages, it responds to sulfonamide treatment. It is a major cause of blindness in Africa and Asia. *See also* Conjunctivitis.

Track and Field, general name for various athletic events. They include competition in foot racing, jumping, hurdling, throwing, and vaulting. Generally, at a track and field meet, the field events (throwing and vaulting) are held within the infield area of the oval track. The field events include the running hop-step-and-jump, the broad jump, the pole vault, the shot put, the discus throw, the hammer throw, the javelin throw, and the high jump. The track events include running races from 60 yards (54.6m) to 10,000 meters, hurdle races from 120 yards (109.2m) to 440 yards (400m), relay races from 400 meters to 4 miles (6.4km), and walking races of 20,000 and 50,000 meters. A combination of both track and field events includes the decathlon (10 events held over a 2-day period) and the pentathlon (5 events in the same day). Scoring for team events is on a point basis. When two teams compete, the scoring is five points for first place, three points for second place, and one point for third place. With more than two teams, the points may range from ten for first place to one for sixth place.

History. Track and field events were held at the original Olympic Games in Greece in 776 BC. The competition was revived in England in the 12th century, and in 1864, Oxford defeated Cambridge in the first college meet. In the United States, the first organized meet was held in 1876. The sport played a major role in the successful resumption of the Olympic Games at Athens in 1896.

Traction, exertion of a pulling force on a part of the skeleton to ensure proper alignment of a fractured bone. The force may be exerted by an elastic device, by pins in the bone, or by rods or wires that can be lengthened or stretched by turning screws.

Tractor, four-wheeled or tracked, self-powered machine designed to pull or push heavy implements over rough terrain. It is commonly used in agriculture, construction, and industry. The tractor replaced draft animals in every phase of modern agriculture. *See also* Farm Machinery.

Tracy, Spencer (1900–67), US film actor, b. Milwaukee, Wis. He was noted first for gangster roles and then for crusty, honorable characters. His nearly 80 films, 9 with Katharine Hepburn (including *Without Love,* 1945, and *The Desk Set,* 1956), are acclaimed for wit and intelligence. His other major films include *Captains Courageous* (1937), *Boys' Town* (1938), for both of which he received Academy Awards, and *The Last Hurrah* (1958).

Trade and Navigation Acts, series of laws that England imposed on its colonies to ensure that trade profits would be kept in England. The acts required that all goods to and from the colonies must be on English ships manned by an English crew (1651); that bounties be placed on colonial goods (1673); and that the admiralty courts enforce the acts (1696).

Trade Barriers, methods a country uses to discourage the importing of goods. Trade barriers include tariffs as well as quotas or absolute bans against importing of certain types of goods. Customs regulations may be so complicated as to constitute an informal trade barrier. Trade barriers are used to protect special interest situations or the perceived national interest of the country.

Trade Winds, or trades, part of the general atmospheric circulation, blowing toward the equator as northeasterlies in the Northern Hemisphere and southeasterlies in the Southern Hemisphere. *See also* Easterlies.

Trafalgar, Battle of (1805), naval engagement in the Napoleonic Wars fought off Cape Trafalgar, Spain. Nelson, the British admiral, divided his 27 ships into two squadrons and broke the Franco-Spanish line of 33 ships under Admiral de Villeneuve. Though Nelson, on board the *Victory,* was killed, the defeat established British naval supremacy in the 19th century.

Traffic Engineering, a branch of highway engineering dealing with the planning and design of streets and highways as well as the safe and economical controls of traffic.

Tragedy, one of the two types of drama. It differs from comedy in its seriousness of style. The story revolves around a central character who struggles to overcome obstacles but is eventually overtaken by disaster. The first tragedies originated in Greece in honor of the god Dionysus in the 5th century BC. *See also* Theater.

Trailing Arbutus, perennial, spreading plant native to central and E United States. This evergreen has thick oval leaves and small, fragrant, pink flowers. Family Ericaceae; species *Epigaea repens.*

Trail of Tears, forced migration of Indians (1829–43) to new reservations west of the Mississippi and Missouri rivers. Bands of Shawnee, Delaware, Wyandot, Cherokee, Seminole, and others were involved and thousands died on the journey from disease, lack of food, or abuse.

Trajan (52?–117), Roman emperor (AD 98–117), adopted son of Nerva, b. Spain. He won military distinction in victories over the Germans (98–99), Dacians (101–06), Parthians (114–16), and Persians and pushed the frontiers of the Roman Empire to their farthest limit. He restored the Appian Way, built a theater, an aqueduct, the Forum of Trajan with noted triumphal column, and partly drained the Pontine Marshes. He died in Cilicia and his ward, Hadrian, succeeded him.

Trajectory, the path of a projectile. On Earth, and in the absence of air resistance, all trajectories would be portions of an ellipse whose focus was at the Earth's center of mass. Since this is 4,000mi (6,440km) deep, the trajectories are virtually indistinguishable from parabolas, whose foci are located at infinity.

Tranquilizers, currently the drugs most important in the treatment of mental illness. Tranquilizers work on the central nervous system to produce relaxation and calm, which in turn often reduces the intensity of many tension-related symptoms. *Minor tranquilizers* are relatively mild, do not produce sedation, and have few side effects. *Major tranquilizers,* which are used to treat psychotic disorders, can calm even those persons who are markedly agitated, but may produce a host of disturbing side effects including drowsiness, tremor, visual difficulties, dry mouth, skin rashes, and jaundice.

Transcaucasia (Transcaucasian Federation or **Transcaucasian Soviet Federated Socialist Republic),** former federated union of the USSR; now the three Soviet Socialist republics of Armenia, Azerbaijan, and Georgia. It was first formed 1917 after the Russian Revolution; soon divided into the above-mentioned separate republics; in 1919–21 Turkish nationalists fought with Bolsheviks for control of this region; in 1922 it was reformed and in 1923 it entered USSR; in 1936 it separated again into three autonomous republics. *See also* Armenia.

Transcendentalism, in literature, philosophic movement prominent in New England from the 1830s to 1860s. A romantic and mystical philosophy, its fundamental basis was the unity of nature and God. Its thought was derived in part from German Romanticism. Transcendentalism encouraged self-expression and individualism. Its proponents included Ralph Waldo Emerson, the movement's chief spokesman; Henry David Thoreau; Jones Very and Christopher Pearse Cranch, poets; Margaret Fuller; Bronson Alcott, and other intellectuals. The transcendentalists published *The Dial* (1840–44), a quarterly magazine expressing their ideas. Many of them participated in the cooperative community, Brook Farm.

Transcendental Meditation (TM), a popular type of meditation taught by Maharishi Mahesh Yogi and practiced twice a day for brief periods, in which the meditator uses his mantra as a vehicle to "transcend," allowing mental activity to decrease. Scientific studies have indicated that TM decreases oxygen consumption and heart rate and increases skin resistance and alpha brain waves, yielding a relaxed mental state differing from sleep or hypnosis.

Transducer, device for converting any nonelectrical signal, such as sound or light, into an electrical signal or vice versa. Examples are microphones, loudspeakers, phonograph pickups, and various measuring instruments used in acoustics. If the transducer derives energy from sources other than the signal itself, it is called an active transducer; if it does not it is passive. The output signal is always a function of the input signal (usually linear).

Transfer Ellipse, or orbit, path followed by a spacecraft while changing from one orbital path to another. The Hohmann, or tangential, ellipse is tangent to the arrival and departure orbits and uses the least energy. Transfer ellipses intersecting the arrival and departure orbits at higher angles use more energy but may be advantageous in other ways.

Transfer Payments, payments made by governments, business firms, or individuals to other individuals, businesses, or governments for which nothing is given in exchange. These payments shift purchasing power to the receiving unit and alter the distribution of earned income. Transfer payments include unemployment compensation, veteran's benefits, and social security payments.

Transfer RNA. *See* Ribonucleic Acid.

Transformer, device for converting alternating current at one voltage to another voltage at the same frequency. It consists of two coils of wire coupled together magnetically. The input current is fed to one coil (the primary), the output being taken from the other coil (the secondary). If core losses are ignored, the ratio of the input voltage to the output voltage is equal to the ratio of the number of turns in the primary coil to the number of turns in the secondary coil.

Transform Fault, a special class of strike-slip fault characteristic of mid-ocean ridges. Because of the transform faults, the Mid-Atlantic Ridge does not run in a straight line but in offset steps. Some geologists think the four major structures of the Earth's crust are mountains, deep-sea trenches, mid-ocean ridges, and strike-slip faults and that they form continuous networks.

Transfusion, Blood, administration of blood, or a blood component such as plasma, directly into a blood vessel.

Transient Situational Character Disorders, temporary disruption of personality as a consequence of a real external stress. The disturbed behavior occurs when the individual attempts to cope with an overwhelming situation. Temporary adjustment reactions during infancy, adulthood, and old age are also included in this category.

Transistor, semiconductor device capable of amplification. It consists of two p-n semiconductor junctions forming either a p-n-p or n-p-n structure. In a p-n-p transistor, the thin central n-region is called the base, one p-region the emitter and the other the collector. The signal to be amplified is fed into the base, a negative voltage being applied to the emitter and a positive voltage to the collector. By suitable design the collector current can be over 100 times as great as the base current. Transistors are very versatile devices that have now replaced electron tubes for most purposes. *See also* Semiconductor.

Transition Elements, metallic elements with chemical properties resembling those of their horizontal neighbors in the periodic table. They have incomplete inner electron shells, and are characterized by variable valences, the formation of colored ions, and a tendency to form stable coordination complexes. They include elements with atomic numbers between 21 (scandium) and 30 (zinc), 39 (yttrium) and 48 (cadmium), 57 (lanthanum) and 80 (mercury), and 89 (actinium) and 103 (lawrencium). The lanthanides and actinides are sometimes called inner transition elements. *See also* Periodic Table.

Transjordan Region, region presently composing the Kingdom of Jordan, in Asia Minor, bounded by Syria (N), Israel (W), Saudi Arabia (S and W), and Iraq (NW). Called Transjordan from early 1900s to 1949, the region passed from a part of the British League of Nations mandate of Palestine (1920) to an independent constitutional state (May 1923). By treaty with Great Britain (1928), British financial assistance to Transjordan continued, accompanied by presence of British military forces in the country; region officially became Hashemite Kingdom of Jordan 1949, when national forces took from Palestine the areas W of the Jordan River which had been named Arab territories by the United Nations. *See also* Jordan.

Transkei, first of the nine black homelands (bantustans) of the Republic of South Africa to be granted independence (1976) under that government's official policy of apartheid ("separation"). Transkei's independence is not recognized by the United Nations or any country other than South Africa. Most of the inhabitants belong to the Xhosa ethnic group, practicing subsistence agriculture and pastoralism except for about 370,000 men who work in South Africa. Area: 15,831sq mi (41,002sq km); Pop. 2,238,000; Capital: Umtata.

Translocation, movement of food materials in solution through plant tissues from one part of a plant to another.

Transmission, Automobile, the device (a gear and shaft or driving chain) for transmitting power from the engine to the live axle. Speed is variable in discrete steps, with gears or chains providing fixed speed ratios. Three general types are in current use: the sliding gear transmission requiring manual operation; the "hydramatic," which combines an automatic clutch with a semi-automatic transmission and allows two or three forward speeds; and the torque-converter, a hydraulic mechanism using engine power, that engages planetary gear trains.

Transmutation, in physics, formation of one isotope from another by radioactive decay or by bombardment with energetic particles.

Transplant, Organ. *See* Organ Transplant.

Transport, in chemistry, movement of measurable entities such as molecules, ions, isotopes, electrical charges, mass, momentum, or energy through or across a medium due to the natural or applied nonuniform conditions existing within it. Transport properties include viscosity, diffusivity, and thermal conductivity. Active transport, in biochemistry, denotes movement of a substance against a concentration gradient.

Transportation, in geology, the movement of particulate matter from a source to an area of deposition. Any movement of material with wind, water, ice, or gravity as the transporting medium falls into this category. Wind, ice, and gravity are mechanical media, whereas water is both a mechanical mover and a solvating medium. *See also* Deposition; Hydrology; Sedimentation.

Transportation, United States Department of (DOT), cabinet-level department within the executive branch. It was established in 1966 to administer transportation programs of the federal government. It also works to develop fast, safe, efficient, low-cost, and convenient transportation. DOT is directed by the secretary who is a cabinet member and appointed by the president.

Transsexualism, act of changing one's sex or the desire to do so. A sex change might be accomplished partially through hormone treatment or through surgery. For a true hermaphrodite, a person born with both male and female characteristics, choice of sex is literally possible. The condition is quite rare, however. Psychological desire to change sex may be exhibited through transvestism.

Trans-Siberian Railroad, major rail line of Asiatic USSR, linking European Russia with the Pacific coast, running between Chelyabinsk and Vladivostok. Built 1892–1905, it first ran generally E through Orm, Novosibirsk, Krasnoyarsk, Irkutsk, Chita, and through Manchuria (Chinese Eastern RR) to Vladivostok; during WWI a Russian line was completed between Chita and Vladivostok, along the Amur and Ussuri rivers. This railroad opened Siberia to settlement and industrialization. Length: 4,600mi (7,406km).

Transubstantiation, Christian doctrine, defined at the Lateran Council in 1215 as *de fide,* stating that there is a change in substance of the eucharistic elements after the consecration. The substance of bread and wine changes to Christ's actual body and blood. The doctrine is opposed by that of consubstantiation. *See also* Consubstantiation; Eucharist.

Transuranium Elements, radioactive elements with atomic numbers in excess of that of uranium (at. no. 92). They are the actinides neptunium, plutonium, americium, curium, berkelium, californium, einsteinium, fermium, mendelevium, nobelium, and lawrencium and the transactinides with atomic numbers 104 and 105. None except neptunium and plutonium occur naturally, and those two only occur in minute amounts as decay products of uranium. *See also* Periodic Table.

Transvaal, province in NE Republic of South Africa, between Limpopo and Vaal rivers. Inhabited by Bantu-speaking black Africans in the early 19th century, it was taken by Boers mid-1830s; the Sand River Convention (1852) recognized the right of Boer self-administration. South African Republic was formed 1856, and Boer leader Martin Pretorius became the first president (1857). Internal problems led to Britain's annexing of the South African Republic 1877; scene of Boers' revolt against British 1880, when it was again proclaimed a republic; Britain granted the republic internal self-government 1881. The discovery of gold (1886) attracted many foreigners, but the Boers imposed heavy taxation and denied political rights to newcomers; at the close of the Boer War (1902), the treaty of Vereeniging made Transvaal a crown colony of the British Empire; it became a founding province of the Union of South Africa 1910. It is the site of University of Pretoria, University of the Witwatersrand, Kruger National Park. Major cities include Pretoria (the capital), Johannesburg, Brakpan. Products: livestock, tobacco, cotton, wheat, citrus fruits. Industries: gold, diamonds, uranium, asbestos, chromium, platinum, explosives, mining equipment, iron, steel. Area: 110,450sq mi (286,066sq km). Pop. 8,717,530.

Transverse Wave, type of wave, such as an electromagnetic wave, in which vibrations of the component electric and magnetic fields or of the particles of the transmitting medium occur at right angles to the direction of wave motion. *See also* Wave.

Transvestism, sexual deviation in which the person identifies with and dresses like the opposite sex. Since sexual arousal or gratification is usually dependent upon the individual's wearing garments of the opposite sex, transvestism can be thought of as a mixture of homosexuality and fetishism.

Transylvania, region in central Romania, surrounded by the Carpathian Mts; belonged to Roman Dacia; became Hungarian in 1003; ruled by Austria 1711–1866; reunited with Hungary 1866; after WWI became part of Romania. Transylvania is rich in iron, lead, gold, copper, manganese, salt, sulfur. Industries: chemicals, textiles, livestock. Area: 21,192sq mi (54,887sq km) Pop. 2,500,000.

Trapdoor Spider, light brown to black spider found worldwide. It digs a tubelike burrow, lined with silk, having a hinged lid covering the entrance. When the spider feels vibrations of passing prey, it rushes out and stuffs the captured prey down its burrow. Length: 0.3–1.2in (8–31mm). Family Ctenizidae. *See also* Spider.

Trapezium. *See* Theta Orionis.

Trapezoid, four-sided plane figure with one pair of opposite sides parallel. The area of a trapezoid is one half the sum of its parallel sides times the perpendicular distance between them.

Trappists, popular name for the Cistercians of the Strict Observance, religious order centered in La Trappe Abbey, France, until moving to Citeaux in 1892. Splitting into three congregations as they spread

Transkei

Transylvania: ceremonial vest

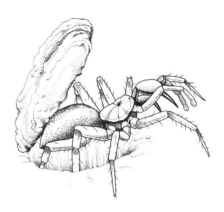

Trap-door spider

worldwide, Trappists were united by papal decree in 1893. Maintaining silence, vegetarianism, and rising for Night Office, manual labor is compulsory for the monks.

Trasimene, Lake, large shallow lake in Umbria, central Italy, site of the battle (217 BC) in which Hannibal defeated the army of the Roman consul Flaminius by ambush, destroying nearly two legions. Also called Lake of Perugia.

Traumatic Neurosis, neurotic disturbance caused by a severe emotional shock such as a close brush with death or an extreme frustration. Symptoms include moodiness, difficulty in concentrating, sleep disturbances (frightening dreams), loss of appetite, and irritability. In acute traumatic neurosis the symptoms may be severe but usually begin to disappear spontaneously in the weeks following the trauma. In chronic traumatic neurosis the symptoms linger indefinitely, recurring from time to time in extreme form (eg, the combat veteran who is awakened many years later by nightmares of battle).

Travelers' Tree, palmlike plant native to Madagascar. The trunk is topped with bananalike leaves. Each cupshaped leaf base holds a quart of water produced by the plant. This is considered a refreshing drink. It has large clusters of white blossoms and blue seeds. Family Strelitziaceae; species *Ravenala madagascariensis.* Height: to 90ft (28m).

Traveling Wave, wave that continuously carries electrical energy, light energy, etc, away from a source. *See also* Wave.

Travis, William Barret (1809–36), US military officer, b. Edgefield co, S.C. Trained as a lawyer, he moved to Texas in 1831 and soon became a leader in the fight for Texas independence from Mexico. When the Alamo was besieged by General Santa Anna's army (1836), Travis, the commander, was killed in its defense.

Trawling, method of catching bottom-dwelling fish, such as cod, and spawning herring, to the depths of 1,968ft (600m). A large net, attached to towboards and pulling cables, is towed by the fishing vessel. This method is generally used only in continental shelf areas. Trawling can be used in deeper waters with an echolocater for finding schools and indicating specific depths.

Treasury, Department of, US cabinet-level department within the executive branch. It is composed of numerous bureaus and divisions that have four basic functions: formulating and recommending financial, tax, and fiscal policies; serving as financial agent for the government; law enforcement; and manufacturing coins and currency. The department is directed by the secretary, who is a cabinet member and a major advisor to the president concerning domestic and international financial policy and tax policy. The Treasury Department was established in 1789.

Treat, Robert (1622?–1710), US soldier and colonial governor, b. England. He arrived in Milford, Conn., in 1639 where he was active in civil and military affairs. From 1667–72 he lived in New Jersey and founded Newark (1666). In 1672 he returned to Connecticut and led troops in King Philip's War (1675–76). He was elected governor of Connecticut in 1683. He opposed the plan for the establishment of the Dominion of New England under Gov. Edmund Andros in 1686 and took part in hiding the charter in the Charter Oak. When Andros was ousted in 1689, Treat resumed the governorship and served until 1698.

Treaty of Paris (1783), agreement between the United States and Great Britain that ended the Revolutionary War. Negotiated by John Adams, Benjamin Franklin, John Jay, and Henry Laurens, the treaty granted the United States independence. Boundary lines were set with the Great Lakes (N), the Mississippi River (W), and the 31st parallel with the Apalachicola and St Mary's rivers (S). Debts were to be recovered, and the restoration of property to Loyalists was recommended. Both countries were granted navigation rights on the Mississippi River. Many of the issues remained controversial and were settled by later treaties.

Treaty of Paris (1898), US agreement with Spain ending the Spanish-American War. Spain was to yield Cuba, cede Puerto Rico and one of the Landrone Islands, and the United States would occupy the Philippines, for which it paid Spain $20,000,000.

Trebbia River (Fiume Trebbia), river in N Italy; rises in Ligurian Apennines; flows N and joins Po River near Piacenza; scene of defeat of Romans by Hannibal 218 BC, and of Russo-Austrian victory over French 1799. Length: approx. 70mi (113km).

Trebizond, Empire of, a Byzantine kingdom located on the Black Sea. It was founded in 1204 by Alexius I (*c.*1180–1222), a member of the Comnenus family. Despite the onslaughts of the Seljuks and the armies of Nicaea and Constantinople, it maintained its autonomy and flourished as a cultural and commercial center. Finally, in 1461 Mohammed II conquered Trebizond and made it part of the Ottoman Empire.

Tree, woody, perennial plant with one main stem or trunk and smaller branches. The trunk increases in diameter each year and leaves are evergreen or deciduous. Trees range in size to the 385ft (117m) redwoods. The giant sequoias live 2,500–3,000 years.

Tree Creeper, or brown creeper, brownish agile bird that scurries up and down trees in cooler areas of the Northern Hemisphere. It uses its long, slightly downcurved bill to probe for insects under bark, bracing itself with its long, spine-tipped, stiff tail. Its eggs (5–8) are laid in a shapeless twig and moss nest behind loose bark. Length: 5in (13cm). Species *Certhia familiaris.*

Tree Cricket, slender, whitish or pale green cricket found worldwide. It lays its eggs in tree or shrub twigs, often causing severe damage. Length: 0.5in (13mm). Family Gryllidae; subfamily Oecanthinae. *See also* Cricket.

Tree Fern, large or small treelike fern. There are 1,500 species. Order Cyatheales. Or, true tree fern growing in tropics of the world, particularly moist mountainous areas. The 80-ft (24-m) trunks are crowned with large fronds, bearing spore cases on lower surfaces. There are 600 species. Family Cyatheaceae; genus *Cyathea.* *See also* Fern.

Tree Frog, frog found worldwide, to 15,000ft (4,575m) above sea level. Most live in trees and have enlarged sucking disks on their toes and long, thin hind legs. Some are non-climbing swamp dwellers. Of 500 species, those common in the United States are the spring peeper, green tree frog, cricket frog, and chorus frog. Family Hylidae.

Tree of Tule, evergreen Mexican bald cypress (*Taxodium mucronatum*) in the churchyard of Tule near Oaxaca, Mexico. It is thought to be the world's oldest living tree. A huge tree for the species, it has a height of 140ft (42.7m) and a diameter of 25ft (7.6m). It may actually be three trees grown together. Age estimates range from 1,500 to 4,000 years old.

Tree Shrew, small mammal ranging from India through SE Asia to Indonesia. It looks like a longsnouted, whiskerless squirrel but is classified as a primitive primate. Tree dwellers, they are dark olive in color and feed on insects and fruit. Family Tupaiidae. *See also* Primates.

Trematoda. *See* Fluke.

Trench, Oceanic, a deep V-shaped depression of the sea floor. In plate tectonic theory they are the places where one plate is being pushed down under the other. The movement causes deep earthquakes. They are the deepest (6mi or 9.7km) and longest (15,000mi or 24,150km) formations on Earth and are found on the borders of the Pacific, North and South Atlantic, and Indian oceans.

Trench Fever, infectious disease caused by a rickettsia transmitted by body lice, characterized by fever and pain in muscles, bones, and joints.

Trench Mouth, infection of the respiratory tract and mouth by a bacillus often in association with a spirochete (*Borrelia vincenti*), producing destructive ulceration of the mucous membranes of the cheeks, gums, and throat.

Trent, Council of (1545–63), ecumenical council of the Roman Catholic Church, convened by Pope Paul III to correct the abuses and defects that had spurred the Protestant Reformation and at the same time to examine church doctrine and to reform certain practices. The council was held in three meetings; 1545–47 under Paul III, 1551–52 under Julius III, and 1562–63 under Pius IV. The causes for the long delays between sessions were disagreement on location, general disinterest of intervening popes, and the political changes in Germany. Major decrees issued by the council involved clerical discipline, education, and obligations; doctrinal revision concentrated on redefining and reexamining teachings, particularly justification, the Mass, the sacraments, and indulgences. These were formulated and published in the Catechism of the Council of Trent, written so explicitly that it is still the basis to understanding the modern Roman Catholic Church.

Trent Affair (1861), diplomatic incident between Britain and the United States. Early in the Civil War Union officers seized two Confederate commissioners (James M. Mason and John Slidell) from the British ship *Trent.* Britain claimed its neutrality was violated and demanded their immediate release. President Lincoln, wishing to avoid war with Britain, released the men.

Trenton, capital city of New Jersey, in W New Jersey, on Delaware River; seat of Mercer co. It was scene of American Revolutionary battle in which Gen. George Washington crossed the Delaware River to capture Hessian troops (Dec. 25–26, 1776); made state capital 1790. Trenton is the site of monument (1893) commemorating Washington's victory, old barracks (1758, now a museum), capitol (1792), William Trent House (1719), Trenton State College (1855), Rider College (1865). Industries: automobile parts, plastics, metal products, rubber goods, steel cables, textiles. Settled 1679 by Friends; inc. 1745 as town and borough; 1792 as city. Pop. (1980) 92,124.

Treponema, a genus of anaerobic, gram-negative spirochetes. Several species are pathogenic in man: *T. pallidum,* causing syphillis, and *T. pertenue,* which causes yaws, an ulcerative skin infection. They are sensitive to penicillin.

Trevelyan, (Sir) George Otto (1838–1928), English historian and statesman. A Liberal member of parliament (1865–97), he spent most of his life in government service. His *The American Revolution* (6 vol., 1899–1914) helped bring about a more sympathetic view of the Revolution among the English. *The Life and Letters of Lord Macauley* (2 vols., 1876) is his finest work.

Trial, the judicial examination of the facts surrounding a case of civil or criminal nature. A jury may or may not be present.

Trial-and Error Learning, in psychology, the process of trying out different solutions to a problem until one works. Original work was done by E.L. Thorndike early in this century using cats as subjects and "puzzle boxes" as problems. The animal could escape from the box by correctly manipulating a latch. Once it had escaped (through trial and error), the cat would know how to escape when next placed in the box. Modern psychology generally subsumes this form of learning under operant conditioning.

Triangle, plane figure bounded by three straight lines. The sum of the interior angles totals 180°. The area is measured by either (1) half the product of one of the sides and the perpendicular onto it from the opposite vertex (½ x base x height), or (2) half the product of two of the sides and the sine of the angle between them.

Triangle Trade, system of trade between New England and Middle Colonies, the West Indies, and African ports. The trade, partly in evasion of British laws, dealt in molasses, rum, and slaves. Imported molasses was made into rum in the colonies; rum was traded for slaves in Africa, slaves were traded for molasses in the West Indies.

Triangulum, or the Triangle, inconspicuous northern constellation situated between Andromeda and Aries. It contains the spiral galaxy M 33 (NGC 598), a member of the Local Group located 2,350,000 light-years from the Milky Way system.

Triangulum Australe, or the Southern Triangle, southern circumpolar constellation situated south of Norma. The three brightest stars Alpha, Beta, and Gamma (all above the third magnitude) form the conspicuous triangular figure.

Triassic Period, the oldest division of the Mesozoic Era, lasting from 225 to 195,000,000 years ago. Following upon a wave of extinctions at the close of the Permian, many new kinds of animals developed. On land lived the first dinosaurs. Mammallike reptiles were common and by the end of the period the first true mammals existed. In the seas lived the first ichthyosaurs, placodonts, and nothosaurs. Also, the first frogs, turtles, crocodilians, and lizards appeared. Although plant life consisted mainly of primitive gymnosperms, the first flowering plants are recorded. The Appalachian Mountains were formed. *See also* Geologic Time; Mesozoic Era.

Tribunes, ten senior Roman officers of the legions elected, often from the plebeian class, to protect plebeians from abuse by magistrates. The tribuneship was reformed by Tiberius Gracchus, repressed by Sulla, and restored by Pompey. It declined during the empire.

Triceratops, large, horned ornithischian dinosaur of late Cretaceous age of W North America. The 8-ft (2.4m) skull carried two 40-in (102-cm) horns above its eyes and a smaller horn at tip of its snout. Length: 20–25ft (6.1–7.6m); height: 8ft (2.4m); weight: 10ton.

Trichinosis, disease of rats, swine, bears, cats, dogs, and humans, caused by infection with the larvae of a parasitic nematode worm *(Trichinella spiralis).* Most human cases originate from eating raw or improperly cooked pork. Symptoms include abdominal pain, vomiting, swelling, and delirium, and permanent heart and eye damage is possible. In its early stages it may be cured by intestinal washing. Thiabendazole is becoming a widely adopted drug treatment.

Trier, city in W West Germany, on Moselle River, near Luxembourg border. Capital of Treveri people of ancient Gaul, it was conquered by Julius Caesar; became part of France 1801 and served as capital of French department of Sarre; awarded to Prussia by Congress of Vienna (1814–15). Notable buildings include 13th-century Gothic cathedral containing coat said to belong to Jesus Christ, Roman amphitheater, imperial palace; seat of Theological Seminary (1773). Industries: leather goods, steel, textiles, wine, beer, cigars. Founded *c.* 15 BC. Pop. 99,600.

Trieste, seaport city in NE Italy, on Gulf of Trieste, 70mi (113km) ENE of Venice; capital of Friuli-Venezia-Giulia region and Trieste prov.; commercial and industrial center. A Roman colony under Julius Caesar, it placed itself under protection of duke of Austria 1382; was made free port 1719 and Austrian crown land 1867; ceded to Italy 1919; occupied by Yugoslavia 1945; Yugoslavia and Italy agreed to territorial compromise 1954, and Trieste was returned to Italy; site of 15th–17th-century cathedral, 14th–17th-century castle. Industries: shipyards, steel, petroleum, textiles. Pop. 266,837.

Trifid Nebula (M20; NGC 6514), emission nebula situated in the constellation Sagittarius. Lanes of dark interstellar matter, superficially resembling a tripod, are situated in space in front of this nebula, against whose shining background they are rendered visible.

Triggerfish, tropical marine fish found in shallow water and identified by an erectile first dorsal fin spine. Its leathery-skinned, compressed body is often beautifully marked and colored. Length: to 17in (43cm). Species include the common *Balistes carolinensis* and the queen *B. vetula.* Family Balistidae.

Triglyceride. *See* Lipid.

Trigonometric Functions, the six ratios of the sides of a right triangle containing a given acute angle—they are the sine, cosine, tangent, cotangent, secant, and cosecant of the angle. These functions can be extended to cover angles of any size by the use of a system of rectangular coordinates. Thus the sine of an angle increases to 1 from 0–90°, decreases to zero from 90–180°, decreases to −1 from 180–270°, and increases again to 0 from 270–360°. Many relationships exist between different trigonometric functions, including the identities $\sin^2 A + \cos^2 A = 1$; $1 + \tan^2 A = \sec^2 A$; and $1 + \cot^2 A = \operatorname{cosec}^2 A$. Trigonometric functions of numbers can also be defined. Thus, the function $\sin x$ is the sine of an angle of x radians.

Trigonometry, use of trigonometric functions of angles in finding the unknown angles or sides of triangles when other angles and/or sides are known. The unknown values are obtained by using simple formulae and tables of sines, cosines, tangents, and other functions of angles. Trigonometry is extensively used in building, surveying, navigation, etc.

Trilobite, any of an extinct group of arthropods found fossilized in marine deposits, ranging in age from Cambrian through Permian times. The body shape is mostly oval, tapering toward the rear. The name refers to the division of the body into three distinct longitudinal segments, consisting of a central axis and two pleural lobes. The head bears eyes on top and a mouth beneath. Transverse divisions show segmentation and bear pairs of jointed limbs. Trilobites were mostly bottom-crawling, shallow-water forms and ranged in adult size from .25in (6mm) to 30in (76cm). Mostly only the hard parts, consisting of mineral-impregnated portions of the chitinous covering, are found as fossils.

Trinidad and Tobago, island republic in West Indies, formed by southernmost two islands of West Indies, separated from Venezuela's NE coast by Gulf of Paris and Serpent's Mouth channel; Trinidad and Tobago islands are separated from each other by Dragon's Mouth channel. Port of Spain is capital. Islands joined politically in 1888 and were members of West Indies Federation 1958–62. They joined to become an independent nation 1962. Trinidad was discovered 1498 by Christopher Columbus and taken in 1797 by British. Tobago was settled 1616 by English, who had to struggle with hostile Carib aboriginals. Sugar, petroleum, and tourism are major industries. Almost half of the people are of black African descent with East Indians making up one-third; remainder are European, Middle Eastern, and Chinese. English is official language, but a French patois is also used. Since 1960 government secondary schools have been free. The University of the West Indies has schools of agriculture and engineering in Trinidad. In 1976, Trinidad and Tobago became an independent country within the Commonwealth of Nations, with a parliamentary government. Since then gradual measures have granted limited internal autonomy to Tobago.

PROFILE

Official name: Republic of Trinidad and Tobago
Area: Trinidad: 1,980sq mi (5,128sq km) Tobago: 116sq mi (300sq km)
Population: 1,156,085
Chief cities: Port of Spain (capital), San Fernando, Scarborough
Government: Republic
Religion: Hinduism, Roman Catholicism, Islam
Language: English (official)
Monetary unit: Trinidad and Tobago dollar
Industries: (major products) sugar, cocoa, petroleum products, asphalt, chemicals, copra, coffee, bananas, citrus fruit, angostura bitters, tourism

Trinitrotoluene. *See* TNT.

Trinity, The, a central doctrine of Christianity, holding that God is three persons, the Father, the Son, and the Holy Spirit (or Holy Ghost). There is only one God, but he exists as "three in one and one in three." Theologians say that the nature of the Trinity is a mystery that cannot be comprehended by humans although they can apprehend some of its meanings. The doctrine of the Trinity was stated in early Christian creeds to counter beliefs such as Gnosticism, which denied that Christ was wholly human during his life on Earth. God the Son was a man, but he is also "of one substance with the Father;" God made man through the power of the Holy Spirit. *See also* Gnosticism.

Trinity River, river in NW California, rises in NE Trinity co; flows SW then NW into the Klamath River, near Eureka; gold has been extracted from the river since gold rush era of mid-19th century. Length: 130mi (209km).

Triple Alliance, War of the, also known as the Paraguayan War, a conflict between Paraguay on one side and Argentina-Brazil-Uruguay on the other (1865–70). Long-standing territorial disputes and Brazilian intervention in the Uruguayan civil war prompted Francisco Solano López of Paraguay to declare war on Brazil in 1865; by May of the same year, the conflict involved four countries. The war devastated Paraguay; 300,000 Paraguayan lives and 55,000sq mi (142,450sq km) of Paraguayan territory were lost.

Triple Entente (1907), fused together earlier Anglo-French and Franco-Russian military agreements to offset the Triple Alliance (1882) of Germany, Austria-Hungary, and Italy. It destroyed the unity of the six great powers by placing them into two rival alliances that would become the power blocs of World War I.

Triple Point, the temperature and pressure at which all three phases (solid, liquid, gas) of a substance can coexist. For water, the triple point occurs at 0°C, and at less than 1% of atmospheric pressure.

Tripoli (Tarabulus ESH Sham), seaport city in Lebanon; captured in 638 by Muslim Arabs, it adopted both the Arabic language and Islam religion; taken 1109 by Raymond de Saint-Gilles, count of Toulouse, who built the castle of Sanjil on its site; the medieval town and modern city grew around the castle; destroyed 1289 by the sultans of Egypt. In 1909 Tripoli's port was enlarged, and a railroad was built connecting it to N Syria and surrounding regions; prospered as terminal of petroleum pipeline. Industries: oil refining, soap, silk, oranges, wool, skins, spinning, tobacco, lemons. Pop. 175,000.

Tripoli (Tarabulus Al-Gharb), city in NW Libya, on Mediterranean Sea, 400mi (644km) W of Benghazi; capital of Libya; captured by Romans 1st century BC, Vandals AD 5th century, Arabs 7th century; developed as important terminus for trans-Saharan caravan routes. Taken 1510 by Spain, it was ruled 1528–51 by the Knights of St John; captured 1553 by Ottoman Turks; seat of Karamanli dynasty 1711–1835; served as base for Barbary pirates, leading to Tripolitan War 1801–05 with the United States. In 1911 Tripoli was taken by Italy and made capital of the Italian colony of Libya; captured 1943 by British; site of 19th-century Gurgi mosque, 1736 Karamanli mosque, remains of Roman walls. Industries: tobacco, textiles, woven goods, processed foods. Founded 7th century BC by Phoenicians. Pop. 551,477.

Tripolitan War (1801–05), conflict between Tripoli and the United States. For several years Tripoli and other Barbary states on the north coast of Africa had interfered with US commerce in the Mediterranean, capturing ships and demanding tribute. In 1801, Tripoli declared war on the United States. After several land and sea battles, Tripoli agreed to leave US ships alone and the United States ransomed all prisoners.

Tristan da Cunha Island, island in S Atlantic Ocean about midway between S Africa and South America. The only inhabitable island of five volcanic islands called Tristan da Cunha Islands, it was discovered 1506 by Portuguese; annexed by Great Britain 1816. In 1938 these islands were made part of dependency of St Helena. In 1961 island of Tristan da Cunha suffered a volcanic eruption that caused evacuation; the islanders returned in 1963. Area: 38sq mi (98sq km). Pop. 271.

Triceratops

Trieste, Italy

Trinidad and Tobago

Trist Mission (1847–48), US peace effort in the Mexican War. Nicholas Trist was a peace commissioner sent to join Gen. Winfield Scott's US troops in the Mexican War. After the first series of negotiations had broken down, President Polk recalled him. Trist, however, stayed on in Mexico and successfully negotiated the treaty ending the war. *See also* Guadalupe Hidalgo, Treaty of.

Tritium, radioactive isotope of hydrogen, the nucleus of which consists of one proton and two neutrons. Only one atom in 10^{17} of natural hydrogen is tritium. Tritiated compounds are used in radioactive tracing. Properties: mass no. 3; atomic mass 3.016; half-life 12.5 years.

Triton, in Greek mythology, a sea god, son of Poseidon and Amphitrite. He was half man, half fish, with a scaled body, sharp teeth and claws, and a forked fishtail. He had power over the waves and possessed the gift of prophecy. Triton blowing his conch seems to have been the personification of the roar of the wild sea.

Triton, large gastropod mollusk found in tropical marine waters near coral reefs. Its shell is used as a religious and martial musical instrument in Shinto temples in Japan. Length: to 16in (40.6cm). Family Cymatiidae; species include brown and pink *Charonia tritonis*.

Trivandrum, seaport city in SW India, on Arabian Sea; capital of Kerala state; served as capital of Travancore kingdom 1745; site of university (1937) and 18th-century fort housing palaces and temples. Industries: tires, tile, plywood, titanium products, textiles. Pop. 409,761.

Trobriand Islanders, aboriginal inhabitants of the Trobriand Islands. The subject of a famous study by Bronislaw Malinowski, their society is divided into totemic clans. Ceremonial gift exchanges *(kula),* following intricate rules, take place regularly, and each village is headed by a chief and a gardener, who has high social status as a magician.

Trochee, metrical foot consisting of a stressed syllable followed by an unstressed syllable, or a long followed by a short, as in the word *happy*. The meter is called trochaic. Trochaic meter is popular in children's verses ("Mary Had a Little Lamb") and in meter expression of the supernatural, as in William Shakespeare's
Double, double, toil and trouble
Fire burn and cauldron bubble.
See also Meter.

Trogon, fragile, brilliantly colored bird of dark tropical forests in America, S Africa, India, Malay, and the Philippines. About 12in (30.5cm) long, they perch motionless and feed on fruits. Both parents incubate the whitish eggs (3–5) in a dead tree limb nest. Family Trogonidae.

Troilus and Cressida (1602), comical satire by William Shakespeare. It bitterly illustrates human failings through the faithless actions of Cressida, who transfers her love from Troilus to the Greek Diomedes during the siege of Troy.

Trois Rivières (Three Rivers), city in S Quebec Canada, on N bank of St Lawrence River, 75mi (120km) NE of Montreal; site of ruins of Les Forges St Maurice, Canada's first iron foundries (1723–1833), University of Quebec (1969), Seminaire of St Joseph (1663). Industries: iron, textiles, shoes, pulp and paper, shipbuilding. Founded by Samuel de Champlain 1634; inc. 1857. Pop. 52,518.

Trojan Asteroids, minor planets, named after Homeric heroes of the *Iliad,* comprising two groups situated in the orbit of Jupiter, one behind the planet and the other ahead of it. In these positions (Lagrangian points), the asteroids are equidistant from both Jupiter and the Sun and are trapped by gravitational forces.

Trojan War, war between the Greeks and Trojans. The war, which lasted 10 years, began when Paris, son of King Priam of Troy, kidnapped Helen, wife of King Menelaus of Sparta. When the Trojans refused to return her, the Greeks formed an army, led by Agamemnon, that included Greek leaders Achilles, Patroclus, Diomedes, Odysseus, Nestor, the two Ajaxes, and Philoctetes. After nine years of fighting the Greeks pretended to sail for home, leaving behind a large hollow, wooden horse in which they concealed some warriors. Sinon persuaded the Trojans to bring the horse within the fortified city walls of Troy, despite the warnings of Cassandra and Laocoön. That night the Greeks returned and when the concealed warriors opened the city gates, Troy was destroyed. Homer wrote about the events of the war in the epic the *Illiad.* Through excavations done at Troy, historians believe that the legend does reflect a real war (c. 1200 BC) between the Greeks and the people of Troas, possibly over the control of the Dardanelles and Black Sea trade.

Troll, in Scandinavian mythology, a grotesque supernatural forest dweller of evil nature but somewhat limited intelligence. They are generally outwitted by their intended victims.

Trolley, an electric-powered street vehicle. Developed by Leo Daft, a US inventor, the trolley was named for its small carriage, or trolley, that ran on two overhead wires, gathering electrical power. Trolleys were popular in several European countries as well as the United States in the late 19th to early 20th centuries, but were then replaced by buses. They had the advantages of quiet operation, avoidance of fumes, and faster acceleration, but had more restricted routes than buses.

Trollope, Anthony (1815–82), widely traveled English novelist. A prolific author, Trollope satirized the upper-middle class in books such as *Barchester Towers* (1857). Later works, including *The Way We Live Now* (1875), are more harshly critical of society.

Trombone, brass wind musical instrument with cylindrical bore, cupped mouthpiece, and flaring bell. It is played with a slide, except for a variant with three valves. The tenor and bass trombones range 2½ octaves. The tone is solemn and mellow, often ribald in glissando flourishes. The trombone has been used since the late 15th century in symphonic and martial music, later in jazz.

Trondheim, city in central Norway, on S shore of Trondheim Fjord; capital of St Trøndelag co; site of many old structures, including an 11th-century cathedral and royal palace; an active seaport. Exports: wood and metal products. Industries: brewing, food processing, shipbuilding, hardware. Founded 997 by Olaf Trygvesson. Pop. 134,889.

Tropical Fish, small fish from the Amazon River Basin and SE Asia kept in captivity by hobbyists in home aquariums. They live in fresh and marine tropical and subtropical waters, generally at temperatures of 75–78 °F (23.9–25.6°C). Hundreds of varieties include the guppy, mollie, swordtail, platy, betta, gourami, tetra, and danie. Exotic types include clown triggerfish, brilliant rasbora, regal angelfish, and yellowtail wrasse. The paradise fish, considered to be earliest tropical aquarium fish, was imported to Paris in 1868. The hobby of keeping tropical fish became popular in the United States during the 1930s. More species became available after World War II.

Tropical Pawpaw. *See* Papaya.

Tropical Year, or solar year, time necessary for the Sun to complete a single one of its apparent journeys along the ecliptic, starting and ending at the First Point of Aries (the vernal equinox). Owing to the westward precession of the equinoxes, the tropical year is about 20 minutes shorter than the sidereal year.

Tropic Bird, black-marked, whitish seabird that flies over warm Atlantic, Pacific, and Indian ocean waters diving for food. They have long, bright bills and long, streamerlike central tail feathers. A single whitish, spotted egg is laid in a hole or crevice and incubated by both parents. Length: to 20in (50cm). Genus *Phaethon;* family Phaethonidae.

Tropic of Cancer, the northernmost parallel of latitude, 23.5° north of the equator, reached by the Sun directly overhead, separating the torrid and north temperate zones. *See also* Solstice.

Tropic of Capricorn, the southernmost parallel of latitude, 23.5° south of the equator, reached by the Sun directly overhead, separating the torrid and south temperate zones. *See also* Solstice.

Tropism, growth or movement of a plant, animal, or part in response to external stimuli, including light, gravity, or temperature. For example, some plants bend toward light; some animals move to warmer areas.

Troposphere, the shell of gases in the atmosphere nearest the Earth. *See also* Atmosphere.

Trotsky, Leon (1879–1940), Russian communist leader, born Leib Davydovich Bronstein. Joining the Social Democratic party, he became a Menshevik (1903). Chairman of the St Petersburg Soviet, he was prominent in the 1905 revolution, after which he escaped abroad. Returning to Russia for the March 1917 revolution, he became a Bolshevik. As head of the Petrograd Soviet he organized the seizure of power. As commissar for foreign affairs (1917–18), he was at Brest-Litovsk, but resigned after the treaty was concluded. As commissar for war (1918–25) he created and led the Red army in the civil war. After V.I. Lenin's death he was outmaneuvered by Joseph Stalin and expelled from the party in 1927 and from the country in 1929 as a leader of the left opposition. He was murdered in Mexico by Stalin's agents in 1940. Fiercely independent, he was a brilliant polemicist and fiery speaker.

Trotskyism, revisionist interpretation of Marxism formulated by Leon Trotsky. Trotsky's principal contribution to Marxist theory was his concept of "permanent revolution." Trotsky rejected the idea that parliamentary democracy and capitalism had to precede the formation of a socialist state. Revolution could begin, he argued, in a pre-capitalist society but could not be completed unless there was a chain reaction in industrialized countries.

Trotting Racing. *See* Horse Racing.

Trout, freshwater sport fish of North America and Europe. Also a good food fish, it is commonly propagated in hatcheries. Trout move upstream to spawn. Those that migrate to ocean between spawnings are called steelheads. Length: to 40.5in (103cm); weight:

37lb (17kg). Types include: the high mountain golden *Salvelinus aguakonita* of W North America, marked by vertical side bars; rainbow trout *Salmo gairdneri* marked by a longitudinal red stripe; brook trout, or char, *Salvelinus fontinalis* of E North America; large European brown trout *Salmo trutta;* and cutthroat *Salmo clarki* of W North America. Family Salmonidae.

Troy, or **Ilium,** ancient city in northwest Asia Minor. Its legend is a frequent theme in Greek literature. The extensive ruins excavated by Heinrich Schliemann in the 1870s have shown at least 10 cities built on the same site, the second and richest dating from the 22nd century BC. The Troy depicted by Homer in his *Iliad* and *Odyssey* was the seventh in chronological order. From the beginning Troy was the seat of a powerful ruler and an important point on the trade route between Europe and Asia. Tradition says Homer's Troy was destroyed by Agamemnon in 1183 BC, but the date is now thought to be in the 14th century. Afterward no major Greek city existed on the site.

Troy, city in SE Michigan, SE of Pontiac. Industries: electronic and automotive parts. Settled 1821; inc. 1955. Pop. (1980) 67,107.

Troy, city in E New York, on E bank of Hudson River, 8mi (13km) NE of Albany; seat of Rensselaer co. Henry Hudson first explored area in 1609; site of Rensselaer Polytechnic Institute (1824), Russell Sage College (1916), and Hudson Valley Community College (1953). Industries: men's clothing, automobile parts, steel, paper. First settled 1780s; inc. as village 1794, as city 1816. Pop. (1980) 56,638.

Troyes, Nicolas de, 16th-century French poet. Of his work only the second part of a manuscript collection of short tales survived, and most of them were borrowed from Boccaccio.

Troyes, city of NE France, 92mi (148km) SE of Paris, on Seine River; Capital of Aube dept. and site of the annual champagne fairs 11th–12th centuries; scene of signing of Treaty of Troyes (1420) between Charles VI and Henry V of England; Joan of Arc expelled English from here in 1429; site of Cathedral of Sts Peter and Paul (13th–16th centuries) and Church of St Urban (1262). Industries: hosiery, needles, flour, automobile parts, tires. Founded in pre-Roman times. Pop. 75,500.

Troyes, Treaty of (1420), truce in the Hundred Years War, between Charles VI of France, Henry V of England, and Philip of Burgundy. It stipulated marriage between Henry and Charles' daughter and stipulated that Henry would be recognized as the heir to the French throne. *See also* Hundred Years War.

Truck, any motor vehicle designed to carry freight or goods. They are powered by gas, diesel, or gasoline engines. Gottlieb Daimler of Germany built the first truck in 1896. Trucks can be either straight, with all the axles on a single frame, or articulated, as in the different types of tractor-trailer combinations. Trucks do the majority of short-distance hauling and also carry a substantial part of long-distance cargoes in most countries.

Trudeau, Pierre Elliott (1919–), Canadian political figure. A student of economics and political science, he became a labor and civil liberties lawyer (1943). He was elected a Liberal member of Parliament in 1965, serving as parliamentary secretary to Prime Minister Lester Pearson until he was appointed minister of justice and attorney general in 1967. He succeeded Pearson as party leader and as prime minister in 1968. He promoted economic and diplomatic independence for Canada, recognizing the People's Republic of China in 1970. Against separatism, in 1970 he had to temporarily impose martial law to combat French separatist terrorism. He favored bilingualism. Defeated in 1979, he was reelected in 1980 and served until 1984 during which time he chaired a 7-nation summit meeting in 1981 that discussed developing nations, the Soviet bloc, and economics. He oversaw the passing into law of Canada's new constitution in 1982.

Truffaut, François (1932–84), French filmmaker. His films are distinguished by sensitivity, charm, and a lyric, intensely personal style. Among his major works are *The 400 Blows* (1959), *Shoot the Piano Player* (1960), *Jules and Jim* (1961), *Stolen Kisses* (1968), *The Wild Child* (1971), *Day for Night* (1973), *The Story of Adele H.* (1975), *Love on the Run* (1979), *The Last Metro* (1981), and *Confidentially Yours* (1984).

Truffle, any of several fungi (family Tuberaceae) that grow underground, mostly among tree roots, and are highly prized edible delicacies. Truffles range in size from pea to potato and in color from black to white. Found in Europe, North Africa, and North America, they are hunted by trained pigs and dogs that can smell them underground.

Trujillo Molina, Rafael Leonidas (1891–1961), dominant figure of the Dominican Republic from 1930 until his death. Initially installed as chief executive by revolutionary coup, Trujillo was several times reelected. As president or maker-of-presidents, Trujillo—together with his family and friends—controlled the nation's institutions for more than a generation.

Truk Islands, island group in E Caroline Islands, W Pacific Ocean; part of US Trust Territory of the Pacific Islands; comprised of about 55 islands and islets, mainly of volcanic origin, surrounded by a reef with navigable passes into natural harbors; inner harbor was site of important Japanese naval base during WWII. Products: fish, copra. Area: 39sq mi (101sq km). Pop. 35,220.

Truman, Harry S. (1884–1972), 33rd president of the United States (1945–53), b. Lamar, Mo. In 1919 he married Elizabeth Wallace; they had one daughter. Unable to attend college, Truman worked at a number of jobs before entering politics. He also commanded an artillery battery in World War I. In 1922, with the support of the Kansas City Democratic machine, he was elected judge (actually, an administrator) of Jackson co; in 1926 he was elected president judge, or chief executive, of the county. In 1935 he went to the US Senate as an ardent New Dealer.

In the Senate, Truman was forced to live down his reputation as a machine politician. He was reelected in 1940, despite strong efforts to unseat him. During World War II, he headed a committee to stop waste in government spending. His success at that task—and his acceptability to all factions of the party—made him Roosevelt's choice for his vice-presidential running mate in 1944. The ticket won easily. Truman was vice president for less than three months; on April 12, 1945, Roosevelt died, and Truman became president. Although ill-prepared, he took quick control of the reins of power. He ordered the bombing of Japanese cities with the atomic bomb, thereby bringing World War II to a victorious end.

The end of the war also saw the end of the alliance with the Soviet Union. The Cold War began, and Truman countered Soviet moves in Europe with such instruments as the Marshall Plan, the Truman Doctrine, the Berlin airlift, and the North Atlantic Treaty Organization. His domestic program, which he named the Fair Deal, was an enlargement of the New Deal programs.

In 1948, Truman was opposed for election by Governor Thomas E. Dewey of New York, who was widely expected to win, and by two splinter tickets of the Democratic party. Despite the opposition, Truman won in one of the great political upsets in US history. Truman's second term was beset by the issue of Communist infiltration of government, particularly by charges leveled by Sen. Joseph McCarthy. His administration was blamed for the "loss" of China to communism. His last years in office were chiefly occupied with waging the Korean War. He chose not to run for reelection in 1952.

Career: judge, Jackson co, Mo., 1922–24; president judge, Jackson co, Mo., 1926–34; US Senate, 1935–45; vice president, 1945; president, 1945–53.

See also Berlin Airlift; Cold War; Korean War; Marshall Plan; Truman Doctrine.

Truman Doctrine (1947), declaration of US foreign policy by Pres. Harry Truman. It stated that the United States would act to prevent the overthrow of democratic institutions by totalitarian governments anywhere in the world. Although the statement was universal in scope, Truman specifically was referring to the protection of Greece and Turkey against Soviet expansion. The doctrine became the primary statement of US policy in the Cold War.

Trumbull, John (1750–1831), US author, b. Westbury, Conn. A poet and essayist, he wrote *The Progress of Dulness* (1773), a long satirical poem, and *M'Fingal* (1782), an anti-British satire. After the American Revolution, he practiced law and was a member of the Connecticut Wits.

Trumbull, John (1756–1843), US painter, b. Lebanon, Conn. His work, mainly portraits and historical subjects, was influenced by Copley and Hogarth. His father and brothers were active patriots in the American Revolution. In 1786 he began a long series of scenes from the American Revolution, as well as portraits of major figures of the Revolution ("Alexander Hamilton," 1792).

Trumbull, Jonathan (1740–1809), US congressman, b. Lebanon, Conn. He sat in the first Congress; was speaker of the second (1791–93); and became a US senator (1795–96). He was Connecticut's governor (1797–1809).

Trumpet, loud, brilliant, brass wind musical instrument of primitive origin. It was used by the Romans for military fanfare. Long-tubed medieval trumpets were folded (*c.*1500), and trumpets were still played only by lip in Bach's time. Piston valves were added (*c.*1820). The common soprano (B♭) trumpet has a 2½-octave range.

Trumpeter Swan, swan with a loud, buglelike call found in Canada and NW United States. Once close to extinction, it is now protected by law and no longer endangered. It is one of the heaviest flying birds in North America. Weight: to 40lb (18kg). Species *Cygnus buccinator. See also* Swan.

Trunkfish, or boxfish, boxlike marine fish found in temperate and tropical seas. It is identified by its fused scales and eye spines. Length: to 24in (61cm). Among 30 species is the common West Indian *Lactophrys trigonus* and smooth *L. triqueter,* which releases a poisonous mucous for killing other fish. Family Ostraciontidae.

Truss Bridge, a bridge supported mainly by trusses, straight pieces of metal or timber, forming a series of triangles lying on a single plane. Individual pieces intersect at truss joints where they are connected by bolts, rivets, or welds. Trusses were first used during the Italian Renaissance for constructing covered bridges. Many beautiful covered truss bridges, built in the early history of North America, are still standing.

Trusts, combinations of companies that handed their stock over to be administered by a central controlling board. Later the term came to refer to business combinations in restraint of trade. In the United States, trusts were started about 1880 to prevent falling prices, which were affecting most businesses. By the early 20th century, trusts had been outlawed through legislation and court action.

Truth, Sojourner (1797?–1883), US abolitionist, b. Ulster co, N.Y. She was freed from slavery in 1827, by the New York Emancipation Act. She took the name Sojourner Truth and traveled, lecturing on emancipation and other social issues. Although illiterate, she spoke forcefully and effectively, winning many converts to her causes. Pres. Abraham Lincoln chose her to be counselor to the freedmen in Washington.

Truth Serum, a misnomer for a sedative/hypnotic drug such as sodium amobarbitol used to facilitate questioning. It is neither a serum, nor does it insure truth.

Trypanosome, animallike flagellate protozoan that is parasitic in the blood of vertebrates. An elongated cell, with long, undulating membrane and flagellum along one side, it is harbored by African game, carried by tsetse fly, and injected into blood of humans causing sleeping sickness. Length: 1/1250in (1/50mm). Class Mastigophora; species *Trypanosoma brucei.*

Trypanosomiasis, a whole array of debilitating diseases in man and domestic animals, caused by several species of parasitic flagellate protozoans of the genus *Trypanosoma.* The vector is usually a fly or other insect. Examples are human sleeping sickness and Chagas' disease, and nagana and surra in cattle and horses.

Trypsin, proteolytic enzyme present in pancreatic juice. It breaks down proteins into short peptides to aid in absorption during digestion.

Tryptophan, colorless crystalline essential amino acid found in proteins. *See* Amino Acid.

Tsetse Fly, brown fly, with a wasplike body, 0.24 to 0.72in (6–18mm) long, found south of the Tropic of Cancer in Africa. It is blood-sucking and transmits African sleeping sickness. Family Muscidae, species *Glossina spp. See also* Diptera.

Tshombe, Moise Kapenda (1919–69), Congolese military leader, secessionist, and politician. He became involved in the government of Katanga (renamed Shaba) and formed a separate nation when the rest of the Congo became independent in 1960. After hostilities with the United Nations, he fled to Europe, but returned as premier of a united Congo (now Zaire) in 1964. He was dismissed (1965), banished for treason, kidnapped, and imprisoned in Algeria (1967), where he died.

Tsinan (Jinan or Chi-nan), city in E China, 225mi (362km) S of Peking, near Yellow River; capital of Shantung prov. An ancient walled city dating from Chou dynasty (1122–256 BC), it has been provincial capital since Ming dynasty (1368–1644); scene of battle during Communist takeover 1948 causing heavy

Harry S. Truman

John Trumbull: Declaration of Independence

Harriet Tubman

loss of Nationalist forces. Industries: textiles, vegetable oils, chemicals, machine shops, food processing, paper, trucks, agricultural machinery, flour, iron, steel. Pop. 1,100,000.

Tsin Dynasty, Chinese dynasty, also known as Chin Dynasty. Established in 265 by Tsin Wu Ti (the Martial Emperor) and known in history as the West Tsin Dynasty, it was destroyed in 316 by the Hsiung-nu or Huns, and survivors fled S of the Yangtze to establish the East Tsin Dynasty (317–419), one of the Six Dynasties in S China. The migration of thousands of high-ranking northern officials to the S aided in development of traditional Chinese style and institutions there.

Tsinghai (Qinghai), province in W central China, bounded by Sinkiang Uighur (N and NE), Kansu (E), Szechwan (SE), Tibet (S and SW), Tibet and Sinkiang Uighur (W); capital is Hsi-ning. Originally part of Tibet, it was annexed to Mongols 14th century; passed to China's control 1724; fell 1949 to Communists, who established numerous autonomous districts; site of Tsinghai Lake, a salt lake giving its name to the province; it is the largest lake in China. Industries: coal, oil, iron ore, salt, borax, potash, Tsinghai horses, grain, potatoes. Area: 250,000sq mi (647,500sq km). Pop. 2,140,000.

Tsingtao (Qingdao, or Ching-tao), seaport city in NE China, in S Shantung Peninsula, on Yellow Sea; occupied by Japanese 1914–22, 1938–45; served as US naval base 1945–49; fell to Communists 1949. Industries: textiles, flour, cotton seed oil, food processing, tobacco, paper, machine shops, railroad cars, chemicals. Pop. 1,300,000.

Tsiolkovskii, Konstantin Eduardovich (1857–1935), Soviet aerospace scientist. He showed early genius in physics. After 1882 he turned his attention to aeronautics, improving dirigibles and airfoils. In 1898 he developed his theory of mass ratio, indicating the possibility of space flight with liquid fuel and booster rockets. He was made a member of the Russian Academy of Sciences (1919).

Tsitsihar (Qiqihaer, or Ch'i-Ch'i-ha-erh), port city in NE China, 170mi (274km) NW of Harbin, on Nen River; former capital of Hokiang and Heilungkiang provs. Industries: locomotives, paper, cement, food processing. Founded 1691. Pop. 1,500,000.

Tsunami, a shallow (3m or 9.8ft), long, sea wave caused by a submarine earthquake, subsidence, or volcanic eruption. Tsunamis spread radially from their source in ever-widening circles. Though rarely detected at sea, in shallow water they build up in force and height, crashing on shore and causing enormous damage. Tsunamis are also called seismic sea waves, but "tidal waves" is erroneous.

Tuatara, nocturnal lizardlike reptile of New Zealand, only survivor of the primitive order Rhynchocephalia. It is brownish-yellow with a unique vestigial third eye on the top of its head, possibly functional in the young, and has a short crest along neck and back. Length: to 2.5ft (76cm). Species *Sphenodon punctatus. See also* Reptile.

Tuba, large brass wind musical instrument in the lowest register. It has a conical bore like the French horn and an oblong shape and cupped mouthpiece like the trumpet. It is held vertically with the bell upward and played with four to five valves. It is made in tenor, bass, and double bass sizes for symphony orchestras. There are also Wagnerian tubas, sousaphones, and other variants in military bands.

Tubal Ligation, a method of sterilizing the female, in which the fallopian tubes leading from the ovaries are tied off with a ligature, preventing the migration of ova to the uterus.

Tuber, short, swollen, fleshy part of an underground stem, such as a potato. New plants develop from the buds, or eyes, growing in the axils of the scale leaves. Tubers are propagated by cutting them into sections containing at least one eye and planting these sections.

Tuberculosis, an infectious disease, usually involving the lungs, caused by several species of bacillus of the genus *Mycobacterium.* In man, the agent is usually the primate or bovine variety. Pulmonary tuberculosis constitutes over 90% of cases, but other parts of the body may also become tuberculous. Individual susceptibility and severity vary. Fatigue, weight loss, persistent coughing, and hemorrhaging from the lungs are progressive symptoms. Modern methods of early detection and chemotherapy have effectively reduced the former high incidence of this disease in densely populated areas.

Tuberose, Mexican perennial bulb plant frequently grown in S United States. The white sweet-scented flowers are so fragrant they should be mixed with other flowers in bouquets and gardens. Height: to 3ft (91.5cm). Family Agavaceae; species *Polianthes tuberosa.*

Tubman, Harriet (*c.* 1820–1913), US abolitionist, b. Dorchester co., Md. A slave, she escaped (1849) through the Underground Railroad; she then became a "conductor" on the Underground Railroad and was able to lead over 300 slaves to freedom. She worked closely with leading abolitionists, including Ralph Waldo Emerson, Wendell Phillips, and John Brown, and aided the Union during the Civil War.

Tucana, or the Toucan, faint southern constellation containing the Small Magellanic Cloud and the globular cluster 47 Tucanae (NGC 104). There is also a smaller globular, NGC 362.

Tucker, Sophie (1884–1966), US entertainer, b. Sophie Kalish in Russia. On stage in *The Ziegfeld Follies* (1909), *Leave It To Me* (1938), and *High Kickers* (1941), her 60-year career also included vaudeville, nightclub, film, radio, and TV performances. The "Last of the Red-hot Mamas" had as her theme song "Some of These Days."

Tucson, city in SE Arizona, 103mi (166km) SE of Phoenix on Santa Cruz River; seat of Pima co. Originally an Indian settlement, it was settled 1776 as the Spanish walled Presidio de San Augustín de Tuguison; transferred to the United States as part of Gadsden Purchase (1853); served as territorial capital 1867–77; prospered with coming of Southern Pacific Railroad (1880). Landmarks include "Old Adobe" (1868), Colossal Cave, Fort Lowell, San Xavier Mission (1783–97), annual rodeo, University of Arizona (1885). Industries: aircraft parts, missiles, dairy products, meat packing, cotton, mining, electronics, tourism. Inc. 1877. Pop. (1980) 330,537.

Tucumán (San Miguel de Tucumán), city in N Argentina, 665mi (1,071km) NW of Buenos Aires; capital of Tucumán prov.; site of first congress (1816) declaring Argentine independence. Industries: agriculture, lumber, sugar. Founded 1565. Pop. 366,000.

Tudor, royal family that ruled England 1485–1603. The dynasty was founded by Owen Tudor (1400?–61), a Welsh squire, who married Henry V's widow Catherine

of Valois. Owen's son Edmund (1430?–56) married Margaret Beaufort, heiress of John of Gaunt. Their son Henry (1457–1509) defeated Richard III at Bosworth (1485) and became Henry VII. Through his marriage (1486) to Edward IV's daughter Elizabeth, Henry united the houses of York and Lancaster. He was succeeded by his son, Henry VIII (1491–1547), who reigned 1509–47; and grandchildren, Edward VI, Mary I, and Elizabeth I. On Elizabeth's death (1603) James VI of Scotland, a Stuart and great-great-grandson of Henry VII, ascended the throne.

Tudor Architecture, English architectural style of the first half of the 16th century, from the time of Henry VII to Mary I.

Tuff, sedimentary rock made up of particles of igneous rock from volcanic eruptions. The particles vary in size from fine to coarse, and may be either stratified or heterogeneous in their arrangement.

Tu Fu (712–70), Chinese poet. Writing during the T'ang dynasty (618–906), China's literary golden age, he is considered one of his nation's greatest poets. His personal life was troubled, but his verse was polished and powerful with an intricate style rich in nuances. His 1405 poems cover such topics as war, corruption, and patriotism.

Tugboat, a small, powerful vessel used primarily for berthing large ships and towing or pushing barges. Some ocean-going tugboats are employed in salvage. First used in the 18th century in Scotland, where they were powered by a steam engine and a paddle wheel, tugboats are now driven by diesel engines.

Tugwell, Rexford Guy (1891–1979), US economist and political leader, b. Sinclairville, N.Y. A professor of economics, he wrote numerous books, including *The Economic Basis of Public Interest* (1922), *Industry's Coming of Age* (1927), critical of laissez-faire economics, and *The Brains Trust* (1968). In 1933 he became an advisor to Pres. Franklin Roosevelt, and a member of the "brain trust." His views on planning helped shape early New Deal policies. He served as assistant secretary of agriculture (1934–37), where he was responsible for the Resettlement Administration (1935–36). He was also governor of Puerto Rico (1941–46) and worked for the Center for the Study of Democratic Institutions (1966–79).

Tularemia, an acute infectious disease resembling plague but less severe, caused by the bacterium *Pasteurella tularensis.* It occurs primarily in wild birds and mammals. Human infection is rare and was first reported in the United States in 1914. Rabbits and hares seem to be the chief agents in transmitting the disease to man; a deerfly can also pass the infection. There are two forms in man: an ulcerative, glandular kind and a less common typhoidlike manifestation. The fatality rate is under 5%. Antibiotic treatment is effective.

Tulip, hardy bulb plants native to Europe, Asia, and North Africa. They have long, pointed leaves growing from the base and elongated cup-shaped flowers that can be almost any color or combination of colors. The bulbs are planted in mid-autumn or spring, depending on climate. They can be planted in pots indoors and forced in winter. The name tulip is derived from the Turkish word for turban. They have been cultivated and hybridized worldwide since the Middle Ages and now vary widely in physical characteristics and blooming times. Family Liliaceae; genus *Tulipa.*

Tulip Tree, or tulip poplar, deciduous tree of North America. It has tulip-shaped, greenish-yellow flowers and long, conelike fruit. Height: 100–200ft (30.5–61m). Family Magnoliaceae; genus *Liriodendron.*

Tull, Jethro (1674–1741), English agriculturist. He invented the agricultural drill (1701), which sowed seeds in drills, or rows, and widely replaced the usual method of sowing by hand. He was also responsible for introducing the practice of pulverizing (breaking down) the soil between rows.

Tulsa, port city in NE Oklahoma, on Arkansas River, seat of Tulsa co. Settled 1830s by Creek Indians, it developed with coming of Atlantic and Pacific Railroad (1882); with discovery of oil (1901), it became booming business center for oil industry; connected to Gulf of Mexico by McClelland-Kerr Waterway (1971). It is site of University of Tulsa (1894), Oral Roberts University, Philbrook Art Center (1938), Old Council Tree, first post office (1879). Industries: oil refining and research, petroleum products, oil field equipment, mining, machinery, aerospace. Inc. 1898. Pop. (1980) 360,919.

Tumbleweed, plant that breaks off near the ground in autumn and is rolled by the wind. The common western tumbleweed is usually white-stemmed and has pale flowers crowded into the leaf axils. Height: 6–20in (15–51cm). Species include *Amaranthus albus* and *A. graecizans.* Family Amaranthaceae.

Tumen (Tyumen), city in Russian SFSR, USSR, on the Tura River, 180mi (290km) E of Sverdlovsk; capital of Tumen oblast. Founded in 1585, it was the first-settled Russian town E of the Urals. Industries: matches, plywood, shipbuilding, tanning, sheepskins, felt boots, meat, flour, woolen milling. Pop. 1,407,000.

Tumor, any uncontrolled, abnormal proliferation of new tissue from pre-existing cells that has no useful function in terms of the body as a whole. Tumors fall into several types and are diagnosed as benign or malignant.

Tuna, mackerellike marine fish found in tropical, temperate, and cold seas. An important commercial fish, it has a blue-black and silvery streamlined body with a large, sharply divided tail. Length: to 14ft (4.3m); weight: 1,800lb (810kg). Types of tuna include bluefin, yellowfin, big eye, skipjack, and bonito. Family Scombridae.

Tundra, a Lapp term for the treeless, level or gently undulating plain characteristic of arctic and subarctic regions. The tundra is marshy with dark mucky soil that supports mosses, lichens, and low shrubs. It has a permanently frozen subsoil known as permafrost.

Tungsten, or wolfram, metallic element (symbol W) of the third transition series, first identified in 1779 and isolated in 1783. Chief ores are wolframite and scheelite. Tungsten has the highest melting point of all metals and is used for filaments in electric light bulbs, electron tubes, etc. It is also used in high-speed steels and other special alloys. The sulfide is used as a lubricant. Chemically, tungsten is fairly unreactive: it oxidizes at high temperatures. Properties: at. no. 74; at. wt. 183.85; sp. gr. 19.3; melt. pt. 6,170°F (3,410°C); boil. pt. 10,701°F (5,921°C); most common isotope W^{184} (30.64%). *See also* Transition Elements.

Tungus, Uralic-Altaic-speaking, Mongoloid people who inhabit E Siberia. Consisting of two main groups, the Evenki and Lamuts, they practice reindeer herding, fishing, and agriculture. Introduction of Russian Orthodoxy resulted in the decline of traditional shamanism.

Tungusic Languages, group of remote languages spoken in the Soviet Union and China, forming part of the Altaic family. A northern branch consists of Evenki (or Tungus) and Even, both spoken in central and E Siberia, while the southern branch consists of Nanai, spoken near the city of Khabarovsk, and Sibo, spoken in northwestern China. Manchu, the language of the Manchus but now nearly extinct, is also a Tungusic language.

Tunicate, or sea squirt, marine, immobile, vase-shaped animal found worldwide. They are solitary or live in colonies. Adults reveal their chordate nature only by numerous gill slits that filter seawater. The tadpole-shaped larvae have well-developed tails, notochords, and nerve cords. Some barrel-shaped tunicates are free-swimming and others are neotenic, retaining their larval shape into maturity. Length: 3/16–11.75in (5mm–30cm). There are 2,000 species. Phylum Chordata; subdivision Urochordata. *See also* Chordate.

Tunis, city in NE Tunisia, N Africa, on Lake of Tunis with canal access to Gulf of Tunis (arm of Mediterranean). A leading industrial and trade center near site of ancient Carthage, the city is divided into Tunisian and European sections; site of museums, Zitouna Mosque (732), medieval walls, University of Tunis (1960). Area was settled by Romans 2nd century BC–AD 5th century; conquered by Muslims 7th century, after which it developed to become 9th-century capital of Tunisia; capital under Hafsid dynasty 13th–16th centuries; occupied by Turks, Spanish, French until independence was recognized 1956. Industries: rail workshops, lead smelting, textiles, carpets, olive oil, chemicals. Pop. 944,000.

Tunisia, independent nation in N Africa. The site of ancient Carthage, and many Roman ruins, it is an agricultural country. Its geographical position makes it politically and economically important.

Land and economy. Between Algeria (W) and Libya (E) on the N coast of Africa, Tunisia extends 1,000mi (1,600km) along the Mediterranean Sea. The N section, source of most agricultural production, is fertile. Livestock grazing and olive groves are in the coastal plains. The S region borders the Sahara Desert and supports grazing and semi-nomadic tribes. Some large farms are state-operated. Although agriculture and pastoralism employ most of the labor force, petroleum is the leading export, earning about half of export earnings. Leading industries are steel, cement, process phosphates, and refined oil.

People. Descended from the Phoenician traders in the 12th century BC Tunisians now consist of about 35% Arabs and 65% Berbers. Arabic is the official and national language; 1% speak Berber. Most of the population is Sunni Muslim with some Andalusian Moors and Jews in the cities. Europeans constitute 1% of the population, the majority being French.

Government. According to the constitution of 1959, Tunisia is a republic led by a popularly-elected president. But in 1963 it became a one-party state, and in 1975 Habib Bourguiba became President for Life.

History. Carthage, the most noted of the Phoenician trading cities, was established in Tunisia. Later, it was a Roman possession; Arabs came in the 7th century when it became an Islamic cultural center. A Turkish invasion occurred in 1574; in 1881 France occupied the land, making it a protectorate. Tunisia's drive for nationalism started after WWI when a constitutional party was formed. In 1934, Habib Bourguiba became its leader. Guerrilla warfare persuaded France to offer internal autonomy followed by an end to the protectorate in 1956. Clashes continued between the two countries, and on July 25, 1957, the Tunisian Constituent Assembly voted to establish a republic. Bourguiba was elected president under the banner of the Destoruian Socialist party. Tunisia is a member of the Arab League, but favors negotiations to settle Arab-Israeli disputes. In 1982 headquarters of the Palestine Liberation Organization (PLO) were established near Tunis. The bombing of PLO headquarters by Israel created tension between the US and Tunisia. Tensions with Libya also increased in 1985.

PROFILE

Official name: Republic of Tunisia
Area: 63,170sq mi (163,610sq km)
Population: 6,218,100
Density: 98per sq mi (38per sq km)
Chief cities: Tunis (capital); Sfax
Government: Republic
Religion: Islam
Language: Arabic (official and national)
Monetary unit: Dinar
Gross national product: $6,950,000,000
Per capita income: $459
Industries: processed foods, wineries, petroleum products, olive oil processing, textiles, clothing, construction materials, leather
Agriculture: cereals, wheat, grains, dates, olives, citrus fruits, almonds, figs, cattle, forests, grapes
Minerals: phosphates, iron ore, oil, lead, zinc
Trading partners: France, Italy, West Germany

Tupelo, or black gum, deciduous tree of moist forests in North America. Its fine-textured wood is used for furniture, mallets, etc. It has lustrous leaves, minute, greenish-white flowers, and dark blue fruit clusters relished by birds. Height: to 100ft (30.5m). Species include the sour gum *(Nyssa sylvatica)* and water tupelo or cotton gum *(N. aquatica).* Family Cornaceae.

Turbellarian. *See* Platyhelminthes.

Turbidity Current, a density current in water, air, or other fluid caused by different amounts of matter in suspension. In the ocean, when sediment along the continental shelves breaks off and rushes downslope, the resulting turbidity current carves out submarine canyons and deposits distinctively bedded layers on the ocean floor.

Turbine, rotary engine that converts the energy of a moving stream of water, steam, or gas into mechanical energy. The basic element in a turbine is a wheel or rotor with blades or buckets arranged on its circumference such that moving water or gas exerts tangential force, which turns the wheel. This mechanical energy is transferred through a drive shaft to operate a machine.

Turbojet Engine, aircraft propulsion unit that produces power through the reaction of expanding gases. Air taken in at the front through a compressor is forced into a combustion chamber, mixed with fuel, and burned, producing a rush of expanding gas that propels the aircraft in a reaction to the rapid outflow. To maintain the cycle the expanding gas also drives a turbine connected to the air compressor.

Turbot, NE Atlantic marine flatfish. A food fish, it has a deep, thick body, short tail shaft, and bony hooks on scales. Colors are marbled gray or brown. Length: 40in (102cm). Family Scopthalmidae (or Pleuronectidae); species *Scophthalmus maximus.*

Turene, Henri de La Tour d'Auvergne, vicomte de (1611–75), French general. He distinguished himself against the Germans in the Thirty Years' War (1618–48) and in the wars of Louis XIV. He was involved in the Fronde (1649–51) but supported the future Louis XIV against the forces of the Prince de Condé and Spain. Killed in battle against the Germans, he was buried with the kings of France.

Turgenev, Ivan (Sergeevich) (1818–83), Russian novelist, playwright, and short-story writer. He was at his most prolific between 1850–60. The play *A Month in the Country,* which would strongly influence Chekhov, appeared in 1850. *A Sportsman's Sketches,* short stories, was published in 1852. Three novels also appeared: *Rudin* (1855), *A Nest of Gentlefolk* (1859), and *On the Eve* (1860). His works received official disapproval because they spoke out against social and political evils. After the appearance of his greatest novel *Fathers and Sons,* about nihilism, he left Russia. Well-known short stories include "First Love" (1870), "A Lear of the Steppe" (1870), and "Torrents of Spring" (1871).

Turgot, Anne Robert Jacques (1727–81), French philosopher, economist, administrator. Chief administrator for Limoges and controller-general of finance (1774–76), he wrote *Reflections on the Formation and Distribution of Riches* (1766). He was considered a physiocrat (agriculture was the ultimate source of real wealth) and a philosophe. He contributed to the French *Encyclopédie* and labored unsuccessfully to set France's fiscal house in order. *See also* Philosophes; Physiocrats.

Turin (Torino), city in NW Italy, 78mi (126km) NW of Genoa, on the Po River; capital of Piedmont region and of Turin province. Founded by the Taurini, it became Roman military colony, and a Lombard duchy 590–636; it was a free commune 12th and 13th centuries; capital of kingdom of Sardinia 1720–1861; 19th-century center of Risorgimento; site of 15th-century cathedral, Palazzo Madama (begun 13th century), university (1404); important center of industry, commerce, and transportation. Industries: automobiles, airplanes, rubber, paper, leather, fashion. Pop. 1,188,689.

Turkey (Türkiye), independent nation in Asia Minor and Europe. Located in a geographically vital position, it became a republic in 1923 under nationalist leader Kemal Ataturk.

Land and economy. Situated in two continents, Asia and Europe, Turkey is bordered by Greece and Bulgaria (N), the USSR and Iran (E), Iraq and Syria (S). The strategically important Turkish straits (the Bosporus, Sea of Marmara, and the Dardanelles) connect the Black Sea and the Mediterranean Sea. The mild, narrow coastal plain supports a variety of crops ranging from tea to cotton. The central inland Anatolian plateau's W section grows wheat; the E portion is mountainous with severe winters. The SW is treeless, with some mountains 10,000ft (3,050m) above sea level, with little population. The Tigris and Euphrates rivers rise in the E and flow S to the Persian Gulf. In 1973 a suspension bridge linked Europe and Asia across the Bosporus. With an agricultural economy, Turkey's main crops are cotton, tobacco, and grains; about 60% of the working population is engaged in farming or allied fields. About half of the economy is made up of government-owned or controlled enterprises. Opium production was halted in 1971 and resumed, for medical purposes, in 1974. Turkey relies on remittances from workers abroad, many in W Europe, as a major source of foreign exchange. With a huge payments deficit, Turkey was virtually bankrupt by 1977 until it received emergency loans from the International Monetary Fund.

People. Turkey's population, 99% Sunni Muslim, lives principally on the Anatolian peninsula in Asia, the rest in the European portion. Once a country of small

Tunisia

Turkey

J. M. W. Turner: Crossing the Stream *(detail)*

villages, the urban centers have drawn villagers, and most cities now have communities of squatter homes surrounding them. There is no officially recognized religion and no legal discrimination against the minority groups of Greeks, Armenians, and Jews. The largest ethnic minority, the Kurds, lives in the remote areas of the E and SE in primitive conditions. Public elementary school is free and compulsory. Literacy is 55%.

Government. A 1961 constitution provides for a bicameral legislature and a president. The premier is chosen from the majority party. Since 1980, however, a military junta has governed the country.

History. In classical times a center of Greek civilization, the region of modern Turkey was subsequently under the Roman, Byzantine, and Ottoman empires. When the 600-year-old rule of the Ottoman Empire collapsed after fighting as one of Germany's allies in WWI, nationalism grew and the trappings of the old empire were abolished. Under the leadership of Kemal Ataturk, Turkey became a republic in 1923, with Ataturk its first president. Turning away from imperial traditions it became westernized with social and economic reforms that were the basis of modern Turkey. Turkey joined the Allies near the end of WWII and under the Truman Doctrine received US military and economic aid. In 1950 the Ataturk party was defeated, and the Democratic party was in power until a 1960 coup d'état. A return to civil government came the following year. Tension with neighboring Greece has been a constant factor in foreign affairs. In 1974 this led to a Turkish invasion of Cyprus, justified by Turkish allegations of mistreatment of the Turkish minority. The invasion strained Turkey's ties with the United States, but relations showed signs of improvement during the early 1980s. Relations with Greece have remained strained. The military government that assumed power in 1980 faced unrest by both left-wing and conservative Muslim extremists and was criticized worldwide for its alleged treatment of political prisoners. A new constitution (1982) and parliamentary elections (1983) paved the way for slight improvements in the economy by the mid-1980s. *See also* Byzantine Empire; Ottoman Empire.

PROFILE

Official name: Republic of Turkey
Area: 301,381sq mi (780,577sq km)
Population: 45,217,556
　Density: 150per sq mi (58per sq km)
Chief cities: Ankara (capital); Istanbul; Izmir
Government: Republic
Religion: Islam
Language: Turkish
Monetary unit: Lira
Gross national product: $58,760,000,000
Per capital income: $576
Industries: chemicals, steel, textiles, olive oil, opium, steel, foundry products, footwear, furniture, cement, paper, glassware, appliances
Agriculture: tobacco, cereals, cotton, olives, sheep, cattle, fruits, nuts, sugar beets, opium, forests
Minerals: antimony, borate, copper, chrome, manganese, lead, zinc, coal, iron, oil, silver, mercury, asbestos
Trading partners: European Economic Community, United States

Turkey, North American game bird now widely domesticated throughout the world. These birds support a food industry, particularly in the United States where turkeys have long been traditional fare for Thanksgiving. A Mexican race with white-tipped tails has been bred into many varieties and is raised commercially. The common wild turkey (*Meleagris gallopavo*), once abundant in Canada, United States, and Mexican highlands, was overhunted and is now protected by wildlife

management measures. The male, or gobbler, is often bearded. He travels in small groups, feeds on forest floor vegetable matter, and, at mating time, displays his feathers and utters courtship noises. The smaller female builds a well concealed nest for the buffy spotted eggs (12–20). Length: 50in (127cm). The ocellated turkey (*Agriocharis ocellata*) of lowland Mexico and adjacent Central American areas has a yellow knob between its eyes, bright metallicky plumage, and a bare, blue, pimple-covered head and neck. Family Meleagrididae.

Turkic Languages, group of languages forming a branch of the Altaic family. Its most important member is Turkish; most of the rest are spoken in the Soviet Union. These include Azerbaijani, Turkmen, Kazakh, Kirgiz, Tatar, Bashkir, Uzbek, Uigur, and a number of others. Azerbaijani and Turkmen are also spoken in Iran.

Turkmen Soviet Socialist Republic (Turkmenskaja Sovetskaja Socialisticeskaja Republik, Turkmenia, Turkmenistan), constituent republic of the USSR, in central Asia; bounded by the Caspian Sea (W), Kazakh and Uzbek republics (N and NE), and Afghanistan and Iran (S), containing the four oblasts of Aschabad, Cardzov, Mary, and Tasauz. Main cities are Aschabad (capital), Krasnovodsk, Mary, Nebit-Dag. The area has been inhabited by Turki tribes since the 10th century; after their 1881 defeat, the region became part of Russian Turkistan; organized as a Soviet Republic 1924, it became a constituent republic of the USSR 1925. Industries: sheep, camels, cotton, guayule, sesame, millet, sweet potatoes, dates, sugar cane, grapes, melons, petroleum, ozocerite, iodine, bromine, salt, sulphur, lignite, potash. Exports: cotton, fruit, silk, karakul, petroleum. Pop. 2,722,000.

Turku, seaport city in SW Finland, at mouth of Aurajoki River on Baltic Sea; capital of Turku ja Pori prov.; site of Finnish university (1917) and Swedish university (1918). Industries: steel, textiles, clothing, shipyards. Founded 1157. Pop. 163,981.

Turner, Frederick Jackson (1861–1932), US historian, b. Portage, Wisc. He gained instant acclaim with his treatise *The Significance of the Frontier in American History* (1893). Growing up in frontier territory, he recognized the influence of the constantly moving frontier on American life. His later works were further developments of his original premise, such as *Rise of the New West* (1906), *The Frontier in American History* (1920), and *The Significance of Sections in American History* (1932) for which he won a Pulitzer Prize (1933).

Turner, J(oseph) M(allord) W(illiam) (1775–1851), English painter. By 1790 he was exhibiting his watercolors at the Royal Academy; although he remained a watercolorist, after 1795 he grew increasingly interested in oil painting. Turner's mature style is evidenced in works such as "Death of Nelson" (1806–08) and "London Seen from Greenwich" (1809). After 1820 he grew increasingly preoccupied with light and intense color. His late works emphasized conflict and turmoil ("Rain, Steam, Speed" 1844) and anticipated the Impressionist style.

Turner, Nat (1800–31), US slave, b. Southampton co, Va., who instigated the "Southampton Insurrection." He said he heard a voice in 1828 saying "the last shall be first." He took this experience plus the solar eclipse of February 1831 as a sign to begin the insurrection in which 85 whites were killed. He was tried, convicted, and hanged.

Turnip, garden vegetable best grown in cool weather. The edible leaves are large and toothed with thick midribs. A biennial, it bears yellow flowers the second year. The edible white, fleshy root is white to purplish-red on the outside; diameter: 3–6in (7.6–15.2cm). It matures in 30–60 days. Height: to 20in (50.8cm). Family Cruciferae; species *Brassica rapa.*

Turnstone, Arctic-nesting, migratory shore bird that uses its curved bill to turn over pebbles in search of food. The vividly marked ruddy turnstone (*Arenaria interpres*) ranges widely in winter; length: 9in (23cm). The larger black turnstone (*Arenaria melanocephala*) favors Pacific North America. Grayish-green spotted eggs (4) are laid in a ground nest.

Turpentine, or gum turpentine, sticky liquid obtained from coniferous trees; it contains rosin and a volatile oil. The volatile oil is obtained by distillation of the gum and is used as a paint thinner, solvent, and in varnishes and lacquers. *See also* Rosin.

Turquoise, a phosphate mineral, hydrous basic copper aluminum phosphate found in veins of aluminum-rich rocks in deserts. Occurs as tiny crystals and dense masses, crusts, and veins. Blue; hardness 5–6; sp gr 2.7. Popular gemstone.

Turtle, reptile found on land or in marine and fresh waters. On the evolutionary scale, turtles have the most ancient lineage, preceding even the dinosaurs. They have a bony, horn-covered, boxlike shell that encloses shoulder and hip girdles and all internal organs. The head, neck, limbs, and tail project through openings in the shell. Horny jaws, resembling those of birds, replace teeth. All lay eggs on land. Terrestrial turtles are frequently called tortoises and some edible species of brackish waters are called terrapins. Marine turtles usually have smaller, lighter shells. Some species are carnivorous, others are herbivorous. There are two major subgroups, the hidden-necked or cryptodires and the side-necked or pleurodires. Length: 2in–7ft (5cm–2m). There are 300 species in 12 families. Order Chelonia. *See also* Green Turtle; Reptile; Soft-shelled Turtle.

Turtle Dove, European dove with a white-edged tail and soft, purring voice. Species *Streptopelia turtur. See also* Dove.

Tuscaloosa, commercial and industrial city in W central Alabama, 50mi (81km) SW of Birmingham; seat of Tuscaloosa co.; site of University of Alabama. Railroad and manufacturing center. Industries: cottonseed oil and products, chemicals, paper products. Settled 1816; inc. 1819. Pop. (1980) 75,143.

Tuscany (Toscana), region in central Italy, on the Tyrrhenian Sea, comprised of the provs. of Massa-Carrara, Lucca, Pistoia, Pisa, Siena, Arezzo, Florence, Grosseto, Leghorn; capital is Florence; chiefly mountainous with fertile areas, particularly in the Arno River Valley. Products: cereal, olives, olive oil, wine, livestock; rich in minerals including lead, zinc, mercury, copper, lignite, marble. Industries: chemicals, metals, textiles, tourism, shipbuilding, handcrafts. Area: 8,876sq mi (22,989sq km). Pop. 3,578,814.

Tuscarora War (1711–13), series of expeditions by colonists from North Carolina, South Carolina, and Virginia against the Tuscarora Indians, who had attacked North Carolina settlers because of encroachments on Indian land. Defeated in 1713, the Tuscaroras moved to western Pennsylvania and became the sixth nation of the Iroquois Confederation.

Tuskegee Institute, nonsectarian private college in Tuskegee, Ala. Founded as a vocational school for blacks (1881), it became a college in 1927. Booker T. Washington was the principal until his death in 1915. It was here that George Washington Carver conducted his agricultural experiments.

Tusk Shell. *See* Tooth Shell.

Tussock Moth, moth whose caterpillar is typically covered with tussocks (tufts) of long hairs. Females of many species, including the gypsy moth, are virtually wingless. Caterpillars of the gypsy moth and some other tussock moths are serious pests of deciduous trees. Family Lymantriidae. *See also* Moth.

Tutankhamen (died *c.* 1340 BC), one of the last kings of the XVIII dynasty of Egypt, whose ascent to the throne was a result of his marriage to the daughter of Akhenaton at the age of 10. During his short, unimpressive reign of 8 years, the god Amon was restored and the capital was moved from Akhetaten back to Thebes. The discovery of his tomb in 1922, still containing most of its royal burial equipment, has made him one of the best known Egyptian pharaohs.

Tutu, Desmond Mpilo (1931–), South African clergyman and anti-apartheid leader. Ordained in 1960, he became the first black Anglican dean of Johannesburg (1975), bishop of Lesotho (1976–78), assistant bishop of Johannesburg (1978–84), and the first black Anglican bishop of Johannesburg (1984–86). He received the Nobel Peace Prize (1984) for his efforts to end apartheid in South Africa. In 1986 he was elected Archbishop of Cape Town, which made him the head of South Africa's Anglican Church.

Tutuola, Amos (1920–), African writer. He tells the traditional tales of the Yoruba people of his native Nigeria. A visionary whose world is a mixture of fantasy and reality, Tutuola has been criticized for not advocating political reform. *The Palm Wine Drinkard* (1952), *My Life in the Bush of Ghosts* (1954), and *Ajaiyi and His Inherited Poverty* (1967) are among his best works.

Tuvalu (formerly Ellice Islands), independent republic in W Pacific Ocean, S of Equator and W of International Date Line, a cluster of nine low-lying coral islands. The first European to discover the islands (1568) was the Spanish navigator Alvaro de Mendaña. The British assumed control in 1892, and it was subsequently administered with the nearby Gilbert Islands (now Kiribati). Tuvalu became a separate self-governing colony in 1975, achieving full independence within the Commonwealth of Nations in 1978. The population, composed of both an indigenous Melanesian minority and Polynesians who invaded during the 16th century, is principally Protestant. Subsistence agriculture dominates the economy with copra and fish the principal products. Capital: Funafuti; area: 10sq mi (26sq km); pop. 10,000.

Twain, Mark (1835–1910), pseud. of Samuel Langhorne Clemens, US journalist, lecturer, and author, b. Florida, Mo. The first US author of world rank to write authentically colloquial novels employing a genuine American idiom. His work, which began as pure humor and developed to bitter satire, was marked by an egalitarian attitude and a strong desire for social justice. "The Celebrated Jumping Frog of Calaveras County" (1865), a short story, brought Twain fame. His reputation was furthered by the travel books *Innocents Abroad* (1869), followed by *Roughing It* (1872).

In 1872 Twain settled in Hartford, Conn., whence he made many successful lecture tours around the United States and the world. He collaborated with Charles Dudley Warner on *The Gilded Age* (1873). *Mark Twain's Sketches, Old and New* (1875) was followed by three of his finest and best-known works, all utilizing material from his boyhood: *The Adventures of Tom Sawyer* (novel, 1876), *Life on the Mississippi* (nonfiction, 1883), and *The Adventures of Huckleberry Finn* (novel, 1885). He published another travel book, *A Tramp Abroad* (1880), and two historical novels, *The Prince and the Pauper* (1882) and *A Connecticut Yankee in King Arthur's Court* (1889), a social satire. Saddened and embittered by personal and financial losses, Twain later wrote such pessimistic works as *The Man That Corrupted Hadleyburg and Other Stories and Sketches* (1900), *What Is Man?* (1905), and *The Mysterious Stranger* (1916). Twain's works revolutionized the language of American fiction and had a great influence on many later American writers.

'Twas the Night Before Christmas (1823), poem by Clement Moore about Santa Claus. It was first published in the Troy (N.Y.) *Sentinel* as "A Visit from St Nicholas."

Tweed, William Marcy (1823–78), US politician, b. New York City. As leader of Tammany, the New York City Democratic political machine, he controlled party nominations. He and his cohorts, known as the Tweed Ring, stole government funds in the 1860s. Finally arrested in 1871, he was sentenced to one year in prison. He was rearrested on other charges, escaped to Spain, but was extradited and jailed.

Twelfth Night (1601), romantic comedy by William Shakespeare. Confusion results when Viola and Sebastian, identical twins, are shipwrecked off the coast of Illyria, and Viola dons male garb to serve as page to Duke Orsino. Mistaken identities complicate the many love interests in this oft-revived and delightful work.

Twelvers. *See* Imamis.

Twelve Tables, basis for Roman law, codified under Theodosius II of Rome (*c.* 450 BC). It was written on tablets, probably of wood, by a committee of decimvirs in response to a plebeian demand for political equality and written law. Compiled from laws of Solon and other Greeks, as well as unwritten Roman laws and customs, only fragments are known today. *See also* Roman Law.

Twelve Tribes of Israel, according to the Bible, the groups of Hebrews descended from Jacob and bearing the names of his sons Reuben, Simeon, Judah, Issachar, Zebulun, Gad, Asher, Benjamin, Dan, and Naphtali. The tribes of Manasseh and Ephraim were named for the sons of Jacob's son, Joseph. The descendants of Jacob's son Levi, the Levites, not counted among the twelve, were devoted to the service of God and acquired no territory in Canaan, but lived among the others. According to the modern critical view, it is unlikely that these tribes all descended from Jacob. *See also* Jacob; Levi.

Twilight, the periods of incomplete darkness following sunset (dusk) and preceding sunrise (dawn), ending or beginning respectively when the Sun is below the horizon by an angle of 6° (civil twilight), 12° (nautical twilight), and 18° (astronomical twilight).

Twins, The. *See* Gemini.

Two Gentlemen of Verona (1592), Shakespearean comedy. Two friends travel to Milan, where they compete for the favors of Silvia, the duke's daughter. Proteus' sweetheart Julia arrives in male garb, and becomes his page. Proteus repents and weds Julia, while Valentine plans to marry Silvia.

Two Noble Kingsmen, The (*c.*1613), 5-act play ascribed to William Shakespeare and John Fletcher. Many scholars attribute the parts of the play that are not obviously written by Fletcher to Shakespeare; others argue that Philip Massinger was Fletcher's collaborator.

Two-Party System, political system with two parties. In the United States and most English-speaking countries, the two political parties compete for power. A two-party system tends to provide greater stability and usually guarantees one party sufficient strength to govern.

Two Sicilies, Kingdom of the, state uniting S Italy with the island of Sicily from the 15th to the 19th centuries. In the 11th century the two areas were united by the Normans and again divided in 1282 between the French Angevins and the Spanish Aragonese. In 1442, Alfonso V of Aragon reunited the two areas and became self-styled king of the Two Sicilies, and in 1816 Ferdinand IV of Naples (Ferdinand III of Sicily) officially merged the kingdoms and became Ferdinand I of the Two Sicilies. In 1861 the kingdom was conquered by and incorporated into the new kingdom of Italy.

Tyler, John (1790–1862), 10th president of the United States (1841–45), b. Charles City co, Va. He graduated from William and Mary College in 1807. In 1813 he married Letitia Christian; after her death he married (1844) Julia Gardiner. He had 14 children. Tyler was admitted to the bar in 1809, the same year his father became governor of Virginia. Two years later he entered the Virginia legislature.

In 1817 he went to the US House of Representatives as a states' rights Democrat. After a term as governor he went to the US Senate (1827). There he formed an uneasy alliance with Andrew Jackson, whom he supported for president. Later, however, he split with Jackson over fiscal policies and joined the new Whig party. In 1836 he resigned from the Senate over a matter of principle.

In 1840 the Whigs chose Tyler as running mate for William Henry Harrison. Harrison died soon after inauguration, and Tyler became the first vice president to succeed to the presidency. Cool to many Whig policies, Tyler was not able to accomplish much during his tenure; the annexation of Texas was a notable exception. In 1844 the Whigs nominated Henry Clay rather than Tyler.

Career: Virginia House of Burgesses, 1811–16, 1823–25; US House of Representatives, 1817–21; governor of Virginia, 1825–27; US Senate, 1827–36; vice president, 1841; president, 1841–45.

Tyler, Wat (died 1381), English rebel. He was the leader of the Peasants' Revolt (1381), a protest against harsh taxation and low wages. Rebels seized Canterbury and, choosing Tyler as their leader, marched to London, plundering John of Gaunt's palace and capturing the Tower of London. Richard II agreed to several demands made by the rebels. When Tyler presented further demands, he was wounded and subsequently beheaded by the lord mayor of London. After his death the rebellion soon ended.

Tyler, city in NE Texas, 85mi (137km) ESE of Dallas; seat of Smith co; site of Butler College, Texas College (1894), Tyler Junior College (1926); scene of Texas Rose Festival. Industries: oil refining, cotton processing, oil, gas, prefabricated homes, agriculture, roses, lumber. Settled 1840; named for President John Tyler; inc. 1846 as town, 1907 as city. Pop. (1980) 70,508.

Tylor, (Sir) Edward Burnett (1832–1917), English anthropologist, often called the founder of cultural anthropology. His observations of travels in the United States and Mexico were published in *Anahuac: or, Mexico and the Mexicans, Ancient and Modern* (1861). His most important work was *Primitive Culture* (1871).

Tyndale, William (1494?–1536), English Bible translator, pamphleteer, and Protestant martyr. After disputes with ecclesiastical authorities, Tyndale fled in 1524 to Germany, where he issued an English Pentateuch and New Testament. Copies introduced into England were destroyed. Their author was captured at Antwerp and strangled. All his work is noted for its sound scholarship.

Tyndall, John (1820–93), Irish physicist who showed that the blue color of the sky is due to dust scattering the Sun's rays. He also studied the magnetic properties of crystals, and light diffusion by dust and large molecules, an effect which bears his name. By 1881, he helped eliminate the idea of spontaneous generation, by showing that germ-free air does not cause food decay.

Type B Blood. *See* Blood Type..

Typhoid Fever, an acute, sometimes epidemic communicable disease marked by fever, chills, prostration, enlargement of the spleen, inflammation of the intestinal tract, and the eruption of pink spots. The bacillus *Salmonella typhosa* is transmitted by contaminated water, milk, and food. Inspection of water supplies, pasteurization of milk, typhoid inoculations, and treatment with chloromycetin have greatly reduced the incidence of this disease.

Typhoon, the name given in the Pacific to a hurricane, a violent tropical cyclone. *See also* Hurricane.

Typhus, or typhus fever, three forms of acute, infectious diseases caused by rickettsial bodies: (1) epidemic human body louse-borne typhus, with mortality of up to 70%. Vaccinations and antibiotic treatment are now very effective against this form. (2) Brill-Zinsser disease, a recrudescent milder form of the same disease. (3) Tropical and semitropical endemic typhus transmitted by the rat flea.

Tyrannosaurus, giant bipedal, carnivorous dinosaur that lived during Late Cretaceous times in W North America and Mongolia. Its four-foot (1.2m) head was armed with a series of daggerlike teeth, some being 6in (15cm) long. The hind legs were enormous, but front legs were so tiny they may have been useless. Length: 45ft (14m); height: 18ft (5.5m). *See also* Theropoda.

Tyre (Sür), town in SW Lebanon, 22mi (35km) S of Sayda. A flourishing city, it was a maritime power by 1100 BC, and Tyre merchants established colonies in Mediterranean areas, including Sicily, Sardinia, France, and Spain; became part of the Roman Empire 64 BC; fell to Crusaders; was destroyed 1291; Roman sites remain. Industries: finance, manufacture, commerce. Founded 1400 BC by Phoenicians. Pop. 35,000.

Tyrosine, white crystalline amino acid found in proteins. *See also* Amino Acid.

Tyrrhenian Sea, part of the Mediterranean Sea, W of Italian mainland, E of Corsica and Sardinia, N of Sicily; site of several small island groups, including Luscan, Lipari, Pontine islands; chief ports are Naples and Palermo. Width: 60–300mi (97–483km). Length: approx. 475mi (765km).

Mark Twain

John Tyler

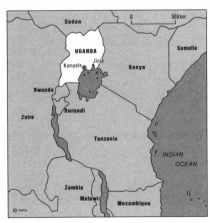

Uganda

Tzu Hsi (1835–1908), the famous empress dowager of the Ch'ing Dynasty, known as the "Old Buddha." She was the real power in China from 1862 to 1908, first as co-regent and then as regent. As imperial concubine she learned the politics of the Manchu court and became one of the most powerful and feared women in Chinese history, an obstinate opponent of the West and modernization.

U

Ubangi. *See* Oubangi.

Uccello, Paolo (1397–1475), Italian painter. Primarily a decorative painter, he strongly influenced the minor Florentine masters. His strongest period was 1436–60, during which he executed "John Hawkwood," a fresco monument commissioned in 1436; "Flood" (*c*. 1450); and the "Battle of San Romano," one of his most famous works. These panels (*c*.1455) were commissioned for the Medici Palace and are primarily decorative. One of Uccello's last works was the predella of the altarpiece in Urbino for the Corpus Domini Society (1465–69).

Ufa, city in Russian SFSR, USSR, at Ufa River mouth, 715mi (1,114km) E of Moscow; capital of the Bashkir Autonomous SSR; site of aviation, medical, agricultural, and teachers' colleges, research institutes, revolutionary, regional, and art museums, famous old cathedral, Baskir State University (1957), Palace of Labor and Art, monument to Lenin. Industries: airplanes, mining machinery, cables, typewriters, clothing, shoes, leather goods, flour, meat, dairy products, cotton milling, clay, gypsum, limestone, lumber and veneer. Pop. 962,000.

Uganda, independent nation in E central Africa, bordered by Kenya (E), Tanzania and Rwanda (S), Zaire (W), and Sudan (N).
 Land and economy. Mostly a plateau 3,000–6,000ft (915–1,830m) above sea level, Uganda sits on the Equator in E central Africa, bordered on the E by Kenya, the S by Tanzania and Rwanda, W by Zaire, and N by Sudan. Lake Victoria, source of the White Nile, is the most important lake. Margherita, in the Ruwenzori range, is the highest peak, 16,763ft (5,113m). Three major national parks preserve Uganda's wildlife. Altitude variations affect the rainfall, which is sparse in the arid N; the SW and W receive about 50in (127cm) annually. Seasonal changes are mild, including two dry spells a year. Coffee provides over 90% of export revenues, although agriculture, forestry, and fishing account for only 22% of gross domestic product (GDP). Principal mineral exports are copper and tin. Textile, steel, and chemical plants have been built, but manufacturing accounts for only 6% of GDP.
 People. Four racial groups are represented: Bantu (the most numerous), Nilotic, Nilo-Hamitic, and Sudanic. The bulk of population, dependent on agriculture, lives in the fertile area S of Lake Kyoga. Nearly half the population is Christian (Roman Catholic predominating), 6% is Muslim, and the remainder are followers of tribal beliefs. Until 1972, when Asians holding British passports (Indians and Pakistanis) were expelled, Uganda had 74,000 Asians, mainly small businessmen. Literacy is estimated at 25%.

Government. Uganda has a parliamentary democracy. Executive power is vested in the president, who represents the majority party in the 126-member national assembly.
 History. When British explorer Capt. John Speke reached Uganda in 1862, he found politically developed African kingdoms. Traders and missionaries followed, and in 1888 the Imperial East Africa Co. made E Africa a British sphere; in 1894 it became a British protectorate. The process leading to independence commenced in 1955, when Africans were granted some representation in the legislature. Full internal self-government came in 1962, and Uganda became fully independent on Oct. 9, 1962, with Dr. Milton Obote the first president. Gen. Idi Amin Dada took power in a 1971 military coup, dissolved parliament, and set up a new government. Under Amin's ruthless, oppressive regime, social and economic order disintegrated. In 1979, Tanzanian troops invaded, successfully overthrowing Amin. In elections held in 1980, Obote was elected president. He faced continuing unrest and disorder, an inflation rate of 500% in 1980, and famine in the N. Although the economy was somewhat stabilized, civil disorder remained, and Obote was overthrown in 1985 in a military coup.

PROFILE

Official name: Republic of Uganda
Area: 91,134sq mi (236,037sq km)
Population: 13,689,200
 Density: 150per sq mi (58per sq km)
Chief city: Kampala (capital)
Government: Parliamentary democracy
Religion: Christian (major)
Language: English (official)
Monetary unit: Uganda shilling
Gross national product: $3,700,000,000
Per capita income: $161
Industries: textiles, steel, chemicals
Agriculture: coffee, cotton, tea, maize, peanuts, sisal, oil seeds, tobacco, sugar, millet, sweet potatoes
Minerals: copper, tin
Trading partners: United States, United Kingdom, Kenya, Japan, India, West Germany

Ugarit, ancient city in W Syria dating as far back as the Neolithic period. It developed as a great commercial center from its trade with Mesopotamia and later from its alliance with Egypt (2nd millennium BC). Its period of highest prosperity occurred during the 15th and 14th cent. BC.

Uinta Mountains, mountain range in NE Utah and SW Wyoming, part of the Rocky Mt system; culminates at Kings Peak, the highest point in Utah, 13,528ft (4,126m).

Uintatherium, archaic, hoofed mammal of Eocene North America. The size of a modern African rhinoceros, it was the giant of its day. Its 2.5-ft (0.75-m) skull bore three pairs of bony outgrowths, one pair above the nose, another before the eyes, and a third toward the rear. Males had tusks. *See also* Dinocerata.

Ujjain, city in W central India, on Sipra River 200mi (322km) E of Ahmadabad. One of the seven holy cities of India, it is a pilgrimage center for thousands of Hindus each year; served as the capital of the Avanti kingdom 6th–4th centuries BC; center of Malwa kingdom 120–395, of Sanskrit learning, and Maratha dynasty of Sindhia (18th century); site of Vikram University (1957) and many notable temples and mosques. Pop. 203,278.

Ukrainian, language spoken in the Ukrainian SSR of the Soviet Union by about 35,000,000 people. Like

Russian and Belorussian, it belongs to the eastern branch of the Slavic languages.

Ukrainian Soviet Socialist Republic (Ukrainskaja Sovetskaja Socialisticeskaja Respublika), constituent republic of the SW European USSR; borders on Poland (NW), Czechoslovakia, Hungary, Romania, and the Moldavian SSR (SW), Black Sea and Sea of Azov (S), Russian SFSR (E and NE), and Belorussian SSR (N); capital is Kiev; Dnieper is main river. It is the 2nd-largest constituent republic of the USSR. A land primarily of fertile steppes, its climate is greatly modified by Black Sea. In the 7th century the Khazars (an ancient Turkish people) held much of the Ukraine; a Varangian dynasty from Scandinavia freed the land from Khazar control 9th century and established a stronghold at Kiev, uniting with the people to form Kievan Russia, a leading Russian principality until 13th century, when Mongols of Golden Horde conquered it. In 1392, Grand Duke of Lithuania seized the Ukraine; in 1569 it came under Polish rule. A Cossack rebellion freed the Ukraine, but the region was unable to stand alone; protection of Muscovy was sought and in 1654 a treaty was signed. Supposedly the Ukraine was internally independent, but this was never accomplished. Conflicts finally resulted in loss of all independence; it became part of Russia 1793. In January 1918 it proclaimed itself an independent country. Four years of war followed and in 1922 USSR reconquered it and made it one of the original constituent republics; it was lost and re-won by USSR in WWII. Industries: iron, steel, tractors, cement, glass, fertilizer, paper, sugar refining. The W Ukraine is mainly agricultural, but there are large petroleum and natural gas fields. Area: 233,089sq mi (603,700sq km). Pop. 49,478,000.

Ulan Bator (Ulaanbaatar), capital city of Mongolian People's Republic; on Tola River; seat of Living Buddhas from mid-17th century–1924, when the last spiritual leader died; center of Mongolian autonomy movement, proclaimed here 1911; occupied by Soviets 1924 during Russian Civil War; industrial development was spurred during Russian influence; site of country's only university (1942); political, cultural, and economic center. Industries: textiles, leather, paper, alcohol, food processing, glassware. Pop. 282,000.

Ulbricht, Walter, (1893–1973), East German Communist party leader and head of the German Democratic Republic. Returning from the Soviet Union in 1945 he played a major role in the establishment of the new Socialist state. As first secretary of the party 1960–71 and chairman of the State Council from 1960 to his death, he effectively crushed opposition to his rigid Stalinist principles.

Ulcers, sores or lesions in the mucosal lining of the gastrointestinal system, frequently caused by abnormally large secretion of gastric juices over a prolonged period. This psychophysiological disorder is often precipitated by emotional stress. Symptoms of ulcers include stomach pains (particularly after eating), nausea, and (in untreated cases) hemorrhaging.

Ulfilas. See Wulfila, Bishop.

Ulna, one of the two forearm bones, extending from the elbow to the wrist. At the head of the ulna, a projection, the olecranon process, fits into a cavity in the humerus, or upper arm bone; at its lower end, there is a small prominence felt on the small-finger side of the wrist.

Ulster, region of NE Ireland, consisting of nine counties. Six form Northern Ireland; Cavan, Donegal, and Monaghan are part of the Republic of Ireland. "Ulster"

also refers to Northern Ireland as a political unit of the United Kingdom. *See also* Ireland, Northern.

Ultrasonics, study of sound with frequencies beyond the range of human hearing, ie, with frequencies in excess of 20,000 hertz. There is no theoretical upper limit, but a practical limit of 5 megahertz is set by existing means of generation. Generation may be mechanical (as in the Galton whistle), by the magnetostrictive effect, or by piezoelectric generators. Applications of ultrasonics include: agitation of liquids to form emulsions, detection of flaws in metals (the ultrasonic wave passed through a metal specimen is reflected by a hairline crack), cleaning small objects by vibrating them ultrasonically in a solvent, echo sounding in deep water, soldering aluminum, and the location of a fetus or tumor.

Ultraviolet Wave, type of electromagnetic wave intermediate in energy between light and X-rays. Wavelength range: 400 nanometers (10^{-9} meter) to about 10 nanometers. *See also* Electromagnetic Spectrum.

Ulysses (1922), stream-of-consciousness novel by James Joyce set in Dublin and relating in intimate detail the events of a day (June 16, 1904) in the life of Leopold Bloom, a Jewish Dubliner. The characters, episodes, and time scheme are enriched by their parallels with those in Homer's *Odyssey*.

Umayyads, or **Ommiads,** Islamic dynasty of 14 caliphs (AD 661–750), the first of whom was Muawiyah. The Umayyad claim to the caliphate originated when a member of their clan, Uthman, became Mohammed's son-in-law and the 3rd caliphate. When the last of the dynasty, Marwan II, was overthrown by the Abbassids, one member escaped to Spain and founded the caliphate of Cordoba (756). This 11-member dynasty developed a brilliant civilization extending over most of Spain and lasting until it was overthrown by the Berbers in 1031.

Umberto I (Eng. Humbert) (1844–1900), king of Italy (1878–1900). Son and successor of Victor Emmanuel II and father of Victor Emmanuel III, he followed nationalistic and imperialistic policies and led Italy into the Triple Alliance (1882) with Germany and Austria. He encouraged Italy's entry into the armaments race and its unsuccessful colonial ventures in Africa. In 1900 an anarchist killed him in the third attempt on his life.

Umberto II (1904–83), prince of Savoy and last king of Italy (1946). The son of Victor Emmanuel III, upon his father's abdication in May 1946, he became king of Italy but went into exile in Portugal after a national vote of June 1946 determined that Italy should henceforth be a republic.

Umbilical Cord, long, thick cord that connects the developing fetus with the placenta, the hormone-secreting structure through which the fetus receives food and oxygen from the mother's bloodstream and gives off waste products. The umbilical cord contains two large arteries and one vein. At birth, the cord is clamped and cut from the placenta; the part of the cord remaining on the baby's abdomen dries and falls off, leaving the scar, known as naval, or belly button.

Umbrella Bird, large tropical American bird with a retractile, black umbrellalike crest and long, often tubular-shaped, feathered wattle on the throat. The typical ornate umbrella bird *(Cephalopterus ornatus),* found from Costa Rica to Brazil, lives high in trees, feeds on fruits, and emits loud piping sounds. During courtship, males display their crests and emit deep sounds.

Umbrella Tree, deciduous tree of North America. It has clusters of long leaves at the ends of the branches, large, white or creamy, foul-smelling flowers, and reddish fruit. Height: 40ft (12m). Family Magnoliaceae; species *Magnolia tripetala*.

Umeå, port city in N Sweden, on Gulf of Bothnia at the mouth of the Ume River; seat of Västerbotten co. Industries: wood products, lumber, machinery. Pop. 54,-530.

UN. *See* United Nations.

Un-American Affairs Committee, House (HUAC), committee established (1938) to investigate subversion. It focused particularly on un-American propaganda activities and worked to formulate legislation against them. The committee, whose first chairman was Martin Dies, was granted permanent status in 1945. The committee began investigating Nazi, Fascist, and Communist organizations, but later turned its attention to organized labor, civil rights organizations, and liberal programs. In the early 1950s it investigated alleged Communists, especially in the film industry. The committee was criticized for demagoguery and is

still considered controversial. In 1960s the name was changed to the House Internal Security Committee.

Unamuno, Miguel de (1864–1936), Spanish philosopher and writer. Twice exiled for his provocative political attitude, he is thought to have inspired many modern thinkers. *The Tragic Sense of Life in Men and Peoples* (1913) is concerned with the tragedy of life manifested in the conflict between faith and reason and in some respects anticipated modern existentialism. Other works include *Mist—a Tragi-comic Novel* (1914) and *The Life of Don Quixote and Sancho* (1905).

Uncas (*c*.1588–*c*.1683), American Indian, chief of the Mohegan Indians. Born in to the Pequot tribe, as a subchief he rebelled and formed the Mohegan tribe. He sought British support and allied with the British during the Pequot War of 1637. Since he was constantly at war with the Narragansett Indians and other tribes, some of which were British allies, Uncas was eventually distrusted by the British.

Uncertainty Principle, principle put forward by Werner Heisenberg (1927) that simultaneous measurement of the position and momentum of a particle, such as an electron, disturbs the system so that there is always an uncertainty in the result.

Uncial Writing. *See* Calligraphy.

Uncle Sam, symbol of the US government. Samuel Wilson (1766–1854), Revolutionary War soldier, supplied meat to the US Army in War of 1812. It was stamped "US," and people said it stood for "Uncle Sam" Wilson.

Uncle Tom's Cabin, or Life Among the Lowly (1852), antislavery novel by Harriet Beecher Stowe. One of the most widely circulated books in literary history, it deals with the trials of Tom, a Christian Negro slave who is sold several times and finally ends up in the hands of a brutal plantation owner, Simon Legree, who has him flogged to death. The novel awakened many people in the North to the horrors of slavery; in the South it was regarded as an inaccurate account of that institution.

Unconformity, in geology, the relation of adjacent rocks or strata showing a distinct break, indicating erosion or nondeposition. Types of unconformity are nonconformity (large intrusion of unstratified material), angular unconformity (two strata at an angle to each other), disconformity (two strata separated by an eroded surface), paraconformity (parallel strata so undifferentiated that they appear to be a single layer).

Unconscious, in psychoanalysis, a term for impulses, ideas, or memories that are generally below the level of awareness but that may affect behavior. Some primitive drives never reach the conscious level. Some thoughts or memories are repressed—pushed below the conscious level—because they seem wrong or threatening. *See also* Id; Repression.

Underground Railroad, network established to help escaping slaves. Beginning about 1804, a group of whites and blacks in the North worked to help fugitive slaves escape from the South. "Conductors" picked up slaves on the plantations and led them north where they passed through a series of hiding places ("stations") until they escaped to safety, often in Canada. One of the most famous conductors was Harriet Tubman.

Underwater Sound. Sound travels in water some 4.5 times faster than it does in air. The velocity of sound in water depends on its density and temperature—in seawater at 15°C it is 1,510 meters per second (compared to 331.4 m/s in air). Devices based on the transmission of sound under water are used to locate submerged objects or to measure depth. The principle is to transmit a sound or ultrasonic wave from a ship on the surface and to measure the time for its reflection to return. *See also* Sonar.

Underwing Moth, noctuid moth with brightly banded underwings and gray or brown front wings with wavy markings. Genus *Catocalla*.

Undset, Sigrid (1882–1949), Norwegian novelist. She became famous with the trilogy *Kristin Lavransdatter* (1920–22), set in medieval Norway. Her other novels, also concerned with woman's role in society, include *The Faithful Wife* (1936), *Madam Dorothea* (1939), and *Return to the Future* (1942). She was awarded the Nobel Prize for literature in 1928.

Unemployment of Labor, inability of workers who are ready, able, and willing to work to find employment. Unemployment is usually expressed as a percentage of the labor force.

Cyclical unemployment exists when the level of aggregate demand in the economy is less than that required to maintain full employment. People are laid off, and their jobs simply disappear.

Structural unemployment exists when jobs are available and workers are seeking jobs, but they cannot fill the jobs that are open for some reason (they lack proper training, live too far away, etc.).

Technological unemployment exists when workers are replaced by machines faster than they can find alternative employment.

Seasonal unemployment occurs when workers are unable to find jobs at certain seasons of the year. Such workers are usually engaged in construction or agriculture.

Underemployment is inefficient use of labor, eg, an employer may keep unneeded workers on the payroll when demand falls in order to have experienced help available when demand increases.

UNESCO. *See* United Nations Educational, Scientific, and Cultural Organization.

Unfair Labor Practices, for unions, are forbidden by the Taft-Hartley Act (1947). Similar practices by employers have been forbidden since the Wagner Act (1935). The purpose of the labor law is to promote peaceful industrial relations, and the unfair practices were held by Congress to discourage successful industrial practices. The lists of banned activities given by the two laws are very similar, and either party can refer a claimed violation to the National Labor Relations Board.

Ungulate, mammals characterized by having hoofed feet. Most ungulates, including cattle, sheep, hogs, and deer, are members of the order *Artiodactyla*. The order *Perissodactyla* consists of horses, tapirs, and rhinoceroses, while the orders *Proboscidea* and *Hyracoidea* contain only elephants and hyraxes, respectively.

UNICEF. *See* United Nations Children's Fund.

Unicorn, mythical animal used as a symbol of purity in the Middle Ages. It resembled a horse or goat with a single horn in the middle of its forehead. The wild and fierce beast could be tamed at a virgin's touch. The ground horn of the unicorn was supposed to have had great salutary properties.

Unicorn, The. *See* Monoceros.

Unified Field Theory, attempt to extend general relativity theory to give a simultaneous representation of both gravitational and electromagnetic fields. A more comprehensive theory would also include the strong and weak interactions. Although some success has been achieved in unifying the electromagnetic and weak interactions, the general problem is still unsolved. *See also* Relativity Theory.

Union, township in NE New Jersey, 5mi (8km) WNW of Elizabeth; site of Newark State College 1855. Industries: paint, lacquer, steel, metal goods, truck farms. Settled *c.* 1749 as Connecticut Farms by colonists from Connecticut. Pop. (1980) 50,184.

Union, Act of (1707), act uniting the kingdoms of England and Scotland under one British Parliament at Westminster, with England and Scotland each retaining its own legal system and national church. By union Scotland hoped to achieve economic equality with England, while England acted to prevent a possible Scottish alliance with France and Roman Catholic succession to the English throne.

Union City, city in NE New Jersey, on Hudson River 3mi (5km) N of and adjoining Jersey City; Lincoln Tunnel links Union City with New York City. Industries: embroidery, perfume, incandescent lamps. Formed 1925 by merging West Hoboken and Union Hill. Pop. (1980) 55,593.

Union of Soviet Socialist Republics, or **Soviet Union,** a federation of 15 union republics, based on socialist ownership of the means of production. The USSR covers one-sixth of the Earth's surface, making it the largest country in the world. The Soviet Union is the world's second industrial power (after the United States) and the leading producer of many minerals, including iron. The Soviet Union is a leader in world politics and dominates affairs of its client states, mostly in E Europe.

Land and economy. Mostly above 50° N latitude, it stretches across Europe and Asia from the Baltic Sea across the Eurasian land mass to the Bering Strait where it is within 3mi (5km) of an island off the coast of Alaska. Its W neighbors are Norway, Finland, Poland, Czechoslovakia, Hungary, and Romania. Border-

Umbrella tree

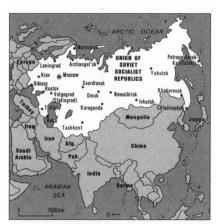

Union of Soviet Socialist Republics

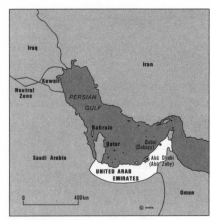

United Arab Emirates

ing it to the S are Turkey, Iran, Afghanistan, China, Mongolia, and North Korea. The European portion, from the Polish border to the Ural Mts, is a broad plain crossed by two major rivers, the Dneiper, leading to the Black Sea, and the Volga, which empties into the Caspian Sea, the world's largest lake in surface area. The low Urals divide European and Asiatic Russia. To the E are enormous Siberian lowlands and the deserts of central Asia; beyond them are the Siberian highlands and the Far Eastern mountains. Along the shores of the Black and Caspian seas is a small subtropical zone. Long, cold winters and short summers mark much of the USSR's climate. N tundra areas record −90°F (−64°C). S of the tundra is a vast forest belt, and S of the forest are the prairies (steppes), where the soil is fertile with plentiful rainfall. The steppes, 12% of the total area, contain 66% of the USSR's arable land. Agriculture is organized into state farms and collective farms; in the latter members share in the income after state obligations have been met. Since 1966, farm wages have been guaranteed, and peasants are allowed to grow crops for sale on land they use but do not own. These plots account for 33% of gross agricultural production. During the late 1970s and early 1980s poor grain harvests resulted in a heavy reliance on imported grains. Operating under a series of 5-year plans, the totally nationalized USSR has become the world's 2nd-largest industrial power. Major problems center about planning and management, increased productivity, efficiency, and modernization. Budget revenues are derived from profits of state enterprises and a levy on all transactions of consumer goods and services. Direct income tax brings in 10% of the total revenue.

People. The indigenous Russians came from two areas. The N primitive forest tribes who fished, used the fur-bearing animals, and cultivated the land are the Slavs, now about half of the population. Indigenous peoples in the S were nomads, living on horseback and in tents and fighting other tribes. Modern ethnic groups are divided into the following units: Indo-European, 36 groups; Caucasian, 40; Semitic, 6; Finno-Ugrian, 16; Nenets, 1; Turkic, 48; Mongo, 3; Tungis-Manchurian, 6; Palaeo-Asiatic, 9; and far E ancient tribes, 4. The first Russian census in 1897 listed 129,800,000 persons. The current population of over 260,000,000 has been affected by large-scale emigration to the United States in 1900–09, increases from areas acquired since 1939, deaths from famine, the high mortality rates in the 1930s and 1940s, and 7,000,000 killed during WWII. In 1897 about 76% of the people could neither read nor write. Literacy is currently estimated at over 98% for those between the ages of 9–49. Soviet schools, planned to serve the needs of the state, aim for 10 years of compulsory education. Admission to universities is highly competitive, based on political background and academic records. Efforts to suppress religion have been sporadic, but persecution of Jews has resulted in widespread protests in Western countries. Some churches, mosques, and synagogues have been allowed a limited function, although anti-religious programs continue.

Government. Power rests in the leaders of the Communist party. Government is patterned on Western democracies, but without checks or balances and little separation of powers. Under the 1932 constitution, the Communist party makes state policy.

History. Annals date the first Russian state in the area of Kiev in the 9th century when the Rus, early Norse pirates and later caravan traders, were asked to mediate the disputes of indigenous tribes. Rus descendants brought Christianity, absentee-landed aristocracy, rich merchants, and lucrative trade. Mongols conquered the country in the 13th century; it had freed itself by 1480. Ivan the Terrible (1533–84) reigned during a period of military and financial reform. Peter the Great (1682–1725) expanded the empire. Catherine

the Great (1762–96) established local legislation, courts, and charters perpetuating the ruling class. The serfs were emancipated in 1861 under Alexander II. This action set the stage for the future political development of Russia. Over the next years the tsars attempted repressive actions, but it was too late. Revolution was in the air, and in 1917 Tsar Nicholas II was forced to abdicate. The succeeding provisional governments were overthrown in November 1917 by the Bolshevik wing of the Russian Social Democratic Labor party. V. I. Lenin was named head of the new Communist government. Land was declared the property of the state; factories, banks, and railroads were nationalized. Joseph Stalin emerged as party leader after Lenin's death in 1924. His rivals, including Leon Trotsky, were executed, and military, political, and cultural leaders were purged in the 1930s. The United States recognized the Soviet Union in 1933. In 1939, Germany and Russia invaded Poland and divided its territory. The Soviets annexed a portion of Finland in March 1940. In June 1940 they added Estonia, Latvia, and Lithuania, and in July they took two provinces of Romania. Adolf Hitler's brief 1940 collaboration with the Soviets ended on June 22, 1941, when Germany attacked the USSR. In four years of fighting, the Germans advanced as far as Moscow, causing enormous USSR casualties and devastation to the E portion of Russia before being defeated in 1945. Following the war, the Soviet Union aided in the creation of Communist governments in its zone of occupation in Eastern Europe, formalized in the creation of the Warsaw Treaty Organization (Warsaw Pact) in 1955. Following the war a decline in relations with the West was marked by the Cold War. After Stalin's death (1953), Nikita S. Khrushchev was installed as first secretary of the Communist party and in 1958 as chairman of the Council of Ministers. Stalin was denounced as a despot, political prisoners were rehabilitated, and limited contact with outside countries was encouraged. Party opposition brought Khrushchev's downfall in 1964, when Leonid I. Brezhnev was named first secretary of the party. Under Brezhnev relations improved with the West during the early 1970s, but by the early 1980s tensions with the United States had increased, partly because the Soviet Union expanded its sphere of influence to include Africa, and Soviet troops invaded Afghanistan in 1979, establishing a Soviet puppet government. Brezhnev's death, in 1982, brought Yuri V. Andropov to the party secretary-general post and eventually the presidency in 1983. Andropov died in 1984 and was succeeded by Konstantin U. Chernenko, who died 13 months after taking office. Mikhail S. Gorbachev, leader since 1985, exemplified a new, young generation of Soviet politicians. The Soviet Union's continuing interest in Eastern Europe was emphasized in 1981–82 when the USSR pressured Poland to take a hard line against labor unrest. In 1984, in retaliation for the US boycott of the 1980 Olympic games in Moscow, the Soviet Union refused to participate in the Los Angeles Summer games. US relations improved when Gorbachev and US Pres. Reagan attended a summit conference in 1985.

PROFILE

Official name: Union of Soviet Socialist Republics
Area: 8,649,512sq mi (22,402,236sq km)
Population: 262,442,000
   Density: 30per sq mi (18per sq km)
Chief cities: Moscow (capital); Leningrad; Kiev; Tashkent; Gorky
Government: People's republic
Religion: Russian Orthodox, Christian, Georgian Orthodox
Language: Russian
Monetary unit: Ruble
Gross national product: $1,082,000,000

Per capita income: $2,000
Industries (major products): chemicals, machines, steel, iron, motor vehicles, railway cars and engines, oil refining, machine tools, tractors, clocks, glass, cameras, cement, textiles, paper, aluminum, electronics, carpets, processed foods, rubber, fertilizers
Agriculture (major products): timber, cattle, hogs, sheep, fish, grains and cereals, sugar beets, potatoes, flax, cotton, tea, tobacco, rice, fruits
Minerals (major): coal, oil, manganese, iron ore, potassium phosphates, salt, copper, zinc, mercury, sulphur, barite, molybdenum, lead, gypsum, chromium
Trading partners: Romania, Bulgaria, Poland, Hungary, Czechoslovakia, East Germany, European countries, Japan

Unitarianism, religious movement first significant in Europe during the early Protestant Reformation. It has no formal creed and strives to be universal. It holds that God is one person and denies the trinity. Members prefer to be called "liberal Christians," distinguishing their ways from those of intolerant Christians. Rejecting any missionary work, the heart and mind must lead men into the fellowship. The first Unitarian churches in the American colonies were established in the late 18th century.

Unitary Government, government in which power is concentrated in a single source and in which local governments act only as administrative agents of the central government. It is the opposite of a federal government in which power is shared with the states.

United Arab Emirates, formerly the Trucial States; union of seven emirates (Dubai, Ajman, Abu Dhabi, Ras alKhaimah, Fujairah, Sharjah, and Umm al-Qaiwain); bordered by Persian Gulf (N), Qatar (NW), Saudi Arabia (W and S), Oman (E). The terrain is flat, consisting mainly of sand and salt flat desert; only in the E does the land rise to any height. The traditional nomad existence is in decline as wealth from oil production attracts people to the towns of the Gulf. Agriculture is limited to the mountain region, oases, and areas where irrigation is provided; main crops are dates and vegetables. Oil production is the economic mainstay of the Union. First produced in 1962 from Abu Dhabi, it now also comes from Dubai and offshore sites, and a little from Sharjah. Government is carried on by the Supreme Council which is made up of the royal families of the emirates; this elects a president. From the 19th century to 1971 Britain was responsible for the area's defense and foreign relations of the Trucial States; the United Arab Emirates was formed when Britain withdrew. The UAE use some of the oil wealth to grant considerable foreign aid to other Arab countries and takes a moderate stand on oil prices and the Arab-Israeli conflict.

PROFILE

Official name: United Arab Emirates
Area: 32,278sq mi (83,600sq km).
Population: 900,000
   Density: 28per sq mi (11per sq km)
Chief cities: Abu Dhabi (capital); Dubai
Government: federation of emirates
Religion: Islam
Language: Arabic
Trading partners (major): Japan, Great Britain, United States

United Arab Republic, political union of Egypt and Syria formed in 1958 with its capital at Cairo and Egypt's Gamal Abdel Nasser as its president. A military coup dissolved the union in 1961 with Syria declaring its independence.

United Empire Loyalists, Canadian organization comprised of descendants of American Loyalists who fled to Canada during the American Revolution. They settled mostly in the Maritime Provinces and Ontario. The organization was formally chartered in 1897 and 1914 and has been a pro-British, conservative force in Canadian politics.

United Kingdom of Great Britain and Northern Ireland. *See* Great Britain.

United Nations (UN), formed in 1945, organization of nations to work together in the cause of international security and peace. Its headquarters are in New York City. As a successor to the League of Nations, it has proved a more durable medium of international cooperation. The principal UN organs are the General Assembly, the Security Council, the Secretariat, the Trusteeship Council, the Economic and Social Council, and the International Court of Justice. The United Nations provides a forum in which almost 160 nations can discuss problems with the hope of peaceful solutions. It has helped find remedies to many international disputes and armed conflicts among its member nations.

The UN Charter was signed in San Francisco on June 16, 1945, by 50 countries. Membership expanded as former colonies gained independence in the decades following World War II. Its first major action came in June 1950 when it voted to help South Korea following an invasion by North Korea and 15 members contributed to a UN force. In its "Uniting for Peace" resolution of November 1950, the General Assembly attempted to develop the power it had already exercised. The resolution stipulated that the General Assembly could hold an emergency session to settle emergency matters that the Security Council was unable to settle because of its members' individual veto power. This new function of the assembly was put to the test in 1956 with the Israeli invasion of Egypt and the subsequent intervention of British and French forces. The assembly met and established the UN Emergency Force, which ultimately provided for the withdrawal of British, French, and Israeli forces. UN teams have also played a peace-keeping role in India and Cyprus. In successive Arab-Israeli conflicts the assembly has applied enough pressure on both sides to force a cease-fire until negotiations began. Since 1978 a UN peacekeeping force has been stationed in S Lebanon. During the early 1980s the assembly continued to pressure the Republic of South Africa to relinquish its disputed control of Namibia. Since the 1960s, when UN forces intervened in the Congo, controversial collective security actions have been avoided, partly because the rise of Afro-Asian, Latin American, and Arab member states has complicated the patterns of power. The range of the Third World's strength was exhibited in 1975 when it successfully forced the passing of a resolution stipulating that Zionism is a form of racism, a resolution directed against Israel. The resolution caused much controversy and was vigorously opposed by the United States. The influence of the Third World nations has also been evident in the economic realm. Special North-South dialogue conferences have focused on the need for cooperation by the developed countries to solve the underdeveloped countries' economic problems, and after 9 years of negotiation, a treaty (1982) on the law of the sea gave special concessions to the developing world for revenues from sea floor exploitation, but many member countries, including the United States, refused to ratify it. During 1985, the Security Council voted to condemn South Africa's apartheid policies. *See also* individual agencies.

UNITED NATIONS MEMBERS

Afghanistan
Albania
Algeria
Antigua and Barbuda
Argentina
Australia
Austria
Bahamas
Bahrain
Bangladesh
Barbados
Belgium
Belize
Belorussian SSR
Benin (Dahomey)
Bhutan
Bolivia
Botswana
Brazil
Brunei
Bulgaria
Burma
Burundi (Urundi)
Cameroon
Canada
Cape Verde
Central African Republic
Chad
Chile
China, People's Republic of
Colombia
Comeros (Comoro Is.)
Congo
Costa Rica
Cuba
Cyprus
Czechoslavakia
Denmark
Dominican Republic
Ecuador
Egypt (UAR)
El Salvador
Equatorial Guinea
Ethiopia
Fiji
Finland
France
Gabon
Gambia
German Democratic Republic
Germany, Federal Republic of
Ghana
Greece
Grenada
Guatemala
Guinea
Guinea-Bissau
Guyana
Haiti
Honduras
Hungary
Iceland
India
Indonesia
Iran
Iraq
Ireland
Israel
Italy
Ivory Coast
Jamaica
Japan
Jordan
Kenya
Khmer Republic (Cambodia)
Kuwait
Laos
Lebanon
Lesotho
Liberia
Libya
Luxembourg
Malagasy Republic
Malawi
Malaysia
Maldives
Mali
Malta
Mauritania
Mauritius
Mexico
Mongolia
Morocco
Mozambique
Nepal
Netherlands
New Zealand
Nicaragua
Niger
Nigeria
Norway
Oman (Muscat and Oman)
Pakistan
Panama
Papua New Guinea
Paraguay
Peru
Philippines
Poland
Portugal
Qatar
Romania
Rwanda
São Tomé and Príncipe
Saudi Arabia
Sengal
Seychelles
Sierra Leone
Singapore
Somalia
South Africa
Soviet Union (USSR)
Spain
Sri Lanka (Ceylon)
Sudan
Surinam
Swaziland
Sweden
Syria
Tanzania
Thailand
Togo
Trinidad and Tobago
Tunisia
Turkey
Uganda
Ukrainian SSR
United Arab Emirates
United Kingdom
United States
Upper Volta (Burkina Faso)
Uruguay
Vanuatu
Venezuela
Western Samoa
Yemen
Yemen, Democratic People's Republic
Yugoslavia
Zaire
Zambia
Zimbabwe

United Nations Children's Fund (UNICEF), organization created by the UN General Assembly (1946) to contribute to the welfare of the world's children through voluntary contributions by governments and individuals. UNICEF is not financed through the UN budget. Its programs include provisions of food, medical care, and disease control. In 1965, UNICEF received the Nobel Peace Prize for its work. UNICEF personnel are members of the UN Secretariat.

United Nations Conference (1945). *See* San Francisco Conference on International Organization.

United Nations Educational, Scientific and Cultural Organization (UNESCO), organization created in 1946 to work in education, the natural sciences, cultural activities, social sciences, and mass communication. Its goal is to promote better understanding of these areas among people throughout the world. Its membership is open to UN member states.

United States, nation in North America. Its official name is the United States of America. It comprises 50 states, of which 48 and the District of Columbia constitute a mass bounded E by the Atlantic Ocean, W by the Pacific, N by Canada, and S by Mexico and the Gulf of Mexico. The state of Alaska, separated from the 48 coterminous states by Canada, is at the NW tip of the continent. The state of Hawaii, an island chain in the Pacific, lies about 2,000mi (3,220km) SW of the mainland. The United States also has sovereignty or jurisdiction over outlying lands, which include the unincorporated territories of Guam and American Samoa, which are islands in the Pacific, and of the US Virgin Islands in the West Indies, and a number of small Pacific islands. Under the United Nations, the United States administers the Trust Territory of the Pacific Islands, which embraces three archipelagoes. Puerto Rico, in the West Indies, is a free commonwealth associated with the United States. The Canal Zone in Panama, through which runs the Panama Canal, is controlled by the US under a treaty with Panama.

Land and economy. The central part is generally a plain, rolling or level, about 1,500mi (2,415km) long and wide, drained by the Mississippi River system, which includes the Missouri and Ohio rivers and scores of tributaries. This is rich agricultural land and also contains valuable mineral deposits. The five Great Lakes, important waterways, lie in the N, forming part of the boundary with Canada. Mountain systems enclose the plain. In the E, behind a narrow level strip along the Atlantic coast, the many parallel ranges of the Appalachian Mts run roughly N to S, reaching a height of 6,600ft (2,013m). W of the plains the ranges of the Rocky Mts run N to S, with 45 peaks over 14,000ft (4,270m). Beyond the Rockies a high plateau, much of it desert land, stretches W to the Sierra Nevada and Cascade ranges, whose altitudes exceed 14,000ft (4,270m) in places. Fertile valleys lie farther W and the low coastal ranges rise along the Pacific shore. The country's vast area and varied climate and terrain permit diversified economic activity in many sections. A transportation complex, based on a national highway network, air freight, railroads, and river and Great Lakes traffic, moves goods and produce rapidly over great distances, and is vital to the economy. Many ports on both coasts handle world commerce, and ports on the Great Lakes have access to the Atlantic through the St Lawrence Seaway. Heavy industry is centered largely in the NE and the Great Lakes region, and in Texas and California. Light industries flourish in most cities and towns. The chief grain lands are in the central plain; cattle ranges are extensive in the W and SW. Truck crops are grown and dairying is carried on in nearly every state. Forests, especially in the NW, support a major timber industry. Coal is mined principally in the Appalachian region and the largest producing petroleum fields are in Louisiana and Texas along the coast of the Gulf of Mexico, but deposits of both fuels are worked in several sections of the country. Metal mining is mostly in E and W mountains. The nation's business and financial structure is broadly based in the large cities.

People. The population is descended largely from European immigrants. The native Indians diminished rapidly as white settlement advanced and live mostly in the SW and W. The earliest pioneers along the Atlantic coast were chiefly from the British Isles. An early mass influx to the country was of blacks from Africa, transported to work the plantations of the S. In the 19th century a tide of immigration began bringing more than 40,000,000 persons into the country up to 1960. Germans, Irish, Italians, and Russians predominated, but every European country was represented. These immigrants spread over the land; their contributions invigorated the nation's life and accelerated its economic growth. Intermarriage produced a population of diverse blood. Nearly 75% of Americans live in urban areas. In the 1970 census, the urban population classification was less than 50% in only seven states. The densest population occurs in the NE. The national density is about 57 persons per square mile (22 per sq km).

Education. There are more than 2,000 institutions of higher education. Every state supports a university, and most of these have many branches. More numerous are privately endowed institutions and those of religious denominations. Enrollments are enormous; the City University of New York has more than 270,000 students and the State University of New York more than 160,000. Some private institutions trace their origins to the 17th century; Harvard University was founded in 1636 and the College of William and Mary in 1693. There are many schools for vocational training. Government and private foundations carry on research, especially in the sciences.

History. The first permanent settlement by Europeans in what is now the United States was made by the Spanish at St Augustine, Fla., in 1565. The English founded Jamestown, Va., in 1607 and Plymouth, Mass., in 1620. The Dutch established New Amsterdam (New York) in 1623. This was taken by the English in 1664 and the spreading communities along the Atlantic coast and inland became British colonies. Having fought off a threat from the French in Canada, the colonists rebelled against British rule in the American Revolution (1775–83), declaring their independence on July 4, 1776. The new nation operated as a confederation of 13 states until 1787, when the national Constitution was drawn up, creating the framework in which the government has continued to function. George Washington was elected the first president in 1788. A federal enclave called the District of Columbia was created in Maryland and Virginia, and the city of Washington was built as the national capital, which was occupied in 1800. Settlements pushed westward into the Mississippi River basin. The Louisiana Purchase from France in 1803 doubled US territory. New states were formed and admitted to the Union. Texas, which had won its independence from Mexico, was annexed in 1845, and after victory in the Mexican War (1846–48), California and what is now New Mexico, Arizona, and Nevada were added to the Union. Old quarrels over slavery and states' rights caused the secession of 11 Southern states in 1861. The four-year Civil War that followed devastated the South but preserved the Union and abolished slavery. The nation expanded quickly. Alaska was purchased from Russia in 1867. Two years

United Nations headquarters

United States

Capitol Building, Washington, D.C.

later the transcontinental railroad linked the Pacific coast with the E. Hawaii was annexed in 1898, and the Philippine Islands were ceded to the United States by Spain after the Spanish-American War in that year. (The Philippines became independent in 1946.) Booming industry and technology spurred the rise of cities and transformed the face and life of the country, especially after the invention of the automobile in the early 20th century. In 1917 the nation joined the Allies in WWI. About 2,000,000 US soldiers were sent to France. After the Allied victory, President Woodrow Wilson played a major role in the peace conferences. The war stimulated US prosperity until the worldwide Great Depression of the 1930s. The Japanese attack on Pearl Harbor, Hawaii, on Dec. 7, 1941, drew the country into WWII. Wartime demands helped to restore the economy. For four years the United States fought a global war against Japan in the Pacific area and against Nazi Germany in Europe, putting 16,000,000 men and women into uniform. After the war, the possession of nuclear bombs thrust the nation into a position of world power and responsibility—as well as frequent conflict with the Soviet Union. New York City was chosen as headquarters of the United Nations. Anticommunist wars were fought in Korea 1950–53 and in Vietnam in the 1960s. Alaska became the 49th state on Jan. 3, 1959, and Hawaii became the 50th on Aug. 21, 1959. The United States won the lead in space exploration, and on July 20, 1969, an American was the first man to walk on the moon. During the mid-1970s and early 1980s the country experienced unprecedented levels of inflation combined with an economic recession; a recovery, which began slowly in 1983, accelerated in the mid–1980s. *See also* American Literature, individual biographies, articles on states, cities, historical events.

PROFILE

Official name: United States of America
Population (including outlying areas): 226,504,825 (1980)
Area (including all areas under US jurisdiction): 3,628,150sq mi (9,396,909sq km)
Capital: Washington, District of Columbia, 637,651 (1980)
Chief cities: New York, 7,071,030; Chicago, 3,005,-072; Los Angeles, 2,966,763; Philadelphia, 1,688,-210
Government: federal republic
Head of State and Chief Executive: President
Legislature: Congress (Senate, 100 members; House of Representatives, 435 members)
Elevations: highest, 20,320ft (6,198m), Mount McKinley, Alaska; lowest, 282ft (86m) below sea level, Death Valley, Calif.
Industries (major products): motor vehicles, aircraft, industrial machinery, electrical equipment and appliances, chemicals, petroleum products, fabricated metals, railroad equipment, processed foods
Agriculture (major products): wheat, corn, rye, barley, oats, soybeans, cattle, dairy products, cotton, tobacco, hogs
Minerals (major): coal, petroleum, natural gas, iron ore, copper, cement, stone, uranium ore
National motto: In God We Trust
National flag: The Stars and Stripes, 7 red, 6 white horizontal stripes; a blue field in the upper left corner containing 50 white 5-pointed stars, one for each state
National anthem: "The Star-Spangled Banner"

United States Air Force Academy, US educational institution. It offers a four-year educational curriculum for Air Force cadets that includes a baccalaureate level education in airmanship, related sciences, and the humanities. It was founded in 1955 and established in Colorado Springs, Colo., in 1958. Graduates normally enter the Air Force as second lieutenants.

United States Military Academy, US educational institution. Formally opened in 1802 and located in West Point, N.Y., the academy is a four-year institution in which Army cadets receive a general education, theoretical and practical training as junior officers. Upon course completion the cadets receive a commission as a second lieutenant in the Army.

United States Naval Academy, US educational institution. It offers a four-year program of academic, military, and professional instruction for the training and education of young people for the naval service. Eighty percent of each class enrolls in engineering, science, or mathematics, the other 20% choose their majors in fields of the humanities or social sciences. Completion of the program normally leads to a commission in the US Navy or the US Marine Corps. It was established in 1845 at Annapolis, Md.

United States v. E.C. Knight Co. (1895), US Supreme Court case holding that the manufacturing process was not a part of "commerce" and therefore could not be regulated by the federal government under the Sherman Antitrust Act. This limited view of the commerce power was abandoned with *U.S.* v. *Darby* and *Heart of Atlanta Motel* v. *U.S.*

Univalve. See Gastropod.

Universal Set, or **Universe,** mathematical set of all the objects that are admissible to that set, such as the set of the seven days of the week or of all the colors of the rainbow. *See also* Sets.

Universe, aggregate of all matter, energy, and space, consisting of vast cold empty regions with a distribution of high-temperature stars and other objects grouped in galaxies. On a large scale the universe is considered uniform: it is identical in every part. It is also known to be expanding at a uniform rate, the galaxies all receding from each other. The origin, evolution, and future characteristics of the universe are considered in several cosmological theories. Recent developments in astronomy imply a finite universe, as postulated in the big-bang theory. *See also* Cosmology; Red Shift.

Unknown, variable with values that are to be found by solving a given equation.

Unterwalden, canton in Switzerland; divided into Nidwalden and Obwalden, half cantons. In 1921 it united with Schwyg and Uri cantons to form league that became the center of the Swiss Confederation. The land is mountainous, forested, and pastoral, with orchards and meadow lands for livestock. Industries: dairying, woodworking, cement, glassworks. Area: 296sq mi (767sq km). Pop. 55,323.

Upanishads, Hindu texts of uncertain authorship, dating from approximately 900 BC. The term Upanishads means "to sit nearby devotedly." Of more than 100 *Upanishads* there are about 10 principal ones. Containing philosophical speculations of many centuries of Indian sages, there is a heterogeneity of thought. The content suggests oral instruction rather than methodical exposition. The metaphysical doctrine of Brahman-Atman, the ultimate unity of design, is a central theme. *See also* Hinduism.

Updike, John (1932–), US author, b. Shillington, Pa. He joined the staff of *The New Yorker* magazine in 1955 but later left to concentrate on his own writing. His works include *The Same Door* (1959), a collection of short stories, and the novels *The Poorhouse Fair* (1959), *Rabbit, Run* (1961), *Centaur* (1962), *Couples* (1968), *Rabbit Redux* (1971), *Marry Me* (1976), *The Coup* (1978), *Rabbit Is Rich* (1981), for which he won a Pulitzer Prize (1982), *Bech Is Back* (1982), and *The Witches of Eastwick* (1984).

Upland, city in S California, 34mi (55km) E of Los Angeles. Industries: processing of citrus fruits, paint, auto parts, feed products. Inc. 1906. Pop. (1980) 47,647.

Upland Plover, short-billed, pleasant-voiced, slender, gray-streaked North American shorebird that has left the shore to breed in pastures of Virginia and northern areas. It often perches on fences. Length: 12in (30cm). Family Charadriidae; species *Bartramia longicauda.*

Upper Canada, the name for the province of Ontario (1791–1841). The name was changed to Canada West (1841–67) and to Ontario after the formation of the Confederation of Canada (1867).

Upper Class, the highest social position in the hierarchically stratified society. Members of the upper class possess in the greatest quantity whatever characteristics society most values: wealth, power, or status. *See also* Hierarchy; Status; Stratification.

Upper Volta, officially **Burkina Faso,** landlocked nation in W Africa. It is bounded on the N by Mali and Niger and to the S by the coastal nations of Ivory Coast, Ghana, Togo, and Benin. A plateau, ranging from 1,000ft (305m) in the N to 650ft (198m) in the S, occupies most of the country. Although three rivers, the Black Volta, the Red Volta, and the White Volta, flow through the country, the land is generally dry and infertile. Over 80% of the population is engaged in agriculture or raising livestock. Irrigation projects, developing the Black and White voltas, promise brighter agricultural prospects for the future. The country is heavily dependent on remittances sent by Upper Voltans working in the Ivory Coast. The country is a member of ECOWAS (Economic Community of West African States), which promotes regional economic unity. Upper Volta was seriously affected by the Sahel drought (1967–74). Much of the population is concentrated in the S and center of the country with 95% living in rural villages. Most of the people are Voltaic or Mande with scattered ethnic minorities. About 75% practice animistic religions; most of the rest are Muslim. Although French is the official language, Moré is the most commonly spoken.

Explored by the French in the late 19th century, Upper Volta, after much colonial manipulation, became a French Overseas Territory in 1947. Becoming autonomous in 1958, it gained its independence in 1960, and formed a bilateral agreement with France in 1961. In 1966 a military coup led by Lt.-Col. Sangoule Lamizana took control of the government, and Lamizana assumed the position of president, which was affirmed in elections held in 1978. In 1980, Lamizana was ousted by a new group of officers, the constitution was suspended, and a military government of National Recovery was established. Another military coup took place in 1982 and another in 1983. In 1984 the country's name was changed to Burkina Faso (land of the honest people). A cease-fire between Burkina Faso and Mali regarding a longtime border dispute was called at the end of 1985.

PROFILE

Official name: Burkina Faso
Area: 105,792sq mi (274,000sq km)
Population: 6,728,000
Density: 64per sq mi (25per sq km)

Chief cities: Ouagadougou, capital; Bobo-Dioulasso
Government: republic
Language: French (official)
Monetary unit: CFA franc
Gross national product: $1,000,000,000
Per capita income: $79
Manufacturing (major products): soap, processed foods, cigarettes
Agriculture (major products): cotton, rice, peanuts
Minerals (major): manganese
Trading partners (major): France, Ivory Coast, Japan

Uppsala (Upsale), city in W Sweden, 40mi (64km) NNW of Stockholm, on Fyrisan River; capital of Uppsala co; pagan capital of Sweden 6th century; site of University of Uppsala (1477), Royal Society of Sciences, Gustav Werner Institute, Victoria Museum, Linnaean Museum, 13th-century Gothic church, and cathedral of Uppsala. Industries: printing, food processing, metal goods, footwear, clothing. Pop. 138,116.

Upwelling, the process that brings water of greater density and lower temperature up to the surface water of the ocean. Upwelling is especially characteristic of the western side of continents where winds blow parallel to the coast and the water carried away by the surface current is replaced by the bottom water.

Ur, ancient Babylonian city and birthplace of Abraham. Settled in the 4th millennium BC, it prospered during its First Dynasty (*c.* 3000–2600 BC), and during its Third Dynasty, it became the richest city in Mesopotamia. A century later it was destroyed by the Elamites only to be rebuilt and destroyed again by the Babylonians. After Babylonia came under the control of Persia, the city was abandoned (3rd cent. BC).

Uralic Languages, family of languages spoken in parts of N and E Europe and the Soviet Union. Its two branches are the Finno-Ugric languages, which include Finnish and Hungarian, and the Samoyed languages, though the former accounts for 99.9% of the 20 million Uralic speakers. Some scholars believe that the Uralic languages are related to the Altaic languages (constituting a Ural-Altaic family), but this remains to be proven conclusively.

Ural Mountains, mountain system in USSR, extends N-S from the Kara Sea to the W Kirgiz Steppe region; densely forested and rich in minerals, including iron ore, copper, chrome, gold, platinum, coal, potassium, and phosphates. Highest peak: Mt Narodnaya 6,214ft (1,895m). Length: approx. 1,640mi (2,640km).

Uraninite, an oxide mineral, uranium oxide (UO_2), found in pegmatites and medium-temperature veins. Cubic system as cubes, octahedrons, and dodecahedrons; when botryoidal (like a bunch of grapes) with radiating structure, called pitchblende. Greasy or dull black; hardness 5–6; sp gr 6.4–9.7. Pitchblende is major source of uranium.

Uranium, radioactive metallic element (symbol U) of the actinide group, identified (1789) by M.H. Klaproth. It occurs in several minerals, the chief ores being pitchblende (oxide), autunite, and tobernite. The element is important because of its use in fission reactors and bombs. The naturally occurring element contains U^{238} (99.28%), U^{235} (0.71%), and U^{234} (0.0058%). U^{235} (half-life 7.1×10^8 yrs) is fissionable and will sustain a neutron chain reaction. Fuels used in reactors are enriched with this isotope by gaseous diffusion, using the volatile hexafluoride, or by a centrifuge. In breeder reactors the isotope U^{238} is converted into Pu^{239} by neutron capture. Chemically uranium is a very reactive metal; it oxidizes in air and reacts with cold water. Properties: at. no. 92; at. wt. 238.029; sp. gr. 18.95; melt. pt. 2,070°F (1,132.3°C); boil. pt. 6,904°F (3,818°C); most stable isotope U^{238} (half-life 4.51×10^9 yrs.

Uranium-Thorium-Lead Dating, a method of assessing geological age up to many millions of years. *See also* Dating, Radioactive.

Uranus, seventh planet from the Sun, discovered in 1781 by William Herschel, encircled by 9 satellites. Impermanent clouds can be seen in its atmosphere, which is gaseous and consists of hydrogen, helium, and methane. Its axis is tilted 98° from the perpendicular position. Mean distance from the Sun, 1,783,000,000mi (2,871,000,000km); mass, 14.6 times that of Earth; diameter, 32,375mi (51,800km); rotation period, 10hr 48min; period of sidereal revolution, 84 years. *See also* Solar System.

Uranus, in Greek mythology, the starry sky, husband and son of Gaea, the broad-bosomed Earth. Together they proceeded to people the Earth. Uranus sired the race of Titans and the Cyclopes and three grotesque monsters. Uranus, in horror, buried these last beneath the ground, incurring the vengeance of Gaea who caused her son Cronus to mutilate his father.

Urban VI, Roman Catholic pope (1378–89), b. Bartolomeo Prignano (c. 1318). The college of cardinals declared his election invalid and appointed an antipope, Clement VII, beginning the Great Schism. His papacy was marked by confusion and financial losses in the papal states. Assumed insane, he is thought to have murdered five cardinals.

Urbana, city in E central Illinois, E of Springfield; seat of Champaign co; site of University of Illinois (1867). Industries: foundries, machine shops, scientific instruments, railroad shops. Founded 1824, inc. 1833, as city 1860. Pop. (1980) 35,978.

Urban Planning, systematic development of new urban areas or altering existing ones to improve quality of life for their inhabitants. Federally assisted urban renewal programs, to clear cities of slums and blighted areas, have had some success, but increasingly complex problems of crime, air pollution, urban sprawl, and municipal bankruptcy have highlighted the need for an integrated approach to city planning. The 1965 Housing Act urged formation of metropolitan and regional agencies for this purpose.

Urban Sociology, sociological study of cities and urban areas. Like its counterpart, rural sociology, it seeks to understand the interplay between a unique environment-type and the social structures within it. Urban sociology examines the effects that such things as high population density, limited space, and heterogeneity have on social organization.

Urdu, the official language of Pakistan, the mother tongue of only about 5 million people there, but used as second language by as much as two-thirds of the population. It is also spoken in India by most of the country's Muslims. Urdu is quite similar to Hindi, the chief difference being that it is written in the Arabic script. Its vocabulary contains many Arabic and Persian borrowings that are absent in Hindi.

Urea, a nitrogen-containing compound in the urine, blood, and lymph, an end product of protein metabolism.

Uremia, toxic condition due to the accumulation of nitrogenous substances in the blood that are normally eliminated in the urine. It is marked by headaches, vomiting, coma, and convulsions.

Ureter, a long narrow duct that connects the kidney to the urinary bladder, transporting urine from the kidney to the bladder where it is stored until voided.

Ureteral Colic. *See* Kidney Stones.

Urethra, duct through which urine is discharged from the body. Urine is produced in the kidney, stored in the bladder until pressure in the bladder triggers specific neural responses that cause urine, under voluntary control, to be released through the urethra. In males the urethra is also the tube through which semen is ejaculated out of the body through the penis.

Urethritis, inflammation of the urethra, most frequently found in males, due to bacterial or viral infection or to mechanical obstruction. Antibiotics or surgical procedures are used for treatment.

Urey, Harold Clayton (1893–1981), US chemist, b. Walkerton, Ind. He became professor at Columbia University and in the same year (1934) was awarded a Nobel prize for his isolation of deuterium. Thereafter he worked on isotope separation at the universities of Chicago and California. Concerned that his work on isotopes had aided the construction of nuclear weapons, he turned in later years to geophysics.

Uri, canton in central Switzerland; an alpine region; capital is Altdorf; contains glaciers, forests, pastures. In 853 it became a fief of the Fraumunster convent at Zurich; after 1098 it was part of the Holy Roman imperial bailiwick of Zurich; in 1231 it was made dependency of Emperor Frederick II; joined the league of cantons 1291, forming center of the Swiss Confederation; Uri rejected the Reformation and joined the Catholic Sonderbund 1845; scene of the William Tell legend. Hydroelectricity has made some industry possible, but agriculture is dominant. Area: 415sq mi (1,075sq km). Pop. 33,400.

Uric Acid, an end product of protein metabolism found in urine, blood, and lymph and also as a salt (urate) in calculi such as kidney stones. Excess amount of uric acid in the blood causes gout, with urate deposits around joints.

Urinalysis, examination of the appearance and condition of the urine both grossly and microscopically, and study of its chemical constituents to detect a wide variety of diseases or conditions and to follow the results of treatment.

Uris, Leon Marcus (1924–), US author, b. Baltimore. He is noted for his historical novels, the most noted of which was *Exodus* (1958), which dealt with the establishment of the state of Israel. It, along with other of his works, has been made into a movie. Among his other books are *Battle Cry* (1953), *Mila 18* (1960), *Armageddon* (1964), and *Trinity* (1976).

Urogenital System, a major system of the body, containing the urinary system and the genital organs, which are part of the reproductive system. The urinary system, the body's excretory system, consists of kidneys, which lie on upper back part of the abdominal cavity on each side; ureters, 10-in (25-cm) tubes that run from kidneys to the bladder; the urinary bladder, lying in the pelvic cavity and storing urine; and the urethra, from which urine passes from the body. In males, the reproductive system includes paired testes that produce sperm cells and hormones and are located in an external pouch, the scrotum; accessory glands; and the penis, the organ through which urine passes and sperm is ejaculated. In females, the reproductive system consists of paired ovaries, found on each side of the pelvic cavity; Fallopian tubes, or oviducts, which connect ovaries to the uterus; the uterus, or womb, located in the pelvic cavity between the bladder and rectum; the cervix, or lower part of the uterus, which opens into the vagina, the opening for intercourse and childbirth. In females, the urethra and vaginal openings are separate but lying close to each other. *See also* articles on various organs.

Urology, that branch of medicine that deals with the diagnosis and treatment of diseases of the urinary tract in women and of the urinary and genital organs in men.

Ursa Major, the Great Bear, the Big Dipper, conspicuous northern circumpolar constellation lying south of Draco and on the opposite side of the north celestial pole from Ursa Minor. Its seven brightest stars form the familiar bowl-and-handle shape, and include the multiple star Mizar, the second star from the end of the handle, and Merak and Dubhe, the last two stars in the bowl, known as the Pointers because they directly indicate Polaris. The constellation, which is known by several other names, including Charles's Wain and the Plow, contains two galaxies M 81 (NGC 3031) and M 82 (NGC 3034) and a planetary nebula, the Owl Nebula (M 97; NGC 3587). Brightest star Alpha Ursae Majoris (Dubhe).

Ursa Minor, the Little Bear, the Little Dipper, northern circumpolar constellation in which the north celestial pole is located, marked by Polaris, the brightest star in the group.

Ursula, Saint, virgin and martyr. Legends about her date from around 1000. A Latin inscription found in Cologne, Germany, probably dating from the 4th century, tells of virgins martyred there. Who they were is not known, but tradition made Ursula their leader and many stories grew. One is that she and her companions were British and were killed by the Huns. The number of martyrs has been set at 11 and at 11,000.

Ursulines, oldest religious order of women in the Roman Catholic Church, named for its patron, St Ursula, and founded by St Angela Merici at Brescia in 1535. The order grew, especially in France and Canada, until interrupted by the French Revolution. Increasing in size again in the 19th century, federations of Roman, Canadian, and German convents were formed.

Uruapan, city in SW Mexico, 60mi (96km) SW of Morelia; manufacturing center for gourd lacquerware crafted by Tarascan Indians. Industries: glassware, woodwork, handcrafts. Founded 1540. Pop. 114,979.

Uruguay, independent nation in Latin America. It is a small republic with state ownership of major utilities and some industry; the country has a high standard of living and well-developed social welfare programs.

Land and economy. Uruguay is located on the E coast of South America, bounded by Argentina and Brazil. With sufficient water and a temperate climate its prairie grasses have made livestock the most significant economic product. Chief crops from the N agricultural areas are wheat and flax. Wool, meat, and leather account for 40% of export revenues. Social welfare programs added to payments deficits and inflation during the 1960s and early 1970s. By the late 1970s the economy had begun to recover, but took a downward turn in 1982 when Argentina, upon whom Uruguay's

Leon Uris

Uruguay

Arches National Park, Utah

economy largely depends, became involved in the Falklands conflict.

People. Uruguay is the only South American country with no uninhabited areas; more than 33% of the people live in Montevideo. Spanish, both in language and culture, predominates, although 25% of the population is Italian. Literacy is 95%. The principal religion is Roman Catholicism. Church and state are completely separated. Primary education is compulsory, and university education is free.

Government. Under a 1966 constitution the president is elected for a five-year term, and the bicameral General Assembly is popularly elected. Suffrage is universal. Since 1973, however, government has been controlled by the military.

History. Struggles with Spain and Portugal, and then with Brazil and Argentina, marked its history until independence was achieved in 1828. Civil wars and foreign intervention plagued the country until the end of the 19th century. Since then Uruguay has been known for its stability as a democracy whose pattern of political and social reform was set by President José Batlle y Ordonez in 1903. In 1973, however, in an effort to stem guerrilla activities of the leftist Tupamaro group, the military took control of the government. In a 1980 plebiscite Uruguayans indicated approval of the current regime. Elections in 1982 and 1984 had returned the country to civilian rule by 1985.

PROFILE

Official name: Eastern Republic of Uruguay
Area: 68,536sq mi (177,508sq km)
Population: 2,878,000
　Density: 42per sq mi (16per sq km)
Chief city: Montevideo (capital)
Government: Republic
Religion: Roman Catholic
Language: Spanish
Monetary unit: New Uruguayan peso
Gross national product: $6,110,000,000
Per capita income: $865
Industries: meat products, wool, hides, construction materials, chemicals, wine
Agriculture: wheat, corn, rice, cattle, sheep, forests, citrus fruits, oats
Trading partners: Western European countries, Argentina, Brazil, United States

Uruguay (Uruguai), river SE South America; rises in S Brazil, and forms part of boundary between Rio Grande do Sul and Santa Catarina states; flows SW to form boundary between Argentina and S Brazil, and Argentina and Uruguay, empties into Rio de la Plata. Important source of hydroelectricity for Argentina and Uruguay. Length: approx. 870mi. (1,401km).

Urumchi (Wulumuqi, or Wu-lu-mu-chi), city in W China, 300mi (483km) E of Kuldja, in Dzungarian basin; capital of Sinkiang Uigur autonomous region; site of Sinkiang University; on caravan routes from USSR, Lanchow, and Kashgar. Industries: printing, tanning, coal, tin, silver, food processing, farm tools. Pop. 500,-000.

Üsküdar, city in NW Turkey, opposite Istanbul across the Bosporus channel; commercial and residential suburb of Istanbul; site of mosques and other early structures. Pop. 133,883.

Usury, lending of money at an unusually high or unlawful rate of interest.

Utah, state in the W United States, in the Rocky Mt region. Its SE corner touches Colorado, New Mexico, and Arizona, the only contact of four states in the country. More than 70% of the inhabitants belong to the

Church of Jesus Christ of Latter-day Saints (Mormonism), and the church exerts a strong influence in Utah.

Land and economy. About 90% of the land is desert or mountains; about 66% is owned by the US government. The Wasatch Range of the Rocky Mts crosses the state from N to S. To the W of this range is a basin of desert land. Great Salt Lake, a saline body of water 72mi (116km) long and 30mi (48km) wide, is in the NE part of the basin. E of the Wasatch Range the Uinta Mts, with 11 peaks over 13,000ft (3,965m), run E and W. Much of the S and E portions of the state are desert plateaus cut by canyons. Agriculture is largely confined to the valleys on the W front of the Wasatch. Irrigation projects have aided production. Manufacturing is concentrated in the area of Ogden-Salt Lake City-Provo. Mining is carried on in many parts of the state. Utah's scenery, especially in the national parks in the S, attracts an important tourist trade.

People. First settlement was by pioneers from other states, whose descendants form the bulk of the population. About 80% live in urban areas.

Education. The University of Utah and Utah State University are state-supported. Brigham Young University is a Mormon church institution.

History. In 1776 two Franciscan friars seeking a way to California crossed the region, which was Mexican territory until ceded to the United States in 1848. The first settlement came in 1847, when Brigham Young led a party of Mormons to the valley between the Wasatch and Great Salt Lake. Through irrigation they created good farmland. Immigrants from Eastern states and Europe established new communities. In 1849 the Mormons organized the State of Deseret and sought admission to the Union, but Congress instead created the Territory of Utah. The transcontinental railroad was completed in 1869 at Promontory Point. A long conflict with federal authorities ended in 1890, when the Mormons agreed to abandon their practice of polygamy. Mining long dominated Utah's economy. Following WWII defense-related manufacturing became important, but the leasing of lands with oil-shale deposits during the 1970s ensured that minerals would continue to play an important role in the state's future.

PROFILE

Admitted to Union: Jan. 4, 1896; rank, 45th
US Congressmen: Senate, 2; House of Representatives, 2
Population: 1,461,037 (1980); rank, 36th
Capital: Salt Lake City, 163,033 (1980)
Chief cities: Salt Lake City; Ogden, 64,407; Provo, 73,907; Bountiful, 32,877
State legislature: Senate, 29; House of Representatives, 75
Area: 84,916sq mi (219,932sq km); rank, 11th
Elevation: highest, 13,528ft (4,126m) Kings Peak; lowest, 2,000ft (610m), Beaverdam Creek
Industries: (major products) missiles, rocket engines, aircraft navigation systems, fabricated steel, food products
Agriculture: sheep, turkeys, apricots, cherries, barley, sugar beets, winter wheat
Minerals (major): copper, gold, silver, lead, petroleum, uranium
State nickname: Beehive State
State motto: Industry
State bird: seagull
State flower: sego lily
State tree: blue spruce

Uterus, or **Womb,** a pear-shaped, hollow muscular organ located in the pelvis between the bladder and rectum in women and in which the fetus is carried and develops. Its upper, wider part, called the body, fundus, or corpus, is connected to an ovary on each side by a Fallopian tube and held in place by broad liga-

ments. Its lower part, called the neck, or cervix, opens into the vagina through which sperm may enter to fertilize an egg and through which menstruation occurs. The lining of the uterus—the endometrium—is shed monthly between puberty and menopause in menstruation when pregnancy does not occur. During pregnancy the uterus gradually increases in size to accommodate the developing fetus and returns to almost pre-pregnancy size after childbirth.

Utica, city in central New York, on the Mohawk River and New York Barge Canal; seat of Oneida co; originally settled 1773 on site of Old Fort Schuyler; site of Utica College of Syracuse University (1946), Mohawk Valley Community College (1946), Munson-Williams-Proctor Institute (Art Museum). Industries: tools, firearms, textiles, electronic and aviation equipment. Inc. as village 1798, as city 1832. Pop. (1980) 75,632.

Utilitarianism, social and ethical doctrine associated with James Mill (1773–1836) and Jeremy Bentham (1749–1832), which asserts that the right act produces the greatest happiness for the greatest number.

Uto-Aztecan Languages, family of American Indian languages spoken in SW United States and in Mexico. It includes Papago, Pima, and Hopi, of Arizona; Ute, of Utah and Colorado; Comanche, of Oklahoma; and Shoshone and Kiowa, spoken in a number of western states. In Mexico there are Nahuatl (the language of the Aztecs), Tarahumara, and Mayo.

Utopia, book by Sir Thomas More, published in Latin in 1516, with the first English edition in 1551. It describes "the best state" found on "the new isle, called Utopia."

Utopianism, a system of political ideas which advocates an ideal state. Among the political theorists who advocated an utopian society were Charles Fourier (1772–1837), Robert Owen (1771–1858), and Karl Marx (1818–83). Marx believed in the overthrow of capitalism and the distribution of goods according to individual needs. Utopian ideals have been the theme of many books. In Sir Thomas More's *Utopia* (1516), a traveler discovers a perfect political, economic, and social state. Other works on Utopianism include *New Atlantis* (1624–29) by Sir Francis Bacon, *Looking Backward* (1888) by Edward Bellamy, and *A Modern Utopia* (1905) by H. G. Wells. Because Utopianism is a reaction to social needs, many of its principles are today called socialistic.

Utrecht, city in central Netherlands, on the Oude Rijn River, approx. 20mi (32km) SSE of Amsterdam; capital of Utrecht prov.; a trade center since medieval times; scene of signing of Union of Utrecht (1579), and Treaty of Utrecht, terminating War of the Spanish Succession (1713); site of university (1636), 15th-century cathedral. Industries: steel, machinery, textiles, electrical equipment, food processing. Chartered 1122. Pop. 250,887.

Utrecht, Peace of, series of treaties (1713–14) concluding the War of the Spanish Succession. It had the effect of ending French expansion and beginning British expansion. Louis XIV confirmed renunciation of claims to French throne of Louis' grandson, Philip V of Spain, France surrendered the Spanish Netherlands, Milan, Naples, and Sardinia to Austria. The treaties also confirmed succession to the British and French thrones. Spain ceded Gibraltar and Minorca to Great Britain, which also was granted sole right of slave traffic with Spanish America. The right bank of the Rhine was restored to the Holy Roman Empire, and

France turned Newfoundland, Nova Scotia, the Hudson's Bay territory, and St Kitts over to Britain. Commercial treaties were also included.

Utrillo, Maurice (1883–1955), French painter. He is known for his scenes of Paris, especially of Montmartre. The son of artist Suzanne Valadon, he began to paint in order to control his alcoholic tendencies. His best works are from his so-called White Period (1908–14) and include "L'Impasse Cottin" (*c.*1910), "Rue Norvins" (1912), and "Place du Tertre" (1911–12). In 1923 he designed the sets and costumes for Sergei Diaghilev's ballet, *Barabau.*

U-2 Incident (1960), international incident precipitated by the downing of a US plane in the USSR. The plane, a U-2 on a photographic reconnaissance mission over the Soviet Union, was shot down and its pilot, Francis Gary Powers, captured. The United States at first claimed the mission was a meteorological one, but US-USSR diplomatic relations were strained when Powers confessed to being a spy. Soviet Premier Khrushchev embarrassed the United States by demanding an apology and canceling a visit scheduled by Pres. Dwight D. Eisenhower to the USSR. Powers was later freed in exchange for the release of a Soviet spy by the United States.

Uxmal, Maya ceremonial and administrative center located on Mexico's Yucatán peninsula. Two pyramids and a grouping of four rectangular buildings called the Nunnery dominated the 160-acre (65-hectares) site. Uxmal flourished AD 600–900 but was abandoned *c.* 1450.

V

Vaal River, river in Republic of South Africa; rises in SE Transvaal, flows W forming border of Transvaal and Orange Free State; empties into Orange River. Length: 720mi (1,159km).

Vaccination, injection of a vaccine in order to produce immunity against a disease. The term most often refers specifically to vaccination against smallpox, in which vaccine is scratched into the skin producing a typical "pox" and leaving a small scar. Vaccines are also injected or administered orally. *See also* Vaccine.

Vaccine, agent used to produce immunity against various diseases without producing serious or fatal symptoms of the disease. The agent may be a live virus but low in virulence or a dead one still able to induce production of antibodies. First of the vaccines to come into general use was the smallpox vaccine, developed in the 19th century. Vaccines against poliomyelitis, influenza, yellow fever, rabies, measles, and other bacterial, viral, and rickettsial diseases are available. Recombinant DNA techniques are being used to produce effective vaccines. The first successful vaccine produced by this method is for hoof-and-mouth disease. *See also* Toxin.

Vacuole, membrane-bound cavity within cell plasma, believed to discharge excess water or wastes.

Vacuum, a state of very low pressure. Interstellar space is an extremely good vacuum, with an average density of about 1 hydrogen atom/cc. Many items of everyday life contain vacuums: electric light bulbs, television picture tubes.

Vacuum Pump, a device that removes air from an enclosure. The rotary oil pump uses an eccentric cylinder rotating in an enclosed space connected to the vessel to be evacuated. At one point in its cycle, air is compressed in an opening and forces a valve to open, thus reducing the air pressure in the vessel.

Vaduz, capital city of Liechtenstein, on the right bank of the Upper Rhine River, approx. 50mi (80km) SE of Zurich, Switzerland. Destroyed in war between Switzerland and the Holy Roman Empire, it was rebuilt in early 16th century; became a possession of the Liechtenstein family 1712; site of Castle of Vaduz, National Library, Post Office, Postal Museum, art gallery. Chief industry is tourism. Pop. 7,500.

Vaginitis, acute infectious inflammation of the vagina caused by a protozoan *Trichonomas vaginalis* and transmitted during sexual intercourse. The male manifestation is usually a mild urethritis.

Valais (Wallis), canton in S Switzerland; extends from Bernese to Pennine Alps; includes upper Rhone valley, Matterhorn, Dufourspitze, Dom, and Weisshorn peaks; capital is Sion. Taken by Romans 57 BC,it passed to Rudolf III of Burgundy in 999, who was made the bishop of Sion, lord of Valais; it was later divided and Lower Valais passed to duke of Savoy; in 1475 Sion defeated the duke of Savoy and Lower Valais was ruled by Upper Valais until 1798, when Valais was made a canton of the Helvetic Republic; became independent 1802; joined the Swiss Confederation 1815. Industries: hydroelectricity, metal products, chemicals, livestock, agriculture, wine. Area: 2,020sq mi (5,232sq km). Pop. 211,600.

Valence, tendency of atoms to join together forming chemical bonds. Valence is also a measure of the "combining power" of a particular element, equal to the number of (single) chemical bonds one atom can form. Thus hydrogen has a valence of 1, carbon 4, and sulfur 2, as seen in compounds such as CH_4, CS_2, and H_2S. Covalence refers to formation of covalent bonds: coordinate valence to coordinate bonds. Many transition elements have two or more different valences. *See also* Oxidation State.

Valence Electron, electron in an atom that is transferred or shared in the formation of a chemical bond. The valence electrons of a nontransition metal are those in the outermost shell (furthest from the nucleus), and in forming compounds the atom tends to attain the stable configuration of a noble gas. Transition metals use both the outer shell and the partially filled penultimate shell in chemical bonding.

Valence Orbital, one of the outer atomic orbitals of an atom, containing the electrons that participate in chemical bonding. In producing ionic bonds electrons are lost or gained by valence orbitals. Covalent bonding involves sharing of electrons between atoms, a process often visualized as overlap of valence orbitals with formation of molecular orbitals.

Valencia, city in E Spain, on the Guadalquivir River, 188mi (303km) ESE of Madrid; capital of Valencia prov. Originally inhabited by Romans, it passed to Visigoths AD 413; conquered by the Moors and made capital of an independent Moorish kingdom 11th century; reconquered 1238 by James of Aragon; served as capital for loyalist government during Spanish civil war 1936–39. It is the site of 15th-century Gothic cathedral, 14th–17th-century Church of San Nicolas, botanical gardens, bullring; processing and distribution center for surrounding region; El Grao serves as the city's port. Industries: shipyards, electrical equipment, chemicals, textiles, machinery. Founded 138 BC by Roman consul Decimus Junius Brutus. Area: (prov.) 4,156sq mi (10,764sq km). Pop. (city) 700,000; (prov.) 1,767,327.

Valencia, city in N Venezuela, 80mi (128km) W of Caracas; capital of Carabobo state. A major industrial and transport center, city was capital of Venezuela 1812 and 1830; scene of Venezuela's proclamation of independence from Greater Colombia 1830. Industries: auto parts, textiles, paper, cement, soap, dairy products, furniture, feed, lumber, food processing. Founded 1555. Pop. 463,418.

Valentine, Saint. The Roman Martyrology lists two saints of this name: Valentine of Rome and Valentine of Terni. Both are said to have been martyred about 269, and both have their feast day on February 14. In the late Middle Ages a custom developed of sending love notes on this date, probably because it was thought to mark the beginning of the mating season for birds.

Valentino, Rudolph (1895–1926), US silent film star, b. Italy. A prototype of the Latin lover, he enhanced many films with sleek, exotic magnetism including *The Sheik* (1921), *The Young Rajah* (1922), *Cobra* (1925), and *Son of the Sheik* (1926). Valentino's early death caused widespread hysteria among his fans.

Valerian, Publius Licinius (died *c.* 269), Roman emperor (253–60). In 257 he revived the persecution of the Christians that had begun under Emperor Decius. Christians were required to perform public acts of worship to the state gods, and penalties were ordered for those who refused. The persecution ended when Valerian was captured by the Persians in 260 while attempting to halt their invasion of Syria and Armenia.

Valéry, Paul Ambroise (1871–1945), French poet and critic. Influenced by Mallarmé, his poems, including *La Jeune Parque* (1917) and *Les Charmes* (1922), are characterized by lyricism and abstract thought. His criticism includes *La Soirée avec Monsieur Teste* (1906) and the five volumes of essays *Varieté* (1924–44). He was elected to the French Academy (1925).

Valhalla, in Norse mythology, the hall where chosen slain warriors live blissfully. The god Odin is the leader of Valhalla and he will lead these warriors to battle against the giants at the time of Ragnarok.

Validity, in statistics and psychometrics, the extent to which a test or method measures what it is supposed to measure. A test's validity may be determined by seeing how well the test predicts some other measure or criterion that is known to be valid. *See also* Statistics.

Valine, white crystalline essential amino acid found in proteins. *See* Amino Acid.

Valium, trademark for diazepam, a sedative drug used in the treatment of anxiety and as an anticonvulsant in epilepsy. Habituation is possible.

Valkyries, in Norse mythology, maidens sent by Odin to choose slain warriors for Valhalla.

Valladolid, city in NW central Spain, on the Pisuerga River, 98mi (157km) NNW of Madrid; capital of Valladolid prov. Liberated by Castilian kings in 10th century, it was scene of marriage of Ferdinand and Isabella (1469); site of 12th-century university and Romanesque cathedral, church of Santa Ana containing paintings by Goya, art museum, monument to Christopher Columbus (who died here 1506), 15th-century home of Cervantes. Industries: chemicals, flour, grain, metal works, textiles, liqueurs, pianos, gloves. First mentioned 1074. Area: (prov.) 3,166sq mi (8,200sq km). Pop. (city) 236,341; (prov.) 412,572.

Vallejo, city in central California, 20mi (32km) N of Oakland; originally constructed on land of Gen. Mariano G. Vallejo to be the state capital; temporary capital 1852–1853; site of California Maritime Academy (1929), Solano College (1945), Mare Island Navy Yard (1854); important port and agricultural trade center. Founded by Admiral David Farragut *c.*1850; inc. 1866. Pop. (1980) 80,188.

Valletta, seaport and capital of Malta, located on NE coast of the island; site of Cathedral of San Giovanni (1576) and Royal University of Malta (1769); heavily damaged during WWII; tourist area. Port was built and named after Jean Parisot de La Valette, grand master of Knights of Malta. Pop. 14,049.

Valley, an elongate, gently sloping depression of the Earth's surface, commonly situated between mountains or hills. It often contains a stream or river that receives the drainage from the surrounding heights. A U-shaped valley was probably formed by a glacier, a V-shaped one by a stream. The term may also be applied to a broad generally flat area that is drained by a large river, like the Mississippi Valley.

Valley Forge, campsite 21mi (34km) north of Philadelphia where American soldiers under George Washington withstood the winter of 1777–78, living in log huts they built, with little food or clothing. The morale of the Americans reached its lowest point here.

Valois Dynasty, royal house of France (1328–1589). Valois kings survived challenges in the Hundred Years War (1337–1453) by England and by Burgundian and Armagnac rivals and consolidated royal strength over feudal lords. They established the crown's sole right to tax and to wage war and extended parlements throughout France. Louis XI (*r.*1461–83) is considered the founder of French royal absolutism. After the death of Henry III (1589), the crown passed to the house of Bourbon.

Valparaíso, city in central Chile; capital of Valparaíso prov. Founded 1536, it was site of treaty signed 1884 by which Bolivia surrendered coastal region with nitrate deposits to Chile; heavily damaged by earthquakes 1906, 1971; principal seaport of Chile; cultural center; site of Chilean Naval Academy, technical university, Catholic university. Industries: chemicals, textiles, sugar, metal products. Pop. 248,972.

Value Added, in economics, value added to the product at each stage of production. A value-added tax taxes products at each stage based upon the value each stage adds to the total value of the product.

Valve, Engine, a device to control admission and rejection of intake and exhaust gases to the engine cylinder.

Vampire, in legend, a corpse that lives at night and sucks the blood of the living to sustain itself. The victim in turn becomes a vampire. The monster can be killed by driving a wooden stake through its heart. Bram Stoker's *Dracula* (1897) drew on the legend of the vampire to produce a masterwork of horror.

Rudolph Valentino

Martin Van Buren

Cornelius Vanderbilt

Vampire Bat, small brown bat inhabiting tropical and subtropical America. It feeds only on fresh blood sucked from resting animals. Length: 3in (7.6cm). Family Desmodontidae. *See also* Bat.

Vanadinite, lead chlorovanadate [$Pb_5(VO_4)_3Cl$] found in upper zone of lead ore deposits. Hexagonal system prisms and needlelike masses. Resinous orange to brown; hardness 2.7–3; sp gr 7. Commercial source of vanadium.

Vanadium, metallic element (symbol V) of the first transition series, discovered in 1801. Chief ores are carnotite, patronite, and vanadinite. The metal is used in special steels and vanadium pentoxide is an important catalyst. Chemically it reacts with oxygen and other nonmetals at high temperature. Properties: at. no. 23; at. wt. 50.9414; sp. gr. 6.11 (18.7°C); melt. pt. 3,288°F (1,890°C); boil. pt. 6,116°F (3,380°C); most common isotope V^{51} (99.76%). *See also* Transition Elements.

Van Allen, James Alfred (1914–   ), US physicist, b. Mount Pleasant, Iowa. During World War II, he invented a radio proximity fuse. After the war he supervised experiments with German V-2 rockets, leading to research with space satellites and his discovery of the two zones of radiation encircling the Earth (commonly known as the Van Allen radiation belts).

Van Allen Radiation Belts, two belts of intense ionizing radiation that surround the Earth in the upper atmosphere, named for their discovery (1953) by US physicist James A. Van Allen. The belts contain particles carrying energies of from approximately 20,000 electron volts to several million electron volts. The inner belt, of protons, centers about 2,000mi (3,220km) above the equator; the outer belt, of electrons, centers at about 11,000mi (17,710km).

Vanbrugh, John (1664–1726), English architect. He was also a dramatist and soldier, who worked with and was influenced by Christopher Wren. His greatest achievement was the design of Blenheim, the monumental palace given to the duke of Marlborough.

Van Buren, Martin (1782–1862), 8th president of the United States (1837–41), b. Kinderhook, N.Y. In 1807 he married Hannah Hoes; they had four sons. He was admitted to the bar in 1803 and soon entered politics, rising to become an important Democratic leader in New York State. After 1824 he was a close political associate of Andrew Jackson, and Jackson chose him as his running mate in 1832. After four years as vice president the Democrats chose Van Buren as their presidential candidate in 1836.

After winning the presidency in a landslide, Van Buren attempted to continue the Jacksonian policies. The Panic of 1837, however, was blamed on his administration, and his effectiveness suffered. The Independent Treasury System was inaugurated during his term. He was defeated for reelection in 1840 by the Whig candidate, William Henry Harrison. He made two later attempts at the presidency: in 1844 on the Democratic ticket again and in 1848 as head of the Free-Soil party.

Career: New York State Senate, 1813–20; New York attorney general, 1815–19; US Senate, 1821–28; governor of New York, 1829; secretary of state, 1829–31; vice president, 1833–37; president, 1837–41. *See also* Free Soil Party.

Vancouver, George (1757–98), English navigator and explorer. First sailing on exploratory expeditions under Captain James Cook, he was made commander of his own expedition in 1791 and ordered to survey the NW

coast of North America and search for a passage from the Pacific to Hudson Bay. He made a detailed survey and found no northern passage to the east, returning by going around Cape Horn in 1794. His journals were published as *A Voyage of Discovery to the North Pacific Ocean and Round the World* (3 vols., 1798).

Vancouver, seaport city in S British Columbia, on S shore of Burrard Inlet; 3rd-largest city in Canada; industrial center of British Columbia, and major port on the Pacific Ocean. First explored 1792 by Capt. George Vancouver aboard the *Discovery;* the first European settlement was est. 1865 as Granville; devastated by forest fire 1886; developed rapidly after completion of transcontinental railroad 1887, Panama Canal 1914. It is the site of annual Vancouver Festival of the Arts (since 1958), Stanley Park, University of British Columbia (1890), Anglican Theological College of British Columbia (1912), Saint Paul's College (1926), Union College of British Columbia (1927), Saint Mark's College (1956), Saint Andrew's Hall (1957), Carey Hall (1960), Simon Fraser University (1963). Exports: forest products, grain, fish and fish products. Industries: lumber, plywood, pulp and paper, shingles, tourism, food processing, chemicals, fishing, shipyards, meat packing. Founded 1881; inc. 1886 as Vancouver. Pop. 396,563.

Vancouver, port city in SW Washington, 8mi (13km) N of Portland, Oregon, on Columbia River; seat of Clark co; important fur center in 19th century; site of Vancouver Barracks (est. 1848, now seat of Oregon Military District), Ulysses S. Grant's house (1852–53) while he was stationed here. Industries: shipyards, lumber, grain elevators, fruit, furniture, wood products. Founded 1824 as Hudson's Bay Co. Post; inc. 1857. Pop. (1980) 42,834.

Vancouver Island, island off SW British Columbia, Canada, in the Pacific Ocean; largest island off W North America; known for its fine harbors, especially Nootka Sound, on inlet on the W coast discovered by Capt. James Cook 1778. Disputed by Spain and Great Britain, the island was chartered 1792 by Capt. George Vancouver; made a British crown colony 1849; became part of British Columbia 1866; site of Pacific Rim National Park and Strathcoma Provincial Park. Industries: lumbering, wood, fishing, tourism, mining. Area: 12,408sq mi (32,137sq km). Pop. 410,188.

Vanda, genus of orchids native from China to N Australia and popular with orchid fanciers. They have leathery leaves and sprays of small flowers. There are many varieties including *V. sanderiana* with 5in (12.7cm) pink and yellow flowers; *V. tricolor* with fragrant yellow and brown-spotted flowers; and *V. coerulea,* one of the few blue orchids. Height: to 3ft (0.9m). Family Orchidaceae.

Vandals, an ancient Germanic people. About AD 170 they migrated from the Baltic shore to the Hungarian plain. Moving westward, they crossed the Rhine in 406 and continued on to Spain. In North Africa, under the leadership of Gaiseric, they set up their own kingdom. They sacked Rome in 455.

Van de Graaff Generator, or electrostatic generator, high-voltage source, used as the voltage supply for a type of electrostatic accelerator (the Van de Graaff accelerator). Positive (or negative) charges, sprayed from a set of high-voltage points onto a moving belt, are conveyed into a large hollow metal sphere to which the charges are carried by a second set of points. As charge accumulates on the outside, the voltage of the sphere increases to many millions of volts.

Vanderbilt, Cornelius (1794–1877), US railroad owner and financier, b. Staten Island, N.Y. Beginning as a boy running a ferry service, he established a steamboat company (1829). He soon won control of most ferries in the New York City area and by 1846 was a millionaire. During the California gold rush (1849), he ran a shipping line between New York and San Francisco, crossing Nicaragua by land. He entered the transoceanic transportation business (1854), but then turned to railroads (1857). During the Civil War he built up a railroad empire by gaining control of existing railroads and in 1873, connected New York and Chicago by rail. His New York Central System had over 4,000 miles (6,440km) of track at the time of his death.

Van der Waals' Forces, weak forces of attraction occurring between atoms and molecules. They result from interactions between dipole moments of adjacent molecules or, if there is no dipole moment, from mutual electrostatic interactions of the electrons and nuclei. Van der Waals forces, so called because they are responsible for the pressure correction term in the Van der Waals equation for an imperfect gas, are much weaker than chemical bonds and fall off sharply with increasing distance. They are the forces holding the molecules together in molecular crystals.

Van DeVanter, Willis (1859–1941), US jurist and lawyer. A Wyoming railroad attorney, assistant US attorney general (1897–1903), and US circuit court judge (1903–10), he was an associate justice of the US Supreme Court (1911–37). An ultra-conservative staunchly opposed to social welfare legislation, and New Deal measures, he wrote few opinions in his 26 years on the court.

Vandyke, or **Van Dyck, Anthony** (1599–1641), Flemish painter. Best known for his elegant portraits of aristocrats, he also painted religious scenes and was an excellent etcher. He worked in Rubens' studio before traveling abroad, first to England in 1620. In Italy, 1621–27, he painted many portraits of the Genoese nobility. Charles I of England appointed him court painter and knighted him in 1632. His many portraits profoundly influenced 17th- and 18th-century portraiture and can be seen in most major museums.

Van Eyck, Hubert (c.1370–c.1426), Flemish painter. The only documentation of his artistic existence is an inscription on the Ghent Altarpiece, which he probably executed with his brother Jan. Two other panels are thought to be his: the "Annunciation" (New York City, Metropolitan Museum of Art) and "The Marys at the Tomb" (Rotterdam, Boymans-Van Beuningen Museum). It is probable that he collaborated with Jan on "The Last Judgment" (New York City, Metropolitan Museum of Art).

Van Eyck, Jan (c.1380–1441), Flemish painter. Often called the father of Flemish painting, he is considered one of the truly original painters of all time. Under his influence oil painting realized a new importance in the north. His earliest signed and dated work is the Ghent Altarpiece, a collaboration with his brother Hubert. "Leal Souvenir" (1432), a threequarter profile of a head (probably a portrait of Gilles Binchois) established a style of portrait painting that was to remain standard for centuries. Other portraits that evidence his growing interest in light and detail are "Incehall Madonna" and "Portrait of a Man in a Red Turban" (both 1433). His mastery of light is further developed in the masterpiece "The Arnolfini Marriage" (1434). "Portrait of a Goldsmith" shows softer shadowing. His last dated work is "Portrait of Margaret Van Eyck" (1439).

Van Gogh, Vincent Willem (1853–1890), Dutch painter and draftsman. He was one of the first to discover the expressive value of color and, as such, was one of the first Expressionists. He did not begin to paint seriously until the 1880s, having clerked in an art gallery and attempted to serve as a self-styled missionary to the poor. His early masterpieces of expressionist flavor include "The Potato Eaters" (1885) and "Shoes with Laces" (1886). In 1887 he met the Impressionists and gradually began to adopt their style and subject matter. His most productive years were 1888 and 1889, when he began to find his own style, producing more than 200 works, including "L'Arlesienne," "The Postman Roulin," "Orchard in Blossom," and "View of Arles with Irises." In 1888 he began to suffer mental conflicts, and until the end of his life he was intermittently hospitalized. It was in an argument with Paul Gauguin in 1888 that van Gogh cut off his own ear. In 1890, while a patient in the hospital of St Remy, he shot himself.

Vanilla, climbing orchid found from Mexico to South America. The vines grow to 50ft (15.2m) and bear greenish-yellow flowers that produce long seed pods. The unripened seeds are the source of the vanillin of commerce, prepared by a fermenting process.

Vanuatu, Republic of (formerly New Hebrides), independent island nation in W. Pacific. Vanuatu is composed of about 80 islands of volcanic origin and some are active. The heavily forested, mountainous regions of the islands' interiors are ringed by narrow coast zones where settlement is concentrated. The two largest are Espiratu Santo and Efate (site of Vila, the capital). During the 19th century the British and French established plantations on the islands, and many of the inhabitants were forcibly recruited to work in Australia and New Zealand. Fighting erupted between the indigenous people and European settlers, and the French and British subsequently established (1906) a joint condominium to rule the islands. Before independence was granted (1980), a separatist rebellion began on Espiratu Santo. After British peace-keeping forces arrived, fighting ended, and Vantuatu was declared independent. Because the Melanesian inhabitants speak many languages a common pidgin, Bislama, is used, as are French and English. The economy is dominated by subsistence agriculture, with yams, coconuts, taro, fruits, and pigs the principal products. Copra, fish, and beef are processed for export. Tourism is of growing importance, and tax incentives have made Vanuatu a center of off-shore banking. Area: 5,700 sq mi (15,000 sq km); Pop. 112,596.

Vapor, a gas. The term is sometimes used to refer to a gas in equilibrium with its liquid phase. The pressure at which this occurs is called the vapor pressure. Vapor pressures always increase with temperature—when the vapor pressure equals the surrounding pressure, the substance boils.

Varanasi (Banaras), formerly Benares; city in N central India, 400mi (644km) WNW of Calcutta on the Ganges River. Considered the holiest city to the Hindus, it is a pilgrimage center with approx. 1,500 shrines, temples, and mosques; Buddha is reputed to have preached his first sermon nearby *c.* 7th century BC; most of the religious buildings date only from *c.* 17th century following Muslim invasion and destruction; site of Benares Hindu University (1916), Golden Temple, Mosque of Aurangzeb, Durga Kund temple housing numerous sacred monkeys. Industries: silk brocade, brassware. Pop. 637,612.

Varangians, Danish and Swedish raiders who invaded eastern Europe during the 9th and 10th centuries while Vikings raided western Europe. They opened routes that crossed Russia. One leader, Rurik, who settled at Novgorod in 862, is the legendary founder of Russia. In the 10th and 11th centuries, Varangians served as mercenaries to Constantinople's emperors and as soldiers to Slavic princes. They eventually merged with the Slavs.

Variable, in statistics, item that may change or vary in the course of a particular discussion, unlike a *constant,* which maintains a given value throughout a particular discussion. An example of a variable would be the grade given to each student in a class of 25, which would change from student to student. The constant in this case would be the number of students in the class.

Variable Star, star that shows regular or irregular fluctuations in brightness. Regular variables include the eclipsing variables and the pulsating stars of the Cepheid or RR Lyrae type. Irregular variables include the novae and the flare stars. Many stars of the red giant or red supergiant class, such as Alpha Orionis (Betelgeuse) or Mira Ceti, show long-period, semi-regular, or totally irregular variability. Except for eclipsing stars, variables are intrinsic, that is, their fluctuations are due to internal disturbances.

Variation, a difference, arising either from heredity or environment, between two members of a species. The difference may be one that is passed on to successive generations, and therefore could be relatively permanent. *See also* Adaptation.

Varicose Veins, veins that are torturous and distended with blood. They can occur anywhere in the body, but are usually found in the legs. Treatments include wearing elastic-type stockings and surgical stripping of the affected veins.

Variscite, a phosphate mineral, hydrous aluminum iron phosphate found with aluminum-rich rocks near surface. Orthorhombic system. Glassy white to green; hardness 3.5–4.5; sp gr 2.5. Used in jewelry, it resembles turquoise, but is greener.

Varna, seaport city of E Bulgaria, on Black Sea, 182mi (293km) NE of Plovdiv; important port while under Turkish rule (1391); taken by Russia 1828; returned to Turkey 1829 by the Peace of Adrianople; ceded to Bulgaria 1878; during Crimean War (1854), it was the major naval base of British and French forces. Industries: textiles, flour, wine, furniture, ceramics, diesel engines, shipbuilding. Founded 580 BC. Pop. 186,591.

Varnish, a liquid preparation that dries by evaporation, forming a hard lustrous coating. Varnish is transparent unless pigments have been added, and serves for decoration and protection. It may be composed of natural or synthetic resins and a base of various oils or spirits.

Varve, term applied to a layer of sediment deposited in a single year in a body of still water. Specifically a varve consists of two layers of sediment, a coarse layer deposited in the summer and a fine layer deposited in the winter in glacial meltwater lakes. Varves have been used to date the age of Pleistocene glacial deposits.

Varying Hare. *See* Snowshoe Rabbit.

Vasa Dynasty (1523–1654), royal dynasty of Sweden. It was established after Gustav Eriksson, a relative of the Stures, revolted against Denmark in 1520, ending the union. He was elected king in 1523 and made Sweden into a national state, stabilized state finances, and confiscated property belonging to the Roman Catholic Church, thus leading to the Reformation in Sweden. The dynasty ended when Christina, daughter of Gustav II, abdicated in 1654.

Vasari, Giorgio (1511–74), Italian painter, architect, and art historiographer. He painted in the Mannerist style and was widely respected in his time, although he is now known mainly for his contributions as a sculptor. His history of Italian art (1550) is an important source of biographical and theoretical information.

Vascular Plant, or tracheophyte, plant with vessels or ducts to carry water and food materials within it. All higher plants—ferns, conifers, and flowering plants—have a vascular system (xylem and phloem). This system exists in roots, stems, and leaves, providing mechanical support and acting as a passageway from the soil.

Vasectomy, a method of sterilizing the male, in which the ductus (vas) deferens, through which the sperm pass to the ejaculatory duct of the testis, is totally or partially removed.

Vasoconstrictor, a chemical compound causing constriction of blood vessels. Decongestants with hydrochlorides act as vasoconstrictors on nasal mucosa.

Vasodilator, compound that opens up blood vessels to permit freer flow of blood. Most frequently used are nitrite preparations to treat angina pectoris.

Vasopressin, or antidiuretic hormone, polypeptide product of the posterior pituitary. It acts on the kidneys to stimulate water and sodium retention; it also constricts blood vessels.

Vassal, in Western European feudalism, a free man who bound himself to another (the lord) by an oath of fealty for mutual protection and maintenance. In exchange for certain obligations, such as military service and loyalty, he would receive direct maintenance in the lord's household or a benefice or fief to work himself. The practice of vassalage is Roman in origin, but became prevalent in the 7th and 8th centuries in France as a result of political upheaval and economic instability. Vassalage became one of the main institutions of feudalism. *See also* Fealty; Feudalism.

Vatican City, an enclave in Italy, 109acres (44hectares), within Rome. It is the smallest sovereign state in the world and is the official home of the pope and the center of the Roman Catholic Church with its own newspaper, railroad system, passports, and stamps.

People. Its population of about 1,000 is mostly Italian and Swiss with citizenship given only to persons who either hold office or are employed in the Vatican, including apostolic delegates and the spiritual staff of the pope. Seventy countries send diplomatic representatives to the Holy See. Italian is the main language; official acts are written in Italian.

Government. Vatican City is governed by a combination of canon law, apostolic constitutions, and laws decreed by the pope.

History. Once a boggy swamp and a charioteers' burial ground, it was made a garden area by AD 59. Popes held sovereignty over mid-Italy (Papal States) until 1861 when conquests shifted much of the papal dominion to the Kingdom of Sardinia; the pope's sovereignty was confined to Rome. In a 1929 treaty, the Holy See and the Italian government agreed to full independence for the Vatican, gave the church special status, and provided compensation for lands taken. *See also* Papacy.

Vatican Council, First (1869–70), 20th ecumenical council of the Roman Catholic Church. Convened by Pope Pius IX to deal with certain contemporary problems, such as rising liberalism and rationalism, the Council is perhaps best remembered for its declaration of papal infallibility, causing widespread protest and minor secessions from the Church. It was cut short by the interference of Italian troops.

Vatican Council, Second, also **Vatican II** (1962–65), 21st ecumenical council of the Roman Catholic Church under Popes John XXIII and Paul VI. Designed to reform and revitalize the Church, the Council redefined the duties of bishops, the relationship of the Catholic to other churches, and the nature of the priesthood and the mass. It condemned anti-Semitism while calling for Christian reunion.

Vaud, canton in W Switzerland; Lausanne is the capital; conquered by Bern and forced to accept the Reformation; independent canton of Leman (1798); joined Switzerland 1803; agricultural area. Area: 1,240sq mi (3,212sq km). Pop. 521,600.

VD. *See* Venereal Disease.

Veblen, Thorstein Bunde (1857–1929), US economist b. Manitowoc co, Wis. He originated the institutionalist school of economics, studying the economy as a whole while emphasizing institutions and their role in the economic system. His two most famous books are *The Theory of Leisure Class* (1899) and the *Theory of Business Enterprise* (1904).

Vector, quantity that has both a magnitude and a direction, as contrasted with a scalar. For example, to specify the velocity of a body, one must give its speed (how fast it is moving) and the direction in which it is moving. Similarly, a force has both magnitude and direction. Mass is a scalar, but weight (the force of gravity on a body) has a magnitude that depends on the body's mass and position in relation to the Earth's center and a direction corresponding to the direction of the Earth's gravitational field at that position. In mathematics, the concept of a vector is generalized to any number of dimensions, and vectors are treated as special cases of tensors. *See also* Scalar.

Vector, in disease, any agent that carries an infectious agent from one host to another. It may be an insect such as a mosquito or flea, or an inanimate object. It also may serve as an intermediate host for the infectious agent.

Vector Analysis, study of the mathematical properties of vectors. Vectors can be added by the parallelogram law: the result of adding two vectors is the diagonal of a parallelogram formed with the two vectors as adjacent sides. Multiplication of a vector by a scalar *a* gives a vector with the same direction but its magnitude multiplied by *a*. Two vectors can also be multiplied, and this may occur in two ways. The scalar, or dot, product of vectors **a** and **b** (written **a.b**) is a scalar given by $ab \cos \theta$, θ being the angle between the vectors and *a* and *b* being their magnitudes (note that symbols for vectors are usually printed in boldface type). For example, work is the scalar product of force and distance. The vector, or cross product, (written **a** $-$**b**) is a vector given by $ab \sin \theta$, directed at right angles to the plane of **a** and **b.** The force on a moving charged particle in a magnetic field is the vector product of field strength and current. Rules also exist for differentiation and integration of vectors.

Vatican City

Venezuela

Venice, Italy: St. Mark's Cathedral

Vedas, ancient sacred books of the Hindus. There are four Vedas: the *Rigveda,* containing priestly tradition originally brought to India by the Aryans; the *Atharvaveda;* the *Samaveda;* and the *Yajurveda.* Each of the four Vedas contains: *Samhitas* or basic verses; *Brahamanas,* rituals and explanations of rituals; and *Upanishads,* philosophical commentaries. The Vedas were composed over a long period, starting around *c.* 1500–900 BC. *See also* Hinduism.

V-E Day (May 8, 1945), the day World War II ended in Europe. The Germans surrendered unconditionally to the United States, England, France, and the USSR.

Veery, thrush of E North America with a reddish-brown back and spotted chest. Species *Turdus fuscescens. See also* Thrush.

Vega, or Alpha Lyrae, white main-sequence star in the constellation of Lyra. Characteristics: apparent mag. 0.03, absolute mag. 0.3; spectral type AO; distance 26 light-years.

Vegetative Reproduction, or vegetative propagation, form of asexual reproduction in higher plants where a piece (leaf, root, stem) of a multicellular organism gives rise to an entire organism. It may occur naturally, as strawberries reproducing by runners, or artificially, as a house plant cutting yielding a new plant.

Veil, Simone (Annie Jacob)(1927–), French political figure. A survivor of the Nazi concentration camp in Auschwitz, Poland, where she was sent along with her mother, who died there, and her sister, she served Pres. Valery Giscard d'Estaing as Health Minister (1974–79) before her election as president of the European Parliament (1979).

Vein, blood vessel that carries blood to the heart. The pulmonary vein carries oxygenated blood to the lungs, but all other veins carry deoxygenated, usually dark purplish, blood from the capillaries back to the heart. The vein walls are thinner than arterial walls, lie closer to the surface, and are not so elastic since blood moves sluggishly, not pulsating. *See also* Artery.

Velázquez, Diego Rodríguez de Silva y (1599–1660), Spanish painter. He is the most representative of the Baroque 17th-century painters. His early genre works (1617–22) include "The Old Cook" and "The Water Carrier of Seville." In 1623 he became court painter to Philip IV, and throughout his career painted many royal portraits. He also executed many portraits of dwarfs and jesters in a sensitive and compassionate manner. "Don Sebastian de Morra" is typical of these psychological portraits. One of his finest works is the portrait of Pope Innocent X (*c.*1650), considered to be one of the greatest portraits in existence. His later works began to merge reality and illusion and include "The Hilanderas" (*c.*1644–48) and "Las Meninas." Velázquez influenced many generations of artists and is still considered one of the finest of all portrait painters.

Velocity, rate of change of a body's position. Average velocity **v** of a body moving from position $\mathbf{x_1}$ to $\mathbf{x_2}$ in a time t is $\mathbf{v} = (\mathbf{x_2} - \mathbf{x_1})/t$. The instantaneous velocity **v** of the body is the value approached by **v** as t becomes small. As a vector, velocity has a direction associated with it; the magnitude of the velocity is called the speed and has no associated direction.

Velvet Worm. *See* Peripatus.

Venda, Republic of, one of the so-called bantustans created by South Africa as part of its policy of apartheid. Although South Africa declared Venda an independent country in 1979 as the third of ten proposed bantustans for the country's black majority population, Venda receives no international recognition as a sovereign state. Venda possesses coal reserves, but the economy remains underdeveloped and two-thirds of the male population works in South Africa. Pop. 358,000.

Vendetta, private family blood feud, characteristic of the Italian Middle Ages and persisting in modern southern Italy. The obligation of kin to avenge wrong done to a relative, the vendetta usually occurs in circumstances in which the family is the only social unit able to ensure security and the state is considered unable or, because of either its insufficient development or perceived disinterest, unwilling to perform equitable justice.

Veneers, thin layers of wood of uniform thickness (usually 1/40–5/16in (0.6–8mm). Most are cut in a lathe by rotating a log against a knife; that used for furniture is cut sheet by sheet from a log section. Logs intended for veneers are softened first in hot water or steam. After production, veneer is dried in a kiln. In addition to furniture, veneers are used for plywood and containers.

Venereal Disease, any of several unrelated diseases transmitted essentially by sexual intercourse. Most widespread are syphilis and gonorrhea. Chancroid, lymphogranuloma venereum, and granuloma inguinale are less common.

Venetian School, Italian school of painting during the Renaissance. Centered in Venice, its art was notable for sumptuousness and radiance of color, a legacy from Byzantine art. Its adherents included the Bellinis, Titian, Giorgione, Guardi, and Tintoretto.

Venezia. *See* Venice.

Venezuela, independent nation in N Latin America. Its petroleum beds make Venezuela the world's fifth-largest oil producer and one of the wealthiest Latin American countries.

Land and economy. Geographically, the country is divided into four regions: the Orinoco River basin, the Andes Mts, Guyana Highlands, plains E and S of the Orinoco, and the N coastal zone bordering Lake Maracaibo, deep enough for ocean-going vessels. The Guyana Highlands contain Angel Fall, the highest waterfall in the world. Venezuela includes 72 islands, the largest of which is Margarita, a center for pearl trade. Venezuela earns 96% of its export revenues from oil; reversion of oil assets to the Venezuelan government will start in 1983. Next to oil, iron ore is the chief export, followed by coffee, cocoa, steel products, sugar, fish, and fruit. Agrarian reform has increased cultivated acreage and resettled 100,000 families on their own land. In Latin America, Venezuela ranks fourth in hydroelectric production. Tourism increases annually.

People. A country shifting from rural to urban, with a population descended from Spanish colonials and Indians, Venezuela also has post-WWII immigrants from Italy, Portugal, and Spain. Spanish is the official language, Roman Catholicism the dominant religion. Literacy is estimated at 80%. Education is free.

Government. The constitution adopted in 1961 guarantees freedom of religion and a strong central government elected by direct, universal suffrage. Voting is mandatory for all citizens over 18 years of age. Executive power is vested in the popularly-elected president; legislative power in the bicameral national congress.

History. Christopher Columbus sighted Venezuela in 1498. It was under Spanish domination until 1810 when Simón Bolívar, Venezuela's native son and national hero, led a revolution for independence. Both in the 19th and 20th centuries it had an unstable history under dictators; Romulo Betancourt was the first elected president to serve his full term (1959–65). Since then, a democratic system has prevailed. During the early 1980s the country's previously rapidly growing economy was troubled by recession in some sectors. In 1982, the dispute with Guyana over border regions on which oil had been discovered flared up. Dropping oil prices due to the world oil glut strained Venezuela's economy through the mid-1980s. Pope John Paul II visited the country in 1985.

PROFILE

Official name: Republic of Venezuela
Area: 352,143sq mi (912,050sq km)
Population: 13,913,218
  Density: 40per sq mi (15per sq km)
Chief cities: Caracas (capital); Maracaibo
Government: presidential democracy
Religion: Roman Catholic
Language: Spanish (official)
Monetary unit: Bolivar
Gross national product: $45,150,000,000
Per capita income: $1,357
Industries: petrochemicals, iron, paper products, canned fish, steel, textiles, tires, shoes, dairy products
Agriculture: coffee, cocoa, citrus fruits, sugar cane, rice, tobacco, bananas, cotton, corn, cattle
Minerals: petroleum, gold, copper, coal, salt, nickel, manganese, asbestos
Trading partners: United States, Federal Republic of Germany, Japan, Canada

Venezuelan Boundary Dispute, boundary controversy between Great Britain and Venezuela. The British Guiana-Venezuela boundary had been in dispute since the British took control of Guiana from the Dutch (1814). The conflict widened when gold was discovered in the area. The United States became involved (1895) when Secretary of State Richard Olney declared that the United States was allowed, by the Monroe Doctrine, to intervene in the settling of such conflicts in the Americas. The British agreed to the United States' suggestion that an independent commission determine the boundary. The boundary was decided in favor of Britain's claims (1899).

Venice (Venezia), city in NE Italy, 162mi (261km) E of Milan; capital of Venezia prov. and Veneto region. Built on 118 islands, it is separated by narrow canals in Lagoon of Venice; joined to mainland by bridge. Settled 5th century, it was a vassal of the Byzantine Empire through 10th century; its merchants traded in parts of E Mediterranean; defeated Genoa 1380. City reached its zenith 15th century; gradually declined and was ceded to Austria 1797; inc. by Napoleon 1805; united with Italy 1866. Venice is site of the Rialto Bridge (1588–91), cathedral of St Mark (begun 830), the Palace of the Doges (14th–15th century), the Academy of Fine Arts, numerous churches, palaces, and public gardens; gondolas and other boats are used for transportation. Industries: glass, tourism, shipbuilding, textiles. Pop. 361,722.

Venizelos, Eleutherios (1864–1936), a Greek statesman. In 1910 he became prime minister and expanded Greek territories during Balkan Wars and World War I. He clashed with Constantine in support of the Allies and resigned (1915). He was recalled and again dismissed but in 1917 took over the government under Alexander, and Greece entered the war on the Allied side. He negotiated for Greek interests at the Versailles peace conference but was voted out of office in 1920. From 1928–35 he was in and out of office as prime minister.

Venn Diagram, diagrammatical representation of the relations and operations between mathematical sets or logical statements (premises or conclusions). The sets or statements are drawn as geometrical figures, usually circles. In set theory, relations, such as subset of a set, are shown by the relative positions of the circles. Operations, such as union or intersection, are indicated by shaded and nonshaded areas. A similar use of the circles is made in logic. *See also* Euler Diagram.

Venom, Snake, toxic substance produced in the poison glands of snakes and injected into their victims through ducts in their fangs. Most venoms are dangerous and can be lethal unless counteracted by immune serum. Three types of toxin are present in venoms, the preponderance of each depending on the type of snake. Cobras produce neurotoxins that paralyze the nerve centers controlling breathing, the rattlesnake produces both hemolysins (toxins that dissolve the red blood cells) and hemotoxins (toxins that cause hemorrhage by perforating the blood vessels). Some venoms also contain substances that coagulate the blood; others contain anticoagulants.

Ventricle, either of the two bottom chambers of the 4-chambered heart. *See also* Heart.

Ventura, city in SW California, 23mi (37km) SE of Santa Barbara; seat of Ventura co; site of San Buenaventura mission founded in 1782. Official name of the city is San Buenaventura. Industries: food packing, oil products, clothing, electronic research. Inc. 1866. Pop. 57,964.

Venus, second planet from the Sun and almost as large as Earth. It has no satellite. Its dense atmosphere is largely carbon dioxide. Mean distance from the Sun, 67,200,000mi (108,190,000km); mass and volume, 0.82 and 0.88 times that of Earth respectively; diameter, 7,500mi (12,100km); rotation period, about 243 Earth days; sidereal period of revolution, 224.70 days; surface temperature, approx. 900°F (485°C). *See also* Solar System.

Venus, in Roman mythology, goddess of spring and fruitfulness. Later identified with the Greek Aphrodite, her name became synonomous with beauty and charm.

Venus of Willendorf. *See* Willendorf, Venus of.

Venus's Flower Basket, sponge found in deep marine waters. Its long cylindrical skeleton is formed from separate silica spicules plus a latticed framework of silica. Length: 10in (25cm). Phylum Porifera; species *Euplectella aspergillum.*

Veracruz, port city in E Mexico, on the Gulf of Mexico; first Spanish colonial post in Mexico (1519); captured by US forces 1847 during Mexican War; occupied again by the United States (1914) during dispute which resulted in the resignation of Mexico's president, Victariano Huerta; site of railroad terminus, 18th-century parish church, bronze statue of former governor Manuel Gutierrez Tamora, colonial fortress of Santiago. Industries: textiles, tiles, shoes, chocolate. Pop. 289, 000.

Verb, the part of speech indicating what action or state of being is described. The tense of the verb indicates the time of the action. Classifications: regular or irregular, transitive or intransitive, or linking.

Verbena, genus of annual and perennial plants native to the Western Hemisphere. Some species are popular garden plants and have pink, white, or purplish flowers. Family Verbenaceae.

Vercingetorix (died 46 BC), leader of the Gauls who united the diverse Gallic tribes against Caesar's Roman armies in 52 BC. A brilliant strategist, he retreated before Caesar's forces, burning towns to destroy a source of supply for the Romans. He halted at the fortress of Alesia where Caesar encircled him, destroyed his Gallic reinforcements, and captured him. Vercingetorix was displayed in Caesar's triumph (46) and then executed.

Verdi, Giuseppe (1813–1901), Italian composer considered one of the greatest of operatic composers. His operas *Rigoletto* (1851), *Aïda* (1871), *La Traviata* (1853), and *Il Trovatore* (1852) are among the most frequently performed in all the operatic literature. He composed three operas based on Shakespeare: *Macbeth* (1847), and two masterpieces of his old age, *Otello* (1887) and *Falstaff* (1893). His *Requiem Mass* (1874) is also highly regarded.

Verdigris River, river in SE Kansas and NE Oklahoma; rises in E central Kansas; flows S across Oklahoma border to the Arkansas River, near Muskogee; used for irrigation. Length: 351mi (565km).

Verdin, titmouse found in the SW United States and N Mexico. It has a yellow head and throat, brownish-gray upperparts, and whitish underparts. It builds a globular nest with a tubular side entrance on a bush branch for its greenish eggs (15). Length: 4.5in (11.4cm). Family Paridae; species *Auriparus flaviceps.*

Verdun, city in S Quebec, Canada, on the St Lawrence River, on S shore of Montreal island; suburb of Montreal; site of Jean-Jacques Olier College (1951). Pop. 68,013.

Verdun, Battle of (Feb.-Sept., 1916), World War I battle at Verdun, an important fortress in NE France. The battle there was longest and bloodiest of World War I, with over 1,000,000 killed. A strong German offensive under Crown Prince Frederick William began on February 21. A British offensive relieved the pressure on Verdun and by December, France had recovered most of lost territory. Over 2,000,000 men fought at Verdun.

Verdun, Treaty of (843), treaty that partitioned Charlemagne's empire among his three grandsons, the sons of Emperor Louis I. It marked the end of political unity in Western Europe. Charles II (the Bald) received the western portion (France); Louis the German the eastern portion (Germany); and Lothair I the central portion (Low Countries, part of Germany and France, much of Italy). Lothair remained Holy Roman emperor.

Vergil, or **Virgil,** or **Publius Vergilius Maro,** (70–19 BC), Roman poet and the author of the *Aeneid,* the *Eclogues, and the Georgics.* Devoting his life solely to his poetry and related studies, he was nevertheless well informed about the current events of his age and was the friend of such men as Octavian and Gallus. Although Epicurean themes appear in his poetry, this trend is replaced by a stoic and neo-Pythagorean attitude. *See also* Aeneid; Eclogues.

Verlaine, Paul (1844–96), French poet. His early poetry, *Poèmes Saturniens* (1866) and *Fêtes galantes* (1869), shows the influence of Baudelaire. An intense relationship with Rimbaud broke up his marriage, and he was eventually imprisoned for shooting Rimbaud. While in jail (1874–76), he wrote *Romance sans paroles* (1874). Returning to Catholicism, his later poetry, such as *Sagesse* (1881) and *Jadis et naguère* (1884), deals with the conflict between the spiritual and the carnal.

Vermeer, Jan (1632–75), Dutch painter. Little is known of his life. His work seems to fall into three stages of style and development. The first (1655–60) is marked by a style close to early Italian Baroque and includes "The Procuress," "A Girl Asleep," and "Christ at the House of Mary and Martha." "Little Street in Delft," with its soft coloring, is typical of this period. His middle period marks his classic phase, in which his works often depict a single figure, marked by precise detail and naturalistic lighting. Works from this period include "Woman with a Red Hat" and "Head of a Young Girl." The third period is one in which Vermeer's style began to fail. His late works, of inferior quality, include "Allegory of the New Testament." In all, fewer than 40 works can be attributed to this great master, and only two can be authentically dated.

Vermiform Appendix. *See* Appendix.

Vermifuge, or **Anthelminthic,** agent that expels worms or parasites from the intestine. Some are toxic and diagnosis of specific parasite should be definite.

Vermont, state in the NE United States, in the New England region.

Land and economy. The N-S ranges of the Green Mts occupy most of the state. A plain lies along Lake Champlain, which forms most of the W boundary. The Connecticut River, along the E border, is the only river important to the state; it is legally in New Hampshire. Dairy farms are found along Lake Champlain and in mountain valleys through the state. Machine tool manufacturing is centered in Springfield. Marble quarries are operated around Rutland, and granite is extracted in the Barre region. Year-round sports facilities have made tourism a major source of income.

People. Vermont was settled by pioneers from other New England states. In the 19th century, numbers of Irish came to build railroads, and Italians, Scots, and Welsh to work the quarries. There is a French-Canadian element in the population. Only about 30% of the inhabitants live in urban areas.

Education. There are about 20 institutions of higher education. The University of Vermont is state-supported.

History. In 1609 the Frenchman Samuel de Champlain discovered the lake that bears his name, but the first permanent settlement was made in 1724 at Fort Drummer in the Connecticut Valley. After the French and Indian Wars ended in 1763, pioneers spread across the region. Land grant disputes with the colonies of New Hampshire and New York persisted for years. At the start of the Revolution, the Green Mountain Boys, an independent force led by Ethan Allen and Seth Warner, took Fort Ticonderoga and Crown Point on Lake Champlain. In 1777, Vermont declared its independence as the republic of New Connecticut and preserved this unrecognized status until its admission to the Union (1791); it was the first state outside the original 13 to be admitted. In the War of 1812, a fleet of small vessels built at Vergennes defeated the British on Lake Champlain. In the Civil War, Confederate agents operating from Canada robbed banks in St Albans in a raid in October 1864. During the late 19th century the state experienced a decline in agriculture and rural population, a trend that continued into the 20th century.

PROFILE

Admitted to Union: March 4, 1791; rank, 14th
US Congressmen: Senate, 2; House of Representatives, 1
Population: 511,456 (1980); rank, 48th
Capital: Montpelier, 8,241 (1980)
Chief cities: Burlington, 37,712; Rutland, 18,436; Bennington, 15,815
State legislature: Senate, 30; House of Representatives, 150
Area: 9,609sq mi (24,887sq km); rank, 43rd
Elevation: highest, 4,393ft (1,340m), Mt Mansfield; lowest, 95ft (28.9m), Lake Champlain
Industries (major products): machine tools, stone products, lumber, furniture
Agriculture (major products): dairy products, maple syrup and sugar, apples
Minerals (major): marble, granite, limestone, asbestos
State nickname: Green Mountain State
State motto: Freedom and Unity
State bird: hermit thrush
State flower: red clover
State tree: sugar maple

Vernal Equinox, equinox occurring when the Sun crosses the celestial equator, moving toward the northern hemisphere, on about March 21. The crossing point on the equator is the First Point of Aries, now actually situated in the constellation Pisces, which is the zero for the celestial coordinate right ascension. *See also* Equinox.

Verne, Jules (1828–1905), French adventure story writer. His early work was published in the magazine *Musée des Familles.* Verne's stories are characterized by fantastic settings and imaginary scientific voyages, and did much to establish science-fiction writing. They include *Journey to the Center of the Earth* (1864), *Twenty Thousand Leagues Under the Sea* (1870), and *Around the World in Eighty Days* (1873). *See also* Around the World in Eighty Days.

Vernier, Pierre (1580–1637) French mathematician. He spent the greater part of his life in the service of the king of Spain in the Low Countries and is remembered for his secondary scale subdividing a primary scale and thus providing a means (vernier scale) of making accurate measurements.

Vernier Rocket, small rocket used not for propulsion but for "fine-tuning" of a rocket's orbit. Types of vernier rockets include retrorockets, to slow craft; and attitude control jets, to correct orientation in space.

Verona, city in NE Italy, 92mi (147km) E of Milan, on the Adige River; capital of Verona prov. Captured by Rome 89 BC, it was a free commune by 12th century; prospered under della Scala family 13th–14th centuries; annexed to Milan 1387, to Venice 1405–1797; held by Austria 1797–1866, when it joined Italy. Verona is site of Roman amphitheater (AD 1st century), church of St Zeno Maggiore (9th–15th centuries), Gothic tombs of the Scaligeri family. Industries: agriculture, textiles, chemicals, paper, printing, wine. Pop. 271,451.

Veronese (Caliari), Paulo (1528–88), Venetian painter and decorator. His earliest dated work is "Christ Among the Doctors" (1548). His mature works include the well-known frescoes at Maser, his largest villa decoration. In 1562 and 1563 he executed a number of large banquet scenes, including "Marriage at Cana," the "Family of Darius before Alexander," and "Cuccina Family Presented to the Virgin," often considered his finest work. A later work is the series for the

Bennington Battle Monument, Vermont

Versailles, France

Amerigo Vespucci

ceiling of Sala del Collegio, containing the famous allegorical "industry."

Veronica, or speedwell, widely distributed genus of annual and perennial plants with small white, blue, or violet flowers, usually in clusters. Height: 3in–5ft (7.6–153cm). Family Scrophulariaceae; genus *Veronica. See also* Figwort.

Verrazano, Giovanni da (1480?–1527), explorer in the service of France, b. Florence, Italy. He explored the Atlantic Coast of North America (1524), discovering the Hudson River and Manhattan Island. He may have been hanged as a pirate by the Spanish.

Verrocchio, Andrea del (1435–88), Florentine sculptor, goldsmith, and painter, b. Andrea di Michele di Francesco di Cioni. He is believed to have been a pupil of Donatello. Although an emphasis on surface finish and elaborate detail prevented his works from achieving the power and monumentality, his finest works are imbued with an easy, rhythmic elegance. Among his sculptural works are the tombs of Piero and Giovanni de Medici in San Lorenzo and a "David" (1476) and "A Boy with a Dolphin" (c. 1480), both in Florence.

Versailles, city in N France, 10mi (16km) WSW of Paris; capital of Yvelines dept.; designed around palace built for Louis XIV, 1665–83. It served as the royal residence until 1793 when it was made a national historic museum. Set in a 20-acre (8-hectare) park, the palace contains king's and queen's apartments, famous Hall of Mirrors, museum of French history; magnificent formal French gardens, Swiss Lake, fountains, Grand Canal, and several outlying buildings complete this magnificent estate. It served as German headquarters during Franco-Prussian War (1870–71); scene of signing of Treaty of Collegio, June 28, 1919, ending WWI. City is also site of Cathedral of St Louis (1743–54). Industries: tourism, metalworks, footwear, brandy. Pop. 97,133.

Versailles, Treaty of (1919), treaty formally ending World War I. The leading figures at the conference were US Pres. Woodrow Wilson, Britian's David Lloyd George, France's Georges Clemenceau, and Italy's Emanuele Orlando. It represented a compromise between Wilson's Fourteen Points and the demands of Britain, France, Italy, and the other Allies for reparations from Germany. It permanently demilitarized and created a triple defense alliance against Germany. It made the former German colonies mandates of the League of Nations; gave Poland a Baltic corridor and Yugoslavia, the Port of Fiume; and created the League of Nations. The Treaty was never ratified by the United States. High reparations levied against Germany in the Treaty contradicted Wilson's program and the newly created League depended on its members' voluntary military support for effectiveness. Based largely on his anti-treaty stand, Warren G. Harding won the 1920 presidential election and made a separate peace with Germany 1921. *See also* Fourteen Points.

Versification, literally the art or practice of composing metrical lines. The terms *verse* and *poetry* are often used interchangeably. When distinctions are made, however, verse is characterized by structure and form, poetry by intensity of feeling and imaginative power. Versification applies particularly to the application of such technical aspects as rhythm, meter, stanzaic pattern, number of syllables in each line, and the distribution of vowels and consonants. The study of versification, especially in its metrical structure, is called prosody. *See also* Meter; Poetry.

Vertebra, one of the small bones making up the vertebral column, also known as the spinal column, or spine. Each vertebra is composed of three parts: a large solid body from the top of which winglike transverse processes project to either side. Behind the body is an opening (vertebral formaen) through which the spinal cord passes, roofed by the spinous and auricular processes of the vertebrae. *See also* Spine.

Vertebrate, animals that have individual disks of bone or cartilage called vertebra surrounding or replacing the embryonic notochord to form a jointed backbone. The head-end of the chordate nerve tube is enlarged into a brain, and the attendent sense organs of smell, taste, sight, hearing, and balance are correspondingly complex. The principal division is between the aquatic, fishlike forms (several extinct and living classes) and the partially (amphibians) and wholly (reptiles, birds, mammals) land-adapted forms.

Four-legged vertebrates are called tetrapods and those with fluid-filled embryonic membranes that permit development on land, amniotes. Birds and mammals are the only vertebrates with circulatory, respiratory, and excretory systems allowing for constant high body temperatures and levels of activity. Their brains and behavior are correspondingly the most complex. Phylum Chordata; subphylum Vertebrata. *See also* Amphibia; Bird; Chordate; Fish; Mammal; Reptile.

Vertigo, condition characterized by dizziness and nausea, attributable to disruption of the functions of equilibrium organs. Vertigo may be produced by rapid body rotation, several diseases, or brain disorder.

Verwoerd, Hendrik Frensch (1901–66), South African prime minister. He studied in Germany and later wrote anti-foreign editorials in South Africa. A nationalist, he held a number of government offices and became prime minister in 1958. An ardent segregationist, he led South Africa out of the British Commonwealth (1961) and was later assassinated.

Vesey Slave Plot (1822), attempted slave insurrection. It was led by Denmark Vesey, a freed black slave who had become influential in the Charleston, S.C., area. Under cover of church meetings, Vesey, a preacher, met with his followers and planned an uprising. The plot was revealed by an informer and the conspirators were all caught. Vesey and about 35 others were hanged, although he maintained his innocence.

Vespasian (AD 9–79), Roman emperor (69–79). He commanded in Germany (42) and Britain (43), was made consul (51), served as governor of Judea under Nero, and conducted the war against the Jews (66). His soldiers proclaimed him emperor when Nero died. He improved Rome's financial state, built the temple of Pax and the Colosseum, and romanized Britain with Agricola (78–79). His son Titus acted as coruler with him in 71.

Vespucci, Amerigo (1451–1512), Italian navigator and explorer. His name was given to America by Martin Waldseemuller, who translated Vespucci's account of his voyages. After service under the Medici, Vespucci made several expeditions along coast of Central and South America (1497–1503) in the service of Spain. He developed a method for computing nearly exact longitude.

Vesta, in Roman religion, goddess of the hearth, identified with the Greek goddess Hestia and associated with the primitive fire deities Cacus and Caca. Vesta was assured of a prominent place in both family and state worship. As goddess of the hearth fire, she was

the patron deity of bakers. Her shrine was in the Forum.

Vestal Virgins, in ancient Rome, the priestesses of the cult of Vesta who tended the sacred fire and officiated at ceremonies in the goddess' honor. The Vestals remained in the service of the temple for 30 years under vows of absolute chastity and were punished severely for breaking those vows. They did, however, enjoy great prestige in the social order of Rome.

Vestigial Organ, organ or part of an organ in a plant or animal that is useless and undersized. It was functional at some time in the past and serves as evidence for evolution.

Vesuvius, Mount (Vesuvio), active volcano in S Italy, on the Bay of Naples; villages and vineyards are located on lower fertile slopes; site of numerous eruptions of varying intensity, especially AD 79 when Pompeii and Herculaneum were destroyed; height changes with each eruption; site of seismological observatory. Height: 4,203ft (1,282m).

Vetch, annual and perennial plants native to temperate and warm areas of the world. Most are tendril climbers and many are grown for food, green manure, or forage. Family Leguminosae; genus *Vicia. See also* Bean.

Veterinary Medicine, medical science of prevention, diagnosis, and treatment of animal diseases and disorders. It was practiced by the Babylonians and Egyptians 4,000 years ago. Late in the 18th century, schools of veterinary medicine were established in Europe. Public health aspects have focused on zoonoses, diseases transmitted to humans by vertebrate animals.

Veto, presidential power to reject legislation. If the president vetoes a bill, it is returned to Congress, where a two-thirds vote of each house is needed to override the veto. The president may also stop legislation by a "pocket veto." If he refuses either to sign or veto a piece of legislation, it will take effect after 10 days of congressional session. If the Congress adjourns before the end of the 10-day period, the legislation is dead.

VHF. *See* Very High Frequency.

Viburnum, genus of flowering shrubs and trees native to North America and Eurasia. All have small, fleshy fruits containing single flat seeds. Flowers are small, fragrant, and clustered. Many are cultivated as ornamentals. Well-known species are wayfaring tree, hobblebush, black haw, arrowwood, highbush cranberry, and snowball. There are 200 species. Family Caprifoliaceae.

Vicenza, industrial city in NE Italy, 40mi (64km) W of Venice; capital of Vicenza province; seat of a Lombard duchy. Est. as free commune and member of Lombard League 12th century, it was taken by Venice 1404; held by Austria 1797–1866, until united with Italy; site of Loggia del Capitanio, Teatro Olimpico (1580–83), Palazzo Chiericato, designed by Andrea Palladio (1508–80). Industries: machinery, chemicals, food processing, printing, agriculture. Pop. 118,994.

Vice President of the United States, second-highest federal official. He is first in line to succeed to the presidency and does so in the event of death, resignation, physical disability, or removal by impeachment of the president. Although not a member, he presides over the Senate and may vote in the case of a tie, although he cannot participate in debates or committees. He participates in cabinet meetings and is a member of the National Security Council. He is elected on the same ticket as the president to serve a four-year term. He is dependent on the president for extraconstitutional responsibilities and, traditionally, is chosen to balance the ticket and for party appeasement or reward. If the office becomes vacant, the president, with the consent of Congress, chooses another vice president.

VICE PRESIDENTS OF THE UNITED STATES

John Adams (1789–97)
Thomas Jefferson (1797–1801)
Aaron Burr (1801–05)
George Clinton (1805–12)
Elbridge Gerry (1813–14)
Daniel Tompkins (1817–25)
John C. Calhoun (1825–32)
Martin Van Buren (1833–37)
Richard M. Johnson (1837–41)
John Tyler (1841)
George M. Dallas (1845–49)
Millard Fillmore (1849–50)
William R. King (1853)
John C. Breckinridge (1857–61)
Hannibal Hamlin (1861–65)
Andrew Johnson (1865)
Schuyler Colfax (1869–73)
Henry Wilson (1873–75)
William A. Wheeler (1877–81)
Chester A. Arthur (1881)
Thomas A. Hendricks (1885)
Levi P. Morton (1889–93)
Adlai E. Stevenson (1893–97)
Garret A. Hobart (1897–1899)
Theodore Roosevelt (1901)
Charles W. Fairbanks (1905–09)
James S. Sherman (1909–12)
Thomas R. Marshall (1913–21)
Calvin Coolidge (1921–23)
Charles G. Dawes (1925–29)
Charles Curtis (1929–33)
John N. Garner (1933–41)
Henry A. Wallace (1941–45)
Harry S. Truman (1945)
Alben W. Barkley (1949–53)
Richard M. Nixon (1953–61)
Lyndon B. Johnson (1961–63)
Hubert H. Humphrey (1965–69)
Spiro T. Agnew (1969–73)
Gerald R. Ford (1973–74)
Nelson A. Rockefeller (1974–77)
Walter F. Mondale (1977–81)
George H. Bush (1981–)

Viceroy Butterfly, large butterfly that has orange-brown wings with black veins and borders, noted for its mimicry of the monarch butterfly. The viceroy can be distinguished from the monarch by its smaller size and a transverse black band on its hind wings. Species *Limenitis archippus. See also* Monarch Butterfly.

Vichy Government (1940–44), collaborationist government of France during World War II from its surrender to Germany to its liberation (1940–44). Under the 1940 armistice agreement, Vichy became the capital of unoccupied France, with Marshal Henri Pétain as premier. Vichy adherents included traditional anti-republicans still longing for pre-Revolutionary France and advocates of modern totalitarianism. Despite the efforts of Pétain and his even more pro-German vice-premier, Pierre Laval, to soften the effects of German occupation, most Frenchmen associated Vichy with capitulation to Germany and agreement to forced labor and payment of occupation costs. After 1942, German troops occupied all of France, leaving the government isolated from the majority, who supported the Free French movement of Charles de Gaulle or remained aloof from affairs of government.

Vicksburg, port city in W Mississippi, on the Mississippi and Yazoo rivers; seat of Warren co; made US possession 1798; Rev. Newitt Vick est. mission 1812; scene of Vicksburg Campaign during Civil War, that resulted in complete Union control of Mississippi River. It is site of many antebellum homes, Vicksburg National Military Park (est. 1899), National Cemetery (est. 1865), US Water Experiment Station; headquarters of US Mississippi River Commission. Industries: lumber and lumber products, tourism, chemicals, fertilizer, food products. Laid out 1819; inc. 1825. Pop. (1980) 25,434.

Vico, Giovanni Battista (1668–1744), Italian historian and philosopher. Although he attended Jesuit school and the University of Naples, he educated himself in the library of a family that he tutored. He was appointed royal historiographer for the new Kingdom of Naples (1735). *New Science* (1725, 1730, 1744), his monumental work, included the idea that history had three stages: the age of the gods, the age of heroes,

and the age of men. His ideas still exercise great influence on modern historians.

Victor Emmanuel II (1820–78), king of Sardinia-Piedmont (1849–61) and first king of united Italy (1861–78). Son and successor of Charles Albert, early in his reign he suppressed the republican left and from 1852 had Camillo Cavour lead his government to Italy's initial consolidation (1861). He also encouraged Giuseppe Garibaldi in the conquest of Sicily and Naples (later part of united Italy). He acquired Venetia in 1866 and Rome in 1870.

Victor Emmanuel III (1869–1947), king of Italy (1900–46), and father of Italy's last monarch, Umberto II. His failure to oppose Benito Mussolini's Fascists in 1922 immediately precipitated Mussolini's seizure of power, and the king became a figurehead. Following Italian military losses, in 1943 he had Mussolini arrested; but with Italy still in difficulty in 1946, he abdicated and a plebiscite established the Italian Republic.

Victoria (1819–1901), queen of Great Britain and Ireland (1837–1901), empress of India (1876–1901). She was the daughter of George III's fourth son, Edward, duke of Kent, and Victoria of Saxe-Coburg. She succeeded William IV to the throne and demonstrated her political acuity by engineering the return as prime minister of Lord Melbourne, her friend and advisor (1839). She married her first cousin, Prince Albert of Saxe-Coburg-Gotha (1840), and had nine children. Pro-Germanic and influenced by Albert in state affairs, she supported the more conservative ministers such as Melbourne and Benjamin Disraeli (who had her crowned empress of India) and particularly disliked William Gladstone's policy for Irish Home Rule. She founded the Victoria Cross (1857) during the Crimean War. She took an active part in state affairs, apart from a period of three years after Albert's death (1861–64), and her reign heightened respect for the monarchy.

Victoria, city in British Columbia, Canada, on SE Vancouver Island; capital, largest city, and chief port of British Columbia; developed during 1858 gold rush as supply base for gold miners; site of the University of Victoria (1902), Royal Roads College (1942), Dominican Astrophysical Observatory; Pacific headquarters of Canadian navy; resort area. Industries: lumber, shipbuilding, fish processing, deep-sea fishing. Founded 1843; became capital 1868. Pop. 62,551.

Victoria, city in S Texas, 125mi (201km) NE of Houston, on Guadalupe River; site of Victoria College (1925), Annunciation College (1959). Industries: aluminum, chemicals, ranching, farming, oil, gas. Settled 1824; inc. 1839. Pop. (1980) 50,695.

Victoria, Lake (Victoria Nyanza), lake in E central Africa; S half is in Tanzania and N half is in Uganda: Indented coastline of 2,000mi (3,200km) provides numerous gulfs and harbors for coastal towns. Lake is the chief reservoir of the Nile River; rainfall is its major water source. The second largest freshwater lake in the world, it supports much of the area's fishing industry. Depth: 265ft (81m). Area: 26,828sq mi (69,485sq km).

Victrola. *See* Phonograph.

Vicuña, graceful, even-toed, hoofed South American mammal found in grasslands of Andes Mountains. It resembles the llama and its silky coat is tawny brown with a yellowish bib under the neck. Its lower incisors, like those of rodents, have enamel on only one side and are constantly growing. The gestation period is 11 months with one young born. It can run 30mph (48kph) at high elevations. Height: 34in (86cm) at shoulder. Family Camelidae; species *Lama vicugna.*

Videotape, a magnetic tape that records television signals. As the FM signals are directed through the heads of a videotape recorder, iron particles on the tape are magnetized. The signals are recovered in the reverse process when the tape passes through a reproducing head, and are then demodulated to produce the output signal. Videotape can be erased and reused.

Vienna (Wien), capital city of Austria, on the Danube River; occupied by the French during Napoleonic Wars (1805–09); after the defeat of Napoleon I, representatives of European powers met for the Congress of Vienna (1814–15). Vienna became the cultural and social center of 19th-century Europe under Emperor Francis Joseph I; suffered economic and political collapse following the defeat of Central Powers in WWI. Chancellor Engelbert Dollfuss established a dictatorship in 1933; in 1938 Hitler's armies invaded Vienna; occupied by joint Soviet-Western forces 1945–55, when Vienna became the free capital of the Second Austrian Republic. City contains St Stephen's Cathe-

dral, the Hofburg (former residence of the Hapsburgs), Capuchin Church, the Winter Palace, Parliament, the State Opera House, Burgtheater, Museum of Art History, the Natural History Museum; also largest central European airport, and headquarters of the International Atomic Energy Agency since 1957; scene of US-USSR disarmament talks of 1970–71. Vienna has been home of composers Mozart, Beethoven, Brahms, and Schubert. Industries: petroleum, metallurgy, chemicals, textiles, furniture, clothing. leather. Settled by Celts; made Roman military station 1st century BC. Pop. 1,614,841.

Vienna, Congress of (1815), assembly of European leaders who reorganized Europe after the defeat of Napoleon. The essential provisions of the treaty lasted for almost a century. With elaborate care and mutual distrust, the four victors—England, Russia, Prussia, and Austria—(plus France) balanced power and territory in Europe, often at the expense of people whose territories were affected. France lost little except the Rhineland to Prussia; Austria received northern Italy; Poland was divided between Russia and Prussia.

Vientiane, administrative capital of Laos, in N central Laos, on the Mekong River; served as capital of Lao kingdom 1707–1827, when it was destroyed by the Siamese; passed to French 1893 and in 1899 became capital of French protectorate; site of canals, several pagodas, architectural museum, teachers' college, royal palace, railroad, international airport. Industries: textiles, hides, forest products. Pop. 150,000.

Vietcong, members of the National Liberation Front of South Vietnam. Formed in 1960 in South Vietnam by Le Duan, a Communist general from North Vietnam, its purpose was to arm and train the people of South Vietnam to overthrow the Diem regime and to eventually unite North and South Vietnam. *See also* Vietnam War.

Vietminh, League for the Independence of Vietnam, founded by Ho Chi Minh in 1941. They fought against the Japanese during World War II and proclaimed the Democratic Republic of Vietnam (North Vietnam) in Hanoi under Ho Chi Minh in 1945. They defeated the French at Dienbienphu in 1954 after eight years of warfare. They refused to accept the Diem regime of South Vietnam and began an insurgency that became the Vietnam War. *See also* Vietnam War.

Vietnam, independent nation in SE Asia. Under Chinese and then French influence for centuries, it was divided into two countries (North and South) in 1954 and was reunited in 1975 after the victory of the Communist forces in the S, assisted by the N.

Land and economy. Located in the Indochinese peninsula, Vietnam is bounded N by China, W by Laos and Cambodia, E and S by the Gulf of Thailand, Gulf of Tonkin, and the South China Sea. The country stretches N and S 1,000mi (1,600km); E and W it ranges from 330mi (531km) to 40mi (64km) at the center. Most of the N portion is a thick, mountainous jungle. In the heavily populated and cultivated Red River delta rice is the main crop. The climate is monsoonal with frequent floods. The S portion of Vietnam is dominated by a flat, marshy, muddy coast—the Mekong River system. Year-round tropical climate and rich soil yield abundant rice harvests. Since 1975 gradual collectivization of agriculture has taken place in the S. The provinces N and E are tropical rain forests and the rugged Annamite Mts. Industry and agriculture were stalled during the war years.

People. The heritage of more than 1,000 years of vassalage to the Chinese exists in language, art, importance of the family, knowledge, and age—the Confucian ethic. It is estimated that N Vietnam has 80%–90% ethnic Vietnamese and many Chinese, principally in the delta region. The S portion, once heavily rural, has several ethnic minorities: Chinese businessmen living in the delta section; Montagnard tribesmen, 30 tribes of farmers and hunters; and Khmers (Cambodians), farmers with a different language and culture. While scientific socialism is the official creed, Buddhist faith is tolerated, especially among the older generation. Approximately 10% of the people are Roman Catholic. Science and vocational training are emphasized in the government-controlled school system. Chinese and Russian are taught and literacy is estimated at 95% in the N, 65% in the S. Vietnamese is the official language.

Government. Legislative power is vested in the national assembly, which elects a Council of State. The ruling Communist Party, through its central committee and politburo, holds real power.

History. Originally dwellers in China's Yellow River valley, the Vietnamese were driven S and inhabited the Red River delta. They were under Chinese rule from the 2nd century BC to 939, when they revolted and founded their own empire. They remained independent until the mid-19th century when the French took control

Vicuña

Vienna: State Opera House

Frederick Vinson

over Indochina—Vietnam, Laos, and Cambodia. Inspired by the success of the Chinese freedom drive under Sun Yat-sen, a nationalist movement in 1930 staged an uprising against the French. The same year Ho Chi Minh organized the Indochinese Communist party. Japan occupied all of Vietnam during WWII, and in 1945, with the war over, a Communist-led revolt in Hanoi proclaimed the Democratic Republic of Vietnam. Ho Chi Minh led the Communists in an eight-year guerrilla war against the French, who were defeated in 1954. Vietnam was divided at the 17th parallel into two countries, Communist N and nationalist S. Vague references to free elections and unification were mentioned in the cease-fire agreement. Ngo Dinh Diem, prime minister in the S, faced a ruined economy, refugee problems, and religious and political factions. The Communists established agrarian reform, rebuilt industries, and embarked on a campaign to overthrow the S. In 1961 the United States sent military advisors and the US role gradually escalated. The South Vietnamese government, backed by the United States, was unable to defeat the insurgent guerrillas, backed by North Vietnam. US air strikes against North Vietnam began in 1964 and US troops eventually numbered about 550,000. Strong US opposition to the war influenced the withdrawal of troops from 1969, when peace talks began. A cease-fire agreement was signed in Paris in 1973. Military pressure against South Vietnam continued, however, and in 1975 the Saigon regime collapsed and the country fell to the Communists. In 1978–79 thousands of "boat people," refugees from the S—many of them ethnic Chinese—fled from Vietnam. In 1978, Vietnamese troops invaded neighboring Cambodia to bring down the regime of Pol Pot; a pro-Vietnamese government was installed, but the invasion led to international criticism and tensions with Vietnam's other neighbors. China launched a brief attack into Vietnam in 1979, and in 1980 conflicts arose with Thailand over Cambodian refugee camps in Thailand. Despite a sagging economy, Vietnam continued its military build up in Cambodia and on the Thailand border through the mid-1980s. Relations with the US had improved slightly by 1985. *See also* Vietnam War.

PROFILE

Official name: Democratic Republic of Vietnam
Area: 128,408sq mi (332,577sq km)
Population: 52,741,766
  Density: 410per sq mi (159per sq km)
Chief cities: Hanoi (capital); Danang; Haiphong; Ho Chi Minh City; Hue
Government: peoples' republic
Religion: Taoism, Buddhism, Roman Catholicism
Language: Vietnamese
Monetary unit: dong
Gross national product: $4,900,000,000
Industries: shellac, processed food, textiles, rubber products, chemicals, cement, metallurgy
Agriculture: rice, rubber, fish, forests, pepper, cattle, corn, tea, coffee, maize, sweet potatoes, tobacco, sugar cane, poultry
Minerals: coal, zinc, tin
Trading partners: USSR, People's Republic of China, Japan

Vietnamese, the national language of Vietnam, spoken by about 35,000,000 people there, or nearly 90% of the country's population. It is known to be related to a minor language of Vietnam called Muong, but its relationship to any of the other major languages of Asia is as yet uncertain.

Vietnam War, military conflict between South Vietnamese government forces aided by the United States, and Communist insurgents (Vietcong) supported by North Vietnam. It was initially a civil war

aimed at reunification of Vietnam following its partition in 1954 into North (Communist) and South (non-Communist). In the early 1960s the United States became militarily involved; by 1969 there were some 550,000 US troops in South Vietnam. North Vietnam received aid from the USSR and China. Despite US armed forces, the South Vietnamese were unable to defeat the Vietcong and North Vietnamese. By the late 1960s pressure developed in the United States for the withdrawal of US troops. Efforts toward negotiated peace were begun in 1969 and a peace treaty was signed in January 1973 by South Vietnam, the United States, North Vietnam, and the National Liberation Front (the Communist provisional revolutionary government in South Vietnam). It provided for an end to hostilities and for the withdrawal of US forces. Fighting between South Vietnamese and Communists continued, however, and in May 1975 the South Vietnamese government fell to the Communists.

Vigée-Lebrun, Marie Anne-Elisabeth (1755–1842), French painter. A protégé of Marie Antoinette, she was strongly influenced by Rubens and occasionally worked in the style of David. One of the most successful portraitists of her time, she maintained one of the great French salons and is best known as a painter of women and children.

Vigeland, Adolf Gustav (1869–1943), Norwegian sculptor. A pupil of Auguste Rodin, he worked in a monumental, highly emotive style that combined realism with romanticism. He is known best for his unfinished magnun opus, an immense "Park of Sculpture" in Osio, Norway.

Vigo, seaport city in NW Spain, on the Vigo Bay, 17mi (27km) S of Pontevedra, near the Portuguese border; divided into new and old sections. Attacked by Francis Drake 1585 and 1589, it was scene of naval battle 1702 between British-Dutch fleet and Spanish galleons carrying gold cargo from the New World; some of the gold sank and is believed to be still at the bottom of the bay; site of ancient palaces. Industries: fishing, fish processing, boats, granite, brandy, tools, soap, machinery. Pop. 197,144.

Viking Mission, exploration of Mars by two US spacecraft landing in the summer of 1976. The mission included experiments to search for evidence of life.

Vikings, Scandinavian pirates. Also called Jarangionsor Norsemen. They conducted raids against areas of Europe and the British Isles during the 10th and 11th centuries. They colonized some of these areas and exerted a great deal of influence on the history of Europe by encouraging the growth of feudalism. They were skilled seafarers and shipbuilders. Their religion was mythological, and their literature grew from heroic legends combined with mythology.

Villa, Francisco "Pancho" (1877–1923), Mexican revolutionary leader, b. Doroteo Arango. He spent his early life as an outlaw before joining Francisco Madero's revolutionary forces (1910). Later he joined Venustiano Carranza's forces when Carranza ousted Madero. Villa broke with Carranza to ally with Emiliano Zapata, and was defeated (1915). After the United States recognized Carranza's government, Villa murdered US citizens in northern Mexico and New Mexico in retaliation. Although Pres. Woodrow Wilson sent troops against him, Villa continued harassment until 1920. *See also* Carranza, Venustiano; Mexican Border Campaign.

Villon, François (1431–after 1463), considered the greatest French poet of the Middle Ages, also known

as François de Montcorbier or François des Loges. He took the name of his tutor and guardian Guillaume de Villon, and received a degree from the Sorbonne in 1452 after a colorful and riotous student life. He associated himself both with the nobility and the criminal element of Paris, and featured prostitutes and thieves in his poetry. After several brawls and thefts, he was sentenced to be hanged in 1462 or 1463 for the murder of a priest during a street fight. The sentence was commuted, and he disappeared while in exile. His most famous works are *Ballade des Pendus* (Ballad of the Hanged) and a lyric beginning "Where are the snows of yesteryear," which popularized the theme of the loss of things past.

Villon, Jacques (1875–1963), pseud. of Gaston Duchamp, French painter. His abstract pictures are based on landscape motifs. He was an early adherent of Cubism. His brothers were the artists Marcel Duchamp and Raymond Duchamp-Villon.

Viña del Mar, city in Chile, near Valparaíso on the Pacific Ocean; seaside resort; site of summer palace of Chilean presidents. Industries: tourism, textiles, paints. Pop. 229,020.

Vincennes, port city in SW Indiana, on Wabash River; seat of Knox co. Fortified by French 1732, it was occupied by British 1763; Americans under George Rogers Clark captured it during American Revolution (1779); capital of Indiana Territory 1800–13; site of Pres. William Harrison's home "Grouseland" and Vincennes University (1804). Industries: agriculture, batteries, glass, wool, paper, seed. Oldest settlement in state, founded 1702; inc. 1856. Pop. (1980) 20,857.

Vincent de Paul, Saint (1581–1660), French priest called the Universal Patron of Works of Charity. As a young man he was captured by Barbary pirates and spent two years as a slave in Tunis. After escaping back to France, he began a mission to the peasantry, founding the Congregation of the Mission (or Lazarists). Showing great organizing ability, he later helped found the Daughters of Charity to minister to the sick, the old, and orphans.

Vinci, Leonardo da. *See* Leonardo da Vinci.

Vindhya, mountain range in India; extends ENE across India to divide the Deccan plateau from the Ganges River basin; historically, it has been used as the dividing line between N and S India. Sandstone extracted from the mountains was used to build the Buddhist stupas at Sanchi (400 BC–AD 11th century), Jain and Brahman temples at Khajraho (11th century), palaces of Gwalior (15th century). Length: 700mi (1,127km).

Vineland, city in SW New Jersey, 11mi (18km) ENE of Bridgeton; site of Vineland Training School (1888) and Cumberland County College (1964). Industries: glassware, chemicals, clothing. Inc. 1952. Pop. (1980) 53,-753.

Vinland (Wineland), area in North America, believed to have been the coast of New England or Newfoundland. In AD 1000 as Leif Eriksson sailed from Norway to Greenland, his ship was blown off course to the S and W. He came to a land first sighted in 985 by Bjarni Herjulfsson, where wild grapes and grain grew. Most scholars accept as fact that the Vikings discovered America. Stories of Vinland voyages are told in Old Norse Sagas.

Vinson, Frederick Moore (1890–1953), US public official and chief justice of US Supreme Court (1946–53), b. Louisa, Ky. He served as congressman (1924–29,

1931–38); associate justice of the US Court of Appeals (1938–42); chief judge of the US Emergency Court Appeals (1942–43). He was also director of the Office of Economic Stabilization (1943–45). Pres. Harry S. Truman named him secretary of treasury (1945–46). Appointed chief justice of the Supreme Court (1946), he was a strong supporter of civil rights but believed in broad powers for the government. This was evident in his dissenting opinion in *Youngstown Sheet and Tube* v. *Sawyer* (1952).

Vinyl Chloride, gas with an etherlike odor (formula CH_2CHCl) manufactured by the chlorination of ethylene. It polymerizes to form polyvinyl chloride (PVC) and is widely used in this form. Properties: sp. gr. (liq. 20°C) 0.9121; melt. pt. −255.4°F (−159.7°C); boil. pt. 7°F (−13.9°C).

Vinyl Plastics, any of several substances (resinous, fibrous, or rubbery) composed of large molecules made by polymerization of vinyl compounds, used in plastic film, upholstery, floor tile, toys, buttons, and fibers. These contain the hydrocarbon vinyl group. The molecules of a single vinyl compound can be made to polymerize; those of two different compounds can also be linked, forming a copolymer. *See also* Polystyrene; Polyvinyl Acetate.

Viola, stringed musical instrument of the violin family, somewhat larger and tuned a fifth lower. It is held horizontally like the violin and played with a horsehair bow, sometimes pizzicato (finger-plucked). The music, written in alto clef, is warm and mellow. The viola is prominent as a solo instrument, in chamber music, and in the string sections of symphony orchestras.

Violet, any of about 850 species of herbs, shrubs, and small trees of the family Violaceae, worldwide in distribution. All cultivated species are of the genus *Viola*. More than 500 species of wild violets have been described; they may be annual or perennial with 5-petaled flowers that grow singly on stalks; usually blue, violet, lilac, yellow, or white. In North America the most common species are the blue, or meadow, violet *(V. papilionacea)* and the bird's foot violet *(V. pedata)*.

Violin, most important stringed musical instrument played by bow. It is a major component of Western chamber and symphony orchestras, ranking with the piano in virtuoso performances. Derived from ancient Asian fiddles and medieval viols it was developed in Italy by the Amati family (*c.*1575–1680), Stradivari (*c.* 1644–1737), and Guarneri (1698–1744). Corelli and Vivaldi (*c.*1700) furthered its performance techniques for their concerti grossi, leading to great violin compositions by Bach, Handel, Haydn, Mozart, Beethoven, and Paganini. The violin, blending well in ensemble, offers a variety of tone colors and dynamics. The body is assembled from curved wooden panels, glued with protruding edges, convex front and back, narrow waist, f-holes, unfretted neck with scroll holding pegs for four strings, which are tuned in fifths and stretched over a bridge. The violin, with a range of 3 to 4 octaves, is held horizontally and played with a horsehair bow, sometimes pizzicato (finger-plucked). *See also* Stringed Musical Instruments.

Viper, or adder, poisonous snake characterized by a pair of long, hollow, venom-injecting fangs in the front of the upper jaw that can be folded back when not in use. There are 150 species. Family Viperidae. Or, true viper of Eurasia and Africa, differing from pit viper in lacking heat-sensitive organs. Also, the common European adder *(Vipera berus)* of Europe and E Asia. Its color varies and it has a dark, zigzag band along its back. It is an aggressive, live-bearing snake. Length: to 24in (61cm). Subfamily Viperinae. *See also* Pit Viper.

Viral Infection. *See* Virus.

Virchow, Rudolf (1821–1902), German pathologist. His finding and succinct statement that "all cells arise from cells" completed the formulation of the cell theory and repudiated spontaneous generation theories. Virchow also studied the nature of disease on a cellular level, establishing the field of cellular pathology.

Vireo, small, American songbird found in forest treetops, city parks, tropical coastline shrubs, and other habitats. They have bristled forehead feathers, slightly down-curved bills, and green, gray, or yellow plumage. They feed on insects and larvae and lay spotted white eggs (3–5) in a complicated cup-shaped nest slung from a tree fork. Family Vireonidae.

Virgil. *See* Vergil.

Virginia, state in E United States, on the Atlantic Ocean, midway between Maine and Florida.

Land and economy. From the coast, the land rises gently to the Blue Ridge Mts. Beyond the Blue Ridge, the Shenandoah Valley is a rich farming region. In the far W, the rugged Allegheny Mts lie along the state boundary. Chesapeake Bay, a large arm of the Atlantic, cuts into the E section; into it flows the James, the York, and the Rappahannock rivers. The Potomac River forms much of the state's N boundary. The rich farmland that long sustained the economy is E of the mountains. Industry is mostly concentrated in the Richmond-Petersburg and the Norfolk areas. Norfolk is a major port. The state's historical shrines are prime attractions for the important tourist industry.

People. Early settlers were English; in the early 18th century numbers of Scots-Irish and Germans arrived, but immigration decreased after 1800. About 63% of the population lives in urban areas.

Education. There are about 70 institutions of higher education. The College of William and Mary, founded in 1693, is the 2nd-oldest in the United States. The state-supported University of Virginia was founded by Thomas Jefferson in 1819.

History. The first permanent settlement in the New World was made at Jamestown in 1607. The General Assembly of 1619 was the first representative local government in America. Virginia became a royal colony in 1624 and developed an aristocratic plantation society in the E, with vast holdings in tobacco acreage. The W was settled by immigrants from overseas and from other colonies in the early 18th century. Virginia's leaders, including Thomas Jefferson, Patrick Henry, and Richard Henry Lee, were foremost in the drive for independence from Great Britain. Jefferson was the principal author of the Declaration of Independence, and George Washington, a Virginian, was commander-in-chief of the Continental army in the Revolution. Lord Cornwallis surrendered his British troops at Yorktown on Oct. 19, 1781. Four of the first five presidents of the United States were Virginians; in all, eight presidents were born in the state. Virginia was one of the last states to join the Confederacy in the Civil War, but Richmond became the Confederate capital. The state was the principal battleground of the war. Gen. Robert E. Lee, the Confederate commander, surrendered his army at Appomattox Court House on April 9, 1865. Social and economic recovery was slow after the war, but was followed by industrial growth during the 20th century. After WWII the Norfolk metropolitan area and Virginia's suburbs outside of Washington, D.C., experienced rapid growth.

PROFILE

Admitted to the Union: June 25, 1788; 10th of the 13 original states to ratify the US Constitution
US Congressmen: Senate, 2: House of Representatives, 10
Population: 5,346,279 (1980); rank, 14th
Capital: Richmond, 219,214 (1980)
Chief cities: Norfolk, 266,979; Richmond; Arlington, 152,599
State legislature: Senate, 40; House of Delegates, 100
Area: 40,817sq mi (105,716sq km); rank, 36th
Elevation: highest, 5,729ft (1,747m), Mt Rogers; lowest, sea level
Industries (major products): chemicals, tobacco products, food products, textiles, apparel, lumber, furniture
Agriculture (major products): tobacco, peanuts, apples, poultry, hogs
Minerals (major): bituminous coal, zinc, limestone
State nickname: Old Dominion
State motto: Sic Semper Tyrannis (Ever Thus to Tyrants)
State bird: cardinal
State flower: American dogwood
State tree: American dogwood

Virginia Beach, city in SE Virginia, on Atlantic Ocean, 18mi (29km) E of Norfolk; site of Cape Henry memorial cross (commemorating first landing of English colonists, 1607, who later founded Jamestown), oldest brick house in the United States built by Adam Thoroughgood 1636; noted tourist center with several recreational facilities and beaches; military complex. Industries: tourism, Guernsey cows, truck farms. Inc. 1906; consolidated with Princess Anne co 1963. Pop. (1980) 262,199.

Virginia City, village in W Nevada, 16mi (26km) SSE of Reno; seat of Storey co. Settled when Comstock Lode was discovered 1859, it grew rapidly into an elegant town with population of 25,000 until the gold and silver ran out *c.* 1886. Now a ghost town with a flourishing tourist business.

Virginia Creeper, or woodbine, American ivy, tendril-climbing vine native to North America, but usually found only in eastern areas. It has leaves divided into five parts, green flower clusters, and blue-black inedible berries. Family Vitaceae; species *Parthenocissus quinquefolia*.

Virginia Deer. *See* White-tailed Deer.

Virginia Plan (1787), a program offered at the Philadelphia Constitutional Convention. Proposed by the Virginia delegation, it consisted of 15 resolutions concerning a structure of government for the union. Among its features were: a bicameral national legislature in which the lower house would be elected by the people and the upper house by the lower chamber, an executive to be chosen by the legislature, and a judiciary with a Supreme Court and lower courts elected by the legislature. The plan favored the large states because representation was based on population and wealth. Some features of this plan were included in the Constitution.

Virginia Resolves, declarations by the House of Burgesses (1765) that the Stamp Act was illegal and void, and that only Virginia and not Parliament could tax Virginia.

Virgin Islands, a group of some 100 islands in the Lesser Antilles between the Caribbean Sea and the Atlantic Ocean. A group of 68, the W cluster known as the Virgin Islands of the United States, is a US possession, administered by the US Department of the Interior. The NE group, about 36 islands, is a British colony, called the British Virgin Islands.

The chain of islands is essentially mountain peaks, rising from the Atlantic Ocean; terrain is difficult for agriculture. Because of the mild climate, Old World architecture, and beautiful bays, the islands have become a popular tourist spot over the past 2 decades; tourism is a major contributor to the economy. Some islands such as the US-held St Croix and St Thomas are used for agriculture and livestock, with sugar cane and rum as major products. The Virgin Islands National Park is located on St John, the third largest of the US islands.

After the last of the islands' native Indian population was eliminated by the Spaniards in the 16th century, immigration brought many nationalities. The slave trade, begun in 1673, brought much of the present population, which today is predominantly black and poor. About 20% of the population is white. Discovered in 1493 by Christopher Columbus, the islands had only sporadic settlements until the Dutch West India Co. came to St Thomas in 1672. The British islands were bought in 1566 from the Dutch, while the US islands were bought in 1917 from Denmark for $25,000,000, because of their strategic position near the Panama Canal. Denmark had claimed St John in 1683 and bought St Croix in 1733 from France, making the group a Danish Royal colony in 1754. The slave trade figures largely in the history of the islands, until violent slave revolts on St John in 1733 and one on St Croix in 1848. The islands were the world's largest slave trading center until the practice was outlawed in 1792 by Denmark. Residents of the US-held islands were made US citizens in 1927, and these islands are administered by a governor appointed by the US president. There is an 11-man elected Senate with a US district judge as chief judicial authority. In 1980 a constitutional convention was convened to draft a charter granting greater autonomy to the islands. The governor of the British islands is appointed by the British Crown, with an executive council and a legislature.

PROFILE

Official name: Virgin Islands of the United States; British Virgin Islands
Area: 133sq mi (344sq km) (US); 59sq mi (153sq km) (British)
Population: 118,960 (US); 11,006 (British)
Chief cities: Charlotte Amalie; Christiansted; Roadtown
Religion: Roman Catholic
Language: English
Monetary unit: US dollar, British pound

Virgin Islands National Park, park in St John, Virgin Islands. This is a park of lush green hills, quiet coves, and white sandy beaches covering 75% of St John Island. There are early Carib indian relics, remains of a Danish colonial sugar plantation, and an underwater swimming trail. Area: 14,419acres (5,840hectares). Est. 1956.

Virgin Mary. *See* Mary, Saint.

Virgo, or the Virgin, equatorial constellation situated on the ecliptic between Leo and Libra; the sixth sign of the zodiac. An extensive star group, Virgo lies south of Coma, located in a part of the sky where galaxies and galaxy clusters are very numerous. Brightest star Alpha Virginis (Spica). The astrological sign for the period Aug. 23–Sept. 22.

Virology, the study of viruses. Unknown until 1892, viruses were first discovered by a Russian bacteriologist, D. Ivonovski, who found that the causative agent

Viper

Flat Top Manor, Blue Ridge Parkway, Virginia

Trunk Bay, Virgin Islands

of tobacco mosaic disease could pass through a porcelain filter impermeable to bacteria. The introduction of the electron microscope in 1940 made it possible to view viruses. *See also* Virus.

Virus, a submicroscopic infectious organism, first discovered when infectious material that had been passed through a fine porcelain filter, which held back bacteria, was still infective (filterable agent). They vary in size from 10 to 300nm (1 nm = 1 billionth of a meter), and contain only genetic material, in the form of deoxyribonucleic acid (DNA) or ribonucleic acid (RNA) enclosed in a protein coat, the capsid. Viruses can grow and reproduce only when they enter another cell, such as a bacterium or animal cell, because they lack energy-producing and protein-synthesizing machinery. When they enter a cell, the host's metabolism is subverted so that viral reproduction is favored. Pathogenesis is the result of cell death or altered metabolism as the virus multiplies. Control of viruses is difficult because harsh measures are required to kill them. The body, however, has devised some protective measures, such as production of interferon and of antibodies directed against specific viruses. One attack of certain viral diseases confers lifetime immunity. Some of the more common virus diseases are: poliomyelitis; influenza virus, causing flu symptoms; rubella virus, causative agent of German measles; ECHO-28 and RS viruses, which cause the common cold; and herpes simplex, which causes cold sores. Where the specific agent can be isolated, vaccines can be developed, but some viruses, such as influenza, change so rapidly that vaccines become ineffective.

Visconti, Italian family that ruled Milan from the 13th century until 1447. Ottone Visconti (1207?–95), appointed (1262) archbishop of Milan by Pope Urban IV, used his position to become the first Visconti lord of Milan. Ghibellines (imperial partisans), the Visconti established their hegemony over Lombardy in the 14th century, and in 1339 they took the hereditary title of duke. From the mid-14th century Visconti-Milanese expansionism met allied resistance from other Italian states such as Florence, Venice, the Papal States, and Savoy. Visconti lordship of Milan passed to the Sforza family after the death of Filippo Maria Visconti in 1447.

Viscosity, the internal friction of a liquid or gas. In the flow of a liquid through a pipe, the central portion moves the fastest and the layers next to the pipe move minimally. Thus layers of the fluid are sliding over one another; the more viscous the liquid, the slower it will flow. Viscosity is large for liquids, small for gases. In liquids, it increases rapidly with decreasing temperature.

Vishnu, in Hindu mythology, one of the supreme triad of Brahma, Siva, and Vishnu. He reigns in heaven with his wife Lakshmi as the most important solar deity. Vishnu is depicted as a young man with four hands holding a shell, wheel, club, and lotus and bearing bow and sword. He was worshiped as a preserver and restorer, as Vishnu, and in his other incarnations, Rama, Krishna, and Radha.

Visigoths, or **West Goths,** an ancient Germanic people. In the 2nd century AD they migrated from their original home on the Baltic to the shores of the Black Sea. There they separated into two groups, divided by the Dniester River: the Visigoths (West Goths) and the Ostrogoths (East Goths). At the end of the 4th century, they began attacking the frontiers of the Roman Empire. The Gothic invasions remained one of the most serious problems of the empire for many years.

Vision, sense concerned with the transformation of light energy into the experience of seeing. Light from an object enters the eye through the transparent cornea, passes through the pupil (the size of which is regulated by the iris), is refracted by the lens, and forms an image on the interior of the eye, a special receptor surface called the retina. The retina is composed of two types of cells: rods, found in the periphery, and cone cells, highly concentrated toward the center (fovea) of the retina. Rods operate in dim illumination and are excellent light detectors; cones function best under brighter illumination and are responsible for color vision and the best acuity (pattern vision).

Receptors connect with bipolar and ganglion cells that in turn form the optic nerve. Before they reach the brain the two optic nerves cross (optic chiasma). The optic nerves synapse at the lateral geniculate body, which in turn sends fibers to the optic cortex, located within the occipital lobes. Vision is not yet explainable in purely anatomical terms, and thus many visual phenomena, eg, visual illusions, are studied by psychologists.

Vistula (Wista), longest river in Poland; rises in Carpathian Mts, SW Poland, flows NE past Krakow, turns NW through Warsaw then flows NW through Toruń, turning N to mouth of the Bay of Danzig at Gdańsk. The major waterway of Poland, it connects a large area through its tributary system, which includes the Bug, San, Wisloka, Dunajec, Bzura, and Pilica rivers; canal systems connect it to still other important rivers; logging is done along lower course. Length: 675mi (1087km).

Visual Purple. *See* Rhodopsin.

Vitamin, organic substance required in small amounts by living organisms for healthy life and growth. Higher animals cannot synthesize vitamins, which must then form part of their diet. Deficiency of a particular vitamin results in a specific vitamin deficiency disease. Vitamins of the B complex and vitamin C are water-soluble. The B complex vitamins are obtained from yeast, liver, etc, and function as coenzymes in metabolic reactions. They include thiamine (B₁), nicotinic acid, riboflavin (B₂), pantothenic acid, pyridoxine (B₆), biotin, and folic acid. Certain other substances, such as choline, may also be considered as belonging to the B complex. Vitamin C (ascorbic acid) is present in certain fruits and green vegetables; lack of it results in scurvy. All the remaining vitamins are fat-soluble. Deficiency of vitamin A (retinal), which occurs in fish-liver oils, causes night blindness; lack of vitamin D, obtained from fish-liver oils, results in rickets in children. The naturally occurring form is produced by the action of sunlight on the skin. Deficiency of vitamin E (tocopherol) may affect fertility, and vitamin K is required for normal blood clotting. *See also* individual vitamins.

Vitamin A, a fat-soluble vitamin found in fish liver and other animal livers, butter, cheese, and vegetables and occurring in two forms: retinol (vitamin A₁) and dehydroretinol (vitamin A₂). Deficiency results in night blindness and various skin disorders.

Vitamin B₁ (thiamine), one of the B complex vitamins; found in green vegetables, corn, beans, liver, egg yolk, and brown rice. Deficiency affects the nervous system, circulation, and gastrointestinal tract and produces such symptoms as sluggish elimination, neuritis, rapid pulse, fluid accumulation, and difficulty in breathing.

Vitamin B₂ (riboflavin), a member of the vitamin B complex group, essential to human nutrition and found in liver, milk, grass, kidneys, eggs, malt, and certain algae. Deficiency causes lesions on the tongue, lips,

and face as well as ocular symptoms. Also called Vitamin G.

Vitamin B₆, a group of vitamins belonging to the vitamin B complex group and including pyridoxine, pyridoxal, and pyridoxamine. They are found in most foods, particularly in meats, liver, vegetables, cereals, and egg yolk, and are important in the metabolism of amino acids, among other metabolic processes. Deficiency of pyridoxine affects the nervous system, resulting in seizures, irritability, and gastrointestinal symptoms, treated by administration of its hydrochloride salt, which is also used in other conditions such as morning sickness.

Vitamin B₁₂ (cyanocobalamin), a vitamin of the B complex group, needed for DNA synthesis and for maturation of red blood cells. It is found especially in liver and eggs and can be produced from cultures of *Streptomyces griseus*, also the source of the antibiotic streptomycin. Deficiency causes pernicious anemia, for which the treatment is administration of the vitamin.

Vitamin B Complex, a large group of water-soluble vitamins that includes riboflavin, thiamine, niacin, nicotinamide, vitamin B₆, cyanocobalamin, biotin, pantothenic acid, folic acid, inositol, and possibly para-aminobenzoic acid and choline. *See also* Vitamin B₁; Vitamin B₂; Vitamin B₆; Vitamin B₁₂; Vitamin H.

Vitamin C (ascorbic acid), a substance found in citrus fruits, strawberries, tomatoes, and other fruits and vegetables and essential to normal metabolism. A deficiency causes the nutritional disorder called scurvy.

Vitamin D, any of several similar compounds related chemically to steroids and essential for normal growth of bone and teeth. They include ergocalciferol and cholecalciferol (vitamin D₂ and D₃) and are found in fish-liver oil and eggs; they can also be made by irradiating ergosterol, a sterol. Deficiency causes such bone diseases as rickets and osteoporosis (thinning of bone).

Vitamin E (alphatocopherol), a vitamin found in beef liver, wheat-germ oil, cereals, and egg yolk and important in reproduction, normal development of muscle, protection of red blood cells, and many other biological processes.

Vitamin G. *See* Vitamin B₂.

Vitamin H (biotin), a B complex vitamin widely distributed in living tissue. Deficiency in experimental animals causes limb paralysis and baldness, as well as graying of fur.

Vitamin K, any of a group of vitamins found in spinach, cabbage, egg yolk, and other sources and important in blood coagulation. The group includes vitamin K₁ (phylloquinone), vitamin K₂ (farnoquinone), and vitamin K₃ (menadione). Vitamins K₁ and K₂ are used to treat hemorrhage, and vitamin K₃, as a vitamin supplement. Deficiency of vitamin K results in prolongation of the clotting time, with subsequent bleeding.

Viticulture, worldwide cultivation of grapes. Most commercially grown grapes in the United States are raised in California and the Finger Lakes region in New York. *See also* Grape.

Vivaldi, Antonio (1680–1743), Italian composer who standardized the three-movement concerto grosso and influenced Johann Sebastian Bach. He composed many concertos, eg, *The Four Seasons* (1725).

Vizsla, pointer and retriever breed of dog (sporting group) with innate hunting ability; also called Hungarian pointer. The breed existed 1,000 years ago on Hungarian plains. Its lean, muscular head tapers to a square muzzle. Rounded, silky ears are low-set and hanging. The body is well-proportioned. Tail is docked by 1/3. Colored rusty gold or dark sandy yellow, the coat is short, smooth, and dense. Average size: 22–24in (56–61cm) high at shoulder; 40–60lb (18–27kg). *See also* Sporting Dog.

V-J Day (Sept. 2, 1945), the day World War II ended in the Pacific. Japan surrendered on the USS *Missouri* in Tokyo Bay.

Vladimir I (956?–1015), Russian ruler and Orthodox saint. In 979, Vladimir's army of Viking mercenaries conquered Polotsk and Kiev. After murdering his brother, he became grand duke of Kiev (980), conquering parts of Poland (981) and Lithuania (983). After his conversion to Christianity in *c*.989, he became the first Christian to rule in Russia. He worked to end heathen practices and built cathedrals and schools on the Byzantine model. He married the sister of Basil II of Constantinople.

Vladimir, city in Russian SFSR, USSR, on N bank of Klyazma River, 110mi (176km) E of Moscow; capital of Vladimir oblast. One of Russia's oldest cities, it served as capital of Grand Duchy of Vladimir-Suzdal 1157–1238; scene of crowning of grand dukes of Moscow in 14th century; site of Assumption cathedral (1158–61), Demetrius Cathedral (1193–97), and Golden Gate (city gate) erected 1164. Industries: chemicals, cotton textiles, plastics, tractors, machine tools. Founded early 12th century by Vladimir II of Kiev. Pop. 291,000.

Vladivostok, seaport city in Russian SFSR, USSR, at S tip of peninsula extending between two bays of Sea of Japan; capital of Primorski Krai (since 1888); a naval base since 1872, it was used as major supply depot by Allies in WWI. They occupied city from 1917–22 following Russian Revolution. During WWII it was major receiving port for lend-lease supplies from the United States; site of Far Eastern University (reopened 1956), Far Eastern branch of Soviet Academy of Sciences, merchant marine college, and an engineering college. Harbor kept open in winter by ice breakers; known as Golden Horn Harbor, it is a base for whaling and fishing fleets. Industries: fish canning, shipbuilding, woodworking, chemicals, food processing. Founded 1860 as a military post. Pop. 548,000.

Vlaminck, Maurice de (1876–1958), French painter. Largely self-taught, he was an early Fauvist. Influenced by Vincent van Gogh, African sculpture, and Paul Cézanne (in that order), he repudiated intellectualism and invested his landscapes with a raw vehemence that was shocking in its time, eg, "Village in the Snow" (Philadelphia Museum of Art). He was also an accomplished novelist, a musician, and an athlete. *See also* Fauvism.

Vltava, longest river in Czechoslovakia; rises in Bohemian Forest of SW Czechoslovakia, flows SE and N to Elbe River at Melnik; supports hydroelectric plants. Length: 267mi (430km).

Vocal Cords. *See* Larynx.

Vocational Education, instruction in an industrial or commercial skill, obtained in trade schools, apprenticeship programs, on-the-job training, some colleges, or through correspondence schools. Such programs answer the great demand for skilled workers inspired by the Industrial Revolution, which lessened the opportunity for informal apprenticeships.

Vojvodina (Voivodina), autonomous province in NE Yugoslavia; bordered by Hungary (N) and Romania (E); Novi Sad is capital; densely populated, fertile agricultural plain. From 1849–60 it was independent crownland of Vojvodina; ceded to Yugoslavia 1920; made autonomous 1946. Industries: fruit, cattle, food processing. Area: 8,301sq mi (21,500sq km). Pop. 1,950,268.

Volcano, a vent from which molten igneous matter (lava), solid rock debris, and gases are erupted. The term also is applied to the pileup of rock around the vent. Central-vent volcanoes, where the material erupts from a single pipe, are of two main types, shield and composite. Fissure volcanoes extrude material along an extensive fracture, building up plains and plateaus.

Volga, river in E European, USSR; longest river in Europe and USSR's principal waterway; rises in the Valdai Hills, flows E past Rzev and Kalinin through Rybinsk Reservoir, to Kazan' where it turns S and continues past Uljanovsk making a hairpin bend at Kuiby-

shev, SW to Volgograd, and SE to Caspian Sea through a wide delta below Astrachan, connected with Baltic Sea by Volga-Baltic Waterway, with Moscow by Moscow Canal, and with Black and Azov seas by Volga-Don Canal. Many dams and hydroelectric plants have been built on the river since 1937; most of river is open from March to mid-December. During May and June it is subject to great floods. Low water in late summer brings on the problem of shoals and sandbars that impede navigation. Its waters carry over half of all river freight in USSR, and are used to irrigate the steppes of the lower Volga region. Navigable for almost all of its 2,293mi (3,692km).

Volga-Baltic Waterway, canal and river system in N European USSR; links Volga River with Baltic Sea and Leningrad industrial area. System was started 1709 to connect St Petersburg with interior; course includes Neva River, canal along S shore of Lake Ladoga, Svir River (partially canalized), canal along S shore of Lake Onega, the Vytegra, Beloye canal, Korzha canal, W and S shores of Beloye Ozero (canalized), Sheksna River through Rybinsk Reservoir to Volga River. Major reconstruction was done in 1960s. Length: 701mi (1,129km).

Volgograd, formerly Stalingrad; seaport in Russian SFSR, USSR, on the Volga River and E terminus of Volga-Don Canal; capital of Volgograd oblast. Cossack rebels took city 1670, and Yemelyan Pugachev captured it 1774; during Russian civil war it was defended by Soviet forces under Joseph Stalin, Kliment Voroshilov, and Semyon Budenny; it was taken by Anton Denikin and the White (anti-bolshevik) troops; scene of bitter fighting in WWII that destroyed most of city; house-to-house fighting between German troops and Red Army ultimately turned in favor of USSR. A major rail and heavy industry center, city contains one of the world's largest hydroelectric stations. Industries: oil refining, shipbuilding, iron, steel, aluminum, flour milling, chemicals, cables, oil field equipment. Founded 1589 as defense point on Volga River and called Tsaritsyn. Pop. 943,000.

Volleyball, a sport played indoors or outdoors. The court is 60ft (18.3m) long and 30ft (9.2m) wide. The court is divided by an upright net, the top of which stands 8 feet (2.4m) from the ground. An inflated rubber or leather ball, about 27 inches (68.6cm) in circumference, is used. Each team has six players, three forwards and three backs, who cover an equal area of the court. The ball, which must be served from behind the back lines of the court, is batted with the open hand or fist (only one attempt is allowed). After clearing the top of the net, it may go into any part of the court. Each team has a maximum of three volley passes (from player to player) before returning the ball to the attacking team; the play continues until the ball is batted out of bounds, into the net, or hits the ground. Players may use any part of their body to hit the ball, but may not catch or hold it. A point is scored only by the team serving, and if the serving team wins the point, it maintains possession of the ball; 15 points are needed to win. If the teams are tied at 14, the first team to score two consecutive points wins. Volleyball was originated in 1895 at Holyoke, Mass., by William G. Morgan.

Volstead Act (1920), US legislation that gave Congress and the states power to enforce the 18th Amendment, prohibiting the manufacture and sale of alcoholic beverages. Insufficient money and labor for enforcement plus general flaunting of the law led to bootlegging and other criminal activities, creating a lawless atmosphere. *See also* Prohibition.

Volsungs, in Scandinavian mythology, a family especially favored by Odin. The founder of the family was Odin's son Sigi; Sigi's grandson was Volsung, a noted warrior. Volsung's son Sigmund won many victories with a sword earned from Odin. Sigmund's son was the hero Siegfried.

Volt, unit of electric potential equal to the difference of potential between two points on a conducting wire carrying a constant current of one ampere when the power dissipated between these points is one watt. The volt is also the unit of electromotive force.

Volta, (Count) Alessandro (1745–1827), Italian physicist who invented the first electric battery (Voltaic pile). He also invented a charge-accumulating machine, the electrophorous, which serves as the basis of modern electrical condensers, and other devices concerned with static electricity. His investigations into electricity led him to correctly interpret Luigi Galvani's experiments with muscle, showing that the metal electrodes and not the tissue generated the current. The unit of electromotive force was named the "volt" in his honor.

Voltaic Cells. *See* Cells, Electrochemical.

Voltaire (1694–1778), French philosopher, historian, and poet, b. François Marie Arouet, Paris. Voltaire is known for his penetrating wit and brilliant style. He left Paris after publication of *Philosophical Letters* (1734). After a stay in Prussia (1750–53) he settled at Ferney (1758), where he added to his literary reputation based on *The Henriade* (1723), *Zaire* (1732), *Mérope* (1743), *Candide* (1759) by conducting a vigorous philosophical campaign in favor of the Enlightenment and against superstition, obscurantism, and metaphysics. His ethical position, expressed in *Essay on Morals* (1756), was founded on toleration and practical humanitarianism as opposed to dogmatic theology. *See also* Candide; Enlightenment, The.

Volta River, main river in Ghana; formed 38mi (61km) NW of Yeji, by the confluence of the Black Volta and White Volta rivers; flows SE to Gulf of Guinea at Ada. Length: approx. 300mi (483km).

Voltmeter, instrument for measuring voltage. The most common type consists of an ammeter with a high resistance connected in series to it and the scale calibrated in volts. An electrostatic voltmeter is essentially a quadrant electrometer.

Voluntary Muscle. *See* Skeletal Muscle.

Volunteers in Service to America (VISTA), a federal program under ACTION. It is comprised of volunteers working on projects to eliminate poverty and poverty-related human, social, and environmental problems in the United States and its territories. Volunteers serve for up to two years providing such services as day care, health and legal aid, education, and city planning. It was established in 1964.

Volvox, a genus of tiny single-celled organisms propelled by a whiplike flagella. *Volvox* forms hollow, spherical colonies, barely visible to the eye. The lashing of the flagellae of the colony's members makes the whole colony turn slowly about a definite axis.

Von Braun, Wernher (1912–77), US engineer, b. Germany. He is known for his role in many aspects of rocketry and space exploration. In 1929 he began experiments with liquid-fuel rockets, and he was instrumental in the development of the German V-2 rocket. In 1945 he was brought to the United States and directed the Redstone rocket program, which launched the first US satellite, Explorer I (1958). In 1970 Von Braun became deputy associate administrator of the National Aeronautics and Space Administration (NASA). He left this post in 1972 to become a business executive. His books include *Across the Space Frontier* (1952), *History of Rocketry and Space Travel* (1966), and *The Rockets' Red Glare* (1976).

Vonnegut, Kurt, Jr. (1922–) US author, b. Indianapolis. Vonnegut's novels and stories protesting the horrors of the 20th century in a black humor vein are particularly popular with college students. Among his novels are *Player Piano* (1951), *Slaughterhouse Five* (1969), *Breakfast of Champions* (1973), *Slapstick: Or Lonesome No More* (1976), *Jailbird* (1979), *Palm Sunday* (1981), and *Deadeye Dick* (1982).

Voodoo, or vodun, religious and magical beliefs and practices found among blacks in the Caribbean, the US South, and Brazil. Voodoo includes elements of West African cults and a supernatural pantheon borrowed largely from Catholicism. Magic, propitiatory rites, and trance play an important role in voodoo. *See also* Obeah.

Vorasilvograd. *See* Lugansk.

Voronezh (Voronez), city and river port in W central Russian USSR, on the Voronezh River, 165mi (266km) NE of Kharkov; capital of the Voronezh oblast. It became a shipbuilding center under Peter I in his campaign against the Turks at Azov (1695–96). During WWII city was almost totally destroyed; most of it has been rebuilt, including the 18th-century Potemkin Palace and Nikolsk church; site of university transferred here from Tartu (1918). Industries: locomotives, machinery, synthetic rubber, oil, food processing, television sets. Founded 1586 as a frontier fortress. Pop. 790,000.

Voroshilovgrad, city in E Ukrainian SSR, USSR, at confluence of Lugan and Olkhov rivers; capital of Voroshilovgrad oblast. Industries: mining equipment, textiles, food products, locomotives. Founded 1795. Pop. 451,000.

Vorster, Balthazar Johannes (1915–83), South African statesman and Nationalist. He served in the legislature and cabinet and succeeded H. F. Verwoerd as prime minister (1966–78), then served briefly as president (1978–79). Although a strict segregationist, he

Vizsla

Alessandro Volta

Richard Wagner

allowed a softening of apartheid policies and met with black African leaders.

Vortex, the eddy or whirlpool observed in fluid motion. Vortices can not occur in ideal (nonviscous) fluid motion, but they are important in the study of real fluids. In particular, the vortices occurring behind air foils are of great interest in aerodynamic design. In the study of turbulence, a major result is the observation that energy is dissipated most efficiently in the smaller vortices.

Voting, process employed to choose candidates for public office or to decide controversial issues. Early forms were by voice or sign, but the written ballot became popular to eliminate the possibility of intimidation and corruption. Absentee voting, or casting a ballot by mail or in advance of the election, originated during the US Civil War for the benefit of military personnel.

VTOL (Vertical Take Off and Landing) Aircraft, experimental airplane designed to perform vertical takeoffs and landings but to maintain flight speed and payload capabilities superior to those of a helicopter. There are designs that permit rotation of the wing and engines from vertical for take-off, to horizontal for high-speed cruising. Another design allows for the diversion downward of the exhaust of fixed jet engines. A third style has two separate systems of thrust for upward and forward movement. *See also* STOL Aircraft.

V2 Rocket, large liquid-fueled rocket developed by the Germans during World War II, the first ballistic missile used in war. The bullet-shaped rocket, 42ft (12.8m) in length and 5ft (1.5m) in diameter, traveled at over 2,000mph (3,200kph). There was no defense against the V2 when it was first fired against England in Sept. 1944. The name was an abbreviation for *Vergeltungswaffe zwei,* German for "Revenge Weapon Two."

Vuillard, Jean-Edouard (1868–1940), French painter, printmaker, and decorator. Drawing on a variety of influences—notably Paul Gauguin, Pierre Puvis de Chavannes, Japanese prints, and his close friend Pierre Bonnard—he developed a distinctive intimist style characterized by simplicity, restraint, calm, and rich surfaces. He specialized in interiors and street scenes.

Vulcan, in Roman religion, the god of fire, particularly in its destructive aspects, such as conflagrations and volcanoes. He was also the god of the thunderbolt and of the Sun. Vulcan finally became the deity who was associated with life-giving warmth. His chief festival, the Volcania, was celebrated on August 23. It is probable that in ancient times human sacrifices were offered to Vulcan.

Vulcanization, chemical process discovered in 1839, of heating sulfur or its compounds with natural or synthetic rubber to improve its durability and resilience. Thin articles, such as balloons or gloves, can be dipped into sulfur chloride; automobile tires, being thicker, take longer.

Vulture, large, keen-sighted, strong-flying bird that feeds on carrion. New World vultures, related to storks and cormorants, are found throughout the Americas and include the condor, turkey buzzard, and king vulture. Family Cathartidae. Old World vultures, related to eagles, are found in Africa, Europe, and Asia and include the griffon vulture. Family Accipitridae. Most vultures lay white or pale eggs (1–3) in a cave, tree hollow, or cliff ledge nest.

W

Waal, river of SW Netherlands, the large S branch of the Rhine River. Formed at fork in lower Rhine near Millingen, the Waal flows WSW across S Netherlands and branches to form the Merwede, Nieuwe, and Oude Mass rivers, before entering North Sea. Length: 52mi (84km).

Waals, Johannes Diderik van der (1837–1923), Dutch physicist who received a Nobel Prize in 1910 for his work involving mathematical equations that described the liquid and gaseous matter states. This research enabled scientists to study temperatures near absolute zero. He introduced into the ideal gas laws two constants (attraction and size), and he derived a more accurate formula, named the van der Waals equation. In tribute to his studies, the weak forces between atoms or molecules are known as van der Waals forces.

Wabanaki. *See* Abnaki.

Wabash, river in Ohio, Indiana, and Illinois; rises in Grand Lake, W Ohio; flows W and SW across Indiana, forms the Indiana-Illinois border before emptying into the Ohio River in SW Indiana; used for irrigation, hydroelectricity, and industrial traffic. Length: 475mi (765km).

Wabash Rate Case (*Wabash, St Louis and Pacific Railway Co.* v. *Illinois*) (1886), US Supreme Court decision. The Court said that a state could not regulate the portion of railroad rates within its borders, reinforcing the right of Congress to regulate interstate commerce.

Wace, Robert (*c.* 1100–1175), Norman poet and chronicler. His works include saints' lives, the *Roman de Rou,* and the *Roman de Brut,* which is based on written and oral accounts of the King Arthur legends.

Waco, city in central Texas, 82mi (144km) S of Fort Worth, on Brazos River; seat of McLennan co; transportation and agricultural center; site of Baylor University (1845), Paul Quinn College (1881), McLennan Community College (1966). Industries: aircraft parts, cotton, grain, tires, furniture, clothing, cottonseed oil products, glass. Settled 1849 on former Waco Indian colony; inc. 1856. Pop. (1980) 101,261.

Wade, Benjamin Franklin (1800–78), US senator and jurist, b. Feeding Hills, Mass. After a successful career in Ohio as a state senator and circuit judge, he became a US senator on the Whig ticket (1851–69). A staunch abolitionist, he opposed the Fugitive Slave Law and the Kansas-Nebraska Act. He denounced President Lincoln's reconstruction plans as too conservative and along with Henry Davis drew up the Wade-Davis Bill (1864), which put the reconstruction plans in the hands of Congress. However, Lincoln vetoed the bill. As president pro tempore of the Senate, Wade would have succeeded to the presidency if Andrew Johnson had been convicted of impeachment charges. In 1869 he retired to Ohio to practice law.

Wade-Davis Bill (1864), act passed by the US Congress to outline the reconstruction process in the South after the Civil War. It stipulated that the government of a seceded state be reorganized only after a majority of white male citizens—exclusive of Confederate of-

ficeholders—had sworn allegiance to the United States. President Lincoln vetoed the measure.

Wading Birds, large number of birds with long legs and at least partially webbed toes. They readily adapt to life of wading through temperate and tropical rivers, lakes, swamps, and lagoons. Includes stork, egret, flamingo, heron, bittern, ibis, and spoonbill. Orders Ciconiformes and Phoenicopteriformes. *See also* individual birds.

Wagner, Richard (1813–83), German composer of operas, b. Leipzig. His wife Cosima was the daughter of Franz Liszt, who sponsored him. His operas are characterized by continuously flowing melody and the use of leitmotivs. His masterpiece is the tetralogy *The Ring of the Nibelungen,* based on legends from German mythology and consisting of the operas *Das Rheingold* (1854), *Die Walküre* (1856), *Siegfried* (1871), and *Das Götterdämmerung* (*The Twilight of the Gods,* 1874).

He also composed *The Flying Dutchman* (1841), *Tannhäuser* (1845), *Lohengrin* (1848), *Tristan und Isolde* (1859), and *Parsifal* (1882). He composed only one comic opera, *Die Meistersinger von Nürnberg* (1867). All of his operas were immensely successful and subsequently influenced many other composers including Arnold Schoenberg, Richard Strauss, and Gustav Mahler.

Wagner, Robert Ferdinand (1877–1953), US political leader, b. Germany. Growing up as a poor immigrant in New York City, he worked in the state legislature (1904–18) to improve workers' conditions. He served on the state supreme court (1919–26). In the US Senate (1926–49), he fought for New Deal legislation, particularly labor bills, helping to establish the National Recovery Administration and social security. He sponsored bills establishing the National Labor Relations Board (1935) and the US Housing Authority (1937).

Wagner Act (1935), US legislation; first modern labor law to be declared constitutional. It represented a positive change in government policy toward labor. The Wagner Act requires that the employer recognize the union, that he bargain collectively with it, and that he do nothing to interfere with employees' rights to join it. The Wagner Act was counterbalanced in 1947 by the Taft-Hartley Act, which restrained the power of organized labor.

Wagner-Steagall Act (1937), US legislation designed to ease the housing shortage. The law established the US Housing Authority (USHA) under the Department of the Interior and gave it power to provide state agencies involved in slum clearing and public housing with long-term, low-interest loans.

Wahhabis, an Islamic sect named after its founder Abd-al-Wahhab (*c.*1703–1791), who opposed all practices, both religious and material, not sanctioned by the Koran. Growing rapidly as a nationalist religious movement, the sect eventually made conquests throughout all of Arabia. Despite two serious setbacks (1818, 1889), the Wahabi movement led by ibn-Saud was able to unify all of its ancestral domains in Arabia under the name Saudia Arabia (1932).

Wahoo, mackerel-type fish found worldwide in tropical marine waters. It is fast-moving with an elongated body. Weight: to 120lb (54kg). Family Scombridae; species *Acanthocybium solanedri.*

Wahusonacook. *See* Powhatan.

Waikato, longest river in New Zealand, in central and NW North Island; rises from Lake Taupo in central mountains; flows NNW into Tasman Sea; provides hydroelectric power for most of North Island; river basin is dairy farming area. Length: 264mi (425km).

Wailing Wall, or Western Wall, a sacred place in Jerusalem for all Jews. It is a remnant of the wall that surrounded Herod's temple and is a place of many pilgrimages to this day. Jews mourn the destruction of their temple at the wall.

Waite, Morrison (1816–88), chief justice of the US Supreme Court (1874–88), b. Lyme, Conn. He gained national prominence as counsel for the United States in the Alabama Claims case (1871–72). Appointed chief justice by President Grant, his major task was interpreting the constitutional amendments that were adopted after the Civil War. He also interpreted the "due process" clause of the 14th Amendment as a means to limit state power. He ruled on the Granger cases (1877), which stipulated that only businesses "clothed with a public interest" were subject to economic regulation by the state, and on the Civil Rights Cases (1883), which stipulated that those who operate inns and places of amusement are agents of the state and discrimination by such people would be considered discrimination by the state.

Waka, a Japanese poetry form consisting of 31 syllables arranged in three 7-syllable and two 5-syllable lines. In the 8th century it became the dominant form; it remained popular, and still is. Contemporary practitioners have been criticized for not saying enough. *Waka* is also called the "Japanese poem."

Wakamatsu. *See* Kitakyushu.

Wakayama, port city in S Honshu, Japan, on Kii Channel, approx. 35mi (56km) SW of Osaka; capital of Wakayama prefecture; forested agricultural region. In feudal times, city was seat of Tokugawa daimyo; site of 16th-century castle of Hideyoshi; suffered earthquake and tidal wave Dec. 21, 1946. Industries: textiles, lumber, laquerware, shipping. Pop. 390,000.

Wake Island, small coral island in W central Pacific Ocean, N of the Marshall Islands and W of Marianas Islands. Sandy and low, the island is actually three islets that form a lagoon; claimed by the United States 1900; site of commercial air base est. 1935; US marine outpost was taken by Japanese 1941; retaken by US forces 1945; US naval base on island remains active. Area: 3sq mi (8sq km).

Waksman, Selman Abraham (1888–1973), US microbiologist, b. Russia. He was awarded the 1952 Nobel Prize in physiology and medicine for his work on antibiotics, a word he coined. He developed screening techniques to search for antibiotics and in 1944 discovered streptomycin. *See also* Antibiotics; Streptomycin.

Wald, George (1906–), US biologist, b. New York City. He shared the 1967 Nobel Prize in physiology and medicine for being "one of the world's greatest authorities on the biochemistry of perception." He studied visual pigments and the effect of light on these pigments. He became an outspoken critic of US policy in Vietnam and lectured against the war throughout the country. Later he became an outspoken critic of DNA research and nuclear safety.

Waldemar IV Atterdag (*c.*1320–75), king of Denmark (1340–75). The disordered kingdom was restored by Waldemar who managed, after years of war and political negotiations, to unite the kingdom by 1361. To reestablish Denmark's control of Baltic trade, he conquered the Swedish island of Gotland. In violation of a treaty with Sweden, he conquered Skane (S Sweden) to gain control of the fishing industry. By conquering their town of Visby he challenged the Hanseatic League, but after trying to restrict them, he made peace in 1370. He married his daughter Margaret, age 6, to the son of Norway's king, hoping to unite the two kingdoms. He was energetic, a skillful politician and unscrupulous.

Walden (1854), narrative by Henry David Thoreau. It is a chronicle of and series of reflections upon his life at Walden Pond near Concord, Mass. In 1845 Thoreau cleared a plot of land belonging to Ralph Waldo Emerson and built a cabin where he lived from July 1845 until September 1847. It was his idea to live simply in order to develop his mind and body. The narrative, derived from journals that he kept during his residence, describes his activities, and reveals his philosophical convictions. The principal tenet of his thought was that each individual should adhere to his inner beliefs regardless of social pressure. His philosophy combined Transcendentalism with his own particular brand of individualism. *See also* Transcendentalism.

Waldenses, small Christian sect founded in the 12th century by Peter Valdes of Lyons. After translating the Bible into French and preaching without authorization, he and his followers were excommunicated and many were executed as heretics. They relied on the Bible and rejected the structure of the Roman Catholic Church. Contact was later made with the Reformation churches, and John Calvin trained some preachers. Waldensians strive to maintain pure Christianity.

Waldheim, Kurt (1918–), Austrian diplomat, secretary-general of the United Nations. (1972–81). He headed Austria's first UN delegation in 1958 and was its permanent representative (1964–68). Waldheim served as foreign minister (1968–70). Unanimously elected as U Thant's successor, he took office as secretary-general in 1972. He was succeeded by Peru's Javier Pérez de Cuéllar.

Wales (Cymru), principality of Great Britain, occupying a broad peninsula in the W of central Britain, bounded by the Irish Sea (N), St George's Channel (W), Bristol Channel (S), and the English counties of Cheshire, Salop, Hereford and Worcester, and Gloucestershire (E).

Land and economy. An upland region, highest in the NW, Wales contains the highest mountain in England and Wales, Snowdon, 3,560ft (1,086m). Lowland areas are confined to the border regions and coastal plains and are widest in the S; principal rivers are Severn, Dee, Wye, Usk Conway, and Teifi. Wrexham is the center of the small N Wales coalfield and industrial region, but S Wales has a major coalfield, heavy industry (iron and steel, engineering, chemicals, metallurgical industries, oil refining), and the main concentration of population. The rest of Wales is mainly agricultural, and tourism is important.

People. The people are of Brythonic Celtic stock. The main religious groups belong to Methodist and other nonconformist churches. About 21% of the population speaks Welsh, and national identity and culture are strong.

Government. Wales sends representatives to Parliament. In 1974 the old Welsh counties were reorganized into eight new counties. The British parliament pledged itself to devolution (limited authority) in Wales, but in 1979, Welsh voters defeated a measure calling for a Welsh regional parliament.

History. The Celtic inhabitants of Britain were little affected by the Roman invasion. The Anglo-Saxons, however, pushed them W and S into what are now Wales and Cornwall. Celtic inhabitants in Wales were temporarily united under one king, Hywel Dda, in the 10th century. With the Norman Conquest (1066), Wales was increasingly threatened by invasion, but the inhabitants managed to resist full conquest until 1282, when Edward I took over the country. A successful but short-lived rebellion was led by Owen Glendower in the 15th century. With the accession of Henry VII, the first Tudor king, Wales began to be assimilated into the political structure of England. The Act of Union (1536) established English law in Wales and made English the official language.

PROFILE

Official name: Principality of Wales
Area: 8,016sq mi (20,764sq km)
Population: 2,774,700
Density: 346per sq mi (134per sq km)
Chief cities: Cardiff (capital); Swansea; Newport
Languages: English, Welsh (official)

Walesa, Lech (1943–), Polish labor leader. In August 1980 he organized Solidarity, an independent self-governing trade union for Polish workers. A strike committee was formed, and a general strike took place. In December 1980 Polish administrators signed an agreement giving the workers the right to organize freely and independently. Walesa became a symbol of the Polish workers' determination to have a greater voice in government affairs. After the government outlawed Solidarity (1981), he was interned until late 1982 as part of the government effort to silence opposition.

Walking Fern, North American evergreen fern found in limy soil. Its long, narrow, five-pointed, arching leaves radiate from the rootstock. When leaf tips touch the ground new plants sprout, hence, its name. Height: to 14in (36cm). Family Aspleniaceae; species *Camptosorus rhizophyllus.*

Walking Stick, or Stick Insect, wingless insect that feeds on leaves found worldwide. These slow moving insects rely on their resemblance to twigs and the ability to squirt a foul-tasting liquid from their thorax to escape predators. Tropical species are the largest. Length: to 13in (32.5cm). Family Phasmatidae. *See also* Leaf Insect, Orthoptera.

Walkowitz, Abraham (1880–1965), US painter, b. Siberia. Chiefly a painter of city life and its surroundings and of figures in landscapes, he was a pupil of Henri Laurens and a participant in the historically significant Armory Show (1913). His style was derived from Cézanne.

Wallace, Alfred Russel (1823–1913), English naturalist and evolutionist. Independent of, but simultaneously with, Charles Darwin, he developed a theory of natural selection. Wallace, who was largely self-taught, conducted several expeditions, including explorative trips to the Amazon and the Malay Archipelago, where the idea of natural selection began to occur to him.

In 1855 Wallace published his article "On the Law Which Has Regulated the Introduction of New Species" and sent his ideas to Darwin. The two men presented their theories to the Linnaean Society in 1858; Wallace's paper was "On the Tendency of Varieties to depart Indefinitely from the Original Type." He later published *Contributions to the Theory of Natural Selection* (1870), which, with Darwin's *Origin of Species,* comprised the fundamental explanation and understanding of the theory of evolution through natural selection.

Wallace, George Corley (1919–), US political leader, b. Clio, Ala. A lawyer and judge (1953–59), he was elected Democratic governor of Alabama in 1962. He attempted unsuccessfully to block federal efforts to integrate Alabama public schools (1962–66). He was succeeded (1966) as governor by his first wife, Lurleen Wallace. He ran for president in 1968 as a third-party candidate for the American Independent party, receiving 13% of the popular vote. He was reelected governor in 1970 and 1974. In 1972, while campaigning for the Democratic presidential nomination, he was shot in an assassination attempt in Maryland. The shot left him paralyzed from the waist down. He campaigned unsuccessfully for the Democratic presidential nomination in 1976 and withdrew from the Senate race in 1978, but was elected governor again in 1982. He announced his retirement in 1986.

Wallace, Henry Agard (1888–1965), US vice president (1941–45) and agriculturalist, b. Adair co, Iowa. He was editor of *Wallace's Farmer,* and later *Iowa Homestead* and *Wallace's Farmer* magazines (1924–33). He was secretary of agriculture from 1933–40, administering the farm price support program. As vice president under Pres. Franklin D. Roosevelt he worked to promote goodwill in Latin America. He also served as head of the Board of Economic Warfare (1942–43). From 1945–46 he was secretary of commerce under Pres. Harry Truman. In 1948 he was the unsuccessful Progressive party candidate for president.

Wallace, Irving (1916–), US author, b. Chicago. He wrote articles and stories for magazines before publishing *The Fabulous Originals* (1955), a nonfiction work. His novels, all popular successes, include *The Chapman Report* (1960), *The Prize* (1962), *The Fan Club* (1974), and *The Second Lady* (1980). Several successful nonfiction books include *The Peoples' Almanac* (1975), *The Peoples' Almanac #2* (1978), *The Book of Lists* (1977), and *The Intimate Sex Lives of Famous People* (1981).

Wallace, Lew(is) (1827–1905), US author, b. Brookville, Ind., best known for his popular, romantic novel *Ben-Hur* (1880). After serving as an officer in both the Mexican and Civil wars, Wallace published *The Fair God* (1873), a story of the Spanish conquest of Mexico, followed by *Ben-Hur,* a story about the Roman Empire and the rise of Christianity, which brought him success. Other works include *The Boyhood of Christ* (1888) and *The Wooing of Malkaton* (1898).

Wallachia, historic region in Romania; former principality between Danube River and Transylvanian Alps; capital and largest city is Bucharest. Principality was est. *c.* 1290 by Rudolf the Black, vassal of Hungary; it secured temporary independence 1330–69; fell to Turks 1387, and remained under Turkish rule until 19th century. In 1829 the Treaty of Adrianpole made Wallachia and Moldavia protectorates of Russia. In 1861 the union of Wallachia and Moldavia formed the nation of Romania; site of Ploesti oil fields, much fought over during WWII. Products: cereals, leguminous plants, fruit, livestock. Industries: oil, handicrafts. Area: 29,575sq mi (76,599sq km).

Wallenstein, Albrecht Eusebius Wenzel von (1583–1634), German general. He sided with the Holy Roman Empire when the Thirty Years War broke out in 1618. He eventually became the commander of the imperial armies, but his ambition led Emperor Ferdinand II to order his capture, and he was murdered by his own officers.

Waller, Fats (1904–43), US jazz and blues pianist and composer, b. Thomas Waller in New York City. Early in his career he accompanied the singers Florence

Kurt Waldheim

Walleye

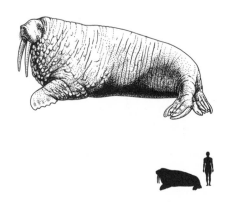

Walrus

Mills and Bessie Smith. He became famous with popular recordings beginning in 1934, displaying his happy, exuberant piano style with humorous vocal renditions. He composed many songs including "Honeysuckle Rose" (1929), "Ain't Misbehavin'" (1929), and "Lonesome Me" (1932).

Walleye, or Walleyed Pike, freshwater game fish of E North America, particularly Lake Erie. Closely related to the sauger and pikeperch, it is mottled greenish-brown with large opaque eyes. Length: to 3ft (91cm); weight: 10–15lb (4.5–6.8kg). Family Percidae; species *Stizostedion vitreum*.

Wallingford, town in S Connecticut, 12mi (19km) N of New Haven; site of a branch of Oneida Community (1851–80), Choate and Putnam preparatory schools; birthplace of Lyman Hall, signer of Declaration of Independence. Industries: silverware, chemicals, hardware, electronic components. Settled 1667; inc. 1670. Pop. (1980) 37,274.

Walloons, term for the French-speaking people who live in the southern provinces of Belgium. The French-speaking south was the industrialized area of Belgium and, therefore, dominated the agricultural, Flemish-speaking north. Because of the rapid economic growth in the 20th century by the north, Walloon dominance has been challenged, and there have been nationalistic conflicts especially over the language to be used in certain regions.

Wallpaper, paper wall coverings that first appeared in Europe in the 16th century as replacements for more expensive cloth wall hangings. Initially the outlines were block printed and the color filled in by brush. By the 18th century paper was glued into a continuous roll before printing. The first large wallpaper factory was started by Jean Papillon in France in 1688, but by the 18th century England was the main producer of wallpaper. By the 19th century wallpaper was being mass produced on roll paper.

Walnut, deciduous tree native to North America, Europe, and Asia. They have smoother bark than hickory trees, to which they are related, and are grown for timber, ornament, and nut production. Height: to 150ft (45.7m). Family Juglandaceae; genus *Juglans*.

Walnut Creek, city in W California, 10mi (16km) N of entrance to Morecambe Bay; site of naval weapons station. Industries: canned foods, walnuts, agriculture. Inc. 1914. Pop. (1980) 53,643.

Walpole, Horace, 4th Earl of Orford (1717–97), English novelist and publisher. A member of Parliament, he wrote and published *The Castle of Otranto* (1764), a supernatural romance, and *Mysterious Mother* (1768), a verse tragedy. His noted letters, some 2,700 in all (1732–97), were published posthumously.

Walpole, (Sir) Hugh (1884–1941), English novelist and critic, b. New Zealand. His novels include *Mr. Perrin and Mr. Traill* (1911), *Fortitude* (1913), *The Dark Forest* (1916), and the tetralogy *The Herries Chronicles* (1930–33). His prose style is colorful and descriptive but of uneven quality.

Walpole, Robert, 1st Earl of Orford (1676–1745), English statesman. He was a Whig member of Parliament (1701–42), led parliamentary opposition to the Tories, and became chancellor of the exchequer and prime minister (1715). Although he resigned (1717) after developing the first sinking fund, he restored order after the South Sea Bubble (1720). He returned

as prime minister (1721–42) and was the first prime minister to develop cabinet government. He transferred power from the House of Lords to the Commons and with royal support strove to unify the cabinet (1733). His financial policies encouraged trade, but he was forced to resign (1742) due to opposition to his noninterventionist foreign policy.

Walras, Léon (1834–1910), French economist. He invented the technique of general equilibrium analysis. Much of economic analysis is devoted to studying equilibrium in one particular market (eg, the supply and demand conditions for wheat). But Walras, through general equilibrium analysis, was concerned with the interrelations among and between all markets. Walras' methodology, consequently, is quite mathematical in approach and abstract in structure.

Walrus, Arctic seal with long tusks resembling a droopy moustache. It feeds on mollusks. It uses its tusks to haul itself onto ice floes and shelves. Its bark resembles a dog's bark or an elephant's trumpeting. Some populations have been hunted almost to extinction by Eskimos. Length: to 12ft (3.7m); weight: to 2,800lb (1,260kg). Species: *Odobenus rosmarus. See also* Pinnipedia; Seal.

Walsall, industrial city in W central England, in Black Country 10mi (16km) NNW of Birmingham. Industries: leather goods, engineering, aircraft parts. Pop. 271,000.

Walsingham, (Sir) Francis (1530?–90), English statesman, secretary of state (1573–90). He was employed on diplomatic missions to France (1570–73; 1581), the Netherlands (1578), and Scotland (1583). Through his efficient espionage system he revealed the Babington plot (1586) and plans for the Spanish Armada (1587). He received little reward from Elizabeth I and died in debt.

Waltham, city in E Massachusetts, on Charles River; site of one of first power looms in United States, designed and built by Francis Cabot Lowell (1813); for the first time all operations of making cotton cloth could be carried on in one building. City was home of Waltham Watch Co. (1854–1950); library has rare collection of these watches; site of Bentley College (1917), and Brandeis University (1947). Industries: electronic components, clothing, paint, varnish. Founded 1636; separated from Watertown 1738; inc. as city 1884. Pop. (1980) 58,200.

Walton, George, (1741–1804), American lawyer and a signer of the Declaration of Independence, b. near Farmville, Va. He was one of Georgia's delegates to the Continental Congress (1776–81) after being captured and released by the British. He was later that state's governor (1779–80, 1789) and a US senator (1795–96).

Walton, Izaak (1593–1683), English biographer and author. His lives of Donne (1640), Sir Henry Wotton (1651), Richard Hooker (1665), George Herbert (1670), and Bishop Sanderson (1678) are the first truly biographical works in English literature. His most famous work, however, is *The Compleat Angler* (1653).

Walton, (Sir) William (1902–83), English composer. Using a largely conservative, post-Romantic style, Walton composed in practically every medium. His best known works are a *Violin Concerto* (1939) and an oratorio, *Belshazzar's Feast* (1931).

Walvis Bay (Walvisbaai), inlet port and surrounding territory on W coast of Namibia (South West Africa);

annexed by Britain 1878, inc. into Cape Colony 1884, now an enclave of South Africa: site of airfield, radio station, railroad terminus. Industries: whaling, fishing, fish processing. Exports: chilled meats. First visited 1487 by Batholomeu Diaz. Area: 43sq mi (1124sq km) Pop. 17,877.

Wampum, or **wampumpeag,** beads used by American Indians as ornaments and as a medium of exchange in early colonial trade. Wampum beads were usually made from clam shells and were colored blue and white. They could also be made up into necklaces or belts.

Wandering Jew, either of two closely related tropical American trailing plants. The white-flowered *Tradescantia fluminensis* normally has bright green leaves. Some varieties have variegated, yellow, or white leaves. The reddish-flowered *Zebrina pendula* has purple-striped, white leaves with reddish-purple undersides. One variety has metallic, green leaves striped with white, green, and red. Family Commelinaceae.

Wanderoo, or lion-tailed macaque, a black monkey of India that has a lionlike ruff of gray fur around its face and a tuft at the tip of its tail. Species *Macaca Silenus*. The purple-faced langur *(Presbytis senex)* of E Asia is also called a wanderoo. *See also* Langur; Macaque.

Wang Mang (33 BC–AD 23), Chinese emperor. A usurper, he attempted the overthrow of the Han Dynasty and proclaimed a Hsin or New Dynasty in AD 8, attempting to carry through a series of drastic changes in the Chinese government and administration. His program led to confusion and anarchy, and the Han was restored by Liu Hsiu. Wang's rule divides Early Han from Later Han China.

Wang Pi (226–249), early Neo-Taoist commentator on the *Lao tzu, Chuang tzu,* and *I Ching*. Making no positive assertions about reality, his most significant idea was his concept of Tao (li) as a "transcendental absolute," which is above all forms and yet unites all things. Wang Pi, along with other Neo-Taoists, kept the true spirit of Taoism alive. *See also* I Ching; Taoism.

Wankel Engine, the most widely used rotary engine. The rotor is an equal-sided triangular piece that rotates in an orbit within a specially constructed casing. Crescent-shaped combustion chambers are created by the rotor that increase and decrease in size as the rotor turns. Sparks ignite the fuel charge from a carburetor at the appropriate time in each chamber.

Wapiti, or **American Elk,** large deer of North America, second only to the moose in size. It is grayish-brown with a yellowish rump. Length: to 7.5ft (2.3m); weight to 770lb (347kg). Its impressive antlers measure over 5ft (1.5m) across. Extensively hunted in the past for their meat and teeth, their range is now greatly restricted. They are commonly seen in groups of 25 or more in national parks. Family Cervidae; species *Cervus canadensis*.

War and Peace (1862–69), novel by Leo Tolstoy. It takes place before, during, and after Napoleon's invasion of Russia. It is both a historical novel, describing the Russian campaign against Napoleon, and a family chronicle examining the lives of several families, centering on the Rostovs. The scope of the work makes it a prose epic.

Warbler, two groups of birds, one of the Old World (Family Sylviidae) and one of New World wood warblers (Family Parulidae). Old World warblers are generally small and related to the thrushes. Excellent songsters, they include the small, brownish grass warblers *(Cisticola);* true warblers *(Sylvia)* of Eurasia and Africa; small, grayish-green leaf warblers; Australian tree warblers *(Gerygone* and *Acanthiza);* and Australian and SW Pacific species. Wood warblers are brightly colored insect-eaters and include the yellow warbler and American redstart. *See also* Wood Warbler.

Warburg, Otto (1883–1970), German biochemist who was awarded the 1931 Nobel Prize in physiology or medicine for his discovery of a respiratory enzyme. He made significant contributions to the understanding of the mechanisms of cellular respiration and energy transfer and of photosynthesis.

War Crimes, conduct that transgresses national or international law in the waging of war, usually relating to treatment of neutrals, prisoners of war, and genocide. After World War II, international military courts were established; high-ranking Germans and Japanese were tried and convicted as war criminals. The statutory period was extended (1969) from 20 to 30 years. Later the Bonn Parliament voted (1979) to do away with the statue of limitations for murder. A one-year limit was set (1980) in the United States for legal action there on 250 cases in its files. Legal proceedings and trials were still being conducted in the 1980s. About 70,000 Germans have been convicted of war crimes in various countries.

Ward, Artemus (1834–67), pseud. of Charles Farrar Browne, popular 19th-century humorist, b. Waterford, Maine. Browne created the character of Artemus Ward to comment on a variety of subjects in books and letters. Browne's lectures as Ward brought him fame.

Ward, Douglas Turner (1930–), US playwright, actor, director, b. Burnside, La. Co-founder of the Negro Ensemble Company, he was an advocate of black-oriented theater. Among his plays are the one-acts *Happy Ending, Day of Absence* (1965); also *The Reckoning* (1969), and *Brotherhood* (1970). He also directed several plays.

War Hawks, name given to a group of Democratic-Republicans who urged expansionism and nationalism. Mainly from the western frontier, this group's continued outcry against British maritime practices helped start the War of 1812 with Britain. Among its leaders were Henry Clay and John C. Calhoun.

Warhol, Andy (1930–), US painter, printmaker, and filmmaker, b. Philadelphia. A leader of the pop art movement of the early 1960s, he is the creator of many of that style's most familiar images: soup cans, packing cartons, faces of film stars, and the like. His style derives from his early career as a commercial illustrator and depends for its distinctive effects on photomechanical techniques and the repeated presentation, with varying degrees of alteration, of single images in series. To a greater extent than any other "serious" artist, he has obliterated the dividing line between the fine arts and the visual data of daily life as recorded by the mass media.

Warlords, regional military leaders in China. From 1912 to 1927, China was torn by the contention for power among the warlords, whose struggles prevented growth and consolidation of national power and left China weak and unable to resist the pressures of imperial Japan. The warlords were backed by different European powers and Japan.

Warner, Charles Dudley (1829–1900), US essayist and novelist, b. Plainfield, Mass. He is best remembered for his collaboration with Mark Twain on *The Gilded Age* (1873). A popular writer in his own time, Warner wrote essays, travel books, biographies, literary criticism, and a trilogy of novels.

Warner, W(illiam) Lloyd (1898–1970), US social anthropologist, b. Redlands, Calif. Using the methods of anthropological fieldwork, Warner and a team of researchers studied Newburyport, Mass., and produced the Yankee City series of books in the 1940s and 50s, which received attention for their concept of class. Among his other books are *A Black Civilization* (1937) and *Social Class in America* (1949).

War of 1812 (1812–15), conflict between the United States and Great Britain. Since the beginning of the French Revolutionary wars in 1793, both France and Great Britain had made depredations on US merchant ships. British impressment of US sailors to serve on British warships was especially galling to the United States, and anti-British sentiments increased. In addition, southern and western politicians looked upon war with Britain as offering a chance to expand US territory into Canada and into Spanish Florida, which was under the protection of Britain. War was also looked upon as

a way of ending British support of western Indian tribes, who were a constant threat to the American settlements in the West. New England, which was economically dependent on trade with Great Britain, was less enthusiastic about the war. The War Hawks—as the followers of John C. Calhoun and Henry Clay were called—prevailed, and on June 18, 1812, Congress declared war on Great Britain. Early efforts by the US forces to take Canada from the British were met with resounding defeats, pointing out to Pres. James Madison the serious weakness of the US army and the ineptitude of its generals. The small US navy, on the other hand, made a better showing for itself, particularly the triumphs of the U.S.S. *Constitution.* US privateers, under government commissions, won impressive prizes of British merchant ships.

By 1813, however, the large and powerful British navy had reasserted itself and had established an efficient blockade of the US coast. That blockade further hurt New England economic interests and aggravated that region's opposition to "Mr. Madison's War." In 1813, however, Commodore Oliver Perry won an impressive naval victory over the British in Lake Erie in September. That in turn led to a land victory by Gen. William Henry Harrison at the Battle of the Thames in Canada. In July 1814 both sides suffered large casualties in the Battle of Lundy's Lake, Ontario.

A more efficient US command was also beginning to be felt in the South. In March 1814, Gen. Andrew Jackson won an impressive victory over the British and their Indian allies at the Battle of Horseshoe Bend in Alabama. In August 1814 a British force landed at Bladensburg, Md., and after a victory there, marched almost unopposed on Washington, D.C. In the most humiliating defeat of the war, the Americans quickly evacuated the capital, with President Madison and the cabinet sent fleeing into the countryside. The British entered and burned the city.

The limited US successes of 1814, however, permitted truce negotiations to begin at Ghent, Belgium, in August 1814. In both nations, organized antiwar groups were becoming more powerful. British shipping interests, continuing to be hurt by the US privateers, pressured the British government to end the war. In New England war opponents, meeting at Hartford, Conn., openly discussed secession from the nation. The Hartford Convention, which they issued, was more moderate in tone but still expressly opposed the war. On Dec. 24, 1814, the negotiators at Ghent reached a truce, but the most spectacular battle of the war was still to take place. On January 8, 1815, before news of the truce had reached the United States, Gen. Andrew Jackson won a resounding victory in the Battle of New Orleans. It was victory that did much to rescue US pride in a war that otherwise had given the Americans more humiliations than victories.

Neither the war nor the Treaty of Ghent settled any of the problems that had originally led to hostilities. Perhaps its only accomplishment, from the US point of view, was that it gave the American people a sense of nationhood and convinced them that the new nation was ready to take its place alongside the major powers of Europe. *See also* Ghent, Treaty of; Hartford Convention; Lake Erie, Battle of.

War of Succession, Austrian. *See* Austrian Succession, War Of The.

War Powers, Presidential, Constitutional powers given to the president as supreme military commander. They include the power to appoint armed forces officers with consent of Senate. Congress alone is empowered to declare war, but presidents have carried out military actions without congressional approval or a formal declaration of war, as in ordering troops into Mexico, Korea, and Vietnam.

Warren, Earl (1891–1974), US jurist and chief justice of the US Supreme Court (1953–69), b. Los Angeles. He was governor of California (1943–53) and was the unsuccessful Republican candidate for vice president with Thomas E. Dewey (1948). Appointed by Pres. Dwight D. Eisenhower (1953) as chief justice of the Supreme Court, he began the "Warren Revolution" that lasted until his retirement (1969). He was less concerned with legal exactitude and more with social justice, and during his tenure brought about many social and political changes. Some of the Warren Court's noteworthy cases made segregation in the public schools unconstitutional, *Brown* v. *Board of Education of Topeka* (1954); established "one-man, one-vote" districts for apportionment in state legislatures, *Reynolds* v. *Simms* (1964); prohibited prayers in public schools, *Engel* v. *Vitale* (1962); made it obligatory that a suspect be informed of his rights, be provided with free state counsel, and given the right to remain silent, *Miranda* v. *Arizona* (1966). *See also* Supreme Court of the United States; Warren Commission.

Warren, Robert Penn (1905–), US poet and novelist, b. Guthrie, Ky. A graduate of Vanderbilt University

(1925), he was a member there of the Fugitives, a literary group that included several notable poets. In his works, he concentrates on Southern themes and characters that are usually related to actual incidents. In *All the King's Men* (1946), for example, the central character resembled Louisiana's Huey Long. The book brought him the Pulitzer Prize for literature (1947). He won the prize again (1958) for poetry for his book *Promises,* then won it a third time (1979) for the book *Now and Then: Poems 1976–1978.* Later works include the novel *A Place to Come To* (1977), *Selected Poems: 1923–1975* (1977), *Talking: Interviews 1950–1978* (1980), and a volume of poetry, *Being Here* (1980). He taught literature at Yale University (1950–56, 1961–73) until his retirement. In 1986 he was named the official poet laureate, a position created by Congress in late 1985.

Warren, city in SE Michigan, adjacent to Detroit on N, 8mi (13km) W of Lake St Clair; site of Detroit Tank Arsenal and General Motors Technical center. Industries: steel, electrical equipment, tools and dies, plastic molding. Inc. as village 1893, as city 1955. Pop. (1980) 161,134.

Warren, city in NE Ohio, 13mi (21km) NW of Youngstown; seat of Trumbull co; fertile farming area; site of Trumbull branch of Kent State University. Industries: steel, electrical equipment, automobile and truck parts, appliance wiring. Founded 1797; inc. as village 1834, as city 1869. Pop. (1980) 56,629.

Warren Commission, US committee to investigate the assassination of Pres. John F. Kennedy. Established in 1963 under the leadership of US Supreme Court Chief Justice Earl Warren, it reported its findings in 1964. The published results were highly criticized by many politicians and citizens. The report concluded that Lee Harvey Oswald acted alone when he shot Kennedy and that there was no conspiracy. In 1976, a second investigation was conducted by a committee headed by Sen. Frank Church. The assassination panel was extended through 1978 to investigate the deaths of both John F. Kennedy and Martin Luther King. The findings by the House committee were that both assassinations were probably plots.

Warrington, industrial town in NW England, on Mersey River. Industries: wire, metal goods, chemicals, soap, brewing, distilling, tanning. Pop. 68,262.

Warsaw (Warszawa), capital city of Poland, in E Poland on the Vistula River; city constitutes separate province, and is capital of Warsaw prov., which surrounds it. The largest city in Poland, its first settlements date from the 11th century. Founded 1300, it quickly became a trade center, and was made capital of Poland 1596; taken by Russia 1813; scene of Polish insurrection 1830–31: occupied by Germans WWI and WWII; returned to Poland following WWII. The Warsaw Pact (Warsaw Treaty Organization) was signed here 1955 joining E European nations in communist bloc; site of Gothic cathedral, medieval castle (Zamek), national theater and museum, University of Warsaw. Industries: heavy machinery, automobiles, chemicals, pharmaceuticals, textiles, food processing. Pop. 1,436,000.

Warsaw, Grand Duchy of, French dependency, created in 1807 by Napoleon I out of the land Prussia had received in the 2nd and 3rd partitions of Poland. Napoleon modeled its constitution on the French one and appointed a grandson of Augustus III as duke. Polish soldiers who fought with Napoleon's army hoped for independence. After Napoleon's defeat in 1815, however, about one-fourth of the area became the Grand Duchy of Poznán under Prussian control, while the rest became Congress Poland.

Warsaw Uprising. On Aug. 1, 1944, the Polish underground of Warsaw attacked the German occupation troops in the city to ensure the postwar authority of the government in exile. The breakthrough of Allied armies in France and the rapid approach of Soviet forces to the outskirts of Warsaw encouraged the resistance soldiers, but the Soviets halted their advance. The unaided Poles fought valiantly for 62 days before they were defeated. The German reprisals were savage, and the city was entirely destroyed.

Wart, raised and well-defined small growth on the outermost surface of the skin, caused by a virus. It is usually painless unless in pressure areas. Warts are considered contagious and are treated locally by chemical and electrical freezing. They often disappear spontaneously even without treatment.

Wart Hog, wild, tusked hog native to forested areas of S and E Africa. It has brownish-black skin with a crest of thin hair along the back and a long thin tail tipped by long hair. The warts, between the eyes and the tusks,

Andy Warhol

Earl Warren

Booker T. Washington

on the cheeks are prominent only on the male. Height: 2–2.5ft (61–76cm) at shoulder; weight: 200lb (90kg). Family Suidae; species *Phacochoerus aethopicus*.

Warwick, Richard Neville, Earl of (1428–71), English statesman and soldier. Known as "the kingmaker," in the Wars of the Roses he helped the Yorkists to victory at St Albans (1455) and captured Henry VI at Northampton (1460). Warwick was the real ruler of England (1461–64) in the first part of the reign of Edward IV, but, losing power, he sided with the Lancastrians and routed Edward (1470), subsequently placing Henry VI on the throne. He was killed by Edward's forces at Barnet. *See also* Roses, Wars of the.

Warwick, city in central Rhode Island, 10mi (16km) S of Providence, on Pawtuxet River and Narragansett Bay. Originally called Shawomet, for the Indian tribe from whom the land was purchased, city was renamed for Earl of Warwick; site of Rocky Point, one of oldest seaside resorts in New England. Industries: tourism, aluminum, clothing, electronic equipment. Founded 1643 by Samuel Gorton; inc. 1644 as town, 1931 as city. Pop. (1980) 87,123.

Warwickshire, county in central England; Warwick is county town; site of Shakespeare Memorial Theatre at Stratford-upon-Avon, Warwick Castle, Merevale and Stoneleigh abbeys. Industries: diversified agriculture, mining, motor vehicles, textiles. Area: 973sq mi (2,520sq mi). Pop. 2,079,799.

Wasatch Range, mountain chain extending from central Utah to SE Idaho; part of Rocky Mt system; rich in mineral deposits. Highest point is Mt Timpanogos, 12,008ft (3,662m).

Wash, The, shallow inlet of the North Sea in NE England, between Lincolnshire and Norfolk. The Witham, Welland, Nene, and Great Ouse rivers empty into it. Two deep-water channels lead to Boston and King's Lynn. Area: 22mi (35km) long by 15mi (24km) wide.

Washington, Booker Taliaferro (1856–1915), noted US educator, b. near Hale's Ford, Va. He worked his way through Hampton Institute and started teaching there in 1879. In 1881 he organized a black normal school that later became Tuskegee Institute, and he headed the school until his death. Washington became an advocate of black vocational education and gradual adjustment rather than political agitation for civil rights.

Washington, George (1732–99), 1st president of the United States, called the "Father of His Country," b. Westmoreland co, Va. In 1759 he married Martha Dandridge Custis, a widow; they had no children. Washington was born into a wealthy planter family. He became a surveyor and charted lands in western Virginia. In 1752, upon the death of his half-brother Lawrence, he inherited large estates, including Mount Vernon. That same year he became an officer in the Virginia militia. He fought in the last of the French and Indian Wars, and by the time he ended (1759) his career in the militia, he had achieved the rank of colonel and the reputation of an astute military commander.

Washington entered (1759) the Virginia House of Burgesses, where he served until 1774, when he went as a delegate to the Continental Congress. The Congress chose Washington as commander in chief of the Continental forces in the American Revolution. Against overwhelming odds, Washington was able finally to triumph over the British and in 1781 General Cornwallis surrendered to him and the independence of the new nation was assured. In 1783, Washington retired to Mount Vernon, but in 1787 he was called back to the Federal Constitutional Convention, over which he pre-

sided. After the new Constitution was adopted and ratified, Washington was elected the country's first president.

Washington's personal prestige and dignity were of incalculable benefit to the new nation. He attempted to govern in a nonpartisan manner and chose for his cabinet men of the various political groups. Soon, however, the factions coalesced into two: the Federalists under the leadership of Alexander Hamilton and the Republicans under Thomas Jefferson. Unanimously reelected, Washington in his second term followed a more conservative, Federalist line, as Hamilton became his most influential adviser. In 1797 Washington retired once more to Mount Vernon, where he died two years later, universally honored as the symbol of the new nation.

Career: Virginia State Militia, 1752–59; Virginia House of Burgesses, 1759–74; Delegate, Continental Congress, 1774–75; commander in chief, Continental forces, 1775–83; presiding delegate, Federal Constitutional Convention, 1787; president, 1789–97.

See also American Revolution; Continental Congress; Washington's Farewell Address.

Washington, state in the NW United States, on the Pacific Ocean and bordered on the N by the province of British Columbia, Canada.

Land and Economy. Puget Sound, an arm of the Pacific, extends about 125mi (201km) into the NW part of the state. It contains hundreds of islands, and its broken shoreline provides many harbors. W of the sound, the Olympic Mts dominate the Olympic Peninsula. The densely forested Cascade Range splits the state from N to S, with an average elevation of 8,000ft (2,440m). E of the Cascades, the land is largely a plateau, farming and grazing country. The Columbia River enters from Canada in the NE and flows S, turning W to form much of the state's S boundary. A number of dams on the river have created huge lakes that provide hydroelectric power and irrigation for vast areas. The Hanford plant in the SE produces nuclear fuels and power. Manufacturing is centered principally in the cities along Puget Sound. Seattle is a major port for communications with Alaska and the Pacific area.

People. Washington was settled by pioneers from other states. Canadians, Norwegians, and Swedes were the chief foreign-born elements. About 72% of the population lives in urban areas, principally in the W.

Education. There are more than 40 institutions of higher education.

History. Bruno Heceta, a Spanish navigator, discovered the mouth of the Columbia River in 1775; he laid claim to the area, and in 1791 a Spanish settlement on the coast survived for a short time. US fur traders established a post at Spokane in 1810 and at the Columbia's mouth the next year. Missionaries came to the site of Walla Walla in 1843. The region's boundary with Canada was fixed by treaty with Great Britain in 1846, and in 1848 Oregon Territory was organized, including the present states of Oregon and Washington. Washington Territory was created separately in 1848. Its natural resources in timber, furs, and fisheries spurred development. The railroad reached the area in 1883, and a few years later Seattle became the supply center for gold-seekers flocking to Alaska. WWI brought a boom to the state, especially in shipbuilding, and before and after WWII huge aircraft plants were established. The aircraft and aerospace industry continue to dominate Washington's industry, resulting in a sometimes unstable economy that the state is attempting to diversify.

PROFILE

Admitted to Union: Nov. 11, 1889; rank, 42nd
US Congressmen: Senate, 2; House of Representatives, 7

Population: 4,130,163 (1980); rank, 20th
Capital: Olympia, 27,447 (1980)
Chief cities: Seattle, 493,846; Spokane, 171,300; Tacoma, 158,501
State legislature: Senate, 49; House of Representatives, 98
Area: 68,192sq mi (176,617sq km); rank, 20th
Elevation: highest, 14,410ft (4,395m), Mt Ranier; lowest, sea level
Industries (major products): aircraft, pulp and paper, aluminum, lumber, metal products, chemicals
Agriculture (major products): wheat, dairy products, pears, apples, cattle, potatoes, sheep, blueberries, apricots
Minerals (major): sand and gravel, zinc, lead
State nickname: Evergreen State
State motto: Alki (By and By)
State bird: willow goldfinch
State flower: coast rhododendron
State tree: western hemlock

Washington, capital city of the United States, on E bank of Potomac River between Maryland and Virginia; coextensive with the District of Columbia; legislative, judicial, and administrative center of the United States. It was chosen 1790 by Pres. George Washington as site of seat of government and was planned by Major Pierre L'Enfant, French engineer. During the War of 1812, it was occupied by the British and almost totally burned. Landmarks include the White House (1792), Capitol (1793), Washington Monument (1848), Lincoln Memorial (1922), Jefferson Memorial (1943), National Archives (1935), Smithsonian Institution (1846), Library of Congress (1897), Pentagon (1943), Supreme Court, Senate, House of Representatives, National Gallery of Art, Constitution Hall, John F. Kennedy Center for the Performing Arts (1971), National Symphony Orchestra, National Shrine of the Immaculate Conception, National Science Foundation, National Aeronautics and Space Administration, numerous embassies, military installations, and professional trade, labor, and professional organization headquarters. Educational facilities include Georgetown University (1789), George Washington University (1821), Catholic University (1887), Howard University (1867), American University (1893). Inc. 1802. Pop. (1980) 637,651.

Washington, Treaty of (1871), agreement between the United States and Great Britain to submit outstanding disputes to an international arbitration commission. The disputes involved included the Alabama claims, the rights of US fishermen in Canadian waters, and the boundary between British Columbia and the state of Washington. *See also* Alabama Claims.

Washington Armament Conference (1921–22), meeting of several nations to discuss disarmament. It convened in Washington, D.C., in the hope that efforts to limit arms might prevent war. Nine treaties resulted from this conference, including the Four-Power Pacific Treaty and the Nine-Power Treaty on China. Among the nations participating were Great Britain, France, Japan, Italy, and the United States.

Washington Peace Convention (1861), effort to avert the Civil War. This convention was called by the Virginia Assembly and met in Washington, D.C. Former Pres. John Tyler chaired the meeting, at which northern, southern, and border states were represented. Its proposals were rejected.

Washington's Farewell Address (1796), speech, dated September 17, but never delivered orally, in which Pres. George Washington gave his reasons for declining a third term. He also warned against the geographical divisions encouraged by the party system and advised the nation to steer clear of permanent alliances with foreign nations. It was written with the help of John Jay and Alexander Hamilton.

Wasp, or **Hornet,** member of the families Vespidae and Sphecidae, with representatives found worldwide. These families have both social and solitary members. Some of the most common in North America are the yellowjacket, paper wasp, and mud dauber wasp. The European hornet, *Vespa crabro,* has become established in the United States. The adults feed on nectar and the larvae are fed insects. They can give a venomous sting, and do so repeatedly. *See also* Hymenoptera; Mud Dauber Wasp.

Wassermann Test, a test for syphilis devised by the German bacteriologist August von Wassermann, in which a specific reaction (the Wassermann reaction) occurring in a mixture of beef heart extract, animal serum, and washed red blood cells, and the patient's serum indicates the presence of the disease.

Waste Disposal, Chemical. Chemical water products of industry contain many toxic substances. The safe disposal of these wastes involves such methods as burial in lined dumps that do not leak. However, no truly safe method of chemical waste disposal has been devised, and there is little agreement about regulating conditions of disposal. The leakage of toxic wastes from the Love Canal dump in New York State was an instance of the inadequacy of waste disposal procedures. *See also* Love Canal.

Waste Disposal, Nuclear. Fission reactors and their fuel preparation plants produce waste residues containing highly radioactive substances. After uranium, plutonium, and any other useful fission products have been removed some long-lived radioactive products remain, such as cesium-137 and strontium-90. These wastes have to be disposed of so that they will not contaminate the earth, seas, or atmosphere. International regulations exist for disposing of the wastes, separate regulations applying to liquids, gases, and solids. In general, disposal consists of burying the materials under controlled conditions in underground tanks, in disused mines, and in the sea.

Waste Land, The (1922), poem by T. S. Eliot. In 434 lines it sums up the disillusionment and moral disgust of the post-World War I generation with the barrenness and corruption of modern civilization. Influenced by the French Symbolist movement, in it Eliot used dense literary and mythological allusions and a difficult structure, as well as providing his own set of explanatory notes. Originally a controversial work, it quickly became an accepted and honored part of modern literature.

Water, odorless colorless liquid that covers about 70% of the Earth's surface and is the most widely used solvent. It is a compound of hydrogen and oxygen (H_2O) with the two H-O links of the molecule forming an angle of 105°. This asymmetry results in polar properties and a force of attraction (hydrogen bond) between opposite ends of neighboring molecules. These forces maintain the substance as a liquid, in spite of its low molecular weight, and account for its unusual property of having its maximum density at 4°C. Properties: sp gr (4°C) 1.0000; melt. pt. 32°F (0°C); boil. pt. 212°F (100°C).

Water Bearer, The. *See* Aquarius.

Water Beetle, aquatic beetle, especially predaceous diving beetle (Family Dytiscidae); water scavenger beetle (Family Hydrophilidae); or whirligig beetle (Family Gyrinidae). *See also* Diving Beetle, Water Scavenger Beetle, Whirligig Beetle.

Water Boatman, aquatic insect, gray to black, found worldwide. It is oval and flat with fringed, oarlike hind legs. It feeds on algae and microorganisms in ponds and streams and is an important fish food. Length: 0.23–0.43in (6–11mm). Family Corixidae. *See also* Hemiptera.

Waterbuck, Kob, or **Lechwe,** large, gregarious, coarse-haired antelope, native to Africa, south of the Sahara, and the Nile Valley. Some species are yellowish, others almost black, many have white markings. Long, ringed horns in males slope backwards, then curve forward at the tip. Length: 4.5–7ft (1.4–2.1m); height: 44–58in (112–147cm) high at shoulder. Family Bovidae; genus *Kobus. See also* Antelope.

Water Buffalo, or **Carabao,** large ox, widely domesticated from Egypt to the Philippines and in Hungary and S Europe; it is wild or feral in N India and Burma. Ash gray to black, with long narrow face, it has stiff, scanty hair and large, splayed hooves. Flat-fronted, ringed horns are widest of any bovid, up to 77in (195.6cm) across. Mainly a draft animal, it is also used for milk; its meat is of poor quality. Length: to 10ft (3m); height: to 6ft (1.8m); weight: to 1,760lb (800kg). Family Bovidae; species *Bubalus bubalis.*

Waterbug, Giant, aquatic bug found worldwide. It preys on other insects, tadpoles, snails, and small fish. It is a strong flier, often attracted to lights. Length: to 4in (102mm). Family Belostomatidae. *See also* Hemiptera.

Waterbury, industrial city in S Connecticut, 18mi (29km) NNW of New Haven; brass center of United States. Industries: clocks, electronics. Settled 1677; inc. 1853. Pop. (1980) 103,266.

Water Chestnut, floating, aquatic weed found in Europe and SE United States. It has diamond-shaped leaves and edible, spiny chestnutlike fruit. Its rapid growth tends to clog streams. Family Hydrocaryaceae; species *Trapa natans.* The water chestnut of Chinese cookery is the tuber of a Chinese sedge, *Eleocharis tuberosus.*

Watercolor, painting technique. In this method finely ground pigments, combined with water-soluble gums, are moistened to produce a transparent stain that is applied in washes to plain or tinted paper. The medium is an ancient one, traceable in its essentials to the papyrus paintings of early Egyptian art and the paintings, on silk or rice paper, of China and Japan.

Although used by Dürer in the late 15th century, and later by such 17th-century artists as Rembrandt and Claude Lorrain (who restricted their efforts to monochrome), its full coloristic range was not exploited in the West until the early 19th century, when it became the principal technique for English topographical painting. Still later, in the hands of such artists as J. R. Cozens, John Sell Cotman, Thomas Girtin, and J. M. W. Turner, it established the English as the great virtuosi of the form. In America, the most notable exponents of the medium were Winslow Homer and John Marin. In its pure form, watercolor painting abjures the use of opaque body colors and scratched-out highlights.

Wateree, river in central South Carolina; rises in North Carolina as Catawba River and enters South Carolina as Wateree River; flows to the Congaree River to form Santee River; used for hydroelectricity. Length: 395mi (636km).

Water Flea, tiny branchiopod crustacean, including freshwater *Daphnia,* commonly used as fish food in aquariums. The head projects from a bivalve carapace. Its long projecting antennae are used for swimming. Order Cladocera. *See also* Arthropod; Crustacean.

Waterford, town in Republic of Ireland, near mouth of Suir River; county town of County Waterford; noted for Waterford cut glass. Industries: beer, paper. Pop. 31,968.

Waterfowl, birds, including ducks, geese, swans, and South American screamers, found throughout most of the world. Large flocks migrate, often in "V"-shaped formations, from cool nesting spots to warm winter homes. All have short bills, short legs, and dense plumage underlaid by down. They engage in a complex courtship and lay large numbers of eggs. Order Anseriformes. *See also* Duck; Goose; Swan.

Watergate Affair (1972–74), US political scandal involving the Nixon administration. It was precipitated by an attempted burglary on Democratic party's national offices, by persons working for President Nixon's reelection committee. The administration's efforts to cover up the connection provoked Senate and Justice Department investigations and ultimately implicated the president. Impeachment proceedings against him were begun (1973). In August 1974, after being forced by a Supreme Court ruling to relinquish tape recordings that attested to his involvement in the coverup, Nixon resigned. Although Nixon was pardoned by his successor, Gerald Ford, other administration members were prosecuted and convicted.

Water Hyacinth, plant of the Pickerelweed family native to tropical America and considered weeds in Florida. They have swollen, floating petioles and spikes of violet flowers. Species *Eichhornia crassipes.*

Waterlily, aquatic plant widely distributed in temperate and tropical regions. They have thick perennial rootstocks and showy flowers of white, pink, red, blue, or yellow. Family Nymphaceae; genera *Nymphaea, Nuphar,* and *Nelumbo.*

Waterloo, town in SE Ontario, Canada; industrial and arts center; site of Waterloo Lutheran College (1910), University of Waterloo (1959). Industries: metal products, furniture, distilleries, plastics, mushrooms. Settled by Mennonites from Pennsylvania 1800–05. Pop. 37,245.

Waterloo, city in NE Iowa, on Cedar River 52mi (84km) NW of Cedar Rapids; seat of Black Hawk co; scene of annual National Dairy Cattle Congress. Industries: tractors, meat packing, dairying. Founded 1845 as Prairie Rapids Crossing; renamed 1851; inc. 1868. Pop. (1980) 75,985.

Waterloo, Battle of (1815), last battle of the Napoleonic Wars. The French under Napoleon and Marshal Ney hoped to defeat the Allies by preventing the Prussians under General von Blücher from joining Arthur Wellesley, future duke of Wellington, and the British. The Prussians were defeated at Ligny, but the British drove back the French at Quatre Bras and took up position near Waterloo, now in Belgium. On June 18, Napoleon delayed his attack on the British until midday. By the evening the Prussians had arrived, and Napoleon was finally routed. *See also* Wellington, Duke of.

Watermelon, trailing annual vine native to tropical Africa and Asia and cultivated in warm areas of the United States. Its fruit has a hard, greenish rind, sweet, red, juicy flesh, and many seeds. Family Cucurbitaceae; species *Citrullus vulgaris. See also* Gourd.

Water Mite, bright red to green aquatic mite found worldwide. The larva is parasitic on aquatic insects and most nymphs and adults are predators. Length: 0.25in (6mm). Order Acari; suborder Prostigmata. *See also* Mite.

Water Moccasin, or cottonmouth, venomous semiaquatic pit viper of SE United States, closely related to the copperheads. It is olive, black, or brown with indistinct bands and a paler belly. It vibrates its tail and holds its white mouth open when excited. Length: to 4ft (1.2m). Family Viperidae; species *Ancistrodon piscivorus.*

Water Monster. *See* Hydra.

Water of Crystallization, definite molecular proportion of water that is chemically combined with certain substances in the crystalline state. Much of this water will be lost on heating to about 100°C but some, the water of constitution, will be retained to a much higher temperature. Cupric sulfate ($CuSO_4 \cdot 5H_2O$), for example, loses four molecules of water at 100°C, becoming $CuSO_4 \cdot H_2O$.

Water Pollution, Oil, the effect of an oil spill from a tanker, an undersea well, or a coastal refinery. It does much damage to sea birds, estuarine ecosystems, and the plankton in the waters which are a major source of global oxygen. There is ongoing research in the areas of prevention and removal of spills.

Water Pollution, Sewage, the result of domestic wastewater discharged directly into waterways. Sewage encompasses all kitchen, body, laundry, and household cleaning wastes. All these waters are rich in nitrogen compounds and bacteria. The result is the spread of waterborne disease and the degradation of the receiving waters.

Water Pollution, Thermal, results from the use of water as a cooling agent in some industrial processes. Increased temperature reduces the capacity of water to carry oxygen. This interferes with organisms living in the water. Thermal pollution becomes a problem when small bodies of water are affected. This is often a problem in nuclear power plant location.

Water Polo, a swimming sport that employs features of basketball, hockey, football, and soccer. It is played by 2 teams of 7 persons each in a pool 57–90ft (17.4–27.5m) long and a maximum of 60ft (18.3m) wide. At each end of the pool is a net-enclosed goal, which one of the players defends. Only one hand may be used to advance the leather-covered ball, which is about 27 inches (68.6cm) in circumference, and the ball must be kept on the surface. It is a rough game where players may be held under water. The game as played in the United States uses six-man teams, a larger pool, and a smaller ball, which is allowed to be carried under water, resulting in much rougher play. The game originated in England in 1870, and was introduced in the United States in 1897. It has been an Olympic Games event since 1900.

Water Power, mechanical power derived from the fall or rush of water striking water-wheel paddles or buckets. It has been used over the years as a means of powering grain and sawmills and some factories. At present, water power is used to turn large electric tur-

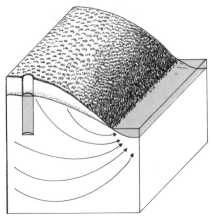

Water table

James Watson

Jean Watteau: Love Disarmed

bine generators. Large, deep reservoirs, such as Grand Coulee and Hoover dams, are established as sources of potential energy for generating power for millions of users. *See also* Hydroelectricity; Power Plant.

Water Scavenger Beetle, oval, dark-colored, aquatic beetle that eats decaying plant and animal matter. It is distinguished from the predaceous diving beetle by its club-shaped antennae. Length: to 2in (5cm). Family Hydrophilidae. *See also* Diving Beetle.

Water Scorpion, brown aquatic bug found worldwide. It has long, slender breathing tubes, grasping front legs, and will bite humans if disturbed. Width: 1–1.5in (25–38mm). Family Nepidae. *See also* Hemiptera.

Watershed, originally a term signifying the line, ridge, or summit of high ground separating two drainage basins. Watershed lines were often used as boundary lines. Watershed has come to mean the region drained by a stream, lake, or other body of water.

Water Skiing, water sport that began in France in the 1920s, in which a person rides on skis on the surface of the water while being towed by a motor-driven boat. Competition skiing usually includes three events—slalom, jumping, and trick riding. Skis must be 4 feet (1.2m) long and 4–8 inches (10.2–20.3cm) wide. In the slalom, skiers are towed through a series of staggered buoys and must ski outside each of them. In jumping, the skiers must ski over an inclined wooden ramp 6 feet (1.8m) high and 20–22 feet (6.1–6.7m) long. Trick riding has no set pattern, and the skiers choose their own intricate routines.

Water Snake, any of numerous races of about 50 species of harmless, semiaquatic snakes found on all continents except South America. Most are heavy-bodied and brown with blotches, streaks, or cross-bands. Length: to 4.5ft (1.4m). Family Colubridae.

Watersnake Constellation. *See* Hydra.

Water Strider, or **pond skater,** dark-brown to black aquatic insect found worldwide. Traveling in groups, it has long legs used to glide on the surface of calm waters. Members of the genus *Halobates* are often found far out at sea. Length: 0.3–1in (8–25mm). Family Gerridae. *See also* Hemiptera.

Water Table, the surface between an upper level, the zone of aeration, and a lower level, the zone of saturation. In the zone of aeration the open spaces are filled mainly with air. In the zone of saturation, a subsurface level, the openings are filled with water. The water table is a subdued imitation of the ground surface.

Waterton Lakes National Park, park in SW Alberta, Canada, on the US border. Park adjoins Glacier National Park in NW Montana; together they form the Waterton-Glacier International Peace Park (est. 1932 by Canadian Parliament and US Congress). The parks are connected by the Chief Mt International Highway and the Continental Divide; terrain is mountainous with numerous lakes, glaciers, hiking trails, birds, and wild flowers. *See also* Glacier National Park.

Water Treatment, the removal of undesirable elements from a water supply. Unpleasant tastes and odors are removed by aeration. Bacteria are destroyed by the addition of chlorine (the taste of chlorine is then removed with sodium sulfite). Hardness is reduced with lime or by using zeolite as a water softener. Other organic and mineral matter is removed with

alum. Fluoride is added to the water supply of many communities to reduce dental caries.

Water Vapor, water in its gaseous state, composing up to 3% by weight of the atmosphere, determining the humidity and forming clouds as it condenses. Most of the atmosphere's water vapor is found in the troposphere, half of it below an altitude of 1.25mi (2km). Water vapor absorbs infrared (long-wave) radiation strongly, holding such radiation in the atmosphere in the greenhouse effect, and plays a vital role in the transfer of energy and the Earth's heat balance.

Watson, James Dewey (1928–), US geneticist and biophysicist, b. Chicago. He is known for his role in the discovery of the molecular structure of DNA (deoxyribonucleic acid), the substance that is the basis of heredity. He shared the Nobel Prize in physiology and medicine in 1962 for his work. Watson later helped break the genetic code of the DNA base sequences and found the RNA (ribonucleic acid) messenger that transfers the DNA code to the cell's protein-forming structures. Writings include *The Double Helix* (1968).

Watson, John B(roadus) (1878–1958), US psychologist, b. Greenville, S.C. He was the founder of behaviorism in the United States. In the early 1900s he rejected mentalism and introspection and advocated a purely objective psychology that would be concerned solely with observable behavior. His work did much to make psychological research more objective and rigorous, and his point of view continues today in the work of B.F. Skinner. Among his major works are *Behaviorism* (1925); and *Psychological Care of the Infant and Child* (1928).

Watt, the unit of power in the metric meter-kilogram-second (mks) system of units. A machine consuming one joule of energy per second has a power output of one watt. One horsepower corresponds to 746 watts.

Watt, James (1736–1819), Scottish inventor. In 1765 he invented a separate condensing vessel for the steam engine. Until this time the cylinder itself was used as a condenser. Watt's invention proved to be very efficient; it used about one third the amount of steam needed in previous steam engines. From 1775–1800 he had a partnership with Matthew Boulton in the Soho Engineering Works. Their company produced steam engines on a large scale—almost 500 engines before 1800. Among Watt's other inventions were the pressure gauge (1790) and the double-action piston (1782). He coined the term *horsepower*. The units *watt* and *kilowatt* were named after him.

Watteau, Jean Antoine (1684–1721), French painter of Flemish parentage. Generally considered the preeminemt French master before the Revolution, he started his career as theatrical designer. His earliest influence was the Flemish painter David Teniers. The Flemish influence showed in pictures whose simple realism contrasted markedly with his more contrived, idealized works. Under the influence of Rubens, Titian, and Paolo Veronese, he invested his pictures with the pearlescent flesh tones and vibrant colors of those masters. His art is of historical importance because it freed French painting from its reliance on academic concepts derived from Italy, giving impetus to a Parisian style that was to prevail in France until the onset of neoclassicism.

Watts, Isaac (1674–1748), English clergyman and author. He is now remembered for his *Divine Songs for Children* (1715) and his hymns, notably "When I Survey the Wondrous Cross" and "O God Our Help in Ages Past." Watts is considered the creator of the

modern English hymn. He also published several religious and educational treatises.

Waugh, Evelyn (Arthur St John) (1903–66), English novelist. His novels, usually considered satiric, include *Decline and Fall* (1928), *Vile Bodies* (1930), *Brideshead Revisited* (1945), *The Loved One* (1948), and a trilogy about World War II: *Men at Arms* (1952), *Officers and Gentlemen* (1955), and *Unconditional Surrender* (1961).

Waukegan, port city in NE Illinois, 40mi (64km) N of Chicago. Industries: outboard motors, wire, steel, gypsum, asbestos, building materials. Founded as Little Fort on old Indian village site 1835; inc. 1849, as city 1859. Pop. (1980) 67,653.

Waukesha, city in SE Wisconsin, on Fox River; seat of Waukesha co; site of Cutler Park, containing three ancient Indian mounds; health resort, noted for mineral water 1870–early 1900s; seat of Carroll College. Industries: electronic equipment, aluminum, internal combustion engines. Settled 1835; inc. 1896. Pop. (1980) 50,319.

Wauwatosa, city in SE Wisconsin; W suburb of Milwaukee, on Menominee River. Industries: chemicals, metal, concrete, lumber. Settled 1835; inc. 1897. Pop. (1980) 51,308.

Wave, in oceanography, a moving disturbance traveling on or through water but which does not move the water itself. Wind causes waves by frictional drag. Waves not under pressure of strong winds are called swells. Waves begin to break on shore or "feel bottom" when they reach a depth shallower than half the wave's length. When the water depth is 1 1/3 times the wave height, the wave front is so steep that the top falls over and the wave breaks. The wave activity between the line of breakers and the shore is called the surf or swash. As the water moves up the beach, it loses its energy and then flows back into the water; the backward flow is called the backwash.

Wave, in physics, vibrating disturbance, either continuous or transient, by which energy is transmitted through a medium at a velocity dependent on the type of wave and on the medium. Electromagnetic waves, such as light, consist of varying magnetic and electric fields vibrating at right angles to each other and to the direction of motion; they are transverse waves. Sound waves are transmitted by the vibrations of the particles of the medium itself, the vibrations being in the direction of wave motion; they are longitudinal waves. Thus sound waves, unlike electromagnetic waves, cannot travel through a vacuum and cannot undergo polarization. Both types of waves can be reflected, refracted, and can give rise to interference phenomena. A wave is characterized by its wavelength or frequency, the velocity of wave motion being the product of wavelength and frequency. The velocity of electromagnetic waves greatly exceeds that of sound.

Wave Amplitude, peak (maximum or minimum) value of a periodically varying quantity, such as an alternating current or voltage or an electromagnetic wave.

Wave Dispersion, variation of the index of refraction of a medium with wavelength. It occurs with all electromagnetic waves but is most obvious at optical wavelengths, causing light to be separated into its component colors. This can be achieved by passing a light beam through a refracting medium, such as a glass prism. As every spectral color has a different wavelength, each color present in the light is refracted by a different amount, red (high wavelength) being bent less than violet (low wavelength), and the emergent beam is colored. Dispersion is used to produce spectra but causes chromatic aberration in lens images.

Wave Frequency (symbol ν or *f*), number of complete oscillations or wave cycles in unit time of a vibrating system; measured in hertz. For a wave it is given by wave velocity divided by wavelength. By quantum theory the frequency of electromagnetic radiation is proportional to the energy of the component photons. The characteristics of electromagnetic radiation depend on the frequency.

Wave Front, contour, which may be plane, spherical, etc, and which is usually at right angles to the direction of wave motion, on which every point is vibrating in step (that is, in phase). Each point is a source of secondary wavelets, the forward vibration limits of which give the wave front position a short time later.

Wave Interference, phenomenon in which two waves of the same wavelength and in step (in phase) at their source interact at a point, having traveled along different paths. The amplitude of the overlapping waves is the sum of the individual amplitudes: two maxima or two minima will reinforce each other and the amplitude is doubled; a maximum and a minimum cancel, producing zero amplitude. With two light waves, such as two identical laser beams, an interference pattern of light and dark bands or rings can be seen on a screen in the overlap region.

Wavelength (symbol λ), distance between two similar and successive points, that is, points having the same phase, of an electromagnetic wave, sound wave, etc, as between two successive points of maximum displacement. It is equal to the wave velocity divided by the wave frequency.

Wavell, Archibald Percival Wavell, 1st Earl of (1883–1950), British field marshal. He fought in South Africa, France, and Palestine. As commander in chief for the Middle East (1939), he defeated the Italians in North and East Africa (1940–41) but was forced back by the Germans under Field Marshal Rommel (1941). He subsequently commanded forces in Southeast Asia but lost Malaya, Singapore, and Burma to the Japanese (1941–42). He became viceroy and governor-general of India (1943–47).

Wax, solid non-greasy insoluble substances of low melting point. They are of three kinds: Animal and vegetable waxes are simple lipids consisting of esters of the higher fatty acids with monohydric alcohols; examples are beeswax and spermaceti (animal) and carnauba and candelilla (vegetable). Mineral waxes, such as paraffin and montan, are esters of the higher hydrocarbons. Synthetic waxes are of diverse origins and include polyethylenes and chloronaphthalenes. They are all used in the manufacture of polishes, cosmetics, candles, etc.

Waxwing. *See* Cedar Waxwing.

Wayne, Anthony (1745–96), US general, b. Waynesboro, Pa. Called "Mad Anthony" because of his daring, he served under George Washington in the Revolutionary War campaigns around New York and Pennsylvania and in 1779 he led the successful night attack on Stony Point, N.Y. In 1781–83 he fought in the South. In the West after the war he defeated the Ohio Indians in the Battle of Fallen Timbers (1794) and signed the Treaty of Greenville, the first treaty in which Indian title to US lands was recognized.

Wayne, John (1907–79), US film star, one of the most successful in film history. He debuted in *Salute* (1929), was a Western player of the 1930s, and became a major Hollywood star in the 1940s. He won a Best Actor Academy Award for *True Grit* (1969), one of the many Western films he is identified with. *The Shootist* (1976) was his last movie.

Weakfish, or squeteague, common sea trout, commercial and game marine fish found in tropical and temperate waters. Dark gray and blue with black spots, soft mouth with a fishing hook easily tearing it. Weight; to 16lb (7.3kg). Family Sciaenidae; species *Cynoscion regalis.*

Weak Interaction. *See* Interaction, Nuclear.

Weaponry. *See* Nuclear Weapons.

Weasel, small, carnivorous, mostly ground-dwelling mammal native to Eurasia, N Africa, and North and South America. Most have small heads, long necks, slender bodies, and short legs. Reddish-brown with light underparts, some turn all white in winter. They are fierce predators and often attack much larger animals. Although they destroy domestic poultry, weasels are one of the most effective forms of rodent control. The dwarf weasel is the smallest, the wolverine the largest. Length: 6–40in (15–102cm). Family Mustelidae; genus *Mustela.*

Weather, the state of the atmosphere in a given locality or over a broad area, particularly as it affects human activities. Weather refers to short-term states of minutes or hours as opposed to long-term climatic conditions. Weather involves such elements as atmospheric temperature, pressure, humidity, precipitation, cloudiness, brightness, visibility, and wind. Many of these are shown on weather maps and are accurately measured by weathermen, or meteorologists, by means of instruments on satellites, balloons, or at radar and weather stations. *See also* Climate; Meteorology; Weather Map; Weather Modification; Weather Observations.

Weather Forecasting, prediction of features and effects of the weather, such as temperature, precipitation, storms and fair weather, travel and sea conditions, by means of data from many observations gathered from weather stations and using a variety of computational and mapping techniques.

Weather Maps, charts made up by meteorologists of weather elements and conditions over wide areas, such as the whole United States or Europe, to assist them in their forecasts and to inform the public. Made up for surface or upper-level atmospheric conditions, such maps often show wind speed and direction, isotherms (lines of constant temperature), isobars (lines of constant pressure) depicting high- and low-pressure areas, ridges, and troughs, various kinds of fronts and the cyclones and anticyclones associated with them, and types of precipitation expected. *See also* Weather; Weather Forecasting.

Weather Modification, changing of natural weather conditions or systems by man, still on a largely experimental basis. Greater knowledge of precipitation has led to many cloud-seeding experiments to increase or decrease rain or snow in local areas. Overseeding of hail-spawning clouds and of thunderstorms has been attempted but reduction in hail or lightning suppression is difficult to measure. Attempts to reduce the severity of hurricanes by seeding the walls around the center have yielded controversial results. Cold fogs can be dissipated somewhat by seeding, however, and warm fogs by heating. Techniques for weather modification are still in their infancy. *See also* Cloud Seeding; Weather.

Weather Observations, furnishing the data required for weather description, analysis, and prediction from thousands of weather stations and instruments around the globe, such as ships and aircraft, balloons, and weather satellites. Weather stations measure and record weather conditions in their vicinity and survey with radar up to 100 to 200 mi. (161 to 320 km). Upper-air conditions are obtained from radiosonde balloons reporting instrument readings, from high-flying aircraft, and from stratospheric balloons operating for long periods at heights up to 20mi. (32km). Weather satellites, in polar orbits covering the whole Earth rotating under them, or observing the development of conditions from stationary orbits above the equator, obtain day and night observations in visible and infrared wavelengths. They provide pictures of cloud cover and storm disturbances as well as data on vertical temperature and moisture profiles of the atmosphere, making more accurate long-term weather forecasts possible.

Weaver, James Baird (1833–1912), US political leader, b. Dayton, Ohio. A Union Army hero in the Civil War, he received the post of federal assessor of internal revenue in Iowa after the war (1867–73). Initially a Republican, he joined the Greenback party and served in the House of Representatives (1879–81; 1885–89). He was the Greenback's presidential candidate (1880) and that of the Populist party (1892), when he polled over 1,000,000 votes.

Weaver, John (1673–1760), English dancer. One of the most prominent figures in the English School of dance and ballet, he was famous for his role as the clown in the English pantomime. He was the first producer of pantomime ballet. His first production was *The Tavern Bilkers,* played at the Drury Lane Theater in 1702.

Weaverbird, short-billed, arboreal, and ground-dwelling birds known for their sophisticated nesting habits. Some build "play" nests, some let foster parents raise their young, and some weave complex nests. The family includes the common house sparrow and other Old World sparrows; African weavers, the destructive red-billed quelea of tropical Africa; and African widow birds whose ornamented males are polygamous. The sociable weaver *(Philetarius socius)* of Africa builds an apartment-house nest. With a group, it erects a canopy high in an isolated grassland tree, weaves straw and grass into retort-shaped chambers for each pair, and constructs vertical tunnels from the egg chambers. Family Ploceidae.

Webb, Sidney (1859–1947), and **Beatrice** (1858–1943), English socialists. The Webbs were cofounders and participants in the Fabian Society of England (1884). Their position was that socialism was the "best" form of political and economic system for society to adopt. Consequently, their efforts were devoted to trying to "educate" people toward preferring socialism to capitalism. *See also* Fabian Society.

Webb-Pomerene Act (1918), US legislation repealing the anti-trust laws for export associations. It enabled US firms to be more competitive in foreign markets against foreign cartels.

Weber, Ernst (1795–1878), German physiologist. He was a pioneer in the study of sensation and perception. He laid the foundations for the branch of psychology called "psychophysics," influenced other thinkers such as Gustav Fechner, and encouraged psychology to be more scientific and methodical.

Weber, Karl Maria von (1786–1826), German composer, conductor, and pianist. He influenced Wagner and helped establish a German national style in his operas *Der Freischütz* (1820) and *Euryanthe* (1823). He also composed piano and chamber music, concertos, and the popular *Invitation to the Dance* (1819).

Weber, Max (1864–1920), German sociologist. He made vital contributions to research in the sociology of religion, the nature of authority, the rationalization of modern life, and the methodology of the social sciences. Disagreeing with the Marxist stress on economics, he emphasized the plurality and interdependence of causative factors in social action, particularly the role of values, ideologies, and individual leaders. He advanced the concept of "ideal types," generalized models of social situations as an analytical tool and insisted that the social sciences should be empirical, based on comparative social history, and free of value judgments. In political sociology he delineated traditional, charismatic, and legal-rational types of leadership. Much of his work was only published in article form in his lifetime, to be collected in book form (such as *Economy and Society,* 1922) after his death. In his most important work, *The Protestant Ethic and the Spirit of Capitalism* (1904–05), he presented the influential and controversial thesis that the asceticism fostered by Calvinism in turn fostered the rise of capitalism. He helped to draft the German constitution of 1920.

Weber, Max (1881–1961), US painter, b. Russia. He was one of the first American artists to recognize the importance of the onset of the modern movement. Early in his career he embraced Fauvist and Cubist devices and theories, but he soon turned to a less radical style derived from Cézanne, a style he later employed to produce colorful, expressionistic, rather fluidly painted scenes of New York Jewish life.

Weber, river in N Utah, rises in Uinta Mts, flows N and NW to join Ogden River at Ogden; together they flow into Great Salt Lake; source of irrigation. Length: 100mi (161km).

Webern, Anton von (1883–1945), Austrian composer, a student of Arnold Schoenberg. He adopted the 12-tone system and though his music contains relatively few works, which have never been generally popular, he influenced many other composers.

Webster, Daniel (1782–1852), US statesman and orator, b. Salisbury, N.H. He was, with John C. Calhoun and Henry Clay, one of the three great political leaders of the mid-19th century. He served in the US House of Representatives (1813–17; 1823–27) where he made his name as an orator. In the Senate (1827–41; 1845–50) and as secretary of state (1841–43; 1850–52), he was influential in maintaining the Union and in dealing with foreign countries. His great disappointment was never becoming president. He negotiated the Webster-Ashburton Treaty (1842) and supported the Compromise of 1850. *See also* Webster-Ashburton Treaty.

Webster, Noah (1758–1843). US lexicographer and author. In 1783 he published his *American Spelling Book* (popularly known as the "Blue-backed Speller"), which became a standard textbook in American schools. In 1828 he completed his monumental *American Dictionary of the English Language,* containing 70,000 words, the largest English dictionary published up to that time.

Webster-Ashburton Treaty (1842), agreement that settled the disputed northeastern boundary between

Daniel Webster

Noah Webster

Webworm

Maine and New Brunswick, named after US Sec. of State Daniel Webster and Britain's Lord Ashburton. It gave the United States about 7,000sq mi (18,130sq km) of the territory in dispute. The United States paid $150,000 to both Maine and Massachusetts to settle their claims, and Britain retained military routes between Quebec and New Brunswick. The United States received rights of navigation on the St John River, and free navigation on the St Lawrence, Detroit, and St Clair rivers. The New York and Vermont boundaries were established along with that between Lake Superior and Lake of the Woods.

Webster-Hayne Debate (1830), debate in the US Senate on the issue of the preservation of the Union. The question of restricting the sale of public land in the West opened debate on the issue of states' rights. Robert Hayne of South Carolina stated the case against federal interference and consolidation of the federal government. Daniel Webster of Massachusetts defended the federal union, saying, "Liberty and Union, now and forever, one and inseparable!"

Webworm, or sod worm, various caterpillars found worldwide in meadows and lawns feeding on grass stems, crowns, and roots. They live on webs at the base of grass. The white to yellow-brown adult moth flies in the evening; length: 0.3–0.5in (7.6–12.7mm). Family Pyralidae.

Wechsler, David (1896–), US psychologist, b. Romania. He developed several widely used intelligence tests—the Wechsler Adult Intelligence Scale (or WAIS, originated in 1939 as the Wechsler-Bellevue) and the Wechsler Intelligence Scale for Children (or WISC, originated in 1949). Among his publications are *The Measurements of Adult Intelligence* (1944) and *Wechsler Preschool and Primary Scale of Intelligence* (1967).

Wechsler Intelligence Scales, widely used intelligence tests devised by psychiatrist David Wechsler. They include the WAIS (Wechsler Adult Intelligence Scale), WISC (Wechsler Intelligence Scale for Children), and WPPSI (Wechsler Preschool and Primary Scale of Intelligence). Each test consists of 11 subtests that reveal the subject's strengths and weaknesses.

Wedgwood, Josiah (1730–95), English potter. A member of the fourth of nine generations of potters in his family, he was responsible for making a major industry of his craft. The developer of a creamy white earthenware (Queen's Ware) that largely supplanted porcelain throughout Europe, he also invented Jasper ware, for which he is best known.

Weed, Thurlow (1797–1882), US journalist and politician, b. Cairo, N.Y. He was an influential writer and became editor of the Rochester *Telegraph* (1822), purchasing the paper three years later. He was powerful in three parties, the Anti-Masons, Whigs, and Republicans. He never held office himself but helped nominate and elect presidents. During the Civil War (1861), he represented the Union cause on diplomatic missions in England and France.

Weed, uncultivated or unwanted plant usually found on wasteland and along roadsides. It produces many seeds, enabling it to colonize rapidly, crowding out other plants. Annual or perennial weeds are a threat to commercial crops because they compete for water and sunlight and harbor pests and diseases that can spread to the crop plants. Common weeds include dodder, poison ivy, poison oak, goldenrod, chickweed, and narrow- and broad-leaved plantain. Edible weeds include purslane and dandelion.

Weeping Willow. *See* Willow.

Weevil, beetle that is an agricultural pest, especially the numerous snout beetles with long, down-curved beaks for boring into plants. There are several thousand weevil species, each typically specialized for feeding on particular parts of particular plants. Family Curculionidae.

Wegener, Alfred Lothar (1880–1930), German geologist, meteorologist, and arctic explorer. In *The Origin of Continents and Oceans* (1915) he set forth his theory of continental drift. He is also noted for his expeditions to Greenland. On one of these he died.

Wei, river in China; originates in W Kansu prov., flows E to join Yellow River at its E bend. The fertile river valley has supported great populations since 1st millennium BC. Length: 537mi (865km).

Weight, the force on a body due to gravity. A body's weight W is the product of its mass and the acceleration due to gravity at that point. Mass remains constant, but weight depends on position on the Earth's surface, decreasing with increasing altitude. *See also* Gravity; Mass.

Weightlessness, the condition of a body in space, when motion is controlled by inertia and the force of gravity is neutralized. Zero gravity is the term used to describe the weightless state. Other than in space flight, weightlessness may be felt in a free-falling elevator or in an airplane flying in unpowered flight along a curved trajectory like that of an artillery shell. Spacecraft pilots have weightlessness problems (called hypogravics) such as decreased circulation of blood, less water retention in tissues and bloodstreams, and loss of muscle tone. Several protective mechanisms have been developed to combat the problems of weightlessness and others are being studied.

Weight Lifting, as a competitive sport, is popular in Europe, Egypt, Japan, Turkey, and the United States. Competitions are conducted according to weight classes that range from bantamweight to super heavyweight. In a weight-lifting meet, each participant uses three standard lifts: two-hand press, clean-and-jerk, and snatch. The man who lifts the greatest combined total of weights wins. Weight lifting was introduced at the Olympic Games in 1896, but did not become a regular event until 1920.

Weights and Measures, a system of basic measurements applied in the areas of mass, volume, length, and area and now extended to temperature, luminosity, pressure, and electric current. Uniformity and unit standards are fundamental. Uniformity requires accurate reliable standards of mass and length. A standard is the physical embodiment of a unit. The system may be evolutionary, growing out of custom, or planned, such as the modern Système International (SI) used by scientists throughout the world. The base units of this system are: length, meter; mass, kilogram; time, second; electric current, ampere; thermodynamic temperature, degrees Kelvin; light intensity, candela. In the United States, the decimal system is the basis of currency, but the metric system introduced in France for other measurements in the early 19th century was rejected in favor of the English system, which used the yard (3 feet) and the avoirdupois pound (7,000 grains), for example. Standards have been fixed throughout all the US since the mid-19th century, having been established by the Office of Standard Weights and Measures, which in 1901 became the National Bureau of Standards (NBS). Within the NBS, the Institute for Basic Standards provides the basis of a consistent system of physical measurements and coordinates that system with those of other nations.

US WEIGHTS AND MEASURES

Linear Measure

12 inches	= 1 foot
3 feet	= 1 yard
5½ yards	= 1 rod
40 rods	= 1 furlong
8 furlongs	= 1 statute mile

Area Measure

144 square inches	= 1 square foot
9 square feet	= 1 square yard
30¼ square yards	= 1 square rod
160 square rods	= 1 acre
640 acres	= 1 square mile
1 mile square	= 1 section of land
6 miles square	= 1 township

Cubic Measure

1728 cubic inches	= 1 cubic foot
27 cubic feet	= 1 cubic yard

Liquid Measure

4 gills	= 1 pint
2 pints	= 1 quart
4 quarts	= 1 gallon

Dry Measure

2 pints	= 1 quart
8 quarts	= 1 peck
4 pecks	= 1 bushel

Avoirdupois Weight

27 11/32 grains	= 1 dram
16 drams	= 1 ounce
16 ounces	= 1 pound
100 pounds	= 1 hundredweight
20 hundredweights	= 1 ton

Troy Weight

24 grains	= 1 pennyweight
20 pennyweights	= 1 ounce troy
12 ounces troy	= 1 pound troy

Apothecaries' Weight

20 grains	= 1 scruple
3 scruples	= 1 dram apothecaries
8 drams apothecaries	= 1 ounce apothecaries
12 ounces apothecaries	= 1 pound apothecaries

Apothecaries' Fluid Measure

60 minims	= 1 fluid dram
8 fluid drams	= 1 fluid ounce
16 fluid ounces	= 1 pint
2 pints	= 1 quart
4 quarts	= 1 gallon

METRIC WEIGHTS AND MEASURES

Linear Measure

10 millimeters	= 1 centimeter
10 centimeters	= 1 decimeter
10 decimeters	= 1 meter
10 meters	= 1 dekameter
10 dekameters	= 1 hectometer
10 hectometers	= 1 kilometer

Area Measure

100 sq. millimeters	= 1 sq. centimeter
10,000 sq. centimeters	= 1 sq. meter
100 sq. meters	= 1 are
100 ares	= 1 hectare
100 hectares	= 1 sq. kilometer

Volume Measure

1000 milliliters	= 1 liter
100 liters	= 1 hectoliter
10 hectoliters	= 1 kiloliter

Cubic Measure

1000 cubic millimeters	= 1 cubic centimeter
1000 cubic centimeters	= 1 cubic decimeter
1000 cubic decimeters	= 1 cubic meter

Weight
1000 milligrams=1 gram
1000 grams=1 kilogram
1000 kilograms=1 metric ton

CONVERSION TABLES

Linear Measure
1 inch=2.5400 centimeters
1 foot=0.3048 meters
1 mile=1.6093 kilometers
1 centimeter=0.3937 inch
1 meter=39.37 inches
3.2808 feet
1 kilometer=0.6214 mile

Area Measure
1 square inch=6.4516 square centimeters
1 square foot=0.0929 square meter
1 square mile=2.5900 square kilometers
1 acre=0.4047 hectare
1 square centimeter=0.1550 square inch
1 square meter=10.7639 square feet
1 hectare=2.4711 acres
1 square kilometer=0.3861 square mile

Cubic Measure
1 cubic inch=16.3871 cubic centimeters
1 cubic yard=0.7646 cubic meter
1 cubic centimeter=0.06102 cubic inch
1 cubic meter=1.3080 cubic yards

Liquid Measure
1 ounce=29.5727 milliliters
1 quart=0.9463 liter
1 milliliter=0.0338 fl. ounce
1 liter=1.0567 quarts

Dry Measure
1 pint=0.5506 liter
1 peck=8.8095 liters
1 liter=1.8162 pints
1 dekaliter=1.1351 pecks

Avoirdupois Weight
1 grain=64.7989 milligrams
1 avoirdupois ounce=28.3495 grams
1 avoirdupois pound=0.4536 kilogram
1 milligram=0.0154 grain
1 gram=0.0353 avoirdupois ounce
1 kilogram=2.2046 avoirdupois pounds

Mariner's Measure
6 feet=1 fathom
1012.7 fathoms=1 nautical mile
3 nautical miles=1 marine league
1 nautical mile per hour=1 knot (measure of speed)

Weil, Simone (1909–43), French philosopher. She became a teacher and also wrote for Socialist and Communist journals. In ill health, she began to study Bible and Hindu teachings, and became a Roman Catholic. She wrote *Waiting for God* (1951) and *Oppression and Liberty* (1958).

Weill, Kurt (1900–50) German composer noted for his satirical operas *The Rise and Fall of the City of Mahagonny* (1927) and *The Threepenny Opera* (1928) done in collaboration with Bertolt Brecht and for the music for a number of Broadway shows.

Weil's Disease. *See* Leptospirosis.

Weimar, city in central East Germany, 13mi (21km) E of Erfurt. City was capital of duchy of Saxe-Weimar 1547–1918; Weimar Republic was est. 1919 by German National Assembly, and abolished by its Chancellor, Adolf Hitler 1933, to establish his dictatorship; cultural center, home of Goethe and Schiller in late 18th century; site of Goethe National Museum, Liszt Museum, Weimar Castle. Industries: farm tools, building materials, chemicals, furniture. Founded 975; chartered 1348. Pop. 63,689.

Weimaraner, hunting dog (sporting group) originally used on big game by nobles of Weimar court; brought to US in 1929. A dog of speed and endurance, it has a long, aristocratic head; light amber, gray, or blue-gray eyes; slightly folded, high-set, lobular ears; medium-length body; straight forelegs and well-angulated hind legs; webbed feet; and tail docked to 6in (15cm). The short, sleek coat is mouse or silver-gray. Average size: 23–27in (58.5–68.5cm) high at shoulder; 55–85lb (25–38.5kg). *See also* Sporting Dog.

Weimar Republic (1919–33), the German federal republic set up after World War I, with a constitution that provided for a democratically elected president and a Reichstag of deputies. Forced by the Allies to agree to the humiliating demands of the Versailles Treaty and financially crippled by demands for reparations that could not be met, the Weimar governments were convulsed by a succession of economic and political crises, which facilitated the rise of extremist groups such as the Nazis. It was abolished by the Nazis in 1933.

Weir, Julian Alden (1852–1919), US painter and etcher, b. West Point, N.Y. An Impressionist, he was the founder of "The Ten," a group of like-minded artists including George Wesley Bellows and John Henry Twachtman.

Weismann, August (1834–1914), German biologist. His book discussing the germ plasm theory, *The Continuity of the Germ Plasm* (1885), proposed the immortality of the germ line cells as opposed to body cells and was influential in the development of modern genetic study.

Weizmann, Chaim (1874–1952), the first president of the State of Israel, was a Zionist leader as well as a noted chemist. He believed Zionism must be political, practical, and cultural. During World War I he had a large role in persuading the British government to agree to the establishment of a Jewish national home in Palestine. From 1920–29 and 1935–46, he served as president of the World Zionist Organization. He was president of Israel from 1949 until his death in 1952. He strove for cooperation with the Arabs.

Weld, Theodore Dwight (1803–95), US abolitionist, b. Hampton, Conn. In 1833 he helped to organize the American Anti-Slavery Society. Trained as a minister, he organized anti-slavery debates that led to his dismissal from the seminary (1834). From the students, he chose a group that he had trained, by 1836, as agents for the American Anti-Slavery Society. In the 1840s he retired from public life, his voice ruined by constant preaching. He taught in Massachusetts and New Jersey and continued to concern himself with social reform issues.

Weld Dye. *See* Dye.

Welding, a technique for joining metallic parts by applying heat or pressure. A number of processes have been developed to accommodate the physical properties of the materials involved and the use to which they are applied. Arc welding, which employs a continuous supply of electric current, is most important for joining steel. Fusion welding involves generating sufficient heat either by electricity or gas to create and maintain a pool of molten metal. Resistance, or spot, welding, a process in which the heat is generated at the interface by the electrical resistance of the joint, requires little time and uses low-voltage, high-current power. Spot welds are made at regular intervals on sheet metal that has an overlap. *See also* Brazing.

Welfare Economics, branch of economics dealing with the maximizing of the total utility or welfare of the society through the economic system, which became a separate discipline with A.C. Pigou's *The Economics of Welfare* (1920). Welfare economics also includes the study of optimizing resource allocations and the distribution of goods and services in order to achieve the maximum level of satisfaction for the sum of all members of society.

Welfare State, nation in which the government assumes the responsibility for the welfare of its citizens. Several European countries are welfare states. Beginning with some of the legislation of the New Deal of Pres. Franklin D. Roosevelt, the United States has had many of the features of a welfare state, such as social security and unemployment insurance. Public medical care, care of the aged and handicapped, retirement benefits, and income redistribution are other characteristics of the welfare state.

Welkom, planned city in Republic of South Africa; commercial center for nearby mines. Founded 1947. Pop. 137,400.

Welland, town in S Ontario, Canada, on the Welland Canal; capital of Welland co. Industries: textiles, fertilizer, wine, iron, stainless steel. Inc. 1917. Pop. 45,047.

Welland Ship Canal, canal in S Ontario, Canada; first built with 25 locks, 1824–33; rebuilt with 8 locks for shipping, 1912–32; connects Port Colborne on Lake Erie to Port Weller on Lake Ontario. Length: 27.6mi (44.4km).

Weller, Thomas Huckle (1915–), US bacteriologist and virologist, b. Ann Arbor, Mich. He shared the 1954 Nobel Prize in physiology or medicine with John F. Enders and Frederick C. Robbins for the discovery of the ability of the poliomyelitis virus to grow in cultures of various types of tissue, a finding that made possible the development of a polio vaccine.

Welles, (George) Orson (1915–85), US actor, director, and filmmaker, b. Kenosha, Wis. He is best known for his brilliant first film *Citizen Kane* (1941), a fictional life of Hearst that revolutionized cinematographic technique. Welles' clash with the studio system limited his directing and forced him to work in Europe. His other notable films include *The Magnificent Ambersons* (1942), *Journey into Fear,* and *Touch of Evil* (1958). He also acted extensively.

Wellington, Arthur Wellesley, Duke of (1769–1852), British general and statesman, b. Dublin. He entered the army in 1787 and fought in India (1796–1805), became Irish secretary (1807), commanded (1809) allied forces in the Peninsular War, and drove the French back over the Pyrenees (1814). Created duke (1814), he represented Britain at the Congress of Vienna (1814–15) and, with the Prussian general von Blücher, defeated Napoleon and the French at Waterloo (1815). He became Tory cabinet minister (1818) and prime minister (1828–30). He supported the Catholic Emancipation Act (1829), but opposed the Reform Bill (1831–32). He joined Robert Peel's cabinet (1834–35, 1841–46), and retired as chief warden of the cinque ports (1851). *See also* Waterloo, Battle of.

Wellington, capital of New Zealand, on S end of North Island, on an inlet of Pacific Ocean near Cook Strait; cultural, governmental, and educational center of New Zealand. Wellington has an excellent harbor with floating docks for ship repair and has been a rail center since the 1870s, growing into a busy commercial and industrial hub of New Zealand. City is surrounded by picturesque suburbs, and is site of National Art Gallery (1936), Dominion Museum, Victoria University of Wellington (1962), Parliament building, and government offices. Industries: textiles, machinery, food processing. Founded 1840; became capital 1865. Pop. 349,628.

Wells, H(erbert) G(eorge) (1866–1946), English author. He is best known for his science fiction, such as the novels *The Time Machine* (1895), *The Invisible Man* (1897), and and *War of the Worlds* (1898). Other novels include *Love and Mr. Lewisham* (1900) and *Tono-Bungay* (1909). He enthusiastically believed in the value of scientific progress, supported various causes, including Fabian socialism, and used fiction as a vehicle for his ideas. His nonfiction includes *The Outline Of History* (1919–1930).

Wells Fargo, an American express company. It was established in 1852 by Henry Wells and William Fargo to serve the banking and shipping needs of California miners. The company took over the failing Pony Express, and in 1866 it operated the largest stagecoach network in America. By 1888, Wells Fargo had a transcontinental rail route. In 1918 it merged with the American Railway Express Company and today operates an armored car service in the eastern United States.

Welsh Pony, light horse breed known since Saxon times in Wales. Usually a mount for older children, it has the physique of a miniature coach horse with good head and neck, short muscular body, and great endurance. Color can be gray, roan, black, bay, brown, and chestnut. Height: 40–56in (102–142cm) high at shoulder; weight: 500lb (225kg).

Welsh Springer Spaniel, water and gun dog (sporting group) found in Wales and western England for several hundred years; able to withstand temperature extremes. This medium-sized dog has a slightly domed head with a square muzzle. The small ears are low-set and hanging; body is strong and muscular; legs medium-length; tail short and low-set. The flat, thick, silky coat is dark red and white. A good guard and gentle with children, it must be trained young. Average size: 17in (43cm) high at shoulder; 30–40lb (13.5–18kg). *See also* Sporting Dog.

Welsh Terrier, sporting dog (terrier group) brought to US in 1888. An old breed also called Old English terrier, the Welsh's flat, long head appears rectangular because of chin whiskers. V-shaped ears are set high and carried forward; dark hazel eyes are small and wide-set. The short, straight body is set on straight, muscular legs; the tail is carried up. Hard, wiry, and abundant, the coat is black and tan or black grizzle, and tan. Average size: 15in (38cm) high at shoulder; 20lb (9kg). *See also* Terrier.

Welty, Eudora (1909–), US author, b. Jackson, Miss. A short-story writer and novelist, many of her works are set in her native Mississippi. Among these are *Delta Wedding* (1946), about a modern plantation family, and *The Ponder Heart* (1954), which deals with small-town life. Collections of her stories include *A Curtain of Green* (1941) and *The Golden Apples* (1949). In 1978 *The Eye of the Story,* a collection of essays and reviews, was published, followed by *Col-*

Weimaraner

Wellington, New Zealand

Franz Werfel

lected Stories of Eudora Welty (1980). Her autobiography, *One Writer's Beginnings*, was published in 1984.

Wenceslaus (1361–1419), Holy Roman emperor (1378–1400) and king of Bohemia (1378–1419), as Wenceslaus IV. His reign was characterized by wars, conspiracies, and periods of anarchy. He was deposed as emperor in 1400 by a group of rebellious princes, and his powers as Bohemian king were undermined by the challenges of his brother Sigismund.

Wen Cheng-ming (1470–1559), Chinese painter of the Ming dynasty. An exponent of *wen-jen hua* (painting of the literati), he was a pupil of Shen Chou and an innovative figure whose combinations of dry brush and wet washes influenced many successors.

Wends, or Sorbs, group of Slavonic tribes who by the Middle Ages had settled in Germany between the Elbe and Oder rivers. Over the centuries their strength was gradually diminished as the Germans either exterminated or Christianized them, although they produced a wealth of national literature at the end of the 19th century.

Werewolf, in legend, a person who can turn himself into a wolf. Throughout the world people believe in the ability possessed by some to change themselves into various animals. In Africa the fierce leopard is object of the metamorphosis, in Haiti, it is a birdlike beast. The ability to change is termed lycanthropy.

Werfel, Franz (1890–1945), Austrian dramatist, novelist, and poet. His religious, historical, and modernist dramas include *The Trojan Women* (1915), *Paulus Among the Jews* (1926), and *Jacobowsky and the Colonel* (1943). *The Forty Days of Musa Dagh* (1933), *Embezzled Heaven* (1939), *The Song of Bernadette* (1941), and *Star of the Unborn* (1946) are among Werfel's most famous novels. His popular expressionist poetry, found in *The Friend of the World* (1911) and *Each Other* (1915), expressed his love for mankind.

Wergeland, Henrik (Arnold) (1808–45), Norwegian poet. Regarded as Norway's national poet, he advocated cultural independence from Denmark. His poetry includes *Creation, Man, and Messiah* (1830), *The Jew* (1842), and *Jan van Huysum's Flowerpiece* (1840).

Werner, Abraham Gottlob (1750–1817), German geologist. He was the first to classify minerals systematically. His theory of the Earth's origins, called neptunism, posited that the Earth was originally a vast ocean from which solid rocks were precipitated to form land.

Werner, Alfred (1866–1916), German-Swiss chemist. After working with Pierre Berthelot in Paris he returned to a professorship at Zurich. In 1913 he was awarded a Nobel Prize for his coordination theory of valency.

Wertheimer, Max (1880–1943), German psychologist. He was one of the founders of the Gestalt psychology movement. His early work was on visual perception. Later he attempted to apply Gestalt principles to thinking and educational problems in such works as *Productive Thinking* (published 1945). *See also* Gestalt Psychology.

Weser, river in West Germany; formed by the junction of the Fulda and Werra rivers at Münden; flows NW to North Sea through a vast estuary near Bremerhaven. Length: 273mi (439km).

Wesley, John (1703–91), English theologian and evangelist who founded Methodism. With his brother Charles, Wesley founded the "Holy Club" at Oxford. The brothers, both clergymen, went to Georgia (1735) where the "first rudiments of the Methodist societies" were formed. There he experienced a conversion, and soon after he was preaching in the fields an extremely emotional personal sense of Christ's saving grace. In *Notes on the New Testament* Wesley's Evangelical Arminianism is clearly indicated. Methodism, as his religious views were called, spread remarkably after his return to England. His *Journal* (1739) records the great extent of his itinerant preaching, which often brought Christianity and organization to many who had not known either before.

Wessex, Anglo-Saxon kingdom, possibly settled by the Saxon Cerdic in 495. During Ceawlin's reign (560–93) it extended from the English Channel to the Thames River, between Berkshire and Devon. Resisting attack by the Danes (865), Alfred of Wessex became king (886) of all England not under Danish rule.

West, Benjamin (1738–1820), US painter. He spent most of his working life abroad, first in Italy and then in England, where he became historical painter to George III and, in 1792, president of the Royal Academy, succeeding Sir Joshua Reynolds. He was the first native-born American artist to achieve recognition in Europe. He supported himself as a portraitist while working on vast historical canvases, notable chiefly for his depictions of figures in modern dress instead of in the ancient costumes favored by the neoclassicists.

West, Morris Langlo (1916–   ), Australian novelist. He became a teacher, later served as secretary to William Morris Hughes, the former prime minister, and finally turned to writing as a career with the publication of *Gallows on the Sand* (1956). West, an award-winning novelist, wrote such international best-sellers as *The Devil's Advocate* (1959), *Shoes of the Fisherman* (1963), *The Ambassador* (1965), and *Tower of Babel* (1968). Later works include *The Navigator* (1976), *Clowns of God* (1981), and *The World is Made of Glass* (1983).

West, Nathanael (1903–40), US author, b. Nathan Weinstein in New York City. He wrote only four novels, which gained critical acclaim after his death. They are: *The Dream Life of Balso Snell* (1931); *Miss Lonelyhearts* (1933), a grimly comic story about the writer of a column for the lovelorn; *A Cool Million* (1934); and *The Day of the Locust* (1939), a macabre, surrealistic story about false dreams and failed lives in Hollywood, where West spent his last years as a scriptwriter.

West, (Dame) Rebecca (1892–1983), pseud. of Cicely Fairfield, English novelist and social and literary critic, b. Ireland. Her novels include *The Thinking Reed* (1936), *The Fountain Overflows* (1956), and *The Birds Fall Down* (1966). Her criticism includes *The Strange Necessity* (1928) and *The Count and the Castle* (1957). Her political writings include *Black Lamb and Grey Falcon* (1942), *The Meaning of Treason* (1947), and *A Train of Powder* (1955).

West Allis, city in SE Wisconsin; W suburb of Milwaukee; site of headquarters of Allis-Chalmers Manufacturing Co., producers of industrial and farm machinery; it gave its name to city 1902; scene of annual Wisconsin State Fair (est. 1892). Industries: electronic equipment, heavy machinery, generators. Settled 1827 as Honey Creek; inc. 1906. Pop. (1980) 63,982.

West Bromwich, urban district in W central England, 5mi (8km) NW of Birmingham. Industries: coal mining, metal goods, chemicals, electrical products. Pop. 166,-626.

West Covina, city in S California, W of Los Angeles. Crops: citrus fruits, walnuts. Inc. 1923. Pop. (1980) 80,094.

Westerlies, any broad currents or persistent patterns of winds from the west, such as the circumpolar and middle-latitude westerlies, reflecting the dominant west-to-east motion of the atmosphere centered over the middle latitudes of both hemispheres. *See also* Easterlies.

Western Reserve, strip of land along Lake Erie in NE Ohio claimed by Connecticut. Most of the original 13 states had claims to western lands that were relinquished. When Connecticut ceded its lands to the federal government (1786), it retained this tract of 4,000,-000 acres (1,618,800 hectares), and in 1792 awarded some of it to citizens whose property had been burned during the American Revolution. The remaining land was bought by the Connecticut Land Company (1795), which established a settlement at Cleveland. It was incorporated into the Ohio Territory (1800), under the provisions of the Northwest Ordinance (1787).

Westerns, type of popular fiction indigenous to the United States. First appearing in 19th-century dime novels and popular magazines, Westerns are adventure stories about the American West and have as principal characters cowboys, Indians, historical persons, frontiersmen, lawmen, and bandits. Owen Wister's *The Virginian* (1902) was the first Western to achieve literary fame. Westerns became very popular in films and on television in the 20th century.

Western Sahara, formerly Spanish Sahara, region in N Africa, bordered by the Atlantic Ocean (W), Morocco (N), Algeria (NE), and Mauritania (E and S). The capital is El Aaiún. A rocky, sandy desert, Western Sahara covers 102,703sq mi (266,000sq km) and contains the world's largest phosphate deposits and rich iron ore lodes. The population of 165,000 is composed of Arabs, Berbers, and black Africans, who are predominantly Muslim. Many inhabitants are pastoralists, raising goats, camels, and sheep; the cultivation of date palms, barley and fishing are also important.

History. Portuguese sailors reached the N coast in 1434, but there was little European contact until 1884, when Spain made the coast a protectorate; the boundaries were enlarged by Franco-Spanish agreements in 1900, 1904, and 1920. In the early 1970s an independence movement began to develop, and Mauritania, Morocco, and Algeria called upon Spain to relinquish control. In 1975, King Hassan II of Morocco organized a so-called Green March of 350,000 unarmed Moroccans into the area. Spain promised to relinquish its claims, and began negotiations with Morocco and Mauritania to take control of the region, despite the existence of an independence movement, the Polisario Front, and a 1974 International Court of Justice ruling calling for self-determination. Spain withdrew from Western Sahara in 1976, and Mauritania annexed the S; Morocco, the remainder. The Polisarios, backed by Algeria, began waging guerrilla war against Moroccan and Mauritanian troops. Mauritania, virtually bankrupted by the war by 1978, signed a peace treaty with the Polisarios, ceding its portion to the group; Morocco also claimed that territory and continued the war, supported with US military equipment. In 1981, King Hassan announced his support for a cease-fire plan drafted by the Organization of African Unity calling for a referendum on Western Sahara's status; fighting continued, however, as both sides disagreed on the specific points of the plan and the referendum, delayed and then promised for February 1986, did not take place.

Western Samoa, independent state in the island group of Samoa; includes Savaii, Apolima, and Manona islands. The chief islands are summits of an underwater volcanic range. The climate is tropical and wet; the islands yield yams, taro, bananas, breadfruit, papayas, coconut palms, pigs, poultry. The main industries include food processing, construction materials, furniture, tourism. The country is heavily dependent upon foreign aid.

The people are overwhelmingly of Polynesian ancestry; society is organized around the family, each larger clan group headed by a chief called a Matai, who are active in the country's central government. Some Samoans have converted to Christianity, many keep their traditional belief of animism. Communication, trade, and W influence in education has brought about social change; New Zealand est. an agricultural school and teacher's college in Western Samoa.

Western Samoa was a German protectorate from 1899 until the end of WWI when New Zealand assumed a League of Nations mandate for the islands. Independence was granted in 1962. The constitution of Western Samoa provides for a parliamentary form of government, with executive power vested in the prime minister. Most representatives to the legislative assembly are selected by the Matai; the remainder are elected by universal suffrage. In 1976, after 14 years of independence, Western Samoa became a UN member. It is a member of the South Pacific Commission and the Commonwealth of Nations.

Area, 1,133sq mi (2,937sq km); pop., 152,000; capital: Apia.

Western Wall. *See* Wailing Wall.

Westfield, city in SW Massachusetts, on Westfield River; site of Westfield State College (1839). Industries: bicycles, school furniture, boilers, textile machinery. Founded as Woronoke (1660); name changed 1669; inc. as city 1920. Pop. (1980) 36,465.

Westfield, town in NE New Jersey, 7mi (11km) W of Elizabeth. Settled as part of Elizabeth prior to 1700; inc. 1903. Pop. (1980) 30,447.

West Goths. *See* Visigoths.

West Hartford, town in central Connecticut; suburb of Hartford; site of St Joseph's College (1925), University of Hartford (1877), American School for Deaf (1817); birthplace of Noah Webster (1758). Industries: tobacco shipping, tools and dies, aircraft accessories, plastics. Settled 1679; inc. 1854. Pop. (1980) 61,301.

West Haven, suburban residential town in S Connecticut, across West River from New Haven. Industries: aircraft products, velvets, beer. Inc. 1921. Pop. (1980) 53,184.

West Highland Terrier, hunting dog (terrier group) bred in Scotland and dating from the time of King James I. Also called Westie and Highlander, this hardy dog has a broad head tapering to a large nose; small, pointed, erect ears; dark eyes under heavy eyebrows; compact, deep-chested body; short legs; and short tail carried up. Bred white to distinguish it from game, the Westie's double coat features a straight, hard outer coat. Average size: 11in (28cm) high at shoulder; 13–20lb (6–9kg). *See also* Terrier.

West Indies Associated States, status held by some British dependencies in the Leeward and Windward Islands of the Caribbean beginning in 1967. The United Kingdom is responsible for defense and foreign affairs but the islands have full internal autonomy. By the early 1980s all but one, St. Kitts-Nevis, had become independent.

West Indies Federation, single nation composed of Britain's Antillean colonies, inaugurated in 1958 with its capital in Trinidad. Political rivalries and ambitions led to the collapse of the federation in 1962.

Westinghouse, George (1846–1914), US inventor, b. Central Bridge, N.Y. During the Civil War he served in the Union navy and became interested in mechanical inventions. His first invention was a railroad "frog," a track junction device. In 1868 he invented the air brake, which made high speed rail travel safe and which is still standard equipment. He formed the Westinghouse Electric Co., a firm holding more than 400 patents dealing with rail transportation.

West Irian. *See* Irian Barat.

West Jersey, colonial proprietorship located in southwestern New Jersey. It was formed after the English seizure of New Netherland (1664), and was originally granted to Lord John Berkeley. The first English settlement was at Fenwick (1675). Besides the Dutch, Swedes, and Puritans, West Jersey also attracted Quakers because Berkeley allowed "freedom of conscience." Acquired by the Quakers (1674), with William Penn becoming part owner (1684), the land was reunited with East Jersey (1702) as royal province. *See also* East Jersey.

Westland, city in SE Michigan, 20mi (32km) W of Detroit. Pop. (1980) 84,603.

Westminster, borough of Greater London, England, comprising the City of Westminster, Paddington, and St Marylebone. The City is the seat of Great Britain's government and contains many historic buildings, such as the Houses of Parliament, Buckingham Palace, and Westminster Abbey. Pop. 214,000.

Westminster, city in S California, SE of Long Beach; near Los Alanitos Naval Air Base. Settled 1870 as a religious commune for Presbyterians; inc. 1957. Pop. (1980) 71,133.

Westminster, Statute of (1931), act of the British Parliament implementing decisions reached at sessions of the Imperial Conference. It gave legislative independence to dominions of the British Empire and declared them autonomous dominions of the Commonwealth of Nations bound together by common allegiance to the British throne.

Westminster Abbey, Anglican cathedral in London. Originally a Benedictine monastery, Elizabeth I rededicated it to St Peter (1560). The present Gothic structure dates mainly from the 13th century. Henry VII's chapel (begun 1503) and Nicholas Hawksmoor's western towers (1722–40) are notable additions. British monarchs are crowned and buried here. In the Poet's Corner (south transept) great poets are buried.

West New York, city in NE New Jersey, on Hudson River 4mi (6.4km) N of Jersey City. Industries: textiles, leather, rubber goods, silk, toys. Settled 1790; inc. 1898. Pop. (1980) 39,194.

Weston, Edward (1886–1958), US photographer, b. Highland Park, Ill. Weston began his enduring portrait of the Western landscape in 1906. He cofounded the *f*/64 group whose sharp, carefully composed images greatly influenced photographic aesthetics. His celebrated photographs of sand dunes, nudes, plants, and other natural forms are rated among the classic works in the medium.

West Orange, town in NE New Jersey, 5mi (8km) NW of Newark; "Glenmont," home of Thomas Alva Edison after 1887 (made a national monument 1961), is in nearby Llewellyn Park. Industries: electrical appliances, truck farming. Separated from Orange 1862; inc. 1900. Pop. (1980) 39,510.

West Palm Beach, winter resort city in SE Florida, on Lake Worth, 65mi (105km) N of Miami. Industries: computers, commercial fisheries. Settled 1893; inc. 1894. Pop. (1980) 62,530.

Westphalia, an area lying roughly between the valleys of the Rhine and Weser rivers, now part of West Germany. Originally belonging to Saxony, it was first separated in 1180. It was ruled as a duchy by the Elector of Cologne until 1803, was later conquered by Napoleon, and after the Congress of Vienna in 1815 was given to Prussia. The Ruhr region was occupied by the French after World War I and after heavy destruction in World War II it was in the British zone of occupation until 1946.

West Point, US military post in SE New York, on W bank of Hudson River, just SE of Storm King and Crow's Nest Mts, approx. 50mi (81km) NW of New York City. First occupied and fortified 1778 by colonists as military post during Revolution, it was site of Benedict Arnold's surrender plot (1780); seat of US Military Academy since 1802; the West Point Museum, Cadet Chapel, and Old Cadet Chapel are noteworthy buildings on post grounds. Area: 3,500acres (1,417hectares).

West River. *See* Hsi.

West Side Story, musical play with lyrics by Stephen Sondheim, music by Leonard Bernstein, book by Arthur Laurents, and choreography by Jerome Robbins, first produced on Broadway in 1959. It transferred Shakespeare's *Romeo and Juliet* story to the setting of modern New York City street gangs. It featured highly praised dance sequences as well as singing and was made into a successful film in 1961.

West Virginia, state in the E United States in the Appalachian Mt region.

Land and Economy. The Allegheny Mt ranges run NE-SW in much of the E half of the state. The W portion is a plateau dropping gradually to the Ohio River, which marks the W boundary. The state's mineral resources supply the manufacturing industries and are the mainstay of the economy. Industries are located principally in the cities along the Ohio River, which is a valuable transportation artery. Agriculture is a minor element in the state.

People. The early settlers came from states to the E. Most were of English, Scots-Irish, and German descent. Later, immigrants from Poland, Hungary, and other central European countries came to work the mines. Less than 40% of the population lives in urban areas.

Education. There are 25 institutions of higher education. West Virginia University, West Virginia State College, and West Virginia Institute of Technology are state-supported.

History. Pioneers from Virginia pushed across the mountains into the region in the late 18th century. Settlement expanded in the early 19th century, especially along the Ohio River. The area was part of the state of Virginia, but political and economic tensions arose between the new settlements and the older society to the E. When Virginia seceded in 1861, a convention of westerners who supported the Union repudiated the act. Later that year they formed a new state named Kanawha, which was admitted to the Union two years later as West Virginia. In later years, the state's fortune depended on the varying prosperity of the coal mining industry. During the 1960s the federal government began an Appalachian aid program, and increased demand led to expansion of coal mining during the early 1980s.

PROFILE

Admitted to Union: June 20, 1863; rank, 35th
US Congressmen: Senate, 2; House of Representatives, 4
Population: 1,949,644 (1980); rank, 34th
Capital: Charleston, 63,968 (1980)
Chief cities: Huntington, 63,684; Charleston; Wheeling, 43,070; Parkersburg, 39,967
State legislature: Senate, 34; House of Delegates, 100
Area: 24,181sq mi (62,629sq km); rank, 41st
Elevation: highest, 4,862ft (1,483m), Spruce Knob; lowest, 240ft (73m), Potomac River
Industries (major products): chemicals, synthetic fibers, plastics, steel, fabricated metals, glass, pottery
Agriculture (major products): poultry, dairy products, apples
Minerals (major): bituminous coal, natural gas, petroleum, salt, stone
State nickname: Mountain State
State motto: Montani Semper Liberi (Mountaineers Are Always Free)
State bird: cardinal
State flower: rhododendron maximum
State tree: sugar maple

Wethersfield, town in central Connecticut, on Connecticut River; adjoins Hartford (N). The oldest permanent settlement in state, it has many preserved buildings; the Webb House was scene of 1781 meeting between George Washington and Comte de Rochambeau to coordinate French aid to American forces. Industries: oil burners, bakery goods, tools, electrical components. Founded 1634 by settlers from Watertown, Mass.; inc. 1637. Pop. (1980) 26,013.

Wetland, marshy ground in an intertidal zone that has prolific vegetation. Coastal wetlands are said to produce more living matter per acre than any other part of the world. Protective laws have recently been passed to stop their destruction for they have come to be recognized as an important part of the oceanic food cycle.

Weyden, Rogier van der (*c.*1400–64), Flemish painter. Among the greatest of the northern European artists of his era, he is believed to have entered the workshop of Robert Campin in 1427 and to have left as an accredited master five years later. Appointed official painter of Brussels in 1435, he spent most of his career there, but in 1450 he traveled to Italy, where his style was influenced somewhat by Renaissance art. In its maturity his style was characterized by clear, subtly modulated colors; great refinement and sensitivity. He influenced the work of Dirk Bouts and Hans Memling.

Weyl, Herman (1885–1955), US mathematician, b. Germany. After holding professorships at Zurich and Göttingen he moved to Princeton University in 1933 with the advent of the Nazis. His work on geometry and relativity led to a unified field theory in which the electromagnetic and gravitational fields appear as geometric properties of space-time. His *Group Theory and Quantum Mechanics* (1928) helped form the modern views of quantum theory.

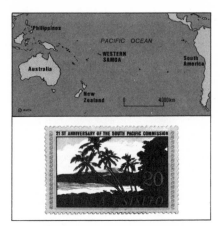

Western Samoa

George Westinghouse

Edith Wharton

Whale, aquatic, generally social mammal inhabiting all oceans and some fresh waters. They have fishlike bodies with paddle-shaped flippers for forelimbs and no external hind limbs. Easily distinguished from large fish by horizontally flattened tail fins, they have no distinct neck or external ears, and nose openings (blowholes) are on top of the head. A few bristles remain of the characteristic mammalian hair and beneath the thick smooth skin is a layer of insulating blubber.

Ranging in size from porpoises to blue whales, they are highly vocal, using sound signals for communication and for sonarlike navigation. Most have teeth and eat chiefly fish. Many large whales with no teeth have a filter of baleen (whalebone) which strains plankton from the water. Length: 4ft (1.25m) to 100ft (30m); weight: to 150 tons. Order Cetacea. *See also* Blue Whale.

Whalebone, or baleen, plates of elastic horny material making up the food-catching filter in the mouth of baleen whales. It was once used for making corset stays.

Whale Shark, largest shark, found worldwide in tropical waters. Brownish to dark gray with white or yellow spots and stripes, this docile, egg-laying fish often travels at water surface in schools. Length: 30ft (9m). Family Rhincodontidae, species *Rhincodon typus. See also* Chondrichthyes; Sharks.

Whaling, begun during the Middle Ages, this industry grew rapidly during the 18th and 19th centuries, when it was dominated by American whalers. The modern whaling era began in the 1850s with the development of harpoons with explosive heads and reached a peak after 1925, when ocean-going factory ships were sent to the Antarctic. During the next 50 years, most larger whale species, including the blue whale, were hunted to near extinction and whalers turned to smaller species. International regulation of the industry is weak, and the outlook for many species of whales is bleak.

Wharton, Edith (Newbold Jones) (1862–1937), US novelist, b. New York City. Of wealthy and socially prominent parents, she married Edward Wharton, a Boston banker in 1885; they were divorced in 1913. Her first novel, *The House of Mirth* (1905) brought her success, which continued with such outstanding works as *Ethan Frome* (1911), *The Custom of the Country* (1913), and *The Age of Innocence* (1920). The latter novel won the Pulitzer Prize in 1921. Although she often wrote of the folly and sterility of New York society, she did not limit herself to that milieu. Her work ranged from the mountain villages of New England to the battlefields of World War I.

Wheat, cereal grass originating in the Middle East. Cultivated there since 7000 BC, it is now cultivated worldwide. It has long, slender leaves, hollow stems, and flowering heads. *Triticum vulgare* is the large-grained variety used for bread; *T. durum* for pasta; and *T. compactum* for cake and pastry flour. Winter wheat is sown in the fall; spring wheat may be planted in spring or fall, depending on the area's climate. It is also used for malt, dextrose, and alcohol. Family Gramineae.

Wheat Jointworm, black, antlike, chalcid wasp, 0.08 to 0.12in (2–3mm) long, that attacks the stems of wheat. It is found in most of the wheat-growing regions of North America. Family Eurytomidae, species *Harmolita tritici. See also* Hymenoptera.

Wheaton, city in NE Illinois, W of Chicago; seat of Du Page co; site of Wheaton College (1853); headquarters of Theosophical Society of America; farming re-

gion. Settled by Jesse and Warren Wheaton 1837; inc. 1859. Pop. (1980) 43,043.

Wheaton, residential city in central Maryland; SW suburb of Baltimore. Pop. 66,247.

Wheel and Axle, a simple machine based on the principle that a small force applied to the rim of a wheel will exert a much larger force on an object attached to the axle. The mechanical advantage, or multiplication factor for the applied force, is the ratio of the diameter of the wheel to that of the axle.

Wheelchair Games, an athletic competition for permanently disabled persons, mostly performed in wheelchairs. The competition includes many track and field events in addition to bowling, basketball, table tennis, archery, swimming, weightlifting, and other specialty events, such as wheelchair slalom. The competition grew out of the many rehabilitation programs initiated for permanently injured veterans returning from World War II. The first National Wheelchair Games were held in 1957, and have since grown to include competition on an international scale where representative countries compete for gold, silver, and bronze medals. In the United States, the National Wheelchair Athletic Association supervises all events.

Wheeler, (Sir) (Robert Eric) Mortimer (1890–1976), British archeologist. A familiar figure on British television, he was noted for his excavations of Roman and pre-Roman settlements in Britain and for his explorations to the Indus Valley of Asia, as well as his contributions to the technological development of archeology. An official and director of the British Academy for many years, and twice trustee of the British Museum, he became professor at the Royal Academy in 1965, and was a fellow at University College, University of London, from 1922 until his death. He was knighted in 1952. His books include the autobiography *Still Digging* (1955) and *Flames Over Persepolis: Turning Point in History* (1968).

Wheeling, city and port of entry in N West Virginia, on Ohio River; seat of Ohio co. Settlement developed around Fort Henry (1774); scene of one of last American Revolution battles (Sept. 11–13, 1782); prospered as W terminus of National Road (1818) and Baltimore and Ohio Railroad (1852); site of Wheeling Conventions (1861–62); served as state capital 1863–70, 1875–85; site of Wheeling College (1954). Industries: steel, iron, nails, coal and natural gas mining, tobacco, plastics, textiles. Settled 1769; inc. 1836. Pop. (1980) 43,070.

Whelk, marine gastropod mollusk found along marine shores. It has a large coiled shell, smooth rim and notch at lower end. Length: 5–7in (127–177.8mm). Family Fasciolariidae; species include Japanese gourmet delicacy *Buccinum tenuissimum* and dog whelk *Nucella.*

Whigs, one of two major US political parties from 1834 to 1852. Formed out of the Federalist party when John Quincy Adams and Henry Clay joined forces against Andrew Jackson it was a coalition party drawing strength from eastern capitalists, western farmers and southern plantation owners. Its principal leaders were Clay and Daniel Webster. The party elected two presidents, William Henry Harrison (1840) and Zachary Taylor (1848). The issue of slavery generated such bitter dispute that the party disintegrated.

Whippet, sporting dog (hound group) bred in England for racing and rabbit coursing. An elegant pet that is capable of running at speeds of 35mph (56.5km); it has

a long, lean head and tapered muzzle; small ears thrown back and folded; a long-backed body with arched loin; long, powerful legs; and a long, tapering tail carried low. The close, smooth coat may be any color. Average size: 19–22in (48–56cm) high at shoulder; 20lb (9kg). *See also* Hound.

Whipple, George Hoyt (1878–76), US pathologist, b. Ashland, N.H.. He shared the 1934 Nobel Prize in physiology or medicine with George R. Minot and William P. Murphy for his work on anemia and its treatment with liver extract. *See also* Anemia.

Whippoorwill, brownish-colored migratory goatsucker that winters in Central America and breeds in E North America. It is known for its repetitive and distinctive "whip-poor-will" call. Species *Camprimulgus vociferus. See also* Goatsucker.

Whipsnake. See Coachwhip Snake.

Whirligig Beetle, medium-sized, dark-colored water beetle often seen resting or gyrating on the surface of a still pool. They prey on small insects. Family Gyrinidae.

Whirlpool, circular motion of a fluid. Whirlpools in rivers occur in regions where waterfalls or sharp breaks in topographic continuity make steady flow impossible. *See also* Vortex.

Whiskey Rebellion (1794), revolt by backwoods farmers in Pennsylvania's western counties. They refused to pay a federal excise tax for the manufacture of whiskey, which they made with surplus grain. US troops put down the riot, but the public reaction damaged the image of the Federalist party, which was responsible for the tax.

Whiskey Ring, group of US public officials and liquor distillers who defrauded the US government of liquor taxes after the Civil War. In 1875, Treasury Department agents broke up the ring and arrested the persons involved. President Grant's secretary, Orville Babcock, was indicted in the scandal but acquitted.

Whist, card game for two sets of partners, played with a standard deck. After the full deck has been distributed, the dealer turns over his last card to indicate trump. Cards rank from ace through 2. The highest card or trump wins the trick. Six tricks make a book, and each trick over the book counts one point. It requires seven points to win in the US game.

Whistler, James Abbott McNeill (1834–1903), US painter and etcher, b. Lowell, Mass. Influenced early in his career by Courbet and Velázquez and later by Japanese woodblock prints, he worked for several years in Paris, then moved to London in 1859, where he soon became known for his dandified, eccentric ways. His painting style combined subtle tonal relationships with a judicious arrangement of forms, and his pictures are characterized by their serenity, as seen in his best-known work, a portrait of his mother (Paris, Louvre). An accomplished and prolific etcher, he produced some 400 plates.

White, Byron Raymond (1917–), US jurist and lawyer, b. Fort Collins, Colo. A college and professional football player, known as "Whizzer White," he studied at Yale Law School while playing with the Detroit Lions (1940–41). Also a Rhodes scholar, he served as a law clerk for Chief Justice Vinson (1946–47), practiced law (1947–61), and served as US deputy attorney general (1961–62). In 1962 he was appointed an associate justice of the US Supreme Court by John

F. Kennedy. On the Court, he has maintained a moderate position. In 1978 he urged Congress to create a new appellate court to decide cases referred by the Supreme Court because of increased workload.

White, Edward Douglass (1845–1921), chief justice of the US Supreme Court (1910–21), b. Lafourche Parish, La. He served in the Confederate army (1861–63), and as state senator (1874–78) before being appointed judge of the state supreme court (1879–80). He served as US senator from Louisiana (1891–94) and was appointed associate justice of the US Supreme Court (1894) by President Cleveland. Appointed chief justice by President Taft, he was considered a conservative, and is best known for his "rule of reason" interpretation of the Sherman Antitrust Act, which dissolved Standard Oil Co. and the American Tobacco Co. (1911). He is also responsible for the decision upholding the constitutionality of the Adamson Act (1916), which set an eight-hour day for railroad workers.

White, E(lwyn) B(rooks) (1899–1985), US essayist and author, b. Mt. Vernon, N.Y. On the staff of *The New Yorker* (1926–1937), he wrote the "Talk of the Town" column. His humorous books for adults include *Is Sex Necessary?* (with James Thurber, 1929) and *One Man's Meat* (1942). His books for children, *Stuart Little* (1945), *Charlotte's Web* (1952) and *The Trumpet of the Swan* (1970) have become classics. Later works include *Essays of E.B. White* (1977). He received a special Pulitzer Prize (1978) "for the full body of his work."

White, Patrick (1912–), Australian writer. His first novel, *The Happy Valley,* appeared in 1939. Many of his novels are set in the Australian outback. His later works, *The Tree of Man* (1955), *Voss* (1957), *Riders in the Chariot* (1961), *The Eye of the Storm* (1974), *The Cockatoos* (1975), *A Fringe of Leaves* (1976), *The Twyborn Affair* (1980), and *Flaws in the Glass* (1982), won universal praise. In 1973 he was awarded the Nobel Prize in literature. He was also a successful dramatist.

White, Walter (1893–1955), US civil rights activist and author, b. Atlanta. As secretary of the NAACP (1918–55), he campaigned for desegregation, voting rights, and antilynching legislation. His books include *Rope and Faggot* (1929), *A Rising Wind* (1945), and the autobiography *A Man Called White* (1948).

White, William A(lanson) (1870–1937), US psychiatrist, b. Brooklyn, N.Y. He was superintendent of St Elizabeth's Hospital in Washington, D.C., from 1903 to 1937. He was a pioneer in the establishment of psychiatric training and research, and he helped psychoanalytic theory to gain acceptance in the United States. Among his works are *Essays on Psychopathology* (1925); *Insanity and the Criminal Law* (1923); and *Crimes and Criminals* (1933).

Whitebait, tropical marine fish found near Australia and New Zealand. Elongated, the scaleless fish has its dorsal fin set far back. Term whitebait is also applied to young of several types of European herring. Length: to 4in (10.2cm). Family Galaxiidae; species *Galaxias attentuatus.*

White Blood Cell. *See* Leukocyte.

White Dwarf Star, very faint hot star of planetary dimensions but with a mass comparable to that of the Sun. The results of gravitational collapse in stars not massive enough to have become supernovae, white dwarfs represent the last stage in the evolution of stars like the Sun, which, having exhausted their fuel, contract under their own weight to become over a million times denser than water. With time white dwarfs cool down to become cold dark globes. They are found on the bottom left of the Hertzsprung-Russell diagram.

White-eye, or spectacle bird, greenish bird of Old World tropical forests with a prominent ring of white feathers around the eye. It has short, rounded wings; squarish tail; straight, pointed bill; and brush-tipped, extensible tongue for feeding on nectar. It also eats insects and fruit. Bluish, greenish, or whitish eggs (3–5) are laid in a grass, spider webbing, and bark basket nest hung in a tree or bush fork. Length: 4–5in (10–12.7cm). Family Zosteropidae.

Whitefield, George (1714–70), English evangelist. An Anglican priest, he preached in the American colonies 1739–41 and figured predominantly in the Great Awakening. In London, he emerged as leader of Calvinistic Methodists (1741), breaking with John Wesley. He made several more trips to the colonies (1744–69). On his last trip he converted his Savannah, Ga., orphanage into Bethesda College (1769).

Whitefish, or **cisco,** freshwater food fish of the Northern Hemisphere, to Arctic waters. It is colored a dull silver. Length: to 59in (150cm); weight: 63lb (29kg). Species include least cisco or lake herring *Coregonus artedii.* Family Salmonidae.

Whitehead, Alfred North (1861–1947), British philosopher and mathematician. He attempted to combine his interests in mathematics, morals, and aesthetics into a comprehensive metaphysical system of scientific cosmology. This system is presented in "An Essay on Cosmology" in his *Process and Reality* (1929). His *Principia Mathematica* (3 vols., written in collaboration with Bertrand Russell, 1910–13) has had a notable influence on contemporary philosophy. Other works include *Adventures of Ideas* (1933), and *Essays in Science and Philosophy* (1947).

Whitehorse, town in Yukon, Canada, 52mi (84km) N of British Columbia border, on the Yukon River; capital of Yukon Territory; developed as trading town during the Klondike gold rush (1897–98); headquarters for the Royal Canadian Mounted Police and Air Force, and N terminus of the Alaska Highway and the White Pass and Yukon Railway. Industries: tourism, copper mining, hunting, fur trapping. Pop. 13,311.

White House, executive mansion and official residence of the US president. On an 18-acre (7.3-hectare) site chosen by George Washington, it was designed by James Hoban, made of Virginia freestone. Its cornerstone was laid in 1792. John Adams was the first president to live there (1800). Restored after being burned by the British in 1814, its name became official when Pres. Theodore Roosevelt had it engraved on his stationery. It contains the offices of the president and his staff, and is used for official entertaining and state occasions.

White Leghorn, chicken breed widely raised for egg production. A small chicken, it has yellow skin, a single comb, and lays white-shelled eggs. Weight: 6lb (2.7kg) cock; 4.5lb (2kg) hen.

White Mountains, part of Appalachian Range in N New Hampshire and SW Maine; consists of two main groups, Presidential Range and Franconia Mts, divided by Crawford Notch. White Mountain National Forest includes much of these ranges. Highest peak is Mt Washington, 6,288ft (1,918m).

White Nile, river in NE Africa; converges with the Blue Nile at Khartoum to form the Nile River; rises in Lake Victoria, flows E with the Sobat River, N through Sudan to Khartoum. Length: 2,172mi (3,497km).

White Plains, city in SE New York, between Bronx and Mamaroneck rivers. New York's provincial congress met here in 1776 to ratify Declaration of Independence; scene of American defeat at Battle of White Plains, Oct. 28, 1776, now a national battlefield site; site of College of White Plains (1923) and Elijah Miller House (George Washington's headquarters). The county seat, it contains government offices, many major corporate offices and large retail stores, and a few light industries. Settled 1683; inc. as village 1866, as city 1916. Pop. (1980) 46,999.

White Potato. *See* Potato.

White River, rises in Boston Mts, NW Arkansas, flows N to SW Missouri, SE across Arkansas to the Mississippi River. Series of dams on river have been built from 1957–65 to provide hydroelectric power. River is navigable for approx. 260mi (419km) of its 690mi (1,111km) length.

White Sands National Monument, area in S New Mexico, in Tularosa Basin between San Andres Mts (W) and Sacramento Mts (E); includes great expanse of white gypsum sand drifting into dunes. Plant and animal life show great adaptation to environment. Est. 1933. Area: 146,535 acres (59,347hectares).

White Sea, large inlet of Barents Sea on N coast of Russian SFSR, USSR, between the Kola Peninsula (W) and Kanin Peninsula (E). Mezen, Northern Dvina, and Onega rivers empty into it. Its chief port is Arkhangelsk, which is kept open by ice breakers from November to May. Herring, cod fishing, and sealing are carried on. White Sea is connected to Baltic Sea by canals. Area: 34,700sq mi (89,873sq km).

White Shark, or **man eater,** great white shark, aggressive, dangerous shark found worldwide in tropical and subtropical marine waters. Known to attack and eat man, it is grayish above and dirty white below. Its teeth are broad and triangular with sawtoothed edges. Length: to 40ft (12.2m); weight: to 7,000lb (3,180kg). Family Isuridae (also called Lamnidae); species *Carcharodon carcharias. See also* Chondrichthyes; Sharks.

White-tailed Deer, or Virginia deer, common deer found from S Canada to N South America. Its antlers have one main beam with minor branches. Full-size antlers are usually attained by the fourth year. These deer do not congregate in herds. They mate in November and December. The gestation period is seven months and two fawns are born. It is a popular game animal. Height: to 3.5ft (1.1m) high at shoulder. Family Cervidae; species *Odocoileus virginianus. See also* Deer.

White Volta, (Volta Blanche) river in W Africa; rises in Upper Volta and flows SW then S into Lake Volta, in Ghana. Length: 550mi (885km).

Whitgift, John (1530–1604). English archbishop of Canterbury. Vice-chancellor of Cambridge University (1570), he helped to revise the university statutes. In 1571 he was appointed dean of Lincoln; in 1577 he became bishop of Worcester and in 1583 archbishop of Canterbury. His vigorous persecution of Puritans enjoyed the approval of Queen Elizabeth.

Whiting, several unrelated food fish. The European whiting *Merlangius merlangus* is a haddocklike cod found in shallow E Atlantic waters from the polar cap to the coast of Spain; length: 23.6–27.6in (60–70cm). The silver hake *(Merluccius bilinearis)* is found along the Atlantic coast of the United States; length: 2.5ft (76.2cm); weight: 5lb (2.3kg). The kingfish *(Menticirrhus saxatilis)* is a dusky silver with dark side bars; length: 17in (43.2cm); weight: 3lb (1.4kg).

Whitman, Walt(er) (1819–92), US poet and essayist, recognized as the poetic spokesman of the American spirit, b. Huntington, N.Y. In 1855 he published *Leaves of Grass,* a collection of poems, the radical form and content of which brought critical disdain and left the poet with a life-long unsavory reputation. Whitman frequently revised and augmented *Leaves of Grass* over the next 35 years.

In 1865, while employed as a government clerk, he published *Drum-Taps,* reissued in 1866 with *Sequel to Drum-Taps;* both included in a later edition of *Leaves of Grass.* A collection of essays, *Democratic Vistas* (1871), was incorporated with more poems in *Two Rivulets* (1876) and published with *Leaves of Grass.* Publicity over an 1881 edition of his poems brought Whitman his first financial success, and only at the time of his death was he beginning to be recognized as an important world poet, whose work had a vital influence on contemporaries and succeeding generations alike.

Whitney, Eli (1765–1825), US inventor, b. Westborough, Mass. He went to Georgia as a teacher and became interested in the cotton industry, which was then limited by the slow, hard work of removing the seeds by hand. Whitney invented a machine to do this task after great difficulties, including manufacturing his own tools (1793). His cotton gin was stolen and patented by others, and although his claims were upheld in 1807, he was denied permission to renew his patent (1812). He received a government contract for firearms (1798) and developed a system in which interchangeable parts were manufactured and assembled by workers with little skill. His factory, in New Haven, Conn., was an early example of mass production.

Whitney, Mount, peak in E California, in the Sierra Nevada at the E edge of Sequoia National Park. Connected to Death Valley by highway. Named for US geologist Josiah D. Whitney who surveyed it in 1864. Second-highest US peak (Mt McKinley in Alaska is first), 14,494ft (4,421m).

Whittier, John Greenleaf (1807–92), US poet and editor, b. Haverhill, Mass. A Quaker, he early became involved in the abolitionist movement and much of his verse is antislavery in theme. He also wrote sentimentally of New England rural life. From 1829 he worked as an editor on various publications to support himself. His works include *Poems Written During the Progress of the Abolition Question* (1838), *Lays of My Home and Other Poems* (1843), *Voices of Freedom* (1846), *Songs of Labor* (1850), and *Among the Hills and Other Poems* (1869). Among his best-known poems are "Maud Muller," regrets for a lost love; "The Barefoot Boy" and "Snowbound," recollections of a rural boyhood; and "Barbara Frietchie," a Civil War poem.

Whittier, city in S California, 12mi (19km) ESE of Los Angeles; hometown of President Richard M. Nixon. Industries: automobile and aircraft parts, oil and steel products. Founded 1887 by Quakers; inc. 1898. Pop. (1980) 68,872.

Whittington, Richard ("Dick") (*c.* 1358–1423), English merchant. The son of a knight, he became

Walt Whitman

Eli Whitney

Thornton Wilder

wealthy dealing in fine cloths and was Lord Mayor of London (1397–99; 1406–07; 1419–20). He made loans to Henry IV and Henry V and endowed many charitable institutions. He is, however, best known as the subject of a legend and pantomime (probably dating from the early 17th century) about a poor boy who makes his fortune with the aid of his cat.

Wholesaling, marketing activity that buys and sells in relatively large quantities. Generally the wholesaler buys directly from the manufacturer and sells to retailers, to other manufacturers, to institutional and commercial users, but not normally to the ultimate consumer.

Whooping Cough, or pertussis, an acute, highly contagious childhood respiratory disease. It is caused by the bacterium *Bordetella pertussis* and marked by spasms of coughing, followed by a long-drawn intake of air, or "whoop," frequently ending with vomiting. Severe manifestations can last up to 6 weeks and serious complications used to be common. Now, immunization vaccinations are routinely administered to infants.

Whooping Crane, North American bird with shrill, buglelike call. Once close to extinction, it became the object of successful intensive preservation efforts. It nests in marshes of W Canada and migrates to winter in S United States. It has large wingspan and black and white plumage. Height: to 5ft (1.5m). Species *Grus americana. See also* Crane.

Whorf, Benjamin Lee (1897–1941), US structural linguist, b. Winthrop, Mass. He formed the Whorf hypothesis (also called Sapir-Whorf hypothesis). The hypothesis states "that the structure of language influences thought processes and our perception of the world around us."

Wichita, city in S central Kansas, 177mi (285km) SW of Kansas City, at the confluence of Arkansas and Little Arkansas rivers; seat of Sedgwick co; largest city in Kansas. Est. 1864 as trading post by James Mead and Jesse Chisholm; it developed with coming of Chisholm Trail and railroad (1872); industrial growth was spurred by discovery of oil (1915) and by development of aircraft industry (1920). It is site of Wichita State University (1892), Friends University (1898), Sacred Heart College (1933), Century II, modern convention and cultural complex. Industries: railroad shops, aircraft, oil refining, grain, meat packing. Inc. 1871 as village, 1886 as city. Pop. (1980) 279,272.

Wichita Falls, city in N Texas, 105mi (169km) NW of Fort Worth, on Wichita River; seat of Wichita co; site of Wichita Falls Junior College (1922). Industries: oil refining, oil-field equipment, textiles, cottonseed and dairy products, electronic components, farm machinery, flour milling, clothing. Settled 1876; inc. 1889. Pop. (1980) 94,201.

Widgeon, river duck with brownish plumage. They feed from the surface and engage in complex courtship displays. Included are the North American *Mareca americana* and European *Mareca penelope. See also* Duck.

Wieland, Christoph Martin (1733–1813), German novelist and poet. His works reveal his pronounced sensuality, and Greece was for him the only land where man could lead a healthy life. His works include prose translations of 22 plays by Shakespeare, the novels *Agathon* (1766), *Peregrinus Proteus* (1791), *Aristipp* (4 vols., 1800–01), and *Der goldene Spiegel* (1772), a verse idyll *Musarion* (1768), and *Oberon*

(1780). He later went to Weimar as a tutor to the duke, and there he edited the influential *Der teutsche Merkur* (1773–1810).

Wiesbaden, city in central West Germany, on Rhine River, 20mi (32km) W of Frankfurt am Main; capital of Hesse state. Made free imperial city *c.* 1242, it was capital of duchy of Nassau 1806–66; headquarters of Rhineland Commission 1918–29; taken by Allies during WWII (March 1945). City contains mineral springs known since Roman times. Industries: tourism, metal goods, concrete, chemicals, plastics, wine, printing. Pop. 249,400.

Wigglesworth, Michael (1631–1705), colonial American poet, b. England. He came to Massachusetts Bay Colony with his parents in 1638. He was a minister and physician. His crude but forceful poetry set forth Puritan theology. His most popular work was *The Day of Doom* (1662).

Wight, Isle of, island county in S England, separated from Hampshire by the Solent and Spithead, a popular holiday resort area. Area: 147sq mi (381sq km). Chief town is Newport. Pop. 109,284.

Wigwam, hut used by Indians from the Great Lakes eastward. Designs vary from semicircular to conical, but most wigwams have arched tops and are constructed of hides, bark, etc, spread over a pole frame.

Wilberforce, William (1759–1833), English social reformer. He served as a member of Parliament for more than 40 years. In 1784, Wilberforce was converted to Evangelical Christianity, and he won recognition for his opposition to the slave trade. He was an officer of the anti-slavery society, but died a month before the Emancipation Bill was passed. The tract *A Practical View* (1797) was immensely popular, and with Hannah More, he worked for the "reformation of manners."

Wilbur, Richard (1921–), US poet, b. New York City. He taught English at Wesleyan University from 1957. His collections of poetry include *Things of This World* (1956), which gained him both the Pulitzer Prize and National Book Award in 1957, *Advice To A Prophet* (1961), *Walking to Sleep* (1969), and *The Mind Reader: New Poems* (1976).

Wild Boar, tusked, cloven-hoofed mammal of the hog family that lives wild in forested areas of Eurasia and Africa. Favorite game animals, wild boars are dangerous when attacked. Now rare in Europe, they were introduced into North America during the 16th century and still roam SE United States. Length: to 5ft (153cm); weight: to 450lb (203kg). Family Suidae; species *Sus scrofa.*

Wildcat Strikes, work stoppages called while a contract is in force, normally without consulting the union leaders, which may result in legal action. Because there is today less suspicion between labor and management and grievance procedures are more efficient, wildcat strikes are less common than in the early days of the labor movement. *See also* Strike.

Wild Coffee. *See* Lemonwood.

Wilde, Oscar Fingal O'Flahertie Wills (1854–1900), Irish poet, dramatist, and wit. After being educated at Trinity College, Dublin, and at Oxford's Magdalen College, where he won the Newdigate Prize in 1878 for his poem *Ravenna,* he became an apostle in the Aesthetic Movement, with its doctrine of "art for art's sake." The flamboyant and witty figure he cut in society was caricatured by Gilbert and Sullivan as the character

Bunthorne in their comic opera *Patience* (1881). In 1882 he embarked on a year's lecture tour of the United States, attracting much notoriety for his eccentric aestheticism. Returning to England, he spent nearly a decade as an editor and critic before publishing *The Picture of Dorian Gray* (1891), his only novel; *Poems* (1891); and *The Duchess of Padua* (1892) in blank verse. There then followed the brilliant, epigrammatic stage comedies, *Lady Windermere's Fan* (1892), *A Woman of No Importance* (1893), *An Ideal Husband* (1895), and *The Importance of Being Earnest* (1895). The exotic drama *Salome,* which Richard Strauss later turned into the opera libretto, appeared in 1893. Tried and imprisoned (1895–97) for his homosexual affair with Lord Alfred Douglas, he wrote the apologia in prose *De Profundis* (published in 1905). He lived out his final years in France, anonymously writing *The Ballad of Reading Gaol* (1898), reflecting on his experiences with inhuman prison conditions.

Wildebeest. *See* Gnu.

Wilder, Laura Ingalls (1867–1957), US author of the "Little House" series of books for children, b. Lake Pepin, Wis. The story of her own childhood, growing up, and marriage in pioneer America is the subject of these famous books. *The Little House in the Big Woods* appeared in 1932 and was followed by seven other titles. The series was reissued in 1953 with fine illustrations by Garth Williams.

Wilder, Thornton Niven (1897–1975), US author and playwright, b. Madison, Wis. Expressing his ideas in a simple, realistic style, he won Pulitzer Prizes for his novel *The Bridge of San Luis Rey* (1928) and the plays *Our Town* (1938) and *Skin of Our Teeth* (1942). His *The Matchmaker* became the popular musical *Helio Dolly*. In 1968 *The Eighth Day* won the National Book Award.

Wilderness, Battle of the (May 1864), US Civil War battle. The opening of Union Gen. Ulysses S. Grant's Richmond Campaign, this was a full-scale battle, complete with trench warfare between Grant's 100,000 men and Robert E. Lee's 60,000 Confederates. Grant lost about 18,000 men; Lee lost close to 8,000.

Wilderness Preservation Act (1964), legislation establishing a National Wilderness Preservation System and Primitive Areas System of more than 14,000,000 acres (5,665,800 hectares) to retain areas "where the Earth and its community of life are untrammeled by man." These areas are open to the public for recreation and study.

Wilderness Road, road through the Appalachian Mountains. Marked out in 1775 by Daniel Boone, it served as an emigrant route from the east coast through the Cumberland Gap to Ohio. It was commissioned by Richard Henderson.

Wild Rice, annual grass native to wetlands of North America. Its stems are crowned with large, open flower clusters. The 1-in (2.5-cm), rodlike grains are dark brown or black. It was an important food for North American Indians. Height: to 10ft (3m). Family Gramineae; species *Zizania aquatica.*

Wilfrid, or **Wilfred, Saint** (634–709), Anglo-Saxon bishop. In his youth he was sent from England to Rome and Lyons to study. Returning to Northumbria, he was named bishop of York, and in that post he improved services and built notable churches. Because he objected to a plan to divide his see of York, Wilfrid was exiled for six years, although he appealed his case to Rome and won a favorable decision. During this time he converted the South Saxons and built a monastery at Selsey. Later he was bishop of Hexham.

Wilkes, Charles (1798–1877), US explorer and admiral, b. New York City. He is credited with discovering the Antarctic continent in 1840; Wilkes Land is named for him. In the Civil War he precipitated the Trent Affair by stopping a British ship and removing two Confederate diplomats. *See also* Trent Affair.

Wilkes, John (1727–97), English political figure and journalist. Elected to Parliament (1757), he opposed Lord Bute's ministry, attacking it in his journal, *The North Briton.* An issue (1763) of this publication carrying a vitriolic article on the king's speech brought about Wilkes' arrest on a general warrant. Subsequent proceedings led to the outlawing of such a warrant, but Wilkes was dismissed from Parliament for his "obscene" *Essay on Woman* (1764). Reelected (1768), he was expelled several times but enjoyed sufficient popularity to regain his seat (1774–90). After 1774, having secured a measure of press freedom, he ceased to be politically important.

Wilkes Barre, city in E Pennsylvania, on Susquehanna River 18mi (29km) SW of Scranton; seat of Luzerne co. The city was burned in 1778 by Indians and British as a result of nearby Wyoming Valley Massacre and again in 1784 during the Yankee-Pennamite Wars; site of Wilkes College (1933), King's College (1946), Luzerne County Community College (1966), and Swetland Homestead (early 1800s); much of city was damaged during flooding of Susquehanna, June 1972. Industries: pencils, clothing, footwear, tobacco products, radios. Settled 1769; named for John Wilkes and Isaac Barre, colonial supporters in Parliament during Revolutionary War; inc. as borough 1806, as city 1871. Pop. (1980) 51,551.

Wilkins, Maurice Hugh Frederick (1916–), English biophysicist. He shared the 1962 Nobel Prize in physiology or medicine with James D. Watson and Francis Crick for his X-ray diffraction studies that helped to determine the molecular structure of DNA (deoxyribonucleic acid) the basic hereditary material of most cells. *See also* Deoxyribonucleic Acid.

Wilkins, Roy (1901–81), US civil rights leader, b. St Louis. He was managing editor of the black weekly, Kansas City *Call* (1923–31), before joining the staff of the National Association for the Advancement of Colored People (NAACP). Rising in the organization, he was executive secretary (1955–65) and executive director (1965–77). He was an opponent of violent tactics, but worked vigorously for black rights until his retirement in 1977 because of failing health.

Wilkinson, James (1757–1825), US general, b. Calvert co, Md. He served in the American Revolution but was forced to resign his commission in 1778 because of his part in the Conway cabal. In 1784 he moved to Kentucky and joined a conspiracy with the Spanish governor of Louisiana to gain trade monopolies for himself and to give Kentucky to Spain. When Indian warfare broke out in Ohio, Wilkinson returned to active service under Anthony Wayne, and upon Wayne's death became ranking officer of the US army (1796). In 1803, Wilkinson officiated at the transfer of Louisiana to US ownership and was Louisiana's governor (1805–06). He then conspired with Aaron Burr to take a large segment of the West to form Burr's own republic. When Burr was brought to trial, Wilkinson was the chief prosecution witness. In 1813 he commanded American forces in Canada and was honorably discharged from the army in 1815.

Willamette River, river in Oregon; rises in Cascade Range, flows N past Eugene, Salem, and Portland to Columbia River NW of Portland; its valley is the most densely populated part of Oregon. Since 1938 a federal project has built dams to provide hydroelectric power, control floods, and improve navigation. River is navigable for most of its 300mi (483km).

Willard, Frances Elizabeth Caroline (1839–98), US social reformer, b. Churchville, N.Y. She left the education field to work for the temperance cause, serving as president of the National Woman's Christian Temperance Union (1879–98). Combining interest in woman suffrage with her temperance work, she was also president of National Council of Women (1888). She organized the WCTU into separate, activist departments involving more women than any other 19th-century organization. She was influential in the Prohibition party. She wrote *Women and Temperance* (1883) and *Glimpses of Fifty Years* (1889).

Willemstad, town on Curacao Island; capital of Netherland Antilles, island group N of Venezuela in Caribbean Sea. A major oil refining and shipping center for Venezuelan oil, city also ships coffee from its fine harbor; tourism is an important industry. Founded 1634. Pop. 152,000.

Willendorf, Venus of, statuette in the Vienna (Austria) Museum of Natural History. Representing a female fertility figure in a highly stylized form, it is quite rotund. Found at Willendorf, Austria, it is one of the earliest known works of Paleolithic art.

William I (1797–1888), German emperor and king of Prussia. He was a symbol of reaction in the Revolution of 1848 and succeeded his brother as king of Prussia in 1861. His belief in the divine right of kings led to constitutional conflict, but Chancellor Bismarck's aggressively expansionist policy largely distracted liberal opposition and resulted in the annexation of many new territories. William's glory was at its peak in 1871 when he was proclaimed German emperor at the palace of Versailles.

William II (1859–1941), German emperor and king of Prussia. Succeeding his father, Frederick III, in 1888, he believed in the absolute powers of the monarchy and attempted to rule on his own initiative, which led to Chancellor Bismarck's resignation in 1890. William made many serious errors of judgment, especially in the area of foreign policy, causing Germany's isolation from former allies and causing him to be blamed by some critics as a cause of World War I. In 1918, with Germany on the brink of collapse, he was forced to abdicate and flee to the Netherlands, where he lived in retirement until his death.

William I, or **William the Conqueror** (1027–87), king of England (1066–87) and duke of Normandy. The illegitimate son of Robert I of Normandy, he was unwillingly accepted as Robert's heir, succeeding to the dukedom of Normandy in 1035. Supported initially by Henry I, king of France, he consolidated his position in Normandy against hostile neighbors throughout the 1050s and expanded his territory in 1060. Having apparently been designated Edward the Confessor's successor as king of England, William secured the agreement of Harold, Earl of Wessex to his accession. Harold's assumption of kingship was the direct cause of William's invasion of England and the ensuing Battle of Hastings (1066). Ruthlessly crushing internal resistance and defeating the invading Danes, he completed his conquest by 1070. He established stable government through astute land distribution and by instituting feudalism in England. One of the greatest achievements of his reign was the compilation of the *Domesday Book* (1086).

William II (1056–1100), king of England (1087–1100), second surviving son of William I. Known as Rufus because of his ruddy complexion, he was of a brutal, warlike temperament, and his rule in England, although stable, was repressive. He ruthlessly quelled two baronial revolts, humbled the Welsh and Scots, and secured Normandy from his elder brother Robert.

William III (1650–1702), king of England, Scotland, and Ireland (1689–1702) and prince of Orange, b. the Netherlands. Born eight days after the death of his father, William II, Prince of Orange, he was prevented from succeeding him as stadholder of Holland until 1672. He commanded the Dutch forces against France, also forming a coalition including England. He married Mary, daughter of the duke of York (later James II of England) in 1677 and concluded the treaty of Nijmegen with France in 1678. Following the Glorious Revolution (1688), he superseded James II (1689), ruling jointly with Mary until her death (1694). He defeated James at the Battle of the Boyne in Ireland (1690), partially reduced Scotland, and carried on a second war with France, also forming the Grand Alliances with European powers. *See also* Glorious Revolution.

William IV (1765–1837), king of Great Britain and Ireland (1830–37) and of Hanover (1830–37). The third son of George III, he at first pursued a naval career, obtaining the rank of rear admiral (1790). He became duke of Clarence (1789) and took as mistress the actress Dorothea Jordan, by whom he had several children before breaking with her (1811). He succeeded his brother George IV as king (1830). His political attitudes were reactionary but did not prevent the passage of the 1832 Reform Act.

William I (1772–1843), king of the Netherlands and grand duke of Luxembourg (1815–40). He commanded the Dutch in the French wars (1793–95). Son of the last stadholder, William V, Prince of Orange, he was first king of the Kingdom of the Netherlands. He granted a fairly liberal constitution, but could not truly unite Belgium and Holland and finally signed treaty of separation (1839). He abdicated (1840) in favor of his son William.

William II (1792–1849), king of the Netherlands and grand duke of Luxembourg (1840–49). Succeeded his father, William I. He fought against France in the Napoleonic Wars and against the Belgian rebels (1830). At first opposed to reforms, he secured a liberal constitution in 1848, despite a conservative states general.

William III (1817–90), king of the Netherlands and grand duke of Luxembourg (1849–90), son of William II. He reluctantly appointed Jan Thorbecke to head the government and accepted his liberal reforms, such as extension of suffrage. He abolished slavery in Dutch West Indies (1862). With his death the male line of Orange ended, and his daughter Wilhelmina succeeded him.

William I, known as **William the Silent** (1533–84), prince of Orange and founder of Dutch Republic. Emperor Charles V appointed him stadholder of northern Holland provinces in 1555. The political and religious persecution of the Dutch by Philip II, Charles' successor in Spain, turned William against Spain, and he opposed the king (1559–67). He fled to Germany (1567). William and his brothers led "War of Liberation" (1568–76) and suffered several defeats but managed to unite the provinces in their resistance. He was first stadholder (1579–84); office made hereditary (1581). He was assassinated by Balthasar Gérard before final victory.

William II (1626–50), prince of Orange, stadholder of the Netherlands (1647–50). He succeeded his father, Frederick Henry, and married Mary, daughter of Charles I of England. William unwillingly made peace with Spain (1648) and negotiated treaty with France (1650). He came into conflict with leaders of the states general and imprisoned some of them (1650), thus weakening the state-rights movement. He was succeeded by his son, William III of England.

Williams, Betty (Smyth) (1943–), Northern Irish peace activist. The daughter of a Roman Catholic mother and a Protestant father, she grew up in an atmosphere of tolerance in a nation torn by prejudice. Deploring the use of violence by both sides in the civil war, she became a founder of the Community of Peace People movement in 1976, to carry out peaceful demonstrations in Northern Ireland and Great Britain. She was awarded the Nobel Peace Prize, with Mairead Corrigan, in 1976.

Williams, Daniel Hale (1856–1931), US surgeon, b. Hollidaysburg, Pa. He performed the first successful heart operation in 1893. He founded Provident Hospital in Chicago, which provided medical training for blacks, and the National Medical Association and was a charter member of the American College of Surgeons.

Williams, George Washington (1849–91), US historian, b. Bedford Springs, Pa. His two-volume *History of the Negro Race in America* (1883) is a classic reference of primary sources. His other books include a history of the governments of Sierra Leone and Liberia and a *History of the Negro Troops in the War of the Rebellion* (1877). He was US minister to Haiti (1885–86).

Williams, John (Towner) (1932–), US composer and conductor, b. New York, N.Y. Williams composed more than 50 motion picture scores, including *Jaws, Close Encounters of the Third Kind, Star Wars, Superman,* and *Raiders of the Lost Ark.* His compositions, which earned three Oscars, reflect the influence of both jazz and classical music. In 1980 he was named conductor of the Boston Pops Orchestra, succeeding Arthur Fiedler.

Williams, Roger (1603–83), advocate of religious freedom and founder of Rhode Island, b. London. After a short term as a chaplain in England, he went to Boston (1631). As a minister at Salem, he had a conflict with the Massachusetts Bay Colony civil authorities, when he stated that a man's conscience was not under state control and that the king had no legal right to Indian land. Banished from the colony (1635), he founded Providence (1636) after buying land from Indians. Williams obtained a patent for Rhode Island, allowing full religious freedom (1644). He served the colony as a civil leader in several posts for many years.

Williams, Tennessee (Thomas Lanier) (1911–83), US playwright, b. Columbus, Miss. His first Broadway play, *The Glass Menagerie* (1945) was awarded the New York Drama Critic's Circle Award. He received the Pulitzer Prize for *A Streetcar Named Desire* (1947) and *Cat on a Hot Tin Roof* (1955). Among his other works were *The Rose Tattoo* (1951), *Camino Real* (1953), *Sweet Bird of Youth* (1959), *The Night of the Iguana* (1961), *A Lovely Sunday for Crève Coeur* (1979), *Clothes for a Summer Hotel* (1980), and *a/k/a*

Roger Williams

Pussy willow

Woodrow Wilson

Tennessee, a drama that included parts from some of his best works. He also wrote poetry, short stories and a novel, and several of his works became motion pictures. Many of his plays were set in the South, where he grew up.

Williams, William Carlos (1883–1963), US author, b. Rutherford, N.J. A practicing physician, he produced numerous poems. He is regarded as the founder of the Objectivist school of poetry. Williams' poems deal with everyday life. His works include *Paterson* (5 vols., 1946–58), a long poem set in Paterson, N.J., and *Pictures from Breughel* (1963; Pulitzer Prize 1964). He also wrote short stories, plays, novels, and the nonfiction work *In the American Grain* (1925).

Williamsburg, historic town in E Virginia, 50mi (80km) SE of Richmond; seat of James co. Settled 1633, it was made state capital 1699–1780, when seat of government moved to Richmond. Williamsburg is visited annually by thousands of tourists and was made part of Colonial National Historic Park (est. 1936). Included in its landmarks are College of William and Mary (1693), Capitol, Public Gaol (1704), Magazine and Guardhouse (1715), Raleigh Tavern, Governor's Palace (1720), Bruton Parish Church (1715), Brush-Everard House (1717), Courthouse (1770). Inc. 1722. Pop. (1980) 9,870.

Williamsport, city in central Pennsylvania, on the Susquehanna River; seat of Lycoming co; site of Lycoming College (1812), Williamsport Area Community College (1920), and national headquarters of Little League Baseball. Industries: paper and lumber products, textiles, chemicals, aircraft engines, valves, wire rope. Settled 1772; chartered as borough 1806; inc. as city 1866. Pop. (1980) 33,401.

William Tell, in Swiss legend, a hero who for his rebellious spirit was forced by the Austrian baliff of Uri to shoot an arrow through an apple on his son's head. Tell later shot the bailiff, signaling a general uprising that led to the beginning of the Swiss Confederation in the early 14th century.

Willkie, Wendell (1892–1944), US lawyer and political leader, b. Elwood, Ind. Becoming president (1933) of a large utilities company, he fought government intervention in business under Pres. Franklin D. Roosevelt, together with projects like the Tennessee Valley Authority (1933). Although formerly a Democrat, he ran against Roosevelt as the Republican (1940) nominee. During World War II, he toured the world in support of Roosevelt's foreign policy. In his book *One World* (1943) he advocated the formation of a post-war world organization.

Willow, deciduous shrubs and trees native to cool or mountainous temperate regions. They have long, pointed leaves and flowers borne on catkins. Familiar species include the weeping willow (*Salix babylonica*) with drooping branches and pussy willow (*Salix discolor*) with fuzzy catkins. Family Salicaceae.

Willow Herb, or **Rosebay,** perennial plants (genus *Epilobium*) with willowlike leaves. Giant willowherb, or fireweed, *(E. angustifolium)* bears spiky terminal clusters of purple flowers; height: to 8ft (2.4m). Family Onagraceae.

Wilmington, city in N Delaware at junction of Delaware and Christina rivers and Brandywine Creek; seat of New Castle co; largest city in Delaware, with shipyards, railroad shops, chemical and manufacturing plants, including DuPont; site of numerous historical buildings, including Fort Christina, built 1638 by

Swedes, now a state park; and 3 junior colleges. Settled 1638; inc. 1832. Pop. (1980) 70,195.

Wilmington, seaport city in SE North Carolina, on Cape Fear River; seat of New Hanover co; scene of resistance to Stamp Act (1765); occupied by Lord Cornwallis before British march on Yorktown; served as port of entry for blockade runners during Civil War; site of Wilmington College (1947), Cornwallis' house (1771), and Greenfield Park, noted for its gardens. Industries: clothing, fertilizer, textiles, paper. Settled *c.* 1730; inc. as town 1740, as city 1866. Pop. (1980) 44,000.

Wilmot Proviso (1846), an attempt to prohibit slavery in territory acquired from Mexico. It was made in the form of an amendment to an appropriations bill by Rep. David Wilmot of Pennsylvania. The proviso passed the House but was defeated twice in the Senate.

Wilson, Charles Thomson Rees (1869–1959), English physicist who won, with A.H. Compton, the Nobel Prize for physics in 1927, for his invention of the Wilson cloud chamber. This device is used in the study of radioactivity, X rays and cosmic rays. He also devised a way of protecting barrage balloons from lightning and published his theory of thunderstorm electricity.

Wilson, Edmund (1895–1972), US author, b. Red Bank, N.J. Primarily a social and literary critic, he was managing editor of *Vanity Fair* (1920–21) and literary editor of *The New Republic* (1926–31). His work examines the social and political implications of literature. His books include *Axel's Castle* (1931), on the Symbolists; *To the Finland Station* (1940), on European revolutionary traditions; and *Patriotic Gore* (1962), on the literature of the American Civil War.

Wilson, Sir (James) Harold (1916–   ), British prime minister (1964–70, 1974–76). A Labourite, he held several academic and government posts before entering Parliament (1945). He was president of the Board of Trade (1947–51). He was Labour party leader from 1963–76 and became prime minister after the elections of 1964 and 1974. He supported Britain's membership in the European Economic Community. He resigned as prime minister in 1976 but remained in Parliament. Later that year he was knighted by Queen Elizabeth.

Wilson, J(ohn) T(uzo) (1908–   ), Canadian geophysicist and geologist. He determined global patterns of faulting and the structure of the continents. His investigations have influenced theories of continental drift, sea-floor spreading, and convection currents within the Earth. *See also* Continental Drift.

Wilson, Woodrow (Thomas Woodrow Wilson) (1856–1924), 28th president of the United States (1913–21), b. Staunton, Va. He graduated from the College of New Jersey (Princeton) in 1879, studied law at the University of Virginia, and was admitted (1882) to the Georgia bar. He married Ellen Axson in 1885, and they had three daughters; in 1915 he married Edith Bolling Galt.

Wilson taught at Bryn Mawr, Wesleyan, and Princeton before becoming president of Princeton in 1902. After a successful tenure there he ran (1910) as a Democrat for the governorship of New Jersey. He won, and his success in that office brought him nationwide attention. In 1912 he was nominated for president. The Republicans were split that year; William Howard Taft and Theodore Roosevelt were both running. As a result, Wilson won but with a minority of the popular vote.

As president, Wilson put through a decrease in the tariff and the Clayton Antitrust Act (1914). The Federal Reserve System (1913) and the Federal Trade Com-

mission (1914) were both instituted during his first term. He waged an aggressive policy toward Latin America; Marines were landed in Mexico, Cuba, the Dominican Republic, and Haiti. Wilson ran for reelection in 1916 and won a narrow victory. Even before Wilson's reelection, World War I was occupying more and more of his attention. US sentiment was decidedly anti-German, but Wilson attempted a neutral stance. Relations deteriorated, however, and war was declared on April 6, 1917.

Wilson assumed wide powers, and he successfully converted the nation to a war footing. In 1918, near the successful end of the war, he issued his Fourteen Points, which were to form the basis for the peace. After an armistice was signed (November 1918), Wilson sailed to Europe to attend the peace conference. He used his enormous prestige to good advantage in drawing up the Treaty of Versailles. At home, isolationists marshalled strong opposition to the League of Nations. Wilson's last years in office were spent in an unsuccessful campaign to win public approval for the League. His health deteriorated, and he suffered a stroke, from which he never fully recovered.

Career: president, Princeton University, 1902–10; governor of New Jersey, 1911–13; president, 1913–21.

See also Fourteen Points; League of Nations; Versailles, Treaty of.

Wilson, city of E North Carolina; seat of Wilson co; site of Atlantic Christian College (1902). Industries: tobacco, agricultural implements, clothing, fertilizer. Settled 1847; inc. 1849. Pop. (1980) 34,424.

Wilt, any of a group of plant diseases characterized by yellowing and wilting of leaves and young stems, often followed by death of the plant. Wilt diseases are caused by bacteria or fungi that grow in the sapwood and plug water-conducting tissues or disrupt the plant's water balance in some other way.

Winchester, city in N Virginia, in Shenandoah Valley, 70mi (112km) WNW of Alexandria. George Washington began his career here as a surveyor (1748); site of Washington's office and the Old Presbyterian church (1790, now an armory), Shenandoah College and Conservatory of Music (1875). Founded 1744; inc. as town 1779, as city 1874. Pop. (1980) 20,217.

Winckelmann, Johann (Ioachim) (1717–68), German archeologist and art historian whose writings helped to popularize ancient art, especially that of Greece, and stimulated the neoclassical revival of the late 18th century. An influential work is *Geschichte der Kunst des Alterthums* ("History of the Art of the Ancients," 1764).

Windaus, Adolf (1876–1959), German chemist. In 1907 he synthesized histamine and in 1928 was awarded a Nobel Prize for his work on steroid structure and the photochemistry of vitamin D.

Windhoek, capital and largest city of Namibia, W Africa; administrative, economic, communications headquarters. City originally served as headquarters of Nana Chief; in 1892 it was made capital of German colony; captured during WWI by South African troops; site of railroad terminus; world's major trade center for karakul sheep skins; city contains three German medieval-style castles. Industries: clothing, meat and bone meal processing. Pop. 62,000.

Windmill. *See* Wind Power.

Windpipe. *See* Trachea.

Wind Power, mechanical power extracted from climatic air currents by windmills. The sails of the windmill are at an angle to the wind and provision is made to keep the sails always facing the wind. Windmills have been used in the past as water pumping devices and for grinding grain. Modern windmills are looked upon as a means of electric power generation for home use.

Winds, air in natural horizontal motion at any speeds relative to the surface of the Earth. Air currents in motion vertical to the surface are usually called updrafts or downdrafts. Winds are named for the direction from which they come relative to the Earth; a west wind blows from west to east, a northeasterly gale from northeast to southwest. Wind direction is indicated by wind or weather vanes, wind speed by anemometers, and wind force by the Beaufort wind scale. Steady, periodic winds around the Earth are named, like the doldrums, the trade winds, and the polar easterlies. Monsoons are seasonal winds in Asia as well as Europe and other regions, caused by excess temperatures and pressures over continents in winter and deficits in summer compared with oceans. Foehns (föhns) are warm, dry winds produced by adiabatic compression as they descend the lee of mountains, yielding arid conditions. Foehns are found in the Alps, are called Chinooks in the Rockies, and occur in nearly all mountainous areas. Siroccos are hot, humid Mediterranean winds often bringing rain and fog to continental Europe. *See also* Doldrums; Easterlies; Trade Winds; Westerlies.

Windsor, name by which the British royal family has been known since 1917. Queen Victoria's descendants in the male line originally belonged to the German house of Saxe-Coburg-Gotha, family of her husband, Prince Albert. During World War I, however, this German connection proved embarrassing. In a proclamation in 1917, George V decreed that British subjects descended from Victoria in the male line take the surname "of Windsor." In 1952, Elizabeth II modified this decree to the effect that all her descendants, in both lines, should take the surname Windsor or Windsor-Mountbatten.

Windsor, city in SE Ontario, Canada, on the Detroit River; seat of Essex co; industrial and transportation center, served by the Canadian National and Canadian Pacific railroads; port of entry; site of Assumption College (1857), Holy Names College (1934), University of Windsor (1963). Industries: automobiles, pharmaceuticals, chemicals, salt. Settled 1749 by French. Pop. 196,526.

Windsor (New Windsor), town in S central England, on Thames River. Windsor Castle has been the chief residence of English monarchs since William the Conqueror. The castle contains the magnificent St George's Chapel, with several royal tombs. Windsor town hall was built by Sir Christopher Wren. Pop. 127,000.

Wind Tunnel, chamber in which aircraft components and scale models are tested by being exposed to mechanically produced wind. The first wind tunnel, built in 1871, used a steam-driven fan. Modern tunnels can reproduce conditions of temperature and pressure that aircraft may encounter and can generate winds far into the hypersonic range.

Windward Islands, S group of Lesser Antilles in West Indies, between Caribbean Sea (W) and Atlantic Ocean (E); chain extends from Leeward Islands (N) to NE coast of Venezuela, and includes French Martinique, Grenada, Dominica, St Lucia, and St Vincent. Barbados, Trinidad, and Tobago are not included in group. The islands are mountainous, of volcanic origin; tropical agricultural center; Rouseau and Kingstown are chief towns; aboriginal Carib inhabitants were forced out with British and French settlements (17th century). English and French disputed possession until Congress of Vienna (1815) fixed ownership with Britain. Industries: bananas, spices, limes, cacao, tourism. Area: approx. 700sq mi (1,813sq km).

Windward Passage, strait in West Indies, between Cuba (W) and Haiti (E); approx. 50mi (81km) wide from Cape Maisi, Cuba, to Cape du Mole, Haiti; links the Caribbean Sea (S) with the Atlantic Ocean (N). It is a direct shipping route between the United States and the Panama Canal.

Wing, specialized, feathered forelimb structure used by birds for flight. The basal and central parts are supported by an upper arm bone and two forearm bones, respectively, with the outer forearm bone bearing long flight feathers. Three fused and modified hand bones support flight quills. *See also* Bird; Flight, Bird.

Wing, Aircraft, an airfoil whose major function is to provide lift. It does this by exploiting the difference in pressure above and below the wing as it moves through the air. *See also* Airfoil.

Winkle. *See* Periwinkle.

Winnebago Lake, lake in E Wisconsin, Fox River flows through it. Wisconsin's largest lake, it is part of water route connecting Great Lakes and Mississippi River. Fond du Lac and Oshkosh are on lake. Recreation site. Area: 215sq mi (557sq km).

Winnipeg, city in Manitoba, Canada, at the junction of Assiniboine and Red rivers; capital of Manitoba prov. City developed in 1880s around the Canadian Pacific Railway; site of University of Winnipeg (1871), University of Manitoba (1877), and Winnipeg Grain Exchange, one of the world's largest. In 1812 the Red River settlement was founded by the Hudson's Bay Co.; the Canadian government took ownership 1870 when the province was est., and Winnipeg was made capital. Industries: cotton, furniture, meat packing, flour, stockyards, food processing. Inc. 1873. Pop. 560,874.

Winnipesaukee, Lake, lake in central New Hampshire; largest lake in the state; summer resort and tourist region. Area: 71sq mi (184sq km)

Winona, city and riverport in SE Minnesota, on the Mississippi River 40mi (64km) E of Rochester; seat of Winona co; site of Winona State College (1858), College of St Teresa (1907), St Mary's College (1912). Industries: flour, cosmetics, pharmaceuticals, fertilizers. Settled 1851; inc. 1857. Pop. (1980) 25,075.

Winston-Salem, city in central North Carolina, 68mi (109km) NNE of Charlotte; seat of Forsyth co. Salem was settled 1766 by Moravians; in 1849 land, later called Winston, was purchased from Moravians for seat of newly est. Forsyth co; the two communities united 1913. City contains Brothers House (1769), Miksch Tobacco Shop (1771), Salem Tavern (1784), Salem Academy (1772), Wake-Forest University (1834), Winston-Salem State University (1892), Salem College (1772). Industries: tobacco, brewing, clothing, textiles, electrical equipment. Salem inc. 1856; Winston inc. 1859. Pop. (1980) 131,885.

Winter Cherry. *See* Chinese Lantern Plant.

Wintergreen, or checkerberry, teaberry, creeping, woody, evergreen shrub native to E North America. It has oval leaves, white or pinkish flowers, and red fruit. An aromatic oil made from its leaves is used as a flavoring. Family Ericaceae; species *Gaultheria procumbens.*

Winter's Tale, The (1611), Shakespearean romance. Leontes, king of Sicily, imprisons his wife Hermione for an imagined indiscretion with his friend Polixenes, and banishes their newborn daughter. All are reunited when his daughter is wooed by Polixenes' son, her true identity is discovered, and Hermione, believed dead, emerges from hiding.

Winterthur, city in N Switzerland, 12mi (19km) NE of Zurich; made a free city (1415) under Holy Roman Empire and bought by Zurich (1467); site of 15th- and 17th-century castles, Gothic church (*c.* 13th–16th centuries), fine art museum. Industries: machinery, diesel engines, locomotives, textiles. Pop. 91,000.

Winthrop, John (1588–1649), Puritan colonist and theocratic governor of the Massachusetts Bay Colony. Originally a London lawyer, as governor he led 700 colonists first to Salem (1630) and later to Charlestown and Boston. He served as governor for 12 years (1630–34; 1637–40; 1642–44; 1646–49). He served as president of the New England Confederation and wrote "History of New England 1630–49." *See also* Massachusetts Bay Colony; New England Confederation.

Winthrop, John (1606–76), colonial governor of Connecticut. Son of John Winthrop, the governor of the Massachusetts Bay Colony, he settled Ipswich, Mass. (1633) and built Fort Saybrook on the Connecticut River (1634). He served as governor (1657–76). He obtained a liberal charter (1662), uniting Connecticut and New Haven and giving the colonists the same rights as Englishmen.

Winthrop, town in E Massachusetts, 4mi (6.4km) ENE of Boston, on a peninsula in Boston Bay. Named for colonial Gov. John Winthrop whose home is preserved here; resort and yachting center. Founded 1635; separated from N Chelsea and inc. 1852. Pop. (1980) 19,294.

Wirehaired Pointing Griffon, pointer and water retriever breed of dog (sporting group) developed in Holland and France at the end of the 19th century; brought to US about 1900. It has a long head and square muzzle; high-set ears hanging flat; and large yellow or light brown eyes. A short-backed body is low-set on very straight forelegs and well-developed hind legs. Its unique coat is harsh, bristly, and unkempt; colors are steel gray, gray-white, dirty white with chestnut, or chestnut. Average size: 21.5–23.5in (54.5–59.5cm) high at shoulder; 45–60lb (20.5–27kg). *See also* Sporting Dog.

Wireworm, long, cylindrical larva of a click beetle. Wireworms are distinctly segmented and usually brown or yellow. Most live in the soil and some cause serious damage to roots of cultivated crops. Family Elateridae. *See also* Click Beetle.

Wirt, William (1772–1834), US lawyer and author, b. Bladensburg, Md. In 1803 he published his first and best work *Letters of a British Spy,* and (1807) was prosecution counsel in the treason trial of Aaron Burr. As US attorney general (1817–29) under presidents Madison, Monroe, and John Quincy Adams, he argued some of the precedent-setting cases in US constitutional history. He initiated the tradition of publishing the opinions of the attorney general. In 1832 Wirt ran for the presidency on the Anti-Masonic party ticket.

Wisconsin, state in the N central United States, in the Great Lakes region, bordered on the E by Lake Michigan and on the N partly by Lake Superior.

Land and Economy. The land is a rolling plain that slopes down from the high ground in the N. The Mississippi River flows along the W boundary; many small rivers are within the state, and there are more than 8,000 lakes. Fertile pasturelands through most of the state support the dairy herds that make Wisconsin the nation's leader in production of milk and dairy products. Manufacturing is chiefly in the cities along Lake Michigan, which gives a water outlet to markets. Milwaukee, Racine, Sheboygan, and Green Bay have developed harbors. In the far NW, Superior is part of the Lake Superior port of Duluth, Minn., center of iron ore shipping.

People. Early settlers came from E states, especially New England. They were followed by New England immigrants, chiefly Germans, Norwegians, and Swedes. Milwaukee became a center of German culture in the nation. About 65% of the population lives in urban areas.

Education. There are about 60 institutions of higher education. The University of Wisconsin is state-supported.

History. Jean Nicolet landed at Green Bay in 1634 and claimed the region for France. French fur trappers were active there through the 18th century. The area was ceded in 1763 to Great Britain, which yielded it to the United States in 1783. Settlement began slowly with exploitation of the lead deposits in the SW. Land was obtained by treaties with the Indians, and the Territory of Wisconsin was created on July 3, 1836. After admission to the Union, the new state was a leader in wheat growing. This declined after 1870, and dairying dominated the economy. In the 20th century, Wisconsin was known for its progressive state governments, which pioneered in many liberal political measures.

PROFILE

Admitted to Union: May 29, 1848; rank, 30th
US Congressmen: Senate, 2; House of Representatives, 9
Population: 4,705,335 (1980); rank, 16th
Capital: Madison, 170,616 (1980)
Chief cities: Milwaukee, 636,212; Madison; Racine, 85,725; Green Bay, 87,899
State legislature: Senate, 33; Assembly, 99
Area: 56,154sq mi (145,439sq km); rank, 26th
Elevation: Highest, 1,952ft (595m), Timms Hill; lowest, 581ft (177m), Lake Michigan
Industries (major products): machinery, food products, beer, motor vehicle parts and equipment, steel, metal products, paper
Agriculture (major products): dairy products, hay, corn, hogs, poultry
Minerals (major): zinc, lime, cement, stone, lead
State nickname: Badger State
State motto: Forward
State bird: robin
State flower: butterfly violet
State tree: sugar maple

Wisconsin River, rises in lake district of NE Wisconsin; flows S through central Wisconsin, turns W and empties into the Mississippi River near Prairie du Chien. Connected to Lake Michigan by canal and Fox River. Hydroelectric projects are on river. Due to shifting sandbars it is navigable for only 200mi (322km) of its 430mi (692km).

Wisdom of Solomon, biblical book of the Old Testament Apocrypha. The first nine chapters deal with the moral and intellectual aspects of the doctrine of Wis-

John Winthrop

Madison, Wisconsin

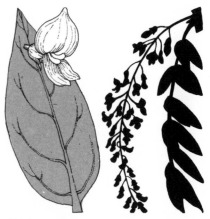

Wisteria

dom, the remaining 10 chapters with the doctrine's place in history.

Wise, Isaac Mayer (1819–1900), US rabbi, founder of Reform Judaism in the United States, b. Bohemia. He moved to New York City in 1846 and later to Ohio, serving as rabbi in both places. He tried to unify Reform Jews and in 1873 founded the Union of American Hebrew Congregations. In 1889 he helped develop the Rabbinic Council of Reform Judaism.

Wise, Stephen Samuel (1874–1949), US rabbi of Reform Judaism and leader of the Zionist movement, b. Hungary. In 1907 he founded the Free Synagogue in New York to create a pulpit free of restraints, stressing democracy. He was a founder of the Zionist Organization of America and of the American Jewish Congress. In 1922 he founded the Jewish Institute of Religion in New York. He vigorously opposed excessive dogmatism in Judaism.

Wister, Owen (1860–1938), US author, b. Philadelphia. He wrote novels, humor, nature studies, poetry, and biographies of three presidents. His novel *The Virginian* (1902) was a great popular success and did much to shape the romantic conception of the cowboy West.

Wisteria, genus of hardy woody vines native to North America, Japan, and China. They have showy, fragrant flower clusters of purplish, white, pink, or blue. Family Leguminosae.

Witchcraft, Primitive. *See* Sorcery.

Witch Doctor, person regarded as supernaturally powerful, especially in Africa. Witch doctors fight or control evil spirits and heal the sick, using herbs and rituals. They wield considerable social power. *See also* Shaman; Sorcery.

Witch Hazel, shrub and small tree of temperate regions that blooms in late autumn or early spring. The common witch hazel (Hamamelis *virginiana*) has yellow flowers and is native to E North America. Family Hamamelidaceae.

Witherite, a carbonate mineral, barium carbonate (BaCO₃), found in low-temperature lead and fluorite ore veins. Orthorhombic system twinned, pseudohexagonal twinned crystals, and in crusts and granular. Glassy white, yellow, or gray; hardness 3–3.5; sp gr 4.5.

Witmer, Lightner (1867–1956), US clinical psychologist, b. Philadelphia. He was the founder of the first psychological clinic in the United States and many throughout the country. He helped create the profession of clinical psychology, devised tests for diagnosing mental disorders, and founded the *Journal of Clinical Psychology* in 1907.

Witt, Jan de (1625–72), Dutch statesman. As burgomaster of Dort, opposed the House of Orange. Grand pensionary from 1653 until his murder in 1672, he led the Dutch in two wars against England and one against France.

Wittelsbach, German family that ruled Bavaria from 1180 to 1918 and was one of the dynasties which shaped the history of Germany. In 1255 the duchy of Bavaria was divided between the dukes of Bavaria at Munich and the counts of the Rhenish Palatinate at Heidelberg. The resulting struggle for power among the different branches of the family eliminated the pos-

sibility of a strong unified Bavaria until 1806, when Maximilian I became sole ruler.

Wittenberg, town in central East Germany, on Elbe River. In 1502, Frederick III founded university here that became center of Protestant Reformation during tenure of Martin Luther and Philip Melanchthon. In 1517 Martin Luther nailed his 95 theses to the door of Schlosskirche (castle church), which still stands, and in 1520 he burned papal bull outside Elster Gate; town passed to Prussia 1815. Industries: machinery, chemicals, rubber products. Founded late 12th century; chartered 1293. Pop. 47,151.

Wittgenstein, Ludwig (1889–1951), Austrian philosopher. A colleague of Bertrand Russell, he was actively involved in the Vienna Circle. In *Tractatus logico-philosophicus* (1921), he analyzed the problem of language and its limits which later influenced the rise of logical positivism and linguistic analysis. *Philosophical Investigations* (1953) and *Remarks on the Foundations of Mathematics* (1956) were published posthumously. *See also* Linguistic Analysis; Logical Positivism.

Witwatersrand, the Rand region in Republic of South Africa, developed in 1880s as one of the richest gold mining regions in the world; site of cities of Johannesburg, Benoni, Boksburg Springs, Germiston. Industries: gold mining, diamond cutting, food processing, steel milling, metallurgy, machines, cement, chemicals. Width: approx. 23mi (37km); Length: 62mi (100km).

Woburn, city in NE Massachusetts; birthplace of horticulturist Loammi Baldwin (1745), for whom the Baldwin apple is named; Charles Goodyear first vulcanized rubber here in 1839; birthplace of inventor Benjamin Rumford (1753), his home is a museum. Industries: leather, chemicals, greenhouses. Founded 1640 as part of Charlestown; inc. as township 1642, as city 1888. Pop. (1980) 36,626.

Wodehouse, (Sir) P(elham) G(renville) (1881–1975), English novelist. In 1910 he began a series of humorous novels and short stories set in the upper-class world of the Edwardian period and the 1920s and created the characters Bertie Wooster and Jeeves. His novels include *Carry on Jeeves* (1925), *The Code of the Woosters* (1938), and *A Pelican at Blandings* (1969). He became an American citizen (1955) and was knighted (1975).

Wöhler, Friedrich (1800–82), German chemist who first isolated aluminum and beryllium and discovered calcium carbide. His synthesis of urea demolished the vitalism of G.E. Stahl and laid the foundation for modern organic chemistry.

Wolcott, Oliver, (1726–97), a signer of the Declaration of Independence. Serving in the Continental Congress (1775–78; 1780–84), he was later lieutenant governor (1787–96), and then governor of Connecticut (1796–97).

Wolf, wild dogs originally native to most of North America and Eurasia. Packs of wolves do kill large mammals, but a large part of the wolf's omnivorous diet consists of rodents and other small animals. Attacks on humans are rare. The gray or timber wolf (Canis lupus) is the largest member of the dog family and an ancestor of domestic dogs. It resembles a large malamute—length: 4ft (1.2m); weight: 115lb (53kg). It is usually gray but the Arctic wolf is mostly white. It is now restricted to thinly populated, mostly northern regions of Europe and North America. The red wolf (Canis niger) of S United States is smaller, more slender, and tawny-gray in color. *See also* Canidae.

Wolfe, James (1727–59), British military officer. He fought in North America during the French and Indian Wars. At Louisbourg (1758), he was given command of the expedition against Quebec. He took 5,000 men down the St Lawrence River where they scaled the heights to the Plains of Abraham, taking the city from Marquis Montcalm and his French forces. Both Wolfe and Montcalm died in this decisive battle that cost France its holdings in Canada.

Wolfe, Thomas (1900–38), US author, b. Asheville, N.C. A graduate of the University of North Carolina (1920), he went to Harvard University to study the writing of plays, but finally realized that his talent was for writing novels. During 1924–30 he taught intermittently at New York University, alternating his teaching with long trips to Europe. His first novel, *Look Homeward, Angel,* a massive fictionalized autobiography, was published in 1929. With it began Wolfe's productive collaboration with Maxwell Perkins, his editor, who also helped cut the voluminous manuscript for *Of Time and the River* (1935).

Subsequent works, all intense and basically autobiographical, include *The Web and the Rock* (1939) and *You Can't Go Home Again* (1940). Both were published after Wolfe's untimely death from complications following pneumonia. Wolfe also wrote *A Portrait of Bascom Hawke* (1932), a short novel, and *From Death to Morning* (1935), a collection of short stories.

Wolff, Christian von (1679–1754), Polish academic philosopher. While professor of mathematics at Halle, Wolff, always a prolific author, acquired a great reputation as a systematizer and popularizer of the thought of W. G. Leibnitz. In the *Radical Thoughts* (1712) Leibnitz's metaphysics was as much distorted as it was simplified. The Wolffian system, known for its rigid and narrow rationalism, was satirized by Voltaire in *Candide.*

Wolframite, a tungstate mineral, iron-manganese tungstate [(Fe,Mn)WO₄], found in high- and medium-temperature quartz veins and in pegmatites. Monoclinic system black bladed crystals embedded in white quartz, or prismatic crystals, or massive granular groups. Black to brown; hardness 4–4.5; sp gr 7.3. Important ore of tungsten.

Wolfram von Eschenbach (c. 1170–c. 1220), German lyric poet and romance writer, b. Eschenbach, Bavaria. Associated with the court of Landgrave Herrman of Thuringia, he probably knew Walther von der Vogelweide and Hartman von Aue. His works include the romances *Parzival, Willehalm,* and *Titurel,* and eight or nine lyric poems. He became a major character, much romanticized, in Wagner's *Tannhäuser. See also* Parzival.

Wolf-Rayet Star, type of very hot blue star of spectral type W, having a temperature of around 80,000°K, which puts them among the hottest stars known. Wolf-Rayet stars, named after the two 19th-century astronomers who first analyzed them systematically, are short-lived phenomena that show several bright emission lines in their spectra due chiefly to neutral and singly ionized helium.

Wolf Spider, common, worldwide spider that is gray to brown and lives under debris or in burrows. The female attaches the egg sac to her spinnerets and, when the eggs hatch, she carries the young spiders on her back. Length: 0.2–1.5in (5–38mm). Family Lycosidae. The hairy European wolf spider (Lycosas tarentula) was formerly thought to be a poisonous tarantula; length: 1in (25mm). *See also* Spider.

Wolgemut, Michael (1434–1519), German painter and designer of woodcuts. He was a pioneer in the use of woodcuts in book illustration. One of the most influential artists of his era, he was responsible for the acceptance of the pure, untinted woodcut as a legitimate, self-sufficient medium. Even more important, it was in his workshop that young Albrecht Dürer was trained as a painter and graphic artist.

Wollaston, William Hyde (1766–1828), English scientist. He developed a method of working platinum, which made him wealthy; discovered palladium and rhodium; and invented a goniometer, the camera lucida, and the double-image prism that bears his name. He observed dark lines in the solar spectrum but failed to understand them and he was a member of the 1819 Royal Commission that delayed metrication in Britain.

Wollongong, city in New South Wales, Australia, 40mi (64km) S of Sydney; major seaport and urban center. Industries: steel, textiles, dairying, brickmaking. Settled 1815. Pop. 211,240.

Wollstonecraft, Mary (1759–97), English author. Family misfortunes, the loss of her best friend, and an unsettled existence marred much of her life. She visited revolutionary France, had an unhappy love affair there, and returned to England, marrying William Godwin (1797) and giving birth to a daughter, the future Mary Shelley. Her *Vindication of the Rights of Woman* (1792) is an early feminist work.

Wolseley, Garnet Joseph Wolseley, 1st Viscount (1833–1913), British military commander. In a career in which he was eventually elevated to commander in chief of the British Army (1895–99), he saw action during the Crimean War, the Indian Mutiny, and the Anglo-French conflict against China. He quelled rebellion in Canada (1871) and held high commands in Cyprus and Africa. Made field marshal in 1894, he is best known for his army reforms, upon which the modern British military system is founded.

Wolsey, Thomas (1475?–1530), English cardinal and statesman. He served as papal legate (1518–30) and lord chancellor of England (1515–29). Of humble birth, he was an ambitious man who rose quickly in church affairs, becoming Henry VII's chaplain and then dean of Lincoln (1509). Appointed a privy councillor (1511) by Henry VIII, he soon virtually controlled English politics. He became archbishop of York and was granted the two bishoprics of Lincoln and Tournai (1514). He aimed to secure international prestige in Europe for both his country and himself. Eventually he incurred the jealousy of the nobility, and his failure to obtain Henry VIII's divorce from Catherine of Aragon finally brought his ruin.

Wolverhampton, industrial city in W central England, in Black Country. Industries: automobiles, tires, rayon, chemicals, hardware, tools. Pop. 269,000.

Wolverine, solitary, ferocious mammal native to pine forests of North America and Eurasia. The largest member of the weasel family, it has brown fur with lighter back and side bands, bushy tail, and large feet. Sometimes called glutton, it eats small animals, birds, berries, and carrion, and often attacks animals much larger than itself. Length: to 40in (1m); weight: to 60lb (27.5kg). Family Mustelidae; species *Gulo gulo.*

Woman's Christian Temperance Union (WCTU), organization formed to oppose the manufacture and use of alcoholic beverages. It was founded in Cleveland, Ohio, in 1874. Its object is to educate the public against the abuses of liquor and it became an important woman's pressure group devoted to many types of social reform. Frances Willard, president of WCTU (1879–98), made it an international society in 1883.

Woman Suffrage, the right of women to vote. The movement to obtain this right for women in the United States got its start at the Seneca Falls Convention for women's rights (1848). In 1869, disappointed over the failure to include women in the 15th Amendment, which enfranchised blacks, Susan B. Anthony and Elizabeth Cady Stanton formed the National Woman Suffrage Association to work for passage of another amendment for women. Also in 1869, Lucy Stone formed the National American Woman Suffrage Association, which united with the Anthony-Cady group in 1890. While some states, notably Wyoming in 1869, granted women the vote, national suffrage was not achieved until the passage of the Constitution's Amendment XIX in 1920. *See also* Constitution of the United States; National Woman Suffrage Association; Seneca Falls Convention.

Womb. *See* Uterus.

Women. *See* Woman Suffrage; Women's Liberation Movement; Women's Rights Movement.

Women's Liberation Movement, resurgent feminist movement that developed in the United States in the 1960s. Under the leadership of the National Organization for Women (NOW) and other groups, the movement fought for abortion reform, equal employment opportunity, equal pay for women, child care facilities, and, in general, for an end to social, economic, and political discrimination on the basis of sex. Pursuant to its goals, the movement supported the Equal Rights Amendment to the US Constitution. *See also* Equal Rights Amendment; National Organization for Women.

Women's Rights Movement, international movement since the early 19th century for the dignity and equality of women. Originally concentrating on women's suffrage (attained in America in 1920), the movement has since worked for equality of employment opportunity and pay, freedom from unjust social, political, and theological expectations, and an awakening of physical, intellectual, and emotional awareness for the female majority of the world's population.

Wonsan, seaport city in SE North Korea, on Sea of Japan; capital of Kangwŏn prov.; made a treaty port 1883; served as Japanese naval base during WWII. Industries: engineering, fishing and fish processing, oil refining, food processing, textiles. Pop. 300,000.

Wood, Grant (1892–1942), US painter, b. Anamosa, Iowa. In a meticulously detailed style, he depicted simple, prosaic aspects of American life and the midwestern landscape, often investing his pictures with mildly satiric overtones, as in his well-known canvas, *American Gothic,* in the Chicago Art Institute.

Wood, the hard substance that forms the trunks of trees, used by man for construction material and fuel. Wood consists of fine cellular tubes, arranged vertically within the trunk, which carry water and minerals from roots to leaves; this accounts for the markings or grain found in all wood. The rings are reflections of growth. In the central portion of the trunk (called the heartwood), the ducts become plugged with resins. Heartwood is usually darker than sapwood. Woods are classified as hardwood, from deciduous trees, or softwood, from conifers. Hardwoods have long, continuous ducts, lacking in softwoods. Most lumber is softwood; hardwood is used mainly for furniture and flooring.

Wood Betony, or lousewort, hardy perennial with dense whorls of small purple flowers. Height: to 3ft (1m). Family Scrophulariaceae; species *Stachys officinalis.*

Woodbine. *See* Virginia Creeper.

Woodchuck, or groundhog, marmot found from Alaska to the Gulf States, having grizzled black-brown hair. Using sharp front teeth and short strong legs, it digs burrows usually having more than one entrance. The woodchuck eats plants, often becoming a garden pest. It feeds heavily in autumn before hibernating. Length: 2ft (61cm); Weight: to 14lb (6.3kg). Species *Marmota monax. See also* Marmot.

Woodcock, shorebird that nests in cool parts of the Northern Hemisphere and winters in warm areas. Both the European *Scolopax rusticola* and American *Philohela minor* are reddish-brown. They insert their long flexible bills into swampy ground to clasp worms. Males make noises with their feathers during elaborate courtship flights. Buff-colored eggs (4) are laid in a grass-lined ground depression. Weight: 0.5lb (225g); Length: 12in (30cm).

Woodcut, oldest printmaking technique. Its simple principle has been in use at least since the 5th century, when relief designs on wooden blocks were used to print fabrics in Asia. The technique did not reach Europe until the early 15th century, when paper came into widespread use there, particularly in Germany. In their simplest form, woodcut prints are produced by tracing a design on a flat wooden surface and cutting away those parts of the wood that are not to be inked. Ink then is applied to the remaining lines and masses and transferred to paper to produce a reverse image. The woodcuts of Albrecht Dürer are unsurpassed in the West. The use of color was perfected by Japanese artists in the 18th century.

Wood Duck, North American perching duck with a long green, purple, and white crest. It perches in forest trees and nests well above the ground. Length: 18in (46cm). Species *Aix sponsa. See also* Duck.

Wood Engraving, printmaking technique. This medium evolved from the woodcut; a design is achieved by pushing a sharp chisel (burin) against the grain of a polished hardwood surface to produce myriad fine incisions, often while the surface is being rotated to facilitate curved contours. Characterized by the density and richness of its effects, the medium was exploited most successfully in the 15th century by Albrecht Dürer.

Wood Frog, true frog found in moist, wooded areas of Canada and NE United States, sometimes far from water. It has a dark patch extending backward from its eyes. Length: to 3in (7.6cm). Family Ranidae; species *Rana sylvatica.*

Woodland, city in N central California, 15mi (24km) WNW of Sacramento; seat of Yolo co; site of many historical homes and a state historical farm. Center of mobile home manufacture; area produces vegetables. Inc. 1871. Pop. (1980) 30,235.

Wood Louse, or **Sowbug,** terrestrial and semi-terrestrial crustacean found worldwide under logs and stones and in houses. It has an oval, segmented body and gills, greatly reduced, for breathing air. The pillbug can roll its body into a tight ball. Length: 0.75in (20mm). Suborder Oniscoidea. *See also* Crustacean.

Wood Nymph, any of several striking butterflies whose caterpillars are brightly colored. Some feed on grape leaves. Family Satyridae.

Woodpecker, tree-climbing birds found worldwide, except in Madagascar and Australia. Emitting a drumming noise as they drill into trees, they have strong chisel-shaped beaks, long protrusible tongues, often equipped with harpoonlike tips for extracting insect larvae, and stiff tail with a spiny end used as a brace when they climb and walk on trees. They have black, red, white, yellow, brown, or green plumage and some are crested. They lay white eggs (2–8) on wood chips in a tree hole nest. Family Picidae.

Woodruff, Hale (1900–), US painter, b. Cairo, Ill. After studying at the Herron Institute of Indianapolis and in Paris he became an art instructor at Atlanta University. His paintings depict landscapes and the conditions of blacks in Georgia.

Woods, Lake of the, resort lake in Manitoba and Ontario, Canada and N Minnesota, United States. Area: 1,695sq mi (4,390sq km).

Wood Sorrel. *See* Oxalis.

Wood Thrush, North American song bird with reddish-brown upperparts and white breast marked with darker spots. It builds an open cup-shaped nest with a core of mud for its whitish or bluish eggs. Length: 8in (20cm). Species *Hylocichla mustelina. See also* Thrush.

Wood Warbler, any of a family (Parulidae) of small, generally colorful birds of the New World with songs considered less pleasant than those of Old World warblers. They feed on insects and sometimes fruit. Most females build open cup-shaped nests in a tree or bush; some build roofed, side-entranced nests for marked whitish eggs (2–5) that they incubate alone. Males help feed the young.

Woodward, Robert Burns (1917–79), US chemist, b. Boston, Mass. He became professor at Harvard in 1950 and was awarded a Nobel Prize in 1965 in recognition of his synthesis of a number of complex organic substances including quinine, cholesterol, cortisone, strychnine, lysergic acid, reserpine, chlorophyll, and tetracycline.

Woodwind Instruments, in the modern symphony orchestra, instruments that are played by blowing over mouth holes (flute, piccolo) or by vibrations of an elastic reed (clarinet, English horn, oboe, bassoon, saxophone). These are contrasted with brass instruments. *See also* Orchestra.

Woodworking Machinery, fixed power tools used to cut, work and join lumber. Use of machinery speeds output and reduces costs. Automated machines permit continuous operation. Included are circular bench saws and radial-arm saws for general cutting such as sawing planks and for ripping, edging and crosscutting; band saws; surface planers for smoothing and reducing timber; mortising machines for making joints; molding cutters for making trim and molding; and sanders for finishing planed surfaces.

Woodworking Tools, implements used by carpenters to cut, work, and join lumber. Hand tools of ancient vintage include planes for smoothing rough surfaces and reducing wood to size; saws for cutting wood; chisels for removing surplus wood or cutting special shapes; and hammers, screwdrivers, awls, gimlets, and pliers. Tri-squares test right angles; bevels test all

Wolverine

Woodchuck

Woodpecker

other angles. Modern powered hand tools include electric drills, saws, and routers.

Woodworth, Robert S(essions) (1869–1962), US psychologist, b. Belchertown, Mass. He was a professor at Columbia University (1903–42). He helped turn US psychology away from the structuralism of Wilhelm Wundt and E.B. Titchener toward a consideration of cause and effect in mental processes, which came to be known as the functionalist school of US psychology. Among his publications are the textbook *Psychology* (1921, 5th ed. 1947) and *Experimental Psychology* (1938).

Wool, soft, curly fibers chiefly obtained from fleece of domesticated sheep, although vicuña, alpaca, goats, and other animals also yield wool. Used extensively in textile manufacturing, it differs from hair, by having scales that cover numerous small fibers that interlock at base. Curl permits resilience. High tensile strength allows wool fabrics to retain shape. *See also* Lanolin.

Woolen Act (1699), English legislation that forbade colonial US wool cloth to be sold outside of place of weaving, protecting English weavers from colonial exports.

Woolf, Virginia (1882–1941), English novelist and critic, daughter of Leslie Stephen, and a member of the Bloomsbury Group. She founded the Hogarth Press (1917) with her husband Leonard. Her novels include *Night and Day* (1919), *Jacob's Room* (1922), *Mrs. Dalloway* (1925), *To the Lighthouse* (1927), *Orlando* (1928), *The Waves* (1931), and *The Years* (1937). They display her experimentation with fictional forms, particularly the stream-of-consciousness technique. *See also* Bloomsbury Group.

Woollcott, Alexander Humphreys (1887–1943), US journalist, b. Phalanx, N.J. He became a reporter for the *New York Times* (1909) and was made drama critic (1914). He wrote criticism for three other New York newspapers (1922–28), was a regular contributor to the *New Yorker* magazine, and conducted a radio interview program (1929–43). He inspired the George S. Kaufman and Moss Hart play *The Man Who Came to Dinner,* in which he played the part of Sheridan Whiteside.

Woolly Bear, tiger moth caterpillar whose body is densely covered with long hairs. The North American banded *Isia isabella* is black in front and behind with a rusty-colored middle band of variable width. Unusually wide rusty bands are said to presage a warm winter and unusually narrow ones, a cold winter.

Woonsocket, city in N Rhode Island, 13mi (21km) NNW of Providence, on Blackstone River. Site was bought from Nipuc Indians 1662; heavy European and Canadian immigration occurred during 19th century due to increased industrial growth. Industries: textiles, electronic components, machine tools, paper, chemicals, clothing. Settled 1666 by John and Richard Arnold; inc. 1871 as town, 1888 as city. Pop. (1980) 45,914.

Worcester, city in central Massachusetts, 37mi (60km) W of Boston on Blackstone River; seat of Worcester co. Industrial development was spurred by canal system down Blackstone River to Providence, R.I. (1828); site of College of the Holy Cross (1843), Worcester Polytechnic Institute (1865), Clark University (1887). Industries: machinery, metal goods, chemicals, pharmaceuticals, electrical equipment, plastics. Settled 1673; inc. 1722 as town, 1848 as city. Pop. (1980) 161,799.

Wordsworth, William (1770–1850), English poet. He spent much of his youth exploring the countryside around Cumberland. He visited France twice (1790–92), sympathizing with the revolutionaries. With his sister Dorothy, to whom he was very close, he settled in Dorsetshire and became friends with Samuel Coleridge, with whom he wrote *Lyrical Ballads* (1798). Disillusioned with politics, Wordsworth explored the correlation between nature and the development of the human mind in poems such as "The Ruined Cottage" (1797), "Tintern Abbey" (1798), "The Prelude" (1805, 1850), "Intimations of Immortality" (1807), and "Resolution and Independence" (1807).

Work, in physics, the energy expended in moving a body against an opposing force. If the opposing force is the body's weight *mg,* the work done in raising it a height *h* is *mgh.* This work has been transferred to the body in the form of potential energy; if the body falls, the kinetic energy at the bottom will equal the work done in raising it.

Works Progress Administration (WPA) (1935), New Deal agency to aid the unemployed. Under Harry Hopkins, the WPA spent billions of dollars and provided work for millions of people. Among its projects were schools, parks, airports, bridges, dams, and sewers. It cleared slums, planted forests, and electrified rural areas. It also employed out-of-work writers, artists, and musicians. After 1939 it was called the Works Projects Administration until it was disbanded in 1943.

World Bank. *See* International Bank for Reconstruction and Development.

World Council of Churches, an ecumenical association formed in 1948 in Amsterdam. It is comprised of Protestant and Orthodox Eastern Churches. The Roman Catholic Church and Russian Orthodox Church are not represented. Unity and renewal of Christianity are central concerns.

World Court, established by the League of Nations (1920) as the Permanent Court of International Justice and as the International Court of Justice by the United Nations in 1945. While the extent of its jurisdiction has been disputed, the World Court has added to the importance, impartiality, and frequency of use of arbitration in international disputes.

World Health Organization (WHO), United Nations agency dealing with health problems in the world. It collects and shares information in medical and scientific areas and promotes the establishment of international standards for drugs and vaccines. It officially became a UN agency in 1948.

World War I (1914–18), primarily European conflict of unprecedented size and brutality, often called the Great War. With the first large-scale use of poison gas, machine guns, aircraft, and other modern devices of war, it led to at least 13,000,000 military deaths and twice that number of wounded. Some of its causes can be found in the Franco-Prussian War (1870–71), when the Prussians and Austrians inflicted a humiliating defeat on France and took Alsace-Lorraine, outraging French nationalists. The Franco-Prussian War itself was an early expression of the rising European nationalism and desire for expansion that accompanied the industrial revolution and the rise of popular government. Territorial conflicts, traditional boundary disputes, the decline of the Ottoman Empire: all came to a head with the assassination of Austrian Archduke Francis Ferdinand by a Serbian nationalist on June 28,

1914, in Sarajevo, Yugoslavia. War broke out on July 28, 1914, and by the end of 1915 the Central Powers of Austria-Hungary, Germany, Bulgaria, and the Ottoman Empire were fighting against the Allied Powers of Great Britain, Russia, Italy, France, Belgium, Serbia, Montenegro, and Japan. In April 1917, the United States was prompted by the sinking of the *Lusitania* to join the Allies, intending, as President Woodrow Wilson said, "to make the world safe for democracy."

The actual fighting of World War I began with the rapid German invasion of France through Belgium in early August 1914. This offensive was stemmed by the battles of the Marne, the Aisne, Ypres, and the Yser, so that by November the Western Front had settled into miserable trench warfare that would consume three long years and millions of lives without an appreciable shift in boundaries.

In the East, the Germans defeated a Russian invasion in August-September 1914, and by late 1915 they and the Austro-Hungarians had occupied most of Poland. The Russian forces, under General Brusilov, were hampered by increasing political conflicts, and after a final great offensive in 1916 were effectively crippled by the Russian Revolution. By March 1918, a peace had been made at Brest-Litovsk, allowing the Germans to concentrate their forces in a new offensive on the Western Front.

Meanwhile, extensive fighting on the Italian Front since May 1915 had resulted in a near Austro-Italian stalemate. The introduction of efficient German troops in the Battle of Caporetto (October-November 1917) resulted in a Central Powers victory, which was offset by the severe Austrian defeat in the Battle of Vittorio Venete almost a year later. An armistice was signed for the Italian Front on Nov. 4, 1918.

In addition to several minor campaigns in Africa and Asia, as well as an extensive naval war, there was considerable fighting of varied outcome between the British and the Turks in Egypt and the Near East, and Russia and the Turks in the Caucasus. The ultimate Allied victory resulted in an armistice on Oct. 31, 1918. The Balkan Campaign, which drew Romania and then Greece to the Allies, involved similar indecisive victories on both sides and resulted in eventual Austrian surrender on Nov. 3, 1918.

The last major campaign of the Western Front came in early 1918, when the truce with the Russians gave the Germans a sudden numerical superiority in the West. Seeking a victory in France before large-scale US involvement, they began the great Somme offensive in March and rapidly advanced 40 miles (64km) under General Ludendorff. This German victory inspired Allied centralization of command under General Foch, and the resulting efficiency, bolstered by a rapid influx of US troops under Gen. John Pershing, led to final defeat of the exhausted German war machine and the signing of an armistice on Nov. 11, 1918.

The Allies quickly occupied the German Rhineland, and peace talks began. The end result was that Germany was forced in 1919 to accept the humiliating terms of the Treaty of Versailles, which limited the German army to 100,000, blamed Germany for the war itself, ceded West Prussia to Poland and Alsace-Lorraine to France, and subjected Germany to other military, economic, and political restrictions and minor losses of land. Other treaties took lands from Austria, Hungary, and Bulgaria, outlawed Austro-German union *(Anschluss),* and imposed such harsh conditions on Turkey that a new treaty was drawn up in 1923. The rigid peace conditions of World War I were a contributing factor to World War II, but the ghastly toll and methods of World War I also created a temporary aversion to war and aided the formation of the League of Nations. *See also* League of Nations; Versailles, Treaty of.

World War II (1939–45), largest conflict in human history, arose from the industrial and nationalistic expansion of the 19th and 20th centuries, and eventually engulfed every occupied continent on the globe. The toll in human life was staggering, with roughly 40,000,000 to 60,000,000 dead, of which at least 20,000,000 were Russians and at least 6,000,000 were Jews executed in Nazi concentration camps.

The causes of the war can be traced in part to the peace terms of World War I. Deprived of valuable territory, demoralized, economically shattered by the war, and forced into the Treaty of Versailles, post-war Germany struggled for survival before the revolutionary leadership of Adolf Hitler. Simultaneously, Japan had completed a rapid transition into a world industrial power and began to feel a pressing need for expanded markets and new sources of raw materials. In addition, the rise of popular government, the extreme economic insecurity of post-war Europe in the Great Depression, and continuing nationalism led to a global rise in demagogic totalitarianism that posed a grave threat to the Communist and democratic nations.

In 1931–32, Japan occupied Manchuria and went on to invade China, then torn by civil war. Adolf Hitler meanwhile engineered a startling rise to power, and after his appointment as chancellor in 1933 he actively rebuilt Germany's economy and armed forces and strengthened the Nazi party for the creation of a new German empire. Allied with fascist Italy and Japan as the Axis powers, Germany suddenly annexed Austria in 1938. Italy, under Benito Mussolini, dissatisfied with the results of World War I, had conquered Ethiopia in 1935 and in 1939 followed the German occupation of Czechoslovakia with the annexation of Albania. The former Allied powers, still weary from World War I, followed a policy of conciliation, seeking appeasement of the expanding fascist powers. The United States held stubornly to its policy of isolation. Yet, with the German invasion of Poland on Sept. 1, 1939, the Allies could no longer deny German intentions; France and the British Commonwealth (except Ireland) declared war on Germany two days later.

The German *Blitzkrieg,* a new style of warfare heavily reliant on armor and aircraft, soon overwhelmed Poland, which was divided with the USSR. The USSR defeated Finland, and in the spring of 1940 the Germans pushed Allied forces from France and Belgium and might have crushed British resistance except for the successful evacuation of British troops at Dunkirk. The French Vichy government of Marshal Pétain was established after a truce with Germany, but British victory in the aerial Battle of Britain prevented German advances on the British Isles, which rallied under Prime Minister Winston Churchill. Meanwhile, the Italians had begun the North African campaign, and by summer of 1941 Germany had overrun Denmark, Norway, Greece, Crete, and Yugoslavia and gained Romania, Hungary, Finland, and Bulgaria as allies in the invasion of the Soviet Union. The Axis powers made rapid advances there and were halted by the Russian winter of 1941–42.

During this time the United States, though providing increasing financial support to Britain, refused to build up its armed forces or threaten active intervention in the European war. Recently recovered from the Great Depression under Pres. Franklin D. Roosevelt, the US answer to Japanese imperialism was restricted US-Japanese trade. Japan responded with the sudden aerial bombardment of Pearl Harbor on Dec. 7, 1941, hoping to so cripple the US Navy as to successfully secure valuable colonies in the Pacific. The United States, the Netherlands, and the British Commonwealth (except Ireland), declared war on Japan the next day, and were followed by China on December 9.

Seriously impaired by the Japanese attack, the inadequate US forces were a small obstacle to Japan's conquest of the Philippines, Indonesia, Malaya, Burma, and various islands of the Pacific. In the summer of 1942 the US Navy stemmed this conquest at Coral Sea and Midway, and Allied troops engaged the Japanese in New Guinea and Guadalcanal. Under Gen. Douglas MacArthur the Allies gradually forced the Japanese from New Guinea, the Solomon and Mariana islands, Okinawa, Iwo Jima, the Philippines, Burma, and other territories, and began intensive bombing of Japan. The Japanese, although unable to withstand the Allied armies, refused surrender, and in a controversial effort to end the war the United States, under the new Pres. Harry S. Truman, dropped an atomic bomb on Hiroshima on Aug. 6, 1945. Three days later Nagasaki was leveled by another blast and the Japanese surrendered (Aug. 14–Sept. 2, 1945).

Four days after the Pearl Harbor disaster, the United States found itself at war in Europe. In 1942 German Field Marshal Rommel (the "Desert Fox") was rapidly conquering North Africa, but the spectacular German offensive in Russia gradually ground to a halt. The Axis powers, greatly outnumbered and lured on by early success, had overextended themselves. Britain's General Montgomery defeated Rommel at El Alamein, and by the summer of 1943, Lt. Gen. Dwight Eisenhower's combined British, American, and Free French had retaken North Africa. In the USSR, following the Battle of Stalingrad and worn out by the Russian winter, the Germans began to retreat before Joseph Stalin's forces in 1943.

The Allies took Sicily in July and August, 1943, and invaded Italy (which surrendered that September). They then turned their attention to France, and invaded the coast of Normandy, with Eisenhower as supreme commander, on June 6, 1944 (D-Day). The Allied forces, led by such men as Omar Bradley, Montgomery, and George Patton, rapidly retook France and entered Germany. The Russians were making tremendous advances in the east, and by May 2, 1945 had taken Berlin. Hitler had committed suicide on April 30. Corresponding Allied victories to the west and south brought an end to the European war on May 9, 1945.

Although treaties with the former Axis powers were concluded in the early 1950s, the world retained a permanent political instability emerging from the vast ramifications of World War II. The war had brought the United States and the USSR to positions of supreme power, positions in part determined by the Yalta and Potsdam conferences. The development and use of the atomic bomb revolutionized modern concepts of warfare. Japan and the Western part of a divided Germany, deprived of military concerns, became flourishing economic powers, partly through US aid, and strong allies against the Soviet Union. World desire for peace led to the founding of the United Nations. *See also* Potsdam Conference; United Nations; Yalta Conference.

Worming, the chemical removal of any of a variety of parasitic worms or their larvae from the lungs, liver, intestines, stomach, or bloodstream of a variety of animals, principally swine, cattle, horses, sheep, dogs, and cats. Worms include roundworms, flukes, spiny-headed worms, screwworms, and tapeworms.

Worms, port city in W West Germany, on Rhine River, 10mi (16km) NNW of Manheim. Made a free imperial city early 13th century, it joined Rhenish Confederation 1255; scene of Diet of Worms (1521), where Martin Luther appeared before Charles V to defend his position on Protestantism; the Edict of Worms (1521) proclaimed Luther a heretic. City was awarded to France 1801; passed to Hess-Darmstadt state 1815; occupied by French 1918–30; taken by Allies 1945; it is setting of epic poem "Nibelungenlied." Industries: leather, machinery, chemicals, paints, ceramics. Pop. 75,500.

Worms, invertebrate animals characterized by elongated shape; many are parasitic. Phyla Platyhelminthes (flatworm), Nemertea (ribbon-worm), Nematoda (roundworm), Acanthocephala (spiny-headed worm), Annelida (segmented worm), Sipunculoida (acorn worm), and Chaetognatha (arrow worm).

Worms, Concordat of (1122), arrangement between Holy Roman Emperor Henry V and Pope Calixtus II which decided the question of investiture for members of the clergy. New church officials were to be elected by the clergy, with the emperor settling electoral disputes. Afterwards the emperor would endow the officials with their due worldly possessions and duties and the church would follow suit with religious concerns.

Worms, Diet of (1521), conference of the Holy Roman Empire, held in Worms, Germany and presided over by Emperor Charles V. Martin Luther was summoned and appeared before the Diet to explain his position and beliefs. Luther refused to renounce his writings, and the Edict of Worms (May 25, 1521) declared him an outlaw.

Worm Snake, harmless snake found in E and central United States. It is brown or purple with a pink belly. Secretive, it lives under moist logs and eats earthworms and insects. Length: to 11in (28cm). Family Colubridae; species *Carphophis amoenus.*

Wormwood, aromatic bitter shrub and herb, including the common wormwood *(Artemisia absinthium),* a European shrub that yields a bitter, dark green oil used to make absinthe. Family Compositae.

Worship, specific acts of devotion that are believed to be owed to Divine Beings. Forms vary according to differing concepts of God and man, and of their roles.

Worthing, seaside resort in S England; site of prehistoric and Roman ruins; grows greenhouse products. Pop. 88,210.

Wouk, Herman (1915–), US author, b. New York City. A radio scriptwriter before turning to writing novels, his works include *The Caine Mutiny* (1951), for which he won a Pulitzer Prize (1952), *Marjorie Morningstar* (1955), *Youngblood Hawke* (1962), *Don't Stop the Carnival* (1965), *The Winds of War* (1971), adapted for television, *War and Remembrance* (1978), and *Inside, Outside* (1985).

Wounded Knee, Massacre at (1890), last engagement between Indians and whites. It took place at Wounded Knee Creek, S. Dak., where over 200 Sioux were cut down by the US 7th cavalry.

Wrack. *See* Rowing.

Wrangel, (Baron) Pëtr N(ikolaevich) (1878–1928), Russian military commander. A field commander in World War I, he joined the White Army and helped capture Volgograd from the Communists in 1919. He led the Whites after 1920, seeking an alliance with Poland, but was defeated in the Ukraine. He helped evacuate 150,000 refugees from Russia before emigrating to Belgium.

Wrangel (Vrangel'a), island of the USSR, in the Arctic Ocean between the East Siberian Sea and the Chukchi Sea. Off NE USSR, it is separated from mainland by 83-mi (134-km) wide Long Strait; discovered by Thomas Long, US whaling captain, in 1867. Since 1924, USSR has controlled island and has a small permanent settlement. Cold winters, and summers barely above freezing make it a breeding ground for polar bears, polar foxes, seals, and lemmings. Area: 2,000sq mi (5180sq km).

Wrasse, brilliantly colored, inshore tropical marine fish. Many are popular aquarium species. They have protrusible mouths and sleep on their sides. Many remove parasites from larger fish. Length: 3in–10ft (7.6–305cm). Among 600 species are the yellowtail *Coris gaimardi* and the rainbow *Labroides dimidiatus.* Family Labridae.

Wren, Sir Christopher (1632–1723), English architect, mathematician, and professor of astronomy. Wren became an architect after the great London fire of 1666. He is best known for his London churches and St Paul's Cathedral. The churches show a considerable and ingenious variety of styles, and St Paul's, with its magnificent dome, is a triumph of structural complexity. Among his other buildings are Chelsea Hospital and Greenwich Hospital, the latter showing Wren's fullest use of the Baroque.

Wren, small, insect-eating song birds of Europe, Asia, and most of the New World. Both sexes sing all year long, sometimes in a duet. During courtship, many males build false nests that are near but more exposed than the true domed nest that has a long side entrance tunnel. The eggs (2–10) range from white to brown, depending on species. Groups often share housekeeping chores and the young help feed the second-generation young. The typical insectivorous winter wren *(Troglodytes troglodytes)* has a slender bill, rounded wings, perky tail, and dark brownish plumage; length: to 4in (10cm). Many species, including wood wrens *(Henicorhina)* of Mexican and South American forests, have white facial lines. Family Troglodytidae.

Wrestling, sport that matches two unarmed opponents in a contest where the object is to try to secure a fall by means of body grips, strength, and adroitness. The most common styles include Greco-Roman, most popular in continental Europe, which permits no tripping or holds below the waist, and free-style, which permits tackling, leg holds, tripping, and other rough features, and is most popular in the United States and England. Other forms include sumo wrestling, popular in Japan; yagli, a Turkish form in which the contestants smear themselves with grease to make the holds difficult; sambo, a Russian form of jacket wrestling similar to judo; and Cumberland-and-Westmoreland, an ancient style of wrestling that continues in England and has the competitors start with their arms clasped behind each other's backs. Amateur wrestling, conducted in free-style and Greco-Roman, is classified by weight and conducted on a mat. A match consists of three periods of three minutes each, with points awarded for falls (pinning both shoulders to the mat) and other maneuvers. Professional wrestling uses the free-style method, but has been lightly regarded since it is no more than planned entertainment.

History. Competitive wrestling has its origins in ancient Greece, where it was regarded as the most important event after discus throwing, in the Olympic Games. Greco-Roman style wrestling was first included in the modern Olympics in 1896, was removed as an event in 1900, and reinstated in 1904 when free-style was also included. *See also* Sumo Wrestling.

Wright, Frank Lloyd (1869–1959), US architect, b. Richland Center, Wis., noted for his great originality. His first independent designs were for domestic houses, which he built with low, horizontal lines in his so-called prairie style; the Robie house, Chicago (1909) is the most famous. He attempted to bring new

World War II: signing of Japanese surrender

Frank Lloyd Wright

Wilbur and Orville Wright

mechanical methods and materials into architectural design, and to create open planning and free-flowing internal space. Notable buildings include the Larkin Office Building, Buffalo (1904), Taliesin, at Spring Green, Wis. (1911, twice rebuilt), the Imperial Hotel, Tokyo (1916), and the Solomon R. Guggenheim Museum, New York City (1945–59).

Wright, Richard (1908–60), US author, b. near Natchez, Miss. A short story writer and novelist, he was the first black American to gain international acclaim as a writer. His works, which deal with racial prejudice in the United States, are realistic and brutal. They include *Native Son* (1940); *Black Boy* (1945), an account of the author's boyhood in the South; and *Twelve Million Black Voices* (1941), a folk history of blacks in America. After World War II Wright resided in Paris.

Wright, Wilbur (1867–1912), b. Millville, Ind., and **Orville** (1871–1948), b. Dayton, Ohio, aviation pioneers. Their first joint venture was a weekly newspaper. They entered bicycle manufacturing in the 1890s, studied aeronautical literature, and experimented with gliders to learn wing control and lateral balancing. The rolling sand dunes and fairly constant winds at Kitty Hawk, N.C. allowed them to test gliders (1900–01). Orville made the first piloted flight in a power-driven plane at Kitty Hawk (1903). Their work was neither believed nor publicized until a reporter, D. Bruce Salley, witnessed their 1000-foot (305-meter) flight (1908). French public recognition preceded US Army's acceptance of their plane (1909). Their success where others had failed usually is attributed to their working as a unit.

Wroclaw, formerly Breslau; industrial city in SW Poland, on the Oder River, approx. 150mi (242km) NW of Krakow; capital of Wroclaw province. Settlement became episcopal see c 1000; it was destroyed by Mongols 1241; rebuilt by Germans and passed to Bohemia 1335; came under Hapsburgs 1526, and under Prussia 1742; grew as a trade center in 19th century; became part of Poland by Potsdam Conference 1945; site of 13th-century cathedral and churches, Gothic structures, university (1702). Industries: railroad cars and repairs, heavy machinery, food processing, textiles, chemicals. Pop. 576,000.

Wrought Iron, a commercial form of smelted iron (the other is cast iron) containing less than 0.3% carbon with 1 or 2% slag mixed with it.

Wuhan (Wu-han), city in central China, at confluence of Han and Yangtze rivers; capital of Hupeh prov.; a municipality inc. (1950) the former cities of Hankow, Hanyang, Wuchang; scene of first uprising (1911) from which the Chinese Republic evolved; site of Hupeh and Wuhan universities. Industries: iron, steel, railroad shops, textiles, food processing, paper, glass, metallurgy. Pop. 2,700,000.

Wundt, Wilhelm (1832–1920), German psychologist. He established the first psychological laboratory in 1879 at Leipzig. Known as "the father of experimental psychology," Wundt did much to convince early psychologists that the mind could be studied with objective, scientific methods. His major publication is *Physiological Psychology* (1880).

Wuppertal, city in W West Germany, on Wupper River, 16mi (26km) ENE of Düsseldorf. As center of ball bearing and chemical production, city was heavily bombed by Allies during WWII. Industries: textiles, pharmaceuticals, paper, chemicals. Formed 1929 by inc. of Barmen, Elberfeld, Vohwinkel, and several villages. Pop. 402,900.

Württemberg, former state in SW West Germany, between Bavaria and Baden states; capital was Stuttgart. States of Baden and Württemberg divided into three states 1945: Baden, Württemberg-Baden, and Württemberg-Hohenzollern. All were inc. into Baden-Württemberg State 1951.

Würzburg, city in central West Germany, on Main River, 60mi (97km) ESE of Frankfurt am Main; made an episcopal see by St Boniface 741; secularized by Treaty of Lunéville 1801; annexed to Bavaria 1803; made an electorate and grand duchy under Ferdinand III of Tuscany (1805); returned to Bavaria 1815; seat of University of Würzburg (1582) whose professors have included Rudolf Virchow, and Wilhelm Roentgen (who discovered the X-ray, 1895). Notable buildings include Marienberg Castle (1201), Romanesque cathedral (11th–13th centuries). Industries: printing, machine tools, chemicals, textiles, brewing. Pop. 112,500.

Würzburg School, a group of psychologists headed by Oswald Külpe (1862–1915) at the University of Würzburg, Germany, who developed a psychological method called "systematic experimental introspection." They concluded that thought can proceed without sensory input. This was an outgrowth of Wilhelm Wundt's studies that saw psychology as the introspective analysis of the contents of immediate experience.

Wu Tao-tzu (*c.*700–*c.*760), Chinese painter of the T'ang dynasty. One of the most revered artists China has produced, he is celebrated as the earliest Chinese figure painter and the inventor of various styles and techniques, including a method of printing designs on silk. His works are known only through copies. His style would seem to have been characterized by monumentality, naturalism, and profound religiosity.

Wyandotte, city in SE Michigan, on Detroit River; site of first US Bessemer steel plant (1864). Industries: chemicals, automobile parts, hardware, detergents. Founded 1818 on site of Wyandotte Indian Village; inc. as city 1867. Pop. (1980) 34,006.

Wyatt, (Sir) Thomas (1503–42), English poet. A courtier, he was sent on many diplomatic missions and imprisoned several times in the Tower of London on charges ranging from immorality to treason. He was a friend and possibly a lover of Anne Boleyn. He introduced the sonnet form into English versification, and 96 of his poems appear in the anthology Tottel's *Miscellany* (1557). He also translated Plutarch and wrote and translated satirical verse. *See also* Sonnet.

Wycliffe, John (?1320–84), English theologian and religious reformer. A cleric, student, and teacher at Oxford (1356–82), he obtained his doctorate in theology in 1372. He came to reject the doctrine of transubstantiation and attacked the formation and hierarchical system of the Roman Catholic Church. He came under the patronage of John of Gaunt and during the 1380s initiated the first English translation of the Bible. He was declared a heretic after his death.

Wyeth, Andrew (Newell) (1917–), US painter, b. Chadds Ford, Pa. He is known for his meticulously detailed portraits, landscapes, and the artifacts of rural and coastal American life. His best known painting is "Christina's World" (1948) in the Museum of Modern Art, New York City. He was trained by his father, the illustrator N.C. Wyeth. Andrew became a member of the French Academy of Fine Arts (1977) and an honorary member of the Soviet Academy of Arts (1978). His son, James (1946–), US painter, b. Wilmington, Del. is a noted painter and artist in the representational tradition of his father and grandfather, James is known

for the high polish of his technique and for his skill as a portraitist.

Wylie, Philip Gordon (1902–71), US author, b. Beverly, Mass. Primarily a short-story writer and novelist, his works often became vehicles for criticism of American society and culture. His novels include *An April Afternoon* (1938), *Opus 21* (1949), and *Triumph* (1963). A noted work of nonfiction is *Generation of Vipers* (1942), a much discussed, bold essay on American customs and beliefs.

Wyoming, state in the NW United States, in the Rocky Mt region.

Land and Economy. The E half of the state is part of the Great Plains, rising to the ranges of the Rocky Mts, which occupy most of the W. High plateaus lie among the ranges. Rivers include the Belle Fourche, Cheyenne, and North Platte, flowing E; the Big Horn and Powder, flowing N; the Snake, flowing NW, and the Green, flowing S. Dams have made reservoirs on many streams. Much of the open country is grazing land. Hay, wheat, barley, and oats are the crops grown, principally under irrigation. Mineral resources supply the greater part of income. Petroleum is mined and refined. Vast reserves of coal and other minerals exist. Wyoming is one of the least industrialized states.

People. Wyoming is sparsely populated, with a density of only 3.4 persons per sq mi (1.3 per sq km). About 60% of the people lives in urban areas.

Education. There are 8 institutions of higher education. The University of Wyoming is state-supported.

History. In the early 19th century US trappers roamed the region, which had been visited by Frenchmen a century before. For 15 years after 1825, the trappers met annually at a rendezvous at Henry's Fork of the Green River in SW Wyoming. Wagon trains bringing supplies to these gatherings were accompanied by scientists and missionaries. Beginning in the 1840s, thousands of immigrants to California and Oregon followed the Oregon Trail through S Wyoming, obtaining supplies at Fort Laramie in the SE and Fort Bridger in the SW, the only posts in the area. Hostile Indians were a threat to settlement until the 1870s. The Union Pacific Railroad was built through S Wyoming in 1867; the cities of Cheyenne, Laramie, Rawlins, and Rock Springs arose along its route. Wyoming Territory was created by Congress in 1868. Later in the 19th century, enmity between cattlemen and sheep ranchers occasionally broke into violence. In the development of nuclear weapons after WWII, the state profited from exploitation of uranium deposits. A missile launching site was located near Cheyenne. During the 1970s increased demand for domestic coal and petroleum resulted in growth for Wyoming's energy-related industries.

PROFILE

Admitted to Union: July 10, 1890; rank, 44th
US Congressmen: Senate, 2; House of Representatives, 1
Population: 470,816 (1980); rank, 49th
Capital: Cheyenne, 47,283 (1980)
Chief cities: Cheyenne; Casper, 51,016; Laramie, 24,410
State legislature: Senate, 30; House of Representatives, 62
Area: 97,914sq mi (253,597sq km); rank, 9th
Elevation: highest, 13,804ft (4,210m), Gannett Peak; lowest, 3,100ft (946m), Belle Fourche River
Industries (major products): refined petroleum, petroleum products, processed foods
Agriculture (major products): cattle, sheep, dairy products

Minerals (major): petroleum, natural gas, coal, uranium, iron ore
State nickname: Equality State
State motto: Equal Rights
State bird: western meadowlark
State flower: Indian paintbrush
State tree: cottonwood.

Wyoming, city in W Michigan, on Grand River. Industries: automobile and aircraft parts, home appliances, aluminum. Settled 1832; inc. 1959. Pop. (1980) 59,616.

Wyszynski, Cardinal Stefan (1901–81), Polish Roman Catholic cardinal. As Polish archbishop of Gniezno and Warsaw, the cardinal protested to Communist authorities against accusations launched against the church during the trial of Bishop Kaczmarek, bishop of Kielce. He was imprisoned from 1953–56. In the late 1970s and early 1980s, as leader of Poland's Roman Catholics, the cardinal played an active mediating role between the workers and government authorities.

Wythe, George, (1726–1806), American patriot and judge and a signer of the Declaration of Independence, b. Elizabeth City co, Va. A legal educator, he taught Thomas Jefferson. He was the first professor of law in the United States at the College of William and Mary (1779–90).

X

Xanthine, a yellow substance found in plants, in most body tissues and fluids, and in urinary tract stones and which can be oxidized to form uric acid. It is a muscle stimulant, particularly of cardiac muscle, and its synthetic derivatives are used to dilate blood vessels and bronchi and as diuretics.

Xanthoma, skin condition causing a disturbance in cholesterol metabolism. Related to liver disease, it is marked by flat, raised, yellowish patches or nodules on eyelids, neck, or back.

Xavier, Francis (1506–52), first Jesuit missionary, called "Apostle of the Indies," a Roman Catholic saint. He helped Ignatius Loyola found the Jesuit order in 1534. Ordained in 1537, he served at Rome until 1540. King John III of Portugal asked him to go to Goa as a missionary, and he spent the rest of his life in the Orient —in Goa and the SW coast of India (1542–45), Malacca and the Moluccas (1545–46), Ceylon (1547), Japan (1549–51). He died while returning to Goa to organize the missionary effort in China.

Xenon, gaseous nonmetallic element (symbol Xe) of the noble-gas group, first discovered (1898) by William Ramsay and M. W. Travers. Xenon is present in the Earth's atmosphere (0.000008% by volume) and is obtained by fractionation of liquid air. It is used in discharge lamps. The element forms several compounds including XeF_2, XeF_4, XeF_6, $XePtF_6$, and XeO_3. Properties: at. no. 54; at. wt. 131.30; density 5.887 g dm^{-3}; melt. pt. −169.42°F (−111.9°C); boil pt. −160.78°F (−107.1°C); most common isotope Xe^{132} (26.89%). *See also* Noble Gases.

Xenophobia, irrational fear of strangers or foreigners. It is often expressed in hatred for the outsider or in stereotyped ideas about persons who are "different."

Xenophon, (430?–?354 BC), Greek historian, essayist, and general. He marched in Cyrus' expedition against Artaxerxes of Persia (401) and rose to leadership in the Greek army. His works include the *Anabasis* (on Cyrus' march), the *Memorabilia* (on Socrates' teachings), and the *Hellenica*. *See also* Anabasis, Hellenica.

Xerophyte, plant able to survive under dry conditions or in areas subject to drought. These plants have a reduced leaf area, thick stems, wax coating to reduce evaporation, and, on desert-living species, spines instead of leaves. Cactus and stonecrop sedum are examples. Cacti make good house plants.

Xerxes, son of Darius, king of Persia (486–465 BC) He carried on his father's punishment of the Greeks, setting out with a large force in 480. He was at first successful, overcoming the Spartans at Thermopylae, but the defeat at Salamis ended the campaign, and he returned to his harem, leaving Mardonius in charge. Xerxes' forces were driven out of Asia Minor by 467, and he was assassinated by a soldier two years later.

Xingu, river in N Brazil; rises in the Serra do Roncador mountains in central Mato Grosso State; flows N into Amazon River at its delta, below Pôrto de Moz. It is only navigable in its lower course for 100mi (160km). Length: 1,230mi (1,980km).

Xi Particle. *See* Hyperon.

Xochimilco, federal district in central Mexico, 10mi (16km) S of Mexico City on Lake Xochimilco; site of Floating Gardens originally built by Aztecs, canals, 16th-century church. Chief industry is tourism. Pop. 117,083.

X-ray Diffractometer, instrument used in the analysis of the atomic arrangement that determines the crystal structure of minerals. X rays, when passing through the symmetrically arranged atoms of a crystal are deflected in a regular pattern, with the atoms acting as a diffraction grating. Photos of these patterns permit deductions of interatomic dimensions, spacing, and bonding arrangements within crystals. *See also* Crystallography.

X-ray Photograph. *See* Radiography; X rays.

X rays, electromagnetic radiation, first observed by W. K. Roentgen (1895), produced by bombarding a target substance, such as tungsten, with a beam of energetic electrons in an evacuated tube. X rays lie between ultraviolet and gamma rays in the electromagnetic spectrum, the wavelength range being about 10^{-8} to 10^{-11} meters. Typically, they have a continuous range of energies (the bremsstrahlung) with more intense sharp peaks at characteristic energies, resulting from electron transitions in the atom. They blacken photographic film and cause ionization along their path.

X rays, in medicine, short-wavelength rays of the electromagnetic spectrum directed toward the body to permit visualization of internal body structures or to destroy diseased or unwanted tissue. Passed through the body onto a photographic plate, X rays reveal such abnormalities as fractures, tumors, foreign bodies, and enlargement of organs. The capacity of X rays to break up cells makes them useful in the treatment of such diseases as cancer. It is also thought that exposure to radiation may increase the risk of cancer.

X-ray Tube, evacuated tube used to provide a source of X rays for medical or other purposes. It consists of an electron gun producing a stream of electrons that strike an anode, part of which is made of a heavy metal such as tungsten. The tungsten emits X rays when it is bombarded by the stream of high-energy electrons.

Xylem, woody vascular tissue of a plant. It usually consists of elongated vessels, tracheids, fibers, and parenchyma. This water-conducting tissue also gives support to stems, leaves, and roots. Xylem cells are thickened with lignin. *See also* Phloem.

Xylophone, melodic percussion instrument similar to the marimba. It has hardwood bars (metal in metallophone) tuned to a 3-octave chromatic scale, framed over cylindrical metal resonators, and played with mallets. A European folk instrument (16th century), it was revived by Gusikov *c.*1830. It is used not only for novelty, but also in major works by Saint-Saens, Shostakovich, de Falla, Khatchaturian, and Stravinsky..

XYZ Affair (1797–98), incident that strained US relations with France. Pres. John Adams sent three representatives, Charles Pinckney, John Marshall, and Elbridge Gerry, to negotiate a treaty with France to end French interference with US commerce. Three French agents, known as X, Y, and Z, demanded that loans and a $240,000 bribe be given to France before discussion could begin. The Americans refused. The revelation of the bribe attempt caused an uproar and the US representatives returned home.

Y

Yachting, a boating sport and recreation. It includes any vessel that employs sail, power, or a combination of power and sail (auxiliary yachts). Sailing yachts, which are usually fore and aft rigged, vary from 20 feet (6.1m) to over 100 feet (30.5m) and include cutters, schooners, ketches, sloops, and yawls, as well as other types. Those fitted with diesel or gasoline engines are usually classified as cruising yachts. Yachts are capable of speeds up to 25 miles (40km) per hour, although the average speed is 10 knots. Although most yachts are used for vacationing and cruising, the sport has been a competitive attraction since 1851 when the Royal Yacht Squadron, formed at Cowes, England, in 1812, offered a silver cup as a prize for a race of 60 miles (97km) around the Isle of Wight. The race was won by the schooner yacht, *America*, owned by the members of the New York Yacht Club (organized 1844), and has since been known as the America's Cup, most prized of all international tournaments. Through 1976, the United States had never lost this trophy. Other famous ocean yacht sailing races include the Newport (R. I.) to Bermuda Race, the Trans-Pacific Race, and the Chicago Yacht Club to Mackinac Island Race.

Yahweh, a personal name for God used in Judaism. It was revealed by God to Moses. It is formed by four Hebrew consonants, YHWH, called the Tetragrammaton. It was replaced after the 3rd century BC, by Adonai, as it was considered too sacred to speak. Its origin is unknown as is its original pronunciation and meaning. Its usage came to be reserved for the high priest.

Yak, large, powerful, long-haired black ox, native to N India and Tibet, with domesticated races throughout central Asia. It inhabits barren heights to 20,000ft (6,000m). Domesticated races are smaller and varied in color. Its horns curve up and forward. Sure-footed beasts of burden, they are also used for meat and milk. Height: to 6.5ft (2m) at shoulders; weight: to 1,200lbs (540kg). Family Bovidae; species *Bos grunniens*. *See also* Cattle.

Yale University, university in New Haven, Conn. It is among the Ivy League schools and operates several colleges of study including divinity, law, medicine, art, theater, and architecture. Its different locations were Killingworth (now Clinton) 1702 and Saybrook (now Old Saybrook) 1717. Chartered in 1701 in Branford, Conn.; current charter 1745.

Yalow, Rosalyn S(ussman) (1921–), US medical physicist. She was trained as a nuclear physicist, and her research (1950–72), with Dr. Solomon A. Berson, in insulin led to the development of radioimmunoassay (RIA), a technique for measuring the concentration of biologically active substances in the blood and other body fluids. She was awarded the Nobel Prize for medicine in 1977 with Roger C. L. Guillemin and Andrew Schally.

Yalta Conference (1945), meeting between US Pres. Franklin D. Roosevelt, Prime Minister Winston Churchill of Britain, and Premier Joseph Stalin of the USSR. It took place at Yalta in the Crimea. They met to plan the final attacks on Germany, its postwar occupation and control, and the punishment of war crimes. A conference to establish what became the United Nations was called to meet at San Francisco. Eastern Poland was awarded to Russia. In return for Far East concessions, Russia agreed to join the war against Japan within three months of Germany's defeat.

Yalu, river in NE China and North Korea; rises in the Ch'ang-pai Shan Mts; flows SW to Korea Bay near Tan-tung; commercially important for production of hydroelectricity at Sunpung Dam and transportation of lumber; site of Communist invasion of North Korea during Korean War. Length: 501mi (807km).

Yam, herbaceous vines native to warm and tropical regions. The large, tuberous roots are sometimes edible and often confused with the sweet potato. Family Dioscoreaceae; genus *Dioscorea*.

Yama, in Indian mythology, lord, guide, and judge of the dead, also a deified hero worshiped as the first mortal man. He and his sister, Yami, are children of Vivasvat, the Sun.

Yamasaki, Minoru (1912–), US architect, b. Seattle. He designed Lambert-St Louis Municipal Airport terminal (1951), noted for its concrete vaults. Other major works include the American consulate in Kobe, Japan (1954); the McGregor Memorial Community Conference Center (1958) and the Reynolds Metal Company (1969), both in Detroit; the US science pavilion at the Seattle Exposition (1962); the Plaza Hotel, Los Angeles (1966); and the Eastern Airlines Terminal, Boston (1968). He was a chief designer of the World Trade Center in New York City (1962–72).

Yamasee War (1715–16), waged by Yamasee Indians angered over land seizures by South Carolina settlers. Indians were driven south into Florida and west to Alabama, opening the way to the settling of Georgia.

Xenophon: sculpture

Yaroslavl, USSR

Yemen

Yamato, term meaning "Great Peace" applied to the Japanese state *c.*400–800. Society then was based on a hierarchy of tribal groups.

Yangtze (Chang, or Ch'ang), river in E central China; the longest and most economically important waterway in the country. Rising in the Kunlun Mts in NE Tibet, it flows E through the central Chinese provinces to the East China Sea at Shanghai. In its upper course it is known as the Kinsha River; navigation is difficult at Yangtze Gorges, between Ichang and Fengkieh; along with its main tributaries, the Yalung, Min, Kialing, Wu, Yü, Han, and Siang, it traverses one of the world's most populated areas, providing fertile land and hydroelectricity. Length: approx. 3,434mi (5,529km).

Yaoundé (Yaunde), capital city of Cameroon, W Africa, 125mi (201km) E of Atlantic coast, on Gulf of Guinea; educational center, site of university (1962). Industries: soap, tile, dairy products, tobacco, coffee, rubber, timber. Founded 1888, became capital 1922. Pop. 180,000.

Yap Islands, island group in W Caroline Islands, W Pacific Ocean, approx. 800mi (1,288km) E of the Philippines; became member of US Trust Territory of the Pacific Islands in 1947. Yap Island is largest of the group, followed by three other large islands and about ten smaller ones. Area: 85sq mi (220sq km). Pop. 8,482.

Yaqui, Indian group concentrated in the Mexican state of Sonora. The Yaqui fiercely resisted Spanish attempts at conquest and colonization and fought guerrilla campaigns against the Mexican authorities until 1918.

Yard. *See* Weights and Measures.

Yaroslavl (Jaroslavl'), city in W central USSR, on Volga River, 160mi (258km) NE of Moscow; capital of Yaroslavl oblast. In 1218 the city was capital of Yaroslavl principality absorbed by Moscow in 1463. From March–July 1612 it served as Russia's capital; site of 12th-century monastery, 17th-century church of St John Chrysostom, and Volkov theater (1911). Industries: linen (since 18th century), diesel engines, construction equipment, oil refining. Founded 1010 by Yaroslavl the Great. Pop. 592,000.

Yarrow, hardy Northern Hemisphere perennial plant. The common yarrow or milfoil *(Achillea millefolium)* has fernlike leaves and flat clusters of white or pink flower heads. Height: to 3ft (91cm). Family Compositae.

Yawl, a two-masted sailboat with the mainmast higher than the mizzenmast, rigged with one or more jib sails, a mainsail, and a mizzen. Unlike the ketch, the yawl has the mizzenmast astern the rudder post. Dinghys and light sailing vessels rigged with lugsails are often referred to as yawls.

Yaws, or frambesia, contagious skin disease found worldwide in the humid tropics. It is caused by a spirochete *(Treponema pertenue)* indistinguishable from the organism causing syphilis. Yaws, however, is not venereal, but is passed along by flies and by direct skin contact with the open raspberry-red sores characteristic of this infection. Unlike syphilis, secondary and tertiary symptoms are not typical, although they can develop.

Yazoo Controversy, dispute over land near the Yazoo River. The land, 35,000,000 acres (14,164,500 hectares) in Alabama and Mississippi, was sold by the

Georgia legislature to land companies (1795). The next year the legislature rescinded the sale.

Yeast, any of a group of single-celled microscopic fungi (class Ascomycetes) that grow wild all over the world in the soil and in organic matter. Yeasts are also produced commercially for use in baking, brewing, wine making, and nutrition. Yeast feeding on sugar can convert it into carbon dioxide (which makes bread rise) and alcohol (which makes wine and beer potent). Yeast is also a rich source of B-complex vitamins. Yeasts reproduce asexually and, like other fungi, must obtain food from their environment. Yeast spores can remain dormant for many years.

Yeats, William Butler (1865–1939), Irish poet, b. Dublin. A founder-member of the Rhymers Club in London (1891), his verse became increasingly austere as he developed a complex symbolism to commemorate public events and private friendships. With his friend Lady Gregory he helped to found the Abbey Theatre in Dublin (1904), for which he wrote plays. He was also involved in Irish nationalist politics and was a skeptical adherent of spiritualism. He married Georglie Hyde-Lees in 1917 and served as a senator of the Irish Free State (1922–28). He received the Nobel Prize for literature in 1923. Among his many memorable poems are "Easter, 1916," "The Second Coming," and "Sailing to Byzantium." *See also* Irish Literary Renaissance.

Yellow (Hwang-Ho), river in N central and E China; rises in Amne Machin Shan; flows across Inner Mongolia, E through gorges along N Honan border. Lower course across Great Plains has shifted often, vitally affecting 35,000,000acres (14,175,000hectares) of rich farmland; construction for dam and reservoir system was begun 1955. Length: 2,903mi (4,673km).

Yellow-Dog Contract, employer anti-union weapon widely used before 1932. The employer would require that the employee, as a condition of employment, sign a contract in which he agreed not to take part in any union activity, including organizing or striking. The yellow-dog contract was banned by the Norris-LaGuardia Act (1932).

Yellow Fever, acute infectious disease marked by sudden onset of headaches, high fever, jaundice, and bloody vomiting. It is caused by a virus transmitted by several species of mosquito, especially in tropical and subtropical regions. Monkeys are also vulnerable. Live-virus vaccines are highly effective.

Yellowhammer, or yellow bunting, small Old World finch known for its pair formation ceremony when males and females drop and pick up small inanimate objects before mating. Species *Emberiza calandra.*

Yellow Jack, tropical marine food fish of the Indo-Pacific. A golden fish, it is marked with 8–12 dark bands. Length: to 3ft (91cm). Family Carangidae; species *Caranx bartholomaei.*

Yellowknife, largest town and capital of Northwest Territories, Canada, on NW shore of Great Slave Lake at mouth of Yellowknife River. Founded 1935 when gold and silver were discovered; site of airport and Royal Canadian Mounted Police post. Pop. 8,256.

Yellow Sea, branch of the Pacific Ocean, N of East China Sea between China's mainland and Korea; the Strait of Chihli connects it to the Chihli and Liaotung gulfs; the Yellow, Huai, Liao, and Yalu rivers empty into it. Depth (max.): 250ft (76m). Area: 180,000sq mi (446,200sq km).

Yellowstone National Park, park in Wyoming, Montana, and Idaho. It is the largest and the oldest of the national parks. It features the world's largest geyser area, with about 3,000 geysers and hot springs. The park is famous for its beautiful scenery, petrified forests, lava formations, and Old Faithful geyser. Bears, bison, moose, elk, and mountain sheep are found. Area: 2,221,772acres (899,818hectares). Est. 1872.

Yellowstone River, river that rises in NW Wyoming; flows N through Yellowstone National Park, across the Montana border, and ENE into the Missouri River near the North Dakota line; after it drains Yellowstone Lake in NW Wyoming it drops 109ft (33m) at the Upper Falls, then another drop of 308ft (94m) at Lower Falls to enter the Grand Canyon of the Yellowstone. River has been used for irrigation since 1860. Length of river: 671mi (1,080km).

Yellowtail, or California yellowtail, popular marine game fish found in the Sea of Cortez off S California coast. A solid-bodied fish with big eyes and scimitar-shaped tail, it is yellow, green, and silver. Weight: to 40lb (18kg). Family Carangidae; species *Seriola dorsalis.*

Yellowthroat, small New World warbler, especially *Geothlypis trichas* that has a brownish back, yellow throat, and, in the male, a black facial mask. The yellow-throated warbler *(Dendroica dominica)* is a wood warbler.

Yemen, People's Democratic Republic of, formerly Southern Yemen, republic on the SE end of the Arabian Peninsula, E of the Yemen Arab Republic; includes the islands of Kamaran, Perim, Socotra; the capital is Aden. Rising from a coastal plain to mountains and highland plateaus (average height 6,500ft/1,983m), the area is generally arid and hot.

Agriculture forms the economic base, heavily relying on foreign aid. Crops include: cotton (main cash crop), tobacco, coffee, millet, grains, and dates. The petroleum refinery (at Little Aden) is the major industry. Other industries include: fishing, textiles, handcrafts, shipbuilding, furniture. Petroleum and food products—mostly live fish—together account for almost 65% of export revenues. Most large enterprises, including the refinery, were nationalized during the 1970s. The people are mostly Arabs, with some mixed African and European influences. There are some nomadic tribes in the N, however Yemenites along the S coast are much more settled and less tribe-oriented.

According to the constitution of 1970 executive authority is vested in the president, who also serves as chairman of the sole legal political party, the Marxist-oriented Yemen Socialist Party. Southern Yemen flourished under the Minaean, Sabaean, and Himyarite empires, and was part of a larger entity called Al-Yemen. It came under Muslim influence in the 600s, and the Ottoman Empire and the imams of Yemen in the 16th century. British occupation began in 1839; by 1914, through the purchase of islands, area mainlands, and treaty agreements with local rulers, a British protectorate was est., leading eventually to the Federation of South Arabia. Terrorist campaigns against British control began in the 1960s, and the National Liberation Front forced the federation's collapse; Southern Yemen became independent November 1967. A new constitution was promulgated 1970, and the name was changed to People's Democratic Republic of Yemen. The country forged close ties with the Soviet Union, which was partly responsible for tensions with neighboring Yemen Arab Republic, which erupted into war briefly in 1972 and again in 1979. Although the two countries subsequently signed a treaty of friendship pledging eventual unification, ideological differences made rapid implementation unlikely. In 1986, civil war broke out between political factions and after 12 days of bloodshed, a new Soviet-backed government emerged to control the country.

PROFILE

Official name: People's Democratic Republic of Yemen
Area: 112,075sq mi (290,274sq km)
Population: 1,853,000
Chief cities: Aden (capital); Mukalla
Religion: Islam
Language: Arabic

Yemen Arab Republic, republic at the SW tip of the Arabian Peninsula, adjacent to Peoples' Democratic Republic of Yemen; earliest seat of Arab culture. The nation consists of the Tihamah, a narrow coastal lowland area, and interior highlands.

Most of the population works in agriculture; chief crops include coffee (shipped worldwide from the Port of Mocha) and gat, a shrub whose leaves yield a narcotic. Much of the farming is at a subsistence level; handcrafts play a major part in the economy. Yemenites are a settled population, unlike their nomadic neighbors, chiefly Arabs, with some Arab-African mixing in the Tihamah; literacy is estimated at about 5%.

An absolute monarchy until 1962, Yemen now is governed by an Army Council, which seized power in 1974. A 1970 constitution est. a presidency and councils. The cradle of three major early civilizations, the Minaeans, Sabaeans, and Himyarites, the area was invaded by Romans in 1st century BC; after subsequent Ethiopian conquests and the rise of Christianity and Judaism, Islam arrived in the 7th century. Following the breakup of the Muslim caliphs the Rassite Dynasty took power, evolving a monarchy that survived until 1962. From 1958–61 Yemen was joined in the nominal United Arab States alliance with Egypt and Syria. In 1962 civil war erupted between royalists, supported by Saudi Arabian troops, and republicans, aided by the Egyptian army. In 1967 fighting ended, with the republicans victorious. In 1974 the military seized control of the government, pledging to unite the country with the Peoples' Democratic Republic of Yemen. A president and constituent assembly were elected in 1978, but the army continues to control the government. Frictions between the two Yemens erupted (1972, 1979) into brief wars, but after the latter both sides pledged themselves to complete unification. An earthquake, killing 2,800 people, struck in 1982.

PROFILE

Official name: Yemen Arab Republic
Area: 75,290sq mi (195,001sq km)
Population: 6,471,893
Chief cities: Sana; Hodeida; Taizz
Religion: Muslim
Language: Arabic
Monetary unit: Riyal

Yen, C. K. (Yen Chia-kan) (1905–), Chinese political leader. He became president (1975–78) of the Republic of China at the death of Chiang Kai-shek. He had served as a key economic minister in bringing about Taiwan's rapid industrial and commercial progress.

Yenan (Yan'an, or Yen-an), town in N central China, on Yen River, 160mi (258km) NNE of Sian. Known as the center of Chinese Communist party (1936–48) during its struggle with the Nationalist forces for control of China and terminus of the Red Eighth Route Army's "Long March," it was captured by Nationalists March 19, 1947; fell to Communists April 22, 1949; site of revolutionary museum, former homes of Mao Tse-tung and Chou En-lai, pagoda built during Sung dynasty (960–1279). Pop. 45,000.

Yenisei (Jenisej), chief river in central Siberia, USSR; formed by confluence of Bolshoi Yenisei and Maly Yenisei; flows W and N through Sayan Mts past Minusinsk into Yenisei Gulf on Kara Sea (arm of Arctic Ocean). Chief tributaries are the Angara, Stony, Tunguska, and Lower Tunguska rivers; connected to Ob River by canals. River is frozen during winter months; ice melting on upper part of river before that on lower river causes severe flooding as water backs up. A large hydroelectric station has been built at Krasnoyarsk. River supports fishing for sturgeon and salmon; lumber, grain and construction materials are shipped. Length: 2,566mi (4,131km).

Yerevan (Jerevan), capital of Armenian SSR, SE European USSR; on Razdan River. In 7th century city was capital of Armenia (under Persian control); site of crossroads of caravan routes between India and Transcaucasia. At different times Persia and Turkey held Yerevan; it was taken by Russia 1827; became capital of Armenian SSR 1920; site of Yerevan State University (1920), Armenian Academy of Sciences (1943), 16th-century Turkish fortress. Industries: chemicals, plastics, synthetic rubber, cables, electrical equipment. Founded AD 7th century. Pop. 982,000.

Yerkes, Robert M(earns) (1876–1956), US biologist and psychologist, b. Breadysville, Pa. He pioneered in the comparative study of apes, the development of methods to test the abilities of animals and humans, and was director of the Yerkes Laboratories of Primate Biology at Yale University (1919–41). Among his many publications are *The Mind of a Gorilla* (1927) and *Chimpanzees: A Laboratory Colony* (1943).

Yerushalayim. *See* Jerusalem.

Yevtushenko, Yevgeny Aleksandrovich (1933–), Soviet poet. An outspoken writer frequently criticized by Soviet authorities, much of his work remains unpublished in the Soviet Union. His verse includes *Zima Junction* (1956), *Babi Yar* (1961), *Precocious Autobiography* (1963), *Stolen Apples* (1971), and *From Desire to Desire* (1976). *Berry Patches* (1982) was a novel.

Yew, evergreen shrubs and trees native to temperate regions of the Northern Hemisphere. They have stiff, narrow, dark green needles, often with pale undersides, and red, berrylike fruits. Height: to 60ft (18.3m). Family Taxaceae; genus *Taxus.*

Yggdrasill, in Norse mythology, a giant ash tree supporting the world. It had three roots; one extending into the underworld, the second, into the land of the giants, and the third, into the home of the gods.

Yiddish, language spoken for centuries by Jews living in central and E Europe and in other countries of the world (including the United States) to which Jews had migrated. It is basically a variety of German, with many Hebrew and Slavic words added, and written in the Hebrew alphabet. More than half of all Yiddish speakers perished during World War II and the number of speakers today is steadily declining.

Yin Dynasty. *See* Shang Dynasty.

Yin-yang, in Chinese philosophy, two cosmic energy modes comprising the Tao or the eternal dynamic way of the universe. A recurrent theme in Taoist and Confucian texts, heaven is yang, or the active, bright, male principle, and Earth is yin, or the passive, dark, female principle. All the things of nature and society are composed of different combinations of the two principles. The trigrams of the *I Ching* embody yin and yang. *See also* I Ching.

Ymir, in Teutonic mythology, the father of all the giants. Bor married one of Ymir's daughters, Bestla. With her he fathered three gods, Odin, Vili, and Ve. These sons killed Ymir and formed the Earth with his inert body. The flesh of Ymir became the land and his blood formed the seas.

Yoga (Sanskrit for "union"), term used for a number of Hindu disciplines to aid the soul's merging with God. Based on the Yoga-sutras of Patañjali (written around the time of Christ), the practice of yoga generally involves moral restraints, meditation, and the awakening of physical energy centers through specific postures *(asanas)* or exercises. Devoted to freeing the soul or self from earthly cares, these ancient practices have become popular in the West as a means of relaxation, self-control, and enlightenment.

Yokohama, seaport and industrial city in SE Honshu, Japan, on W shore of Tokyo Bay, approx. 18mi (29km) SSW of Tokyo; capital of Kanagawa prefecture. It is main port for Tokyo, Kawasaki, Yokohama industrial region; grew from a small fishing village to a major port after being visited 1854 by Comm. Matthew C. Perry; it was opened to foreign trade 1859; site of Yokohama Municipal University and Yokohama National University (both 1949). Industries: steel, automobiles, oil refining, silk textiles, machinery, chemicals, shipbuilding, fish canning, electronic equipment. Pop. 2,622,000.

Yom Kippur, the Day of Atonement in Judaism. It is the last of the Ten Days of Penitence that begin the new year. On this solemn day set aside for prayer and fasting, man is called to account for his sins and reconcile himself with God and man. It is described as the Sabbath of Sabbaths.

Yonkers, city in SE New York, on Hudson River, adjoining greater New York City. Land was originally purchased from Indians in 1639 by Dutch West India Co.; site of St Joseph's College and Seminary (1839), Elizabeth Seton College (1961), Philipse Manor (17th century), and Hudson River Museum. Industries: elevators (since 1852), chemicals, cables, telephone parts, art supplies. Inc. as village 1855, as city 1872. Pop. (1980) 195,351.

York, Richard Plantagenet, 3rd Duke of (1411–60), contender for the English throne during the Wars of the Roses, father of Edward IV and Richard III. Succeeding his uncle, Edward, as duke of York (1415), he became Edward III's heir by primogeniture (1425). Loyal to Henry VI, he protected the realm during the king's illness (1453–54), but conflicted with the jealous Edmund Beaufort, duke of Somerset, and Margaret of Anjou. Rivalry flared into war (1455). After some initial successes, York was killed in battle at Wakefield (1460).

York, House of, branch of the Plantagenet family—an English royal family—descended from Edmund of Langley, 1st duke of York (1341–1402), fourth surviving son of Edward III. The duke of York's hereditary claim to the English throne was strengthened when it became linked to that of the descendants of Lionel, duke of Clarence, Edmund's elder brother. Upon the deposition of Richard II (1399), the crown reverted to the House of Lancaster, in the person of Henry IV. Minor demonstrations of disloyalty by the Yorkists followed, becoming more marked under Henry VI, and culminating in the outbreak of the Wars of the Roses (1455), after which Henry Tudor ascended the throne as Henry VII (1485).

York, city in N England, at confluence of Ouse and Foss rivers; rail center, makes confectionery and other products. As Eboracum, city was the chief Roman military base and has been an ecclesiastical center of N England since the 7th century; site of York Minster cathedral (1154); 8th-century educational center. Pop. 102,700.

York, city in S Pennsylvania, 23mi (37km) S of Harrisburg; seat of York co; scene of the Continental Congress 1777–78; occupied briefly by Confederates 1863; rich farm region in Pennsylvania Dutch country; site of York College of Pennsylvania (1941); Friends Meeting house (1765); and several colonial houses. Industries: refrigerators, stoves, roofing materials, paper products. Founded 1741; inc. as borough 1787, as city 1887. Pop. (1980) 44,619.

Yorkshire, former county of N England, now divided into the nonmetropolitan counties of Cleveland, North Yorkshire, West Yorkshire, South Yorkshire, and Humberside. The region is bounded by the North Sea (E), Tees River (N), the Pennines (W), and the Humber (SE); famous for its coal, iron, steel, wool, and textiles from such industrial centers as Middlesbrough, Bradford, Leeds, and Sheffield.

Yorkshire Terrier, long-haired dog (toy group) bred in Lancashire and Yorkshire, England, about 1860 as Scotch terrier; brought to US 1880. Its small head with short muzzle is carried high. Small, V-shaped ears are erect. The compact body has a short, straight back. Straight legs are hidden under the coat. The docked tail is carried high. The straight, fine, silky coat is floor length; colors are blue and tan. Average size: 9in (23cm) high at shoulder; 4–7lb (2–3kg). *See also* Toy Dog.

Yorktown Campaign (1781), final military campaign of the American Revolution. British Gen. Lord Cornwallis had fortified the Virginia community of Yorktown to protect entry to the York River. Gen. George Washington, with the help of French soldiers and the French fleet, laid siege to the town and, in October after less than two weeks, forced Cornwallis to capitulate (Oct. 19, 1781).

Yoruba, Negroid people of SW Nigeria. They are mainly agriculturalists, crops include yams, maize, and cocoa. Many Yoruba live in towns built around the palace of an *oba,* or chief, and commute to their outlying farms. Religions include Christianity and Islam; traditional deities are also still worshiped.

Yosemite National Park, park in central California. It is a mountainous, glacial area of outstanding beauty. It features the nation's highest waterfall, Yosemite Valley, and other breathtaking gorges. There are three groves of giant redwood trees. Area: 761,320acres (308,335hectares). Est. 1890.

Young, Andrew Jackson, Jr. (1932–), US political leader and diplomat, b. New Orleans, La. He became a minister in the United Church of Christ in 1955, after graduating from the Hartford Theological Seminary. He served as a key aide to Martin Luther King, Jr., and in 1972 became the first black elected to Congress from an Atlanta district, serving three terms. Pres.

Yugoslavia (Jugoslavija)

Yorkshire terrier

Brigham Young

Thomas Young

Jimmy Carter appointed him ambassador to the United Nations in 1977. His controversial term of service terminated with his resignation (1979) over a private meeting with a Palestine Liberation Organization representative. In 1981 he was elected mayor of Atlanta, Ga.

Young, Brigham (1801–77), US religious leader, b. Whittingham, Vt. An early convert (1832) to the Church of Jesus Christ of Latter-Day Saints, Young took over the leadership when Joseph Smith, the church founder, was killed by a mob (1844) in Illinois. A strong leader, Young held the group together through persecutions and led them in their great westward migration (1846–47). In Utah he directed the settlement that became Salt Lake City. He was governor of Utah territory (1850–57), but was replaced when the Morman practice of polygamy brought them into conflict with the federal government. As head of the Mormon church he remained the effective ruler in Utah until his death.

Young, Thomas (1773–1829), English physicist and physician who did pioneer work in the accommodation of the eye and who detailed the cause of astigmatism. In 1803 he showed the wave nature of light and computed the visible light wavelength. He also helped present the Young-Helmholtz three-color theory; explained that double refraction was due to the transverse state of light waves; and worked with elastic substances.

Young, Whitney Jr. (1921–71), US black leader, b. Lincoln Ridge, Ky. A leader in the civil rights movement, he advocated improvement in economic opportunities, housing, and welfare. He was executive director of the National Urban League (1961–71). His books include *To Be Equal* (1964).

Younger Brothers, American outlaws, four brothers, James (d. 1902), Robert (d. 1889), Cole (1844–1916), and John (d. 1874) Younger. As members of the outlaw gang of Jesse James, John was shot by a Pinkerton detective (1874), and the others were arrested during an attempted bank robbery in Northfield, Minn. (1876). Sentenced to life imprisonment, Robert died in prison (1889), Cole and James were paroled 1901; James committed suicide, and Cole joined a Wild West show.

Young Men's Christian Association (YMCA), Christian community organization with programs that seek the improvement of conditions and opportunities for young men of all races and economic backgrounds. The YMCA stresses physical training and fitness and tries to develop cultural, intellectual, social, and vocational interests. First organized in London in 1844 by Sir George Williams, the association spread to North America by 1851.

Youngstown, city in NE Ohio, on Mahoning River 43mi (69km) E of Akron; seat of Mahoning co. One of the largest US steel producing centers, it is the site of Youngstown University (1908), First Presbyterian Church (1799), and the modern gothic St Columba's Cathedral (1958). Industries: iron, steel, office equipment, electric light bulbs, plastics, paper products. Founded 1797 when John Young bought area from Western Reserve Land Co.; inc. as town 1848; chartered as city 1867. Pop. (1980) 115,436.

Youngstown Sheet and Tube Company v. Sawyer (1952), noted US Supreme Court decision holding that President Truman had exceeded his powers in nationalizing a steel company to avert a strike that would have affected the Korean War effort. The court held

that other avenues were open to keep the company operating and that an executive order was improper.

Young Women's Christian Association (YWCA), organization dedicated to the welfare and needs of women and girls, whose programs offer growth in their spiritual, intellectual, social, vocational, and physical development. It was first organized in London in 1855 by Lady Kinnaird, and officially became the YWCA 1877. The organization spread to North America where a New York City prayer group, started by Mrs. Marshall O. Roberts (1858), is considered the first US YWCA.

Ypsilanti, city in SE Michigan, on Huron River; site of Eastern Michigan University (1849) and Cleary College (1883). Industries: automobile parts, paper, ladders. Settled 1825; inc. as village 1832, as city 1858. Pop. (1980) 24,031.

Ytterbium, metallic element (symbol Yb) of the lanthanide group, first isolated in 1878 along with lutetium. Chief ore is monazite (phosphate). The element has few commercial uses. Properties: at. no. 70; at. wt. 173.04; sp gr 6.965 (δ), 6.54 (β); melt. pt. 1,515°F (824°C); boil. pt. 2,179°F (1,193°C); most common isotope Yb^{174} (31.84%). *See also* Lanthanide Elements.

Yttrium, metallic element (symbol Y) of group IIIB of the periodic table, first isolated in 1828 by Friedrich Wohler. It is found associated with the lanthanides in monazite (phosphate) and bastnasite (fluorocarbonate) and resembles the lanthanides in its chemistry. The element has few commercial uses. Properties: at. no. 39; at. wt. 88.9059; sp gr 4.469; melt. pt. 2,773°F (1,523°C); boil pt. 6,039°F (3,337°C); most common isotope Y^{89} (100%).

Yüan Dynasty (1264–1368), Chinese dynasty, the period of Mongol rule in China by the descendants of Genghis Khan. Kublai Khan, known as the Chinese Emperor Shih-tsu, was able to conquer all of China and eliminate the last Sung Dynasty pretender in 1279. Mongol rulers sent expeditions to attempt to conquer Japan and to SE Asia and brought China into contact with areas of Europe and the Middle East. The Yüan period became the golden age of Chinese drama.

Yucatán, peninsula consisting of SE Mexico, British Honduras, and N Guatemala, separates the Gulf of Mexico from the Caribbean Sea; includes Campeche and Yucatán states, and the territory of Quintana Roo, Mexico. The terrain is mostly low-lying limestone region, with beautiful beaches along the coast, and dense tropical forests chiefly in Guatemala and British Honduras. The peninsula was the seat of the ancient Maya civilization; site of several ruined cities, temples, and pyramids. Area: approx. 70,000sq mi (181,300sq km).

Yucatán, state in SE Mexico, on N end of Yucatán Peninsula; seat of ancient Maya civilization; conquered 1546 by Francisco de Montejo. Terrain is flat plains, sparse hills, and forest lands. Products: lumber, tobacco, tropical fruit, honey, corn, sugar. Industries: fishing, tourism, sisal hemp, shoes, bags, hats. Area: approx. 14,900sq mi (38,600sq km). Pop. 904,000.

Yucca Moth, small white moth that has a symbiotic relationship with the yucca plant. Yucca plant flowers are pollinated exclusively by yucca moths and the moth larvae feed only on yucca plant seeds. Genus *Tegeticula.*

Yugoslavia (Jugoslavija), independent nation in SE Europe. With historical ethnic and religious differences

among Yugoslavia's six republics and two autonomous regions, it has proven difficult to forge a national identity in this Communist—yet staunchly nonaligned—country.

Land and economy. Located in SE Europe, it is bordered by Italy and the Adriatic Sea (W), Austria, Hungary, and Romania (N), Bulgaria (E), and Greece and Albania (S). Politically it is divided into the republics of Bosnia and Herzegovina, Croatia, Macedonia, Montenegro, Serbia, Slovenia, and the autonomous regions of Vojvodina and Kossovo. Geographically, it is divided into two regions. Agricultural plains, low hills, and a few mountain ranges outline the area from Zagreb in the NW to Nis in the SE, including about 35% of the country. Minerals, timber, and sheep raising are in the mountainous section, which covers the remaining 65% of the country. The Danube River, the major water route between central and E Europe, flows through Yugoslavia. In the interior the climate is moderate; summers are hot, winters mild, and it is rainy along the Adriatic. Wars and drought have hindered the economy; most industry is socialized and managed by workers' councils. Private farms are restricted to 25acres (10hectares). Tourism is a major factor in the economy. In 1965, Yugoslavia attempted to increase production by shifting its centrally controlled economy to a decentralized system, incorporating worker self-management.

People. Great diversity marks the Yugoslav population. The main nationality groups are: Serbs 42%; Croats 23%; Slovenes 8%; Macedonians, Albanians, and Bosnian Muslims 6% each; Montenegrins 3%; Hungarians 2%; and Turks 1%. Religious preferences are based mainly on ethnic divisions. Seven million Serbs, Montenegrins, and Macedonians belong to the Eastern Orthodox Church, while 5,000,000 Croats, Slovenes, and Hungarians belong to the Roman Catholic Church. Three languages are officially approved—Slovenian, Macedonian, and Serbo-Croatian. Education is free and compulsory to age 14. Literacy is 80%.

Government. According to the constitution of 1974, executive power is vested in a collective state presidency composed of one representative from each of the republics and autonomous regions; chairmanship rotates among the members. The only legal political party is the League of Communists.

History. Yugoslavia's history has been characterized by ethnic and religious crises. Centuries as an Ottoman Empire vassal were followed by territorial expansion after the 1913 Balkan Wars and the 1914 Sarejevo assassination of Austrian Archduke Ferdinand, which precipitated WWI. A monarchy was established in 1918. Serb and Croat nationalist demands erupted in 1928 when a Croatian leader was assassinated, and King Alexander established a royal dictatorship in 1929. At the start of WWII, pro-Allied Serb elements staged a coup d'etat and replaced Prince Paul, who had become regent in 1934, with King Peter. The Axis powers then invaded Yugoslavia, and the government went into exile. Yugoslav resistance forces were divided between those loyal to the monarchy and those allied with the National Liberation Army (Partisans) led by Marshal Tito. At the close of WWII the Partisans were in power. A 1945 constitution made Yugoslavia a republic, and Marshal Tito became head of the government. Initially a Soviet satellite, Yugoslavia broke with Joseph Stalin and the USSR in 1948 and subsequently followed an independent policy that brought increased contacts with the West. Despite fears to the contrary, leadership of the country succeeded smoothly to the collective presidency following Tito's death in 1980, and the country continued its nonaligned policy. However, the 1980s brought splits in the party leadership, economic woes, and tense relations with Albania over Albanians residing in Yugoslavia's Kosovo province who were demanding republic status.

PROFILE

Official name: Socialist Federal Republic of Yugoslavia
Area: 98,766sq mi (255,804sq km)
Population: 22,299,027
Density: 226per sq mi (87per sq km)
Chief cities: Belgrade (capital); Zagreb; Skopje
Government: Federated republic
Religion: Eastern Orthodox and Roman Catholic
Language: Slovenian, Macedonian, Serbo-Croatian; all government recognized
Monetary unit: Dinar
Gross national product: $53,790,000,000
Per capita income: $859
Industries: wood products, iron, steel, processed foods, chemicals, machinery, textiles
Agriculture: maize, wheat, barley, rye, tobacco, oats, hops, fruits, sugar beets, fish, cattle, potatoes
Minerals: coal, iron, copper, chrome, antimony, manganese, lead, mercury, salt, bauxite
Trading partners: West Germany, Italy, United Kingdom, USSR, Czechoslovakia

Yukon River, third-longest river in North America; rises at the confluence of the Lewes and Pelly rivers in SW Yukon Territory, Canada; flows NW across the border into Alaska, then SW across central Alaska to the Bering Sea S of Norton Sound. Lower course of river was first explored by Russians in 1836–37; upper course by Robert Campbell 1843. Navigable for three months of year up to Whitehorse, Alaska, *c.* 1,775mi (2,858km) of its 2,000mi (3,220km).

Yukon Territory, territory of extreme NW Canada, bordered on the W and SW by the state of Alaska, and on the N by the Arctic Ocean.

Land and economy. The highest peaks in Canada are in the St Elias Mts in the SW. Most of the region is a rough plateau, broken by mountains and deep river valleys. The Yukon River, which flows W into Alaska, and its tributaries form the principal river system and are a potential source of great hydroelectric power. Most of the S and central portions are forested, but transportation problems have hampered exploitation of the timber. The famous gold deposits have now been supplanted by copper, lead, silver, and zinc mining. Arable land lies in some river valleys, but its use has been limited to farming for local use. Some fishing and hunting for furs takes place, but after mining, tourism is the second-leading source of income.

People and education. The population consists largely of immigrants from Canada and the United States, concentrated around Whitehorse, the capital. A few Indians are scattered about the territory. The territorial government directs the education of children. There are no institutions of higher education.

History. Fur traders of the Hudson's Bay Co. and surveyors explored the region, then part of the Northwest Territories, after 1840. Small strikes of gold were discovered beginning in 1873 and in 1896 a rich find occurred on a tributary of the Klondike River. Prospectors stampeded to the territory, swelling its population to more than 22,000 by 1901. More than $100,000,000 in gold was taken from the diggings in 10 years. The gold rush subsided; by 1921 the population was just over 4,000 and in 1941 it was only 4,914. Defense needs in WWII stimulated the territory. The Alaska Highway to S Canada and the United States, a chain of airfields, and a pipeline to carry oil from the Northwest Territories to a refinery constructed at Whitehorse were built. The pipeline and the refinery were closed after the war but the highway and the airfields were kept in operation. The improved transportation network has encouraged the growth of mining.

PROFILE

Created territory: 1898
National Parliament representatives: Senate, 0; House of Commons, 1
Population: 16,000
Chief city: Whitehorse (capital)
Provincial legislature: Territorial Council, 12
Area: 207,076sq mi (536,327sq km)
Elevation: highest, 19,850ft (6,054m), Mt Logan; lowest, sea level
Economy: mining (gold, copper, silver, lead, zinc), furs
Floral emblem: fireweed

Yunnan, province in S China, bounded by Tibet autonomous region and Szechwan prov. (N), Laos and Vietnam (S), Kweichow prov. and Kwangsi autonomous region (E), Burma (W); capital is Kunming. Beseiged by Kublai Khan 1253; became part of China 1659; scene of Muslim revolt 1855–72; fell to Communists 1950. Crops: rice, corn, sweet potatoes, wheat, soybeans, tea, sugar cane, tobacco, cotton. Industries: livestock, lumber, tin, iron, coal, copper, zinc, gold, mercury, silver, antimony, sulfur. Area: 168,417sq mi (436,200sq km). Pop. 20,510,000.

Z

Zabrze, formerly Hindenburg; city in S Poland, W of Katowice, in Katowice mining district. Founded 1300, it grew rapidly in 19th century as a mining center; named Hindenburg after German occupation 1915; passed to Poland 1945. Industries: coal mining, iron founding, chemicals. Pop. 203,000.

Zafrullah Khan, Muhammad (1893–1985), Pakistani statesman and diplomat. He was a member of the Punjab Legislative Council 1926–35; and president of the All-India Muslim League 1931–32. In 1939 he acted as leader of the Indian delegation to the League of Nations. He led the Pakistani delegation to the United Nations (1947–54). He was a member of the International Court of Justice (1954–61) and again became Pakistan's UN representative (1961–64) and served as president of the UN General Assembly 1962–63. He once more became a member of the International Court of Justice (1964) and served as its president, (1970).

Zagreb, city in NW Yugoslavia, on Sava River; 2nd-largest city in Yugoslavia, and capital of Croatia; industrial and trade center; site of St Stephen's Cathedral, Yugoslav Academy of Arts and Sciences (1861), nuclear energy institute, university (1669), botanical gardens. The ancient Roman town of Andautonia, it was chief city of Croatia and Slavonia late 13th century; became center of nationalist (Yugoslav) movement in 19th century. Industries: textiles, chemicals, leather goods, machinery. Pop. 566,084.

Zagros, mountain range in S and SW Iran; extends from Soviet-Turkish border to the Persian Gulf; topography varies from rugged peaks (N), to ridges and valleys (central), to lowland marshes and rock (S). The nomadic Kurds inhabit the Zagros, graze their sheep and goats in central and lower parts; one of world's most productive oil fields is located in W foothills. Sabalan is the highest peak, 14,921ft (4,551m). Length: approx. 1,000mi (1,610km).

Zaharias, Babe Didrikson. *See* Didrikson, (Mildred) Babe.

Zaibatsu, great industrial combines of modern Japan. Aided by subsidies and favorable tax laws, several family-controlled banking and industrial firms, such as Mitsui, Sumitomo and Mitsubishi, became economically and politically very powerful.

Zaire, independent nation in W central Africa. Formerly known as the Belgian Congo and, after independence, as the Democratic Republic of the Congo, it changed its name to Zaire ("river") in 1971. Zaire's vast resources give it great potential for economic growth.

Land and economy. With only a narrow strip of land offering access to the sea, Zaire is located on the equator in W central Africa bounded W by the People's Republic of the Congo, N by the Central African Republic and Sudan; E by Uganda, Rwanda, Burundi, and Tanzania; S by Angola and Zambia. The central area is a large, low, rain forest plateau surrounded by mountains (W), plateaus (S and SW), and grasslands (NW). High ranges, the Mts of the Moon, cover the E section, including Mt Margherita, 16,763ft (5,113m) above sea level. One of the longest rivers in the world, the Zaire (Congo) rises near the Zambian border. It is one of the most economically developed countries in Africa. Most of the agricultural revenue comes from large European-owned plantations producing coffee, palm kernels and oil, and rubber. Zairians are mainly subsistence farmers (80%). The country is the world's leading source of industrial diamonds, possesses 65% of the world's cobalt reserves, and is the world's third-largest producer of copper. Nevertheless, the country has suffered serious economic problems following falling copper prices in 1974—including a huge foreign debt and inflation—that were partially alleviated by loans from the International Monetary Fund in 1979.

People. The Zairian population is divided into three groups: Pygmies, believed to be the first inhabitants of the Zaire River basin; Negroid people, classified as either Bantu, Sudanese, or Nilotics; and Hamites. About 200 languages are spoken, with 4 dominant sets: Lingala, Kingwana, Kikongo, and Tshiluba. French is the official language. Literacy is estimated at 35%. Regional religions—monotheism, animism, vitalism, ancestor worship, and witchcraft—are practiced by about half the population; the other half is Christian.

Government. The government is a strong, centralized presidential form, with both the president and unicameral National Assembly elected by universal suffrage.

History. The country was settled in the 9th and 10th centuries by Bantus from Nigeria. The Portuguese navigator Diego Cao explored the mouth of the Zaire in 1482; Belgian influence came in 1877 when Henry Morton Stanley penetrated the region for Belgium, whose undisputed control over the region lasted until 1907. Opposition to colonial domination grew, culminating in riots and then independence in 1960. Patrice Lumumba, elected first premier, formed a coalition government, put down attempted secession of copper-rich Katanga prov. (now Shaba) and was himself removed. Leftist uprisings precipitated several government changes before 1965, when Lt. Col. Mobuto Sese Seko seized control in a military coup. Becoming president in 1970, he was able to introduce stability largely by crushing opposition, including another uprising in Shaba province (1977–78). Border tensions with Zambia and economic woes plagued Zaire through the mid-1980s.

PROFILE

Official name: Republic of Zaire
Area: 905,063sq mi (2,344,113sq km)
Population: 27,535,000
Density: 30per sq mi (12per sq km)
Chief cities: Kinshasa (capital); Luluabourg; Lubumbashi
Government: Republic
Religion: Christian and tribal (evenly divided)
Language: French (official)
Monetary unit: Zaire
Gross national product: $7,020,000,000
Per capita income: $147
Industries: palm oil, processed foods, clothing, textiles, soap
Agriculture: forests, bananas, coffee, rubber, rice, sugar cane, mangoes, plantain
Minerals: copper, cobalt, diamonds, cadmium, gold, silver, tin, zinc, iron, tungsten, manganese, uranium
Trading partners: Belgium (major), United Kingdom

Zaire River. *See* Congo (Zaire).

Zama, name of one or more ancient towns on the N coast of Africa (in modern Tunisia), traditionally the site of the last battle of the Second Punic War in which the Roman general Scipio Africanus Major defeated Hannibal of Carthage in 202 BC.

Zambezi, river in S central Africa; rises in NW Zambia and flows E through Angola and along the Zambia-Rhodesia border; empties into the Mozambique Channel in the Indian Ocean. Because navigable stretches are separated by rapids, it is used for local transportation only; has great hydroelectric potential. River was first explored by David Livingstone 1851–53. Length: 1,700mi (2,737km).

Zambia, independent nation in S Africa. Formerly the British colony of Northern Rhodesia, it was the first British territory to become a republic immediately after independence. Its economy is dependent on copper.

Land and economy. A land-locked plateau crossed by streams flowing into two of Africa's greatest rivers, the Zaire (Congo) and the Zambesi, Zambia is bordered by Zaire and Tanzania (N); Malawi and Mozambique (E); Zimbabwe, Botswana, and Namibia (S); and Angola (W). Victoria Falls, on the Zambesi River, is twice as wide and more than twice the height of Niagara Falls. The climate is subtropical with rainfall 25–30in (63–76cm) annually. Copper and cobalt mining dominate the economy, together providing 98% of export revenue. In 1970 the government acquired a 51% interest in copper mines and other major industries and in 1973 assumed complete control of the two largest copper-mining complexes.

People. Although copper mining has brought many rural Zambians into the N copper belt, the majority remain subsistence farmers. Ninety-nine percent of the population is African and Bantu, divided into some 70 tribes speaking 8 tongues. English is the official language. Animism is the dominant religion with a Christian minority. Literacy is rated between 15%–20%.

Government. The republic is headed by a president with broad powers, who also serves as chairman of the sole legal political party. Legislative power is vested in the 135-seat unicameral National Assembly, both elected by universal suffrage. Tribal interests are represented by the House of Chiefs, an advisory body.

History. It is probable that immigrants into Zambia came about 2,000 years ago, displaced the Stone Age hunters and were themselves absorbed by waves of Bantu-speaking immigrants. European missionaries and traders came in the 19th century. David Livingstone saw Victoria Falls in 1855, and in 1888 Cecil Rhodes obtained mineral concessions and led the way for British commercial interests, proclaiming both Northern and Southern Rhodesia as British spheres of influence. Northern Rhodesia became a British protec-

Yugoslavia

Zaire

Zanzibar

torate in 1924 and remained one until 1953 when it became part of the Federation of Rhodesia and Nyasaland with Southern Rhodesia and Nyasaland (now Malawi). After years of nationalist turmoil directed against white domination, a 1962 election allowed Northern Rhodesia to secede. On Oct. 24, 1964, it became the Republic of Zambia, under the leadership of Dr. Kenneth Kaunda. Zambia's economy was seriously disrupted by instability in neighboring Rhodesia (now Zimbabwe), but with that country's independence in 1980, Zambia's economy was able to recuperate somewhat. However, it took a downturn in 1982 due to poor crop yields and earnings from mining. Under Kaunda, Zambia has been a prominent "front-line state" opposed to the segregationist policies of the Republic of South Africa. During the mid-1980s ties were strengthened with the United States and Egypt.

PROFILE

Official name: Republic of Zambia
Area: 290,585sq mi (752,615sq km)
Population: 5,834,000
 Density: 20per sq mi (8per sq km)
Chief city: Lusaka
Government: Republic
Religion: Animist (major)
Language: English (official)
Monetary unit: Kwacha
Gross national product: $2,790,000,000
Per capita income: $503
Industries: timber, metal refining, sugar refining
Agriculture: sugarcane, maize, cassava, peanuts, cattle,
Minerals: copper, zinc, cobalt, gold, lead, coal
Trading partners: United Kingdom, Japan, West Germany, South Africa, United States

Zanesville, city in central Ohio, on Muskingum River 50mi (81km) E of Columbus; seat of Muskingum co; served as state capital 1810–1812; birthplace of novelist Zane Grey (1875). Industries: batteries, radiators, cement, farm machinery. Founded 1797 by Ebenezer Zane; inc. as village 1814, as city 1850. Pop. (1980) 28,655.

Zanzibar, major island of Tanzania, E Africa, in the Indian Ocean. The first inhabitants date to *c.* AD 1000; under Arab domination until *c.* 1505 when controlled by Portuguese; taken by Arabs from Oman 1698; made a British protectorate 1890; inc. into German East Africa 1895; gained self-government 1963; became part of Tanzania 1964. Island economy is based mainly on agriculture; Zanzibar is the largest producer of cloves in the world. Industries: copra, spices, coconuts, cacao. fishing. Area: 641sq mi (1,660sq km). Pop. 421,000.

Zanzibar, city in Tanzania, on the coast of Zanzibar Island, 45mi (72km) N of Dar es Salaam; center of East African trade. Capital was transferred here in 1832; political and commercial importance has declined with the rise of competing ports. Industries: cloves, citrus fruits, chilies, copra, mangrove bark, clove oil, soap, coconut oil, handcrafts. Pop. 69,000.

Zapata, Emiliano (*c.* 1879–1919), leader of the Mexican Revolution, champion of agrarian reform in his native Morelos. Of middle-class background, Zapata steadfastly demanded that successive revolutionary governments abide by his Plan of Ayala, issued in 1911, which called for dividing the sugar plantations of Morelos and restoring the land to the Indians. He allied himself with Villa in capturing Mexico City in 1914, but soon retreated to his stronghold in the south. Led into a trap by forces loyal to Carranza, Zapata was captured and executed.

Zápolya, John (1487–1540), governor of Transylvania (1511–26), regent for Louis II (1516–26); elected king of Hungary in 1526. He was supported by the Turks in his struggle against Holy Roman Emperor Ferdinand I of Germany, who also claimed to be king of Hungary, a dispute settled by the Treaty of Nagyvarad in 1526. Zápolya was king of Hungary 1526–40, but was subservient to the Ottoman Empire.

Zapopan, city in W Mexico, approx. 10mi (16km) W of Guadalajara; trade center for agricultural products; site of 17th-century church. Products: fertilizer, flour, textiles. Pop. 182,934.

Zaporozhye (Zaporožje), city in Ukrainian republic, USSR, on W bank of Dnieper River, 45mi (72km) S of Dnepropetrovsk; originally settled 16th century as a Cossack stronghold; the historic site on islands downstream from present-day city has been almost obliterated by the construction of a dam and large hydroelectric plant (1927–32). The new city dates from 1930s as an industrial site. Industries: steel, coke, aluminum, magnesium, chemicals, soap, farm machinery. Old city was founded 1770 on site of Cossack camp and called Aleksandrovsk until 1921. Pop. 784,000.

Zapotec, Indian group inhabiting a section of the Mexican state of Oaxaca. The Zapotec built great pre-conquest urban centers at Mitla and Monte Albán. They sought contact with the Spaniards in order to preserve their independence from the rival Mixes and Aztecs; their numbers were drastically reduced as a result of Spanish labor demands. Benito Juárez, president of Mexico, was a full-blooded Zapotec.

Zaragoza (Saragossa), city in NE Spain, on Ebro River, approx. 170mi (274km) NE of Madrid; capital of Zaragoza prov.; commercial and industrial center; site of Gothic cathedrals and churches. City was taken by Rome 1st century BC, by Moors early 8th century; taken by Alfonso I of Aragon and made capital of Aragon 1118. Industries: heavy machinery, building materials, textiles. Area: (prov.) 6,639sq mi (17,195sq km). Pop. (city) 479,845; (prov.) 760,186.

Zarathustra. *See* Zoroaster.

Zealots, a sect of Jewish extremists originating as early as the 2nd century BC. Driven by their religious fanaticism and intense hatred for foreign paganism, this faction organized into a political party during the reign of Herod the Great (37–4 BC). For nearly a century, they conducted acts of violence in opposition to Roman rule, ultimately prompting a revolt in which Jerusalem was destroyed (AD 70).

Zebra, common equine of African plains. More like an ass than a horse, it has long ears, short stiff mane, tufted tail, narrow hooves, and white coat striped with black, patterned according to species. Gestation period is 345–390 days; one colt is born. Varieties of true zebra are mountain, cape, cape mountain, Hartmann's, and plains. Height: 46–55in (118–140cm) at shoulder; weight: 600lb (270kg). Family Equidae; subgenus *Hippotigris;* species *Equus zebra.* Grevy's zebra is larger and has larger ears. Height: 55.1–63in (140–160cm) at shoulder. Family Equidae; subgenus *Dolichohippus;* species *Equus grevyi.*

Zebu, or Brahman cattle, numerous domestic varieties of a single species of ox, native to India, used extensively in Asia and Africa, and recently introduced in the New World.

Zechariah, biblical author and 11th of the 12 minor prophets. He was Haggai's contemporary and shared his concern for rebuilding the Temple in Jerusalem.

Zeeman, Pieter (1865–1943), Dutch physicist. He shared a Nobel Prize in 1902 with his teacher Hendrik Lorentz for their discovery (1896) of the Zeeman effect, the splitting of spectral lines when a light source is placed in a strong magnetic field. He also detected the magnetic fields at the surface of the Sun.

Zen, a Japanese school of Buddhism initially developed in China. Instead of doctrines and scriptures, mind-to-mind instruction from master to disciple is emphasized in order to achieve *satori,* or awakening of the Buddha-nature inherent in everyone. There are two major Zen sects. One called Rinzai, introduced to Japan from China in 1191, emphasizes sudden shock and meditation on paradoxical statements. The other, the Soto sect, also transmitted from China (in 1227), prefers the method of quiet sitting. In its secondary emphasis on mental tranquillity, fearlessness, and spontaneity, Zen has had a great influence on Japanese culture. Zen priests inspired art, literature, the tea ceremony, and the No play. Over the last several decades, a number of Zen groups have formed in the United States and several European countries.

Zenger, John Peter (1697–1746), American printer and journalist, b. Germany. Editor of the *New York Weekly Journal* (1733) he attacked Gov. William Cosby and was jailed for libel (1734). He was later tried by a jury and acquitted. His case established the truth of statements made as a defense for libel and made Zenger a symbol of freedom of the press. He was public printer of New York (1737) and New Jersey (1738).

Zenobia, (*fl.* 3rd century AD), queen of Palmyra, a part of the Roman Empire in the East. After the death (267) of her husband Odenathus, she secured power for herself in the name of her young son Vaballathus. Under her leadership, in 271 Palmyra broke off from the Roman Empire and became an independent state. She was defeated (272) by Aurelian, taken to Rome, but later pardoned.

Zephaniah, biblical author and ninth of the 12 minor prophets. He condemned Israel's religious and political corruption and stressed the certainty of God's judgment against Israel.

Zeppelin, Ferdinand, Count von (1838–1917), German army officer and designer-builder of large-scale rigid dirigible balloons.

Zero, integer, denoted by 0, that symbolizes the concept of emptiness, absence of something. It can be added to or subtracted from a number, etc, so as to leave the number unchanged: $x + 0 = x; x - 0 = x$; also $x \times 0 = 0; 0 \div x = 0; x^0 = 1$.

Zero Gravity or **Zero g,** the condition of experiencing no net gravitational force. It may be attained by airplane pilots for a few minutes during free fall, or by astronauts in satellites or lunar probes. Physiological accompaniments include some muscle wastage and lower blood pressure, but no major harmful effects have yet been noted. *See also* Weightlessness.

Zero Population Growth, social movement that urges families to have no more than two children, thereby maintaining the present population. The movement was initiated by Paul R. Ehrlich, an American biologist, whose book *The Population Bomb* (rev. ed. 1971) stated that overpopulation was causing a depletion of food supplies.

Zeus, in the mythology of the Greeks, the sky god, lord of the wind, clouds, rain, and thunder. Later he was the supreme deity, omnipresent, omniscient, omnipotent. Zeus ruled from Mt Olympus, where he dwelt with all the gods, and consorted with gods and men as he pleased. He was depicted as a mature, strong man with stern features and thick hair and beard, bearing the sceptre in one hand and in the other, the thunderbolt. The centers of his worship were at Dodona, Mount Lycaeus in Arcadia, and the temples at Olympia and Athens, though he was honored throughout the country.

Zhengzhou (Chengchow), city in N China, 10mi (16km) S of Yellow River; capital of Honan prov.; railroad junction. Industries: cotton, food processing, agricultural tools, thermal power. Pop. 1,500,000.

Zhukov, Georgi K(onstantinovich) (1894–1974), Soviet military commander and political figure. A draftee in World War I, he joined the Communists in 1918 as a cavalry commander. He studied in Germany and commanded successfully in Manchuria (1938). In World War II he led the defense of Moscow (1941), broke the German sieges of Stalingrad and Leningrad, and led the final assault on Berlin (1945). He became defense minister in 1955, helping to modernize the Soviet armed forces. He was a member of the Presidium (1957) and received the Order of Lenin (1971).

Zia-ul-Haq, Mohammad (1924–), President of Pakistan. Born in Punjab and trained in the Indian military, Zia was appointed (1966) to the Command and Staff College in Quetta, Pakistan. In 1976, Prime Minister Bhutto made him chief of staff of the army; he ousted Bhutto in a coup in 1977, establishing Pakistan's fourth military dictatorship since 1947. Zia became president of his country in 1978. During his administration better relations between Pakistan and India were fostered. In late 1986, his rule was seriously challenged by Bhutto's daughter Benazir.

Ziggurat, a temple in Babylonian and Assyrian architecture, constructed as a truncated pyramid in diminishing tiers, usually square or rectangular. The shrine at the top was reached by a series of ramps. Ziggurats date from 3000 to 600 BC.

Zimbabwe, independent nation in S central Africa. Following years of rule by the white minority as Rhodesia, the independent nation of Zimbabwe—with a black-led government—was proclaimed in 1980.

Land and Economy. A high inland plateau country in S central Africa, its neighbors are Zambia (N), Mozambique (E), Republic of South Africa (S), and Botswana (W). Crossing the country NE to SW is a 4,000–5,000-ft (1,220–1,525-m) high plateau with land sloping to the Zambesi River. Victoria Falls, 335ft (102m) high and 5,580ft (1,702m) wide, were discovered by David Livingstone in 1855. About 65% of the labor force is engaged in agriculture, and the country is largely self-sufficient in food supplies. Manufacturing employs about 15% of the labor force, contributing about 25% of the gross domestic product. The Lake Cariba Dam meets most of the country's power needs. During the late 1970s and early 1980s, Zimbabwe lost much of its skilled labor force with the emigration of whites. Climate is subtropical.

People. About 96% of the population is composed of black Africans, and most are Bantu. The two largest ethnic groups are the Shona and Matabele. Most of the remainder of the population are white, but there is also a small Asian minority. Literacy rates vary from almost 100% among whites to only about 30% among blacks.

Government. According to the constitution of 1980, legislative power is vested in the bicameral parliament. Of the 100 seats in the house of representatives, 20 are reserved for whites. Executive authority is held by the prime minister, who leads the majority party or coalition in parliament.

History. Exploration of ruins at Zimbabwe has revealed an impressive trading culture between the 9th and 13th centuries. Portuguese traders came in the 16th century, and the hinterlands were explored 300 years later by missionaries and traders. Meanwhile, waves of equatorial Bantus came to the region. In 1888, Cecil Rhodes started the British South Africa Co. to exploit the region's mineral resources. Britain took over the company in 1923 and granted internal self-government, with control in the hands of the white minority. A 1961 constitution extended privileges, with voting restricted to keep whites in power. In 1965, Rhodesia, rejecting Britain's demand for progress toward majority rule, made a unilateral declaration of independence condemned by the United Nations and Great Britain. The United Nations subsequently declared economic sanctions against Rhodesia. By the early 1970s black nationalist groups had begun waging a guerrilla campaign. Prime Minister Ian Smith attempted to reach a settlement with moderate black groups, and in 1979 they agreed on the transition to a black-led government that incorporated entrenched safeguards for the white minority. The settlement was not recognized by the most influential guerrilla groups, the United Nations, or Great Britain, and fighting between guerrillas and the Rhodesian army intensified. In 1979 a constitutional convention was convened in London; a cease-fire agreement was reached, Rhodesia reverted to its former status of a British colony, and preparations were made to elect a new government to lead the independent nation of Zimbabwe. Robert Mugabe became prime minister of the new country and, to discourage the white minority from leaving, pledged a policy of gradual Africanization. His desire for a one-party state led to violence across the country and a falling out with Joshua Nkomo, head of the Zimbabwe African People's Union, in 1982. In 1985, Mugabe was reelected in a landslide victory and opposition supporters were victims of violence.

PROFILE

Official name: Zimbabwe
Area: 150,803sq mi (390,580sqkm)
Population: 7,147,000
Density: 47per sq mi (18per sq km)
Chief cities: Salisbury(capital); Bulawayo
Government: Parliamentary democracy
Religion: Christian (major)
Monetary unit: Zimbabwean dollar
Gross national product: $3,330,000,000
Per capita income: $406
Industries: food processing, metals, engineering, textiles
Agriculture: tobacco, tea, cotton, wheat, maize, peanuts, cattle
Minerals: gold, nickel, coal, tin, silver, iron

Zimbabwe, ruined city in SE Zimbabwe, near Fort Victoria. Name means "houses of stone" and refers to the large, well preserved buildings. Ruins were discovered in 1868 and indicate the first inhabitants may have lived during Iron Age. Construction of stone monuments began in 1450; most noted are the famous Elliptical Building, Conical tower, and Acropolis.

Zimmerman Note (1917), cable intercepted by British intelligence from German Foreign Minister. It stated Germany's intent to wage unrestricted submarine warfare and proposed that Mexico be offered three US states if it allied herself with Germany. Because it violated the *Sussex* Pledge, President Wilson severed diplomatic relations with Germany, which led to US entry into World War I.

Zinc, metallic element (symbol Zn) of group IIB of the periodic table, known from early times. Chief ores are zinc blende (sulfide), smithsonite (carbonate), and calamine (silicate). The element is used in many alloys, including brass, bronze, nickel, silver, and soft solder. It is also used in galvanizing iron and in producing zinc compounds. Properties: at. no. 30; at. wt. 65.38; sp gr 7.133 (25°C); melt. pt. 787.2°F (419.58°C); boil. pt. 1,665°F (907°C); most common isotope Zn^{64} (48.89%).

Zinc Oxide, white powder used in ointments as a mild antiseptic, astringent, and protectant against drying in cases of eczema and other skin conditions.

Zinnia, genus of chiefly annual plants native to North and South America. Most garden zinnias are varieties of *Z. elegans,* that has flower heads of all colors but blue and green. Height: to 3ft (91cm); flower diameter: to 6in (15cm). Family Compositae.

Zinoviev, Grigori E(vseevich) (1883–1936), Soviet political leader. He was a close collaborator of V.I. Lenin in exile (1908–17) and supported a coalition government after the 1917 revolution. His support of pluralistic government led to his arrest during Stalin's purge trials (1934) and execution (1936).

Zion (Sion), height in E part of Jerusalem, Israel; center of Jewish spiritual life; site of Temple of David; referred to in Bible as the City of David.

Zionism, a movement within Judaism which advocates the return to the land of Israel (Zion). It is based on the conception of the coming of the Messiah connected with the land of the fathers, Israel. In 1897, Theodor Herzl developed the movement into an organized body. Zionism gained momentum in the 19th century as the Jews developed a sense of nationalism and as actual movement to Israel began. Practical, political, and cultural Zionism developed. Herzl believed that only through public law would Zionist aims be achieved. Conflicts developed within the leadership and outside the movement. Hebrew was revived as a modern, daily language and in 1948 when the state of Israel was founded, Hebrew became its official language. Zionism continues as an effective movement, combating anti-Semitism and improving conditions of Jewish life.

Zion National Park, park in SW Utah. It is famous for its scenic trails, canyons, colorful cliffs, and mesas. There is evidence of past volcanic activity. The outstanding feature is a deep, many colored gorge cut by the Virgin River. Area: 147,034acres (59,549hectares). Est. 1909.

Zircon, an orthosilicate mineral, zirconium silicate ($ZrSiO_4$) found in igneous rocks and metamorphosed limestones and in sand and gravel. Tetragonal system prismatic crystals. Brilliant, colorless or of varied hues; hardness 7.5; sp gr 4.6. Used widely as a gemstone because of its high refractive index.

Zirconium, metallic element (symbol Zr) of the second transition series, first discovered (1789) by M. H. Klaproth. Chief source is the gemstone zircon (silicate). It has a number of minor commercial uses. Chemically it is similar to titanium. Properties: at. no. 40; at. wt. 91.22; sp gr 6.506; melt pt. 3,366°F (1,852°C); boil. pt. 7,911°F (4,377°C); most common isotope Zr^{90} (51.46%). *See also* Transition Elements.

Zither, stringed musical instrument from ancient China via the Near East to medieval Europe. It is still popular for folk music in Austria, Bavaria, and the rural United States. The flat wooden sound box holds 30 to 40 strings, the five nearest stretched over a fretted board for melody, and plucked with fingers or a plectrum. *See also* Psaltery.

Zodiac, region of the sky extending either side of the ecliptic and containing the 12 constellations through which the Sun appears to move. Ancient astrologers divided it into 12 equal signs or houses, roughly coincident with these constellations. But owing to the Earth's precession, the constellations have now shifted eastward and lag behind the signs. *See also* Astrology.

Zodiacal Light, a faint, cone-shaped sky glow extending upward on the ecliptic from the horizon in the west after sunset and in the east before sunrise, probably caused by scattering of sunlight from dust particles in the plane of the solar system. Observations transmitted from Earth satellites have shown that this light does not vary as previously believed.

Zog I, original name **Ahmed Bey Zogu** (1895–1961), king of Albania (1928–39). Son of a Muslim chieftain, he was prominent in the struggle for independence, 1912–14, supporting William of Wied. Zogu was premier 1922–24. When Albania was proclaimed a republic in 1925, Zogu was elected president. In 1928 he was proclaimed king. As head of state, he consistently championed modernization and reforms. His rule became autocratic, however, and he was ineffectual in resisting the Fascist takeover in 1939.

Zoisite, an orthosilicate mineral, hydrous calcium aluminum silicate, found in metamorphic rocks. Orthorhombic system prismatic crystals and masses. Glassy, transparent gray, white, brown, green, or pink; hardness 6–6.5; sp gr 3.2. A vivid blue variety, tanzanite, of Tanzania is a gemstone.

Zola, Émile (1840–1902), French novelist. A leader of the naturalist school, his novels include *L'Assommoir* (1877), *Nana* (1880), *Germinal* (1885), and *Le Docteur Pascal* (1893), which were published under the collective title of *Les Rougon-Macquart.* He was tried for writing a letter *J'accuse* (1898), in support of Alfred Dreyfus, and fled to a short exile in England.

Zone Refining, method of purifying crystals, especially for use in semiconductor devices. The material is placed in a long tube and passed through a furnace in which hot and cold zones alternate. As the rod moves through the furnace, impurities remain in the molten state while melting and recrystallization of the material takes place; the impurities are thus transferred to one end of the tube.

Zoogeography, or animal geography, study of the geographic distribution of animals. Formerly, the approach of this science was descriptive. Presently, it utilizes various data, including isotope dating and ocean-bottom core sampling.

Zoological Garden, or zoo, public or private institution in which living animals are kept and exhibited. Organized zoos, sometimes called menageries or aquariums, open to the general public, have been operating for over 400 years in Europe. Currently, nonprofit organizations or zoological societies run most zoos in a scientific manner. Some outstanding examples are the zoological societies of San Diego, New York, Philadelphia, London, Antwerp, and Munich. Most zoos are run

Zimbabwe: Prime Minister Robert Mugabe

Émile Zola

Zoological Garden: puma in natural setting

for public recreation as well as for scientific and educational purposes. Worldwide representations of animal groups and rarities are frequently displayed. Present emphasis is on exhibiting animals in natural settings. Conservation programs are undertaken by some zoological societies, as is the breeding of rare species.

Zoology, study of animals. When combined with botany, it comprises the science of biology. Various subdivisions of zoological study include: taxonomy, classification of animals; zoogeography, distribution of animals; ecology, relationship of animals to each other and to their environment; paleontology, fossils; anthropology, man; evolution, origin of species and changes through history; anatomy, structure of body and its organs; morphology, functions of structure; embryology, development from conception to birth; genetics, heredity; physiology, function; pathology, abnormal function and structure; and psychology, behavior.

Zoonosis, an infection or infestation of lower animals that can be transmitted to man. Examples include some parasites such as fleas or canine tapeworms, and bacteria such as *Bacillis anthracis,* a primary cause of disease of sheep and cows.

Zoroaster, or **Zarathustra** (*c.*628–*c.*551 BC), Persian religious figure, founder of Zoroastrianism. Zoroaster is believed to have been born in western Persia. Persian religion at the time was a polytheism in a state of decadence; it was run by a hereditary priesthood and numerous animal sacrifices were required. Zoroaster, after a series of revelations, preached a new religion in which a single Wise Lord, Ahura Mazda, was recognized as the creator of the universe. Pitted against Ahura Mazda was Ahriman and the forces of evil. Unable to convert the petty chieftains of his native area, Zoroaster traveled to the east, where in Chorasmia (now in Khorasan province in northeastern Iran) he converted the royal family, including King Vishtaspa. By the time of Zoroaster's death, his new religion had spread to a large part of Persia. Parts of the Avesta, the holy scripture of Zoroastrianism, are believed to have been written by Zoroaster himself.

Zoroastrianism, religion originated by Zoroaster in the 6th century BC, which became the state religion of Persia in the period from 229–652. Viewing the world

as divided between the spirits of good and evil, Zoroastrians worship Ahura Mazda as the Supreme Deity. Islam's conquest in the 7th century led to the decline and near disappearance of the religion in Persia. Today the Parsis of India comprise most of the 125,000 followers of Zoroastrianism. *See also* Ahura Mazda; Parsi; Zoroaster.

Zuccarelli, Francesco (1702–88), Italian painter of the Venetian School. He was the leading landscapist of Venice in his time. Very popular with English patrons, he spent many years in London and became a charter member of the Royal Academy. Influenced by Marco Ricci, his brilliantly atmospheric landscapes in turn influenced several British painters, notably Richard Wilson. *See also* Venetian School.

Zucchini, variety of summer squash. A bushy annual plant, it produces a cucumber-shaped, dark green fruit with a smooth rind. Family Cucurbitaceae.

Zuider Zee (Zuyder Zee), former landlocked inlet of the North Sea on the N coast of the Netherlands. Since the completion of the dike of IJsselmeer (1932), this area is divided between the saline Wadden Zee and freshwater IJsselmeer Lake. *See also* IJsselmeer.

Zulu, Negroid people of South Africa, living mainly in Natal. They are closely related to the Swazi and the Xhosa. Traditionally agriculturalists, concentrating on grain production but also possessing large herds of cattle, which perform the function of status symbols, the Zulus have a patriarchal, polygynous society with a strong militaristic tradition. Unified under their leader Shaka in the 19th century, they fiercely resisted the encroachments of white colonialists. Today many Zulu males work as migrant laborers in the mines of South Africa or on white-owned farms. The predominant religion is now Christianity, although traditional ancestor worship, sorcery, and fetishism are still common.

Zululand, an historical region of NE Natal province, E Republic of South Africa; site of intense battles between native Zulu tribes and British and Boers in late 19th century; region now comprised of native reserves (Kwazulu). Sugarcane is economic staple. Area: 10,362sq mi (26,838sq km). Pop. 570,160.

Zuñi, major tribe of Pueblo Indians speaking an individual tongue, occupying a village area in McKinley and Valencia counties, New Mexico. They were the first Indian village visited by Coronado on his famed *entrada* in 1541 in search of the Seven Cities of Cíbola. Noted for their fine jewelry making, about 5,100 people live today in the village area.

Zürich, capital city of Zurich canton in Switzerland, on Limmat River, at NW end of Lake Zurich, in the foothills of the Alps; largest city in Switzerland. Conquered by Romans 58 BC, it passed to Alemanni, Franks, Swabia after 5th century; became free imperial city 1218; joined Swiss Confederation 1351; starting point of Swiss Reformation 16th century; site of Swiss National Museum, 11th- and 13th-century Protestant cathedrals, 13th-century St Peter's Church, University of Zurich, Federal Institute of Technology. Industries: automobiles, banking, travel, machinery, paper, trade, textiles, publishing, beer, chemicals. Pop. 389,600.

Zwingli, Ulrich or **Huldreich** (1484–1531), Swiss theologian. Ordained in 1506, he studied the New Testament in Erasmus' editions. He preached reformed doctrine in Zurich and made that city a center of the Reformation. More radical than Luther, he saw communion as symbolic and commemorative. The *First Helvetic Confession* (1536), compiled by his followers, was based on his opinions. Zwingli died as a chaplain in battle with Roman Catholics at Kappel.

Zworykin, Vladimir Kosma (1889–1982), US electronic engineer and inventor, b. Mourom, Russia. He emigrated to the United States in 1919 and went to work for the Westinghouse Electric Corporation. His inventions of a television transmission tube and a television receiver were patented in the early 1920s, after which he became director of electronic development for RCA. In 1967 he received the National Medal of Science for his inventions and contributions to medical research.

Zygote, cell formed by fusion of male and female gametes. The fertilized egg contains a diploid number of chromosomes, half contributed by the sperm, half by the ovum.

CREDITS